LIFE APPLICATION BIBLE

LIFE APPLICATION BIBLE

THE LIVING BIBLE

TYNDALE HOUSE PUBLISHERS, INC.
AND
YOUTH FOR CHRIST/USA
WHEATON, ILLINOIS

Third printing. October 1988

Life Application Bible
© 1988 by Tyndale House
Publishers, Inc., Wheaton,
IL 60189.

The *Life Application Bible*
is a trademark of Tyndale
House Publishers, Inc.

The text of the *Life Application Bible* is from *The
Living Bible* © 1971 owned
by assignment to Illinois
Regional Bank N.A.,
Elmhurst, IL. All rights
reserved.

Living History of Israel
© 1970, *Living Books of
Moses* © 1969, *Living
Lessons of Life and Love*
© 1968, *Living Psalms and
Proverbs* © 1967, *Living
Gospels* © 1966, *Living
Prophecies* © 1965, *Living
Letters* © 1962 owned by
assignment to Illinois
Regional Bank N.A. All
rights reserved.

New Testament Life
Application Notes and
Bible Helps © 1986 owned
by assignment to Tyndale
House Publishers, Inc.,
Wheaton, IL 60189. Har-
mony of the Gospels
© 1986 by James C.
Galvin. Maps © 1986 by
Tyndale House Publishers,
Inc. All rights reserved.

ISBN 0-8423-2551-4
Cloth
ISBN 0-8423-2559-X
Black Bonded Leather
ISBN 0-8423-2560-3
Burgundy Bonded Leather
ISBN 0-8423-2561-1
Navy Blue Bonded Leather
ISBN 0-8423-2566-2
Gray Bonded Leather
Library of Congress
Catalog Card Number
88-050035

Printed in the United
States of America

CONTENTS

Senior Editorial Team
Dr. Bruce B. Barton
Ronald A. Beers
Dr. James C. Galvin
LaVonne Neff
Linda Chaffee Taylor
David R. Veerman

General Editor
Ronald A. Beers

Book Introductions
David R. Veerman

Book Outlines, Blueprints, Harmony
Dr. James C. Galvin

Megathemes
Dr. Bruce B. Barton

Map Development & Computer Operation
Linda Chaffee Taylor

Charts & Diagrams
Neil S. Wilson
Ronald A. Beers
David R. Veerman

Personality Profiles
Neil S. Wilson

Design & Development Team
Dr. Bruce B. Barton
Ronald A. Beers
Dr. James C. Galvin
David R. Veerman

Tyndale House Senior Bible Editor
Philip W. Comfort

Tyndale House Bible Editors
Virginia Muir
Robert Brown
Del Lankford
Mark Norton

Tyndale House Production
Marlene Muller
Joan Major
Edythe Draper

Tyndale House Graphic Design
Timothy R. Botts

A Chronology of Bible Events and World Events
Dr. David Maas

Theological Reviewers

Dr. Kenneth S. Kantzer
General Theological Reviewer
Dean Emeritus and
Distinguished Professor of Bible
and Systematic Theology
Trinity Evangelical Divinity School

Dr. V. Gilbert Beers
Senior Editor
Christianity Today, Inc.

Dr. Barry Beitzel
Associate Academic Dean
and Professor of Old Testament
and Semitic Languages
Trinity Evangelical Divinity School

Dr. Edwin A. Blum
Associate Professor of
Historical Theology
Dallas Theological Seminary

Dr. Geoffrey W. Bromiley
Professor
Fuller Theological Seminary

Dr. George K. Brushaber
President
Bethel College & Seminary

Dr. L. Russ Bush
Associate Professor,
Philosophy & Religion
Southwestern Baptist
Theological Seminary

C. Donald Cole
Pastor, Moody Radio Network

Mrs. Naomi E. Cole
Speaker & Seminar Leader

Dr. Walter A. Elwell
Dean,
Wheaton College Graduate School

Dr. Gerald F. Hawthorne
Professor of Greek
Wheaton College

Dr. Howard G. Hendricks
Professor-at-Large
Chairman,
Center for Christian Leadership
Dallas Theological Seminary

Dr. Grant R. Osborne
Professor of New Testament
Trinity Evangelical Divinity School

A special thanks to the nationwide
staff of Youth for Christ/USA for
their suggestions and field-testing,
and to the following additional
contributing writers: V. Gilbert
Beers, Neil Wilson, John Crosby,
Joan Young, Jack Crabtree, Philip
Craven, Bob Black, Bur Schilling,
Arthur Deyo, Annie Lafrentz,
Danny Sartin, William Hanawalt,
William Bonikowsky, Brian
Rathbun, Pamela Barden, Thomas
Stobie, Robert Arnold, Greg
Monaco, Larry Dunn, Lynn
Zeigenfuss, Mitzie Barton, Mari-
jean Hamilton, Larry Kreider, Gary
Dausey, William Roland, Kathy
Howell, Philip Steffeck, James
Coleman, Marty Grasley, O'Ann
Steere, Julia Amstutz.

A special thanks also to the following people whose personal counsel,
encouragement, and determination
helped make this product a reality:

Dr. Kenneth N. Taylor
Translator of *The Living Bible*
Chairman of the Board
Tyndale House Publishers

Mark D. Taylor
President
Tyndale House Publishers

Dr. Wendell C. Hawley
Editor-In-Chief
Tyndale House Publishers

Virginia Muir
Assistant Editor-In-Chief
Tyndale House Publishers

Richard R. Wynn
President, Youth for Christ/USA

Dr. Jay L. Kesler
President, Taylor University

A CHRONOLOGY OF BIBLE EVENTS AND WORLD EVENTS

Creation
undated

Noah
builds
the ark
undated

Abraham
born
2166

Abraham
enters
Canaan
2091

2500 B.C.
Egyptians
discover
papyrus
and ink
for writing
and build
the first
libraries;
iron objects
manufactured
in the ancient
Near East

2400
Egyptians
import gold
from Africa

2331
Semitic
chieftain,
Sargon,
conquers Sumer
to become first
"world conqueror"

2300
Horses
domesticated
in Egypt;
chickens
domesticated
in Babylon;
bows & arrows
used in wars

2100
Glass made
by the
Mesopotamians;
Ziggurats
(like the tower
of Babel)
built in
Mesopotamia;
Earliest
discovered drug,
Ethyl alcohol,
used to
alleviate pain

Have you ever opened your Bible and asked the following:

- What does this passage really mean?
- How does it apply to my life?
- Why does some of the Bible seem irrelevant?
- What do these ancient cultures have to do with today?
- I love God; why can't I understand what he is saying to me through his Word?
- What's going on in the lives of these Bible people?

Many Christians do not read the Bible regularly. Why? Because in the pressures of daily living they cannot find a connection between the timeless principles of Scripture and the ever-present problems of day-by-day living.

God urges us to apply his Word (Isaiah 42:23, 1 Corinthians 10:11; 2 Thessalonians 3:4), but too often we stop at accumulating Bible knowledge. This is why the *Life Application Bible* was developed—to show how to put into practice what we have learned.

Applying God's Word is a vital part of one's relationship with God; it is the evidence that we are obeying him. The difficulty in applying the Bible is not with

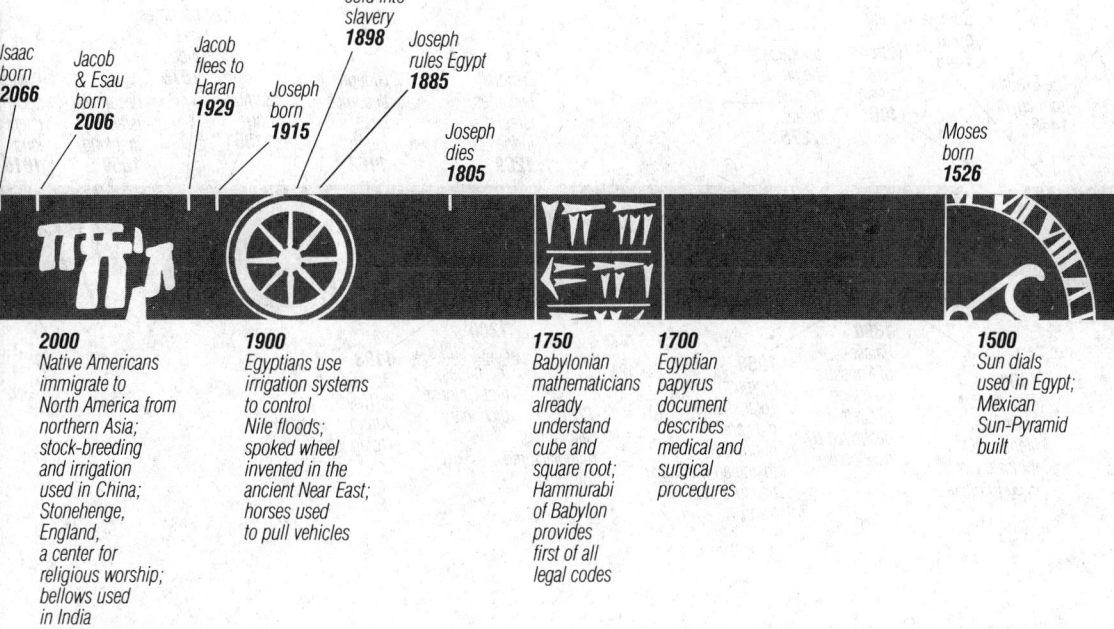

Isaac
born
2066

Jacob
& Esau
born
2006

Jacob
flees to
Haran
1929

Joseph
born
1915

Joseph
sold into
slavery
1898

Joseph
rules Egypt
1885

Joseph
dies
1805

Moses
born
1526

2000
Native Americans
immigrate to
North America from
northern Asia;
stock-breeding
and irrigation
used in China;
Stonehenge,
England,
a center for
religious worship;
bellows used
in India
allowing for
higher furnace
temperatures

1900
Egyptians use
irrigation systems
to control
Nile floods;
spoked wheel
invented in the
ancient Near East;
horses used
to pull vehicles

1750
Babylonian
mathematicians
already
understand
cube and
square root;
Hammurabi
of Babylon
provides
first of all
legal codes

1700
Egyptian
papyrus
document
describes
medical and
surgical
procedures

1500
Sun dials
used in Egypt;
Mexican
Sun-Pyramid
built

the Bible itself, but with the reader's inability to bridge the gap between the past and present, the conceptual and practical. When we don't or can't do this, spiritual dryness, shallowness, and indifference are the results.

The words of Scripture itself cry out to us, "Won't even one of you apply these lessons . . .?" (Isaiah 42:23). The *Life Application Bible* does just that. Developed by an interdenominational team of pastors, scholars, family counselors, and a national organization dedicated to promoting God's Word and spreading the Gospel, the *Life Application Bible* took many years to complete, and all the work was reviewed by several renowned theologians under the directorship of Dr. Kenneth Kantzer.

The *Life Application Bible* does what a good resource Bible should—it helps you understand the context of a passage, gives important background and historical information, explains difficult words and phrases, and helps you see the interrelationships within Scripture. But it does much more. The *Life Application Bible* goes deeper into God's Word, helping you discover the timeless truth being communicated, see the relevance for your life, and make a personal application. While some study Bibles attempt application, over 75% of this Bible is application-oriented. The notes answer the questions, "So what?" and "What does this passage mean to me, my family, my friends, my job, my neighborhood, my church, my country?"

Imagine reading a familiar passage of Scripture and gaining fresh insight, as if it were the first time you had ever read it. How much richer your life would be if you left each Bible reading with a new perspective and a small change for the better. A small change every day adds up to a changed life—and that is the very purpose of Scripture.

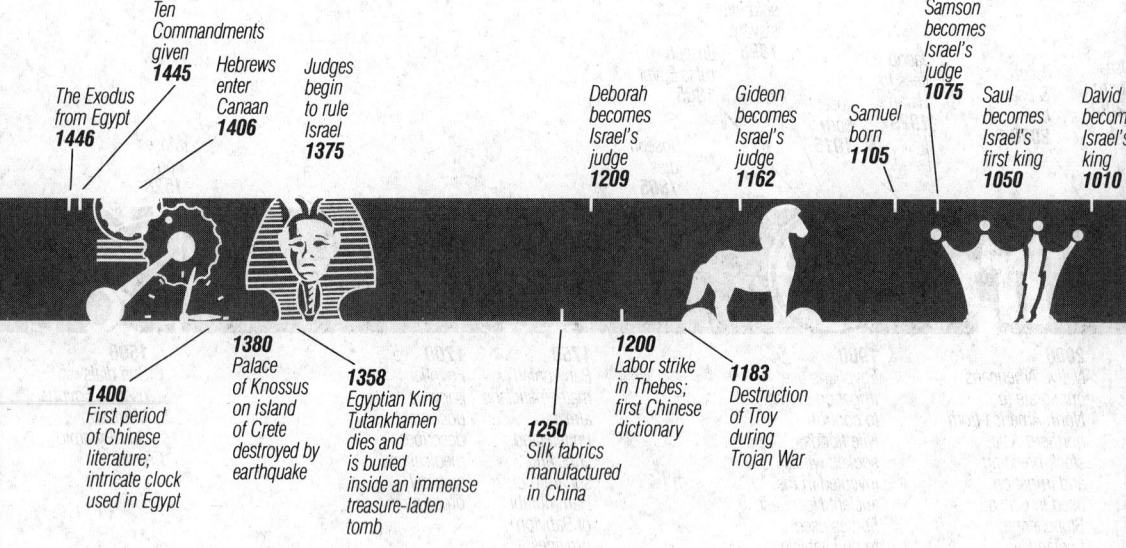

The best way to define application is to first determine what it is *not*. Application is *not* just accumulating knowledge. This helps us discover and understand facts and concepts, but it stops there. History is filled with philosophers who knew what the Bible said, but failed to apply it to their lives, keeping them from believing and changing. Many think that understanding is the end goal of Bible study, but it is really only the beginning.

Application is *not* just illustration. Illustration only tells us how someone else handled a similar situation. While we may empathize with that person, we still have little direction for our personal situation.

Application is *not* just making a passage "relevant." Making the Bible relevant only helps us to see that the same lessons that were true in Bible times are true today; it does not show us how to apply them to the problems and pressures of our individual lives.

What, then, is application? Application begins by knowing and understanding God's Word and its timeless truths. *But you cannot stop there.* If you do, God's Word may not change your life, and it may become dull, difficult, tedious, and tiring. A good application focuses the truth of God's Word, shows the reader what to do about what is being read, and motivates the reader to respond to what God is teaching. All three are essential to application.

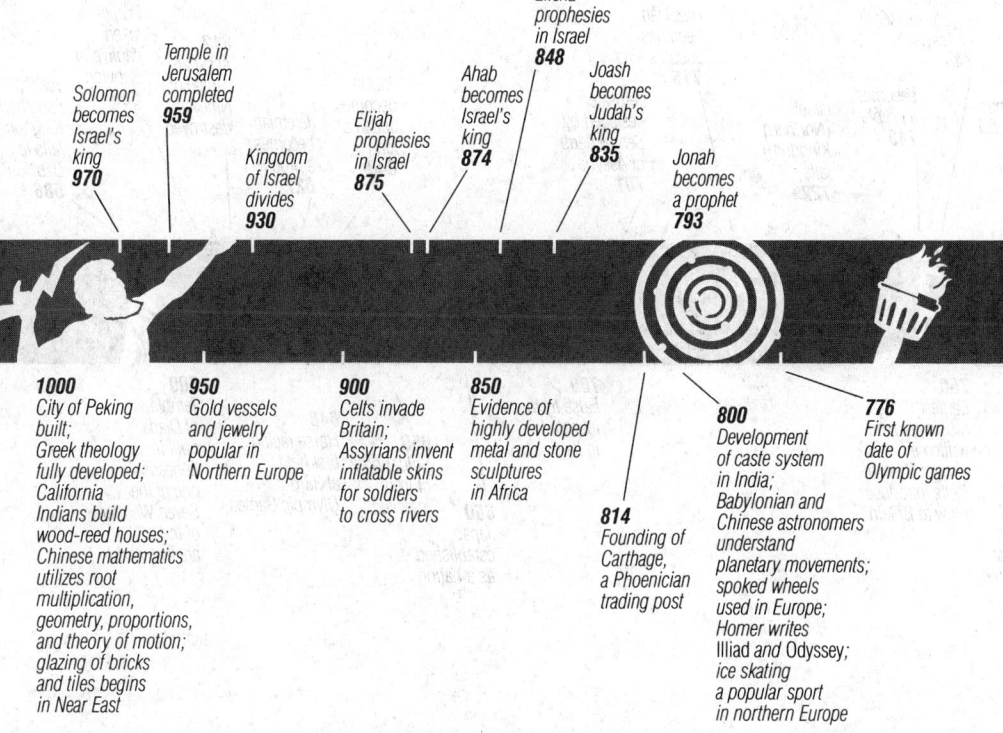

Solomon
becomes
Israel's
king
970

Temple in
Jerusalem
completed
959

Kingdom
of Israel
divides
930

Elijah
prophesies
in Israel
875

Ahab
becomes
Israel's
king
874

Elisha
prophesies
in Israel
848

Joash
becomes
Judah's
king
835

Jonah
becomes
a prophet
793

1000
City of Peking
built;
Greek theology
fully developed;
California
Indians build
wood-reed houses;
Chinese mathematics
utilizes root
multiplication,
geometry, proportions,
and theory of motion;
glazing of bricks
and tiles begins
in Near East

950
Gold vessels
and jewelry
popular in
Northern Europe

900
Celts invade
Britain;
Assyrians invent
inflatable skins
for soldiers
to cross rivers

850
Evidence of
highly developed
metal and stone
sculptures
in Africa

814
Founding of
Carthage,
a Phoenician
trading post

800
Development
of caste system
in India;
Babylonian and
Chinese astronomers
understand
planetary movements;
spoked wheels
used in Europe;
Homer writes
Illiad and Odyssey;
ice skating
a popular sport
in northern Europe

776
First known
date of
Olympic games

Application is putting into practice what we already know (see Mark 4:24 and Hebrews 5:14) and answering the question, "So what?" by confronting us with the right questions and motivating us to take action (see 1 Timothy 4:8 and James 2:20). Application is deeply personal—unique for each individual. It is making a relevant truth a personal truth, and involves developing a strategy and action plan to live your life in harmony with the Bible. It is the biblical "how to" of life.

You may ask, "How can your application notes be relevant to my life?" Each application note has three parts: (1) an *explanation* that ties the note directly to the Scripture passage and sets up the truth that is being taught, (2) the *bridge* which explains the timeless truth and makes it relevant for today, (3) the *application* which shows you how to take the timeless truth and apply it to your personal situation. No note, by itself, can apply Scripture directly to your life. It can only teach, direct, lead, guide, inspire, recommend, and urge. It can give you the resources and direction you need to apply the Bible; but only you can take these resources and put them into practice.

A good note, therefore, should not only give you knowledge and understanding, but point you to application. Before you buy any kind of resource Bible, you should evaluate the notes and ask the following questions: (1) Does the note contain enough information to help me understand the point of the Scripture passage? (2) Does the note assume I know too much? (3) Does the note avoid denominational bias? (4) Do the notes touch most of life's experiences? (5) Does the note help me *apply* God's Word?

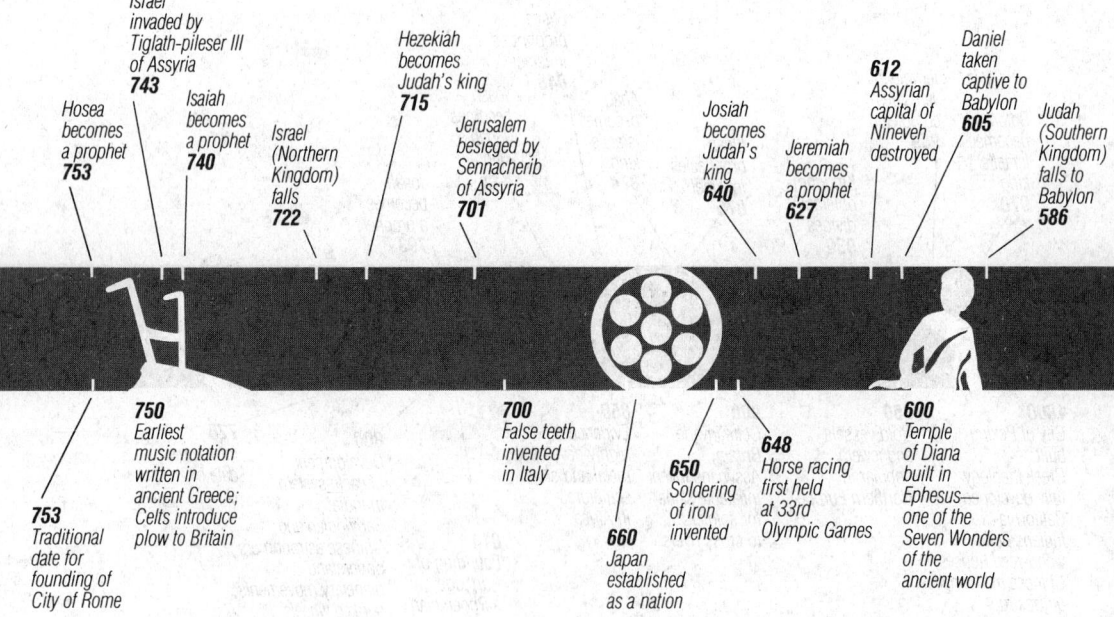

Israel invaded by Tiglath-pileser III of Assyria **743**

Hezekiah becomes Judah's king **715**

Daniel taken captive to Babylon **605**

Hosea becomes a prophet **753**

Isaiah becomes a prophet **740**

Israel (Northern Kingdom) falls **722**

Jerusalem besieged by Sennacherib of Assyria **701**

Josiah becomes Judah's king **640**

Jeremiah becomes a prophet **627**

612 Assyrian capital of Nineveh destroyed

Judah (Southern Kingdom) falls to Babylon **586**

750 Earliest music notation written in ancient Greece; Celts introduce plow to Britain

700 False teeth invented in Italy

650 Soldering of iron invented

648 Horse racing first held at 33rd Olympic Games

600 Temple of Diana built in Ephesus— one of the Seven Wonders of the ancient world

753 Traditional date for founding of City of Rome

660 Japan established as a nation

NOTES

In addition to providing the reader with many application notes, the *Life Application Bible* offers several explanatory notes, which are notes that help the reader understand culture, history, context, difficult-to-understand passages, background, places, theological concepts, and the relationship of various passages in Scripture to other passages. Maps, charts, and diagrams are also found on the same page as the passages to which they relate. For an example of an application note, see Mark 15:47. For an example of an explanatory note, see Mark 11:1, 2.

BOOK INTRODUCTIONS

The Book Introductions are divided into several easy-to-find parts:

Timeline. This puts the Bible book into its historical setting. It lists the key events of each book and the date when they occurred.

Vital Statistics. This is a list of straight facts about the book—those pieces of information you need to know at a glance.

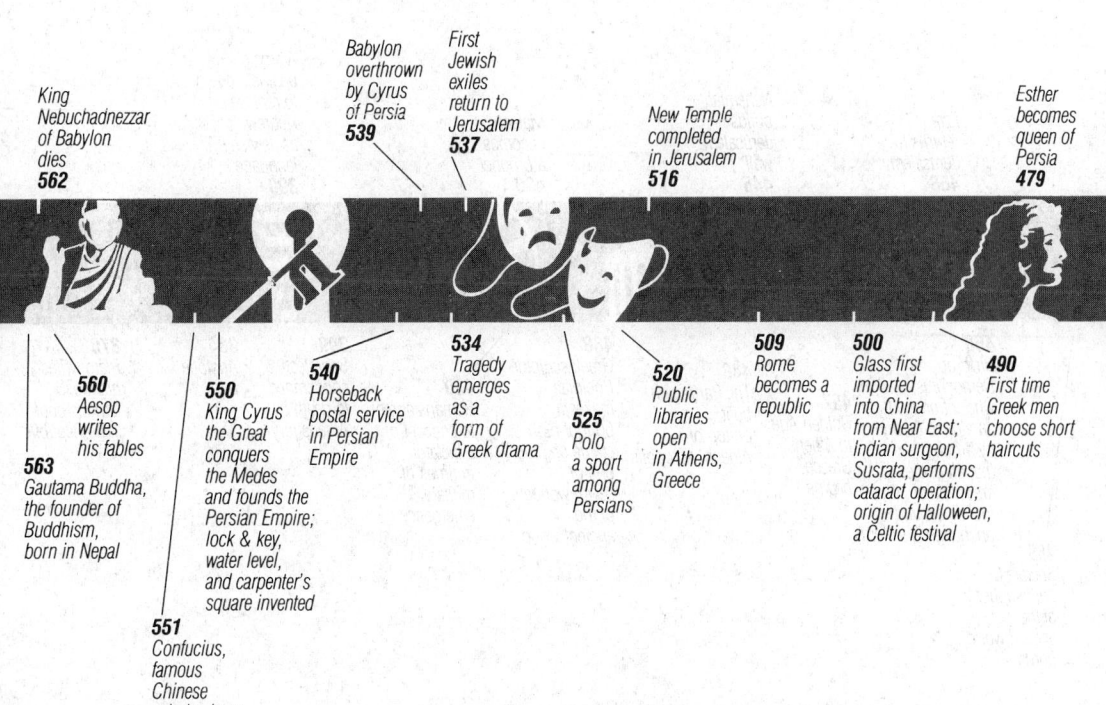

King Nebuchadnezzar of Babylon dies
562

Babylon overthrown by Cyrus of Persia
539

First Jewish exiles return to Jerusalem
537

New Temple completed in Jerusalem
516

Esther becomes queen of Persia
479

560 Aesop writes his fables

563 Gautama Buddha, the founder of Buddhism, born in Nepal

550 King Cyrus the Great conquers the Medes and founds the Persian Empire; lock & key, water level, and carpenter's square invented

551 Confucius, famous Chinese scholar, born

540 Horseback postal service in Persian Empire

534 Tragedy emerges as a form of Greek drama

525 Polo a sport among Persians

520 Public libraries open in Athens, Greece

509 Rome becomes a republic

500 Glass first imported into China from Near East; Indian surgeon, Susrata, performs cataract operation; origin of Halloween, a Celtic festival

490 First time Greek men choose short haircuts

Overview. This is a summary of the book with general lessons and applications that can be learned from the book as a whole.

Blueprint. This is the outline of the book. It is printed in easy-to-understand language and is designed for easy memorization. To the right of each main heading is a key lesson that is taught in that particular section.

Megathemes. This section gives the main themes of the Bible book, explains their significance, and then tells why they are still important for us today.

Map. This shows the key places found in that book and retells the story of the book from a geographical point of view.

OUTLINE

The *Life Application Bible* has a new, custom-made outline that was designed specifically from an application point of view. Several unique features should be noted:

1. To avoid confusion and to aid memory work, each book outline has only three levels for headings. Main outline heads are marked with a capital letter. Subheads are marked by a number. Minor, explanatory heads have no letter or number.

2. Each main outline head marked by a letter also has a brief paragraph below it summarizing the Bible text and offering a general application.

3. Parallel passages are listed where they apply in the Gospels.

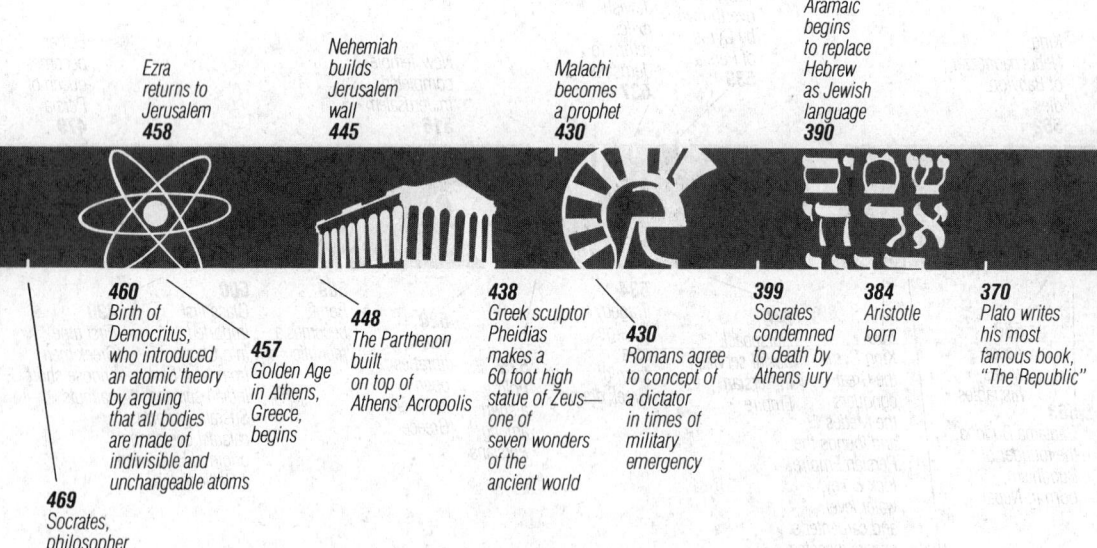

Ezra returns to Jerusalem
458

Nehemiah builds Jerusalem wall
445

Malachi becomes a prophet
430

Aramaic begins to replace Hebrew as Jewish language
390

460 Birth of Democritus, who introduced an atomic theory by arguing that all bodies are made of indivisible and unchangeable atoms

469 Socrates, philosopher of the ancient world, born

457 Golden Age in Athens, Greece, begins

448 The Parthenon built on top of Athens' Acropolis

438 Greek sculptor Pheidias makes a 60 foot high statue of Zeus— one of seven wonders of the ancient world

430 Romans agree to concept of a dictator in times of military emergency

399 Socrates condemned to death by Athens jury

384 Aristotle born

370 Plato writes his most famous book, "The Republic"

HARMONY OF THE GOSPELS

A harmony of the Gospels was developed specifically for this Bible. It is the first harmony that has ever been incorporated into the Bible text. Through a unique and simple numbering system, you can read any Gospel account and see just where you are in relation to the entire life of Christ. The harmony is located after the Gospel of John and explained in detail there.

PROFILE NOTES

Another unique feature of this Bible is the profiles of many Bible people, including their strengths and weaknesses, greatest accomplishments and mistakes, and key lessons from their lives. The profiles of these people are found in the Bible books where their stories occur.

MAPS

The *Life Application Bible* has more maps than any other Bible. A thorough and comprehensive Bible atlas is built right into each Bible book. There are two kinds of maps: (1) A book introduction map, telling the story of that Bible book. (2) Thumbnail maps in the notes, plotting most geographic movements in the Bible.

CHARTS AND DIAGRAMS

Hundreds of charts and diagrams are included to help the reader better visualize difficult concepts or relationships. Most charts not only present the needed information, but show the significance of the information as well.

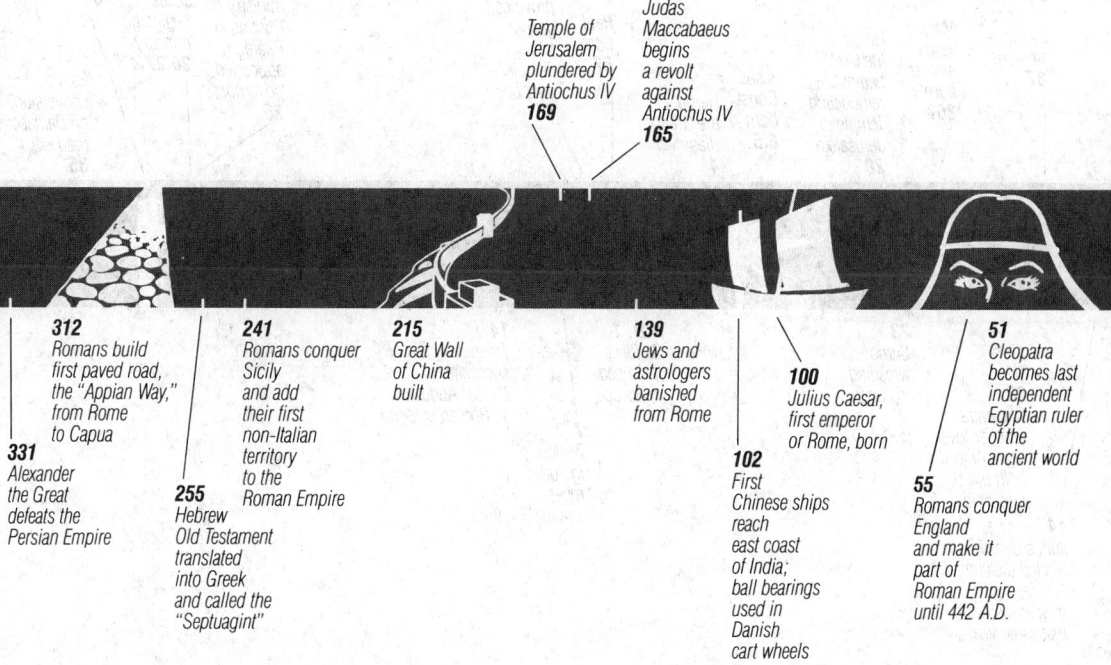

Temple of
Jerusalem
plundered by
Antiochus IV
169

Judas
Maccabaeus
begins
a revolt
against
Antiochus IV
165

312
Romans build
first paved road,
the "Appian Way,"
from Rome
to Capua

331
Alexander
the Great
defeats the
Persian Empire

241
Romans conquer
Sicily
and add
their first
non-Italian
territory
to the
Roman Empire

255
Hebrew
Old Testament
translated
into Greek
and called the
"Septuagint"

215
Great Wall
of China
built

139
Jews and
astrologers
banished
from Rome

102
First
Chinese ships
reach
east coast
of India;
ball bearings
used in
Danish
cart wheels

100
Julius Caesar,
first emperor
or Rome, born

55
Romans conquer
England
and make it
part of
Roman Empire
until 442 A.D.

51
Cleopatra
becomes last
independent
Egyptian ruler
of the
ancient world

CROSS REFERENCES
An updated, exhaustive cross reference system in the margins of the Bible text helps the reader find related passages quickly.

TEXTUAL NOTES
Directly related to *The Living Bible* text, the textual notes provide explanations on certain wording in the translation, alternate translations, and information about readings in the ancient manuscripts.

INDEX
This book contains a complete index to all the notes, charts, maps, and personality profiles. With its emphasis on application it is helpful for group Bible study, sermon preparation, teaching, or personal study.

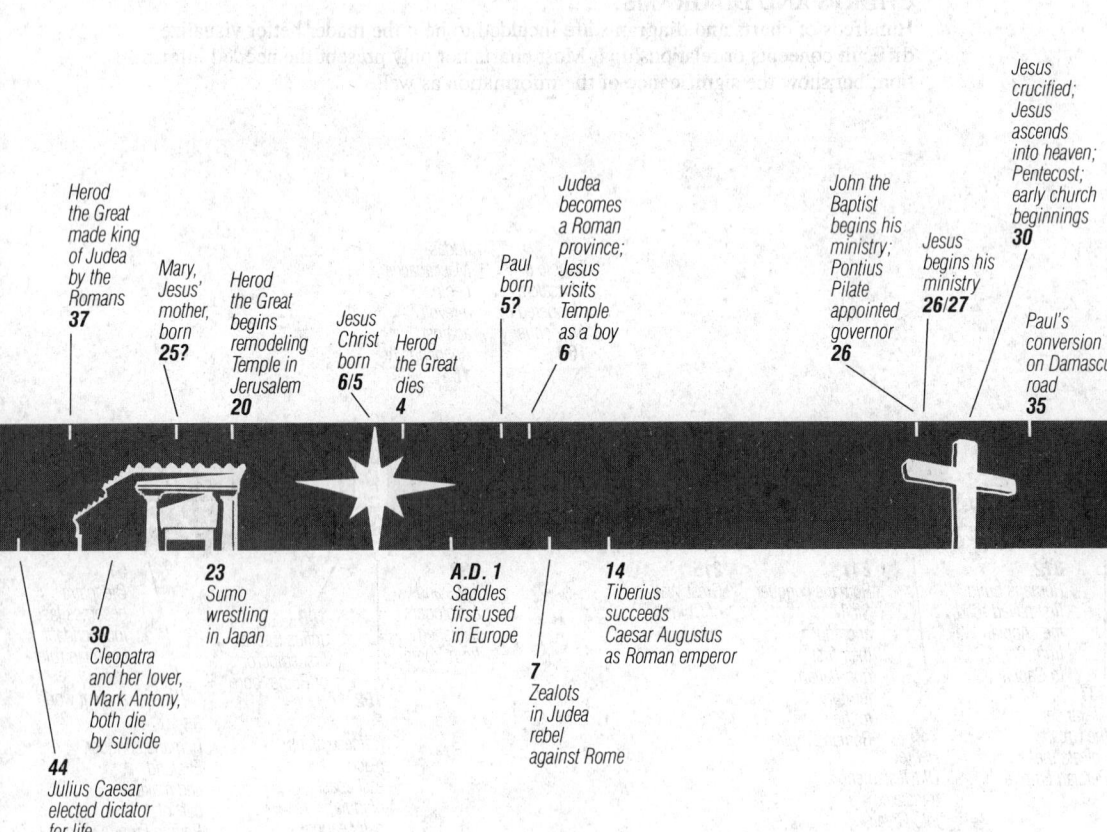

Herod the Great made king of Judea by the Romans **37**

Mary, Jesus' mother, born **25?**

Herod the Great begins remodeling Temple in Jerusalem **20**

Jesus Christ born **6/5**

Herod the Great dies **4**

Paul born **5?**

Judea becomes a Roman province; Jesus visits Temple as a boy **6**

John the Baptist begins his ministry; Pontius Pilate appointed governor **26**

Jesus begins his ministry **26/27**

Jesus crucified; Jesus ascends into heaven; Pentecost; early church beginnings **30**

Paul's conversion on Damascus road **35**

30 Cleopatra and her lover, Mark Antony, both die by suicide

23 Sumo wrestling in Japan

A.D. 1 Saddles first used in Europe

14 Tiberius succeeds Caesar Augustus as Roman emperor

7 Zealots in Judea rebel against Rome

44 Julius Caesar elected dictator for life, then assasinated that same year

Paul
writes
Romans;
Paul
imprisoned
in Caesarea
57

Paul
writes
"prison
epistles"
60

960 Jews
commit
mass
suicide
at Masada
while under
Roman
attack
73

Paul's
voyage
to Rome
59

Paul
released
from
prison
62

Romans
destroy
Jerusalem
70

Herod
Agrippa
appointed
king of
Judea
40

Paul
begins
first
missionary
journey
46

Paul
martyred
67?

Apostle
John
writes
Revelation
95

43
London
founded;
first definite
reference
to diamonds

50
Romans
begin
using
soap

54
Emperor
Claudius
poisoned
by order
of his wife;
Nero
becomes
emperor

66
Painting
on canvas

74
China opens
silk trade
with the west

79
Mt. Vesuvius
in Italy erupts,
killing 30,000 people
and burying cities
of Pompeii and
Herculaneum

64
Fire burns
much of Rome.
Nero blames
Christians
for setting it

68
Romans destroy
a Jewish
religious commune
of the Essene sect.
Before the Essenes
were captured
they hid their library
of Bible manuscripts
in a cave in Qumram
by the Dead Sea
(discovered in 1948).

75
Rome begins
construction of
famous Colosseum

THE OLD TESTAMENT

GENESIS

VITAL STATISTICS

PURPOSE:
To record God's creation of the world and his desire to have a people set apart to worship him

AUTHOR:
Moses

TO WHOM WRITTEN:
The people of Israel

DATE WRITTEN:
1450–1410 B.C.

SETTING:
The region presently known as the Middle East

KEY VERSES:
"So God made man like his Maker. Like God did God make man; man and maid did he make them" (1:27). "God had told Abram, . . . I will cause you to become the father of a great nation; I will bless you and make your name famous, and you will be a blessing to many others" (12:2, 3).

KEY PEOPLE:
Adam, Eve, Noah, Abraham, Sarah, Isaac, Rebekah, Jacob, Joseph

BEGIN . . . start . . . commence . . . open. . . . There's something refreshing and optimistic about these words, whether they refer to the dawn of a new day, the birth of a child, the prelude of a symphony, or the first miles of a family vacation. Free of problems and full of promise, beginnings stir hope and imaginative visions of the future. Genesis means "beginnings" or "origin," and it unfolds the record of the beginning of the world, of human history, of family, of civilization, of salvation. It is the story of God's purpose and plan for his creation. As the book of beginnings, Genesis sets the stage for the entire Bible. It reveals the person and nature of God (Creator, Sustainer, Judge, Redeemer); the value and dignity of human beings (made in God's image, saved by grace, used by God in the world); the tragedy and consequences of sin (the fall, separation from God, judgment); and the promise and assurance of salvation (covenant, forgiveness, promised Messiah). Read Genesis and be encouraged. There is hope! No matter how dark the world situation seems, God has a plan. No matter how insignificant or useless you feel, God loves you and wants to use you in his plan. No matter how sinful and separated from God you are, his salvation is available. Read Genesis . . . and hope!

God. That's where Genesis begins. All at once we see him creating the world in a majestic display of power and purpose, culminating with a man and woman made like himself (1:26, 27). But before long sin entered the world and Satan was unmasked. Bathed in innocence, creation was shattered by the fall (the willful disobedience of Adam and Eve). Fellowship with God was broken, and evil began weaving its destructive web. In rapid succession, we read how Adam and Eve were expelled from the beautiful garden, their first son turned murderer, and evil bred evil until God finally destroyed everyone on earth except a small family led by Noah, the only godly person left.

As we come to Abraham on the plains of Canaan, we discover the beginning of God's covenant people and the broad strokes of his salvation plan: salvation comes by faith, Abraham's descendants will be God's people, and the Savior of the world will come through this chosen nation. The stories of Isaac, Jacob, and Joseph which follow are more than interesting biographies. They emphasize the promises of God and the proof that he is faithful. The people we meet in Genesis are simple ordinary people, yet through them, God did great things. These are vivid pictures of how God can and does use all kinds of people to accomplish his good purposes . . . even people like you and me.

THE BLUEPRINT

A. THE STORY OF CREATION (1:1—2:3)

Because God created people, we have dignity and worth.

B. THE STORY OF ADAM (2:4—5:32)
1. Adam and Eve
2. Cain and Abel
3. Adam's descendants

Through Adam and Eve we learn about the destructive power of sin and its bitter consequences.

C. THE STORY OF NOAH (6:1—11:32)
1. The great flood
2. Repopulating the earth
3. The tower of Babel

Just as God protected Noah and his family, he protects those who are faithful to him today.

Pride is making ourselves more important than God.

D. THE STORY OF ABRAHAM (12:1—25:18)
1. God promises a nation to Abraham
2. Abraham and Lot
3. God promises a son to Abraham
4. Sodom and Gomorrah
5. Birth and near sacrifice of Isaac
6. Isaac marries Rebekah
7. Abraham dies

Through sharp testing, Abraham remained faithful to God. Abraham's example teaches us how to live a life of faith.

We are to trust God completely, even when it hurts.

E. THE STORY OF ISAAC (25:19—28:9)
1. Jacob and Esau, Isaac's twin sons
2. Isaac and King Abimelech
3. Isaac blesses Jacob instead of Esau

Isaac did not resist when he was about to be sacrificed, and he gladly accepted a wife chosen for him by others. We must put God's will ahead of our own as Isaac did.

F. THE STORY OF JACOB (28:10—36:43)
1. Jacob starts a family
2. Jacob returns home

Although Jacob made many mistakes, his hard work teaches us about living a life of service for our Lord.

God is in the business of changing lives, despite our inadequacies.

G. THE STORY OF JOSEPH (37:1—50:26)
1. Joseph is sold into slavery
2. Judah and Tamar (a parenthesis)
3. Joseph is thrown into jail
4. Joseph is placed in charge of Egypt
5. Joseph and his brothers meet in Egypt
6. Jacob's family moves to Egypt
7. Jacob and Joseph die in Egypt

Through Joseph, we learn that suffering, no matter how unfair, can develop in us a strong character.

God can turn even our greatest defeats into victory.

MEGATHEMES

THEME	EXPLANATION	IMPORTANCE
Beginnings	Genesis explains how many important realities began: the universe, earth, people, sin, and God's plan of salvation.	Genesis teaches us that the earth is well made and good. Mankind is special to God and unique. God creates and sustains all life.
Disobedience	People are always facing great choices. Disobedience occurs when people choose not to follow God's plan of living.	Genesis explains why men are evil: they choose to do wrong. Even great Bible heroes failed God and disobeyed.
Sin	Sin ruins people's lives. It happens when we disobey God.	Living God's way makes life productive and fulfilling.
Promises	God makes promises to help and protect mankind. This kind of promise is called a "covenant."	God kept his promises then, and he keeps them now. He promises to love us, accept us, forgive us.
Obedience	The opposite of sin is obedience. Obeying God restores our relationship to him.	The only way to enjoy the benefits of God's promises is to obey him.

Prosperity	Prosperity is deeper than mere material wealth. True prosperity and fulfillment come as a result of obeying God.	When people obey God, they find peace with him, with others, and with themselves.
Israel	God started the nation of Israel in order to have a dedicated people who would (1) keep his ways alive in the world, (2) proclaim to the world what he is really like, and (3) prepare the world for the birth of Christ.	God is looking for people today to follow him. We are to proclaim God's truth and love to all nations, not just our own.

KEY PLACES IN GENESIS

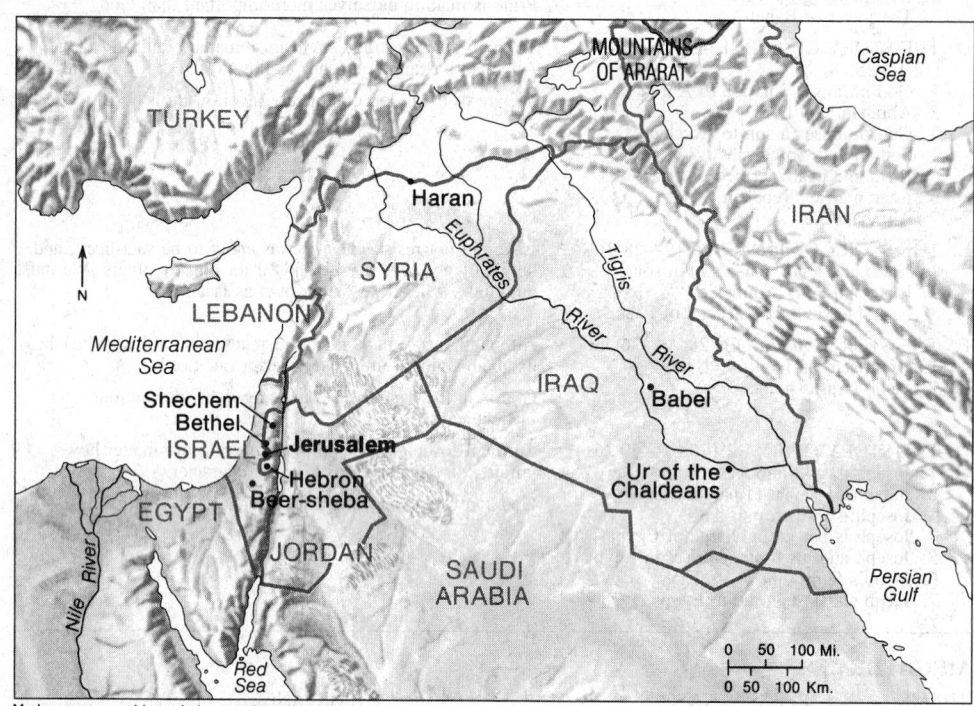

Modern names and boundaries are shown in gray.

God created the universe and the earth. Then he made man and woman, giving them a home in a beautiful garden. Unfortunately, Adam and Eve disobeyed God and were expelled from the garden (3:24).

1 Mountains of Ararat Adam and Eve's sin brought sin into the human race. Years later, sin had run rampant and God decided to destroy the earth with a great flood. But Noah, his family, and two of each animal were safe in a huge boat. When the floods receded, the boat rested on the Mountains of Ararat (8:4).

2 Babel People never learn. Again sin abounded and the pride of the people led them to build a huge tower as a monument to their own greatness—obviously they had no thought of God. As punishment, God scattered the people by giving them different languages (11:8, 9).

3 Ur of the Chaldeans Abram, a descendant of Shem, was born in this great city (11:27).

4 Haran Terah, Lot, Abram, and Sarai left Ur and, following the fertile crescent of the Euphrates River, headed toward the land of Canaan. Along the way, they settled in the city of Haran for a while (11:31).

5 Shechem God urged Abram to leave Haran and go to a place where he would become the father of a great nation (12:1, 2). So Abram, Lot, and Sarai traveled to the land of Canaan and settled near a city called Shechem (12:6).

6 Hebron Abraham moved on to Hebron, by the "oaks at Moreh," where he put down his deepest roots. Abraham, Isaac, and Jacob all lived and were buried there.

7 Beer-sheba A well was dug here as a sign of an oath between Abraham and the army of King Abimelech (21:31). Years later, as Isaac was moving from place to place, God appeared to him here and passed on to him the covenant he had made with his father, Abraham (26:23–25).

8 Bethel   After deceiving his brother out of both his birthright and his blessing, Jacob left Beer-sheba and fled to Haran to find a wife. Along the way God revealed himself to Jacob in a dream and again passed on the covenant he had made with Abraham and Isaac (28:10–22). Jacob lived in Haran, worked for Laban and married Leah and Rachel (29:15–28). After a tense meeting with his brother Esau, Jacob returned to Bethel.

9 Egypt   Jacob had 12 sons, including Joseph, Jacob's favorite. The other brothers grew jealous, until one day, out in the fields, the brothers sold him to Ishmaelite traders who were going to Egypt. Eventually, Joseph rose from Egyptian slave to Pharaoh's "right hand man," saving Egypt and the surrounding country from famine. His entire family moved from Canaan to Egypt and settled there during the severe famine.

A. THE STORY OF CREATION (1:1—2:3)

We sometimes wonder how our world came to be. But here we find the answer. God created the earth and everything in it, and made man like himself. Although we may not understand the complexity of just how he did it, it is clear that God did create all life. This shows not only God's authority over humanity, but his deep love for all people.

1:1
Ps 33:6; 89:11
Isa 42:5; 48:13
Jn 1:1-3
1:2
Job 26:13
Ps 104:30
1:3
Ps 33:9; 104:2
2 Cor 4:6
1:4,5
Ps 74:16

1 When God began creating the heavens and the earth, 2the earth was a shapeless, chaotic mass, with the Spirit of God brooding over the dark vapors. 3Then God said, "Let there be light." And light appeared. 4, 5And God was pleased with it, and divided the light from the darkness. He called the light "daytime," and the darkness "nighttime." Together they formed the first day.

6And God said, "Let the vapors separate to form the sky above and the oceans below." 7, 8So God made the sky, dividing the vapor above from the water below. This all happened on the second day.

1:1 *When God began creating,* or, "In the beginning God created . . ." **1:2** *The earth was,* or, "The earth became . . ." a shapeless, chaotic mass, or, "shapeless and void." *over the dark vapors,* or, "over the cloud of darkness," or, "over the darkness and waters," or even, "over the dark gaseous mass." There is no "right" way to translate these words. **1:4, 5** *Together they formed the first day,* literally, "And there was evening and there was morning, one day (or, 'period of time')." **1:6** *Let the vapors separate,* literally, "Let there be a dome to divide the waters." **1:7, 8** *This all happened on the second day,* literally, "There was evening and there was morning, a second day (or, 'period of time')."

1:1   The simple statement that God created the heavens and the earth is one of the most challenging concepts confronting the modern mind. The vast galaxy we live in is spinning at the incredible speed of 490,000 miles an hour.

But even at this breakneck speed, our galaxy still needs 200 million years to make one rotation. And there are over one billion other galaxies just like ours.

Some scientists say that the number of stars in creation is equal to all the grains of all the sands on all the beaches of the world. Yet this complex sea of spinning stars functions with remarkable order and efficiency. To say that the universe "just happened" or "evolved" requires more faith than to believe that God is behind these amazing statistics. God did create a wonderful universe.

God did not *need* to create the universe; he *chose* to create it. Why? God is love, and love is best expressed toward something or someone else—so God created the world and people as an expression of his love. We should avoid reducing God's creation to only scientific terms while forgetting that God created the universe because he loved us.

1:1ff   The creation story teaches us much about God and ourselves. First, we learn about God: (1) he is creative; (2) as the Creator he is distinct from his creation; (3) he is eternal and in control of the world. We also learn about ourselves: (1) since God chose to create us, we are valuable in his eyes; (2) we are given a place above the animals.

1:1ff   Did God create the world? If so, just how did he do it? This is still a subject of great debate. Some say there was a sudden explosion and the universe appeared. Others say God got it all started and the rest evolved over billions of years. Almost every ancient religion has its own story to explain how the world came to be. And almost every scientist has an opinion on the origin of the universe. But only the Bible shows one supreme God creating the earth out of his great love and giving all people a special place in it.

We will never know all the answers to how God created the world. But the Bible tells us that God did create it. That fact alone brings worth and dignity to all people.

1:2   Who created God? To ask that question, we have to assume there was another creator before God. At some time, however, we are forced to stop asking that question and realize that there had to be a Being who has always existed.

God is that infinite Being who has always been and who was created by no one. This is difficult to understand, for finite minds cannot comprehend what is infinite. For example, what is the highest number? It doesn't even exist and there is no point in trying to discover it. Likewise, we must stop thinking of the infinite God in finite terms.

1:2   The statement "the earth was a shapeless, chaotic mass" can also be translated "the earth was formless and void." This statement provides the setting for the creation narrative that follows. During the second and third days of creation, God gave *form* to the universe; during the next three days, God *filled* the earth with living beings. And the light that was created on the first day dispelled the darkness.

1:2   The image of the Spirit of God brooding over the dark vapors (or, over the surface of the deep waters) likens God's Spirit to a bird caring for and protecting its young (see Deuteronomy 32:11; Isaiah 31:5). God's Spirit was actively involved in the creation of the world (see Job 33:4; Psalm 104:30).

1:3—2:7   How long did it take God to create the world? There are two basic views about the days of creation: (1) each day was a literal 24-hour period; (2) each day represents an indefinite period of time (even millions of years).

The Bible does not mention which theory is true. But the real question is not how long God took, but how he did it. God created the world in an orderly fashion (he did not make plants before light); and he created men and women as unique beings capable of communication with him. No other part of creation can claim that remarkable privilege. The important point is not how long it took God to create the world—a few days or a few billion years. The point, Scripture says, is that he created it just the way he wanted.

9, 10Then God said, "Let the water beneath the sky be gathered into oceans so that the dry land will emerge." And so it was. Then God named the dry land "earth," and the water "seas." And God was pleased. 11, 12And he said, "Let the earth burst forth with every sort of grass and seed-bearing plant, and fruit trees with seeds inside the fruit, so that these seeds will produce the kinds of plants and fruits they came from." And so it was, and God was pleased. 13This all occurred on the third day.

14, 15Then God said, "Let bright lights appear in the sky to give light to the earth and to identify the day and the night; they shall bring about the seasons on the earth, and mark the days and years." And so it was. 16For God had made two huge lights, the sun and moon, to shine down upon the earth—the larger one, the sun, to preside over the day and the smaller one, the moon, to preside through the night; he had also made the stars. 17And God set them in the sky to light the earth, 18and to preside over the day and night, and to divide the light from the darkness. And God was pleased. 19This all happened on the fourth day.

20Then God said, "Let the waters teem with fish and other life, and let the skies be filled with birds of every kind." 21, 22So God created great sea animals, and every sort of fish and every kind of bird. And God looked at them with pleasure, and blessed them all. "Multiply and stock the oceans," he told them, and to the birds he said, "Let your numbers increase. Fill the earth!" 23That ended the fifth day.

24And God said, "Let the earth bring forth every kind of animal—cattle and reptiles and wildlife of every kind." And so it was. 25God made all sorts of wild animals and cattle and reptiles. And God was pleased with what he had done.

26Then God said, "Let us make a man—someone like ourselves, to be the master of all life upon the earth and in the skies and in the seas."

1:9
Job 26:7
Ps 24:1-2; 95:5
Prov 8:9
Jer 5:22
2 Pet 3:5

1:10
Gen 1:4
Gen 1:12

1:14,15
Gen 8:22
Deut 4:19
Ps 74:16; 104:19

1:16
Ps 8:3; 19:1-6
Ps 136:7-9
1 Cor 15:41
Rev 21:23

1:18
Jer 31:35

1:20
Gen 8:17
Ps 104:24,25
Ps 148:7

1:21,22
Gen 6:20
8:17,19; 35:11
Lev 26:9

1:25
Gen 2:19,20
Job 12:7-9
Jer 27:5

1:26
Gen 5:1; 9:6
Ps 8:6-8
Eph 4:24
Col 3:10
Jas 3:9

1:13 *This all occurred on the third day,* literally, "And there was evening and there was morning, a third day (or, 'period of time')."   **1:19** *This all happened on the fourth day,* literally, "And there was evening and there was morning, a fourth day (or, 'period of time')."   **1:23** *That ended the fifth day,* literally, "And there was evening and there was morning, a fifth day (or, 'period of time')."   **1:26** *a man,* literally, "men." *someone like ourselves,* literally, "Let us make man in our image, in our likeness."

The Bible does not discuss the subject of evolution. Rather, its world view assumes God created the world. The biblical view of creation is not in conflict with science or with various evolutionary theories; it is in conflict with any world view that starts with no creator.

BEGINNINGS

Equally committed and sincere Christians have struggled with the subject of beginnings and come to differing conclusions. This, of course, is to be expected since the evidence is very old and, due to the ravages of the ages, quite fragmented. Students of the Bible and of science should avoid polarizations and black/white thinking. Students of the Bible must be careful not to make the Bible say things it doesn't say, and students of science must not make science say things it doesn't say.

The most important aspect of the continuing discussion is not the *process* of creation, but the *origin* of creation. The world is not a product of blind chance and probability; God created it.

The Bible not only tells us that the world was created by God; more important, it tells us who this God is. It reveals God's personality, his character, and his plan for his creation. It also reveals God's deepest desire: to relate to and fellowship with the people he created. God took the ultimate step toward fellowship with us through his historic visit to this planet in the person of his Son, Jesus Christ. We can know this God who created the universe in a very personal way.

The heavens and the earth are here. We are here. God created all that we see and experience. The book of Genesis begins, "God began creating the heavens and the earth."

Here we begin the most exciting and fulfilling journey imaginable.

1:25 The fact that "God was pleased" indicates his capacity for pleasure. People sometimes feel guilty for having a good time or for feeling good about an accomplishment. This need not be so. Just as God was pleased with his work, we can be pleased with ours. However, we cannot be pleased with our work if God would not be pleased with it. What are you doing that makes both you *and* God happy?

1:26 Why does God use the plural form when he says, "Let *us* make man . . . like *ourselves*"? One view says this is a reference to the Trinity—God, the Father; Jesus Christ, his Son; and the Holy Spirit—all of whom are God. It is difficult to prove (and understand) the existence of the Trinity in Genesis. But see John 14:26 where God, Jesus, and the Holy Spirit are all represented in one verse. Another view states that the plural wording is used to denote

1:27
Mt 19:4
1 Cor 11:8,9

27So God made man like his Maker.
Like God did God make man;
Man and maid did he make them.

1:29
Gen 9:3
Ps 115:16
Ps 136:25;
145:15
1:30
Ps 104:14
1:31
Ps 19:1; 104:24

28And God blessed them and told them, "Multiply and fill the earth and subdue it; you are masters of the fish and birds and all the animals. 29And look! I have given you the seed-bearing plants throughout the earth, and all the fruit trees for your food. 30And I've given all the grass and plants to the animals and birds for their food." 31Then God looked over all that he had made, and it was excellent in every way. This ended the sixth day.

2:1
Ps 136:5-9
Isa 42:5
2:2
Ex 31:17
Heb 4:4

2 Now at last the heavens and earth were successfully completed, with all that they contained. 2So on the seventh day, having finished his task, God ceased from this work he had been doing, 3and God blessed the seventh day and declared it holy, because it was the day when he ceased this work of creation.

B. THE STORY OF ADAM (2:4—5:32)

Learning about our ancestors often helps us understand ourselves. Adam and Eve, our first ancestors, were the highlight of God's creation—the very reason God made the world. But they didn't always live the way God intended. Through their mistakes, we can learn important lessons on how to live rightly. Adam and Eve teach us much about the nature of sin and its consequences.

1. Adam and Eve

2:4
Gen 1:3-31; 5:1;
6:9
Gen 10:1

4Here is a summary of the events in the creation of the heavens and earth when the Lord God made them.

5There were no plants or grain sprouting up across the earth at first, for the Lord

1:31 *This ended the sixth day*, literally, "And there was evening and there was morning, a sixth day (or, 'period of time')."

DAYS OF CREATION		
First Day	Light (so there was light and darkness)	
Second Day	Sky and water (vapors separated)	
Third Day	Sea and earth (waters gathered)	
Fourth Day	Sun, moon, and stars (to preside over day and night, to bring about the seasons, and mark days and years)	
Fifth Day	Fish and birds (to fill the waters and the sky)	
Sixth Day	Animals (to fill the earth) Man and woman (to care for the earth and commune with God)	
Seventh Day	God rested and was pleased	

majesty—today many kings still use the plural form in speaking of themselves.

1:26 How are we made like God? The phrase "Let us make man . . . like ourselves" does not mean that God created us exactly like himself, especially in a physical sense. Instead, we are reflections of God's glory. God is sinless, eternal, and unlimited. Although we are given the potential to be sinless and eternal, we are also given the choice to fall short. We will never be totally like God, because he is our supreme Creator. Our best hope is to reflect his character in our love, patience, forgiveness, kindness, and faithfulness.

We are made like God and therefore share many of his characteristics and emotions. Knowing this provides the basis for self-worth. Self-worth is not defined by possessions, achievements, physical attractiveness, or public acclaim. Self-worth is knowing that God created us in his likeness. Criticizing or downgrading ourselves is criticizing what God has made. Because we are like God we can feel positive about ourselves and our abilities. Knowing that you are a person of infinite worth gives you the freedom to love God, know him personally, and make a valuable contribution to those around you.

1:27 God made both man and woman in his image. Neither man nor woman is made more in the image of God than the other. From the beginning we see the Bible placing both men and women at the pinnacle of God's creation. Neither is depreciated.

1:28 God worked like a master craftsman in creating the earth. Now he watches over his creation like a loving master. Just as God "masters" the earth with his loving care, we too are to "master" it. God's charge to man to subdue the earth implies responsibility to the environment and to the other creatures that share our planet. God was careful how he made this earth. We must not be careless about how we take care of it.

1:31 God was pleased with all he created, for it was excellent in every way. You are part of God's creation,and he is pleased with how he made you. At times you may feel worthless or of little value. Remember that God made you for a good reason. You are valuable to him.

2:2, 3 We live in a world that is action-oriented! Yet God demonstrated that rest is appropriate and right. If God himself rested from his work, then it should not amaze us that we need rest as well. Jesus demonstrated this principle in the New Testament when he and the disciples left in a boat to get away from the press of the crowd (see Mark 6:31, 32). Our times of rest refresh us for times of service.

God hadn't sent any rain; nor was there anyone to farm the soil. 6(However, water welled up from the ground at certain places and flowed across the land.)

7The time came when the Lord God formed a man's body from the dust of the ground and breathed into it the breath of life. And man became a living person.

The Garden of Eden

8Then the Lord God planted a garden in Eden, to the east, and placed in the garden the man he had formed. 9The Lord God planted all sorts of beautiful trees there in the garden, trees producing the choicest of fruit. At the center of the garden he placed the Tree of Life, and also the Tree of Conscience, giving knowledge of Good and Bad. 10A river from the land of Eden flowed through the garden to water it; afterwards the river divided into four branches. 11, 12One of these was named the Pishon; it winds across the entire length of the land of Havilah, where nuggets of pure gold are found, also beautiful bdellium and even lapis lazuli. 13The second branch is called the Gihon, crossing the entire length of the land of Cush. 14The third branch is the Tigris, which flows to the east of the city of Asher. And the fourth is the Euphrates.

15The Lord God placed the man in the Garden of Eden as its gardener, to tend and care for it. 16, 17But the Lord God gave the man this warning: "You may eat any fruit in the garden except fruit from the Tree of Conscience—for its fruit will open your eyes to make you aware of right and wrong, good and bad. If you eat its fruit, you will be doomed to die."

Eve is created

18And the Lord God said, "It isn't good for man to be alone; I will make a companion for him, a helper suited to his needs." 19, 20So the Lord God formed from the soil every kind of animal and bird, and brought them to the man to see what he would call them; and whatever he called them, that was their name. But still there was no proper helper for the man. 21Then the Lord God caused the man to fall into a deep sleep, and took one of his ribs and closed up the place from which

2:7 from the dust of the ground, or, "from a lump of soil," or, "from clods in the soil," or, "from a clod of clay."

Cross-references:

2:7
Gen 3:19,23
Job 33:4
Ps 103:14
Ezek 37:5
Jn 20:22

2:8
Gen 3:23; 13:10
Isa 51:3
Ezek 28:13
Joel 2:3

2:9
Gen 3:22
Ezek 47:12
Rev 2:7
22:2,14

2:10
Rev 22:1,17

2:14
Gen 15:18
Deut 1:7
Dan 10:4

2:16
Deut 30:15,19
2:17
Gen 3:1,16,17
Rom 5:2; 6:23
Jas 1:15

2:18
Gen 3:12
Prov 18:22

2:19
Gen 1:20-25
6:20

2:7 "From the dust of the ground" implies that there is nothing specially good about the chemical elements from which we are made. Water, dirt, a little protein—there is really not much to our physical bodies. The body is a lifeless shell until God brings it alive with his "breath of life." When God removes his life-giving breath, our bodies once again return to dust. Therefore, man's life and worth come from God's Spirit. This graphically portrays our need for God. Many boast of their significant achievements, only to fail soon after. Others have no achievements to boast about. But the reality is that life and worth come from the God of the universe, and he chose to give you that mysterious and miraculous gift. Value it, as he does.

2:8-14 The Garden of Eden was a showcase of the magnificent beauty God intended for his creation. Eden was no accident. It was a place to be fully enjoyed.

2:9 Other translations call the "Tree of Conscience" the "Tree of the Knowledge of Good and Evil." The name of this tree implies that evil had already occurred, if not in the garden, then at the time of Satan's fall.

2:9, 16, 17 Were the Tree of Life and the Tree of Conscience real trees? Two different views are often expressed:
(1) The trees were real, but symbolic. Eternal life with God was symbolized by eating from the Tree of Life.
(2) The trees were real, possessing special properties. By eating the fruit from the Tree of Life, Adam and Eve could have had eternal life, enjoying a permanent relationship as children of God.
In either case, Adam and Eve's sin separated them from the Tree of Life and thus kept them from obtaining eternal life. Interestingly, the Tree of Life again appears in Revelation 22 where people will enjoy eternal life with God.

2:15-17 God gave Adam responsibility for the garden and told him not to eat from the Tree of Conscience. Rather than physically preventing him from eating, God gave Adam a choice, even though Adam might choose wrongly. God still gives us choices today, and we, too, often choose wrongly. These wrong choices may cause us pain and irritation, but they can help us learn and grow and make better choices in the future. Living with the consequences of our choices is one of the best ways to become more responsible.

2:16, 17 Why would God place a tree in the garden and then forbid Adam to eat from it? God wanted Adam to obey, but he gave him the freedom to choose. Without choice, Adam would have been a prisoner forced to obey. The two trees presented an exercise in choice, with rewards for choosing to obey or consequences for choosing to disobey.

2:18-24 God's creative work was not complete until he made woman. He could have made her from the dust of the ground, as he made man. He chose, however, to make her from the man's bone and flesh. In so doing, he illustrated for us that in marriage man and woman symbolically become one flesh. This is a mystical union of the couple's hearts and lives. Throughout the Bible, God treats this special union seriously. If you are married or planning to be married, are you willing to keep the commitment which, in fact, makes the two of you one? The goal in marriage should be more than friendship; it should be oneness.

2:21-23 God styles and equips men and women for various tasks, but all lead to the same goal—honoring God. Man gives life to woman; woman gives life to the world. Each role carries exclusive privileges that should eliminate any attitudes about an inferior or superior sex.

2:22
1 Cor 11:8
1 Tim 2:13
2:23
Gen 29:14
Eph 5:28-30
2:24
Mt 19:5
Eph 5:31

he had removed it, 22and made the rib into a woman, and brought her to the man.

23"This is it!" Adam exclaimed. "She is part of my own bone and flesh! Her name is 'woman' because she was taken out of a man." 24This explains why a man leaves his father and mother and is joined to his wife in such a way that the two become one person. 25Now although the man and his wife were both naked, neither of them was embarrassed or ashamed.

Adam and Eve sin

3:1
1 Chron 21:1
Ezek 28:12-17
Mt 4:3,6,9
Rev 12:9; 20:2
3:2,3
Gen 2:16
Ex 19:12

3 The serpent was the craftiest of all the creatures the Lord God had made. So the serpent came to the woman. "Really?" he asked. *"None* of the fruit in the garden? God says you mustn't eat *any* of it?"

2, 3"Of course we may eat it," the woman told him. "It's only the fruit from the tree at the *center* of the garden that we are not to eat. God says we mustn't eat it or even touch it, or we will die."

2:24 *the two become one person,* literally, "one flesh."

WHAT THE BIBLE SAYS ABOUT MARRIAGE

Genesis 2:18–24	Marriage is God's idea
Genesis 24:58–60	Commitment is essential to a successful marriage
Genesis 29:10, 11	Romance is important
Jeremiah 7:34	Marriage holds times of great joy
Malachi 2:14, 15	Marriage creates the best environment for raising children
Matthew 5:32	Unfaithfulness breaks the bond of trust, the foundation of all relationships
Matthew 19:6	Marriage is permanent
Romans 7:2, 3	Ideally, only death should dissolve marriage
Ephesians 5:21–33	Marriage is based on the principled practice of love, not on feelings
Ephesians 5:23, 32	Marriage is a living symbol of Christ and the church
Hebrews 13:4	Marriage is good and honorable

2:24 God gave marriage as a gift to Adam and Eve. They were perfectly created for each other. Marriage was not just for convenience, nor was it brought about by any culture. It was instituted by God and has three basic aspects: (1) the man "leaves" his father and mother and, in a public act, promises himself to his wife; (2) the man and woman are joined together by taking responsibility for each other's welfare and loving their mate above all others; (3) the two become "one person" or "one flesh" in the intimacy and commitment of sexual union which is reserved for marriage. Strong marriages today include all three of these aspects.

2:25 Have you ever noticed how a little child can run naked through a room full of strangers without embarrassment? He is not aware of his nakedness, just as Adam and Eve were not embarrassed in their innocence. But after Adam and Eve sinned, embarrassment, shame, and awkwardness followed—creating barriers between themselves and God. We often experience these same barriers in marriage. Ideally, a husband and wife should have no barriers, feeling no shame exposing themselves to each other or to God. Like Adam and Eve (3:7), we put on fig leaves (barriers) because we have areas we don't want our spouse (or God) to know about. Then we hide—just as Adam and Eve hid from God. In marriage, lack of spiritual, emotional, and intellectual intimacy usually precedes a breakdown of physical intimacy. In the same way, when we fail to expose our sins and secret thoughts to God, we shut down the lines of communication we have with him.

3:1 Disguised as a crafty serpent, Satan came to tempt Eve.

Satan at one time was an angelic being who rebelled against God and was thrown out of heaven. God makes it clear that Satan is a created being and thus has limitations. Although Satan is trying to tempt everyone away from God, he will not be the final victor—in Genesis 3:14, 15 God promises that Satan will be crushed.

3:1–6 Why does Satan tempt us? Temptation is Satan's invitation to give in to his kind of life and give up on God's kind of life. Satan tempted Eve and succeeded in getting her to sin. He's been busy getting people to sin ever since—he even tempted Jesus (Matthew 4:11).

How could Eve have resisted temptation? By following the same guidelines we can follow. First, we must realize that *being tempted* is not a sin. We have not sinned until we *give in* to the temptation. Then, to resist temptation, we must: (1) pray for strength to resist, (2) run (sometimes literally), and (3) say no when confronted with what we know is wrong. James 1:12 tells of the blessings and rewards for those who don't give in when tempted.

3:2–6 The serpent (Satan) tempted Eve by getting her to doubt God's goodness. He suggested that God was strict, stingy, and selfish for not wanting Eve to share his knowledge of good and evil. Satan made Eve forget all that God had given her and focus on the one thing she couldn't have. We fall into trouble, too, when we focus on the few things we don't have rather than on the countless things God has given us. The next time you are feeling sorry for yourself over what you don't have, consider all you do have and thank God.

⁴"That's a lie!" the serpent hissed. "You'll not die! ⁵God knows very well that the instant you eat it you will become like him, for your eyes will be opened—you will be able to distinguish good from evil!"

⁶The woman was convinced. How lovely and fresh looking it was! And it would make her so wise! So she ate some of the fruit and gave some to her husband, and he ate it too. ⁷And as they ate it, suddenly they became aware of their nakedness, and were embarrassed. So they strung fig leaves together to cover themselves around the hips.

⁸That evening they heard the sound of the Lord God walking in the garden; and they hid themselves among the trees. ⁹The Lord God called to Adam, "Why are you hiding?"

3:9 *Why are you hiding?*, or, "Where are you?"

3:4
Jn 8:44
2 Cor 2:11
11:3

3:5
Gen 2:17
3:22

3:6
2 Cor 11:3
1 Tim 2:14
Jas 1:14
1 Jn 2:16

3:8
Lev 26:12
Deut 23:14
Job 31:33

		SATAN'S PLAN
Doubt	Makes you question God's Word and his goodness	
Discouragement	Makes you look at your problems rather than at God	
Diversion	Makes the wrong things seem attractive so you will want them more than the right things	
Defeat	Makes you feel like a failure, so you don't even try	
Delay	Makes you put off doing something so it never gets done	

3:5 Adam and Eve got what they wanted: an intimate knowledge of both good and evil. But they got it in a distorted and painful way. Satan had twisted their thinking by telling them they could know the difference between good and evil by *doing* evil. We sometimes have the illusion that "freedom" is doing anything we want. God says true freedom comes from obedience and knowing what *not* to do. The restrictions he gives us are for our good, showing us how to avoid evil. We have the freedom to walk in front of a speeding car, but we don't need to be hit to realize it would be a foolish thing to do. Don't listen to Satan's temptations to experience evil in order to learn more about life.

3:5 Satan used a sincere motive to tempt Eve—'You will become like God!" To become more like God is the highest goal of humanity. It is what we are supposed to do. But Satan misled Eve on the right way to accomplish this goal. He told her that you become more like God by defying God's authority, by taking God's place and deciding for yourself what is best for your life. You become your own "god."

But Scripture clearly states that to become like God is not to be God himself. Rather, it is to reflect his characteristics and recognize his authority over your life. Like Eve, we often have a worthy goal but try to achieve it the wrong way. It's like paying off an election judge to be voted into office. Serving the people is no longer the highest goal.

The ultimate goal of self-exaltation is rebellion against God. As soon as we begin to leave God out of our plans, we are placing ourselves above him, which is exactly what Satan wants us to do.

3:6 Satan tried to show Eve that sin is "lovely." A knowledge of both good and evil seemed desirable and harmless to Eve. People usually choose wrong things because they have become convinced that those things are good, at least for themselves. Our sins do not always appear ugly to us, and the "lovely" sins are the hardest to avoid. So prepare yourself for the attractive temptations that may come your way. First Corinthians 10:13 says that although we cannot always prevent temptation, we can always resist.

3:6, 7 Notice what Eve did: she looked, then took, then ate, then gave. The battle is often lost at the first look. Temptation often begins by simply seeing something we want. Are you struggling with temptation because you have not learned that looking is the first step toward sin? We would win over temptation more often if we followed Paul's advice to run from those things that produce evil thoughts (2 Timothy 2:22).

3:6, 7 One of the realities of sin is that its effect spreads. After Eve sinned, she involved Adam in her wrongdoing. When we do something wrong, often our first relief from guilt comes by involving someone else. Like poison spilled in a river, sin swiftly spreads and becomes impossible to recapture. Recognize and confess your sin to God before you are tempted to pollute those around you.

3:7 Adam and Eve chose their course of action (disobedience), and now God chose his. As a holy God, he could respond only in a way that was consistent with his perfect moral nature. He could not allow sin to go unchecked; he had to punish it. If the consequences of Adam and Eve's sin seem extreme, remember that their sin set in motion the world's constant tendency toward disobeying God. That is why we sin today: every human being ever born has inherited the sinful nature of Adam and Eve (Romans 5:12–21). Adam and Eve's punishment (3:16-24) reflects how seriously God views sin of any kind.

3:7, 8 After sinning, Adam and Eve felt guilt and embarrassment over their nakedness. Their guilty feelings made them run from God and try to hide. Guilt (or a guilty conscience) is a warning signal God placed inside you that goes off when you've done wrong. The worst thing we could do is to eliminate the guilty feelings without eliminating the cause. That is like using a pain killer but not addressing the disease. Be glad those guilty feelings are there—they make you aware of your sin so you can ask God to forgive you and correct your wrongdoing.

3:8 After sinning, Adam and Eve tried to hide from God. The thought of two humans covered with fig leaves trying to hide from an all-seeing, all-knowing God is humorous. How could they be so silly as to think they could actually hide? Yet we do the same when we try to hide things from God. Share all you do and think with him and don't try to hide—it can't be done.

3:8 This verse shows God's desire for our fellowship. It also shows why we are afraid to have fellowship with him. Adam and Eve hid from God when they heard him approaching. God wanted to be with them, but because of their sin, Adam and Eve were afraid to show themselves to him. Sin had broken their fellowship with God. Sin has broken our fellowship with God as well. But through Jesus Christ, God's Son, the way has been opened for us to renew our fellowship with him. God longs to be with us. He is actively offering us his unconditional love. Our natural response is fear, for we know we can't live up to his standards. But recognizing that he loves us, regardless of our faults, can help remove that dread.

3:10
Job 23:15
1 Jn 3:20
3:11
Gen 4:10

¹⁰And Adam replied, "I heard you coming and didn't want you to see me naked. So I hid."

¹¹"Who told you you were naked?" the Lord God asked. "Have you eaten fruit from the tree I warned you about?"

ADAM

We can hardly imagine what it must have been like to be the first and only person on earth. It's one thing for us to be lonely; it was another for Adam, who had never known another human being. He missed much that makes us who we are—he had no childhood, no parents, no family or friends. He had to learn to be human on his own. Fortunately, God didn't let him struggle too long before presenting him with an ideal companion and mate, Eve. Theirs was a complete, innocent, and open oneness, without a hint of shame.

One of Adam's first conversations with his delightful new companion must have been about the rules of the garden. Before God made Eve he had already given Adam complete freedom in the garden, with the responsibility to tend and care for it. But one tree was off limits, the Tree of Conscience. Adam would have told Eve all about this. She knew, when Satan approached her, that the tree's fruit was not to be eaten. However, she decided to eat the forbidden fruit. Then she offered some to Adam. At that moment, the fate of creation was on the line. Sadly, Adam didn't pause to consider the consequences. He went ahead and ate.

In that moment of small rebellion something large, beautiful, and free was shattered . . . the perfect creation of God. Man was separated from God by his desire to act on his own. The effect on a plate glass window is the same whether a pebble or a boulder is hurled at it—the thousands of fragments can never be regathered.

In the case of man's sin, however, God already had a plan in motion to overcome the effects of the rebellion. The entire Bible is the story of how that plan unfolds, ultimately leading to God's own visit to earth through his Son, Jesus. His sinless life and death made it possible for God to offer forgiveness to all who want it. Our small and large acts of rebellion prove that we are descendants of Adam. Only by asking forgiveness of Jesus Christ can we become children of God.

Strengths and accomplishments:
- The first zoologist—namer of animals
- The first landscape architect, placed in the garden to tend and care for it
- Father of the human race
- The first person made in the image of God, and the first human to share an intimate personal relationship with God

Weaknesses and mistakes:
- Avoided responsibility and blamed others; chose to hide rather than to confront; made excuses rather than admitting the truth
- Greatest mistake: teamed up with Eve to bring sin into the world

Lessons from his life:
- As Adam's descendants, we all reflect to some degree the image of God
- God wants people who are free to do wrong to choose instead to love him
- We should not blame others for our own faults
- We cannot hide from God

Vital statistics:
- Where: Garden of Eden
- Occupation: Caretaker, gardener, farmer
- Relatives: Wife: Eve. Sons: Cain, Abel, Seth. Numerous other children. The only man who never had an earthly mother or father.

Key verses:
"But it was the woman you gave me who brought me some, and I ate it" (Genesis 3:12).
"Everyone dies because all of us are related to Adam, being members of his sinful race, and wherever there is sin, death results. But all who are related to Christ will rise again" (1 Corinthians 15:22).

Adam's story is told in Genesis 1:26—4:26. He is also mentioned in 1 Chronicles 1:1; Job 31:33; Luke 3:38; Romans 5:14; 1 Corinthians 15:22, 45; 1 Timothy 2:13, 14.

3:11-13 Adam and Eve failed to heed God's warning in 2:16, 17. God's command not to eat from the Tree of Conscience showed the essential nature of obedience to God. Most commands of God are obviously for our own good. But more important, the reason for obeying God is that he tells us to, and that must be reason enough.

¹²"Yes," Adam admitted, "but it was the woman you gave me who brought me some, and I ate it."

¹³Then the Lord God asked the woman, "How could you do such a thing?" "The serpent tricked me," she replied.

¹⁴So the Lord God said to the serpent, "This is your punishment: You are singled out from among all the domestic and wild animals of the whole earth—to be cursed. You shall grovel in the dust as long as you live, crawling along on your belly. ¹⁵From now on you and the woman will be enemies, as will your offspring and hers. You will strike his heel, but he will crush your head."

¹⁶Then God said to the woman, "You shall bear children in intense pain and suffering; yet even so, you shall welcome your husband's affections, and he shall be your master."

¹⁷And to Adam, God said, "Because you listened to your wife and ate the fruit when I told you not to, I have placed a curse upon the soil. All your life you will struggle to extract a living from it. ¹⁸It will grow thorns and thistles for you, and you shall eat its grasses. ¹⁹All your life you will sweat to master it, until your dying day. Then you will return to the ground from which you came. For you were made from the ground, and to the ground you will return."

²⁰The man named his wife Eve (meaning "The life-giving one"), for he said, "She shall become the mother of all mankind"; ²¹and the Lord God clothed Adam and his wife with garments made from skins of animals.

²²Then the Lord said, "Now that the man has become as we are, knowing good from bad, what if he eats the fruit of the Tree of Life and lives forever?" ²³So the Lord God banished him forever from the Garden of Eden, and sent him out to farm the ground from which he had been taken. ²⁴Thus God expelled him, and placed mighty angels at the east of the Garden of Eden, with a flaming sword to guard the entrance to the Tree of Life.

2. Cain and Abel
Cain kills Abel

4 Then Adam had sexual intercourse with Eve his wife, and she conceived and gave birth to a son, Cain (meaning "I have created"). For, as she said, "With God's help, I have created a man!" ²Her next child was his brother, Abel.

3:13
2 Cor 11:3
1 Tim 2:14

3:14
Deut 28:15
Isa 65:25

3:15
Jn 8:44
Acts 13:10
Rom 16:20
Gal 4:4
1 Jn 3:8-10
Rev 12:7

3:16
Gen 35:16
1 Cor 7:4; 11:3
Eph 5:22
Tit 2:5

3:17
Job 5:6,7
Rom 8:20-22

3:18
Heb 6:8

3:19
Gen 2:7
Ps 90:3; 104:29
Eccles 12:7
Rom 5:12
1 Cor 15:21,22

3:20
1 Tim 2:13

3:21
2 Cor 5:2,3

3:22
Jn 6:48

3:24
Rev 2:7; 22:2,14

4:2
Lk 11:50,51

3:12, 13 When God asked Adam about his sin, Adam blamed Eve. Then Eve blamed the serpent. How easy it is to excuse our sins by blaming someone else. We often fall into the trap of blaming others or circumstances for our personal failures. But God knows the truth! And he holds each of us responsible for what we do (see verses 14–19). Admit sin and apologize to God. Don't try to get away with sin by blaming someone else.

3:14-19 Adam and Eve learned by painful experience that since God is holy and hates sin, he must punish sinners. The rest of the book of Genesis recounts painful stories of lives ruined as a result of sin. Disobedience is sin and it breaks our fellowship with God. Fortunately, when we disobey, God can forgive us, restoring our relationship with him.

3:15 Satan is our enemy—he'll do anything he can to get us to follow his evil, deadly path. The phrase "You will strike at his heel" refers to Satan's repeated attempts to defeat Christ during his life on earth. "He shall strike you on your head" foreshadows Satan's defeat when Christ rose from the dead. A bruise on the heel is not deadly, but a strike on the head is. Already God was revealing his plan to defeat Satan and offer salvation to the world through his Son, Jesus Christ.

3:16-19 Adam and Eve's disobedience affected all of creation, including the environment. Years ago people thought nothing of polluting streams with chemical wastes and garbage. This seemed so insignificant, so small. Now we know that just two or three parts per million of certain chemicals can damage human health. Sin in our lives is strangely similar to toxic wastes. Even small amounts are deadly.

3:22-24 Life in the Garden of Eden was like living in heaven. Everything was perfect.

When God first placed Adam and Eve in the garden, he made it clear that complete obedience would be rewarded by immortal life (living forever in the paradise of Eden). But after disobeying, Adam and Eve no longer deserved to live there. So God told them to leave. If they had continued to live in the garden, and if they had eaten from the Tree of Life, they would have lived forever. But eternal life in a state of sin would mean forever trying to hide from God. Like Adam and Eve, all of us have sinned and are separated from fellowship with God. God is preparing a new earth as the place of eternal paradise for all his people (Revelation 22).

3:24 This is how Adam and Eve broke their relationship with God: (1) they became convinced their way was better than God's; (2) they became self-conscious and hid; (3) they tried to excuse and defend themselves. To build a relationship with God, we must reverse those steps, doing the opposite of Adam and Eve: (1) drop our excuses and self-defenses; (2) stop trying to hide from God; (3) become convinced that God's way is better than our way.

4:2 No longer was everything provided for Adam and Eve as in the Garden of Eden. Although they worked to care for the garden, their tasks were probably fun and delightful. But now Adam and his family had to struggle to fight the elements in order to grow their own food and spin wool for their clothes. Adam's oldest son, Cain, became a farmer, while Abel, the younger, was a shepherd.

4:3
Lev 2:1
Num 18:12
4:4
Ex 13:12
Lev 3:15,16
Heb 11:4
4:5
Mt 20:15
4:7
Lk 11:35
Rom 6:12
Jas 1:15

Abel became a shepherd, while Cain was a farmer. ³At harvest time Cain brought the Lord a gift of his farm produce, ⁴and Abel brought the fatty cuts of meat from his best lambs, and presented them to the Lord. And the Lord accepted Abel's offering, ⁵but not Cain's. This made Cain both dejected and very angry, and his face grew dark with fury.

⁶"Why are you angry?" the Lord asked him. "Why is your face so dark with rage? ⁷It can be bright with joy if you will do what you should! But if you refuse to obey, watch out. Sin is waiting to attack you, longing to destroy you. But you can conquer it!"

We know very little about Eve, the first woman in the world, yet she is the mother of us all. She was the final piece in the intricate and amazing puzzle of God's creation. Adam now had another human being with whom to fellowship—someone with an equal share in God's image. Here was someone alike enough for companionship, yet different enough for relationship. Together, they were greater than either could have been alone.

Eve was approached by Satan in the Garden of Eden, where she and Adam lived. He questioned her contentment. How could she be happy when she was not allowed to eat from one of the fruit trees? Satan helped Eve shift her focus from all that God had done and given to the one thing he had withheld. And Eve was willing to accept Satan's viewpoint without checking with God.

Sound familiar? How often is our attention drawn from the much which is ours to the little that isn't? We get that "I've got to have it" feeling. Eve was typical of us all—and we consistently show we are her descendants by repeating her mistakes. Our desires, like Eve's, can be quite easily manipulated. They are not the best basis for actions. We need to keep God in our decision-making process always. His Word, the Bible, is our guidebook in decision-making.

Strengths and accomplishments:
● First wife and mother
● First female. As such she shared a special relationship with God, had co-responsibility with Adam over creation, and displayed certain characteristics of God

Weaknesses and mistakes:
● Allowed her contentment to be undermined by Satan
● Acted impulsively without talking either to God or to her mate
● Not only sinned, but shared her sin with her mate
● When confronted, blamed others

Lessons from her life:
● The female shares in the image of God (1:27)
● The necessary ingredients for a strong marriage are commitment to each other, companionship with each other, complete oneness, absence of shame (2:24, 25)
● The basic human tendency to sin goes back to the beginning of the human race

Vital statistics:
● Where: Garden of Eden
● Occupation: Wife/helper/companion/co-manager of Eden
● Relatives: Husband: Adam. Sons: Cain, Abel, Seth. Numerous other children.

Key verse:
"And the Lord God said, 'It isn't good' for man to be alone; I will make a companion for him, a helper suited to his needs' " (Genesis 2:18).

Eve's story is told in Genesis 2:19—4:26. Her death is not mentioned in Scripture.

Farming and shepherding are the two oldest occupations on earth, and in the Middle East today their jobs have changed little over the centuries.

4:3, 4 We are not told why God rejected Cain's sacrifice. Perhaps Cain's attitude was improper, or perhaps his offering was not up to God's standards. God evaluates both our motives and the quality of what we offer him. When we give to God and others, we should have a joyful heart because of what we are able to give. When we give, we should not worry about how much we are giving up; for all things are God's in the first place. Instead, we should joyfully give

to God our best in time, money, possessions, and talents.

4:6, 7 How do you react when someone suggests you have done something wrong? Do you move to correct the mistake or deny that you need to correct it? After Cain's sacrifice was rejected, God gave him the chance to right his wrong and try again. God even encouraged him to do this! But Cain refused, and the rest of his life is a startling example of what happens to those who refuse to admit their mistakes. The next time someone suggests you are wrong, take an honest look at yourself and choose God's way instead of Cain's.

8One day Cain suggested to his brother, "Let's go out into the fields." And while they were together there, Cain attacked and killed his brother.

9But afterwards the Lord asked Cain, "Where is your brother? Where is Abel?" "How should I know?" Cain retorted. "Am I supposed to keep track of him wherever he goes?"

10But the Lord said, "Your brother's blood calls to me from the ground. What have you done? 11You are hereby banished from this ground which you have defiled with your brother's blood. 12No longer will it yield crops for you, even if you toil on it forever! From now on you will be a fugitive and a tramp upon the earth, wandering from place to place."

13Cain replied to the Lord, "My punishment is greater than I can bear. 14For you have banished me from my farm and from you, and made me a fugitive and a tramp; and everyone who sees me will try to kill me."

15The Lord replied, "They won't kill you, for I will give seven times your punishment to anyone who does." Then the Lord put an identifying mark on Cain as a warning not to kill him. 16So Cain went out from the presence of the Lord and settled in the land of Nod, east of Eden.

Cain's descendants

17Then Cain's wife conceived and presented him with a baby son named Enoch; so when Cain founded a city, he named it Enoch, after his son.

18Enoch was the father of Irad; Irad was the father of Mehujael; Mehujael was the father of Methusael; Methusael was the father of Lamech;

19Lamech married two wives—Adah and Zillah. 20To Adah was born a baby named Jabal. He became the first of the cattlemen and those living in tents. 21His brother's name was Jubal, the first musician—the inventor of the harp and flute. 22To Lamech's other wife, Zillah, was born Tubal-cain. He opened the first foundry forging instruments of bronze and iron.

23One day Lamech said to Adah and Zillah, "Listen to me, my wives. I have killed a youth who attacked and wounded me. 24If anyone who kills Cain will be punished seven times, anyone taking revenge against me for killing that youth should be punished seventy-seven times!"

3. Adam's descendants

25Later on Eve gave birth to another son and named him Seth (meaning "Granted"); for, as Eve put it, "God has granted me another son for the one Cain killed." 26When Seth grew up, he had a son and named him Enosh. It was during his lifetime that men first began to call themselves "the Lord's people."

4:18 or, "the ancestor of," and so also in the remainder of the verse. **4:21** *the inventor of,* literally, "He was the father of all such as handle the harp and pipe." **4:22** *He opened the first foundry,* literally, "He was the father of all metal workers in bronze and iron." **4:26** *men first began to call themselves "the Lord's people,"* literally, "This man was the first to invoke the name of Jehovah."

Cross-references (right margin):
4:8 Heb 12:24; 1 Jn 3:12
4:9 Ps 9:12; 10:13,14
4:10 Heb 12:24
4:11 Deut 27:15-26; Gal 3:10
4:12 Lev 26:20; Deut 28:15-24,
4:14 Gen 9:6; Job 15:22
4:15 Rev 14:9
4:16 2 Kgs 13:23; 24:20; Jer 23:39; 52:3
4:17 Ps 49:11
4:23 Lev 19:18; Deut 32:35
4:25 Gen 4:8; 5:3; 1 Chron 1:1; Lk 3:38
4:26 Gen 12:8

4:8-10 This is the first murder—taking a life by the shedding of human blood. Blood represents life (Leviticus 17:10–14). If blood is removed from a living person, he will die. Since God created life and gave it to man, only God should take life away.

4:8-10 Adam and Eve's disobedience brought sin into the human race. They may have thought their sin (eating a "harmless" piece of fruit) wasn't very bad, but notice how quickly their sinful nature developed in the lives of their children. Simple disobedience suddenly degenerated into outright murder. Adam and Eve acted only against God, but Cain acted against both God and man. A small sin has a way of growing out of control. Let God help you with your little sins before they turn into tragedies.

4:12-15 Cain was severely punished for this murder. God judges all sins and punishes appropriately, but not simply out of anger or vengeance. Rather, God's punishment is meant to correct us and restore our fellowship with him. When you're corrected, don't resent it, but renew your fellowship with God.

4:14 We have heard about only four people so far—Adam, Eve, Cain, and Abel. So two questions arise: (1) why was Cain worried about being killed by others, and (2) where did he get his wife?

Adam and Eve had numerous children—they had been told to "fill the earth" (1:28). Cain's guilt and fear over killing his brother were heavy, and he probably feared repercussions from his family. If he was capable of killing, so were they. The wife Cain chose may have been one of his sisters or a niece. The human race was still genetically pure and there was little fear of side effects from marrying relatives.

4:19-26 Unfortunately, when left to themselves, people tend to get worse instead of better. This short narrative about Lamech and his family shows us the variety of talent and ability God gives man. But it also presents the continuous development of sin as time passes. Another murder has occurred, presumably in self-defense. Violence is on the rise. Two distinct groups are now appearing: (1) those who show indifference to sin and evil, and (2) those who are called "people of God" (the descendants of Seth, 4:26). Seth will take Abel's place as leader of a line of God's faithful people.

5:1
Gen 1:26; 6:9
5:2
Gen 1:27
Mk 10:6
5:3
Gen 4:25
5:4
1 Chron 1:1
5:5
Gen 3:19
Heb 9:27
5:6
1 Chron 1:1
Lk 3:38
5:9
1 Chron 1:1
Lk 3:37
5:12
1 Chron 1:1
Lk 3:37

5 Here is a list of some of the descendants of Adam—the man who was like God from the day of his creation. ²God created man and woman and blessed them, and called them Man from the start.

3, 4, 5*Adam:* Adam was 130 years old when his son Seth was born, the very image of his father in every way. After Seth was born, Adam lived another 800 years, producing sons and daughters, and died at the age of 930.

6, 7, 8*Seth:* Seth was 105 years old when his son Enosh was born. Afterwards he lived another 807 years, producing sons and daughters, and died at the age of 912.

9, 10, 11*Enosh:* Enosh was ninety years old when his son Kenan was born. Afterwards he lived another 815 years, producing sons and daughters, and died at the age of 905.

12, 13, 14*Kenan:* Kenan was seventy years old when his son Mahalalel was born. Afterwards he lived another 840 years, producing sons and daughters, and died at the age of 910.

15, 16, 17*Mahalalel:* Mahalalel was sixty-five years old when his son Jared was

5:1 *Here is a list of some of the descendants of Adam,* literally, "This is the roll of Adam's descendants." *the man who was like God,* literally, "in the likeness of God."   **5:3-5** *when his son,* or, by Hebrew usage, "When his son, the ancestor (of Seth) was born." So also in verses 6, 9, 15, 18, 21, 25, 28, 32. *the very image of his father in every way,* literally, "In his own likeness, after his image." *After Seth was born,* or, by Hebrew usage, "After this ancestor of Seth was born."

ABEL

Abel was the second child born into the world, but the first one to obey God. All we know about this man is that his parents were Adam and Eve, he was a shepherd, he presented pleasing sacrifices to God, and his short life was ended at the hands of his jealous older brother, Cain.

The Bible doesn't tell us why God liked Abel's gift and disliked Cain's, but both Cain and Abel knew what God expected. Only Abel obeyed. Throughout history, Abel is remembered for his obedience and faith (Hebrews 11:4), and he is called "righteous" (Matthew 23:35).

The Bible is filled with God's general guidelines and expectations for our lives. It is also filled with more specific directions. Like Abel, we must obey regardless of the cost, and trust God to make things right.

Strengths and accomplishments:
• First member of the Hall of Faith in Hebrews 11:4
• First shepherd
• First martyr for truth (Matthew 23:35)

Lessons from his life:
• God hears those who come to him
• God recognizes the innocent person, and sooner or later judges the guilty

Vital statistics:
• Where: Just outside of Eden
• Occupation: Shepherd
• Relatives: Parents: Adam and Eve. Brother: Cain.

Key verse:
"God accepted Abel and proved it by accepting his gift; and though Abel is long dead, we can still learn lessons from him about trusting God" (Hebrews 11:4).

Abel's story is told in Genesis 4:1–8. He is also mentioned in Matthew 23:35; Luke 11:51; Hebrews 11:4 and 12:24.

5:1ff The Bible contains several lists of ancestors, called *genealogies.* There are two basic views concerning these lists: (1) they are complete, recording the entire history of a family, tribe, or nation; or (2) they are not intended to be exhaustive and may include only famous people or the heads of families. In the original Hebrew genealogies, the phrase "was the son of" can also mean "was the descendant of."

Why are genealogies included in the Bible? The Hebrews carried on their beliefs through oral tradition. Writing was still primitive and, in many places, nonexistent. Stories were told to children, who passed them on to their children. Genealogies gave a skeletal outline that helped people remember the stories. For centuries these genealogies were added to and passed down from family to family. Even more important than family tradition,

genealogies were included to confirm the Bible's promise that the coming Messiah, Jesus Christ, would be born into the line of Abraham.

Genealogies point out an interesting characteristic of God. People are important to him as individuals, not just as masses. Therefore God refers to people by name, mentioning their lifespan and descendants. The next time you feel overwhelmed in a vast crowd, remember that the focus of God's attention and love is on the individual.

5:3–5 In the most general sense, all human beings are related, going back to Adam and Eve. Actually, we are a family of mankind, sharing one flesh and blood. Remember this when prejudice enters your mind or hatred invades your feelings. Each person is a valuable and unique creation of God, just like you.

born. Afterwards he lived 830 years, producing sons and daughters, and died at the age of 895.

18, 19, 20*Jared:* Jared was 162 years old when his son Enoch was born. Afterwards he lived another 800 years, producing sons and daughters, and died at the age of 962.

21-24*Enoch:* Enoch was sixty-five years old when his son Methuselah was born. Afterwards he lived another 300 years in fellowship with God, and produced sons and daughters; then, when he was 365, and in constant touch with God, he disappeared, for God took him!

25, 26, 27*Methuselah:* Methuselah was 187 years old when his son Lamech was born; afterwards he lived another 782 years, producing sons and daughters, and died at the age of 969.

28-31*Lamech:* Lamech was 182 years old when his son Noah was born. Lamech named him Noah (meaning "Relief") because he said, "He will bring us relief from the hard work of farming this ground which God has cursed." Afterwards Lamech lived 595 years, producing sons and daughters, and died at the age of 777.

32*Noah:* Noah was 500 years old and had three sons, Shem, Ham, and Japheth.

5:18
1 Chron. 1:1
Lk 3:37
Jude 14

5:22
Gen 6:9; 24:20; 48:15
Heb 11:5
Jude 14

5:24
2 Kgs 2:11
Ps 49:5; 73:24

5:29
Gen 3:17; 8:21
Rom 8:20

5:32
Gen 7:6
Gen 9:18

C. THE STORY OF NOAH (6:1—11:32)

Earth was no longer the perfect paradise that God had intended. It is frightening to see how quickly all of humanity forgot about God. Incredibly, in all the world, only one man and his family still worshiped God. That man was Noah. Because of his faithfulness and obedience, God saved him and his family from a vast flood that destroyed every other human being on earth. This section shows us how God hates sin and judges those who enjoy it.

1. The great flood

6 Now a population explosion took place upon the earth. It was at this time that beings from the spirit world looked upon the beautiful earth women and took any they desired to be their wives. 3Then Jehovah said, "My Spirit must not forever be disgraced in man, wholly evil as he is. I will give him 120 years to mend his ways."

4In those days, and even afterwards, when the evil beings from the spirit world were sexually involved with human women, their children became giants, of whom so many legends are told. 5When the Lord God saw the extent of human wickedness, and that the trend and direction of men's lives were only towards evil, 6he was sorry he had made them. It broke his heart.

6:1
Gen 1:28
6:2
2 Pet 2:14
6:3
Ps 78:39
1 Pet 3:20

6:4
Num 13:33
6:5
Ps 14:2,3
6:6
Ex 32:14
Num 23:19

6:1, 2 *beings from the spirit world,* literally, "sons of God."

5:25–27 How did these people live for so long? Some believe that the ages listed were lengths of family dynasties rather than ages of individual men. Those who believe these were actual ages state three main possibilities. (1) The human race was genetically purer in this early time period so there was less disease to shorten the lifespan. (2) No rain had yet fallen on the earth and the "vapor above" (1:7, 8) kept out harmful cosmic rays. Thus, the environmental factors that cause aging were less pronounced. (3) God gave people longer lives so they would have time to "fill the earth" (1:28) and make a significant impact for God.

6:1–4 The "beings from the spirit world," more literally, "the sons of God," were probably not angels, because angels cannot marry or reproduce (Matthew 22:30; Mark 12:25). Some experts believe that this phrase refers to the sons of Seth (called "the Lord's people" in 4:26), but they were no longer godly. Therefore, these verses tell of intermarriage between Seth's godly descendants and Cain's evil descendants. This would have weakened the godly line and increased moral depravity in the world. The resulting population explosion brought an explosion of evil.

6:3 What patience God showed, allowing the people of Noah's day a great deal of time (120 years) to change their sinful ways. God demonstrates his great patience with us as well. He is giving

us time to quit living our way and begin living his way, the way he shows us in his Word. While 120 years may seem like a long time for God to wait, time did run out one day, and the flood waters swept across the earth. Your time also may be running out. Turn to God to forgive your sins. You can't see the stopwatch of God's patience, and there is no bargaining for additional time.

6:4 The giants mentioned here were probably large people sometimes reaching nine or ten feet in height. These may have been the same people mentioned in Numbers 13:33. Goliath, a man nine feet tall, appears in 1 Samuel 17. They used their physical advantage to oppress the people around them.

6:6, 7 Does this mean God was sorry for creating humanity? Was he admitting he had made a mistake? No, God does not change his mind (1 Samuel 15:29). Instead, this was God's expression of sorrow for what the people had done to themselves—the same feeling a parent might have over a rebellious child. God was sorry that the people chose sin and death instead of a relationship with him.

6:6–8 The sin of the people "broke God's heart." Our sins break God's heart as much as sin did in Noah's day. Noah, however, was a pleasure to God. Although we are far from perfect, we can follow Noah's example and be a pleasure to God in the midst of the sin that surrounds us.

6:7
Deut 29:19,20

6:9
Ezek 14:14

6:11
Deut 31:29
Judg 2:19
Ezek 8:17

6:12
Gen 8:21
Ps 14:1-3;
53:2,3
Rom 3:23

6:13
Isa 34:1-4
Ezek 7:2,3

6:14
Ex 2:3

7And he said, "I will blot out from the face of the earth all mankind that I created. Yes, and the animals too, and the reptiles and the birds. For I am sorry I made them."

8But Noah was a pleasure to the Lord. Here is the story of Noah: 9, 10He was the only truly righteous man living on the earth at that time. He tried always to conduct his affairs according to God's will. And he had three sons—Shem, Ham, and Japheth.

11Meanwhile, the crime rate was rising rapidly across the earth, and, as seen by God, the world was rotten to the core.

12, 13As God observed how bad it was, and saw that all mankind was vicious and depraved, he said to Noah, "I have decided to destroy all mankind; for the earth is filled with crime because of man. Yes, I will destroy mankind from the earth. 14Make a boat from resinous wood, sealing it with tar; and construct decks and

---

CAIN

In spite of parents' efforts and worries, conflicts between children in a family seem inevitable. Sibling relationships allow both competition and cooperation. In most cases, the mixture of loving and fighting eventually creates a strong bond between brothers and sisters. It isn't unusual, though, to hear parents say, "They fight so much I hope they don't kill each other before they grow up"' In Cain's case, the troubling potential became a tragedy. And while we don't know many details of this first child's life, his story can still teach us.

Cain got angry. Furious. Both he and his brother Abel had made sacrifices to God, and his had been rejected. Cain's reaction gives us a clue that his attitude was probably wrong from the start. Cain had a choice to make. He could correct his attitude about his sacrifice to God, or he could take out his anger on his brother. His decision is a clear reminder of how often we are aware of opposite choices, yet choose the wrong just as Cain did. We may not be choosing to murder, but we are still intentionally choosing what we shouldn't.

The feelings motivating our behavior can't always be changed by simple thought-power. But here we can begin to experience God's willingness to help. Asking for his help to do what is right can prevent us from setting into motion actions which we will later regret.

Strengths and accomplishments:
- First human child
- First to follow in father's profession, farming

Weaknesses and mistakes:
- When disappointed, reacted out of anger and discouragement
- Took the negative option even when a positive possibility was offered
- Was the first murderer

Lessons from his life:
- Anger is not the sin. It is what we get angry about or actions motivated by anger that can be sinful. Anger must be the energy behind good action, not evil action.
- What we offer to God must be from the heart—the best we are and have
- The consequences of sin are sometimes for life

Vital statistics:
- Where: Near Eden, which was probably located in the present-day countries of Iraq or Iran
- Occupation: Farmer at first, later nomad
- Relatives: Parents: Adam and Eve. Brothers: Abel, Seth, and others not mentioned by name.

Key verse:
"Your face . . . can be bright with joy if you will do what you should! But if you refuse to obey, watch out. Sin is waiting to attack you, longing to destroy you. But you can conquer it!" (Genesis 4:7).

Cain's story is told in Genesis 4:1–17. He is also mentioned in Hebrews 11:4; 1 John 3:12; Jude 11.

6:9, 10 Although Noah lived among evil people, he tried to do what pleased God by conducting his affairs according to God's will. For a lifetime he walked step by step in faith, a living example to his generation. Like Noah, we live in a world filled with evil. Are we being an influence on others, or are we being influenced? Either the two- or three-foot space around us is becoming more like us, or we are becoming more like it.

stalls throughout the ship. ¹⁵Make it 450 feet long, 75 feet wide, and 45 feet high. ¹⁶Construct a skylight all the way around the ship, eighteen inches below the roof; and make three decks inside the boat—a bottom, middle, and upper deck—and put a door in the side.

¹⁷"Look! I am going to cover the earth with a flood and destroy every living being—everything in which there is the breath of life. All will die. ¹⁸But I promise to keep you safe in the ship, with your wife and your sons and their wives. ¹⁹, ²⁰Bring a pair of every animal—a male and a female—into the boat with you, to keep them alive through the flood. Bring in a pair of each kind of bird and animal and reptile. ²¹Store away in the boat all the food that they and you will need." ²²And Noah did everything as God commanded him.

6:17
Lev 26:28
Ps 29:10
Isa 54:9
2 Pet 2:5
6:21
Gen 1:29
6:22
Gen 7:5
Ex 40:16

7 Finally the day came when the Lord said to Noah, "Go into the boat with all your family, for among all the people of the earth, I consider you alone to be righteous. ²Bring in the animals, too—a pair of each, except those kinds I have chosen for eating and for sacrifice: take seven pairs of each of them, ³and seven pairs of every kind of bird. Thus there will be every kind of life reproducing again after the flood has ended. ⁴One week from today I will begin forty days and nights of rain; and all the animals and birds and reptiles I have made will die."

7:1
Job 5:19
Prov 11:8
Isa 26:20
Mt 24:38
Lk 17:26
Heb 11:17
1 Pet 3:20
7:2
Lev 11:2-47
Deut 14:3-20
Ezek 44:23

⁵So Noah did everything the Lord commanded him. ⁶He was 600 years old when the flood came. ⁷He boarded the boat with his wife and sons and their wives, to escape the flood. ⁸, ⁹With him were all the various kinds of animals—those for eating and sacrifice, and those that were not, and the birds and reptiles. They came into the boat in pairs, male and female, just as God commanded Noah.

7:11
Ps 78:23
Ezek 26:19
Mal 3:10

¹⁰, ¹¹, ¹²One week later, when Noah was 600 years, two months, and seventeen days old, the rain came down in mighty torrents from the sky, and the subterranean waters burst forth upon the earth for forty days and nights. ¹³But Noah had gone into the boat that very day with his wife and his sons, Shem, Ham, and Japheth, and their wives. ¹⁴, ¹⁵With them in the boat were pairs of every kind of animal—domestic and wild—and reptiles and birds of every sort. ¹⁶Two by two they came, male and female, just as God had commanded. Then the Lord God closed the door and shut them in.

7:12
Ex 24:18
Deut 9:9
1 Kgs 19:8
Mt 4:2
7:13
Heb 11:7
1 Pet 3:20
2 Pet 2:5
7:15
Gen 6:19; 7:8

¹⁷For forty days the roaring floods prevailed, covering the ground and lifting the boat high above the earth. ¹⁸As the water rose higher and higher above the ground, the boat floated safely upon it; ¹⁹until finally the water covered all the high mountains under the whole heaven, ²⁰standing twenty-two feet and more above the highest peaks. ²¹And all living things upon the earth perished—birds, domestic and wild animals, and reptiles and all mankind— ²²everything that breathed and lived upon dry land. ²³All existence on the earth was blotted out—man and animals alike, and reptiles and birds. God destroyed them all, leaving only Noah alive, and those with him in the boat. ²⁴And the water covered the earth 150 days.

7:18
Ex 14:28
Ps 69:14,15
7:19
Ps 46:2,3
2 Pet 3:6
7:20
Ps 104:6
7:23
Mt 24:37-39
1 Pet 3:20
2 Pet 2:5
7:24
Gen 7:11; 8:4

8 God didn't forget about Noah and all the animals in the boat! He sent a wind to blow across the waters, and the floods began to disappear, ²for the subterranean water sources ceased their gushing, and the torrential rains subsided. ³, ⁴So the flood gradually receded until, 150 days after it began, the boat came to rest

8:1
a) Ex 2:24
2 Pet 2:5
b)Ex 14:21
8:4
Isa 37:38

7:3 *seven pairs*, literally, "the male and female."   **7:16** *the Lord God*, literally, "Jehovah."

6:15 The boat Noah built was no canoe! Picture yourself building a boat the length of one and a half football fields and as high as a four-story building. The "ark" (as it is commonly called) was exactly six times longer than it was wide—the same ratio used by modern shipbuilders. This huge boat was probably built miles from any body of water by only a few faithful men who trusted God and believed his promises.

6:18 Noah got right to work when God told him to build the ark. The other people must have been warned about the coming disaster (1 Peter 3:20), but apparently they did not expect it to

happen. Today things haven't changed much. Each day thousands of people are warned of God's inevitable judgment, yet most of them don't really believe it will happen. Don't expect people to welcome or accept your message of God's coming judgment on sin. Those who don't believe in God will deny his judgment and try to get you to deny God as well. But remember God's promise to Noah to keep him safe. This can inspire you to trust God for deliverance in the judgment that is sure to come.

7:1 Pairs of every animal joined Noah in the ark; seven pairs were taken of those animals used for sacrifice. Many scholars estimate that almost 45,000 animals could have fit into the ark.

upon the mountains of Ararat. 5Three months later, as the waters continued to go down, other mountain peaks appeared.

6After another forty days, Noah opened a porthole 7and released a raven that flew back and forth until the earth was dry. 8Meanwhile he sent out a dove to see if it could find dry ground, 9but the dove found no place to light, and returned to Noah, for the water was still too high. So Noah held out his hand and drew the dove back into the boat.

10Seven days later Noah released the dove again, 11and this time, towards evening, the bird returned to him with an olive leaf in her beak. So Noah knew that

8:6
Gen 6:16

8:7
Lev 11:15
Deut 14:14
1 Kgs 17:4
Lk 12:24

8:8
Isa 60:8
Hos 11:11
Mt 10:16

8:5 three months later, *literally, "on the first day of the tenth month."*

NOAH

The story of Noah's life involved not one, but two great and tragic floods. The world in Noah's day was flooded with evil. The number of those who remembered the God of creation, perfection, and love had dwindled to one. Of God's people, only Noah was left. God's response to the severe situation was a 120-year-long last chance, during which he had Noah build a graphic illustration of the message of his life. Nothing like a huge boat, built on dry land, to make a point! For Noah, obedience meant a long-term commitment to a project.

Many of us have trouble sticking to any project, whether or not it is directed by God. It is interesting that the length of Noah's obedience was greater than today's expected lifetime. Our only comparable long-term project is our very lives. But perhaps this is one great challenge Noah's life gives us: to live, in acceptance of God's grace, an entire lifetime of obedience and gratitude.

Strengths and accomplishments:
- Only follower of God left in his generation
- Second father of the human race
- Man of patience, consistence, and obedience
- First major shipbuilder in history

Lessons from his life:
- God is faithful to those who obey him
- God does not always protect us from trouble, but cares for us in spite of trouble
- Obedience is a long-term commitment
- A man may be faithful, but his sinful nature always travels with him

Vital statistics:
- Where: We're not told how far from the Garden of Eden location people had settled
- Occupation: Farmer, shipbuilder, preacher
- Relatives: Grandfather: Methuselah. Father: Lamech. Sons: Ham, Shem, and Japheth.

Key verse:
"Noah did everything as God commanded him" (Genesis 6:22).

Noah's story is told in Genesis 5:29—10:32. He is also mentioned in 1 Chronicles 1:4; Isaiah 54:9; Ezekiel 14:14, 20; Matthew 24:37, 38; Luke 3:36; 17:26, 27; Hebrews 11:7; 1 Peter 3:20; 2 Peter 2:5.

7:16 Many have wondered how this animal kingdom roundup happened. Did Noah and his sons spend years collecting them? In reality, the creation, along with Noah, was doing just as God had commanded. There seemed to be no problem gathering the animals—God took care of the details of that job while Noah was doing his part, building the ark. Often we do just the opposite of Noah. We worry about details in our lives over which we have no control, while neglecting specific areas that *are* under our control (like attitudes, relationships, responsibilities). Try to be more like Noah, concentrating on those things God has given you to do, and leaving the rest to him.

7:17–21 Was the flood a local event, or did it cover the entire earth? A universal flood was certainly possible. There is enough water on the earth to cover all dry land (the earth began that way in Genesis 1:9, 10). Afterwards, God promised never again to destroy the earth with a flood. Thus, this flood must either have covered the entire earth or destroyed all the inhabited parts of the earth. Remember, God's reason for sending the flood was to destroy all the earth's wickedness. It would have taken a major flood to accomplish this.

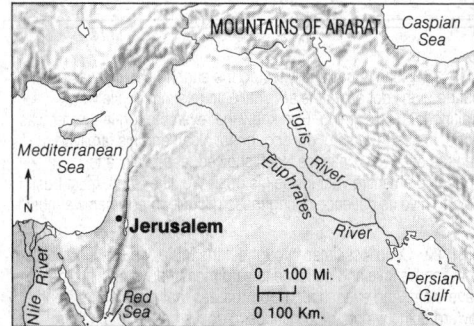

MOUNTAINS OF ARARAT The boat touched land in the Mountains of Ararat located in present-day Turkey near the Russian border. There it rested for almost eight months before Noah, his family, and the animals stepped onto dry land.

the water was almost gone. ¹²A week later he released the dove again, and this time she didn't come back.

¹³Twenty-nine days after that, Noah opened the door to look, and the water was gone. ¹⁴Eight more weeks went by. Then at last the earth was dry. ¹⁵, ¹⁶Then God told Noah, "You may all go out. ¹⁷Release all the animals, birds, and reptiles, so that they will breed abundantly and reproduce in great numbers." ¹⁸, ¹⁹So the boat was soon empty. Noah, his wife, and his sons and their wives all disembarked, along with all the animals, reptiles, and birds—all left the ark in pairs and groups.

²⁰Then Noah built an altar and sacrificed on it some of the animals and birds God had designated for that purpose. ²¹And Jehovah was pleased with the sacrifice and said to himself, "I will never do it again—I will never again curse the earth, destroying all living things, even though man's bent is always toward evil from his earliest youth, and even though he does such wicked things. ²²As long as the earth remains, there will be springtime and harvest, cold and heat, winter and summer, day and night."

8:13
Gen 7:11
8:15
Gen 6:13; 7:1
8:17
Gen 7:8,14
8:19
Gen 7:2,3,8,9
8:20
Gen 4:4; 12:7
13:18; 22:2
8:21
Gen 3:17; 5:29
Lev 1:9
Isa 54:9
8:22
Gen 45:6
Ps 74:16,17

2. Repopulating the earth

9 God blessed Noah and his sons and told them to have many children and to repopulate the earth.

², ³"All wild animals and birds and fish will be afraid of you," God told him; "for I have placed them in your power, and they are yours to use for food, in addition to grain and vegetables. ⁴But never eat animals unless their life-blood has been drained off. ⁵, ⁶And murder is forbidden. Man-killing animals must die, and any man who murders shall be killed; for to kill a man is to kill one made like God. ⁷Yes, have many children and repopulate the earth and subdue it."

9:2
Gen 1:26
Ps 8:6-8
9:4
Lev 3:17
7:26,27; 17:10
9:5
Ex 21:12,28,29
Lev 19:17
9:6
Ex 20:13

The rainbow

⁸Then God told Noah and his sons, ⁹, ¹⁰, ¹¹"I solemnly promise you and your children and the animals you brought with you—all these birds and cattle and wild animals—that I will never again send another flood to destroy the earth. ¹²And I seal this promise with this sign: ¹³I have placed my rainbow in the clouds as a sign of my promise until the end of time, to you and to all the earth. ¹⁴When I send clouds over the earth, the rainbow will be seen in the clouds, ¹⁵and I will remember my promise to you and to every being, that never again will the floods come and destroy all life. ¹⁶, ¹⁷For I will see the rainbow in the cloud and remember my eternal promise to every living being on the earth."

9:11
Isa 54:9
2 Pet 3:6
9:12
Gen 17:11
Mt 26:26-28
9:13
Ezek 1:28
9:15
Gen 6:18
8:21,22
Deut 7:9

Noah's descendants

¹⁸The names of Noah's three sons were Shem, Ham, and Japheth. (Ham is the

8:13 *Twenty-nine days after that,* literally, "in the 601st year, in the first month, the first day of the month."
8:20 *some of the animals and birds God had designated,* literally, "Clean," i.e., ritually approved by God.
8:21 *Jehovah was pleased with the sacrifice,* literally, "and Jehovah smelled the delicious odor and said . . ."
9:9-11 *promise you and your children,* literally, "your seed."

8:15, 16 Noah occasionally tested the earth to see if it was dry, but he didn't get out of the ark until God told him to. He was waiting for God's timing. God knew that even though the water was gone, the earth was not dry enough for Noah and his family to venture out. What patience Noah showed, especially after spending an entire year inside his boat! We, like Noah, must trust God to give us patience during those difficult times when we must wait.

8:21, 22 Countless times throughout the Bible, we see God showing his love and patience toward men and women in order to save them. And even though God realizes that people are "bent" toward doing wrong, he continues to do his part to reach them. When we sin or fall away from God, we surely deserve to be destroyed by his judgment. But God has now promised never again to destroy everything on earth with a curse of judgment until the day Jesus Christ returns to destroy evil forever. Now every change of season is a reminder of his promise.

9:5, 6 Here God explains why murder is so wrong: to kill a person is to kill one made like God. Since all people are made like God, all people possess the qualities that differentiate us from the animals—morality, reason, creativity, and self-worth. When we interact with others, we are interacting with beings made like God, beings who will live eternally. God intended for us to recognize these special qualities in all people.

9:8-13 Noah stepped out of the ark onto an earth deserted of human life. But God gave him a reassuring promise. This promise, or covenant, had three parts: (1) never again will a flood do such destruction; (2) as long as the earth remains, the seasons of the year will always come as expected; (3) a rainbow will shine when it rains as a sign to all that God will keep his promises. To this day, God has kept his promises. The earth's order and seasons are still preserved, and rainbows still remind us of his faithfulness to his Word.

ancestor of the Canaanites.) ¹⁹From these three sons of Noah came all the nations of the earth.

²⁰, ²¹Noah became a farmer and planted a vineyard, and he made wine. One day as he was drunk and lay naked in his tent, ²²Ham, the father of Canaan, saw his father's nakedness and went outside and told his two brothers. ²³Then Shem and Japheth took a robe and held it over their shoulders and, walking backwards into the tent, let it fall across their father to cover his nakedness as they looked the other way. ²⁴, ²⁵When Noah awoke from his drunken stupor, and learned what had happened and what Ham, his younger son, had done, he cursed Ham's descendants:

"A curse upon the Canaanites," he swore.
"May they be the lowest of slaves
To the descendants of Shem and Japheth."

²⁶, ²⁷Then he said,

"God bless Shem,
And may Canaan be his slave.
God bless Japheth,
And let him share the prosperity of Shem,
And let Canaan be his slave."

²⁸Noah lived another 350 years after the flood, ²⁹and was 950 years old at his death.

10 These are the families of Shem, Ham, and Japheth, who were the three sons of Noah; for sons were born to them after the flood. ²The sons of Japheth were: Gomer, Magog, Madai, Javan, Tubal, Meshech, Tiras. ³The sons of Gomer: Ashkenaz, Riphath, Togarmah. ⁴The sons of Javan: Elishah, Tarshish, Kittim, Dodanim. ⁵Their descendants became the maritime nations in various lands, each with a separate language. ⁶The sons of Ham were: Cush, Mizraim, Put, Canaan. ⁷The sons of Cush were: Seba, Havilah, Sabtah, Raamah, Sabteca. The sons of Raamah were: Sheba, Dedan.

⁸One of the descendants of Cush was Nimrod, who became the first of the kings. ⁹He was a mighty hunter, blessed of God, and his name became proverbial. People would speak of someone as being "like Nimrod—a mighty hunter, blessed of

9:20,21
Gen 19:32
Prov 20:1
9:22
Prov 30:17
Heb 2:15
9:23
Ex 20:12
9:24
Deut 27:16
9:25
Judg 1:28

9:26
Gen 14:20; 27:40
9:27
Gen 10:2-5
Isa 66:19

9:29
Gen 5:32; 7:11

10:1
Gen 6:9; 9:18
1 Chron 1:4
10:2
1 Chron 1:5-7
Isa 66:19
Ezek 27:13
38:2,3,6
10:3
Jer 51:27
Ezek 27:14
10:4
1 Chron 1:6,7
10:6
1 Chron 1:8,9
10:7
Isa 43:3
Ezek 27:15,20,22

9:24, 25 *he cursed Ham's descendants,* literally, "cursed be Canaan." **9:26, 27** *God bless Shem, and may Canaan be his slave,* or, "Blessed be Jehovah, the God of Shem . . . and may the Canaanites be Shem's slaves." **10:2** *The sons,* or, "descendants." **10:8** *One of the descendants,* or, "the son of Cush." **10:9** *a mighty hunter, blessed of God,* or, "a mighty hunter against the Lord."

BIBLE NATIONS DESCENDED FROM NOAH'S SONS	*Shem*	*Ham*	*Japheth*	Shem's descendants were called Semites.
	Hebrews	Canaanites	Greeks	Abraham, David, and Jesus descended
	Chaldeans	Egyptians	Thracians	from Shem. Ham's descendants settled in
	Assyrians	Philistines	Scythians	Canaan, Egypt, and the rest of Africa.
	Persians	Hittites		Japheth's descendants settled for the
	Syrians	Amorites		most part in Europe and Asia Minor.

9:20-27 Noah, the great hero of faith, was drunk—a poor example of godliness to his sons. Perhaps this story is included to show us that even godly men can sin and that their bad influence affects their families. Though the wicked people on the earth had been killed, the possibility of evil still existed in the hearts of Noah and his family. Ham's mocking attitude revealed a severe lack of respect for his father and for God.

9:25 This verse has been used by many to support racial prejudice and even slavery. Noah's curse wasn't directed toward any particular race of people, but rather at the Canaanite nation (a nation that God knew would become wicked and evil). The curse

was fulfilled when the Israelites entered the Promised Land and drove the Canaanites out (see the book of Joshua).

10:8-12 Who was Nimrod? Not much is known about him except that he was a mighty, powerful man and "blessed of God." But people given great blessings can let their gifts go to their heads. This is probably what happened to Nimrod. Although he was called "blessed of God," he is also considered by some to be the founder of the great, godless Babylonian Empire. The Bible mentions some of his building projects (10:11, 12). Perhaps Nimrod realized that religion could unify people for his own political purposes.

God." 10The heart of his empire included Babel, Erech, Accad, and Calneh in the land of Shinar. 11, 12From there he extended his reign to Assyria. He built Nineveh, Rehoboth-Ir, Calah, and Resen (which is located between Nineveh and Calah), the main city of the empire.

13, 14Mizraim was the ancestor of the people inhabiting these areas: Ludim, Anamim, Lehabim, Naphtuhim, Pathrusim, Casluhim (from whom came the Philistines), and Caphtorim.

15-19Canaan's oldest son was Sidon, and he was also the father of Heth; from Canaan descended these nations: Jebusites, Amorites, Girgashites, Hivites, Arkites, Sinites, Arvadites, Zemarites, Hamathites. Eventually the descendants of Canaan spread from Sidon all the way to Gerar, in the Gaza strip; and to Sodom, Gomorrah, Admah, and Zeboiim, near Lasha.

20These, then, were the descendants of Ham, spread abroad in many lands and nations, with many languages.

21Eber descended from Shem, the oldest brother of Japheth. 22Here is a list of Shem's other descendants: Elam, Asshur, Arpachshad, Lud, Aram.

23Aram's sons were: Uz, Hul, Gether, Mash.

24Arpachshad's son was Shelah, and Shelah's son was Eber.

25Two sons were born to Eber: Peleg (meaning "Division," for during his lifetime the people of the world were separated and dispersed), and Joktan (Peleg's brother).

26-30Joktan was the father of Almodad, Sheleph, Hazarmaveth, Jerah, Hadoram, Uzal, Diklah, Obal, Abima-el, Sheba, Ophir, Havi-lah, Jobab. These descendants of Joktan lived all the way from Mesha to the eastern hills of Sephar.

31These, then, were the descendants of Shem, classified according to their political groupings, languages, and geographical locations.

32All of the men listed above descended from Noah, through many generations, living in the various nations that developed after the flood.

3. The tower of Babel

11 At that time all mankind spoke a single language. 2As the population grew and spread eastward, a plain was discovered in the land of Babylon, and was soon thickly populated. 3, 4The people who lived there began to talk about building a great city, with a temple-tower reaching to the skies—a proud, eternal monument to themselves.

"This will weld us together," they said, "and keep us from scattering all over the world." So they made great piles of hardburned brick, and collected bitumen to use as mortar.

5But when God came down to see the city and the tower mankind was making, 6he said, "Look! If they are able to accomplish all this when they have just *begun* to exploit their linguistic and political unity, just think of what they will do later! Nothing will be unattainable for them! 7Come, let us go down and give them different languages, so that they won't understand each other's words!"

8So, in that way, God scattered them all over the earth; and that ended the building of the city. 9That is why the city was called Babel (meaning "confusion"),

10:13, 14 *ancestor,* or, "father." **10:23** *sons,* or, "descendants." **10:26-30** *father,* or "ancestor." **11:2** *the land of Babylon,* literally, "the land of Shinar," located at the mouth of the Persian Gulf. *and was soon thickly populated,* literally, "and they settled there."

10:10
Gen 11:9
10:11
a)Mic 5:6
b)Num 4:22,24
Ezra 4:2
10:13
1 Chron 1:11,12
Jer 46:9
10:15
Gen 15:19-21;
23:3
1 Chron 1:13
Jer 47:4
10:16
Gen 15:19-21
10:19
Gen 14:2,3
10:22
Gen 11:10-26
2 Kgs 15:29
1 Chron 1:17-23
Isa 66:19
10:23
Job 1:1
Jer 25:30
10:24
Lk 3:35

10:32
Gen 9:19; 10:1

11:2
Gen 10:10; 14:1
Isa 11:11
Dan 1:2
Zech 5:11
11:3
Gen 14:10
11:4
2 Sam 8:13
Ps 49:11-13
11:5
Gen 18:21
Ex 19:11
11:6
Gen 9:19; 11:1
11:7
Gen 1:26; 3:22
Job 5:12
11:8
Gen 10:25,32
11:9
Gen 10:10
1 Cor 14:23

11:3, 4 This tower of Babel was most likely a ziggurat, a common structure in the area at this time. Most often built as temples, they looked like pyramids with steps or ramps leading up the sides. Ziggurats stood as high as 300 feet and were often just as wide, making them the focal point of the city. The people of this story built their tower as a monument to their own greatness, something for the whole world to see.

11:4 The tower of Babel was a great human achievement—a wonder of the world. But it was a monument to the people themselves rather than to God. We often build monuments to ourselves (expensive clothes, big house, fancy car, important job) to call attention to our achievements. These may not be wrong in themselves, but when we use them to give us identity and self-worth, they take God's place in our lives.

because it was there that Jehovah confused them by giving them many languages, thus widely scattering them across the face of the earth.

Shem's descendants

11:10
Gen 10:22-25

10, 11Shem's line of descendants included Arpachshad, born two years after the flood when Shem was 100 years old; after that he lived another 500 years, and had many sons and daughters.

11:13
1 Chron 1:17

12, 13When Arpachshad was thirty-five years old, his son Shelah was born, and after that he lived another 403 years, and had many sons and daughters.

14, 15Shelah was thirty years old when his son Eber was born, living 403 years after that, and had many sons and daughters.

16, 17Eber was thirty-four years old when his son Peleg was born. He lived another 430 years afterwards, and had many sons and daughters.

18, 19Peleg was thirty years old when his son Reu was born. He lived another 209 years afterwards, and had many sons and daughters.

20, 21Reu was thirty-two years old when Serug was born. He lived 207 years after that, with many sons and daughters.

22, 23Serug was thirty years old when his son Nahor was born. He lived 200 years afterwards, with many sons and daughters.

11:24
Josh 24:2

24, 25Nahor was twenty-nine years old at the birth of his son Terah. He lived 119 years afterwards, and had sons and daughters.

11:26
Gen 22:20
1 Chron 1:26,27

26By the time Terah was seventy years old, he had three sons, Abram, Nahor, and Haran.

11:29
Gen 17:15
20:12; 22:20
31:53

27And Haran had a son named Lot. 28But Haran died young, in the land where he was born (in Ur of the Chaldeans), and was survived by his father.

11:30
Gen 15:2; 16:1
18:11; 25:21
1 Sam 1:5
Luke 1:7

29Meanwhile, Abram married his half-sister Sarai, while his brother Nahor married their orphaned niece Milcah, who was the daughter of their brother Haran; and she had a sister named Iscah. 30But Sarai was barren; she had no children.

11:31
Gen 27:43
Josh 24:2
Heb 11:8
Acts 7:2

31Then Terah took his son Abram, his grandson Lot (his son Haran's child), and his daughter-in-law Sarai, and left Ur of the Chaldeans to go to the land of Canaan; but they stopped instead at the city of Haran and settled there. 32And there Terah died at the age of 205.

11:12, 13 *his son,* or, by Hebrew usage, "there was born to him the ancestor of Shelah, and after that . . ." So also throughout the remainder of the chapter. **11:29** *half-sister,* implied. (See 20:12.) *orphaned niece Milcah,* implied. **11:32** *age of 205,* implied. The Samaritan Pentateuch says that Terah died when he was 145 years old, so that his death occurred in the year of Abraham's departure from Haran. This is more consistent with 11:26 and 12:4. See also Acts 7:4.

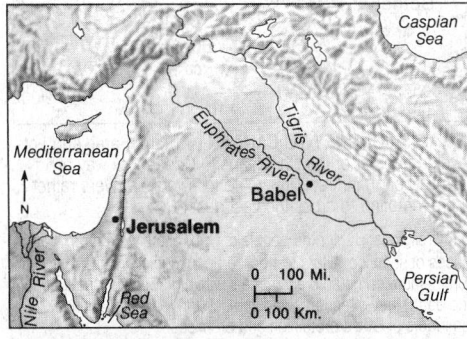

THE TOWER OF BABEL The plain between the Tigris and Euphrates rivers offered a perfect location for the "temple-tower reaching to the skies."

11:26–28 Abram grew up in Ur of the Chaldeans—an important city in the ancient world. Archeologists have discovered evidence of a flourishing civilization there in Abram's day. The city carried on an extensive trade with its neighbors and had a vast library. Growing up in Ur, Abram was probably well educated.

11:10-27 In Genesis 9:24-27 we read Noah's curse of Ham's descendants and his blessing on Shem and Japheth's descendants. Note the beginning of the fulfillment of Noah's words: one of Ham's sons is Canaan (10:6). Shem's descendants are listed here and in 10:22-31. The curse was on Ham's descendants who became the evil Canaanites; a blessing was on Shem's descendants from whom came Abram and the entire Jewish nation which would eventually conquer the land of Canaan in the days of Joshua.

11:31 Terah left Ur to go to Canaan, but settled in Haran instead. Why did he stop half way? It may have been his health, the climate, or even fear. But this did not change Abram's calling ("God had told Abram"—12:1). He had respect for his father's leadership, but when Terah died, Abram moved on to Canaan. God's will may come in stages. As the time in Haran was a transition period for Abram, so God may give us transition periods and times of waiting to help us depend on him and trust his timing. If we patiently do his will during the transition times, we will be better prepared to serve him as we should when he calls us.

D. THE STORY OF ABRAHAM (12:1—25:18)

Despite God's swift judgment of sin, most people ignored him and continued to sin. But a handful of people really tried to follow him. One of these was Abraham. God appeared to Abraham one day and promised to make his descendants into a great nation. Abraham's part of the agreement was to obey God. Through sharp testing and an incident that almost destroyed his family, Abraham remained faithful to God. Throughout this section we discover how to live a life of faith.

1. God promises a nation to Abraham

12 God had told Abram, "Leave your own country behind you, and your own people, and go to the land I will guide you to. ²If you do, I will cause you to become the father of a great nation; I will bless you and make your name famous, and you will be a blessing to many others. ³I will bless those who bless you and curse those who curse you; and the entire world will be blessed because of you."

⁴So Abram departed as the Lord had instructed him, and Lot went too; Abram was seventy-five years old at that time. ⁵He took his wife Sarai, his nephew Lot, and all his wealth—the cattle and slaves he had gotten in Haran—and finally arrived in Canaan. ⁶Traveling through Canaan, they came to a place near Shechem, and set up camp beside the oak at Moreh. (This area was inhabited by Canaanites at that time.)

⁷Then Jehovah appeared to Abram and said, "I am going to give this land to your descendants." And Abram built an altar there to commemorate Jehovah's visit. ⁸Afterwards Abram left that place and traveled southward to the hilly country between Bethel on the west and Ai on the east. There he made camp, and made an altar to the Lord and prayed to him. ⁹Thus he continued slowly southward to the Negeb, pausing frequently.

¹⁰There was at that time a terrible famine in the land: and so Abram went on down to Egypt to live. ¹¹, ¹², ¹³But as he was approaching the borders of Egypt, he asked Sarai his wife to tell everyone that she was his sister! "You are very

12:1 Gen 15:7 Acts 7:3 Heb 11:8
12:2 Gen 13:16 15:5; 17:5 18:18; 22:17 Zech 8:13
12:3 Gen 22:18 26:4; 27:29 Ex 23:22 Acts 3:25 Gal 3:8
12:7 Gen 13:15 17:1; 18:1 Isa 41:8; 44:3 Gal 3:16
12:8 Gen 4:26; 8:20 22:9
12:9 Gen 13:1; 20:1
12:10 Gen 26:1; 42:5
12:11 Gen 26:7; 29:17

12:2 *you will be a blessing to many others*, or, "I will make your name so famous that it will be used to pronounce blessings on others." **12:3** *the entire world will be blessed because of you*, or, "the nations will bless themselves because of you." **12:8** *traveled southward*, implied.

12:1-3 Abram moved out in faith from Ur to Haran and finally to Canaan. God then established a covenant with Abram, telling him that he would be the founder of a great nation. Not only would this great nation be blessed, God said, but the other nations of the world would be blessed too—all because of Abram.

Israel, the nation that would come from Abram, was to be a people who followed God and influenced those with whom it came in contact. We, too, are to extend God's love to all nations, not just our own. Through Abram's family tree, Jesus Christ was born to save humanity. Through Christ, all people and all nations can have a personal relationship with God and be blessed beyond measure. As you read the rest of the book of Genesis, notice how people (Esau, Laban, Lot) and nations (Egypt) were blessed because of their association with those in Abram's direct line of descendants.

12:2 God promised to bless Abram and make him great. But there was one condition. Abram had to do what God wanted him to do. This meant leaving his home and friends and traveling to a new land where God promised to build a great nation from Abram's family. Abram obeyed, walking away from his home for God's promise of even greater things in the future. God may be trying to lead you to a place of greater service and usefulness for him. Don't let the comfort and security of your present position make you miss God's plan for you.

12:5 God planned to develop a nation of people he would call his own. He called Abram from the godless, man-centered city of Ur to a fertile region called Canaan, where a God-centered, moral nation could be established. Though small in dimension, the land of Canaan was the focal point for most of the history of Israel as well as for the rise of Christianity. This small land given to one man, Abram, has had a tremendous impact on world history.

12:7 Abram built an altar to God. Altars of worship were used in

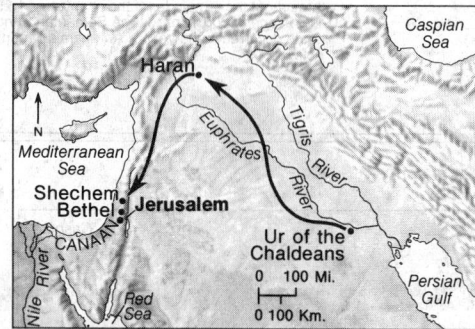

ABRAM'S JOURNEY TO CANAAN Abram, Sarai, and Lot traveled from Ur of the Chaldeans to Canaan by way of Haran. Though indirect, this route followed the rivers rather than attempting to cross the vast desert.

many religions. But for the people of God, altars were more than places of sacrifice. Altars symbolized communion with God and commemorated notable encounters with him. Built of rough stones and earth, they often remained in place for years as continual reminders of God's protection and promises.

Abram regularly built altars to God for two reasons: (1) for prayer and worship, and (2) to remember God's promise to bless him. He couldn't survive spiritually without regularly renewing his love and loyalty to God. These occasions of altar-building helped Abram remember that God was at the center of his life. Without regular worship, it is difficult to remember what God desires and even more difficult to obey.

beautiful," he told her, "and when the Egyptians see you they will say, 'This is his wife. Let's kill him and then we can have her!' But if you say you are my sister, then the Egyptians will treat me well because of you, and spare my life!" ¹⁴And sure enough, when they arrived in Egypt everyone spoke of her beauty. ¹⁵When the palace aides saw her, they praised her to their king, the Pharaoh, and she was taken into his harem. ¹⁶Then Pharaoh gave Abram many gifts because of her—sheep, oxen, donkeys, men and women slaves, and camels.

¹⁷But the Lord sent a terrible plague upon Pharaoh's household on account of her being there. ¹⁸Then Pharaoh called Abram before him and accused him sharply. "What is this you have done to me?" he demanded. "Why didn't you tell me she was your wife? ¹⁹Why were you willing to let me marry her, saying she was your sister? Here, take her and be gone!" ²⁰And Pharaoh sent them out of the country under armed escort—Abram, his wife, and all his household and possessions.

2. Abraham and Lot
Abraham and Lot separate

13 So they left Egypt and traveled north into the Negeb—Abram with his wife, and Lot, and all that they owned, for Abram was very rich in livestock, silver, and gold. ³, ⁴Then they continued northward toward Bethel where he had camped before, between Bethel and Ai—to the place where he had built the altar. And there he again worshiped the Lord.

⁵Lot too was very wealthy, with sheep and cattle and many servants. ⁶But the land could not support both Abram and Lot with all their flocks and herds. There were too many animals for the available pasture. ⁷So fights broke out between the

12:12
Gen 20:11
12:13
Gen 20:2,12
12:16
Gen 13:2
20:14; 24:35
12:17
1 Chron 16:21
Ps 105:14
12:18
Gen 3:13; 4:10
20:9

13:1
Gen 12:9; 20:1
13:2
Gen 12:16
20:14; 24:35
13:3
Gen 12:8; 28:19
13:5
Gen 12:4,5
13:6
Gen 36:6,7

12:15 *she was taken into his harem,* literally, "into the household of Pharaoh." **13:5** *many servants,* implied. Literally, "many tents." **13:7** *despite the danger they all faced,* implied.

ABRAM'S JOURNEY TO EGYPT
A famine could cause the loss of a shepherd's wealth. So Abram traveled through the Negeb Desert to Egypt, where there was plenty of food and good land for his flocks.

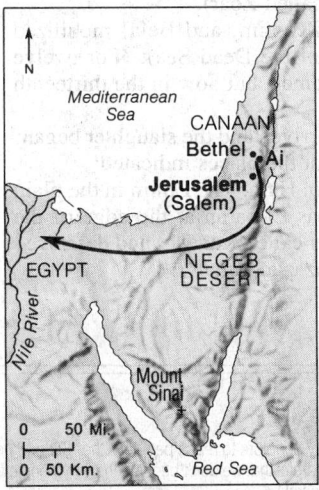

they knew the truth, they would kill him to get Sarai. Sarai would have been a desirable addition to Pharaoh's harem because of her wealth, beauty, and potential for political alliance. As her brother, Abram would have been given a place of honor. As her husband, however, his life would be in danger, for Sarai could not enter Pharaoh's harem unless Abram were dead. So Abram told only half the truth and showed a lack of faith in God's protection, even after all God had promised him. This is also a lesson in how lying compounds the effects of sin. When he lied, Abram's problem didn't become easier, but more complex.

13:1, 2 In Abram's day, shepherds could acquire great wealth. Abram was a shepherd. His wealth included not only money, but also sheep. Sheep were a valuable commodity used for food, clothing, tent material, and sacrifices. Sheep were often traded for other goods and services. Abram was able to watch his wealth grow and multiply daily.

13:5–9 Facing a potential conflict with his nephew Lot, Abram took the initiative in settling the dispute. He gave Lot first choice, even though Abram, being older, had the right to choose first. Abram also showed a willingness to risk being cheated. Abram's example shows us how to respond to difficult family situations: (1) take the initiative in resolving conflicts; (2) let others have first choice, even if that means not getting what we want; (3) put family peace above personal desires.

13:7, 8 Surrounded by hostile neighbors, the herdsmen of Abram and Lot should have pulled together. Instead, they let petty jealousy tear them apart. A similar situation exists today. Many Christian people argue and fight, while Satan is at work all around them.

Rivalries, arguments, and disagreements among believers can be destructive in three ways: (1) they damage good will, trust, and peace—the foundations of human relationships; (2) they hamper progress toward important goals; (3) they make us self-centered rather than love-centered. Jesus understood how destructive this could be. In his final prayer before being betrayed and arrested, Jesus asked God that his followers be "of one heart and mind" (John 17:21).

12:10 When famine struck, Abram continued to Egypt where there was food. Why would there be a famine in the land to which God had just called Abram? This was a test of Abram's faith. Abram didn't question God's leading when he faced this difficulty. Many believers find that when they determine to follow God, they immediately encounter great obstacles. The next time you face such a test, don't try to second-guess what God is doing. Use the intelligence God gave you (as Abram did when he temporarily moved to Egypt, a land with plenty of food) and wait for new opportunities.

12:11–13 Abram, acting out of fear, asked Sarai to tell a half-truth by saying she was his sister. She *was* Abram's half sister, but she was also his wife (11:29).

Abram's intent was to deceive the Egyptians. He feared that if

herdsmen of Abram and Lot, despite the danger they all faced from the tribes of Canaanites and Perizzites present in the land. 8Then Abram talked it over with Lot. "This fighting between our men has got to stop," he said. "We can't afford to let a rift develop between our clans. Close relatives such as we are must present a united front! 9I'll tell you what we'll do. Take your choice of any section of the land you want, and we will separate. If you want that part over there to the east, then I'll stay here in the western section. Or, if you want the west, then I'll go over there to the east."

10Lot took a long look at the fertile plains of the Jordan River, well watered everywhere (this was before Jehovah destroyed Sodom and Gomorrah); the whole section was like the Garden of Eden, or like the beautiful countryside around Zoar in Egypt. 11So that is what Lot chose—the Jordan valley to the east of them. He went there with his flocks and servants, and thus he and Abram parted company. 12For Abram stayed in the land of Canaan, while Lot lived among the cities of the plain, settling at a place near the city of Sodom. 13The men of this area were unusually wicked, and sinned greatly against Jehovah.

14After Lot was gone, the Lord said to Abram, "Look as far as you can see in every direction, 15for I am going to give it all to you and your descendants. 16And I am going to give you so many descendants that, like dust, they can't be counted! 17Hike in all directions and explore the new possessions I am giving you." 18Then Abram moved his tent to the oaks of Mamre, near Hebron, and built an altar to Jehovah there.

Abraham rescues Lot

14 Now war filled the land—Amraphel, king of Shinar, Arioch, king of Ellasar, Ched-or-laomer, king of Elam, and Tidal, king of Goiim 2Fought against: Bera, king of Sodom,Birsha, king of Gomorrah, Shinab, king of Admah, Shemeber, king of Zeboiim, and The king of Bela (later called Zoar).

3These kings (of Sodom, Gomorrah, Admah, Zeboiim, and Bela) mobilized their armies in Siddim Valley (that is, the valley of the Dead Sea). 4For twelve years they had all been subject to King Ched-or-laomer, but now in the thirteenth year, they rebelled.

5, 6One year later, Ched-or-laomer and his allies arrived and the slaughter began. For they were victorious over the following tribes at the places indicated:

The Rephaim in Ashteroth-karnaim; The Zuzim in Ham; The Emim in the plain of Kiriathaim; The Horites in Mount Seir, as far as El-paran at the edge of the desert. 7Then they swung around to Enmishpat (later called Kadesh) and destroyed the Amalekites, and also the Amorites living in Hazazan-tamar.

13:10 *Garden of Eden*, literally, "the Garden of Jehovah."

13:8
Mt 5:9
Heb 12:14

13:9
Gen 20:15

13:10
Gen 2:8
14:2,8
19:22,30
Deut 34:3

13:13
Gen 18:20
Deut 32:32
Isa 1:9; 3:9
Rom 9:29
2 Pet 2:7

13:14
Gen 28:14
Deut 3:27
34:1-4

13:15
Gen 12:2,7
15:18; 17:7,8

13:16
Gen 15:5; 28:14
Num 23:10

13:17
Num 13:17-24

13:18
Gen 8:20; 12:7
14:13; 18:1

14:1
Jer 48:34
Dan 8:2
Acts 2:9

14:2
13:10; 19:24
Deut 29:23

14:3
Num 34:12
Deut 3:17
Josh 3:16

14:5
Deut 1:4
2:10,20; 3:11
Josh 13:19

14:7
Gen 16:14; 20:1
Num 13:26
Deut 1:19
2 Chron 20:2

13:10, 11 Lot's character is revealed by the nature of his choices. He took the best share of the land even though it meant living near Sodom, a city known for its sin. He was greedy for the best, without thinking about his uncle Abram's needs or what was fair.

Our lives are a series of choices. We too can choose the best while ignoring the needs and feelings of others. This kind of choice, as Lot's life shows, leads to problems. When we stop making choices in God's direction, all that is left is to make choices in the wrong direction.

13:12 Good pasture and available water seemed like a wise choice to Lot at first. But he failed to recognize that the wicked influence of Sodom could provide temptations strong enough to destroy his family. Have you chosen to live or work in a "Sodom"? Even though you may be strong enough to resist the temptations, other members of your family may not. While we are commanded

by Scripture to reach people in the "Sodom" near us, we must be careful that we don't become the very people we are trying to reach.

14:4–16 Who was Ched-or-laomer, and why was he important? In Abram's time, most cities had their own kings. Wars and rivalries were common. A conquered city paid tribute to the victorious king. Nothing is known about Ched-or-laomer except what we read in the Bible. Apparently he was quite powerful. Five cities including Sodom had paid tribute (taxes) to him for twelve years. The five cities formed an alliance and rebelled by withholding tribute. Ched-or-laomer reacted swiftly and reconquered them all. When he defeated Sodom, he captured Lot, his family, and his possessions. Abram, with only 318 men, chased Ched-or-laomer's army and attacked him near Damascus. With God's help, he defeated them and recovered Lot, his family, and their possessions.

14:8
Gen 13:10; 14:2

14:12
Gen 11:27
13:6,12

14:13
Gen 10:16
13:18; 39:14

8, 9But now the other army, that of the kings of Sodom, Gomorrah, Admah, Zeboiim, and Bela (Zoar), unsuccessfully attacked Ched-or-laomer and his allies as they were in the Dead Sea Valley (four kings against five). 10As it happened, the valley was full of asphalt pits. And as the army of the kings of Sodom and Gomorrah fled, some slipped into the pits, and the remainder fled to the mountains. 11Then the victors plundered Sodom and Gomorrah and carried off all their wealth and food, and went on their homeward way, 12taking with them Lot—Abram's nephew who lived in Sodom—and all he owned. 13One of the men who escaped came and told Abram the Hebrew, who was camping among the oaks belonging to Mamre the Amorite (brother of Eshcol and Aner, Abram's allies).

14:8, 9 *unsuccessfully,* implied.   **14:11** *the victors plundered,* implied.   **14:12** *Abram's nephew,* literally, "Abram's brother's son."

Some people simply drift through life. Their choices, when they can muster the will to choose, tend to follow the course of least resistance. Lot, Abram's nephew, was such a person.

While still young, Lot lost his father. Although this must have been hard on him, he was not left without strong role models in his grandfather Terah and his uncle Abram, who raised him. Still, Lot's life shows his pattern of being tentative in his actions, so caught up in the present moment that he seems to have been incapable of seeing the consequences of his actions. It is hard to imagine what his life would have been like without Abram's careful attention and God's intervention.

By the time Lot drifted out of the picture, his life had taken an ugly turn. He had so blended into the sinful culture of his day that he did not want to leave it. Then his daughters committed incest with him. His drifting finally led him in a very specific direction—destruction.

Lot, however, is called good in the New Testament (2 Peter 2:7). Ruth, the descendant of Moab, was an ancestor of Jesus Christ, even though Moab was a result of Lot's incestuous relationship with one of his daughters.

This gives hope to us that God forgives and often brings about positive circumstances from evil.

What is the direction of your life? Are you headed toward God or away from him? If you're a drifter, the choice for God may seem difficult, but it is the one choice that puts all other choices in a different light.

Strengths and accomplishments:
● He was a successful businessman
● Peter calls him a good man (2 Peter 2:7, 8)

Weaknesses and mistakes:
● When faced with decisions, he tended to put off deciding, then chose the easiest course of action
● When given a choice, his first reaction was to think of himself

Lesson from his life:
● God wants us to do more than drift through life. He wants people to be an influence for him.

Vital statistics:
● Where: Lived first in Ur of the Chaldeans, then moved to Canaan with Abram. Eventually, he moved to the wicked city of Sodom.
● Occupation: Wealthy sheep and cattle rancher. Also a city official.
● Relatives: Father: Haran. Adopted by Abram when his father died. The name of his wife, who turned into a pillar of salt, is not mentioned.

Key verse:
"When Lot still hesitated, the angels seized his hand" (Genesis 19:16).

Lot's story is told in Genesis 11—14; 19. He is also mentioned in Deuteronomy 2:9; Luke 17:28–32; 2 Peter 2:7.

14:12 Lot's greed for the best of everything led him into sinful surroundings. His burning desire for possessions and success cost him his freedom and enjoyment. As a captive to King Ched-or-laomer, he faced torture, slavery, or death. In much the same way, we can be enticed into doing something or going somewhere we shouldn't. The prosperity we long for is captivating: it can both entice us and enslave us if our motives are not in line with God's desires.

¹⁴When Abram learned that Lot had been captured, he called together the men born into his household, 318 of them in all, and chased after the retiring army as far as Dan. ¹⁵He divided his men and attacked during the night from several directions, and pursued the fleeing army to Hobah, north of Damascus, ¹⁶and recovered everything—the loot that had been taken, his relative Lot, and all of Lot's possessions, including the women and other captives.

¹⁷As Abram returned from his strike against Ched-or-laomer and the other kings at the Valley of Shaveh (later called King's Valley), the king of Sodom came out to meet him, ¹⁸and Melchizedek, the king of Salem (Jerusalem), who was a priest of the God of Highest Heaven, brought him bread and wine. ¹⁹, ²⁰Then Melchizedek blessed Abram with this blessing:

"The blessing of the supreme God, Creator of heaven and earth, be upon you, Abram; and blessed be God, who has delivered your enemies over to you."

Then Abram gave Melchizedek a tenth of all the loot.

²¹The king of Sodom told him, "Just give me back my people who were captured; keep for yourself the booty stolen from my city."

²²But Abram replied, "I have solemnly promised Jehovah, the supreme God, Creator of heaven and earth, ²³that I will not take so much as a single thread from you, lest you say, 'Abram is rich because of what I gave him!' ²⁴All I'll accept is what these young men of mine have eaten; but give a share of the loot to Aner, Eshcol, and Mamre, my allies."

3. God promises a son to Abraham

15 Afterwards Jehovah spoke to Abram in a vision, and this is what he told him: "Don't be fearful, Abram, for I will defend you. And I will give you great blessings."

14:14 Gen 12:5 / Deut 34:1
14:15 Gen 15:2 / 1 Kgs 15:8 / Acts 9:2
14:16 Gen 14:12,14
14:17 Gen 14:5 / 2 Sam 18:18
14:18 Ps 7:17; 50:14 / 76:2; 110:4 / Heb 5:6,10; 7:1
14:19 Gen 27:25; 48:9 / Mk 10:16
14:20 Gen 9:26; 24:27 / Ps 44:3 / 72:17-19 / Heb 7:4,6
14:22 Gen 1:1
14:23 2 Kgs 5:16
14:24 Gen 14:13
15:1 Gen 21:17 / 26:24; 46:2 / Num 12:6

LOT'S RESCUE Having conquered Sodom, Ched-or-laomer left for his home country, taking many captives with him. Abram learned what had happened and chased Ched-or-laomer past Dan and beyond Damascus. There he defeated the king and rescued the captives, among them Lot.

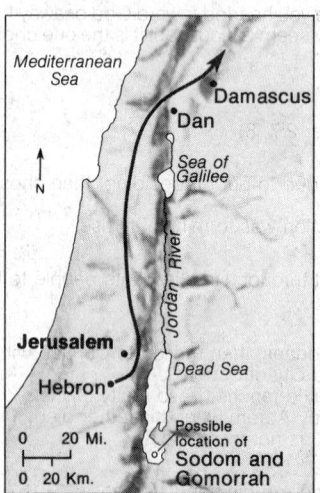

situation in order to help others. We should be willing to act immediately when others need our help.

14:18 Who was Melchizedek? He was obviously a godly man, for his name means "king of justice" and "king of peace" (Hebrews 7:2). He was a priest of "the God of highest heaven." He recognized God as Creator of heaven and earth. What else is known about him? Four main theories have been suggested. (1) Melchizedek was a respected king of that region. Abram was simply showing him the respect he deserved. (2) The name Melchizedek may have been a standing title for all the kings of Salem (Jerusalem). (3) Melchizedek was a "type" of Christ (Hebrews 7:3). A type is an Old Testament event or teaching that is so closely related to what Christ did that it illustrates a lesson about Christ. Hebrews 7 calls Melchizedek a type of Christ and discusses him in more detail. (4) Melchizedek was the appearance on earth of the pre-incarnate Christ in a temporary bodily form. Many scholars support this view.

14:20 Abram gave one-tenth of the booty to Melchizedek. Even in some pagan religions, it was traditional to give a tenth of one's "earnings" to the gods. Abram followed accepted tradition. However, Abram refused to take any booty from the king of Sodom. Even though this huge amount would significantly increase what he could have given to God, he chose to reject it for more important reasons—he didn't want the ungodly people of Sodom to say, "Look what we have done to make Abram great." Instead, Abram wanted them to look at his life and say, "Look what *God* has done for Abram." In this case, accepting the gifts would have focused everyone's attention on Abram rather than on God, who really won the victory. When people look at us, they need to see what God has accomplished in our lives.

14:14–16 These incidents portray two of Abram's characteristics: (1) He had courage that came from God. He faced a powerful foe and attacked. (2) He was prepared. He had taken time to train his men for a potential conflict. We never know when we will be called upon to complete difficult tasks. Like Abram, we should prepare for those times and then take courage from God when they come.

14:14–16 When Abram learned that Lot was a prisoner, he immediately tried to help his nephew. It is easier and safer not to become involved. But with Lot in serious trouble, Abram acted at once. Sometimes we must get involved in a messy or painful

15:1 God told Abram not to be afraid. Why would Abram be afraid? Perhaps he feared revenge from the kings he had just defeated (14:15). God then gave Abram two good reasons for courage: (1) he promised to defend Abram and be at his side

15:3
Gen 14:14
15:4
Gen 17:16
Gal 4:28
15:5
Gen 12:2
22:17; 32:12
Rom 4:18

2, 3But Abram replied, "O Lord Jehovah, what good are all your blessings when I have no son? For without a son, some other member of my household will inherit all my wealth."

4Then Jehovah told him, "No, no one else will be your heir, for you will have a son to inherit everything you own."

5Then God brought Abram outside beneath the nighttime sky and told him, "Look up into the heavens and count the stars if you can. Your descendants will be

15:2, 3 *some other member of my household* was Eliezer of Damascus.

MELCHIZEDEK

Do you like a good mystery? History is full of them! They usually involve people. One of the most mysterious people in the Bible is the King of Peace, Melchizedek. He appeared one day in the life of Abraham (then Abram) and was never heard from again. What happened that day, however, was to be remembered throughout history and eventually became a subject of a New Testament letter (Hebrews).

This meeting between Abram and Melchizedek was most unusual. Though the two men were strangers and foreigners to each other, they shared a most important characteristic: both worshiped and served the one God who made heaven and earth. This was a great moment of triumph for Abram. He had just defeated an army and regained the freedom of a large group of captives. If there was any doubt in his mind about whose victory it was, Melchizedek set the record straight by reminding Abram, "Blessed be God, who has delivered your enemies over to you." Abram recognized that this man worshiped the same God he did.

Melchizedek was one of a small group of godly people throughout the Old Testament who came in contact with the Jews (Israelites), but were not Jews themselves. This seems to indicate that the requirement to be a follower of God is not genetic (a Jew, an Israelite). Instead, it means faithfully obeying his teachings and recognizing his greatness.

Do you let God speak to you through other people? Does your evaluation of others place a high priority on where God fits into their lives? Are you more aware of the little differences between you or the big similarities you share? Do you know the God of the Bible well enough to know if you truly worship him? Allow Melchizedek, Abraham, David, and Jesus, along with many other persons in the Bible, to tell you about and show you this great God, Creator of heaven and earth. He wants you to know how much he loves you; he wants you to know him personally.

Strengths and accomplishments:
- The first priest/king of Scripture—a leader with a heart tuned to God
- Good at encouraging others to serve God wholeheartedly
- A man whose character obviously reflected his love for God
- A person in the Old Testament who reminds us of Jesus and who some believe really was Jesus

Lessons from his life:
- Live for God and you're likely to be at the right place at the right time. To see if you can serve God, his first test is to examine your heart. To whom or what is your greatest loyalty? If you answered *God*, you pass the test and all other factors are unimportant.

Vital statistics:
- Where: Ruled in Salem, site of the future Jerusalem
- Occupation: King of Salem and Priest of the Most High God

Key verse:
"This Melchizedek was king of the city of Salem, and also a priest of the Most High God" (Hebrews 7:1).

Melchizedek's story is told in Genesis 14:17–20. He is also mentioned in Psalm 110:4; Hebrews 5—7.

during difficulties, and (2) he promised to give Abram "great blessings." When you fear what lies ahead, remember that God won't desert you in difficult times and has promised you great blessings.

15:2, 3 Eliezer was Abram's most trusted servant, maybe acting as household administrator (Genesis 24). According to custom, if Abram were to die without a son of his own, his eldest servant would become his heir. Though Abram loved his servant, he wanted a son of his own to carry on the family line.

15:5 Abram wasn't promised wealth or fame—he already had that. Instead God promised descendants that would be like the stars in the sky—"too many to count." To appreciate the vast number of stars scattered through the sky, you need to be, like Abram, away from any interfering lights or buildings. Or pick up a handful of sand and try to count the grains—it can't be done! Just when Abram was despairing over having no heir, God promised descendants too numerous to imagine!

like that—too many to count!" 6And Abram believed God; then God considered him righteous on account of his faith.

7And he told him, "I am Jehovah who brought you out of the city of Ur of the Chaldeans, to give you this land."

8But Abram replied, "O Lord Jehovah, how can I be sure that you will give it to me?" 9Then Jehovah told him to take a three-year-old heifer, a three-year-old female goat, a three-year-old ram, a turtledove and a young pigeon, 10and to slay them and to cut them apart down the middle, and to separate the halves, but not to divide the birds. 11And when the vultures came down upon the carcasses, Abram shooed them away.

12That evening as the sun was going down, a deep sleep fell upon Abram, and a vision of terrible foreboding, darkness, and horror.

13Then Jehovah told Abram, "Your descendants will be oppressed as slaves in a foreign land for 400 years. 14But I will punish the nation that enslaves them, and at the end they will come away with great wealth. 15(But you will die in peace, at a ripe old age.) 16After four generations they will return here to this land; for the wickedness of the Amorite nations living here now will not be ready for punishment until then."

17As the sun went down and it was dark, Abram saw a smoking fire-pot and a flaming torch that passed between the halves of the carcasses. 18So that day Jehovah made this covenant with Abram: "I have given this land to your descendants from the Wadi-el-Arish to the Euphrates River. 19, 20, 21And I give to them these nations: Kenites, Kenizzites, Kadmonites, Hittites, Perizzites, Rephaim, Amorites, Canaanites, Girgashites, Jebusites."

Abraham's second wife

16 But Sarai and Abram had no children. So Sarai took her maid, an Egyptian girl named Hagar, 2, 3and gave her to Abram to be his second wife.

"Since the Lord has given me no children," Sarai said, "you may sleep with my servant girl, and her children shall be mine."

And Abram agreed. (This took place ten years after Abram had first arrived in the land of Canaan.) 4So he slept with Hagar, and she conceived; and when she

15:16 *Amorite nations living here now,* implied. 15:18 *Wadi-el-Arish,* literally, "River of Egypt," at the southern border of Judah.

15:6
Ps 106:31
Rom 4:3
Gal 3:6
15:7
Gen 12:1; 13:15
Acts 7:2-4
15:8
Judg 6:17
Lk 1:18
15:9
Lev 1:2
15:12
Gen 2:21; 28:11
1 Sam 26:12
15:13
Ex 12:40
Acts 7:6
Gal 3:17
15:14
Ex 6:5
15:15
Gen 25:7,8
15:16
Ex 33:2
15:18
Num 34:1-15
Deut 1:7,8
15:19
Num 24:21
15:21
Gen 10:15
Ex 23:23,28

16:1
Gen 11:30
15:2; 21:9
Gal 4:24,25
16:2
Gen 30:3
Ex 21:4
16:3
Gen 13:1

15:6 Although Abram had been demonstrating his faith through his actions, it was faith, not actions, that made Abram right with God (Romans 4:1–5). We too can have a right relationship with God by trusting him with our lives. Our outward actions—church attendance, prayer, good deeds—will not by themselves make us right with God. A right relationship is based on faith—the confidence that God is who he says he is and does what he says he will do. Right actions follow naturally as a by-product.

15:6 We have read of Abram's mistakes, and we know he was only human. How could God call him righteous? Though human and sinful, Abram believed and trusted in God. It was faith, not perfection, that made him right in God's eyes. This same principle holds for all of us. Our first response must be to believe in God. When we do, he declares us "righteous."

15:13, 14 The book of Exodus tells the story of this incredible journey.

15:16 The Amorites were one of the nations living in Canaan, the land God promised to Abram. God knew the people would grow more wicked and would someday need to be punished. Part of that punishment would involve taking away their land and giving it to Abram's descendants. God, in his mercy, was giving the Amorites plenty of time to repent, but he already knew they would not. At the right time, they would be "ready for punishment." Everything God does is true to his character. He is merciful, knows all, and acts justly—and his timing is perfect.

15:17 Why did God send this strange vision to Abram? God's

covenant with Abram was serious business. It represented an incredible promise from God and a huge responsibility for Abram. To confirm his promise, God gave Abram a sign—the smoking fire-pot and flaming torch. God took the initiative, gave the confirmation, and followed through on his promises. The sign to Abram was a visible assurance to him that the covenant God had made was real.

16:1–3 Sarai gave Hagar to Abram as a substitute wife, a common practice of that time. A married woman who could not have children was shamed by her peers and was often required to give a female servant to her husband in order to produce heirs. The children born to the servant woman were considered the children of the wife. Abram was acting in line with the custom of the day. But his action showed a lack of faith in God to fulfill his promise that Abram and *Sarai* would have a child (15:4).

16:3 Sarai took matters into her own hands by giving Hagar to Abram. Like Abram, she had trouble believing God's promise, which was apparently directed specifically toward Abram and Sarai. Out of this lack of faith came a series of problems. This invariably happens when we take over for God, trying to make a promise of his come true through efforts that are not in line with God's specific directions. In this case, time was the greatest test of Abram and Sarai's willingness to allow God to supply their needs. Sometimes we too must simply wait. When we ask God for something, and it is clear that we must wait, the temptation increases to do something ourselves to make it happen in the wrong way.

realized she was pregnant, she became very proud and arrogant toward her mistress Sarai.

16:5
Gen 31:53

5Then Sarai said to Abram, "It's all your fault. For now this servant girl of mine despises me, though I myself gave her the privilege of being your wife. May the Lord judge you for doing this to me!"

6"You have my permission to punish the girl as you see fit," Abram replied. So Sarai beat her and she ran away.

16:7
Gen 21:17
22:11

7The Angel of the Lord found her beside a desert spring along the road to Shur.

16:5 *May the Lord judge you for doing this to me,* literally, "Let the Lord judge between me and you."

ISHMAEL

Have you ever wondered if you were born into the wrong family? We don't know much about how Ishmael viewed life, but that question must have haunted him at times. His life, his name, and his position were bound up in a conflict between two jealous women. Sarah, impatient with God's timetable, had taken matters into her own hands, deciding to have a child through another woman. Hagar, servant that she was, submitted to being used this way. But her pregnancy gave birth to strong feelings of superiority toward Sarah. Into this tense atmosphere, Ishmael was born.

For 16 years, Abraham thought Ishmael's birth had fulfilled God's promise. He was surprised to hear God say that the child he would work through would be Abraham and Sarah's very own. Sarah's pregnancy and Isaac's birth must have had a devastating impact on Ishmael. Until then he had been treated as a son, but this latest arrival made his future uncertain. During Isaac's weaning celebration, Sarah caught Ishmael teasing his half brother. As a result, Hagar and Ishmael were permanently expelled from Abraham's family.

Much of what happened throughout his life cannot be blamed on Ishmael. He was caught in a process much bigger than himself. However, his own actions showed that he had chosen to become part of the problem and not part of the solution. He chose to live out his circumstances instead of living above them.

The choice he made is one we all must make. There are circumstances over which we have no control (heredity, for instance), but there are others over which we do have control (decisions we make). At the heart of the matter is the sin-oriented nature we have all inherited. It can be partly controlled, although not overcome, by human effort. In the context of history, Ishmael's life represents the mess we make when we don't try to change those things that we can change. The God of the Bible has offered a solution. His answer is not control, but a changed life freely given by God. To have a changed life, turn to God, trust him to forgive your sinful past, and begin to change your attitude toward him and others.

Strengths and accomplishments:
- One of the first to experience the physical sign of God's covenant, circumcision
- Known for his ability as an archer and hunter
- Fathered twelve sons who became leaders of warrior tribes

Weakness and mistake:
- Failed to recognize the place of his half brother, Isaac, and mocked him

Lesson from his life:
- God's plans incorporate people's mistakes

Vital statistics:
- Where: Canaan and Egypt
- Occupation: Archer/Hunter/Warrior
- Relatives: Parents: Hagar and Abraham. Half brother: Isaac.

Key verses:
"Hagar, what's wrong? Don't be afraid! For God has heard the lad's cries as he is lying there. Go and get the boy and comfort him, for I will make a great nation from his descendants" (Genesis 21:17, 18).

Ishmael's story is told in Genesis 16—17, 25—28, and 36. He is also mentioned in 1 Chronicles 1:28–31; Galatians 4:28, 29.

16:5 Sarai arranged for Hagar to have a child by Abram and then blamed Abram for going along with the plan. Sarai blamed someone else for her situation just as Adam and Eve did in Genesis 3:12, 13. It is easier to strikeout in frustration and point the finger at someone else than to admit an error and ask forgiveness.

16:6 Did Sarai really beat Hagar? After Sarai blamed Abram for her problems, he gave her authority to punish Hagar as she pleased. Sarai took out her anger against Abram and herself on Hagar. Although Sarai may not literally have beaten her, the treatment was harsh enough to cause Hagar to run away. Anger, especially when it arises out of our own shortcomings, can be dangerous.

[8]*The Angel:* "Hagar, Sarai's maid, where have you come from, and where are you going?"

Hagar: "I am running away from my mistress."

[9-12]*The Angel:* "Return to your mistress and act as you should, for I will make you into a great nation. Yes, you are pregnant and your baby will be a son, and you are to name him Ishmael ('God hears'), because God has heard your woes. This son of yours will be a wild one—free and untamed as a wild ass! He will be against everyone, and everyone will feel the same towards him. But he will live near the rest of his kin."

[13]Thereafter Hagar spoke of Jehovah—for it was he who appeared to her—as "the God who looked upon me," for she thought, "I saw God and lived to tell it." [14]Later that well was named "The Well of the Living One Who Sees Me." It lies between Kadesh and Bered.

[15]So Hagar gave Abram a son, and Abram named him Ishmael. [16](Abram was eighty-six years old at this time.)

The terms of the promise

17 When Abram was ninety-nine years old, God appeared to him and told him, "I am the Almighty; obey me and live as you should. [2, 3, 4]I will prepare a contract between us, guaranteeing to make you into a mighty nation. In fact you shall be the father of not only one nation, but a multitude of nations!" Abram fell face downward in the dust as God talked with him.

[5]"What's more," God told him, "I am changing your name. It is no longer 'Abram' ('Exalted Father'), but 'Abraham' ('Father of Nations')—for that is what you will be. I have declared it. [6]I will give you millions of descendants who will form many nations! Kings shall be among your descendants! [7, 8]And I will continue this agreement between us generation after generation, forever, for it shall be between me and your children as well. It is a contract that I shall be your God and the God of your posterity. And I will give all this land of Canaan to you and them, forever. And I will be your God.

16:13 *Thereafter,* implied.

Cross references (right margin):

16:8 Gen 3:9; 4:9
16:9 Gen 21:12; Eccles 10:4; Eph 6:5; Tit 2:9
16:10 Gen 17:20
16:11 Gen 16:15; Ex 3:7,8
16:12 Gen 21:20; Job 39:5-8
16:13 Gen 12:8; 32:30
16:14 Gen 14:7
16:15 Gen 21:9; 25:12
16:16 Gen 12:4; 16:3
17:1 Gen 12:7; 28:3
17:2 Gen 13:16; 15:5; 17:2
17:3 Gen 17:17; 18:2; Ex 3:6
17:5 Neh 9:7; Rom 4:17
17:6 Gen 35:11
17:7 Gen 12:7; 13:15; Lev 11:45; 26:12; Ps 105:8-11

16:8 Hagar was running away from her mistress and her problem. The Angel of the Lord gave her this advice: (1) to return and face Sarai, the cause of her problem, and (2) to act as she should. This suggests that she needed to work on her attitude toward Sarai, no matter how justified it may have been. Running from our problems rarely solves them. With Hagar we learn that it is wise to return to our problems, face them squarely, accept God's promise of help, correct our attitudes, and act as we should, not as we would like to.

16:9–12 The statement that Ishmael would be "free and untamed as a wild ass" was actually a compliment, something Hagar could take pride in. In Abram's culture, the ass or donkey was a highly valued animal.

16:13 We have watched three people make serious mistakes: (1) Sarai, who took matters into her own hands and gave her servant girl to Abram; (2) Abram, who went along with the plan but who, when things began to go wrong, refused to get involved in solving the problem; and (3) Hagar, who ran away from the problem. In spite of this messy situation, God demonstrates how he is not limited by the complications in our lives. He can bring good out of any situation. Sarai and Abram still received the son they so desperately wanted, and God solved Hagar's problem despite Abram's refusal to get involved. No problem in your life is too complicated for God if you are willing to allow him to help you.

17:1 The Lord told Abram: "I am God; therefore obey me and live as you should." God has the same message for us today. We are to obey him because he is God. That is reason enough. If you don't think the benefits are worth it, consider first who God is—the only one who has the power and ability to meet your every need.

17:2–4 Why did God repeat his covenant to Abram? Twice before, God had mentioned this agreement (Genesis 12 and15). Now, however, God was bringing it into focus and preparing to carry it out. God now revealed to Abram several specific parts of his covenant: (1) God would make Abram the father of a mighty nation; (2) many nations and kings would come from his descendants; (3) God would continue to reveal himself to those descending from Abraham; (4) God would give Abram's descendants the land of Canaan.

17:5 God changes Abram's name to Abraham to reflect his new position as the father of a nation. From this point on he is always referred to as Abraham.

17:5–8 God was making an agreement, or contract, between himself and Abraham. The terms were very simple. Abraham's part was to believe in God and obey him. God's part was to give him heirs, property, power, and wealth. Most contracts we make with others are even trades. We give something and in return receive something of equal value. But when we make the agreement to become part of God's family, the blessings far outweigh what we must give up.

17:9
Ex 19:5; 26:5
Ps 25:10
17:10
Acts 7:8
17:11
Ex 12:48
Deut 10:16
17:12
Gen 21:4
Lev 12:3
Lk 1:59; 2:21
Phil 3:5
17:13
Ex 12:44
17:14
Ex 30:33
Lev 7:20
17:16
Gen 18:10

9, 10"Your part of the contract," God told him, "is to obey its terms. You personally and all your posterity have this continual responsibility: that every male among you shall be circumcised; 11the foreskin of his penis shall be cut off. This will be the proof that you and they accept this covenant. 12Every male shall be circumcised on the eighth day after birth. This applies to every foreign-born slave as well as to everyone born in your household. This is a permanent part of this contract, and it applies to all your posterity. 13All must be circumcised. Your bodies will thus be marked as participants in my everlasting covenant. 14Anyone who refuses these terms shall be cut off from his people; for he has violated my contract."

15Then God added, "Regarding Sarai your wife—her name is no longer 'Sarai' but 'Sarah' ('Princess'). 16And I will bless her and give you a son from her! Yes, I will bless her richly, and make her the mother of nations! Many kings shall be among your posterity."

ABRAHAM

We all know that there are consequences to any action we take. What we do can set into motion a series of events that may still be going on long after we're gone. Unfortunately, when we are making a decision most of us think only of the immediate consequences. These are often misleading because they are short-lived.

Abraham had a choice to make. His decision was between setting out with his family and belongings for parts unknown or staying right where he was. He had to decide between the security of what he already had and the uncertainty of traveling under God's direction. All he had to go on was God's promise to guide and bless him. Abraham could hardly have been expected to visualize how much of the future was resting on his decision of whether to go or to stay. But his obedience affected the history of the world. His decision to follow God set into motion the development of the nation that God would eventually use as his own when he visited earth himself. When Jesus Christ came to earth, God's promise was fulfilled: through Abraham the entire world was blessed.

You probably don't know the long-term effects of most decisions you make. But shouldn't the fact that there will be long-term results cause you to think carefully and seek God's guidance as you make choices and take action today?

Strengths and accomplishments:
- His faith pleased God
- Became the founder of the Jewish nation
- Was respected by others and courageous in defending his family at any cost
- Was not only a caring father to his own family, but practiced hospitality to others
- Was a successful and wealthy rancher
- He usually avoided conflicts, but when they were unavoidable, he allowed his opponent to set the rules for settling the disputes

Weakness and mistake:
- Under direct pressure, he distorted the truth

Lessons from his life:
- God desires dependence, trust, and faith in him—not faith in our ability to please him
- God's plan from the beginning has been to make himself known to all people

Vital statistics:
- Where: Born in Ur of the Chaldeans; spent most of his life in the land of Canaan
- Occupation: Wealthy livestock owner
- Relatives: Brothers: Nahor and Haran. Father: Terah. Wife: Sarah. Nephew: Lot. Sons: Ishmael and Isaac.
- Contemporaries: Abimelech, Melchizedek

Key verse:
"And Abram believed God; then God considered him righteous on account of his faith" (Genesis 15:6).

Abraham's story is told in Genesis 11—25. He is also mentioned in Exodus 2:24; Acts 7:2–8; Romans 4; Galatians 3; Hebrews 6, 7, 11.

17:9, 10 Why did God require circumcision? (1) As a sign of obedience to him in all matters. (2) As a sign of belonging to his covenant people. Once circumcised, there was no turning back. The man would be identified as a Jew forever. (3) As a symbol of "cutting off" the old life of sin, purifying one's heart toward God, and dedicating oneself to God and his promises. (4) Possibly as a health measure.

Circumcision more than any other practice tended to separate God's people from their heathen neighbors. In Abraham's day, this was essential to develop the pure worship of the one true God.

¹⁷Then Abraham threw himself down in worship before the Lord, but inside he was laughing in disbelief! "Me, be a father?" he said in amusement. "Me—100 years old? And Sarah, to have a baby at 90?"

¹⁸And Abraham said to God, "Yes, do bless Ishmael!"

¹⁹"No," God replied, "that isn't what I said. *Sarah* shall bear you a son; and you are to name him Isaac ('Laughter'), and I will sign my covenant with him forever, and with his descendants. ²⁰As for Ishmael, all right, I will bless him also, just as you have asked me to. I will cause him to multiply and become a great nation. Twelve princes shall be among his posterity. ²¹But my contract is with Isaac, who will be born to you and Sarah next year at about this time."

²²That ended the conversation and God left. ²³Then, that very day, Abraham took Ishmael his son and every other male—born in his household or bought from outside—and cut off their foreskins, just as God had told him to. ²⁴⁻²⁷Abraham was ninety-nine years old at that time, and Ishmael was thirteen. Both were circumcised the same day, along with all the other men and boys of the household, whether born there or bought as slaves.

17:17
Gen 17:3; 18:13

17:19
Gen 21:1,2
26:3-5

17:20
Gen 21:13
25:16

17:21
Gen 17:7,19

17:22
Gen 18:33
35:13

17:23
Gen 14:14

17:24
Gen 16:16; 17:1
Rom 4:11

17:25
Gen 16:16

4. Sodom and Gomorrah
Three angels visit Abraham

18 The Lord appeared again to Abraham while he was living in the oak grove at Mamre. This is the way it happened: One hot summer afternoon as he was sitting in the opening of his tent, ²he suddenly noticed three men coming toward him. He sprang up and ran to meet them and welcomed them.

³,⁴"Sirs," he said, "please don't go any further. Stop awhile and rest here in the shade of this tree while I get water to refresh your feet, ⁵and a bite to eat to strengthen you. Do stay awhile before continuing your journey."

"All right," they said, "do as you have said."

⁶Then Abraham ran back to the tent and said to Sarah, "Quick! Mix up some pancakes! Use your best flour, and make enough for the three of them!" ⁷Then he ran out to the herd and selected a fat calf and told a servant to hurry and butcher it. ⁸Soon, taking them cheese and milk and the roast veal, he set it before the men and stood beneath the trees beside them as they ate.

⁹"Where is Sarah, your wife?" they asked him.

"In the tent," Abraham replied.

¹⁰Then the Lord said, "Next year I will give you and Sarah a son!" (Sarah was listening from the tent door behind him.) ¹¹Now Abraham and Sarah were both very old, and Sarah was long since past the time when she could have a baby. ¹²So Sarah laughed silently. "A woman my age have a baby?" she scoffed to herself. "And with a husband as old as mine?"

¹³Then God said to Abraham, "Why did Sarah laugh? Why did she say 'Can an old woman like me have a baby?' ¹⁴Is anything too hard for God? Next year, just as I told you, I will certainly see to it that Sarah has a son."

18:1
Gen 12:7; 13:18
Gen 14:13

18:2
Gen 19:1; 23:7
33:3,6,7
Josh 5:13-15

18:3
Gen 19:2; 24:31

18:5
Judg 6:18; 13:15,
16

18:7
Judg 13:15

18:8
Deut 32:14

18:10
Gen 22:15
Judg 13:3
Rom 9:9

18:11
Gen 17:17

18:12
1 Pet 3:6

18:14
Gen 18:10
Jer 32:17,27
Lk 1:37

17:17 *inside he was laughing in disbelief*, implied. **18:6** *pancakes*, probably some sort of *tortilla.* **18:10** *next year*, literally, "when life would be due."

17:17–27 How could Abraham doubt God? Abraham, the man God considered "righteous" because of his faith, had trouble believing God's promise to him. However, in spite of his doubts, Abraham proceeded to follow God's commands (17:22–27). Even those of great faith may have doubts. When God seems to want the impossible and you begin to doubt his leading, be like Abraham. Focus on God's commitment to fulfill his promises to you, and then continue to obey.

18:2–5 Abraham was eager to show hospitality to these men, as was Lot in Genesis 19:2. In Abraham's day, a person's reputation was largely connected to his hospitality—the sharing of home and food. Even strangers were to be treated as highly honored guests.

Meeting another's need for food or shelter was and still is one of the most immediate and practical ways to obey God and do his will. It is also a time-honored relationship-builder. Hebrews 13:2 suggests that we, like Abraham, might actually entertain angels. This thought should be on our minds the next time we have the opportunity to meet the needs of any stranger.

18:14 "Is anything too hard for God?" This question reveals much about God. Make it a habit to insert your specific needs into this question. "Is this day in my life too hard for God?" "Is this habit I'm trying to break too hard for God?" "Is the communication problem I'm having too hard for God?" Asking the question in this way reminds you that God is personally involved in your life and offers his power to help you.

¹⁵But Sarah denied it. "I didn't laugh," she lied, for she was afraid.

18:16
Gen 18:22; 19:1
¹⁶Then the men stood up from their meal and started on toward Sodom; and Abraham went with them part of the way.

18:17
Gen 19:24
18:18
Gen 12:2,3
Gal 3:18
18:19
Neh 9:7
¹⁷"Should I hide my plan from Abraham?" God asked. ¹⁸"For Abraham shall become a mighty nation, and he will be a source of blessing for all the nations of the earth. ¹⁹And I have picked him out to have godly descendants and a godly household—men who are just and good—so that I can do for him all I have promised."

SARAH

There probably isn't anything harder to do than to wait, whether we are expecting something good, something bad, or an unknown.

One way we often cope with a long wait (or even a short one) is to begin helping God get his plan into action. Sarah tried this approach. She was too old to expect to have a child of her own, so she thought God must have something else in mind. From Sarah's limited point of view this could only be to give Abraham a son through another woman—a common practice in her day. The plan seemed harmless enough. Abraham would sleep with Sarah's slave girl who would then give birth to a child. Sarah would take the child as her own. The plan worked beautifully—at first. But as you read about the events that followed, you will be struck by how often Sarah must have regretted the day she decided to push God's timetable ahead.

Another way we cope with a long wait is to gradually conclude that what we're waiting for is never going to happen. Sarah waited ninety years for a baby! When God told her she would finally have one of her own, she laughed, not so much from a lack of faith in what God could do, but from doubt about what he could do *through her*. When confronted about her laughter, she lied—as she had seen her husband do from time to time. She probably didn't want her true feelings to be known.

What parts of your life seem to be "on hold" right now? Do you understand that this may be part of God's plan for you? The Bible has more than enough clear direction to keep us busy while we're waiting for some particular part of life to move ahead.

Strengths and accomplishments:
- Was intensely loyal to her own child
- Became the mother of a nation and an ancestor of Jesus
- Was a woman of faith. She is the first woman listed in the Hall of Faith in Hebrews 11.

Weaknesses and mistakes:
- Had trouble believing God's promises to her
- Attempted to work problems out on her own, without consulting God
- Tried to cover her own faults by blaming others

Lessons from her life:
- God responds to faith even in the midst of failures
- God is not bound by what usually happens. He can stretch the limits and cause unheard-of events to occur.

Vital statistics:
- Where: Married Abram in Ur of the Chaldeans, then moved with him to Canaan
- Occupation: Wife, mother, household manager
- Relatives: Father: Terah. Husband: Abraham. Brothers: Nahor and Haran. Nephew: Lot. Son: Isaac.

Key verse:
"Sarah, too, had faith, and because of this she was able to become a mother in spite of her old age, for she realized that God, who gave her his promise, would certainly do what he said" (Hebrews 11:11).

Sarah's story is told in Genesis 11—25. She is also mentioned in Isaiah 51:2; Romans 4:19; 9:9; Hebrews 11:11; 1 Peter 3:6.

18:15 Sarah lied because she was afraid of being discovered. Fear is the most common motive for lying. We are afraid that our inner thoughts and emotions will be exposed or our wrongdoings discovered. But lying causes greater complications than telling the truth. If God can't be trusted with our innermost thoughts and fears, we are in greater trouble than we first imagined.

Abraham prays for Sodom

20So the Lord told Abraham, "I have heard that the people of Sodom and Gomorrah are utterly evil, and that everything they do is wicked. 21I am going down to see whether these reports are true or not. Then I will know."

22,23So the other two went on toward Sodom, but the Lord remained with Abraham a while. Then Abraham approached him and said, "Will you kill good and bad alike? 24Suppose you find fifty godly people there within the city—will you destroy it, and not spare it for their sakes? 25That wouldn't be right! Surely you wouldn't do such a thing, to kill the godly with the wicked! Why, you would be treating godly and wicked exactly the same! Surely you wouldn't do that! Should not the Judge of all the earth be fair?"

26And God replied, "If I find fifty godly people there, I will spare the entire city for their sake."

27Then Abraham spoke again. "Since I have begun, let me go on and speak further to the Lord, though I am but dust and ashes. 28*Suppose there are only forty-five?* Will you destroy the city for lack of five?"

And God said, "I will not destroy it if I find forty-five."

29Then Abraham went further with his request. *"Suppose there are only forty?"*

And God replied, "I won't destroy it if there are forty."

30"Please don't be angry," Abraham pleaded. "Let me speak: *suppose only thirty are found there?"*

And God replied, "I won't do it if there are thirty there."

31Then Abraham said, "Since I have dared to speak to God, let me continue—*Suppose there are only twenty?"*

And God said, "Then I won't destroy it for the sake of the twenty."

32Finally, Abraham said, "Oh, let not the Lord be angry; I will speak but this once more! *Suppose only ten are found?"*

And God said, "Then, for the sake of the ten, I won't destroy it."

33And the Lord went on his way when he had finished his conversation with Abraham. And Abraham returned to his tent.

God rescues Lot

19 That evening the two angels came to the entrance of the city of Sodom, and Lot was sitting there as they arrived. When he saw them he stood up to meet them, and welcomed them.

18:20-33 Did Abraham change God's mind? Of course not. The more likely answer is that God changed Abraham's mind. Abraham knew that God is just and that he punishes sin. But he may have wondered about God's mercy. Abraham seemed to be probing God's mind to see how merciful he really was. He left his conversation with God convinced that God was both kind and fair. Our prayers may not change God's mind, but they may change ours just as Abraham's prayer changed his. Prayer is the means through which we can better comprehend the mind of God.

18:20-33 Why did God let Abraham question his justice and intercede for a wicked city? Abraham knew God must punish sin, but he also knew from experience that God is merciful to sinners. God knew there were not ten righteous people in the city, but he was merciful enough to allow Abraham to intercede. He was also merciful enough to help Lot, Abraham's nephew, get out of Sodom before it was destroyed. God does not take pleasure in destroying the wicked, but he must punish sin. He is both just and merciful. We must be thankful that God's mercy extends to us.

18:21 God gave a fair test to the men of Sodom. He was not ignorant of all the wicked things going on, but, in his fairness and long-suffering, gave the people of Sodom one last chance to turn to him. God is still waiting with the hope that all people will turn to him (2 Peter 3:9). The wise will turn to him before his patience wears out.

18:25 Was God being unfair to the people of Sodom? Did he really plan to destroy the good with the wicked? On the contrary, God's fairness stood out: (1) he agreed to spare the entire city if only ten godly people lived there; (2) he showed great mercy toward Lot, apparently the only man in the city who had any kind of relationship with him (and even that was questionable). God went so far as to almost force Lot to leave Sodom before it was destroyed. Remember God's patience when you are tempted to think he is unfair. Even the most godly people deserve his justice. We should be glad God doesn't direct his justice toward us as he did toward Sodom.

18:33 God showed Abraham that asking for anything is allowed, with the understanding that God's answers come from God's perspective. They are not always in harmony with our expectations, for only he knows the whole story. Are you missing God's answer to a prayer of yours because you haven't considered any possible answer other than the one you expect?

19:1 The city gate was the meeting place for city officials and others to discuss current events and transact business. It was a place of authority and status where you could see and be seen. Evidently Lot held an important position in the government or associated with those who did, for the angels found him at the city gate when they arrived. Perhaps this is why Lot was so reluctant to leave (19:16, 18-22).

19:2
Gen 18:3
Lk 24:28

2"Sirs," he said, "come to my home as my guests for the night; you can get up as early as you like and be on your way again."

"Oh, no thanks," they said, "we'll just stretch out here along the street."

19:3
Gen 18:6-8

3But he was very urgent, until at last they went home with him, and he set a great feast before them, complete with freshly baked unleavened bread. After the meal, 4as they were preparing to retire for the night, the men of the city—yes, Sodomites,

19:4
Gen 13:13; 18:20
Prov 4:16

young and old from all over the city—surrounded the house 5and shouted to Lot, "Bring out those men to us so we can rape them."

19:5
Lev 18:22; 20:13
Judg 19:22
19:8
Deut 23:17

6Lot stepped outside to talk to them, shutting the door behind him. 7"Please, fellows," he begged, "don't do such a wicked thing. 8Look—I have two virgin daughters, and I'll surrender them to you to do with as you wish. But leave these men alone, for they are under my protection."

19:9
Ex 2:14
Prov 9:7,8

9"Stand back," they yelled. "Who do you think you are? We let this fellow settle among us and now he tries to tell us what to do! We'll deal with you far worse than with those other men." And they lunged at Lot and began breaking down the door.

19:10
Gen 19:1
19:11
Deut 28:28
2 Kgs 6:18
Acts 9:8

10But the two men reached out and pulled Lot in and bolted the door, 11and temporarily blinded the men of Sodom so that they couldn't find the door.

12"What relatives do you have here in the city?" the men asked. "Get them out of this place—sons-in-law, sons, daughters, or anyone else. 13For we will destroy the city completely. The stench of the place has reached to heaven and God has sent us to destroy it."

19:13
Gen 18:20
1 Chron 21:15
Jude 7

14So Lot rushed out to tell his daughters' fiancés, "Quick, get out of the city, for the Lord is going to destroy it." But the young men looked at him as though he had lost his senses.

19:14
Ex 9:21
Jer 5:11,12
43:1-3

15At dawn the next morning the angels became urgent. "Hurry," they said to Lot, "take your wife and your two daughters who are here and get out while you can, or you will be caught in the destruction of the city."

19:16
Ps 119:60

16When Lot still hesitated, the angels seized his hand and the hands of his wife and two daughters and rushed them to safety, outside the city, for the Lord was merciful.

19:17
Gen 13:10
19:26
1 Sam 19:11
Jer 48:6

17"Flee for your lives," the angels told him. *"And don't look back.* Escape to the mountains. Don't stay down here on the plain or you will die."

18, 19, 20"Oh no, sirs, please," Lot begged, "since you've been so kind to me and saved my life, and you've granted me such mercy, let me flee to that little village over there instead of into the mountains, for I fear disaster in the mountain. See, the village is close by and it is just a small one. Please, please, let me go there instead. Don't you see how small it is? And my life will be saved."

19:21
Ps 102:17
145:19

21"All right," the angel said, "I accept your proposition and won't destroy that

---

19:8 How could any father give his daughters to be savaged by a mob of perverts, just to protect two strangers? Possibly Lot was scheming to save both the girls and the visitors, hoping the girls' fiances (19:14) would rescue them or that the homosexual men would be uninterested in the girls and simply go away. Although it was the custom of the day to protect your guests at *any* cost, this terrible suggestion reveals how deeply sin had been absorbed into Lot's life. He had become hardened to evil acts in an evil city. Whatever Lot's motives were, we see here an illustration of Sodom's terrible wickedness—a wickedness so great that God had to destroy the entire city.

19:13 God promised to spare Sodom if only ten godly people lived there (18:32). Obviously not even ten could be found, for the angels arrived to destroy the city. Archeological evidence points to an advanced civilization in this area during Abraham's day. Most researchers also confirm some kind of sudden and devastating destruction. It is now widely thought that the buried city lies covered beneath the waters of the southern end of the Dead Sea. The sins of Sodom reveal that the people of Lot's day had to deal with the same kinds of repulsive sins the world faces today.

19:14 Lot had lived so long and so contented among ungodly

people that he was no longer a believable witness for God. He had allowed his environment to shape him, rather than shaping his environment. Do those who know you see you as a witness for God, or are you just one of the crowd, blending in unnoticed? Lot had compromised to the point that he had become almost useless to God. When he finally did make a stand, no one listened. Have you, too, become useless to God because you are too much like your environment? To make a difference, you first must decide to be different.

19:16 Lot hesitated and the angel seized his hand and rushed him to safety. He did not want to abandon the wealth and comfort he enjoyed in Sodom. It is easy to criticize Lot for being hypnotized by his attraction to Sodom when the choice seems so clear to us. To be wiser than Lot, we must see that our hesitation to obey stems from the false attractions of the pleasures of our culture.

19:16, 29 Notice how God's mercy toward Abraham extended to Lot and his family. Because Abraham pleaded for Lot, God was merciful and saved Lot from the fiery death that engulfed Sodom. A godly person can often affect others for good. James says the prayer of a godly person is powerful (James 5:16). All Christians should follow Abraham's example and pray for others to be saved.

little city. 22But hurry! For I can do nothing until you are there." (From that time on that village was named Zoar, meaning "Little City.")

23The sun was rising as Lot reached the village. 24Then the Lord rained down fire and flaming tar from heaven upon Sodom and Gomorrah, 25and utterly destroyed them, along with the other cities and villages of the plain, eliminating all life—people, plants, and animals alike. 26But Lot's wife looked back as she was following along behind him, and became a pillar of salt.

27That morning Abraham was up early and hurried out to the place where he had stood before the Lord. 28He looked out across the plain to Sodom and Gomorrah and saw columns of smoke and fumes, as from a furnace, rising from the cities there. 29So God heeded Abraham's plea and kept Lot safe, removing him from the maelstrom of death that engulfed the cities.

The sin of Lot's daughters

30Afterwards Lot left Zoar, fearful of the people there, and went to live in a cave in the mountains with his two daughters. 31One day the older girl said to her sister, "There isn't a man anywhere in this entire area that our father would let us marry. And our father will soon be too old for having children. 32Come, let's fill him with wine and then we will sleep with him, so that our clan will not come to an end." 33So they got him drunk that night, and the older girl went in and had sexual intercourse with her father; but he was unaware of her lying down or getting up again.

34The next morning she said to her younger sister, "I slept with my father last night. Let's fill him with wine again tonight, and you go in and lie with him, so that our family line will continue." 35So they got him drunk again that night, and the younger girl went in and lay with him, and, as before, he didn't know that anyone was there. 36And so it was that both girls became pregnant from their father. 37The older girl's baby was named Moab; he became the ancestor of the nation of the Moabites. 38The name of the younger girl's baby was Benammi; he became the ancestor of the nation of the Ammonites.

Abraham deceives the king

20 Now Abraham moved south to the Negeb, and settled between Kadesh and Shur. One day, when visiting the city of Gerar, 2he declared that Sarah was his sister! Then King Abimelech sent for her, and had her brought to him at his palace.

19:22
Gen 13:10
19:30
Isa 15:5

19:24
Lk 17:29
2 Pet 2:6
Jude 7

19:25
Deut 29:23
Isa 3:9; 13:19
2 Pet 2:6

19:26
Gen 19:17
Lk 17:32

19:29
2 Pet 2:7,8

19:30
Gen 13:10
1 Sam 22:1
1 Kgs 18:4

19:31
Gen 19:14
Gen 38:8,9,18

19:32
Prov 23:31-33
Hab 2:15

19:33
Gen 9:21
Lev 18:6
Prov 20:1

19:37
Gen 36:35
Ex 15:15
Num 21:29
Deut 2:9
Ruth 1:1

19:38
Num 21:24
Deut 2:19

20:1
Gen 13:1; 14:7
26:1

20:2
Gen 12:13
20:12; 26:7

19:24 In the story of Sodom and Gomorrah, we see two facets of God's character: his great patience (considering sparing a wicked city for ten good men) and his fierce anger (destroying both cities). As we grow spiritually, we should find ourselves developing both a deeper fear of God (because of his anger toward sin) and a deeper love for God (because of his patience when we sin).

19:26 Lot's wife turned back to look at the smoldering city of Sodom. Clinging to the comforts of the past, she was unwilling to turn completely from sin. Are you looking back longingly at sin while trying to move forward with God? You can't make progress with God as long as you are holding onto pieces of your old life. Jesus said it this way in Matthew 6:24: "You cannot serve two masters."

19:30–38 In this pitiful sequel to the story of the destruction of Sodom, we see two women compelled to preserve their family line. They were not driven by lust, but by desperation—they feared they would never marry. Lot's tendency to compromise and refusal to act reached its peak. He should have found right partners for his daughters long before this—Abraham's family wasn't far away. Now the two daughters stooped to incest, showing their acceptance of the morals learned in Sodom. When we are desperate for what we feel we must have, we are most likely to sin.

19:30–38 Why doesn't the Bible openly condemn these sisters for what they did? In many cases, the Bible does not judge people for

their actions. It simply reports the events. However, incest is clearly condemned in other parts of Scripture (Leviticus 18:6–18; 20:11, 12, 17, 19–21; Deuteronomy 22:30; 27:20–23; Ezekiel 22:11; 1 Corinthians 5:1). Perhaps the consequence of their actions (Moab and Ammon became enemies of Israel) was God's way of judging their sin.

19:37, 38 Moab and Benammi were the products of incest. They became the fathers of two of Israel's greatest enemies, the Moabites and Ammonites. These nations settled east of the Jordan River, and Israel never conquered them. Because of the family connection, Moses was forbidden to attack them (Deuteronomy 2:9). Ruth, great-grandmother of King David and an ancestor of Jesus, was from Moab.

20:2 Abraham had used this same trick before to protect himself and Sarah (12:11–13). Though Abraham is one of our heroes of faith, he did not learn his lesson well enough the first time. In fact, by giving in to the temptation again he risked turning a sinful act into a sinful pattern—lying whenever he suspected his life was in danger.

However godly we may be, certain temptations are especially difficult to resist. These are the vulnerable spots in our spiritual armor. As we struggle with these weaknesses, we can be encouraged to know that God is watching out for us just as he did with Abraham.

20:3
Gen 28:12
31:24,37:5

20:4
Gen 18:23-25

20:5
Gen 12:17
1 Kgs 9:4
Ps 7:8; 26:6

20:6
Gen 15:1; 31:7
Ps 84:11

20:7
Ex 7:1
1 Sam 7:5
Job 42:8

20:9
Gen 12:18

20:11
Gen 12:12
22:12; 42:18

20:13
Gen 11:31; 12:1

20:14
Gen 12:16

20:15
Gen 47:6

20:16
Gen 23:15

20:17
Num 12:13; 21:7

20:18
Gen 12:17

21:1
Gen 17:16,21

21:5
Rom 4:19

21:6
Gen 18:12

21:7
Gen 18:14
Lk 1:37

³But that night God came to him in a dream and told him, "You are a dead man, for that woman you took is married."

⁴But Abimelech hadn't slept with her yet, so he said, "Lord, will you slay an innocent man? ⁵He told me, 'She is my sister,' and she herself said, 'Yes, he is my brother.' I hadn't the slightest intention of doing anything wrong."

⁶"Yes, I know," the Lord replied. "That is why I held you back from sinning against me; that is why I didn't let you touch her. ⁷Now restore her to her husband, and he will pray for you (for he is a prophet) and you shall live. But if you don't return her to him, you are doomed to death along with all your household."

⁸The king was up early the next morning, and hastily called a meeting of all the palace personnel and told them what had happened. And great fear swept through the crowd.

⁹, ¹⁰Then the king called for Abraham. "What is this you've done to us?" he demanded. "What have I done that deserves treatment like this, to make me and my kingdom guilty of this great sin? Who would suspect that you would do a thing like this to me? Whatever made you think of this vile deed?"

¹¹, ¹²"Well," Abraham said, "I figured this to be a godless place. 'They will want my wife and will kill me to get her,' I thought. And besides, she *is* my sister—or at least a half-sister (we both have the same father)—and I married her. ¹³And when God sent me traveling far from my childhood home, I told her, 'Have the kindness to mention, wherever we come, that you are my sister.' "

¹⁴Then King Abimelech took sheep and oxen and servants—both men and women—and gave them to Abraham, and returned Sarah his wife to him.

¹⁵"Look my kingdom over, and choose the place where you want to live," the king told him. ¹⁶Then he turned to Sarah. "Look," he said, "I am giving your 'brother' a thousand silver pieces as damages for what I did, to compensate for any embarrassment and to settle any claim against me regarding this matter. Now justice has been done."

¹⁷Then Abraham prayed, asking God to cure the king and queen and the other women of the household, so that they could have children; ¹⁸for God had stricken all the women with barrenness to punish Abimelech for taking Abraham's wife.

5. Birth and near sacrifice of Isaac

21 Then God did as he had promised, and Sarah became pregnant and gave Abraham a baby son in his old age, at the time God had said; ³and Abraham named him Isaac (meaning "Laughter!"). ⁴, ⁵Eight days after he was born, Abraham circumcised him, as God required. (Abraham was 100 years old at that time.)

⁶And Sarah declared, "God has brought me laughter! All who hear about this shall rejoice with me. ⁷For who would have dreamed that I would ever have a baby? Yet I have given Abraham a child in his old age!"

20:6 Abimelech had unknowingly taken a married woman to his wife and was about to commit adultery. But God somehow prevented him from touching Sarah and held him back from sinning. What mercy on God's part. How many times has God done the same for us, holding us back from sin in ways we can't even detect? We have no way of knowing—we just know from this story that he can. God works just as often in ways we can't see as in ways we can.

20:11, 12 Abraham *assumed* that Abimelech was a wicked and ungodly man. He made a quick judgment based on an assumption that may not have been true. Abraham then resorted to a half-truth, deceiving Abimelech instead of trusting God to work in the king's life. Don't assume that God will not work in a situation that has potential problems. He may intervene when you least expect it.

20:17, 18 Why did God condemn Abimelech when it was Abraham who told the lie? Two reasons are suggested. (1) Abimelech was politically motivated to ally himself with

Abraham. To place Sarah in his harem would strengthen Abimelech's international position. (2) God was telling Abimelech that he wouldn't be punished if he simply did what was right. God was giving him the chance to prevent an unwarranted alliance and a sinful sexual relationship.

21:1–7 Who could believe Abraham would have a son at 100 years of age—and live to raise him to adulthood? But doing the impossible is everyday business for God. Our big problems may not seem so impossible if we let God handle them.

21:7 "Who would have dreamed!" After several promises, a visit by two angels, and the appearance of the Lord himself, Sarah finally cried out with surprise and joy at the birth of her son. Because of her doubt, worry, and fear, she had forfeited the peace she could have felt in God's wonderful promise to her. The way to bring peace to a troubled heart and mind is to focus on the promises of God. Trust him to do what he says.

Hagar and Ishmael sent away

⁸Time went by and the child grew and was weaned; and Abraham gave a party to celebrate the happy occasion. ⁹But when Sarah noticed Ishmael—the son of Abraham and the Egyptian girl Hagar—teasing Isaac, ¹⁰she turned upon Abraham and demanded, "Get rid of that slave girl and her son. He is not going to share your property with my son. I won't have it."

¹¹This upset Abraham very much, for after all, Ishmael too was his son.

¹²But God told Abraham, "Don't be upset over the boy or your slave-girl wife; do as Sarah says, for Isaac is the son through whom my promise will be fulfilled. ¹³And I will make a nation of the descendants of the slave-girl's son, too, because he also is yours."

¹⁴So Abraham got up early the next morning, prepared food for the journey, and strapped a canteen of water to Hagar's shoulders and sent her away with their son. She walked out into the wilderness of Beersheba, wandering aimlessly.

¹⁵When the water was gone she left the youth in the shade of a bush ¹⁶and went off and sat down a hundred yards or so away. "I don't want to watch him die," she said, and burst into tears, sobbing wildly.

¹⁷Then God heard the boy crying, and the Angel of God called to Hagar from the sky, "Hagar, what's wrong? Don't be afraid! For God has heard the lad's cries as he is lying there. ¹⁸Go and get him and comfort him, for I will make a great nation from his descendants."

¹⁹Then God opened her eyes and she saw a well; so she refilled the canteen and gave the lad a drink. ²⁰, ²¹And God blessed the boy and he grew up in the wilderness of Paran, and became an expert archer. And his mother arranged a marriage for him with a girl from Egypt.

A treaty by a well

²²About this time King Abimelech, and Phicol, commander of his troops, came to Abraham and said to him, "It is evident that God helps you in everything you do; ²³swear to me by God's name that you won't defraud me or my son or my grandson, but that you will be on friendly terms with my country, as I have been toward you."

²⁴Abraham replied, "All right, I swear to it!" ²⁵Then Abraham complained to the king about a well the king's servants had taken violently away from Abraham's servants.

²⁶"This is the first I've heard of it," the king exclaimed, "and I have no idea who is responsible. Why didn't you tell me before?"

²⁷Then Abraham gave sheep and oxen to the king, as sacrifices to seal their pact. ²⁸, ²⁹But when he took seven ewe lambs and set them off by themselves, the king inquired, "Why are you doing that?"

³⁰And Abraham replied, "They are my gift to you as a public confirmation that this well is mine."

³¹So from that time on the well was called Beer-sheba ("Well of the Oath"), because that was the place where they made their covenant. ³²Then King Abimelech, and Phicol, commander of his army, returned home again. ³³And Abraham planted a tamarisk tree beside the well, and prayed there to the Lord, calling upon the Eternal God. ³⁴And Abraham lived in the Philistine country for a long time.

21:9 *teasing*, or "mocking," whether in innocent fun or otherwise is not clear in the text.

21:8
1 Sam 1:22
21:9
Gal 4:29
21:10
Gen 16:4,5
Gal 4:30
21:12
Rom 9:7
Heb 11:18
21:13
Gen 16:10; 21:18
Gen 25:12-18
21:14
Gen 16:7
21:16
Jer 6:26
21:17
Ex 3:7
Deut 26:7
Ps 6:8
21:18
Gen 16:1-12;
25:12
21:19
Isa 48:15
21:20
Gen 28:15
21:21
Gen 14:6; 25:18
21:22
Gen 26:26
21:23
Gen 24:2
21:24
Gen 14:22
21:25
Gen 13:7; 26:15
21:27
Gen 26:31
Prov 18:16
21:14
21:30
Gen 31:44
21:31
Gen 21:14
26:33
Josh 15:28
21:33
1 Sam 22:6
31:13
Ps 90:2
Isa 9:6; 40:28
21:34
Gen 22:19

21:18 What happened to Ishmael, and who were his descendants? Ishmael became the ruler of a large tribe or nation. The Ishmaelites were nomads living in the wilderness of Sinai and Paran (south of Israel). One of Ishmael's daughters married Esau, Ishmael's nephew (28:9). The Bible pictures them as hostile to Israel and to God (Psalm 83:6).

21:31 Beer-sheba, the southernmost city of Israel, lay on the edge of a vast wilderness that stretched as far as Egypt to the southwest and Mount Sinai to the south. The phrase "from Dan to Beer-sheba" was often used to describe the traditional boundaries of the Promised Land (2 Samuel 17:11). Beer-sheba's southern location and the presence of several wells in the area may explain why Abraham settled there. Beer-sheba was also the home of Isaac, Abraham's son.

God tests Abraham's obedience

22:1
Ex 15:25; 16:4
Deut 8:2
Prov 17:3

22 Later on, God tested Abraham's [faith and obedience].
"Abraham!" God called.
"Yes, Lord?" he replied.

22:1 *faith and obedience,* implied.

ISAAC

A name carries great authority. It sets you apart. It triggers memories. The sound of it calls you to attention anywhere.

Many Bible names accomplished even more. They were often descriptions of important facts about one's past and hopes for the future. The choice of the name *Isaac,* "laughter," for Abraham and Sarah's son must have created a variety of feelings in them each time it was spoken. At times it must have recalled their shocked laughter at God's announcement that they would be parents in their old age. At other times, it must have brought back joyful feelings of receiving their long-awaited answer to prayer for a child. Most important, it was a testimony to God's power in making his promise a reality.

In a family of forceful initiators, Isaac was the quiet, "mind-my-own-business" type unless he was specifically called on to take action. He was the protected only child from the time Sarah got rid of Ishmael until Abraham arranged his marriage to Rebekah.

In his own family, Isaac had the patriarchal position, but Rebekah had the power. Rather than stand his ground, Isaac found it easier to compromise or lie to avoid confrontations.

In spite of these shortcomings, Isaac was part of God's plan. The model his father gave him included a great gift of faith in the one true God. God's promise to create a great nation through which he would bless the world was passed on by Isaac to his twin sons.

It is usually not hard to identify with Isaac in his weaknesses. But consider for a moment that God works through people in spite of their shortcomings and, often, through them. As you pray, put into words your desire to be available to God. You will discover that his willingness to use you is even greater than your desire to be used.

Strengths and accomplishments:
- He was the miracle child born to Sarah when she was 90 years old and Abraham when he was 100 years old
- He was the first descendant in fulfillment of God's promise to Abraham
- He seems to have been a caring and consistent husband, at least until his sons were born
- He demonstrated great patience

Weaknesses and mistakes:
- Under pressure he tended to imitate his father and lie
- In conflict he sought to avoid confrontation
- He played favorites between his sons and alienated his wife

Lessons from his life:
- Patience often brings rewards
- Both God's plans and his promises are larger than people
- God keeps his promises! He remains faithful though we are often faithless
- Playing favorites is sure to bring family conflict

Vital statistics:
- Where: The area called Negeb, in the southern part of Palestine, between Kadesh and Shur (Genesis 20:1)
- Occupation: Wealthy livestock owner
- Relatives: Parents: Abraham and Sarah. Half brother: Ishmael. Wife: Rebekah. Sons: Jacob and Esau.

Key verse:
"Sarah shall bear you a son; and you are to name him Isaac ('Laughter'), and I will sign my covenant with him forever, and with his descendants" (Genesis 17:19).

Isaac's story is told in Genesis 17:15—35:29. He is also mentioned in Romans 9:7, 8; Hebrews 11:17–20; James 2:21–24.

22:1 God gave Abraham a test. The purpose of this test was not to trip Abraham and watch him fall. Rather, God's real purpose was to deepen Abraham's capacity to obey God, and thus to develop his character. Just as fire refines ore to extract precious metals, God refines us through difficult circumstances. When we are tested we can complain, or we can try to see how God is stretching us to develop our character.

2"Take with you your only son—yes, Isaac whom you love so much—and go to the land of Moriah and sacrifice him there as a burnt offering upon one of the mountains which I'll point out to you!"

22:2
2 Kgs 3:27
2 Chron 3:1
Jn 3:16

3The next morning Abraham got up early, chopped wood for a fire upon the altar, saddled his donkey, and took with him his son Isaac and two young men who were his servants, and started off to the place where God had told him to go. 4On the third day of the journey Abraham saw the place in the distance.

22:3
Mt 10:37

5"Stay here with the donkey," Abraham told the young men, "and the lad and I will travel yonder and worship, and then come right back."

6Abraham placed the wood for the burnt offering upon Isaac's shoulders, while he himself carried the knife and the flint for striking a fire. So the two of them went on together.

22:7
Gen 8:20
Ex 29:38
Jn 1:29
Rev 13:7

7"Father," Isaac asked, "we have the wood and the flint to make the fire, but where is the lamb for the sacrifice?"

8"God will see to it, my son," Abraham replied. And they went on.

22:8
Gen 18:14
Mt 19:26
1 Pet 1:19
Rev 5:6

9When they arrived at the place where God had told Abraham to go, he built an altar and placed the wood in order, ready for the fire, and then tied Isaac and laid him on the altar over the wood. 10And Abraham took the knife and lifted it up to plunge it into his son, to slay him.

22:9
Gen 12:7
Heb 11:17
Jas 2:21

11At that moment the Angel of God shouted to him from heaven, "Abraham! Abraham!"

"Yes, Lord!" he answered.

22:11
Gen 16:7; 21:17
Ex 3:2

12"Lay down the knife; don't hurt the lad in any way," the Angel said, "for I know that God is first in your life—you have not withheld even your beloved son from me."

22:12
Heb 11:17

22:13
Gen 8:20

22:15
Gen 22:11

13Then Abraham noticed a ram caught by its horns in a bush. So he took the ram and sacrificed it, instead of his son, as a burnt offering on the altar. 14Abraham named the place "Jehovah provides"—and it still goes by that name to this day.

22:16
49:13
Heb 6:13
Lk 1:73,74

15Then the Angel of God called again to Abraham from heaven. 16"I, the Lord, have sworn by myself that because you have obeyed me and have not withheld even your beloved son from me, 17I will bless you with incredible blessings and multiply

22:17
Gen 12:12
13:16; 15:15
17:5

ABRAHAM'S TRIP TO MOUNT MORIAH
Abraham and Isaac traveled the 50 or 60 miles from Beer-sheba to Mount Moriah in about three days. This was a very difficult three days for Abraham who was on his way to sacrifice his beloved son, Isaac.

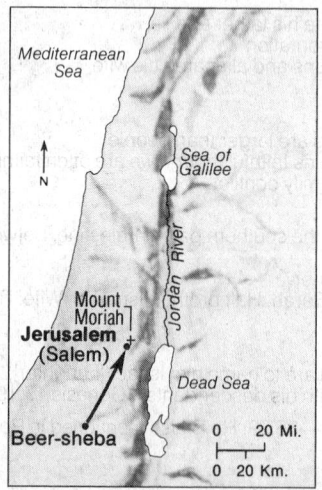

We should not always expect our obedience to God to be easy or come naturally.

22:7, 8 Why did God ask Abraham to perform human sacrifice? Heathen nations practiced human sacrifice, but God himself condemned this as a terrible sin (Leviticus 20:1–5). God did not want the physical death of Isaac, but he wanted Abraham to "sacrifice" Isaac in his heart so Abraham would be convinced that he loved God more than he loved his promised and long-awaited son. God was really testing Abraham. The purpose of testing is to strengthen our character and deepen our commitment to God. Through this difficult experience, Abraham learned about his commitment to obey God. He also learned about God's ability to provide.

22:13 Notice the parallel between the ram offered on the altar as a substitute for Isaac and Christ himself offered on the cross as a substitute for us. Whereas God stopped Abraham from sacrificing his son, God did not spare his own Son, Jesus, from dying on the cross. If Jesus had lived, the rest of mankind would have died. God sent his only Son to die for us so that we can be spared from the eternal death we deserve, and instead receive eternal life.

22:17, 18 Abraham received incredible blessings because he obeyed God. But what is God's idea of an incredible blessing? First, God promised Abraham children and grandchildren who would grow up to honor and obey God. Second, God gave Abraham the ability to face his enemies and ultimately conquer them. Third, God gave Abraham the opportunity of being a positive influence upon others. Their lives would be changed as a result of knowing Abraham. Most often we think of blessings as gifts to be enjoyed. But God's ideas of a blessing also extend to others.

22:3 The next morning Abraham began one of the greatest acts of obedience known to man. Over the years he had learned many tough lessons about the importance of obeying God. This time his obedience was prompt and complete. Obeying God is often a struggle, because it may mean giving up something we truly want.

your descendants into countless thousands and millions, like the stars above you in the sky, and like the sands along the seashore. They will conquer their enemies, ¹⁸and your offspring will be a blessing to all the nations of the earth—all because you have obeyed me."

¹⁹So they returned to his young men, and traveled home again to Beer-sheba. ²⁰⁻²³After this, a message arrived that Milcah, the wife of Abraham's brother Nahor, had borne him eight sons. Their names were: Uz, the oldest, Buz, the next oldest, Kemuel (father of Aram), Chesed, Hazo, Pildash, Jidlaph, Bethuel (father of Rebekah).

²⁴He also had four other children from his concubine, Reumah: Tebah, Gaham, Tahash, Maacah.

Abraham buries Sarah

23 When Sarah was 127 years old, she died in Hebron in the land of Canaan; there Abraham mourned and wept for her. ³Then, standing beside her body, he said to the men of Heth:

22:18 *your offspring*, or, "your seed."

22:18
Gen 18:18
Acts 3:25
Gal 3:8,16

22:19
Gen 21:31

22:20
Gen 11:29
31:53

22:23
Gen 24:15

23:2
Josh 14:15

23:3
Gen 10:15

HAGAR

Escape of some kind is usually the most tempting solution to our problems. In fact, it can become a habit. Hagar was a person who used that approach. When the going got tough, she usually got going—in the other direction.

However, it is worthwhile to note that the biggest challenges Hagar faced were brought on by *other* people's choices. Sarah chose her to be a substitute child-bearer—Hagar probably had little to say in the matter.

It isn't hard to understand how Hagar's pregnancy caused her to look down on Sarah. But that brought on hard feelings and Sarah consequently punished Hagar. This motivated her first escape. When she returned to the family and gave birth to Ishmael, Sarah's continued barrenness must have contributed to bitterness on both sides.

When Isaac was finally born, Sarah looked for any excuse to have Hagar and Ishmael sent away. She found it when she caught Ishmael teasing Isaac. In the desert, out of water and facing the death of her son, Hagar once again tried to escape. She walked away so she wouldn't have to watch her son die. Once again, God graciously intervened.

Have you noticed how patiently God operates to make our escape attempts fail? Have you begun to learn that escape is only a temporary solution? God's continual desire is for us to face our problems with his help. We experience his help most clearly in and through the conflicts and difficulties, not away from them. Are there problems in your life for which you've been using the "Hagar solution"? Choose one of those problems, ask for God's help, and begin to face it today.

Strength and accomplishment:
● Mother of Abraham's first child, Ishmael, who became founder of the Arab nations

Weaknesses and mistakes:
● When faced with problems, she tended to run away
● Her pregnancy brought out strong feelings of pride and arrogance

Lessons from her life:
● God is faithful to his plan and promises, even when humans complicate the process
● God shows himself as one who knows us and wants to be known by us
● The New Testament uses Hagar as a symbol of those who would pursue favor with God by their own efforts, rather than by trusting in his mercy and forgiveness

Vital statistics:
● Where: Canaan and Egypt
● Occupation: Slave/Maid/Single Parent
● Relatives: Son: Ishmael

Key verse:
"Return to your mistress and act as you should, for I will make you into a great nation" (Genesis 16:9).

Hagar's story is told in Genesis 16—21. She is also mentioned in Galatians 4:24, 25.

23:1-4 In Abraham's day, death and burial were steeped in rituals and traditions. Failing to honor a dead person demonstrated the greatest possible lack of respect. If someone didn't receive a proper burial, it was taken as a curse. Mourning was an essential part of the death ritual. Friends and relatives let out loud cries for the whole neighborhood to hear. Since there were no funeral homes or undertakers, these same friends and relatives helped prepare the body for burial, which usually took place on the same day because of the warm climate.

⁴"Here I am, a visitor in a foreign land, with no place to bury my wife. Please sell me a piece of ground for this purpose."

⁵, ⁶"Certainly," the men replied, "for you are an honored prince of God among us; it will be a privilege to have you choose the finest of our sepulchres, so that you can bury her there."

⁷Then Abraham bowed low before them and said, ⁸"Since this is your feeling in the matter, be so kind as to ask Ephron, Zohar's son, ⁹to sell me the cave of Mach-pelah, down at the end of his field. I will of course pay the full price for it, whatever is publicly agreed upon, and it will become a permanent cemetery for my family."

¹⁰Ephron was sitting there among the others, and now he spoke up, answering Abraham as the others listened, speaking publicly before all the citizens of the town: ¹¹"Sir," he said to Abraham, "please listen to me. I will give you the cave and the field without any charge. Here in the presence of my people, I give it to you free. Go and bury your dead."

¹²Abraham bowed again to the men of Heth, ¹³and replied to Ephron, as all listened: "No, let me buy it from you. Let me pay the full price of the field, and then I will bury my dead."

¹⁴, ¹⁵"Well, the land is worth 400 pieces of silver," Ephron said, "but what is that between friends? Go ahead and bury your dead."

¹⁶So Abraham paid Ephron the price he had suggested—400 pieces of silver, as publicly agreed. ¹⁷, ¹⁸This is the land he bought: Ephron's field at Mach-pelah, near Mamre, and the cave at the end of the field, and all the trees in the field. They became his permanent possession, by agreement in the presence of the men of Heth at the city gate. ¹⁹, ²⁰So Abraham buried Sarah there, in the field and cave deeded to him by the men of Heth as a burial plot.

6. Isaac marries Rebekah

24 Abraham was now a very old man, and God blessed him in every way. ²One day Abraham said to his household administrator, who was his oldest servant, ³"Swear by Jehovah, the God of heaven and earth, that you will not let my son

23:4
Lev 25:23
1 Chron 29:15
Ps 39:12
Heb 11:9

23:6
Gen 13:2; 21:22
23:7
Gen 18:2; 19:1
23:9
Gen 25:9

23:10
Ruth 4:11

23:13
Gen 14:23
2 Sam 24:24

23:15
Ex 30:13
23:16
Ezra 8:25
Jer 32:9
23:17,18
Gen 25:9
49:29; 50:13

24:1
Gen 12:2
18:11; 24:35
24:3
Gen 21:23
26:34; 28:1

23:4–6 Abraham was in a foreign land looking for a place to bury his wife. Strangers offered to help him, because he was "an honored prince of God," and they felt it would be a privilege to assist him. Abraham's reputation as a man of God had preceded him. Those who invest their time and money in obeying God will receive a good reputation as a pleasant return on that investment.

23:14, 15 The polite interchange between Abraham and Ephron was typical of bargaining at that time. Ephron graciously offered to give his land to Abraham at no charge; Abraham insisted on paying for it; Ephron politely mentioned the price but said, in effect, that it wasn't important; Abraham paid the 400 pieces of silver. Both men knew what was going on, but went through the bargaining process. If Abraham had accepted the land as a free gift when it was offered, he would have insulted Ephron, who then would have rescinded his offer.

Many shopkeepers in the Middle East still follow this ritual with their customers. But the customer would find himself in jail if he took the shopkeeper up on his initial offer.

23:16 Four hundred pieces of silver was a high price for the piece of property Abraham bought. The Hittites who lived in the land weren't thrilled about foreigners buying up lots of property, so Abraham had little bargaining leverage.

Ephron asked an outrageous price. The custom of the day was to ask double the fair market value of the land, fully expecting the buyer to offer half the stated price. The worth of a piece of silver was determined by its weight, but because the standards varied so often at this time, it is impossible to know exactly what Abraham

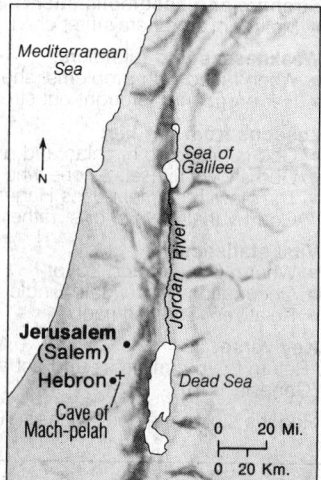

CAVE OF MACH-PELAH
Sarah died in Hebron. Abraham bought the Cave of Mach-pelah, near Hebron, as her burial place. Abraham was also buried there, as were two of his descendants, Isaac and Jacob.

paid for the land by today's standards. Even though God had promised the land to Abraham, he did not just strip it away from Ephron.

24:4
Gen 12:1

24:5
Gen 24:58

24:7
Gen 12:7; 15:18
Gen 16:17; 22:11
Ex 23:20,23

24:10
Gen 11:22
22:20
Deut 23:4

24:11
Gen 24:43

24:12
Gen 24:27,48

24:14
a)Judg 6:17
1 Sam 14:9,10
Prov 19:14
b)Gen 15:8
Ex 4:1-9

24:15
Gen 22:20-24
25:20

24:16
Gen 12:11
26:7; 29:17

24:17
1 Kgs 17:10
Jn 4:7

24:19
Gen 24:14,45,
46

marry one of these local girls, these Canaanites. ⁴Go instead to my homeland, to my relatives, and find a wife for him there."

⁵"But suppose I can't find a girl who will come so far from home?" the servant asked. "Then shall I take Isaac there, to live among your relatives?"

⁶"No!" Abraham warned. "Be careful that you don't do that under any circumstance. ⁷For the Lord God of heaven told me to leave that land and my people, and promised to give me and my children this land. He will send his angel on ahead of you, and he will see to it that you find a girl from there to be my son's wife. ⁸But if you don't succeed, then you are free from this oath; but under no circumstances are you to take my son there."

⁹So the servant vowed to follow Abraham's instructions.

¹⁰He took with him ten of Abraham's camels loaded with samples of the best of everything his master owned, and journeyed to Iraq, to Nahor's village. ¹¹There he made the camels kneel down outside the town, beside a spring. It was evening, and the women of the village were coming to draw water.

¹²"O Jehovah, the God of my master," he prayed, "show kindness to my master Abraham and help me to accomplish the purpose of my journey. ¹³See, here I am, standing beside this spring, and the girls of the village are coming out to draw water. ¹⁴This is my request: When I ask one of them for a drink and she says, 'Yes, certainly, and I will water your camels too!'—let her be the one you have appointed as Isaac's wife. That is how I will know."

¹⁵, ¹⁶As he was still speaking to the Lord about this, a beautiful young girl named Rebekah arrived with a water jug on her shoulder and filled it at the spring. (Her father was Bethuel the son of Nahor and his wife Milcah.) ¹⁷Running over to her, the servant asked her for a drink.

¹⁸"Certainly, sir," she said, and quickly lowered the jug for him to drink. ¹⁹Then she said, "I'll draw water for your camels, too, until they have enough!"

24:15, 16 *a beautiful young girl,* literally, "a virgin." *the son of Nahor,* Abraham's brother.

ELIEZER:	24:3, 9	Accepted the challenge
PROFILE OF A	24:5	Examined alternatives
TRUE SERVANT	24:9	Promised to follow instructions
Have you ever	24:12–14	Made a plan
approached a	24:12–14	Submitted the plan to God
responsibility with	24:12–14	Prayed for guidance
this kind of	24:12–14	Devised a strategy with room for God to operate
singlemindedness	24:21	Waited
and careful	24:21	Watched carefully
planning, while	24:26	Accepted the answer thankfully
ultimately	24:34–49	Explained the situation to concerned parties
depending on	24:56	Refused unnecessary delay
God?	24:66	Followed through with entire plan

24:4 Abraham wanted Isaac to marry within the family tribe. This was acceptable at this time to avoid intermarrying with heathen neighbors. A son's wife was usually chosen by the parents. It was common for a woman to be married at age 12 or 13, although Rebekah was probably older than this.

24:9 Literally, "put his hand under the thigh of Abraham his master and swore to him that. . . ." This was the cultural way of binding a promise—much like the handshake is today.

24:11 The well, people's chief source of water, was usually found outside town along the main road. Many people had to walk a mile or more for their water. They could use only what they could carry home. Rebekah would have visited the well twice daily to draw water for her family. Farmers and shepherds would come from nearby fields to draw water for their animals. It was the best place to meet new friends and chat with old ones.

24:14 Was it right for Abraham's servant to ask God for such a specific sign? The "sign" he requested was not out of the ordinary. The hospitality of the day required women at the well to offer water to weary travelers, but not to their animals. Eliezer was simply asking God to show him a woman with an attitude of true service—someone who would go beyond the expected. An offer to water his camels would indicate that kind of servant attitude. Eliezer did not ask for a woman with looks or wealth—he knew the importance of having the right heart. And he knew the importance of asking God to help him with his task.

24:15, 16 Rebekah had physical beauty, but the servant was looking for a sign that revealed inner beauty. Appearance is important to us, and we spend time and money improving it. But how much effort do we put into developing our inner beauty? Patience, kindness, and joy are the beauty treatments that help us become truly lovely—on the inside.

24:18–20 Rebekah's "servant spirit" was clearly demonstrated as she willingly and quickly drew water for Eliezer and his camels. The pots used for carrying water were large and heavy. It took a lot of water to satisfy a thirsty camel (up to 25 gallons per camel after a week of travel). Eliezer was seeing a live demonstration of someone with a heart for doing far more than was expected.

²⁰So she emptied the jug into the watering trough and ran down to the spring again and kept carrying water to the camels until they had enough. ²¹The servant said no more, but watched her carefully to see if she would finish the job, so that he would know whether she was the one. ²²Then at last, when the camels had finished drinking, he produced a quarter-ounce gold earring and two five-ounce gold bracelets for her wrists.

²³"Whose daughter are you, miss?" he asked. "Would your father have any room to put us up for the night?"

²⁴"My father is Bethuel," she replied. "My grandparents are Milcah and Nahor. ²⁵Yes, we have plenty of straw and food for the camels, and a guest room."

²⁶The man stood there a moment with head bowed, worshiping Jehovah. ²⁷"Thank you, Lord God of my master Abraham," he prayed; "thank you for being so kind and true to him, and for leading me straight to the family of my master's relatives."

²⁸The girl ran home to tell her folks, ²⁹, ³⁰and when her brother Laban saw the ring, and the bracelets on his sister's wrists, and heard her story, he rushed out to the spring where the man was still standing beside his camels, and said to him, ³¹"Come and stay with us, friend; why stand here outside the city when we have a room all ready for you, and a place prepared for the camels!"

³²So the man went home with Laban, and Laban gave him straw to bed down the camels, and feed for them, and water for the camel drivers to wash their feet. ³³Then supper was served. But the old man said, "I don't want to eat until I have told you why I am here."

"All right," Laban said, "tell us your errand."

³⁴"I am Abraham's servant," he explained. ³⁵"And Jehovah has overwhelmed my master with blessings so that he is a great man among the people of his land. God has given him flocks of sheep and herds of cattle, and a fortune in silver and gold, and many slaves and camels and donkeys.

³⁶"Now when Sarah, my master's wife, was very old, she gave birth to my master's son, and my master has given him everything he owns. ³⁷And my master made me promise not to let Isaac marry one of the local girls, ³⁸but to come to his relatives here in this far-off land, to his brother's family, and to bring back a girl from here to marry his son. ³⁹'But suppose I can't find a girl who will come?' I asked him. ⁴⁰'She will,' he told me—'for my Lord, in whose presence I have walked, will send his angel with you and make your mission successful. Yes, find a girl from among my relatives, from my brother's family. ⁴¹You are under oath to go and ask. If they won't send anyone, then you are freed from your promise.'

⁴²"Well, this afternoon when I came to the spring I prayed this prayer: 'O Jehovah, the God of my master Abraham, if you are planning to make my mission a success, please guide me in this way: ⁴³Here I am, standing beside this spring. I will say to some girl who comes out to draw water, "Please give me a drink of water!" ⁴⁴And she will reply, "Certainly! And I'll water your camels too!" Let that girl be the one you have selected to be the wife of my master's son.'

⁴⁵"Well, while I was still speaking these words, Rebekah was coming along with her water jug upon her shoulder; and she went down to the spring and drew water and filled the jug. I said to her, 'Please give me a drink.' ⁴⁶She quickly lifted the jug down from her shoulder so that I could drink, and told me, 'Certainly, sir, and I will water your camels too!' So she did! ⁴⁷Then I asked her, 'Whose family are you from?' And she told me, 'Nahor's. My father is Bethuel, the son of Nahor and his wife Milcah.' So I gave her the ring and the bracelets. ⁴⁸Then I bowed my head and worshiped and blessed Jehovah, the God of my master Abraham, because he had led me along just the right path to find a girl from the family of my master's brother. ⁴⁹So tell me, yes or no. Will you or won't you be kind to my master and do what is right? When you tell me, then I'll know what my next step should be, whether to move this way or that."

24:21 2 Sam 7:18-20
24:22 Gen 24:47
24:24 Gen 24:15
24:26 Ex 4:31
24:27 Gen 14:20 24:12,48
24:28 Gen 29:12
24:29 Gen 24:50 25:20; 29:5
24:30 Gen 24:22,47
24:31 Gen 18:3-5 19:2
24:34 Gen 24:2
24:35 Gen 12:2; 13:2
24:36 Gen 21:1-7 25:5
24:37 Gen 24:3; 28:1
24:40 Gen 24:7
24:45 1 Sam 1:13
24:47 Gen 24:23,24
24:49 Gen 32:10 47:29

24:21 *to see if she would finish the job,* implied. **24:22** *gold earring,* literally, "nose-ring." **24:31** *friend,* literally, "blessed of Jehovah." **24:37** *local girls,* literally, "daughters of the Canaanites." **24:38** *to his brother's family,* literally, "go into my father's house." **24:48** *a girl from the family of my master's brother,* literally, "my master's brother's daughter."

24:50
Ps 118:23
Mt 21:42

24:51
Gen 20:15

24:52
Gen 24:26

24:54
Gen 28:6; 30:25

24:55
Judg 19:4

24:58
Ps 45:10

24:59
Gen 35:8

24:60
Gen 17:16
22:17
Dan 7:10

⁵⁰Then Laban and Bethuel replied, "The Lord has obviously brought you here, so what can we say? ⁵¹Take her and go! Yes, let her be the wife of your master's son, as Jehovah has directed."

⁵²At this reply, Abraham's servant fell to his knees before Jehovah. ⁵³Then he brought out jewels set in solid gold and silver for Rebekah, and lovely clothing; and he gave many valuable presents to her mother and brother. ⁵⁴Then they had supper, and the servant and the men with him stayed there overnight. But early the next morning he said, "Send me back to my master!"

⁵⁵"But we want Rebekah here at least another ten days or so!" her mother and brother exclaimed. "Then she can go."

⁵⁶But he pleaded, "Don't hinder my return; the Lord has made my mission successful, and I want to report back to my master."

⁵⁷"Well," they said, "we'll call the girl and ask her what she thinks."

⁵⁸So they called Rebekah. "Are you willing to go with this man?" they asked her. And she replied, "Yes, I will go."

⁵⁹So they told her good-bye, sending along the woman who had been her childhood nurse, ⁶⁰and blessed her with this blessing as they parted:

REBEKAH

Some people are initiators. They help get the ball rolling. Rebekah would easily stand out in this group. Her life was characterized by initiative. When she saw a need she took action—even though the action was not always right.

It was Rebekah's initiative that first caught the attention of Eliezer, the servant Abraham sent to find a wife for Isaac. It was common courtesy to give a drink to a stranger, but it took added character to also fetch water for ten thirsty camels. Later, after hearing the details of Eliezer's mission, Rebekah was immediately willing to be Isaac's bride.

Several later events help us see how initiative can be misdirected. Rebekah was aware that God's plan would be channeled through Jacob, not Esau (Genesis 25:23). So not only did Jacob become her favorite; she actually planned ways to ensure that he would overshadow his older twin. Meanwhile, Isaac had a preference for Esau. This created a conflict between the couple. She felt justified in deceiving her husband when the time came to bless the sons. Her ingenious plan was carried out to perfection.

Most of the time we try to justify the things we choose to do. Often we attempt to add God's approval to our actions. While it is true that our actions will not spoil God's plan, it is also true that we are responsible for our actions and must always be cautious about our motives. When thinking about a course of action, are you simply seeking God's stamp of approval on something you've already decided to do? Or are you willing to set the plan aside if the principles and commands of God's Word are against the action? Initiative and action are admirable and right when they are controlled by God's wisdom.

Strengths and accomplishments:
- When confronted with a need, she took immediate action
- She was accomplishment-oriented

Weaknesses and mistakes:
- Her initiative was not always balanced by wisdom
- She favored one of her sons
- She deceived her husband

Lessons from her life:
- Our actions must be guided by God's Word
- God even makes use of our mistakes in his plan
- Parental favoritism hurts a family

Vital statistics:
- Where: Haran, Canaan
- Occupation: Wife, mother, household manager
- Relatives: Parents: Bethuel and Milcah. Husband: Isaac. Brother: Laban. Twin sons: Esau and Jacob.

Key verses:
"And Isaac brought Rebekah into his mother's tent, and she became his wife. He loved her very much, and she was a special comfort to him after the loss of his mother" (Genesis 24:67).

". . . and Rebekah's favorite was Jacob" (Genesis 25:28).

Rebekah's story is told in Genesis 24—27. She is also mentioned in Romans 9:10.

> "Our sister,
> May you become
> The mother of many millions!
> May your descendants
> Overcome all your enemies."

61So Rebekah and her servant girls mounted the camels and went with him.

62Meanwhile, Isaac, whose home was in the Negeb, had returned to Beer-lahai-roi. 63One evening as he was taking a walk out in the fields, meditating, he looked up and saw the camels coming. 64Rebekah noticed him and quickly dismounted.

65"Who is that man walking through the fields to meet us?" she asked the servant.

And he replied, "It is my master's son!" So she covered her face with her veil. 66Then the servant told Isaac the whole story.

67And Isaac brought Rebekah into his mother's tent, and she became his wife. He loved her very much, and she was a special comfort to him after the loss of his mother.

7. Abraham dies

25 Now Abraham married again. Keturah was his new wife, and she bore him several children: Zimran, Jokshan, Medan, Midian, Ishbak, Shuah. 3Jokshan's two sons were Sheba and Dedan. Dedan's sons were Asshurim, Letushim, and Leummim. 4Midian's sons were Ephah, Epher, Hanoch, Abida, and Eldaah.

5Abraham deeded everything he owned to Isaac; 6however, he gave gifts to the sons of his concubines and sent them off into the east, away from Isaac.

7,8Then Abraham died, at the ripe old age of 175, 9, 10and his sons Isaac and Ishmael buried him in the cave of Mach-pelah near Mamre, in the field Abraham had purchased from Ephron the son of Zohar, the Hethite, where Sarah, Abraham's wife was buried.

11After Abraham's death, God poured out rich blessings upon Isaac. (Isaac had now moved south to Beer-lahai-roi in the Negeb.)

12-15Here is a list, in the order of their births, of the descendants of Ishmael, who was the son of Abraham and Hagar the Egyptian, Sarah's slave girl: Nebaioth, Kedar, Abdeel, Mibsam, Mishma, Dumah, Massa, Hadad, Tema, Jetur, Naphish, Kedemah.

16These twelve sons of his became the founders of twelve tribes that bore their names. 17Ishmael finally died at the age of 137, and joined his ancestors. 18These descendants of Ishmael were scattered across the country from Havilah to Shur (which is a little way to the northeast of the Egyptian border in the direction of Assyria). And they were constantly at war with one another.

E. THE STORY OF ISAAC (25:19—28:9)
Isaac inherited everything from his father, including God's promise to make his descendants into a great nation. As a boy, Isaac did not resist as his father prepared to sacrifice him, and as a man, he gladly accepted the wife that others chose for him. Through Isaac, we learn how to let God guide our life and place his will ahead of our own.

1. Jacob and Esau, Isaac's twin sons

19This is the story of Isaac's children: 20Isaac was forty years old when he married Rebekah, the daughter of Bethuel the Aramean from Paddam-aram. Rebekah was the sister of Laban. 21Isaac pleaded with Jehovah to give Rebekah a child, for even after many years of marriage she had no children. Then at last she

24:62 Gen 16:14 25:11
24:63 Ps 119:15,27, 47,48
24:66 Mk 6:30
24:67 Gen 23:2 25:20; 29:18
25:1 1 Chron 1:32
25:5 Gen 24:36
25:7 Gen 12:4
25:8 Gen 25:17 35:29; 49:29,33
25:9,10 Gen 23:17 49:29; 50:13
25:11 Gen 24:62; 26:3
25:12 Gen 16:15 1 Chron 1:28-31
25:13 Gen 17:20
25:17 Gen 25:8
25:18 a)Gen 20:1 b)Gen 16:12
25:19 Gen 21:3 1 Chron 1:34
25:21 Gen 21:2

24:65 *It is my master's son,* literally, "It is my master." **25:4** *and Eldaah.* The text adds, "all these were the children of Keturah." **25:17** *joined his ancestors,* literally, "and was gathered to his people." **25:21** *even after many years of marriage,* implied in vss 20 and 26.

25:21 As Isaac pleaded with God for something as precious as children, so we are encouraged throughout the Bible to ask, and even plead, for our most personal and important requests. God wants to give us good things, but he wants us to ask for them.

Even then, as Isaac learned, God may decide to withhold his answer for a while in order to (1) deepen our insight into what we really need, (2) broaden our appreciation for his answers, or (3) allow us to mature so we can use his gifts more wisely.

became pregnant. ²²And it seemed as though children were fighting each other inside her!

"I can't endure this," she exclaimed. So she asked the Lord about it.

25:23
Gen 17:2-4
27:29; 48:19
Num 20:14
Deut 2:4,8
Rom 9:12

²³And he told her, "The sons in your womb shall become two rival nations. One will be stronger than the other; and the older shall be a servant of the younger!"

²⁴And sure enough, she had twins. ²⁵The first was born so covered with reddish hair that one would think he was wearing a fur coat! So they called him "Esau."

25:25
Gen 27:11

²⁶Then the other twin was born with his hand on Esau's heel! So they called him Jacob (meaning "Grabber"). Isaac was sixty years old when the twins were born.

25:26
Hos 12:3

Esau sells his birthright

²⁷As the boys grew, Esau became a skillful hunter, while Jacob was a quiet sort who liked to stay at home. ²⁸Isaac's favorite was Esau, because of the venison he brought home, and Rebekah's favorite was Jacob.

²⁹One day Jacob was cooking stew when Esau arrived home exhausted from the hunt.

25:30
Gen 36:1,9
Ex 15:15

³⁰*Esau:* "Boy, am I starved! Give me a bite of that red stuff there!" (From this came his nickname "Edom," which means "Red Stuff.")

25:25 which sounds a little like the Hebrew word for "hair."

Common sense isn't all that common. In fact, the common thread in many decisions is that they don't make sense. Esau's life was filled with choices he must have regretted bitterly. He appears to have been a person who found it hard to consider consequences. He reacted to the need of the moment without realizing what he was giving up to meet that need. Trading his birthright for a bowl of stew was the clearest example of this weakness. He also chose wives in direct opposition to his parents' wishes.

What are you willing to trade for the things you want? Do you find yourself, at times, willing to negotiate *anything* for what you feel you need *now*? Do your family, spouse, integrity, body, or soul get included in these deals? Do you sometimes feel that the important parts of life escaped while you were grabbing for something else?

If so, your initial response, like Esau's, may be deep anger. In itself that isn't wrong, as long as you direct the energy of that anger toward a solution and not toward yourself or others as the cause of the problem. Your greatest need is to find a focal point other than "what I need now." The only worthy focal point is God. A relationship with him will not only give an ultimate purpose to your life, but will also be a daily guideline for living.

Strengths and accomplishments:
- Ancestor of the Edomites
- Known for his archery skill
- Able to forgive after explosive anger

Weaknesses and mistakes:
- When faced with important decisions, tended to choose according to the immediate need rather than the long-range effect
- Angered his parents by poor marriage choices

Lessons from his life:
- God allows certain events in our lives to accomplish his overall purposes, but we are still responsible for our actions
- Consequences are important to consider
- It is possible to have great anger and yet not sin

Vital statistics:
- Where: Canaan
- Occupation: Skillful hunter
- Relatives: Parents: Isaac and Rebekah. Brother: Jacob. Wives: Judith, Basemath, and Mahalath.

Key verses:
"Watch out that no one becomes involved in sexual sin or becomes careless about God as Esau did: he traded his rights as the oldest son for a single meal. And afterwards, when he wanted those rights back again, it was too late, even though he wept bitter tears of repentance. So remember, and be careful" (Hebrews 12:16, 17).

Esau's story is told in Genesis 25—36. He is also mentioned in Malachi 1:2; Romans 9:13; Hebrews 12:16, 17.

³¹*Jacob:* "All right, trade me your birthright for it!

³²*Esau:* "When a man is dying of starvation, what good is his birthright?"

³³*Jacob:* "Well then, vow to God that it is mine!"

And Esau vowed, thereby selling all his eldest-son rights to his younger brother. ³⁴Then Jacob gave Esau bread, peas, and stew; so he ate and drank and went on about his business, indifferent to the loss of the rights he had thrown away.

25:31
Deut 21:15-17

25:33
Gen 27:36
Heb 12:16

2. Isaac and King Abimelech

26 Now a severe famine overshadowed the land, as had happened before, in Abraham's time, and so Isaac moved to the city of Gerar where Abimelech, king of the Philistines, lived.

²Jehovah appeared to him there and told him, "Don't go to Egypt. ³Do as I say and stay here in this land. If you do, I will be with you and bless you, and I will give all this land to you and to your descendants, just as I promised Abraham your father. ⁴And I will cause your descendants to become as numerous as the stars! And I will give them all of these lands; and they shall be a blessing to all the nations of the earth. ⁵I will do this because Abraham obeyed my commandments and laws."

26:1
Gen 12:10
20:1,2; 41:54

26:2
Gen 12:1,7

26:3
Gen 12:7; 15:8;

26:4
Gen 15:15
22:17
Ex 32:13
Gal 3:8

Isaac deceives the king

⁶So Isaac stayed in Gerar. ⁷And when the men there asked him about Rebekah, he said, "She is my sister!" For he feared for his life if he told them she was his wife; he was afraid they would kill him to get her, for she was very attractive. ⁸But sometime later, King Abimelech, king of the Philistines, looked out of a window and saw Isaac and Rebekah making love.

⁹Abimelech called for Isaac and exclaimed, "She is your wife! Why did you say she is your sister?"

26:7
Gen 12:11,12
20:12

26:8
Prov 5:18,19
Eccles 9:9

25:34 *indifferent to the loss of the rights he had thrown away,* literally, "thus did Esau consider his birthright to be of no value."

25:31 A birthright was a special honor given to the first-born son. It included a double portion of the family inheritance along with the honor of one day becoming the family leader. The oldest son could sell his birthright or give it away if he chose. But in so doing, he forfeited his position as family leader. Esau was within his rights to trade his birthright. But he showed complete disregard for the spiritual blessings that would have come his way if he had kept it.

25:32, 33 Esau traded the lasting benefits of his birthright for the immediate pleasure of food. He acted on impulse, satisfying his immediate desires without pausing to consider the long-range consequences of what he was about to do. We can fall into the same trap. When we see something we want, our first impulse is to get it. At first we feel intensely satisfied and sometimes even powerful because we have obtained what we set out to get. But immediate pleasure often loses sight of the future. We can avoid Esau's mistake by comparing the short-term satisfaction with its long-range consequences—before we act.

Esau exaggerated his hunger. "I'm dying of starvation," he said. This thinking made his choice much easier, for if he was starving, what good was an inheritance anyway? The pressure of the moment twisted his perspective and made his decision seem urgent. We often experience similar situations. For example, when we feel sexual pressure, a marriage license may not seem so important. We sometimes feel such great pressure in one area that nothing else seems to matter. The pressure of the moment makes us lose our perspective. Getting through that short, pressure-filled moment is often the hardest part of overcoming a temptation.

26:1 The Philistines were a tribe of people who were to become one of Israel's fiercest enemies. "Philistine" means "Sea People," for they originally were sailors from the Mediterranean Sea. These people, living along the southwest coast of Palestine, were few but ferocious in battle. Although friendly to Isaac, this small group was

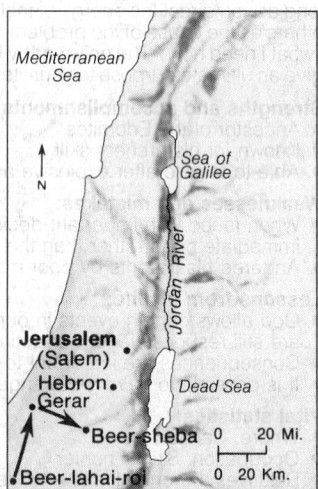

Mediterranean
Sea

Sea of
Galilee

N

Jordan River

Jerusalem
(Salem)
Hebron
Gerar

Dead Sea

Beer-sheba   0   20 Mi.

Beer-lahai-roi   0   20 Km.

**ISAAC'S MOVE
TO GERAR**
Isaac had settled in Beer-lahai-roi, where his sons, Jacob and Esau, were born. A famine drove him to Gerar. But when he became wealthy, his jealous neighbors asked him to leave. From Gerar he moved to Beersheba.

the forerunner of the nation that would plague Israel during the time of Joshua, the Judges, and King David.

26:7-11 Isaac was afraid that the men in Gerar would kill him to get his beautiful wife, Rebekah. So he lied, claiming that Rebekah was his sister. Where did he learn that trick? Evidently, Isaac knew about the actions of his father, Abraham (see Genesis 12:10-14 and 20:1-4). Parents help shape the future of their world by the way they shape the lifestyle and values of their children. The first step toward helping children live right is to have parents who live right. Your actions are often copied by those closest to you.

"Because I was afraid I would be murdered," Isaac replied. "I thought someone would kill me to get her from me."

26:10
Gen 20:7-10
26:11
Prov 6:29

10"How could you treat us this way?" Abimelech exclaimed. "Someone might carelessly have raped her, and we would be doomed." 11Then Abimelech made a public proclamation: "Anyone harming this man or his wife shall die."

JACOB

Abraham, Isaac, and Jacob are among the most significant people in the Old Testament. It is important to realize that this significance is not based upon their personal characters, but upon the character of God. They were all men who earned the grudging respect and even fear of their peers; they were wealthy and powerful, and each was capable of lying, deceit, and selfishness. They were not the perfect heroes we might have expected; instead, they were just like us, trying to please God, yet often falling short.

Jacob was the third link in God's plan to start a nation from Abraham. The success of that plan was more often in spite of than because of Jacob's life. Before Jacob was born, God promised that his plan would be worked out through Jacob and not his twin brother, Esau. Although Jacob's methods were not always respectable, his skill, determination, and patience have to be admired. As we follow him from birth to death, we are able to see God's work.

Jacob's life had four stages, each marked by a personal encounter with God. In the first stage, Jacob lived up to his name, "Grabber." He grabbed Esau's heel at birth and by the time he fled from home, he had also grabbed his brother's birthright and blessing. On his flight, God first appeared to him. Not only did God confirm to Jacob his blessing, but he awakened in Jacob a personal knowledge of himself. In the second stage, Jacob experienced life from the other side, being manipulated and deceived by Laban. But we note a curious fact: the Jacob of stage one would simply have left Laban; the Jacob of stage two decided to leave, but waited six years for God's permission. In the third stage, Jacob was in a new role as grabber. This time, by the Jordan River, he grabbed on to God and wouldn't let go. He realized his dependence on the God who had continued to bless him. His relationship to God became essential to his life, and his name was changed to Israel. Jacob's last stage of life was to *be* grabbed—God achieved a firm hold on him. In responding to Joseph's invitation to come to Egypt, Jacob was clearly unwilling to make a move without God's approval.

Can you think of times when God has made himself known to you? Do you allow yourself to meet him as you study his Word? What difference have these experiences made in your life? Are you more like the young Jacob, forcing God to track you down in the wilderness of your own plans and mistakes? Or are you more like the Jacob who placed his desires and plans before God for his approval before taking any action?

Strengths and accomplishments:
- Father of the twelve tribes of Israel
- Third in the Abrahamic line of God's plan
- Determined, willing to work long and hard for what he wanted
- Wealthy livestock owner

Weaknesses and mistakes:
- When faced with conflict, relied on his own resources rather than going to God for help
- Tended to accumulate wealth for its own sake

Lessons from his life:
- Security does not lie in the accumulation of goods
- All human intentions and actions—for good or for evil—are woven by God into his ongoing plan

Vital statistics:
- Where: Canaan
- Occupation: Shepherd/Livestock owner
- Relatives: Parents: Isaac and Rebekah. Brother: Esau. Father-in-law: Laban. Wives: Rachel and Leah. Twelve sons and one daughter are named in the Bible.

Key verse:
"What's more, I am with you, and will protect you wherever you go, and will bring you back safely to this land; I will be with you constantly until I have finished giving you all I am promising" (Genesis 28:15).

Jacob's story is told in Genesis 25—50. He is also mentioned in Hosea 12:3–5; Matthew 1:2; 22:32; Acts 3:13; 7:46; Romans 9:11–13; Hebrews 11:9, 20–21.

Isaac refuses to fight

12That year Isaac's crops were tremendous—100 times the grain he sowed. For Jehovah blessed him. 13He was soon a man of great wealth, and became richer and richer. 14He had large flocks of sheep and goats, great herds of cattle, and many servants. And the Philistines became jealous of him. 15So they filled up his wells with earth—all those dug by the servants of his father Abraham.

16And King Abimelech asked Isaac to leave the country. "Go somewhere else," he said, "for you have become too rich and powerful for us."

17So Isaac moved to Gerar Valley and lived there instead. 18And Isaac redug the wells of his father Abraham, the ones the Philistines had filled after his father's death, and gave them the same names they had had before, when his father had named them. 19His shepherds also dug a new well in Gerar Valley, and found a gushing underground spring.

20Then the local shepherds came and claimed it. "This is our land and our well," they said, and argued over it with Isaac's herdsmen. So he named the well, "The Well of Argument!" 21Isaac's men then dug another well, but again there was a fight over it. So he called it, "The Well of Anger." 22Abandoning that one, he dug again, and the local residents finally left him alone. So he called it, "The Well of Room Enough for Us at Last!" "For now at last," he said, "the Lord has made room for us and we shall thrive."

23When he went to Beer-sheba, 24Jehovah appeared to him on the night of his arrival. "I am the God of Abraham your father," he said. "Fear not, for I am with you and will bless you, and will give you so many descendants that they will become a great nation—because of my promise to Abraham, who obeyed me." 25Then Isaac built an altar and worshiped Jehovah; and he settled there, and his servants dug a well.

26One day Isaac had visitors from Gerar. King Abimelech arrived with his advisor, Ahuzzath, and also Phicol, his army commander.

27"Why have you come?" Isaac asked them. "This is obviously no friendly visit, since you kicked me out in a most uncivil way."

28"Well," they said, "we can plainly see that Jehovah is blessing you. We've decided to ask for a treaty between us. 29Promise that you will not harm us, just as we have not harmed you, and in fact, have done only good to you and have sent you away in peace; we bless you in the name of the Lord."

30So Isaac prepared a great feast for them, and they ate and drank in preparation for the treaty ceremonies. 31In the morning, as soon as they were up, they each took solemn oaths to seal a non-aggression pact. Then Isaac sent them happily home again.

32That very same day Isaac's servants came to tell him, "We have found water"—in the well they had been digging. 33So he named the well, "The Well of the Oath," and the city that grew up there was named "Oath," and is called that to this day.

26:20 *The Well of Argument*, i.e., Ezek. **26:21** *The Well of Anger*, i.e., Sitnah. **26:22** *The Well of Room Enough for Us at Last*, i.e., Rehoboth. **26:33** *The Well of the Oath*, i.e., Shibah. *Oath*, i.e., Beer-sheba.

Cross references (margin):

26:12 Gen 26:3
26:13 Gen 24:35; 25:5
26:15 Gen 21:15
26:16 Ex 1:9
26:19 Jn 4:10,11
26:22 Ps 4:1; 18:19; 118:5 Isa 54:2
26:23 Gen 21:31; 46:1
26:24 Gen 12:1,2 17:1-7 Ex 3:6
26:25 Gen 12:7 13:3,4
26:26 Gen 21:22,23
26:27 Gen 26:14,16
26:28 Gen 26:3,12-16
26:29 Ps 115:15
26:30 Gen 21:8; 31:54
26:31 Gen 14:22 21:31; 31:55
26:33 Gen 21:31

26:12-16 God kept his promise to bless Isaac. The neighboring Philistines grew jealous because everything Isaac did seemed to go right. So they plugged his wells and tried to get rid of him. Jealousy is a dividing force strong enough to tear apart the mightiest of nations or the closest of friends. It forces you to separate yourself from what you were longing for in the first place. When you find yourself becoming jealous of others try thanking God for their good fortune.

26:17-22 Three times Isaac and his men dug new wells. When the first two disputes arose, Isaac moved on. Finally there was enough room for everyone. Rather than start a huge conflict, Isaac compromised for the sake of peace. Would you be willing to forsake an important position or valuable possession to keep peace? Ask God for the wisdom to know when to withdraw and when to stand and fight.

26:18 The area of Gerar was a desolate place on the edge of the wilderness. Water was as precious as gold. If someone dug a well, he was staking a claim to the land. Some wells had locks to keep thieves from stealing the water. To plug up someone's well was an act of war; it was one of the most serious crimes in the land. Isaac had every right to fight back when the Philistines ruined his wells. Yet he chose not to fight. In the end, the Philistines respected him for his patience and efforts for peace.

26:26-29 With his enemies wanting to make peace, Isaac was quick to respond, turning the occasion into a greater celebration. We should be just as receptive to those who want to patch things up with us. When the godliness in our lives begins to attract people—even enemies—we must let it be an opportunity to reach out to them with God's love.

3. Isaac blesses Jacob instead of Esau

26:34
Gen 28:6-8
26:35
Gen 27:46

34Esau, at the age of forty, married a girl named Judith, daughter of Be-eri the Hethite; and he also married Basemath, daughter of Elon the Hethite. **35**But Isaac and Rebekah were bitter about his marrying them.

27:1
Gen 25:25
48:10

27 One day, in Isaac's old age when he was almost blind, he called for Esau his oldest son.

Isaac: "My son?"
Esau: "Yes, father?"

27:2
Gen 47:29
27:3
Gen 25:28
27:4
Gen 24:60
27:19; 48:9

2, 3, 4*Isaac:* "I am an old man now, and expect every day to be my last. Take your bow and arrows out into the fields and get me some venison, and prepare it just the way I like it—savory and good—and bring it here for me to eat, and I will give you the blessings that belong to you, my first-born son, before I die."

27:6
Gen 25:28
27:8
Gen 27:13,43

5But Rebekah overheard the conversation. So when Esau left for the field to hunt for the venison, **6, 7**she called her son Jacob and told him what his father had said to his brother.

27:9
Judg 13:15

8, 9, 10*Rebekah:* "Now do exactly as I tell you. Go out to the flocks and bring me two young goats, and I'll prepare your father's favorite dish from them. Then take it to your father, and after he has enjoyed it he will bless *you* before his death, instead of Esau!"

27:11
Gen 25:25
27:12
Gen 9:25
27:21,22
27:13
Gen 27:8,43

11, 12*Jacob:* "But mother! He won't be fooled that easily. Think how hairy Esau is, and how smooth my skin is! What if my father feels me? He'll think I'm making a fool of him, and curse me instead of blessing me!"

13*Rebekah:* "Let his curses be on me, dear son. Just do what I tell you. Go out and get the goats."

27:15
Gen 27:27

14So Jacob followed his mother's instructions, bringing the dressed kids, which she prepared in his father's favorite way. **15**Then she took Esau's best clothes—they were there in the house—and instructed Jacob to put them on. **16**And she made him a pair of gloves from the hairy skin of the young goats, and fastened a strip of the hide around his neck; **17**then she gave him the meat, with its rich aroma, and some fresh-baked bread. **18**Jacob carried the platter of food into the room where his father was lying.

Jacob: "Father?"
Isaac: "Yes? Who is it, my son—Esau or Jacob?"

27:2-4 *that belong to you, my first-born son,* implied. **27:8-10** *instead of Esau,* implied. **27:11, 12** *He won't be fooled that easily,* implied.

26:34, 35 Esau married heathen women. This upset his parents greatly. Most parents have a lifetime of insight into the character of their children. They can be a storehouse of good advice. You may not agree with everything your parents say. But at least talk with them and listen carefully. This will help avoid the hard feelings Esau experienced.

27:5–10 When Rebekah learned that Isaac was preparing to bless Esau, she quickly devised a plan to trick him into blessing Jacob instead. Although God had already told her that Jacob would become the family leader (Genesis 25:23–26), Rebekah took matters into her own hands. She resorted to doing something wrong to try to bring about what God had already said would happen. For Rebekah, the end justified the means. No matter how good we think our goals may be, we should not attempt to achieve them unjustly.

27:11, 12 How we react to a dilemma often exposes our real motives. Frequently we are more worried about getting caught than about doing what is right. Jacob did not seem concerned about the deceitfulness of his mother's plan. Instead he was afraid of getting caught while carrying it out. If you are worried about getting caught, you may already be in a position that is less than honest.

Let your fear of getting caught be a warning to do right. Jacob paid a huge price for carrying out his dishonest plan.

27:11–13 Jacob hesitated when he heard Rebekah's deceitful plan. Although he questioned his mother's plan for the wrong reason (fear of getting caught), he protested and thus gave Rebekah one last chance to consider her actions. But Rebekah had become so wrapped up in her plan that she could no longer see clearly what she was doing. Sin had trapped her and was now degrading her character. Correcting yourself in the middle of doing wrong can bring hurt and disappointment, but it also brings freedom from the control of sin.

27:14 Although Jacob got the blessing he wanted, deceiving his father cost him dearly. These are some of the consequences of his actions: (1) he never saw his mother again; (2) his brother wanted to kill him; (3) he was deceived by his own uncle, Laban; (4) his family became torn by strife; (5) Esau became the founder of a nation of eternal enemies; (6) he was exiled from his family for years. Ironically, Jacob would have received the birthright and blessing anyway (Genesis 25:23). Imagine how different his life would have been had he and his mother allowed God to do things his way, in his time!

¹⁹*Jacob:* "It's Esau, your oldest son. I've done as you told me to. Here is the delicious venison you wanted. Sit up and eat it, so that you will bless me with all your heart!"

27:19
Gen 27:21,24, 31

²⁰*Isaac:* "How were you able to find it so quickly, my son?"
Jacob: "Because Jehovah your God put it in my path!"

²¹*Isaac:* "Come over here. I want to feel you, and be sure it really is Esau!"

27:21
Gen 27:12

₂₂(Jacob goes over to his father. He feels him!)

Isaac: (to himself) "The voice is Jacob's, but the hands are Esau's!"

₂₃(The ruse convinces Isaac and he gives Jacob his blessings):

27:23
Gen 27:4,16

²⁴*Isaac:* "Are you really Esau?"
Jacob: "Yes, of course."

27:24
Prov 12:19,22

²⁵*Isaac:* "Then bring me the venison, and I will eat it and bless you with all my heart."

27:25
Gen 27:4

(Jacob takes it over to him and Isaac eats; he also drinks the wine Jacob brings him.)

²⁶*Isaac:* "Come here and kiss me, my son!"

(Jacob goes over and kisses him on the cheek. Isaac sniffs his clothes, and finally seems convinced.)

²⁷, ²⁸, ²⁹*Isaac:* "The smell of my son is the good smell of the earth and fields that Jehovah has blessed. May God always give you plenty of rain for your crops, and good harvests and grapes. May many nations be your slaves. Be the master of your brothers. May all your relatives bow low before you. Cursed are all who curse you, and blessed are all who bless you."

27:27
Ps 65:9,10
Heb 11:20

27:28
Gen 27:39
45:18
Deut 7:13; 33:13, 28
Zech 8:12

27:29
Gen 9:25; 12:3
22:17; 49:8
Num 24:9
Isa 45:14

³⁰(As soon as Isaac has blessed Jacob, and almost before Jacob leaves the room, Esau arrives, coming in from his hunting. ³¹He also has prepared his father's favorite dish and brings it to him.)

Esau: "Here I am, father, with the venison. Sit up and eat it so that you can give me your finest blessings!"

27:31
Gen 27:4,19

³²*Isaac:* "Who is it?"
Esau: "Why, it's me, of course! Esau, your oldest son!"

27:32
Gen 27:18

₃₃(Isaac begins to tremble noticeably.)

27:33
Gen 27:35
Ps 55:5

Isaac: "Then who is it who was just here with venison, and I have already eaten it and blessed him with irrevocable blessing?"

₃₄(Esau begins to sob with deep and bitter sobs.)

27:34
Heb 12:17

Esau: "O my father, bless me, bless me too!"

27:35
Gen 27:12, 19-23

³⁵*Isaac:* "Your brother was here and tricked me and has carried away your blessing."

27:36
Gen 25:26
32:28

³⁶*Esau:* (bitterly) "No wonder they call him 'The Cheater.' For he took my

27:36 *The Cheater.* "Jacob" means "Cheater."

27:33–37 Before the father died, he performed a ceremony called "the blessing," in which he officially handed over the birthright to the rightful heir. Although the firstborn son was entitled to the birthright, it was not actually his until the blessing was pronounced. Before the blessing was given, the father could take the birthright away from the oldest son and give it to someone more deserving. But after the blessing was given, the birthright could no longer be taken away. This is why fathers usually waited until late in life to give away this irrevocable blessing. Although Jacob had been given the birthright by his older brother years ago, he still needed his father's blessing to make it binding.

birthright, and now he has stolen my blessing. Oh, haven't you saved even one blessing for me?"

27:37
Gen 27:27-29
2 Sam 8:14

37*Isaac:* "I have made him your master, and have given him yourself and all of his relatives as his servants. I have guaranteed him abundance of grain and wine—what is there left to give?"

27:38
Gen 27:34
Heb 12:17

38*Esau:* "Not one blessing left for me? O my father, bless me too."

(Isaac says nothing as Esau weeps.)

27:39
Heb 11:20
27:40
2 Kgs 8:20
2 Chron 21:8

39, 40*Isaac:* "Yours will be no life of ease and luxury, but you shall hew your way with your sword. For a time you will serve your brother, but you will finally shake loose from him and be free."

27:41
Gen 32:6
35:29; 37:4
Deut 34:8

41So Esau hated Jacob because of what he had done to him. He said to himself, "My father will soon be gone, and then I will kill Jacob." 42But someone got wind of what he was planning, and reported it to Rebekah. She sent for Jacob and told him that his life was being threatened by Esau.

27:43
Gen 11:31
12:4; 27:8,13
28:10
27:44
Gen 31:41
27:45
Prov 20:21

43"This is what to do," she said. "Flee to your Uncle Laban in Haran. 44Stay there with him awhile until your brother's fury is spent, 45and he forgets what you have done. Then I will send for you. For why should I be bereaved of both of you in one day?"

27:46
Gen 26:34,35

46Then Rebekah said to Isaac, "I'm sick and tired of these local girls. I'd rather die than see Jacob marry one of them."

28:1
Gen 24:3,4

28 So Isaac called for Jacob and blessed him and said to him, "Don't marry one of these Canaanite girls. 2Instead, go at once to Paddan-aram, to the house

27:38 *Isaac says nothing.* This appears in some versions, not in others. **28:2** *your grandfather,* literally, "your mother's father." *your Uncle Laban,* literally, "your mother's brother."

JACOB'S FAMILY TREE

Marrying within the extended family was common and acceptable in this day. Had Jacob married outside his family, he would have married someone who didn't believe in God. So Jacob married his cousins, Rachel and Leah.

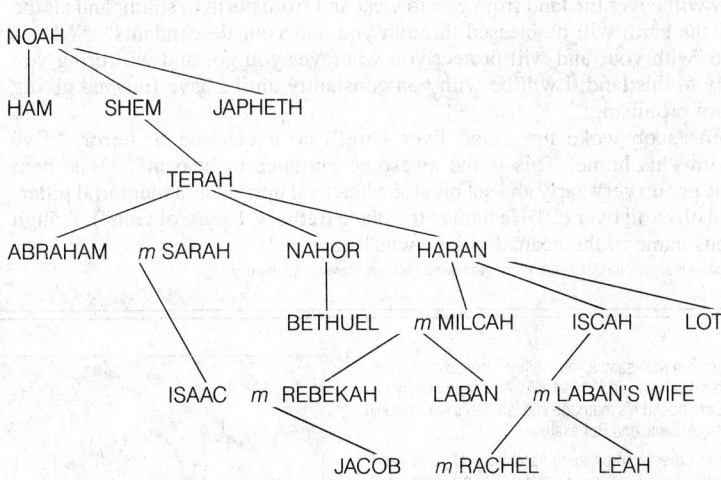

NOAH

HAM   SHEM   JAPHETH

TERAH

ABRAHAM   *m* SARAH   NAHOR   HARAN

BETHUEL   *m* MILCAH   ISCAH   LOT

ISAAC   *m* REBEKAH   LABAN   *m* LABAN'S WIFE

JACOB   *m* RACHEL   LEAH

m: married

27:41 Esau was so angry at Jacob that he failed to see his own wrong in giving away the birthright in the first place. Jealous anger pollutes clear thinking by blinding us to the good things we have and making us dwell on what we don't have.

27:41 When Esau lost the valuable family blessing, his future suddenly changed. Reacting in anger, he decided to kill Jacob.

When you lose something of great value, or if others conspire against you and succeed, anger is the first and most natural reaction. But you can control your feelings by (1) recognizing your reaction for what it is, (2) praying for strength, and (3) asking God for help to see the opportunities that your bad situation may provide.

of your grandfather Bethuel, and marry one of your cousins—your Uncle Laban's daughters. ³God Almighty bless you and give you many children; may you become a great nation of many tribes! ⁴May God pass on to you and to your descendants the mighty blessings promised to Abraham. May you own this land where we now are foreigners, for God has given it to Abraham."

⁵So Isaac sent Jacob away, and he went to Paddan-aram to visit his Uncle Laban, his mother's brother—the son of Bethuel the Aramean. ⁶, ⁷, ⁸Esau realized that his father despised the local girls, and that his father and mother had sent Jacob to Paddan-aram, with his father's blessing, to get a wife from there, and that they had strictly warned him against marrying a Canaanite girl, and that Jacob had agreed and had left for Paddan-aram. ⁹So Esau went to his Uncle Ishmael's family and married another wife from there, besides the wives he already had. Her name was Mahalath, the sister of Nebaioth, and daughter of Ishmael, Abraham's son.

28:3
Gen 17:1-4
27:4,7
35:11

28:4
Gen 12:1-3
15:7; 35:11
48:3

28:7
Gen 27:8

28:8
Gen 26:34

28:9
Gen 36:3

F. THE STORY OF JACOB (28:10—36:43)

Jacob did everything, both right and wrong, with great zeal. He deceived his own brother Esau and his father Isaac. He wrestled with an angel and worked fourteen years to marry the woman he loved. Through Jacob we learn how a strong leader can also be a servant. We also see how wrong actions will always come back to haunt us.

1. Jacob starts a family
Jacob's dream

¹⁰So Jacob left Beer-sheba and journeyed toward Haran. ¹¹That night, when he stopped to camp at sundown, he found a rock for a headrest and lay down to sleep, ¹²and dreamed that a staircase reached from earth to heaven, and he saw the angels of God going up and down upon it.

¹³At the top of the stairs stood the Lord. "I am Jehovah," he said, "the God of Abraham, and of your father Isaac. The ground you are lying on is yours! I will give it to you and to your descendants. ¹⁴For you will have descendants as many as dust! They will cover the land from east to west and from north to south; and all the nations of the earth will be blessed through you and your descendants. ¹⁵What's more, I am with you, and will protect you wherever you go, and will bring you back safely to this land; I will be with you constantly until I have finished giving you all I am promising."

¹⁶, ¹⁷Then Jacob woke up. "God lives here!" he exclaimed in terror. "I've stumbled into his home! This is the awesome entrance to heaven!" ¹⁸The next morning he got up very early and set his stone headrest upright as a memorial pillar, and poured olive oil over it. ¹⁹He named the place Bethel ("House of God"), though the previous name of the nearest village was Luz.

28:10
Gen 12:4,5
26:23; 46:1

28:12
Gen 20:3
32:1,2; 37:5
Num 12:6
Jn 1:51

28:13
Gen 15:18

28:14
Gen 12:2
13:14,16; 22:18

28:15
Gen 26:3; 48:21
Deut 7:9; 31:6,8

28:16
Ex 3:5

28:17
2 Chron 5:14

28:18
Gen 35:14

28:19
Gen 12:8; 35:6

28:12 *a staircase,* literally, "ladder."   **28:19** *of the nearest village,* literally, "of the city."

28:9 Uncle Ishmael was Isaac's half brother. He was the son of Hagar, Abraham's servant girl (16:1–4, 15). After marrying two foreign girls, Esau hoped his marriage into Ishmael's family would please his parents, Isaac and Rebekah.

28:10–15 God's covenant promise to Abraham and Isaac was offered to Jacob as well. But it was not enough to be Abraham's grandson—Jacob had to establish his own personal relationship with God. God has no grandchildren, just children. Each of us must have a personal relationship with him. It is not enough to hear wonderful stories about Christians in your family. You need to become part of the story yourself (see Galatians 3:6, 7).

28:19 Bethel was about ten miles north of Jerusalem and 60 miles north of Beersheba, where Jacob left his family. This was where Abraham made one of his first sacrifices to God when he entered the land. Later Bethel became a center of idol worship, and the prophet Hosea condemned its evil practices.

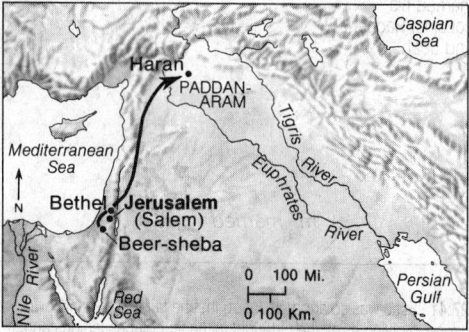

JACOB'S TRIP TO HARAN After Jacob deceived Esau, he literally ran for his life, traveling more than 400 miles to Haran where an uncle, Laban, lived. In Haran, Jacob married and started a family.

28:21
Gen 35:3
Ex 15:2
28:22
Gen 14:20; 35:7
Deut 14:22

20And Jacob vowed this vow to God: "If God will help and protect me on this journey and give me food and clothes, 21and will bring me back safely to my father, then I will choose Jehovah as my God! 22And this memorial pillar shall become a place for worship; and I will give you back a tenth of everything you give me!"

Jacob meets Rachel

29:1
Judg 6:3,33
29:2
Gen 24:11

29 Jacob traveled on, finally arriving in the land of the East. 2He saw in the distance three flocks of sheep lying beside a well in an open field, waiting to be watered. But a heavy stone covered the mouth of the well. 3(The custom was that the stone was not removed until all the flocks were there. After watering them, the stone was rolled back over the mouth of the well again.) 4Jacob went over to the shepherds and asked them where they lived.

29:4
Gen 11:31
28:10

"At Haran," they said.

29:5
Gen 24:29

5"Do you know a fellow there named Laban, the son of Nahor?"

"We sure do."

29:6
Gen 37:14
43:27

6"How is he?"

"He's well and prosperous. Look, there comes his daughter Rachel with the sheep."

7"Why don't you water the flocks so they can get back to grazing?" Jacob asked. "They'll be hungry if you stop so early in the day!"

8"We don't roll away the stone and begin the watering until all the flocks and shepherds are here," they replied.

29:10
Ex 2:16
29:11
Gen 27:26; 33:4
29:12
Gen 28:5

9As this conversation was going on, Rachel arrived with her father's sheep, for she was a shepherdess. 10And because she was his cousin—the daughter of his mother's brother—and because the sheep were his uncle's, Jacob went over to the well and rolled away the stone and watered his uncle's flock. 11Then Jacob kissed Rachel and started crying! 12, 13He explained about being her cousin on her father's side, and that he was her Aunt Rebekah's son. She quickly ran and told her father, Laban, and as soon as he heard of Jacob's arrival, he rushed out to meet him and greeted him warmly and brought him home. Then Jacob told him his story.

29:14
Judg 9:2
2 Sam 5:1

14"Just think, my very own flesh and blood," Laban exclaimed.

Jacob marries two sisters

29:15
Gen 30:28
31:7,41
29:16
Gen 29:25,26
29:17
Gen 12:11; 26:7
1 Sam 25:3
29:18
Gen 24:67
Hos 12:12
29:20
Song 8:6,7
1 Cor 13:7

After Jacob had been there about a month, 15Laban said to him one day, "Just because we are relatives is no reason for you to work for me without pay. How much do you want?" 16Now Laban had two daughters, Leah, the older, and her younger sister, Rachel. 17Leah had lovely eyes, but Rachel was shapely, and in every way a beauty. 18Well, Jacob was in love with Rachel. So he told her father, "I'll work for you seven years if you'll give me Rachel as my wife."

19"Agreed!" Laban replied. "I'd rather give her to you than to someone outside the family."

20So Jacob spent the next seven years working to pay for Rachel. But they seemed to him but a few days, he was so much in love. 21Finally the time came for him to marry her.

28:20–22 Was Jacob trying to bargain with God? It is possible that Jacob, in his ignorance of how to worship and serve God, treated God like a servant who would perform a service for a tip. Or it is possible that Jacob was not really bargaining, but pledging his future to God. In effect he was saying, "Since you have blessed me, even though I don't deserve it, I will promise to follow you." Whether Jacob was bargaining or pledging, God blessed him. But God also had some difficult lessons for him to learn.

29:18–27 It was the custom of the day for the man to pay a gift or "dowry" to the family of his future wife. This was done to compensate the family for the loss of the girl. Jacob's dowry was not a material possession—instead he agreed to work seven years for Laban. But there was another custom of the land that Laban did

not tell Jacob. The oldest daughter had to be married first. Thus, Laban deceived Jacob into giving him seven free years of hard work.

29:20–28 People often wonder if waiting a long time for something they truly desire is worth it. Jacob waited seven years to marry Rachel. After being tricked, he agreed to work seven more years for her! The most important goals and desires are worth waiting and paying for. Movies and television have created the illusion that people have to wait only an hour or two to solve their problems or get what they want. Don't be trapped into thinking the same is true in real life. Patience is hardest when we need it the most, but it is the key to achieving our goals.

"I have fulfilled my contract," Jacob said to Laban. "Now give me my wife, so that I can sleep with her."

22So Laban invited all the men of the settlement to celebrate with Jacob at a big party. 23Afterwards, that night, when it was dark, Laban took Leah to Jacob, and he slept with her. 24(And Laban gave to Leah a servant girl, Zilpah, to be her maid.) 25But in the morning—it was Leah!

"What sort of trick is this?" Jacob raged at Laban. "I worked for seven years for Rachel. What do you mean by this trickery?"

26"It's not our custom to marry off a younger daughter ahead of her sister," Laban replied smoothly. 27"Wait until the bridal week is over and you can have Rachel too—if you promise to work for me another seven years!"

28So Jacob agreed to work seven more years. Then Laban gave him Rachel, too. 29And Laban gave to Rachel a servant girl, Bilhah, to be her maid. 30So Jacob slept with Rachel, too, and he loved her more than Leah, and stayed and worked the additional seven years.

29:22 Judg 14:10
29:23 Gen 24:65 38:14
29:24 Gen 30:9
29:25 Gen 12:18 27:35
29:27 Lev 18:18 Judg 14:10,12
29:29 Gen 30:3-8
29:30 Gen 29:17

Jacob's many sons

31But because Jacob was slighting Leah, Jehovah let her have a child, while Rachel was barren. 32So Leah became pregnant and had a son, Reuben (meaning "God has noticed my trouble"), for she said, "Jehovah has noticed my trouble—now my husband will love me." 33She soon became pregnant again and had another son and named him Simeon (meaning "Jehovah heard"), for she said, "Jehovah heard that I was unloved, and so he has given me another son." 34Again she became pregnant and had a son, and named him Levi (meaning "Attachment") for she said, "Surely now my husband will feel affection for me, since I have given him three sons!" 35Once again she was pregnant and had a son and named him Judah (meaning "Praise"), for she said, "Now I will praise Jehovah!" And then she stopped having children.

29:31 Gen 20:18 Deut 21:15 Mal 1:2,3
29:32 Gen 35:23 37:21; 42:22 46:8,9
29:33 Gen 30:6
29:34 Gen 49:5
29:35 Gen 49:8

30 Rachel, realizing she was barren, became envious of her sister. "Give me children or I'll die," she exclaimed to Jacob.

2Jacob flew into a rage. "Am I God?" he flared. "He is the one who is responsible for your barrenness."

3Then Rachel told him, "Sleep with my servant-girl Bilhah, and her children will be mine." 4So she gave him Bilhah to be his wife, and he slept with her, 5and she became pregnant and presented him with a son. 6Rachel named him Dan (meaning "Justice"), for she said, "God has given me justice, and heard my plea and given me a son." 7Then Bilhah, Rachel's servant-girl, became pregnant again and gave

30:1 1 Sam 1:4-7 Eccles 4:4
30:2 Gen 25:21 31:36
30:3 Gen 16:2
30:4 Gen 22:24 35:22
30:6 Gen 29:32

29:26 *Laban replied smoothly,* implied from context.   **30:6** *Dan* (meaning "Justice"). The meaning is not of the actual Hebrew name, but of a Hebrew word sounding like the name. The name given is a Hebrew pun. An example in English might be, "Because of the large hospital bill the child was named 'Bill.'"

29:23-25 Jacob flew into a rage when he learned that Laban had tricked him. The deceiver of Esau was now deceived himself. How natural it is for us to become enraged at an injustice done to us while closing our eyes to the injustices we do to others. Sin has a way of coming back to haunt us.

29:28-30 Although Jacob was tricked by Laban, he kept his part of the bargain. There was more at stake than just Jacob's hurt. There was Rachel to think about, as well as God's plan for his life. When we are tricked by others, keeping our part of the bargain may still be wise. "Nursing our wounds" or plotting revenge keeps us from seeing God's perspective.

29:32 Today parents usually give their children names that sound good or have sentimental appeal. But the Old Testament portrays a more dynamic use of names. Parents hoped their children would fulfill the meaning of the names given them. Later the parents could look back and see if their grown children had lived up to their names. Sometimes a person's name was changed because his or her character and name did not match. This happened to Jacob. His name (meaning "grabber") was changed to Israel

(meaning "one who has power with God"). Jacob's character had changed to the point that he was no longer seen as a deceiver, but rather as a godly man.

30:3 Each of the three great patriarchs (Abraham, Isaac, and Jacob) had wives who had difficulty conceiving children. It is interesting to note how each man reacted to his wife's predicament. Abraham had relations with Sarah's servant girl in order to have his own child. This relationship only caused bitterness and jealousy. Isaac, however, prayed to God when his wife was barren. God eventually answered his prayers and Rebekah had twin sons. But Jacob followed his grandfather's example. He too had relations with his wives' servant girls, leading to sad and sometimes bitter consequences.

30:4-12 Rachel and Leah were locked in a cruel contest. In their race to have more children, they both gave their servant girls to Jacob as concubines. Jacob would have been wise to refuse, even though this was an accepted custom of the day. The fact that a custom is socially acceptable does not mean it is wise. You will be spared much heartbreak if you look at the potential consequences, to you or to others, of your actions.

30:8
Gen 32:24
Mt 4:13

30:11
Gen 35:26
46:16; 49:19

30:14
Song 7:13

30:17
Gen 29:31; 30:6
Ex 3:7

Jacob a second son. 8Rachel named him Naphtali (meaning "Wrestling"), for she said, "I am in a fierce contest with my sister and I am winning!"

9Meanwhile, when Leah realized that she wasn't getting pregnant anymore, she gave her servant-girl Zilpah to Jacob, to be his wife, 10and soon Zilpah presented him with a son. 11Leah named him Gad (meaning "My luck has turned!").

12Then Zilpah produced a second son, 13and Leah named him Asher (meaning "Happy"), for she said, "What joy is mine! The other women will think me blessed indeed!"

14One day during the wheat harvest, Reuben found some mandrakes growing in a field and brought them to his mother Leah. Rachel begged Leah to give some of them to her.

15But Leah angrily replied, "Wasn't it enough to steal my husband? And now will you steal my son's mandrakes too?"

Rachel said sadly, "He will sleep with you tonight because of the mandrakes."

16That evening as Jacob was coming home from the fields, Leah went out to meet him. "You must sleep with me tonight!" she said; "for I am hiring you with some mandrakes my son has found!" So he did. 17And God answered her prayers and she

30:14 Mandrakes were a leafy plant eaten by peasant women who supposed this would aid them in becoming pregnant.

RACHEL

History seems to repeat itself here. Twice a town well at Haran was the site of significant events in one family's story. It was here that Rebekah met Eliezer, Abraham's servant, who had come to find a wife for Isaac. Some 40 years later, Rebekah's son Jacob returned the favor by serving his cousin Rachel and her sheep from the same well. The relationship that developed between them not only reminds us that romance is not a modern invention, but also teaches us a few lessons about patience and love.

Jacob's love for Rachel was both patient and practical. Jacob had the patience to wait seven years for her, but he kept busy in the meantime. His commitment to Rachel kindled a strong loyalty within her. In fact, her loyalty to Jacob got out of hand and became self-destructive. She was frustrated by her barrenness and desperate to compete with her sister for Jacob's affection. She was trying to gain from Jacob what he had already given: devoted love.

Rachel's attempts to earn the unearnable are a picture of a much greater error we can make. Like her, we find ourselves trying somehow to earn love—God's love. But apart from his Word, we end up with one of two false ideas. Either we think we've been good enough to deserve his love, or we recognize we aren't able to earn his love and assume that it cannot be ours. If the Bible makes no other point, it shouts this one: God loves us! His love had no beginning and is incredibly patient. All we need to do is respond, not try to earn what is freely offered. God has said in many ways, "I love you. I have demonstrated that love to you by all I've done for you. I have even sacrificed my Son, Jesus, to pay the price for what is unacceptable about you (your sin). Now, live because of my love. Respond to me; love me with your whole being; give yourself to me in thanks, not as payment. Live life fully, in the freedom of knowing you are loved."

Strengths and accomplishments:
● She showed great loyalty to her family
● She mothered Joseph and Benjamin after being barren for many years

Weaknesses and mistakes:
● Her envy and competitiveness marred her relationship with her sister, Leah
● She was capable of dishonesty by taking her loyalty too far
● She failed to recognize that Jacob's devotion was not dependent on her ability to have children

Lessons from her life:
● Loyalty must be controlled by what is true and right
● Love is accepted, not earned

Vital statistics:
● Where: Haran
● Occupation: Shepherdess/Housewife
● Relatives: Father: Laban. Aunt: Rebekah. Sister: Leah. Husband: Jacob. Sons: Joseph and Benjamin.

Key verse:
"So Jacob spent the next seven years working to pay for Rachel. But they seemed to him but a few days, he was so much in love" (Genesis 29:20).

Rachel's story is told in Genesis 29—35:20. She is also mentioned in Ruth 4:11.

became pregnant again, and gave birth to her fifth son. ¹⁸She named him Issachar (meaning "Wages"), for she said, "God has repaid me for giving my slave-girl to my husband." ¹⁹Then once again she became pregnant, with a sixth son. ²⁰She named him Zebulun (meaning "Gifts"), for she said, "God has given me good gifts for my husband. Now he will honor me, for I have given him six sons." ²¹Afterwards she gave birth to a daughter and named her Dinah.

²²Then God remembered about Rachel's plight, and answered her prayers by giving her a child. ²³, ²⁴For she became pregnant and gave birth to a son. "God has removed the dark slur against my name," she said. And she named him Joseph (meaning "May I also have another!"), for she said, "May Jehovah give me another son."

Jacob becomes wealthy

²⁵Soon after the birth of Joseph to Rachel, Jacob said to Laban, "I want to go back home. ²⁶Let me take my wives and children—for I earned them from you—and be gone, for you know how fully I have paid for them with my service to you."

²⁷"Please don't leave me," Laban replied, "for a fortune-teller that I consulted told me that the many blessings I've been enjoying are all because of your being here. ²⁸How much of a raise do you need to get you to stay? Whatever it is, I'll pay it."

²⁹Jacob replied, "You know how faithfully I've served you through these many years, and how your flocks and herds have grown. ³⁰For it was little indeed you had before I came, and your wealth has increased enormously; Jehovah has blessed you from everything I do! But now, what about me? When should I provide for my own family?"

³¹, ³²"What wages do you want?" Laban asked again.

Jacob replied, "If you will do one thing, I'll go back to work for you. Let me go out among your flocks today and remove all the goats that are speckled or spotted, and all the black sheep. Give them to me as my wages. ³³Then if you ever find any white goats or sheep in my flock, you will know that I have stolen them from you!"

³⁴"All right!" Laban replied. "It shall be as you have said!"

³⁵, ³⁶So that very day Laban went out and formed a flock for Jacob of all the male goats that were ringed and spotted, and the females that were speckled and spotted with any white patches, and all of the black sheep. He gave them to Jacob's sons to take them three days' distance, and Jacob stayed and cared for Laban's flock. ³⁷Then Jacob took fresh shoots from poplar, almond, and sycamore trees, and peeled white streaks in them, ³⁸and placed these rods beside the watering troughs so that Laban's flocks would see them when they came to drink; for that is when they mated. ³⁹, ⁴⁰So the flocks mated before the white-streaked rods, and their offspring were streaked and spotted, and Jacob added them to his flock. Then he divided out the ewes from Laban's flock and segregated them from the rams, and let them mate only with Jacob's black rams. Thus he built his flocks from Laban's. ⁴¹Moreover, he watched for the stronger animals to mate, and placed the peeled branches before them, ⁴²but didn't with the feebler ones. So the less healthy lambs were Laban's and the stronger ones were Jacob's! ⁴³As a result, Jacob's flocks increased rapidly and he became very wealthy, with many servants, camels, and donkeys.

30:27 *a fortune-teller that I consulted*, literally, "I have learned by divination."

30:18
Gen 35:23
49:14,15
30:20
Mt 4:13

30:22
1 Sam 1:19
30:23
Lk 1:25

30:24
Gen 35:17

30:26
Gen 29:18,27
Hos 12:12

30:27
Gen 18:3
39:2-5
30:28
Gen 29:15; 31:7

30:30
Gen 30:43

30:32
Gen 31:8,10,12

30:37
Gen 31:9-13

30:43
Gen 13:2
24:35; 26:13
33:11

30:22-24 Eventually the Lord answered Rachel's prayers and gave her a child of her own. She caused herself many heartaches by taking matters into her own hands (giving Bilhah to Jacob). Trusting God when nothing seems to happen is difficult. But it is harder still to live with the consequences of taking matters into our own hands. Resist the temptation to feel that God has forgotten you. Have patience and courage to wait for God to act.

2. Jacob returns home

31:1
Prov 27:4

31:2
Gen 31:36
1 Sam 18:9

31:3
Gen 28:15; 32:9

31:5
Gen 31:42,53

31:6
Gen 30:29

31:7
Gen 29:15
30:28; 31:41

31:8
Gen 30:32

31 But Jacob learned that Laban's sons were grumbling, "He owes everything he owns to our father. All his wealth is at our father's expense." 2Soon Jacob noticed a considerable cooling in Laban's attitude towards him.

3Jehovah now spoke to Jacob and told him, "Return to the land of your fathers, and to your relatives there; and I will be with you."

4So one day Jacob sent for Rachel and Leah to come out to the field where he was with the flocks, 5to talk things over with them.

"Your father has turned against me," he told them, "and now the God of my fathers has come and spoken to me. 6You know how hard I've worked for your father, 7but he has been completely unscrupulous and has broken his wage contract with me again and again and again. But God has not permitted him to do me any harm! 8For if he said the speckled animals would be mine, then all the flock produced speckled; and when he changed and said I could have the streaked ones,

---

LABAN

We're all selfish, but some of us have a real corner on the weakness. Laban's whole life was stamped by self-centeredness. His chief goal was to look out for himself. The way he treated others was controlled by that goal. He made profitable arrangements for his sister Rebekah's marriage to Isaac, and used his daughters' lives as bargaining chips. Jacob eventually outmaneuvered Laban, but the older man was unwilling to admit defeat. His hold on Jacob was broken, but he still tried to maintain some kind of control by getting Jacob to promise to be gone for good. He realized that Jacob and Jacob's God were more than he could handle.

On the surface, we may find it difficult to identify with Laban. But his selfishness is one point we have in common. Like him, we often have a strong tendency to control people and events to our benefit. Our "good" reasons for treating others the way we do may simply be a thin cover over the motive of self-centeredness. We may not recognize our selfishness, however. One way to discover it is to examine our willingness to admit we're wrong. Laban could not bring himself to do this. If you find yourself amazed by what you sometimes say and do to avoid facing wrong actions, you are on the right road back to God.

Strengths and accomplishments:
- Controlled two generations of marriages in the Abrahamic family (Rebekah, Rachel, Leah)
- Possessed a quick wit

Weaknesses and mistakes:
- Manipulated and used others for his own benefit
- Unwilling to admit wrongdoing
- Benefited financially from using Jacob but never received the full benefit he could have gained by knowing and worshiping the God of Jacob

Lessons from his life:
- Those who set out to use people will eventually find themselves used
- God's plan cannot be stopped

Vital statistics:
- Where: Haran
- Occupation: Wealthy shepherd
- Relatives: Father: Bethuel. Sister: Rebekah. Brother-in-law: Isaac. Daughters: Rachel and Leah. Son-in-law: Jacob.

Key verse:
"In fact, except for the grace of God—The God of my grandfather Abraham, even the glorious God of Isaac, my father—you would have sent me off without a penny to my name. But God has seen your cruelty and my hard work, and that is why he appeared to you last night" (Genesis 31:42).

Laban's story is told in Genesis 27:43—31:55.

31:1-3 Jacob's wealth made Laban's sons jealous. It is sometimes difficult to be happy when others are doing well. To compare our success with that of others is a dangerous way to judge the quality of our life. By comparing ourselves to others, we may be giving jealousy a foothold. We can avoid jealousy by rejoicing in others' success (see Romans 12:15).

31:4-13 Although Laban treated Jacob unfairly, God still increased Jacob's prosperity. God's power is not limited by lack of fair play. He has the ability to meet our needs and make us thrive even though others treat us unfairly. To give in and play unfairly in return is to be no different from your enemies.

then all the lambs were streaked! ⁹In this way God has made me wealthy at your father's expense.

¹⁰"And at the mating season, I had a dream, and saw that the he-goats mating with the flock were streaked, speckled, and mottled. ¹¹Then, in my dream, the Angel of God called to me ¹²and told me that I should mate the white female goats with streaked, speckled, and mottled male goats. 'For I have seen all that Laban has done to you,' the Angel said. ¹³I am the God you met at Bethel,' he continued, 'the place where you anointed the pillar and made a vow to serve me. Now leave this country and return to the land of your birth.' "

¹⁴Rachel and Leah replied, "That's fine with us! There's nothing for us here—none of our father's wealth will come to us anyway! ¹⁵He has reduced our rights to those of foreign women; he sold us, and what he received for us has disappeared. ¹⁶The riches God has given you from our father were legally ours and our children's to begin with! So go ahead and do whatever God has told you to."

Laban pursues Jacob

¹⁷⁻²⁰So one day while Laban was out shearing sheep, Jacob set his wives and sons on camels, and fled without telling Laban his intentions. He drove the flocks before him—Jacob's flocks he had gotten there at Paddan-aram—and took everything he owned and started out to return to his father Isaac in the land of Canaan. ²¹So he fled with all of his possessions (and Rachel stole her father's household gods and took them with her) and crossed the Euphrates River and headed for the territory of Gilead.

²²Laban didn't learn of their flight for three days. ²³Then, taking several men with him, he set out in hot pursuit and caught up with them seven days later, at Mount Gilead. ²⁴That night God appeared to Laban in a dream.

"Watch out what you say to Jacob," he was told. "Don't give him your blessing

31:9
Gen 31:1,16

31:10
Gen 31:24

31:11
Gen 16:7-13
18:1; 22:1,11

31:12
Gen 30:37-43
Ex 3:7
Lev 19:13
Deut 24:14,15

31:13
Gen 28:13-19
35:7

31:15
Gen 29:20,27
30:26-28

31:18
Gen 24:29
25:20

31:20
Gen 31:27

31:21
Gen 15:18
Num 32:1
Deut 3:12
Judg 17:4,5
18:20

31:22
Gen 30:36

31:24
Gen 25:20
31:10

31:12 and told me that I should mate the white female goats with streaked, speckled, and mottled male goats, implied. Literally, "notice that all the mating males are speckled, streaked, and mottled."

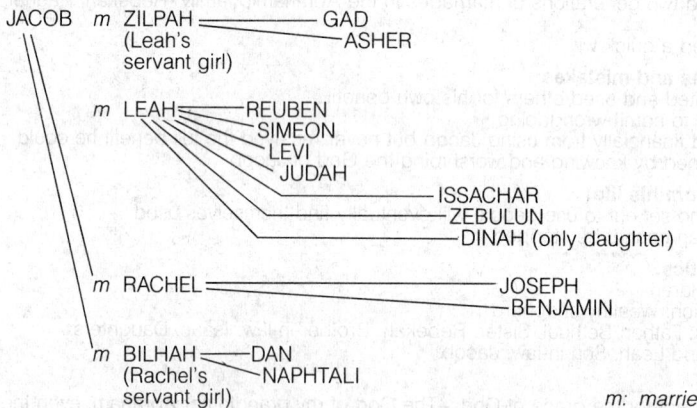

```
JACOB   m  ZILPAH ————————— GAD
            (Leah's          ‾‾ASHER
            servant girl)

         m  LEAH ═════ REUBEN
              ‾‾‾‾‾‾‾‾ SIMEON
                     ‾ LEVI
                      ‾ JUDAH
                                    ————————— ISSACHAR
                                    ‾‾‾‾‾‾‾‾‾‾ ZEBULUN
                                    ————————— DINAH (only daughter)

         m  RACHEL ═══════════════ JOSEPH
                                   ‾‾BENJAMIN

         m  BILHAH ———— DAN
            (Rachel's   ‾‾NAPHTALI
            servant girl)                        m: married
```

JACOB'S CHILDREN
This chart shows from left to right Jacob's children in the order in which they were born.

Jacob's many wives (two wives and two "substitute" wives) led to sad and bitter consequences among the children. Anger, resentment, and jealousy were common among Jacob's sons. It is interesting to note that the worst fighting and rivalry occurred between Leah's children and Rachel's children, and among the tribes that descended from them.

31:14, 15 Leaving home was not difficult for Rachel and Leah because their father had treated them as poorly as he had Jacob. According to custom, they were supposed to receive the benefits of Jacob's dowry, which was fourteen years of hard work. When Laban did not give them what was rightfully theirs, they knew they would never inherit anything from their father.

31:21 Many people kept small wooden or metal idols in their homes. These idols were called teraphim, and they were thought to protect the home and offer advice in times of need. They had legal significance as well, for when they were passed on to an heir, the

31:25
Gen 33:18

and don't curse him." 25Laban finally caught up with Jacob as he was camped at the top of a ridge; Laban, meanwhile, camped below him in the mountains.

26"What do you mean by sneaking off like this?" Laban demanded. "Are my daughters prisoners, captured in a battle, that you have rushed them away like this?

31:28
Gen 29:13
31:55
Ex 4:27

27Why didn't you give me a chance to have a farewell party, with singing and orchestra and harp? 28Why didn't you let me kiss my grandchildren and tell them good-bye? This is a strange way to act. 29I could crush you, but the God of your father appeared to me last night and told me, 'Be careful not to be too hard on Jacob!' 30But see here—though you feel you must go, and long so intensely for your childhood home—why have you stolen my idols?"

31:29
Gen 31:24,42

31:30
Gen 31:21

31:31
Gen 20:11

31"I sneaked away because I was afraid," Jacob answered. "I said to myself, 'He'll take his daughters from me by force.' 32But as for your household idols, a curse upon anyone who took them. Let him die! If you find a single thing we've stolen from you, I swear before all these men, I'll give it back without question." For Jacob didn't know that Rachel had taken them.

31:32
Gen 44:9
1 Sam 12:3

33Laban went first into Jacob's tent to search there, then into Leah's, and then searched the two tents of the concubines, but didn't find them. Finally he went into Rachel's tent. 34Rachel, remember, was the one who had stolen the idols; she had stuffed them into her camel saddle and now was sitting on them! So although Laban searched the tents thoroughly, he didn't find them.

31:35
Gen 18:11

35"Forgive my not getting up, father," Rachel explained, "but I'm having my monthly period." So Laban didn't find them.

31:36
Gen 30:2
Num 16:15

36, 37Now Jacob got mad. "What did you find?" he demanded of Laban. "What is my crime? You have come rushing after me as though you were chasing a criminal and have searched through everything. Now put everything I stole out here in front of us, before your men and mine, for all to see and to decide whose it is! 38Twenty years I've been with you, and all that time I cared for your ewes and goats so that they produced healthy offspring, and I never touched one ram of yours for food. 39If any were attacked and killed by wild animals, did I show them to you and ask you to reduce the count of your flock? No, I took the loss. You made me pay for every animal stolen from the flocks, whether I could help it or not. 40I worked for you through the scorching heat of the day, and through the cold and sleepless nights. 41Yes, twenty years—fourteen of them earning your two daughters, and six years to get the flock! And you have reduced my wages ten times! 42In fact, except for the grace of God—the God of my grandfather Abraham, even the glorious God of Isaac, my father—you would have sent me off without a penny to my name. But

31:37
Gen 31:32
Josh 7:23

31:38
Gen 31:41

31:39
Ex 22:10-13

31:41
Gen 29:27
30:27-32

31:42
Gen 28:13-15,
20; 31:29

31:35 *but I'm having my monthly period,* implied. Literally, "The manner of women is upon me." She was pregnant with Benjamin, but was falsely claiming her menstrual period, which, under the later Mosaic law, caused ceremonial defilement of all that she sat upon. See Lev 15. **31:39** *whether I could help it or not,* literally, "stolen by day or by night."

---

person who received them could rightfully claim the greatest amount of the family inheritance. No wonder Laban was concerned when he realized his idols were missing. Most likely Rachel stole her father's idols because she was afraid Laban would consult them and learn where she and Jacob had gone, or perhaps she wanted to claim the family inheritance.

31:32 Can you remember feeling absolutely sure about something? Jacob was so sure that no one had stolen Laban's idols that he vowed to kill the offender. Since Rachel took them, this statement put his wife's safety in serious jeopardy. Even when we are absolutely sure about a matter, it is safer to avoid rash statements. Someone may hold you to them.

31:38-42 Jacob worked hard even after several pay cuts. Jacob's diligence eventually paid off: his flocks began to multiply. Making a habit of doing more than expected can pay off by (1) pleasing God, (2) earning recognition and advancement, (3) enhancing your reputation, (4) building others' confidence in you, (5) giving you more experience and knowledge, and (6) developing your spiritual maturity.

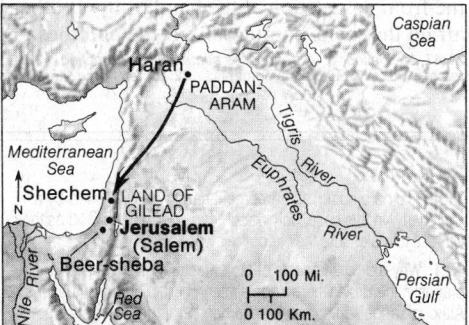

JACOB'S RETURN TO CANAAN God told Jacob to leave Haran and return to his homeland. Jacob took his family, crossed the Euphrates River, and headed first for the land of Gilead. Laban caught up with him there.

God has seen your cruelty and my hard work, and that is why he appeared to you last night."

43Laban replied, "These women are my daughters, and these children are mine, and these flocks and all that you have—all are mine. So how could I harm my own daughters and grandchildren? 44Come now and we will sign a peace pact, you and I, and will live by its terms."

45So Jacob took a stone and set it up as a monument, 46and told his men to gather stones and make a heap, and Jacob and Laban ate together beside the pile of rocks. 47, 48They named it "The Witness Pile"—"Jegar-sahadutha," in Laban's language, and "Galeed" in Jacob's.

"This pile of stones will stand as a witness against us [if either of us trespasses across this line]," Laban said. 49So it was also called "The Watchtower" (Mizpah). For Laban said, "May the Lord see to it that we keep this bargain when we are out of each other's sight. 50And if you are harsh to my daughters, or take other wives, I won't know, but God will see it. 51, 52This heap," Laban continued, "stands between us as a witness of our vows that I will not cross this line to attack you and you will not cross it to attack me. 53I call upon the God of Abraham and Nahor, and of their father, to destroy either one of us who does."

So Jacob took oath before the mighty God of his father Isaac, to respect the boundary line. 54Then Jacob presented a sacrifice to God there at the top of the mountain, and invited his companions to a feast, and afterwards spent the night with them on the mountain. 55Laban was up early the next morning and kissed his daughters and grandchildren, and blessed them, and returned home.

Jacob takes gifts to Esau

32 So Jacob and his household started on again. And the angels of God came to meet him. When he saw them he exclaimed, "God lives here!" So he named the place "God's territory!"

3Jacob now sent messengers to his brother Esau in Edom, in the land of Seir, 4with this message: "Hello from Jacob! I have been living with Uncle Laban until recently, 5and now I own oxen, donkeys, sheep, goats, and many servants, both men and women. I have sent these messengers to inform you of my coming, hoping that you will be friendly to us."

6The messengers returned with the news that Esau was on the way to meet Jacob—with an army of 400 men! 7Jacob was frantic with fear. He divided his household, along with the flocks and herds and camels, into two groups; 8for he said, "If Esau attacks one group, perhaps the other can escape."

9Then Jacob prayed, "O God of Abraham my grandfather, and of my father Isaac—O Jehovah who told me to return to the land of my relatives, and said that you would do me good— 10I am not worthy of the least of all your lovingkindnesses shown me again and again just as you promised me. For when I left home I owned nothing except a walking stick! And now I am two armies! 11O Lord, please deliver me from destruction at the hand of my brother Esau, for I am frightened—terribly afraid that he is coming to kill me and these mothers and my children. 12But you

31:44 Gen 21:27 26:28-31
31:45 Gen 28:18 Josh 24:26,27
31:46 Gen 35:14 Josh 4:5
31:48 Gen 21:30 Deut 4:26
31:49 Judg 10:17 11:11,29
31:50 Judg 11:10 1 Sam 12:5 Jer 29:23; 42:5
31:52 Gen 31:29,42
31:53 Gen 28:13 31:29
31:54 Gen 26:30 Ex 18:12
31:55 Gen 31:28; 33:4
32:1 Gen 16:7 18:1,2; 19:1 22:11; 31:11 2 Kgs 6:16,17 Ps 34:7
32:2 Josh 13:26 21:38 2 Sam 2:8
32:3 Gen 14:5,6 25:30; 27:41 Mal 3:1
32:4 Gen 31:17,18
32:8 Gen 33:1-3
32:9 Gen 28:13-15 31:13
32:10 Gen 24:27
32:11 Gen 27:41; 33:4
32:12 Gen 28:14,15

31:47, 48 *if either of us trespasses across this line,* implied.   **32:1, 2** *So Jacob and his household,* implied. *God's territory,* literally, "Two encampments."   **32:10** *left home,* literally, "passed over this Jordan."

31:49 To be binding, an agreement had to be witnessed by a third party. In this case, both Jacob and Laban used God as their witness to make sure they kept their word.

32:1 Why did these angels of God meet Jacob? There are many places in the Bible where angels intervened in human situations. Although angels often came in human form, these angels must have looked different, for Jacob recognized them at once.

32:3 The last time Jacob had seen Esau, his brother was ready to kill him for stealing the family blessing (Genesis 25:29—27:42).

Esau was so angry he had vowed to kill Jacob as soon as their father, Isaac, died (27:41). Afraid of their reunion, Jacob sent a messenger ahead with gifts, hoping to buy Esau's favor.

32:9–12 How would you feel, knowing you were about to meet the person whom you had cheated out of his most precious possession? Jacob had taken Esau's birthright (25:33) and his blessing (27:27–29). Now he was about to meet his brother for the first time in twenty years, and he was frantic with fear. He collected his thoughts, however, and decided to pray. When we face a difficult or urgent conflict, we can run about frantically or we can pause to pray. Which approach will be more effective?

promised to do me good, and to multiply my descendants until they become as the sands along the shores—too many to count."

13, 14, 15Jacob stayed where he was for the night, and prepared a present for his brother Esau: 200 female goats, 20 male goats, 200 ewes, 20 rams, 30 milk camels, with their colts, 40 cows, 10 bulls, 20 female donkeys, 10 male donkeys. 16He instructed his servants to drive them on ahead, each group of animals by itself, separated by a distance between. 17He told the men driving the first group that when they met Esau and he asked, "Where are you going? Whose servants are you? Whose animals are these?"— 18they should reply: "These belong to your servant Jacob. They are a present for his master Esau! He is coming right behind us!"

19Jacob gave the same instructions to each driver, with the same message. 20Jacob's strategy was to appease Esau with the presents before meeting him face to face! "Perhaps," Jacob hoped, "he will be friendly to us." 21So the presents were sent on ahead, and Jacob spent that night in the camp.

Jacob wrestles with an angel

22, 23, 24But during the night he got up and wakened his two wives and his two concubines and eleven sons, and sent them across the Jordan River at the Jabbok ford with all his possessions, then returned again to the camp and was there alone; and a Man wrestled with him until dawn. 25And when the Man saw that he couldn't win the match, he struck Jacob's hip, and knocked it out of joint at the socket.

26Then the Man said, "Let me go, for it is dawn."

But Jacob panted, "I will not let you go until you bless me."

27"What is your name?" the Man asked.

"Jacob," was the reply.

28"It isn't anymore!" the Man told him. "It is Israel—one who has power with God. Because you have been strong with God, you shall prevail with men."

29"What is your name?" Jacob asked him.

"No, you mustn't ask," the Man told him. And he blessed him there.

30Jacob named the place "Peniel" ("The Face of God"), for he said, "I have seen God face to face, and yet my life is spared." 31The sun rose as he started on, and he was limping because of his hip. 32(That is why even today the people of Israel don't eat meat from near the hip, in memory of what happened that night.)

The brothers make peace

33 Then, far in the distance, Jacob saw Esau coming with his 400 men. 2Jacob now arranged his family into a column, with his two concubines and their children at the head, Leah and her children next, and Rachel and Joseph last. 3Then Jacob went on ahead. As he approached his brother he bowed low seven times before him. 4And then Esau ran to meet him and embraced him affectionately and kissed him; and both of them were in tears!

32:22, 23, 24 and wakened, implied.

32:18
Gen 32:4,5

32:20
Gen 43:11,12
1 Sam 25:18
Prov 21:14

32:22
Deut 3:16
Josh 12:2

32:24
Gen 18:3
Hos 12:3,4

32:26
Ex 32:10
1 Chron 4:10
Ps 67:1,6,7

32:28
Gen 35:10
1 Kgs 18:31

32:29
Ex 3:13
Judg 13:17

32:30
Gen 16:13
Ex 24:10; 33:20
Num 12:8
Deut 5:24; 34:10
Judg 6:22
Jn 1:18

32:31
Judg 8:8,9,17

33:1
Gen 32:6,16

33:3
Gen 18:2; 42:6
Prov 6:3

33:4
Gen 45:14
46:29

32:26 Jacob continued this wrestling match all night just to be blessed. He was persistent. God encourages persistence in all areas of our lives, including the spiritual. We should be aware of areas in our spiritual lives where we need to be more persistent. Strong character results from struggling under tough conditions.

32:27–29 God gave many Bible people new names (Abraham, Sarah, Jacob, Peter, Paul). Their new names were a symbol of how God had changed their lives. Here we see how Jacob's character had changed. Jacob, the ambitious deceiver, had now become Israel, the man who persistently clings to God.

33:1–11 It is refreshing to see Esau's change of heart when Jacob and Esau meet again. The bitterness over losing his birthright and blessing seems gone (Genesis 25:29–34). Instead we see Esau happy and content with what he has. Jacob even exclaims how great it is to see his brother's friendly smile (33:10).

Life can deal us some bad situations. We can feel cheated, as Esau did, but we don't have to remain bitter. We can remove the bitterness from our lives by honestly expressing our feelings to God, forgiving those who have wronged us, and being content with what we have.

33:3 Bowing low seven times was the sign of respect given to a king. Jacob was taking every precaution as he met Esau, hoping to dispel any thoughts of revenge.

33:4 Esau met his brother, Jacob, and greeted him with a great hug. Imagine how hard this was for Esau, who at one time had actually plotted his brother's death (27:41). But time away from each other allowed the bitter wounds to heal. With the passing of time each brother was able to see that their relationship was more important than their real estate.

⁵Then Esau looked at the women and children and asked, "Who are these people with you?"

"My children," Jacob replied. ⁶Then the concubines came forward with their children, and bowed low before him. ⁷Next came Leah with her children, and bowed, and finally Rachel and Joseph came and made their bows.

⁸"And what were all the flocks and herds I met as I came?" Esau asked. And Jacob replied, "They are my gifts, to curry your favor!"

⁹"Brother, I have plenty," Esau laughed. "Keep what you have."

¹⁰"No, but please accept them," Jacob said, "for what a relief it is to see your friendly smile! I was as frightened of you as though approaching God! ¹¹Please take my gifts. For God has been very generous to me and I have enough." So Jacob insisted, and finally Esau accepted them.

¹²"Well, let's be going," Esau said. "My men and I will stay with you and lead the way."

¹³But Jacob replied, "As you can see, some of the children are small, and the flocks and herds have their young, and if they are driven too hard, they will die. ¹⁴So you go on ahead of us and we'll follow at our own pace and meet you at Seir."

¹⁵"Well," Esau said, "at least let me leave you some of my men to assist you and be your guides."

"No," Jacob insisted, "we'll get along just fine. Please do as I suggest." ¹⁶So Esau started back to Seir that same day. ¹⁷Meanwhile Jacob and his household went as far as Succoth. There he built himself a camp, with pens for his flocks and herds. (That is why the place is called Succoth, meaning "huts.") ¹⁸Then they arrived safely at Shechem, in Canaan, and camped outside the city. ¹⁹(He bought the land he camped on from the family of Hamor, Shechem's father, for 100 pieces of silver. ²⁰And there he erected an altar and called it "El-Elohe-Israel," "The Altar to the God of Israel.")

Jacob's sons take revenge

34 One day Dinah, Leah's daughter, went out to visit some of the neighborhood girls, ²but when Shechem, son of King Hamor the Hivite, saw her, he took her and raped her. ³He fell deeply in love with her, and tried to win her affection.

⁴Then he spoke to his father about it. "Get this girl for me," he demanded. "I want to marry her."

⁵Word soon reached Jacob of what had happened, but his sons were out in the

33:10 *I was as frightened of you as though approaching God,* literally, "forasmuch as I have seen your face as one sees the face of God." 33:13 *as you can see,* implied.

33:11 Why did Jacob send gifts ahead for Esau? In Bible times, gifts were given for several reasons. (1) As a bribe. Even today, gifts are given to win someone over or buy his or her support. Esau may first have refused Jacob's gifts (33:9) because he didn't want or need to accept a bribe. He had already forgiven Jacob, and he had ample wealth of his own. (2) As an expression of affection. (3) Gifts were often exchanged before a meeting of two people. The gifts were often related to a person's occupation. This explains why Jacob sent Esau, who was a herdsman, sheep, goats, and cattle.

34:1-4 Shechem may have been a victim of "love at first sight," but he acted on it with an impulsive, evil act. Not only did he sin against Dinah, he sinned against her entire family (34:6, 7), which brought about severe consequences (34:25-31). Even Shechem's declared love for Dinah could not excuse the evil he did by forcefully raping her. Don't allow sexual passion to boil over into evil actions. Passion must be controlled.

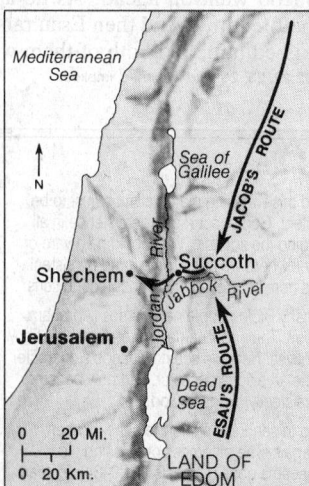

JACOB'S JOURNEY TO SHECHEM After a joyful reunion with his brother Esau (who journeyed from Edom), Jacob set up camp in Succoth. Later he moved on to Shechem where his daughter, Dinah, was raped and two of his sons took revenge on the city.

33:5 Gen 48:8,9
33:8 Gen 32:5,13-16
33:9 Gen 27:39
33:10 Gen 19:19 47:29; 50:4
33:11 Gen 32:13-15
33:14 Gen 32:3 Deut 2:1
33:17 Josh 13:27 Judg 8:5 Ps 60:6
33:18 Gen 12:6 25:20; 28:6,7
33:19 Gen 23:17
33:20 Josh 24:32 Jn 4:5
34:1 Gen 30:21
34:2 Deut 21:14 22:29 2 Sam 11:2
34:4 Judg 14:2,6

34:7
2 Sam 13:12

fields herding cattle, so he did nothing until their return. 6, 7Meanwhile King Hamor, Shechem's father, went to talk with Jacob, arriving just as Jacob's sons came in from the fields, too shocked and angry to overlook the insult, for it was an outrage against all of them.

34:9
Gen 24:3; 28:1

8Hamor told Jacob, "My son Shechem is truly in love with your daughter, and longs for her to be his wife. Please let him marry her. 9, 10Moreover, we invite you folks to live here among us and to let your daughters marry our sons, and we will give our daughters as wives for your young men. And you shall live among us wherever you wish and carry on your business among us and become rich!"

34:11
Gen 33:10

34:12
Gen 24:53
29:18; 31:41
Ex 22:16

11Then Shechem addressed Dinah's father and brothers. "Please be kind to me and let me have her as my wife," he begged. "I will give whatever you require. 12No matter what dowry or gift you demand, I will pay it—only give me the girl as my wife."

34:13
Gen 27:35
31:7; 34:31

34:14
Gen 17:13,14
Josh 5:2

13Her brothers then lied to Shechem and Hamor, acting dishonorably because of what Shechem had done to their sister. 14They said, "We couldn't possibly. For you are not circumcised. It would be a disgrace for her to marry such a man. 15I'll tell you what we'll do—if every man of you will be circumcised, 16then we will intermarry with you and live here and unite with you to become one people. 17Otherwise we will take her and be on our way."

34:19
Gen 29:20

18, 19Hamor and Shechem gladly agreed, and lost no time in acting upon this request, for Shechem was very much in love with Dinah, and could, he felt sure, sell the idea to the other men of the city—for he was highly respected and very popular. 20So Hamor and Shechem appeared before the city council and presented their request.

34:20
Gen 23:10
Deut 17:5

21"Those men are our friends," they said. "Let's invite them to live here among us and ply their trade. For the land is large enough to hold them, and we can intermarry with them. 22But they will only consider staying here on one condition—that every one of us men be circumcised, the same as they are. 23But if we do this, then all they have will become ours and the land will be enriched. Come on, let's agree to this so that they will settle here among us."

34:22
Gen 34:15

34:24
Gen 17:23
Josh 5:2

34:25
Gen 49:5,6
Josh 5:8

24So all the men agreed, and all were circumcised. 25But three days later, when their wounds were sore and sensitive to every move they made, two of Dinah's brothers, Simeon and Levi, took their swords, entered the city without opposition, and slaughtered every man there, 26including Hamor and Shechem. They rescued Dinah from Shechem's house and returned to their camp again. 27Then all of Jacob's sons went over and plundered the city because their sister had been dishonored there. 28They confiscated all the flocks and herds and donkeys—everything they could lay their hands on, both inside the city and outside in the fields, 29and took all the women and children, and wealth of every kind.

34:28
Josh 7:21

34:30
Gen 13:7
Gen 49:5-7
Ex 5:21
1 Chron 16:19

30Then Jacob said to Levi and Simeon, "You have made me stink among all the people of this land—all the Canaanites and Perizzites. We are so few that they will come and crush us, and we will all be killed."

31"Should he treat our sister like a prostitute?" they retorted.

34:20 *appeared before the city council,* literally, "came into the gate of their city."

34:24-31 Why did Simeon and Levi take such harsh action against the city of Shechem? Jacob's family saw themselves as "set apart" from others. That is what God wanted. They were to remain separate from their heathen neighbors. But the brothers wrongly thought that being set apart also meant being better. This arrogant attitude led to the terrible slaughter of innocent people.

34:27-29 When Shechem raped Dinah, the consequences were far greater than he could have imagined. Dinah's brothers were outraged and took revenge. Pain, lying, deceit, and murder followed. Sexual sin is no more sinful than any other sin, but its

consequences may be more devastating.

34:30, 31 In seeking revenge against Prince Shechem, Simeon and Levi lied, murdered, and stole. Their desire for justice was right. Their ways of achieving it were wrong. Because of their sin, their own father cursed them with his dying breath (49:5-7). Generations later, Simeon's descendants lost part of the Promised Land allotted to them. When tempted to return evil for evil, leave revenge to God and spare yourself the dreadful consequences of sin.

Rachel and Isaac die

35 "Move on to Bethel now, and settle there," God said to Jacob, "and build an altar to worship me—the God who appeared to you when you fled from your brother Esau."

2So Jacob instructed all those in his household to destroy the idols they had brought with them, and to wash themselves and to put on fresh clothing. 3"For we are going to Bethel," he told them, "and I will build an altar there to the God who answered my prayers in the day of my distress, and was with me on my journey."

4So they gave Jacob all their idols and their earrings, and he buried them beneath the oak tree near Shechem. 5Then they started on again. And the terror of God was upon all the cities they journeyed through, so that they were not attacked. 6Finally they arrived at Luz (also called Bethel), in Canaan. 7And Jacob erected an altar there and named it "The altar to the God who met me here at Bethel" because it was there at Bethel that God appeared to him when he was fleeing from Esau.

8Soon after this Rebekah's old nurse Deborah died and was buried beneath the oak tree in the valley below Bethel. And ever after it was called "The Oak of Weeping."

9Upon Jacob's arrival at Bethel, en route from Paddan-aram, God appeared to him once again and blessed him. 10And God said to him, "You shall no longer be called Jacob ('Grabber'), but Israel ('One who prevails with God'). 11I am God Almighty," the Lord said to him, "and I will cause you to be fertile and to multiply and to become a great nation, yes, many nations; many kings shall be among your descendants. 12And I will pass on to you the land I gave to Abraham and Isaac. Yes, I will give it to you and to your descendants."

13, 14Afterwards Jacob built a stone pillar at the place where God had appeared to him; and he poured wine over it as an offering to God, and then anointed the pillar with olive oil. 15Jacob named the spot Bethel ("House of God"), because God had spoken to him there.

16Leaving Bethel, he and his household traveled on toward Ephrath (Bethlehem). But Rachel's pains of childbirth began while they were still a long way away. 17After a very hard delivery, the midwife finally exclaimed, "Wonder-

35:1 Gen 12:1; 22:1 28:19; 31:3
35:2 Gen 31:19
35:3 Gen 28:15-22
35:4 Ex 32:2 Josh 24:23-26 Judg 8:24 Hos 2:13
35:5 Gen 34:30 Ex 15:16
35:6 Gen 12:8 28:19; 48:3
35:7 Gen 28:19
35:8 Gen 24:59
35:9 Gen 26:2 28:13; 48:3
35:10 Gen 17:5,15 32:28
35:11 Gen 12:1 17:1,5; 28:3
35:12 Gen 13:15 28:13
35:13 Judg 6:21; 13:20
35:14 Gen 28:18,19
35:16 Ruth 4:11
35:17 Gen 30:23,24 1 Sam 4:19,20

35:7 *the God who met me here at Bethel,* literally, "The God of Bethel." **35:8** *Soon after this,* implied.

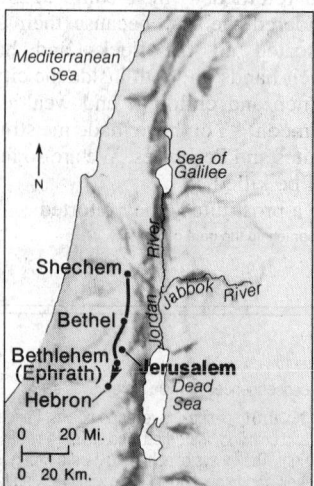

JACOB'S JOURNEY BACK TO HEBRON
After Jacob's sons Simeon and Levi destroyed Shechem, God told Jacob to move to Bethel, where Jacob's name was changed to *Israel*. He then traveled to Hebron, but along the way, his dear wife Rachel died in Ephrath (Bethlehem).

idols should have no place in his household. He wanted no good-luck charms to divert the spiritual focus of his family.

Jacob ordered his household to destroy all their idols. An idol is anything we put before God. Unless we remove idols from our lives, they can ruin our faith. Idols don't have to be physical objects. They can be thoughts or desires. Like Jacob, we should begin to remove the idols from our lives at once.

35:4 Why did the people give Jacob their earrings? Jewelry, in itself, was not evil. In Jacob's day, however, earrings were often worn by people in neighboring cultures as good-luck charms in order to ward off evil. The people had to cleanse away all heathen influences including reminders of foreign gods.

35:10 God reminded Jacob of his new name, Israel, which meant "one who has power with God" or "one who prevails with God." Jacob's life was littered with difficulties and trials. Yet his new name was a tribute to his desire to stay close to God despite life's disappointments.

Many people believe that Christianity should offer a problem-free life. Consequently, as life gets tough, they draw back disappointed. Instead, they should determine to prevail with God through the storms of life. Troubles and difficulties are painful but inevitable. Look at them as opportunities for growth. You can't prevail with God without troubles to prevail over.

35:2 Why did the people have these idols? Idols were sometimes seen more as good-luck charms than as gods. Some Israelites, even though they worshiped God, had idols in their homes, just as some Christians today own good-luck trinkets. Jacob believed that

35:13, 14 Anointing oil was olive oil of the finest grade of purity. It was expensive and very valuable. Anointing something with this precious oil showed the high value placed on the anointed object. Jacob was showing the greatest respect for the place where he met with God.

35:18
Gen 46:19
49:27

35:19
Gen 48:7

35:22
Gen 49:4
Lev 18:8
1 Chron 5:1

35:23
Gen 29:32-35
46:8-14

35:24
Gen 30:22-24

35:25
Gen 30:4-8
46:23-25

35:26
Gen 30:9-13
46:16-18

35:27
Gen 13:18
23:2; 37:14

35:28
Gen 23:1; 25:7
25:20; 47:28
50:26

ful—another boy!" 18And with Rachel's last breath (for she died) she named him "Ben-oni" ("Son of my sorrow"); but his father called him "Benjamin" ("Son of my right hand").

19So Rachel died, and was buried near the road to Ephrath (also called Bethlehem). 20And Jacob set up a monument of stones upon her grave, and it is there to this day.

21Then Israel journeyed on and camped beyond the Tower of Eder. 22It was while he was there that Reuben slept with Bilhah, his father's concubine, and someone told Israel about it.

Here are the names of the twelve sons of Jacob:

23The sons of Leah: Reuben, Jacob's oldest child, Simeon, Levi, Judah, Issachar, Zebulun.

24The sons of Rachel: Joseph, Benjamin.

25The sons of Bilhah, Rachel's servant-girl: Dan, Naphtali.

26The sons of Zilpah, Leah's servant-girl: Gad, Asher.

All these were born to him at Paddan-aram.

27So Jacob came at last to Isaac his father at Mamre in Kiriath-arba (now called Hebron), where Abraham too had lived. 28, 29Isaac died soon afterwards, at the ripe old age of 180. And his sons Esau and Jacob buried him.

Esau's descendants

36:1
Gen 25:25-34
32:3-7
1 Chron 1:35

36:2
Gen 26:34
36:10,14

36:3
Gen 25:13

36:4
Gen 36:10,11,
13

36:5
Gen 36:18

36:7
Gen 13:6

36:8
Gen 14:6
25:30; 32:3

36:9
Gen 36:43
1 Kgs 11:1

36:10
1 Chron 1:35

36:11
1 Chron 1:36

36 Here is a list of the descendants of Esau (also called Edom): 2, 3Esau married three local girls from Canaan:

Adah (daughter of Elon the Hethite),
Oholibamah (daughter of Anah and granddaughter of Zibeon the Hivite),
Basemath (his cousin—she was a daughter of Ishmael—the sister of Nebaioth).

4Esau and Adah had a son named Eliphaz. Esau and Basemath had a son named Reuel.

5Esau and Oholibamah had sons named Jeush, Jalam, and Korah. All these sons were born to Esau in the land of Canaan.

6, 7, 8Then Esau took his wives, children, household servants, cattle and flocks—all the wealth he had gained in the land of Canaan—and moved away from his brother Jacob to Mount Seir. (For there was not land enough to support them both because of all their cattle.)

9Here are the names of Esau's descendants, the Edomites, born to him in Mount Seir:

10, 11, 12Descended from his wife Adah, born to her son Eliphaz were:

Teman, Omar, Zepho, Gatam, Kenaz, Amalek (born to Timna, Eliphaz' concubine).

13, 14Esau also had grandchildren from his wife Basemath. Born to her son Reuel were:

Nahath, Zerah, Shammah, Mizzah.

36:2, 3 *Basemath (his cousin . . .),* implied. Literally, Basemath "the daughter of Ishmael." **36:13, 14** Verse 14 is a repetition of the names listed in verse 5.

35:22 Reuben's sin was costly, although not immediately. As the oldest son, he stood to receive a double portion of the family inheritance and a place of leadership among his people. Reuben may have thought he got away with his sin. No more was mentioned of it until Jacob, on his deathbed, assembled his family for the final blessing. Suddenly, Jacob took away Reuben's double portion and gave it to someone else. The reason? "You slept with one of my wives . . ." (Genesis 49:4).

Sin's consequences can plague us long after the sin is committed. When we do something wrong we may think we can escape unnoticed, only to discover later that the sin has been quietly breeding serious consequences.

36:9 The Edomites were descendants of Esau who lived south and east of the Dead Sea. The country featured rugged mountains and desolate wilderness. Several major roads led through Edom, for it was rich in natural resources. During the Exodus, God told Israel to leave the Edomites alone (Deuteronomy 2:5) because they were "brothers." But Edom refused to let them enter the land, and later they became bitter enemies of King David. The nations of Edom and Israel shared the same ancestor (Isaac) and the same border. Israel looked down on the Edomites because they intermarried with the Canaanites.

15, 16Esau's grandchildren became the heads of clans, as listed here: The clan of Teman, The clan of Omar, The clan of Zepho, The clan of Kenaz, The clan of Korah, The clan of Gatam, The clan of Amalek.

The above clans were the descendants of Eliphaz, the oldest son of Esau and Adah.

17The following clans were the descendants of Reuel, born to Esau and his wife Basemath while they lived in Canaan: The clan of Nahath, The clan of Zerah, The clan of Shammah, The clan of Mizzah.

18, 19And these are the clans named after the sons of Esau and his wife Oholiba-mah (daughter of Anah): The clan of Jeush, The clan of Jalam, The clan of Korah.

20, 21These are the names of the tribes that descended from Seir, the Horite—one of the native families of the land of Seir: The tribe of Lotan, The tribe of Shobal, The tribe of Zibeon, The tribe of Anah, The tribe of Dishon, The tribe of Ezer, The tribe of Dishan.

22The children of Lotan (the son of Seir) were Hori and Heman. (Lotan had a sister, Timna.)

23The children of Shobal: Alvan, Manahath, Ebal, Shepho, Onam.

24The children of Zibeon: Aiah, Anah. (This is the boy who discovered a hot springs in the wasteland while he was grazing his father's donkeys.)

25The children of Anah: Dishon, Oholibamah.

26The children of Dishon: Hemdan, Eshban, Ithran, Cheran.

27The children of Ezer: Bilhan, Zaavan, Akan.

28, 29, 30 The children of Dishan: Uz, Aran.

31-39These are the names of the kings of Edom (before Israel had her first king):

King Bela (son of Beor), from Dinhabah in Edom.

Succeeded by: King Jobab (son of Zerah), from the city of Bozrah.

Succeeded by: King Husham, from the land of the Temanites.

Succeeded by: King Hadad (son of Bedad), the leader of the forces that defeated the army of Midian when it invaded Moab. His city was Avith.

Succeeded by: King Samlah, from Masrekah.

Succeeded by: King Shaul, from Rehoboth-by-the-River.

Succeeded by: King Baal-hanan (son of Achbor).

Succeeded by: King Hadad, from the city of Paul.

King Hadad's wife was Mehetabel, daughter of Matred and granddaughter of Mezahab.

40-43Here are the names of the sub-tribes of Esau, living in the localities named after themselves: The clan of Timna, The clan of Alvah, The clan of Jetheth, The clan of Oholibamah, The clan of Elah, The clan of Pinon, The clan of Kenaz, The clan of Teman, The clan of Mibzar, The clan of Magdiel, The clan of Iram.

These, then, are the names of the subtribes of Edom, each giving its name to the area it occupied. (All were Edomites, descendants of Esau.)

G. THE STORY OF JOSEPH (37:1—50:26)

Joseph, one of Jacob's twelve sons, was obviously the favorite. Hated by his brothers for this, Joseph was sold to slave traders only to emerge as ruler of all Egypt. Through Joseph, we learn how suffering, no matter how unfair, develops strong character and deep wisdom.

1. Joseph is sold into slavery

37 So Jacob settled again in the land of Canaan, where his father had lived. 2Jacob's son Joseph was now seventeen years old. His job, along with his half-brothers, the sons of his father's wives Bilhah and Zilpah, was to shepherd his father's flocks. But Joseph reported to his father some of the bad things they were doing. 3Now as it happened, Israel loved Joseph more than any of his other children, because Joseph was born to him in his old age. So one day Jacob gave him

36:18
1 Chron 1:35

36:19
Gen 36:1,9

36:20
Gen 14:6
Deut 2:12,22
1 Chron 1:38-42

36:22
1 Chron 1:39

36:23
1 Chron 1:40

36:25
Gen 36:2,5,14,18
1 Chron 1:41

36:27
1 Chron 1:38,42

36:29,30
Gen 36:20

36:31
Gen 17:6,16
20:14
1 Chron 1:43

36:35
1 Chron 1:46

36:37
1 Chron 1:48

36:40
1 Chron 1:51

37:1
Gen 17:8; 28:4

37:2
Gen 6:9
35:22-26; 41:46

37:3
Gen 37:23,32
44:20

36:15, 16 *grandchildren,* implied.　36:29, 30 These verses repeat the names listed in vss 20, 21.
36:31-39 *succeeded by,* more literally, "succeeded at his death by. . . ." *from the city,* implied.　37:3 *a brightly colored coat,* more literally, "an ornamented tunic," or "long-sleeved tunic."

37:4
Gen 27:41
37:5
Gen 28:12
Num 12:6
Dan 2:1
37:7
Gen 42:6,9
43:26
37:8
Ex 2:14
Deut 33:16
37:9
Gen 41:25,32

a special gift—a brightly-colored coat. ⁴His brothers of course noticed their father's partiality, and consequently hated Joseph; they couldn't say a kind word to him. ⁵One night Joseph had a dream and promptly reported the details to his brothers, causing even deeper hatred.

⁶"Listen to this," he proudly announced. ⁷"We were out in the field binding sheaves, and my sheaf stood up, and your sheaves all gathered around it and bowed low before it!"

⁸"So you want to be our king, do you?" his brothers derided. And they hated him both for the dream and for his cocky attitude.

⁹Then he had another dream and told it to his brothers. "Listen to my latest

JOSEPH

As a youngster, Joseph was overconfident. His natural self-assurance, increased by being Jacob's favorite son and by knowing of God's designs on his life, was unbearable to his ten older brothers, who eventually conspired against him. But this self-assurance, molded by pain and combined with a personal knowledge of God, allowed him to survive and prosper where most would have failed. He added quiet wisdom to his confidence and won the hearts of everyone he met—Potiphar, the jailer, other prisoners, the king, and after many years, even those ten brothers.

Perhaps you can identify with one or more of these hardships Joseph experienced: he was betrayed and deserted by his family, was exposed to sexual temptation, was punished for doing the right thing, endured a long imprisonment, was forgotten by those he helped. As you read his story, note what Joseph did in each case. His positive response transformed each setback into a step forward. He didn't spend much time asking, "Why?" His approach was, "What shall I do now?" Those who saw his life were aware that wherever Joseph went and whatever he did, God was with him. When you're facing a setback, the beginning of a Joseph-like attitude is to acknowledge that God is with you. There is nothing like the reality of his presence to shed new light on a dark situation.

Strengths and accomplishments:
- Rose in power from slave to ruler of Egypt
- Was known for his personal integrity
- Was a man of spiritual sensitivity
- Prepared a nation to survive a famine

Weakness and mistake:
- His youthful pride caused friction with his brothers

Lessons from his life:
- What matters is not so much the events or circumstances of life, but our response to them
- With God's help any situation can be used for good, even when others intend it for evil

Vital statistics:
- Where: Canaan, Egypt
- Occupation: Shepherd, Slave, Convict, Ruler
- Relatives: Parents: Jacob and Rachel. Eleven brothers. Wife: Asenath. Sons: Manasseh and Ephraim.

Key verses:
"Joseph's suggestions were well received by Pharaoh and his assistants. As they discussed who should be appointed for the job, Pharaoh said, 'Who could do it better than Joseph? For he is a man who is obviously filled with the Spirit of God' " (Genesis 41:37, 38).

Joseph's story is told in Genesis 37—50. He is also mentioned in Hebrews 11:22.

37:3 In Joseph's day, everyone had a cloak. It was used to warm oneself, to bundle up belongings for a trip, to wrap babies, to sit on, or to serve as security for a loan. Most cloaks were plain, knee-length and short-sleeved. In contrast, Joseph's was probably the type of cloak royalty wore—long-sleeved, ankle-length, and colorful. This shows the favoritism Jacob showed Joseph.

It was obvious to the other boys that Joseph was Jacob's favorite son, especially when Joseph received the brightly-colored cloak. This gift aggravated the already strained relations between Joseph and his brothers. Favoritism in families may be unavoidable, but its divisive effects should be minimized. Parents

may not be able to change their feelings toward a favorite child, but they can change their actions toward the others.

37:6–11 Joseph's brothers were already angry over the possibility of being ruled by their little brother. Joseph then fueled the fire with his immature attitude and boastful manner. No one enjoys a braggart. If you want to tell others about things you have done, share your successes in a way that gives the glory to God. Young Joseph learned his lesson the hard way. His angry brothers sold him into slavery to get rid of him. But later, in Genesis 41:16, Joseph does give God the credit for his successes.

dream," he boasted. "The sun, moon, and eleven stars bowed low before me!"
¹⁰This time he told his father as well as his brothers; but his father rebuked him.
"What is this?" he asked. "Shall I indeed, and your mother and brothers come and
bow before you?" ¹¹His brothers were fit to be tied concerning this affair, but his
father gave it quite a bit of thought and wondered what it all meant.

¹²One day Joseph's brothers took their father's flocks to Shechem to graze them
there. ¹³, ¹⁴A few days later Israel called for Joseph, and told him, "Your brothers
are over in Shechem grazing the flocks. Go and see how they are getting along, and
how it is with the flocks, and bring me word."

"Very good," Joseph replied. So he traveled to Shechem from his home at
Hebron Valley. ¹⁵A man noticed him wandering in the fields.

"Who are you looking for?" he asked.

¹⁶"For my brothers and their flocks," Joseph replied. "Have you seen them?"

¹⁷"Yes," the man told him, "they are no longer here. I heard your brothers say
they were going to Dothan." So Joseph followed them to Dothan and found them
there. ¹⁸But when they saw him coming, recognizing him in the distance, they
decided to kill him!

¹⁹, ²⁰"Here comes that master-dreamer," they exclaimed. "Come on, let's kill
him and toss him into a well and tell father that a wild animal has eaten him. Then
we'll see what will become of all his dreams!"

²¹, ²²But Reuben hoped to spare Joseph's life. "Let's not kill him," he said; "we'll
shed no blood—let's throw him alive into this well here; that way he'll die without
our touching him!" (Reuben was planning to get him out later and return him to his
father.) ²³So when Joseph got there, they pulled off his brightly-colored robe, ²⁴and
threw him into an empty well—there was no water in it. ²⁵Then they sat down for
supper. Suddenly they noticed a string of camels coming towards them in the
distance, probably Ishmaelite traders who were taking gum, spices, and herbs from
Gilead to Egypt.

²⁶, ²⁷"Look there," Judah said to the others. "Here come some Ishmaelites. Let's
sell Joseph to them! Why kill him and have a guilty conscience? Let's not be
responsible for his death, for, after all, he is our brother!" And his brothers agreed.
²⁸So when the traders came by, his brothers pulled Joseph out of the well and sold
him to them for twenty pieces of silver, and they took him along to Egypt. ²⁹Some
time later, Reuben (who was away when the traders came by) returned to get

37:28 *traders*, literally, "Midianites."   37:29 *who was away when the traders came by*, implied.

37:10
Gen 27:29
Isa 60:14
Phil 2:10
37:11
Ps 106:16
Isa 11:13
Mt 27:18
Acts 7:9
37:12
Gen 33:18; 37:1
37:14
Gen 29:6; 35:27

37:17
2 Kgs 6:13

37:20
Gen 37:33
Prov 1:11
37:21
Gen 42:22
37:22
Gen 37:29
37:23
Gen 37:3
37:24
Jer 38:6
37:25
Gen 25:16-18
31:23; 37:28
Jer 8:22; 46:11
37:27
Ex 21:16
Neh 5:8
37:28
Gen 39:1; 45:4
Lev 27:5
Judg 8:22-24
Acts 7:9
37:29
Gen 37:34
44:13
Num 14:6

**JOSEPH GOES
TO MEET
HIS BROTHERS**
Jacob asked
Joseph to go find
his brothers, who
were grazing their
flocks near She-
chem. When
Joseph arrived, he
learned that his
brothers had gone
on to Dothan,
which lay along a
major trade route
to Egypt. There
the jealous broth-
ers sold Joseph
as a slave to a
group of Ishmael-
ite traders on their
way to Egypt.

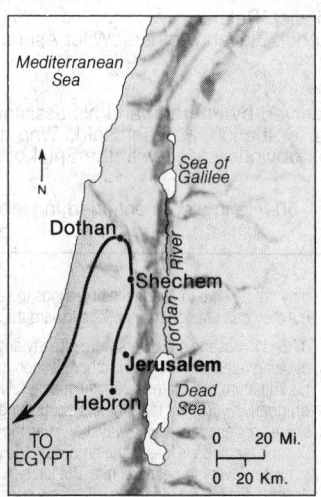

37:19, 20 Can your jealousy toward someone make you feel like
killing him? Before you say, "Of course not," look at what
happened in this story. Ten men were suddenly willing to kill their
own brother over a colored coat. Their deep jealousy had grown
into ugly rage, blinding them completely to what was right.
Jealousy can be hard to recognize because our reasons for it
seem to make sense. Left unchecked, jealousy can grow quickly
and lead to more serious sins. The longer you let jealous feelings
exist, the harder it is to correct them. The time to deal with jealousy
is when you notice yourself keeping score of what others have.

37:26, 27 The brothers were worried about having the guilt of
Joseph's death on them. Judah suggested an option that was not
right, but would leave them guiltless of murder. Sometimes we
jump at a solution because it is "the lesser of two evils," but it still is
not the right action to take. When people propose a seemingly
workable solution, first ask the question, "Is it right?"

37:28 Although Joseph's brothers didn't kill him outright, they
thought he was as good as dead (or at least out of their lives) when
they sold him to slave traders. They were quite willing to shift the
blame to these cruel men. Joseph faced a 30-day journey through
the desert, probably chained and on foot. He would be treated like
baggage and, once in Egypt, would be sold as a piece of
merchandise.

Joseph out of the well. When Joseph wasn't there, he ripped at his clothes in anguish and frustration.

37:30
Gen 5:24
42:13,32,36
³⁰"The child is gone; and I, where shall I go now?" he wept to his brothers. ³¹Then the brothers killed a goat and spattered its blood on Joseph's coat, ³²and
37:32
Lk 15:30
took the coat to their father and asked him to identify it.

37:33
Gen 37:20
44:28
"We found this in the field," they told him. "Is it Joseph's coat or not?" ³³Their father recognized it at once.

37:34
Gen 37:29
44:13
"Yes," he sobbed, "it is my son's coat. A wild animal has eaten him. Joseph is without doubt torn in pieces."

37:35
Gen 31:43
44:29
2 Sam 12:17
Ps 77:2
³⁴Then Israel tore his garments and put on sackcloth and mourned for his son in deepest mourning for many weeks. ³⁵His family all tried to comfort him, but it was no use.

37:36
Gen 39:1; 40:4
"I will die in mourning for my son," he would say, and then break down and cry. ³⁶Meanwhile, in Egypt, the traders sold Joseph to Potiphar, an officer of the

Parents are usually the best judges of their children's character. Jacob summarized the personality of his son Reuben by comparing him to wild waves. Except when frozen, water has no stable shape of its own. It always shapes itself to its container or environment. Reuben usually had good intentions but seemed unable to stand against a crowd. His instability made him hard to trust. He had both private and public values, but these contradicted each other. He went along with his brothers in their action against Joseph while hoping to counteract the evil in private. The plan failed. Compromise has a way of destroying convictions. Without convictions, lack of direction will destroy life. It would seem that Reuben's action in sleeping with his father's concubine showed how little he had left of the integrity he had displayed earlier in life.

How consistent are your public and private lives? We may want to think they are separate, but we can't deny they affect each other. What convictions are present in your life at all times? How closely does Jacob's description of his son—"unstable as the wild waves"—describe your life?

Strengths and accomplishments:
• Saved Joseph's life by talking the other brothers out of murder
• Showed intense love for his father by offering his own sons as a guarantee that Benjamin's life would be safe

Weaknesses and mistakes:
• Gave in quickly to group pressure
• Did not directly protect Joseph from his brothers, although as eldest son he had the authority to do so
• Slept with his father's concubine

Lessons from his life:
• Public and private integrity must be the same, or one will destroy the other
• Punishment for sin may not be immediate, but it is certain

Vital statistics:
• Where: Canaan, Egypt
• Occupation: Shepherd
• Relatives: Parents: Jacob and Leah. Eleven brothers.

Key verse:
"But you are unruly as the wild waves of the sea, and you shall be first no longer. I am demoting you, for you slept with one of my wives and thus dishonored me" (Genesis 49:4).

Reuben's story is told in Genesis 29—50.

37:30 Reuben returned to the pit to find Joseph, but Joseph was gone. His first response was "What is going to happen to me?" rather than "What is going to happen to Joseph?" When you get into a tough situation, are you always concerned first about yourself? Consider the person who is most affected by the problem. This may clear up the problem for you as well.

37:33, 34 To cover their evil action, Jacob's sons deceived their father into thinking Joseph was dead. Jacob himself had deceived others many times (even *his* father, in 27:35). Now, though blessed by God, he still had to face the consequences of his sins. God may not have punished Jacob immediately for his sins of deceit, but the consequences came nevertheless and stayed with him for the rest of his life.

37:36 Imagine the culture shock Joseph experienced upon arriving in Egypt. Joseph had lived as a nomad, traveling the countryside with his family, caring for sheep. Suddenly he was thrust into the world's most advanced civilized society with great pyramids, beautiful homes, sophisticated people, and a new language. While Joseph saw Egypt's skill and intelligence at their best, he also saw the Egyptians' spiritual blindness: they worshiped countless gods pertaining to every facet of life.

Pharaoh—the king of Egypt. Potiphar was captain of the palace guard, the chief executioner.

2. Judah and Tamar

38 About this time, Judah left home and moved to Adullam and lived there with a man named Hirah. 2There he met and married a Canaanite girl—the daughter of Shua. 3, 4, 5They lived at Chezib and had three sons, Er, Onan, and Shelah. These names were given to them by their mother, except for Er, who was named by his father.

6When his oldest son Er grew up, Judah arranged for him to marry a girl named Tamar. 7But Er was a wicked man, and so the Lord killed him.

8Then Judah said to Er's brother, Onan, "You must marry Tamar, as our law requires of a dead man's brother; so that her sons from you will be your brother's heirs."

9But Onan was not willing to have a child who would not be counted as his own, and so, although he married her, whenever he went in to sleep with her, he spilled the sperm on the bed to prevent her from having a baby which would be his brother's. 10So far as the Lord was concerned, it was very wrong of him [to deny a child to his deceased brother], so he killed him, too. 11Then Judah told Tamar, his daughter-in-law, not to marry again at that time, but to return to her childhood home and to her parents, and to remain a widow there until his youngest son Shelah was old enough to marry her. (But he didn't really intend for Shelah to do this, for fear God would kill him, too, just as he had his two brothers.) So Tamar went home to her parents.

12In the process of time Judah's wife died. After the time of mourning was over, Judah and his friend Hirah, the Adullamite, went to Timnah to supervise the shearing of his sheep. 13When someone told Tamar that her father-in-law had left for the sheep-shearing at Timnah, 14and realizing by now that she was not going to be permitted to marry Shelah, though he was fully grown, she laid aside her widow's clothing and covered herself with a veil to disguise herself, and sat beside the road at the entrance to the village of Enaim, which is on the way to Timnah. 15Judah noticed her as he went by and thought she was a prostitute, since her face was veiled. 16So he stopped and propositioned her to sleep with him, not realizing of course that she was his own daughter-in-law.

"How much will you pay me?" she asked.

17"I'll send you a young goat from my flock," he promised.

"What pledge will you give me, so that I can be sure you will send it?" she asked.

18"Well, what do you want?" he inquired.

"Your identification seal and your walking stick," she replied. So he gave them to her and she let him come and sleep with her; and she became pregnant as a result.

38:9 *although he married her,* implied. *he spilled the sperm on the bed,* literally, "spilled it on the ground."

38:1	Josh 12:15 / 15:35 / 1 Sam 22:1
38:2	Gen 24:3; 34:2 / 38:12
38:3	Gen 46:12 / Num 26:19
38:6	Mt 1:3
38:7	Gen 6:5,13:13 / 19:13; 38:10 / 2 Chron 33:6
38:8	Lev 18:16 / Num 36:8 / Deut 25:5-10 / Mt 22:24
38:10	2 Sam 11:27 / 1 Chron 21:7
38:11	Ruth 1:13
38:12	Gen 31:19 / Josh 13:23-27 / 1 Sam 25:4 / 2 Sam 13:23-27
38:14	Gen 23:10 / Josh 15:34
38:15	Gen 24:65
38:16	2 Sam 13:11 / Deut 23:18 / Ezek 16:33
38:17	Gen 38:20,25
38:18	Gen 41:42 / Hos 4:11

38:1ff This chapter vividly portrays the immoral character of Judah in contrast to the moral character of Joseph. Judah's character was tainted by jealousy and immorality. He was soon to learn some difficult lessons. In the following chapter, we see Joseph's godliness. His integrity and wise choices reflected his godly character. His faithfulness was rewarded with blessings greater than he could imagine.

38:8-10 This law about marrying a widow "in the family" is explained in Deuteronomy 25:5-10. The reason for the law was to ensure that a widow with no children would have an heir to whom she could pass on her inheritance. Because Judah's son (Tamar's husband) had no children, there was no family line through which the inheritance and the blessing of the covenant could continue. God killed Onan because he refused to fulfill his obligation to God's law and to Tamar.

38:11-26 When Tamar revealed she was pregnant, Judah (who unknowingly had gotten her pregnant) moved to have her killed. Judah had concealed his own sin, yet he came down harshly on Tamar. Often the sins we are trying to cover up in our lives are the ones that anger us most when we see them in others. If you find yourself feeling indignant at the sins of others, you may have a similar tendency to sin which you do not wish to face.

38:15-23 Why does this story seem to take a light view of prostitution? Prostitutes were common in heathen cultures such as Canaan. Public prostitutes served heathen goddesses and were common elements of the religious cults. They were more highly respected than private prostitutes who were sometimes punished when caught. Tamar was driven to prostitution because of her intense desire to have children; Judah was driven to prostitution because of lust. Neither case was justified.

38:18 A seal was a form of identification much like a fingerprint. It was usually a unique design carved in stone and worn on a ring or necklace that was inseparable from its owner. Persons of wealth or prestige used seals to make marks in clay or wax as a signature. Obviously, since Tamar had Judah's seal, she could prove he had been with her.

19Afterwards she resumed wearing her widow's clothing as usual. 20Judah asked his friend Hirah the Adullamite to take the young goat back to her, and to pick up the pledges he had given her, but Hirah couldn't find her!

21So he asked around of the men of the city, "Where does the prostitute live who was soliciting out beside the road at the entrance of the village?"

"But we've never had a public prostitute here," they replied. 22So he returned to Judah and told him he couldn't find her anywhere, and what the men of the place had told him.

38:23
Prov 6:32,33

23"Then let her keep them!" Judah exclaimed. "We tried our best. We'd be the laughingstock of the town to go back again."

38:24
Gen 34:31
Lev 20:10; 21:9
Eccles 7:26

24About three months later word reached Judah that Tamar, his daughter-in-law, was pregnant, obviously as a result of prostitution.

"Bring her out and burn her," Judah shouted.

38:25
Gen 37:32

25But as they were taking her out to kill her she sent this message to her father-in-law: "The man who owns this identification seal and walking stick is the father of my child. Do you recognize them?"

38:26
1 Sam 24:17
Ezek 16:52

26Judah admitted that they were his and said, "She is more in the right than I am, because I refused to keep my promise to give her to my son Shelah." But he did not marry her.

38:27
Gen 25:24
38:29
Gen 46:12
Num 26:20
Ruth 4:12
1 Chron 2:4
Mt 1:3
Lk 3:33

27In due season the time of her delivery arrived and she had twin sons. 28As they were being born, the midwife tied a scarlet thread around the wrist of the child who appeared first, 29but he drew back his hand and the other baby was actually the first to be born. "Where did *you* come from!" she exclaimed. And ever after he was called Perez (meaning "Bursting Out"). 30Then, soon afterwards, the baby with the scarlet thread on his wrist was born, and he was named Zerah.

3. Joseph is thrown into jail

39:1
Acts 7:9

39 When Joseph arrived in Egypt as a captive of the Ishmaelite traders, he was purchased from them by Potiphar, a member of the personal staff of Pharaoh, the king of Egypt. Now this man Potiphar was the captain of the king's

39:2
Gen 21:22
26:24,28; 28:15
39:4
Gen 32:5; 41:40
Prov 14:35
17:2; 27:18
39:5
Deut 28:3-6

bodyguard and his chief executioner. 2The Lord greatly blessed Joseph there in the home of his master, so that everything he did succeeded. 3Potiphar noticed this and realized that the Lord was with Joseph in a very special way. 4So Joseph naturally became quite a favorite with him. Soon he was put in charge of the administration of Potiphar's household, and all of his business affairs. 5At once the Lord began

---

WOMEN IN JESUS' FAMILY TREE			
Tamar	Canaanite	Genesis 38:1–30	
Rahab	Canaanite	Joshua 6:22–25	
Ruth	Moabite	Ruth 4:13–22	
Bath-sheba	Israelite	2 Samuel 12:24, 25	

38:29, 30 Perez was born as a result of incest and prostitution, gross sins to the Israelites. Yet he became an ancestor of Christ, who would die for the sins of everyone (Matthew 1:3).

39:1 The exact date of Joseph's arrival in Egypt is highly debated. Many scholars believe he arrived during the period of the Hyksos rulers. The Hyksos were foreigners who came from the region of Canaan. They invaded Egypt and controlled the land for almost 150 years. Although the dates for the Hyksos rule are usually placed after the reign of Joseph as stated in the Genesis chronology, those dates are uncertain. If Joseph did arrive in the period of the Hyksos, they would have had no problems promoting a brilliant young foreigner up the royal ladder since they were foreigners themselves.

39:1 Ancient Egypt was a land of great contrasts. People were either rich beyond measure or poverty stricken. There wasn't much middle ground. Joseph found himself serving Potiphar, an extremely rich member of Pharaoh's cabinet. Rich families like

Potiphar's had elaborate homes two or three stories tall with beautiful gardens and balconies. They enjoyed live entertainment at home as they chose delicious fruit from expensive bowls. They were surrounded by alabaster vases of flowers, paintings, beautiful rugs, and hand-carved chairs. Dinner was served on golden tableware, and their rooms were lit with gold candlesticks. The servants, such as Joseph, worked on the first floor, while the family occupied the upper stories.

39:2ff As a prisoner and slave, Joseph could have seen his situation as hopeless. Instead, he did his best with each small task given him. His diligence and positive attitude were soon noticed by the jail warden, who promoted him to prison administrator. Are you in the midst of a seemingly hopeless predicament? At work, at home, or at school, follow Joseph's example by taking each small task and doing your best. Remember how God turned Joseph's situation around. He will see your efforts and can reverse even overwhelming odds.

blessing Potiphar for Joseph's sake. All his household affairs began to run smoothly, his crops flourished and his flocks multiplied. 6So Potiphar gave Joseph the complete administrative responsibility over everything he owned. He hadn't a worry in the world with Joseph there, except to decide what he wanted to eat! Joseph, by the way, was a very handsome young man.

7One day at about this time Potiphar's wife began making eyes at Joseph, and suggested that he come and sleep with her.

8Joseph refused. "Look," he told her, "my master trusts me with everything in the entire household; 9he himself has no more authority here than I have! He has held back nothing from me except you yourself because you are his wife. How can I do such a wicked thing as this? It would be a great sin against God."

10But she kept on with her suggestions day after day, even though he refused to listen, and kept out of her way as much as possible. 11Then one day as he was in the house going about his work—as it happened, no one else was around at the time—12she came and grabbed him by the sleeve demanding, "Sleep with me." He tore himself away, but as he did, his jacket slipped off and she was left holding it as he fled from the house. 13When she saw that she had his jacket, and that he had fled, 14, 15she began screaming; and when the other men around the place came running in to see what had happened, she was crying hysterically. "My husband had to bring in this Hebrew slave to insult us!" she sobbed. "He tried to rape me, but when I screamed, he ran, and forgot to take his jacket."

16She kept the jacket, and when her husband came home that night, 17she told him her story.

"That Hebrew slave you've had around here tried to rape me, 18and I was only saved by my screams. He fled, leaving his jacket behind!"

19Well, when her husband heard his wife's story, he was furious. 20He threw Joseph into prison, where the king's prisoners were kept in chains. 21But the Lord was with Joseph there, too, and was kind to him by granting him favor with the chief jailer. 22In fact, the jailer soon handed over the entire prison administration to Joseph, so that all the other prisoners were responsible to him. 23The chief jailer had no more worries after that, for Joseph took care of everything, and the Lord was with him so that everything ran smoothly and well.

Joseph interprets two dreams

40 Some time later it so happened that the king of Egypt became angry with both his chief baker and his chief butler, so he jailed them both in the prison where Joseph was, in the castle of Potiphar, the captain of the guard, who was the chief executioner. 4They remained under arrest there for quite some time, and Potiphar assigned Joseph to wait on them. 5One night each of them had a dream. 6The next morning Joseph noticed that they looked dejected and sad.

7"What in the world is the matter?" he asked.

39:12 *sleeve.* The Hebrew word is not specific.

Marginal references (right column):

39:6 Gen 29:17 / Ex 2:2 / 1 Sam 16:12,18 / Lk 16:10 / Acts 7:20
39:7 Ps 119:37 / Prov 2:16; 5:3 / 7:13 / Ezek 23:5
39:8 Gen 39:5 / Prov 1:10 / 6:23,24
39:9 2 Sam 12:13 / Ps 51:4
39:10 1 Cor 6:18 / 15:33 / 1 Thess 5:22 / 2 Tim 2:22
39:12 Prov 7:13 / Eccles 7:26 / Ezek 16:30
39:14 Isa 54:17
39:17 Ex 20:16; 23:1 / Ps 37:14; 55:3
39:19 Prov 6:34; 18:17
39:20 Gen 40:1-3,15 / 41:12,14 / Ps 105:18
39:21 Gen 39:2,3 / 49:25 / Acts 7:9
39:22 Gen 39:4; 41:40
39:23 Gen 39:3 / Ps 1:3
40:1 Neh 1:11
40:4 Gen 37:36; 39:1
40:5 Gen 20:3 / 37:5-10; 40:8 / 41:1-7,11

39:9 Potiphar's wife failed to seduce Joseph, who resisted this temptation by saying, "It would be a great sin against God." Joseph didn't say, "I'd be hurting you," or "I'd be sinning against Potiphar," or "I'd be sinning against myself." When under pressure, those kinds of excuses are easily rationalized away. Remember that sexual sin is not just between two consenting adults. It is an act of disobedience to God.

39:10–15 Joseph avoided Potiphar's wife as much as possible. He refused her advances and finally *ran* from her. Sometimes merely trying to avoid temptation is not enough; we must turn and run, especially when the temptations are too great for us. This is often the case in sexual temptations.

39:20 Prisons were grim places with vile conditions. They were used to house forced laborers or those accused and awaiting trial like Joseph. In ancient days, prisoners were guilty until proven innocent. Many prisoners never made it to court, for trials were held at the whim of the ruler. Joseph was in prison two years before appearing before Pharaoh, and then he was called out to interpret a dream, not to stand trial.

40:1 "Pharaoh" was the general name for all the kings of Egypt. It was a title like "Mr. President," used to address the country's leader. The Pharaohs in Genesis and Exodus were not the same man.

40:1–3 The baker and wine taster (cupbearer) were two of the most trusted men in Pharaoh's kingdom. The baker was in charge of making the king's food, and the wine-taster tasted all the king's food and drink *before* giving it to Pharaoh, in case any of it was contaminated or poisoned. These trusted men must have been suspected of a serious wrong to be thrown into prison. Perhaps Pharaoh suspected the men of conspiring against him. Later the wine taster was released and the baker executed.

40:8
Gen 41:15,16
Job 33:15,16
Dan 2:28

40:9
Gen 37:5
Judg 7:13

40:12
Gen 41:12
Judg 7:14
Dan 2:36

40:13
Gen 40:19,20

40:14
Josh 2:12
1 Sam 20:13,14

40:15
Gen 37:28
39:1,20

40:16
Gen 40:1,2

40:18
Gen 40:12
41:13

40:19
Gen 40:22
41:13
Deut 21:22

40:20
Gen 40:13,18
2 Kgs 25:27-30
Jer 52:31-34

40:22
Gen 40:19

40:23
Gen 40:14; 41:9

8And they replied, "We both had dreams last night, but there is no one here to tell us what they mean."

"Interpreting dreams is God's business," Joseph replied. "Tell me what you saw."

9, 10The butler told his dream first. "In my dream," he said, "I saw a vine with three branches that began to bud and blossom, and soon there were clusters of ripe grapes. 11I was holding Pharaoh's wine cup in my hand, so I took the grapes and squeezed the juice into it, and gave it to him to drink."

12"I know what the dream means," Joseph said. "The three branches mean three days! 13Within three days Pharaoh is going to take you out of prison and give you back your job again as his chief butler. 14And please have some pity on me when you are back in his favor, and mention me to Pharaoh, and ask him to let me out of here. 15For I was kidnapped from my homeland among the Hebrews, and now this—here I am in jail when I did nothing to deserve it."

16When the chief baker saw that the first dream had such a good meaning, he told his dream to Joseph, too.

"In my dream," he said, "there were three baskets of pastries on my head. 17In the top basket were all kinds of bakery goods for Pharaoh, but the birds came and ate them."

18, 19"The three baskets mean three days," Joseph told him. "Three days from now Pharaoh will take off your head and impale your body on a pole, and the birds will come and pick off your flesh!"

20Pharaoh's birthday came three days later, and he held a party for all of his officials and household staff. He sent for his chief butler and chief baker, and they were brought to him from the prison. 21Then he restored the chief butler to his former position; 22but he sentenced the chief baker to be impaled, just as Joseph had predicted. 23Pharaoh's wine taster, however, promptly forgot all about Joseph, never giving him a thought.

PARALLELS BETWEEN JOSEPH AND JESUS
Genesis 37-50

Joseph	Parallels	Jesus
37:3	His father loved him dearly	Matthew 3:17
37:2	A shepherd of his father's sheep	John 10:11, 27–29
37:13, 14	Sent by father to brothers	Hebrews 2:11
37:4	Hated by brothers	John 7:4, 5
37:20	Others plotted to harm them	John 11:53
39:7	Tempted	Matthew 4:1
37:26	Taken to Egypt	Matthew 2:14, 15
37:23	Robes taken from them	John 19:23, 24
37:28	Sold for the price of a slave	Matthew 26:15
39:20	Bound in chains	Matthew 27:2
39:16–18	Falsely accused	Matthew 26:59, 60
40:2, 3	Placed with two other prisoners, one who was saved and the other lost	Luke 23:32
41:46	Both 30 years old at the beginning of public recognition	Luke 3:23
41:41	Exalted after suffering	Philippians 2:9–11
45:1–15	Forgave those who wronged them	Luke 23:34
45:7	Saved their nation	Matthew 1:21
50:20	What men did to hurt them God turned to good	1 Corinthians 2:7, 8

40:8 When the subject of dreams came up, Joseph focused everyone's attention on God. Rather than use the situation to make himself look good, he turned it into a powerful witness for God. One of the secrets of effective witnessing is to recognize opportunities to relate God to the other person's experience. When the opportunity comes, we must have the courage to speak, as Joseph did.

40:23 When Pharaoh's wine taster was freed from prison, he forgot about Joseph, even though he had Joseph to thank for his freedom. It was two full years before Joseph had another opportunity to be freed (41:1). Yet Joseph's faith was deep and he would be ready when the next chance occurred. When we feel passed by, overlooked, or forgotten, we shouldn't be surprised that people are often ungrateful. In situations like this, work at trusting God as Joseph did. More opportunities may be waiting.

4. Joseph is placed in charge of Egypt
Pharaoh's strange dream

41 One night two years later, Pharaoh dreamed that he was standing on the bank of the Nile River, ²when suddenly, seven sleek, fat cows came up out of the river and began grazing in the grass. ³Then seven other cows came up from the river, but they were very skinny and all their ribs stood out. They went over and stood beside the fat cows. ⁴Then the skinny cows ate the fat ones! At which point, Pharaoh woke up!

⁵Soon he fell asleep again and had a second dream. This time he saw seven heads of grain on one stalk, with every kernel well formed and plump. ⁶Then, suddenly, seven more heads appeared on the stalk, but these were shriveled and withered by the east wind. ⁷And these thin heads swallowed up the seven plump, well-formed heads! Then Pharaoh woke up again and realized it was all a dream. ⁸Next morning, as he thought about it, he became very concerned as to what the dreams might mean; he called for all the magicians and sages of Egypt and told them about it, but not one of them could suggest what his dreams meant. ⁹Then the king's wine taster spoke up. "Today I remember my sin!" he said. ¹⁰"Some time ago when you were angry with a couple of us and put me and the chief baker in jail in the castle of the captain of the guard, ¹¹the chief baker and I each had a dream one night. ¹²We told the dreams to a young Hebrew fellow there who was a slave of the captain of the guard, and he told us what our dreams meant. ¹³And everything happened just as he said: I was restored to my position of wine taster, and the chief baker was executed, and impaled on a pole."

¹⁴Pharaoh sent at once for Joseph. He was brought hastily from the dungeon, and after a quick shave and change of clothes, came in before Pharaoh.

¹⁵"I had a dream last night," Pharaoh told him, "and none of these men can tell me what it means. But I have heard that you can interpret dreams, and that is why I have called for you."

¹⁶"I can't do it by myself," Joseph replied, "but God will tell you what it means!"

¹⁷So Pharaoh told him the dream. "I was standing upon the bank of the Nile River," he said, ¹⁸"when suddenly, seven fat, healthy-looking cows came up out of the river and began grazing along the river bank. ¹⁹But then seven other cows came up from the river, very skinny and bony—in fact, I've never seen such poor-looking specimens in all the land of Egypt. ²⁰And these skinny cattle ate up the seven fat ones that had come out first, ²¹and afterwards they were still as skinny as before! Then I woke up.

²²"A little later I had another dream. This time there were seven heads of grain on one stalk, and all seven heads were plump and full. ²³Then, out of the same stalk, came seven withered, thin heads. ²⁴And the thin heads swallowed up the fat ones! I told all this to my magicians, but not one of them could tell me the meaning."

²⁵"Both dreams mean the same thing," Joseph told Pharaoh. "God was telling you what he is going to do here in the land of Egypt. ²⁶The seven fat cows (and also the seven fat, well-formed heads of grain) mean that there are seven years of prosperity ahead. ²⁷The seven skinny cows (and also the seven thin and withered heads of grain) indicate that there will be seven years of famine following the seven years of prosperity.

²⁸"So God has showed you what he is about to do: ²⁹The next seven years will be

41:2
Job 8:11
Isa 19:7

41:3
Gen 41:20,21

41:4
1 Kgs 3:15

41:6
Ezek 17:10
19:12

41:8
Ex 7:11
Dan 2:1-3; 4:5
Mt 2:1

41:9
Gen 40:14,23

41:10
Gen 40:2

41:11
Gen 40:5-8

41:12
Gen 40:12-19

41:13
Gen 40:22

41:14
Ex 10:16
Ps 105:16-22

41:15
Gen 41:8
Dan 2:25

41:16
Gen 40:8
Num 12:6
Dan 2:28-30
Acts 3:12

41:17
Gen 41:1-7,
26,27

41:18
Gen 41:28,32

41:26
Gen 40:12,18

41:27
Gen 41:30,54
2 Sam 24:13
2 Kgs 8:1

41:29
Gen 41:47

41:8 Magicians and sages were common in the palaces of ancient rulers. Their job description included studying sacred arts and sciences, reading the stars, interpreting dreams, predicting the future, and performing magic. These men had power (see Exodus 7:11, 12), but their power was satanic. They were unable to interpret Pharaoh's dream, but God had revealed it to Joseph in prison.

41:14 Our most important opportunities may come when we least expect them. Joseph was brought hastily from the dungeon and pushed before Pharaoh. Did he have time to prepare? Yes and no. He had no warning that he would be suddenly pulled from prison and questioned by the king. Yet Joseph was ready for almost anything because of his right relationship with God. It was not Joseph's knowledge of dreams that helped him interpret their meaning. It was his knowledge of God. Be ready for opportunities by getting to know more about God. Then you will be ready to take on almost anything that comes your way.

41:28–36 After interpreting Pharaoh's dream, Joseph gave the

41:30
Gen 47:13

41:32
Gen 37:9
Job 33:14
Isa 14:24; 46:10

41:33
Gen 41:39
Dan 4:27

41:34
Ex 18:19
Deut 1:13
2 Chron 34:12

41:36
Gen 47:13

a period of great prosperity throughout all the land of Egypt; 30but afterwards there will be seven years of famine so great that all the prosperity will be forgotten and wiped out; famine will consume the land. 31The famine will be so terrible that even the memory of the good years will be erased. 32The double dream gives double impact, showing that what I have told you is certainly going to happen, for God has decreed it, and it is going to happen soon. 33My suggestion is that you find the wisest man in Egypt and put him in charge of administering a nation-wide farm program. 34, 35Let Pharaoh divide Egypt into five administrative districts, and let the officials of these districts gather into the royal storehouses all the excess crops of the next seven years, 36so that there will be enough to eat when the seven years of famine come. Otherwise, disaster will surely strike."

Joseph becomes a ruler

41:37
Prov 25:11
Acts 7:10

41:38
Job 32:8
Dan 4:8,18
Dan 5:11,14

41:39
Gen 41:28,33

41:40
Gen 39:4,22
42:6; 45:8
Ps 105:21
Prov 22:29
Acts 7:10

41:41
Esth 10:3
Prov 17:2
Dan 6:3

41:42
Esth 3:10
Esth 6:8

41:44
Gen 45:8
Ps 105:21,22

41:45
Ezek 30:17

41:46
Gen 37:2; 50:22

41:47
Gen 26:12

41:48
Gen 47:21

41:49
Judg 6:5; 7:12
1 Sam 13:5

41:50
Gen 46:20

41:51
Gen 48:5
Deut 33:17
Prov 31:7

37Joseph's suggestions were well received by Pharaoh and his assistants. 38As they discussed who should be appointed for the job, Pharaoh said, "Who could do it better than Joseph? For he is a man who is obviously filled with the Spirit of God." 39Turning to Joseph, Pharaoh said to him, "Since God has revealed the meaning of the dreams to you, you are the wisest man in the country! 40I am hereby appointing you to be in charge of this entire project. What you say goes, throughout all the land of Egypt. I alone will outrank you."

41, 42Then Pharaoh placed his own signet ring on Joseph's finger as a token of his authority, and dressed him in beautiful clothing and placed the royal gold chain about his neck and declared, "See, I have placed you in charge of all the land of Egypt."

43Pharaoh also gave Joseph the chariot of his second-in-command, and wherever he went the shout arose, "Kneel down!" 44And Pharaoh declared to Joseph, "I, the king of Egypt, swear that you shall have complete charge over all the land of Egypt."

45Pharaoh gave him a name meaning "He has the god-like power of life and death!" And he gave him a wife, a girl named Asenath, daughter of Potiphera, priest of Heliopolis. So Joseph became famous throughout the land of Egypt. 46He was thirty years old as he entered the service of the king. Joseph went out from the presence of Pharaoh, and began traveling all across the land.

47And sure enough, for the next seven years there were bumper crops everywhere. 48During those years, Joseph requisitioned for the government a portion of all the crops grown throughout Egypt, storing them in nearby cities. 49After seven years of this, the granaries were full to overflowing, and there was so much that no one kept track of the amount.

50During this time before the arrival of the first of the famine years, two sons were born to Joseph by Asenath, the daughter of Potiphera, priest of the sun god Re of Heliopolis. 51Joseph named his oldest son Manasseh (meaning "Made to Forget"—what he meant was that God had made up to him for all the anguish of his youth, and for the loss of his father's home). 52The second boy was named Ephraim

41:34, 35 Let Pharaoh divide Egypt into five administrative districts, or, "Let Pharaoh appoint officials to collect a fifth of all the crops . . ."

---

king a survival plan for the next 14 years. The only way to prevent starvation was through careful planning; without a "famine plan" Egypt would have turned from might to ruin. Many find detailed planning boring or unnecessary. But believers must recognize that planning is a responsibility, not an option. Joseph was able to save a nation by translating God's plan for Egypt into practical actions (implementation). We must take time to translate God's plan for us into practical actions too.

41:38–40 Joseph rose quickly to the top, from prison walls to Pharaoh's palace. His training for this important position involved being a slave first and then a prisoner. In each situation he learned the importance of serving God and others. Whatever your situation, no matter how undesirable, consider it part of your training program for future service to God.

41:45 Pharaoh may have been trying to acculturate Joseph by giving him an Egyptian name and wife. He probably wanted to (1) play down the fact that Joseph was a nomadic shepherd, an occupation disliked by the Egyptians, (2) make Joseph's name easier for Egyptians to pronounce and remember, and (3) demonstrate how highly he was honored by giving him the daughter of a prominent Egyptian official.

41:46 Joseph was 30 years old when he became governor of Egypt. He was 17 when he was sold into slavery by his brothers. Therefore, he had spent 11 years as an Egyptian slave and two years in prison.

(meaning "Fruitful"—"For God has made me fruitful in this land of my slavery," he said). 53So at last the seven years of plenty came to an end. 54Then the seven years of famine began, just as Joseph had predicted. There were crop failures in all the surrounding countries too, but in Egypt there was plenty of grain in the storehouses. 55The people began to starve. They pleaded with Pharaoh for food, and he sent them to Joseph. "Do whatever he tells you to," he instructed them.

56, 57So now, with severe famine all over the world, Joseph opened up the storehouses and sold grain to the Egyptians and to those from other lands who came to Egypt to buy grain from Joseph.

41:54
Gen 41:27
45:11
Acts 7:11

41:55
Gen 41:40,41,
49
Jer 14:1

41:57
Gen 42:5; 50:20
Ps 105:16

5. Joseph and his brothers meet in Egypt

42 When Jacob heard that there was grain available in Egypt he said to his sons, "Why are you standing around looking at one another? 2I have heard that there is grain available in Egypt. Go down and buy some for us before we all starve to death."

3So Joseph's ten older brothers went down to Egypt to buy grain. 4However, Jacob wouldn't let Joseph's younger brother Benjamin go with them, for fear some harm might happen to him [as it had to his brother Joseph]. 5So it was that Israel's sons arrived in Egypt along with many others from many lands to buy food, for the famine was as severe in Canaan as it was everywhere else.

6Since Joseph was governor of all Egypt, and in charge of the sale of the grain, it was to him that his brothers came, and bowed low before him, with their faces to the earth. 7Joseph recognized them instantly, but pretended he didn't.

"Where are you from?" he demanded roughly.

"From the land of Canaan," they replied. "We have come to buy grain."

8, 9Then Joseph remembered the dreams of long ago! But he said to them, "You are spies. You have come to see how destitute the famine has made our land."

10"No, no," they exclaimed. "We have come to buy food. 11We are all brothers and honest men, sir! We are not spies!"

12"Yes, you are," he insisted. "You have come to see how weak we are."

13"Sir," they said, "there are twelve of us brothers, and our father is in the land of Canaan. Our youngest brother is there with our father, and one of our brothers is dead."

14"So?" Joseph asked. "What does that prove? You are spies. 15This is the way I will test your story: I swear by the life of Pharaoh that you are not going to leave Egypt until this youngest brother comes here. 16One of you go and get your brother! I'll keep the rest of you here, bound in prison. Then we'll find out whether your story is true or not. If it turns out that you don't have a younger brother, then I'll know you are spies."

17So he threw them all into jail for three days.

42:1
Acts 7:12

42:2
Gen 43:2; 45:9

42:3
Gen 42:13

42:4
Gen 43:8

42:5
Gen 41:57
Acts 7:11

42:6
Ps 105:16-21

42:7
Gen 42:14-17

42:8
Gen 37:2,6-9

42:9
Gen 42:16,
30-34

42:10
Gen 27:29
37:8; 42:2

42:11
Gen 42:19,
31-34

42:13
Gen 37:30
42:4; 43:7
44:20; 46:8-26

42:14
Gen 42:9

42:15
Gen 42:34

42:17
Gen 40:4

42:3 *ten older,* implied.   **42:4** *[as it had to his brother Joseph],* implied.   **42:14** *What does that prove?* Literally, "It is as I said: you are spies."

41:54 Famine was a catastrophe in ancient times. Almost perfect conditions were needed to produce good crops, because there were no chemical fertilizers or pesticides. Any variances in the delicate balance of rain or insects could cause crop failure and great hunger, for the people relied almost exclusively on their own crops for food. Lack of storage, refrigeration, or transportation turned an average famine into a desperate situation. The famine Joseph prepared for was described as "terrible." Without God's intervention, the Egyptian nation would have crumbled.

42:1 Why was grain so valuable in those days? As a food source it was universal and used in nearly everything eaten. It could be dried and stored much longer than any vegetables, milk products, or meat. It was so important that it was even used as money.

42:4 Jacob was especially fond of Benjamin because (1) he was the only true brother of Joseph, and (2) he was the only other son of his beloved wife, Rachel. Benjamin was Jacob's youngest son and a child of his old age.

42:7 Joseph could have revealed his identity to his brothers at once. But Joseph's last memory of them was of staring in horror at their faces as Ishmaelite slave traders carried him away. Were his brothers still evil and treacherous, or had they changed over the years? Joseph decided to put them through a few tests to find out.

42:8, 9 Joseph remembered the dreams he had had as a boy about his brothers bowing down to him (37: 9). Those dreams were coming true! As a young boy, Joseph was boastful about his dreams. As a man, he no longer flaunted his superior status. He did not feel the need to say "I told you so." It was not yet time to reveal his identity, so he kept quiet. Sometimes it is best for us to remain quiet, even when we would like to have the last word.

42:15 Joseph was testing his brothers to make sure they had not been as cruel to Benjamin as they had been to him. Benjamin was his only full brother and he wanted to see him face to face.

42:18
Gen 20:11
Lev 25:43

42:20
Gen 42:34
43:15

42:21
Gen 37:23-28
41:9
Num 32:23

42:22
Gen 9:6
37:21,22
Lk 23:41

42:24
Gen 43:14,23,
30; 45:14

42:25
Gen 44:1

42:27
Gen 43:21
Ex 4:24

42:28
Gen 27:33
Isa 45:7
Lam 3:37

42:30
Gen 42:7

42:31
Gen 42:11

42:32
Gen 42:13

42:33
Gen 42:19

42:34
Gen 42:20

42:35
Gen 42:27
43:12,21

42:36
Gen 43:14
44:20-22

42:37
Gen 43:9; 44:32

42:38
Gen 37:35
44:20-22,29
1 Kgs 2:6

43:1
Gen 41:5,6,7
42:5

43:2
Gen 43:15

43:3
Gen 42:15
44:23

18The third day Joseph said to them, "I am a God-fearing man and I'm going to give you an opportunity to prove yourselves. 19I'm going to take a chance that you are honorable; only one of you shall remain in chains in jail, and the rest of you may go on home with grain for your families; 20but bring your youngest brother back to me. In this way I will know whether you are telling me the truth; and if you are, I will spare you." To this they agreed.

21Speaking among themselves, they said, "This has all happened because of what we did to Joseph long ago. We saw his terror and anguish and heard his pleadings, but we wouldn't listen."

22"Didn't I tell you not to do it?" Reuben asked. "But you wouldn't listen. And now we are going to die because we murdered him."

23Of course they didn't know that Joseph understood them as he was standing there, for he had been speaking to them through an interpreter. 24Now he left the room and found a place where he could weep. Returning, he selected Simeon from among them and had him bound before their eyes. 25Joseph then ordered his servants to fill the men's sacks with grain, but also gave secret instructions to put each brother's payment at the top of his sack! He also gave them provisions for their journey. 26So they loaded up their donkeys with the grain and started for home. 27But when they stopped for the night and one of them opened his sack to get some grain to feed the donkeys, there was his money in the mouth of the sack!

28"Look," he exclaimed to his brothers, "my money is here in my sack." They were filled with terror. Trembling, they exclaimed to each other. "What is this that God has done to us?" 29So they came to their father Jacob in the land of Canaan and told him all that had happened.

30"The king's chief assistant spoke very roughly to us," they told him, "and took us for spies. 31'No, no,' we said, 'we are honest men, not spies. 32We are twelve brothers, sons of one father; one is dead, and the youngest is with our father in the land of Canaan.' 33Then the man told us, 'This is the way I will find out if you are what you claim to be. Leave one of your brothers here with me and take grain for your families and go on home, 34but bring your youngest brother back to me. Then I shall know whether you are spies or honest men; if you prove to be what you say, then I will give you back your brother and you can come as often as you like to purchase grain.'"

35As they emptied out the sacks, there at the top of each was the money paid for the grain! Terror gripped them, as it did their father.

36Then Jacob exclaimed, "You have bereaved me of my children—Joseph didn't come back, Simeon is gone, and now you want to take Benjamin too! Everything has been against me."

37Then Reuben said to his father, "Kill my two sons if I don't bring Benjamin back to you. I'll be responsible for him."

38But Jacob replied, "My son shall not go down with you, for his brother Joseph is dead and he alone is left of his mother's children. If anything should happen to him, I would die."

Jacob lets Benjamin go

43 But there was no relief from the terrible famine throughout the land. 2When the grain they had brought from Egypt was almost gone, their father said to them, "Go again and buy us a little food."

3, 4, 5But Judah told him, "The man wasn't fooling one bit when he said, 'Don't ever come back again unless your brother is with you.' We cannot go unless you let Benjamin go with us."

42:19 *I'm going to take a chance that you are honorable*, literally, "If you are forthright men."

43:1 Jacob and his sons had no relief from the famine. They could not see God's overall plan of sending them to Egypt to be reunited with Joseph and fed from Egypt's storehouses. If you are praying for relief from suffering or pressure and God is not bringing it as quickly as you would like, remember that God may be leading you to special treasures.

6"Why did you ever tell him you had another brother?" Israel moaned. "Why did you have to treat me like that?"

7"But the man specifically asked us about our family," they told him. "He wanted to know whether our father was still living and he asked us if we had another brother, so we told him. How could we know that he was going to say, 'Bring me your brother'?"

43:7
Gen 42:13
43:27

8Judah said to his father, "Send the lad with me and we will be on our way; otherwise we will all die of starvation—and not only we, but you and all our little ones. 9I guarantee his safety. If I don't bring him back to you, then let me bear the blame forever. 10For we could have gone and returned by this time if you had let him come."

43:8
Gen 42:2
44:26; 45:18,19

43:9
Gen 42:37
44:32
Heb 7:22

11So their father Israel finally said to them, "If it can't be avoided, then at least do this. Load your donkeys with the best products of the land. Take them to the man as gifts—balm, honey, spices, myrrh, pistachio nuts, and almonds. 12Take double money so that you can pay back what was in the mouths of your sacks, as it was probably someone's mistake, 13and take your brother and go. 14May God Almighty give you mercy before the man, so that he will release Simeon and return Benjamin. And if I must bear the anguish of their deaths, then so be it."

43:11
Gen 32:13
37:25; 43:25

43:12
Gen 42:35

43:13
Gen 42:38; 43:4

43:14
Gen 39:21
42:36
Ps 106:46

15So they took the gifts and double money and went to Egypt, and stood before Joseph. 16When Joseph saw that Benjamin was with them he said to the manager of his household, "These men will eat with me this noon. Take them home and prepare a big feast." 17So the man did as he was told and took them to Joseph's palace. 18They were badly frightened when they saw where they were being taken.

43:16
Gen 31:54; 44:1

43:18
Gen 42:28,35

"It's because of the money returned to us in our sacks," they said. "He wants to pretend we stole it and seize us as slaves, with our donkeys."

19As they arrived at the entrance to the palace, they went over to Joseph's household manager, 20and said to him, "O sir, after our first trip to Egypt to buy food, 21as we were returning home, we stopped for the night and opened our sacks, and the money was there that we had paid for the grain. Here it is; we have brought it back again, 22along with additional money to buy more grain. We have no idea how the money got into our sacks."

43:21
Gen 42:27,35
43:12

43:22
Gen 42:25

23"Don't worry about it," the household manager told them; "your God, even the God of your fathers, must have put it there, for we collected your money all right."

43:23
Gen 42:24

Then he released Simeon and brought him out to them. 24They were then conducted into the palace and given water to refresh their feet; and their donkeys were fed. 25Then they got their presents ready for Joseph's arrival at noon, for they were told that they would be eating there. 26When Joseph came home they gave him their presents, bowing low before him.

43:24
Gen 18:4; 24:32
Lk 7:44

43:26
Gen 42:6

43:27
Gen 43:7; 45:3
Ex 18:7

27He asked how they had been getting along. "And how is your father—the old man you spoke about? Is he still alive?"

28"Yes," they replied. "He is alive and well." Then again they bowed before him.

43:28
Ex 18:7

29Looking at his brother Benjamin, he asked, "Is this your youngest brother, the one you told me about? How are you, my son? God be gracious to you." 30Then Joseph made a hasty exit, for he was overcome with love for his brother and had to

43:29
Num 6:25
Ps 67:1

43:30
Gen 42:24
45:2,14,15
46:29

43:29 Looking at his brother Benjamin, literally, "his brother Benjamin, his mother's son."

43:9 Judah accepted full responsibility for Benjamin's safety. He did not know what that might mean for him, but he was determined to carry it out. In the end it was Judah's stirring words that caused Joseph to break down and reveal himself to his brothers (44:18–34). Accepting and fulfilling responsibilities is difficult, but it builds character and confidence, earns others' respect, and motivates us to complete our work. When you have been given an assignment to complete or a responsibility to fulfill, commmit yourself to seeing it through.

43:11 These gifts of balm, honey, spices, myrrh, pistachio nuts,

and almonds were highly valuable. They were specialty items not common in Egypt. Because of the famine, they were even more rare.

43:12 Joseph's brothers arrived home from Egypt only to find in their grain sacks the money they had used to pay for the grain. Some months later, when it was time to return to Egypt for more food, Jacob paid back double the cost of the grain to maintain his integrity. We should follow Jacob's example and guard our integrity. A reputation for honesty and integrity is worth far more than whatever we may spend earning and keeping it.

43:31
Gen 43:25; 45:1
Isa 42:14
43:32
Gen 46:34
Ex 8:26
43:33
Gen 44:12

go out and cry. Going into his bedroom, he wept there. 31Then he washed his face and came out, keeping himself under control. "Let's eat," he said.

32Joseph ate by himself, his brothers were served at a separate table, and the Egyptians at still another; for Egyptians despise Hebrews and never eat with them. 33He told each of them where to sit, and seated them in the order of their ages, from the oldest to the youngest, much to their amazement! 34Their food was served to them from his own table. He gave the largest serving to Benjamin—five times as much as to any of the others! They had a wonderful time bantering back and forth, and the wine flowed freely!

44:1
Gen 42:25
43:16

44 When his brothers were ready to leave, Joseph ordered his household manager to fill each of their sacks with as much grain as they could carry—and to put into the mouth of each man's sack the money he had paid! 2He was also told to put Joseph's own silver cup at the top of Benjamin's sack, along with the grain money. So the household manager did as he was told. 3The brothers were up at dawn and on their way with their loaded donkeys.

44:4
Prov 17:13

4But when they were barely out of the city, Joseph said to his household manager, "Chase after them and stop them and ask them why they are acting like this when their benefactor has been so kind to them? 5Ask them, 'What do you

44:5
Gen 30:27
Lev 19:26
Deut. 18:10-14

mean by stealing my lord's personal silver drinking cup, which he uses for fortune telling? What a wicked thing you have done!' " 6So he caught up with them and spoke to them along the lines he had been instructed.

7"What in the world are you talking about?" they demanded. "What kind of people do you think we are, that you accuse us of such a terrible thing as that?

44:8
Gen 43:21
Ex 20:15
44:9
Gen 31:32
44:16
Ps 7:3-5

8Didn't we bring back the money we found in the mouth of our sacks? Why would we steal silver or gold from your master's house? 9If you find his cup with any one of us, let that one die. And all the rest of us will be slaves forever to your master."

10"Fair enough," the man replied, "except that only the one who stole it will be a slave, and the rest of you can go free."

44:12
Gen 44:2
44:13
Gen 37:29,34
Num 14:6
44:14
Gen 43:26
44:15
Gen 41:38; 44:5

11They quickly took down their sacks from the backs of their donkeys and opened them. 12He began searching the oldest brother's sack, going on down the line to the youngest. And the cup was found in Benjamin's! 13They ripped their clothing in despair, loaded the donkeys again, and returned to the city. 14Joseph was still home when Judah and his brothers arrived, and they fell to the ground before him.

15"What were you trying to do?" Joseph demanded. "Didn't you know such a man as I would know who stole it?"

44:16
Gen 42:21
43:8,9
Num 32:23
Ezra 9:10

16And Judah said, "Oh, what shall we say to my lord? How can we plead? How can we prove our innocence? God is punishing us for our sins. Sir, we have all returned to be your slaves, both we and he in whose sack the cup was found."

17"No," Joseph said. "Only the man who stole the cup, he shall be my slave. The rest of you can go on home to your father."

44:18
Gen 37:7,8
41:40

18Then Judah stepped forward and said, "O sir, let me say just this one word to you. Be patient with me for a moment, for I know you can doom me in an instant, as though you were Pharaoh himself.

44:1 *When his brothers were ready to leave,* implied.

43:32 Why did Joseph eat by himself? Eating alone followed the law of the ancient caste system. Egyptians considered themselves highly intelligent and sophisticated. They looked upon shepherds and nomads as uncultured and even vulgar. As foreigners and shepherds, Joseph's brothers were lower in rank than any Egyptian citizens. And Joseph could not even eat with fellow Egyptians who were lower than he in rank.

44:2 Joseph's silver cup was a symbol of his authority. It was thought to have supernatural powers, and to steal it was a serious crime. Such goblets were used for predicting the future. A person poured water into the cup and interpreted the reflections, ripples, and bubbles. Joseph wouldn't have needed his cup—God told

him everything he needed to know about the future.

44:13 The ripping of clothing was an expression of deep sorrow and a customary manner of showing grief. The brothers were deeply upset that Benjamin might be harmed.

44:16-34 When Judah was younger, he showed no regard for his brother Joseph or his father, Jacob. First he convinced his brothers to sell Joseph as a slave (37:26); then he lied to his father about Joseph's fate (37:32). But what a change took place in Judah! Now the man was so concerned for his father and younger brother, Benjamin, that he was willing to die for them. When you are ready to give up hope on yourself or others, remember that God can work a complete change in even the most selfish personality.

19"Sir, you asked us if we had a father or a brother, 20and we said, 'Yes, we have a father, an old man, and a child of his old age, a little one. And his brother is dead, and he alone is left of his mother's children, and his father loves him very much.' 21And you said to us, 'Bring him here so that I can see him.' 22But we said to you, 'Sir, the lad cannot leave his father, for his father would die.' 23But you told us, 'Don't come back here unless your youngest brother is with you.' 24So we returned to our father and told him what you had said. 25And when he said, 'Go back again and buy us a little food,' 26we replied, 'We can't, unless you let our youngest brother go with us. Only then may we come.' 27"Then my father said to us, 'You know that my wife had two sons, 28and that one of them went away and never returned—doubtless torn to pieces by some wild animal; I have never seen him since. 29And if you take away his brother from me also, and any harm befalls him, I shall die with sorrow.' 30And now, sir, if I go back to my father and the lad is not with us—seeing that our father's life is bound up in the lad's life— 31when he sees that the boy is not with us, our father will die; and we will be responsible for bringing down his gray hairs with sorrow to the grave. 32Sir, I pledged my father that I would take care of the lad. I told him, 'If I don't bring him back to you, I shall bear the blame forever.' 33Please sir, let me stay here as a slave instead of the lad, and let the lad return with his brothers. 34For how shall I return to my father if the lad is not with me? I cannot bear to see what this would do to him."

44:19
Gen 42:13-16
43:7

44:21
Gen 42:20,34
43:7

44:22
Gen 42:38

44:23
Gen 42:20

44:24
Gen 42:29-34

44:25
Gen 43:2

44:26
Gen 43:4,5

44:27
Gen 46:19

44:28
Gen 37:33

44:29
Gen 42:38

44:30
1 Sam 18:1

44:32
Gen 43:9

Joseph sends for Jacob

45 Joseph could stand it no longer. "Out, all of you," he cried out to his attendants, and he was left alone with his brothers. 2Then he wept aloud. His sobs could be heard throughout the palace, and the news was quickly carried to Pharaoh's palace.

45:1
Gen 42:24
43:30

3"I am Joseph!" he said to his brothers. "Is my father still alive?" But his brothers couldn't say a word, they were so stunned with surprise.

45:3
Gen 50:17-19
Mt 14:27
Acts 7:13

4"Come over here," he said. So they came closer. And he said again, "I am Joseph, your brother whom you sold into Egypt! 5But don't be angry with yourselves that you did this to me, for God did it! He sent me here ahead of you to preserve your lives. 6These two years of famine will grow to seven, during which there will be neither plowing nor harvest. 7God has sent me here to keep you and your families alive, so that you will become a great nation. 8Yes, it was God who sent me here, not you! And he has made me a counselor to Pharaoh, and manager of this entire nation, ruler of all the land of Egypt.

45:4
Gen 37:28

45:5
Gen 50:20

45:6
Gen 41:29,30
47:18,23

45:8
Gen 41:39
Judg 17:10
Ps 105:21
Jn 15:16; 19:11

9"Hurry, return to my father and tell him, 'Your son Joseph says, "God has made me chief of all the land of Egypt. Come down to me right away! 10You shall live in the land of Goshen so that you can be near me with all your children, your grandchildren, your flocks and herds, and all that you have. 11, 12I will take care of you there" ' (you men are witnesses of my promise, and my brother Benjamin has heard me say it) ' "for there are still five years of famine ahead of us. Otherwise you will come to utter poverty along with all your household." ' 13Tell our father about all my power here in Egypt, and how everyone obeys me. And bring him to me quickly."

45:9
Acts 7:14

45:10
Gen 46:28,34
47:6
Ex 8:22

45:11
Gen 45:8; 47:12

45:13
Acts 7:14

14Then, weeping with joy, he embraced Benjamin and Benjamin began weeping

45:14
Gen 43:30
46:29

44:32 In Genesis 43:9, Judah promised Jacob that he would guarantee the safety of young Benjamin. Now Judah had a chance to keep that promise. Though becoming a slave was a terrible fate, Judah was determined to keep his word to his father. He showed great courage in carrying out his promise. Accepting a responsibility means carrying it out with determination and courage, regardless of the personal sacrifice.

44:33 Joseph wanted to see if his brothers' attitudes had changed for the better, so he tested the way they treated each other. Judah had stepped forward with the plan to sell Joseph (37:26). In this situation, Judah stepped forward to take Benjamin's

punishment so Benjamin could return to their father. This courageous act convinced Joseph that his brothers had changed for the better—in a dramatic way.

45:4-8 Although Joseph's brothers had wanted to get rid of him (Genesis 37:26-36), God's ultimate plan was being fulfilled through their evil actions. He sent Joseph ahead to preserve their lives, save Egypt, and prepare the way for the beginning of the nation of Israel. God is sovereign. His plans are not dictated by human actions. When others intend evil for your life, remember that they are only God's tools. In Genesis 50:20 Joseph said, "As far as I am concerned, God turned into good what you meant for evil."

45:16
Acts 7:13

45:17
Gen 42:25; 44:1

45:18
Gen 27:28; 47:6

45:19
Gen 45:27; 46:5

45:20
Gen 20:15

45:22
Gen 43:34
Judg 14:12
2 Kgs 5:5

45:23
Gen 43:11

45:24
Gen 37:22
42:21
Ps 133:1-3

too. 15And he did the same with each of his brothers, who finally found their tongues! 16The news soon reached Pharaoh—"Joseph's brothers have come"; and Pharaoh was very happy to hear it, as were his officials.

17Then Pharaoh said to Joseph, "Tell your brothers to load their pack animals and return quickly to their homes in Canaan, 18and to bring your father and all of your families and come here to Egypt to live. Tell them, 'Pharaoh will assign to you the very best territory in the land of Egypt. You shall live off the fat of the land!' 19And tell your brothers to take wagons from Egypt to carry their wives and little ones, and to bring your father here. 20Don't worry about your property, for the best of all the land of Egypt is yours."

21So Joseph gave them wagons, as Pharaoh had commanded, and provisions for the journey, 22and he gave each of them new clothes—but to Benjamin he gave five changes of clothes and three hundred pieces of silver! 23He sent his father ten donkey-loads of the good things of Egypt, and ten donkeys loaded with grain and all kinds of other food, to eat on his journey. 24So he sent his brothers off.

"Don't quarrel along the way!" was his parting shot! 25And leaving, they returned to the land of Canaan, to Jacob their father.

JUDAH

People who are leaders stand out. They don't necessarily act or look a certain way until the need for their action is apparent. Among their skills are outspokenness, decisiveness, action, and control. These skills can be used for great good or great evil. Jacob's fourth son, Judah, was a natural leader. The events of his life provided many opportunities to exercise those skills. Unfortunately Judah's decisions were often shaped more by the pressures of the moment than by a conscious desire to cooperate with God's plan. But when he did recognize his mistakes, he was willing to admit them. His experience with Tamar and the final confrontation with Joseph are both examples of Judah's willingness to bear the blame when confronted. It was one of the qualities he passed on to his descendant David.

Whether or not we have Judah's natural leadership qualities, we do share with him a tendency to be blind toward our own sin. But too often we don't share his willingness to admit our mistakes. From Judah we can learn that it is not wise to wait until our errors force us to admit to wrongdoing. It is far better to openly admit our mistakes, shoulder the blame, and seek forgiveness.

Strengths and accomplishments:
- Was a natural leader—outspoken and decisive
- Thought clearly and took action in pressure situations
- Was willing to stand by his word and put himself on the line when necessary
- Was the fourth son of 12, through whom God would eventually bring King David and Jesus, the Messiah

Weaknesses and mistakes:
- Suggested to his brothers they sell Joseph into slavery
- Failed to keep his promise to his daughter-in-law, Tamar

Lessons from his life:
- God is in control far beyond the immediate situation
- Procrastination often brings about a worse result
- Judah's offer to substitute his life for Benjamin's is a picture of what his descendant Jesus would do for all men

Vital statistics:
- Where: Canaan and Egypt
- Occupation: Shepherd
- Relatives: Parents: Jacob and Leah. Wife: Bathshua. Daughter-in-law: Tamar. Eleven brothers and at least five sons (Genesis 29:31—30:24).

Key verses:
"Judah, your brothers shall praise you. You shall destroy your enemies. Your father's sons shall bow before you. Judah is a young lion that has finished eating its prey. He has settled down as a lion—who will dare to rouse him?" (Genesis 49:8, 9).

Judah's story is told in Genesis 29:35—50:26. He is also mentioned in 1 Chronicles 2—4.

45:17-20 Joseph was rejected, kidnaped, enslaved, and imprisoned. Although his brothers had been unfaithful to him, he graciously forgave them and shared his prosperity. Joseph demonstrated how God forgives us and showers us with goodness even though we have sinned against him. This same forgiveness and blessing are ours if only we ask for them.

26"Joseph is alive," they shouted to him. "And he is ruler over all the land of Egypt!" But Jacob's heart was like a stone; he couldn't take it in. 27But when they had given him Joseph's messages, and when he saw the wagons filled with food that Joseph had sent him, his spirit revived.

28And he said, "It must be true! Joseph my son is alive! I will go and see him before I die."

6. Jacob's family moves to Egypt

46 So Israel set out with all his possessions, and came to Beer-Sheba, and offered sacrifices there to the God of his father Isaac. 2During the night God spoke to him in a vision.

"Jacob! Jacob!" he called.

"Yes?" Jacob answered.

3, 4"I am God," the voice replied, "the God of your father. Don't be afraid to go down to Egypt, for I will see to it that you become a great nation there. And I will go down with you into Egypt and I will bring your descendants back again; but you shall die in Egypt with Joseph at your side."

5So Jacob left Beer-sheba, and his sons brought him to Egypt, along with their little ones and their wives, in the wagons Pharaoh had provided for them. 6They brought their livestock too, and all their belongings accumulated in the land of Canaan, and came to Egypt—Jacob and all his children, 7sons and daughters, grandsons and granddaughters—all his loved ones.

8-14Here are the names of his sons and grandchildren who went with him into Egypt:

Reuben, his oldest son;

Reuben's sons: Hanoch, Pallu, Hezron, and Carmi.

Simeon and his sons: Jemuel, Jamin, Ohad, Jachin, Zohar, and Shaul (Shaul's mother was a girl from Canaan).

Levi and his sons: Gershon, Kohath, Merari.

Judah and his sons: Er, Onan, Shelah, Perez, Zerah (however, Er and Onan died while still in Canaan, before Israel went to Egypt).

The sons of Perez were Hezron and Hamul.

Issachar and his sons: Tola, Puvah, Iob, Shimron.

Zebulun and his sons: Sered, Elon, Jahleel.

15So these descendants of Jacob and Leah, not including their daughter Dinah, born to Jacob in Paddan-aram, were thirty-three in all.

45:26
Gen 37:31-35
45:27
Gen 45:19,21
Judg 15:19
1 Sam 30:12
45:28
Gen 46:30
Lk 2:28-30
46:1
Gen 21:14
26:22
28:10,13
31:42; 33:20
35:7
46:2
Gen 22:11
31:11
Num 12:6
46:3
Gen 15:1; 17:1
26:2
Isa 41:10
46:4
Gen 28:15
48:21; 50:5
Ex 3:8
46:5
Gen 45:19
46:6
Num 20:15
Deut 10:22; 26:5
Acts 7:14,15
46:8
Gen 29:32
35:23; 49:3
46:9
1 Chron 5:3
46:10
1 Chron 4:24
46:11
1 Chron 6:1
46:12
1 Chron 2:3
46:13
1 Chron 7:1
46:14
Gen 30:20
49:13
46:15
Gen 30:21

45:26, 27 Jacob needed some evidence before he could believe the incredible news that Joseph was alive. Similarly, Thomas refused to believe that Jesus had risen from the dead until he could see and touch him (John 20:25). It is hard to change what you believe without all the facts—or sometimes even with the facts. Good news can be hard to believe. Don't ever give up hope that God has wonderful news in store for you.

46:3, 4 God told Jacob to leave his home and travel to a strange and faraway land. But God reassured him by promising to go with him and take care of him. When new situations or surroundings frighten or worry you, recognize that experiencing fear is normal. To be paralyzed by fear, however, is an indication that you question God's ability to take care of you.

46:32-34 Jacob moved his whole family to Egypt, but they wanted to live apart from the Egyptians. To ensure this, Joseph told them to let Pharaoh know they were shepherds. Although Pharaoh may have been sympathetic to shepherds (for he was probably a nomadic king from the Hyksos line), the Egyptian culture looked down on shepherds and was not yet ready to accept them. The strategy worked and Jacob's family was able to benefit from Pharaoh's generosity and from the prejudice of the Egyptians.

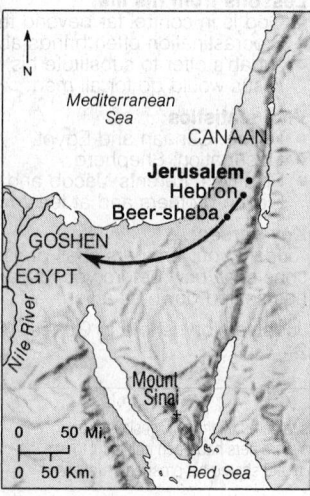

JACOB MOVES TO EGYPT
After hearing the joyful news that Joseph was alive, Jacob packed up and moved his family to Egypt. Stopping first in Beer-sheba, Jacob offered sacrifices and received assurance from God that Egypt was where he should go. Jacob and his family settled in the land of Goshen, in the northeastern part of Egypt.

46:16
Gen 30:11
35:26; 49:19
Num 26:15
1 Chron 5:11

16, 17Also accompanying him were:

Gad and his sons: Ziphion, Haggi, Shuni,
Ezbon, Eri, Arodi, and Areli.

46:17
Gen 30:13
49:20
Num 26:44
1 Chron 7:30

Asher and his sons: Imnah, Ishvah, Ishvi,
Beriah, and a sister, Serah.
Beriah's sons were Heber and Malchiel.

18These sixteen persons were the sons of Jacob and Zilpah, the slave-girl given to
Leah by her father, Laban.

46:19
Gen 30:24
35:18

19-22Also in the total of Jacob's household were these fourteen sons and descendants of Jacob and Rachel:

46:20
Gen 41:45,
50-52

Joseph and Benjamin;

46:21
Num 26:38
1 Chron 7:6

Joseph's sons, born in the land of Egypt, were Manasseh and Ephraim (their
mother was Asenath, the daughter of Potiphera, priest of Heliopolis);

46:22
Gen 35:24

Benjamin's sons: Bela, Becher, Ashbel, Gera, Naaman, Ehi, Rosh, Muppim,
Huppim, and Ard.

46:23
Gen 30:6
35:25; 49:16
Num 26:42

23, 24, 25Also in the group were these seven sons and descendants of Jacob and
Bilhah, the slave-girl given to Rachel by her father, Laban:

46:24
Gen 30:8; 49:21
Num 26:48
1 Chron 7:13

Dan and his son: Hushim.
Naphtali and his sons: Jahzeel, Guni, Jezer, and Shillem.

46:25
Gen 35:25

46:27
Ex 1:5; 24:1
Deut 10:22
Acts 7:14

26So the total number of those going to Egypt, of his own descendants, not
counting the wives of Jacob's sons, was sixty-six. 27With Joseph and his two sons
included, this total of Jacob's household there in Egypt totaled seventy.

46:28
Gen 43:8
45:10; 47:1

28Jacob sent Judah on ahead to tell Joseph that they were on the way, and would
soon arrive in Goshen—which they did. 29Joseph jumped into his chariot and

46:29
Gen 33:4
45:10,14
Lk 15:20

journeyed to Goshen to meet his father and they fell into each other's arms and wept
a long while.

46:30
Gen 45:28
Lk 2:29

30Then Israel said to Joseph, "Now let me die, for I have seen you again and
know you are alive."

46:31
Gen 45:16; 47:1

31And Joseph said to his brothers and to all their households, "I'll go and tell
Pharaoh that you are here, and that you have come from the land of Canaan to join

46:32
Gen 37:2,14
47:3

me. 32And I will tell him, 'These men are shepherds. They have brought with them
their flocks and herds and everything they own.' 33So when Pharaoh calls for you

46:33
Gen 47:2

and asks you about your occupation, 34tell him, 'We have been shepherds from our
youth, as our fathers have been for many generations.' When you tell him this, he

46:34
Gen 13:7
43:32; 47:4

will let you live here in the land of Goshen." For shepherds were despised and hated
in other parts of Egypt.

47:1
Gen 46:31

47 Upon their arrival, Joseph went in to see Pharaoh.
"My father and my brothers are here from Canaan," he reported, "with all

47:2
Acts 7:13

their flocks and herds and possessions. They wish to settle in the land of Goshen."
2He took five of his brothers with him, and presented them to Pharaoh.

47:3
Gen 46:33
Amos 7:14

3Pharaoh asked them, "What is your occupation?"
And they replied, "We are shepherds like our ancestors. 4We have come to live

47:4
Gen 15:13
43:1; 46:34
Deut 26:5

here in Egypt, for there is no pasture for our flocks in Canaan—the famine is very
bitter there. We request permission to live in the land of Goshen."
5, 6And Pharaoh said to Joseph, "Choose anywhere you like for them to live.

46:34 The Israelites did become a great nation, and Jacob's
descendants did eventually return to Canaan. The book of Exodus
recounts the story of Israel's slavery in Egypt for 400 years
(fulfilling God's words to Abram in 15:13-16), and the book of
Joshua tells the exciting account of the Israelites entering and
conquering Canaan, the "Promised Land."

Give them the best land of Egypt. The land of Goshen will be fine. And if any of
them are capable, put them in charge of my flocks, too."

7Then Joseph brought his father Jacob to Pharaoh. And Jacob blessed Pharaoh.
8"How old are you?" Pharaoh asked him.

9Jacob replied, "I have lived 130 long, hard years, and I am not nearly as old as
many of my ancestors." 10Then Jacob blessed Pharaoh again before he left.

11So Joseph assigned the best land of Egypt—the land of Rameses—to his father
and brothers, just as Pharaoh had commanded. 12And Joseph furnished food to
them in accordance with the number of their dependents.

13The famine became worse and worse, so that all the land of Egypt and Canaan
were starving. 14Joseph collected all the money in Egypt and Canaan in exchange
for grain, and he brought the money to Pharaoh's treasure-houses. 15When the
people were out of money, they came to Joseph crying again for food.

"Our money is gone," they said, "but give us bread; for why should we die?"
16"Well then," Joseph replied, "give me your livestock. I will trade you food in
exchange."

17So they brought their cattle to Joseph in exchange for food. Soon all the horses,
flocks, herds, and donkeys of Egypt were in Pharaoh's possession.

18The next year they came again and said, "Our money is gone, and our cattle are
yours, and there is nothing left but our bodies and land. 19Why should we die? Buy
us and our land and we will be serfs to Pharaoh. We will trade ourselves for food,
then we will live, and the land won't be abandoned."

20So Joseph bought all the land of Egypt for Pharaoh; all the Egyptians sold him
their fields because the famine was so severe. And the land became Pharaoh's.
21Thus all the people of Egypt became Pharaoh's serfs. 22The only land he didn't
buy was that belonging to the priests, for they were assigned food from Pharaoh
and didn't need to sell.

23Then Joseph said to the people, "See, I have bought you and your land for
Pharaoh. Here is grain. Go and sow the land. 24And when you harvest it, a fifth of
everything you get belongs to Pharaoh. Keep four parts for yourselves to be used
for next year's seed, and as food for yourselves and for your households and little
ones."

25"You have saved our lives," they said. "We will gladly be the serfs of
Pharaoh."

26So Joseph made it a law throughout the land of Egypt—and it is still the
law—that Pharaoh should have as his tax twenty percent of all the crops except
those produced on the land owned by the temples.

7. Jacob and Joseph die in Egypt
Jacob blesses Joseph

27So Israel lived in the land of Goshen in Egypt, and soon the people of Israel
began to prosper, and there was a veritable population explosion among them.
28Jacob lived seventeen years after his arrival, so that he was 147 years old at the
time of his death. 29As the time drew near for him to die, he called for his son
Joseph and said to him, "Swear to me most solemnly that you will honor this, my
last request: do not bury me in Egypt. 30But when I am dead, take me out of Egypt
and bury me beside my ancestors." And Joseph promised. 31"Swear that you will
do it," Jacob insisted. And Joseph did. Soon afterwards Jacob took to his bed.

48 One day not long after this, word came to Joseph that his father was failing
rapidly. So, taking with him his two sons, Manasseh and Ephraim, he went
to visit him. 2When Jacob heard that Joseph had arrived, he gathered his strength
and sat up in the bed to greet him, 3and said to him, "God Almighty appeared to me
at Luz in the land of Canaan and blessed me, 4and said to me, 'I will make you a

Cross-references (right margin)
47:6 Gen 45:18; 46:34; 47:11; Ex 18:21
47:7 Gen 47:10; Ex 12:32; Num 6:23
47:9 Gen 35:28; 1 Chron 29:15
47:10 Gen 14:19
47:11 Ex 1:11; 12:37
47:12 Gen 45:11; 47:24
47:13 Gen 41:30; Jer 14:1-6; Acts 7:11
47:14 Gen 41:56; 1 Cor 4:2
47:15 Gen 47:18, 19,24
47:17 Ex 9:3; 1 Kgs 10:28
47:19 Neh 5:2; Job 2:4; Lam 1:11; Mt 16:26
47:22 Gen 41:45; Deut 12:19
47:23 Gen 45:6; Prov 11:26
47:24 Gen 41:34; Lev 27:32
47:25 Gen 33:15; 45:7; 50:20; Ruth 2:13
47:26 Gen 47:22
47:27 Gen 13:16; 46:3; Ex 1:7
47:29 Gen 24:2,49; 50:24,25; Acts 7:15,16; Heb 11:21
47:30 Gen 15:15; 23:19; 25:9; 49:29
48:1 Gen 41:50-52; 46:20; Heb 11:21
48:3 Gen 28:3, 12-19; 35:9-15

47:29-31 Jacob had Joseph promise to bury him in his
homeland. Few things were written in this culture, so a person's
word carried as much force as a written contract. People today
seem to find it easy to say, "I didn't mean that." God's people,
however, are to speak the truth and live the truth. Let your words
be as binding as a written contract.

great nation and I will give this land of Canaan to you and to your children's children, for an everlasting possession.' 5And now, as to these two sons of yours, Ephraim and Manasseh, born here in the land of Egypt before I arrived, I am adopting them as my own, and they will inherit from me just as Reuben and Simeon will. 6But any other children born to you shall be your own, and shall inherit Ephraim's and Manasseh's portion from you. 7For your mother Rachel died after only two children when I came from Paddan-aram, as we were just a short distance from Ephrath, and I buried her beside the road to Bethlehem." 8Then Israel looked over at the two boys. "Are these the ones?" he asked.

9"Yes," Joseph told him, "these are my sons whom God has given me here in Egypt."

And Israel said, "Bring them over to me and I will bless them."

10Israel was half blind with age, so that he could hardly see. So Joseph brought the boys close to him and he kissed and embraced them.

11And Israel said to Joseph, "I never thought that I would see you again, but now God has let me see your children too."

12, 13Joseph took the boys by the hand, bowed deeply to him, and led the boys to their grandfather's knees—Ephraim at Israel's left hand and Manasseh at his right. 14But Israel crossed his arms as he stretched them out to lay his hands upon the boys' heads, so that his right hand was upon the head of Ephraim, the younger boy, and his left hand was upon the head of Manasseh, the older. He did this purposely.

15Then he blessed Joseph with this blessing: "May God, the God of my fathers Abraham and Isaac, the God who has shepherded me all my life, wonderfully bless these boys. 16He is the Angel who has kept me from all harm. May these boys be an honor to my name and to the names of my fathers Abraham and Isaac; and may they become a mighty nation."

17But Joseph was upset and displeased when he saw that his father had laid his right hand on Ephraim's head; so he lifted it to place it on Manasseh's head instead. 18"No, father," he said. "You've got your right hand on the wrong head! This one over here is the older. Put your right hand on him!"

19But his father refused. "I know what I'm doing, my son," he said. "Manasseh too shall become a great nation, but his younger brother shall become even greater."

20So Jacob blessed the boys that day with this blessing: "May the people of Israel bless each other by saying, 'God make you as prosperous as Ephraim and Manasseh.' " (Note that he put Ephraim before Manasseh.)

21Then Israel said to Joseph, "I am about to die, but God will be with you and will bring you again to Canaan, the land of your fathers. 22And I have given the choice land of Shekem to you instead of to your brothers, as your portion of that land which I took from the Amorites with my sword and with my bow."

48:7 *after only two children*, implied.

Marginal references (left column):

48:5 Gen 46:20,27

48:6 Josh 14:4

48:7 Gen 35:19; 1 Sam 10:2; Mt 2:18

48:9 Gen 27:4; 33:5; 49:28

48:10 Gen 27:1

48:11 Gen 37:33,34; 42:36

48:12 Gen 33:3; 42:6

48:14 Gen 41:51,52; Ex 15:6; Ps 110:1

48:15 Gen 17:1; 27:4; 28:20,21; 49:24,28

48:16 Gen 22:11; 28:13; 31:11; 32:28; Deut 28:11

48:19 Gen 28:14; 46:3; Deut 1:10

48:20 Gen 28:3; Ruth 4:11

48:21 Gen 28:15; 46:4; 50:24

48:22 Gen 15:16; Josh 17:17,18; 24:32; Jn 4:5

48:9-20 Jacob gave Ephraim, instead of his older brother Manasseh, the greater blessing. When Joseph objected, Jacob scolded him, for God had told him that Ephraim would become greater. God often works in unexpected ways. When he chooses people to fulfill his plans, he always goes deeper than appearance, tradition, or position. He sometimes surprises us by choosing the less obvious person—at least by human reasoning. God can use you to carry out his plans, even if you don't think you have all the qualifications.

48:11 When Joseph became a slave (37:30), Jacob thought he was dead and wept in despair. But eventually God's plan allowed Jacob to regain not only his son, but grandchildren as well. Circumstances are never so bad that they are beyond God's help. Jacob regained his son. In like manner, Job regained a new family (Job 42:10-17), and Mary regained her brother Lazarus (John

11:1-44). We need not despair, because we belong to a loving God. We never know what good he will bring out of a seemingly hopeless situation.

48:15 Jacob spoke of God as one who had "shepherded" him all his life. He pictured himself as a sheep who needed a shepherd's wisdom and guidance to lead him along the best path. This marks a total attitude change from his scheming and dishonest youth. To develop an attitude like Jacob's, you must begin by recognizing that God's advice for living is what you need most. Follow the voice of the Good Shepherd, and he will lead you.

48:20-22 Jacob was giving these young boys land occupied by the Philistines and Canaanites. But Jacob's gift became reality when the tribe of Ephraim and the half-tribe of Manasseh occupied the east and west sides of the Jordan River (Joshua 16).

Jacob's prophecies

49 Then Jacob called together all his sons and said, "Gather around me and I will tell you what is going to happen to you in the days to come. ²Listen to me, O sons of Jacob; listen to Israel your father.

³"Reuben, you are my oldest son, the child of my vigorous youth. You are the head of the list in rank and in honor. ⁴But you are unruly as the wild waves of the sea, and you shall be first no longer. I am demoting you, for you slept with one of my wives and thus dishonored me.

⁵"Simeon and Levi are two of a kind. They are men of violence and injustice. ⁶O my soul, stay away from them. May I never be a party to their wicked plans. For in their anger they murdered a man, and maimed oxen just for fun. ⁷Cursed be their anger, for it is fierce and cruel. Therefore, I will scatter their descendants throughout Israel.

⁸"Judah, your brothers shall praise you. You shall destroy your enemies. Your father's sons shall bow before you. ⁹Judah is a young lion that has finished eating its prey. He has settled down as a lion—who will dare to rouse him? ¹⁰The scepter shall not depart from Judah until Shiloh comes, whom all people shall obey. ¹¹He has chained his steed to the choicest vine, and washed his clothes in wine. ¹²His eyes are darker than wine and his teeth are whiter than milk.

¹³"Zebulun shall dwell on the shores of the sea and shall be a harbor for ships, with his borders extending to Sidon.

¹⁴"Issachar is a strong beast of burden resting among the saddle bags. ¹⁵When he saw how good the countryside was, how pleasant the land, he willingly bent his shoulder to the task and served his masters with vigor.

¹⁶"Dan shall govern his people like any other tribe in Israel. ¹⁷He shall be a serpent in the path that bites the horses' heels, so that the rider falls off. ¹⁸I trust in your salvation, Lord.

¹⁹"A marauding band shall stamp upon Gad, but he shall rob and pursue them!

²⁰"Asher shall produce rich foods, fit for kings!

²¹"Naphtali is a deer let loose, producing lovely fawns.

²²"Joseph is a fruitful tree beside a fountain. His branches shade the wall. ²³He has been severely injured by those who shot at him and persecuted him, ²⁴but their weapons were shattered by the Mighty One of Jacob, the Shepherd, the Rock of Israel. ²⁵May the God of your fathers, the Almighty, bless you with blessings of

49:3
Num 26:5
Deut 21:17
1 Chron 2:1; 5:1
49:4
Gen 35:22
Deut 27:20
49:5
Gen 29:33,34
34:25
49:6
Gen 34:30
49:7
Josh 1:9
21:1-42
49:8
Deut 33:7
Judg 1:1,2
20:18; Heb 7:14
49:9
Num 24:9
Mic 5:8
49:10
Num 24:17
Ps 2:6-9; 60:7
49:13
Deut 33:19
Josh 19:10
49:14
Josh 19:17
Judg 5:16
49:16
Deut 33:22
Judg 13:2; 15:20
Judg 18:26
49:19
Deut 33:20
49:20
Deut 33:24
49:21
Deut 33:23
49:22
Deut 33:13-17
49:23
Gen 37:4,18
49:24
Isa 28:16; 49:26

49:7 *I will scatter their descendants throughout Israel.* That is, the tribes of Simeon and Levi were not given land holdings, as were their brother-tribes.   **49:11** *washed his clothes in wine.* Showing wealth and extravagance.

49:3-28 Jacob blessed each of his sons, then gave a prediction about their future. The way they had lived their past played an important part in the way Jacob predicted their future. The same is true for us. By sunrise tomorrow, our actions of today will have become part of our past. Yet at the same time they begin shaping our future. What actions can you choose or avoid today that will positively shape your future?

49:4 The oldest child was supposed to receive twice the inheritance. But Reuben lost his special honor. Wild and uncontrollable, especially in his younger days, he had gone so far as to sleep with one of his father's wives. Jacob could not give an honored blessing to such a dishonorable son.

49:8-12 Why was Judah, one of Jacob's most wicked sons, so greatly blessed? God had chosen Judah to be the ancestor of Israel's royal line of kings (referred to as the "scepter" in these verses). This may have been due to Judah's dramatic change of character (44:33, 34). Judah's line would also produce the promised Messiah, Jesus Christ.

49:10 What does Shiloh mean? This is a difficult passage to understand and the meaning is disputed. Shiloh may be used as another name for the Messiah, for translated literally it means, "until he to whom it belongs comes, whom all people shall obey." Shiloh might also refer to the Tabernacle set up at the city of Shiloh in Joshua 18:1.

49:18 In the middle of his prophecy to Dan, Jacob exclaimed, "I trust in your salvation, Lord." He was emphasizing to Dan that he would be a strong leader, but only if his trust was in God, not in his natural strength or ability. Those who are strong, attractive, or talented often find it easier to trust in themselves than in God, who gave them these gifts. Remember to thank God for what you are and have so your trust does not become misplaced.

49:22 Joseph was indeed a "fruitful tree" with some heroic descendants. Among them Joshua (who will lead the Israelites into the Promised Land, Joshua 1:10, 11); Deborah (a judge of Israel, Judges 4:4); Gideon (a judge of Israel, Judges 6:11,12); and Samuel (a great prophet of Israel, 1 Samuel 3:19).

49:24 Jacob summarized God's work in Joseph's life with the phrase, "their weapons were shattered by the Mighty One." This was his way of expressing how God had come to the rescue when Joseph was attacked by those who hated him. So often we struggle and strain without thinking that God is able to help us fight our battles, whether they are against men with weapons or against spiritual forces. Joseph was able to draw closer to God as adversity mounted. To trust God to rescue you shows great faith. Can you trust him to shatter the weapons of injury or persecution directed at you? Such spiritual battles require teamwork between courageous, faithful people and a mighty God.

heaven above and of the earth beneath—blessings of the breasts and of the womb,

49:26
Num 6:2
Deut 33:15,16

26blessings of the grain and flowers, blessings reaching to the utmost bounds of the everlasting hills. These shall be the blessings upon the head of Joseph who was exiled from his brothers.

49:27
Deut 33:12
Judg 3:15

27"Benjamin is a wolf that prowls. He devours his enemies in the morning, and in the evening divides the loot."

49:29
Gen 23:16
25:8,9; 35:29
47:29; 50:5

28So these are the blessings that Israel their father blessed his twelve sons with.

29, 30Then he told them, "Soon I will die. You must bury me with my fathers in the land of Canaan, in the cave in the field of Mach-pelah, facing Mamre—the field Abraham bought from Ephron the Hethite for a burial ground. 31There they buried Abraham and Sarah his wife; there they buried Isaac and Rebekah his wife; and there I buried Leah. 32It is the cave which my grandfather Abraham purchased from the sons of Heth." 33Then, when Jacob had finished his prophecies to his sons, he lay back in the bed, breathed his last, and died.

49:31
Gen 23:19
25:9; 35:29

49:33
Gen 25:8,17
35:29
Acts 7:15
Heb 11:21

Jacob is buried in Canaan

50:1
Gen 23:2
46:4,29

50 Joseph threw himself upon his father's body and wept over him and kissed him. 2Afterwards he commanded his morticians to embalm the body. 3The embalming process required forty days, with a period of national mourning of seventy days. 4Then, when at last the mourning was over, Joseph approached Pharaoh's staff and requested them to speak to Pharaoh on his behalf.

50:2
Gen 50:26

50:3
Num 20:29
Deut 34:8

50:5
Gen 47:29
48:21

5"Tell his majesty," he requested them, "that Joseph's father made Joseph swear to take his body back to the land of Canaan, to bury him there. Ask his majesty to permit me to go and bury my father; assure him that I will return promptly."

6Pharaoh agreed. "Go and bury your father, as you promised," he said.

50:8
Ex 10:9
Num 32:24

7So Joseph went, and a great number of Pharaoh's counselors and assistants—all the senior officers of the land, 8as well as all of Joseph's people—his brothers and their families. But they left their little children and flocks and herds in the land of Goshen. 9So a very great number of chariots, cavalry, and people accompanied Joseph.

50:9
Gen 41:43
46:29
Ex 14:7

10When they arrived at Atad (meaning "Threshing Place of Brambles"), beyond the Jordan River, they held a very great and solemn funeral service, with a seven-day period of lamentation for Joseph's father. 11The local residents, the Canaanites, renamed the place Abel-mizraim (meaning "Egyptian Mourners") for

50:10 *Atad.* Located just west of the Jordan River, near Jericho.

JACOB'S SONS	REUBEN	none
AND THEIR	SIMEON	none
NOTABLE	LEVI	Aaron, Moses, Eli, John the Baptist
DESCENDANTS	JUDAH	David, Jesus
Jacob's 12 sons	DAN	Samson
were the	NAPHTALI	Barak, Elijah (?)
ancestors of the	GAD	Jephthah (?)
12 tribes of Israel.	ASHER	none
The entire nation	ISSACHAR	none
of Israel came	ZEBULUN	none
from these men.	JOSEPH	Joshua, Gideon, Samuel
	BENJAMIN	Saul, Esther, Paul

50:1–11 When Jacob died at the age of 147, Joseph wept and mourned for months. When someone close to us dies, we need a long period of time to work through our grief. Crying and sharing our feelings with others helps us recover and go on with life. Allow yourself and others the freedom to grieve over the loss of a loved one and a long enough time to bring grieving to completion.

50:2, 3 Embalming was typical for Egyptians but unusual for these nomadic shepherds. Believing that the dead went to the next world in their physical bodies, the Egyptians embalmed a body to preserve it so it could function in the world to come. Jacob's family allowed him to be embalmed as a sign of courtesy and respect to the Egyptians.

50:5 Joseph had proven himself trustworthy as Pharaoh's advisor. Because of Joseph's record, Pharaoh had little doubt that he would return to Egypt as promised after burying his father in Canaan. Privileges and freedom often result when we have demonstrated our trustworthiness. Since trust must be built gradually over time, take every opportunity to prove your reliability no matter how unimportant the occasion may seem.

they said, "It is a place of very deep mourning by these Egyptians." 12, 13So his sons did as Israel commanded them, and carried his body into the land of Canaan and buried it there in the cave of Mach-pelah—the cave Abraham had bought in the field of Ephron the Hethite, close to Mamre.

50:12
Ex 20:12
Acts 7:16
50:13
Gen 23:16-18

Joseph treats his brothers kindly

14Then Joseph returned to Egypt with his brothers and all who had accompanied him to the funeral of his father. 15But now that their father was dead, Joseph's brothers were frightened.

"Now Joseph will pay us back for all the evil we did to him," they said. 16, 17So they sent him this message: "Before he died, your father instructed us to tell you to forgive us for the great evil we did to you. We servants of the God of your father beg you to forgive us." When Joseph read the message, he broke down and cried.

18Then his brothers came and fell down before him and said, "We are your slaves."

19But Joseph told them, "Don't be afraid of me. Am I God, to judge and punish you? 20As far as I am concerned, God turned into good what you meant for evil, for he brought me to this high position I have today so that I could save the lives of many people. 21No, don't be afraid. Indeed, I myself will take care of you and your families." And he spoke very kindly to them, reassuring them.

50:15
Gen 42:17,22
50:16
Prov 29:25
50:17
Gen 45:5
Deut 32:35
Mt 6:12
Lk 6:27
Rom 12:19
50:18
Gen 37:7-11
42:6; 44:14
50:19
Gen 30:2
50:20
Gen 37:26
Ps 76:10
105:17-19
50:21
Gen 45:11

Joseph dies

22So Joseph and his brothers and their families continued to live in Egypt. Joseph was 110 years old when he died. 23He lived to see the birth of his son Ephraim's children, and the children of Machir, Manasseh's son, who played at his feet.

24"Soon I will die," Joseph told his brothers, "but God will surely come and get you, and bring you out of this land of Egypt and take you back to the land he promised to the descendants of Abraham, Isaac and Jacob." 25Then Joseph made his brothers promise with an oath that they would take his body back with them when they returned to Canaan. 26So Joseph died at the age of 110, and they embalmed him, and his body was placed in a coffin in Egypt.

50:23
Gen 16:3; 30:3
50:24
Gen 13:15
28:13; 35:12
48:21; 49:29
50:25
Gen 47:29
Ex 13:19
Josh 24:32
Heb 11:22

50:12, 13 Abraham had purchased the Cave of Mach-pelah as a burial place for his wife, Sarah (23:1–9). It was to be a burial place for his entire family. Jacob was Abraham's grandson, and Jacob's sons returned to Canaan to bury him in this cave along with Abraham and Isaac. Their desire to be buried in this cave expressed their faith in God's promise to give their descendants the land of Canaan.

50:15–21 Now that Jacob was dead, the brothers expected revenge from Joseph. Could he really forgive them for selling him into slavery (Genesis 37)? But to their surprise, Joseph not only forgave them but offered to care for them and their families. Joseph's forgiveness was complete. Joseph demonstrates how God graciously accepts us even though we don't deserve it. Realizing that God forgives us, even when we have ignored or rejected him, will motivate us to forgive others.

50:20 Even when powerful people plotted to cause him harm, Joseph saw God bring good from it. The experiences in Joseph's life taught him that God brings good from evil for those who trust him. Do you trust God enough to wait patiently for him to bring good from the bad that happens to you? You can trust him because, as Joseph learned, God can transform evil into good.

50:24 Joseph was ready to die. But he had no doubts that God would keep his promise and one day bring the Israelites back to their homeland. What a tremendous example! The secret of that kind of faith is a lifetime of trusting God. Our faith is like a muscle—it grows with exercise, gaining strength over time. After a lifetime of exercising trust, our faith can be as strong as Joseph's. Then at our death, we can be confident that God will fulfill all his promises to us and to those who come after.

50:24 This verse is a vivid statement of what will begin to happen in Exodus and come to completion in Joshua. God was going to make Jacob's family into a great nation, lead them out of Egypt, and bring them into the land he had promised them. The nation would rely heavily on this promise, and Joseph emphasized his belief that God would do what he promised.

50:26 The book of Genesis gives us rich descriptions of the lives of many great men and women who walked with God. They sometimes succeeded and often failed. Yet we learn much by reading the biographies of these famous people and key historical figures. But where did they get their inspiration? They got it by realizing that God was with them despite their inadequacies. Knowing this should inspire us to maintain our walk with God and reach for the potential he has given us.

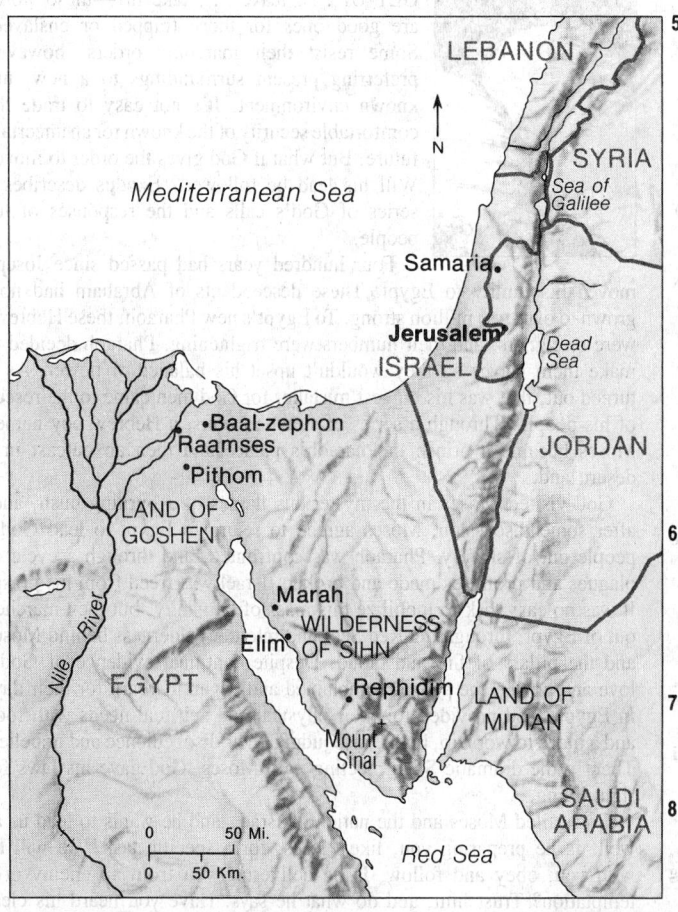

5 Baal-zephon Slavery was not to last, because God planned to deliver his people. After choosing Moses and Aaron to be his spokesmen to Pharaoh, God worked a series of dramatic miracles in the land of Egypt to convince Pharaoh to let the Hebrews go (5:1—12:33). When finally freed, the entire nation set out with the riches of Egypt (12:34–36). One of their first stops was at Baal-zephon (14:1), where Pharaoh, who had changed his mind, chased the Hebrews and trapped them against the Red Sea. But God parted the waters and led the people through the sea on dry land. When Pharaoh's army tried to pursue, the waters collapsed around them, and they were drowned (14:5–31).

6 Marah Moses now led the people southward. The long trek across the desert brought hot tempers and parched throats for this mass of people. At Marah, the water they found was bitter, but God sweetened it (15:22–25).

7 Elim As they continued their journey, the Hebrews (now called Israelites) came to Elim, an oasis with twelve springs (15:27).

8 Wilderness of Sihn Leaving Elim, the people headed into the Wilderness of Sihn. Here the people became hungry, so God provided them with manna that came from heaven and covered the ground each morning (16:1, 13–15). The people ate this manna until they entered the Promised Land.

9 Rephidim Moses led the people to Rephidim where they found no water. But God miraculously provided water from a rock (17:1, 5, 6). Here the Israelites encountered their first test in battle: the Amalekites attacked and were defeated (17:9–13). Moses' father-in-law, Jethro, then arrived on the scene with some sound advice on delegating responsibilities (18).

10 Mount Sinai God had previously appeared to Moses on this mountain and commissioned him to lead Israel (3:1, 2). Now Moses returned with the people God had asked him to lead. For almost a year the people camped at the foot of Mount Sinai. During this time God gave them his Ten Commandments as well as other laws for right living. He also provided the blueprint for building the Tabernacle (19–40).

God was forging a holy nation, prepared to live for and serve him alone.

1 Land of Goshen This area was given to Jacob and his family when they moved to Egypt (Genesis 47:5, 6). It became the Hebrews' homeland for 400 years, and remained separate from the main Egyptian centers, for Egyptian culture looked down upon shepherds and nomads. As the years passed, Jacob's family grew into a large nation (1:7).

2, 3 Pithom and Raamses After 400 years, a Pharaoh came to the throne who had no respect for these descendants of Joseph and feared their large numbers. He forced them into slavery in order to oppress and subdue them. Out of their slave labor, the store-cities of Pithom and Raamses were built (1:11).

4 Land of Midian Moses, an Egyptian prince who was born a Hebrew, killed an Egyptian task master and fled for his life to the land of Midian. There he became a shepherd and married a woman named Zipporah. It was while he was here that God commissioned him for the job of leading the Hebrew people out of Egypt (2:15—4:31).

EXODUS

VITAL STATISTICS

PURPOSE:
To record the events of Israel's deliverance from Egypt and development as a nation

AUTHOR:
Moses

DATE WRITTEN:
1450–1410 B.C., approximately the same as Genesis

WHERE WRITTEN:
In the wilderness during Israel's wanderings, somewhere in the Sinai Peninsula

SETTING:
Egypt. God's people, once highly favored in the land, are now slaves. A God of great miracles is about to set them free.

KEY VERSES:
"I have seen the deep sorrows of my people . . . I am going to send you to . . . lead my people . . . out" (3:7–10).

KEY PEOPLE:
Moses, Miriam, Pharaoh, Pharaoh's daughter, Jethro, Aaron, Joshua, Bezalel

KEY PLACES:
Egypt, Goshen, Nile River, Land of Midian, Red Sea, Sinai Peninsula, Mount Sinai

SPECIAL FEATURES:
Exodus relates more miracles than any other Old Testament book and is noted for containing the Ten Commandments

GET UP . . . leave . . . take off—these words are good ones for those trapped or enslaved. Some resist their marching orders, however, preferring present surroundings to a new, unknown environment. It's not easy to trade the comfortable security of the known for an uncertain future. But what if God gives the order to move? Will his lead be followed? Exodus describes a series of God's calls and the responses of his people.

Four hundred years had passed since Joseph moved his family to Egypt. These descendants of Abraham had now grown to over two million strong. To Egypt's new Pharaoh, these Hebrews were foreigners, and their numbers were frightening. Pharaoh decided to make them slaves so they wouldn't upset his balance of power. As it turned out, that was his biggest mistake, for God then came to the rescue of his people. Through a series of strange events, a Hebrew boy named Moses became a prince in Pharaoh's palace and then an outcast in a desert land.

God visited Moses in the mysterious flames of a burning bush, and, after some discussion, Moses agreed to return to Egypt to lead God's people out of slavery. Pharaoh was confronted, and through a cycle of plagues and promises made and broken, Israel was freed from his grasp. It was no easy task to mobilize this mass of humanity, but they marched out of Egypt, through the Red Sea, and into the wilderness behind Moses and the pillars of fire and cloud. Despite continual evidence of God's love and power, the people complained and began to yearn for their days in Egypt. God provided for their physical and spiritual needs with food and a place to worship, but he also judged their disobedience and unbelief. Then in the dramatic Sinai meeting with Moses, God gave his laws for right living.

God called Moses and the nation of Israel, and he wants to lead us as well. Is he preparing you, like Moses, for a specific task? He will be with you; obey and follow. Is he delivering you from an enemy or a temptation? Trust him, and do what he says. Have you heard his clear moral directions? Read, study, and obey his Word. Is he calling you to true worship? Discover God's presence in your life, in your home, and in the body of assembled believers. Exodus is the exciting story of God's guidance. Read with the determination to follow God wherever he leads.

THE BLUEPRINT

A. ISRAEL IN EGYPT (1:1—12:36)
   1. Slavery in Egypt
   2. God chooses Moses
   3. God sends Moses to Pharaoh
   4. Plagues strike Egypt
   5. The Passover

God heard the cries of his people in Egypt; he hears our cries and answers us too.

Just as God prepared Moses for his work, God is still preparing leaders today.

B. ISRAEL IN THE WILDERNESS (12:37—18:27)
   1. Escape from Egypt
   2. Rescue through the Red Sea
   3. Complaining in the wilderness

God's rescuing the Israelites from Egypt teaches us much about how he delivers Christians from sin and death.

The events here parallel the Christian's life after salvation. Christians still have struggles.
Complaining and dissatisfaction come easy for us.

C. ISRAEL AT SINAI (19:1—40:38)
   1. Giving the Law
   2. Tabernacle instructions
   3. Breaking the Law
   4. Tabernacle construction

Israel's experiences at Sinai show us the beginning of a relationship between God and man.

Through God's Law, we have a way to expose and identify sin and the standard for righteous living.

MEGATHEMES

THEME	EXPLANATION	IMPORTANCE
Slavery	The Israelites were slaves for 400 years. Pharaoh, the king of Egypt, oppressed them cruelly.	Physical slavery is like slavery to sin. After being slaves so long, it is hard to be free. We need both human and divine leadership to do it. After their escape, the memory of slavery helped Israel learn to treat others generously.
Rescue/ Redemption	God rescued Israel through the leader Moses and through mighty miracles. The Passover celebration was an annual reminder of their escape from slavery.	God delivers us from slavery to sin. Jesus Christ celebrated the Passover with his disciples at the Last Supper and then went on to rescue us from sin by dying in our place.
Guidance	God guided Israel out of slavery by using the plagues, Moses' heroic courage, the miracle of the Red Sea, and the Ten Commandments.	Although God can do miracles, he normally leads us by wise leadership and community effort. His words give us the wisdom to make daily decisions and govern our lives.
Ten Commandments	God's law system had three parts. The Ten Commandments were the first part, containing the absolutes of spiritual and moral life. The civil law was the second part, giving the people rules to manage their lives. The ceremonial law was the third part, showing them patterns for building the Tabernacle and regular worship.	God was teaching Israel the importance of choice and responsibility. When they obeyed the conditions of the Law, he blessed them; if they forgot or disobeyed, he punished them or allowed calamities to come. Many great countries of the world base their laws on the moral system set up in the book of Exodus.
The Nation	God founded the nation of Israel to be the source of truth and salvation to all the world. His relationship to his people was loving yet firm. The Israelites had no army, schools, governors, mayors, or police when they left Egypt. God had to instruct them in their constitutional laws and daily practices. He showed them how to worship and how to have national holidays.	Israel's newly formed nation had all the behavioral characteristics of Christians today. We are often disorganized, sometimes rebellious, and sometimes victorious. God's Person and Word are still our only guide.

A. ISRAEL IN EGYPT (1:1—12:36)

Joseph brought his family to Egypt and protected them there. But after Joseph's death, as they multiplied into a nation, they were forced into slavery. God then prepared Moses to free his people from slavery and lead them out of Egypt. To help Moses, God unleashed ten plagues upon the land. After the tenth plague, Pharaoh let the people go. On the night before the great exodus, God's new nation celebrated the Passover. Just as God delivered Israel from Egypt, he delivers us from sin, death, and evil.

1. Slavery in Egypt

1 This is the list of the sons of Jacob who accompanied him to Egypt, with their families: Reuben, Simeon, Levi, Judah, Issachar, Zebulun, Benjamin, Dan, Naphtali, Gad, Asher.

5So the total number who went with him was seventy (for Joseph was already there). 6In due season Joseph and each of his brothers died, ending that generation. 7Meanwhile, their descendants were very fertile, increasing rapidly in numbers; there was a veritable population explosion so that they soon became a large nation, and they filled the land of Goshen.

8Then, eventually, a new king came to the throne of Egypt who felt no obligation to the descendants of Joseph.

9He told his people, "These Israelis are becoming dangerous to us because there are so many of them. 10Let's figure out a way to put an end to this. If we don't, and war breaks out, they will join our enemies and fight against us and escape out of the country."

11So the Egyptians made slaves of them and put brutal taskmasters over them to wear them down under heavy burdens while building the cities of Pithom and Raamses as supply centers for the king. 12But the more the Egyptians mistreated and oppressed them, the more the Israelis seemed to multiply! The Egyptians became alarmed, 13, 14and made the Hebrew slavery more bitter still, forcing them to toil long and hard in the fields and to carry heavy loads of mortar and brick.

15, 16Then Pharaoh, the king of Egypt, instructed the Hebrew midwives (their names were Shiphrah and Puah) to kill all Hebrew boys as soon as they were born, but to let the girls live. 17But the midwives feared God and didn't obey the king—they let the boys live too.

1:1 Gen 46:8-26 49:3-27 1 Chron 2:1,2 Rev 7:4-8
1:2 Ex 6:14-16
1:5 Gen 46:27 Ex 24:1 Deut 10:22 Judg 8:30 Acts 7:14
1:6 Gen 50:26 Acts 7:15,16
1:7 Gen 1:27; 12:2 35:11; 46:3 47:27; 48:4 Ex 12:37 Acts 7:17
1:8 Acts 7:18
1:9 Ps 105:24
1:10 Ps 105:25 Acts 7:19
1:11 Ex 2:11; 3:7
1:14 Ex 2:23
1:16 Acts 7:19

1:8 *eventually, a new king came,* implied. This incident occurred about four hundred years after Joseph's death. *who felt no obligation to the descendants of Joseph,* literally, "who did not know Joseph."

1:1 Jacob's family arrived in Egypt during the glory days of the Pharaohs. Over the years, this Hebrew family grew into a large nation. But, as foreigners and newcomers, their lives were in marked contrast to those of the Egyptians. The Hebrews worshiped one God; the Egyptians worshiped many gods. The Hebrews were wanderers; the Egyptians had a deeply rooted culture. The Hebrews were shepherds; the Egyptians were builders. Hebrew women kept to the background; Egyptian women occupied a prominent place in society. In addition to being so different, the Hebrews were also physically separated from the rest of the Egyptians: they lived in Goshen, north of the great Egyptian centers.

1:9, 10 Pharaoh was afraid the Israelites were becoming so numerous that they would organize and threaten his kingdom. He made them slaves to kill their spirit and stop their growth. Slavery was an ancient practice used by almost all nations to "employ" conquered people and other captives. The great pyramids of Egypt were most likely built with slave labor. Although Israel was not a conquered nation, the people were considered uncultured, less intelligent, and generally lower in status.

1:11 There were levels of slavery in Egypt. Some slaves worked long hours in mud pits while others were skilled carpenters, jewelers, and craftsmen. Regardless of the specific skill or level, all slaves were kept under the eye of ruthless taskmasters. The name *taskmaster* means "chief of burden" or "oppressor," and their assignment was to keep the slaves working as fast as possible. They were specialists at making a slave's life miserable.

1:11 The Bible says the Hebrew slaves built the store-cities of Pithom and Raamses. Ancient records indicate these cities were built in 1290 B.C. But many scholars insist the Hebrews left Egypt in 1446 B.C. How could they build two cities 150 years *after* they left? Two theories have been proposed: (1) The Exodus really occurred around 1290 B.C. This is called the "late exodus theory." (2) Raamses, the Pharaoh in 1290 B.C., did not build the store-cities of Pithom and Raamses. He renamed them. It was a common practice for an Egyptian ruler to make improvements on a city and then take credit for building it, thus wiping out all records of previous founders. See note on Exodus 13:17, 18.

1:12 The Egyptians tried to wear down the Hebrew people by forcing them into slavery and mistreating them. Instead, the Hebrews multiplied and grew stronger. When we are burdened or mistreated, we may feel defeated. But our burdens can make us stronger and develop qualities in us that will prepare us for the future. One cannot overcome without troubles to come over. Thank God for the hard times, because even the worst situations can make us better people in the long run.

1:15–17 Hebrew midwives helped women give birth and cared for the baby until the mother was stronger. When Pharaoh ordered the midwives to kill the Hebrew baby boys, he was asking the wrong people. Most midwives were friends, neighbors, or relatives of the mother. These women showed great courage and love for God by risking their lives to disobey Pharaoh's command.

1:17–21 Against Pharaoh's orders, the midwives spared the lives of the Hebrew babies. Their faith in God gave them the courage to

¹⁸The king summoned them before him and demanded, "Why have you disobeyed my command and let the baby boys live?"

¹⁹"Sir," they told him, "the Hebrew women have their babies so quickly that we can't get there in time! They are not slow like the Egyptian women!"

²⁰And God blessed the midwives [because they were God-fearing women]. So the people of Israel continued to multiply and to become a mighty nation. ²¹And because the midwives revered God, he gave them children of their own. ²²Then Pharaoh commanded all of his people to throw the newborn Hebrew boys into the Nile River. But the girls, he said, could live.

2. God chooses Moses
Moses is born

2 There were at this time a Hebrew fellow and girl of the tribe of Levi who married and had a family, and a baby son was born to them. When the baby's mother saw that he was an unusually beautiful baby, she hid him at home for three months. ³Then, when she could no longer hide him, she made a little boat from papyrus reeds, waterproofed it with tar, put the baby in it, and laid it among the reeds along the river's edge. ⁴The baby's sister watched from a distance to see what would happen to him.

⁵Well, this is what happened: A princess, one of Pharaoh's daughters, came down to bathe in the river, and as she and her maids were walking along the river bank, she spied the little boat among the reeds and sent one of the maids to bring it to her. ⁶When she opened it, there was a baby! And he was crying. This touched her heart. "He must be one of the Hebrew children!" she said.

⁷Then the baby's sister approached the princess and asked her, "Shall I go and find one of the Hebrew women to nurse the baby for you?"

⁸"Yes, do!" the princess replied. So the little girl rushed home and called her mother!

1:20 *because they were God-fearing women,* implied from vs 21.

Marginal references:

1:19
Josh 2:4
2 Sam 17:20
1:20
Ex 1:12
1:22
Mt 2:16

2:1
Ex 6:16,20
Num 26:59
2:2
Acts 7:20
Heb 11:23
2:3
Gen 6:14
Ex 1:22
Isa 18:2; 19:6
2:4
Ex 15:20
Num 26:59
Mic 6:4
2:5
Ex 8:20
Acts 7:21
2:6
Ps 106:46

---

take a stand for what they knew was right. In this situation, disobeying the authority was proper. God does not expect us to obey those in authority when they ask us to disobey him or his Word. The Bible is filled with examples of those who were willing to sacrifice their very lives in order to obey God or save the lives of others. Esther and Mordecai (Esther 3:2; 4:13–16), and Shadrach, Meshach, and Abednego (Daniel 3:16–18) are some of the people who took a bold stand for what was right.

Whole nations can be caught up in immorality (racial hatred, slavery, prison cruelty), but following the majority or the authority is not always right. When we are ordered to act in disobedience to God's Word, we must take a stand to obey God rather than man.

1:19–21 Did God bless the Hebrew midwives for lying to Pharaoh? God blessed them not because they lied, but because they saved the lives of innocent children. This doesn't mean that a lie was necessarily the best way to answer Pharaoh. The midwives were blessed, however, for not violating the higher law of God which forbids the senseless slaughter of innocent lives.

2:1, 2 Although a name is not mentioned yet, the baby in this story was Moses. Moses' mother and father were named Jochebed and Amram. His brother was Aaron and his sister, Miriam.

2:3ff Moses' mother knew how wrong it would be to destroy her child. But there was little she could do to change Pharaoh's new law. Her only alternative was to hide the child and later place him in a tiny reed basket on the river. God used her small but courageous act to place her son, the Hebrew of his choice, in the house of Pharaoh. Do you sometimes feel surrounded by evil and frustrated by how little you can do about it? What seems a small and futile act to you may be just what God will use to change a situation. When faced with evil, look for ways to act against it. Then

trust God to use your act, however small, in his war against evil.

2:3 This tiny boat made of papyrus reeds was fashioned by a woman who knew what she was doing. Egyptian river boats were made with these same reeds and waterproofed with tar. These reeds (often called bulrushes) could be gathered in swampy areas along the Nile and grew as tall as sixteen feet. Thus, a tiny basket hidden among the reeds would be well insulated from the weather and difficult to see.

2:5 Who was Pharaoh's daughter? There are two popular explanations. (1) Some think that Hatshepsut was the woman who pulled Moses from the river. Her husband was the Pharaoh Thutmose II. Apparently Hatshepsut could not have children, so Thutmose had a son by another woman who became heir to the throne. Hatshepsut would have considered Moses a "gift from the gods," for now she had her own son who would be the legal heir to the throne. (2) Many think the princess who rescued baby Moses was the daughter of Raamses II, an especially cruel Pharaoh who would have made life miserable for the Hebrew slaves.

2:7, 8 Miriam, the baby's sister, saw that Pharaoh's daughter had discovered Moses. Quickly she took the initiative to suggest a nurse (her mother) who might care for the baby. The Bible doesn't say if Miriam was afraid to approach the Egyptian princess, or if the princess was suspicious of the Hebrew girl. But Miriam *did* approach her, and she bought the services of Miriam and her mother. Their family was reunited. Special opportunities often come our way unexpectedly. Don't let the fear of what might happen cause you to miss an opportunity when it comes. Be alert for the opportunities God gives you and take full advantage of them.

⁹"Take this child home and nurse him for me," the princess instructed the baby's mother, "and I will pay you well!" So she took him home and nursed him.

¹⁰Later, when he was older, she brought him back to the princess and he became her son. She named him Moses (meaning "to draw out") because she had drawn him out of the water.

Moses runs away

¹¹One day, many years later when Moses had grown up and become a man, he went out to visit his fellow Hebrews and saw the terrible conditions they were under. During his visit he saw an Egyptian knock a Hebrew to the ground—one of his own Hebrew brothers! ¹²Moses looked this way and that to be sure no one was watching, then killed the Egyptian and hid his body in the sand.

¹³The next day as he was out visiting among the Hebrews again, he saw two of them fighting. "What are you doing, hitting your own Hebrew brother like that?" he said to the one in the wrong.

¹⁴"And who are you?" the man demanded. "I suppose you think you are *our* prince and judge! And do you plan to kill me as you did that Egyptian yesterday?" When Moses realized that his deed was known, he was frightened. ¹⁵And sure enough, when Pharaoh heard about it he ordered Moses arrested and executed. But Moses ran away into the land of Midian. As he was sitting there beside a well, ¹⁶seven girls who were daughters of the priest of Midian came to draw water and fill the water troughs for their father's flocks. ¹⁷But the shepherds chased the girls away. Moses then came to their aid and rescued them from the shepherds and watered their flocks.

¹⁸When they returned to their father Reuel he asked, "How did you get the flocks watered so quickly today?"

¹⁹"An Egyptian defended us against the shepherds," they told him; "he drew water for us and watered the flocks."

²⁰"Well, where is he?" their father demanded. "Did you just leave him there? Invite him home for supper."

²¹Moses eventually decided to accept Reuel's invitation to live with them, and Reuel gave him one of the girls, Zipporah, as his wife. ²²They had a baby named

2:10 The name *Moses* sounds like another Hebrew word meaning "to draw out."   **2:11** *many years later*, implied.

2:10
1 Sam 1:20
2 Sam 22:17

2:11
Acts 7:23,24
Heb 11:24

2:12
Acts 7:24

2:13
Acts 7:26-28
2:14
Gen 19:9; 37:8
Num 16:3
Acts 7:28,33
2:15
Gen 24:11; 29:2
1 Kgs 19:1-3
Acts 7:29
2:16
Gen 14:18
24:11
Ex 3:1; 18:7,12
2:17
Gen 29:10

2:18
Num 10:29
2:20
Gen 18:5; 24:31
Job 31:32
2:21
Ex 4:25; 18:2
Acts 7:29
2:22
Gen 23:4
Ex 4:20; 18:3
Heb 11:13

2:9 Moses' mother was reunited with her baby! God used her small act of courage to overcome almost impossible human circumstances. God doesn't need much from us to accomplish his plan for our lives. Focusing on our human predicament may paralyze us because the situation may appear humanly impossible. But concentrating on God and his power helps us see the way out. Right now you may feel you're in the "reeds" of life, unable to see out of your troubles. Focus instead on trusting God for the way out. That is all he needs to begin his work in you.

2:12–14 Moses tried to make sure no one was watching before he killed the Egyptian. But as it turned out, someone did see, and Moses had to flee the country. Sometimes we mistakenly think that we can get away with doing wrong if no one sees or catches us. Sooner or later, however, doing wrong will catch up with us as it did with Moses. Even if we are not caught in this life, we will still have to face God's evaluation of our actions.

2:17 How did Moses handle these shepherds so easily? As an Egyptian prince, Moses would have been well trained in the Egyptian military, the most advanced army in the world. Even a large group of shepherds would have been no match for the sophisticated fighting techniques of this trained warrior.

2:22 To escape punishment for killing the Egyptian, Moses ran away to the land of Midian. He became a stranger in a foreign land, separated from his home and family. It took many years after this incident for Moses to be ready to serve God. But he trusted God instead of fearing the king (Hebrews 11:27). We often feel

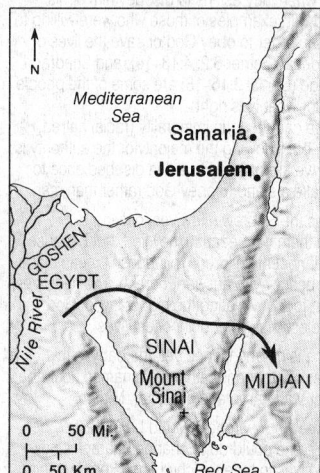

MOSES FLEES TO MIDIAN
After murdering an Egyptian, Moses escaped into the land of Midian. There he married Zipporah and became a shepherd.

abandoned, away from home, or isolated because of something we have done. But though we feel afraid and separated, we should not give up. Moses didn't. He trusted God to deliver him, no matter how dark his past or bleak his future.

2:23
Ex 6:5,9
Deut 26:7
Acts 7:34
Jas 5:4
2:24
Gen 22:16-18
26:2,3; 28:13
46:3,4
Ps 105:8,42

Gershom (meaning "foreigner"), for he said, "I am a stranger in a foreign land."

23Several years later the king of Egypt died. The Israelis were groaning beneath their burdens, in deep trouble because of their slavery, and weeping bitterly before the Lord. He heard their cries from heaven, 24and remembered his promise to Abraham, Isaac, and Jacob [to bring their descendants back into the land of Canaan]. 25Looking down upon them, he knew that the time had come for their rescue.

The burning bush

3:2
Acts 7:30
3:3
Acts 7:31
3:5
Gen 28:16,17
Ex 19:12
Josh 5:15
Acts 7:33
3:6
Gen 31:42; 32:9
Mt 22:32
Mk 12:26
Lk 20:37
Acts 7:32
3:7
Acts 7:34
3:8
a)Gen 15:16
46:4; 50:24
b)Gen 15:19
Ex 3:17
Deut 6:3; 8:7-9
11:9; 26:9
3:10
Acts 7:34; 12:6
3:11
Ex 4:10; 6:12
3:12
Ex 4:12; 19:2
Acts 7:7

3 One day as Moses was tending the flock of his father-in-law Jethro, the priest of Midian, out at the edge of the desert near Horeb, the mountain of God, 2suddenly the Angel of Jehovah appeared to him as a flame of fire in a bush. When Moses saw that the bush was on fire and that it didn't burn up, 3, 4he went over to investigate. Then God called out to him,

"Moses! Moses!"

"Who is it?" Moses asked.

5"Don't come any closer," God told him. "Take off your shoes, for you are standing on holy ground. 6I am the God of your fathers—the God of Abraham, Isaac, and Jacob." (Moses covered his face with his hands, for he was afraid to look at God.)

7Then the Lord told him, "I have seen the deep sorrows of my people in Egypt, and have heard their pleas for freedom from their harsh taskmasters. 8I have come to deliver them from the Egyptians and to take them out of Egypt into a good land, a large land, a land 'flowing with milk and honey'—the land where the Canaanites, Hittites, Amorites, Perizzites, Hivites, and Jebusites live. 9Yes, the wail of the people of Israel has risen to me in heaven, and I have seen the heavy tasks the Egyptians have oppressed them with. 10Now I am going to send you to Pharaoh, to demand that he let you lead my people out of Egypt."

11"But I'm not the person for a job like that!" Moses exclaimed.

12Then God told him, "I will certainly be with you, and this is the proof that I am

2:24 *to bring their descendants back into the land of Canaan,* implied.　**2:25** *knew that the time had come for their rescue,* literally, "knew their condition."　**3:1** *his father-in-law Jethro.* Moses' father-in-law goes under two names in these chapters, Jethro and Reuel.

2:23–25 God's rescue doesn't always come the moment we want it. God had promised to bring the Hebrew slaves out of Egypt (Genesis 15:16; 46:3, 4). The people had waited a long time for that promise to be kept, but God rescued them when he knew the right time had come. God knows the best time to act. When you feel that God has forgotten you in your troubles, remember that God has a time schedule we can't see.

3:1 What a contrast between Moses' life as an Egyptian prince and his life as a Midianite shepherd! As a prince he had everything done for him; he was the famous son of an Egyptian princess. As a shepherd he had to do everything for himself. He was holding the very job he had been taught to despise (Genesis 43:32; 46:32–34), and he lived as an unknown foreigner. What a humbling experience this must have been for Moses! But God was preparing Moses for leadership. Living the life of a shepherd and nomad, Moses learned about the ways of the people he would be leading and also about life in the wilderness. Moses couldn't see this himself, but God was getting him ready to free Israel from Pharaoh's grasp.

3:2 God spoke to Moses from an unexpected source: a burning bush. When Moses saw it, he went to investigate. God often uses unexpected sources when working in our lives too. Be willing to investigate. Whether he uses people, thoughts, or experiences, be ready for God's surprises. He may have guidance for you that can come when you are ready to listen to a "burning bush."

3:3, 4 Moses "saw" God in a burning bush and spoke with him. Many people in the Bible experienced appearances of God in

visible (not necessarily human) form. Abraham saw the smoking fire-pot and flaming torch (Genesis 15:17); Jacob wrestled with a Man (Genesis 32:24–29). When the slaves were freed from Egypt, God led them by a pillar of cloud and fire. These appearances occurred mostly in Old Testament times. God made such appearances to encourage his new nation and prove the reliability of his verbal message.

3:5, 6 God commanded Moses to take off his shoes because he was standing on holy ground. Moses obeyed and covered his face as well. Taking off his shoes was an act of reverence, conveying his own unworthiness before God. God is our friend, but he is also our sovereign Lord. To approach him frivolously shows a lack of respect and sincerity. When you come to God in worship, do you approach him casually or as though you were an invited guest before a king? At times we must adjust our attitude so it is suitable for approaching a holy God.

3:10–12 Moses made excuses because he felt inadequate for the job God asked him to do. It was natural for him to feel that way. He *was* inadequate all by himself. But God wasn't asking Moses to work alone. He offered other resources to help (God himself, Aaron, and the special gift to do miracles). God often calls us to tasks that seem too difficult, but he doesn't ask us to do them alone. God offers us his resources, just as he did Moses. We should not hide behind our inadequacies, as Moses did, but look beyond ourselves to the great resources available. Then we can allow God to use our unique contributions.

the one who is sending you: When you have led the people out of Egypt, you shall worship God here upon this mountain!"

[13]But Moses asked, "If I go to the people of Israel and tell them that their fathers' God has sent me, they will ask, 'Which God are you talking about?' What shall I tell them?"

3:13
Ex 15:3

[14]" 'The Sovereign God,' " was the reply. "Just say, 'I Am has sent me!' [15]Yes, tell them, 'Jehovah, the God of your ancestors Abraham, Isaac, and Jacob, has sent me to you.' (This is my eternal name, to be used throughout all generations.)

3:14
Ex 6:3
Jn 8:58
Rev 1:8; 4:8

[16]"Call together all the elders of Israel," God instructed him, "and tell them about Jehovah appearing to you here in this burning bush and that he said to you, 'I have visited my people, and have seen what is happening to them there in Egypt. [17]I promise to rescue them from the drudgery and humiliation they are undergoing, and to take them to the land now occupied by the Canaanites, Hittites, Amorites, Perizzites, Hivites, and Jebusites, a land "flowing with milk and honey." ' [18]The elders of the people of Israel will accept your message. They must go with you to the king of Egypt and tell him, 'Jehovah, the God of the Hebrews, has met with us and instructed us to go three days' journey into the desert to sacrifice to him. Give us your permission.'

3:15
Ps 72:17
102:12; 135:13
145:1
Acts 7:32
3:16
Ex 4:29; 18:12
3:17
Ex 3:8
Josh 24:11
3:18
Ex 4:31; 5:1,3
Num 23:4,16

[19]"But I know that the king of Egypt will not let you go except under heavy pressure. [20]So I will give him all the pressure he needs! I will destroy Egypt with my miracles, and then at last he will let you go. [21]And I will see to it that the Egyptians load you down with gifts when you leave, so that you will by no means go out empty-handed! [22]Every woman will ask for jewels, silver, gold, and the finest of clothes from her Egyptian master's wife and neighbors. You will clothe your sons and daughters with the best of Egypt!"

3:19
Ex 5:2; 6:1; 7:4
Deut 6:22
3:20
Ex 11:1; 12:31
15:11
Neh 9:10
Acts 7:36
3:21
Ex 11:3; 12:36
3:22
Ex 11:2; 12:35

Moses asks for help

4 But Moses said, "They won't believe me! They won't do what *I* tell them to. They'll say, 'Jehovah never appeared to you!' "

4:1
Ex 3:11,13-16

[2]"What do you have there in your hand?" the Lord asked him.
And he replied, "A shepherd's rod."

4:2
Ex 4:17,20

[3]"Throw it down on the ground," the Lord told him. So he threw it down—and it became a serpent, and Moses ran from it!

4:3
Ex 7:10-12

3:14 *the Sovereign God,* or, "the Living God." Literally, "I am what I am," or "I will be what I will be." **3:15** *Jehovah.* Properly the name should be pronounced "Yahweh," as it is spelled in many modern versions. In this paraphrase "Yahweh" is translated either "Jehovah" or "Lord."

3:13–15 The Egyptians had many gods by many different names. Moses wanted to know God's name so the Hebrew people would know exactly who had sent him to them. God called himself *I Am,* an appellation describing his eternal power and unchangeable character. In a world where values, morals, and laws change constantly, we can find stability and security in our unchanging God. The God who appeared to Moses is the same God who can live in us today. Hebrews 13:8 says God is the same "yesterday, today, and forever." As God's nature is trustworthy, we are free to enjoy him rather than spend our time trying to figure him out.

3:14 Jehovah, or Yahweh, means *I Am.* By using this name, God was reminding Moses of his covenant promises to Abraham (Genesis 12:1–3; 15; 17), Isaac (Genesis 26:2–5), and Jacob (Genesis 28:13–15). When Moses later used it with the elders (4:29-31), he was invoking national pride in a promise almost 500 years old.

3:16–18 God instructed Moses to tell the people what he saw and heard at the burning bush. Our God is a God who acts and speaks. One of the most convincing ways to tell others about him is to describe what he has done and how he has spoken to his people. If you are trying to explain God to others, talk about what he has done in your life or in the lives of those in the Bible.

3:17 The land "flowing with milk and honey" is a poetic word picture that expresses the beauty and productivity of the Promised Land.

3:18–20 The leaders of Israel would accept God's message, and the leaders of Egypt would reject it. God knew what both reactions would be before they happened. This is more than good psychology—God knows the future. Any believer can trust his or her future to God, because God already knows what is going to happen.

4:1 Moses' fear was caused by overanticipation. He was worried about how the people might respond to him. We often overanticipate events and then panic over what might go wrong. God does not ask us to go where he has not provided the means to help. Go where he leads, trusting him to supply courage, confidence, and resources at the right moment.

4:2–4 A shepherd's staff was commonly a three- to six-foot wooden rod with a curved hook at the top. The shepherd used it for walking, guiding his sheep, killing snakes, and many other tasks. Still, it was just a stick. But God used the simple shepherd's rod Moses carried to teach him an important lesson. God sometimes takes joy in using ordinary things for extraordinary purposes. What are the ordinary things in your life—your voice, a pen, a hammer, a broom, a musical instrument? While it is easy to assume God can use only special skills, you must not hinder his use of the everyday contributions you can make. Little did Moses imagine the power his simple staff would yield when it became the rod of God.

⁴Then the Lord told him, "Grab it by the tail!" He did, and it became a rod in his hand again!

4:5
Ex 4:30,31; 19:9

⁵"Do that and they will believe you!" the Lord told him. "Then they will realize that Jehovah, the God of their ancestors Abraham, Isaac, and Jacob, has really appeared to you. ⁶Now reach your hand inside your robe, next to your chest." And when he did, and took it out again, it was white with leprosy! ⁷"Now put it in again," Jehovah said. And when he did, and took it out again, it was normal, just as before! ⁸"If they don't believe the first miracle, they will the second," the Lord said, ⁹"and if they don't accept you after these two signs, then take water from the Nile River and pour it upon the dry land, and it will turn to blood."

4:6
Ex 12:10
Num 12:10
4:7
Num 12:13,14
Deut 32:39
2 Kgs 5:14
Mt 8:3
Lk 17:12-14
4:9
Ex 7:19
4:10
Jer 1:6
Acts 7:22

¹⁰But Moses pleaded, "O Lord, I'm just not a good speaker. I never have been, and I'm not now, even after you have spoken to me, for I have a speech impediment."

4:10 *I have a speech impediment,* literally, "my speech is slow and halting."

JETHRO

People such as Jethro and Melchizedek—not Hebrews, but nevertheless worshipers of the true God—played an important role in the Old Testament. They remind us of God's commitment to the world. God chose one nation through whom to work; but his love and concern are for all nations!

Jethro's religious background prepared him for, rather than prevented him from, faith in God. When he saw and heard what God had done for the Israelites, his response was wholehearted worship. But we can also guess that for 40 years as Moses' father-in-law, Jethro had been watching God at work, molding a leader. Their relationship must have been close, for Moses readily accepted his advice. Both benefited from knowing each other. Jethro met God through Moses, and Moses received hospitality, his wife, and wisdom from Jethro.

The greatest gift one person can give another is faith in God. But that gift is hindered if the believer's attitude is, "I have the greatest gift to pass on to you, while you have nothing to give to me." Real friends give to and receive from each other. The importance of passing on the gift of a relationship with God does not make the other person's gift to us insignificant. Rather, we discover that in introducing another person to God, we increase our own awareness of what knowing God means to us. As we give God away, he gives himself even more to us.

Is all you know about God a miscellaneous collection of trivia, or do you have a living, vital relationship? Only with a vital relationship can you pass on to others the excitement of allowing God to guide your life. Have you reached the point of saying, with Jethro, "I know now that the Lord is greater than any other God because he delivered his people . . ." (Exodus 18:11)?

Strengths and accomplishments:
• Father-in-law to Moses, he came to recognize the one true God
• He was a practical troubleshooter and organizer

Lessons from his life:
• Supervision and administration are a team effort
• God's plan includes all nations

Vital statistics:
• Where: The land of Midian and the Sinai desert
• Occupation: Shepherd, Priest
• Relatives: Daughter: Zipporah. Son-in-law: Moses. Son: Hobab.

Key verse:
"I know now that the Lord is greater than any other God because he delivered his people from the proud and cruel Egyptians" (Exodus 18:11).

Jethro's story is told in Exodus 2:15—3:2; 18:1-27. He is also mentioned in Judges 1:16; 4:11.

4:6 Leprosy was one of the most feared diseases of this time. There was no cure, and a great deal of suffering preceded eventual death. Moses learned that God could cause or cure any kind of problem. Moses saw that God indeed had all power and was commissioning him to exercise that power to lead the Hebrews out of Egypt.

4:10-12 Moses pleaded with God to let him out of his mission. After all, he was not a good speaker and would probably embarrass both himself and God. But God looked at Moses' problem quite differently. All Moses needed was some help, and who better than God could help him say and do the right things. It is easy for us to focus on our weaknesses, but if God asks us to do something, then he will help us get the job done. If the job involves some of our weak areas, then we can trust that he will provide words, strength, courage, and ability where needed.

11"Who makes mouths?" Jehovah asked him. "Isn't it I, the Lord? Who makes a man so that he can speak or not speak, see or not see, hear or not hear? 12Now go ahead and do as I tell you, for I will help you to speak well, and I will tell you what to say."

13But Moses said, "Lord, please! Send someone else."

14Then the Lord became angry. "All right," he said, "your brother Aaron is a good speaker. And he is coming here to look for you, and will be very happy when he finds you. 15So I will tell you what to tell him, and I will help both of you to speak well, and I will tell you what to do. 16He will be your spokesman to the people. And you will be as God to him, telling him what to say. 17And be sure to take your rod along so that you can perform the miracles I have shown you."

Moses and Aaron go to Egypt

18Moses returned home and talked it over with Jethro, his father-in-law. "With your permission," Moses said, "I will go back to Egypt and visit my relatives. I don't even know whether they are still alive."

"Go with my blessing," Jethro replied.

19Before Moses left Midian, Jehovah said to him, "Don't be afraid to return to Egypt, for all those who wanted to kill you are dead."

20So Moses took his wife and sons and put them on a donkey, and returned to the land of Egypt, holding tightly to the "rod of God"!

21Jehovah told him, "When you arrive back in Egypt you are to go to Pharaoh and do the miracles I have shown you, but I will make him stubborn so that he will not let the people go. 22Then you are to tell him, 'Jehovah says, "Israel is my eldest son, 23and I have commanded you to let him go away and worship me, but you have refused: and now see, I will slay your eldest son." ' "

24As Moses and his family were traveling along and had stopped for the night, Jehovah appeared to Moses and threatened to kill him. 25, 26Then Zipporah his wife took a flint knife and cut off the foreskin of her young son's penis, and threw it against Moses' feet, remarking disgustedly, "What a blood-smeared husband you've turned out to be!"

Then God let him alone.

27Now Jehovah said to Aaron, "Go into the wilderness to meet Moses." So Aaron traveled to Mount Horeb, the mountain of God, and met Moses there, and they greeted each other warmly. 28Moses told Aaron what God had said they must do, and what they were to say, and told him about the miracles they must do before Pharaoh.

4:11
Ps 94:9
Isa 35:6
Mt 11:5

4:14
Ex 4:27; 6:7
4:15
Num 22:38
Jer 1:9
4:16
Ex 7:1; 18:19
4:17
Ex 14:16; 17:9

4:18
Ex 3:1; 18:5

4:19
Ex 2:15,23
4:20
Ex 4:17; 18:3
Mt 2:20
4:21
Ex 7:3,13; 9:12
Deut 2:30
Jn 12:40
4:22
Isa 63:17; 64:8
Jer 31:9
Hos 11:1
Rom 9:4
4:23
Ex 5:1; 6:11
7:16; 12:29
4:24
Num 22:22
1 Chron 21:16
4:25,26
Gen 17:14
Josh 5:2

4:27
Ex 4:14

4:28
Ex 4:15,16

4:14 *your brother Aaron,* literally, "your brother the Levite."

4:14 God finally agreed to let Aaron speak for Moses. Moses' feelings of inadequacy were so strong that he could not trust even God's ability to help him. Moses had to deal with his deep sense of inadequacy many times. When we face situations which are too difficult or frightening, we must be willing to let God help us.

4:17–20 Moses clung tightly to the shepherd's rod as he left for Egypt to face the greatest challenge of his life. The rod was his assurance of God's presence and power. In the midst of uncertainty, some people need something to stabilize and reassure them. For assurance in the midst of great trials, God has given promises from his Word and examples from great heroes of faith. Any Christian may cling tightly to these.

4:24 God threatened to kill Moses because Moses had not circumcised his son. Why hadn't Moses done this? Remember that Moses had spent half his life in Pharaoh's palace and half his life in the Midianite desert. He might not have been too familiar with God's laws, especially since all the requirements of God's covenant with Israel (Genesis 17) had not been actively carried out

in over 400 years. In addition, many scholars believe that Moses' wife, due to her background, was opposed to the circumcision.

But Moses could not effectively serve as God's deliverer until he had fulfilled the conditions of God's covenant, and one of those conditions was circumcision. Before they could go any further, Moses and his family had to follow God's commands completely.

In the Old Testament law, failing to circumcise your son was to cut yourself and your family off from God's blessings. Moses would soon learn that disobeying God was even more dangerous than tangling with an Egyptian Pharaoh.

4:25, 26 Why did Zipporah perform the circumcision? Many scholars believe that it may have been Zipporah who, as a Midianite unfamiliar with the circumcision requirement, had persuaded Moses not to circumcise their son. If she prevented the action, now she would have to perform it. It is also possible that Moses fell ill as a result of permitting disobedience and that Zipporah had to perform the circumcision herself to save both her husband and son. This would not have made her happy—hence, her unflattering comment to Moses.

4:29
Ex 3:16
4:30
Ex 4:16,17
4:31
Ex 3:18; 12:27

29So Moses and Aaron returned to Egypt and summoned the elders of the people of Israel to a council meeting. 30Aaron told them what Jehovah had said to Moses, and Moses performed the miracles as they watched. 31Then the elders believed that God had sent them, and when they heard that Jehovah had visited them and had seen their sorrows, and had decided to rescue them, they all rejoiced and bowed their heads and worshiped.

3. God sends Moses to Pharaoh

5:1
Ex 3:18; 4:21
10:9

5 After this presentation to the elders, Moses and Aaron went to see Pharaoh. They told him, "We bring you a message from Jehovah, the God of Israel. He says, 'Let my people go, for they must make a holy pilgrimage out into the wilderness, for a religious feast, to worship me there.' "

5:2
Ex 3:19
2 Kgs 18:35
Job 21:15

2"Is that so?" retorted Pharaoh. "And who is Jehovah, that I should listen to him, and let Israel go? I don't know Jehovah and I will not let Israel go."

5:3
Ex 3:18
Deut 28:21

3But Aaron and Moses persisted. "The God of the Hebrews has met with us," they declared. "We must take a three days' trip into the wilderness and sacrifice there to Jehovah our God; if we don't obey him, we face death by plague or sword."

Bricks without straw

5:4,5
Ex 1:11; 2:11
Jer 38:4
Amos 7:10
5:6
Ex 3:7; 5:10,14
5:7
Gen 11:13

4, 5"Who do you think you are," Pharaoh shouted, "distracting the people from their work? Get back to your jobs!" 6That same day Pharaoh sent this order to the taskmasters and officers he had set over the people of Israel: 7, 8"Don't give the people any more straw for making bricks! However, don't reduce their production quotas by a single brick, for they obviously don't have enough to do or else they wouldn't be talking about going out into the wilderness and sacrificing to their God. 9Load them with work and make them sweat; that will teach them to listen to Moses' and Aaron's lies!"

10, 11So the taskmasters and officers informed the people: "Pharaoh has given orders to furnish you with no more straw. Go and find it wherever you can; but you must produce just as many bricks as before!" 12So the people scattered everywhere to gather straw.

5:14
Ex 5:6
Isa 10:24

13The taskmasters were brutal. "Fulfill your daily quota just as before," they kept demanding. 14Then they whipped the Israeli work-crew bosses. "Why haven't you fulfilled your quotas either yesterday or today?" they roared.

MOSES RETURNS TO EGYPT
God appeared to Moses in a mysterious burning bush on Mount Sinai (also called Mount Horeb). Later Aaron met Moses at the mountain and together they returned to Egypt, a 200-mile trip.

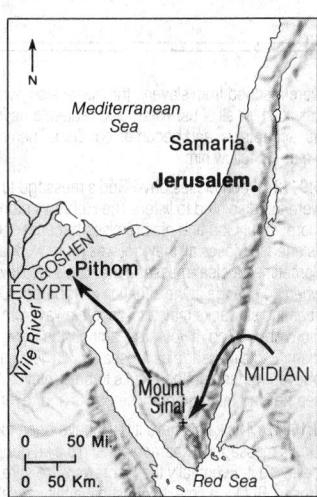

5:1, 2 Pharaoh was familiar with many gods (Egypt was filled with them), but he had never heard of Jehovah. And if Jehovah was the God of the Hebrew slaves, he couldn't be too powerful, Pharaoh thought. At first then, Pharaoh was not at all concerned that Moses' message was from Jehovah, for he had not yet seen any evidence of his power.

5:3 Pharaoh would not listen to Moses and Aaron because he did not know or respect God. People who do not know God may not listen to his Word or his messengers. Like Moses and Aaron, we need to persist. When others reject you or your faith, don't be surprised or discouraged. Continue to tell them about God, trusting him to open minds and soften stubborn hearts.

5:4–9 Moses and Aaron took their message to Pharaoh just as God directed. The unhappy result was harder work and more oppression for the Hebrews. Sometimes hardship comes as a result of obeying God. Are you following God, but still suffering—or suffering even worse than before? If your life is miserable, don't assume you have fallen out of God's favor. You may be suffering for doing good in an evil world.

5:7, 8 Mixing straw with mud made bricks stronger and more durable. Pharaoh had supplied the slaves with straw, but now he made them find their own straw and increase their production of bricks as well.

15These foremen went to Pharaoh and pleaded with him. "Don't treat us like this," they begged. 16"We are given no straw and told to make as many bricks as before, and we are beaten for something that isn't our fault—it is the fault of your taskmasters for making such unreasonable demands."

17But Pharaoh replied, "You don't have enough work, or else you wouldn't be saying, 'Let us go and sacrifice to Jehovah.' 18Get back to work. No straw will be given you, and you must deliver the regular quota of bricks."

5:17
Ex 5:8

19Then the foremen saw that they were indeed in a bad situation. 20When they met Moses and Aaron waiting for them outside the palace, as they came out from their meeting with Pharaoh, 21they swore at them. "May God judge you for making us stink before Pharaoh and his people," they said, "and for giving them an excuse to kill us."

5:21
Gen 16:5; 34:30
Ex 14:11; 15:24

22Then Moses went back to the Lord. "Lord," he protested, "how can you mistreat your own people like this? Why did you ever send me, if you were going to do this to them? 23Ever since I gave Pharaoh your message, he has only been more and more brutal to them, and you have not delivered them at all!"

5:22
Num 11:11
Jer 4:10; 20:7

5:23
Ex 3:8,19

The Hebrews refuse to listen to Moses

6 "Now you will see what I shall do to Pharaoh," the Lord told Moses. "For he must be forced to let my people go; he will not only let them go, but will *drive them out of his land!* 2, 3I am Jehovah, the Almighty God who appeared to Abraham, Isaac, and Jacob—though I did not reveal my name, Jehovah, to them. 4And I entered into a solemn covenant with them; under its terms I promised to give them and their descendants the land of Canaan where they were living. 5And now I have heard the groanings of the people of Israel, in slavery now to the Egyptians, and I remember my promise.

6:1
Ex 3:19,20
11:1; 12:31

6:2,3
Gen 15:7
Ex 3:14; 14:18
Ps 83:18
Isa 42:8; 52:6
Ezek 37:6,13
Jn 8:58

6:4
Gen 15:18

6:5
Ex 2:24
Deut 6:12
Ps 105:8

6"Therefore tell the descendants of Israel that I will use my mighty power and perform great miracles to deliver them from slavery, and make them free. 7And I will accept them as my people and be their God. And they shall know that I am Jehovah their God who has rescued them from the Egyptians. 8, 9I will bring them into the land I promised to give to Abraham, Isaac, and Jacob. It shall belong to my people."

6:6
Ex 3:17; 7:4
Deut 26:8

6:7
Ex 16:12
Deut 4:20
Isa 60:16

6:8
Num 14:30
Josh 24:13

So Moses told the people what God had said, but they wouldn't listen any more because they were too dispirited after the tragic consequence of what he had said before.

10Now the Lord spoke to Moses again and told him, 11"Go back again to Pharaoh and tell him that he *must* let the people of Israel go."

6:11
Ex 5:1; 7:2

6:8, 9 *because they were too dispirited after the tragic consequence of what he had said before,* literally, "because of their broken spirit and the cruel bondage."

5:22, 23 Pharaoh had just increased the Hebrews' workload. Moses protested that God was mistreating his people by not delivering them. He expected faster results and fewer problems. When God is at work, however, suffering, setbacks, and hardship may still occur. In James 1:2–4, we read that we should be happy when difficulties come our way. Problems exercise our patience and character by teaching us to (1) trust God to do what is best for us, (2) look for ways to honor God in our present situation, (3) remember that God will not abandon us, and (4) watch for God's plan in our life.

6:6 Small problems only need small answers. But when we face great problems, God has an opportunity to exercise his great power. As the Hebrews' troubles grew steadily worse, God planned to intervene with his mighty power and perform great miracles to deliver them. How big are your problems? Big problems put you in a perfect position to watch God give big answers.

6:6–8 God's promises in these verses were fulfilled to the letter when the Hebrews left Egypt. He delivered them from slavery, became their God, and accepted them as his people. Then he led them toward the land he had promised them. When the Hebrews

were rescued from slavery, they were also portraying the drama of salvation for all of us. When God redeems us from sin he delivers us, accepts us, and becomes our God. Then he leads us to a new life as we follow him.

6:9–12 When Moses gave God's message to the people, they were too dispirited to listen. The Hebrews didn't want to hear any more about God and his promises because the last time they listened to Moses all they got was more work and greater suffering. Sometimes a clear message from God is followed by a period when no change in the situation is apparent. During that time, seeming setbacks may turn people away from wanting to hear more about God. If you are leading, don't give up. Keep bringing them God's message as Moses did. By focusing on the God to be obeyed rather than the results to be achieved, good leaders can see beyond the temporary setbacks and reversals.

6:10–12 Think how hard it must have been for Moses to bring God's message to Pharaoh when his own people had trouble believing it. Eventually the Hebrews were sure that God had sent Moses. But for a time, he must have felt very alone. Moses did obey God, however, and what a difference it made! When the chances for success appear slim, remember that anyone can obey

6:12
Ex 4:10; 6:30
[12]"But look," Moses objected, "my own people won't even listen to me any more; how can I expect Pharaoh to? I'm no orator!"

[13]Then the Lord ordered Moses and Aaron to return to the people of Israel and to Pharaoh, king of Egypt, demanding that the people be permitted to leave.

A genealogy

6:14
Gen 46:9
Num 26:5
[14]These are the names of the heads of the clans of the various tribes of Israel: The sons of Reuben, Israel's oldest son: Hanoch, Pallu, Hezron, Carmi.

6:15
Gen 46:10
Num 26:12
[15]The heads of the clans of the tribe of Simeon: Jemuel, Jamin, Ohad, Jachin, Zohar, Shaul (whose mother was a Canaanite).

6:16
Gen 46:11
Num 3:18
1 Chron 6:1,16
[16]These are the names of the heads of the clans of the tribe of Levi, in the order of their ages: Gershon, Kohath, Merari. (Levi lived 137 years.)

6:17
Num 3:18-20
[17]The sons of Gershon were: Libni, Shime-i, (and their clans).

6:18
Num 3:25-30
1 Chron 6:17
[18]The sons of Kohath: Amram, Izhar, Hebron, Uzziel. (Kohath lived 133 years.)

6:19
Num 3:33-35
[19]The sons of Merari: Mahli, Mushi.

The above are the families of the Levites, listed according to their ages.

6:20
Ex 2:1,2
Num 1:7; 2:3; 3:2
Num 26:59
[20]And Amram married Jochebed, his father's sister; and Aaron and Moses were their sons.

Amram lived to the age of 137.

6:21
Num 16:1; 26:10
[21]The sons of Izhar: Korah, Nepheg, Zichri.

6:22
Lev 10:4
[22]The sons of Uzziel: Misha-el, Elzaphan, Sithri.

6:23
Ex 24:1
Ruth 4:19,20
Lk 1:5
[23]Aaron married Elisheba, the daughter of Amminadab and sister of Nahshon. Their children were: Nadab, Abihu, Eleazar, Ithamar.

6:24
Ex 6:21
Num 16:1
[24]The sons of Korah: Assir, Elkanah, Abiasaph.

These are the families within the clan of Korah.

6:25
Num 25:7,11
Josh 22:13
[25]Aaron's son Eleazar married one of the daughters of Puti-el, and Phinehas was one of his children. These are all the names of the heads of the clans of the Levites, and the families within the clans.

6:26
Ex 6:13
Josh 24:5
[26]Aaron and Moses, included in that list, are the same Aaron and Moses to whom Jehovah said, "Lead all the people of Israel out of the land of Egypt," [27]and who

6:28,29
Ex 6:2; 7:16
went to Pharaoh to ask permission to lead the people from the land, [28, 29]and to whom the Lord said, "I am Jehovah. Go in and give Pharaoh the message I have given you."

6:30
Ex 4:10; 6:12
[30]This is that Moses who argued with the Lord, "I can't do it; I'm no speaker—why should Pharaoh listen to *me?*"

Moses' rod becomes a serpent

7:1
Ex 4:16; 18:19
7 Then the Lord said to Moses, "See, I have appointed you as my ambassador to Pharaoh, and your brother Aaron shall be your spokesman. [2]Tell Aaron

7:3
Ex 4:21; 8:19
9:16,34
everything I say to you, and he will announce it to Pharaoh, demanding that the people of Israel be allowed to leave Egypt. [3]But I will cause Pharaoh to stubbornly

7:4
Ex 11:9; 12:51
refuse, and I will multiply my miracles in the land of Egypt. [4]Yet even then Pharaoh won't listen to you; so I will crush Egypt with a final major disaster and

7:5
Ex 8:10,19
then lead my people out. [5]The Egyptians will find out that I am indeed God when I show them my power and force them to let my people go."

7:7
Deut 31:2; 34:7
Acts 7:23,30
[6]So Moses and Aaron did as the Lord commanded them. [7]Moses was eighty years old and Aaron eighty-three at this time of their confrontation with Pharaoh.

7:9
Ex 4:3
Isa 7:11
[8]Then the Lord said to Moses and Aaron, [9]"Pharaoh will demand that you show

6:16 *in the order of their ages*, literally, "according to their generations." So also in verse 19. **6:20** *Amram.* See verse 18.

God when the task is easy and everyone is behind it. Only those with persistent faith can obey when the task seems impossible.

7:1 God called Moses his ambassador. An ambassador represents another country, another type of people, and often another point of view. We are each God's ambassadors—representing to the world that Christians are a different people with a different lifestyle. Much of the world knows nothing about God except what it sees in the lives of God's people. What kind of God would they think you represent? Taking note of how you come across to others gives you a good indication of how well you are representing God.

him a miracle to prove that God has sent you; when he does, Aaron is to throw down his rod, and it will become a serpent."

¹⁰So Moses and Aaron went in to see Pharaoh, and performed the miracle, as Jehovah had instructed them—Aaron threw down his rod before Pharaoh and his court, and it became a serpent. ¹¹Then Pharaoh called in his sorcerers—the magicians of Egypt—and they were able to do the same thing with their magical arts! ¹²Their rods became serpents, too! But Aaron's serpent swallowed their serpents! ¹³Pharaoh's heart was still hard and stubborn, and he wouldn't listen, just as the Lord had predicted. ¹⁴The Lord pointed this out to Moses, that Pharaoh's heart had been unmoved, and that he would continue to refuse to let the people go.

7:11
Gen 41:8
Ex 8:7,18
Dan 2:4
2 Tim 3:8,9
7:12
Ex 8:19
7:13
Ex 4:21
Deut 2:30
Zech 7:11
7:14
Ex 7:4; 8:15

4. Plagues strike Egypt
The river turns to blood

¹⁵"Nevertheless," the Lord said, "go back to Pharaoh in the morning, to be there as he goes down to the river. Stand beside the river bank and meet him there, holding in your hand the rod that turned into a serpent. ¹⁶Say to him, 'Jehovah, the God of the Hebrews, has sent me back to demand that you let his people go to worship him in the wilderness. You wouldn't listen before, ¹⁷and now the Lord says this: "You are going to find out that I am God. For I have instructed Moses to hit the water of the Nile with his rod, and the river will turn to blood! ¹⁸The fish will die and the river will stink, so that the Egyptians will be unwilling to drink it." ' "

¹⁹Then the Lord instructed Moses: "Tell Aaron to point his rod toward the waters of Egypt: all its rivers, canals, marshes, and reservoirs, and even the water stored in bowls and pots in the homes will turn to blood."

²⁰So Moses and Aaron did as the Lord commanded them. As Pharaoh and all of his officials watched, Aaron hit the surface of the Nile with the rod, and the river turned to blood. ²¹The fish died and the water became so foul that the Egyptians couldn't drink it; and there was blood throughout the land of Egypt. ²²But then the magicians of Egypt used their secret arts and they, too, turned water into blood; so Pharaoh's heart remained hard and stubborn, and he wouldn't listen to Moses and Aaron, just as the Lord had predicted, ²³and he returned to his palace, unimpressed. ²⁴Then the Egyptians dug wells along the river bank to get drinking water, for they couldn't drink from the river.

²⁵A week went by.

7:15
Ex 2:5; 8:20
7:16
Ex 4:23; 8:1
7:17
Ex 7:20
Rev 11:6; 16:4-6

7:19
Ex 8:5,16; 9:22

7:20
Ps 78:44; 105:28, 29

7:22
Ex 8:7

7:23
Ex 9:21

Hordes of frogs

8 Then the Lord said to Moses, "Go in again to Pharaoh and tell him, 'Jehovah says, "Let my people go and worship me. ²If you refuse, I will send vast hordes of frogs across your land from one border to the other. ³, ⁴The Nile River will

8:1
Ex 5:1
8:3
Ps 105:30

7:11 How were these sorcerers and magicians able to duplicate Moses' miracles? Some of their feats involved trickery or illusion. But some may have used Satanic power, since worshiping gods of the underworld was part of their religion. Ironically, whenever the sorcerers duplicated one of Moses' plagues, it only made matters worse. If the magicians had been as powerful as God, they would have reversed the plagues, not added to them.

7:12 God performed a miracle by turning Aaron's rod into a serpent. But Pharaoh's magicians were able to duplicate the act through trickery or sorcery. Although miracles can help us believe, it is dangerous to rely on them alone. Satan can imitate some parts of God's work and lead people astray. Pharaoh focused on the miracle rather than the message. We can avoid this error by letting the Word of God be the basis of our faith. No miracle from God would endorse any message that is contrary to the teachings of his Word.

7:17 God dramatically turned the waters of the Nile into blood to show Pharaoh who he was. Do you sometimes wish for miraculous signs so you can be sure about God? God has given you the miracle of eternal life through your faith in him, something Pharaoh

never obtained. This is a quiet miracle and, while less evident right now, is just as extraordinary as water turned to blood. The desire for spectacular signs may cause us to ignore the more subtle miracles God is working every day.

7:20 Egypt was a large country, but the bulk of the population was centered along the banks of the Nile River. This 3,000-mile waterway was truly a river of life for Egyptians. It made life possible in a land that was mostly desert by providing water for drinking, farming, bathing, and fishing. Egyptian society was a ribbon of civilization lining the banks of this life source, rarely reaching very far into the surrounding desert. Without the Nile's water, Egypt could not have existed. Imagine Pharaoh's dismay when Moses turned this sacred river to blood!

8:3ff Moses predicted that every house in Egypt would be filled with frogs. The poor of Egypt lived in small, mud-brick houses of one or two rooms with palm-trunk roofs. The homes of the rich, however, were often two or three stories high, surrounded by landscaped gardens and enclosed by a high wall. Servants lived and worked on the first floor while the family occupied the upper floors. Thus, if the frogs got into the royal bedrooms, they had

swarm with them, and they will come out into your houses, even into your bedrooms and right into your beds! Every home in Egypt will be filled with them. They will fill your ovens and your kneading bowls; you and your people will be immersed in them!" ' "

8:5
Ex 7:19; 8:16

5Then the Lord said to Moses, "Instruct Aaron to point the rod toward all the rivers, streams, and pools of Egypt, so that there will be frogs in every corner of the land." 6Aaron did, and frogs covered the nation. 7But the magicians did the same with their secret arts, and they, too, caused frogs to come up upon the land.

8:6
Ps 78:45;
105:30

8:7
Ex 7:11; 8:18

8Then Pharaoh summoned Moses and Aaron and begged, "Plead with God to take the frogs away, and I will let the people go and sacrifice to him."

8:8
Ex 5:2; 9:28
10:10,17

9"Be so kind as to tell me when you want them to go," Moses said, "and I will pray that the frogs will die at the time you specify, everywhere except in the river."

10"Do it tomorrow," Pharaoh said.

8:10
Ex 9:14,29
15:11
Deut 4:35
Ps 83:18
Isa 46:9

"All right," Moses replied, "it shall be as you have said; then you will know that there is no one like the Lord our God. 11All the frogs will be destroyed, except those in the river."

8:12
Ex 8:30; 9:33;
10:18

12So Moses and Aaron went out from the presence of Pharaoh, and Moses pleaded with the Lord concerning the frogs he had sent. 13And the Lord did as Moses promised—dead frogs covered the countryside and filled the nation's homes. 14They were piled into great heaps, making a terrible stench throughout the land. 15But when Pharaoh saw that the frogs were gone, he hardened his heart and refused to let the people go, just as the Lord had predicted.

8:15
Ex 7:22; 9:34
14:5
Prov 29:1
Eccles 8:11

The dust becomes lice

8:16
Ex 8:5; 9:22

16Then the Lord said to Moses, "Tell Aaron to strike the dust with his rod, and it will become lice, throughout all the land of Egypt." 17So Moses and Aaron did as God commanded, and suddenly lice infested the entire nation, covering the Egyptians and their animals. 18Then the magicians tried to do the same thing with their secret arts, but this time they failed.

8:17
Ps 105:31

8:18
Ex 7:11; 9:11

8:19
Ex 7:5; 8:15
1 Sam 6:9

19"This is the finger of God," they exclaimed to Pharaoh. But Pharaoh's heart was hard and stubborn, and he wouldn't listen to them, just as the Lord had predicted.

Swarms of flies

8:20
Ex 7:15

20Next the Lord told Moses, "Get up early in the morning and meet Pharaoh as he comes out to the river to bathe, and say to him, 'Jehovah says, "Let my people go and worship me. 21If you refuse I will send swarms of flies throughout Egypt. Your homes will be filled with them and the ground will be covered with them. 22But it will be very different in the land of Goshen where the Israelis live. No flies will be there; thus you will know that I am the Lord God of all the earth, 23for I will make a distinction between your people and my people. All this will happen tomorrow." ' "

8:22
Ex 8:10; 9:4
10:23

8:24
Ps 78:45
105:31

24And Jehovah did as he had said, so that there were terrible swarms of flies in Pharaoh's palace and in every home in Egypt.

8:25
Gen 46:34
Ex 8:8; 10:8

25Pharaoh hastily summoned Moses and Aaron and said, "All right, go ahead and sacrifice to your God, but do it here in the land. Don't go out into the wilderness."

---

infiltrated even the upper floors. There would be no place in Egypt that was safe from them.

8:15 After repeated warnings, Pharaoh still refused to obey God. His stubborn disobedience brought suffering upon himself and his entire country. Avoid disobedience, because the consequences may spill over onto those who are closest to us.

8:19 Some people think, "If only I could see a miracle, I could believe in God." God gave Pharaoh just such an opportunity. When lice infested Egypt, even the magicians agreed that this was God's work—but Pharaoh refused to believe. He was stubborn, and

stubbornness can blind a person to the truth. Rid stubbornness from your life and you may be surprised by the evidences of God's hand in your life that you begin to see around you.

8:25–29 Pharaoh wanted a compromise. "All right, sacrifice, but do it here," he said. Then he said, "Go, but don't go far away." But God's condition was firm: the Hebrews had to leave Egypt. Sometimes others will want to compromise on the commands God gives believers. But commitment and obedience to God cannot be negotiated. When it comes to obeying God, half-way obedience won't do.

26But Moses replied, "That won't do! Our sacrifices to God are hated by the Egyptians, and if we do this right here before their eyes, they will kill us. 27We must take a three-day trip into the wilderness and sacrifice there to Jehovah our God, as he commanded us."

8:26
Ex 3:18; 9:3
8:27
Ex 10:26

28"All right, go ahead," Pharaoh replied, "but don't go too far away. Now, hurry and plead with God for me."

8:28
Ex 8:8; 9:28
1 Kgs 13:6

29"Yes," Moses said, "I will ask him to cause the swarms of flies to disappear. But I am warning you that you must never again lie to us by promising to let the people go and then changing your mind."

30So Moses went out from Pharaoh and asked the Lord to get rid of the flies. 31, 32And the Lord did as Moses asked and caused the swarms to disappear, so that not one remained. But Pharaoh hardened his heart again and did not let the people go!

8:30
Ex 8:12
8:31,32
Ex 7:13; 9:12

Animals destroyed

9 "Go back to Pharaoh," the Lord commanded Moses, "and tell him, 'Jehovah, the God of the Hebrews, demands that you let his people go to sacrifice to him. 2If you refuse, 3the power of God will send a deadly plague to destroy your cattle, horses, donkeys, camels, flocks, and herds. 4But the plague will affect only the cattle of Egypt; none of the Israeli herds and flocks will even be touched!' "

9:1
Ex 8:1; 10:3
9:3
Ex 7:4; 9:18
9:4
Ex 8:22; 9:26

5The Lord announced that the plague would begin the very next day, 6and it did. The next morning all the cattle of the Egyptians began dying, but not one of the Israeli herds was even sick. 7Pharaoh sent to see whether it was true that none of the Israeli cattle were dead, yet when he found out that it was so, even then his mind remained unchanged and he refused to let the people go.

9:5
Ex 8:23; 10:4
9:7
Ex 7:14; 8:32
9:35

Ashes cause boils

8Then Jehovah said to Moses and Aaron, "Take ashes from the kiln. Moses, toss it into the sky as Pharaoh watches. 9It will spread like fine dust over all the land of Egypt and cause boils to break out upon people and animals alike, throughout the land."

9:8
Ex 8:16
9:9
Lev 13:18
Rev 16:2

10So they took ashes from the kiln and went to Pharaoh; as he watched, Moses tossed it toward the sky, and it became boils that broke out on men and animals alike throughout all Egypt. 11And the magicians couldn't stand before Moses because of the boils, for the boils appeared upon them too. 12But Jehovah hardened Pharaoh in his stubbornness, so that he refused to listen, just as the Lord had predicted to Moses.

9:11
Ex 8:18
9:12
Ex 7:13; 10:1

A terrible hail storm

13Then the Lord said to Moses, "Get up early in the morning and stand before Pharaoh and tell him, 'Jehovah the God of the Hebrews says, "Let my people go to worship me. 14This time I am going to send a plague that will really speak to you and to your servants and to all the Egyptian people, and prove to you there is no

9:13
Ex 8:20
9:14
Ex 8:10; 5:11

9:1 This was the fifth time God sent Moses back to Pharaoh with the demand, "Let my people go!" Moses may have been tired and discouraged by this time, but God kept sending him back and Moses continued to obey. Is there a difficult conflict you must face again and again? Don't give up when you know what is right to do. As Moses discovered, persistence will be rewarded.

9:6 As each gloomy plague descended upon the land, the Egyptian people realized how powerless their own gods were to stop it. Hapi, the "powerful" god of the Nile River, could not prevent the waters from turning to blood. Hathor, the crafty cow-goddess, was helpless as Egyptian cattle died in droves. Amon-Ra, the sun god and chief of the Egyptian gods, could not stop an eerie darkness from covering the land for three full days. God was proving to both the Hebrews and the Egyptians that he alone was the living and all-powerful God.

9:7 The Egyptian gods were (1) centered around nonpersonal images like the sun or the river, (2) many in number, and (3) worshiped along with many other gods. But the God of the Hebrews was (1) a living personal Being, (2) the only true God, and (3) the only God who should be worshiped.

9:12 God gave Pharaoh many opportunities to heed Moses' warnings. But finally God seemed to say, "All right, Pharaoh, have it your way," and Pharaoh's heart became permanently hardened. Did God intentionally harden Pharaoh's heart and overrule his free will? No, he simply confirmed that Pharaoh freely chose a life of resisting God. Similarly, after a lifetime of resisting God, you may find it impossible to turn to him. Don't wait until "just the right time" before turning to God. Do it now while you still have the chance. If you continually ignore God's voice, eventually you will be unable to hear it at all.

9:15
Ex 11:6; 14:28
9:16
Ex 14:4,17
18:11
Rom 9:17
9:17
Job 9:4; 15:25
Isa 37:23
9:18
Ex 9:5; 10:4
9:20
Prov 13:13
Heb 11:7
9:22
Ex 8:5
9:23
Ex 19:16
Josh 10:11
Ps 18:13; 78:47
105:32
Rev 8:3; 16:21

other God in all the earth. 15I could have killed you all by now, 16but I didn't, for I wanted to demonstrate my power to you and to all the earth. 17So you still think you are so great, do you, and defy my power, and refuse to let my people go? 18Well, tomorrow about this time I will send a hailstorm across the nation such as there has never been since Egypt was founded! 19Quick! Bring in your cattle from the fields, for every man and animal left out in the fields will die beneath the hail!'." "

20Some of the Egyptians, terrified by this threat, brought their cattle and slaves in from the fields; 21but those who had no regard for the word of Jehovah left them out in the storm.

22Then Jehovah said to Moses, "Point your hand toward heaven and cause the hail to fall throughout all Egypt, upon the people, animals, and trees."

23So Moses held out his hand, and the Lord sent thunder and hail and lightning. 24It was terrible beyond description. Never in all the history of Egypt had there been a storm like that. 25All Egypt lay in ruins. Everything left in the fields, men and animals alike, was killed, and the trees were shattered and the crops were

THE PLAGUES	Reference	Plague	What Happened	Result
	7:14–24	Blood	Fish die, the river smells, the people are without water	Pharaoh's magicians duplicate the miracle by "secret arts" so Pharaoh is unmoved
	8:1–15	Frogs	Frogs come up from the water and completely cover the land	Again Pharaoh's magicians duplicate the miracle by sorcery and Pharaoh is unmoved.
	8:16–19	Lice	All the dust of Egypt becomes a massive swarm of lice	Magicians are unable to duplicate this and say it is the "finger of God," But Pharaoh's heart remains hard
	8:20–32	Flies	Swarms of flies cover the land	Pharaoh promises to let the Hebrews go, but then hardens his heart and refuses
	9:1–7	Livestock	All the Egyptian livestock dies—but none of Israel's is even sick	Pharaoh still refuses to let the people go
	9:8–12	Boils	Horrible boils break out on everyone in Egypt	Magicians cannot respond as they are struck down with boils as well—Pharaoh refuses to listen
	9:13–35	Hail	Hailstorms kill all the slaves and animals left out or unprotected and strip or destroy almost every plant	Pharaoh admits his sin, but then changes his mind and refuses to let Israel go
	10:1–20	Locusts	Locusts cover Egypt and eat everything left by the hail	Everyone advises Pharaoh to let the Hebrews go, but God hardens Pharaoh's heart and he refuses
	10:21–29	Darkness	Total darkness covers Egypt for three days so no one can even move—except the Hebrews, who have light as usual	Pharaoh again promises to let Israel go, but again changes his mind
	11:1—12:33	Death of Firstborn	The firstborn of all the people and cattle of Egypt die—but Israel is spared	Pharaoh and the Egyptians urge Israel to leave quickly; but after they are gone, Pharaoh again changes his mind and chases after them

destroyed. 26The only spot in all Egypt without hail that day was the land of Goshen where the people of Israel lived.

9:26
Ex 8:22; 10:23

27Then Pharaoh sent for Moses and Aaron. "I finally see my fault," he confessed. "Jehovah is right, and I and my people have been wrong all along. 28Beg God to end this terrifying thunder and hail, and I will let you go at once."

9:27
2 Chron 12:6
Ps 129:4

9:28
Ex 8:8; 10:17

29"All right," Moses replied, "as soon as I have left the city I will spread out my hands to the Lord, and the thunder and hail will stop. This will prove to you that the earth is controlled by Jehovah. 30But as for you and your officials, I know that even yet you will not obey him." 31All the flax and barley were knocked down and destroyed (for the barley was ripe, and the flax was in bloom), 32but the wheat and the emmer were not destroyed, for they were not yet out of the ground.

9:29
Deut 10:14
Ps 24:1
1 Cor 10:26,28

9:30
Ex 8:29; 11:9

33So Moses left Pharaoh and went out of the city and lifted his hands to heaven to the Lord, and the thunder and hail stopped, and the rain ceased pouring down. 34When Pharaoh saw this, he and his officials sinned yet more by their stubborn refusal to do what they had promised; 35so Pharaoh refused to let the people leave, just as the Lord had predicted to Moses.

9:34
Ex 8:15; 11:9

Locusts cover the land

10 Then the Lord said to Moses, "Go back again and make your demand upon Pharaoh; but I have hardened him and his officials, so that I can do more miracles demonstrating my power. 2What stories you can tell your children and grandchildren about the incredible things I am doing in Egypt! Tell them what fools I made of the Egyptians, and how I proved to you that I am Jehovah."

10:1
Ex 4:21; 7:13
14:17

10:2
Ex 13:8
Deut 4:9
Ps 44:1

3So Moses and Aaron requested another audience with Pharaoh and told him: "Jehovah, the God of the Hebrews, asks, 'How long will you refuse to submit to me? Let my people go so they can worship me. 4, 5If you refuse, tomorrow I will cover the entire nation with a thick layer of locusts so that you won't even be able to see the ground, and they will finish destroying everything that escaped the hail. 6They will fill your palace, and the homes of your officials, and all the houses of Egypt. Never in the history of Egypt has there been a plague like this will be!' " Then Moses stalked out.

10:3
Ex 4:23; 16:28

10:4,5
Ex 9:18; 11:4,5
Joel 1:4; 2:25

7The court officials now came to Pharaoh and asked him, "Are you going to destroy us completely? Don't you know even yet that all Egypt lies in ruins? Let the *men* go and serve Jehovah their God!"

10:7
Ex 5:1; 12:33

8So Moses and Aaron were brought back to Pharaoh. "All right, go and serve Jehovah your God!" he said. "But just who is it you want to go?"

10:8
Ex 5:1; 8:25

9"We will go with our sons and daughters, flocks and herds," Moses replied. "We will take everything with us; for we must all join in the holy pilgrimage."

10:9
Ex 12:37

10"In the name of God I will not let you take your little ones!" Pharaoh retorted. "I can see your plot! 11Never! You that are men, go and serve Jehovah, for that is what you asked for." And they were driven out from Pharaoh's presence.

10:10
Gen 50:8
Ex 12:31

10:11
Ex 10:28; 11:8

12Then the Lord said to Moses, "Hold out your hand over the land of Egypt to bring locusts—they will cover the land and eat everything the hail has left."

10:12
Ex 7:19; 9:22

13So Moses lifted his rod and Jehovah caused an east wind to blow all that day and night; and when it was morning, the east wind had brought the locusts. 14And the locusts covered the land of Egypt from border to border; it was the worst locust plague in all Egyptian history; and there will never again be another like it. 15For the locusts covered the face of the earth and blotted out the sun so that the land was darkened; and they ate every bit of vegetation the hail had left; there remained not one green thing—not a tree, not a plant throughout all the land of Egypt.

10:13
Ps 78:46
105:34

10:14
Joel 1:4,7
2:1,11

10:15
Ex 10:5
Ps 78:46
105:35

9:27-34 After promising to let the Hebrews go, Pharaoh immediately broke his promise and brought even more trouble upon the land. His actions revealed that his repentance was not real. We do damage to ourselves and to others if we pretend to change but don't mean it.

10:2 What stories Moses had to tell! Living out one of the greatest dramas in biblical history, Moses witnessed events few people would ever see. God told Moses that his miraculous experiences with Pharaoh should be retold to his descendants. It is important to tell our children about God's work in our past and to help them see what he is doing right now. What are the turning points in your life where God intervened? What is God doing for you now? The stories you share will lay the foundations of your children's belief in God.

10:16
Ex 8:8; 9:27

10:17
Ex 8:28
Num 21:7
1 Sam 15:25

10:18
Ex 8:30

10:20
Ex 4:21; 9:12
11:10

16Then Pharaoh sent an urgent call for Moses and Aaron and said to them, "I confess my sin against Jehovah your God, and against you. 17Forgive my sin only this once, and beg Jehovah your God to take away this deadly plague. I solemnly promise that I will let you go as soon as the locusts are gone."

18So Moses went out from Pharaoh and entreated the Lord, 19and he sent a very strong west wind that blew the locusts out into the Red Sea, so that there remained not one locust in all the land of Egypt! 20But the Lord hardened Pharaoh's heart and he did not let the people go.

Three days of darkness

10:21
Ex 9:22
Deut 28:29

10:22
Ex 20:21
Ps 105:28
Joel 2:2

10:23
Ex 8:22; 9:4
14:20

10:24
Ex 8:28; 10:8

10:26
Ex 10:9; 12:32

10:27
Ex 4:21; 9:12
11:10; 14:4

10:28
Ex 10:11

10:29
Heb 11:27

21Then Jehovah said to Moses, "Lift your hands to heaven, and darkness without a ray of light will descend upon the land of Egypt." 22So Moses did, and there was thick darkness over all the land for three days. 23During all that time the people scarcely moved—but all the people of Israel had light as usual.

24Then Pharaoh called for Moses and said, "Go and worship Jehovah—but let your flocks and herds stay here; you can even take your children with you."

25"No," Moses said, "we must take our flocks and herds for sacrifices and burnt offerings to Jehovah our God. 26Not a hoof shall be left behind; for we must have sacrifices for the Lord our God, and we do not know what he will choose until we get there."

27So the Lord hardened Pharaoh's heart and he would not let them go.

28"Get out of here and don't let me ever see you again," Pharaoh shouted at Moses. "The day you do, you shall die."

29"Very well," Moses replied. "I will never see you again."

The firstborn will die

11:1
Ex 3:20,21
12:31

11:2
Ex 12:35

11 Then the Lord said to Moses, "I will send just one more disaster on Pharaoh and his land, and after that he will let you go; in fact, he will be so anxious to get rid of you that he will practically throw you out of the country. 2Tell all the men and women of Israel to ask their Egyptian neighbors for gold and silver jewelry."

11:3
Deut 34:10-12

3(For God caused the Egyptians to be very favorable to the people of Israel, and Moses was a very great man in the land of Egypt and was revered by Pharaoh's officials and the Egyptian people alike.)

11:4
Ex 12:29
Amos 4:10

11:5
Ex 4:23; 12:12
13:15

11:6
Ex 12:30
Amos 5:17

11:7
Ex 8:22; 10:23

11:8
Ex 12:31
Heb 11:27

4Now Moses announced to Pharaoh, "Jehovah says, 'About midnight I will pass through Egypt. 5And all the oldest sons shall die in every family in Egypt, from the oldest child of Pharaoh, heir to his throne, to the oldest child of his lowliest slave; and even the firstborn of the animals. 6The wail of death will resound throughout the entire land of Egypt; never before has there been such anguish, and it will never be again.

7" 'But not a dog shall move his tongue against any of the people of Israel, nor shall any of their animals die. Then you will know that Jehovah makes a distinction between Egyptians and Israelis.' 8All these officials of yours will come running to me, bowing low and begging, 'Please leave at once, and take all your people with you.' Only then will I go!" Then, red-faced with anger, Moses stomped from the palace.

11:4 *to Pharaoh,* implied.   **11:8** *Moses stomped from the palace,* literally, "he went out from Pharaoh."

10:27, 28 Why was Pharaoh so reluctant to let the people go? The Hebrews were Egypt's free labor—the builders of their great cities. As Egypt's leader, Pharaoh would not easily let such a great resource go.

11:7 Moses told Pharaoh that God made a distinction between the Hebrews and the Egyptians. At this time the distinction was very clear in God's mind: he knew the Hebrews would become his chosen people. The distinction was taking shape in Moses' mind also. But the Hebrews still saw the distinction only in terms of slave and free. Later, when they were in the desert, God would teach them the laws, principles, and values that would make them distinct as his people. It is comforting to know that God sees us in terms of what we will become and not just what we are right now.

9The Lord had told Moses, "Pharaoh won't listen, and this will give me the opportunity of doing mighty miracles to demonstrate my power." 10So, although Moses and Aaron did these miracles right before Pharaoh's eyes, the Lord hardened his heart so that he wouldn't let the people leave the land.

5. The Passover

12 Then the Lord said to Moses and Aaron, 2"From now on, this month will be the first and most important of the entire year. 3, 4Annually, on the tenth day of this month (announce this to all the people of Israel) each family shall get a lamb (or, if a family is small, let it share the lamb with another small family in the neighborhood; whether to share in this way depends on the size of the families). 5This animal shall be a year-old male, either a sheep or a goat, without any defects.

6"On the evening of the fourteenth day of this month, all these lambs shall be killed, 7and their blood shall be placed on the two side-frames of the door of every home and on the panel above the door. Use the blood of the lamb eaten in that home. 8Everyone shall eat roast lamb that night, with unleavened bread and bitter herbs. 9The meat must not be eaten raw or boiled, but roasted, including the head, legs, heart, and liver. 10Don't eat any of it the next day; if all is not eaten that night, burn what is left.

11"Eat it with your traveling clothes on, prepared for a long journey, wearing your walking shoes and carrying your walking sticks in your hands; eat it hurriedly. This observance shall be called the Lord's Passover. 12For I will pass through the land of Egypt tonight and kill all the oldest sons and firstborn male animals in all the land of Egypt, and execute judgment upon all the gods of Egypt—for I am Jehovah. 13The blood you have placed on the doorposts will be proof that you obey me, and when I see the blood I will pass over you and I will not destroy your firstborn children when I smite the land of Egypt.

14"You shall celebrate this event each year (this is a permanent law) to remind you of this fatal night. 15The celebration shall last seven days. For that entire period

11:9 Ex 7:4; 10:1
11:10 Ex 4:21 Rom 2:2; 9:17
12:2 Ex 12:14; 13:4 23:15; 34:18
12:3,4 Lev 1:5 Jn 12:1 1 Cor 5:7
12:5 Lev 22:18-20 Heb 9:14
12:6 Lev 23:5 Num 9:3; 28:16 Deut 16:1 Mk 14:12
12:7 Ex 12:22 Heb 9:13,14
12:8 Ex 13:3; 34:25 Num 9:11 Deut 16:7
12:10 Ex 23:18; 29:34 Lev 7:15
12:11 Num 28:16
12:12 Ex 11:4,5 Num 33:4
12:13 Heb 11:28

12:3, 4 The Hebrew word here translated "lamb" can also mean "kid"—a baby goat.   **12:9** *liver,* literally, 'inner parts."

11:9, 10 You may wonder how Pharaoh could be so foolish as to see God's miraculous power and still not listen to Moses. But Pharaoh had his mind made up long before the plagues started. He couldn't believe that someone was greater than he. This stubborn unbelief led to a heart so hard that even a major catastrophe couldn't budge him. Finally, it took the greatest of all calamities, the loss of his son, to force him to recognize God's authority. But even then he wanted God to leave, not to rule his country. We must not wait for great calamities to drive us to God, but must open our hearts and minds to his direction now.

11:10 Did God really harden Pharaoh's heart and force him to do wrong? Before the ten plagues began, Moses and Aaron announced what God would do if Pharaoh didn't let the people go. But their message only made Pharaoh stubborn—he was hardening his own heart. In so doing, he defied both God and his messengers.

Through the first six plagues, Pharaoh's heart grew even more stubborn. After the sixth plague, God passed judgment. Sooner or later, evil people will be punished for their sins. Proverbs 29:1 says that the man who is often reproved, but refuses to accept criticism, will suddenly be broken and never have another chance. When it became evident he wouldn't change, God confirmed Pharaoh's prideful decision and set the painful consequences of his actions in motion.

God didn't force Pharaoh to reject him; rather, he gave him every opportunity to change his mind. In Ezekiel 33:11, God says "I have no pleasure in the death of the wicked."

12:1–3 Certain holidays were instituted by God himself. Passover was a holiday designed to celebrate Israel's deliverance from Egypt and to remind the people what God had done. Holidays can be important today, too, as annual reminders of what God has

done for us. Develop traditions in your family to highlight the religious significance of certain holidays. These serve as reminders to the older people and learning experiences for the younger ones.

12:3, 4 Why did the Hebrews sacrifice a lamb? The significance of the sacrifice was that innocent blood was shed. For the Israelites to be spared from the plague of death, a lamb with no defects had to be killed and its blood placed on the doorframes of each home. The lamb was a sacrifice, a substitute for the person who was supposed to die. From this point on, the Hebrew people would have a clear understanding that being spared from death meant that another life had to be sacrificed in their place.

12:6–11 The Feast of the Passover was to be an annual holiday to remember the night when the angel of the Lord "passed over" the homes of the Israelites. The Hebrews followed God's instructions by placing the blood of a lamb on the doorposts of their homes. That night the firstborn son of every family who did not have blood on the doorposts was killed. The lamb had to be killed in order to get the blood that would protect them. (This foreshadowed the blood of Christ, the Lamb of God, who gave his blood for the sins of all people.) Inside their homes, the Israelites ate a Passover meal of roast lamb, unleavened bread, and bitter herbs. Unleavened bread could be made quickly because the dough did not have to rise. Thus they could be ready to leave at any time. Bitter herbs signified the bitterness of slavery. Today the Passover feast is still celebrated to bring in the Hebrew new year.

12:11 Eating the Passover feast while wearing traveling clothes was a sign of the Hebrews' faith. Though they were not yet free, they were to prepare themselves, for God had said he would lead them out of Egypt. Their preparation was an act of faith. Preparing ourselves for the fulfillment of God's scriptural promises, however unlikely they may seem, demonstrates our faith.

12:15
Ex 13:6; 34:18
Lev 23:5-8
Deut 16:3
12:16
Ex 20:10
Num 28:18

12:17
Ex 13:3
Num 9:4; 28:16
Josh 5:10
2 Kgs 23:21
Ezra 6:20
Mk 14:12-16
12:19
Ex 12:15

12:21
Ex 3:16; 17:5
Heb 11:28
12:22
Lev 14:6
Num 19:18
Ps 51:7
Heb 9:13,14
11:28

you are to eat only bread made without yeast. Anyone who disobeys this rule at any time during the seven days of the celebration shall be excommunicated from Israel. 16On the first day of the celebration, and again on the seventh day, there will be special religious services for the entire congregation, and no work of any kind may be done on those days except the preparation of food.

17"This annual 'Celebration with Unleavened Bread' will cause you always to remember today as the day when I brought you out of the land of Egypt; so it is a law that you must celebrate this day annually, generation after generation. 18Only bread without yeast may be eaten from the evening of the fourteenth day of the month until the evening of the twenty-first day of the month. 19For these seven days there must be no trace of yeast in your homes; during that time anyone who eats anything that has yeast in it shall be excommunicated from the congregation of Israel. These same rules apply to foreigners who are living among you just as much as to those born in the land. 20Again I repeat, during those days you must not eat anything made with yeast; serve only yeastless bread."

21Then Moses called for all the elders of Israel and said to them, "Go and get lambs from your flocks, a lamb for one or more families depending upon the number of persons in the families, and kill the lamb so that God will pass over you and not destroy you. 22Drain the lamb's blood into a basin, and then take a cluster of hyssop branches and dip them into the lamb's blood, and strike the hyssop

---

THE HEBREW CALENDAR

A Hebrew month began in the middle of a month on our calendar today. Crops are planted in November and December and harvested in March and April.

Month		Today's Calendar	Bible Reference	Israel's Holidays
1	Nisan (Abib)	March–April	Exodus 13:4; 23:15; 34:18; Deuteronomy 16:1	Passover (Leviticus 23:5) Unleavened Bread (Leviticus 23:6) Firstfruits (Leviticus 23:10)
2	Iyyar (Ziv)	April–May	1 Kings 6:1, 37	
3	Sivan	May–June	Esther 8:9	Pentecost (Leviticus 23:15)
4	Tammuz	June–July		
5	Ab	July–August		
6	Elul	August–September	Nehemiah 6:15	
7	Tishri (Ethanim)	September–October	1 Kings 8:2	Trumpets (Numbers 29:1; Leviticus 23:24) Day of Atonement (Leviticus 23:27) Tabernacles (Leviticus 23:34)
8	Marchesvan (Bul)	October–November	1 Kings 6:38	
9	Chislev	November–December	Nehemiah 1:1	Dedication (John 10:22)
10	Tebeth	December–January	Esther 2:16	
11	Shebat	January–February	Zechariah 1:7	
12	Adar	February–March	Esther 3:7	

12:17, 23 Passover became an annual remembrance of how God delivered the Hebrews from Egypt. Each year the people would pause to remember the day when God's angel of death (the Destroyer) passed over their homes. They gave thanks to God for saving them from death and bringing them out of a land of slavery and sin. Believers today have experienced a day of deliverance as well—the day we were delivered from spiritual death and slavery to sin. The Lord's Supper is our "Passover remembrance" of our new life and freedom from sin. The next time struggles and trials come, focus on how God has delivered you in the past and on his promise of new life with him.

against the lintel above the door and against the two side panels, so that there will be blood upon them, and none of you shall go outside all night.

23"For Jehovah will pass through the land and kill the Egyptians; but when he sees the blood upon the panel at the top of the door and on the two side pieces, he will pass over that home and not permit the Destroyer to enter and kill your firstborn. 24And remember, this is a permanent law for you and your posterity. 25And when you come into the land that the Lord will give you, just as he promised, and when you are celebrating the Passover, 26and your children ask, 'What does all this mean? What is this ceremony about?' 27you will reply, 'It is the celebration of Jehovah's passing over us, for he passed over the homes of the people of Israel, though he killed the Egyptians; he passed over our houses and did not come in to destroy us.' " And all the people bowed their heads and worshiped.

28So the people of Israel did as Moses and Aaron had commanded.

The firstborn die

29And that night, at midnight, Jehovah killed all the firstborn sons in the land of Egypt, from Pharaoh's oldest son to the oldest son of the captive in the dungeon; also all the firstborn of the cattle. 30Then Pharaoh and his officials and all the people of Egypt got up in the night; and there was bitter crying throughout all the land of Egypt, for there was not a house where there was not one dead.

31And Pharaoh summoned Moses and Aaron during the night and said, "Leave us; please go away, all of you; go and serve Jehovah as you said. 32Take your flocks and herds and be gone; and oh, give me a blessing as you go." 33And the Egyptians were urgent upon the people of Israel, to get them out of the land as quickly as possible. For they said, "We are as good as dead."

34The Israelis took with them their bread dough without yeast, and bound their kneading troughs into their spare clothes, and carried them on their shoulders. 35And the people of Israel did as Moses said and asked the Egyptians for silver and gold jewelry, and for clothing. 36And the Lord gave the Israelis favor with the Egyptians, so that they gave them whatever they wanted. And the Egyptians were practically stripped of everything they owned!

12:23 *he will pass over. . . .* or, "He will pause at the door of that home and not permit the Destroyer to enter. . . ."
12:32 *give me a blessing as you go,* literally, "say farewell to me forever."

12:23 Ex 12:12; 2 Sam 24:16; Isa 37:36 **12:24** Gen 17:8 **12:25** Gen 50:24; Ex 3:8; Deut 4:5; 12:9 **12:26** Ex 13:8; Deut 6:7; Josh 4:6; Ps 78:5 **12:27** a)Deut 16:2; 1 Cor 5:7; b)Ex 4:31 **12:29** Ex 4:23; Ps 78:51; 105:36 **12:30** Ex 11:6 **12:31** Ex 3:19; 10:9,29; 11:8; Ps 105:38 **12:33** Gen 20:3; Ex 11:1; Num 17:12 **12:35** Ex 3:22 **12:36** Gen 39:21; Ex 11:3; Ps 105:37

12:28-30 Every firstborn child of the Egyptians died, but all the Israelite children were spared. Because the blood of the lamb had been placed on their doorposts, the people were saved. So began the story of redemption, the central theme of the Bible. Redemption, as it is used in the Bible, means to be freed from our slavery to sin. All of us have sinned and will sin again; that makes us slaves to sin. We cannot deliver ourselves from its consequences. That's where redemption comes in. It involves two parts: (1) a ransom, a cost paid for the penalty of sin, and (2) a substitute who pays the penalty for us. In this story, the lamb was sacrificed as a substitute for the lives of the Israelites. Its life was the penalty paid. In the Old Testament, animal sacrifice was the method used by God to forgive and take away one's sin. The individual sacrificed a valuable animal to demonstrate that sin's penalty must be paid.

In the New Testament, Jesus performed the ultimate act of redemption by sacrificing his life on the cross for our sins. This made animal sacrifice no longer necessary. He was the substitute and his blood was the cost paid for the penalty of our sins (1 Peter 1:18, 19). Only Jesus could redeem all people from slavery to sin because only he had lived a life that was perfect in every way (Hebrews 7:26, 27; 1 John 3:5). Since only he lived up to the demands of God, only he had the right to release us from our "sentence," which was death due to our sin. Jesus substituted his

life for ours so that we could be restored to God.

We must recognize that if we want to be freed from the deadly consequences of our sin, a tremendous price must be paid. But *we* don't have to pay it. Jesus Christ (our substitute) already did by his death on the cross. All we must do is totally trust him and accept the fact that our sins have been paid for and that the way is cleared for us to begin a bright new relationship with God (Titus 2:14; Hebrews 9:13-15, 23-26).

12:31, 32 Who was this Pharaoh who tangled with God and Moses? If the Exodus from Egypt occurred between 1500 and 1400 B.C., Amenhotep II would probably have been Egypt's leader. If the Exodus occurred between 1300 and 1200 B.C., Raamses II, an especially brutal Pharaoh, would have reigned during Moses' boyhood years and could have easily oppressed the Hebrew slaves without a guilty conscience. Raamses' successor, Merneptah, was a weak ruler who would have let the Hebrews go after experiencing the power of God's plagues.

12:34 A kneading trough was a large bowl made of wood, bronze, or pottery and used for kneading dough. Bread was made by mixing water and flour in the trough with a small piece of leaven saved from bread dough made the day before. Bread was basic to life, and thus it was vital to bring the trough along. It could be easily carried over the shoulder.

B. ISRAEL IN THE WILDERNESS (12:37—18:27)

As Egypt buried its dead, the Hebrew slaves left the country, a free people at last. Pharaoh made one last attempt to bring them back, but the people escaped when God miraculously parted the waters of the Red Sea. But on the other side, the people soon became dissatisfied and complained bitterly to Moses and Aaron about their trek through the wilderness. Through these experiences of the Hebrews, we learn that the Christian life is not always trouble-free. We still have struggles and often complain bitterly to God about conditions in our lives.

1. Escape from Egypt

37That night the people of Israel left Rameses and started for Succoth; there were six hundred thousand of them, besides all the women and children, going on foot. 38People of various sorts went with them; and there were flocks and herds—a vast exodus of cattle. 39When they stopped to eat, they baked bread from the yeastless dough they had brought along. It was yeastless because the people were pushed out of Egypt and didn't have time to wait for bread to rise to take with them on the trip.

40, 41The sons of Jacob and their descendants had lived in Egypt 430 years, and it was on the last day of the 430th year that all of Jehovah's people left the land. 42This night was selected by the Lord to bring his people out from the land of Egypt; so the same night was selected as the date of the annual celebration of God's deliverance.

Passover instructions

43Then Jehovah said to Moses and Aaron, "These are the rules concerning the observance of the Passover. No foreigners shall eat the lamb, 44but any slave who has been purchased may eat it if he has been circumcised. 45A hired servant or a visiting foreigner may not eat of it. 46You shall, all of you who eat each lamb, eat it together in one house, and not carry it outside; and you shall not break any of its bones. 47All the congregation of Israel shall observe this memorial at the same time.

48"As to foreigners, if they are living with you and want to observe the Passover with you, let all the males be circumcised, and then they may come and celebrate with you—then they shall be just as though they had been born among you; but no uncircumcised person shall ever eat the lamb. 49The same law applies to those born in Israel and to foreigners living among you."

50So the people of Israel followed all of Jehovah's instructions to Moses and Aaron. 51That very day the Lord brought out the people of Israel from the land of Egypt, wave after wave of them crossing the border.

The firstborn are dedicated to God

13 The Lord instructed Moses, "Dedicate to me all of the firstborn sons of Israel, and every firstborn male animal; they are mine!"

3Then Moses said to the people, "This is a day to remember forever—the day of leaving Egypt and your slavery; for the Lord has brought you out with mighty miracles. Now remember, during the annual celebration of this event you are to use no yeast; don't even have any in your homes. 4, 5Celebrate this day of your exodus, at the end of March each year, when Jehovah brings you into the land of the Canaanites, Hittites, Amorites, Hivites, and Jebusites—the land he promised your fathers, a land 'flowing with milk and honey.' 6, 7For seven days you shall eat only bread without yeast, and there must be no yeast in your homes, or anywhere within the borders of your land! Then, on the seventh day, a great feast to the Lord shall be held.

8"During those celebration days each year you must explain to your children why

12:37 Ex 1:11; 38:26 Num 1:46
12:38 Num 11:4 Deut 3:19 Zech 8:23
12:39 Ex 6:1; 11:1
12:40,41 Gen 15:13,16 Acts 7:6 Gal 3:16,17
12:42 Ex 13:3 Deut 16:1
12:43 Num 9:14
12:44 Gen 17:12,13 Lev 22:11
12:46 a)1 Cor 12:12 Eph 2:19 b)Num 9:12 Jn 19:33,36
12:48 Gen 17:12 Num 9:14; 15:15 Gal 3:28
12:49 Lev 24:22
12:50 Ex 12:28 Deut 4:1,2 12:32
13:1,2 Ex 13:11; 22:29 34:19 Lev 27:26 Num 3:13 Deut 15:19 Lk 2:23
13:3 Ex 12:42; 23:15 Deut 5:15
13:4,5 Gen 17:7,8 Ex 3:8,17 34:11 Deut 7:1
13:6 Ex 12:15,19

12:38 *People of various sorts,* literally, "a mixed multitude." **12:51** *wave after wave of them crossing the border,* or, "... from the land of Egypt, all of the communities of them." **13:1, 2** *all of the firstborn sons,* literally, "all the firstborn." **13:4, 5** *the end of March,* literally, "at the appointed time each year."

12:37, 38 The total number of people leaving Egypt is estimated to have been about two million. The phrase "people of various sorts" may refer to Egyptians and others who were drawn to the Hebrews by God's mighty works and who decided to leave Egypt with them.

you are celebrating—it is a celebration of what the Lord did for you when you left Egypt. 9This annual memorial week will brand you as his own unique people, just as though he had branded his mark of ownership upon your hands or your forehead.

10"So celebrate the event annually in late March. 11And remember, when the Lord brings you into the land he promised to your ancestors long ago, where the Canaanites are now living, 12all firstborn sons and firstborn male animals belong to the Lord, and you shall give them to him. 13A firstborn donkey may be purchased back from the Lord in exchange for a lamb or baby goat; but if you decide not to trade, the donkey shall be killed. However, you *must* buy back your firstborn sons.

14"And in the future, when your children ask you, 'What is this all about?' you shall tell them, 'With mighty miracles Jehovah brought us out of Egypt from our slavery. 15Pharaoh wouldn't let us go, so Jehovah killed all the firstborn males throughout the land of Egypt, both of men and animals; that is why we now give all the firstborn males to the Lord—except that all the eldest sons are always bought back.' 16Again I say, this celebration shall identify you as God's people, just as much as if his brand of ownership were placed upon your foreheads. It is a reminder that the Lord brought us out of Egypt with great power."

Pillar of cloud, pillar of fire

17, 18So at last Pharaoh let the people go.

God did not lead them through the land of the Philistines, although that was the most direct route from Egypt to the Promised Land. The reason was that God felt the people might become discouraged by having to fight their way through, even though they had left Egypt armed; he thought they might return to Egypt. Instead, God led them along a route through the Red Sea wilderness.

19Moses took the bones of Joseph with them, for Joseph had made the sons of

13:10 *in late March,* literally, "in its season from year to year."

13:9
Ex 12:14
Num 15:39
Deut 6:8
13:10
Ex 12:14; 23:15
Lev 23:6-8
Deut 16:3,4
13:12
Ex 13:2; 22:29
Num 8:17
Deut 15:19
13:13
Ex 34:20
Num 18:15
Rev 14:4
13:14
Ex 12:26; 13:8
Deut 6:20
13:15
Ex 12:29; 13:12
13:16
Ex 12:13; 13:9
Deut 6:7-9
11:18

13:17,18
Ex 14:11; 16:12
Num 14:1-4
Deut 17:16
Josh 1:14; 4:12, 13
13:19
Gen 50:24,25
Josh 24:32
Acts 7:15,16

13:9 This memorial week marked the Hebrews as a unique people—as though they were branded with God's trademark. What do you do that marks you as a follower of God? The way you raise your children, demonstrate love for others, show concern for the poor, and live in devotion to God—what you do in these areas will leave visible marks for all to see. While national groups are marked by customs and traditions, Christians are marked by loving one another (John 13:34, 35).

13:12-14 What did it mean when God said, "You must buy back your firstborn sons"? During the first Passover, God spared the oldest Hebrew sons if the house in which they lived had blood brushed on the doorposts. Because God saved their lives, he owned them and had a rightful claim to them. But God commanded the Israelites to buy their sons back from him. This ritual served three main purposes: (1) it was a reminder to the people of how God had spared their sons from the angel of death and freed them all from slavery; (2) it showed God's high respect for human life by distinguishing his people from the heathen religions which sacrificed human lives to make peace with their gods; (3) it looked forward to the day when Jesus Christ would buy us back by paying the price of sin once and for all.

13:17, 18 God doesn't always work in the way that seems best to us. Instead of guiding the Israelites along the direct route from Egypt to the Promised Land, he took them by a longer route to avoid fighting with the Philistines. If God does not lead you along the shortest path to your goal, don't complain or resist. Follow him willingly and trust him to lead you safely around unseen obstacles. He can see the end of your journey from the beginning, and he knows the safest and best route.

13:17, 18 When did the Hebrews leave Egypt? There are two theories. The "early" theory says the Exodus occurred around 1446-1445 B.C. The "late" theory suggests the Exodus happened between 1300 and 1200 B.C. Those who hold to the earlier date point to 1 Kings 6:1, where the Bible clearly states that King

THE EXODUS
The Israelites left Succoth and camped first at Etham before going toward Baal-zephon to camp "along the shore" (14:2). God miraculously brought them across the sea, into the wilderness of Shur (15:22). After stopping at the oasis of Elim, the people moved into the wilderness of Sihn (16:1).

Solomon began building his temple 480 years after the Hebrews left Egypt. Since almost all scholars agree that Solomon began building the Temple in 966, this puts the Exodus in the year 1446. But those who hold to the later date suggest that the 480 years cannot be taken literally. They point to Exodus 1:11, which says that the Hebrews built the store-cities of Pithom and Raamses, named after the Pharaoh Raamses, who reigned around 1290 B.C.

Regardless of which date is correct, the fact is that God led the Hebrews out of Egypt, just as he had promised. This showed his great power and his great love for his people.

13:20
Ex 12:37
Num 33:5,6

13:21
Ex 14:19,20
33:9,10
Ps 105:39
1 Cor 10:1

Israel vow before God that they would take his bones with them when God led them out of Egypt—as he was sure God would.

20Leaving Succoth, they camped in Etham at the edge of the wilderness. 21The Lord guided them by a pillar of cloud during the daytime, and by a pillar of fire at night. So they could travel either by day or night. 22The cloud and fire were never out of sight.

14 Jehovah now instructed Moses, 2"Tell the people to turn toward Piha-hiroth between Migdol and the sea, opposite Baal-zephon, and to camp there along the shore. 3For Pharaoh will think, 'Those Israelites are trapped now, between the desert and the sea!' 4And once again I will harden Pharaoh's heart and he will chase after you. I have planned this to gain great honor and glory over Pharaoh and all his armies, and the Egyptians shall know that I am the Lord."

14:2
Ex 13:17
Num 33:3,7
Jer 44:1

14:4
Ex 4:21; 7:3
14:17
Rom 9:17,22

So they camped where they were told.

The Egyptian army pursues the people of Israel

14:5
Ex 12:33
Ps 105:25
Jer 34:10

5When word reached the king of Egypt that the Israelis were not planning to return to Egypt after three days, but to keep on going, Pharaoh and his staff became bold again. "What is this we have done, letting all these slaves get away?" they asked. 6So Pharaoh led the chase in his chariot, 7followed by the pick of Egypt's chariot corps—600 chariots in all—and other chariots driven by Egyptian officers.

14:7
Ex 14:23; 15:4

14:8
Ex 15:9

14:9
Ex 14:2
Josh 24:6

8He pursued the people of Israel, for they had taken much of the wealth of Egypt with them. 9Pharaoh's entire cavalry—horses, chariots, and charioteers—was used in the chase; and the Egyptian army overtook the people of Israel as they were camped beside the shore near Piha-hiroth, across from Baal-zephon.

14:10
Josh 24:7
Neh 9:9

10As the Egyptian army approached, the people of Israel saw them far in the distance, speeding after them, and they were terribly frightened, and cried out to the Lord to help them.

14:11
Ex 5:21; 15:24
Ps 106:6,7
Acts 7:39

11And they turned against Moses, whining, "Have you brought us out here to die in the desert because there were not enough graves for us in Egypt? Why did you make us leave Egypt? 12Isn't this what we told you, while we were slaves, to leave us alone? We said it would be better to be slaves to the Egyptians than dead in the wilderness."

14:13
Gen 15:1
Ex 14:30; 20:20

14:14
Ex 15:3
Deut 1:30; 3:22
Isa 30:15; 31:4,5

13But Moses told the people, "Don't be afraid. Just stand where you are and watch, and you will see the wonderful way the Lord will rescue you today. The Egyptians you are looking at—you will never see them again. 14The Lord will fight for you, and you won't need to lift a finger!"

14:14 *you won't need to lift a finger,* or, "you will be speechless with amazement."

13:21, 22 God gave the Hebrews a pillar of cloud and fire so they would know day and night that God was with them on their journey to the Promised Land. What has he given us so that we can have the same assurance? The Bible—something the Israelites did not have. Look to God's Word for reassurance of his presence. As the Hebrews looked to the pillar of cloud and fire, we can look to God's Word day and night to know he is with us, helping us on our journey.

13:21, 22 The pillar of fire and cloud was an example of a *theophany*—God appearing in a physical form. In this form, God lighted Israel's path, protected them from their enemies, provided reassurance, controlled their movements, and symbolized the burning zeal that Israel should have for her God.

14:6-9 Six hundred Egyptian war chariots were bearing down on the helpless Israelites, who were trapped between the mountains and the sea. These war chariots carried two people—one to drive and one to fight. They were made of a wood or leather cab placed over two wheels and pulled by horses. These were the armored tanks of Bible times. But even their power was no match for God, who destroyed both the chariots and their soldiers.

14:10, 11 Trapped against the sea, the Israelites faced the Egyptian army sweeping in for the kill. The Israelites thought they were doomed. After watching God's powerful hand deliver them from Egypt, their only response was fear, whining, and despair. Where was their trust in God? Israel had to learn from repeated experience that God was able to provide for them.

God has preserved these examples in Scripture so that we can learn to trust him the first time. By focusing on God's faithfulness in the past we can avoid responding to crises with fear and complaining.

14:11 This is the first of constant grumbling and complaining by the Israelites. Their lack of faith in God is startling. Yet how often do we find ourselves doing the same thing—grumbling or complaining over inconveniences or discomforts? The Israelites were about to learn some tough lessons. Had they trusted God, they would have been spared much grief.

14:13 The people were hostile and despairing, but Moses encouraged them to watch the wonderful way God would rescue them. Moses had a positive attitude! When it looked as if they were trapped, Moses called upon God to intervene. We may not be chased by an army, but we may still feel trapped. While our first reaction could be despair, we should adopt Moses' attitude to "watch and see what God will do."

2. Rescue through the Red Sea

15Then the Lord said to Moses, "Quit praying and get the people moving! Forward, march! 16Use your rod—hold it out over the water, and the sea will open up a path before you, and all the people of Israel shall walk through on dry ground! 17I will harden the hearts of the Egyptians and they will go in after you and you will see the honor I will get in defeating Pharaoh and all his armies, chariots, and horsemen. 18And all Egypt shall know that I am Jehovah."

19Then the Angel of God, who was leading the people of Israel, moved the cloud around behind them, 20and it stood between the people of Israel and the Egyptians. And that night, as it changed to a pillar of fire, it gave darkness to the Egyptians but light to the people of Israel! So the Egyptians couldn't find the Israelis!

21Meanwhile, Moses stretched his rod over the sea, and the Lord opened up a path through the sea, with walls of water on each side; and a strong east wind blew all that night, drying the sea bottom. 22So the people of Israel walked through the sea on dry ground! 23Then the Egyptians followed them between the walls of water along the bottom of the sea—all of Pharaoh's horses, chariots, and horsemen. 24But in the early morning Jehovah looked down from the cloud of fire upon the array of the Egyptians, and began to harass them. 25Their chariot wheels began coming off, so that their chariots scraped along the dry ground. "Let's get out of here," the Egyptians yelled. "Jehovah is fighting for them and against us."

26When all the Israelites were on the other side, the Lord said to Moses, "Stretch out your hand again over the sea, so that the waters will come back over the Egyptians and their chariots and horsemen." 27Moses did, and the sea returned to normal beneath the morning light. The Egyptians tried to flee, but the Lord drowned them in the sea. 28The water covered the path and the chariots and horsemen. And of all the army of Pharaoh that chased after Israel through the sea, not one remained alive.

29The people of Israel had walked through on dry land, and the waters had been walled up on either side of them. 30Thus Jehovah saved Israel that day from the Egyptians; and the people of Israel saw the Egyptians dead, washed up on the seashore. 31When the people of Israel saw the mighty miracle the Lord had done for them against the Egyptians, they were afraid and revered the Lord, and believed in him and in his servant Moses.

Songs to the Lord

15 Then Moses and the people of Israel sang this song to the Lord:

I will sing to the Lord, for he has triumphed gloriously;
He has thrown both horse and rider into the sea.

14:26 When all the Israelites were on the other side, implied.

Cross-references (right margin):

14:15 Josh 7:10
14:16 Ex 4:2; 7:9 Num 20:8
14:18 Ex 7:5; 14:25
14:19 Gen 24:7 Ex 13:21,22 23:20
14:20 Ps 18:11
14:21 Ex 7:19 Ps 106:9 114:3,5 136:13 Isa 63:12,13
14:22 Num 33:8 Ps 66:6; 78:13 Isa 11:15 Heb 11:29
14:26 Ex 7:19; 14:21
14:27 Ex 15:1,7 Deut 11:4 Josh 4:18
14:28 Ex 15:10 Neh 9:11 Ps 78:53 106:11
14:29 Ps 66:6 Isa 11:15 Ps 58:10 106:10 Isa 63:11
14:31 Ex 4:31; 19:9 2 Chron 20:20 Ps 106:12
15:1 Ps 106:12 Isa 12:5; 42:10-12 Jer 51:21 Rev 15:3

14:15 The Lord told Moses to stop praying and get moving! Prayer must have a vital place in our lives, but there is also a place for action. Sometimes we know what to do, but we pray for more guidance as an excuse to justify our failure to act. If we know what we should do, then it is time to get moving.

14:21 There was no apparent way of escape, but the Lord opened up a dry path through the sea. Sometimes we find ourselves caught in a problem and see no way out. Don't panic; God can open up a way.

14:21, 22 Some scholars believe the Israelites did not really cross the main body of the Red Sea but one of the shallow lakes or marshes north of it. These often dry up at certain times of the year. But the Bible clearly states that "the Lord opened up a path through the sea with walls of water on each side . . . drying the sea bottom (14:21; see also Joshua 3:15, 16; and 2 Kings 2:13, 14). Others have suggested that the Israelites crossed the Sea of Reeds, a much smaller body of water also located north of the Red Sea, where the water would have been shallow enough to wade across. Still others have maintained that the Red Sea extended much farther north in ancient times. Today's lakes are simply

remnants of the sea's western arm (presently called the Gulf of Aqaba). The point is that the God who created the earth and water performed a mighty miracle at exactly the right time to demonstrate his great power and love for his people.

14:27, 28 No evidence of this great Exodus has been discovered in Egyptian history records. It was a common practice for Egyptian Pharaohs not to record their defeats. They even went so far as to take existing records and delete the names of traitors and political adversaries. Pharaoh would have been especially anxious not to record that his great army was destroyed chasing a band of runaway slaves. Since the Egyptians either failed to record the Exodus or the record has not yet been found, it is impossible to place a precise date on it.

15:1 Music played an important part in Israel's worship and celebration. Singing was an expression of love and thanks, and it was a creative way to pass down oral traditions. Some say this song of Moses is the oldest recorded song in the world. It was a festive epic poem celebrating God's victory, lifting the hearts and voices of the people outward and upward. Psalms and hymns can be great ways to express relief, praise, and thanks.

15:2
Ex 3:15,16
Deut 10:21
2 Sam 22:47,51
Ps 18:1,2
140:7
Isa 12:2

15:3
Ex 6:2; 14:14
Ps 24:8

15:4
Ex 14:6,7, 27,28

15:5
Neh 9:11
Ezek 27:34
Jonah 2:2

15:6
Ex 3:20
Ps 17:7; 118:15

15:7
Ex 9:16; 14:24
Ps 78:49,50

15:8
Ex 14:22,29
2 Sam 22:16
Ps 78:13; 114:5;
118:15
Hab 3:8-10

15:9
Ex 14:5,8,9

15:10
Ex 14:27
Ps 74:13
147:18

15:11
Ex 8:10
Deut 3:24
1 Sam 2:2
2 Sam 7:22
Ps 22:3
Isa 6:3; 57:15
Jer 23:9
Mic 7:18
Rev 4:8

15:12
Ex 15:6

15:13
Neh 9:12
Ps 77:14,15,20
Jer 2:6

15:14
Num 14:14
Deut 2:25
Isa 14:29

15:15
Num 22:3
Deut 2:4
Josh 2:11

15:17
Ex 23:20; 32:34
Ps 2:6
78:54,68
Isa 5:1,2
Jer 2:21

15:18
Ps 10:16; 29:10
Isa 57:15
Rev 11:15

15:19
Ex 14:22,23,29
15:5,10
Heb 11:29

15:20
Ex 2:4
Num 26:59
1 Sam 18:6
Ps 150:4

2The Lord is my strength, my song, and my salvation.
  He is my God, and I will praise him.
  He is my father's God—I will exalt him.
3The Lord is a warrior—
  Yes, Jehovah is his name.
4He has overthrown Pharaoh's chariots and armies,
  Drowning them in the sea.
  The famous Egyptian captains are dead beneath the waves.
5The water covers them.
  They went down into the depths like a stone.
6Your right hand, O Lord, is glorious in power;
  It dashes the enemy to pieces.
7In the greatness of your majesty
  You overthrew all those who rose against you.
  You sent forth your anger, and it consumed them as fire consumes straw.
8At the blast of your breath
  The waters divided!
  They stood as solid walls to hold the seas apart.
9The enemy said, "I will chase after them,
  Catch up with them, destroy them.
  I will cut them apart with my sword
  And divide the captured booty."
10But God blew with his wind, and the sea covered them.
  They sank as lead in the mighty waters.
11Who else is like the Lord among the gods?
  Who is glorious in holiness like him?
  Who is so awesome in splendor,
  A wonder-working God?
12You reached out your hand and the earth swallowed them.
13You have led the people you redeemed.
  But in your lovingkindness
  You have guided them wonderfully
  To your holy land.
14The nations heard what happened, and they trembled.
  Fear has gripped the people of Philistia.
15The leaders of Edom are appalled,
  The mighty men of Moab tremble;
  All the people of Canaan melt with fear.
16Terror and dread have overcome them.
  O Lord, because of your great power they won't attack us!
  Your people whom you purchased
  Will pass by them in safety.
17You will bring them in and plant them on your mountain,
  Your own homeland, Lord—
  The sanctuary you made for them to live in.
18Jehovah shall reign forever and forever.
19The horses of Pharaoh, his horsemen, and his chariots
  Tried to follow through the sea;
  But the Lord let down the walls of water on them
  While the people of Israel walked through on dry land.

  20Then Miriam the prophetess, the sister of Aaron, took a tambourine and led the
women in dances.

15:20 Miriam was called a prophetess not only because she received revelations from God (Exodus 15:20; Micah 6:4) but also for her musical skill. Prophecy and music were often closely related in the Bible (1 Samuel 10:5; 1 Chronicles 25:1). Miriam's timbrel was an instrument shaped like a circle and ringed with brass pieces. It was similar to the tambourine.

21And Miriam sang this song:

Sing to the Lord, for he has triumphed gloriously.
The horse and rider have been drowned in the sea.

3. Complaining in the wilderness
The people complain about bitter water

22Then Moses led the people of Israel on from the Red Sea, and they moved out into the wilderness of Shur and were there three days without water. 23Arriving at Marah, they couldn't drink the water because it was bitter (that is why the place was called Marah, meaning "bitter").

24Then the people turned against Moses. "Must we die of thirst?" they demanded.

25Moses pleaded with the Lord to help them, and the Lord showed him a tree to throw into the water, and the water became sweet.

It was there at Marah that the Lord laid before them the following conditions, to test their commitment to him: 26"If you will listen to the voice of the Lord your God, and obey it, and do what is right, then I will not make you suffer the diseases I sent on the Egyptians, for I am the Lord who heals you." 27And they came to Elim where there were twelve springs and seventy palm trees; and they camped there beside the springs.

15:21
Ex 15:1
Judg 5:3
Rev 5:9

15:22
Gen 16:7; 25:18
Ex 3:18

15:23
Num 33:8
Ruth 1:20

15:24
Ex 14:11; 16:2
17:3
Ps 106:13

15:25
Ex 14:10; 16:4
17:4

15:26
Ex 19:5; 20:2-17
Deut 7:15; 12:28
Ps 103:3

15:27
Num 33:9

Where	Purpose of Song	
Exodus 15:1–21	Moses' song of victory and praise after God led Israel out of Egypt and saved them by parting the Red Sea; Miriam joined in the singing too	**FAMOUS SONGS IN THE BIBLE**
Numbers 21:17–18	Israel's song of praise to God for giving them water in the wilderness	
Deuteronomy 32:1–43	Moses' song of Israel's history with thanksgiving and praise as the Hebrews were about to enter the Promised Land	
Judges 5:2–31	Deborah and Barak's song of praise thanking God for Israel's victory over King Jabin's army at Mount Tabor	
2 Samuel 22:1–51	David's song of thanks and praise to God for rescuing him from Saul and his other enemies	
Song of Solomon	Solomon's song of love celebrating the union of husband and wife	
Isaiah 26:1	Isaiah's prophetic song about how the redeemed will sing in the New Jerusalem	
Ezra 3:11	Israel's song of praise at the completion of the Temple's foundation	
Luke 1:46–55	Mary's song of praise to God for the conception of Jesus	
Luke 1:68–79	Zechariah's song of praise for the promise of a son	
Acts 16:25	Paul and Silas sang hymns in prison	
Revelation 5:9–10	The "new song" of the 24 elders acclaiming Christ as worthy to break the seven seals of God's scroll	
Revelation 14:3	The song of the 144,000 redeemed from the earth	
Revelation 15:3–4	The song of all the redeemed in praise of the Lamb who redeemed them	

15:26 God promised that if the people obeyed him they would be free from the diseases that plagued the Egyptians. Little did they know that many of the moral laws he later gave them were designed to keep them free from sickness. For example, God's law against prostitution kept them free of venereal disease. God's laws for us are often designed to keep us from harm. A man and a woman are complex beings. Our physical, emotional, and spiritual lives are intertwined. Modern medicine is now acknowledging what these laws assumed. If we want God to care for us, we need to submit to his directions for living.

16:1 The Wilderness of Sihn was a vast and hostile environment of sand and stone. Its barren surroundings provided the perfect place for God to test and shape the character of his people.

16:2 It happened again. As the Israelites encountered danger, shortages, and inconvenience, they complained bitterly and longed to be back in Egypt. But as always, God provided for their needs.

Difficult circumstances can cause stress. When that happens, complaining is the natural response. The Israelites didn't really want to be back in Egypt; they just wanted life to get a little easier.

God provides meat and bread

16:1
Ex 17:1; 19:1
Num 33:10
16:2
Ex 14:11
Acts 7:39
1 Cor 10:10

16 Now they left Elim and journeyed on into the Sihn Wilderness, between Elim and Mt. Sinai, arriving there on the fifteenth day of the second month after leaving Egypt. 2There too, the people spoke bitterly against Moses and Aaron.

3"Oh, that we were back in Egypt," they moaned, "and that the Lord had killed

MOSES

Some people can't stay out of trouble. When conflict breaks out, they always manage to be nearby. Reaction is their favorite action. This was Moses. He seemed drawn to what needed to be righted. Throughout his life, he was at his finest and his worst responding to the conflicts around him. Even the burning bush experience was an illustration of his character. Having spotted the fire and seen that the bush did not burn, he had to investigate. Whether jumping into a fight to defend a Hebrew slave or trying to referee a fight between two kinsmen, when Moses saw conflict, he reacted.

The amazing thing about the change in Moses' character is not that he stopped reacting, but that he learned to react correctly. The kaleidoscopic action going on each day as two million people traveled in the wilderness was more than enough challenge for Moses' reacting ability. Much of the time he was actually a buffer between God and the people. At one moment he had to respond to God's anger at the people's stubbornness and forgetfulness. At another moment, he had to react to the people's bickering and complaining. At still another moment, he had to react to their unjustified attacks on his character.

Leadership often involves reaction. Learning to react with instincts consistent with God's will requires that we develop habits of obedience to God. Consistent obedience to God is best developed in times of less stress. Then when stress comes, our natural reaction is to obey God's desires as we confront a difficult situation.

In our age of lowering moral standards, we find it almost impossible to believe that God would punish Moses for the one time he disobeyed outrightly. What we fail to see, however, is that God did not reject Moses; Moses simply disqualified himself from being able to enter the Promised Land. Personal greatness does not make a person immune to error or its consequences.

In Moses we see an outstanding personality shaped by God. But we must not miss what God actually did. He did not change *who* or *what* Moses was; he worked on how Moses was. Moses' abilities and strengths were not changed; how Moses used them was changed.

Does knowing this make a difference in your understanding of God's purpose in your life? He is trying to take what he created in the first place and invest that creation in the way he intended to invest it all along. The next time you talk with God, don't ask, "What should I be?" but "How should I be?"

Strengths and accomplishments:
- Egyptian education; desert training
- Greatest Jewish leader; set the Exodus in motion
- Prophet and lawgiver; recorder of the Ten Commandments
- Author of the Pentateuch

Weaknesses and mistakes:
- Failed to enter the Promised Land because of disobedience to God
- Did not always recognize and use the talents of others

Lessons from his life:
- God prepares, then he uses—his timetable is life-sized
- God does his greatest work through frail people

Vital statistics:
- Where: Egypt, Midian, Sinai Desert
- Occupation: Prince, Shepherd, Leader of the Israelites
- Relatives: Sister: Miriam. Brother: Aaron. Wife: Zipporah. Son: Gershom.

Key Verse:
"And it was because he trusted God that he left the land of Egypt and wasn't afraid of the king's anger. Moses kept right on going; it seemed as though he could see God right there with him" (Hebrews 11:27).

Moses' story is told in the books of Exodus through Deuteronomy. He is also mentioned in Acts 7:22–37; Hebrews 11:23–29.

In the pressure of the moment, they could not focus on the cause of their stress (in this case, lack of trust in God). They could only think about the quickest way of escape.

When pressure comes your way, resist the temptation to make a quick escape. Instead, focus on God's power and wisdom to help you deal with the *cause* of your stress.

us there! For there we had plenty to eat. But now you have brought us into this wilderness to kill us with starvation."

4Then the Lord said to Moses, "Look, I'm going to rain down food from heaven for them. Everyone can go out each day and gather as much food as he needs. And I will test them in this, to see whether they will follow my instructions or not. 5Tell them to gather twice as much as usual on the sixth day of each week."

6Then Moses and Aaron called a meeting of all the people of Israel and told them, "This evening you will realize that it was the Lord who brought you out of the land of Egypt. 7, 8, 9In the morning you will see more of his glory; for he has heard your complaints against him (for you aren't really complaining against us—who are we?). The Lord will give you meat to eat in the evening, and bread in the morning. Come now before Jehovah, and hear his reply to your complaints."

10So Aaron called them together and suddenly, out toward the wilderness, from within the guiding cloud, there appeared the awesome glory of Jehovah.

11, 12And Jehovah said to Moses, "I have heard their complaints. Tell them, 'In the evening you will have meat and in the morning you will be stuffed with bread, and you shall know that I am Jehovah your God.' "

13That evening vast numbers of quail arrived and covered the camp, and in the morning the desert all around the camp was wet with dew; 14and when the dew disappeared later in the morning it left thin white flakes that covered the ground like frost. 15When the people of Israel saw it they asked each other, "What is it?"

And Moses told them, "It is the food Jehovah has given you. 16Jehovah has said for everyone to gather as much as is needed for his household—about two quarts for each person."

17So the people of Israel went out and gathered it—some getting more and some less before it melted on the ground, 18and there was just enough for everyone. Those who gathered more had nothing left over and those who gathered little had no lack! Each home had just enough.

19And Moses told them, "Don't leave it overnight."

20But of course some of them wouldn't listen, and left it until morning; and when they looked, it was full of maggots and had a terrible odor; and Moses was very angry with them. 21So they gathered the food morning by morning, each home according to its need; and when the sun became hot upon the ground, the food melted and disappeared. 22On the sixth day there was twice as much as usual on the ground—four quarts instead of two; the leaders of the people came and asked Moses why this had happened.

23And he told them, "Because the Lord has appointed tomorrow as a day of seriousness and rest, a holy Sabbath to the Lord when we must refrain from doing our daily tasks. So cook as much as you want to today, and keep what is left for tomorrow."

24And the next morning the food was wholesome and good, without maggots or odor. 25Moses said, "This is your food for today, for today is the Sabbath to Jehovah and there will be no food on the ground today. 26Gather the food for six days, but the seventh is a Sabbath, and there will be none there for you on that day."

27But some of the people went out anyway to gather food, even though it was the Sabbath, but there wasn't any.

28, 29"How long will these people refuse to obey?" the Lord asked Moses. "Don't

16:4
Ex 15:25
Deut 8:2,16
Ps 78:24
105:40
Jn 6:31
1 Cor 10:3

16:5
Ex 16:22; 35:2

16:6
Ex 12:51; 16:28

16:7-9
Ex 16:12
Num 14:27
17:5; 21:7
1 Sam 8:7
Mt 9:4

16:10
Ex 13:21; 40:34
Num 14:10

16:11,12
Ex 4:5; 16:6

16:13
Ex 16:31-33
Ps 78:27-29
105:40

16:14
Num 11:7-9
Deut 8:3

16:15
Ex 16:31
Josh 5:12
Neh 9:5
Jn 6:31

16:16
Ex 16:18,33,36

16:18
2 Cor 8:15

16:19
Ex 12:10; 23:18
Mt 6:34

16:20
Num 16:15

16:22
Ex 16:5; 34:31
Lev 25:11,12,22

16:23
Gen 2:2
Ex 20:8; 23:12
31:14,15
Neh 9:14
Mk 2:27

16:24
Ex 16:20,33

16:26
Deut 5:13

16:28,29
Num 14:11
Ps 78:10,18-24

16:16 about two quarts, literally, "an omer." The exact measure is not known.

16:4, 5 God promised to meet the Hebrews' need for food in the wilderness, but he decided to test their obedience. God wanted to see if they would obey his detailed instructions. We can only learn to follow by following. We can only learn obedience by obeying.

16:14-16 Manna appeared on the ground each day as a fresh white grain the size of a pearl. The people gathered it, ground it like grain, folded it, and made it into honey-tasting tortillas. For the Israelites the manna was a free gift—it came every day and was just what they needed. It satisfied their temporary physical need.

The word manna is used by Christ in John 6:48, 49 to portray his own person. Christ is our daily bread who satisfies our eternal, spiritual need.

16:23 The Israelites were not to work on the Sabbath—not even to cook food. Why? God knew that the busy routine of daily living could distract people from worshiping him. It is so easy to let work, family responsibilities, and recreation crowd our schedules so tightly that we don't take time for God. Guard jealously your time with God.

they realize that I am giving them twice as much on the sixth day, so that there will be enough for two days? For the Lord has given you the seventh day as a day of Sabbath rest; stay in your tents and don't go out to pick up food from the ground that day." 30So the people rested on the seventh day.

31And the food became known as "manna" (meaning "What is it?"); it was white, like coriander seed, and flat, and tasted like honey bread.

32Then Moses gave them this further instruction from the Lord: they were to take two quarts of it to be kept as a museum specimen forever, so that later generations could see the bread the Lord had fed them with in the wilderness, when he brought them from Egypt. 33Moses told Aaron to get a container and put two quarts of manna in it and to keep it in a sacred place from generation to generation. 34Aaron did this, just as the Lord had instructed Moses, and eventually it was kept in the Ark in the Tabernacle.

35So the people of Israel ate the manna forty years until they arrived in the land of Canaan, where there were crops to eat. 36The omer—the container used to measure the manna—held about two quarts; it is approximately a tenth of a bushel.

The people complain about lack of water

17 Now, at God's command, the people of Israel left the Sihn desert, going by easy stages to Rephidim. But upon arrival, there was no water!

2So once more the people growled and complained to Moses. "Give us water!" they wailed.

"Quiet!" Moses commanded. "Are you trying to test God's patience with you?"

3But, tormented by thirst, they cried out, "Why did you ever take us out of Egypt? Why did you bring us here to die, with our children and cattle too?"

4Then Moses pleaded with Jehovah. "What shall I do? For they are almost ready to stone me."

5, 6Then Jehovah said to Moses, "Take the elders of Israel with you and lead the people out to Mt. Horeb. I will meet you there at the rock. Strike it with your rod—the same one you struck the Nile with—and water will come pouring out, enough for everyone!" Moses did as he was told, and the water gushed out! 7Moses named the place Massah (meaning "tempting Jehovah to slay us"), and sometimes they referred to it as Meribah (meaning "argument" and "strife!")—for it was there that the people of Israel argued against God and tempted him to slay them by saying, "Is Jehovah going to take care of us or not?"

17:5, 6 *Strike it with your rod,* implied.   **17:7** *to slay them,* implied.

16:30
Lev 23:3
Deut 5:12

16:31
Ex 16:15
Num 11:6
Deut 8:3,16

16:32
Ps 111:4,5

16:33
Heb 9:4
Rev 2:17

16:34
Ex 25:16; 30:6
Num 1:50

16:35
Josh 5:12
Neh 9:15,20,21
Ps 78:24

17:1
Ex 16:1; 19:2
Num 33:14

17:2
Ex 5:21; 14:11
15:24; 16:2
Num 14:22; 20:2
Deut 6:16

17:3
Ex 16:3
Num 11:4,5

17:4
Ex 15:25
Num 11:11
14:10; 16:19

17:5,6
Ex 3:1,16; 7:20
Num 20:8-10
Neh 9:15
Ps 78:15
105:41
1 Cor 10:4

17:7
Deut 6:16; 9:22
Ps 81:7; 95:8
Heb 3:8

JOURNEY TO MOUNT SINAI
God miraculously supplied food and water in the wilderness for the Israelites. In the Sihn wilderness, he provided manna (16). At Rephidim, he provided water from a rock (17:1-7). Finally God brought them to the foot of Mount Sinai, where he gave them his holy laws.

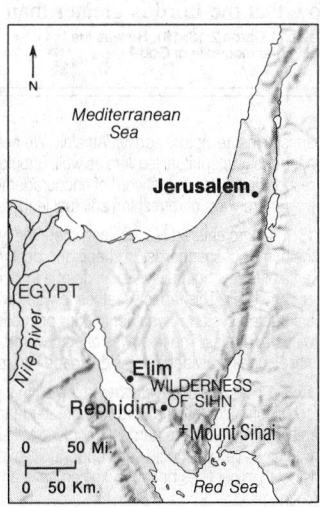

16:32 The Hebrews put some manna in a special jar as a reminder of the way God provided for them in the wilderness. Symbols can be an important part of Christian worship. We use special objects as symbols to remind us of God's work in our lives. Such symbols can be valuable aids to our worship as long as we are careful to keep them from becoming objects of worship.

17:2 Again the people complained about their problem instead of praying. Some problems can be solved by careful thought or by rearranging our lives. Some can be solved by discussion and good counsel. But some problems can be solved only by prayer. We should make a determined effort to pray when we feel like complaining because complaining only raises our feelings of stress.

8But now the warriors of Amalek came to fight against the people of Israel at Rephidim. 9Moses instructed Joshua to issue a call to arms to the Israelites, to fight the army of Amalek.

"Tomorrow," Moses told him, "I will stand at the top of the hill, with the rod of God in my hand!"

10So Joshua and his men went out to fight the army of Amalek. Meanwhile Moses, Aaron, and Hur went to the top of the hill. 11And as long as Moses held up the rod in his hands, Israel was winning; but whenever he rested his arms at his sides, the soldiers of Amalek were winning. 12Moses' arms finally became too tired to hold up the rod any longer; so Aaron and Hur rolled a stone for him to sit on, and they stood on each side, holding up his hands until sunset. 13As a result, Joshua and his troops crushed the army of Amalek, putting them to the sword.

14Then the Lord instructed Moses, "Write this into a permanent record, to be remembered forever, and announce to Joshua that I will utterly blot out every trace of Amalek." 15, 16Moses built an altar there and called it "Jehovah-nissi" (meaning "Jehovah is my flag").

"Raise the banner of the Lord!" Moses said. "For the Lord will be at war with Amalek generation after generation."

Jethro visits Moses

18 Word soon reached Jethro, Moses' father-in-law, the priest of Midian, about all the wonderful things God had done for his people and for Moses, and how the Lord had brought them out of Egypt.

2Then Jethro took Moses' wife, Zipporah, to him (for he had sent her home), 3along with Moses' two sons, Gershom (meaning "foreigner," for Moses said when he was born, "I have been wandering in a foreign land") 4and Eliezer (meaning "God is my help," for Moses said at his birth, "The God of my fathers was my helper, and delivered me from the sword of Pharaoh"). 5, 6They arrived while Moses and the people were camped at Mt. Sinai.

"Jethro, your father-in-law, has come to visit you," Moses was told, "and he has brought your wife and your two sons."

7Moses went out to meet his father-in-law and greeted him warmly; they asked about each other's health and then went into Moses' tent to talk further. 8Moses related to his father-in-law all that had been happening and what the Lord had done to Pharaoh and the Egyptians in order to deliver Israel, and all the problems there had been along the way, and how the Lord delivered his people from all of them. 9Jethro was very happy about everything the Lord had done for Israel, and about his bringing them out of Egypt.

10"Bless the Lord," Jethro said, "for he has saved you from the Egyptians and from Pharaoh, and has rescued Israel. 11I know now that the Lord is greater than

17:8
Gen 36:12,16
Num 24:20
Deut 25:17
1 Sam 15:2
17:9
Ex 24:13
Num 11:28
17:10
Ex 24:14; 31:2
1 Chron 2:18,19
17:11,12
Heb 12:12

17:14
Ex 24:4; 34:27
Num 33:2
Deut 25:19
17:15,16
Gen 22:14
Ps 60:4

18:1
Ex 2:16,18; 3:1
18:2
Ex 2:21; 4:25
18:3
Ex 2:22; 4:20
Acts 7:29
Heb 11:13
18:4
Gen 28:13
49:25
Ps 46:1
Isa 50:7
18:5,6
Ex 3:1; 4:27
18:7
Gen 43:26
18:8
Ex 15:4,8,22
Num 20:14
Neh 9:9-15
18:9
Isa 44:23; 63:7
18:10
1 Kgs 8:56
Ps 68:19
106:44-46
18:11
Ex 10:2; 15:11

17:10 *Hur.* Hur was a man of Judah, of the family of Hezron, house of Caleb (1 Chron 2:18, 19). He was the grandfather of Bezalel (31:1, 2). **18:5, 6** *Mt. Sinai*, or, "Mt. Horeb." Literally, "the mountain of God."

17:8 The Amalekites were descendants of Amalek, a grandson of Esau. They were a fierce nomadic nation or tribe who lived in the desert region of the Dead Sea. Part of their livelihood was made by conducting frequent raids on other settlements and carrying off booty. They killed for pleasure. One of the greatest insults in Israelite culture was to call someone "a friend of Amalek."

When the Israelites entered the region, the Amalekites saw this as a perfect opportunity for both pleasure and profit. But this hostile tribe was moving in on the wrong people—a people led by God. For the Israelite slaves to defeat such a warlike nation was more than enough proof that God was with them as he had promised to be.

17:9 Here we meet Joshua for the first time. Later he became the great leader who brought God's people into the Promised Land. As a general of the Israelite army, he was gaining valuable experience for the greater battles to come.

17:10–13 Aaron and Hur stood by Moses' side and held up his

arms to insure victory against Amalek. We need to "lift up the hands" of our spiritual leaders as well. Shouldering some responsibility, lending a word of encouragement, or offering a prayer are ways of refreshing spiritual leaders in their work.

18:7 Jethro entered Moses' tent where the two talked. Tents were the homes of shepherds. In shape and design, they resembled the tents of today, but they were made of a thick cloth woven from goat or camel hair. This fabric breathed in warm weather and contracted in stormy weather to offer protection from the winter winds and rains. The floor was often covered with animal-skin rugs, while curtains divided the inside space into rooms.

18:8–11 Moses told his father-in-law all that God had done, convincing him that the Lord was greater than any other god. Our relatives are often the hardest people to tell about our relationship with God. Yet we should seek opportunities to tell them what God is doing in our lives because we can have an important influence on them.

18:12
Gen 31:54
Ex 24:5
Job 1:5

any other god because he delivered his people from the proud and cruel Egyptians.

12Jethro offered sacrifices to God, and afterwards Aaron and the leaders of Israel came to meet Jethro, and they all ate the sacrificial meal together before the Lord.

Jethro's wise advice

13The next day Moses sat as usual to hear the people's complaints against each other, from morning to evening.

14When Moses' father-in-law saw how much time this was taking, he said, "Why are you trying to do all this alone, with people standing here all day long to get your help?"

18:15,16
Lev 24:12-14
Num 9:6-8
15:34
Deut 17:8-13
2 Sam 15:3

15, 16"Well, because the people come to me with their disputes, to ask for God's decisions," Moses told him. "I am their judge, deciding who is right and who is wrong, and instructing them in God's ways. I apply the laws of God to their particular disputes."

18:18
Num 11:14
Deut 1:9
Acts 6:1-4

17"It's not right!" his father-in-law exclaimed. 18"You're going to wear yourself out—and if you do, what will happen to the people? Moses, this job is too heavy a burden for you to try to handle all by yourself. 19, 20Now listen, and let me give you a word of advice, and God will bless you: Be these people's lawyer—their representative before God—bringing him their questions to decide; you will tell them his decisions, teaching them God's laws, and showing them the principles of godly living.

18:19,20
Deut 1:17; 4:1

18:21
Deut 1:12-15
16:18
1 Kgs 3:9
Ps 15:1-5

21"Find some capable, godly, honest men who hate bribes, and appoint them as judges, one judge for each 1000 people; he in turn will have ten judges under him, each in charge of a hundred; and under each of them will be two judges, each responsible for the affairs of fifty people; and each of these will have five judges beneath him, each counseling ten persons. 22Let these men be responsible to serve the people with justice at all times. Anything that is too important or complicated can be brought to you. But the smaller matters they can take care of themselves. That way it will be easier for you because you will share the burden with them. 23If you follow this advice, and if the Lord agrees, you will be able to endure the pressures, and there will be peace and harmony in the camp."

18:22
Num 15:33
27:2; 36:1
Deut 17:8

24Moses listened to his father-in-law's advice, and followed this suggestion. 25He chose able men from all over Israel and made them judges over the people—thousands, hundreds, fifties, and tens. 26They were constantly available to administer justice. They brought the hard cases to Moses but judged the smaller matters themselves.

18:25
Deut 1:15; 16:18

18:26
Deut 17:8

27Soon afterwards Moses let his father-in-law return to his own land.

18:27
Num 10:29,30

C. ISRAEL AT SINAI (19:1—40:38)

After escaping through the Red Sea, the Hebrews traveled through the wilderness and arrived at Sinai, God's holy mountain. There they received the Ten Commandments, as well as instructions for building a Tabernacle as a center of worship. Through Israel's experiences at Mount Sinai, we learn about the importance of obedience in our relationship with God. His laws help expose sin, and they give standards for righteous living.

1. Giving the Law

19:1
Ex 12:51; 16:1

19 The Israelis arrived in the Sinai peninsula three months after the night of their departure from Egypt. 2, 3After breaking camp at Rephidim, they came to the

18:12 *sacrifices,* literally, "a burnt offering and sacrifices for God."

18:12 The Israelites frequently shared a sacrificial meal among themselves. A burnt offering was sacrificed to God, and then the meal taken from the sacrifice was dedicated to God and eaten ceremonially as a type of fellowship dinner.

18:13-26 Moses was spending so much time and energy hearing the Hebrews' complaints that he could not get to other important work. Jethro suggested that Moses delegate most of this work to others and focus his efforts on jobs only he could do. People in positions of responsibility sometimes feel they are the only ones who can do necessary tasks, but others are capable of handling

part of the load. Delegation relieved Moses' stress and improved the quality of the people's lives as well.

19:2, 3 Mount Sinai is one of the most sacred locations in Israel's history. Located in the south-central Sinai peninsula, this mountain is where Moses met God in a burning bush, God made his covenant with Israel, and Elijah heard God in "the sound of a gentle whisper." Here God's people learned the potential blessings of obedience (Exodus 24:9-18) and the tragic consequences of disobedience (Exodus 32).

base of Mt. Sinai and set up camp there. Moses climbed the rugged mountain to meet with God, and from somewhere in the mountain God called to him and said,

"Give these instructions to the people of Israel. Tell them, 4'You have seen what I did to the Egyptians, and how I brought you to myself as though on eagle's wings. 5Now if you will obey me and keep your part of my contract with you, you shall be my own little flock from among all the nations of the earth; for all the earth is mine. 6And you shall be a kingdom of priests to God, a holy nation.' "

7Moses returned from the mountain and called together the leaders of the people and told them what the Lord had said.

8They all responded in unison, "We will certainly do everything he asks of us." Moses reported the words of the people to the Lord.

9Then he said to Moses, "I am going to come to you in the form of a dark cloud, so that the people themselves can hear me when I talk with you, and then they will always believe you. 10Go down now and see that the people are ready for my visit. Sanctify them today and tomorrow, and have them wash their clothes. 11Then, the day after tomorrow, I will come down upon Mt. Sinai as all the people watch. 12Set boundary lines the people may not pass, and tell them, 'Beware! Do not go up into the mountain, or even touch its boundaries; whoever does shall die— 13no hand shall touch him, but he shall be stoned or shot to death with arrows, whether man or animal.' Stay away from the mountain entirely until you hear a ram's horn sounding one long blast; then gather at the foot of the mountain!"

14So Moses went down to the people and sanctified them and they washed their clothing.

15He told them, "Get ready for God's appearance two days from now, and do not have sexual intercourse with your wives."

16On the morning of the third day there was a terrific thunder and lightning storm, and a huge cloud came down upon the mountain, and there was a long, loud blast as from a ram's horn; and all the people trembled. 17Moses led them out from the camp to meet God, and they stood at the foot of the mountain. 18All Mt. Sinai was covered with smoke because Jehovah descended upon it in the form of fire; the smoke billowed into the sky as from a furnace, and the whole mountain shook with a violent earthquake. 19As the trumpet blast grew louder and louder, Moses spoke and God thundered his reply. 20So the Lord came down upon the top of Mt. Sinai and called Moses up to the top of the mountain, and Moses ascended to God.

21But the Lord told Moses, "Go back down and warn the people not to cross the boundaries. They must not come up here to try to see God, for if they do, many of them will die. 22Even the priests on duty must sanctify themselves, or else I will destroy them."

23"But the people won't come up into the mountain!" Moses protested. "You told them not to! You told me to set boundaries around the mountain, and to declare it off limits because it is reserved for God.

24But Jehovah said, "Go down, and bring Aaron back with you, and don't let the

19:22 *the priests on duty,* literally, "the priests who come near to Jehovah."

19:4
Deut 4:9; 32:11
Isa 40:31; 63:9
Rev 12:14
19:5
Ex 15:26; 23:22
24:7
Deut 4:20; 14:2
Isa 41:8
19:6
Lev 11:44 ,45
Deut 33:2-4
Isa 61:6
1 Pet 2:5,9
Rev 1:6; 5:10
19:7
Ex 4:29,30
24:9
19:8
Ex 4:31; 24:3,7
Deut 5:27; 26:17
19:9
Ex 14:31; 19:16
Deut 4:11
Ps 99:7
1 Kgs 8:12
19:10
Gen 35:2
Josh 3:5
Heb 10:22
Rev 7:14; 22:14
19:11
Ex 19:16; 34:5
19:13
Heb 12:20
19:15
1 Sam 21:4
Mt 3:2
1 Cor 7:5
19:16
Ex 9:23; 20:18
Heb 12:18,19
19:17
Deut 4:10; 5:5
19:18
Ex 24:17
Deut 5:4
Ps 68:7,8
104:32
19:19
Ps 81:7
19:20
Ex 24:12
Neh 9:13
19:21
Ex 3:5; 33:20
19:22
Lev 10:2,3
21:5-8
19:24
Ex 24:1,9,12

19:4-6 God had a reason for rescuing the Israelites from slavery. Now he was ready to tell them what it was: Israel was to become a holy people, a nation of priests in which anyone could approach God freely. It didn't take long, however, for the people to corrupt God's plan. God then established the Levites as priests, representing what the entire nation should have been (Leviticus 8—9). But with the coming of Jesus Christ, God has once again extended his plan to all believers. We are to become holy, a changed people "filled with God." The death and resurrection of Christ has allowed each of us to approach God freely once again.

19:5 Why did God choose Israel as his nation? God knew that no nation on earth was good enough to deserve to be called his people. He chose Israel, not because of anything they had done, but *in spite of* the wrong things they had done and would do. Why

did he want to have a special nation on earth? To represent his ways and to be a saving presence in the world. Abraham's descendants were to "be a source of blessing for all the nations of the earth" (Genesis 18:18). "All nations will come to your light," Isaiah predicted (Isaiah 60:3).God chose one nation and put it through a rigorous training program, so that one day it could be a channel for his blessings to the whole world.

19:5-8 In Genesis 15 and 17, God made a covenant with Abraham, promising to make his descendants into a great nation. Now that promise was being realized as God restated his agreement with the Israelite nation, the descendants of Abraham. God promised to bless and care for them. The people promised to obey him. The covenant was thus sealed. But the good intentions of the people quickly wore off. Have you made a commitment to God? How are you holding up your end of the bargain?

priests and the people break across the boundaries to try to come up here, or I will punish them."

25So Moses went down to the people and told them what God had said.

The Ten Commandments

20:3
Ex 15:11; 20:23
Deut 5:7; 6:14

20:4
Lev 26:1
Deut 4:15-20

20:5
Ex 23:24; 34:14
Num 14:18
Deut 4:24; 5:9

20 Then God issued this edict:

2"I am Jehovah your God who liberated you from your slavery in Egypt.

3"You may worship no other god than me.

4"You shall not make yourselves any idols: no images of animals, birds, or fish.

5You must never bow or worship it in any way; for I, the Lord your God, am very possessive. I will not share your affection with any other god!

"And when I punish people for their sins, the punishment continues upon the

---

JESUS AND THE TEN COMMAND-MENTS

The Ten Commandments said . . .	Jesus said . . .
Exodus 20:3 "Worship no other gods"	Matthew 4:10 "Worship only the Lord God. Obey only him"
Exodus 20:4 "You shall not make any idols"	Luke 16:13 "Neither you nor anyone else can serve two masters"
Exodus 20:7 "You shall not use the name of . . . God irreverently, nor use it to swear"	Matthew 5:34 "But I say, 'Don't make any vows! And even to say, By heavens, is a sacred vow to God"
Exodus 20:8–10 "Observe the Sabbath as a holy day . . . on that day you are to do no work"	Mark 2:27–28 "The Sabbath was made to benefit man, and not man to benefit the Sabbath. And I, the Messiah, have authority even to decide what men can do on Sabbath days!"
Exodus 20:12 "Honor your father and mother"	Matthew 10:37 "If you love your father and mother more than you love me, you are not worthy of being mine"
Exodus 20:13 "You must not murder"	Matthew 5:22 ". . . If you are only angry. . .you are in danger of judgment"
Exodus 20:14 "You must not commit adultery"	Matthew 5:28 "Anyone who even looks at a woman with lust in his eye has already committed adultery with her in his heart"
Exodus 20:15 "You must not steal"	Matthew 5:40 "If your shirt is taken, give your coat too"
Exodus 20:16 "You must not lie"	Matthew 12:36 "You must give an account on Judgment Day for every idle word you speak"
Exodus 20:17 "You must not be envious"	Luke 12:15 "Beware! Don't always be wishing for what you don't have"

20:1 Why was the Law necessary for God's new nation? At the foot of Mount Sinai, God showed his people the true function and beauty of the Law. The Law was designed to lead Israel to a life of *practical* holiness. Its commands and guidelines were intended to direct the community to meet the needs of each individual in a loving and responsible manner. By Jesus' time, however, most people looked at the Law the wrong way. They saw it as a means to salvation. To obey every law was the ticket to eternal life, they thought. But here God shows that the Law is a blueprint for living, not a method of salvation.

20:1, 2 The Israelites had just come from Egypt, a land of many idols and many gods. Since each god represented a different aspect of a person's life, it was common to worship many gods in order to have the most fulfilled life. When God told his people to worship and believe in him, that wasn't so hard for them—he was

just one more god to add to the list. But when he said, "worship no other god than me," that was hard for the people to accept. But if they didn't learn that the God who led them out of Egypt was the only true God, they could not be his people—no matter how faithfully they kept the other nine commandments. Thus, God made this his first commandment and emphasized it more than the others.

Today we can allow certain values to become gods to us. Money, fame, work, or pleasure can become gods when we concentrate too much on them for meaning and security. No one sets out with the intention of worshiping these things. But by the amount of time they occupy in our lives, they can grow into gods that ultimately control our thoughts and energies. Letting God hold the central place in our lives keeps these things from turning into gods.

children, grandchildren, and great-grandchildren of those who hate me; 6but I lavish my love upon thousands of those who love me and obey my commandments.

7"You shall not use the name of Jehovah your God irreverently, nor use it to swear to a falsehood. You will not escape punishment if you do.

8"Remember to observe the Sabbath as a holy day. 9Six days a week are for your daily duties and your regular work, 10but the seventh day is a day of Sabbath rest before the Lord your God. On that day you are to do no work of any kind, nor shall your son, daughter, or slaves—whether men or women—or your cattle or your house guests. 11For in six days the Lord made the heaven, earth, and sea, and everything in them, and rested the seventh day; so he blessed the Sabbath day and set it aside for rest.

12"Honor your father and mother, that you may have a long, good life in the land the Lord your God will give you.

13"You must not murder.

14"You must not commit adultery.

15"You must not steal.

16"You must not lie.

17"You must not be envious of your neighbor's house, or want to sleep with his wife, or want to own his slaves, oxen, donkeys, or anything else he has."

18All the people saw the lightning and the smoke billowing from the mountain, and heard the thunder and the long, frightening trumpet blast; and they stood at a distance, shaking with fear.

19They said to Moses, "You tell us what God says and we will obey, but don't let God speak directly to us, or it will kill us."

20"Don't be afraid," Moses told them, "for God has come in this way to show you his awesome power, so that from now on you will be afraid to sin against him!"

21As the people stood in the distance, Moses entered into the deep darkness where God was.

22And the Lord told Moses to be his spokesman to the people of Israel. "You are witnesses to the fact that I have made known my will to you from heaven.

20:6
Ex 34:6,7
Deut 7:9

20:7
Lev 19:12
Deut 5:11; 6:13

20:8
Gen 2:3
Ex 16:23;
31:12-15
Deut 5:12

20:9
Ex 23:12; 34:21
Deut 5:13

20:11
Gen 2:2,3
Mk 2:27

20:12
Lev 19:1-3
Deut 5:16,33
Mt 15:4; Eph 6:2

20:13
Gen 4:8-12; 9:5
Deut 5:17
Mt 5:21,22

20:14
Lev 20:10
Mt 5:27,28

20:15
Lev 6:1-7
19:11,13
Mt 15:19; 19:18

20:16
Deut 5:20
19:15-21

20:18
Heb 12:18

20:19
Gen 32:30
Ex 33:20

20:21
Deut 5:22
Ps 97:2

20:7 use the name of Jehovah your God irreverently, or, "you must not use the name of the Lord your God to swear falsely." **20:11** blessed the Sabbath day and set it aside for rest, or, "hallowed it." **20:16** You must not lie, or, "You must not give false testimony in court."

20:7 God's name is special, for it carries his personal identity. Using it frivolously or in a curse is so common today that we may fail to realize how serious it is. The way we use God's name conveys how we really feel about him. We should respect his name and use it appropriately, speaking it in praise or worship rather than in curse or jest. We will not be found blameless if we dishonor his name.

20:8-11 The Sabbath was a day set aside for rest and worship. God commanded a Sabbath because we need to spend unhurried time in worship and rest each week. A God who is concerned enough to provide a day each week for us to rest is indeed a wonderful God. To observe a regular time of rest and worship in our hurried world demonstrates the importance of God in our lives while having the extra benefit of refreshing our spirits.

20:12 This is the first commandment with a promise. To live in peace for generations in the Promised Land, the Israelites would need to respect authority and build strong families. But what does it mean to "honor" parents? Partly, "honoring" means speaking well of them and politely to them. It also means acting in a way that shows them courtesy and respect (but we are not to follow them in acts of disobedience to God). Parents have a special place in God's sight. Even those who find it difficult to get along with their parents are still commanded to honor them.

20:16 Lying is an attempt to deceive. We deceive others by leaving something out of a story, by telling a half-truth, by twisting the facts, or by inventing a falsehood. God warns us against these kinds of deceptions. Even though deception is a way of life for many people, we must resist it!

20:17 God says we must not envy the possessions of others. He knows that possessions cannot make us happy.You can admire someone else's possessions and even think, "I'd like to have one of those," without being envious. Envy comes when you resent the fact that others have what you don't. Resentment and envy go hand-in-hand.

Since only God can supply all our needs, true contentment is found in him. When you begin to feel envious, try to determine if there is a more basic need you have that stands behind that envy. For example, you may be envious of someone's success not because you want to take away his success, but because you have a more basic need to feel appreciated by others. If this is the case, pray that God will bring you through your envy and help you meet those basic needs.

20:18 Sometimes God speaks to his people with a majestic display of power; at other times he speaks quietly. Why the difference? God speaks in the way that best accomplishes his purposes. At Sinai, the awesome display of light and sound was necessary to show Israel God's great power and authority. Only then would they listen to Moses and Aaron.

20:20 Throughout the Bible we find this phrase, "Don't be afraid!" God wasn't trying to scare the people. He was showing his mighty power so the Israelites would know he was the true God and would therefore obey him. God wants us to follow him out of love rather than fear. To overcome fear, we must think more about his love. 1 John 4:18 says, "We need have no fear of someone who loves us perfectly."

20:23
Ex 20:4; 32:4
Deut 29:17

20:24
Ex 10:25; 18:12
24:5; 27:1-8
Deut 12:4,5

20:25
Deut 27:5
Josh 8:31

20:26
Ex 28:42

21:1
Lev 18:4,5,26
Deut 5:1,31

21:2
Lev 25:39-43
Deut 15:12
Neh 5:1,2
Jer 34:9-11

21:5
Deut 15:16

21:6
Ex 18:21
21:7
Neh 5:5
21:8
Deut 21:11-14
21:10
1 Cor 7:2-6
21:11
Ex 20:2,3
21:12
Gen 9:5
Ex 20:13
Lev 24:21
21:13
Num 35:9-29,32
Deut 19:1-10
Josh 20:1-10
21:14
Ex 20:13
Num 35:30,31
Deut 19:11-13
1 Kgs 2:28-34
21:15
Ex 20:12
Deut 21:18
Prov 30:11,17
21:16
Deut 24:7
1 Tim 1:10
21:17
Lev 20:9
Deut 27:16
Mt 15:4
Mk 7:10
21:18
Num 35:16,17

23Remember, you must not make or worship idols made of silver or gold or of anything else!

24"The altars you make for me must be simple altars of earth. Offer upon them your sacrifices to me—your burnt offerings and peace offerings of sheep and oxen. Build altars only where I tell you to, and I will come and bless you there. 25You may also build altars from stone, but if you do, then use only uncut stones and boulders. Don't chip or shape the stones with a tool, for that would make them unfit for my altar. 26And don't make steps for the altar, or someone might look up beneath the skirts of your clothing and see your nakedness.

Laws concerning people

21 "Here are other laws you must obey:
2"If you buy a Hebrew slave, he shall serve only six years and be freed in the seventh year, and need pay nothing to regain his freedom.

3"If he sold himself as a slave before he married, then if he married afterwards, only he shall be freed; but if he was married before he became a slave, then his wife shall be freed with him at the same time. 4But if his master gave him a wife while he was a slave, and they have sons or daughters, the wife and children shall still belong to the master, and he shall go out by himself free.

5"But if the man shall plainly declare, 'I prefer my master, my wife, and my children, and I would rather not go free,' 6then his master shall bring him before the judges and shall publicly bore his ear with an awl, and after that he will be a slave forever.

7"If a man sells his daughter as a slave, she shall not be freed at the end of six years as the men are. 8If she does not please the man who bought her, then he shall let her be bought back again; but he has no power to sell her to foreigners, since he has wronged her by no longer wanting her after marrying her. 9And if he arranges an engagement between a Hebrew slave-girl and his son, then he may no longer treat her as a slave-girl, but must treat her as a daughter. 10If he himself marries her and then takes another wife, he may not reduce her food or clothing, or fail to sleep with her as his wife. 11If he fails in any of these three things, then she may leave freely without any payment.

12"Anyone who hits a man so hard that he dies shall surely be put to death. 13But if it is accidental—an act of God—and not intentional, then I will appoint a place where he can run and get protection. 14However, if a man deliberately attacks another, intending to kill him, drag him even from my altar, and kill him.

15"Anyone who strikes his father or mother shall surely be put to death.

16"A kidnapper must be killed, whether he is caught in possession of his victim or has already sold him as a slave.

17"Anyone who reviles or curses his mother or father shall surely be put to death.

18"If two men are fighting, and one hits the other with a stone or with his fist and injures him so that he must be confined to bed, but doesn't die, 19if later he is able to walk again, even with a limp, the man who hit him will be innocent except that

21:2 *If you buy a Hebrew slave,* that is, "If he owes you money and defaults in the payment, and thus becomes your slave." **21:19** *if later he is able to walk again, even with a limp,* literally, "if he walks abroad with his staff."

20:24-26 Why were specific directions given for building altars? God's people had no Bible and few religious traditions to learn from. God had to start from scratch and teach them how to worship him. God gave specific instructions about building altars because he wanted to control the way sacrifices were offered. To prevent idolatry from creeping into worship, God did not allow the altar stones to be cut or shaped into any form. Nor did God let the people build an altar just anywhere. This was designed to prevent them from starting their own religions or making changes in the way God wanted things done.

21:1ff These laws were given because everything we do has consequences. It is vital to think before acting, to consider the effects of our choices. Think of the things you are planning to do

today and consider what their long-range results will be. As we deal with others, we should keep the principles of these laws in mind. We should act responsibly and justly with all people—friends and enemies alike.

21:2 The Hebrews, though freed from slavery, had slaves themselves. A person could become a slave because of poverty, debt, or even crime. But Hebrew slaves were treated as humans, not property, and were allowed to work their way to freedom. The Bible acknowledged the existence of slavery but never encouraged it. Today, as in Moses' day, some people cannot have physical freedom. But they can be free from spiritual death by following God's laws for living.

he must pay for the loss of his time until he is thoroughly healed, and pay any medical expenses.

20"If a man beats his slave to death—whether the slave is male or female—that man shall surely be punished. 21However, if the slave does not die for a couple of days, then the man shall not be punished—for the slave is his property.

21:21
Lev 25:44-46

22"If two men are fighting, and in the process hurt a pregnant woman so that she has a miscarriage, but she lives, then the man who injured her shall be fined whatever amount the woman's husband shall demand, and as the judges approve. 23But if any harm comes to the woman and she dies, he shall be executed.

21:23
Ex 20:13; 21:12
21:24,25
Lev 24:20-22
Deut 19:21
Mt 5:38

24"If her eye is injured, injure his; if her tooth is knocked out, knock out his; and so on—hand for hand, foot for foot, 25burn for burn, wound for wound, lash for lash.

26"If a man hits his slave in the eye, whether man or woman, and the eye is blinded, then the slave shall go free because of his eye. 27And if a master knocks out his slave's tooth, he shall let him go free to pay for the tooth.

21:26
Job 31:13

28"If an ox gores a man or woman to death, the ox shall be stoned and its flesh not eaten, but the owner shall not be held— 29unless the ox was known to gore people in the past, and the owner had been notified and still the ox was not kept under control; in that case, if it kills someone, the ox shall be stoned and the owner also shall be killed. 30But the dead man's relatives may accept a fine instead, if they wish. The judges will determine the amount.

21:28
Gen 9:5

21:30
Num 30:11,12
35:31

31"The same law holds if the ox gores a boy or a girl. 32But if the ox gores a slave, whether male or female, the slave's master shall be given thirty pieces of silver, and the ox shall be stoned.

21:32
Gen 37:28
Zech 11:12
Mt 26:15; 27:3,9

Laws about property

33"If a man digs a well and doesn't cover it, and an ox or a donkey falls into it, 34the owner of the well shall pay full damages to the owner of the animal, and the dead animal shall belong to him.

21:34
Ex 22:5

35"If a man's ox injures another, and it dies, then the two owners shall sell the live ox and divide the price between them—and each shall also own half of the dead ox. 36But if the ox was known from past experience to gore, and its owner has not kept it under control, then there will not be a division of the income; but the owner of the living ox shall pay in full for the dead ox, and the dead one shall be his.

22 "If a man steals an ox or sheep and then kills or sells it, he shall pay a fine of five to one—five oxen shall be returned for each stolen ox. For sheep, the fine shall be four to one—four sheep returned for each sheep stolen.

22:1
Lev 6:1-7
2 Sam 12:6
Prov 6:31
Lk 19:8

2"If a thief is caught in the act of breaking into a house and is killed, the one who killed him is not guilty. 3But if it happens in the daylight, it must be presumed to be murder and the man who kills him is guilty.

22:2
Num 35:26,27
22:3
Ex 20:13
21:2,14

"If a thief is captured, he must make full restitution; if he can't, then he must be sold as a slave for his debt.

4"If he is caught in the act of stealing a live ox or donkey or sheep or whatever it is, he shall pay double value as his fine.

22:4
Prov 6:30
Jer 2:26
Jn 12:6

21:30 Literally, verse 30 reads: "But if a ransom is laid upon him, he shall give for the redemption of his life whatever is laid upon him."

21:24, 25 The "eye for an eye" rule was instituted as a guide for judges—not as a rule for personal relationships. This rule fit the punishment to the crime, thereby preventing the cruel and barbaric punishments that characterized many ancient countries.

Jesus took this principle a step further in Matthew 5:38-48. Whether as a parent or as a judge, you must make fitting decisions in order for discipline to be effective. A punishment too harsh is unfair, and one too lenient is powerless to teach. Ask God for wisdom before you judge.

22:1 These are not merely a collection of picky laws but are examples of what is today called a *case study*. God was taking potential situations and showing how his laws would work in the everyday lives of Israelites.

These case studies had these objectives: (1) to protect the nation, (2) to organize the nation, (3) to focus Israel's attention on God. The laws listed here do not cover every possible situation, since each law could apply to an endless number of variations.

22:3 Throughout chapter 22 we find the principle of restitution—making right our wrongs. For example, if a man stole an animal, he had to repay double the beast's market value. If you have done someone wrong, perhaps you should go beyond what is expected to make things right. This will (1) help ease any pain you've caused, (2) help the other person be more forgiving, and (3) make you more likely not to repeat your mistake.

22:5
Ex 21:34

22:7
Lev 6:1-7
Prov 6:30,31
22:8
Ex 21:6
Deut 1:17
22:9
Num 5:7
Deut 25:1
2 Chron 19:10

22:12
Lev 6:2

22:13
Gen 37:33

22:14
Deut 23:19
Neh 5:4
Ps 37:21

22:16
Deut 22:28,29
22:17
Deut 7:3
22:18
Lev 19:26; 20:27
Deut 18:10
22:19
Lev 18:23; 20:15
22:20
Ex 32:8; 34:15
22:21
Lev 19:33,34
22:22
Deut 24:17

22:25
Lev 25:36
Deut 23:19
22:26
Deut 24:6,10-13

5"If someone deliberately lets his animal loose and it gets into another man's vineyard; or if he turns it into another man's field to graze, he must pay for all damages by giving the owner of the field or vineyard an equal amount of the best of his own crop.

6"If the field is being burned off and the fire gets out of control and goes into another field so that the shocks of grain, or the standing grain, are destroyed, the one who started the fire shall make full restitution.

7"If someone gives money or goods to anyone to keep for him, and it is stolen, the thief shall pay double if he is found. 8But if no thief is found, then the man to whom the valuables were entrusted shall be brought before God to determine whether or not he himself has stolen his neighbor's property.

9"In every case in which an ox, donkey, sheep, clothing, or anything else is lost, and the owner believes he has found it in the possession of someone else who denies it, both parties to the dispute shall come before God for a decision, and the one whom God declares guilty shall pay double to the other.

10"If a man asks his neighbor to keep a donkey, ox, sheep, or any other animal for him, and it dies, or is hurt, or gets away, and there is no eyewitness to report just what happened to it, 11then the neighbor must take an oath that he has not stolen it, and the owner must accept his word, and no restitution shall be made for it. 12But if the animal or property has been stolen, the neighbor caring for it must repay the owner. 13If it was attacked by some wild animal, he shall bring the torn carcass to confirm the fact, and shall not be required to make restitution.

14"If a man borrows an animal (or anything else) from a neighbor, and it is injured or killed, and the owner is not there at the time, then the man who borrowed it must pay for it. 15But if the owner is there, he need not pay; and if it was rented, then he need not pay, because this possibility was included in the original rental fee.

General laws

16"If a man seduces a girl who is not engaged to anyone, and sleeps with her, he must pay the usual dowry and accept her as his wife. 17But if her father utterly refuses to let her marry him, then he shall pay the money anyway.

18"A sorceress shall be put to death.

19"Anyone having sexual relations with an animal shall certainly be executed.

20"Anyone sacrificing to any other god than Jehovah shall be executed.

21"You must not oppress a stranger in any way; remember, you yourselves were foreigners in the land of Egypt.

22"You must not exploit widows or orphans; 23if you do so in any way, and they cry to me for my help, I will surely give it. 24And my anger shall flame out against you, and I will kill you with enemy armies, so that your wives will be widows and your children fatherless.

25"If you lend money to a needy fellow-Hebrew, you are not to handle the transaction in an ordinary way, with interest. 26If you take his clothing as a pledge

22:16 *girl,* literally, "a virgin." *usual dowry,* more literally, "customary marriage present to the bride's parents."
22:20 *shall be executed,* literally, "shall be utterly destroyed."

22:18 Why did God's laws speak so strongly against sorcery (Leviticus 19:31; 20:6, 27; Deuteronomy 18:10–12)? Sorcery was punishable by death, because it was a crime against God himself. To invoke evil powers violated the first commandment to "have no other gods." Sorcery was in rebellion against God and his authority. In essence, it was teaming up with Satan instead of God.

22:21 God warned the Israelites not to treat strangers unfairly, for they themselves were once strangers in Egypt. It is not easy coming to a new environment where you feel alone and out of place. Are there strangers in your corner of the world? Refugees? New arrivals at school? Immigrants from another country? Be sensitive to their struggles, and express God's love by your actions.

22:22–27 The Hebrew law code is noted for its fairness toward the poor and less fortunate. God insisted that the poor and powerless be well treated and given the chance to restore their fortunes. We should reflect God's concern for the poor by helping those less fortunate than ourselves.

22:26 Why did the law insist on returning a person's cloak by evening? Cloaks were one of an Israelite's most valuable possessions. Making clothing was difficult and time-consuming. As a result, cloaks were expensive. Most people owned only one. The cloak was used as a blanket, a sack to carry things in, a place to sit, a pledge for a debt, and, of course, as clothing.

of his repayment, you must let him have it back at night. [27]For it is probably his only warmth; how can he sleep without it? If you don't return it, and he cries to me for help, I will hear and be very gracious to him [at your expense], for I am very compassionate.

[28]"You shall not blaspheme God, nor curse government officials—your judges and your rulers.

[29]"You must be prompt in giving me the tithe of your crops and your wine, and the redemption payment for your oldest son.

[30]"As to the firstborn of the oxen and the sheep, give it to me on the eighth day, after leaving it with its mother for seven days.

[31]"And since you yourselves are holy—my special people—do not eat any animal that has been attacked and killed by a wild animal. Leave its carcass for the dogs to eat.

23 "Do not pass along untrue reports. Do not cooperate with an evil man by affirming on the witness stand something you know is false.

[2, 3]"Don't join mobs intent on evil. When on the witness stand, don't be swayed in your testimony by the mood of the majority present, and do not slant your testimony in favor of a man just because he is poor.

[4]"If you come upon an enemy's ox or donkey that has strayed away, you must take it back to its owner. [5]If you see your enemy trying to get his donkey onto its feet beneath a heavy load, you must not go on by, but must help him.

[6]"A man's poverty is no excuse for twisting justice against him.

[7]"Keep far away from falsely charging anyone with evil; never let an innocent person be put to death. I will not stand for this.

[8]"Take no bribes, for a bribe makes you unaware of what you clearly see! A bribe hurts the cause of the person who is right.

[9]"Do not oppress foreigners; you know what it's like to be a foreigner; remember your own experience in the land of Egypt.

[10]"Sow and reap your crops for six years, [11]but let the land rest and lie fallow during the seventh year, and let the poor among the people harvest any volunteer crop that may come up; leave the rest for the animals to enjoy. The same rule applies to your vineyards and your olive groves.

[12]"Work six days only, and rest the seventh; this is to give your oxen and donkeys a rest, as well as the people of your household—your slaves and visitors.

[13]"Be sure to obey all of these instructions; and remember—never mention the name of any other god.

[14]"There are three annual religious pilgrimages you must make.

[15]"The first is the Pilgrimage of Unleavened Bread, when for seven days you are not to eat bread with yeast, just as I commanded you before. This celebration is to be an annual event at the regular time in March, the month you left Egypt; everyone must bring me a sacrifice at that time. [16]Then there is the Harvest Pilgrimage, when

22:27
Ex 2:23
Ps 34:6; 72:12
Isa 19:20

22:28
Lev 24:15
Acts 23:5

22:29
Ex 13:2
23:16,19
34:19,20
Deut 26:2

22:30
Gen 17:12
Lev 12:3; 22:27

22:31
Ex 19:6
Lev 7:24; 17:15
22:8

23:1
Deut 5:20; 19:16

23:2,3
Deut 1:17; 16:19

23:4
Deut 22:1-4

23:6
Ex 22:21-24
Deut 27:19

23:7
Ex 20:13,16
Deut 27:15

23:8
Deut 16:19
1 Sam 8:3; 12:3

23:9
Ex 22:21
Lev 19:33,34

23:10
Lev 25:1

23:11
Lev 26:34,35

23:12
Ex 20:8-11
Deut 5:13

23:13
Deut 4:9,23

23:14
Ex 34:22
Lev 23:4
Deut 16:16

23:15
Ex 12:2; 13:4
Lev 23:5
Num 9:2

23:16
Ex 34:22
Lev 23:9,34
Deut 16:9,13

22:27 *at your expense,* implied.   **23:7** *I will not stand for this,* literally, "I will not acquit the wicked."   **23:13** *never mention the name of any other god,* in prayer, or in taking an oath.   **23:14** *pilgrimages you must make,* or, "feasts you must celebrate."

22:29 The Israelites were to be prompt in giving God their tithes. It was part of God's law that the tithe was to be paid first, right away. Since God doesn't send payment overdue notices, it is easy to take care of other financial responsibilities while letting our tithe slide. Giving to God first out of what he has allowed you to have demonstrates that he has first priority in your life.

23:1 Passing along untrue reports was strictly forbidden by God. Untrue reports and false witnessing undermined families, strained neighborhood cooperation, and made chaos of the justice system. Destructive gossip still causes problems. Even if we do not start a false rumor or initiate a lie, we become responsible if we pass it along. To participate in these activities is to participate in a lie. Make rumor-squelching a mark of your life.

23:2, 3 Frequently rich people bought their acquittal by bribing false witnesses or buying the public's support. The Israelites were

warned against buckling under such pressure. Peer pressure remains a strong force in our lives, pushing us to conform regardless of the direction God would have us go. We can withstand the pressure of the crowd by remembering that popularity and success are temporary while the things God offers remain forever.

23:4, 5 The thought of being kind to enemies was new and startling in a world where revenge was the common form of justice. God not only introduced this idea to the Israelites, he made it law! If a man found a lost animal owned by his enemy, he was to return it at once, even if his enemy would use it to harm him.

Jesus clearly taught in Luke 10:30–37 to reach out to all people in need, even our enemies. Following the laws of right living is hard enough with friends. To apply God's laws of fairness and kindness to our enemies shows we are truly different from the world.

you must bring to me the first of your crops. And, finally, the Pilgrimage of Ingathering at the end of the harvest season. ¹⁷At these three times each year, every man in Israel shall appear before the Lord God.

23:17
Deut 12:5; 16:16

¹⁸"No sacrificial blood shall be offered with leavened bread; no sacrificial fat shall be left unoffered until the next morning.

23:18
Ex 12:10; 34:25
Lev 2:11; 7:15

¹⁹"As you reap each of your crops, bring me the choicest sample of the first day's harvest; it shall be offered to the Lord your God.

23:19
Ex 22:29; 34:26
Lev 23:10

"Do not boil a young goat in its mother's milk.

Instructions regarding enemies

²⁰"See, I am sending an Angel before you to lead you safely to the land I have prepared for you. ²¹Reverence him and obey all of his instructions; do not rebel against him, for he will not pardon your transgression; he is my representative—he bears my name. ²²But if you are careful to obey him, following all my instructions, then I will be an enemy to your enemies. ²³For my Angel shall go before you and bring you into the land of the Amorites, Hittites, Perizzites, Canaanites, Hivites, and Jebusites, to live there. And I will destroy those people before you.

23:20
Ex 3:2; 14:19
23:21
Ex 3:14; 34:5
Num 14:10,11
23:22
Num 24:9
Deut 30:7
23:23
Gen 15:19-21
Deut 7:1
Josh 24:11

²⁴"You must not worship the gods of these other nations, nor sacrifice to them in any way, and you must not follow the evil example of these heathen people; you must utterly conquer them and break down their shameful idols.

23:24
Ex 20:5; 34:13

²⁵"You shall serve the Lord your God only; then I will bless you with food and with water, and I will take away sickness from among you. ²⁶There will be no miscarriages nor barrenness throughout your land, and you will live out the full quota of the days of your life.

23:25
Ex 15:26
Lev 26:3
Deut 7:15
28:1-14

²⁷"The terror of the Lord shall fall upon all the people whose land you invade, and they will flee before you; ²⁸and I will send hornets to drive out the Hivites, Canaanites, and Hittites from before you. ²⁹I will not do it all in one year, for the land would become a wilderness, and the wild animals would become too many to control. ³⁰But I will drive them out a little at a time, until your population has increased enough to fill the land. ³¹And I will set your enlarged boundaries from the Red Sea to the Philistine coast, and from the southern deserts as far as the Euphrates River; and I will cause you to defeat the people now living in the land, and you will drive them out ahead of you.

23:27
Gen 35:5
Ex 15:16
Deut 2:25
23:28
Deut 7:20
23:30
Deut 7:22
Josh 15:63
16:10; 17:12
23:31
Gen 15:18
Josh 21:44
24:12,18

³²"You must make no covenant with them, nor have anything to do with their gods. ³³Don't let them live among you! For I know that they will infect you with their sin of worshiping false gods, and that would be an utter disaster to you."

23:32
Deut 7:2
23:33
Deut 7:16; 12:30

The people promise to obey

24 The Lord now instructed Moses, "Come up here with Aaron, Nadab, Abihu, and seventy of the elders of Israel. All of you except Moses are to worship at a distance. ²Moses alone shall come near to the Lord; and remember, none of the ordinary people are permitted to come up into the mountain at all."

24:1
Ex 6:23; 19:24

24:2
Ex 20:21

³Then Moses announced to the people all the laws and regulations God had given him; and the people answered in unison, "We will obey them all."

24:3
Ex 19:8; 24:7
Deut 5:27; 11:1

⁴Moses wrote down the laws; and early the next morning he built an altar at the foot of the mountain, with twelve pillars around the altar because there were twelve tribes of Israel. ⁵Then he sent some of the young men to sacrifice the burnt

24:4
Deut 31:9
24:5
Ex 18:12
Lev 1:2; 7:11

23:19 *it shall be offered to the Lord your God,* literally, "you shall bring (it) into the house of Jehovah thy God."
23:21 *he is my representative—he bears my name,* literally, "my name is in him."

23:20 Who was this angel that went with the Israelites? Most likely the angel was God. This verse may be referring to the presence of God in the pillar of cloud and fire (Exodus 13:21, 22).

23:24, 25 If you're in the furnace, it's easy to catch fire. God warned the Israelites about their neighbors, whose beliefs and actions could turn them away from him. We also live with neighbors who often have completely different values. We are called to maintain a lifestyle that shows our faith. This can be a struggle,

especially if our Christian lifestyle differs from the norm. Our lives should show that we put our faith before the values of society.

23:32, 33 God continually warned the people to avoid false religions and their idols. In Egypt they had been surrounded by idols, but leaving that idolatrous land did not mean they were free from idols. The land of Canaan was just as infested with idol worship. God knew his people needed extra strength, so he continually emphasized guarding against the influence of idols.

offerings and peace offerings to the Lord. 6Moses took half of the blood of these animals, and drew it off into basins. The other half he splashed against the altar.

7And he read to the people the Book he had written—the Book of the Covenant—containing God's directions and laws. And the people said again, "We solemnly promise to obey every one of these rules."

8Then Moses threw the blood from the basins towards the people and said, "This blood confirms and seals the covenant the Lord has made with you in giving you these laws."

9Then Moses, Aaron, Nadab, Abihu, and seventy of the elders of Israel went up into the mountain. 10And they saw the God of Israel; under his feet there seemed to be a pavement of brilliant sapphire stones, as clear as the heavens.

11Yet, even though the elders saw God, he did not destroy them; and they had a meal together before the Lord.

12And the Lord said to Moses, "Come up to me into the mountain, and remain until I give you the laws and commandments I have written on tablets of stone, so that you can teach the people from them." 13So Moses and Joshua, his assistant, went up into the mountain of God.

14He told the elders, "Stay here and wait for us until we come back; if there are any problems while I am gone, consult with Aaron and Hur."

15Then Moses went up the mountain and disappeared into the cloud at the top. 16And the glory of the Lord rested upon Mt. Sinai and the cloud covered it six days; the seventh day he called to Moses from the cloud. 17Those at the bottom of the mountain saw the awesome sight: the glory of the Lord on the mountain top looked like a raging fire. 18And Moses disappeared into the cloud-covered mountain top, and was there for forty days and forty nights.

2. Tabernacle instructions

25 Jehovah said to Moses, "Tell the people of Israel that everyone who wants to may bring me an offering from this list: Gold, silver, bronze, blue cloth,

24:6
Ex 12:7; 29:16

24:7
Ex 19:8; 24:3
Deut 5:27

24:8
Lev 8:30
Zech 9:11
Mt 26:28
1 Cor 11:25

24:10
Ex 33:20
Num 12:8
Isa 6:5
Ezek 1:26

24:12
Ex 31:18
Jer 31:33

24:13
Ex 17:9; 32:17
33:11

24:15
Ex 19:9
2 Chron 6:1

24:16
Lev 9:23
Num 14:10

24:17
Ex 3:2; 16:10
Deut 4:24,36
Ezek 1:27
Heb 12:29

24:18
Ex 19:20,34:28
Deut 9:9; 10:10
1 Kgs 19:8

25:1
Ex 35:5-9
1 Chron 29:2-5

Verse	Theophany
Genesis 16:7	The Angel of the Lord appeared to Sarah's maid, Hagar, announcing the birth of Abraham's son, Ishmael
Genesis 18:1–11	The Lord appeared to Abraham, foretelling Isaac's birth
Genesis 22:11, 12	The Angel of the Lord stopped Abraham from sacrificing Isaac
Exodus 3:2	The Angel of the Lord appeared to Moses as a flame in a bush
Exodus 14:19	God appeared to Israel in a pillar of cloud and fire to guide them through the wilderness
Exodus 33:11	The Lord spoke to Moses face to face
Daniel 3:25	God appeared as the fourth man in Shadrach, Meshach, and Abednego's fiery furnace

THEOPHANIES IN THE SCRIPTURE
At the foot of Mount Sinai, God appeared to the people of Israel in a physical form. This is called a *theophany*. Here are some of the other times God appeared to Bible people.

24:6–8 Why did Moses throw the blood toward the people, and how did this blood "confirm and seal the covenant" God had made with them?

God is the sovereign judge of the universe. He is also absolutely holy. As the holy judge of all, he condemns sin and judges it worthy of death. In the Old Testament God accepted the death of an animal as a substitute for the sinner. The animal's shed blood was proof that one life had been given for another. So on the one hand blood symbolized the death of the animal, but on the other hand it symbolized the life that was spared as a result. Of course the death of the animal that brought forgiveness in the Old Testament was only a temporary provision, looking forward to the death of Jesus Christ (Hebrews 9:9—10:24).

In this ceremony that Moses conducted, half the blood from the

sacrificed animals was thrown against the altar to show that the sinner could once again approach God because something had died in his place. The other half of the blood from the sacrifice was placed in bowls or basins. This blood was then thrown toward the people to show that their penalty for sin had been paid and they could be reunited with God. Through this symbolic act God's promises to Israel were reaffirmed and spiritual lessons were taught about the future sacrificial death (or atonement) of Jesus Christ.

25:1 Chapters 25 through 31 record God's directions for building the Tabernacle. Chapters 35 through 39 tell how these instructions were actually carried out. But what can all these ancient, complicated details of construction show us today? Several things: first, the high quality of the precious materials making up the

purple cloth, scarlet cloth, fine linen, goat's hair, red-dyed ram's skins, goat-skins, acacia wood, olive oil for the lamps, spices for the anointing oil and for the fragrant incense, onyx stones, stones to be set in the ephod and in the breastplate.

25:8
Ex 29:45; 36:1
Deut 12:11
Rev 21:3

8"For I want the people of Israel to make me a sacred Temple where I can live among them.

25:9
Acts 7:44
Heb 8:5

9"This home of mine shall be a tent pavilion—a Tabernacle. I will give you a drawing of the construction plan, and the details of each furnishing.

The Ark

25:10
Ex 37:1-5
25:12
Ex 26:29; 27:7
37:5; 38:7
25:13
Ex 30:5; 37:4
40:20
25:15
1 Kgs 8:8
25:16
Ex 16:34; 30:6
Heb 9:4
25:17
Ex 37:6; 40:20
Lev 16:13
Rom 3:25
Heb 9:5
25:18
Ex 37:7
25:20
1 Kgs 8:7
Heb 9:5
25:22
Ex 30:6,36
Lev 1:1

10"Using acacia wood, make an Ark 3¾ feet long, 2¼ feet wide, and 2¼ feet high. 11Overlay it inside and outside with pure gold, with a molding of gold all around it. 12Cast four rings of gold for it and attach them to the four lower corners, two rings on each side. 13, 14Make poles from acacia wood overlaid with gold, and fit the poles into the rings at the sides of the Ark, to carry it. 15These carrying poles shall never be taken from the rings, but are to be left there permanently. 16When the Ark is finished, place inside it the tablets of stone I will give you, with the Ten Commandments engraved on them.

17"And make a lid of pure gold, 3¾ feet long and 2¼ feet wide. This is the place of mercy for your sins. 18Then make two statues of Guardian Angels using beaten gold, and place them at the two ends of the lid of the Ark. 19They shall be one piece with the mercy place, one at each end. 20The Guardian Angels shall be facing each other, looking down upon the place of mercy, and shall have wings spread out above the gold lid. 21Install the lid upon the Ark, and place within the Ark the tablets of stone I shall give you. 22And I will meet with you there and talk with you from above the place of mercy between the Guardian Angels; and the Ark will contain the laws of my covenant. There I will tell you my commandments for the people of Israel.

The table

25:23
Ex 37:10; 40:22

25:29
Ex 37:16
Num 4:7

25:30
Ex 35:13; 39:36
40:23
Lev 24:5
Num 4:7
2 Chron 13:11

23"Then make a table of acacia wood three feet long, 1½ feet wide, and 2¼ feet high. 24Overlay it with pure gold, and run a rib of gold around it. 25Put a molding four inches wide around the edge of the top, and a gold ridge along the molding, all around. 26, 27Make four gold rings and put the rings at the outside corner of the four legs, close to the top; these are rings for the poles that will be used to carry the table. 28Make the poles from acacia wood overlaid with gold. 29And make gold dishes, spoons, pitchers, and flagons; 30and always keep the special Bread of the Presence on the table before me.

The lampstand

25:31
Ex 37:17; 40:24
1 Kgs 7:49
Heb 9:2

31"Make a lampstand of pure, beaten gold. The entire lampstand and its decorations shall be one piece—the base, shaft, lamps, and blossoms. 32, 33It will have three branches going out from each side of the center shaft, each branch decorated with three almond flowers. 34, 35The central shaft itself will be decorated with four almond flowers—one placed between each set of branches; also, there will be one flower above the top set of branches and one below the bottom set. 36These decorations and branches and the shaft are all to be one piece of pure, beaten gold.

25:37
Ex 37:23
Zech 4:2
Rev 1:4,12,20
4:5

37Then make seven lamps for the lampstand, and set them so that they reflect their light forward. 38The snuffers and trays are to be made of pure gold. 39You will need about 107 pounds of pure gold for the lampstand and its accessories.

25:16 *place inside it the tablets of stone I will give you, with the Ten Commandments engraved on them,* implied. Literally, "Put into the Ark the Testimony which I shall give you." **25:17** *the place of mercy for your sins,* literally, "mercy seat" or "place of making propitiation for your sins." **25:18** *Guardian Angels,* literally, "cherubim." **25:39** *about 107 pounds of pure gold,* literally, "a [gold] talent." The exact weight is not known.

Tabernacle shows God's greatness and transcendence. Second, the veil surrounding the Holy of Holies shows God's holiness as symbolized by his separation from the common and unclean. Third, the portable nature of the Tabernacle shows God's desire to be with his people.

25:10 Much of the Tabernacle and its furniture was made of acacia wood. Acacia trees flourished in barren regions and were fairly common in Old Testament times. The wood was brownish-orange and very hard, making it an excellent material for furniture. Acacia wood is still used in furniture-making today.

40"Be sure that everything you make follows the pattern I am showing you here on the mountain.

25:40
Acts 7:44
Heb 8:5

The tent

26 "Make the tabernacle-tent from ten colored sheets of fine linen, forty-two feet long and six feet wide, dyed blue, purple, and scarlet, with figures of Guardian Angels embroidered on them. 3Join five sheets end to end for each side of the tent, forming two long pieces, one for each side. 4, 5Use loops at the edges to join these two long pieces together side by side. There are to be fifty loops on each side, opposite each other. 6Then make fifty gold clasps to fasten the loops together, so that the Tabernacle, the dwelling place of God, becomes a single unit.

26:1
Ex 36:8-19

7, 8"The roof of the Tabernacle is made of goat's hair tarpaulins. There are to be eleven of these tarpaulins, each forty-five feet across and six feet wide. 9Connect five of these tarpaulins into one wide section; and use the other six for another wide section. (The sixth tarpaulin will hang down to form a curtain across the front of the sacred tent.) 10, 11Use fifty loops along the edges of each of these two wide pieces, to join them together with fifty bronze clasps. Thus the two widths become one. 12There will be a 1½-foot length of this roof-covering hanging down from the back of the tent, 13and a 1½-foot length at the front. 14On top of these blankets is placed a layer of rams' skins, dyed red, and over them a top layer of goatskins. This completes the roof-covering.

26:7
Ex 35:26; 36:14

26:14
Ex 36:19

15, 16"The framework of the sacred tent shall be made from acacia wood, each frame-piece being fifteen feet high and 2¼ feet wide, standing upright, 17with grooves on each side to mortise into the next upright piece. 18, 19Twenty of these frames will form the south side of the sacred tent, with forty silver bases for the frames to fit into—two bases under each piece of the frame. 20On the north side there will also be twenty of these frames, 21with their forty silver bases, two bases for each frame, one under each edge. 22On the west side there will be six frames, 23and two frames at each corner. 24These corner frames will be connected at the bottom and top with clasps. 25So, in all, there will be eight frames on that end of the building with sixteen silver bases for the frames—two bases under each frame.

26:15
Ex 36:20
40:18,19
Num 4:31

26, 27"Make bars of acacia wood to run across the frames, five bars on each side of the Tabernacle. Also five bars for the rear of the building, facing westward. 28The middle bar, halfway up the frames, runs all the way from end to end of the Tabernacle. 29Overlay the frames with gold, and make gold rings to hold the bars; and also overlay the bars with gold. 30Set up this Tabernacle-tent in the manner I showed you on the mountain.

26:30
Ex 25:40; 39:42
Num 8:4
Acts 7:44
Heb 8:5

The curtains

31"[Inside the Tabernacle], make a curtain from fine linen, with blue, purple, and scarlet Guardian Angels embroidered into the cloth. 32Hang this curtain on gold hooks set into four pillars made from acacia wood overlaid with gold. The pillars are to be set in silver bases. 33Behind this curtain place the Ark containing the stone tablets engraved with God's laws. The curtain will separate the Holy Place and the Most Holy Place.

26:31
Ex 36:35; 40:3
2 Chron 3:14
Mt 27:51
Heb 9:3; 10:20

26:33
Ex 25:16; 40:21

34"Now install the mercy place—the golden lid of the Ark—in the Most Holy Place. 35Place the table and lampstand across the room from each other on the outer side of the veil, the lampstand on the south and the table on the north.

26:34
Ex 25:17; 37:6

36"As a screen for the door of the sacred tent, make another curtain from fine

26:36
Ex 40:28

26:31 Inside the Tabernacle, implied.

26:31 The veil separated the two sacred rooms in the Tabernacle—the Holy Place and the Holy of Holies. The priest entered the Holy Place each day to commune with God and tend to the altar of incense, the lampstand, and the table for the bread. The Holy of Holies was the place where God himself dwelt, his presence resting on the place of mercy which covered the Ark of the Covenant. Only the High Priest could enter the Holy of Holies. Even he could do so only once a year (on the Day of Atonement) to make atonement for the sins of the nation as a whole.

When Jesus Christ died on the cross, the veil in the Temple (which had replaced the Tabernacle) tore from top to bottom (Mark 15:38), symbolizing our free access to God because of Jesus' death. No longer did people have to approach God through priests and sacrifices.

linen, skillfully embroidered in blue, purple, and scarlet. 37Hang this curtain on gold hooks set into posts made from acacia wood overlaid with gold. The posts are to rest on bronze bases.

The altar

27:1
Ex 20:24; 38:1
40:10,29
Ezek 43:13
Heb 13:10
27:2
Ex 29:12
Lev 4:7; 16:18
Num 16:38
27:8
Ex 25:40; 26:30

27 "Using acacia wood, make a square altar 7½ feet wide, and 4½ feet high. 2Make horns for the four corners of the altar, attach them firmly, and overlay everything with bronze. 3The ash buckets, shovels, basins, carcass-hooks, and fire pans are all to be made of bronze. 4Make a bronze grating, with a metal ring at each corner, 5and fit the grating halfway down into the fire box, resting it upon the ledge built there. 6For moving the altar, make poles from acacia wood overlaid with bronze. 7To carry it, put the poles into the rings at each side of the altar. 8The altar is to be hollow, made from planks, just as was shown you on the mountain.

The courtyard

27:9
Ex 38:9-20; 40:8
1 Kgs 6:36; 8:64

9, 10"Then make a courtyard for the Tabernacle, enclosed with curtains made from fine-twined linen. On the south side the curtains will stretch for 150 feet, and be held up by twenty posts, fitting into twenty bronze post holders. The curtains will be held up with silver hooks attached to silver rods, attached to the posts. 11It will be the same on the north side of the court—150 feet of curtains held up by twenty posts fitted into bronze sockets, with silver hooks and rods. 12The west side of the court will be seventy-five feet wide, with ten posts and ten sockets. 13The east side will also be seventy-five feet. 14, 15On each side of the entrance there will be 22½ feet of curtain, held up by three posts imbedded in three sockets.

16"The entrance to the court will be a thirty-foot-wide curtain, made of beautifully embroidered blue, purple, and scarlet fine-twined linen, and attached to four posts imbedded in their four sockets. 17All the posts around the court are to be connected by silver rods, using silver hooks, the posts being imbedded in solid bronze bases. 18So the entire court will be 150 feet long, and 75 feet wide, with curtain walls 7½ feet high, made from fine-twined linen.

27:20
Ex 35:8
Lev 24:2
Zech 4:11,12
27:21
Lev 24:3
Ps 134:1

19"All utensils used in the work of the Tabernacle, including all the pins and pegs for hanging the utensils on the walls, will be made of bronze.

20"Instruct the people of Israel to bring you pure olive oil to use in the lamps of the Tabernacle, to burn there continually. 21Aaron and his sons shall place this eternal flame in the outer holy room, tending it day and night before the Lord, so that it never goes out. This is a permanent rule for the people of Israel.

The clothing for the priests

28:1
Ex 24:1-9
Ps 99:6
Heb 5:4
28:2
Ex 29:5; 31:10
39:1
Lev 8:7,30
Num 20:26

28 "Consecrate Aaron your brother, and his sons Nadab, Abihu, Eleazar, and Ithamar, to be priests, to minister to me. 2Make special clothes for Aaron, to indicate his separation to God—beautiful garments that will lend dignity to his work. 3Instruct those to whom I have given special skill as tailors to make the garments that will set him apart from others, so that he may minister to me in the priest's office. 4This is the wardrobe they shall make: a chestpiece, an ephod, a

---

28:1 God was teaching his people how to worship him. As he did so, he needed ministers to oversee the operations of the Tabernacle and help the people maintain their relationship with God. These men were called priests and Levites, and they could be descendants only of the tribe of Levi.

Exodus 28 and 29 give some details about priests. A priest not only was from the tribe of Levi, but also was a descendant of Aaron, Israel's first High Priest. As such, priests had more responsibilities than Levites.

As High Priest, Aaron was in charge of all the priests and Levites. Only a direct descendant of Aaron could become a High Priest.

The priests performed the daily sacrifices, maintained the

Tabernacle, and counseled the people on how to follow God. They were the people's representatives before God, and as such were required to live lives worthy of their office.

Jesus is now our High Priest (Hebrews 8). Daily sacrifices are no longer required, because he sacrificed himself on the cross for our sins. Ministers today no longer sacrifice animals. Instead they lead us in prayer and teach us about both the blessings and sacrifices that come from our new life as Christians.

28:3 Tailors used their special skills to help with the work in God's house. All of us have special skills. God wants us to use these for his glory. Think about your special talents and abilities and the ways you could use them for God's work in the world. A talent must be used and polished or it will tarnish.

robe, an embroidered shirt, a turban, and a sash. They shall also make special garments for Aaron's sons.

5, 6"The ephod shall be made by the most skilled of the workmen, using gold, blue, purple, and scarlet threads of fine linen. 7It will consist of two pieces, front and back, joined at the shoulders. 8And the sash shall be made of the same material—threads of gold, blue, purple, and scarlet fine-twined linen. 9Take two onyx stones, and engrave on them the names of the tribes of Israel. 10Six names shall be on each stone, so that all the tribes are named in the order of their births. 11When engraving these names, use the same technique as in making a seal; and mount the stones in gold settings. 12Fasten the two stones upon the shoulders of the ephod, as memorial stones for the people of Israel: Aaron will carry their names before the Lord as a constant reminder. 13, 14Two chains of pure, twisted gold shall be made and attached to gold clasps on the shoulder of the ephod.

28:5
Ex 39:2
Lev 8:7

28:12
Ex 39:7

15"Then, using the most careful workmanship, make a chestpiece to be used as God's oracle; use the same gold, blue, purple, and scarlet threads of fine-twined linen as you did in the ephod. 16This chestpiece is to be of two folds of cloth, forming a pouch nine inches square. 17Attach to it four rows of stones: A ruby, a topaz, and an emerald shall be in the first row. 18The second row will be carbuncle, a sapphire, and a diamond. 19The third row will be an amber, an agate, and an amethyst. 20The fourth row will be an onyx, a beryl, and a jasper—all set in gold settings. 21Each stone will represent one of the tribes of Israel and the name of that tribe will be engraved upon it like a seal.

28:15
Ex 39:8

28:17
Ex 39:10

22, 23, 24"Attach the top of the chestpiece to the ephod by means of two twisted cords of pure gold. One end of each cord is attached to gold rings placed at the outer top edge of the chestpiece. 25The other ends of the two cords are attached to the front edges of the two settings of the onyx stones on the shoulder of the ephod. 26Then make two more gold rings and place them on the two lower, inside edges of the chestpiece; 27also make two other gold rings for the bottom front edge of the ephod at the sash. 28Now attach the bottom of the chestpiece to the bottom rings of the ephod by means of blue ribbons; this will prevent the chestpiece from coming loose from the ephod. 29In this way Aaron shall carry the names of the tribes of Israel on the chestpiece over his heart (it is God's oracle) when he goes in to the Holy Place; thus Jehovah will be reminded of them continually. 30, 31Insert into the pocket of the chestpiece the Urim and Thummim, to be carried over Aaron's heart when he goes in before Jehovah. Thus Aaron shall always be carrying the oracle over his heart when he goes in before the Lord.

"The ephod shall be made of blue cloth, 32with an opening for Aaron's head. It shall have a woven band around this opening, just as on the neck of a coat of mail, so that it will not fray. 33, 34The bottom edge of the ephod shall be embroidered with blue, purple, and scarlet pomegranates, alternated with gold bells. 35Aaron shall wear the ephod whenever he goes in to minister to the Lord; the bells will tinkle as he goes in and out of the presence of the Lord in the Holy Place, so that he will not die.

28:31
Ex 39:22

36"Next, make a plate of pure gold and engrave on it, just as you would upon a seal, 'Consecrated to Jehovah.' 37, 38This plate is to be attached by means of a blue ribbon to the front of Aaron's turban. In this way Aaron will be wearing it upon his forehead, and thus bear the guilt connected with any errors regarding the offerings of the people of Israel. It shall always be worn when he goes into the presence of the Lord, so that the people will be accepted and forgiven.

28:36
Ex 39:30

28:37,38
Lev 8:9
Lev 10:17; 22:16
Num 18:1

39"Weave Aaron's embroidered shirt from fine-twined linen, using a checkerboard pattern; make the turban, too, of this linen; and make him an embroidered sash.

40"Then, for Aaron's sons, make robes, sashes, and turbans to give them honor and respect. 41Clothe Aaron and his sons with these garments, and then dedicate these men to their ministry by anointing their heads with olive oil, thus sanctifying them as the priests, my ministers. 42Also make linen undershorts for them, to be worn beneath their robes next to their bodies, reaching from hips to knees. 43These are to be worn whenever Aaron and his sons go into the Tabernacle or to the altar

28:40
Ex 39:27
Lev 8:13

28:42
Ex 20:26

in the Holy Place, lest they be guilty and die. This is a permanent ordinance for Aaron and his sons.

The dedication of the priests

29:1
Lev 8:1,2; 9:2
16:3

29:2
Lev 2:4; 6:19

29 "This is the ceremony for the dedication of Aaron and his sons as priests: get a young bull and two rams with no defects, 2and bread made without yeast, and thin sheets of sweetened bread mingled with oil, and unleavened wafers with oil poured over them. (The various kinds of bread shall be made with finely ground wheat flour.) 3, 4Place the bread in a basket and bring it to the entrance of the Tabernacle, along with the young bull and the two rams.

29:5
Ex 28:4,8,15,
31,39

29:6
Ex 28:36

29:7
Ex 28:41
Lev 8:10; 10:7
Ps 133:2

29:9
Ex 40:15
Num 3:10; 18:7
25:13
Deut 18:5
Heb 5:4

29:10
Lev 1:4; 3:2
8:14

29:12
Ex 27:2
Lev 8:15,16

29:13
Lev 3:3-5

29:14
Lev 4:11,12,21
Heb 13:11,12

29:15
Ex 29:10
Lev 1:4

29:18
Gen 8:21
Lev 2:2,9; 6:15

29:21
Ex 30:25,31

"Bathe Aaron and his sons there at the entrance. 5Then put Aaron's robe on him, and the embroidered shirt, ephod, chestpiece, and sash, 6and place on his head the turban with the gold plate. 7Then take the anointing oil and pour it upon his head. 8Next, dress his sons in their robes, 9with their woven sashes, and place caps on their heads. They will then be priests forever; thus you shall consecrate Aaron and his sons.

10"Then bring the young bull to the Tabernacle, and Aaron and his sons shall lay their hands upon its head; 11and you shall kill it before the Lord, at the entrance of the Tabernacle. 12Place its blood upon the horns of the altar, smearing it on with your finger, and pour the rest at the base of the altar. 13Then take all the fat that covers the inner parts, also the gall bladder and two kidneys, and the fat on them, and burn them upon the altar. 14Then take the body, including the skin and the dung, outside the camp and burn it as a sin offering.

15, 16"Next, Aaron and his sons shall lay their hands upon the head of one of the rams as it is killed. Its blood shall also be collected and sprinkled upon the altar. 17Cut up the ram and wash off the entrails and the legs; place them with the head and the other pieces of the body, 18and burn it all upon the altar; it is a burnt offering to the Lord, and very pleasant to him.

19, 20"Now take the other ram, and Aaron and his sons shall lay their hands upon its head as it is killed. Collect the blood and place some of it upon the tip of the right ear of Aaron and his sons, and upon their right thumbs and the big toes of their right feet; sprinkle the rest of the blood over the altar. 21Then scrape off some of the blood from the altar and mix it with some of the anointing oil and sprinkle it upon Aaron and his sons and upon their clothes; and they and their clothing shall be sanctified to the Lord.

22"Then take the fat of the ram, including the fat tail and the fat that covers the insides, also the gall bladder and the two kidneys and the fat surrounding them, and the right thigh—for this is the ram for ordination of Aaron and his sons— 23and one loaf of bread, one cake of shortening bread, and one wafer from the basket of unleavened bread that was placed before the Lord: 24Place these in the hands of Aaron and his sons, to wave them in a gesture of offering to the Lord. 25Afterwards, take them from their hands and burn them on the altar as a fragrant burnt offering to him. 26Then take the breast of Aaron's ordination ram and wave it before the Lord in a gesture of offering; afterwards, keep it for yourself.

29:23
Lev 8:26

29:24
Lev 7:30

29:26
Lev 7:31; 8:29
9:21

29:27
Lev 7:31-33
Num 18:11,18
Deut 18:3

27"Give the breast and thigh of the consecration ram 28to Aaron and his sons. The

---

29:1–26 Why did God set up the priesthood? God had originally intended that his chosen people be a "nation of priests" with both the nation as a whole and each individual dealing directly with God. But the people's sin prevented this from happening, because a sinful person is not worthy to approach a perfect God. God then appointed priests from the tribe of Levi to carry out the intent of his original desire. The people could only approach God now through the priests and the system of sacrifices. Sacrifices had to be made in order to forgive the people's sin. The priests administered the sacrifices on behalf of the people.

Through these priests and their work, God wished to prepare all people for the coming of Jesus Christ, who would once again offer a direct relationship with God for anyone who desired it. But until

Christ came, the priests were the people's representatives before God. Through this Old Testament system, we can better understand the significance of what Christ did for us (see Hebrews 10:1–14).

29:10–41 Why the detailed rituals surrounding these sacrifices? Partly, it was for "quality control"—a centralized, standardized form of worship prevented problems which could arise from individuals worshiping on their own. Also, it differentiated the Hebrews from the pagan Canaanites they would meet in the Promised Land. These heathens performed sacrifices to their gods wherever, however, and whenever they wanted. Finally, it showed Israel that God was serious about his relationship with them.

people of Israel must always contribute this portion of their sacrifices—whether peace offerings or thanksgiving offerings—as their contribution to the Lord.

29"These sacred garments of Aaron shall be preserved for the consecration of his son who succeeds him, from generation to generation, for his anointing ceremony. 30Whoever is the next High Priest after Aaron shall wear these clothes for seven days before beginning to minister in the Tabernacle and the Holy Place.

31"Take the ram of consecration—the ram used in the ordination ceremony—and boil its meat in a sacred area. 32Aaron and his sons shall eat the meat, also the bread in the basket, at the door of the Tabernacle. 33They alone shall eat those items used in their atonement (that is, in their consecration ceremony). The ordinary people shall not eat them, for these things are set apart and holy. 34If any of the meat or bread remains until the morning, burn it; it shall not be eaten, for it is holy.

35"This, then, is the way you shall ordain Aaron and his sons to their offices. This ordination shall go on for seven days. 36Every day you shall sacrifice a young bull as a sin offering for atonement; afterwards, purge the altar by making atonement for it; pour olive oil upon it to sanctify it. 37Make atonement for the altar and consecrate it to God every day for seven days. After this the altar shall be exceedingly holy, so that whatever touches it shall be set apart for God.

38"Each day offer two yearling lambs upon the altar, 39one in the morning and the other in the evening. 40With one of them offer three quarts of finely ground flour mixed with 2½ pints of oil, pressed from olives; also 2½ pints of wine, as an offering.

41Offer the other lamb in the evening, along with the flour and the wine as in the morning, for a fragrant offering to the Lord, an offering made to the Lord by fire.

42"This shall be a perpetual daily offering at the door of the Tabernacle before the Lord, where I will meet with you and speak with you. 43And I will meet with the people of Israel there, and the Tabernacle shall be sanctified by my glory. 44Yes, I will sanctify the Tabernacle and the altar and Aaron and his sons who are my ministers, the priests. 45And I will live among the people of Israel and be their God, 46and they shall know that I am the Lord their God. I brought them out of Egypt so that I could live among them. I am Jehovah their God.

The procedures to prepare for worship

30 "Then make a small altar for burning incense. It shall be made from acacia wood. 2It is to be eighteen inches square and three feet high, with horns carved from the wood of the altar—they are not to be merely separate parts that are attached. 3Overlay the top, sides, and horns of the altar with pure gold, and run a gold molding around the entire altar. 4Beneath the molding, on each of two sides, construct two gold rings to hold the carrying poles. 5The poles are to be made of acacia wood overlaid with gold. 6Place the altar just outside the veil, near the place of mercy that is above the Ark containing the Ten Commandments. I will meet with you there.

7"Every morning when Aaron trims the lamps, he shall burn sweet spices on the altar, 8and each evening when he lights the lamps he shall burn the incense before the Lord, and this shall go on from generation to generation. 9Offer no unauthorized incense, burnt offerings, meal offerings, or wine offerings.

10"Once a year Aaron must sanctify the altar, placing upon its horns the blood of

29:36 *afterwards,* implied. **29:37** *shall be set apart for God,* or, "shall become holy," or, "only those who are holy may touch it." **30:10** *must sanctify the altar,* literally, "shall make an atonement for the altar."

29:29
Num 20:26,28

29:30
Lev 8:35

29:33
Lev 22:10
Num 1:51
3:10,38

29:37
Mt 23:19

29:38,39
Num 28:3; 29:6
1 Chron 16:40
Ezra 3:3
Dan 12:11

29:41
1 Kgs 29:36
2 Kgs 16:15
Ezra 9:4
Ps 141:2

29:45
Ex 25:8
Lev 26:5
Num 5:3
Ps 68:18
Zech 2:10
Rev 21:3

29:46
Ex 20:2
Jer 31:33

30:1
Ex 27:1; 37:25
Lev 4:7
1 Kgs 6:22
Rev 8:3

30:7
Ex 27:20; 30:34
1 Sam 2:28
Lk 1:9

30:10
Lev 16:8

29:45, 46 God's action in bringing the Israelites out of Egypt showed his great desire to be with them and protect them. Throughout the Bible, God shows that he is not an absentee landlord. He wants to live among us, even in our hearts. Don't exclude God from your life. Allow him to be your God as you obey his Word and communicate with him in prayer. Let him be your resident landlord.

30:10 This once-a-year ceremony was called the Day of

Atonement. On this day a sacrifice was made for the sins of the entire Israelite nation. This was the only day the High Priest could enter the Holy of Holies, the innermost room of the Tabernacle. Here he asked God to forgive the people.

The Day of Atonement served as a reminder that the daily, weekly, and monthly sacrifices could cover sins only temporarily. It pointed toward Jesus Christ, the perfect atonement, who could remove sins forever.

the sin offering for atonement. This shall be a regular, annual event from generation to generation, for this is the Lord's supremely holy altar."

30:11,12
Ex 38:25
Num 1:2; 26:2
2 Sam 24:1
Mt 20:28
1 Pet 1:18,19

11, 12And Jehovah said to Moses, "Whenever you take a census of the people of Israel, each man who is numbered shall give a ransom to the Lord for his soul, so that there will be no plague among the people when you number them. 13His payment shall be half a dollar. 14All who have reached their twentieth birthday shall give this offering. 15The rich shall not give more and the poor shall not give less, for it is an offering to the Lord to make atonement for yourselves. 16Use this money for the care of the Tabernacle; it is to bring you, the people of Israel, to the Lord's attention, and to make atonement for you."

30:13
Mt 17:24

30:15
Prov 22:2

30:17
Ex 31:9; 38:8
Lev 8:11

17, 18And the Lord said to Moses, "Make a bronze basin with a bronze pedestal. Put it between the Tabernacle and the altar, and fill it with water. 19Aaron and his sons shall wash their hands and feet there, 20when they go into the Tabernacle to appear before the Lord, or when they approach the altar to burn offerings to the Lord. They must always wash before doing so, or they will die. 21These are instructions to Aaron and his sons from generation to generation."

30:19
Ex 40:31

30:21
Ex 28:43

30:22
Ps 45:8

22, 23Then the Lord told Moses to collect the choicest of spices—eighteen pounds of pure myrrh; half as much of cinnamon and of sweet cane; 24the same amount of cassia as of myrrh; and 1½ gallons of olive oil. 25The Lord instructed skilled perfumemakers to compound all this into a holy anointing oil.

30:25
Ex 37:29; 40:9
Lev 8:10

30:26
Num 7:1

26, 27"Use this," he said, "to anoint the Tabernacle, the Ark, the table and all its instruments, the lampstand and all its utensils, the incense altar, 28the burnt offering altar with all its instruments, and the washbasin and its pedestal. 29Sanctify them, to make them holy; whatever touches them shall become holy. 30Use it to anoint Aaron and his sons, sanctifying them so that they can minister to me as priests. 31And say to the people of Israel, 'This shall always be my holy anointing oil. 32It must never be poured upon an ordinary person, and you shall never make any of it yourselves, for it is holy, and it shall be treated by you as holy. 33Anyone who compounds any incense like it or puts any of it upon someone who is not a priest shall be excommunicated.' "

30:33
Gen 17:4
Ex 12:15
Lev 7:20,21

34These were the Lord's directions to Moses concerning the incense: "Use sweet spices—stacte, onycha, galbanum, and pure frankincense, weighing out the same amounts of each, 35using the usual techniques of the incensemaker, and seasoning it with salt; it shall be a pure and holy incense. 36Beat some of it very fine and put some of it in front of the Ark where I meet with you in the Tabernacle; this incense is most holy. 37Never make it for yourselves, for it is reserved for the Lord and you must treat it as holy. 38Anyone making it for himself shall be excommunicated."

Craftsmen given special skill

31:1
Ex 35:30,36:1
37:1
1 Chron 2:20

31 The Lord also said to Moses, "See, I have appointed Bezalel (son of Uri, and grandson of Hur, of the tribe of Judah), 3and have filled him with the Spirit of God, giving him great wisdom, ability, and skill in constructing the Tabernacle and everything it contains. 4He is highly capable as an artistic designer of objects made of gold, silver, and bronze. 5He is skilled, too, as a jeweler and in carving wood.

31:3
1 Kgs 7:14

31:6
Ex 35:34; 36:1

6"And I have appointed Oholiab (son of Ahisamach of the tribe of Dan) to be his assistant; moreover, I have given special skill to all who are known as experts, so

30:13 *half a dollar*, literally, "half a shekel after the shekel of the sanctuary [the shekel is twenty gerahs], half a shekel for an offering to Jehovah." **30:29** *shall become holy*, or, "shall be set apart for God," or, "only what is holy may touch them."

30:11–15 Whenever a census took place, everyone, both rich and poor, was required to pay a ransom. God does not discriminate between people on the basis of race, sex, wealth, or even past performance. All of us need mercy and forgiveness because of the sinful ways in which we act. There is no way the rich person can buy off God, and no way the poor can avoid paying. God's demand is that all of us come humbly before him to be forgiven and restored to his family.

30:34–38 The Israelites often burned incense on special occasions, but only holy incense could be burned in the Tabernacle. Here God gives the recipe for this special incense. The sweet-smelling incense was burned in shallow dishes called censers and was used as a symbol of honor and reverence to God. It was also a vital part of the sacred ceremony on the Day of Atonement, when the High Priest carried his smoking censer into the Holy of Holies.

that they can make all the things I have instructed you to make: 7the Tabernacle; the
Ark with the place of mercy upon it; all the furnishings of the Tabernacle; 8the table
and its instruments; the pure gold lampstand with its instruments; the altar of
incense; 9the burnt offering altar with its instruments; the laver and its pedestal;
10the beautifully made, holy garments for Aaron the priest, and the garments for his
sons, so that they can minister as priests; 11the anointing oil; and the sweet-spice
incense for the Holy Place. They are to follow exactly the directions I gave you."

31:7
Ex 25:9
31:8
Ex 25:31
Lev 24:4

Resting on the Sabbath

12, 13The Lord then gave these further instructions to Moses: "Tell the people of
Israel to rest on my Sabbath day, for the Sabbath is a reminder of the covenant
between me and you forever; it helps you to remember that I am Jehovah who
makes you holy. 14, 15Yes, rest on the Sabbath, for it is holy. Anyone who does not
obey this command must die; anyone who does any work on that day shall be
killed. 16, 17Work six days only, for the seventh day is a special day to remind you
of my covenant—a weekly reminder forever of my promises to the people of Israel.
For in six days the Lord made heaven and earth, and rested on the seventh day, and
was refreshed."

18Then, as God finished speaking with Moses on Mount Sinai, he gave him the
two tablets of stone on which the Ten Commandments were written with the finger
of God.

31:12
Ex 20:8,12
Lev 19:30; 26:2
Deut 5:12
31:14
Ex 16:23; 35:2
Jn 7:21
31:16
Ex 20:9
Deut 5:13
31:17
Gen 2:2,3
Ex 20:11
Heb 4:4
31:18
Ex 24:12
34:1,28; 32:15

3. Breaking the Law
The golden calf

32 When Moses didn't come back down the mountain right away, the people
went to Aaron. "Look," they said, "make us a god to lead us, for this fellow
Moses who brought us here from Egypt has disappeared; something must have
happened to him."

2, 3"Give me your gold earrings," Aaron replied.

So they all did—men and women, boys and girls. 4Aaron melted the gold, then
molded and tooled it into the form of a calf. The people exclaimed, "O Israel, this
is the god that brought you out of Egypt!"

5When Aaron saw how happy the people were about it, he built an altar before
the calf and announced, "Tomorrow there will be a feast to Jehovah!"

32:1
Ex 24:18
Deut 9:10
Acts 7:40
32:2
Ex 12:35; 35:22
32:4
Ex 20:23
Deut 9:16
Ps 106:19
Acts 7:41
32:5
Hos 8:11

31:12–17 The Sabbath had two purposes: it was a time to rest
and a time to remember what God had done. We need rest.
Without time out from the bustle, life becomes a rut filled with
activity but void of meaning. In our day as in Moses' day, taking
time out is not easy, but God reminds us that without it we will
forget what all of the activity is for and lose the balance crucial to a
faithful life. Make sure your Sabbath provides a time of both
refreshment and remembrance of God.

31:18 The Ten Commandments were not the only code of laws in
the ancient world. Other law codes had come into existence when
a city or nation decided that there must be standards of judgment,
ways to correct specific wrongs. But God's laws for Israel were
unique in that they alleviated the arbitrary judgments typical of the
day. The poor and the powerful received the same punishment. In
addition, the laws did not separate religious and social law. All law
rested on God's authority.

32:1–10 Idols again! Even though Israel had seen the invisible
God in action, they still wanted the familiar gods they could see
and shape into whatever image they desired. How much like them
we are! Our great temptation is still to shape God to our liking, to
make him convenient to obey or ignore. God responds in great
anger when his mercy is trampled on. Idols blind us to the love he
would prefer to shower on us. They stop God from living within us,
for he will not share us with any other god. Are any idols in your life
preventing God from living in you?

32:4, 5 The cow, or calf, was one of the most popular idols in
Egypt. Hapi and Hathor, two of the most worshiped cow gods,
were symbols of power and fertility. Therefore they were closely
connected to immoral sexual practices.

When the Israelites forged their calf-idol, some of the people
may have truly believed that they were worshiping God, for they
had made the idol to represent God himself. Just as Hapi was the
Egyptian god of the Nile River, this golden calf was the god of
Israel. They had simply borrowed the idea for their own purposes.

Though some of the Israelites may have been sincere, they
were clearly not worshiping God the right way. They were violating
God's command not to make or worship any idols or images
(20:4, 5), as well as the command to worship him alone.

Even more disastrous, they were no longer worshiping the true
God, for they had made God conform to their own image of him,
shaping him to fit their expectations, desires, and present
circumstances. They had invented a twisted image of God to justify
their immoral behavior. This demonstrates how easy it is for us to
"make God in our own image," shaping our understanding of his
Word to agree with our actions and beliefs. Sincerity isn't enough
because there is always the danger of creating him in the image of
our needs, desires, or latest ideas. He is always greater than any
concept or label we use. If you attempt to justify your immoral
behavior by saying God doesn't know or care, you have forced
God into the role of a controllable idol. Respect for God's Word
and a desire to keep on knowing the true God of the Bible keeps
us from false images.

32:6
Num 25:2
Acts 7:41
1 Cor 10:7

32:7
Ex 19:24; 33:1
Deut 9:12

32:8
Ex 22:20; 34:15
Deut 32:17

32:9
Ex 33:5
Num 14:11
Acts 7:42,51

32:10
Gen 18:32
Deut 9:13,14

32:11
Num 14:17-19
Deut 9:18,26
Ps 106:23

32:12
Deut 9:28
Josh 7:9

32:13
Gen 15:5
22:16-18
Ex 13:5,11
Lev 26:42

6So they were up early the next morning and began offering burnt offerings and peace offerings to the calf-idol; afterwards they sat down to feast and drink at a wild party, followed by sexual immorality.

7Then the Lord told Moses, "Quick! Go on down, for your people that you brought from Egypt have defiled themselves, 8and have quickly abandoned all my laws. They have molded themselves a calf, and worshiped it, and sacrificed to it, and said, 'This is your god, O Israel, that brought you out of Egypt.' "

9Then the Lord said, "I have seen what a stubborn, rebellious lot these people are. 10Now let me alone and my anger shall blaze out against them and destroy them all; and I will make you, Moses, into a great nation instead of them."

11But Moses begged God not to do it. "Lord," he pleaded, "why is your anger so hot against your own people whom you brought from the land of Egypt with such great power and mighty miracles? 12Do you want the Egyptians to say, 'God tricked them into coming to the mountains so that he could slay them, destroying them from off the face of the earth'? Turn back from your fierce wrath. Turn away from this terrible evil you are planning against your people! 13Remember your promise to your servants—to Abraham, Isaac, and Israel. For you swore by your own self, 'I will multiply your posterity as the stars of heaven, and I will give them all of this land I have promised to your descendants, and they shall inherit it forever.' "

AARON

Effective teamwork happens when each team member uses his or her special skills. Ideally, each member's strengths will contribute something important to the team effort. In this way, members make up for one another's weaknesses. Aaron made a good team with Moses. He provided Moses with one skill he lacked, effective public speaking. But while Aaron was necessary to Moses, he needed Moses as well. Without a guide, Aaron had little direction of his own. There was never doubt as to who God's chosen and trained leader was. The pliability that made Aaron a good follower made him a weak leader. The major failures of his life were caused by his inability to stand alone. His yielding to public pressure in making an idol was a good example of this weakness.

Most of us have more of the follower than the leader in us. We may even be good followers. We may be following a good leader. But no leader is perfect, and no human deserves our complete allegiance. Only God is capable of deserving our complete loyalty and obedience. We need to be effective team members in using the skills and abilities God has given us. But if the team or the leader goes against God's Word, we must be willing to stand alone.

Strengths and accomplishments:
• First High Priest of God in Israel
• Effective communicator; he was Moses' mouthpiece

Weaknesses and mistakes:
• Pliable personality; gave in to people's demands for a golden calf
• Joined with Moses in disobeying God's orders about the water-giving rock
• Joined sister Miriam in complaining against Moses

Lessons from his life:
• God gives special abilities to individuals which he weaves together for his use
• The very skills that make a good team player sometimes also make a poor leader

Vital statistics:
• Where: Egypt, Sinai Peninsula
• Occupation: Priest/Second in command
• Relatives: Brother: Moses. Sister: Miriam. Sons: Nadab, Abihu, Eleazar, and Ithamar.

Key verse:
"Then the Lord became angry. 'All right,' he said, 'your brother Aaron is a good speaker. And he is coming here to look for you, and will be very happy when he finds you' " (Exodus 4:14).

Aaron's story is told in Exodus—Deuteronomy 10:6. He is also mentioned in Hebrews 7:11.

32:9-14 God was ready to destroy the whole nation because of their sin. But Moses pleaded for mercy, and God spared them. This is one of the countless examples in Scripture of how prayer can make a difference. Don't neglect prayer because the situation seems irreversible. Make a daily prayer list and spend time praying for others. Prayer can change things.

¹⁴So the Lord changed his mind and spared them.

¹⁵Then Moses went down the mountain, holding in his hands the Ten Commandments written on both sides of two stone tablets. ¹⁶(God himself had written the commandments on the tablets.)

¹⁷When Joshua heard the noise below them, of all the people shouting, he exclaimed to Moses, "It sounds as if they are preparing for war!"

¹⁸But Moses replied, "No, it's not a cry of victory or defeat, but singing."

¹⁹When they came near the camp, Moses saw the calf and the dancing, and in terrible anger he threw the tablets to the ground and they lay broken at the foot of the mountain. ²⁰He took the calf and melted it in the fire, and when the metal cooled, he ground it into powder and spread it upon the water and made the people drink it.

²¹Then he turned to Aaron. "What in the world did the people do to you," he demanded, "to make you bring such a terrible sin upon them?"

²²"Don't get so upset," Aaron replied. "You know these people and what a wicked bunch they are. ²³They said to me, 'Make us a god to lead us, for something has happened to this fellow Moses who led us out of Egypt.' ²⁴Well, I told them, 'Bring me your gold earrings.' So they brought them to me and I threw them into the fire, and . . . well . . . this calf came out!"

²⁵When Moses saw that the people had been committing adultery—at Aaron's encouragement, and much to the amusement of their enemies— ²⁶he stood at the camp entrance and shouted, "All of you who are on the Lord's side, come over here and join me." And all the Levites came.

²⁷He told them, "Jehovah the God of Israel says, 'Get your swords and go back and forth from one end of the camp to the other and kill even your brothers, friends, and neighbors.' " ²⁸So they did, and about three thousand men died that day.

²⁹Then Moses told the Levites, "Today you have ordained yourselves for the service of the Lord, for you obeyed him even though it meant killing your own sons and brothers; now he will give you a great blessing."

Moses pleads for the people

³⁰The next day Moses said to the people, "You have sinned a great sin, but I will return to the Lord on the mountain—perhaps I will be able to obtain his forgiveness for you."

³¹So Moses returned to the Lord and said, "Oh, these people have sinned a great sin, and have made themselves gods of gold. ³²Yet now if you will only forgive their sin—and if not, then blot *me* out of the book you have written."

³³And the Lord replied to Moses, "Whoever has sinned against me will be blotted out of my book. ³⁴And now go, lead the people to the place I told you about, and I assure you that my Angel shall travel on ahead of you; however, when I come to visit these people, I will punish them for their sins."

³⁵And the Lord sent a great plague upon the people because they had worshiped Aaron's calf.

The people mourn

33 The Lord said to Moses, "Lead these people you brought from Egypt to the land I promised Abraham, Isaac, and Jacob; for I said, 'I will give this land to your descendants.' ²I will send an Angel before you to drive out the Canaanites, Amorites, Hittites, Perizzites, Hivites, and Jebusites. ³It is a land 'flowing with milk and honey'; but I will not travel among you, for you are a stubborn, unruly people, and I would be tempted to destroy you along the way."

32:32 then blot me *out of the book you have written,* or "then kill me instead of them."

32:14
Gen 6:5,6
1 Sam 15:35
2 Sam 24:16
Ps 106:45

32:15
Ex 24:18
Deut 9:15

32:16
Ex 31:18; 34:1
Deut 9:9

32:19
Ex 32:6
Deut 9:16,17

32:20
Deut 9:21

32:22
Deut 9:6,24
31:27

32:23
Ex 32:1

32:25
1 Kgs 12:25

32:26
2 Sam 20:11

32:27
Num 25:5

32:28
Num 16:32; 25:9

32:29
Deut 13:6; 33:9

32:31
Ex 20:23

32:32
Deut 9:14
Ps 139:16
Isa 4:3
Dan 12:1
Mal 3:16
Rev 3:5

32:33
Deut 29:20
Ps 9:5; 69:28
Ezek 18:4

32:34
Ex 3:17; 23:20
33:2
Num 20:16

33:1
Gen 12:7; 22:16
Ex 32:13,34

33:2
Ex 23:23,27

33:3
Ex 3:8; 13:5
32:9,10,14

32:14 How could God change his mind? God did not change his mind in the same way as a parent who decides not to discipline a child. Instead, God changed his behavior to remain consistent with his nature. When God first wanted to destroy the people, he was acting consistently with his justice. When Moses interceded for the people, God "changed" in order to act consistently with his mercy. God had often told the people that if they changed their ways he would not condemn them. They changed, and God did as he promised.

33:4
Num 14:1,3,9

33:5
Num 16:45

4When the people heard these stern words, they went into mourning and stripped themselves of their jewelry and ornaments.

5For the Lord had told Moses to tell them, "You are an unruly, stubborn people. If I were there among you for even a moment, I would exterminate you. Remove your jewelry and ornaments until I decide what to do with you." 6So, after that, they wore no jewelry.

The sacred tent

33:7
Ex 18:26; 29:43

7Moses always erected the sacred tent (the "Tent for Meeting with God," he called it) far outside the camp, and everyone who wanted to consult with Jehovah went out there.

33:8
Num 16:27

33:9
Ex 13:21; 19:9
25:22
Ps 99:7

33:11
Gen 32:30
Num 12:8
Deut 34:10

8Whenever Moses went to the Tabernacle, all the people, when they saw it, stood and would rise and stand in their tent doors. 9As he entered, the pillar of cloud would come down and stand at the door while the Lord spoke with Moses. 10Then all the people worshiped from their tent doors, bowing low to the pillar of cloud. 11Inside the tent the Lord spoke to Moses face to face, as a man speaks to his friend. Afterwards Moses would return to the camp, but the young man who assisted him, Joshua (son of Nun), stayed behind in the Tabernacle.

Moses asks to see God

33:12
Ex 3:10; 32:34

33:13
Ex 3:10; 5:1
Ps 25:4; 27:11

33:14
Ex 13:21
Josh 22:4
Isa 63:9

12Moses talked there with the Lord and said to him, "You have been telling me, 'Take these people to the Promised Land,' but you haven't told me whom you will send with me. You say you are my friend, and that I have found favor before you; 13please, if this is really so, guide me clearly along the way you want me to travel so that I will understand you and walk acceptably before you. For don't forget that this nation is your people."

14And the Lord replied, "I myself will go with you and give you success."

33:15
Ps 80:3,7,19

33:16
Ex 8:22
Lev 20:24,26
Num 14:14

15For Moses had said, "If you aren't going with us, don't let us move a step from this place. 16If you don't go with us, who will ever know that I and my people have found favor with you, and that we are different from any other people upon the face of the earth?"

33:17
Gen 19:21
Ex 33:12

17And the Lord had replied to Moses, "Yes, I will do what you have asked, for you have certainly found favor with me, and you are my friend."

33:18
Ps 4:6
2 Cor 3:18

18Then Moses asked to see God's glory.

33:20
Ex 24:10
Isa 6:5
Jn 1:18
1 Tim 6:16

33:22
Ps 18:2
Isa 2:21; 49:2
51:16

19The Lord replied, "I will make my goodness pass before you, and I will announce to you the meaning of my name Jehovah, the Lord. I show kindness and mercy to anyone I want to. 20But you may not see the glory of my face, for man may not see me and live. 21However, stand here on this rock beside me. 22And when my glory goes by, I will put you in the cleft of the rock and cover you with my hand until I have passed. 23Then I will remove my hand and you shall see my back, but not my face."

The Ten Commandments written again

34:1
Ex 24:12; 31:18
Deut 10:1

34 The Lord told Moses, "Prepare two stone tablets like the first ones and I will write upon them the same commands that were on the tablets you broke. 2Be ready in the morning to come up into Mount Sinai and present yourself to me on the

33:12 *You say you are my friend,* literally, "You have said you know me by name." **33:13** *guide me clearly along the way you want me to travel,* or, "show me your ways," or "show me your majesty." **33:17** *you are my friend,* literally, "I know you by name." **33:19** *I will announce to you the meaning of my name,* literally, "I will proclaim before you my name." His name, *Jehovah,* means, "I will be what I will be." (See Ex 3:14.)

33:5, 6 This ban on jewelry was not a permanent law, but a symbol of repentence and mourning. In Exodus 35:22 the people still had their jewelry.

33:11–17 God told Moses, "You are my friend." Why did Moses find such favor with God? It certainly was not because he was perfect, gifted, or powerful. Moses was God's friend because friends trust each other, talk to each other, and have common interests. No one can drive wedges between them. Moses never knew where he was going with God, and it didn't matter. He knew

with whom he was going, and that was all that mattered.

33:14, 15 God spoke to Moses face to face as we would speak to a friend. Moses' passionate devotion to and reliance on God's wisdom and direction brought him to this close working relationship. This special relationship was a true privilege for Moses, out of reach for the other Hebrews of that time. But this special relationship is not out of reach for us today. We too can become friends of God through our passionate devotion to him and through the forgiveness he offers us.

top of the mountain. 3No one shall come with you and no one must be anywhere on
the mountain. Do not let the flocks or herds feed close to the mountain."

4So Moses took two tablets of stone like the first ones, and was up early and
climbed Mount Sinai, as the Lord had told him to, taking the two stone tablets in his
hands.

5, 6Then the Lord descended in the form of a pillar of cloud and stood there with
him, and passed in front of him and announced the meaning of his name. "I am
Jehovah, the merciful and gracious God," he said, "slow to anger and rich in
steadfast love and truth. 7I, Jehovah, show this steadfast love to many thousands by
forgiving their sins; or else I refuse to clear the guilty, and require that a father's
sins be punished in the sons and grandsons, and even later generations."

8Moses fell down before the Lord and worshiped. 9And he said, "If it is true that
I have found favor in your sight, O Lord, then please go with us to the Promised
Land; yes, it is an unruly, stubborn people, but pardon our iniquity and our sins,
and accept us as your own."

10The Lord replied, "All right, this is the contract I am going to make with you.
I will do miracles such as have never been done before anywhere in all the earth,
and all the people of Israel shall see the power of the Lord—the terrible power I will
display through you. 11Your part of the agreement is to obey all of my commandments; then I will drive out from before you the Amorites, Canaanites, Hittites,
Perizzites, Hivites, and Jebusites.

12"Be very, very careful never to compromise with the people there in the land
where you are going, for if you do, you will soon be following their evil ways.
13Instead, you must break down their heathen altars, smash the obelisks they
worship, and cut down their shameful idols. 14For you must worship no other gods,
but only Jehovah, for he is a God who claims absolute loyalty and exclusive
devotion.

15"No, do not make a peace treaty of any kind with the people living in the land,
for they are spiritual prostitutes, committing adultery against me by sacrificing to
their gods. If you become friendly with them and one of them invites you to go with
him and worship his idol, you are apt to do it. 16And you would accept their
daughters, who worship other gods, as wives for your sons—and then your sons
would commit adultery against me by worshiping their wives' gods. 17You must
have nothing to do with idols.

18"Be sure to celebrate the Feast of Unleavened Bread for seven days, just as I
instructed you, at the dates appointed each year in March; that was the month you
left Egypt.

19"Every firstborn male is mine—cattle, sheep, and goats. 20The firstborn colt of
a donkey may be redeemed by giving a lamb in its place. If you decide not to
redeem it, then its neck must be broken. But your sons must all be redeemed. And
no one shall appear before me without a gift.

21"Even during plowing and harvest times, work only six days, and rest on the
seventh.

22"And you must remember to celebrate these three annual religious festivals: the
Festival of Weeks, the Festival of the First Wheat, and the Harvest Festival. 23On
each of these three occasions all the men and boys of Israel shall appear before the

34:3
Ex 19:12
Lev 16:17

34:5,6
Ex 19:9; 33:9
Num 14:17,18
Neh 9:17
Ps 86:15; 103:8
34:7
Ex 20:5,6; 23:7
Deut 5:10
Neh 1:5

34:9
Num 14:19
Deut 4:20; 32:9
Ps 25:11
34:10
Ex 8:10
Deut 4:35
Ps 72:18; 136:4
34:11
Ex 33:2
Deut 4:1,40; 6:3
34:12
Ex 23:32,33
Deut 7:1-4
34:13
Ex 23:24
Deut 7:5; 12:2
16:21
2 Chron 34:4
34:14
Ex 20:3,4
Deut 4:24
34:15
Num 25:1,2
Deut 31:16
34:16
Deut 7:3
Josh 23:12
34:17
Lev 19:3,4
Deut 29:17
34:18
Ex 12:2,15,17
23:15
Deut 16:1
34:19
Ex 13:2
22:29,30
34:20
Ex 13:13
Num 3:45
Lk 2:23
34:21
Ex 20:8; 31:15
35:2
34:22
Ex 23:16
Lev 23:4
34:23
Ex 23:14-17
Deut 16:16

34:5, 6 *announced the meaning of his name,* literally, "proclaimed the name of Jehovah." **34:7** *forgiving their sins,*
literally, "forgiving iniquity and transgression and sin." *or else,* implied. **34:13** *Asherim, or shameful idols.* They were
carved statues of male and female genital organs. **34:15** *committing adultery against me,* literally, "they play the
harlot worshiping their gods." **34:19** *Every firstborn male,* literally, "all that opens the womb."

34:7 God delivered a frightening thought to Moses: the sins of a
father could be punished in future generations. Children still suffer
for the sins of their parents. Consider child abuse or alcoholism for
example. While these sins are obvious, sins like selfishness and
greed can be passed along as well. The dire consequences of sin
are not limited to the individual family member. Be careful not to
treat sin casually, but repent and turn from it. You may feel little
pain now, but your sin could sting in a most tender area of your life

later—your children and grandchildren.

34:12-14 God told the Israelites not to compromise with the sinful
people around them, but to give their absolute loyalty and
exclusive devotion to him. As we compromise, our sensitivity to sin
becomes dulled. Are you beginning to accept lower standards
regarding the things you do or think about? This could lead to a
downhill slide you won't be able to stop. The way you act shows
where your true allegiance lies.

34:24
Ex 23:27; 33:2

34:25
Ex 12:10,20
23:18
Lev 2:11

34:26
Ex 23:19
Deut 26:2

34:27
Ex 17:14; 24:4
Deut 1:5; 31:9

34:28
Ex 24:18
Deut 4:13; 10:4

34:29
Ex 32:15
Mt 17:2
Acts 6:15
2 Cor 3:7

34:31
Ex 4:29; 24:1

34:33
2 Cor 3:13

34:34
2 Cor 3:16

Lord. 24No one will attack and conquer your land when you go up to appear before the Lord your God those three times each year. For I will drive out the nations from before you and enlarge your boundaries.

25"You must not use leavened bread with your sacrifices to me, and none of the meat of the Passover lamb may be kept over until the following morning. 26And you must bring the best of the first of each year's crop to the Tabernacle of the Lord your God. You must not cook a young goat in its mother's milk."

27And the Lord said to Moses, "Write down these laws that I have given you, for they represent the terms of my covenant with you and with Israel."

28Moses was up on the mountain with the Lord for forty days and forty nights, and in all that time he neither ate nor drank. At that time God wrote out the Covenant—the Ten Commandments—on the stone tablets.

29Moses didn't realize as he came back down the mountain with the tablets that his face glowed from being in the presence of God. 30Because of this radiance upon his face, Aaron and the people of Israel were afraid to come near him. 31But Moses called them over to him, and Aaron and the leaders of the congregation came and talked with him. 32Afterwards, all the people came to him, and he gave them the commandments the Lord had given him upon the mountain. 33When Moses had finished speaking with them, he put a veil over his face; 34but whenever he went into the Tabernacle to speak with the Lord, he removed the veil until he came out again; then he would pass on to the people whatever instructions God had given him, 35and the people would see his face aglow. Afterwards he would put the veil on again until he returned to speak with God.

4. Tabernacle construction

35:1
Ex 25:1; 34:32

35:2
Ex 16:23; 20:8
23:12; 34:21
Num 15:32
Deut 5:13,14

35 Now Moses called a meeting of all the people and told them, "These are the laws of Jehovah you must obey.

2"Work six days only; the seventh day is a day of solemn rest, a holy day to be used to worship Jehovah; anyone working on that day must die. 3Don't even light the fires in your homes that day."

Gathering the material

35:5-9
Ex 25:1-7

4Then Moses said to all the people, "This is what the Lord has commanded: 5-9All of you who wish to, all those with generous hearts, may bring these offerings to Jehovah:

Gold, silver, and bronze;
Blue, purple, and scarlet cloth, made of fine-twined linen or of goat's hair;
Tanned rams' skins and specially treated goatskins;
Acacia wood;
Olive oil for the lamps;
Spices for the anointing oil and for the incense;
Onyx stones and stones to be used for the ephod and chestpiece.

35:10-19
Ex 39:32-41

10-19"Come, all of you who are skilled craftsmen having special talents, and construct what God has commanded us:

34:27 *Write down these laws,* that is, the preceding laws in vss 12-26. **34:28** *At that time God,* implied. See 34:1; Deut 10:1-4. **34:33** *put a veil over his face.* So that the people would not see the glory fade. See 2 Cor 3:13.

34:28-35 Moses' face actually glowed after spending time with God. The people could clearly see the presence of God reflected in him. How often do you spend time alone with God? Although your face won't light up a room, time spent in prayer, reading the Bible, and meditating should have such an effect on your life that people will see the difference.

35:5-21 God did not require these special offerings, but he appealed to those with generous hearts. Only those who were *willing* to give were invited to participate. God loves cheerful givers

(2 Corinthians 9:7). Our giving should be from a generous heart, not a guilty conscience.

35:10-19 Moses asked people with various abilities to help with the Tabernacle. Every one of God's people has been given special abilities. We are responsible to develop these abilities—even the ones not considered "religious"—and to use them for God's glory. We can become skilled through study, by watching others, and through practice. Take note of skills or abilities you have which you could use to help your church, work, or community.

The Tabernacle tent, and its coverings, clasps, frames, bars, pillars, and bases;
The Ark and its poles;
The place of mercy;
The curtain to enclose the Holy Place;
The table, its carrying poles, and all of its utensils;
The Bread of the Presence;
Lamp holders, with lamps and oil;
The incense altar and its carrying poles;
The anointing oil and sweet incense;
The curtain for the door of the Tabernacle;
The altar for the burnt offerings;
The bronze grating of the altar, and its carrying poles and utensils;
The basin with its pedestal;
The drapes for the walls of the court;
The pillars and their bases;
Drapes for the entrance to the court;
The posts of the Tabernacle court, and their cords;
The beautiful clothing for the priests, to be used when ministering in the Holy
    Place;
The holy garments for Aaron the priest, and for his sons."

20So all the people went to their tents to prepare their gifts. 21Those whose hearts
were stirred by God's Spirit returned with their offerings of materials for the
Tabernacle, its equipment, and for the holy garments. 22Both men and women
came, all who were willing-hearted. They brought to the Lord their offerings of
gold, jewelry—earrings, rings from their fingers, necklaces—and gold objects of
every kind. 23Others brought blue, purple, and scarlet cloth made from the fine-
twined linen or goat's hair; and ram skins dyed red, and specially treated goatskins.
24Others brought silver and bronze as their offering to the Lord; and some brought
the acacia wood needed in the construction.

25The women skilled in sewing and spinning prepared blue, purple, and scarlet
thread and cloth, and fine-twined linen, and brought them in. 26Some other women
gladly used their special skill to spin the goat's hair into cloth. 27The leaders
brought onyx stones to be used for the ephod and the chestpiece; 28and spices, and
oil—for the light, and for compounding the anointing oil and the sweet incense.
29So the people of Israel—every man and woman who wanted to assist in the work
given to them by the Lord's command to Moses—brought their freewill offerings
to him.

30, 31And Moses told them, "Jehovah has specifically appointed Bezalel (the son
of Uri and grandson of Hur of the tribe of Judah) as general superintendent of the
project. 32He will be able to create beautiful workmanship from gold, silver, and
bronze; 33he can cut and set stones like a jeweler, and can do beautiful carving; in
fact, he has every needed skill. 34And God has made him and Oholiab gifted
teachers of their skills to others. (Oholiab is the son of Ahisamach, of the tribe of
Dan.) 35God has filled them both with unusual skills as jewelers, carpenters,
embroidery designers in blue, purple, and scarlet on linen backgrounds, and as
weavers—they excel in all the crafts we will be needing in the work.

35:21
Ex 25:2; 35:5

35:25
Ex 28:3; 31:6;
36:1
35:27
1 Chron 29:6
Ezra 2:68

35:29
1 Chron 29:9

35:30,31
Ex 31:1; 38:22
1 Chron 2:20
1 Cor 3:10
35:32
1 Kgs 7:13
2 Chron 2:14

35:35
Ex 31:3
1 Kgs 3:12; 7:13
2 Chron 2:14
Isa 28:26

35:20–24 Where did the Israelites, who were once Egyptian
slaves, get all this gold and jewelry? When the Hebrews left Egypt,
they took with them the spoils from the land—all the booty they
could carry (Exodus 12:35). This included gold, silver, jewels,
linen, skins, and other valuables.

35:21 Those whose hearts were stirred by God gave cheerfully to
the Tabernacle. With great enthusiasm they gave because they
knew how important their giving was to the completion of God's
house. Airline pilots have certain test buttons they push to see if
their equipment is functioning properly. God has a quick test

button he can push to see the level of our commitment—our
pocketbooks. Generous people aren't necessarily faithful to God.
But faithful people are always generous.

35:26 Those who sewed and spun cloth made a beautiful
contribution to the Tabernacle. Good workers take pride in both the
quality and beauty of their work. God is concerned with both the
quality and beauty of what you do as well. If your work was painted
in a picture, would the picture be beautiful? Whether you are a
corporate executive or a drug store cashier, your work should
reflect the creative abilities God has given you.

36 "All the other craftsmen with God-given abilities are to assist Bezalel and Oholiab in constructing and furnishing the Tabernacle." So Moses told Bezalel and Oholiab and all others who felt called to the work to begin. 3Moses gave them the materials donated by the people and additional gifts were received each morning.

36:2
1 Chron 29:5

4-7But finally the workmen all left their task to meet with Moses and told him, "We have more than enough materials on hand now to complete the job!" So Moses sent a message throughout the camp announcing that no more donations were needed. Then at last the people were restrained from bringing more!

36:5
2 Chron 31:10
2 Cor 8:2,3

36:7
1 Kgs 8:64

Building the Tabernacle

36:8-38
Ex 26:1-37

8,9The skilled weavers first made ten sheets from fine linen, then embroidered into them blue, purple, and scarlet Guardian Angels. Each sheet was forty-two feet long and six feet wide. 10Five of these sheets were attached end to end, then five others similarly attached, forming two long roofsheets. 11, 12Fifty blue ribbons were looped along the edges of these two long sheets, each loop being opposite its

KEY TABERNACLE PIECES	Name	Function and Significance
	Ark of the Covenant	• A golden rectangular box that contained the Ten Commandments • Symbolized God's covenant with Israel's people • Located in the Holy of Holies
	Place of Mercy (Mercy Seat)	• The lid to the Ark of the Covenant • Symbolized the presence of God among his people
	Veil	• The curtain that divided the two sacred rooms of the Tabernacle—the Holy Place and the Holy of Holies • Symbolized how the people are separated from God because of sin
	Table (of Showbread)	• A wooden table located in the Holy Place of the Tabernacle. The Bread of the Presence and various utensils were kept on this table
	Bread of the Presence (Showbread)	• Twelve loaves of baked bread, one for each tribe of Israel • Symbolized the spiritual nourishment God offers his people
	Lampholders and Lamps	• A golden lampstand located in the Holy Place, which held seven burning oil lamps • The lampstand lighted the Holy Place for the priests
	Incense Altar	• An altar in the Holy Place in front of the veil • Used for burning God's special incense and symbolic of acceptable prayer
	Anointing Oil	• A special oil used to anoint the priests and all the pieces in the Tabernacle • A sign of being set apart for God
	Altar for the Burnt Offerings	• The bronze altar outside the Tabernacle used for the sacrifices • Symbolized how sacrifice restored one's relationship with God
	Basin (Laver)	• A large wash basin outside the Tabernacle used by the priests to cleanse themselves before performing their duties • Symbolized the need for spiritual cleansing

36:8, 9 Making cloth (spinning and weaving) took a great deal of time in Moses' day. To own more than two or three changes of clothes was a sign of wealth. The effort involved in making enough cloth for a building like the Tabernacle was staggering. It demonstrated a tremendous community effort. Churches and neighborhoods today often require this same kind of community effort. Without it, many essential services just wouldn't get done.

mate on the other long sheet. ¹³Then fifty clasps of gold were made to connect the loops, thus tying the two long sheets together to form the ceiling of the Tabernacle.

¹⁴, ¹⁵Above the ceiling was a second layer formed by eleven draperies made of goat's hair (uniformly forty-five feet long and six feet wide). ¹⁶Bezalel coupled five of these draperies together to make one long piece, and six others to make another long piece. ¹⁷Then he made fifty loops along the end of each, ¹⁸and fifty small bronze clasps to couple the loops so that the draperies were firmly attached to each other.

36:14
Ex 26:7; 35:26

¹⁹The top layer of the roof was made of rams' skins, dyed red, and tanned goat skins.

²⁰For the sides of the Tabernacle he used frames of acacia wood standing on end. ²¹The height of each frame was fifteen feet and the width 2¼ feet. ²²Each frame had two clasps joining it to the next. ²³There were twenty frames on the south side, ²⁴with the bottoms fitting into forty silver bases. Each frame was connected to its base by two clasps. ²⁵, ²⁶There were also twenty frames on the north side of the Tabernacle, with forty silver bases, two for each frame. ²⁷The west side of the Tabernacle, which was its rear, was made from six frames, ²⁸plus another at each corner. ²⁹These frames, including those at the corners, were linked to each other at both top and bottom by rings. ³⁰So, on the west side, there were a total of eight frames with sixteen silver bases beneath them, two for each frame.

36:20-34
Ex 26:15-29
40:18,19
Num 4:31

³¹, ³²Then he made five sets of bars from acacia wood to tie the frames together along the sides, five for each side of the Tabernacle. ³³The middle bar of the five was halfway up the frames, along each side, running from one end to the other. ³⁴The frames and bars were all overlaid with gold, and the rings were pure gold.

³⁵The blue, purple, and scarlet inner curtain was made from woven linen, with Guardian Angels skillfully embroidered into it. ³⁶The curtain was then attached to four gold hooks set into four posts of acacia wood, overlaid with gold and set into four silver bases.

36:35-38
Ex 26:31-37;
40:3
Lev 16:2

³⁷Then he made a drapery for the entrance to the Tabernacle; it was woven from finespun linen, embroidered with blue, purple, and scarlet. ³⁸This drapery was connected by five hooks to five posts. The posts and their capitals and rods were overlaid with gold; their five bases were molded from bronze.

Building the Ark

37 Next Bezalel made the Ark. This was constructed of acacia wood and was 3¾ feet long, 2¼ feet wide, and 2¼ feet high. ²It was plated with pure gold inside and out, and had a molding of gold all the way around the sides. ³There were four gold rings fastened into its four feet, two rings at each end. ⁴Then he made poles from acacia wood, and overlaid them with gold, ⁵and put the poles into the rings at the sides of the Ark, to carry it.

37:1-9
Ex 25:10-20;
26:33
Deut 10:3

⁶Then, from pure gold, he made a lid called "the place of mercy"; it was 3¾ feet long and 2¼ feet wide. ⁷He made two statues of Guardian Angels of beaten gold, and placed them at the two ends of the gold lid. ⁸They were molded so that they were actually a part of the gold lid—it was all one piece. ⁹The Guardian Angels faced each other, with outstretched wings that overshadowed the place of mercy, looking down upon it.

¹⁰Then he made a table, using acacia wood, three feet long, 1½ feet wide and 2¼ feet high. ¹¹It was overlaid with pure gold, with a gold molding all around the edge. ¹²A rim four inches high was constructed around the edges of the table, with a gold molding along the rim. ¹³Then he cast four rings of gold and placed them into the

37:10-16
Ex 25:23-29;
40:22

36:35 *inner,* implied.

37:1 The Ark (also called the Ark of the Covenant) was built to hold the tablets of the Ten Commandments. It symbolized God's covenant with his people. Two gold angels called cherubim ("Guardian Angels") were placed on its top. The Ark was the most sacred article of Israel and was kept in the holiest place in the Tabernacle. Only once each year, the High Priest entered the Holy of Holies to sprinkle blood on the top of the Ark (called the Mercy Seat) to atone for the sins of the entire nation.

four table legs, ¹⁴close to the molding, to hold the carrying poles in place. ¹⁵He made the carrying poles of acacia wood covered with gold. ¹⁶Next, using pure gold, he made the bowls, flagons, dishes, and spoons to be placed upon this table.

Building the lampstand

37:17-24
Ex 25:31-39;
40:24

¹⁷Then he made the lampstand, again using pure, beaten gold. Its base, shaft, lamp-holders, and decorations of almond flowers were all of one piece. ¹⁸The lampstand had six branches, three from each side. ¹⁹Each of the branches was decorated with identical carvings of blossoms. ²⁰, ²¹The main stem of the lampstand was similarly decorated with almond blossoms, a flower on the stem beneath each pair of branches; also a flower below the bottom pair and above the top pair, four in all. ²²The decorations and branches were all one piece of pure, beaten gold. ²³, ²⁴Then he made the seven lamps at the ends of the branches, the snuffers, and the ashtrays, all of pure gold. The entire lampstand weighed 107 pounds, all pure gold.

Building the incense altar

37:25-29
Ex 30:1-5
Lev 4:7
1 Kgs 6:22

²⁵The incense altar was made of acacia wood. It was eighteen inches square and three feet high, with its corner-horns made as part of the altar so that it was all one piece. ²⁶He overlaid it all with pure gold and ran a gold molding around the edge. ²⁷Two gold rings were placed on each side, beneath this molding, to hold the carrying poles. ²⁸The carrying poles were gold-plated acacia wood.

37:29
Ex 30:22,23
40:9
Lev 8:10

²⁹Then, from sweet spices, he made the sacred oil for anointing the priests, and the pure incense, using the techniques of the most skilled perfumers.

Building the burnt-offering altar

38:1-7
Ex 20:24; 27:1-8
40:10,29
Heb 13:10

38 The burnt-offering altar was also constructed of acacia wood; it was 7½ feet square at the top, and 4½ feet high. ²There were four horns at the four corners, all of one piece with the rest. This altar was overlaid with bronze. ³Then he made bronze utensils to be used with the altar—the pots, shovels, basins, meat hooks, and fire pans. ⁴Next he made a bronze grating that rested upon a ledge about halfway up [in the fire box]. ⁵Four rings were cast for each side of the grating, to insert the carrying poles. ⁶The carrying poles themselves were made of acacia wood, overlaid with bronze. ⁷The carrying poles were inserted into the rings at the side of the altar. The altar was hollow, with plank siding.

38:8
Ex 30:18; 31:9
Lev 8:11

⁸The bronze washbasin and its bronze pedestal were cast from the solid bronze mirrors donated by the women who assembled at the entrance to the Tabernacle.

Building the courtyard

38:9-20
Ex 27:9-19; 40:8
1 Kgs 6:36; 8:64

⁹Then he constructed the courtyard. The south wall was 150 feet long; it consisted of drapes woven from fine-twined linen thread. ¹⁰There were twenty posts to hold drapes, with bases of bronze and with silver hooks and rods. ¹¹The north wall was also 150 feet long, with twenty bronze posts and bases and with silver hooks and rods. ¹²The west side was seventy-five feet wide; the walls were made from drapes supported by ten posts and bases, and with silver hooks and rods. ¹³The east side was also seventy-five feet wide.

¹⁴, ¹⁵The drapes at either side of the entrance were 22½ feet wide, each with three posts and three bases. ¹⁶All the drapes making up the walls of the court were woven of fine-twined linen. ¹⁷Each post had a bronze base, and all the hooks and rods were silver; the tops of the posts were overlaid with silver, and the rods to hold up the drapes were solid silver.

¹⁸The drapery covering the entrance to the court was made of fine-twined linen, beautifully embroidered with blue, purple, and scarlet thread.

It was thirty feet long and 7½ feet wide, just the same as the drapes composing the walls of the court. ¹⁹It was supported by four posts, with four bronze bases, and with silver hooks and rods; the tops of the posts were also silver.

²⁰All the nails used in constructing the Tabernacle and court were bronze.

38:4 *in the fire box,* implied.

²¹This summarizes the various steps in building the Tabernacle to house the Ark, so that the Levites could carry on their ministry. All was done in the order designated by Moses and was supervised by Ithamar, son of Aaron the priest. ²²Bezalel (son of Uri and grandson of Hur, of the tribe of Judah) was the master craftsman, ²³assisted by Oholiab (son of Ahisamach of the tribe of Dan); he too was a skilled craftsman and also an expert at engraving, weaving, and at embroidering blue, purple, and scarlet threads into fine linen cloth.

The materials used

²⁴The people brought gifts of 3,140 pounds of gold, all of which was used throughout the Tabernacle.

²⁵, ²⁶The amount of silver used was 9,575 pounds, which came from the fifty-cent head tax collected from all those registered in the census who were twenty years old or older, a total of 603,550 men. ²⁷The bases for the frames of the sanctuary walls and for the posts supporting the veil required 9,500 pounds of silver, ninety-five pounds for each socket. ²⁸The silver left over was used for the posts and to overlay their tops, and for the rods and hooks.

38:25,26
Ex 12:37
30:11-16
Num 1:2,46
26:2,51

²⁹, ³⁰, ³¹The people brought 7,540 pounds of bronze, which was used for casting the bases for the posts at the entrance to the Tabernacle, and for the bronze altar, the bronze grating, the altar utensils, the bases for the posts supporting the drapes enclosing the court, and for all the nails used in the construction of the Tabernacle and the court.

The priests' garments

39 Then, for the priests, the people made beautiful garments of blue, purple, and scarlet cloth—garments to be used while ministering in the Holy Place. This same cloth was used for Aaron's sacred garments, in accordance with the Lord's instructions to Moses. ²The ephod was made from this cloth too, woven from fine-twined linen thread. ³Bezalel beat gold into thin plates and cut it into wire threads, to work into the blue, purple, and scarlet linen; it was a skillful and beautiful piece of workmanship when finished.

39:2
Ex 28:6
Lev 8:7

⁴, ⁵The ephod was held together by shoulder straps at the top, and was tied down by an elaborate one-piece woven sash made of the same gold, blue, purple, and scarlet cloth cut from fine-twined linen thread, just as God had directed Moses. ⁶, ⁷The [two] onyx stones, attached to the [two] shoulder straps of the ephod, were set in gold, and the stones were engraved with the names of the tribes of Israel, just as initials are engraved upon a ring. These stones were reminders to Jehovah concerning the people of Israel; all this was done in accordance with the Lord's instructions to Moses.

⁸The chestpiece was a beautiful piece of work, just like the ephod, made from the finest gold, blue, purple, and scarlet linen. ⁹It was a piece nine inches square, doubled over to form a pouch; ¹⁰there were four rows of stones across it. In the first row were a sardius, a topaz, and a carbuncle; ¹¹in the second row were an emerald, a sapphire, and a diamond. ¹²In the third row were a jacinth, an agate, and an amethyst. ¹³In the fourth row, a beryl, an onyx, and a jasper—all set in gold

39:8-21
Ex 28:15-28

38:27 *ninety-five pounds,* literally, "a [silver] talent." The exact weight cannot be ascertained. 39:6, 7 *two . . . two,* implied. *reminders to Jehovah concerning the people of Israel,* literally, "to be stones of memorial for the children of Israel."

38:21 In building the Tabernacle, Moses laid out the steps, but Ithamar supervised the project. We all have different talents and abilities. God didn't ask Moses to build the Tabernacle but to motivate the experts to do it. Look for the areas where God has gifted you and then seek opportunities to allow God to use them.

39:2-21 The priests had to wear a uniform to the Tabernacle each day. Some of the pieces of their uniform were not only beautiful but also significant. Two parts of the High Priest's uniform were the ephod and chestpiece. The ephod looked like a vest and

was worn over the outer clothing. The chestpiece was fitted to the ephod (and sometimes was called the ephod).

The chestpiece was made of colored linens about nine inches square. On its front were attached twelve precious stones, each inscribed with the name of a tribe of Israel. This symbolized how the High Priest represented all the people before God.

The chestpiece also contained pockets that held two stones or plates called the Urim and Thummim. Somehow the High Priest could determine God's will for the nation by consulting the Urim and Thummim.

39:14
Rev 21:12

filigree. 14The stones were engraved like a seal, with the names of the twelve tribes of Israel.

15-18[To attach the chestpiece to the ephod], a gold ring was placed at the top of each shoulder strap of the ephod, and from these gold rings, two strands of twined gold attached to gold clasps on the top corners of the chestpiece. 19Two gold rings were also set at the lower edge of the chestpiece, on the under side, next to the ephod. 20Two other gold rings were placed low on the shoulder straps of the ephod, close to where the ephod joined its beautifully woven sash. 21The chestpiece was held securely above the beautifully woven sash of the ephod by tying the rings of the chestpiece to the rings of the ephod, with a blue ribbon.

All this was commanded to Moses by the Lord.

39:22
Ex 28:31

22The main part of the ephod was woven, all of blue, 23and there was a hole at the center just as in a coat of mail, for the head to go through, reinforced around the edge so that it would not tear. 24Pomegranates were attached to the bottom edge of the robe; these were made of linen cloth, embroidered with blue, purple, and scarlet. 25, 26Bells of pure gold were placed between the pomegranates along the bottom edge of the skirt, with bells and pomegranates alternating all around the edge. This robe was worn when Aaron ministered to the Lord, just as the Lord had commanded Moses.

39:27
Ex 28:40
Lev 8:13

27Robes were now made for Aaron and his sons from fine-twined linen thread. 28, 29The chestpiece, the beautiful turbans, and the caps and the underclothes were all made of this linen, and the linen belt was beautifully embroidered with blue,

39:30
Ex 38:36
Lev 8:9

purple, and scarlet threads, just as Jehovah had commanded Moses. 30Finally they made the holy plate of pure gold to wear on the front of the turban, engraved with the words, "Consecrated to Jehovah." 31It was tied to the turban with a blue cord, just as the Lord had instructed.

32And so at last the Tabernacle was finished, following all of the Lord's instructions to Moses.

Moses inspects the work

33-40Then they brought the entire Tabernacle to Moses:

Furniture; clasps; frames; bars;
Posts; bases; layers of covering for the roof and sides—the rams' skins dyed
    red, the specially tanned goat skins, and the entrance drape; the Ark with
    the Ten Commandments in it;
The carrying poles;
The place of mercy;
The table and all its utensils;
The Bread of the Presence;
The pure [gold] lampstand with its lamps, utensils, and oil;
The gold altar;
The anointing oil;
The sweet incense;
The curtain-door of the Tabernacle;
The bronze altar;
The bronze grating;
The poles and the utensils;
The washbasin and its base;
The drapes for the walls of the court and the posts holding them up;
The bases and the drapes at the gate of the court;
The cords and nails;
All the utensils used there in the work of the Tabernacle.

39:15-18 *to the ephod,* implied.   **39:24** *embroidered,* implied.   **39:33-40** *gold,* implied.

39:32 The Tabernacle was finally complete to the last detail. God was keenly interested in every minute part. The Creator of the universe was concerned about even the little things. Matthew 10:30 says that God actually knows the number of hairs on our heads. This shows that God is greatly interested in you. Don't be afraid to talk with him about any of your concerns—no matter how small or unimportant they might seem.

41They also brought for his inspection the beautifully tailored garments to be worn while ministering in the Holy Place, and the holy garments for Aaron the priest and those for his sons, to be worn when on duty.

42So the people of Israel followed all the Lord's instructions to Moses. 43And Moses inspected all their work and blessed them because it was all as the Lord had instructed him.

39:43
Lev 9:22,23
Num 6:23
Josh 22:6
1 Kgs 8:14
2 Chron 30:27

Putting the Tabernacle together

40 The Lord now said to Moses, 2"Put together the Tabernacle on the first day of the first month. 3In it, place the Ark containing the Ten Commandments; and install the veil to enclose the Ark within the Holy of Holies. 4Then bring in the table and place the utensils on it, and bring in the lampstand and light the lamps.

40:2
Ex 12:1; 19:1
40:17
Num 1:1; 7:1

40:3
Ex 25:9,10
Num 4:5

5"Place the gold altar for the incense in front of the Ark. Set up the drapes at the entrance of the Tabernacle, 6and place the altar for burnt offerings in front of the entrance. 7Set the washbasin between the Tabernacle-tent and the altar, and fill it with water. 8Then make the courtyard around the outside of the tent, and hang the curtain-door at the entrance to the courtyard.

9"Take the anointing oil and sprinkle it here and there upon the Tabernacle and everything in it, upon all of its utensils and parts, and all the furniture, to hallow it; and it shall become holy. 10Sprinkle the anointing oil upon the altar of burnt offering and its utensils, sanctifying it; for the altar shall then become most holy. 11Then anoint the washbasin and its pedestal, sanctifying it.

12"Now bring Aaron and his sons to the entrance of the Tabernacle and wash them with water; 13and clothe Aaron with the holy garments and anoint him, sanctifying him to minister to me as a priest. 14Then bring his sons and put their robes upon them, 15and anoint them as you did their father, that they may minister to me as priests; their anointing shall be permanent from generation to generation: all their children and children's children shall forever be my priests."

40:12
Ex 28:41; 29:1
Lev 8:1-13

40:15
Ex 29:9
Num 3:10
Deut 18:5
Heb 5:4

16So Moses proceeded to do all as the Lord had commanded him. 17On the first day of the first month, in the second year, the Tabernacle was put together. 18Moses erected it by setting its frames into their bases and attaching the bars. 19Then he spread the coverings over the framework, and put on the top layers, just as the Lord had commanded him.

40:17
Ex 40:2
Num 7:1

20Inside the Ark he placed the stones with the Ten Commandments engraved on them, and attached the carrying poles to the Ark and installed the gold lid, the place of mercy. 21Then he brought the Ark into the Tabernacle and set up the curtain to screen it, just as the Lord had commanded.

40:20
Deut 10:5
1 Kgs 8:9
Heb 9:4

22Next he placed the table at the north side of the room outside the curtain, 23and set the Bread of the Presence upon the table before the Lord, just as the Lord had commanded.

40:23
Ex 25:30; 35:13
Lev 24:5

24And he placed the lampstand next to the table, on the south side of the Tabernacle. 25Then he lighted the lamps before the Lord, following all the instructions, 26and placed the gold altar in the Tabernacle next to the curtain, 27and burned upon it the incense made from sweet spices, just as the Lord had commanded.

28He attached the curtain at the entrance of the Tabernacle, 29and placed the outside altar for the burnt offerings near the entrance, and offered upon it a burnt offering and a meal offering, just as the Lord had commanded him.

30Next he placed the washbasin between the tent and the altar, and filled it with

---

39:43 Moses had learned his management lesson well. He gave important responsibilities to others and then trusted them to do the job. Great leaders, like Moses, give plans and direction while letting others participate on the team. If you are a leader, trust your assistants with a piece of the action.

39:43 Moses inspected the finished work, saw that it was done the way God wanted, and then blessed the people. A good leader follows up on assigned tasks and gives rewards for good work. In whatever responsible position you find yourself, follow up to make sure tasks are completed as intended, and show your appreciation to the people who have helped.

40:16 God told Moses how to build the Tabernacle, and Moses did it. God allows people to participate with him in carrying out his will. Your task is not just to sit and watch God work, but to give your best efforts when labor is called for.

40:31
Ex 30:19

water so that the priests could use it for washing. 31Moses and Aaron and Aaron's sons washed their hands and feet there. 32Whenever they walked past the altar to enter the Tabernacle, they stopped and washed, just as the Lord had commanded Moses.

33Then he erected the enclosure surrounding the tent and the altar, and set up the curtain-door at the entrance of the enclosure. So at last Moses finished the work.

The glory of the Lord

40:34
1 Kgs 8:10,11
Hag 2:7,9
40:35
1 Kgs 8:1
40:36
Num 9:17; 10:11
40:37,38
Num 9:15-23

34Then the cloud covered the Tabernacle and the glory of the Lord filled it. 35Moses was not able to enter because the cloud was standing there, and the glory of the Lord filled the Tabernacle. 36Whenever the cloud lifted and moved, the people of Israel journeyed onward, following it. 37But if the cloud stayed, they stayed until it moved. 38The cloud rested upon the Tabernacle during the daytime, and at night there was fire in the cloud so that all the people of Israel could see it. This continued throughout all their journeys.

40:33 The physical care of the Tabernacle required a long list of tasks, but each was important to the work of God's house. This principle is equally important to remember today, when God's house is the church. There are many seemingly unimportant tasks that must be done to keep your church building maintained. Washing dishes, painting walls, or shoveling snow may not seem very spiritual. But they are vital to the ministry of the church and have an important role in our worship of God.

40:34 The Tabernacle was God's home on earth. He filled it with his presence and glory. Almost 500 years later, Solomon built the Temple, which replaced the Tabernacle as the central place of worship. God also filled the Temple with his glory (2 Chronicles 5:13, 14). But when Israel turned from God, his glory and presence departed from the Temple, and it was destroyed by invading armies (2 Kings 25). The Temple was rebuilt in 516 B.C., and God's glory returned in even greater splendor nearly five centuries later when Jesus Christ, God's Son, entered it and taught. When Jesus was crucified, God's glory again left the Temple. However, God no longer needed a physical building after Jesus rose from the dead. God's Temple now is his church, the body of believers.

40:38 The Israelites were once Egyptian slaves making bricks without straw. Now they were following the cloud of fire, carrying the Tabernacle they had built for God. Exodus begins in gloom and ends in glory, which parallels our progress through the Christian life. We begin as slaves to sin, are redeemed by God, and end our pilgrimage living with God forever. The lessons the Israelites learned along the way are practical lessons for us, too.

VITAL STATISTICS

PURPOSE:
A handbook for the Levites outlining their priestly duties in worship, and a guidebook of holy living for the Hebrews

AUTHOR:
Moses

DATE OF EVENTS:
1445–1444 B.C.

SETTING:
At the foot of Mount Sinai. God is teaching the Israelites how to live as holy people.

KEY VERSE:
"You must be holy, because I, the Lord your God, am holy" (19:2).

KEY PEOPLE:
Moses, Aaron, Nadab, Abihu, Eleazar, Ithamar

KEY PLACE:
Mount Sinai

SPECIAL FEATURE:
Holiness is mentioned more times (152) than in any other book of the Bible.

GOD seems so far away . . . if only I could see or hear him." When have you felt this way—struggling with loneliness, burdened by despair, riddled with sin, overwhelmed by problems? Made in God's image, we were created to have a close relationship with him; and when fellowship is broken, we are incomplete and need restoration. Communion with the living God is the essence of worship. It is vital, touching the very core of our lives. Perhaps this is why a whole book of the Bible is dedicated to worship.

After Israel's dramatic exit from Egypt, the nation was camped at the foot of Mount Sinai for two years to listen to God (Exodus 19 to Numbers 10). It was a time of resting, teaching, building, and meeting with him face to face. Redemption in Exodus is the foundation for cleansing, worship, and service in Leviticus.

The overwhelming message of Leviticus is the holiness of God—"You must be holy, because I, the Lord your God, am holy" (19:1, 2). But how can unholy people approach a holy God? The answer—first sin must be dealt with. Thus the opening chapters of Leviticus give detailed instructions for offering sacrifices, which were the active symbols of repentance and obedience. Whether bulls, grain, goats, or sheep, the sacrificial offerings had to be perfect, with no defects or bruises—pictures of the ultimate sacrifice to come, Jesus, the Lamb of God. Jesus has come and opened the way to God by giving up his life as the final sacrifice in our place. True worship and oneness with God begin as we confess our sin and accept Christ as the only one who can redeem us from sin and help us approach God.

In Leviticus, sacrifices, priests, and the sacred Day of Atonement opened the way for the Israelites to come to God. God's people were also to worship him with their lives. Thus we read of purity laws (11—15) and rules for daily living concerning family responsibilities, sexual conduct, relationships, worldliness (18—20), and vows (27). These instructions involve one's holy walk with God, and the patterns of spiritual living still apply today. Worship, therefore, has a horizontal aspect—that is, God is honored by our lives as we relate to others.

The final emphasis in Leviticus is celebration. The book gives instructions for the festivals. These were special and regular occasions for remembering what God had done, giving thanks to him, and rededicating lives to his service (23). Our Christian traditions and holidays are different, but they are necessary ingredients of worship. We too need special days of worship and celebration with our brothers and sisters to remember God's goodness in our lives. As you read Leviticus, rededicate yourself to holiness, worshiping God in private confession, public service, and group celebration.

THE BLUEPRINT

A. WORSHIPING A HOLY GOD
   (1:1—17:16)
   1. Instructions for the offerings
   2. Instructions for the priests
   3. Instructions for the people
   4. Instructions for the altar

B. LIVING A HOLY LIFE
   (18:1—27:34)
   1. Standards for the people
   2. Standards for the priests
   3. Seasons and festivals
   4. Receiving God's blessing

God's instructions for worship provide guidelines about our attitude toward worship today.

Through the offerings we learn of the seriousness of sin and the importance of bringing our sins to God for forgiveness.

The Day of Atonement foreshadows how Christ became the sacrifice for our sins.

Seeing how God combated sin in the nation of Israel shows us how God wants to remove sin from our lives.

God made a distinction between the Israelites and the heathen nations around them. Christians today are to be separated from sin and dedicated to God.

All people, including priests, had to perform a special cleansing ceremony before they could approach God. From this we learn about the purity and holiness of God.

MEGATHEMES

THEME	EXPLANATION	IMPORTANCE
Sacrifice/Offering	There are five kinds of offerings that fulfill two main purposes: one to show praise, thankfulness, and devotion; the other for atonement, the covering and removal of guilt and sin.	The sacrifices (offerings) were for worship and forgiveness of sin. Through them we learn about the cost of sin, for we see that we cannot forgive ourselves. God's system says that a life must be given for a life. In the Old Testament, an animal's life was given to save the life of a person. But this was only a temporary measure until Jesus' death paid the penalty of sin for all people forever.
Worship	Seven feasts were designated religious and national holidays. These events teach us much about worshiping God in both celebration and quiet dedication.	God's rules about worship set up an orderly, regular pattern of fellowship with him. It allowed times for celebration and thanksgiving as well as for reverence and rededication. Our worship should follow the same pattern.
Health	Civil rules for handling food, disease, and sex were taught. In these physical principles, many spiritual principles were suggested. Israel was to be different from the surrounding nations. God was preserving Israel from disease and genetic problems.	We are to be different morally and spiritually from the unbelievers around us. Principles for healthy living are as important today as in Moses' time. A healthy environment and a healthy body make our service to God more effective.
Holiness	Holy means "separated" or "devoted." God removed his people from Egypt; now he was removing Egypt from the people. He was showing them how to exchange Egyptian ways of living for his ways.	We must devote every area of life to God. God desires absolute obedience in motives as well as practices. Though we do not observe all the worship practices of Israel, we are to have the same spirit of preparation and devotion.
Levites	The Levites and priests instructed the people in their worship. They were the ministers of their day. They also regulated the moral, civil, and ceremonial laws and supervised the health, justice, and welfare of the nation.	The Levites were servants who showed Israel the way to God. They provide the historical backdrop for Christ, who is our High Priest and yet our servant.

A. WORSHIPING A HOLY GOD (1:1—17:16)

The Israelites have arrived safely at the foot of Mount Sinai, and the Tabernacle has been completed. The people will spend a great deal of time here as God shows them a new way of life with clear instructions on how sinful people can relate to a holy God. These instructions help us avoid taking our relationship with the same holy God too lightly. We learn about the holiness and majesty of the God with whom we are allowed to have a personal relationship.

1. Instructions for the offerings

The burnt offering

1 The Lord now spoke to Moses from the Tabernacle, 2, 3and commanded him to give the following instructions to the people of Israel: "When you sacrifice to the Lord, use animals from your herds and flocks.

"If your sacrifice is to be an ox given as a burnt offering, use only a bull with no physical defects. Bring the animal to the entrance of the Tabernacle where the priests will accept your gift for the Lord. 4The person bringing it is to lay his hand

1:1
Ex 25:22
Num 7:89

1:2
Lev 6:9-13
17:1-8
22:19,20-25
Heb 9:14

1:4 *as the penalty for his sins,* literally, "to make atonement for him."

THE ISRAELITES AT MOUNT SINAI
Throughout the book of Leviticus, the Israelites were camped at the foot of Mount Sinai. It was time to regroup as a nation and learn the importance of following God as they prepared to march toward the Promised Land.

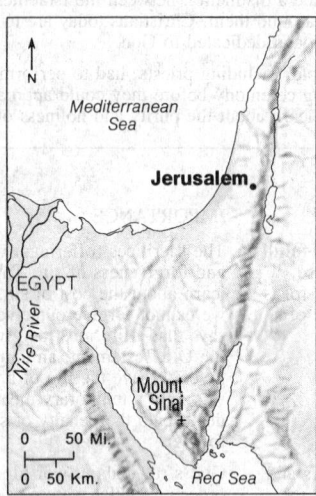

1:1 The book of Leviticus begins where the book of Exodus ends—at the foot of Mount Sinai. The Tabernacle has just been completed (Exodus 35—40). Now God is ready to teach the people how to worship him.

1:1ff We may be tempted to dismiss Leviticus as a record of bizarre rituals of a different age. But its practices made sense to the people of the day and now offer important insights for us into God's nature and character.

Animal sacrifice is repulsive to many sensitive modern people. Doubtless this was true in biblical times as well. This is part of the point—sin is serious. People seeing the intensity of the sacrifice were sensitized to the importance of their behavior. Today the casual attitude toward violence in our culture produces a casual view of pain and sin.

Although many of the rituals of Leviticus were fitted to the culture of the day, their purpose was to reveal a high and holy God who should be loved and worshiped. God's laws and sacrifices were intended to bring out devotion of the heart. The ceremonies and rituals were simply the best way for these people to focus their hearts on him.

1:2, 3 Was there any difference between a sacrifice and an offering? In Leviticus the words are interchanged. Usually a specific sacrifice was called an offering (burnt offering, grain offering, thank offering). Offerings in general were called sacrifices. The point is that each person *offered* a gift to God by

sacrificing it on the altar. In the Old Testament, the sacrifice was the only way to approach God and restore a relationship with him.

1:2, 3 When God taught his people to worship him, he placed great emphasis on sacrifices. Why? It was God's way in the Old Testament for people to ask forgiveness for their sins. Since the first sin of mankind, God made it clear that sin separated people from him and that those who sinned deserved to die. Since all people have sinned (Romans 3:23), God designed the sacrifice as a way to seek forgiveness and restore a relationship with him.

Because he is a God of love and mercy, God decided from the very first that he would come down into our world and die to pay the penalty for all humans. This he did in his Son who, while still God, took the form and characteristics of a human being. In the meantime, before God made this ultimate sacrifice to send his Son, he instructed all people to kill an animal as their sacrifice for sin. The animal sacrifice accomplished two things: (1) the animal symbolically took the sinner's place and paid the penalty for sin, and (2) the animal's death represented one life given so that another life could be saved.

This method of sacrifice continued throughout Old Testament times. It was effective in teaching, guiding, and bringing the people back to God. But in New Testament times, Christ's death became the last sacrifice needed. He took our punishment once and for all. Animal sacrifice was no longer required. All people can now be freed from the penalty of sin by simply believing in Jesus and accepting the forgiveness he offers.

1:2, 3 There was more than one kind of offering or sacrifice. The variety of sacrifices made them more meaningful, because each one related to a specific situation in a person's life. Sacrifices were given in praise, worship, and thanksgiving, as well as for forgiveness and fellowship. The first seven chapters of Leviticus describe the variety of offerings and how the people used them.

1:2, 3 The first of the offerings God described was the burnt offering. A person who had sinned brought an animal with no defects to a priest. The unblemished animal symbolized the moral perfection demanded by a holy God and the perfect nature of the real sacrifice to come—Jesus Christ.

The person then laid his hand on the head of the animal while it was slain by the priest. This symbolized the person's complete identification with the animal as his substitute. He was transferring his sorrow for his sins to the animal, and thus his sins were taken away. Finally the animal (except for the blood and skin) was burned on the altar, signifying the person's complete dedication to God.

God required more than a sacrifice, of course. He also asked the sinner to have an attitude of repentance. The outward symbol (the sacrifice) and the inner change (repentance) were to work together. But it is important to remember that neither sacrifice nor repentance actually caused the sin to be taken away. God alone

1:4
Ex 29:10,15,19
Lev 4:13-35
Num 8:10-12;
15:25
2 Chron 29:23,
24

1:5
Lev 1:11; 3:7,8
16:15
Heb 12:24

1:6
Lev 7:8
Neh 13:31

1:8
Ex 29:17
Lev 3:3,4,5

1:9
Gen 8:21
Ex 29:17,18
Num 15:8,9
Eph 5:2
Phil 4:18

upon its head, and it then becomes his substitute: the death of the animal will be accepted by God instead of the death of the man who brings it, as the penalty for his sins. ⁵The man shall then kill the animal there before the Lord, and Aaron's sons, the priests, will present the blood before the Lord, sprinkling it upon all sides of the altar at the entrance of the Tabernacle. 6, ⁷Then the priests will skin the animal and quarter it, and build a wood fire upon the altar, ⁸and put the sections of the animal and its head and fat upon the wood. ⁹The internal organs and the legs are to be washed, then the priests will burn them upon the altar, and they will be an acceptable burnt offering with which the Lord is pleased.

10"If the animal used as a burnt offering is a sheep or a goat, it too must be a male, and without any blemishes. ¹¹The man who brings it will kill it before the Lord on the north side of the altar, and Aaron's sons, the priests, will sprinkle its blood back and forth upon the altar. ¹²Then the man will quarter it, and the priests will lay the pieces, with the head and the fat, on top of the wood on the altar. ¹³But the internal organs and the legs shall first be washed with water. Then the priests shall burn it all upon the altar as an offering to the Lord; for burnt offerings give much pleasure to the Lord.

1:6, 7 *the priests will skin,* literally, "he shall skin . . ." **1:9** *they will be an acceptable burnt offering with which the Lord is pleased,* literally, "it will be a sweet savor unto the Lord."

THE OFFERINGS
Listed here are the five key offerings the Israelites made to God. The Jews made these offerings in order to have their sins forgiven and to restore their fellowship with God. The death of Jesus Christ made these sacrifices unnecessary. Because of his death our sins were completely forgiven and fellowship with God has been restored.

Offering	Purpose	Significance	Christ, the Perfect Offering
Burnt Offering (Lev. 1— voluntary)	To make payment for sins in general	Showed a person's devotion to God	Christ's death was the perfect offering
Grain Offering (Lev. 2— voluntary)	To show honor and respect to God in worship	Acknowledged that all we have belongs to God	Christ was the perfect man, who gave all of himself to God and others
Peace Offering (Lev. 3— voluntary)	To express gratitude to God	Symbolized peace and fellowship with God	Christ is the only way to fellowship with God
Sin Offering (Lev. 4— required)	To make payment for unintentional sins of uncleanness, neglect, or thoughtlessness	Restored the sinner to fellowship with God; showed seriousness of sin	Christ's death restores our fellowship with God
Guilt Offering (Lev. 5— required)	To make payment for sins against God and others. A sacrifice was made to God and the injured person repaid or compensated	Provided compensation for injured parties	Christ's death takes away the deadly consequences of sin

---

forgives sin. Fortunately for us, forgiveness is part of God's loving nature.

1:3ff What did sacrifices teach the people? (1) By requiring perfect animals and holy priests, they taught reverence for a holy God. (2) By the exact obedience they demanded, they taught total trust in God's laws. (3) By requiring an animal, something of great value in Bible times, they showed the high cost of sin and demonstrated the sincerity of the offerer's commitment to God.

1:4ff Israel was not the only nation to sacrifice animals—many heathen religions did it as well to try to please their gods. They sometimes even included human sacrifice, which was strictly forbidden by God. However, the meaning behind Israel's animal sacrifices was clearly different. Israelites sacrificed animals, not to

appease God, but as a substitute for the punishment they deserved for their sins. A sacrifice showed faith in God and commitment to his laws. Most important, this system foreshadowed the day when the Lamb of God (Jesus Christ) would die and conquer sin once and for all.

1:4-13 Why such detailed regulations for each offering? God had a purpose in giving these commands. He was starting from scratch, teaching his people a whole new system of government, restoring true worship of himself, and cleansing them from the many heathen practices they had learned in Egypt. The strict details kept Israel from slipping back into their old lifestyle. In addition, each law paints a graphic, orderly picture of the seriousness of sin and of God's great mercy in forgiving sinners.

14"If anyone wishes to use a bird as his burnt offering, he may choose either turtledoves or young pigeons. 15, 16, 17A priest will take the bird to the altar and wring off its head, and the blood shall be drained out at the side of the altar. Then the priest will remove the crop and the feathers and throw them on the east side of the altar with the ashes. Then, grasping it by the wings, he shall tear it apart, but not completely. And the priest shall burn it upon the altar, and the Lord will have pleasure in this sacrifice.

1:14
Gen 15:9
Lev 12:8
1:15
Lev 5:9

The grain offering

2 "Anyone who wishes to sacrifice a grain offering to the Lord is to bring fine flour and is to pour olive oil and incense upon it. 2Then he is to take a handful, representing the entire amount, to one of the priests to burn, and the Lord will be fully pleased. 3The remainder of the flour is to be given to Aaron and his sons as their food; but all of it is counted as a holy burnt offering to the Lord.

2:1
Ex 29:2
Lev 6:14-18
24:7
Num 15:4-21
2:2
Lev 2:9
5:12,13
6:15-18
2:3
Lev 10:12,13
Num 8:8-11
2:4
Ex 29:2
Lev 7:12

4"If bread baked in the oven is brought as an offering to the Lord, it must be made from finely ground flour, baked with olive oil but without yeast. Wafers made without yeast and spread with olive oil may also be used as an offering. 5If the offering is something from the griddle, it shall be made of finely ground flour without yeast, and mingled with olive oil. 6Break it into pieces and pour oil upon it—it is a form of grain offering. 7If your offering is cooked in a pan, it too shall be made of fine flour mixed with olive oil.

8"However it is prepared—whether baked, fried, or grilled—you are to bring this grain offering to the priest and he shall take it to the altar to present it to the Lord.

2:9
Gen 8:21
Ex 29:18
Lev 2:2; 6:15
2:10
Lev 2:3
2:11
Lev 6:16,17
2:12
Lev 7:13
23:9-14
2:13
Num 18:19
2 Chron 13:5
Ezek 43:24
Mk 9:49
2:14
Lev 23:9-14
2 Kgs 4:42
2:16
Lev 2:1,2

9"The priests are to burn only a representative portion of the offering, but all of it will be fully appreciated by the Lord. 10The remainder belongs to the priests for their own use, but it is all counted as a holy burnt offering to the Lord.

11"Use no yeast with your offerings of flour; for no yeast or honey is permitted in burnt offerings to the Lord. 12You may offer yeast bread and honey as thanksgiving offerings at harvest time, but not as burnt offerings.

13"Every offering must be seasoned with salt, because the salt is a reminder of God's covenant.

14"If you are offering from the first of your harvest, remove the kernels from a fresh ear, crush and roast them, then offer them to the Lord. 15Put olive oil and incense on the offering, for it is a grain offering. 16Then the priests shall burn part of the bruised grain mixed with oil and all of the incense as a representative portion before the Lord.

The peace offering

3 "When anyone wants to give an offering of thanksgiving to the Lord, he may use either a bull or a cow, but the animal must be entirely without defect if it

3:1
Lev 1:2; 7:11-21

1:17 *the Lord will have pleasure in this sacrifice,* literally, "it will be a sweet savor unto the Lord." **2:2** *representing the entire amount,* literally, "shall burn the memorial portion thereof upon the altar, an offering made by fire." **2:9** *a representative portion,* literally, "the memorial." **2:12** *but not as burnt offerings,* literally, "but not for a sweet savor on the altar." **2:13** *seasoned with salt.* In many of the languages of the ancient Near East, the word "salt" is a homonym of the word "good." It was used symbolically for "goodness" in making covenants.

2:1ff The grain offering accompanied all burnt offerings and was a gift of thanks to God. It reminded the people that their food came from God and that therefore they owed their lives to him. Three kinds of grain offerings are listed: (1) fine flour with oil and frankincense, (2) baked cakes of fine flour and oil, (3) roasted heads of grain with oil and frankincense. The absence of leaven symbolized the absence of sin, and the oil symbolized God's presence. Part of the grain offering was burned on the altar as a gift to God, and the rest was eaten by the priests. The offerings helped support them in their work.

2:11 Why was no yeast (leaven) allowed in the grain offerings? Yeast is a bacterial fungus or mold, the active ingredient in leaven. Yeast, therefore, was an appropriate symbol for sin. It grows in bread just as sin grows in a life. A little yeast will affect the whole

loaf, just as a little sin can ruin a whole life. Jesus continued this analogy by warning about the leaven of the Pharisees (Matthew 16:6; Mark 8:15).

2:13 Their offering was seasoned with salt as a reminder of the people's covenant (contract) with God. Salt is a good symbol of God's activity in a person's life, because it penetrates, preserves, and aids in healing. God wants to be active in your life. Let him become part of you, penetrating every aspect of your life, preserving you from the evil all around, and healing you of your sins and shortcomings.

3:1ff A person gave a thank (or peace) offering as an expression of gratitude and a means of establishing fellowship between himself and God. Because it symbolized peace with God, part of the offering could be eaten by the person presenting it.

is to be offered to the Lord! ²The man who brings the animal shall lay his hand upon its head and kill it at the door of the Tabernacle. Then Aaron's sons shall throw the blood against the sides of the altar, ³, ⁴, ⁵and shall burn before the Lord the fat that covers the inward parts, the two kidneys and the loin-fat on them, and the gall bladder. And it will give the Lord much pleasure.

⁶"If a goat or sheep is used as a thank-offering to the Lord, it must have no defect and may be either a male or female.

⁷, ⁸"If it is a lamb, the man who brings it shall lay his hand upon its head and kill it at the entrance of the Tabernacle; the priests shall throw the blood against the sides of the altar, ⁹, ¹⁰, ¹¹and shall offer upon the altar the fat, the tail removed close to the backbone, the fat covering the internal organs, the two kidneys with the loin-fat on them, and the gall bladder, as a burnt offering to the Lord.

¹²"If anyone brings a goat as his offering to the Lord, ¹³he shall lay his hand upon its head and kill it at the entrance of the Tabernacle. The priest shall throw its blood against the sides of the altar, ¹⁴and shall offer upon the altar, as a burnt offering to the Lord, the fat which covers the insides, ¹⁵, ¹⁶the two kidneys and the loin-fat on them, and the gall bladder. This burnt offering is very pleasing to the Lord. All the fat is Jehovah's. ¹⁷This is a permanent law throughout your land, that you shall eat neither fat nor blood."

The sin offering

4 Then the Lord gave these further instructions to Moses:

²"Tell the people of Israel that these are the laws concerning anyone who unintentionally breaks any of my commandments. ³If a priest sins unintentionally, and so brings guilt upon the people, he must offer a young bull without defect as a sin offering to the Lord. ⁴He shall bring it to the door of the Tabernacle, and shall lay his hand upon its head and kill it there before Jehovah. ⁵Then the priest shall take the animal's blood into the Tabernacle, ⁶and shall dip his finger in the blood and sprinkle it seven times before the Lord in front of the veil that bars the way to the Holy of Holies. ⁷Then the priest shall put some of the blood upon the horns of the incense altar before the Lord in the Tabernacle; the remainder of the blood shall be poured out at the base of the altar for burnt offerings, at the entrance to the Tabernacle. ⁸Then he shall take all the fat on the entrails, ⁹the two kidneys and the loin-fat on them, and the gall bladder, ¹⁰and shall burn them on the altar of burnt offering, just as in the case of a bull or cow sacrificed as a thank-offering. ¹¹, ¹²But the remainder of the young bull—the skin, meat, head, legs, internal organs, and intestines—shall be carried to a ceremonially clean place outside the camp—a place where the ashes are brought from the altar—and burned there on a wood fire.

¹³"If the entire nation of Israel sins without realizing it, and does something that Jehovah has said not to do, all the people are guilty. ¹⁴When they realize it, they shall offer a young bull for a sin offering, bringing it to the Tabernacle ¹⁵where the leaders of the nation shall lay their hands upon the animal's head and kill it before the Lord. ¹⁶Then the priest shall bring its blood into the Tabernacle, ¹⁷and shall dip his finger in the blood and sprinkle it seven times before the Lord, in front of the veil. ¹⁸Then he shall put blood upon the horns of the altar there in the Tabernacle before the Lord, and all the remainder of the blood shall be poured out at the base of the burnt offering altar, at the entrance to the Tabernacle. ¹⁹All the fat shall be removed and burned upon the altar. ²⁰He shall follow the same procedure as for a

4:15 *leaders,* literally, "elders."

4:1, 2ff Have you ever done something wrong without realizing it until later? Although your sin was unintentional, it was still sin. One of the purposes of God's law was to make the Israelites aware of their unintentional sins so they would not repeat them and so they could be forgiven for them.

The opposite of love is not hate but indifference. A casual approach to life often leads to unintentional sins—those we commit without even knowing it. Leviticus 4 and 5 mention some of these unintentional sins and the way the Israelites could be forgiven for them. As you read more of God's laws, keep in mind that they were meant to teach and guide the people.

4:2 The sin offering was for those who (1) committed a sin without realizing it or (2) committed a sin out of weakness or negligence as opposed to outright rebellion against God. Different animals were sacrificed for the different kinds of sin. The death of Jesus Christ was the final sin offering in the Bible (2 Corinthians 5:21).

sin offering; in this way the priest shall make atonement for the nation, and everyone will be forgiven. 21The priest shall then cart the young bull outside the camp and burn it there, just as though it were a sin offering for an individual, only this time it is a sin offering for the entire nation.

22"If one of the leaders sins without realizing it and is guilty of disobeying one of God's laws, 23as soon as it is called to his attention he must bring as his sacrifice a male goat without any physical defect. 24He shall lay his hand upon its head and kill it at the place where the burnt offerings are killed, and present it to the Lord. This is his sin offering. 25Then the priest shall take some of the blood of this sin offering and place it with his finger upon the horns of the altar of burnt offerings, and the rest of the blood shall be poured out at the base of the altar. 26All the fat shall be burned upon the altar, just as if it were the fat of the sacrifice of a thank-offering; thus the priest shall make atonement for the leader concerning his sin, and he shall be forgiven.

27"If any one of the common people sins and doesn't realize it, he is guilty. 28But as soon as he does realize it, he is to bring as his sacrifice a female goat without defect to atone for his sin. 29He shall bring it to the place where the animals for burnt offerings are killed, and there lay his hand upon the head of the sin offering and kill it. 30And the priest shall take some of the blood with his finger and smear it upon the horns of the burnt offering altar. Then the priest shall pour out the remainder of the blood at the base of the altar. 31All the fat shall be taken off, just as in the procedure for the thank-offering sacrifice, and the priest shall burn it upon the altar; and the Lord will appreciate it. Thus the priest shall make atonement for that man, and he shall be forgiven.

32"However, if he chooses to bring a lamb as his sin offering, it must be a female without physical defect. 33He shall bring it to the place where the burnt offerings are killed, and lay his hand upon its head and kill it there as a sin offering. 34The priest shall take some of the blood with his finger and smear it upon the horns of the burnt offering altar, and all the rest of the blood shall be poured out at the base of the altar. 35The fat shall be used just as in the case of a thank-offering lamb—the priest shall burn the fat on the altar as in any other sacrifice made to Jehovah by fire; and the priest shall make atonement for the man, and his sin shall be forgiven.

5 "Anyone refusing to give testimony concerning what he knows about a crime is guilty.

2"Anyone touching anything ceremonially unclean—such as the dead body of an animal forbidden for food, wild or domesticated, or the dead body of some forbidden insect—is guilty, even though he wasn't aware of touching it. 3Or if he touches human discharge of any kind, he becomes guilty as soon as he realizes that he has touched it.

4"If anyone makes a rash vow, whether the vow is good or bad, when he realizes what a foolish vow he has taken, he is guilty. 5"In any of these cases, he shall confess his sin 6and bring his guilt offering to the Lord, a female lamb or goat, and the priest shall make atonement for him, and he shall be freed from his sin, and need not fulfill the vow.

7"If he is too poor to bring a lamb to the Lord, then he shall bring two turtledoves or two young pigeons as his guilt offering; one of the birds shall be his sin offering

4:21
Lev 4:11

4:22
Lev 4:2,13

4:24
Lev 6:25-30
9:2-11

4:25
Lev 4:7

4:26
Lev 4:8-12

4:27
Lev 4:23

4:28
Lev 1:2-4

4:30
Lev 9:9-11

4:31
Gen 8:21
Ex 29:18
Lev 2:2; 4:8; 6:15

4:32
Lev 4:28

4:35
Lev 3:3

5:2
Lev 11:4-11,
24-39
Num 19:11-16
Deut 14:3-21

5:4
Judg 11:31
1 Sam 14:24,25
Acts 23:12

5:5
Lev 16:21
Num 5:7
Josh 7:19
Ezra 10:11

5:6
Lev 4:28,32
7:1-10

5:7
Lk 2:24

4:26 thank-offering, literally, "peace offering." Also in vss 31, 35. **5:6** he shall be freed from his sin, and need not fulfill the vow, implied.

5:4 Have you ever sworn to do or not do something (made a vow), and then realized what a foolish thing you had done? God's people are called to keep their word, even if they make a promise that is tough to keep. Jesus said, "Your word is enough. To strengthen your promise with a vow shows that something is wrong" (Matthew 5:37). The only kind of promises we ought not to keep are promises that lead to sin. A wise and self-controlled person avoids making rash vows.

5:5, 6 The entire system of sacrifices was worthless unless the offerer came with an attitude of repentance and a willingness to confess sin. Today, because of Christ's death on the cross, we do not have to sacrifice animals. But it is still vital to confess sin, because such confession shows realization of sin, awareness of God's holiness, humility before God, and willingness to turn from this sin (Psalm 51:16, 17). Even Jesus' death can be of little value to us if we do not appropriate its meaning for our lives. It is like a vaccine for a dangerous disease—it is of little value unless it has entered the bloodstream.

5:8
Lev 1:15-17

5:9
Lev 4:7; 7:2

5:10
Lev 1:14-17

and the other his burnt offering. ⁸The priest shall offer as the sin sacrifice which-ever bird is handed to him first, breaking its neck, but not severing its head from its body. ⁹Then he shall sprinkle some of the blood at the side of the altar and the rest shall be drained out at the base of the altar; this is the sin offering. ¹⁰He shall offer the second bird as a burnt offering, following the customary procedures that have been set forth; so the priest shall make atonement for him concerning his sin and he shall be forgiven.

5:11
Lev 14:21
Num 15:3-9
5:15

5:12
Lev 6:25-30

¹¹"If he is too poor to bring turtledoves or young pigeons as his sin offering, then he shall bring a tenth of a bushel of fine flour. He must not mix it with olive oil or put any incense on it, because it is a sin offering. ¹²He shall bring it to the priest and the priest shall take out a handful as a representative portion, and burn it on the altar just as any other offering to Jehovah made by fire; this shall be his sin offering. ¹³In this way the priest shall make atonement for him for any sin of this kind, and he shall be forgiven. The rest of the flour shall belong to the priest, just as was the case with the grain offering."

The guilt offering

5:15
Ex 30:13
Lev 6:6; 7:1-10
22:14-16
27:3,25

5:16
Lev 6:4-6
22:15; 27:13

¹⁴And the Lord said to Moses, ¹⁵"If anyone sins by unintentionally defiling what is holy, then he shall bring a ram without defect, worth whatever fine you charge against him, as his guilt offering to the Lord. ¹⁶And he shall make restitution for the holy thing he has defiled, or the tithe omitted, by paying for the loss, plus a twenty percent penalty; he shall bring it to the priest, and the priest shall make atonement for him with the ram of the guilt offering, and he shall be forgiven.

5:17
Lev 5:17,19

¹⁷,¹⁸"Anyone who disobeys some law of God without realizing it is guilty anyway, and must bring his sacrifice of a value determined by Moses. This sacrifice shall be a ram without blemish taken to the priest as a guilt offering; with it the priest shall make atonement for him, so that he will be forgiven for whatever it is he has done without realizing it. ¹⁹It must be offered as a guilt offering, for he is certainly guilty before the Lord."

6:2
Ex 22:7-15
Num 5:6
Col 3:9

6:3
Lev 19:12
Deut 22:1-3

6:4
Ex 22:1,4,7,9
Lev 5:16
Prov 6:31
Jer 7:9
Zech 5:4
Lk 19:8

6 And the Lord said to Moses, ²"If anyone sins against me by refusing to return a deposit on something borrowed or rented, or by refusing to return something entrusted to him, or by robbery, or by oppressing his neighbor, ³or by finding a lost article and lying about it, swearing that he doesn't have it— ⁴, ⁵on the day he is found guilty of any such sin, he shall restore what he took, adding a twenty percent fine, and give it to the one he has harmed; and on the same day he shall bring his guilt offering to the Tabernacle. ⁶His guilt offering shall be a ram without defect, and must be worth whatever value you demand. He shall bring it to the priest, ⁷and the priest shall make atonement for him before the Lord, and he shall be forgiven."

Burnt offerings

6:9
Ex 29:38-42
Lev 1:2-17
Num 28:1-25

6:10
Ex 28:39-43
Lev 16:4

6:11
Lev 16:23-25

⁸Then the Lord said to Moses, ⁹*"Give Aaron and his sons these regulations concerning the burnt offering:*

"The burnt offering shall be left upon the hearth of the altar all night, with the altar fire kept burning. ¹⁰(The next morning) the priest shall put on his linen undergarments and his linen outer garments and clean out the ashes of the burnt offering and put them beside the altar. ¹¹Then he shall change his clothes and carry

5:15 *worth whatever fine,* literally, "using the standard of the shekel of the sanctuary." **5:16** *guilt offering (asham). or the tithe omitted,* implied in remainder of the verse.

5:16 The guilt offering was another way of taking care of sin committed unknowingly. It was especially for those who thought they might have committed a sin but weren't sure. If the sin was against God (like forgetting a tithe), a ram with no defects had to be sacrificed. If the sin was against another person, not only did the ram have to be sacrificed, but those harmed by the sin had to be compensated for their loss, plus a 20% penalty. Even though

Christ's death has made guilt offerings unnecessary, we still need to make things right with those we hurt.

6:1-7 Here we discover that stealing involves more than just taking from someone. Finding something and not returning it or refusing to return something borrowed are other forms of stealing. These are sins against God and not just your neighbor. Apologize to the owner, confess your sin to God, and return the stolen items.

the ashes outside the camp to a place that is ceremonially clean. [12]Meanwhile, the fire on the altar must be kept burning—it must not go out. The priest shall put on fresh wood each morning, and lay the daily burnt offering on it, and burn the fat of the daily peace offering. [13]The fire must be kept burning upon the altar continually. It must never go out.

6:12
Lev 3:3; 6:9

6:13
Ex 27:20,21
Lev 6:9,12
24:1-4

Grain offerings

[14]*"These are the regulations concerning the grain offering:*

"Aaron's sons shall stand in front of the altar to offer it before the Lord. [15]The priest shall then take out a handful of the finely ground flour with the olive oil and the incense mixed into it, and burn it upon the altar as a representative portion for the Lord; and it will be received with pleasure by the Lord. [16]After taking out this handful, the remainder of the flour will belong to Aaron and his sons for their food; it shall be eaten without yeast in the courtyard of the Tabernacle. [17](Stress this instruction, that if it is baked it must be without yeast.) I have given to the priests this part of the burnt offerings made to me. However, all of it is most holy, just as is the entire sin offering and the entire guilt offering. [18]It may be eaten by any male descendant of Aaron, any priest, generation after generation. But only the priests may eat these offerings made by fire to the Lord."

6:14
Lev 2:1-16

6:15
Lev 2:1,2,9

6:16
Lev 10:12-15
Num 18:8-11

6:17
Ex 29:33,34,37
Lev 2:11
6:26,29; 10:17

6:18
Lev 6:29
Num 18:10
1 Cor 9:13

[19, 20]And Jehovah said to Moses, "On the day Aaron and his sons are anointed and inducted into the priesthood, they shall bring to the Lord a regular grain offering—a tenth of a bushel of fine flour, half to be offered in the morning and half in the evening. [21]It shall be cooked on a griddle, using olive oil, and should be well cooked, then brought to the Lord as an offering that pleases him very much. [22, 23]As the sons of the priests replace their fathers, they shall be inducted into office by offering this same sacrifice on the day of their anointing. This is a perpetual law. These offerings shall be entirely burned up before the Lord; none of it shall be eaten."

6:19
Ex 29:40
Lev 8:12

6:21
Lev 2:5,8; 7:9

6:22,23
Ex 29:25

Sin offerings

[24]Then the Lord said to Moses, [25]*"Tell Aaron and his sons that these are the instructions concerning the sin offering:*

"This sacrifice is most holy, and shall be killed before the Lord at the place where the burnt offerings are killed. [26]The priest who performs the ceremony shall eat it in the courtyard of the Tabernacle. [27]Only those who are sanctified—the priests—may touch this meat; if any blood sprinkles onto their clothing, it must be washed in a holy place. [28]Then the clay pot in which the clothing is boiled shall be broken; or if a bronze kettle is used, it must be scoured and rinsed out thoroughly. [29]Every male among the priests may eat this offering, but only they, for it is most holy. [30]No sin offering may be eaten by the priests if any of its blood is taken into the Tabernacle, to make atonement in the Holy Place. That carcass must be entirely burned with fire before the Lord.

6:25
Lev 4:24,29

6:27
Ex 29:37
30:29,30
Lev 6:18

6:28
Lev 11:33; 15:12

6:29
Lev 6:18
Num 18:10

6:30
Lev 16:27
Heb 9:11; 13:11

Guilt offerings

7 *"Here are the instructions concerning the most holy offering for guilt:*
[2]"The sacrificial animal shall be killed at the place where the burnt offering sacrifices are slain, and its blood shall be sprinkled back and forth upon the altar. [3]The priest will offer upon the altar all its fat, including the tail, the fat that covers the insides, [4]the two kidneys and the loin-fat, and the gall bladder—all shall be set aside for sacrificing. [5]The priests will burn them upon the altar as a guilt offering to the Lord. [6]Only males among the priests may then eat the carcass, and it must be eaten in a holy place, for this is a most holy sacrifice.

7:1
Lev 5:14-19
6:1-7
Num 6:12

7:2
Lev 4:29

7:3
Lev 3:3,9

7:6
Lev 6:18,29

6:18 *But only the priests,* literally, "[only] whoever is holy may touch them," or "whoever touches them shall become holy."

6:12, 13 The holy fire on the altar had to keep burning because God had started it. This represented God's eternal presence in the sacrificial system. It showed the people that only by God's gracious favor could man's sacrifice be acceptable. God's fire is present in each believer's life today, and we must keep our dedication to him burning in our hearts.

7:7
Lev 14:13

7:9
Lev 2:5,8
Num 18:9
Ezek 44:29

7:11
Lev 3:1-17
22:21-25
Ezek 45:15

7:12
Lev 2:4
Num 6:15

7:13
Lev 2:12; 23:17

7:14
Ex 29:27

7:15
Lev 22:29,30

7:16
Lev 19:5-8
22:18-21

7:17
Ex 29:14

7:19
Lev 11:47

7:20
Gen 17:14
Lev 22:3-7
Num 19:13
1 Cor 11:27,28

7:21
Lev 5:2,3
Deut 14:8

7:23
Lev 3:17

7:24
Ex 22:31
Lev 17:15
Deut 14:21

7:26
Gen 9:4
Lev 3:17;
17:10-14
Ezek 33:25
John 6:53
Acts 15:20,29

7:29
Ezek 45:15

7:30
Ex 29:24,27
Lev 8:27; 9:21
Num 6:20

7:31
Lev 7:34
Num 18:18

7"The same instructions apply to both the sin offering and the guilt offering—the carcass shall be given to the priest who is in charge of the atonement ceremony, for his food. 8(When the offering is a burnt sacrifice, the priest who is in charge shall also be given the animal's hide.) 9The priests who present the people's grain offerings to the Lord shall be given whatever remains of the sacrifice after the ceremony is completed. This rule applies whether the sacrifice is baked, fried, or grilled. 10All other grain offerings, whether mixed with olive oil or dry, are the common property of all sons of Aaron.

Peace offerings

11*"Here are the instructions concerning the sacrifices given to the Lord as special peace offerings:*

12"If it is an offering of thanksgiving, unleavened short bread shall be included with the sacrifice, along with unleavened wafers spread with olive oil and loaves from a batter of flour mixed with olive oil. 13This thanksgiving peace offering shall be accompanied with loaves of leavened bread. 14Part of this sacrifice shall be presented to the Lord by a gesture of waving it before the altar, then it shall be given to the assisting priest, the one who sprinkles the blood of the animal presented for the sacrifice. 15After the animal has been sacrificed and presented to the Lord as a peace offering to show special appreciation and thanksgiving to him, its meat is to be eaten that same day, and none left to be eaten the next day.

16"However, if someone brings a sacrifice that is not for thanksgiving, but is because of a vow or is simply a voluntary offering to the Lord, any portion of the sacrifice that is not eaten the day it is sacrificed may be eaten the next day. 17, 18But anything left over until the third day shall be burned. For if any of it is eaten on the third day, the Lord will not accept it; it will have no value as a sacrifice, and there will be no credit to the one who brought it to be offered; and the priest who eats it shall be guilty, for it is detestable to the Lord, and the person who eats it must answer for his sin.

19"Any meat that comes into contact with anything that is ceremonially unclean shall not be eaten, but burned; and as for the meat that may be eaten, it may be eaten only by a person who is ceremonially clean. 20Any priest who is ceremonially unclean but eats the thanksgiving offering anyway, shall be cut off from his people, for he has defiled what is sacred. 21Anyone who touches anything that is ceremonially unclean, whether it is uncleanness from man or beast, and then eats the peace offering, shall be cut off from his people, for he has defiled what is holy."

22Then the Lord said to Moses, 23"Tell the people of Israel never to eat fat, whether from oxen, sheep, or goats. 24The fat of an animal that dies of disease, or is attacked and killed by wild animals, may be used for other purposes, but never eaten. 25Anyone who eats fat from an offering sacrificed by fire to the Lord shall be outlawed from his people.

26, 27"Never eat blood, whether of birds or animals. Anyone who does shall be excommunicated from his people."

28And the Lord said to Moses, 29"Tell the people of Israel that anyone bringing a thanksgiving offering to the Lord must bring it personally with his own hands. 30He shall bring the offering of the fat and breast, which is to be presented to the Lord by waving it before the altar. 31Then the priest shall burn the fat upon the altar,

7:12 *unleavened short bread,* literally, "unleavened loaves mingled with oil." **7:20** *he has defiled what is sacred,* literally, "it pertains unto Jehovah."

7:28, 29 God told the people of Israel to bring their thanksgiving offerings *personally,* with their own hands. They were to take time and effort to express thanks to God. You are the only person who can express your thankfulness to God and to others. Do you leave it to others to express thanks for what people have done? Do you rely on the one leading the prayer to say it for you? Take time yourself to express thanks both to God and to those important to you.

7:30–36 The offering that was waved before the altar was called the wave offering. The part of the offering the priests waved was theirs to keep. The waving motion toward and away from the altar symbolized the offering of the sacrifice to God and his returning it to the priests.

These offerings helped to care for the priests, who cared for God's house. The New Testament teaches that ministers should be paid by the people they serve (1 Corinthians 9:10). Similarly, we should give to those who minister to us.

but the breast shall belong to Aaron and his sons, ³², ³³while the right thigh shall be given to the officiating priest. ³⁴For I have designated the breast and thigh as donations from the people of Israel to the sons of Aaron. Aaron and his sons must always be given this portion of the sacrifice. ³⁵This is their pay! It is to be set apart from the burnt offerings, and given to all who have been appointed to minister to the Lord as priests—to Aaron and to his sons. ³⁶For on the day the Lord anointed them, he commanded that the people of Israel give these portions to them; it is their right forever throughout all their generations."

³⁷These were the instructions concerning the burnt offering, grain offering, sin offering, and guilt offering, and concerning the consecration offering and the peace offering; ³⁸these instructions were given to Moses by the Lord on Mount Sinai, to be passed on to the people of Israel so that they would know how to offer their sacrifices to God in the Sinai desert.

2. Instructions for the priests
Moses consecrates the priests

8 The Lord said to Moses, "Now bring Aaron and his sons to the entrance of the Tabernacle, together with their garments, the anointing oil, the young bull for the sin offering, the two rams, and the basket of bread made without yeast; and summon all Israel to a meeting there."

⁴So all the people assembled, ⁵and Moses said to them, "What I am now going to do has been commanded by Jehovah."

⁶Then he took Aaron and his sons and washed them with water, ⁷and he clothed Aaron with the special coat, sash, robe, and the ephod-jacket with its beautifully woven belt. ⁸Then he put on him the chestpiece and deposited the Urim and the Thummim inside its pouch; ⁹and placed on Aaron's head the turban with the sacred gold plate at its front—the holy crown—as the Lord had commanded Moses. ¹⁰Then Moses took the anointing oil and sprinkled it upon the Tabernacle itself

7:32
Num 18:18
7:34
Ex 29:28
Lev 7:31; 10:14, 15
Deut 18:3
7:36
Ex 29:22-34
40:13-15

7:38
Lev 26:46

8:1
Ex 29:1-4
8:2
Ex 28:1

8:6
Ex 29:3,4
8:8
Ex 28:30,31
Ezra 2:62,63
8:9
Ex 28:4,36-38
29:6; 39:27-31
Zech 6:11-14
8:10
Ex 30:26-33
40:9-11

7:38 God gave his people many rituals and instructions to follow. All the rituals in Leviticus were meant to teach the people valuable lessons. But over time, the people became indifferent to the meanings of these rituals. As a result, the people began to lose touch with God.

When your church appears to be conducting dry, meaningless rituals, try rediscovering the original meaning and purpose behind each practice. This helps you understand why your worship service is arranged as it is.

8:1ff Why did Aaron and his sons need to be cleansed and sanctified? Though all the men from the tribe of Levi were dedicated for service to God, only Aaron's descendants could be priests. They alone had the honor and responsibility of performing the sacrifices. These priests had to cleanse and dedicate themselves before they could help the people do the same.

The ceremony described in Leviticus 8 and 9 was their ordination ceremony. Blood was placed on the priests to show that the entire person was set apart for service to God. This showed that holiness came from God alone, not from the role of being a priest. Similarly, we are not spiritually cleansed because we have a religious position. Spiritual cleansing comes only from God.

8:1ff Why were priests needed in Israel? In Exodus 19:6, the Israelites were instructed to be a kingdom of priests; they would all be holy and relate to God. Before that time, the heads of households (like Abraham and Job) were priests of the house or clan and made sacrifices for the family. At the first Passover, all the firstborn of the tribes were dedicated to God. Later, because of special service, the Levites were selected by God to stand in the place of each tribe's firstborn. Out of the Levites, the descendants of Aaron were chosen to serve as the priests for the nation.

The priests stood in the gap between God and man. They were the spiritual leaders, overseers of offerings, and the first scholars. The system of sacrifice and worship required full-time service. In many ways, the priestly system was a concession to man's inability

to confront and relate to God individually and corporately. In Christ, this imperfect system was transformed. All believers can individually approach God, and Jesus Christ is our High Priest.

8:8 What were the Urim and Thummim? Little is known about them, but they were probably some kind of precious stones or flat objects that God used to give guidance to his people. The priest kept them in a pouch attached to his chestpiece. Some scholars think the Urim may have been the "no" answer and the Thummim the "yes" answer. The priest would shake one of the stones out of the pouch, and God would cause the proper one to fall out.

Another view is that the Urim and Thummim were small flat objects, each with a "yes" side and a "no" side. The priest spilled both from his pouch. If both landed on their "yes" sides, God's answer was positive. Two "no" sides were negative. A "yes" and a "no" meant no reply.

God had a specific purpose for using this method of guidance, as he was teaching a nation the principles of following him. Our situation is not the same, however, so we must not assume God will guide us in ways like this today.

8:10–13 Why were there so many specific guidelines for the priests? The Israelites would have been quite familiar with priests from Egypt. Egyptian priests were mainly interested in politics. They viewed religion as a way to gain power. Thus the Israelites would have been suspicious of the establishment of a new priestly order. But God wanted his priests to serve him and the people. They could not own land or take money from anyone. Their duties were religious—to help people draw near to God and worship him. All these specific guidelines reassured the people and helped the priests accomplish their purpose.

8:12 What was the significance of anointing Aaron as High Priest? The High Priest had special duties that no other priest had. He alone could enter the Holy of Holies in the Tabernacle on the Day of Atonement to atone for the sins of the nation. Therefore he was

8:11
Ex 29:37
Lev 16:14

8:12
Ex 28:41; 30:30
Lev 21:10-12

8:13
Ex 28:36-38

8:14
Ex 29:10-14
Lev 16:6

8:15
Ex 30:10
Lev 4:7

8:17
Lev 4:11
Num 19:9

8:18
Ex 29:15-19

8:22
Ex 29:31
8:23
Ex 29:19,20

8:25
Ex 29:22
Lev 3:9-11

8:26
Ex 29:23

8:27
Ex 29:24

8:28
Ex 29:25

8:29
Ex 29:26
Lev 8:22

8:30
Ex 29:21

8:31
Ex 29:31,32
1 Sam 2:12-17
8:32
Lev 7:17,18

8:33
Ex 29:35

8:35
Lev 8:33

and on each item in it, sanctifying them. ¹¹When he came to the altar he sprinkled it seven times, and also sprinkled the utensils of the altar and the washbasin and its pedestal, to sanctify them. ¹²Then he poured the anointing oil upon Aaron's head, thus setting him apart for his work. ¹³Next Moses placed the robes on Aaron's sons, with the belts and caps, as the Lord had commanded him.

¹⁴Then he took the young bull for the sin offering, and Aaron and his sons laid their hands upon its head ¹⁵, ¹⁶as Moses killed it. He smeared some of the blood with his finger upon the four horns of the altar, and upon the altar itself, to sanctify it, and poured out the rest of the blood at the base of the altar; thus he sanctified the altar, making atonement for it. He took all the fat covering the entrails, the fatty mass above the liver, and the two kidneys and their fat, and burned them all on the altar. ¹⁷The carcass of the young bull, with its hide and dung, was burned outside the camp, as the Lord had commanded Moses.

¹⁸Then he presented to the Lord the ram for the burnt offering. Aaron and his sons laid their hands upon its head, ¹⁹and Moses killed it and sprinkled the blood back and forth upon the altar. ²⁰Next he quartered the ram and burned the pieces, the head and the fat. ²¹He then washed the insides and the legs with water, and burned them upon the altar, so that the entire ram was consumed before the Lord; it was a burnt offering that pleased the Lord very much, for Jehovah's directions to Moses were followed in every detail.

²²Then Moses presented the other ram, the ram of consecration; Aaron and his sons laid their hands upon its head. ²³Moses killed it and took some of its blood and smeared it upon the lobe of Aaron's right ear and the thumb of his right hand and upon the big toe of his right foot. ²⁴Next he smeared some of the blood upon Aaron's sons—upon the lobes of their right ears, upon their right thumbs, and upon the big toes of their right feet. The rest of the blood he sprinkled back and forth upon the altar.

²⁵Then he took the fat, the tail, the fat upon the inner organs, the gall bladder, the two kidneys with their fat, and the right shoulder, ²⁶and placed on top of these one unleavened wafer, one wafer spread with olive oil, and a slice of bread, all taken from the basket which had been placed there before the Lord. ²⁷All this was placed in the hands of Aaron and his sons to present to the Lord by a gesture of waving them before the altar. ²⁸Moses then took it all back from them and burned it upon the altar, along with the burnt offering to the Lord; and Jehovah was pleased by the offering. ²⁹Now Moses took the breast and presented it to the Lord by waving it before the altar; this was Moses' portion of the ram of consecration, just as the Lord had instructed him.

³⁰Next he took some of the anointing oil and some of the blood that had been sprinkled upon the altar, and sprinkled it upon Aaron and upon his clothes and upon his sons and upon their clothes, thus consecrating to the Lord's use Aaron and his sons and their clothes.

³¹Then Moses said to Aaron and his sons, "Boil the meat at the entrance of the Tabernacle, and eat it along with the bread that is in the basket of consecration, just as I instructed you to do. ³²Anything left of the meat and bread must be burned."

³³Next he told them not to leave the Tabernacle entrance for seven days, after which time their consecration would be completed—for it takes seven days. ³⁴Then Moses stated again that all he had done that day had been commanded by the Lord in order to make atonement for them. ³⁵And again he warned Aaron and his sons to stay at the entrance of the Tabernacle day and night for seven days. "If you leave," he told them, "you will die—this is what the Lord has said."

³⁶So Aaron and his sons did all that the Lord had commanded Moses.

8:24 *The rest of the blood he sprinkled back and forth upon the altar,* literally, "Moses threw the blood upon the altar round about." **8:28** *along with the burnt offering,* literally, "upon the burnt offering."

---

in charge of all the other priests. The High Priest was a picture of Jesus Christ, who is our High Priest (Hebrews 7:26–28).

8:36 Aaron and his sons did all that the Lord told them to do. Considering all the detailed lists of Leviticus, that was a

remarkable feat. They knew what God wanted, how he wanted it done, and with what attitude it was to be carried out. We also should obey God this carefully. God wants us to be special and holy people, not a rough approximation.

The priests present the offerings

9 On the eighth day (of the consecration ceremonies), Moses summoned Aaron and Aaron's sons and the elders of Israel, 2and told Aaron to take a bull calf from the herd for a sin offering, and a ram without bodily defect for a burnt offering, and to offer them before the Lord.

3"And tell the people of Israel," Moses instructed, "to select a male goat for their sin offering, also a yearling calf and a yearling lamb, all without bodily defect, for their burnt offering. 4In addition, the people are to bring to the Lord a peace offering sacrifice—an ox and a ram, and a grain offering—flour mingled with olive oil. For today," Moses said, "Jehovah will appear to them."

5So they brought all these things to the entrance of the Tabernacle, as Moses had commanded, and the people came and stood there before the Lord.

6Moses told them, "When you have followed the Lord's instructions, his glory will appear to you."

7Moses then told Aaron to proceed to the altar and to offer the sin offering and the burnt offering, making atonement for himself first, and then for the people, as the Lord had commanded. 8So Aaron went up to the altar and killed the calf as a sacrifice for his own sin; 9his sons caught the blood for him, and he dipped his finger in it and smeared it upon the horns of the altar, and poured out the rest at the base of the altar. 10Then he burned upon the altar the fat, kidneys, and gall bladder from this sin offering, as the Lord had commanded Moses, 11but he burned the meat and hide outside the camp.

12Next he killed the burnt offering animal, and his sons caught the blood and he sprinkled it back and forth upon the altar; 13they brought the animal to him piece by piece, including the head, and he burned each part upon the altar. 14Then he washed the insides and the legs, and offered these also upon the altar as a burnt offering.

15Next he sacrificed the people's offering; he killed the goat and offered it in just the same way as he had the sin offering for himself. 16Thus he sacrificed their burnt offering to the Lord, in accordance with the instructions God had given.

17Then he presented the grain offering, taking a handful and burning it upon the altar in addition to the regular morning offering.

18Next he killed the ox and ram—the people's peace offering sacrifice; and Aaron's sons brought the blood to him and he sprinkled it back and forth upon the altar. 19Then he collected the fat of the ox and the ram—the fat from their tails and the fat covering the inner organs—and the kidneys and gall bladders. 20The fat was placed upon the breasts of these animals, and Aaron burned it upon the altar; 21but he waved the breasts and right shoulders slowly before the Lord as a gesture of offering it to him, just as Moses had commanded.

22Then, with hands spread out towards the people, Aaron blessed them and came down from the altar. 23Moses and Aaron went into the Tabernacle, and when they came out again they blessed the people; and the glory of the Lord appeared to the whole assembly. 24Then fire came from the Lord and consumed the burnt offering and fat on the altar; and when the people saw it, they all shouted and fell flat upon the ground before the Lord.

9:15 *the sin offering for himself.* See vss 8-11.

9:2
Ex 29:24

9:3
Ezra 6:17

9:4
Ex 29:43
Lev 2:4

9:6
Ex 40:34
Lev 9:23

9:7
Heb 5:1-3; 7:27
9:7

9:9
Lev 4:6,7
Heb 9:22

9:15
Lev 4:27-31; 9:3
Heb 5:1-3; 7:27
9:7

9:16
Lev 1:3-10
8:18-21

9:17
Ex 29:38-42
Lev 2:1-16
6:14-18

9:18
Lev 3:1-11
7:11-18

9:19
Lev 3:3; 9:10

9:21
Lev 7:30,32

9:22
Num 6:24-26

9:23
Num 16:19,42

9:24
Gen 15:17
1 Kgs 18:38

9:22, 23 In Leviticus 9:6 Moses said to the people, "When you have followed the Lord's instructions, then his glory will appear to you." Moses, Aaron, and the people then got to work and completed the instructions. Soon after, the glory of the Lord did appear. Often we look for God's glorious acts without concern for following his instructions. Do you serve God in the daily routines of life, or do you wait for him to do a mighty act? If you depend on his glorious acts, you may find yourself sidestepping your regular duty to obey.

9:24 As a display of his mighty power, God sent fire from the sky to consume Aaron's offering. The people fell to the ground in awe. Some people today wonder if God really exists, because they don't see his activity in the world. But God is at work in today's world as he was in Moses' world. When there is a large body of believers who are active for him, God tends not to display his power in the form of mighty physical acts. Instead he works to change people's lives through the work of these believers. When you realize that, you will begin to see acts of love and faith in your life that are just as spectacular as anything recorded in Leviticus.

Aaron's sons destroyed by fire

10:1
Ex 6:23
Num 3:2

10:2
Lev 16:1
Num 26:61

10:3
Ex 19:22
30:29,30
Ezek 38:16
Rom 14:11

10:4
Ex 6:18
Num 3:25-30

10 But Nadab and Abihu, the sons of Aaron, placed unholy fire in their censers, laid incense on the fire, and offered the incense before the Lord—contrary to what the Lord had just commanded them! 2So fire blazed forth from the presence of the Lord and destroyed them.

3Then Moses said to Aaron, "This is what the Lord meant when he said, 'I will show myself holy among those who approach me, and I will be glorified before all the people.' " And Aaron was speechless.

4Then Moses called for Misha-el and Elzaphon, Aaron's cousins, the sons of Uzziel, and told them, "Go and get the charred bodies from before the Tabernacle, and carry them outside the camp."

10:1 *and offered the incense before the Lord,* or "placed fire in their censors . . . and offered unholy fire . . ."

NADAB/ABIHU

When it comes to trouble, brothers seem to follow one of two courses: either they get each other in trouble, or they get into trouble together. This has been illustrated over and over in the development of the human race, from its early days in Genesis with Cain and Abel, through Abraham's family with Jacob and Esau, and Jacob's twelve sons, and now in another tragic case with Nadab and Abihu.

Although little is known of their early years, there's an abundance of information about the environment in which they grew up. Born in Egypt, they were eyewitnesses of God's mighty acts of the Exodus. They saw their father, Aaron, and their uncle, Moses, in action many times. They had firsthand knowledge of God's holiness as few men have ever had, and for a while at least, they followed God wholeheartedly (Leviticus 8:36). But at a crucial moment they chose to treat with indifference the clear instructions from God. The consequences of their sin was fiery, instant, and shocking to all.

We are in danger of making the same mistake as these brothers when we treat lightly the justice and holiness of God. We must draw near to God while realizing that there is a proper fear of God. Don't forget that the opportunity to know God personally is his gracious invitation to an always unworthy people, not a gift to be taken for granted. Do your thoughts about God include a humble recognition of his great holiness?

Strengths and accomplishments:
• Oldest sons of Aaron
• Primary candidates to become High Priest after their father
• Involved with the original consecration of the Tabernacle
• Commended in Scripture for "doing all that the Lord had commanded them" (Leviticus 8:36)

Weakness and mistake:
• Treated lightly God's direct commands

Lesson from their lives:
• Sin does have deadly consequences

Vital Statistics:
• Where: The Sinai Peninsula
• Occupation: Priests-in-training
• Relatives: Father: Aaron. Uncle and Aunt: Moses and Miriam. Brothers: Eleazar and Ithmar.

Key verses:
"But Nadab and Abihu, the sons of Aaron, placed unholy fire in their censers, laid incense on the fire, and offered the incense before the Lord—contrary to what the Lord had just commanded them! So fire blazed forth from the presence of the Lord and destroyed them" (Leviticus 10:1, 2).

The story of Nadab and Abihu is told in Leviticus 8—10. They are also mentioned in Exodus 24:1, 9; 28:1; Numbers 3:2–4; 26:61.

10:1 What was the unholy fire that Nadab and Abihu offered before God? Leviticus 6:12, 13 mentions that the fire on the altar of burnt offering was never to go out, implying that it was holy. It is possible that Nadab and Abihu brought coals of fire to the altar from another source, making the sacrifice unholy. It has also been suggested that the two priests gave an offering at an unprescribed time. Whatever explanation is correct, the point is that Nadab and Abihu abused their office as priests in a flagrant act of disrespect to God, who had just reviewed with them precisely how they were to conduct worship. As leaders, they had special responsibility to

obey God because they were in a position where they could easily lead many people astray.

10:1, 2 Aaron's sons were careless about following the laws for sacrifices. In response, God destroyed them with a blast of fire. Performing the sacrifices was an act of obedience. Doing them correctly showed respect for God. It is easy for us to grow careless about obeying God. Some of God's commands are simple to obey. Others require more careful attention. God can tell when we are just acting religious. Disobedience to God always brings correction.

5So they went over and got them, and carried them out in their coats as Moses had told them to.

6Then Moses said to Aaron and his sons Eleazar and Ithamar, "Do not mourn—do not let your hair hang loose as a sign of your mourning, and do not tear your clothes. If you do, God will strike you dead too, and his wrath will come upon all the people of Israel. But the rest of the people of Israel may lament the death of Nadab and Abihu, and mourn because of the terrible fire the Lord has sent. 7But you are not to leave the Tabernacle under penalty of death, for the anointing oil of Jehovah is upon you." And they did as Moses commanded.

8, 9Now the Lord instructed Aaron, "Never drink wine or strong drink when you go into the Tabernacle, lest you die; and this rule applies to your sons and to all your descendants from generation to generation. 10Your duties will be to arbitrate for the people, to teach them the difference between what is holy and what is ordinary, what is pure and what is impure; 11and to teach them all the laws Jehovah has given through Moses."

12Then Moses said to Aaron and to his sons who were left, Eleazar and Ithamar, "Take the grain offering—the food that remains after the handful has been offered to the Lord by burning it on the altar—make sure there is no leaven in it, and eat it beside the altar. The offering is most holy; 13therefore you must eat it in the sanctuary, in a holy place. It belongs to you and to your sons, from the offerings to Jehovah made by fire; for so I am commanded. 14But the breast and the thigh, which have been offered to the Lord by the gesture of waving it before him, may be eaten in any holy place. It belongs to you and to your sons and daughters for your food. It is your portion of the peace offering sacrifices of the people of Israel.

15"The people are to bring the thigh that was set aside, along with the breast that was offered when the fat was burned, and they shall be presented before the Lord by the gesture of waving them. And afterwards they shall belong to you and your family, for the Lord has commanded this."

16Then Moses searched everywhere for the goat of the sin offering and discovered that it had been burned! He was very angry about this with Eleazar and Ithamar, the remaining sons of Aaron.

17"Why haven't you eaten the sin offering in the sanctuary, since it is most holy, and God has given it to you to take away the iniquity and guilt of the people, to make atonement for them before the Lord?" he demanded. 18"Since its blood was not taken inside the sanctuary, you should certainly have eaten it there, as I ordered you."

19But Aaron interceded with Moses. "They offered their sin offering and burnt offering before the Lord," he said, "but if I had eaten the sin offering on such a day as this, would it have pleased the Lord?" 20And when Moses heard that, he was satisfied.

3. Instructions for the people
Clean and unclean animals

11 Then the Lord said to Moses and Aaron,
2, 3"Tell the people of Israel that the animals which may be used for food include any animal with cloven hooves which chews its cud. 4-7This means that the following may *not* be eaten:

Cross-reference margin notes:

10:6 Lev 21:1-15; Num 1:53; Deut 33:9; Josh 7:1

10:7 Lev 21:12

10:8,9 Ezek 44:21

10:10 Lev 11:47; Ezek 22:26

10:11 Deut 6:4-9; 33:10

10:12 Lev 2:1-3; 21:22; Num 3:2

10:13 Lev 16:14-18

10:14 Lev 7:28-36

10:15 Lev 7:30-34

10:16 Lev 6:25-30; 9:3

10:17 Lev 7:6

10:18 Lev 6:29,30

11:2-19 Deut 14:3-21

10:8-11 The priests could not drink wine or other liquor when going into the Tabernacle in order to prevent their senses from being dulled as they offered sacrifices or taught the people.

10:10, 11 This passage (along with 19:1, 2) provides the focus of Leviticus. The Ten Commandments recorded in Exodus 20 were the fundamental laws God taught his people. Leviticus put these laws into practice, providing guidelines and principles that gave them meaning.

10:16-20 The priest who offered the sin offering was supposed to eat a portion of the animal and then burn the rest (Leviticus 6:24-30). Moses was angry because Eleazar and Ithamar burned the sin offering, but did not eat any of it. Aaron explained to Moses that his two sons did not feel it appropriate to eat the sacrifice after their two brothers, Nadab and Abihu, had just been killed for sacrificing wrongly. Moses then understood that Eleazar and Ithamar were not trying to disobey God. They were simply afraid and upset over what had just happened to their brothers.

11:8 God had strictly forbidden eating the meat of certain animals; to make sure, he forbade even touching them. He wanted

11:4
Ezek 4:14
Dan 1:8
Mt 15:11
Acts 10:14
Rom 14:2,3
Heb 9:10; 13:9
11:7
Isa 65:4; 66:3,17
11:8
Mk 7:15,18
Acts 10:14,15
1 Cor 8:8
Heb 9:10

The camel (it chews the cud but does not have cloven hooves);

The coney, or rock badger (because although it chews the cud, it does not have cloven hooves);

The hare (because although it chews the cud, it does not have cloven hooves);

The swine (because although it has cloven hooves, it does not chew the cud).

8"You may not eat their meat or even touch their dead bodies; they are forbidden foods for you.

9"As to fish, you may eat whatever has fins and scales, whether taken from rivers or from the sea; 10but all other water creatures are strictly forbidden to you. 11You mustn't eat their meat or even touch their dead bodies. 12I'll repeat it again—any water creature that does not have fins or scales is forbidden to you.

13-19"Among the birds, these are the ones you may *not* eat: the eagle, the metire, the osprey, the falcon (all kinds), the kite, the raven (all kinds), the ostrich, the nighthawk, the seagull, the hawk (all kinds), the owl, the cormorant, the ibis, the marsh hen, the pelican, the vulture, the stork, the heron (all kinds), the hoopoe, the bat.

11:22
Mt 3:4
Mk 1:6

20"No insects may be eaten, 21, 22with the exception of those that jump; locusts of all varieties—ordinary locusts, bald locusts, crickets, and grasshoppers—may be eaten. 23All insects that fly and walk or crawl are forbidden to you.

11:25
Lev 11:28,40
Num 19:11-13

24"Anyone touching their dead bodies shall be defiled until the evening, 25and must wash his clothes immediately. He must also quarantine himself until nightfall, as being ceremonially defiled.

26"You are also defiled by touching any animal with only semi-parted hoofs, or any animal that does not chew the cud. 27Any animal that walks on paws is forbidden to you as food. Anyone touching the dead body of such an animal shall be defiled until evening. 28Anyone carrying away the carcass shall wash his clothes and be ceremonially defiled until evening; for it is forbidden to you.

29, 30"These are the forbidden small animals which scurry about your feet or crawl upon the ground: the mole, the rat, the great lizard, the gecko, the mouse, the lizard, the snail, the chameleon.

11:32
Lev 15:12

31"Anyone touching their dead bodies shall be defiled until evening, 32and anything upon which the carcass falls shall be defiled—any article of wood, or of clothing, a rug, or a sack; anything it touches must be put into water, and is defiled until evening. After that it may be used again. 33If it falls into a pottery bowl,

11:33
Lev 6:28
2 Tim 2:20,21

anything in the bowl is defiled, and you shall smash the bowl. 34If the water used to cleanse the defiled article touches any food, all of it is defiled. Any drink which is in the defiled bowl is also contaminated.

35"If the dead body of such an animal touches any clay oven, it is defiled and must be smashed. 36If the body falls into a spring or cistern where there is water, that water is not defiled; yet anyone who pulls out the carcass is defiled. 37And if the carcass touches grain to be sown in the field, it is not contaminated; 38but if the seeds are wet and the carcass falls upon it, the seed is defiled.

39"If an animal which you are permitted to eat dies of disease, anyone touching

11:40
Lev 11:25; 17:15
Deut 14:21
Ezek 4:14; 44:31

the carcass shall be defiled until evening. 40Also, anyone eating its meat or carrying away its carcass shall wash his clothes and be defiled until evening.

11:41
Lev 11:20,23
Deut 14:19,20

41, 42"Animals that crawl shall not be eaten. This includes all reptiles that slither along upon their bellies as well as those that have legs. No crawling thing with many feet may be eaten, for it is defiled. 43Do not defile yourselves by touching it.

---

the people to be totally separated from those things he had forbidden. So often we flirt with temptation, rationalizing that at least we are technically keeping the commandment not to commit it. But God says we are to separate ourselves completely from all sin and tempting situations.

11:25 In order to worship, people need to be prepared. There were some acts of disobedience, some natural acts (such as childbirth, menstruation, or sex), or some accidents (such as touching a dead or diseased body) that would make a person

ceremonially defiled and thus forbidden to participate in worship. This chapter describes many of the intentional or accidental occurrences that would disqualify a person from worship until they were "cleansed" or straightened out. One had to be *prepared* for worship. We cannot live any way we want during the week then rush into God's presence on Sunday. Our relationship with him must be one of constant repentance and cleansing so we are prepared for worship.

44"I am the Lord your God. Keep yourselves pure concerning these things, and be holy, for I am holy; therefore do not defile yourselves by touching any of these things that crawl upon the earth. 45For I am the Lord who brought you out of the land of Egypt to be your God. You must therefore be holy, for I am holy." 46These are the laws concerning animals, birds, and whatever swims in the water or crawls upon the ground. 47These are the distinctions between what is ceremonially clean and may be eaten, and what is ceremonially defiled and may not be eaten, among all animal life upon the earth.

11:44
Ex 19:6; 20:2
Lev 19:2
20:7,26
Isa 6:3,4
Amos 3:3
Mt 5:48
1 Thess 4:7
1 Pet 1:16
Rev 4:8; 22:11

11:47
Lev 10:10

Purification after childbirth

12 The Lord told Moses to give these instructions to the people of Israel: 2"When a baby boy is born, the mother shall be ceremonially defiled for seven days, and under the same restrictions as during her monthly menstrual periods. 3On the eighth day, her son must be circumcised. 4Then, for the next thirty-three days, while she is recovering from her ceremonial impurity, she must not touch anything sacred, nor enter the Tabernacle.

12:2
Lev 15:19; 18:19

12:3
Gen 17:12-14
Josh 5:2-7
Lk 1:59; 2:21
Phil 3:5

5"When a baby girl is born, the mother's ceremonial impurity shall last two weeks, during which time she will be under the same restrictions as during menstruation. Then for a further sixty-six days she shall continue her recovery.

6"When these days of purification are ended (the following instructions are applicable whether her baby is a boy or girl), she must bring a yearling lamb as a burnt offering, and a young pigeon or a turtledove for a sin offering.

12:6
Lev 14:21,22
Lk 2:22

"She must take them to the door of the Tabernacle to the priest; 7and the priest will offer them before the Lord and make atonement for her; then she will be ceremonially clean again after her bleeding at childbirth.

"These then, are the procedures after childbirth. 8But if she is too poor to bring a lamb, then she must bring two turtledoves or two young pigeons. One will be for a burnt offering and the other for a sin offering. The priest will make atonement for her with these, so that she will be ceremonially pure again."

12:8
Lev 5:7
15:29-31
Lk 2:24

Rules about leprosy

13 The Lord said to Moses and Aaron, "If anyone notices a swelling in his skin, or a scab or boil or pimple with transparent skin, leprosy is to be suspected.

12:5 *shall continue her recovery,* literally, "shall continue in her blood of purification."

11:44, 45 There is more to this passage than eating right. These verses provide a key to understanding all the laws and regulations in Leviticus. God wanted his people to be holy, just like himself. His desire hasn't changed. God wants us to be holy too. Holiness means to be wholly devoted to God and to be wholly set aside for God.

Holy people are separate and distinct from ungodly people. The laws and restrictions we find here and elsewhere in Leviticus show God's desire to help the Israelites become a people separate—both socially and spiritually—from the rampant wickedness all around them. God called Israel out of the mass of idolatrous worldly nations and sought to make them a unique nation, dedicated to serve him and lead holy lives. They were to be holy because of their association with God, cooperation with God, and devotion to God. They were not to be contaminated by beliefs and habits that God would not approve of. To grow in holiness is the pathway God wants us to follow. This is no easy task and requires strenuous efforts on our part. Even so, we find ourselves doing things we know we shouldn't. But as we become more holy, we become more like God.

11:47 Clean and unclean (or defiled) had little to do with the physical habits of animals. These words were simply used to define the kind of animals the Israelites could and could not eat. There were several reasons for this restricted diet: (1) To insure the health of the nation. The forbidden foods were usually scavenging animals that fed on dead animals; thus disease could be

transmitted through them. (2) To visibly distinguish Israel from other nations. The pig, for example, was a common sacrifice of heathen religions. (3) To avoid objectionable associations. "Creeping things," for example, were reminiscent of serpents, which were often symbolic of sin.

12:1-4 Why was a woman considered defiled (unclean) after the wonderful miracle of childbirth? Probably it was due to the bodily emissions and secretions occurring during and after childbirth. These were considered unclean and made the woman unprepared to enter the pure surroundings of the Tabernacle.

12:1-4 Defiled did not mean "sinful," implying that sex or childbirth is dirty. Instead it meant "not appropriate to make sacrifice." In Canaan, prostitution and fertility rites were part of worship. By contrast, in Israel, anything related to the sexual was avoided when worshiping God.

13:1-3 Leprosy was one of the most feared diseases of Bible times. The Israelites first came in contact with it in Egypt. There were different types of diseases that went by the name leprosy in the Hebrew language. Only one of these was the disease we call leprosy today. Some were contagious. The worst type of leprosy slowly ruined the body. In most cases, there was no cure for it. Those who had leprosy were separated from family and friends and confined outside the camp.

Since priests were responsible for the health and sanitation of the camp, it was their duty to expel leprous people. If someone's

13:2,3
Lev 13:38; 14:56
Deut 24:8
Lk 17:14

He must be brought to Aaron the priest or to one of his sons 3for the spot to be examined. If the hair in this spot turns white, and if the spot looks to be more than skin-deep, it is leprosy, and the priest must declare him a leper.

4"But if the white spot in the skin does not seem to be deeper than the skin, and the hair in the spot has not turned white, the priest shall quarantine him for seven days. 5At the end of that time, on the seventh day, the priest will examine him again, and if the spot has not changed and has not spread in the skin, then the priest must quarantine him seven days more. 6Again on the seventh day the priest will examine him, and if the marks of the disease have become fainter and have not spread, then the priest shall pronounce him cured; it was only a scab, and the man need only wash his clothes and everything will be normal again. 7But if the spot spreads in the skin after he has come to the priest to be examined, he must come back to the priest again, 8and the priest shall look again, and if the spot has spread, then the priest must pronounce him a leper.

13:6
Lev 11:25

13:9,10
Num 12:10
2 Kgs 5:27

9, 10"When anyone suspected of having leprosy is brought to the priest, the priest is to look to see if there is a white swelling in the skin with white hairs in the spot, and an ulcer developing. 11If he finds these symptoms, it is an established case of leprosy, and the priest must pronounce him defiled. The man is not to be quarantined for further observation, for he is definitely diseased. 12But if the priest sees that the leprosy has erupted and spread all over his body from head to foot wherever he looks, 13then the priest shall pronounce him cured of leprosy, for it has all turned white; he is cured. 14, 15But if there is raw flesh anywhere, the man shall be declared a leper. It is proved by the raw flesh. 16, 17But if the raw flesh later changes to white, the leper will return to the priest to be examined again. If the spot has indeed turned completely white, then the priest will pronounce him cured.

13:18
Ex 9:9

18"In the case of a man who has a boil in his skin which heals, 19but which leaves a white swelling or a bright spot, sort of reddish white, the man must go to the priest for examination. 20If the priest sees that the trouble seems to be down under the skin, and if the hair at the spot has turned white, then the priest shall declare him defiled, for leprosy has broken out from the boil. 21But if the priest sees that there are no white hairs in this spot, and the spot does not appear to be deeper than the skin, and if the color is gray, then the priest shall quarantine him for seven days. 22If during that time the spot spreads, the priest must declare him a leper. 23But if the bright spot grows no larger and does not spread, it is merely the scar from the boil, and the priest shall declare that all is well.

24"If a man is burned in some way, and the burned place becomes bright reddish white or white, 25then the priest must examine the spot. If the hair in the bright spot turns white, and the problem seems to be more than skin-deep, it is leprosy that has broken out from the burn, and the priest must pronounce him a leper. 26But if the priest sees that there are no white hairs in the bright spot, and the brightness appears to be no deeper than the skin and is fading, the priest shall quarantine him for seven days, 27and examine him again the seventh day. If the spot spreads in the skin, the priest must pronounce him a leper. 28But if the bright spot does not move or spread in the skin, and is fading, it is simply a scar from the burn, and the priest shall declare that he does not have leprosy.

13:27
Deut 24:8

29, 30"If a man or woman has a sore on the head or chin, the priest must examine him; if the infection seems to be below the skin and yellow hair is found in the sore, the priest must pronounce him a leper. 31But if the priest's examination reveals that the spot seems to be only in the skin but there is healthy hair in it, then he shall be quarantined for seven days, 32and examined again on the seventh day. If the spot has not spread and no yellow hair has appeared, and if the infection does not seem to be deeper than the skin, 33he shall shave off all the hair around the spot (but not

13:33
Lev 14:9

13:3 *must declare him a leper,* literally, *"shall declare him unclean."* **13:25** *must pronounce him a leper,* literally, *"pronounce him unclean."* Also vs 27.

---

leprosy appeared to go away, only the priest could decide if he was truly cured. Leprosy is often used in the Bible as an illustration of sin because sin is contagious and destructive and leads to separation.

on the spot itself) and the priest shall quarantine him for another seven days. 34He shall be examined again on the seventh day, and if the spot has not spread, and it appears to be no deeper than the skin, the priest shall pronounce him well, and after washing his clothes, he is free. 35But if, later on, this spot begins to spread, 36then the priest must examine him again and, without waiting to see if any yellow hair develops, declare him a leper. 37But if it appears that the spreading has stopped and black hairs are found in the spot, then he is healed and is not a leper, and the priest shall declare him healed.

38"If a man or a woman has white, transparent areas in the skin, 39but these spots are growing dimmer, this is not leprosy, but an ordinary infection that has broken out in the skin.

40"If a man's hair is gone, this does not make him a leper even though he is bald! 41If the hair is gone from the front part of his head, he simply has a bald forehead, but this is not leprosy. 42However, if in the baldness there is a reddish white spot, it may be leprosy breaking out. 43In that case the priest shall examine him, and if there is a reddish white lump that looks like leprosy, 44then he is a leper, and the priest must pronounce him such.

45"Anyone who is discovered to have leprosy must tear his clothes and let his hair grow in wild disarray, and cover his upper lip and call out as he goes, "I am a leper, I am a leper." 46As long as the disease lasts, he is defiled and must live outside the camp.

47, 48"If leprosy is suspected in a woolen or linen garment or fabric, or in a piece of leather or leather-work, 49and there is a greenish or a reddish spot in it, it is probably leprosy, and must be taken to the priest to be examined. 50The priest will put it away for seven days 51and look at it again on the seventh day. If the spot has spread, it is a contagious leprosy, 52and he must burn the clothing, fabric, linen or woolen covering, or leather article, for it is contagious and must be destroyed by fire.

53"But if when he examines it again on the seventh day the spot has not spread, 54the priest shall order the suspected article to be washed, then isolated for seven more days. 55If after that time the spot has not changed its color, even though it has not spread, it is leprosy and shall be burned, for the article is infected through and through. 56But if the priest sees that the spot has faded after the washing, then he shall cut it out from the garment or leather goods or whatever it is in. 57However, if it then reappears, it is leprosy and he must burn it. 58But if after washing it there is no further trouble, it can be put back into service after another washing."

59These are the regulations concerning leprosy in a garment or anything made of skin or leather, indicating whether to pronounce it leprous or not.

Purification after leprosy

14 And the Lord gave Moses these regulations concerning a person whose leprosy disappears:

3"The priest shall go out of the camp to examine him. If the priest sees that the leprosy is gone, 4he shall require two living birds of a kind permitted for food, and shall take some cedar wood, a scarlet string, and some hyssop branches, to be used for the purification ceremony of the one who is healed. 5The priest shall then order one of the birds killed in an earthenware pot held above running water. 6The other bird, still living, shall be dipped in the blood, along with the cedar wood, the scarlet thread, and the hyssop branch. 7Then the priest shall sprinkle the blood seven times

13:34 Lev 14:8
13:45 Lam 4:15 Ezek 24:17,22 Mic 3:7
13:46 Num 5:1-4; 12:14 2 Kgs 7:3; 15:5 2 Chron 26:21 Lk 17:12
13:51 Lev 14:44
14:2 Mt 8:4 Mk 1:40-45 Lk 5:12-14 17:12-14
14:3 Lev 13:36
14:4 Lev 14:6,49-53 Num 19:6
14:6 Ps 51:7 Heb 9:19

13:34 *he is free,* literally, "he is clean." **13:45** *I am a leper, I am a leper,* literally, "unclean, unclean." **13:55** *through and through,* literally, "whether the bareness be within or without," or "whether it be bald in the head thereof or in the forehead thereof."

13:45, 46 A person with leprosy had to perform this strange ritual to protect others from coming too near. Since leprosy was often a contagious disease, it was important that people stay away from those who had it.

upon the man cured of his leprosy, and the priest shall pronounce him cured, and shall let the living bird fly into the open field.

14:8
Lev 14:9
Num 8:7

14:9
Lev 13:33; 14:8
Num 6:9

8"Then the man who is cured shall wash his clothes, shave off all his hair, and bathe himself, and return to live inside the camp; however, he must stay outside his tent for seven days. 9The seventh day he shall again shave all the hair from his head, beard, and eyebrows, and wash his clothes and bathe, and shall then be declared fully cured of his leprosy.

14:10
Lev 23:12,13
Num 6:14,15

10"The next day, the eighth day, he shall take two male lambs without physical defect, one yearling ewe-lamb without physical defect, ten quarts of finely ground flour mixed with olive oil, and a pint of olive oil; 11then the priest who examines him shall place the man and his offerings before the Lord at the entrance of the

14:12
Ex 29:24

Tabernacle. 12The priest shall take one of the lambs and the pint of olive oil and offer them to the Lord as a guilt offering by the gesture of waving them before the

14:13
Lev 1:11-13
4:4-12
6:1—7:10

altar. 13Then he shall kill the lamb at the place where sin offerings and burnt offerings are killed, there at the Tabernacle; this guilt offering shall then be given to the priest for food, as in the case of a sin offering. It is a most holy offering.

14:14
Ex 29:19-21
Lev 8:23,24

14The priest shall take the blood from this guilt offering and smear some of it upon the tip of the right ear of the man being cleansed, and upon the thumb of his right hand, and upon the big toe of his right foot.

15"Then the priest shall take the olive oil and pour it into the palm of his left hand, 16and dip his right finger into it, and sprinkle it with his finger seven times before the Lord. 17Some of the oil remaining in his left hand shall then be placed by the priest upon the tip of the man's right ear and the thumb of his right hand and the big

14:18
Lev 8:30

toe of his right foot—just as he did with the blood of the guilt offering. 18The remainder of the oil in his hand shall be used to anoint the man's head. Thus the priest shall make atonement for him before the Lord.

14:19
Lev 6:24-30

19"Then the priest must offer the sin offering and again perform the rite of atonement for the person being cleansed from his leprosy; and afterwards the priest

14:20
Lev 23:12,13

shall kill the burnt offering, 20and offer it along with the grain offering upon the altar, making atonement for the man, who shall then be pronounced finally cleansed.

14:21
Lev 5:7,11
12:8

21"If he is so poor that he cannot afford two lambs, then he shall bring only one, a male lamb for the guilt offering, to be presented to the Lord in the rite of atonement by waving it before the altar; and only three quarts of fine white flour, mixed with olive oil, for a grain offering, and a pint of olive oil.

14:22
Lev 5:7

22"He shall also bring two turtledoves or two young pigeons—whichever he is able to afford—and use one of the pair for a sin offering and the other for a burnt

14:23
Lev 14:11

offering. 23He shall bring them to the priest at the entrance of the Tabernacle on the eighth day, for his ceremony of cleansing before the Lord. 24The priest shall take the lamb for the guilt offering, and the pint of oil, and wave them before the altar

14:25
Lev 14:14

as a gesture of offering to the Lord. 25Then he shall kill the lamb for the guilt offering and smear some of its blood upon the tip of the man's right ear—the man on whose behalf the ceremony is being performed—and upon the thumb of his right hand and on the big toe of his right foot.

26"The priest shall then pour the olive oil into the palm of his own left hand, 27and with his right finger he is to sprinkle some of it seven times before the Lord. 28Then he must put some of the olive oil from his hand upon the tip of the man's right ear, and upon the thumb of his right hand, and upon the big toe of his right foot, just as he did with the blood of the guilt offering. 29The remaining oil in his hand shall be placed upon the head of the man being cleansed, to make atonement for him before the Lord.

30"Then he must offer the two turtledoves or two young pigeons (whichever pair he is able to afford). 31One of the pair is for a sin offering and the other for a burnt offering, to be sacrificed along with the grain offering; and the priest shall make atonement for the man before the Lord."

32These, then, are the laws concerning those who are cleansed of leprosy but are not able to bring the sacrifices normally required for the ceremony of cleansing.

14:19 *and again,* implied.

33, 34Then the Lord said to Moses and Aaron, "When you arrive in the land of Canaan which I have given you, and I place leprosy in some house there, 35then the owner of the house shall come and report to the priest, 'It seems to me that there may be leprosy in my house!'

14:35
Ps 91:10
Zech 5:4

36"The priest shall order the house to be emptied before he examines it, so that everything in the house will not be declared contaminated if he decides that there is leprosy there. 37If he finds greenish or reddish streaks in the walls of the house which seem to be beneath the surface of the wall, 38he shall close up the house for seven days, 39and return the seventh day to look at it again. If the spots have spread in the wall,

14:39
Lev 13:6-8

40then the priest shall order the removal of the spotted section of wall, and the material must be thrown into a defiled place outside the city. 41Then he shall order the inside walls of the house scraped thoroughly, and the scrapings dumped in a defiled place outside the city. 42Other stones shall be brought to replace those that have been removed, new mortar used, and the house replastered.

43"But if the spots appear again, 44the priest shall come again and look, and if he sees that the spots have spread, it is leprosy, and the house is defiled. 45Then he shall order the destruction of the house—all its stones, timbers, and mortar shall be carried out of the city to a defiled place. 46Anyone entering the house while it is closed shall be defiled until evening. 47Anyone who lies down or eats in the house shall wash his clothing.

14:45
Lev 14:41-45

48"But if, when the priest comes again to look, the spots have not reappeared after the fresh plastering, then he will pronounce the house cleansed, and declare the leprosy gone. 49He shall also perform the ceremony of cleansing, using two birds, cedar wood, scarlet thread, and hyssop branches. 50He shall kill one of the birds over fresh water in an earthenware bowl, 51, 52and dip the cedar wood, hyssop branch, and scarlet thread, as well as the living bird, into the blood of the bird that was killed over the fresh water, and shall sprinkle the house seven times. In this way the house shall be cleansed. 53Then he shall let the live bird fly away into an open field outside the city. This is the method for making atonement for the house and cleansing it."

14:49
Lev 14:4-7
Num 19:6

54These, then, are the laws concerning the various places where leprosy may appear: 55in a garment or in a house, 56or in any swelling in one's skin, or a scab from a burn, or a bright spot. 57In this way you will know whether or not it is actually leprosy. That is why these laws are given.

14:57
Deut 24:8
Ezek 44:23

Purification after bodily discharges

15 The Lord told Moses and Aaron to give the people of Israel these further instructions:

"Any man who has a genital discharge is ceremonially defiled. 3This applies not only while the discharge is active, but also for a time after it heals. 4Any bed he lies on and anything he sits on is contaminated: 5so anyone touching the man's bed is

15:1-3
Lev 22:4
Num 5:2

15:4
Lev 15:20-23

15:2 *a genital discharge,* literally, "an issue out of his flesh."

14:33–53 Could leprosy really infect one's clothing or house? The Hebrew word for leprosy included a variety of skin diseases as well as other molds and fungi. The "leprosy" found on clothing or house walls was more like a mold, fungus, or bacteria. Like mildew, this fungus could spread rapidly and promote disease. It was therefore important to check its spread as soon as possible. In extreme cases, if the fungus had done enough damage, the clothing was burned or the house destroyed.

14:54–57 God told the Israelites how to diagnose leprosy so they could avoid it or treat it. These laws were given for the people's health and protection. They helped the Israelites avoid diseases that were serious threats in that time and place. Although they wouldn't have understood the medical reasons for some of these laws, their obedience to them made them healthier.

Many of God's laws must have seemed strange to the Israelites. His laws, however, helped them avoid not only physical

contamination, but moral and spiritual infection as well. The Word of God still provides a pattern for living physically, spiritually, and morally healthy lives. We may not always understand the wisdom of God's laws. But if we obey them, we will thrive.

Does this mean we are to follow the Old Testament health and dietary restrictions? In general, the basic principles of health and cleanliness are just as applicable for us today as they were then. But it would be legalistic, if not wrong, to adhere to each specific restriction today. Some of these regulations were intended to mark the Israelites as different from the wicked people around them. Others were given to prevent God's people from becoming involved in pagan religious practices, one of the most serious problems of the day. Still others related to quarantines in a culture where exact medical diagnosis was impossible. Today, for example, we can determine medically the different forms of leprosy and which ones are contagious.

ceremonially defiled until evening, and must wash his clothes and bathe himself. 6Anyone sitting on a seat the man has sat upon while defiled is himself ceremonially impure until evening, and must wash his clothes and bathe himself. 7The same instructions apply to anyone touching him. 8Anyone he spits on is ceremonially impure until evening, and must wash his clothes and bathe himself. 9Any saddle he rides on is defiled. 10Anyone touching or carrying anything else that was beneath him shall be defiled until evening, and must wash his clothes and bathe himself. 11If the defiled man touches anyone without first rinsing his hands, that person must wash his clothes and bathe himself and be defiled until evening. 12Any earthen pot touched by the defiled man must be broken, and every wooden utensil must be rinsed in water.

13"When the discharge stops, he shall begin a seven-day cleansing ceremony by washing his clothes and bathing in running water. 14On the eighth day he shall take two turtledoves or two young pigeons and come before the Lord at the entrance of the Tabernacle, and give them to the priest. 15The priest shall sacrifice them there, one for a sin offering and the other for a burnt offering; thus the priest shall make atonement before the Lord for the man because of his discharge.

16"Whenever a man's semen goes out from him, he shall take a complete bath and be ceremonially impure until the evening. 17Any clothing or bedding the semen spills on must be washed and remain ceremonially defiled until evening. 18After sexual intercourse, the woman as well as the man must bathe, and they are ceremonially defiled until the next evening.

19"Whenever a woman menstruates, she shall be in a state of ceremonial defilement for seven days afterwards, and during that time anyone touching her shall be defiled until evening. 20Anything she lies on or sits on during that time shall be defiled. 21, 22, 23Anyone touching her bed or anything she sits upon shall wash his clothes and bathe himself and be ceremonially defiled until evening. 24A man having sexual intercourse with her during this time is ceremonially defiled for seven days, and every bed he lies upon shall be defiled.

25"If the menstrual flow continues after the normal time, or at some irregular time during the month, the same rules apply as indicated above, 26so that anything she lies upon during that time is defiled, just as it would be during her normal menstrual period, and everything she sits on is in a similar state of defilement. 27Anyone touching her bed or anything she sits on shall be defiled, and shall wash his clothes and bathe and be defiled until evening. 28Seven days after the menstruating stops, she is no longer ceremonially defiled.

29"On the eighth day, she shall take two turtledoves or two young pigeons and bring them to the priest at the entrance of the Tabernacle, 30and the priest shall offer one for a sin offering and the other for a burnt offering, and make atonement for her before the Lord, for her menstrual defilement. 31In this way you shall cleanse the people of Israel from their defilement, lest they die because of defiling my Tabernacle that is among them."

32This, then, is the law for the man who is defiled by a genital disease or by a seminal emission; 33and for a woman's menstrual period; and for anyone who has sexual intercourse with her while she is in her period of defilement afterwards.

15:32 is defiled by a genital disease, literally, "has an issue."

15:12
Lev 6:28; 11:33

15:13
Num 19:11,12

15:15
Lev 14:22

15:16
Lev 15:5; 22:6
Deut 23:10,11

15:18
Ex 19:15
1 Sam 21:4

15:19
Lev 12:2-5

15:20
Lev 15:4,5

15:24
Lev 15:33
18:19; 20:18
Ezek 18:6; 22:10

15:25
Mt 9:20
Mk 5:25
Lk 8:43,44

15:30
Lev 5:7; 14:22
15:15

15:31
Num 5:3; 19:13,
20

15:18 This verse is not implying that sex is dirty or disgusting. God created sex, both for the enjoyment of married couples, as well as for continuing the race and continuing the covenant. Everything must be seen and done with a view toward God's love and control. Sex is not separate from spirituality and God's care. God is concerned about our sexual habits. We tend to separate our physical and spiritual lives, but there is an inseparable intertwining. God must be Lord over our whole selves—including our private lives.

15:32, 33 God is concerned about health, the dignity of the person, the dignity of the body, and the dignity of the sexual experience. His commands call the people to avoid unhealthy practices and promote healthy ones. To wash was the physical health response; to be purified or cleansed was the spiritual dignity response. This shows God's high regard for sex and sexuality. In our day, sex has been degraded by publicity; it has become public domain, not private celebration. We are called to have the same high regard for sex, both in good health and purity.

4. Instructions for the altar
The Day of Atonement for sin

16 After Aaron's two sons died before the Lord, the Lord said to Moses, "Warn your brother Aaron not to enter into the Holy Place behind the veil, where the Ark and the place of mercy are, just whenever he chooses. The penalty for intrusion is death. For I myself am present in the cloud above the place of mercy.

³"Here are the conditions for his entering there: He must bring a young bull for a sin offering, and a ram for a burnt offering. ⁴He must bathe himself and put on the sacred linen coat, shorts, belt, and turban. ⁵The people of Israel shall then bring him two male goats for their sin offering, and a ram for their burnt offering. ⁶First he shall present to the Lord the young bull as a sin offering for himself, making atonement for himself and his family. ⁷Then he shall bring the two goats before the Lord at the entrance of the Tabernacle, ⁸and cast lots to determine which is the Lord's and which is to be sent away. ⁹The goat allotted to the Lord shall then be sacrificed by Aaron as a sin offering. ¹⁰The other goat shall be kept alive and placed before the Lord. The rite of atonement shall be performed over it, and it shall then be sent out into the desert as a scapegoat.

¹¹"After Aaron has sacrificed the young bull as a sin offering for himself and his family, ¹²he shall take a censer full of live coals from the altar of the Lord, and fill his hands with sweet incense beaten into fine powder, and bring it inside the veil. ¹³There before the Lord he shall put the incense upon the coals, so that a cloud of incense will cover the mercy place above the Ark (containing the stone tablets of the Ten Commandments); thus he will not die. ¹⁴And he shall bring some of the blood of the young bull and sprinkle it with his finger upon the east side of the mercy place, and then seven times in front of it.

¹⁵"Then he must go out and sacrifice the people's sin offering goat, and bring its blood within the veil, and sprinkle it upon the place of mercy and in front of it, just as he did with the blood of the young bull. ¹⁶Thus he shall make atonement for the holy place because it is defiled by the sins of the people of Israel, and for the Tabernacle, located right among them and surrounded by their defilement. ¹⁷Not another soul shall be inside the Tabernacle when Aaron enters to make atonement in the Holy Place—not until after he comes out again and has made atonement for himself and his household and for all the people of Israel. ¹⁸Then he shall go out to the altar before the Lord and make atonement for it. He must smear the blood of the young bull and the goat on the horns of the altar, ¹⁹and sprinkle blood upon the altar seven times with his finger, thus cleansing it from the sinfulness of Israel, and making it holy.

²⁰"When he has completed the rite of atonement for the Holy Place, the entire Tabernacle, and the altar, he shall bring the live goat and, ²¹laying both hands upon

16:1,2 Ex 25:17-22
30:10
Lev 10:1,2
Heb 9:7,25

16:3 Lev 16:6,7
Num 29:7-11

16:4 Ex 28:39-43
39:27-29
Lev 6:10
Ezek 44:17-19

16:6 Lev 9:7
Heb 5:1-3; 7:27,
28; 9:7

16:10 Isa 53:4-10

16:11 Lev 9:7
Heb 9:7

16:12 Ex 30:34-38
Num 16:18,46
Isa 6:6,7
Rev 8:3-5

16:13 Ex 25:21; 30:1,
7,8
Lev 22:9

16:14 Lev 4:17

16:15 Heb 6:19; 9:3,7,
12

16:16 Ex 30:10
Ezek 45:18
Heb 9:22,23

16:17 Lk 1:10

16:18 Lev 4:7,17,25
Ezek 43:20

16:19 Lev 4:6; 16:14

16:21 Lev 5:5
Num 5:7

16:8, 10 *sent away* and *sent out . . . as a scapegoat,* literally, "for Azazel" or "for removing." **16:15** *Then he must go out,* implied. **16:19** *making it holy,* literally, "hallowing it."

16:1ff This was the greatest day of the year for Israel. The Hebrew word for *atone* means "to cover." Old Testament sacrifices could not actually remove sins, only cover them. On this day, the people confessed their sins as a nation, and the High Priest went into the Holy of Holies to make atonement for them. Sacrifices were made and blood was shed so that the people's sins could be "covered" until Christ's sacrifice on the cross gave all people the opportunity to remove sin from their lives forever. The Israelites, with their limited perspective of God's plan, did not understand the distinction between "covered" sins and sins that were cleansed and completely removed.

16:1–25 Aaron had to spend hours preparing himself to meet God. But we can approach God anytime (Hebrews 4:16). What a privilege! We are offered easier access to God than the High Priests of Old Testament times! Still, we must never forget that God is holy nor let this privilege cause us to approach God thoughtlessly. The way to God has been opened to us by Christ. But easy access to God does not eliminate our need to prepare our hearts as we draw near in prayer.

16:5–28 This event with the two goats occurred on the Day of Atonement. The two goats represented the two ways God was dealing with the Israelites' sin: (1) he was forgiving their sin through the first goat, which was sacrificed, and (2) he was removing their guilt through the second goat, the scapegoat, which was sent into the wilderness. This symbolized how God carried away the sins of the people. The same ritual had to be repeated every year. Jesus Christ's death replaced this system once and for all. At any time we can have our sins forgiven and guilt removed by placing our trust in Christ, our permanent "scapegoat" (Hebrews 10:1–4).

16:12 A censer was a dish or shallow bowl that hung by a chain or was carried with tongs. Inside the censer were placed incense (a combination of sweet-smelling spices) and live coals from the altar. On the Day of Atonement, the High Priest entered the Holy of Holies carrying a smoking censer. The smoke shielded him from the Ark of the Covenant and the presence of God—otherwise he would die. Incense may also have had a very practical purpose. The sweet smell drew the people's attention to the morning and evening sacrifices and helped to cover their sometimes foul smell.

its head, confess over it all the sins of the people of Israel. He shall lay all their sins upon the head of the goat and send it into the desert, led by a man appointed for the task. 22So the goat shall carry all the sins of the people into a land where no one lives, and the man shall let it loose in the wilderness.

23"Then Aaron shall go into the Tabernacle again and take off the linen garments he wore when he went behind the veil, and leave them there in the Tabernacle. 24Then he shall bathe in a sacred place, put on his clothes again, and go out and sacrifice his own burnt offering for the people, making atonement for himself and for them. 25He shall also burn upon the altar the fat for the sin offering.

26"(The man who took the goat out into the desert shall afterwards wash his clothes and bathe himself and then come back into the camp.) 27And the young bull and the goat used for the sin offering (their blood was taken into the Holy Place by Aaron, to make atonement) shall be carried outside the camp and burned, including the hides and internal organs. 28Afterwards, the person doing the burning shall wash his clothes and bathe himself and then return to camp.

29, 30"This is a permanent law: You must do no work on the twenty-fifth day of September, but must spend the day in self-examination and humility. This applies whether you are born in the land or are a foreigner living among the people of Israel; for this is the day commemorating the atonement, cleansing you in the Lord's eyes from all of your sins. 31It is a Sabbath of solemn rest for you, and you shall spend the day in quiet humility; this is a permanent law. 32This ceremony, in later generations, shall be performed by the anointed High Priest, consecrated in place of his ancestor Aaron; he shall be the one to put on the holy linen garments, 33and make atonement for the holy sanctuary, the Tabernacle, the altar, the priests, and the people. 34This shall be an everlasting law for you, to make atonement for the people of Israel once each year, because of their sins."

And Aaron followed all these instructions that the Lord gave to Moses.

Warnings against improper sacrifice

17 The Lord gave to Moses these additional instructions for Aaron and the priests and for all the people of Israel:

16:22 *where no one lives,* literally, "a solitary land." **16:26** *the goat out into the desert,* literally, "for Azazel" or "for removal." **16:29, 30** *on the twenty-fifth day of September* (which was "on the tenth day of the seventh month" of the Hebrew calendar). **16:31** *in quiet humility,* or, "in fasting."

Marginal references (left column):

16:22
Isa 53:4-7

16:23
Ex 28:39-43
Lev 16:4
16:24
Ex 29:3-9

16:26
Num 19:7
16:27
Lev 4:11,12
8:17

16:28
Lev 16:26

16:29
Lev 23:26-32
Num 27:7
Ps 51:7

16:31
Ex 12:16; 20:10
Lev 23:32
Ezra 8:21

16:32
Ex 28:39-43

16:34
Ex 30:10
Lev 23:14,21,
30,31
Heb 9:7

OLD/NEW SYSTEMS OF SACRIFICE	Old System of Sacrifice	New System of Sacrifice
	Was temporary (Hebrews 7:21)	Is permanent (Hebrews 7:20)
	Aaron first High Priest (Leviticus 16:32)	Jesus only High Priest (Hebrews 4:14)
	From tribe of Levi (Hebrews 7:16)	From tribe of Judah (Hebrews 7:14)
	Ministered on earth (Hebrews 8:5)	Ministers in heaven (Hebrews 8:12)
	Used blood of animals (Leviticus 16:15)	Uses blood of Christ (Hebrews 10:5)
	Required many sacrifices (Leviticus 22:19)	Requires one sacrifice (Hebrews 9:28)
	Needed perfect animals (Leviticus 22:19)	Needs perfect life (Hebrews 5:9)
	Required careful approach to Tabernacle (Leviticus 16:3)	Encourages bold approach to Throne (Hebrews 4:16)
	Looked forward to new system (Hebrews 10:1)	Cancels old system (Hebrews 10:9)

17:1ff Leviticus 17—26 is often called the Holiness Code because it focuses on what it means to live a holy life. The central verse is 19:1, "You must be holy because I, the Lord your God, am holy."

3, 4"Any Israelite who sacrifices an ox, lamb, or goat anywhere except at the Tabernacle is guilty of murder and shall be excommunicated from his nation. 5The purpose of this law is to stop the people of Israel from sacrificing in the open fields, and to cause them to bring their sacrifices to the priest at the entrance of the Tabernacle, and to burn the fat as a savor the Lord will appreciate and enjoy— 6for in this way the priest will be able to sprinkle the blood upon the altar of the Lord at the entrance of the Tabernacle, and to burn the fat as a savor the Lord will appreciate and enjoy— 7instead of the people's sacrificing to evil spirits out in the fields. This shall be a permanent law for you, from generation to generation. 8, 9I repeat: Anyone, whether an Israelite or a foreigner living among you who offers a burnt offering or a sacrifice anywhere other than at the entrance of the Tabernacle, where it will be sacrificed to the Lord, shall be excommunicated.

10"And I will turn my face against anyone, whether an Israelite or a foreigner living among you, who eats blood in any form. I will excommunicate him from his people. 11For the life of the flesh is in the blood, and I have given you the blood to sprinkle upon the altar as an atonement for your souls; it is the blood that makes atonement, because it is the life. 12That is the reasoning behind my decree to the people of Israel, that neither they, nor any foreigner living among them, may eat blood. 13Anyone, whether an Israelite or a foreigner living among you, who goes hunting and kills an animal or bird of a kind permitted for food, must pour out the blood and cover it with dust, 14for the blood is the life. That is why I told the people of Israel never to eat it, for the life of every bird and animal is its blood. Therefore, anyone who eats blood must be excommunicated.

15"And anyone—native born or foreigner—who eats the dead body of an animal that dies a natural death, or is killed by wild animals, must wash his clothes and bathe himself and be defiled until evening; after that he shall be declared cleansed. 16But if he does not wash his clothes and bathe, he shall suffer the consequence."

17:3,4
Lev 1:2,3
Deut 12:5-7

17:5
Deut 12:4-7

17:6
Ex 29:18

17:7
Ex 22:20; 32:8
Deut 32:17
2 Chron 11:15
1 Cor 10:20

17:9
Lev 17:3,4
Deut 12:4-7

17:10
Lev 3:17; 19:26
Deut 12:23

17:11
Gen 9:4
Lev 17:14
Matt 26:28
Rom 3:25
Eph 1:7
Col 1:14,20
Heb 9:22
1 Pet 1:2
1 Jn 1:7

17:13
Deut 12:16,24,
25; 15:23
Ezek 24:7

17:14
Lev 7:26,27
17:11

17:15
Lev 7:24
11:24,39
Num 19:8

B. LIVING A HOLY LIFE (18:1—27:34)

After the sacrificial system for forgiving sins was in place, the people were instructed on how to live as forgiven people. Applying these standards to our lives helps us grow in obedience and live a life pleasing to God.

1. Standards for the people

Sexual perversions forbidden

18 The Lord then told Moses to tell the people of Israel, "I am Jehovah your God, 3so don't act like heathen—like the people of Egypt

18:1
Ex 20:2

17:3, 4 *sacrifices*, literally, "slaughters." **17:7** *evil spirits*, literally, "hairy ones." **17:11** *because it is the life*, implied. **17:14** *every bird and animal*, literally, "every creature."

17:3–9 Why were the Israelites prohibited from sacrificing outside the Tabernacle area? God had established specific times and places for sacrifices, and each occasion was permeated with symbolism. If people sacrificed on their own, not only would it demonstrate a callous disregard for God, but it would also encourage people to add to or subtract from God's laws to fit their own lifestyle. Since many heathen religions allowed every individual priest to set his own rules, this law helped the Israelites resist the temptation to follow the heathen pattern. It is interesting that when the people did slip into idolatry, it was because "everyone did whatever he wanted to—whatever seemed right in his own eyes" (Judges 17:6).

17:11–14 How does blood make atonement for sin? When offered with the right attitude, the sacrifice and the blood shed from it made forgiveness of sin possible.

On the one hand, blood represented the sinner's life, infected by his sin and headed for death. On the other hand, the blood represented the innocent life of the animal that was sacrificed in place of the guilty person making the offering. The death of the animal (of which the blood was proof) fulfilled the penalty of death. God therefore granted forgiveness to the sinner.

17:14 Why was eating or drinking blood prohibited? The

prohibition against eating blood can be traced all the way back to Noah (Genesis 9:4). Eating blood was a common pagan practice. It was often done in hopes of gaining the characteristics of the slain animal (strength, speed, etc.).

God prohibited the eating or drinking of blood for several reasons. (1) Israel was to have practices that were separate and distinct from those of the heathen nations around them. (2) Blood symbolized the life of the animal that was sacrificed in the sinner's place. To drink it would change the symbolism of the sacrificial penalty (blood taken in instead of blood shed). (3) The shedding of blood was the price that had to be paid if a person was to become right with God. It was proof that a life had been sacrificed in the sinner's place. To drink it would have destroyed the evidence of the sacrifice.

This is why people in the New Testament were so upset when Jesus told them to "drink my blood" (John 6:54, 55). Of course, he did not mean this literally. But Jesus, as God himself and the last sacrifice ever needed for sins, was asking believers to identify with him completely. He wants us to take his life into us and he wants to participate in our lives as well.

18:3 The Israelites moved from one idol-infested country to another. As God helped them form a new culture, he warned them

18:4
Lev 19:37; 20:22
Deut 4:1; 6:1
Ezek 20:11

18:7
Lev 20:11

18:8
Gen 35:22
Lev 20:10
Deut 27:20

18:9
Lev 20:17

18:12
Lev 20:19

18:14
Lev 20:20

18:15
Lev 20:15
Ezek 22:11

18:16
Lev 20:21
Deut 25:5
Mt 22:24

18:17
Lev 20:14

18:19
Lev 15:24; 20:18
Ezek 18:6; 22:10

18:20
Ex 20:14
Deut 5:18
22:22-27

18:21
Lev 19:12
20:1-5; 21:6
Deut 12:31
2 Kgs 23:10
Mal 1:12

18:22
Gen 19:4-8
Lev 20:13
Judg 19:22-24
Rom 1:26,27
1 Tim 1:10

18:23
Ex 22:19
Lev 20:15,16
Deut 27:21

18:24
Deut 12:31

18:25
Lev 20:22,23
Deut 9:5

where you lived so long, or the people of Canaan where I am going to take you. 4, 5You must obey only my laws, and you must carry them out in detail, for I am the Lord your God. If you obey them you shall live. I am the Lord.

6"None of you shall marry a near relative, for I am the Lord. 7Do not disgrace your father by having intercourse with your mother, 8nor any other of your father's wives. 9Do not have intercourse with your sister or half-sister, whether the daughter of your father or your mother, whether brought up in the same household or elsewhere.

10"You shall not have intercourse with your granddaughter—the daughter of either your son or your daughter—for she is a close relative. 11You may not have intercourse with a half-sister—your father's wife's daughter; 12nor your aunt—your father's sister—because she is so closely related to your father; 13nor your aunt—your mother's sister—because she is a close relative of your mother; 14nor your aunt—the wife of your father's brother.

15"You may not marry your daughter-in-law—your son's wife; 16nor your brother's wife, for she is your brother's. 17You may not marry both a woman and her daughter or granddaughter, for they are near relatives, and to do so is horrible wickedness. 18You shall not marry two sisters, for they will be rivals. However, if your wife dies, then it is all right to marry her sister.

19"There must be no sexual relationship with a woman who is menstruating; 20nor with anyone else's wife, to defile yourself with her.

21"You shall not give any of your children to Molech, burning them upon his altar; never profane the name of your God, for I am Jehovah.

22"Homosexuality is absolutely forbidden, for it is an enormous sin. 23A man shall have no sexual intercourse with any female animal, thus defiling himself; and a woman must never give herself to a male animal, to mate with it; this is a terrible perversion.

24"Do not defile yourselves in any of these ways, for these are the things the heathen do; and because they do them I am going to cast them out from the land into which you are going. 25That entire country is defiled with this kind of activity; that is why I am punishing the people living there, and will throw them out of the land. 26You must strictly obey all of my laws and ordinances, and you must not do any of these abominable things; these laws apply both to you who are born in the nation of Israel and to foreigners living among you.

27"Yes, all these abominations have been done continually by the people of the land where I am taking you, and the land is defiled. 28Do not do these things or I will throw you out of the land, just as I will throw out the nations that live there now. 29, 30Whoever does any of these terrible deeds shall be excommunicated from

18:4, 5 *shall live,* literally, "shall live in them" or "shall live by them." **18:6** *marry,* literally, "uncover the nakedness of," that is "have sexual intercourse with." **18:10** *for she is a close relative,* literally, "for theirs is your own nakedness." **18:14** *nor your aunt—the wife of your father's brother.* This prohibition applied not only while her husband lived, but also after his death. **18:16** *for she is your brother's.* Except when the brother died and left no heir, in which case his wife was left to a brother to beget children for her to carry on the name and inheritance of the deceased. See Deut 25:5. **18:25** *and will throw them out of the land,* literally, "the land vomits out her inhabitants." **18:28** *or I will throw you out of the land, just as I will throw out,* literally, "that the land vomit not you out also . . . as it vomited out . . .'"

---

to leave all aspects of their heathen background behind. He also warned them how easy it would be to slip into the heathen culture of Canaan where they were going. The society and religions of Canaan appealed to carnal desires, especially sexual immorality and drunkenness. The Israelites were to keep themselves pure and set apart for God. God did not want his people to be absorbed into the surrounding culture and environment. Society may pressure us to conform to its way of life and thought, but yielding to that pressure will (1) create confusion as to which side we should be on and (2) eliminate our effectiveness. Follow God, and don't let the culture around you mold how you think or what you believe.

18:6-18 Marrying relatives was prohibited by God for physical, social, and moral reasons. Children born to near relatives may experience a greater frequency of health problems. Without these specific laws, sexual promiscuity would have been more likely, first

in the families, then outside. When improper sexual relations begin, family life is destroyed.

18:6-27 Several abominations, or wicked things, are listed here: (1) marrying close relatives, (2) having sex with someone else's wife, (3) burning children, (4) homosexuality, (5) sex with animals. These practices were quite common to pagan religions and it is easy to see why God dealt harshly with those who began to follow them. Such practices are not only a source of disease; more important, they are extremely disruptive to family and social life. They reveal a low regard for the value of oneself and of others.

Society today takes some of these practices lightly, even trying to make them acceptable. But they are sins in God's eyes. If you consider them acceptable, you are not judging by God's standards.

this nation. So be very sure to obey my laws, and do not practice any of these horrible customs. Do not defile yourselves with the evil deeds of those living in the land where you are going. For I am Jehovah your God."

Commands for daily life

19 The Lord also told Moses to tell the people of Israel, "You must be holy because I, the Lord your God, am holy. You must respect your mothers and fathers, and obey my Sabbath law, for I am the Lord your God. 3, 4Do not make or worship idols, for I am Jehovah your God.

5"When you sacrifice a peace offering to the Lord, offer it correctly so that it will be accepted: 6Eat it the same day you offer it, or the next day at the latest; any remaining until the third day must be burned. 7For any of it eaten on the third day is repulsive to me, and will not be accepted. 8If you eat it on the third day you are guilty, for you profane the holiness of Jehovah, and you shall be excommunicated from Jehovah's people.

9"When you harvest your crops, don't reap the corners of your fields, and don't pick up stray grains of wheat from the ground. 10It is the same with your grape crop—don't strip every last piece of fruit from the vines, and don't pick up the grapes that fall to the ground. Leave them for the poor and for those traveling through, for I am Jehovah your God.

11"You must not steal nor lie nor defraud. 12You must not swear to a falsehood, thus bringing reproach upon the name of your God, for I am Jehovah.

13"You shall not rob nor oppress anyone, and you shall pay your hired workers promptly. If something is due them, don't even keep it overnight.

14"You must not curse the deaf nor trip up a blind man as he walks. Fear your God; I am Jehovah!

15"Judges must always be just in their sentences, not noticing whether a person is poor or rich; they must always be perfectly fair.

16"Don't gossip. Don't falsely accuse your neighbor of some crime, for I am Jehovah.

17"Don't hate your brother. Rebuke anyone who sins; don't let him get away with it, or you will be equally guilty. 18Don't seek vengeance. Don't bear a grudge; but love your neighbor as yourself, for I am Jehovah.

19"Obey my laws: Do not mate your cattle with a different kind; don't sow your field with two kinds of seed; don't wear clothes made of half wool and half linen.

20"If a man seduces a slave girl who is engaged to be married, they shall be tried in a court but not put to death, because she is not free. 21The man involved shall bring his guilt offering to the Lord at the entrance of the Tabernacle; the offering shall be a ram. 22The priest shall make atonement with the ram for the sin the man has committed, and it shall be forgiven him.

23"When you enter the land and have planted all kinds of fruit trees, do not eat the first three crops, for they are considered ceremonially defiled. 24And the fourth year the entire crop shall be devoted to the Lord, and shall be given to the Lord in praise to him. 25Finally, in the fifth year, the crop is yours.

26"I am Jehovah your God! You must not eat meat with undrained blood nor use fortune telling or witchcraft.

19:1
Ex 20:8-11
Lev 11:44,45
19:3
Ex 20:3-5,23
Lev 26:1
Deut 27:15
19:5
Lev 3:1-17
7:11-21,28-38
19:8
Num 15:31
19:9
Lev 23:22
Deut 24:19-22
19:11
Ex 20:15,16
Deut 5:19,20
19:13
Ex 22:7-15,
21-27; 23:4-9
Deut 24:14,15
Prov 22:22
Mal 3:5
19:14
Deut 27:18
19:15
Ex 23:2,3,6
Deut 1:17
16:19,20
Prov 24:23
Jas 2:1-7
19:16
Ex 23:1,7
Prov 20:19
Ezek 22:9
Mt 26:60,61
Acts 6:11-14
19:17
Prov 9:7,8
27:5,6
Mt 17:17,18
1 Jn 3:15
19:18
Ex 23:4,5
Deut 32:35
Ps 103:9
Mt 5:43; 19:19
Mk 12:31-33
Lk 10:27-37
Rom 12:17-21
Gal 5:14
Heb 10:30
19:19
Deut 22:9-11
19:20
Ex 21:20,21
19:21
Lev 5:14-19
19:26
Ex 22:18

19:16 Don't falsely accuse your neighbor of some crime, literally, "neither shall you stand against the blood of your neighbor." 19:20 slave girl, literally, "not yet redeemed, nor given her freedom." 19:23 for they are considered ceremonially defiled, literally, "you shall count the fruit thereof as their uncircumcision."

19:9, 10 This law was a protection for the poor and a reminder that God owned the land; the people were only caretakers. Laws such as this showed the generosity and liberality inherent in God's character. As people of God, Israel was to reflect his nature and characteristics in their attitudes and actions. Ruth and Naomi were two people who benefited from this merciful law (Ruth 2:2).

19:9, 10 God instructed the Hebrews to provide for those in need. He required that the people leave the corners of their fields unharvested, providing food for travelers and the poor. It is easy to ignore the poor or forget about those who have less than we do. But God desires generosity. In what ways can you leave "the corners of your fields" for those in need?

19:18 Don't, don't, don't. Some people think that is all the Bible is, a book of don'ts. But Jesus neatly summarized all these rules when he said to love God with all your heart, and your neighbor as yourself. He called these the greatest commandments (or rules) of all (Matthew 22:34–40). If we carried out Jesus' simple statement, we would find ourselves following all of God's other laws.

19:27
Ezek 44:20

19:28
Deut 14:1
Jer 16:6; 48:37

19:29
Lev 21:9
Deut 23:17,18
Hos 4:13

19:30
Ex 20:8-11
Lev 26:2

19:31
Lev 19:26

19:32
1 Tim 5:1,2

19:34
Lev 19:18

19:35
Deut 25:13-16
Prov 11:1
16:11; 20:10
Amos 8:5
Mic 6:11

27"You must not trim off your hair on your temples or clip the edges of your beard, as the heathen do. 28You shall not cut yourselves nor put tattoo marks upon yourselves in connection with funeral rites; I am the Lord.

29"Do not violate your daughter's sanctity by making her a prostitute, lest the land become full of enormous wickedness.

30"Keep my Sabbath laws and reverence my Tabernacle, for I am the Lord.

31"Do not defile yourselves by consulting mediums and wizards, for I am Jehovah your God.

32"You shall give due honor and respect to the elderly, in the fear of God. I am Jehovah.

33"Do not take advantage of foreigners in your land; do not wrong them. 34They must be treated like any other citizen; love them as yourself, for remember that you too were foreigners in the land of Egypt. I am Jehovah your God.

35, 36"You must be impartial in judgment. Use accurate measurements—lengths, weights, and volumes—and give full measure, for I am Jehovah your God who brought you from the land of Egypt. 37You must heed all of my commandments and ordinances, carefully obeying them, for I am Jehovah."

Punishments for sin

20:2
Lev 18:21
24:13,14,23
Deut 13:10
17:5-7

20:3
Lev 18:21
Num 19:20
Ezek 5:11; 23:38,
39

20:5
Lev 17:10

20:6
Lev 19:26,31

20:7
Lev 11:44

20:9
Ex 21:17
Deut 27:16
Mt 15:4

20:10
Ex 20:14
Deut 22:22-24

20 The Lord gave Moses these further instructions for the people of Israel: "Anyone—whether an Israelite or a foreigner living among you—who sacrifices his child as a burnt offering to Molech shall without fail be stoned by his peers. 3And I myself will turn against that man and cut him off from all his people, because he has given his child to Molech, thus making my Tabernacle unfit for me to live in, and insulting my holy name. 4And if the people of the land pretend they do not know what the man has done, and refuse to put him to death, 5then I myself will set my face against that man and his family and cut him off, along with all others who turn to other gods than me.

6"I will set my face against anyone who consults mediums and wizards instead of me and I will cut that person off from his people. 7So sanctify yourselves and be holy, for I am the Lord your God. 8You must obey all of my commandments, for I am the Lord who sanctifies you.

9"Anyone who curses his father or mother shall surely be put to death—for he has cursed his own flesh and blood.

10"If a man commits adultery with another man's wife, both the man and woman

19:27 *as the heathen do,* implied.   **20:3** *my Tabernacle,* literally, "my sanctuary . . ."

19:32 It's sometimes easy to dismiss the opinions of the elderly and avoid taking time to visit with them. But the fact that God commanded the Israelites to respect and honor the elderly shows how seriously we should take this responsibility.

19:33, 34 How do you feel when you encounter foreigners, especially those who don't speak your language? Are you impatient? Do you think or act as if they should go back where they came from? Are you tempted to take advantage of them? God says to treat foreigners as you'd treat a fellow countryman, to love them as you love yourself. In reality, we are all foreigners in this world, because it is only our temporary home. View strangers, newcomers, and foreigners as opportunities to demonstrate God's love.

20:1–3 Sacrificing children to the gods was a common practice in ancient religions. The Ammonites, Israel's neighbors, made child sacrifice to Molech (their national god) a vital part of their religion. They saw this as the greatest gift they could offer to ward off evil or appease angry gods. God made it clear that this practice was detestable and strictly forbidden because it (1) was murder, and thus against his laws, (2) was a tragic waste of human life, and (3) was connected to idol worship.

20:6 Everyone is interested in what the future holds, and we often look to others for guidance. But God warned about looking to the occult for advice. Mediums, wizards, and astrologers were outlawed because God was not the source of their information and

therefore they could not be trusted. Claiming to have supernatural information, they are either fakes making false claims, or they are offering supernatural information that is evil. God has given us the Bible so that we may obtain supernatural knowledge that is trustworthy and true.

20:10–21 This list of commands against sexual sins includes extremely harsh punishments. Why? The detestable acts listed were very common in the heathen nations of Canaan; their religions were rampant with sex goddesses, temple prostitution, and other gross sins. The Canaanite culture was destructive, and its people would not benefit the world. On the other hand, God was building a nation to make a positive influence on the world. So he prepared the people for what they would face in the Promised Land and commanded them against falling into the trap of such sexual sins.

Sexual sins were dealt with swiftly and harshly in the Old Testament. God had no tolerance for such acts for the following reasons: (1) they shatter the mutual commitment of married partners; (2) they destroy the sanctity of the family; (3) they twist people's mental well-being; and (4) they spread disease. Sexual sin has always been widely available. The glorification of sex between people who are not married to each other often hides the fact that deep tragedy and hurt exist behind the scenes. When society portrays sexual sins as attractive, it is easy to forget what God said and why he said it.

shall be put to death. ¹¹If a man sleeps with his father's wife, he has defiled what is his father's; both the man and the woman must die, for it is their own fault. ¹²And if a man has sexual intercourse with his daughter-in-law, both shall be executed: they have brought it upon themselves by defiling each other. ¹³The penalty for homosexual acts is death to both parties. They have brought it upon themselves. ¹⁴If a man has sexual intercourse with a woman and with her mother, it is a great evil. All three shall be burned alive to wipe out wickedness from among you.

¹⁵"If a man has sexual intercourse with an animal, he shall be executed and the animal killed. ¹⁶If a woman has sexual intercourse with an animal, kill the woman and the animal, for they deserve their punishment.

¹⁷"If a man has sexual intercourse with his sister, whether the daughter of his father or of his mother, it is a shameful thing, and they shall publicly be cut off from the people of Israel. He shall bear his guilt. ¹⁸If a man has sexual intercourse with a woman during her period of menstruation, both shall be excommunicated, for he has uncovered the source of her flow, and she has permitted it.

¹⁹"Sexual intercourse is outlawed between a man and his maiden aunt—whether the sister of his mother or of his father—for they are near of kin; they shall bear their guilt. ²⁰If a man has intercourse with his uncle's wife, he has taken what belongs to his uncle; their punishment is that they shall bear their sin and die childless. ²¹If a man marries his brother's wife, this is impurity; for he has taken what belongs to his brother, and they shall be childless.

²²"You must obey all of my laws and ordinances so that I will not throw you out of your new land. ²³You must not follow the customs of the nations I cast out before you, for they do all these things I have warned you against; that is the reason I abhor them. ²⁴I have promised you their land; I will give it to you to possess it. It is a land 'flowing with milk and honey.' I am the Lord your God who has made a distinction between you and the people of other nations.

²⁵"You shall therefore make a distinction between the birds and animals I have given you permission to eat and those you may not eat. You shall not contaminate yourselves and make yourselves hateful to me by eating any animal or bird which I have forbidden, though the land teem with them. ²⁶You shall be holy to me, for I the Lord am holy, and I have set you apart from all other peoples, to be mine.

²⁷"A medium or a wizard—whether man or woman—shall surely be stoned to death. They have caused their own doom."

2. Standards for the priests

21 The Lord said to Moses: "Tell the priests never to defile themselves by touching a dead person, ², ³unless it is a near relative—a mother, father, son, daughter, brother, or unmarried sister for whom he has special responsibility since she has no husband. ⁴For the priest is a leader among his people and he may not ceremonially defile himself as an ordinary person can.

⁵"The priests shall not clip bald spots in their hair or beards, nor cut their flesh. ⁶They shall be holy unto their God, and shall not dishonor and profane his name; otherwise they will be unfit to make food offerings by fire to the Lord their God. ⁷A priest shall not marry a prostitute, nor a woman of another tribe, and he shall not marry a divorced woman, for he is a holy man of God. ⁸The priest is set apart to offer the sacrifices of your God; he is holy, for I, the Lord who sanctifies you, am holy. ⁹The daughter of any priest who becomes a prostitute, thus violating her father's holiness as well as her own, shall be burned alive.

20:11 Lev 18:7,8; Deut 27:20
20:12 Lev 18:15
20:13 Gen 19:5; Lev 18:22; Deut 23:17; Judg 19:22
20:14 Lev 18:17; Deut 27:23
20:15 Lev 18:23; Deut 27:21
20:17 Lev 18:9
20:18 Lev 15:24; 18:19
20:19 Lev 18:12,13
20:20 Lev 18:14
20:21 Lev 18:16
20:22 Lev 18:28
20:23 Lev 18:1-3, 24-30; Deut 9:5
20:24 Gen 15:16; Ex 3:17; 6:8,9; Deut 6:3; 8:7-9; 11:9; 26:9; 27:3; Josh 5:6; 24:11
20:25 Lev 11:1-47; Deut 14:3-5
20:26 Lev 11:44
20:27 Lev 19:26,31; Deut 18:10-12
21:1 Lev 21:11; Num 19:14,16; Ezek 44:25
21:2 Lev 21:11
21:5 Lev 19:27,28; Deut 14:1; Jer 16:6; 48:37
21:6 Ex 29:44; Lev 10:3
21:7 Lev 21:14; Ezek 44:22
21:8 Lev 11:44

20:16 *for they deserve their punishment,* literally, "their blood shall be upon them." **20:21** *his brother's wife.* However, marriage to his brother's widow was required if she had no children. See Deut 25:5. **20:22** *so that I will not throw you out of your new land,* literally, "that the land I give you will not vomit you out again." **21:2, 3** *unmarried,* literally, "a virgin."

20:22, 23 God gave many rules to his people—but not without reason. He did not withhold good from them; he only prohibited those acts that would bring them to ruin. All of us understand God's physical laws of nature. For example, those who jump off a ten-story building will die because of the law of gravity. But some of us don't understand how God's spiritual laws work. God forbids us to do certain things because he wants to keep us from self-destruction. We must beware of desiring these forbidden pleasures because the consequences are suffering, death, and separation from the God who is trying to help us.

¹⁰"The High Priest—anointed with the special anointing oil and wearing the special garments—must not let his hair hang loose in mourning, nor tear his clothing, ¹¹nor be in the presence of any dead person—not even his father or mother. ¹²He shall not leave the sanctuary [when on duty], nor treat my Tabernacle like an ordinary house, for the consecration of the anointing oil of his God is upon him; I am Jehovah. ¹³He must marry a virgin. ¹⁴, ¹⁵He may not marry a widow, nor a woman who is divorced, nor a prostitute. She must be a virgin from his own tribe, for he must not be the father of children of mixed blood—half priestly and half ordinary."

¹⁶, ¹⁷And the Lord said to Moses, "Tell Aaron that any of his descendants from generation to generation who have any bodily defect may not offer the sacrifices to God. ¹⁸For instance, if a man is blind or lame, or has a broken nose or any extra fingers or toes, ¹⁹or has a broken foot or hand, ²⁰or has a humped back, or is a dwarf, or has a defect in his eye, or has pimples or scabby skin, or has imperfect testicles— ²¹although he is a descendant of Aaron—he is not permitted to offer the fire sacrifices to the Lord because of his physical defect. ²²However, he shall be fed with the food of the priests from the offerings sacrificed to God, both from the holy and most holy offerings. ²³But he shall not go in behind the veil, nor come near the altar, because of the physical defect; this would defile my sanctuary, for it is Jehovah who sanctifies it."

²⁴So Moses gave these instructions to Aaron and his sons and to all the people of Israel.

22 The Lord told Moses, "Instruct Aaron and his sons to be very careful not to defile my holy name by desecrating the people's sacred gifts; for I am Jehovah. ³From now on and forever, if a priest who is ceremonially defiled sacrifices the animals brought by the people or handles the gifts dedicated to Jehovah, he shall be discharged from the priesthood. For I am Jehovah!

⁴"No priest who is a leper or who has a running sore may eat the holy sacrifices until healed. And any priest who touches a dead person, or who is defiled by a seminal emission, ⁵or who touches any reptile or other forbidden thing, or who touches anyone who is ceremonially defiled for any reason— ⁶that priest shall be defiled until evening, and shall not eat of the holy sacrifices until after he has bathed that evening. ⁷When the sun is down, then he shall be purified again and may eat the holy food, for it is his source of life. ⁸He may not eat any animal that dies of itself or is torn by wild animals, for this will defile him. I am Jehovah. ⁹Warn the priests to follow these instructions carefully, lest they be declared guilty and die for violating these rules. I am the Lord who sanctifies them.

¹⁰"No one may eat of the holy sacrifices unless he is a priest; no one visiting the priest, for instance, nor a hired servant, may eat this food. ¹¹However, there is one exception—if the priest buys a slave with his own money, that slave may eat it, and any slave children born in his household may eat it. ¹²If a priest's daughter is married outside the tribe, she may not eat the sacred offerings. ¹³But if she is a widow or divorced and has no son to support her, and has returned home to her father's household, she may eat of her father's food again. But otherwise, no one who is not in the priestly families may eat this food.

¹⁴"If someone should eat of the holy sacrifices without realizing it, he shall return to the priest the amount he has used, with twenty percent added; ¹⁵for the holy sacrifices brought by the people of Israel must not be defiled by being eaten by

21:11 *not even his father or mother.* Note this rule applied to the High Priest, while the contrary instructions in vs 1 applied to ordinary priests. **21:12** *when on duty,* implied. **21:15** *for he must not be the father of children of mixed blood—half priestly and half ordinary,* literally, "he must not profane his offspring among his people." **22:12** *the sacred offerings,* literally, "the elevation of the holy things."

21:16–23 Was God unfairly discriminating against handicapped people when he said they were unqualified to offer sacrifices? Just as God demanded that no imperfect animals be used for sacrifice, he required that no "imperfect" priests offer sacrifices. This was not an insult to their handicap. Rather, it had to do with the fact that the priest must in some way match the perfect God he served. Of course, such perfection was not fully realized until Jesus Christ came. As Levites, the handicapped priests were protected and provided for with food from the sacrifices. They were not abandoned, for they still performed many essential services within the Tabernacle.

unauthorized persons, for these sacrifices have been offered to the Lord. [16]Anyone who violates this law is guilty and is in great danger because he has eaten the sacred offerings; for I am Jehovah who sanctifies the offerings."

22:16
Lev 22:9

Acceptable animals for sacrifice

[17, 18]And the Lord said to Moses, "Tell Aaron and his sons and all the people of Israel that if an Israelite or other person living among you offers a burnt offering sacrifice to the Lord—whether it is to fulfill a promise or is a spontaneous free will offering— [19]it will only be acceptable to the Lord if it is a male animal without defect; it must be a young bull or a sheep or a goat. [20]Anything that has a defect must not be offered, for it will not be accepted.

22:19
Lev 1:2; 4:3
22:20
Lev 22:22-25
Deut 15:21

[21]"Anyone sacrificing a peace offering to the Lord from the herd or flock, whether to fulfill a vow or as a voluntary offering, must sacrifice an animal that has no defect, or it will not be accepted: [22]An animal that is blind or disabled or mutilated, or which has sores or itch or any other skin disease, must not be offered to the Lord; it is not a fit burnt offering for the altar of the Lord. [23]If the young bull or lamb presented to the Lord has anything superfluous or lacking in its body parts, it may be offered as a free will offering, but not for a vow. [24]An animal that has injured genitals—crushed or castrated—shall not be offered to the Lord at any time. [25]This restriction applies to the sacrifices made by foreigners among you as well as those made by yourselves, for no defective animal is acceptable for this sacrifice."

22:22
Lev 22:20
Mal 1:8

22:25
Num 15:15,16
Mal 1:14

[26, 27]And the Lord said to Moses, "When a bullock, sheep, or goat is born, it shall be left with its mother for seven days, but from the eighth day onward it is acceptable as a sacrifice by fire to the Lord. [28]You shall not slaughter a mother animal and her offspring the same day, whether she is a cow or ewe. [29, 30]When you offer the Lord a sacrifice of thanksgiving, you must do it in the right way, eating the sacrificial animal the same day it is slain. Leave none of it for the following day. I am the Lord.

22:26
Ex 22:30

22:28
Deut 22:6
22:29
Ex 16:19
Lev 7:15

[31]"You must keep all of my commandments, for I am the Lord. [32, 33]You must not treat me as common and ordinary. Revere me and hallow me, for I, the Lord, made you holy to myself and rescued you from Egypt to be my own people! I am Jehovah!"

22:31
Ex 20:2
Lev 18:4

22:33
Lev 22:31

3. Seasons and festivals

23 The Lord said to Moses, "Announce to the people of Israel that they are to celebrate several annual festivals of the Lord—times when all Israel will assemble and worship me. [3](These are in addition to your Sabbaths—the seventh day of every week—which are always days of rest in every home, times for assembling to worship, and for resting from the normal business of the week.) [4]These are the holy festivals which are to be observed each year:

23:1
Ex 23:17; 34:22
Lev 23:4,37,44
Num 29:39
23:3
Ex 20:8-11
23:12; 31:15
Deut 5:13,14
Lk 13:14

The Passover and Festival of Unleavened Bread

[5]*"The Passover of the Lord:* This is to be celebrated on the first day of April, beginning at sundown.

[6]*"The Festival of Unleavened Bread:* This is to be celebrated beginning the day

23:5
Ex 12:3-20
Mt 26:17
Mk 14:12

23:3 your Sabbaths, implied. **23:5** *This is to be celebrated on the first day of April,* literally, "on the fourteenth day of the first month" (of the Hebrew calendar). This corresponds approximately to our April first.

22:19–25 Animals with defects were not acceptable as sacrifices, because they did not match God's holy nature. Furthermore, the animal had to be without blemish in order to foreshadow the perfect, sinless life of Jesus Christ. When we give our best time, talent, and treasure to God, rather than what is tarnished or common, we show the true meaning of worship and testify to God's supreme worth.

23:1ff Feasts (or festivals) played a major role in Israel's culture. Israel's feasts were different from those of any other nation because they were ordained by God and were times of celebrating

with him, not times of moral depravity. God wanted to set aside special days for the people to come together for rest, refreshment, and remembering with thanksgiving all he had done for them.

23:1–4 God established several national holidays each year for celebration, fellowship, and worship. Much can be learned about people by observing the holidays they celebrate and the way they celebrate them. Take note of your holiday traditions. What do they say about you and the way you live?

23:6 The Festival of Unleavened Bread reminded Israel of their escape from Egypt. For seven days they ate unleavened bread,

23:6
Mk 14:1-12
Lk 22:1

23:7
Ex 12:6
Num 28:18

following the Passover, and for seven days you must not eat any bread made with yeast. 7On the first day of this festival, you shall gather the people for worship, and all ordinary work shall cease. 8You shall do the same on the seventh day of the festival. On each of the intervening days you shall make an offering by fire to the Lord.

The Festival of First Fruits

23:9-11
Ex 23:16,19
34:22
Num 15:17-21
28:26-31
Deut 16:9-12
Rom 11:16
Jas 1:18
Rev 14:4

23:13
Lev 6:14-23
Num 15:3-10

23:14
Lev 3:17

9, 10, 11*"The Festival of First Fruits:* When you arrive in the land I will give you, and you reap your first harvest, bring the first sheaf of the harvest to the priest on the day after the Sabbath. He shall wave it before the Lord in a gesture of offering, and it will be accepted by the Lord as your gift. 12That same day you shall sacrifice to the Lord a male yearling lamb without defect as a burnt offering. 13A grain offering shall accompany it, consisting of a fifth of a bushel of finely ground flour mixed with olive oil, to be offered by fire to the Lord; this will be very pleasant to him. Also offer a drink offering consisting of three pints of wine. 14Until this is done you must not eat any of the harvest for yourselves—neither fresh kernels nor bread nor parched grain. This is a permanent law throughout your nation.

The Festival of Pentecost

23:15,16
Lev 23:9-14
Num 28:26-31
Acts 2:1

15, 16*"The Harvest Festival (Festival of Pentecost):* Fifty days later you shall bring to the Lord an offering of a sample of the new grain of your later crops. 17This shall consist of two loaves of bread from your homes to be waved before the Lord

23:7 *all ordinary work shall cease,* literally, "you shall do no hard work." **23:17** *It is an offering to the Lord of the first sampling of your later crops,* literally, "as first fruits to the Lord."

THE FEASTS
Besides enjoying one Sabbath day of rest each week, the Israelites also enjoyed 19 days when national holidays were celebrated.

Feast	What It Celebrated	Its Importance
Passover One day (Leviticus 23:5)	When God spared the lives of Israel's firstborn children in Egypt and freed the Hebrews from slavery	Reminded the people of God's deliverance
Unleavened Bread Seven days (Leviticus 23:6–8)	The Exodus from Egypt	Reminded the people they were leaving the old life behind and entering a new way of living
First Fruits One day (Leviticus 23:9–14)	The first crops of the barley harvest	Reminded the people how God provided for them
Pentecost One day (Leviticus 23:15–22)	The end of the barley harvest and beginning of the wheat harvest	Showed joy and thanksgiving over the bountiful harvest
Trumpets One day (Leviticus 23:23–25)	The beginning of the seventh month (civil new year)	Expressed joy and thanksgiving to God
Day of Atonement One day (Leviticus 23:26–32)	The removal of sin from the people and the nation	Restored fellowship with God
Tabernacles Seven days (Leviticus 23:33–43)	God's protection and guidance in the wilderness	Renewed Israel's commitment to God and trust in his guidance and protection

---

just as they had eaten it back then (Exodus 12:15). Unleavened bread was made without yeast, and its symbolism became important to the Israelites. First, because the bread was unique, it illustrated Israel's uniqueness as a nation. Second, it taught rejection of sin, since yeast (an agent that changed the nature of bread dough) was a symbol of sin. Third, it reminded them to obey quickly, for the flight from Egypt was hurried—there was no time to

put yeast into the dough and wait for the bread to rise.

23:9–14 The Festival of First Fruits required that the first crops harvested be given as an offering to God. The Israelites could not even eat the food from their harvest until their first crops had been offered. Today God still expects us to set aside his portion *first*, not last. Giving leftovers to God is no way to express thanks.

in a gesture of offering. Bake this bread from a fifth of a bushel of fine flour containing yeast. It is an offering to the Lord of the first sampling of your later crops. 18Along with the bread and the wine, you shall sacrifice as burnt offerings to the Lord seven yearling lambs without defects, one young bull, and two rams. All are fire offerings, very acceptable to Jehovah. 19And you shall offer one male goat for a sin offering, and two male yearling lambs for a peace offering.

23:19
Lev 16:15

20"The priests shall wave these offerings before the Lord along with the loaves representing the first sampling of your later crops. They are holy to the Lord, and will be given to the priests as food. 21That day shall be announced as a time of sacred convocation of all the people; don't do any work that day. This is a law to be honored from generation to generation. 22(When you reap your harvests, you must not thoroughly reap all the corners of the fields, nor pick up the fallen grain; leave it for the poor and for foreigners living among you who have no land of their own; I am Jehovah your God!)

23:20
Num 18:12
Deut 18:4

23:22
Lev 19:9,10
Deut 24:19-21
Prov 11:24,25

The Festival of Trumpets

23, 24"*The Festival of Trumpets:* Mid-September is a time for all the people to meet together for worship; it is a time of remembrance, and is to be announced by loud blowing of trumpets. 25Don't do any hard work on that day, but offer a sacrifice by fire to the Lord.

23:23,24
Num 10:10
29:1-6

23:25
Lev 23:7

The Day of Atonement

26, 27"*The Day of Atonement* follows nine days later: All the people are to come together before the Lord, saddened by their sin; and they shall offer sacrifices by fire to the Lord. 28Don't do any work that day, for it is a special day for making atonement before the Lord your God. 29Anyone who does not spend the day in repentance and sorrow for sin shall be excommunicated from his people. 30, 31And I will put to death anyone who does any kind of work that day. This is a law of Israel from generation to generation. 32For this is a Sabbath of rest, and in it you shall go without food and be filled with sorrow; this time for atonement begins in the evening and continues through the next day.

23:26
Lev 16:3-34
Num 29:7-11

23:28
Lev 23:7

23:29
Lev 23:32

23:32
Lev 16:29-31

The Festival of Tabernacles

33, 34"*The Festival of Shelters:* Five days later, on the last day of September, is the Festival of Shelters to be celebrated before the Lord for seven days. 35On the first day there will be a sacred assembly of all the people; don't do any hard work that day. 36On each of the seven days of the festival you are to sacrifice an offering by fire to the Lord. The eighth day requires another sacred convocation of all the people, at which time there will again be an offering by fire to the Lord. It is the closing assembly, and no regular work is permitted.

23:33,34
Ex 23:16
Lev 23:39-43
Num 29:12-39
Deut 16:13-16
Ezra 3:4
Neh 8:14
Zech 14:16
Jn 7:2

23:35
Lev 23:7

37"(These, then, are the regular annual festivals—sacred convocations of all people—when offerings to the Lord are to be made by fire. 38These annual festivals are in addition to your regular Sabbaths—the weekly days of holy rest. The sacrifices made during the festivals are to be in addition to your regular giving and normal fulfillment of your vows.)

23:36
Lev 23:34
Neh 8:18
Jn 7:39

23:37
Ex 34:22
Deut 16:16

39"This last day of September, at the end of your harvesting, is the time to begin to celebrate this seven-day festival before the Lord. Remember that the first and

23:38
Num 29:39

23:18 *very acceptable to Jehovah,* literally, "of a sweet odor to the Lord." **23:23, 24** *Mid-September,* literally, "the first day of the seventh month" (of the Hebrew calendar). **23:26, 27** *nine days later, literally, "on the tenth day of the seventh month" (of the Hebrew calendar).* **23:33, 34** *on the last day of September,* literally, "on the fifteenth day of the seventh month" (of the Hebrew calendar). *Festival of Shelters,* literally, "Feast of Tabernacles."

23:23 Worship involves both celebration and confession. But in Israel's national holidays, the balance seems heavily tipped in favor of celebration—five joyous occasions to two solemn occasions. The God of the Bible encourages joy! God did not intend for religion to be only meditation and introspection. He also wants us to celebrate. Serious reflection and immediate confession

of sin is essential, of course. But this should be balanced by celebrating who God is and what he has done for his people.

23:23, 24 The word trumpet is literally "ram's horn," for most of Israel's trumpets were made of animal horns. Some of the more special trumpets were made of beaten silver. They were blown to announce the beginning of each month as well as the start of festivals.

last days of the festival are special days of rest. 40On the first day, take boughs of fruit trees laden with fruit, and palm fronds, and the boughs of leafy trees—such as willows that grow by the brooks—and [build shelters with them], rejoicing before the Lord your God for seven days. 41This seven-day annual feast is a law from generation to generation. 42During those seven days, all of you who are native Israelites are to live in these shelters. 43The purpose of this is to remind the people of Israel, generation after generation, that I rescued you from Egypt, and caused you to live in shelters. I am Jehovah your God."

44So Moses announced these annual festivals of the Lord to the people of Israel.

The Memorial Offering

24 The Lord said to Moses, "Tell the people of Israel to bring you pure olive oil for an eternal flame 3, 4in the lampstand of pure gold which stands outside the veil that secludes the Holy of Holies. Each morning and evening Aaron shall supply it with fresh oil and trim the wicks. It will be an eternal flame before the Lord from generation to generation.

5-8"Every Sabbath day the High Priest shall place twelve loaves of bread in two rows upon the gold table that stands before the Lord. These loaves shall be baked from finely ground flour, using a fifth of a bushel for each. Pure frankincense shall be sprinkled along each row. This will be a memorial offering made by fire to the Lord, in memory of his everlasting covenant with the people of Israel. 9The bread shall be eaten by Aaron and his sons, in a place set apart for the purpose. For these are offerings made by fire to the Lord under a permanent law of God, and are most holy."

The penalty for cursing God

10Out in the camp one day, a young man whose mother was an Israelite and whose father was an Egyptian, got into a fight with one of the men of Israel. 11During the fight the Egyptian man's son cursed God, and was brought to Moses for judgment. (His mother's name was Shelomith, daughter of Dibri of the tribe of Dan.) 12He was put in jail until the Lord would indicate what to do with him.

13, 14And the Lord said to Moses, "Take him outside the camp and tell all who heard him to lay their hands upon his head; then all the people are to execute him by stoning. 15, 16And tell the people of Israel that anyone who curses his God must pay the penalty: he must die. All the congregation shall stone him; this law applies to the foreigner as well as to the Israelite who blasphemes the name of Jehovah. He must die.

17"Also, all murderers must be executed. 18Anyone who kills an animal [that isn't his] shall replace it. 19The penalty for injuring anyone is to be injured in exactly the same way: 20fracture for fracture, eye for eye, tooth for tooth. Whatever anyone does to another shall be done to him.

21"To repeat, whoever kills an animal must replace it, and whoever kills a man must die. 22You shall have the same law for the foreigner as for the home-born citizen, for I am Jehovah your God.

23So they took the youth out of the camp and stoned him until he died, as Jehovah had commanded Moses.

Rest every seventh year

25 While Moses was on Mount Sinai, the Lord gave him these instructions for the people of Israel:

23:40 *build shelters with them,* implied. **24:11** *the Egyptian man's son,* literally, "the Israelite woman's son." *cursed God,* literally, "blasphemed the Name." **24:18** *that isn't his,* implied. *shall replace it,* literally, "shall make it good, life for life."

23:42
Neh 8:14-18
23:43
Ex 13:14-18
Deut 13:31
Ps 78:1-8
23:44
Lev 23:37

24:1
Ex 27:20,21
24:3
Ex 25:31-39
37:17-24

24:5
Ex 25:30
37:10-13; 40:23
Lev 2:9,16
5:12; 6:15
Heb 9:2
24:9
Lev 6:16-18
Mt 12:4

24:11
Ex 22:28
Job 1:5,11,22
Ps 74:18
24:13
Lev 4:15
Deut 13:9; 17:7
21:21
24:15,16
Ex 22:28
24:17
Gen 9:5
Ex 20:13
21:12,14
Num 35:30,31
Deut 19:11-13
24:18
Ex 21:33-36
Lev 24:21
24:20
Ex 21:24,25
Deut 19:21
Mt 5:38
24:21
Lev 24:18
24:22
Ex 12:49
Num 15:15,
16,29

23:43 Israel's festivals were special family outings. Passover, Pentecost, and the Feast of Tabernacles all required family participation. They taught family members of all ages about God's nature and what he had done for them. They were a time of renewed commmitment to God. Our families also need rituals of celebration to renew our faith and to pass it on to our children. In addition to Christmas and Easter, we should select other special days in which to commemorate God's goodness.

"When you come into the land I am going to give you, you must let the land rest before the Lord every seventh year. 3For six years you may sow your field and prune your vineyards and harvest your crops, 4but during the seventh year the land is to lie fallow before the Lord, uncultivated. Don't sow your crops and don't prune your vineyards during that entire year. 5Don't even reap for yourself the volunteer crops that come up, and don't gather the grapes for yourself; for it is a year of rest for the land. 6, 7Any crops that do grow that year shall be free to all—for you, your servants, your slaves, and any foreigners living among you. Cattle and wild animals alike shall be allowed to graze there.

The Year of Jubilee

8"Every fiftieth year, 9on the Day of Atonement, let the trumpets blow loud and long throughout the land. 10For the fiftieth year shall be holy, a time to proclaim liberty throughout the land to all enslaved debtors, and a time for the canceling of all public and private debts. It shall be a year when all the family estates sold to others shall be returned to the original owners or their heirs.

11"What a happy year it will be! In it you shall not sow, nor gather crops nor grapes; 12for it is a holy Year of Jubilee for you. That year your food shall be the volunteer crops that grow wild in the fields. 13Yes, during the Year of Jubilee everyone shall return home to his original family possession; if he has sold it, it shall be his again! 14, 15, 16Because of this, if the land is sold or bought during the preceding forty-nine years, a fair price shall be arrived at by counting the number of years until the Jubilee. If the Jubilee is many years away, the price will be high; if few years, the price will be low; for what you are really doing is selling the number of crops the new owner will get from the land before it is returned to you.

17, 18"You must fear your God and not overcharge! For I am Jehovah. Obey my laws if you want to live safely in the land. 19When you obey, the land will yield bumper crops and you can eat your fill in safety. 20But you will ask, 'What shall we eat the seventh year, since we are not allowed to plant or harvest crops that year?' 21, 22The answer is, 'I will bless you with bumper crops the sixth year that will last you until the crops of the eighth year are harvested!' 23And remember, the land is mine, so you may not sell it permanently. You are merely my tenants and share-croppers!

24"In every contract of sale there must be a stipulation that the land can be redeemed at any time by the seller. 25If anyone becomes poor and sells some of his land, then his nearest relatives may redeem it. 26If there is no one else to redeem it, and he himself gets together enough money, 27then he may always buy it back at a price proportionate to the number of harvests until the Jubilee, and the owner must accept the money and return the land to him. 28But if the original owner is not able to redeem it, then it shall belong to the new owner until the Year of Jubilee; but at the Jubilee year it must be returned again.

29"If a man sells a house in the city, he has up to one year to redeem it, with full right of redemption during that time. 30But if it is not redeemed within the year, then it will belong permanently to the new owner—it does not return to the original owner in the Year of Jubilee. 31But village houses—a village is a settlement without fortifying walls around it—are like farmland, redeemable at any time, and are always returned to the original owner in the Year of Jubilee.

32"There is one exception: The homes of the Levites, even though in walled cities, may be redeemed at any time, 33and must be returned to the original owners

25:9 *on the Day of Atonement*, literally, "the tenth day of the seventh month (of the Hebrew calendar). 25:29 *in the city*, literally, "in a walled city." 25:33 *and the surrounding fields*, implied.

25:8–10 The Year of Jubilee was meant to be celebrated every 50 years. It included canceling all debts and returning all land that had been sold. There is no indication in the Bible that the Year of Jubilee was ever carried out. If Israel had followed this practice faithfully, a society without permanent poverty would have resulted.

25:23 In God's plan, only God's ownership was absolute. He wanted his people to avoid materialism. If you have the attitude that you are taking care of the Lord's property, you will make what you have more available to others. This is difficult to do if you have an attitude of ownership. Think of yourself as a manager, not as an owner.

25:2
Ex 23:11
Lev 26:33-35,43

25:3
Ex 23:10

25:4
Lev 25:1,20-23

25:5
2 Kgs 19:29

25:6
Lev 25:20-22

25:9
Num 10:10

25:10
Lev 25:8-16,
28-54
Isa 61:1,2
Jer 34:8,15,17
Lk 4:17-20

25:12
Lev 25:5

25:13
Lev 25:10,24-31

25:14
Lev 25:17,51,52

25:17
Lev 25:14-16

25:21
Lev 25:3,4

25:23
Ex 19:5
2 Chron 7:20
Ezek 48:14

25:25
Lev 25:35
Ruth 2:20; 4:4,6
Jer 32:6-8

25:27
Lev 25:50-53

25:28
Lev 25:10,13

in the Year of Jubilee; for the Levites will not be given farmland like the other tribes, but will receive only houses in their cities, and the surrounding fields. 34The Levites are not permitted to sell the fields of common land surrounding their cities, for these are their permanent possession, and they must belong to no one else.

35"If your brother becomes poor, you are responsible to help him; invite him to live with you as a guest in your home. 36Fear your God and let your brother live with you; and don't charge him interest on the money you lend him. 37Remember—no interest; and give him what he needs, at your cost: don't try to make a profit! 38For I, the Lord your God, brought you out of the land of Egypt to *give* you the land of Canaan, and to be your God.

39"If a fellow Israelite becomes poor and sells himself to you, you must not treat him as an ordinary slave, 40but rather as a hired servant or as a guest; and he shall serve you only until the Year of Jubilee. 41At that time he can leave with his children, and return to his own family and possessions. 42For I brought you from the land of Egypt, and you are my servants; so you may not be sold as ordinary slaves, 43or treated harshly; fear your God.

44"However, you may purchase slaves from the foreign nations living around you, 45and you may purchase the children of the foreigners living among you, even though they have been born in your land. 46They will be permanent slaves for you to pass on to your children after you; but your brothers, the people of Israel, shall not be treated so.

47"If a foreigner living among you becomes rich, and an Israelite becomes poor and sells himself to the foreigner or to the foreigner's family, 48he may be redeemed by one of his brothers, 49his uncle, nephew, or anyone else who is a near relative. He may also redeem himself if he can find the money. 50The price of his freedom shall be in proportion to the number of years left before the Year of Jubilee—whatever it would cost to hire a servant for that number of years. 51If there are still many years until the Jubilee, he shall pay almost the amount he received when he sold himself; 52if the years have passed and only a few remain until the Jubilee, then he will repay only a small part of the amount he received when he sold himself. 53If he sells himself to a foreigner, the foreigner must treat him as a hired servant rather than as a slave or as property. 54If he has not been redeemed by the time the Year of Jubilee arrives, then he and his children shall be freed at that time. 55For the people of Israel are *my* servants; I brought them from the land of Egypt; I am the Lord your God.

4. Receiving God's blessing

26 "You must have no idols; you must never worship carved images, obelisks, or shaped stones, for I am the Lord your God. 2You must obey my Sabbath laws of rest, and reverence my Tabernacle, for I am the Lord.

Cross-references (margin)

25:34 Num 35:2-5

25:35 Lev 25:25 Deut 15:7-11 Prov 14:21 19:17

25:36 Ex 22:25 Deut 23:19,20 Neh 5:10

25:38 Ex 20:2 Lev 11:45

25:39 Ex 21:2-11 Deut 15:12-18

25:40 Lev 25:53

25:42 Rom 6:22 1 Cor 7:23

25:43 Eph 6:9

25:46 Lev 25:40,53

25:47 Lev 25:39

25:48 Neh 5:5

25:49 Lev 25:26

25:50 Lev 25:27 Job 7:1

25:53 Lev 25:40,46

25:54 Ex 21:3-6 Lev 25:41

26:1 Ex 20:4; 34:17

26:2 Ex 20:8-11

25:35-37 God said that neglecting the poor was a sin. Poverty was not allowed in Israel. Individuals were responsible to help and house those in need. Many times we do nothing, not because we lack compassion, but because we are overwhelmed by the size of the problem and don't know where to begin. God doesn't expect you to eliminate poverty, nor does he expect you to neglect your family while providing for others. He does, however, expect that when you see an individual in need you will reach out with whatever help you can offer.

25:35 The Bible places great emphasis on assisting the poor in every way. Orphans, widows, and the handicapped were most likely to be poor and unable to help themselves. In Israelite society, no paid work was available to women. A widow and her children thus had no livelihood. Neither was there work available for the seriously handicapped among these farmers and sheepherders. The poor were to be helped without charging any interest. Personal responsibility to care for the poor was crucial since there was no government aid.

25:44 Why did God allow the Israelites to purchase slaves? Under Hebrew laws, slaves were treated differently than in other nations. They were to be looked upon as human beings with dignity, and not as animals. Nowhere does the Bible condone slavery, but it recognizes its existence. God's laws offered many guidelines for treating slaves properly. This is evident in that Hebrew slaves took part in the religious festivals and rested on the Sabbath.

26:1 The people of the Old Testament were warned over and over against worshiping idols. We wonder how they could be deceived by these objects of wood and stone. Yet God could well give us the same warning, for we are prone to put idols before him. Idolatry is making anything more important than God, and our lives are full of that temptation. Money, looks, success, reputation, security . . . the list becomes suddenly much more relevant than the idols we read about here. As you look at these false gods, which promise everything you want but nothing you need, does idolatry seem so far removed?

Rewards for obedience

3"If you obey all of my commandments, 4, 5I will give you regular rains, and the land will yield bumper crops, and the trees will be loaded with fruit long after the normal time! And grapes will still be ripening when sowing time comes again. You shall eat your fill, and live safely in the land, 6for I will give you peace, and you will go to sleep without fear. I will chase away the dangerous animals. 7You will chase your enemies; they will die beneath your swords. 8Five of you will chase a hundred, and a hundred of you, ten thousand! You will defeat all of your enemies. 9I will look after you, and multiply you, and fulfill my covenant with you. 10You will have such a surplus of crops that you won't know what to do with them when the new harvest is ready! 11And I will live among you, and not despise you. 12I will walk among you and be your God, and you shall be my people. 13For I am the Lord your God who brought you out of the land of Egypt, so that you would be slaves no longer; I have broken your chains so that you can walk with dignity.

Results of obedience

14"But if you will not listen to me or obey me, 15but reject my laws, 16this is what I will do to you: I will punish you with sudden terrors and panic, and with tuberculosis and burning fever; your eyes shall be consumed and your life shall ebb away; you will sow your crops in vain, for your enemies will eat them. 17I will set my face against you and you will flee before your attackers; those who hate you will rule you; you will even run when no one is chasing you!

18"And if you still disobey me, I will punish you seven times more severely for your sins. 19I will break your proud power and make your heavens as iron, and your earth as bronze. 20Your strength shall be spent in vain; for your land shall not yield its crops, nor your trees their fruit.

21"And if even then you will not obey me and listen to me, I will send you seven times more plagues because of your sins. 22I will send wild animals to kill your children and destroy your cattle and reduce your numbers so that your roads will be deserted.

23"And if even this will not reform you, but you continue to walk against my wishes, 24then I will walk against your wishes, and I, even I, will personally smite you seven times for your sin. 25I will revenge the breaking of my covenant by bringing war against you. You will flee to your cities, and I will send a plague among you there; and you will be conquered by your enemies. 26I will destroy your food supply so that one oven will be large enough to bake all the bread available for ten entire families; and you will still be hungry after your pittance has been doled out to you.

27"And if you still won't listen to me or obey me, 28then I will let loose my great anger and send you seven times greater punishment for your sins. 29You shall eat your own sons and daughters, 30and I will destroy the altars on the hills where you worship your idols, and I will cut down your incense altars, leaving your dead bodies to rot among your idols; and I will abhor you. 31I will make your cities desolate, and destroy your places of worship, and will not respond to your incense

26:4
Lev 25:19-22
Deut 11:14,15
Amos 9:13
26:8
Deut 28:7; 32:30
26:9
Ex 6:4,5
Deut 28:2-6
26:10
Lev 26:5
26:11
Ex 29:45,46
26:12
Ex 6:7
Jer 32:38
26:13
Ex 20:2

26:15
Num 15:30,31
26:16
Deut 28:22,33, 65-67; 32:25
Jer 5:17
26:17
Deut 28:25
Neh 9:27-30
Ps 106:41,42
26:19
Deut 28:23
Isa 25:11; 26:5
26:20
Ps 127:1
Hab 2:13
26:22
Deut 32:24
26:23
Isa 1:18-20
26:25
Deut 28:21,22, 27-29; 32:35
26:26
Isa 3:1; 9:19,20
Ezek 4:16
26:29
Deut 28:53-57
2 Kgs 6:26-30
26:30
1 Kgs 13:2-5
Isa 27:9
26:31
2 Kgs 25:4-10
Isa 24:10-13
Jer 52:13

26:4, 5 *long after the normal time,* literally, "until the grape harvest."   **26:13** *so that you can walk with dignity,* literally, "and make you go upright," or "walk with heads held high."

26:3–5 If the Israelites obeyed, there was peace in the land. If they disobeyed, there was disaster. God used the consequences of sin to draw them to repentance, not to get back at them.

Today sin's consequences are not always so apparent. When calamity strikes us we may not know the reason. It may be (1) the result of our own disobedience, (2) the result of someone else's sin, (3) the result of natural disaster. Since we don't know, we are to "search our hearts" to see if we are at peace with God. His Spirit, like a great searchlight, will reveal those areas we need to deal with. Since calamity is not always the result of wrongdoing, we

must guard against assigning or accepting blame for every tragedy we encounter. Misplaced guilt is one of Satan's favorite weapons against believers.

26:13 Imagine the joy of a slave set free. God took the children of Israel out of bitter slavery and gave them freedom and dignity. We too are set free when we accept Christ's payment to buy us out of sin's slavery. We no longer need to be bogged down in shame over our past sins but can walk with dignity because God has forgiven us and forgotten them. But just as the Israelites were still in danger of returning to a slave mentality, we need to beware of the temptation to return to our old lives of sin.

26:32
Deut 28:37
29:23
Jer 12:11; 18:16
Ezek 33:28
Dan 9:2

26:33
Deut 28:64-68

26:34
2 Chron 36:21
Jer 29:10

26:36
Deut 28:65,67
Ezek 21:7

26:38
Deut 4:25-27
Jer 42:17,18

26:39
Ezek 20:43
33:10

26:40
Deut 30:1-3
2 Chron 7:17
Ezek 36:31
Mt 23:12
Lk 14:11
1 Jn 1:9

26:42
Gen 12:1-3
15:1-4,13-16
26:2-5
28:13-15

26:44
Deut 4:29-31
Neh 9:31
Rom 11:2,26

26:45
Ex 2:24; 20:2
Lev 22:32,33
Lk 1:72,73

26:46
Lev 27:34
Deut 6:1; 12:1

27:3
Ex 30:13
Lev 5:15; 27:25

27:6
Num 3:46-48
18:14-16

27:8
Lev 14:21,22

27:10
Lev 27:14-33

offerings. 32Yes, I will desolate your land; your enemies shall live in it, utterly amazed at what I have done to you.

33"I will scatter you out among the nations, destroying you with war as you go. Your land shall be desolate and your cities destroyed. 34, 35Then at last the land will rest and make up for the many years you refused to let it lie idle; for it will lie desolate all the years that you are captives in enemy lands. Yes, then the land will rest and enjoy its Sabbaths! It will make up for the rest you didn't give it every seventh year when you lived upon it.

36"And for those who are left alive, I will cause them to be dragged away to distant lands as prisoners of war, and slaves. There they will live in constant fear. The sound of a leaf driven in the wind will send them fleeing as though chased by a man with a sword; they shall fall when no one is pursuing them. 37Yes, though none pursue they shall stumble over each other in flight, as though fleeing in battle, with no power to stand before their enemies. 38You shall perish among the nations and be destroyed among your enemies. 39Those left shall pine away in enemy lands because of their sins, the same sins as those of their fathers.

40, 41"But at last they shall confess their sins and their fathers' sins of treachery against me. (Because they were against me, I was against them, and brought them into the land of their enemies.) When at last their evil hearts are humbled and they accept the punishment I send them for their sins, 42then I will remember again my promises to Abraham, Isaac, and Jacob, and I will remember the land (and its desolation). 43For the land shall enjoy its Sabbaths as it lies desolate. But then at last they shall accept their punishment for rejecting my laws and for despising my rule. 44But despite all they have done, I will not utterly destroy them and my covenant with them, for I am Jehovah their God. 45For their sakes I will remember my promises to their ancestors, to be their God. For I brought their forefathers out of Egypt as all the nations watched in wonder. I am Jehovah."

46These were the laws, ordinances, and instructions that Jehovah gave to the people of Israel, through Moses, on Mount Sinai.

Payments to the Lord

27 The Lord said to Moses, "Tell the people of Israel that when a person makes a special vow to give himself to the Lord, he shall give these payments instead: 3A man from the age of twenty to sixty shall pay twenty-five dollars; 4a woman from the age of twenty to sixty shall pay fifteen dollars; 5a boy from five to twenty shall pay ten dollars; a girl, five dollars. 6A boy one month to five years old shall have paid for him two and a half dollars; a girl, one and a half dollars. 7A man over sixty shall pay seven and a half dollars; a woman, five dollars. 8But if the person is too poor to pay this amount, he shall be brought to the priest and the priest shall talk it over with him, and he shall pay as the priest shall decide.

9"But if it is an animal that is vowed to be given to the Lord as a sacrifice, it must be given. 10The vow may not be changed; the donor may neither change his mind about giving it to the Lord, nor substitute good for bad or bad for good; if he does, both the first and the second shall belong to the Lord! 11, 12But if the animal given to the Lord is not a kind that is permitted as a sacrifice, the owner shall bring it to

27:3 *shall pay twenty-five dollars.* Note: The actual value by today's standards is uncertain. The above figures are approximate.

26:33–35 Because God is all-knowing he can see the future. He knew that the Israelites would disobey him and be exiled to foreign lands for many years. In 2 Kings 17 and 25 the warning pronounced in these verses came true. The people were conquered and carried off to the lands of Assyria and Babylon.

26:40–45 When the Israelites faced suffering, God offered them hope. One key to holding onto hope in God is to maintain his perspective on all of life while looking at our present experiences. Our day-to-day experiences and hardships are sometimes overwhelming; unless we can see that God's purpose is to bring about continual growth in us, we may despair. The hope we need

is best expressed in Jeremiah 29:11: " 'For I know the plans I have for you,' says the Lord. 'They are plans for good and not for evil, to give you a future and a hope.' " To retain hope in the midst of suffering shows we have an eternal perspective on our present difficulties.

27:9, 10 God taught the Israelites that when they made a vow to him, they must not go back on their promise even if it turned out to cost more than expected. God takes our promises seriously. If you vow to give 10% of your income and suddenly some unexpected bills come along, your faithful stewardship will be costly but will not go unnoticed by God.

the priest to value it, and he shall be told how much to pay instead. ¹³If the animal is a kind that may be offered as a sacrifice, but the man wants to redeem it, then he shall pay twenty percent more than the value set by the priest.

¹⁴, ¹⁵"If someone donates his home to the Lord and then wishes to redeem it, the priest will decide its value and the man shall pay that amount plus twenty percent, and the house will be his again.

¹⁶"If a man dedicates any part of his field to the Lord, value it in proportion to its size, as indicated by the amount of seed required to sow it. A section of land that requires ten bushels of barley seed for sowing is valued at twenty-five dollars. ¹⁷If a man dedicates his field in the Year of Jubilee, then the whole estimate shall stand; ¹⁸but if it is after the Year of Jubilee, then the value shall be in proportion to the number of years remaining until the next Year of Jubilee. ¹⁹If the man decides to redeem the field, he shall pay twenty percent in addition to the priest's valuation, and the field will be his again. ²⁰But if he decides not to redeem the field, or if he has sold the field to someone else [and has given to the Lord his rights to it at the Year of Jubilee], it shall not be returned to him again. ²¹When it is freed in the Year of Jubilee, it shall belong to the Lord as a field devoted to him, and it shall be given to the priests.

²²"If a man dedicates to the Lord a field he has bought, but which is not part of his family possession, ²³the priest shall estimate the value until the Year of Jubilee, and he shall immediately give that estimated value to the Lord, ²⁴and in the Year of Jubilee the field shall return to the original owner from whom it was bought. ²⁵All the valuations shall be stated in standard money.

²⁶"You may not dedicate to the Lord the firstborn of any ox or sheep, for it is already his. ²⁷But if it is the firstborn of an animal that cannot be sacrificed because it is not on the list of those acceptable to the Lord, then the owner shall pay the priest's estimate of its worth, plus twenty percent; or if the owner does not redeem it, the priest may sell it to someone else. ²⁸However, anything utterly devoted to the Lord—people, animals, or inherited fields—shall not be sold or redeemed, for they are most holy to the Lord. ²⁹No one sentenced by the courts to die may pay a fine instead; he shall surely be put to death.

³⁰"A tenth of the produce of the land, whether grain or fruit, is the Lord's, and is holy. ³¹If anyone wants to buy back this fruit or grain, he must add a fifth to its value. ³²And the Lord owns every tenth animal of your herds and flocks and other domestic animals, as they pass by for counting. ³³The tenth given to the Lord shall not be selected on the basis of whether it is good or bad, and there shall be no substitutions; for if there is any change made, then both the original and the substitution shall belong to the Lord, and may not be bought back!"

³⁴These are the commandments the Lord gave to Moses for the people of Israel on Mount Sinai.

27:18
Lev 25:14-16

27:21
Lev 25:8-54
Num 18:14
Ezek 44:29

27:24
Lev 27:21

27:25
Ex 30:13
Lev 5:15
Num 3:47; 18:16
Ezek 45:12

27:26
Ex 13:2,12
22:30

27:28
Lev 27:21
Jos 6:17-19

27:30
Gen 28:22
Num 18:21,24
2 Chron 31:5,6
Neh 3:12
Mal 3:8

27:33
Lev 27:10

27:34
Lev 26:46

27:13 *If the animal is a kind that may be offered as a sacrifice,* implied.   27:20 *and has given to the Lord his rights to it at the Year of Jubilee,* implied.   27:25 *All the valuations shall be stated in standard money,* literally, "and all your estimations shall be according to the shekel of the sanctuary: twenty gerahs shall be the shekel."   27:29 *No one sentenced by the courts to die may pay a fine instead; he shall surely be put to death,* literally, "no one who is under the ban of God to be put to death may be ransomed."

27:33 Many of the principles regarding sacrifices and tithes were intended to encourage inward attitudes as well as outward actions. If a person gives grudgingly, he shows that he has a stingy heart. God wants us to be cheerful givers (2 Corinthians 9:7) who give with grateful eyes turned on him, the object of our giving.

27:34 The Book of Leviticus is filled with the commands God gave his people at the foot of Mount Sinai. From these commands we can learn much about the nature and character of God. At first glance, Leviticus seems irrelevant to our high-tech world. But digging a little deeper, we realize that the book still speaks to us today because God has not changed. As people and society change, we need constantly to search for ways to apply the principles of God's law to our present circumstances. God was the same in Leviticus as he is today and will be forever (Hebrews 13:8).

In the New Testament, Jesus performed the ultimate act of redemption by sacrificing his life on the cross for our sins. This made animal sacrifice no longer necessary. He was the substitute and his blood was the cost paid for the penalty of our sins (1 Peter 1:18, 19). Only Jesus could redeem all people from slavery to sin because only he had lived a life that was perfect in every way (Hebrews 7:26, 27; 1 John 3:5). Since only he lived up to the demands of God, only he had the right to release us from our "sentence" which was death due to our sin. Jesus substituted his life for ours so that we could be restored to God.

Jesus clearly taught in Luke 10:30–37 to reach out to all people in need, even our enemies. Following the laws of right living is hard enough with friends. To apply God's laws of fairness and kindness to our enemies shows we are truly different from the world.

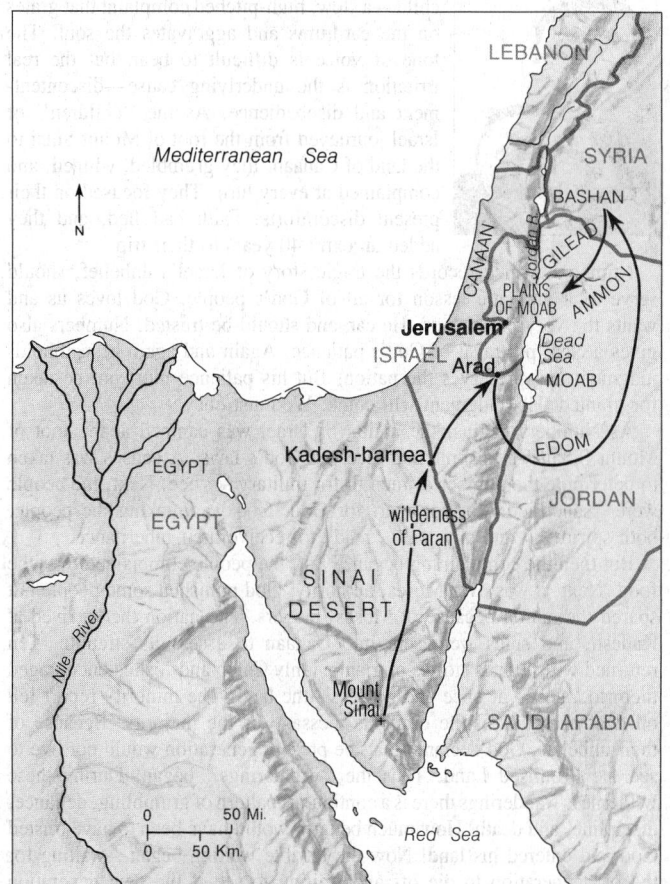

Modern names and boundaries are shown in gray.

made to wander in the desert for 40 years (12:16—19:22).

3 Kadesh-barnea With the years of wandering nearing an end, the Israelites set their sights once again on the Promised Land. Kadesh-barnea was the oasis where they spent most of their wilderness years. Miriam died here. And it was here that Moses angrily struck the rock, which kept him from entering the Promised Land (20).

4 Arad When the king of Arad heard that Israel was on the move, he attacked, but he was soundly defeated. Moses then led the people southward and eastward around the Dead Sea (21:1-3).

5 Edom The Israelites wanted to travel through Edom, but the king of Edom refused them passage (20:14-22). So they traveled around Edom and became very discouraged. The people complained, and God sent poisonous snakes to punish them. Only by looking at a bronze serpent on a pole could those bitten be healed (21:4-9).

6 Ammon Next, King Sihon of the Amorites refused Israel passage. When he attacked, Israel defeated Ammon (21:21-32).

7 Bashan After capturing the Amorite country, Moses sent spies to Bashan. King Og attacked, but he was also defeated (21:33-35).

1 Mount Sinai Numbers begins at Mount Sinai with Moses taking a census of the men eligible for battle. As the battle preparations began, the people also prepared for the spiritual warfare they would face. The Promised Land was full of wicked people who would try to entice the Israelites to sin. God, therefore, taught Moses and the Israelites how to live rightly (1:1—12:15).

2 Wilderness of Paran After a full year at Mount Sinai, the Israelites broke camp and began their march toward the Promised Land by moving into the wilderness of Paran. From there, one leader from each tribe was sent to spy out the new land. After 40 days they returned, and all but Joshua and Caleb were too afraid to enter. Because of their lack of faith, the Israelites were

8 Plains of Moab The people camped on the Plains of Moab, east of the Jordan River opposite Jericho. They were on the verge of entering the Promised Land (22:1).

9 Moab King Balak of Moab, terrified of the "mob" of Israelites, called upon Balaam, a famous sorcerer, to curse Israel from the mountains above where the Israelites camped. But the Lord caused Balaam to bless them instead (22:2—24:25).

10 Gilead The tribes of Reuben and Gad decided to settle in the fertile country of Gilead east of the Jordan River because it was a good land for their sheep. But first they promised to help the other tribes conquer the land west of the Jordan River (32).

NUMBERS

VITAL STATISTICS

PURPOSE:
To tell the story of how Israel prepared to enter the Promised Land, how they sinned and were punished, and how they prepared to try again

AUTHOR:
Moses

TO WHOM WRITTEN:
The people of Israel

DATE WRITTEN:
1450–1410 B.C.

SETTING:
The vast desert of the Sinai region, as well as lands just south and east of Canaan

KEY VERSES:
"Not one . . . of the men who . . . refused to trust me and obey me . . . shall even see the land I promised" (14:22, 23).

KEY PEOPLE:
Moses, Aaron, Miriam, Joshua, Caleb, Eleazar, Korah, Balaam

KEY PLACES:
Mount Sinai, Promised Land (Canaan), Kadesh-barnea, Mount Hor, plains of Moab

EVERY parent knows the shrill whine of a young child—a slow, high-pitched complaint that grates on the eardrums and aggravates the soul. The tone of voice is difficult to bear, but the real irritation is the underlying cause—discontent-ment and disobedience. As the "children" of Israel journeyed from the foot of Mount Sinai to the land of Canaan, they grumbled, whined, and complained at every turn. They focused on their present discomforts. Faith had fled, and they added an extra 40 years to their trip.

Numbers, which records the tragic story of Israel's unbelief, should serve as a dramatic lesson for all of God's people. God loves us and wants the very best for us. He can and should be trusted. Numbers also gives a clear portrayal of God's patience. Again and again he withholds judgment and preserves the nation. But his patience must not be taken for granted. His judgment will come. We must obey.

As Numbers begins, the nation of Israel was camped at the foot of Mount Sinai. The people had received God's laws. A census was taken to determine the number of men fit for military service. Next, the people were "sanctified," or set apart for God. God was making the people, both spiritually and physically, ready to receive their inheritance.

But then the complaining began. First, the people complained over the food. Next, it was over Moses' authority. God punished some people but spared the nation because of Moses' prayers. The nation then arrived at Kadesh, and spies were sent into Canaan to assess its strength. Ten returned with fearful stories of giants. Only Caleb and Joshua encouraged them to "go up at once and possess" the land! The minority report fell on deaf ears full of the ominous message of the majority. Because of their unbelief, God declared that the present generation would not live to see the Promised Land. Thus the "wanderings" began. During these wilderness wanderings there is a continuous pattern of grumbling, defiance, discipline, and death. How much better it would have been to have trusted God and entered his land! Now the terrible waiting began—waiting for the old generation to die off and waiting to see if the new generation could faithfully obey God.

Numbers ends as it begins, with preparation. This new generation of Israelites are numbered and sanctified. After defeating numerous armies, they settle the east side of the Jordan River. Now they face their greatest test: they must cross the river and possess the beautiful land God promised them.

THE BLUEPRINT

A. PREPARING FOR THE JOURNEY (1:1—10:10)
  1. The first numbering of the nation
  2. The role of the Levites
  3. Maintaining purity in the camp
  4. Receiving guidance for the journey

God abundantly provided for the Israelites on their journey to the Promised Land. He supplies all that we need for our journey through life too.
The Lord gave strict guidelines to the Israelites regarding purity in the camp. We, too, need to concern ourselves with purity in the church.

B. FIRST APPROACH TO THE PROMISED
   LAND (10:11—14:45)
   1. The people complain
   2. Miriam and Aaron criticize Moses
   3. The spies incite rebellion

When the people complained and criticized Moses, they were severely punished. We must guard against complaining and criticizing our leaders.
The Israelites were prevented from entering the Promised Land because of their unbelief. We must prevent unbelief from gaining a foothold in our lives, for it will keep us from enjoying the blessings which God has promised.

C. WANDERING IN THE WILDERNESS
   (15:1—21:35)
   1. Additional regulations
   2. Many leaders rebel against Moses
   3. Directions to the priests and Levites
   4. The new generation

After years of wandering in the wilderness, Israel developed a stronger relationship with God. The hard times in our lives help make us better and stronger Christians.
Over 14,000 people died in the rebellion against Moses. Dissatisfaction and discontent, if allowed to remain in our lives, can easily lead to disaster.

D. SECOND APPROACH TO THE
   PROMISED LAND (22:1—36:13)
   1. The story of Balaam
   2. The second numbering of the nation
   3. Instructions concerning offerings
   4. The war against Midian
   5. Two and a half tribes receive their land
   6. Camped on the plains of Moab

Balaam was a man who knew what was right, but gave in to the temptation of material rewards, and sinned. Knowing what is right is not enough, we must also do what is right.
Two and a half tribes chose the land they could see over the land they were promised. We sometimes think we can make better choices than the Lord can, but he can see farther than we can, and he has our spiritual well-being in mind.

MEGATHEMES

THEME	EXPLANATION	IMPORTANCE
Census	Moses counted the Israelites twice. The first census organized the people into marching units to better defend themselves. The second prepared them to conquer the country east of the Jordan River.	People have to be organized, trained, and led to be effective in great movements. It is always wise to count the cost before setting out on some great undertaking. When we are aware of the obstacles before us we can more easily avoid the pitfalls which lie ahead. In God's work, we must remove any obstacles which may hinder our relationships with others so that our effectiveness is not diminished.
Rebellion	At Kadesh-barnea, 12 spies were sent out into the land of Canaan to see what the fortifications of the enemies looked like. When the spies returned, ten said that they should give up and go back to Egypt. As a result, the people refused to enter the land. Faced with the choice, Israel rebelled against God. Rebellion did not start with an uprising, but with griping and murmuring against Moses and God.	Rebellion against God is always a serious matter. It is not something to take lightly, for God's punishment for sin is often very severe. Our rebellion does not usually begin with all-out warfare, but in subtle ways—with griping and criticizing.
Wandering	Because they rebelled, the Israelites wandered 40 years in the wilderness. This shows how severely God can punish sin. Forty years was enough time for all those who held on to Egypt's customs and values to die off. It gave time to train up a new generation in the ways of God.	God judges sin harshly because he is holy. The wanderings in the wilderness demonstrate how serious God considers flagrant disobedience of his commands.
Canaan	Canaan is the Promised Land. It was the land God had promised to Abraham, Isaac, and Jacob—the land of the covenant. Canaan was to be the dwelling place of God's people, those set apart for true spiritual worship.	Although God's punishment for sin is often severe, he offers reconciliation even in the midst of punishment—his love is truly amazing. Just as God's love and law led Israel to the Promised Land, God desires to give purpose and destiny to our lives.

A. PREPARING FOR THE JOURNEY (1:1—10:10)

At Mount Sinai, the Israelites received specific directions for their lifestyle in the new land God would give to them. A census was taken and the second Passover was celebrated, marking one year of freedom from slavery in Egypt. The people were now prepared to continue their journey to the Promised Land. Just as the Lord prepared the Israelites, he prepares us for our journey through life.

1. The first numbering of the nation

The Lord orders a census

1 It was on the fifteenth day of April of the second year after the Israelis left Egypt that the Lord issued the following instructions to Moses. (He was in the Tabernacle at the camp of Israel on the Sinai peninsula at the time.)

2-15"Take a census of all the men twenty years old and older who are able to go to war, indicating their tribe and family. You and Aaron are to direct the project, assisted by these leaders from each tribe:"

Tribe	Leader
Reuben	Elizur (son of Shedeur)
Simeon	Shelumi-el (son of Zurishaddai)
Judah	Nahshon (son of Amminadab)
Issachar	Nethanel (son of Zuar)
Zebulun	Eliab (son of Helon)
Ephraim (son of Joseph)	Elishama (son of Ammihud)
Manasseh (son of Joseph)	Gamaliel (son of Pedahzur)
Benjamin	Abidan (son of Gideoni)
Dan	Ahiezer (son of Ammishaddai)
Asher	Pagiel (son of Ochran)
Gad	Eliasaph (son of Deuel)
Naphtali	Ahira (son of Enan)

16These were the tribal leaders elected from among the people.

17, 18, 19On the same day Moses and Aaron and the above-named leaders summoned all the men of Israel who were twenty years old or older to come and register, each man indicating his tribe and family, as the Lord had commanded Moses. 20-46Here is the final tabulation:

Tribe	Total
Reuben (the oldest son of Jacob)	46,500
Simeon	59,300
Gad	45,650
Judah	74,600
Issachar	54,400
Zebulun	57,400

Cross-references:
1:2 Ex 25:22; 30:11, 12 38:26 Num 26:2-4, 63-65 2 Sam 24:1-3 1 Chron 21:2
1:16 Num 1:2-15 7:2; 26:3-51 1 Chron 27:16-22
1:17 Num 1:2 Ezra 2:59 Neh 7:61
1:20 Num 2:32,33 26:5-51

1:1 *fifteenth day of April,* literally, "on the first day of the second month" (of the Jewish calendar). So also for verse 17, *On the same day.* 1:17-19 Added in the Hebrew text is this sentence: "So he numbered them in the wilderness of Sinai."

1:2 God wanted the people performing the tedious work of the census to know why their task was important. He wanted them to see the bigger picture. When our daily tasks seem to get dull or tedious, identifying the purpose and importance of our work can breathe new life into an otherwise boring job. Just as Moses needed to know the number of men available to fight or do God's work, so we need to take inventory of our resources. Setting aside time to take a "census" of all you have—your possessions, relationships, spiritual condition, use of time, and goals—will help you serve God more effectively.

1:2-15 Taking such a census was long and tedious, but it wasn't just a time-filler or a useless task. The fighting men had to be counted to determine Israel's military strength before entering the Promised Land. In addition, the tribes had to be organized to

determine the amount of land each would need, as well as to provide genealogical records. Without such a census, the task of conquering and organizing the Promised Land would have been more difficult.

1:20-46 If there were 603,550 men, there must have been a total population of more than two million Israelites. How could such a large population grow from Jacob's family of 70 who moved down to Egypt? The record in Exodus chapter one tells us that the Israelites who descended from Jacob's family had a population explosion. Since they remained in Egypt more than 400 years, they had more than enough time to grow into a large group of people. Once they left Egypt, they were able to survive in the desert because God miraculously provided the needed food and water. Numbers 22:3 says that the leaders of Moab were terrified because of the large number of Israelites.

Ephraim (son of Joseph)	40,500
Manasseh (son of Joseph)	32,200
Benjamin	35,400
Dan	62,700
Asher	41,500
Naphtali	53,400

Grand Total: 603,550

1:47-49
Num 2:32,33
26:62
1:50
Num 3:6-10,
25-37; 4:25-48
1:51
Num 3:38; 18:22
1:52
Num 2:1
1:53
Num 1:50
1:54
Ex 39:43

47, 48, 49This total does not include the Levites, for the Lord had said to Moses, "Exempt the entire tribe of Levi from the draft, and do not include their number in the census. 50For the Levites are assigned for the work connected with the Tabernacle and its transportation. They are to live near the Tabernacle, 51and whenever the Tabernacle is moved, the Levites are to take it down and set it up again; anyone else touching it shall be executed. 52Each tribe of Israel shall have a separate camping area with its own flag. 53The Levites' tents shall be clustered around the Tabernacle as a wall between the people of Israel and God's wrath—to protect them from his fierce anger against their sins."

54So all these instructions of the Lord to Moses were put into effect.

Where the tribes camped

2:1
Num 1:52

2 The Lord gave these further instructions to Moses and Aaron: "Each tribe will have its own tent area, with its flagpole and tribal banner; and at the center of these tribal compounds will be the Tabernacle." 3-31Here are the tribal locations:

Tribe:	Leader:	Location:	Census:
Judah	Nahshon (son of Amminadab)	East side of the Tabernacle	74,600
Issachar	Nethanel (son of Zuar)	Next to Judah	54,400
Zebulun	Eliab (son of Helon)	Next to Issachar	57,400

So the total of all those on Judah's side of the camp was 186,400. These three tribes led the way whenever the Israelites traveled to a new campsite.

**ARRANGE-
MENT OF
TRIBES
AROUND THE
TABERNACLE
WHILE
IN THE
WILDERNESS**

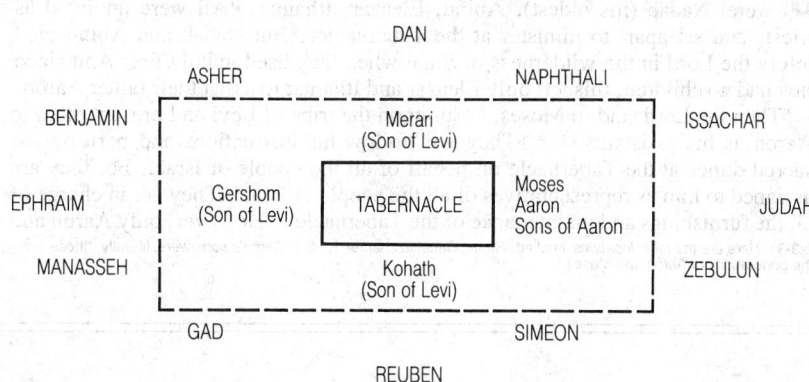

1:54 The very organization of the Israelite camp was ordered by God! By obeying God's commands and methods of organization, even when the reason for them was not apparent, the people became more effective. When a group becomes a mere collection of individuals each going his or her own way, the ability to be used by God is diminished. But if the group looks to God for direction and organization, it will be more effective.

2:2 The nation of Israel was organized according to tribes for several reasons. (1) It was an effective way to manage and govern such a large group. (2) It made dividing the Promised Land easier.

(3) It was part of their culture and heritage (people were not known by their last name, but by their family, clan, and tribe). (4) Detailed genealogies were easier to keep when tribes stuck together. Genealogies were the only way to prove that you were a legitimate member of God's chosen people. (5) Travel was made much more efficient. Every person knew what his or her tribal standard looked like. A standard was a symbol made of cloth, feathers, or other materials which were placed on a pole and raised in the air while traveling. The people followed the tribe's standard to stay together and keep from getting lost.

Reuben	Elizur (son of Shedeur)	South side of the Tabernacle	46,500
Simeon	Shelumi-el (son of Zurishaddai)	Next to Reuben	59,300
Gad	Eliasaph (son of Reuel)	Next to Simeon	45,650

So the total of the Reuben side of the camp was 151,450. These three tribes were next in line whenever the Israelis traveled.

Next in the line of march was the Tabernacle, with the Levites. When traveling, each tribe stayed together under its own flag, just as each was separate from the others in camp.

Ephraim	Elishama (son of Ammihud)	West side of Tabernacle	40,500
Manasseh	Gamaliel (son of Pedahzur)	Next to Ephraim	32,200
Benjamim	Abidan (son of Gideoni)	Next to Manasseh	35,400

So the total on the Ephraim side of the camp was 108,100, and they were next in the line of march.

Dan	Ahiezer (son of Ammishaddai)	North side of the Tabernacle	62,700
Asher	Pagiel (son of Ochran)	Next to Dan	41,500
Naphtali	Ahira (son of Enan)	Next to Asher	53,400

So the total on Dan's side of the camp was 157,600. They brought up the rear whenever Israel traveled. 32, 33In summary, the armies of Israel totaled 603,550 (not including the Levites, who were exempted by Jehovah's commandment to Moses). 34So the people of Israel set up their camps, each tribe under its own banner, in the locations indicated by the Lord to Moses.

2:32
Ex 12:37; 38:26
Num 1:20
11:21; 26:51
2:34
Num 1:54

2. The role of the Levites

3 At the time when the Lord spoke to Moses on Mount Sinai, 2Aaron's sons were: Nadab (his oldest), Abihu, Eleazar, Ithamar. 3All were anointed as priests and set apart to minister at the Tabernacle. 4But Nadab and Abihu died before the Lord in the wilderness of Sinai when they used unholy fire. And since they had no children, this left only Eleazar and Ithamar to assist their father Aaron.

5Then the Lord said to Moses, 6"Summon the tribe of Levi and present them to Aaron as his assistants. 7, 8, 9They will follow his instructions and perform the sacred duties at the Tabernacle on behalf of all the people of Israel. For they are assigned to him as representatives of all the people of Israel. They are in charge of all the furnishings and maintenance of the Tabernacle. 10However, only Aaron and

3:2
Lev 10:1,2,6
Num 26:60
3:3
Ex 29:1-37
3:4
Lev 10:1,2
Num 26:61
3:6
Num 8:6-15,
22-26; 18:2-6
Deut 33:10
3:7
Num 3:11,12,
41; 8:16-18

2:3-3-31 *Here are the tribal locations,* implied. *Reuel.* Deuel in chapter 1. **3:2** *Aaron's sons were,* literally, "these are the generations of Aaron and Moses."

2:34 This must have been one of the biggest camp sites the world has ever seen! It would have taken about twelve square miles to set up tents for just the 600,000 fighting men—not to mention the women and children. Moses must have had a difficult time managing such a group. In the early stages of the journey and at Mount Sinai, the people were obedient to both God and Moses. Everything went smoothly. But when the people left Mount Sinai, they suddenly began to complain, grumble, and disobey. Soon problems erupted, and Moses could no longer effectively manage the Israelites. The books of Exodus, Leviticus, and Numbers present a striking contrast between how much we can accomplish when we obey God and how little we can accomplish when we don't.

3:4 See Leviticus 10:1, 2 for the story of Nadab and Abihu.

3:10 There is a tremendous contrast between the priesthood of Aaron in the Old Testament and the priesthood of Christ in the New Testament. Aaron and his descendants were the only ones who could carry out the duties of the priests and approach the dwelling place of God. Now that Christ is our high priest—our intermediary with God—anyone who follows him is also called a priest (1 Peter 2:5, 9). All Christians may now come into God's presence without fear, for God's own Son encourages his followers to do so. The guilt of sin can be put behind us when we realize the special relationship we can have with God based on what Christ has done for us.

his sons may carry out the duties of the priesthood; anyone else who presumes to assume this office shall be executed."

3:11
Num 3:7,41,45
3:13
Ex 13:2,12,15
Lev 27:26
Num 8:16,17
Lk 2:23

11, 12And the Lord said to Moses, "I have accepted the Levites in substitution for all the oldest sons of the people of Israel. The Levites are mine 13in exchange for all the oldest sons. From the day I killed all the oldest sons of the Egyptians, I took for myself all the firstborn in Israel of both men and animals! They are mine; I am Jehovah."

Census of Levi's tribes

3:14
Num 26:57-62
3:16
Ex 16:16-22

14, 15The Lord now spoke again to Moses at the Sinai peninsula, telling him, "Take a census of the tribe of Levi, indicating each person's clan; count every male down to one month old." 16–24So Moses did:

Levi's son	Levi's grandsons (clan names)	Census	Leader	Camp Location
Gershon	Libni Shime-i	7,500	Elisaph (son of Lael)	West side of Tabernacle

3:25
Num 1:50
4:25-28

25-30Responsibilities:

The responsibility of these two clans of Levites was the care of the Tabernacle: its coverings, its entry drapes, the drapes covering the fence surrounding the courtyard, the screen at the entrance of the courtyard surrounding the Tabernacle, the altar, and all the ropes used in tying the Tabernacle together.

Levi's son	Levi's grandsons (clan names)	Census	Leader	Camp Location
Kohath	Amran Izhar Hebron Uzziel	8,600	Elizaphan (son of Uzziel)	South side of Tabernacle

31-35Responsibilities:

The responsibility of these four clans of Levites was the care of the Ark, the table, the lampstand, the altars, the various utensils used in the Tabernacle, the veil, and any repairs needed on any of these items. (Note: Eleazar, Aaron's son, shall be the chief administrator over the leaders of the Levites, with special responsibility for the oversight of the sanctuary.)

Levi's son	Levi's grandsons (clan names)	Census	Leader	Camp Location
Merari	Mahli Mushi	6,200	Zuriel (son of Abihail)	North side of Tabernacle

36, 37Responsibilities:

3:38
Num 1:51; 3:10

The responsibility of these two clans was the care of the frames of the Tabernacle building; the posts; the bases for the posts, and all of the equipment needed for their use; the posts around the courtyard and their bases, pegs, and ropes. 38The area east of the Tabernacle was reserved for the tents of Moses and of Aaron and his sons, who had the final responsibility for the Tabernacle on behalf of the people of Israel.

3:11–13 At the time of the first Passover, God instructed every Israelite family to dedicate its firstborn sons (Exodus 13:2) to him. They were set apart to assist Moses and Aaron in ministering to the people. This was only a temporary measure, however. Here God chooses all the men from the tribe of Levi to replace the firstborn sons from every Israelite tribe. These men, called Levites, were required to go into "full-time service." They assumed the responsibilities of ministering to the people. Once the Tabernacle

was built, it was their job to maintain it and assist with the sacrifices. All the priests had to belong to the tribe of Levi.

3:25–28 The tribe of Levi was set apart to minister at the altar, to burn sacrifices, and to teach the law. They represented Israel in its relationship to God and were a visible reminder to the people of all that God required of them. The Levites were to be 25 years old before entering service. They probably received five years of on-the-job training before being admitted to full service at age 30.

(Anyone who was not a priest or Levite, but came into the Tabernacle, was to be executed.)

³⁹So all the Levites, as numbered by Moses and Aaron at the command of the Lord, were 22,000 males one month old and older.

3:39
Num 26:62

Census of Israel's firstborn males

⁴⁰Then the Lord said to Moses, "Now take a census of all the eldest sons in Israel who are one month old and older, and register each name. ⁴¹The Levites shall be mine (I am Jehovah) as substitutes for the eldest sons of Israel; and the Levites' cattle are mine as substitutes for the firstborn cattle of the whole nation."

3:40
Num 1:2
3:41
Num 3:11,13,45

⁴²So Moses took a census of the eldest sons of the people of Israel, as the Lord had commanded, ⁴³and found the total number of eldest sons one month old and older to be 22,273.

3:43
Num 3:39

⁴⁴Now the Lord said to Moses, ⁴⁵"Give me the Levites instead of the eldest sons of the people of Israel; and give me the cattle of the Levites instead of the firstborn cattle of the people of Israel; yes, the Levites shall be mine; I am Jehovah. ⁴⁶To redeem the 273 eldest sons in excess of the number of Levites, ⁴⁷, ⁴⁸pay five dollars for each one to Aaron and his sons."

3:45
Num 3:11,13,41
3:46
Ex 13:13,15
Num 18:14-16
3:47,48
Lev 27:1-8
Num 18:16

⁴⁹So Moses received redemption money for the 273 eldest sons of Israel who were in excess of the number of Levites. (All the others were redeemed because the Levites had been given to the Lord in their place.) ⁵⁰The money collected came to a total of $1,365. ⁵¹And Moses gave it to Aaron and his sons as the Lord had commanded.

3:50
Lev 25:25
Ezek 45:12

Duties of Kohath division

4 Then the Lord said to Moses and Aaron, "Take a census of the Kohath division of the Levite tribe. ³This census will be of all males from ages thirty to fifty who are able to work in the Tabernacle. ⁴These are their sacred duties:

4:1
Num 3:25-30
4:3
Num 4:21-23
8:23,24

⁵"When the camp moves, Aaron and his sons will enter the Tabernacle first and take down the veil and cover the Ark with it. ⁶Then they will cover the veil with goatskin leather, cover the goatskins with a blue cloth, and place the carrying poles of the Ark in their rings.

4:5
Num 4:15
4:6
Ex 26:31
Num 4:25

⁷"Next they must spread a blue cloth over the table where the Bread of the Presence is displayed, and place the dishes, spoons, bowls, cups, and the Bread upon the cloth. ⁸They will spread a scarlet cloth over that, and finally a covering of goatskin leather on top of the scarlet cloth. Then they shall insert the carrying poles into the table.

4:7
Ex 37:10-16
Lev 24:5-8
4:8
Num 4:25

⁹"Next they must cover with a blue cloth the lampstand, the lamps, snuffers, trays, and the reservoir of olive oil. ¹⁰This entire group of objects shall then be covered with goatskin leather, and the bundle shall be placed upon a carrying frame.

4:9
Ex 25:37,38

¹¹"They must then spread a blue cloth over the gold altar, cover it with a covering of goatskin leather, and insert the carrying poles into the altar. ¹²All of the remaining utensils of the Tabernacle are to be wrapped in a blue cloth, covered with goatskin leather, and placed on the carrying frame.

¹³"The ashes are to be removed from the altar, and the altar shall be covered with a purple cloth. ¹⁴All of the altar utensils are to be placed upon the cloth—the firepans, hooks, shovels, basins, and other containers—and a cover of goatskin leather will be spread over them. Finally, the carrying poles are to be put in place. ¹⁵When Aaron and his sons have finished packing the sanctuary and all the utensils, the clan of Kohath shall come and carry the units to wherever the camp is traveling; but they must not touch the holy items, lest they die. This, then, is the sacred work of the sons of Kohath.

4:15
Num 3:38
4:5,17-19

¹⁶"Aaron's son Eleazar shall be responsible for the oil for the light, the sweet incense, the daily grain offering, and the anointing oil—in fact, the supervision of the entire Tabernacle and everything in it will be his responsibility."

4:16
Ex 25:1-7
30:22-38

¹⁷, ¹⁸, ¹⁹Then the Lord said to Moses and Aaron, "Don't let the families of Kohath destroy themselves! This is what you must do so that they will not die when they

4:17
Num 4:15

3:50 *$1,365*, literally, "1365 shekels after the shekel of the sanctuary."

carry the most holy things: Aaron and his sons shall go in with them and point out what each is to carry. 20Otherwise they must never enter the sanctuary for even a moment, lest they look at the sacred objects there and die."

Duties of Gershon division

4:21
Num 3:3,
14-24,35

21, 22, 23And the Lord said to Moses, "Take a census of the Gershonite division of the tribe of Levi, all of the men between the ages of thirty and fifty who are eligible for the sacred work of the Tabernacle. 24These will be their duties:

4:25
Num 3:25-30

25"They will carry the curtains of the Tabernacle, the Tabernacle itself with its coverings, the goatskin leather roof, and the curtain for the Tabernacle entrance. 26They are also to carry the drapes covering the courtyard fence, and the curtain across the entrance to the courtyard that surrounds the altar and the Tabernacle. They will also carry the altar, the ropes, and all of the accessories. They are fully responsible for the transportation of these items. 27Aaron or any of his sons may assign the Gershonites' tasks to them, 28but the Gershonites will be directly responsible to Aaron's son Ithamar.

Duties of Merari division

4:29
Num 3:31-35
4:30-32
Ex 26:15,16
Num 4:3

29"Now take a census of the Merari division of the Levite tribe, all of the men from thirty to fifty who are eligible for the Tabernacle service. 30, 31When the Tabernacle is moved, they are to carry the frames of the Tabernacle, the bars, the bases, 32the frames for the courtyard fence with their bases, pegs, cords, and everything else connected with their use and repair.

"Assign duties to each man by name. 33The Merari division will also report to Aaron's son Ithamar."

Census of men eligible for Tabernacle service

4:35
Num 3:3,21,35

34So Moses and Aaron and the other leaders took a census of the Kohath division, 35including all of the men thirty to fifty years of age who were eligible for the Tabernacle service, 36and found that the total number was 2,750. 37All this was done to carry out the Lord's instructions to Moses. 38-41A similar census of the Gershon division totaled 2,630. 42-45And of the Merari division, 3,200.

4:46
Num 3:39

46, 47, 48Thus Moses and Aaron and the leaders of Israel found that the total of all the Levites who were thirty to fifty years old and who were eligible for the

4:49
Num 1:47-49
3:14,15

Tabernacle service and transportation, was 8,580. 49This census was taken in response to the Lord's instructions to Moses.

3. Maintaining purity in the camp

5:1
Lev 13:45,46
15:1-5
Num 19:11

5 These are further instructions from the Lord to Moses: "Inform the people of Israel that they must expel all lepers from the camp, and all who have open sores, or who have been defiled by touching a dead person. 3This applies to men

5:3
Lev 11:24,25
14:8; 26:11,12
2 Cor 6:16

and women alike. Remove them so that they will not defile the camp where I live among you." 4These instructions were put into effect.

5:5
Lev 6:1-3

5, 6Then the Lord said to Moses, "Tell the people of Israel that when anyone, man or woman, betrays the Lord by betraying a trust, it is sin. 7He must confess his sin

5:7
Lev 5:5,16
6:4,5; 16:21

and make full repayment for what he has stolen, adding twenty percent and returning it to the person he took it from. 8But if the person he wronged is dead, and there is no near relative to whom the payment can be made, it must be given to the

5:7 for what he has stolen, literally, "for his wrong." **5:8** But if the person he wronged is dead, implied.

4:27, 28 The Gershonites could receive directions from any of Aaron's sons, but they were directly responsible to Aaron only. The lines of authority and accountability were clearly communicated to all. As you function with others, make sure the lines of authority between you and those you work with are clearly understood.

5:5–8 God included restitution, a unique concept for that day, as part of his law for Israel. When someone was robbed, the guilty person was required to restore to the victim what had been taken and pay an additional interest penalty. When we have wronged others, we ought to look for ways to set things right, in addition to apologizing. Even if we are the one who has been wronged, we should still seek restoration. When we have been wronged, we can look for ways to restore peace rather than striking out in vengeance.

priest, along with a lamb for atonement. 9, 10When the people of Israel bring a gift to the Lord it shall go to the priests."

5:9
Ex 29:27,28
Lev 6:17,18

A test to uncover adultery

11, 12And the Lord said to Moses, "Tell the people of Israel that if a man's wife commits adultery, 13but there is no proof, there being no witness, 14and he is jealous and suspicious, 15the man shall bring his wife to the priest with an offering for her of a tenth of a bushel of barley meal without oil or frankincense mingled with it—for it is a suspicion offering—to bring out the truth as to whether or not she is guilty.

5:11
Ex 20:14
Lev 18:20; 20:10
Num 5:4,29
5:15
Num 15:1-10

16"The priest shall bring her before the Lord, 17and take holy water in a clay jar and mix into it dust from the floor of the Tabernacle. 18He shall unbind her hair and place the suspicion offering in her hands to determine whether or not her husband's suspicions are justified. The priest shall stand before her holding the jar of bitter water that brings a curse. 19He shall require her to swear that she is innocent, and then he shall say to her, 'If no man has slept with you except your husband, be free from the effects of this bitter water that causes the curse. 20But if you have committed adultery, 21, 22then Jehovah shall make you a curse among your people, for he will make your thigh rot away and your body swell.' And the woman shall be required to say, 'Yes, let it be so.' 23Then the priest shall write these curses in a book and wash them off into the bitter water. 24(When he requires the woman to drink the water, it becomes bitter within her [if she is guilty].)

5:21
2 Chron 21:15
Neh 10:29
Jer 29:22
Isa 65:16

25"Then the priest shall take the suspicion offering from the woman's hand and wave it before Jehovah, and carry it to the altar. 26He shall take a handful, representing all of it, and burn the handful upon the altar, and then require the woman to drink the water. 27If she has been defiled, having committed adultery against her husband, the water will become bitter within her, and her body will swell and her thigh will rot, and she shall be a curse among her people. 28But if she is pure and has not committed adultery, she shall be unharmed and will soon become pregnant. 29"This, then, is the law concerning a wayward wife—or a husband's suspicions against his wife—

5:26
Lev 5:12; 6:15
5:27
Num 5:11,21
Jer 29:18; 42:18
44:12
5:29
Num 5:11

30to determine whether or not she has been unfaithful to him. He shall bring her before the Lord and the priest shall handle the situation as outlined above. 31Her husband shall not be brought to trial for causing her horrible disease, for she is responsible."

5:30
Num 5:15,16

Rules for the Nazirite vow

6 The Lord gave Moses these further instructions for the people of Israel: "When either a man or a woman takes the special vow of a Nazirite, consecrating himself to the Lord in a special way, 3, 4he must not thereafter, during the entire period of his special consecration to the Lord, taste strong drink or wine or even fresh wine, grape juice, grapes, or raisins! He may eat nothing that comes from grape vines, not even the seeds or skins!

6:1,2
Lev 20:26
Num 6:3-8
Judg 13:4,5
16:16,17
Amos 2:11,12
6:3
Lev 10:8,9
Jer 35:6-8

5:15 *a suspicion offering—to bring out the truth,* literally, "an offering of remembrance." 5:24 *if she is guilty,* implied.

5:11–31 This test for adultery served to remove a jealous husband's suspicion. Trust between husband and wife had to be completely eroded for a man to bring his wife to the priest for this type of test. Today priests and pastors help restore marriages by counseling couples who have lost faith in each other. Whether justified or not, suspicion must still be removed for a marriage to survive and for trust to be restored.

5:27 Today we are unsure what the bitter water and the rotting thigh were. But the intent of the procedure is still clear. In the absence of positive proof, the procedure was an appeal to God to determine the guilt or innocence of the accused person.

6:1, 2 In Moses' day, a personal vow was as binding as a written

contract. It was one thing to say you were going to do something, but it was considered much more serious when you made a solemn vow to do it. God invented the Nazirite vow for those who wanted to devote some time exclusively to serving him. Taking this vow was a way of making this devoted attitude strong and binding. A Nazirite vow could be taken for as little as 30 days or as long as a lifetime. It was voluntary, with one exception—parents could take the vow for their young children, making them Nazirites for life. The vow included three distinct restrictions: (1) the hair could not be cut and the beard could not be shaved; (2) wine and strong drink could never be tasted; and (3) touching a dead body was prohibited. The purpose of the Nazirite vow was to raise up a group of leaders devoted completely to God. Samson, Samuel, and John the Baptist were probably Nazirites for life.

6:5
Num 1:1
1 Sam 1:11
6:6
Lev 21:1-3
Num 19:11-22

6:9
Num 6:18
Acts 18:18
21:23,24

6:11
Lev 5:7; 12:6-8

6:12
Lev 7:1-10
14:24,25

6:14
Lev 1:2-17
7:1-10
6:15
Num 15:1-7

6:18
Num 6:9

6:20
Lev 7:28-34
Num 18:18

6:21
Num 6:1-5

6:22
Deut 21:5; 33:1
Josh 8:33
1 Chron 23:13
6:24-26
Deut 28:3-6
Ps 4:6; 17:8
29:11
44:3; 80:3,7,19

7:1
Ex 40:9-11
Lev 8:10

7:2
Num 1:2-16

5"Throughout that time he must never cut his hair, for he is holy and consecrated to the Lord; that is why he must let his hair grow.

6, 7"And he may not go near any dead body during the entire period of his vow, even if it is the body of his father, mother, brother, or sister; for his vow of consecration remains in effect, 8and he is consecrated to the Lord throughout the entire period. 9If he is defiled by having someone fall dead beside him, then seven days later he shall shave his defiled head; he will then be cleansed from the contamination of being in the presence of death. 10The next day, the eighth day, he must bring two turtledoves or two young pigeons to the priest at the entrance of the Tabernacle. 11The priest shall offer one of the birds for a sin offering, and the other for a burnt offering, and make atonement for his defilement. And he must renew his vows that day and let his hair begin to grow again. 12The days of his vow that were fulfilled before his defilement no longer count. He must begin all over again with a new vow, and must bring a male lamb a year old for a guilt offering.

13"At the conclusion of the period of his vow of separation to the Lord, he must go to the entrance of the Tabernacle 14and offer a burnt sacrifice to the Lord, a year-old lamb without defect. He must also offer a sin offering, a yearling ewe lamb without defect; a peace offering, a ram without defect; 15a basket of bread made without yeast; pancakes made of fine flour mixed with olive oil; unleavened wafers spread with oil; and the accompanying grain offering and drink offerings. 16The priest shall present these offerings before the Lord: first the sin offering and the burnt offering; 17then the ram for a peace offering, along with the basket of bread made without yeast; and finally the grain offering along with the drink offering.

18"Then the Nazirite shall shave his long hair—the sign of his vow of separation. This shall be done at the entrance of the Tabernacle, after which the hair shall be put in the fire under the peace offering sacrifice. 19After the man's head has been shaved, the priest shall take the roasted shoulder of the lamb, one of the pancakes (made without yeast), and one of the wafers (also made without yeast), and put them all into the man's hands. 20The priest shall then wave it all back and forth before the Lord in a gesture of offering; all of it is a holy portion for the priest, as are the rib piece and shoulder that were waved before the Lord. After that the Nazirite may again drink wine, for he is freed from his vow.

21"These are the regulations concerning a Nazirite and his sacrifices at the conclusion of his period of special dedication. In addition to these sacrifices he must bring any further offering he promised at the time he took his vow to become a Nazirite."

How to bless the people

22, 23Now the Lord said to Moses, "Tell Aaron and his sons that they are to give this special blessing to the people of Israel: 24, 25, 26'May the Lord bless and protect you; may the Lord's face radiate with joy because of you; may he be gracious to you, show you his favor, and give you his peace.' 27This is how Aaron and his sons shall call down my blessings upon the people of Israel; and I myself will personally bless them."

Gifts for the dedication of the Tabernacle

7 Moses anointed and sanctified each part of the Tabernacle, including the altar and its utensils, on the day he finished setting it up. 2Then the leaders of Israel—the chiefs of the tribes, the men who had organized the census—brought their offerings. 3They brought six covered wagons, each drawn by two oxen—a

6:27 *shall call down my blessings,* literally, "shall put my name upon the people of Israel."

6:24-26 A blessing was one way of asking for God's divine favor to rest upon others. The ancient blessing in these verses helps us understand what a blessing was supposed to do. Its five parts conveyed hope that God would (1) bless and protect, (2) radiate with joy (be pleased) because of us, (3) be gracious (merciful and compassionate) to us, (4) show favor to us, (5) give us peace. When you ask God to bless others or yourself, you are asking him to do these five things. The blessing you offer will not only help the one receiving it; it will also demonstrate love, encourage others, and provide a model of caring to those who watch.

wagon for every two leaders and an ox for each one; and they presented them to the Lord in front of the Tabernacle.

4, 5"Accept their gifts," the Lord told Moses, "and use these wagons for the work of the Tabernacle. Give them to the Levites for whatever needs they may have."

6So Moses presented the wagons and the oxen to the Levites. 7Two wagons and four oxen were given to the Gershon division for their use, 8and four wagons and eight oxen were given to the Merari division, which was under the leadership of Ithamar, Aaron's son. 9None of the wagons or teams was given to the Kohath division, for they were required to carry their portion of the Tabernacle upon their shoulders.

7:7
Num 4:26
7:8
Num 4:33
7:9
Num 4:5-15

10The leaders also presented dedication gifts on the day the altar was anointed, placing them before the altar. 11The Lord said to Moses, "Let each of them bring his gift on a different day for the dedication of the altar."

12So Nahshon, the son of Amminadab of the tribe of Judah, brought his gift the first day. 13It consisted of a silver platter weighing three pounds and a silver bowl of about two pounds, both filled with grain offerings of fine flour mixed with oil. 14He also brought a tiny gold box of incense which weighed only about four ounces. 15He brought a young bull, a ram, and a male yearling lamb as burnt offerings; 16male goat for a sin offering; 17and for the peace offerings two oxen, five rams, five male goats, and five male yearling lambs.

7:15
Lev 6:9-13
7:16
Lev 6:25-30
7:17
Lev 7:11-21

18-23The next day Nethanel, the son of Zuar, chief of the tribe of Issachar, brought his gifts and offerings. They were exactly the same as Nahshon had presented on the previous day.

24-29On the third day Eliab, the son of Helon, chief of the tribe of Zebulun, came with his offerings—the same as those presented on the previous days.

30-35On the fourth day the gifts were presented by Elizur, son of Shedeur, chief of the tribe of Reuben; his gifts and offerings were the same as those given on the previous days.

36-41On the fifth day came Shelumi-el, the son of Zuri-shaddai, chief of the tribe of Simeon, with the same gifts.

42-47The next day it was Eliasaph's turn, son of Deuel, chief of the tribe of Gad. He, too, offered the same gifts and sacrifices.

48-53On the seventh day, Elishama, the son of Ammihud, chief of the tribe of Ephraim, brought his gifts, the same as those presented on the previous days.

54-59Gamaliel, son of Pedahzur, prince of the tribe of Manasseh, came the eighth day with the same offerings.

60-65On the ninth day it was Abidan the son of Gideoni, chief of the tribe of Benjamin, with his gifts, the same as those offered by the others.

66-71Ahiezer, the son of Ammishaddai, brought his gifts on the tenth day. He was the chief of the tribe of Dan and his offerings were the same as those on the previous days.

72-77Pagiel, son of Ochran, chief of the tribe of Asher, brought his gifts on the eleventh day—the same gifts and offerings as the others.

78-83On the twelfth day came Ahira, son of Enan, chief of the tribe of Naphtali, with his offerings; they were identical to those brought by the others.

84, 85, 86So, beginning the day the altar was anointed, it was dedicated by these gifts from the chiefs of the tribes of Israel. Their combined offerings were as follows:

7:84
Num 7:10

12 silver platters (each weighing about three pounds);
12 silver bowls (each weighing about two pounds); so the total weight of the silver was about sixty pounds);
12 gold trays (the trays weighing about four ounces apiece); (so the total weight of gold was about three pounds).

87For the burnt offerings they brought:

7:87
Lev 1:2-17
6:9-13

12 bulls, 12 rams,
12 yearling male goats (with the grain offerings that accompanied them).

7:14 *tiny*, implied. **7:18-83** The original text repeats the lists of the offerings recorded in verses 13-17.

For sin offerings they brought:

12 male goats.

7:88
Num 7:17

88For the peace offerings they brought:

24 young bulls,
60 rams, 60 male goats,
60 male lambs one year old.

7:89
Ex 25:22
33:9-11
Lev 1:1
Ps 80:1; 99:1

89When Moses went into the Tabernacle to speak with God, he heard the Voice speaking to him from above the place of mercy over the Ark, between the statues of the two Guardian Angels.

Setting up the lamps

8:2
Ex 25:37

8 The Lord said to Moses, 2"Tell Aaron that when he lights the seven lamps in the lampstand, he is to set them so that they will throw their light forward."

8:4
Ex 25:18,31-36,
40; 37:17-22
Heb 8:5

3So Aaron did this. 4The lampstand, including the floral decorations on the base and branches, was made entirely of beaten gold. It was constructed according to the exact design the Lord had shown Moses.

The Levites are dedicated

8:7
Ex 19:10
Lev 14:8,9
15:6; 16:28
8:8
Num 15:3-12
8:10
Lev 4:15
8:11
Num 3:5-9

5, 6Then the Lord said to Moses, "Now set apart the Levites from the other people of Israel. 7Do this by sprinkling water of purification upon them, then having them shave their entire bodies and wash their clothing and themselves. 8Have them bring a young bull and a grain offering of fine flour mingled with oil, along with another young bull for a sin offering. 9Then bring the Levites to the door of the Tabernacle as all the people watch. 10There the leaders of the tribes shall lay their hands upon them, 11and Aaron, with a gesture of offering, shall present them to the Lord as a gift from the entire nation of Israel. The Levites will represent all the people in serving the Lord.

8:12
Ex 29:10-14
Lev 16:20-22
Num 8:10

12"Next, the Levite leaders shall lay their hands upon the heads of the young bulls and offer them before the Lord; one for a sin offering and the other for a burnt offering, to make atonement for the Levites. 13Then the Levites are to be presented to Aaron and his sons, just as any other gift to the Lord is given to the priests! 14In this way you will dedicate the Levites from among the rest of the people of Israel, and the Levites shall be mine. 15After you have sanctified them and presented them in this way, they shall go in and out of the Tabernacle to do their work.

8:14
Num 8:11

8:16
Num 3:13

16"They are mine from among all the people of Israel, and I have accepted them in place of all the firstborn children of the Israelites: I have taken the Levites as their substitutes. 17For all the firstborn among the people of Israel are mine, both men and animals; I claimed them for myself the night I killed all the firstborn Egyptians. 18Yes, I have accepted the Levites in place of all the eldest sons of Israel. 19And I will give the Levites as a gift to Aaron and his sons. The Levites will carry out the sacred duties required of the people of Israel in the Tabernacle, and will offer the people's sacrifices, making atonement for them. There will be no plague among the Israelites—as there would be if the ordinary people entered the Tabernacle."

8:17
Ex 13:12,13

8:19
Num 1:53

8:10 *There the leaders,* implied. Also in vs 12.

7:89 Imagine hearing the very voice of God! Moses must have trembled at the sound. Yet we have God's words recorded for us in the Bible, and we should have no less reverence and awe for them. Before the Bible was written, God sometimes spoke directly to his people to tell them the proper way to live. The Bible records these conversations to give us insights into God's character. Like Moses, we have the privilege of talking directly to God, but God answers us differently—through his written Word and through the guidance of his Holy Spirit. To receive this guidance we need to seek to know God as Moses did.

8:1-4 The lampstand provided light for the priests as they carried out their duties. The light was also an expression of God's presence. Jesus said, "I am the light of the world" (John 8:12). The golden lampstand is still one of the major symbols of the Jewish faith.

20So Moses and Aaron and all the people of Israel dedicated the Levites, carefully following Jehovah's instructions to Moses. 21The Levites purified themselves and washed their clothes, and Aaron presented them to the Lord in a gesture of offering. He then performed the rite of atonement over them to purify them. 22After that they went into the Tabernacle as assistants to Aaron and his sons; everything was done just as the Lord had commanded Moses.

23, 24The Lord also instructed Moses, "The Levites are to begin serving in the Tabernacle at the age of twenty-five, and are to retire at the age of fifty. 25, 26After retirement they can assist with various light duties in the Tabernacle, but will have no regular responsibilities."

8:23
Num 4:3

The second Passover

9 Jehovah gave these instructions to Moses while he and the rest of the Israelis were on the Sinai peninsula, during the first month of the second year after leaving Egypt:

9:1
Ex 40:2,17

2, 3"The people of Israel must celebrate the Passover annually on April first, beginning in the evening. Be sure to follow all of my instructions concerning this celebration."

9:2
Ex 12:1-6

4, 5So Moses announced that the Passover celebration would begin on the evening of April first, there in the Sinai peninsula, just as the Lord had commanded. 6, 7But as it happened, some of the men had just attended a funeral, and were ceremonially defiled by having touched the dead, so they couldn't eat the Passover lamb that night. They came to Moses and Aaron and explained their problem and protested at being forbidden from offering their sacrifice to the Lord at the time he had appointed.

9:6
Lev 21:1-4

8Moses said he would ask the Lord about it, 9and this was God's reply:

10"If any of the people of Israel, now or in the generations to come, are defiled at Passover time because of touching a dead body, or if they are on a journey and cannot be present, they may still celebrate the Passover, but one month later, 11on May first, beginning in the evening. They are to eat the lamb at that time, with unleavened bread and bitter herbs. 12They must not leave any of it until the next morning, and must not break a bone of it, and must follow all the regular instructions concerning the Passover.

9:12
Ex 12:1-50
Lev 23:5-14
Num 28:16-25
Jn 19:36

13"But anyone who is not defiled, and anyone who is not away on a trip, and yet refuses to celebrate the Passover at the regular time, shall be excommunicated from the people of Israel for refusing to sacrifice to Jehovah at the proper time; he must bear his guilt. 14And if a foreigner is living among you and wants to celebrate the Passover to the Lord, he shall follow all these same instructions. There is one law for all."

9:13
Ex 12:15
Num 15:30,31

9:14
Ex 12:48,49

9:2, 3 *on April first,* literally, "on the fourteenth day of the first month" (of the Hebrew calendar). This corresponds approximately to our first day of April. **9:11** *May first,* literally, "on the fourteenth day of the second month" (of the Hebrew calendar).

8:23, 24 Why were the Levites supposed to retire at the age of 50? The reasons were probably more practical than theological. (1) Moving the Tabernacle and its furniture through the wilderness required strength. The younger men were more suited for the work of lifting the heavy articles. (2) The Levites over 50 did not stop working altogether, but they took on fewer duties. This helped the younger men assume more responsibilities, and it allowed the older men to be in a position to advise and counsel them.

9:6–12 Several men came to Moses because of the predicament they faced: attendance at a funeral would prevent them from participating in the Passover meal because it had made them unclean. Notice that God did not adjust the requirements of the Passover. The standards of holiness were maintained, and the men were not allowed to participate. But God did make an exception and allowed the men to celebrate the Passover at a later date. This upheld the sacred requirements of the Passover while allowing the

men to participate in the feast—a duty for all Israelite men. We sometimes face true predicaments where the most obvious solution might cause us to compromise God's standards. Like Moses, we must use wisdom and prayer to reach a workable solution.

9:14 One reaction to all the detailed Old Testament laws is to say they applied only to the Israelites. If they were man-made, this would be true. They would be historically and culturally bound to a time and place. But since they came from God, their moral principles are timeless and true for all people. The often repeated phrase, "There is one law for all," emphasizes that non-Israelites were also subject to God's commands and promises. God singled out Israel for a special purpose—to be an example of how one nation could, and should, worship him. His aim, however, was to have all people obey and worship him. Although God gave these laws only to Israel, the principles behind them are applicable to all believers today.

4. Receiving guidance for the journey
The pillar of cloud and fire

9:15
Ex 14:20,24
40:2,18
Num 14:14
Neh 9:12,19
Ps 78:14

¹⁵On the day the Tabernacle was raised, the Cloud covered it; and that evening the Cloud changed to the appearance of fire, and stayed that way throughout the night. ¹⁶It was always so—the daytime Cloud changing to the appearance of fire at night. ¹⁷When the Cloud lifted, the people of Israel moved on to wherever it

9:17
Ex 40:36-38
Num 10:11,33,
34

stopped, and camped there. ¹⁸In this way they journeyed at the command of the Lord and stopped where he told them to, then remained there as long as the Cloud stayed. ¹⁹If it stayed a long time, then they stayed a long time. But if it stayed only a few days, then they remained only a few days; for so the Lord had instructed them. ^{20, 21}Sometimes the fire-cloud stayed only during the night and moved on the next morning. But day or night, when it moved, the people broke camp and followed. ²²If the Cloud stayed above the Tabernacle two days, a month, or a year, that is how long the people of Israel stayed; but as soon as it moved, they moved.

9:23
Josh 22:2,3

²³So it was that they camped or traveled at the commandment of the Lord; and whatever the Lord told Moses they should do, they did.

The silver trumpets

10:2
Lev 25:9
2 Kgs 12:13

10 Now the Lord said to Moses, "Make two trumpets of beaten silver to be used for summoning the people to assemble and for signaling the breaking of camp. ³When both trumpets are blown, the people will know that they are to gather at the entrance of the Tabernacle. ⁴But if only one is blown, then only the chiefs of

10:5,7
Ex 19:13
Judg 3:27
Joel 2:1

the tribes of Israel shall come to you. ^{5, 6, 7}"Different trumpet blasts will be necessary to distinguish between the summons to assemble and the signal to break camp and move onward. When the travel signal is blown, the tribes camped on the east side of the Tabernacle shall leave first; at the second signal, the tribes on the

10:8
Num 31:6
Josh 6:3-9
2 Chron 5:11,12

south shall go. ⁸Only the priests are permitted to blow the trumpets. This is a permanent instruction to be followed from generation to generation.

10:9
Judg 3:27
Ezek 33:3
Joel 2:1
Zeph 2:5

⁹"When you arrive in the Promised Land and go to war against your enemies, God will hear you and save you from your enemies when you sound the alarm with these trumpets. ¹⁰Use the trumpets in times of gladness, too, blowing them at your

10:10
Lev 23:33,34
Num 29:1
Ezra 3:10
Ps 81:3-5

annual festivals and at the beginning of each month to rejoice over your burnt offerings and peace offerings. And God will be reminded of his covenant with you. For I am Jehovah, your God."

B. FIRST APPROACH TO THE PROMISED LAND (10:11—14:45)
As the Israelites approached the Promised Land, Moses sent leaders to spy out the land and its people. But the spies returned with a discouraging report—"It is a magnificent country, but the people living there are too powerful." Although Joshua and Caleb disagreed, the Israelites had already made up their minds and began to complain. As punishment for their lack of faith, God condemned them to wander in the wilderness for forty years. Our obedience must be complete and timely.

1. The people complain
¹¹The Cloud lifted from the Tabernacle on the twentieth day of the second month

10:5-7 *and the signal to break the camp and move onward,* more literally, vs 7 reads: "But when the Assembly is to be gathered together, you shall blow but you shall not sound the alarm." **10:11** *on the twentieth day of the second month,* (of the Hebrew Calendar), this was approximately May 5.

9:15–22 A pillar of cloud by day and a pillar of fire by night guided and protected the Israelites as they traveled across the wilderness. This was a vehicle of God's presence and a visible sign of his moving and directing his people. Some have said this pillar may have been a burning bowl of pitch whose smoke was visible during the day and whose fire could be seen at night. However, a bowl of pitch would not have lifted itself up and moved ahead of the people. A mere human instrument would not have been an adequate representation of God's presence. The Bible is clear that the cloud and fire moved in accordance with God's will.

9:23 The Hebrews traveled and camped as God guided. Guidance means knowing you are where God wants you, whether you're moving or staying in one place. You are physically somewhere right now. Instead of praying, "God, what do you want me to do next?" ask, "God, what do you want me to do while I'm right here?" Direction from God is not just for your next big move. He has a purpose in placing you where you are right now. Begin to understand God's purpose for your life by discovering what it is he desires you to do now!

of the second year of Israel's leaving Egypt; 12so the Israelites left the Sinai wilderness, and followed the Cloud until it stopped in the wilderness of Paran. 13This was their first journey after having received the Lord's travel instructions to Moses.

10:12
Gen 21:20,21
Num 12:16
13:3,26
10:13
Deut 1:6

A good start

14At the head of the march was the tribe of Judah grouped behind its flag, and led by Nahshon, the son of Amminadab. 15Next came the tribe of Issachar, led by Nethanel, the son of Zuar, 16and the tribe of Zebulun, led by Eliab, the son of Helon.

10:14
Num 2:3-31

17The Tabernacle was taken down and the men of the Gershon and Merari divisions of the tribe of Levi were next in the line of march, carrying the Tabernacle upon their shoulders. 18Then came the flag of the camp of Reuben, with Elizur the son of Shedeur leading his people. 19Next was the tribe of Simeon headed by Shelumi-el, the son of Zuri-shaddai; 20and the tribe of Gad led by Eliasaph, the son of Deuel.

10:17
Num 4:21-23
10:18
Num 2:3-31
26:5-18

21Next came the Kohathites carrying the items from the inner sanctuary. (The Tabernacle was already erected in its new location by the time they arrived.) 22Next in line was the tribe of Ephraim behind its flag, led by Elishama, the son of Ammihud; 23and the tribe of Manasseh led by Gamaliel the son of Pedahzur; 24and the tribe of Benjamin, led by Abidan the son of Gideoni. 25Last of all were the tribes headed by the flag of the tribe of Dan under the leadership of Ahiezer, the son of Ammishaddai; 26the tribe of Asher, led by Pagiel, the son of Ochran; 27and the tribe of Naphtali, led by Ahira, the son of Enan. 28That was the order in which the tribes traveled.

10:21
Num 4:1-20
10:22
Num 2:3-31

29One day Moses said to his brother-in-law Hobab (son of Reuel, the Midianite), "At last we are on our way to the Promised Land. Come with us and we will do you good; for the Lord has given wonderful promises to Israel!"

30But his brother-in-law replied, "No, I must return to my own land and kinfolk."

31"Stay with us," Moses pleaded, "for you know the ways of the wilderness and will be a great help to us. 32If you come, you will share in all the good things the Lord does for us."

10:29
Ex 2:18-21; 3:1
18:1,5-27
Judg 1:16; 4:11
10:32
Num 10:29
Ps 67:5-7
10:33
Josh 3:2-6,
11-17
10:34
Ex 14:20,24
Num 9:15-22
10:35
Ps 68:1,2
132:8
Isa 51:9

33They traveled for three days after leaving Mount Sinai, with the Ark at the front of the column to choose a place for them to stop. 34It was daytime when they left, with the Cloud moving along ahead of them as they began their march. 35As the Ark was carried forward, Moses cried out, "Arise, O Lord, and scatter your

10:31 *for you know the ways of the wilderness and will be a great help to us,* literally, "you know how we are to encamp in the wilderness, and you will serve as eyes for us." **10:33** *Mount Sinai,* literally, "the mount of Jehovah."

10:21 Those who travel, move, or face new challenges know what it is to be uprooted. Life is full of changes, and few things remain stable. The Israelites were constantly moving through the wilderness. They were able to handle change only because God's presence in the Tabernacle was always with them. The portable Tabernacle signified how God and his people move together. For us, stability does not mean lack of change, but moving with God in every circumstance.

10:29-32 By complimenting his wilderness skills, Moses let Hobab know he was needed. Others cannot know you appreciate them if you do not tell them they are important to you. Complimenting those who deserve it builds lasting relationships and helps others know they are valued by others. Think about those who have helped you this month. What can you do to let them know how much you need and appreciate them?

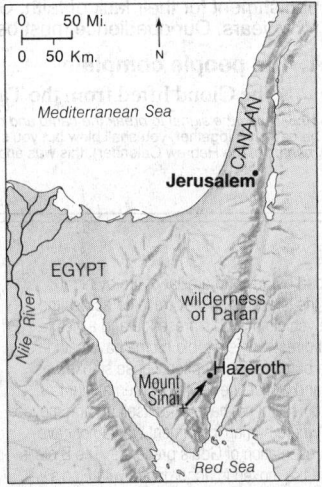

```
0        50 Mi.
|---|---|
0        50 Km.           N

        Mediterranean Sea

                              CANAAN

          Jerusalem

EGYPT

                    wilderness
                    of Paran

    Nile River
                          Hazeroth
            Mount
            Sinai

              Red Sea
```

ISRAEL'S DEPARTURE FROM SINAI
It has been two years since Israel left Egypt. Having received God's travel instructions through Moses, Israel set out from Mount Sinai into the wilderness of Paran on their way toward the Promised Land.

10:36
Deut 1:10,11
Ps 90:13-17

enemies; let them flee before you." 36And when the Ark was set down he said, "Return, O Lord, to the millions of Israel."

God sends fire upon the complaining people

11:1
Ex 16:2-9
17:2,3
Lev 10:1,2
Num 14:2
16:35; 17:5
20:2-5
Deut 32:22

11 The people were soon complaining about all their misfortunes, and the Lord heard them. His anger flared out against them because of their complaints, so the fire of the Lord began destroying those at the far end of the camp. 2They screamed to Moses for help, and when he prayed for them the fire stopped. 3Ever after, the area was known as "The Place of Burning," because the fire from the Lord burned among them there.

God sends meat to the complaining people

11:4
Ex 12:38
Lev 24:10,11
Ps 78:18
106:14
1 Cor 10:6

4, 5Then the Egyptians who had come with them began to long for the good things of Egypt. This added to the discontent of the people of Israel and they wept, "Oh, for a few bites of meat! Oh, that we had some of the delicious fish we enjoyed so much in Egypt, and the wonderful cucumbers and melons, leeks, onions, and

11:3 *The Place of Burning,* literally, "Taberah."

ISRAEL'S COMPLAINING	Reference	Complaint	Sin	Result
	11:1	About their misfortunes	Complained about their problems instead of praying to God about them	Thousands of people were destroyed when God sent a plague of fire to punish them
	11:4	About the lack of meat	Lusted after things they didn't have	God sent quail; but as the people began to eat, God struck them with a plague that killed many
	14:1–4	About being stuck in the wilderness, facing the giants of the Promised Land, and wishing to return to Egypt	Openly rebelled against God's leaders and failed to trust in his promises	All who complained were not allowed to enter the Promised Land, being doomed to wander in the wilderness until they died
	16:3	About Moses' and Aaron's authority and leadership	Were greedy for more power and authority	The families, friends, and possessions of Korah, Dathan, and Abiram were swallowed up by the earth. Fire then burned up the 250 other men who rebelled.
	16:41	That Moses and Aaron caused the deaths of Korah and his conspirators	Blamed others for their own troubles	God began to destroy Israel with a plague. Moses and Aaron made atonement for the people, but 14,700 of them were killed.
	20:3	About the lack of water	Refused to believe that God would provide as he has promised	Moses sinned along with the people. For this he was barred from entering the Promised Land.
	21:5	That God and Moses brought them into the wilderness	Failed to recognize that their problems were brought on by their own disobedience	God sent poisonous snakes which killed many people and seriously injured many others

11:1, 11–15 The Israelites complained, and then Moses complained. But God responded positively to Moses and negatively to the rest of the people. Why? The people complained *to one another*—and nothing was accomplished. Moses took his complaint *to God,* who can solve any problem. Many of us are good at complaining to each other. We need to learn to take our problems to the One who can do something about them.

11:4–6 Dissatisfaction comes when our attention shifts from what we have to what we don't have. The people of Israel didn't seem to notice what God was doing for them—setting them free, making

them a nation, giving them a new land—because they were so wrapped up in what God wasn't doing for them. They could think of nothing but the delicious Egyptian melons they had left behind. Somehow they forgot that the brutal whip of Egyptian slavery was the cost of eating those melons. Before we judge the Israelites too harshly, it's helpful to think about what occupies our attention most of the time. Are we grateful for the things God has given us, or are we always thinking about new things we would like to have? We should not allow our unfulfilled desires to cause us to forget God's gifts of life, food, health, work, and friends.

garlic! 6But now our strength is gone, and day after day we have to face this manna!"

11:6
Num 21:5

7The manna was the size of small seeds, whitish yellow in color. 8The people gathered it from the ground and pounded it into flour, then boiled it, and then made pancakes from it—they tasted like pancakes fried in vegetable oil. 9The manna fell with the dew during the night.

11:7
Ex 16:14,31

11:9
Ex 16:13
Ps 78:23-25

10Moses heard all the families standing around their tent doors weeping, and the anger of the Lord grew hot; Moses too was highly displeased.

11:10
Num 11:1
14:1,2; 16:27

11Moses said to the Lord, "Why pick on me, to give me the burden of a people like this? 12Are they *my* children? Am I their father? Is that why you have given me the job of nursing them along like babies until we get to the land you promised their ancestors? 13Where am I supposed to get meat for all these people? For they weep to me saying, 'Give us meat!' 14I can't carry this nation by myself! The load is far too heavy! 15If you are going to treat me like this, please kill me right now; it will be a kindness! Let me out of this impossible situation!"

Deut 32:22
Isa 5:25

11:11
Ex 17:4
Num 11:15

11:12
Gen 13:14-17
26:3; 50:24,25
Ex 13:4,5
Isa 49:15

11:14
Ex 18:18
Deut 1:9-13

11:15
Ex 32:32

16Then the Lord said to Moses, "Summon before me seventy of the leaders of Israel; bring them to the Tabernacle, to stand there with you. 17I will come down and talk with you there and I will take of the Spirit which is on you and will put it upon them also; they shall bear the burden of the people along with you, so that you will not have the task alone.

11:16
Ex 4:29; 24:1,9
Lk 10:1,17

11:17
Ex 34:5,6
Num 11:25; 12:5

18"And tell the people to purify themselves, for tomorrow they shall have meat to eat. Tell them, 'The Lord has heard your tearful complaints about all you left behind in Egypt, and he is going to give you meat. You shall eat it, 19, 20not for just a day or two, or five or ten or even twenty! For one whole month you will have meat until you vomit it from your noses; for you have rejected the Lord who is here among you, and you have wept for Egypt.' "

11:18
Ex 19:10,14,15
Josh 7:13

21But Moses said, "There are 600,000 men alone [besides all the women and children], and yet you promise them meat for a whole month! 22If we butcher all our flocks and herds it won't be enough! We would have to catch every fish in the ocean to fulfill your promise!"

11:21
Ex 12:37
Num 1:20-46
2:32,33

23Then the Lord said to Moses, "When did I become weak? Now you shall see whether my word comes true or not!"

11:23
Gen 18:14

24So Moses left the Tabernacle and reported Jehovah's words to the people; and he gathered the seventy elders and placed them around the Tabernacle. 25And the Lord came down in the Cloud and talked with Moses, and the Lord took of the Spirit that was upon Moses and put it upon the seventy elders; and when the Spirit rested upon them, they prophesied for some time.

11:25
Num 11:16,17
Isa 50:2

26But two of the seventy—Eldad and Medad—were still in the camp, and when the Spirit rested upon them, they prophesied there. 27Some young men ran and told Moses what was happening, 28and Joshua (the son of Nun), one of Moses' personally chosen assistants, protested, "Sir, make them stop!"

11:28
Josh 1:1
Mk 9:38-40

11:8 *vegetable oil,* literally, "olive oil."   11:21 *besides all the women and children,* implied.

11:7-12 Every morning the Israelites drew back their tent doors and witnessed a miracle. Covering the ground was white, fluffy manna—food from heaven. But soon that wasn't enough. "Oh, for a few bites of meat!" they complained to Moses. "Give us some of the good things we had in Egypt." God gave them what they asked for, but they paid dearly for it (see 11:18-20, 31-34). They were punished for their lust. Feeling it was their right to have more, they forgot what they already had. They didn't ask God to fill their need, they demanded that meat be given to them, and they stopped trusting God to care for them. The next time you ask something of God, he may grant your request. But if you approach him with a sinful attitude, getting what you want may prove costly.

11:21, 22 Moses had witnessed God's power in spectacular miracles, yet at this time he questioned God's ability to feed the wandering Israelites. If Moses doubted God's power, how much easier it is for us to do the same. But completely depending upon

God is essential, regardless of our level of spiritual maturity. When we begin to rely on our own understanding, we are in danger of ignoring God's assessment of the situation. By remembering his past works and his present power, we can be sure that we are not cutting off his potential help.

11:23 How strong is God? It is easy to trust God when we see his mighty acts (the Israelites saw many), but after a while his strength may appear to weaken in the routine of our daily problems. God doesn't change, but our view of him often does. The monotony of day-by-day living lulls us into forgetting the powerful things God can do in our lives. God's strength is always present and, as Moses learned, always available.

11:26-29 This incident is similar to a story told in Mark 9:38-41. The disciples wanted Jesus to forbid others to cast out demons because they were not part of the disciples' group. But this type of narrow attitude was condemned by both Moses and Jesus.

29But Moses replied, "Are you jealous for my sake? I only wish that all of the Lord's people were prophets, and that the Lord would put his Spirit upon them all!" 30Then Moses returned to the camp with the elders of Israel.

11:31
Ex 16:13
Ps 78:26-33
105:40

31The Lord sent a wind that brought quail from the sea, and let them fall into the camp and all around it! As far as one could walk in a day in any direction, there were quail flying three or four feet above the ground. 32So the people caught and killed quail all that day and through the night and all the next day too! The least anyone gathered was 100 bushels! Quail were spread out all around the camp. 33But

11:33
Num 11:10

as everyone began eating the meat, the anger of the Lord rose against the people and he killed large numbers of them with a plague. 34So the name of that place was called, "The Place of the Graves Caused by Lust," because they buried the people there who had lusted for meat and for Egypt. 35And from that place they journeyed to Hazeroth, where they stayed awhile.

11:34
Num 33:15-37
Deut 9:22

11:35
Num 12:16

2. Miriam and Aaron criticize Moses

12:1
Ex 2:21; 15:20
12:2
Num 16:3
Mic 6:4

12 One day Miriam and Aaron were criticizing Moses because his wife was a Cushite woman, 2and they said, "Has the Lord spoken only through Moses? Hasn't he spoken through us, too?"

12:3
Num 16:16-21

But the Lord heard them. 3, 4Immediately he summoned Moses, Aaron, and Miriam to the Tabernacle: "Come here, you three," he commanded. So they stood before the Lord. (Now Moses was the humblest man on earth.)

12:5
Num 11:25
12:6
Gen 15:1
31:10; 46:2
1 Kgs 3:5
Ezek 1:1
Dan 8:2
Mt 1:20
2:12,13,19
Acts 22:17,18

5Then the Lord descended in the Cloud and stood at the entrance of the Tabernacle. "Aaron and Miriam, step forward," he commanded; and they did. 6And the Lord said to them, "Even with a prophet, I would communicate by visions and dreams; 7, 8but that is not how I communicate with my servant Moses. He is completely at home in my house! With him I speak face to face! And he shall see the very form of God! Why then were you not afraid to criticize him?"

12:7,8
Ex 33:11
Num 14:14
Deut 18:15-19
34:10
Acts 3:21-23
Heb 3:2,5
12:10
Deut 24:9

9Then the anger of the Lord grew hot against them, and he departed. 10As the Cloud moved from above the Tabernacle, Miriam suddenly became white with leprosy. When Aaron saw what had happened, 11he cried out to Moses, "Oh, sir, do not punish us for this sin; we were fools to do such a thing. 12Don't let her be as one dead, whose body is half rotted away at birth."

13And Moses cried out to the Lord, "Heal her, O God, I beg you!"

11:31 *there were quail flying three or four feet above the ground,* or, "The ground was covered with them, three feet thick." **11:32** *quail were spread out all around.* To cure them by drying. **11:34** *The Place of the Graves caused by Lust,* literally, "Kibroth-hattaavah." **12:1** *Cushite woman,* literally "because of the Cushite woman he had married." Apparently they were referring to his wife Zipporah, the Midianite daughter of Reuel (Ex 2:21); for the land of Midian from which she came was sometimes called Cush. But areas of Ethiopia and Babylon were also known as Cush, so it is possible that the reference is to a second wife of Moses. It is indeterminate from the text whether she was criticized for being a Gentile, or (if she was a Cushite from Ethiopia) because of her color.

11:29 When it comes to serving God, there is plenty of room for everyone. Moses was recognized as Israel's leader, yet when others showed leadership ability, he was overjoyed. Joshua, however, was so faithful to Moses' leadership that he forgot the objective—creating a nation of faithful people. As a result, he tried to restrict God's work in order to keep Moses in the limelight. Focusing on individuals and their abilities may cause us to lose sight of our overall objective. In God's service, shared accomplishments are more important than individual achievements.

11:34 Lust is more than inappropriate sexual desire. Lust can be an unnatural or greedy desire for anything (sports, knowledge, possessions, influence over others). In this circumstance, God punished the Israelites for lusting after good food! It was not their desire for good things that was lust; it was allowing that desire to turn into greed that made it wrong. They felt it was their right to have fine food, and they could think of nothing else. When you become preoccupied with something until it affects your perspective on everything else, you may be moving from desire to lust.

12:1 Disagreements are often over symptoms and not real issues.

Such was the case when Miriam and Aaron came to Moses with a complaint. The real issue was their growing jealousy of Moses' position and influence. Since they could not find fault with the way Moses was leading the people, they chose to criticize his wife. Rather than face the problem squarely by dealing with their envy and pride, they chose to create a smoke-screen that was really a diversion from the real issue at hand. When you are in the midst of a disagreement, stop and ask yourself if you are arguing over the real issue or if you have introduced a smoke-screen by attacking someone's character. If you are unjustly criticized, remember that your critics may be afraid to face the real problem. Don't take this type of criticism personally. Ask God to help you identify the real issue and deal with it.

12:11 Aaron cried out, "We were fools to do such a thing." It is easy to look back at our mistakes and recognize their foolishness. It is much harder to recognize foolish plans before we become too involved, because while we are doing them, they somehow seem appropriate. To get rid of foolish ideas before they turn into foolish actions requires ridding our lives of wrong thoughts and motives. Failing to do this caused Miriam and Aaron much grief.

14And the Lord said to Moses, "If her father had but spit in her face she would be defiled seven days. Let her be banished from the camp for seven days, and after that she can come back again."

15So Miriam was excluded from the camp for seven days, and the people waited until she was brought back in before they traveled again. 16Afterwards they left Hazeroth and camped in the wilderness of Paran.

3. The spies incite rebellion
The spies are sent out

13 Jehovah now instructed Moses, 2"Send spies into the land of Canaan—the land I am giving to Israel; send one leader from each tribe." 3-15(The Israelis were camped in the wilderness of Paran at the time.) Moses did as the Lord had commanded and sent these twelve tribal leaders:

Shammu-a, son of Zaccur, from the tribe of Reuben;
Shaphat, son of Hori, from the tribe of Simeon;
Caleb, son of Jephunneh, from the tribe of Judah;
Igal, son of Joseph, from the tribe of Issachar;
Hoshea, son of Nun, from the half-tribe of Ephraim;
Palti, son of Raphu, from the tribe of Benjamin;
Gaddiel, son of Sodi, from the tribe of Zebulun;
Gaddi, son of Susi, from the tribe of Joseph (actually, the half-tribe of Manasseh);
Ammiel, son of Gemalli, from the tribe of Dan;
Sethur, son of Michael, from the tribe of Asher;
Nahbi, son of Vophsi, from the tribe of Naphtali;
Geuel, son of Machi, from the tribe of Gad.

16It was at this time that Moses changed Hoshea's name to Joshua.

The spies explore the land

17Moses sent them out with these instructions: "Go northward into the hill country of the Negeb, 18and see what the land is like; see also what the people are like who live there, whether they are strong or weak, many or few; 19and whether the land is fertile or not; and what cities there are, and whether they are villages or are fortified; 20whether the land is rich or poor, and whether there are many trees. Don't be afraid, and bring back some samples of the crops you see." (The first of the grapes were being harvested at that time.)

21So they spied out the land all the way from the wilderness of Zin to Rehob near Hamath. 22Going northward, they passed first through the Negeb and arrived at Hebron. There they saw the Ahimanites, Sheshites, and Talmites, all families descended from Anak. (By the way, Hebron was very ancient, having been founded seven years before Tanis in Egypt). 23Then they came to what is now known as the Valley of Eshcol where they cut down a single cluster of grapes so large that it took two of them to carry it on a pole between them! They also took some samples of the pomegranates and figs. 24The Israelis named the valley "Eshcol" at that time (meaning "Cluster") because of the cluster of grapes they found!

Cross-references (margin):

12:14 Lev 14:8,9; 15:8; Num 5:1-3; Deut 25:9

12:16 Num 11:35

13:2 Ex 18:25; Num 11:16; 32:8; Deut 1:22-25; Josh 2:1

13:3 Num 1:2-15; 12:16; 13:26; 34:16-28

13:16 Num 13:3-15; Acts 7:45

13:17 Gen 12:9; 13:1; Num 13:22; Josh 15:1

13:20 Num 13:23,24

13:21 Num 20:1; 27:14; Josh 19:28; Judg 1:31,32; 2 Sam 8:9; Amos 6:2

13:22 Num 13:33; Josh 11:21; 15:14; Judg 1:10

13:23 Num 13:24; 32:9; Deut 1:24,25

13:3-15 Hoshea, or, "Joshua." See verse 16.   13:16 Moses changed Hoshea's name to Joshua. "Hoshea" means "salvation;" "Joshua" means "Jehovah is salvation." Joshua is the same name in Hebrew as the Greek name "Jesus." 13:22 Zoan or Tanis, also known as Avaris, was built ca. 1700 B.C.

12:14 Spitting in someone's face was considered the ultimate insult. The religious leaders spat in Jesus' face to insult him (Matthew 26:67). A parent spat in a child's face as a sign of punishment. God punished Miriam for her smug attitude toward not only Moses' authority, but also God's. He struck her with leprosy, then ordered her out of the camp for a week. This punishment was actually quite lenient. A week was the length of time she would have been excluded if her father had spat in her face. How much more she deserved for wronging God! Once again, God blended mercy with effective discipline.

13:17-20 Moses decided what information was needed before the people could enter the Promised Land, and he took careful steps to get that information. When you are making decisions or assuming new responsibilities, these are two important steps to remember. Ask yourself what you need to know about the opportunity, and then take steps to obtain that knowledge. This kind of common sense is a valuable aid in accomplishing God's purposes.

The people rebel at the spies' report

13:26
Num 12:16
13:3; 20:1; 32:8
Deut 1:19
Josh 14:6

²⁵After forty days of exploration they returned from their tour. ²⁶They made their report to Moses, Aaron, and all the people of Israel in the wilderness of Paran at Kadesh, and they showed the fruit they had brought with them.

²⁷This was their report: "We arrived in the land you sent us to see, and it is indeed

---

Ask older brothers or sisters what their greatest test in life is and they will often answer, "My younger brother (or sister)!" This is especially true when the younger sibling is more successful than the older. The bonds of family loyalty can be strained to the breaking point.

When we first meet Miriam she is involved in one of history's most unusual babysitting jobs. She is watching her infant brother float down the Nile River in a waterproof cradle. Miriam's quick thinking allowed Moses to be raised by his own mother. Her protective superiority, reinforced by that event, must have been hard to give up as she watched her little brother rise to greatness.

Eventually Moses' choice of a wife gave Miriam an opportunity to criticize. It was natural for her insecurity to break out over this issue. With Moses married, Miriam was clearly no longer the most important woman in his life. The real issue, however, was not the kind of woman Moses had married. It was the fact that he was now the most important man in Israel. "Has the Lord spoken only through Moses?" asked Miriam and her brother Aaron. "Hasn't he spoken through us, too?" No mention is made of Moses' response, but God had a quick answer for Miriam and Aaron. Without denying their role in his plan, God clearly pointed out his special relationship with Moses. Miriam was stricken with leprosy, a deadly disease, as punishment for her insubordination. But Moses, true to his character, intervened for his sister, so that God healed Miriam of her leprosy.

Before criticizing someone else, we need to pause long enough to discover our own motives. Failing to do this can bring disastrous results. What is often labeled "constructive criticism" may actually be destructive jealousy. The easiest way to raise our status is to bring someone else down. Are you willing to question your motives before you offer criticism? Does the critical finger you point need to be pointed first toward yourself?

Strengths and accomplishments:
- Quick thinker under pressure
- Able leader
- Song writer
- Prophetess

Weaknesses and mistakes:
- Was jealous of Moses' authority
- Openly criticized Moses' leadership

Lesson from her life:
- The motives behind criticism are often more important to deal with than the criticism itself

Vital statistics:
- Where: Egypt, Sinai Peninsula
- Relatives: Brothers: Aaron and Moses

Key verse:
"And Miriam sang this song: Sing to the Lord, for he has triumphed gloriously . . . " (Exodus 15:21).

Miriam's story is told in Exodus 2 and 15; Numbers 12 and 20. She is also mentioned in Deuteronomy 24:9; 1 Chronicles 6:3; Micah 6:4.

13:25–29 God told the Israelites that the Promised Land was rich and plentiful. Not only that, he promised that this bountiful land would be theirs. When the spies reported back to Moses, they gave plenty of good reasons for entering the land, but they couldn't stop focusing on the bad things that might happen. Talk of giants and walled cities made it easy to forget about God's promise to help. When facing a tough decision, don't let the negatives cause you to lose sight of the positives. Weigh the two carefully. Don't let potential difficulties blind you to God's power to help and his promise to guide.

13:26 Although Kadesh was only a desert oasis, it was a crossroads in Israel's history. When the spies returned to Kadesh from scouting the new land, the people had to decide either to enter the land or to retreat. They chose to retreat and were condemned to wander 40 years in the wilderness. It was also at Kadesh that Moses disobeyed God (Numbers 20:11, 12). For this, he too was denied entrance into the Promised Land. Aaron and Miriam died there, for they could not enter the new land either. Geographically, Kadesh was near Canaan's southern borders. But because of the Israelites' lack of faith, they needed more than a lifetime to go from Kadesh to the Promised Land.

13:27 The Promised Land, also called the land of Canaan, was indeed magnificent, as the 12 spies discovered. The Bible often calls it the "land flowing with milk and honey." Although the land was relatively small—150 miles long and 60 miles wide—its lush hillsides were covered with figs, dates, and nuts. It was the land God had promised to the Abraham, Isaac, and Jacob.

a magnificent country—a land 'flowing with milk and honey.' Here is some fruit we have brought as proof. 28But the people living there are powerful, and their cities are fortified and very large; and what's more, we saw Anakim giants there! 29The Amalekites live in the south, while in the hill country there are the Hittites, Jebusites, and Amorites; down along the coast of the Mediterranean Sea and in the Jordan River valley are the Canaanites."

30But Caleb reassured the people as they stood before Moses. "Let us go up at once and possess it," he said, "for we are well able to conquer it!"

31"Not against people as strong as they are!" the other spies said. "They would crush us!"

32So the majority report of the spies was negative: "The land is full of warriors, the people are powerfully built, 33and we saw some of the Anakim there, descendants of the ancient race of giants. We felt like grasshoppers before them, they were so tall!"

14 Then all the people began weeping aloud, and they carried on all night. 2Their voices rose in a great chorus of complaint against Moses and Aaron. "We wish we had died in Egypt," they wailed, "or even here in the wilderness, 3rather than be taken into this country ahead of us. Jehovah will kill us there, and our wives and little ones will become slaves. Let's get out of here and return to Egypt!"

4The idea swept the camp. "Let's elect a leader to take us back to Egypt!" they shouted.

13:29
Gen 15:19-21
Ex 3:8,17
17:8-16
Num 14:43
13:30
Num 14:6-9
Josh 14:6-8
Isa 41:10-16
13:31
Num 32:9
Josh 14:8
Heb 3:19
13:32
Num 14:36,37
Deut 1:28
13:33
1 Sam 17:4-7
2 Sam 21:20-22
1 Chron 11:23

14:2
Ex 15:24; 16:3
Num 11:1,5
16:41; 20:3,4
21:5
14:3
Ex 5:21; 16:3
Num 14:31
Deut 1:39

13:28, 29 The fortified cities the spies talked about were surrounded by high walls as much as 20 feet thick and 25 feet tall. Guards were often stationed on top, where there was a commanding view of the countryside. The inhabitants, said the spies, were formidable men—seven to nine feet tall—so that the Israelites felt like grasshoppers next to them. The walled cities and the giants struck fear into the hearts of most of the spies.

13:30 Imagine standing before a crowd and loudly voicing an unpopular opinion! Caleb was willing to take the unpopular stand to do as God had commanded. To be effective when you go against the crowd, you must (1) have the facts (Caleb had seen the land himself); (2) have the right attitude (Caleb trusted God's promise to give Israel the land); and (3) state clearly what you believe ("We are well able to conquer it!").

13:31, 32 The Israelites didn't trust God—they believed victory was impossible. From their perspective, their decision seemed to make sense. But they failed to realize that God doesn't always operate from a human perspective. A promise from God is a sure thing, no matter how unlikely it seems. God's Word isn't subject to majority opinion. His truth is set apart from feelings, situations, or opinions. Caleb stood for the truth he knew about God, apart from what he saw. He knew that God's Word had always been true. God had said very plainly that he would help the people conquer the Promised Land. But the other spies forgot what they knew about God and made their decision on the basis of what they knew of themselves. Are you willing to stand against the pressure of popular opinion to do what God's Word says?

13:33—14:4 The negative opinion of ten men caused a great rebellion among the people. Because it is human nature to accept opinion as fact, we must be especially careful when voicing our negative opinions. What we say may heavily influence the actions of those who are trusting us to give sound advice.

14:1–4 When the chorus of despair went up, everyone joined in. Losing their perspective, the people became caught up in the emotion of the moment, forgetting what they knew about the character of God. What if the people had spent as much energy moving forward as they did moving back? The Promised Land would have been conquered much sooner and with less effort.

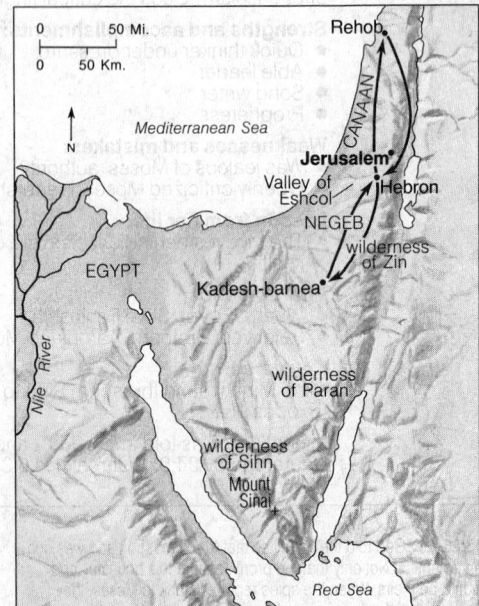

ROUTE OF THE SPIES The spies traveled from Kadesh-barnea at the northern edge of the wilderness of Paran to Rehob at the northern end of the Jordan Valley and back, a round trip of about 300 miles.

When a cry of despair goes up around you, consider the larger perspective before you join in. You probably have better things to do with your energy.

14:5–9 With great miracles, God led the Israelites out of slavery, through the desolate wilderness, and up to the very edge of the

Moses prays for the rebellious people

14:5
Gen 17:3
Lev 9:24
Num 16:22,45
Josh 5:14

14:7
Num 13:27
Deut 1:25
6:10,11; 8:7-9

14:8
Ex 3:8
Num 13:27

14:9
Deut 1:21,29
7:18; 9:7,23,24

14:10
Ex 16:7,10
17:4; 24:16,17
32:9-13
Lev 9:23
Num 20:6
1 Sam 30:6

14:12
Ex 32:10
Lev 26:25
Num 16:46-49
Deut 28:21

14:13
Ex 9:28; 32:12

14:14
Ex 13:21; 33:11
Num 9:15-21
Deut 5:4; 34:10

14:15
Ex 32:12
Num 14:13

14:17
Ex 20:5; 34:6,7
Ps 103:8

14:19
Ex 32:32; 34:9

⁵Then Moses and Aaron fell face downward on the ground before the people of Israel. ⁶Two of the spies, Joshua (the son of Nun), and Caleb (the son of Jephunneh), ripped their clothing ⁷and said to all the people, "It is a wonderful country ahead, ⁸and the Lord loves us. He will bring us safely into the land and give it to us. It is *very* fertile, a land 'flowing with milk and honey'! ⁹Oh, do not rebel against the Lord, and do not fear the people of the land. For they are but bread for us to eat! The Lord is with us and he has removed his protection from them! Don't be afraid of them!"

¹⁰, ¹¹But the only response of the people was to talk of stoning them. Then the glory of the Lord appeared, and the Lord said to Moses, "How long will these people despise me? Will they *never* believe me, even after all the miracles I have done among them? ¹²I will disinherit them and destroy them with a plague, and I will make you into a nation far greater and mightier than they are!"

¹³"But what will the Egyptians think when they hear about it?" Moses pleaded with the Lord. "They know full well the power you displayed in rescuing your people. ¹⁴They have told this to the inhabitants of this land, who are well aware that you are with Israel and that you talk with her face to face. They see the pillar of cloud and fire standing above us, and they know that you lead and protect us day and night. ¹⁵Now if you kill all your people, the nations that have heard your fame will say, ¹⁶'The Lord had to kill them because he wasn't able to take care of them in the wilderness. He wasn't strong enough to bring them into the land he swore he would give them.'

¹⁷, ¹⁸"Oh, please, show the great power [of your patience] by forgiving our sins and showing us your steadfast love. Forgive us, even though you have said that you don't let sin go unpunished, and that you punish the father's fault in the children to the third and fourth generation. ¹⁹Oh, I plead with you, pardon the sins of this people because of your magnificent, steadfast love, just as you have forgiven them all the time from when we left Egypt until now."

God condemns the people to wander for forty years

14:20
Num 14:28
Deut 32:40
Mic 7:18-20

²⁰, ²¹Then the Lord said, "All right, I will pardon them as you have requested. But I vow by my own name that just as it is true that all the earth shall be filled with the glory of the Lord, ²²so it is true that not one of the men who has seen my glory

14:17 *of your patience,* implied.

Promised Land. He protected them, fed them, and fulfilled every promise. Yet when encouraged to take that last step of faith and enter the land, the people refused. After witnessing so many miracles, why did they stop trusting God? Why did they refuse to enter the Promised Land when that had been their goal since leaving Egypt? How often we do the same thing. We trust God to handle the smaller things but doubt his ability to take care of the tough decisions, the frightening situations, and the big problems. Don't stop trusting God just as you are ready to reach your goal. If he has brought you this far, why would he let you down now? We can continue trusting God by remembering all he has done for us.

14:10 Two wise men, Joshua and Caleb, encouraged the people to act on God's promise and move ahead into the land. The people rejected their advice and even talked of killing them. Don't be too quick to reject advice you don't like. Evaluate it carefully and weigh it against the teaching in God's Word. Those who offer the advice may be giving God's advice.

14:13–16 They didn't deserve it, but Moses pleaded for his people because he was concerned about God's reputation among unbelievers. Think of the reputation you give God by your life. What your friends and neighbors think about God is more important than what they think about you.

14:17–20 Moses pleaded with God, asking him to forgive his people. His plea reveals several characteristics of God: (1) God is immensely patient; (2) God's love is one thing we can always count

on; (3) God forgives again and again; and (4) God is merciful, listening to and answering our requests. God has not changed since Moses' day. Like Moses, we can rely on God's love, patience, forgiveness, and mercy.

14:20–23 The people of Israel had a clearer view of God than any people before them, for they had both his laws and his physical presence. Their refusal to follow God after witnessing his miraculous deeds and listening to his Word made the judgment against them more severe. Increased opportunity brings increased responsibility. As Jesus said: "Much is required from those to whom much is given, for their responsibility is greater" (Luke 12:48). How much greater is our responsibility to obey and serve God, for we have the whole Bible and we know God's Son, Jesus Christ.

14:22 God wasn't exaggerating when he said that the Israelites had already failed ten times to trust and obey him. Here is a list of their ten failures: (1) lacking trust at the crossing of the Red Sea (Exodus 14:11, 12); (2) complaining over bitter water at Marah (Exodus 15:24); (3) complaining in the Sihn Wilderness (Exodus 16:3); (4) collecting more than the daily quota of manna (Exodus 16:20); (5) collecting manna on the Sabbath (Exodus 16:27–29); (6) complaining over lack of water at Rephidim (Exodus 17:2,3); (7) committing idolatry with a golden calf (Exodus 32:7–10); (8) complaining at Taberah (Numbers 11:1); (9) more complaining over the lack of delicious food (Numbers 11:4); (10) failing to trust God and enter the Promised Land (Numbers 14:1–4).

and the miracles I did both in Egypt and in the wilderness—and ten times refused to trust me and obey me— 23shall even see the land I promised to this people's ancestors. 24But my servant Caleb is a different kind of man—he has obeyed me fully. I will bring him into the land he entered as a spy, and his descendants shall have their full share in it. 25But now, since the people of Israel are so afraid of the Amalekites and the Canaanites living in the valleys, tomorrow you must turn back into the wilderness in the direction of the Red Sea."

26, 27Then the Lord said to Moses and to Aaron, "How long will this wicked nation complain about me? For I have heard all that they have been saying. 28Tell them, 'The Lord vows to do to you what you feared: 29You will all die here in this wilderness! Not a single one of you twenty years old and older, who has complained against me, 30shall enter the Promised Land. Only Caleb (son of Jephunneh) and Joshua (son of Nun) are permitted to enter it.

31" 'You said your children would become slaves of the people of the land. Well, instead I will bring *them* safely into the land and they shall inherit what you have despised. 32But as for you, your dead bodies shall fall in this wilderness. 33You must wander in the desert like nomads for forty years. In this way you will pay for your faithlessness, until the last of you lies dead in the desert.

34, 35" 'Since the spies were in the land for forty days, you must wander in the wilderness for forty years—a year for each day, bearing the burden of your sins. I will teach you what it means to reject me. I, Jehovah, have spoken. Every one of you who has conspired against me shall die here in this wilderness.' "

36, 37, 38Then the ten spies who had incited the rebellion against Jehovah by striking fear into the hearts of the people were struck dead before the Lord. Of all the spies, only Joshua and Caleb remained alive. 39What sorrow there was throughout the camp when Moses reported God's words to the people!

The people try to enter the Promised Land on their own

40They were up early the next morning, and started towards the Promised Land. "Here we are!" they said. "We realize that we have sinned, but now we are ready to go on into the land the Lord has promised us."

41But Moses said, "It's too late. Now you are disobeying the Lord's orders to return to the wilderness. 42Don't go ahead with your plan or you will be crushed by your enemies, for the Lord is not with you. 43Don't you remember? The Amalekites and the Canaanites are there! You have deserted the Lord, and now he will desert you."

44But they went ahead into the hill country, despite the fact that neither the Ark nor Moses left the camp. 45Then the Amalekites and the Canaanites who lived in the hills came down and attacked them and chased them to Hormah.

14:23
Num 26:65
32:11
Deut 1:35

14:24
Num 13:30
14:6; 26:65
Josh 14:6-15

14:25
Num 13:29

14:26
Num 11:1

14:28
Num 14:21
Heb 3:17

14:29
Num 1:17-19
26:2

14:30
Num 14:24,38
32:12

14:31
Num 14:3

14:32
Num 14:29
26:64; 32:13
1 Cor 10:5

14:33
Num 33:38
Deut 2:7; 8:2

14:36
Num 13:26-29,
31-33; 16:49
25:9

14:39
Ex 33:4

14:40
Deut 1:41-44

14:44
Num 10:33; 31:6

14:45
Num 21:3
Judg 1:17

14:24 The fulfillment of this verse is recorded in Joshua 14:6-15, when Caleb received his inheritance in the Promised Land.

14:34, 35 God's judgment came in a form the people feared most. The people were afraid of dying in the wilderness, so God punished them by making them wander in the wilderness until they died. Now they wished they had the problem of facing the giants and the fortified cities of the Promised Land. Failing to trust God often brings even greater problems than we had in the first place. Was this judgment—wandering 40 years in the wilderness—too harsh? Not compared to the instant death that God first threatened (14:12). Instead, God allowed the people to live. God had brought his people to the edge of the Promised Land, just as he said he would. He was ready to give them the rich land, but the people

didn't want it (14:1, 2). By this time, God had put up with a lot. At least ten times the people had refused to trust and obey him (14:22). The whole nation (except for Joshua, Caleb, Moses, and Aaron) showed contempt and distrust of God. But God's punishment was not permanent. In 40 years, a new generation would have a chance to enter (Joshua 1—3).

14:40-44 When the Israelites realized their foolish mistake, they were suddenly ready to return to God. But God didn't confuse their admission of guilt with true repentance, because he knew their hearts. Sure enough, they soon went their own way again. Sometimes good actions or intentions come too late. We must not only do the right things; we must do them at the right time. Otherwise, we have to face the consequences. The kind of obedience God desires is complete and instant.

C. WANDERING IN THE WILDERNESS (15:1—21:35)

After their disobedience and unsuccessful attempt to enter the Promised Land, the Israelites are condemned to wander forty years in the desert. Even in the midst of this punishment, the people continued to rebel and thus God continued to punish them. But the hearts of the people remained hard and rebellious. Hard hearts toward God may bring similar calamity to us.

1. Additional regulations

For offerings

15:3
Lev 1:1; 2:1-16
6:9-11
6:14-21; 22:21
23:37,38; 27:2
Deut 12:6,17
16:16

15:5
Num 15:5-10
28:7

15 The Lord told Moses to give these instructions to the people of Israel: "When your children finally live in the land I am going to give them, 3, 4and they want to please the Lord with a burnt offering or any other offering by fire, their sacrifice must be an animal from their flocks of sheep and goats, or from their herds of cattle. Each sacrifice—whether an ordinary one, or a sacrifice to fulfill a vow, or a free-will offering, or a special sacrifice at any of the annual festivals—must be accompanied by a grain offering. If a lamb is being sacrificed, use three quarts of fine flour mixed with three pints of oil, 5accompanied by three pints of wine for a drink offering.

6"If the sacrifice is a ram, use six quarts of fine flour mixed with four pints of oil, 7and four pints of wine for a drink offering. This will be a sacrifice that is a pleasing fragrance to the Lord.

15:8
Lev 3:1; 7:11-18
15:10
Num 15:5

8, 9"If the sacrifice is a young bull, then the grain offering accompanying it must consist of nine quarts of fine flour mixed with three quarts of oil, 10plus three quarts of wine for the drink offering. This shall be offered by fire as a pleasing fragrance to the Lord.

11, 12"These are the instructions for what is to accompany each sacrificial bull,

---

The voice of the minority is not often given a hearing. Nevertheless, truth cannot be measured by numbers. On the contrary, it often stands against majority opinion. Truth remains unchanged because it is guaranteed by the character of God. God is truth; what he says is the last word. At times, a person must even stand alone on the side of truth.

Caleb was not so much a man of great faith as a man of faith in a great God! His boldness rested on his understanding of God, not on his confidence in Israel's abilities to conquer the land. He could not agree with the majority, for that would be to disagree with God.

We, on the other hand, often base our decisions on what everyone else is doing. Few of us are first-order cowards like the ten spies. We are more like the people of Israel, getting our cowardice secondhand. Our search for right and wrong usually starts with questions such as "What do the experts say?" or "What do my friends say?" The question we most often avoid is "What does God say?" The principles we learn as we study the Bible provide a dependable road map for life. They draw us into a personal relationship with the God whose Word is the Bible. The God who gave Caleb his boldness is the same God who offers us the gift of eternal life through his Son, Jesus. That's truth worth believing!

Strengths and accomplishments:
- One of the spies sent by Moses to survey the land of Canaan (Numbers 13, 14)
- One of the only two adults who left Egypt and entered the Promised Land
- Voiced the minority opinion in favor of conquering the land
- Expressed faith in God's promises, in spite of apparent obstacles

Lessons from his life:
- Numbers are not an accurate measurement of right and wrong
- Boldness based on God's faithfulness is appropriate
- For courage and faith to be effective, they must combine words and actions

Vital statistics:
- Where: From Egypt to the Sinai Peninsula to the Promised Land
- Occupation: Spy, soldier, shepherd

Key verse:
"But my servant Caleb is a different kind of man—he has obeyed me fully. I will bring him into the land he entered as a spy, and his descendants shall have their full share in it" (Numbers 14:24).

Caleb's story is told in Numbers 13, 14 and Joshua 14, 15. He is also mentioned in Judges 1 and 1 Chronicles 4:13–15.

ram, lamb, or young goat. 13, 14These instructions apply both to native-born Israelis and to foreigners living among you who want to please the Lord with sacrifices offered by fire; 15, 16for there is the same law for all, native-born or foreigner, and this shall be true forever from generation to generation; all are the same before the Lord. Yes, one law for all!"

15:15
Ex 12:49
Lev 24:22
Num 9:14; 15:29

17, 18The Lord also said to Moses at this time, "Instruct the people of Israel that when they arrive in the land that I am going to give them, 19, 20, 21they must present to the Lord a sample of each year's new crops by making a loaf, using coarse flour from the first grain that is cut each year. This loaf must be waved back and forth before the altar in a gesture of offering to the Lord. It is an annual offering from your threshing floor, and must be observed from generation to generation.

15:19
Lev 23:10,17
Num 18:12

22"If by mistake you or future generations fail to carry out all of these regulations which the Lord has given you over the years through Moses, 23, 24then when the people realize their error, they must offer one young bull for a burnt offering. It will be a pleasant odor before the Lord, and must be offered along with the usual grain offering and drink offering, and one male goat for a sin offering. 25And the priest shall make atonement for all of the people of Israel and they shall be forgiven; for it was an error, and they have corrected it with their sacrifice made by fire before the Lord, and by their sin offering. 26All the people shall be forgiven, including the foreigners living among them, for the entire population is involved in such error and forgiveness.

15:23
Lev 4:2,22,27
5:15,18

15:25
Lev 4:20

27"If the error is made by a single individual, then he shall sacrifice a one-year-old female goat for a sin offering, 28and the priest shall make atonement for him before the Lord, and he shall be forgiven. 29This same law applies to individual foreigners who are living among you.

15:29
Num 15:15

30"But anyone who deliberately makes the 'mistake,' whether he is a native Israeli or a foreigner, is blaspheming Jehovah, and shall be cut off from among his people. 31For he has despised the commandment of the Lord and deliberately failed to obey his law; he must be executed, and die in his sin."

15:30
Num 14:40-44
Deut 1:43
17:12,13

For breaking the Sabbath

32One day while the people of Israel were in the wilderness, one of them was caught gathering wood on the Sabbath day. 33He was arrested and taken before Moses and Aaron and the other judges. 34They jailed him until they could find out the Lord's mind concerning him.

15:32
Ex 31:14,15
35:2,3

35Then the Lord said to Moses, "The man must die—all the people shall stone him to death outside the camp."

15:35
Lev 24:14,23
Deut 21:21

36So they took him outside the camp and killed him as the Lord had commanded.

For clothing

37, 38The Lord said to Moses, "Tell the people of Israel to make tassels for the hems of their clothes (this is a permanent regulation from generation to generation) and to attach the tassels to their clothes with a blue cord. 39The purpose of this regulation is to remind you, whenever you notice the tassels, of the commandments of the Lord, and that you are to obey his laws instead of following your own desires and going your own ways, as you used to do in serving other gods. 40It will remind you to be holy to your God. 41For I am Jehovah your God who brought you out of the land of Egypt; yes, I am the Lord, your God."

15:37,38
Deut 22:12
Mt 9:20; 23:5
Lk 8:44
15:39
Ex 13:9
Deut 6:12; 8:11
Jude 16
15:40
1 Pet 1:15,16
15:41
Ex 20:1

15:15, 16 *all are the same before the Lord,* literally, "as you are, so shall the foreigner be before Jehovah."
15:31 *he must be executed,* literally, "that soul shall be utterly cut off; his iniquity shall be upon him." **15:33** *before Moses and Aaron and the other judges,* literally, "to all the congregation."

15:30, 31 God was willing to forgive those who made unintentional errors if they realized their mistakes quickly and corrected them. However, those who deliberately sinned received a harsher judgment. Intentional sin grows out of an improper attitude toward God. A child who knowingly disobeys his parents challenges their authority and dares them to respond. Both the act and the attitude have to be dealt with.

15:39 Idol worship is self-centered, focusing on what a person can get from serving an idol. Good luck, prosperity, long life, and success in battle were expected from the gods. So were power and prestige. The worship of God is in striking contrast. Believers are to be selfless rather than self-centered. Instead of expecting God to serve us, we are to serve him, expecting nothing in return. We serve God for who he is, not for what we get out of him.

2. Many leaders rebel against Moses
Rebellion in the camp

16:1
Ex 6:21
Num 26:9,10
Deut 11:6
Jude 11

16:2
Num 1:16

16:3
Ex 19:6
Num 16:7; 35:34

16:4
Num 14:5
16:45; 20:6

16:5
Lev 10:3
21:6-8,12-15
Jn 15:16

16:7
Num 16:3

16:10
Num 3:6-10
16:11
Num 16:3
1 Sam 8:7

16:13
Ex 16:3,17
Num 11:5
14:2,3; 20:3,4
16:14
Ex 22:5
Num 20:5

16:15
Gen 4:4
1 Sam 12:3

16:19
Lev 9:6
Num 12:5
14:10; 16:42
20:6
16:21
Ex 32:10
Num 14:12

16 One day Korah (son of Izhar, grandson of Kohath, and a descendant of Levi) conspired with Dathan and Abiram (the sons of Eliab) and On (the son of Peleth), all three from the tribe of Reuben, 2to incite a rebellion against Moses. Two hundred and fifty popular leaders, all members of the Assembly, were involved.

3They went to Moses and Aaron and said, "We have had enough of your presumption; you are no better than anyone else; everyone in Israel has been chosen of the Lord, and he is with all of us. What right do you have to put yourselves forward, claiming that we must obey you, and acting as though you were greater than anyone else among all these people of the Lord?"

4When Moses heard what they were saying he fell face downward to the ground. 5Then he said to Korah and to those who were with him, "In the morning the Lord will show you who are his, and who is holy, and whom he has chosen as his priest. 6, 7Do this: You, Korah, and all those with you, take censers tomorrow and light them, and put incense upon them before the Lord, and we will find out whom the Lord has chosen. You are the presumptuous ones, you sons of Levi."

8, 9Then Moses spoke again to Korah: "Does it seem a small thing to you that the God of Israel has chosen you from among all the people of Israel to be near to himself as you work in the Tabernacle of Jehovah, and to stand before the people to minister to them? 10Is it nothing to you that he has given this task to only you Levites? And now are you demanding the priesthood also? 11, 12That is what you are really after! That is why you are revolting against Jehovah. And what has Aaron done, that you are dissatisfied with him?" Then Moses summoned Dathan and Abiram (the sons of Eliab), but they refused to come.

13"Is it a small thing," they mimicked, "that you brought us out of lovely Egypt to kill us here in this terrible wilderness, and that now you want to make yourself our king? 14What's more, you haven't brought us into the wonderful country you promised, nor given us fields and vineyards. Whom are you trying to fool? We refuse to come."

15Then Moses was very angry and said to the Lord, "Do not accept their sacrifices! I have never stolen so much as a donkey from them, and have not hurt one of them."

16And Moses said to Korah, "Come here tomorrow before the Lord with all your friends; Aaron will be here too. 17Be sure to bring your censers with incense on them; a censer for each man, 250 in all; and Aaron will also be here with his."

18So they did. They came with their censers and lit them and placed the incense on them, and stood at the entrance of the Tabernacle with Moses and Aaron. 19Meanwhile, Korah had stirred up the entire nation against Moses and Aaron, and they all assembled to watch. Then the glory of Jehovah appeared to all the people, 20and Jehovah said to Moses and Aaron, 21"Get away from these people so that I may instantly destroy them."

16:6, 7 *whom the Lord has chosen,* literally, "whom Jehovah chooses to be the holy one." **16:13** *mimicked,* literally, "said."

16:2, 3 Korah and his associates had seen the advantages of the priesthood in Egypt. Egyptian priests had great wealth and political influence, something Korah desired for himself. Korah might have assumed that Moses, Aaron, and his sons were trying to make the Israelite priesthood the same kind of political machine. He wanted to be a part of it. He did not understand that Moses' main ambition was to serve God rather than control others.

16:8-10 Like Korah, we often desire the special qualities God has given others. Korah had significant, worthwhile abilities and responsibilities of his own. In the end, however, his ambition for more caused him to lose everything. Inappropriate ambition is greed in disguise. Concentrate on seeking from God the special purpose he has for you, instead of wishing you were in someone else's shoes.

16:13, 14 One of the easiest ways to fall short of following God is to look at our present problems and inflate their unpleasantness. Dathan and Abiram did just that when they began to long for better food and more pleasant surroundings. Egypt, the place they had longed to leave, was now looking better and better—not because of slavery and taskmasters, of course, but because of its mouth-watering food! These two men and their followers had completely lost their perspective. They no longer knew where they were going and what awaited them if they got there. When we take our eyes off God and start looking at ourselves and our problems, we begin to lose our perspective as well. Overrating problems can hinder our relationship with God. Don't let difficulties make you lose sight of God's purpose for your life.

22But Moses and Aaron fell face downward to the ground before the Lord. "O God, the God of all mankind," they pleaded, "must you be angry with all the people when one man sins?"

16:22
Gen 18:23-32

Punishment for the rebellion

23, 24And the Lord said to Moses, "Then tell the people to get away from the tents of Korah, Dathan, and Abiram."

16:24
Num 16:45

25So Moses rushed over to the tents of Dathan and Abiram, followed closely by the 250 Israeli leaders. 26"Quick!" he told the people, "get away from the tents of these wicked men, and don't touch anything that belongs to them, lest you be included in their sins [and be destroyed with them]."

16:26
Gen 19:12-17
Deut 13:17

27So all the people stood back from the tents of Korah, Dathan, and Abiram. And Dathan and Abiram came out and stood at the entrances of their tents with their wives and sons and little ones.

28And Moses said, "By this you shall know that Jehovah has sent me to do all these things that I have done—for I have not done them on my own. 29If these men die a natural death or from some ordinary accident or disease, then Jehovah has not sent me. 30But if the Lord does a miracle and the ground opens up and swallows them and everything that belongs to them, and they go down alive into Sheol, then you will know that these men have despised the Lord."

16:28
Ex 3:12; 4:1-9
7:9
Deut 18:22

31He had hardly finished speaking the words when the ground suddenly split open beneath them, 32and a great fissure swallowed them up, along with their tents and families and the friends who were standing with them, and everything they owned. 33So they went down alive into Sheol and the earth closed upon them, and they perished. 34All of the people of Israel fled at their screams, fearing that the earth would swallow them too. 35Then fire came from Jehovah and burned up the 250 men who were offering incense.

16:32
Num 16:30
26:10

16:35
Lev 10:2
Num 11:1; 16:2
26:10

36, 37And the Lord said to Moses, "Tell Eleazar the son of Aaron the priest to pull those censers from the fire; for they are holy, dedicated to the Lord. He must also scatter the burning incense 38from the censers of these men who have sinned at the cost of their lives. He shall then beat the metal into a sheet as a covering for the altar, for these censers are holy because they were used before the Lord; and the altar sheet shall be a reminder to the people of Israel."

39So Eleazar the priest took the 250 bronze censers and beat them out into a sheet of metal to cover the altar, 40to be a reminder to the people of Israel that no unauthorized person—no one who is not a descendant of Aaron—may come before the Lord to burn incense, lest the same thing happen to him as happened to Korah and his associates. Thus the Lord's directions to Moses were carried out.

16:40
Num 1:51
3:10,38

41But the very next morning all the people began muttering again against Moses and Aaron, saying, "You have killed the Lord's people."

16:41
Num 16:3

42Soon a great, sullen mob formed; suddenly, as they looked toward the Tabernacle, the Cloud appeared and the awesome glory of the Lord was seen. 43, 44Moses and Aaron came and stood at the entrance of the Tabernacle, and the Lord said to Moses,

16:42
Ex 24:16
40:34,35
Num 14:10
16:19

45"Get away from these people so that I can instantly destroy them." But Moses and Aaron fell face downward to the earth before the Lord.

16:45
Num 16:21,24

16:26 and be destroyed with them, implied.

16:22–27 Moses and Aaron asked God to have mercy on the very people who rebelled against them. They prayed for those with whom they were most angry and frustrated. Do you pray for those who try to hurt you? Or do you seek revenge, asking God to help you to get even? Only men and women who have a deep relationship with God can remain firm under pressure and pray for their attackers. They understand that the God who called them to their task will take the responsibility to settle the score with those who rebel. It is not the child's job to discipline a sibling, but the parents'. In the same way, it is not our job to seek revenge against those who wrong us. God will make certain that, in the end, justice is carried out.

16:26 The Israelites were told not even to touch the belongings of the wicked rebels. In this case, doing so would have shown sympathy to their cause and agreement with their principles. Korah, Dathan, and Abiram were directly challenging Moses and God. Moses clearly stated what God intended to do to the rebels (16:28–30). He did this so that everyone would have to choose between following Korah or following Moses, God's chosen leader. This story does not mean that touching something a wicked person owns will make you wicked. What it means is that God asks us to

16:46
Ex 30:7-10
Lev 10:6
Num 8:19; 18:5
25:13
Deut 9:22

⁴⁶And Moses said to Aaron, "Quick, take a censer and place fire in it from the altar; lay incense on it, and carry it quickly among the people and make atonement for them; for God's anger has gone out among them—the plague has already begun.

KORAH

Some notorious historical figures might have remained anonymous if they hadn't tried to grab onto more than they could hold. But by refusing to be content with what they had, and by trying to get more than they deserved, they often ended up with nothing. Korah, one of the Israelite leaders, was such a person.

Korah was a Levite who served as a special assistant in the daily functions of the Tabernacle. Shortly after Israel's great rebellion against God (Numbers 13, 14), Korah instigated his own mini-rebellion. He recruited a grievance committee and confronted Moses and Aaron. Their list of complaints boils down to three statements: (1) you are no better than anyone else; (2) everyone in Israel has been chosen of the Lord; (3) we don't need to obey you. It is amazing to see how Korah twisted the first two statements—both true—to reach the wrong conclusions.

Moses would have agreed that he was no better than anyone else. He would also have agreed that all Israelites were God's chosen people. But Korah's application of these truths was wrong. Not all Israelites were chosen to lead. Korah's hidden claim was this: "I have as much right to lead as Moses does." His error cost him not only his job—a position of service which he enjoyed—but also his life.

Korah's story gives us numerous warnings: (1) Don't let desire for what someone else has make you discontented with what you already have. (2) Don't try to raise your own self-esteem by attacking someone else. (3) Don't use part of God's Word to support what you want; rather, allow Scripture as a whole to shape your wants. (4) Don't expect to find satisfaction in power and position; God may want to work through you in a position that seems unimportant.

Strengths and accomplishments:
• Popular leader; influential figure during the Exodus
• Mentioned among the chief men of Israel (Exodus 6)
• One of the first Levites appointed for special service in the Tabernacle
• His descendants became psalm writers (Psalms 42—49, 84, 85, 87, 88), singers in the Temple choir (2 Chronicles 20:19), and faithful ministers

Weaknesses and mistakes:
• Failed to recognize the significant position God had placed him in
• Forgot that his fight was against someone greater than Moses
• Allowed greed to blind his common sense

Lessons from his life:
• There is sometimes a fine line between goals and greed
• If we are discontented with what we have, we may lose it without gaining anything better

Vital statistics:
• Where: Egypt, Sinai Peninsula
• Occupation: Levite, Tabernacle assistant

Key verses:
"Then Moses spoke again to Korah: 'Does it seem a small thing to you that the God of Israel has chosen you from among all the people of Israel to be near to himself as you work in the Tabernacle of Jehovah, and to stand before the people to minister to them? Is it nothing to you that he has given this task to only you Levites? And now are you demanding the priesthood also'?" (Numbers 16:8–10).

Korah's story is told in Numbers 16:1–40. He is also mentioned in Numbers 26:9; Jude 11.

---

make a fundamental choice between siding with wicked people or siding with him.

16:33 Sheol, in this case, is used as another word for the grave. In other words, Korah and the other rebels were buried alive when the earth split open. God executed swift and final judgment against those who had rejected him.

16:41 Just one day after Korah and his followers were executed for grumbling and complaining against God, the Israelites started all over with more muttering and complaining. Their negative attitude only caused them to rebel even more and to bring about

even greater trouble. It eroded their faith in God and encouraged thoughts of giving up and turning back. The path to open rebellion against God begins with dissatisfaction and skepticism, then moves to grumbling about both God and present circumstances. Next comes bitterness and resentment, followed finally by rebellion and open hostility. If you are often dissatisfied, skeptical, complaining, or bitter—beware! These attitudes lead to rebellion and separation from God. Any choice to side against God is a step in the direction of letting go of him completely and making your own way through life.

47Aaron did as Moses had told him to, and ran among the people, for the plague had indeed already begun; and he put on the incense and made atonement for them. 48And he stood between the living and the dead, and the plague was stopped, 49but not before 14,700 people had died (in addition to those who had died the previous day with Korah). 50Then Aaron returned to Moses at the entrance of the Tabernacle; and so the plague was stopped.

16:47
Num 16:36
25:7,8,13
Deut 33:10
16:49
Num 16:32-35
25:9
1 Chron 21:14

Aaron's budding rod proves his authority

17 Then the Lord said to Moses, "Tell the people of Israel that each of their tribal chiefs is to bring you a wooden rod with his name inscribed upon it. Aaron's name is to be on the rod of the tribe of Levi. 4Put these rods in the inner room of the Tabernacle where I meet with you, in front of the Ark. 5I will use these rods to identify the man I have chosen: for buds will grow on his rod! Then at last this murmuring and complaining against you will stop!"

17:4
Ex 25:16-22
Num 17:10
17:5
Num 16:5; 17:8
Heb 9:4

6So Moses gave the instructions to the people, and each of the twelve chiefs (including Aaron) brought him a rod. 7He put them before the Lord in the inner room of the Tabernacle, 8and when he went in the next day, he found that Aaron's rod, representing the tribe of Levi, had budded and was blossoming, and had ripe almonds hanging from it!

17:7
Num 18:2
17:8
Num 17:5
Heb 9:4

9When Moses brought them out to show the others, they stared in disbelief! Then each man except Aaron claimed his rod. 10The Lord told Moses to place Aaron's rod permanently beside the Ark as a reminder of this rebellion. He was to [bring it out and show it to the people again] if there were any further complaints about Aaron's authority; this would ward off further catastrophe to the people. 11So Moses did as the Lord commanded him.

17:10
Num 17:4
Deut 9:7,24

12, 13But the people of Israel only grumbled the more. "We are as good as dead," they whined. "Everyone who even comes close to the Tabernacle dies. Must we all perish?"

17:12
Num 1:51-53
18:4-7; 26:11
Isa 6:5

3. Directions to the priests and Levites

18 The Lord now spoke to Aaron: "You and your sons and your family are responsible for any desecration of the sanctuary," he said, "and will be held liable for any impropriety in your priestly work.

18:1
Ex 28:38

2, 3"Your kinsmen, the tribe of Levi, are your assistants; but only you and your sons may perform the sacred duties in the Tabernacle itself. The Levites must be careful not to touch any of the sacred articles or the altar, lest I destroy both them and you. 4No one who is not a member of the tribe of Levi shall assist you in any way. 5Remember, only the priests are to perform the sacred duties within the sanctuary and at the altar. If you follow these instructions the wrath of God will never again fall upon any of the people of Israel for violating this law. 6I say it again—your kinsmen the Levites are your assistants for the work of the Tabernacle. They are a gift to you from the Lord. 7But you and your sons, the priests, shall personally handle all the sacred service, including the altar and all that is within the veil, for the priesthood is your special gift of service. Anyone else who attempts to perform these duties shall die."

18:2
Num 1:51
3:5-10
4:15-20
8:19,22; 18:7
18:5
Num 8:19; 16:46
18:6
Num 3:9
8:16-19
18:7
Ex 29:9
Num 1:51; 3:10

8The Lord gave these further instructions to Aaron: "I have given the priests all the gifts which are brought to the Lord by the people; all these offerings presented to the Lord by the gesture of waving them before the altar belong to you and your sons, by permanent law. 9The grain offerings, the sin offerings, and the guilt offerings are yours, except for the sample presented to the Lord by burning upon

18:8
Lev 7:28-34
Deut 12:6
18:9
Lev 2:2; 4:22
6:25-30
10:12,13

17:10 bring it out and show it to the people again, implied.

17:12, 13 After witnessing spectacular miracles, seeing the Egyptians punished by the plagues, and experiencing the actual presence of God, the Israelites still complained and rebelled. We wonder how they could be so blind and ignorant, and yet we often repeat this same pattern. We have centuries of evidence, the Bible in many translations, and the convincing results of archeological and historical studies. But people today continue to disobey God and do things their own way. Like the Israelites, we pay more attention to our physical condition than to our spiritual condition. We can escape this pattern only through serving God with our whole heart. A halfhearted approach doesn't get us half way there—it gets us nowhere.

the altar. All these are most holy offerings. ¹⁰They are to be eaten only in a most holy place, and only by males. ¹¹All other gifts presented to me by the gesture of waving them before the altar are for you and your families, sons and daughters alike. For all the members of your families may eat these unless anyone is ceremonially impure at the time.

¹²"Yours also are the first-of-the-harvest gifts the people bring as offerings to the Lord—the best of the olive oil, wine, grain, ¹³and every other crop. Your families may eat these unless they are ceremonially defiled at the time. ¹⁴, ¹⁵So everything that is dedicated to the Lord shall be yours, including the firstborn sons of the people of Israel, and the firstborn of their animals. ¹⁶However, you may never accept the firstborn sons, nor the firstborn of any animals that I do not permit for food. Instead, there must be a payment of two and a half dollars made for each firstborn child. It is to be brought when he is one month old.

¹⁷"However, the firstborn of cows, sheep, or goats may not be bought back; they must be sacrificed to the Lord. Their blood is to be sprinkled upon the altar, and their fat shall be burned as a fire offering; it is very pleasant to the Lord. ¹⁸The meat of these animals shall be yours, including the breast and right thigh that are presented to the Lord by the gesture of waving before the altar. ¹⁹Yes, I have given to you all of these 'wave offerings' brought by the people of Israel to the Lord; they are for you and your families as food; this is a permanent contract between the Lord and you and your descendants.

²⁰"You priests may own no property, nor have any other income, for I am all that you need.

²¹As for the tribe of Levi, your relatives, they shall be paid for their service with the tithes from the entire land of Israel.

²²"From now on, Israelites other than the priests and Levites shall not enter the sanctuary, lest they be judged guilty and die. ²³Only the Levites shall do the work there, and they shall be guilty if they fail. This is a permanent law among you, that the Levites shall own no property in Israel, ²⁴for the people's tithes, offered to the Lord by the gesture of waving before the altar, shall belong to the Levites; these are their inheritance, and so they have no need for property."

²⁵, ²⁶The Lord also said to Moses, "Tell the Levites to give to the Lord a tenth of the tithes they receive—a tithe of the tithe, to be presented to the Lord by the gesture of waving before the altar. ²⁷The Lord will consider this as your first-of-the-harvest offering to him of grain and wine, as though it were from your own property. ²⁸, ²⁹This tithe of the tithe shall be selected from the choicest part of the tithes you receive as the Lord's portion, and shall be given to Aaron the priest. ³⁰It shall be credited to you just as though it were from your own threshing floor and wine press. ³¹Aaron and his sons and their families may eat it in their homes or anywhere they wish, for it is their compensation for their service in the Tabernacle. ³²You Levites will not be held guilty for accepting the Lord's tithes if you then give the best tenth to the priests. But beware that you do not treat the holy gifts of the people of Israel as though they were common, lest you die."

Purification after defilement

19 The Lord said to Moses and Aaron, "Here is another of my laws: "Tell the people of Israel to bring you a red heifer without defect, one that

18:17 *they must be sacrificed to the Lord*, literally, "they are holy." 18:19 *a permanent contract*, literally, "a covenant of salt."

Cross-references (left margin):

18:11 Lev 22:2,3, 11-13
18:12 Ex 22:29 Num 15:19-21 Deut 18:4
18:14 Lev 27:28
18:19 2 Chron 13:5
18:20 Num 18:23 Deut 10:9; 18:2 Josh 13:33 Ezek 44:28
18:21 Lev 27:30-33
18:23 Num 18:1,20
18:25,26 Num 18:28 Neh 10:38
18:28 Num 18:25
18:31 Mt 10:10 Lk 10:7 1 Cor 9:13 1 Tim 5:18
18:32 Lev 22:2,15,16

18:25, 26 Even the Levites, who were ministers, had to tithe to support the work of the Tabernacle. No one was exempt from returning to God a portion of what was received from him. Though the Levites owned no land and operated no great enterprises, they were to treat their income the same as everyone else did by giving a portion to care for the needs of the other Levites and of the Tabernacle. The tithing principle is still relevant today. God expects all his followers to supply the material needs of those who devote themselves to meeting the spiritual needs of the community of faith.

18:32 Gifts dedicated to God were to be treated with respect. Churches today also have the responsibility to manage carefully the money and time people have dedicated to God. If you are involved in raising or handling your church's money, insist that people show respect for gifts made to God by their careful management and responsible stewardship of his resources.

has never been yoked. Give her to Eleazar the priest and he shall take her outside the camp and someone shall kill her as he watches. ⁴Eleazar shall take some of her blood upon his finger and sprinkle it seven times towards the front of the Tabernacle. ⁵Then someone shall burn the heifer as he watches—her hide, meat, blood, and dung. ⁶Eleazar shall take cedar wood and hyssop branches and scarlet thread, and throw them into the burning pile.

⁷"Then he must wash his clothes, and bathe, and afterwards return to the camp and be ceremonially defiled until the evening. ⁸And the one who burns the animal must wash his clothes, and bathe, and he too shall be defiled until evening. ⁹Then someone who is not ceremonially defiled shall gather up the ashes of the heifer and place them in some purified place outside the camp, where they shall be kept for the people of Israel as a source of water for the purification ceremonies, for removal of sin. ¹⁰And the one who gathers up the ashes of the heifer must wash his clothes and be defiled until evening; this is a permanent law for the benefit of the people of Israel and any foreigners living among them.

¹¹"Anyone who touches a dead human body shall be defiled for seven days, ¹²and must purify himself the third and seventh days with water [run through the ashes of the red heifer]; then he will be purified; but if he does not do this on the third day, he will continue to be defiled even after the seventh day. ¹³Anyone who touches a dead person and does not purify himself in the manner specified, has defiled the Tabernacle of the Lord, and shall be excommunicated from Israel. The cleansing water was not sprinkled upon him, so the defilement continues.

¹⁴"When a man dies in a tent, these are the various regulations: Everyone who enters the tent, and those who are in it at the time, shall be defiled seven days. ¹⁵Any container in the tent without a lid over it is defiled.

¹⁶"If someone out in a field touches the corpse of someone who has been killed in battle, or who has died in any other way, or if he even touches a bone or a grave, he shall be defiled seven days. ¹⁷To become purified again, ashes from the red heifer sin offering are to be added to spring water in a kettle. ¹⁸Then a person who is not defiled shall take hyssop branches and dip them into the water and sprinkle the water upon the tent and upon all the pots and pans in the tent, and upon anyone who has been defiled by being in the tent, or by touching a bone, or touching someone who has been killed or is otherwise dead, or has touched a grave. ¹⁹This shall take place on the third and seventh days; then the defiled person must wash his clothes and bathe himself, and that evening he will be out from under the defilement.

²⁰"But anyone who is defiled and doesn't purify himself shall be excommunicated, for he has defiled the sanctuary of the Lord, and the water to cleanse him has not been sprinkled upon him; so he remains defiled. ²¹This is a permanent law. The man who sprinkles the water must afterwards wash his clothes; and anyone touching the water shall be defiled until evening. ²²And anything a defiled person touches shall be defiled until evening."

4. The new generation
Moses strikes the rock and is judged

20 The people of Israel arrived in the wilderness of Zin in April and camped at Kadesh, where Miriam died and was buried. ²There was not enough water to

19:2 Lev 10:6 22:20-25 Num 3:4 Deut 21:3
19:4 Lev 4:6,17 16:14
19:6 Lev 14:4,6,49
19:7 Lev 11:25,40 16:26-28
19:9 Num 8:7 19:13,20,21
19:10 Num 19:7,8,19
19:11 Lev 11:27,31 21:1,11
19:12 Num 19:17-19
19:13 Lev 7:20,21 15:31; 20:3 22:3-7
19:16 Num 19:11 31:19
19:17 Num 19:9
19:19 Num 19:9 Ps 51:7 Ezek 36:25-27
19:20 Num 15:30 19:13
19:21 Lev 11:25,40 16:26-28 Num 19:7
19:22 Lev 5:2,3; 7:21
20:1 Num 13:21

19:12 *run through the ashes of the red heifer,* implied. See verse 17. **19:17** *ashes from the red heifer sin offering,* literally, "ashes of the burnt sin offering." **20:1** *in April,* literally, "the first month."

19:9, 10 What is the significance of the red heifer's ashes? When a person touched a dead body, he was considered unclean or defiled (i.e., unable to approach God in worship). This ritual purified the unclean person so that once again he could offer sacrifices and worship God. Death was the strongest of defilements because it was the final result of sin. Thus a special sacrifice—a red heifer—was required. It had to be offered by someone who was not unclean. When it had been burned on the altar, its ashes were used as a filter through which water was poured in order to be purified—not so much literally as symbolically. The unclean person then washed himself, and often his clothes and belongings, with this purified water as an act of becoming clean again.

20:2
Ex 17:1-4

20:3
Ex 17:2
Num 11:1,
33,34
14:1,2,36,37
16:31-35

20:5
Num 16:14

20:8
Ex 4:2,17
Num 21:18

20:11
Ex 17:6
Ps 78:16
Isa 48:21
1 Cor 10:4

20:12
Lev 10:3
Num 20:24
Ezek 36:23

20:13
Ex 17:7
Deut 32:51

drink at that place, so the people again rebelled against Moses and Aaron. A great mob formed, 3and they held a protest meeting.

"Would that we too had died with our dear brothers the Lord killed!" they shouted at Moses. 4"You have deliberately brought us into this wilderness to get rid of us, along with our flocks and herds. 5Why did you ever make us leave Egypt and bring us here to this evil place? Where is the fertile land of wonderful crops—the figs, vines, and pomegranates you told us about? Why, there isn't even water enough to drink!"

6Moses and Aaron turned away and went to the entrance of the Tabernacle, where they fell face downward before the Lord; and the glory of Jehovah appeared to them.

7And he said to Moses, 8"Get Aaron's rod; then you and Aaron must summon the people. As they watch, speak to that rock over there and tell it to pour out its water! You will give them water from a rock, enough for all the people and all their cattle!"

9So Moses did as instructed. He took the rod from the place where it was kept before the Lord; 10then Moses and Aaron summoned the people to come and gather at the rock; and he said to them, "Listen, you rebels! Must we bring you water from this rock?"

11Then Moses lifted the rod and struck the rock twice, and water gushed out; and the people and their cattle drank.

12But the Lord said to Moses and Aaron, "Because you did not believe me and did not sanctify me in the eyes of the people of Israel, you shall not bring them into the land I have promised them!"

13This place was named Meribah (meaning "Rebel Waters"), because it was where the people of Israel fought against Jehovah, and where he showed himself to be holy before them.

20:8 *Get Aaron's rod,* literally, "get the rod." **20:12** *did not believe me,* literally, "did not sanctify me." The Lord had said to *speak* to the rock. Moses *struck* it, not once, but *twice.*

EVENTS AT KADESH
After wandering in the wilderness for 40 years, Israel arrived at Kadesh, where Miriam died. There was not enough water for the people, and they complained bitterly. Moses struck a rock, and it gave enough water for everyone. The king of Edom refused Israel passage through his land, forcing them to travel around his country.

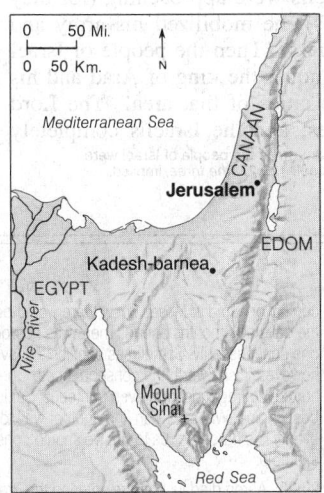

to enter the Promised Land. Moses, Aaron, Joshua, and Caleb were among the few who remained from those who had left Egypt. Once again they camped at Kadesh, the site of the first spy mission that had ended in disaster. Now Moses hoped the people were ready for a fresh start.

20:3-5 After 37 years in the wilderness, the Israelites forgot that their wanderings were a result of their own sin. They could not accept the fact that they brought their problems upon themselves, so they blamed Moses for their condition. Often our troubles result from our own disobedience or lack of faith. We cannot blame God for our sins. Until we face this fact, there will be little peace and no spiritual growth in our lives.

20:12 The Lord had told Moses to speak to the rock; Moses struck it, not once, but twice. For this he was forbidden to enter the Promised Land. Was God's punishment of Moses too harsh? After all, the people had nagged him, slandered him, and rebelled against both him and God. Now they were at it again (20:5). But Moses was the leader and model for the entire nation. Because of this great responsibility to the people, he could not be let off lightly. By striking the rock, Moses disobeyed God's direct command and dishonored God in the presence of his people.

20:1 It had been 37 years since Israel's first spy mission into the Promised Land (Numbers 13, 14) and 40 years since the exodus from Egypt. The Bible is virtually silent about those 37 years of aimless wandering. The generation of those who had lived in Egypt had almost died off, and the new generation would soon be ready

Edom refuses to let Israel pass through

14While Moses was at Kadesh he sent messengers to the king of Edom: "We are the descendants of your brother Israel," he declared. "You know our sad history, 15how our ancestors went down to visit Egypt and stayed there so long, and became slaves of the Egyptians. 16But when we cried to the Lord he heard us and sent an Angel who brought us out of Egypt, and now we are here at Kadesh, encamped on the borders of your land. 17Please let us pass through your country. We will be careful not to go through your planted fields, nor through your vineyards; we won't even drink water from your wells, but will stay on the main road and not leave it until we have crossed your border on the other side."

18But the king of Edom said, "Stay out! If you attempt to enter my land I will meet you with an army!"

19"But, sir," protested the Israeli ambassadors, "we will stay on the main road and will not even drink your water unless we pay whatever you demand for it. We only want to pass through, and nothing else."

20But the king of Edom was adamant. "Stay out!" he warned, and, mobilizing his army, he marched to the frontier with a great force. 21, 22Because Edom refused to allow Israel to pass through their country, Israel turned back and journeyed from Kadesh to Mount Hor.

Aaron dies

23Then the Lord said to Moses and Aaron at the border of the land of Edom, 24"The time has come for Aaron to die—for he shall not enter the land I have given the people of Israel, for the two of you rebelled against my instructions concerning the water at Meribah. 25Now take Aaron and his son Eleazar and lead them up onto Mount Hor. 26There you shall remove Aaron's priestly garments from him and put them on Eleazar his son; and Aaron shall die there."

27So Moses did as the Lord commanded him. The three of them went up together into Mount Hor as all the people watched. 28When they reached the summit, Moses removed the priestly garments from Aaron and put them on his son Eleazar; and Aaron died on the top of the mountain. Moses and Eleazar returned, 29and when the people were informed of Aaron's death, they mourned for him for thirty days.

Israel defeats the king of Arad

21 When the king of Arad heard that the Israelis were approaching (for they were traveling the same route as the spies), he mobilized his army and attacked Israel, taking some of the men as prisoners. 2Then the people of Israel vowed to the Lord that if he would help them conquer the king of Arad and his people, they would completely annihilate all the cities of that area. 3The Lord heeded their request and defeated the Canaanites; and the Israelis completely

20:14 your brother Israel. The people of Edom were descended from Esau, while the people of Israel were descended from his brother Jacob, whose name was later changed to Israel. **20:27** the three, implied.

Cross-references (margin)

20:14 Gen 36:31-39; Josh 2:10; 9:9,10
20:16 Ex 3:2-6; 14:19; 23:30
20:21 Num 20:1,14; 21:4; Deut 2:8,29; Judg 11:17
20:25 Num 3:4; 19:3,4
20:26 Num 20:24
20:28 Num 33:38
21:1 Num 33:40; Josh 12:14; Judg 1:16
21:3 Num 14:45; 1 Sam 30:30

20:14 Two brothers became the ancestors of two nations. The Edomites descended from Esau; the Israelites from Jacob. Thus the Edomites were "brothers" to the Israelites. Israel sent a brotherly message to Edom requesting passage through their land on the main road, a well-traveled trade route. Israel promised to stay on the road, thus harmlessly bypassing Edom's fields, vineyards, and wells. However, Edom refused because they did not trust Israel's word. They were afraid that this great horde of people would either attack them or devour their crops (Deuteronomy 2:4, 5). Since "brothers" should not fight, God told the Israelites to turn back and travel by a different route to the Promised Land.

20:17 Moses negotiated and reasoned with the Edomite king. When nothing worked, he was left with two choices—force a conflict or avoid it. Moses knew there would be enough barriers in the days and months ahead. There was no point in adding another one unnecessarily. Sometimes conflict is unavoidable. Sometimes, however, it isn't worth the consequences. Open warfare may seem heroic, courageous, and even righteous, but it is not always the best choice. When we can find another way to solve our problems, even if it is harder for us to do, we should consider Moses' example.

20:28 Aaron died just before entering the Promised Land, probably as punishment for his sin of rebellion (Exodus 32; Numbers 12:1–9). Thus this was the first time that a new High Priest was appointed. The priestly clothing was removed from Aaron and placed on his son Eleazar, following the commands from the book of Leviticus.

destroyed them and their cities. The name of the region was thereafter called Hormah (meaning "Utterly Destroyed").

The bronze snake

21:4
Deut 2:8

21:5
Ex 16:15
Num 11:1-9
14:1-4; 16:13

21:6
Deut 8:15

4Then the people of Israel returned to Mount Hor, and from there continued southward along the road to the Red Sea in order to go around the land of Edom. The people were very discouraged; 5they began to murmur against God and to complain against Moses. "Why have you brought us out of Egypt to die here in the wilderness?" they whined. "There is nothing to eat here, and nothing to drink, and we hate this insipid manna."

6So the Lord sent poisonous snakes among them to punish them, and many of them were bitten and died.

An understudy must know the lead role completely and be willing to step into it at a moment's notice. Eleazar was an excellent understudy, well trained for his eventual leading role. However, his moments in the spotlight were painful. On one occasion, he watched his two older brothers burn to death for failing to take God's holiness seriously. Later, as his father was dying, he was made High Priest, surely one of the most responsible—and therefore potentially the most stressful—positions in Israel.

An understudy benefits from having both the script and a human model of the role. Ever since childhood, Eleazar had been able to observe Moses and Aaron. Now he could learn from watching Joshua. In addition, he had God's laws to guide him as he worked as priest and adviser to Joshua.

Strengths and accomplishments:
- Succeeded his father, Aaron, as High Priest
- Completed his father's work by helping lead the people into the Promised Land
- Teamed up with Joshua
- Acted as God's spokesman to the people

Lessons from his life:
- Concentrating on our present challenges and responsibilities is the best way to prepare for what God has planned for our future
- God's desire is consistent obedience throughout our lives

Vital statistics:
- Where: Sinai Wilderness, Promised Land
- Occupation: Priest and High Priest
- Relatives: Father: Aaron. Brothers: Nadab and Abihu. Aunt and Uncle: Miriam and Moses.
- Contemporaries: Joshua, Caleb

Key verse:
"He [Joshua] shall be the one to consult with Eleazar the priest in order to get directions from the Lord. The Lord will speak to Eleazar through the use of the Urim, and Eleazar will pass on these instructions to Joshua and the people. In this way the Lord will continue to give them guidance" (Numbers 27:21).

Eleazar is mentioned in Exodus 6:23; Leviticus 10:16–20; Numbers 4:16; 16:37–39; 26:1, 3, 63; 27:2, 15–23; 32:2; 34:17; Deuteronomy 10:6; Joshua 14:1; 17:4.

21:5 In Psalm 78, we learn the sources of Israel's complaining: (1) they forgot the miracles God did for them, (2) they demanded more than what God had given them, (3) their repentance was insincere, and (4) they were ungrateful for what God had done for them. Our complaining often has its roots in one of these thoughtless actions and attitudes. If we can cut off the source of complaining, it will not take hold and grow in our lives.

21:6 God used poisonous snakes to punish the people for their unbelief and complaining. The Sinai desert has a variety of snakes. Some hide in the sand and attack without warning. Both the Israelites and Egyptians had a great fear of snakes. A bite by a poisonous snake often meant a slow death with intense suffering.

⁷Then the people came to Moses and cried out, "We have sinned, for we have spoken against Jehovah and against you. Pray to him to take away the snakes." So Moses prayed for the people.

⁸Then the Lord told him, "Make a bronze replica of one of these snakes and attach it to the top of a pole; anyone who is bitten shall live if he simply looks at it!"

21:8
Isa 14:29
Jn 3:14,15

⁹So Moses made the replica, and whenever anyone who had been bitten looked at the bronze snake, he recovered!

21:9
2 Kgs 18:4
Jn 3:14; 12:32

¹⁰Israel journeyed next to Oboth and camped there. ¹¹Then they went on to Iyeabarim, in the wilderness, a short distance east of Moab, ¹²and from there they traveled to the valley of the brook Zared and set up camp. ¹³Then they moved to the far side of the Arnon River, near the borders of the Amorites. (The Arnon River is the boundary line between the Moabites and the Amorites. ¹⁴This fact is mentioned in *The Book of the Wars of Jehovah,* where it is stated that the valley of the Arnon River, and the city of Waheb, ¹⁵lie between the Amorites and the people of Moab.)

21:15
Num 21:28
Deut 2:9

¹⁶Then Israel traveled to Beer (meaning "A Well"). This is the place where the Lord told Moses, "Summon the people, and I will give them water." ¹⁷, ¹⁸What happened is described in this song the people sang:

21:16
Judg 9:21
Jn 4:14

Spring up, O well!
Sing of the water!
This is a well
The leaders dug.
It was hollowed
With their staves
And shovels.

Then they left the desert and proceeded on through Mattanah, ¹⁹Naha-liel, and

21:8 *Make a bronze replica,* literally, "Make a fiery serpent."

21:8, 9 When the bronze snake was hung on the pole, the Israelites couldn't have understood the fuller meaning Jesus Christ would bring to this event (see John 3:14, 15). Jesus explained that just as the Israelites were healed of their sickness by looking at the snake on the pole, all believers today can be saved from the sickness of sin by looking to Jesus' death on the cross. It was not the snake that healed the people, but their belief that God could heal them. This belief was demonstrated by their obedience in following God's instructions (see Hebrews 12:2).

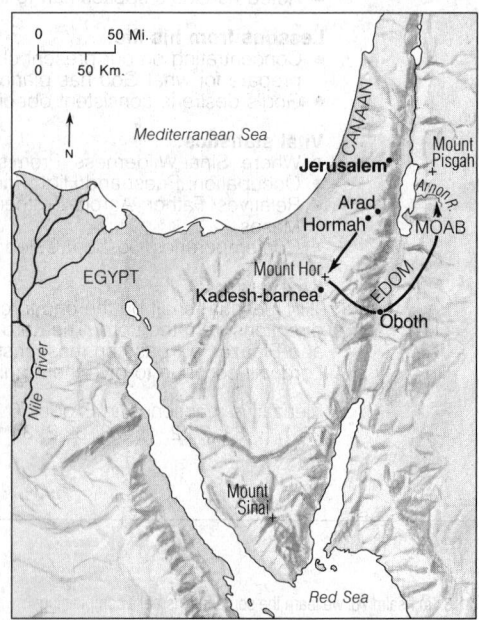

EVENTS IN THE WILDERNESS Israel next met resistance from the king of Arad, but soundly defeated him. The next stop was Mount Hor (where Aaron had died); then they traveled south and east around Edom. After camping at Oboth, they moved toward the Arnon River and onto the plains of Moab near Mount Pisgah.

Bamoth; 20then to the valley in the plateau of Moab, which overlooks the desert with Mount Pisgah in the distance.

Israel defeats King Sihon

21Israel now sent ambassadors to King Sihon of the Amorites.

22"Let us travel through your land," they requested. "We will not leave the road until we have passed beyond your borders. We won't trample your fields or touch your vineyards or drink your water."

23But King Sihon refused. Instead he mobilized his army and attacked Israel in the wilderness, battling them at Jahaz. 24But Israel slaughtered them and occupied their land from the Arnon River to the Jabbok River, as far as the borders of the Ammonites; but they were stopped there by the rugged terrain.

25, 26So Israel captured all the cities of the Amorites and lived in them, including the city of Heshbon, which had been King Sihon's capital. 27–30The ancient poets had referred to King Sihon in this poem:

Come to Heshbon,
King Sihon's capital,
For a fire has flamed forth
And devoured
The city of Ar in Moab,
On the heights of the Arnon River.
Woe to Moab!
You are finished,
O people of Chemosh;
Your sons have fled,
And your daughters are captured

21:24 *but they were stopped there by the rugged terrain,* literally, "For the border of the children of Ammon was strong." Deuteronomy 2:19 indicates that God had promised the land of the Ammonites to the descendants of Lot.

21:21
Deut 2:26-28
Judg 11:19-21
21:22
Num 20:17
21:23
Num 20:21
Deut 2:32
Judg 11:20
21:24
Deut 2:19,31-37
Josh 12:1-3
13:8-10
21:25,26
Neh 9:22
Ps 135:9,10
136:19
Amos 2:9
21:27
Num 21:15
Deut 2:9,18
Judg 11:24
1 Kgs 11:33
Jer 48:45,46

THE SERPENT IN THE WILDERNESS
Compare the texts for yourself: Numbers 21:7–9 and John 3:14, 15.

Israelites	*Christians*
Bitten by snakes	Bitten by sin
Little initial pain, then intense suffering	Little initial pain, then intense suffering
Physical death from snakes' poison	Spiritual death from sin's poison
Bronze snake lifted up in the wilderness	Christ lifted up on the cross
Looking to the snake spared one's life	Looking to Christ saves from eternal death

---

BATTLES WITH SIHON AND OG
King Sihon refused passage to the Israelites through his land, and he attacked Israel at Jahaz. Israel defeated him, occupying the land between the Arnon and Jabbok Rivers, including the capital city, Heshbon. As they moved north, they defeated King Og of Bashan at Edrei.

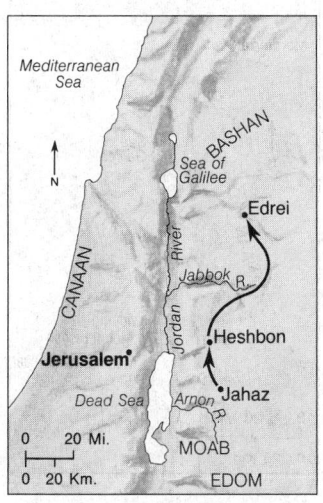

21:23 How could a horde of Israelite slaves fight against King Sihon's well-organized army? (1) The Israelites had already engaged in several military encounters (Exodus 17:8; Numbers 21:1); (2) Moses was well trained in warfare from his days as an Egyptian prince; (3) the people were prepared for war (Numbers 1); (4) God promised the land of the Ammonites to Lot's descendants, not to Sihon; (5) God had given the Promised Land to Isreal. Any country who got in their way would be destroyed. For God, who is mightier than any army, was with his people. King Sihon was outmatched without knowing it.

21:27-30 Chemosh (or Baal-peor), the national god of Moab and Ammon, was worshiped as a god of war. This false god, however, was no help to these nations when they fought against Israel. Israel's God was stronger than any of Canaan's war gods.

By King Sihon of the Amorites.
He has destroyed
The little children
And the men and women
As far as Dibon, Nophah, and Medeba.

Israel defeats King Og

31, 32While Israel was there in the Amorite country, Moses sent spies to look over the Jazer area; he followed up with an armed attack, capturing all of the towns and driving out the Amorites. 33They next turned their attention to the city of Bashan, but King Og of Bashan met them with his army at Edrei. 34The Lord told Moses not to fear—that the enemy was already conquered! "The same thing will happen to King Og as happened to King Sihon at Heshbon," the Lord assured him. 35And sure enough, Israel was victorious and killed King Og, his sons, and his subjects, so that not a single survivor remained; and Israel occupied the land.

21:31
Num 32:1,35
Isa 16:8,9
Jer 48:32

21:33
Deut 32:14

D. SECOND APPROACH TO THE PROMISED LAND (22:1—36:13)

Now the old generation has died and a new generation stands poised at the border, ready to enter the Promised Land. Neighboring nations, however, cause Israel to begin worshiping other gods. Without Moses' quick action, the nation may never have entered Canaan. We must never let down our guard in resisting sin.

1. The story of Balaam

22 The people of Israel now traveled to the plains of Moab and camped east of the Jordan River opposite Jericho. 2, 3When King Balak of Moab (the son of Zippor) realized how many of them there were, and when he learned what they had done to the Amorites, he and his people were terrified. 4They quickly consulted with the leaders of Midian.

"This mob will eat us like an ox eats grass," they exclaimed.

22:1
Num 33:48,49

22:2
Ex 15:15
Deut 2:25

22:4
Num 22:7
25:15-18

Balaam asked to curse Israel

So King Balak 5, 6sent messengers to Balaam (son of Beor) who was living in his native land of Pethor, near the Euphrates River. He begged Balaam to come and help him.

"A vast horde of people has arrived from Egypt, and they cover the face of the earth and are headed toward me," he frantically explained. "Please come and curse them for me, so that I can drive them out of my land; for I know what fantastic

22:5
Num 22:17
23:7,8; 24:9
Deut 23:4

21:34 God assured Israel that their enemy was conquered even before the battle began! God wants to give us victory over our enemies (which are usually problems related to sin rather than armed soldiers). But first we must believe that he can help us. Secondly, we must trust him to help us.

22:4-6 Balaam was a sorcerer, one called upon to place curses on others. Belief in curses and blessings was common in Old Testament times. Sorcerers were thought to have power with the gods. Thus the king of Moab wanted Balaam to use his powers with the God of Israel to place a curse on Israel—hoping that, by magic, Jehovah would turn against his people. Neither Balaam nor Balak had any idea whom they were dealing with!

22:9 Why would God speak through a sorcerer like Balaam? God wanted to give a message to the Moabites, and they had already chosen to employ Balaam. So Balaam was available for God to use, much as he used the wicked Pharaoh to accomplish his will in Egypt (Exodus 10:1). Balaam entered into his prophetic role seriously, but his heart was mixed. He had some knowledge of God, but not enough to forsake his magic and turn wholeheartedly to God. Although this story leads us to believe he turned completely to God, later passages in the Bible show that Balaam couldn't resist the tempting pull of money and idolatry (Numbers 31:16; 2 Peter 2:15; Jude 11).

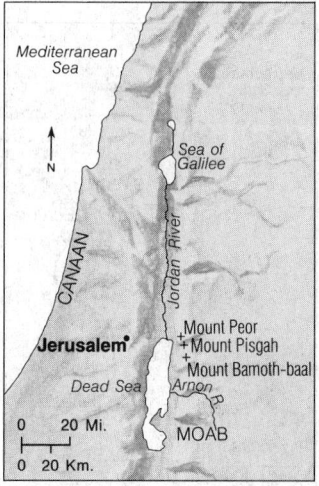

THE STORY OF BALAAM
At King Balak's request Balaam traveled nearly 400 miles to curse Israel. Balak took Balaam to Mount Bamoth-baal, then to Mount Pisgah, and finally to Mount Peor. Each mountain looked over the Plains of Moab where the Israelites were camped. But to the king's dismay, Balaam was used by God to bless, not curse, Israel.

blessings fall on those whom you bless, and I also know that those whom you curse are doomed."

22:7
1 Sam 9:7,8
Isa 56:11

7The messengers he sent were some of the top leaders of Moab and Midian. They went to Balaam with money in hand, and urgently explained to him what Balak wanted.

8"Stay here overnight," Balaam said, "and I'll tell you in the morning whatever the Lord directs me to say." So they did.

9That night God came to Balaam and asked him, "Who are these men?"

10"They have come from King Balak of Moab," he replied. 11"The king says that a vast horde of people from Egypt has arrived at his border, and he wants me to go at once and curse them, in the hope that he can battle them successfully."

22:12
Num 23:13-15

12"Don't do it!" God told him. "You are not to curse them, for I have blessed them!

13The next morning Balaam told the men, "Go on home! The Lord won't let me do it."

14So King Balak's ambassadors returned without him and reported his refusal.
15Balak tried again. This time he sent a larger number of even more distinguished

---

BALAAM

Balaam was one of those noteworthy Old Testament characters who, though not one of God's chosen people, was willing to acknowledge that Jehovah was indeed a powerful God. But he did not believe in Jehovah as the only true God. His story exposes the deception of maintaining an outward facade of spirituality over a corrupt inward life. Balaam was a man ready to obey God's command as long as he could profit from doing so. This mixture of motives—obedience and profit—eventually led to Balaam's death. Though he realized the awesome power of Israel's God, his heart was occupied with the wealth he could gain in Moab. There he returned to die when the armies of Israel invaded.

Eventually, each of us lives through the same process. Who and what we are will somehow come to the surface, destroying any masks we may have put on to cover up our real selves. Efforts spent on keeping up appearances would be much better spent on finding the answer to sin in our lives. We can avoid Balaam's mistake by facing ourselves and realizing that God is willing to accept, forgive, and literally make us over from within. Don't miss this great discovery that eluded Balaam.

Strengths and accomplishments:
• Widely known for his effective curses and blessings
• Obeyed God and blessed Israel, in spite of King Balak's bribe

Weaknesses and mistakes:
• Encouraged the Israelites to worship idols (Numbers 31:16)
• Returned to Moab and was killed in war

Lessons from his life:
• Motives are just as important as actions
• Your treasure is where your heart is

Vital statistics:
• Where: Lived near Euphrates River, traveled to Moab
• Occupation: Prophet
• Relatives: Father: Beor
• Contemporaries: Balak (King of Moab), Moses, Aaron

Key verses:
"They have gone off the road and become lost like Balaam, the son of Beor, who fell in love with the money he could make by doing wrong; but Balaam was stopped from his mad course when his donkey spoke to him with a human voice, scolding and rebuking him" (2 Peter 2:15, 16).

Balaam's story is told in Numbers 22:1—24:25. He is also mentioned in Numbers 31:16; Deuteronomy 23:4, 5; Joshua 24:9, 10; Nehemiah 13:2; Micah 6:5; 2 Peter 2:15, 16; Jude 11; Revelation 2:14.

ambassadors than the former group. 16, 17They came to Balaam with this message: "King Balak pleads with you to come. He promises you great honors plus any payment you ask. Name your own figure! Only come and curse these people for us."

18But Balaam replied, "If he were to give me a palace filled with silver and gold, I could do nothing contrary to the command of the Lord my God. 19However, stay here tonight so that I can find out whether the Lord will add anything to what he said before."

20That night God told Balaam, "You may get up and go with these men, but be sure to say only what I tell you to."

Balaam's donkey speaks

21So the next morning he saddled his donkey and started off with them. 22, 23But God was angry about Balaam's eager attitude, so he sent an angel to stand in the road to kill him. As Balaam and two servants were riding along, Balaam's donkey suddenly saw the angel of the Lord standing in the road with a drawn sword. She bolted off the road into a field, but Balaam beat her back onto the road. 24Now the angel of the Lord stood at a place where the road went between two vineyard walls. 25When the donkey saw him standing there, she squirmed past by pressing against the wall, crushing Balaam's foot in the process. So he beat her again. 26Then the angel of the Lord moved farther down the road and stood in a place so narrow that the donkey couldn't get by at all.

27So she lay down in the road! In a great fit of temper Balaam beat her again with his staff.

28Then the Lord caused the donkey to speak! "What have I done that deserves your beating me these three times?" she asked.

29"Because you have made me look like a fool!" Balaam shouted. "I wish I had a sword with me, for I would kill you."

30"Have I ever done anything like this before in my entire life?" the donkey asked.

"No," he admitted.

31Then the Lord opened Balaam's eyes and he saw the angel standing in the roadway with drawn sword, and he fell flat on the ground before him.

32"Why did you beat your donkey those three times?" the angel demanded. "I have come to stop you because you are headed for destruction. 33Three times the donkey saw me and shied away from me; otherwise I would certainly have killed you by now, and spared her."

34Then Balaam confessed, "I have sinned. I didn't realize you were there. I will go back home if you don't want me to go on."

35But the angel told him, "Go with the men, but say only what I tell you to say." So Balaam went on with them. 36When King Balak heard that Balaam was on the way, he left the capital and went out to meet him at the Arnon River, at the border of his land.

22:22, 23 *God was angry about Balaam's eager attitude,* literally, "God was angry because he went." He said much more than God had told him to. See Num 25:1-3; 31:16.

22:16
Num 22:6

22:18
Num 23:26
24:13

22:20
Num 22:35
23:12,26

22:21
2 Pet 2:15

22:28
2 Pet 2:16

22:31
Num 24:4
Josh 5:13-15

22:34
Ex 9:27
1 Sam 15:24
22:35
Num 22:20,21

22:21-23 God let Balaam go with King Balak's messengers, but he was angry about Balaam's greedy attitude. Balaam claimed that he would not go against God just for money, but his resolve was beginning to slip. His greed for the wealth offered by the king blinded him so that he could not see how God was trying to stop him. Though we may know what God wants us to do, we too can become blinded by our greedy desire for money, possessions, or prestige. We can avoid Balaam's mistake by looking past the allure of fame or fortune to the long-range benefits of following God.

22:27 Donkeys were the all-purpose vehicles in ancient society.

They were used for transportation, carrying loads, grinding grain, and plowing fields. Donkeys were usually highly dependable, which explains why Balaam became so angry when his donkey refused to move.

22:29 The donkey saved Balaam's life but made him look foolish in the process. So Balaam lashed out at the donkey to satisfy his anger and wounded pride. We sometimes strike out at blameless people who get in our way because we are embarrassed or our pride is hurt. Lashing out at others can be a sign that something is wrong in our heart.

Balaam's first blessing

22:37,38
Num 22:18

37"Why did you delay so long?" he asked Balaam. "Didn't you believe me when I said I would give you great honors?"

38Balaam replied, "I have come, but I have no power to say anything except what God tells me to say; and that is what I shall speak." 39Balaam accompanied the king to Kiriathhuzoth, 40where King Balak sacrificed oxen and sheep, and gave animals

22:41
Num 21:19,20
23:13

to Balaam and the ambassadors for their sacrifices. 41The next morning Balak took Balaam to the top of Mount Bamoth-baal, from which he could see the people of Israel spread out before him.

23 Balaam said to the king, "Build seven altars here, and prepare seven young bulls and seven rams for sacrifice."

2Balak followed his instructions, and a young bull and a ram were sacrificed on each altar.

3, 4Then Balaam said to the king, "Stand here by your burnt offerings and I will see if the Lord will meet me; and I will tell you what he says to me." So he went up to a barren height, and God met him there. Balaam told the Lord, "I have prepared

23:5
Num 22:20,35
23:16

seven altars, and have sacrificed a young bull and a ram on each." 5Then the Lord gave Balaam a message for King Balak.

6When Balaam returned, the king was standing beside the burnt offerings with all the princes of Moab. 7–10This was Balaam's message:

23:7-10
Gen 10:22
13:16; 22:17
28:14
Ex 19:5,6
33:16
Num 22:5,6,11,
12,17
Deut 33:28
Ps 37:37
Isa 57:1,2

"King Balak, king of Moab, has brought me
From the land of Aram,
From the eastern mountains.
'Come,' he told me, 'curse Jacob for me!
Let your anger rise on Israel.'
But how can I curse
What God has not cursed?
How can I denounce
A people God has not denounced?
I see them from the cliff tops,
I watch them from the hills.
They live alone,
And prefer to remain distinct
From every other nation.
They are as numerous as dust!
They are beyond numbering.
If only I could die as happy as an Israelite!
Oh, that my end might be like theirs!"

23:12
Num 22:38
23:20,26

11"What have you done to me?" demanded King Balak. "I told you to curse my enemies, and now you have blessed them!"

12But Balaam replied, "Can I say anything except what Jehovah tells me to?"

Balaam's second blessing

13Then Balak told him, "Come with me to another place; there you will see only a portion of the nation of Israel. Curse at least that many!"

14So King Balak took Balaam into the fields of Zophim at the top of Mount Pisgah, and built seven altars there; and he offered up a young bull and a ram on each altar.

23:16
Num 22:35

15Then Balaam said to the king, "Stand here by your burnt offering while I go to meet the Lord." 16And the Lord met Balaam and told him what to say. 17So he returned to where the king and the princes of Moab were standing beside their burnt offerings.

"What has Jehovah said?" the king eagerly inquired.

18-24And he replied,

23:18-24
Ex 3:12; 20:1,2
Num 22:18,38
Deut 31:23
1 Sam 15:29
Isa 40:8; 43:13
55:11

"Rise up, Balak, and hear:
Listen to me, you son of Zippor.

God is not a man, that he should lie;
He doesn't change his mind like humans do.
Has he ever promised,
Without doing what he said?
Look! I have received a command to bless them,
For God has blessed them,
And I cannot reverse it!
He has not seen sin in Jacob.
He will not trouble Israel!
Jehovah their God is with them.
He is their king!
God has brought them out of Egypt.
Israel has the strength of a wild ox.
No curse can be placed on Jacob,
And no magic shall be done against him.
For now it shall be said of Israel,
'What wonders God has done for them!'
These people rise up as a lion;
They shall not lie down
Until they have eaten what they capture
And have drunk the blood of the slain!"

25"If you aren't going to curse them, at least don't *bless* them!" the king exclaimed to Balaam.

23:25,26
Num 22:18,38

26But Balaam replied, "Didn't I tell you that I must say whatever Jehovah tells me to?"

Balaam's third blessing

27Then the king said to Balaam, "I will take you to yet another place. Perhaps it will please God to let you curse them from there."

28So King Balak took Balaam to the top of Mount Peor, overlooking the desert. 29Balaam again told the king to build seven altars, and to prepare seven young bulls and seven rams for the sacrifice. 30The king did as Balaam said, and offered a young bull and ram on every altar.

23:28
Num 31:16
Josh 22:17,18

24 Balaam realized by now that Jehovah planned to bless Israel, so he didn't even go to meet the Lord as he had earlier. Instead, he went at once and looked out toward the camp of Israel 2which stretched away across the plains, divided by tribal areas.

Then the Spirit of God came upon him, 3–9and he spoke this prophecy concerning them:

"Balaam the son of Beor says—
The man whose eyes are open says—
'I have listened to the word of God,
I have seen what God Almighty showed me;
I fell, and my eyes were opened:
Oh, the joys awaiting Israel,
Joys in the homes of Jacob.
I see them spread before me as green valleys,
And fruitful gardens by the riverside;
As aloes planted by the Lord himself;
As cedar trees beside the waters.

24:1
Num 23:3,15

24:2
Num 11:25-29
1 Sam 10:10
2 Chron 15:1

24:3-9
Gen 12:3
15:1,2; 27:29
49:9
Ex 20:1,2
Num 12:6; 14:9
22:20
23:7-10,18-24
24:15-24
Deut 7:1
1 Sam 15:8
Ps 45:8
145:11-13
Dan 8:26,27

23:27 King Balak took Balaam to several places to try to entice him to curse the Israelites. He thought a change of scenery might help change Balaam's mind. But changing locations won't change God's will. We must learn to face the source of the problem.

Moving to escape the problem only complicates the solution. Problems that are rooted in us are not solved by a change of scenery. To make a change in geography or a change in jobs may only cloud the need for a change in heart.

They shall be blessed with an abundance of water,
And they shall live in many places.
Their king will be greater than Agag;
Their kingdom is exalted.
God has brought them from Egypt.
Israel has the strength of a wild ox,
And shall eat up the nations that oppose him;
He shall break their bones in pieces,
And shall shoot them with many arrows.
Israel sleeps as a lion or a lioness—
Who dares arouse him?
Blessed is everyone who blesses you, O Israel,
And curses shall fall upon everyone who curses you.' "

10King Balak was livid with rage by now. Striking his hands together in anger and disgust he shouted, "I called you to curse my enemies and instead you have blessed them three times. 11Get out of here! Go back home! I had planned to promote you to great honor, but Jehovah has kept you from it!"

Balaam's fourth blessing

24:13
Num 22:18,20

12Balaam replied, "Didn't I tell your messengers 13that even if you gave me a palace filled with silver and gold, I could not go beyond the words of Jehovah, and could not say a word of my own? I said that I would say only what Jehovah says! 14Yes, I shall return now to my own people. But first, let me tell you what the Israelites are going to do to your people!"

24:15
Gen 49:10
Num 21:29
Isa 15:1—16:4
Amos 9:11,12
Mt 2:2
Rev 22:16

15-19So he spoke this prophecy to him:

"Balaam the son of Beor is the man
Whose eyes are open!
He hears the words of God
And has knowledge from the Most High;
He sees what Almighty God has shown him;
He fell, and his eyes were opened:
I see in the future of Israel,
Far down the distant trail,
That there shall come a star from Jacob!
This ruler of Israel
Shall smite the people of Moab,
And destroy the sons of Sheth.
Israel shall possess all Edom and Seir.
They shall overcome their enemies.
Jacob shall arise in power
And shall destroy many cities."

24:20
Ex 17:14

20Then Balaam looked over at the homes of the people of Amalek and prophesied:

"Amalek was the first of the nations,
But its destiny is destruction!"

24:11 Though Balaam's motives were not correct, in this moment he acted with integrity. God's message had so filled him that Balaam spoke the truth. In so doing, he forfeited the promotion that had lured him to speak in the first place. Staying true to God's Word may cost us promotions and advantages in the short run. But those who choose God over money will one day acquire heavenly wealth beyond measure (Matthew 6:19–21).

24:15–19 In verse 17 the star from Jacob is often interpreted to be a prophecy of the coming Messiah. It was probably this prophecy that convinced the wise men to travel to Israel to search for the baby Jesus (see Matthew 2:1, 2). It seems strange that God would use a sorcerer like Balaam to foretell the coming of the Messiah. But this teaches us that God can use anything or anyone to accomplish his plans. By using a sorcerer, God is not suggesting that sorcery is acceptable; in fact, Scripture condemns it in several places (Exodus 22:18; 2 Chronicles 33:6; Revelation 18:23). Rather, it shows that God is ultimately sovereign over good and evil.

21, 22Then he looked over at the Kenites:

"Yes, you are strongly situated,
Your nest is set in the rocks!
But the Kenites shall be destroyed,
And the mighty army of the king of Assyria
   shall deport you from this land!"

23, 24He concluded his prophecies by saying:

"Alas, who can live when God does this?
Ships shall come from the coasts of Cyprus,
And shall oppress both Eber and Assyria.
They too must be destroyed."

25So Balaam and Balak returned to their homes.

The Israelites worship Baal

25 While Israel was camped at Acacia, some of the young men began going to wild parties with the local Moabite girls. 2These girls also invited them to attend the sacrifices to their gods, and soon the men were not only attending the feasts, but also bowing down and worshiping the idols. 3Before long all Israel was joining freely in the worship of Baal, the god of Moab; and the anger of the Lord was hot against his people.

4He issued the following command to Moses:

"Execute all the tribal leaders of Israel. Hang them up before the Lord in broad daylight, so that his fierce anger will turn away from the people."

5So Moses ordered the judges to execute all who had worshiped Baal.

6But one of the Israeli men insolently brought a Midianite girl into the camp, right before the eyes of Moses and all the people, as they were weeping at the door of the Tabernacle. 7When Phinehas (son of Eleazar and grandson of Aaron the priest) saw this, he jumped up, grabbed a spear, 8and rushed after the man into his tent, where he had taken the girl. He thrust the spear all the way through the man's body and into her stomach. So the plague was stopped, 9but only after 24,000 people had already died.

10, 11Then the Lord said to Moses, "Phinehas (son of Eleazar and grandson of Aaron the priest) has turned away my anger for he was angry with my anger, and

24:21
Gen 15:19
Judg 1:16
Ezra 4:2

24:23
Gen 10:4,21-25
Dan 9:26,27

25:1
Num 33:49
Josh 2:1

25:2
Ex 34:15,16

25:3
Num 25:5
Deut 4:3,4

25:6
Num 22:4
31:2,9-16

25:7
Ex 6:25
Josh 22:30,31

25:9
1 Cor 10:8

24:25 *So Balaam and Balak returned to their homes.* But not before Balaam gave insidious advice that brought about the situation described in 25:1-3. See 31:16.

25:1 This verse shows the great challenge Israel had to face. The most dangerous problem for Moses and Joshua was not the hostile army of Jericho, but the subtle temptation to form alliances with the heathen Canaanite religions and cultures. Alliances would lead to familiarity, and familiarity to compromise.

25:1, 2 Attending a local party with the Moabite girls may have seemed harmless enough. But for these young Israelite men, "fun" turned into tragedy. At first, they didn't think about worshiping idols. They just wanted to go to the party and have a good time. Before long, they started attending local feasts and family celebrations that involved idol worship. Soon they were in over their heads, absorbed into the practices of the heathen culture. Their desire for fun and companionship caused them to loosen their spiritual commitment. What about your favorite recreations—do they help you grow in faith, or do they push you to relax your standards?

25:1–3 This combination of sexual sin and idolatry, it turns out, was Balaam's idea (see 31:16; Revelation 2:14)—the same Balaam who had just blessed Israel and who appeared to be on their side. It is easy to see how the Israelites were misled, for Balaam seemed to say and do all the right things—at least for a while (Numbers 22—24). Not until Balaam had inflicted great damage on their

personal lives and on their nation did the Israelites realize that he was greedy, that he used sorcery, and that he was deeply involved in heathen religious practices. We must be careful to weigh both the words and the deeds of those who claim to offer spiritual help.

25:3 Baal was the most popular god in Canaan, the land Israel was about to enter. Baal was represented by a bull, symbol of strength and fertility. He was the god of the rains and harvest. The Israelites were continually attracted to Baal worship throughout their years in Canaan. Prostitution was a large part of Baal worship. Since Baal was so popular, his name was often used as a generic title for all the local gods.

25:10, 11 It is clear from Phinehas' story that some anger is proper and justified. But how can we know when our anger is appropriate and when it should be restrained? Ask these questions when you become angry: (1) Why am I angry? (2) Whose rights are being violated (mine or another's)? (3) Is the truth (a principle of God) being violated? If only your rights are at stake, it may be wiser to keep angry feelings under control. But if the truth is at stake, anger is often justified, although violence and retaliation are usually the wrong way to express it (Phinehas' case was unique). If we are becoming more and more like God, we should be angered by sin.

25:12
Ex 29:9; 32:30
40:15
Num 16:46
Isa 54:10
Ezek 37:26

25:15
Num 25:18; 31:8
Josh 13:21

25:16
Num 31:2

25:18
Num 25:15

26:1
Num 25:6-9

26:2
Num 1:2-15
4:1-4

26:5
Gen 46:8-14
Num 1:20-46
16:1
1 Chron 5:1-5

26:12
1 Chron 4:24-43

would not tolerate the worship of any God but me. So I have stopped destroying all Israel as I had intended. 12, 13Now because of what he has done—because of his zeal for his God, and because he has made atonement for the people of Israel by what he did—I promise that he and his descendants shall be priests forever."

14The name of the man who was killed with the Midianite girl was Zimri, son of Salu, a leader of the tribe of Simeon. 15The girl's name was Cozbi, daughter of Zur, a Midianite prince.

16, 17Then the Lord said to Moses, "Destroy the Midianites, 18for they are destroying you with their wiles. They are causing you to worship Baal, and they are leading you astray, as you have just seen by the death of Cozbi."

2. The second numbering of the nation

26 After the plague had ended, Jehovah said to Moses and to Eleazar (son of Aaron the priest), 2"Take a census of all the men of Israel who are twenty years old or older, to find out how many of each tribe and clan are able to go to war."

3, 4So Moses and Eleazar issued census instructions to the leaders of Israel. (The entire nation was camped in the plains of Moab beside the Jordan River, opposite Jericho.) Here are the results of the census:

5-11*The tribe of Reuben:* 43,730.

(Reuben was Israel's oldest son.) In this tribe were the following clans, named after Reuben's sons:

The Hanochites, named after their ancestor Hanoch.
The Palluites, named after their ancestor Pallu. (In the sub-clan of Eliab—who was one of the sons of Pallu—were the families of Nemu-el, Abiram, and Dathan. This Dathan and Abiram were the two leaders who conspired with Korah against Moses and Aaron, and in fact challenged the very authority of God! But the earth opened and swallowed them; and 250 men were destroyed by fire from the Lord that day, as a warning to the entire nation.)
The Hezronites, named after their ancestor Hezron.
The Carmites, named after their ancestor Carmi.

12, 13, 14*The tribe of Simeon:* 22,200.

In this tribe were the following clans, founded by Simeon's sons:

The Nemu-elites, named after their ancestor Nemu-el.
The Jaminites, named after their ancestor Jamin.
The Jachinites, named after their ancestor Jachin.
The Zerahites, named after their ancestor Zerah.
The Shaulites, named after their ancestor Shaul.

15-18*The tribe of Gad:* 40,500

In this tribe were the following clans founded by the sons of Gad:

The Zephonites, named after their ancestor Zephon.
The Haggites, named after their ancestor Haggi.
The Shunites, named after their ancestor Shuni.
The Oznites, named after their ancestor Ozni.
The Erites, named after their ancestor Eri.
The Arodites, named after their ancestor Arod.
The Arelites, named after their ancestor Areli.

26:2 This is the second great census in the book of Numbers. Both were taken to count the number of men able to go to war. The first census (Numbers 1, 2) counted the Hebrews who had left Egypt. When the old generation died in the wilderness, another census was needed to count the new generation ready to enter the Promised Land. The new census revealed that although over 600,000 men (not counting women and children) had died in the wilderness, the new generation had increased by almost the same amount. The census was one of the first major steps in preparing the people to enter the land they had waited so long to possess.

19-22*The tribe of Judah:* 76,500
In this tribe were the following clans named after the sons of Judah—but not including Er and Onan who died in the land of Canaan:

26:19
1 Chron 4:1-4

The Shelanites, named after their ancestor Shelah.
The Perezites, named after their ancestor Perez.
The Zerahites, named after their ancestor Zerah.
This census also included the subclans of Perez: The Hezronites, named after their
ancestor Hezron. The Hamulites, named after their ancestor Hamul.

23, 24, 25*The tribe of Issachar:* 64,300.
In this tribe were the following clans named after the sons of Issachar:

26:23
1 Chron 7:1-5

The Tolaites, named after their ancestor Tola.
The Punites, named after their ancestor Puvah.
The Jashubites, named after their ancestor Jashub.
The Shimronites, named after their ancestor Shimron.

26, 27*The tribe of Zebulun:* 60,500.
In this tribe were the following clans named after the sons of Zebulun:

The Seredites, named after their ancestor Sered.
The Elonites, named after their ancestor Elon.
The Jahleelites, named after their ancestor Jahleel.

28-37*The tribe of Joseph:* 32,500 *in the half-tribe of Ephraim; and* 52,700 *in the half-tribe of Manasseh.*
In the half-tribe of Manasseh was the following clan of Machirites, named after their ancestor Machir.

26:28
Gen 46:19-22
1 Chron 7:14-40

The sub-clan of the Machirites was the Gileadites, named after their ancestor
Gilead.
The tribes of the Gileadites:
The Jezerites, named after their ancestor Jezer.
The Helekites, named after their ancestor Helek.
The Asrielites, named after their ancestor Asriel.
The Shechemites, named after their ancestor Shechem.
The Shemidaites, named after their ancestor Shemida.
The Hepherites, named after their ancestor Hepher. (Hepher's son, Zelophehad,
had no sons. Here are the names of his daughters: Mahlah, Noah, Hoglah,
Milcah, Tirzah.

The 32,500 registered in the half-tribe of Ephraim included the following clans, named after the sons of Ephraim:

The Shuthelahites, named after their ancestor Shuthelah. (A sub-clan of the Shu-
thelahites was the Eranites, named after their ancestor Eran, a son of Shuthelah.)
The Becherites, named after their ancestor Becher.
The Tahanites, named after their ancestor Tahan.

38-41*The tribe of Benjamin:* 45,600.
In this tribe were the following clans named after the sons of Benjamin:

26:38
Gen 46:19-22
1 Chron 7:6-12
8:1-40

The Bela-ites, named after their ancestor Bela.
Sub-clans named after sons of Bela were:
The Ardites, named after their ancestor Ard.
The Naamites, named after their ancestor Naaman.
The Ashbelites, named after their ancestor Ashbel.
The Ahiramites, named after their ancestor Ahiram.
The Shuphamites, named after their ancestor Shephupham.
The Huphamites, named after their ancestor Hupham.

26:42
Gen 46:23-25

42, 43*The tribe of Dan:* 64,400.

In this tribe was the clan of the Shuhamites, named after Shuham, the son of Dan.

26:44
Gen 46:16,17

44-47*The tribe of Asher:* 53,400.

In this tribe were the following clans named after the sons of Asher:

The Imnites, named after their ancestor Imnah.
The Ishvites, named after their ancestor Ishvi.
The Beriites, named after their ancestor Beriah.
Sub-clans named after the sons of Beriah were:
 The Heberites, named after their ancestor Heber.
 The Malchi-elites, named after their ancestor Malchi-el.

Asher also had a daughter named Serah.

26:48
1 Chron 7:13

48, 49, 50*The tribe of Naphtali:* 45,400.

In this tribe were the following clans, named after the sons of Naphtali:

The Jahzeelites, named after their ancestor Jahzeel.
The Gunites, named after their ancestor Guni.
The Jezerites, named after their ancestor Jezer.
The Shillemites, named after their ancestor Shillem.

26:51
Num 2:32,33
26:5
26:54
Num 33:54

51So the total number of the men of draft age throughout Israel was 601,730.

52, 53Then the Lord told Moses to divide the land among the tribes in proportion to their population, as indicated by the census— 54the larger tribes to be given more land, the smaller tribes less land.

26:55
Num 33:54
34:13
Josh 14:2; 17:14

55, 56"Let the representatives of the larger tribes have a lottery, drawing for the larger sections," the Lord instructed, "and let the smaller tribes draw for the smaller sections."

26:57
Num 3:16-38
1 Chron 6:1

57These are the clans of the Levites numbered in the census:

The Gershonites, named after their ancestor Gershon.
The Kohathites, named after their ancestor Kohath.
The Merarites, named after their ancestor Merari.

26:58
Num 3:16-35

58, 59These are the families of the tribe of Levi: The Libnites, the Hebronites, The Mahlites, the Mushites, The Korahites.

While Levi was in Egypt, a daughter, Jochebed, was born to him and she became the wife of Amram, son of Kohath. They were the parents of Aaron, Moses, and Miriam. 60To Aaron were born Nadab, Abihu, Eleazar, and Ithamar. 61But Nadab and Abihu died when they offered unauthorized incense before the Lord.

26:60
Num 3:2,8
26:61
Lev 10:1,2
Num 3:4
26:62
Num 3:39
4:46-48
Deut 10:9

62*The total number of Levites in the census* was 23,000, counting all the males a month old and upward. But the Levites were not included in the total census figure of the people of Israel, for the Levites were given no land when it was divided among the tribes.

26:64
Num 14:20-43
Deut 2:14,15

63So these are the census figures as prepared by Moses and Eleazar the priest, in the plains of Moab beside the Jordan River, across from Jericho. 64, 65Not one person in this entire census had been counted in the previous census taken in the

26:64, 65 *Not one person . . . had been counted in the previous census . . .* Forty years earlier, at the time of the first census, they had been under twenty years of age, and so were not counted. All who at that time were older than twenty years of age were now dead.

26:64 A new census for a new generation. Thirty-eight years had elapsed since the first great census in Numbers chapter one. During that time, every Israelite man and woman over 20 years of age—except Caleb, Joshua, and Moses—had died, and yet God's laws and the spiritual character of the nation were still intact. Numbers records some dramatic miracles. This is a quiet but powerful miracle often overlooked: a whole nation moves from one land to another, loses its entire adult population, yet manages to maintain its spiritual direction. Sometimes we wonder why God isn't working dramatic miracles in our lives. But God often works in quiet ways to bring about his long-range purposes.

wilderness of Sinai! For all who had been counted then had died, as the Lord had decreed when he said of them, "They shall die in the wilderness." The only exceptions were Caleb (son of Jephunneh) and Joshua (son of Nun).

The inheritance for daughters

27 One day the daughters of Zelophehad came to the entrance of the Tabernacle to give a petition to Moses, Eleazar the priest, the tribal leaders, and others who were there. The names of these women were Mahlah, Noah, Hoglah, Milcah and Tirzah. They were members of the half-tribe of Manasseh (a son of Joseph). Their ancestor was Machir, son of Manasseh. Manasseh's son Gilead was their great-grandfather, his son Hepher was their grandfather, and his son Zelophehad was their father.

27:1
Num 26:28-37
36:1-4
Josh 17:3,4

3, 4"Our father died in the wilderness," they said, "and he was not one of those who perished in Korah's revolt against the Lord—it was a natural death, but he had no sons. Why should the name of our father disappear just because he had no son? We feel that we should be given property along with our father's brothers." 5So Moses brought their case before the Lord.

6, 7And the Lord replied to Moses, "The daughters of Zelophehad are correct. Give them land along with their uncles; give them the property that would have been given to their father if he had lived. 8Moreover, this is a general law among you, that if a man dies and has no sons, then his inheritance shall be passed on to his daughters. 9And if he has no daughter, it shall belong to his brothers. 10And if he has no brother, then it shall go to his uncles. 11But if he has no uncles, then it shall go to the nearest relative."

27:6,7
Num 36:1-4
Josh 17:5,6

27:11
Lev 25:25,49

Moses appoints Joshua as his successor

12One day the Lord said to Moses, "Go up into Mount Abarim and look across the river to the land I have given to the people of Israel. 13After you have seen it, you shall die as Aaron your brother did, 14for you rebelled against my instructions in the wilderness of Zin. When the people of Israel rebelled, you did not glorify me before them by following my instructions to order water to come out of the rock." He was referring to the incident at the waters of Meribah ("Place of Strife") in Kadesh, in the wilderness of Zin.

27:12
Num 33:47
Deut 32:49

27:13
Deut 32:50,51
34:1-6

27:14
Num 20:9-13
Deut 32:48-52
34:1-6

15Then Moses said to the Lord, 16"O Jehovah, the God of the spirits of all mankind, [before I am taken away] please appoint a new leader for the people, 17a man who will lead them into battle and care for them, so that the people of the Lord will not be as sheep without a shepherd."

27:17
1 Kgs 22:17
Ezek 34:1-24
Zech 10:2
Mt 9:36

18The Lord replied, "Go and get Joshua (son of Nun), who has the Spirit in him, 19and take him to Eleazar the priest, and as all the people watch, charge him with the responsibility of leading the people. 20Publicly give him your authority so that all the people of Israel will obey him. 21He shall be the one to consult with Eleazar the priest in order to get directions from the Lord. The Lord will speak to Eleazar through the use of the Urim, and Eleazar will pass on these instructions to Joshua and the people. In this way the Lord will continue to give them guidance." 22So Moses did as Jehovah commanded, and took Joshua to Eleazar the priest.

27:18
Deut 3:28
31:7,8; 34:9

27:20
Deut 31:3

27:21
Ex 28:30
Lev 8:8
Deut 33:8
1 Sam 28:6

27:14 *you did not glorify me,* implied. **27:16** *before I am taken away,* implied.

27:3, 4 Up to this point, the Hebrew law gave sons alone the right to inherit. The daughters of Zelophehad, having no brothers, came to Moses to ask for their father's possessions. God told Moses that if a man died without sons, his inheritance would go to his daughters (27:8). But the daughters could keep it only as long as they married within their own tribe (36:5–12).

27:15–20 Moses did not want to leave his work without making sure a new leader was ready to replace him. First he asked God to help him find a replacement. Then, when Joshua was selected, Moses gave him a variety of tasks to ease him into his new job. Moses also told the people that Joshua had the authority and the ability to handle the job of leading the nation. Displaying such confidence in Joshua was good for both Joshua and the people. Anyone in a leadership position should train others to carry on his duties should he suddenly or eventually have to leave. There would rarely be a leadership gap if this principle were practiced. Before a leadership crisis occurs, follow Moses' pattern: pray, select, develop, and commission.

27:16, 17 Moses asked God to appoint a leader who was both courageous (could lead in battle) and caring. The Lord responded by appointing Joshua. Many people want to be known as leaders. Some are very capable of leading in battle and reaching their goal. Others care deeply for the people in their charge. A good leader is both goal-oriented and people-oriented.

As the people watched, 23Moses laid his hands upon him and dedicated him to his responsibilities, as the Lord had commanded.

3. Instructions concerning offerings

28 The Lord gave Moses these instructions to give to the people of Israel: "The offerings which you burn on the altar for me are my food, and are a pleasure to me; so see to it that they are brought regularly and are offered as I have instructed you.

Daily offerings

28:3
Ex 29:38-41
Ezek 46:13-15
28:4
Lev 6:19,20
28:5
Num 15:3-12
28:7
Ex 29:41
Lev 23:12-14
Num 28:31

3"When you make offerings by fire, you shall use yearling male lambs—each without defect. Two of them shall be offered each day as a regular burnt offering. 4One lamb shall be sacrificed in the morning, the other in the evening. 5With them shall be offered a grain offering of three quarts of finely ground flour mixed with three pints of oil. 6This is the burnt offering ordained at Mount Sinai, to be regularly offered as a fragrant odor, an offering made by fire to the Lord. 7Along with it shall be the drink offering, consisting of three pints of strong wine with each lamb, poured out in the holy place before the Lord. 8Offer the second lamb in the evening with the same grain offering and drink offering. It too is a fragrant odor to the Lord, an offering made by fire.

Sabbath offerings

9, 10"On the Sabbath day, sacrifice two yearling male lambs—both without defect—in addition to the regular offerings. They are to be accompanied by a grain offering of six quarts of fine flour mixed with oil, and the usual drink offering.

Monthly offerings

28:11
Num 10:10
28:19
1 Chron 23:31
2 Chron 2:4
Ezra 3:5
Neh 10:33
Isa 1:12,13
Ezek 46:6,7
Col 2:16
28:12
Num 15:4-12
28:5
28:14
Num 28:7
28:15
Lev 6:8-13
Num 28:3

11"Also, on the first day of each month there shall be an extra burnt offering to the Lord of two young bulls, one ram, and seven male yearling lambs—all without defect. 12Accompany them with nine quarts of finely ground flour mixed with oil as a grain offering with each bull; and six quarts of finely ground flour mixed with oil as a grain offering for the ram; 13and for each lamb, three quarts of finely ground flour mixed with oil for a grain offering. This burnt offering shall be presented by fire, and will please the Lord very much. 14Along with each sacrifice shall be a drink offering—six pints of wine with each bull, four pints for a ram, and three pints for a lamb. This, then, will be the burnt offering each month throughout the year.

15"Also on the first day of each month you shall offer one male goat for a sin offering to the Lord. This is in addition to the regular daily burnt offering and its drink offering.

Offerings for The Festival of Unleavened Bread

28:16
Ex 23:15
Lev 23:5-14
Num 9:3-5
Deut 16:1-8
28:19
Num 29:11

16"On April first, you shall celebrate the Passover—[when the death angel passed over the oldest sons of the Israelites in Egypt, leaving them unharmed]. 17On the following day, a great, joyous seven-day festival will begin, but no leavened bread shall be served. 18On the first day of the festival all the people shall be called together before the Lord. No hard work shall be done on that day. 19You shall offer as burnt sacrifices to the Lord two young bulls, one ram, and seven

28:16 *on April first,* literally, "on the fourteenth day of the first month" (of the Hebrew calendar). *when the death angel passed over . . . leaving them unharmed,* implied.

28:1, 2 Offerings had to be brought regularly and carried out a certain way under the supervision of the priests. The people had to undergo a period of preparation to insure that their hearts were ready for worship. By spending this much time and preparation in worshiping God, they gave idolatry little time to influence their lives. God is pleased today when we allow nothing to come between him and us. He also is delighted by hearts that are prepared to receive his guidance.

28:9, 10 Why were extra offerings made on the Sabbath day? The Sabbath was a special day of rest and worship commemorating both creation (Exodus 20:8–11) and the deliverance from Egypt (Deuteronomy 5:12–15). Because of the significance of this special day, it was only natural to offer extra sacrifices.

yearling male lambs—all without defect. 20, 21With each bull there shall be a grain offering of nine quarts of fine flour mixed with oil; with the ram there shall be six quarts; and with each of the seven lambs there shall be three quarts of fine flour. 22You must also offer a male goat as a sin offering, to make atonement for yourselves. 23These offerings shall be in addition to the usual daily sacrifices. 24This same sacrifice shall be offered on each of the seven days of the feast; they will be very pleasant to the Lord. 25On the seventh day there shall again be a holy and solemn assembly of all the people, and during that day you may do no hard work.

Offerings for The Festival of First Fruits

26"On the first day of the Harvest Festival, all the people must come before the Lord for a special, solemn assembly to celebrate the new harvest. On that day you are to present the first of the new crop of grain as a grain offering to the Lord; there is to be no regular work by anyone on that day. 27A special burnt offering, very pleasant to the Lord, shall be offered that day. It shall consist of two young bulls, one ram, and seven yearling male lambs. 28, 29These shall be accompanied by your grain offering of nine quarts of fine flour mixed with oil with each bull, six quarts with the ram, and three quarts with each of the seven lambs. 30Also offer one male goat to make atonement for yourselves. 31These special offerings are in addition to the regular daily burnt offerings and grain offerings and drink offerings. Make sure that the animals you sacrifice are without defect.

28:26
Ex 23:16
Lev 23:9-22
Deut 16:16
Acts 2:1

28:31
Num 28:3

Offerings for The Festival of Trumpets

29 The Festival of Trumpets shall be celebrated on the fifteenth day of September each year; there shall be a solemn assembly of all the people on that day, and no hard work may be done. 2On that day you shall offer a burnt sacrifice consisting of one young bull, one ram, and seven yearling male lambs—all without defect. These are sacrifices which the Lord will appreciate and enjoy. 3, 4A grain offering of nine quarts of fine flour mingled with oil shall be offered with the bull, six quarts with the ram, and three quarts with each of the seven lambs. 5In addition, there shall be a male goat sacrificed as a sin offering, to make atonement for you. 6These special sacrifices are in addition to the regular monthly burnt offering for that day, and also in addition to the regular daily burnt sacrifices, which are to be offered with the respective grain offerings and drink offerings, as specified by the ordinances governing them.

29:1
Lev 23:23-25
Num 10:10

29:6
Num 28:3

Offerings for The Day of Atonement

7"Ten days later another convocation of all the people shall be held. This will be a day of solemn humility before the Lord, and no work of any kind may be done. 8On that day you shall offer a burnt sacrifice to the Lord—it will be very pleasant to him—of one young bull, one ram, seven yearling male lambs—each without

29:7
Lev 16:29-31
23:23-27

28:26 *The Harvest Festival,* also called Pentecost, the Feast of Weeks, and the Day of Firstfruits. **29:1** *fifteenth day of September,* literally, "upon the first day of the seventh month" (of the Hebrew calendar). **29:6** *regular monthly burnt offering for that day,* literally, "burnt offerings of the new moon." **29:7** *Ten days later,* literally, "On the tenth day of the seventh month" (of the Hebrew calendar).

29:1ff God placed many holidays on Israel's calendar. The Festival of Trumpets was one of three great holidays celebrated in the seventh month (the Feast of Tabernacles and Day of Atonement were the other two). These holidays provided a time to refresh the mind and body and to renew one's commitment to God. If you feel tired or far from God, try taking a "spiritual holiday"—separate yourself from your daily routine and concentrate on renewing your commitment to God.

29:1, 2 The Festival of Trumpets demonstrated four important principles of worship: (1) The people gathered together to celebrate and worship. There is something special about worshiping with other believers. (2) God ordered that no hard work be done during this special day. It takes time to worship, and setting aside a special day gives us the time to worship God as we should. (3) The people gave God something of value by sacrificing one of their own animals as a burnt offering to him. True worship involves giving something of value to God to show our commitment to him. (4) Spending time away from the normal routine of life was symbolic of giving themselves to God and demonstrating their dedication. These same principles should appear in our worship.

defect— 9, 10and their accompanying grain offerings. Nine quarts of fine flour mixed with oil are to be offered with the bull; six with the ram; and three with each of the seven lambs. 11You are also to sacrifice one male goat for a sin offering. This is in addition to the sin offering of the Day of Atonement [offered annually on that day], and in addition to the regular daily burnt sacrifices, grain offerings, and drink offerings.

29:11
Lev 16:1-35
23:26-32

Offerings for The Festival of Tabernacles

12"Five days later there shall be yet another assembly of all the people, and on that day no hard work shall be done; it is the beginning of a seven-day festival before the Lord. 13Your special burnt sacrifice that day, which will give much pleasure to the Lord, shall be thirteen young bulls, two rams, and fourteen male yearling lambs—each without defect— 14accompanied by the usual grain offerings—nine quarts of fine flour mingled with oil for each of the thirteen young bulls; six quarts for each of the two rams; 15and three quarts for each of the fourteen lambs. 16There must also be a male goat sacrificed for a sin offering, in addition to the regular daily burnt sacrifice with its accompanying grain offerings and drink offerings.

29:12
Lev 23:33-43
Deut 16:13,14
Ezek 45:25

17"On the second day of this seven-day festival you shall sacrifice twelve young bulls, two rams, and fourteen male yearling lambs—each without defect— 18accompanied by the usual grain offerings and drink offerings. 19Also, in addition to the regular daily burnt sacrifice, you are to sacrifice a male goat with its accompanying grain offering and drink offering for a sin offering.

29:19
Num 28:3,11,31

20"On the third day of the festival, offer eleven young bulls, two rams, fourteen male yearling lambs—each without defect— 21and the usual grain offering and drink offering with each sacrifice. 22And in addition to the regular daily burnt sacrifices, sacrifice a male goat for a sin offering, with its accompanying grain offering and drink offering.

23"On the fourth day of the festival, you are to sacrifice ten young bulls, two rams, and fourteen male yearling lambs—each without defect— 24each with its accompanying grain offering and drink offering; 25also a male goat as a sin offering (along with the usual grain and drink offerings) in addition to the regular daily sacrifices.

26, 27"On the fifth day of the festival, sacrifice nine young bulls, two rams, and fourteen male yearling lambs—each without defect—accompanied by the usual grain offerings and drink offerings; 28also sacrifice a male goat with the usual grain and drink offerings, as a special sin offering, in addition to the usual daily sacrifices.

29"On the sixth day of the festival, you must sacrifice eight young bulls, two rams, and fourteen male yearling lambs—each without defect— 30along with their usual grain and drink offerings. 31In addition to the usual daily sacrifices, sacrifice a male goat and the usual grain and drink offerings as a sin offering.

32"On the seventh day of the festival, sacrifice seven young bulls, two rams, and fourteen male yearling lambs—each without defect— 33each with its customary grain and drink offerings; 34also sacrifice an extra sin offering of one male goat, with the usual grain and drink offerings, in addition to the regular daily sacrifices.

35"On the eighth day summon the people to another solemn assembly; you must do no hard work that day. 36Sacrifice a burnt offering—they are very pleasant to the Lord—of one young bull, one ram, seven male yearling lambs—each without defect— 37and the customary grain and drink offerings. 38Sacrifice also one male goat with the usual grain and drink offerings for a sin offering, in addition to the regular daily sacrifices. 39These offerings are compulsory at the times of your annual feasts, and are in addition to sacrifices and offerings you present in connection with vows, or as free-will offerings, burnt sacrifices, grain offerings, drink offerings, or peace offerings."

29:35
Lev 23:3,7,
21,36

29:39
Lev 22:20,21
2 Chron 31:3
Ezra 3:5
Neh 10:33

40So Moses gave all of these instructions to the people of Israel.

29:11 *offered annually on that day,* implied. **29:12** *Five days later,* literally, "On the fifteenth day of the seventh month" (of the Hebrew calendar).

Rules about vows

30 Now Moses summoned the leaders of the tribes and told them, "The Lord has commanded that when anyone makes a promise to the Lord, either to do something or to quit doing something, that vow must not be broken: the person making the vow must do exactly as he has promised.

30:1,2
Lev 5:4; 27:2-13
Deut 23:21-25
Judg 11:30-35
Eccles 5:4

3"If a woman promises the Lord to do or not do something, and she is still a girl at home in her father's home, 4and her father hears that she has made a vow with penalties, but says nothing, then her vow shall stand. 5But if her father refuses to let her make the vow, or feels that the penalties she has agreed to are too harsh, then her promise will automatically become invalid. Her father must state his disagreement on the first day he hears about it; and then Jehovah will forgive her because her father would not let her do it.

6"If she takes a vow or makes a foolish pledge, and later marries, 7and her husband learns of her vow and says nothing on the day he hears of it, her vow shall stand. 8But if her husband refuses to accept her vow or foolish pledge, his disagreement makes it void, and Jehovah will forgive her.

30:6
Judg 11:30,31

9"But if the woman is a widow or is divorced, she must fulfill her vow.

10"If she is married and living in her husband's home when she makes the vow, 11and her husband hears of it and does nothing, the vow shall stand; 12but if he refuses to allow it on the first day he hears of it, her vow is void and Jehovah will forgive her. 13So her husband may either confirm or nullify her vow, 14but if he says nothing for a day, then he has already agreed to it. 15If he waits more than a day and then refuses to permit the vow, whatever penalties to which she agreed shall come upon him—he shall be responsible."

16These, then, are the commandments the Lord gave Moses concerning relationships between a man and his wife and between a father and his daughter who is living at home.

30:16
Num 5:29

4. The war against Midian

31 Then the Lord said to Moses, "Take vengeance on the Midianites for leading you into idolatry, and then you must die."

31:1,2
Num 25:6-18
Deut 32:35

3Moses said to the people, "Some of you must take arms to wage Jehovah's war against Midian. 4, 5Conscript 1,000 men from each tribe." So this was done; and out of the many thousands of Israel, 12,000 armed men were sent to battle by Moses. 6Phinehas (son of Eleazar the priest) led them into battle, accompanied by the Ark, with trumpets blaring. 7And every man of Midian was killed. 8Among

31:6
Num 10:10
Josh 6:4-6
1 Sam 4:4,5,17
2 Chron 13:12-15

31:8
Josh 13:21,22

31:6 *accompanied by the Ark,* literally, "with the vessels of the sanctuary."

30:1-3 Moses reminded the people that their promises to God and others must be kept. In ancient times, people did not sign written contracts. A person's word was as binding as a signature. To make a vow even more binding, an offering was given along with it. No one was forced by law to make a vow; but once made, vows had to be fulfilled. Children could not make vows without the consent of their parents, and a concerned parent could nullify a rash vow made by a child. Keeping a vow signified the sincerity and faithfulness of a life devoted to pleasing God. Breaking a vow signified a broken trust and a broken relationship. Trust is still the basis of our relationships with God and others. Thus a broken promise today is just as harmful as it was in Moses' day.

30:3-8 In the Israelite law, parents could overrule their children's vows. This helped young people avoid making foolish promises or costly commitments. From this law comes an important principle for both parents and children. Young people still living at home should seek their parents' help in avoiding foolish decisions. A parent's experience could save a child from a serious mistake. Parents, however, should exercise their spiritual authority and responsibility to guide their children with caution and grace.

31:1ff The Midianites were a nomadic people who descended from Abraham and his second wife, Keturah. The land of Midian lay far south of Canaan, but large bands of Midianites roamed many miles from their homeland, searching for grazing areas for their flocks. Such a group was near the Promised Land when the Israelites arrived. These Midianites were responsible for enticing Israel into Baal worship. In Numbers 25:16-18, God commanded the Israelites to destroy the Midianites for leading them into idolatry. When Moses fled from Egypt (Exodus 2), he took refuge in the land of Midian. His wife and father-in-law were Midianites. But despite this alliance, the Israelites and Midianites were always bitter enemies. The Lord commanded the Israelites to take vengeance on the Midianites for leading them into the sin of worshiping idols. But their destruction of the sinful culture was a lukewarm effort, probably because of the tempting enticements of the Midianites' sinful lifestyle. When we discover sin in our lives, our first mistake is to allow it to remain there. Our second mistake is to deal with it in a half-hearted manner. When the Israelites later entered the Promised Land, it was an indifferent attitude toward sin that eventually ruined them. Like Moses, we should hate sin and ruthlessly remove it from our lives.

those killed were all five of the Midianite kings—Evi, Rekem, Zur, Hur, and Reba. Balaam, the son of Beor, was also killed.

9, 10, 11Then the Israeli army took as captives all the women and children, and seized the cattle and flocks and a lot of miscellaneous booty. All of the cities, towns, and villages of Midian were then burned. 12The captives and other war loot were brought to Moses and Eleazar the priest, and to the rest of the people of Israel who were camped on the plains of Moab beside the Jordan River, across from Jericho. 13Moses and Eleazar the priest and all the leaders of the people went out to meet the victorious army, 14but Moses was very angry with the army officers and battalion leaders.

15"Why have you let all the women live?" he demanded. 16"These are the very ones who followed Balaam's advice and caused the people of Israel to worship idols on Mount Peor, and they are the cause of the plague that destroyed us. 17Now kill all the boys and all the women who have had sexual intercourse. 18Only the little girls may live; you may keep them for yourselves. 19Now stay outside of the camp for seven days, all of you who have killed anyone or touched a dead body. Then purify yourselves and your captives on the third and seventh days. 20Remember also to purify all your garments and everything made of leather, goat's hair, or wood."

21Then Eleazar the priest said to the men who were in the battle, "This is the commandment Jehovah has given Moses: 22'Anything that will stand heat—such as gold, silver, bronze, iron, tin, or lead— 23shall be passed through fire in order to be made ceremonially pure; it must then be further purified with the purification water. But anything that won't stand heat shall be purified by the water alone.' 24On the seventh day you must wash your clothes and be purified, and then you may come back into the camp."

25And the Lord said to Moses, 26"You and Eleazar the priest and the leaders of the tribes are to make a list of all the loot, including the people and animals; 27then divide it into two parts. Half of it is for the men who were in the battle, and the other half is to be given to the people of Israel. 28But first, the Lord gets a share of all the captives, oxen, donkeys, and flocks kept by the army. His share is one out of every five hundred. 29Give this share to Eleazar the priest to be presented to the Lord by the gesture of waving before the altar. 30Also levy a two percent tribute of all the captives, flocks, and cattle that are given to the people of Israel. Present this to the Levites in charge of the Tabernacle, for it is the Lord's portion."

31So Moses and Eleazar the priest did as the Lord commanded. 32–35The total booty (besides the jewelry, clothing, etc., which the soldiers kept for themselves) was 675,000 sheep; 72,000 oxen; 61,000 donkeys; and 32,000 young girls.

36–40So the half given to the army totaled: 337,500 sheep (of which 675 were given to the Lord); 36,000 oxen (of which 72 were given to the Lord); 30,500 donkeys (of which 61 were given to the Lord); 16,000 girls (of whom 32 went to the Levites).

41All of the Lord's portion was given to Eleazar the priest, as the Lord had directed Moses.

42–46The half of the booty assigned to the people of Israel—Moses had separated it from the half belonging to the warriors—amounted to: 337,500 sheep, 36,000

31:36-40 *of whom 32 went to the Levites,* literally, "were the Lord's portion."

31:16
Num 25:1-18
Deut 4:3
Josh 22:17,18
2 Pet 2:15,16

31:17
Judg 21:10-12
Deut 7:2
20:16-18

31:20
Lev 13:52

31:24
Lev 11:25; 14:9
Num 19:19

31:27
Josh 22:8
1 Sam 30:23,24

31:28
2 Sam 8:11,12

31:29
Num 18:25,26

31:16 Balaam's story is found in Numbers 22—24. That story, taken alone, would lead us to believe that Balaam was an honest and godly man. But here is the first of much biblical evidence indicating that Balaam was not the godly man he appeared to be. For more on Balaam see notes in Numbers 22:9 and 25:1–3, and Balaam's Profile in Numbers 22.

31:22, 23 The Israelites could purify certain captured possessions by passing them through a fire. If the material goods passed through without being destroyed, they could be used and enjoyed by God's people. There are some worldly things we should never have in our possession. But here we learn that some things, if purified through dedication to God, can be used for his service.

31:28–30 Moses told the Israelites to give a portion of the war spoils to God. Another portion was to go to the people who remained behind. Similarly, the money we earn is not ours alone. Everything we possess comes directly or indirectly from God and ultimately belongs to him. We should return a portion to him and also share what we have been given with those in need.

oxen, 30,500 donkeys, and 16,000 girls 47In accordance with the Lord's directions, Moses gave two percent of these to the Levites.

48, 49Then the officers and battalion leaders came to Moses and said, "We have
accounted for all the men who went out to battle, and not one of us is missing! 50So
we have brought a special thank-offering to the Lord from our loot—gold jewelry,
bracelets, anklets, rings, earrings, and necklaces. This is to make atonement for
our souls before the Lord."

51, 52Moses and Eleazar the priest received this special offering from the captains
and battalion leaders and company commanders, and found its total value to be
more than $300,000. 53(The soldiers had also kept personal loot for themselves.)
54The offering was taken into the Tabernacle and kept there before the Lord as a
memorial of the people of Israel.

31:53
Deut 20:14

5. Two and a half tribes receive their land

32 When Israel arrived in the land of Jazar and Gilead, the tribes of Reuben and
Gad (who had large flocks of sheep) noticed what wonderful sheep country
it was. 2So they came to Moses and Eleazar the priest and the other tribal leaders
and said, 3, 4"The Lord has used Israel to destroy the population of this whole
countryside—Ataroth, Dibon, Jazer, Nimrah, Heshbon, Elealeh, Sebam, Nebo,
and Beon. And it is all wonderful sheep country, ideal for our flocks. 5Please let us
have this land as our portion instead of the land on the other side of the Jordan
River."

32:1
Num 21:32
Josh 13:25
2 Sam 24:5

32:3
Num 32:33-42
Josh 13:17-19
Isa 15:2-6; 16:8

6"You mean you want to sit here while your brothers go across and do all the
fighting?" Moses demanded. 7"Are you trying to discourage the rest of the people
from going across to the land that the Lord has given them? 8This is the same kind
of thing your fathers did! I sent them from Kadesh-barnea to spy out the land, 9but
when they finished their survey and returned from the valley of Eshcol, they
discouraged the people from going on into the Promised Land. 10, 11And the Lord's
anger was hot against them, and he swore that of all those he had rescued from
Egypt, no one over twenty years of age would ever see the land he promised
Abraham, Isaac, and Jacob, for they had refused to do what he wanted them to.

32:8
Num 13:2-26
14:2
Deut 1:19-21

32:9
Num 13:23,24,
27-33; 14:1-12

32:10,11
Num 14:28-30
Deut 1:34,35

12"The only exceptions were Caleb (son of Jephunneh the Kenizzite) and Joshua
(son of Nun)—for they wholeheartedly followed the Lord and urged the people to
go on into the Promised Land.

32:12
Num 14:6,24,30
Deut 1:36
Josh 14:8,9

13"The Lord made us wander back and forth in the wilderness for forty years until
all that evil generation died. 14But here you are, a brood of sinners doing exactly the

32:13
Num 14:31-39
Deut 2:14,15

31:48–50 After carefully accounting for all their men, the officers
discovered that not one soldier was lost or killed in the battle. At
once they thanked God. After going through tough times, we
should be quick to thank God for what was not lost as well as for
what was gained.

32:1ff Three tribes (Reuben, Gad, and the half-tribe of Manasseh)
wanted to live east of the Jordan River on land they had already
conquered. Moses immediately assumed they had selfish motives
and were trying to avoid helping the others fight for the land across
the river. But Moses jumped to the wrong conclusion. In dealing
with people, we must find out all the facts before making up our
minds. We shouldn't automatically assume that their motives are
wrong, even if their plans sound suspicious.

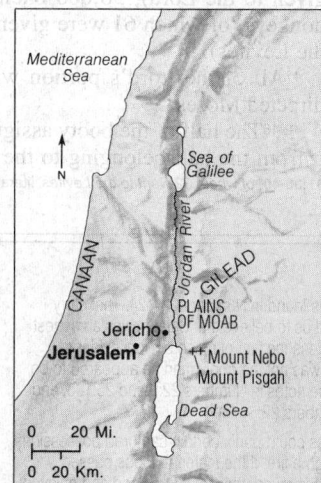

**PREPARING TO
ENTER THE
PROMISED
LAND**
The Israelites had
been camped in
the Plains of
Moab, opposite
Jericho. From this
position, they
were ready to en-
ter the Promised
Land.

same thing! Only there are more of you, so Jehovah's anger against Israel will be even fiercer this time. [15]If you turn away from God like this, he will make the people stay even longer in the wilderness, and you will be responsible for destroying his people and bringing disaster to this entire nation!"

32:15
Deut 30:17
Josh 22:16

[16]"Not at all!" they explained. "We will build sheepfolds for our flocks and cities for our little ones, [17]but we ourselves will go over armed, ahead of the rest of the people of Israel, until we have brought them safely to their inheritance. But first we will need to build walled cities here for our families, to keep them safe from attack by the local inhabitants. [18]We will not settle down here until all the people of Israel have received their inheritance. [19]We don't want land on the other side of the Jordan; we would rather have it on this side, on the east."

32:17
Deut 3:18-20
Josh 4:12,13

32:18,19
Josh 13:8; 22:4

[20]Then Moses said, "All right, if you will do what you have said and arm yourselves for Jehovah's war, [21]and keep your troops across the Jordan until the Lord has driven out his enemies, [22]then, when the land is finally subdued before the Lord, you may return. Then you will have discharged your duty to the Lord and to the rest of the people of Israel. And the land on the eastern side shall be your possession from the Lord. [23]But if you don't do as you have said, then you will have sinned against the Lord, and you may be sure that your sin will catch up with you. [24]Go ahead and build cities for your families and sheepfolds for your sheep, and do all you have said."

32:21
Deut 3:18
Josh 1:12-18

32:22
Deut 3:20
Josh 2:4-9

32:24
Num 30:2

[25]"We will follow your instructions exactly," the people of Gad and Reuben replied. [26]"Our children, wives, flocks, and cattle shall stay here in the cities of Gilead. [27]But all of us who are conscripted will go over to battle for the Lord, just as you have said."

[28]So Moses gave his approval by saying to Eleazar, Joshua, and the tribal leaders of Israel, [29]"If all the men of the tribes of Gad and Reuben who are conscripted for the Lord's battles go with you over Jordan, then, when the land is conquered, you must give them the land of Gilead; [30]but if they refuse, then they must accept land among the rest of you in the land of Canaan."

[31]The tribes of Gad and Reuben said again, "As the Lord has commanded, so we will do— [32]we will follow the Lord fully armed into Canaan, but our own land shall be here on this side of the Jordan."

[33]So Moses assigned the territory of King Sihon of the Amorites, and of King Og of Bashan—all the land and cities—to the tribes of Gad, Reuben, and the half-tribe of Manasseh (son of Joseph).

32:33
Num 21:23-26
32:22; 34:14,15
Deut 2:32-37
3:8-17
Josh 12:1-6

[34,35,36]The people of Gad built these cities: Dibon, Ataroth, Aroer, Atroth-shophan, Jazer, Jogbehah, Beth-nimrah, Beth-haran. They were all fortified cities with sheepfolds.

[37,38]The children of Reuben built the following cities: Heshbon, Elealeh, Kiriathaim, Nebo, Baal-meon, Sibmah. (The Israelites later changed the names of some of these cities they had conquered and rebuilt.)

[39]Then the clan of Machir of the tribe of Manasseh went to Gilead and conquered it, and drove out the Amorites who were living there. [40]So Moses gave Gilead to the Machirites, and they lived there. [41]The men of Jair, another clan of the tribe of Manasseh, occupied many of the towns in Gilead, and changed the name of their area to Havroth-jair. [42]Meanwhile, a man named Nobah led an army to Kenath and

32:41
Deut 3:14
Josh 13:30
1 Chron 2:22

32:42 *led an army,* implied.

32:16 A sheepfold was a shelter for enclosing and protecting sheep. A simple sheepfold had four roughly built stone walls, high enough to keep wild animals out. Sometimes the top of the wall was lined with thorns to further discourage predators and thieves. The fold's single entrance made it easier for a shepherd to guard his flock. Often several shepherds used a single fold and took turns guarding the entrance. Mingling the animals was no problem since each flock responded readily to its own shepherd's voice. The three tribes who chose to remain east of the Jordan River wanted to build sheepfolds to protect their flocks and cities to

protect their families before the men crossed the river to help the rest of the tribes conquer the Promised Land.

32:16–19 The land on the east side of the Jordan had been conquered. The hard work was done by all of the tribes together. But the tribes of Reuben and Gad and the half-tribe of Manasseh did not stop after their land was cleared. They promised to keep working with the others until everyone's land was conquered. After others have helped you, do you find excuses for being unable to help them? Finish the whole job, even those parts that may not benefit you directly.

its surrounding villages, and occupied them, and he called the area Nobah, after his own name.

6. Camped on the plains of Moab
Israel's travel route

33 This is the itinerary of the nation of Israel from the time Moses and Aaron led them out of Egypt. ²Moses had written down their movements as the Lord had instructed him. ³,⁴They left the city of Rameses, Egypt, on the first day of April, the day after the night of the Passover. They left proudly, hurried along by the Egyptians who were burying all their eldest sons, killed by the Lord the night before. The Lord had certainly defeated all the gods of Egypt that night!

⁵,⁶After leaving Rameses, they stayed in Succoth, Etham (at the edge of the wilderness), and ⁷Pihahiroth (near Baal-zephon, where they camped at the foot of Mount Migdol). ⁸From there they went through the middle of the Red Sea and on for three days into the Etham wilderness, camping at Marah.

⁹Leaving Marah, they came to Elim, where there are twelve springs of water and seventy palm trees; they stayed there for quite a long time.

¹⁰Leaving Elim, they camped beside the Red Sea, ¹¹and then in the wilderness of Sihn.

¹²Next was Dophkah, ¹³and then Alush; ¹⁴then on to Rephidim (where there was no water for the people to drink).

¹⁵⁻³⁷From Rephidim they went to the wilderness of Sinai; from the wilderness of Sinai to Kibroth-hattaavah;

From Kibroth-hattaavah to Hazeroth;
From Hazeroth to Rithmah;
From Rithmah to Rimmon-parez;
From Rimmon-parez to Libnah;
From Libnah to Rissah;
From Rissah to Kehelathah;
From Kehelathah to Mount Shepher;
From Mount Shepher to Haradah;
From Haradah to Makheloth;
From Makheloth to Tahath;
From Tahath to Terah;
From Terah to Mithkah;
From Mithkah to Hashmonah;
From Hashmonah to Moseroth;
From Moseroth to Bene-jaakan;
From Bene-jaakan to Hor-haggidgad;
From Hor-haggidgad to Jotbathah;
From Jotbathah to Abronah;
From Abronah to Ezion-geber;
From Ezion-geber to Kadesh (in the wilderness of Zin);
From Kadesh to Mount Hor (at the edge of the land of Edom).

³⁸,³⁹While they were at the foot of Mount Hor, Aaron the priest was directed by the Lord to go up into the mountain, and there he died. This occurred during the fortieth year after the people of Israel had left Egypt. The date of his death was July 15, when he was 123 years old.

33:3, 4 *on the first day of April,* literally, "on the fifteenth day of the first month" (of the Hebrew calendar).
33:38, 39 *The date of his death was July 15,* literally, "the first day of the fifth month" (of the Hebrew calendar).

33:3 Ex 12:11-51
33:5 Ex 13:20
33:7 Ex 14:2,9
33:8 Ex 14:21,22
33:9 Ex 15:27; 16:1
33:11 Ex 16:1; 17:1
33:14 Ex 17:1-8 19:2,3
33:15 Num 11:34,35 13:21; 20:1 Deut 2:2-8 10:6,7; 32:51 1 Kgs 9:26 2 Chron 20:36
33:38 Num 20:28

33:1ff Look at the map in the introduction to the book of Numbers to see the travels of the Israelites.

33:2 Moses recorded the movements of the Israelites as God instructed him. But it was probably intended to be a record of their spiritual progress more than their geographic progress. Have you made spiritual progress lately? A valuable aid to spiritual growth can be found in recording your thoughts about God and some lessons you have learned over a period of time. Before long, you will have a record of your spiritual pilgrimage which will let you check up on your progress and avoid repeated mistakes.

33:40
Num 21:1
33:42
Num 21:10,11
33:47
Num 27:12
33:48
Num 22:1
33:49
Num 25:1
Josh 2:1
Joel 13:18
Mic 6:5

40It was then that the Canaanite king of Arad, who lived in the Negeb, in the land of Canaan, heard that the people of Israel were approaching his land. 41After dealing with him, the Israelis journeyed from Mount Hor and camped in Zalmonah, 42then at Punon, 43then at Oboth, 44then Iyeabarim (at the border of Moab). 45From there they went to Dibon-gad, 46and then to Almon-diblathaim, 47and on into the mountains of Abarim, near Mount Nebo, 48and finally to the plains of Moab beside the river Jordan, opposite Jericho. 49While in that area they camped at various places along the Jordan River, from Bethjeshimoth as far as Abel-shittim, on the plains of Moab.

How to settle and conquer the new land

33:52
Ex 23:24
34:12-17
Deut 7:2-5,25,
26
Josh 23:7
Judg 2:2
33:54
Num 26:53-56
33:55
Ex 23:33
Deut 7:4,16-20
Ps 106:34-36
33:56
Deut 28:63

50, 51It was while they were camped there that the Lord told Moses to tell the people of Israel, "When you pass across the Jordan River into the land of Canaan, 52you must drive out all the people living there and destroy all their idols—their carved stones, molten images, and the open-air sanctuaries in the hills where they worship their idols. 53I have given the land to you; take it and live there. 54You will be given land in proportion to the size of your tribes. The larger sections of land will be divided by lot among the larger tribes, and the smaller sections will be allotted to the smaller tribes. 55But if you refuse to drive out the people living there, those who remain will be as cinders in your eyes and thorns in your sides. 56And I will destroy you as I had planned for you to destroy them."

The boundaries of Canaan

34:2
Gen 17:8
Deut 1:7,8
Ezek 47:14
34:3
Ex 23:31
Josh 15:1-4
34:4
Num 34:4
34:7
Josh 13:5
15:5-11
Ezek 47:15-17

34 The Lord told Moses to tell the people of Israel, "When you come into the land of Canaan (I am giving you the entire land as your homeland), 3the southern portion of the country will be the wilderness of Zin, along the edge of Edom. The southern boundary will begin at the Dead Sea, 4and will continue south past Scorpion Pass in the direction of Zin. Its southernmost point will be Kadesh-barnea, from which it will go to Hazaraddar, and on to Azmon. 5From Azmon the boundary will follow the Brook of Egypt down to the Mediterranean Sea.

6"Your western boundary will be the coastline of the Mediterranean Sea.

7, 8, 9"Your northern border will begin at the Mediterranean Sea and will proceed

34:4 *Scorpion Pass*, literally, "ascent of Akrabbim."

33:50–53 God told Moses that before the Israelites settled in the Promised Land, they were to drive out the wicked people and destroy their idols. In Colossians chapter three, Paul encourages us to live the Christian life in the same manner. We are to throw away our old way of living and move ahead into our new life of obedience to God and faith in Jesus Christ. Like the Israelites moving into the Promised Land, we can destroy the wickedness in our lives or we can settle down and live with it. To move in and possess the new life, we must drive out the sinful habits that would keep us from entering.

33:50–56 Why were the Israelites told to destroy the people living in Canaan? Wasn't this unjust? No, because it was God's command. The Israelites were to obey the command as a sign of loyalty to God, the Commander-in-chief of all armies. (1) God was stamping out the wickedness of an extremely sinful nation. The Canaanites brought on their own punishment. Idol worship was the outward practice of their deepest evil desires, for it ultimately led to the worship of Satan and the total rejection of God. (2) God was using Moses and Israel to judge Canaan for its sins as fulfillment of the prophecy in Genesis 9:24, 25. (3) God wanted to remove all trace of pagan beliefs and practices from the land. He did not want his people to mix or compromise with idolatry in any way. We are to obey God's Word without question because we know it is just, even if we cannot fully understand his overall purposes.

33:55 If you don't do the job right the first time, it often comes back to haunt you. God promised that if the Israelites did not drive

the wicked inhabitants out of the Promised Land, they would become a source of great irritation later on. That is exactly what happened. Just as the Israelites were hesitant to clear out all the wicked people, we are sometimes hesitant to clear out all the sin in our lives, either because we are afraid of it (as the Israelites feared the "giants"), or because it seems harmless and attractive (as sexual sin seemed to the Israelites). But Hebrews 12:1, 2 tells us to throw off those sins that wrap themselves tightly around our feet and trip us up. We all have an "idol" we don't want to let go of (a bad habit, an unhealthy relationship, a certain lifestyle). If we allow these idols to remain in our lives, they will cause serious problems later on.

33:55, 56 God never goes back on a promise, and this is one promise the Israelites should not have taken lightly. God made his message perfectly clear: "Drive the wicked people out of the Promised Land—every one of them. If you don't, you will become as wicked as they are, and I will have to destroy you too." For some reason the people did not take God seriously. The Israelites did not drive all the wicked nations out, and soon they began to assimilate their evil religious beliefs and practices. After a while, an Israelite was no different from a Canaanite. God fulfilled his warning in these verses during the period of the judges, and in a fuller sense during the time of the kings when he sent the Babylonians (2 Kings 25) and the Assyrians (2 Kings 17) to destroy Israel and carry the people away as captives. The Israelites learned that God's Word should not be taken lightly.

eastward to Mount Hor, then to Lebo-Hamath, and on through Zedad and Ziphron to Hazar-enan.

10, 11"The eastern border will be from Hazar-enan south to Shepham, then on to Riblah at the east side of Ain. From there it will make a large half-circle, first going south and then westward until it touches the southernmost tip of the Sea of Galilee, 12and then along the Jordan River, ending at the Dead Sea."

13"This is the territory you are to apportion among yourselves by lot," Moses said. "It is to be divided up among the nine and one-half tribes, 14, 15for the tribes of Reuben and Gad and the half-tribe of Manasseh have already been assigned land on the east side of the Jordan, opposite Jericho."

16-28And the Lord said to Moses, "These are the names of the men I have appointed to handle the dividing up of the land: Eleazar the priest, Joshua (son of Nun), and one leader from each tribe, as listed below:

Tribe	Leader
Judah	Caleb (son of Jephunneh)
Simeon	Shemuel (son of Ammihud)
Benjamin	Elidad (son of Chislon)
Dan	Bukki (son of Jogli)
Manasseh	Hanniel (son of Ephod)
Ephraim	Kemuel (son of Shiphtan)
Zebulun	Elizaphan (son of Parnach)
Issachar	Paltiel (son of Azzan)
Asher	Ahihud (son of Shelomi)
Naphtali	Pedahel (son of Ammihud)

29These are the names of the men I have appointed to oversee the dividing of the land among the tribes."

The cities for the Levites

35 While Israel was camped beside the Jordan on the plains of Moab, opposite Jericho, the Lord said to Moses,

2"Instruct the people of Israel to give to the Levites as their inheritance certain cities and surrounding pasture lands. 3These cities are for their homes, and the surrounding lands for their cattle, flocks, and other livestock. 4, 5Their gardens and vineyards shall extend 1500 feet out from the city walls in each direction, with an additional 1500 feet beyond that for pastureland.

6"You shall give the Levites the six Cities of Refuge where a person who has

34:10
Deut 3:17
Josh 15:5,12
2 Kgs 23:33
25:6
Jer 52:9
Mt 14:34
Lk 5:1
Jn 6:1

34:13
Josh 14:1,2

34:14
Num 32:33

34:16
Num 1:2-15
2:3-21

35:2
Lev 25:32-34
Josh 14:3,4
Ezek 45:1; 48:8

35:6
Deut 4:41-43
Josh 20:2-9
21:3,13,21-38

THE BORDERS OF THE PROMISED LAND

The borders of the Promised Land stretched from the wilderness of Zin and Kadesh-barnea in the south to Lebo-hamath and Riblah in the north, and from the Mediterranean sea coast on the west to the Jordan River on the east. The land of Gilead was also part of the Promised Land.

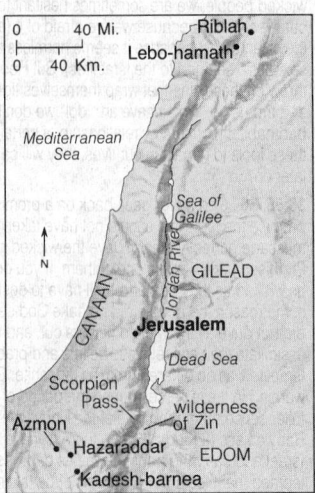

THE BORDERS OF THE PROMISED LAND
0   40 Mi.
0   40 Km.
Riblah
Lebo-hamath
Mediterranean Sea
Sea of Galilee
GILEAD
Jerusalem
Dead Sea
Scorpion Pass
Azmon
wilderness of Zin
Hazaraddar
EDOM
Kadesh-barnea
CANAAN
Jordan River
N

34:16-29 In God's plan for settling the land, he (1) explained what to do, (2) communicated this clearly to Moses, and (3) assigned specific people to oversee the apportionment of the land. No plan is complete until each job is assigned and everyone understands his or her responsibilities. When you have a job to do, determine what must be done, give clear instructions, and put specific people in charge of each part.

35:2-4 The Levites were ministers. They earned a living from the tithes of the people, who were required to support them and supply their needs. The people of Israel gave the Levites homes, flocks, and pastureland. Today, we have a great responsibility to support our churches, ministers, and missionaries so that their needs are supplied.

35:6 A man who accidentally killed someone was permitted to hide from his avengers in a designated City of Refuge. He was safe there, but he had to remain until the death of the current High Priest. At that time, he was allowed to go free. He could start a new life without worrying about avengers. Of the 48 cities given to the Levites by the people, six were Cities of Refuge. These six cities were probably put under the Levites' supervision because they would be the most impartial judges. Such cities were needed because the ancient custom of justice called for revenge

accidentally killed someone can run and be safe, and forty-two other cities besides. ⁷In all, there shall be forty-eight cities with the surrounding pastureland given to the Levites. ⁸These cities shall be in various parts of the nation; the larger tribes with many cities will give several to the Levites, while the smaller tribes will give fewer."

35:7
Josh 21:3-42
1 Chron 6:54-81

35:8
Num 26:54

The Cities of Refuge

⁹, ¹⁰And the Lord said to Moses, "Tell the people that when they arrive in the land, ¹¹Cities of Refuge shall be designated for anyone to flee into if he has killed someone accidentally. ¹²These Cities will be places of protection from the dead man's relatives who want to avenge his death; for the slayer must not be killed unless a fair trial establishes his guilt. ¹³, ¹⁴Three of these six Cities of Refuge are

35:11
Num 35:6

35:12
Num 35:16-29

PRIESTS IN ISRAEL'S HISTORY
Numbers 35:25–28 mentions the death of a High Priest. Each new High Priest had to come from the lineage of Aaron. Listed here are the ones whose stories are told elsewhere in the Bible.

Priest	Importance	Reference
Aaron	Moses' brother and first priest	Exodus 28:1–3
Eleazar	Watched two of his brothers die in a fire from God because they did not follow God's instructions. He obeyed God and became chief administrator of the Tabernacle.	Leviticus 10 Numbers 3:32
Phinehas	Executed a young Israeli idol worshiper and his Midianite mistress to end a plague. He was then promised that his priestly line would never end.	Numbers 25:1–15
Ahitub	A priest during King Saul's reign	1 Samuel 14:3
Zadok	A faithful High Priest under King David. He and Nathan anointed Solomon as the next king.	2 Samuel 8:17 1 Kings 1:38, 39
Ahima-az	Carried the message of Absalom's death to King David, but was apparently afraid to tell about it.	2 Samuel 18:19–29
Azariah	High Priest under King Solomon	1 Kings 4:2
Azariah	High Priest under Uzziah. He rebuked the king for burning incense himself.	2 Chronicles 26:17–21
	When Hezekiah became king he reopened the Temple. Azariah again served as High Priest.	2 Chronicles 31:10
Amariah	King Jehoshaphat appointed him to judge religious disputes.	2 Chronicles 19:11
Hilkiah	Found the book of the Law during Josiah's reign	2 Kings 22:3–13 2 Chronicles 34:14–21
Azariah	Probably one of the first to return to Israel from Babylon	1 Chronicles 9:10, 11
Seraiah	The father of Ezra	Ezra 7:1–5

(2 Samuel 14:7). The Levites would hold a preliminary hearing outside the gates; then the accused person was kept in the city until the time of his trial. If the killing was accidental, the person stayed in the city until the death of the High Priest. If it was not accidental, the person was delivered to the slain person's avengers. This system of justice shows how God's law and God's mercy go hand in hand.

35:11–21 If anyone was found dead, it was often assumed the person had been murdered; but it was wrong to assume that the murder suspect was actually guilty. The people were to be intolerant of the sin, yet impartial to the accused so that he or she could have a fair trial. This demonstrates the balance between God's justice and God's mercy. God's laws about the consequences of murder show his justice. The Cities of Refuge represented God's concern and provision for justice in a culture that did not always protect the innocent. When you suspect wrongdoing, don't dismiss it or you risk becoming tolerant of sin. Listen carefully to all sides of the story, or you will risk becoming unjust yourself.

to be located in the land of Canaan, and three on the east side of the Jordan River. 15These are not only for the protection of Israelites, but also for foreigners and travelers.

16"But if someone is struck and killed by a piece of iron, it must be presumed to be murder, and the murderer must be executed. 17Or if the slain man was struck down with a large stone, it is murder, and the murderer shall die. 18The same is true if he is killed with a wooden weapon. 19The avenger of his death shall personally kill the murderer when he meets him. 20So, if anyone kills another out of hatred by throwing something at him, or ambushing him, 21or angrily striking him with his fist so that he dies, he is a murderer; and the murderer shall be executed by the avenger.

22, 23"But if it is an accident—a case in which something is thrown unintentionally, or in which a stone is thrown without anger, without realizing it will hit anyone, and without wanting to harm an enemy—yet the man dies, 24then the people shall judge whether or not it was an accident, and whether or not to hand the killer over to the avenger of the dead man. 25If it is decided that it was accidental, then the people shall save the killer from the avenger; the killer shall be permitted to stay in the City of Refuge; and he must live there until the death of the High Priest.

26"If the slayer leaves the City, 27and the avenger finds him outside and kills him, it is not murder, 28for the man should have stayed inside the City until the death of the High Priest. But after the death of the High Priest, the man may return to his own land and home. 29These are permanent laws for all Israel from generation to generation.

30"All murderers must be executed, but only if there is more than one witness; no man shall die with only one person testifying against him. 31Whenever anyone is judged guilty of murder, he must die—no ransom may be accepted for him. 32Nor may a payment be accepted from a refugee in a City of Refuge, permitting him to return to his home before the death of the High Priest. 33In this way the land will not be polluted, for murder pollutes the land, and no atonement can be made for murder except by the execution of the murderer. 34You shall not defile the land where you are going to live, for I, Jehovah, will be living there."

35:16
Ex 21:12-14
Lev 24:17
Deut 19:11-13

35:19
Deut 19:6,7,12
Josh 20:3,5

35:30
Deut 17:6,7
19:15
Mt 18:16
2 Cor 13:1
Heb 10:28

35:34
Lev 18:25
Deut 21:1-8
2 Kgs 24:4
Ezek 22:24-27

The inheritance of each tribe to remain secure

36 Then the heads of the sub-clan of Gilead (of the clan of Machir, of the tribe of Manasseh, one of the sons of Joseph) came to Moses and the leaders of Israel with a petition: "The Lord instructed you to divide the land by lot among the people of Israel," they reminded Moses, "and to give the inheritance of our brother

36:1,2
Num 27:1-11
Josh 17:3,4

35:33 Murderers were to be executed, for they polluted and corrupted the land. But Jesus startles us by saying that even becoming angry at someone for no reason is a sin like murder (Matthew 5:21, 22). Murder and anger stem from the same root; and while one seems a lesser sin, it will often lead to the greater sin if left unchecked. If bitterness and anger continue, they will pollute us by arousing our evil thoughts and motives, and will ultimately destroy us. We need to deal with any bitterness and anger we feel before it festers and corrupts our lives.

36:13 The book of Numbers covers 39 years and closes with the Israelites poised near the banks of the Jordan River with the Promised Land in sight. The wanderings in the wilderness had come to an end, and the people were preparing for their next big move—the conquest of the land. The Apostle Paul said that the events in Numbers are examples that warn Christians and help them avoid the same mistakes (1 Corinthians 10:1-12). From the Israelites' experiences we learn that unbelief is disastrous. We also learn not to long for the sinful pleasures of the past, to avoid complaining, and to stay away from all forms of compromise. If we choose to let God lead our lives, we should not ignore the book of Numbers.

Mediterranean Sea

N

Kedesh

Sea of Galilee

Golan

Ramoth-gilead

Shechem

Jordan River

CANAAN

Jerusalem

Hebron

Bezer

Dead Sea

0   20 Mi.

0   20 Km.

CITIES OF REFUGE
Six of the Levites' cities were designated as Cities of Refuge. They were spaced throughout the land and protected those who had accidentally committed a crime or who were awaiting trial.

Zelophehad to his daughters. ³But if they marry into another tribe, their land will go with them to the tribe into which they marry. In this way the total area of our tribe will be reduced, ⁴and will not be returned at the Year of Jubilee."

⁵Then Moses replied publicly, giving them these instructions from the Lord: "The men of the tribe of Joseph have a proper complaint. ⁶This is what the Lord has further commanded concerning the daughters of Zelophehad: 'Let them be married to anyone they like, so long as it is within their own tribe. ⁷In this way none of the land of the tribe will shift to any other tribe, for the inheritance of every tribe is to remain permanently as it was first allotted. ⁸The girls throughout the tribes of Israel who are heiresses must marry within their own tribe, so that their land won't leave the tribe. ⁹In this way no inheritance shall move from one tribe to another.' "

¹⁰The daughters of Zelophehad did as the Lord commanded Moses. ¹¹, ¹²These girls, Mahlah, Tirzah, Hoglah, Milcah, and Noah, were married to men in their own tribe of Manasseh (son of Joseph); so their inheritance remained in their tribe.

¹³These are the commandments and ordinances which the Lord gave to the people of Israel through Moses, while they were camped on the plains of Moab beside the Jordan River, across from Jericho.

36:6
Gen 24:3,57,58

36:8
1 Chron 23:22

36:11
Num 27:1-11
36:1

36:13
Lev 7:37,38
27:34

Joseph
dies
1850 B.C.

S L A V E R Y I N E G Y P T

Exodus
from
Egypt
1446

Ten
Command-
ments
given
1445

WILDERNESS WANDERINGS

VITAL STATISTICS

PURPOSE:
To remind the people of what God has done and encourage them to rededicate their lives to him

AUTHOR:
Moses (except for the final summary which was probably written after Moses' death by Joshua)

TO WHOM WRITTEN:
Israel (the new generation entering the Promised Land)

DATE WRITTEN:
About 1407/6 B.C.

SETTING:
The east side of the Jordan River, in view of the Promised Land

KEY VERSE:
"The Lord your God is the faithful God" (7:9).

KEY PEOPLE:
Moses, Joshua

KEY PLACE:
The Valley of Arabah in Moab, east of the Jordan River

CLASS reunions, scrapbooks and photo albums, familiar songs, and old neighborhoods—like long-time friends they awaken our memories and stir our emotions. The past is a kaleidoscope of promises, failures, victories, and embarrassments. Sometimes we want to forget memories that are too painful. However, as the years pass, memories of unpleasant events usually fade into our subconscious. But there is a time to remember: mistakes should not be repeated; commitments made must be fulfilled; and the memory of special events can encourage us and move us to action.

The book of Deuteronomy calls Israel to remember who God is and what he has done. Lacking faith, the old generation wandered for 40 years and died in the wilderness. They left Egypt behind, but never knew the Promised Land. Now on the east bank of the Jordan River, Moses prepares the sons and daughters of that faithless generation to possess the land. After a brief history lesson emphasizing God's great acts on behalf of his people, Moses reviews the Law. Then he restates the covenant—God's contract with his people. The lessons are clear. Because of what God has done, Israel should have hope and follow him; because of what he expects, they should listen and obey; because of who he is, they should love him completely. Obeying these lessons will prepare them to possess the Promised Land.

As you hear the message of Deuteronomy, remember how God has expressed his kindness in your life, and then commit yourself anew to trust, love, and obey him.

THE BLUEPRINT

A. WHAT GOD HAS DONE FOR US: MOSES' FIRST ADDRESS (1:1—4:43)

Moses reviewed the mighty acts of God for the nation of Israel. Remembering God's special involvement in our lives gives us hope and encouragement for the future.

B. PRINCIPLES FOR GODLY LIVING: MOSES' SECOND ADDRESS (4:44—28:68)

Moses reviews God's commands and applies them to specific situations. Knowing what God requires is not enough. We must put God's Word into action, making it a part of our lives.

1. Review of the Ten Commandments
2. Love God and obey his commandments
3. Laws for proper worship
4. Laws for ruling the nation
5. Laws for human relationships
6. Consequences of obedience and disobedience

Obeying God's laws brought blessings to the Israelites and disobeying brought misfortune. This was part of the written agreement God made with his people. Although we are not part of this covenant, the principle holds true: obedience and disobedience carry inevitable consequences in this life and the next.

Moses'
Death;
Israelites
enter
Canaan
1406

Judges
begin
to rule
1375

United
Kingdom
under
Saul
1050

C. A CALL FOR COMMITMENT TO GOD:
    MOSES' THIRD ADDRESS (29:1—30:20)

Moses called the people to commitment. God still calls us to be committed to love him with all our heart, soul, mind, and strength.

D. THE CHANGE IN LEADERSHIP:
    MOSES' LAST DAYS (31:1—34:12)

Although Moses made some serious mistakes, he had lived uprightly and carried out God's commands. Moses died with integrity. We too may make some serious mistakes, but that should not stop us from living with integrity and godly commitment.

MEGATHEMES

THEME	EXPLANATION	IMPORTANCE
History	Moses reviews the mighty acts of God through which he liberated Israel from slavery in Egypt.	By reviewing God's promises and mighty acts, we can learn about his character. We come to know God more intimately through understanding how he has acted in the past. We can also avoid mistakes in our own lives through learning from Israel's past failures.
Laws	God reviews his laws with the people. The legal contract between God and his people had to be renewed for the new generation about to enter the Promised Land.	Commitment to God and his truth cannot be taken for granted. Each generation and each person must respond afresh to God's call.
Love	God's faithful and patient love is portrayed more often than his punishment. God shows his love by being faithful to his people and his promises. In response, God desires love from the heart and not mere legalistic adherence to his law.	God's love forms the foundation for our trust in him. We trust him because he loves us. God's love should form the basis for our attitude toward justice and the rights of others.
Choices	God reminded his people that in order to ratify his agreement they must choose the path of obedience. Personal choice to obey could bring benefits to their lives; rebellion would bring severe calamity.	Our choices make a difference. Choosing to follow God produces good results in our lives and in our relationships with others. Choosing to abandon God's ways brings harm to ourselves and others.
Teaching	God commanded the Israelites to teach their children his ways. They were to use ritual, instruction, and memorization to make sure their children understood God's principles and passed them on to the next generation.	It is important to pass on God's truth in our traditions to future generations. But God desires that his truth be in our hearts and minds and not merely in our traditions.

A. WHAT GOD HAS DONE FOR US: MOSES' FIRST ADDRESS (1:1—4:43)

God has led his people out of Egypt and across the great wilderness. Now they stand ready to enter the Promised Land. But before the Israelites go into the land, Moses has some important advice to give them. He delivers his advice in three parts. In the first part, Moses reviews the history of God's previous care for the people of Israel. Through God's actions in the past, we can learn about the God we serve today.

1 This book records Moses' address to the people of Israel when they were camped in the valley of the Arabah in the wilderness of Moab, east of the Jordan River. (Cities in the area included Suph, Paran, Tophel, Laban, Hazeroth, and Dizahab.) The speech was given on February 15, forty years after the people of Israel left Mount Horeb—though it takes only eleven days to travel by foot from Mount Horeb to Kadesh-barnea, going by way of Mount Seir! At the time of this address, King Sihon of the Amorites had already been defeated at Heshbon, and King Og of Bashan had been defeated at Ashtaroth, near Edre-i. Here, then, is Moses' address to Israel, stating all the laws God had commanded him to pass on to them:

1:1
Gen 32:3
Num 21:24,33
Deut 2:8,24
3:3; 4:1,44-46

Leaders chosen from each tribe

6"It was forty years ago, at Mount Horeb, that Jehovah our God told us, 'You have stayed here long enough. 7Now go and occupy the hill country of the Amorites, the valley of the Arabah, and the Negeb, and all the land of Canaan and Lebanon—the entire area from the shores of the Mediterranean Sea to the Euphrates River. 8I am giving all of it to you! Go in and possess it, for it is the land the Lord promised to your ancestors Abraham, Isaac, and Jacob, and all of their descendants.'

9"At that time I told the people, 'I need help! You are a great burden for me to

1:6
Ex 19:1
Num 10:11-13
33:38
1:7
Gen 15:18-21
Deut 4:49
Josh 10:5,40
1:8
Gen 12:7; 26:3
Ex 33:1

1:1-5 *February 15th,* literally, "the first day of the eleventh month" (of the Hebrew calendar). *eleven days to travel by foot from Mount Horeb to Kadesh-barnea.* Kadesh-barnea was at the southern edge of the Promised Land.

EVENTS IN DEUTERONOMY
The book of Deuteronomy opens with Israel camped east of the Jordan River in the Arabah Valley in the land of Moab. Just before the people crossed the river into the Promised Land, Moses delivered an inspirational speech indicating how they were to live.

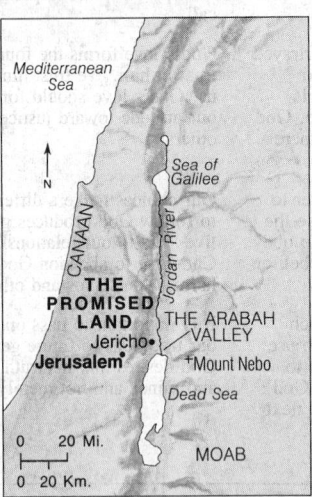

fallen, sinful, prone to rebellion and doubt. He gave his rebellious people the Law to help them understand how to relate to their God. Your spiritual pilgrimage may be lengthy and your life may be full of pain, discouragement, and difficulties. But remember that God isn't just trying to keep you alive. He wants to prepare you to live in service and devotion to him.

1:1–5 The 40 years of desert wandering come to an end in this book. The events of Deuteronomy cover only a week or two of the eleventh month of the 40th year (1:3). The twelfth and last month was spent in mourning for Moses (34:8). The Israelites then entered the Promised Land the first month of the 41st year after the Exodus (Joshua 4:19).

1:6 Notice that Moses' summary of Israel's forty-year journey begins at Mount Horeb (Sinai), not at Egypt. Why did Moses leave out the first part of the Exodus? Moses was not giving a trip itinerary—he was summarizing the nation's development. In Moses' mind the nation of Israel began at the base of Mount Sinai, not in Egypt, for it was at Mount Sinai that God gave his covenant to the people (Exodus 19, 20). Along with this covenant came knowledge and responsibility. After the people chose to follow God (and it was their choice), they had to know how to follow him. Therefore, God gave them a comprehensive set of laws and guidelines that showed them God's idea of how life should be lived (these are found in the books of Exodus, Leviticus, and Numbers). The people could no longer say they didn't know the difference between right and wrong. Now that the people had promised to follow God and knew how to follow him, they had a responsibility to do it. Moses probably gave his first speech at Mount Sinai to remind the people of this responsibility as they faced their biggest challenge to date—finally entering the Promised Land and starting a nation that was to obey God and be a light and example to others.

1:1ff The Israelites spent 40 years on a journey that should have lasted 11 days. It wasn't distance that stood between them and the Promised Land. It was the condition of their hearts. God's purpose went deeper than simply transporting a huge group of people to the Promised Land. He was preparing them to live in obedience to him once they arrived. What good was the Promised Land if the Israelites were just as wicked as the nations already living there? The journey was a painful but necessary part of their preparation. Through it God taught the Israelites who he was: the living God, the Leader of their nation. He also taught them what they were:

1:9–13 It was a tremendous burden for Moses to lead the nation by himself. He could not accomplish the task single-handedly. As

carry all by myself, 10for the Lord has multiplied you to become as many as the stars! 11And may he multiply you a thousand times more, and bless you as he promised, 12but what can one man do to settle all your quarrels and problems? 13So choose some men from each tribe who are wise, experienced, and understanding, and I will appoint them as your leaders.'

14"They agreed to this; 15I took the men they selected, some from every tribe, and appointed them as administrative assistants in charge of thousands, hundreds, fifties, and tens to decide their quarrels and assist them in every way. 16I instructed them to be perfectly fair at all times, even to foreigners. 17'When giving your decisions,' I told them, 'never favor a man because he is rich; be fair to great and small alike. Don't fear their displeasure, for you are judging in the place of God. Bring me any cases too difficult for you, and I will handle them.' 18And I gave them other instructions at that time, also.

19, 20, 21"Then we left Mount Horeb and traveled through the great and terrible desert, finally arriving among the Amorite hills to which the Lord our God had directed us. We were then at Kadesh-barnea [on the border of the Promised Land] and I said to the people, 'The Lord God has given us this land. Go and possess it as he told us to. Don't be afraid! Don't even doubt!'

22"But they replied, 'First let's send out spies to discover the best route of entry, and to decide which cities we should capture first.'

23"This seemed like a good idea, so I chose twelve spies, one from each tribe. 24, 25They crossed into the hills and came to the Valley of Eshcol, and returned with samples of the local fruit. One look was enough to convince us that it was indeed a good land the Lord our God had given us.

Rebellion against God

26But the people refused to go in, and rebelled against the Lord's command. 27"They murmured and complained in their tents and said, 'The Lord must hate us, bringing us here from Egypt to be slaughtered by these Amorites. 28What are we getting into? Our brothers who spied out the land have frightened us with their report. They say that the people of the land are tall and powerful, and that the walls of their cities rise high into the sky! They have even seen giants there—the descendants of the Anakim!'

1:19-21 *on the border of the Promised Land,* implied.

---

churches and families grow, they become more complex. Needs, conflicts, and quarrels arise. No longer can one leader make all the decisions. Like Moses, you may have a natural tendency to try to do all the work alone. You may be afraid or embarrassed to ask for help. Moses made a wise decision to share the leadership with others. Rather than trying to handle larger responsibilities alone, look into ways of sharing the load so that others may exercise their God-given gifts and abilities.

1:14-18 Moses identified some of the inner qualities of good leaders: (1) fairness, (2) impartiality, (3) character strength, and (4) the ability to recognize their limitations. These characteristics differ markedly from the ones that often help elect leaders today: good looks, wealth, popularity, willingness to do anything to get to the top. The qualities Moses identified should be evident in our lives as we lead, and we should look for them in the lives of those we elect to positions of leadership.

1:19-21 God gave the Promised Land to his people and told them to take possession of it. By remaining outside the land the Israelites were being disobedient. When God offers a gift, he offers it in good faith. Often, however, when he opens up opportunities we have doubts and are afraid of failure. Seize your opportunities to grow, to share your faith, and to live in a manner pleasing to God. He will lead the way and give you strength.

1:22 The spies were not sent into the Promised Land to determine whether they should enter, but where they should enter. Upon returning, however, most of the spies decided that the risk might

not be worth the obstacles they would encounter. God gave the Israelites the power to conquer the Promised Land, but they failed to enter because they were afraid and did not trust God. God gives us the power to conquer our obstacles, but like the Israelites, we often let obstacles control our lives because of fear and skepticism. Following God regardless of the obstacles and difficulties is what faith is all about.

1:27, 28 Moses retold the story of the spy mission into the Promised Land (Numbers 13, 14). When the spies returned with reports of giants and walled cities, the people were too afraid to move ahead and began to complain about their predicament. But the minority report of Joshua and Caleb pointed out that the land was fertile with abundant crops, the enemy was vulnerable, and God was on their side. We become fearful and immobile by focusing on the negative aspects of a situation. How much better to focus on the positive—God's direction and promises. When you are confronted with an important decision and you know what you should do, move out in faith. Discover and develop the positives while trusting God to overcome the negatives. Problems don't have to rob you of the victory.

1:28 This was a land with giants and imposing city walls. The "giants" the spies talked about were descendants of Anak and may have been seven to nine feet tall. Many of the land's fortified cities had walls as high as 30 feet. The Israelites' fear was understandable, but not justified, for the all-powerful God had already promised them victory.

29"But I said to them, 'Don't be afraid! 30The Lord God is your leader, and he will fight for you with his mighty miracles, just as you saw him do in Egypt. 31And you know how he has cared for you again and again here in the wilderness, just as a father cares for his child!' 32But nothing I said did any good.

"They refused to believe the Lord our God 33who had led them all the way, and had selected the best places for them to camp, and had guided them by a pillar of fire at night and a pillar of cloud during the day.

34, 35"Well, the Lord heard their complaining and was very angry. He vowed that not one person in that entire generation would live to see the good land he had promised their fathers, 36except Caleb (the son of Jephunneh), who, because he had wholly followed the Lord, would receive as his personal inheritance some of the land he had walked over.

37"And the Lord was even angry with me because of them and said to me, 'You shall not enter the Promised Land! 38Instead, your assistant, Joshua (the son of Nun), shall lead the people. Encourage him as he prepares to take over the leadership. 39I will give the land to the children they said would die in the wilderness. 40But as for you of the older generation, turn around now and go on back across the desert toward the Red Sea.'

41"Then they confessed, 'We have sinned! We will go into the land and fight for it as the Lord our God has told us to.' So they strapped on their weapons and thought it would be easy to conquer the whole area.

42"But the Lord said to me, 'Tell them not to do it, for I will not go with them; they will be struck down before their enemies.'

43"I told them, but they wouldn't listen. Instead, they rebelled again against the Lord's commandment and went on up into the hill country to fight. 44But the Amorites who lived there came out against them, and chased them like bees and killed them from Seir to Hormah. 45Then they returned and wept before the Lord, but he wouldn't listen. 46So they stayed there at Kadesh for a long time.

Review of the wanderings

2 "Then we turned back across the wilderness toward the Red Sea, for so the Lord had instructed me. For many years we wandered around in the area of Mount Seir. 2Then at last the Lord said,

3" 'You have stayed here long enough. Turn northward. 4Inform the people that they will be passing through the country belonging to their brothers the Edomites, the descendants of Esau who live in Seir; the Edomites will be nervous, so be careful. 5Don't start a fight! For I have given them all the Mount Seir hill country as their permanent possession, and I will not give you even a tiny piece of their land. 6Pay them for whatever food or water you use. 7The Lord your God has watched over you and blessed you every step of the way for all these forty years as you have wandered around in this great wilderness; and you have lacked nothing in all that time.'

8"So we passed through Edom where our brothers lived, crossing the Arabah Road that goes south to Elath and Ezi-on-geber, and traveling northward toward the Moab desert.

9"Then the Lord warned us, 'Don't attack the Moabites either, for I will not give you any of their land; I have given it to the descendants of Lot.'

10"(The Emim used to live in that area, a very large tribe, tall as the giants of Anakim; 11both the Emim and the Anakim are often referred to as the Rephaim, but the Moabites call them Emim. 12In earlier days the Horites lived in Seir, but they were driven out and displaced by the Edomites, the descendants of Esau, just as

1:29
Deut 3:22; 7:18
Josh 8:1

1:30
Ex 14:14
Deut 20:4

1:31
Deut 32:11
Isa 40:11
Acts 13:18

1:33
Ex 13:21
Num 9:15-23
10:33-36

1:34
Num 14:28-30
32:8-12
Deut 2:14

1:36
Num 14:24
Josh 14:6

1:37
Num 20:12
27:18

1:38
Num 34:16-28
Deut 3:28; 31:7

1:39
Num 14:3,31

1:40
Num 14:25

1:41
Num 14:40

1:42
Num 14:41-43

1:43
Num 14:44

1:44
Num 14:45

2:1
Num 21:4

2:4
Ex 15:15
Num 20:14
Judg 11:17

2:5
Deut 23:7

2:6
Num 20:19

2:7
Deut 8:2; 29:5

2:8
Num 20:20

2:9
Gen 19:37
Deut 1:1-5

2:10
Num 13:28
Josh 14:12

2:11
Deut 2:20
3:11,13
Josh 12:4

2:12
Gen 14:5,6
Num 21:25,35
Deut 2:22

2:4-6 When the Israelites passed through Edom, God advised them to be careful. The Israelites were looked upon as warriors, and the Edomites would be understandably nervous as the great crowd passed through their land. God warned the Israelites not to start a fight, to respect the territory of the Edomites, and to pay for whatever they used. God wanted the Israelites to deal justly with their neighbors. We must also act justly in dealing with others. Recognize the rights of others, even your opponents. By behaving wisely and justly you may be able to establish a relationship, or restore a damaged one.

Israel would displace the peoples of Canaan, whose land had been assigned to Israel by the Lord.)

13" 'Now cross Zered Brook,' the Lord said; and we did.

2:14,15
Num 14:29-35
26:64,65
Deut 2:7
Ps 106:26
1 Cor 10:5
Jude 5

14, 15"So it took us thirty-eight years to finally get across Zered Brook from Kadesh! For the Lord had decreed that this could not happen until all the men, who thirty-eight years earlier were old enough to bear arms, had died. Yes, the hand of the Lord was against them until finally all were dead.

16, 17"Then at last the Lord said to me,

2:18
Num 21:15
Deut 2:9

18" 'Today Israel shall cross the borders of Moab at Ar, 19into the land of the Ammonites. But do not attack them, for I will not give you any of their land. I have given it to the descendants of Lot.'

2:20
Deut 2:11

20"(That area, too, used to be inhabited by the Rephaim, called 'Zamzummim' by the Ammonites. 21They were a large and powerful tribe, as tall as the Anakim; but Jehovah destroyed them as the Ammonites came in, and the Ammonites lived there in their place. 22The Lord had similarly helped the descendants of Esau at Mount Seir, for he destroyed the Horites who were living there before them.

2:23
Gen 10:13,14
1 Chron 1:11,12
Jer 47:4
Amos 9:7

23Another similar situation occurred when the people of Caphtor invaded and destroyed the tribe of Avvim living in villages scattered across the countryside as far away as Gaza.)

Review of battles

2:24
Num 21:13
Judg 11:18
2:25
Ex 15:14-16
23:27
Deut 11:25
Josh 2:9

24"Then the Lord said, 'Cross the Arnon River into the land of King Sihon the Amorite, king of Heshbon. War against him and begin to take possession of his land. 25Beginning today I will make people throughout the whole earth tremble with fear because of you, and dread your arrival.'

2:26
Num 21:21
Deut 20:10-13
Judg 11:19

26"Then from the wilderness of Kedemoth I sent ambassadors to King Sihon of Heshbon with a proposal of peace. 27'Let us pass through your land,' we said. 'We will stay on the main road and won't turn off into the fields on either side. 28We will not steal food as we go, but will purchase every bite we eat and everything we drink; all we want is permission to pass through. 29The Edomites at Seir allowed us to go through their country, and so did the Moabites, whose capital is at Ar. We are on our way across the Jordan into the land the Lord our God has given us.'

2:29
Deut 2:8,9; 23:3

2:30
Ex 11:10
Num 21:23
Josh 11:20

30"But King Sihon refused because Jehovah your God made him obstinate, so that he could destroy Sihon by the hands of Israel, as has now been done. 31"Then the Lord said to me, 'I have begun to give you the land of King Sihon; when you possess it, it shall belong to Israel forever.'

32"King Sihon then declared war on us and mobilized his forces at Jahaz.

2:33
Num 21:24-30
Deut 3:6; 29:7
2:35,36
Num 31:9-11
Deut 3:7,10
Ps 44:3

33, 34But the Lord our God crushed him, and we conquered all his cities, and utterly destroyed everything, including the women and babies. We left nothing alive 35, 36except the cattle, which we took as our reward, along with the booty gained from ransacking the cities we had taken. We conquered everything from Aroer to Gilead—from the edge of the Arnon River valley, and including all the cities in the valley. Not one city was too strong for us, for the Lord our God gave all of them to us. 37However, we stayed away from the people of Ammon and from the Jabbok River and the hill country cities, the places Jehovah our God had forbidden us to enter.

2:37
Deut 3:16

3:1
Num 21:33-35
Deut 1:1-5

3 "Next we turned toward King Og's land of Bashan. He immediately mobilized his army and attacked us at Edre-i. But the Lord told me not to be afraid of him.

2:14, 15 Israel did not have to spend 40 years en route to the Promised Land. God sentenced them to desert wanderings because they rebelled against his love, ignored his commands for right living, and willfully broke their end of the agreement made in Exodus 19:8 and 24:3–8. In short, they disobeyed God. We often make life's journey more difficult than necessary by disobedience. Accept God's love, read and follow his commands in the Bible, and make a promise to stick with God regardless of your situation.

2:25 God told Moses he would make the enemy nations afraid of

the Israelites. By worldly standards, Israel's army was not intimidating, but Israel had God on their side. The important issue is not whether you are the biggest or strongest, but whether or not you are on God's side.

3:1–3 The Israelites faced a big problem—the well-trained army of King Og. But they won because God fought for them. God can help his people regardless of the problems they face. No matter how insurmountable the obstacles may seem, remember that God is sovereign and he will keep his promises.

'All his people and his land are yours,' the Lord told me. 'You will do to him as you did to King Sihon of the Amorites, at Heshbon.' 3So the Lord helped us fight against King Og and his people, and we killed them all. 4We conquered all sixty of his cities, the entire Argob region of Bashan. 5These were well-fortified cities with high walls and barred gates. Of course we also took all of the unwalled towns. 6We utterly destroyed the kingdom of Bashan just as we had destroyed King Sihon's kingdom at Heshbon, killing the entire population—men, women, and children alike. 7But we kept the cattle and loot for ourselves.

8"We now possessed all the land of the two kings of the Amorites east of the Jordan River—all the land from the valley of the Arnon to Mount Hermon. 9(The Sidonians called Mount Hermon 'Sirion,' while the Amorites called it 'Senir.') 10We had now conquered all the cities on the plateau, and all of Gilead and Bashan as far as the cities of Salecah and Edre-i.

11"Incidentally, King Og of Bashan was the last of the giant Rephaim. His iron bedstead is kept in a museum at Rabbah, one of the cities of the Ammonites, and measures thirteen and a half feet long by six feet wide.

Dividing the land

12"At that time I gave the conquered land to the tribes of Reuben, Gad, and the half-tribe of Manasseh. To the tribes of Reuben and Gad I gave the area beginning at Aroer on the Arnon River, plus half of Mount Gilead, including its cities. 13The half-tribe of Manasseh received the remainder of Gilead and all of the former kingdom of King Og, the Argob region. (Bashan is sometimes called 'The Land of the Rephaim.') 14The clan of Jair, of the tribe of Manasseh, took over the whole Argob region (Bashan) to the borders of the Geshurites and Ma-acathites. They renamed their country after themselves, calling it Havvoth-jair (meaning 'Jair's Villages') as it is still known today. 15Then I gave Gilead to the clan of Machir. 16The tribes of Reuben and Gad received the area extending from the Jabbok River in Gilead (which was the Ammonite frontier) to the middle of the valley of the Arnon River. 17They also received the Arabah (or, wasteland), bounded by the Jordan River on the west, from Chinnereth to Mount Pisgah and the Dead Sea (also called the Sea of the Arabah).

18"At that time I reminded the tribes of Reuben and Gad and the half-tribe of Manasseh, that although the Lord had given them the land, they could not begin settling down until their armed men led the other tribes across the Jordan to the land the Lord was giving them.

19" 'But your wives and children,' I told them, 'may live here in the cities the Lord has given you, caring for your many cattle 20until you return after the Lord has given victory to the other tribes, too. When they conquer the land the Lord your God has given them across the Jordan River, then you may return here to your own land.'

Moses' prayer to God

21"Then I said to Joshua, 'You have seen what the Lord your God has done to those two kings. You will do the same to all the kingdoms on the other side of the Jordan. 22Don't be afraid of the nations there, for the Lord your God will fight for you.'

23, 24, 25"At that time I made this plea to God: 'O Lord God, please let me cross over into the Promised Land—the good land beyond the Jordan River with its rolling hills—and Lebanon. I want to see the result of all the greatness and power you have been showing us; for what God in all of heaven or earth can do what you have done for us?'

3:3
Josh 9:10
3:4
Num 32:33-42
Josh 12:4
3:6
Num 21:2
Deut 2:33,34
20:16
Josh 11:11
Ps 135:10-12
3:7
Josh 8:27
3:8
Num 32:33-42
Josh 12:1-6
13:8-13
Amos 3:9,10
3:9
Deut 4:48
Josh 11:17
Ps 29:5,6
3:12
Num 32:33-42
Deut 2:35,36
Josh 13:8-13
3:13
Num 32:41
Judg 10:4
3:15
Num 32:40
3:17
Josh 13:27
3:18
Num 32:20
Josh 1:12,13
4:12,13
3:19
Num 32:26
Deut 20:5-8
Josh 1:14
3:21
Num 27:18
3:22
Deut 1:30; 20:4
Josh 10:25
3:23
Jer 15:1

3:21, 22 "Don't be afraid . . . God will fight for you." What encouraging news for Joshua, who was to lead his men against the persistent forces of evil occupying the Promised Land. And God promised to help him win every battle. Our battles may not be against godless armies, but they are just as real. Whether we are resisting temptation or battling fear, God has promised to fight with and for us as we obey him.

3:26
Num 20:12
27:14
Deut 1:37; 32:51

3:27
Num 23:14
27:12
Deut 1:37

3:28
Num 27:18

4:1
Lev 19:37
Deut 5:32,33
8:1; 16:20
30:16
Ezek 11:20
20:11
Rom 10:5

4:2
Mt 5:18

4:3
Num 25: 1-9
Deut 3:29

4:5
Lev 26:46; 27:34

4:6
Deut 32:46,47
Ps 19:7,8

4:7
Ps 148:14

4:8
Ps 89:14,15

4:9
Ex 13:8
Josh 4:6

4:10
Ex 19:7-9,16

26"But the Lord was angry with me because of you, and would not let me cross over. 'Speak of it no more,' he ordered, 27'but go to the top of Mount Pisgah where you can look out in every direction, and there you will see the land in the distance. But you shall not cross the Jordan River. 28Commission Joshua to replace you, and then encourage him, for he shall lead the people across to conquer the land you will see from the mountaintop.'

29"So we remained in the valley near Beth-peor.

Moses urges the people to obey

4 "And now, O Israel, listen carefully to these laws I teach you, and obey them if you want to live and enter into and possess the land given you by the Lord God of your ancestors. 2Do not add other laws or subtract from these; just obey them, for they are from the Lord your God. 3You have seen what the Lord did to you at Baalpeor, where he destroyed many people for worshiping idols. 4But all of you who were faithful to the Lord your God are still alive today.

5"These are the laws for you to obey when you arrive in the land where you will live. They are from the Lord our God. He has given them to me to pass on to you. 6If you obey them they will give you a reputation for wisdom and intelligence. When the surrounding nations hear these laws they will exclaim, 'What other nation is as wise and prudent as Israel!' 7For what other nation, great or small, has God among them, as the Lord our God is here among us whenever we call upon him? 8And what nation, no matter how great, has laws as fair as these I am giving you today?

9"But watch out! Be very careful never to forget what you have seen God doing for you. May his miracles have a deep and permanent effect upon your lives! Tell your children and your grandchildren about the glorious miracles he did. 10Tell them especially about the day you stood before the Lord at Mount Horeb, and he told me, 'Summon the people before me and I will instruct them, so that they will

---

3:28 God had made it clear that Moses would not enter the Promised Land (Numbers 20:12). So God told Moses to commission Joshua as the new leader and encourage him in this new role. This is a good example to churches and organizations who must eventually replace their leaders. Good leaders prepare their people to function without them by discovering those with leadership potential, providing the training they need, and looking for ways to encourage them.

4:2 What is meant by "Do not add other laws or subtract from these"? These laws were the Word of God and therefore complete. How could mankind, with limited wisdom and knowledge, do an editing job on God's perfect laws? To add to the laws would make them a burden; to subtract from the laws would make them incomplete. Thus the basic laws were to remain unchanged. To presume to make changes in God's law is to assume a position of authority over God who gave the laws (Matthew 5:17–19; 15:3–9; Revelation 22:18, 19). The religious leaders at the time of Christ did exactly this; they elevated their own laws to the same level as God's. Jesus rebuked them for this (Matthew 23:1–4).

4:6 Some people work hard to make others think they are smart. The books they carry and the facts they quote are impressive. But Moses said that a reputation for wisdom comes by obeying God's Word. This may not be the easiest or most glamorous way to earn a reputation, but it is the most authentic. Do you fall into the trap of trying to make others think you are intelligent because of what you know or pretend to know? Obeying God's Word will give you a far greater reputation, because it's not just what you know, but what you do that counts.

4:8 Do the laws God gave to the Israelites still apply to Christians today? God's laws were designed to guide all people toward healthy, upright, and godly living. Their purpose was to point out sin (or potential sin) and show the proper course of action needed

to deal with that sin. The Ten Commandments, the heart of God's law, are just as applicable today as they were 3,000 years ago because they proclaim a lifestyle endorsed by God. They are the perfect expression of (1) who God is and (2) how he wants people to live.

But God gave other laws besides the Ten Commandments. Are these just as important? God never issued a law that didn't have a purpose. However, many of the laws we read in the Pentateuch were directed specifically to people of that time and culture. Although the specific law may not apply to us, the timeless truth or principle behind the law does. For example, most contemporary cultures do not have animal sacrifices. However, the principles behind the sacrifices—purity and holiness in worship—still apply. The sacrifices pointed to the ultimate sacrifice made for us by Jesus Christ. The New Testament says that with the death and resurrection of Jesus Christ the Old Testament laws were fulfilled. This means that while the Old Testament laws help us recognize our sins and correct our wrongdoings, Jesus Christ has taken our sins away. Jesus is now our primary example to follow because he alone perfectly obeyed the Law and modeled its true intent. Although many of the specific Old Testament laws are no longer necessary, Jesus showed that the spirit of these laws is no less applicable today, because the principles they uphold still point us to God.

4:9 Moses wanted to make sure that the people did not forget all they had seen God do, so he urged parents to tell their children about God's great miracles. This helped parents remember God's faithfulness and it provided the means for passing on from one generation to the next the stories recounting the great acts of God. It is easy to forget the wonderful ways God has worked in the lives of his people. But you can remember God's great acts of faithfulness by telling your children, friends, or associates what you have seen him do.

learn always to reverence me, and so that they can teach my laws to their children.'
¹¹You stood at the foot of the mountain, and the mountain burned with fire; flames shot far into the sky, surrounded by black clouds and deep darkness. ¹²And the Lord spoke to you from the fire; you heard his words but didn't see him. ¹³He proclaimed the laws you must obey—the Ten Commandments—and wrote them on two stone tablets. ¹⁴Yes, it was at that time that the Lord commanded me to issue the laws you must obey when you arrive in the Promised Land.

4:11
Ex 19:18
Heb 12:18
4:13
Ex 31:18
34:1,28
Deut 10:4

Moses' warning against idols

¹⁵"But beware! You didn't see the form of God that day as he spoke to you from the fire at Mount Horeb, ¹⁶, ¹⁷so do not defile yourselves by trying to make a statue of God—an idol in any form, whether of a man, woman, animal, bird, ¹⁸a small animal that runs along the ground, or a fish. ¹⁹And do not look up into the sky to worship the sun, moon, or stars. The Lord may permit other nations to get away with this, but not you. ²⁰The Lord has rescued you from prison—Egypt—to be his special people, his own inheritance; this is what you are today. ²¹, ²²But he was angry with me because of you; he vowed that I could not go over the Jordan River into the good land he has given you as your inheritance. I must die here on this side of the river. ²³Beware lest you break the contract the Lord your God has made with you! You will break it if you make any idols, for the Lord your God has utterly forbidden this. ²⁴He is a devouring fire, a jealous God.

4:15
Ex 19:9,18,21
4:16
Ex 20:4,5; 32:8
4:19
Acts 7:43
4:20
1 Kgs 8:51
Jer 11:4
4:21
Num 27:14
Deut 1:37
4:23
Josh 23:11
4:24
Ex 24:17; 34:14
Heb 12:29

²⁵"In the future, when your children and grandchildren are born and you have been in the land a long time, and you have defiled yourselves by making idols, and the Lord your God is very angry because of your sin, ²⁶heaven and earth are witnesses that you shall be quickly destroyed from the land. Soon, now, you will cross the Jordan River and conquer that land. But your days there will be brief; you will then be utterly destroyed. ²⁷For the Lord will scatter you among the nations, and you will be but few in number. ²⁸There, far away, you will worship idols made from wood and stone, idols that neither see nor hear nor eat nor smell.

4:25
Deut 4:16; 31:29
4:26
Deut 7:4; 8:19
31:29
4:27
Deut 28:64
4:28
Deut 28:36,64
29:17
Ps 115:4-8

²⁹"But you will also begin to search again for Jehovah your God, and you shall find him when you search for him with all your hearts and souls. ³⁰When those bitter days have come upon you in the latter times, you will finally return to the Lord your God and listen to what he tells you. ³¹For the Lord your God is merciful—he will not abandon you nor destroy you nor forget the promises he has made to your ancestors.

4:29
Deut 6:5; 10:12
30:1-3
2 Chron 15:4
Neh 1:8,9
4:31
Deut 31:6,8
Josh 1:5
Heb 13:5

4:19 God was not excusing the other nations for their idol worship. He was simply saying that while judgment might be delayed for those other nations, it would be swift and complete for Israel because they knew God's laws. We must keep in mind that idol worship was not just keeping statues around the house—harmless lumps of clay, wood, or iron. It was the commitment to certain beliefs and principles which the idol represented (such as murder, prostitution, cruelty in war, self-centeredness). Because God had so clearly revealed himself in Israel's history, the Israelites had no excuse for worshiping anyone but the true God.

4:24 God is a devouring fire. Because he is morally perfect, he hates sin and cannot accept those who practice it. Moses' sin kept him from entering the Promised Land, and no sacrifice could remove that judgment. Sin kept us from entering God's presence, but Jesus Christ paid the penalty for our sin and removed God's judgment forever by his death. Trusting in Jesus Christ will save you from God's anger and will allow you to begin a personal relationship with him.

4:24 Jealousy is a demand for someone else's exclusive affection or loyalty. Some jealousy is bad. It is destructive for a man to get upset when his wife talks pleasantly with another man. But other

jealousy is good. It is right for a man to demand that his wife treat him, and only him, as her husband. Usually we use the word "jealousy" when referring to the bad kind. But God's jealousy is appropriate and good. He makes strong, exclusive demands on us: we must treat only Jehovah—and no one else in all the universe—as God.

4:25-28 This warning eventually came true. Time and again, the Israelites turned from God; but God, in his great patience, gave them time to recognize their wrongs and return to him. Finally God's patience had been spent, so he allowed the Israelites to be captured and carried off to foreign lands. The warnings in the book of Deuteronomy were clear enough to help them, but they failed to heed them. A clear warning is not enough to make people obey—they need to take God's warnings to heart.

4:29 Do you want to know God? This passage promised the Israelites that they would find God when they searched with all their hearts and souls. God is knowable and wants to be known—but we have to want to know him. Acts of service and worship must be accompanied by sincere devotion of the heart. As Hebrews 11:6 says, "Anyone who wants to come to God must believe that there is a God and that he rewards those who sincerely look for him." God will reward those who pursue a relationship with him.

There is no other God

4:32
Gen 1:27
4:33
Ex 20:22
Deut 5:24,26
4:34
Ex 14:30
Deut 5:15; 6:21
7:19; 33:29
Ps 136:12
4:35
Ex 8:10; 9:14
Deut 4:39
1 Sam 17:46
Mk 12:29
4:36
Ex 19:9,19
Neh 9:13
4:37
Deut 7:7,8
Ps 105:5-11
4:38
Ex 23:27-30
Num 32:3,4
4:40
Ex 23:26

32"In all history, going back to the time when God created man upon the earth, search from one end of the heavens to the other to see if you can find anything like this: 33An entire nation heard the voice of God speaking to it from fire, as you did, and lived! 34Where else will you ever find another example of God's removing a nation from its slavery by sending terrible plagues, mighty miracles, war, and terror? Yet that is what the Lord your God did for you in Egypt, right before your very eyes. 35He did these things so you would realize that Jehovah is God, and that there is no one else like him. 36He let you hear his voice instructing you from heaven, and he let you see his great pillar of fire upon the earth; you even heard his words from the center of the fire.

37"It was because he loved your ancestors and chose to bless their descendants that he personally brought you out from Egypt with a great display of power. 38He drove away other nations greater by far than you, and gave you their land as an inheritance, as it is today. 39This is your wonderful thought for the day: Jehovah is God both in heaven and down here upon the earth; and there is no God other than him! 40You must obey these laws that I will tell you today, so that all will be well with you and your children, and so that you will live forever in the land the Lord your God is giving you."

Cities of refuge

4:41
Num 35:6
Deut 19:1-13
Josh 20:7

41Then Moses instructed the people of Israel to set apart three cities east of the Jordan River, 42where anyone who accidentally killed someone could flee for safety. 43These cities were Bezer, on the plateau in the wilderness, for the tribe of Reuben; Ramoth, in Gilead, for the tribe of Gad; and Golan, in Bashan, for the tribe of Manasseh.

B. PRINCIPLES FOR GODLY LIVING: MOSES' SECOND ADDRESS (4:44—28:68)

After reviewing the history of Israel's journey, Moses recounts the Ten Commandments and the other laws given to the Israelites at Mount Sinai. He urges them to obey the Law and reminds them of the consequences of disobeying God's laws. The Ten Commandments and all of God's laws point out to us where we fall short and show us how we should act as God's people.

44, 45, 46Listed below are the laws Moses issued to the people of Israel when they left Egypt, and as they were camped east of the Jordan River near the city of Beth-peor. (This was the land formerly occupied by the Amorites under King Sihon, whose capital was Heshbon; he and his people were destroyed by Moses and the Israelis. 47Israel conquered his land and that of King Og of Bashan—they were two Amorite kings east of the Jordan. 48Israel also conquered all the area from Aroer at the edge of the Arnon River valley to Mount Sirion, or Mount Hermon, as it is sometimes called; 49and all the Arabah east of the Jordan River over to the Dead Sea, below the slopes of Mount Pisgah.)

4:48
Deut 2:35,36

1. Review of the Ten Commandments

5:1
Deut 6:4; 9:1
20:3; 27:9

5 Moses continued speaking to the people of Israel and said, "Listen carefully now to all these laws God has given you; learn them, and be sure to obey them!

4:40 Was Israel guaranteed prosperity for obeying God's laws? Yes—but we have to look carefully at what that means. God's laws were designed to make his chosen nation healthy, just, and merciful. When they followed those laws, they prospered. This does not mean, however, that no sickness, no poverty, and no misunderstandings existed among them. Rather, it means that as a nation they prospered, and that individuals' problems were handled as fairly as possible. Today God's promise of prosperity—his constant presence, comfort, and the resources to live as we should—extends to all believers. We will face trials, Jesus assured us of that. But we will avoid the misery that directly results from intentional sin, and we will know that a great heavenly treasure awaits us if we are faithful.

5:1 The people had entered into a covenant with God, and Moses commanded them to listen, learn, and obey. Christians also have entered into a covenant with God (through Jesus Christ) and should be sensitive to what God expects. Moses' threefold command to the Israelites is excellent advice for all God's followers. Listening is absorbing and accepting the information we read and hear about God. Learning is understanding its meaning and implications. Obeying is putting into action all we have learned and understood. All three parts are essential to a growing relationship with God.

2, 3"The Lord our God made a contract with you at Mount Horeb—*not with your ancestors, but with you who are here alive today*. 4He spoke with you face to face from the center of the fire, there at the mountain. 5I stood as an intermediary between you and Jehovah, for you were afraid of the fire and did not go up to him on the mountain. He spoke to me and I passed on his laws to you. This is what he said:

6" 'I am Jehovah your God who rescued you from slavery in Egypt.

7" 'Never worship any god but me.

8" 'Never make idols; don't worship images, whether of birds, animals, or fish. 9, 10You shall not bow down to any images nor worship them in any way, for I am the Lord your God. I am a jealous God, and I will bring the curse of a father's sins upon even the third and fourth generation of the children of those who hate me; but I will show kindness to a thousand generations of those who love me and keep my commandments.

11" 'You must never use my name to make a vow you don't intend to keep. I will not overlook that.

12" 'Keep the Sabbath day holy. This is my command. 13Work the other six days, 14but the seventh day is the Sabbath of the Lord your God; no work shall be done that day by you or by any of your household—your sons, daughters, servants, oxen, donkeys, or cattle; even foreigners living among you must obey this law. Everybody must rest as you do. 15Why should you keep the Sabbath? It is because you were slaves in Egypt, and the Lord your God brought you out with a great display of miracles.

16" 'Honor your father and mother (remember, this is a commandment of the Lord your God); if you do so, you shall have a long, prosperous life in the land he is giving you.

17" 'You must not murder.

18" 'You must not commit adultery.

19" 'You must not steal.

20" 'You must not tell lies.

21" 'You must not burn with desire for another man's wife, nor envy him for his home, land, servants, oxen, donkeys, nor anything else he owns.'

22"The Lord has given these laws to each one of you from the heart of the fire,

5:2
Ex 19:5
Num 26:64,65
5:4
Num 14:14
5:5
Ex 19:16,25
5:6
Ex 20:2-17
5:7
Ex 20:3
Mt 4:10
5:8
Ex 20:4
Lev 26:1
Deut 4:16,17
5:9,10
Ex 20:4-6
5:11
Deut 6:13; 10:20
Mt 5:33
5:12
Ex 20:8-11
Lev 26:2
5:15
Ex 20:11
Deut 15:15
16:12
5:16
Ex 20:12; 21:17
Eph 6:2,3
5:17
Ex 20:13
Mt 5:21
5:18
Ex 20:14
Lk 18:20
Jas 2:11
5:19
Ex 20:15
Rom 13:9
5:20
Ex 20:16
5:21
Rom 7:7; 13:9
5:22
Ex 19:16-19

5:11 *never use my name to make a vow you don't intend to keep,* literally, "You must not utter the name of the Lord your God to misuse it." **5:22** *the only commandments he gave you at that time,* literally, "and he added no more."

5:7 A "god" is whatever people put first in their lives. Some people literally worship other gods by joining cults or other strange religions. In a more subtle way, many of us worship other gods by building our lives around something other than the one true God. If your greatest desire is for friendships, popularity, or money, you are devoting yourself to something other than God. To put God first, (1) recognize what is taking his place in your life; (2) renounce this "substitute god" as unworthy of such devotion; (3) ask God for forgiveness; (4) restructure your priorities so that love for God is the motive for everything you do; and (5) examine yourself daily to be sure you are giving God first place.

5:8-10 How would you feel if someone took a picture of you, framed it, stared at it a lot, showed it to others, but completely ignored the real you? God does not want to be treated this way either. He wants a genuine relationship with us, not mere ritual. He wants us to know him. God knows that if we put anything other than him at the center of our lives, we will not reach the potential he created in us.

5:16 Obeying our parents is our main task when we are young, but respect for them should continue even beyond their death. One way to honor parents is to provide for them in times of financial need or when they are ill and unable to care for themselves. Perhaps the best way to honor them is to pass on their godly values to your children. Honoring involves all that sons and

daughters do with their lives—the way they work and talk, the values they hold, and the morals they practice. What are you doing to honor your parents? Are you living in a way that brings honor to them?

5:17 "But I don't murder people," you may say. Good. That fulfills the letter of the law. But Jesus explained that hateful anger breaks this commandment (Matthew 5:21, 22). Have you ever been so angry with someone who mistreated you that for a moment you wished that person were dead? Have you ever fantasized that you could "do someone in"? Jesus' teaching concerning this law demonstrates that we are capable of murder in our hearts. Even if we are legally innocent, we are all morally guilty of murder and need to ask God's forgiveness. We need to commit ourselves to the opposite of hatred and anger—love and reconciliation.

5:21 We are not to envy anyone for anything. Not only can envy make us miserable, it can also lead us to other sins such as adultery and stealing. Envy is a useless emotion because God is able to provide everything we really need, even if he does not always give us everything we want. To drive out envy, we need to practice being content with what we have. The apostle Paul emphasizes the significance of contentment in Philippians 4:11. It's a matter of perspective. Instead of thinking about what we don't have, we should thank God for what is ours and strive to be content. After all, our most important possession is free and available to everyone—eternal life through Christ.

surrounded by the clouds and thick darkness that engulfed Mount Sinai. Those were the only commandments he gave you at that time, and he wrote them out on two stone tablets and gave them to me. 23But when you heard the loud voice from the darkness, and saw the terrible fire at the top of the mountain, all your tribal leaders came to me 24and pleaded, 'Today the Lord our God has shown us his glory and greatness; we have even heard his voice from the heart of the fire. Now we know that a man may speak to God and not die; 25but we will surely die if he speaks to us again. This awesome fire will consume us. 26, 27What man can hear, as we have, the voice of the living God speaking from the heart of the fire, and live? You go and listen to all that God says, then come and tell us, and we will listen and obey.'

28"And the Lord agreed to your request, and said to me, 'I have heard what the people have said to you, and I agree. 29Oh, that they would always have such a heart for me, wanting to obey my commandments. Then all would go well with them in the future, and with their children throughout all generations! 30Go and tell them to return to their tents. 31Then you come back and stand here beside me, and I will give you all my commandments, and you shall teach them to the people; and they will obey them in the land I am giving to them.' "

32So Moses told the people, "You must obey all the commandments of the Lord your God, following his directions in every detail, going the whole way he has laid out for you; 33only then will you live long and prosperous lives in the land you are to enter and possess.

2. Love God and obey his commandments

6 "The Lord your God told me to give you all these commandments which you are to obey in the land you will soon be entering, where you will live. 2The purpose of these laws is to cause you, your sons, and your grandsons to reverence the Lord your God by obeying all of his instructions as long as you live; if you do, you will have long, prosperous years ahead of you. 3Therefore, O Israel, listen

5:25
Ex 20:18,19
Deut 18:16
Heb 12:19

5:26
Ex 24:3

5:28
Deut 18:17

5:29
Deut 5:16,33
Ps 81:13
Isa 48:18
Mt 23:37
Lk 19:42

5:31
Ex 24:12
Deut 5:1
6:1,2; 11:1,2
Ezek 20:11

5:32
Deut 17:20
28:14
Josh 1:7; 23:6

5:33
Ex 20:12
Deut 4:1,40
5:16; 6:2
25:13-15

6:1
Deut 5:1; 12:1

6:2
Deut 4:9; 10:12

6:3
Ex 3:8,17
Deut 5:33

BROKEN COMMAND-MENTS
The Ten Commandments were God's standards for right living. To obey them was to obey God. Yet throughout the Old Testament, we can see how each commandment was broken. As you read the stories, notice the tragic consequences that occurred as a result of violating God's Law.

Ten Commandments	*Notable Violations*
"Never worship any god but me."	Solomon (1 Kings 11)
"Never make idols. . . .You shall not bow down to any images nor worship them in any way."	The golden calf-idol incident (Exodus 32); generations after Joshua (Judges 2:10–14; 2 Kings 21:1–15; Jeremiah 1:16)
"You must never use my name to make a vow you don't intend to keep."	Zedekiah (Ezekiel 18:15–21)
"Keep the Sabbath day holy."	Judah (2 Chronicles 36:21)
"Honor your father and mother."	Eli's sons—Hophni and Phinehas (1 Samuel 2:12, 23–25)
"You must not murder."	Hazael (2 Kings 8:15)
"You must not commit adultery."	David (2 Samuel 11:2–5)
"You must not steal."	Ahab (1 Kings 21:1–19)
"You must not tell lies."	Saul (1 Samuel 15:13–25)
"You must not burn with desire for another man's wife, nor envy him for his home, land, servants, oxen, donkeys, nor anything else he owns."	Achan (Joshua 7:19–26)

5:29 The Lord said to Moses that he wanted the people to have a heart for him—to want to obey him. There is a difference between doing something because it is required and doing something because we want to. God is not interested in forced religious exercises. He wants our lives dedicated to him.

6:3 For a nation that had wandered 40 years in a parched desert, a land "flowing with milk and honey" sounded like paradise. It brought to mind rich crops, rushing streams, gentle rains, and lush fields filled with livestock. The Israelites could have had all that 40 years earlier. Numbers 13 and 14 explain how the people missed their chance. Now Moses was determined to help the people avoid the same mistake by whetting their appetite for the beautiful land and then clearly explaining the conditions for entering the land.

closely to each command and be careful to obey it, so that all will go well with you, and so that you will have many children. If you obey these commands you will become a great nation in a glorious land 'flowing with milk and honey,' even as the God of your fathers promised you.

Teach your children to obey God

4"O Israel, listen: Jehovah is our God, Jehovah alone. 5You must love him with *all* your heart, soul, and might. 6And you must think constantly about these commandments I am giving you today. 7You must teach them to your children and talk about them when you are at home or out for a walk; at bedtime and the first thing in the morning. 8Tie them on your finger, wear them on your forehead, 9and write them on the doorposts of your house!

10, 11, 12"When the Lord your God has brought you into the land he promised your ancestors, Abraham, Isaac, and Jacob, and when he has given you great cities full of good things—cities you didn't build, wells you didn't dig, and vineyards and olive trees you didn't plant—and when you have eaten until you can hold no more, then beware lest you forget the Lord who brought you out of the land of Egypt, the land of slavery. 13When you are full, don't forget to be reverent to him and to serve him and to use *his* name alone to endorse your promises.

14"You must not worship the gods of the neighboring nations, 15for Jehovah your God who lives among you is a jealous God, and his anger may rise quickly against you, and wipe you off the face of the earth. 16You must not provoke him and try his patience as you did when you complained against him at Massah. 17You must actively obey him in everything he commands. 18Only then will you be doing what is right and good in the Lord's eyes. If you obey him, all will go well for you, and you will be able to go in and possess the good land which the Lord promised your ancestors. 19You will also be able to throw out all the enemies living in your land, as the Lord agreed to help you do.

20"In the years to come when your son asks you, 'What is the purpose of these laws which the Lord our God has given us?' 21you must tell him, 'We were Pharaoh's slaves in Egypt, and the Lord brought us out of Egypt with great power 22and mighty miracles—with terrible blows against Egypt and Pharaoh and all his people. We saw it all with our own eyes. 23He brought us out of Egypt so that he could give us this land he had promised to our ancestors. 24And he has commanded us to obey all of these laws and to reverence him so that he can preserve us alive as he has until now. 25For it always goes well with us when we obey all the laws of the Lord our God.'

6:4,5
Deut 4:35,39
Mt 22:37
Mk 12:29,30
Lk 10:27
1 Cor 8:4,6

6:6
Deut 10:12
11:13
Josh 1:8

6:7
Ex 12:26
Deut 4:9
Ps 78:4-6

6:8
Ex 13:9
Deut 11:18

6:9
Deut 11:20

6:10
Deut 8:10; 9:1
Josh 24:13

6:13
Mt 4:10
Lk 4:8

6:15
Deut 4:24
5:9,10
11:16,17

6:16
Ex 17:7
Mt 4:7
Lk 4:12
1 Cor 10:9

6:17
Ex 15:26
Deut 11:22

6:18
Deut 4:40; 8:11
12:24,25

6:20
Ex 13:8,14

6:24
Deut 6:17; 10:12

6:4 "Jehovah alone" is sometimes translated, "the Lord is one." This verse shows that there were not many gods, as many ancient religions believed. Jehovah (or Yahweh) is the only true God. This was an important insight for the nation of Israel, because they were about to enter a land with many gods. Both then and today, there are people who prefer to place their trust in many different "gods." But the day is coming when God will be recognized as the only one. He will be the King over all the earth (Zechariah 14:9).

6:4-8 This passage is often said to be the central theme of Deuteronomy. It sets a pattern that helps us relate the Word of God to our daily lives. We are to love God, think constantly about his commandments, teach his commandments to our children, and live our daily lives by the guidelines of his Word. God emphasized the importance of parents teaching Scripture to their children. The church and Christian schools cannot be used to escape from this responsibility. Scripture provides so many opportunities for object lessons and practical teaching that it would be a shame to study it only one day a week. Eternal truths are most effectively learned in the loving environment of a God-fearing home.

6:5 Jesus said that loving God with all your heart, soul, and might is the first and greatest commandment (Matthew 22:37–39). This command, combined with the command to love your neighbor, encompasses all the other Old Testament laws.

6:7 The Hebrews were extremely successful at making religion an integral part of life. The reason for their success was that religious education was life-oriented, not information-oriented. They used the context of daily life to teach about God. The key to teaching your children to love God is stated simply and clearly in these verses. If you want your children to follow God, you must make God a part of your everyday life. You must teach your children to see God in all aspects of life, not just those that are church related.

6:10-13 Moses warned the people not to forget God when they entered the Promised Land and became prosperous. Prosperity, more than poverty, can dull our spiritual vision, because it tends to focus our thoughts on "more and better" rather than on "here and now." Rather than being content with what we have or what God has done, we wish for what might have been or desire what we could have. We then become driven by our need to have more of everything except God. The same thing can happen in the church. Once it becomes successful in terms of numbers, programs, and buildings, it can easily become less sensitive to its need for God. This leads it to concentrate on self-preservation rather than thankfulness and service to God.

6:25 Does this verse mean that we can expect only prosperity and no suffering when we obey God? What is promised here is a right relationship with God for those who strive to love him with all

Conquer the enemy nations

7:1
Ex 3:8
Deut 20:17
Josh 3:10
Acts 13:19

7:2
Ex 23:32

7:3
Josh 23:12

7:5
Ex 23:24; 34:13

7:6
Ex 19:5,6
Deut 14:2; 26:18
Amos 3:2
1 Pet 2:9

7:7
Deut 4:37
Jn 15:16

7:8
Lk 1:55,72,73

7:9
Ex 20:6,34:7
Deut 4:39
5:9,10
1 Cor 1:9
2 Cor 1:18
2 Thess 3:3
2 Tim 2:13
Heb 11:11

7:12
Lev 26:3
Deut 28:1

7:13
Lev 26:9
Deut 28:2-6
30:5,6

7 "When the Lord brings you into the Promised Land, as he soon will, he will destroy the following seven nations, all greater and mightier than you are: The Hittites, the Girgashites, the Amorites, the Canaanites, the Perizzites, the Hivites, the Jebusites.

2"When the Lord your God delivers them over to you to be destroyed, do a complete job of it—don't make any treaties or show them mercy; utterly wipe them out. 3Do not intermarry with them, nor let your sons and daughters marry their sons and daughters. 4That would surely result in your young people's beginning to worship their gods. Then the anger of the Lord would be hot against you and he would surely destroy you.

5"You must break down the heathen altars and shatter the obelisks and cut up the shameful images and burn the idols.

6"For you are a holy people, dedicated to the Lord your God. He has chosen you from all the people on the face of the whole earth to be his own chosen ones. 7He didn't choose you and pour out his love upon you because you were a larger nation than any other, for you were the smallest of all! 8It was just because he loves you, and because he kept his promise to your ancestors. That is why he brought you out of slavery in Egypt with such amazing power and mighty miracles.

9"Understand, therefore, that the Lord your God is the faithful God who for a thousand generations keeps his promises and constantly loves those who love him and who obey his commands. 10But those who hate him shall be punished publicly and destroyed. He will deal with them personally. 11Therefore, obey all these commandments I am giving you today. 12Because of your obedience, the Lord your God will keep his part of the contract which, in his tender love, he made with your fathers. 13And he will love you and bless you and make you into a great nation. He

---

DANGER IN PLENTY	*Person*	*Reference*	*Comment*
"... And when you have eaten until you can hold no more, then beware lest you forget the Lord ..." (Deuteronomy 6:12). It is often most difficult to follow God when life is easy—we can fall prey to temptation and fall away from God. Here are some notable examples of this truth.	Adam	Genesis 3	Adam lived in a perfect creation and had a perfect relationship with God. His needs were met; he had everything. But he fell to Satan's deception.
	Noah	Genesis 9	Noah and his family had survived the flood and the whole world was theirs. They were prosperous, and life was easy. Noah shamed himself by becoming drunk and cursed his son Ham.
	The nation of Israel	Judges 2	God had given Israel the Promised Land—rest at last with no more wandering. But as soon as brave and faithful Joshua died, they fell into the idolatrous practices of the Canaanites.
	David	2 Samuel 11	David ruled well, and Israel was a dominant nation, politically, economically, and militarily. In the midst of prosperity and success, he committed adultery with Bath-sheba and had her husband Uriah murdered.
	Solomon	1 Kings 11	Solomon truly had it all: power, wealth, fame, and wisdom. But his very abundance was the source of his downfall. He loved his pagan, idolatrous wives so much that he allowed himself and Israel to copy their detestable religious rites.

---

their heart. This verse, then, is speaking of a relationship with God, not material prosperity or lack of physical suffering. God's view of wellness is a strong and vital relationship with him. Obeying God is the first step toward establishing this kind of relationship.

7:2 God instructed the Israelites to utterly wipe out their enemies. How could a God of love and mercy wipe out everyone, even children? Although God is loving and merciful, he is also just. These enemy nations were as much a part of God's creation as Israel was, but God does not allow evil to continue unchecked. The

command to destroy these nations was both a judgment and a safety measure. On one hand, the people living in the land were being judged for their sin, and Israel was God's instrument of judgment—just as God would one day use other nations to judge Israel for its sin (2 Chronicles 36:17; Isaiah 10:12). On the other hand, God's command was designed to protect the nation of Israel from being ruined by the idolatry and immorality of its enemies. To think that God is too "nice" to judge sin is faulty thinking.

will make you fertile and give fertility to your ground and to your animals, so that you will have large crops of grain, grapes, and olives, and great flocks of cattle, sheep, and goats when you arrive in the land he promised your fathers to give you. 14You will be blessed above all the nations of the earth; not one of you, whether male or female, shall be barren, not even your cattle. 15And the Lord will take away all your sickness and will not let you suffer any of the diseases of Egypt you remember so well; he will give them all to your enemies!

16"You must destroy all the nations which the Lord your God delivers into your hands. Have no pity, and do not worship their gods; if you do, it will be a sad day for you. 17Perhaps you will think to yourself, 'How can we ever conquer these nations that are so much more powerful than we are?' 18But don't be afraid of them! Just remember what the Lord your God did to Pharoah and to all the land of Egypt. 19Do you remember the terrors the Lord sent upon them—your parents saw it with their own eyes—and the mighty miracles and wonders, and the power and strength of Almighty God which he used to bring you out of Egypt? Well, the Lord your God will use this same might against the people you fear. 20Moreover, the Lord your God will send hornets to drive out those who hide from you!

21"No, do not be afraid of those nations, for the Lord your God is among you, and he is a great and awesome God. 22He will cast them out a little at a time; he will not do it all at once, for if he did, the wild animals would multiply too quickly and become dangerous. 23He will do it gradually, and you will move in against those nations and destroy them. 24He will deliver their kings into your hands, and you will erase their names from the face of the earth. No one will be able to stand against you.

25"Burn their idols and do not touch the silver or gold they are made of. Do not take it or it will be a snare to you, for it is horrible to the Lord your God. 26Do not bring an idol into your home and worship it, for then your doom is sealed. Utterly detest it, for it is a cursed thing.

Do not forget God

8 "You must obey all the commandments I give you today. If you do, you will not only live, you will multiply and will go in and take over the land promised to your fathers by the Lord. 2Do you remember how the Lord led you through the wilderness for all those forty years, humbling you and testing you to find out how you would respond, and whether or not you would really obey him? 3Yes, he humbled you by letting you go hungry and then feeding you with manna, a food previously unknown to both you and your ancestors. He did it to help you realize that food isn't everything, and that real life comes by obeying every command of God. 4For all these forty years your clothes haven't grown old, and your feet haven't been blistered or swollen. 5So you should realize that, as a man punishes his son, the Lord punishes you to help you.

6"Obey the laws of the Lord your God. Walk in his ways and fear him. 7For the Lord your God is bringing you into a good land of brooks, pools, gushing springs, valleys, and hills; 8it is a land of wheat and barley, of grape vines, fig trees, pomegranates, olives, and honey; 9it is a land where food is plentiful, and nothing

7:14
Ex 23:26
Deut 33:29
Ps 147:19,20

7:15
Ex 15:26; 23:26

7:16
Ex 23:32
Deut 7:2

7:17
Deut 8:17

7:18
Num 14:9
Deut 1:19,20,
21; 8:2

7:19
Deut 4:34; 8:17
11:3,4
Neh 9:10

7:20
Ex 23:28
Josh 24:12

7:21
Ex 29:45
Lev 26:11
Ps 68:18

7:22
Ex 23:27-30

7:24
Deut 11:25
Josh 1:5; 6:2
10:8; 23:9

7:25
Deut 7:2; 12:3
Josh 7:1,21

7:26
Deut 13:17
Josh 6:18,19

8:1
Lev 26:3
Deut 4:1; 7:11

8:2
Ex 15:25
Deut 13:3
Job 33:16-18
Ps 81:7

8:3
Ps 78:24

8:4
Deut 29:5
Neh 9:21

8:5
Ps 89:30-32
Prov 3:11,12
Heb 12:6

8:7
Deut 10:7
11:9-15
Jer 2:7

8:8
Deut 32:13

7:21–24 Moses told the Israelites that God would cast their enemies out of the Promised Land, but not all at once. God had the power to destroy those nations instantly, but he chose to do it in stages. In the same way and with the same power, God could miraculously and instantaneously change your life. Usually, however, he chooses to help you gradually, teaching you one lesson at a time. Rather than expect instant spiritual maturity and solutions to all your problems, slow down and work one step at a time, trusting God to make up the difference between where you should be and where you are now. You'll soon look back and see that a miraculous transformation has occurred.

8:3 How do you find "real life"? Many people think it comes from

how they look, what they eat or drink, where they go, or what they do in their leisure time. If they can earn enough money to dress, eat, and play in high style, they think they are living "the good life." But such things satisfy only our appetites, not our deepest longings. In the end they leave us empty and dissatisfied. Real life, according to Moses, comes from total commitment to God, the one who created life itself. It requires discipline, sacrifice, and hard work, and that's why most people never find it. At first it may not seem to be as much fun as the world's way of living, but gradually, as our friendship with God deepens, it leads to strength of character, peace of mind, and deep satisfaction. The long-term rewards of obeying God are greater than anything the world has to offer.

is lacking; it is a land where iron is as common as stone, and copper is abundant in the hills. [10]When you have eaten your fill, bless the Lord your God for the good land he has given you.

[11]"But that is the time to be careful! Beware that in your plenty you don't forget the Lord your God and begin to disobey him. [12, 13]For when you have become full and prosperous and have built fine homes to live in, and when your flocks and herds have become very large, and your silver and gold have multiplied, [14]that is the time to watch out that you don't become proud, and forget the Lord your God who brought you out of your slavery in the land of Egypt. [15]Beware that you don't forget the God who led you through the great and terrible wilderness with the dangerous snakes and scorpions, where it was so hot and dry. He gave you water from the rock! [16]He fed you with manna in the wilderness (it was a kind of bread unknown before) so that you would become humble and so that your trust in him would grow, and he could do you good. [17]He did it so that you would never feel that it was your own power and might that made you wealthy. [18]Always remember that it is the Lord your God who gives you power to become rich, and he does it to fulfill his promise to your ancestors.

[19]"But if you forget about the Lord your God and worship other gods instead, and follow evil ways, you shall certainly perish, [20]just as the Lord has caused other nations in the past to perish. That will be your fate, too, if you don't obey the Lord your God.

Do not forget God's mercy

9 "O Israel, listen! Today you are to cross the Jordan River and begin to dispossess the nations on the other side. Those nations are much greater and more powerful than you are! They live in high walled cities. Among them are the famed Anak giants, against whom none can stand! [3]But the Lord your God will go

8:11 Beware that in your plenty, implied.

8:10
Ps 103:2

8:11
Deut 4:9,23
6:10-12

8:12
Prov 3:9
Hos 13:6

8:15
Ex 17:6
Num 20:11; 21:6
Deut 1:19-21
32:13
Ps 78:15; 114:8

8:16
Ex 16:15
Deut 8:2
Jn 6:30,31

8:18
Prov 10:22
Hos 2:8

8:19
Deut 4:26; 30:18

8:20
Dan 9:11,12

9:1
Num 13:27-30
Deut 2:18; 12:10
Josh 1:10; 11:21

9:3
Ps 78:52,53

OBEDIENCE		
Deuteronomy 8:1 tells us to obey God's commandments. We do this by obeying God with . . .	OUR HEART	By loving him more than any relationship, activity, achievement, or possession.
	OUR WILL	By committing ourselves completely to him.
	OUR MIND	By seeking to know him and his Word, so his principles and values form the foundation of all we think and do.
	OUR BODY	By recognizing that our strengths, talents, and sexuality are given to us by God to be used for pleasure and fulfillment according to his rules, not ours.
	OUR FINANCES	By deciding that all of the resources we have ultimately come from God, and that we are to be managers of them and not owners.
	OUR FUTURE	By deciding to make service to God and man the main purpose of our life's work.

8:10 The Israelites were to bless the Lord after eating their fill in the Promised Land. This verse is traditionally cited as the reason we say grace before or after meals. The purpose here was not just to provide a time for prayer, but to warn the Israelites not to forget God when their needs and wants were satisfied. Let your table prayers serve as a constant reminder of the Lord's goodness to you.

8:11-19 In times of plenty, it is easy to take credit for your prosperity and begin to feel that your own hard work and cleverness have made you rich. It is easier yet to get so busy collecting and managing your wealth that you soon find God has been pushed right out of your life. But it is God who blesses us with abundance, and it is God who asks us to manage it for him. Don't forget God in your abundance, or you will eventually lose all you have (8:19). Remember that the most valuable things in life—your relationship with God and eternal life—are free.

9:2, 3 The Anak giants, or Anakim, were enormous. Some rose to a height of almost ten feet. Goliath, probably a descendant of this race, was over nine feet tall (1 Samuel 17:4-7). Unfortunately, these great men used their size as a means of intimidation rather than for noble causes. Their appearance alone frightened the Israelite spies (Numbers 13:28), and their bad reputation may have been the deciding factor that kept the Israelites out of the land 40 years earlier (Numbers 13, 14). Moses used all his persuasive power to convince his people that God could handle these bullies. He used the illustration of God as a devouring fire, for not even a giant could stand up to that.

9:3 God promised to go before the Israelites as a "devouring fire" to help them conquer their enemies. Fire was a symbol of holiness and purification, illustrating God's desire to purify the land of wicked people in order to make Israel a holy nation.

before you as a devouring fire to destroy them, so that you will quickly conquer them and drive them out.

4"Then, when the Lord has done this for you, don't say to yourselves, 'The Lord has helped us because we are so good!' No, it is because of the wickedness of the other nations that he is doing it. 5It is not at all because you are such fine, upright people that the Lord will drive them out from before you! I say it again, it is only because of the wickedness of the other nations, and because of his promises to your ancestors, Abraham, Isaac, and Jacob, that he will do it. 6I say it yet again: *Jehovah your God is not giving you this good land because you are good, for you are not*—you are a wicked, stubborn people.

7"Don't you remember (oh, never forget it!) how continually angry you made the Lord your God out in the wilderness, from the day you left Egypt until now? For all this time you have constantly rebelled against him.

8"Don't you remember how angry you made him at Mount Horeb? He was ready to destroy you. 9I was on the mountain at the time, receiving the contract which Jehovah had made with you—the stone tablets with the laws inscribed upon them. I was there for forty days and forty nights, and all that time I ate nothing. I didn't even take a drink of water. 10, 11At the end of those forty days and nights the Lord gave me the contract, the tablets on which he had written the commandments he had spoken from the fire-covered mountain while the people had watched below.

12He told me to go down quickly because the people I had led out of Egypt had defiled themselves, quickly turning away from the laws of God, and had made an idol from molten metal.

13, 14" 'Let me alone that I may destroy this evil, stubborn people!' the Lord told me, 'and I will blot out their name from under heaven, and I will make a mighty nation of you, mightier and greater than they are.'

15"I came down from the burning mountain, holding in my hands the two tablets inscribed with the laws of God. 16There below me I could see the calf you had made in your terrible sin against the Lord your God. How quickly you turned away from him! 17I lifted the tablets high above my head and dashed them to the ground! I smashed them before your eyes! 18Then, for another forty days and nights I lay before the Lord, neither eating bread nor drinking water, for you had done what the Lord hated most, thus provoking him to great anger. 19How I feared for you—for the Lord was ready to destroy you. But that time, too, he listened to me. 20Aaron was in great danger because the Lord was so angry with him; but I prayed, and the Lord spared him. 21I took your sin—the calf you had made—and burned it and ground it into fine dust, and threw it into the stream that cascaded out of the mountain.

22"Again at Taberah and once again at Massah you angered the Lord, and yet again at Kibroth-hattaavah. 23At Kadesh-barnea, when the Lord told you to enter the land he had given you, you rebelled and wouldn't believe that he would help you; you refused to obey him. 24Yes, you have been rebellious against the Lord from the first day I knew you. 25That is why I fell down before him for forty days and nights when the Lord was ready to destroy you.

26"I prayed to him, 'O Lord God, don't destroy your own people. They are your inheritance saved from Egypt by your mighty power and glorious strength. 27Don't

9:4
Lev 18:23-30
Deut 7:24
12:31; 18:9-14
31:27

9:6
Deut 9:13,14
10:16; 31:27
Ps 78:17,40

9:7
Ex 14:11
Num 11:4,5
14:20-22
Deut 8:2; 31:27
32:5,6

9:8
Ex 32:7
Ps 106:19,20

9:9
Ex 24:18
Deut 9:18

9:12
Ex 32:7,8

9:13
Ex 32:10

9:15
Ex 32:15

9:16
Ex 32:19
Acts 7:40,41

9:17
Ex 32:19

9:18
Ex 34:8,9,28
Deut 9:9; 10:10

9:19
Ex 32:10,11
Heb 12:21

9:20
Ex 32:2,3,21

9:21
Ex 32:20

9:22
Ex 17:7
Num 11:3,34

9:24
Ex 32:9
Deut 9:7; 31:27

9:25
Ex 34:8
Deut 9:18

9:26
Ex 32:11-13
34:9
Num 14:13

9:27
Ex 32:31
Ps 78:7,8

9:5, 6 If the Israelites were so wicked and stubborn (9:6), why did God make such wonderful promises to them? There are two good reasons: (1) A bargain is a bargain. God and Israel had made a treaty (Genesis 15, 17; Exodus 19, 20). God promised to be faithful to them and they promised to obey him. The agreement was irrevocable and for all time. Even though the Israelites rarely upheld their end of the bargain, God would always be faithful to his part. (Although he has punished them several times, he has always remained faithful.) (2) God's mercy is unconditional. No matter how many times the people turned from God, he was always there to restore them. It is comforting to know that despite our

inconsistencies and sins, God loves us unconditionally. Eternal life is not achieved on the merit system, but on the mercy system, understanding that God loves us no matter who we are and what we have done.

9:23 The Israelites did not believe God would be able to help them—in spite of all he had already done. They would not follow, because they were looking around to others for help instead of to God. Unbelief is the root of many sins and problems in life. When you feel lost, it may be because you're looking everywhere but to God for your help and guidance. (See Psalm 81:6–12; 95:8; 106:13–20; Hebrews 3.)

notice the rebellion and stubbornness of these people, but remember instead your promises to your servants Abraham, Isaac, and Jacob. Oh, please overlook the awful wickedness and sin of these people. 28For if you destroy them the Egyptians will say, "It is because the Lord wasn't able to bring them to the land he promised them," or "He destroyed them because he hated them: he brought them into the wilderness to slay them." 29They are your people and your inheritance which you brought from Egypt by your great power and your mighty arm.'

Do not forget to fear God

10 "At that time the Lord told me to cut two more stone tablets like the first ones, and to make a wooden Ark to keep them in, and to return to God on the mountain. 2He said he would rewrite on the tablets the same commandments that were on the tablets I had smashed, and that I should place them in the Ark. 3So I made an Ark of acacia wood and hewed out two stone tablets like the first two, and took the tablets up on the mountain to God. 4He again wrote the Ten Commandments on them and gave them to me. (They were the same commandments he had given you from the heart of the fire on the mountain as you all watched below.) 5Then I came down and placed the tablets in the Ark I had made, where they are to this day, just as the Lord commanded me.

6"The people of Israel then journeyed from Be-eroth of Bene-jaakan to Moserah, where Aaron died and was buried. His son Eleazar became the next priest.

7"Then they journeyed to Gudgodah, and from there to Jotbathah, a land of brooks and water. 8It was there that Jehovah set apart the tribe of Levi to carry the Ark containing the Ten Commandments of Jehovah, and to stand before the Lord and to do his work and to bless his name, just as is done today. 9(That is why the tribe of Levi does not have a portion of land reserved for it in the Promised Land, as their brother tribes do; for as the Lord told them, he himself is their inheritance.)

10"As I said before, I stayed on the mountain before the Lord for forty days and nights the second time, just as I had the first, and the Lord again yielded to my pleas and didn't destroy you.

11"But he said to me, 'Arise and lead the people to the land I promised their fathers. It is time to go in and possess it.'

Do not forget to obey God

12, 13"And now, Israel, what does the Lord your God require of you except to listen carefully to all he says to you, and to obey for your own good the commandments I am giving you today, and to love him, and to worship him with all your hearts and souls? 14Earth and highest heaven belong to the Lord your God. 15And yet he rejoiced in your fathers and loved them so much that he chose you, their children, to be above every other nation, as is evident today. 16Therefore, cleanse your sinful hearts and stop your stubbornness.

17"Jehovah your God is God of gods and Lord of lords. He is the great and

---

9:29
Deut 4:34

10:1
Ex 25:10; 34:1

10:2
Ex 25:16
Deut 4:13
Heb 9:4

10:3
Ex 34:4; 37:1

10:4
Ex 34:28
Deut 4:13

10:5
Ex 40:20

10:6
Num 20:25,26
33:15-38

10:8
Num 3:6; 18:1
Deut 18:5; 21:5
31:9

10:9
Num 18:20,24
26:62
Deut 18:2
Josh 14:3,4
Ezek 44:28

10:10
Deut 9:18

10:11
Ex 32:34; 33:1

10:12
Deut 6:5
Jer 7:22,23

10:14
Ps 68:33
115:16

10:16
Lev 26:41,42
Deut 30:6

10:17
Ps 136:2

10:5 "Where they are to this day" refers to the time when this book was written (1407/6 B.C.). However, as late as the reign of Solomon (971 B.C.), the stone tablets were still kept in the Ark of the Covenant (1 Kings 8:9).

10:12, 13 Often we ask, "What does God expect of me? What is essential in my commitment to him?" Here Moses gives us a summary of what God expects. It is simple in form and easy to remember. Here are the essentials: (1) Listen carefully to what God says. (2) Obey his commands. (3) Love and worship him with all your heart. How often we complicate faith with man-made rules, regulations, and requirements. Are you frustrated and burned out from trying hard to please God? Concentrate on his real requirements and find peace. Listen, obey, and love.

10:16 Human nature is basically stubborn—we want to do things our way. Moses urged the people to stop doing what comes naturally (being stubborn) and start making an effort to clean up

their sinful hearts. If our hearts are right with God, if the vertical relationship between us and God has been made right—then our horizontal relationships with other people can be made right too. When your heart has been cleansed and you have been reconciled to God, it will be natural for you to love others.

10:17 Moses said that Jehovah is God of gods and Lord of lords. He was distinguishing the true God from all of the local gods worshiped throughout the Promised Land. Then Moses went a step further, calling God a God of terror. Fear God, he told the people, because only then can you learn about his mercy. God is a God of terror in that he has such awesome power and justice that people cannot stand before him without his mercy. When people begin to grasp the extent of God's mercy towards them, they see what true love is and how deeply God loves them. Although our sins deserve severe judgment, God has chosen to show love and mercy to all who seek him.

mighty God, the God of terror who shows no partiality and takes no bribes. 18He gives justice to the fatherless and widows. He loves foreigners and gives them food and clothing. 19(You too must love foreigners, for you yourselves were foreigners in the land of Egypt.) 20You must fear the Lord your God and worship him and cling to him and take oaths by his name alone. 21He is your praise and he is your God, the one who has done mighty miracles you yourselves have seen. 22When your ancestors went down into Egypt there were only seventy of them, but now the Lord your God has made you as many as the stars in the sky!

11 "You must love the Lord your God and obey every one of his commands. 2Listen! I am not talking now to your children who have never experienced the Lord's punishments or seen his greatness and his awesome power. 3They weren't there to see the miracles he did in Egypt against Pharaoh and all his land. 4They didn't see what God did to the armies of Egypt and to their horses and chariots—how he drowned them in the Red Sea as they were chasing you, and how the Lord has kept them powerless against you until this very day! 5They didn't see how the Lord cared for you time and again through all the years you were wandering in the wilderness, until your arrival here. 6They weren't there when Dathan and Abiram (the sons of Eliab, descendants of Reuben) sinned, and the earth opened up and swallowed them, with their households and tents and all their belongings, as all Israel watched!

Choose between blessings and curses

7"But *you* have seen these mighty miracles! 8How carefully, then, you should obey these commandments I am going to give you today, so that you may have the strength to go in and possess the land you are about to enter. 9If you obey the commandments, you will have a long and good life in the land the Lord promised to your ancestors and to you, their descendants—a wonderful land 'flowing with milk and honey'! 10For the land you are about to enter and possess is not like the land of Egypt where you have come from, where irrigation is necessary. 11It is a land of hills and valleys with plenty of rain— 12a land that the Lord your God personally cares for! His eyes are always upon it, day after day throughout the year!

13"And if you will carefully obey all of his commandments that I am going to give you today, and if you will love the Lord your God with all your hearts and souls, and will worship him, 14then he will continue to send both the early and late rains that will produce wonderful crops of grain, grapes for your wine, and olive oil. 15He will give you lush pastureland for your cattle to graze in, and you yourselves shall have plenty to eat and be fully content.

16"But beware that your hearts do not turn from God to worship other gods. 17For if you do, the anger of the Lord will be hot against you, and he will shut the heavens—there will be no rain and no harvest, and you will quickly perish from the good land the Lord has given you. 18So keep these commandments carefully in mind. Tie them to your hand to remind you to obey them, and tie them to your forehead between your eyes! 19Teach them to your children. Talk about them when you are sitting at home, when you are out walking, at bedtime, and before breakfast! 20Write them upon the doors of your houses and upon your gates, 21so that as long as there is sky above the earth, you and your children will enjoy the good life awaiting you in the land the Lord has promised you.

11:6 *descendants*, literally, "sons." **11:21** *promised you*, literally, "your fathers."

10:18
Ex 22:22
Deut 27:19
Ps 68:5; 103:6

10:19
Ex 22:21
Lev 19:34

10:21
Ex 15:2

10:22
Gen 46:27

11:1
Lev 18:29,30
Deut 6:5,6
10:12,13
11:8,31; 28:1

11:2
Deut 5:2,3
7:19; 8:3

11:4
Ex 14:28; 15:4
Ps 106:6-11

11:5
Ps 77:19,20

11:6
Num 16:31
26:5-11

11:8
Deut 26:17
31:6,7,23
Josh 1:6,7

11:9
Deut 4:40; 5:33
6:2
Ps 34:12
Prov 3:1,2

11:11
Deut 8:7-9
Ps 104:10-13
Jer 2:7

11:13
Deut 4:29; 6:5
8:6

11:14
Lev 26:4,5
Deut 28:12

11:15
Deut 6:10-12
8:10
Joel 2:19

11:16
Deut 8:19; 30:17

11:17
Deut 4:26; 28:24
Josh 23:13

11:18
Ex 13:16
Ps 119:11

11:19
Deut 4:9; 6:7
Ps 78:5,6

10:19 Just as the Israelites' ancestors were at one time foreigners in a strange land, so they were to be friends to foreigners who were seeking a new life. Likewise, we are commanded to love those who are foreigners. By showing genuine love, we may bring those who are not yet Christians to Christ. We must remember that it took the love of another to lead us to him.

11:7 Israel had strong reasons to believe in God and obey his commandments. They had witnessed a barrage of mighty miracles

that demonstrated God's love and care for them. Incredibly, they still had trouble remaining faithful. Since few of us have seen such dramatic miracles, it may seem even more difficult for us to obey God and remain faithful. However, we do have the Bible, the written record of God's acts throughout history. Reading God's Word gives us a panoramic view of both the miracles Israel saw and others they didn't see. The lessons from the past, the instructions for the present, and the glimpses into the future give us many opportunities to strengthen our faith in God.

22"If you carefully obey all the commandments I give you, loving the Lord your God, walking in all his ways, and clinging to him, 23then the Lord will drive out all the nations in your land, no matter how much greater and stronger than you they might be. 24Wherever you go, the land is yours. Your frontiers will stretch from the southern Negeb to Lebanon, and from the Euphrates River to the Mediterranean Sea. 25No one will be able to stand against you, for the Lord your God will send fear and dread ahead of you wherever you go, just as he has promised.

26"I am giving you the choice today between God's blessing or God's curse! 27There will be blessing if you obey the commandments of the Lord your God which I am giving you today, 28and a curse if you refuse them and worship the gods of these other nations. 29When the Lord your God brings you into the land to possess it, a blessing shall be proclaimed from Mount Gerizim, and a curse from Mount Ebal! 30(Gerizim and Ebal are mountains west of the Jordan River, where the Canaanites live, in the wasteland near Gilgal, where the oaks of Moreh are.) 31For you are to cross the Jordan and live in the land the Lord is giving you. 32But you must obey all the laws I am giving you today.

3. Laws for proper worship

12 "These are the laws you must obey when you arrive in the land which Jehovah, the God of your fathers, has given you forever:

Only one altar for sacrifice

2"You must destroy all the heathen altars wherever you find them—high in the mountains, up in the hills, or under the trees. 3Break the altars, smash the obelisks, burn the shameful images, cut down the metal idols, and leave nothing even to remind you of them!

4, 5"You must not make sacrifices to your God just anywhere, as the heathen sacrifice to their gods. Rather, you must build a sanctuary for him at a place he himself will select as his home. 6There you shall bring to the Lord your burnt offerings and other sacrifices—your tithes, your offerings presented by the gesture of waving before the altar, your offerings to fulfill your vows, your free-will offerings, and your offerings of the firstborn animals of your flocks and herds. 7There you and your families shall feast before the Lord your God, and shall rejoice in all he has done for you.

8"You will no longer go your own way as you do now, everyone doing whatever he thinks is right; 9(for these laws don't go into effect until you arrive in the place of rest the Lord will give to you). 10But when you cross the Jordan River and live in the Promised Land, and the Lord gives you rest and keeps you safe from all your enemies, 11then you must bring all your burnt sacrifices and other offerings to his

---

11:26 It is amazing that God offered the Israelites a choice between blessings and curses. It is even more amazing that most of them actually chose the curses through their disobedience. We have the same fundamental choice today. We can live for ourselves or live in service to God. To choose our own way is to travel on a dead-end road, but to choose God is to receive eternal life (John 5:24).

11:26 What is God's curse? It is not a magician's spell. Instead it refers to the conditions of the treaty between God and Israel. Both parties had agreed to the terms. The blessings were to benefit Israel if they kept their part of the treaty—they would receive the Promised Land, live there forever, have fruitful crops, and expel their enemies. The curse was the warning of the consequences to Israel if the treaty was broken—punishment, discipline, and judgment. Joshua later reviewed these blessings and curses with the entire nation (Joshua 8:34).

12:2, 3 When taking over a nation, the Israelites were to destroy every heathen altar and idol in the land. God knew it would be easy for them to change their beliefs if they started using those altars, so nothing was to remain that might remind them of

idolatrous worship. We too should be ruthless in finding and removing any "heathen altars" we have in our lives. They may be activities, attitudes, possessions, relationships, places, or habits—anything that reminds us and tempts us to do wrong. These can turn our hearts from God. We should never flatter ourselves by thinking we're too strong to be tempted. Israel learned that lesson. They also learned that it took time to remove all the altars. It will take us time too, but we can begin by tearing down those within our reach.

12:4, 5 God continued to separate himself and his people from the practices of the heathen. In Canaan, pagan sacrifice could be carried out anywhere, in any way. But the Israelites were to worship one God, one way, at one specified place. This was a type of "quality control" to keep the people from falling into their own ways of worshiping, which could lead to idolatry and other perverted forms of devotion to God. This does not denounce individual and spontaneous worship. Instead, it emphasizes the importance of a body of believers gathering together at a specified place and time to worship God.

sanctuary, the place he will choose as his home. 12You shall rejoice there before the Lord with your sons and daughters and servants; and remember to invite the Levites to feast with you, for they have no land of their own.

13"You are not to sacrifice your burnt offerings just anywhere; 14you may only do so in the place the Lord will choose. He will pick a place in the territory allotted to one of the tribes. Only there may you offer your sacrifices and bring your offerings. 15However, the meat you eat may be butchered anywhere, just as you do now with gazelle and deer. Eat as much of this meat as you wish and as often as you are able to obtain it, because the Lord has prospered you. Those who are ceremonially defiled may eat it, too. 16The only restriction is that you are not to eat the blood—pour it out on the ground, like water.

17"But none of the offerings may be eaten at home. Neither the tithe of your grain and new wine and olive oil, nor the firstborn of your flocks and herds, nor anything you have vowed to give the Lord, nor your freewill offerings, nor the offerings to be presented to the Lord by waving them before his altar. 18All these must be brought to the central altar where you, your children, and the Levites shall eat them before the Lord your God. He will tell you where this altar must be located. Rejoice before the Lord your God in everything you do. 19(By the way, be very careful not to forget about the Levites. Share with them.)

20-23"If, when the Lord enlarges your borders, the central altar is too far away from you, then your flocks and herds may be butchered on your own farms, just as you do now with gazelle and deer. And even persons who are ceremonially defiled may eat them. The only restriction is never to eat the blood, for the blood is the life, and you shall not eat the life with the meat. 24, 25Instead, pour the blood out upon the earth. If you do, all will be well with you and your children. 26, 27Only your gifts to the Lord, and the offerings you have promised in your vows, and your burnt offerings need be taken to the central altar. These may only be sacrificed upon the altar of the Lord your God. The blood will be poured out upon the altar, and you will eat the meat.

28"Be careful to obey all of these commandments. If you do what is right in the eyes of the Lord your God, all will go well with you and your children forever. 29When he destroys the nations in the land where you will live, 30don't follow their example in worshiping their gods. Do not ask, 'How do these nations worship their gods?' and then go and worship as they do! 31You must not insult the Lord your God like that! These nations have done horrible things that he hates, all in the name of their religion. They have even roasted their sons and daughters in front of their gods. 32Obey all the commandments I give you. Do not add to or subtract from them.

Warnings against worshiping other gods

13 "If there is a prophet among you, or one who claims to foretell the future by dreams, 2and if his predictions come true but he says, 'Come, let us worship

12:12
Deut 10:9
12:7,18,19
26:11

12:13
Deut 12:4,5

12:15
Deut 12:20-23
14:3-5

12:16
Lev 17:10-12
Deut 15:23

12:17
Deut 12:26
14:22; 26:12

12:18
Deut 12:4,5,26

12:20
Lev 11:2,3
Deut 12:16
15:23; 18:3-5

12:24
Deut 4:40

12:26
Lev 3:1
Deut 12:20

12:28
Deut 4:40

12:30
Rom 16:19

12:31
Lev 18:21
Deut 9:5; 18:10
Ps 106:37,38

12:32
Deut 4:2

13:1,2
Num 12:6
Deut 18:20-22

12:12, 18 The Hebrews placed great emphasis on family worship. Whether offering a sacrifice or attending a great feast, the family was often together. This gave the children a healthy attitude toward worship, and it put extra meaning into it for the adults. Watching a family member confess his or her sin was just as important as celebrating a great holiday. Although there are appropriate times to separate people by ages, some of the most meaningful worship can only be experienced as a family.

12:16 Eating blood was forbidden for several reasons: (1) it was an integral part of the pagan practices of the land the Israelites were about to enter; (2) it was a sign of life; (3) it was a symbol of the sacrifice that had to be made for sin. (For more on why eating blood was prohibited see the note on Leviticus 17:14.)

12:30, 31 God did not want the Israelites even to ask about the heathen religions surrounding them. Idolatry completely permeated the land of Canaan. It was too easy to get drawn into the subtle temptations of seemingly harmless practices. Sometimes knowledge hinders. Knowledge of evil can often be harmful because the evil we are learning about can become too tempting to resist. To avoid knowledge of certain harmful areas shows discretion and obedience.

12:32 Some people want to add to or subtract from God's commands. Subtracting is looking for an easy way around them. Adding sounds religious, but it can crush people with unnecessary requirements. Strangely enough, when we add one command we often wind up subtracting another. For example, the Pharisees in Jesus' day added many restrictions to the Sabbath commandment. But by trying to keep Jesus from healing on the Sabbath (see John 9), they were breaking God's commandment to "love your

13:3
Deut 6:5; 8:2,16
Ps 81:7

13:4
Deut 10:20
Jer 7:23

13:5
Deut 7:4; 13:9
17:5; 22:21
Jer 14:15
Zech 13:3

13:6,7
Deut 13:2
17:2-7; 29:18
Mic 7:5

13:8
Deut 7:2
Ezek 9:5

13:9
Lev 24:13,14
Deut 13:5; 17:7

13:10
Lev 24:15
Num 15:35
Josh 7:25

13:11
Deut 17:13
19:20

13:12
Deut 13:2
Josh 22:11

13:16
Num 21:2
Deut 7:25,26
Josh 6:24

13:17
Ex 32:12
Num 25:4
Deut 7:13; 30:3

13:18
Deut 12:28
Mt 6:33,34

14:1
Lev 19:27,28
21:5
Jer 16:6

14:2
Ex 19:5

the gods of the other nations,' ³don't listen to him. For the Lord is testing you to find out whether or not you really love him with all your heart and soul. ⁴You must *never* worship any God but Jehovah; obey only his commands and cling to him.

⁵"The prophet who tries to lead you astray must be executed, for he has attempted to foment rebellion against the Lord your God who brought you out of slavery in the land of Egypt. By executing him you will clear out the evil from among you.

⁶, ⁷If your nearest relative or closest friend, even a brother, son, daughter, or beloved wife whispers to you to come and worship these foreign gods, ⁸do not consent nor listen, and have no pity: Do not spare that person from the penalty; don't conceal his horrible suggestion. ⁹Execute him! Your own hand shall be the first upon him to put him to death, then the hands of all the people. ¹⁰Stone him to death because he has tried to draw you away from the Lord your God who brought you from the land of Egypt, the place of slavery. ¹¹Then all Israel will hear about his evil deed, and will fear such wickedness as this among you.

¹², ¹³, ¹⁴"If you ever hear it said about one of the cities of Israel that some worthless rabble have led their fellow citizens astray with the suggestion that they worship foreign gods, first check the facts to see if the rumor is true. If you find that it is, that it is certain that such a horrible thing is happening among you in one of the cities the Lord has given you, ¹⁵you must without fail declare war against that city and utterly destroy all of its inhabitants, and even all of the cattle. ¹⁶Afterwards you must pile all the booty into the middle of the street and burn it, then put the entire city to the torch, as a burnt offering to Jehovah your God. That city shall forever remain a lifeless mound and may never be rebuilt. ¹⁷Keep none of the booty! Then the Lord will turn from his fierce anger and be merciful to you, and have compassion upon you, and make you a great nation just as he promised your ancestors.

¹⁸"Of course, the Lord your God will be merciful only if you have been obedient to him and to his commandments which I am giving you today, and if you have been doing that which is right in the eyes of the Lord.

Clean and unclean foods

14 "Since you are the people of God, never cut yourselves [as the heathen do when they worship their idols] nor shave the front halves of your heads for funerals. ²You belong exclusively to the Lord your God, and he has chosen you to be his own possession, more so than any other nation on the face of the earth.

14:1 *as the heathen do when they worship idols,* implied.

---

neighbor as yourself" (Leviticus 19:18). God gave his laws for a reason. Making them simpler or more difficult than they really are only confuses their real purpose—to point us to him.

13:1-3 Good leaders are not always godly leaders. Moses warned the Israelites against false prophets who encouraged worship that was not directed to the true God. Often new ideas from inspiring people look attractive, but we must judge them by whether or not they are consistent with God's Word. When people claim to speak for God today, we should check them in these areas: Are they telling the truth? Is their focus on God? Are their words consistent with what you already know to be true? Do they speak the truth while directing you toward God, or do they speak persuasively while directing you toward themselves? Someone may say the right things but still lead you in the wrong direction. God is not against new ideas, but he is for discernment. When you hear a new, attractive idea, ask these questions before getting too excited. False prophets are still around today. The wise person will carefully test ideas against the truth of God's Word.

13:5-11 The Israelites were warned not to listen to false prophets or to anyone else who tried to get them to worship other

gods—even if this person was a close friend or family member. The temptation to abandon God's commands often sneaks up on us. It may not come with a loud shout but in a whispering doubt. And whispers can be very persuasive, especially if they come from loved ones. But love for relatives should not take precedence over devotion to God. We can overcome whispered temptations by pouring out our hearts to God in prayer and by diligently studying his Word.

13:12-14 A city that completely rejected God was to be destroyed so as not to lead the rest of the nation astray. But Israel was not to take action against a city until the rumor about its rejecting God was proven true. This guideline saved many lives when the leaders of Israel wrongly accused three tribes of falling away from their faith (Joshua 22). If we hear of friends who have wandered from the Lord or of entire churches that have fallen away, we should check the facts and find the truth before doing or saying anything that could prove harmful. There are times, of course, when God wants us to take action—to rebuke a wayward friend, to discipline a child, to reject false teaching—but first we must be sure we have all the facts straight.

3, 4, 5"You are not to eat any animal I have declared to be ceremonially defiled. These are the animals you may eat: The ox, the sheep, the goat, the deer, the gazelle, the roebuck, the wild goat, the ibex, the antelope, and the mountain sheep.

6"Any animal that has cloven hooves and chews the cud may be eaten, 7but if the animal doesn't have both, it may not be eaten. So you may not eat the camel, the hare, or the coney.

"They chew the cud but do not have cloven hooves. 8Pigs may not be eaten because, although they have cloven hooves, they don't chew the cud. You may not even touch the dead bodies of such animals.

9"Only sea animals with fins and scales may be eaten; 10all other kinds are ceremonially defiled.

11-18"You may eat any bird except the following: The eagle, the vulture, the osprey, the buzzard, the falcon (any variety), the raven (any variety), the ostrich, the nighthawk, the sea gull, the hawk (any variety), the screech owl, the great owl, the horned owl, the pelican, the vulture, the cormorant, the stork, the heron (any variety), the hoopoe, the bat.

19, 20"With certain exceptions, insects are a defilement to you and may not be eaten.

21"Don't eat anything that has died a natural death. However, a foreigner among you may eat it. You may give it or sell it to him, but don't eat it yourself, for you are holy to the Lord your God.

"You must not boil a young goat in its mother's milk.

Tithes

22"You must tithe all of your crops every year. 23Bring this tithe to eat before the Lord your God at the place he shall choose as his sanctuary; this applies to your tithes of grain, new wine, olive oil, and the firstborn of your flocks and herds. The purpose of tithing is to teach you always to put God first in your lives. 24If the place the Lord chooses for his sanctuary is so far away that it isn't convenient to carry your tithes to that place, 25then you may sell the tithe portion of your crops and herds and take the money to the Lord's sanctuary. 26When you arrive, use the money to buy an ox, a sheep, some wine, or beer, to feast there before the Lord your God, and to rejoice with your household.

27"Don't forget to share your income with the Levites in your community, for they have no property or crops as you do.

28"Every third year you are to use your entire tithe for local welfare programs: 29Give it to the Levites who have no inheritance among you, or to foreigners, or to

14:19, 20 *With certain exceptions.* See Lev 11:20-23.

14:3
Lev 11:2-43
Ezek 4:14
Acts 10:12-14

14:21
Ex 23:19; 34:26
Lev 17:15; 22:8
Deut 14:2
Ezek 4:14

14:22
Deut 12:6,17
26:12
14:23
Deut 4:10; 12:4
14:24
Deut 12:20

14:26
Deut 12:18
14:27
Num 18:20
Deut 10:9; 12:12
14:28
Deut 26:12
14:29
Deut 16:11,14
24:19

14:3–21 Why was Israel forbidden to eat certain foods? There are several reasons: (1) Predatory animals ate the blood of other animals. Since the people could not eat blood, they could not eat such animals. (2) Some animals in the Israelite culture had bad associations, as bats, snakes, and spiders do for some people today. Every culture has its own food taboos. The animals that were forbidden represented sin or unhealthy habits to the Israelite culture. Some may have been used in heathen religious practices (Isaiah 66:17). (3) Perhaps some restrictions were given to Israel just to remind them continually that they were a different and separate people committed to God. Although we no longer must follow these laws about food (Acts 10:9–16), we can still learn from them the lesson that holiness is to be carried into all parts of life. We can't restrict holiness only to the spiritual part of our life, but we must also be holy in the everyday practical part of life as well. Health practices, finances, use of leisure—all provide opportunities to put "holy living" into "daily living."

14:22, 23 The Bible makes the purpose of tithing very clear—to put God first in our lives. We are to give God the first and best of what we earn. For example, what we do first with our money shows what we value most. Giving the first part of our paycheck to God immediately focuses our attention on him. It also reminds us that all we have belongs to him. A habit of regular tithing can keep God at the top of our priority list and give us a proper perspective on everything else we have.

14:28, 29 The Bible supports an organized system of caring for the poor. God told his people to use their tithe every third year for those who were helpless, hungry, or poor. These regulations were designed to prevent the country from sinking under crushing poverty and oppression. It was everyone's responsibility to care for those less fortunate. Families were to help other family members, and towns were to help members of their community. National laws protected the rights of the poor, but helping the poor was also an active part of religious life. God counts on believers to provide for the needy, and we should use what God has given us to aid those less fortunate. Look beyond your regular giving and think of ways to help the needy. This will help you to show your regard for God as Creator of all people, share God's goodness with others, and draw them to him. It is a practical and essential way to make faith work in everyday life.

widows and orphans within your city, so that they can eat and be satisfied; and then Jehovah your God will bless you and your work.

Lending money

15 "At the end of every seventh year there is to be a canceling of all debts! ²Every creditor shall write 'Paid in full' on any promissory note he holds against a fellow Israelite, for the Lord has released everyone from his obligation. ³(This release does not apply to foreigners.) ⁴, ⁵No one will become poor because of this, for the Lord will greatly bless you in the land he is giving you if you obey this command. The only prerequisite for his blessing is that you carefully heed all the commands of the Lord your God that I am giving you today. ⁶He will bless you as he has promised. You shall lend money to many nations but will never need to borrow! You shall rule many nations, but they shall not rule over you!

⁷"But if, when you arrive in the land the Lord will give you, there are any among you who are poor, you must not shut your heart or hand against them; ⁸you must lend them as much as they need. ⁹Beware! Don't refuse a loan because the year of debt cancellation is close at hand! If you refuse to make the loan and the needy man cries out to the Lord, it will be counted against you as a sin. ¹⁰You must lend him what he needs, and don't moan about it either! For the Lord will prosper you in everything you do because of this! ¹¹There will always be some among you who are poor; that is why this commandment is necessary. You must lend to them liberally.

Hebrew slaves

¹²"If you buy a Hebrew slave, whether a man or woman, you must free him at the end of the sixth year you have owned him, ¹³and don't send him away empty-handed! ¹⁴Give him a large farewell present from your flock, your olive press, and your wine press. Share with him in proportion as the Lord your God has blessed you. ¹⁵Remember that you were slaves in the land of Egypt and the Lord your God rescued you! That is why I am giving you this command.

¹⁶"But if your Hebrew slave doesn't want to leave—if he says he loves you and enjoys your pleasant home and gets along well with you— ¹⁷then take an awl and pierce his ear into the door, and after that he shall be your slave forever. Do the same with your women slaves. ¹⁸But when you free a slave you must not feel bad, for remember that for six years he has cost you less than half the price of a hired hand! And the Lord your God will prosper all you do because you have released him!

Firstborn animals

¹⁹"You shall set aside for God all the firstborn males from your flocks and herds. Do not use the firstborn of your herds to work your fields, and do not shear the firstborn of your flocks of sheep and goats. ²⁰Instead, you and your family shall eat these animals before the Lord your God each year at his sanctuary. ²¹However, if this firstborn animal has any defect such as being lame or blind, or if anything else is wrong with it, you shall not sacrifice it. ²²Instead, use it for food for your family at home. Anyone, even if ceremonially defiled at the time, may eat it, just as anyone may eat a gazelle or deer. ²³But don't eat the blood; pour it out upon the ground like water.

15:1 Deut 31:10,11
15:2 Neh 5:7 Amos 8:4-8
15:3 Deut 23:20
15:4 Deut 14:29 28:1-8
15:6 Deut 28:12,13
15:7 Deut 15:11 Prov 19:11
15:9 Ex 22:22,23 Deut 15:1 24:14,15 Job 34:28
15:10 2 Cor 9:7
15:11 Jn 12:8
15:12 Ex 21:2 Lev 25:39 Jer 34:14
15:15 Ex 20:2 Deut 5:15; 16:12
15:16 Ex 21:5,6
15:17 Lev 25:39
15:19 Ex 13:1; 34:19 Lev 27:26 Num 3:13
15:20 Lev 7:15 Deut 12:7
15:21 Lev 22:19 Mal 1:7,8
15:22 Deut 12:15

15:7-11 God told the Israelites to help the poor among them when they arrived in the Promised Land. This was an important part of possessing the land. Many people conclude that people are poor through some fault of their own. This kind of reasoning makes it easy to shut our hearts and hands against them. But we are not to invent reasons for not helping the poor. We are to respond to the needs of the poor no matter who or what was responsible for their condition. Who are the poor in your commmunity? How could your church help them? If your church does not have a program to identify the poor and assist in fulfilling their needs, why not help start one?

15:12-14 The Israelites were to release their slaves after six years, sending them away with enough food so that they would be amply supplied until their needs could be met by some other means. This humanitarian act recognized that God created each person with dignity and worth. It also reminded the Israelites that they, too, had once been slaves in Egypt, and that their present freedom was a gift from God. Today, we must be sure to treat our employees with respect and economic fairness.

Celebrations

16 "Always remember to celebrate the Passover during the month of April, for that was when Jehovah your God brought you out of Egypt by night. 2Your Passover sacrifice shall be either a lamb or an ox, sacrificed to the Lord your God at his sanctuary. 3Eat the sacrifice with unleavened bread. Eat unleavened bread for seven days as a reminder of the bread you ate as you escaped from Egypt. This is to remind you that you left Egypt in such a hurry that there was no time for the bread to rise. Remember that day all the rest of your lives! 4For seven days no trace of yeast shall be in your homes, and none of the Passover lamb shall be left until the next morning.

5"The Passover is not to be eaten in your homes. 6It must be eaten at the place the Lord shall choose as his sanctuary. Sacrifice it there on the anniversary evening just as the sun goes down. 7Roast the lamb and eat it, then start back to your homes the next morning. 8For the following six days you shall eat no bread made with yeast. On the seventh day there shall be a quiet gathering of the people of each city before the Lord your God. Don't do any work that day.

9"Seven weeks after the harvest begins, 10there shall be another festival before the Lord your God called the Festival of Weeks. At that time bring to him a free-will offering proportionate in size to his blessing upon you as judged by the amount of your harvest. 11It is a time to rejoice before the Lord with your family and household. And don't forget to include the local Levites, foreigners, widows, and orphans. Invite them to accompany you to the celebration at the sanctuary. 12Remember! You were a slave in Egypt, so be sure to carry out this command.

13"Another celebration, the Festival of Shelters, must be observed for seven days at the end of the harvest season, after the grain is threshed and the grapes have been pressed. 14This will be a happy time of rejoicing together with your family and servants. And don't forget to include the Levites, foreigners, orphans, and widows of your town.

15"This feast will be held at the sanctuary, which will be located at the place the Lord will designate. It is a time of deep thanksgiving to the Lord for blessing you with a good harvest and in so many other ways; it shall be a time of great joy.

16"Every man in Israel shall appear before the Lord your God three times a year at the sanctuary for these festivals:

The Festival of Unleavened Bread,
The Festival of Weeks,
The Festival of Shelters.

"On each of these occasions bring a gift to the Lord. 17Give as you are able, according as the Lord has blessed you.

4. Laws for ruling the nation
Justice in the courts

18"Appoint judges and administrative officials for all the cities the Lord your God is giving you. They will administer justice in every part of the land. 19Never

---

16:1 Ex 12:2
Lev 23:5
Num 9:2,3
28:16
16:2 Ex 12:5
16:3 Ex 12:8,15
34:18
16:4 Ex 13:6,7
34:25
16:6 Deut 12:4,5
2 Kgs 23:21-23
Jn 2:13; 11:55
16:7 2 Chron 35:13
16:9 Ex 23:16; 34:22
Lev 23:15
Num 28:26
16:10 Lev 5:7; 12:8
16:11 Deut 12:7,12
14:29; 24:19
16:12 Ex 21:2
Deut 15:15
16:13 Lev 23:40
Ezek 45:25
16:16 Ex 22:29
23:14; 34:20,
22-24
16:17 Deut 16:10
16:18 Ex 18:25
Deut 1:17

16:1 *the month of April*, literally, "Abib"—the first month of the Hebrew calendar. **16:3** *you left Egypt in such a hurry that there was no time for the bread to rise*, literally, "for you left Egypt in hurried flight."

16:16, 17 Three times a year every male was to make a journey to the sanctuary located in the city designated as the religious capital of Israel. At these festivals, each participant was encouraged to give what he could in proportion to what God had given him. God does not expect us to give more than we can, but we are blessed when we are able to give cheerfully. For some of us, 10 percent may be a burden. For most of us, it is far too little. Look around at what you have, then give in proportion to what you have been given.

16:18–20 These verses anticipate a great problem the Israelites

would face when they arrived in the Promised Land. Though they had Joshua as their national leader, they failed to complete the task and choose other spiritual leaders who would guide the tribes, districts, and cities with justice and godliness. Because they did not appoint wise judges and godly administrators, rebellion and injustice plagued their communities. It is the responsibility of the people to carefully appoint or elect officials who are wise and just. In your sphere of influence—home, church, school, job—are you ensuring that justice and godliness prevail? Failing to choose leaders who uphold justice can lead to much trouble, as Israel would discover.

16:19
Ex 23:2,3
Lev 19:15

16:20
Deut 25:13-15

16:21
Ex 34:13

16:22
Lev 26:1

twist justice to benefit a rich man, and never accept bribes. For bribes blind the eyes of the wisest and corrupt their decisions. 20Justice must prevail.

"That is the only way you will be successful in the land which the Lord your God is giving you.

21"Never, under any circumstances, are you to erect shameful images beside the altar of the Lord your God. 22And never set up stone pillars to worship them, for the Lord hates them!

17:1
Lev 22:20
Deut 15:21

17:2
Deut 4:19,23
29:26
Josh 22:16
2 Kgs 21:3-5
Acts 7:43

17:4
Deut 13:12-14
19:18

17:5
Deut 13:10
21:21

17:6
Num 35:30
Deut 19:15

17:7
Lev 24:13,14
Deut 13:9

17:8
Deut 1:17; 19:17

17:11
Deut 25:1

17:13
Deut 13:11
19:20

17 "Never sacrifice a sick or defective ox or sheep to the Lord your God. He doesn't feel honored by such gifts!

2, 3"If anyone, whether man or woman, in any village throughout your land violates your covenant with God by worshiping other gods, the sun, moon, or stars—which I have strictly forbidden— 4first check the rumor very carefully; if there is no doubt it is true, 5then that man or woman shall be taken outside the city and shall be stoned to death. 6However, never put a man to death on the testimony of only one witness; there must be at least two or three. 7The witnesses shall throw the first stones, and then all the people shall join in. In this way you will purge all evil from among you.

8"If a case arises that is too hard for you to decide—for instance, whether someone is guilty of murder when there is insufficient evidence, or whether someone's rights have been violated—you shall take the case to the sanctuary of the Lord your God, 9to the priests and Levites, and the chief judge on duty at the time will make the decision. 10His decision is without appeal and is to be followed to the letter. 11The sentence he imposes is to be fully executed. 12If the defendant refuses to accept the decision of the priest or judge appointed by God for this purpose, the penalty is death. Such sinners must be purged from Israel. 13Then everyone will hear about what happened to the man who refused God's verdict, and they will be afraid to defy a court's judgment.

Guidelines for the king

17:14
Deut 11:31
Josh 21:43

17:16
1 Kgs 4:26

17:17
2 Sam 5:13
1 Kgs 11:3,4

14"When you arrive in the land the Lord your God will give you, and have conquered it, and begin to think, 'We ought to have a king like the other nations around us'— 15be sure that you select as king the man the Lord your God shall choose. He must be an Israelite, not a foreigner. 16Be sure that he doesn't build up a large stable of horses for himself, nor send his men to Egypt to raise horses for him there, for the Lord has told you, 'Never return to Egypt again.' 17He must not

---

17:1 The fact that this command was included probably indicates that some Israelites were sacrificing imperfect or deformed animals to God. Then, as now, it is difficult and expensive to offer God our best (i.e., the first part of what we earn). It is always tempting to shortchange God, because we don't seem to get caught. But our giving shows our real priorities. When we give God the leftovers, he is obviously not at the center of our lives. Give God the honor of having first claim on your money, your time, and your talents.

17:2, 3 It was common not only to worship idols of wood and stone, but the sun, moon, and stars as well. This was simply another form of idol worship—bowing down to a created thing, rather than the Creator himself.

17:7 A person was not put to death on the testimony of only one witness. On the witness of two or three, a person could be condemned and then sentenced to death by stoning. The condemned person was taken outside the city gates, and the witnesses were the first to throw heavy stones down on him or her. Bystanders would then pelt the dying person with stones. This system would "purge all evil" by putting the idolater to death. At the same time, it protected the rights of accused persons two ways. First, by requiring several witnesses, it prevented any angry individual from "bearing false witness." Second, by requiring the accusers to throw the first stones, it made them think twice about accusing unjustly. They were responsible to finish what they had started.

17:8-13 Sometimes a case came up that was too difficult for the local community to decide. Perhaps there were no witnesses, or the evidence was insufficient, or unusual circumstances made the truth hard to see. When this happened, the case was to be taken to God's sanctuary. There the priest in charge of judging these special cases would make a decision. His word was final. This was the fairest way to settle the matter once and for all. It was vitally important to have a just and godly man in this position.

17:14-20 God was not encouraging Israel to appoint a king to rule their nation. He was actually against the idea because he was their king, and the people were to obey and follow him. But God knew that the people would one day demand a king for selfish reasons—they would want to be like the nations around them (1 Samuel 8). If they insisted on having a king, he wanted to make sure they chose the right person for the job. That is why he included these instructions both for the people's benefit as they chose their king and for the king himself as he sought to lead the nation according to God's laws.

17:16, 17 Israel's kings did not heed this warning, and their behavior led to their downfall. King Solomon had everything going for him, but when he became rich, built up a large army, and married many wives, his heart turned from God. Out of Solomon's sin came Israel's disobedience, division, and captivity.

have too many wives, lest his heart be turned away from the Lord, neither shall he be excessively rich. 18"And when he has been crowned and sits upon his throne as king, then he must copy these laws from the book kept by the Levite-priests. 19That copy of the laws shall be his constant companion. He must read from it every day of his life so that he will learn to respect the Lord his God by obeying all of his commands. 20This regular reading of God's laws will prevent him from feeling that he is better than his fellow citizens. It will also prevent him from turning away from God's laws in the slightest respect, and will ensure his having a long, good reign. His sons will then follow him upon the throne.

17:18
Deut 31:9,24
2 Kgs 11:12; 22:8

17:19
Deut 6:6; 11:18
Ps 119

Offerings for the priests and Levites

18 "Remember that the priests and all the other members of the Levite tribe will not be given property like the other tribes. So the priests and Levites are to be supported by the sacrifices brought to the altar of the Lord and by the other offerings the people bring to him. 2They don't need to own property, for the Lord is their property! That is what he promised them! 3The shoulder, the cheeks, and the stomach of every ox or sheep brought for sacrifice must be given to the priests. 4In addition, the priests shall receive the harvest samples brought in thanksgiving to the Lord—the first of the grain, the new wine, the olive oil, and of the fleece at shearing time. 5For the Lord your God has chosen the tribe of Levi, of all the tribes, to minister to the Lord from generation to generation.

6, 7"Any Levite, no matter where he lives in the land of Israel, has the right to come to the sanctuary at any time and minister in the name of the Lord, just like his brother Levites who work there regularly. 8He shall be given his share of the sacrifices and offerings as his right, not just if he is in need.

18:1
Deut 10:9
1 Cor 9:13

18:2
Deut 12:12
Ps 16:5

18:3
Lev 7:32
Num 18:11

18:4
Ex 22:29; 23:19

18:5
Ex 28:1
Num 3:10
Deut 10:8

18:6
Num 35:2,3

18:8
Lev 27:30
Num 18:21

Warnings against unholy practices

9"When you arrive in the Promised Land you must be very careful lest you be corrupted by the horrible customs of the nations now living there. 10For example, any Israeli who presents his child to be burned to death as a sacrifice to heathen
18:10 Implied.

18:9
Lev 18:26
Deut 9:5
12:29,30

17:18-20 The king was to be a man of God's Word. He was to (1) have a copy of the law made for his personal use, (2) keep it with him all the time, (3) read from it every day, and (4) obey it completely. By this process he would learn respect for God, keep himself from feeling more important than others, and avoid neglecting God in times of prosperity. We can't know what God wants unless we read his Word, and his Word won't affect our lives unless we read and think about it regularly. With the abundant availability of the Scriptures today, it is not difficult to gain access to the source of the king's wisdom. What is more of a challenge is to follow what God demanded of the king.

18:1-8 The priests and Levites served much the same function as our ministers today. Their duties included (1) teaching the people about God, (2) setting an example of godly living, (3) caring for the sanctuary and its workers, and (4) distributing the offerings. Since priests could not own property or pursue outside business interests, God made special arrangements so the people would not take advantage of them. Often churches take advantage of the men and women God has brought to lead them. For example, pastors may not be paid in accordance with their skills or the time they put in. Or maybe they are expected to attend every evening meeting, even if this continual absence is harmful to their families. As you look at your own church in light of God's Word, in what ways can you honor the leaders that God has given you?

18:9 God warned the Israelites that their problems wouldn't all disappear just because they were entering the Promised Land. God did not insulate them from the evils they would face, but he gave them the support they needed to live in the land and conquer

the enemy. Earth has no trouble-free environments. There will always be problems as long as the world is filled with sinful people. Not even Christian churches, schools, ministries, or homes are problem free. But you can deal with your problem-filled environment by applying God's Word to your situation. Rather than looking for a safe, secure retreat from corrupting influences, we must look to God for the courage to deal with our problem-filled environment and the power to conquer it.

18:10 Child sacrifice, magic, and divination were strictly forbidden by God. These practices were common among heathen religions. Israel's own neighbors actually sacrificed their children to the god Molech (Leviticus 20:2-5). Other neighboring religions used supernatural means, such as magic and contacting the spirit world, to foretell the future and gain guidance. Because of these wicked practices, God would drive out the heathen nations (18:12). The Israelites were to replace their evil practices with the worship of the one true God.

18:10-13 Just as most of us are naturally curious about a magic trick, the Israelites were curious about the occult practices of the Canaanite religions. But Satan is behind the occult, and God flatly forbade Israel to have anything to do with it. Today people are still fascinated by horoscopes, fortune-telling, witchcraft, and bizarre cults. Often their interest comes from a desire to know and control the future. But Satan is no less dangerous today than he was in Moses' time. In the Bible, God tells us all we need to know about what is going to happen. The information Satan offers is likely to be distorted or completely false. With the trustworthy guidance of the Holy Spirit through the Scriptures and the church, we don't need to turn to occult sources for faulty information about our futures.

18:10
Ex 22:18
Lev 19:26,31
Deut 12:31
Jer 27:9,10

18:13
Gen 6:7-10
17:1
Job 1:1
Mt 5:48

gods, must be killed. No Israeli may practice black magic, or call on the evil spirits for aid, or be a fortune teller, 11or be a serpent charmer, medium, or wizard, or call forth the spirits of the dead. 12Anyone doing these things is an object of horror and disgust to the Lord, and it is because the nations do these things that the Lord your God will displace them. 13You must walk blamelessly before the Lord your God. 14The nations you replace all do these evil things, but the Lord your God will not permit you to do such things.

Advice concerning prophets

18:15
Lk 24:19
Jn 1:21,24,25
6:14; 7:52
Acts 3:20-22
7:37
Heb 3:2

18:16
Deut 5:23-27

18:18
Acts 3:21-23

18:19
Deut 17:12
Heb 12:25

18:20
Deut 13:1-4
Jer 28:15,16

18:22
Isa 41:22
Jer 28:9

15"Instead, he will raise up for you a Prophet like me, an Israeli, a man to whom you must listen and whom you must obey. 16For this is what you yourselves begged of God at Mount Horeb. There at the foot of the mountain you begged that you might not have to listen to the terrifying voice of God again, or see the awesome fire on the mountain, lest you die.

17" 'All right,' the Lord said to me, 'I will do as they have requested. 18I will raise up from among them a Prophet, an Israeli like you. I will tell him what to say, and he shall be my spokesman to the people. 19I will personally deal with anyone who will not listen to him and heed his messages from me. 20But any prophet who falsely claims that his message is from me, shall die. And any prophet who claims to give a message from other gods must die.' 21If you wonder, 'How shall we know whether the prophecy is from the Lord or not?' 22this is the way to know: If the thing he prophesies doesn't happen, it is not the Lord who has given him the message; he has made it up himself. You have nothing to fear from him.

Cities of refuge

19:1
Deut 6:10-12
17:14

19:2,3
Num 35:6
Deut 4:41,42
Josh 20:7

19:4
Num 35:9-34

19:8
Deut 11:24
12:20-24

19:9
Deut 6:15; 11:22

19:10
Num 35:33
Deut 21:1-9

19

"When the Lord your God has destroyed the nations you will displace, and when you are living in their cities and homes, 2, 3you must set apart three Cities of Refuge so that anyone who accidentally kills someone may flee to safety. Divide the country into three districts, with one of these cities in each district; and keep the roads to these cities in good repair.

4"Here is an example of the purpose of these cities: 5If a man goes into the forest with his neighbor to chop wood, and the axe head flies off the handle and kills the man's neighbor, he may flee to one of those cities and be safe. 6, 7Anyone seeking to avenge the death will not be able to. These cities must be scattered so that one of them will be reasonably close to everyone; otherwise the angry avenger might catch and kill the innocent slayer, even though he should not have died since he had not killed deliberately.

8"If the Lord enlarges your boundaries as he promised your ancestors, and gives you all the land he promised 9(whether he does this depends on your obedience to all these commandments I am giving you today—loving the Lord your God and walking his paths), then you must designate three additional Cities of Refuge. 10In

---

18:15 Who is this Prophet? Stephen used this verse to support his claim that Jesus Christ really is God's Son, the Messiah (Acts 7:37). The coming of Jesus Christ to earth was not an afterthought, but part of God's original plan.

18:21, 22 As in the days of ancient Israel, some people today claim to have messages from God. God still speaks to his people, but we must be cautious before saying that the Lord has spoken through a prophet. How can we tell when people are speaking for the Lord? (1) We can see whether or not their prophecies come true—the ancient test for judging prophets. (2) We can check their words against Scripture. God never contradicts himself, so if someone says something contrary to the Bible, we can know that this is not God's word. We should give our trust carefully and in accordance with what we already know about God from the church and Scripture.

19:2 Every society must deal with the problem of murder. But how should society treat those who have innocently or accidentally killed someone? God had an answer for the Israelites. Since

revenge was common and swift in Moses' day, God had the Israelites appoint some of their cities as "Cities of Refuge." Anyone who claimed to have accidentally killed someone could flee to one of these cities until he could have a fair trial. If he was found innocent of intentional murder, he could remain in that city and be safe from those seeking revenge. This is a beautiful example of how God blended his justice and mercy toward his people. (For more information on Cities of Refuge see the note on Numbers 35:6.)

19:2, 3 The Cities of Refuge would have been ineffective if the roads that led to them were in disrepair. Many who came to the cities were literally running for their lives. A well-maintained road could have meant the difference between life and death. "Repair" meant continued maintenance, because these were dirt roads that could easily be washed away, covered by sand, or crisscrossed with deep ruts. It was important not only to initiate this system of justice, but to provide the necessary means of maintaining it.

this way you will be able to avoid the death of innocent people, and you will not be held responsible for unjustified bloodshed.

11"But if anyone hates his neighbor and springs out of hiding and kills him, and then flees into one of the Cities of Refuge, 12the elders of his home town shall send for him and shall bring him home and deliver him over to the dead man's avenger, to kill him. 13Don't pity him! Purge all murderers from Israel! Only then will all go well with you.

14"When you arrive in the land the Lord your God is giving you, remember that you must never steal a man's land by moving the boundary marker.

15"Never convict anyone on the testimony of one witness. There must be at least two, and three is even better. 16If anyone gives false witness, claiming he has seen someone do wrong when he hasn't, 17both men shall be brought before the priests and judges on duty before the Lord at the time. 18They must be closely questioned, and if the witness is lying, 19his penalty shall be the punishment he thought the other man would get. In this way you will purge out evil from among you. 20Then those who hear about it will be afraid to tell lies on the witness stand. 21You shall not show pity to a false witness. Life for life, eye for eye, tooth for tooth, hand for hand, foot for foot; this is your rule in such cases.

Instructions for soldiers

20 "When you go to war and see before you vast numbers of horses and chariots, an army far greater than yours, don't be frightened! The Lord your God is with you—the same God who brought you safely out of Egypt! 2Before you begin the battle, a priest shall stand before the Israeli army and say,

3" 'Listen to me, all you men of Israel! Don't be afraid as you go out to fight today! 4For the Lord your God is going with you! He will fight for you against your enemies, and he will give you the victory!'

5"Then the officers of the army shall address the men in this manner: 'Has anyone just built a new house, but not yet dedicated it? If so, go home! For you might be killed in the battle, and someone else would dedicate it! 6Has anyone just planted a vineyard but not yet eaten any of its fruit? If so, go home! You might die in battle and someone else would eat it! 7Has anyone just become engaged? Well, go home and get married! For you might die in the battle, and someone else would marry your fiancée. 8And now, is anyone afraid? If you are, go home before you frighten the rest of us!' 9When the officers have finished saying this to their men, they will announce the names of the battalion leaders.

10"As you approach a city to fight against it, first offer it a truce. 11If it accepts the truce and opens its gates to you, then all its people shall become your servants. 12But if it refuses and won't make peace with you, you must besiege it. 13When the Lord your God has given it to you, kill every male in the city; 14but you may keep for yourselves all the women, children, cattle, and booty. 15These instructions apply only to distant cities, not to those in the Promised Land itself.

16"For in the cities within the boundaries of the Promised Land you are to save no one; destroy every living thing. 17Utterly destroy the Hittites, the Amorites, the Canaanites, the Perizzites, the Hivites, and the Jebusites. This is the command-

20:15 *not to those in the Promised Land itself,* literally, "which are not of the cities of these nations."

Cross-references (right margin):

19:11 Deut 27:24
19:12 Num 35:21,24
19:13 Deut 7:16; 13:8
19:14 Deut 27:17 / Prov 23:10,11
19:15 Num 35:30 / Deut 17:16 / Mt 18:16 / 2 Cor 13:1
19:16 Ex 23:1 / Prov 14:5,25
19:17 Deut 17:9; 21:5
19:19 Deut 13:5; 17:7 / Prov 19:5,9
19:21 Ex 21:23 / Lev 24:17,20 / Mt 5:38
20:1 Deut 1:29,30 / 3:22; 7:18 / 31:6,7 / Josh 11:6
20:2 Num 10:8; 31:6
20:3 Ps 27:1-3 / Isa 35:4; 41:10
20:5 Neh 12:27
20:6 Lev 19:23
20:7 Deut 24:5
20:8 Judg 7:3
20:10 2 Sam 20:17-21
20:13 Num 31:7-11 / 1 Kgs 11:15
20:14 Josh 8:2 / 11:14 / 2 Chron 14:13-15
20:16 Ex 23:31 / Deut 7:1,2

19:21 This attitude toward punishment may seem primitive, but it was a actually a breakthrough for justice and fairness in these ancient times when most nations used arbitrary methods to punish criminals. This guideline reflects a concern for evenhandedness and justice—ensuring that those who violated the law were not punished more severely than their particular crime deserved. In the same way, a false witness was to receive the same punishment the accused person would have suffered. The principle of making the punishment fit the crime should still be observed today.

20:1 Just like the Israelites, we sometimes face overwhelming opposition. Whether at school, at work, or even at home, we can feel outnumbered and helpless. God bolstered the Israelites' confidence by reminding them that he was always with them and that he had already saved them from the potential danger. We too can feel secure when we consider that God is able to overcome even the most difficult odds.

20:13–18 How could a merciful and just God order the destruction of entire population centers? He did this to protect his people from idol worship, which was certain to bring ruin to Israel (20:18). In fact, because Israel did not completely destroy these evil people as God commanded, Israel was constantly oppressed by them and experienced greater bloodshed and destruction than if they had followed God's instructions in the first place.

20:18
Deut 7:4; 9:5
12:31

20:19,20
2 Chron 26:15

21:5
Deut 10:8; 17:9
19:17

21:6,7
Ps 26:6
Mt 27:24

21:8
Num 35:33,34
Jonah 1:14

21:9
Deut 19:13

21:10
Deut 20:1

21:11
Deut 20:14

21:12
Lev 14:8,9
Num 6:9

21:13
Ps 45:10

21:14
Ex 21:8,11
Deut 22:19

21:17
Gen 49:3

21:18
Deut 27:16
Prov 28:24
30:11,12

21:21
Lev 20:2,27
24:13,14
Num 15:35

ment of the Lord your God. 18The purpose of this command is to prevent the people of the land from luring you into idol worship and into participation in their loathsome customs, thus sinning deeply against the Lord your God.

19"When you besiege a city, don't destroy the fruit trees. Eat all the fruit you wish; just don't cut down the trees. They aren't enemies who need to be slaughtered! 20But you may cut down trees that aren't valuable for food. Use them for the siege [to make ladders, portable towers, and battering rams].

5. Laws for human relationships
Forgiveness for an unsolved murder

21 "If, when you arrive in the Promised Land, a murder victim is found lying in a field and no one has seen the murder, 2the elders and judges shall measure from the body to the nearest city. 3Then the elders of that city shall take a heifer that has never been yoked, 4and lead it to a valley where there is running water—a valley neither plowed nor sowed—and there break its neck.

5"Then the priests shall come (for the Lord your God has chosen them to minister before him and to pronounce his blessings and decide lawsuits and punishments), 6and shall wash their hands over the heifer, 7and say, 'Our hands have not shed this blood, neither have our eyes seen it. 8O Lord, forgive your people Israel whom you have redeemed, and do not charge them with murdering an innocent man. Forgive us the guilt of this man's blood.' 9In this way you will put away the guilt from among you by following the Lord's directions.

Marriage and family

10"When you go to war and the Lord your God delivers your enemies to you, 11and you see among the captives a beautiful girl you want as your wife, 12take her home with you. She must shave her head and pare her nails 13and change her clothing, laying aside that which she was wearing when she was captured, then remain in your home in mourning for her father and mother for a full month. After that you may marry her. 14However, if after marrying her you decide you don't like her, you must let her go free—you may not sell her or treat her as a slave, for you have humiliated her.

15"If a man has two wives but loves one and not the other, and both have borne him children, and the mother of his oldest son is the wife he doesn't love, 16he may not give a larger inheritance to his younger son, the son of the wife he loves. 17He must give the customary double portion to his oldest son, who is the beginning of his strength and who owns the rights of a firstborn son, even though he is the son of the wife his father doesn't love.

18"If a man has a stubborn, rebellious son who will not obey his father or mother, even though they punish him, 19then his father and mother shall take him before the elders of the city 20and declare, 'This son of ours is stubborn and rebellious and won't obey; he is a worthless drunkard.' 21Then the men of the city shall stone him to death. In this way you shall put away this evil from among you, and all the young men of Israel will hear about what happened and will be afraid.

20:20 *to make ladders, portable towers, and battering rams,* implied.

20:19, 20 To keep from destroying the land, the people were warned against needlessly cutting down valuable fruit trees. Israel remained a fruitful, fertile land until medieval times, when the Crusaders destroyed most of the trees and thus prevented the land from replenishing itself. This is the very thing God was warning against.

20:20 Archaeologists have uncovered the remnants of many well-fortified cities in Canaan. Some had tall walls (up to 30 feet high), ramparts, moats, and towers. Accustomed to fighting on the open plains, the Israelites were going to have to learn new battle strategies to conquer these massive fortresses.

21:1–9 When a crime was committed and the criminal got away,

the whole community was held responsible. In much the same way, if a city has a dangerous intersection and someone is killed there, the community may be held responsible for both damages and repairs. God was pointing to the need for the whole community to feel a keen sense of responsibility for what was going on around them and to move to correct any situations that are potentially harmful—physically, socially, or morally.

21:18–21 Disobedient and rebellious children were to be brought before the elders of the city and stoned to death. There is no biblical or archeological record that this punishment was ever carried out, but the point was that disobedience and rebellion were not to be tolerated in the home or allowed to continue unchecked.

Burying criminals

22"If a man has committed a crime worthy of death, and is executed and then hanged on a tree, 23his body shall not remain on the tree overnight. You must bury him the same day, for anyone hanging on a tree is cursed of God. Don't defile the land the Lord your God has given you.

21:22
2 Sam 21:5,6,9
Mt 26:65,66
Mk 14:63,64

21:23
Gal 3:13

Helping neighbors

22 "If you see someone's ox or sheep wandering away, don't pretend you didn't see it; take it back to its owner. 2If you don't know who the owner is, take it to your farm and keep it there until the owner comes looking for it, and then give it to him. 3The same applies to donkeys, clothing, or anything else you find. Keep it for its owner.

4"If you see someone trying to get an ox or donkey onto its feet when it has slipped beneath its load, don't look the other way. Go and help!

22:1
Ex 23:4
Lev 20:4

Various rules

5"A woman must not wear men's clothing, and a man must not wear women's clothing. This is abhorrent to the Lord your God.

6"If a bird's nest is lying on the ground, or if you spy one in a tree, and there are young ones or eggs in it with the mother sitting in the nest, don't take the mother with the young. 7Let her go, and take only the young. The Lord will bless you for it.

8"Every new house must have a guardrail around the edge of the flat rooftop to prevent anyone from falling off and bring guilt to both the house and its owner.

9"Do not sow other crops in the rows of your vineyard. If you do, both the crops and the grapes shall be confiscated by the priests.

10"Don't plow with an ox and a donkey harnessed together.

11"Don't wear clothing woven from two kinds of thread: for instance, wool and linen.

12"You must sew tassels on the four corners of your cloaks.

22:6
Lev 22:28

22:9
Lev 19:19

22:10
2 Cor 6:14

22:12
Num 15:37-39
Mt 23:5

Violations of marriage laws

13, 14"If a man marries a girl, then after sleeping with her accuses her of having had premarital intercourse with another man, saying, 'She was not a virgin when I married her,' 15then the girl's father and mother shall bring the proof of her virginity to the city judges.

16"Her father shall tell them, 'I gave my daughter to this man to be his wife, and now he despises her, 17, 18and has accused her of shameful things, claiming that she was not a virgin when she married; yet here is the proof.' And they shall spread before the judges the blood-stained sheet from her marriage bed. The judges shall

22:13
Deut 24:1

22:4 *when it has slipped beneath its load,* implied. **22:9** *the grapes shall be confiscated by the priests,* literally, "lest the fulness of the fruit be consecrated."

22:1–3 The Hebrews were to care for and return lost animals or possessions to their rightful owner. The way of the world, by contrast, is "Finders keepers, losers weepers." To go beyond the finders-keepers rule by protecting the property of others keeps us from being lustful and greedy.

22:5 This verse commands men and women not to reverse their sexual roles. It is not a statement about clothing styles. Today role rejections are common—there are men who want to become women and women who want to become men. It's not the clothing style that offends God, but using the style to act out a different sex role. God had a purpose in making us uniquely male and female.

22:8–11 These are practical laws, helpful for establishing good habits for everyday living. Verse 8: Since people used their flat roofs as porches, a guardrail was a wise safety precaution.

Verse 9: If you plant two different crops side by side, one of them will not survive since, the stronger, taller one will block the sunlight and take most of the vital nutrients from the soil. Verse 10: A donkey and an ox, due to differences in strength and size, could not pull a plow evenly. Verse 11: Two different kinds of thread wear unevenly and wash differently. Combining them would reduce the life of the garment. Don't think of God's laws as arbitrary restrictions. Look for the reason behind the law. They are not made just to teach or restrict, but also to protect.

22:13–30 Why did God include all these laws about sexual sins? Instructions about sexual behavior would have been vital for three million people on a forty-year camping trip. But they would be equally important when they entered the Promised Land and settled down as a nation. Paul, in Colossians 3:5–8, recognized the importance of strong rules about sex for believers, because sexual

sentence the man to be whipped, ¹⁹and fine him one hundred dollars to be given to the girl's father, for he has falsely accused a virgin of Israel. She shall remain his wife and he may never divorce her. ²⁰But if the man's accusations are true, and she

22:21
Lev 19:29; 21:9
Deut 23:17,18

was not a virgin, ²¹the judges shall take the girl to the door of her father's home where the men of the city shall stone her to death. She has defiled Israel by flagrant crime, being a prostitute while living at home with her parents; and such evil must be cleansed from among you.

22:22
Lev 20:10
Ezek 16:38
Jn 8:5

²²"If a man is discovered committing adultery, both he and the other man's wife must be killed; in this way evil will be cleansed from Israel. ²³, ²⁴If a girl who is

22:23
Lev 19:20
Deut 20:7

engaged is seduced within the walls of a city, both she and the man who seduced her shall be taken outside the gates and stoned to death—the girl because she didn't scream for help, and the man because he has violated the virginity of another man's fiancée. ²⁵, ²⁶, ²⁷In this way you will reduce crime among you. But if this deed takes place out in the country, only the man shall die. The girl is as innocent as a murder victim; for it must be assumed that she screamed, but there was no one to

22:28
Ex 22:16

hear and rescue her out in the field. ²⁸, ²⁹If a man rapes a girl who is not engaged, and is caught in the act, he must pay a fine to the girl's father and marry her; he may

22:30
Lev 18:8; 20:11
Deut 27:20

never divorce her. ³⁰A man shall not sleep with his father's widow since she belonged to his father.

The sanctuary

23:1
Lev 21:20; 22:24

23 "If a man's testicles are crushed or his penis cut off, he shall not enter the sanctuary. ²A bastard may not enter the sanctuary, nor any of his descen-

23:3
Deut 7:1

dants for ten generations.

23:4
Num 23:4,7-10
Neh 13:1
2 Pet 2:15
Jude 11

³"No Ammonite or Moabite may ever enter the sanctuary, even after the tenth generation. ⁴The reason for this law is that these nations did not welcome you with food and water when you came out of Egypt; they even tried to hire Balaam, the son of Beor from Pethor, Mesopotamia, to curse you. ⁵But the Lord wouldn't listen to

23:5
Num 22:35
24:3-9

Balaam; instead, he turned the intended curse into a blessing for you, because the Lord loves you. ⁶You must never, as long as you live, try to help the Ammonites

23:7
Lev 19:34
Num 20:14
Deut 10:19

or the Moabites in any way. ⁷But don't look down on the Edomites and the Egyptians; the Edomites are your brothers and you lived among the Egyptians. ⁸The grandchildren of the Egyptians who came with you from Egypt may enter the

23:8
Num 11:4

sanctuary of the Lord.

The camps

⁹, ¹⁰"When you are at war, the men in the camps must stay away from all evil. Any man who becomes ceremonially defiled because of a seminal emission during

23:11
Lev 15:5,16

the night must leave the camp, ¹¹and stay outside until the evening; then he shall bathe himself and return at sunset. ¹²The toilet area shall be outside the camp. ¹³Each man must have a spade as part of his equipment; after every bowel

23:14
Lev 26:12

movement he must dig a hole with the spade and cover the excrement. ¹⁴The camp must be holy, for the Lord walks among you to protect you and to cause your enemies to fall before you; and the Lord does not want to see anything indecent lest he turn away from you.

Various rules

23:15
1 Sam 22:2
25:10

¹⁵, ¹⁶"If a slave escapes from his master, you must not force him to return; let him live among you in whatever town he shall choose, and do not oppress him.

22:19 *one hundred dollars,* literally, "a hundred shekels of silver." The exact value cannot be determined. **22:28, 29** *he must pay a fine,* literally, "shall pay her father fifty shekels of silver." **22:30** *a man shall not sleep with his father's widow,* literally, "his father's wife." The general law against adultery protected her and other wives while their husbands were living.

---

sins had the power to disrupt and destroy the church. Sins involving sex are not innocent dabblings in forbidden pleasures, as so often portrayed, but powerful destroyers of relationships. They

confuse and tear down the climate of respect, trust, and credibility so essential for solid marriages and secure children.

17, 18"No prostitutes are permitted in Israel, either men or women; you must not bring to the Lord any offering from the earnings of a prostitute or a homosexual, for both are detestable to the Lord your God.

19"Don't demand interest on loans you make to a brother Israelite, whether it is in the form of money, food, or anything else. 20You may take interest from a foreigner, but not from an Israeli. For if you take interest from a brother, an Israeli, the Lord your God won't bless you when you arrive in the Promised Land.

21"When you make a vow to the Lord, be prompt in doing whatever it is you promised him, for the Lord demands that you promptly fulfill your vows; it is a sin if you don't. 22(But it is not a sin if you refrain from vowing!) 23Once you make the vow, you must be careful to do as you have said, for it was your own choice, and you have vowed to the Lord your God.

24"You may eat your fill of the grapes from another man's vineyard, but do not take any away in a container. 25It is the same with someone else's grain—you may eat a few handfuls of it, but don't use a sickle.

24 "If a man doesn't like something about his wife, he may write a letter stating that he has divorced her, give her the letter, and send her away. 2If she then remarries, 3and the second husband also divorces her, or dies, 4the former husband may not marry her again, for she has been defiled; this would bring guilt upon the land the Lord your God is giving you.

5"A newly married man is not to be drafted into the army nor given any other special responsibilities; for a year he shall be free to be at home, happy with his wife.

6"It is illegal to take a millstone as a pledge, for it is a tool by which its owner gains his livelihood. 7If anyone kidnaps a brother Israelite, and treats him as a slave or sells him, the kidnapper must die, in order to purge the evil from among you.

8"Be very careful to follow the instructions of the priest in cases of leprosy, for I have given him rules and guidelines you must obey to the letter: 9Remember what the Lord your God did to Miriam as you were coming from Egypt.

10"If you lend anything to another man, you must not enter his house to get his security. 11Stand outside! The owner will bring it out to you. 12, 13If the man is poor and gives you his cloak as security, you are not to sleep in it. Take it back to him at sundown so that he can use it through the night and bless you; and the Lord your God will count it as righteousness for you.

14, 15"Never oppress a poor hired man, whether a fellow Israelite or a foreigner

23:17
Lev 18:22; 20:13
Deut 22:21

23:19
Ex 22:25
Lev 25:36

23:20
Deut 28:12

23:21
Lev 5:4
Num 15:4
30:1,2
Eccles 5:4
Mt 5:33

23:25
Mt 12:1,2
Mk 2:23
Lk 6:1

24:1
Num 5:12-28
Deut 22:13-21
Jer 3:1
Mal 2:16
Mt 5:31; 19:7
Mk 10:4

24:5
Deut 20:7

24:8
Lev 13:1,59

24:9
Num 12:10

24:10
Deut 15:8

24:12
Ex 22:26

24:14
Lev 19:13
Mt 20:8
1 Tim 5:18
Jas 5:4

23:17, 18 Prostitution was not winked at in God's law—it was strictly forbidden. To forbid this practice may seem obvious to us, but it may not have been so obvious to the Israelites. Almost every other religion known to them included this immoral act. In fact, it was an integral part of many heathen worship services. Prostitution makes a mockery of God's original idea for sex. It treats sex as an isolated physical act rather than an act of commitment to another. Outside of marriage, sex destroys relationship. Within marriage, if approached with the right attitude, it can be a relationship builder. God frequently had to warn the people against the practice of extramarital sex. Today we still need to hear his warnings; young people need to be reminded about premarital sex and adults need to be reminded about sexual fidelity.

24:1–4 Many look at verse 1 as supporting divorce, but that is not the case. It simply recognizes a practice that already existed in Israel. The intent is not to suggest that a man divorce his spouse for any whim or reason. All four verses must be read to understand the point of the passage. Divorce was a permanent and final act for the couple. Once divorced, they could never be remarried if they had established a new relationship with someone else after their divorce (24:4). This restriction was to prevent casual remarriage after a frivolous separation.

24:5 Newly married couples were to remain together their first year. This was to avoid placing an excessive burden upon a new,

unproven relationship and give it a chance to mature and strengthen before confronting it with numerous social responsibilities. A gardener starts a tiny seedling in a small pot and allows it to take root before planting it in the field. Let your marriage grow strong by protecting your relationship from too much outside pressure and distraction—especially in the beginning. And don't expect or demand so much from newlyweds that they have inadequate time or energy to establish their marriage.

24:10–22 Throughout the Old Testament God told his people to treat the poor with justice. The powerless and the unattractive are often looked upon as incompetent or lazy when, in fact, they are often victims of oppression and circumstance. God says we must do all we can to help these needy ones. His justice did not permit the Israelites to insist on profits or quick payment from those who were less fortunate. Instead, his laws gave the poor every opportunity to better their situation, while giving many provisions to help those who couldn't. None of us is completely isolated from the poor. When our lives touch, we are called to do our part to treat them fairly and see that their needs are met.

24:12, 13 The Israelites were not to take advantage of others when seeking justice for themselves. Whenever we demand our own legal rights, we must also be concerned about the needs of our opponent. If we seek justice for others, we may find that we too are being treated more fairly.

living in your town. Pay him his wage each day before sunset, for since he is poor he needs it right away; otherwise he may cry out to the Lord against you and it would be counted as a sin against you.

16"Fathers shall not be put to death for the sins of their sons nor the sons for the sins of their fathers; every man worthy of death shall be executed for his own crime.

17"Justice must be given to migrants and orphans and you must never accept a widow's garment in pledge of her debt. 18Always remember that you were slaves in Egypt, and that the Lord your God rescued you; that is why I have given you this command. 19If, when reaping your harvest, you forget to bring in a sheaf from the field, don't go back after it. Leave it for the migrants, orphans, and widows; then the Lord your God will bless and prosper all you do. 20When you beat the olives from your olive trees, don't go over the boughs twice; leave anything remaining for the migrants, orphans, and widows. 21It is the same for the grapes in your vineyard; don't glean the vines after they are picked, but leave what's left for those in need. 22Remember that you were slaves in the land of Egypt—that is why I am giving you this command.

25 "If a man is guilty of a crime, and the penalty is a beating, the judge shall command him to lie down and be beaten in his presence with up to forty stripes in proportion to the seriousness of the crime; but no more than forty stripes may be given lest the punishment seem too severe, and your brother be degraded in your eyes.

4"Don't muzzle an ox as it treads out the grain.

5"If a man's brother dies without a son, his widow must not marry outside the family; instead, her husband's brother must marry her and sleep with her. 6The first son she bears to him shall be counted as the son of the dead brother, so that his name will not be forgotten. 7But if the dead man's brother refuses to do his duty in this matter, refusing to marry the widow, then she shall go to the city elders and say to them, 'My husband's brother refuses to let his brother's name continue—he refuses to marry me.' 8The elders of the city will then summon him and talk it over with him, and if he still refuses, 9the widow shall walk over to him in the presence of the elders, pull his sandal from his foot and spit in his face. She shall then say, 'This is what happens to a man who refuses to build his brother's house.' 10And ever afterwards his house shall be referred to as 'the home of the man who had his sandal pulled off!'

11"If two men are fighting and the wife of one intervenes to help her husband by grabbing the testicles of the other man, 12her hand shall be cut off without pity.

13, 14, 15"In all your transactions you must use accurate scales and honest measurements, so that you will have a long, good life in the land the Lord your God is giving you. 16All who cheat with unjust weights and measurements are detestable to the Lord your God.

17"You must never forget what the people of Amalek did to you as you came

24:16
2 Kgs 14:6
2 Chron 25:4
Ezek 18:4,20

24:17
Ex 22:21,22
23:2,3
Deut 1:17; 10:17

24:18
Deut 5:15; 24:22

24:19
Lev 19:9,10
Deut 14:28,29

24:20
Lev 19:10

24:22
Deut 15:15
16:12

25:1-3
Deut 17:11
Acts 16:33
2 Cor 11:24

25:4
1 Cor 9:9
1 Tim 5:18

25:5
Gen 38:8
Ruth 1:11,12
Mt 22:24
Mk 12:19
Lk 20:28

25:6
Ruth 4:5

25:9,10
Ruth 4:7,8

25:12
Deut 7:2

25:13
Lev 19:35
Prov 11:1; 16:11
Ezek 45:10,11

25:16
Deut 18:12; 22:5

25:17
Ex 17:8-16

24:19–21 Ruth obtained food for herself and Naomi by gleaning behind the reapers in Boaz's field, picking up the leftovers (Ruth 2:2). Because this law was being obeyed years after it was written, Ruth, a woman in Christ's lineage, was able to find food.

25:1–3 At first glance these verses appear irrelevant today. But a closer look reveals some important principles about discipline. Are you responsible for the discipline of a child, a student, or an employee? Three important points will help you carry out your responsibility: (1) let the punishment follow quickly after the offense; (2) let the degree of punishment reflect the seriousness of the offense; and (3) don't overdo the punishment. Discipline that is swift, just, and restrained makes its point while preserving the dignity of the offender.

25:4 What is the point of this Old Testament regulation? Oxen were often used to tread out the grain on a threshing floor. The animal was attached by poles to a large millstone. As it walked around the millstone, its hooves trampled the grain, separating the

kernel from the chaff. At the same time, the millstone ground the grain into flour. To muzzle the ox would prevent it from eating while it was working. Paul used this illustration in the New Testament in referring to those in Christian work (I Corinthians 9:9, 10; I Timothy 5:17, 18). Paul's emphasis was this: people productive in Christian work should not be denied its benefits—those in Christian service should receive financial support. The fact that one is in Christian ministry doesn't mean he or she should be unfairly paid. There is also a broader application: don't be stingy with those who work for you.

25:5–10 This law describes a "levirate" marriage, the marriage of a widow to the brother of her dead husband. The purpose of such a marriage was to carry on the dead man's name and inheritance. Family ties were an important aspect of Israelite culture. The best way to be remembered was through your line of descendants. If a widow married someone outside the family, her first husband's line would come to an end. Tamar fought for this right in Genesis 38.

from Egypt. 18Remember that they fought with you and struck down those who were faint and weary and lagging behind, with no respect or fear of God. 19Therefore, when the Lord your God has given you rest from all your enemies in the Promised Land, you are utterly to destroy the name of Amalek from under heaven. Never forget this.

25:19
Deut 12:9

Prayers to God

26 "When you arrive in the land and have conquered it and are living there, 2, 3you must present to the Lord at his sanctuary the first sample from each annual harvest. Bring it in a basket and hand it to the priest on duty and say to him, 'This gift is my acknowledgment that the Lord my God has brought me to the land he promised our ancestors.' 4The priest will then take the basket from your hand and set it before the altar. 5You shall then say before the Lord your God, 'My ancestors were migrant Arameans who went to Egypt for refuge. They were few in number, but in Egypt they became a mighty nation. 6, 7The Egyptians mistreated us and we cried to the Lord God. He heard us and saw our hardship, toil, and oppression, 8and brought us out of Egypt with mighty miracles and a powerful hand. He did great and awesome miracles before the Egyptians, 9and has brought us to this place and given us this land "flowing with milk and honey!" 10And now, O Lord, see, I have brought you a token of the first of the crops from the ground you have given me.' Then place the samples before the Lord your God, and worship him. 11Afterwards, go and feast on all the good things he has given you. Celebrate with your family and with any Levites or migrants living among you.

12"Every third year is a year of special tithing. That year you are to give all your tithes to the Levites, migrants, orphans, and widows, so that they will be well fed. 13Then you shall declare before the Lord your God, 'I have given all of my tithes to the Levites, the migrants, the orphans, and the widows, just as you commanded me; I have not violated or forgotten any of your rules. 14I have not touched the tithe while I was ceremonially defiled (for instance, while I was in mourning), nor have I offered any of it to the dead. I have obeyed the Lord my God and have done everything you commanded me. 15Look down from your holy home in heaven and bless your people and the land you have given us, as you promised our ancestors; make it a land "flowing with milk and honey"!'

Keeping God's laws

16"You must wholeheartedly obey all of these commandments and ordinances which the Lord your God is giving you today. 17You have declared today that he is your God, and you have promised to obey and keep his laws and ordinances, and to heed all he tells you to do. 18And the Lord has declared today that you are his very own people, just as he promised, and that you must obey all of his laws. 19If you do, he will make you greater than any other nation, allowing you to receive praise, honor, and renown; but to attain this honor and renown you must be a holy people to the Lord your God, as he requires."

26:1
Deut 6:1
26:2
Ex 22:29
23:16,19

26:5
Gen 43:1; 46:27
Deut 1:10; 10:22
26:6
Ex 1:11,12
Deut 4:20
26:8
Deut 4:34
26:9
Ex 3:8,17
Deut 27:2-4
Josh 5:6

26:11
Deut 12:7,12

26:12
Deut 14:28,29
Heb 7:5,9,10

26:15
1 Kgs 8:30
2 Chron 30:27
Zech 2:13

26:16
Deut 6:5,17
26:17
Ex 24:3
Lev 18:4,5
Deut 5:1
26:18
Deut 7:6
26:19
Deut 28:1,13

6. Consequences of obedience and disobedience
A monument for God's laws

27 Then Moses and the elders of Israel gave the people these further instructions to obey:

26:2, 3 *from each annual,* implied. **27:1** *gave the people these further instructions to obey,* literally, "Keep all the commandments I enjoin on you today."

26:1–3 The Feast of the First Fruits (Leviticus 23:9–14) was a reminder to the people of all God had provided for them. When they arrived in the Promised Land, the people were to recite a confession that would retell the story of their small beginnings in Egypt, their growth into a mighty nation, and their journey to conquer and claim the land given them by God.

26:5–10 In Israelite tradition, each person was required to recite the history of God's dealings with his people. What is the history of your relationship with God? Can you put into clear and concise words what God has done for you? Find a friend with whom you can share your spiritual journey. Take turns telling your stories. This will help you get a firm grip on your personal spiritual history, as well as encouraging and inspiring you both.

27:2
Deut 26:9
Josh 8:30-32

2, 3, 4"When you cross the Jordan River and go into the Promised Land—a land 'flowing with milk and honey'—take out boulders from the river bottom and immediately pile them into a monument on the other side, at Mount Ebal. Face the stones with a coating of lime and then write the laws of God in the lime. 5, 6And build an altar there to the Lord your God. Use uncut boulders, and on the altar offer burnt offerings to the Lord your God. 7Sacrifice peace offerings upon it also, and feast there with great joy before the Lord your God. 8Write all of these laws plainly [upon the monument].''

27:7
Lev 7:11
Num 6:14; 7:88

27:9
Deut 26:17

9Then Moses and the Levite-priests addressed all Israel as follows: "O Israel, listen! Today you have become the people of the Lord your God, 10so today you must begin to obey all of these commandments I have given you.''

The Levites shout twelve curses

27:12
Deut 11:26
Josh 8:33-35

11That same day Moses gave this charge to the people:

27:15
Ex 20:4,23
34:17
Lev 19:3,4
Deut 4:16; 5:8

12"When you cross into the Promised Land, the tribes of Simeon, Levi, Judah, Issachar, Joseph, and Benjamin shall stand upon Mount Gerizim to proclaim a blessing, 13and the tribes of Reuben, Gad, Asher, Zebulun, Dan, and Naphtali shall stand upon Mount Ebal to proclaim a curse. 14Then the Levites standing between them shall shout to all Israel,

27:16
Ex 21:15
Lev 20:9
Deut 21:18
Ezek 22:7

15" 'The curse of God be upon anyone who makes and worships an idol, even in secret, whether carved of wood or made from molten metal—for these handmade gods are hated by the Lord.' And all the people shall reply, 'Amen.'

27:17
Deut 19:14

16" 'Cursed is anyone who despises his father or mother.' And all the people shall reply, 'Amen.'

27:18
Lev 19:14

17" 'Cursed is he who moves the boundary marker between his land and his neighbor's.' And all the people shall reply, 'Amen.'

27:19
Ex 22:21
Lev 19:33
Deut 10:18
24:17
Ezek 22:7

18" 'Cursed is he who takes advantage of a blind man.' And all the people shall reply, 'Amen.'

19" 'Cursed is he who is unjust to the foreigner, the orphan, and the widow.' And all the people shall reply, 'Amen.'

27:20
Lev 18:8; 20:11
Deut 22:30

20" 'Cursed is he who commits adultery with one of his father's wives, for she belongs to his father.' And all the people shall reply, 'Amen.'

27:21
Ex 22:19
Lev 18:23; 20:15

21" 'Cursed is he who has sexual intercourse with an animal.' And all the people shall reply, 'Amen.'

27:22
Lev 18:9; 20:17

22" 'Cursed is he who has sexual intercourse with his sister, whether she be a full sister or a half-sister.' And all the people shall reply, 'Amen.'

27:23
Lev 18:17; 20:14

23" 'Cursed is he who has sexual intercourse with his widowed mother-in-law.' And all the people shall reply, 'Amen.'

27:24
Ex 21:12
Lev 24:17
Num 35:30
Deut 19:13
Ps 64:4

24" 'Cursed is he who secretly slays another.' And all the people shall reply, 'Amen.'

27:25
Ex 23:8
Deut 10:17

25" 'Cursed is he who accepts a bribe to kill an innocent person.' And all the people shall reply, 'Amen.'

27:2-4 *with a coating of lime,* literally, "plaster them with plaster." **27:8** *upon the monument,* implied. See vss 1-4. **27:14** *Then the Levites standing between,* implied. **27:23** *widowed,* implied. If she were still married, no special law would be needed to prohibit adultery.

27:9, 10 Moses said that because the Israelites were now God's people, they needed to start obeying God's commands. If we decide to believe in God, we must also decide to follow his ways. What we do shows what we really believe. Examine yourself and ask if people are able to discern that you are a member of God's family.

27:15–26 These curses were actually a series of oaths, spoken by the priests, by which the people promised to stay away from wrong actions. Not only did the people hear the laws; they responded by saying Amen, "So be it." By doing this, they took responsibility for their actions. Sometimes looking at a list of curses like this gives us the idea that God has a bad temper and is out to crush anyone who steps out of line. But we need to see these restrictions not as threats, but as loving warnings about the plain

facts of life. Just as we warn children to stay away from hot stoves and busy streets, God warns us to stay away from dangerous actions. The natural law of his universe makes it clear that wrongdoing toward man or God has tragic consequences. God is merciful enough to tell us this truth plainly. Motivated by love and not anger, his strong words are necessary to warn of the serious consequences that will result from choosing to neglect God or wrong others. But God does not leave us with only curses or consequences. Immediately following these curses, we discover the great blessings (positive consequences) that come from living for God (28:1–14). These give us extra incentive to obey God's laws. While all these blessings may not come in our lifetime on earth, those who obey God will experience the fullness of his blessing when he establishes the new heavens and the new earth.

26" 'Cursed is anyone who does not obey these laws.' And all the people shall reply, 'Amen.'

27:26
Deut 5:1; 28:15
Gal 3:10

Blessings for obedience

28 "If you fully obey all of these commandments of the Lord your God, the laws I am declaring to you today, God will transform you into the greatest nation in the world. 2–6These are the blessings that will come upon you:

28:1
Ex 15:26; 23:22
Lev 26:3
Deut 7:12; 11:13
28:2
Lev 26:9
Deut 28:8
Ps 107:36-38
Amos 9:13

Blessings in the city,
Blessings in the field;
Many children,
Ample crops,
Large flocks and herds;
Blessings of fruit and bread;
Blessings when you come in,
Blessings when you go out.

7"The Lord will defeat your enemies before you; they will march out together against you but scatter before you in seven directions! 8The Lord will bless you with good crops and healthy cattle, and prosper everything you do when you arrive in the land the Lord your God is giving you. 9He will change you into a holy people dedicated to himself; this he has promised to do if you will only obey him and walk in his ways. 10All the nations in the world shall see that you belong to the Lord, and they will stand in awe.

28:7
Lev 26:7
Deut 32:30
Josh 10:10
Ps 89:23
28:8
Lev 25:21,22
26:4,5
28:9
Ex 19:5
Deut 7:6; 26:18

11"The Lord will give you an abundance of good things in the land, just as he promised: many children, many cattle, and abundant crops. 12He will open to you his wonderful treasury of rain in the heavens, to give you fine crops every season. He will bless everything you do; and you shall lend to many nations, but shall not borrow from them. 13If you will only listen and obey the commandments of the Lord your God that I am giving you today, he will make you the head and not the tail, and you shall always have the upper hand. 14But each of these blessings depends on your not turning aside in any way from the laws I have given you; and you must never worship other gods.

28:11
Lev 26:9
Deut 28:2-6,8
30:9
28:12
Lev 26:4
Deut 11:14
23:20
28:13
Deut 28:1,44
28:14
Deut 5:32,33
19:9

Curses for disobedience

15-19"If you won't listen to the Lord your God and won't obey these laws I am giving you today, then all of these curses shall come upon you:

28:15
Lev 26:14
Deut 27:15
28:1-6
Josh 23:15,16

Curses in the city,
Curses in the fields,
Curses on your fruit and bread,
The curse of barren wombs,
Curses upon your crops,
Curses upon the fertility of your cattle and flocks,
Curses when you come in,
Curses when you go out.

20"For the Lord himself will send his personal curse upon you. You will be confused and a failure in everything you do, until at last you are destroyed because of the sin of forsaking him. 21He will send disease among you until you are destroyed from the face of the land which you are about to enter and possess. 22He will send tuberculosis, fever, infections, plague, and war. He will blight your crops, covering them with mildew. All these devastations shall pursue you until you perish.

28:20
Deut 8:11; 28:25
28:21
Lev 26:25
Num 14:12
1 Kgs 8:37
Amos 4:10
28:23
Lev 26:19
28:24
Deut 11:17
1 Kgs 17:1
Jer 14:1
28:25
Lev 26:17,36
2 Chron 29:8
Isa 30:17
Jer 15:4

23"The heavens above you will be as unyielding as bronze, and the earth beneath will be as iron. 24The land will become as dry as dust for lack of rain, and dust storms shall destroy you.

25"The Lord will cause you to be defeated by your enemies. You will march out to battle gloriously, but flee before your enemies in utter confusion; and you will be

28:26
Ps 79:2
Jer 7:33; 16:4
19:7; 34:20

28:27
Ex 9:9; 15:26
Lev 13:1,2
Deut 7:15
1 Sam 5:6,9,12

28:28
Isa 19:14

28:29
Ex 10:21
Job 5:14
Ps 69:23
Isa 59:10

28:30
Deut 20:6,7
Job 31:10
Isa 65:21
Jer 8:10
Amos 5:11

28:32
2 Chron 29:9
Neh 5:2,5

28:34
Deut 28:28

28:35
Job 2:7
Isa 3:17

28:36
Deut 4:28
2 Kgs 17:4,6
24:12,14
25:7,11

28:37
Deut 29:22

28:38
Lev 26:20
Isa 5:10
Joel 1:4
Mic 6:15

28:39
Amos 5:11
Mic 6:15

28:41
Deut 28:32

28:42
Deut 28:38
Amos 7:11

28:44
Deut 28:12,13

28:45
Lev 26:28
Deut 4:25,26
29:20

28:47
Lev 26:13
Deut 28:36
Jer 28:14
Lam 1:3

28:49
Deut 28:36
Isa 5:26; 7:18
Jer 5:15

28:52
2 Kgs 19:30
25:1
2 Chron 32:1
Jer 10:17,18
Zeph 1:14,15

28:53
Lev 26:29

tossed to and fro among all the nations of the earth. 26Your dead bodies will be food to the birds and wild animals, and no one will be there to chase them away.

27"He will send upon you Egyptian boils, tumors, scurvy, and itch, for none of which there will be a remedy. 28He will send madness, blindness, fear, and panic upon you. 29You shall grope in the bright sunlight just as the blind man gropes in darkness. You shall not prosper in anything you do; you will be oppressed and robbed continually, and nothing will save you.

30"Someone else will marry your fiancée; someone else will live in the house you build; someone else will eat the fruit of the vineyard you plant. 31Your oxen shall be butchered before your eyes, but you won't get a single bite of the meat. Your donkeys will be driven away as you watch, and will never return to you again. Your sheep will be given to your enemies. And there will be no one to protect you. 32You will watch as your sons and daughters are taken away as slaves. Your heart will break with longing for them, but you will not be able to help them. 33A foreign nation you have not even heard of will eat the crops you will have worked so hard to grow. You will always be oppressed and crushed. 34You will go mad because of all the tragedy you see around you. 35The Lord will cover you with boils from head to foot.

36"He will exile you and the king you will choose, to a nation to whom neither you nor your ancestors gave a second thought; and while in exile you shall worship gods of wood and stone! 37You will become an object of horror, a proverb and a byword among all the nations, for the Lord will thrust you away.

38"You will sow much but reap little, for the locusts will eat your crops. 39You will plant vineyards and care for them, but you won't eat the grapes or drink the wine, for worms will destroy the vines. 40Olive trees will be growing everywhere, but there won't be enough olive oil to anoint yourselves! For the trees will drop their fruit before it is matured. 41Your sons and daughters will be snatched away from you as slaves. 42The locusts shall destroy your trees and vines. 43Foreigners living among you shall become richer and richer while you become poorer and poorer. 44They shall lend to you, not you to them! They shall be the head and you shall be the tail!

45"All these curses shall pursue and overtake you until you are destroyed—all because you refuse to listen to the Lord your God. 46These horrors shall befall you and your descendants as a warning: 47, 48You will become slaves to your enemies because of your failure to praise God for all that he has given you. The Lord will send your enemies against you, and you will be hungry, thirsty, naked, and in want of everything. A yoke of iron shall be placed around your neck until you are destroyed!

49"The Lord will bring a distant nation against you, swooping down upon you like an eagle; a nation whose language you don't understand— 50a nation of fierce and angry men who will have no mercy upon young or old. 51They will eat you out of house and home until your cattle and crops are gone. Your grain, new wine, olive oil, calves, and lambs will all disappear. 52That nation will lay siege to your cities and knock down your highest walls—the walls you will trust to protect you. 53You will even eat the flesh of your own sons and daughters in the terrible days of siege that lie ahead. 54The most tenderhearted man among you will be utterly callous toward his own brother and his beloved wife and his children who are still alive. 55He will refuse to give them a share of the flesh he is devouring—the flesh of his own children—because he is starving in the midst of the siege of your cities. 56, 57The most tender and delicate woman among you—the one who would not so

---

28:34 One of the curses for those who rejected God was that they would go mad from seeing all the tragedy around them. Do you ever feel that you will go crazy if you hear about one more rape, kidnaping, murder, or war? Much of the world's evil is a result of people's failure to acknowledge and serve God. When you hear bad news, don't groan helplessly as do unbelievers who have no

hope for the future. Remind yourself that in spite of it all, God has ultimate control and will one day come back to make everything right.

28:36 This is a prediction of the days when Assyria and Babylon would take the Israelites captive to their lands (2 Kings 17:23; 25:11).

much as touch her feet to the ground—will refuse to share with her beloved husband, son, and daughter. She will hide from them the afterbirth and the new baby she has borne, so that she herself can eat them: so terrible will be the hunger during the siege and the awful distress caused by your enemies at your gates.

58, 59"If you refuse to obey all the laws written in this book, thus refusing reverence to the glorious and fearful name of Jehovah your God, then Jehovah will send perpetual plagues upon you and upon your children. 60He will bring upon you all the diseases of Egypt which you feared so much, and they shall plague the land. 61And that is not all! The Lord will bring upon you every sickness and plague there is, even those not mentioned in this book, until you are destroyed. 62There will be few of you left, though before you were as numerous as stars. All this if you do not listen to the Lord your God.

63"Just as the Lord has rejoiced over you and has done such wonderful things for you and has multiplied you, so the Lord at that time will rejoice in destroying you; and you shall disappear from the land. 64For the Lord will scatter you among all the nations from one end of the earth to the other. There you will worship heathen gods that neither you nor your ancestors have known, gods made of wood and stone! 65There among those nations you shall find no rest, but the Lord will give you trembling hearts, darkness, and bodies wasted from sorrow and fear. 66Your lives will hang in doubt. You will live night and day in fear, and will have no reason to believe that you will see the morning light. 67In the morning you will say, 'Oh, that night were here!' And in the evening you will say, 'Oh, that morning were here!' You will say this because of the awesome horrors surrounding you. 68Then the Lord will send you back to Egypt in ships, a journey I promised you would never need to make again; and there you will offer to sell yourselves to your enemies as slaves—but no one will even want to buy you."

28:58
Lev 26:14
Deut 28:15

28:60
Deut 28:21,27

28:62
Deut 1:10

28:63
Deut 30:9
Jer 45:4

28:64
Lev 26:33
Deut 4:27; 32:17
Neh 1:8
Jer 16:13
Lk 21:24

28:65
Lam 1:3

28:66
Heb 10:27

28:67
Deut 28:34

28:68
Deut 17:16

C. A CALL FOR COMMITMENT TO GOD: MOSES' THIRD ADDRESS (29:1—30:20)

After reviewing God's laws, Moses calls for commitment, urging the people to honor the contract they had previously made with God. Knowing God's Word is not enough, we must obey it.

Moses restates God's contract

29 It was on the plains of Moab that Moses restated the covenant which the Lord had made with the people of Israel at Mount Horeb. 2, 3He summoned all Israel before him and told them,

"You have seen with your own eyes the great plagues and mighty miracles that the Lord brought upon Pharaoh and his people in the land of Egypt. 4But even yet the Lord hasn't given you hearts that understand or eyes that see or ears that hear! 5For forty years God has led you through the wilderness, yet your clothes haven't become old, and your shoes haven't worn out! 6The reason he hasn't let you settle down to grow grain for bread or grapes for wine and strong drink, is so that you would realize that it is the Lord your God who has been caring for you.

7"When we came here, King Sihon of Heshbon and King Og of Bashan came out against us in battle, but we destroyed them, 8and took their land and gave it to the tribes of Reuben and Gad and to the half-tribe of Manasseh as their inheritance. 9Therefore, obey the terms of this covenant so that you will prosper in everything you do. 10All of you—your leaders, the people, your judges, and your administra-

29:1
Lev 27:34
Deut 1:1-5; 5:1

29:2
Lev 8:1
Num 1:17-19

29:4
Isa 6:9,10
Acts 28:26
Rom 11:8

29:5
Deut 8:2,4

29:7
Num 21:21
Deut 1:2-5; 2:26

29:8
Num 32:31
Deut 3:12

29:9
Ex 19:5
Deut 4:6
Josh 1:7

28:64 This severe warning tragically came true when Israel was defeated and carried away into captivity by Assyria (722 B.C.), and Judah to Babylon (586 B.C.). Later, in A.D. 70, Roman oppression forced many Jews to flee their homeland. Thus, the people were dispersed throughout the various nations.

29:1ff At Mount Sinai, 40 years earlier, God and Israel had made a covenant (Exodus 19, 20). Although there were many parts to the covenant (read the books of Exodus, Leviticus, and Numbers), its purpose can be summed up in one sentence: God promised to bless the Israelites by making them the nation through whom the

rest of the world could know God. The Israelites promised to love and obey God in order to receive physical and spiritual blessings. Here Moses reviews this covenant. God was still keeping his part of the bargain (and he always would), but the Israelites were already neglecting their part. Moses restated the covenant to warn the people that if they did not keep their part of the agreement, they would experience severe discipline.

29:18 Moses cautioned that the day the Hebrews chose to turn from God, a root would be planted that would produce bitter fruit.

29:11
Josh 9:21,23,27

29:12
Deut 5:2

29:13
Gen 17:7
Ex 6:7
Deut 7:6; 26:18

29:14
Jer 31:31
Heb 8:7

29:16
Deut 2:4

29:17
Ex 20:23
Deut 4:28; 28:36

29:18
Deut 13:6; 32:32
Jer 9:15
Hos 10:4
Heb 12:15

29:19
Num 15:30,39
Ps 10:4-6
49:18,19
Prov 29:1
Jer 5:12

29:20
Deut 9:14
2 Kgs 14:27
Ps 74:1; 80:4

29:22
Jer 19:8

29:23
Gen 19:24
Isa 1:7; 34:9
64:11

29:24
1 Kgs 9:8
2 Chron 7:21
Jer 22:8
Lam 2:15

29:25
2 Kgs 17:9
2 Chron 36:13
Jer 40:2,3; 50:7

29:27
Deut 29:20

29:28
1 Kgs 14:15
Ezek 19:12

29:29
Job 11:6,7
Ps 25:14; 78:2-7

30:1
Lev 26:40,41
Deut 4:30; 11:26

tive officers—are standing today before the Lord your God, 11along with your little ones and your wives and the foreigners that are among you—those who chop your wood and carry your water. 12You are standing here to enter into a contract with Jehovah your God, a contract he is making with you today. 13He wants to confirm you today as his people, and to confirm that he is your God, just as he promised your ancestors, Abraham, Isaac, and Jacob. 14, 15This contract is not with you alone as you stand before him today, but with all future generations of Israel as well.

16"Surely you remember how we lived in the land of Egypt, and how as we left, we came safely through the territory of enemy nations. 17And you have seen their heathen idols made of wood, stone, silver, and gold. 18The day that any of you—man or woman, family or tribe of Israel—begins to turn away from the Lord our God and desires to worship these gods of other nations, that day a root will be planted that will grow bitter and poisonous fruit.

19"Let no one blithely think, when he hears the warnings of this curse, 'I shall prosper even though I walk in my own stubborn way!' 20For the Lord will not pardon! His anger and jealousy will be hot against that man. And all the curses written in this book shall lie heavily upon him, and the Lord will blot out his name from under heaven. 21The Lord will separate that man from all the tribes of Israel, to pour out upon him all the curses (which are recorded in this book) that befall those who break this contract. 22Then your children and the generations to come and the foreigners that pass by from distant lands shall see the devastation of the land and the diseases the Lord will have sent upon it. 23They will see that the whole land is alkali and salt, a burned over wasteland, unsown, without crops, without a shred of vegetation—just like Sodom and Gomorrah and Admah and Zeboiim, destroyed by the Lord in his anger.

24" 'Why has the Lord done this to his land?' the nations will ask. 'Why was he so angry?'

25"And they will be told, 'Because the people of the land broke the contract made with them by Jehovah, the God of their ancestors, when he brought them out of the land of Egypt. 26For they worshiped other gods, violating his express command. 27That is why the anger of the Lord was hot against this land, so that all his curses (which are recorded in this book) broke forth upon them. 28In great anger the Lord rooted them out of their land and threw them away into another land, where they still live today!'

29"There are secrets the Lord your God has not revealed to us, but these words which he has revealed are for us and our children to obey forever.

Returning to the Lord

30 "When all these things have happened to you—the blessings and the curses I have listed—you will meditate upon them as you are living among the

---

When we decide to do what we know is wrong, we plant an evil seed that begins to grow out of control, eventually yielding a crop of sorrow and pain. But we can prevent those seeds of sin from taking root. If you have done something wrong, confess it to God and others immediately. If the seed never finds fertile soil, its bitter fruit will never ripen.

29:29 There are some things God has chosen not to reveal to us, possibly for the following reasons: (1) our finite minds cannot understand some of the infinite aspects of God's universe; (2) some things are unnecessary for us to know; and (3) since God is infinite and all-knowing, it is simply impossible for us to know everything he does. This verse shows that although God has not told us everything there is to know about obeying him, he has told us enough. Thus, disobedience comes from an act of the will, not from a lack of knowledge. Through God's Word we know enough about what to do. Our next step is to make the necessary effort.

30:1-6 The theme of verses 1-6 is frequently found in the writings of the prophets. Although the Israelites will be punished for their

sin, made captives, and exiled to distant lands, God will let them return one day to their homeland. This prediction was fulfilled in part when many Israelites returned from 70 years of captivity in Babylon (Ezra 1, 2). It will be fulfilled completely at the Second Coming of Jesus Christ. Then all believers, Jews and non-Jews, will be gathered from the ends of the earth to worship Christ in his new kingdom.

30:1-6 Moses told the Hebrews that when they were ready to return to God, he would be ready to receive them. God's mercy is unbelievable. It goes far beyond what we can imagine. Even if the Jews deliberately walked away from him and ruined their lives, God would still take them back. God wants to forgive us and bring us back to himself too. Some people will not learn until their world has crashed in around them. Then the sorrow and pain seem to open their eyes to what God has been saying all along. Are you separated from God by sin? This verse assures us that no matter how far we have wandered, God promises a fresh beginning if only we will turn to him.

nations where the Lord your God will have driven you. 2If at that time you want to return to the Lord your God, and you and your children have begun wholeheartedly to obey all of the commandments I have given you today, 3then the Lord your God will rescue you from your captivity! He will have mercy upon you and come and gather you out of all the nations where he will have scattered you. 4Though you are at the ends of the earth, he will go and find you and bring you back again 5to the land of your ancestors. You shall possess the land again, and he will do you good and bless you even more than he did your ancestors! 6He will cleanse your hearts and the hearts of your children and of your children's children so that you will love the Lord your God with all your hearts and souls, and Israel shall come alive again!

7, 8"If you return to the Lord and obey all the commandments that I command you today, the Lord your God will take his curses and turn them against your enemies—against those who hate you and persecute you. 9The Lord your God will prosper everything you do and give you many children and much cattle and wonderful crops; for the Lord will again rejoice over you as he did over your fathers. 10He will rejoice if you but obey the commandments written in this book of the law, and if you turn to the Lord your God with all your hearts and souls.

The choice of life or death

11"Obeying these commandments is not something beyond your strength and reach; 12for these laws are not in the far heavens, so distant that you can't hear and obey them, and with no one to bring them down to you; 13nor are they beyond the ocean, so far that no one can bring you their message; 14but they are very close at hand—in your hearts and on your lips—so obey them.

15"Look, today I have set before you life and death, depending on whether you obey or disobey. 16I have commanded you today to love the Lord your God and to follow his paths and to keep his laws, so that you will live and become a great nation, and so that the Lord your God will bless you and the land you are about to possess. 17But if your hearts turn away and you won't listen—if you are drawn away to worship other gods— 18then I declare to you this day that you shall surely perish; you will not have a long, good life in the land you are going in to possess.

19"I call heaven and earth to witness against you that today I have set before you life or death, blessing or curse. Oh, that you would choose life; that you and your children might live! 20Choose to love the Lord your God and to obey him and to cling to him, for he is your life and the length of your days. You will then be able to live safely in the land the Lord promised your ancestors, Abraham, Isaac, and Jacob."

30:2
Lev 26:3
Deut 26:16
Neh 1:8,9
30:3
Gen 28:15
48:21
Ps 106:45-47
Isa 56:8
Mt 23:37
Jn 12:51,52
30:4
Isa 43:5,6
48:20; 62:11
30:5
Deut 13:17
Jer 29:14; 30:3
30:7
Ex 23:22
Deut 25:19
28:7; 30:2
30:9
Deut 15:10; 29:9
30:10
Deut 4:29
Ezek 18:21
30:11-14
Isa 45:19
Rom 16:25-27
30:12-14
Rom 10:6-8
30:15
Deut 11:26
Jer 21:8
Mt 7:13,14
30:16
Deut 4:1; 6:5
30:6
30:17
Deut 28:15,36,
64; 29:18
30:18
Deut 25:13-15
31:29
30:19
Deut 4:26
31:28; 32:1
Isa 1:2
30:20
Deut 10:20; 13:4
Josh 22:5

D. THE CHANGE IN LEADERSHIP: MOSES' LAST DAYS (31:1—34:12)

Realizing that he is about to die, Moses commissions Joshua, records the laws in a permanent form, and teaches a special song to the Israelites. Thus Moses prepared the people for his departure. Similarly, we should not allow others to become dependent upon us for their spiritual growth, but help them to become dependent upon God.

Moses commissions Joshua

31 After Moses had said all these things to the people of Israel, 2he told them, "I am now 120 years old! I am no longer able to lead you, for the Lord has told me that I shall not cross the Jordan River. 3But the Lord himself will lead you, and will destroy the nations living there, and you shall overcome them. Joshua is your new commander, as the Lord has instructed. 4The Lord will destroy the

31:2
Deut 1:37; 34:7
Acts 7:23,30
31:3
Num 27:18
Deut 3:28; 34:9
Josh 1:2; 3:7

31:2 *I am no longer able to lead you,* literally, "I am no longer able to go out and come in."

30:11-14 God has called us to obey his commandments, while reminding us that his laws are not too difficult to follow. Have you ever said you would obey God if you knew what he wanted? Have you ever complained that obedience is too difficult for a mere human? These are unacceptable excuses. God's laws are written in the Bible and are clearly evident in the world around us. Obeying them is reasonable, sensible, and beneficial. The most difficult part of obeying God's laws is simply deciding to do so.

30:19, 20 Moses reminded Israel of all that God had done for them. He challenged them to choose to obey God and therefore continue to experience his blessings. God doesn't force his will on anyone. He lets us decide whether to follow him or reject him. This decision, however, is a life or death matter. God wants us to realize this, for he would like us all to choose life. Daily, with each new circumstance of life, we must decide again.

nations living in the land, just as he destroyed Sihon and Og, the kings of the Amorites. 5The Lord will deliver over to you the people living there, and you shall destroy them as I have commanded you. 6Be strong! Be courageous! Do not be afraid of them! For the Lord your God will be with you. He will neither fail you nor forsake you."

31:6
Deut 20:1
Heb 13:5

7Then Moses called for Joshua and said to him, as all Israel watched, "Be strong! Be courageous! For you shall lead these people into the land promised by the Lord to their ancestors; see to it that they conquer it. 8Don't be afraid, for the Lord will go before you and will be with you; he will not fail nor forsake you."

31:7
Deut 1:38; 3:28

Moses records the laws

9Then Moses wrote out the laws he had already delivered to the people and gave them to the priests, the sons of Levi, who carried the Ark containing the Ten Commandments of the Lord. Moses also gave copies of the laws to the elders of Israel. 10, 11The Lord commanded that these laws be read to all the people at the end of every seventh year—the Year of Release—at the Festival of Tabernacles, when all Israel would assemble before the Lord at the sanctuary.

31:9
Num 4:5,6
Deut 10:8

31:10
Deut 12:4,5
15:1

12"Call them all together," the Lord instructed, "—men, women, children, and foreigners living among you—to hear the laws of God and to learn his will, so that you will reverence the Lord your God and obey his laws. 13Do this so that your little children who have not known these laws will hear them and learn how to revere the Lord your God as long as you live in the Promised Land."

31:12
Deut 4:10; 29:11

Israel's disobedience predicted

14Then the Lord said to Moses, "The time has come when you must die. Summon Joshua and come into the Tabernacle where I can give him his instructions." So Moses and Joshua came and stood before the Lord.

31:14
Num 27:13
Deut 34:5

15He appeared to them in a great cloud at the Tabernacle entrance, 16and said to Moses, "You shall die and join your ancestors. After you are gone, these people will begin worshiping foreign gods in the Promised Land. They will forget about me and break the contract I have made with them. 17Then my anger will flame out against them and I will abandon them, hiding my face from them, and they shall be destroyed. Terrible trouble will come upon them, so that they will say, 'God is no longer among us!' 18I will turn away from them because of their sins in worshiping other gods.

31:15
Ex 16:10
31:16
Deut 4:25; 32:50
Judg 2:11; 10:6
31:17
Judg 2:12-14

19"Now write down the words of this song, and teach it to the people of Israel as my warning to them. 20When I have brought them into the land I promised their ancestors—a land 'flowing with milk and honey'—and when they have become fat and prosperous, and worship other gods and despise me and break my contract, 21and great disasters come upon them, then this song will remind them of the reason for their woes. (For this song will live from generation to generation.) I know now, even before they enter the land, what these people are like."

31:20
Deut 6:10-12
8:10,19
11:16,17

31:21
Lev 26:40,41

22So, on that very day, Moses wrote down the words of the song and taught it to the Israelites. 23Then he charged Joshua (son of Nun) to be strong and courageous, and said to him, "You must bring the people of Israel into the land the Lord promised them; for the Lord says, 'I will be with you.'"

31:10–13 The laws were read to the whole assembly so that everyone, including the children, could hear them. Every seven years the entire nation gathered together and listened to a priest read the Law to them. There were no books, Bibles, or newsstands to spread God's Word, so the people had to rely on word of mouth and an accurate memory. Memorization was an important part of worship, for if everyone knew the law, ignorance would be no excuse for breaking it. To fulfill the purpose and will of God in our lives, we need the content and substance of his Word in our hearts and minds. For the Hebrews, this process began in childhood. Teaching our children and new believers should be one of our top priorities. Our finest teachers, best resources, and most careful thought should be directed toward showing them how to follow God in all life's situations.

31:23 Joshua had been appointed to take over the leadership of Israel and guide the people into the Promised Land (Moses could not enter the land due to his disobedience—Numbers 20:12). Joshua, first mentioned in Exodus 17:9, had been Moses' assistant for many years (Joshua 1:1). One of his key qualifications was his faith. As one of the twelve spies to first enter Canaan, only he and Caleb believed that God could help Israel conquer the land (Numbers 13:1—14:30). He was strong and courageous because he knew God was with him, and he had faith that God would do all he had promised Israel.

24When Moses had finished writing down all the laws that are recorded in this book, 25he instructed the Levites who carried the Ark containing the Ten Commandments 26to put this book of the law beside the Ark, as a solemn warning to the people of Israel.

31:25
Deut 31:9

27"For I know how rebellious and stubborn you are," Moses told them. "If even today, while I am still here with you, you are defiant rebels against the Lord, how much more rebellious will you be after my death! 28Now summon all the elders and officers of your tribes so that I can speak to them, and call heaven and earth to witness against them. 29I know that after my death you will utterly defile yourselves and turn away from God and his commands; and in the days to come evil will crush you for you will do what the Lord says is evil, making him very angry."

31:27
Deut 9:6,7,13, 14

31:28
Deut 30:19; 32:1

31:29
Deut 32:5

Moses' song

30So Moses recited this entire song to the whole assembly of Israel:

32 "Listen, O heavens and earth!
    Listen to what I say!
2My words shall fall upon you
  Like the gentle rain and dew,
  Like rain upon the tender grass,
  Like showers on the hillside.
3I will proclaim the greatness of the Lord.
  How glorious he is!
4He is the Rock. His work is perfect.
  Everything he does is just and fair.
  He is faithful, without sin.
5But Israel has become corrupt,
  Smeared with sin. They are no longer his;
  They are a stubborn, twisted generation.
6Is this the way you treat Jehovah?
  O foolish people,
  Is not God your Father?
  Has he not created you?
  Has he not established you and made you strong?
7Remember the days of long ago!
  (Ask your father and the aged men;
  They will tell you all about it.)
8When God divided up the world among the nations,
  He gave each of them a supervising angel!
9But he appointed none for Israel;
  For Israel was God's own personal possession!
10God protected them in the howling wilderness
   As though they were the apple of his eye.
11He spreads his wings over them,
   Even as an eagle overspreads her young.
   She carries them upon her wings—
   As does the Lord his people!
12When the Lord alone was leading them,
   And they lived without foreign gods,

32:1
Deut 4:26
Isa 1:2

32:2
Ps 72:6
Isa 55:10

32:3
Gen 18:25
Ex 34:5,6
Deut 3:23-25
5:24

32:4
Gen 49:24
Deut 32:18
2 Sam 22:2

32:5
Deut 4:25; 31:27
Mt 17:17

32:6
Deut 1:31; 32:28

32:7
Deut 7:18,19
8:2

32:9
Deut 1:19-21
1 Kgs 8:51
Jer 10:16

32:10
Ps 17:8

32:11
Ex 19:4
Ps 17:8; 91:4

32:12
Deut 4:36
Isa 43:12

31:27-29 Moses knew that the Israelites, in spite of all they had seen of God's work, were rebellious at heart. They deserved God's punishment, although they often received his mercy instead. We too are stubborn and rebellious by nature. Throughout our lives we struggle with sin. Repentance once a month or once a week is not enough. We must continually confess our sins to God and let his mercy save us.

32:1ff Moses was not only a great prophet but a songleader as well. After three sermons, he changed the form of his message to singing. Sometimes reciting something in a different form makes it easier to remember. This song gives a brief history of Israel. It reminds them of their mistakes, warns them to avoid repetition of those mistakes, and offers hope that is found only in trusting God.

32:13
Job 29:6
Ps 81:16

13God gave them fertile hilltops,
  Rolling, fertile fields,
  Honey from the rock,
  And olive oil from stony ground!

32:14
Ps 147:14

14He gave them milk and meat—
  Choice Bashan rams, and goats—
  And the finest of the wheat;
  They drank the sparkling wine.

32:15
Judg 10:6

15But Israel was soon overfed;
  Yes, fat and bloated;
  Then, in plenty, they forsook their God.
  They shrugged away the Rock of their salvation.

32:16
Ps 78:58
106:29

16Israel began to follow foreign gods,
  And Jehovah was very angry;
  He was jealous of his people.

32:17
Lev 17:7
1 Cor 10:20

17They sacrificed to heathen gods,
  To new gods never before worshiped.

32:18
Ps 106:21
Deut 8:11; 32:4

18They spurned the Rock who had made them,
  Forgetting it was God who had given them birth.

32:19
Lev 26:30
Ps 106:40

19God saw what they were doing,
  And detested them!
  His sons and daughters were insulting him.

32:20
Deut 32:5
Mt 17:17

20He said, 'I will abandon them;
  See what happens to them then!
  For they are a stubborn, faithless generation.

32:21
1 Kgs 16:13,26
Rom 10:19

21They have made me very jealous of their idols,
  Which are not gods at all.
  Now I, in turn, will make them jealous
  By giving my affections
  To the foolish Gentile nations of the world.

32:22
Lev 26:20
Ps 18:7,8

22For my anger has kindled a fire
  That burns to the depths of the underworld,
  Consuming the earth and all of its crops,
  And setting its mountains on fire.

32:23
Lev 26:18
Deut 28:15-19
2 Sam 22:15
Ps 85:5

23I will heap evils upon them
  And shoot them down with my arrows.

32:24
Deut 28:53
Ps 91:6

24I will waste them with hunger,
  Burning fever, and fatal disease.
  I will devour them! I will set wild beasts upon them,
  To rip them apart with their teeth;
  And deadly serpents
  Crawling in the dust.

32:25
2 Chron 36:17
Lam 1:20; 2:21
Ezek 7:15

25Outside, the enemies' sword—
  Inside, the plague—
  Shall terrorize young men and girls alike;

32:13 *oil from stony ground*, or, "oil from flinty rocks." **32:15** *Israel*, literally, "Jeshurun." **32:25** *the plague*, implied.

VARIETY IN WORSHIP
Israel's worship involved all of the senses. This reinforced the meaning of the ceremony and painted a dramatic picture that worship touches *all* of life.

SIGHT	the beauty and symbolism of the tabernacle; every color and hue had a meaning
HEARING	the use of music; there were instructions for the use of a variety of instruments, and the Bible records many songs
TOUCH	at the sacrifice, they were to touch the head of the animal symbolizing the fact that it was taking their place
SMELL	the sacrifices were burned, emitting a familiar aroma
TASTE	Israel's feasts were celebrations and memorials—much of the food was symbolic

The baby nursing at the breast,
And aged men.
26I had decided to scatter them to distant lands,
So that even the memory of them
Would disappear.

32:26
Deut 4:27; 28:64

27But then I thought,
"My enemies will boast,
'Israel is destroyed by our own might;
It was not the Lord
Who did it!' " '
28Israel is a stupid nation;
Foolish, without understanding.
29Oh, that they were wise!
Oh, that they could understand!
Oh, that they would know what they are getting into!

32:29
Deut 5:29

30How could one single enemy chase a thousand of them,
And two put ten thousand to flight,
Unless their Rock had abandoned them,
Unless the Lord had destroyed them?

32:30
Lev 26:7,8
Josh 23:10
Judg 7:22
Deut 32:4,18

31But the rock of other nations
Is not like our Rock;
Prayers to their gods are valueless.
32They act like men of Sodom and Gomorrah:
Their deeds are bitter with poison;

32:32
Gen 19:4,5
Deut 29:18

33They drink the wine of serpent venom.
34But Israel is my special people,
Sealed as jewels within my treasury.
35Vengeance is mine,
And I decree the punishment of all her enemies:
Their doom is sealed.

32:35
Jer 23:12
Ezek 7:5
Rom 12:19

36The Lord will see his people righted,
And will have compassion on them when they slip.
He will watch their power ebb away,
Both slave and free.

32:36
Lev 26:44,45
Deut 30:2,3
Heb 10:30

37Then God will ask,
'Where are their gods—
The rocks they claimed to be their refuge?

32:37
Jer 2:28

38Where are these gods now,
To whom they sacrificed their fat and wine?
Let those gods arise,
And help them!

32:38
Num 25:1,2
Jer 11:12

39Don't you see that I alone am God?
I kill and make live.
I wound and heal—
No one delivers from my power.

32:39
1 Sam 2:6
Ps 50:22
Isa 41:4; 43:10

40, 41I raise my hand to heaven
And vow by my existence,
That I will whet the lightning of my sword!
And hurl my punishments upon my enemies!

32:40
Num 8:21
Ps 65:5
Isa 1:24; 34:6
Jer 12:12
46:10; 50:28-32

42My arrows shall be drunk with blood!
My sword devours the flesh and blood
Of all the slain and captives.
The heads of the enemy
Are gory with blood.'
43Praise his people,
Gentile nations,
For he will avenge his people,

32:32 *deeds,* literally, "grapes." **32:34** Implied.

Taking vengeance on his enemies,
Purifying his land
And his people.

44, 45When Moses and Joshua had recited all the words of this song to the people, 46Moses made these comments:

"Meditate upon all the laws I have given you today, and pass them on to your children. 47These laws are not mere words—they are your life! Through obeying them you will live long, plentiful lives in the land you are going to possess across the Jordan River.

Moses is told he is about to die

48That same day, the Lord said to Moses, 49"Go to Mount Nebo in the Abarim mountains, in the land of Moab across from Jericho. Climb to its heights, and look out across the land of Canaan, the land I am giving to the people of Israel. 50After you see the land you must die and join your ancestors, just as Aaron your brother died in Mount Hor and joined them. 51For you dishonored me among the people of Israel at the springs of Meribah-kadesh, in the wilderness of Zin. 52You will see spread out before you the land I am giving the people of Israel, but you will not enter it."

Moses blesses all the tribes

33 This is the blessing Moses, the man of God, gave to the people of Israel before his death:

2"The Lord came to us at Mount Sinai,
And dawned upon us from Mount Seir;
He shone from Mount Paran,
Surrounded by ten thousands of holy angels,
And with flaming fire at his right hand.
3How he loves his people—
His holy ones are in his hands.
They followed in your steps, O Lord.
They have received their directions from you.
4The laws I have given
Are your precious possession.
5The Lord became king in Jerusalem,
Elected by a convocation of the leaders of the tribes!
6Let Reuben live forever
And may his tribe increase!"

7And Moses said of Judah:

"O Lord, hear the cry of Judah
And unite him with Israel;
Fight for him against his enemies."

8Then Moses said concerning the tribe of Levi:

33:2 *holy angels,* literally, "holy ones."

Cross-references (left margin):

32:46
Deut 4:9
Ezek 40:4; 44:5
32:47
Deut 4:40; 8:3
30:20

32:49
Num 27:12
Deut 3:27
32:50
Gen 25:17
Num 27:13,14
Deut 31:16
32:51
Num 20:12
32:52
Deut 1:37; 3:27

33:1
1 Sam 2:27

33:2
Ex 19:18,20
Judg 5:4
Ps 68:8,17
Dan 7:10
Hab 3:3
Gal 3:19

33:3
Deut 4:37
6:1-9; 7:6; 14:2

33:4
Deut 4:2
Ps 119:111
33:5
Num 23:18-24
Ps 10:16; 22:28
33:6
Gen 49:3

33:7
Gen 49:8-12

33:8
Ex 17:7
Lev 8:8
Num 20:13,24
Deut 6:16

32:46, 47 Moses urged the people to think about God's Word and teach it to their children. The Bible can sit on your bookshelf and gather dust, or you can make it a vital part of your life by regularly setting aside time to study it. When you discover the wisdom of God's message, you will want to apply it to your life and pass it on to your family and others. The Bible is not merely good reading—it's real life.

33:6-25 Note the difference in blessings God gave each tribe. To one he gave the best land, to another strength, to another wisdom. Too often we see someone with a particular strength and think that God must love that person more than others. Think rather that God draws out in all people their unique talents. All these gifts are needed to complete his plan. Don't be jealous of the gifts others have. Instead, look for the gifts God has given you, and resolve to do the tasks he has uniquely qualified you to do.

"Give to godly Levi
Your Urim and your Thummim.
You tested Levi at Massah and at Meribah;
9He obeyed your instructions
[and destroyed many sinners],
Even his own children, brothers, fathers, and mothers.
10The Levites shall teach God's laws to Israel
And shall work before you at the incense altar
And the altar of burnt offering.
11O Lord, prosper the Levites
And accept the work they do for you.
Crush those who are their enemies;
Don't let them rise again."

12Concerning the tribe of Benjamin, Moses said:

"He is beloved of God
And lives in safety beside him.
God surrounds him with his loving care,
And preserves him from every harm."

13Concerning the tribe of Joseph, he said:

"May his land be blessed by God
With the choicest gifts of heaven
And of the earth that lies below.
14May he be blessed
With the best of what the sun makes grow;
Growing richly month by month,
15With the finest of mountain crops
And of the everlasting hills.
16May he be blessed with the best gifts
Of the earth and its fullness,
And with the favor of God who appeared
In the burning bush.
Let all these blessings come upon Joseph,
The prince among his brothers.
17He is a young bull in strength and splendor,
With the strong horns of a wild ox
To push against the nations everywhere;
This is my blessing on the multitudes of Ephraim
And the thousands of Manasseh."

18Of the tribe of Zebulun, Moses said:

"Rejoice, O Zebulun, you outdoorsmen,
And Issachar, you lovers of your tents;
19They shall summon the people
To celebrate their sacrifices with them.
Lo, they taste the riches of the sea
And the treasures of the sand."

20Concerning the tribe of Gad, Moses said:

33:9 and destroyed many sinners, implied.

33:9 Ex 32:27; Lev 10:6; 21:11; Mt 10:37
33:10 Lev 10:11; 16:12,13; Deut 17:9; 31:9
33:12 Gen 49:27; Deut 12:10; 32:11
33:13 Gen 27:27-29; 49:22
33:14 Deut 28:8
33:16 Ps 24:1; 50:12; 89:11
33:17 Num 23:22; 24:8; 1 Kgs 22:11
33:18 Gen 49:13
33:19 Deut 32:13; Ps 4:5; 51:19
33:20 Gen 49:19

33:20, 21 The tribe of Gad received the best of the new land because they obeyed God by executing his punishment on the Canaanites. Punishment is unpleasant for both the giver and the receiver, but it is a necessary part of growth. If you are in a position that sometimes requires you to punish, don't hold back from fulfilling your task. Understand that realistic discipline is important to character development. Always strive to be both just and merciful, keeping in mind the best interests of the person who must receive the punishment.

"A blessing upon those who help Gad.
He crouches like a lion,
With savage arm and face and head.

33:21
Num 32:1
34:14,15
Josh 4:12; 22:1

21He chose the best of the land for himself
Because it is reserved for a leader.
He led the people
Because he carried out God's penalties for Israel."

33:22
Gen 49:16
Josh 19:47,48
Ezek 19:2

22Of the tribe of Dan, Moses said:

"Dan is like a lion's cub
Leaping out from Bashan."

33:23
Gen 49:21
Isa 9:1,2

23Of the tribe of Naphtali, Moses said:

"O Naphtali, you are satisfied
With all the blessings of the Lord;
The Mediterranean coast and the Negeb
Are your home."

33:24
Gen 49:20
Job 29:6

24Of the tribe of Asher:

"Asher is a favorite son,
Esteemed above his brothers;
He bathes his feet in oil.

33:25
Ps 147:13

25May you be protected with strong bolts
Of iron and bronze,
And may your strength match the length of your days!

33:26
Ex 15:11
Deut 4:35
Ps 68:33

26There is none like the God of Jerusalem—
He descends from the heavens
In majestic splendor to help you.

33:27
Gen 49:24
Deut 7:2
Josh 24:18
Ps 90:1

27The eternal God is your Refuge,
And underneath are the everlasting arms.
He thrusts out your enemies before you;
It is he who cries, 'Destroy them!'

33:28
Gen 27:27-29,
37
Deut 33:12,13

28So Israel dwells safely,
Prospering in a land of corn and wine,
While the gentle rains descend from heaven.

33:29
Gen 15:1
Deut 4:32
2 Sam 22:3
Ps 66:3; 115:11

29What blessings are yours, O Israel!
Who else has been saved by the Lord?
He is your shield and your helper!
He is your excellent sword!
Your enemies shall bow low before you,
And you shall trample on their backs!"

Moses dies

34:1
Num 21:20
27:12
Deut 32:49,52

34 Then Moses climbed from the plains of Moab to Pisgah Peak in Mount Nebo, across from Jericho. And the Lord pointed out to him the Promised Land, as they gazed out across Gilead as far as Dan:

34:2
Ex 23:31
Deut 11:24
Josh 19:32

2"There is Naphtali; and there is Ephraim and Manasseh; and across there, Judah, extending to the Mediterranean Sea; 3there is the Negeb; and the Jordan Valley; and Jericho, the city of palm trees; and Zoar," the Lord told him.

33:27 Moses' song declares that God is our refuge, our only true security. How often we entrust our lives to other things—perhaps money, career, a noble cause, or a lifelong dream. But our only true refuge is the eternal God, who always holds out his arms to catch us when the shaky things we trust in collapse and we fall. No storm can destroy us when we take refuge in him. The ungodly, however, must forever be cautious. One mistake could wipe them out. Living a godly life in this world may look like risky business. But it is the godless who are on shaky ground. Because God is our refuge, we can dare to be bold.

4"It is the Promised Land," the Lord told Moses. "I promised Abraham, Isaac, and Jacob that I would give it to their descendants. Now you have seen it, but you will not enter it."

5So Moses, the disciple of the Lord, died in the land of Moab as the Lord had said. 6The Lord buried him in a valley near Beth-Peor in Moab, but no one knows the exact place.

7Moses was 120 years old when he died, yet his eyesight was perfect and he was as strong as a young man. 8The people of Israel mourned for him for thirty days on the plains of Moab.

9Joshua (son of Nun) was full of the spirit of wisdom, for Moses had laid his hands upon him; so the people of Israel obeyed him, and followed the commandments the Lord had given to Moses.

10There has never been another prophet like Moses, for the Lord talked to him face to face. 11, 12And at God's command he performed amazing miracles which have never been equaled.

34:4
Gen 12:7; 26:3
Ps 105:10,11

34:5
Num 12:7,8
Deut 32:50

34:6
Deut 3:29
4:44-46
Jude 9

34:7
Deut 31:2
Acts 7:23,30

34:9
Ex 31:3
Num 27:18

34:10
Num 12:7,8
Acts 3:22,23

34:11
Deut 4:34; 7:19

34:4, 10 Moses was the only person who ever spoke with God face to face. He was called Israel's greatest prophet. Yet even this great man was not allowed to enter the Promised Land, because he disobeyed God (Numbers 20:12). No matter how good we are, or how much we've done for God, we sometimes disobey him. The result of our disobedience will be discipline. God disciplined Moses severely, yet still called him his friend. When you experience the sting of God's discipline, do what Moses did. Turn toward God with love, understanding, and a desire to do better. Don't turn away in anger, embarrassment, or with feelings of failure and inadequacy.

34:10 Moses, the man who did not want to be sent to Egypt because he had "a speech impediment" (Exodus 4:10), delivered the three addresses to Israel that make up the book of Deuteronomy. God gave him the power to develop from a stuttering shepherd into a national leader and powerful orator. His courage, humility, and wisdom molded the Hebrew slaves into a nation. But Moses was one person who did not let success go to his head. In the end, God was still Moses' best friend. His love, respect, and awe for God had grown daily throughout his life. Moses knew that it was not his own greatness that made him successful; it was the greatness of the God in whom he believed.

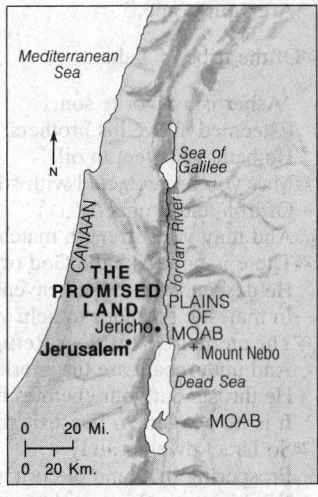

THE DEATH OF MOSES
Just before Moses died, he climbed Mount Nebo. Although he could not enter the Promised Land, God showed him its beauty from Mount Nebo's peak.

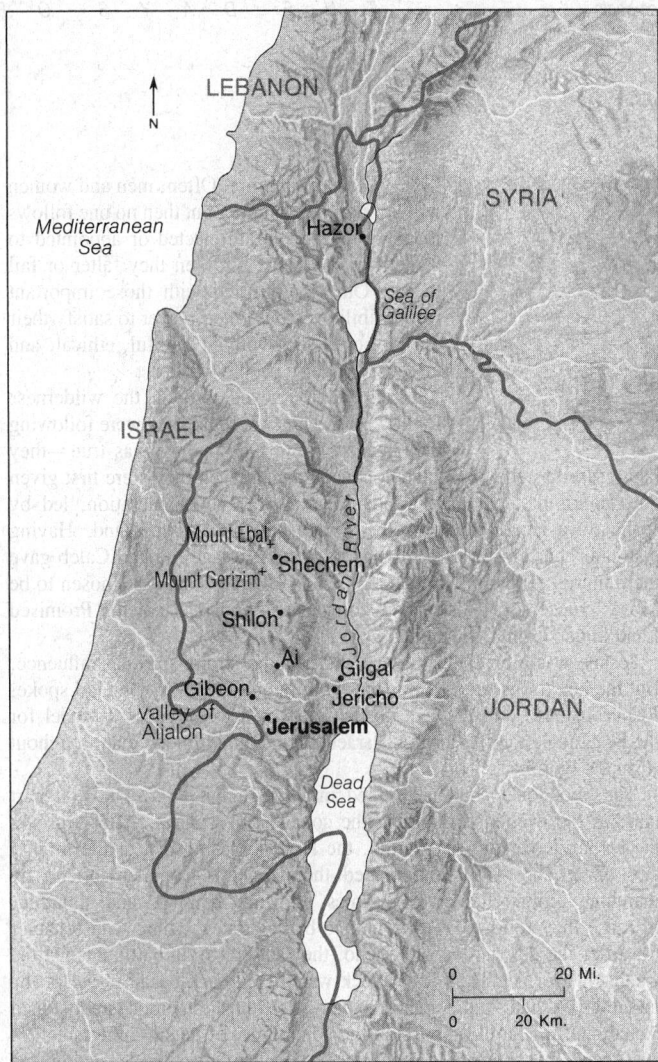

Modern names and boundaries are shown in gray.

1 **Acacia** The story of Joshua begins with the Israelites camping at Acacia. The Israelites under Joshua were ready to enter and conquer Canaan. But before the nation moved out, Joshua received instructions from God (1:1–18).

2 **Jordan River** The entire nation prepared to cross this river, which was swollen from spring rains. After the spies returned from Jericho with a positive report, Joshua prepared the priests and people for a miracle. As the priests carried the Ark into the Jordan River, the water stopped flowing and the entire nation crossed on dry ground into the Promised Land (2:1—4:24).

3 **Gilgal** After crossing the Jordan River, the Israelites camped at Gilgal where they renewed their commitment to God and celebrated the Passover, the feast commemorating their deliverance from Egypt (see Exodus). As Joshua made plans for the attack on Jericho, an angel appeared to him (5:1–15).

4 **Jericho** The walled city of Jericho seemed a formidable enemy. But when Joshua followed God's plans, the great walls were no obstacle. The city was conquered with only the obedient marching of the people (6:1–27).

5 **Ai** Victory could not continue without obedience to God. That is why the disobedience of one man, Achan, brought defeat to the entire nation in the first battle against Ai. But once the sin was recognized and punished, God told Joshua to take heart and try Ai once again. This time the city was taken (7:1—8:29).

6 **The Mountains of Ebal and Gerizim** After the defeat of Ai, Joshua built an altar at Mount Ebal. Then the people divided themselves, half at the foot of Mount Ebal, half at the foot of Mount Gerizim. The priests stood between the mountains holding the Ark of the Covenant as Joshua read God's Law to all the people (8:30–35).

7 **Gibeon** It was just after the Israelites reaffirmed their covenant with God that their leaders made a major mistake in judgment: they were tricked into making a peace treaty with the city of Gibeon. The Gibeonites pretended that they had traveled a long distance and asked for the Israelites for a treaty. The leaders made the agreement without consulting God. The trick was soon discovered, but because the treaty had been made Israel could not go back on its word. As a result, the Gibeonites saved their own lives, but they were forced to become Israel's slaves (9:1–27).

8 **Valley of Aijalon** The king of Jerusalem was very angry at Gibeon (7) for making a peace treaty with the Israelites. He gathered armies from four other cities to attack the city. Gibeon summoned Joshua for help. Joshua took immediate action. Leaving Gilgal (3), he attacked the coalition by surprise. As the battle waged on and moved into the valley of Aijalon, Joshua prayed for the sun to stand still until the enemy could be destroyed (10:1–43).

9 **Hazor** Up north in Hazor, King Jabin mobilized the kings of the surrounding cities to unite and crush Israel. But God gave Joshua and Israel victory. Joshua conquered the entire federation (11:1–23).

10 **Shiloh** After the armies of Canaan were conquered, Israel gathered at Shiloh to set up the Tabernacle. This movable building had been the nation's center of worship during their years of wandering. The seven tribes who had not received their land were given their allotments (18:1—19:51).

11 **Shechem** Before Joshua died he called the entire nation together at Shechem to remind them that it was God who had given them their land and that only with God's help could they keep it. The people vowed to follow God. As long as Joshua was alive, the land was at rest from war and trouble (24:1–33).

JOSHUA

VITAL STATISTICS

PURPOSE:
To give the history of Israel's conquest of the Promised Land

AUTHOR:
Joshua, except for the ending which may have been written by the High Priest Phinehas, an eyewitness to the events recounted there

SETTING:
Canaan, also called the Promised Land, which occupied the same general geographical territory of modern-day Israel

KEY VERSE:
"In three days we will go across and conquer and live in the land which God has given us" (1:11).

KEY PEOPLE:
Joshua, Rahab, Achan, Phinehas, Eleazar

KEY PLACES:
Jericho, Ai, Mount Ebal, Mount Gerizim, Gibeon, Gilgal, Shiloh, Shechem

SPECIAL FEATURE:
Out of over a million people, Joshua and Caleb were the only two who left Egypt and entered the Promised Land.

GREAT leaders are rare. Often, men and women will lay claim to that title, but then no one follows them. Some people are elected or appointed to leadership positions, but then they falter or fail to act. Others, entrusted with those important responsibilities, abuse their power to satisfy their massive egos. But without faithful, ethical, and effective leaders, people wander.

Israel had journeyed through the wilderness for 40 years, but not because they were following their leader. Quite the opposite was true—they had refused to obey God and conquer Canaan when they were first given the opportunity. So they wandered. Now the new generation, led by Joshua, was ready to cross the Jordan and possess the land. Having distinguished himself as a man of faith and courage (he and Caleb gave the minority report in Numbers 13:30—14:10), Joshua was chosen to be Moses' successor. This book records Israel's conquest of the Promised Land under Joshua's leadership.

Joshua was a brilliant military leader and a strong spiritual influence. But the key to his success was his submission to God. When God spoke, Joshua listened and obeyed. Joshua's obedience served as a model for the Israelite nation. As a result, Israel remained faithful to God throughout Joshua's lifetime.

The book of Joshua is divided into two main parts. The first part narrates the events surrounding the conquest of Canaan. After crossing the Jordan River on dry ground, the Israelites camped near the mighty city of Jericho. God commanded the people to conquer Jericho by marching around the city 13 times, blowing trumpets and shouting. Because they followed God's unique battle strategy, they won (chapter 6). After the destruction of Jericho, they set out to do battle against the small town of Ai. Their first attack was driven back because one of the Israelites (Achan) had sinned (chapter 7). After the men of Israel stoned Achan and his family—purging the community of its sin—the Israelites succeeded in capturing Ai (chapter 8). In their next battle against the Amorites, God even made the sun stand still to aid the Israelites in their victory (chapter 10). Finally, after defeating other miscellaneous Canaanites led by Jabin and his allies (chapter 11), they possessed a good portion of the land.

Part two of the book of Joshua records the assignment and settlement of the captured territory (chapters 13—22). The book concludes with Joshua's farewell address and his death (chapters 23, 24).

Joshua was committed to obeying God, and this book is about obedience. Whether conquering enemies or settling the land, God's people were required to do it God's way. Joshua underscored the importance of obedience to God in his final message to the people. "So be very careful to keep on loving him [the Lord]" (23:11), and "decide today whom you will obey. . . . But as for me and my family, we will serve the Lord" (24:15). Read Joshua and make a fresh commitment to obey God today. Decide to follow your Lord wherever he leads and whatever it costs.

THE BLUEPRINT

A. ENTERING THE PROMISED LAND
(1:1—5:12)
1. Joshua leads the nation
2. The nation crosses the Jordan River

Joshua demonstrated his faith in God as he took up the challenge to lead the nation. The Israelites reaffirmed their commitment to God by obediently setting out across the Jordan River to possess the land. As we live the Christian life, we need to cross over from the old life to the new, put off our selfish desires, and press on to possess all God has planned for us. Like Joshua and Israel, we need courageous faith to live the new life.

B. CONQUERING THE PROMISED LAND
(5:13—12:24)
1. Joshua attacks the center of the land
2. Joshua attacks the southern kings
3. Joshua attacks the northern kings
4. Summary of conquests

Joshua and his army moved from city to city, cleansing the land of its wickedness by destroying every trace of idol worship. Conflict with evil is inevitable, and we should be as merciless as Israel in destroying sin in our lives.

C. DIVIDING THE PROMISED LAND
(13:1—24:33)
1. The tribes receive their land
2. Special cities are set aside
3. The eastern tribes build an altar
4. Joshua's last message

Joshua urged the Israelites to continue to follow the Lord and worship him alone. The people had seen God deliver them from many enemies and miraculously provide for all their needs, but they were prone to wandering from the Lord. Even though we may have experienced God at work in our lives, we too must continually renew our commitment to obey him above all other authority and to worship him alone.

MEGATHEMES

THEME	EXPLANATION	IMPORTANCE
Success	God gave success to the Israelites when they obeyed his master plan, not when they followed their own desires. Victory came when they trusted in him rather than in their military power, money, muscle, or mental capacity.	God's work done in God's way will bring success. The standard for success, however, is not to be set by the society around us but by God's Word. We must adjust our minds to God's way of thinking in order to see his standard for success.
Faith	The Israelites demonstrated their faith by trusting God daily to save and guide them. By noticing how God fulfilled his promises in the past, they developed strong confidence that he would be faithful in the future.	Our strength to do God's work comes from trusting him. His promises reassure us of his love and that he will be there to guide us in the decisions and struggles we face.
Guidance	God gave instructions to Israel for every aspect of their lives. His law guided their daily living and his specific marching orders gave them victory in battle.	Guidance from God for daily living can be found in his Word. By staying in touch with God, we will have the needed wisdom to meet the great challenges of life.
Leadership	Joshua was an example of an excellent leader. He was confident in God's strength, courageous in the face of opposition, and willing to seek God's advice.	To be a strong leader like Joshua we must be ready to listen and to move quickly when God instructs us. Once we have his instructions, we must be diligent in carrying them out. Strong leaders are led by God.
Conquest	God commanded his people to conquer the Canaanites and take all their land. Completing this mission would have fulfilled God's promise to Abraham and brought judgment on the evil people living there. Unfortunately, Israel never finished the job.	Israel was faithful in accomplishing their mission at first, but their commitment faltered. To love God means more than being enthusiastic about him. We must complete all the work he gives us and apply his instructions to every corner of our lives.

A. ENTERING THE PROMISED LAND (1:1—5:12)

After wandering for forty years in the wilderness, a new generation is ready to enter Canaan. But first God prepares both Joshua and the nation by teaching them the importance of courageous and consistent faith. The nation then miraculously crosses the Jordan River to begin the long-awaited conquest of the Promised Land. Like Joshua, we too need faith to begin and continue living the Christian life.

1. Joshua leads the nation

God's charge to Joshua

1 After the death of Moses, the Lord's disciple, God spoke to Moses' assistant, whose name was Joshua (the son of Nun), and said to him, 2"Now that my disciple is dead, [you are the new leader of Israel]. Lead my people across the Jordan River into the Promised Land. 3I say to you what I said to Moses: 'Wherever you go will be part of the land of Israel— 4all the way from Negeb desert in the south to the Lebanon mountains in the north, and from the Mediterranean Sea in the west to the Euphrates River in the east, including all the land of the Hittites.' 5No one will be able to oppose you as long as you live, for I will be with you just as I was with Moses; I will not abandon you or fail to help you.

1:1 Num 13:16 Deut 34:7,8
1:2 Num 12:7,8 Deut 34:9 1 Kgs 8:56
1:3 Deut 11:24
1:5 Deut 7:24 31:6-8 Heb 13:5

1:2 *you are the new leader of Israel,* implied.

Genesis 12:1–3	God promised to bless Abraham and make his descendants into a great nation	**TAKE THE LAND**
Genesis 15:16	God would choose the right time for Israel to enter Canaan because the nations living there then would be wicked and ripe for judgment	God told Joshua to lead the Israelites into the Promised Land
Genesis 17:7, 8	God promised to give all the land of Canaan to Abraham's descendants	(also called Canaan) and conquer it. This was not an act of
Exodus 33:1–3	God promised to help the Israelites drive out all the evil nations from Canaan	imperialism or aggression, but an
Deuteronomy 4:5–8	The Israelites were to be an example of right living to the whole world; this would not work if they intermingled with the wicked Canaanites	act of judgment. Here are some of the earlier
Deuteronomy 7:1–5	The Israelites were to utterly wipe the Canaanites out because of their wickedness and because of Israel's call to purity	passages in the Bible where God promised to give
Deuteronomy 12:2	The Israelites were to completely destroy the Canaanite altars so nothing would tempt them away from worshiping God alone	this land to the Israelites and the reasons for doing so.

1:1 As the book of Joshua opens, the Israelites are camped along the east bank of the Jordan River at the very edge of the Promised Land. Thirty-nine years earlier (after spending a year at Mount Sinai receiving God's law), the Israelites had an opportunity to enter the Promised Land, but they failed to trust God. As a result, God did not allow them to enter the land, but made them wander in the wilderness until the disobedient generation had all died.

During their wilderness wanderings, the Israelites obeyed God's laws. They also taught the new generation to obey God's laws so that they might enter the Promised Land (also called Canaan). As the children grew, they were often reminded that faith and obedience to God brought victory, while unbelief and disobedience brought tragedy. When the last of the older generation had died and the new generation had become adults, the Israelites prepared to cross the river and claim the long-awaited Promised Land.

1:1–5 Joshua succeeded Moses as Israel's leader. What qualifications did he have to become the leader of a nation? (1) God appointed him (Numbers 27:18–23). (2) He was one of only two living eyewitnesses to the Egyptian plagues and the Exodus from Egypt. (3) He had been Moses' personal assistant for forty years. (4) Of the twelve spies, only he and Caleb showed

complete confidence that God would help them conquer the land.

1:2 Because Joshua had assisted Moses for many years, he was well prepared to take over the leadership of the nation. Changes in leadership are common in many organizations. At such times, a smooth transition is essential for the establishment of the new administration. This doesn't happen unless new leaders are trained. If you are currently in a leadership position, begin preparing someone to take your place. Then, when you leave or are promoted, operations can continue to run efficiently. If you desire to be in a leadership position, learn from other leaders so you will be prepared to lead when the opportunity comes.

1:5 Joshua's new job consisted of leading more than a million people into a strange new land and conquering it. What a challenge—even for a man of Joshua's caliber! Every new job is a challenge. Without God it can be frightening. With God it can be a great adventure. Just as God assured Joshua he would be with him, he is with us as we face our new challenges. We may not conquer nations, but every day we face tough situations, difficult people, and temptations. However, God promises that he will never abandon us or fail to help us, regardless of how we feel. By asking God to direct us, as Joshua did, we too can conquer many of life's challenges.

1:7
Deut 5:29,32
28:14; 29:9

1:8
Deut 6:6,7
11:18; 17:19
Ps 1:1-3

⁶"Be strong and brave, for you will be a successful leader of my people; and they shall conquer all the land I promised to their ancestors. ⁷You need only to be strong and courageous and to obey to the letter every law Moses gave you, for if you are careful to obey every one of them you will be successful in everything you do. ⁸Constantly remind the people about these laws, and you yourself must think about them every day and every night so that you will be sure to obey all of them. For only

One of the greatest challenges to leadership is training others to become leaders. Many outstanding accomplishments have been started by someone with great ability whose life or career ended before the vision became reality. The fulfillment of that dream then became the responsibility of that person's successor. Death is the ultimate deadline for leadership. One of the best tests of our leadership is our willingness and ability to train another for our position.

Moses made an excellent decision when he chose Joshua as his assistant. That choice was later confirmed by God himself when he instructed Moses to commission Joshua as his successor (Numbers 27:15–21). Joshua had played a key role in the Exodus story. Introduced as the field general of Israel's army, he was the only person allowed to accompany Moses partway up the mountain when Moses received the Law. Joshua and Caleb were the only two among the 12 spies to bring back an encouraging report after being sent into the Promised Land the first time. Other references show him to have been Moses' constant shadow. His basic training was living with Moses— experiencing firsthand what it meant to lead God's people. This was modeling at its best!

Who is your Moses? Who is your Joshua? You are part of the chain of God's ongoing work in the world. You are modeling yourself after others, and others are patterning their lives after you. How important is God to those you want to be like? Do those who are watching you see God reflected in every area of your life? Ask God to lead you to a trustworthy Moses. Ask him to make you a good Joshua.

Strengths and accomplishments:
• Moses' assistant and successor
• One of only two adults who experienced Egyptian slavery and lived to enter the Promised Land
• Led the Israelites into their God-given homeland
• Brilliant military strategist
• Faithful to ask God's direction in the challenges he faced

Weakness and mistake:
• He was unable to complete the task of possessing all the land

Lessons from his life:
• Effective leadership is often the product of good preparation and encouragement
• The persons after whom we pattern ourselves will have a definite effect on us
• A person committed to God provides the best model for us

Vital statistics:
• Where: Joshua lived in Egypt, the Sinai Wilderness, and Canaan (the Promised Land)
• Occupation: Special assistant to Moses, warrior, leader
• Relatives: Father: Nun
• Contemporaries: Moses, Caleb, Miriam, Aaron

Key verses:
"So Moses did as Jehovah commanded, and took Joshua to Eleazar the priest. As the people watched, Moses laid his hands upon him and dedicated him to his responsibilities, as the Lord had commanded" (Numbers 27:22, 23).

Joshua is also mentioned in Exodus 17, 24, 32, 33; Numbers 11:28; 13; 14; 26:65; 27:18, 22; 32:12, 28; 34:17; Deuteronomy 1:38; 3:21, 28; 31:3, 7, 14, 23; 34:9; Joshua; Judges 2; 1 Kings 16:34, and Hebrews 4:8.

1:6–8 Many people think success is based on wealth, power, influential personal contacts, and a relentless desire to get ahead. But the strategy for success which God taught Joshua goes against such criteria. He told Joshua that to succeed he must (1) be strong and brave because the task ahead would not be easy, (2) obey God's Word, (3) constantly remind the people of the truths in God's Word, and (4) daily read and study God's Word. To be successful, follow God's words to Joshua. You may not succeed by the world's standards, but you will be a success in God's eyes, and his opinion lasts forever.

1:7 How strange to equate success with obedience. For many, success is controlling others; for Joshua it meant being controlled by God. God told Joshua that to succeed he must obey the rules for living found in God's law. Often we can't see what the results or future benefits of following God will be. When we are not sure what to do, obedience to what God has revealed in the Scriptures is the only sure step we can take. Resolve to set aside time each day to read and think about God's Word. Remind yourself of God's words day and night. Act today on what you know God has said, and God will assure your success in carrying out his purposes.

then will you succeed. ⁹Yes, be bold and strong! Banish fear and doubt! For remember, the Lord your God is with you wherever you go."

1:9
Deut 31:6,8

Joshua prepares the people to enter

¹⁰,¹¹Then Joshua issued instructions to the leaders of Israel to tell the people to get ready to cross the Jordan River. "In three days we will go across and conquer and live in the land which God has given us!" he told them.

1:10
Deut 3:2-4,
15-17

¹²,¹³Then he summoned the leaders of the tribes of Reuben, Gad, and the half-tribe of Manasseh and reminded them of their agreement with Moses: "The Lord your God has given you a homeland here on the east side of the Jordan River," Moses had told them, ¹⁴"so your wives and children and cattle may remain here, but your troops, fully armed, must lead the other tribes across the Jordan River to help them conquer their territory on the other side; ¹⁵stay with them until they complete the conquest. Only then may you settle down here on the east side of the Jordan."

1:12
Num 32:20
Deut 3:18
Josh 22:1

1:15
Josh 22:4

¹⁶To this they fully agreed, and pledged themselves to obey Joshua as their commander-in-chief.

1:16
Num 32:25

¹⁷,¹⁸"We will obey you just as we obeyed Moses," they assured him, "and may the Lord your God be with you as he was with Moses. If anyone, no matter who, rebels against your commands, he shall die. So lead on with courage and strength!"

1:17
Ex 19:8; 24:3
Deut 5:27

Rahab protects the spies

2 Then Joshua sent two spies from the Israeli camp at Acacia to cross the river and check out the situation on the other side, especially at Jericho. They arrived at an inn operated by a woman named Rahab, who was a prostitute. They were planning to spend the night there, ²but someone informed the king of Jericho that two Israelis who were suspected of being spies had arrived in the city that evening. ³He dispatched a police squadron to Rahab's home, demanding that she surrender them.

2:1
Num 13:2
Mt 1:5

"They are spies," he explained. "They have been sent by the Israeli leaders to discover the best way to attack us."

⁴But she had hidden them, so she told the officer in charge, "The men were here

2:4
Ex 1:19
2 Sam 17:20

1:12, 13 During the previous year, the tribes of Reuben and Gad and the half-tribe of Manasseh had asked Moses if they could settle just east of the Promised Land. The area was excellent pastureland for their large flocks. Moses agreed to give them the land on one condition—that they help their fellow tribes enter and conquer the Promised Land. Only after the land was conquered could they return to their homes. Now it was time for these three tribes to live up to their agreement.

1:16 What would have happened if everyone had tried to conquer the Promised Land his own way? Chaos would have resulted. In order to complete the enormous task of conquering the land, everyone had to agree with the leader's plan and be willing to support and obey him. If we are going to complete the tasks God has given us, we must fully agree to his plan and pledge ourselves to obey it by putting his principles into action. Agreeing to God's plan means both knowing his plan for us as found in Scripture and committing ourselves to carrying it out in daily living.

2:1 Why would the spies stop at the house of Rahab the prostitute? (1) It was a good place to gather information and have no questions asked in return. (2) Rahab's house was in an ideal location for a quick escape because it was built into the city wall. (3) God directed the spies to Rahab's house because he knew her heart was open to him and that she would be instrumental in the Israelite victory over Jericho. God often uses people with simple faith to accomplish his great purposes, no matter what kind of past they have had or how insignificant they seem to be.

2:4, 5 Was Rahab justified in lying to save the lives of the spies? Although the Bible does not speak negatively about her lie, it is

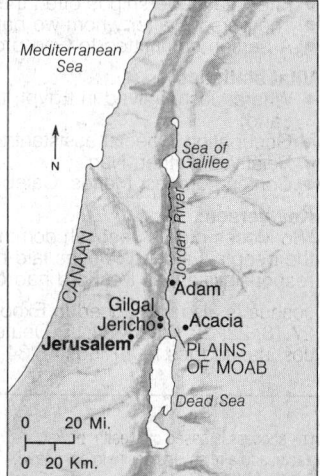

SPY MISSION TO JERICHO
Two spies left the Israelite camp at Acacia, crossed the Jordan River, and slipped into Jericho. The city was built around an oasis in the midst of a hot and desolate valley 840 feet below sea level. Jericho was the first major city the Israelites set out to conquer.

clear that lying is sin. In Hebrews 11:31, however, Rahab is commended for her faith in God. Her lie is not mentioned. Several explanations have been offered: (1) God forgave Rahab's lie because of her faith; (2) Rahab was simply deceiving the enemy, a normal and acceptable practice in wartime; (3) since Rahab was not a Jew, she could not be held responsible for keeping the moral

earlier, but I didn't know they were spies. 5They left the city at dusk as the city gates were about to close, and I don't know where they went. If you hurry you can probably catch up with them!"

2:6
Jas 2:25

6But actually she had taken them up to the roof and hidden them beneath piles of flax that were drying there. 7So the constable and his men went all the way to the Jordan River looking for them; meanwhile, the city gates were kept shut. 8Rahab went up to talk to the men before they retired for the night.

2:9
Ex 23:27
Deut 2:25
Josh 9:24
Heb 11:31

2:10
Ex 14:21-31
Num 21:21
Deut 2:30; 3:1

9"I know perfectly well that your God is going to give my country to you," she told them. "We are all afraid of you; everyone is terrified if the word *Israel* is even mentioned. 10For we have heard how the Lord made a path through the Red Sea for you when you left Egypt! And we know what you did to Sihon and Og, the two

RAHAB

Rahab was a survivor. She was accustomed to figuring the odds. As a prostitute, she lived on the edge of society, one stop short of rejection. Her inn, built right into the city walls, provided both lodging and favors to travelers. It was a natural place for the Israelite spies to stay. These were undoubtedly not the first men she had hidden from the police. Her lie to the authorities was a calculated risk: she hoped it would guarantee her (and her guests) immediate safety and also set into motion her plan for long-term survival. By protecting the spies, Rahab hoped that her future safety would be secure.

Stories about the Israelites had been circulating for some time, but now it was evident that they were about to invade. Living on the wall, Rahab felt especially vulnerable. Yet while she shared the general mood of fear with the rest of the population, she alone looked for a way of survival. Her faith began with the thought, "If we can't beat them, maybe I can join them." Rahab knew her position was dangerous. In harboring the spies, she was in danger of being caught and killed. She knew that siding with the strangers was risky business: they might lose the battle, or they might refuse to guarantee her safety. Against these real dangers, Rahab sensed that the Israelites relied on a God worth trusting.

God works through people—like Rahab—who we are inclined to reject. We remember her because of her moral failure; God remembers her because of her faith! If at times you feel like a failure, remember that Rahab rose above her situation through her trust in God. You can do the same!

Strengths and accomplishments:
• Mother of Boaz, ancestor of David and Jesus
• One of only two women listed in the Hall of Faith in Hebrews 11
• Resourceful, willing to help others at great cost to herself

Weakness and mistake:
• She was a prostitute

Lesson from her life:
• She did not let fear affect her faith in God's ability to deliver

Vital statistics:
• Where: Jericho
• Occupation: Prostitute, innkeeper, later became a wife
• Relatives: Husband: Salmon. Son: Boaz. Daughter-in-law: Ruth.
• Contemporaries: Joshua

Key verse:
"By faith—because she believed in God and his power—Rahab the harlot did not die with all the others in her city when they refused to obey God, for she gave a friendly welcome to the spies" (Hebrews 11:31).

Rahab's story is told in Joshua 2 and 6. She is also mentioned in Matthew 1:5, Hebrews 11:31, and James 2:25.

standards set forth in God's Law; (4) Rahab broke a lesser principle—telling the truth—to uphold a higher principle—protecting God's people.

There may have been another way to save the lives of the Israelite spies. But under the pressure of the moment, Rahab had to make a choice. Most of us will face dilemmas at one time or another. We may feel that there is no perfect solution to our problem. Fortunately, God does not demand that our judgment be perfect in all situations. He simply asks us to put our trust in him and to do the best we know how. Rahab did that and was commended for her faith.

2:6 Flax was harvested in the fields and piled high on the rooftops to dry. It was then made into yarn which was used to make linen cloth. Flax grows to a height of three or four feet. Stacked on the roof, it made an excellent hiding place for the spies.

2:9-13 Many would assume that Rahab—a heathen, a Canaanite, and a prostitute—would never be interested in God. Yet Rahab was willing to risk everything she had for a God she barely knew. We must not gauge a person's interest in God by their background, life-style, or appearance. We should let nothing get in the way of telling people about the God in whom we believe.

Amorite kings east of the Jordan, and how you ruined their land and completely destroyed their people. ¹¹No wonder we are afraid of you! No one has any fight left in him after hearing things like that, for your God is the supreme God of heaven, not just an ordinary god. ¹², ¹³Now I beg for this one thing: Swear to me by the sacred name of your God that when Jericho is conquered you will let me live, along with my father and mother, my brothers and sisters, and all their families. This is only fair after the way I have helped you."

¹⁴The men agreed. "If you won't betray us, we'll see to it that you and your family aren't harmed," they promised. ¹⁵"We'll defend you with our lives." Then, since her house was on top of the city wall, she let them down by a rope from a window.

¹⁶"Escape to the mountains," she told them. "Hide there for three days until the men who are searching for you have returned; then go on your way."

¹⁷, ¹⁸But before they left, the men had said to her, "We cannot be responsible for what happens to you unless this rope is hanging from this window and unless all your relatives—your father, mother, brothers, and anyone else—are here inside the house. ¹⁹If they go out into the street we assume no responsibility whatsoever; but we swear that no one inside this house will be killed or injured. ²⁰However, if you betray us, then this oath will no longer bind us in any way."

²¹"I accept your terms," she replied. And she left the scarlet rope hanging from the window.

²²The spies went up into the mountains and stayed there three days, until the men who were chasing them had returned to the city after searching everywhere along the road without success. ²³Then the two spies came down from the mountain and crossed the river and reported to Joshua all that had happened to them.

²⁴"The Lord will certainly give us the entire land," they said, "for all the people over there are scared to death of us."

2. The nation crosses the Jordan River

3 Early the next morning Joshua and all the people of Israel left Acacia, and arrived that evening at the banks of the Jordan River, where they camped for a few days before crossing.

², ³, ⁴On the third day, officers went through the camp giving these instructions: "When you see the priests carrying the Ark of God, follow them. You have never before been where we are going now, so they will guide you. However, stay about a half mile behind, with a clear space between you and the Ark; be sure that you don't get any closer."

⁵Then Joshua told the people to purify themselves. "For tomorrow," he said, "the Lord will do a great miracle."

3:2-4 *the Ark of God*, literally, "the Ark of the covenant of the Lord."

2:11
Deut 4:39
1 Kgs 8:60
Ps 83:18

2:12
Josh 6:22,23
9:14,15,18

2:15
Josh 2:17,18,21

2:16
Jas 2:25

2:24
Josh 5:1; 9:24

3:1
Josh 2:1

3:2
Deut 31:9
Josh 1:10,11

3:5
Ex 19:10
Josh 7:13

2:11 Rahab recognized something that many of the Israelites had not—the God of heaven is not an ordinary god! He is all-powerful. The people of Jericho were afraid, for they had heard the news of God's extraordinary power in defeating the armies across the Jordan River.

Today we can worship this same powerful, miracle-working God: He is powerful enough to destroy mighty, wicked armies, as he did with Jericho. He is also powerful enough to save us from certain death, as he did with Rahab.

2:15 In Joshua's day it was common to build houses on city walls. Many cities had two walls about 12 to 15 feet apart. Houses were built on wooden logs laid across the tops of the two walls. Rahab may have lived in such a house with a window that looked out over the outside wall.

2:23, 24 This was not the first time spies were sent into the Promised Land. Thirty-nine years earlier, another spy mission had been conducted (Numbers 13, 14). Then, however, most of the

spies came back afraid. They doubted God's ability to help them conquer the land. Joshua was one of those spies; only he and Caleb encouraged the people to follow God's plan. This time Joshua sent spies secretly. He did not want the possibility of another negative report to stir up the people to revolt.

3:2–4 The Ark of God (also called the Ark of the Covenant) was Israel's most sacred treasure. It was a symbol of God's presence and power. The Ark was a golden rectangular box with two cherubim facing each other on the lid. Inside the Ark were the Ten Commandments Moses received from God, a jar of manna (the bread God miraculously sent from heaven), and Aaron's staff (the symbol of the high priest's authority). According to God's law, only the Levites, who were descendants of Aaron, could carry the Ark. The Ark was constructed at the same time as the Tabernacle (Exodus 37:1–9), and placed in the sanctuary's most sacred room.

3:5 Before entering the Promised Land, the Israelites were to perform a "purification ceremony." This was often done before

6In the morning Joshua ordered the priests, "Take up the Ark and lead us across the river!" And so they started out.

3:7
Josh 4:14
3:8
Josh 3:13,14

7"Today," the Lord told Joshua, "I will give you great honor, so that all Israel will know that I am with you just as I was with Moses. 8Instruct the priests who are carrying the Ark to stop at the edge of the river."

3:10
Gen 15:19,
20,21
Deut 7:1

9Then Joshua summoned all the people and told them, "Come and listen to what the Lord your God has said. 10Today you are going to know for sure that the living God is among you and that he will, without fail, drive out the Canaanites, Hittites, Hivites, Perizzites, Girgashites, Amorites, and Jebusites—all the people who now live in the land you will soon occupy. 11Think of it! The Ark of God, who is Lord of the whole earth, will lead you across the river!

The people miraculously cross the Jordan River

3:12
Josh 4:2,3
3:13
Ex 15:8

3:15,16
1 Chron 12:15
Ps 66:6; 74:15
114:3,5

3:17
Ex 14:21,22,29
Josh 3:6-8
2 Kgs 2:8

12"Now select twelve men, one from each tribe, for a special task. 13, 14When the priests who are carrying the Ark touch the water with their feet, the river will stop flowing as though held back by a dam, and will pile up as though against an invisible wall!" Now it was the harvest season and the Jordan was overflowing all its banks; but as the people set out to cross the river and as the feet of the priests who were carrying the Ark touched the water at the river's edge, 15, 16suddenly, far up the river at the city of Adam, near Zarethan, the water began piling up as though against a dam! And the water below that point flowed on to the Dead Sea until the riverbed was empty. Then all the people crossed at a spot where the river was close to the city of Jericho, 17and the priests who were carrying the Ark stood on dry ground in the middle of the Jordan and waited as all the people passed by.

3:12 *for a special task.* Their duties are explained in 4:2-7.

---

making a sacrifice or, as in this case, before seeing a great act of God. God's Law stated that many things could make a person unclean—certain foods (Leviticus 11), childbirth (Leviticus 12), disease (Leviticus 13, 14), touching a dead person (Numbers 19:11-22). God used these various outward signs of uncleanness to illustrate man's inward uncleanness, which comes as a result of sin. The purification ceremony pictured the importance of approaching God with a pure heart. Like the Israelites, we must take care of the sin in our lives when we approach God.

3:9 Just before crossing over into the Promised Land, Joshua gathered the people to hear what the Lord their God had said. Their excitement was high. No doubt they wanted to rush on, but Joshua made them stop and listen. We live in a fast-paced age. We feel we have to rush just to keep up. It is easy to get caught up in our tasks, becoming too busy for what God says is most important—taking time to hear from him. Before making your schedule, take time to focus on what God wants from all your activities. Knowing what God has said before you rush into your day may help you avoid foolish mistakes.

3:10 Why would God help the Israelites drive out these nations from their native land? Genesis 15:13-16 states that the people of Canaan were wicked and deserved to be punished for their many sins. Israel was to be a vehicle for this punishment. More important was the fact that Israel, as a holy nation, could not live among such evil and idolatrous people. To do so would be to invite sin into their lives. The only way to prevent Israel from being infected by evil religions was to drive out those who practiced them from the land. Israel, however, failed to drive everyone out as God had told them to do. It wasn't long before Israel was following the evil practices of the Canaanites.

3:11 As the Israelites prepared to enter the Promised Land and divide up the territory, Joshua reminded them that God is Lord of the whole earth, not just one part of it. Understanding this truth

delivers us from thinking of *our* church, *our* nation, *our* family, or *ourselves* as the central figures on God's stage. We are not central, God is. Though we are infinitely valuable in God's sight, we must realize that he is weaving a grand design much larger than our personal interests. God doesn't exist to grant us personal success in all we do. We exist to serve him and fulfill his desires.

3:13, 14 The Israelites were eager to enter the Promised Land, conquer nations, and live peacefully. But first they had to cross the flood-level waters of the Jordan River. God gave them specific instructions: in order to cross, they had to step into the water. What if they had been afraid to take the first step? Often God provides no solution to our problems until we trust him and move ahead with what we know we should do. What are the rivers, or obstacles, in your life? In obedience to God, take that first step into the water.

3:13-17 God had parted the waters of the Red Sea to let the people out of Egypt (Exodus 14), and now he parts the Jordan River to let them enter Canaan. These miracles showed Israel that God keeps his promises. God's presence among his people and his faithfulness to them made the entire journey from Egypt to the Promised Land possible. He was with them at the end of their wanderings just as he was with them in the beginning.

3:15, 16 The Israelites crossed the Jordan River in the spring, when it was overflowing its banks. God chose the time when the river was at its highest to demonstrate his power—parting the waters so that the entire nation could cross on dry ground. Some say that God used a natural occurrence (such as a landslide) to stop the waters of the Jordan; others say he did it by a supernatural act. In either case, God showed his great power by working a miracle of timing and location to bring Israel into the Promised Land. This testimony of God's power served to build the Israelites' hope in God and to give them a great reputation with their enemies, even though they were outnumbered.

The people build a monument

4 When all the people were safely across, the Lord said to Joshua, 2, 3"Tell the twelve men chosen for a special task, one from each tribe, each to take a stone from where the priests are standing in the middle of the Jordan, and to carry them out and pile them up as a monument at the place where you camp tonight."

4So Joshua summoned the twelve men, 5and told them, "Go out into the middle of the Jordan where the Ark is. Each of you is to carry out a stone on your shoulder—twelve stones in all, one for each of the twelve tribes. 6We will use them to build a monument so that in the future, when your children ask, 'What is this monument for?' 7you can tell them, 'It is to remind us that the Jordan River stopped flowing when the Ark of God went across!' The monument will be a permanent reminder to the people of Israel of this amazing miracle."

8So the men did as Joshua told them. They took twelve stones from the middle of the Jordan river—one for each tribe, just as the Lord had commanded Joshua. They carried them to the place where they were camped for the night and constructed a monument there. 9Joshua also built another monument of twelve stones in the middle of the river, at the place where the priests were standing; and it is there to this day. 10The priests who were carrying the Ark stood in the middle of the river until all these instructions of the Lord, which had been given to Joshua by Moses, had been carried out. Meanwhile, the people had hurried across the riverbed, 11and when everyone was over, the people watched the priests carry the Ark up out of the riverbed.

12, 13The troops of Reuben, Gad, and the half-tribe of Manasseh—fully armed as Moses had instructed, and forty thousand strong—led the other tribes of the Lord's army across to the plains of Jericho.

14It was a tremendous day for Joshua! The Lord made him great in the eyes of all the people of Israel, and they revered him as much as they had Moses, and respected him deeply all the rest of his life. 15, 16For it was Joshua who, at the Lord's command, issued the orders to the priests carrying the Ark.

"Come up from the riverbed," the Lord now told him to command them.

17So Joshua issued the order. 18And as soon as the priests came out, the water poured down again as usual and overflowed the banks of the river as before! 19This miracle occurred on the 25th of March. That day the entire nation crossed the Jordan River and camped in Gilgal at the eastern edge of the city of Jericho; 20and there the twelve stones from the Jordan were piled up as a monument.

21Then Joshua explained again the purpose of the stones: "In the future," he said, "when your children ask you why these stones are here and what they mean, 22you are to tell them that these stones are a reminder of this amazing miracle—that the nation of Israel crossed the Jordan River on dry ground! 23Tell them how the Lord

4:6
Ex 12:26; 13:14
Deut 6:20
Josh 4:20,21

4:8
Josh 1:16

4:9
Josh 5:8,9

4:12
Num 32:1,17,25
Josh 1:12,13

4:14
Josh 24:31
1 Chron 29:25

4:15
Josh 3:8

4:19
Ex 12:3

4:22
Josh 3:17

4:19 *the 25th of March,* literally, "The tenth day of the first month" (of the Jewish calendar). **4:23** *forty years ago,* implied.

4:1 After the people safely crossed the river, what would be next? Conquering the land? Not yet. First, God directed them to build a monument from 12 stones drawn from the river by 12 men, one from each tribe. This may seem like an insignificant step in their mission of conquering the land, but God did not want his people to plunge into something unprepared. They were to focus on him and remember who was guiding them. As you are busy doing your God-given tasks, set aside quiet moments, times to "pile stones and build an altar." Too much activity can shift your focus away from God.

4:2-7 Joshua and the nation erected a monument to commemorate the end of their wandering and the beginning of their new life and new land. While monuments are usually erected to commemorate great events or acknowledge heroic deeds, individual lives also have special monuments, though often less visible—a special event, an answered prayer, a miracle. Think back over what God has done in your life. Let your memories serve

as monuments, reminders of God's work in your life and of his care for you.

4:14 Joshua was respected in the eyes of the people for his role in leading the Israelites across the Jordan River. He, like Moses, would receive Israel's praises generation after generation. Although Israel was not a world power in Joshua's day, his reputation for handling things God's way brought him greater glory than if he had been a hero in a "super-power" nation.

4:21 The monument of 12 stones was to be a constant reminder of the moment when the Israelites crossed the Jordan River on dry ground. Their children would see the stones, hear the story, and learn about God. Do you have traditions—special dates or special places—to help your children learn about God's work in your life? Do you take time to tell them what God has done for you—forgiving and saving you, answering your prayers, supplying your needs? Retelling your story will help keep memories of God's faithfulness alive in your family.

our God dried up the river right before our eyes, and then kept it dry until we were all across! It is the same thing the Lord did forty years ago at the Red Sea! 24He did this so that all the nations of the earth will realize that Jehovah is the mighty God, and so that all of you will worship him forever."

4:24
Ex 7:3

The nation reaffirms its commitment to God

5 When the nations west of the Jordan River—the Amorites and Canaanites who lived along the Mediterranean coast—heard that the Lord had dried up the Jordan River so the people of Israel could cross, their courage melted away completely and they were paralyzed with fear.

5:1
Num 13:29
Josh 2:9-11

2, 3The Lord then told Joshua to set aside a day to circumcise the entire male population of Israel. (It was the second time in Israel's history that this was done.) The Lord instructed them to manufacture flint knives for this purpose. The place where the circumcision rite took place was named "The Hill of the Foreskins." 4, 5The reason for this second circumcision ceremony was that although when Israel left Egypt all of the men who had been old enough to bear arms had been circumcised, that entire generation had died during the years in the wilderness, and none of the boys born since that time had been circumcised. 6For the nation of Israel had traveled back and forth across the wilderness for forty years until all the men who had been old enough to bear arms when they left Egypt were dead; they had not obeyed the Lord, and he vowed that he wouldn't let them enter the land he had promised to Israel—a land that "flowed with milk and honey." 7So now Joshua circumcised their children—the men who had grown up to take their fathers' places.

5:2,3
Gen 17:9,10,23

5:4
Deut 2:14

5:6
Num 14:29-35
26:64,65
Deut 2:7

5:7
Deut 1:39

8, 9And the Lord said to Joshua, "Today I have ended your shame of not being circumcised." So the place where this was done was called Gilgal (meaning, "to end"), and is still called that today. After the ceremony the entire nation rested in camp until the raw flesh of their wounds had been healed.

10While they were camped at Gilgal on the plains of Jericho, they celebrated the Passover during the evening of April first. 11, 12The next day they began to eat from the gardens and grain fields which they invaded, and they made unleavened bread.

5:10
Ex 12:18
Josh 4:19

5:11
Ex 16:35
Neh 9:20

5:8, 9 *your shame of not being circumcised,* literally "the shame of Egypt." *to end,* literally, "to roll" (away).
5:10 *April first,* literally, "the fourteenth day of the first month" (of the Hebrew calendar).

5:1 The Israelites spent 39 years in the wilderness unnecessarily because they were terrified of the Canaanites. They underestimated God's ability. Their first attempt to enter the Promised Land had failed (Numbers 13, 14). Now Israel saw that the Canaanites were terrified of their army. They had heard about Israel's great victories through God (Joshua 2:9–11). Their last hope was that the Jordan River would slow Israel down or discourage them from entering the land. But news that the Israelites had crossed the Jordan on dry land caused any courage the Canaanites still had to melt away.

Don't underestimate God. If we are faithful to God as the Israelites were, God can cause great opposition to melt away. He can change the attitudes of those who oppose him.

5:1 The Canaanites and Amorites were the two major groups living in Canaan at the time of Israel's invasion. The Canaanites worshiped a variety of gods, but Baal was their favorite. The Israelites continually turned to Baal after entering Canaan. The Amorite gods also infected Israel's worship and turned people away from worshiping the true God. Worshiping these false gods eventually brought about Israel's downfall.

5:2, 3 The rite of circumcision marked Israel's position as God's covenant people. When God made the original covenant with Abraham, he required that each male be circumcised as a sign of cutting off the old life and beginning a new life with God (Genesis 17:13). Other cultures at that time used circumcision as a sign of entry into adulthood, but only Israel used it as a sign of following God.

5:8, 9 Located about two miles northeast of Jericho, Gilgal was Israel's base camp and temporarily the center of government and worship during their conquest of Canaan. Here the people renewed their commitment and covenant with God before attempting to conquer the new land. At Gilgal the angelic commander of God's army appeared to Joshua with further instructions for battle and encouragement for the conquest. After the conquest, Gilgal continued to be an important place in Israel. It was here that Israel's first king, Saul, was crowned (1 Samuel 11:14, 15).

5:10 This joyous Passover was the first to be celebrated in the Promised Land and only the third celebrated by Israel since the Exodus from Egypt. This celebration reminded Israel of God's mighty miracles that brought them out of Egypt. There they had to eat in fear and haste; now they ate in celebration of God's blessings and promises. (See Exodus 12 for a description of the night the angel "passed over" Israel.)

5:11, 12 God had miraculously supplied manna to the hungry Israelites during their 40 years in the wilderness (Exodus 16:14–31). In the bountiful Promised Land they no longer needed this daily food supply because the land was ready for planting and harvesting. God had miraculously provided food for the Israelites while they were in the desert; now he provided food from the land itself. Prayer is not an alternative to preparation, and faith is not a substitute for hard work. God can and does provide miraculously for his people as needed, but he also expects them to use their God-given talents and resources to provide for themselves.

The following day no manna fell, and it was never seen again! So from that time on they lived on the crops of Canaan.

B. CONQUERING THE PROMISED LAND (5:13—12:24)

After crossing the Jordan River, the Israelites begin to conquer Canaan. Jericho is the first to fall. Then Israel suffers its first defeat because of one man's disobedience. After the people remove the sin from their community, they strike again—this time with success. Soon great kings attack from the north and south, but they are defeated because God is with Israel. Evil could not be tolerated in the Promised Land, nor can it be tolerated in our lives. We, like Israel, must ruthlessly remove sin from our lives before it takes control of us.

1. Joshua attacks the center of the land

Joshua meets an angel

13As Joshua was sizing up the city of Jericho, a man appeared nearby with a drawn sword. Joshua strode over to him and demanded, "Are you friend or foe?" 14"I am the Commander-in-Chief of the Lord's army," he replied.

Joshua fell to the ground before him and worshiped him and said, "Give me your commands."

15"Take off your shoes," the Commander told him, "for this is holy ground." And Joshua did.

The walls of Jericho fall

6 The gates of Jericho were kept tightly shut because the people were afraid of the Israelis; no one was allowed to go in or out.

2But the Lord said to Joshua, "Jericho and its king and all its mighty warriors are already defeated, for I have given them to you! 3, 4Your entire army is to walk around the city once a day for six days, followed by seven priests walking ahead of the Ark, each carrying a trumpet made from a ram's horn. On the seventh day you are to walk around the city seven times, with the priests blowing their trumpets. 5Then, when they give one long, loud blast, all the people are to give a mighty shout and the walls of the city will fall down; then move in upon the city from every direction."

6-9So Joshua summoned the priests and gave them their instructions: the armed men would lead the procession followed by seven priests blowing continually on their trumpets. Behind them would come the priests carrying the Ark, followed by a rear guard.

10"Let there be complete silence except for the trumpets," Joshua commanded. "Not a single word from any of you until I tell you to shout; then *shout!*"

11The Ark was carried around the city once that day, after which everyone

5:13
Gen 18:2
32:22,23,24
Ex 23:23
Num 22:31
Judg 13:9
5:14
Ex 3:5

6:1
Josh 5:1

6:2
Deut 7:24
Josh 10:8
6:3
Lev 25:9

6:6
Josh 1:10; 3:2

5:14, 15 This was an angel of superior rank, the Commander-in-Chief of heaven's army. Some say he was Christ himself as he appeared before his birth on earth. As a sign of respect, Joshua took off his shoes. Although Joshua was Israel's leader, he was still subordinate to God, the absolute leader. Awe and respect are the responses due to God who is holy. How can we show respect for God? By our attitudes and actions. We should recognize God's power, authority, and deep love. Our actions must model our attitudes before others. Respect for God is just as important today as it was in Joshua's day, even though removing sandals is no longer our cultural way of showing it.

6:1 The city of Jericho, built thousands of years before Joshua was born, was one of the oldest cities in the world. In some places it had fortified walls up to 25 feet high and 20 feet thick. Soldiers standing guard on top of the walls could see for miles. Jericho was a symbol of military power and strength—the Canaanites considered it invincible.

Israel would attack this city first, and its destruction would put the fear of Israel into the hearts of every person in Canaan. The Canaanites saw Israel's God as a nature god because he parted the Jordan and as a war god because he defeated Sihon and Og.

But the Canaanites did not consider him a "fortress god"—one who could prevail against a walled city. The defeat of Jericho showed that Israel's God was not only superior to the Canaanite gods, but he was also invincible.

6:2–5 God told Joshua that the enemy was already defeated! What confidence Joshua must have had as he went into battle! Christians must also fight against a defeated enemy. Our enemy, Satan, has been defeated by Christ (Romans 8:37–39; Hebrews 2:14, 15; 1 John 3:8). Although we still fight battles every day, we have the assurance that the war has already been won. We do not have to be paralyzed by the power of a defeated enemy; we can overcome temptation through the power of Christ.

6:3–5 Why did the Lord give Joshua all these complicated instructions for the battle? Several answers are possible: (1) God was making it undeniably clear that the battle would depend upon him, and not upon Israel's weapons and expertise. This is why the priests who carried the Ark led the Israelites into battle, not soldiers. (2) God's method of taking the city accentuated the terror already felt in Jericho (2:9). (3) This strange military maneuver was a test of the Israelites' faith and their willingness to follow God completely.

6:12
Josh 6:3,4

returned to the camp again and spent the night there. 12, 13, 14At dawn the next morning they went around again, and returned again to the camp. They followed this pattern for six days.

15At dawn of the seventh day they started out again, but this time they went around the city not once, but seven times. 16The seventh time, as the priests blew a long, loud trumpet blast, Joshua yelled to the people, *"Shout!* The Lord has given us the city!"

6:17
Josh 2:15; 6:22

6:18
Deut 20:17
Josh 7:1

6:19
Num 31:22,23

17(He had told them previously, "Kill everyone except Rahab the prostitute and anyone in her house, for she protected our spies. 18Don't take any loot, for everything is to be destroyed. If it isn't, disaster will fall upon the entire nation of Israel. 19But all the silver and gold and the utensils of bronze and iron will be dedicated to the Lord, and must be brought into his treasury.")

6:20
Heb 11:30

6:21
Deut 20:16

20So when the people heard the trumpet blast, they shouted as loud as they could. And suddenly the walls of Jericho crumbled and fell before them, and the people of Israel poured into the city from every side and captured it! 21They destroyed everything in it—men and women, young and old; oxen; sheep; donkeys—everything.

The spies rescue Rahab's family

6:22
Josh 2:15
Judg 1:25

22Meanwhile Joshua had said to the two spies, "Keep your promise. Go and rescue the prostitute and everyone with her."

6:23
Heb 11:31

23The young men found her and rescued her, along with her father, mother, brothers, and other relatives who were with her. Arrangements were made for them to live outside the camp of Israel. 24Then the Israelis burned the city and everything in it except that the silver and gold and the bronze and iron utensils were kept for the Lord's treasury. 25Thus Joshua saved Rahab the prostitute and her relatives who were with her in the house, and they still live among the Israelites because she hid the spies sent to Jericho by Joshua.

6:25
Josh 2:6
Heb 11:31

6:26
2 Sam 10:5
1 Kgs 16:34

26Then Joshua declared a terrible curse upon anyone who might rebuild Jericho, warning that when the foundation was laid, the builder's oldest son would die, and when the gates were set up, his youngest son would die.

6:27
Deut 31:7

27So the Lord was with Joshua, and his name became famous everywhere.

Achan's sin of disobedience

7:1
Josh 6:17-19
1 Chron 2:7

7 But there was sin among the Israelis. God's command to destroy everything except that which was reserved for the Lord's treasury was disobeyed. For

---

6:14–20 It must have seemed strange to the Israelites that, instead of going to battle, they were going to march around the city for a week! But this was God's plan, and the Israelites had a guaranteed victory if they would follow it (6:2). As strange as the plan sounded, it worked. God's instructions may require you to do things that don't make sense at first. Even as you follow him, you may wonder how things can possibly work out. Like the Israelites, take one day at a time and follow step by step. You may not see the logic of God's plan until after you have obeyed.

6:21 Why did God demand that the Israelites destroy almost everyone and everything in Jericho? He was carrying out severe judgment against the wickedness of the Canaanites. This judgment, or "ban," usually required that everything be destroyed (Deuteronomy 12:2, 3; 13:12–18). Because of their evil practices and their idolatry, the Canaanites were a stronghold of rebellion against God. This threat to right living had to be removed. If not, it would affect all Israel like a cancerous growth (which is the sad story of the book of Judges). A few people and some items in Jericho were not destroyed. Rahab and her household were saved because she had faith in God and because she helped the Israelite spies. The silver and gold were kept, not to enrich the people, but to beautify the Tabernacle and its services.

God's purpose in all this was to keep the people's faith and religion uncontaminated. He did not want the loot to cause Israel to be reminded of Canaanite practices. God desires purity in each of

us as well. We must not let the desire for personal gain distract us from our spiritual purpose. We must also reject any objects that commemorate a life lived in rebellion to God. (For more information on how Israel handled its booty, see the note on Numbers 31:22, 23.)

6:22 In return for information, Joshua's spies had promised to protect Rahab and her family from the battle (Joshua 2:14, 15). Rahab kept her part of the promise, and Joshua took time from the battle to tell the spies to keep their part.

6:26 This curse was fulfilled in 1 Kings 16:34 when a man rebuilt Jericho and consequently lost his oldest and youngest sons.

7:1 Notice the results of Achan's sin: (1) many men died (7:5); (2) Israel's army was paralyzed with fear (7:5); (3) the leaders faltered and were confused (7:7–9); (4) God said he might withdraw his presence from the people (7:12); (5) Achan and his family had to be destroyed (7:24–26).

When Israel eliminated the sin in their community, these were the results: (1) encouragement from God (8:1); (2) God's guidance and promise of victory (8:2); (3) God's presence in battle (8:2); (4) God's permission to keep the loot from the battle for themselves (8:2).

Throughout Israel's history, blessings came when the people got rid of their sin. You will experience victory when you rid your life of sin.

Achan (the son of Carmi, grandson of Zabdi, and great-grandson of Zerah, of the tribe of Judah) took some loot for himself, and the Lord was very angry with the entire nation of Israel because of this.

²Soon after Jericho's defeat, Joshua sent some of his men to spy on the city of Ai, east of Bethel.

7:2
Gen 28:19
Josh 16:2

³Upon their return they told Joshua, "It's a small city and it won't take more than two or three thousand of us to destroy it; there's no point in all of us going there."

⁴So approximately three thousand soldiers were sent—and they were soundly defeated. ⁵About thirty-six of the Israelis were killed during the attack, and many others died while being chased by the men of Ai as far as the quarries. The Israeli army was paralyzed with fear at this turn of events. ⁶Joshua and the elders of Israel tore their clothing and lay prostrate before the Ark of the Lord until evening, with dust on their heads.

7:5
Josh 8:1

7:6
Job 2:12; 42:6
Lam 2:10

⁷Joshua cried out to the Lord, "O Jehovah, why have you brought us over the Jordan River if you are going to let the Amorites kill us? Why weren't we content with what we had? Why didn't we stay on the other side? ⁸O Lord, what am I to do now that Israel has fled from her enemies! ⁹For when the Canaanites and the other nearby nations hear about it, they will surround us and attack us and wipe us out. And then what will happen to the honor of your great name?"

7:7
Ex 14:11; 17:3

7:9
Ex 32:12
Deut 9:28

¹⁰, ¹¹But the Lord said to Joshua, "Get up off your face! Israel has sinned and disobeyed my commandment and has taken loot when I said it was not to be taken; and they have not only taken it, they have lied about it and have hidden it among their belongings. ¹²That is why the people of Israel are being defeated. That is why your men are running from their enemies—for they are cursed. I will not stay with you any longer unless you completely rid yourselves of this sin.

7:10
Ex 14:15
1 Sam 15:22
16:1

¹³"Get up! Tell the people, 'Each of you must undergo purification rites in preparation for tomorrow, for the Lord your God of Israel says that someone has stolen from him, and you cannot defeat your enemies until you deal with this sin. ¹⁴In the morning you must come by tribes, and the Lord will point out the tribe to which the guilty man belongs. And that tribe must come by its clans and the Lord will point out the guilty clan; and the clan must come by its families, and then each member of the guilty family must come one by one. ¹⁵And the one who has stolen that which belongs to the Lord shall be burned with fire, along with everything he

7:13
Ex 19:10
Joel 2:16,17
Zeph 2:1-3

7:12 *for they are cursed,* literally, they have become "something which must be totally destroyed" or else become totally God's.

7:6 Joshua and the elders "tore their clothing" and put "dust on their heads" as signs of deep mourning before God. They were confused by their defeat at the small city of Ai after the spectacular Jericho victory, so they went before God in deep humility and sorrow to receive his instructions. Like Joshua and the elders, we should humble ourselves before God so that we will be able to hear his word and receive direction for our lives.

7:7 When Joshua first went against Ai (7:3), he did not consult God but relied on the strength of his army to defeat the small city. Only after Israel was defeated did he turn to God and ask, "What happened?"

Too often we rely on our own skills and strength, especially when the task before us seems easy. We go to God only when the obstacles seem too great. However, only God knows what lies ahead. Consulting him, even when we are on a winning streak, may save us from grave mistakes or misjudgments.

7:7-9 Imagine praying this way to God. This is not a formal church prayer; it is the prayer of a man who is afraid and confused by what is happening around him. Joshua poured out his real thoughts to God. Hiding your needs from God is ignoring the only one who can really help. God welcomes your honest prayers and wants you to express your true feelings to him. Any believer can become more honest in prayer by remembering that God is all-knowing and all-powerful.

7:10, 11 Once Achan started covering up, he couldn't stop until it

was too late. Covering his sin only led to further sinning. First Achan stole the possessions, then he hid them, then he lied. When you sin, beware of compounding your problems by deceit.

7:12 Why did Achan's sin bring judgment on the entire nation? Though it was one man's failure, God saw it as national disobedience to a national law. God needed the entire nation to be committed to the job they had agreed to do—conquer the land. Thus, when one person failed, everyone failed. If Achan's sin went unpunished, unlimited looting would break out. The nation as a whole had to take responsibility for preventing this.

Achan's sin was not the mere act of keeping some of the booty (which was allowed in some cases), but the disobedience to God's explicit command to destroy everything connected with *this* city. His sin was indifference to the evil and idolatry of the city, not just a desire for extra money. God would not protect Israel's army again until the sin was removed and the army returned to obeying him without reservation.

God is not content with people doing what is right some of the time. He wants all of us to do what is right all the time. We are under orders from him to rid our lives of anything that hinders our devotion to him.

7:13 These purification rites are the same as those mentioned in Joshua 3:5 when the Israelites were preparing to cross the Jordan River. Such rites prepared the people to approach God and constantly reminded them of their sinfulness and his holiness.

has, for he has violated the covenant of the Lord and has brought calamity upon all of Israel.' "

16So, early the next morning, Joshua brought the tribes of Israel before the Lord, and the tribe of Judah was indicated. 17Then he brought the clans of Judah, and the clan of Zerah was singled out. Then the families of that clan were brought before the Lord and the family of Zabdi was indicated. 18Zabdi's family was brought man by man, and his grandson Achan was found to be the guilty one.

19Joshua said to Achan, "My son, give glory to the God of Israel and make your confession. Tell me what you have done."

20Achan replied, "I have sinned against the Lord, the God of Israel. 21For I saw a beautiful robe imported from Babylon, and some silver worth $200, and a bar of gold worth $500. I wanted them so much that I took them, and they are hidden in the ground beneath my tent, with the silver buried deeper than the rest."

22So Joshua sent some men to search for the loot. They ran to the tent and found the stolen goods hidden there just as Achan had said, with the silver buried beneath the rest. 23They brought it all to Joshua and laid it on the ground in front of him. 24Then Joshua and all the Israelites took Achan, the silver, the robe, the wedge of gold, his sons, his daughters, his oxen, donkeys, sheep, his tent, and everything he had, and brought them to the valley of Achor.

25Then Joshua said to Achan, "Why have you brought calamity upon us? The Lord will now bring calamity upon you."

And the men of Israel stoned them to death and burned their bodies, 26and piled a great heap of stones upon them. The stones are still there to this day, and even today that place is called "The Valley of Calamity." And so the fierce anger of the Lord was ended.

Israel destroys the city of Ai

8 Then the Lord said to Joshua, "Don't be afraid or discouraged; take the entire army and go to Ai, for it is now yours to conquer. I have given the king of Ai and all of his people to you. 2You shall do to them as you did to Jericho and her king; but this time you may keep the loot and the cattle for yourselves. Set an ambush behind the city."

3, 4Before the main army left for Ai, Joshua sent thirty thousand of his bravest troops to hide in ambush close behind the city, alert for action.

5"This is the plan," he explained to them. "When our main army attacks, the men of Ai will come out to fight as they did before, and we will run away. 6We will let them chase us until they have all left the city; for they will say, 'The Israelis are

7:19
Jer 13:16
Jn 9:24

7:20
Ex 10:16

7:24
Josh 15:7

7:25
Deut 13:17
24:16
Josh 6:18

7:26
Gen 31:46,
51,52
Josh 8:28,29
Isa 65:10
Hos 2:15

8:1
Deut 1:19,20,
21; 31:8
Josh 1:9; 6:2
10:8

8:2
Josh 6:18; 8:27

8:6
Josh 7:5

7:24, 25 Achan underestimated God and didn't take his commands seriously (6:18). It may have seemed a small thing to Achan, but the effects of his sin were felt by the entire nation, especially his family. Like Achan, our actions affect more people than just ourselves. Beware of the temptation to rationalize your sins by saying they are too small or too personal to hurt anyone but you.

7:24–26 Why did Achan's entire family pay for his sin? The biblical record does not tell us if they were accomplices to his crime. But in the ancient world, the family was treated as a whole. Achan, as the head of his family, was like a king. If he prospered, the family prospered with him. If he suffered, so did they. Many Israelites had already died in battle because of Achan's sin. Now he was to be completely cut off from Israel.

His entire family was to be stoned along with him, so that no trace of Achan would remain in Israel. In our individualistic culture we have a hard time understanding such a decree, but in ancient cultures it was a common punishment. The punishment fit the crime: Achan had disobeyed God's command to destroy everything in Jericho; thus everything that belonged to Achan would be destroyed.

8:1 Now that Israel was cleansed from Achan's sin, Joshua

prepared to attack Ai again—this time to win. Joshua had learned some lessons which we can follow in our daily lives: (1) seek God first each day (7:7); (2) confess your sins when God reveals them to you (7:19–21); (3) when you fail, refocus on God, deal with the problem, and move on (7:7, 22–25; 8:1). God wants the cycle of sin, repentance, and forgiveness to strengthen us, not weaken us. The lessons we learn from our failures should make us better able to handle the same situation the second time around. Since God is eager to give us cleansing, forgiveness, and strength, the only way to lose is to give up. We can tell what kind of people we are by what we do on the second and third attempts.

8:2 Why did God allow the Israelites to keep the loot this time? Israel's laws for handling the spoils of war covered two situations. (1) Cities like Jericho which were under God's "ban" (judgment for idolatry) could not be looted. God's people were to be kept holy and separate from every influence of idolatry. (2) The distribution of loot from cities not under the "ban" was a normal part of warfare. It provided the army and the nation with the necessary food, flocks, and weapons needed to sustain itself in wartime. Ai was not under the ban. The conquering army needed the food and equipment. Since soldiers were not paid, the loot was part of their incentive and reward for going to war.

running away again just as they did before!' 7Then you will jump up from your ambush and enter the city, for the Lord will give it to you. 8Set the city on fire, as the Lord has commanded. You now have your instructions."

9So they left that night and lay in ambush between Bethel and the west side of Ai; but Joshua and the rest of the army remained in the camp at Jericho. 10Early the next morning Joshua roused his men and started toward Ai, accompanied by the elders of Israel, 11, 12, 13and stopped at the edge of a valley north of the city. That night Joshua sent another five thousand men to join the troops in ambush on the west side of the city. He himself spent the night in the valley.

14The King of Ai, seeing the Israelis across the valley, went out early the next morning and attacked at the Plain of Arabah. But of course he didn't realize that there was an ambush behind the city. 15Joshua and the Israeli army fled across the wilderness as though badly beaten, 16and all the soldiers in the city were called out to chase after them; so the city was left defenseless; 17there was not a soldier left in Ai or Bethel and the city gates were left wide open.

18Then the Lord said to Joshua, "Point your spear toward Ai, for I will give you the city." Joshua did. 19And when the men in ambush saw his signal, they jumped up and poured into the city and set it on fire. 20, 21When the men of Ai looked behind them, smoke from the city was filling the sky, and they had nowhere to go. When Joshua and the troops who were with him saw the smoke, they knew that their men who had been in ambush were inside the city, so they turned upon their pursuers and began killing them. 22Then the Israelis who were inside the city came out and began destroying the enemy from the rear. So the men of Ai were caught in a trap and all of them died; not one man survived or escaped, 23except for the king of Ai, who was captured and brought to Joshua.

24When the army of Israel had finished slaughtering all the men outside the city, they went back and finished off everyone left inside. 25So the entire population of Ai, twelve thousand in all, was wiped out that day. 26For Joshua kept his spear pointed toward Ai until the last person was dead. 27Only the cattle and the loot were not destroyed, for the armies of Israel kept these for themselves. (The Lord had told Joshua they could.) 28So Ai became a desolate mound of refuse, as it still is today.

29Joshua hanged the king of Ai on a tree until evening, but as the sun was going down, he took down the body and threw it in front of the city gate. There he piled a great heap of stones over it, which can still be seen.

Joshua reads the law to the entire nation

30Then Joshua built an altar to the Lord God of Israel at Mount Ebal, 31as Moses had commanded in the book of his laws: "Make me an altar of boulders that have neither been broken nor carved," the Lord had said concerning Mount Ebal. Then the priests offered burnt sacrifices and peace offerings to the Lord on the altar. 32And as the people of Israel watched, Joshua carved upon the stones of the altar each of the Ten Commandments.

33Then all the people of Israel—including the elders, officers, judges, and the foreigners living among them—divided into two groups, half of them standing at the foot of Mount Gerizim and half at the foot of Mount Ebal. Between them stood the priests with the Ark, ready to pronounce their blessing. (This was all done in accordance with the instructions given long before by Moses.) 34Joshua then read to them all of the statements of blessing and curses that Moses had written in the book of God's laws. 35Every commandment Moses had ever given was read before the entire assembly, including the women and children and the foreigners who lived among the Israelis.

8:8 Josh 6:24; 8:20,21
8:14 Deut 1:1; 4:49; Josh 11:1
8:17 Josh 12:8-24
8:18 Ex 14:16; 17:9; Josh 8:26
8:22 Num 21:35; Deut 3:6
8:25 Deut 20:16
8:26 Ex 17:11; Josh 8:18
8:27 Josh 8:2
8:28 Josh 7:26
8:29 Deut 21:22,23
8:30 Gen 8:20; 12:7,8; Josh 22:10; Judg 6:24
8:31 Ex 20:25; Deut 27:5,6
8:33 Deut 27:12,13
8:34 Deut 11:26; 28:2-6,15-19

8:11-13 *another five thousand men.* These were evidently additional to the thirty thousand men already hiding there. Perhaps the additional five thousand were to intercept the forces expected from Bethel (vs 17). **8:31** *as Moses had commanded.* See Deut 27:2-8. **8:32** *each of the Ten Commandments,* literally, "the law of Moses."

8:32 See Exodus 20 for a list of the Ten Commandments that Joshua carved into the altar. These were the heart of all God's laws, and they are still relevant today.

8:33, 35 After Israel's military victory, Joshua obeyed God's command by gathering the people together and reminding them of God's laws (1:8). First he reminded them of the Ten

2. Joshua attacks the southern kings

9:1
Num 13:17,29
Deut 1:7
Josh 3:10
10:40; 11:16

9 When the kings of the surrounding area heard what had happened to Jericho, they quickly combined their armies to fight for their lives against Joshua and the Israelis. These were the kings of the nations west of the Jordan River, along the shores of the Mediterranean as far north as the Lebanon mountains—the Hittites, Amorites, Canaanites, Perizzites, Hivites, and Jebusites.

The people of Gibeon trick Joshua

9:3
Josh 10:2,7
11:19
Prov 13:17

3, 4, 5But when the people of Gibeon heard what had happened to Jericho and Ai, they resorted to trickery to save themselves. They sent ambassadors to Joshua wearing worn-out clothing, as though from a long journey, with patched shoes, weatherworn saddlebags on their donkeys, old, patched wine-skins and dry, moldy bread. 6When they arrived at the camp of Israel at Gilgal, they told Joshua and the men of Israel, "We have come from a distant land to ask for a peace treaty with you."

9:7
Ex 23:32
Josh 11:19

7The Israelis replied to these Hivites, "How do we know you don't live nearby? For if you do, we cannot make a treaty with you."

8They replied, "We will be your slaves."

"But who are you?" Joshua demanded. "Where do you come from?"

9:9
Josh 2:9
9:16,17

9And they told him, "We are from a very distant country; we have heard of the might of the Lord your God and of all that he did in Egypt, 10and what you did to the two kings of the Amorites—Sihon, king of Heshbon, and Og, king of Bashan. 11So our elders and our people instructed us, 'Prepare for a long journey; go to the people of Israel and declare our nation to be their servants, and ask for peace.' 12This bread was hot from the ovens when we left, but now as you see, it is dry and moldy; 13these wineskins were new, but now they are old and cracked; our clothing and shoes have become worn out from our long, hard trip."

9:14
Ex 23:32
Num 27:21

14, 15Joshua and the other leaders finally believed them. They did not bother to ask the Lord, but went ahead and signed a peace treaty. And the leaders of Israel ratified the agreement with a binding oath.

9:17
Josh 18:15,25,
26; 15:9,60
1 Sam 7:1,2
1 Chron 13:5,6

16Three days later the facts came out—these men were close neighbors. 17The Israeli army set out at once to investigate, and reached their cities in three days. (The names of the cities were Gibeon, Chephirah, Be-eroth, and Kiriath-jearim.)

THE BATTLE FOR AI
Under the cover of night, Joshua sent one detachment of soldiers to the west of Ai to lie in wait. The next morning he led a second group north of Ai. When the army of Ai attacked, the Israelites to the north pretended to scatter, only to turn on the enemy as the men lying in ambush moved in and burned the city.

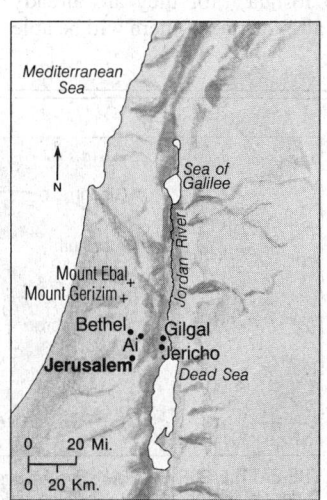

Mediterranean Sea
N
Sea of Galilee
Jordan River
Mount Ebal
Mount Gerizim
Bethel
Ai
Gilgal
Jerusalem
Jericho
Dead Sea
0   20 Mi.
0   20 Km.

most other books—once through quickly. We should read it daily as a constant reminder of who God is and what we can become.

9:1–5 As the news about their victory became widespread, the Israelites experienced opposition in two forms: direct (kings in the area began to unite against them); and indirect (the Gibeonites resorted to trickery). We can expect the same kinds of opposition as we obey God's commands. To guard against these pressures, we must rely on God and communicate daily with him. He will give us strength to endure the direct pressures and wisdom to see through the indirect trickery.

9:14, 15 After the promise had been made and the treaty ratified, the facts came out—Israel's leaders had been deceived. God had specifically instructed Israel to make no treaties with the inhabitants of Canaan (Exodus 23:32; 34:12; Numbers 33:55; Deuteronomy 7:2; 20:17, 18). As a strategist, Joshua knew enough to ask God before leading his troops into battle. But the peace treaty seemed innocent enough, so Joshua and the leaders made this decision on their own. By failing to seek God's guidance and rushing ahead with their own plans, they had to deal with angry people and an awkward alliance.

Successful people may feel they can "go it on their own." Feeling they have all the facts and understand the situation, they may not seek advice in untried ventures. But seeking God's advice before entering into agreements can keep minor matters from becoming major headaches.

Commandments; then he read the rest of the laws to them. God knows how easily we forget. We, like the Israelites, constantly need to review what God says. We should not read the Bible as we do

18But the cities were not harmed because of the vow which the leaders of Israel had made before the Lord God. The people of Israel were angry with their leaders because of the peace treaty.

19But the leaders replied, "We have sworn before the Lord God of Israel that we will not touch them, and we won't. 20We must let them live, for if we break our oath the wrath of Jehovah will be upon us."

9:20
2 Sam 21:1

21So they became servants of the Israelis, chopping their wood and carrying their water.

9:21
Gen 9:25

22Joshua summoned their leaders and demanded, "Why have you lied to us by saying that you lived in a distant land, when you were actually living right here among us? 23Now a curse shall be upon you! From this moment you must always furnish us with servants to chop wood and carry water for the service of our God."

24They replied, "We did it because we were told that Jehovah instructed his disciple Moses to conquer this entire land and destroy all the people living in it. So we feared for our lives because of you; that is why we have done it. 25But now we are in your hands; you may do with us as you wish."

9:24
Deut 7:1
20:16,17
Josh 2:24; 5:1

26So Joshua would not allow the people of Israel to kill them, 27but they became wood-choppers and water-carriers for the people of Israel and for the altar of the Lord—wherever it would be built (for the Lord hadn't yet told them where to build it). This arrangement is still in force at the time of this writing.

9:27
Deut 12:4,5,6

The sun stands still

10 When Adoni-zedek, the king of Jerusalem, heard how Joshua had captured and destroyed Ai and had killed its king, the same as he had done at Jericho, and how the people of Gibeon had made peace with Israel and were now their allies, 2he was very frightened. For Gibeon was a great city—as great as the royal cities and much larger than Ai—and its men were known as hard fighters. 3So King Adoni-zedek of Jerusalem sent messengers to several other kings: King Hoham of Hebron, King Piram of Jarmuth, King Japhia of Lachish, King Debir of Eglon.

10:1
Josh 8:25
9:14,15

10:2
1 Kgs 3:4,5
9:2,3
1 Chron 21:29
2 Chron 1:2,3

4"Come and help me destroy Gibeon," he urged them, "for they have made peace with Joshua and the people of Israel."

5So these five Amorite kings combined their armies for a united attack on Gibeon. 6The men of Gibeon hurriedly sent messengers to Joshua at Gilgal.

10:5
Num 13:29
Josh 9:1

"Come and help your servants!" they demanded. "Come quickly and save us! For all the kings of the Amorites who live in the hills are here with their armies."

7So Joshua and the Israeli army left Gilgal and went to rescue Gibeon.

8"Don't be afraid of them," the Lord said to Joshua, "for they are already defeated! I have given them to you to destroy. Not a single one of them will be able to stand up to you."

10:8
Josh 1:5,9; 6:2
8:1

9:19, 20 Joshua and his advisors had made a mistake. But since they had vowed to protect the Gibeonites, they would keep their word. The vow was not nullified by the Gibeonites' trickery. God had commanded that vows be kept (Leviticus 5:4; 27:9, 10), and breaking a vow was serious. This encourages us not to take vows lightly.

10:1-9 The Israelites, who were supposed to have destroyed the Gibeonites, were now allied with them. Even though this was a big mistake, God would remain faithful to his promise and help Israel defeat the coalition of nations now on the attack. God forgives sin and helps us move on, but he does not cancel its consequences. Even so, God can use our bad situations for his purposes.

10:5-8 This alliance of enemy kings from the south actually helped Joshua and his army. Because the enemies were united and making an attack on Gibeon, Joshua didn't have to spend the time and resources required to wage separate campaigns against each fortified city represented in the coalition. Joshua confidently confronted this coalition of armies and defeated them in a single battle because he trusted God to give Israel the victory.

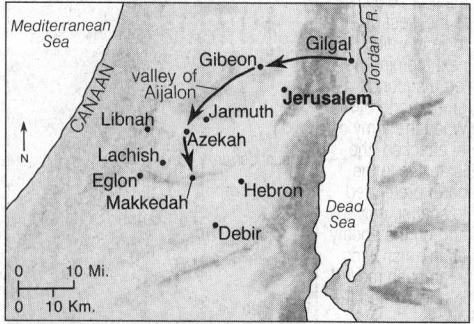

THE BATTLE FOR GIBEON Five Amorite kings conspired to destroy Gibeon. Israel came to the aid of the Gibeonites. The Israelites attacked the enemy armies outside of Gibeon and chased them through the Aijalon Valley as far as Makkedah and Azekah.

10:10
Judg 4:15

⁹Joshua traveled all night from Gilgal and took the enemy armies by surprise. ¹⁰Then the Lord threw them into a panic so that the army of Israel slaughtered great numbers of them at Gibeon and chased the others all the way to Beth-horon and Azekah and Makkedah, killing them along the way. ¹¹And as the enemy was racing down the hill to Beth-horon, the Lord destroyed them with a great hailstorm that continued all the way to Azekah; in fact, more men died from the hail than by the swords of the Israelis.

¹²As the men of Israel were pursuing and harassing the foe, Joshua prayed aloud, "Let the sun stand still over Gibeon, and let the moon stand in its place over the valley of Aijalon!"

10:13
Isa 38:8

¹³And the sun and the moon didn't move until the Israeli army had finished the destruction of its enemies! This is described in greater detail in *The Book of Jashar*. So the sun stopped in the heavens and stayed there for almost twenty-four hours!

10:14
Ex 14:14
Deut 1:30
10:15
Josh 10:6,43

¹⁴There had never been such a day before, and there has never been another since, when the Lord stopped the sun and moon—all because of the prayer of one man. But the Lord was fighting for Israel. ¹⁵(Afterwards Joshua and the Israeli army returned to Gilgal.)

The five kings are killed

10:16
Josh 10:28

¹⁶During the battle the five kings escaped and hid in a cave at Makkedah. ¹⁷When the news was brought to Joshua that they had been found, ¹⁸he issued a command that a great stone be rolled against the mouth of the cave and that guards be placed there to keep the kings inside.

¹⁹Then Joshua commanded the rest of the army, "Go on chasing the enemy and cut them down from the rear. Don't let them get back to their cities, for the Lord will help you to completely destroy them."

10:20
Deut 20:16
10:21
Josh 10:16

²⁰So Joshua and the Israeli army continued the slaughter and wiped out the five armies except for a tiny remnant that managed to reach their fortified cities. ²¹Then the Israelis returned to their camp at Makkedah without having lost a single man! And after that no one dared to attack Israel.

10:22
Deut 7:24
1 Sam 15:32,33

²²,²³Joshua now instructed his men to remove the stone from the mouth of the cave and to bring out the five kings—of Jerusalem, Hebron, Jarmuth, Lachish, and Eglon. ²⁴Joshua told the captains of his army to put their feet on the kings' necks.

10:25
Josh 10:8

²⁵"Don't ever be afraid or discouraged," Joshua said to his men. "Be strong and courageous, for the Lord is going to do this to all of your enemies."

10:26
Josh 8:29

²⁶With that, Joshua plunged his sword into each of the five kings, killing them. He then hanged them on five trees until evening.

10:27
Deut 21:22,23

²⁷As the sun was going down, Joshua instructed that their bodies be taken down and thrown into the cave where they had been hiding; and a great pile of stones was placed at the mouth of the cave. (The pile is still there today.)

Israel destroys cities in the south

²⁸On that same day Joshua destroyed the city of Makkedah and killed its king and

---

10:12 How did the sun stand still? Of course, in relation to the earth the sun always stands still—it is the earth that travels around the sun. But the terminology used in Joshua should not cause us to doubt the miracle. After all, we are not confused when someone tells us the sun rises or sets. The point is that the day was prolonged, not that God used a particular method to prolong it.

Two explanations have been given for how this event occurred: (1) A slowing of the earth's normal rotation gave Joshua more time, as the original Hebrew language seems to indicate. (2) Some unusual refraction of the sun's rays gave additional hours of light. Regardless of God's chosen method, the Bible is clear that the day was prolonged by a miracle, and that God's intervention turned the tide of battle for his people.

10:13 *The Book of Jashar* was probably a collection of historical events put to music. Many parts of the Bible contain quotations

from previous books, songs, poems, or other spoken and written materials. Because God guided the writer to select this material, his message comes with divine authority.

10:24 Placing a foot on the neck of a captive was a common military practice in the ancient Near East. It symbolized the victor's domination of his captives.

10:25 With God's help, Israel won the battle against five armies without losing a single soldier. Such a triumph was part of God's daily business as he worked with his people for victory. Joshua told his men never to be afraid, because God would give them similar victories over all their enemies. God has often protected us and won victories in our lives. The same God who empowered Joshua and who has led us in the past will help us with our present and future needs. Reminding ourselves of his help in the past will give us hope for the struggles that lie ahead.

everyone in it. Not one person in the entire city was left alive. 29Then the Israelis went to Libnah. 30There, too, the Lord gave them the city and its king. Every last person was slaughtered, just as at Jericho.

31From Libnah they went to Lachish and attacked it. 32And the Lord gave it to them on the second day; here, too, the entire population was slaughtered, just as at Libnah.

33During the attack on Lachish, King Horam of Gezer arrived with his army to try to help defend the city, but Joshua's men killed him and destroyed his entire army.

34, 35The Israeli army then captured Eglon on the first day and, as at Lachish, they killed everyone in the city. 36After leaving Eglon they went to Hebron, 37and captured it and all of its surrounding villages, slaughtering the entire population. Not one person was left alive. 38Then they turned back to Debir, 39which they quickly captured with all of its outlying villages. And they killed everyone just as they had at Libnah.

40So Joshua and his army conquered the whole country—the nations and kings of the hill country, the Negeb, the lowlands, and the mountain slopes. They destroyed everyone in the land, just as the Lord God of Israel had commanded, 41slaughtering them from Kadesh-barnea to Gaza, and from Goshen to Gibeon. 42This was all accomplished in one campaign, for the Lord God of Israel was fighting for his people. 43Then Joshua and his army returned to their camp at Gilgal.

3. Joshua attacks the northern kings

11 When King Jabin of Hazor heard what had happened, he sent urgent messages to the following kings:

King Jobab of Madon;
The king of Shimron;
The king of Achshaph;
All the kings of the northern hill country;
The kings in the Arabah, south of Chinneroth;
Those in the lowland;
The kings in the mountain areas of Dor, on the west;
The kings of Canaan, both east and west;
The kings of the Amorites;
The kings of the Hittites;

10:29
Num 33:15-37
Josh 12:8-24

10:36
Josh 10:3

10:40
Deut 1:7; 7:24
20:16
10:41
Josh 11:16
15:48-62

10:43
Josh 10:6

11:1
Josh 10:3,4
11:10; 12:8-24
19:35-39
Judg 4:2,17

10:40 God had commanded Joshua to rid the land of sin so God's people could occupy it. Joshua did his job thoroughly. When God orders us to eliminate sin from our lives, we must not pause to debate, consider the options, negotiate a compromise, or rationalize. Instead, like Joshua, our response must be swift and complete. We must be ruthless in removing sin from our lives.

11:1-4 There were two kings of Hazor named Jabin. The other, apparently a weak ruler, is mentioned in Judges 4:2, 3. The King Jabin of this story was quite powerful, for he was able to build an alliance with dozens of kings. By all appearances, Jabin had a clear advantage over Joshua and his outnumbered forces. But those who honor God can be victorious regardless of the odds.

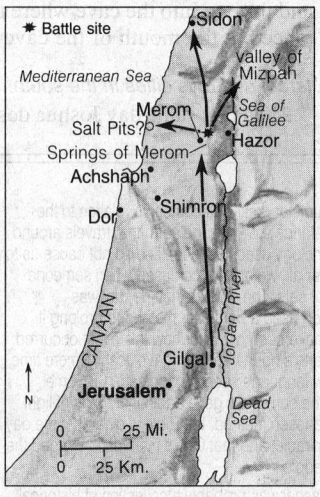

THE BATTLE FOR HAZOR Kings from the north joined together to battle the Israelites who controlled the southern half of the land of Canaan. They gathered by the Springs of Merom, but Joshua attacked them by surprise—the enemies' chariots were useless in the dense forests. Hazor, the largest Canaanite center in Galilee, was destroyed.

The kings of the Perizzites;
The kings in the Jebusite hill country;
The Hivite kings in the cities on the slopes of Mount Hermon, in the land of
  Mizpah.

11:4
Josh 11:20

4All these kings responded by mobilizing their armies, and uniting to crush Israel. Their combined troops, along with a vast array of horses and chariots, covered the landscape around the Springs of Merom as far as one could see; 5for they established their camp at the Springs of Merom.

11:6
Josh 8:1; 10:8
2 Sam 8:4

6But the Lord said to Joshua, "Don't be afraid of them, for by this time tomorrow they will all be dead! Hamstring their horses and burn their chariots." 7Joshua and his troops arrived suddenly at the Springs of Merom and attacked. 8And the Lord gave all that vast army to the Israelis, who chased them as far as Great Sidon and a place called the Salt Pits, and eastward into the valley of Mizpah; so not one enemy troop survived the battle. 9Then Joshua and his men did as the Lord had instructed, for they hamstrung the horses and burned all the chariots.

11:10
Judg 4:2,3
1 Sam 12:9
1 Kgs 9:15
2 Kgs 15:29

10On the way back, Joshua captured Hazor and killed its king. (Hazor had at one time been the capital of the federation of all those kingdoms.) 11Every person there was killed and the city was burned.

11:11
Deut 20:16
Josh 8:8,20,21
10:28,30

12Then he attacked and destroyed all the other cities of those kings. All the people were slaughtered, just as Moses had commanded long before. 13(However, Joshua did not burn any of the cities built on mounds except for Hazor.) 14All the loot and cattle of the ravaged cities were taken by the Israelis for themselves, but they killed all the people. 15For so the Lord had commanded his disciple Moses; and Moses had passed the commandment on to Joshua, who did as he had been told: he carefully obeyed all of the Lord's instructions to Moses.

11:14
Josh 8:27

11:15
Ex 34:11
Deut 31:7

4. Summary of conquests

11:16
Josh 10:40,41

11:17
Deut 7:24
Josh 12:7

16So Joshua conquered the entire land—the hill country, the Negeb, the land of Goshen, the lowlands, the Arabah, and the hills and lowlands of Israel. 17The Israeli territory now extended all the way from Mount Halak, near Seir, to Baal-gad in the valley of Lebanon, at the foot of Mount Hermon. And Joshua killed all the kings of those territories. 18It took seven years of war to accomplish all of this. 19None of the cities was given a peace treaty except the Hivites of Gibeon; all of the others were destroyed. 20For the Lord made the enemy kings want to fight the Israelis instead of asking for peace; so they were mercilessly killed, as the Lord had commanded Moses.

11:19
Josh 9:3-15

11:20
Ex 14:17
Deut 20:16
Josh 11:4

11:18 *It took seven years,* implied in other text. Literally, "a long time."

11:10–13 Victorious invaders usually kept captured cities intact, moving into them and making them centers of commerce and defense. For example, Moses predicted in Deuteronomy 6:10–12 that Israel would occupy cities they themselves had not built. Hazor, however, was burned. As a former capital of the land, it symbolized the wicked culture Israel had come to destroy. In addition, its capture and destruction broke the backbone of the federation and weakened the rest of the people's will to resist.

11:15 Joshua followed every detail of God's commands to Moses. It is usually difficult to complete someone else's project, but Joshua stepped into Moses' job, building upon what Moses had started, and brought it to completion. A new person starting a new job usually brings a new style and personality to that job. But the church or any other organization cannot work effectively if every change of personnel means starting from scratch. True servants will step in and continue or complete good work that others have started.

11:15 Joshua carefully obeyed all the instructions given by God.

This theme of obedience is repeated frequently in the book of Joshua, partly because obedience is one aspect of life the individual believer can control. We can't always control understanding because we may not have all the facts. We can't control what other people do or how they treat us. However, we can control our response to life's situations when we *choose* to obey God. Whatever new challenges we may face, the Bible contains relevant instructions which we can choose to ignore or choose to follow.

11:18 The conquest of Canaan seems to have happened quickly (we can read about it in one sitting), but it actually took seven years. We often expect quick changes in our lives and quick victories over sin. But our journey with God is a lifelong process, and the changes and victories may take time. It is easy to grow impatient with God and feel like giving up hope because things are moving too slowly. When we are close to a situation, it is difficult to see progress. But when we look back we can see that God never stopped working.

21During this period Joshua routed all of the giants—the descendants of Anak who lived in the hill country in Hebron, Debir, Anab, Judah, and Israel; he killed them all and completely destroyed their cities. 22None was left in all the land of Israel, though some still remained in Gaza, Gath, and Ashdod.

23So Joshua took the entire land just as the Lord had instructed Moses; and he gave it to the people of Israel as their inheritance, dividing the land among the tribes. So the land finally rested from its war.

11:21
Num 13:33
Deut 9:1,2
Josh 14:12
15:13

11:23
Deut 1:38
12:9,10; 25:19
Heb 4:8

A list of the conquered kings

12 Here is the list of the kings on the east side of the Jordan River whose cities were destroyed by the Israelis: (The area involved stretched all the way from the valley of the Arnon River to Mount Hermon, including the cities of the eastern desert.)

12:1
Num 32:33
Deut 3:8
Josh 11:1-3

2King Sihon of the Amorites, who lived in Heshbon. His kingdom extended from Aroer, on the edge of the Arnon Valley, and from the middle of the valley of the Arnon River to the Jabbok River, which is the boundary of the Ammonites. This includes half of the present area of Gilead, which lies north of the Jabbok River. 3Sihon also controlled the Jordan River valley as far north as the western shores of the Lake of Galilee; and as far south as the Dead Sea and the slopes of Mount Pisgah.

12:2
Num 21:23
Deut 2:35

4King Og of Bashan, the last of the Rephaim, who lived at Ashtaroth and Edre-i: 5He ruled a territory stretching from Mount Hermon in the north to Salecah on Mount Bashan in the east, and on the west, extending to the boundary of the kingdoms of Geshur and Ma-acah. His kingdom also stretched south to include the northern half of Gilead where the boundary touched the border of the kingdom of Sihon, king of Heshbon. 6Moses and the people of Israel had destroyed these people, and Moses gave the land to the tribes of Reuben and the half-tribe of Manasseh.

12:4
Num 21:33
Josh 13:12

7Here is a list of the kings destroyed by Joshua and the armies of Israel on the west side of the Jordan. (This land which lay between Baal-gad in the Valley of Lebanon and Mount Halak, west of Mount Seir, was allotted by Joshua to the other tribes of Israel. 8-24The area included the hill country, the lowlands, the Arabah, the mountain slopes, the Judean Desert, and the Negeb. The people who lived there were the Hittites, the Amorites, the Canaanites, the Perizzites, the Hivites, and the Jebusites):

12:7
Josh 11:17

12:8
Num 21:1-3
Deut 7:24
Josh 11:16

The king of Jericho; the king of Ai, near Bethel; the king of Jerusalem; the king of Hebron; the king of Jarmuth; the king of Lachish; the king of Eglon; the king of Gezer; the king of Debir; the king of Geder; the king of Hormah; the king of Arad; the king of Libnah; the king of Adullam; the king of Makkedah; the king of Bethel; the king of Tappu-ah; the king of Hepher; the king of Aphek; the king of Lasharon; the king of Madon; the king of Hazor; the king of Shimron-meron; the king of Achshaph; the king of Taanach; the king of Megiddo; the king of Kedesh; the king of Jokne-am, in Carmel; the king of Dor in the city of Naphathdor; the king of Goiim in Gilgal; the king of Tirzah. So in all, thirty-one kings and their cities were destroyed.

11:21 These were the same tribes of giants the Israelite spies described when they gave their negative report on the Promised Land (Numbers 13, 14). This time the people did not let their fear of the giants prevent them from engaging in battle and claiming the land God had promised.

12:1 Chapter 12 is a summary of the first half of Joshua. It lists the kings and nations conquered by Joshua both to the east and west of the Jordan River. As long as the people trusted and obeyed God, one evil nation after another fell in defeat.

13:1 Joshua was getting old—he was between 85 and 100 years of age at this time. God, however, still had work for him to do. Our culture often glorifies the young and strong and seems to set aside those who are older. Yet older people are filled with the wisdom that comes with experience. They are very capable of serving if given the chance and should be encouraged to do so. Believers are never allowed to retire from God's service. And those past retirement age should not assume that age alone excuses them from serving in God's work.

C. DIVIDING THE PROMISED LAND (13:1—24:33)

After seven years of battle, Israel gained control of the land, which was then divided and allotted to the tribes. Joshua dismisses the army, for it was now each tribe's responsibility to clear out the remaining enemies from their own areas. Joshua continues to encourage the people to remain faithful to God so they can remain in the land. The Promised Land was Israel's earthly inheritance. But Israel also had a spiritual inheritance in which we can share when we live a life of faithfulness to God.

1. The tribes receive their land

Areas still to be occupied:

13:1
Josh 14:10

13:2
Josh 12:3
Judg 3:1-3

13 Joshua was now an old man. "You are growing old," the Lord said to him, "and there are still many nations to be conquered. 2-7Here is a list of the areas still to be occupied:

All the land of the Philistines;

The land of the Geshurites;

The territory now belonging to the Canaanites from the brook of Egypt to the southern boundary of Ekron;

Five cities of the Philistines: Gaza, Ashdod, Ashkelon, Gath, Ekron;

The land of the Avvim in the south;

In the north, all the land of the Canaanites, including Me-arah (which belongs to the Sidonians), stretching northward to Aphek at the boundary of the Amorites;

The land of the Gebalites on the coast and all of the Lebanon mountain area from Baal-gad beneath Mount Hermon in the south to the entrance of Hamath in the north;

All the hill country from Lebanon to Misrephoth-maim, including all the land of the Sidonians.

I am ready to drive these people out from before the nation of Israel, so include all this territory when you divide the land among the nine tribes and the half-tribe of Manasseh as I have commanded you."

13:2-7 *In the north, stretching northward, on the coast,* implied.

THE LAND YET TO BE CONQUERED
Canaan was now controlled by the Israelites, although much land and several cities still needed to be conquered. Joshua told the people to include both conquered and unconquered lands in the territorial allotments (13:7). He was certain the people would complete the conquest as God had commanded.

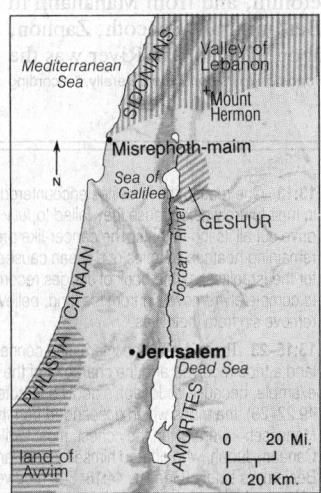

13:2ff The following chapters describe how the Promised Land was divided among the 12 tribes. First, the tribe of Levi was not to have any land because they were to spend all their energies serving the people, not their own interests (13:14; 21). Second, the tribes of Reuben and Gad and the half-tribe of Manasseh had already received land east of the Jordan River, which had been

given to them by Moses (Numbers 32). Third, the tribes of Judah and Joseph (Ephraim and the other half-tribe of Manasseh) received land that their ancestor Jacob had promised them 450 years earlier (Genesis 48:22; Joshua 15—17). The rest of the tribes divided up the remaining land by throwing sacred dice (chapter 18).

In Jacob's original blessing of his sons (Genesis 49) and in Moses' blessing of the 12 tribes (Deuteronomy 33), the type of land each tribe would receive was already known. The two blessings were prophetic, for although Joshua threw dice to determine the land to be given to each of the remaining tribes, the allotments came out just as Jacob and Moses had predicted.

13:7 Much of the land was unconquered at this point, but God's plan was to go ahead and include that land in the divisions among the tribes. God's desire was that it would eventually be conquered by the Israelites. God knows the future, and as he leads you he already knows about the victories that lie ahead. But just as the Israelites still had to go to battle and fight, we must still face the trials and fight the battles of our unconquered land.

What are our unconquered lands today? They may be overseas missionary territories, new languages in which to translate the Bible, new missionary areas in our neighborhoods, interest groups or institutions that need redemptive work, unchallenged public problems or ethical issues, unconfessed sin in our lives, or underdeveloped talents and resources. What territory has God given you to conquer? This territory is our "Promised Land." Our inheritance will be a new heaven and a new earth (Revelation 21:1), if we, like Israel, fulfill the mission God has given us to do.

Assignment of the land east of the Jordan

⁸The other half of the tribe of Manasseh, and the tribes of Reuben and Gad, had already received their inheritance on the east side of the Jordan, for Moses had previously assigned this land to them. ⁹Their territory ran from Aroer, on the edge of the valley of the Arnon River, included the city in the valley, and crossed the tableland of Medeba to Dibon; ¹⁰it also included all the cities of King Sihon of the Amorites, who reigned in Heshbon, and extended as far as the borders of Ammon. ¹¹It included Gilead; the territory of the Geshurites and the Ma-acathites; all of Mount Hermon; Mount Bashan with its city of Salecah; ¹²and all the territory of King Og of Bashan, who had reigned in Ashtaroth and Edre-i. (He was the last of the Rephaim, for Moses had attacked them and driven them out. ¹³However, the people of Israel had not driven out the Geshurites or the Ma-acathites, who still live there among the Israelites to this day.)

¹⁴**The Territorial Assignments**

The Land Given to the Tribe of Levi: Moses hadn't assigned any land to the tribe of Levi: instead, they were given the offerings brought to the Lord.

¹⁵*The Land Given to the Tribe of Reuben:* Fitting the size of its territory to its size of population, Moses had assigned the following area to the tribe of Reuben: ¹⁶Their land extended from Aroer on the edge of the valley of the Arnon River, past the city of Arnon in the middle of the valley, to beyond the tableland near Medeba. ¹⁷It included Heshbon and the other cities on the plain—Dibon, Bamoth-baal, Beth-baal-meon, ¹⁸Jahaz, Kedemoth, Mepha-ath, ¹⁹Kiriathaim, Sibmah, Zereth-shahar on the mountain above the valley, ²⁰Beth-peor, Beth-jeshimoth, and the slopes of Mount Pisgah.

²¹The land of Reuben also included the cities of the tableland and the kingdom of Sihon. Sihon was the king who had lived in Heshbon and was killed by Moses along with the other chiefs of Midian—Evi, Rekem, Zur, Hur, and Reba. ²²The people of Israel also killed Balaam the magician, the son of Beor. ²³The Jordan River was the western boundary of the tribe of Reuben.

²⁴*The Land Given to the Tribe of Gad:* Moses also assigned land to the tribe of Gad in proportion to its population. ²⁵This territory included Jazer, all the cities of Gilead and half of the land of Ammon as far as Aroer near Rabbah. ²⁶It also extended from Heshbon to Ramath-mizpeh and Betonim, and from Mahanaim to Lodebar. ²⁷, ²⁸In the valley were Beth-haram, and Beth-nimrah, Succoth, Zaphon, and the rest of the kingdom of King Sihon of Heshbon. The Jordan River was the

13:8
Num 32:33
Deut 3:12

13:12
Josh 12:4

13:13
Josh 6:25; 13:13

13:14
Deut 18:1

13:15
Josh 18:7

13:21
Num 31:8

13:22
Num 22:5
32:34-36

13:27
Deut 3:17

13:15 *size of population,* literally, "according to its families." **13:24** *in proportion to its population,* literally, "according to its families."

THE TRIBES EAST OF THE JORDAN

Joshua assigned territory to the tribes of Reuben, Gad, and the half-tribe of Manasseh on the east side of the Jordan where they had chosen to remain because of the wonderful sheep country (Numbers 32:1–5).

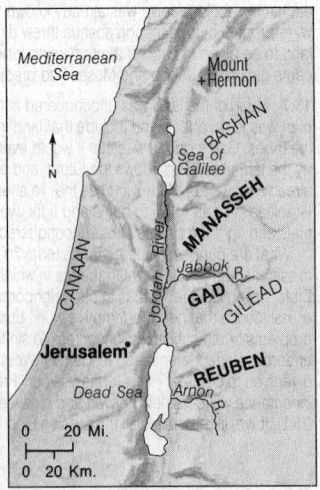

13:13 One reason the Israelites encountered so many problems in their future was because they failed to *fully* conquer the land and drive out all its inhabitants. The cancer-like presence of the remaining heathen peoples of Canaan caused unending difficulties for the Israelites, as the book of Judges records. Just as they failed to completely remove sin from the land, believers often fail to remove sin from their lives.

13:15–23 There is often an interesting connection between the land a tribe received and the character of the tribe's founder. For example, because of Joseph's godly character (Genesis 49:22–26), the tribes which descended from him—Ephraim and Manasseh—were given the richest, most fertile land in all of Canaan. Judah, who offered himself in exchange for his brother Benjamin's safety (Genesis 44:18–34), received the largest portion of land, which eventually became the Southern Kingdom and the seat of the dynasty of King David. Reuben, who slept with one of his father's wives (Genesis 49:4), was given desert land.

13:29 The tribe of Manasseh was divided into two half-tribes. This occurred when many people from the tribe wanted to settle east of the Jordan River in an area that was especially suited for their flocks (Numbers 32:33). The rest of the tribe still preferred to settle west of the Jordan River in the land of Canaan.

western border, extending as far as the Lake of Galilee; then the border turned east from the Jordan River.

²⁹*The Land Given to the Half-Tribe of Manasseh:* Moses had assigned the following territory to the half-tribe of Manasseh in proportion to its needs: ³⁰Their territory extended north from Mahanaim, included all of Bashan, the former kingdom of King Og, and the sixty cities of Jair in Bashan. ³¹Half of Gilead and King Og's royal cities of Ashtaroth and Edre-i were given to half of the clan Machir, who was Manasseh's son.

³²That was how Moses divided the land east of the Jordan River where the people were camped at that time across from Jericho. ³³But Moses had given no land to the

13:33
Josh 13:14

13:29 *in proportion to its needs,* literally, "according to its families."

THE CONQUERED LAND
Joshua displayed brilliant military strategy in the way he went about conquering the land of Canaan. He first captured the well-fortified Jericho to gain a foothold in Canaan and to demonstrate the awesome might of the God of Israel. Then he gained the hill country around Bethel and Gibeon. From there he subdued towns in the lowlands. Then his army conquered important cities in the north, such as Hazor. In all, Israel conquered land both east (12:1–6) and west (12:7–24) of the Jordan River; from Mount Hermon in the north to beyond the Negeb to Mount Halak in the south. Thirty-one kings and their cities had been defeated. The Israelites had over-powered the Hittites, the Amorites, the Canaanites, the Perizzites, the Hivites, and the Jebusites. Other peoples living in Canaan were yet to be conquered.

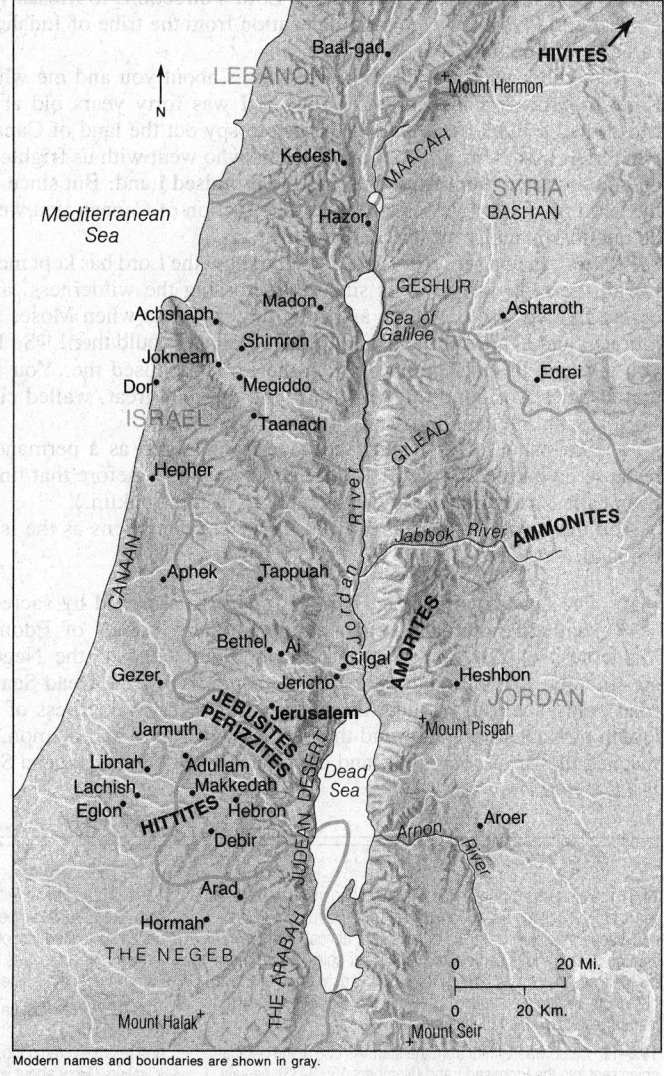

Modern names and boundaries are shown in gray.

13:33 The Levites were dedicated to serving God. They needed more time and mobility than a landowner could possibly have. Giving them land would mean saddling them with responsibilities and loyalties that would hinder their service to God. Instead, God arranged for the other tribes to meet the Levites' needs through donations. (See Numbers 35:2–4 for how the Levites were to receive cities within each tribal territory.)

tribe of Levi for, as he had explained to them, the Lord God was their inheritance. He was all they needed. He would take care of them in other ways.

Assignment of the land west of the Jordan

14 The conquered lands of Canaan were allotted to the remaining nine and a half tribes of Israel. The decision as to which tribe would receive which area was decided by throwing dice before the Lord, and he caused them to turn up in the ways he wanted. Eleazar the priest, Joshua, and the tribal leaders supervised the lottery.

14:1
Num 34:10-29
Josh 18:5,6

3, 4(Moses had already given land to the two and a half tribes on the east side of the Jordan River. The tribe of Joseph had become two separate tribes, Manasseh and Ephraim, and the Levites were given no land at all, except cities in which to live and the surrounding pasturelands for their cattle. 5So the distribution of the land was in strict accordance with the Lord's directions to Moses.)

14:3
Num 32:33
Josh 13:14

6*The Land Given to Caleb:* A delegation from the tribe of Judah, led by Caleb, came to Joshua in Gilgal.

14:6
Num 13:30
14:6,24,30
Josh 15:13

"Remember what the Lord said to Moses about you and me when we were at Kadesh-barnea?" Caleb asked Joshua. 7"I was forty years old at the time, and Moses had sent us from Kadesh-barnea to spy out the land of Canaan. I reported what I felt was the truth, 8but our brothers who went with us frightened the people and discouraged them from entering the Promised Land. But since I had followed the Lord my God, 9Moses told me, 'The section of Canaan you were just in shall belong to you and your descendants forever.'

14:9
Deut 1:36

10"Now, as you see, from that time until now the Lord has kept me alive and well for all these forty-five years since crisscrossing the wilderness, and today I am eighty-five years old. 11I am as strong now as I was when Moses sent us on that journey, and I can still travel and fight as well as I could then! 12So I'm asking that you give me the hill country which the Lord promised me. You will remember that as spies we found the Anakim living there in great, walled cities, but if the Lord is with me I shall drive them out of the land."

14:12
Num 13:33

13, 14So Joshua blessed him and gave him Hebron as a permanent inheritance because he had followed the Lord God of Israel. 15(Before that time Hebron had been called Kiriath-arba, after a great hero of the Anakim.)

And there was no resistance from the local populations as the Israelis resettled the land.

14:15
Gen 35:27
Josh 15:48-62
20:7
Judg 1:10

15 The land given *to the Tribe of Judah* (as assigned by sacred lot): Judah's southern boundary began at the northern border of Edom, crossed the Wilderness of Zin, and ended at the northern edge of the Negeb. 2, 3, 4More specifically, this boundary began at the south bay of the Dead Sea, ran along the road going south of Mount Akrabbim, on into the Wilderness of Zin to Hezron (south of Kadesh-barnea), and then up through Karka and Azmon, until it finally reached the Brook of Egypt, and along that to the Mediterranean Sea.

15:1
Num 34:3,4
Deut 32:51
Josh 15:13
19:1,36

14:2 *by throwing dice,* literally, "by lot."

14:5 The land was divided exactly as God had instructed Moses years before. Joshua did not change a word. He followed God's commands precisely. Often we believe that "almost" is close enough. And this idea can carry over into our spiritual lives. For example, we may follow God's Word as long as we agree with it, but ignore it when the demands seem harsh. But God is looking for leaders who follow instructions precisely.

14:6–12 Caleb was faithful from the start. As one of the original spies sent into the Promised Land (Numbers 13:30–33), he saw great cities and giants, yet he knew God would help the people conquer the land. Because of his faith, God promised him a personal inheritance of land (Numbers 14:24; Deuteronomy 1:34–36). Now, 45 years later, the land was given to him. His faith was still unwavering. Although his inherited land still had giants, he knew the Lord would help him conquer them. Like Caleb, we must be faithful to God, not only at the start of our walk with him, but through our entire lives. We must never allow ourselves to rest on our past accomplishments or reputations.

14:6–12 When Joshua gave Caleb his land, it fulfilled a promise God had made to Caleb 45 years earlier. We expect such integrity and reliability from God, but do we expect the same from his followers? How about you? Is your word this reliable? Would you honor a 45-year-old promise? God would—and does. Even today he is honoring promises he made *thousands* of years ago. In fact, some of his greatest promises are yet to be fulfilled. This gives us much to look forward to. Let your faith grow as you realize how God keeps his word.

15:5
Josh 18:15

⁵The eastern boundary extended along the Dead Sea to the mouth of the Jordan River.

The northern boundary began at the bay where the Jordan River empties into the Salt Sea, ⁶crossed to Beth-hoglah, then proceeded north of Beth-arabah to the stone of Bohan (son of Reuben). ⁷From that point it went through the Valley of Achor to Debir, where it turned northwest toward Gilgal, opposite the slopes of Adummim on the south side of the valley. From there the border extended to the springs at Enshemesh and on to En-rogel. ⁸The boundary then passed through the Valley of Hinnom, along the southern shoulder of Jebus (where the city of Jerusalem is located), then west to the top of the mountain above the Valley of Hinnom and on up to the northern end of the Valley of Rephaim. ⁹From there the border extended from the top of the mountain to the spring of Nephtoah, and from there to the cities of Mount Ephron before it turned northward to circle around Baalah (which is another name for Kiriath-jearim). ¹⁰, ¹¹Then the border circled west of Baalah to Mount Seir, passed along to the town of Chesalon on the northern shoulder of Mount Jearim, and went down to Beth-shemesh. Turning northwest again, the boundary line proceeded past the south of Timnah to the shoulder of the hill north of Ekron, where it bent to the left, passing south of Shikkeron and Mount Baalah. Turning again to the north, it passed Jabneel and ended at the Mediterranean Sea. ¹²The western border was the shoreline of the Mediterranean.

15:8
Josh 15:63

15:13
Josh 14:13-15
Judg 1:12-15

15:14
Num 13:33
Deut 9:2
Josh 11:21,22

¹³*The Land Given to Caleb:* The Lord instructed Joshua to assign some of Judah's territory to Caleb (son of Jephunneh), so he was given the city of Arba (also called Hebron), which had been named after Anak's father. ¹⁴Caleb drove out the descendants of the three sons of Anak: Talmai, Sheshai, and Ahiman. ¹⁵Then he fought against the people living in the city of Debir (formerly called Kiriath-sepher).

15:17
Judg 1:13; 3:9

¹⁶Caleb said that he would give his daughter Achsah to be the wife of anyone who would go and capture Kiriath-sepher. ¹⁷Othni-el (son of Kenaz), Caleb's nephew, was the one who conquered it, so Achsah became Othni-el's wife. ¹⁸, ¹⁹As she was leaving with him, she urged him to ask her father for an additional field as a wedding present. She got off her donkey to speak to Caleb about this.

"What is it? What can I do for you?" he asked.

And she replied, "Give me another present! For the land you gave me is a desert. Give us some springs, too!" Then he gave her the upper and lower springs. ²⁰So this was the assignment of land to the tribe of Judah:

15:21
Gen 21:31
35:21
1 Sam 27:6
30:1
2 Kgs 14:19

²¹⁻³²The cities of Judah which were situated along the borders of Edom in the Negeb, namely: Kabzeel, Eder, Jagur, Kinah, Dimonah, Adadah, Kedesh, Hazor, Ithnan, Ziph, Telem, Be-aloth, Hazor-hadattah, Keri-oth-hezron (or, Hazor), Amam, Shema, Moladah, Hazar-gaddah, Heshmon, Beth-pelet, Hazar-shual, Beer-sheba, Biziothiah, Baalah, Iim, Ezem, Eltolad, Chesil, Hormah, Ziklag, Madmannah, Sansannah, Lebaoth, Shilhim, Ain, and Rimmon. In all, there were twenty-nine of these cities with their surrounding villages.

15:33
Judg 13:25
16:31
1 Sam 22:1

³³⁻³⁶The following cities situated in the lowlands were also given to Judah: Eshtaol, Zorah, Ashnah, Zanoah, En-gannim, Tappu-ah, Enam, Jarmuth, Adullam, Socoh, Azekah, Sha-araim, Adithaim, Gederah, and Gederothaim. In all, there were fourteen of these cities with their surrounding villages.

15:37
Josh 10:3
2 Kgs 14:19

³⁷⁻⁴⁴The tribe of Judah also inherited twenty-five other cities with their villages: Zenan, Hadashah, Migdal-gad, Dilean, Mizpeh, Jokthe-el, Lachish, Bozkath, Eglon, Cabbon, Lahmam, Chitlish, Gederoth, Beth-dagon, Naamah, Makkedah, Libnah, Ether, Ashan, Iphtah, Ashnah, Nezib, Keilah, Achzib, and Mareshah.

⁴⁵The territory of the tribe of Judah also included all the towns and villages of Ekron. ⁴⁶From Ekron the boundary extended to the Mediterranean, and included

15:18, 19 *as a wedding present,* implied. **15:37-44** *The tribe of Judah also inherited twenty-five other cities with their villages,* implied. See verses 41 and 44.

15:16–19 Othniel became Israel's first judge after Joshua's death (Judges 1:13; 3:9–11). He played an important role in reforming Israel by chasing away an oppressive enemy army and bringing peace back to the land.

the cities along the borders of Ashdod with their nearby villages; 47also the city of
Ashdod with its villages, and Gaza with its villages as far as the Brook of Egypt;
also the entire Mediterranean coast from the mouth of the Brook of Egypt on the
south, to Tyre on the north.

48-62Judah also received these forty-four cities in the hill country with their
surrounding villages: Shamir, Jattir, Socoh, Dannah, Kiriath-sannah (or Debir),
Anab, Eshtemoh, Anim, Goshen, Holon, Giloh, Arab, Dumah, Eshan, Janim,
Beth-tappu-ah, Aphekah, Humtah, Kiriath-arba (or, Hebron), Zior, Maon, Car-
mel, Ziph, Juttah, Jezreel, Jokde-am, Zanoah, Kain, Gibe-ah, Timnah, Halhul,
Beth-zur, Gedor, Maarath, Beth-anoth, Eltekon, Kiriath-baal (also known as
Kiriath-jearim), Rabbah, Beth-arabah, Middin, Secacah, Nibshan, The City of
Salt, and En-gedi.

63But the tribe of Judah could not drive out the Jebusites who lived in the city of
Jerusalem, so the Jebusites live there among the people of Judah to this day.

16 The southern boundary *of the Tribes of Joseph* (Ephraim and the half-tribe of
Manasseh): This boundary extended from the Jordan River at Jericho
through the wilderness and the hill country to Bethel. It then went from Bethel to
Luz, then on to Ataroth, in the territory of the Archites; and west to the border of
the Japhletites as far as Lower Beth-horon, then to Gezer and on over to the
Mediterranean.

5, 6*The Land Given to the Tribe of Ephraim:* The eastern boundary began at
Ataroth-addar. From there it ran to Upper Beth-horon, then on to the Mediterranean Sea. The northern boundary began at the Sea, ran east past Michmethath,
then continued on past Taanath-shiloh and Janoah. 7From Janoah it turned southward to Ataroth and Naarah, and touched Jericho, and ended at the Jordan River.
8[The western half of the northern boundary] went from Tappu-ah, and followed
along Kanah Brook to the Mediterranean Sea. 9Ephraim was also given some of the
cities in the territory of the half-tribe of Manasseh. 10The Canaanites living in
Gezer were never driven out, so they still live as slaves among the people of
Ephraim.

17 The land given *to the Half-tribe of Manasseh* (Joseph's oldest son): The clan
of Machir (Manasseh's oldest son who was the father of Gilead) had already
been given the land of Gilead and Bashan [on the east side of the Jordan River], for
they were great warriors. 2So now, land on the west side of the Jordan was given
to the clans of Abiezer, Helek, Asriel, Shechem, Shemida, and Hepher.

3However, Hepher's son Zelophehad (grandson of Gilead, great-grandson of
Machir, and great-great-grandson of Manasseh) had no sons. He had only five
daughters whose names were Mahlah, Noah, Hoglah, Milcah, and Tirzah. 4These
women came to Eleazar the priest and to Joshua and the Israeli leaders and
reminded them,

"The Lord told Moses that we were to receive as much property as the men of our
tribe."

5, 6So, as the Lord had commanded through Moses, these five women were given
an inheritance along with their five great-uncles, and the total inheritance came to
ten sections of land (in addition to the land of Gilead and Bashan across the Jordan
River).

15:47
Josh 13:2-7

15:63
Judg 1:21
2 Sam 5:6

16:1
Josh 8:15
10:33; 18:13
1 Kgs 9:17

16:5
Josh 17:7; 18:13

16:8
Josh 17:8

16:10
Josh 13:13
15:63; 17:12,13
Judg 1:29
1 Kgs 9:16

17:1
Josh 13:8

17:3
Num 26:28-37
27:1-7; 36:1-12

17:5
Josh 13:30

15:48-62 *Judah also received these forty-four cities in the hill country with their surrounding villages,* implied in vss
51, 54, 57, 59, 60, and 62, where the original text indicates sub-totals of the number of cities assigned to Judah.
16:8 *The western half of the northern boundary,* implied. **17:1** *on the east side of the Jordan River,* implied.

16:1 Though Joseph was one of Jacob's twelve sons, he did not
have a tribe named after him. This was because Joseph, as the
oldest son of Jacob's wife Rachel, received a double portion of the
inheritance. This double portion was given to Joseph's two sons,
Ephraim and Manasseh, whom Jacob considered as his own
(Genesis 48:5). The largest territory and the greatest influence in
northern Israel belonged to Ephraim and Manasseh.

17:3, 4 Although women did not traditionally receive property as
inheritance in Israelite society, Moses put justice ahead of tradition
and gave these five women the land they deserved (see Numbers
27:3–11). In fact, God told Moses to add a law that would help
other women in similar circumstances inherit property as well.
Joshua was now carrying out this law. It is easy to refuse to honor
a reasonable request because "things have never been done that
way before." But it is best to look carefully at the purpose of the law
and the merits of each case before deciding.

7The northern boundary of the tribe of Manasseh extended southward from the border of Asher to Michmethath, which is east of Shechem. On the south the boundary went from Michmethath to the Spring of Tappu-ah. 8(The land of Tappu-ah belonged to Manasseh, but the city of Tappu-ah, on the border of Manasseh's land, belonged to the tribe of Ephraim.) 9From the spring of Tappu-ah the border of Manasseh followed the north bank of the Brook of Kanah to the Mediterranean Sea. (Several cities south of the brook belonged to the tribe of Ephraim, though they were located in Manasseh's territory.) 10The land south of the brook and as far west as the Mediterranean Sea was assigned to Ephraim, and the land north of the brook and east of the sea went to Manasseh. Manasseh's northern boundary was the territory of Asher and the eastern boundary was the territory of Issachar.

17:11
1 Chron 7:29

11The half-tribe of Manasseh was also given the following cities which were situated in the areas assigned to Issachar and Asher: Beth-shean, Ible-am, Dor, En-dor, Taanach, Megiddo (where there are the three cliffs), with their respective villages. 12But since the descendants of Manasseh could not drive out the people who lived in those cities, the Canaanites remained. 13Later on, however, when the Israelis became strong enough, they forced the Canaanites to work as slaves.

17:12
Josh 16:10
Judg 1:27

17:14
Num 26:28-37

14Then the two tribes of Joseph came to Joshua and asked, "Why have you given us only one portion of land when the Lord has given us such large populations?"

15"If the hill country of Ephraim is not large enough for you," Joshua replied, "and if you are able to do it, you may clear out the forest land where the Perizzites and Rephaim live."

17:16
Judg 1:19
4:3,13

16, 17, 18"Fine," said the tribes of Joseph, "for the Canaanites in the lowlands around Beth-shean and the Valley of Jezreel have iron chariots and are too strong for us."

"Then you shall have the mountain forests," Joshua replied, "and since you are such a large, strong tribe you will surely be able to clear it all and live there. And I'm sure you can drive out the Canaanites from the valleys, too, even though they are strong and have iron chariots."

Scouts survey the unconquered territory

18:1
Gen 49:10
Deut 12:10,11
Judg 21:19

18 After the conquest—although seven of the tribes of Israel had not yet entered and conquered the land God had given them—all Israel gathered at Shiloh to set up the Tabernacle.

17:14, 15 Notice the two contrasting attitudes toward settling the Promised Land. Caleb took what God gave him and moved ahead to fulfill God's plan for him (14:12). He was confident that God would help him drive out the wicked inhabitants and that he would soon fully occupy his land (15:14, 15). In contrast, the two tribes of Joseph were given rich land and lots of it, but they were afraid to drive out the inhabitants and take full possession of it. Instead, they begged for more land. But Joshua asked them to prove their sincerity first by clearing the unclaimed forest areas (17:15). They agreed, but they failed to carry through (Judges 1:27).

18:1, 2 With most of the conquest behind them, Israel moved its religious center from Gilgal (see note on Joshua 5:8, 9) to Shiloh. This was probably the first place where the Tabernacle was set up permanently. The Tabernacle was where God lived among his people (Exodus 25:8). Its central location in the Promised Land made it easier for the people to attend the special worship services and yearly feasts.

Samuel, a great priest and prophet, often traveled to Shiloh as a boy (1 Samuel 1:3, 22). The Tabernacle remained in Shiloh through the period of the judges (about 300 years). Apparently the city was destroyed by the Philistines when the Ark of the Covenant was captured (1 Samuel 4—5). Shiloh never lived up to its reputation as Israel's religious center, for later references in the Bible point to the wickedness and idolatry in the city (Psalm 78:56–60; Jeremiah 7:12–15).

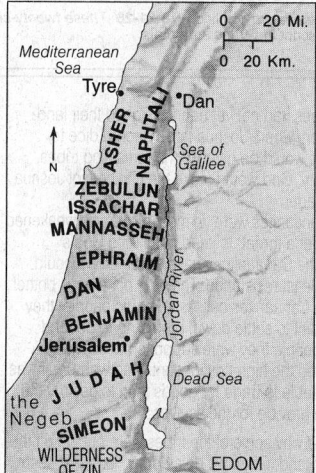

THE TRIBES WEST OF THE JORDAN
Judah, Ephraim, and the other half-tribe of Manasseh were the first tribes to receive land west of the Jordan because of their past acts of faith. The remaining seven tribes—Benjamin, Zebulun, Issachar, Asher, Naphtali, Simeon, and Dan—were slow to conquer and possess the land allotted to them.

3Then Joshua asked them, "How long are you going to wait before clearing out the people living in the land which the Lord your God has given to you? 4Select three men from each tribe and I will send them to scout the unconquered territory and bring back a report of its size and natural divisions so that I can divide it for you. 5, 6The scouts will map it into seven sections, and then I will throw the sacred dice to decide which section will be assigned to each tribe. 7However, remember that the Levites won't receive any land; they are priests of the Lord. That is their wonderful heritage. And of course the tribes of Gad and Reuben and the half-tribe of Manasseh won't receive any more, for they already have land on the east side of the Jordan where Moses promised them that they could settle."

8So the scouts went out to map the country and to bring back their report to Joshua. Then the Lord could assign the sections of land to the tribes by the throw of the sacred dice. 9The men did as they were told and divided the entire territory into seven sections, listing the cities in each section. Then they returned to Joshua and the camp at Shiloh. 10There at the Tabernacle at Shiloh the Lord showed Joshua by the sacred lottery which tribe should have each section:

11*The Land Given to the Tribe of Benjamin:* The section of land assigned to the families of the tribe of Benjamin lay between the territory previously assigned to the tribes of Judah and Joseph.

12The northern boundary began at the Jordan River, went north of Jericho, then west through the hill country and the Wilderness of Beth-aven. 13From there the boundary went south to Luz (also called Bethel) and proceeded down to Ataroth-addar in the hill country south of Lower Beth-horon. 14There the border turned south, passing the mountain near Beth-horon and ending at the village of Kiriath-baal (sometimes called Kiriath-jearim), one of the cities of the tribe of Judah. This was the western boundary.

15The southern border ran from the edge of Kiriath-baal, over Mount Ephron to the spring of Naphtoah, 16and down to the base of the mountain beside the valley of Hinnom, north of the valley of Rephaim. From there it continued across the valley of Hinnom, crossed south of the old city of Jerusalem where the Jebusites lived, and continued down to En-rogel. 17From En-rogel the boundary proceeded northeast to En-shemesh and on to Geliloth (which is opposite the slope of Adummim). Then it went down to the Stone of Bohan (who was a son of Reuben), 18where it passed along the north edge of the Arabah. The border then went down into the Arabah, 19ran south past Beth-hoglah, and ended at the north bay of the Dead Sea—which is the southern end of the Jordan River.

20The eastern border was the Jordan River. This was the land assigned to the tribe of Benjamin. 21-28These twenty-six cities were included in the land given to the

18:16 *the old city of Jerusalem,* implied. 18:21-28 *These twenty-six cities,* implied in verses 24 and 28, where the original Hebrew manuscript indicates sub-totals.

18:3 Josh 14:1

18:7 Num 18:7,20 Josh 13:32,33

18:8 Judg 1:22

18:10 Num 34:16-29 Josh 19:51

18:14 Josh 15:9,48-62

18:3 Seven of the tribes had not yet been assigned their land. They gathered at Shiloh, where Joshua threw sacred dice to determine which areas would be given to the remaining tribes. Using the sacred lottery, God would make the choice, not Joshua or any other human leader.

By this time, the Canaanites were, in most places, so weakened that they were no longer a threat. Instead of fulfilling God's command to destroy the Canaanites, these seven tribes would often take the path of least resistance. They did not always bother to drive the rest of the Canaanites out. As nomadic people, they may have been reluctant to settle down, preferring to depend economically on the people they were supposed to eliminate. Others may have feared the high cost of continued warfare. It was easier and more profitable to trade for goods than to destroy the suppliers and have to provide for themselves.

18:3–6 Joshua asked why some of the tribes were putting off the job of clearing out the land. Often we delay doing jobs that seem large, difficult, boring, or disagreeable. But to continue putting

them off shows lack of discipline, poor stewardship of time, and in some cases disobedience to God. Jobs we don't look forward to require concentration, teamwork, twice as much time, lots of encouragement, and accountability. We must apply these characteristics to any tasks that cause us or others to procrastinate.

18:8 Making decisions by the method of casting lots, here called "throwing dice," was a common practice among the Hebrews. Little is known about the actual method used in Joshua's day. Dice may have been used. Another possibility is that two urns were used: one containing tribal names; the other, the divisions of the land. Drawing one name from each urn matched a tribe to a region. The Urim and Thummim (see Exodus 28:30, 31) may also have been used. No matter how it was done, the process removed human choice from the decision-making process and allowed God to match tribes and lands as he saw fit.

18:11 The tribe of Benjamin was given a narrow strip of land that served as a buffer zone between Judah and Ephraim, the two tribes that would come to dominate the land.

tribe of Benjamin: Jericho, Beth-hoglah, Emek-keziz, Beth-arabah, Zimaraim, Bethel, Avvim, Parah, Ophrah, Chephar-ammoni, Ophni, Geba, Gibeon, Ramah, Be-eroth, Mizpeh, Chephirah, Mozah, Rekem, Irpeel, Taralah, Zela, Ha-eleph, Jebus (or Jerusalem), Gibe-ah, and Kiriath-jearim. All of these cities and their surrounding villages were given to the tribe of Benjamin.

19 *The land given to the Tribe of Simeon:* The tribe of Simeon received the next assignment of land—including part of the land previously assigned to Judah. 2-7Their inheritance included these seventeen cities with their respective villages: Beer-sheba, Sheba, Moladah, Hazar-shual, Balah, Ezem, Eltolad, Bethul, Hormah, Ziklag, Beth-marcaboth, Hazar-susah, Beth-lebaoth, Sharuhen, En-rimmon, Ether, and Ashan. 8The cities as far south as Baalath-beer (also known as Ramah-in-the-Negeb) were also given to the tribe of Simeon. 9So the Simeon tribe's inheritance came from what had earlier been given to Judah, for Judah's section had been too large for them.

10*The Land Given to the Tribe of Zebulun:* The third tribe to receive its assignment of land was Zebulun. Its boundary started on the south side of Sarid. 11From there it circled to the west, going near Mareal and Dabbesheth until it reached the brook east of Jeokne-am. 12In the other direction, the boundary line went east to the border of Chisloth-tabor, and from there to Daberath and Japhia; 13then it continued east of Gath-hepher, Ethkazin, and Rimmon and turned toward Neah. 14The northern boundary of Zebulun passed Hannathon and ended at the Valley of Iphtahel. 15, 16The cities in these areas, besides those already mentioned, included Kattath, Nahalal, Shimron, Idalah, Bethlehem, and each of their surrounding villages. Altogether there were twelve of these cities.

17-23*The Land Given to the Tribe of Issachar:* The fourth tribe to be assigned its land was Issachar. Its boundaries included the following cities: Jezreel, Chesulloth, Shunem, Hapharaim, Shion, Anaharath, Rabbith, Kishion, Ebez, Remeth, En-gannim, En-haddah, Beth-pazzez, Tabor, Shahazumah, and Beth-shemesh—sixteen cities in all, each with its surrounding villages. The boundary of Issachar ended at the Jordan River.

24, 25, 26*The Land Given to the Tribe of Asher:* The fifth tribe to be assigned its land was Asher. The boundaries included these cities: Helkath, Hali, Beten, Achshaph, Allammelech, Amad, and Mishal.

The boundary on the west side went from Carmel to Shihor-libnath, 27turned east toward Beth-dagon, and ran as far as Zebulun in the Valley of Iphtahel, running north of Beth-emek and Neiel. It then passed to the east of Kabul, 28Ebron, Rehob, Hammon, Kanah, and Greater Sidon. 29Then the boundary turned toward Ramah and the fortified city of Tyre and came to the Mediterranean Sea at Hosah. The territory also included Mahalab, Achzib, 30, 31Ummah, Aphek, and Rehob—an overall total of twenty-two cities and their surrounding villages.

32*The Land Given to the Tribe of Naphtali:* The sixth tribe to receive its assignment was the tribe of Naphtali. 33Its boundary began at Judah, at the oak in Zaanannim, and extended across to Adami-nekeb, Jabneel, and Lakkum, ending at the Jordan River. 34The western boundary began near Heleph and ran past Aznoth-tabor, then to Hukkok, and coincided with the Zebulun boundary in the south, and with the boundary of Asher on the west, and with the Jordan River at the east. 35-39The fortified cities included in this territory were: Ziddim, Zer, Hammath, Rakkath, Chinnereth, Adamah, Ramah, Hazor, Kedesh, Edre-i, Enhazor, Yiron, Migdal-el, Horem, Beth-anath, and Beth-shemesh.

So altogether the territory included nineteen cities with their surrounding villages.

40*The Land Given to the Tribe of Dan:* The last tribe to be assigned its land was Dan. 41–46The cities within its area included: Zorah, Eshta-ol, Ir-shemesh, Sha-alabbin, Aijalon, Ithlah, Elon, Timnah, Ekron, Eltekeh, Gibbethon, Baalath, Jehud, Bene-berak, Gath-rimmon, Me-jarkon, and Rakkon, also the territory near

19:2-7 *these seventeen cities.* Totaled from verses 6 and 7 of the original manuscripts, where sub-totals are indicated. **19:15, 16** *besides those already mentioned,* implied.

Joppa. 47, 48But some of this territory proved impossible to conquer, so the tribe of Dan captured the city of Leshem, slaughtered its people, and lived there; and they called the city "Dan," naming it after their ancestor.

Land is given to Joshua

49So all the land was divided among the tribes, with the boundaries indicated; and the nation of Israel gave a special piece of land to Joshua, 50for the Lord had said that he could have any city he wanted. He chose Timnath-serah in the hill country of Ephraim; he rebuilt it and lived there.

51Eleazar the priest, Joshua, and the leaders of the tribes of Israel supervised the sacred lottery to divide the land among the tribes. This was done in the Lord's presence at the entrance of the Tabernacle at Shiloh.

2. Special cities are set aside
Cities of Refuge named

20 The Lord said to Joshua, 2"Tell the people of Israel to designate now the Cities of Refuge, as I instructed Moses. 3If a man is guilty of killing someone unintentionally, he can run to one of these cities and be protected from the relatives of the dead man, who may try to kill him in revenge. 4When the innocent killer reaches any of these cities, he will meet with the city council and explain what happened, and they must let him come in and must give him a place to live among them. 5If a relative of the dead man comes to kill him in revenge, the innocent slayer must not be released to him for the death was accidental. 6The man who caused the accidental death must stay in that city until he has been tried by the judges and found innocent, and must live there until the death of the High Priest who was in office at the time of the accident. But then he is free to return to his own city and home."

7The cities chosen as Cities of Refuge were Kedesh of Galilee in the hill country of Naphtali; Shechem, in the hill country of Ephraim; and Kiriath-arba (also known as Hebron) in the hill country of Judah. 8The Lord also instructed that three cities be set aside for this purpose on the east side of the Jordan River, across from Jericho. They were Bezer, in the wilderness of the land of the tribe of Reuben;

20:2 *as I instructed Moses.* See Numbers 35 and 1 Chronicles 6.

Margin references:
19:50 Josh 24:30; Judg 2:7-9
19:51 Josh 14:1; 18:10
20:2 Num 35:6; Deut 4:41; 19:2,3; 1 Chron 6:58,59
20:7 Josh 21:9-16,32; 1 Chron 6:76; Lk 1:39

19:47, 48 Some of the land looked impossible to conquer for the tribe of Dan. They were not familiar with the territory, and the local inhabitants were fierce. Although God had given Israel victory in even worse situations, the tribe of Dan chose to migrate north to avoid the intense opposition. Anyone can trust God when the going is easy. It is when everything looks impossible that our faith and courage are put to the test. Have faith that God is great enough to tackle your most difficult situations.

19:49 There were several good reasons for establishing these well-set boundaries instead of turning the Promised Land into a single undivided nation. (1) The boundaries gave each tribe ownership of an area, promoting loyalty and unity which would strengthen each tribe. (2) The boundaries delineated areas of responsibility and privilege which would help each tribe develop and mature. (3) The boundaries reduced conflicts that might have broken out if everyone had wanted to live in the choicest areas. (4) The boundaries fulfilled the promised inheritance to each tribe given as early as the days of Jacob (Genesis 48:21, 22).

20:6 Along with a new nation of people in a new land came the need for a new government. Many years earlier God had told Moses how this government should function. One of the things God wanted the Israelites to do when they entered the Promised Land was to designate certain cities as "Cities of Refuge." These were to be scattered throughout the land. Their purpose was to prevent injustice, especially in cases of revenge. For example, if someone accidently killed another person, he could flee to the City of Refuge where he was safe until he could have a fair trial. The

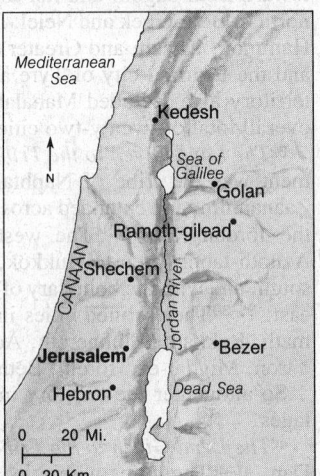

THE CITIES OF REFUGE A City of Refuge was just that— refuge for someone who committed an un-intentional murder which would evoke revenge from the victim's friends and rela-tives. The six cit-ies of Refuge were spaced throughout the land so that a person was never too far from one.

Map labels: Mediterranean Sea; Kedesh; Sea of Galilee; Golan; N; Ramoth-gilead; Shechem; CANAAN; Jordan River; Jerusalem; Bezer; Hebron; Dead Sea; 0   20 Mi.; 0   20 Km.

Levites were in charge of each City of Refuge. This may have been done to make it even more likely that God's principles of justice and fairness would be kept. (For more on Cities of Refuge, see the notes on Numbers 35:6; 35:11–21.)

Ramoth of Gilead, in the territory of the tribe of Gad; and Golan of Bashan, in the land of the tribe of Manasseh. 9These Cities of Refuge were for foreigners living in Israel as well as for the Israelis themselves, so that anyone who accidentally killed another man could run to that place for a trial, and not be killed in revenge.

Cities given to the Levites

21:1
Josh 14:1; 17:4

21:2
Num 35:1,2
1 Chron 6:54

21 Then the leaders of the tribe of Levi came to Shiloh to consult with Eleazar the priest and with Joshua and the leaders of the various tribes.

2"The Lord instructed Moses to give cities to us Levites for our homes, and pastureland for our cattle," they said.

3So they were given some of the recently conquered cities with their pasturelands. 4Thirteen of these cities had been assigned originally to the tribes of Judah, Simeon, and Benjamin. These were given to some of the priests of the Kohath division (of the tribe of Levi, descendants of Aaron). 5The other families of the Kohath division were given ten cities from the territories of Ephraim, Dan, and the half-tribe of Manasseh. 6The Gershon division received thirteen cities, selected by sacred lot in the area of Bashan. These cities were given by the tribes of Issachar, Asher, Naphtali, and the half-tribe of Manasseh. 7The Merari division received twelve cities from the tribes of Reuben, Gad, and Zebulun. 8So the Lord's command to Moses was obeyed, and the cities and pasturelands were assigned by the toss of the sacred dice.

9-16First to receive their assignment were the priests—the descendants of Aaron, who was a member of the Kohath division of the Levites. The tribes of Judah and Simeon gave them the nine cities listed below, with their surrounding pasturelands:

Hebron, in the Judean hills, as a City of Refuge—it was also called Kiriatharba (Arba was the father of Anak)—although the fields beyond the city and the surrounding villages were given to Caleb, the son of Jephunneh; Libnah, Jattir, Eshtemoa, Holon, Debir, Ain, Juttah, and Beth-shemesh.

17, 18The tribe of Benjamin gave them these four cities and their pasturelands: Gibeon, Gaba, Anathoth, and Almon. 19So in all, thirteen cities were given to the priests—the descendants of Aaron.

20, 21, 22The other families of the Kohath division received four cities and pasturelands from the tribe of Ephraim: Shechem (a City of Refuge), Gezer, Kibza-im, and Beth-horon.

23, 24The following four cities and pasturelands were given by the tribe of Dan: Elteke, Gibbethon, Aijalon, and Gath-rimmon.

25The half-tribe of Manasseh gave the cities of Taanach and Gath-rimmon with their surrounding pasturelands. 26So the total number of cities and pasturelands given to the remainder of the Kohath division was ten.

27The descendants of Gershon, another division of the Levites, received two cities and pasturelands from the half-tribe of Manasseh: Golan, in Bashan (a City of Refuge), and Be-eshterah.

28, 29The tribe of Issachar gave four cities: Kishion, Daberath, Jarmuth, and Engannim.

30, 31The tribe of Asher gave four cities and pasturelands: Mishal, Abdon, Helkath, and Rehob.

32The tribe of Naphtali gave: Kedesh, in Galilee (a City of Refuge), Hammoth-dor, and Kartan.

33So thirteen cities with their pasturelands were assigned to the division of Gershon.

34, 35The remainder of the Levites—the Merari division—were given four cities by the tribe of Zebulun: Jokne-am, Kartah, Dimnah, and Nahalal.

21:9-16 *the nine cities,* implied in verse 16, where a sub-total is indicated in the original text. **21:20-22** *four cities,* implied in verse 22, where the total appears in the text.

21:2 The Levites were to minister before God on behalf of all the people, so they were given cities scattered throughout the land. Although Jerusalem was far away from the homes of many Israelites, almost no one lived more than a day's journey from a levitical city.

36, 37Reuben gave them: Bezer, Jahaz, Kedemoth, and Mepha-ath.

38, 39Gad gave them four cities with pasturelands: Ramoth (a City of Refuge), Mahanaim, Heshbon, and Jazer.

40So the Merari division of the Levites was given twelve cities in all.

41, 42The total number of cities and pasturelands given to the Levites came to forty-eight.

21:41
Num 35:7

The Lord gives the nation peace

43So in this way the Lord gave to Israel all the land he had promised to their ancestors, and they went in and conquered it and lived there. 44And the Lord gave them peace, just as he had promised, and no one could stand against them; the Lord helped them destroy all their enemies. 45Every good thing the Lord had promised them came true.

21:43
Num 33:53
Deut 11:31
17:14; 34:4
21:44
Ex 23:31
Deut 7:24

3. The eastern tribes build an altar

22 Joshua now called together the troops from the tribes of Reuben, Gad, and the half-tribe of Manasseh, 2, 3and addressed them as follows:

"You have done as the Lord's disciple Moses commanded you, and have obeyed every order I have given you—every order of the Lord your God. You have not deserted your brother tribes, even though the campaign has lasted for such a long time. 4And now the Lord our God has given us success and rest as he promised he would. So go home now to the land given you by the Lord's servant Moses, on the other side of the Jordan River. 5Be sure to continue to obey all of the commandments Moses gave you. Love the Lord and follow his plan for your lives. Cling to him and serve him enthusiastically."

22:1
Num 32:29-41
22:2
Josh 1:12-18

22:4
Num 32:18
Deut 3:20
22:5
Deut 5:1

6So Joshua blessed them and sent them home. 7, 8(Moses had assigned the land of Bashan to the half-tribe of Manasseh, although the other half of the tribe was given land on the west side of the Jordan.) As Joshua sent away these troops, he blessed them and told them to share their great wealth with their relatives back home—their loot of cattle, silver, gold, bronze, iron, and clothing.

22:7
Num 32:33
Josh 17:1

9So the troops of Reuben, Gad, and the half-tribe of Manasseh left the army of Israel at Shiloh in Canaan and crossed the Jordan River to their own homeland of Gilead. 10Before they went across, while they were still in Canaan, they built a large monument for everyone to see, in the shape of an altar.

11But when the rest of Israel heard about what they had done, 12they mustered an army at Shiloh and prepared to go to war against their brother tribes. 13First, however, they sent a delegation led by Phinehas, the son of Eleazar the priest. They

22:10
Deut 12:5
22:11
Deut 13:12-14
22:13
Num 25:7,10,
11; 31:6

21:43–45 God proved faithful in fulfilling every promise he had given to Israel. Fulfillment of some promises took several years, but "every good thing the Lord had promised them came true" (21:45). His promises will be fulfilled according to his timetable, not ours, but we know that his Word is sure. The more we learn of those promises God has fulfilled and continues to fulfill, the easier it is to hope for those yet to come.

22:2–4 Before the conquest had begun, these tribes were given land on the east side of the Jordan River. But before they could settle down they had to first promise to help the other tribes conquer the land on the west side (Numbers 32:20–22). They had patiently and diligently carried out their promised duties. Joshua now commended them for doing just that. At last they are permitted to return to their families and build their cities. Follow-through is vital in God's work. Beware of the temptation to quit early and leave God's work undone.

22:5 Here Joshua briefly restated the central message Moses gave the people in Deuteronomy: obedience should be based on love for God rather than fear of God. Although the Israelites had completed their military responsibility, Joshua reminded them of their spiritual responsibility. Sometimes we think so much about

what we are to do that we neglect thinking about who we are to be. We must not let daily service crowd spiritual growth out of our lives.

22:8 Joshua's parting counsel to these tribes was to share their new wealth with the relatives back home. We often neglect this vital part of the Christian life—sharing what we have been given. This does not mean, "When I'm wealthy, I'll share." It means being willing to share what we have right now. It means being willing to share whatever we have with those not fortunate enough to enjoy the same blessings.

22:11–34 When the tribes of Reuben, Gad, and the half-tribe of Manasseh built an altar at the Jordan River, the rest of Israel was afraid that these tribes were starting their own religion and rebelling against God. But before beginning an all-out war, Phinehas led a delegation to learn the truth. He was prepared to negotiate rather than fight if a battle was not necessary. When he learned that the altar was for a memorial rather than for heathen sacrifice, war was averted and unity restored.

As nations and as individuals, we would benefit from a similar approach to resolving conflicts. Assuming the worst about the intentions of others only brings trouble. Israel averted the threat of civil war by asking before assaulting. Beware of reacting before you hear the whole story.

crossed the river and talked to the tribes of Reuben, Gad, and Manasseh. 14In this delegation were ten high officials of Israel, one from each of the ten tribes, and each a clan leader. 15When they arrived in the land of Gilead they said to the tribes of Reuben, Gad, and the half-tribe of Manasseh,

22:17
Num 25:1-9

16"The whole congregation of the Lord demands to know why you are sinning against the God of Israel by turning away from him and building an altar of rebellion against the Lord. 17, 18Was our guilt at Peor—from which we have not even yet been cleansed despite the plague that tormented us—so little that you must rebel again? For you know that if you rebel today the Lord will be angry with all of us tomorrow. 19If you need the altar because your land is defiled, then join us on our side of the river where the Lord lives among us in his Tabernacle, and we will share our land with you. But do not rebel against the Lord by building another altar

22:20
Josh 7:1

in addition to the only true altar of our God. 20Don't you remember that when Achan, the son of Zerah, sinned against the Lord, the entire nation was punished in addition to the one man who had sinned?"

21This was the reply of the people of Reuben, Gad, and the half-tribe of Manasseh to these high officials:

22:22
Deut 12:1,2

22, 23"We swear by Jehovah, the God of gods, that we have not built the altar in rebellion against the Lord. He knows (and let all Israel know it too) that we have not built the altar to sacrifice burnt offerings or grain offerings or peace offerings—may the curse of God be on us if we did. 24, 25We have done it because we love the Lord and because we fear that in the future your children will say to ours, 'What right do you have to worship the Lord God of Israel? The Lord has placed the Jordan River as a barrier between our people and your people! You have no part in the Lord.' And your children may make our children stop worshiping him. 26, 27So we decided to build the altar as a symbol to show our children and your children that we, too, may worship the Lord with our burnt offerings and peace offerings and sacrifices, and your children will not be able to say to ours, 'You have no part in the Lord our God.' 28If they say this, our children can reply, 'Look at the altar of the Lord which our fathers made, patterned after the altar of Jehovah. It is not for burnt offerings or sacrifices but is a symbol of the relationship with God that both of us have.' 29Far be it from us to turn away from the Lord or to rebel against him by building our own altar for burnt offerings, grain offerings, or sacrifices. Only the altar in front of the Tabernacle may be used for that."

30When Phinehas the priest and the high officials heard this from the tribes of Reuben, Gad, and Manasseh, they were very happy.

31Phinehas replied to them, "Today we know that the Lord is among us because you have not sinned against the Lord as we thought; instead, you have saved us from destruction!"

32Then Phinehas and the ten ambassadors went back to the people of Israel and told them what had happened, 33and all Israel rejoiced and praised God and spoke

22:34
Gen 31:47-49

no more of war against Reuben and Gad. 34The people of Reuben and Gad named the altar "The Altar of Witness," for they said, "It is a witness between us and them that Jehovah is our God, too."

4. Joshua's last message
Joshua addresses the leaders

23:1
Josh 21:44
23:2
Deut 31:28
Josh 24:1

23 Long after this, when the Lord had given success to the people of Israel against their enemies and when Joshua was very old, 2he called for the leaders of Israel—the elders, judges, and officers—and said to them, "I am an old man now, 3and you have seen all that the Lord your God has done for you during

---

22:20 For the story of Achan, a man who allowed greed to get the best of him, see Joshua 7.

22:26, 27 The tribes were concerned that future generations might see conflict between the people on the two sides of the Jordan without some visible sign of their unity. The altar, patterned

after the altar of Jehovah, was to remind these people that they all worshiped the same God. Often we need to be reminded of the faith of our fathers. What actions demonstrate to your children your reliance on God and what he has done? Take the time to establish family traditions that will help your children remember.

my lifetime. He has fought for you against your enemies and has given you their land. 4, 5And I have divided to you the land of the nations yet unconquered as well as the land of those you have already destroyed. All the land from the Jordan River to the Mediterranean Sea shall be yours, for the Lord your God will drive out all the people living there now, and you will live there instead, just as he has promised you.

6"But be very sure to follow all the instructions written in the book of the laws of Moses; do not deviate from them the least little bit. 7Be sure that you do not mix with the heathen people still remaining in the land; do not even mention the names of their gods, much less swear by them or worship them. 8But follow the Lord your God just as you have until now. 9He has driven out great, strong nations from before you, and no one has been able to defeat you. 10Each one of you has put to flight a thousand of the enemy, for the Lord your God fights for you, just as he has promised. 11So be very careful to keep on loving him.

12"If you don't, and if you begin to intermarry with the nations around you, 13then know for a certainty that the Lord your God will no longer chase those nations from your land. Instead, they will be a snare and a trap to you, a pain in your side and a thorn in your eyes, and you will disappear from this good land which the Lord your God has given you.

14"Soon I will be going the way of all the earth—I am going to die.

"You know very well that God's promises to you have all come true. 15, 16But as certainly as the Lord has given you the good things he promised, just as certainly he will bring evil upon you if you disobey him. For if you worship other gods he will completely wipe you out from this good land which the Lord has given you. His anger will rise hot against you, and you will quickly perish."

Joshua addresses all the people

24 Then Joshua summoned all the people of Israel to him at Shechem, along with their leaders—the elders, officers, and judges. So they came and presented themselves before God.

2Then Joshua addressed them as follows: "The Lord God of Israel says, 'Your ancestors, including Terah the father of Abraham and Nahor, lived east of the Euphrates River; and they worshiped other gods. 3But I took your father Abraham from that land across the river and led him into the land of Canaan and gave him many descendants through Isaac his son. 4Isaac's children, whom I gave him, were Jacob and Esau. To Esau I gave the area around Mount Seir while Jacob and his children went into Egypt.

5"Then I sent Moses and Aaron to bring terrible plagues upon Egypt; and afterwards I brought my people out as free men. 6But when they arrived at the Red Sea, the Egyptians chased after them with chariots and cavalry. 7Then Israel cried out to me and I put darkness between them and the Egyptians; and I brought the sea crashing in upon the Egyptians, drowning them. You saw what I did. Then Israel lived in the wilderness for many years.

8"Finally I brought you into the land of the Amorites on the other side of the Jordan; and they fought against you, but I destroyed them and gave you their land. 9Then King Balak of Moab started a war against Israel, and he asked Balaam, the

23:6–13 Joshua knew the nation's weak spots. Before dying, he called the people together and gave commands to them in areas where they were most likely to slip: (1) follow all Moses' instructions without deviating; (2) don't mix with the heathen nations or be tempted to worship their idols; (3) don't intermarry with the heathen nations. These temptations were right in their backyard. Similar temptations are in our backyards as well. It's wise to identify weak spots in our lives *before* we break down. Then we can develop strategies to overcome these obstacles before we are overcome by them.

23:12–14 This chilling prediction about the consequences of intermarriage with the Canaanite nations eventually became a reality. Numerous stories in the book of Judges show what Israel had to suffer because of failure to follow God wholeheartedly. God showed Israel supreme love and patience, just as he does to believers today. But we must not confuse his patience with approval. Beware of wanting your own way, because eventually you may get it—along with all its painful consequences.

24:2–13 Joshua reminded the people of God's goodness and his provision for them by reviewing past times when God blessed them. Reviewing past blessings can encourage us to continue to serve God faithfully. When you need a reminder of God's love, review how God has blessed you in the past. Then turn to the Scriptures and notice how unchanging his love is.

son of Beor, to curse you. ¹⁰But I wouldn't listen to him. Instead I made him bless you; and so I delivered Israel from him.

24:11
Ex 23:23,31
Deut 7:1
Josh 3:15-17

¹¹"Then you crossed the Jordan River and came to Jericho. The men of Jericho fought against you, and so did many others—the Perizzites, the Canaanites, the Hittites, the Girgashites, the Hivites, and the Jebusites. Each in turn fought against you but I destroyed them all. ¹²And I sent hornets ahead of you to drive out the two kings of the Amorites and their people. It was not your swords or bows that brought you victory! ¹³I gave you land you had not worked for and cities you did not build—these cities where you are now living. I gave you vineyards and olive groves for food, though you did not plant them.'

24:12
Ex 23:28
Deut 7:20
Ps 44:3

24:13
Deut 6:10-12

24:14
Deut 10:12,13
18:13
1 Sam 12:24
Ps 111:10

¹⁴"So revere Jehovah and serve him in sincerity and truth. Put away forever the idols your ancestors worshiped when they lived beyond the Euphrates River and in Egypt. Worship the Lord alone. ¹⁵But if you are unwilling to obey the Lord, then decide today whom you will obey. Will it be the gods of your ancestors beyond the Euphrates or the gods of the Amorites here in this land? But as for me and my family, we will serve the Lord."

24:15
Ruth 1:15,16
1 Kgs 18:21

The nation promises to worship and obey the Lord

¹⁶And the people replied, "We would never forsake the Lord and worship other gods! ¹⁷For the Lord our God is the one who rescued our fathers from their slavery in the land of Egypt. He is the God who did mighty miracles before the eyes of Israel, as we traveled through the wilderness, and preserved us from our enemies when we passed through their land. ¹⁸It was the Lord who drove out the Amorites and the other nations living here in the land. Yes, we choose the Lord, for he alone is our God."

24:19
Ex 20:5; 23:21
34:14
Lev 19:1,2
20:7,26

¹⁹But Joshua replied to the people, "You can't worship the Lord God, for he is holy and jealous; he will not forgive your rebellion and sins. ²⁰If you forsake him and worship other gods, he will turn upon you and destroy you, even though he has taken care of you for such a long time."

24:20
Deut 4:25
Josh 23:12
Acts 7:42

²¹But the people answered, "We choose the Lord!"

²²"You have heard yourselves say it," Joshua said—"you have chosen to obey the Lord."

"Yes," they replied, "we are witnesses."

²³"All right," he said, "then you must destroy all the idols you now own, and you must obey the Lord God of Israel."

JOSHUA'S FINAL SPEECH
Joshua called all the Israelites to Shechem to hear his final words. He challenged the people to make a conscious choice to always serve God. Soon afterwards, Joshua died and was buried in his hometown of Timnath-serah.

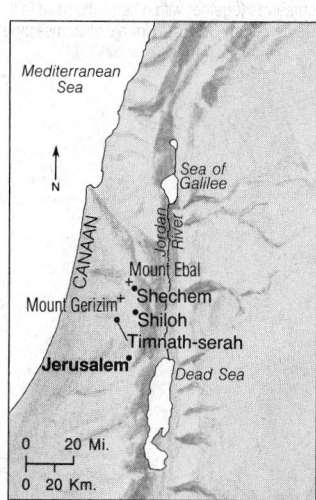

Mediterranean Sea

N

CANAAN

Jordan River

Sea of Galilee

Mount Ebal
Mount Gerizim Shechem
Shiloh
Timnath-serah
Jerusalem Dead Sea

0　　20 Mi.

0　20 Km.

which were only man-made idols. It's easy to slip into a quiet rebellion—going about life in our own way. But the time comes when we have to choose who or what will control us. Will it be God, our own limited personality, or another imperfect substitute? Once we have chosen to be controlled by God's Spirit, we need to reaffirm our choice every day.

24:15 In taking a definite stand for the Lord, Joshua again displayed his spiritual leadership. Regardless of what others decided, Joshua had made a commitment to God and he was willing to set the example of living by that decision. The way we live shows others the strength of our commitment to serving God.

24:16 All the people of the nation boldly claimed that they would never forsake the Lord. But they did not keep that promise. Very soon God would charge them with breaking their contract with him (Judges 2:3). Yet the nation followed God through Joshua's lifetime, a great tribute to Joshua's godliness and powerful leadership.

24:23 Joshua told the Israelites to destroy their idols. To follow God requires destroying whatever gets in the way of worshiping him. Like the Israelites, we have idols in our lives—greed, wrong priorities, jealousies, prejudices—that get in the way of worshiping God. God is not satisfied if we merely hide these idols. We must completely remove them from our lives.

24:15 The people had to decide whether they would obey the Lord, who had proven his trustworthiness, or obey the local gods,

24The people replied to Joshua, "Yes, we will worship and obey the Lord alone."

25So Joshua made a covenant with them that day at Shechem, committing them to a permanent and binding contract between themselves and God. 26Joshua recorded the people's reply in the book of the laws of God, and took a huge stone as a reminder and rolled it beneath the oak tree that was beside the Tabernacle.

27Then Joshua said to all the people, "This stone has heard everything the Lord said, so it will be a witness to testify against you if you go back on your word."

28Then Joshua sent the people away to their own sections of the country.

Leaders are buried in the Promised Land

29Soon after this he died at the age of 110. 30He was buried on his own estate at Timnath-serah, in the hill country of Ephraim, on the north side of the mountains of Gaash.

31Israel obeyed the Lord throughout the lifetimes of Joshua and the other old men who had personally witnessed the amazing deeds the Lord had done for Israel.

32The bones of Joseph, the people of Israel had brought them along when they left Egypt—were buried in Shechem, in the parcel of ground Jacob had bought from the sons of Hamor. (The land was located in the territory assigned to the tribes of Joseph.)

33Eleazar, the son of Aaron, also died; he was buried in the hill country of Ephraim, at Gibe-ah, the city which had been given to his son Phinehas.

24:32 *had bought*, literally, "had bought for 100 pieces of silver."

24:24
Ex 19:8; 24:3,7
Deut 5:26,27

24:25
Ex 24:8

24:27
Ex 22:26,27

24:29
Judg 2:7-9

24:30
Josh 19:50

24:32
Gen 50:25
Ex 13:19
Acts 7:16
Heb 11:22

24:33
Judg 19:12,13
1 Sam 10:26

24:24-26 The permanent contract between Israel and God was that the people would "worship and obey the Lord alone." Their purpose was to become a holy nation that would influence the rest of the world for God. The conquest of Canaan was a means to achieve this purpose, but Israel became preoccupied with the land and lost sight of the Lord God.

The same can happen in our lives. We can spend so much time on the means that we forget the end—to glorify God. Churches may make this mistake as well. For example, the congregation may pour all of its energies into a new facility, only to become self-satisfied or fearful of letting certain groups use it. If this happens, they have focused on the building and lost sight of its purpose—to bring others to God. Just as Joshua set up a stone to be a reminder of Israel's ultimate purpose, so we should set up reminders to keep us aware of the reason for everything we do.

24:29-31 The book of Joshua opens with a new leader being handed a seemingly impossible task—to take over the land of

Canaan. By following God closely, Joshua led the people through military victories and faithful spiritual obedience. In 24:16 we read that the people "would never forsake the Lord." The response of the whole nation during these many years is a tribute both to Joshua's leadership and to the God he faithfully served.

24:33 Joshua and Eleazar had died, but not before laying before the people the fundamentals of what it means to have faith in God. We are to revere and worship the Lord alone (24:14). This is based on a choice: to decide to obey or not to obey him (24:15). We are incapable, however, of properly worshiping him because of our rebellion and sin (24:19). By choosing God as Lord we enter into a covenant with God (24:25) whereby he promises not only to forgive and love us, but also to enable us by his Spirit to do his work here on earth. It also means we must renounce the principles and practices of the culture around us that are hostile to God's plan (24:23). This is not to be done alone or in a vacuum, but by binding ourselves together with others who have faith in him. (See Deuteronomy 30:15-20 for a similar message from Moses.)

JUDGES

REAL heroes are hard to find these days. Modern research and the media have made the foibles and weaknesses of our leaders very apparent; we search in vain for men and women to emulate. The music, movie, and sports industries produce a steady stream of "stars" who shoot to the top and then quickly fade from view.

Judges is a book about heroes—12 men and women who delivered Israel from her oppressors. These judges were not perfect; in fact, they included an assassin, a sexually promiscuous man, and a person who broke all the laws of hospitality. But they were submissive to God, and God used them.

Judges is also a book about sin and its consequences. Like a minor cut or abrasion which becomes infected when left untreated, sin grows and soon poisons the whole body. The book of Joshua ends with the nation taking a stand for God, ready to experience all the blessings of the Promised Land. After settling in Canaan, however, the Israelites lost their spiritual commitment and motivation. When Joshua and the elders died, the nation experienced a leadership vacuum, leaving them without a strong central government. Instead of enjoying freedom and prosperity in the Promised Land, Israel entered the dark ages of her history.

Simply stated, the reason for this rapid decline was sin—individual and corporate. The first step away from God was incomplete obedience (1:1—2:5); the Israelites refused to eliminate the enemy completely from the land. This led to intermarriage and idolatry (2:6—3:7) and everyone doing "whatever seemed right in his own eyes" (17:6). Before long the Israelites became captives. Out of their desperation they begged God to rescue them. In faithfulness to his promise and out of his lovingkindness, God would raise up a judge to deliver his people and, for a time, there would be peace. Then complacency and disobedience would set in, and the cycle would begin again.

The book of Judges spans a period of over 325 years, recording six successive periods of oppression and deliverance, and the careers of 12 deliverers. Their captors included the Mesopotamians, Moabites, Philistines, Canaanites, Midianites, and Ammonites. A variety of deliverers—from Othniel to Samson—were used by God to lead his people to freedom and true worship. God's deliverance through the judges is a powerful demonstration of his love and mercy towards his people.

As you read the book of Judges, take a good look at these heroes from Jewish history. Take note of their dependence on God and obedience to his commands. Observe Israel's repeated downward spiral into sin, refusing to learn from history and living only for the moment. But most of all, stand in awe of God's mercy as he delivers his people over and over again.

VITAL STATISTICS

PURPOSE:
To show that God's judgment against sin is certain, and his forgiveness of sin and restoration to relationship is just as certain for those who repent

AUTHOR:
Probably Samuel

SETTING:
The land of Canaan, later called Israel. God had helped the Israelites conquer Canaan, which had been inhabited by a host of wicked nations. But they were in danger of losing this Promised Land because they compromised their convictions and disobeyed God.

KEY VERSE:
"For in those days Israel had no king, so everyone did whatever he wanted to—whatever seemed right in his own eyes" (17:6).

KEY PEOPLE:
Othniel, Ehud, Deborah, Gideon, Abimelech, Jephthah, Samson, Delilah

SPECIAL FEATURE:
Records Israel's first civil war

THE BLUEPRINT

A. THE MILITARY FAILURE OF ISRAEL
(1:1—3:4)
1. Incomplete conquest of the land
2. Religious rebellion of the people

The tribes had compromised God's command to drive out the inhabitants of the land. Incomplete removal of evil often means disaster in the end. We must beware of compromising with wickedness.

B. THE RESCUE OF ISRAEL BY THE
JUDGES (3:5—16:31)
1. First period: Othniel
2. Second period: Ehud and Shamgar
3. Third period: Deborah and Barak
4. Fourth period: Gideon, Tola, and Jair
5. Fifth period: Jephthah, Ibzan, Elon, and
Abdon
6. Sixth period: Samson

Repeatedly we see the nation of Israel sinning against God and God allowing suffering to come upon the land and the people. Sin always has its consequences. Where there is sin we can expect suffering to follow. Rather than living in an endless cycle of abandoning God and then crying out to him for rescue, we should seek to live a consistent life of faithfulness.

C. THE MORAL FAILURE OF ISRAEL
(17:1—21:25)
1. Idolatry in the tribe of Dan
2. War against the tribe of Benjamin

Despite the efforts of Israel's judges, the people still would not turn wholeheartedly to God. They all did whatever they thought was best for themselves. The result was the spiritual, moral, and political decline of the nation. Our lives will also fall into decline and decay unless we live by the guidelines God has given us.

MEGATHEMES

THEME	EXPLANATION	IMPORTANCE
Decline/ Compromise	The people faced decline and failure because they compromised their high spiritual purpose in many ways. They abandoned their mission to drive all the people out of the land, and they adopted the customs of the people living around them.	Society offers many rewards to those who compromise their faith: wealth, acceptance, recognition, power, and influence. When God gives us a mission, it must not be polluted by a desire for approval from society.
Decay/Apostasy	Israel's moral downfall had its roots in the fierce independence that each tribe cherished. It led to everyone doing whatever seemed good in his own eyes. There was no unity in government or in worship. Law and order broke down. Finally idol worship and man-made religion led to the complete abandoning of faith in God.	We can expect decay when we value anything more highly than God. If we value our own independence more than God, we have placed an idol in our hearts, and soon our lives become temples to that god. We must constantly regard God's first claim on our lives and all our desires.
Defeat/ Oppression	God used evil oppressors to punish the Israelites for their sin, to bring them to the point of repentance, and to test their allegiance to him.	Rebellion against God leads to disaster. God may use oppression to bring wandering hearts back to him.
Repentance	Decline, decay, and defeat caused the people to cry out for help. They vowed to turn from idolatry and to turn to God for mercy and deliverance.	Idolatry gains a foothold in our hearts when we make anything more important than God. We must identify modern idols in our hearts, renounce them, and turn to God for his love and mercy.
Deliverance/ Heroes	Because Israel repented, God raised up heroes to deliver his people from their path of sin and the oppression it brought. He used many kinds of people to accomplish this purpose.	God's love and mercy are available to all people. Anyone who is dedicated to God can be used for his service. Real heroes recognize the futility of human effort without God's leading.

A. THE MILITARY FAILURE OF ISRAEL (1:1—3:4)

By faithfully obeying the Lord, Joshua led the Israelites to military victory. After his death, however, the tribes failed to clear the inhabitants from the land, so the Lord withdrew his promise to help drive the people out and bless the Israelites in battle. The new generation abandoned God and worshiped idols. This part of Judges shows what can happen when we neglect to teach our children to follow the Lord.

1. Incomplete conquest of the land

Israel begins clearing out the land

1:1
Num 27:21

1 After Joshua died, the nation of Israel went to the Lord to receive his instructions.

"Which of our tribes should be the first to go to war against the Canaanites?" they inquired.

1:2
Gen 49:8

1:3
Josh 19:1

1:4
Gen 13:7; 34:30
1 Sam 11:8

2God's answer came, "Judah. And I will give them a great victory."

3The leaders of the tribe of Judah, however, asked help from the tribe of Simeon. "Join us in clearing out the people living in the territory allotted to us," they said, "and then we will help you conquer yours." So the army of Simeon went with the army of Judah. 4, 5, 6And the Lord helped them defeat the Canaanites and Perizzites, so that ten thousand of the enemy were slain at Bezek. King Adoni-bezek escaped, but the Israeli army soon captured him and cut off his thumbs and big toes.

7"I have treated seventy kings in this same manner and have fed them the scraps under my table!" King Adoni-bezek said. "Now God has paid me back." He was taken to Jerusalem, and died there.

1:8
Josh 15:63

1:10
Josh 15:14
20:7; 21:9-16

8(Judah had conquered Jerusalem, and massacred its people, setting the city on fire.) 9Afterward the army of Judah fought the Canaanites in the hill country and in the Negeb, as well as on the coastal plains. 10Then Judah marched against the

---

1:1 The people of Israel had finally entered and taken control of the land promised to their ancestors (Genesis 12:7; Exodus 3:16, 17). The book of Judges continues this story of the conquest which began in the book of Joshua. By God's strength, Israel had conquered many enemies and overcome many difficulties, but their work was not yet finished. They had been effective in overcoming the political and military challenges they faced, but overcoming their spiritual challenges was more difficult. The unholy but attractive life-style of the Canaanites proved to be more dangerous than their military might. The Israelites gave in to the pressure and compromised their faith. If we attempt to overcome life's challenges with human effort alone, we will find the pressures and temptations around us too great to resist.

1:1 Soon after Joshua died, Israel began to lose its firm grip on the land. Although Joshua was a great commander, the people missed his spiritual leadership even more than his military skill, for he had kept the people focused on God and his purposes. Joshua had been the obvious successor to Moses, but there was no obvious successor to Joshua. During this crisis of leadership, Israel had to learn that no matter how powerful and wise the current leader was, their real leader was God. We often focus our hope and confidence on some influential leader, failing to realize that in reality it is God who is in command. Acknowledge God as your commander in chief, and avoid the temptation of relying too heavily on human leaders, regardless of their spiritual wisdom.

1:1 Everyone wants guidance in making tough decisions. The Israelites were no different. Although Joshua was dead, they learned well from his example—at least in the beginning. With his words of encouragement still ringing in their ears (Joshua 24), the people asked God about their next step. In asking for this national guidance, the elders probably gathered at the Tabernacle in Shiloh as they had done when the land was divided (Joshua 18). There they may have used the Urim and Thummim to seek God's answers. These were two stones or plates which were made according to God's instructions and used to seek his guidance in special situations that involved the entire nation. They were used to take away the possibility of human error and allow God to decide.

1:1 The Canaanites were all the people who lived in Canaan (the Promised Land). They lived in city-states where each city had its own government, army, and laws. One reason Canaan was so difficult to conquer was that each city had to be defeated individually. There was no single king who could surrender the entire country into the hands of the Israelites. However, Canaan's greatest threat to Israel was not its military, but its religion. Canaanite religion idealized evil traits: cruelty in war, sexual immorality, selfish greed, and materialism. It was a "me first, anything goes" society. Obviously, the religions of Israel and Canaan could not coexist.

1:2 The book of Joshua tells of a swift and thorough conquest of enemy armies and cities, while the book of Judges seems to suggest a more lengthy and gradual conquest. When the Israelites first entered the Promised Land (Joshua 1—12), they united as one army to crush the inhabitants until they were too weak to retaliate. Then, after the land was divided up among the 12 tribes (Joshua 13—24), each tribe was responsible for clearing out the remaining enemy from its own territory. The book of Judges tells of their failure to do this.

Some tribes succeeded better than others. Under Joshua, they all began strong, but soon most became sidetracked by fear, weariness, lack of discipline, or pursuit of their own interests. As a result their faith began to fade away, and "everyone did whatever he wanted to—whatever seemed right in his own eyes" (Judges 17:6). In order for our faith to survive, it must be lived day by day. It must penetrate every aspect of our lives. Beware of starting out strong and then getting sidetracked from your real purpose— loving God and living for him.

1:6 The Israelites cut off the thumbs and big toes of King Adoni-bezek to humiliate him and to make him ineffective in battle. According to God's instructions for conquering the Promised Land, he should have been killed.

1:8 Although the Israelites conquered Jerusalem, they did not occupy the city until the days of David (2 Samuel 5:6–10).

KEY PLACES IN JUDGES

1 **Bochim** The book of Judges opens with the Israelites continuing their conquest of the Promised Land. Their failure to obey God and destroy all the evil inhabitants soon comes back to haunt them in two ways: (1) the enemies reorganized and counterattacked, and (2) Israel turned away from God, adopting the evil and idolatrous practices of the inhabitants of the land. The Angel of the Lord appeared at Bochim to inform the Israelites that their sin and disobedience had broken their agreement with God and would result in punishment through oppression (1:1—3:10).

2 **Jericho** The nation of Moab was one of the first to oppress Israel. Moab's King Eglon conquered much of Israel— including the city of Jericho— and forced the people to pay unreasonable taxes. The messenger chosen to deliver this tax money to King Eglon was named Ehud. But he had more than money to deliver, for he drew his hidden sword and killed the Moabite king. Ehud then escaped, only to return with an army that chased the Moabites out of the land and freed Israel from its oppressors (3:11—31).

3 **Hazor** After Ehud's death, King Jabin of Hazor conquered Israel and oppressed the people for 20 years. Then Deborah became Israel's leader. She summoned Barak to fight General Sisera, the leader of King Jabin's army. Together Deborah and Barak led their army into battle against Jabin's forces in the land between Mount Tabor and the Kishon River and conquered them (4:1—5:31).

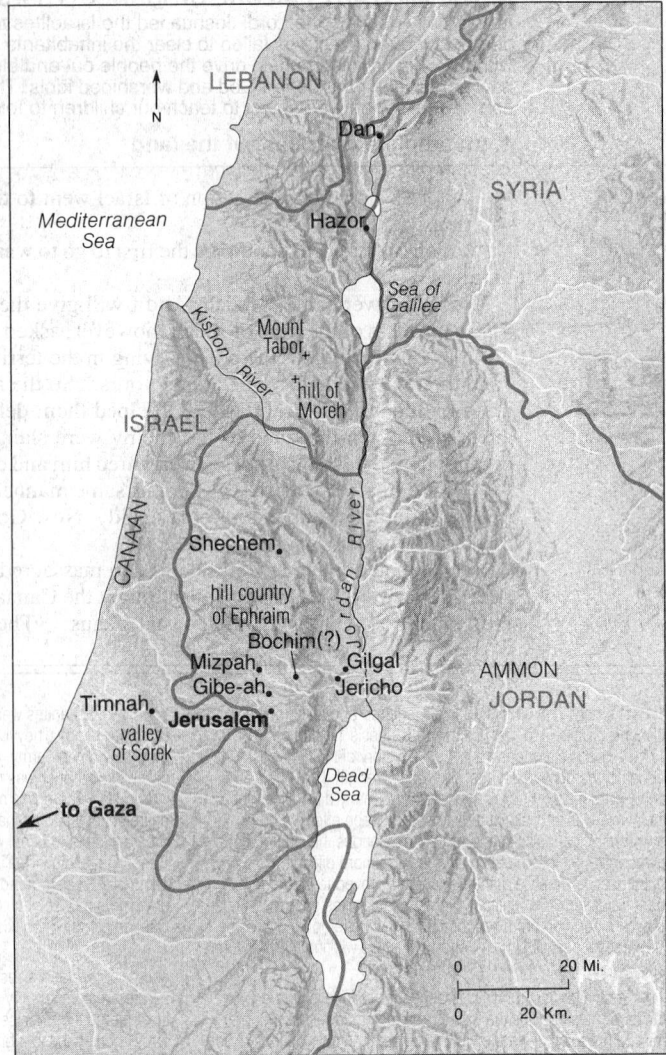

Modern names and boundaries are shown in gray.

4 **Hill of Moreh** After 40 years of peace, the Midianites began to harass the Israelites by destroying their flocks and crops. When the Israelites finally cried out to God, he chose Gideon, a poor and humble farmer, to be their deliverer. After struggling with doubt and feelings of inferiority, Gideon took courage and knocked down his town's altar to Baal, causing a great uproar among the citizens. Filled with the Spirit of God, he attacked the vast army of Midian which was camped near the hill of Moreh. With just a handful of men he sent the enemy running away in confusion (6:1—7:25).

5 **Shechem** Even great leaders make mistakes. Gideon's relations with a concubine in Shechem resulted in the birth of a son named Abimelech. Abimelech turned out to be treacherous and power hungry—stirring up the people to proclaim him king. To carry out his plan, he went so far as to kill 69 of his 70 half brothers. Eventually some men of Shechem rebelled against Abimelech, but he gathered together an army and defeated them. His lust for power led him to ransack two other cities, but he

was killed by a woman who dropped a millstone onto his head (8:28—9:57).

6 **Land of Ammon** Again Israel turned completely from God; so God turned from them. But when the Ammonites mobilized their army to attack, Israel threw away her idols and called upon God once again. Jephthah, a prostitute's son who had been run out of Israel, was asked to return and lead Israel's forces against the enemy. After defeating the Ammonites, Jephthah became involved in a war with the tribe of Ephraim over a misunderstanding (10:1—12:15).

7 **Timnah** Israel's next judge, Samson, was a miracle child promised by God to a barren couple. He was the one who would begin to free Israel from their next and most powerful oppressor, the Philistines. According to God's command, Samson was to be a Nazirite—one who took a vow to be set apart for special service to God. One of the stipulations of the vow was that Samson's hair could never be cut. But when Samson grew up, he did not always take his special responsibility

1:11
Josh 15:15

Canaanites in Hebron (formerly called Kiriath-arba), destroying the cities of She-shai, Ahiman, and Talmai. ¹¹Later they attacked the city of Debir (formerly called Kiriath-sepher).

1:12
Josh 15:16

¹²"Who will lead the attack against Debir?" Caleb challenged them. "Whoever conquers it shall have my daughter Achsah as his wife!"

1:13
Judg 3:9

¹³Caleb's nephew, Othni-el, son of his younger brother Kenaz, volunteered to lead the attack; and he conquered the city and won Achsah as his bride. ¹⁴As they were leaving for their new home, she urged him to ask her father for an additional piece of land. She dismounted from her donkey to speak to Caleb about it.

"What do you wish?" he asked.

¹⁵And she replied, "You have been kind enough to give me land in the Negeb, but please give us springs of water too."

So Caleb gave her the upper and lower springs.

Israel fails to drive out the enemy

1:16
Deut 34:3
Judg 3:13; 4:11

¹⁶When the tribe of Judah moved into its new land in the Negeb wilderness south of Arad, the descendants of Moses' father-in-law—members of the Kenite tribe—accompanied them. They left their homes in Jericho, "The City of Palm Trees," and the two tribes lived together after that. ¹⁷Afterwards the army of Judah joined Simeon's and they fought the Canaanites at the city of Zephath and massacred all its people. So now the city is named Hormah (meaning, "massacred"). ¹⁸The army of Judah also conquered the cities of Gaza, Ashkelon, and Ekron, with

1:17
Num 21:3

1:14 *As they were leaving for their new home,* literally, "when she came to him." *for an additional,* implied.

---

to God seriously. He even fell in love with a Philistine girl in Timnah and asked to marry her. Before the wedding, Samson held a party for some men in the city, using a riddle to place a bet with them. The men, however, forced Samson's fiancée into giving the answer. Furious at being tricked, Samson paid his bet with the lives of 30 Philistines who lived in the nearby city of Ashkelon (13:1—14:20).

8 Valley of Sorek Samson killed thousands of Philistines with his incredible strength. The nation's leaders looked for a way to stop him. They got their chance when another Philistine woman stole Samson's heart. Her name was Delilah, and she lived in the Valley of Sorek. In exchange for a great sum of money, Delilah deceived Samson into confiding in her the secret of his strength. One night while he slept, Delilah cut off his hair. As a result, Samson fell helplessly into the hands of the enemy (15:1—16:20).

9 Gaza Samson was blinded and led captive to a prison in Gaza. There his hair began to grow again. After a while, the Philistines held a great festival to celebrate Samson's imprisonment and to humiliate him before the crowds. When he was brought out as the entertainment, he literally brought down the house when he pushed on the main pillars of the banquet hall and killed the thousands trapped inside. The prophecy that he would begin to free Israel from the Philistines had come true (16:21–31).

10 Hill Country of Ephraim In the hill country of Ephraim lived a man named Micah. Micah hired his own priest to perform priestly duties in the shrine which housed his collection of idols. He thought he was pleasing God with all his religiosity! Like many of the Israelites, Micah assumed that his own opinions of what was right would agree with God's (17:1–13).

11 Dan The tribe of Dan migrated north in order to find new territory. They sent spies ahead of them to scout out the land. One night the spies stopped at Micah's home. Looking for some assurance of victory, the spies stole Micah's idols and priest. Rejoining the tribe, they came upon the city of Laish and slaughtered the unarmed and innocent citizens, renaming the conquered city Dan. Micah's idols were then set up in the city and became the focal point of the tribe's worship for many years (18:1–31).

12 Gibeah The extent to which many people had fallen away from God became clear in Gibeah, a village in the territory of Benjamin. A man and his concubine were traveling north toward the hill country of Ephraim. They stopped for the night in Gibeah, thinking they would be safe. But some perverts in the city gathered around the home where they were staying and demanded that the man come out to have sexual relations with them. Instead, the man and his host pushed the concubine out the door. She was raped and abused all night. When the man found her lifeless body the next morning, he cut it into 12 pieces and sent the parts to each tribe of Israel. This tragic event demonstrated that the nation had sunk to its lowest spiritual level (19:1–30).

13 Mizpah The leaders of Israel came to Mizpah to decide how to punish the wicked men from the city of Gibeah. When the city leaders refused to turn the criminals over, the whole nation of Israel took vengeance upon both Gibeah and the tribe of Benjamin where the city was located. When the battle ended, the entire tribe had been destroyed except for a handful of men who took refuge in the hills. Israel had become morally depraved. The stage was now set for the much-needed spiritual renewal that would come under the prophet Samuel (20:1—21:25).

1:12–15 This same event is recorded in Joshua 15:16–19. Caleb was one of the original spies who scouted out the Promised Land

(Numbers 13, 14) and, with Joshua, encouraged the people to conquer it. For his faithfulness, he was given the land of his choice.

their surrounding villages. 19The Lord helped the tribe of Judah exterminate the people of the hill country, though they failed in their attempt to conquer the people of the valley, who had iron chariots.

20The city of Hebron was given to Caleb as the Lord had promised; so Caleb drove out the inhabitants of the city; they were descendants of the three sons of Anak.

21The tribe of Benjamin failed to exterminate the Jebusites living in their part of the city of Jerusalem, so they still live there today, mingled with the Israelis.

22, 23As for the tribe of Joseph, they attacked the city of Bethel, formerly known as Luz, and the Lord was with them. First they sent scouts, 24who captured a man coming out of the city. They offered to spare his life and that of his family if he would show them the entrance passage through the wall. 25So he showed them how to get in, and they massacred the entire population except for this man and his family. 26Later the man moved to Syria and founded a city there, naming it Luz, too, as it is still known today.

27The tribe of Manasseh failed to drive out the people living in Beth-shean, Taanach, Dor, Ibleam, Megiddo, with their surrounding towns; so the Canaanites stayed there. 28In later years when the Israelis were stronger they put the Canaanites to work as slaves, but never did force them to leave the country. 29This was also true of the Canaanites living in Gezer; they still live among the tribe of Ephraim.

30And the tribe of Zebulun did not massacre the people of Kitron or Nahalol, but made them their slaves; 31, 32nor did the tribe of Asher drive out the residents of Acco, Sidon, Ahlab, Achzib, Helbah, Aphik, or Rehob; so the Israelis still live among the Canaanites, who were the original people of that land. 33And the tribe of Naphtali did not drive out the people of Beth-shemesh or of Beth-anath, so these people continue to live among them as servants.

34As for the tribe of Dan, the Amorites forced them into the hill country and wouldn't let them come down into the valley; 35but when the Amorites later spread

1:24 *the passage through the wall*, literally, "the way into the city." Obviously, this does not mean via the city gates.

Cross references (right margin):

1:19
Josh 17:16
Judg 4:2,3

1:20
Josh 14:6-9
15:14

1:21
Josh 15:63
2 Sam 5:6

1:22
Gen 28:19
Josh 14:3,4

1:24
Josh 6:22

1:25
Josh 6:25

1:27
Josh 17:11,12

1:29
Josh 16:10

1:34
Josh 19:47
Judg 18:1

1:19 Why did God order the Israelites to exterminate the Canaanites? Although the command seems cruel, the Israelites were under God's order to execute judgment on the wicked people of the land. Over 700 years earlier God had told Abraham that when the Israelites entered the Promised Land, the gross evil of the native people would be ready for judgment (Genesis 15:16). But God wasn't playing favorites with the Israelites, for eventually they too would be severely punished for becoming as evil as the people they were ordered to drive out (2 Kings 17, 25; Jeremiah 6:18, 19; Ezekiel 8). God is not partial, all people are eligible for God's gracious forgiveness as well as his firm justice.

1:19 Canaanite chariots pulled by horses were some of the most sophisticated weapons of the day. Israelite foot soldiers were absolutely powerless when a speeding iron chariot bore down upon them. This is why Israel preferred to fight in the hills where chariots couldn't venture.

1:20 Caleb was given land "as the Lord had promised." In a world where promises are often broken, it is encouraging to know that God keeps his promises. The Bible is filled with promises from God, and to discover them is an exciting adventure. As you discover God's promises, don't be worried when a promise seems slow in being fulfilled. God will keep his every promise to you just as he did to Caleb.

1:21ff Tribe after tribe failed to drive the evil Canaanites from their land. Why didn't they follow through and completely obey God's commands? (1) They had been fighting for a long time and were tired. Although the goal was in sight, they lacked the discipline and energy to reach it. (2) They were afraid the enemy was too strong—the iron chariots seemed invincible. (3) Spiritual decay had infected them from within. They thought they could handle the

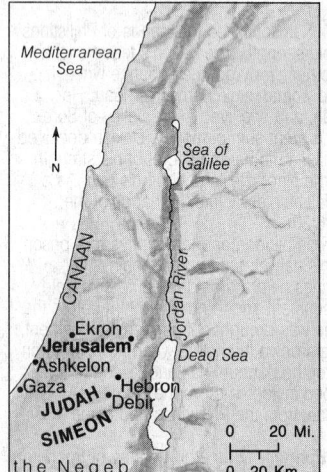

JUDAH FIGHTS FOR ITS LAND
The tribe of Judah wasted no time beginning their conquest of the territory allotted to them. With help from the tribe of Simeon, Jerusalem was conquered, as were the the Canaanites dwelling in the Negeb and along the coast. Hebron and Debir fell to Judah, and later Gaza, Ashkelon, and Ekron.

temptation and be more prosperous by doing business with the Canaanites.

We, too, often fail to drive out sin from our lives. Most often we know what to do, but we just don't follow through. Our failure to follow through results in a gradual deterioration of our relationship with God. In our battles, we may grow tired and want rest, but we need more than the absence of work. We need to know that God loves us and has given us a purpose in life. Victory comes from living according to his purpose.

into Mount Heres, Aijalon, and Sha-albim, the tribe of Joseph conquered them and made them their slaves. 36The boundary of the Amorites begins at the ascent of Scorpion Pass, runs to a spot called The Rock, and continues upward from there.

An angel announces that the covenant is broken

2 One day the Angel of the Lord arrived at Bochim, coming from Gilgal, and announced to the people of Israel, "I brought you out of Egypt into this land which I promised to your ancestors, and I said that I would never break my covenant with you, 2if you, on your part, would make no peace treaties with the people living in this land; I told you to destroy their heathen altars. Why have you not obeyed? 3And now since you have broken the contract, it is no longer in effect, and I no longer promise to destroy the nations living in your land; rather, they shall be thorns in your sides, and their gods will be a constant temptation to you."

2:1
Ex 20:2
Josh 3:10
Judg 6:11

2:2
Gen 17:7,8
Ex 23:32
34:12,13

2:3
Num 33:55,56
Deut 29:25

THE JUDGES OF ISRAEL	Judge	Years of Judging	Memorable Act(s)	Reference
	OTHNIEL	40	He captured a powerful Canaanite city	Judges 3:7–11
	EHUD	80	He killed Eglon and defeated the Moabites	Judges 3:12–30
	SHAMGAR	unrecorded	He killed 600 Philistines with an ox goad	Judges 3:31
	DEBORAH (w/Barak)	40	She defeated General Sisera and the Canaanites and later sang a victory song with Barak	Judges 4 and 5
	GIDEON	40	He destroyed his family idols, used a fleece to determine God's will, raised an army of 10,000, and defeated 135,000 Midianites with 300 troops	Judges 6–8
	TOLA	23	He judged Israel for 23 years	Judges 10:1, 2
	JAIR	22	He had 30 sons	Judges 10:3–5
	JEPHTHAH	6	He made a rash vow, defeated the Ammonites, and later battled jealous Ephraim	Judges 10:6—12:17
	IBZAN	7	He had 30 sons and 30 daughters	Judges 12:8–10
	ELON	10	unrecorded	Judges 12:11, 12
	ABDON	8	He had 40 sons and 30 grandsons each of whom had his own donkey	Judges 12:13–15
	SAMSON	20	He was a Nazirite, killed a lion with his bare hands, burned the Philistine wheat fields, killed 1,000 Philistines with an ass' jawbone, tore off an iron gate, was betrayed by Delilah, destroyed thousands of Philistines in one last mighty act	Judges 13—16

2:1–3 This event marks a significant change in Israel's relationship with God. At Mount Sinai, God made a sacred and binding agreement with the Israelites called a covenant (Exodus 19:5–8). God's part was to make Israel a special nation (see the note on Genesis 12:1–3), to protect them, and to give them unique blessings for following him. Israel's part was to love God and obey his laws. But because they rejected and disobeyed God, the agreement to protect them was no longer in effect. However, God wasn't going to abandon his people. They would receive wonderful blessings if they asked God to forgive them and sincerely followed him once again.

Although God's agreement to help Israel conquer the land was no longer in effect, his promise to make Israel a nation through whom the whole world would be blessed (fulfilled in the Messiah's coming) remained valid. God still wanted the Israelites to be a holy people (just as he wants us to be holy), and he often used oppression to bring them back to him, just as he said he would (Leviticus 26; Deuteronomy 28). The book of Judges records a number of instances where God allowed his people to be oppressed so that they would repent of their sins and return to him.

2:1 The Angel of the Lord was either (1) a special divine messenger sent by God, or (2) God appearing in a human form. In either case, the message was so important that God used a special visitation to communicate the seriousness of breaking the agreement with him.

Did this angel speak to all two million Israelites at once? One possible answer is that the angel spoke only to the tribal leaders as representatives of the entire nation. (We say, "the President addressed the nation," even though he doesn't speak to each individual.) Possibly, by miraculous means, every Israelite actually heard the speech. But it is certain that God wanted all the people to know the consequences of their sins.

2:3 No one can escape the consequences of disobeying God. The Israelites not only disobeyed, but often rejected him. Numbers 33:55 is one of several verses predicting what would happen if Israel disobeyed God. Israel could not say they hadn't been warned. We have also been warned. We can learn to obey God's clear warnings in Scripture, or we can experience the devastating consequences of our wrong actions. If we choose to disobey God's commands, we can be certain that the consequences will be regrettable.

4The people broke into tears as the Angel finished speaking; 5so the name of that **2:5** Josh 7:26
place was called "Bochim" (meaning, "the place where people wept"). Then they
offered sacrifices to the Lord.

The death of Joshua

6When Joshua finally disbanded the armies of Israel, the tribes moved into their **2:6** Josh 24:28
new territories and took possession of the land. 7, 8, 9Joshua, the man of God, died **2:7** Josh 24:29
at the age of 110, and was buried at the edge of his property in Timnath-heres, in
the hill country of Ephraim, north of Mount Gaash. The people had remained true
to the Lord throughout Joshua's lifetime, and as long afterward as the old men of
his generation were still living—those who had seen the mighty miracles the Lord
had done for Israel.

2. Religious rebellion of the people

10But finally all that generation died; and the next generation did not worship **2:10** Ps 81:11
Jehovah as their God, and did not care about the mighty miracles he had done for
Israel. 11They did many things which the Lord had expressly forbidden, including **2:11** Judg 4:1; 6:1 8:33; 10:6
the worshiping of heathen gods. 12, 13, 14They abandoned Jehovah, the God loved **2:12** Deut 28:25
and worshiped by their ancestors—the God who had brought them out of Egypt. 31:16,17; 32:30
Instead, they were worshiping and bowing low before the idols of the neighboring Judg 10:6
nations. So the anger of the Lord flamed out against all Israel. He left them to the Ps 106-40
mercy of their enemies, for they had departed from Jehovah and were worshiping
Baal and the Ashtaroth idols.

15So now when the nation of Israel went out to battle against its enemies, the
Lord blocked their path. He had warned them about this, and in fact had vowed that **2:16** Judg 6:6
he would do it. But when the people were in this terrible plight, 16the Lord raised Ps 106:43-45
up judges to save them from their enemies. **2:17** Ps 81:11,12

17Yet even then Israel would not listen to the judges, but broke faith with

---

2:4 The people of Israel knew they had sinned, and they responded with deep sorrow. Doing wrong comes naturally, and God knows that perfection is unattainable. Repentance is therefore the true measure of spiritual integrity. Repentance is asking God to forgive us and turning from our sinful ways. But we cannot do this sincerely unless we are truly sorry for our sinful actions. When we are aware of wrongdoing in our lives, we should admit it plainly to God rather than trying to cover it up or hoping to get away with it.

2:7–9 The account of Joshua's death is found here as well as at the end of the book of Joshua (24:29). Either this account is a summary of what happened earlier, or the account in the book of Joshua omitted the events in the first chapter of Judges. (For more on Joshua see his Profile in Joshua 1.)

2:10ff One generation died, and the next did not follow God. Judges 2:10—3:7 is a brief preview of the cycle of sin, judgment, and repentance which Israel experienced again and again. Each generation failed to teach the next generation to love and follow God. Yet this was at the very center of God's Law (Deuteronomy 6:4–9). Likewise, it is tempting to leave the job of teaching the Christian faith to the church or Christian school. Yet God says that the greatest responsibility for this task belongs to the family. Because children learn so much by example, faith must be a family matter. We should take the responsibility of building faith into the lives of our children seriously.

2:11–14 This generation of Israelites abandoned the faith of their parents and began worshiping the gods of their neighbors. Many things can tempt us to abandon what we know is right. The desire to be accepted by our neighbors can pressure us into behavior that is unacceptable to God. Don't let anyone pressure you into disobeying God.

2:12–14 God often saved his harshest criticism and punishment for those who worshiped idols. Why were idols so bad in God's sight? To worship an idol violated two of the Ten Commandments

(Exodus 20:3, 4). Bowing to an idol meant that a person did not believe God was the one true God. The Canaanites had gods for almost every season, activity, or place. To them, Jehovah was just another god to add to their collection of gods. Israel, by contrast, was to worship only Jehovah. Idol worship reduces God to the level of what he created, attributing his unique qualities to what he made. Idols represent sensual, carnal, and immoral aspects of human nature. God's nature, however, is spiritual and moral. Adding the worship of idols to the worship of God could not be tolerated.

2:12–14 God was angry with Israel, and he allowed them to be punished by their enemies. Anger, in itself, is not a sin. God's anger was the reaction of his holy nature to sin. One side of God's nature is his anger against sin; the other side is his love and mercy toward sinners. We cannot fully appreciate God's mercy without understanding his fierce wrath.

2:15, 16 Despite Israel's disobedience, God showed his great mercy to Israel by providing judges to save the people from their oppressors. Mercy has been defined as "not giving a person what he deserves." This is exactly what God did for Israel and what he does for us. Our disobedience demands judgment! But God shows mercy toward us by providing an escape from sin's penalty through Jesus Christ, who alone saves us from sin. When we pray for forgiveness, we are asking for what we do not deserve. Yet when we take this step and trust in Christ's redemptive work on our behalf, we can experience God's forgiveness.

2:17 Why would the people of Israel turn so quickly from their faith in God? Simply put, the Canaanite religion appeared more attractive and offered more short-range benefits. One of its most attractive features was that people could remain selfish and yet fulfill their religious requirements. They could do almost anything they wished and still be obeying at least one of the many Canaanite gods. Sex outside of marriage, selfishness, oppression

Jehovah by worshiping other gods instead. How quickly they turned away from the true faith of their ancestors, for they refused to obey God's commands. ¹⁸Each judge rescued the people of Israel from their enemies throughout his lifetime, for the Lord was moved to pity by the groaning of his people under their crushing oppressions; so he helped them as long as that judge lived. ¹⁹But when the judge died, the people turned from doing right and behaved even worse than their ancestors had. They prayed to heathen gods again, throwing themselves to the ground in humble worship. They stubbornly returned to the evil customs of the nations around them.

²⁰Then the anger of the Lord would flame out against Israel again. He declared, "Because these people have violated the treaty I made with their ancestors, ²¹I will no longer drive out the nations left unconquered by Joshua when he died. ²²Instead, I will use these nations to test my people, to see whether or not they will obey the Lord as their ancestors did."

²³So the Lord left those nations in the land and did not drive them out, nor let Israel destroy them.

3 Here is a list of the nations the Lord left in the land to test the new generation of Israel who had not experienced the wars of Canaan. For God wanted to give opportunity to the youth of Israel to exercise faith and obedience in conquering their enemies: The Philistines (five cities), the Canaanites, the Sidonians, the Hivites living in Mount Lebanon, from Baal-hermon to the entrance of Hamath. ⁴These people were a test to the new generation of Israel, to see whether they would obey the commandments the Lord had given to them through Moses.

B. THE RESCUE OF ISRAEL BY THE JUDGES (3:5—16:31)

The Israelites began a series of cycles of sinning, worshiping idols, being punished, crying out for help, being rescued by a judge sent from God, obeying God for a while, then falling back into idolatry. They were conquered by Syria, Moab, Canaan, Midian, Ammon, and Philistia. They even faced the threat of civil war. Just as God sent help to the people when they cried out to him, he will deliver us when we call on him.

1. First period: Othniel

⁵So Israel lived among the Canaanites, Hittites, Hivites, Perizzites, Amorites, and Jebusites. ⁶But instead of destroying them, the people of Israel intermarried with them. The young men of Israel took their girls as wives, and the Israeli girls married their men. And soon Israel was worshiping their gods. ⁷So the people of

3:1-3 *youth of Israel to exercise faith and obedience,* implied in 2:22 and 3:4, *in conquering their enemies,* literally, "that . . . the people might know war . . ."

2:19
Judg 3:11,12
4:1; 8:33
2 Chron 24:17,
18
Ps 78:8

2:21
Josh 23:13
2:22
2 Chron 32:31

3:1
Ps 78:7
Josh 11:19

3:4
Deut 8:2
Judg 2:22

3:5
Judg 1:29-32
3:6
Ex 34:15,16
Deut 7:3,4

---

of the helpless—these were not only allowed, but encouraged as forms of worship.

Faith in the one true God, however, does not offer short-range benefits that appeal to our sinful human nature. The essence of sin is selfishness; the essence of faith in God is selflessness.

2:17-19 Throughout this period of history Israel went through seven cycles of (1) rebelling against God, (2) being overrun by enemy nations, (3) being delivered by a godly judge, (4) remaining loyal to God under that judge, and (5) again forgetting God when the judge died. We tend to follow the same cycle—remaining loyal to God as long as we are near those who are devoted to him. But when we are on our own, the pressure to be drawn away from God increases. Determine to be faithful to God despite the difficult situations you may find yourself in.

3:1-3 We learn from chapter one that these enemy nations were still in the land because the Israelites had failed to obey God and drive them out. Now God would allow the enemies to remain in order to test the Israelites, so they could "exercise faith and obedience." By now the younger generation which had not fought in the great battles of conquest was coming of age. It was their job to complete the conquest of the land. There were many obstacles yet to be overcome in their new homeland. How they handled these obstacles would be a test of their faith.

Perhaps God has left obstacles in your life—hostile people,

difficult situations, baffling problems—for the purpose of allowing you to develop faith and obedience.

3:5-7 The Israelites discovered that relationships affect faith. The men and women of the surrounding nations were attractive to the Israelites. Soon they intermarried, and the Israelites accepted their pagan gods. This was clearly prohibited by God (Exodus 34:15-17; Deuteronomy 7:1-4). By accepting these gods into their homes, the Israelites gradually began to accept the immoral practices associated with them. Most Israelites didn't start out determined to be idolaters. But before long they found themselves absorbed in pagan worship.

A similar problem faces us. We desire to befriend those who don't know God, but in those friendships we can become entangled in unhealthy practices. Friendships with unbelievers are important, but we are to accept people without accepting their patterns of behavior. We must claim God's help to avoid the compromises with our society that can entangle us in sinful practices.

3:7 Archaelogists have uncovered many Baal idols in Israel. It is difficult to imagine the people of Israel trading worship of the Lord for worship of idols of wood, stone, and iron. But we do the same when we forsake worshiping God for other things. Our idols are not made of wood or stone, but they are every bit as sinful.

Israel were very evil in God's sight, for they turned against Jehovah their God and worshiped Baal and the Asheroth idols.

8Then the anger of the Lord flamed out against Israel, and he let King Cushan-rishathaim of eastern Syria conquer them. They were under his rule for eight years. 9But when Israel cried out to the Lord, he gave them Caleb's nephew, Othni-el (son of Kenaz, Caleb's younger brother) to save them. 10The Spirit of the Lord took control of him and he reformed and purged Israel so that when he led the forces of Israel against the army of King Cushan-rishathaim, the Lord helped Israel conquer him completely.

11Then, for forty years under Othni-el, there was peace in the land. But when Othni-el died,

3:8
Ex 22:24
Deut 29:20
Judg 2:12-14,20

3:9
Judg 1:13

3:10
Num 11:17
27:18
Judg 6:34; 11:29
1 Sam 10:6

3:11
Judg 5:31; 8:28

2. Second period: Ehud and Shamgar

12the people of Israel turned once again to their sinful ways, so God helped King Eglon of Moab to conquer part of Israel at that time. 13Allied with him were the armies of the Ammonites and the Amalekites. These forces defeated the Israelis and took possession of Jericho, often called "The City of Palm Trees." 14For the next eighteen years the people of Israel were required to pay crushing taxes to King Eglon.

3:12
Judg 2:19
Hos 6:4

3:13
Judg 1:16

Worshiping God	Worshiping idols	**WHY DID ISRAEL WANT TO WORSHIP IDOLS?**
long-range benefits	short-range benefits	
gratification postponed	self-gratification immediate	
morality required	sensuality approved	
high ethical standards demanded	low ethical standards tolerated	
neighbors' sins disapproved	neighbors' sins approved	
unseen God worshiped	visible deities worshiped	
unselfishness expected	selfishness condoned	
business relations hindered	business relations improved	
strict religious practices maintained	religious practices loosely regulated	
changed life demanded	changed life not demanded	
ethical stand expected	compromise and cooperation practiced	
concern for others taught	no concern for others expected	

The temptation to follow false gods because of short-term benefits, good feelings, easy "rules," or convenience is always present. *But the benefits are deceptive because the gods are false.* We worship God because he is the one and only true God.

3:9 Othniel was Israel's first judge. In Judges 1:13 he volunteered to lead an attack against a fortified city. Now he is to lead the nation back to God. Othniel had a rich spiritual heritage, for his uncle was Caleb, a man with unwavering faith in God (Numbers 13:30; 14:24). Othniel's godly leadership brought the people back to God and freed them from the oppression of the king of Syria. But after his death it didn't take the Israelites long to fall back into the sinful ways of their neighbors.

3:10 This phrase, "the Spirit of the Lord took control of him," is spoken of Gideon, Jephthah, Samson, and other judges of Israel. It expresses a temporary and spontaneous increase of physical, spiritual, and mental strength. Other translations say that "the Spirit of the Lord came upon" them. This was an extraordinary and supernatural occurrence for the special task at hand. Because the Holy Spirit is available to each believer today, we still see special cases in which the Spirit comes upon believers in an extraordinary way for special tasks.

3:12, 13 The Moabites, Ammonites, and Amalekites were nomadic tribes that lived near each other. They were located southeast of Canaan. These tribes were notorious raiders, possessing great military skill. This was the first time nations outside of Canaan attacked the Israelites in their own land.

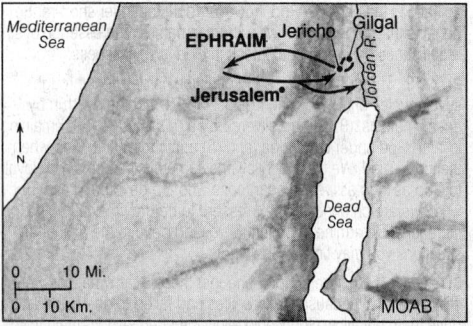

EHUD FREES ISRAEL FROM MOAB When King Eglon of Moab conquered part of Israel, he set up his throne in the city of Jericho. Ehud was chosen to take Israel's tribute there. After delivering Israel's tribute, Ehud killed King Eglon and escaped into the hill country of Ephraim. From there he gathered together an army to cut off any Moabites trying to escape across the Jordan River.

Ehud

3:15
Judg 3:9; 20:16
1 Chron 12:2

15But when they cried to the Lord, he sent them a savior, Ehud (son of Gera, a Benjaminite), who was left-handed. Ehud was the man chosen to carry Israel's annual tax money to the Moabite capital. 16Before he went on this journey he made himself a double-edged dagger eighteen inches long and hid it in his clothing, strapped against his right thigh. 17, 18, 19After delivering the money to King Eglon (who, by the way, was very fat!) he started home again. But outside the city, at the quarries of Gilgal, he sent his companions on and returned alone to the king.

"I have a secret message for you," he told him.

The king immediately dismissed all those who were with him so that he could have a private interview. 20Ehud walked over to him as he was sitting in a cool upstairs room and said to him, "It is a message from God!"

King Eglon stood up at once to receive it, 21whereupon Ehud reached beneath his robe with his strong left hand, pulled out the double-bladed dagger strapped against his right thigh, and plunged it deep into the king's belly. 22, 23The hilt of the dagger disappeared beneath the flesh, and the fat closed over it as the entrails oozed out. Leaving the dagger there, Ehud locked the doors behind him and escaped across an upstairs porch.

3:24
1 Sam 24:3

24When the king's servants returned and saw that the doors were locked, they

---

At first glance, Ehud's career as a judge in Israel may not seem relevant to us. He clearly lived in another time. He took radical and violent action to free his people. His murder of King Eglon shocks us. His war on Moab was swift and deadly. His life is difficult to relate to. But our commitment to God's Word challenges us not to ignore this leader. As we read about his life, some questions come to mind: (1) When was the last time God showed me something wrong in my life and I took immediate and painful action to correct the error? (2) When was the last time I asked God to show me how he could use something unique about me (such as left-handedness)? (3) When was the last time I made a plan to obey God in some specific area of my life and then followed through on that plan? (4) When was the last time my life was an example to others of obedience to God?

The enemies we face are as real as Ehud's, but they are most often within ourselves. The battles we fight are not against other people but against the power of sin. We need God's help in doing battle against sin. We also need to remember that he has already won the war. He has defeated sin at the cross of his Son, Jesus. His help is in each success, and his forgiveness is sufficient for each failure.

Strengths and accomplishments
- Second judge of Israel
- A man of direct action, a front-line leader
- Used a perceived weakness (left-handedness) to do a great work for God
- Led the revolt against Moabite domination; gave Israel 80 years of peace

Lessons from his life:
- Some conditions call for radical action
- God responds to the cry of repentance
- God is ready to use our unique qualities to accomplish his work

Vital statistics:
- Where: Born during the last of the wilderness wanderings or during Israel's early years in the Promised Land
- Occupation: Bonded messenger, judge
- Relatives: Father: Gera
- Contemporaries: King Eglon of Moab

Key verse:
"But when they cried to the Lord, he sent them a savior, Ehud (son of Gera, a Benjaminite), who was left-handed" (Judges 3:15).

His story is told in Judges 3:11–30.

3:15 Ehud is called a "savior." Other translations call him a "deliverer." In the broadest sense, all the judges can be looked upon as foreshadowing the perfect Savior, Jesus Christ. While Ehud saved Israel from its enemies, Jesus saves us from sin, our greatest enemy.

3:15-21 This is a strange story, but it teaches us that God can use us just the way he made us. Being left-handed in Ehud's day was considered a handicap or, at best, an abnormality. But Ehud's perceived weakness was used by God to give Israel victory. Let God use you the way you are to accomplish his work.

waited, thinking that perhaps he was using the bathroom. 25But when, after a long time, he still didn't come out, they became concerned and got a key. And when they opened the door, they found their master dead on the floor.

26Meanwhile Ehud had escaped past the quarries to Se-irah. 27When he arrived in the hill country of Ephraim, he blew a trumpet as a call to arms and mustered an army under his own command.

28"Follow me," he told them, "for the Lord has put your enemies, the Moabites, at your mercy!"

3:28
Judg 7:24; 12:5

The army then proceeded to seize the fords of the Jordan River near Moab, preventing anyone from crossing. 29Then they attacked the Moabites and killed about ten thousand of the strongest and most skillful of their fighting men, letting not one escape. 30So Moab was conquered by Israel that day, and the land was at peace for the next eighty years.

Shamgar

31The next judge after Ehud was Shamgar (son of Anath). He once killed six hundred Philistines with an ox goad, thereby saving Israel from disaster.

3:31
Judg 5:6

3. Third period: Deborah and Barak

4 After Ehud's death the people of Israel again sinned against the Lord, 2, 3so the Lord let them be conquered by King Jabin of Hazor, in Canaan. The commander-in-chief of his army was Sisera, who lived in Harosheth-ha-goiim. He had nine hundred iron chariots, and made life unbearable for the Israelis for twenty years. But finally they begged the Lord for help.

4:1
Judg 2:19
4:2
Josh 11:1
Ps 83:9

3:28–30 Ehud's courageous faith brought peace to the nation of Israel for 80 years. Genuine faith becomes stronger in the face of opposition. By bravely following God, we can present an inspiring example that helps others stand up for him.

3:31 To kill 600 Philistines with an ox goad was quite a feat. A goad was a long stick with a small flat piece of iron on one side and a sharp point on the other. The sharp side was used to drive the oxen during the times of plowing, and the flat end was used to clean the mud off the plow. Ancient ox goads have been found that were as long as eight feet. In times of crisis they could easily be used as spears, as in Shamgar's case. Ox goads are still used in the Middle East to drive oxen.

4:1 When Israel sinned it was "against the Lord." Our sins harm both ourselves and others, but all sin is ultimately against God because it disregards his commands and his authority over our lives. When confessing his sin David prayed, "It is against you and you alone I sinned" (Psalm 51:4). Recognizing the seriousness of sin may be the first step towards removing it from our lives.

4:2, 3 Nothing is known about King Jabin. Joshua had defeated a king by that name years earlier (Joshua 11:1–11). Joshua had also burned the city of Hazor to the ground. The city was either rebuilt by this time, or Jabin was hoping to rebuild it.

This is the only time during the period of the judges when the Israelites' enemies came from within their land. The Israelites had failed to drive out all the Canaanites, and they had regrouped and were attempting to restore their lost power. If the Israelites had obeyed God in the first place and driven the Canaanites from the land, this incident would probably not have happened.

4:2, 3 Chariots were the tanks of the ancient world. Made of iron or wood, they were pulled by one or two horses and were the most feared and powerful weapons of the day. Some chariots even had razor sharp knives extending from the wheels designed to mutilate helpless foot soldiers. The Canaanite army had 900 of these iron chariots. It was not within Israel's power to defeat such an

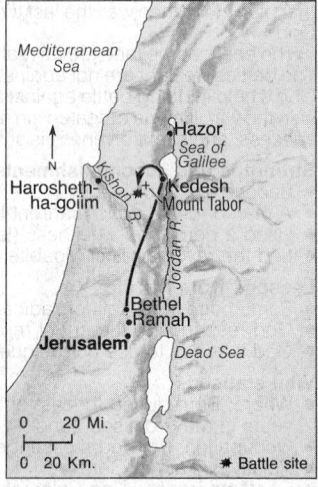

KING JABIN IS DEFEATED
Deborah traveled from her home between Ramah and Bethel to march with Barak and the Israelite army from Kedesh to do battle with the army of Hazor. Sisera, commander of Hazor's army, assembled his men at Harosheth-ha-goiim. In spite of Sisera's 900 chariots and expertly trained army, Israel was victorious.

invincible army. With such power King Jabin and General Sisera had no trouble oppressing the people until a faithful woman named Deborah called upon God.

4:3 After 20 years of unbearable circumstances, the Israelites finally turned to God for help. But God should be the first place we turn when we are facing struggles or dilemmas. The Israelites did things their way and got into a mess. We often do the same. Trying to control our own lives without God's help often leads to struggle and confusion. Keeping in daily contact with God helps eliminate some of the painful circumstances we create. This is a lesson the Israelites never fully learned. When struggles come our way, God wants us to seek him first, giving him top priority in our lives.

Deborah and Barak

⁴Israel's leader at that time, the one who was responsible for bringing the people back to God, was Deborah, a prophetess, the wife of Lappidoth. ⁵She held court at a place now called "Deborah's Palm Tree," between Ramah and Bethel, in the hill country of Ephraim; and the Israelites came to her to decide their disputes.

4:6
1 Sam 12:11
Heb 11:32

⁶One day she summoned Barak (son of Abinoam), who lived in Kedesh, in the land of Naphtali, and said to him, "The Lord God of Israel has commanded you to mobilize ten thousand men from the tribes of Naphtali and Zebulun. Lead them to Mount Tabor, ⁷to fight King Jabin's mighty army with all his chariots, under General Sisera's command. The Lord says, 'I will draw them to the Kishon River, and you will defeat them there.'"

4:7
Ps 83:9

⁸"I'll go, but only if you go with me!" Barak told her.

⁹"All right," she replied, "I'll go with you; but I'm warning you now that the honor of conquering Sisera will go to a woman instead of to you!" So she went with him to Kedesh.

4:10
Judg 5:18

4:11
Josh 19:33
Judg 1:16

¹⁰When Barak summoned the men of Zebulun and Naphtali to mobilize at Kedesh, ten thousand men volunteered. And Deborah marched with them. ¹¹(Heber, the Kenite—the Kenites were the descendants of Moses' father-in-law Hobab—had moved away from the rest of his clan, and had been living in various places as far away as the Oak of Za-anannim, near Kedesh.) ¹²When General Sisera was told that Barak and his army were camped at Mount Tabor ¹³he mobilized his entire army, including the nine hundred iron chariots, and marched from Harosheth-ha-goiim to the Kishon River.

¹⁴Then Deborah said to Barak, "Now is the time for action! The Lord leads on! He has already delivered Sisera into your hand!"

So Barak led his ten thousand men down the slopes of Mount Tabor into battle.

4:15
Josh 10:10
Judg 7:21

4:16
Judg 4:2,3
Ps 83:9

¹⁵Then the Lord threw the enemy into a panic, both the soldiers and the charioteers, and Sisera leaped from his chariot and escaped on foot. ¹⁶Barak and his men chased the enemy and the chariots as far as Harosheth-ha-goiim, until all of Sisera's army was destroyed; not one man was left alive. ¹⁷Meanwhile, Sisera had escaped to the tent of Jael, the wife of Heber the Kenite, for there was a mutual-assistance agreement between King Jabin of Hazor and the clan of Heber.

4:5 *came to her to decide their disputes,* or, "to listen to her speak to them about God."

THE JUDGES' FUNCTIONS
Regardless of an individual judge's leadership style, each one demonstrated that God's judgement follows apostasy, while repentance brings restoration.

Judges of Israel could be:

saviors (deliverers) and redeemers (Gideon)	or mediators and administrators (Tola)
providers of rest and peace (Ehud and Jair)	or rude, petty dictators (Jephthah)
famous and powerful (Samson)	or hardworking yet unsung (Elon and Abdon)
leaders of the nation (Othniel and Deborah)	or local heroes (Shamgar and Ibzan)

4:4ff The Bible records few women in national leadership positions, but Deborah was obviously the best person for the job, and God chose her to lead Israel. God can choose anyone to lead his people, young or old, man or woman. Don't let your prejudices get in the way of those God may have chosen to lead you.

4:6–8 Was Barak cowardly or just in need of support? We don't know Barak's character, but we see the character of a great leader in Deborah, who took charge as God directed. Deborah told Barak that God would be with him in battle, but that was not enough for Barak. He wanted Deborah to go with him. We cannot expect honor, respect, or praise if God alone is not enough for us. Our desire for support shouldn't become a crutch.

4:9 How did Deborah command such respect? She was responsible for leading the people into battle, but more than that,

she influenced the people to live for God after the battle was over. She had a personality that drew people together and commanded the respect of even Barak, a military general. She was also a prophetess, whose main role was to encourage the people to obey God. Those who lead must not forget about the spiritual condition of those being led. A true leader is concerned for persons, not just success.

4:11 Heber was Jael's husband (4:17). He was from the Kenite tribe who had long been Israel's ally. But for some reason, Heber decided to side with Jabin, maybe because Jabin's army appeared to have the military advantage. It was probably Heber who told General Sisera that the Israelites were camped near Mount Tabor (4:12; see map). Although Heber put in his lot with Jabin and his forces, his wife Jael did not (4:21).

18Jael went out to meet Sisera and said to him, "Come into my tent, sir. You will be safe here in our protection. Don't be afraid." So he went into her tent and she covered him with a blanket.

19"Please give me some water," he said, "for I am very thirsty." So she gave him some milk and covered him again.

4:19
Judg 5:25

20"Stand in the door of the tent," he told her, "and if anyone comes by, looking for me, tell them that no one is here."

21Then Jael took a sharp tent peg and a hammer and, quietly creeping up to him as he slept, she drove the peg through his temples and into the ground; and so he died, for he was fast asleep from weariness.

22When Barak came by looking for Sisera, Jael went out to meet him and said, "Come, and I will show you the man you are looking for."

So he followed her into the tent and found Sisera lying there dead, with the tent peg through his temples. 23So that day the Lord used Israel to subdue King Jabin of Canaan. 24And from that time on Israel became stronger and stronger against King Jabin, until he and all his people were destroyed.

Song of Deborah and Barak

5 Then Deborah and Barak sang this song about the wonderful victory:

5:1
Ex 15:1,21
Num 21:17,18
1 Sam 2:1

2"Praise the Lord!
Israel's leaders bravely led;
The people gladly followed!
Yes, bless the Lord!

5:2
Ps 110:3

3Listen, O you kings and princes,
For I shall sing about the Lord,
The God of Israel.

4When you led us out from Seir,
Out across the fields of Edom,
The earth trembled
And the sky poured down its rain.

5:4
Deut 33:2
Hab 3:3

5Yes, even Mount Sinai quaked
At the presence of the God of Israel!

5:5
Ex 19:18; 20:18
Ps 97:5; 114:6
Isa 64:3

6In the days of Shamgar and of Jael,
The main roads were deserted.
Travelers used the narrow, crooked side paths.

5:6
Judg 3:31; 4:17

7Israel's population dwindled,
Until Deborah became a mother to Israel.

8When Israel chose new gods,
Everything collapsed.
Our masters would not let us have
A shield or spear.

5:8
Deut 32:17
1 Sam 13:22

4:18-21 Sisera couldn't have been more pleased when Jael offered him her tent as a hiding place. First, because Jael was the wife of Heber, a man loyal to Sisera's forces (see the note on 4:11), she could certainly be trusted. Second, men were never allowed to enter a woman's tent; no one would think to look for Sisera there.

Even though Heber was loyal to Sisera's forces, Jael certainly was not. Since women of that day were in charge of pitching the tents, Jael had no problem driving the tent peg into Sisera's head while he slept. Deborah's prediction was thus fulfilled: she had said that the honor of conquering Sisera would go to a woman (4:9).

5:1ff Music and singing were a cherished part of Israelite history. Chapter five is a song, possibly composed by Deborah and Barak and sung by them as well. It sets to music the events of Israel's great victory recounted in chapter four. This victory song was accompanied by great celebration. It proclaimed the greatness of

God by giving him credit for the victory. It was an excellent way to preserve and retell this wonderful story from generation to generation. (Other songs in the Bible are listed in the chart in Exodus 15.)

5:1ff In victory, Barak and Deborah sang praises to God. Songs of praise focus our attention on God, give us an outlet for spiritual celebration, and remind us of God's faithfulness and character. Whether you are in the midst of a great victory or a major dilemma, singing praises to God can have a positive effect on your attitude.

5:8 Israel's world fell apart when the people chose to follow false gods. Pressure from without became greater than power from within. Though God had given Israel clear directions, the people failed to put into practice God's words. Instead they lived on a false foundation of values that soon collapsed. If you are letting a desire for recognition, craving for power, or love of money rule your life, you may find your world collapsing because you lack the solid foundation that comes only from God.

Among forty thousand men of Israel,
Not a weapon could be found!
9How I rejoice
In the leaders of Israel
Who offered themselves so willingly!
Praise the Lord!

5:10
Judg 10:4; 12:14

10Let all Israel, rich and poor,
Join in his praises—
Those who ride on white donkeys
And sit on rich carpets,
And those who are poor and must walk.

5:11
Gen 24:11
1 Sam 12:7

11The village musicians
Gather at the village well
To sing of the triumphs of the Lord.
Again and again they sing the ballad
Of how the Lord saved Israel
With an army of peasants!
The people of the Lord
Marched through the gates!
12Awake, O Deborah, and sing!
Arise, O Barak!
O son of Abino-am, lead away your captives!

DEBORAH

Wise leaders are rare. They accomplish great amounts of work without direct involvement because they know how to work through other people. They are able to see the big picture which often escapes those directly involved, so they make good mediators, advisers, and planners. Deborah fit this description perfectly. She had all these leadership skills, and she had a remarkable relationship with God. The insight and confidence God gave this woman placed her in a unique position in the Old Testament. Deborah is among the outstanding women of history.

Her story shows that she was not power hungry. She wanted to serve God. Whenever praise came her way, she gave God the credit. She didn't deny or resist her position in the culture as a woman and wife, but she never allowed herself to be hindered by it either. Her story shows that God can accomplish great things through people who are willing to be led by him.

Deborah's life challenges us in several ways. She reminds us of the need to be available both to God and to others. She encourages us to spend our efforts on what we can do rather than on worrying about what we can't do. Deborah challenges us to be wise leaders. She demonstrates what a person can accomplish when God is in control.

Strengths and accomplishments:
• Fourth and only female judge of Israel
• Special abilities as a mediator, adviser, and counselor
• When called on to lead, was able to delegate, plan, and direct
• Known for her prophetic power
• A writer of songs

Lessons from her life:
• God chooses leaders by his standards, not ours
• Wise leaders choose good helpers

Vital statistics:
• Where: Canaan
• Occupation: Prophetess and judge
• Relatives: Husband: Lappidoth
• Contemporaries: Barak, Jael, King Jabin (of Hazor in Canaan), Sisera (army commander)

Key verse:
"Israel's leader at that time, the one who was responsible for bringing the people back to God, was Deborah, a prophetess, the wife of Lappidoth" (Judges 4:4).

Her story is told in Judges 4, 5.

13, 14Down from Mount Tabor marched the noble remnant.
The people of the Lord
Marched down against great odds.
They came from Ephraim and Benjamin,
From Machir and from Zebulun.
15Down into the valley
Went the princes of Issachar
With Deborah and Barak.
At God's command they rushed into the valley.
(But the tribe of Reuben didn't go.
16Why did you sit at home among the sheepfolds,
Playing your shepherd pipes?
Yes, the tribe of Reuben has an uneasy conscience.
17Why did Gilead remain across the Jordan,
And why did Dan remain with his ships?
And why did Asher sit unmoved
Upon the seashore,
At ease beside his harbors?)
18But the tribes of Zebulun and Naphtali
Dared to die upon the fields of battle.
19The kings of Canaan fought in Taanach
By Megiddo's springs,
But did not win the victory.
20The very stars of heaven
Fought Sisera.
21The rushing Kishon River
Swept them away.
March on, my soul, with strength!
22Hear the stamping
Of the horsehoofs of the enemy!
See the prancing of his steeds!
23But the Angel of Jehovah
Put a curse on Meroz.
'Curse them bitterly,' he said,
'Because they did not come to help the Lord
Against his enemies.'
24Blessed be Jael,
The wife of Heber the Kenite—
Yes, may she be blessed
Above all women who live in tents.
25He asked for water
And she gave him milk in a beautiful cup!
26Then she took a tent pin and a workman's hammer
And pierced Sisera's temples,
Crushing his head.
She pounded the tent pin through his head.
27He sank, he fell, he lay dead at her feet.
28The mother of Sisera watched through the window
For his return.
'Why is his chariot so long in coming?
Why don't we hear the sound of the wheels?'

5:16
Num 32:24

5:17
Josh 13:25; 22:9

5:19
Josh 11:1,2
Judg 1:27

5:21
Judg 4:7

5:22
Job 39:19-25

5:13, 14 Even against great odds, God's people marched into battle. If you are struggling with something greater than you can handle, turn to the Scripture for God's encouragement. When the odds seem stacked against us, God can turn them to our favor.

5:15–17 Four tribes—Reuben, Gilead (either Gad or Manasseh), Dan, and Asher—were accused of not lending a helping hand in the battle. No reasons are given for their refusal to help their fellow Israelites, but they may be the same ones that stopped them from driving out the Canaanites in the first place: (1) lack of faith in God, (2) lack of effort, (3) fear of the enemy, (4) fear of antagonizing those with whom they did business. This disobedience showed a lack of enthusiasm for God's plan.

29But her ladies-in-waiting—and she herself—replied,

5:30
Ex 15:9

30'There is much loot to be divided,
And it takes time.
Each man receives a girl or two;
And Sisera will get gorgeous robes,
And he will bring home
Many gifts for me.'

5:31
Ps 68:1,2
92:8,9

31O Lord, may all your enemies
Perish as Sisera did,
But may those who love the Lord
Shine as the sun!"

After that there was peace in the land for forty years.

4. Fourth period: Gideon, Tola, and Jair

6:1
Num 22:4
25:15; 31:1
Judg 2:11-14

6 Then the people of Israel began once again to worship other gods, and once again the Lord let their enemies harass them. This time it was by the people of Midian, for seven years. 2The Midianites were so cruel that the Israelis took to the mountains, living in caves and dens. 3, 4When they planted their seed, marauders from Midian, Amalek, and other neighboring nations came and destroyed their crops and plundered the countryside as far away as Gaza, leaving nothing to eat, and taking away all their sheep, oxen, and donkeys. 5These enemy hordes arrived on droves of camels too numerous to count and stayed until the land was completely stripped and devastated. 6, 7So Israel was reduced to abject poverty because of the Midianites. Then at last the people of Israel began to cry out to the Lord for help.

6:3
Isa 21:2

6:5
1 Sam 30:17

6:6
Deut 28:43

6:8
Ex 18:9
Judg 2:1,2,18
10:12

8However, the Lord's reply through the prophet he sent to them was this: "The Lord God of Israel brought you out of slavery in Egypt, 9and rescued you from the Egyptians and from all who were cruel to you, and drove out your enemies before you, and gave you their land. 10He told you he is the Lord your God, and you must not worship the gods of the Amorites who live around you on every side. But you have not listened to him."

6:10
Josh 24:15

God commissions Gideon

6:11
Judg 13:2,3
Heb 11:32

11But one day the Angel of the Lord came and sat beneath the oak tree at Ophrah, on the farm of Joash the Abiezrite. Joash's son, Gideon, had been threshing wheat by hand in the bottom of a grape press—a pit where grapes were pressed to make wine—for he was hiding from the Midianites.

5:23 Meroz was probably a city near the scene of the great battle between the Canaanites and Israelites. It must have been an Israelite city, because it was cursed for not sending help against Sisera's forces.

6:2 The Midianites were desert people descended from Abraham's second wife, Keturah (Genesis 25:1, 2). From this relationship came a nation that was always in conflict with Israel. Years earlier the Israelites, while still wandering in the wilderness, battled the Midianites and almost destroyed them completely (Numbers 31:1–20). Because of their failure to do so, the tribe repopulated. Now they were once again oppressing Israel.

6:6, 7 Again Israel hits rock bottom before turning back to God. How much suffering they could have avoided if they had trusted God! Turning to God shouldn't be a last resort, we should look to him for help each day. This isn't to say life will always be easy. There will be struggles, but God will give us the strength to endure them. Don't wait until you're at the end of your rope. Call upon God first in every situation you face.

6:8 Scripture does not say who this prophet was. Prophets were those who brought God's messages to the people. Their main role was not to tell about the future but to urge the people to turn away from their sins and back to God. This is what this prophet did.

6:11 The Old Testament records several appearances of an Angel of the Lord: Genesis 16:7; 22:11; 31:11; Exodus 3:2; 14:19; Judges 2:1; 13:2; Zechariah 3:1–6. It is not known whether the same Angel appeared in each of these references. The Angel mentioned here in Judges appears to be separate from God in one place (6:12) and yet the same as God in another place (6:14). This has led many to believe that the Angel was a physical appearance of Jesus prior to his mission on earth as recorded in the New Testament. It is also possible that as a special messenger from God, the Angel had authority to speak for God. In either case, God sent a special messenger to deliver a message to Gideon.

6:11 Threshing was the process of separating the grains of wheat from the useless outer shell called chaff. This was normally done in a large area, often on a hill, where the wind could blow away the lighter chaff when the farmer tossed the beaten wheat into the air. If Gideon had done this, however, he would have been an easy target for the bands of raiders who were overrunning the land. Therefore, he was forced to thresh his wheat in a winepress, a pit that was probably hidden from view and that would not be suspected as a place to find a farmer's crops.

12The Angel of the Lord appeared to him and said, "Mighty soldier, the Lord is with you!"

13"Stranger," Gideon replied, "if the Lord is with us, why has all this happened to us? And where are all the miracles our ancestors have told us about—such as when God brought them out of Egypt? Now the Lord has thrown us away and has let the Midianites completely ruin us."

14Then the Lord turned to him and said, "I will make you strong! Go and save Israel from the Midianites! I am sending you!"

15But Gideon replied, "Sir, how can *I* save Israel? My family is the poorest in the whole tribe of Manasseh, and I am the least thought of in the entire family!"

16Whereupon the Lord said to him, "But I, Jehovah, will be with you! And you shall quickly destroy the Midianite hordes!"

17Gideon replied, "If it is really true that you are going to help me like that, then do some miracle to prove it! Prove that it is really Jehovah who is talking to me! 18But stay here until I go and get a present for you."

"All right," the Angel agreed. "I'll stay here until you return."

19Gideon hurried home and roasted a young goat, and baked some unleavened bread from a bushel of flour. Then, carrying the meat in a basket and broth in a pot, he took it out to the Angel, who was beneath the oak tree, and presented it to him.

20The Angel said to him, "Place the meat and the bread upon that rock over there, and pour the broth over it.

"When Gideon had followed these instructions, 21the Angel touched the meat and bread with his staff, and fire flamed up from the rock and consumed them! And suddenly the Angel was gone!

22When Gideon realized that it had indeed been the Angel of the Lord, he cried out, "Alas, O Lord God, for I have seen the Angel of the Lord face to face!"

23"It's all right," the Lord replied. "Don't be afraid! You shall not die."

Gideon destroys idols

24And Gideon built an altar there and named it "The Altar of Peace with Jehovah." (The altar is still there in Ophrah in the land of the Abiezrites.) 25That night the Lord told Gideon to hitch his father's best ox to the family altar of Baal, and pull it down, and to cut down the wooden idol of the goddess Asherah that stood nearby.

6:13
Deut 31:17
2 Chron 15:2
Ps 44:9

6:15
Ex 3:11

6:17
Isa 38:7

6:19
Gen 18:8

6:21
Lev 9:24

6:22
Gen 16:13
32:30
Ex 33:20
Judg 13:22

6:25
Ex 34:13
Deut 7:5

6:16 *But I, Jehovah,* literally, "I Am will be with you." The same name is used here as in Exodus 3:14. God is telling Gideon that the same one who appeared to Moses and rescued Israel from Egypt (much on Gideon's mind: see vs 13) will now do it again, rescuing Israel from Midian.

6:13 Gideon questioned God about the problems he and his nation faced and about God's apparent lack of help. What he didn't acknowledge was the fact that the people had brought calamity upon themselves when they decided to disobey and neglect God. How easy it is to overlook personal accountability and blame our problems on God and others. Unfortunately this does not solve our problems. It brings us no closer to God, and it escorts us to the very edge of rebellion and backsliding.

When problems come, the first place to look is within. Our first action should be confession to God for sins that may have had a part in creating our problems.

6:13 Gideon had heard about the great miracles God had done for his people, but he hadn't seen any. It had been almost 250 years since the ten plagues and the parting of the Red Sea (Exodus 7–14), and 200 years had passed since the last great miracle, the parting of the Jordan River (Joshua 3). Because of this lack of miracles, Gideon wrongly assumed that God had given up on his people. But it was the people who had given up on God. They knew what God expected of them. They had his laws and they no longer needed great miracles as proof that God was their leader. If we are growing in God as we should, there is rarely a need for great miracles.

6:14–16 "I am sending you!" God told Gideon, and God promised to give him the strength he needed to overcome the opposition. In spite of this clear calling and promise for strength, Gideon made excuses. He saw only his limitations and weaknesses. He failed to see how God could work through him.

Like Gideon, we are called to serve God in specific ways. Although God promises us the tools and strength we need, we often make excuses too. But reminding God of our limitations only implies that he does not know all about us or that he has made a mistake in evaluating our character. Don't spend time making excuses. Instead spend it doing what God wants.

6:25–30 After God called Gideon to be Israel's deliverer, he immediately asked him to tear down the altar of the god Baal—an act that would test Gideon's faith and commitment. The real test of faith is how it stands up under pressure. Canaanite religion was very political, so an attack on a god was often seen as an attack on the local government which supported that god. If caught, Gideon would face serious social problems and probable physical attack.

Gideon took a great risk by following God's higher law which specifically states that idol worship is forbidden (Exodus 20:1–5). After learning what Gideon had done, the townspeople wanted to kill him. Many of those people were fellow Israelites. This shows how immoral God's people had become. God said in Deuteronomy 13:6–11 that idolaters must be stoned to death. But these Israelites wanted to stone Gideon for tearing down an idol and worshiping God!

26"Replace it with an altar for the Lord your God, built here on this hill, laying the stones carefully. Then sacrifice the ox as a burnt offering to the Lord, using the wooden idol as wood for the fire on the altar."

27So Gideon took ten of his servants and did as the Lord had commanded. But he did it at night for fear of the other members of his father's household, and for fear of the men of the city; for he knew what would happen if they found out who did it! 28Early the next morning, as the city began to stir, someone discovered that the altar of Baal was knocked apart, the idol beside it was gone, and a new altar had been built instead, with the remains of a sacrifice on it.

29"Who did this?" everyone demanded. Finally they learned that it was Gideon, the son of Joash.

30"Bring out your son," they shouted to Joash. "He must die for insulting the altar of Baal, and for cutting down the Asherah idol."

31But Joash retorted to the whole mob, "Does Baal need *your* help? What an insult to a god! You are the ones who should die for insulting Baal! If Baal is really a god, let him take care of himself and destroy the one who broke apart his altar!"

32From then on Gideon was called "Jerubbaal," a nickname meaning "Let Baal take care of himself!"

Gideon puts out the fleece

6:33
Josh 17:16-18
Judg 7:1,12,13
6:34
Judg 3:10

33Soon afterward the armies of Midian, Amalek, and other neighboring nations united in one vast alliance against Israel. They crossed the Jordan and camped in the valley of Jezreel. 34Then the Spirit of the Lord came upon Gideon, and he blew a trumpet as a call to arms, and the men of Abiezer came to him. 35He also sent

6:32 *Let Baal take care of himself,* literally, "Let Baal bring charges," or used mockingly, "Let Baal be honored!"

GOD USES COMMON PEOPLE	Person	Known as	Task	Reference
God uses all sorts of people to do his work— like you and me!	JACOB	A liar	To "father" the Israelite nation	Genesis 27
	JOSEPH	A slave	To save his family	Genesis 39ff
	MOSES	Shepherd in exile (and murderer)	To lead Israel out of bondage, to the Promised Land	Exodus 3
	GIDEON	A farmer	To deliver Israel from Midian	Judges 6
	JEPHTHAH	Son of a prostitute	To deliver Israel from the Ammonites	Judges 11
	HANNAH	A housewife	To be the mother of Samuel	I Samuel 1
	DAVID	A shepherd boy and last-born of the family	To be Israel's greatest king	I Samuel 16
	EZRA	A scribe	To lead the return to Judah and to write some of the Bible	Ezra, Nehemiah
	ESTHER	A slave girl	To save her people from massacre	Esther
	MARY	A peasant girl	To be the mother of Christ	Luke 1:26–38
	MATTHEW	A tax-collector	To be an apostle and Gospel writer	Matthew 9:9
	LUKE	A Greek physician	To be a companion of Paul and a Gospel writer	Colossians 4:14
	PETER	A fisherman	To be an apostle, a leader of the early church, and a writer of two New Testament epistles	Matthew 4:18–20

6:33 The armies of Midian and Amalek camped in the valley of Jezreel. Since the valley was surrounded by mountains, it was the agricultural center for the area. Whoever controlled the rich and fertile land of the valley controlled the people who lived in and around it. Because of its vast resources, many of the major trade routes converged at the pass which led into the valley. This made the Jezreel valley the site of many great battles. Gideon's men attacked the enemy armies from the hills, and the only escape route was through the pass toward the Jordan River. That is why Gideon urged some of his troops to take control of the river's crossing points (7:24).

messengers throughout Manasseh, Asher, Zebulun, and Naphtali, summoning their fighting forces, and all of them responded.

36Then Gideon said to God, "If you are really going to use me to save Israel as you promised, 37prove it to me in this way: I'll put some wool on the threshing floor tonight, and if, in the morning, the fleece is wet and the ground is dry, I will know you are going to help me!"

38And it happened just that way! When he got up the next morning he pressed the fleece together and wrung out a whole bowlful of water!

39Then Gideon said to the Lord, "Please don't be angry with me, but let me make one more test: this time let the fleece remain dry while the ground around it is wet!"

40So the Lord did as he asked; that night the fleece stayed dry, but the ground was covered with dew!

Gideon selects an army and defeats Midian

7 Jerubbaal (that is, Gideon—his other name) and his army got an early start and went as far as the spring of Harod. The armies of Midian were camped north of them, down in the valley beside the hill of Moreh.

2The Lord then said to Gideon, "There are too many of you! I can't let all of you fight the Midianites, for then the people of Israel will boast to me that they saved themselves by their own strength! 3Send home any of your men who are timid and frightened."

So twenty-two thousand of them left, and only ten thousand remained who were willing to fight.

4But the Lord told Gideon, "There are still too many! Bring them down to the spring and I'll show you which ones shall go with you and which ones shall not."

5, 6So Gideon assembled them at the water. There the Lord told him, "Divide them into two groups decided by the way they drink. In Group 1 will be all the men who cup the water in their hands to get it to their mouths and lap it like dogs. In Group 2 will be those who kneel, with their mouths in the stream."

Only three hundred of the men drank from their hands; all the others drank with their mouths to the stream.

6:35
Judg 7:24; 9:31

6:36
Judg 6:14

6:39
Gen 18:32

7:1
Gen 12:6
Deut 11:30
Judg 6:32

7:2
Deut 8:18
Isa 10:13
Ezek 28:2,17

7:3
Deut 20:8

7:4
1 Sam 14:6

6:37 Was Gideon really testing God, or was he simply asking God for more encouragement? In either case it is clear that Gideon's motive was right (to obey God and defeat the enemy), but his method was less than ideal. Gideon seems to have known that his requests might displease God (6:39). In addition, Gideon had witnessed not one but three miracles as proof of his mission (6:21, 38, 40). After asking for a miracle and receiving it, he still did not believe (6:39). It is true that to make good decisions we need facts. Gideon had all the facts, but still he hesitated. He delayed his obedience because he wanted even more proof.

Demanding extra signs was an indication of unbelief. Fear often makes us wait for more confirmation when we should be obedient. Visible signs are unnecessary if they are only confirming what we already know is true.

Today the greatest sign of God's guidance is his Word. Unlike Gideon, we have God's complete, revealed Word to humankind. If you want to have more of God's guidance, don't ask for signs; study God's Word (2 Timothy 3:16, 17).

6:39 After seeing the miracle of the wet fleece, why did Gideon ask for another miracle? Perhaps he thought the results of the first test could have happened naturally. A thick woolen fleece could retain moisture long after the sun had dried the surrounding ground. "Putting out fleeces" is a poor decision-making method. Those who do this put limitations on God. They ask him to fit their expectations. The results of such experiments are usually inconclusive and thus fail to make us any more confident about our choices. Don't let a "fleece" become a substitute for the wisdom of God that comes through Bible study and prayer.

7:2 Self-sufficiency is an enemy when it causes us to believe we can always do what needs to be done in our own strength. To

GIDEON'S BATTLE
In spite of Deborah and Barak's victory, the Canaanites still caused trouble in this fertile region. God appeared to Gideon at Ophrah and called him to defeat them. With only 300 fighting men, Gideon routed thousands of Midianites, chasing them to Zererah and Abel-meholah.

prevent this attitude among Gideon's soldiers, God reduced their number from 32,000 to 300. With an army this small, there could be no doubt that any victory was from God. The men could not take the credit. Like Gideon, we must recognize the danger of fighting in our own strength. We can only be confident of victory if we put our confidence in God and not ourselves.

7:8
Josh 2:24; 10:8
11:6
Judg 3:28; 4:14

7:12
Josh 11:4
Judg 6:5; 8:10

7:21
Ex 14:25
2 Kgs 7:7

7:24
Judg 3:28; 12:5

7"I'll conquer the Midianites with these three hundred!" the Lord told Gideon. "Send all the others home!"

8, 9So after Gideon had collected all the clay jars and trumpets they had among them, he sent them home, leaving only three hundred men with him.

During the night, with the Midianites camped in the valley just below, the Lord said to Gideon, "Get up! Take your troops and attack the Midianites, for I will cause you to defeat them! 10But if you are afraid, first go down to the camp alone—take along your servant Purah if you like— 11and listen to what they are saying down there! You will be greatly encouraged and be eager to attack!"

So he took Purah and crept down through the darkness to the outposts of the enemy camp. 12, 13The vast armies of Midian, Amalek, and the other nations of the Mideast were crowded across the valley like locusts—yes, like the sand upon the seashore—and there were too many camels even to count! Gideon crept up to one of the tents just as a man inside had wakened from a nightmare and was telling his tent-mate about it.

"I had this strange dream," he was saying, "and there was this huge loaf of barley bread that came tumbling down into our camp. It hit our tent and knocked it flat!"

14The other soldier replied, "Your dream can mean only one thing! Gideon, the son of Joash, the Israeli, is going to come and massacre all the allied forces of Midian!"

15When Gideon heard the dream and the interpretation, all he could do was just stand there worshiping God! Then he returned to his men and shouted, "Get up! For the Lord is going to use you to conquer all the vast armies of Midian!"

16He divided the three hundred men into three groups and gave each man a trumpet and a clay jar with a torch in it. 17Then he explained his plan.

"When we arrive at the outer guardposts of the camp," he told them, "do just as I do. 18As soon as I and the men in my group blow our trumpets, you blow yours on all sides of the camp and shout, 'We fight for God and for Gideon!' "

19, 20It was just after midnight and the change of guards when Gideon and the hundred men with him crept to the outer edge of the camp of Midian.

Suddenly they blew their trumpets and broke their clay jars so that their torches blazed into the night. Then the other two hundred of his men did the same, blowing the trumpets in their right hands, and holding the flaming torches in their left hands, all shouting, "For the Lord and for Gideon!"

21Then they just stood and watched as the whole vast enemy army began rushing around in a panic, shouting and running away. 22For in the confusion the Lord caused the enemy troops to begin fighting and killing each other from one end of the camp to the other, and they fled into the night to places as far away as Beth-shittah near Zererah, and to the border of Abel-meholah near Tabbath.

23Then Gideon sent for the troops of Naphtali, Asher, and Manasseh and told them to come and chase and destroy the fleeing army of Midian. 24Gideon also sent messengers throughout the hill country of Ephraim summoning troops who seized the fords of the Jordan River at Beth-barah, thus preventing the Midianites from

7:19, 20 "For the Lord and for Gideon!" literally, "A sword for the Lord and for Gideon."

7:10, 11 Facing overwhelming odds, Gideon was afraid. God understood his fear, but he didn't excuse Gideon from his task. Instead he allowed Gideon to slip into the enemy camp and overhear a conversation that would give him courage (7:12–15). Are you facing a battle? God can give you the strength you need for any situation. And don't be startled by the way he helps you. Like Gideon, you must listen to God and be ready to take the first step. Only after you begin to obey God will you find the courage to move ahead.

7:12, 13 An enemy soldier dreamed of a huge loaf of barley bread tumbling into camp. Barley grain was only half the value of wheat, and the bread made from it was considered inferior. In the same way, Israel's tiny band of men was considered inferior to the vast forces of Midian and Amalek. But God would make the

underdog Israelites seem invincible.

7:15 Gideon stood just outside the enemy camp "worshiping God." Rituals, motions, and loud praise would have announced his presence to the enemy, so Gideon's worship was a silent attitude of joy, thanksgiving, and praise to God. Worship is not limited to a particular form or building. We can worship anywhere by changing our focus from life's struggles to a God who cares. True worship begins with a worshipful attitude.

7:21 Gideon's army simply watched as the army of Midian fell into panic, confusion, and disordered retreat—not one man had to draw a sword to defeat the enemy. Gideon's small army could never have brought about such a victory in their own strength. God wanted to demonstrate to Israel that victory depends not on strength or numbers, but on obedience and commitment to him.

escaping by going across. 25Oreb and Zeeb, the two generals of Midian, were captured. Oreb was killed at the rock now known by his name, and Zeeb at the winepress of Zeeb, as it is now called; and the Israelis took the heads of Oreb and Zeeb across the Jordan to Gideon.

7:25
Judg 8:2,3
Ps 83:11
Isa 10:26

Gideon punishes those who refuse to help

8 But the tribal leaders of Ephraim were violently angry with Gideon. "Why didn't you send for us when you first went out to fight the Midianites?" they demanded.

8:1
Judg 12:1

2, 3But Gideon replied, "God let you capture Oreb and Zeeb, the generals of the army of Midian! What have I done in comparison with that? Your actions at the end of the battle were more important than ours at the beginning!" So they calmed down.

4Gideon now crossed the Jordan River with his three hundred men. They were very tired, but still chasing the enemy. 5He asked the men of Succoth for food. "We are weary from chasing after Zebah and Zalmunna, the kings of Midian," he said.

8:5
Gen 33:17
Judg 8:15

6But the leaders of Succoth replied, "You haven't caught them yet! If we feed you and you fail, they'll return and destroy us."

7Then Gideon warned them, "When the Lord has delivered them to us, I will return and tear your flesh with the thorns and briars of the wilderness."

8:7
Judg 4:14; 7:15

8Then he went up to Penuel and asked for food there, but got the same answer. 9And he said to them also, "When this is all over, I will return and break down this tower."

8:8
Gen 32:30
1 Kgs 12:25

10By this time King Zebah and King Zalmunna with a remnant of fifteen thousand troops were in Karkor. That was all that was left of the allied armies of the east; for one hundred twenty thousand had already been killed. 11Then Gideon circled around by the caravan route east of Nobah and Jogbehah, striking at the Midianite army in surprise raids. 12The two kings fled, but Gideon chased and captured them, routing their entire force. 13Later, Gideon returned by way of Heres Pass. 14There he captured a young fellow from Succoth and demanded that he write down the names of all the seventy-seven political and religious leaders of the city.

8:10
Ps 83:9
Isa 9:4

15He then returned to Succoth. "You taunted me that I would never catch King Zebah and King Zalmunna, and you refused to give us food when we were tired and hungry," he said. "Well, here they are!"

8:15
Judg 8:7

16Then he took the leaders of the city and scraped them to death with wild thorns and briars. 17He also went to Penuel and knocked down the city tower and killed the entire male population.

8:17
Judg 8:8

18Then Gideon asked King Zebah and King Zalmunna, "The men you killed at Tabor—what were they like?"

They replied, "They were dressed just like you—like sons of kings!"

8:2, 3 *at the beginning,* more literally, "Are not the last grapes of Ephraim better than the entire crop of Abiezer?" **8:6** *they'll return and destroy us,* literally, "are Zebah and Zalmunna already in your hand . . . ?" **8:16** *and scraped them to death,* literally, "he taught the men of Succoth."

8:1–3 Ephraim's leaders felt left out because Gideon had not called them to join the battle, but had left them in place to "clean up" the escaping Midianites. As Gideon diplomatically pointed out, this rear guard had managed to capture the enemy's generals, thus cutting off the leaders from their army. Not every necessary job is a highly visible leadership role. Much of the necessary labor of any large enterprise is considered by many to be dirty work. But such work is vital to getting any big task done. Engineers and millionaires may design and finance a huge skyscraper, but it is the bricklayers who get the work done. Pride causes us to want recognition. Are you content to be God's bricklayer, or do you resent the work God has given you?

8:5, 6 The leaders of Succoth refused to help Gideon, fearing Midian's revenge should he fail. They should have realized that victory was certain because God was with Gideon. But they were so worried about saving themselves that they never thought about God's power to save.

Because of fear or overconcern for ourselves, we may fail to recognize God's presence in other people or situations and therefore miss participating in the victory God brings. Then we must face the often bitter consequences of failing to join forces with those God has chosen to do his work. Since God's work will prevail with or without you, be quick to join others who are engaged in godly work, lending support with your time, money, talents, or prayer.

8:15–17 Gideon carried out the threat he had made in 8:7. It is difficult to determine whether this act of revenge was justified or whether he should have left the punishment up to God. Gideon was God's appointed leader, but the officials of Succoth and Penuel refused to help him in any way because they feared the enemy. They showed no faith and respect for God and the man he had chosen to save them. We should help others because it is right, moral, and ethical, regardless of whether we will benefit personally.

¹⁹"They must have been my brothers!" Gideon exclaimed. "I swear that if you hadn't killed them I wouldn't kill you."

²⁰Then, turning to Jether, his oldest son, he instructed him to kill them. But the boy was only a lad and was afraid to.

Most of us want to know God's plan for our lives, but we're not always sure how to find it. One common misunderstanding is the idea that God's guidance will come to us out of the blue, that it has nothing to do with what we're involved in. But if we're always looking around for God's next assignment, we run the risk of ruining whatever we're working on right now. Fortunately, the Bible points to a kind of guidance that does not put our current projects in jeopardy. In the Bible's descriptions of how God guided many people, we can see that often God's call came while people were completely immersed in the challenge of the moment. A good example of this kind of guidance is seen in Gideon's life.

Gideon had a limited vision, but he was committed to it. His challenge was to obtain food for his family even though hostile invaders were making the growing, gathering, and preparation of the food almost impossible. Gideon was resourceful. He put a wine-pressing pit to double duty by turning it into a sunken threshing floor. It lacked ventilation to blow the chaff away, but at least it was hidden from the Midianites. Gideon was working in his threshing floor when God sent him a messenger with a challenge.

Gideon was surprised by what God told him to do. He did not want to jump into a task for which he was ill prepared. The angel had to overcome three objections before Gideon was convinced: (1) Gideon's feelings of responsibility for his family's welfare, (2) his doubts about the call itself, and (3) his feelings of inadequacy for the job. Once Gideon was convinced, however, he obeyed with zest, resourcefulness, and speed. He dedicated those personality traits to the God of his people, with whom he was now personally acquainted.

Gideon had his weak moments and failures, but he was still God's servant. If you can easily see yourself in the first half of that last sentence, can you also see yourself in the second half? Remember Gideon as a man who obeyed God by giving his attention to the task at hand. Then give your full attention to believing God will prepare you for tomorrow when it comes.

Strengths and accomplishments:
- Israel's fifth judge
- A military strategist who was expert at surprise
- A member of the Hall of Faith in Hebrews
- Defeated the Midianite army
- Was offered the title of king by the men of Israel
- Though slow to be convinced, acted on his convictions

Weaknesses and mistakes:
- Feared that his own limitations would prevent God from working
- Collected Midianite gold and made a symbol which became an object of worship
- Through a sexual relationship outside marriage, fathered a son who would bring great grief and tragedy to both Gideon's family and the nation of Israel
- Failed to establish his family in God's ways; after he died they all went back to idol worship

Lessons from his life:
- God expands and uses the abilities he has already built into us
- God uses us in spite of our limitations and failures
- Even those who make great spiritual progress can easily fall into sin if they don't consistently follow God

Vital statistics:
- Where: Ophrah, valley of Jezreel, Spring of Harod
- Occupation: Farmer, warrior, and judge
- Relatives: Father: Joash. Son: Abimelech.
- Contemporaries: King Zebah, King Zalmunna

Key verses:
"But Gideon replied, 'Sir, how can *I* save Israel? My family is the poorest in the whole tribe of Manasseh, and I am the least thought of in the entire family!' Whereupon the Lord said to him, 'But I, Jehovah, will be with you! And you shall quickly destroy the Midianite hordes!' " (Judges 6:15, 16).

His story is told in Judges 6—8. He is also mentioned in Hebrews 11:32.

GIDEON

8:20, 21 For a general to be killed by a boy was humiliating. The two men wanted to avoid that disgrace, as well as the slower and more painful death which an inexperienced swordsman might inflict.

²¹Then Zebah and Zalmunna said to Gideon, "You do it; we'd rather be killed by a man!" So Gideon killed them and took the ornaments from their camels' necks.

Gideon refuses to become king

²²Now the men of Israel said to Gideon, "Be our king! You and your sons and all your descendants shall be our rulers, for you have saved us from Midian."

²³, ²⁴But Gideon replied, "I will not be your king, nor shall my son; the Lord is your King! However, I have one request. Give me all the earrings collected from your fallen foes,"—for the troops of Midian, being Ishmaelites, all wore gold earrings.

²⁵"Gladly!" they replied, and spread out a sheet for everyone to throw in the gold earrings he had gathered. ²⁶Their value was estimated at $25,000, not including the crescents and pendants or the royal clothing of the kings, or the chains around the camels' necks. ²⁷Gideon made an ephod from the gold and put it in Ophrah, his home town. But all Israel soon began worshiping it, so it became an evil deed that Gideon and his family did.

8:27
Ex 28:5,6
Judg 17:4,5

Gideon dies

²⁸That is the true account of how Midian was subdued by Israel. Midian never recovered, and the land was at peace for forty years—all during Gideon's lifetime. ²⁹He returned home, ³⁰and eventually had seventy sons, for he married many wives. ³¹He also had a concubine in Shechem, who presented him with a son named Abimelech. ³²Gideon finally died, an old, old man, and was buried in the sepulcher of his father Joash in Ophrah, in the land of the Abiezrites.

8:30
Judg 9:2,5
8:31
Judg 9:1,2

³³But as soon as Gideon was dead, the Israelis began to worship the idols Baal and Baal-berith. ³⁴They no longer considered the Lord as their God, though he had rescued them from all their enemies on every side. ³⁵Nor did they show any kindness to the family of Gideon despite all he had done for them.

8:33
Judg 2:11
8:34
Deut 4:9
Judg 3:7

Abimelech tries to become king of Israel

9 One day Gideon's son Abimelech visited his uncles—his mother's brothers—in Shechem. ²"Go and talk to the leaders of Shechem," he requested, "and ask them whether

8:21 *we'd rather be killed by a man,* literally, "For as a man is, so is his strength." Perhaps the meaning is, "A quick death is less painful." **8:27** The ephod was usually a linen pouch worn by the priests on their chests. In this case the ephod evidently was highly decorated with gold, and probably, because of its weight, hung upon a wall. **9:2** *meaning me, your own flesh and blood.* Of all Gideon's wives, only Abimelech's mother was from Shechem (8:30, 31), so Abimelech felt his close kinship there.

8:21 Those who were very wealthy put jewelry on their camels as a way of displaying their wealth. Women wore vast amounts of jewelry as well, often up to 15 pairs of earrings. Jewelry was also worn for good luck. After Gideon's rise to power, he seems to have become carried away with this accumulation of wealth. Eventually it led the Israelites to idolatry (8:27).

8:23 The people wanted to make Gideon their king, but Gideon stressed that God was their true King. Despite his inconsistencies, Gideon never lost sight of the fact that the key to life, for both a nation and an individual, is putting God first. Is God first in your life?

8:27 We do not know why Gideon made the golden ephod. An ephod was a linen garment worn by priests over their chests. It was considered holy (Exodus 28:5–35; 39:2–24; Leviticus 8:7, 8). Gideon probably had good motives for making the ephod (a visible remembrance commemorating the victory). Unfortunately, the people began to worship the ephod as an idol. Sadly, many decisions that stem from good motives have negative results. Perhaps no one stops to ask, "What might go wrong?" or "Is there a possibility of negative consequences?" In plans and decisions you are involved with, take time to anticipate how a good idea might turn into a potential problem.

8:31 This relationship between Gideon and a concubine

produced a son who tore apart Gideon's family and caused tragedy for the nation. Gideon illustrates the fact that heroes in battle are not always heroic in day-to-day living. Gideon led the nation but could not lead his family. No matter who you are, moral laxness will cause problems. Just because you have won a single battle with temptation does not mean you will automatically overcome the next. We need to be constantly watchful against temptation.

9:1 With Gideon dead, Abimelech wanted to take his father's place. To set his plan in motion he went to the city of Shechem, his mother's hometown, to drum up support. Here he felt close kinship with the residents. This is why he referred to himself as the peoples' "own flesh and blood."

9:1 Abimelech was declared ruler of Israel at Shechem, the site of other key Bible events. It was one of Abraham's first stops upon arriving in Canaan (Genesis 12:6, 7). When Jacob lived there, two of his sons killed all the men in Shechem because the crown prince raped their sister (Genesis 34). Joseph's bones were buried in Shechem (Joshua 24:32). Israel renewed its covenant with God at Shechem (Joshua 24), and the kingdom of Israel split apart at this same city (1 Kings 12).

9:2–5 Israel's king was to be the Lord and not a man. But Abimelech wanted to usurp the position which had been reserved

they want to be ruled by seventy kings—Gideon's seventy sons—or by one man—meaning me, your own flesh and blood!"

³So his uncles went to the leaders of the city and proposed Abimelech's scheme; and they decided that since his mother was a native of their town they would go along with it. ⁴They gave him money from the temple offerings of the idol Baal-berith, which he used to hire some worthless loafers who agreed to do whatever he told them to. ⁵He took them to his father's home at Ophrah and there, upon one stone, they slaughtered all seventy of his half-brothers, except for the youngest, Jotham, who escaped and hid. ⁶Then the citizens of Shechem and Beth-millo called a meeting under the oak beside the garrison at Shechem, and Abimelech was acclaimed king of Israel.

⁷When Jotham heard about this, he stood at the top of Mount Gerizim and shouted across to the men of Shechem, "If you want God's blessing, listen to me!

9:4
Judg 8:33; 9:46

9:5
Judg 6:11; 8:32

9:6
Josh 24:26

9:7
Deut 11:29
27:12
Jn 4:20

ABIMELECH

People who desire power always outnumber those who are able to use power wisely once they have it. Perhaps this is because power has a way of taking over and controlling the person using it. This is especially true in cases of inherited but unmerited power. Abimelech's life shows us what happens when hunger for power corrupts judgment.

Abimelech's position in Gideon's family as the son of a concubine must have created great tension between him and Gideon's many other sons. One against 70: such odds can either crush a person or make him ruthless. It is obvious which direction Abimelech chose. Gideon's position as warrior and judge had placed Abimelech in an environment of power; Gideon's death provided an opportunity for this son to seize power. Once the process began, the disastrous results were inevitable. A person's thirst for power is not satisfied when he gets power—it only becomes more intense. Abimelech's life was consumed by that thirst. Eventually, he could not tolerate any threat to his power.

By this time, ownership had changed: Abimelech no longer had power—power had him. One of the lessons we can learn from his life is that our goals control our actions. The amount of control is related to the importance of the goal. Abimelech's most important goal was to have power. His lust for power led him to wipe out not only his brothers, but also whole cities that refused to submit to him. Nothing but death could stop his bloodthirsty drive to conquer. The contrast between Abimelech and the great people of Scripture is great. He wanted to control the nation; the great people of Scripture were willing to be controlled by God.

Strengths and accomplishments:
- The first self-declared king of Israel
- Qualified tactical planner and organizer

Weaknesses and mistakes:
- Power hungry and ruthless
- Overconfident
- Took advantage of his father's position without imitating his character
- Had 70 half brothers killed

Vital statistics:
- Where: Shechem, Arumah, Thebez
- Occupation: Self-acclaimed king, judge, political troublemaker
- Relatives: Father: Gideon. Only surviving brother: Jotham.

Key verses:
"Thus God punished both Abimelech and the men of Shechem for their sin of murdering Gideon's seventy sons" (Judges 9:56, 57).

His story is told in Judges 8:31—9:57. He is also mentioned in 2 Samuel 11:21.

---

for God alone. In his selfish quest, he killed all but one of his 70 half brothers. People with selfish desires often seek to fulfill them in ruthless ways. Examine your ambitions to see if they are self-centered or God-centered. Be sure you always seek to meet your desires in a way God would approve.

9:4 Politics played a major part in heathen religions as in the worship of Baal-berith. Governments often went so far as to hire temple prostitutes to bring in additional monies. In many cases a religious system was set up and supported by the government so the offerings could fund community projects. Religion became a profit-making business. In Israel's religion, this was strictly forbidden. God's system of religion was designed to come from an attitude of the heart, not from calculated plans and business opportunites. It was also designed to serve people and help those in need, not to oppress the needy.

9:7–15 In Jotham's parable the trees represented Gideon's 70 sons, and the thorn bush represented Abimelech. Jotham's point was that if the person chosen as king was a "fruitful tree," then good fruit would come from his reign. But if a "thorn bush" was chosen, it would catch fire and burn. Abimelech, like a thorn bush, could offer Israel no real protection or security. Jotham's parable came true when Abimelech destroyed the city of Shechem (9:45), burned the city of Migdal (9:49), and was finally killed (9:53, 54).

8Once upon a time the trees decided to elect a king. First they asked the olive tree, 9but it refused.

" 'Should I quit producing the olive oil that blesses God and man, just to wave to and fro over the other trees?' it asked.

10"Then they said to the fig tree, 'You be our king!'

11"But the fig tree also refused. 'Should I quit producing sweetness and fruit just to lift my head above all the other trees?' it asked.

12"Then they said to the grapevine, 'You reign over us!'

13"But the grapevine replied, 'Shall I quit producing the wine that cheers both God and man, just to be mightier than all the other trees?'

14"Then all the trees finally turned to the thorn bush. 'You be our king!' they explained.

15"And the thorn bush replied, 'If you really want me, come and humble yourselves beneath my shade! If you refuse, let fire flame forth from me and burn down the great cedars of Lebanon!'

16"Now make sure that you have done the right thing in making Abimelech your king, that you have done right by Gideon and all of his descendants. 17For my father fought for you and risked his life and delivered you from the Midianites, 18yet you have revolted against him and killed his seventy sons upon one stone. And now you have chosen his slave girl's son, Abimelech, to be your king just because he is your relative. 19If you are sure that you have done right by Gideon and his descendants, then may you and Abimelech have a long and happy life together. 20But if you have not been fair to Gideon, then may Abimelech destroy the citizens of Shechem and Beth-millo; and may they destroy Abimelech!"

21Then Jotham escaped and lived in Beer for fear of his brother Abimelech.

22, 23Three years later God stirred up trouble between King Abimelech and the citizens of Shechem, and they revolted. 24In the events that followed, both Abimelech and the citizens of Shechem who aided him in butchering Gideon's seventy sons were given their just punishment for these murders. 25For the men of Shechem set an ambush for Abimelech along the trail at the top of the mountain. (While they were waiting for him to come along, they robbed everyone else who passed that way.) But someone warned Abimelech about their plot.

26At that time Gaal (the son of Ebed) moved to Shechem with his brothers, and he became one of the leading citizens. 27During the harvest feast at Shechem that year, held in the temple of the local god, the wine flowed freely and everyone began cursing Abimelech.

28"Who is Abimelech," Gaal shouted, "and why should he be our king? Why

9:8
2 Kgs 14:9
Ezek 17:3
Dan 4:10

9:18
Judg 9:5

9:22
1 Sam 16:14
9:24
Num 35:33
Deut 27:25

9:27
Judg 8:33

ABIMELECH'S FALL
Gideon's illegitimate son killed 69 of his half brothers in Ophrah and returned to Shechem to be acclaimed king. But three years later, Shechem rebelled. From Arumah, Abimelech attacked Shechem, Migdal, and Thebez, only to be killed at Thebez.

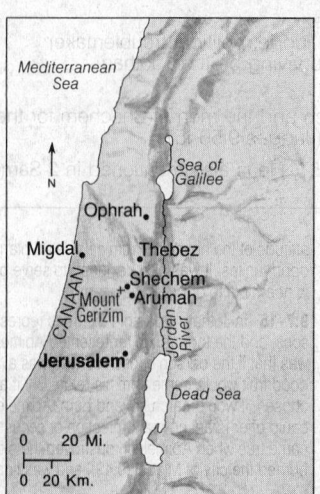

Mediterranean Sea

Sea of Galilee

N

Ophrah

Migdal   Thebez

Shechem

Mount Gerizim   Arumah

CANAAN

Jerusalem

Jordan River

Dead Sea

0   20 Mi.

0   20 Km.

9:16 Jotham told the story about the trees in order to help the people set good priorities. He did not want them to appoint a leader of low character. As we serve in leadership positions, we should examine our motives. Do we just want praise, prestige, or power? In the parable, the good trees chose to be productive and to provide blessings. Make sure these are your priorities as you aspire to leadership.

9:22-24 Abimelech was the opposite of what God wanted in a judge, but it was three years before God moved against him, fulfilling Jotham's parable. Those three years must have seemed like forever to Jotham. Why wasn't Abimelech punished sooner for his evil ways?

We are not alone when we wonder why evil seems to prevail (Job 10:3; 21:1-18; Jeremiah 12:1; Habakkuk 1:2-4, 12-17). God promises to deal with sin, but in his time, not ours. Actually it is good news that God doesn't punish us immediately, for we all have sinned and deserve God's punishment. God, in his mercy, often spares us from immediate punishment and allows us time to turn from our sins and turn to him in repentance. Trusting God for justice means that (1) we must first recognize our own sins and repent, and (2) we may face a difficult time of waiting for the wicked to be punished. But in God's time, all evil will be destroyed.

should we be his servants? He and his friend Zebul should be *our* servants. Down with Abimelech! 29Make me your king and you'll soon see what happens to Abimelech! I'll tell Abimelech, 'Get up an army and come on out and fight!' "

30But when Zebul, the mayor of the city, heard what Gaal was saying, he was furious. 31He sent messengers to Abimelech in Arumah telling him, "Gaal, son of Ebed, and his relatives have come to live in Shechem, and now they are arousing the city to rebellion against you. 32Come by night with an army and hide out in the fields; 33and in the morning, as soon as it is daylight, storm the city. When he and those who are with him come out against you, you can do with them as you wish!"

9:33
1 Sam 10:7

34So Abimelech and his men marched through the night and split into four groups, stationing themselves around the city. 35The next morning as Gaal sat at the city gates, discussing various issues with the local leaders, Abimelech and his men began their march upon the city.

36When Gaal saw them, he exclaimed to Zebul, "Look over at that mountain! Doesn't it look like people coming down?"

"No!" Zebul said. "You're just seeing shadows that look like men!"

37"No, look over there," Gaal said. "I'm sure I see people coming towards us. And look! There are others coming along the road past the oak of Meonenim!"

38Then Zebul turned on him triumphantly. "Now where is that big mouth of yours?" he demanded. "Who was it who said, 'Who is Abimelech, and why should he be our king?' The men you taunted and cursed are right outside the city! Go on out and fight!"

39So Gaal led the men of Shechem into the battle and fought with Abimelech, 40but was defeated, and many of the men of Shechem were left wounded all the way to the city gate. 41Abimelech was living at Arumah at this time, and Zebul drove Gaal and his relatives out of Shechem, and wouldn't let them live there any longer.

42The next day the men of Shechem went out to battle again. However, someone had told Abimelech about their plans, 43so he had divided his men into three groups hiding in the fields. And when the men of the city went out to attack, he and his men jumped up from their hiding places and began killing them. 44Abimelech stormed the city gate to keep the men of Shechem from getting back in, while his other two groups cut them down in the fields. 45The battle went on all day before Abimelech finally captured the city, killed its people, and leveled it to the ground. 46The people at the nearby town of Migdal saw what was happening and took refuge in the fort next to the temple of Baal-berith.

9:46
Judg 8:33

9:47
Ps 68:14

47, 48When Abimelech learned of this, he led his forces to Mount Zalmon where he began chopping a bundle of firewood, and placed it upon his shoulder. "Do as I have done," he told his men. 49So each of them quickly cut a bundle and carried it back to the town where, following Abimelech's example, the bundles were piled against the walls of the fort and set on fire. So all the people inside died, about a thousand men and women.

50Abimelech next attacked the city of Thebez, and captured it. 51However, there was a fort inside the city and the entire population fled into it, barricaded the gates, and climbed to the top of the roof to watch. 52But as Abimelech was preparing to burn it, 53a woman on the roof threw down a millstone. It landed on Abimelech's head, crushing his skull.

9:53
2 Sam 11:19-21

54"Kill me!" he groaned to his youthful armor bearer. "Never let it be said that a woman killed Abimelech!"

So the young man pierced him with his sword, and he died. 55When his men saw

---

9:53 In times of battle, women were sometimes asked to join the men at the city wall to drop heavy objects on the soldiers below. A millstone would have been an ideal object for this purpose. It was a round stone about two feet in diameter with a hole in the center. It weighed several hundred pounds. Millstones were used to grind grain into flour. The grain was placed between two millstones. The top millstone was turned, crushing the grain.

Abimelech's death was especially humiliating: he was killed by a woman, not by fighting; and he was killed by a farm implement instead of a weapon. Abimelech therefore asked his armor bearer to stab him with his sword before he died from the blow of the millstone.

that he was dead, they disbanded and returned to their homes. 56, 57Thus God punished both Abimelech and the men of Shechem for their sin of murdering Gideon's seventy sons. So the curse of Jotham, Gideon's son, came true.

Tola and Jair

10 After Abimelech's death, the next judge of Israel was Tola (son of Puah and grandson of Dodo). He was from the tribe of Issachar, but lived in the city of Shamir in the hill country of Ephraim. 2He was Israel's judge for twenty-three years. When he died, he was buried in Shamir, 3and was succeeded by Jair, a man from Gilead, who judged Israel for twenty-two years. 4His thirty sons rode around together on thirty donkeys, and they owned thirty cities in the land of Gilead which are still called "The Cities of Jair." 5When Jair died he was buried in Kamon.

10:4
Num 32:41

5. Fifth period: Jephthah, Ibzan, Elon, and Abdon

6Then the people of Israel turned away from the Lord again, and worshiped the heathen gods Baal and Ashtaroth, and the gods of Syria, Sidon, Moab, Ammon and Philistia. Not only this, but they no longer worshiped Jehovah at all. 7, 8This made Jehovah very angry with his people, so he immediately permitted the Philistines and the Ammonites to begin tormenting them. These attacks took place east of the Jordan River in the land of the Amorites (that is, in Gilead), 9and also in Judah, Benjamin, and Ephraim. For the Ammonites crossed the Jordan to attack the Israelis. This went on for eighteen years. 10Finally the Israelis turned to Jehovah again and begged him to save them.

10:6
Judg 4:1; 6:1
10:16; 13:1
2 Kgs 17:7
2 Chron 7:21,22

10:7
Judg 4:2
1 Sam 12:9

10:10
Judg 3:9
Ps 106:43

"We have sinned against you and have forsaken you as our God and have worshiped idols," they confessed.

11But the Lord replied, "Didn't I save you from the Egyptians, the Amorites, the Ammonites, the Philistines, 12the Sidonians, the Amalekites, and the Maonites? Has there ever been a time when you cried out to me that I haven't rescued you? 13Yet you continue to abandon me and to worship other gods. So go away; I won't save you any more. 14Go and cry to the new gods you have chosen! Let them save you in your hour of distress!"

10:11
Judg 2:1-3
1 Kgs 9:9

10:14
Deut 32:37

15But they pleaded with him again and said, "We have sinned. Punish us in any way you think best, only save us once more from our enemies."

10:15
2 Sam 12:13

16Then they destroyed their foreign gods and worshiped only the Lord; and he was grieved by their misery. 17The armies of Ammon were mobilized in Gilead at that time, preparing to attack Israel's army at Mizpah.

10:16
Deut 32:43
Josh 24:23
2 Chron 7:14
15:8; 33:15
Jer 18:7,8

9:56, 57 Gideon, Abimelech's father, succeeded in military battles, but sometimes failed in his personal struggles. Gideon was not condemned for taking a concubine (8:31), but the family problems that resulted from this relationship are clearly stated.

In the end, Abimelech killed his 70 half brothers, tore apart a nation, and then was killed himself. From Gideon's life we learn that no matter how much good we do for God's kingdom, sin in our lives will still produce powerful, damaging consequences.

9:56, 57 Jotham's curse is found in Judges 9:16-20.

10:1-6 In five verses we read about two judges. The most that was said about these judges is this: Tola—"was Israel's judge for twenty-three years" (10:2); Jair—"judged Israel for twenty-two years. His thirty sons rode around together on thirty donkeys" (10:3, 4). What are you doing for God that is worth noting? When your life is over, will people remember more than just what was in your bank account or the number of years you lived?

10:7-10 God permitted the heathen nations to oppress the Israelites because of their sin (Judges 2:1-3). Because God is just, he will punish sin (Leviticus 26). God allows problems and pressures to enter our lives in order to lovingly draw us back into relationship with him. When problems arise, before you ask, "Why me?" ask "Is God trying to say something to me through this?"

10:9, 10 Once again the Israelites suffered for many years before

they gave up their sinful ways and called out to God for help (see 4:1-3; 6:1-7). Notice that when the Israelites were at the end of their rope they did not look to their heathen gods for help, but to the only One who was really able to help.

Is God your last resort? So much unnecessary suffering takes place because we don't call on God until we've used up all other resources. Rather than waiting until the situation becomes desperate, turn to God first. He has all the necessary resources to meet every kind of problem.

10:11-16 These verses show how difficult it can be to follow God over the long haul. The Israelites always seemed to forget God when things were going well. But despite being rejected by his own people, God never failed to rescue them when they called out to him in repentance. God never fails to rescue us either. It is tempting to say that the Israelites were blind or simply stupid to ignore God's Law, but we do the same when we put God outside our daily events instead of at the center of them. Just as a loving parent feels great rejection when a child rebels, so God feels great rejection when we ignore or neglect him (1 Samuel 8:1-9; 10:17-19; John 12:44-50). We should strive to stay close to God rather than see how far we can go before judgment comes.

10:17, 18 The power of the Ammonite nation was at its peak during the period of the judges. The people were descendants of

¹⁸"Who will lead our forces against the Ammonites?" the leaders of Gilead asked each other. "Whoever volunteers shall be our king!"

Jephthah defeats the Ammonites

11:1
1 Sam 12:11
20:30
Heb 11:32

11 Now Jephthah was a great warrior from the land of Gilead, but his mother was a prostitute. His father (whose name was Gilead) had several other sons by his legitimate wife, and when these half brothers grew up, they chased Jephthah out of the country.

"You son of a whore!" they said. "You'll not get any of our father's estate."

11:3
Judg 9:4; 12:4
1 Sam 22:2
30:22
2 Sam 10:6,8
11:4
Judg 10:9

³So Jephthah fled from his father's home and lived in the land of Tob. Soon he had quite a band of malcontents as his followers, living off the land as bandits. ⁴It was about this time that the Ammonites began their war against Israel. ⁵The leaders of Gilead sent for Jephthah, ⁶begging him to come and lead their army against the Ammonites.

⁷But Jephthah said to them, "Why do you come to me when you hate me and have driven me out of my father's house? Why come now when you're in trouble?"

⁸"Because we need you," they replied. "If you will be our commander-in-chief against the Ammonites, we will make you the king of Gilead."

11:10
Gen 21:23
31:51-53

⁹"Sure!" Jephthah exclaimed. "Do you expect me to believe that?"

¹⁰"We swear it," they replied. "We promise with a solemn oath."

RASH VOWS	Person	Vow	Result	Reference
Proverbs 20:25 says, "It is foolish and rash to make a promise to the Lord before counting the cost." Scripture records the vows of many men and women. Some of these vows proved to be rash and unwise, and others, though extreme, were kept to the letter by those who made them. Let us learn from the Proverbs and from the examples in God's Word not to make rash vows.	JACOB	To "choose" the true God and to give back a tenth to him if he kept him safe	God protected Jacob, who kept his vow to follow God	Genesis 28:20
	JEPHTHAH	To offer to the Lord whoever came out to meet him after battle (it turned out to be his daughter)	He lost his daughter	Judges 11:30, 31
	HANNAH	To give her son back to God, if God would give her a son	When Samuel was born, she dedicated him to God	1 Samuel 1:11
	SAUL	To kill anyone who ate before evening (Jonathan, his son, had not heard the command and broke it)	Saul would have killed Jonathan if soldiers had not intervened	1 Samuel 14:24-45
	DAVID	To be kind to Jonathan's family	Mephibosheth, Jonathan's son, was treated royally by David	2 Samuel 9:7
	ITTAI	To remain loyal to David	He became one of the great men in David's army	2 Samuel 15:21
	MICAIAH	To say only what God told him to say	He was put in prison	1 Kings 22:14
	JOB	That he was not rebelling against God	His fortunes were restored	Job 27:2
	HEROD ANTIPAS	To give Herodias' daughter anything she requested	Herod was forced to order John the Baptist's death	Mark 6:22
	PAUL	To offer a sacrifice of thanksgiving in Jerusalem	He made the sacrifice despite the danger	Acts 18:18

Ammon, conceived when Lot's daughter slept with her drunk father (Genesis 19:30–38). The land of Ammon was located just east of the Jordan River across from Jerusalem. South of Ammon lay the land of Moab, the nation born when Lot's other daughter slept with her father. Moab and Ammon were usually allies. It was a formidable task to defeat these nations.

11:1, 2 Jephthah, an illegitimate son of Gilead, was chased out of the country by his half brothers. He suffered as a result of another's decision and not for any wrong he had done. Yet in spite of his brothers' rejection, God used him. If you are suffering from unfair rejection, don't blame others and become discouraged. Remember how God used Jephthah despite his unjust

circumstances, and realize that he is able to use you as well.

11:3 Circumstances beyond his control forced Jephthah away from his people and into life as an outcast. Today, both believers and nonbelievers may drive away those who do not fit the norms dictated by our society, neighborhoods, or churches. Often, as in Jephthah's case, great potential is wasted because of prejudice—a refusal to look beyond ill-conceived stereotypes. Look around you to see if there are potential Jephthahs being kept out due to factors beyond their control. As a Christian you know that everyone can have a place in God's family. Is there anything you can do to help these people gain acceptance for their character and abilities?

¹¹So Jephthah accepted the commission and was made commander-in-chief and king. The contract was ratified before the Lord in Mizpah at a general assembly of all the people. ¹²Then Jephthah sent messengers to the king of Ammon, demanding to know why Israel was being attacked. ¹³The king of Ammon replied that the land belonged to the people of Ammon; it had been stolen from them, he said, when the Israelis came from Egypt; the whole territory from the Arnon River to the Jabbok and the Jordan was his, he claimed.

"Give us back our land peaceably," he demanded.

^{14, 15}Jephthah replied, "Israel did not steal the land. ¹⁶What happened was this: When the people of Israel arrived at Kadesh, on their journey from Egypt after crossing the Red Sea, ¹⁷they sent a message to the king of Edom asking permission to pass through his land. But their petition was denied. Then they asked the king of Moab for similar permission. It was the same story there, so the people of Israel stayed in Kadesh.

¹⁸"Finally they went around Edom and Moab through the wilderness, and traveled along the eastern border until at last they arrived beyond the boundary of Moab at the Arnon River; but they never once crossed into Moab. ¹⁹Then Israel sent messengers to King Sihon of the Amorites, who lived in Heshbon, and asked permission to cross through his land to get to their destination.

²⁰"But King Sihon didn't trust Israel, so he mobilized an army at Jahaz and attacked them. ^{21, 22}But the Lord our God helped Israel defeat King Sihon and all your people, so Israel took over all of your land from the Arnon River to the Jabbok, and from the wilderness to the Jordan River.

²³"So you see, it was the Lord God of Israel who took away the land from the Amorites and gave it to Israel. Why, then, should we return it to you? ²⁴You keep whatever your god Chemosh gives you, and we will keep whatever Jehovah our God gives us! ²⁵And besides, just who do you think you are? Are you better than King Balak, the king of Moab? Did he try to recover his land after Israel defeated him? No, of course not. ²⁶But now after three hundred years you make an issue of this! Israel has been living here for all that time, spread across the land from Heshbon to Aroer, and all along the Arnon River. Why have you made no effort to recover it before now? ²⁷No, I have not sinned against you; rather, you have wronged me by coming to war against me; but Jehovah the Judge will soon show which of us is right—Israel or Ammon."

²⁸But the king of Ammon paid no attention to Jephthah's message.

²⁹At that time the Spirit of the Lord came upon Jephthah and he led his army across the land of Gilead and Manasseh, past Mizpah in Gilead, and attacked the army of Ammon. ^{30, 31}Meanwhile Jephthah had vowed to the Lord that if God

11:11
Judg 9:14,15

11:13
Josh 13:10

11:16
Num 20:1-22

11:17
Josh 24:9

11:18
Num 21:4
Deut 2:8,9,18,
19

11:19
Num 21:21-32

11:21
Deut 2:19,37
3:3

11:24
Num 21:27-30
1 Kgs 11:7

11:29
Judg 3:10; 6:34
13:25

11:14ff Jephthah sent a dispatch to the king of Ammon wanting to know why the Israelites in the land of Gilead were being attacked (11:12). The king replied that Israel had stolen this land and he wanted it back (11:13).

Jephthah sent another message to the king (11:14–27). In it he gave three arguments against the king's claim: (1) Gilead was never the king's land in the first place (11:16–22) because Israel took it from the Amorites, not the Ammonites; (2) God gave Israel this land—it was part of his purpose (11:23–25); (3) no one had contested Israel's ownership of the land since its conquest 300 years earlier (11:26).

To Jephthah's credit, he tried to solve the problem without bloodshed. But the king of Ammon ignored his message and prepared his troops for battle.

11:27 Over the years, Israel had many judges to lead them. But Jephthah recognized God as the people's true Judge, the only One who could really lead them and help them conquer the invading enemies.

11:29 The Spirit of the Lord came upon Jephthah as he did with many of the Old Testament judges, kings, and prophets. Generally when the Spirit came upon a person in the Old Testament, it

referred to a special empowering of the Holy Spirit for a specific task or mission. Many believe that it wasn't until Pentecost (Acts 2) that God sent the Holy Spirit to live permanently in the lives of all those who believe in Jesus Christ.

11:30, 31 In God's Law, a vow was a promise to God that should not be broken (Numbers 30:1, 2; Deuteronomy 23:21–23). It carried as much force as a written contract. Many people made vows in biblical times. Some, like Jephthah's, were very foolish.

11:30, 31 Did Jephthah really vow to sacrifice a person in exchange for victory in battle? Scholars are evenly divided over the issue. Those who say Jephthah was considering human sacrifice use the following arguments: (1) He was from an area where heathen religion and human sacrifice were common. In his eyes, it may not have seemed like such a serious sin. (2) Jephthah may not have had a background in religious law. Perhaps he was ignorant of God's command against human sacrifice. (3) The Bible text clearly says a "burnt offering."

Those who say Jephthah could not have been thinking about human sacrifice point to other evidence: (1) Some other translations say *whatever* comes out of my house rather than *whoever*. (2) As leader of the people, Jephthah must have been

would help Israel conquer the Ammonites, then when he returned home in peace, the first person coming out of his house to meet him would be sacrificed as a burnt offering to the Lord!

32So Jephthah led his army against the Ammonites, and the Lord gave him the victory. 33He destroyed the Ammonites with a terrible slaughter all the way from Aroer to Minnith, including twenty cities, and as far away as Vineyard Meadow. Thus the Ammonites were subdued by the people of Israel.

34When Jephthah returned home his daughter—his only child—ran out to meet him, playing on a tambourine and dancing for joy. 35When he saw her he tore his clothes in anguish.

"Alas, my daughter!" he cried out. "You have brought me to the dust. For I have made a vow to the Lord and I cannot take it back."

36And she said, "Father, you must do whatever you promised the Lord, for he has given you a great victory over your enemies, the Ammonites. 37But first let me

11:34
Ex 15:20
1 Sam 18:6
Jer 31:4

11:35
Num 30:1,2
Eccles 5:4,5

JEPHTHAH

It's hard not to admire people whose word can be depended on completely and whose actions are consistent with their words. For such people, talking is not avoiding action; it is the beginning of action. People like this can make excellent negotiators. They approach a conflict with the full intention of settling issues verbally, but they do not hesitate to use other means if verbal attempts fail. Jephthah was this kind of person.

In most of his conflicts, Jephthah's first move was to talk. In the war with the Ammonites, his strategy was negotiation. He clarified the issues so that everyone knew the cause of the conflict. His opponent's response determined his next action.

The fate of Jephthah's daughter is difficult to understand. We are not sure what Jephthah meant by his vow recorded in Judges 11:31. In any case, his vow was unnecessary. We do not know what actually happened to his daughter—whether she was burned as an offering or set apart as a virgin, thus denying Jephthah any hope of descendants since she was his only child. What we do know is that Jephthah was a person of his word, even when it was a word spoken in haste, and even when keeping his word cost him great pain.

How do you approach conflicts? There is a big difference between trying to settle a conflict through words and simply counterattacking someone verbally. How dependable are the statements you make? Do your children, friends, and fellow workers know you to be a person of your word? The measure of your trustworthiness is your willingness to take responsibility, even if you must pay a painful price because of something you said.

Strengths and accomplishments:
• Listed in the Hall of Faith in Hebrews
• Controlled by God's Spirit
• Brilliant military strategist who negotiated before fighting

Weaknesses and mistakes:
• Was bitter over the treatment he received from his half brothers
• Made a rash and foolish vow that was costly

Lesson from his life:
• A person's background does not prevent God from working powerfully in his or her life

Vital statistics:
• Where: Gilead
• Occupation: Warrior, judge
• Relatives: Father: Gilead

Key verse:
"So Jephthah led his army against the Ammonites, and the Lord gave him the victory" (Judges 11:32).

His story is told in Judges 11:1—12:7. He is also mentioned in 1 Samuel 12:11 and Hebrews 11:32.

familiar with God's Law; human sacrifice was clearly forbidden (Leviticus 18:21; 20:1–5). (3) No legitimate priest would have helped Jephthah carry out his vow. (4) If the girl was to die, she would not have spent her last two weeks in the mountains. (5) God would not have honored a vow based on a wicked practice. (6) 11:39 said she never married, not that she died, implying that she was set apart for service to God, not killed.

11:34, 35 Jephthah's rash vow brought him unspeakable grief. In the heat of emotion or personal turmoil it is easy to make foolish promises to God. These promises may sound very spiritual when we make them, but they may produce only guilt and frustration when we are forced to fulfill them. Making spiritual "deals" only brings disappointment. God does not want promises for the future, but obedience for today.

go up into the hills and roam with my girl friends for two months, weeping because I'll never marry."

38"Yes," he said. "Go."

And so she did, bewailing her fate with her friends for two months. 39Then she returned to her father, who did as he had vowed. So she was never married. And after that it became a custom in Israel, 40that the young girls went away for four days each year to lament the fate of Jephthah's daughter.

Jephthah attacks the tribe of Ephraim

12 Then the tribe of Ephraim mobilized its army at Zaphon and sent this message to Jephthah: "Why didn't you call for us to help you fight against Ammon? We are going to burn down your house, with you in it!"

2"I summoned you, but you refused to come!" Jephthah retorted. "You failed to help us in our time of need, 3so I risked my life and went to battle without you, and the Lord helped me to conquer the enemy. Is that anything for you to fight us about?"

4Then Jephthah, furious at the taunt of Ephraim that the men of Gilead were mere outcasts and the scum of the earth, mobilized his army and attacked the army of Ephraim. 5He captured the fords of the Jordan behind the army of Ephraim, and whenever a fugitive from Ephraim tried to cross the river, the Gilead guards challenged him.

"Are you a member of the tribe of Ephraim?" they asked. If the man replied that he was not, 6then they demanded, "Say 'Shibboleth.'" But if he couldn't pronounce the H and said, "Sibboleth" instead of "Shibboleth," he was dragged away and killed. So forty-two thousand people of Ephraim died there at that time.

7Jephthah was Israel's judge for six years. At his death he was buried in one of the cities of Gilead.

Ibzan

8The next judge was Ibzan, who lived in Bethlehem. 9, 10He had thirty sons and thirty daughters. He married his daughters to men outside his clan, and brought in thirty girls to marry his sons. He judged Israel for seven years before he died, and was buried at Bethlehem.

11:39 *So she was never married.* It is not clear whether he killed her or satisfied his vow by consecrating her to perpetual virginity.   **12:4** *the men of Gilead were mere outcasts,* literally, "fugitives of Ephraim . . ."

12:1
Judg 8:1

12:3
1 Sam 19:5
Job 13:14

12:4
Judg 11:3
1 Sam 22:2
12:5-7
Josh 2:7
Judg 3:28; 7:24

12:1ff Israel had just won a great battle, but instead of joy, there was pettiness and quarreling. The tribe of Ephraim was angry and jealous that they were not invited to join in the fighting (although Jephthah said he had invited them). The insults of the Ephraimites enraged Jephthah, who called out his troops and killed 42,000 men from Ephraim.

Jephthah usually talked before he acted, but this time his revenge was swift. It cost Israel dearly, and it might have been avoided. Insults and jealousy are not the right response when we feel left out. But revenge for an insult is just as wrong, and very costly.

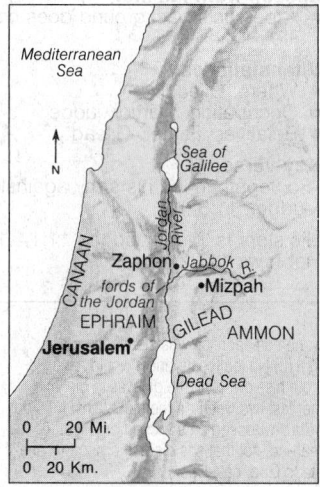

JEPHTHAH'S VICTORY
The Ephraimites mobilized an army in Zaphon because they were angry at not being included in the battle against Ammon. They planned to attack Jephthah at his home in Gilead. Jephthah captured the fords of the Jordan at the Jabbok River and killed the Ephraimites who tried to cross.

Elon

11, 12The next judge was Elon from Zebulun. He judged Israel for ten years and was buried at Aijalon in Zebulun.

Abdon

13Next was Abdon (son of Hillel) from Pirathon. 14He had forty sons and thirty grandsons, who rode on seventy donkeys. He was Israel's judge for eight years. 15Then he died and was buried in Pirathon, in Ephraim, in the hill country of the Amalekites.

6. Sixth period: Samson
The birth of Samson

13:1
Judg 2:11; 3:8
4:2,3; 10:6-8
13:2
Gen 16:7; 17:17
Judg 2:1
6:11,12
13:4
Num 6:1-4
Judg 13:13,14
13:5
Judg 16:16,17

13 Once again Israel sinned by worshiping other gods, so the Lord let them be conquered by the Philistines, who kept them in subjection for forty years. 2, 3Then one day the Angel of the Lord appeared to the wife of Manoah, of the tribe of Dan, who lived in the city of Zorah. She had no children, but the Angel said to her, "Even though you have been barren so long, you will soon conceive and have a son! 4Don't drink any wine or beer, and don't eat any food that isn't kosher. 5Your son's hair must never be cut, for he shall be a Nazirite, a special servant of God from the time of his birth; and he will begin to rescue Israel from the Philistines."

6The woman ran and told her husband, "A man from God appeared to me and I think he must be the Angel of the Lord, for he was almost too glorious to look at. I didn't ask where he was from, and he didn't tell me his name, 7but he told me, 'You are going to have a baby boy!' And he told me not to drink any wine or beer, and not to eat food that isn't kosher, for the baby is going to be a Nazirite—he will be dedicated to God from the moment of his birth until the day of his death!"

8Then Manoah prayed, "O Lord, please let the man from God come back to us again and give us more instructions about the child you are going to give us." 9The Lord answered his prayer, and the Angel of God appeared once again to his wife as she was sitting in the field. But again she was alone—Manoah was not with her— 10so she quickly ran and found her husband and told him, "The same man is here again!"

11Manoah ran back with his wife and asked, "Are you the man who talked to my wife the other day?"

"Yes," he replied, "I am."

12So Manoah asked him, "Can you give us any special instructions about how we should raise the baby after he is born?"

13:13
Judg 13:4

13, 14And the Angel replied, "Be sure that your wife follows the instructions I

13:1 The Philistines lived on the west side of Canaan, along the Mediterranean seacoast. From Samson's day until the time of David they were the major enemy force in the land and a constant threat to Israel. The Philistines were fierce warriors; they had the advantage over Israel in numbers, tactical expertise, and technology. They knew the secret of making weapons out of iron (1 Samuel 13:19–22). But none of that mattered when God was fighting for Israel.

13:1ff Once again the cycle of sin, judgment, and repentance begins (Judges 3:8, 9; 3:14, 15; 4:1–4; 6:1–14; 10:6—11:11). The Israelites would not turn to God unless they had been stunned by suffering, oppression, and death. This suffering was not caused by God, but resulted from the fact that the people ignored God as their judge and ruler. What will it take for you to follow God? The warnings in God's Word are clear: if we continue to harden our hearts against God, we can expect the same fate as Israel.

13:2, 3 The Angel of the Lord could have been a special divine messenger sent from God or a physical appearance of Jesus Christ. The reason for the Angel's visit was to give Samson's parents the vital news that Samson would begin to rescue Israel

from the Philistines. (For more on the Angel see the notes on 2:1 and 6:11.)

13:5 Samson was to be a Nazirite—a person who took a vow to be set apart for God's service. Samson's parents made the vow for him. A Nazirite vow was usually temporary, but in Samson's case, it was for life. As a Nazirite, Samson could not cut his hair, touch a dead body, or drink anything containing alcohol.

Although Samson often used poor judgment and sinned terribly, he accomplished much when he determined to be set apart for God. In this way he was like the nation Israel. As long as the Israelites remained set apart for God, the nation thrived. But they fell into terrible sin when they ignored God.

13:5 Manoah's wife was told that her son would *begin* to rescue the Israelites from the Philistines' oppression. It wasn't until David's day that the Philistine opposition was completely crushed (2 Samuel 8:1). Samson's part in subduing the Philistines was just the beginning, but it was important nonetheless. It was the task God had given Samson to do. Be faithful in following God even if you don't see instant results, because you might be beginning an important job which others will finish.

gave her. She must not eat grapes or raisins, or drink any wine or beer, or eat anything that isn't kosher."

15Then Manoah said to the Angel, "Please stay here until we can get you something to eat."

16"I'll stay," the Angel replied, "but I'll not eat anything. However, if you wish to bring something, bring an offering to sacrifice to the Lord." (Manoah didn't yet realize that he was the Angel of the Lord.)

17Then Manoah asked him for his name. "When all this comes true and the baby is born," he said to the Angel, "we will certainly want to tell everyone that you predicted it!"

18"Don't even ask my name," the Angel replied, "for it is a secret."

19Then Manoah took a young goat and a grain offering and offered it as a sacrifice to the Lord; and the Angel did a strange and wonderful thing, 20for as the flames from the altar were leaping up toward the sky, and as Manoah and his wife watched, the Angel ascended in the fire! Manoah and his wife fell face downward to the ground, 21and that was the last they ever saw of him. It was then that Manoah finally realized that it had been the Angel of the Lord.

22"We will die," Manoah cried out to his wife, "for we have seen God!"

23But his wife said, "If the Lord were going to kill us he wouldn't have accepted our burnt offerings and wouldn't have appeared to us and told us this wonderful thing and done these miracles."

24When her son was born they named him Samson, and the Lord blessed him as he grew up. 25And the Spirit of the Lord began to excite him whenever he visited the parade grounds of the army of the tribe of Dan, located between the cities of Zorah and Eshta-ol.

Samson asks a riddle

14 One day when Samson was in Timnah, he noticed a certain Philistine girl, 2and when he got home he told his father and mother that he wanted to marry her. 3They objected strenuously.

13:15
Gen 18:3,4
Judg 6:18

13:17
Gen 32:29

13:19
Judg 6:19

13:22
Gen 32:30
Ex 33:20
Judg 6:22

13:24
Heb 11:32
13:25
Judg 3:10; 6:34
14:6
1 Sam 10:6,10

14:3
Deut 7:3
Josh 23:12

13:18 Why did the Angel keep his name a secret? There was a belief in those days that if you knew someone's name, you knew his character and how to control him. By keeping his name a secret, the Angel was saying it was a mystery beyond understanding and too wonderful to imagine. Manoah asked the Angel for an answer that he wouldn't have understood. Sometimes we ask God questions and then receive no answer. This may not be because God is saying no. It may be that we have asked for knowledge beyond our ability to understand or accept.

13:19 Manoah sacrificed a *grain offering* to the Lord. A grain offering was grain, oil, and flour shaped into a cake and burned on the altar along with the *burnt offering* (the young goat). The grain offering, described in Leviticus 2, was offered as a sign of honor, respect, and worship to God. It was an acknowledgment that because the Israelites' food came from God, they owed their lives to him. With the grain offering, Manoah showed his desire to serve God and demonstrated his respect.

13:25 Samson's tribe, Dan, continued to wander in their inherited land (18:1) which was yet unconquered (Joshua 19:47, 48). Samson must have grown up with the yearnings of his warlike tribe—for a permanent and settled territory—burning in his heart. Thus his visits to the tribal "parade grounds" stirred his heart, and God's Spirit began preparing him for his role as judge against the Philistines.

Perhaps there are things that stir your heart. These may indicate areas where God wants to use you. God uses a variety of means to develop and prepare us: hereditary traits, environmental influences, and personal experiences. As with Samson, this preparation often begins long before adulthood.

14:3 Samson's parents objected to his marrying the Philistine

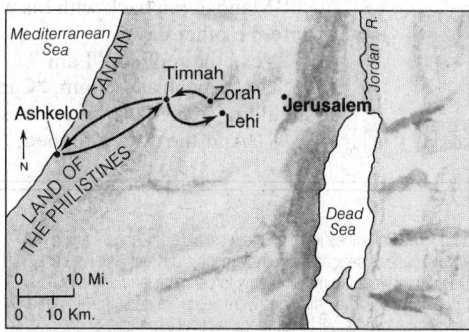

SAMSON'S VENTURES Samson grew up in Zorah and wanted to marry a Philistine girl from Timnah. Tricked at his own wedding feast, he went to Ashkelon and killed some Philistine men and stole their coats to pay off a bet. Samson then let himself be captured and brought to Lehi where he snapped his ropes and killed 1,000 people.

woman for several reasons: (1) It was against God's law (Exodus 34:15–17; Deuteronomy 7:1–4). A stark example of what happened when the Israelites married those from pagan nations can be found in 3:5–7. (2) The Philistines were Israel's greatest enemies. Marriage to a hated Philistine would be a disgrace to Samson's family. But Samson's father gave in to Samson's demand and allowed the marriage, even though he had the right to refuse his son.

"Why don't you marry a Jewish girl?" they asked. "Why must you go and get a wife from these heathen Philistines? Isn't there one girl among all the people of Israel you could marry?"

But Samson told his father, "She is the one I want. Get her for me."

14:4
Josh 11:20
1 Kgs 12:15

⁴His father and mother didn't realize that the Lord was behind the request, for God was setting a trap for the Philistines, who at that time were the rulers of Israel.

⁵As Samson and his parents were going to Timnah, a young lion attacked Samson in the vineyards on the outskirts of the town. ⁶At that moment the Spirit of the Lord came mightily upon him and since he had no weapon, he ripped the lion's jaws apart, and did it as easily as though it were a young goat! But he didn't tell his father or mother about it. ⁷Upon arriving at Timnah he talked with the girl and found her to be just what he wanted, so the arrangements were made.

14:6
Judg 11:29
13:25; 15:14
1 Sam 17:34-36

⁸When he returned for the wedding, he turned off the path to look at the carcass of the lion. And he found a swarm of bees in it, and some honey! ⁹He took some of the honey with him, eating as he went, and gave some of it to his father and mother. But he didn't tell them where he had gotten it.

14:7 *so the arrangements were made,* implied.

SAMSON

It is sad to be remembered for what one might have been. Samson had tremendous potential. Not many people have started life with credentials like his. Born as a result of God's plan in the lives of Manoah and his wife, Samson was to be "a special servant of God." He was to "begin to rescue Israel from the Philistines." To help him accomplish God's plan, he was given enormous physical strength.

Because Samson wasted his strength on practical jokes and getting out of scrapes, and because he eventually gave it up altogether to satisfy the woman he loved, we tend to see him as a failure. We remember him as the judge in Israel who spent his last days grinding grain in an enemy prison, and we say, "What wasted potential!"

Yes, Samson wasted his life. He could have strengthened his nation. He could have returned his people to the worship of God. He could have wiped out the Philistines. But even though he did none of those things, Samson still accomplished the purpose announced by the Angel who visited his parents before his birth. In his final act, Samson began to rescue Israel from the Philistines.

Interestingly, the New Testament does not mention Samson's failures or his heroic feats of strength. In Hebrews, he is simply called one who "trusted God and . . . received what God had promised." In the end, Samson recognized his dependence on God. When he died, God turned his failures and defeats into victory. Samson's story teaches us that it is never too late to start over. However badly we may have failed in the past, today is not too late for us to put our complete trust in God.

Strengths and accomplishments:
● Dedicated to God from birth as a Nazirite
● Known for his feats of strength
● Listed in the Hall of Faith in Hebrews
● Began to free Israel from Philistine oppression

Weaknesses and mistakes:
● Violated his vow and God's laws on many occasions
● Was controlled by sensuality
● Confided in the wrong people
● Used his gifts and abilities unwisely

Lessons from his life:
● Great strength in one area of life does not make up for weaknesses in other areas
● God's presence does not overwhelm a person's will
● God can use people of faith in spite of their mistakes

Vital statistics:
● Where: Zorah, Timnah, Ashkelon, Gaza, valley of Sorek
● Occupation: Judge
● Relatives: Father: Manoah
● Contemporaries: Delilah; Samuel, who might have been born while Samson was a judge

Key verse:
"Your son's hair must never be cut, for he shall be a Nazirite, a special servant of God from the time of his birth; and he will begin to rescue Israel from the Philistines" (Judges 13:5).

His story is told in Judges 13—16. He is also mentioned in Hebrews 11:32.

10, 11As his father was making final arrangements for the marriage, Samson threw a party for thirty young men of the village, as was the custom of the day. 12When Samson asked if they would like to hear a riddle, they replied that they would.

"If you solve my riddle during these seven days of the celebration," he said, "I'll give you thirty plain robes and thirty fancy robes. 13But if you can't solve it, then you must give the robes to me!"

"All right," they agreed, "let's hear it."

14This was his riddle: "Food came out of the eater, and sweetness from the strong!" Three days later they were still trying to figure it out.

15On the fourth day they said to his new wife, "Get the answer from your husband, or we'll burn down your father's house with you in it. Were we invited to this party just to make us poor?"

16So Samson's wife broke down in tears before him and said, "You don't love me at all; you hate me, for you have told a riddle to my people and haven't told me the answer!"

"I haven't even told it to my father or mother; why should I tell you?" he replied.

17So she cried whenever she was with him and kept it up for the remainder of the celebration. At last, on the seventh day, he told her the answer and she, of course, gave the answer to the young men. 18So before sunset of the seventh day they gave him their reply.

"What is sweeter than honey?" they asked, "and what is stronger than a lion?"

"If you hadn't plowed with my heifer, you wouldn't have found the answer to my riddle!" he retorted.

19Then the Spirit of the Lord came upon him and he went to the city of Ashkelon, killed thirty men, took their clothing, and gave it to the young men who had told him the answer to his riddle. But he was furious about it and abandoned his wife and went back home to live with his father and mother. 20So his wife was married instead to the fellow who had been best man at Samson's wedding.

Samson kills many enemies

15 Later on, during the wheat harvest, Samson took a young goat as a present to his wife, intending to sleep with her; but her father wouldn't let him in.

2"I really thought you hated her," he explained, "so I married her to your best man. But look, her sister is prettier than she is. Marry her instead."

3Samson was furious. "You can't blame me for whatever happens now," he shouted.

4So he went out and caught three hundred foxes and tied their tails together in pairs, with a torch between each pair. 5Then he lit the torches and let the foxes run through the fields of the Philistines, burning the grain to the ground along with all the sheaves and shocks of grain, and destroying the olive trees.

6"Who did this?" the Philistines demanded.

"Samson," was the reply, "because his wife's father gave her to another man." So the Philistines came and got the girl and her father and burned them alive.

7"Now my vengeance will strike again!" Samson vowed. 8So he attacked them

14:12
Gen 29:27
Dan 5:12
Ezek 17:2

14:15
Judg 15:6

14:19
Judg 14:6; 15:14

14:20
Jn 3:29

15:6
Judg 14:15

14:18 "If you hadn't plowed with my heifer" means "If you hadn't manipulated my wife." A heifer is a young female; plowing in the fields was usually done with male animals. Samson was saying that if they hadn't threatened his wife, they wouldn't have learned the answer to his riddle.

14:19 Throughout these chapters, Samson impulsively uses the special gift God had given to him for selfish purposes. Today, God distributes abilities and skills throughout the church (1 Corinthians 12:1ff). The apostle Paul states that these gifts are to be used to build up "the church . . . to a position of strength and maturity" (Ephesians 4:12). To use these abilities for selfish purposes is to rob the church and fellow believers of strength. As you use the gifts God has given you, be sure you are helping others, not just yourself.

15:1ff Samson's reply in 15:11 tells the story of this chapter: "I only paid them back for what they did to me." It is a tale of action, reaction, and chain reaction based on anger, hatred, hurt, and revenge. Revenge is an uncontrollable monster. Each vengeful act of retaliation brings another. It is a boomerang which cannot be thrown without cost to the thrower. Don't allow revenge to get your life in its grasp. The cycle of revenge can be halted only by forgiveness.

15:7 God had given all the land of the Philistines to Israel (Joshua 13:2), but Israel had failed to drive the Philistines out and were now dominated by them. God used Samson and his short temper to judge these oppressors. God can cause even "man's futile wrath" to bring himself glory (Psalm 76:10). He is not limited by our weaknesses.

with great fury and killed many of them. Then he went to live in a cave in the rock of Etam. 9The Philistines in turn sent a huge posse into Judah and raided Lehi.

10"Why have you come here?" the men of Judah asked.

And the Philistines replied, "To capture Samson and do to him as he has done to us."

15:11
Judg 13:1; 15:20

11So three thousand men of Judah went down to get Samson at the cave in the rock of Etam.

"What are you doing to us?" they demanded of him. "Don't you realize that the Philistines are our rulers?"

But Samson replied, "I only paid them back for what they did to me."

12, 13"We have come to capture you and take you to the Philistines," the men of Judah told him.

"All right," Samson said, "but promise me that you won't kill me yourselves."

"No," they replied, "we won't do that."

15:14
Judg 14:6,19

So they tied him with two new ropes and led him away. 14As Samson and his captors arrived at Lehi, the Philistines shouted with glee; but then the strength of the Lord came upon Samson, and the ropes with which he was tied snapped like thread and fell from his wrists! 15Then he picked up a donkey's jawbone that was lying on the ground and killed a thousand Philistines with it. 16, 17Tossing away the jawbone, he remarked,

> "Heaps upon heaps,
> All with a donkey's jaw!
> I've killed a thousand men,
> All with a donkey's jaw!"

(The place has been called "Jawbone Hill" ever since.)

15:19
Gen 45:27
1 Sam 30:11

18But now he was very thirsty and he prayed to the Lord and said, "You have given Israel such a wonderful deliverance through me today! Must I now die of thirst, and fall to the mercy of these heathen?" 19So the Lord caused water to gush out from a hollow in the ground and Samson's spirit was revived as he drank. Then he named the place "The Spring of the Man Who Prayed," and the spring is still there today.

15:20
Judg 13:1,5
16:31
Heb 11:32

20Samson was Israel's leader for the next twenty years, but the Philistines still controlled the land.

Samson reveals his secret to Delilah

16:1
Josh 15:47

16 One day Samson went to the Philistine city of Gaza and spent the night with a prostitute. 2Word soon spread that he had been seen in the city, so the police were alerted and many men of the city lay in wait all night at the city gate to capture him if he tried to leave.

"In the morning," they thought, "when there is enough light, we'll find him and kill him."

3Samson stayed in bed with the girl until midnight, then went out to the city gates

---

15:14-17 The Lord's strength came upon Samson, but he was proud and saw only his own strength. "I've killed a thousand men" he said, and later asked God to refresh him because of *his* accomplishments (15:18). Pride can cause us to take credit for things we've done only with God's strength.

15:18 Samson was physically and emotionally exhausted. After a great personal victory, his attitude declined quickly into self-pity—"Must I now die of thirst?" Emotionally, we are most vulnerable after a great effort or when faced with real physical needs. Severe depression often follows great achievements, so don't be surprised if you feel drained after a personal victory.

During these times of vulnerability, avoid the temptation to think that God owes you for your efforts. It was *his* strength that gave you victory. Concentrate on keeping your attitudes, actions, and

words focused on God instead of yourself.

15:20 Apparently Samson was appointed as Israel's judge after this victory over the Philistines. He was a judge for 20 years (16:31).

16:3 Samson was set apart for special service to God from birth. But for the most part he ignored his vow of devotion and depended more and more on his own strength rather than on God's. For the first time, the Spirit of the Lord is not mentioned as directly affecting one of Samson's great feats of strength (14:6, 19; 15:14).

If we become successful using our God-given gifts, we must not forget who gave us these gifts, skills, and abilities or the moral purpose that directs the use of those gifts. Notice what happened when Samson forgot (16:20, 21). We must always remember that all our gifts and abilities come from God.

and lifted them, with the two gateposts, right out of the ground. He put them on his shoulders and carried them to the top of the mountain across from Hebron!

⁴Later on he fell in love with a girl named Delilah over in the valley of Sorek. ⁵The five heads of the Philistine nation went personally to her and demanded that she find out from Samson what made him so strong, so that they would know how to overpower and subdue him and put him in chains.

"Each of us will give you a thousand dollars for this job," they promised.

⁶So Delilah begged Samson to tell her his secret. *"Please* tell me, Samson, why you are so strong," she pleaded. "I don't think anyone could ever capture you!"

⁷"Well," Samson replied, "if I were tied with seven raw-leather bowstrings, I would become as weak as anyone else."

⁸So they brought her the seven bowstrings, and while he slept she tied him with them. ⁹Some men were hiding in the next room, so as soon as she had tied him up she exclaimed,

"Samson! The Philistines are here!"

Then he snapped the bowstrings like cotton thread, and so his secret was not discovered.

¹⁰Afterward Delilah said to him, "You are making fun of me! You told me a lie! *Please* tell me how you can be captured!"

¹¹"Well," he said, "if I am tied with brand new ropes which have never been used, I will be as weak as other men."

¹²So that time, as he slept, Delilah took new ropes and tied him with them. The men were hiding in the next room, as before. Again Delilah exclaimed,

"Samson! The Philistines have come to capture you!"

But he broke the ropes from his arms like spiderwebs!

¹³"You have mocked me again, and told me more lies!" Delilah complained. "Now tell me how you can *really* be captured."

"Well," he said, "if you weave my hair into your loom . . . !"

¹⁴So while he slept, she did just that and then screamed, "The Philistines have come, Samson!" And he woke up and yanked his hair away, breaking the loom.

¹⁵"How can you say you love me when you don't confide in me?" she whined. "You've made fun of me three times now, and you still haven't told me what makes you so strong!"

16, ¹⁷She nagged at him every day until he couldn't stand it any longer and finally told her his secret.

16:15
Judg 14:16

16:16
Num 6:5
Judg 13:5

16:8 *and while he slept,* implied in vs 14. **16:9** *he snapped the bowstrings like cotton thread,* literally, "like a string of tow snaps when it touches the fire." **16:12** *as he slept,* implied.

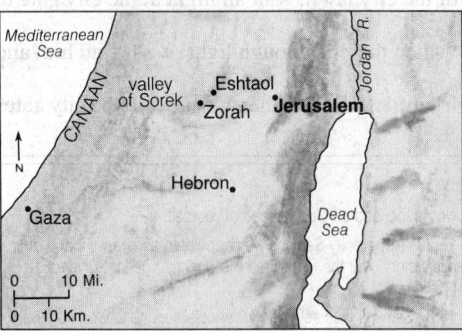

SAMSON AND DELILAH Samson was seduced by a Philistine woman named Delilah who lived in the valley of Sorek. She betrayed the secret of his strength to the Philistines who captured him and led him away in chains to Gaza. There he died. His relatives buried him between Zorah and Eshtaol.

16:5 The Philistines were ruled by five leaders, not just one. Each leader ruled from a different city—Ashdod, Ashkelon, Ekron, Gath, and Gaza. Each of these cities was an important center for trade and commerce. Given Delilah's character, it is little wonder that she betrayed Samson when these rich and powerful men paid her a personal visit.

16:15 Samson was deceived because he wanted to believe Delilah's lies. Although he could strangle a lion, he could not smother his burning lust and see Delilah for what she really was. How can you keep your desire for love and sexual pleasure from deceiving you into believing a lie? (1) You must decide what kind of a person you will love *before* passion takes over. Determine whether a person's character and faith in God are as desirable as his or her physical appearance. (2) Since most of the time you do not spend with your spouse will *not* involve sex, your companion's personality, temperament, and commitment to solve problems must be as gratifying as his or her kisses. (3) Be willing to exercise patience. The second look often reveals what is beneath the pleasant appearance and attentive touch.

16:16, 17 Delilah kept asking Samson for the secret of his strength until he finally grew tired of hearing her nagging and gave in. What a pitiful excuse for disobedience. Don't allow anyone, no matter how attractive or persuasive, to talk you into doing wrong.

"My hair has never been cut," he confessed, "for I've been a Nazirite to God since before my birth. If my hair were cut, my strength would leave me, and I would become as weak as anyone else."

18Delilah realized that he had finally told her the truth, so she sent for the five Philistine leaders.

"Come just this once more," she said, "for this time he has told me everything."

So they brought the money with them. 19She lulled him to sleep with his head in her lap, and they brought in a barber and cut off his hair. Delilah began to hit him, but she could see that his strength was leaving him.

16:20
1 Sam 16:14
18:11,12

20Then she screamed, "The Philistines are here to capture you, Samson!" And he woke up and thought, "I will do as before; I'll just shake myself free." But he didn't realize that the Lord had left him. 21So the Philistines captured him and gouged out his eyes and took him to Gaza, where he was bound with bronze chains and made to grind grain in the prison. 22But before long his hair began to grow again.

DELILAH

A person's greatest accomplishment may well be helping others accomplish great things. Likewise, a person's greatest failure may be preventing others from achieving greatness. Delilah played a minor role in Samson's life, but her effect was devastating, for she influenced him to betray his special calling from God. Motivated by greed, Delilah used her persistence to wear down Samson. His infatuation with her made Samson a vulnerable target. For all his physical strength, he was no match for her and he paid a great price for giving in to her. Delilah is never mentioned again in the Bible. Her unfaithfulness to Samson brought ruin to his life and to her people.

Are people helped by knowing you? Do they find that knowing you challenges them to be the best they can be? Even more important, does knowing you help their relationship to God? What do your demands for their time and attention tell them about your real care for them? Are you willing to be God's instrument in the lives of others?

Strength and accomplishment:
• Persistent when faced with obstacles

Weaknesses and mistakes:
• Valued money more than relationships
• Betrayed the man who trusted her

Lesson from her life:
• We need to be careful to place our trust only in people who are trustworthy

Vital statistics:
• Where: valley of Sorek
• Contemporary: Samson

Key verses:
"She nagged at him every day until he couldn't stand it any longer and finally told her his secret" (Judges 16:16, 17).

Her story is told in Judges 16.

16:19 Delilah was a deceitful woman with honey on her lips and poison in her heart. Cold and calculating, she toyed with Samson, pretending to love him while looking for personal gain. How could Samson be so foolish? Four times Delilah took advantage of him. If he didn't realize what was happening after the first or second experience, surely he should have understood the situation by the fourth time! We think Samson is foolish; but how many times do we allow ourselves to be deceived by flattery and give in to temptation and wrong beliefs? Avoid falling prey to deceit by asking God to help you distinguish between deception and truth.

16:20 Samson's relationship with God had deteriorated so much that he didn't even realize God had left him. He took his leadership abilities as well as God's presence for granted. God offered Samson all he would ever need, yet Samson chose instead to put himself into Delilah's deceitful hands. As a result he lost his strength. We must be careful not to put our lives into the wrong hands. Our only true security is found in God.

16:21 Samson, the mighty warrior, became a slave. Rather than kill him, the Philistines preferred to humiliate him by gouging out his eyes and making him grind grain. Samson now had plenty of time to wonder if Delilah's charms were worth spending the rest of his life in humiliation.

Although God did not completely abandon Samson (16:28–30), he allowed Samson's decision to stand, and the consequences of his decision followed naturally. We may choose to be close to God or to go our own way, but there are consequences resulting from our choice. Samson didn't choose to be captured, but he chose to be with Delilah, and he could not escape the consequences of his decision.

16:21 Blinded and without strength, Samson was taken to Gaza where he would spend the rest of his short life. Gaza was one of the five capital cities of the Philistines. Known for its many wells, Gaza was a vital stop along a great caravan route that connected Egypt to the south with Syria to the north. The Philistines probably showed off their prize captive Samson to many dignitaries passing through.

Ironically, it was in Gaza that Samson had earlier demonstrated his great strength by uprooting the city gates (16:1–3). Now he was an example of weakness.

Samson triumphs in death

23, 24The Philistine leaders declared a great festival to celebrate the capture of Samson. The people made sacrifices to their god Dagon and excitedly praised him.

"Our god has delivered our enemy Samson to us!" they gloated as they saw him there in chains. "The scourge of our nation who killed so many of us is now in our power!" 25, 26Half drunk by now, the people demanded, "Bring out Samson so we can have some fun with him!"

So he was brought from the prison and made to stand at the center of the temple, between the two pillars supporting the roof. Samson said to the boy who was leading him by the hand, "Place my hands against the two pillars. I want to rest against them."

27By then the temple was completely filled with people. The five Philistine leaders were there as well as three thousand people in the balconies who were watching Samson and making fun of him.

28Then Samson prayed to the Lord and said, "O Lord Jehovah, remember me again—please strengthen me one more time, so that I may pay back the Philistines for the loss of at least one of my eyes."

29Then Samson pushed against the pillars with all his might.

30"Let me die with the Philistines," he prayed.

And the temple crashed down upon the Philistine leaders and all the people. So those he killed at the moment of his death were more than those he had killed during his entire lifetime. 31Later, his brothers and other relatives came down to get his body, and they brought him back home and buried him between Zorah and Eshta-ol, where his father, Manoah, was buried. He had led Israel for twenty years.

16:23
1 Sam 5:1,2

16:28
Judg 15:18

C. THE MORAL FAILURE OF ISRAEL (17:1—21:25)

This section shows Israel falling into idolatry, moral decline, and petty fighting. Israel, the nation that was to set the example for spiritual living, had instead become morally depraved. When Israel did serve God, and that was seldom, it was often from selfish motives. Selfish obedience does not bring us far. Genuine obedience is motivated by a love and reverence for God himself.

1. Idolatry in the tribe of Dan

Micah collects idols

17 In the hill country of Ephraim lived a man named Micah.

2One day he said to his mother, "That thousand dollars you thought was stolen from you, and you were cursing about—well, I stole it!"

"God bless you for confessing it," his mother replied. 3So he returned the money to her.

"I am going to give it to the Lord as a credit for your account," she declared. "I'll have an idol carved for you and plate it with the silver."

17:3
Ex 20:4,23
34:17
Deut 12:3
Judg 10:10
18:31

16:27 *people in the balconies,* literally, "on the roof."

16:23, 24 Dagon was the chief god of the Philistines, the god of grain and harvest. Many temples were built to Dagon, and the worship there included human sacrifice. The temples were also the local entertainment centers. Just as people today crowd into theaters, Philistine townspeople crowded into the local temple. They sat on the flat temple roof and looked into the courtyard below. What they often saw was the torture and humiliation of prisoners.

Since the Philistines had control over the Israelites, they thought their god was stronger. But when the Ark of God was placed before Dagon in a similar temple, the idol fell over and broke into pieces (1 Samuel 5:1-7). God's strength goes beyond numbers or physical might.

16:28–30 In spite of Samson's past, God still heard and answered his prayer, destroying the heathen temple and worshipers. God still loved him. He was willing to hear Samson's prayer of confession and repentance and use him this final time. One of the effects of sin in our lives is to keep us from feeling like

praying. But perfect moral behavior is not a condition for prayer. Don't let guilt feelings over sin keep you from your only means of restoration. No matter how long you have been away from God, he is ready to hear from you and restore you to a right relationship. Every situation in life can be salvaged if you are willing to turn again to him. If God could still work in Samson's situation, he can certainly make something worthwhile out of yours.

17:2 Micah and his mother seemed to be good and moral and may have sincerely desired to worship God, but they disobeyed God by following their own desires instead of doing what God wanted. The attitude that prevailed in Micah's day was this: "Everyone did whatever he wanted to—whatever seemed right in his own eyes" (17:6). This is remarkably similar to the attitudes that prevail today. But God has given us standards. He has not left our conduct up to us and our opinions. We can avoid conforming to society's prevailing attitudes by taking God's commands seriously and applying them to life. Independence and self-reliance are positive traits, but only within the framework of God's standards.

17:4
Judg 8:27
1 Sam 19:13

17:6
Deut 12:8
Judg 18:1; 19:1
21:25

17:7
Judg 19:1
Ruth 1:1,2
Mic 5:2
Mt 2:1

17:12
Num 16:10
Judg 18:30
1 Kgs 12:31

4, 5So his mother took a fifth of it to a silversmith, and the idol he made from it was placed in Micah's shrine. Micah had many idols in his collection, also an ephod and some teraphim, and he installed one of his sons as the priest. 6(For in those days Israel had no king, so everyone did whatever he wanted to—whatever seemed right in his own eyes.)

7, 8One day a young priest from the town of Bethlehem, in Judah, arrived in that area of Ephraim, looking for a good place to live. He happened to stop at Micah's house as he was traveling through.

9"Where are you from?" Micah asked him.

And he replied, "I am a priest from Bethlehem, in Judah, and I am looking for a place to live."

10, 11"Well, stay here with me," Micah said, "and you can be my priest. I will give you one hundred dollars a year plus a new suit and your board and room." The young man agreed to this, and became as one of Micah's sons. 12So Micah consecrated him as his personal priest.

13"I know the Lord will really bless me now," Micah exclaimed, "because now I have a genuine priest working for me!"

The Danites steal Micah's idols

18:1
Josh 19:40
Judg 17:6; 21:25

18:2
Judg 13:2,3,25

18 As has already been stated, there was no king in Israel at that time. The tribe of Dan was trying to find a place to settle, for they had not yet driven out the people living in the land assigned to them. 2So the men of Dan chose five army heroes from the cities of Zorah and Eshta-ol as scouts to go and spy out the land they were supposed to settle in. Arriving in the hill country of Ephraim, they stayed at Micah's home. 3Noticing the young Levite's accent, they took him aside and

17:7, 8 *a young man*, "a Levite."   **17:13** *now I have a genuine priest working for me*, literally, "a Levite as a priest."

17:4, 5 Micah may have felt religious because of his collection of idols, his confession of wrongdoing, and the appointment of his son as a priest. He obviously wanted to maintain a religious influence in his home, but he went about it the wrong way. His apparently good intentions were not enough; he needed to follow God's laws and not his own ideas of what was right. If Micah truly loved God, he would have desired to know what God had communicated to his people and what he should do about it. Instead, Micah set up his own religious system for his own benefit. Don't think sincerity and good intentions are enough; you may be in danger of thinking that you need no instruction from God's Word or anyone else.

17:6 Today, as in Micah's day, everyone seems to put his or her own interests first. Time has not changed human nature. Most people still reject God's right way of living. The people in Micah's time replaced the true worship of God with a homemade version of worship. As a result, justice was soon replaced by evil and chaos. Ignoring God's direction led to confusion and destruction. Anyone who is not submitted to God will end up doing whatever seems right at the time. This tendency is present in all of us. Drawing closer to God and his Word reminds us of what is really right.

17:7-12 Apparently the Israelites no longer supported the priests and Levites with their tithes, because so many of the people no longer worshiped God. The young priest in this story probably left his home in Bethlehem because the money he received from the people there was not enough to live on. But Israel's moral decay had even crept into the priesthood. This man accepted money (17:10, 11), idols (18:20), and position (17:12) in a way that was inconsistent with God's laws. While Micah illustrated the religious downfall of the individual Israelites, this priest illustrated the religious downfall of the priesthood.

18:1 The tribe of Dan had been assigned land that was sufficient

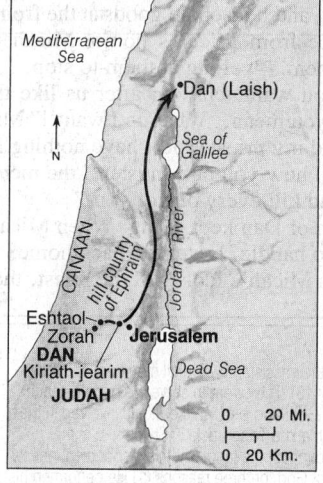

THE TRIBE OF DAN MOVES NORTH Troops from the tribe of Dan traveled from Zorah and Eshtaol into the hill country of Ephraim where they persuaded Micah's priest to come with them. They continued north to Laish where they ruthlessly butchered its citizens. The city was renamed Dan and the priest's idols became the focus of their worship.

for their needs (Joshua 19:40–48). However, because they failed to trust God to help them conquer their territory, the Amorites forced them into the hill country and wouldn't let them settle in the plains (Judges 1:34). Rather than fight for their allotted territory, they preferred to look for new land in the north where resistance from the enemy wouldn't be so tough. It was while they were traveling north that some of their men passed the home of Micah and stole some of his idols.

asked him, "What are you doing here? Why did you come?" ⁴He told them about his contract with Micah, and that he was his personal priest.

18:4
Judg 17:10,11

⁵"Well, then," they said, "ask God whether or not our trip will be successful."

⁶"Yes," the priest replied, "all is well. The Lord is taking care of you."

⁷So the five men went on to the town of Laish, and noticed how secure everyone felt. Their manner of life was Phoenician, and they were wealthy. They lived quietly, and were unprepared for an attack, for there were no tribes in the area strong enough to try it. They lived a great distance from their relatives in Sidon, and had little or no contact with the nearby villages. ⁸So the spies returned to their people in Zorah and Eshta-ol.

18:7
Josh 19:47,48

"What about it?" they were asked. "What did you find?"

⁹, ¹⁰And the men replied, "Let's attack! We have seen the land and it is ours for the taking—a broad, fertile, wonderful place—a real paradise. The people aren't even prepared to defend themselves! Come on, let's go! For God has given it to us!"

¹¹So six hundred armed troops of the tribe of Dan set out from Zorah and Eshtaol. ¹²They camped first at a place west of Kiriath-jearim in Judah (which is still called "The Camp of Dan"), ¹³then they went on up into the hill country of Ephraim.

As they passed the home of Micah, ¹⁴the five spies told the others. "There is a shrine in there with an ephod, some teraphim, and many plated idols. It's obvious what we ought to do!"

18:14
Judg 17:4,5

¹⁵, ¹⁶So the five men went over to the house and with all of the armed men standing just outside the gate, they talked to the young priest, and asked him how he was getting along. ¹⁷Then the five spies entered the shrine and took the idols, the ephod, and the teraphim.

¹⁸"What are you doing?" the young priest demanded when he saw them carrying them out.

¹⁹"Be quiet and come with us," they said. "Be a priest to all of us. Isn't it better for you to be a priest to a whole tribe in Israel instead of just to one man in his private home?"

18:19
Judg 17:10,11

²⁰The young priest was then quite happy to go with them, and he took along the ephod, the teraphim, and the idols. ²¹They started on their way again, placing their children, cattle, and household goods at the front of the column. ²²When they were quite a distance from Micah's home, Micah and some of his neighbors came chasing after them, ²³yelling at them to stop.

18:21
Gen 33:2
Ex 12:37

"What do you want, chasing after us like this?" the men of Dan demanded.

²⁴"What do you mean, 'What do I want'!" Micah retorted. "You've taken away all my gods and my priest, and I have nothing left!"

²⁵"Be careful how you talk, mister," the men of Dan replied. "Somebody's apt to get angry and kill every one of you."

²⁶So the men of Dan kept going. When Micah saw that there were too many of them for him to handle, he turned back home.

²⁷Then, with Micah's idols and the priest, the men of Dan arrived at the city of

---

18:4-6 Priests and their assistants were all members of the tribe of Levi (Numbers 3:5–13). They were to serve the people, teach them how to worship God, and perform the rituals involved in the worship services both at the Tabernacle in Shiloh and in the designated cities throughout the land. But this disobedient priest showed disrespect for God for three reasons (1) He performed his duties in a house. Priestly duties were to be performed only in the Tabernacle or a designated city. This requirement was intended to prevent God's laws from being changed or adapted. (2) He carried idols with him (18:20). (3) He claimed to speak for God when God had not spoken through him (18:6).

18:11–26 Through this entire incident, the desire on the part of all involved was not to worship God, but to use God for selfish gain. Today some people go to church to feel better, be accepted, relieve guilt, and gain business contacts or friends. Beware of

following God for selfish gain rather than selfless service.

18:24 Micah made idols and hired a priest to run his personal religion. When the men of Dan took his idols and priest, nothing remained. What an empty spiritual condition! An idol is anything that takes God's place in a person's life. Some people invest their whole lives in things like money, success, possessions or a career. If these idols are taken away, only an empty shell is left. The only way to protect yourself against such emptiness is to invest your life in the living God whom you can never lose.

18:27 Did the tribe of Dan have the right to kill the citizens of Laish? No. God had commanded Israel to clean out and destroy certain cities because of their idolatry and wickedness. But Laish did not fall under that judgment. It was not within the assigned boundaries of Dan, and its people were peaceful in contrast to the warlike Canaanites. But the tribe of Dan had no regard for God's

18:28
2 Sam 10:6

Laish. There weren't even any guards, so they went in and slaughtered all the people and burned the city to the ground. 28There was no one to help the inhabitants, for they were too far away from Sidon, and they had no local allies, for they had no dealings with anyone. This happened in the valley next to Beth-rehob. Then the people of the tribe of Dan rebuilt the city and lived there. 29The city was named "Dan" after their ancestor, Israel's son, but it had originally been called Laish.

18:30
Ex 2:22; 18:3

30Then they set up the idols and appointed a man named Jonathan (son of Gershom and grandson of Moses!) and his sons as their priests. This family continued as priests until the city was finally conquered by its enemies. 31So Micah's idols were worshiped by the tribe of Dan as long as the Tabernacle remained at Shiloh.

2. War against the tribe of Benjamin
The runaway concubine

19:1
Judg 17:6; 21:25

19 At this time before Israel had a king, there was a man of the tribe of Levi living on the far side of the hill country of Ephraim, who brought home a girl from Bethlehem in Judah to be his concubine. 2But she became angry with him and ran away, and returned to her father's home in Bethlehem, and was there about four months. 3Then her husband, taking along a servant and an extra donkey, went to

19:3
Gen 34:3

see her to try to win her back again. When he arrived at her home, she let him in and introduced him to her father, who was delighted to meet him. 4Her father urged him to stay awhile, so he stayed three days, and they all had a very pleasant time.

19:5
Gen 18:5

5On the fourth day they were up early, ready to leave, but the girl's father insisted on their having breakfast first. 6Then he pleaded with him to stay one more day, as they were having such a good time. 7At first the man refused, but his father-in-law kept urging him until finally he gave in. 8The next morning they were

---

Law. Ironically, God's Law said to destroy a city for idolatry (Deuteronomy 13:12–15). The Danites themselves were guilty of this sin. This story shows how far some of the tribes had wandered from God's Law.

18:27 Just because the Danites successfully defeated Laish doesn't mean they were right in their actions. Their idolatry showed that God was not guiding them. Today many justify their wrong actions by outward signs of success. They think that wealth, popularity, or lack of suffering is an indication of God's blessing. They say, "Let's go! For God has given it to us" (18:10). But Scripture is clear that evil and earthly success often go hand in hand (2 Kings 14:23–29). Success doesn't indicate God's approval. Don't allow personal success to become a measuring rod of whether or not you are pleasing God.

18:30, 31 The tribe of Dan had stolen Micah's idols, and now they set them up in Laish. Although the Danites were actually denying God by worshiping these images (Exodus 20:1–5), they probably assumed they were worshiping God through them (see the note on Exodus 32:4, 5). Worshiping images of God is *not* worshiping God, even if it resembles true worship in some ways. People repeat the same mistake today when they give the appearance of godliness without really believing in God's power. Claiming to follow God, they fail to change their lives to conform to his expectations. Godliness cannot be merely an appearance. It must be a reality within our hearts.

18:31 Shiloh was probably destroyed during the events reported in 1 Samuel 4 and 5, not long after the time described here. Because Shiloh was the religious center for Israel, all adult males were required to travel there for certain religious feasts. The tribe of Dan, however, set up idols and priests in the new territory they conquered. The fact that they were over 80 miles away from Shiloh may have been their excuse for not fulfilling the requirements of the Law. This act was a further demonstration of their disregard for God.

18:31 The true worship of God should have been maintained through the the levitical priests scattered throughout the land and the influence of the Tabernacle in Shiloh. This story shows how pagan influences and moral depravity had crept into every corner of Israelite culture. Although 300 years had passed since they entered the Promised Land, they still had not destroyed the idolatry and evil practices within it.

There may be a tendency in your life to allow "harmless" habits to have their own small corners, but they can become dominating forces. The values, attitudes, and practices you have adopted from the world's system can be exposed by applying the light of God's truth to them. Once you see them for what they are, you can begin to uproot them.

19:1—21:25 What is the significance of this tragic story? When the Israelites' faith in God disintegrated, their unity as a nation also disintegrated. They could have taken complete possession of the land if they had obeyed God and trusted him to keep his promises. But when they forgot to include him in their lives, they lost their purpose, and soon "every man did whatever he thought was right" (21:25). When they stopped letting God lead them, they became no better than the evil people around them. When they made their own laws for their own benefit, they set standards far below God's. When you leave God out of your life you will shock even yourself at what you are capable of doing (19:30).

19:1 Having concubines was an accepted part of Israelite society, though this is not what God intended (Genesis 2:24). A concubine had the duties, but not the privileges of being a wife. Although she was legally attached to one man, she and her children usually did not have the inheritance rights of the legal wife and legitimate children. Her primary purpose was giving the man sexual pleasure, bearing additional children, and contributing more help to the household or estate. Concubines were often foreign prisoners of war. But they could also be Israelites, as was probably the case in this story.

up early again, and again the girl's father pleaded, "Stay just today and leave sometime this evening." So they had another day of feasting.

9That afternoon as he and his wife and servant were preparing to leave, his father-in-law said, "Look, it's getting late. Stay just tonight, and we will have a pleasant evening together and tomorrow you can get up early and be on your way."

10But this time the man was adamant, so they left, getting as far as Jerusalem (also called Jebus) before dark.

19:10
Josh 15:8
18:21-28
1 Chron 11:4

11His servant said to him, "It's getting too late to travel; let's stay here tonight."

12, 13"No," his master said, "we can't stay in this heathen city where there are no Israelites—we will go on to Gibe-ah, or possibly Ramah."

19:12
Josh 24:33
Judg 20:4

14So they went on. The sun was setting just as they came to Gibe-ah, a village of the tribe of Benjamin, 15so they went there for the night. But as no one invited them in, they camped in the village square. 16Just then an old man came by on his way home from his work in the fields. (He was originally from the hill country of Ephraim, but was living now in Gibe-ah, even though it was in the territory of Benjamin.) 17When he saw the travelers camped in the square, he asked them where they were from, and where they were going.

19:17
Esth 4:6

18"We're on the way home from Bethlehem, in Judah," the man replied. "I live on the far edge of the Ephraim hill country, near Shiloh. But no one has taken us in for the night, 19even though we have fodder for our donkeys, and plenty of food and wine for ourselves."

20"Don't worry," the old man said, "be my guests; for you mustn't stay here in the square. It's too dangerous."

21So he took them home with him. He fed their donkeys while they rested, and afterward they had supper together. 22Just as they were beginning to warm to the occasion, a gang of sex perverts gathered around the house and began beating at the door and yelling at the old man to bring out the man who was staying with him, so they could rape him. 23The old man stepped outside to talk to them.

19:21
Gen 18:4; 19:2
24:32

19:22
Gen 19:4,5

19:23
2 Sam 13:12

"No, my brothers, don't do such a dastardly act," he begged, "for he is my guest. 24Here, take my virgin daughter and this man's wife. I'll bring them out and you can do whatever you like to them—but don't do such a thing to this man."

19:24
Gen 19:8

25But they wouldn't listen to him. Then the girl's husband pushed her out to them, and they abused her all night, taking turns raping her until morning. Finally, just at dawn, they let her go. 26She fell down at the door of the house and lay there until it was light. 27When her husband opened the door to be on his way, he found her there, fallen down in front of the door with her hands digging into the threshold.

28"Well, come on," he said. "Let's get going."

But there was no answer, for she was dead; so he threw her across the donkey's back and took her home. 29When he got there he took a knife and cut her body into twelve parts and sent one piece to each tribe of Israel. 30Then the entire nation was roused to action against the men of Benjamin because of this awful deed.

"There hasn't been such a horrible crime since Israel left Egypt," everyone said. "We've got to do something about it."

19:24 Nowhere is the unwritten law of hospitality stronger than in the Middle East. Protecting a guest at any cost ranked at the top of a man's code of honor. But here the hospitality code turned to fanaticism. The rape and abuse of a daughter and companion was preferable to the *possibility* of a conflict between a guest and a neighbor. The two men were selfish (they didn't want to get hurt themselves), they lacked courage (they didn't want to face a conflict even when lives were at stake), and they disobeyed God's Law (they allowed deliberate abuse and murder). What drastic consequences can result when social protocol carries more authority than moral convictions!

19:29, 30 Although this was a terrible deed, it effectively communicated the horror of the crime and called the people to action. Saul used a similar method in 1 Samuel 11:7. Ironically, the man who alerted Israel to the murder of his concubine was just as guilty for her death as the men who actually killed her.

19:30 The horrible crime described in this chapter wasn't Israel's worst offense. Even worse was the nation's failure to establish a government based upon God's moral principles, where the Law of God was the law of the land. As a result, laws were usually unenforced and crime was ignored. The sexual perversion and lawlessness were a by-product of Israel's disobedience to God. The Israelites weren't willing to speak up until events had gone too far.

Whenever we get away from God and his Word, all sorts of evil can follow. Our drifting away from God may be slow and almost imperceptible, with the ultimate results affecting a future generation. We must continually call ourselves and our nation back to God and work toward the establishment of God's moral and spiritual reign in the heart of every person.

Israel attacks the tribe of Benjamin

20:1
1 Sam 7:5
2 Sam 19:14

20 Then the entire nation of Israel sent their leaders and 450,000 troops to assemble with one mind before the Lord at Mizpah. They came from as far away as Dan and Beersheba, and everywhere between, and from across the Jordan in the land of Gilead. 3(Word of the mobilization of the Israeli forces at Mizpah soon reached the land of Benjamin.) The chiefs of Israel now called for the murdered woman's husband and asked him just what had happened.

4"We arrived one evening at Gibe-ah, a village in Benjamin," he began. 5"That night the men of Gibe-ah surrounded the house, planning to kill me, and they raped my wife until she was dead. 6So I cut her body into twelve pieces and sent the pieces throughout the land of Israel, for these men have committed a terrible crime. 7Now then, sons of Israel, express your mind and give me your counsel!"

8, 9, 10And as one man they replied, "Not one of us will return home until we have punished the village of Gibe-ah. A tenth of the army will be selected by lot as a supply line to bring us food, and the rest of us will destroy Gibe-ah for this horrible deed."

11So the whole nation united in this task.

12Then messengers were sent to the tribe of Benjamin, asking, "Did you know about the terrible thing that was done among you? 13Give up these evil men from the city of Gibe-ah so that we can execute them and purge Israel of her evil." But

20:14
Num 2:23

the people of Benjamin wouldn't listen. 14, 15Instead, twenty-six thousand of them arrived in Gibe-ah to join the seven hundred local men in their defense against the

20:16
Judg 3:15

rest of Israel. 16(Among all these there were seven hundred men who were left-handed sharpshooters. They could hit a target within a hair's breadth, never missing!) 17The army of Israel, not counting the men of Benjamin, numbered 400,000 men.

20:18
Num 27:21
Judg 1:1

18Before the battle the Israeli army went to Bethel first to ask counsel from God. "Which tribe shall lead us against the people of Benjamin?" they asked.

And the Lord replied, "Judah shall go first."

19, 20So the entire army left early the next morning to go to Gibe-ah, to attack the men of Benjamin. 21But the men defending the village stormed out and killed

20:22
Josh 7:6,7

twenty-two thousand Israelis that day. 22, 23, 24Then the Israeli army wept before the Lord until evening and asked him, "Shall we fight further against our brother Benjamin?"

And the Lord said, "Yes." So the men of Israel took courage and went out again the next day to fight at the same place. 25And that day they lost another eighteen thousand men, all experienced swordsmen.

20:26
Judg 21:4
1 Sam 13:9
2 Sam 24:25

20:27
Judg 7:9

26Then the entire army went up to Bethel and wept before the Lord and fasted until evening, offering burnt sacrifices and peace offerings. 27, 28(The Ark of God was in Bethel in those days. Phinehas, the son of Eleazar and grandson of Aaron, was the priest.)

The men of Israel asked the Lord, "Shall we go out again and fight against our brother Benjamin, or shall we stop?"

20:1, 2 Dan was the northernmost city in Israel and Beersheba the southernmost. The two were often mentioned together as a reference to the entire nation.

20:13 Perhaps the Benjamite leaders had been given distorted facts about the serious crime in their territory, or perhaps they were too proud to admit that some of their people had stooped so low. In either case, they would not listen to the rest of Israel and hand over the accused criminals. They were more loyal to their own tribe than to God's Law.

By covering for their kinsmen, the entire tribe of Benjamin sank to a level of immorality as low as the criminals'. Through this act, we get a glimpse of how thoroughly the nation's moral fabric had unraveled. The book of Judges ends in a bloody civil war that sets the stage for the spiritual renewal to come under Samuel.

20:13 Israel called for the execution of the perverted men who had committed rape and murder. Since the entire nation was responsible for the acts of its individuals (Deuteronomy 13:12–15; Joshua 7:10–12), the nation stood guilty until justice was served.

20:27, 28 This is the only place in Judges where the Ark of God (also called the Ark of the Covenant) is mentioned. This probably indicates how seldom the people consulted God.

Phinehas, the High Priest, was also the High Priest under Joshua (Joshua 22:13). The reference to Phinehas as High Priest and the location of the Tabernacle in Bethel instead of Shiloh probably indicate that the events of this story occurred during the early years of the judges.

And the Lord said, "Go, for tomorrow I will see to it that you defeat the men of Benjamin."

29So the Israeli army set an ambush all around the village, 30and went out again on the third day and set themselves in their usual battle formation. 31When the army of Benjamin came out of the town to attack, the Israeli forces retreated and Benjamin was drawn away from the town as they chased after Israel. And as they had done previously, Benjamin began to kill the men of Israel along the roadway running between Bethel and Gibe-ah, so that about thirty of them died.

32Then the army of Benjamin shouted, "We're defeating them again!" But the armies of Israel had agreed in advance to run away so that the army of Benjamin would chase them and be drawn away from the town. 33But when the main army of Israel reached Baal-tamar, it turned and attacked, and the ten thousand men in ambush west of Geba jumped up from where they were, 34and advanced against the rear of the army of Benjamin, who still didn't realize the impending disaster. 35-39So the Lord helped Israel defeat Benjamin, and the Israeli army killed 25,100 men of Benjamin that day, leaving but a tiny remnant of their forces.

Summary of the Battle: The army of Israel retreated from the men of Benjamin in order to give the ambush more room for maneuvering. When the men of Benjamin had killed about thirty of the Israelis, they were confident of a massive slaughter just as on the previous days. But then the men in ambush rushed into the village and slaughtered everyone in it, and set it on fire. The great cloud of smoke pouring into the sky was the signal for the Israeli army to turn around and attack the army of Benjamin, 40, 41who now looked behind them and were terrified to discover that their city was on fire, and that they were in serious trouble. 42So they ran toward the wilderness, but the Israelis chased after them, and the men who had set the ambush came out and joined the slaughter from the rear. 43They encircled the army of Benjamin east of Gibe-ah, and killed most of them there. 44Eighteen thousand of the Benjamin troops died in that day's battle. 45The rest of the army fled into the wilderness toward the rock of Rimmon, but five thousand were killed along the way, and two thousand more near Gidom.

46, 47So the tribe of Benjamin lost twenty-five thousand brave warriors that day, leaving only six hundred men who escaped to the rock of Rimmon, where they lived for four months. 48Then the Israeli army returned and slaughtered the entire population of the tribe of Benjamin—men, women, children, and cattle—and burned down every city and village in the entire land.

Wives for the men of Benjamin

21 The leaders of Israel had vowed at Mizpah never to let their daughters marry a man from the tribe of Benjamin. 2And now the Israeli leaders met at Bethel and sat before God until evening, weeping bitterly.

3"O Lord God of Israel," they cried out, "why has this happened, that now one of our tribes is missing?"

4The next morning they were up early and built an altar, and offered sacrifices and peace offerings on it. 5And they said among themselves, "Was any tribe of Israel not represented when we held our council before the Lord at Mizpah?" For at that time it was agreed by solemn oath that anyone who refused to come must die. 6There was deep sadness throughout all Israel for the loss of their brother tribe, Benjamin.

Marginal references:
20:31 Josh 8:16
20:33 Josh 8:19
20:42 Josh 8:15,24
20:45 Judg 21:13
21:1 Judg 20:1
21:2 Judg 20:31
21:19
21:4 Deut 12:4,5
2 Sam 24:25

20:29ff After their first battle against the Benjamites had failed, Israel used the battle plan Joshua had devised against Ai (Joshua 8). However, the ambush would not have defeated the tribe of Benjamin without God's promise of victory (20:28).

20:46-48 The effects of the horrible rape and murder should never have been felt outside the community where it happened. The local people should have brought the men responsible to justice and corrected the laxness that originally permitted the crime. Instead, first the town and then the entire tribe defended this wickedness, going so far as to go to war over it.

To prevent unresolved problems from turning into major conflicts, firm action must be taken quickly, wisely, and forcefully *before* the situation gets out of hand.

20:48 The tribe of Benjamin eventually recovered from this slaughter. Saul, Israel's first king, was from this tribe (1 Samuel 9:21). So were Queen Esther (Esther 2:5-7) and the apostle Paul (Romans 11:1).

"Gone," they kept saying to themselves, "gone—an entire tribe of Israel has been cut off, and is gone. 7And how shall we get wives for the few who remain, since we have sworn by the Lord that we will not give them our daughters?"

8, 9Then they thought again of their oath to kill anyone who refused to come to Mizpah, and discovered that no one had attended from Jabesh-gilead. 10, 11, 12So they sent twelve thousand of their best soldiers to destroy the people of Jabesh-gilead. All the men, married women, and children were slain, but the young virgins of marriageable age were saved. There were four hundred of these, and they were brought to the camp at Shiloh.

13Then Israel sent a peace delegation to the little remnant of the men of Benjamin at Rimmon Rock. 14The four hundred girls were given to them as wives, and they returned to their homes; but there were not enough of these girls for all of them. 15(What a sad time it was in Israel in those days, because the Lord had made a breach in the tribes of Israel.)

16"What shall we do for wives for the others, since all the women of the tribe of Benjamin are dead?" the leaders of Israel asked. 17"There must be some way to get wives for them, so that an entire tribe of Israel will not be lost forever. 18But we can't give them our own daughters. We have sworn with a solemn oath that anyone who does this shall be cursed of God."

19Suddenly someone thought of the annual religious festival held in the fields of Shiloh, between Lebonah and Bethel, along the east side of the road that goes from Bethel to Shechem.

20They told the men of Benjamin who still needed wives, "Go and hide in the vineyards, 21and when the girls of Shiloh come out for their dances, rush out and catch them and take them home with you to be your wives! 22And when their fathers and brothers come to us in protest, we will tell them, 'Please be understanding and let them have your daughters, for we didn't find enough wives for them when we destroyed Jabesh-gilead, and you couldn't have given your daughters to them without being guilty.'"

23So the men of Benjamin did as they were told and kidnapped the girls who took part in the celebration, and carried them off to their own land. Then they rebuilt their cities and lived in them. 24So the people of Israel returned to their homes.

25(There was no king in Israel in those days, and every man did whatever he thought was right.)

21:10 Num 31:18
21:13 Deut 20:10
21:19 Josh 18:1 / Judg 18:31 / 1 Sam 1:3
21:21 Ex 15:20 / Judg 11:34
21:23 Judg 20:48

21:8-12 The Israelites moved from one mess to another. Because of a rash vow made in the heat of emotion (21:5), they now destroyed another town. Israel probably justified their action with the following arguments: (1) An oath could not be broken, and Israel had vowed that anyone who did not help them fight the Benjamites would be killed. (2) Since all the women from Benjamin had been killed, the few remaining men needed wives to prevent the tribe from disappearing. To spare the unmarried women from Jabesh-gilead seemed the right solution.

We do not know all the circumstances behind the brutal massacre at Jabesh-gilead, but it seems that the rest of Israel followed Benjamin's pattern. They put tribal loyalties above God's commands, and they justified wrong actions to correct past mistakes.

21:25 During the time of the judges, the people of Israel experienced trouble because everyone became his own authority and acted on his own opinions of right and wrong. This produced horrendous results. Our world is similar. Individuals, groups, and societies have made themselves the final authorities without reference to God. When people selfishly seek to satisfy their personal desires at all cost, everyone pays the price.

It is the ultimate heroic act to submit all our plans, desires, and motives to God. Men like Gideon, Jephthah, and Samson are known for their heroism in battle. But their personal lives were far from heroic. To be truly heroic, we must go into battle each day in our home, job, church, and society to make God's kingdom a reality. Our weapons are the standards, morals, truths, and convictions we receive from God's Word. We will lose the battle if we gather the spoils of earthly treasures rather than seeking the treasures of heaven.

VITAL STATISTICS

PURPOSE:
To show how three people remained strong in character and true to God even when the society around them was collapsing

AUTHOR:
Unknown. Some think it was Samuel, but internal evidence suggests that it was written after his death.

DATE WRITTEN:
Sometime after the period of the judges (1375–1050 B.C.)

SETTING:
A dark time in Israel's history when people lived to please themselves, not God (Judges 17:6)

KEY VERSE:
"But Ruth replied, 'Don't make me leave you, for I want to go wherever you go, and to live wherever you live; your people shall be my people, and your God shall be my God' " (1:16).

KEY PEOPLE:
Ruth, Naomi, Boaz

KEY PLACES:
Moab, Bethlehem

WHEN someone says, "Let me tell you about my mother-in-law," we expect some kind of negative statement or humorous anecdote. The mother-in-law caricature has been a standard centerpiece of ridicule or comedy. In the book of Ruth, however, a different story is told. Ruth loved her mother-in-law, Naomi. Recently widowed, she begged to stay with Naomi wherever she went. In heart-felt words Ruth said, "Your people shall be my people, and your God shall be my God" (1:16). Naomi agreed and Ruth traveled with her to Bethlehem.

Not much is said about Naomi except that she loved and cared for Ruth. Obviously, Naomi's life was a powerful witness to the reality of God. Ruth was drawn to her—and to the God she worshiped. In the succeeding months and years, God led this young Moabite widow to a man named Boaz, whom she eventually married. As a result, she became the great-grandmother of David and a descendant in the line of the Messiah. What a profound impact was made by Naomi's life!

The book of Ruth is also the story of God's grace in the midst of difficult circumstances. Ruth's story occurred during the time of the judges—a time marked by disobedience, idolatry, and violence. Even in times of crisis and deepest despair, there are those who follow God and through whom God works. No matter how discouraging or antagonistic the world may seem, there are always people who follow God. And he will use anyone who is open to him to achieve his purposes. Ruth was a Moabitess and Boaz was a descendant of Rahab, a former prostitute from Jericho. Nevertheless, their offspring continued the family line through which the Messiah came into our world.

Read this book and be encouraged. God is at work in the world and he wants to use you. God could use you, as he used Naomi, to bring family and friends to him.

THE BLUEPRINT

1. Ruth remains loyal to Naomi (1:1–22)
2. Ruth gleans in Boaz's field (2:1–23)
3. Ruth follows Naomi's plan (3:1–18)
4. Ruth and Boaz are married (4:1–22)

When we first meet Ruth, she is a destitute widow. We follow her as she joins God's people, gleans in the grain fields, and risks her honor at the threshing floor of Boaz. In the end, we see Ruth becoming the wife of Boaz. What a picture of how we come to faith in Christ. We begin with no hope and are rebellious aliens with no part in the Kingdom of God. Then as we risk everything by putting our faith in Christ, God saves us, forgives us, rebuilds our lives, and gives us blessings which will last through eternity. Boaz's redeeming of Ruth is a picture of Christ redeeming us.

MEGATHEMES

THEME	EXPLANATION	IMPORTANCE
Faithfulness	Ruth's faithfulness to Naomi as a daughter-in-law and friend is a great example of love and loyalty. Ruth, Naomi, and Boaz are also faithful to God and his laws. Throughout the story we see how God is faithful in return.	Ruth's life was guided by faithfulness toward God and showed itself in loyalty toward the people she knew. To be loyal and loving in relationships, we must imitate God's faithfulness in our relationships with others.
Kindness	Ruth showed great kindness to Naomi. In turn, Boaz showed kindness to Ruth—a despised Moabite woman with no money. God showed his kindness to Ruth, Naomi, and Boaz by bringing them together for his purposes.	Just as Boaz showed his kindness by buying back land to guarantee Ruth and Naomi's inheritance, so Christ showed his kindness by purchasing us to guarantee our eternal life. God's kindness motivates us to love and honor him.
Integrity	Ruth showed high moral character by being loyal to Naomi, by her clean break from her former land and customs, and by her hard work in the fields. Boaz showed integrity in his moral standards, his honesty, and by following through on his commitments.	When we have experienced God's faithfulness and kindness, we should respond by living a godly life. Just as the values which Ruth and Boaz lived by were in sharp contrast to those of the culture portrayed in Judges, so our lives should stand out from the world around us.
Protection	We see God's care and protection over the lives of Naomi and Ruth. His supreme control over circumstances brings them safety and security. He guides the minds and activities of people to fulfill his purpose.	No matter how devastating our present situation may be, we can hope in God. His resources are infinite. We must believe that he can work in the life of any person—whether that person is a king or a stranger in a foreign land.
Prosperity/Blessing	Ruth and Naomi came to Bethlehem as poor widows, but they soon became prosperous through Ruth's marriage to Boaz. Ruth became the great-grandmother of King David. Yet the greatest blessing was not the money, the marriage, or the child; it was the quality of love and respect between Ruth, Boaz, and Naomi.	We tend to think of blessings in terms of prosperity rather than the high-quality relationships God makes possible for us. No matter what our economic situation, we can love and respect the people God has brought into our lives. In so doing, we give and receive blessings.

1. Ruth remains loyal to Naomi
Naomi's husband and sons die

1:1
Judg 2:16-18

1 Long ago when judges ruled in Israel, a man named Elimelech, from Bethlehem, left the country because of a famine and moved to the land of Moab. With him were his wife, Naomi, and his two sons, Mahlon and Chilion. ³During the time

1:1 *from Bethlehem,* literally, "They were Ephrathites from Bethlehem in Judah."

1:1 The story of Ruth takes place sometime during the period of the judges. These were dark days for Israel, when "everyone did whatever he wanted to—whatever seemed right in his own eyes" (Judges 17:6; 21:25). Perversion and moral depravity were the rule, not the exception. But in the midst of those dark and evil times, there were still some who followed God. This book tells of two such people, Naomi and Ruth. They are a beautiful picture of loyalty, friendship, and commitment—to God and to each other.

1:1, 2 Moab was the land east of the Dead Sea. It was one of the nations that oppressed Israel during the period of the judges (Judges 3:12ff). The famine must have been quite severe in Israel for Elimelech to move his family there. Even if Israel had already defeated Moab, there still would have been tensions between the two nations.

of their residence there, Elimelech died and Naomi was left with her two sons.

4, 5These young men, Mahlon and Chilion, married girls of Moab, Orpah and Ruth. But later, both men died, so that Naomi was left alone, without her husband or sons. 6, 7She decided to return to Israel with her daughters-in-law, for she had heard that the Lord had blessed his people by giving them good crops again.

1:6
Ex 4:31

8But after they had begun their homeward journey, she changed her mind and said to her two daughters-in-law, "Why don't you return to your parents' homes instead of coming with me? And may the Lord reward you for your faithfulness to your husbands and to me. 9And may he bless you with another happy marriage." Then she kissed them and they all broke down and cried.

10"No," they said. "We want to go with you to your people."

11But Naomi replied, "It is better for you to return to your own people. Do I have younger sons who could grow up to be your husbands? 12No, my daughters, return to your parents' homes, for I am too old to have a husband. And even if that were possible, and I became pregnant tonight, and bore sons, 13would you wait for them to grow up? No, of course not, my daughters; oh, how I grieve for you that the Lord has punished me in a way that injures you."

1:11
Deut 25:5

14And again they cried together, and Orpah kissed her mother-in-law good-bye, and returned to her childhood home; but Ruth insisted on staying with Naomi.

Ruth decides to go with Naomi to Bethlehem

15"See," Naomi said to her, "your sister-in-law has gone back to her people and to her gods; you should do the same."

16But Ruth replied, "Don't make me leave you, for I want to go wherever you go, and to live wherever you live; your people shall be my people, and your God shall

---

SETTING FOR THE STORY

Elimelech, Naomi, and their sons traveled from Bethlehem to the land of Moab because of a famine. After her husband and sons died, Naomi returned to Bethlehem with her daughter-in-law Ruth.

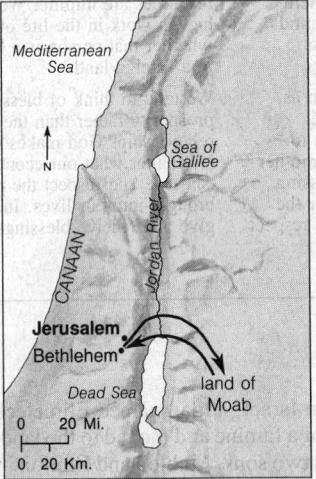

Mediterranean Sea

Sea of Galilee

CANAAN

Jordan River

N

Jerusalem
Bethlehem

Dead Sea

land of Moab

0   20 Mi.

0   20 Km.

1:4, 5 Friendly relationships with the Moabites were discouraged (Deuteronomy 23:6), but probably not forbidden since the Moabites lived outside the Promised Land. Marrying a Canaanite, however, was against God's Law (Deuteronomy 7:3). Moabites were not allowed to worship at the Tabernacle because they had not let the Israelites pass through their land during the Exodus from Egypt (Deuteronomy 23:3, 4).

As God's chosen nation, Israel should have set the standards of high moral living for the other nations. Ironically it was Ruth, a Moabitess, whom God used as an example of genuine spiritual character. This shows just how bleak life had become in Israel during those days.

1:8, 9 There was almost nothing worse than being a widow in the ancient world. Widows were taken advantage of or ignored. They were almost always poverty-stricken. The Law, therefore, provided that the nearest relative of the dead husband should care for the widow; but Naomi had no relatives in Moab, and she did not know if any of her relatives were alive in Israel.

In her desperate situation, Naomi had a very selfless attitude. Although she had decided to return to Israel, she encouraged Ruth and Orpah to stay in Moab and start their lives over, even though this would mean hardship for herself. Like Naomi, we must consider the needs of others and not just our own. As Naomi discovered, when you reach out to others, they often reach back to you.

1:11 Naomi's comment here refers to *levirate marriage,* the obligation of a dead man's brother to care for his widow (Deuteronomy 25:5–10). This law kept the widow from poverty and it provided a way for the family name of the dead husband to continue.

Naomi, however, had no other sons for Ruth or Orpah to marry, so she encouraged them to remain in their homeland and remarry. Orpah agreed, which was her right. But Ruth was willing to give up the possibility of security and children in order to care for Naomi.

1:16 Ruth was a Moabitess, but that didn't stop her from worshiping the true God, nor did it stop God from accepting her worship and heaping great blessings upon her. The Jews were not the only people God loved. God chose the Jews to be the people through whom the rest of the world would come to know him. This was fulfilled when Jesus Christ was born as a Jew. Through him, the entire world can come to know God. Acts 10:34 says that "the Jews are not God's only favorites." He accepts all those who worship him, working through all people regardless of their race, sex, or nationality. Ruth is a perfect example of God's impartiality. Although she belonged to a race often despised by Israel, she was blessed because of her faithfulness. She became a great-grandmother of King David and a direct ancestor of Jesus.

be my God; 17I want to die where you die, and be buried there. May the Lord do terrible things to me if I allow anything but death to separate us."

18And when Naomi saw that Ruth had made up her mind and could not be persuaded otherwise, she stopped urging her. 19So they both came to Bethlehem and the entire village was stirred by their arrival.

"Is it really Naomi?" the women asked.

1:20
Job 6:4

20But she told them, "Don't call me Naomi. Call me Mara," (Naomi means "pleasant"; Mara means "bitter") "for Almighty God has dealt me bitter blows. 21I went out full and the Lord has brought me home empty; why should you call me Naomi when the Lord has turned his back on me and sent such calamity!"

22(Their return from Moab and arrival in Bethlehem was at the beginning of the barley harvest.)

RUTH & NAOMI

The stories of several people in the Bible are woven together so well that they are almost inseparable. We know more about their relationship than we know about them as individuals. And in an age that worships individualism, their stories become helpful models of good relationships. Naomi and Ruth are beautiful examples of this blending of lives. Their cultures, family backgrounds, and ages were very different. As mother-in-law and daughter-in-law, they probably had many opportunities for tension as well as tenderness. And yet they were bound to each other.

They gave each other freedom in their commitment to one another. Naomi was willing to let Ruth return to her family. Ruth was willing to leave her homeland to go to Israel. Naomi even helped arrange Ruth's marriage to Boaz although it would change their relationship.

God was at the center of their intimate communication. Ruth came to know the God of Israel through Naomi. The older woman allowed Ruth to see, hear, and feel all the joy and anguish of her relationship to God. How often do you feel that your thoughts and questions about God should be left out of a close relationship? How often do you share your unedited thoughts about God with your spouse or friends? Sharing openly about our relationship with God can bring depth and intimacy to our relationships with others.

Strengths and accomplishments:
• A relationship where the greatest bond was their faith in God
• A relationship of strong mutual commitment
• A relationship in which each person tried to do what was best for the other

Lesson from their lives:
• God's living presence in a relationship overcomes differences that might otherwise create division and disharmony

Vital statistics:
• Where: Moab, Bethlehem
• Occupations: Wives, widows, gleaners
• Relatives: Elimelech, Mahlon, Chilion, Orpah, Boaz

Key verse:
"But Ruth replied, 'Don't make me leave you, for I want to go wherever you go, and to live wherever you live; your people shall be my people, and your God shall be my God' " (Ruth 1:16).

Their story is told in the book of Ruth. Matthew 1:5 also mentions Ruth.

1:20, 21 Naomi had experienced severe hardships. She had left Israel married and secure; she returned widowed and poor. Naomi changed her name to express the bitterness and pain she felt. Naomi was not rejecting God by openly expressing the pain she felt. However, she seems to have lost sight of the tremendous resources she had in her relationship with Ruth and with God. When you face bitter times, God welcomes your honest prayers, but be careful not to overlook the love, strength, and resources that he provides in relationships. And don't allow bitterness and

disappointment to blind you to positive opportunities.

1:22 Because Israel's climate is quite moderate, there are two harvests each year, in the spring and in the fall. The barley harvest took place in the spring, and it was during this time of hope and plenty that Ruth and Naomi returned to Bethlehem. Bethlehem was a farming community, and because it was the time of the harvest, there was plenty of leftover grain in the fields. This grain could be collected, or "gleaned," and then made into food. (See the note on 2:2 for more information on gleaning.)

2. Ruth gleans in Boaz's field

2 Now Naomi had an in-law there in Bethlehem who was a very wealthy man. His name was Boaz.

2One day Ruth said to Naomi, "Perhaps I can go out into the fields of some kind man to glean the free grain behind his reapers."

And Naomi said, "All right, dear daughter. Go ahead."

3So she did. And as it happened, the field where she found herself belonged to Boaz, this relative of Naomi's husband.

4, 5Boaz arrived from the city while she was there. After exchanging greetings with the reapers he said to his foreman, "Hey, who's that girl over there?"

6And the foreman replied, "It's that girl from the land of Moab who came back with Naomi. 7She asked me this morning if she could pick up the grains dropped by the reapers, and she has been at it ever since except for a few minutes' rest over there in the shade."

8, 9Boaz went over and talked to her. "Listen, my child," he said to her. "Stay right here with us to glean; don't think of going to any other fields. Stay right behind my women workers; I have warned the young men not to bother you; when you are thirsty, go and help yourself to the water."

10, 11She thanked him warmly. "How can you be so kind to me?" she asked. "You must know I am only a foreigner."

"Yes, I know," Boaz replied, "and I also know about all the love and kindness you have shown your mother-in-law since the death of your husband, and how you left your father and mother in your own land and have come here to live among strangers. 12May the Lord God of Israel, under whose wings you have come to take refuge, bless you for it."

13"Oh, thank you, sir," she replied. "You are so good to me, and I'm not even one of your workers!

14At lunch time Boaz called to her, "Come and eat with us."

So she sat with his reapers and he gave her food, more than she could eat. 15And

2:2
Lev 19:9,10
23:22

2:12
Ruth 1:16

2:14 *he gave her food,* literally, "ate the parched grain and dipped her morsels of food in the wine."

2:1 Bethlehem was about five miles southwest of Jerusalem. The town was surrounded by lush fields and olive groves. Its harvests were abundant.

Ruth and Naomi's return to Bethlehem was certainly part of God's plan, for in this town King David would be born (1 Samuel 16:1); and, as predicted by the prophet Micah (Micah 5:2), Jesus Christ would also be born there. This move, then, was more than merely convenient for Ruth and Naomi, it led to the fulfillment of the Scriptures.

2:2 When the wheat and barley were ready to be harvested, reapers were hired to cut down the stalks and tie them into bundles. Israelite law demanded that the corners of the fields not be harvested. In addition, any grain that was dropped was also to be left for the gleaners, poor people who were free to pick up the leftover grain (Leviticus 19:9; 23:22; Deuteronomy 24:19). The purpose of this law was to provide food for the poor and prevent the owners from hoarding. This law served as a type of welfare program in Israel. Because she was a widow with no means of providing for herself, Ruth went into the fields to glean the grain.

2:2, 3 Ruth made her home in a foreign land. Instead of depending on Naomi or waiting for good fortune to happen, she took the initiative. She went to work. She was not afraid of admitting her need or working hard to supply it. When Ruth went out to the fields, God provided for her. If you are waiting for God to provide, consider this: he may be waiting for you to take the first step to demonstrate just how important your need is.

2:7 Ruth's task, though menial, tiring, and perhaps degrading, was done faithfully. What is your attitude when the task you have been given is not up to your true potential? The task at hand may be all we can do, or it may be the work God wants us to do. Or, as in Ruth's case, it may be a test of our character that can open

up new doors of opportunity for us.

2:8, 9 Not only did Ruth take the initiative to work, she worked hard. There are times in our lives when hard work with little rest is our only option. Boaz noticed Ruth's hard work. Had she considered herself too proud or embarrassed to glean, she would have missed the opportunity of meeting Boaz, changing her life, and becoming the ancestor of a king and the Messiah.

2:10, 11 Foreigners were not always warmly welcomed in Israel, but Boaz gladly welcomed Ruth, because she had gained a reputation for showing kindness and generosity to others. Boaz was so impressed with Ruth that he let her follow directly behind his reapers in order to pick up the choicest grain that was dropped.

Ruth's past actions were a report card by which others judged her. Her good reputation was her most valuable asset. It came as a result of her hard work, her strong moral character, and her sensitivity, kindness, and loyalty to Naomi. A good reputation is built upon godly character and kindness towards others.

2:10–12 Ruth's life exhibited admirable qualities: she was hardworking, loving, kind, faithful, and brave. These qualities gained for her a good reputation, but only because she displayed them *consistently* in all areas of her life. Wherever Ruth went or whatever she did, her character remained the same.

Your reputation is formed by the people who watch you at work, in town, at home, in church. A good reputation comes by *consistently* living out the qualities you believe in—no matter what group of people or surroundings you are in.

2:15, 16 The book of Ruth is a classic example of good people in action. Boaz went far beyond the intent of the gleaners' law in demonstrating his kindness and generosity. Not only did he let Ruth glean in his field; he also told his workers to purposely snap

when she went back to work again, Boaz told his young men to let her glean right among the sheaves without stopping her, 16and to snap off some heads of barley and drop them on purpose for her to glean, and not to make any remarks. 17So she worked there all day, and in the evening when she had beaten out the barley she had gleaned, it came to a whole bushel! 18She carried it back into the city and gave it to her mother-in-law, with what was left of her lunch.

19"So much!" Naomi exclaimed. "Where in the world did you glean today? Praise the Lord for whoever was so kind to you." So Ruth told her mother-in-law all about it, and mentioned that the owner of the field was Boaz.

20"Praise the Lord for a man like that! God has continued his kindness to us as well as to your dead husband!" Naomi cried excitedly. "Why, that man is one of our closest relatives!"

21"Well," Ruth told her, "he said to come back and stay close behind his reapers until the entire field is harvested."

22"This is wonderful!" Naomi exclaimed. "Do as he has said. Stay with his girls right through the whole harvest; you will be safer there than in any other field!"

23So Ruth did, and gleaned with them until the end of the barley harvest, and then the wheat harvest, too.

3. Ruth follows Naomi's plan

3 One day Naomi said to Ruth, "My dear, isn't it time that I try to find a husband for you, and get you happily married again? 2The man I'm thinking of is Boaz! He has been so kind to us, and is a close relative. I happen to know that he will be winnowing barley tonight out on the threshing-floor. 3Now do what I tell you—bathe and put on some perfume and some nice clothes and go on down to the threshing-floor, but don't let him see you until he has finished his supper. 4Notice where he lies down to sleep; then go and lift the cover off his feet and lie down there, and he will tell you what to do concerning marriage."

2:20 *that man* (Boaz) *is one of our closest relatives,* literally, "a near relative, one of our redeemers."

3:2
Deut 25:5-10

---

off some grain and let it drop in her path. Out of his abundance, he provided for the needy. How often do we go beyond the accepted patterns of providing for those less fortunate?

2:19, 20 Naomi had felt bitter (1:20, 21), but her faith in God was still alive, and she praised God for guiding Ruth to the field of Boaz. In the midst of her sorrows, she still trusted God and acknowledged his goodness. We may feel bitter about a situation, but we must never despair about God's work in our lives.

2:20 Though Ruth may not have always recognized God's guidance in her life, he had been with her every step of the way. She went to glean and "just happened" to end up in the field owned by Boaz who "just happened" to be a close relative. This was more than mere coincidence. As you go about your daily tasks, God is working in your life in ways you may not even notice. We must not close the door on what God can do. For the believer, events do not occur by luck or coincidence. We have faith that God is directing our lives for his purpose.

3:1 As widows, Ruth and Naomi could only look forward to difficult times. (See the note on 1:8, 9 for more on a widow's life.) But when Naomi heard the news about Boaz, her hope for the future was renewed (2:20). Typical of her character, she thought first of Ruth, encouraging her to see if Boaz would take the responsibility of being a "kinsman-redeemer."

A kinsman-redeemer was a relative who volunteered to take responsibility for the extended family. Because Ruth's husband had died, the Law (Deuteronomy 25:5–10) provided that she could marry a brother of her dead husband (one of Naomi's sons). But Naomi had no more sons. In that case, the nearest relative to Ruth's husband could become a kinsman-redeemer and marry Ruth. The nearest relative did not have to marry the widow. If he chose not to, the next nearest relative could take his place. If no

one chose to help the widow, she would probably live in poverty the rest of her life, because in Israelite culture the inheritance was passed on to the son or nearest male relative, not to the wife. To take the sting out of these inheritance rules, there were laws for gleaning and kinsman-redeemers.

We have a kinsman-redeemer in Jesus Christ, who though he was God, came to earth as a man in order to save us. By his death on the cross, he has redeemed us from sin and hopelessness and thereby purchased us to be his own possession (1 Peter 1:18, 19). This guarantees our eternal inheritance.

3:2 The threshing floor was the place where the grain was separated from the harvested wheat. The wheat stalks were crushed, either by hand or by oxen, and the valuable grain (inner kernels) separated from the worthless chaff (the outside shell). The floor was made from rock or soil and located outside the village, usually on an elevated site where the winds would blow away the lighter chaff when the crushed wheat was thrown into the air (or winnowed). Boaz spent the night beside the threshing floor for two reasons: (1) to prevent theft, and (2) to wait for his turn to thresh grain. (Threshing was often done at night, because daylight hours were spent harvesting.)

3:4 Naomi's advice seems strange, but she was not suggesting a seductive act. Actually, Naomi was instructing Ruth to act in accordance with Israelite custom and law. It was common for servants to lie at the feet of their master and even share a part of his covering. Ruth was to apply this custom to the kinsman-redeemer law and thus inform Boaz of his responsibility to find someone to marry her or to marry her himself. It was family business, nothing romantic. But the story later became beautifully romantic as Ruth and Boaz developed an unselfish love and deep respect for each other.

5And Ruth replied, "All right. I'll do whatever you say."

Ruth approaches Boaz at the threshing floor

6,7So she went down to the threshing-floor that night and followed her mother-in-law's instructions. After Boaz had finished a good meal, he lay down very contentedly beside a heap of grain and went to sleep. Then Ruth came quietly and lifted the covering off his feet and lay there. 8Suddenly, around midnight, he wakened and sat up, startled. There was a woman lying at his feet!

9"Who are you?" he demanded.

"It's I, sir—Ruth," she replied. "Make me your wife according to God's law, for you are my close relative."

10"Thank God for a girl like you!" he exclaimed. "For you are being even kinder to Naomi now than before. Naturally you'd prefer a younger man, even though poor. But you have put aside your personal desires. 11Now don't worry about a thing, my child; I'll handle all the details, for everyone knows what a wonderful person you are. 12But there is one problem. It's true that I am a close relative, but there is someone else who is more closely related to you than I am. 13Stay here tonight, and in the morning I'll talk to him, and if he will marry you, fine; let him do his duty; but if he won't, then I will, I swear by Jehovah; lie down until the morning."

3:11
Prov 31:10

14So she lay at his feet until the morning and was up early, before daybreak, for he had said to her, "Don't let it be known that a woman was here at the threshing-floor."

15-18"Bring your shawl," he told her. Then he tied up a bushel and a half of barley in it as a present for her mother-in-law, and laid it on her back. Then she returned to the city.

"Well, what happened, dear?" Naomi asked her when she arrived home. She told Naomi everything and gave her the barley from Boaz, and mentioned his remark that she mustn't go home without a present.

Then Naomi said to her, "Just be patient until we hear what happens, for Boaz won't rest until he has followed through on this. He'll settle it today."

4. Ruth and Boaz are married
Boaz speaks to the nearest relative

4 So Boaz went down to the marketplace and found the relative he had mentioned.

"Say, come over here," he called to him. "I want to talk to you a minute."

So they sat down together. 2Then Boaz called for ten of the chief men of the village, and asked them to sit as witnesses.

3Boaz said to his relative, "You know Naomi, who came back to us from Moab.

4:3
Lev 25:25

4:1 *went down to the marketplace,* literally, "the gate" of the city.

3:5 As a foreigner, Ruth may have thought that Naomi's advice was odd. But Ruth followed the advice, because she knew Naomi was kind, trustworthy, and filled with moral integrity. Each of us knows a parent, older friend, or relative who is always looking out for our best interests. The experience and knowledge of such a person can be invaluable. Imagine what Ruth's life would have been like had she ignored her mother-in-law.

3:10 Boaz was an unselfish man. He had much to lose by honoring Ruth's request, especially since their first child would be Naomi's heir, not his. But Boaz focused on Ruth's virtuous qualities and was honored that she had come to him. This was remarkable in a culture that looked upon women, especially foreign women, more as property than as human beings.

3:12 Ruth and Naomi must have assumed that Boaz was their closest relative. Boaz, too, must have already considered marrying Ruth, because his answer to her shows he had been thinking

about it. One man in the city was a closer relative than Boaz, and this man had the first right to take Ruth as his wife. If he chose not to, then Boaz could marry Ruth (3:13).

3:18—4:1 Naomi said Boaz would follow through with his promise at once. He obviously had a reputation for keeping his word. He did not rest until his task was completed. Such reliable people stand out in any age and culture. Do others regard you as one who will do what you say? Keeping your word and following through on assignments should be high on anyone's priority list. Building a reputation for integrity, however, must be done one brick at a time.

4:1 Boaz knew where to find his relative—at the city gate. This was the center of activity. No one could enter or leave the city without traveling through the gate. Merchants set up their temporary shops near the gate which also served as "city hall." Here city officials gathered to transact business. Since there was so much activity, it was a good place to find witnesses (4:2) and an appropriate place for Boaz to make his transaction.

She is selling our brother Elimelech's property. ⁴I felt that I should speak to you about it so that you can buy it if you wish, with these respected men as witnesses. If you want it, let me know right away, for if you don't take it, I will. You have the first right to purchase it and I am next."

The man replied, "All right, I'll buy it."

⁵Then Boaz told him, "Your purchase of the land from Naomi requires your marriage to Ruth so that she can have children to carry on her husband's name, and to inherit the land."

4:6
Lev 25:25

⁶"Then I can't do it," the man replied. "For her son would become an heir to my property, too; you buy it."

4:7
Deut 25:8-10

⁷In those days it was the custom in Israel for a man transferring a right of purchase to pull off his sandal and hand it to the other party; this publicly validated the transaction. ⁸So, as the man said to Boaz, "You buy it for yourself," he drew off his sandal.

⁹Then Boaz said to the witnesses and to the crowd standing around, "You have seen that today I have bought all the property of Elimelech, Chilion, and Mahlon,

4:4 *if you want it,* literally, "if you want to redeem it." **4:6** *"For her son would become an heir to my property, too,"* or, "that would ruin my own inheritance."

Heroes are easier to admire than to define. They are seldom conscious of their moments of heroism, and others may not recognize their acts as heroic. Heroes simply do the right thing at the right time, whether or not they realize the impact their action will have. Perhaps the one quality they share is a tendency to think of others before they think of themselves. Boaz was a hero.

In his dealings with other people, he was always sensitive to their needs. His words to his employees, relatives, and others were colored with kindness. He offered help openly, not grudgingly. When he discovered who Ruth was, he took several steps to help her because she had been faithful to his relative Naomi. When Naomi advised Ruth to request his protection, he was ready to marry her if the legal complications could be worked out.

Boaz not only did what was right; he also did it right away. Of course he could not foresee all that his actions would accomplish. He could not have known that the child he would have by Ruth would be an ancestor of King David and Jesus. He only met the challenge of taking the right action in the situation facing him.

We are faced with this challenge in our daily choices. Like the closer relative, we are often more concerned with making the easy choice than with making the right one. Yet more often than not, the right choice is clear. Ask God to give you a special awareness in your choices today, as well as renewed commitment to make the right ones.

Strengths and accomplishments:
- A man of his word
- Sensitive to those in need, caring for his workers
- A keen sense of responsibility, integrity, doing things the right way
- A successful and shrewd businessman

Lessons from his life:
- It can be heroic to do what must be done and to do it right
- God often uses little decisions to carry out his big plan

Vital statistics:
- Where: Bethlehem
- Occupation: Wealthy farmer
- Relatives: Elimelech, Naomi, Ruth

Key verse:
"I have purchased Ruth the Moabitess, the widow of Mahlon, to be my wife, so that she can have a son to carry on the family name of her dead husband" (Ruth 4:10).

His story is told in the book of Ruth. He is also mentioned in Matthew 1:5.

4:3 Boaz cleverly presented his case to the relative. First he brought in new information not yet mentioned in the story— Elimelech, Naomi's former husband, still had some property in the area that was now for sale. As the nearest relative, this man had the first right to buy the land, which he agreed to do (Leviticus 25:25). But then Boaz said that according to the Law, if the relative bought the property he also had to marry the widow (probably because Mahlon, Ruth's former husband and Elimelech's son, had inherited the property). With this stipulation, the relative backed down. He did not want to complicate the inheritance he was leaving for his own sons. He may have feared that if he had a son through Ruth, some of his estate would transfer away from his family to the family of Elimelech. Whatever his reason, the way was now clear for Boaz to marry Ruth.

from Naomi, ¹⁰and that with it I have purchased Ruth the Moabitess, the widow of Mahlon, to be my wife, so that she can have a son to carry on the family name of her dead husband."

¹¹And all the people standing there, and the witnesses replied, "We are witnesses. May the Lord make this woman, who has now come into your home, as fertile as Rachel and Leah, from whom all the nation of Israel descended! May you be a great and successful man in Bethlehem, ¹²and may the descendants the Lord will give you from this young woman be as numerous and honorable as those of our ancestor Perez, the son of Tamar and Judah."

4:11
Gen 29:25-30

4:12
Gen 38:29
46:12

The descendants of Boaz and Ruth

¹³So Boaz married Ruth, and when he slept with her, the Lord gave her a son.

¹⁴And the women of the city said to Naomi, "Bless the Lord who has given you this little grandson; may he be famous in Israel. ¹⁵May he restore your youth and take care of you in your old age; for he is the son of your daughter-in-law who loves you so much, and who has been kinder to you than seven sons!"

¹⁶, ¹⁷Naomi took care of the baby, and the neighbor women said, "Now at last Naomi has a son again!"

And they named him Obed. He was the father of Jesse and grandfather of King David.

¹⁸⁻²²This is the family tree of Boaz, beginning with his ancestor Perez: Perez, Hezron, Ram, Amminadab, Nashon, Salmon, Boaz, Obed, Jesse, David.

4:18-22
Mt 1:3-6

4:12 Of all the ancestors (including Abraham) they could have named, why did these men mention Perez? The birth of Perez was an example of the "levirate" practice, whereby the brother or relative of the dead husband married his widow (Genesis 38). Boaz, as kinsman-redeemer, was following this levirate practice since Ruth's former husband had no brothers. (See the note on 3:1.) The descendants of Perez made Judah a prominent tribe. Boaz, David, and all the Judean kings were descendants of Perez.

4:15 Ruth's kindness was known and recognized throughout the city. From the beginning of the book of Ruth to the end, her kindness toward others remained unchanged.

4:15 God brought great blessings out of Naomi's tragedy, even greater blessings than "seven sons" (indicating the great blessing of an abundance of heirs). Throughout her tough times, Naomi continued to trust God. And God, in his time, blessed her greatly. Even in our sorrow and calamity, God can bring great blessings.

Be like Naomi, and don't turn your back on God when tragedy strikes. Don't ask "How can God allow this to happen to me?" Instead, trust him. He will be with you even in the hard times.

4:16, 17 To some, the book of Ruth may be just a nice story about a girl who got lucky. But in reality, the whole series of events recorded in Ruth were part of God's preparations for the birth of King David and for Jesus Christ, the promised Messiah. Just as Ruth was unaware of this larger purpose in her life, we will never know the full purpose and importance of our lives until we are able to look back on the whole picture from the perspective of eternity. We must make our choices with God's eternal values in mind. Because of Ruth's faithful obedience, her life and legacy carried great significance even though she couldn't see the end result. Live in faithfulness to God, knowing that the significance of your life will extend beyond your lifetime.

KEY PLACES IN 1 SAMUEL

1 Ramah Samuel was born in Ramah. Before his birth, Samuel's mother Hannah made a promise to God that she would dedicate her son to serve God alongside the priests in the Tabernacle at Shiloh (1:1—2:11).

2 Shiloh The focal point of Israel's worship was at Shiloh where the Tabernacle and the Ark of the Covenant resided. Eli was the High Priest, but his sons, Hophni and Phinehas, were evil men who took advantage of the

people. Samuel, however, served God faithfully and God blessed him as he grew (2:12—3:21).

3 Kiriath-jearim Israel was constantly at odds with the Philistines, and another battle was brewing. Hophni and Phinehas brought the Ark of the Covenant from Shiloh to the battlefield, believing that its mere presence would bring the Israelites victory. The Israelites were defeated by the Philistines at Ebenezer and the Ark was captured. However, the Philistines soon found out that the Ark was

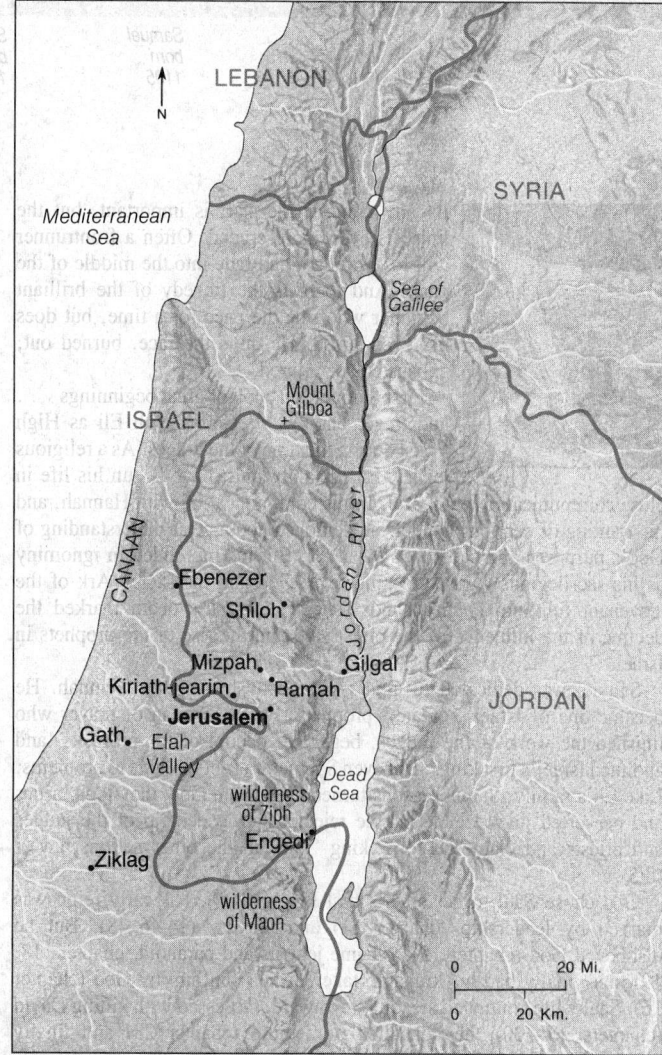

Modern names and boundaries are shown in gray.

6 **Elah Valley** Saul won many other battles, but over time he proved to be arrogant, sinful, and rebellious until God finally rejected him as king. Unknown to Saul, a young shepherd and musician named David was anointed to be Israel's next king. But it would be many years before David sat upon the throne. Ironically, Saul hired David to play the harp in his palace. Saul grew to like David so much that he made him his personal bodyguard. In one particular battle with the Philistines in the Elah Valley, David killed Goliath, the Philistines' mightiest soldier. But this victory was the beginning of the end of Saul's love for David. The Israelites praised David more than Saul, causing Saul to become so jealous that he plotted to kill David (12:1—22:23).

7 **The Wilderness** Even anointed kings are not exempt from troubles. David literally ran for his life from King Saul, hiding with his band of followers in the wilderness of Ziph (where the men of Ziph constantly betrayed him), the wilderness of Maon, and the caves of Engedi. Though he had opportunities to kill Saul, David refused to do so because Saul was God's anointed king (23:1—26:25).

8 **Gath** David moved his men and family to Gath, the Philistine city where King Achish lived. Saul then stopped chasing him. The Philistines seemed to welcome this famous fugitive from Israel (27:1–4).

9 **Ziklag** Desiring privacy in return for his pretended loyalty to King Achish, David asked for a city in which to house his men and family. Achish gave him Ziklag. From there David conducted raids against the cities of the Geshurites, Girzites, and Amalekites, making sure no one escaped to tell the tale (27:5–12). David later conquered the Amalekites after they raided Ziklag (30:1–31).

10 **Mount Gilboa** War with the Philistines broke out again in the north, near Mount Gilboa. Saul, who no longer relied on God, consulted a witch in a desperate attempt to contact Samuel for help. In the meantime, David was sent back to Ziklag because the Philistine commanders did not trust his loyalty in battle against Israel. The Philistines slaughtered the Israelites on Mount Gilboa, killing King Saul and his three sons, including David's loyal friend Jonathan. Without God, Saul led a bitter and misguided life. The consequences of his sinful actions not only affected him, but hurt his family and the entire nation (28:1—31:13).

not quite the great battle trophy they expected. For God sent plagues upon every Philistine city into which the Ark was brought. Finally, the Philistines sent it back to Kiriath-jearim in Israel (4:1—7:4).

4 **Mizpah** The Israelites' defeat made them realize that God was no longer blessing them. Samuel called the people together at Mizpah and asked them to fast and pray in sorrow for their sins. The convocation at Mizpah was a tempting target for the confident Philistines who advanced for an attack. But God intervened and routed their mighty army. Meanwhile, Samuel was judging cases throughout Israel. But as Samuel grew old, the people came to him at Ramah (his home base) demanding a king in order to be like the other nations. At Mizpah, Saul was chosen by sacred lot to be Israel's first king with the blessing, but not the approval, of God and Samuel (7:5—10:27).

5 **Gilgal** A battle with the Ammonites proved Saul's leadership abilities to the people of Israel. He protected the people of Jabesh-gilead and scattered the Ammonite army. Samuel and the people crowned Saul as king of Israel at Gilgal (11:1–15).

1 SAMUEL

VITAL STATISTICS

PURPOSE:
To record the life of Samuel, Israel's last judge; the reign and decline of Saul, the first king; and the choice and preparation of David, Israel's greatest king

AUTHOR:
Probably Samuel, but also includes writings from the prophets Nathan and Gad (1 Chronicles 29:29)

SETTING:
The book begins in the days of the judges and describes Israel's transition from a theocracy (led by God) to a monarchy (led by a king).

KEY VERSES:
" 'Do as they say,' the Lord replied, 'for I am the one they are rejecting, not you—they don't want me to be their king any longer. . . . but warn them about what it will be like to have a king!' " (8:7, 9).

KEY PEOPLE:
Eli, Hannah, Samuel, Saul, Jonathan, David

IN any contest, the start is important, but the finish is even more crucial. Often a frontrunner will lose strength and fade into the middle of the pack. And there is the tragedy of the brilliant beginner who sets the pace for a time, but does not even finish. He quits the race, burned out, exhausted, or injured.

First Samuel is a book of great beginnings . . . and tragic endings. It begins with Eli as High Priest during the time of the judges. As a religious leader, Eli certainly must have begun his life in close communication with God. In his communication with Hannah, and his training of her son Samuel, he demonstrated a clear understanding of God's purposes and call (chapters 1, 3). But his life ended in ignominy as his sacrilegious sons were judged by God and the sacred Ark of the Covenant fell into enemy hands (chapter 4). Eli's death marked the decline of the influence of the priesthood and the rise of the prophets in Israel.

Samuel was dedicated to God's service by his mother, Hannah. He became one of Israel's greatest prophets. He was a man of prayer who finished the work of the judges, began the school of the prophets, and anointed Israel's first kings. But even Samuel was not immune to problems. Like Eli's family, Samuel's sons turned away from God; they took bribes and perverted justice. The people rejected the leadership of the judges and priests and clamored for a king "like all the other nations have" (8:5).

God chose Saul to be Israel's first king (10:24). His early reign was marked by leadership (chapter 11) and bravery (14:46–48). But he disobeyed God (chapter 15), became jealous and paranoid (chapters 18, 19), and finally had his kingship taken away from him by God (chapter 16). Saul's life continued steadily downward. Obsessed with killing David (chapters 20—30), he consulted a medium (chapter 28) and finally committed suicide (chapter 31).

As you read 1 Samuel, note the transition from theocracy to monarchy, exult in the classic stories of David and Goliath, David and Jonathan, David and Abigail, and watch the rise of the influence of the prophets. But in the midst of reading all the history and adventure, determine to run your spiritual race from start to finish.

THE BLUEPRINT

A. ELI AND SAMUEL (1:1—7:17)
1. Samuel's birth and childhood
2. War with the Philistines

We see a vivid contrast between young Samuel and Eli's sons. Eli's sons were selfish, but Samuel was helpful. Eli's sons defrauded people, but Samuel grew in wisdom and gave the people messages from God. As an adult, Samuel became a prophet, priest, and judge over Israel. A person's actions reflect his character. This was true of Samuel and Eli's sons. It is also true of us. Strive, like Samuel, to keep your heart pure before God.

B. SAMUEL AND SAUL (8:1—15:35)
1. Saul becomes king of Israel
2. God rejects Saul for disobedience

Saul showed great promise. He was strong, tall, and modest. God's Spirit came upon him and Samuel was his counselor. But Saul deliberately disobeyed God and became an evil king. We must not base our hopes or future on our potential. Instead, we must consistently obey God in all areas of life. God evaluates obedience, not potential.

C. SAUL AND DAVID (16:1—31:13)
1. Samuel anoints David as king
2. David and Goliath
3. David and Jonathan's friendship
4. Saul pursues David
5. Saul's defeat and death

David quickly killed Goliath, but waited patiently for God to deal with Saul. Although David was anointed to be Israel's next king, he had to wait years to realize this promise. The difficult circumstances in life and the times of waiting often refine, teach, and prepare us for the future responsibilities God has for us.

MEGATHEMES

THEME	EXPLANATION	IMPORTANCE
King	Because Israel had corrupt priests and judges, the people wanted a king. They wanted to be organized like the surrounding nations. Though it was against his original purpose, God chose a king for them.	Establishing a monarchy did not solve Israel's problems. What God desires is the genuine devotion of each person's mind and heart to him. No government or set of laws can substitute for the rule of God in your heart and life.
God's Control	Israel prospered as long as the people regarded God as their true king. When the leaders strayed from God's Law, God intervened in their personal lives and overruled their actions. In this way, God maintained ultimate control over Israel's history.	God is always at work in this world, even when we can't see what he is doing. No matter what kinds of pressures we must endure or how many changes we must face, God is ultimately in control of our situation. Being confident of God's sovereignty, we can face the difficult situations in our lives with boldness.
Leadership	God guided his people using different forms of leadership: judges, priests, prophets, kings. Those whom he chose for these different offices, such as Eli, Samuel, Saul, and David, portrayed different styles of leadership. Yet the success of each leader depended on his devotion to God, not his position, leadership style, wisdom, age, or strength.	When Eli, Samuel, Saul, and David disobeyed God, they faced tragic consequences. Sin affected what they accomplished for God and how some of them raised their children. Being a real leader means letting God guide all aspects of your activities, values, and goals, including the way you raise your children.
Obedience	To God, "obedience is far better than sacrifice" (15:22). God wanted his people to obey, serve, and follow him with a whole heart rather than to maintain a superficial commitment based on tradition or ceremonial systems.	Although we are free from the sacrificial system of the Jewish law, we may still rely on outward observances to substitute for inward commitment. God desires that all our work and worship be motivated by genuine, heart-felt devotion to him.
God's Faithfulness	God faithfully kept the promises he made to Israel. He responded to his people with tender mercy and swift justice. In showing mercy, he faithfully acted in the best interest of his people. In showing justice, he was faithful to his word and perfect moral nature.	Because God is faithful, he can be counted on to be merciful towards us. Yet God is also just and he will not tolerate rebellion against him. His faithfulness and unselfish love should inspire us to dedicate ourselves to him completely. We must never take his mercy for granted.

A. ELI AND SAMUEL (1:1—7:17)

Israel has been ruled by judges for over 200 years. Eli and Samuel are the last of those judges. Samuel is born near the end of Eli's life. He grows up in the Tabernacle as a priest-in-training under Eli and is well qualified to serve Israel as both a priest and judge. Although the nation has fallen away from God, it is clear that God is preparing Samuel from the very beginning to lead the nation back to right living. God is always in control; he is able to bring his people back to him.

1. Samuel's birth and childhood

God answers Hannah's prayer for a son

1 This is the story of Elkanah, a man of the tribe of Ephraim who lived in Ramathaim-zophim, in the hills of Ephraim.

His father's name was Jeroham,
His grandfather was Elihu,
His great-grandfather was Tohu,
His great-great-grandfather was Zuph.

²He had two wives, Hannah and Peninnah. Peninnah had some children, but Hannah didn't.

³Each year Elkanah and his families journeyed to the Tabernacle at Shiloh to worship the Lord of the heavens and to sacrifice to him. (The priests on duty at that time were the two sons of Eli—Hophni and Phinehas.) ⁴On the day he presented his sacrifice, Elkanah would celebrate the happy occasion by giving presents to Peninnah and her children; ⁵but although he loved Hannah very much, he could give her only one present, for the Lord had sealed her womb; so she had no children to give presents to. ⁶Peninnah made matters worse by taunting Hannah because of her barrenness. ⁷Every year it was the same—Peninnah scoffing and laughing at her as they went to Shiloh, making her cry so much she couldn't eat.

1:1
1 Chron
6:22-28
6:33-38

1:2
Gen 29:30; 30:1
Deut 21:15-17

1:3
Ex 34:22,23
Deut 12:4-7
Josh 18:1,2
1 Sam 2:12
4:4,11
Lk 2:41,42

1:5
Gen 20:18; 30:2

1:1 The book of 1 Samuel begins in the days when the judges still ruled Israel, possibly during the closing years of Samson's life. Samuel was Israel's last judge, and the first priest and prophet to serve during the time of a king. He was the best example of what a good judge should be, governing the people by God's Word and not by his own impulses. Samuel was the man who anointed Saul as Israel's first king.

1:2 Although many great leaders in the Old Testament had more than one wife (such as Abraham, Jacob, and David), this was not God's original intention for marriage. Genesis 2:24 states that in marriage, two people become one flesh. Why then did polygamy exist among God's people? First, it was to produce more offspring to help in the man's work and to assure the continuation of the man's family line. Numerous children were a symbol of status and wealth. Second, in societies where many young men were killed in battle, polygamy became an accepted way of supporting women who otherwise would have remained unmarried and, very likely, destitute. Nevertheless, polygamy often caused serious family problems, as we see in this story of Hannah and Peninnah.

1:3 The Tabernacle was located at Shiloh, the religious center of the nation. Three times a year all Israelite men were required to attend a religious feast held at the Tabernacle: the Passover, the Feast of Shelters, and the Feast of Weeks (Deuteronomy 16:16). Elkanah made this pilgrimage regularly to fulfill God's commands. (See Exodus 23:14–17 for the regulations concerning the pilgrimage, and see the note on Exodus 40:34 for more on the Tabernacle.)

1:6 Hannah had been unable to conceive children, and in Old Testament times, a barren woman was thought to be a failure. Her barrenness was a social embarrassment for her husband. Children were a very important part of the economic structure of society. They were a source of labor for the family and it was their duty to care for their parents in their old age. If a wife could not bear children she was often obligated, by ancient Middle Eastern

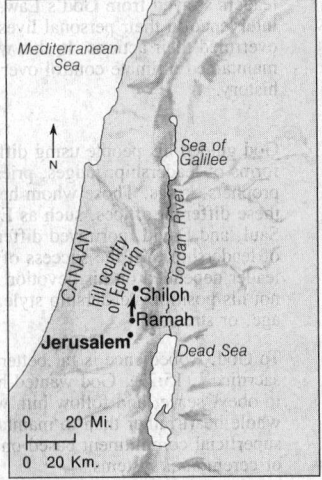

THE JOURNEY TO SHILOH
Each year El-kanah and his family traveled from their home at Ramah to Shiloh, where they worshiped and sacrificed at God's Tabernacle.

custom, to give one of her servant girls to her husband to bear children for her. Although Elkanah could have left Hannah (a husband was permitted to divorce a barren wife), he remained lovingly devoted to her despite social criticism and his rights under civil law.

1:7 Part of God's plan for Hannah involved postponing her years of childbearing. While Peninnah and Elkanah looked at Hannah's outward circumstances, God was moving ahead with his plan. Can you think of others who are struggling with the way God is working in their lives and who need your support? By supporting those who are struggling, you may be helping them remain obedient to God and confident in his plan for their lives.

1:8
Ruth 4:15

8"What's the matter, Hannah?" Elkanah would exclaim. "Why aren't you eating? Why make such a fuss over having no children? Isn't having me better than having ten sons?"

9One evening after supper, when they were at Shiloh, Hannah went over to the Tabernacle. Eli the priest was sitting at his customary place beside the entrance. 10She was in deep anguish and was crying bitterly as she prayed to the Lord.

1:11
Gen 29:32
Num 6:1-6
30:6-11
Judg 13:5
Lk 1:15

11And she made this vow: "O Lord of heaven, if you will look down upon my sorrow and answer my prayer and give me a son, then I will give him back to you, and he'll be yours for his entire lifetime, and his hair shall never be cut."

12, 13Eli noticed her mouth moving as she was praying silently and, hearing no sound, thought she had been drinking.

1:14
Acts 2:13

14"Must you come here drunk?" he demanded. "Throw away your bottle."

1:15
Ps 42:4
142:1,2
Lam 2:19

15, 16"Oh, no, sir!" she replied, "I'm not drunk! But I am very sad and I was pouring out my heart to the Lord. Please don't think that I am just some drunken bum!"

1:17
Ps 20:3

17"In that case," Eli said, "cheer up! May the Lord of Israel grant you your petition, whatever it is!"

18"Oh, thank you, sir!" she exclaimed, and went happily back, and began to take her meals again.

1:19
Gen 21:1,2
30:22
Ex 2:24
Ps 106:45

19, 20The entire family was up early the next morning and went to the Tabernacle to worship the Lord once more. Then they returned home to Ramah, and when Elkanah slept with Hannah, the Lord remembered her petition; in the process of time, a baby boy was born to her. She named him Samuel (meaning "asked of God") because, as she said, "I asked the Lord for him."

Hannah fulfills her promise to God

1:21
Lk 2:22

21, 22The next year Elkanah and Peninnah and her children went on the annual trip to the Tabernacle without Hannah, for she told her husband, "Wait until the baby is weaned, and then I will take him to the Tabernacle and leave him there."

23"Well, whatever you think best," Elkanah agreed. "May the Lord's will be done."

1:19, 20 *named him Samuel (meaning "asked of God").* This was a play on words. The word *Samuel* in Hebrew sounds like the word "to ask."

1:8 Hannah knew her husband loved her, but even his encouragement could not comfort her. She could not keep from listening to Peninnah's jeers and letting her words erode her self-confidence. Although we cannot keep others from unjustly criticizing us, we can choose how we will react to the criticism. Rather than dwelling upon our problems, we can enjoy the loving relationships God has brought into our lives.

1:10 Hannah had good reason to feel discouraged. She was unable to bear children; she shared her husband with a woman who ridiculed her (1:7); her loving husband could offer little encouragement (1:8); and even the High Priest misunderstood her motives (1:14). But instead of retaliating or giving up hope, Hannah prayed. She brought her problem honestly before God.

Each of us may face times of "barrenness" in our lives when nothing "comes to birth" in our work, service, or relationships. It is difficult to pray in faith when we feel so ineffective. But prayer opens the way for God to work, as Hannah discovered (1:19, 20).

1:11 In return for conceiving a son, Hannah vowed to dedicate him to God for lifetime service. Hannah may have been making a Nazirite vow which parents could take for their unborn children. The Nazirite vow was a promise to be set apart for special service to God. (See the notes on Numbers 6:1, 2 and Judges 13:5.) As long as the vow was in effect, the person's hair could not be cut. Although some vows were temporary, Hannah's vow was for life.

1:11 Be careful what you promise in prayer because God may

take you up on it. Hannah so desperately wanted her prayer to be answered that she was willing to strike a bargain with God. God took her up on her promise, and to Hannah's credit, she followed through on her part, even though it must have been very painful (1:27, 28).

Although we are not in a position to barter with God, he may still choose to answer a prayer which has an attached promise. When you pray, ask yourself, "Will I follow through on any promises I make to God if he grants my request?" It is dishonest and dangerous to ignore a promise, especially to God.

1:12–14 When you notice something is wrong with another person, what is your first reaction? Eli made a snap judgment before he knew all the facts. It is easy to misunderstand motives and actions. Be sensitive to the fact that, like Hannah, someone may be facing tremendous burdens.

1:18 Earlier Hannah had been discouraged to the point of being physically sick and unable to eat. Here she returns home well and happy. The change in her attitude may be attributed to three factors: (1) her honest prayer to God (1:11), (2) her resolve to leave the problem with God (1:18), and (3) the encouragement she received from Eli. This is the antidote for discouragement: tell God how you really feel and leave your problems with him. Then rely upon the support of good friends.

So she stayed home until the baby was weaned. ²⁴Then, though he was still so small, they took him to the Tabernacle in Shiloh, along with a three-year-old bull for the sacrifice, and a bushel of flour and some wine. ²⁵After the sacrifice they took the child to Eli.

²⁶"Sir, do you remember me?" Hannah asked him. "I am the woman who stood here that time praying to the Lord! ²⁷I asked him to give me this child, and he has given me my request; ²⁸and now I am giving him to the Lord for as long as he lives." So she left him there at the Tabernacle for the Lord to use.

Hannah's prayer of thanks

2 This was Hannah's prayer:

"How I rejoice in the Lord!
How he has blessed me!
Now I have an answer for my enemies,
For the Lord has solved my problem.
How I rejoice!
²No one is as holy as the Lord!
There is no other God,
Nor any Rock like our God.
³Quit acting so proud and arrogant!
The Lord knows what you have done,
And he will judge your deeds.
⁴Those who were mighty are mighty no more!
Those who were weak are now strong.
⁵Those who were well are now starving;
Those who were starving are fed.
The barren woman now has seven children;
She with many children has no more!
⁶The Lord kills,
The Lord gives life.
⁷Some he causes to be poor
And others to be rich.
He cuts one down
And lifts another up.

1:24
Num 15:8,9,10

2:1
Ex 15:1,2
Deut 32:3,4
Isa 12:2,3
Lk 1:47,68

2:2
Ex 15:11
Deut 4:35
32:30,31
1 Sam 2:2
2 Sam 22:32
Ps 18:2

2:3
1 Sam 16:7
1 Kgs 8:39
Prov 8:13; 16:2
29:11,12

2:4
Ps 37:15
46: 7-9

2:5
Ruth 4:15
Ps 113:9
Jer 15:9
Lk 1:53

2:6
Deut 32:39
2 Kgs 5:7
Rev 1:17,18

2:7
Deut 8:17,18
Job 1:21
5:10,11
Eccl 2:24-26
Jas 4:10

1:24, 25 At each of the great annual feasts, several different types of sacrifices were offered to God. Some required animal sacrifices for the forgiveness of sins, some required food or grain offerings for praise and thanksgiving, and some required a liquid to be poured out at the base of the altar for dedication. Elkanah and Hannah took a bull, some flour, and some wine to the annual feast in order to offer several types of sacrifices, including one to dedicate their child Samuel to God. (See Numbers 15:1–10 for more on the different types of offerings.)

1:24, 25 To follow through on her promise (1:11), Hannah gave up what she wanted most—her son—and presented him to Eli to serve God in the Tabernacle. In dedicating her son to God, Hannah was dedicating her entire life and future to God. Since Samuel's life was from God, Hannah was not really giving him up. Rather, she was returning him to God who had given him to Hannah in the first place. These verses show us the nature of the gifts we are to give to God. Are they gifts which cost us little (Sunday mornings, a comfortable tithe), or are they gifts of sacrifice? Are you presenting God with tokens, or are you presenting him with your entire life?

1:28 Samuel was probably three years old—the customary age for weaning—when his mother left him at the Tabernacle. She did not, of course, forget her much-wanted son. She visited him regularly. And each year she brought him a linen robe just like Eli's (2:19). In later years, Samuel lived in Ramah (7:17), the

hometown of his parents (1:19, 20).

2:1–10 Hannah praised God for his answer to her prayer for a son. The theme of her "poetic prayer" was her confidence in God's sovereignty and her thankfulness for his blessings. Mary, the mother of Jesus, modeled her own praise song, called the Magnificat, after Hannah's prayer (Luke 1:46–55). Like Hannah and Mary, we should be confident of God's ultimate control over the events in our lives, and we should be thankful for the ways he has blessed us. By praising him for all good gifts, we are acknowledging his ultimate control over all the affairs of life.

2:2 Hannah praises God for being a Rock—firm, strong, and unchanging. In our fast-paced world, friends come and go and circumstances change. It's difficult to find a solid foundation that will not change. Those who devote their lives to people, causes, possessions, or other finite things are trusting their security to that which is transitory. The goals and possessions for which we work so hard will all pass away. However, God is always present and ready to help, even when all else seems to be falling apart.

2:3–5 Most likely, in these verses Hannah was referring to Peninnah's arrogance and chiding. Hannah did not have to get even with her, however, because she understood that God is all-knowing, and that he will judge sin and arrogance even if it is well-hidden. No one can get away with sin, and so Hannah wisely left judgment up to God. Resist the temptation to take judgment into your own hands.

2:8
Job 36:7
38:4-7; 42:10
Ps 75:6,7
Jas 2:5

8He lifts the poor from the dust—
Yes, from a pile of ashes—
And treats them as princes
Sitting in the seats of honor.
For all the earth is the Lord's
And he has set the world in order.

2:9
Ps 33:16,17
Jer 9:23,24
Zech 4:6
Mt 8:12

9He will protect his godly ones,
But the wicked shall be silenced in darkness.
No one shall succeed by strength alone.

2:10
Ex 15:6; 19:18
1 Sam 7:10
Ps 18:13
21:1,7; 96:13

10Those who fight against the Lord shall be broken;
He thunders against them from heaven.
He judges throughout the earth.
He gives mighty strength to his King,
And gives great glory to his anointed one.

11So they returned home to Ramah without Samuel; and the child became the Lord's helper, for he assisted Eli the priest.

HANNAH

Hannah's prayer shows us that all we have and receive is on loan from God. Hannah might have had many excuses for being a possessive mother. But when God answered her prayer, she followed through on her promise to dedicate Samuel to God's service.

She discovered that the greatest joy in having a child is to give that child fully and freely back to God. She entered motherhood prepared to do what all mothers must eventually do—let go of their children.

When children are born, they are completely dependent upon their parents for all their basic necessities. This causes some parents to forget that those same children will grow towards independence within the span of a few short years. Being sensitive to the different stages of that healthy process will greatly strengthen family relationships; resistance or denial of that process will cause great pain. We must gradually let go of our children in order to allow them to become mature, interdependent adults.

Strengths and accomplishments:
• Mother of Samuel, Israel's greatest judge
• Fervent in worship; effective in prayer
• Willing to follow through on even a costly commitment

Weakness:
• Struggled with her sense of self-worth because she was unable to have children

Lessons from her life:
• God hears and answers prayer
• Our children are gifts from God
• God is concerned for the oppressed and afflicted

Vital statistics:
• Where: Ephraim
• Occupation: Homemaker
• Relatives: Husband: Elkanah. Son: Samuel. Later, three other sons and two daughters.
• Contemporaries: Eli, the priest

Key verses:
"I am the woman who stood here that time praying to the Lord! I asked him to give me this child, and he has given me my request; and now I am giving him to the Lord for as long as he lives" (1 Samuel 1:26–28).

Her story is told in 1 Samuel 1, 2.

2:10 Living in a world where the threat of a nuclear holocaust is always present and where evil abounds can cause us to forget that God is sovereign over all things. Hannah saw God as (1) solid as a rock (2:2); (2) the one who watches what we do (2:3); (3) sovereign over all the affairs of people (2:4–8); and (4) the supreme judge who administers perfect justice (2:10).

2:11 As Eli's assistant, Samuel's responsibilities would have included opening the Tabernacle doors each morning (3:15),

cleaning the furniture, and sweeping the floors. As he grew older, Samuel would have assisted Eli in the offering of sacrifices. The fact that he was wearing a linen ephod (a garment worn only by priests) shows that he was a priest-in-training (2:18). Because Samuel was Eli's helper, Scripture says he was God's helper too. When you serve others—even in carrying out ordinary tasks—you are serving God. Remembering that ultimately it is God whom we serve, gives dignity to every job.

Samuel serves the Lord

12Now the sons of Eli were evil men who didn't love the Lord. 13, 14It was their regular practice to send out a servant whenever anyone was offering a sacrifice, and while the flesh of the sacrificed animal was boiling, the servant would put a three-pronged fleshhook into the pot and demand that whatever it brought up be given to Eli's sons. They treated all of the Israelites in this way when they came to Shiloh to worship. 15Sometimes the servant would come even before the rite of burning the fat on the altar had been performed, and he would demand raw meat before it was boiled, so that it could be used for roasting.

16If the man offering the sacrifice replied, "Take as much as you want, but the fat must first be burned," [as the law requires], then the servant would say,

"No, give it to me now or I'll take it by force."

17So the sin of these young men was very great in the eyes of the Lord; for they treated the people's offerings to the Lord with contempt.

18Samuel, though only a child, was the Lord's helper and wore a little linen robe just like the priest's. 19Each year his mother made a little coat for him and brought it to him when she came with her husband for the sacrifice. 20Before they returned home Eli would bless Elkanah and Hannah and ask God to give them other children to take the place of this one they had given to the Lord. 21And the Lord gave Hannah three sons and two daughters. Meanwhile Samuel grew up in the service of the Lord.

22Eli was now very old, but he was aware of what was going on around him. He knew, for instance, that his sons were seducing the young women who assisted at the entrance of the Tabernacle.

23, 24, 25"I have been hearing terrible reports from the Lord's people about what you are doing," Eli told his sons. "It is an awful thing to make the Lord's people sin. Ordinary sin receives heavy punishment, but how much more this sin of yours

2:16 *as the law requires,* implied. **2:18** *a little linen robe just like the priest's,* literally, "wore a linen ephod."

2:12	1 Sam 1:3
	4:4,11
	Jer 2:8; 9:3,6
2:13	Lev 7:20,28-36
2:15	Lev 3:2-5; 7:30
2:17	Mal 2:7-9
2:19	1 Sam 1:3
2:21	Gen 21:1
	1 Sam 3:19-21
	Lk 2:40
2:23	Num 15:30
	Deut 1:17

2:12ff It was stipulated in the Law that the needs of all the Levites were to be met through the tithes of the people (Numbers 18:20–24; Joshua 13:14, 33). Since Eli's sons were priests, they were to be taken care of in this way. But Eli's sons took advantage of their position of trust to satisfy their lust for power, possessions, and control. Their contempt and arrogance toward the people and the worship of God endangered the integrity of the whole priesthood.

Eli knew his sons were evil, but he did little to correct or stop them, even when the integrity of God's sanctuary was threatened. As the High Priest, Eli should have executed his sons (Numbers 15:22–31). No wonder Eli chose not to confront the situation. By giving in to their selfish actions, Eli let his sons ruin their own lives and the lives of many others. There are times when serious problems must be confronted, even if the consequences might be painful.

2:13, 14 The fleshhook was a utensil used in the Tabernacle for administering sacrifices. This bronze instrument (Exodus 27:3) usually had three prongs which were used to hook the meat to be offered on the altar. Eli's sons used the fleshhook to take more meat from the pot than was due them according to God's Law.

2:13–17 What were Eli's sons doing wrong? They were taking parts of the sacrifices *before* they were offered to God on the altar. They were also eating meat before the fat was burned off. This was against God's Law (Leviticus 3:3–5). In effect, Eli's sons were treating God's offerings with contempt. Offerings were given to show honor and respect to God while seeking forgiveness for sins, but Eli's sons were actually sinning while making the offerings, demonstrating irreverence to God. To add to their sins, they were

also seducing young women in the Tabernacle (2:22).

Like Eli's sons, some people today treat the faith which others have in God and their "offerings" to him with contempt. God harshly judges those who mislead his people astray or scorn that which is holy (Numbers 18:32).

2:18 Samuel was a young child, and yet he was called "the Lord's helper." Children can often serve God just as effectively as adults. God will use anyone who is willing to learn from him and serve him. He has no age limits. Don't discount the faith of a child or let your age keep you from serving God.

2:18 Samuel wore a linen robe called an *ephod.* An ephod was a long sleeveless vest made of plain linen worn by all priests. The ephod of the High Priest carried special significance. It was embroidered with a variety of bright colors. Attached to it was the chestpiece, a bib-like garment with gold embroidered shoulder straps. Twelve precious gemstones were attached to the chestpiece; each stone representing one of the tribes of Israel. A pouch was attached to the ephod which held the Urim and Thummim, two small objects which were used to determine God's will in certain national matters.

2:21 God honored the desires of faithful Hannah. We never hear about Peninnah or her children again, but Samuel was used mightily by God. God also gave Hannah five more children besides Samuel. God often blesses us in ways we do not expect. Hannah never expected a child at her age, much less six children! God's blessings might not be immediate, but they will come if we are faithful to do what God says in his Word.

2:23–25 Eli's sons knew better, but they continued to disobey God and rebel against him by deliberately cheating, seducing, and

which has been committed against the Lord!" But they wouldn't listen to their father, for the Lord was already planning to kill them.

2:26
Lk 1:80
2:40,52

26Little Samuel was growing in two ways—he was getting taller, and he was becoming everyone's favorite (and he was a favorite of the Lord's, too!).

A prophet speaks to Eli

2:27
Ex 13:16
Deut 6:21
Jos 2:10
Judg 6:8

27One day a prophet came to Eli and gave him this message from the Lord: "Didn't I demonstrate my power when the people of Israel were slaves in Egypt? 28Didn't I choose your ancestor Levi from among all his brothers to be my priest, and to sacrifice upon my altar, and to burn incense, and to wear a priestly robe as he served me? And didn't I assign the sacrificial offerings to you priests? 29Then why are you so greedy for all the other offerings which are brought to me? Why have you honored your sons more than me—for you and they have become fat from the best of the offerings of my people!

2:28
Ex 28: 1-4
30:7,8
Deut 10:9

2:29
Mt 10:37

2:30
Num 25: 12,13
Ps 50:23
Mal 2:7-9

30"Therefore, I, the Lord God of Israel, declare that although I promised that your branch of the tribe of Levi could always be my priests, it is ridiculous to think that what you are doing can continue. I will honor only those who honor me, and I will despise those who despise me. 31I will put an end to your family, so that it will no longer serve as priests. Every member will die before his time. None shall live to be old. 32You will envy the prosperity I will give my people, but you and your family will be in distress and need. Not one of them will live out his days. 33Those who are left alive will live in sadness and grief; and their children shall die by the sword. 34And to prove that what I have said will come true, I will cause your two sons, Hophni and Phinehas, to die on the same day!

2:31
1 Sam 4:11
22:17-20

2:34
1 Sam 4:11,17

35"Then I will raise up a faithful priest who will serve me and do whatever I tell him to do. I will bless his descendants, and his family shall be priests to my kings forever. 36Then all of your descendants shall bow before him, begging for money and food. 'Please,' they will say, 'give me a job among the priests so that I will have enough to eat.' "

2:27 *a prophet*, literally, "a man of God."   **2:28** *wear a priestly robe*, literally, "wear an ephod."

---

robbing the people. Therefore, God planned to kill them. Any sin is wrong, but sin carried out deliberately and deceitfully is even worse. Even when we sin out of ignorance, we can expect punishment. But when we sin intentionally, the consequences will be more severe. Don't ignore God's warnings about sin.

2:25 Does a loving God really plan to kill people? Look at the situation in the Tabernacle. A person made an offering in order to have his sins forgiven, and Eli's sons were stealing these offerings and making a sham of the person's repentant attitude. God, in his love for Israel, could not permit this situation to continue. He allowed them to die as a result of their own boastful presumption. They took the Ark into battle, thinking it would protect them. But God withdrew his protection and the wicked sons of Eli were killed.

2:29 Eli had a difficult time trying to rear his sons. He apparently did not take any strong disciplinary action with his sons when he became aware of their wrongdoing. But Eli was not just a father trying to handle his rebellious sons; he was the High Priest overlooking the sins of priests under his jurisdiction. As a result, *the Lord* took the necessary disciplinary action that Eli would not.

Eli was guilty of honoring his sons above God by letting them continue in sin. Is there something in your life, family, or work that you allow to continue even though you know it is wrong? If so, you may become as guilty as those engaged in the wrong act. Honor

God more highly than anything else, and don't wait for God to intervene for you.

2:31–34 God is just, and he accounts for all sin. Eli's sons had sinned by despising God, and Eli had sinned by allowing them to continue in their sin. As religious leaders, they may have thought they would get away with it, or that God would ignore it, but God brought judgment.

If you are in a position of authority, don't rationalize away God's standards for right living. God expects leaders to lead fairly and to eliminate evil practices. God will not overlook those who sin or those who ignore sin.

2:31, 35, 36 For the fulfillment of this prediction see 1 Kings 2:26, 27, when Abiathar was expelled from his position by King Solomon. Abiathar's expulsion ended Eli's line. The faithful priest that God raised up was Zadok, a priest under David and then the High Priest under Solomon. Zadok's line was probably still in place as late as the days of Ezra.

2:35 God is looking for faithfulness. He doesn't *need* us to get his work done, but he wants us to be faithful. Eli and his sons were not faithful, so God said he would choose someone else who *was* faithful. When God has given you a job—in your family, church, community, or career—do it faithfully, or God may find someone else to do it in your place.

God calls Samuel to serve him

3 Meanwhile little Samuel was helping the Lord by assisting Eli. Messages from the Lord were very rare in those days, ², ³but one night after Eli had gone to bed (he was almost blind with age by now), and Samuel was sleeping in the Temple near the Ark, ⁴, ⁵the Lord called out, "Samuel! Samuel!"

"Yes?" Samuel replied. "What is it?" He jumped up and ran to Eli. "Here I am. What do you want?" he asked.

"I didn't call you," Eli said. "Go on back to bed." So he did. ⁶Then the Lord called again, "Samuel!" And again Samuel jumped up and ran to Eli.

"Yes?" he asked. "What do you need?"

"No, I didn't call you, my son," Eli said. "Go on back to bed."

⁷(Samuel had never had a message from Jehovah before.) ⁸So now the Lord called the third time, and once more Samuel jumped up and ran to Eli.

"Yes?" he asked. "What do you need?"

Then Eli realized it was the Lord who had spoken to the child. ⁹So he said to Samuel, "Go and lie down again, and if he calls again, say, 'Yes, Lord, I'm listening.' " So Samuel went back to bed.

¹⁰And the Lord came and called as before, "Samuel! Samuel!"

And Samuel replied, "Yes, I'm listening."

¹¹Then the Lord said to Samuel, "I am going to do a shocking thing in Israel. ¹²I am going to do all of the dreadful things I warned Eli about. ¹³I have continually threatened him and his entire family with punishment because his sons are blaspheming God, and he doesn't stop them. ¹⁴So I have vowed that the sins of Eli and of his sons shall never be forgiven by sacrifices and offerings."

¹⁵Samuel stayed in bed until morning, then opened the doors of the Temple as usual, for he was afraid to tell Eli what the Lord had said to him. ¹⁶, ¹⁷But Eli called him.

"My son," he said, "what did the Lord say to you? Tell me everything. And may God punish you if you hide anything from me!"

¹⁸So Samuel told him what the Lord had said.

"It is the Lord's will," Eli replied; "let him do what he thinks best."

¹⁹As Samuel grew, the Lord was with him and people listened carefully to his advice. ²⁰And all Israel from one end of the land to the other knew that Samuel was going to be a prophet of the Lord. ²¹, ⁴:¹Then the Lord began to give messages to him there at the Tabernacle in Shiloh, and he passed them on to the people of Israel.

3:7 *Samuel never had a message from God before,* literally, "did not yet know Jehovah."

3:1
1 Sam 3:21
Isa 1:1
Jer 1:1
Ezek 13:17
3:4
Isa 6:8

3:11
Deut 31:21
2 Kgs 21:12
Isa 29:14
Jer 19:3
3:14
Lev 15:31
1 Sam 2:25
Ps 51:16,17
Isa 22:14
Jer 7:16
3:15
Jer 1:8
3:18
2 Sam 16:10
Job 2:10
Ps 39:9
Isa 39:8
3:19
Gen 21:22
Judg 13:24
Lk 1:80
2:40,52
3:20
Judg 20:1
2 Sam 3:9,10
17:11

3:1-5 Although this was the era when God still gave direct and audible messages to his people, such messages became rare in the days of Eli. Why? Look at the attitude of Eli's sons. They either refused to listen to God or allowed greed to get in the way of any communication with him.

Listening and responding is vital in a relationship with God. Although God may not use the sound of a human voice, he speaks just as clearly today through his Word. To receive his messages, we must be ready to listen and to act upon what he tells us. Like Samuel, be ready to say "Here I am" when God calls you to action.

3:2, 3 The Ark of the Covenant was kept in the Holy of Holies, the innermost room of the Tabernacle where only the High Priest could enter once a year. Surrounding the Holy of Holies was the Holy Place, a small room where the other sacred furniture of the Tabernacle was kept (the Altar of Incense, the Table of Showbread, the Lampstand). Just outside the Holy Place was a court with small rooms where the priests were to stay. Samuel probably slept here with the other priests, only a few yards away from the Ark.

3:8, 9 One would naturally expect an audible message from God to be given to the priest Eli and not to the child Samuel. Eli was older and more experienced, and he held the proper position. But God's chain of command is based on faith. His view of authority and ability is not based on age or position. In finding faithful followers, God may use unexpected channels. Be prepared for the Lord to work at any place, at any time, and through anyone he chooses.

3:13 Eli had spent his entire life in service to God. He had the mission and great responsibility to oversee all of the worship in Israel. But in pursuing this great mission he neglected the responsibilities in his own home. Don't let your desire to do God's work cause you to neglect God's will at home. If you do, your mission may degenerate into a quest for personal importance, and your family will suffer the consequences of your neglect.

3:20 The phrase "from one end of the land to the other" is literally "from Dan to Beer-sheba." Dan was one of the northernmost cities in the land, and Beer-sheba one of the cities farthest south. In this context, it was a way of emphasizing that *everyone* in Israel knew that Samuel was called to be a prophet.

2. War with the Philistines

The Philistines capture the Ark

4:1
Josh 13:2-7
Judg 13:1
1 Sam 29:1

4:2
Josh 7:5,12
Ps 44:9,10

4:3
Num 10:35; 31:6
Josh 7:7
1 Sam 14:18

4:4
1 Sam 1:3; 4:11
2 Sam 6:2
2 Kgs 19:15
Ps 80:1

4:5
Josh 6:5

4:7
Ex 14:25; 15:14

4:9
Judg 13:1
2 Sam 10:12

4:10
Deut 28:15,25
Ps 78:9

4:11
1 Sam 2:34
Ps 78:60,61

4:12
Josh 7:6
2 Sam 1:1,2
13:19
Neh 9:1

4 At that time Israel was at war with the Philistines. The Israeli army was camped near Ebenezer, the Philistines at Aphek. 2And the Philistines defeated Israel, killing four thousand of them. 3After the battle was over, the army of Israel returned to their camp and their leaders discussed why the Lord had let them be defeated.

"Let's bring the Ark here from Shiloh," they said. "If we carry it into battle with us, the Lord will be among us and he will surely save us from our enemies."

4So they sent for the Ark of the Lord of heaven who is enthroned above the angels. Hophni and Phinehas, the sons of Eli, accompanied it into the battle. 5When the Israelis saw the Ark coming, their shout of joy was so loud that it almost made the ground shake!

6"What's going on?" the Philistines asked. "What's all the shouting about over in the camp of the Hebrews?"

When they were told it was because the Ark of the Lord had arrived, 7they panicked.

"God has come into their camp!" they cried out. "Woe upon us, for we have never had to face anything like this before! 8Who can save us from these mighty gods of Israel? They are the same gods who destroyed the Egyptians with plagues when Israel was in the wilderness. 9Fight as you never have before, O Philistines, or we will become their slaves just as they have been ours."

10So the Philistines fought desperately and Israel was defeated again. Thirty thousand men of Israel died that day and the remainder fled to their tents. 11And the Ark of God was captured and Hophni and Phinehas were killed.

12A man from the tribe of Benjamin ran from the battle and arrived at Shiloh the

---

4:1 The Philistines, descendants of Noah's son Ham, settled along the southeastern Mediterranean coast between Egypt and Gaza. They were originally called "Sea People" because they migrated to the middle East in ships from across the Mediterranean Sea. By Samuel's time, these warlike people were well established in the southwest part of Canaan and were constantly pressing inland against the Israelites. Throughout this book, the Philistines were Israel's major enemy.

4:3 The Ark of the Covenant contained the Ten Commandments given by God to Moses. The Ark was supposed to be kept in the Holy of Holies, a sacred part of the Tabernacle that only the High Priest could enter once a year. Hophni and Phinehas desecrated the room by unlawfully entering it and removing the Ark.

The Israelites rightly recognized the great holiness of the Ark, but they thought that the Ark itself—the wood and metal box—was their source of power. They began to use it as a good luck charm, expecting it to protect them from their enemies. Their attitude toward the Ark came perilously close to idol worship. When the Ark was captured by their enemies, they thought that Israel's glory was gone (4:19–22) and that God had deserted them (7:1, 2).

4:4 "The Ark of the Lord of Heaven who is enthroned above the angels" is another way of saying that the presence of God rested on the Ark of the Covenant between the two golden angels (or cherubim) attached to its lid. The people believed that this symbol of the presence of Almighty God would bring victory when carried into battle by Hophni and Phinehas.

4:5–8 The Philistines were frightened by their recollection of stories from the past of how God intervened for Israel when they left Egypt. But Israel had turned away from God and now only clung to a form of godliness.

People, churches, and organizations often try to live on the memories of God's blessings. Israel wrongly assumed that since God had given them victory in the past, he would do it again, even though they had strayed far from him. Today, spiritual victories come through continually renewing our relationship with God. Don't

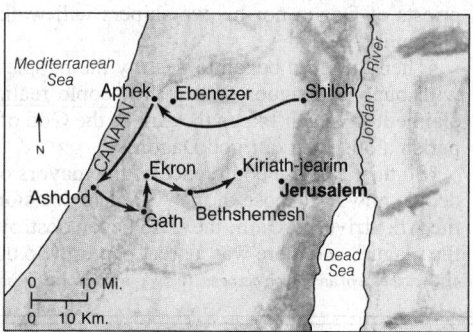

THE ARK'S TRAVELS Eli's sons took the Ark from Shiloh to the battlefield on the lower plains at Ebenezer and Aphek. The Philistines captured the Ark and took it to Ashdod, Gath, and Ekron. Plagues forced the people to send the Ark back to Israel, where it finally was taken by cattle-driven carts on route to Bethshemesh and on to the home of Eleazar in Kiriath-jearim.

live off the past. Keep your relationship with God new and fresh.

4:11 This is a fulfillment of the prophecy in 2:34 which stated that Eli's sons, Hophni and Phinehas, would "die on the same day."

4:12 At this time, the city of Shiloh was the religious center of Israel (Joshua 18:1; 1 Samuel 4:3). The Tabernacle was permanently set up there. Since Israel did not have a civil capital—a seat of national government—Shiloh was the natural place for a messenger to come to deliver the sad news from the battle. Many scholars believe that it was during this battle that Shiloh was destroyed (Jeremiah 7:12; 26:2–6; also see the note on 7:1).

same day with his clothes torn and dirt on his head. 13Eli was waiting beside the road to hear the news of the battle, for his heart trembled for the safety of the Ark of God. As the messenger from the battlefront arrived and told what had happened, a great cry arose throughout the city.

14"What is all the noise about?" Eli asked. And the messenger rushed over to Eli and told him what had happened. 15(Eli was ninety-eight years old and was blind.)

16"I have just come from the battle—I was there today," he told Eli, 17"and Israel has been defeated and thousands of the Israeli troops are dead on the battlefield. Hophni and Phinehas were killed too, and the Ark has been captured."

18When the messenger mentioned what had happened to the Ark, Eli fell backward from his seat beside the gate and his neck was broken by the fall and he died (for he was old and fat). He had judged Israel for forty years.

19When Eli's daughter-in-law, Phinehas's wife, who was pregnant, heard that the Ark had been captured and that her husband and father-in-law were dead, her labor pains suddenly began. 20Just before she died, the women who were attending her told her that everything was all right and that the baby was a boy. But she did not reply or respond in any way. 21, 22Then she murmured, "Name the child 'Ichabod,' for Israel's glory is gone." (Ichabod means "there is no glory." She named him this because the Ark of God had been captured and because her husband and her father-in-law were dead.)

God punishes the Philistines

5 The Philistines took the captured Ark of God from the battleground at Ebenezer to the temple of their idol Dagon in the city of Ashdod. 3But when the local citizens went to see it the next morning, Dagon had fallen with his face to the ground before the Ark of Jehovah! They set him up again, 4but the next morning the same thing had happened—the idol had fallen face down before the Ark of the Lord again. This time his head and hands had been cut off and were lying in the doorway; only the trunk of his body was left intact. 5(That is why to this day neither the priests of Dagon nor his worshipers will walk on the threshold of the temple of Dagon in Ashdod.)

6Then the Lord began to destroy the people of Ashdod and the nearby villages with bubonic plague. 7When the people realized what was happening, they exclaimed, "We can't keep the Ark of the God of Israel here any longer. We will all perish along with our god Dagon."

8So they called a conference of the mayors of the five cities of the Philistines to decide how to dispose of the Ark. The decision was to take it to Gath. 9But when the Ark arrived at Gath, the Lord began destroying its people, young and old, with the plague, and there was a great panic. 10So they sent the Ark to Ekron, but when

4:12 *clothes torn and dirt on his head.* This was a common expression of grief in that day.

4:14
2 Sam 1:4

4:15
Gen 27:1
1 Sam 3:2

4:17
1 Sam 2:34
4:11

4:20
Gen 35:17,18

4:21
1 Sam 14:3
Ps 78:61
106:19,20

5:1
Josh 13:3
Judg 16:23-30
1 Sam 4:11,17
1 Chron 10:8-10
Ps 78:61

5:3
Isa 19:1
46:1,2,7

5:6
Ex 9:3
Deut 28:27
1 Sam 6:4,5

5:7
Ex 8:8; 12:33
1 Sam 6:20

5:9
1 Sam 7:13
12:15

5:10
Josh 15:45
Judg 1:18
2 Kgs 1:2

4:18 Eli was Israel's judge and High Priest. His death marked the end of the dark period of the judges when most of the nation ignored God. Although Samuel was also a judge, his career saw the transition from Israel's rule by judges to the nation's monarchy. He began the great revival that Israel would experience for the next century. The Bible does not say who became the next High Priest (Samuel was not eligible because he was not a direct descendant of Aaron), but Samuel acted as High Priest at this time by offering the important sacrifices throughout Israel.

4:19–22 This incident illustrates the spiritual darkness and decline of Israel. This young boy Ichabod was supposed to succeed his father Phinehas in the priesthood, but his father had been killed because he was an evil man who desecrated the Tabernacle. The terror of God leaving his people overshadowed the joy of childbirth.

5:1 Dagon was the chief god of the Philistines. They believed this god sent rain and assured a bountiful harvest. But the Philistines, like most of their heathen neighbors, worshiped many gods. The more gods they could have on their side, the more secure they felt.

That was why they wanted the Ark. They thought that if it helped the Israelites, it could help them too. However, when the people living nearby began to get sick and die, the Philistines realized that for them, the Ark was not a good omen. It was a source of more power than they had ever seen—power they could not control.

5:6, 7 Although the Philistines had just witnessed a great victory by Israel's God over their idol, Dagon, they didn't act upon that insight until they were personally afflicted with boils. Similarly, many people don't respond to biblical truth until they experience personal pain. Are you willing to listen to God for truth's sake, or do you turn to him only when you are personally afflicted?

5:7 The Philistines thought they had defeated God because they had beaten Israel and captured the Ark. They soon learned that no one defeats God. Their sweet victory turned sour as God began to destroy them with a plague.

5:8 The Philistines were governed by five rulers. Each ruler lived in a different city—Gath, Ekron, Ashdod, Ashkelon, Gaza. The Ark was taken to three of these capital cities, but in each case it brought great trouble to the citizens.

the people of Ekron saw it coming they cried out, "They are bringing the Ark of the God of Israel here to kill us too!"

11So they summoned the mayors again and begged them to send the Ark back to its own country, lest the entire city die. For the plague had already begun and great fear was sweeping across the city. 12Those who didn't die were deathly ill; and there was weeping everywhere.

The Philistines return the Ark

6:1
1 Sam 5:1

6:2
Gen 41:8
Dan 2:1; 5:7

6 The Ark remained in the Philistine country for seven months in all. 2Then the Philistines called for their priests and diviners and asked them, "What shall we do about the Ark of God? What sort of gift shall we send with it when we return it to its own land?"

Eli was one Old Testament person with a very modern problem. The recognition and respect he earned in public were not a result of the way he handled his private affairs. He may have been an excellent priest, but he was a poor parent. His sons brought him grief and ruin. He lacked two important qualities needed for effective parental discipline: firm resolve and corrective action.

Eli responded to situations rather than solving them. But even his responses tended to be weak. God pointed out his sons' errors, but Eli did little to correct them. The contrast between God's dealing with Eli and Eli's dealing with his sons is clear—God gave warning, spelled out the consequences of disobedience, and then acted. Eli only warned. Children need to learn that their parents' words and actions go together. Both love and discipline must be spoken as well as acted out.

But Eli had another problem. He was more concerned with the symbols of his religion than with the God they represented. For Eli, the Ark of the Covenant had become a relic to be protected rather than a reminder of the Protector. His faith shifted from the Creator to the created.

It may be easier to worship things we can see, whether buildings, people, or Scripture itself, but such tangible things have no power in themselves. This book you hold is either merely a respectable religious relic, or it is the sharp and effective Word of God. Your attitude toward it is largely shaped by your relationship to the God from whom it comes. A relic or antique has to be carefully stored away; God's Word has to be used and obeyed. Which attitude accurately describes your approach to the Word of God?

Strengths and accomplishments:
- Judged Israel for 40 years
- Spoke with Hannah, the mother of Samuel, and assured her of God's blessing
- Raised and trained Samuel, the greatest judge of Israel

Weaknesses and mistakes:
- Failed to discipline his sons or correct them when they sinned
- Tended to react to situations rather than take decisive action
- Saw the Ark of the Covenant as a relic to be cherished, rather than as a symbol of God's presence with Israel

Lessons from his life:
- Parents need to be responsible in the disciplining of their children
- Life is more than simply reacting, it demands action

Vital statistics:
- Where: Shiloh
- Occupation: High Priest and judge of Israel
- Relatives: Sons: Hophni and Phinehas
- Contemporaries: Samuel

Key verses:
"Then the Lord said to Samuel, 'I am going to do a shocking thing in Israel. I am going to do all of the dreadful things I warned Eli about. I have continually threatened him and his entire family with punishment because his sons are blaspheming God, and he doesn't stop them. So I have vowed that the sins of Eli and of his sons shall never be forgiven by sacrifices and offerings' " (1 Samuel 3:11–14).

His story is told in 1 Samuel 1—4. He is also mentioned in 1 Kings 2:26, 27.

6:2 The Philistines had ample evidence that the God of Israel was greater than all gods. Their leaders gave him some token gifts, not out of worship, but in order to remove the plague. We need to offer God true, heartfelt devotion, not token gifts.

³"Yes, send it back with a gift," they were told. "Send a guilt offering so that the plague will stop. Then, if it doesn't, you will know God didn't send the plague upon you after all."

⁴,⁵"What guilt offering shall we send?" they asked.

And they were told, "Send five gold models of the tumor caused by the plague, and five gold models of the rats that have ravaged the whole land—the capital cities and villages alike. If you send these gifts and then praise the God of Israel, perhaps he will stop persecuting you and your god. ⁶Don't be stubborn and rebellious as Pharaoh and the Egyptians were. They wouldn't let Israel go until God had destroyed them with dreadful plagues. ⁷Now build a new cart and hitch to it two cows that have just had calves—cows that never before have been yoked—and shut their calves away from them in the barn. ⁸Place the Ark of God on the cart beside a chest containing the gold models of the rats and tumors, and let the cows go wherever they want to. ⁹If they cross the border of our land and go into Beth-shemesh, then you will know that it was God who brought this great evil upon us; if they don't, [but return to their calves,] then we will know that the plague was simply a coincidence and was not sent by God at all."

¹⁰So these instructions were carried out. Two cows with newborn calves were hitched to the cart and their calves were shut up in the barn. ¹¹Then the Ark of the Lord and the chest containing the gold rats and tumors were placed upon the cart. ¹²And sure enough, the cows went straight along the road toward Beth-shemesh, lowing as they went; and the Philistine mayors followed them as far as the border of Beth-shemesh. ¹³The people of Beth-shemesh were reaping wheat in the valley, and when they saw the Ark they went wild with joy!

¹⁴The cart came into the field of a man named Joshua and stopped beside a large rock. So the people broke up the wood of the cart for a fire and killed the cows and sacrificed them to the Lord as a burnt offering. ¹⁵Several men of the tribe of Levi lifted the Ark and the chest containing the gold rats and tumors from the cart and laid them on the rock. And many burnt offerings and sacrifices were offered to the Lord that day by the men of Beth-shemesh.

¹⁶After the five Philistine mayors had watched for awhile, they returned to Ekron that same day. ¹⁷The five gold models of tumors which had been sent by the Philistines as a guilt offering to the Lord were gifts from the mayors of the capital cities, Ashdod, Gaza, Ashkelon, Gath, and Ekron. ¹⁸The gold rats were to placate God for the other Philistine cities, both the fortified cities and the country villages controlled by the five capitals. (By the way, that large rock at Beth-shemesh can still be seen in the field of Joshua.) ¹⁹But the Lord killed seventy of the men of

6:9 *return to their calves,* implied.

6:3
Lev 5:15,16
7:1-7
1 Sam 6:9

6:6
Ex 8:15,31,32
12:31

6:7
Deut 21:3
2 Sam 6:3

6:9
Josh 15:10,11
Judg 1:33
1 Sam 6:3

6:11
2 Sam 6:3
1 Chron 13:7

6:14
Judg 6:26
1 Kgs 18:30
2 Sam 24:22

6:15
Josh 3:2-4

6:17
1 Sam 6:4,5

6:18
Num 4:1,15,20
Deut 3:5
2 Sam 6:7

6:3 What was this guilt offering supposed to accomplish? This was a typical heathen reaction to trouble. The Philistines thought their problems came because one of their gods was angry. They recognized their guilt in taking the Ark and now were trying everything they could to placate Israel's God. The diviners (6:2) probably helped choose the gift they thought would placate Jehovah. But the offering consisted of images of tumors and rats, not the kind of guilt offering prescribed in God's laws (Leviticus 5:14—6:7; 7:1–10). How easy it is to design our own methods of acknowledging God rather than committing ourselves to serve him in the way that he requires.

6:7-12 The Philistine priests and diviners devised a test to see if God was really the one who had caused all their recent troubles. Two cows who had just given birth to calves were hitched to a cart and sent toward Israel's border carrying the Ark of the Covenant. For a cow to leave her calves, she would have to go against all her motherly instincts. Only God, who has power over the natural order, could cause this to happen. God sent the cows to Israel, not to pass the Philistine's test, but to show them his mighty power.

6:9 The Philistines acknowledged the existence of the Hebrew God, but only as one of many deities whose favor they sought.

Thinking of God in this way made it easy for them to ignore his demand that people worship him alone. Many people "worship" God this way. They see God as just one ingredient in a successful life. But God is not an ingredient—he is the source of life itself. Are you a "Philistine," seeing God's favor as an ingredient of the good life?

6:15 The men of Beth-shemesh sacrificed a burnt offering to God. Wherever there is a burnt offering in Scripture, it represents a renewing of a person's relationship with God. Although some of the people were insincere (6:19) when the people of Beth-shemesh made burnt offerings to God, they were rededicating their lives to him and demonstrating their willingness to start over with him as their leader.

6:19 Why were people killed for looking into the Ark? The Israelites had made an idol of the Ark. They had tried to harness God's power, to use it for their own purposes (victory in battle). But the Lord of the universe cannot be controlled by humans. To protect the Israelites from his power, he had warned them not even to look at the sacred sanctuary objects in the Most Holy Place or they would die (Numbers 4:20). Because of their disobedience, God carried out his promised judgment.

Beth-shemesh because they looked into the Ark. And the people mourned because of the many people whom the Lord had killed.

6:20
Lev 11:44,45
2 Sam 6:9

20"Who is able to stand before Jehovah, this holy God?" they cried out. "Where can we send the Ark from here?"

6:21
Josh 15:9,60

21So they sent messengers to the people at Kiriath-jearim and told them that the Philistines had brought back the Ark of the Lord.

"Come and get it!" they begged.

7:1
2 Sam 6:3,4

7:2
Judg 2:3

7 So the men of Kiriath-jearim came and took the Ark to the hillside home of Abinadab; and installed his son Eleazar to be in charge of it. 2The Ark remained there for twenty years, and during that time all Israel was in sorrow because the Lord had seemingly abandoned them.

ISRAELITES VS. PHILISTINES	Location of the Battle	Winner	Comments	Reference
The Israelites and Philistines were archenemies and constantly fighting. Here are some of their confrontations found in 1 and 2 Samuel. When Israel trusted God for the victory, they always won.	Aphek to Ebenezer	Philistines	The Ark was captured and Eli's sons killed	1 Samuel 4:1–11
	Mizpah	Israelites	After the Ark was returned, the Philistines planned to attack again, but God confused them. Israel chased the Philistines back to Beth-car	1 Samuel 7:7–14
	Geba	Israelites under Jonathan	One garrison destroyed	1 Samuel 13:3, 4
	Gilgal	A standoff	The Israelites lost their nerve and hid	1 Samuel 13:6–17
	Michmash	Israelites	Jonathan and his bodyguard said it didn't matter how many enemies there were. If God was with them, they would win. They began the battle, and the army completed it	1 Samuel 14:1–23
	Elah	Israelites	David and Goliath	1 Samuel 17:1–58
	?	Israelites	David killed 200 Philistines to earn a wife	1 Samuel 18:17–30
	Keilah	Israelites under David	David protected the threshing floors from Philistine robbers	1 Samuel 23:1–5
	Aphek, Jezreel, to Mount Gilboa	Philistines	Saul and Jonathan killed	1 Samuel 29:1; 31:1–13
	Baal-perazim	Israelites	The Philistines tried to capture King David	2 Samuel 5:17–25
	Gath	Israelites	There was very little trouble with the Philistines after this defeat in their largest city	2 Samuel 8:1
	?	Israelites	Abishai saved David from a Philistine giant	2 Samuel 21:15–17
	Gob	Israelites	Other giants were killed, including Goliath's brother	2 Samuel 21:18–22

God could not allow the people to think they could use his power for their own ends. He could not permit them to disregard his warnings and come into his presence lightly. He did not want the cycle of disrespect, disobedience, and defeat to start all over again. God did not kill the men of Beth-shemesh just to be cruel. He killed them because overlooking their presumptuous sin would lead the whole nation of Israel into overlooking God.

7:1 The Ark was taken to Kiriath-jearim—a city near the battlefield—for safekeeping. Why wasn't the Ark taken back to the Tabernacle at Shiloh? Shiloh had probably been captured and destroyed by the Philistines in an earlier battle (4:1–18; Jeremiah 26:2–6) because of the evil deeds of its priests (2:12–17). The Tabernacle and its furniture were apparently saved, because we read that it was set up in Nob during Saul's reign (21:1–6) and in Gibeon during the reigns of David and Solomon (1 Chronicles

16:39; 21:29, 30; 2 Chronicles 1). Shiloh, however, is never again mentioned in the historical books of the Old Testament. Samuel's new home became Ramah (7:15–17; 8:4), his birthplace (further evidence of Shiloh's destruction).

7:2, 3 Sorrow gripped Israel for 20 years. The Ark was put away like an unwanted box in an attic, and it seemed as if the Lord had abandoned his people. Samuel, now a grown man, roused them to action by saying that if they were truly sorry, they should do something about it. How easy it is for us to complain about our problems, even to God, while we refuse to act, to change, and to do what he requires. We don't even take the advice he has already given us. Do you ever feel as if God has abandoned you? Check to see if there is anything he has already told you to do. You may not be able to receive new guidance until you have acted on his previous directions.

Samuel becomes a judge

3At that time Samuel said to them, "If you are really serious about wanting to return to the Lord, get rid of your foreign gods and your Ashtaroth idols. Determine to obey only the Lord; then he will rescue you from the Philistines."

7:3
Deut 6:13; 13:4
Josh 24:14,23
Judg 2:12-14
10:16
2 Chron 19:13
Joel 2:12-14

4So they destroyed their idols of Baal and Ashtaroth and worshiped only the Lord.

5Then Samuel told them, "Come to Mizpah, all of you, and I will pray to the Lord for you."

7:5
1 Sam 12:17-19
1 Kgs 18:24

6So they gathered there and, in a great ceremony, drew water from the well and poured it out before the Lord. They also went without food all day as a sign of sorrow for their sins. So it was at Mizpah that Samuel became Israel's judge.

7:6
Judg 10:10
Neh 9:1
Lam 2:19

7When the Philistine leaders heard about the great crowds at Mizpah, they mobilized their army and advanced. The Israelis were badly frightened when they learned that the Philistines were approaching.

7:7
1 Sam 13:6

8"Plead with God to save us!" they begged Samuel.

9So Samuel took a suckling lamb and offered it to the Lord as a whole burnt offering and pleaded with him to help Israel. And the Lord responded. 10Just as Samuel was sacrificing the burnt offering, the Philistines arrived for battle, but the Lord spoke with a mighty voice of thunder from heaven, and they were thrown into confusion, and the Israelis routed them, 11and chased them from Mizpah to Beth-car, killing them all along the way. 12Samuel then took a stone and placed it between Mizpah and Jeshanah and named it Ebenezer (meaning, "the Stone of Help"), for he said, "The Lord has certainly helped us!" 13So the Philistines were subdued and didn't invade Israel again at that time, because the Lord was against them throughout the remainder of Samuel's lifetime. 14The Israeli cities between Ekron and Gath, which had been conquered by the Philistines, were now returned to Israel, for the Israeli army rescued them from their Philistine captors. And there was peace between Israel and the Amorites in those days.

7:8
1 Sam 12:19
Isa 37:4

7:9
Lev 22:26,27
Jer 15:1

7:10
1 Sam 2:10
2 Sam 22:14
Ps 18:14

7:12
Gen 28:18
35:13-15
Josh 4:9; 24:26

7:13
Judg 13:1
1 Sam 13:5

7:15
1 Sam 7:6
12:11

15Samuel continued as Israel's judge for the remainder of his life. 16He rode circuit annually, setting up his court first at Bethel, then Gilgal, and then Mizpah, and cases of dispute were brought to him in each of those three cities from all the surrounding territory. 17Then he would come back to Ramah, for his home was there, and he would hear cases there, too. And he built an altar to the Lord at Ramah.

7:16
Gen 28:19
Josh 5:8; 11:1
1 Sam 7:5

7:17
1 Sam 1:1,19
2:11; 15:34
16:13

7:3 Samuel told the people they had to "determine to obey only the Lord." To determine means to set your mind on a course of action. This kind of commitment means that you don't back out, but you work toward the goal you have set. If you have made a decision to follow God, don't allow excuses, distractions, or second thoughts to deter you from your goal.

7:3 Samuel urged the Israelites to get rid of their foreign gods and idols. Idols today are much more subtle, but just as dangerous. Whatever holds first place in our lives or controls us becomes our god. Money, success, material goods, pride, or anything else can be an idol if it takes the place of God in our lives. There is no difference between commitment to these idols and commitment to those made of wood and stone. The Lord alone is worthy of our service and worship, and we must let nothing rival him. If we have "foreign gods" in our lives, we need to ask God to help us dethrone them, making the true God our first priority.

7:5 Mizpah held special significance for the Israelite nation. It was at Mizpah where the Israelites had earlier gathered to mobilize against the tribe of Benjamin (Judges 20:1). Samuel was appointed to be judge there (7:6), and Saul, Israel's first king, was crowned there (10:17ff).

7:6 Pouring water on the ground "before the Lord" was a sign of repentance for sin, turning from idols, and determining to obey the Lord alone.

7:6 Samuel became the last in the long line of Israel's judges that began in the days when Israel first conquered the Promised Land. For a list of these judges see the chart in the book of Judges. A judge was both a political and a religious leader. God was Israel's true leader, while the judge was to be God's spokesman to the people and administrator of justice throughout the land. While some of Israel's judges relied more on their own judgment than on God's, Samuel's obedience and dedication to God made him one of the better judges in Israel's history. (For more on Samuel as a judge, see the note on 4:18.)

7:12 The Israelites had great difficulty with the Philistines, but God rescued them. In response, the people set up a rock as a memorial to remind them of God's great deliverance. During tough times, we may need to remember the crucial turning points in our past to help us through the present. While we must be careful that memorials do not become idols, they can help us to remember God's past victories and gain confidence and strength for the present.

7:14 In the days of Joshua, the Amorites were a powerful tribe occupying the east side of the Jordan River opposite the Dead Sea. In the context of this verse, however, "Amorites" is another general name for all the inhabitants of Canaan who were not Israelites.

8:1-3 By this time, Samuel was an old man. He appointed his

B. SAMUEL AND SAUL (8:1—15:35)

Samuel judges Israel well, saves them from the Philistines, and leads them back to God. But when he retires, the nation does not want another judge, instead they demand to be given a king in order to be like the nations around them. Although God is unhappy with their request, he tells Samuel to anoint Saul as Israel's first king. Saul is a skillful soldier who successfully leads the nation into many battles against their enemies. But in God's eyes Saul is a failure because he constantly disobeys and does things his own way. God eventually rejected Saul as king. Sometimes we want to go our own way rather than follow the ways of God. This will always end in ruin as it did for Saul.

1. Saul becomes king of Israel

The people demand a king

8:1
Deut 16:18,19

8 In his old age, Samuel retired and appointed his sons as judges in his place. ²Joel and Abijah, his oldest sons, held court in Beer-sheba; ³but they were not

---

We often wonder about the childhoods of great people. We have little information about the early years of most of the people mentioned in the Bible. One delightful exception is Samuel; he came as a result of God's answer to Hannah's prayer for a child. (In fact, the name "Samuel" comes from the Hebrew expression, "asked of God.") God shaped Samuel from the start. Like Moses, Samuel was called to fill many different roles: judge, priest, prophet, counselor, and God's man at a turning point in the history of Israel. God worked through Samuel because Samuel was willing to be one thing: God's servant.

Samuel showed that those whom God finds faithful in small things will be trusted with greater things. He grew up assisting the High Priest (Eli) in the Temple, and did what he could until God directed him to other responsibilities. God was able to use Samuel because he was genuinely dedicated to God.

Samuel moved ahead because he was listening to God's directions. Too often we ask God to control our lives without giving up the goals for which we strive. We ask God to help us get where *we* want to go. The first step in correcting this tendency is to turn over both the control and destination of our lives to him. The second step is to be obedient to what we *already* know God requires of us. The third step is to listen for further direction from his Word—God's map for life.

Strengths and accomplishments:
- Used by God to assist Israel's transition from a loosely governed tribal people to a monarchy
- Anointed the first two kings of Israel
- Was the last and most effective of Israel's judges
- Is listed in the Hall of Faith in Hebrews 11

Weakness and Mistake:
- Was unable to instill in his sons the same relationship he had with God

Lessons from his life:
- The significance of what people accomplish in life is directly related to their relationship with God.
- The kind of person we are is more important than anything we might do.

Vital statistics:
- Where: Ephraim
- Occupation: Judge, prophet, priest
- Relatives: Mother: Hannah. Father: Elkanah. Sons: Joel and Abijah.
- Contemporaries: Eli, Saul, David

Key verses:
"As Samuel grew, the Lord was with him and people listened carefully to his advice. And all Israel from Dan to Beer-sheba knew that Samuel was going to be a prophet of the Lord" (1 Samuel 3:19, 20).

His story is told in 1 Samuel 1—28. He is also mentioned in Psalm 99:6; Jeremiah 15:1; Acts 3:24; 13:20; Hebrews 11:32.

---

sons to be judges over Israel in his place, but they turned out to be corrupt, much like Eli's sons (2:12). We don't know why Samuel's sons were bad, but we do know that Eli was held responsible for his own sons' corruption (2:29–34).

It is impossible to know if Samuel was a bad parent. His children were old enough to be on their own. We need to be careful not to blame ourselves for the sins of our children. On the other hand, parenthood is an awesome responsibility, and nothing

should take greater priority than molding and shaping the lives of our children.

If your grown children are not following God's ways, realize that you can't control them any longer. Don't blame yourself for what you can no longer be responsible for. But if your children are still in your care, realize that what you do and what you teach will have a profound effect upon your children that will last the rest of their lives.

like their father, for they were greedy for money. They accepted bribes and were very corrupt in the administration of justice. 4Finally the leaders of Israel met in Ramah to discuss the matter with Samuel. 5They told him that since his retirement things hadn't been the same, for his sons were not good men.

"Give us a king like all the other nations have," they pleaded. 6Samuel was terribly upset and went to the Lord for advice.

7"Do as they say," the Lord replied, "for I am the one they are rejecting, not you—they don't want me to be their king any longer. 8Ever since I brought them from Egypt they have continually forsaken me and followed other gods. And now they are giving you the same treatment. 9Do as they ask, but warn them about what it will be like to have a king!"

10So Samuel told the people what the Lord had said:

11"If you insist on having a king, he will conscript your sons and make them run before his chariots; 12some will be made to lead his troops into battle, while others will be slave laborers; they will be forced to plow in the royal fields, and harvest his crops without pay; and make his weapons and chariot equipment. 13He will take your daughters from you and force them to cook and bake and make perfumes for him. 14He will take away the best of your fields and vineyards and olive groves and give them to his friends. 15He will take a tenth of your harvest and distribute it to his favorites. 16He will demand your slaves and the finest of your youth and will use your animals for his personal gain. 17He will demand a tenth of your flocks, and you shall be his slaves. 18You will shed bitter tears because of this king you are demanding, but the Lord will not help you."

19But the people refused to listen to Samuel's warning.

"Even so, we still want a king," they said, 20"for we want to be like the nations around us. He will govern us and lead us to battle."

21So Samuel told the Lord what the people had said, 22and the Lord replied again, "Then do as they say and give them a king."

So Samuel agreed and sent the men home again.

Saul hunts for his father's donkeys

9 Kish was a rich, influential man from the tribe of Benjamin. He was the son of Abiel, grandson of Zeror, great-grandson of Becorath, and great-great-grandson of Aphiah. 2His son Saul was the most handsome man in Israel. And he was head and shoulders taller than anyone else in the land!

Cross-references (right margin):

8:4 — 1 Sam 7:17
8:5 — Deut 17:14,15 / 1 Sam 12:19
8:6 — 1 Sam 12:17 / 15:11
8:7 — Ex 16:8
8:8 — Ex 14:11; 16:3 / Deut 9:24 / Judg 2:1,2 / 1 Sam 10:18,19
8:11 — Deut 17:14-20 / 1 Sam 10:24 / 14:52 / 2 Sam 15:1 / 1 Kgs 1:5
8:12 — 1 Sam 22:7 / 1 Kgs 4:7
8:14 — 1 Sam 22:7 / 1 Kgs 21:7 / Ezek 46:18
8:18 — Job 27:9 / Prov 1:25-28 / Isa 8:21 / Mic 3:4
8:19 — 1 Sam 8:5
9:1 — 1 Chron 8:33 / 9:36-39
9:2 — 2 Sam 14:25

8:4-9 Israel wanted a king for several reasons: (1) Samuel's sons were not fit to lead Israel. (2) The 12 tribes of Israel continually had problems working together because each tribe had its own leader and territory. It was hoped that a king would unite the tribes into one nation and one army. (3) The people wanted to be like the neighboring nations. This is exactly what God didn't want. Having a king would make it easy to forget who their real leader was. It was not wrong for Israel to want a king; God had mentioned the possibility in Deuteronomy 17:14-20. Yet God was disappointed because the people were rejecting him as their leader. The Israelites wanted laws, an army, and a human monarch in the place of God. They were seeking a human solution to goals that were beyond human ability to achieve.

8:5, 6 Israel's 12 tribes were weak and disorganized. They attributed this problem to the lack of a united army, central capital, and ruling authority. The people clamored for a king, thinking that a new system of government would bring about a change in the nation. But since their real problem was disobedience to God, their problems would only continue under the new administration.

Had the Israelites submitted to God's leadership, they would have thrived beyond their expectations (Deuteronomy 28:1). You, too, can choose your leader, but you must also live with the consequences.

8:18 Samuel warned the people that they would regret their decision to have a king. Israel (including the future Northern and Southern Kingdoms) eventually had 41 kings over a period of 450 years. Only 11 kings followed God at all, and seven of those forgot God at the end of their reigns. It was the spiritual rebellion of the kings that caused the later captivities by foreign nations (2 Kings 17, 25).

8:19, 20 Samuel carefully explained all the negative consequences of having a king, but the Israelites refused to listen. When you have an important decision to make, weigh the positives and negatives carefully, considering everyone who might be affected by your choice. When you want something badly enough, it is difficult to see the potential negative consequences. But don't discount the negatives. Unless you have a plan to handle each one, they will cause you great difficulty later.

8:19, 20 Israel was called to be a holy nation, separate from and unique among all others (Leviticus 20:26). The Israelites' motive in asking for a king was to be like the nations around them. This was in total opposition to God's original plan. It was not their desire for a king that was wrong, but their reasons for wanting a king.

Often we let the values and actions of others dictate our attitudes and behavior. Have you ever made a wrong choice because you wanted to be like everyone else? Be careful that the values of your friends or "heroes" don't pull you away from what God says is right. When God's people want to be like unbelievers, they are heading for spiritual decline (3 John 11).

9:3
1 Sam 10:2,14

³One day Kish's donkeys strayed away, so he sent Saul and a servant to look for them. ⁴They traveled all through the hill country of Ephraim, the land of Shalisha, the Shaalim area, and the entire land of Benjamin, but couldn't find them anywhere. ⁵Finally, after searching in the land of Zuph, Saul said to the servant, "Let's go home; by now my father will be more worried about us than about the donkeys!"

9:5
1 Sam 1:1

9:6
Deut 18:20,21
1 Sam 3:19,20
2 Kgs 5:8

⁶But the servant said, "I've just thought of something! There is a prophet who lives here in this city; he is held in high honor by all the people because everything he says comes true; let's go and find him and perhaps he can tell us where the donkeys are."

9:7
1 Kgs 14:3
2 Kgs 5:15
8:8,9
Ezek 13:19

⁷"But we don't have anything to pay him with," Saul replied. "Even our food is gone and we don't have a thing to give him."

⁸"Well," the servant said, "I have a dollar! We can at least offer it to him and see what happens!"

9:9
Ex 2:16
1 Chron 26:28

⁹, ¹⁰, ¹¹"All right," Saul agreed, "let's try it!"

So they started into the city where the prophet lived. As they were climbing a hill toward the city, they saw some young girls going out to draw water and asked them if they knew whether the seer was in town. (In those days prophets were called seers. "Let's go and ask the seer," people would say, rather than, "Let's go and ask the prophet," as we would say now.)

9:12
Lk 9:16
Jn 6:11

¹², ¹³"Yes," they replied, "stay right on this road. He lives just inside the city gates. He has just arrived back from a trip to take part in a public sacrifice up on the

---

THE PROBLEMS WITH HAVING A KING	Problems (warned by Samuel)	Reference	Fulfillment
	Conscripting young men into the army	8:11, 12	14:52—"Whenever Saul saw any brave, strong young man, he conscripted him into his army."
	Having the young men "run before his [the king's] chariots"	8:11	2 Samuel 15:1—"Absalom . . . hired fifty footmen to run ahead of him."
	Making slave laborers	8:12, 17	2 Chronicles 2:17—Solomon conscripted laborers to build the Temple.
	Taking the "best of your fields and vineyards"	8:14	1 Kings 21:5–16—Jezebel stole Naboth's vineyard.
	Using your property for his personal gain	8:14–16	1 Kings 9:10–15—Solomon gave away 20 cities to Hiram of Tyre.
	Demanding a tenth of your harvest and flocks	8:15, 17	1 Kings 12:1–19—Rehoboam was going to demand heavier taxation than Solomon.

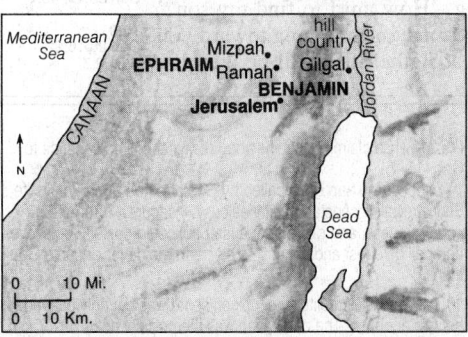

SAUL CHOSEN AS KING Saul and a servant searched for their lost donkeys in the hill country of Ephraim and the territory of Benjamin. They went to Ramah, looking for help from Samuel the prophet. While Saul was there, he found himself unexpectedly anointed by Samuel as Israel's first king. Samuel called Israel together at Mizpah to tell them God's choice for their king.

9:3 Saul was sent by his father on an important mission—to find their stray donkeys. Donkeys were all-purpose animals, the "pick-up trucks" of Bible times. Used for transportation, hauling, and farming, they were considered necessities. Even the poorest family owned one. To own many donkeys was a sign of wealth, and to lose them was a disaster. Saul's father was wealthy (9:1). His many donkeys were evidence of that wealth.

9:3ff Often we think that events just happen to us, but as we learn from this story about Saul, God often uses common occurences to lead us where he wants. It is important to evaluate all situations as potential "divine appointments" designed to shape our lives. Think of all the good and bad circumstances that have affected you lately. Can you see God's purpose in them? Perhaps he is building a certain quality in your life or leading you to serve him in a new area.

9:6 The city where the servant said the prophet lived was probably Ramah because Samuel moved there after the Philistine battle near Shiloh (7:17). Saul's lack of knowledge about Samuel showed his ignorance of spiritual matters. Saul and Samuel even lived in the same territory, Benjamin.

hill. So hurry, because he'll probably be leaving about the time you get there; the guests can't eat until he arrives and blesses the food."

14So they went into the city, and as they were entering the gates they saw Samuel coming out toward them to go up the hill. 15The Lord had told Samuel the previous day,

9:15
1 Sam 15:1
Acts 13:21

16"About this time tomorrow I will send you a man from the land of Benjamin. You are to anoint him as the leader of my people. He will save them from the Philistines, for I have looked down on them in mercy and have heard their cry."

9:16
Ex 3:7,9
Ps 106:44

17When Samuel saw Saul the Lord said, "That's the man I told you about! He will rule my people."

9:17
1 Sam 10:1
12:13; 16:12

18Just then Saul approached Samuel and asked, "Can you please tell me where the seer's house is?"

19"I am the seer!" Samuel replied. "Go on up the hill ahead of me and we'll eat together; in the morning I will tell you what you want to know and send you on your way. 20And don't worry about those donkeys that were lost three days ago, for they have been found. And anyway, you own all the wealth of Israel now!"

9:20
1 Sam 9:6
1 Sam 10:16

21"Pardon me, sir," Saul replied. "I'm from the tribe of Benjamin, the smallest in Israel, and my family is the least important of all the families of the tribe! You must have the wrong man!"

9:21
Judg 20:46-48
1 Sam 15:17

22Then Samuel took Saul and his servant into the great hall and placed them at the head of the table, honoring them above the thirty special guests. 23Samuel then instructed the chef to bring Saul the choicest cut of meat, the piece that had been set aside for the guest of honor. 24So the chef brought it in and placed it before Saul.

9:23
Gen 43:34

"Go ahead and eat it," Samuel said, "for I was saving it for you, even before I invited these others!"

So Saul ate with Samuel. 25After the feast, when they had returned to the city, Samuel took Saul up to the porch on the roof and talked with him there. 26, 27At daybreak the next morning, Samuel called up to him, "Get up; it's time you were on your way!"

9:25
Deut 22:8
2 Kgs 4:10
Neh 8:16
Acts 10:9,10

So Saul got up and Samuel accompanied him to the edge of the city. When they reached the city walls Samuel told Saul to send the servant on ahead. Then he told him, "I have received a special message for you from the Lord."

Samuel anoints Saul to be king

10 Then Samuel took a flask of olive oil and poured it over Saul's head and kissed him on the cheek and said,

"I am doing this because the Lord has appointed you to be the king of his people, Israel! 2When you leave me, you will see two men beside Rachel's tomb at Zelzah, in the land of Benjamin; they will tell you that the donkeys have been found and that your father is worried about you and is asking, 'How am I to find my son?' 3And when you get to the oak of Tabor you will see three men coming toward you who are on their way to worship God at the altar at Bethel; one will be bringing

10:1
Ex 30:22-25
Lev 8:12
1 Sam 9:16
16:13; 26:9
2 Sam 1:14

10:2
Gen 35:19; 48:7

10:3
Gen 28:16,22
35:1,3,7

9:18-21 Saul looked pessimistically at his circumstances and did not realize the resources he now had with God's help. He was so intent on finding the lost animals that he did not understand that he soon would have all the wealth of Israel. Remember that God sees you in light of your potential, as you rely upon him for strength. Don't let your past experiences or present pressures keep you from seeing your new self and new life in light of God's available resources.

9:21 "You must have the wrong man!" Saul's outburst reveals a problem he would face repeatedly—insecurity. Saul was like a leaf tossed about by the wind, vacillating between his feelings and convictions. Everything he said and did was for selfish motives, because he lived for himself. For example, Saul said his family was "the least important" in the "smallest" tribe in Israel, but 9:1 said just the opposite. Saul didn't want to face the responsibility to which God had called him. In another situation, Saul kept some war booty he shouldn't have and then tried to blame his soldiers

(15:21) while claiming that they had really taken it to sacrifice to God (15:15).

Although he had been called by God and had a mission in life, Saul struggled constantly with jealousy, insecurity, arrogance, impulsiveness, and deceit. Because Saul could not let God's love and call give rest and security to his heart, he never became God's man.

10:1 When an Israelite king took office he was not only crowned, he was anointed. The coronation was the political act of establishing the king as ruler; the anointing was the religious act of making the king God's representative to the people. A king was always anointed by a priest or prophet. The special anointing oil was a mixture of olive oil, myrrh, and other expensive spices. It was poured over the king's head to symbolize the presence and power of the Holy Spirit of God in his life. This anointing ceremony was to remind the king of his great responsibility to lead his people by God's wisdom and not his own.

three young goats, another will have three loaves of bread, and the third will have a bottle of wine. 4They will greet you and offer you two of the loaves, which you are to accept. 5After that you will come to Gibeath-elohim, also known as "God's Hill," where the garrison of the Philistines is. As you arrive there you will meet a band of prophets coming down the hill playing a psaltery, a timbrel, a flute, and a harp, and prophesying as they come.

6"At that time the Spirit of the Lord will come mightily upon you, and you will prophesy with them and you will feel and act like a different person. 7From that time on your decisions should be based on whatever seems best under the circumstances, for the Lord will guide you. 8Go to Gilgal and wait there seven days for me, for I will be coming to sacrifice burnt offerings and peace offerings. I will give you further instructions when I arrive."

9As Saul said good-bye and started to go, God gave him a new attitude, and all of Samuel's prophecies came true that day. 10When Saul and the servant arrived at the Hill of God they saw the prophets coming toward them, and the Spirit of God came upon him, and he too began to prophesy.

11When his friends heard about it, they exclaimed, "What? Saul a prophet?" 12And one of the neighbors added, "With a father like his?" So that is the origin of the proverb, "Is Saul a prophet, too?"

13When Saul had finished prophesying he climbed the hill to the altar.

14"Where in the world did you go?" Saul's uncle asked him.

And Saul replied, "We went to look for the donkeys, but we couldn't find them; so we went to the prophet Samuel to ask him where they were."

15"Oh? And what did he say?" his uncle asked.

10:5
1 Sam 19:20
2 Kgs 2:3,5,15
1 Chron 25:1

10:6
Num 11:25,29
Judg 3:10; 14:6
1 Sam 16:13
19:23,24

10:8
1 Sam 7:16
11:14,15; 13:7
15:33

10:9
1 Sam 10:6

10:11
1 Sam 19:24
Amos 7:14,15
Mt 13:54-57

10:14
1 Sam 9:3

RELIGIOUS AND POLITICAL CENTERS OF ISRAEL

GILGAL	Joshua 4:19; Judges 2:1; Hosea 4:15; Micah 6:5
SHILOH	Joshua 18:1–10; 19:51; Judges 18:31; 1 Samuel 1:3; Jeremiah 7:12–14
SHECHEM	Joshua 24:1
RAMAH	1 Samuel 7:17; 8:4
MIZPAH	Judges 11:11; 20:1; 1 Samuel 10:17
BETHEL	Judges 20:18, 26; 1 Samuel 10:3; Hosea 4:15
GIBE-AH (political center only)	1 Samuel 10:26
GIBEON (religious center only)	1 Kings 3:4; 2 Chronicles 1:2, 3
JERUSALEM	1 Kings 8:1ff; Psalm 48:1

During the period of the Judges, Israel may have had more than one capital. This may explain why the Scriptures overlap with reference to some cities.

Samuel called the Israelites together at Mizpah where he would anoint Saul as their first king. Up to this point, the political seat of the nation seems to have been the religious center of the nation as well. Above are the cities which probably served as both the religious and political centers of Israel since the days of Joshua. Saul may have been the first Israelite leader to separate the nation's religious center (probably Mizpah at this time) from its political center (Gibe-ah—1 Samuel 11:4; 26:1). Politically, the nation grew strong for a while. But when Saul and his officials stopped seeking God's will, internal jealousies and strife soon began to decay the nation from within. When David became king he brought the Ark of the Covenant back to Jerusalem, his capital. King Solomon then completely united the religious and political centers at Jerusalem.

10:6 How could Saul be so filled with the Spirit and later commit such evil acts? Throughout the Old Testament, God's Spirit "came upon" a person temporarily so that God could use him or her for great acts. This happened frequently to Israel's judges when they were called by God to rescue the nation (Judges 3:8–10). This was not a permanent, abiding influence, but a temporary manifestation of the Holy Spirit. In many ways it corresponds to the "filling" of the Holy Spirit in the New Testament. Yet, at times in the Old Testament, the Spirit even came upon unbelievers to enable them to do unusual tasks (Numbers 24; 2 Chronicles 36:22, 23). Saul, in his early years as king, had a "new attitude" (10:1–10) as a result of the Holy Spirit's work in him. But as Saul's power grew, so did

his pride. After a while he refused to seek God, the Spirit left him (16:14), and his good attitude melted away. The Spirit was "taking control" not "taking residence." The Holy Spirit can use anyone to accomplish his will, but takes residence *only* in those who have put their faith in Jesus Christ, trusting in his sacrifice for their salvation.

10:10, 11 A prophet is someone who speaks God's words. While God told many prophets to predict certain events, what God wanted most was for them to instruct and inspire people to live in faithfulness to God. When Saul's friends heard inspired words coming from Saul they exclaimed, "What? Saul a prophet?" This was an expression of surprise at worldly Saul becoming religious. It is equivalent to "What? Has he got religion?"

The people accept Saul as king

16"He said the donkeys had been found!" Saul replied. (But he didn't tell him that he had been anointed as king!)

10:16
1 Sam 9:20

17Samuel now called a convocation of all Israel at Mizpah, 18, 19and gave them this message from the Lord God: "I brought you from Egypt and rescued you from the Egyptians and from all of the nations that were torturing you. But although I have done so much for you, you have rejected me and have said, 'We want a king instead!' All right, then, present yourselves before the Lord by tribes and clans."

10:17
Judg 20:1
1 Sam 7:5,6

10:18
Josh 24:5
Judg 6:8
1 Sam 8:6,7

20So Samuel called the tribal leaders together before the Lord, and the tribe of Benjamin was chosen by sacred lot. 21Then he brought each family of the tribe of Benjamin before the Lord, and the family of the Matrites was chosen. And finally, the sacred lot selected Saul, the son of Kish. But when they looked for him, he had disappeared!

10:20
Josh 7:16
1 Sam 14:41
Acts 1:24,25

22So they asked the Lord, "Where is he? Is he here among us?"
And the Lord replied, "He is hiding in the baggage."

10:22
Num 27:21

23So they found him and brought him out, and he stood head and shoulders above anyone else.

10:23
1 Sam 9:2; 16:7

24Then Samuel said to all the people, "This is the man the Lord has chosen as your king. There isn't his equal in all of Israel!"
And all the people shouted, "Long live the king!"

10:24
1 Kgs 1:25,
34,39
2 Kgs 11:12

25Then Samuel told the people again what the rights and duties of a king were; he wrote them in a book and put it in a special place before the Lord. Then Samuel sent the people home again.

10:25
Deut 17:15
1 Sam 8:11-18

26When Saul returned to his home at Gibe-ah, a band of men whose hearts the Lord had touched became his constant companions. 27There were, however, some bums and loafers who exclaimed, "How can this man save us?" And they despised him and refused to bring him presents, but he took no notice.

10:27
1 Kgs 10:24
Ps 72:10

10:19 Israel's true king was God, but the nation demanded another. Imagine wanting a person instead of God as their guide and leader! Men and women have rejected God throughout history, and they continue to do it today. Are you rejecting God by pushing him aside and acknowledging other people or things as your "king" or top priority? Learn from the rejections you have experienced, and become sensitive to the moments when you reject God.

10:20 The Israelites chose their first king by "sacred lot," probably by using the Urim and Thummim, two plates or flat stones carried by the High Priest. The fact that Saul was chosen may seem like luck, but it was really the opposite. For God had instructed the Israelites to make the Urim and Thummim for the specific purpose of consulting him in times such as this (Exodus 28:30, 31; Numbers 27:12–21). By using the Urim and Thummin, the Israelites were taking the decision out of their own hands and turning it over to God.

Only the High Priest could use the Urim and Thummim which were designed to give only yes or no answers. It is not clear in the Bible whether Samuel was the priest in charge at Saul's coronation or whether there was a High Priest in office at this time.

10:22 When the king was to be chosen, Saul already knew that he was the one (10:1). Instead of coming forward, however, he hid in the baggage. Often we hide from important responsibilities because we are afraid of failure, afraid of what others will think, or perhaps unsure about how to proceed.

10:24 Saul, who not long ago was a farmer searching for donkeys, was now king. Although he was tall, handsome, and wealthy, it seems surprising that he was God's first choice to be king, especially since he lacked any great spiritual heritage and

was probably not a deeply religious man. But God does not always choose people according to human expectations. He may not even choose the one best qualified for the task, but rather the one who will best fulfill his larger purpose. Sometimes this means choosing a poor leader to teach people a valuable lesson. God may want to use you for a great work, or he may choose someone else who seems unfit. In either case, try to look for God's greater purpose.

10:25 The kings of Israel, unlike kings of other nations, had specific duties outlined for them (Deuteronomy 17:14–20). Heathen kings were considered gods; they made their own laws and answered to no one. Israel's king, by contrast, had to answer to a higher authority—the Lord of heaven and earth. The Israelites now had a king like everyone else, just as they wanted. But God, in his charge to both the king and the people, wanted to make sure that Israel's king would rule differently than his pagan counterparts.

10:26 Since Israel had no political capital at this time, Saul returned to Gibe-ah, his hometown, which eventually became the first capital of the united kingdom. Saul's move to Gibe-ah marked the first time that the political center of Israel was separated from the religious center. During this time, the religious center was in Ramah.

10:26, 27 Some men became Saul's constant companions, while others despised him. Criticism will always be directed toward those who lead, because they are in a vulnerable position. At this time, Saul took no notice of those who seemed to be against him, although later he would become consumed with this thought (18:14–16; 19:1–3; 26:17–21). As you lead, listen to constructive criticism, but don't spend valuable time and energy worrying about those who may oppose you. Instead, focus your attention on those who are ready and willing to help.

Saul defeats the Ammonite army

11:1
Judg 11:4-6
21:8
1 Sam 31:11

11

At this time Nahash led the army of the Ammonites against the Israeli city of Jabesh-gilead. But the citizens of Jabesh asked for peace. "Leave us alone and we will be your servants," they pleaded.

2"All right," Nahash said, "but only on one condition: I will gouge out the right eye of every one of you as a disgrace upon all Israel!"

3"Give us seven days to see if we can get some help!" replied the elders of Jabesh. "If none of our brothers will come and save us, we will agree to your terms."

11:4
1 Sam 10:26
14:2; 30:4

4When a messenger came to Gibe-ah, Saul's home town, and told the people about their plight, everyone broke into tears.

11:5
1 Kgs 19:19

5Saul was plowing in the field, and when he returned to town he asked, "What's the matter? Why is everyone crying?"

11:6
Judg 3:10; 6:34
1 Sam 10:6,
7,10

So they told him about the message from Jabesh. 6Then the Spirit of God came strongly upon Saul and he became very angry. 7He took two oxen and cut them into pieces and sent messengers to carry them throughout all Israel.

11:7
Judg 19:29; 20:1

"This is what will happen to the oxen of anyone who refuses to follow Saul and Samuel to battle!" he announced. And God caused the people to be afraid of Saul's anger, and they came to him as one man. 8He counted them in Bezek and found that there were three hundred thousand of them in addition to thirty thousand from Judah.

11:8
Judg 1:4-6

9So he sent the messengers back to Jabesh-gilead to say, "We will rescue you before tomorrow noon!" What joy there was throughout the city when that message arrived!

10The men of Jabesh then told their enemies, "We surrender. Tomorrow we will come out to you and you can do to us as you wish."

11:11
Judg 7:16; 9:43

11But early the next morning Saul arrived, having divided his army into three detachments, and launched a surprise attack against the Ammonites and slaughtered them all morning. The remnant of their army was so badly scattered that no two of them were left together.

11:12
1 Sam 10:27
Lk 19:27

12Then the people exclaimed to Samuel, "Where are those men who said that Saul shouldn't be our king? Bring them here and we will kill them!"

11:13
Ex 14:13
1 Sam 14:45
19:5
2 Sam 19:22

13But Saul replied, "No one will be executed today; for today the Lord has rescued Israel!"

11:1 At this time, Israel was very susceptible to invasion by marauding tribes such as these Ammonites from east of the Jordan River. Saul's leadership in battle against this warlike tribe helped unify the nation and proved that he was a worthy military ruler. Saul's kingship was solidified by saving the nation from disgrace and sparing the people who had criticized him.

11:3 Why would Nahash give the city of Jabesh-gilead seven days to find an army to help them? Because Israel was still disorganized, Nahash was betting that no one would come to the city's aid. He was hoping to take the city without a fight and avoid a battle. He also may not have been prepared to attack the city because a siege against the walls could last weeks or months.

11:6 Anger is a powerful emotion. Often it is used wrongly to hurt others with words or physical violence. But anger directed at sin and the mistreatment of others is not wrong. Saul was angered by the Ammonites' threat to humiliate and mistreat his fellow Israelites. God used Saul's anger to bring justice and freedom. When injustice or sin makes you angry, ask God how you can channel that anger in constructive ways to help bring about a positive change.

11:8 Judah, one of the 12 tribes of Israel, is often mentioned separately from the other 11. There are several reasons for this. Judah was the largest tribe (Numbers 1:20–46), and it was the tribe from which most of Israel's kings would come (Genesis 49:8–12). Later, Judah would be one of the few tribes to return to God after a century of captivity under a hostile foreign power.

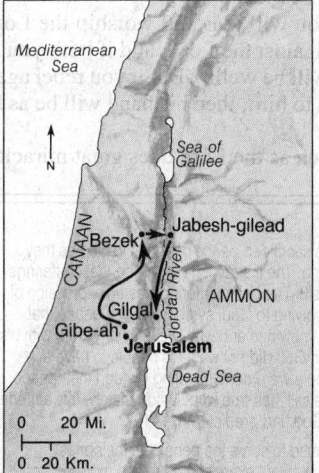

SAUL DEFEATS THE AMMONITES
The Ammonites prepared to attack Jabesh-gilead. The people of Jabesh sent messengers to Saul in Gibe-ah asking for help. Saul mobilized an army at Bezek and then attacked the Ammonites. After the battle, the Israelites returned to Gilgal to crown Saul as king.

Judah would also be the tribe through which the Messiah would come (Micah 5:2).

14Then Samuel said to the people, "Come, let us all go to Gilgal and reconfirm
Saul as our king."

15So they went to Gilgal and in a solemn ceremony before the Lord they crowned
him king. Then they offered peace offerings to the Lord, and Saul and all Israel
were very happy.

Samuel reminds the people of God's blessing

12 Then Samuel addressed the people again:
"Look," he said, "I have done as you asked. I have given you a king. 2I have
selected him ahead of my own sons and now I stand here, an old, grey-haired man
who has been in public service from the time he was a lad. 3Now tell me as I stand
before the Lord and before his anointed king—whose ox or donkey have I stolen?
Have I ever defrauded you? Have I ever oppressed you? Have I ever taken a bribe?
Tell me and I will make right whatever I have done wrong."

4"No," they replied, "you have never defrauded or oppressed us in any way and
you have never taken even one single bribe."

5"The Lord and his anointed king are my witnesses," Samuel declared, "that you
can never accuse me of robbing you."

"Yes, it is true," they replied.

6"It was the Lord who appointed Moses and Aaron," Samuel continued. "He
brought your ancestors out of the land of Egypt.

7"Now stand here quietly before the Lord as I remind you of all the good things
he has done for you and for your ancestors:

8"When the Israelites were in Egypt and cried out to the Lord, he sent Moses and
Aaron to bring them into this land. 9But they soon forgot about the Lord their God,
so he let them be conquered by Sisera, the general of King Hazor's army, and by
the Philistines and the king of Moab.

10"Then they cried to the Lord again and confessed that they had sinned by
turning away from him and worshiping the Baal and Ashtaroth idols. And they
pleaded, 'We will worship you and you alone if you will only rescue us from our
enemies.' 11Then the Lord sent Gideon, Barak, Jephthah, and Samuel to save you,
and you lived in safety.

12"But when you were afraid of Nahash, the king of Ammon, you came to me
and said that you wanted a king to reign over you. But the Lord your God was
already your King, for he has always been your King. 13All right, here is the king
you have chosen. Look him over. You have asked for him, and the Lord has
answered your request.

14"Now if you will fear and worship the Lord and listen to his commandments
and not rebel against the Lord, and if both you and your king follow the Lord your
God, then all will be well. 15But if you rebel against the Lord's commandments and
refuse to listen to him, then his hand will be as heavy upon you as it was upon your
ancestors.

16"Now watch as the Lord does great miracles. 17You know that it does not rain

11:14
1 Sam 10:1,8

12:2
1 Sam 3:10,19,
20; 8:1,5

12:3
Ex 23:8
Num 16:15
Deut 16:19

12:4
1 Sam 8:3

12:5
Ex 22:4
Ps 17:3

12:6
Ex 6:26

12:7
Deut 4:9
Judg 5:11
Ps 78:4
Mic 6:4

12:8
Ex 2:23-25
3:10; 4:14-16

12:9
Deut 32:18
Judg 3:7; 10:7
13:1
Ps 106:21

12:10
Judg 3:15
10:10,15,16

12:11
Judg 4:6; 6:32
11:1
1 Sam 1:19,20
Heb 11:32

12:12
Judg 8:23,24

12:13
Hos 13:11

12:14
Josh 24:14,20
Ps 81:12-15
Isa 3:10

12:15
Deut 28:15
Josh 24:20
Isa 1:2,20

12:17
Josh 10:12
Ps 99:6
Jer 15:1

11:15 The Israelites sacrificed peace offerings to God as they
crowned their first king. The instructions for giving these offerings
are given in Leviticus 3. The peace offering was an expression of
gratitude and thanksgiving to God, symbolizing the peace that
comes to those who know him and who live in accordance with his
commands. Although God did not want his people to have a
human king, the people were demonstrating through their peace
offerings that he was still their true king. Unfortunately, this attitude
did not last, just as God had predicted (8:7–19).

12:1 Samuel continued to serve the people as their priest,
prophet, and judge, but Saul exercised more and more political
and military control over the tribes (see 7:15).

12:1–3 By asking the Israelites to point out any wrongs he had
committed during his time as Israel's judge, Samuel was reminding
them that he could be trusted to tell the truth. He was also

reminding them that having a king was their idea, not his. Samuel
was setting the stage for the miraculous thunderstorm recorded in
12:16–19, so that the people could not blame him when God
punished them for their selfish motives.

12:12–15 God granted the nation's request for a king, but his
commandments and requirements for their lives remained the
same. God was to be their true king, and both Saul and the people
were to be subject to his law. No person is ever exempt from God's
law. No human involvement is outside of his jurisdiction. God is the
true king of every area of life. We must recognize his kingship and
submit to him in obedience.

12:17 The wheat harvest came near the end of the dry season
during the months of May and June. Since rain rarely fell during
this period, a great thunderstorm was considered a miraculous
event. But rain during the wheat harvest could damage the crops

12:20
Ex 20:20
Deut 11:16

12:21
Isa 41:29
Hab 2:18
1 Cor 8:4

12:22
Ex 32:12
Num 14:13
Deut 7:6; 31:6
1 Pet 2:9

12:23
Prov 4:11
Rom 1:9
Col 1:9
1 Thess 3:10

12:24
Deut 10:21
Eccles 12:13
Rom 12:1

12:25
Isa 1:20
Hos 10:3

at this time of the year, during the wheat harvest; I will pray for the Lord to send thunder and rain today, so that you will realize the extent of your wickedness in asking for a king!"

18So Samuel called to the Lord, and the Lord sent thunder and rain; and all the people were very much afraid of the Lord and of Samuel.

19"Pray for us lest we die!" they cried out to Samuel. "For now we have added to all our other sins by asking for a king."

20"Don't be frightened," Samuel reassured them. "You have certainly done wrong, but make sure now that you worship the Lord with true enthusiasm, and that you don't turn your back on him in any way. 21Other gods can't help you. 22The Lord will not abandon his chosen people, for that would dishonor his great name. He made you a special nation for himself—just because he wanted to!

23"As for me, I will certainly not sin against the Lord by ending my prayers for you; and I will continue to teach you those things which are good and right. 24"Trust the Lord and sincerely worship him; think of all the tremendous things he has done for you. 25But if you continue to sin, you and your king will be destroyed."

2. God rejects Saul for disobedience
Saul disobeys God by wrongly making a sacrifice

13:2
1 Sam 10:26
13:23
14:2,5,52

13:3
Judg 3:27; 6:34
2 Sam 2:28
20:1

13:5
Josh 11:4

13:6
Judg 6:2
1 Sam 14:11
23:19

13 By this time Saul had reigned for one year. In the second year of his reign, 2he selected three thousand special troops and took two thousand of them with him to Michmash and Mount Bethel while the other thousand remained with Jonathan, Saul's son, in Gibe-ah in the land of Benjamin. The rest of the army was sent home. 3, 4Then Jonathan attacked and destroyed the garrison of the Philistines at Geba. The news spread quickly throughout the land of the Philistines, and Saul sounded the call to arms throughout Israel. He announced that he had destroyed the Philistine garrison and warned his men that the army of Israel stank to high heaven as far as the Philistines were concerned. So the entire Israeli army mobilized again and joined at Gilgal. 5The Philistines recruited a mighty army of three thousand chariots, six thousand horsemen, and so many soldiers that they were as thick as sand along the seashore; and they camped at Michmash east of Beth-aven.

6When the men of Israel saw the vast mass of enemy troops, they lost their nerve entirely and tried to hide in caves, thickets, coverts, among the rocks, and even in

13:1 *Saul had reigned for one year.* The Hebrew, from which the numbers have evidently dropped out in copying, reads: "Saul was . . . years old when he began to reign, and he reigned . . . and two years over Israel."

---

and cause them to rot quickly. This unusual occurrence demonstrated God's displeasure with Israel's demand for a king.

12:22 Why did God make Israel a special nation? God did not choose them because they deserved it (Deuteronomy 7:7, 8), but in order that they might become the means by which God would bless all people through the Messiah (Genesis 12:1–3). God would never abandon his people; but because they were his special nation, he would often punish them for their disobedience.

12:23 Is failing to pray for others a sin? Samuel's words seem to indicate that such a failure is sin. Samuel's actions illustrate two responsibilities which God's people should be concerned about: (1) they should pray consistently for others (Ephesians 6:18), and (2) they should teach others the right way to God (2 Timothy 2:2). Samuel disagreed with the Israelites' demand for a king, but he assured them that he would continue to pray for them and teach them. We may disagree with someone, but we shouldn't stop praying for him or her. Samuel also became irritated with Saul because he was always looking for a military answer to his problems instead of a spiritual one. Saul often performed spiritual functions out of duty rather than from his heart. Samuel was hoping that God would answer his prayers and change Saul.

12:24 This is the second time in this chapter that Samuel reminded the people to take time to recall all the good things God had done for them (see 12:7). Taking time for reflection allows us to focus our attention upon God's goodness and strengthens our

faith. Sometimes we fail to take time to reflect on all that God has already done. Make it a practice to review what God has done for you so that you may move ahead with a grateful attitude.

12:25 If we continue in sin, we will not enjoy fellowship with God and we will end up destroying ourselves. Persisting in destructive habits, immoral thoughts, harbored resentments, and failing to heed God's Word are examples of "continuing in sin."

13:3, 4 Jonathan attacked and destroyed the Philistine garrison, but Saul took all the credit for it. Although this was normal in that culture, it didn't make his action right. Saul's growing pride started out small—taking credit for a battle which was won by his son. Left unchecked, his pride grew into an ugly obsession which threatened the well-being of the nation. Taking credit for the accomplishments of others indicates that there is pride in your life. When you notice pride taking a foothold, take immediate steps to put it in check by giving credit to those who deserve it.

13:6 When we forget who is on our side, or see only our own resources, we tend to panic at the sight of the opposition. The Israelites became terrified and hid when they saw the mighty Philistine army. They forgot that God was on their side and that he couldn't be defeated. As you face problems and temptations, focus your attention on God and his resources, trusting him to help you (Romans 8:31–37).

tombs and cisterns. ⁷Some of them crossed the Jordan River and escaped to the land of Gad and Gilead. Meanwhile, Saul stayed at Gilgal, and those who were with him trembled with fear at what awaited them. ⁸Samuel had told Saul earlier to wait seven days for his arrival, but when he still didn't come, and Saul's troops were rapidly slipping away, ⁹he decided to sacrifice the burnt offering and the peace offerings himself. ¹⁰But just as he was finishing, Samuel arrived. Saul went out to meet him and to receive his blessing, ¹¹but Samuel said, "What is this you have done?"

"Well," Saul replied, "when I saw that my men were scattering from me, and that you hadn't arrived by the time you said you would, and that the Philistines were at Michmash, ready for battle, ¹²I said, 'The Philistines are ready to march against us and I haven't even asked for the Lord's help!' So I reluctantly offered the burnt offering without waiting for you to arrive."

¹³"You fool!" Samuel exclaimed. "You have disobeyed the commandment of the Lord your God. He was planning to make you and your descendants kings of Israel forever, ¹⁴but now your dynasty must end; for the Lord wants a man who will obey him. And he has discovered the man he wants and has already appointed him as king over his people; for you have not obeyed the Lord's commandment."

Saul's military hindrances

¹⁵Samuel then left Gilgal and went to Gibe-ah in the land of Benjamin.

When Saul counted the soldiers who were still with him, he found only six hundred left! ¹⁶Saul and Jonathan and these six hundred men set up their camp in

13:8	1 Sam 10:8
13:9	2 Sam 24:25 / 1 Kgs 3:4
13:10	1 Sam 15:13
13:11	2 Sam 3:23,24
13:13	1 Sam 15:22,28 / 2 Chron 16:9
13:14	Acts 13:22
13:16	1 Sam 14:2

Reference	Message	**GLOOM**
3:11–14	Judgment will come to the house of Eli.	**AND DOOM**
7:1–4	The nation must turn from idol worship.	
8:10–22	Your kings will bring you nothing but trouble.	
12:25	If you continue in sin, you will be destroyed by God.	
13:13, 14	Saul's kingdom will not continue.	
15:17–31	Saul, you have sinned before God.	

It wasn't easy being a prophet. Most of the messages they had to give were very unpleasant to hear. They preached of repentance, judgment, impending destruction, sin, and in general, how displeased God was over the behavior of his people. Prophets were not the most popular people in town (unless they were *false* prophets and said just what the people wanted to hear). But popularity was not the bottom line for true prophets of God—it was obedience to God and faithfully proclaiming his word. Samuel is a good example of a faithful prophet.

God has words for us to proclaim as well. And although his messages are loaded with "Good News," there is also "bad news" to give. May we, like true prophets, faithfully deliver *all* God's words, regardless of their popularity or lack of it.

13:9 Rather than wait for a priest, Saul offered the sacrifice himself. This was against the law (Numbers 18:5). Under pressure from the approaching Philistines, he took matters into his own hands and disobeyed God. He was doing a good thing (offering a sacrifice to God before a crucial battle), but he did it at the wrong time and in the wrong way. Our true spiritual character is revealed under pressure, as was Saul's. The methods we use to accomplish our goals are as important as the attainment of those goals.

13:11, 12 One of the most difficult times to trust God is when you feel your resources slipping away. When Saul felt that time was running out, his impatience caused him to act against God's will. Thinking that the ritual of the sacrifice alone was enough to help, he confused the sacrifice with the God of the sacrifice.

When you are faced with a difficult decision, make sure that impatience does not drive you to do what is not in agreement with God's Word. When you know what God wants, don't go against that plan regardless of the circumstances. God often uses delays to test our obedience and patience.

13:12 Saul had plenty of excuses for his disobedience. But Samuel zeroed in on the real issue: "You have disobeyed the commandment of the Lord your God" (13:13). Like Saul, we often gloss over our mistakes and sins, trying to justify and spiritualize our actions because of our "special" circumstances. Our excuses, however, are nothing more than disobedience. God knows our true motives. He forgives, restores, and blesses only when we are honest about our sins. By trying to hide his sins behind excuses, Saul lost his kingship (13:14).

13:13 Why did Samuel react to Saul's disobedience in such a harsh way? Saul could offer a sacrifice only in the presence of a priest. By offering the sacrifice himself, he directly violated God's law (Numbers 18:5).

Saul was already ignoring the charge which Samuel had given to him in 12:14, 15. Almost at once he began to work independent of God's law, priests, and prophets. Such actions disqualified him from his real task, which was to be God's representative. Leaders who disobey God must face the consequences. God wants servants who will obey.

13:17
1 Sam 11:11

13:18
1 Kgs 9:17
Neh 11:31-35

13:19
Judg 5:8
1 Sam 17:47
2 Kgs 24:14
Jer 24:1

Geba in the land of Benjamin; but the Philistines stayed at Michmash. ¹⁷Three companies of raiders soon left the camp of the Philistines; one went toward Ophrah in the land of Shual, ¹⁸another went to Beth-horon, and the third moved toward the border above the valley of Zeboim near the desert.

¹⁹There were no blacksmiths at all in the land of Israel in those days, for the Philistines wouldn't allow them for fear of their making swords and spears for the Hebrews. ²⁰So whenever the Israelites needed to sharpen their plowshares, discs, axes, or sickles, they had to take them to a Philistine blacksmith. ²¹(The schedule of charges was as follows:

For sharpening a plow point, 60¢
For sharpening a disc, 60¢
For sharpening an axe, 30¢

SAUL

First impressions can be deceiving, especially when the image created by a person's appearance is contradicted by their qualities and abilities. Saul was the ideal visual image of a king, but the tendencies of his personality often went contrary to God's commands for a king. He was God's chosen leader, but God's choice did not imply that Saul was capable of being king on his own.

During his reign, Saul had his greatest successes when he obeyed God. His greatest failures resulted from acting on his own. Saul had the raw materials to be a good leader—appearance, courage, and action. Even his weaknesses could have been used by God if Saul had recognized them and left them in God's hands. His own choices cut him off from God and eventually alienated him from his own people.

From Saul we learn that while our strengths and abilities make us useful, it is our weaknesses that make us useable. Our skills and talents make us tools, but our failures and shortcomings remind us that we need a Craftsman in control of our lives. Whatever we accomplish on our own is only a hint of what God could do through our lives. Does he control your life?

Strengths and accomplishments:
- First God-appointed king of Israel
- Known for his personal courage and generosity
- Stood tall, with a striking appearance

Weaknesses and mistakes:
- His leadership abilities did not match the expectations created by his appearance
- Impulsive by nature, he tended to overstep his bounds
- Jealous of David, he tried to kill him
- He specifically disobeyed God on several occasions

Lessons from his life:
- God wants obedience from the heart, not mere acts of religious ritual
- Obedience always involves sacrifice, but sacrifice is not always obedience
- God wants to make use of our strengths and weaknesses
- Weaknesses should help us remember our need for God's guidance and help

Vital statistics:
- Where: The land of Benjamin
- Occupation: King of Israel
- Relatives: Father: Kish. Sons: Jonathan and Ish-bosheth. Wife: Ahi-noam. Daughters: Merab and Michal.

Key verses:
"Samuel replied, 'Has the Lord as much pleasure in your burnt offerings and sacrifices as in your obedience? Obedience is far better than sacrifice. He is much more interested in your listening to him than in your offering the fat of rams to him. For rebellion is as bad as the sin of witchcraft, and stubbornness is as bad as worshiping idols. And now because you have rejected the word of Jehovah, he has rejected you from being king' " (1 Samuel 15:22, 23).

His story is told in 1 Samuel 9—31. He is also mentioned in Acts 13:21.

13:19–21 Israel was in no position to conquer anyone. The army had no weapons, and there were no facilities for turning their tools into weapons. In fact, if an Israelite wanted to sharpen his tools, he had to pay a Philistine blacksmith to do it, because the Philistines had a carefully guarded monopoly on iron and blacksmithing. Their tight control over the technology, along with their surprise raids, were designed to demoralize the Israelites.

Against such superiority, the Israelites were at a serious disadvantage. How could they hope to rout their oppressors? Only with God's help. God wanted to give Israel victory without swords; then the victory would be his alone.

For sharpening a sickle, 30¢
For sharpening an ox goad, 30¢)

22So there was not a single sword or spear in the entire "army" of Israel that day, except for Saul's and Jonathan's. 23The mountain pass at Michmash had meanwhile been secured by a contingent of the Philistine army.

13:23
1 Sam 14:5,31
Isa 10:28

Jonathan's brave plan

14 A day or so later, Prince Jonathan said to his young bodyguard, "Come on, let's cross the valley to the garrison of the Philistines." But he didn't tell his father that he was leaving.

14:1
1 Sam 13:2,22
14:39-45; 18:1

2Saul and his six hundred men were camped at the edge of Gibe-ah, around the pomegranate tree at Migron. 3Among his men was Ahijah the priest (the son of Ahitub, Ichabod's brother; Ahitub was the son of Phinehas and the grandson of Eli, the priest of the Lord in Shiloh).

14:2
1 Sam 13:16
14:3
1 Sam 1:3
4:21,22
22:11,12

No one realized that Jonathan had gone. 4To reach the Philistine garrison, Jonathan had to go over a narrow pass between two rocky crags which had been named Bozez and Seneh. 5The crag on the north was in front of Michmash and the southern one was in front of Geba.

14:5
1 Sam 13:23

6"Yes, let's go across to those heathen," Jonathan had said to his bodyguard. "Perhaps the Lord will do a miracle for us. For it makes no difference to him how many enemy troops there are!"

14:6
Judg 7:4
2 Chron 14:11

7"Fine!" the youth replied. "Do as you think best; I'm with you heart and soul, whatever you decide."

8"All right, then this is what we'll do," Jonathan told him. 9"When they see us, if they say, 'Stay where you are or we'll kill you!' then we will stop and wait for them. 10But if they say, 'Come on up and fight!' then we will do just that; for it will be God's signal that he will help us defeat them!"

14:10
Gen 24:14
Judg 6:36
14:11
1 Sam 13:6

11When the Philistines saw them coming they shouted, "Look! The Israelis are crawling out of their holes!" 12Then they shouted to Jonathan, "Come on up here and we'll show you how to fight!"

14:12
Judg 5:14; 7:15
2 Sam 5:24

14:1ff In this chapter we read about Saul's failure as Israel's leader: (1) he had no communication with Jonathan (14:1, 17); (2) he was unprepared to follow up when Jonathan routed the enemy (14:19); (3) he didn't ask God's help ahead of time (14:19); (4) he made a rash vow (14:24); and (5) he ignored the well-being of his own soldiers (14:31). Saul's poor leadership was not a result of personality traits, but of decaying spiritual character. What we do is often a direct result of our spiritual condition. We cannot ignore the importance of spiritual character in becoming an effective leader.

14:1 Why would Jonathan go alone to attack the Philistines? Jonathan may have been weary of the long, hopeless standoff in the battle; he trusted God to give the victory and wanted to act on that trust. He also knew that the number of Philistines was no problem for God. Perhaps he didn't tell his father about his mission because he thought Saul would not let him go.

14:6 Jonathan and his bodyguard weren't much of a force to attack the huge Philistine army. But while everyone else was afraid, they trusted God, knowing that the size of the enemy army had no relationship to God's ability to help them. God honored the faith and brave action of these two men with a tremendous victory.

Have you ever felt surrounded by the "enemy" or faced overwhelming odds? God is never intimidated by the size of the enemy or the complexity of a problem. With him, there are always enough resources to resist the pressures and win your battles. If God has called you to action, then bravely commit what few resources you have to God and rely upon him to give you the victory.

14:12 Jonathan did not have the authority to lead all the troops

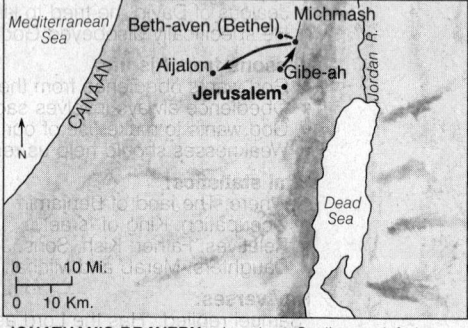

JONATHAN'S BRAVERY Jonathan, Saul's son, left the camp at Gibe-ah and crept to the Philistine camp at Michmash. With God's help, Jonathan and his bodyguard surprised the Philistine army who panicked and began killing each other! Saul's army heard the commotion and chased the Philistines as far as Beth-aven and Aijalon.

into battle, but he could start a small skirmish in one corner of the enemy camp. When he did, panic broke out among the Philistines, the Hebrews who were drafted into the Philistine army revolted, and the men who hid in the hills regained their courage and returned to fight.

When you are facing an obstacle that is beyond your control, ask yourself, "What steps can I take now to work toward a solution?" A few small steps may be just what is needed to begin

"Come on, climb right behind me," Jonathan exclaimed to his bodyguard, "for the Lord will help us defeat them!"

13So they clambered up on their hands and knees, and the Philistines fell back as Jonathan and the lad killed them right and left, 14about twenty men in all, and their bodies were scattered over about half an acre of land. 15Suddenly panic broke out throughout the entire Philistine army, and even among the raiders. And just then there was a great earthquake, increasing the terror.

16Saul's lookouts in Gibe-ah saw a strange sight—the vast army of the Philistines began to melt away in all directions.

17"Find out who isn't here," Saul ordered. And when they had checked, they found that Jonathan and his bodyguard were gone. 18"Bring the Ark of God," Saul shouted to Ahijah. (For the Ark was among the people of Israel at that time.) 19But while Saul was talking to the priest, the shouting and the tumult in the camp of the Philistines grew louder and louder. "Quick! What does God say?" Saul demanded.

20Then Saul and his six hundred men rushed out to the battle and found the Philistines killing each other, and there was terrible confusion everywhere. 21And now the Hebrews who had been drafted into the Philistine army revolted and joined with the Israelis. 22Finally even the men hiding in the hills joined the chase when they saw that the Philistines were running away. 23So the Lord saved Israel that day, and the battle continued out beyond Beth-aven.

Saul's foolish order to eat nothing

24, 25Saul had declared, "A curse upon anyone who eats anything before evening—before I have full revenge on my enemies." So no one ate anything all day, even though they found honeycomb on the ground in the forest, 26for they all feared Saul's curse. 27Jonathan, however, had not heard his father's command; so he dipped a stick into a honeycomb, and when he had eaten the honey he felt much better. 28Then someone told him that his father had laid a curse upon anyone who ate food that day, and everyone was weary and faint as a result.

29"That's ridiculous!" Jonathan exclaimed. "A command like that only hurts us. See how much better I feel now that I have eaten this little bit of honey. 30If the people had been allowed to eat freely from the food they found among our enemies, think how many more we could have slaughtered!"

31But hungry as they were, they chased and killed the Philistines all day from Michmash to Aijalon, growing more and more faint. 32That evening they flew upon the battle loot and butchered the sheep, oxen, and calves, and ate the raw, bloody meat. 33Someone reported to Saul what was happening, that the people were sinning against the Lord by eating blood.

"That is very wrong," Saul said. "Roll a great stone over here, 34and go out among the troops and tell them to bring the oxen and sheep here to kill and drain them, and not to sin against the Lord by eating the blood." So that is what they did.

14:32 *that evening,* implied.

14:15
Josh 2:9
1 Sam 7:10
2 Kgs 7:6

14:18
1 Sam 4:3
23:9; 30:7

14:19
Num 27:21

14:20
Judg 7:21
2 Chron 20:23

14:21
1 Sam 29:4

14:22
1 Sam 13:6
31:7

14:23
Ex 14:30
2 Chron 32:22

14:24
Josh 6:26

14:31
Josh 10:12

14:32
Gen 9:4
Lev 17:10
1 Sam 15:19
Acts 15:20

---

the chain of events leading to your eventual victory.

14:18 This is the only time in the Old Testament when the Ark of the Covenant was used as a means of consulting with God. Usually the Urim and Thummim were used to consult with God (see the note on 10:20). During Saul's reign the Ark was kept in a private home in the town of Kiriath-jearim (7:1). Again Saul showed his impulsiveness by going ahead with his battle plans before God gave him an answer (14:19, 20).

14:24, 25 Saul made a vow without thinking through the implications. The results? (1) His men were too tired to fight; (2) they were so hungry that they ate raw meat that still contained blood, which was against God's laws; (3) Saul almost killed his own son (14:42–44).

Saul's impulsive vow sounded heroic, but its disastrous side effects made it little more than "shooting off at the mouth." If you

are in the middle of a conflict, guard against impulsive statements that you may be forced to honor.

14:29 Saul had issued a ridiculous command and had driven his men to sin, and still he wouldn't back down even if it meant killing his son. When we make ridiculous statements, it is difficult to admit we are wrong. We stick to our story just to save face, which only compounds the problem. We should realize that it takes more courage to admit a mistake than to resolutely hold to an error.

14:32–34 One of the oldest and strongest Hebrew food laws was the prohibition against eating raw meat containing the animal's blood (Leviticus 7:26, 27). This law began in Noah's day (Genesis 9:4) and was still observed by the early Christians (Acts 15:27–29). It was wrong to eat blood because blood represented life. (For further explanation see Leviticus 17:10–14.)

³⁵And Saul built an altar to the Lord——his first.

³⁶Afterwards Saul said, "Let's chase the Philistines all night and destroy every last one of them."

"Fine!" his men replied. "Do as you think best."

But the priest said, "Let's ask God first."

³⁷So Saul asked God, "Shall we go after the Philistines? Will you help us defeat them?" But the Lord made no reply all night.

³⁸Then Saul said to the leaders, "Something's wrong! We must find out what sin was committed today. ³⁹I vow by the name of the God who saved Israel that though the sinner be my own son Jonathan, he shall surely die!" But no one would tell him what the trouble was.

⁴⁰Then Saul proposed, "Jonathan and I will stand over here, and all of you stand over there." And the people agreed.

⁴¹Then Saul said, "O Lord God of Israel, why haven't you answered my question? What is wrong? Are Jonathan and I guilty, or is the sin among the others? O Lord God, show us who is guilty." And Jonathan and Saul were chosen by sacred lot as the guilty ones, and the people were declared innocent.

⁴²Then Saul said, "Now draw lots between me and Jonathan." And Jonathan was chosen as the guilty one.

⁴³"Tell me what you've done," Saul demanded of Jonathan.

"I tasted a little honey," Jonathan admitted. "It was only a little bit on the end of a stick; but now I must die."

⁴⁴"Yes, Jonathan," Saul said, "you must die; may God strike me dead if you are not executed for this."

⁴⁵But the troops retorted, "Jonathan, who saved Israel today, shall die? Far from it! We vow by the life of God that not one hair on his head will be touched, for he has been used of God to do a mighty miracle today." So the people rescued Jonathan.

Saul's military successes

⁴⁶Then Saul called back the army, and the Philistines returned home. ⁴⁷And now, since he was securely in the saddle as king of Israel, Saul sent the Israeli army out in every direction against Moab, Ammon, Edom, the kings of Zobah, and the

14:38 *Something's wrong,* implied.

14:35
1 Sam 7:12,17
14:36
Josh 10:14

14:37
1 Sam 23:4
28:5,6; 30:7,8

14:38
Josh 7:10-12
14:39
1 Sam 14:24-44
19:6

14:41
Prov 16:33
Acts 1:24

14:43
Josh 7:19
1 Sam 14:27

14:44
Gen 38:24
1 Sam 3:17
14:39; 25:22
2 Sam 12:5
14:45
2 Sam 14:11
Lk 21:18
Acts 27:34

14:35, 36 After being king for several years, Saul finally built his first altar to God, but only as a last resort. Throughout Saul's reign he consistently approached God only after he had tried everything else. This was in sharp contrast to Ahijah the priest, who suggested that God be consulted *first* (14:36).

How much better if Saul had gone to God first, building an altar as his first official act as king. God is too great to be an afterthought. When we turn to him first, we will never have to turn to him as a last resort.

14:38, 39 Instead of recognizing and admitting his faults, Saul tried to cover them up by blaming everyone but himself. When things are in a mess, stop and consider whether *your* actions and attitudes may be a big part of the problem.

14:39 Saul made the first of his two rash vows (14:24-26) because he was overly anxious to defeat the Philistines and wanted to give his soldiers an incentive to finish the battle quickly. In the Bible, God never asked people to make vows, but if they did, he expected them to be kept (Leviticus 5:4; Numbers 30).

Saul's vow was not something God would have approved of, but still it was a vow. And Jonathan, although he didn't know about Saul's vow, was nevertheless guilty of breaking it. Like Jephthah (Judges 11), Saul made a vow that risked the life of his own child. Fortunately for Saul, the people intervened and spared Jonathan's life.

14:42 The lots cast in this incident were probably the Urim and Thummim, which were designed to give only a yes or no answer.

When God controlled them, the innocent were eliminated by the "no" answer and the guilty exposed by the "yes" answer. A similar incident occurred in Joshua 7:14-18. (For more on the Urim and Thummim see the notes on 2:18 and 10:20.)

14:43 Jonathan's spiritual character was a striking contrast to Saul's. Jonathan admitted what he had done, he did not try to make excuses. Even though he was unaware of Saul's order, Jonathan was willing to accept the consequences of his actions. When you do wrong, even unintentionally, respond more like Jonathan than like Saul.

14:44, 45 Saul made another foolish statement, this time because he was more concerned about saving face than being right. To spare Jonathan's life would require him to admit he had acted foolishly, an embarrassment for a king. Saul was really more interested in protecting his image than in enforcing his vow. Don't be like Saul. Admit your mistakes and show that you are more interested in what is right than in looking good.

14:47 Why was Saul so successful right after he had disobeyed God and been told that his reign would end (13:13, 14)? Success is not a result of godliness, but of God's provision. God could give Saul success for the sake of the people, not the king. The timing of God's plans and promises are known only to him. He may have left Saul on the throne for a while to utilize his military talents so that David, Israel's next king, could spend more time focusing on the nation's spiritual battles. Regardless of God's reasons for delaying Saul's demise, his reign ended exactly the way God had foretold.

14:48
1 Sam 15:3,7

14:49
1 Sam 18:17,20,
27; 19:11,12
31:2
2 Sam 6:20
1 Chron 10:2

14:50
1 Sam 17:55
2 Sam 2:8

14:52
1 Sam 8:11
1 Kgs 9:22

15:1
1 Sam 9:16
10:1

15:2
Ex 17:8-16
Num 24:20
Deut 25:17

15:3
Deut 20:16-18
Josh 6:17,18

15:6
Num 24:21,22
Judg 1:16; 4:11

15:7
Gen 16:7; 25:18
Ex 15:22
1 Sam 27:8

15:8
Num 24:7

15:9
1 Sam 15:15,21

15:11
Gen 6:6,7
Ex 32:9,11,14
2 Sam 24:16
Luke 6:12

Philistines. And wherever he turned, he was successful. 48He did great deeds and conquered the Amalekites and saved Israel from all those who had been their conquerors.

49Saul had three sons, Jonathan, Ishvi, and Malchishua; and two daughters, Merab and Michal. 50, 51Saul's wife was Ahino-am, the daughter of Ahima-az. And the general-in-chief of his army was his cousin Abner, his uncle Ner's son. (Abner's father, Ner, and Saul's father, Kish, were brothers; both were the sons of Abiel.)

52The Israelis fought constantly with the Philistines throughout Saul's lifetime. And whenever Saul saw any brave, strong young man, he conscripted him into his army.

Saul disobeys God by keeping plunder

15 One day Samuel said to Saul, "I crowned you king of Israel because God told me to. Now be sure that you obey him. 2Here is his commandment to you: 'I have decided to settle accounts with the nation of Amalek for refusing to allow my people to cross their territory when Israel came from Egypt. 3Now go and completely destroy the entire Amalek nation—men, women, babies, little children, oxen, sheep, camels, and donkeys.' "

4So Saul mobilized his army at Telaim. There were two hundred thousand troops in addition to ten thousand men from Judah. 5The Amalekites were camped in the valley below them. 6Saul sent a message to the Kenites, telling them to get out from among the Amalekites or else die with them. "For you were kind to the people of Israel when they came out of the land of Egypt," he explained. So the Kenites packed up and left.

7Then Saul butchered the Amalekites from Havilah all the way to Shur, east of Egypt. 8He captured Agag, the king of the Amalekites, but killed everyone else. 9However, Saul and his men kept the best of the sheep and oxen and the fattest of the lambs—everything, in fact, that appealed to them. They destroyed only what was worthless or of poor quality.

10Then the Lord said to Samuel, 11"I am sorry that I ever made Saul king, for he has again refused to obey me."

Samuel was so deeply moved when he heard what God was saying, that he cried to the Lord all night. 12Early the next morning he went out to find Saul. Someone said that he had gone to Mount Carmel to erect a monument to himself, and had then gone on to Gilgal. 13When Samuel finally found him, Saul greeted him cheerfully.

"Hello there," he said. "Well, I have carried out the Lord's command!"

15:2–5 Why did God command such utter destruction? The Amalekites were a band of guerilla terrorists. They lived by attacking other nations and carrying off their wealth and their families. They were the first to attack the Israelites as they entered the Promised Land, and they continued to raid Israelite camps at every opportunity. God knew that the Israelites could never live peacefully in the Promised Land as long as the Amalekites existed. He also knew that their corrupt, idolatrous religious practices threatened Israel's relationship with him. The only way to protect the Israelites' bodies and souls was to utterly destroy the people of this evil nation, and all their possessions, including their idols.

15:9 Saul and his men did not destroy all the booty from the battle as God commanded (15:3). The law of devoting something—setting it aside—entirely for destruction was well known to the Israelites. Anything under God's "ban" was to be completely destroyed (Deuteronomy 20:16–18). To break this law was equivalent to idolatry and was punishable by death (Joshua 7). It showed disrespect and disregard for God because it directly violated his command and it involved taking what was not devoted to him.

When we gloss over sin in order to protect what we have or for material gain, we aren't being shrewd; we are disobeying God's law. Selective obedience is just another form of disobedience.

15:11 When God said he was sorry for making Saul king, was he saying he had made a mistake? God's comment was an expression of sorrow, not an admission of error (Genesis 6:5–7). An omniscient God cannot make a mistake; therefore, God did not change his mind. He did, however, change his attitude toward Saul when Saul changed. Saul's heart no longer belonged to God, but to his own interests.

15:13, 14 Saul thought he had won a great victory over the Amalekites, but God saw it as a great failure because Saul had disobeyed him and then lied to Samuel about the results of the battle. Saul may have thought his lie wouldn't be detected, or that what he did was not wrong.

Dishonest people soon begin to believe the lies they construct around themselves. Then they lose the ability to tell the difference between telling the truth and lying. By believing your own lies, you will begin a life of alienation from God. That is why honesty is so important in our relationships, both with God and with others.

¹⁴"Then what was all the bleating of sheep and lowing of oxen I heard?" Samuel demanded.

¹⁵"It's true that the army spared the best of the sheep and oxen," Saul admitted, "but they are going to sacrifice them to the Lord your God; and we have destroyed everything else."

¹⁶Then Samuel said to Saul, "Stop! Listen to what the Lord told me last night!"

"What was it?" Saul asked.

¹⁷And Samuel told him, "When you didn't think much of yourself, God made you king of Israel. ¹⁸And he sent you on an errand and told you, 'Go and completely destroy the sinners, the Amalekites, until they are all dead.' ¹⁹Then why didn't you obey the Lord? Why did you rush for the loot and do exactly what God said not to?"

²⁰"But I *have* obeyed the Lord," Saul insisted. "I did what he told me to; and I brought King Agag but killed everyone else. ²¹And it was only when my troops demanded it that I let them keep the best of the sheep and oxen and loot to sacrifice to the Lord."

²²Samuel replied, "Has the Lord as much pleasure in your burnt offerings and sacrifices as in your obedience? Obedience is far better than sacrifice. He is much more interested in your listening to him than in your offering the fat of rams to him. ²³For rebellion is as bad as the sin of witchcraft, and stubbornness is as bad as worshiping idols. And now because you have rejected the word of Jehovah, he has rejected you from being king."

Saul pleads for forgiveness

²⁴"I have sinned," Saul finally admitted. "Yes, I have disobeyed your instructions and the command of the Lord, for I was afraid of the people and did what they demanded. ²⁵Oh, please pardon my sin now and go with me to worship the Lord."

²⁶But Samuel replied, "It's no use! Since you have rejected the commandment of the Lord, he has rejected you from being the king of Israel."

²⁷As Samuel turned to go, Saul grabbed at him to try to hold him back, and tore his robe.

²⁸And Samuel said to him, "See? The Lord has torn the kingdom of Israel from you today and has given it to a countryman of yours who is better than you are. ²⁹And he who is the glory of Israel is not lying, nor will he change his mind, for he is not a man!"

³⁰Then Saul pleaded again, "I have sinned; but oh, at least honor me before the leaders and before my people by going with me to worship the Lord your God."

Cross-references (right margin):

15:15 Gen 3:12,13 / 1 Sam 15:9,21

15:17 Judg 6:15 / 1 Sam 9:21 / 10:22

15:19 1 Sam 14:32

15:21 1 Sam 15:9,15

15:22 Ps 40:6-8 / 51:16-17 / Isa 1:11 / Jer 7:22 / Hos 6:6 / Mic 6:7,8 / Mk 12:33

15:23 Deut 18:10 / 1 Sam 13:14

15:24 Num 22:34 / 2 Sam 12:13 / Ps 51:4

15:25 Ex 10:17

15:27 1 Kgs 11:30,31

15:28 1 Sam 28:17,18

15:29 Num 23:19 / Ezek 24:14 / 2 Tim 2:13

15:30 Isa 29:13

15:15 Saul was told to destroy everything, but he kept part of the spoils, including the choicest cattle. When Samuel arrived, he could see and hear the evidence of Saul's wrong actions. When confronted, Saul said the spoils taken were to be sacrificed to God. This is like saying, "But I only stole the money so I could put it in the offering plate!" Obedience to God is always better than seemingly noble deeds.

15:22, 23 This is the first of numerous places in Scripture where the theme "obedience is better than sacrifice" is repeated (Psalm 40:6-8; 51:16, 17; Proverbs 21:3; Isaiah 1:11-17; Jeremiah 7:21-23; Hosea 6:6; Micah 6:6-8; Matthew 12:7). Was Samuel saying that sacrifice is unimportant? No, he was urging Saul to look at his reasons for making the sacrifice, rather than at the sacrifice itself. A sacrifice was a ritual transaction between man and God that physically demonstrated a relationship between them. But if the person's heart was not truly repentant or if he did not truly love God, the sacrifice was a hollow ritual. Religious ceremonies or rituals are empty unless they are performed with an attitude of love and obedience. "Being religious" (going to church, praying, giving to charity) is not enough if we do not act out of devotion and obedience to God.

15:23 Rebellion and stubbornness are serious sins. They involve

far more than being independent and strong-minded. Scripture equates them with witchcraft and idol worship, sins worthy of death (Exodus 22:18; Leviticus 20:6; Deuteronomy 13:12-15; 18:10; Micah 5:10-14).

Since Saul became both rebellious and stubborn, it is little wonder that God finally rejected him and took away his kingdom. Rebellion against God is more than a choice, privilege, or option; it is a serious sin that robs people of the joys and benefits of life with God.

15:26 "It's no use." Saul's excuses had come to an end. The time of reckoning had come. God wasn't rejecting Saul as a person; the king could still seek forgiveness and restore his relationship with God, but it was too late to get his kingdom back. If you are not responsibly looking after what God has entrusted to you, you will eventually run out of excuses. All of us must one day give an account for our actions (Romans 14:10-13).

15:30 Saul was more concerned about what others would think of him than he was about the status of his relationship with God. He begged Samuel to go with him to worship as a public demonstration that Samuel still supported him. If Samuel had refused, the people probably would have lost all confidence in Saul.

31So Samuel finally agreed and went with him.

32Then Samuel said, "Bring King Agag to me." Agag arrived all full of smiles, for he thought, "Surely the worst is over and I have been spared!" 33But Samuel said, "As your sword has killed the sons of many mothers, now your mother shall be childless." And Samuel chopped him in pieces before the Lord at Gilgal. 34Then Samuel went home to Ramah, and Saul returned to Gibe-ah. 35Samuel never saw Saul again, but he mourned constantly for him; and the Lord was sorry that he had ever made Saul king of Israel.

C. SAUL AND DAVID (16:1—31:13)

While Saul is still on the throne, Samuel anoints David as Israel's next king. Young David then bravely conquers Goliath, the Philistine champion, and establishes a lifelong friendship with Jonathan, Saul's son. When Saul realizes that David would become king one day, he grows very jealous and tries to kill David on several occasions. David escapes into Philistine territory until Saul is killed in battle. When treated unjustly, we should not take matters into our own hands. God, who is faithful and just, sees all that is happening and will judge all evil.

1. Samuel anoints David as king

Samuel goes to Bethlehem

16 Finally the Lord said to Samuel, "You have mourned long enough for Saul, for I have rejected him as king of Israel. Now take a vial of olive oil and go to Bethlehem and find a man named Jesse, for I have selected one of his sons to be the new king."

2But Samuel asked, "How can I do that? If Saul hears about it, he will kill me."

"Take a heifer with you," the Lord replied, "and say that you have come to make a sacrifice to the Lord. 3Then call Jesse to the sacrifice and I will show you which of his sons to anoint."

4So Samuel did as the Lord had told him to. When he arrived at Bethlehem, the elders of the city came trembling to meet him.

"What is wrong?" they asked. "Why have you come?"

5But he replied, "All is well. I have come to sacrifice to the Lord. Purify yourselves and come with me to the sacrifice."

And he performed the purification rite on Jesse and his sons, and invited them too. 6When they arrived, Samuel took one look at Eliab and thought, "Surely this is the man the Lord has chosen!"

7But the Lord said to Samuel, "Don't judge by a man's face or height, for this is not the one. I don't make decisions the way you do! Men judge by outward appearance, but I look at a man's thoughts and intentions."

8Then Jesse told his son Abinadab to step forward and walk in front of Samuel. But the Lord said, "This is not the right man either."

9Next Jesse summoned Shammah, but the Lord said, "No, this is not the one." In the same way all seven of his sons presented themselves to Samuel and were rejected.

10, 11"The Lord has not chosen any of them," Samuel told Jesse. "Are these all there are?"

15:33
Gen 9:5,6
Judg 1:7

15:34
1 Sam 7:17
11:4; 15:35
1 Sam 15:11

16:1
Ruth 4:18-22
1 Sam 9:16
13:13; 14
2 Kgs 9:1,2

16:2
1 Sam 20:28,29

16:3
Deut 17:14,15

16:4
1 Sam 16:18
Lk 2:4

16:5
Gen 35:2
Ex 19:10
Josh 3:5

16:7
1 Sam 9:2
1 Kgs 8:39
1 Chron 28:9
Lk 16:15

16:8
1 Sam 17:13

16:10
2 Sam 7:8
1 Chron 17:7

15:35 Samuel had to confront Saul with his disobedience and give him the news of God's judgment. He and Saul were not the best of friends. Saul had wronged and hurt both God and Samuel deeply. In spite of this, Samuel mourned for Saul when God promised to take his kingdom away. This is a great example of love. Never give up on people. Even if you'll never see them again, continue to pray for their repentance and eventual blessing.

16:5 This purification rite was a special ceremony performed to prepare a person to come before God in worship or to offer a sacrifice. (For more on the purification ceremony, see Genesis 35:2 and the note on Joshua 3:5.)

16:7 Saul was tall and handsome; he was an impressive looking man. Samuel may have been trying to find someone who looked

like Saul to be Israel's next king, but God warned him against judging by appearance alone. When people judge by outward appearance, they may overlook individuals who lack the particular physical qualities society currently admires. But appearance doesn't reveal what people are really like or their true value.

Fortunately, God judges by character, not appearances. And because only God can see on the inside, only he can accurately judge people. While we spend hours each week maintaining our outward appearance, we should do even more to develop our inner character. While everyone can see your face, only you and God know what your heart really looks like. Which is the more attractive part of you?

"Well, there is the youngest," Jesse replied. "But he's out in the fields watching the sheep."

"Send for him at once," Samuel said, "for we will not sit down to eat until he arrives."

¹²So Jesse sent for him. He was a fine looking boy, ruddy-faced, and with pleasant eyes. And the Lord said, "This is the one; anoint him."

16:12
Gen 39:6
Ex 2:1,2
1 Sam 9:17
Acts 7:20

¹³So as David stood there among his brothers, Samuel took the olive oil he had brought and poured it upon David's head; and the Spirit of Jehovah came upon him and gave him great power from that day onward. Then Samuel returned to Ramah.

16:13
1 Sam 10:6,
9,10

David joins Saul's staff

¹⁴But the Spirit of the Lord had left Saul, and instead, the Lord had sent a tormenting spirit that filled him with depression and fear. ^{15, 16}Some of Saul's aides suggested a cure.

16:14
1 Sam 11:6
18:10-12; 19:9
1 Kgs 22:22

"We'll find a good harpist to play for you whenever the tormenting spirit is bothering you," they said. "The harp music will quiet you and you'll soon be well again."

16:15
2 Kgs 3:15

¹⁷"All right," Saul said. "Find me a harpist."

¹⁸One of them said he knew a young fellow in Bethlehem, the son of a man named Jesse, who was not only a talented harp player, but was handsome, brave, and strong, and had good, solid judgment. "What's more," he added, "the Lord is with him."

16:18
1 Sam 3:19
18:11,12

¹⁹So Saul sent messengers to Jesse, asking that he send his son David the shepherd. ²⁰Jesse responded by sending not only David but a young goat and a donkey carrying a load of food and wine. ²¹From the instant he saw David, Saul admired and loved him; and David became his bodyguard.

16:21
1 Sam 22:14

²²Then Saul wrote to Jesse, "Please let David join my staff, for I am very fond of him."

²³And whenever the tormenting spirit from God troubled Saul, David would play the harp and Saul would feel better, and the evil spirit would go away.

2. David and Goliath
Goliath challenges Israel

17 The Philistines now mustered their army for battle and camped between Socoh in Judah and Azekah in Ephes-dammim. ²Saul countered with a buildup of forces at Elah Valley. ³So the Philistines and Israelis faced each other on opposite hills, with the valley between them.

17:1
1 Sam 13:5
1 Chron 11:13
17:2
1 Sam 21:9

⁴⁻⁷Then Goliath, a Philistine champion from Gath, came out of the Philistine ranks to face the forces of Israel. He was a giant of a man, measuring over nine feet tall! He wore a bronze helmet, a two-hundred-pound coat of mail, bronze leggings,

17:4
Josh 11:21,22
2 Sam 21:19

16:13 David was anointed king, but it was done in secret; he was not crowned until much later (2 Samuel 2:4; 5:3). Saul was still legally the king, but God was preparing David for his future responsibilities. The anointing oil poured over David's head stood for holiness. It was used to set people or objects apart for God's service. Each king and high priest of Israel was anointed with oil. This commissioned them as God's representatives to the nation. Although God rejected Saul's kingship by not allowing any of his descendants to sit on Israel's throne, Saul himself remained in his position until his death.

16:14 What was this tormenting spirit the Lord sent? There are several possibilities: (1) Saul was simply depressed; (2) the Holy Spirit had left Saul and God allowed an evil spirit (a demon) to torment him as judgment for his disobedience (this would demonstrate God's power over the spirit world—1 Kings 22:19–23); (3) a good angel was sent to torment Saul by convicting him of his coming judgment. Either way, Saul was driven to madness, which led him to attempt to murder David.

16:15, 16 Harps were popular musical instruments in Saul's day,

and their music is still known for its soothing qualities. The simplest harps were merely two pieces of wood fastened at right angles to each other. The strings are stretched between the wood to give the harp a triangular shape. Simple strings could be made of twisted grasses, but better strings were made of dried animal intestine. Harps could have up to 40 strings and were louder than the smaller three- or four-stringed instruments called lyres. David, known for his shepherding skills and bravery, was also an accomplished harpist and musician who would eventually write many of the Psalms found in the Bible.

16:19–21 When Saul asked David to join his palace staff, he obviously did not know that David had been secretly anointed king (16:12). Saul's invitation presented an excellent opportunity for the young future king to gain firsthand information about leading a nation.

Sometimes our plans—even the ones we think God has approved—have to be put on hold indefinitely. Like David, we can use this waiting time profitably. We can choose to learn and grow in our present circumstances, whatever they may be.

and carried a bronze javelin several inches thick, tipped with a twenty-five-pound iron spearhead, and his armor bearer walked ahead of him with a huge shield.

⁸He stood and shouted across to the Israelis, "Do you need a whole army to settle this? I will represent the Philistines, and you choose someone to represent you, and we will settle this in single combat! ⁹If your man is able to kill me, then we will be your slaves. But if I kill him, then you must be our slaves! ¹⁰I defy the armies of Israel! Send me a man who will fight with me!"

17:9
2 Sam 2:12-16

¹¹When Saul and the Israeli army heard this, they were dismayed and frightened. ¹²David (the son of aging Jesse, a member of the tribe of Judah who lived in Bethlehem) had seven older brothers. ¹³The three oldest—Eliab, Abinadab, and Shammah—had already volunteered for Saul's army to fight the Philistines. ¹⁴, ¹⁵David was the youngest son, and was on Saul's staff on a part-time basis. He went back and forth to Bethlehem to help his father with the sheep. ¹⁶For forty days, twice a day, morning and evening the Philistine giant strutted before the armies of Israel.

17:12
Gen 35:19
Ruth 4:18-22
1 Chron 2:13

¹⁷One day Jesse said to David, "Take this bushel of roasted grain and these ten loaves of bread to your brothers. ¹⁸Give this cheese to their captain and see how the boys are getting along; and bring us back a letter from them!"

17:17
1 Sam 25:18
17:18
Gen 37:13,14

¹⁹(Saul and the Israeli army were camped at the valley of Elah.)

²⁰So David left the sheep with another shepherd and took off early the next morning with the gifts. He arrived at the outskirts of the camp just as the Israeli army was leaving for the battlefield with shouts and battle cries. ²¹Soon the Israeli and Philistine forces stood facing each other, army against army. ²²David left his luggage with a baggage officer and hurried out to the ranks to find his brothers. ²³As he was talking with them, he saw Goliath the giant step out from the Philistine troops and shout his challenge to the army of Israel. ²⁴As soon as they saw him the Israeli army began to run away in fright.

17:20
1 Sam 26:5,7

²⁵"Have you seen the giant?" the soldiers were asking. "He has insulted the entire army of Israel. And have you heard about the huge reward the king has offered to anyone who kills him? And the king will give him one of his daughters for a wife, and his whole family will be exempted from paying taxes!"

17:25
Josh 15:16
1 Sam 18:17

²⁶David talked to some others standing there to verify the report. "What will a man get for killing this Philistine and ending his insults to Israel?" he asked them. "Who is this heathen Philistine, anyway, that he is allowed to defy the armies of the living God?" ²⁷And he received the same reply as before.

17:26
1 Sam 14:6
2 Kgs 19:4

²⁸But when David's oldest brother, Eliab, heard David talking like that, he was

17:28
Gen 37:4,8

17:18 *bring back a letter*, literally, "take their pledge."

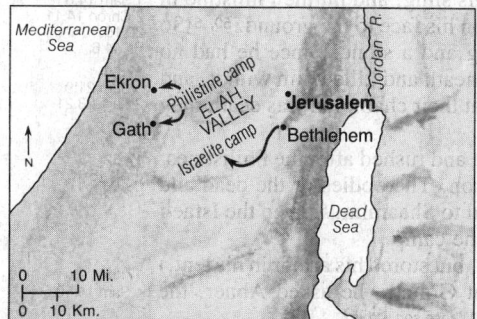

DAVID AND GOLIATH The armies of Israel and Philistia faced each other across the Elah Valley. David arrived from Bethlehem and offered to fight the giant Goliath. After David defeated Goliath, the Israelite army chased the Philistines to Ekron and Gath (Goliath's hometown).

17:4-7 In the days of the Exodus, most of the Israelites had been afraid to enter the Promised Land because of the giants living

there (Numbers 13:32, 33). King Og of Bashan needed a bed over 13 feet long (Deuteronomy 3:11). Now the nine-foot tall Goliath taunted Israel's soldiers, and King Saul may have been especially worried because he was the tallest of the Israelites. In God's eyes, however, Goliath was no different than anyone else.

17:9 An army often avoided the high cost of battle by pitting its strongest warrior against the strongest warrior of the enemy. This avoided great bloodshed. Goliath had the definite advantage against David from a human standpoint. But Goliath didn't realize that in fighting David, he also had to fight God.

17:26 What a difference perspective can make. Saul saw only a giant and a young boy. David, however, saw a mortal man defying almighty God. He knew he would not be alone when he faced Goliath; God would fight with him. He looked at his situation from God's point of view. Viewing impossible situations from God's point of view helps us to put giant problems in perspective.

17:28-32 Criticism couldn't stop David. While the rest of the army stood around, he knew the importance of taking action—with God to fight for him there was no reason to wait. People may try to discourage you with negative comments or mockery, but you must continue to do what you know is right. By doing what is right, you will be pleasing God, whose opinion matters most.

angry. "What are you doing around here, anyway?" he demanded. "What about the sheep you're supposed to be taking care of? I know what a cocky brat you are; you just want to see the battle!"

29"What have I done now?" David replied. "I was only asking a question!" 30And he walked over to some others and asked them the same thing and received the same answer. 31When it was finally realized what David meant, someone told King Saul, and the king sent for him.

David kills Goliath

32"Don't worry about a thing," David told him. "I'll take care of this Philistine!"
33"Don't be ridiculous!" Saul replied. "How can a kid like you fight with a man like him? You are only a boy and he has been in the army *since* he was a boy!"

34But David persisted. "When I am taking care of my father's sheep," he said, "and a lion or a bear comes and grabs a lamb from the flock, 35I go after it with a club and take the lamb from its mouth. If it turns on me I catch it by the jaw and club it to death. 36I have done this to both lions and bears, and I'll do it to this heathen Philistine too, for he has defied the armies of the living God! 37The Lord who saved me from the claws and teeth of the lion and the bear will save me from this Philistine!"

Saul finally consented, "All right, go ahead," he said, "and may the Lord be with you!"

38, 39Then Saul gave David his own armor—a bronze helmet and a coat of mail. David put it on, strapped the sword over it, and took a step or two to see what it was like, for he had never worn such things before. "I can hardly move!" he exclaimed, and took them off again. 40Then he picked up five smooth stones from a stream and put them in his shepherd's bag and, armed only with his shepherd's staff and sling, started across to Goliath. 41, 42Goliath walked out towards David with his shield bearer ahead of him, sneering in contempt at this nice little red-cheeked boy!

43"Am I a dog," he roared at David, "that you come at me with a stick?" And he cursed David by the names of his gods. 44"Come over here and I'll give your flesh to the birds and wild animals," Goliath yelled.

45David shouted in reply, "You come to me with a sword and a spear, but I come to you in the name of the Lord of the armies of heaven and of Israel—the very God whom you have defied. 46Today the Lord will conquer you and I will kill you and cut off your head; and then I will give the dead bodies of *your* men to the birds and wild animals, and the whole world will know that there is a God in Israel! 47And Israel will learn that the Lord does not depend on weapons to fulfill his plans—he works without regard to human means! He will give you to us!"

48, 49As Goliath approached, David ran out to meet him and, reaching into his shepherd's bag, took out a stone, hurled it from his sling, and hit the Philistine in the forehead. The stone sank in, and the man fell on his face to the ground. 50, 51So David conquered the Philistine giant with a sling and a stone. Since he had no sword, he ran over and pulled Goliath's from its sheath and killed him with it, and then cut off his head. When the Philistines saw that their champion was dead, they turned and ran.

52Then the Israelis gave a great shout of triumph and rushed after the Philistines, chasing them as far as Gath and the gates of Ekron. The bodies of the dead and wounded Philistines were strewn all along the road to Shaaraim. 53Then the Israeli army returned and plundered the deserted Philistine camp.

54(Later David took Goliath's head to Jerusalem, but stored his armor in his tent.)
55As Saul was watching David go out to fight Goliath, he asked Abner, the

17:55 *What sort of family does this young fellow come from?* Literally, "Whose son is this?"

17:32
Deut 20:1
Ps 27:3

17:35
Amos 3:12

17:36
1 Sam 17:26

17:37
1 Sam 20:13
Ps 18:16,17
2 Tim 4:17

17:42
1 Sam 16:12

17:43
2 Sam 3:8; 9:8
16:9
1 Kgs 20:10

17:45
2 Chron 32:8
Ps 124:8
Prov 18:10
Heb 11:34

17:46
Ex 7:5
Josh 4:24
2 Kgs 19:19
Isa 37:20
Dan 2:47

17:47
1 Sam 14:6
2 Chron 14:11
20:15
Ps 44:6

17:50
1 Sam 21:9
2 Sam 23:21

17:52
Josh 15:10,11,
33-36

17:55
1 Sam 14:50,51

17:55–58 Although David had played his harp many times in front of Saul, Saul's question to Abner seems to show he didn't know David very well. There are several explanations to this confusing passage: (1) since David was scheduled to marry Saul's daughter if he was successful (17:25), Saul wanted to know more about his family; (2) Saul's unstable mental condition (16:14) may have prevented him from recognizing David; (3) David was still only a part-time staff member at Saul's palace (17:14, 15), and Saul may not have bothered to get to know him or learn much about him.

general of his army, "Abner, what sort of family does this young fellow come from?"

"I really don't know," Abner said.

56"Well, find out!" the king told him.

57After David had killed Goliath, Abner brought him to Saul with the Philistine's head still in his hand.

17:58
1 Sam 16:18

58"Tell me about your father, my boy," Saul said.

And David replied, "His name is Jesse and we live in Bethlehem."

When we think of David, we think: shepherd, poet, giant-killer, king, ancestor of Jesus, in short, one of the greatest men in the Old Testament. But alongside that list stands another: betrayer, liar, adulterer, murderer. The first list gives qualities we all might like to have; the second, qualities that might be true of any one of us. The Bible makes no effort to hide David's failures. Yet he is remembered and respected for his godliness. Knowing how much more we share in David's failures than in his greatness, we should be curious to find out what made God refer to David as a man who would obey him.

David, more than anything else, had an unchangeable belief in the faithful and forgiving nature of God. He was a man who lived with great zest. He sinned many times, but he was quick to confess his sins. His confessions were from the heart and his repentance was genuine. David never took God's forgiveness lightly or his blessing for granted. In return, God never held back from David either his forgiveness or the consequences of his actions. David experienced the joy of forgiveness even when he had to suffer the consequences of his sins.

We tend to get these two reversed. Too often we would rather avoid the consequences than experience forgiveness. One big difference between us and David is that while he sinned greatly, he did not sin repeatedly. He learned from his mistakes because he accepted the suffering they brought. Often we don't seem to learn from our mistakes or the consequences that result from those mistakes. What changes would it take for God to find this kind of obedience in you?

Strengths and accomplishments:
- Greatest king of Israel
- Ancestor of Jesus Christ
- Listed in the Hall of Faith in Hebrews 11
- A man described by God himself as "a man who will obey" (1 Samuel 13:14)

Weaknesses and mistakes:
- Commited adultery with Bath-sheba
- Arranged the murder of Uriah, Bath-sheba's husband
- Directly disobeyed God in taking a census of the people

Lessons from his life:
- Willingness to honestly admit our mistakes is the first step in dealing with them
- Forgiveness does not remove the consequences of sin
- God greatly desires our complete trust and worship

Vital statistics:
- Where: Bethlehem, Jerusalem
- Occupation: Shepherd, musician, poet, soldier, king
- Relatives: Father: Jesse. Wives included: Michal, Ahino-am, Bath-sheba, Abigail. Sons: Absalom, Amnon, Solomon, Adonijah. Daughter: Tamar. Seven brothers.
- Contemporaries: Saul, Jonathan, Samuel, Nathan

Key verses:
"For you are indeed God, and your words are truth; and you have promised me these good things—so do as you have promised! Bless me and my family forever! May our dynasty continue on and on before you; for you, Lord God, have promised it" (2 Samuel 7:28, 29).

His story is told in 1 Samuel 16—1 Kings 2. He is also mentioned in Amos 6:5; Matthew 1:1; 22:43-45; Luke 1:32; Romans 1:3; Hebrews 11:32.

3. David and Jonathan become friends
Saul is jealous of David

18 After King Saul had finished his conversation with David, David met Jonathan, the king's son, and there was an immediate bond of love between them. Jonathan swore to be his blood brother, 4and sealed the pact by giving him his robe, sword, bow, and belt.

King Saul now kept David with him and wouldn't let him return home any more. 5He was Saul's special assistant, and he always carried out his assignments successfully. So Saul made him commander of his troops, an appointment which was applauded by the army and general public alike. 6But something had happened when the victorious Israeli army was returning home after David had killed Goliath. Women came out from all the towns along the way to celebrate and to cheer for King Saul, and were singing and dancing for joy with tambourines and cymbals.

7However, this was their song: "Saul has slain his thousands, and David his ten thousands!"

8Of course Saul was very angry. "What's this?" he said to himself. "They credit David with ten thousands and me with only thousands. Next they'll be making him their king!"

9So from that time on King Saul kept a jealous watch on David. 10The very next day, in fact, a tormenting spirit from God overwhelmed Saul, and he began to rave like a madman. David began to soothe him by playing the harp, as he did whenever this happened. But Saul, who was fiddling with his spear, 11, 12suddenly hurled it at David, intending to pin him to the wall. But David jumped aside and escaped. This happened another time, too, for Saul was afraid of him and jealous because the Lord had left him and was now with David. 13Finally Saul banned him from his presence and demoted him to the rank of captain. But the controversy put David more than ever in the public eye.

14David continued to succeed in everything he undertook, for the Lord was with him. 15, 16When King Saul saw this, he became even more afraid of him; but all Israel and Judah loved him, for he was as one of them.

David kills 200 Philistines as a dowry

17One day Saul said to David, "I am ready to give you my oldest daughter Merab as your wife. But first you must prove yourself to be a real soldier by fighting the Lord's battles." For Saul thought to himself, "I'll send him out against the Philistines and let them kill him rather than doing it myself."

18"Who am I that I should be the king's son-in-law?" David exclaimed. "My father's family is nothing!"

19But when the time arrived for the wedding, Saul married her to Adriel, a man

18:1
1 Sam 20:8
23:18
2 Sam 1:26; 9:1

18:4
Gen 41:42
Esther 6:8

18:6
Judg 11:34
Ps 68:24; 149:3

18:7
1 Sam 21:11
29:5

18:8
1 Sam 15:28
16:13

18:10
1 Sam 16:14,23

18:13
2 Sam 5:2

18:14
1 Sam 14:47
16:18; 18:30
2 Sam 5:10

18:17
1 Sam 17:25
25:28

18:18
Ex 3:11
1 Sam 9:21
2 Sam 7:18

18:19
2 Sam 21:8

18:1-4 When David and Jonathan met, they became close friends at once. Although Jonathan was probably somewhat older than David, their friendship is one of the deepest and closest recorded in the Bible because they (1) based their friendship on commitment to God, not just each other; (2) let nothing come between them, not even career or family problems; (3) drew closer together when their friendship was tested; and (4) were able to remain friends to the end.

Jonathan, the prince of Israel, later realized that David, and not he, would be king (23:17). But that did not weaken his love for David. Jonathan would much rather lose the throne of Israel than lose his closest friend.

18:8 Saul's appreciation for David turned to jealousy as people began to applaud David's exploits. In a jealous rage, Saul attempted to murder David by hurling his spear at him (18:11, 12).

Jealousy may not seem to be a major sin, but in reality, it is one step short of murder. It begins by destroying a person on the inside, then it manifests itself in harmful actions. Beware of letting jealousy get a foothold in your life.

18:10 The note on 16:14 gives several explanations for what this tormenting spirit might have been.

18:11, 12 Saul tried to kill David because he was jealous of David's popularity, yet David continued to protect and comfort Saul. Perhaps people have been jealous of you and have even attacked you in some way. They may be intimidated by your strengths or made aware of their own shortcomings. It would be natural to strike back or to avoid them. A better response is to befriend them (Matthew 5:43, 44) and to ask God for the strength to continue to love them, as David kept on loving Saul.

18:15-18 While Saul's popularity made him proud and arrogant, David remained humble even when the entire nation praised him. Although David succeeded in almost everything he tried and became famous throughout the land, he refused to use his popular support to his advantage against Saul. Don't allow popularity to twist your perception of your own importance. It's easier to be humble when you're not on center stage, but how will you react to praise and honor?

from Meholath, instead. 20In the meantime Saul's daughter Michal had fallen in love with David, and Saul was delighted when he heard about it.

21"Here's another opportunity to see him killed by the Philistines!" Saul said to himself. But to David he said, "You can be my son-in-law after all, for I will give you my youngest daughter."

22Then Saul instructed his men to say confidentially to David that the king really liked him a lot, and that they all loved him and thought he should accept the king's proposition and become his son-in-law.

18:23
Gen 29:20
34:12

23But David replied, "How can a poor man like me from an unknown family find enough dowry to marry the daughter of a king?"

24When Saul's men reported this back to him, 25he told them, "Tell David that the only dowry I need is one hundred dead Philistines! Vengeance on my enemies is all I want." But what Saul had in mind was that David would be killed in the fight.

18:27
2 Sam 3:14

26David was delighted to accept the offer. So, before the time limit expired, 27he and his men went out and killed two hundred Philistines and presented their foreskins to King Saul. So Saul gave Michal to him.

28When the king realized how much the Lord was with David and how immensely popular he was with all the people, 29he became even more afraid of him, and grew to hate him more with every passing day. 30Whenever the Philistine army attacked, David was more successful against them than all the rest of Saul's officers. So David's name became very famous throughout the land.

18:30
1 Sam 18:14

David escapes from Saul

19:1
1 Sam 18:1-3

19 Saul now urged his aides and his son Jonathan to assassinate David. But Jonathan, because of his close friendship with David, 2told him what his father was planning. "Tomorrow morning," he warned him, "you must find a hiding place out in the fields. 3I'll ask my father to go out there with me, and I'll talk to him about you; then I'll tell you everything I can find out."

19:3
1 Sam 20:9

18:25 one hundred dead Philistines, literally, "one hundred foreskins of the Philistines."

SIMPLE OBJECTS
God often uses simple, ordinary objects to accomplish his tasks in the world. It is important, only, that it be dedicated to him for his use. What do you have that God can use? Anything and everything is a possible "instrument" for him.

Object	Reference	Who used it?	How was it used?
a rod	Exodus 4:2–4	Moses	To work miracles before Pharaoh
trumpets	Joshua 6:3–5	Joshua	To flatten the walls of Jericho
a fleece	Judges 6:36–40	Gideon	To confirm God's will
trumpets, jars, and torches	Judges 7:19–22	Gideon	To defeat the Midianites
jawbone	Judges 15:15	Samson	To kill 1,000 Philistines
small stone	1 Samuel 17:40	David	To slay Goliath
oil	2 Kings 4:1–7	Elisha	To demonstrate God's power to provide
a river	2 Kings 5:9–14	Elisha	To heal a man of leprosy
loincloth	Jeremiah 13:1–11	Jeremiah	As an object lesson of God's wrath
pottery	Jeremiah 19:1–13	Jeremiah	As an object lesson of God's wrath
iron plate, water, and food	Ezekiel 4:1–17	Ezekiel	As an object lesson of judgment
five loaves of bread and two fish	Mark 6:30–44	Jesus	To feed a crowd of over 5,000 people

19:1, 2 Is it ever right to disobey your father, as Jonathan did here? It is clearly a principle of Scripture that when a father instructs a son to break God's law, the son should obey God rather than man. This principle assumes that the son is old enough to be accountable and see through any deception. A son's role is to be respectful, helpful, and obedient to his father (Ephesians 6:1–3), but not to follow commands or accept values that violate God's law.

4The next morning as Jonathan and his father were talking together, he spoke well of David and begged him not to be against David.

"He's never done anything to harm you," Jonathan pleaded. "He has always helped you in any way he could. 5Have you forgotten about the time he risked his life to kill Goliath, and how the Lord brought a great victory to Israel as a result? You were certainly happy about it then. Why should you now murder an innocent man? There is no reason for it at all!"

6Finally Saul agreed, and vowed, "As the Lord lives, he shall not be killed."

7Afterwards Jonathan called David and told him what had happened. Then he took David to Saul and everything was as it had been before. 8War broke out shortly after that and David led his troops against the Philistines and slaughtered many of them, and put to flight their entire army.

9, 10But one day as Saul was sitting at home, listening to David playing the harp, suddenly the tormenting spirit from the Lord attacked him. He had his spear in his hand, and hurled it at David in an attempt to kill him. But David dodged out of the way and fled into the night, leaving the spear imbedded in the timber of the wall. 11Saul sent troops to watch David's house and kill him when he came out in the morning.

"If you don't get away tonight," Michal warned him, "you'll be dead by morning."

12So she helped him get down to the ground through a window. 13Then she took an idol and put it in his bed, and covered it with blankets, with its head on a pillow of goat's hair. 14When the soldiers came to arrest David and take him to Saul, she told them he was sick and couldn't get out of bed. 15Saul said to bring him in his bed, then, so that he could kill him. 16But when they came to carry him out, they discovered that it was only an idol!

17"Why have you deceived me and let my enemy escape?" Saul demanded of Michal.

"I had to," Michal replied. "He threatened to kill me if I didn't help him."

18In that way David got away and went to Ramah to see Samuel, and told him all that Saul had done to him. So Samuel took David with him to live at Naioth. 19When the report reached Saul that David was at Naioth in Ramah, 20he sent soldiers to capture him; but when they arrived and saw Samuel and the other prophets prophesying, the Spirit of God came upon them and they also began to prophesy. 21When Saul heard what had happened, he sent other soldiers, but they too prophesied! The same thing happened a third time! 22Then Saul himself went to Ramah and arrived at the great well in Secu.

"Where are Samuel and David?" he demanded.

Someone told him they were at Naioth. 23But on the way to Naioth the Spirit of God came upon Saul, and he too began to prophesy! 24He tore off his clothes and lay naked all day and all night, prophesying with Samuel's prophets. Saul's men were incredulous!

"What!" they exclaimed. "Is Saul a prophet, too?"

19:5
Deut 19:10-13
1 Sam 17:49,50
Ps 94:21

19:7
1 Sam 16:21

19:9
1 Sam 16:14
18:10-12

19:11
Judg 16:2
Ps 59 (title),vss
3,4,6

19:13
Judg 17:4,5
18:14,17

19:18
1 Sam 7:17
15:34; 19:22

19:20
Num 11:24,25
1 Sam 10:5,
6,10
Joel 2:28

19:22
1 Sam 19:18

19:23
1 Sam 19:20

19:24
1 Sam 10:10-12
2 Sam 6:20
Mic 1:8

19:4 *the next morning,* implied.   **19:13** *an idol,* literally, "teraphim."   **19:14** *When the soldiers came to arrest David and take him to Saul,* implied.   **19:24** *Is Saul a prophet, too?* implied. Literally, "Hence it is said, 'Is Saul also among the prophets?' " (See 10:10-12.)

19:20-24 This was the second time that Saul surprised everyone by joining a band of prophets and prophesying. The first time (chapter 10) happened right after he was anointed king and did not want to accept the responsibility. This time Saul was consumed with jealousy over David's growing popularity, but the Spirit of God immobilized him so he was unable to harm David. In both cases, Saul spoke God's words (he "prophesied"), although he was far from thinking God's thoughts.

19:23 Jonathan spoke up for David (19:4); Michal helped him escape (19:11-17); Samuel gave him a place to hide (19:18); and the Spirit of God interrupted Saul's manhunt (19:23). Each of these events protected David from harm or death. They were more than coincidence; God was at work. When you are spared from harm, recognize that God may be protecting you because he has a purpose for you.

Jonathan saves David's life

20:1
1 Sam 24:9,
11,17

20 David now fled from Naioth in Ramah, and found Jonathan. "What have I done?" he exclaimed. "Why is your father so determined to kill me?"

2"That's not true!" Jonathan protested. "I'm sure he's not planning any such thing, for he always tells me everything he's going to do, even little things, and I know he wouldn't hide something like this from me. It just isn't so."

20:3
Deut 6:13
2 Kgs 2:6,7
Jer 4:2

3"Of course you don't know about it!" David fumed. "Your father knows perfectly well about our friendship, so he has said to himself, 'I'll not tell Jonathan—why should I hurt him?' But the truth is that I am only a step away from death! I swear it by the Lord and by your own soul!"

4"Tell me what I can do," Jonathan begged.

20:5
Num 10:10
28:11-17
20:6
1 Sam 16:2
17:58; 20:28

5And David replied, "Tomorrow is the beginning of the celebration of the new moon. Always before, I've been with your father for this occasion, but tomorrow I'll hide in the field and stay there until the evening of the third day. 6If your father asks where I am, tell him that I asked permission to go home to Bethlehem for an annual family reunion. 7If he says, 'Fine!' then I'll know that all is well. But if he

20:8
1 Sam 18:1-3
23:18
2 Sam 1:26

is angry, then I'll know that he is planning to kill me. 8Do this for me as my sworn brother. Or else kill me yourself if I have sinned against your father, but don't betray me to him!"

20:9
1 Sam 19:2

9"Of course not!" Jonathan exclaimed. "Look, wouldn't I say so if I knew that my father was planning to kill you?"

10Then David asked, "How will I know whether or not your father is angry?"

11"Come out to the field with me," Jonathan replied. And they went out there together.

12Then Jonathan told David, "I promise by the Lord God of Israel that about this time tomorrow, or the next day at the latest, I will talk to my father about you and let you know at once how he feels about you. 13If he is angry and wants you killed,

20:13
Ruth 1:17
1 Sam 3:17
14:44; 18:11,12
1 Chron 28:20

then may the Lord kill me if I don't tell you, so you can escape and live. May the Lord be with you as he used to be with my father. 14And remember, you must demonstrate the love and kindness of the Lord not only to me during my own lifetime, 15but also to my children after the Lord has destroyed all of your enemies."

20:15
1 Sam 24:21
2 Sam 9:1; 21:7
20:16
Deut 23:21
1 Sam 25:22

16So Jonathan made a covenant with the family of David, and David swore to it with a terrible curse against himself and his descendants, should he be unfaithful to his promise. 17But Jonathan made David swear to it again, this time by his love for him, for he loved him as much as he loved himself.

20:5 At the beginning of each month, the Israelites gathered to celebrate the Festival of the New Moon. While this was mainly a time to be enjoyed, it was also a way to dedicate the next month to God. Other nations had celebrations during the full moon and worshiped the moon itself. The Israelites, however, celebrated their festival during the new moon, when the moon was not visible in the sky. This was an added precaution against false worship.

20:15 Jonathan asked David to keep a promise to treat his children kindly in the future. Years later David took great pains to fulfill this promise: he invited Jonathan's son Mephibosheth into his palace to live (2 Samuel 9).

DAVID'S ESCAPE David learned of Saul's plans to kill him, and fled to Samuel at Ramah. Returning to Gibe-ah to say good-bye to Jonathan, he then escaped to Nob where he received food and a sword from the priest. He then fled to Gath in Philistine territory. When the Philistines became suspicious, he escaped to a cave near Adullam where many men joined him.

18Then Jonathan said, "Yes, they will miss you tomorrow when your place at the table is empty. 19By the day after tomorrow, everyone will be asking about you, so be at the hideout where you were before, over by the stone pile. 20I will come out and shoot three arrows in front of the pile as though I were shooting at a target. 21Then I'll send a lad to bring the arrows back. If you hear me tell him, 'They're on this side,' then you will know that all is well and that there is no trouble. 22But if I tell him, 'Go farther—the arrows are still ahead of you,' then it will mean that you must leave immediately. 23And may the Lord make us keep our promises to each other, for he has witnessed them."

20:23
Gen 31:49,53

24, 25So David hid himself in the field.

When the new moon celebration began, the king sat down to eat at his usual place against the wall. Jonathan sat opposite him and Abner was sitting beside Saul, but David's place was empty. 26Saul didn't say anything about it that day, for he supposed that something had happened so that David was ceremonially impure. Yes, surely that must be it! 27But when his place was still empty the next day, Saul asked Jonathan, "Why hasn't David been here for dinner either yesterday or today?"

20:26
Lev 7:21
Num 19:16
1 Sam 16:5

28, 29"He asked me if he could go to Bethlehem to take part in a family celebration," Jonathan replied. "His brother demanded that he be there, so I told him to go ahead."

20:28
1 Sam 20:6

30Saul boiled with rage. "You fool!" he yelled at him. "Do you think I don't know that you want this son of a nobody to be king in your place, shaming yourself and your mother? 31As long as that fellow is alive, you'll never be king. Now go and get him so I can kill him!"

20:30
Judg 11:1

20:31
1 Sam 26:16
2 Sam 12:5

32"But what has he done?" Jonathan demanded. "Why should he be put to death?"

33Then Saul hurled his spear at Jonathan, intending to kill him; so at last Jonathan realized that his father really meant it when he said David must die. 34Jonathan left the table in fierce anger and refused to eat all that day, for he was crushed by his father's shameful behavior toward David.

20:33
1 Sam 18:11
19:10,11

35The next morning, as agreed, Jonathan went out into the field and took a young boy with him to gather his arrows.

36"Start running," he told the boy, "so that you can find the arrows as I shoot them." So the boy ran and Jonathan shot an arrow beyond him. 37When the boy had almost reached the arrow, Jonathan shouted, "The arrow is still ahead of you. 38Hurry, hurry, don't wait." So the boy quickly gathered up the arrows and ran back to his master. 39He, of course, didn't understand what Jonathan meant; only Jonathan and David knew. 40Then Jonathan gave his bow and arrows to the boy and told him to take them back to the city.

20:36
1 Sam 20:20,21

41As soon as he was gone, David came out from where he had been hiding near the south edge of the field. Both of them were crying as they said goodbye, especially David. 42At last Jonathan said to David, "Cheer up, for we have entrusted each other and each other's children into God's hands forever." So they parted, David going away and Jonathan returning to the city.

20:42
1 Sam 20:14,
15; 23:18

20:23 *for he has witnessed them,* literally, "The Lord is our mediator forever." **20:30** *You fool,* literally, "Son of a perverse, rebellious woman." *this son of a nobody,* literally, "son of Jesse." **20:41** *Both of them were crying . . . especially David,* literally, "David . . . bowed himself three times and they kissed each other and wept until David exceeded."

20:26 Because the Festival of the New Moon involved making a sacrifice to God (Numbers 28:11–15), those attending the feast had to be ceremonially clean according to God's law (Exodus 19:10; Leviticus 15; Numbers 19:11–22; also see the note on Joshua 3:5). This cleansing involved washing the body and clothes before approaching God to offer a sacrifice. The outward cleansing was a symbol of the inward desire for a purified heart and right relationship with God.

20:31, 32 Saul was still trying to secure his throne for future generations even though he had already been told his dynasty would end with him (13:13, 14). Even worse, he was trying to do this by human means, because he knew he would get no help from God. Jonathan could have made a move to become the next king by killing his rival, but he bypassed this opportunity because of his love for both God and David (23:16–18).

4. Saul pursues David
David asks for holy bread

21:1
1 Sam 22:19
Neh 11:32
Mk 2:25,26

21:2
1 Sam 19:17

21:4
Ex 19:14,15
Lev 24:5-8
Mt 12:4

21 David went to the city of Nob to see Ahimelech, the priest. Ahimelech trembled when he saw him.

"Why are you alone?" he asked. "Why is no one with you?"

²"The king has sent me on a private matter," David lied. "He told me not to tell anybody why I am here. I have told my men where to meet me later. ³Now, what is there to eat? Give me five loaves of bread, or anything else you can."

⁴"We don't have any regular bread," the priest replied, "but there is the holy bread, which I guess you can have if only your young men have not slept with any women for awhile."

⁵"Rest assured," David replied. "I never let my men run wild when they are on an expedition, and since they stay clean even on ordinary trips, how much more so on this one!"

JONATHAN

Loyalty is one of life's most costly qualities; it is the most selfless part of love. To be loyal, you cannot live only for yourself. Loyal people not only stand by their commitments, they are willing to suffer for them. Jonathan is a shining example of loyalty. Sometimes he was forced to deal with a conflict of loyalties: to his father Saul or to his friend David. His solution to that conflict teaches us both how to be loyal and what must guide loyalty. In Jonathan, truth always guided loyalty.

Jonathan realized the source of truth was the God who demanded his ultimate loyalty. It was his relationship with God that gave Jonathan the ability to deal effectively with the complicated situations in his life. He was loyal to Saul because Saul was his father and the king. He was loyal to David because David was his friend. His loyalty to God guided him through the conflicting demands of his human relationships.

The conflicting demands of our relationships can be great challenges to us as well. If we attempt to settle these conflicts only at the human level, we will be constantly dealing with a sense of betrayal. But if we communicate to our friends that our ultimate loyalty is to God and his truth, many of our choices will be much clearer. The truth in his Word, the Bible, will bring light to our decisions. Do those closest to you know who has your greatest loyalty?

Strengths and accomplishments:
- Brave, loyal, and a natural leader
- The closest friend David ever had
- Did not put his personal well-being ahead of those he loved
- Depended on God

Lessons from his life:
- Loyalty is one of the strongest aspects of courage
- An allegiance to God puts all other relationships in perspective
- Great friendships are costly

Vital statistics:
- Occupation: Military leader
- Relatives: Father: Saul. Mother: Ahino-am. Brothers: Abinadab and Malchishua. Sisters: Merab and Michal. Son: Mephibosheth.

Key verse:
"How I weep for you, my brother Jonathan; How much I loved you! And your love for me was deeper than the love of women!" (2 Samuel 1:26).

His story is told in 1 Samuel 13—31. He is also mentioned in 2 Samuel 9.

21:1ff This is the first time Ahimelech is mentioned. Either he was the Ahijah mentioned in 14:3, 18, or, more likely, he was the successor to Ahijah. In either case, Ahimelech had to go against the law to give the Bread of the Presence to David, because the bread was supposed to be given only to the priests (Leviticus 24:5-9). But Ahimelech put David's need and life ahead of religious ceremony and fed him the holy food. This upheld a higher law of charity (Leviticus 19:18). Centuries later, Jesus would refer to this incident to show that God's law should not be applied legalistically. To do good and to save life is God's greater law (Matthew 12:1-8; Luke 6:1-5).

21:2 David lied to protect himself from Saul (21:10). Some excuse this lie because a war was going on and it is the duty of a good soldier to deceive the enemy. But nowhere is David's lie condoned. In fact, the opposite is true because his lie led to the death of 85 priests (22:9-19). David's small lie seemed harmless enough, but it led to tragedy. The Bible makes it very clear that lying is wrong (Leviticus 19:11). Lying, like every other sin, is serious in God's sight and may lead to all sorts of harmful consequences. Don't minimize or categorize sins. All sins must be avoided regardless of whether or not we can foresee their potential consequences.

6So, since there was no other food available, the priest gave him the holy bread—the Bread of the Presence that was placed before the Lord in the Tabernacle. It had just been replaced that day with fresh bread.

21:6
Mt 12:3,4
Mk 2:25,26
Lk 6:4

7(Incidentally, Doeg the Edomite, Saul's chief herdsman, was there at that time for ceremonial purification.)

21:7
1 Sam 22:9
Ps 52:1

8David asked Ahimelech if he had a spear or sword he could use. "The king's business required such haste, and I left in such a rush that I came away without a weapon!" David explained.

9"Well," the priest replied, "I have the sword of Goliath, the Philistine—the fellow you killed in the valley of Elah. It is wrapped in a cloth in the clothes closet. Take that if you want it, for there is nothing else here."

21:9
1 Sam 17:2,
50,51

"Just the thing!" David replied. "Give it to me!"

David pretends insanity

10Then David hurried on, for he was fearful of Saul, and went to King Achish of Gath. 11But Achish's officers weren't happy about his being there. "Isn't he the top leader of Israel?" they asked.

21:10
1 Sam 27:1-3
28:1

21:11
1 Sam 18:7
29:5

"Isn't he the one the people honor at their dances, singing, 'Saul has slain his thousands and David his ten thousands'?"

12David heard these comments and was afraid of what King Achish might do to him, 13so he pretended to be insane! He scratched on doors and let his spittle flow down his beard, 14, 15until finally King Achish said to his men.

"Must you bring me a madman? We already have enough of them around here! Should such a fellow as this be my guest?"

Saul executes the priests

22 So David left Gath and escaped to the cave of Adullam, where his brothers and other relatives soon joined him. 2Then others began coming—those who were in any kind of trouble, such as being in debt, or merely discontented—until David was the leader of about four hundred men.

22:1
Josh 15:33-36
2 Sam 23:13

22:2
Judg 9:4; 11:3

22:3
Judg 11:29

22:5
2 Sam 24:11
1 Chron 21:9
29:29
2 Chron 29:25,
26

22:6
Judg 4:5
1 Sam 14:2

22:7
1 Sam 8:14
1 Chron 12:16

22:8
1 Sam 23:21

3(Later David went to Mizpeh in Moab to ask permission of the king for his father and mother to live there under royal protection until David knew what God was going to do for him. 4They stayed in Moab during the entire period when David was living in the cave.)

5One day the prophet Gad told David to leave the cave and return to the land of Judah. So David went to the forest of Hereth. 6The news of his arrival in Judah soon reached Saul. He was in Gibe-ah at the time, sitting beneath an oak tree playing with his spear, surrounded by his officers.

7"Listen here, you men of Benjamin!" Saul exclaimed when he heard the news. "Has David promised you fields and vineyards and commissions in his army? 8Is

21:7 *was there at that time for ceremonial purification,* literally, "detained before the Lord." **21:9** *wrapped in a cloth in the clothes closet,* literally, "behind the ephod."

21:6 Once a week on the Sabbath, a priest entered the Holy Place of the Tabernacle and placed 12 freshly baked loaves of bread on a small table. This bread, called Bread of the Presence, symbolized God's presence among his people as well as his loving providence that met their physical needs. The bread that was replaced was to be eaten only by the priests on duty.

21:10-15 Why did the Philistines accept their archenemy, David, into their camp? The Philistines may have been initially happy to accept a defector who was a high military leader. Any enemy of Saul would have been a friend of theirs. They could not have known David had been anointed Israel's next king (16:13). Soon, however, the Philistines became nervous about David's presence. After all, he had slain thousands of their own people (18:7). David then protected himself by acting insane, for it was the custom not to harm mentally unstable people.

22:2 Outlaws, malcontents, and troublemakers joined David, who

himself was an outlaw. These people were outcasts themselves and could only improve their lot by helping David become king. David's control over this band of men again shows his resourcefulness and ability to lead and motivate others. It is difficult enough to build an army out of good men, but it takes great leadership to mold together the kind of men that followed David. This group eventually formed the core of his military leadership and became known as "the heroic men in David's army" (2 Samuel 23:8ff).

22:3, 4 While Israel was not on friendly terms with Moab (14:47), David may have been able to secure permission from the king because of family ties. His great-grandmother, Ruth, was from Moab (Ruth 1:4; 4:13–22).

22:7, 8 Why did Saul address his officers as "men of Benjamin"? Apparently Saul's key officers were from the tribe of Benjamin, just as he was. David was from the neighboring tribe of Judah. Saul was appealing to tribal loyalty to maintain his hold on the throne.

that why you are against me? For not one of you has ever told me that my own son is on David's side. You're not even sorry for me. Think of it! My own son—encouraging David to come and kill me!"

22:9
1 Sam 21:1,7
Ps 52:1

9, 10Then Doeg the Edomite, who was standing there with Saul's men, spoke up. "When I was at Nob," he said, "I saw David talking to Ahimelech the priest. Ahimelech consulted the Lord to find out what David should do, and then gave him food and the sword of Goliath the Philistine."

22:11
1 Sam 14:3

11, 12King Saul immediately summoned Ahimelech and all his family and all the other priests at Nob. When they arrived Saul shouted at him, "Listen to me, you son of Ahitub!"

"What is it?" quavered Ahimelech.

13"Why have you and David conspired against me?" Saul demanded. "Why did you give him food and a sword and talk to God for him? Why did you encourage him to revolt against me and to come here and attack me?"

22:14
1 Sam 19:4; 5
20:32; 24:11
22:15
2 Sam 5:19,23

14"But sir," Ahimelech replied, "is there anyone among all your servants who is as faithful as David your son-in-law? Why, he is the captain of your bodyguard and a highly honored member of your own household! 15This was certainly not the first time I had consulted God for him! It's unfair for you to accuse me and my family in this matter, for we knew nothing of any plot against you."

16"You shall die, Ahimelech, along with your entire family!" the king shouted.

22:17
1 Sam 14:45
2 Kgs 10:25

17He ordered his bodyguards, "Kill these priests, for they are allies and conspirators with David; they knew he was running away from me, but they didn't tell me!"

But the soldiers refused to harm the clergy.

22:18
1 Sam 2:30-33

18Then the king said to Doeg, "You do it."

So Doeg turned on them and killed them, eighty-five priests in all, all wearing their priestly robes. 19Then he went to Nob, the city of the priests, and killed the priests' families—men, women, children, and babies, and also all the oxen, donkeys, and sheep. 20Only Abiathar, one of the sons of Ahimelech, escaped and fled to David.

22:20
1 Sam 2:30-33
23:9; 30:7
1 Kgs 2:26,27

21When he told him what Saul had done, 22David exclaimed, "I knew it! When I saw Doeg there, I knew he would tell Saul. Now I have caused the death of all of your father's family. 23Stay here with me, and I'll protect you with my own life. Any harm to you will be over my dead body."

Mediterranean Sea · Jordan R. · Gibe-ah · **Jerusalem** · Adullam · forest of Hereth · Keilah · Dead Sea · Ziph · Engedi · Maon · Horesh · 0 10 Mi. · 0 10 Km. · —— David · ---- Saul · N

DAVID FLEES FROM SAUL David and his men attacked the Philistines at Keilah from the forest of Hereth. Saul came from Gibe-ah to attack David, but David escaped into the wilderness of Ziph. At Horesh he met Jonathan who encouraged him. Then he fled into the wilderness of Maon and into the caves of Engedi.

22:18 Why would Saul have his own priests killed? Saul suspected a conspiracy among Jonathan, David, and the priests.

His suspicion came from Doeg's report of seeing David talking to Ahimelech, the High Priest, and receiving food and a weapon from him (22:9, 10). Saul's action showed his mental and emotional instability and how far he had strayed from God.

By destroying everything in Nob, Saul was placing the city under the "ban" described in Deuteronomy 13:12–17, which was supposed to be used only in cases of idolatry and rebellion against God. But it was Saul, not the priests, who had rebelled against God.

22:18, 19 Why did God allow 85 innocent priests to be killed? Scripture does not give a specific answer to this question, but it gives insights into the issue.

Serving God is not a ticket to wealth, success, or health. While God does not promise to protect good people from evil in this world, we can find comfort in knowing that he does promise that ultimately all evil will be abolished. Those who have remained faithful through their trials will experience untold blessings in the age to come (Matthew 5:11, 12; Revelation 21:1–7; 22:1–21).

22:20 Abiathar escaped to David with the ephod (23:6) which contained the Urim and Thummim, two objects David used to consult God. Saul destroyed Israel's priesthood, but when David became king, he installed Abiathar as the new High Priest. Abiathar remained in that position during David's entire reign.

Saul chases David

23 One day news came to David that the Philistines were at Keilah robbing the threshing floors.

2David asked the Lord, "Shall I go and attack them?"

"Yes, go and save Keilah," the Lord told him.

3But David's men said, "We're afraid even here in Judah; we certainly don't want to go to Keilah to fight the whole Philistine army!"

4David asked the Lord again, and the Lord again replied, "Go down to Keilah, for I will help you conquer the Philistines."

5They went to Keilah and slaughtered the Philistines and confiscated their cattle, and so the people of Keilah were saved. 6(Abiathar the priest went to Keilah with David, taking his ephod with him to get answers for David from the Lord.) 7Saul soon learned that David was at Keilah.

"Good!" he exclaimed. "We've got him now! God has delivered him to me, for he has trapped himself in a walled city!"

8So Saul mobilized his entire army to march to Keilah and besiege David and his men. 9But David learned of Saul's plan and told Abiathar the priest to bring the ephod and to ask the Lord what he should do.

10"O Lord God of Israel," David said, "I have heard that Saul is planning to come and destroy Keilah because I am here. 11Will the men of Keilah surrender me to him? And will Saul actually come, as I have heard? O Lord God of Israel, please tell me."

And the Lord said, "He will come."

12"And will these men of Keilah betray me to Saul?" David persisted.

And the Lord replied, "Yes, they will betray you."

13So David and his men—about six hundred of them now—left Keilah and began roaming the countryside. Word soon reached Saul that David had escaped, so he didn't go there after all. 14, 15David now lived in the wilderness caves in the hill country of Ziph. One day near Horesh he received the news that Saul was on the way to Ziph to search for him and kill him. Saul hunted him day after day, but the Lord didn't let him find him.

16(Prince Jonathan now went to find David; he met him at Horesh and encouraged him in his faith in God.

17"Don't be afraid," Jonathan reassured him. "My father will never find you! You are going to be the king of Israel and I will be next to you, as my father is well aware." 18So the two of them renewed their pact of friendship; and David stayed at Horesh while Jonathan returned home.)

23:1
Josh 15:44
Neh 3:17
23:2
1 Sam 22:15
23:9; 30:8
2 Sam 5:19,23
23:4
Josh 8:7
Judg 7:7
2 Sam 5:19
2 Kgs 3:18
23:9
1 Sam 22:15
23:2; 30:7
23:13
1 Sam 22:2
25:13
2 Sam 15:20
23:14
Josh 15:55
1 Sam 26:1
2 Chron 11:8
23:17
1 Sam 20:31
24:20
23:18
1 Sam 20:16

23:1 The threshing floor was an open, circular area where the grain kernels were separated from their husks. In order to separate the grain from the husk, farmers would toss their grain into the air allowing the wind to blow the husks away to leave only the grain. This process is called winnowing. Robbing the threshing floor meant the Philistines were robbing Keilah's citizens of all the results of their farming—that is, of all their food stores. (For more on threshing see the note on Ruth 3:2.)

23:2 David sought the Lord's guidance *before* he took action, probably through the Urim and Thummim that Abiathar the priest had brought (23:6). He listened to God's directions and then proceeded accordingly. Rather than trying to find God's will *after* the fact or having to ask God to undo the results of our hasty decisions, we should take time to discern God's will beforehand. We can hear him speak through the counsel of others, his Word, and the leading of his Spirit in our hearts, as well as through circumstances.

23:6 An ephod was a sleeveless, linen vest worn by priests. The ephod of the High Priest was brightly colored and had a chestpiece with 12 gemstones representing each tribe. The Urim and Thummim were kept within a pouch of the High Priest's ephod. (See the second note on 2:18 for a more detailed explanation of the ephod.)

23:7 When Saul heard that David was trapped in a walled city, he thought God was putting David at his mercy. Saul wanted to kill David so badly that he would have interpreted any sign as God's approval to move ahead with his plan. Had Saul known God better, he would have known what God wanted and would not have misread the situation as God's approval for murder.

Not every opportunity is sent from God. We may want something so much that we assume any opportunity to obtain it is from God. As we see from Saul's case, however, this may not be true. An opportunity to do something against God's will can never be from God, because God does not tempt us. When ripe opportunities come your way, double-check your motives. Make sure you are following God's desires, and not just your own.

23:16—18 This may have been the last time David and Jonathan were together. As true friends they were more than just companions who enjoyed each other's company. They encouraged each other's faith in God and trusted each other with their deepest thoughts and closest confidences. These are the marks of true friendship.

As Jonathan prepared to leave David, he not only promised to be David's friend to the end, but he also encouraged David to remember God's faithfulness. As a friend, remember that you have far more to offer than companionship.

23:19
1 Sam 22:6
26:1

19But now the men of Ziph went to Saul in Gibe-ah and betrayed David to him. "We know where he is hiding," they said. "He is in the caves of Horesh on Hachilah Hill, down in the southern part of the wilderness. 20Come on down, sir, and we will catch him for you and your fondest wish will be fulfilled!"

23:21
1 Sam 22:8

21"Well, praise the Lord!" Saul said. "At last someone has had pity on me! 22Go and check again to be sure of where he is staying and who has seen him there, for I know that he is very crafty. 23Discover his hiding places and then come back and give me a more definite report. Then I'll go with you. And if he is in the area at all, I'll find him if I have to search every inch of the entire land!"

23:24
Josh 15:55

23:26
Ps 17:9; 22:12

24, 25So the men of Ziph returned home. But when David heard that Saul was on his way to Ziph, he and his men went even further into the wilderness of Maon in the south of the desert. But Saul followed them there. 26He and David were now on opposite sides of a mountain. As Saul and his men began to close in, David tried his best to escape, but it was no use. 27But just then a message reached Saul that the Philistines were raiding Israel again, 28so Saul quit the chase and returned to fight the Philistines. Ever since that time the place where David was camped has been called, "The Rock of Escape!" 29David then went to live in the caves of Engedi.

23:29
Josh 15:62
2 Chron 20:2

David spares Saul's life

24:2
1 Sam 13:2
26:2

24 After Saul's return from his battle with the Philistines, he was told that David had gone into the wilderness of Engedi; 2so he took three thousand special troops and went to search for him among the rocks and wild goats of the desert. 3At the place where the road passes some sheepfolds, Saul went into a cave to go to the bathroom, but as it happened, David and his men were hiding in the cave!

24:4
1 Sam 26:8

4"Now's your time!" David's men whispered to him. "Today is the day the Lord was talking about when he said, 'I will certainly put Saul into your power, to do with as you wish'!" Then David crept forward and quietly slit off the bottom of Saul's robe! 5But then his conscience began bothering him.

24:5
2 Sam 24:10
24:6
1 Sam 26:11
2 Sam 1:14
24:7
1 Kgs 1:31

6"I shouldn't have done it," he said to his men. "It is a serious sin to attack God's chosen king in any way."

7, 8These words of David persuaded his men not to kill Saul.

After Saul had left the cave and gone on his way, David came out and shouted after him, "My lord the king!" And when Saul looked around, David bowed low before him. 9, 10Then he shouted to Saul, "Why do you listen to the people who say I am trying to harm you? This very day you have seen it isn't true. For the Lord placed you at my mercy back there in the cave and some of my men told me to kill you, but I spared you. For I said, 'I will never harm him—he is the Lord's chosen king.' 11See what I have in my hand? It is the hem of your robe! I cut it off, but I didn't kill you! Doesn't this convince you that I am not trying to harm you and that I have not sinned against you, even though you have been hunting for my life? 12"The Lord will decide between us. Perhaps he will kill you for what you are

24:9
1 Sam 26:19
Ps 7:3,4

24:11
1 Sam 23:14,
23; 26:20

24:12
Gen 31:53
Judg 11:27

24:3 A sheepfold was a large enclosure with a wall or fence around it which was used at night to protect sheep from thieves and wild animals. Thorn branches were sometimes placed on top of the walls, which were high enough to prevent most wild animals from getting in. There was only one entrance to the sheepfold, and the shepherd often slept in front of it.

24:3 David and his 600 men found the wilderness of Engedi a good place to hide because of the many caves in the area. These caves were used by local people for housing and as tombs. For David's men they were places of refuge. These caves can still be seen today. Some are large enough to hold thousands of people.

24:4 Scripture does not record any such statement being made by God to David or his men. The men were probably offering their own interpretation of some previous event such as David's anointing (16:13) or Jonathan's prediction that David would become king (23:17). When David's men saw Saul entering their cave, they wrongly assumed that this was an indication from God that they should act.

24:5 David had great respect for Saul, even though Saul was trying to kill him. Although Saul was in a state of sin and rebellion against God, David still respected the position he held as God's anointed king. David knew he would one day be king, and he also knew it was not right to strike down the man God had placed on the throne. If he assassinated Saul he would be setting a precedent for his own opponents to remove him some day.

Romans 13:1–7 teaches that God has placed the government and its leaders in power. We may not know why, but, like David, we are to respect the positions and roles of those to whom God has given authority. There is one exception, however. Since God is our highest authority, we should not allow a leader to force us to violate God's Law.

trying to do to me, but I will never harm you. ¹³As that old proverb says, 'Wicked is as wicked does,' but despite your wickedness, I'll not touch you. ¹⁴And who is the king of Israel trying to catch, anyway? Should he spend his time chasing one who is as worthless as a dead dog or a flea? ¹⁵May the Lord judge as to which of us is right and punish whichever one of us is guilty. He is my lawyer and defender, and he will rescue me from your power!"

¹⁶Saul called back, "Is it really you, my son David?" Then he began to cry. ¹⁷And he said to David, "You are a better man than I am, for you have repaid me good for evil. ¹⁸Yes, you have been wonderfully kind to me today, for when the Lord delivered me into your hand, you didn't kill me. ¹⁹Who else in all the world would let his enemy get away when he had him in his power? May the Lord reward you well for the kindness you have shown me today. ²⁰And now I realize that you are surely going to be king, and Israel shall be yours to rule. ²¹Oh, swear to me by the Lord that when that happens you will not kill my family and destroy my line of descendants!"

²²So David promised, and Saul went home, but David and his men went back to their cave.

Nabal's rudeness angers David

25 Shortly afterwards, Samuel died and all Israel gathered for his funeral and buried him in his family plot at Ramah.

Meanwhile David went down to the wilderness of Paran. ²A wealthy man from Maon owned a sheep ranch there, near the village of Carmel. He had three thousand sheep and a thousand goats, and was at his ranch at this time for the sheep shearing. ³His name was Nabal and his wife, a beautiful and very intelligent woman, was named Abigail. But the man, who was a descendant of Caleb, was uncouth, churlish, stubborn, and ill-mannered.

⁴When David heard that Nabal was shearing his sheep, ⁵he sent ten of his young men to Carmel to give him this message: ⁶"May God prosper you and your family and multiply everything you own. ⁷I am told that you are shearing your sheep and goats. While your shepherds have lived among us, we have never harmed them, nor stolen anything from them the whole time they have been in Carmel. ⁸Ask your young men and they will tell you whether or not this is true. Now I have sent my men to ask for a little contribution from you, for we have come at a happy time of holiday. Please give us a present of whatever is at hand."

⁹The young men gave David's message to Nabal and waited for his reply. ¹⁰"Who is this fellow David?" he sneered. "Who does this son of Jesse think he is? There are lots of servants these days who run away from their masters. ¹¹Should I take my bread and my water and my meat that I've slaughtered for my shearers and give it to a gang who comes from God knows where?"

¹²So David's messengers returned and told him what Nabal had said.

¹³"Get your swords!" was David's reply as he strapped on his own. Four hundred of them started off with David and two hundred remained behind to guard their gear.

24:13
Mt 7:16-20
12:33; 15:19

24:14
1 Sam 26:20

24:15
1 Sam 26:17
Ps 35:1; 84:9

24:17
1 Sam 26:21
Mt 5:44

24:19
1 Sam 26:23

24:20
1 Sam 13:14
20:31; 23:17

24:21
Gen 21:23
1 Sam 20:14-17
2 Sam 21:7

25:1
Num 10:12; 13:3
1 Sam 2:11
7:17; 15:35
28:3

25:2
Josh 15:55
1 Sam 27:2; 3
1 Kgs 18:19

25:3
Gen 24:15,16
29:17
Josh 15:13
1 Sam 30:14

25:7
1 Sam 15:21

25:10
Ex 5:2
Judg 9:28

25:13
1 Sam 23:13
25:13

24:16–19 The means we use to accomplish a goal is just as important as the goal we are trying to accomplish. David's goal was to become king, so his men urged him to kill Saul when he had the chance. David's refusal was not an example of cowardice but of courage—the courage to stand against the group and do what he knew was right. Don't compromise your moral standards by giving in to group pressure or taking the easy way out.

24:21, 22 David kept his promise—he never took revenge on Saul's family or descendants. Most of Saul's sons were killed later, however, by the Gibeonites (2 Samuel 21:1–14). David had promised to be kind to the descendants of Saul's son Jonathan (20:14-17), and he kept this promise when he invited Mephibosheth to live in his palace (2 Samuel 9).

25:1 Saul was king, but Samuel was the nation's spiritual leader. As a young boy and an older man, he was always careful to listen (3:10; 9:14–17) and obey (3:21; 10:1, 2) the Lord. With Samuel gone, Israel would be without this spiritual leadership until David became king. (For more on Samuel, read his Profile in chapter 8.)

25:4–8 Nabal rudely refused David's request to feed his 600 men. If we sympathize with Nabal, it is because customs are so different today. First, simple hospitality demanded that travelers—any number of them—be fed. Nabal was very rich and could have easily afforded to meet David's request. Second, David wasn't asking for a handout. He and his men had been protecting Nabal's work-force, and part of Nabal's prosperity was due to David's vigilance. We should reward those who protect us and help us prosper, even if we are not obligated to do so by law or custom.

¹⁴Meanwhile, one of Nabal's men went and told Abigail, "David sent men from the wilderness to talk to our master, but he insulted them and railed at them. ¹⁵, ¹⁶But David's men were very good to us and we never suffered any harm from them; in fact, day and night they were like a wall of protection to us and the sheep, and nothing was stolen from us the whole time they were with us. ¹⁷You'd better think fast, for there is going to be trouble for our master and his whole family—he's such a stubborn lout that no one can even talk to him!"

25:18
2 Sam 16:1
1 Chron 12:40

¹⁸Then Abigail hurriedly took two hundred loaves of bread, two barrels of wine, five dressed sheep, two bushels of roasted grain, one hundred raisin cakes, and two hundred fig cakes, and packed them onto donkeys.

25:19
Gen 32:16,20

¹⁹"Go on ahead," she said to her young men, "and I will follow." But she didn't tell her husband what she was doing. ²⁰As she was riding down the trail on her donkey, she met David coming towards her.

²¹David had been saying to himself, "A lot of good it did us to help this fellow. We protected his flocks in the wilderness so that not one thing was lost or stolen,

25:22
1 Sam 3:17
14:44

but he has repaid me bad for good. All that I get for my trouble is insults. ²²May God curse me if even one of his men remains alive by tomorrow morning!"

Abigail intercedes for Nabal

²³When Abigail saw David, she quickly dismounted and bowed low before him. ²⁴"I accept all blame in this matter, my lord," she said. "Please listen to what I want to say. ²⁵Nabal is a bad-tempered boor, but please don't pay any attention to what he said. He is a fool—just like his name means. But I didn't see the

25:26
2 Sam 18:32

messengers you sent. ²⁶Sir, since the Lord has kept you from murdering and taking vengeance into your own hands, I pray by the life of God, and by your own life too,

25:27
Gen 33:11
1 Sam 30:26
2 Kgs 5:15

that all your enemies shall be as cursed as Nabal is. ²⁷And now, here is a present I have brought to you and your young men. ²⁸Forgive me for my boldness in coming

25:28
2 Sam 7:16

out here. The Lord will surely reward you with eternal royalty for your descendants, for you are fighting his battles; and you will never do wrong through-

25:29
1 Sam 2:9
Ps 66:9

out your entire life. ²⁹Even when you are chased by those who seek your life, you are safe in the care of the Lord your God, just as though you were safe inside his purse! But the lives of your enemies shall disappear like stones from a sling!

25:30
Gen 40:14
1 Sam 13:14

³⁰, ³¹When the Lord has done all the good things he promised you and has made you king of Israel, you won't want the conscience of a murderer who took the law into

---

LIFE OF DAVID VS. LIFE OF SAUL

Life of David	Life of Saul
David was God's kind of king (2 Samuel 7:8–16)	Saul was man's kind of king (1 Samuel 10:23)
David was a man after God's heart (Acts 13:22)	Saul was a man after people's praise (1 Samuel 18:6–13)
David's kingship was eternal (through Jesus) (2 Samuel 7:27)	Saul's kingship was rejected (1 Samuel 15:23)
David was kind and benevolent (2 Samuel 9; 1 Chronicles 19:2, 3)	Saul was cruel (1 Samuel 20:30–34; 22:11–19)
David was forgiving (1 Samuel 26)	Saul was unforgiving (1 Samuel 14:44; 18:9)
David repented (2 Samuel 12:13; 24:10)	When confronted, Saul lied (1 Samuel 15:10–31)
David was courageous (1 Samuel 17; 1 Chronicles 18)	Saul was fearful (1 Samuel 17:11; 18:9–13)
David was at peace with God (Psalm 37:11; 119:165)	Saul was separated from God (1 Samuel 16:14)

25:24 David was in no mood to listen when he set out for Nabal's ranch (25:13, 22). Nevertheless, he stopped to hear what Abigail had to say. If he had ignored her, he would have been guilty of taking vengeance into his own hands. No matter how right we think we are, we must always be careful to stop and listen to what others have to say. The extra time and effort can save us much pain and trouble in the long run.

his own hands! And when the Lord has done these great things for you, please remember me!"

32David replied to Abigail, "Bless the Lord God of Israel who has sent you to meet me today! 33Thank God for your good sense! Bless you for keeping me from murdering the man and carrying out vengeance with my own hands. 34For I swear by the Lord, the God of Israel who has kept me from hurting you, that if you had not come out to meet me, not one of Nabal's men would be alive tomorrow morning."

25:32
Ex 18:10
1 Sam 24:19
26:9,10

35Then David accepted her gifts and told her to return home without fear, for he would not kill her husband. 36When she arrived home she found that Nabal had thrown a big party. He was roaring drunk, so she didn't tell him anything about her meeting with David until the next morning. 37, 38By that time he was sober, and when his wife told him what had happened, he had a stroke and lay paralyzed for about ten days, then died, for the Lord killed him.

25:35
Gen 19:21

39When David heard that Nabal was dead, he said, "Praise the Lord! God has paid back Nabal and kept me from doing it myself; he has received his punishment for his sin."

25:39
2 Sam 3:28,29

Then David wasted no time in sending messengers to Abigail to ask her to become his wife. 40When the messengers arrived at Carmel and told her why they had come, 41she readily agreed to his request. 42Quickly getting ready, she took along five of her serving girls as attendants, mounted her donkey, and followed the men back to David. So she became his wife.

25:42
Gen 24:61

25:43
1 Sam 27:2,3
30:5
2 Sam 2:2; 3:2

43David also married Ahino-am from Jezreel. 44King Saul, meanwhile, had forced David's wife Michal, Saul's daughter, to marry a man from Gallim named Palti (the son of Laish).

25:44
1 Sam 18:27
2 Sam 3:14,15

David again spares Saul's life

26 Now the men from Ziph came back to Saul at Gibe-ah to tell him that David had returned to the wilderness and was hiding on Hachilah Hill. 2So Saul took his elite corps of three thousand troops and went to hunt him down. 3, 4Saul camped along the road at the edge of the wilderness where David was hiding, but David knew of Saul's arrival and sent out spies to watch his movements.

26:1
1 Sam 23:19

26:2
1 Sam 13:2
24:2

26:3
1 Sam 23:19

5, 6, 7David slipped over to Saul's camp one night to look around. King Saul and General Abner were sleeping inside a ring formed by the slumbering soldiers.

26:5
Judg 7:10,11
1 Sam 14:50,51
2 Sam 3:29
1 Chron 2:15,16

"Any volunteers to go down there with me?" David asked Ahimelech (the Hittite) and Abishai (Joab's brother and the son of Zeruiah).

"I'll go with you," Abishai replied. So David and Abishai went to Saul's camp and found him asleep, with his spear in the ground beside his head.

8"God has put your enemy within your power this time for sure," Abishai whispered to David. "Let me go and put that spear through him. I'll pin him to the earth with it—I'll not need to strike a second time!"

26:8
1 Sam 24:4

9"No," David said. "Don't kill him, for who can remain innocent after attacking the Lord's chosen king? 10Surely God will strike him down some day, or he will die in battle or of old age. 11But God forbid that I should kill the man he has chosen to be king! But I'll tell you what—we'll take his spear and his jug of water and then get out of here!"

26:9
1 Sam 24:6
2 Sam 1:14,16

12So David took the spear and jug of water, and they got away without anyone seeing them or even waking up, because the Lord had put them sound asleep. 13They climbed the mountain slope opposite the camp until they were at a safe distance.

26:12
Gen 2:21; 15:12
Isa 29:10

25:37, 38 *he had a stroke and lay paralyzed*, literally, "his heart died within him and he became as stone."

25:44 The story of David and Michal does not end here. (See 2 Samuel 3:12–16 for the next episode.)

26:5–7 Abishai showed great courage when he volunteered to go into Saul's camp with David. In the heat of emotion, Abishai wanted to kill Saul, but David restrained him. Although Abishai was only trying to protect David, his leader, David could not hurt Saul

because of his respect for Saul's authority and position as God's anointed king. Abishai may have disagreed with David, but he also respected the one in authority over him. Eventually he became the greatest warrior in David's army (2 Samuel 23:18, 19).

26:8ff The strongest moral decisions are the ones we make before temptation strikes. David was determined to follow God and

26:14
1 Sam 14:50
17:55

26:16
2 Sam 12:5

¹⁴Then David shouted down to Abner and Saul, "Wake up, Abner!"
"Who is it?" Abner demanded.
¹⁵"Well, Abner, you're a great fellow, aren't you?" David taunted. "Where in all Israel is there anyone as wonderful? So why haven't you guarded your master the king when someone came to kill him? ¹⁶This isn't good at all! I swear by the Lord

ABIGAIL

Some men don't deserve their wives. Abigail was probably the best woman Nabal could afford, and he got even more than he bargained for when he arranged to marry her. She was beautiful and more suited than he was to manage his wealth. But Nabal took this wife for granted.

In spite of his shortcomings, Nabal's household did what they could to keep him out of trouble. This loyalty must have been inspired by Abigail. Although her culture and her husband placed a low value on her, she made the most of her skills and opportunities. When Nabal died, she could have inherited both wealth and position. Instead, she gave herself and all she owned to David. Evidently she was more interested in being a certain kind of person than in having a certain position.

She was an effective counselor to both of the men in her life, working hard to prevent them from making rash moves. By her swift action and skillful negotiation, she kept David from taking vengeance upon Nabal. She saw the big picture and left plenty of room for God to get involved.

How do your goals compare with Abigail's? Do you think more about the things you want to have or the person you want to be? What challenge or responsibility do you face today that needs a person under God's control?

Strengths and accomplishments:
● Sensible and capable manager of a large estate
● A persuasive speaker, able to see beyond herself

Lessons from her life:
● Life's tough situations bring out the best in people
● One does not need a prestigious title to perform a significant role
● Every life has certain responsibilities which present worthwhile challenges

Vital statistics:
● Where: Carmel
● Occupation: Homemaker, estate manager
● Relatives: First husband: Nabal. Second husband: David. Son: Chileab (Daniel).
● Contemporaries: Saul, Michal, Ahino-am

Key verses:
"David replied to Abigail, 'Bless the Lord God of Israel who has sent you to meet me today! Thank God for your good sense! Bless you for keeping me from murdering the man and carrying out vengeance with my own hands'" (1 Samuel 25:32, 33).

Her story is told in 1 Samuel 25—2 Samuel 2. She is also mentioned in 1 Chronicles 3:1.

this carried over into his decision not to murder God's anointed king, Saul, even when his men and the circumstances seemed to make it a feasible option. Who would you have been like in such a situation—David or David's men? To be like David and follow God, we must realize that we can't do wrong in order to execute justice. Even when our closest friends counsel us to a certain action that seems right, we must always put God's commands first.

26:9 Why did David refuse to kill Saul? God had placed Saul in power and had not yet removed him. David did not want to run ahead of God's timing. We are in similar stiuations when we have leaders in church or government who are unfaithful or incompetent. It may be easy for us to criticize or move against a leader without regard to God's hidden purposes and timing. Determining not to do wrong, David left Saul's destiny in God's hands. While we should not ignore sin or sit back and allow evil leaders to carry on their wickedness, neither should we take actions that are against God's laws. We should work for righteousness while trusting God.

26:15, 16 David could have killed Saul and Abner and made a point, but he would have disobeyed God and set into motion unknown consequences. Instead, he took a water jug and sword, showing that he had had the opportunity to do evil but had not done it. And he made the point that he had great respect for both God and God's anointed king. When you need to make a point,

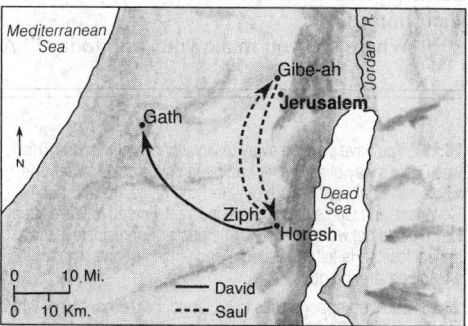

SAUL CHASES DAVID The men of Ziph again betrayed David to Saul, who was in his palace in Gibe-ah. Saul took three thousand troops to Horesh in order to find David. David could have killed Saul, but he refused. Saul, feeling foolish at David's kindness, returned to Gibe-ah and David went to Gath.

look for creative, God-honoring ways to do so. It will have a more significant impact.

that you ought to die for your carelessness. Where is the king's spear and the jug of water that was beside his head? Look and see!"

17, 18Saul recognized David's voice and said, "Is that you, my son David?" And David replied, "Yes, sir, it is. Why are you chasing me? What have I done? What is my crime? 19If the Lord has stirred you up against me, then let him accept my peace offering. But if this is simply the scheme of a man, then may he be cursed by God. For you have driven me out of my home so that I can't be with the Lord's people, and you have sent me away to worship heathen gods. 20Must I die on foreign soil, far from the presence of Jehovah? Why should the king of Israel come out to hunt my life like a partridge on the mountains?"

21Then Saul confessed, "I have done wrong. Come back home, my son, and I'll no longer try to harm you; for you saved my life today. I have been a fool, and very, very wrong."

22"Here is your spear, sir," David replied. "Let one of your young men come over and get it. 23The Lord gives his own reward for doing good and for being loyal, and I refused to kill you even when the Lord placed you in my power. 24Now may the Lord save my life, even as I have saved yours today. May he rescue me from all my troubles."

25And Saul said to David, "Blessings on you, my son David. You shall do heroic deeds and be a great conqueror."

Then David went away and Saul returned home.

5. Saul's defeat and death
David lives among the Philistines

27 But David kept thinking to himself, "Some day Saul is going to get me. I'll try my luck among the Philistines until Saul gives up and quits hunting for me; then I will finally be safe again."

2, 3So David took his six hundred men and their families to live at Gath under the protection of King Achish. He had his two wives with him—Ahino-am of Jezreel and Abigail of Carmel, Nabal's widow. 4Word soon reached Saul that David had fled to Gath, so he quit hunting for him.

5One day David said to Achish, "My lord, if it is all right with you, we would rather live in one of the country towns instead of here in the royal city."

6So Achish gave him Ziklag (which still belongs to the kings of Judah to this day), 7and they lived there among the Philistines for a year and four months. 8He and his men spent their time raiding the Geshurites, the Girzites, and the Amalekites—people who had lived near Shur along the road to Egypt ever since ancient times. 9They didn't leave one person alive in the villages they hit, and took for themselves the sheep, oxen, donkeys, camels, and clothing before returning to their homes.

10"Where did you make your raid today?" Achish would ask.

26:17
1 Sam 24:16

26:19
1 Sam 24:9
2 Sam 16:11

26:21
1 Sam 15:24
24:17

26:23
1 Sam 24:19
2 Sam 22:21

26:24
Ps 54:7

27:1
1 Sam 17:52
28:1

27:2
1 Sam 21:10
25:42,43
2 Sam 2:2,3
1 Kgs 2:39

27:6
Josh 15:31
2 Sam 1:1
Neh 11:28

27:7
1 Sam 29:3

27:8
Ex 17:8
Josh 13:2-7,13
1 Sam 15:7,8

27:9
1 Sam 15:3

27:10
Judg 1:16; 4:11
1 Sam 30:27-31
1 Chron 2:9,25

26:19 "You have sent me away to worship heathen gods." This was David's way of saying he had been driven out of Israel. The whole earth belongs to God, but the Tabernacle, the Ark of the Covenant, and God's people were in Israel. Forced to leave Israel, David could not worship at the Tabernacle or participate in the annual feasts. He felt separated, living among people who worshiped strange gods.

26:25 Saul had opportunities to kill David, but he never did. Why? First, every time David and Saul were face to face, David did something generous for Saul. The king did not want to respond to David's kindness with cruelty in front of all his men. Second, David had a large following in Israel. By killing him, Saul would risk his hold on the kingdom. Third, God had appointed David to become king of Israel and was protecting him.

27:2, 3 For the second time, David sought refuge from Saul in Philistine territory (21:10–15). Once the great conqueror of

Philistines, he now had permission to live under the protection of King Achish of Gath. Achish certainly would have known about the split between Saul and David and would have been glad to shelter this Israelite traitor. In return, Achish would have expected military support from David and his 600 warriors. David further strengthened his position with Achish by conducting fake raids on Israel and by pretending loyalty to the Philistine ruler.

27:4 Saul finally stopped pursuing David. His army was not strong enough to invade Philistine territory just to seek one man. Besides, the immediate threat to Saul's throne was gone while David was out of the country.

27:5–7 Gath was one of five capital cities in Philistia, and Achish was one of five co-rulers. David may have wanted to move out of this royal city to avoid potential skirmishes or attacks upon his family. He may also have wanted to escape the close scrutiny of the Philistine officials. Achish let David move to Ziklag, where he lived until Saul's death (2 Samuel 2:1).

And David would reply, "Against the south of Judah and the people of Jerahmeel and the Kenites."

¹¹No one was left alive to come to Gath and tell where he had really been. This happened again and again while he was living among the Philistines. ¹²Achish believed David and thought that the people of Israel must hate him bitterly by now. "Now he will have to stay here and serve me forever!" the king thought.

Saul consults a witch

28 About that time the Philistines mustered their armies for another war with Israel.

"Come and help us fight," King Achish said to David and his men.

²"Good," David agreed. "You will soon see what a help we can be to you."

"If you are, you shall be my personal bodyguard for life," Achish told him.

³(Meanwhile, Samuel had died and all Israel had mourned for him. He was buried in Ramah, his home town. King Saul had banned all mediums and wizards from the land of Israel.)

⁴The Philistines set up their camp at Shunem, and Saul and the armies of Israel were at Gilboa. ⁵, ⁶When Saul saw the vast army of the Philistines, he was frantic with fear and asked the Lord what he should do. But the Lord refused to answer him, either by dreams, or by Urim, or by the prophets. ⁷, ⁸Saul then instructed his aides to try to find a medium so that he could ask her what to do, and they found one at Endor. Saul disguised himself by wearing ordinary clothing instead of his royal robes. He went to the woman's home at night, accompanied by two of his men.

"I've got to talk to a dead man," he pleaded. "Will you bring his spirit up?"

⁹"Are you trying to get me killed?" the woman demanded. "You know that Saul has had all of the mediums and fortune-tellers executed. You are spying on me."

¹⁰But Saul took a solemn oath that he wouldn't betray her.

28:1
1 Sam 21:10
27:1-3

28:3
Lev 19:31
Deut 18:10
1 Sam 15:23
25:1

28:4
1 Sam 31:1
2 Sam 1:6

28:5
Ex 28:30,31
Num 12:6

28:7
2 Chron 18:29
35:22
Ps 83:10
Isa 8:19
Acts 16:16

THE BATTLE AT GILBOA
David pretended loyalty to Achish, but when war broke out with Israel, he was sent to Ziklag from Aphek. The Philistines defeated the Israelites at Mount Gilboa. David returned to Ziklag to find that the Amalekites had destroyed Ziklag. So David and his men pursued the Amalekite raiders and slaughtered them, recovering all that was taken.

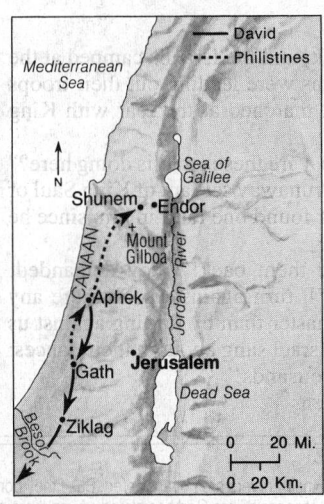

— David
----- Philistines

Mediterranean Sea

N

Sea of Galilee

Shunem •Endor
Mount Gilboa
•Aphek

CANAAN

Jordan River

•Gath **Jerusalem**
Dead Sea

Besor Brook
•Ziklag

0   20 Mi.
0   20 Km.

agreed, once again pretending loyalty to the Philistines (28:1ff). Whether he would have actually fought Saul's army we can't know, but we can be sure that his ultimate loyalty was to God and not to Achish or Saul.

28:1, 2 Achish's request put David in a difficult position. To refuse to help Achish fight the Israelites would give away David's loyalty to Israel and endanger the lives of his soldiers and family. But to agree to fight his own people would be to hurt the very people he loved and would soon lead. David, however, never had to solve his dilemma. The other Philistine leaders objected to his presence in battle; thus, he did not have to fight his countrymen.

28:3–8 It was Saul who had banned all mediums and wizards from Israel, but in desperation he turned to one for counsel. Although he had removed the sin of witchcraft from the land, he did not remove it from his heart. We may make a great show of denouncing sin, but if our heart does not change, the sins will return. Knowing what is right and condemning what is wrong does not take the place of *doing* what is right.

28:5, 6 The Urim, along with the Thummim, was used by the High Priest to determine God's guidance in certain matters. (See the notes on 2:18 and 10:20 for further information on the use of the Urim and Thummim.)

28:7, 8 God had strictly forbidden the Israelites to have anything to do with black magic, fortune tellers, witches, wizards, or anyone who claimed to bring forth spirits from the dead (Deuteronomy 18:9–14). In fact, sorcerers were to be put to death (Exodus 22:18). Occult practices were carried on in the name of pagan gods and people turned to the occult for answers that God would not give.

Practitioners of the occult have Satan and demons as the source of their information; God does not reveal his will to them. Instead he spoke through the prophets and still speaks today through his Word.

27:8, 9 David probably conducted these guerrilla-style raids because these three tribes were known for their surprise attacks and cruel treatment of innocent people. These desert tribes were a danger not just to the Philistines, but especially to the Israelites, the people David would one day be leading.

27:10–12 Was David wrong in falsely reporting his activities to Achish? No doubt David was lying, but he may have felt his strategy was justified in a time of war against a pagan enemy. David knew he would one day be Israel's king. The Philistines were still his enemies, but this was an excellent place to hide from Saul. When Achish asked David to go into battle against Israel, David

11Finally the woman said, "Well, whom do you want me to bring up?"

"Bring me Samuel," Saul replied.

12When the woman saw Samuel, she screamed, "You've deceived me! You are Saul!"

13"Don't be frightened!" the king told her. "What do you see?"

"I see a specter coming up out of the earth," she said.

14"What does he look like?"

"He is an old man wrapped in a robe."

Saul realized that it was Samuel and bowed low before him.

15"Why have you disturbed me by bringing me back?" Samuel asked Saul. **28:15** 1 Sam 16:13, 14; 28:4-6

"Because I am in deep trouble," he replied. "The Philistines are at war with us, and God has left me and won't reply by prophets or dreams; so I have called for you to ask you what to do."

16But Samuel replied, "Why ask me if the Lord has left you and has become your enemy? 17He has done just as he said he would and has taken the kingdom from you **28:17** 1 Sam 15:28 16:13 and given it to your rival, David. 18All this has come upon you because you did not obey the Lord's instructions when he was so angry with Amalek. 19What's more, **28:19** 1 Sam 31:2,6 the entire Israeli army will be routed and destroyed by the Philistines tomorrow, and you and your sons will be here with me."

20Saul now fell full length upon the ground, paralyzed with fright because of **28:20** 1 Sam 25:37,38 Samuel's words. He was also faint with hunger, for he had eaten nothing all day. 21When the woman saw how distraught he was, she said, "Sir, I obeyed your command at the risk of my life. 22Now do what I say, and let me give you something to eat so you'll regain your strength for the trip back."

23But he refused. The men who were with him added their pleas to that of the **28:23** 2 Kgs 5:13 woman until he finally yielded and got up and sat on the bed. 24The woman had **28:24** Gen 18:6,7 been fattening a calf, so she hurried out and killed it and kneaded dough and baked unleavened bread. 25She brought the meal to the king and his men, and they ate it. Then they went out into the night.

The Philistines distrust David

29 The Philistine army now mobilized at Aphek, and the Israelis camped at the **29:1** Josh 12:18 springs in Jezreel. 2As the Philistine captains were leading out their troops 1 Sam 4:1 by battalions and companies, David and his men marched at the rear with King 2 Kgs 9:30 Achish.

3But the Philistine commanders demanded, "What are these Israelis doing here?" **29:3** 1 Sam 27:1-6

And King Achish told them, "This is David, the runaway servant of King Saul of 1 Chron 12:19, Israel. He's been with me for years, and I've never found one fault in him since he 20 arrived."

4But the Philistine leaders were angry. "Send them back!" they demanded. "They aren't going into the battle with us—they'll turn against us. Is there any better way for him to reconcile himself with his master than by turning against us in the battle? 5This is the same man the women of Israel sang about in their dances: **29:5** 1 Sam 18:7 'Saul has slain his thousands and David his ten thousands!' " 21:11

6So Achish finally summoned David and his men. **29:6** 1 Sam 27:12

28:12 Did Samuel really come back from the dead at the medium's call? The medium shrieked at the appearance of Samuel—she knew too well that her efforts to make contact with the dead were either contrived or satanic. Somehow Samuel's appearance revealed to her that she was dealing with a power far greater than she had known. She did not call up Samuel by trickery or by the power of Satan; God brought Samuel back to give Saul a prediction regarding his fate, a message Saul already knew. This in no way justifies efforts to contact the dead today. God is against all such practices (Galatians 5:19-21).

28:13 A specter is a ghost-like figure.

28:15 God did not answer Saul's appeals because Saul had not followed God's previous directions. Sometimes people wonder why

their prayers are not answered. But if they don't fulfill the responsibilities God has already given them, they should not be surprised when he does not give further guidance.

28:20 Saul was overwhelmed at the sight of the Philistine army. Instead of turning to God, however, he turned to the occult. Let life's difficulties and obstacles push you in God's direction and make you depend upon him. As we see from Saul's story, turning to anything or anyone else leads only to disaster.

28:23-25 This paragraph highlights Saul's grim condition. He was frightened, faint, and depressed by the news Samuel had given him. In his grief over God's rejection, he had gone without food all day and had to be forced to eat. What an unhappy demise for one so gifted and honored by God in the beginning.

"I swear by the Lord," he told them, "you are some of the finest men I've ever met, and I think you should go with us, but my commanders say no. 7Please don't upset them, but go back quietly."

8"What have I done to deserve this treatment?" David demanded. "Why can't I fight your enemies?"

9But Achish insisted, "As far as I'm concerned, you're as perfect as an angel of God. But my commanders are afraid to have you with them in the battle. 10Now get up early in the morning and leave as soon as it is light."

11So David headed back into the land of the Philistines while the Philistine army went on to Jezreel.

David destroys the Amalekites

30 Three days later, when David and his men arrived home at their city of Ziklag, they found that the Amalekites had raided the city and burned it to the ground, 2carrying off all the women and children. 3As David and his men looked at the ruins and realized what had happened to their families, 4they wept until they could weep no more. 5(David's two wives, Ahino-am and Abigail, were among those who had been captured.) 6David was seriously worried, for in their bitter grief for their children, his men began talking of killing him. But David took strength from the Lord.

7Then he said to Abiathar the priest, "Bring me the oracle!" So Abiathar brought it.

8David asked the Lord, "Shall I chase them? Will I catch them?"

And the Lord told him, "Yes, go after them; you will recover everything that was taken from you!"

9, 10So David and his six hundred men set out after the Amalekites. When they reached Besor Brook, two hundred of the men were too exhausted to cross, but the other four hundred kept going. 11, 12Along the way they found an Egyptian youth in a field and brought him to David. He had not had anything to eat or drink for three days and nights, so they gave him part of a fig cake, two clusters of raisins, and some water, and his strength soon returned.

13"Who are you and where do you come from?" David asked him.

"I am an Egyptian—the servant of an Amalekite," he replied. "My master left me behind three days ago because I was sick. 14We were on our way back from raiding the Cherethites in the Negeb, and had raided the south of Judah and the land of Caleb, and had burned Ziklag."

15"Can you tell me where they went?" David asked.

The young man replied, "If you swear by God's name that you will not kill me or give me back to my master, then I will guide you to them."

16So he led them to the Amalekite encampment. They were spread out across the fields, eating and drinking and dancing with joy because of the vast amount of loot they had taken from the Philistines and from the men of Judah. 17David and his men rushed in among them and slaughtered them all that night and the entire next day until evening. No one escaped except four hundred young men who fled on camels. 18, 19David got back everything they had taken. The men recovered their families and all of their belongings, and David rescued his two wives. 20His troops rounded

30:7 *Bring me the oracle,* literally, "Bring me the ephod." See Ex 28.

29:9
2 Sam 14:17,
20; 19:27

30:1
1 Sam 15:7
27:6,8; 30:26

30:5
1 Sam 25:39,
43; 30:18,19
2 Sam 2:2; 3:2

30:6
Ex 17:4
1 Sam 23:16
Ps 18:2

30:7
1 Sam 23:9

30:8
Judg 20:18
1 Sam 23:2,4
2 Sam 5:19

30:9
1 Sam 27:2

30:11
Judg 15:19

30:14
1 Sam 30:1
2 Sam 1:1
15:17,18
1 Chron 18:17

30:15
Josh 2:12; 9:19

30:17
1 Sam 15:3

30:6 Faced with the tragedy of losing their families, David's soldiers began to turn against him and even talked about killing him. Instead of planning a rescue, they looked for someone to blame. But David began looking for a solution rather than a scapegoat. When facing problems, remember that it is useless to look for someone to blame or criticize. Instead of looking for a scapegoat, consider how you can help find a solution.

30:7 When David called for the ephod he was really asking the High Priest to bring the Urim and Thummim, which were kept in a pouch attached to the ephod. Only the High Priest could carry and

use the Urim and Thummim. (For more information on the ephod and its contents, see the note on Exodus 39:2.)

30:11-15 The Amalekites cruelly left this slave to die, but God used him to lead David and his men to the Amalekite camp. David and his men treated the young man kindly and he returned the kindness by leading them to the enemy. Treat those you meet with respect and dignity no matter how insignificant they may seem. You never know how God will use them to help you or haunt you, depending upon your response to them.

up all the flocks and herds and drove them on ahead of them. "These are all yours personally, as your reward!" they told David.

21When they reached Besor Brook and the two hundred men who had been too exhausted to go on, David greeted them joyfully. 22But some of the ruffians among David's men declared, "They didn't go with us, so they can't have any of the loot. Give them their wives and their children and tell them to be gone."

23But David said, "No, my brothers! The Lord has kept us safe and helped us defeat the enemy. 24Do you think that anyone will listen to you when you talk like this? We share and share alike—those who go to battle and those who guard the equipment."

25From then on David made this a law for all of Israel, and it is still followed.

26When he arrived at Ziklag, he sent part of the loot to the elders of Judah. "Here is a present for you, taken from the Lord's enemies," he wrote them. 27-31The gifts were sent to the elders in the following cities where David and his men had been: Bethel, South Ramoth, Jattir, Aroer, Siphmoth, Eshtemoa, Racal, the cities of the Jerahmeelites, the cities of the Kenites, Hormah, Borashan, Athach, Hebron.

Saul dies on the battlefield

31 Meanwhile the Philistines had begun the battle against Israel, and the Israelis fled from them and were slaughtered wholesale on Mount Gilboa. 2The Philistines closed in on Saul, and killed his sons Jonathan, Abinidab, and Malchishua.

3, 4Then the archers overtook Saul and wounded him badly. He groaned to his armor bearer, "Kill me with your sword before these heathen Philistines capture me and torture me." But his armor bearer was afraid to, so Saul took his own sword and fell upon the point of the blade, and it pierced him through. 5When his armor bearer saw that he was dead, he also fell upon his sword and died with him. 6So Saul, his armor bearer, his three sons, and his troops died together that same day.

7When the Israelis on the other side of the valley and beyond the Jordan heard that their comrades had fled and that Saul and his sons were dead, they abandoned their cities; and the Philistines lived in them.

8The next day when the Philistines went out to strip the dead, they found the bodies of Saul and his three sons on Mount Gilboa. 9They cut off Saul's head and

30:21
1 Sam 30:10,11

30:24
Num 31:27
Josh 22:7,8

30:26
Gen 33:11
1 Sam 25:27
2 Kgs 5:15

31:1
1 Sam 28:4
1 Chr 10:1-12

31:3
Judg 9:54
2 Sam 1:6,10

31:9
Judg 16:23,24
2 Sam 1:20

30:25 David made a law that those who guarded the equipment were to be treated equally with those who fought in battle. Today it takes several people to provide the support services needed for every soldier in battle. In the church and other organizations, we need to treat those who provide support services equally with those on the front lines. Without bookkeepers, secretaries, trainers, and administrators, those with a public ministry would be unable to do their jobs. Are you on the front lines? Don't forget those who are backing you up. Are you in the support group? Realize that your position, although it may be less glamorous or exciting, is vital to the work of the entire group.

30:26 Why did David send part of the battle spoils to the tribe of Judah? (1) David was from the tribe of Judah. (2) David was recognizing that Judah was the largest tribe of Israel and represented the greatest authority. (3) After Saul's death, the tribe of Judah split off from the rest of the tribes (2 Samuel 2:4) because they refused to recognize Saul's son as king. David may have anticipated this split. If so, he was preparing the leaders of Judah to accept him as their king.

31:3, 4 The Philistines had a well-earned reputation for torturing their captives. Saul no doubt knew about Samson's fate (Judges 16:18-31) and did not want to risk physical mutilation or other abuse. When his armor bearer refused to kill him, he took his own life.

31:3, 4 Saul was tall, handsome, strong, rich, and powerful. But all of this was not enough to make him someone we should emulate. He was tall physically, but he was small in God's eyes. He was handsome, but his sin made him ugly. He was strong, but his lack of faith made him weak. He was rich, but he was spiritually bankrupt. He could give orders to many, but he couldn't command their respect or allegiance. Saul looked good on the outside, but he was decaying on the inside. Godly character is much more valuable than a good-looking exterior.

31:3, 4 Saul's armor bearer faced a moral dilemma—should he carry out a sinful order from a man he was supposed to obey? He knew he should obey his master, the king, but he also knew murder was wrong. He decided not to kill Saul.

There is a difference between following an order with which you don't agree and following one you know is wrong. It is never right or ethical to carry out a wrong act, no matter who gives the order or what the consequences for disobedience may be. What shapes your choice when you face a moral dilemma? Have the courage to follow God's law above human commands.

31:4 Saul faced death the same way he faced life. He took matters into his own hands without thinking of God or asking for his guidance. If our lives aren't the way we would like them to be now, we can't assume that change will come more easily later. When nearing death, we will respond to God the same way we have been responding all along. Coming face to face with death only shows us what we are *really* like. How do you want to face death? Start facing life that way right now.

stripped off his armor and sent the wonderful news of Saul's death to their idols and to the people throughout their land.

31:10
Josh 17:11
Judg 2:12-14
1 Sam 7:3
2 Sam 21:12-14

10His armor was placed in the temple of Ashtaroth, and his body was fastened to the wall of Beth-shan.

31:11
1 Sam 11:1-13

11But when the people of Jabesh-gilead heard what the Philistines had done, 12warriors from that town traveled all night to Beth-shan and took down the bodies of Saul and his sons from the wall and brought them to Jabesh, where they cremated them. 13Then they buried their remains beneath the oak tree at Jabesh and fasted for seven days.

31:12
2 Sam 2:4-7

31:13 Consider the difference between the last judge of Israel and its first king. Saul, the king, was characterized by inconsistency, disobedience, and self-will. He did not have a heart for God. Samuel, the judge, was characterized by consistency, obedience, and a deep desire for God's will. He had a genuine desire for God.

When God called Samuel, he said, "Yes, Lord, I'm listening" (3:10). But when God called Saul, he replied, "You must have the wrong man" (9:21). Saul was dedicated to himself; Samuel was dedicated to God.

31:13 Saul's death was also the death of an ideal—Israel could

no longer believe that having a king like the other nations would solve all their troubles. The real problem was not the form of government, but the sinful king. Saul tried to please God by spurts of religiosity, but real spirituality takes a lifetime of consistent obedience.

Heroic spiritual lives are built by stacking days of obedience one on top of the other. Like a brick, each obedient act is small in itself, but in time the acts will pile up and a huge wall of strong character will be built—a great defense against temptation. We should strive for consistent obedience each day.

2 SAMUEL

Judges
begin
to rule
1375 B.C.

Saul
becomes
king
1050

VITAL STATISTICS

PURPOSES:
(1) to record the history of David's reign;
(2) to demonstrate effective leadership under God;
(3) to reveal that one person *can* make a difference;
(4) to show the personal qualities that please God;
(5) to depict David as an ideal leader of an imperfect kingdom, and foreshadow Christ who will be the ideal leader of a new and perfect kingdom (chapter 7).

AUTHOR:
Unknown. Some have suggested that Nathan's son Zabud may have been the author (1 Kings 4:5). The book also includes the writings of Nathan and Gad (1 Chronicles 29:29).

DATE WRITTEN:
930 B.C.; written soon after David's reign, 1050–970 B.C.

SETTING:
The land of Israel under David's rule

KEY VERSE:
"David now realized why the Lord had made him the king and blessed his kingdom so greatly—it was because God wanted to pour out his kindness on Israel, his chosen people" (5:12).

SPECIAL FEATURES:
This book was named after the prophet who anointed David and guided him in godly living.

MODELS . . . everyone has them . . . people we emulate, people who are our ideals. Unconsciously perhaps, we copy their actions and adopt their ideas.

Among all the godly role models mentioned in the Bible, there is probably no one who stands out more than King David. Born halfway between Abraham and Jesus, he becomes God's leader for all of Israel and the ancestor of the Messiah. David is "a man about whom God said, 'David (son of Jesse) is a man after my own heart' " (Acts 13:22). What are the personal qualities David possessed that pleased God?

The book of 2 Samuel tells David's story. You will be filled with excitement as he is crowned king of Judah and then king over all of Israel (5:1–5), praising God as he brings the Ark of the Covenant back to the Tabernacle (6:1–23) and exulting as he leads his armies to victory over all their enemies and completes the conquest of the Promised Land begun by Joshua (8—10). David was a man who accomplished many great things.

But David was human, and there were some dark times when he stumbled and fell into sin. The record of lust, adultery, and murder is not easy to read (11—13) and reveals to us that even great people who try to follow God are susceptible to temptation and sin.

Godliness does not guarantee an easy and carefree life. David had family problems—his own son incited the entire nation to rebellion and crowned himself king (14:1—18:33). And greatness can cause pride, as we see in David's sinful act of taking a census in order to glory in the strength of his nation (24:1–25). But the story of this fallen hero does not end in tragedy. Through repentance, his fellowship and peace with God were restored, but he had to face the consequences of the sins he committed (12—20). These consequences stayed with him the rest of his life as a reminder of his sinful deeds and his need for God.

As you read 2 Samuel, look for David's God-like characteristics—his faithfulness, patience, courage, generosity, commitment, honesty—as well as other God-honoring characteristics such as modesty and penitence. Valuable lessons can be learned from his sins and from his repentance. You, like David, can become a person after God's own heart.

THE BLUEPRINT

A. DAVID'S SUCCESSES (1:1—10:19)
  1. David becomes king of Judah
  2. David becomes king of all Israel
  3. David conquers the surrounding nations

David took the fractured kingdom which Saul had left behind and built a strong united power. Forty years later, David would turn this kingdom over to his son Solomon. David had a heart for God. He was a king who governed God's people by God's principles, and God blessed him greatly. We may not have David's earthly success, but following God is, ultimately, the most successful decision we can make.

B. DAVID'S STRUGGLES (11:1—24:25)
  1. David and Bath-sheba
  2. Turmoil in David's family
  3. National rebellion against David
  4. The later years of David's rule

David sinned with Bath-sheba and then tried to cover his sin by having her husband killed. Although he was forgiven for his sin, the consequences remained—he experienced trouble and distress, both with his family and with the nation. God is always ready to forgive, but we must live with the consequences of our actions. Covering up our sin will only multiply sin's painful consequences.

MEGATHEMES

THEME	EXPLANATION	IMPORTANCE
Kingdom Growth	Under David's leadership, Israel's kingdom grew rapidly. With the growth came many changes: from tribal independence to centralized government, from the leadership of judges to a monarchy, from decentralized worship to worship at Jerusalem.	No matter how much growth or how many changes we experience, God provides for us if we love him and highly regard his principles. God's work done in God's way never lacks God's supply of wisdom and energy.
Personal Greatness	David's popularity and influence increased greatly. He realized that the Lord was behind his success because he wanted to pour out his kindness on Israel.	God graciously pours out his favor on us because of what Christ has done. God does not regard personal greatness as something to be used selfishly, but as an instrument to carry out his work among his people. The greatness we should desire is to love others as God loves us.
Justice	King David showed justice, mercy, and fairness to Saul's family, enemies, rebels, allies, and close friends alike. His just rule was grounded in his faith in and knowledge of God.	Although David was the most just of all Israel's kings, he was still imperfect. His use of justice offered hope for a heavenly, ideal kingdom. This hope will never be satisfied in the heart of man until Christ, the Son of David, comes to rule in perfect justice forever.
Consequences of Sin	Because David sinned with Bath-sheba, he experienced the consequences of his sin which ruined both his family and the nation. David's prosperity and ease led from triumph to trouble.	Temptation quite often comes when a person's life is aimless. We sometimes think that sinful pleasures and freedom from God's restraint will bring us a feeling of vitality; but sin creates a cycle of suffering that is not worth the fleeting pleasures it offers.
Feet of Clay	David not only sinned with Bath-sheba, he murdered an innocent man. He neglected to discipline his sons when they got involved in rape and murder. This great hero showed a lack of character in many of his personal decisions. The man of iron had feet of clay.	Sin should never be considered as a mere weakness or flaw. Sin is fatal and must be eradicated from our lives. David's life teaches us to have compassion for all men, including those whose sinful nature leads them into sinful acts. It serves as a warning to us not to excuse sin in our own lives, even in times of success.

KEY PLACES IN 2 SAMUEL

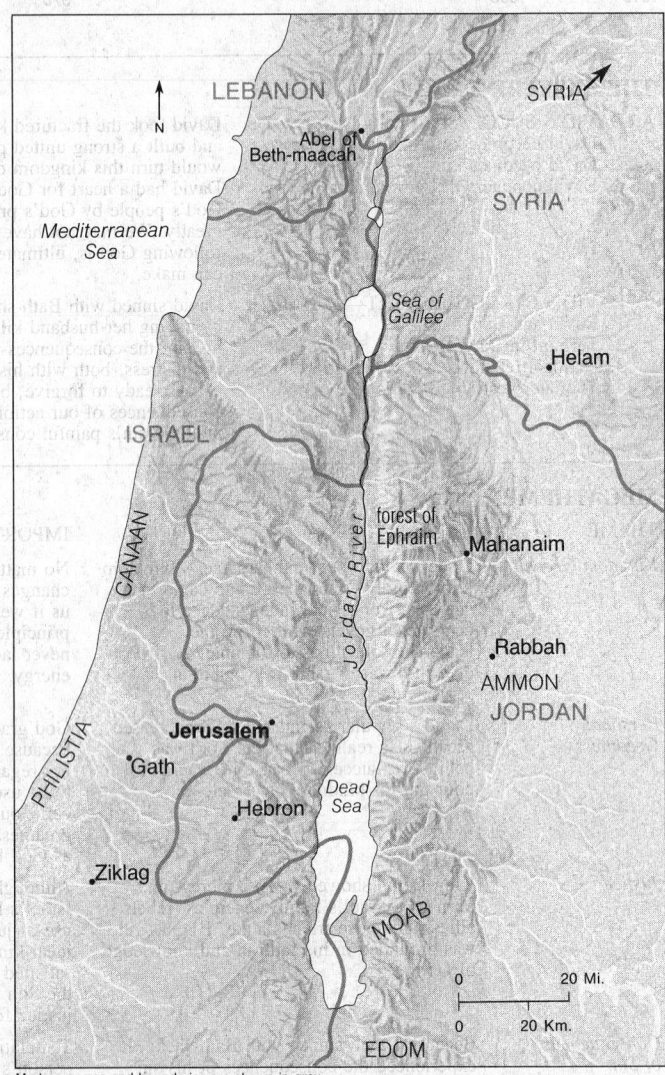

Modern names and boundaries are shown in gray.

1 **Hebron** After Saul's death, David moved from the Philistine city of Ziklag to Hebron, where the tribe of Judah crowned him king. But the rest of Israel's tribes backed Saul's son Ish-bosheth, and crowned him king at Mahanaim. As a result, there was war between Judah and the rest of the tribes of Israel until Ish-bosheth was assassinated. Then all of Israel pledged loyalty to David as their king (1:1—5:5).

2 **Jerusalem** One of David's first battles as king occurred at the fortress city of Jerusalem. David and his troops took the city by surprise and it became his capital. It was here that David brought the Ark of the Covenant and made a special agreement with God (5:6—7:29).

3 **Gath** The Philistines were Israel's constant enemy, though they did give David sanctuary when he was hiding from Saul (1 Samuel 27). But when Saul died and David became king, the Philistines planned to defeat him. In a battle near Jerusalem, David and his troops routed the Philistines (5:17–25), but they were not completely subdued until David conquered Gath, their largest city (8:1).

4 **Moab** During the time of the judges, Moab controlled many cities in Israel and demanded heavy taxes (Judges 3:8–30). David conquered Moab and, in turn, levied tribute from them (8:2).

5 **Edom** Though the Edomites and the Israelites traced their ancestry back to the same man, Isaac (Genesis 25:19–23), they were longstanding enemies. David defeated Edom and forced them to pay tribute also (8:13–18).

6 **Rabbah** The Ammonites insulted David's ambassadors and turned a peacemaking mission into angry warfare. The Ammonites called troops from Syria, but David defeated this alliance first at Helam, then at Rabbah, the capital city (9:1—12:31).

7 **Mahanaim** David had victory in the field, but problems at home. His son, Absalom, incited a rebellion and crowned himself king at Hebron. David and his men fled to Mahanaim. Acting on bad advice, Absalom mobilized his army to fight David (13:1—17:29).

8 **Forest of Ephraim** The armies of Absalom and David fought in the forest of Ephraim. Absalom's hair got caught in a tree and Joab, David's general, found and killed him. With Absalom's death, the rebellion died and David was welcomed back to Jerusalem (18:1—19:43).

9 **Abel** A man named Sheba also incited a rebellion against David. He fled to Abel, but Joab and a small troop besieged the city. The citizens of Abel killed Sheba themselves (20:1–26). David's victories laid the foundation for the peaceful reign of his son, Solomon.

A. DAVID'S SUCCESSES (1:1—10:19)

After years of running from Saul, David is finally crowned king over the tribe of Judah. The rest of Israel, however, followed Ish-bosheth, Saul's son. David did not attempt to take the tribes by force, but placed the matter in God's hands. After a few years Ish-bosheth was assassinated and the rest of the tribes finally put their support behind David. David moved the capital to Jerusalem, defeated the surrounding nations, and even showed kindness to Saul's family. We may not understand why God seems to move slowly at times, but we must trust him and be faithful with what he has given us.

1. David becomes king of Judah

David mourns for Saul and Jonathan

1:1
1 Sam 30:1,17,
26; 31:6
2 Sam 4:9,10

1 Saul was dead and David had returned to Ziklag after slaughtering the Amalek- ites. Three days later a man arrived from the Israeli army with his clothes torn and with dirt on his head as a sign of mourning. He fell to the ground before David in deep respect.

3"Where do you come from?" David asked.

"From the Israeli army," he replied.

1:4
1 Sam 4:16
31:2-4
1 Chron 10:1

4"What happened?" David demanded. "Tell me how the battle went."

And the man replied, "Our entire army fled. Thousands of men are dead and wounded on the field, and Saul and his son Jonathan have been killed."

5"How do you know they are dead?"

1:6
1 Sam 28:4
31:1

6"Because I was on Mount Gilboa and saw Saul leaning against his spear with the enemy chariots closing in upon him. 7When he saw me he cried out for me to come to him.

1:8
1 Sam 15:3
30:1,13

8" 'Who are you?' he asked.

" 'An Amalekite,' I replied.

9" 'Come and put me out of my misery,' he begged, 'for I am in terrible pain but life lingers on.'

1:10
1 Sam 31:3,4

10"So I killed him, for I knew he couldn't live. Then I took his crown and one of his bracelets to bring to you, my lord."

1:11
Gen 37:29,34

11David and his men tore their clothes in sorrow when they heard the news. 12They mourned and wept and fasted all day for Saul and his son Jonathan, and for the Lord's people, and for the men of Israel who had died that day.

13Then David said to the young man who had brought the news, "Where are you from?"

1:14
1 Sam 24:6
26:9,11

And he replied, "I am an Amalekite."

14"Why did you kill God's chosen king?" David demanded.

1:1 David was a man who had great faith in God. He waited for God to fulfill his promises. The book of 1 Samuel tells of David's struggles as he waited to become king of Israel (Samuel had anointed David as king of Israel many years earlier). Saul became jealous of David because the people were heaping great praise upon David for his accomplishments. Eventually, Saul's jealousy became so intense that he tried to kill David. As a result, David had to run away and hide. For many years David hid from Saul in enemy territory and in the barren wilderness south and east of Jerusalem. David may have wondered if God's promise that he would be king would ever come true, but his struggles prepared him for the great responsibilities he would later face. The book of 2 Samuel tells how David was finally rewarded for his patience and consistent faith in God.

1:1 When Saul died, David and his men were still living in Ziklag, a Philistine city. Because Saul had driven him out of Israel, David pretended loyalty to Achish, a Philistine ruler (1 Samuel 27). There he was safe from Saul.

1:11, 12 David and his men were visibly shaken over Saul's death: "They mourned and wept and fasted all day." This showed their genuine sorrow over the loss of their king, their friend Jonathan, and the other soldiers of Israel who died that day. They were not ashamed to grieve. Today, expressing our emotions outwardly is considered by some to be a sign of weakness. Those who wish to appear strong try to hide their grief. But mourning can help us deal with our intense sorrow when a loved one dies.

1:13 The man identified himself as an Amalekite, but 1:1 states that he was from Israel's army. Obviously he was lying about his identity and about what happened on the battlefield. Because he had Saul's crown with him, something the Philistines wouldn't have left behind, we can infer that he found Saul dead on the battlefield before the Philistines arrived (1 Samuel 31:8).

A life of deceit leads to disaster. The man lied to gain some personal reward for killing David's rival, but he misread David's character. If David had rewarded him for murdering the king, David would have shared his guilt. Instead, David had the messenger killed—most likely for something he did not do.

1:13 The Amalekites were a fierce nomadic tribe that frequently conducted surprise raids on Canaan's towns. They had been Israel's enemies since Moses' time. David had just destroyed an Amalekite band of raiders (1 Samuel 30:1–20). This man was probably unaware of David's recent confrontations with Amalekites; thus he incurred David's wrath by posing as an enemy of Israel and claiming to kill God's chosen king.

1:14–16 Although Saul had been trying to kill him for many years, David did not rejoice upon learning of Saul's death. David main- tained respect for Saul's position as God's anointed servant. When looking at our own leaders, we may be tempted to become angry, despairing, or fearful. However, in spite of the shortcomings of our leaders, we should maintain respect for the positions they hold.

15Then he said to one of his young men, "Kill him!" So he ran him through with
his sword and he died.

16"You die self-condemned," David said, "for you yourself confessed that you
killed God's appointed king."

1:15
2 Sam 4:10,12

1:16
1 Sam 26:9
2 Sam 1:10

David's song for Saul and Jonathan

17, 18Then David composed a dirge for Saul and Jonathan and afterward commanded that it be sung throughout Israel. It is quoted here from the book, *Heroic
Ballads*.

1:17
Josh 10:13
2 Chron 35:27

19O Israel, your pride and joy lies dead upon the hills;
Mighty heroes have fallen.
20Don't tell the Philistines, lest they rejoice.
Hide it from the cities of Gath and Ashkelon,
Lest the heathen nations laugh in triumph.
21O Mount Gilboa,
Let there be no dew nor rain upon you,
Let no crops of grain grow on your slopes.
For there the mighty Saul has died;
He is God's appointed king no more.
22Both Saul and Jonathan slew their strongest foes,
And did not return from battle empty-handed.
23How much they were loved, how wonderful they were—
Both Saul and Jonathan!
They were together in life and in death.
They were swifter than eagles, stronger than lions.
24But now, O women of Israel, weep for Saul;
He enriched you
With fine clothing and gold ornaments.
25These mighty heroes have fallen in the midst of the battle.
Jonathan is slain upon the hills.
26How I weep for you, my brother Jonathan;
How much I loved you!
And your love for me was deeper
Than the love of women!
27The mighty ones have fallen,
Stripped of their weapons, and dead.

1:19
2 Sam 3:38

1:20
1 Sam 6:17
31:8

1:21
1 Sam 31:1
Ezek 31:15

1:23
Judg 14:18
Prov 31:29-31

1:25
2 Sam 1:19

1:26
1 Sam 18:1
19:1; 20:17

Judah crowns David king

2 David then asked the Lord, "Shall I move back to Judah?"
And the Lord replied, "Yes."
"Which city shall I go to?"

2:1
Josh 14:13,14
1 Sam 23:2,4,9
2 Sam 5:19

1:21 *let no crops of grain grow on your slopes.* The text is uncertain in the original manuscripts.

1:15, 16 Why did David consider it a crime to kill the king, even
though Saul was his enemy? David believed that only God could
remove from office the one he had anointed. Thus, it was God's
job, not his, to judge the sins of Saul (Leviticus 19:18). We must
realize that God has placed rulers in authority over us. We are to
respect their positions (Romans 13:1-5).

1:16, 17 Saul had caused much trouble for David, but when he
died, David composed a poem for the king and his son. David had
every reason to hate Saul, yet he chose not to. He chose to look at
the good Saul had done and ignore the times when Saul had
attacked him. It takes courage to lay aside hatred and hurt in order
to show respect for another person—especially an enemy.

1:17, 18 David was a talented musician. He played the harp
(1 Samuel 16:23), he brought music into the worship services of
the Temple (1 Chronicles 25), and he wrote many of the Psalms.
Here we are told that he wrote a poem in memory of King Saul and

his son Jonathan, David's closest friend. Music played an
important role in Israel's history. (For other famous songs in the
Bible see the chart in Exodus 15.)

1:26 David was not implying that he had a sexual relationship with
Jonathan. Homosexual acts were absolutely forbidden in Israel.
Leviticus 18:22 calls homosexuality "an enormous sin," and
Leviticus 20:13 decrees the death penalty for those who practice
homosexuality. David was simply restating the deep brotherhood
and faithful friendship he had with Jonathan. (For more on their
friendship, see the note on 1 Samuel 18:1-4.)

2:1 Although David knew he would become king (1 Samuel 16:13;
23:17; 24:20), and although the time seemed right (now that Saul
was dead), David still asked God if he should move back to Judah,
the territory of his home tribe. Before moving ahead with what
seems obvious, first bring the matter to God, who alone knows the
best timing.

2:3
1 Sam 22:2
2 Sam 3:19; 4:8
1 Chron 12:1
2:4
1 Sam 16:13
2:5
1 Sam 24:19
25:32

And the Lord replied, "Hebron."

²So David and his wives—Ahino-am from Jezreel and Abigail the widow of Nabal from Carmel— ³and his men and their families all moved to Hebron. ⁴Then the leaders of Judah came to David and crowned him king of the Judean confederacy.

When David heard that the men of Jabesh-gilead had buried Saul, ⁵he sent them

ABNER

The honest compliments of an opponent are often the best measure of someone's greatness. Although Abner and David frequently saw each other across battle lines, the Bible gives a glimpse of the respect they had for each other. As a young man, David had served under Abner. But later, Saul's campaign to kill David was carried out by Abner. After Saul's death, Abner temporarily upheld the power of the king's family. But the struggle between Abner and Saul's heir, Ish-bosheth, brought about Abner's decision to support David's claim to the throne. It was during his efforts to unite the kingdom that Abner was murdered by Joab.

Several years earlier, in a battle between Ish-bosheth's army under Abner and David's forces under Joab, Abner fled and was pursued by Joab's brother, Asahel. Abner told Asahel twice to stop following him, but the eager young soldier refused, so Abner killed him. Joab was determined to avenge his brother.

Abner realized Saul's family was doomed to defeat and that David would be the next king, so he decided to change sides. He hoped that in exchange for delivering Saul's kingdom, David would make him commander-in-chief of his army. David's willingness to accept this proposal was probably another reason for Joab's action.

Abner lived by his wits and his will. To him, God was someone with whom he would cooperate if it suited his plans. Otherwise he did what seemed best for him at the time. We can identify with Abner's tendency to give God conditional cooperation. Obedience is easy when the instructions in God's Word fit in with our plans. But our allegiance to God is tested when his plans are contrary to ours. What action should you take today in obedience to God's Word?

Strengths and accomplishments:
- Commander-in-chief of Saul's army and a capable military leader
- Held Israel together for several years under the weak king Ish-bosheth
- Recognized and accepted God's plan to make David king over all Israel

Weaknesses and mistakes:
- He was motivated selfishly in his effort to reunite Judah and Israel rather than by godly conviction
- He slept with one of the royal concubines after Saul's death

Lesson from his life:
- God requires more than conditional, half-hearted cooperation

Vital statistics:
- Where: Territory of Benjamin
- Occupation: Commander of the armies under Saul, Ish-bosheth, and David
- Relatives: Father: Ner. Cousin: Saul. Son: Jaasiel.
- Contemporaries: David, Asahel, Joab, Abishai

Key verse:
"And David said to his people, 'A great leader and a great man has fallen today in Israel' " (2 Samuel 3:38).

Abner's story is told in 1 Samuel 14:50—2 Samuel 4:12. He is also mentioned in 1 Kings 2:5, 32; 1 Chronicles 26:28; 27:16–22.

2:1 God told David to return to Hebron, where he would soon be crowned king of Judah. David made Hebron his capital because: (1) it was the largest city in Judah at that time; (2) it was secure against attack; (3) it was located near the center of Judah's territory; and (4) many key trade routes converged at Hebron, making it difficult for supply lines to be cut off.

2:4 The tribe of Judah publicly crowned David as their king. David had been anointed king by Samuel years earlier (1 Samuel 16:13), but the anointing had taken place in private. This coronation was like inaugurating a public official who has already been elected to office. The rest of Israel, however, didn't accept David's kingship for seven and one-half years (2:10, 11).

2:4-7 David sent a message thanking the men of Jabesh-gilead

who had risked their lives to bury Saul's body (1 Samuel 31:11–13). In his message, he also suggested they acknowledge him as their king. Jabesh-gilead was to the north in the land of Gilead, and David was seeking to gain support among the ten remaining tribes who had not yet recognized him as king.

2:5, 6 In spite of great danger, the men of Jabesh-gilead took the bodies of their king and his sons and gave them a proper burial. Saul had rescued Jabesh-gilead from certain defeat when Nahash the Ammonite surrounded the city (1 Samuel 11), and now these citizens were showing their gratitude and loyalty. Loyalty often brings no material reward and sometimes makes us vulnerable as well. But it is a sign of true devotion, friendship, and love (1 Corinthians 13:7).

this message: "May the Lord bless you for being so loyal to your king and giving him a decent burial. 6May the Lord be loyal to you in return, and reward you with many demonstrations of his love! And I too will be kind to you because of what you have done. 7And now I ask you to be my strong and loyal subjects, now that Saul is dead. Be like the tribe of Judah who have appointed me as their new king."

Abner crowns Ish-bosheth king

8But Abner, Saul's commander-in-chief, had gone to Mahanaim to crown Saul's son Ish-bosheth as king. 9His territory included Gilead, Ashuri, Jezreel, Ephraim, the tribe of Benjamin, and all the rest of Israel. 10, 11Ish-bosheth was forty years old at the time. He reigned in Mahanaim for two years; meanwhile, David was reigning in Hebron and was king of the Judean confederacy for seven and one-half years.

Civil war begins

12One day General Abner led some of Ish-bosheth's troops to Gibeon from Mahanaim, 13and General Joab (the son of Zeruiah) led David's troops out to meet them. They met at the pool of Gibeon, where they sat facing each other on opposite sides of the pool. 14Then Abner suggested to Joab, "Let's watch some sword play between our young men!"

Joab agreed, 15so twelve men were chosen from each side to fight in mortal combat. 16Each one grabbed his opponent by the hair and thrust his sword into the other's side, so that all of them died. The place has been known ever since as Sword Field.

17The two armies then began to fight each other, and by the end of the day Abner and the men of Israel had been defeated by Joab and the forces of David. 18Joab's brothers, Abishai and Asahel, were also in the battle. Asahel could run like a deer, 19and he began chasing Abner. He wouldn't stop for anything, but kept on, singleminded, after Abner alone.

20When Abner looked behind and saw him coming, he called out to him, "Is that you, Asahel?"

2:17 by Joab, implied.

2:6
Ex 34:5,6

2:8
1 Sam 14:50
17:55; 26:14
2 Sam 2:29
17:24

2:10
2 Sam 5:4,5

2:12
Josh 10:12
2 Sam 19:5
21:5,6

2:13
2 Sam 8:16
1 Chron 2:16
11:5,6

2:17
2 Sam 3:1

2:18
1 Chron 2:16
11:26; 12:8

JOAB VS. ABNER
David was crowned king of Judah in Hebron; Ish-bosheth was crowned king of Israel in Maha-naim. The oppos-ing armies of Judah and Israel met at Gibeon for battle—Judah un-der Joab, Israel under Abner.

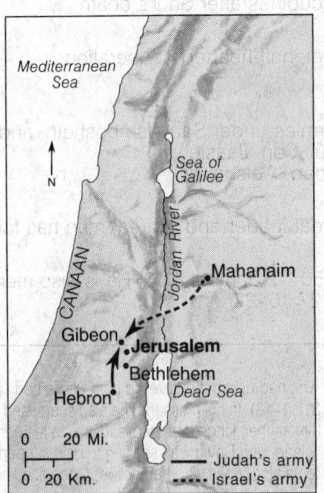

Judah pledged allegiance to David (2:4) because (1) he was from their own tribe; (2) he kept close ties with Judah; and (3) he had protected their land and shared battle spoils with them (1 Samuel 30:26). In addition, the elders of Judah may have known that David had been anointed by Samuel as Israel's next king and, therefore, was God's choice (1 Samuel 16:13).

2:10, 11 David ruled over Judah for seven and one-half years, while Ish-bosheth reigned in Israel for only two years. The five-year gap may be due to Ish-bosheth's not assuming the throne immediately after Saul's death. Because of constant danger from the Philistines in the northern part of Israel, five years may have passed before Ish-bosheth could begin his reign. During that time, Abner, his general, probably played a principal role in driving out the Philistines and leading the northern confederacy.

2:12ff With Israel divided, there was constant tension between north and south. David's true rival in the north, however, was not Ish-bosheth but Abner. In this incident Abner suggested a "sword game" between the champions of his army and the champions of David's army, led by Joab. The fact that this confrontation occurred at the pool of Gibeon (located in Saul's home territory of Benjamin) suggests that Joab's men were pushing northward, gaining more territory. Abner may have suggested this confron-tation hoping to stop Joab's advance.

Twelve men from each side were supposed to fight each other, and the side with the most survivors would be declared the winner. The confrontation between David and Goliath (1 Samuel 17) was a similar battle strategy—one way of avoiding terrible bloodshed from an all-out war. In this case, however, all 24 champions were killed before either side could claim victory. Nothing was accomplished, and the civil war continued.

2:8 The nation of Israel split in two after Saul's death. Ten tribes followed Ish-bosheth, one of Saul's surviving sons; two tribes (Judah and Simeon) followed David. Abner, Saul's general, rallied Israel around Ish-bosheth; he was no doubt afraid that he, as the opposing general, would be killed if David became king of all Israel.

"Yes," he called back, "it is."

21"Go after someone else!" Abner warned. But Asahel refused and kept on coming.

22Again Abner shouted to him, "Get away from here. I could never face your brother Joab if I have to kill you!"

23But he refused to turn away, so Abner pierced him through the belly with the butt end of his spear. It went right through his body and came out his back. He stumbled to the ground and died there, and everyone stopped when they came to the place where he lay.

24Now Joab and Abishai set out after Abner. The sun was just going down as they arrived at Ammah Hill near Giah, along the road into the Gibeon desert. 25Abner's troops from the tribe of Benjamin regrouped there at the top of the hill, 26and Abner shouted down to Joab, "Must our swords continue to kill each other forever? How long will it be before you call off your people from chasing their brothers?"

27Joab shouted back, "I swear by God that even if you hadn't spoken, we would all have gone home tomorrow morning." 28Then he blew his trumpet and his men stopped chasing the troops of Israel.

29That night Abner and his men retreated across the Jordan Valley, crossed the river, and traveled all the next morning until they arrived at Mahanaim. 30Joab and the men who were with him returned home too, and when he counted his casualties, he learned that only nineteen men were missing, in addition to Asahel. 31But three hundred and sixty of Abner's men (all from the tribe of Benjamin) were dead. 32Joab and his men took Asahel's body to Bethlehem and buried him beside his father; then they traveled all night and reached Hebron at daybreak.

David becomes stronger

3 That was the beginning of a long war between the followers of Saul and of David. David's position now became stronger and stronger, while Saul's dynasty became weaker and weaker.

2Several sons were born to David while he was at Hebron. The oldest was

Cross-references (margin):

2:24 — 1 Sam 26:5-7 / 2 Sam 10:10
2:25 — 2 Sam 2:9
2:29 — 2 Sam 2:8
2:32 — 1 Sam 17:58
3:1 — 1 Kgs 14:30 / 15:16,32,33
3:2 — 2 Sam 13:1 / 1 Chron 3:1

CHARACTERS IN THE DRAMA
It can be confusing to keep track of all the characters introduced in the first few chapters of 2 Samuel. Here is some help.

Character	Relation	Position	Whose side?
Joab	Son of Zeruiah, David's half sister	One of David's generals and later, commander-in-chief	David's
Abner	Saul's cousin	Saul's commander-in-chief	Saul and Ish-bosheth's, but made overtures to David
Abishai	Joab's brother	High officer in David's army—chief of "The Thirty"	Joab and David's
Asahel	Joab and Abishai's brother	High officer—one of David's 30 select warriors	Joab and David's
Ish-bosheth	Saul's son	Saul and Abner's selection as king	Saul's

---

2:21-23 Abner repeatedly warned Asahel to turn back or risk losing his life, but Asahel refused to turn from his self-imposed duty. Persistence is a good trait if it is for a worthy cause. But if the goal is only personal honor or gain, persistence may be no more than stubbornness. Asahel's stubbornness not only cost his life, but also spurred unfortunate disunity in David's army for years to come (3:26, 27; 1 Kings 2:28-35). Before you decide to pursue a goal, make sure it is worthy of your devotion.

2:28 This battle ended with a victory for Joab's troops (2:17), but war in the divided nation continued until David was finally crowned king of all Israel (5:1-5).

3:1 The events of chapter 2 led to a long war between David's followers and those loyal to Abner and Ish-bosheth. Civil war rocked the country at great cost to both sides. This war occurred because Israel and Judah had lost sight of God's vision and

purpose: to settle the land (Genesis 12:7), to drive out the Canaanites (Deuteronomy 7:1-4), and to obey God's laws (Deuteronomy 8:1). Instead of uniting to accomplish these goals, they fought each other. When you face conflict, step back from the hostilities and consider: Is it possible that you and your enemy have common goals that are bigger than your differences?

3:2-4 David suffered much heartache because of his many wives. Owning a harem was a socially acceptable practice for kings at this time, although God specifically warned against it (Deuteronomy 17:14-17). Sadly, the numerous sons born to David's wives caused him great trouble. Murder (13:28), rebellion (15:13), and greed (1 Kings 1:5, 6) all resulted from the jealous rivalries among the half-brothers. Solomon, one of David's sons and his successor to the throne, also took many wives, and they eventually turned him away from God (1 Kings 11:3, 4).

Amnon, born to his wife Ahino-am. ³His second son, Chileab, was born to Abigail, the widow of Nabal of Carmel. The third was Absalom, born to Maacah, the daughter of King Talmai of Geshur. ⁴The fourth was Adonijah, who was born to Haggith. Then Shephatiah was born to Abital, and ⁵Ithream was born to Eglah.

3:3
1 Sam 25:39
2 Sam 13:20
1 Chron 3:2
3:4
1 Chron 3:2,3

Abner negotiates with David

⁶As the war went on, Abner became a very powerful political leader among the followers of Saul. ⁷He took advantage of his position by sleeping with one of Saul's concubines, a girl named Rizpah. But when Ish-bosheth accused Abner of this, ⁸Abner was furious.

3:7
2 Sam 21:8

"Am I a Judean dog to be kicked around like this?" he shouted. "After all I have done for you and for your father by not betraying you to David, is this my reward—to find fault with me about some woman? ⁹, ¹⁰May God curse me if I don't do everything I can to take away the entire kingdom from you, all the way from Dan to Beersheba, and give it to David, just as the Lord predicted."

3:8
1 Sam 24:14
2 Sam 9:8; 16:9
3:9
1 Sam 3:16,17
14:44

¹¹Ish-bosheth made no reply, for he was afraid of Abner.

¹²Then Abner sent messengers to David to discuss a deal—to surrender the kingdom of Israel to him in exchange for becoming commander-in-chief of the combined armies of Israel and Judah.

¹³"All right," David replied, "but I will not negotiate with you unless you bring me my wife Michal, Saul's daughter." ¹⁴David then sent this message to Ish-bosheth: "Give me back my wife Michal, for I bought her with the lives of one hundred Philistines."

3:13
1 Sam 18:20
1 Chron 15:29
3:14
1 Sam 18:26,27

¹⁵So Ish-bosheth took her away from her husband Palti. ¹⁶He followed along behind her as far as Behurim, weeping as he went. Then Abner told him, "Go on home now." So he returned.

3:15
1 Sam 25:44
3:16
2 Sam 16:5

¹⁷Meanwhile, Abner consulted with the leaders of Israel and reminded them that for a long time they had wanted David as their king.

¹⁸"Now is the time!" he told them. "For the Lord has said, 'It is David by whom I will save my people from the Philistines and from all their other enemies.' "

3:18
1 Sam 9:16
15:28

¹⁹Abner also talked to the leaders of the tribe of Benjamin; then he went to Hebron and reported to David his progress with the people of Israel and Benjamin. ²⁰Twenty men accompanied him, and David entertained them with a feast.

3:19
1 Sam 10:20

²¹As Abner left, he promised David, "When I get back I will call a convention of

---

3:6, 7 To sleep with any of the king's wives or concubines was to make a claim to the throne, and it was considered treason. Because Ish-bosheth was a weak ruler, Abner was running the country; thus he may have felt justified in sleeping with Saul's concubine. Ish-bosheth, however, saw that Abner's power was getting out of hand.

3:7 Ish-bosheth was right to speak out against Abner's behavior, but he didn't have the moral strength to maintain his authority (3:11). Lack of moral backbone became the root of Israel's troubles over the next four centuries. Only four of the next forty kings of Israel were called "good." It takes courage and strength to stand firm in your convictions to confront wrongdoing in the face of opposition. When you believe something is wrong, do not let yourself be talked out of your position. Firmly attack the wrong and uphold the right.

3:8 By saying, "Am I a Judean dog?" Abner was really saying, "Am I a traitor for Judah?" He may have been refuting the accusation that he was trying to take over the throne, or he may have been angry that Ish-bosheth scolded him after Abner had helped put him on the throne in the first place. Prior to this conversation, Abner might have realized that he could not successfully keep David from eventually taking over Israel. Because he was angry at Ish-bosheth, Abner devised a plan to turn over the kingship of Israel to David in return for being made general of David's army.

3:12 By now Abner realized that it was useless to fight for the weak ruler, Ish-bosheth. Nothing could prevent David from becoming king of all Israel, because God was with him (3:18). The deal Abner made with David was designed to prevent David's men from seeking revenge against him for being the general of both Saul's army (1 Samuel 26:5–7) and the northern confederacy (2:8).

3:13 In an effort to reunite all Israel, David agreed to Abner's deal. Ish-bosheth was not God's appointed king as Saul had been; therefore, David accepted Abner's terms of handing Ish-bosheth over to him.

3:13, 14 Michal had been married to David. King Saul had arranged the marriage as acts of bravery as a reward for David's (1 Samuel 17:25; 18:24–27). Later, however, in one of his jealous fits, Saul took Michal away from David and forced her to marry Palti (1 Samuel 25:44). Now David wanted his wife back before he would begin to negotiate peace with the northern tribes. Perhaps David still loved her (but see 6:20–23 for the tension in their relationship). More likely, he thought that marriage to Saul's daughter would strengthen his claim to rule all Israel and demonstrate that he had no animosity toward Saul's house. Palti was the unfortunate victim caught in the web of Saul's jealousy.

3:19 Because Saul, Ish-bosheth, and Abner were all from the tribe of Benjamin, the support of the elders of that tribe meant that Abner was serious about his offer and that there was a strong possibility of overcoming tribal jealousies and uniting the kingdom.

all the people of Israel, and they will elect you as their king, as you've so long desired." So David let Abner return in safety.

Joab kills Abner

3:22
1 Sam 27:8

3:24
1 Sam 29:3

22But just after Abner left, Joab and some of David's troops returned from a raid, bringing much loot with them. 23When Joab was told that Abner had just been there visiting the king and had been sent away in peace, 24, 25he rushed to the king, demanding, "What have you done? What do you mean by letting him get away? You know perfectly well that he came to spy on us and that he plans to return and attack us!"

26Then Joab sent messengers to catch up with Abner and tell him to come back. They found him at the well of Sirah and he returned with them; but David knew

3:27
2 Sam 2:23
20:8-10
1 Kgs 2:5

nothing about it. 27When Abner arrived at Hebron, Joab took him aside at the city gate as if to speak with him privately; but then he pulled out a dagger and killed him in revenge for the death of his brother Asahel.

3:29
Lev 13:45,46
Deut 21:7,8
1 Kgs 2:31

28When David heard about it he declared, "I vow by the Lord that I and my people are innocent of this crime against Abner. 29Joab and his family are the guilty ones. May each of his children be victims of cancer, or be lepers, or be sterile, or die of starvation, or be killed by the sword!"

3:30
2 Sam 2:23

30So Joab and his brother Abishai killed Abner because of the death of their brother Asahel at the battle of Gibeon.

3:31
Gen 37:34
Judg 11:35
2 Sam 1:11

31Then David said to Joab and to all those who were with him, "Go into deep mourning for Abner." And King David accompanied the bier to the cemetery. 32They buried Abner in Hebron. And the king and all the people wept at the graveside.

33, 34"Should Abner have died like a fool?" the king lamented.

"Your hands were not bound,
Your feet were not tied—
You were murdered—
The victim of a wicked plot."

3:35
2 Sam 1:12
12:17

And all the people wept again for him. 35, 36David had refused to eat anything the day of the funeral, and now everyone begged him to take a bite of supper. But David vowed that he would eat nothing until sundown. This pleased his people, just as everything else he did pleased them! 37Thus the whole nation, both Judah and Israel, understood from David's actions that he was in no way responsible for Abner's death.

3:39
1 Sam 26:5-7
2 Sam 8:16
19:5
1 Chron 11:5,6

38And David said to his people, "A great leader and a great man has fallen today in Israel; 39and even though I am God's chosen king, I can do nothing with these

---

3:26–29 Joab took revenge for the death of his brother, but that revenge backfired on him (1 Kings 2:31–34). God "will repay those who deserve it" (Romans 12:19). Refuse to rejoice when your enemies suffer, and don't seek revenge.

3:27 Abner killed Joab's brother Asahel in self-defense. Joab then killed Abner to avenge his brother's death and also to save his position, since David had agreed to appoint Abner as general. Men who killed in self-defense were supposed to be safe in a City of Refuge (Numbers 35:22–25). It is ironic that Joab killed Abner out of revenge in Hebron, a City of Refuge (Joshua 20:7).

3:29 Why did David say such harsh things about Joab? David was upset over Abner's death for several reasons. (1) He was grieved over the loss of a skilled military officer. (2) He wanted to make sure that the guilt of Abner's murder was placed on Joab, not himself. (3) He was on the verge of becoming king over the entire nation, and Abner seemed the key to his success. Abner's death could have revived the civil war. (4) David's agreement to protect Abner had been violated. Joab's murderous act ruined David's plans, and David was especially angry that his own

general had committed the crime.

3:31ff David ordered Joab to mourn, possibly because few people were aware that Joab had committed the crime and because David did not want any further trouble. If this was true, David was thinking more about strengthening his kingdom than about justice.

3:39 Joab and Abishai were the two sons of Zeruiah David mentioned. David had an especially hard time controlling Joab because, although he was intensely loyal, he was strong-willed, preferring to do things his own way. In exchange for his loyalty, however, David was willing to give him the flexibility he craved.

Joab's murder of Abner is an example of his fierce independence. While David opposed the murder, he allowed it to remain unpunished because (1) to punish Joab could cause the troops to rebel; (2) Joab was David's nephew, and any harsh treatment could cause family problems; (3) Joab was from the tribe of Judah, and David didn't want rebellion from his own tribe; (4) to get rid of Joab would mean losing a skilled and competent general who had been invaluable in strengthening his army.

two sons of Zeruiah. May the Lord repay wicked men for their wicked deeds."

The murder of Ish-bosheth

4 When King Ish-bosheth heard about Abner's death at Hebron, he was paralyzed with fear, and his people too were badly frightened. 2, 3The command of the Israeli troops then fell to two brothers, Baanah and Rechab, who were captains of King Ish-bosheth's raiding bands. They were the sons of Rimmon, who was from Be-eroth in Benjamin. (People from Be-eroth are counted as Benjaminites even though they fled to Gittaim, where they now live.)

4(There was a little lame grandson of King Saul's named Mephibosheth, who was the son of Prince Jonathan. He was five years old at the time Saul and Jonathan were killed at the battle of Jezreel. When the news of the outcome of the battle reached the capital, the child's nurse grabbed him and fled, but she fell and dropped him as she was running, and he became lame.)

5Rechab and Baanah arrived at King Ish-bosheth's home one noon as he was taking a nap. 6, 7They walked into the kitchen as though to get a sack of wheat, but then sneaked into his bedroom and murdered him and cut off his head. Taking his head with them, they fled across the desert that night and escaped. 8They presented the head to David at Hebron.

"Look!" they exclaimed. "Here is the head of Ish-bosheth, the son of your enemy Saul who tried to kill you. Today the Lord has given you revenge upon Saul and upon his entire family!"

9But David replied, "I swear by the Lord who saved me from my enemies, 10that when someone told me, 'Saul is dead,' thinking he was bringing me good news, I killed him; that is how I rewarded him for his 'glad tidings.' 11And how much more shall I do to wicked men who kill a good man in his own house and on his bed! Shall I not demand your lives?"

12So David ordered his young men to kill them, and they did. They cut off their hands and feet and hanged their bodies beside the pool in Hebron. And they took Ish-bosheth's head and buried it in Abner's tomb in Hebron.

2. David becomes king of all Israel

5 Representatives of all the tribes of Israel now came to David at Hebron and gave him their pledge of loyalty.

"We are your blood brothers," they said. 2"And even when Saul was our king you were our real leader. The Lord has said that you should be the shepherd and leader of his people."

3So David made a contract before the Lord with the leaders of Israel there at Hebron, and they crowned him king of Israel. 4, 5(He had already been the king of

4:3 *to Gittaim,* which is not in Benjamin.

4:1
2 Sam 3:27
4:2
Josh 9:17; 18:25
Neh 11:33
4:4
1 Sam 31:1-4
2 Sam 9:3,5,6
1 Chron 8:34
4:5
2 Sam 2:8
4:6
1 Sam 17:54
31:9
2 Kgs 10:6
Mt 14:11
4:9
2 Sam 22:20
1 Kgs 1:29
4:10
2 Sam 1:1,2,
4,15
4:11
Gen 9:5
1 Kgs 2:32
Ps 9:12
4:12
2 Sam 1:15
3:32
5:1
1 Chron 11:1
5:2
1 Sam 18:5,14
5:3
1 Sam 16:1,13
5:4
1 Kgs 2:11
Lk 3:23

4:1 Ish-bosheth was a man who took his courage from another man (Abner) rather than from God. When Abner deserted him, Ish-bosheth was left with nothing. In crisis and under pressure, he collapsed in fear. Fear can paralyze us, but faith and trust in God can overcome fear (2 Timothy 1:6–8; Hebrews 13:6). If we trust in God, we will be free to respond boldly to the events around us.

4:4 The rest of Mephibosheth's story is told in 2 Samuel 9; 16:1–4; and 19:24–30.

4:5-11 This situation is almost identical to the one in 1:1–16 where a man proudly announced to David that he had killed King Saul. Baanah and Rechab undoubtedly were seeking a reward or great recognition for killing David's rival, but they misjudged David's character.

4:11 David called Ish-bosheth a "good man." As Saul's son, Ish-bosheth had reason to think he was in line for the throne. He was not wicked for wanting to be king; rather, he was simply too weak to stand against injustice. Although David knew Ish-bosheth was not the strong leader needed to unite Israel, he had no

intention of killing him. God had promised the kingship to David, and he knew that God would fulfill his promise.

When David learned of Ish-bosheth's death, he was angry. He had never harmed Saul, and he thought the assassins' method was cowardly. David wanted to unite Israel, not drive a permanent wedge between him and Ish-bosheth's supporters. To show that he had nothing to do with the extermination of Saul's royal line, he ordered the assassins killed. Ish-bosheth was given a proper burial. All the tribes of Israel, recognizing in David the strong leader they needed, pledged their loyalty to him. No doubt the Philistine threat and David's military reputation (1 Samuel 18:7) also had a unifying effect on the people.

5:3-5 This was the third time David was anointed king. First he was privately anointed by Samuel (1 Samuel 16:13). Then he was crowned king over the tribe of Judah (2 Samuel 2:4). Finally he was crowned king over all Israel. When he was an outlaw, life had looked bleak for him, but God's promise to make him king over all Israel was now being fulfilled. Although the kingdom would be divided once again in less than 75 years, David's dynasty would reign over Judah, the Southern Kingdom, for over 400 years.

Judah for seven years, since the age of thirty. He then ruled thirty-three years in Jerusalem as king of both Israel and Judah; so he reigned for forty years altogether.)

David conquers Jerusalem

5:6
Josh 15:63
Judg 1:21
1 Chron 11:4

5:7
1 Kgs 2:10

6David now led his troops to Jerusalem to fight against the Jebusites who lived there.

"You'll never come in here," they told him. "Even the blind and lame could keep you out!" For they thought they were safe. 7But David and his troops defeated them and captured the stronghold of Zion, now called the City of David.

8When the insulting message from the defenders of the city reached David, he told his troops, "Go up through the water tunnel into the city and destroy those 'lame' and 'blind' Jebusites. How I hate them." (That is the origin of the saying, "Even the blind and the lame could conquer you!")

5:9
1 Kgs 9:15,24

5:10
1 Sam 18:14
2 Sam 3:1

5:11
1 Kgs 5:10,18
1 Chron 14:1

5:12
Deut 7:14
2 Sam 7:15
1 Kgs 10:9

9So David made the stronghold of Zion (also called the City of David) his headquarters. Then, beginning at the old Millo section of the city, he built northward toward the present city center. 10So David became greater and greater, for the Lord God of heaven was with him.

11Then King Hiram of Tyre sent cedar lumber, carpenters, and masons to build a palace for David. 12David now realized why the Lord had made him the king and blessed his kingdom so greatly—it was because God wanted to pour out his kindness on Israel, his chosen people.

5:13
Deut 17:17
1 Chron 3:9
14:3

5:14
1 Chron 3:5-8
14:4-7

13After moving from Hebron to Jerusalem, David married additional wives and concubines, and had many sons and daughters. 14, 15, 16These are his children who were born at Jerusalem: Shammu-a, Shobab, Nathan, Solomon, Ibhar, Elishu-a, Nepheg, Japhia, Elishama, Eliada, Eliphelet.

David defeats the Philistines

17When the Philistines heard that David had been crowned king of Israel, they

---

5:4, 5 David did not become king of all Israel until he was 37 years old, although he had been promised the kingship many years earlier (1 Samuel 16:13). During those years, David had to wait patiently for the fulfillment of God's promise. If you feel pressured to achieve instant results and success, remember David's patience. Just as his time of waiting prepared him for his important task, a waiting period may help prepare you by strengthening your spiritual character.

5:6 The fortress city of Jerusalem was located on a high ridge near the center of the united Israelite kingdom. It was considered neutral territory because it stood on the border of the territory of the tribes of Benjamin and Judah and it was still occupied by the Jebusites, a Canaanite tribe that had never been expelled from the land (Judges 1:21). Because of its strategic advantages, David made Jerusalem his capital.

5:6, 7 The Jebusites had a clear military advantage and boasted of their security behind the impregnable walls of Jerusalem. But soon they would discover that their walls would not help them.

Only in God are we truly safe and secure. Anything else is false security. Whether you are surrounded by mighty walls of stone, a comfortable home, or a secure job, don't be so sure it will be there tomorrow. Our relationship with God is the only security we have or need.

5:12 Although the heathen kingdoms based their greatness on conquest, power, armies, and wealth, David knew that his greatness came only from God. To be great meant to keep a close relationship with God personally and nationally. To do this, David had to keep his ambition under control. Although he was famous, successful, and well-liked, he gave God first place in his life and served the people according to God's purpose. Do you seek greatness from God or from men? In the drive for success, remember to keep your ambition under God's control.

5:13 Although David sincerely sought after God, he had

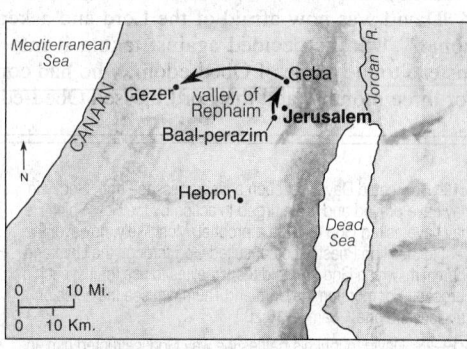

DAVID DEFEATS THE PHILISTINES The Philistines camped in the valley of Rephaim. David defeated them at Baal-perazim, but they remained in the valley. He attacked again, and chased them from Geba to Gezer.

weaknesses like any other person. One of those weaknesses was his desire for many wives. Sadly, the children born to these wives caused David and the kingdom much grief. David also set an unhealthy pattern for his son Solomon. (For more on the problems caused by David's many wives see the note on 3:2-4.)

5:17 The Philistine oppression of Israel began in the days of Samson (Judges 13—16). The Philistines were still Israel's most powerful enemy. Because they occupied much of Israel's northern territory, they apparently did not bother David while he was king of Judah to the south. But when they learned that David was trying to unite all Israel, they tried to stop him.

tried to capture him; but David was told that they were coming and went into the stronghold. 18The Philistines arrived and spread out across the valley of Rephaim.

19Then David asked the Lord, "Shall I go out and fight against them? Will you defeat them for me?"

And the Lord replied, "Yes, go ahead, for I will give them to you."

20So David went out and fought with them at Baal-perazim, and defeated them. "The Lord did it!" he exclaimed. "He burst through my enemies like a raging flood." So he named the place "Bursting." 21At that time David and his troops confiscated many idols which had been abandoned by the Philistines. 22But the Philistines returned and again spread out across the valley of Rephaim.

23When David asked the Lord what to do, he replied, "Don't make a frontal attack. Go behind them and come out by the balsam trees. 24When you hear a sound like marching feet in the tops of the balsam trees, attack! For it will signify that the Lord has prepared the way for you and will destroy them."

25So David did as the Lord had instructed him and destroyed the Philistines all the way from Geba to Gezer.

5:18
Josh 15:8; 18:16
2 Sam 23:13

5:19
1 Sam 23:2
30:8

5:20
Num 33:3,4
1 Chron 14:11

5:24
Judg 4:14; 7:15
2 Kgs 7:6

5:25
Josh 12:12
21:20-22

David brings the Ark to Jerusalem

6 Then David mobilized thirty thousand special troops and led them to Baal-judah to bring home the Ark of the Lord of heaven who is en-throned above the Guardian Angels. 3The Ark was placed upon a new cart and taken from the hillside home of Abinadab. It was driven by Abinadab's sons, Uzzah and Ahio. 4Ahio was walking in front, 5and was followed by David and the other leaders of Israel, who were joyously waving branches of juniper trees and playing every sort of musical instrument before the Lord—lyres, harps, tambourines, castanets, and cymbals.

6But when they arrived at the threshing floor of Nacon, the oxen stumbled and Uzzah put out his hand to steady the Ark. 7Then the anger of the Lord flared out against Uzzah and he killed him for doing this, so he died there beside the Ark. 8David was angry at what the Lord had done, and named the spot "The Place of Wrath upon Uzzah" (which it is still called to this day).

9David was now afraid of the Lord and asked, "How can I ever bring the Ark home?" 10So he decided against taking it into the City of David, but carried it instead to the home of Obed-edom, who had come from Gath. 11It remained there for three months, and the Lord blessed Obed-edom and all his household.

6:1
Ex 25:22
1 Sam 7:1
2 Kgs 19:15
1 Chron 13:5,6

6:3
Num 7:9
1 Sam 6:7; 7:1

6:5
1 Sam 10:5
16:16
1 Chron 13:7,8
16:5

6:6
Num 4:15
1 Chron 13:9

6:7
Lev 10:1,2
1 Sam 6:19

6:10
1 Chron 13:13
26:4; 5

5:19 How could David get such a clear message from God? He may have prayed and been urged to action by the Holy Spirit. He may have asked God through a prophet. Most likely, however, he went to the High Priest, who consulted God through the Urim and Thummim, which God had told the Israelites to use for just such a purpose. (For more on the Urim and Thummim see the notes on Leviticus 8:8 and 1 Samuel 10:20.)

5:19–25 David fought his battles the way God instructed him. In each instance he (1) asked if he should fight or not; (2) followed instructions carefully; and (3) gave God the glory. We can err in our "battles" by ignoring these steps and instead (1) doing what we want without considering God's will; (2) doing things our way and ignoring advice in the Bible or from other wise people; and (3) taking the glory ourselves or giving it to someone else without acknowledging the help we received from God. All of these responses are sin.

5:25 After David became king, his first order of business was to subdue his enemies—a task the nation had failed to complete when they first entered the land (Judges 2:1–4). David knew this had to be done in order to: (1) protect the nation, (2) unify the kingdom, and (3) prepare for the building of the Temple (which would unify religion under God and help abolish idolatrous influences from other nations).

6:3 The Ark of the Covenant was Israel's national treasure. This most sacred object in the land was ordinarily kept in the Tabernacle. When the Ark was returned to Israel after a brief

Philistine captivity (1 Samuel 4—6), it was kept in Abinadab's home for 20 years. David saw how Abinadab was blessed, and he wanted to bring the Ark to Jerusalem in order to bless the entire nation. (See the notes on Exodus 37:1 and Joshua 3:2–4 for more information on the Ark.)

6:7 Was God's anger against Uzzah just? Uzzah was only trying to protect the Ark. According to Numbers 4:5–15, the Ark was to be moved only by the Levites, who were to carry it using the carrying poles—they were *never* to touch the Ark itself. To touch it was a capital offense under Jewish law. God's action was directed against both David and Uzzah. David placed the Ark on a cart, following the Philistine's example (1 Samuel 6:7, 8) rather than God's commands. Uzzah, though sincere in his desire to protect the Ark, had to face the consequences of the sin of touching it. Also, Uzzah may not have been a Levite. As David sought to bring Israel back into a relationship with God, God had to remind the nation dramatically that enthusiasm must be accompanied by obedience to his laws. The next time David tried to bring the Ark to Jerusalem, he was careful to handle it correctly (1 Chronicles 15:1–15).

6:11–13 David was angry that a well-meaning man had been killed and that his plans for a joyous return of the Ark had been spoiled (6:8). He undoubtedly knew that the fault was his own for transporting the Ark carelessly. After cooling down, he had the Ark put into temporary storage while he waited to see if the Lord would allow him to bring it to Jerusalem. This also gave David time to

6:12
1 Kgs 8:1
1 Chron 15:1-3,
25

6:14
Ex 15:20
1 Sam 2:18,28

6:16
1 Sam 18:27
2 Sam 3:14

12When David heard this, he brought the Ark to the City of David with a great celebration. 13After the men who were carrying it had gone six paces, they stopped and waited so that he could sacrifice an ox and a fat lamb. 14And David danced before the Lord with all his might, and was wearing priests' clothing. 15So Israel brought home the Ark of the Lord with much shouting and blowing of trumpets.

16(But as the procession came into the city, Michal, Saul's daughter, watched from a window and saw King David leaping and dancing before the Lord; and she was filled with contempt for him.)

6:14 *was wearing priests' clothing,* literally, "David was girded with a linen ephod."

MICHAL

Sometimes love is not enough—especially if that love is little more than the strong emotional attraction that grows between a hero and an admirer. To Michal, Saul's daughter, the courageous young David must have seemed like a dream come true. Her feelings about this hero gradually became obvious to others, and eventually, her father heard about her love for David. He saw this as an opportunity to get rid of his rival. He promised Michal's hand in marriage in exchange for David's success in the impossible task of killing one hundred Philistines. But David was victorious. As a result, Saul lost a daughter and David became even more popular with the people.

Michal's love for David did not have time to be tested by the realities of marriage. Instead, she became involved in saving David's life. Her quick thinking helped him escape, but it cost her Saul's anger and her separation from David. Her father gave her to another man, Palti, but David eventually took her back.

Unlike her brother, Jonathan, Michal did not have the kind of deep relationship with God which would have helped her come through the difficulties in her life. Instead she became bitter. She could not share David's joyful worship of God, so she hated it. As a result, she never bore David any children.

Beyond feeling sorry for her, we need to see Michal as a person mirroring our own tendencies. How quickly and easily we become bitter with life's unexpected turns. But bitterness cannot change the bad things that have happened. Often bitterness only makes a bad situation worse. On the other hand, a willingness to respond to God gives him the opportunity to bring good out of the difficult situations. That willingness has two parts: asking God for his guidance and looking for that guidance in his Word.

Strengths and accomplishments:
• Loved David and became his first wife
• Saved David's life
• Could think and act quickly when it was needed

Weaknesses and mistakes:
• Lied under pressure
• Allowed herself to become bitter over her circumstances
• In her unhappiness, hated David for loving God

Lessons from her life:
• We are not as responsible for what happens to us as we are for how we respond to our circumstances
• Disobedience to God almost always harms us as well as others

Vital statistics:
• Occupation: Daughter of one king, Saul, and wife of another, David
• Relatives: Parents: Saul and Ahino-am. Brothers: Abinadab, Jonathan, Malchishua. Sister: Merab. Husbands: David and Palti.

Key verse:
"But as the procession came into the city, Michal, Saul's daughter, watched from a window and saw King David leaping and dancing before the Lord; and she was filled with contempt for him" (2 Samuel 6:16).

Michal's story is told in 1 Samuel 14—2 Samuel 6. She is also mentioned in 1 Chronicles 15:29.

consider the right way to transport the Ark. The fact that God blessed the home of Obed-edom was a sign to David that he could try once again to move the Ark to Jerusalem.

6:16ff Michal was David's first wife, but here she is simply called Saul's daughter, possibly to show how similar her attitude was to her father's. Her contempt for David probably did not start with David's grand entrance into the city. Perhaps she thought it was undignified to be so concerned with public worship at a time when it was so unimportant in the kingdom. Or maybe she thought it was not fitting for a king to display such emotion. Whatever the reason, this contempt she felt toward her spouse escalated into a difficult confrontation, and Michal ended up childless for life. Feelings of bitterness and resentment that go unchecked are very destructive to a relationship. They must be dealt with before they escalate into open warfare. Don't wait until contempt overcomes you to deal with your feelings.

17The Ark was placed inside the tent which David had prepared for it; and he sacrificed burnt offerings and peace offerings to the Lord. 18Then he blessed the people in the name of the Lord of heaven, 19and gave a present to everyone—men and women alike—of a loaf of bread, some wine, and a cake of raisins. When it was all over, and everyone had gone home, 20David returned to bless his family.

But Michal came out to meet him and exclaimed in disgust, "How glorious the king of Israel looked today! He exposed himself to the girls along the street like a common pervert!"

21David retorted, "I was dancing before the Lord who chose me above your father and his family and who appointed me as leader of Israel, the people of the Lord! So I am willing to act like a fool in order to show my joy in the Lord. 22Yes, and I am willing to look even more foolish than this, but I will be respected by the girls of whom you spoke!"

23So Michal was childless throughout her life.

God promises eternal blessing to David

7 When the Lord finally sent peace upon the land, and Israel was no longer at war with the surrounding nations, 2David said to Nathan the prophet, "Look! Here I am living in this beautiful cedar palace while the Ark of God is out in a tent!"

3"Go ahead with what you have in mind," Nathan replied, "for the Lord is with you."

4But that night the Lord said to Nathan, 5"Tell my servant David not to do it! 6For

7:5 *Tell my servant David not to do it!* Literally, "Shall you build me a house to dwell in?"

6:17
1 Kgs 8:62
1 Chron 15:1
2 Chron 1:4

7:1
Josh 21:44; 23:1
1 Kgs 5:4
2 Chron 14:7
7:2
1 Kgs 8:17,18
1 Chron 17:1
29:29
Acts 7:46

Person/Situation	Result	Reference	
Miriam: Mocked Moses because he had a Cushite wife	Stricken with leprosy	Numbers 12	**CRITICIZING GOD'S LEADERS**
Korah and followers: Led the people of Israel to rebel against Moses' leadership	Swallowed by the earth	Numbers 16	It is dangerous to criticize God's leaders. Consider the consequences for these men and women.
Michal: Had contempt for David because he danced before the Lord	Remained childless	2 Samuel 6	
Shime-i: Cursed and threw stones at David	Executed at Solomon's order	2 Samuel 16 1 Kings 2	
Young men: Mocked Elisha and laughed at his baldness	Killed by bears	2 Kings 2	
Sanballat and Tobiah: Spread rumors and lies to stop the building of Jerusalem's walls	Frightened and humiliated	Nehemiah 2, 4, 6	
Hananiah: Contradicted Jeremiah's prophecies with false predictions	Died two months later	Jeremiah 28	
Bar-Jesus, a sorcerer: Lied about Paul in an attempt to turn the governor against him	Stricken with blindness	Acts 13	

6:17 Only a priest could place the sacrifices on the altar. Leviticus 1:10–13 seems to indicate that anyone who was ceremonially clean could assist a priest in offering the sacrifice (see the notes on Joshua 3:5; 1 Samuel 20:26). Therefore, David probably offered these sacrifices to God with the aid of a priest.

6:20 Michal was so concerned about David's undignified actions that she did not rejoice in the Ark's return to the city. She emphasized outward appearances while David emphasized the inward condition of his heart before God. He was willing to look foolish in the eyes of some in order to worship God fully and honestly. Godly people may worship in ways that look foolish to us because they have a different culture or tradition. But we should accept their heartfelt expressions of worship. And we should not be afraid to express our feelings toward God, even when others are present.

7:1ff This chapter records the covenant which God made with David, promising to carry on David's line forever. This promise would be fully realized in the birth of Jesus Christ. Although the word *covenant* or *agreement* is not specifically stated here, it is used elsewhere to describe this occasion (23:5; Psalm 89:3, 4, 28, 34–37).

7:2 This is the first time that Nathan the prophet is mentioned. God made certain that a prophet was living during the reign of each of the kings of Israel. The prophet's main tasks were to urge the people to follow God and to communicate God's laws and plans to the king. Most of the kings rejected the prophets God sent. But God gave them the opportunity to listen and obey. In earlier years, judges and priests had the role of prophets. Samuel served as judge, priest, and prophet, bridging the gap between the period of the judges and the monarchy.

I have never lived in a temple. My home has been a tent ever since the time I brought Israel out of Egypt. 7And I have never once complained to Israel's leaders, the shepherds of my people. Have I ever asked them, 'Why haven't you built me a beautiful cedar temple?'

8"Now go and give this message to David from the Lord of heaven: 'I chose you to be the leader of my people Israel when you were a mere shepherd, tending your sheep in the pastureland. 9I have been with you wherever you have gone and have destroyed your enemies. And I will make your name greater yet, so that you will be one of the most famous men in the world! 10, 11I have selected a homeland for my people from which they will never have to move. It will be their own land where the heathen nations won't bother them as they did when the judges ruled my people. There will be no more wars against you; and your descendants shall rule this land for generations to come! 12For when you die, I will put one of your sons upon your throne and I will make his kingdom strong. 13He is the one who shall build me a temple. And I will continue his kingdom into eternity. 14I will be his father and he shall be my son. If he sins, I will use other nations to punish him, 15but my love and kindness shall not leave him as I took it from Saul, your predecessor. 16Your family shall rule my kingdom forever.' "

17So Nathan went back to David and told him everything the Lord had said.

David's prayer of acceptance

18Then David went into the Tabernacle and sat before the Lord and prayed, "O Lord God, why have you showered your blessings on such an insignificant

7:7
1 Chron 17:6
7:8
1 Sam 16:10
2 Sam 5:2
Ps 78:70
7:10
1 Sam 12:9-11
Ps 89:22
Isa 60:18
7:12
1 Kgs 2:1; 5:4
7:13
1 Kgs 6:11,12
8:19
Isa 9:7
Acts 7:46,47
7:14
Ps 89:26
Heb 1:5,6
7:15
1 Sam 15:23
16:14
Ps 89:35,36
7:16
1 Sam 25:28
7:18
1 Sam 18:18
Ps 8:4

COVENANTS	Name and Reference	God's Promise	Sign
A covenant is a legally binding obligation (promise). Throughout history God has made covenants with his people— he would keep his side if they would keep theirs. Below are seven covenants found in the Bible.	In Eden Genesis 3:15	Satan and mankind will be enemies	Pain of childbirth
	Noah Genesis 9:8–11	God would never again destroy the earth with a flood	Rainbow
	Abraham Genesis 15:12–21; 17:1–14	Abraham's descendants would become a great nation if they obeyed God. God would be their God forever	Smoking fire-pot and flaming torch
	At Mount Sinai Exodus 19:5, 6	Israel would be God's special people, a holy nation. But they would have to keep their part of the covenant—obedience	The Exodus
	The Priesthood Numbers 25:10–13	Aaron's descendants would be priests forever	The Aaronic priesthood
	David 2 Samuel 7:13; 23:5	Salvation would come through David's line through the birth of the Messiah	David's line continued and the Messiah was born a descendant of David
	New Covenant Hebrews 8:6–12	Forgiveness and salvation is available through faith in Christ	Christ's resurrection

7:5 Why didn't God want David to build a Temple for him? God told David that his job was to unify and lead Israel and to destroy its enemies. This task would require David to shed a great deal of blood. In 1 Chronicles 28:3, we learn that God did not want his Temple built by a warrior. Therefore, David made the plans and collected the materials so that his son Solomon could begin work on the Temple as soon as he became king (1 Kings 5—7). David accepted this role in God's plan and did not try to go beyond it. We, too, should be satisfied to accept the roles which God gives us.

7:8-16 David's request was good, but God said no. This does not mean that God rejected David. In fact, God was planning to do something even greater in David's life than allowing him the prestige of building the Temple. Although God turned down David's request, he promised to continue the house (or dynasty) of

David forever. David's earthly dynasty ended four centuries later, but Jesus Christ, a direct descendant of David, was the ultimate fulfillment of this promise (Acts 2:22–36). He will reign for eternity—first in his spiritual kingdom, and ultimately on earth in the New Jerusalem (Luke 1:30–33; Revelation 21). Have you prayed with good intentions, only to have God say no? This is not rejection, but God's way of fulfilling a greater purpose in your life.

7:18ff This section records David's prayer in which he expressed his humble acceptance of God's desire to extend his dynasty forever. David realized that these blessings were bestowed upon him and his descendants in order that Israel might also be blessed. They would help fulfill God's greater purpose and promises for the whole nation and ultimately the whole world (Genesis 12:1–3).

person as I am? 19And now, in addition to everything else, you speak of giving me an eternal dynasty! Such generosity is far beyond any human standard! Oh, Lord God! 20What can I say? For you know what I am like! 21You are doing all these things just because you promised to and because you want to! 22How great you are, Lord God! We have never heard of any other god like you. And there is no other god. 23What other nation in all the earth has received such blessings as Israel, your people? For you have rescued your chosen nation in order to bring glory to your name. You have done great miracles to destroy Egypt and its gods. 24You chose Israel to be your people forever, and you became our God.

25"And now, Lord God, do as you have promised concerning me and my family. 26And may you be eternally honored when you have established Israel as your people and have established my dynasty before you. 27For you have revealed to me, O Lord of heaven, God of Israel, that I am the first of a dynasty which will rule your people forever; that is why I have been bold enough to pray this prayer of acceptance. 28For you are indeed God, and your words are truth; and you have promised me these good things— 29so do as you have promised! Bless me and my family forever! May our dynasty continue on and on before you; for you, Lord God, have promised it."

7:19	1 Chron 17:17
	Isa 55:8,9
7:20	Ps 139:1
	Jn 21:17
7:22	Ex 10:2; 15:11
	1 Sam 2:2
	Ps 48:1
7:23	Deut 4:32; 10:21
	Ps 40:5; 65:5
7:24	Gen 17:7,8
	Ex 6:7
	Deut 32:6
	1 Chron 17:22
7:26	1 Chron 17:23
	Ps 89:35,36
7:28	Ex 34:5,6
	Jn 17:17
7:29	Num 6:24-26

3. David conquers the surrounding nations

8 After this David subdued and humbled the Philistines by conquering Gath, their largest city. 2He also devastated the land of Moab. He divided his victims by making them lie down side by side in rows. Two-thirds of each row, as measured with a tape, were butchered, and one-third were spared to become David's servants—they paid him tribute each year.

3He also destroyed the forces of King Hadadezer (son of Rehob) of Zobah in a battle at the Euphrates River, for Hadadezer had attempted to regain his power. 4David captured seventeen hundred cavalry and twenty thousand infantry; then he lamed all of the chariot horses except for one hundred teams. 5He also slaughtered twenty-two thousand Syrians from Damascus when they came to help Hadadezer. 6David placed several army garrisons in Damascus, and the Syrians became David's subjects and brought him annual tribute money. So the Lord gave him victories wherever he turned. 7David brought the gold shields to Jerusalem which King Hadadezer's officers had used. 8He also carried back to Jerusalem a very large amount of bronze from Hadadezer's cities of Betah and Berothai.

9When King Toi of Hamath heard about David's victory over the army of Hadadezer, 10he sent his son Joram to congratulate him, for Hadadezer and Toi were enemies. He gave David presents made from silver, gold, and bronze. 11, 12David dedicated all of these to the Lord, along with the silver and gold he had taken from Syria, Moab, Ammon, the Philistines, Amalek, and King Hadadezer.

13So David became very famous. After his return he destroyed eighteen thousand Edomites at the Valley of Salt, 14and then placed garrisons throughout Edom, so that the entire nation was forced to pay tribute to Israel—another example of the way the Lord made him victorious wherever he went.

15David reigned with justice over Israel and was fair to everyone. 16The general

8:1	1 Chron 18:1
8:2	Num 24:15-19
	1 Kgs 4:21
	2 Kgs 3:4; 17:3
8:3	1 Sam 14:47
	2 Sam 10:19
	1 Kgs 11:23
	Ps 60 Title
8:4	Josh 11:6
8:6	2 Sam 3:18
	2 Chron 17:2
	26:8
8:7	1 Kgs 10:16
	14:26
	1 Chron 18:7
8:8	Ezek 47:16
8:11	1 Sam 27:8
	1 Kgs 7:51
	1 Chron 18:11
8:13	2 Kgs 14:7
	1 Chron 18:12
8:14	Gen 27:30,37
8:16	2 Sam 3:39
	19:5
	1 Kgs 4:1

8:13 *Edomites,* literally, "Syrians."

7:28 David knew that God's words were true, and he based his life on them. People search many places seeking truth on which to base their lives. Yet, as David knew, God's Word is the only trustworthy foundation upon which to build your life.

8:1–5 Part of God's covenant with David included the promise that Israel's enemies would be brought under control and would no longer oppress them (7:10, 11). God fulfilled this promise by helping David defeat the opposing nations. Several enemies are listed in this chapter: (1) *The Moabites*—descendants of Lot who lived east of the Dead Sea. They posed a constant military and religious threat to Israel (Numbers 25:1–3; Judges 3:11–30;

1 Samuel 14:47). David seemed to have a good relationship with the Moabites at one time (see the note on 1 Samuel 22:3, 4). (2) *King Hadadezer of Zobah*—his defeat at David's hands fulfilled God's promise to Abraham that Israel would control the land as far north as the Euphrates River (Genesis 15:18). (3) *The Edomites*—descendants of Esau (Genesis 36:1) who were also archenemies of Israel (see 2 Kings 8:20; Jeremiah 49:7–22; Ezekiel 25:12; and the note on Genesis 36:9).

8:6 A tribute was a tax levied on conquered nations. The tax helped to support Israel's government and demonstrated that the conquered nation was under Israel's control.

of his army was Joab (son of Zeruiah), and his secretary of state was Jehoshaphat (son of Ahilud). ¹⁷Zadok (son of Ahitub) and Ahimelech (son of Abiathar) were the High Priests, and Seraiah was the king's private secretary. ¹⁸Benaiah (son of Jehoiada) was captain of his bodyguard, and David's sons were his assistants.

8:18
2 Sam 20:7,23
1 Kgs 1:38
1 Chron 18:17

David is kind to Mephibosheth

9:1
1 Sam 20:14,
42; 23:18

9:2
2 Sam 16:1
19:17

9 One day David began wondering if any of Saul's family was still living, for he wanted to be kind to them, as he had promised Prince Jonathan. ²He heard about a man named Ziba who had been one of Saul's servants, and summoned him.

"Are you Ziba?" the king asked.

"Yes, sir, I am," he replied.

9:3
2 Sam 4:4

³The king then asked him, "Is anyone left from Saul's family? If so, I want to fulfill a sacred vow by being kind to him."

"Yes," Ziba replied, "Jonathan's lame son is still alive."

9:4
2 Sam 17:27

⁴"Where is he?" the king asked.

"In Lo-debar," Ziba told him. "At the home of Machir."

9:5
2 Sam 19:24
21:7
1 Chron 8:34

⁵, ⁶So King David sent for Mephibosheth—Jonathan's son and Saul's grandson. Mephibosheth arrived in great fear and greeted the king in deep humility, bowing low before him.

9:7
2 Sam 19:28
2 Kgs 25:29

⁷But David said, "Don't be afraid! I've asked you to come so that I can be kind to you because of my vow to your father Jonathan. I will restore to you all the land of your grandfather Saul, and you shall live here at the palace!"

⁸Mephibosheth fell to the ground before the king. "Should the king show kindness to a dead dog like me?" he exclaimed.

9:9
2 Sam 16:4
19:29

⁹Then the king summoned Saul's servant Ziba. "I have given your master's grandson everything that belonged to Saul and his family," he said. ¹⁰, ¹¹"You and your sons and servants are to farm the land for him, to produce food for his family; but he will live here with me."

9:10
2 Sam 19:28

8:18 *captain of his bodyguard,* literally, "the Cherethites and Pelethites." *were his assistants,* literally, "were priests." See 1 Chron 18:17.

DAVID'S ENEMIES
David wanted to complete the conquest of Canaan begun by Joshua. He defeated the Jebusites at Jerusalem, and the Philistines at Gath. The Ammonites, Syrians, and Moabites became his subjects. He placed garrisons in Edom, and levied a tax upon them.

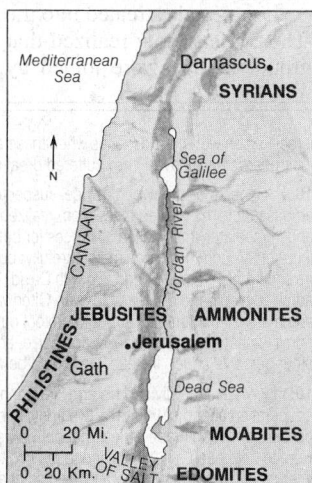

your convictions will be highly respected by both God and man.

8:15 King David's reign was characterized by justice. Is it any wonder that almost everyone trusted and followed him? Why was it good for David to pursue justice? (1) It was God's command (Deuteronomy 16:18-20). His laws were meant to establish a just society. (2) It was in the nation's best interest because times would arise when each individual would need to rely on it. Justice should characterize the way you relate to others. Make sure that you are just in the decisions you make.

9:1ff Most kings in David's day tried to wipe out the families of their rivals in order to prevent any descendants from seeking the throne. But David showed kindness to Mephibosheth, whose father was prince Jonathan and whose grandfather was King Saul. David was kind partly because of his loyalty to God's previously anointed king (see the note on 1 Samuel 24:5); partly for political reasons—to unite Judah and Israel (see the notes on 3:13, 14 and 3:29); and mainly because of his vow to show kindness to all of Jonathan's descendants (1 Samuel 20:14-17).

9:3 How Mephibosheth became lame is recorded in 4:4. Mephibosheth was five years old when Saul and Jonathan died.

9:5, 6 Mephibosheth was afraid to visit the king, who was treating him like a prince. Although he felt unworthy, that didn't mean David's gifts should be refused. When God graciously offers us forgiveness of sins and a place in heaven, we may feel unworthy, but we will receive these gifts if we accept them. A reception even warmer than the one David gave Mephibosheth is waiting for all who are willing to receive God's gifts through trusting Jesus Christ; not because they deserve it, but because of God's promise (Ephesians 2:8, 9).

8:15 Everything David did pleased the people (3:35, 36), not because he tried to please them, but because he tried to please God. Often those who try the hardest to become popular never make it. But "the praise of men" is not that important. Don't spend your time devising ways to please others in order to become accepted in the public eye. Instead, strive to do what is right and

Ziba, who had fifteen sons and twenty servants, replied, "Sir, I will do all you have commanded."

And from that time on, Mephibosheth ate regularly with King David, as though he were one of his own sons. 12Mephibosheth had a young son, Mica. All the household of Ziba became Mephibosheth's servants, 13but Mephibosheth (who was lame in both feet) moved to Jerusalem to live at the palace.

David defeats the Syrians

10 Some time after this the Ammonite king died and his son Hanun replaced him.

10:1
1 Chron 19:1-19

2"I am going to show special respect for him," David said, "because his father Nahash was always so loyal and kind to me." So David sent ambassadors to express regrets to Hanun about his father's death.

3But Hanun's officers told him, "These men aren't here to honor your father! David has sent them to spy out the city before attacking it!"

4So Hanun took David's men and shaved off half their beards and cut their robes off at the buttocks and sent them home half naked. 5When David heard what had happened he told them to stay at Jericho until their beards grew out; for the men were very embarrassed over their appearance.

10:4
Isa 15:2; 20:4
47:2,3
Jer 41:5

6Now the people of Ammon realized how seriously they had angered David, so they hired twenty thousand Syrian mercenaries from the lands of Rehob and Zobah, one thousand from the king of Maacah, and ten thousand from the land of Tob. 7, 8When David heard about this, he sent Joab and the entire Israeli army to attack them. The Ammonites defended the gates of their city while the Syrians from Zobah, Rehob, Tob, and Maacah fought in the fields. 9When Joab realized that he would have to fight on two fronts, he selected the best fighters in his army, placed them under his personal command, and took them out to fight the Syrians in the fields. 10He left the rest of the army to his brother Abishai, who was to attack the city.

10:6
2 Kgs 7:6

10:7
Judg 11:3

10:10
2 Sam 2:18
16:9

11"If I need assistance against the Syrians, come out and help me," Joab instructed him. "And if the Ammonites are too strong for you, I will come and help you. 12Courage! We must really act like men today if we are going to save our people and the cities of our God. May the Lord's will be done."

10:12
Deut 31:6
1 Sam 3:18
1 Cor 16:13

13And when Joab and his troops attacked, the Syrians began to run away. 14Then, when the Ammonites saw the Syrians running, they ran too, and retreated into the city. Afterwards Joab returned to Jerusalem. 15, 16The Syrians now realized that they were no match for Israel. So when they regrouped, they were joined by

10:13
1 Kgs 20:20
1 Chron 19:14

10:15
2 Sam 8:3
1 Chron 19:16

DAVID AND THE AMMONITES
Ammon gathered together their troops from the north; Joab brought the Israelite army to attack them near Rabbah. Joab returned to Jerusalem victorious, but the enemy recruited additional forces and regrouped at Helam. David himself led the next victorious attack.

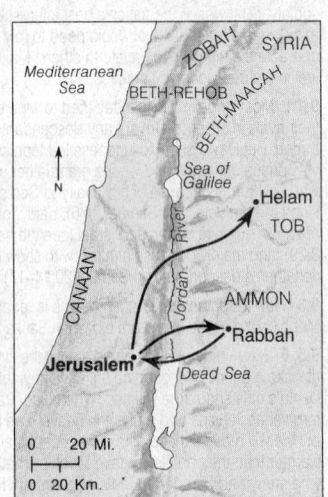

Israelite men wore beards. Thus when these ambassadors had their beards half shaved, they suffered great indignity.

10:6 Hanun took the wrong advice, suspected the motives of the ambassadors, humiliated these men, realized David was angry, and immediately marshalled his forces for battle. He should have thought through the advice more carefully; but even if he had not, he should have tried to negotiate with David. Instead, he refused to admit any fault and got ready for war. Often we respond in anger and marshall our forces in order to protect ourselves rather than admit we have made a mistake, apologize, and try to diffuse the other person's anger. Instead, we should be willing to seek peace.

10:11 When Joab divided his army in two, he arranged for cooperation ahead of time. The two fronts in battle were clearly divided, but Joab made it clear that both divisions of the army were to help each other if either one ran into trouble. The spirit of interdependency and cooperation should characterize families, church staffs, and your attitude at your place of work.

10:12 There must be a balance in life between our actions and our faith in God. David here says, "Courage!" In other words, do what you can. Plan the battle strategy, use your mind to figure out the best techniques, and use your resources. But he also says, "The Lord's will be done." He knew that the outcome was in God's hands. In the same way, we are to use our minds and our

10:4, 5 In Israelite culture, a beard was a sign of maturity—all

additional Syrian troops summoned by Hadadezer from the other side of the Euphrates River. These troops arrived at Helam under the command of Shobach, the commander-in-chief of all of Hadadezer's forces.

17When David heard what was happening, he personally led the Israeli army to Helam, where the Syrians attacked him. 18But again the Syrians fled from the Israelis, this time leaving seven hundred charioteers dead on the field, also forty thousand cavalrymen, including General Shobach. 19When Hadadezer's allies saw that the Syrians had been defeated, they surrendered to David and became his servants. And the Syrians were afraid to help the Ammonites anymore after that.

10:18
1 Chron 19:17, 18
10:19
2 Sam 8:6

B. DAVID'S STRUGGLES (11:1—24:25)

After restoring the nation to peace and great military power, David's personal life becomes entangled in sin. He commits adultery with Bath-sheba and then orders her husband killed in an attempted cover-up. David deeply regretted what he had done and sought God's forgiveness, but the child of his sinful act died. We may be forgiven by God for our sins, but we will often experience harsh consequences.

1. David and Bath-sheba
David sins with Bath-sheba

11:1
1 Chron 20:1
Jer 49:2
11:2
1 Sam 9:25
Acts 10:9,10
11:3
1 Chron 3:5
2 Sam 23:39
11:4
Lev 15:19; 18:19
Ps 51 Title
11:5
Lev 20:10
Deut 22:22

11 In the spring of the following year, at the time when wars begin, David sent Joab and the Israeli army to destroy the Ammonites. They began by laying siege to the city of Rabbah. But David stayed in Jerusalem.

2One night he couldn't get to sleep and went for a stroll on the roof of the palace. As he looked out over the city, he noticed a woman of unusual beauty taking her evening bath. 3He sent to find out who she was and was told that she was Bath-sheba, the daughter of Eliam and the wife of Uriah. 4Then David sent for her and when she came he slept with her. (She had just completed the purification rites after menstruation.) Then she returned home. 5When she found that he had gotten her pregnant she sent a message to inform him.

David tries to cover his sin

11:8,9
Job 5:12

6So David dispatched a memo to Joab: "Send me Uriah the Hittite." 7When he arrived, David asked him how Joab and the army were getting along and how the war was prospering. 8Then he told him to go home and relax, and he sent a present to him at his home. 9But Uriah didn't go there. He stayed that night at the gateway of the palace with the other servants of the king.

10When David heard what Uriah had done, he summoned him and asked him,

11:2 *he couldn't get to sleep,* literally, "arose from his bed."

---

resources to obey God, while at the same time living by faith and trusting God for the outcome.

11:1ff In the episode with Bath-sheba, David allowed himself to fall deeper and deeper into sin. (1) David abandoned his purpose by staying home from battle (11:1). (2) He focused on his own desires (11:3). (3) When temptation came he looked into it instead of turning away from it (11:4). (4) He sinned deliberately (11:4). (5) He tried to cover up his sin by deceiving others (11:6–15). (6) He committed murder to continue the cover-up (11:15, 17). (7) His sin was exposed (12:9). (8) His sin was punished (12:10–14). (9) The consequences of his sin affected many others (12:11, 14, 15).

David could have chosen to stop and turn from evil at any stage along the way. But once the progression of sin gets started it is difficult to stop (James 1:14, 15). The deeper the mess, the less we want to admit having caused it. It's much easier to stop sliding down a hill when you are near the top rather than halfway down. The best solution is to stop sin before it starts.

11:1 Winter is the rainy season in Israel, the time when crops were planted. Spring was a good time to go to war because the roads were dry, making travel easier for wagons and chariots. In Israel, many crops were ready to be harvested in the spring. These crops were an important food source for traveling armies.

11:1 This successful siege (see 12:26, 27) put an end to the Ammonites' power. From this time on, the Ammonites were subject to Israel.

11:3 See 1 Kings 1 for the Profile note on Bath-sheba.

11:3, 4 As David gazed from his palace roof, he saw a beautiful woman bathing, and lust filled his heart. He should have left the roof and fled from the temptation. Instead, he entertained the temptation by inquiring about Bath-sheba. The results of letting temptation stay in his heart were devastating.

To flee temptation: (1) Ask God in earnest prayer to help you stay away from people, places, and situations that offer temptation. (2) Memorize and meditate on portions of Scripture that combat your specific weaknesses. At the root of most temptation is a real need or desire that God can fill. (3) Find another believer with whom you can openly share your temptations, and call this person for help when temptation strikes.

11:4 The sentence in parentheses is one of the most significant statements in the story because it shows that Bath-sheba couldn't have already been pregnant by her own husband when David slept with her. It may also be included to show that Bath-sheba was just as guilty of adultery as David. (Leviticus 15:19–30 gives more information on the purification rites Bath-sheba had to perform.)

"What's the matter with you? Why didn't you go home to your wife last night after being away for so long?"

11Uriah replied, "The Ark and the armies and the general and his officers are camping out in open fields, and should I go home to wine and dine and sleep with my wife? I swear that I will never be guilty of acting like that."

11:11
2 Sam 7:2; 20:6

12"Well, stay here tonight," David told him, "and tomorrow you may return to the army."

So Uriah stayed around the palace. 13David invited him to dinner and got him drunk; but even so he didn't go home that night, but again he slept at the entry to the palace.

14Finally the next morning David wrote a letter to Joab and gave it to Uriah to deliver. 15The letter instructed Joab to put Uriah at the front of the hottest part of the battle—and then pull back and leave him there to die! 16So Joab assigned Uriah to a spot close to the besieged city where he knew that the enemies' best men were fighting; 17and Uriah was killed along with several other Israeli soldiers.

11:15
2 Sam 12:9

18When Joab sent a report to David of how the battle was going, 19, 20, 21he told his messenger, "If the king is angry and asks, 'Why did the troops go so close to the city? Didn't they know there would be shooting from the walls? Wasn't Abimelech killed at Thebez by a woman who threw down a millstone on him?'—then tell him, 'Uriah was killed, too.'"

11:19
Judg 9:53

22So the messenger arrived at Jerusalem, and gave the report to David.

23"The enemy came out against us," he said, "and as we chased them back to the city gates, 24the men on the wall attacked us; and some of our men were killed, and Uriah the Hittite is dead too."

25"Well, tell Joab not to be discouraged," David said. "The sword kills one as well as another! Fight harder next time, and conquer the city; tell him he is doing well."

26When Bath-sheba heard that her husband was dead, she mourned for him; 27then, when the period of mourning was over, David sent for her and brought her to the palace and she became one of his wives; and she gave birth to his son. But the Lord was very displeased with what David had done.

11:26
Gen 50:10
Deut 34:8
1 Sam 31:13
11:27
1 Sam 3:2-5
Ps 51:4,5

Nathan accuses David of sin

12 So the Lord sent the prophet Nathan to tell David this story: "There were two men in a certain city, one very rich, owning many flocks of sheep and herds of goats; 3and the other very poor, owning nothing but a little lamb he had managed to buy. It was his children's pet and he fed it from his own plate and let it drink from his own cup; he cuddled it in his arms like a baby daughter. 4Recently a guest arrived at the home of the rich man. But instead of killing a lamb

12:1
2 Sam 7:2,17
1 Kgs 20:35
Ps 51 Title

11:25 *The sword kills one as well as another*, literally, "the sword devours now one and now another."

11:15 David put both Bath-sheba and Joab in a difficult situation. Bath-sheba knew it was wrong to commit adultery, but to refuse a king's request could mean punishment or death. Joab did not know why Uriah was to die, but it was obvious the king wanted him killed. We sometimes face situations with only two apparent choices, and both seem wrong. When that happens, we must not lose sight of what God wants. The answer may be to seek out more choices. By doing this, we are likely to find one that honors God.

11:17 Uriah and several other soldiers died as a result of David's scheme. Sin sometimes hurts innocent bystanders. When you are tempted to do wrong, thinking about the people who could be hurt by your sin may motivate you to avoid it.

11:25 David's response to Uriah's death seems flippant and insensitive. While he grieved deeply for Saul and Abner, his rivals (2 Samuel 1; 3:31–39), he showed no grief for Uriah, a good man with strong spiritual character. Why? David had become callous to his own sin. The only way he could cover up his first sin (adultery)

was to sin again, and soon he no longer felt guilt for his wrong actions. Deliberate, repeated sinning had dulled David's sensitivity to God's law and others' rights. The more you try to cover up a sin, the more insensitive you become toward it. Don't become hardened to sin, as was David. Confess your wrong actions to God right away, before you forget they are sin.

11:27 King David abused his position of authority to get what he wanted. Today we often see abuse of power in government and business. God is especially hard on leaders who misuse their positions to exploit, manipulate, or compromise those under their authority. This breaks the trust between them and those they serve.

12:1ff As a prophet, Nathan was required to confront sin, even the sin of a king. It took great courage, skill, and tact to speak to David in a way that would make him aware of his wrong actions. When you have to confront someone with unpleasant news, pray for courage, skill, and tact. If you want that person to respond constructively, how you present your message may be as important as what you say. Season your words with wisdom.

12:5
1 Sam 26:16
1 Kgs 20:39

12:6
Ex 22:1

12:7
1 Sam 16:13

12:8
2 Sam 7:2; 9:7

12:9
1 Sam 15:23

12:10
2 Sam 13:29
18:14
1 Kgs 2:23

12:11
2 Sam 16:21
15:6,10

from his own flocks for food for the traveler, he took the poor man's lamb and roasted it and served it."

5David was furious. "I swear by the living God," he vowed, "any man who would do a thing like that should be put to death; 6he shall repay four lambs to the poor man for the one he stole, and for having no pity."

7Then Nathan said to David, *"You* are that rich man! The Lord God of Israel says, 'I made you king of Israel and saved you from the power of Saul. 8I gave you his palace and his wives and the kingdoms of Israel and Judah; and if that had not been enough, I would have given you much, much more. 9Why, then, have you despised the laws of God and done this horrible deed? For you have murdered Uriah and stolen his wife. 10Therefore murder shall be a constant threat in your family from this time on, because you have insulted me by taking Uriah's wife. 11I vow that because of what you have done I will cause your own household to rebel

12:11 *with them in public view,* literally, "under this sun."

NATHAN

This prophet lived up to the meaning of his name, "God has given." He was a necessary and helpful gift from God to King David. He served as God's spokesman to David and proved himself to be a fearless friend and counselor, always willing to speak the truth, even when he knew great pain would result.

In confronting David's multiple sin of coveting, theft, adultery, and murder in his affair with Bath-sheba, Nathan was able to help David see his own wrongdoing by showing that he would not have tolerated such actions from anyone else. David's repentance allowed Nathan to comfort him with the reality of God's forgiveness, and at the same time remind him of the painful consequences his sin would bring.

Nathan's approach helps us judge our actions. How often do we make choices that we would condemn others for making? It is beneficial to ask ourselves how God and others view our actions. Unfortunately, we have a huge capacity to lie to ourselves. God still provides two safeguards against self-deception: his Word, and true friends. In each case, we get a view beyond ourselves. You are holding God's Word. Let it speak to you about yourself, even if the truth is painful. If you don't have a friend like Nathan, ask God for one. And ask God to use you as a suitable Nathan for someone else.

Strengths and accomplishments:
• A trusted advisor to King David
• A prophet of God
• A fearless, but careful confronter
• One of God's controls in David's life

Weakness:
• His eagerness to see David build a Temple for God in Jerusalem made him speak without God's instructions

Lessons from his life:
• We should not be afraid to tell the truth to those we care about
• A trustworthy companion is one of God's greatest gifts
• God cares enough to find a way to communicate to us when we are in the wrong

Vital statistics:
• Occupation: Prophet, royal advisor
• Contemporaries: David, Bath-sheba, Solomon, Zadok, Adonijah

Key verse:
"So Nathan went back to David and told him everything the Lord had said" (2 Samuel 7:17).

Nathan's story is told in 2 Samuel 7—1 Kings 1. He is also mentioned in 1 Chronicles 17:15; 2 Chronicles 9:29; 29:25, 26.

12:5-7 David had become so insensitive to his own sins that he didn't realize he was the villain in Nathan's story. The qualities we condemn in others are often our own character flaws. Which friends, associates, or family members do you find easy to criticize and hard to accept? Instead of trying to change them, ask God to help you understand their feelings and see your own flaws more clearly. You may discover that in condemning others, you have been condemning yourself.

12:10-14 The predictions in these verses came true. Because David murdered Uriah and stole his wife, (1) murder was a

constant threat in his family (13:29, 30; 18:14, 15; 1 Kings 2:23-25); (2) his household rebelled against him (15:13); (3) his wives were given to another in public view (16:20-23); (4) his child through Bath-sheba died (12:18). If David had known the painful consequences of his sin, he might not have pursued the pleasures of the moment. Remember that the consequences of your actions reach farther and deeper than you can ever foresee. Because sin has consequences, God has set up moral guidelines to help us avoid sin in the first place.

against you. I will give your wives to another man, and he will go to bed with them in public view. ¹²You did it secretly, but I will do this to you openly, in the sight of all Israel.' "

¹³"I have sinned against the Lord," David confessed to Nathan.

Then Nathan replied, "Yes, but the Lord has forgiven you, and you won't die for this sin. ¹⁴But you have given great opportunity to the enemies of the Lord to despise and blaspheme him, so your child shall die."

David and Bath-sheba's baby dies

¹⁵Then Nathan returned to his home. And the Lord made Bath-sheba's baby deathly sick. ¹⁶David begged him to spare the child, and went without food and lay all night before the Lord on the bare earth. ¹⁷The leaders of the nation pleaded with him to get up and eat with them, but he refused. ¹⁸Then, on the seventh day, the baby died. David's aides were afraid to tell him.

"He was so broken up about the baby being sick," they said, "what will he do to himself when we tell him the child is dead?"

¹⁹But when David saw them whispering, he realized what had happened.

"Is the baby dead?" he asked.

"Yes," they replied, "he is." ²⁰Then David got up off the ground, washed himself, brushed his hair, changed his clothes, and went into the Tabernacle and worshiped the Lord. Then he returned to the palace and ate. ²¹His aides were amazed.

"We don't understand you," they told him. "While the baby was still living, you wept and refused to eat; but now that the baby is dead, you have stopped your mourning and are eating again."

²²David replied, "I fasted and wept while the child was alive, for I said, 'Perhaps the Lord will be gracious to me and let the child live.' ²³But why should I fast when he is dead? Can I bring him back again? I shall go to him, but he shall not return to me."

²⁴Then David comforted Bath-sheba; and when he slept with her, she conceived and gave birth to a son and named him Solomon. And the Lord loved the baby, ²⁵and sent congratulations and blessings through Nathan the prophet. David nicknamed the baby Jedidiah (meaning, "Beloved of Jehovah") because of the Lord's interest.

12:25 *and sent congratulations,* literally, "Jehovah sent word by Nathan the prophet." *because of the Lord's interest,* literally, "because of the Lord."

Cross-references (right margin):

12:13 Lev 20:10; 24:17 / 2 Sam 11:5 / 24:10 / Prov 28:13 / Mic 7:18 / Lk 18:13

12:14 Isa 52:5 / Rom 2:23

12:16 2 Sam 1:12 / 13:31 / Ps 69:10

12:17 2 Sam 3:35

12:22 Isa 38:1-5 / Jonah 3:9

12:23 Job 7:9-10

12:24 1 Chron 22:9

12:13 During this incident, David wrote Psalm 51, giving valuable insight into his character and offering hope for us as well. No matter how miserable guilt makes you feel or how terribly you have sinned, you can pour out your heart to God and seek his forgiveness as David did. David also wrote Psalm 32, which expresses the joy he felt after he was forgiven.

12:14 David repented of his sin (12:13), but God's judgment was that his child would die. The consequences of David's sin were irreversible. Sometimes an apology isn't enough. When God forgives us and restores our relationship to him, he doesn't eliminate all the consequences of our wrongdoing. We may be tempted to say, "If this is wrong, I can always apologize to God," but we must remember that we may set into motion events whose consequences cannot be reversed.

12:14 Why did this child have to die? This was not a judgment on the child for being born out of wedlock, but a judgment on David for his sin. David and Bath-sheba deserved to die, but God spared their lives and took the child instead. God still had work for David to do in building the kingdom. Perhaps the child's death was a greater punishment for David than his own death would have been.

It is also possible that had the child lived, God's name would have been dishonored among Israel's heathen neighbors. What

would they have thought of a God who rewards murder and adultery by giving a king an heir? A baby's death is tragic, but despising God brings death to entire nations. While God readily forgave David's sin, he did not negate all its consequences.

12:15 Nathan, a prophet of great wisdom, bravery, obedience, and loyalty, gave three crucial messages at three critical times in David's life. (1) He told David that his son would build the Temple and that David's dynasty would last forever (2 Samuel 7:1–17). (2) He confronted David with his sin of adultery (2 Samuel 12:1–14). (3) He helped David place Solomon on the throne (1 Kings 1:11–53).

12:20, 21 David did not continue to dwell on his sin; he returned to God and God forgave him, opening the way to begin life anew. Even the nickname David gave Solomon was a reminder of God's grace (12:25). When we return to God, accept his forgiveness, and change our ways, he gives us a fresh start.

12:22, 23 Perhaps the most bitter experience in life is the death of one's child. For comfort in such difficult circumstances, see Psalms 16:9–11; 17:15; 139; Isaiah 40:11.

12:24 Solomon was the fourth son of David and Bath-sheba (1 Chronicles 3:5). Therefore, several years passed between the death of their first child and Solomon's birth.

David conquers the Ammonites

12:26
Deut 3:11
2 Sam 11:1
1 Chron 20:1

26, 27Meanwhile Joab and the Israeli army were successfully ending their siege of Rabbah the capital of Ammon. Joab sent messengers to tell David, "Rabbah and its beautiful harbor are ours! 28Now bring the rest of the army and finish the job, so that you will get the credit for the victory instead of me."

12:29
1 Chron 20:2,3

29, 30So David led his army to Rabbah and captured it. Tremendous amounts of loot were carried back to Jerusalem, and David took the king of Rabbah's crown—a $50,000 treasure made from solid gold set with gems—and placed it on his own head. 31He made slaves of the people of the city and made them labor with saws, picks, and axes and work in the brick kilns; that is the way he treated all of the cities of the Ammonites. Then David and the army returned to Jerusalem.

2. Turmoil in David's family
Amnon rapes Tamar

13:1
2 Sam 3:2,3
1 Chron 3:2,9

13 Prince Absalom, David's son, had a beautiful sister named Tamar. And Prince Amnon (her half brother) fell desperately in love with her. 2Amnon became so tormented by his love for her that he became ill. He had no way of talking to her, for the girls and young men were kept strictly apart. 3But Amnon had a very crafty friend—his cousin Jonadab (the son of David's brother Shime-ah).

4One day Jonadab said to Amnon, "What's the trouble? Why should the son of a king look so haggard morning after morning?"

So Amnon told him, "I am in love with Tamar, my half sister."

5"Well," Jonadab said, "I'll tell you what to do. Go back to bed and pretend you

12:26, 27 *Rabbah and its beautiful harbor are ours,* or, "I have taken the City of Waters." **12:31** *made them labor with saws, picks, and axes and work in the brick kilns,* or "killed them with saws and iron harrows, and in the brick kilns." **13:2** *for the girls and young men were kept strictly apart,* literally, "for she was a virgin, and it seemed impossible to Amnon to do anything to her."

DAVID'S FAMILY TROUBLES	Wife	Children	What happened
David's many wives caused him much grief. And as a result of David's sin with Bath-sheba, God said that murder would be a constant threat in his family, his family would rebel, and someone else would sleep with his wives. All this happened as the prophet Nathan had predicted. The consequences of sin affect not only us, but those we know and love. Remember that the next time you are tempted to sin.	Michal (Saul's daughter)	She was childless, but adopted five of her sister Merab's sons	David gave her five nephews to the Gibeonites to be killed because of Saul's sins
	Ahinoam (from Jezreel)	Amnon, David's first-born	He raped Tamar, his half sister, and was later murdered by Absalom in revenge
	Maacah (daughter of King Talmai of Geshur)	Absalom, third son Tamar, the only daughter mentioned by name	Absalom killed Amnon for raping Tamar, and then fled to Geshur. Later he returned, only to rebel against David. He set up a tent on his roof and slept with ten of his father's wives there. His pride led to his death
	Haggith	Adonijah, fourth son. He was very handsome, but it is recorded that he was never disciplined	He set himself up as king before David's death. His plot was exposed and David spared his life, but his half brother Solomon, later had him executed
	Bath-sheba	Unnamed son	Died in fulfillment of God's punishment for David and Bath-sheba's adultery
	Bath-sheba	Solomon	Became the next king of Israel. Ironically, Solomon's many wives caused his downfall

---

13:1ff David now faced sins in his own family similar to those he himself had committed earlier. The sin in his life was magnified in the lives of his children. If you are a parent you can't always control what your children will do, but you can live by God's standards, giving them a good example to follow.

13:3–5 Amnon was encouraged by his own cousin Jonadab to commit sexual sin. We may be more vulnerable to the advice of our relatives because we are close to them. However, we must make sure that every piece of advice we are given passes through the filter of God's standards.

are sick; when your father comes to see you, ask him to let Tamar come and prepare some food for you. Tell him you'll feel better if she feeds you."

6So Amnon did. And when the king came to see him, Amnon asked him for this favor—that his sister Tamar be permitted to come and cook a little something for him to eat. 7David agreed, and sent word to Tamar to go to Amnon's quarters and prepare some food for him. 8So she did, and went into his bedroom so that he could watch her mix some dough; then she baked some special bread for him. 9But when she set the serving tray before him, he refused to eat!

"Everyone get out of here," he told his servants; so they all left the apartment.

10Then he said to Tamar, "Now bring me the food again here in my bedroom and feed it to me." So Tamar took it to him. 11But as she was standing there before him, he grabbed her and demanded, "Come to bed with me, my darling."

12"Oh, Amnon," she cried. "Don't be foolish! Don't do this to me! You know what a serious crime it is in Israel. 13Where could I go in my shame? And you would be called one of the greatest fools in Israel. Please, just speak to the king about it, for he will let you marry me.

14But he wouldn't listen to her; and since he was stronger than she, he forced her. 15Then suddenly his love turned to hate, and now he hated her more than he had loved her.

"Get out of here!" he snarled at her.

16"No, no!" she cried. "To reject me now is a greater crime than the other you did to me."

But he wouldn't listen to her. 17, 18He shouted for his valet and demanded, "Throw this woman out and lock the door behind her."

So he put her out. She was wearing a long robe with sleeves, as was the custom in those days for virgin daughters of the king. 19Now she tore the robe and put ashes on her head and with her head in her hands went away crying.

13:12 Lev 18:9,11 20:17

13:17 Gen 37:3,32

13:19 Gen 37:29 2 Sam 1:11 Esth 4:1

Absalom murders Amnon

20Her brother Absalom asked her, "Is it true that Amnon raped you? Don't be so upset, since it's all in the family anyway. It's not anything to worry about!"

So Tamar lived as a desolate woman in her brother Absalom's quarters.

21-24When King David heard what had happened, he was very angry, but Absalom said nothing one way or the other about this to Amnon. However, he hated him with a deep hatred because of what he had done to his sister. Then, two years later, when Absalom's sheep were being sheared at Baal-hazor in Ephraim, Absalom invited his father and all his brothers to come to a feast to celebrate the occasion.

25The king replied, "No, my boy; if we all came, we would be too much of a burden on you."

13:12 *You know what a serious crime it is in Israel,* literally, "No such thing ought to be done in Israel; do not this folly."

13:14, 15 Love and lust are very different. After Amnon raped his half-sister, his "love" turned to hate. Although he had claimed to be in love, he was actually overcome by lust. Love is patient; lust requires immediate sexual satisfaction. Love is kind; lust is harsh. Love does not demand its own way; lust does. You can read about the characteristics of real love in 1 Corinthians 13.

13:16 The crimes Amnon committed were rape and incest, both strictly forbidden by God (Leviticus 18:6–9; 20:17). Why was rejecting Tamar an even greater crime? By throwing her out, Amnon made it look as if Tamar had made a shameful proposition to him, and there were no witnesses on her behalf because he had gotten rid of the servants. His crime destroyed any chance of marriage for her—because she was no longer a virgin, she could not be given in marriage (Deuteronomy 22:23–29).

13:20 Absalom tried to comfort Tamar and persuade her not to turn the incident into a public scandal. Secretly, he planned to take revenge against Amnon himself. This he did two years later (13:20–33). Absalom tried to comfort Tamar by saying the crime was only a "family matter." But God's standards for moral conduct are not suspended when dealing with family matters.

13:21–24 David was angry with Amnon for his incest; however, David did not punish him. According to God's law, David should have had Amnon banished for this sin (Leviticus 20:17). David probably hesitated because (1) Amnon was his eldest son (1 Chronicles 3:1) and therefore next in line to be king, and (2) David was guilty of a similar sin himself in his adultery with Bath-sheba. While David was unsurpassed as a king and military leader, he lacked skill and sensitivity as a husband and father.

13:21–24 Hatred leads to disaster. Absalom had reason to be angry with Amnon, but instead of confronting Amnon with his sin, he allowed his anger to turn into hatred. This produced revenge

Absalom pressed him, but he wouldn't come, though he sent his thanks.

26"Well, then," Absalom said, "if you can't come, how about sending my brother Amnon instead?"

"Why Amnon?" the king asked.

27Absalom kept on urging the matter until finally the king agreed, and let all of his sons attend, including Amnon.

28Absalom told his men, "Wait until Amnon gets drunk, then, at my signal, kill him! Don't be afraid. I'm the one who gives the orders around here, and this is a command. Take courage and do it!"

29, 30So they murdered Amnon. Then the other sons of the king jumped on their mules and fled. As they were on the way back to Jerusalem, the report reached David: "Absalom has killed all of your sons, and not one is left alive!"

31The king jumped up, ripped off his robe, and fell prostrate to the ground. His aides also tore their clothes in horror and sorrow.

32, 33But just then Jonadab (the son of David's brother Shime-ah) arrived and said, "No, not all have been killed! It was only Amnon! Absalom has been plotting this ever since Amnon raped Tamar. No, no! Your sons aren't all dead! It was only Amnon."

34Meanwhile Absalom escaped. Now the watchman on the Jerusalem wall saw a great crowd coming toward the city along the road at the side of the hill.

35"See!" Jonadab told the king. "There they are now! Your sons are coming, just as I said."

36They soon arrived, weeping and sobbing, and the king and his officials wept with them. 37, 38, 39Absalom fled to King Talmai of Geshur (the son of Ammihud) and stayed there three years. Meanwhile David, now reconciled to Amnon's death, longed day after day for fellowship with his son Absalom.

A woman intercedes for Absalom

14 When General Joab realized how much the king was longing to see Absalom, 2, 3he sent for a woman of Tekoa who had a reputation for great wisdom and told her to ask for an appointment with the king. He told her what to say to him.

"Pretend you are in mourning," Joab instructed her. "Wear mourning clothes, and dishevel your hair as though you have been in deep sorrow for a long time."

4When the woman approached the king, she fell face downward on the floor in front of him, and cried out, "O king! Help me!"

5, 6"What's the trouble?" he asked.

"I am a widow," she replied, "and my two sons had a fight out in the field, and since no one was there to part them, one of them was killed. 7Now the rest of the family is demanding that I surrender my other son to them to be executed for murdering his brother. But if I do that, I will have no one left, and my husband's name will be destroyed from the face of the earth."

8"Leave it with me," the king told her, "I'll see to it that no one touches him."

9"Oh, thank you, my lord," she replied. "And I'll take the responsibility if you are criticized for helping me like this."

10"Don't worry about that!" the king replied. "If anyone objects, bring him to me; I can assure you he will never complain again!"

11Then she said, "Please swear to me by God that you won't let anyone harm my son. I want no more bloodshed."

"I vow by God," he replied, "that not a hair of your son's head shall be disturbed!"

12"Please let me ask one more thing of you!" she said.

"Go ahead," he replied. "Speak!"

13"Why don't you do as much for all the people of God as you have promised to do for me?" she asked. "You have convicted yourself in making this decision,

13:28
2 Sam 3:27
11:13

13:29
2 Sam 18:9

13:31
2 Sam 1:11
12:16
13:32
2 Sam 13:4,14

13:34
2 Sam 18:24

13:37
2 Sam 3:3
12:21; 14:23,32

14:2
2 Chron 11:5-10
Amos 1:1

14:4
2 Sam 12:1,2

14:7
Num 35:19
Deut 19:12,13

14:9
Gen 43:9
1 Sam 25:24

14:11
Num 35:19,21
Deut 19:4-10
1 Sam 14:45

14:13
2 Sam 12:7
13:37-39
1 Kgs 20:40-42

instead of resolution. When you have been wronged or are angry at a wrong done to someone else, try to solve the problem, not get even.

13:37-39 Absalom fled to Geshur because King Talmai was his grandfather (1 Chronicles 3:2), and he knew he would be welcomed as family.

because you have refused to bring home your own banished son. ¹⁴All of us must die eventually; our lives are like water that is poured out on the ground—it can't be gathered up again. But God will bless you with a longer life if you will find a way to bring your son back from his exile. ¹⁵, ¹⁶But I have come to plead with you for my son because my life and my son's life have been threatened, and I said to myself, 'Perhaps the king will listen to me and rescue us from those who would end our existence in Israel. ¹⁷Yes, the king will give us peace again.' I know that you are like the angel of God and can discern good from evil. May God be with you."

¹⁸"I want to know one thing," the king replied.

"Yes, my lord?" she asked.

¹⁹"Did Joab send you here?"

And the woman replied, "How can I deny it? Yes, Joab sent me and told me what to say. ²⁰He did it in order to place the matter before you in a different light. But you are as wise as an angel of God, and you know everything that happens!"

²¹So the king sent for Joab and told him, "All right, go and bring back Absalom."

²²Joab fell to the ground before the king and blessed him and said, "At last I know that you like me! For you have granted me this request!"

²³Then Joab went to Geshur and brought Absalom back to Jerusalem.

²⁴"He may go to his own quarters," the king ordered, "but he must never come here. I refuse to see him."

Absalom demands to see David

²⁵Now no one in Israel was such a handsome specimen of manhood as Absalom, and no one else received such praise. ²⁶He cut his hair only once a year—and then only because it weighed three pounds and was too much of a load to carry around! ²⁷He had three sons and one daughter, Tamar, who was a very beautiful girl.

²⁸After Absalom had been in Jerusalem for two years and had not yet seen the king, ²⁹he sent for Joab to ask him to intercede for him; but Joab wouldn't come. Absalom sent for him again, but again he refused to come.

³⁰So Absalom said to his servants, "Go and set fire to that barley field of Joab's next to mine," and they did.

³¹Then Joab came to Absalom and demanded, "Why did your servants set my field on fire?"

³²And Absalom replied, "Because I wanted you to ask the king why he brought me back from Geshur if he didn't intend to see me. I might as well have stayed there. Let me have an interview with the king; then if he finds that I am guilty of murder, let him execute me."

³³So Joab told the king what Absalom had said. Then at last David summoned Absalom, and he came and bowed low before the king, and David kissed him.

3. National rebellion against David

Absalom plots to overthrow David

15 Absalom then bought a magnificent chariot and chariot horses, and hired fifty footmen to run ahead of him. ²He got up early every morning and went

14:14 *bring your son back from his exile,* or, "God does not sweep life away, but has made provision to bring back those he banishes, so that they will not be forever exiles."

Side references:

14:14 Job 34:14,15 Heb 9:27

14:17 1 Sam 29:9 2 Sam 19:27

14:23 2 Sam 13:37-39

14:27 2 Sam 13:1

14:28 2 Sam 14:24

14:32 1 Sam 20:8

14:33 Gen 27:26; 33:4 Lk 15:20

15:1 1 Kgs 1:5

14:33 David only made half-hearted efforts to raise his children. In 13:21–39, David did not punish Amnon for his sin, nor did he deal decisively with Absalom's murder of Amnon. When he finally allowed Absalom back, he did not speak to him for two years. Such indecisiveness became David's undoing. When sin is ignored, it will result in greater pain than if it is dealt with immediately.

15:1ff David wrote several Psalms during the days of Absalom's rebellion. Some of them are Psalms 39, 41, 55, 61, 62, and 63.

15:1 A group of footmen or "runners" often served as traffic police to clear a path before the chariot of an important person when he was traveling through crowded or narrow streets. Sometimes they also announced this person's name. This procedure was an excellent attention-getting device.

15:2 The city gate was like city hall and a shopping center combined. Because Jerusalem was the nation's capital, both local and national leaders met there daily to transact business and conduct government affairs. The city gate was the perfect spot for this because government and business transactions needed witnesses to be legitimate, and anyone entering or leaving the city had to enter through the gate. Merchants set up their tent-shops near the gate for the same reason. Absalom, therefore, went to the city gate to try to win the hearts of Israel's leaders as well as those of the common people.

out to the gate of the city; and when anyone came to bring a case to the king for trial, Absalom called him over and expressed interest in his problem.

15:4
Judg 9:1-3

³He would say, "I can see that you are right in this matter; it's unfortunate that the king doesn't have anyone to assist him in hearing these cases. ⁴I surely wish I were the judge; then anyone with a lawsuit could come to me, and I would give him justice!"

15:5
2 Sam 14:33

⁵And when anyone came to bow to him, Absalom wouldn't let him, but shook his hand instead! ⁶So in this way Absalom stole the hearts of all the people of Israel.

15:7
Gen 28:20,21
2 Sam 13:37-39

⁷,⁸After four years, Absalom said to the king, "Let me go to Hebron to sacrifice to the Lord in fulfillment of a vow I made to him while I was at Geshur—that if he would bring me back to Jerusalem, I would sacrifice to him."

⁹"All right," the king told him, "go and fulfill your vow."

15:5 *shook his hand instead,* literally, "took hold of him and kissed him."

ABSALOM

A father's mistakes are often reflected in the lives of his children. In Absalom, David saw a bitter replay and amplification of many of his own past sins. God had predicted that David's family would suffer because of his sin against Bath-sheba and Uriah. His heart was broken as he realized that God's predictions were coming true. God forgave David, but he did not cancel the consequences of David's sin. David was horrified as he saw his son's strengths run wild without the controls God had built into his own life.

By most casual evaluations, Absalom would have made an excellent king. The people loved him. But he lacked the inner character and control needed in a good leader. His appearance, skill, and position did not make up for his lack of personal integrity.

David's sins took him away from God, but repentance brought him back. But Absalom sinned and kept on sinning. Although he relied heavily on the advice of others, he was not wise enough to evaluate the counsel he received.

Can you identify with Absalom? Do you find yourself on a fast track toward self-destruction? Absalom wasn't able to say, "I was wrong. I need forgiveness." God offers forgiveness, but we will not experience that forgiveness until we genuinely confess our sin to God. Absalom rejected his father's love and ultimately God's love. How often do you miss entering back into God's love through the door of forgiveness?

Weaknesses and mistakes:
● Avenged the rape of his sister Tamar by killing his half-brother Amnon
● Plotted against his father to take away the throne
● Consistently listened to the wrong advice

Lessons from his life:
● The sins of parents are often repeated and amplified in the children
● A smart man gets a lot of advice; a wise man evaluates the advice he gets
● Actions against God's plans will fail, sooner or later

Vital statistics:
● Where: Hebron
● Occupation: Prince
● Relatives: Father: David. Mother: Maacah. Brothers: Amnon, Chileab, Solomon, and others. Sister: Tamar.
● Contemporaries: Nathan, Jonadab, Joab, Ahithophel, Hushai

Key verse:
"But while he was there [in Hebron], he sent spies to every part of Israel to incite rebellion against the king. 'As soon as you hear the trumpets,' his message read, 'you will know that Absalom has been crowned in Hebron' " (2 Samuel 15:10).

Absalom's story is told in 2 Samuel 13—19. He is also mentioned in 2 Samuel 3:3.

15:6 Absalom's political strategy was to steal the hearts of the people with his good looks, grand entrances, a public position of justice, and friendly embraces. Most were fooled and switched their allegiance. Later, however, Absalom proved to be an evil and pathetic ruler.

We need to evaluate our leaders to make sure their charisma is not a mask covering craft, deception, or hunger for power. Make sure that underneath their style and charm, they are able to make good decisions and handle people wisely.

15:9 Absalom went to Hebron because it was his hometown (3:2, 3). Hebron was David's first capital as well, and there Absalom could expect to find loyal friends who would be proud of him.

So Absalom went to Hebron. [10]But while he was there, he sent spies to every part of Israel to incite rebellion against the king. "As soon as you hear the trumpets," his message read, "you will know that Absalom has been crowned in Hebron." [11]He took two hundred men from Jerusalem with him as guests, but they knew nothing of his intentions. [12]While he was offering the sacrifice, he sent for Ahithophel, one of David's counselors who lived in Giloh. Ahithophel declared for Absalom, as did more and more others. So the conspiracy became very strong.

15:10
1 Kgs 1:34
2 Kgs 9:13

15:12
2 Sam 16:20
17:14

David flees from Absalom

[13]A messenger soon arrived in Jerusalem to tell King David, "All Israel has joined Absalom in a conspiracy against you!"

15:13
Judg 9:3

[14]"Then we must flee at once or it will be too late!" was David's instant response to his men. "If we get out of the city before he arrives, both we and the city of Jerusalem will be saved."

15:14
2 Sam 12:11
Ps 3 Title

[15]"We are with you," his aides replied. "Do as you think best."

[16]So the king and his household set out at once. He left no one behind except ten of his young wives to keep the palace in order. [17, 18]David paused at the edge of the city to let his troops move past him to lead the way—six hundred Gittites who had come with him from Gath, and the Cherethites and Pelethites.

15:16
2 Sam 16:21

15:17
1 Sam 23:13
25:13; 30:9
2 Sam 8:18
18:1,2

[19, 20]But suddenly the king turned to Ittai, the captain of the six hundred Gittites, and said to him, "What are you doing here? Go on back with your men to Jerusalem, to your king, for you are a guest in Israel, a foreigner in exile. It seems but yesterday that you arrived, and now today should I force you to wander with us, who knows where? Go on back and take your troops with you, and may the Lord be merciful to you."

15:19
1 Sam 23:13
Ruth 1:16

[21]But Ittai replied, "I vow by God and by your own life that wherever you go, I will go, no matter what happens—whether it means life or death."

[22]So David replied, "All right, come with us." Then Ittai and his six hundred men and their families went along.

[23]There was deep sadness throughout the city as the king and his retinue passed by, crossed Kidron Brook, and went out into the country. [24]Abiathar and Zadok and the Levites took the Ark of the Covenant of God and set it down beside the road until everyone had passed. [25, 26]Then, following David's instructions, Zadok took the Ark back into the city. "If the Lord sees fit," David said, "he will bring me back to see the Ark and the Tabernacle again. But if he is through with me, well, let him do what seems best to him."

15:23
1 Kgs 15:13
2 Chron 15:16
29:16

15:24
Num 4:15
1 Sam 4:4
2 Sam 8:17
20:25

15:25
1 Sam 3:18

15:27
2 Sam 17:17
18:19

[27]Then the king told Zadok, "Look, here is my plan. Return quietly to the city

---

ABSALOM'S REBELLION
Absalom crowned himself king in Hebron. David and his men fled from Jerusalem, crossed the Jordan, and went to Mahanaim. Absalom and his army followed, only to be defeated in the forest of Ephraim, where Absalom was killed.

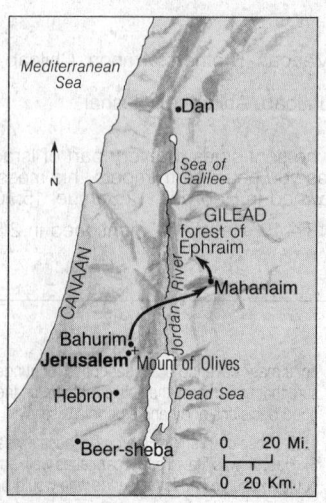

15:14 Had David not escaped from Jerusalem, the ensuing fight might have destroyed both him and the innocent inhabitants of the city. Some fights that we think necessary may be costly and destructive to those around us. In such cases, it may be wise to back down and save the fight for another day—even if doing so hurts our pride. It takes courage to stand and fight, but it also takes courage to back down when you must for the sake of others.

15:14 Why couldn't David just crush this rebellion? There were several reasons he chose to flee: (1) The rebellion was widespread (15:10–13), and would not have been easily suppressed; (2) David did not want the city of Jerusalem to be destroyed; (3) David still cared for his son and did not want to hurt him. We know that David expected to return to Jerusalem soon, because he left ten of his wives to keep the palace in order (15:16).

15:17, 18 David had many loyal non-Israelites in his armed forces. The Gittites from the Philistine city of Gath were apparently friends David had acquired while hiding from Saul. The Cherethites and Pelethites were also from Philistine territory. Although Israel was supposed to destroy wicked enemies, the nation was to welcome foreigners who came on friendly terms (Exodus 23:9; Deuteronomy 10:19) and to try to show them the importance of obeying God.

15:28
Judg 3:28; 7:4
12:5
2 Sam 17:16

with your son Ahima-az and Abiathar's son Jonathan. 28I will stop at the ford of the Jordan River and wait there for a message from you. Let me know what happens in Jerusalem before I disappear into the wilderness."

29So Zadok and Abiathar carried the Ark of God back into the city and stayed there.

15:30
Ezek 24:23

30David walked up the road that led to the Mount of Olives, weeping as he went. His head was covered and his feet were bare as a sign of mourning. And the people who were with him covered their heads and wept as they climbed the mountain.

15:31
2 Sam 15:12
16:23; 17:14,23

15:32
2 Sam 16:16
17:5

31When someone told David that Ahithophel, his advisor, was backing Absalom, David prayed, "O Lord, please make Ahithophel give Absalom foolish advice!" 32As they reached the spot at the top of the Mount of Olives where people worshiped God, David found Hushai the Archite waiting for him with torn clothing and earth upon his head.

15:33
2 Sam 16:19

15:35
2 Sam 16:15
17:15
1 Chron 27:33

33, 34But David told him, "If you go with me, you will only be a burden; return to Jerusalem and tell Absalom, 'I will counsel you as I did your father.' Then you can frustrate and counter Ahithophel's advice. 35, 36Zadok and Abiathar, the priests, are there. Tell them the plans that are being made to capture me, and they will send their sons Ahima-az and Jonathan to find me and tell me what is going on."

37So David's friend Hushai returned to the city, getting there just as Absalom arrived.

Ziba joins David

16:1
2 Sam 9:2

16 David was just past the top of the hill when Ziba, the manager of Mephibosheth's household, caught up with him. He was leading two donkeys loaded with two hundred loaves of bread, one hundred clusters of raisins, one hundred bunches of grapes, and a small barrel of wine.

16:2
Judg 5:10; 10:4
2 Sam 17:28

2"What are these for?" the king asked Ziba.

And Ziba replied, "The donkeys are for your people to ride on, and the bread and summer fruit are for the young men to eat; the wine is to be taken with you into the wilderness for any who become faint."

16:3
2 Sam 9:9
19:26,27

3"And where is Mephibosheth?" the king asked him.

"He stayed at Jerusalem," Ziba replied. "He said, 'Now I'll get to be king! Today I will get back the kingdom of my father, Saul.' "

HIGHS AND LOWS OF DAVID'S LIFE

The Bible calls David a man after God's own heart (Acts 13:22), but that didn't mean his life was free of troubles. David's life was full of highs and lows. Some of David's troubles were a result of his sins; some were a result of the sins of others. We can't always control our ups and downs, but we can trust God every day. We can be certain that he will help us through our trials, just as he helped David. In the end, he will reward us for our consistent faith.

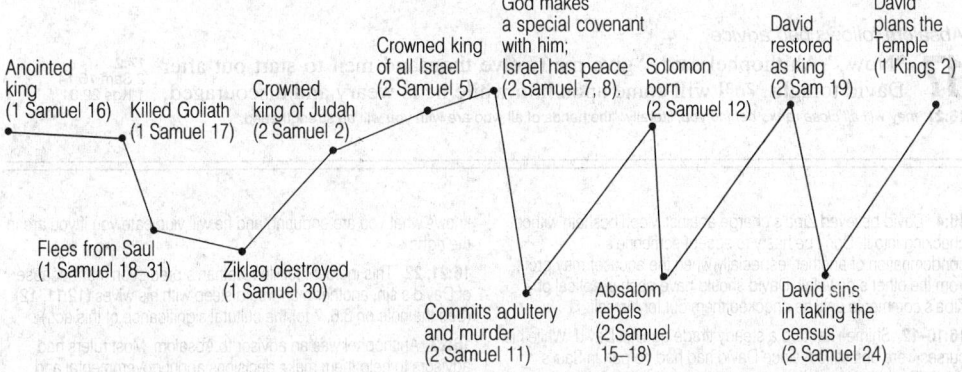

God makes a special covenant with him; Israel has peace (2 Samuel 7, 8).

Crowned king of all Israel (2 Samuel 5)

David restored as king (2 Sam 19)

David plans the Temple (1 Kings 2)

Anointed king (1 Samuel 16)

Killed Goliath (1 Samuel 17)

Crowned king of Judah (2 Samuel 2)

Solomon born (2 Samuel 12)

Flees from Saul (1 Samuel 18–31)

Ziklag destroyed (1 Samuel 30)

Commits adultery and murder (2 Samuel 11)

Absalom rebels (2 Samuel 15–18)

David sins in taking the census (2 Samuel 24)

16:3 King Saul was Mephibosheth's grandfather. Most likely Ziba was lying, hoping to receive a reward from David. (See 19:24–30 for Mephibosheth's side of the story.) Contrary to Ziba's report, Mephibosheth apparently remained loyal to David.

4"In that case," the king told Ziba, "I give you everything he owns."
"Thank you, thank you, sir," Ziba replied.

Shime-i curses David

5As David and his party passed Bahurim, a man came out of the village cursing them. It was Shime-i, the son of Gera, a member of Saul's family. 6He threw stones at the king and the king's officers and all the mighty warriors who surrounded them!

16:5
Ex 22:28
1 Sam 17:43
2 Sam 3:16
17:18; 19:16
1 Kgs 2:8

7, 8"Get out of here, you murderer, you scoundrel!" he shouted at David. "The Lord is paying you back for murdering King Saul and his family; you stole his throne and now the Lord has given it to your son Absalom! At last you will taste some of your own medicine, you murderer!"

16:7
2 Sam 12:9
21:1

9"Why should this dead dog curse my lord the king?" Abishai demanded. "Let me go over and strike off his head!"

16:9
Ex 22:28
1 Sam 26:8
2 Sam 19:21

10"No!" the king said. "If the Lord has told him to curse me, who am I to say no? 11My own son is trying to kill me, and this Benjaminite is merely cursing me. Let him alone, for no doubt the Lord has told him to do it. 12And perhaps the Lord will see that I am being wronged and will bless me because of these curses."

16:10
2 Sam 3:39
19:22
Jn 18:11
Rom 9:20

13So David and his men continued on, and Shime-i kept pace with them on a nearby hillside, cursing as he went and throwing stones at David and tossing dust into the air. 14The king and all those who were with him were weary by the time they reached Bahurim, so they stayed there awhile and rested.

16:11
Gen 45:5
1 Sam 26:19
2 Sam 12:11

16:12
Deut 23:5
Rom 8:28

Absalom seizes the throne

15Meanwhile, Absalom and his men arrived at Jerusalem, accompanied by Ahithophel. 16When David's friend, Hushai the Archite, arrived, he went immediately to see Absalom.

16:15
2 Sam 15:12,37

16:16
1 Sam 10:24
2 Sam 15:33
17:5
2 Kgs 11:12

"Long live the king!" he exclaimed. "Long live the king!"

17"Is this the way to treat your friend David?" Absalom asked him. "Why aren't you with him?"

18"Because I work for the man who is chosen by the Lord and by Israel," Hushai replied. 19"And anyway, why shouldn't I? I helped your father and now I will help you!"

16:19
2 Sam 15:33,34

20Then Absalom turned to Ahithophel and asked him, "What shall I do next?"

21Ahithophel told him, "Go and sleep with your father's wives, for he has left them here to keep the house. Then all Israel will know that you have insulted him beyond the possibility of reconciliation, and they will all close ranks behind you."

16:21
2 Sam 15:16

22So a tent was erected on the roof of the palace where everybody could see it, and Absalom went into the tent to lie with his father's wives. 23(Absalom did whatever Ahithophel told him to, just as David had; for every word Ahithophel spoke seemed as wise as though it had come directly from the mouth of God.)

16:22
2 Sam 12:11
20:3

16:23
2 Sam 15:12
17:14

Absalom follows bad advice

17 "Now," Ahithophel said, "give me twelve thousand men to start out after David tonight. 2, 3I will come upon him while he is weary and discouraged,

17:2
2 Sam 16:14
1 Kgs 22:31

16:21 *they will all close ranks behind you,* literally, "the hands of all who are with you will be strengthened."

16:4 David believed Ziba's charge against Mephibosheth without checking into it. Don't be hasty to accept someone's condemnation of another, especially when the accuser may profit from the other's downfall. David should have been skeptical of Ziba's comments until he checked them out for himself.

16:10–12 Shime-i kept up a steady tirade against David. While his curses were unjustified, since David had had no part in Saul's death, David and his followers quietly tolerated the abuse. Maintaining your composure in the face of unjustified criticism can be a trying experience and an emotional drain, but if you can't stop criticism, it is best just to ignore it. Like David, remember that God

knows what you are enduring and he will vindicate you if you are in the right.

16:21, 22 This incident fulfilled Nathan's prediction that because of David's sin, another man would sleep with his wives (12:11, 12). (See the note on 3:6, 7 for the cultural significance of this act.)

16:23 Ahithophel was an advisor to Absalom. Most rulers had advisors to help them make decisions about governmental and political matters. They probably arranged the king's marriages as well, since these were usually politically motivated unions. But God made Ahithophel give foolish advice to Absalom, just as David had prayed (15:31; 17:14).

and he and his troops will be thrown into a panic and everyone will run away; and I will kill only the king, and let all those who are with him live, and restore them to you."

17:5
2 Sam 15:33,
34; 16:16

4Absalom and all the elders of Israel approved of the plan, 5but Absalom said, "Ask Hushai the Archite what he thinks about this."

6When Hushai arrived, Absalom told him what Ahithophel had said.

"What is your opinion?" Absalom asked him. "Should we follow Ahithophel's advice? If not, speak up."

17:7
2 Sam 16:21
17:8
2 Kgs 2:24
Hos 13:8
17:9
1 Sam 22:2
23:19

7"Well," Hushai replied, "this time I think Ahithophel has made a mistake. 8You know your father and his men; they are mighty warriors and are probably as upset as a mother bear who has been robbed of her cubs. And your father is an old soldier and isn't going to be spending the night among the troops; 9he has probably already hidden in some pit or cave. And when he comes out and attacks and a few of your men fall, there will be panic among your troops and everyone will start shouting that your men are being slaughtered. 10Then even the bravest of them, though they have hearts of lions, will be paralyzed with fear; for all Israel knows what a mighty man your father is and how courageous his soldiers are.

17:11
1 Sam 3:20
2 Sam 3:9,10
1 Chron 21:2
17:13
Mic 1:6

11"What I suggest is that you mobilize the entire army of Israel, bringing them from as far away as Dan and Beer-sheba, so that you will have a huge force. And I think that you should personally lead the troops. 12Then when we find him we can destroy his entire army so that not one of them is left alive. 13And if David has escaped into some city, you will have the entire army of Israel there at your command, and we can take ropes and drag the walls of the city into the nearest valley until every stone is torn down."

17:14
2 Sam 15:33,
34; 16:23

14Then Absalom and all the men of Israel said, "Hushai's advice is better than Ahithophel's." For the Lord had arranged to defeat the counsel of Ahithophel, which really was the better plan, so that he could bring disaster upon Absalom!

17:15
2 Sam 15:35,36

15Then Hushai reported to Zadok and Abiathar, the priests, what Ahithophel had said and what he himself had suggested instead.

17:16
2 Sam 15:28
17:21

16"Quick!" he told them. "Find David and urge him not to stay at the ford of the Jordan River tonight. He must go across at once into the wilderness beyond; otherwise he will die, and his entire army with him."

17:17
Josh 15:7
2 Sam 15:27,35,
36; 18:19
17:18
2 Sam 16:5
19:16
17:19
Josh 2:4-6

17Jonathan and Ahima-az had been staying at En-rogel so as not to be seen entering and leaving the city. Arrangements had been made for a servant girl to carry to them the messages they were to take to King David. 18But a boy saw them leaving En-rogel to go to David, and he told Absalom about it. Meanwhile, they escaped to Bahurim where a man hid them inside a well in his backyard. 19The man's wife put a cloth over the top of the well with grain on it to dry in the sun; so no one suspected they were there.

17:20
Ex 1:19
Lev 19:11
1 Sam 19:14

20When Absalom's men arrived and asked her if she had seen Ahima-az and Jonathan, she said they had crossed the brook and were gone. They looked for them without success and returned to Jerusalem. 21Then the two men crawled out of the well and hurried on to King David. "Quick!" they told him, "cross the Jordan tonight!" And they told him how Ahithophel had advised that he be captured and killed. 22So David and all the people with him went across during the night and were all on the other bank before dawn.

17:23
1 Sam 31:4,5
2 Sam 15:1,2
1 Kgs 16:18
2 Kgs 20:1
Mt 27:5
17:24
2 Sam 2:8
19:31,32

23Meanwhile, Ahithophel—publicly disgraced when Absalom refused his advice—saddled his donkey, went to his home town, set his affairs in order, and hanged himself; so he died and was buried beside his father.

17:25
2 Sam 19:13
20:12
1 Kgs 2:5
1 Chron 2:16,17

24David soon arrived at Mahanaim. Meanwhile, Absalom had mobilized the entire army of Israel and was leading the men across the Jordan River. 25Absalom had appointed Amasa as general of the army, replacing Joab. (Amasa was Joab's second cousin; his father was Ithra, an Ishmaelite, and his mother was Abigail, the

---

17:11 Hushai appealed to Absalom through flattery, and Absalom's vanity became his own trap. Hushai predicted great glory for Absalom if he personally led the entire army against David. "Pride ends in destruction" (Proverbs 18:12) is an appropriate comment on Absalom's condition.

daughter of Nahash, who was the sister of Joab's mother Zeruiah.) 26Absalom and the Israeli army now camped in the land of Gilead.

27When David arrived at Mahanaim, he was warmly greeted by Shobi (son of Nahash of Rabbah, an Ammonite) and Machir (son of Ammiel of Lodebar) and Barzillai (a Gileadite of Rogelim). 28, 29They brought him and those who were with him mats to sleep on, cooking pots, serving bowls, wheat and barley flour, parched grain, beans, lentils, honey, butter, and cheese. For they said, "You must be very tired and hungry and thirsty after your long march through the wilderness."

17:27
2 Sam 9:4
10:1,2; 12:26
1 Kgs 2:7

17:28
2 Sam 16:2

Joab kills Absalom

18 David now appointed regimental colonels and company commanders over his troops. 2A third were placed under Joab's brother, Abishai (the son of Zeruiah); and a third under Ittai, the Gittite. The king planned to lead the army himself, but his men objected strongly.

18:1
Ex 18:25
1 Sam 8:12
22:7

3"You mustn't do it," they said, "for if we have to turn and run, and half of us die, it will make no difference to them—they will be looking only for you. You are worth ten thousand of us, and it is better that you stay here in the city and send us help if we need it."

18:2
1 Sam 11:11
2 Sam 15:19

18:3
2 Sam 17:2,3
21:17
1 Kgs 22:31

4"Well, whatever you think best," the king finally replied. So he stood at the gate of the city as all the troops passed by.

18:4
2 Sam 18:24

5And the king commanded Joab, Abishai, and Ittai, "For my sake, deal gently with young Absalom." And all the troops heard the king give them this charge.

6So the battle began in the forest of Ephraim, 7and the Israeli troops were beaten back by David's men. There was a great slaughter and twenty thousand men laid down their lives that day. 8The battle raged all across the countryside, and more men disappeared in the forest than were killed. 9During the battle Absalom came upon some of David's men and as he fled on his mule, it went beneath the thick boughs of a great oak tree, and his hair caught in the branches. His mule went on, leaving him dangling in the air. 10One of David's men saw him and told Joab.

18:6
Josh 17:15

18:7
2 Sam 2:17

18:9
2 Sam 14:26

11"What? You saw him there and didn't kill him?" Joab demanded. "I would have rewarded you handsomely and made you a commissioned officer."

18:11
2 Sam 3:27
11:15; 14:20

12"For a million dollars I wouldn't do it," the man replied. "We all heard the king say to you and Abishai and Ittai, 'For my sake, please don't harm young Absalom.' 13And if I had betrayed the king by killing his son (and the king would certainly find out who did it), you yourself would be the first to accuse me."

14"Enough of this nonsense," Joab said. Then he took three daggers and plunged them into the heart of Absalom as he dangled alive from the oak. 15Ten of Joab's young armor bearers then surrounded Absalom and finished him off. 16Then Joab blew the trumpet, and his men returned from chasing the army of Israel. 17They threw Absalom's body into a deep pit in the forest and piled a great heap of stones over it. And the army of Israel fled to their homes.

18:16
2 Sam 2:28
20:22

18(Absalom had built a monument to himself in the King's Valley, for he said, "I have no sons to carry on my name." He called it "Absalom's Monument," as it is still known today.)

18:18
1 Sam 15:12
2 Sam 14:27

David mourns Absalom's death

19Then Zadok's son Ahima-az said, "Let me run to King David with the good news that the Lord has saved him from his enemy Absalom."

18:19
2 Sam 15:35,
36; 17:17

20"No," Joab told him, "it wouldn't be good news to the king that his son is dead. You can be my messenger some other time."

21Then Joab said to a man from Cush, "Go tell the king what you have seen." The man bowed and ran off.

18:9 *as he fled,* implied. **18:11** *made you a commissioned officer,* literally, "given you ten pieces of silver and a belt." There is no way of knowing the value of the silver. The belt was probably that worn by a commissioned officer.

18:1 David took command as he had in former days. In the later years, his life had been characterized by indecisiveness and moral paralysis. Now he began to take charge and do his duty.

18:21–23 Joab wanted the Cushite to bring the news of Absalom's death, not Ahima-az. Joab may have been afraid David would react violently to the dreadful news (see 1:15; 4:12).

REBELLION

The Bible records many rebellions. Many were against God's chosen leaders. They were doomed for failure. Others were begun by wicked men against wicked men. While these were sometimes successful, the rebel's life usually came to a violent end. Still other rebellions were made by good people against the wicked or unjust actions of others. This kind of rebellion is sometimes good in freeing the common people from oppression and giving them the freedom to turn back to God.

Who rebelled?	Who they rebelled against	What happened	Reference
Adam and Eve	God	Expelled from Eden	Genesis 3
Israelites	God, Moses	Forced to wander in desert for 40 years	Numbers 14
Korah	Moses	Swallowed by the earth	Numbers 16
Israelites	God	God took away his special promise of protection	Judges 2
Absalom (David's son)	David	Killed in battle	2 Samuel 15—18
Sheba	David	Killed in battle	2 Samuel 20
Adonijah (David's son)	David, Solomon	Killed for treason	1 Kings 1, 2
Joab	David, Solomon	Supported Adonijah's kingship without seeking God's choice. Killed for treason	1 Kings 1, 2
Ten Tribes of Israel	Rehoboam	The kingdom was divided. The ten tribes forgot about God, became wicked, and were eventually taken into captivity	1 Kings 12:16—20
Baasha, king of Israel	Nadab, king of Israel	Overthrew the throne and became king. God destroyed his descendants	1 Kings 15:27—16:7
Zimri, king of Israel	Elah, king of Israel	Overthrew the throne, but killed himself when his rule was not accepted	1 Kings 16:8—16
Jehu, king of Israel	Joram, king of Israel; Ahaziah, king of Judah	Killed both kings. Later turned from God and his dynasty was wiped out	2 Kings 9, 10
Joash, king of Judah; Jehoida, a priest	Athaliah, queen of Judah	Athaliah, a wicked queen was overthrown. This was a "good" rebellion	2 Kings 11
Shallum, king of Israel	Zechariah, king of Israel	Overthrew the throne, but was assassinated in return	2 Kings 15:8—15
Menahem, king of Israel	Shallum, king of Israel	Overthrew the throne, but then invaded by Assyrian army	2 Kings 15:17—22
Hoshea, king of Israel	Assyria	The city of Samaria was destroyed, the nation of Israel taken into captivity	2 Kings 17
Zedekiah, king of Judah	Nebuchadnezzar, king of Babylon	The city of Jerusalem destroyed, the nation of Judah taken into captivity	2 Kings 24, 25

22But Ahima-az pleaded with Joab, "Please let me go, too."

"No, we don't need you now, my boy." Joab replied. "There is no further news to send."

23"Yes, but let me go anyway," he begged.

And Joab finally said, "All right, go ahead." Then Ahima-az took a short cut across the plain and got there ahead of the man from Cush. 24David was sitting at the gate of the city. When the watchman climbed the stairs to his post at the top of the wall, he saw a lone man running towards them.

18:24
2 Sam 13:34
18:4; 19:8-10
2 Kgs 9:17

25He shouted the news down to David, and the king replied, "If he is alone, he has news."

As the messenger came closer, 26the watchman saw another man running towards them. He shouted down, "Here comes another one."

And the king replied, "He will have more news."

27"The first man looks like Ahima-az, the son of Zadok," the watchman said. "He is a good man and comes with good news," the king replied.

18:27
1 Kgs 1:42

28Then Ahima-az cried out to the king, "All is well!" He bowed low with his face to the ground and said, "Blessed be the Lord your God who has destroyed the rebels who dared to stand against you."

18:28
1 Sam 17:46
25:23

29"What of young Absalom?" the king demanded. "Is he all right?"

"When Joab told me to come, there was a lot of shouting; but I didn't know what was happening," Ahima-az answered.

30"Wait here," the king told him. So Ahima-az stepped aside.

31Then the man from Cush arrived and said, "I have good news for my lord the king. Today Jehovah has rescued you from all those who rebelled against you."

18:31
Judg 5:31

32"What about young Absalom? Is he all right?" the king demanded.

And the man replied, "May all of your enemies be as that young man is!"

33Then the king broke into tears, and went up to his room over the gate, crying as he went. "O my son Absalom, my son, my son Absalom. If only I could have died for you! O Absalom, my son, my son."

18:33
2 Sam 19:4
Rom 9:1-3

Joab scolds David

19 Word soon reached Joab that the king was weeping and mourning for Absalom. 2As the people heard of the king's deep grief for his son, the joy of that day's wonderful victory was turned into deep sadness. 3The entire army crept back into the city as though they were ashamed and had been beaten in battle.

19:1
2 Sam 18:5,14

4The king covered his face with his hands and kept on weeping, "O my son Absalom! O Absalom my son, my son!"

19:4
2 Sam 15:30
18:33

5Then Joab went to the king's room and said to him, "We saved your life today and the lives of your sons, your daughters, your wives and concubines; and yet you act like this, making us feel ashamed, as though we had done something wrong. 6You seem to love those who hate you, and hate those who love you. Apparently we don't mean anything to you; if Absalom had lived and all of us had died, you would be happy. 7Now go out there and congratulate the troops, for I swear by Jehovah that if you don't, not a single one of them will remain here during the night; then you will be worse off than you have ever been in your entire life."

19:5
2 Sam 3:39
20:8-10

18:29 Although he reached the city first, Ahima-az was afraid to tell the king the truth about the death of his son Absalom.

18:33 Why was David so upset over the death of his rebel son? (1) David realized that he, in part, was responsible for Absalom's death. Nathan, the prophet, had said that because David had killed Uriah, his own sons would rebel against him. (2) David was angry at Joab and his officers for killing Absalom against his wishes. (3) David truly loved his son. Absalom did nothing to deserve David's love. Just as God bestows undeserved grace upon us, David was gracious to Absalom.

19:4-7 At times we must reprove those in authority over us. Joab knew he was risking the king's displeasure by confronting him, but he saw what had to be done. Joab told David that there would be dreadful consequences if he didn't commend the troops for their victory. Joab's actions are a helpful example to us when we must reprove those in authority over us.

19:8-10 Just a few days before, Absalom had turned the hearts of Israel away from David. Now the people wanted David back as their king. Because crowds are known to be fickle, there must be a higher moral code to follow than the pleasure of the majority. Following the moral principles given in God's Word will help you avoid being swayed by the popular opinions of the crowd.

David returns to Jerusalem

19:8
2 Sam 8:1
15:2; 18:24

8, 9, 10So the king went out and sat at the city gates, and as the news spread throughout the city that he was there, everyone went to him.

Meanwhile, there was much discussion and argument going on all across the nation: "Why aren't we talking about bringing the king back?" was the great topic everywhere. "For he saved us from our enemies, the Philistines; and Absalom, whom we made our king instead, chased him out of the country, but now Absalom is dead. Let's ask David to return and be our king again."

Joab, the great military leader, had two brothers who were also famous soldiers: Abishai and Asahel. Joab proved to be the greatest leader of the three, and was the commander of David's army throughout most of David's reign. There is no record that his troops ever lost a battle.

Joab was a fearless fighter like his brothers. But, unlike them, he was also a brilliant and ruthless strategist. His plans usually worked, but he was seldom concerned about those hurt or killed by them. He did not hesitate to use treachery or murder to accomplish his goals. His career is a story of great accomplishments and shameful acts. He conquered Jerusalem and the surrounding nations, defeated Abner, and reconciled Absalom and David. But he also murdered Abner, Amasa, and Absalom, took part in Uriah's murder, and plotted with Adonijah against Solomon. That plot led to his execution.

Joab set his own standards—he lived by them, and died because of them. There is little evidence that Joab ever acknowledged God's standards. On one occasion he confronted David about the danger of taking a census without God's command, but this may have been little more than a move to protect himself. Joab's self-centeredness eventually destroyed him. He was loyal only to himself, even willing to betray his lifelong relationship with David to preserve his power.

Joab's life illustrates the disastrous results of having no source of direction outside of oneself. Brilliance and power are self-destructive without God's guidance. Only God can give the direction we need. For that reason, he has made available his Word, the Bible, and he is willing to be personally present in the lives of those who will admit their need for him.

Strengths and accomplishments:
● Brilliant planner and strategist
● Fearless fighter and resourceful commander
● Confident leader who did not hesitate to confront even the king
● Helped to reconcile David and Absalom

Weaknesses and mistakes:
● Repeatedly showed himself to be a ruthless, violent, vengeful man
● Carried out David's scheme to have Uriah, Bath-sheba's husband, killed
● Avenged his brother's death by murdering Abner
● Killed Absalom against David's orders
● Plotted with Adonijah against David and Solomon

Lessons from his life:
● Those who live by violence often die by violence
● Even brilliant leaders need guidance

Vital statistics:
● Occupation: Commander-in-chief of David's army
● Relatives: Mother: Zeruiah. Brothers: Abishai, Asahel. Uncle: David.
● Contemporaries: Saul, Abner, Absalom

Key verses:
"Then Jehovah will hold him personally responsible for the murders of two men who were better than he. For my father was no party to the deaths of General Abner, commander-in-chief of the army of Israel, and General Amasa, commander-in-chief of the army of Judah. May Joab and his descendants be forever guilty of these murders, and may the Lord declare David and his descendants guiltless concerning their deaths" (1 Kings 2:32, 33).

Joab's story is told in 1 Samuel 22—1 Kings 2. He is also mentioned in 1 Chronicles 2:16; 11:5–39; 19:8–10; 20:1; 21:2–6; 26:28, and in the title of Psalm 60.

^{11, 12}Then David sent Zadok and Abiathar the priests to say to the elders of Judah, "Why are you the last ones to reinstate the king? For all Israel is ready, and only you are holding out. Yet you are my own brothers, my own tribe, my own flesh and blood!"

¹³And he told them to tell Amasa, "Since you are my nephew, may God strike me dead if I do not appoint you as commander-in-chief of my army in place of Joab." ¹⁴Then Amasa convinced all the leaders of Judah, and they responded as one man. They sent word to the king, "Return to us and bring back all those who are with you."

¹⁵So the king started back to Jerusalem. And when he arrived at the Jordan River, it seemed as if everyone in Judah had come to Gilgal to meet him and escort him across the river! ¹⁶Then Shime-i (the son of Gera the Benjaminite), the man from Bahurim, hurried across with the men of Judah to welcome King David. ¹⁷A thousand men from the tribe of Benjamin were with him, including Ziba, the servant of Saul, and Ziba's fifteen sons and twenty servants; they rushed down to the Jordan to arrive ahead of the king. ¹⁸They all worked hard ferrying the king's household and troops across, and helped them in every way they could.

As the king was crossing, Shime-i fell down before him, ¹⁹and pleaded, "My lord the king, please forgive me and forget the terrible thing I did when you left Jerusalem; ²⁰for I know very well how much I sinned. That is why I have come here today, the very first person in all the tribe of Joseph to greet you."

²¹Abishai asked, "Shall not Shime-i die, for he cursed the Lord's chosen king!"

²²"Don't talk to me like that!" David exclaimed. "This is not a day for execution but for celebration! I am once more king of Israel!"

²³Then, turning to Shime-i, he vowed, "Your life is spared."

^{24, 25}Now Mephibosheth, Saul's grandson, arrived from Jerusalem to meet the king. He had not washed his feet or clothes nor trimmed his beard since the day the king left Jerusalem.

"Why didn't you come with me, Mephibosheth?" the king asked him.

²⁶And he replied, "My lord, O king, my servant Ziba deceived me. I told him, 'Saddle my donkey so that I can go with the king.' For as you know I am lame. ²⁷But Ziba has slandered me by saying that I refused to come. But I know that you are as an angel of God, so do what you think best. ²⁸I and all my relatives could expect only death from you, but instead you have honored me among all those who eat at your own table! So how can I complain?"

²⁹"All right," David replied. "My decision is that you and Ziba will divide the land equally between you."

³⁰"Give him all of it," Mephibosheth said. "I am content just to have you back again!"

^{31, 32}Barzillai, who had fed the king and his army during their exile in Mahanaim, arrived from Rogelim to conduct the king across the river. He was very old now, about eighty, and very wealthy.

³³"Come across with me and live in Jerusalem," the king said to Barzillai. "I will take care of you there."

19:27 *saying that I refused to come,* implied.

19:11	2 Sam 5:1
19:13	2 Sam 8:16; 17:25; 20:23; 1 Chron 2:16,17
19:15	Josh 5:8,9; 1 Sam 11:14
19:16	2 Sam 16:5; 1 Kgs 2:8
19:17	2 Sam 9:2; 16:1
19:19	1 Sam 26:21; 2 Sam 16:6-9; 1 Kgs 1:31
19:21	Ex 22:28; 1 Sam 24:6; 1 Kgs 21:10
19:22	1 Sam 11:13; 2 Sam 3:39
19:23	1 Kgs 2:8
19:24	2 Sam 9:5,6; 21:7
19:26	2 Sam 9:3,13
19:27	2 Sam 14:17, 20; 16:3,4
19:28	2 Sam 9:7, 10,13
19:31	2 Sam 17:27; 1 Kgs 2:7

19:11-13 Why was the tribe of Judah hesitant to bring David back as king? Apparently the elders of Judah had consented to Absalom's rebellion. It is not surprising that leaders who had backed Absalom would hesitate before inviting David back.

David's appointment of Amasa was a shrewd political move. First, Amasa had been commander of Absalom's army; by making Amasa his commander, David would secure the allegiance of the rebel army. Second, by replacing Joab as commander-in-chief, David punished him for his previous crimes (3:26–29). Third, Amasa had a great deal of influence over the leaders of Judah (19:14). All of these moves would help to unite the kingdom.

19:19, 20 By admitting his wrong and asking David's forgiveness, Shime-i was trying to save his own life. His plan worked for a while. But we read in 1 Kings 2:8, 9 that David advised Solomon to execute Shime-i.

19:21ff David showed tremendous mercy and generosity in his return to Jerusalem. He spared Shime-i, restored Mephibosheth, and rewarded faithful Barzillai. David's fairness sets a standard for government that will be fully realized in Christ's righteous rule in the coming kingdom.

19:24-30 David could not be certain if Mephibosheth or Ziba was in the right, and Scripture leaves the question unanswered. (For the whole story on Mephibosheth, see 9:1–13, 16:1–4, and 19:24–30.)

19:35
Ps 90:10,13

19:37
1 Kgs 2:7

19:39
Gen 31:55
Ruth 1:14
2 Sam 14:33

19:43
2 Sam 5:1

20:1
1 Sam 16:7,8
1 Kgs 12:16
2 Chron 10:16

20:2
2 Sam 19:15,41

20:3
2 Sam 15:16
16:21,22

20:4
2 Sam 17:25
19:13

20:6
2 Sam 18:2,12
21:7

20:7
2 Sam 8:18
15:17,18
1 Kgs 1:38

20:8
2 Sam 2:13
3:27
1 Kgs 2:5
Mt 26:49

34"No," he replied, "I am far too old for that. 35I am eighty years old today, and life has lost its excitement. Food and wine are no longer tasty, and entertainment is not much fun; I would only be a burden to my lord the king. 36Just to go across the river with you is all the honor I need! 37Then let me return again to die in my own city, where my father and mother are buried. But here is Chimham. Let him go with you and receive whatever good things you want to give him."

38"Good," the king agreed. "Chimham shall go with me, and I will do for him whatever I would have done for you."

39So all the people crossed the Jordan with the king; and after David had kissed and blessed Barzillai, he returned home. 40The king then went on to Gilgal, taking Chimham with him. And most of Judah and half of Israel were there to greet him. 41But the men of Israel complained to the king because only men from Judah had ferried him and his household across the Jordan.

42"Why not?" the men of Judah replied. "The king is one of our own tribe. Why should this make you angry? We have charged him nothing—he hasn't fed us or given us gifts!"

43"But there are ten tribes in Israel," the others replied, "so we have ten times as much right in the king as you do; why didn't you invite the rest of us? And, remember, we were the first to speak of bringing him back to be our king again."

The argument continued back and forth, and the men of Judah were very rough in their replies.

Sheba rebels against David

20 Then a hot-head whose name was Sheba (son of Bichri, a Benjaminite) blew a trumpet and yelled, "We want nothing to do with David. Come on, you men of Israel, let's get out of here. He's not our king!"

2So all except Judah and Benjamin turned around and deserted David and followed Sheba! But the men of Judah stayed with their king, accompanying him from the Jordan to Jerusalem. 3When he arrived at his palace in Jerusalem, the king instructed that his ten wives he had left to keep house should be placed in seclusion. Their needs were to be cared for, he said, but he would no longer sleep with them as his wives. So they remained in virtual widowhood until their deaths.

4Then the king instructed Amasa to mobilize the army of Judah within three days and to report back at that time. 5So Amasa went out to notify the troops, but it took him longer than the three days he had been given.

6Then David said to Abishai, "That fellow Sheba is going to hurt us more than Absalom did. Quick, take my bodyguard and chase after him before he gets into a fortified city where we can't reach him."

7So Abishai and Joab set out after Sheba with an elite guard from Joab's army and the king's own bodyguard. 8, 9, 10As they arrived at the great stone in Gibeon, they came face to face with Amasa. Joab was wearing his uniform with a dagger strapped to his side. As he stepped forward to greet Amasa, he stealthily slipped the dagger from its sheath. "I'm glad to see you, my brother," Joab said, and took him by the beard with his right hand as though to kiss him. Amasa didn't notice the dagger in his left hand, and Joab stabbed him in the stomach with it, so that his bowels gushed out onto the ground. He did not need to strike again, and he died there. Joab and his brother Abishai left him lying there and continued after Sheba.

19:35 *life has lost its excitement,* literally, "can I discern between good and bad?" **19:37** *Chimham.* According to Josephus, Chimham was Barzillai's son.

19:41–43 Although Israel was a united kingdom, it was still made up of 12 separate tribes. These tribes often had difficulty agreeing on the goals of the nation as a whole. Tribal jealousies had originally kept Israel from completely conquering the Promised Land (read the book of Joshua), and now tribal jealousies were threatening the stability of David's reign by giving Sheba an opportunity to rebel.

20:7–10 Once again Joab's murderous treachery went unpunished, just as it did when he killed Abner (3:26, 27). Eventually, however, justice caught up with him (1 Kings 2:28–35). It may seem that sin and treachery often go unpunished, but God's justice is not limited to this life's rewards. Even if Joab had died of old age, he would have to face the Judgment.

¹¹One of Joab's young officers shouted to Amasa's troops, "If you are for David, come and follow Joab."

¹²But Amasa lay in his blood in the middle of the road, and when Joab's young officers saw that a crowd was gathering around to stare at him, they dragged him off the road into a field and threw a garment over him. ¹³With the body out of the way, everyone went on with Joab to capture Sheba.

¹⁴Meanwhile Sheba had traveled across Israel to mobilize his own clan of Bichri at the city of Abel in Beth-maacah. ¹⁵When Joab's forces arrived, they besieged Abel and built a mound to the top of the city wall and began battering it down. ¹⁶But a wise woman in the city called out to Joab, "Listen to me, Joab. Come over here so I can talk to you."

20:15
2 Kgs 19:32
Ezek 4:2

¹⁷As he approached, the woman asked, "Are you Joab?"

And he replied, "I am."

¹⁸So she told him, "There used to be a saying, 'If you want to settle an argument, ask advice at Abel.' For we always give wise counsel. ¹⁹You are destroying an ancient, peace-loving city, loyal to Israel. Should you destroy what is the Lord's?"

20:19
Deut 20:10
2 Sam 14:15,16

²⁰And Joab replied, "That isn't it at all. ²¹All I want is a man named Sheba from the hill country of Ephraim, who has revolted against King David. If you will deliver him to me, we will leave the city in peace."

20:21
Josh 24:33
2 Sam 20:2

"All right," the woman replied, "we will throw his head over the wall to you."

²²Then the woman went to the people with her wise advice, and they cut off Sheba's head and threw it out to Joab. And he blew the trumpet and called his troops back from the attack, and they returned to the king at Jerusalem.

20:22
2 Sam 2:28
8:16

²³Joab was commander-in-chief of the army, and Benaiah was in charge of the king's bodyguard. ²⁴Adoram was in charge of the forced labor battalions, and Jehoshaphat was the historian who kept the records. ²⁵Sheva was the secretary, and Zadok and Abiathar were the chief priests. ²⁶Ira the Jairite was David's personal chaplain.

20:24
1 Kgs 12:18

20:26
2 Sam 23:34

4. The later years of David's rule
The execution of Saul's sons

21 There was a famine during David's reign that lasted year after year for three years, and David spent much time in prayer about it. Then the Lord said,

21:1
Gen 12:10
26:1; 42:5

20:23 *the king's bodyguard,* literally, "the Cherithites and Pelethites."

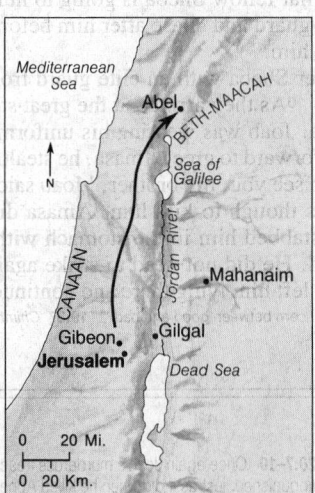

SHEBA'S REBELLION
After defeating Absalom, David returned to Jerusalem from Mahanaim. But Sheba incited a rebellion against David. So David sent Joab, Abishai, and a small army after him. Joab and his troops beseiged Abel, Sheba's hideout, until the people of Abel killed Sheba themselves.

Map labels: Mediterranean Sea; Abel; BETH-MAACAH; Sea of Galilee; CANAAN; Jordan River; Mahanaim; Gibeon; Gilgal; Jerusalem; Dead Sea; N; 0 20 Mi.; 0 20 Km.

quiet in public, this woman spoke out. She stopped Joab's attack not with weapons, but with wise words and a plan of action. Sometimes the courage to speak a few sensible words can prevent great disaster.

20:23 Benaiah was the captain of King David's bodyguard and a famous member of that special group of mighty men called "The Thirty" (23:24–39). He remained loyal to David during Absalom's rebellion. Later he helped establish Solomon as king (1 Kings 1:32–40; 2:28–34) and eventually replaced Joab as commander of Israel's army (1 Kings 2:35).

21:1ff The next four chapters are an appendix to the book. The events described are not presented in chronological order. They tell of David's exploits at various times during his reign.

21:1 Farmers relied heavily on spring and fall rains for their crops. If the rains stopped or came at the wrong time, or if the plants became insect-infested, drastic food shortages could occur in the coming year. Agriculture at that time was completely dependent upon natural conditions. There were no irrigation methods, fertilizers, or pesticides. Even moderate variations in rainfall or insect activity could destroy an entire harvest.

21:1–14 Although the Bible does not record Saul's act of vengeance against the Gibeonites, it was apparently a serious crime. Still, why were Saul's sons killed for the murders their father committed? In many Near Eastern cultures, including Israel's, an entire family was held guilty for the crime of the father because the family was considered an indissoluble unit. Saul broke the vow

20:16ff Joab's men were attacking the city, and it looked as if it would be destroyed. Though women in that society were usually

"The famine is because of the guilt of Saul and his family, for they murdered the Gibeonites."

21:2
Ex 34:11
Josh 9:15-20
1 Sam 7:14

²So King David summoned the Gibeonites. They were not part of Israel, but were what was left of the nation of the Amorites. Israel had sworn not to kill them; but Saul, in his nationalistic zeal, had tried to wipe them out.

³David asked them, "What can I do for you, to rid ourselves of this guilt and to induce you to ask God to bless us?"

21:4
Num 35:31

⁴"Well, money won't do it," the Gibeonites replied, "and we don't want to see Israelites executed in revenge."

"What can I do, then?" David asked. "Just tell me and I will do it for you."

21:5
Num 25:4
2 Sam 21:1

⁵, ⁶"Well, then," they replied, "give us seven of Saul's sons—the sons of the man who did his best to destroy us. We will hang them before the Lord in Gibeon, the city of King Saul."

"All right," the king said, "I will do it."

21:7
1 Sam 18:1-3
20:14,15; 23:18
2 Sam 4:4

⁷He spared Jonathan's son Mephibosheth, who was Saul's grandson, because of the oath between himself and Jonathan. ⁸But he gave them Saul's two sons Armoni and Mephibosheth, whose mother was Rizpah, the daughter of Aiah. He also gave them the five adopted sons of Michal that she brought up for Saul's daughter Merab, the wife of Adri-el. ⁹The men of Gibeon impaled them in the mountain

21:8
1 Sam 18:19
2 Sam 3:7

ABISHAI

Most great leaders struggle with a few followers who try too hard. For David, Abishai was that kind of follower. His fierce loyalty to David had to be kept from becoming destructive—he was too willing to leap to his leader's defense. David never put down Abishai's eager loyalty. Instead, he patiently tried to direct its powerful energy. This approach, while not completely successful, saved David's life on at least one occasion. On at least three other occasions, however, Abishai would have killed for the king if David had not stopped him.

Abishai was an excellent soldier, but he was better at taking orders than giving them. When he wasn't carrying out David's orders, Abishai was usually under the command of his younger brother Joab. The two brothers helped each other accomplish great military feats as well as shameful acts of violence—Abishai helped Joab murder Abner and Amasa. When he was an effective leader, he led mostly by example. But all too often he did not think before he acted.

We should be challenged by Abishai's admirable qualities of fearlessness and loyalty; we should also avoid his tendency to act without thinking. It is not enough to be strong and effective, we must also have the self-control and wisdom that God can give us. We are to follow and obey with our hearts and our minds.

Strengths and accomplishments:
- Known as one of the heroes among David's fighting men
- A fearless and willing volunteer, fiercely loyal to David
- Saved David's life

Weaknesses and mistakes:
- Tended to act without thinking
- Helped Joab murder Abner and Amasa

Lessons from his life:
- The most effective followers combine careful thought and action
- Blind loyalty can cause great evil

Vital statistics:
- Occupation: Soldier
- Relatives: Mother: Zeruiah. Brothers: Joab and Asahel. Uncle: David.

Key verses:
"Of those three men, Abishai, the brother of Joab (son of Zeruiah), was the greatest. Once he took on three hundred of the enemy singlehanded and killed them all. It was by such feats that he earned a reputation equal to The Three, though he was not actually one of them. But he was the greatest of The Thirty—the top-ranking officers of the army—and was their leader" (2 Samuel 23:18, 19).

Abishai's story is told in 2 Samuel 2:18—23:19. He is also mentioned in 1 Samuel 26:1–13; 1 Chronicles 2:16; 11:20; 18:12; 19:11, 15.

---

which the Israelites made to the Gibeonites (Joshua 9:16–20). This was a serious offense against God's law (Numbers 30:1, 2).

21:9, 10 Rizpah guarded the men's bodies during the entire harvest season, which lasted from April to October.

before the Lord. So all seven of them died together at the beginning of the barley harvest.

10Then Rizpah, the mother of two of the men, spread sackcloth upon a rock and stayed there through the entire harvest season to prevent the vultures from tearing at their bodies during the day and the wild animals from eating them at night. 11When David learned what she had done, 12, 13, 14he arranged for the men's bones to be buried in the grave of Saul's father, Kish. At the same time he sent a request to the men of Jabesh-gilead, asking them to bring him the bones of Saul and Jonathan. They had stolen their bodies from the public square at Beth-shan where the Philistines had impaled them after they had died in battle on Mount Gilboa. So their bones were brought to him. Then at last God answered prayer and ended the famine.

21:10
Deut 21:23
1 Sam 17:44

21:12
2 Sam 2:4,5
24:25

Giants killed by David's men

15Once when the Philistines were at war with Israel, and David and his men were in the thick of the battle, David became weak and exhausted. 16Ishbi-benob, a giant whose speartip weighed more than twelve pounds and who was sporting a new suit of armor, closed in on David and was about to kill him. 17But Abishai the son of Zeruiah came to his rescue and killed the Philistine. After that David's men declared, "You are not going out to battle again! Why should we risk snuffing out the light of Israel?"

21:15
2 Sam 5:17
21:16
Num 13:28
Deut 1:28
21:17
2 Sam 18:2
20:6

18Later, during a war with the Philistines at Gob, Sibbecai the Hushathite killed Saph, another giant. 19At still another time and at the same place, Elhanan killed the brother of Goliath the Gittite, whose spearhandle was as huge as a weaver's beam! 20, 21And once when the Philistines and the Israelis were fighting at Gath, a giant with six fingers on each hand and six toes on each foot defied Israel, and David's nephew Jonathan—the son of David's brother Shime-i—killed him. 22These four were from the tribe of giants in Gath, and were killed by David's troops.

21:18
1 Chron 11:29
20:4-8; 27:11
21:19
1 Sam 17:4-7

21:22
1 Chron 20:8

David's song of praise

22 David sang this song to the Lord after he had rescued him from Saul and from all his other enemies:

22:1
Ex 15:1
Deut 31:30
Judg 5:1
Ps 18 Title

2"Jehovah is my rock,
My fortress and my Savior.
3I will hide in God,
Who is my rock and my refuge.
He is my shield
And my salvation,
My refuge and high tower.
Thank you, O my Savior,
For saving me from all my enemies.
4I will call upon the Lord,
Who is worthy to be praised;
He will save me from all my enemies.
5The waves of death surrounded me;
Floods of evil burst upon me;
6I was trapped, and bound
By hell and death;
7But I called upon the Lord in my distress,

22:2
Deut 32:4
1 Sam 2:2
Ps 31:3; 71:3

22:3
Gen 15:1
Deut 33:29
Ps 3:3; 9:9
Lk 1:69

22:4
Ps 66:2,3; 96:4

22:5
Ps 69:14; 93:4
Jonah 2:3
22:6
Ps 116:3,4

21:19 the brother of Goliath the Gittite, literally, "slew Goliath of Gath." (See 1 Chron 20:5.)

21:18 For more information on Goliath and giants, see 1 Samuel 17:4–7 and the note on Genesis 6:4.

22:1ff David was a skilled musician who played his harp for King Saul (1 Samuel 16:23), instituted the music programs in the Temple (1 Chronicles 25), and wrote more of the book of Psalms than anyone else. Writing a song like this was not unusual for David. This royal hymn of thanksgiving is almost identical to Psalm 18. (For other songs in the Bible, see the chart in Exodus 15.)

And he heard me from his Temple.
My cry reached his ears.

22:8
Judg 5:4
Job 26:11
Ps 97:4

8Then the earth shook and trembled;
The foundations of the heavens quaked
Because of his wrath.

22:9
Ex 15:7; 19:18
Deut 32:22
Heb 12:29

9Smoke poured from his nostrils;
Fire leaped from his mouth
And burned up all before him,
Setting fire to the world.

22:10
Ex 20:21
1 Kgs 8:12,13
Ps 97:2
Nah 1:3

10He bent the heavens down and came to earth;
He walked upon dark clouds.

11He rode upon the glorious—
On the wings of the wind.

22:11
Ps 68:17,18

22:12
Ps 18:11,12
97:2

12Darkness surrounded him,
And clouds were thick around him;
13The earth was radiant with his brightness.

22:14
Ex 19:19
Job 37:2
Ps 29:3

14The Lord thundered from heaven;
The God above all gods gave out a mighty shout.

22:15
Deut 32:23
Josh 10:10
1 Sam 7:10

15He shot forth his arrows of lightning
And routed his enemies.

22:16
Ex 15:8
Nah 1:4

16By the blast of his breath
Was the sea split in two.
The bottom of the sea appeared.

22:17
Ps 144:7

17From above, he rescued me.
He drew me out from the waters;

22:18
Ps 23:4

18He saved me from powerful enemies,
From those who hated me
And from those who were too strong for me.

19They came upon me
In the day of my calamity,
But the Lord was my salvation.

22:20
2 Sam 4:9
1 Kgs 1:29
Ps 31:8; 118:5

20He set me free and rescued me,
For I was his delight.

22:21
1 Sam 26:23
Ps 24:5; 128:1

21The Lord rewarded me for my goodness,
For my hands were clean;
22And I have not departed from my God.

22:23
Deut 6:6
Ps 119:6

23I knew his laws,
And I obeyed them.

22:24
Gen 6:9,10; 7:1
Job 1:8; 9:20

24I was perfect in obedience
And kept myself from sin.

22:25
Isa 3:10

25That is why the Lord has done so much for me,
For he sees that I am clean.

22:9 *setting fire to the world,* literally, "coals were kindled by it."

David reveals many truths about God in his song of praise	*David says, "God is my . . ."*	Rock, Fortress, Savior, Refuge, Shield, Salvation, High Tower, Light
	David names these characteristics of God. He is:	Saving, Worthy of Praise, Hearing, Wrathful (against enemies), Rescuing, Rewarding, Seeing, Merciful, Showing (revealing) himself, Destroying (evil), Powerful, Strong, Perfect, True, Shielding (us from enemies), Giving, Gentle, Preserving, Living, Delivering

---

22:22-24 David was not saying that he had never sinned. Psalm 51 shows his tremendous anguish over his sin against Uriah and Bath-sheba. But David understood God's faithfulness and was writing this hymn from God's perspective. He knew that God had made him clean again—"whiter than snow," (Psalm 51:7) with a

"new, clean heart" (Psalm 51:10). Through the death and resurrection of Jesus Christ, we also are made clean and perfect. Our sin is replaced with his purity and forgiveness, and God no longer sees our sin.

26You are merciful to the merciful;
You show your perfections
To the blameless.
27To those who are pure,
You show yourself pure;
But you destroy those who are evil.
28You will save those in trouble,
But you bring down the haughty;
For you watch their every move.
29O Lord, you are my light!
You make my darkness bright.
30By your power I can crush an army;
By your strength I leap over a wall.
31As for God, his way is perfect;
The word of the Lord is true.
He shields all who hide behind him.
32Our Lord alone is God;
We have no other Savior.
33God is my strong fortress;
He has made me safe.
34He causes the good to walk a steady tread
Like mountain goats upon the rocks.
35He gives me skill in war
And strength to bend a bow of bronze.
36You have given me the shield of your salvation;
Your gentleness has made me great.
37You have made wide steps for my feet,
To keep them from slipping.
38I have chased my enemies
And destroyed them.
I did not stop till all were gone.
39I have destroyed them
So that none can rise again.
They have fallen beneath my feet.
40For you have given me strength for the battle
And have caused me to subdue
All those who rose against me.
41You have made my enemies
Turn and run away;
I have destroyed them all.
42They looked in vain for help;
They cried to God,
But he refused to answer.
43I beat them into dust;
I crushed and scattered them
Like dust along the streets.
44You have preserved me
From the rebels of my people;
You have preserved me
As the head of the nations.
Foreigners shall serve me
45And shall quickly submit to me
When they hear of my power.
46They shall lose heart
And come, trembling,
From their hiding places.
47The Lord lives.

22:32 *We have no other Savior,* literally, "Who is a rock save our God?"

22:26
Mt 5:7
Jas 2:13

22:27
Lev 26:23,24
Deut 28:58,59
Ps 125:4,5
Mt 5:8

22:28
Ex 3:7,8
Ps 72:12,13
Isa 2:11,12,17
5:15

22:29
Ps 27:1; 84:11

22:30
Ps 18:29

22:31
Deut 32:4
2 Sam 22:3
Ps 12:6
119:140
Prov 30:5
Mt 5:48

22:32
1 Sam 2:2
Isa 44:6,8

22:34
Ps 18:33

22:35
Ps 144:1

22:36
2 Sam 22:3
Eph 6:16

22:37
Ps 18:36; 31:8
66:9

22:38
2 Sam 8:1,2
Ps 18:37
21:8-10; 110:1

22:39
Mal 4:3

22:40
Ps 18:32
Isa 45:5

22:41
Ex 23:27
Ps 18:40,41

22:42
1 Sam 28:5,6
Job 27:9
Isa 1:15

22:43
Ps 18:42
Isa 10:6
Mic 7:10

22:44
2 Sam 3:1; 5:1
8:1
19:8-10

22:45
Ps 66:3; 72:8-10
Isa 55:5; 60:12

22:46
Isa 2:19
Mic 7:17

22:47
2 Sam 22:2,32
Ps 89:26

Blessed be my Rock.
Praise to him—
The Rock of my salvation.

22:48
1 Sam 24:12
25:39
2 Sam 18:19
Ps 94:1; 144:2

48Blessed be God
Who destroys those who oppose me
49And rescues me from my enemies.
Yes, you hold me safe above their heads.

22:49
Ps 44:5
140:1,4,11

You deliver me from violence.
50No wonder I give thanks to you, O Lord, among the nations,
And sing praises to your name.

22:50
Ps 18:49
Rom 15:9

51He gives wonderful deliverance to his king,
And shows mercy to his anointed—

22:51
2 Sam 7:12
Ps 18:50; 89:20
144:10

To David and his family,
Forever."

David's last words

23:1
Gen 49:1
Deut 33:1
Josh 23:2
1 Sam 16:12,13
2 Sam 7:8,9
Ps 78:70-72
89:20

23 These are the last words of David:

"David, the son of Jesse, speaks.
David, the man to whom God gave such wonderful success;
David, the anointed of the God of Jacob;
David, sweet psalmist of Israel:

23:2
2 Pet 1:20,21

2The Spirit of the Lord spoke by me,
And his word was on my tongue.

DAVID'S MIGHTY MEN

One way to understand David's success is to notice the kind of men who followed him. During the time he was being hunted by Saul, David gradually built a fighting force of several hundred men. Some were relatives, others were outcasts of society, many were in trouble with the law. They all shared at least one thing in common—complete devotion to David. Their achievements made them famous. Among these men were elite military groups like "The Three" and "The Thirty." They were true heroes.

Scripture gives the impression that these men were motivated to greatness by the personal qualities of their leader. David inspired them to achieve beyond their goals and meet their true potential. Likewise, the leaders we follow and the causes to which we commit ourselves will affect our lives. David's effectiveness was clearly connected with his awareness of God's leading. He was a good leader when he was following *his* Leader. Do you know who the people you respect most are following? Your answer should help you decide whether they deserve your loyalty. Do you also recognize God's leading in your life? No one can lead you to excellence like your Creator.

Strengths and accomplishments:
● Able soldiers and military leaders
● Shared many special skills
● Though frequently outnumbered, were consistently victorious
● Loyal to David

Weakness:
● Often had little in common beyond their loyalty to David and their military expertise

Lessons from their lives:
● Greatness is often inspired by the quality and character of leadership
● Even a small force of able and loyal men can accomplish great feats

Vital statistics:
● Where: They came from all over Israel (primarily Judah and Benjamin), and from some of the other surrounding nations as well
● Occupations: Various backgrounds—almost all were fugitives

Key verses:
"So David left Gath and escaped to the cave of Adullam, where his brothers and other relatives soon joined him. Then others began coming—those who were in any kind of trouble, such as being in debt, or merely discontented—until David was the leader of about four hundred men" (1 Samuel 22:1, 2).

Their stories are told in 1 Samuel 22—2 Samuel 23:39. They are also mentioned in 1 Chronicles 11, 12.

3The Rock of Israel said to me:
'One shall come who rules righteously,
Who rules in the fear of God.
4He shall be as the light of the morning;
A cloudless sunrise
When the tender grass
Springs forth upon the earth;
As sunshine after rain.'
5And it is my family
He has chosen!
Yes, God has made
An everlasting covenant with me;
His agreement is eternal, final, sealed.
He will constantly look after
My safety and success.
6But the godless are as thorns to be thrown away,
For they tear the hand that touches them.
7One must be armed to chop them down;
They shall be burned.

23:3
2 Sam 22:2,32
2 Chron 19:7,9
Ps 72:1
Isa 11:3,4

23:4
Deut 32:2
Judg 5:31
Ps 72:6; 110:3

23:5
2 Sam 7:12
Ps 89:29
Isa 55:3

23:6
Mt 13:41,42

23:7
Mt 3:10; 13:30
Heb 6:8

David's mighty men

8These are the names of the Top Three—the most heroic men in David's army: the first was Josheb-basshebeth from Tah-chemon, known also as Adino, the Eznite. He once killed eight hundred men in one battle.

9Next in rank was Eleazar, the son of Dodo and grandson of Ahohi. He was one of the three men who, with David, held back the Philistines that time when the rest of the Israeli army fled. 10He killed the Philistines until his hand was too tired to hold his sword; and the Lord gave him a great victory. (The rest of the army did not return until it was time to collect the loot!)

11, 12After him was Shammah, the son of Agee from Harar. Once during a Philistine attack, when all his men deserted him and fled, he stood alone at the center of a field of lentils and beat back the Philistines; and God gave him a great victory.

13One time when David was living in the cave of Adullam and the invading Philistines were at the valley of Rephaim, three of The Thirty—the top-ranking officers of the Israeli army—went down at harvest time to visit him. 14David was in the stronghold at the time, for Philistine marauders had occupied the nearby city of Bethlehem.

15David remarked, "How thirsty I am for some of that good water in the city well!" (The well was near the city gate.)

16So the three men broke through the Philistine ranks and drew water from the well and brought it to David. But he refused to drink it! Instead, he poured it out before the Lord.

17"No, my God," he exclaimed, "I cannot do it! This is the blood of these men who have risked their lives."

23:8
1 Chron 11:11
27:2

23:9
1 Chron 11:12
27:4

23:13
1 Sam 22:1
2 Sam 5:18

23:16
Gen 35:13
1 Sam 7:6

23:5 *My safety and success,* literally, "He will cause my help and my desire to sprout."

23:3 In the style of a prophet, David spoke of a coming righteous ruler. This will be fulfilled in Jesus Christ when he returns to rule in perfect justice and peace. For similar prophecies see Isaiah 11:1–10; Jeremiah 23:5, 6; 33:15–18; Zechariah 9:9, 10. For the fulfillment of some of these prophecies see Matthew 4:14–16; Luke 24:25–27, 44–49; John 5:45–47; 8:28, 29.

23:8–39 These verses tell of some of the exploits which the special corps of David's army carried out. There were two elite groups of men: "The Thirty" and "The Three" (23:18–39; 1 Chronicles 11:11–25). To become a member of such a group a man had to show unparalleled courage in battle as well as wisdom in leadership. "The Three" was the most elite group. The list of "The

Thirty" actually contains 37 names, but it mentions some warriors known to be dead (Uriah, for example, in 23:39). Apparently new members were appointed to replace those who had fallen in battle.

23:16 David poured out the water as an offering to God because he was so moved by the sacrifice it represented. When Hebrews offered sacrifices, they never consumed the blood. It represented life, and they poured it out before God. David would not drink this water which represented the lives of his soldiers. Instead, he offered it to God.

24:1–3 What was wrong with taking a census? A census was taken in Numbers to prepare an army for conquering the Promised Land (Numbers 1:2; 26:2). The land was now at peace, so there

23:18
2 Sam 10:10
18:2
1 Chron 11:20

18, 19Of those three men, Abishai, the brother of Joab (son of Zeruiah), was the greatest. Once he took on three hundred of the enemy singlehanded and killed them all. It was by such feats that he earned a reputation equal to The Three, though he was not actually one of them. But he was the greatest of The Thirty—the top-ranking officers of the army—and was their leader.

23:20
Josh 15:21
2 Sam 8:18
20:23
1 Kgs 4:1-6

20There was also Benaiah (son of Jehoiada), a heroic soldier from Kabzeel. Benaiah killed two giants, sons of Ariel of Moab. Another time he went down into a pit and, despite the slippery snow on the ground, took on a lion that was caught there and killed it. 21Another time, armed only with a staff, he killed an Egyptian warrior who was armed with a spear; he wrenched the spear from the Egyptian's hand and killed him with it. 22These were some of the deeds that gave Benaiah almost as much renown as the Top Three. 23He was one of the greatest of The Thirty, but was not actually one of the Top Three. And David made him chief of his bodyguard.

24-39Asahel, the brother of Joab, was also one of The Thirty. Others were:

Elhanan (son of Dodo) from Bethlehem;
Shammah from Harod;
Elika from Harod;
Helez from Palti;
Ira (son of Ikkesh) from Tekoa;
Abi-ezer from Anathoth;
Mebunnai from Hushath;
Zalmon from Ahoh;
Maharai from Netophah;
Heleb (son of Baanah) from Netophah;
Ittai (son of Ribai) from Gibe-ah, of the tribe of Benjamin;
Benaiah of Pirathon;
Hiddai from the brooks of Gaash;
Abi-albon from Arbath;
Azmaveth from Bahurim;
Eliahba from Sha-albon;
The sons of Jashen;
Jonathan;
Shammah from Harar;
Ahiam (the son of Sharar) from Harar;
Eliphelet (son of Ahasbai) from Maacah;
Eliam (the son of Ahithophel) from Gilo;
Hezro from Carmel;
Paarai from Arba;
Igal (son of Nathan) from Zobah;
Bani from Gad;
Zelek from Ammon;
Naharai from Be-eroth, the armor bearer of Joab (son of Zeruiah);
Ira from Ithra;
Gareb from Ithra;
Uriah the Hittite—thirty-seven in all.

David takes a census

24:1
2 Sam 6:7
1 Kgs 16:33

24 Once again the anger of the Lord flared against Israel, and he caused David to harm them by taking a national census. "Go and count the people of Israel and Judah," the Lord told him.

23:20 *two giants.* The meaning of the Hebrew word is uncertain.

was no need for a census. Israel had extended its borders and become a recognized power. David's sin was in counting the people so that he could glory in the size of his nation and army, its power and defenses. By doing this, he put his faith in the size of his army rather than in God's ability to protect them regardless of their number. Even Joab knew a census was wrong, but David did not heed his advice. We sin in a similar way when we place our security in money, possessions, or even the might of our nation.

2So the king said to Joab, commander-in-chief of his army, "Take a census of all the people from one end of the nation to the other, so that I will know how many of them there are."

24:2
Judg 20:1
2 Sam 3:9,10

3But Joab replied, "God grant that you will live to see the day when there will be a hundred times as many people in your kingdom as there are now! But you have no right to rejoice in their strength."

24:3
Deut 1:11

4But the king's command overcame Joab's remonstrance; so Joab and the other army officers went out to count the people of Israel. 5First they crossed the Jordan and camped at Aroer, south of the city that lies in the middle of the valley of Gad, near Jazer; 6then they went to Gilead in the land of Tahtim-hodshi and to Dan-jaan and around to Sidon; 7and then to the stronghold of Tyre, and all the cities of the Hivites and Canaanites, and south to Judah as far as Beer-sheba. 8Having gone through the entire land, they completed their task in nine months and twenty days. 9And Joab reported the number of the people to the king—800,000 men of conscription age in Israel and 500,000 in Judah.

24:5
Num 21:32
32:34-36
Josh 13:9,16

24:6
Gen 31:21,47
Josh 19:28
2 Sam 17:26

24:9
Num 1:20-46
1 Chron 21:5

David submits to judgment

10But after he had taken the census, David's conscience began to bother him, and he said to the Lord, "What I did was very wrong. Please forgive this foolish wickedness of mine."

24:10
1 Sam 24:5
2 Sam 12:13
1 Chron 21:8

11The next morning the word of the Lord came to the prophet Gad, who was David's contact with God.

The Lord said to Gad, 12"Tell David that I will give him three choices."

24:11
1 Sam 22:5
1 Chron 29:29
2 Chron 29:25,
26

13So Gad came to David and asked him, "Will you choose seven years of famine across the land, or to flee for three months before your enemies, or to submit to three days of plague? Think this over and let me know what answer to give to God."

24:13
1 Chron 21:12

14"This is a hard decision," David replied, "but it is better to fall into the hand of the Lord (for his mercy is great) than into the hands of men."

24:14
Ps 51:1
130:3,4

15So the Lord sent a plague upon Israel that morning, and it lasted for three days; and seventy thousand men died throughout the nation. 16But as the death angel was preparing to destroy Jerusalem, the Lord was sorry for what was happening and told him to stop. He was by the threshing floor of Araunah the Jebusite at the time.

24:15
Num 16:46; 24:9
1 Sam 6:19
1 Chron 21:14
27:24

17When David saw the angel, he said to the Lord, "Look, I am the one who has sinned! What have these sheep done? Let your anger be only against me and my family."

24:16
Ex 12:23; 32:14
2 Kgs 19:35
2 Chron 32:21

24:17
2 Sam 7:8
1 Kgs 22:17
Ps 74:1

18That day Gad came to David and said to him, "Go and build an altar to the Lord on the threshing floor of Araunah the Jebusite." 19So David went to do what the Lord had commanded him. 20When Araunah saw the king and his men coming towards him, he came forward and fell flat on the ground with his face in the dust.

24:18
1 Chron 21:15
2 Chron 3:1

21"Why have you come?" Araunah asked.

And David replied, "To buy your threshing floor, so that I can build an altar to the Lord, and he will stop the plague."

22"Use anything you like," Araunah told the king. "Here are oxen for the burnt offering, and you can use the threshing instruments and ox yokes for wood to build a fire on the altar. 23I will give it all to you, and may the Lord God accept your sacrifice."

24:22
1 Sam 6:14
1 Kgs 19:21

24:12–14 Both David and the Israelites were guilty of sin (24:1). David's sin was pride, but the Bible does not say why God was angry with the people of Israel. Perhaps it was due to their support of the rebellions of Absalom (chapters 15—18) and Sheba (chapter 20), or perhaps they put their security in things rather than God, as David did. In any event, a nation shares corporately in the sins of its leaders.

God gave David three choices. Each was a form of punishment God had told the people they could expect if they disobeyed his laws (disease—Deuteronomy 28:20–22; famine—28:23, 24; war—28:25, 26). David wisely chose the form of punishment that came most directly from God. He knew how brutal and harsh men in war could be, and he also knew God's great mercy. When you sin greatly, turn back to God. To be punished by him is far better than to take your chances without him.

24:18 Many believe that this threshing floor is the location where Abraham nearly sacrificed his son Isaac (Genesis 22:1–18). After David's death, Solomon built the Temple on this spot. Centuries later, Jesus would teach and preach here.

24:24
Gen 23:16
1 Chron 21:24

²⁴But the king said to Araunah, "No, I will not have it as a gift. I will buy it, for I don't want to offer to the Lord my God burnt offerings that have cost me nothing."

So David paid him for the threshing floor and the oxen. ²⁵And David built an altar there to the Lord and offered burnt offerings and peace offerings. And the Lord answered his prayer, and the plague was stopped.

24:24 *So David paid him,* literally, "paid him fifty shekels of silver."

24:25 The book of 2 Samuel describes David's reign. Since the Israelites first entered the Promised Land under Joshua, they had been struggling to unite the nation and drive out the wicked inhabitants. Now, after more than 400 years, Israel was finally at peace. David had accomplished what no leader before him, judge or king, had done. His administration was run on the principle of dedication to God and to the well-being of the people. Yet David also sinned. Despite his sins, however, the Bible calls David a man after God's own heart (Acts 13:22) because when he sinned he recognized it and confessed it before God. David committed his life to God and remained loyal to God throughout his lifetime. Reading the Psalms gives an even deeper insight into David's love for God.

1 KINGS

| David becomes king 1010 B.C. | Solomon becomes king 970 | Temple completed 959 | The kingdom divides 930 | Shishak invades Jerusalem 925 |

VITAL STATISTICS

PURPOSE:
To contrast the lives of those who live for God and those who refuse to do so through the history of the kings of Israel and Judah

AUTHOR:
Unknown. Possibly Jeremiah or a group of prophets

SETTING:
The once great nation of Israel turns into a land divided, not only physically, but also spiritually.

KEY VERSES:
"And if you live in honesty and truth as your father David did, always obeying me, then I will cause your descendants to be the kings of Israel forever, just as I promised your father David when I told him, 'One of your sons shall always be upon the throne of Israel' " (9:4, 5).

KEY PEOPLE:
David, Solomon, Rehoboam, Jeroboam, Elijah, Ahab, Jezebel

SPECIAL FEATURE:
The books of 1 and 2 Kings were originally one book.

"I DON'T CARE what anyone says, I'm going to do it!" he yells at his mother as he storms out of the house.

This is a familiar scene in our society. The words change, but the essential message is the same . . . the person is *not* open to advice because his mind is closed. Some advice may be sought, but it is heeded only if it reinforces the decision already made or is an easier path to take. It is human nature to reject help and to do things *our* way.

A much wiser approach is to seek, hear, and heed the advice of good counselors. Solomon, the world's wisest man, urges this in Proverbs (see 11:14; 15:22; 24:6). How ironic that his son and successor, Rehoboam, listens instead to foolish advice, with devastating results. At Rehoboam's inauguration, he is petitioned by the people to be a kind and generous ruler. The older men counsel him to "give them a pleasant reply and agree to be good to them and serve them well" (12:7). But Rehoboam agrees to the cruel words of his peers who urge him to be harsh. As a result, Rehoboam splits the kingdom. Learn from Rehoboam's mistake. Commit yourself to seeking and following wise counsel.

The main events of 1 Kings are David's death, Solomon's reign, the division of the kingdom, and Elijah's ministry. As Solomon ascends the throne, David charges him to obey God's laws and "follow all his ways" (2:3). This Solomon does; and when given the choice of gifts from God, he humbly asks for wisdom (3:9). As a result, Solomon's reign begins with great success, including the construction of the Temple—his greatest achievement. Unfortunately, Solomon takes many pagan wives and concubines who eventually turn his heart away from the Lord to their false gods (11:1–4).

Rehoboam succeeds Solomon and has the opportunity to be a wise, compassionate, and just king. Instead, he accepts the poor advice of his young friends and attempts to rule with an iron hand. But the people rebel, and the kingdom splits with ten tribes in the north (Israel) ruled by Jeroboam, and only Judah and Benjamin remaining with Rehoboam. Both kingdoms weave a path through the reigns of corrupt and idolatrous kings with only the clear voice of the prophets continuing to warn and call the nation back to God.

Elijah is surely one of the greatest prophets who ever lived, and chapters 17 through 22 feature his conflict with wicked Ahab and Jezebel in Israel. In one of the most dramatic confrontations in history, Elijah defeats the prophets of Baal at Mount Carmel. In spite of incredible opposition, Elijah stands for God and proves that *one plus God* is a majority. If God is on our side, no one can stand against us (Romans 8:31).

THE BLUEPRINT

A. THE UNITED KINGDOM (1:1—11:43)
1. Solomon becomes king
2. Solomon's wisdom
3. Solomon builds the Temple
4. Solomon's greatness and downfall

Solomon was a botanist, zoologist, architect, poet, and philosopher. He was the wisest king in the history of Israel, but his wives led to the introduction of false gods and false worship in Israel. It is good for us to have wisdom, but that is not enough. The highest goal in life is to obey the Lord. Patient obedience to God should characterize our lives.

B. THE DIVIDED KINGDOM (12:1—22:53)
1. Revolt of the northern tribes
2. Kings of Israel and Judah
3. Elijah's ministry
4. Kings of Israel and Judah

When the Northern Kingdom of Israel was being led by wicked kings, God raised up a prophet to proclaim his messages. Elijah single-handedly challenged the priesthood of the state religion and had them removed in one day. Through the dividing of the kingdom and the sending of Elijah, God dealt with the people's sin in powerful ways. Sin in our lives is graciously forgiven by God. However, the sin of an unrepentant person will be handled harshly. We must turn from sin and turn to God to be saved from judgment.

MEGATHEMES

THEME	EXPLANATION	IMPORTANCE
The King	Solomon's wisdom, power, and achievements brought honor to the Israelite nation and to God. All the kings of Israel and Judah were told to obey God and to govern according to his laws. But their tendency to abandon God's Word and to worship other gods led them to change the religion and government to meet their personal desires. This neglect of God's Law led to their downfall.	Wisdom, power, and achievement do not ultimately come from any human source; they are from God. No matter what we lead or govern, we can't do well when we ignore God's guidelines. Whether or not we are leaders, effectiveness depends upon listening and obeying God's Word.
The Temple	Solomon's Temple was a beautiful place of worship and prayer. This sanctuary was the center of Jewish religion. It was the place of God's special presence and housed the Ark of the Covenant containing the Ten Commandments.	A beautiful house of worship doesn't always indicate that the people gathered there are offering heartfelt worship to God. Providing opportunities for true worship doesn't guarantee that it will happen. God wants to live in our hearts, not just meet us in a sanctuary.
Other gods	Although the Israelites had God's Law and experienced his presence among them, they became attracted to other gods. When this happened, their hearts became cold to God's Law, resulting in the ruin of families and government, and eventually leading to the destruction of the nation.	Through the years, the people took on the false qualities of the false gods they worshiped. They became cruel, power-hungry, and sexually perverse. We tend to become what we worship. Unless we serve the true God, we will become slaves to whatever takes his place.
The Prophet's Message	The prophet's responsibility was to confront and correct any deviation from God's Law. Elijah was a bolt of judgment against Israel. His messages and miracles were a warning to the evil and rebellious kings and people.	The Bible, the truth in sermons, and the wise counsel of believers are warnings to us. Anyone who points out how we deviate from obeying God's Word is a blessing to us. Changing our lives in order to obey God and get back on track often takes painful discipline and hard work.
Sin and Repentance	Each king had God's Word, a priest or prophet, and the lessons of the past to draw him back to God. All the people had the same resources. Whenever they repented and returned to God, God heard their prayers and forgave them.	God hears and forgives us when we pray— if we are willing to trust him and turn from sin. Then he will give us a fresh start and a new desire to live for him.

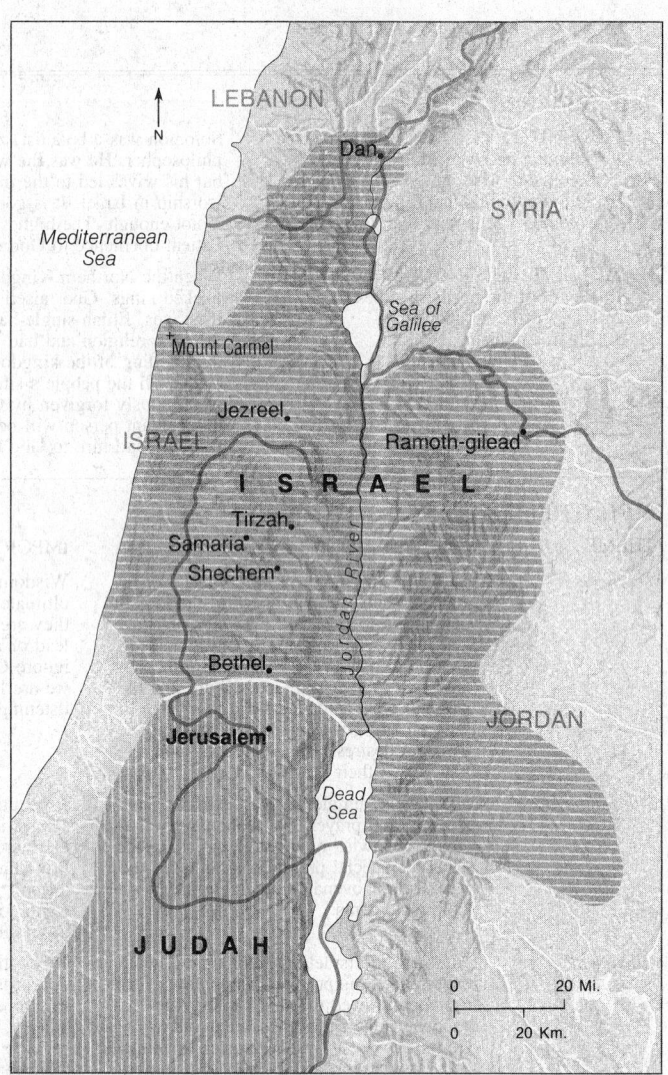

Solomon, David's son, brought Israel into its golden age. His wealth and wisdom were acclaimed worldwide. But he ignored God in his later years (1:1—11:25).

1 **Shechem** After Solomon's death, Israel assembled at Shechem to inaugurate his son Rehoboam. However, Rehoboam foolishly angered the people by threatening even higher taxes, causing a revolt (11:26—12:19).

2 **Israel** Jeroboam, leader of the rebels, was made king of Israel, now called the Northern Kingdom. Jeroboam made Shechem his capital city (12:25).

3 **Judah** Only the tribes of Judah and Benjamin remained loyal to Rehoboam. These two tribes became the Southern Kingdom. Rehoboam returned to Judah from Shechem and prepared to force the rebels into submission, but a prophet's message halted these plans (12:21–24).

4 **Jerusalem** Jerusalem was the capital city of Judah. Its temple, built by Solomon, was the focal point of Jewish worship. This worried Jeroboam. How could he keep his people loyal if they were constantly going to Rehoboam's capital to worship (12:26, 27)?

5 **Dan** Jeroboam's solution was to set up his own worship centers. Two calf-idols were made and proclaimed to be Israel's gods. One was placed in Dan, and the people were told that they could go there instead of to Jerusalem to worship (12:28, 29).

Modern names and boundaries are shown in gray.

6 **Bethel** The other idol was placed in Bethel. The people of the Northern Kingdom had two convenient locations for worship in their own country, but their sin displeased God. In Jerusalem, meanwhile, Rehoboam was also allowing idolatry to creep in. The two nations were constantly at war (12:29—15:26).

7 **Tirzah** Baasha became king of Israel after assassinating Nadab. He moved the capital from Shechem to Tirzah (15:27—16:22).

8 **Samaria** Israel continued to gain and lose kings through plots, assassinations, and warfare. When Omri became king, he bought a hill on which he built a new capital city, Samaria. Omri's son, Ahab, became the most wicked king of Israel. His wife Jezebel worshiped Baal. Ahab erected a temple to Baal in Samaria (16:23–34).

9 **Mount Carmel** Great evil often brings great people who oppose it. Elijah challenged the prophets of Baal and Asherah at Mount Carmel, where he would prove that they were false prophets. There Elijah humiliated these prophets and then executed them (17:1—18:46).

10 **Jezreel** Elijah returned to Jezreel. But Queen Jezebel, furious at the execution of her prophets, vowed to kill Elijah. He ran for his life, but God cared for and encouraged him. During his travels he anointed the future kings of Syria and Israel, as well as Elisha, his own replacement (19:1–21).

11 **Ramoth-gilead** The king of Syria declared war on Israel and was defeated in two battles. But the Syrians occupied Ramoth-gilead. Ahab and Jehoshaphat joined forces to recover the city. In this battle, Ahab was killed. Jehoshaphat later died (20:1—22:53).

A. THE UNITED KINGDOM (1:1—11:43)

When Solomon is appointed king, he eliminates all opposition to the throne, builds the Temple, establishes a strong army, and becomes the richest and wisest king in the history of Israel. But his heathen wives lead him into idolatry and, as a result, he leads the nation into spiritual decline. No matter what position in life we attain, we are always ripe for a downfall and must never let our guard down against sin and temptation.

1. Solomon becomes king
Adonijah tries to seize the throne

1 In his old age King David was confined to his bed; but no matter how many blankets were heaped upon him, he was always cold.

Bath-sheba was the unlikely link between Israel's two most famous kings—David and Solomon. She was lover and wife to one, mother to the other. Her adultery with David almost brought an end to the family through which God planned to physically enter his world. Out of the ashes of that sin, however, God brought good. Eventually Jesus Christ, the salvation of mankind, was born to a descendant of David and Bath-sheba.

David and Bath-sheba's story illustrates that little wrong decisions often lead to big mistakes. It is likely that neither was where he or she should have been. Bath-sheba may have been rash in bathing where she might be seen; David should have been at war with his army. Each decision contributed to the beginning of a very sad series of events.

Bath-sheba must have been devastated by the chain of events—unfaithfulness to her husband, discovery of pregnancy, death of her husband, death of her child. We are told that David comforted her (2 Samuel 12:24), and she lived to see another son, Solomon, sit on the throne.

From her life we see that the little day-to-day choices we make are very important. They prepare us to make the right choices when the big decisions come. The wisdom to make right choices in small and large matters is a gift from God. Understanding this should make us more conscious of the decisions we make and more willing to include God in our decision making. Have you asked for his help with today's decisions?

Strengths and accomplishments:
* Became influential in the palace alongside her son, King Solomon
* Was the mother of Israel's wisest king and the ancestor of Jesus Christ

Mistake:
* Committed adultery

Lessons from her life:
* Although we may feel caught up in a chain of events, we are still responsible for the way that we participate in those events
* A sin may seem like one small seed, but the harvest of consequences is beyond measure
* In the worst possible situations, God is still able to bring about good when people truly turn to him
* While we must live with the natural consequences of our sins, God's forgiveness of sin is complete

Vital statistics:
* Where: Jerusalem
* Occupation: Queen and queen mother
* Relatives: Father: Elim. Husbands: Uriah and David. Son: Solomon.
* Contemporaries: Nathan, Joab, Adonijah

Key verses:
"When Bath-sheba heard that her husband was dead, she mourned for him; then, when the period of mourning was over, David sent for her and brought her to the palace and she became one of his wives; and she gave birth to his son. But the Lord was very displeased with what David had done" (2 Samuel 11:26, 27).

Her story is told in 2 Samuel 11, 12 and 1 Kings 1, 2. A related passage is Psalm 51.

1:1 Israel was near the end of the golden years of David's reign. The book of 1 Kings begins with a unified kingdom, glorious and God-centered; it ends with a divided kingdom, degraded and idolatrous. The reason for Israel's decline appears simple to us—they failed to obey God. But we are vulnerable to the same forces that brought about Israel's decay—greed, jealousy, lust for power, weakening of marriage vows, and superficiality in our devotion to God. As we read about these tragic events in Israel's history, we must see ourselves in the mirror of their experiences.

2"The cure for this," his aides told him, "is to find a young virgin to be your concubine and nurse. She will lie in your arms and keep you warm."

3, 4So they searched the country from one end to the other to find the most beautiful girl in all the land. Abishag, from Shunam, was finally selected. They brought her to the king and she lay in his arms to warm him (but he had no sexual relations with her).

5At about that time, David's son Adonijah (his mother was Haggith) decided to crown himself king in place of his aged father. So he hired chariots and drivers and recruited fifty men to run down the streets before him as royal footmen. 6Now his father, King David, had never disciplined him at any time—not so much as by a single scolding! He was a very handsome man, and was Absalom's younger brother. 7He took General Joab and Abiathar the priest into his confidence, and they agreed to help him become king. 8But among those who remained loyal to King David and refused to endorse Adonijah were the priests Zadok and Benaiah, the prophet Nathan, Shime-i, Rei, and David's army chiefs.

9Adonijah went to En-rogel where he sacrificed sheep, oxen, and fat young goats at the Serpent's Stone. Then he summoned all of his brothers—the other sons of King David—and all the royal officials of Judah, requesting that they come to his

1:3
1 Sam 28:4
1 Kgs 2:17

1:5
2 Sam 3:4
1 Chron 3:2

1:7
1 Sam 22:20
2 Sam 20:25
1 Kgs 2:28

1:8
2 Sam 8:18
12:1; 20:25
23:20

1:5 Implied

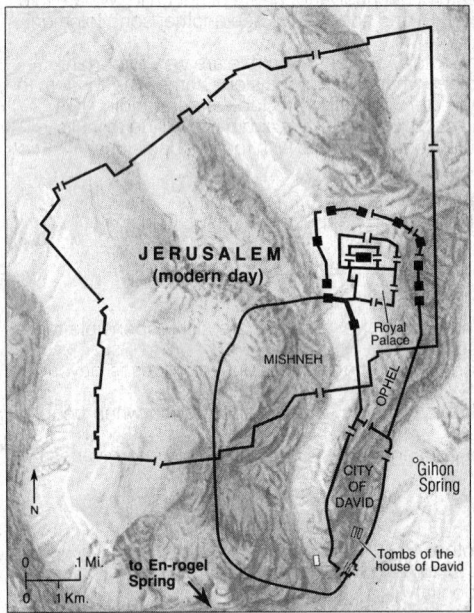

JERUSALEM (modern day)

Royal Palace

MISHNEH

OPHEL

CITY OF DAVID

Gihon Spring

Tombs of the house of David

N

0   1 Mi.   **to En-rogel Spring**
0   1 Km.

TWO CORONATIONS As David lay on his deathbed, his son Adonijah crowned himself king at the En-rogel Spring outside Jerusalem. When the news reached David, he declared that Solomon was to be the next ruler. Solomon was anointed at Gihon Spring. It may have been more than coincidence that Gihon Spring was not only within shouting distance of En-rogel Spring, but also closer to the royal palace.

1:5 Adonijah was David's fourth son and the logical choice to succeed him as king. David's first son, Amnon, had been killed by Absalom for having raped his sister (2 Samuel 13:20–33). His second son, Daniel, is mentioned only in the genealogy of 1 Chronicles 3:1 and had probably died by this time. David's third

son, Absalom, died in an earlier rebellion (2 Samuel 18:1–18). Although many people expected Adonijah to be the next king (2:13–25), David (and God) had other plans (1:29, 30).

1:5 Adonijah decided to seize the throne without David's knowledge. He knew that Solomon was David's first choice to be the next king (1:17). This was why he did not invite Solomon and David's loyal advisers to his "coronation" (1:9, 10). As the oldest living son, Adonijah was the heir apparent to the throne, and many Israelites expected him to be crowned (2:15). But his deceptive plans to gain the throne were unsuccessful. The proud Adonijah was self-exalted and self-defeated.

1:6 God-fearing people like David and Samuel were used by God to lead nations, but they nevertheless had problems in family relationships. Godly leaders cannot take for granted the spiritual well-being of their children. They are used to having others follow their orders, but they cannot expect their children to manufacture faith upon request. Moral and spiritual character takes years to build, and it requires continual attention and patient discipline.

David served God well as a king, but as a parent he often failed both God and his children. Don't let even your service to God in leadership positions take up so much of your time and energy that you neglect your other God-given responsibilities.

1:6 Because David had not disciplined his son, Adonijah did not know how to work within limits. The result was that he always wanted his own way, regardless of how it affected others. Adonijah did whatever he wanted and paid no respect to God's wishes. An undisciplined child may look cute to his or her parents, but an undisciplined adult destroys himself and others. As you set limits for your children, you make it possible for them to develop the self-restraint they will need in order to control themselves later. Discipline your children carefully while they are young, so that they will grow into self-disciplined adults.

1:7 See Joab's Profile in 2 Samuel 19 for a more complete picture of his life. For more information on Abiathar, see the note on 1 Samuel 22:20.

1:9 Sacrifices were traditionally offered when a new king was crowned. They were called peace offerings, and they showed the nation's joy over their newly appointed leader. A priest had to offer the sacrifices, showing that the king's power was from God. To make his coronation seem legitimate, Adonijah wanted sacrifices offered. But Adonijah was not God's choice to succeed David. Sealing an action with religious ceremony does not make it God's will.

1:10
2 Sam 12:24

coronation. ¹⁰But he didn't invite Nathan the prophet, Benaiah, the loyal army officers, or his brother Solomon.

¹¹Then Nathan the prophet went to Bath-sheba, Solomon's mother, and asked her, "Do you realize that Haggith's son, Adonijah, is now the king and that our lord David doesn't even know about it? ¹²If you want to save your own life and the life of your son Solomon—do exactly as I say! ¹³Go at once to King David and ask him,

1:13
1 Chron 22:9

'My lord, didn't you promise me that my son Solomon would be the next king and would sit upon your throne? Then why is Adonijah reigning?' ¹⁴And while you are still talking with him, I'll come and confirm everything you've said."

¹⁵So Bath-sheba went into the king's bedroom. He was an old, old man now, and Abishag was caring for him. ¹⁶Bath-sheba bowed low before him.

"What do you want?" he asked her.

¹⁷She replied, "My lord, you vowed to me by the Lord your God that my son Solomon would be the next king and would sit upon your throne. ¹⁸But instead, Adonijah is the new king, and you don't even know about it. ¹⁹He has celebrated his coronation by sacrificing oxen, fat goats, and many sheep and has invited all your sons and Abiathar the priest and General Joab. But he didn't invite Solomon.

1:20
2 Sam 7:12

²⁰And now, my lord the king, all Israel is waiting for your decision as to whether Adonijah is the one you have chosen to succeed you. ²¹If you don't act, my son

---

Who joined Adonijah's conspiracy and who remained loyal to David?
Contrast the fate of those who rebelled and those who remained loyal to David, God's appointed leader. Adonijah, the leader of the conspiracy, met a violent death (2:25). Those who rebel against God's leaders rebel against God.

Joined Adonijah

JOAB (1:7)
Brilliant military general and commander of David's army. He continually demonstrated his belief that cold-blooded murder was as acceptable as a fairly fought battle. Solomon later had him executed.

ABIATHAR (1:7)
One of two High Priests under David. He was a son of Ahimelech who had helped David, and David promised to protect him. Abiathar repaid David with his treachery. Solomon later had him banished, fulfilling the prophecy that Eli's priestly line would end (1 Samuel 2:31).

JONATHAN (1:42)
Abiathar's son. He helped David stop Absalom's rebellion (2 Samuel 17:17–22), but supported this rebellion by another of David's sons.

CHARIOTEERS (1:5)
Hired by Adonijah, apparently more loyal to money than to their king.

50 RUNNERS (1:5)
Recruited to give Adonijah a "royal" appearance.

Remained with David

ZADOK (1:8)
The other High Priest under David. His loyalty gave him the privilege of crowning Solomon. He became the sole High Priest under King Solomon.

BENAIAH (1:8)
Distinguished himself as a great warrior. Commanded a division of David's army—over 24,000 troops. One of The Thirty, he was also placed in charge of David's bodyguard. Solomon later made him chief commander of the army.

NATHAN (1:8)
God's prominent prophet during David's reign. The Bible says he wrote a history of David and Solomon.

SHIME-I (1:8)
This man was probably the Shime-i who was rewarded by Solomon and appointed official of the tribe of Benjamin (4:18). (He was not the same person who cursed David at Bahurim and brought on his own death under Solomon.)

REI (1:8)
Only mentioned here. Possibly he was an army officer. The word means "friend."

ARMY CHIEFS (1:10)
David's army was highly organized with several different divisions of troops. It is enough to know that many of his leaders remained true to their king.

1:11 For more on Bath-sheba, David's wife, read 2 Samuel 11, 12. As mother of the king, Bath-sheba was highly influential in the royal palace.

1:11–14 When Nathan learned of Adonijah's conspiracy, he immediately tried to stop it. He was a man of both faith and action. He knew the right course to take—that Solomon should be king—and moved quickly when he saw someone trying to block

what was right. We often know what is right but don't act on it. Perhaps we don't want to get involved, or maybe we are lazy. Don't stop with prayer, good intentions, or angry feelings. Take the action needed to correct the situation.

1:13 The Bible does not record David's promise that Solomon would be Israel's next king, but it is clear that Solomon was the choice of both David (1:17, 30) and God (1 Chronicles 22:9).

Solomon and I will be arrested and executed as criminals as soon as you are dead."

22, 23While she was speaking, the king's aides told him, "Nathan the prophet is here to see you."

Nathan came in and bowed low before the king, 24and asked, "My lord, have you appointed Adonijah to be the next king? Is he the one you have selected to sit upon your throne? 25Today he celebrated his coronation by sacrificing oxen and fat goats and many sheep, and has invited your sons to attend the festivities. He also invited General Joab and Abiathar the priest; and they are feasting and drinking with him and shouting, 'Long live King Adonijah!' 26But Zadok the priest and Benaiah and Solomon and I weren't invited. 27Has this been done with your knowledge? For you haven't said a word as to which of your sons you have chosen to be the next king."

1:25
1 Sam 10:24
2 Sam 24:24
1 Kgs 1:9

David declares Solomon king

28"Call Bath-sheba," David said. So she came back in and stood before the king.

29And the king vowed, "As the Lord lives who has rescued me from every danger, 30I decree that your son Solomon shall be the next king and shall sit upon my throne, just as I swore to you before by the Lord God of Israel."

1:29
2 Sam 4:9
22:20

31Then Bath-sheba bowed low before him again and exclaimed, "Oh, thank you, sir. May my lord the king live forever!"

32"Call Zadok the priest," the king ordered, "and Nathan the prophet, and Benaiah."

1:32ff
2 Sam 19:19

When they arrived, 33he said to them, "Take Solomon and my officers to Gihon. Solomon is to ride on my personal mule, 34and Zadok the priest and Nathan the prophet are to anoint him there as king of Israel. Then blow the trumpets and shout, 'Long live King Solomon!' 35When you bring him back here, place him upon my throne as the new king; for I have appointed him king of Israel and Judah."

1:34
1 Sam 10:1
16:3,12
2 Sam 15:10
2 Kgs 9:13
11:13,14

36"Amen! Praise God!" replied Benaiah, and added, 37"May the Lord be with Solomon as he has been with you, and may God make Solomon's reign even greater than yours!"

1:37
Josh 1:5,17
1 Sam 20:13
1 Chron 28:20

38So Zadok the priest, Nathan the prophet, Benaiah, and David's bodyguard took Solomon to Gihon, riding on King David's own mule. 39At Gihon, Zadok took a flask of sacred oil from the Tabernacle and poured it over Solomon; and the trumpets were blown and all the people shouted, "Long live King Solomon!"

1:39
1 Sam 16:3,13
1 Kgs 1:34
1 Chron 16:39
29:22

40Then they all returned with him to Jerusalem, making a joyous and noisy celebration all along the way.

1:40
1 Sam 11:15
2 Kgs 11:13,14

41Adonijah and his guests heard the commotion and shouting just as they were finishing their banquet.

"What's going on?" Joab demanded. "Why is the city in such an uproar?"

42And while he was still speaking, Jonathan, the son of Abiathar the priest, rushed in.

1:42
2 Sam 18:27

"Come in," Adonijah said to him, "for you are a good man; you must have good news."

43"Our lord King David has declared Solomon as king!" Jonathan shouted. 44, 45"The king sent him to Gihon with Zadok the priest and Nathan the prophet and Benaiah, protected by the king's own bodyguard; and he rode on the king's own mule. And Zadok and Nathan have anointed him as the new king! They have just returned, and the whole city is celebrating and rejoicing. That's what all the noise is. 46, 47Solomon is sitting on the throne, and all the people are congratulating King David, saying, 'May God bless you even more through Solomon than he has

1:31 *bowed low before him*, literally, "did reverence to the king."

1:33 Today, mules are the brunt of many jokes, but in David's time they were prized animals, ridden by the wealthy and powerful. As a sign that he had been chosen king, Solomon was given David's personal mule to ride. Riding a king's mule was an honor as great as that of traveling in a royal limousine today.

1:39 The sacred oil was used to anoint Israel's kings and High Priests, as well as to dedicate certain objects to God. The Tabernacle where the oil was kept was probably the tent David set up to shelter the Ark of the Covenant (2 Samuel 6:17). It was not the Tabernacle Moses carried in the wilderness; that Tabernacle was still at Gibeon (see the note on 1 Samuel 7:1 for more details). The recipe and uses for the sacred oil are found in Exodus 30:22–33. For more on anointing, see the notes on 1 Samuel 10:1 and 16:13.

1:48
2 Sam 7:12
1 Kgs 3:6

1:49
1 Kgs 2:28

2:1
Josh 23:14
Job 16:22; 30:23
Ps 89:48

2:3
Deut 18:18,19
Josh 1:7
1 Chron 22:12

2:4
2 Sam 7:12
1 Kgs 8:25; 9:5
1 Chron 17:11

2:5
2 Sam 3:27
20:10

blessed you personally! May God make Solomon's reign even greater than yours!' And the king is lying in bed, acknowledging their blessings. 48He is saying, 'Blessed be the Lord God of Israel who has selected one of my sons to sit upon my throne while I am still alive to see it.' "

49, 50Then Adonijah and his guests jumped up from the banquet table and fled in panic; for they were fearful for their lives. Adonijah rushed into the Tabernacle and caught hold of the horns of the sacred altar. 51When word reached Solomon that Adonijah was claiming sanctuary in the Tabernacle, and pleading for clemency, 52Solomon replied, "If he behaves himself, he will not be harmed; but if he does not, he shall die." 53So King Solomon summoned him, and they brought him down from the altar. He came to bow low before the king; and then Solomon curtly dismissed him.

"Go on home," he said.

David's charge to Solomon

2 As the time of King David's death approached, he gave this charge to his son Solomon:

2"I am going where every man on earth must some day go. I am counting on you to be a strong and worthy successor. 3Obey the laws of God and follow all his ways; keep each of his commands written in the law of Moses so that you will prosper in everything you do, wherever you turn. 4If you do this, then the Lord will fulfill the promise he gave me, that if my children and their descendants watch their step and are faithful to God, one of them shall always be the king of Israel—my dynasty will never end.

5"Now listen to my instructions. You know that Joab murdered my two generals, Abner and Amasa. He pretended that it was an act of war, but it was done in a time

---

TRAITS OF DAVID, SOLOMON, AND CHRIST	*David*	*Solomon*	*Christ*
	Warlike	Peace-loving	Peace-loving
	Faithful	Fell into idol worship	Faithful
	Kind	Exploitive	Kind
	Obedient to God	Disobedient to God	Obedient to God
	A heart after God	A heart after wealth	A heart after God
	Served his people	Ruled his people	Serves his people

David and Solomon were two of the most renowned kings in Israel's history. Compare the characteristics of Jesus Christ, the perfect eternal king, to the characteristics of David and Solomon.

1:49, 50 Sometimes it takes getting caught before someone is willing to give up his scheme. When Adonijah learned that his plans had been exposed, he ran in panic to the sacred altar, the highest symbol of God's mercy and forgiveness. He went there, however, *after* his plans for treason were exposed. If Adonijah had first considered what God wanted, he might have avoided trouble. Don't wait until you have made a mess of things to run to God; how much better to seek God's guidance *before* you act.

1:49–51 Both Adonijah and his general, Joab, thought they would be safe by clutching the horns (or corner posts) of the sacred Altar of Burnt Offering in the Tabernacle court. They hoped to place themselves under God's protection. Solomon granted Adonijah a reprieve, but he later had Joab killed right at the altar (2:28–34). This punishment was appropriate justice for a cold-blooded murderer such as Joab (Exodus 21:14).

1:52, 53 While Adonijah feared for his life and expected the severest punishment, Solomon simply dismissed his brother and sent him home. As a new king, Solomon had the power to kill his rivals, something Adonijah would have done had his conspiracy succeeded. But Solomon acted as if he had nothing to prove, thus showing his authority and power. Sometimes forgiving a personal attack shows more strength than lashing out in revenge. Trying to prove one's power and authority often proves only one's fear and self-doubt. Only after Adonijah made another attempt to secure

royal power was Solomon forced to have him executed (2:13–25).

2:3, 4 David stressed to Solomon the need to make God and his laws the center of personal life and government in order to preserve the kingdom, as God had promised to do (2 Samuel 7). This promise from God had two parts: one part was conditional and depended upon the actions of the present king. The other part was unconditional.

God's conditional promise was that David and his descendants would remain in office as kings *only* when they honored and obeyed him. When David's descendants failed to do this, they lost the throne (2 Kings 25). God's unconditional promise was that David's ancestral line would go on forever. This was fulfilled in the birth of Jesus Christ, a descendant of David who was also the eternal Son of God (Romans 1:3, 4). David, whose life exemplified obedience, gave well-seasoned advice to his son, the next king. It would be up to Solomon to follow it.

2:5–7 Joab epitomizes those who are ruthless in accomplishing their goals. His strength was his only code and winning the battle his only law. He wanted to get power for himself and protect it. In contrast, Barzillai stands for those who are loyal to God and live by his standards. When offered glory, for example, he unselfishly asked that it be given to his son. Is your leadership self-serving or God-serving?

of peace. 6You are a wise man and will know what to do—don't let him die in peace. 7But be kind to the sons of Barzillai the Gileadite. Make them permanent guests of the king, for they took care of me when I fled from your brother Absalom. 8And do you remember Shime-i, the son of Gera the Benjaminite from Bahurim? He cursed me with a terrible curse as I was going to Mahanaim; but when he came down to meet me at the Jordan River I promised I wouldn't kill him. 9But that promise doesn't bind you! You are a wise man, and you will know how to arrange a bloody death for him."

2:7
2 Sam 17:27

2:8
2 Sam 16:5-8
19:16

2:10
2 Sam 5:7
1 Chron 29:28
Acts 2:29; 13:36

10Then David died and was buried in Jerusalem. 11He had reigned over Israel for forty years, seven of them in Hebron and thirty-three in Jerusalem. 12And Solomon became the new king, replacing his father David; and his kingdom prospered.

2:11
2 Sam 5:4,5

2:12
1 Chron 29:23
2 Chron 1:1

Solomon removes the opposition

13One day Adonijah the son of Haggith came to see Solomon's mother, Bath-sheba.

"Have you come to make trouble?" she asked him.

"No," he replied, "I come in peace. 14As a matter of fact, I have a favor to ask of you."

"What is it?" she asked.

15"Everything was going well for me," he said, "and the kingdom was mine: everyone expected me to be the next king. But the tables are turned, and everything went to my brother instead; for that is the way the Lord wanted it. 16But now I have just a small favor to ask of you; please don't turn me down."

"What is it?" she asked.

17He replied, "Speak to King Solomon on my behalf (for I know he will do anything you request) and ask him to give me Abishag, the Shunammite, as my wife."

18"All right," Bath-sheba replied, "I'll ask him."

19So she went to ask the favor of King Solomon. The king stood up from his throne as she entered and bowed low to her. He ordered that a throne for his mother be placed beside his; so she sat at his right hand.

20"I have one small request to make of you," she said. "I hope you won't turn me down."

"What is it, my mother?" he asked. "You know I won't refuse you."

21"Then let your brother Adonijah marry Abishag," she replied.

22"Are you crazy?" he demanded. "If I were to give him Abishag, I would be giving him the kingdom too! For he is my older brother! He and Abiathar the priest and General Joab would take over!" 23, 24Then King Solomon swore with a great oath, "May God strike me dead if Adonijah does not die this very day for this plot against me! I swear it by the living God who has given me the throne of my father David and this kingdom he promised me."

2:23
Ruth 1:17
1 Sam 14:44
1 Kgs 20:10

2:25
2 Sam 8:18

2:26
Josh 21:17,18
1 Sam 22:20

25So King Solomon sent Benaiah to execute him, and he killed him with a sword.

26Then the king said to Abiathar the priest, "Go back to your home in Anathoth.

26:16
2 Sam 15:24
Jer 1:1

2:6–9 David had some harsh advice for Solomon concerning his enemies. This advice was designed to help the young king secure his throne, and it was directed only toward blatant enemies—those who opposed God by opposing God's appointed king. Legally, David was asking Solomon to give his enemies the punishment they deserved. It was against both civil law and God's law for Shime-i to curse a king (Exodus 22:28).

2:10 David died at about age 70 (2 Samuel 5:4, 5). See David's Profile in 1 Samuel 17 for more on his life.

2:22 This was not a case of thwarted love, although Adonijah probably hoped Bath-sheba would think so. Adonijah wanted Abishag because she had been David's last mistress. To sleep with the king's mistress was equivalent to claiming the throne. Absalom had done the same thing in his rebellion against David.

Solomon well understood what Adonijah was trying to do.

2:23, 24 In this plot against Solomon, all the conspirators lost. Adonijah and Joab were killed, and the priest, Abiathar, lost his job. They all thought they would gain something by their alliance: influence, position, recognition, authority. But they had a poor leader and wrong motives. Consider your motives carefully before making alliances with others.

2:26, 27 As a young man, Abiathar was the only one to escape when King Saul massacred all the priests in the city of Nob (1 Samuel 22:11–23). Abiathar then became the High Priest under David and remained loyal to him throughout his reign. When he supported Adonijah's wrongful claim to the throne after David's death (1:7), Solomon forced him to give up the priesthood, fulfilling the prophecy of 1 Samuel 2:27–36 that Eli's descendants would not continue to serve as priests.

You should be killed, too, but I won't do it now. For you carried the Ark of the Lord during my father's reign, and you suffered right along with him in all of his troubles."

2:27
1 Sam 2:30,31

27So Solomon forced Abiathar to give up his position as the priest of the Lord, thereby fulfilling the decree of Jehovah at Shiloh concerning the descendants of Eli.

2:28
2 Sam 17:25
1 Kgs 1:49

28When Joab heard about Adonijah's death (Joab had joined Adonijah's revolt, though not Absalom's) he ran to the Tabernacle for sanctuary and caught hold of the horns of the altar. 29When news of this reached King Solomon, he sent Benaiah to execute him.

30Benaiah went into the Tabernacle and said to Joab, "The king says to come out!"

"No," he said, "I'll die here."

So Benaiah returned to the king for further instructions.

2:31
Ex 21:14
Num 35:33
Deut 19:13

2:32
Gen 9:5,6
Judg 9:24,56,57
2 Sam 3:27
20:8-10

2:33
2 Sam 3:29
Prov 25:5

31"Do as he says," the king replied. "Kill him there beside the altar and bury him. This will remove the guilt of his senseless murders from me and from my father's family. 32Then Jehovah will hold him personally responsible for the murders of two men who were better than he. For my father was no party to the deaths of General Abner, commander-in-chief of the army of Israel, and General Amasa, commander-in-chief of the army of Judah. 33May Joab and his descendants be forever guilty of these murders, and may the Lord declare David and his descendants guiltless concerning their deaths."

34So Benaiah returned to the Tabernacle and killed Joab; and he was buried beside his house in the desert.

2:35
1 Chron 29:22

35Then the king appointed Benaiah as commander-in-chief, and Zadok as priest instead of Abiathar.

2:36
2 Sam 16:5
1 Kgs 2:8

36,37The king now sent for Shime-i and told him, "Build a house here in Jerusalem, and don't step outside the city on pain of death. The moment you go beyond Kidron Brook, you die; and it will be your own fault."

38"All right," Shime-i replied, "whatever you say." So he lived in Jerusalem for a long time.

39But three years later two of Shime-i's slaves escaped to King Achish of Gath. When Shime-i learned where they were, 40he saddled a donkey and went to Gath to visit the king. And when he had found his slaves, he took them back to Jerusalem.

41When Solomon heard that Shime-i had left Jerusalem and had gone to Gath and returned, 42he sent for him and demanded, "Didn't I command you in the name of God to stay in Jerusalem or die? You replied, 'Very well, I will do as you say.'

2:44
1 Sam 25:39
2 Sam 16:5

2:45
2 Sam 7:13
Isa 9:7

2:46
2 Chron 1:1

43Then why have you not kept your agreement and obeyed my commandment? 44And what about all the wicked things you did to my father, King David? May the Lord take revenge on you, 45but may I receive God's rich blessings, and may one of David's descendants always sit upon this throne."

46Then, at the king's command, Benaiah took Shime-i outside and killed him.

So Solomon's grip upon the kingdom became secure.

2:28 To understand why Joab clutched the horns of the altar, see the note on 1:49–51.

2:31 Joab had spent his life trying to defend his position as David's general. Twice David tried to replace him, and both times Joab treacherously killed his rivals before they could assume command (2 Samuel 3:12–30; 19:13—20:10). Because Joab was in his service, David was ultimately responsible for these senseless deaths. But for political and military reasons (see the note on 2 Samuel 3:39), David decided not to publicly punish Joab. Instead he put a personal curse on Joab and his family (2 Samuel 3:29, 39). Solomon, in punishing Joab, was publicly declaring that David was not part of Joab's crimes, thus removing the guilt from David and placing it on Joab where it belonged.

2:35 Abiathar the High Priest and Joab the army commander were key men in David's kingdom. But when they conspired

against Solomon, they were replaced with Zadok and Benaiah. Zadok, a descendant of Aaron, had been a prominent priest during David's reign. He was put in charge of the Ark of the Covenant (2 Samuel 15:24ff). He was also loyal to Solomon after David's death. His descendants were in charge of the Temple until its destruction. At one time, Benaiah had been one of David's mighty men (2 Samuel 23:20–23) and the captain of David's bodyguards.

2:46 Solomon ordered the executions of Adonijah, Joab, and Shime-i, forced Abiathar out as priest, and then appointed new men to take their places. He did these things swiftly, and his grip on the kingdom became secure. By executing justice and tying up loose ends that could affect the future stability of his kingdom, Solomon was promoting peace, not bloodshed. He was a man of peace in two ways: he did not go to war, and he put an end to internal rebellion.

2. Solomon's wisdom

3 Solomon made an alliance with Pharoah, the king of Egypt, and married one of his daughters. He brought her to Jerusalem to live in the City of David until he could finish building his palace and the Temple and the wall around the city. ²At that time the people of Israel sacrificed their offerings on altars in the hills, for the Temple of the Lord hadn't yet been built.

Solomon asks for wisdom

³(Solomon loved the Lord and followed all of his father David's instructions except that he continued to sacrifice in the hills and to offer incense there.) ⁴The most famous of the hilltop altars was at Gibeon and now the king went there and sacrificed one thousand burnt offerings! ⁵The Lord appeared to him in a dream that night and told him to ask for anything he wanted, and it would be given to him!

⁶Solomon replied, "You were wonderfully kind to my father David because he was honest and true and faithful to you, and obeyed your commands. And you have continued your kindness to him by giving him a son to succeed him. ⁷O Lord my God, now you have made me the king instead of my father David, but I am as a little child who doesn't know his way around. ⁸And here I am among your own chosen people, a nation so great that there are almost too many people to count! ⁹Give me an understanding mind so that I can govern your people well and know the difference between what is right and what is wrong. For who by himself is able to carry such a heavy responsibility?"

¹⁰The Lord was pleased with his reply and was glad that Solomon had asked for wisdom. ¹¹So he replied, "Because you have asked for wisdom in governing my people, and haven't asked for a long life or riches for yourself, or the defeat of your enemies— ¹²yes, I'll give you what you asked for! I will give you a wiser mind than anyone else has ever had or ever will have! ¹³And I will also give you what you didn't ask for—riches and honor! And no one in all the world will be as rich and famous as you for the rest of your life! ¹⁴And I will give you a long life if you follow me and obey my laws as your father David did."

¹⁵Then Solomon woke up and realized it had been a dream. He returned to Jerusalem and went into the Tabernacle. And as he stood before the Ark of the

3:1
1 Kgs 7:8; 9:24

3:2
Lev 17:3-5
Deut 12:13,14
1 Kgs 5:2,3

3:3
1 Kgs 9:4
11:4,6,38

3:4
1 Chron 16:39
21:29
2 Chron 1:2,3

3:5
1 Kgs 9:2,3
2 Chron 1:7

3:6
2 Sam 7:8; 12:7
2 Chron 1:8

3:7
1 Chron 22:9
29:1

3:8
Gen 13:16
15:5; 22:17

3:9
2 Sam 14:17
1 Kgs 3:12,13
2 Chron 1:10
Prov 2:3-5,9
Jas 1:5

3:12
1 Kgs 4:29; 5:12

3:13
1 Kgs 3:28
4:20; 10:23

3:14
Deut 5:16
25:13-15

3:15
1 Kgs 8:63

3:1 Marriage between royal families was a common practice in the ancient Near East because it secured peace. Although Solomon's marital alliances built friendships with surrounding nations, they were also the beginning of his downfall. These relationships became inroads for pagan ideas and practices. Solomon's foreign wives brought their idols to Jerusalem and eventually lured him into idolatry (11:1–8).

It is easy to minimize religious differences in order to encourage the development of a friendship, but seemingly small differences can have an enormous impact upon a relationship. God gives us standards to follow for all our relationships, including marriage. If we follow God's will, we will not be lured away from our true focus.

3:2, 3 God's law said that the Israelites could make sacrifices only in specified places (Deuteronomy 12:13, 14). This was to prevent the people from instituting their own methods of worship and allowing heathen practices to creep into their worship. But many Israelites, including King Solomon, made sacrifices in the surrounding hills. Solomon loved God, but this act was sin. It took the offerings out of the watchful care of priests and ministers loyal to God and opened the way for false teaching to be tied to these sacrifices.

3:6–9 When given a chance to have anything in the world, Solomon asked for wisdom in order to lead well and to make right decisions. We can ask God for this same wisdom (James 1:5). Notice that Solomon asked for wisdom to carry out his job. He did not ask God to do the job for him. We should not ask God to do *for*

us what he wants to do *through* us. Instead we should ask God to give us the wisdom to know what to do and the courage to follow through on it.

3:10 Solomon received great wisdom from God, but it was up to him to apply that wisdom to all areas of his life. He was obviously wise in governing the nation, but foolish in running his household. Wisdom is both the discernment to know what is best and the strength of character to act upon that knowledge. While Solomon remained wise all his life, he did not always act upon his wisdom (11:6).

3:11–14 Solomon asked for wisdom, not wealth, but God gave him riches and long life as well. While God does not promise riches to those who follow him, he gives us what we need if we put his kingdom, his interests, and his principles first in our lives (Matthew 6:31–33). Setting your sights on riches will only leave you dissatisfied, because even if you get the riches you crave, you will still desire something more. But if you put God and his work first, he will satisfy your deepest needs.

3:12 Solomon prayed for wisdom, and God made him wiser than anyone else had ever been. In Proverbs 1:1–9, we read Solomon's definition of wisdom: "to trust and reverence the Lord." No other human being has had the wisdom of Solomon, yet many have remained more faithful to the Lord throughout their lives. Solomon is remembered for his wisdom, but not for his faithfulness to God. We need wisdom, but even more we need a steadfast relationship with God, the source of all wisdom. Not everyone has great wisdom, but all have the opportunity to be faithful to God.

Covenant of the Lord, he sacrificed burnt offerings and peace offerings. Then he invited all of his officials to a great banquet.

Solomon shows great wisdom

16Soon afterwards two young prostitutes came to the king to have an argument settled.

17, 18"Sir," one of them began, "we live in the same house, just the two of us, and recently I had a baby. When it was three days old, this woman's baby was born too. 19But her baby died during the night when she rolled over on it in her sleep and smothered it. 20Then she got up in the night and took my son from beside me while I was asleep, and laid her dead child in my arms and took mine to sleep beside her. 21And in the morning when I tried to feed my baby it was dead! But when it became light outside, I saw that it wasn't my son at all."

SOLOMON

Wisdom is only effective when it is put into use. Early in his life, Solomon had the sense to recognize his need for wisdom. But by the time Solomon asked for wisdom to rule his kingdom, he had already started a habit which would make his wisdom ineffective for his own life—he sealed a pact with Egypt by marrying Pharaoh's daughter. She was the first of hundreds of wives married for similar reasons. In doing this, Solomon went against not only his father's last words, but also God's direct commands. His action reminds us how easy it is to know what is right and yet not do it.

It is clear that God's gift of wisdom to Solomon did not mean that he couldn't make mistakes. He had been given great possibilities as the king of God's chosen people, but with them came great responsibilities—he tended to pursue the former and neglect the latter. While becoming famous as a builder of temples and palaces, he became infamous as a leader who excessively taxed and worked his people. Visitors from distant lands came to admire this wise king, while his own people were gradually alienated from him.

Little is mentioned in the Bible about the last decade of Solomon's reign. Ecclesiastes probably records his last reflections on life. In that book we find a man proving through bitter experience that finding meaning to life apart from God is a vain pursuit. Security and contentment are only found in a personal relationship with God. The contentment we find in the opportunities and successes of this life is temporary. The more we expect them to be permanent, the more quickly they are gone. Be sure to balance your pursuit of the possibilities in life with reliable fulfillment of your responsibilities.

Strengths and accomplishments:
● Third king of Israel, David's chosen heir
● The wisest man who ever lived
● Author of *Ecclesiastes* and *Song of Solomon,* as well as many of the Proverbs and some of the Psalms
● Built God's Temple in Jerusalem
● Diplomat, trader, collector, patron of the arts

Weaknesses and mistakes:
● Sealed many foreign agreements by marrying heathen women
● Allowed his wives to affect his loyalty to God
● Excessively taxed his people and drafted them into a labor force

Lessons from his life:
● Effective leadership can be nullified by an ineffective personal life
● Solomon failed to obey God, but did not learn the lesson of repentance until late in life
● Knowing what actions are required of us means little without the will to perform those actions

Vital Statistics:
● Where: Jerusalem
● Occupation: King of Israel
● Relatives: Father: David. Mother: Bath-sheba. Brothers: Absalom, Adonijah. Sister: Tamar. Son: Rehoboam.

Key verse:
" 'Wasn't this exactly King Solomon's problem?' I demanded. 'There was no king who could compare with him, and God loved him and made him the king over all Israel; but even so he was led into idolatry by foreign women' " (Nehemiah 13:26).

Solomon's story is told in 2 Samuel 12:24—1 Kings 11:43. He is also mentioned in 1 Chronicles 28, 29; 2 Chronicles 1—9; Nehemiah 13:26; Psalm 72; and Matthew 6:29; 12:42.

²²Then the other woman interrupted, "It certainly was her son, and the living child is mine."

"No," the first woman said, "the dead one is yours and the living one is mine." And so they argued back and forth before the king.

²³Then the king said, "Let's get the facts straight: both of you claim the living child, and each says that the dead child belongs to the other. ²⁴All right, bring me a sword." So a sword was brought to the king. ²⁵Then he said, "Divide the living child in two and give half to each of these women!"

²⁶Then the woman who really was the mother of the child, and who loved him very much, cried out, "Oh, no, sir! Give her the child—don't kill him!"

3:26
Isa 49:15

But the other woman said, "All right, it will be neither yours nor mine; divide it between us!"

²⁷Then the king said, "Give the baby to the woman who wants him to live, for she is the mother!"

²⁸Word of the king's decision spread quickly throughout the entire nation, and all the people were awed as they realized the great wisdom God had given him.

3:28
1 Kgs 3:9; 4:29

Solomon's cabinet members

4 Here is a list of King Solomon's cabinet members:

Azariah (son of Zadok) was the High Priest;

Elihoreph and Ahijah (sons of Shisha) were secretaries;

Jehoshaphat (son of Ahilud) was the official historian and in charge of the archives;

Benaiah (son of Jehoiada) was commander-in-chief of the army;

Zadok and Abiathar were priests;

Azariah (son of Nathan) was secretary of state;

Zabud (son of Nathan) was the king's personal priest and special friend;

Ahishar was manager of palace affairs;

Adoniram (son of Abda) was superintendent of public works.

⁷There were also twelve officials of Solomon's court—one man from each tribe—responsible for requisitioning food from the people for the king's household. Each of them arranged provisions for one month of the year.

⁸⁻¹⁹The names of these twelve officers were:

Ben-hur, whose area for this taxation was the hill country of Ephraim;

Ben-deker, whose area was Makaz, Sha-albim, Beth-shemesh, and Elon-beth-hanan;

Ben-hesed, whose area was Arubboth, including Socoh and all the land of Hepher;

Ben-abinadab (who married Solomon's daughter, the princess Taphath), whose area was the highlands of Dor;

Baana (son of Ahilud), whose area was Taanach and Megiddo, all of Beth-shean near Zarethan below Jezreel, and all the territory from Beth-shean to Abel-meholah and over to Jokmeam;

Ben-geber, whose area was Ramoth-gilead, including the villages of Jair (the son of Manasseh) in Gilead; and the region of Argob in Bashan, including sixty walled cities with bronze gates;

Ahinadab (the son of Iddo), whose area was Mahanaim;

4:1ff Solomon was well organized, with eleven cabinet members, 12 district officers (one for each of the tribes), and a general manager. Each person had a specific responsibility or territory to manage. This organization was essential to maintain the government's effectiveness: it was a wise move by a wise man. It is good stewardship to be well organized. Good organization helps people work together in harmony and insures that the desired goal will be reached.

4:7 A census was often taken for tax purposes. Israel was made up of 12 tribes and, during Solomon's reign, each tribe was responsible for supporting the king for one month. The census counted all the people in each tribe who were eligible to pay the taxes. The prophet Samuel had warned the people of heavy taxation when they came to him begging to have a king (1 Samuel 8:11–18).

Ahima-az (who married Princess Basemath, another of Solomon's daughters),
   whose area was Naphtali;
Baana (son of Hushai), whose areas were Asher and Bealoth;
Jehoshaphat (son of Paruah), whose area was Issachar;
Shime-i (son of Ela), whose area was Benjamin;
Geber (son of Uri), whose area was Gilead, including the territories of King
   Sihon of the Amorites and King Og of Bashan.

A general manager supervised these officials and their work.

Solomon's dominion

4:20
Gen 32:12
Prov 14:28

4:21
2 Sam 8:2,6
2 Chron 9:26
Ps 68:29
72:10,11

4:24
1 Kgs 5:4
1 Chron 22:9

4:25
Isa 60:18
Jer 23:5,6
Mic 4:4
Zech 3:10

4:26
1 Kgs 10:26
2 Chron 1:14

20Israel and Judah were a wealthy, populous, contented nation at this time.
21King Solomon ruled the whole area from the Euphrates River to the land of the
Philistines, and down to the borders of Egypt. The conquered peoples of those
lands sent taxes to Solomon and continued to serve him throughout his lifetime.
22The daily food requirements for the palace were 195 bushels of fine flour, 390
bushels of meal, 2310 oxen from the fattening pens, 20 pasture-fed cattle, 100
sheep, and, from time to time, deer, gazelles, roebucks, and plump fowl.
24His dominion extended over all the kingdoms west of the Euphrates River,
from Tiphsah to Gaza. And there was peace throughout the land.
25Throughout the lifetime of Solomon, all of Judah and Israel lived in peace and
safety; and each family had its own home and garden.
26Solomon owned forty thousand chariot horses and employed twelve thousand
charioteers. 27Each month the tax officials provided food for King Solomon and his
court; 28also the barley and straw for the royal horses in the stables.

Solomon is famous for wisdom

4:29
1 Kgs 3:9,28

4:30
Isa 19:11
Acts 7:22

4:32
Prov 1:1
Eccles: 12:9
Song 1:1

4:34
1 Kgs 10:1
2 Chron 9:23

29God gave Solomon great wisdom and understanding, and a mind with broad
interests. 30In fact, his wisdom excelled that of any of the wise men of the East,
including those in Egypt. 31He was wiser than Ethan the Ezrahite and Heman,
Calcol, and Darda, the sons of Mahol; and he was famous among all the surrounding nations. 32He was the author of 3,000 proverbs and wrote 1,005 songs. 33He
was a great naturalist, with interest in animals, birds, snakes, fish, and trees—from
the great cedars of Lebanon down to the tiny hyssop which grows in cracks in the
wall. 34And kings from many lands sent their ambassadors to him for his advice.

3. Solomon builds the Temple
Preparation for the Temple

5:1
2 Sam 5:11
1 Chron 14:1
2 Chron 14:1

5 King Hiram of Tyre had always been a great admirer of David, so when he
learned that David's son Solomon was the new king of Israel, he sent ambassadors to extend congratulations and good wishes. 2, 3Solomon replied with a

---

SOLOMON'S KINGDOM Solomon's kingdom spread from
the Euphrates River in the north to the borders of Egypt. The
entire land was at peace under his rule.

4:20–25 Throughout most of his reign, Solomon applied his
wisdom well because he sought after God. The fruits of this
wisdom were peace, security, and prosperity for the nation.
Solomon's era is often looked upon as the ideal of what any nation
can become when united in trust and obedience to God.

4:32 The book of Proverbs records many of these 3,000 wise
proverbs. Other biblical writings of Solomon include Psalms 72 and
127 and the books of *Ecclesiastes* and the *Song of Solomon*.

5:2, 3 When David offered to build a temple, God said "no"
through the prophet Nathan (2 Samuel 7:1–17). God wanted a
peacemaker, not a warrior, to build his house of prayer
(1 Chronicles 28:2, 3).

proposal about the Temple of the Lord he wanted to build. His father David, Solomon pointed out to Hiram, had not been able to build it because of the numerous wars going on, and he had been waiting for the Lord to give him peace.

4"But now," Solomon said to Hiram, "the Lord my God has given Israel peace on every side; I have no foreign enemies or internal rebellions. 5So I am planning to build a Temple for the Lord my God, just as he instructed my father that I should do. For the Lord told him, 'Your son, whom I will place upon your throne, shall build me a Temple.' 6Now please assist me with this project. Send your woodsmen to the mountains of Lebanon to cut cedar timber for me, and I will send my men to work beside them, and I will pay your men whatever wages you ask; for as you know, no one in Israel can cut timber like you Sidonians!"

7Hiram was very pleased with the message from Solomon. "Praise God for giving David a wise son to be king of the great nation of Israel," he said. 8Then he sent this reply to Solomon: "I have received your message and I will do as you have asked concerning the timber. I can supply both cedar and cypress. 9My men will bring the logs from the Lebanon mountains to the Mediterranean Sea and build them into rafts. We will float them along the coast to wherever you need them; then we will break the rafts apart and deliver the timber to you. You can pay me with food for my household."

10So Hiram produced for Solomon as much cedar and cypress timber as he desired, 11and in return Solomon sent him an annual payment of 125,000 bushels of wheat for his household and 96 gallons of pure olive oil. 12So the Lord gave great wisdom to Solomon just as he had promised. And Hiram and Solomon made a formal alliance of peace.

13Then Solomon drafted thirty thousand laborers from all over Israel, 14and rotated them to Lebanon, ten thousand a month, so that each man was a month in Lebanon and two months at home. Adoniram was the general superintendent of this labor camp. 15Solomon also had seventy thousand additional laborers, eighty thousand stonecutters in the hill country, 16and thirty-three hundred foremen. 17The stonecutters quarried and shaped huge blocks of stone—a very expensive job—for the foundation of the Temple. 18Men from Gebal helped Solomon's and Hiram's builders in cutting the timber and making the boards, and in preparing the stone for the Temple.

Solomon begins to build the Temple

6 It was in the spring of the fourth year of Solomon's reign that he began the actual construction of the Temple. (This was 480 years after the people of Israel left their slavery in Egypt.) 2The Temple was ninety feet long, thirty feet wide, and forty-five feet high. 3All along the front of the Temple was a porch thirty feet long and fifteen feet deep. 4Narrow windows were used throughout.

5An annex of rooms was built along the full length of both sides of the Temple against the outer walls. 6These rooms were three stories high, the lower floor being 7½ feet wide, the second floor 9 feet wide, and the upper floor 10½ feet wide. The rooms were connected to the walls of the Temple by beams resting on blocks built out from the wall—so the beams were not inserted into the walls themselves. 7The stones used in the construction of the Temple were prefinished at the

5:4
1 Kgs 4:24
1 Chron 22:9

5:5
2 Sam 7:12,13
1 Chron 17:12

5:9
2 Chron 2:16
Ezra 3:7

5:12
1 Kgs 3:12; 4:29

6:1
Judg 11:26
2 Chron 3:1
Acts 7:47

6:2
1 Chron 28:11
Ezek 40:5

6:7
Ex 20:25
Deut 27:5,6

5:8 Solomon asked Hiram to send cedar and cypress wood for the Temple because he knew these were precious woods considered the best for building. These woods were coarse grained, very hard, and rot resistant. They were also beautiful and had a fragrant scent. The logs were tied into rafts and floated down the seacoast from Tyre to a port in Israel, from which they were carried overland to Jerusalem.

5:13, 14 Solomon drafted three times the number of workers needed for the Temple project and then arranged their schedules so they didn't have to be away from home for long periods of time. This showed his concern for the welfare of his workers and the

importance he placed on family life. The strength of a nation is in direct proportion to the strength of its families. Solomon wisely recognized that the family should always be a top priority. As you structure your own work or arrange the schedules of others, watch for the impact of your plans upon your family and those of others.

6:1ff For more information on the purpose of the Temple, see the note on 2 Chronicles 5:1ff.

6:7 In honor of God, the Temple in Jerusalem was built without the sound of a hammer or any tool at the building site. This meant cutting the stone miles away at the quarry. The people's honor and respect for God extended to every aspect of constructing this

quarry, so the entire structure was built without the sound of hammer, axe, or any other tool at the building site.

8The bottom floor of the side rooms was entered from the right side of the Temple, and there were winding stairs going up to the second floor; another flight of stairs led from the second to the third. 9After completing the Temple, Solomon paneled it all, including the beams and pillars, with cedar. 10As already stated, there was an annex on each side of the building, attached to the Temple walls by cedar timbers. Each story of the annex was 7½ feet high.

11, 12Then the Lord sent this message to Solomon concerning the Temple he was building: "If you do as I tell you to and follow all of my commandments and instructions, I will do what I told your father David I would do: 13I will live among the people of Israel and never forsake them."

14At last the Temple was finished. 15The entire inside, from floor to ceiling, was paneled with cedar, and the floors were made of cypress boards. 16The thirty-foot inner room at the far end of the Temple—the Most Holy Place—was also paneled from the floor to the ceiling with cedar boards. 17The remainder of the Temple—other than the Most Holy Place—was sixty feet long. 18Throughout the Temple the cedar paneling laid over the stone walls was carved with designs of rosebuds and open flowers.

19The inner room was where the Ark of the Covenant of the Lord was placed. 20This inner sanctuary was thirty feet long, thirty feet wide, and thirty feet high. Its walls and ceiling were overlaid with pure gold, and Solomon made a cedar-wood altar for this room. 21, 22Then he overlaid the interior of the remainder of the Temple—including the cedar altar—with pure gold; and he made gold chains to protect the entrance to the Most Holy Place.

23-28Within the inner sanctuary Solomon placed two statues of Guardian Angels made from olive wood, each fifteen feet high. They were placed so that their outspread wings reached from wall to wall, while their inner wings touched each other at the center of the room; each wing was 7½ feet long, so each angel measured fifteen feet from wing tip to wing tip. The two angels were identical in all dimensions, and each was overlaid with gold.

29Figures of angels, palm trees, and open flowers were carved on all the walls of both rooms of the Temple, 30and the floor of both rooms was overlaid with gold.

31The doorway to the inner sanctuary was a five-sided opening, 32and its two olive-wood doors were carved with Guardian Angels, palm trees, and open flowers, all overlaid with gold.

33Then he made square doorposts of olive wood for the entrance to the Temple. 34There were two folding doors of cypress wood, and each door was hinged to fold back upon itself. 35Angels, palm trees, and open flowers were carved on these doors and carefully overlaid with gold.

36The wall of the inner court had three layers of hewn stone and one layer of cedar beams.

37The foundation of the Temple was laid in the month of May in the fourth year of Solomon's reign, 38and the entire building was completed in every detail in November of the eleventh year of his reign. So it took seven years to build.

6:23-28 *two statues of Guardian Angels,* literally, "he made two cherubim."

6:9
2 Sam 7:7
1 Kgs 6:14,38

6:11
1 Kgs 3:14

6:13
Ex 25:8
Deut 31:6
Josh 1:5

6:16
Ex 26:33
Lev 16:1,2
2 Chron 3:8

6:21
Ex 30:1

6:23
Ex 25:20; 37:7
2 Chron 3:10

6:34
Ezek 41:23

6:37
2 Chron 3:3

---

building in which to worship him. This detail is recorded not to teach us how to build a church, but to show us the importance of demonstrating care, concern, honor, and respect for God and his sanctuary.

6:13 This verse summarizes the main purpose of the Temple. God promised that his eternal presence would never leave the Temple as long as one condition was met: the Israelites had to follow God's Law. Knowing how many laws they had to follow, we may think this condition was difficult. But the Israelites' situation was

much like ours today. They were not cut off from God for failing to keep some small subpoint of a law. Forgiveness was amply provided for all their sins, no matter how large or small. As you read the history of the kings, you will see that lawbreaking was the result, not the cause, of estrangement from God. The kings abandoned God in their hearts first and *then* failed to keep his laws. When we close our hearts to God, the power of his presence soon leaves us.

Solomon builds his palace

7 Then Solomon built his own palace, which took thirteen years to construct. **2**One of the rooms in the palace was called the Hall of the Forest of Lebanon. It was huge—measuring 150 feet long, 75 feet wide, and 45 feet high. The great cedar ceiling beams rested upon four rows of cedar pillars. **3, 4**There were forty-five windows in the hall, set in three tiers, one tier above the other, five to a tier, facing each other from three walls. **5**Each of the doorways and windows had a square frame.

6Another room was called the Hall of Pillars. It was seventy-five feet long and forty-five feet wide, with a porch in front covered by a canopy which was supported by pillars.

7There was also the Throne Room or Judgment Hall, where Solomon sat to hear legal matters; it was paneled with cedar from the floor to the rafters.

8His cedar-paneled living quarters surrounded a courtyard behind this hall. (He designed similar living quarters, the same size, in the palace which he built for Pharaoh's daughter—one of his wives.) **9**These buildings were constructed entirely from huge, expensive stones, cut to measure. **10**The foundation stones were twelve to fifteen feet across. **11**The huge stones in the walls were also cut to measure, and were topped with cedar beams. **12**The Great Court had three courses of hewn stone in its walls, topped with cedar beams, just like the inner court of the Temple and the porch of the palace.

Equipment for the Temple

13King Solomon then asked for a man named Hiram to come from Tyre, for he was a skilled craftsman in bronze work. **14**He was half Jewish, being the son of a widow of the tribe of Naphtali, and his father had been a foundry worker from Tyre. So he came to work for King Solomon.

15He cast two hollow bronze pillars, each twenty-seven feet high and eighteen feet around, with three-inch-thick walls. **16-22**At the tops of the pillars he made two lily-shaped capitals from molten bronze, each 7½ feet high. The upper part of each capital was shaped like a lily, six feet high. Each capital was decorated with seven sets of bronze, chain-designed lattices and four hundred pomegranates in two rows. Hiram set these pillars at the entrance of the Temple. The one on the south was named the Jachin Pillar, and the one on the north, the Boaz Pillar.

23Then Hiram cast a round bronze tank, 7½ feet high and 15 feet from brim to brim; 45 feet in circumference. **24**On the underside of the rim were two rows of ornaments an inch or two apart, which were cast along with the tank. **25**It rested on twelve bronze oxen standing tail to tail, three facing north, three west, three south, and three east. **26**The sides of the tank were four inches thick; its brim was shaped like a goblet, and it had a twelve thousand gallon capacity.

27-30 Then he made ten four-wheeled movable stands, each 6 feet square and 4½ feet high. They were constructed with undercarriages braced with square crosspieces. These crosspieces were decorated with carved lions, oxen, and angels. Above and below the lions and oxen were wreath decorations. Each of these movable stands had four bronze wheels and bronze axles, and at each corner of the stands were supporting posts made of bronze and decorated with wreaths on each side. **31**The top of each stand was a round piece 1½ feet high. Its center was concave, 2¼ feet deep, decorated on the outside with wreaths. Its panels were square, not round.

32The stands rode on four wheels which were connected to axles that had been

7:1
1 Kgs 3:1; 9:10
2 Chron 8:1

7:2
1 Kgs 10:17
2 Chron 9:16

7:7
1 Kgs 6:9

7:8
1 Kgs 3:1; 7:8
2 Chron 8:11

7:13
1 Kgs 7:40
2 Chron 2:13

7:15
2 Kgs 25:13
2 Chron 3:15
4:12
Jer 52:17

7:27
2 Kgs 16:17

7:22 *Jachin Pillar* and *Boaz Pillar.* Jachin means "to establish," and Boaz means "strength." **7:24** *an inch or two apart,* literally, "ten in a cubit." **7:25** *bronze,* implied. **7:27** *square,* implied in vs 31.

7:13 This is not King Hiram mentioned in chapter 5, but a craftsman. Second Chronicles 2:13, 14 calls this man Huramabi.

7:23 This enormous tank was called the *laver.* Designed and used for the priests' ceremonial washings, it was placed in the Temple court near the altar of burnt offering. Priests washed

themselves before offering sacrifices or entering the Temple (Exodus 30:17–20).

7:27-37 These vats of water were used for washing the various parts of the animal sacrifices. Each vat was placed on a movable stand so it could be used where needed.

cast as part of the stands. The wheels were twenty-seven inches high, 33and were similar to chariot wheels. All the parts of the stands were cast from molten bronze, including the axles, spokes, rims, and hubs. 34There were supports at each of the four corners of the stands, and these, too, were cast with the stands. 35A nine-inch rim surrounded the tip of each stand, banded with lugs. All was cast as one unit with the stand. 36Guardian Angels, lions, and palm trees surrounded by wreaths were engraved on the borders of the band wherever there was room. 37All ten stands were the same size and were made alike, for each was cast from the same mold.

7:38
2 Kgs 25:14
2 Chron 4:6

38Then he made ten brass vats, and placed them on the stands. Each vat was six feet square and contained 240 gallons of water. 39Five of these vats were arranged on the left and five on the right-hand side of the room. The tank was in the southeast corner, on the right-hand side of the room. 40Hiram also made the necessary pots, shovels, and basins and at last completed the work in the Temple of the Lord which had been assigned to him by King Solomon.

7:41
2 Chron 4:12

41-46Here is a list of the items he made:

Two pillars;
A capital at the top of each pillar;
Latticework covering the bases of the capitals of each pillar;
Four hundred pomegranates in two rows on the latticework, to cover the bases of
   the two capitals;
Ten movable stands holding ten vats;
One large tank and twelve oxen supporting it;
Pots;
Shovels;
Basins.

7:47
1 Chron 22:3,14

All these items were made of burnished bronze, and were cast at the plains of the Jordan River between Succoth and Zarethan. 47The total weight of these pieces was not known because they were too heavy to weigh!

7:48
Ex 37:10,15,16

48All the utensils and furniture used in the Temple were made of solid gold. This included the altar, the table where the Bread of the Presence of God was displayed,

7:49
Ex 25:31; 37:14
7:50
2 Kgs 25:14,15

49the lampstands (five on the right-hand side and five on the left, in front of the Most Holy Place), the flowers, lamps, tongs, 50cups, snuffers, basins, spoons, firepans, the hinges of the doors to the Most Holy Place, and the main entrance doors of the Temple. Each of these was made of solid gold.

7:51
2 Sam 8:11
2 Chron 5:1

51When the Temple was finally finished, Solomon took into the treasury of the Temple the silver, the gold, and all the vessels dedicated for that purpose by his father David.

The Ark is brought to the Temple

8:1
2 Sam 5:7; 6:17

8 Then Solomon called a convocation at Jerusalem of all the leaders of Israel—the heads of the tribes and clans—to observe the transferring of the Ark of the Covenant of the Lord from the Tabernacle in Zion, the City of David, to the Temple. 2This celebration occurred at the time of the Tabernacle Festival in the month of October. 3,4During the festivities the priests carried the Ark to the

8:2
2 Chron 5:3; 7:8
8:3
Num 7:9

7:40 These other utensils had the same use in the Temple as they had in the Tabernacle (Exodus 35). Kept in the inner court, they were designed to help the priests with all the work connected with the sacrifices.

7:41–46 Hiram's items of bronze and brass would look strange in today's churches, but some Christians use other articles to enhance worship. Stained-glass windows, crosses, pulpits, hymnbooks, baptistries, and communion tables serve as aids to worship. While the instruments of worship may change, the purpose should never change—to give honor and praise to God.

7:41–46 Pomegranates were used to decorate the Tabernacle of

Moses' day as well as the Temple. They symbolized fruitfulness.

8:1ff What was the difference between the Temple and the Tabernacle, and why did the Israelites change from one to the other? The Tabernacle was a portable place of worship designed for the people as they were traveling toward the Promised Land. The word *tabernacle* means tent. The Temple was a permanent place to worship God after the Israelites entered Canaan.

8:3, 4 The palace and the Temple were built close together because Israel's king was to be both a political and a religious leader. Guiding the political, judicial, and military affairs of the nation was not to be done apart from God.

Temple, along with all the sacred vessels which had previously been in the Tabernacle. ⁵King Solomon and all the people gathered before the Ark, sacrificing uncounted sheep and oxen.

⁶Then the priests took the Ark into the inner sanctuary of the Temple—the Most Holy Place—and placed it under the wings of the statues of the mighty angels. ⁷The angels had been constructed in such a manner that their wings spread out over the spot where the Ark would be placed; so now their wings overshadowed the Ark and its carrying poles. ⁸The poles were so long that they stuck out past the angels and could be seen from the next room, but not from the outer court; and they remain there to this day. ⁹There was nothing in the Ark at that time except the two stone tablets which Moses had placed there at Mount Horeb at the time the Lord made his covenant with the people of Israel after they left Egypt.

¹⁰*Look! As the priests are returning from the inner sanctuary, a bright cloud fills the Temple!* ¹¹*The priests have to go outside because the glory of the Lord is filling the entire building!*

¹²,¹³Now King Solomon prayed this invocation:

"The Lord has said that he would live in the thick darkness;
But, O Lord, I have built you a lovely home on earth, a place for you to live
    forever.

¹⁴Then the king turned around and faced the people as they stood before him, and blessed them.

¹⁵"Blessed be the Lord God of Israel," he said, "who has done today what he promised my father David: ¹⁶for he said to him, 'When I brought my people from Egypt, I didn't appoint a place for my Temple, but I appointed a man to be my people's leader.' ¹⁷This man was my father, David. He wanted to build a Temple for the Lord God of Israel, ¹⁸but the Lord told him not to. 'I am glad you want to do it,' he said, ¹⁹'but your son is the one who shall build my Temple.' ²⁰And now the Lord has done what he promised; for I have followed my father as king of Israel, and now this Temple has been built for the Lord God of Israel. ²¹And I have prepared a place in the Temple for the Ark which contains the covenant made by the Lord with our fathers, at the time that he brought them out of the land of Egypt."

Solomon dedicates the Temple

²²,²³Then, as all the people watched, Solomon stood before the altar of the Lord with his hands spread out towards heaven and said, "O Lord God of Israel, there is no god like you in heaven or earth, for you are loving and kind and you keep your promises to your people if they do their best to do your will. ²⁴Today you have fulfilled your promise to my father David, who was your servant; ²⁵and now, O Lord God of Israel, fulfill your further promise to him: that if his descendants follow your ways and try to do your will as he did, one of them shall always sit upon the throne of Israel. ²⁶Yes, O God of Israel, fulfill this promise too.

²⁷"But is it possible that God would really live on earth? Why, even the skies and the highest heavens cannot contain you, much less this Temple I have built! ²⁸And yet, O Lord my God, you have heard and answered my request: ²⁹Please watch over this Temple night and day—this place you have promised to live in—and as

8:5
1 Kgs 8:62,63
2 Chron 1:5,6

8:8
Ex 25:13,14
37:4,5
8:9
Ex 24:7; 25:16
Deut 4:13,14
10:2
Heb 9:4
8:10
Ex 40:34
2 Chron 7:1

8:12
2 Sam 7:13
22:10
2 Chron 6:1
Ps 97:2; 132:14

8:15
2 Sam 7:12
1 Kgs 8:24
1 Chron 22:10
29:10
8:16
Deut 12:4,5,11
1 Sam 16:1
8:17
2 Sam 7:2,3
1 Chron 17:1
8:19
2 Sam 7:12,13
1 Chron 17:11,
12; 22:8; 28:6
8:20
Neh 9:8
Jer 29:10

8:22
Deut 7:9
1 Sam 2:2
2 Sam 7:22
2 Chron 6:12
Neh 1:5; 9:32
8:24
1 Kgs 8:15
8:25
2 Sam 7:12,16
1 Kgs 2:4
1 Chron 17:23

8:27
2 Chron 6:18
Ps 139:7
Isa 66:1
Jer 23:24
Acts 7:48,49

8:16 For 480 years after Israel's escape from Egypt, God did not ask them to build a Temple for him. Instead he emphasized the importance of his presence among them and their need for spiritual leaders. It is easy to think of a building as the focus of God's presence and power, but God chooses and uses people to do his work. He can use you more than he can use a building of wood and stone. Building or enlarging our place of worship may be necessary, but it should never take priority over developing spiritual leaders.

8:24 Solomon was referring to the promise God made to David

that one of his sons would build the Temple (2 Samuel 7:12-15).

8:27 Solomon declared that even the highest heavens cannot contain God. Isn't it amazing that, though the heavens can't contain him, he is willing to live in the hearts of those who love him? The God of the universe takes up residence in the lives of his people.

8:29 Did God really live in the Temple? God is everywhere—he does not need a home in which to live. The Temple was a visible symbol of the invisible presence of God. Yet God was specially present in the Temple. Today God does not need a Temple because he lives in his people!

I face toward the Temple and pray, whether by night or by day, please listen to me and answer my requests. ³⁰Listen to every plea of the people of Israel whenever they face this place to pray; yes, hear in heaven where you live, and when you hear, forgive.

³¹"If a man is accused of doing something wrong and then, standing here before your altar, swears that he didn't do it, ³²hear him in heaven and do what is right; judge whether or not he did it.

8:30
Neh 1:5-7

8:31
Ex 22:8
Lev 5:1

SOLOMON'S TEMPLE
960–586 B.C.

Solomon's Temple was a beautiful sight. It took over seven years to build and was a magnificent building containing gold, silver, bronze, and cedar. This house for God was without equal. The blueprint is found in 2 Chronicles.

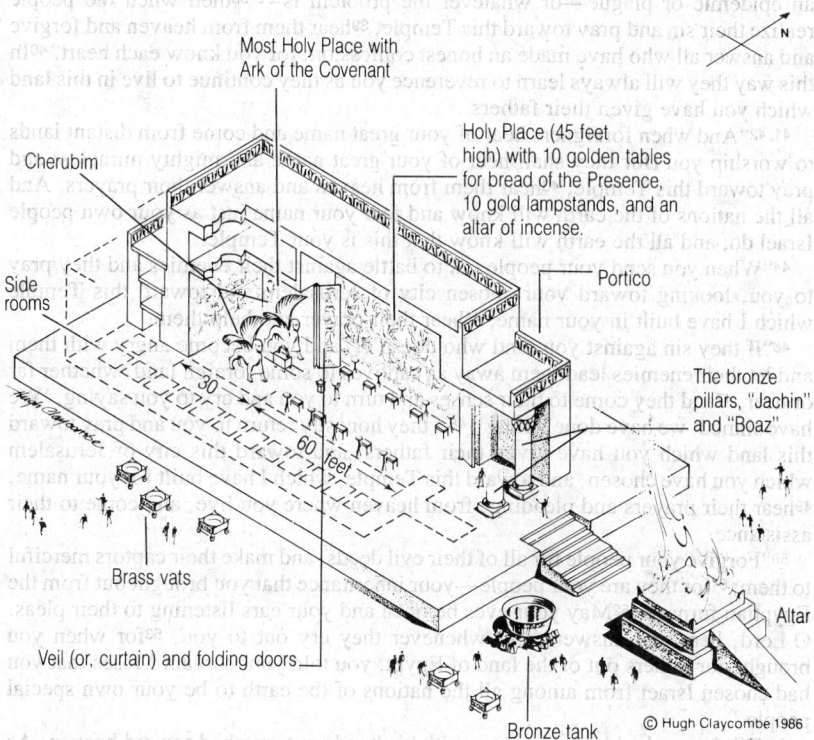

Most Holy Place with Ark of the Covenant

Holy Place (45 feet high) with 10 golden tables for bread of the Presence, 10 gold lampstands, and an altar of incense.

Cherubim

Side rooms

Portico

The bronze pillars, "Jachin" and "Boaz"

Brass vats

Altar

Veil (or, curtain) and folding doors

Bronze tank

© Hugh Claycombe 1986

FURNISHINGS

Cherubim: represented heavenly beings, symbolized God's presence and holiness (gold-plated, 15 feet wide)

Ark of the Covenant: contained the law written on two tablets, symbolized God's presence with Israel (wood overlaid with gold)

Veil: separated the Holy Place from the Most Holy Place (fine linen of red and blue, embroidered with depictions of angels)

Folding doors: between Holy Place and Most Holy Place (wood overlaid with gold)

Golden tables (wood overlaid with gold), *golden lampstands* (with seven lamps on each stand), and *altar of incense* (wood overlaid with gold): instruments for priestly functions in the Holy Place

Bronze pillars: named Jachin (meaning "sustainer") and Boaz (meaning "strength")—taken together they could mean "God provides the strength"

Altar: for burning of sacrifices (bronze)

Bronze tank: for priests' washing (had 12,000 gallon capacity)

Brass vats: for washing the sacrifices (tanks on wheeled bases)

This reconstruction uses known archaeological parallels to supplement the text, and assumes interior dimensions from 1 Kings 6:17-20. © Hugh Claycombe.

33, 34"And when your people sin and their enemies defeat them, hear them from heaven and forgive them if they turn to you again and confess that you are their God. Bring them back again to this land which you have given to their fathers.

35, 36"And when the skies are shut up and there is no rain because of their sin, hear them from heaven and forgive them when they pray toward this place and confess your name. And after you have punished them, help them to follow the good ways in which they should walk, and send rain upon the land which you have given your people.

37"If there is a famine in the land caused by plant disease or locusts or caterpillars, or if Israel's enemies besiege one of her cities, or if the people are struck by an epidemic or plague—or whatever the problem is— 38then when the people realize their sin and pray toward this Temple, 39hear them from heaven and forgive and answer all who have made an honest confession; for you know each heart. 40In this way they will always learn to reverence you as they continue to live in this land which you have given their fathers.

41, 42"And when foreigners hear of your great name and come from distant lands to worship you (for they shall hear of your great name and mighty miracles) and pray toward this Temple, 43hear them from heaven and answer their prayers. And all the nations of the earth will know and fear your name just as your own people Israel do; and all the earth will know that this is your Temple.

44"When you send your people out to battle against their enemies and they pray to you, looking toward your chosen city of Jerusalem and toward this Temple which I have built in your name, 45hear their prayer and help them.

46"If they sin against you (and who doesn't?) and you become angry with them and let their enemies lead them away as captives to some foreign land, whether far or near, 47and they come to their senses and turn to you and cry to you saying, 'We have sinned, we have done wrong'; 48if they honestly return to you and pray toward this land which you have given their fathers, and toward this city of Jerusalem which you have chosen, and toward this Temple, which I have built for your name, 49hear their prayers and pleadings from heaven where you live, and come to their assistance.

50"Forgive your people for all of their evil deeds, and make their captors merciful to them; 51for they are your people—your inheritance that you brought out from the Egyptian furnace. 52May your eyes be open and your ears listening to their pleas. O Lord, hear and answer them whenever they cry out to you, 53for when you brought our fathers out of the land of Egypt, you told your servant Moses that you had chosen Israel from among all the nations of the earth to be your own special people."

54, 55Solomon had been kneeling with his hands outstretched toward heaven. As he finished this prayer, he rose from before the altar of Jehovah and cried out this blessing upon all the people of Israel:

56"Blessed be the Lord who has fulfilled his promise and given rest to his people Israel; not one word has failed of all the wonderful promises proclaimed by his

8:33
Lev 26:14-17,
40,41
Deut 28:25,
47,48

8:35
Lev 26:19
Deut 11:16,17
28:23
1 Sam 12:23
2 Sam 21:1
1 Kgs 18:41

8:37
Lev 26:16,25
Deut 28:21,31
2 Kgs 6:25

8:39
1 Sam 2:3
1 Chron 28:9
Jer 17:10
Jn 2:24

8:41
1 Kgs 10:1
2 Chron 6:32

8:43
1 Sam 17:46
2 Kgs 19:19

8:44
2 Chron 14:11

8:46
2 Kgs 17:6,18
25:21
2 Chron 6:36
Ps 130:3,4

8:47
Lev 26:40
Ezra 9:5,6
Neh 1:6,7
Ps 106:6,7
Dan 9:5

8:48
Deut 4:29
1 Sam 7:3
Jer 29:12

8:50
2 Chron 30:9
Ezra 7:6
Neh 1:11
Ps 106:46

8:51
Ex 32:11
Deut 4:20; 9:26
1 Sam 8:8
Jer 11:4

8:53
Ex 19:5,6
33:16
Deut 4:34

8:54
1 Kgs 8:22

8:56
Josh 21:45
23:14
2 Kgs 10:9,10
Lk 1:54

8:33, 34 After Solomon's reign, the people continually turned away from God. The rest of the kingdom era is a vivid picture of what Solomon described in these verses. As a result of the people's sin, God let them be overrun by enemies several times. Then, in desperation, they cried out to God for forgiveness, and God restored them.

8:41-43 God chose Israel to be a blessing to the whole world (Genesis 12:1-3). This blessing found its fulfillment in Jesus—a descendant of Abraham and David (Galatians 3:8, 9)—who became the Messiah for all people, Jew and non-Jew. When the Israelites first entered the Promised Land, they were ordered to clear out several wicked nations; thus we read of many wars in the Old Testament. But we should not conclude that war was Israel's first duty. After subduing the evil people, Israel was to become a light to the surrounding nations. But Israel's own sin and spiritual

blindness prevented them from reaching out to the rest of the world with God's love. Jesus came to do what the nation of Israel failed to do.

8:46-49 Solomon, who seemed to have prophetic insight into the future captivities of his people (2 Kings 17, 25), asked God to be merciful to them when they cried out to him to return them to their homeland. Reference to their return is made in Ezra 1, 2; Nehemiah 1, 2.

8:56-61 Solomon blessed the people and prayed for them. His prayer can be a pattern for our prayers. He had five basic requests: (1) for God's presence (8:57); (2) for the desire to do God's will in everything (8:58); (3) for help with daily needs (8:59); (4) for the desire to live good and perfect lives (8:61); (5) for the ability to obey God's laws and commandments (8:61). These prayer requests are just as applicable today as in Solomon's time.

8:57
Josh 1:5
1 Sam 12:22
Isa 41:17
Heb 13:5

8:58
Ps 119:36
Jer 31:33

8:59
2 Chron 6:40

8:60
Deut 4:35
1 Sam 17:46
1 Kgs 18:39
Jer 10:10

8:61
Deut 18:13
1 Kgs 20:3

8:62
2 Sam 6:17
2 Chron 7:4

8:64
2 Chron 7:7

servant Moses. 57May the Lord our God be with us as he was with our fathers; may he never forsake us. 58May he give us the desire to do his will in everything, and to obey all the commandments and instructions he has given our ancestors. 59And may these words of my prayer be constantly before him day and night, so that he helps me and all of Israel in accordance with our daily needs. 60May people all over the earth know that the Lord is God, and that there is no other god at all. 61O my people, may you live good and perfect lives before the Lord our God; may you always obey his laws and commandments, just as you are doing today."

62, 63Then the king and all the people dedicated the Temple by sacrificing peace offerings to the Lord—a total of 22,000 oxen and 120,000 sheep and goats! 64As a temporary measure the king sanctified the court in front of the Temple for the burnt offerings, grain offerings, and the fat of the peace offerings: for the bronze altar was too small to handle so much. 65The celebration lasted for fourteen days, and a great crowd came from one end of the land to the other. 66Afterwards Solomon sent the people home, happy for all the goodness that the Lord had shown to his servant David and to his people Israel. And they blessed the king.

4. Solomon's greatness and downfall
God's warning to Solomon

9:1
1 Kgs 7:1
2 Chron 8:6

9:2
1 Kgs 3:5; 11:9

9:4
1 Kgs 3:14; 11:4

9:5
2 Sam 7:12
1 Kgs 8:25

9:6
2 Sam 7:14
1 Chron 28:9
2 Chron 7:19

9:7
Lev 18:24
Deut 4:26,27
2 Kgs 17:23
Jer 7:4

9:8
Deut 29:24
2 Chron 7:21
Jer 22:8

9:9
Deut 29:25
2 Chron 7:22

9 When Solomon had finished building the Temple and the palace and all the other buildings he had always wanted, 2, 3the Lord appeared to him the second time (the first time had been at Gibeon) and said to him,

"I have heard your prayer. I have hallowed this Temple which you have built and have put my name here forever. I will constantly watch over it and rejoice in it. 4And if you live in honesty and truth as your father David did, always obeying me, 5then I will cause your descendants to be the kings of Israel forever, just as I promised your father David when I told him, 'One of your sons shall always be upon the throne of Israel.'

6"However, if you or your children turn away from me and worship other gods and do not obey my laws, 7then I will take away the people of Israel from this land which I have given them. I will take them from this Temple which I have hallowed for my name and I will cast them out of my sight; and Israel will become a joke to the nations and an example and proverb of sudden disaster. 8This Temple will become a heap of ruins, and everyone passing by will be amazed and will whistle with astonishment, asking, 'Why has the Lord done such things to this land and this Temple?' 9And the answer will be, 'The people of Israel abandoned the Lord their God who brought them out of the land of Egypt; they worshiped other gods instead. That is why the Lord has brought this evil upon them.'"

Solomon's other achievements

9:10
1 Kgs 6:37

9:11
1 Kgs 5:4
2 Chron 2:4

10At the end of the twenty years during which Solomon built the Temple and the palace, 11, 12he gave twenty cities in the land of Galilee to King Hiram of Tyre as payment for all the cedar and cypress lumber and gold he had furnished for the construction of the palace and Temple. Hiram came from Tyre to see the cities, but he wasn't at all pleased with them.

13"What sort of deal is this, my brother?" he asked. "These cities are a wasteland!" (And they are still known as "The Wasteland" today.) 14For Hiram had sent gold to Solomon valued at $3,500,000!

8:61 Solomon gathered the people not just to dedicate the Temple, but to rededicate themselves to God's service. Solomon could well be speaking these words to us today: "May you live good and perfect lives before the Lord our God; may you always obey his laws and commandments."

9:4–7 For more on the conditions of God's great promise to David and his descendants, see the note on 2:3, 4.

9:11–14 Was Solomon being unfair to Hiram? It is not clear from these verses whether Solomon gave these cities to Hiram, or whether they were collateral until he could repay Hiram for the gold he had lent. Second Chronicles 8:1, 2 implies that the cities were returned to Solomon. In either case, Hiram probably preferred a piece of land on the coast more suitable for trade. But in the end, he was repaid many times over through his trade partnerships with Solomon (2 Chronicles 9:10, 21). Because Phoenicia was on friendly terms with Israel and dependent on it for grain and oil, Hiram's relationship with Solomon was more important than a feud over some cities.

15Solomon had conscripted forced labor to build the Temple, his palace, Fort Millo, the wall of Jerusalem, and the cities of Hazor, Megiddo, and Gezer. 16Gezer was the city the king of Egypt conquered and burned, killing the Israeli population; later he had given the city to his daughter as a dowry—she was one of Solomon's wives. 17, 18So now Solomon rebuilt Gezer along with Lower Beth-horon, Baalath, and Tamar, a desert city. 19He also built cities for grain storage, cities in which to keep his chariots, cities for homes for his cavalry and chariot drivers, and resort cities near Jerusalem and in the Lebanon mountains and elsewhere throughout the land.

20, 21Solomon conscripted his labor forces from those who survived in the nations he conquered—the Amorites, Hittites, Perizzites, Hivites, and Jebusites. For the people of Israel had not been able to wipe them out completely at the time of the invasion and conquest of Israel, and they continue as slaves even today. 22Solomon didn't conscript any Israelis for this work, although they became soldiers, officials, army officers, chariot commanders, and cavalrymen. 23And there were 550 men of Israel who were overseers of the labor forces.

Miscellaneous Notes:

24King Solomon moved Pharaoh's daughter from the City of David—the old sector of Jerusalem—to the new quarters he had built for her in the palace. Then he built Fort Millo.

25After the Temple was completed, Solomon offered burnt offerings and peace offerings three times a year on the altar he had built. And he also burned incense upon it.

26King Solomon had a shipyard in Ezion-geber near Eloth on the Red Sea in the land of Edom, where he built a fleet of ships.

27, 28King Hiram supplied experienced sailors to accompany Solomon's crews. They used to sail back and forth from Ophir, bringing gold to King Solomon, the total value of which was several million dollars each trip.

The Queen of Sheba visits Solomon

10 When the Queen of Sheba heard how wonderfully the Lord had blessed Solomon with wisdom, she decided to test him with some hard questions. 2She arrived in Jerusalem with a long train of camels carrying spices, gold, and jewels; and she told him all her problems. 3Solomon answered all her questions; nothing was too difficult for him, for the Lord gave him the right answers every

10:1 *the Lord had blessed Solomon with wisdom,* literally, "heard of the fame of Solomon concerning the name of the Lord." **10:3** *the Lord gave him the right answers every time,* literally, "there was nothing hidden from the king which he could not explain to her."

9:15
2 Sam 5:9
1 Kgs 6:38; 7:1
2 Chron 8:1,2

9:20
Gen 9:24,25
Josh 15:63
Judg 1:28,35

9:24
1 Kgs 3:1; 7:8
11:1,27
2 Chron 32:5

9:25
Ex 23:14
Deut 16:16
2 Chron 8:13

9:27
1 Kgs 10:11
1 Chron 29:4

10:1
2 Chron 9:1
Ps 72:10,15
Isa 60:6
Mt 12:42

9:16 At this time, Israel and Egypt were the world powers in the Near East. During Solomon's reign the Egyptian king captured Gezer. To make peace, Solomon married one of Pharaoh's daughters. Intermarriage among royal families was common, but it was not endorsed by God (Deuteronomy 17:17). Because the princess' dowry included the city of Gezer, which the Egyptian king had conquered earlier, it was returned to Israel.

9:24 Millo was an older section of Jerusalem already in use by the Jebusites before David captured the city (2 Samuel 5:9). It was rebuilt by Solomon and again restored by Hezekiah over two centuries later (2 Chronicles 32:5).

Mediterranean Sea

Hazor • Sea of Galilee

Megiddo •

SOLOMON'S KINGDOM

Gezer • Lower Beth-horon
Baalath • **Jerusalem**

Dead Sea

0   20 Mi.
0   20 Km.

to Tamar

SOLOMON'S BUILDING PROJECTS
Solomon became known as one of the great builders in Israel's history. He built Hazor, Megiddo, and Gezer as fortress cities at key points during his reign. He also rebuilt the cities of Lower Beth-horon, Baalath, and Tamar.

time. 4She soon realized that everything she had ever heard about his great wisdom was true. She also saw the beautiful palace he had built, 5and when she saw the wonderful foods on his table, the great number of servants and aides who stood around in splendid uniforms, his cupbearers, and the many offerings he sacrificed by fire to the Lord—well, there was no more spirit in her!

6She exclaimed to him, "Everything I heard in my own country about your wisdom and about the wonderful things going on here is all true. 7I didn't believe it until I came, but now I have seen it for myself! And really! The half had not been told me! Your wisdom and prosperity are far greater than anything I've ever heard of! 8Your people are happy and your palace aides are content—but how could it be otherwise, for they stand here day after day listening to your wisdom! 9Blessed be the Lord your God who chose you and set you on the throne of Israel. How the Lord must love Israel—for he gave you to them as their king! And you give your people a just, good government!"

10:9
2 Sam 8:15
23:3
1 Kgs 5:7
2 Chron 2:11

10Then she gave the king a gift of $3,500,000 in gold, along with a huge quantity of spices and precious gems; in fact, it was the largest single gift of spices King Solomon had ever received.

10:11
1 Kgs 9:27

11(And when King Hiram's ships brought gold to Solomon from Ophir, they also brought along a great supply of algum trees and gems. 12Solomon used the algum wood to make pillars for the Temple and the palace, and for harps and harpsichords for his choirs. Never before or since has there been such a supply of beautiful wood.)

13In exchange for the gifts from the Queen of Sheba, King Solomon gave her everything she asked him for, besides the presents he had already planned. Then she and her servants returned to their own land.

FRIENDS AND ENEMIES
Solomon's reputation brought acclaim and riches from many nations, but he disobeyed God, marrying heathen women and worshiping their idols. So God raised up enemies like Hadad from Edom and Rezin from Zobah (modern-day Syria). Jeroboam from Zeredah was another enemy who would eventually divide this mighty kingdom.

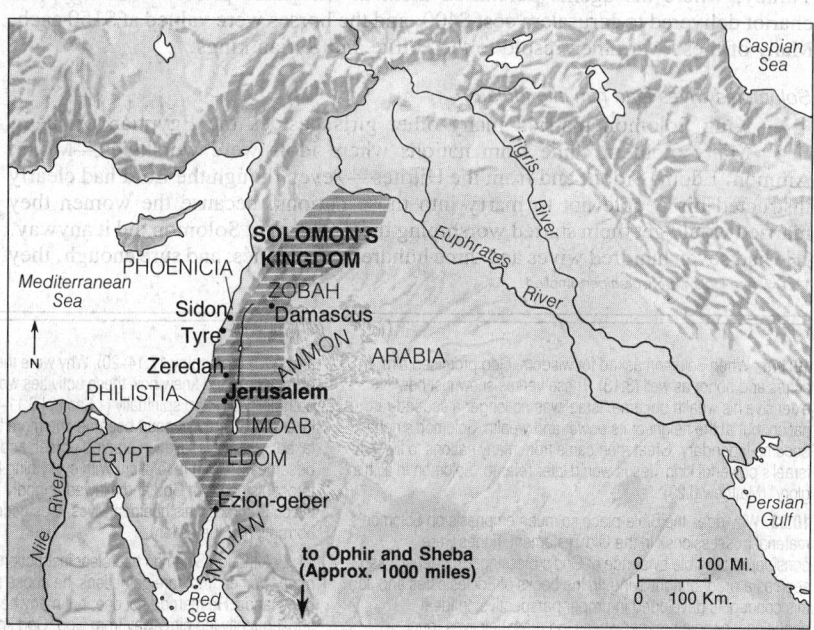

10:5 The Queen of Sheba came to see for herself if everything she had heard about Solomon was true. Contests using riddles or proverbs were often used to test wisdom. The queen may have used some of these as she questioned Solomon (10:3). When she realized the extent of his riches and wisdom, there was "no more spirit in her." In other words, she no longer disputed his power or wisdom. No longer a competitor, she became an admirer. Most

likely, her experience was repeated by many kings and foreign dignitaries who paid honor to Solomon.

10:8 Because of Solomon's wisdom, the people were happy and the palace aides content. Wisdom's quality is shown by how well it works. In James 3:17, 18 we learn that wisdom helps plant the seeds of peace. Are you seeking the kind of wisdom that establishes peace in your relationships?

Solomon's great riches

14Each year Solomon received gold worth a quarter of a billion, 15besides sales taxes and profits from trade with the kings of Arabia and the other surrounding territories. 16, 17Solomon had some of the gold beaten into two hundred pieces of armor (gold worth $6,000 went into each piece) and three hundred shields ($1,800 worth of gold in each). And he kept them in his palace in the Hall of the Forest of Lebanon.

18He also made a huge ivory throne and overlaid it with pure gold. 19It had six steps and a rounded back, with arm rests; and a lion standing on each side. 20And there were two lions on each step—twelve in all. There was no other throne in all the world so splendid as that one.

21All of King Solomon's cups were of solid gold, and in the Hall of the Forest of Lebanon his entire dining service was made of solid gold. (Silver wasn't used because it wasn't considered to be of much value!)

22King Solomon's merchant fleet was in partnership with King Hiram's, and once every three years a great load of gold, silver, ivory, apes, and peacocks arrived at the Israeli ports.

23So King Solomon was richer and wiser than all the kings of the earth. 24Great men from many lands came to interview him and listen to his God-given wisdom. 25They brought him annual tribute of silver and gold dishes, beautiful cloth, myrrh, spices, horses, and mules.

26Solomon built up a great stable of horses with a vast number of chariots and cavalry—1,400 chariots in all, and 12,000 cavalrymen who lived in the chariot cities and with the king at Jerusalem. 27Silver was as common as stones in Jerusalem in those days, and cedar was of no greater value than the common sycamore! 28Solomon's horses were brought to him from Egypt and southern Turkey, where his agents purchased them at wholesale prices. 29An Egyptian chariot delivered to Jerusalem cost $400, and the horses were valued at $150 each. Many of these were then resold to the Hittite and Syrian kings.

Solomon's wives lead him into idolatry

11 King Solomon married many other girls besides the Egyptian princess. Many of them came from nations where idols were worshiped—Moab, Ammon, Edom, Sidon, and from the Hittites— 2even though the Lord had clearly instructed his people not to marry into those nations, because the women they married would get them started worshiping their gods. Yet Solomon did it anyway. 3He had seven hundred wives and three hundred concubines; and sure enough, they

11:1 *where idols were worshiped,* implied.

10:14
2 Chron 9:13

10:16
1 Kgs 14:26
2 Chron 9:15
12:9

10:21
1 Kgs 7:2

10:23
1 Kgs 3:12,13
4:30
2 Chron 9:22

10:27
2 Chron 1:15
9:27

10:28
2 Chron 1:16
9:28

10:29
2 Kgs 7:7

11:1
1 Kgs 3:1; 7:8
9:24
Neh 13:26

11:2
Ex 23:32,33
34:12-14
Deut 7:3,4

10:14ff When Solomon asked for wisdom, God promised him riches and honor as well (3:13). These verses show just how extensive his wealth became. Israel was no longer a second-rate nation, but at the height of its power and wealth. Solomon's riches became legendary. Great men came from many nations to listen to Israel's powerful king. Jesus would later refer to "Solomon in all his glory" (Matthew 6:29).

10:23 Why does the Bible place so much emphasis on Solomon's material possessions? In the Old Testament, riches were considered tangible evidence of God's blessing. Prosperity was seen as a proof of right living. In the books of Ecclesiastes and Job this concept is developed in proper perspective. In ideal conditions, people prosper when God runs their lives, but prosperity is not guaranteed. It does not prove that a person is living rightly before God.

In fact, a greater evidence that one is living for God is the presence of suffering and persecution (Mark 10:29, 30; 13:13). The most important "treasure" is not earthly, but heavenly (Matthew 6:19–21; 19:21; 1 Timothy 6:17–19). The gift of greatest worth has no price tag—it is the free gift of salvation offered by God to all.

10:26—11:2 In accumulating great horse stables, a huge harem, and incredible wealth, Solomon was violating God's commands for

a king (Deuteronomy 17:14–20). Why were these things prohibited? God knew how these activities would hurt the nation both politically and spiritually (1 Samuel 8:11–18). The more luxurious Solomon's court became, the more the people were taxed. Excessive taxation created unrest, and soon conditions became ripe for a revolution. With everything he wanted, Solomon forgot his need for God and allowed ungodly influences to enter his court through his heathen wives, thus accelerating the spiritual corruption of the nation.

11:2 Although Solomon had clear instructions from God *not* to marry women from foreign nations, he chose to disregard God's commands. He married not one, but many heathen wives, who subsequently led him away from God. God knows our human strengths and weaknesses, and his commands are always for our good. Some people ignore God's commands, but there are inevitable negative consequences resulting from such action. It is not enough to know God's Word or even to believe it; we must follow it and apply it to life's daily activities and decisions. Take God's commands seriously. Like Solomon, the "wisest man who ever lived," we are not as strong as we may think.

11:3 For all his wisdom, Solomon had some weak spots. He could not say "no" to compromise or to lustful desires. Whether he

11:3
2 Sam 5:13

11:5
Judg 2:12-14
10:6
1 Sam 7:3,4
12:10
1 Kgs 11:33
2 Kgs 23:13

11:7
Lev 20:2
Num 21:27-30
Judg 11:24
2 Kgs 23:10,13

11:9
1 Kgs 3:5; 9:2,3

11:11
1 Sam 2:30
1 Kgs 6:11,12
11:31

11:12
1 Kgs 21:29

11:15
2 Sam 8:13,14
1 Chron 18:12

11:16
Num 10:12

turned his heart away from the Lord, 4especially in his old age. They encouraged him to worship their gods instead of trusting completely in the Lord as his father David had done. 5Solomon worshiped Ashtoreth, the goddess of the Sidonians, and Milcom, the horrible god of the Ammonites. 6Thus Solomon did what was clearly wrong and refused to follow the Lord as his father David did. 7He even built a temple on the Mount of Olives, across the valley from Jerusalem, for Chemosh, the depraved god of Moab, and another for Molech, the unutterably vile god of the Ammonites. 8Solomon built temples for these foreign wives to use for burning incense and sacrificing to their gods.

9, 10Jehovah was very angry with Solomon about this, for now Solomon was no longer interested in the Lord God of Israel who had appeared to him twice to warn him specifically against worshiping other gods. But he hadn't listened, 11so now the Lord said to him, "Since you have not kept our agreement and have not obeyed my laws, I will tear the kingdom away from you and your family and give it to someone else. 12, 13However, for the sake of your father David, I won't do this while you are still alive. I will take the kingdom away from your son. And even so I will let him be king of one tribe, for David's sake and for the sake of Jerusalem, my chosen city."

Solomon's adversaries

14So the Lord caused Hadad the Edomite to grow in power. And Solomon became apprehensive, for Hadad was a member of the royal family of Edom. 15Years before, when David had been in Edom with Joab to arrange for the burial of some Israeli soldiers who had died in battle, the Israeli army had killed nearly every male in the entire country. 16, 17, 18It took six months to accomplish this, but they finally killed all except Hadad and a few royal officials who took him to Egypt (he was a very small child at the time). They slipped out of Midian and went to Paran, where others joined them and accompanied them to Egypt, and Pharaoh had given them homes and food.

19Hadad became one of Pharaoh's closest friends, and he gave him a wife—the sister of Queen Tahpenes. 20She presented him with a son, Genubath, who was

married to strengthen political alliances or to gain personal pleasure, these foreign wives led him into idolatry. You may have strong faith, but you have weak spots—and it is at these places where temptation usually strikes. Strengthen and protect your weaker areas because a chain is only as strong as its weakest link. If a person as strong and wise as Solomon could fall, so can we.

11:4 Solomon handled great pressures in running the government, but he could not handle the pressures from his wives who wanted him to worship their gods. In marriage and other close friendships, it is difficult to resist pressure to compromise. Our love leads us to identify with the desires of those we care about.

Faced with such pressure, Solomon at first *resisted* it, maintaining pure faith. Then he *tolerated* a more widespread practice of idolatry. Finally he himself became involved in idolatrous worship; he *rationalized* away the potential danger to himself and the kingdom. It is because we naturally wish to identify with those we love that God asked Solomon (and asks us) not to marry those who do not share our commitment to him.

11:5–8 Ashtoreth was a goddess who symbolized reproductive power—a mistress of the god Baal. Milcom may be another name for Molech, the national god of the Ammonites, called a "horrible god" because his worship rites included child sacrifice. Chemosh was the Moabites' national god. The Israelites were warned against worshiping all other gods in general and Molech in particular (Exodus 20:1–6; Leviticus 18:21; 20:1–5).

11:6 If Solomon was so wise, why did he turn from God? While Solomon applied his wisdom to political affairs, he did not always apply it to his spiritual life. He knew the right way to live, but he did

not always have the will to do it. Many people have enough wisdom to know the difference between right and wrong, but they don't always do right. We need to develop not only the wisdom to do right, but the *will* to do it. In his later years, Solomon was still wise, but he was no longer godly.

11:9, 10 Solomon didn't turn away from God all at once or in a brief moment. His spiritual coldness started with a minor departure from God's law (3:1). Over the years, that little sin grew until it resulted in Solomon's downfall. A little sin can be the first step in turning away from God. It is not the sins we don't know about, but the sins we excuse that cause us the greatest trouble. We must never let any sin go unchallenged. In your life, is there an unchallenged sin that is spreading like a deadly cancer? Don't excuse it. Confess it to God and ask him for strength to resist the temptation.

11:9–11 Solomon's powerful and glorious kingdom, which could have been blessed for all time, was instead approaching its end. Solomon had God's promises, guidance, and answers to prayer, and yet he allowed sin to remain all around him. Eventually it corrupted him to the point where he was "no longer interested in the Lord God." In Psalm 127, Solomon wrote, "Unless the Lord builds a house, the builders' work is useless." Solomon had begun by laying the foundation with God, but he did not follow through in his later years. As a result he lost everything. It is not enough to get off to a right start in building our lives on God's principles; we must endure with God to the end (Mark 13:13). God must be in control of our lives from start to finish.

brought up in Pharaoh's palace among Pharaoh's own sons. ²¹When Hadad, there in Egypt, heard that David and Joab were both dead, he asked Pharaoh for permission to return to Edom.

²²"Why?" Pharaoh asked him. "What do you lack here? How have we disappointed you?"

"Everything is wonderful," he replied "but even so, I'd like to go back home."

²³Another of Solomon's enemies whom God raised to power was Rezon, one of the officials of King Hadad-ezer of Zobah who had deserted his post and fled the country. ²⁴He had become the leader of a gang of bandits—men who fled with him to Damascus (where he later became king) when David destroyed Zobah. ²⁵During Solomon's entire lifetime, Rezon and Hadad were his enemies, for they hated Israel intensely.

²⁶Another rebel leader was Jeroboam (the son of Nebat), who came from the city of Zeredah in Ephraim; his mother was Zeruah, a widow. ²⁷, ²⁸Here is the story back of his rebellion: Solomon was rebuilding Fort Millo, repairing the walls of this city his father had built. Jeroboam was very able, and when Solomon saw how industrious he was, he put him in charge of his labor battalions from the tribe of Joseph.

²⁹One day as Jeroboam was leaving Jerusalem, the prophet Ahijah from Shiloh (who had put on a new robe for the occasion) met him and called him aside to talk to him. And as the two of them were alone in the field, ³⁰Ahijah tore his new robe into twelve parts, ³¹and said to Jeroboam, "Take ten of these pieces, for the Lord God of Israel says, 'I will tear the kingdom from the hand of Solomon and give ten of the tribes to you! ³²But I will leave him one tribe for the sake of my servant David and for the sake of Jerusalem, which I have chosen above all the other cities of Israel. ³³For Solomon has forsaken me and worships Ashtoreth, the goddess of the Sidonians; and Chemosh, the god of Moab; and Milcom, the god of the Ammonites. He has not followed my paths and has not done what I consider right; he has not kept my laws and instructions as his father David did. ³⁴I will not take the kingdom from him now, however; for the sake of my servant David, my chosen one who obeyed my commandments, I will let Solomon reign for the rest of his life.

³⁵" 'But I will take away the kingdom from his son and give ten of the tribes to you. ³⁶His son shall have the other one so that the descendants of David will continue to reign in Jerusalem, the city I have chosen to be the place for my name to be enshrined. ³⁷And I will place you on the throne of Israel, and give you absolute power. ³⁸If you listen to what I tell you and walk in my path and do whatever I consider right, obeying my commandments as my servant David did, then I will bless you; and your descendants shall rule Israel forever. (I once made this same promise to David. ³⁹But because of Solomon's sin I will punish the descendants of David—though not forever.)' "

⁴⁰Solomon tried to kill Jeroboam, but he fled to King Shishak of Egypt and stayed there until the death of Solomon.

Solomon's death

⁴¹The rest of what Solomon did and said is written in the book *The Acts of Solomon.* ⁴²He ruled in Jerusalem for forty years, ⁴³and then died and was buried in the city of his father David; and his son Rehoboam reigned in his place.

11:21
1 Kgs 2:10,34

11:23
2 Sam 8:3
10:15,16
11:24
2 Sam 10:7,8

11:26
1 Kgs 13:1
2 Chron 13:6
11:27
Prov 22:29

11:29
1 Kgs 12:15
14:2
2 Chron 10:15
11:30
1 Sam 15:27
11:31
1 Kgs 11:11

11:33
1 Kgs 11:5,7

11:35
1 Kgs 12:16
11:36
1 Kgs 15:4
2 Kgs 8:19
2 Chron 21:7
11:38
2 Sam 7:11,27
1 Kgs 14:7-9

11:40
1 Kgs 12:2-4
14:25
2 Chron 12:2

11:41
2 Chron 9:29
11:43
2 Chron 9:31

11:31-33 The prophet Ahijah predicted the division of the kingdom of Israel. Ten of Israel's twelve tribes would follow Jeroboam. The other two tribes, Judah and Benjamin, would remain loyal to David. Judah, the largest tribe, and Benjamin, the smallest, were often mentioned as one tribe because they shared the same border. Both Jeroboam and Ahijah were from Ephraim, the most prominent of the ten rebel tribes. (For more on the divided kingdom see the note on 12:20.)

12:1 Rehoboam's coronation was held at Shechem, about 35 miles north of Jerusalem. The crowning of a king would normally be held in Jerusalem, the capital city. Rehoboam saw trouble brewing with Jeroboam and went north to try to maintain good relations with the northern tribes. He probably chose Shechem because it was an ancient location for making covenants (Joshua 24:1). When the kingdom divided, Shechem became the capital of the Northern Kingdom for a short time (12:25).

B. THE DIVIDED KINGDOM (12:1—22:53)

After Solomon's death, the northern tribes revolt, forming two separate nations. Each nation experiences disastrous consequences from having evil kings. Elijah appears on the scene, confronting these kings for their sin. God deals with sin in powerful ways. Although judgment may appear to be slow, God will judge evil harshly.

1. Revolt of the northern tribes
Rebellion against Rehoboam

12:1
Josh 20:7; 24:1
Judg 9:1,6
2 Chron 10:1

12:2
1 Sam 8:18

12 Rehoboam's inauguration was at Shechem, and all Israel came for the coronation ceremony. 2, 3, 4Jeroboam, who was still in Egypt where he had fled from King Solomon, heard about the plans from his friends. They urged him to attend, so he joined the rest of Israel at Shechem, and was the ringleader in getting the people to make certain demands upon Rehoboam.

"Your father was a hard master," they told Rehoboam. "We don't want you as our king unless you promise to treat us better than he did."

12:5
1 Kgs 12:12

5"Give me three days to think this over," Rehoboam replied. "Come back then for my answer." So the people left.

6Rehoboam talked it over with the old men who had counseled his father Solomon.

"What do you think I should do?" he asked them.

7And they replied, "If you give them a pleasant reply and agree to be good to them and serve them well, you can be their king forever."

8But Rehoboam refused the old men's counsel and called in the young men with whom he had grown up.

12:9
2 Chron 10:8
18:3-5

9"What do you think I should do?" he asked them.

10And the young men replied, "Tell them, 'If you think my father was hard on you, well, I'll be harder! 11Yes, my father was harsh, but I'll be even harsher! My father used whips on you, but I'll use scorpions!' "

12:12
1 Kgs 12:5

12:15
Deut 2:30
Judg 14:4
2 Chron 10:15
22:7
Amos 3:6

12:16
2 Sam 20:1

12So when Jeroboam and the people returned three days later, 13, 14the new king answered them roughly. He ignored the old men's advice and followed that of the young men; 15so the king refused the people's demands. (But the Lord's hand was in it—he caused the new king to do this in order to fulfill his promise to Jeroboam, made through Ahijah, the prophet from Shiloh.)

16, 17When the people realized that the king meant what he said and was refusing

---

THE KINGDOM DIVIDES
Rehoboam's threat of higher taxes caused a rebellion and divided the nation. Rehoboam ruled the Southern Kingdom; Jeroboam ruled the Northern Kingdom. Jeroboam set up idols in Dan and Bethel to discourage worship in Jerusalem. At the same time Syria, Ammon, Moab, and Edom claimed independence from the divided nation.

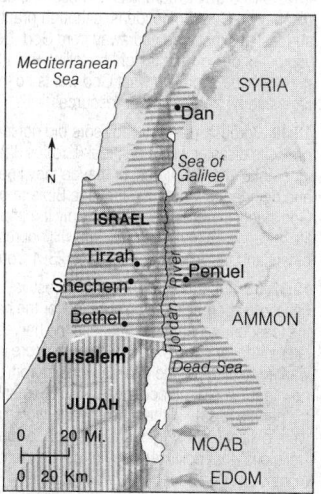

12:6-8 Rehoboam asked for advice, but he didn't carefully evaluate that advice. If he had, he would have realized that the advice offered by the older men was wiser than that of his peers. To evaluate advice, ask if it is realistic, workable, and consistent with the Bible. Determine if the results of following the advice will be fair, make improvements, and give a positive solution or direction. Seek counsel from those more experienced and wiser. Advice is helpful only if we evaluate it with God's standards in mind.

12:15-19 Both Jeroboam and Rehoboam did what was good for themselves, not what was good for their people. Rehoboam was harsh and did not listen to what the people said; Jeroboam established new places of worship to keep his people from traveling to Jerusalem, Rehoboam's capital. Both actions backfired. Rehoboam's move divided the nation, and Jeroboam's turned the people from God. Good leaders put the best interests of the people above their own. Making decisions only for yourself will backfire and cause you to lose more than if you had kept the welfare of others in mind.

to listen to them, they began shouting, "Down with David and all his relatives! Let's go home! Let Rehoboam be king of his own family!"

And they all deserted him except for the tribe of Judah, who remained loyal and accepted Rehoboam as their king. 18When King Rehoboam sent Adoram (who was in charge of the draft) to conscript men from the other tribes, a great mob stoned him to death. But King Rehoboam escaped by chariot and fled to Jerusalem. 19And Israel has been in rebellion against the dynasty of David to this day.

20When the people of Israel learned of Jeroboam's return from Egypt, he was asked to come before an open meeting of all the people; and there he was made king of Israel. Only the tribe of Judah continued under the kingship of the family of David.

21When King Rehoboam arrived in Jerusalem, he summoned his army—all the able-bodied men of Judah and Benjamin: 180,000 special troops—to force the rest of Israel to acknowledge him as their king. 22But God sent this message to Shemaiah, the prophet:

23, 24"Tell Rehoboam the son of Solomon, king of Judah, and all the people of Judah and Benjamin that they must not fight against their brothers, the people of Israel. Tell them to disband and go home, for what has happened to Rehoboam is according to my wish." So the army went home as the Lord had commanded.

Jeroboam leads Israel into idolatry

25Jeroboam now built the city of Shechem in the hill country of Ephraim, and it became his capital. Later he built Penuel. 26Jeroboam thought, "Unless I'm careful, the people will want a descendant of David as their king. 27When they go to Jerusalem to offer sacrifices at the Temple, they will become friendly with King Rehoboam; then they will kill me and ask him to be their king instead."

28So on the advice of his counselors, the king had two gold calf-idols made and told the people, "It's too much trouble to go to Jerusalem to worship; from now on these will be your gods—they rescued you from your captivity in Egypt!"

29One of these calf-idols was placed in Bethel and the other in Dan. 30This was of course a great sin, for the people worshiped them. 31He also made shrines on the hills and ordained priests from the rank and file of the people—even those who were not from the priest-tribe of Levi. 32, 33Jeroboam also announced that the

12:32, 33 *on the first of November,* literally, "on the fifteenth day of the eighth month" of the Hebrew calendar.

12:18
2 Sam 20:24

12:19
2 Kgs 17:21
2 Chron 10:19
Isa 7:17

12:20
1 Kgs 12:2-4

12:21
2 Chron 11:1

12:22
2 Chron 11:2
12:5

12:25
Judg 8:8,17

12:27
Deut 12:4,5

12:28
Ex 32:4
2 Kgs 10:29
2 Chron 11:15
Hos 8:5

12:29
Gen 28:19; 35:1
Judg 20:1

12:31
Num 3:10
2 Kgs 17:32
2 Chron 11:13,
14; 13:9

12:20 This marks the beginning of the divided kingdom which was to last for centuries. Ten of Israel's twelve tribes followed Jeroboam and called their new nation Israel, or the Northern Kingdom. The other two tribes remained loyal to Rehoboam and called their nation Judah, or the Southern Kingdom. The kingdom did not split overnight. It was already dividing as early as the days of the judges because of tribal jealousies, especially between Ephraim, the most influential tribe of the north, and Judah, the chief tribe of the south.

Before the days of Saul and David, the religious center of Israel was located, for the most part, in the territory of Ephraim. When Solomon built the Temple, he moved the religious center of Israel to Jerusalem. This eventually brought tribal rivalries to the breaking point. (For more information on tribal jealousies and how they affected Israel see Judges 12:1ff; 2 Samuel 2:8–12; 19:41–43.)

12:28 Jeroboam shrewdly placed his calf-idols in Bethel and Dan, strategic locations. Bethel was just ten miles north of Jerusalem on the main road, enticing the citizens from the north to stop there instead of traveling the rest of the way to Jerusalem. Dan was the northernmost city in Israel, so people living in the north far from Jerusalem were attracted to its convenient location. As leader of the Northern Kingdom, Jeroboam wanted to establish his own worship centers; otherwise his people would make regular trips to Jerusalem, and his authority would be undermined. Soon this substitute religion had little in common with true faith in God.

12:28 All Jewish men were required to travel to the Temple three times each year (Deuteronomy 16:16), but Jeroboam set up his own worship centers and told his people it was too much trouble to travel all the way to Jerusalem. Those who obeyed Jeroboam were disobeying God. Some ideas, although practical, may include suggestions that lead you away from God. Don't let anyone talk you out of doing what is right by telling you that your actions are not worth the effort. Do what God wants no matter what the cost in time, energy, reputation, or resources.

12:30 Jeroboam and his advisors did not learn from Israel's previous disaster with a calf-idol (Exodus 32). Perhaps they were ignorant of the Scriptures, or maybe they knew about the event and decided to ignore it. Study the Bible to become aware of God's acts in history, and then apply the important lessons to your life. If you learn from the past, you will not repeat the mistakes of others and face disaster (Isaiah 42:23; 1 Corinthians 10:11).

12:32, 33 "The annual Tabernacle Festival" was probably the Feast of Tabernacles, a celebration for the harvest. Jeroboam set the feast one month later because the harvest was several weeks later in the far north than in the south. More important, Jeroboam wanted to differentiate Israel's worship from Judah's. He hoped his new feast would replace the feasts in Jerusalem and encourage his people to stay in their own land to worship. His real motives were political, not religious. Don't rush to support everything "religious" that politicians say or do. Leaders today still use religious customs for political advantage.

12:32, 33 In the days of Israel's founding fathers, the city of

12:32
Lev 23:33,34

annual Tabernacle Festival would be held at Bethel on the first of November (a date he decided upon himself), similar to the annual festival at Jerusalem; he himself offered sacrifices upon the altar to the calves at Bethel, and burned incense to them. And it was there at Bethel that he ordained priests for the shrines on the hills.

2. Kings of Israel and Judah
A prophet dies for disobedience

13:1
2 Kgs 23:17
13:2
2 Kgs 23:15,16

13 As Jeroboam approached the altar to burn incense to the gold calf-idol, a prophet of the Lord from Judah walked up to him. ²Then, at the Lord's command, the prophet shouted, "O altar, the Lord says that a child named Josiah shall be born into the family line of David, and he shall sacrifice upon you the priests from the shrines on the hills who come here to burn incense; and men's bones shall be burned upon you."

13:3
2 Kgs 20:8

³Then he gave this proof that his message was from the Lord: "This altar will split apart, and the ashes on it will spill to the ground."

⁴The king was very angry with the prophet for saying this. He shouted to his guards, "Arrest that man!" and shook his fist at him. Instantly the king's arm became paralyzed in that position; he couldn't pull it back again! ⁵At the same moment a wide crack appeared in the altar and the ashes poured out, just as the prophet had said would happen. For this was the prophet's proof that God had been speaking through him.

13:6
Ex 8:8,28; 9:28
Jer 37:3
Acts 8:24

⁶"Oh, please, please," the king cried out to the prophet, "beg the Lord your God to restore my arm again."

So he prayed to the Lord, and the king's arm became normal again.

13:7
1 Sam 9:7
2 Kgs 5:15

⁷Then the king said to the prophet, "Come to the palace with me and rest awhile and have some food; and I'll give you a reward because you healed my arm."

⁸But the prophet said to the king, "Even if you gave me half your palace, I

TRIBAL JEALOUSIES

Although the kingdom of Israel was "united" under David and Solomon, the tensions between north and south were never resolved. The jealousy and animosity behind this civil war didn't begin with Rehoboam and Jeroboam, but had its roots in the days of the judges, when the people were more interested in tribal loyalty than in national unity. Note how easily tension arose between Ephraim, the most prominent tribe in the north, and Judah, the prominent tribe of the south.

- Ephraim claimed the promises in Genesis 48:17–22 and 49:22–26 for its leadership role.
- Joshua (Hoshea), who conquered the Promised Land, was an Ephraimite (Numbers 13:8).
- Samuel, Israel's greatest judge, was from Ephraim (1 Samuel 1:1ff).
- Ephraim allied with Ish-bosheth in revolt against David, who was from the tribe of Judah (2 Samuel 2:8–11).
- David, a shepherd from the tribe of Judah, became king over all Israel, including Ephraim, who no longer had a claim to leadership.
- Although David helped to smooth over the bad feelings, the high taxes under Solomon and Rehoboam led the northern tribes to the breaking point.

Such tension developed because Ephraim was the key tribe in the north. They resented Judah's role in leadership under David, and resented that the nation's capital and center of worship were located in Jerusalem.

Bethel was a symbol of commitment to God, because it was there that Jacob had rededicated his life to God (Genesis 28:16–19). But Jeroboam turned the city into Israel's chief religious center, intending it to compete with Jerusalem. But Bethel's religion centered on an idol, and this led to the eventual downfall of Israel. During the period of the kings, Bethel developed a reputation as a wicked and idolatrous city. The prophets Hosea and Amos recognized the sins of Bethel and condemned the city for its godless ways (Hosea 4:15–17; 10:8; Amos 5:4–6).

13:2 Three hundred years later, this prophecy was fulfilled in

every detail when Josiah killed the pagan priests at their own altars. The story is found in 2 Kings 23:1–20.

13:7–31 This prophet had been given strict orders from God not to eat or drink anything while on his mission (13:9). He died because he listened to a man who claimed to have a message from God, rather than to God himself. This prophet should have followed God's Word instead of hearsay. Trust what Scripture says rather than what someone claims is true. And disregard what others claim to be messages from God if their words contradict the Bible.

wouldn't go into it; nor would I eat or drink even water in this place! ⁹For the Lord has given me strict orders not to eat anything or drink any water while I'm here, and not to return to Judah by the road I came on."

¹⁰So he went back another way.

¹¹As it happened, there was an old prophet living in Bethel, and his sons went home and told him what the prophet from Judah had done and what he had said to the king.

¹²"Which way did he go?" the old prophet asked. So they told him.

¹³"Quick, saddle the donkey," the old man said. And when they had saddled the donkey for him, ¹⁴he rode after the prophet and found him sitting under an oak tree.

"Are you the prophet who came from Judah?" he asked him.

"Yes," he replied, "I am."

¹⁵Then the old man said to the prophet, "Come home with me and eat."

¹⁶, ¹⁷"No," he replied, "I can't; for I am not allowed to eat anything or to drink any water at Bethel. The Lord strictly warned me against it; and he also told me not to return home by the same road I came on."

¹⁸But the old man said, "I am a prophet too, just as you are; and an angel gave me a message from the Lord. I am to take you home with me and give you food and water."

But the old man was lying to him. ¹⁹So they went back together, and the prophet ate some food and drank some water at the old man's home.

²⁰Then, suddenly, while they were sitting at the table, a message from the Lord came to the old man, ²¹, ²²and he shouted at the prophet from Judah, "The Lord says that because you have been disobedient to his clear command, and have come here, and have eaten and drunk water in the place he told you not to, therefore your body shall not be buried in the grave of your fathers."

²³After finishing the meal, the old man saddled the prophet's donkey, ²⁴, ²⁵and the prophet started off again. But as he was traveling along, a lion came out and killed him. His body lay there on the road, with the donkey and the lion standing beside it. Those who came by and saw the body lying in the road and the lion standing quietly beside it, reported it in Bethel where the old prophet lived.

²⁶When he heard what had happened he exclaimed, "It is the prophet who disobeyed the Lord's command; the Lord fulfilled his warning by causing the lion to kill him."

²⁷Then he said to his sons, "Saddle my donkey!" And they did.

²⁸He found the prophet's body lying in the road; and the donkey and lion were still standing there beside it, for the lion had not eaten the body nor attacked the donkey. ²⁹So the prophet laid the body upon the donkey and took it back to the city to mourn over it and bury it.

³⁰He laid the body in his own grave, exclaiming, "Alas, my brother!"

³¹Afterwards he said to his sons, "When I die, bury me in the grave where the prophet is buried. Lay my bones beside his bones. ³²For the Lord told him to shout against the altar in Bethel, and his curse against the shrines in the cities of Samaria shall surely be fulfilled."

³³Despite the prophet's warning, Jeroboam did not turn away from his evil ways; instead, he made more priests than ever from the common people, to offer sacrifices to idols in the shrines on the hills. Anyone who wanted to could be a priest. ³⁴This was a great sin, and resulted in the destruction of Jeroboam's kingdom and the death of all of his family.

13:9
Num 22:18
24:13

13:21
1 Sam 15:26

13:24
1 Kgs 20:36

13:31
2 Kgs 23:17

13:33
2 Chron 13:9

13:34
1 Kgs 14:10
15:29
2 Kgs 17:21

13:24, 25 Lions were well known in Old Testament times and common enough to be a threat both to people and to their flocks. Samson (Judges 14:5, 6), David (1 Samuel 17:34–37), and Benaiah (2 Samuel 23:20) all faced wild lions.

13:33, 34 Under penalty of death, God had forbidden anyone to be a priest who was not from the tribe of Levi (Numbers 3:10). Levites were assured of lifetime support from the tithe, so they did not have to spend time farming, worrying about tribal interests, or fearing for their financial futures. Jeroboam's new priests were financed by the king and his fees. They had to mix priestly and secular duties, and they quickly fell into party politics. Because they didn't have job security, they were easily corrupted by bribes. Jeroboam's disobedience was the downfall of true religion in the Northern Kingdom.

God's judgment on Jeroboam

14:2
1 Sam 28:7,8
2 Sam 14:2,3
2 Chron 18:29

14:3
1 Sam 9:7,8
2 Kgs 4:42

14:4
1 Sam 3:2,3
4:15

14 Jeroboam's son Abijah now became very sick. ²Jeroboam told his wife, "Disguise yourself so that no one will recognize you as the queen, and go to Ahijah the prophet at Shiloh—the man who told me that I would become king. ³Take him a gift of ten loaves of bread, some fig bars, and a jar of honey and ask him whether the boy will recover."

⁴So his wife went to Ahijah's home at Shiloh. He was an old man now, and could no longer see. ⁵But the Lord told him that the queen, pretending to be someone else, would come to ask about her son, for he was very sick. And the Lord told him what to tell her.

⁶So when Ahijah heard her at the door, he called out, "Come in, wife of Jeroboam! Why are you pretending to be someone else?" Then he told her, "I have

Even clear warnings are hard to obey. The Bible is filled with people who had direction from God and yet chose their own way. Their disobedience was rarely due to ignorance of what God wanted; rather, it was out of stubborn selfishness. Jeroboam was a consistent example of this all too human trait.

During the construction of Fort Millo, Solomon noticed young Jeroboam's natural leadership skills and made him a special project foreman. Shortly after this, God contacted Jeroboam through the prophet Ahijah. He told Jeroboam that God would punish David's dynasty by tearing the kingdom from Solomon's son and that Jeroboam would rule the ten northern tribes. And God made it clear that the same fate would destroy Jeroboam's family if they refused to obey God. Apparently, Solomon heard about these events and tried to have Jeroboam killed. The future king escaped to Egypt, where he stayed until Solomon died.

When Rehoboam, Solomon's heir, took the throne, Jeroboam returned. He represented the people in demanding that the new king be more lenient than his father. Rehoboam's unwise choice to reject his people's request led to their rejecting him as king. Only Judah and the annexed tribe of Benjamin remained loyal to David's dynasty. The other ten tribes made Jeroboam king.

Rather than seeing this fulfillment of God's promise to him as motivation to obey God, Jeroboam decided to do whatever he could to secure his position. He led his kingdom away from the God who had allowed him to reign. The consequences of this action had already been stated by God—his family was eventually wiped out. And Jeroboam set into motion events that would lead to the destruction of the Northern Kingdom.

Sin's consequences are guaranteed in God's Word. When we do something directly opposed to God's commands, and there isn't immediate disaster, we are often fooled into believing we got away with disobedience. But that is a dangerous assumption. Jeroboam's life should make us recognize our frequent need to admit our disobedience and ask God to forgive us.

Strengths and accomplishments:
- An effective leader and organizer
- First king of the ten tribes of Israel in the divided kingdom
- A charismatic leader with much popular support

Weaknesses and mistakes:
- Erected idols in Israel to keep people away from the Temple in Jerusalem
- Appointed priests from outside the tribe of Levi
- Depended more on his own cunning than on God's promises

Lessons from his life:
- Great opportunities are often destroyed by small decisions
- Careless efforts to correct another's errors often lead to the same errors
- Mistakes always occur when we attempt to take over God's role in a situation

Vital Statistics:
- Where: The Northern Kingdom of Israel
- Occupation: Project foreman, king of Israel
- Relatives: Father: Nebat. Mother: Zeruah. Sons: Abijah and Nadab.
- Contemporaries: Solomon, Nathan, Ahijah, Rehoboam

Key verses:
"Despite the prophet's warning, Jeroboam did not turn away from his evil ways; instead, he made more priests than ever from the common people, to offer sacrifices to idols in the shrines on the hills. Anyone who wanted to could be a priest. This was a great sin, and resulted in the destruction of Jeroboam's kingdom and the death of all of his family" (1 Kings 13:33, 34).

Jeroboam's story is told in 1 Kings 11:26—14:20. He is also mentioned in 2 Chronicles 10—13.

JEROBOAM

sad news for you. 7Give your husband this message from the Lord God of Israel: 'I promoted you from the ranks of the common people and made you king of Israel. 8I ripped the kingdom away from the family of David and gave it to you, but you have not obeyed my commandments as my servant David did. His heart's desire was always to obey me and to do whatever I wanted him to. 9But you have done more evil than all the other kings before you; you have made other gods and have made me furious with your gold calves. And since you have refused to acknowledge me, 10I will bring disaster upon your home and will destroy all of your sons—this boy who is sick and all those who are well. I will sweep away your family as a stable hand shovels out manure. 11I vow that those of your family who die in the city shall be eaten by dogs, and those who die in the field shall be eaten by birds.' "

12Then Ahijah said to Jeroboam's wife, "Go on home, and when you step into the city, the child will die. 13All of Israel will mourn for him and bury him, but he is the only member of your family who will come to a quiet end. For this child is the only good thing which the Lord God of Israel sees in the entire family of Jeroboam. 14And the Lord will raise up a king over Israel who will destroy the family of Jeroboam. 15Then the Lord will shake Israel like a reed whipped about in a stream; he will uproot the people of Israel from this good land of their fathers and scatter them beyond the Euphrates River, for they have angered the Lord by worshiping idol-gods. 16He will abandon Israel because Jeroboam sinned and made all of Israel sin along with him."

17So Jeroboam's wife returned to Tirzah; and the child died just as she walked through the door of her home. 18And there was mourning for him throughout the land, just as the Lord had predicted through Ahijah.

19The rest of Jeroboam's activities—his wars and the other events of his reign—are recorded in *The Annals of the Kings of Israel.* 20Jeroboam reigned twenty-two years, and when he died, his son Nadab took the throne.

Rehoboam rules Judah

21Meanwhile, Rehoboam the son of Solomon was king in Judah. He was forty-one years old when he began to reign, and he was on the throne seventeen years in Jerusalem, the city which, among all the cities of Israel, the Lord had chosen to live in. (Rehoboam's mother was Naamah, an Ammonite woman.) 22During his reign the people of Judah, like those in Israel, did wrong and angered the Lord with their sin, for it was even worse than that of their ancestors. 23They built shrines and obelisks and idols on every high hill and under every green tree. 24There was homosexuality throughout the land, and the people of Judah became as depraved as the heathen nations which the Lord drove out to make room for his people.

25In the fifth year of Rehoboam's reign, King Shishak of Egypt attacked and conquered Jerusalem. 26He ransacked the Temple and the palace and stole everything, including all the gold shields Solomon had made. 27Afterwards Rehoboam

14:10 *this boy who is sick and all those who are well,* literally, "every male, both bond and free."

14:7
1 Kgs 11:28,31
12:20

14:8
1 Kgs 11:30,33
15:5

14:9
Ex 34:17
1 Kgs 13:33
2 Chron 11:15
Ps 50:17
Ezek 23:35

14:10
1 Kgs 21:22
2 Kgs 9:8

14:11
1 Kgs 16:4-7
21:24

14:12
1 Kgs 14:17

14:14
1 Kgs 15:27,29

14:15
Ex 34:17
Deut 12:3
1 Sam 12:25
Ps 52:5

14:17
1 Kgs 15:21
16:9

14:19
1 Kgs 14:29
15:7,23,31
16:4-7,14,20
1 Chron 9:1

14:21
1 Kgs 11:32,36
2 Kgs 21:7
2 Chron 12:13

14:22
2 Chron 12:1,14

14:23
Deut 16:22
2 Kgs 17:10
Jer 2:20
Ezek 16:24

14:24
Deut 23:17,18
2 Kgs 23:7

14:25
2 Chron 12:2,9

14:26
1 Kgs 7:51
10:16,17; 15:18

14:14 Who was this king who would "destroy the family of Jeroboam"? His name was Baasha, and he would kill all of Jeroboam's descendants (15:27–30).

14:19 Three books are mentioned in 1 and 2 Kings— *The Annals of the Kings of Israel, The Annals of the Kings of Judah* (14:19, 29), and *The Acts of Solomon* (11:41). These books were historical records of Israel and Judah and were the main sources of material God directed the author to use to write 1 and 2 Kings. No copies of these books have been found.

14:25 When Rehoboam came to power, he inherited a mighty kingdom. Everything he could ever want was handed over to him. But apparently he did not recognize why he had so much or how it had been obtained. To teach Rehoboam a lesson, God allowed

King Shishak of Egypt to invade Judah and Israel. Egypt was no longer the world power it had once been, and Shishak, possibly resenting Solomon's enormous success, was determined to change that. Shishak's army was not strong enough to destroy Judah and Israel, but he weakened them so much that they were never the same again.

14:25 Just five years after Solomon died, the Temple and palace were ransacked by foreign invaders. How quickly the glory, power, and money disappeared! When the people became spiritually corrupt and immoral (14:24), it was just a short time until they lost everything. Their possessions and wealth had become more important to them than God. When we remove God from our lives, everything else becomes useless, no matter how valuable it seems.

made bronze shields as substitutes, and the palace guards used these instead. [28]Whenever the king went to the Temple, the guards paraded before him and then took the shields back to the guard chamber.

[29]The other events in Rehoboam's reign are written in *The Annals of the Kings of Judah*. [30]There was constant war between Rehoboam and Jeroboam. [31]When Rehoboam died—his mother was Naamah the Ammonitess—he was buried among his ancestors in Jerusalem, and his son Abijam took the throne.

14:30
1 Kgs 15:6
2 Chron 12:15

Abijam rules Judah

15:1
2 Chron 13:1
15:3
1 Kgs 11:4
15:4
2 Chron 21:7
15:5
2 Sam 11:4,15
1 Kgs 9:4; 14:8
15:7
2 Chron 13:1,2
15:8
1 Chron 3:10-14
2 Chron 14:1

15 Abijam began his three-year reign as king of Judah in Jerusalem during the eighteenth year of Jeroboam's reign in Israel. (Abijam's mother was Maacah, the daughter of Abishalom.) [3]He was as great a sinner as his father was, and his heart was not right with God, as King David's was. [4]But despite Abijam's sin, the Lord remembered David's love and did not end the line of David's royal descendants. [5]For David had obeyed God during his entire life except for the affair concerning Uriah the Hittite. [6]During Abijam's reign there was constant war between Israel and Judah. [7]The rest of Abijam's history is recorded in *The Annals of the Kings of Judah*. [8]When he died he was buried in Jerusalem, and his son Asa reigned in his place.

Asa rules Judah

[9]Asa became king of Judah, in Jerusalem, in the twentieth year of the reign of Jeroboam over Israel, [10]and reigned forty-one years. (His grandmother was

15:4 *The Lord remembered David's love,* literally, "for David's sake." **15:6** *between Israel and Judah,* literally, "between Rehoboam and Jeroboam."

THE APPEAL OF IDOLS		*The appeal of Idols*	*Modern parallel*
On the surface, the lives of the kings don't make sense. How could they run to idolatry so fast when they had God's Word (at least some of it), prophets, and the example of David? Here are some of the reasons for the enticement of idols:	POWER	The people wanted freedom from the authority of both God and the priests. They wanted religion to fit their life-style, not have their life-style fit their religion.	People do not want to answer to a greater authority. Instead of having power *over* others, God wants us to have the Holy Spirit's power to *help* others.
	PLEASURE	Idol worship exalted sensuality without responsibility or guilt. People acted out the vicious and sensuous personalities of the gods they worshiped, thus gaining approval for their degraded lives.	People deify pleasure, seeking it at the expense of everything else. Instead of seeking pleasure that leads to long-range disaster, God calls us to seek the kind of pleasure that leads to long-range rewards.
	PASSION	Mankind was reduced to little more than animals. The people did not have to be viewed as unique individuals, but could be exploited sexually, politically, and economically.	Today man is being reinterpreted as an animal where sinful drives and passions are condoned. Instead of seeking passion that exploits others, God calls us to redirect our passions to areas that build others up.
	PRAISE AND POPULARITY	The high and holy nature of God was replaced by gods who were more a reflection of human nature, thus more culturally suitable to the people. These gods no longer required sacrifice, just a token of appeasement.	Sacrifice is seen as self-inflicted punishment, making no sense. Success is to be sought at all costs. Instead of seeking praise for ourselves, God calls us to praise him and those who honor him.

As societies change and evolve, they often throw out norms and values no longer considered necessary or acceptable. Believers must be careful not to follow society's example if it discards God's Word. When society does that, only godlessness and evil remain.

15:1 Abijam is called Abijah in 2 Chronicles 13:1.
15:5 See 2 Samuel 11 for the story of David and Uriah.

15:9 See Asa's Profile in 2 Chronicles 14 for more information on this king.

Maacah, the daughter of Abishalom.) [11]He pleased the Lord like his ancestor King David. [12]He executed the male prostitutes and removed all the idols his father had made. [13]He deposed his grandmother Maacah as queen-mother because she had made an idol—which he cut down and burned at Kidron Brook. [14]However, the shrines on the hills were not removed, for Asa did not realize that these were wrong. [15]He made permanent exhibits in the Temple of the bronze shields his grandfather had dedicated, along with the silver and gold vessels he himself had donated.

[16]There was lifelong war between King Asa of Judah and King Baasha of Israel. [17]King Baasha built the fortress city of Ramah in an attempt to cut off all trade with Jerusalem. [18]Then Asa took all the silver and gold left in the Temple treasury and all the treasures of the palace, and gave them to his officials to take to Damascus, to King Ben-hadad of Syria, with this message:

[19]"Let us be allies just as our fathers were. I am sending you a present of gold and silver. Now break your alliance with King Baasha of Israel so that he will leave me alone."

[20]Ben-hadad agreed and sent his armies against some of the cities of Israel; and he destroyed Ijon, Dan, Abel-beth-maacah, all of Chinneroth, and all the cities in the land of Naphtali. [21]When Baasha received word of the attack, he discontinued building the city of Ramah and returned to Tirzah. [22]Then King Asa made a proclamation to all Judah, asking every able-bodied man to help demolish Ramah and haul away its stones and timbers. And King Asa used these materials to build the city of Geba in Benjamin and the city of Mizpah.

[23]The rest of Asa's biography—his conquests and deeds and the names of the cities he built—is found in *The Annals of the Kings of Judah*. In his old age his feet became diseased, [24]and when he died he was buried in the royal cemetery in Jerusalem. Then his son Jehoshaphat became the new king of Judah.

Nadab rules Israel

[25]Meanwhile, over in Israel, Nadab the son of Jeroboam had become king. He reigned two years, beginning in the second year of the reign of King Asa of Judah. [26]But he was not a good king; like his father, he worshiped many idols and led all of Israel into sin.

[27]Then Baasha (the son of Ahijah, from the tribe of Issachar) plotted against him and assassinated him while he was with the Israeli army laying siege to the Philistine city of Gibbethon. [28]So Baasha replaced Nadab as the king of Israel in Tirzah, during the third year of the reign of King Asa of Judah. [29]He immediately killed all of the descendants of King Jeroboam, so that not one of the royal family was left, just as the Lord had said would happen when he spoke through Ahijah, the prophet from Shiloh. [30]This was done because Jeroboam had angered the Lord God of Israel by sinning and leading the rest of Israel into sin.

Baasha rules Israel

[31]Further details of Baasha's reign are recorded in *The Annals of the Kings of Israel*.

[32, 33]There was continuous warfare between King Asa of Judah and King Baasha of Israel. Baasha reigned for twenty-four years, [34]but all that time he continually

15:11 2 Chron 14:2 15:17
15:12 Deut 23:17,18 1 Kgs 22:46 2 Chron 15:3
15:13 2 Chron 15:16
15:14 1 Kgs 22:43 2 Kgs 12:3; 14:4
15:15 1 Kgs 14:27
15:17 2 Chron 16:1
15:18 1 Kgs 14:26 20:1-5 2 Kgs 12:18
15:19 2 Chron 16:7
15:21 2 Chron 16:5
15:22 2 Chron 16:6
15:23 1 Kgs 15:7,31 2 Chron 16:11
15:24 1 Kgs 22:41 2 Chron 16:13, 14; 17:1
15:25 1 Kgs 14:20
15:26 1 Kgs 12:28 13:33; 14:16
15:27 Josh 21:23,24
15:29 1 Kgs 14:14
15:31 1 Kgs 14:19 16:4-7,14
15:32 2 Chron 15:19

15:14 *Asa did not realize that these were wrong,* literally, "nevertheless, the heart of Asa was perfect toward Jehovah all his days." **15:15** *the bronze shields his grandfather had dedicated,* literally, "the dedicated objects of his grandfather." See 14:27.

15:16 King Baasha seized the throne from Nadab (15:27, 28), who had replaced his father, Jeroboam, as king.

15:29 See 1 Kings 14:12–14 for Ahijah's prediction of this event.

15:30 All the descendants of Jeroboam were killed because he led Israel into sin. Sin is always judged harshly, but the worst sinners are those who lead others into sin. Jesus said it would be better if such people had a millstone tied around their necks and were thrown into the sea (Mark 9:42). If you have taken the responsibility of leading others, remember the consequences of leading them astray. Teaching the truth is a responsibility that goes hand in hand with the privilege of leadership.

disobeyed the Lord. He followed the evil paths of Jeroboam, for he led the people of Israel into the sin of worshiping idols.

16:1
1 Kgs 16:12
2 Chron 19:2
20:34

16:2
1 Sam 2:8
1 Kgs 14:7

16:3
1 Kgs 14:10
15:29; 21:21

16:4
1 Kgs 14:11
15:31; 16:14
21:19
Isa 66:24

16 A message of condemnation from the Lord was delivered to King Baasha at this time by the prophet Jehu:

2"I lifted you out of the dust," the message said, "to make you king of my people Israel; but you have walked in the evil paths of Jeroboam. You have made my people sin, and I am angry! 3So now I will destroy you and your family, just as I did the descendants of Jeroboam. 4-7Those of your family who die in the city will be eaten by dogs, and those who die in the fields will be eaten by the birds."

The message was sent to Baasha and his family because he had angered the Lord by all his evil deeds. He was as evil as Jeroboam despite the fact that the Lord had destroyed all of Jeroboam's descendants for their sins.

The rest of Baasha's biography—his deeds and conquests—are written in *The Annals of the Kings of Israel*.

Elah rules Israel

16:9
2 Kgs 9:31

8Elah, Baasha's son, began reigning during the twenty-sixth year of the reign of King Asa of Judah, but he reigned only two years. 9Then General Zimri, who had charge of half the royal chariot troops, plotted against him. One day King Elah was half drunk at the home of Arza, the superintendent of the palace, in the capital city of Tirzah. 10Zimri simply walked in and struck him down and killed him. (This occurred during the twenty-seventh year of the reign of King Asa of Judah.) Then Zimri declared himself to be the new king of Israel.

16:11
1 Kgs 14:10
15:29

11He immediately killed the entire royal family—leaving not a single male child.

KINGS TO DATE AND THEIR ENEMIES

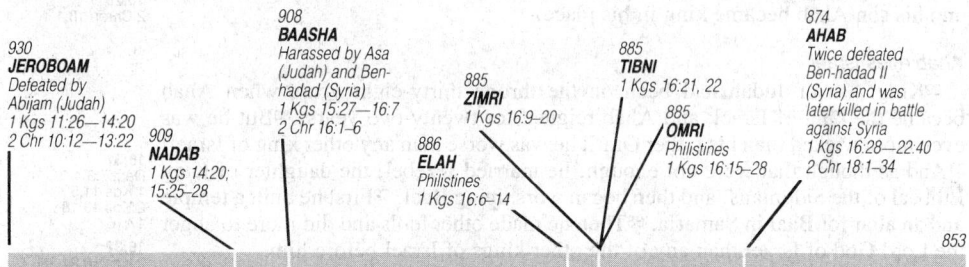

930
JEROBOAM
Defeated by
Abijam (Judah)
1 Kgs 11:26—14:20
2 Chr 10:12—13:22

909
NADAB
1 Kgs 14:20;
15:25–28

908
BAASHA
Harassed by Asa
(Judah) and Ben-
hadad (Syria)
1 Kgs 15:27—16:7
2 Chr 16:1–6

886
ELAH
Philistines
1 Kgs 16:6–14

885
ZIMRI
1 Kgs 16:9–20

885
TIBNI
1 Kgs 16:21, 22

885
OMRI
Philistines
1 Kgs 16:15–28

874
AHAB
Twice defeated
Ben-hadad II
(Syria) and was
later killed in battle
against Syria
1 Kgs 16:28—22:40
2 Chr 18:1–34

853

I S R A E L

J U D A H

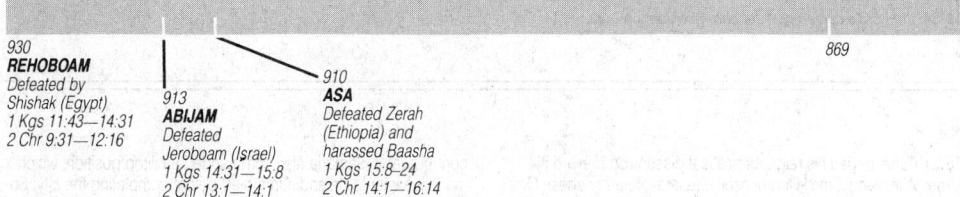

930
REHOBOAM
Defeated by
Shishak (Egypt)
1 Kgs 11:43—14:31
2 Chr 9:31—12:16

913
ABIJAM
Defeated
Jeroboam (Israel)
1 Kgs 14:31—15:8
2 Chr 13:1—14:1

910
ASA
Defeated Zerah
(Ethiopia) and
harassed Baasha
1 Kgs 15:8–24
2 Chr 14:1—16:14

869

All dates are B.C.
For all the kings of Israel and Judah, see the chart between the books of 1 and 2 Kings.

16:1-7 God destroyed Jeroboam's descendants for their flagrant sins, and yet King Baasha repeated the same mistakes. He did not learn from the example of those who went before him; he did not stop to think that his sin would be punished. Make sure you learn the lessons from your own past, the lives of others, and the lives of those whose stories are told in the Bible. Don't repeat their mistakes.

He even destroyed distant relatives and friends. 12This destruction of the descendants of Baasha was in line with what the Lord had predicted through the prophet Jehu. 13The tragedy occurred because of the sins of Baasha and his son Elah; for they had led Israel into worshiping idols and the Lord was very angry about it. 14The rest of the history of Elah's reign is written in *The Annals of the Kings of Israel*.

16:12
1 Kgs 16:1

16:13
Deut 32:21
1 Kgs 15:30

16:14
1 Kgs 16:4-7,20,
28,30

Zimri rules Israel

15, 16But Zimri lasted only seven days; for when the army of Israel, which was then engaged in attacking the Philistine city of Gibbethon, heard that Zimri had assassinated the king, they decided on General Omri, commander-in-chief of the army, as their new ruler. 17So Omri led the army of Gibbethon to besiege Tirzah, Israel's capital. 18When Zimri saw that the city had been taken, he went into the palace and burned it over him and died in the flames. 19For he, too, had sinned like Jeroboam; he had worshiped idols and had led the people of Israel to sin with him. 20The rest of the story of Zimri and his treason are written in *The Annals of the Kings of Israel*.

16:18
1 Sam 31:4,5
2 Sam 17:23

16:19
1 Kgs 12:28
14:6

16:20
1 Kgs 16:14,27

Omri rules Israel

21But now the kingdom of Israel was split in two; half the people were loyal to General Omri, and the other half followed Tibni, the son of Ginath. 22But General Omri won and Tibni was killed; so Omri reigned without opposition.

23King Asa of Judah had been on the throne thirty-one years when Omri began his reign over Israel, which lasted twelve years, six of them in Tirzah. 24Then Omri bought the hill now known as Samaria from its owner, Shemer, for $4,000 and built a city on it, calling it Samaria in honor of Shemer. 25But Omri was worse than any of the kings before him; 26he worshiped idols as Jeroboam had, and led Israel into this same sin. So God was very angry. 27The rest of Omri's history is recorded in *The Annals of the Kings of Israel*. 28When Omri died he was buried in Samaria, and his son Ahab became king in his place.

16:24
1 Kgs 13:32
18:2
Jn 4:4

16:25
1 Kgs 14:9
Mic 6:16

16:26
1 Kgs 13:33,34

16:27
1 Kgs 16:20
22:39

16:28
2 Chron 18:1

Ahab rules Israel

29King Asa of Judah had been on the throne thirty-eight years when Ahab became the king of Israel; and Ahab reigned for twenty-two years. 30But he was even more wicked than his father Omri; he was worse than any other king of Israel! 31And as though that were not enough, he married Jezebel, the daughter of King Ethbaal of the Sidonians, and then began worshiping Baal. 32First he built a temple and an altar for Baal in Samaria. 33Then he made other idols and did more to anger the Lord God of Israel than any of the other kings of Israel before him.

34(It was during his reign that Hiel, a man from Bethel, rebuilt Jericho. When he laid the foundations, his oldest son, Abiram, died; and when he finally completed it by setting up the gates, his youngest son, Segub, died. For this was the Lord's curse upon Jericho as declared by Joshua, the son of Nun.)

16:31
Deut 7:3,4
1 Kgs 11:5
2 Kgs 10:18
17:16

16:32
2 Kgs 10:21,26

16:33
1 Kgs 21:19,25
2 Kgs 13:6

16:34
Josh 6:26

16:34 *the Lord's curse upon Jericho.* See Joshua 6:26.

16:21 Omri began his reign as political dissension brewed in Israel. After King Zimri killed himself, the Israelite army chose Omri, their general, as the next ruler. To gain the support of the whole nation, Omri killed his chief rival to the throne, Tibni, and then began his evil reign. During his 12-year rule over Israel, he was a shrewd and capable leader. He organized the building of his new capital city, Samaria, while strengthening the nation politically and militarily. But he did not care about the nation's spiritual condition (Micah 6:16), and he purposely led Israel farther from God in order to put more power in his own hands.

16:24 Omri's new capital, Samaria, offered some political advantages. The city was his personal property, so he had total

control over it. Samaria also commanded a hilltop position, which made it easier to defend. Omri died before completing the city. So his son, Ahab, completed it, building not only the beautiful ivory palace (1 Kings 22:39; Amos 3:13–15), but also a temple to the god Baal. Samaria served as the capital city for the rest of Israel's dynasties until it fell to the Assyrians in 722 B.C. (2 Kings 17:5).

16:31 Ahab's evil wife, Jezebel, came from the Phoenician city of Tyre where her father had been a high priest and eventually king. Jezebel worshiped the god Baal. In order to please her, Ahab "built a temple and an altar for Baal" (16:32), thus promoting idolatry and leading the entire nation into sin. (For more about Baal, see the note on 18:18.)

3. Elijah's ministry
Elijah predicts drought

17:1
Judg 12:4
1 Kgs 22:14
Lk 4:25
Jas 5:17

17:4
1 Kgs 19:5

17:8
Obad 20
Lk 4:25,26

17:10
Gen 24:17
Jn 4:7

17:12
2 Kgs 4:2
Mt 15:33

17 Then Elijah, the prophet from Tishbe in Gilead, told King Ahab, "As surely as the Lord God of Israel lives—the God whom I worship and serve—there won't be any dew or rain for several years until I say the word!"

²Then the Lord said to Elijah, ³"Go to the east and hide by Cherith Brook at a place east of where it enters the Jordan River. ⁴Drink from the brook and eat what the ravens bring you, for I have commanded them to feed you."

⁵So he did as the Lord had told him to, and camped beside the brook. ⁶The ravens brought him bread and meat each morning and evening, and he drank from the brook. ⁷But after awhile the brook dried up, for there was no rainfall anywhere in the land.

Elijah miraculously supplies food

⁸,⁹Then the Lord said to him, "Go and live in the village of Zarephath, near the city of Sidon. There is a widow there who will feed you. I have given her my instructions."

¹⁰So he went to Zarephath. As he arrived at the gates of the city he saw a widow gathering sticks; and he asked her for a cup of water.

¹¹As she was going to get it, he called to her, "Bring me a bite of bread, too."

¹²But she said, "I swear by the Lord your God that I haven't a single piece of bread in the house. And I have only a handful of flour left and a little cooking oil in the bottom of the jar. I was just gathering a few sticks to cook this last meal, and then my son and I must die of starvation."

¹³But Elijah said to her, "Don't be afraid! Go ahead and cook that 'last meal,' but bake me a little loaf of bread first; and afterwards there will still be enough food for you and your son. ¹⁴For the Lord God of Israel says that there will always be plenty of flour and oil left in your containers until the time when the Lord sends rain, and the crops grow again!"

¹⁵So she did as Elijah said, and she and Elijah and her son continued to eat from

17:1 *The prophet, implied.*

17:1 Elijah was one of the first in a long line of important prophets God sent to both Israel and Judah. Israel, the Northern Kingdom, had no faithful kings throughout its history. Each king was wicked, actually leading the people in worshiping heathen gods. There were few priests left from the tribe of Levi—most had gone to Judah—and the priests appointed by Israel's kings were corrupt and ineffective. With no king or priests to bring God's Word to the people, God called prophets to try to rescue Israel from its moral and spiritual decline. For the next 300 years these men and women would play vital roles in both nations, encouraging the people and leaders to turn back to God.

17:1 Those who worshiped Baal believed he was the god who brought the rains and bountiful harvests. So when Elijah walked into the presence of this Baal-worshiping king and told him there would be no rain for several years, Ahab was shocked. Ahab had built a strong military defense, but it would be no help against drought. He had many Baal priests, but they could not bring rain. Elijah bravely confronted the man who led his people into evil, and he told of a power far greater than any heathen god—the Lord God of Israel. When rebellion and heresy were at an all-time high in Israel, God responded not only with words but with action.

17:10ff In a nation that was required by law to care for its prophets, it is ironic that God turned to ravens (unclean birds) and a widow (a foreigner from Jezebel's home territory) to care for Elijah. God has help where we least expect it. He provides for us in ways that go beyond our narrow definitions or expectations. No matter how bitter our trials or how seemingly hopeless our situation, we should look for God's hand of care. We may find his providence in some strange places!

17:13–16 When the widow of Zarephath met Elijah, she thought

ELIJAH HIDES FROM AHAB
Elijah prophesied a drought, and then hid from King Ahab by the Cherith Brook where he was fed by ravens. When the brook dried up, God sent him to Zarephath in Phoenicia where a widow and her son fed him and gave him lodging.

she was preparing her last meal. But a simple act of faith produced a miracle. Faith is the step between promise and assurance. Miracles seem so out of reach for our feeble faith. But every miracle, large or small, begins with an act of obedience. We may not see the solution until we take the first step of faith.

her supply of flour and oil as long as it was needed. 16For no matter how much they used, there was always plenty left in the containers, just as the Lord had promised through Elijah!

Elijah restores a boy to life

17But one day the woman's son became sick and died.

18"O man of God," she cried, "what have you done to me? Have you come here to punish my sins by killing my son?"

19"Give him to me," Elijah replied. And he took the boy's body from her and carried it upstairs to the guest room where he lived, and laid the body on his bed, 20and then cried out to the Lord, "O Lord my God, why have you killed the son of this widow with whom I am staying?"

21And he stretched himself upon the child three times, and cried out to the Lord, "O Lord my God, please let this child's spirit return to him."

22And the Lord heard Elijah's prayer; and the spirit of the child returned, and he became alive again! 23Then Elijah took him downstairs and gave him to his mother.

"See! He's alive!" he beamed.

24"Now I know for sure that you are a prophet," she told him afterward, "and that whatever you say is from the Lord!"

Elijah rebukes King Ahab

18 It was three years later that the Lord said to Elijah, "Go and tell King Ahab that I will soon send rain again!"

2So Elijah went to tell him. Meanwhile the famine had become very severe in Samaria.

3, 4The man in charge of Ahab's household affairs was Obadiah, who was a devoted follower of the Lord. Once when Queen Jezebel had tried to kill all of the Lord's prophets, Obadiah had hidden one hundred of them in two caves—fifty in each—and had fed them with bread and water.

5That same day, while Elijah was on the way to see King Ahab, the king said to Obadiah, "We must check every stream and brook to see if we can find enough grass to save at least some of my horses and mules. You go one way and I'll go the other, and we will search the entire land."

6So they did, each going alone. 7Suddenly Obadiah saw Elijah coming toward him! Obadiah recognized him at once and fell to the ground before him.

"Is it really you, my lord Elijah?" he asked.

8"Yes, it is," Elijah replied. "Now go and tell the king I am here."

9"Oh, sir," Obadiah protested, "what harm have I done to you that you are sending me to my death? 10For I swear by God that the king has searched every nation and kingdom on earth from end to end to find you. And each time when he was told 'Elijah isn't here,' King Ahab forced the king of that nation to swear to the truth of his claim. 11And now you say, 'Go and tell him Elijah is here'! 12But as soon as I leave you, the Spirit of the Lord will carry you away, who knows where, and when Ahab comes and can't find you, he will kill me; yet I have been a true servant of the Lord all my life. 13Has no one told you about the time when Queen Jezebel was trying to kill the Lord's prophets, and I hid a hundred of them in two caves and fed them with bread and water? 14And now you say, 'Go tell the king that Elijah is here'! Sir, if I do that, I'm dead!"

15But Elijah said, "I swear by the Lord God of the armies of heaven, in whose presence I stand, that I will present myself to Ahab today."

17:24 *she told him afterward,* implied. **18:5** *while Elijah was on the way to see King Ahab,* implied.

17:21
2 Kgs 4:34
Acts 20:10-12
17:23
2 Kgs 4:36
Lk 7:15
Acts 9:41
Heb 11:35
17:24
Jn 2:11; 3:1,2
11:15

18:1
Jas 5:18

18:2
1 Kgs 16:24

18:3
1 Kgs 18:16

18:12
2 Kgs 2:16
Ezek 3:12
Acts 8:39

18:13
1 Kgs 18:3; 4

17:17 Even when God has done a miracle in our lives, our troubles may not be over. The famine was a terrible experience, but the worst was yet to come. God's provision is never given in order to let us rest upon it. We are to depend on him as each new trial faces us.

17:24 Chapter 17 presents Elijah's credentials in order to establish the authority of his ministry.

18:3, 4 Although Elijah was alone in his confrontation with Ahab and Jezebel, he was not the only one in Israel who believed in God. Obadiah had been faithful in hiding 100 prophets still true to the Lord.

Elijah's contest with the evil prophets

¹⁶So Obadiah went to tell Ahab that Elijah had come; and Ahab went out to meet him.

18:17
Josh 7:25

¹⁷"So it's you, is it?—the man who brought this disaster upon Israel!" Ahab exclaimed when he saw him.

18:18
1 Kgs 9:9; 21:25
2 Chron 15:5

¹⁸"You're talking about yourself," Elijah answered. "For you and your family have refused to obey the Lord, and have worshiped Baal instead. ¹⁹Now bring all

ELIJAH

Elijah's singleminded commitment to God shocks and challenges us. He was sent to confront, not comfort, and he spoke God's words to a king who often rejected his message. Elijah chose to carry out his ministry for God alone and paid for that decision by experiencing isolation.

It is interesting to think about the amazing miracles God accomplished through Elijah, but we would do well to focus on the relationship they shared. All that happened in Elijah's life began with the same miracle that is available to us—he responded to the miracle of being able to know God.

For example, after God worked an overwhelming miracle through Elijah in defeating the prophets of Baal, Queen Jezebel retaliated by threatening Elijah's life. And Elijah ran. He felt afraid, depressed, and abandoned. Despite God's provision of food and shelter in the desert, Elijah wanted to die. So God presented Elijah with an "audio-visual display" and a message he needed to hear. Elijah witnessed a windstorm, an earthquake, and God's fire from heaven. But the Lord was not in any of those powerful things. Instead, God displayed his presence in a soft whisper.

Elijah, like us, struggled with his feelings even after this comforting message from God. So God confronted Elijah's emotions and commanded action. He told Elijah what to do next and informed him that part of his loneliness was based on ignorance: 7,000 others in Israel were still faithful to God.

Even today, God often speaks through the quiet and obvious rather than the spectacular and unusual. God has work for us to do even when we feel fear and failure. And God always has more resources and people than we know. Although we might wish to do amazing miracles for God, we should instead focus on having a relationship with him. The real miracle of Elijah's life was his very personal relationship with God.

Strengths and accomplishments:
- The most famous and dramatic of Israel's prophets
- Predicted the beginning and end of a three-year drought
- Was used by God to restore a dead child to his mother
- God's representative in a showdown with priests of Baal and Asherah
- Appeared with Moses and Jesus in the New Testament transfiguration scene

Weaknesses and mistakes:
- Chose to work alone and paid for it through isolation
- Fled in fear from Jezebel when she threatened his life

Lessons from his life:
- We are never closer to defeat than in our moments of greatest victory
- We are never as alone as we may feel; God is always there
- God speaks more frequently in persistent whispers than in shouts

Vital statistics:
- Where: Gilead
- Occupation: Prophet
- Contemporaries: Ahab, Jezebel, Ahaziah, Obadiah, Jehu, Hazael

Key verses:
"At the customary time for offering the evening sacrifice, Elijah walked up to the altar and prayed, 'O Lord God of Abraham, Isaac, and Israel, prove today that you are the God of Israel and that I am your servant; prove that I have done all this at your command. . . . Then, suddenly, fire flashed down from heaven" (1 Kings 18:36, 38).

Elijah's story is told in 1 Kings 17:1—2 Kings 2:11. He is also mentioned in 2 Chronicles 21:12–15; Malachi 4:5, 6; Matthew 11:14; 16:14; 17:3–13; 27:47–49; Luke 1:17; 4:25, 26; John 1:19–25; Romans 11:2–4; James 5:17, 18.

18:18 Instead of worshiping the true God, Ahab and his wife Jezebel worshiped Baal, the most popular Canaanite god. Baal idols were usually molded into the shape of a bull, representing strength and fertility and reflecting lust for power and sexual pleasure.

18:19 Ahab brought 850 heathen prophets to Mount Carmel to match wits and power with Elijah. These prophets were also called priests because they were in charge of the heathen religious worship. Evil kings hated God's prophets because they spoke against sin and idolatry and undermined their control over the people. With the wicked kings' backing, many heathen prophets sprang up to counter the words of God's prophets. But Elijah showed the people that speaking a prophecy wasn't enough. One needed the power of a living God to fulfill it.

the people of Israel to Mount Carmel, with all 450 prophets of Baal and the 400 prophets of Asherah who are supported by Jezebel."

20So Ahab summoned all the people and the prophets to Mount Carmel.

21Then Elijah talked to them. "How long are you going to waver between two opinions?" he asked the people. "If the Lord is God, *follow* him! But if Baal is God, then follow *him!*"

18:21
Josh 24:15
2 Kgs 17:41
Zeph 1:5

22Then Elijah spoke again. "I am the only prophet of the Lord who is left," he told them, "but Baal has 450 prophets. 23Now bring two young bulls. The prophets of Baal may choose whichever one they wish and cut it into pieces and lay it on the wood of their altar, but without putting any fire under the wood; and I will prepare the other young bull and lay it on the wood on the Lord's altar, with no fire under it. 24Then pray to your god, and I will pray to the Lord; and the god who answers by sending fire to light the wood is the true God!" And all the people agreed to this test.

18:22
1 Kgs 19:10,14

18:24
1 Sam 7:5
1 Chron 21:26

25Then Elijah turned to the prophets of Baal. "You first," he said, "for there are many of you; choose one of the bulls and prepare it and call to your god; but don't put any fire under the wood."

26So they prepared one of the young bulls and placed it on the altar; and they called to Baal all morning, shouting, "O Baal, hear us!" But there was no reply of any kind. Then they began to dance around the altar. 27About noontime, Elijah began mocking them.

18:26
Ps 115:5
Jer 10:5
1 Cor 12:2

"You'll have to shout louder than that," he scoffed, "to catch the attention of your god! Perhaps he is talking to someone, or is out sitting on the toilet, or maybe he is away on a trip, or is asleep and needs to be wakened!"

28So they shouted louder and, as was their custom, cut themselves with knives and swords until the blood gushed out. 29They raved all afternoon until the time of the evening sacrifice, but there was no reply, no voice, no answer.

18:28
Lev 19:28
Deut 14:1

30Then Elijah called to the people, "Come over here."

And they all crowded around him as he repaired the altar of the Lord which had been torn down. 31He took twelve stones, one to represent each of the tribes of Israel, 32and used the stones to rebuild the Lord's altar. Then he dug a trench about three feet wide around the altar. 33He piled wood upon the altar and cut the young bull into pieces and laid the pieces on the wood.

18:30
1 Kgs 19:10,14

18:31
Josh 4:2,3

18:33
Gen 22:9

18:31 *one to represent each of the tribes of Israel,* literally, "each of the tribes of the sons of Jacob to whom the Lord had said, 'Israel shall be your name.'" **18:32** *three feet wide,* literally, "as great as would contain two measures of seed."

18:21 Elijah challenged the people to take a stand—to follow whoever was the true God. Why did so many people waver between the two choices? Perhaps some were not sure. Many, however, knew that the Lord was God, but they enjoyed the sinful pleasures and other benefits that came with following Ahab and his idolatrous worship. It is important to take a stand for the Lord. If we just drift along with whatever is pleasant and easy, we will someday discover that we have been worshiping a false god—ourselves.

18:29 Although the prophets of Baal raved all afternoon, "there was no reply, no voice, no answer." Their god was silent because it was not real. The "gods" we may be tempted to follow are not idols of wood or stone, but they are just as false and dangerous because they cause us to depend on something other than God. Power, status, appearance, or material possessions can become our gods if we devote our lives to them. But when we reach times of crisis and desperately call out to these "gods," there will only be silence. They can offer no true answers, no guidance, and no wisdom.

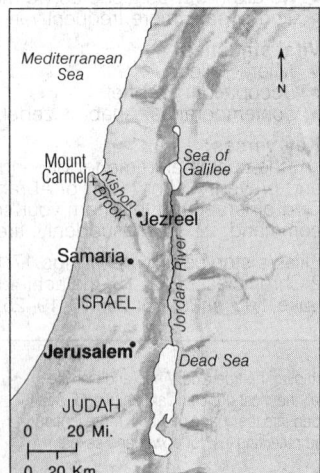

THE SHOWDOWN AT CARMEL
In a showdown with the false prophets of Baal at Mount Carmel, Elijah set out to prove to evil Ahab that only the Lord is God. Elijah then killed the false prophets beside the Kishon Brook and fled back to Jezreel.

"Fill four barrels with water," he said, "and pour the water over the carcass and the wood."

After they had done this he said, 34"Do it again." And they did.

"Now, do it once more!" And they did; 35and the water ran off the altar and filled the trench.

18:36
Ex 3:6; 4:5
Num 16:28
1 Sam 17:46
2 Kgs 19:19
1 Chron 29:18

36At the customary time for offering the evening sacrifice, Elijah walked up to the altar and prayed, "O Lord God of Abraham, Isaac, and Israel, prove today that you are the God of Israel and that I am your servant; prove that I have done all this at your command. 37O Lord, answer me! Answer me so these people will know that you are God and that you have brought them back to yourself."

18:38
Gen 15:17
Lev 9:24; 10:1
2 Kgs 1:12
Job 1:16
18:39
1 Kgs 8:60
18:40
Deut 13:5; 18:20
2 Kgs 10:24

38Then, suddenly, fire flashed down from heaven and burned up the young bull, the wood, the stones, the dust, and even evaporated all the water in the ditch!

39And when the people saw it, they fell to their faces upon the ground shouting, "Jehovah is God! Jehovah is God!"

40Then Elijah told them to grab the prophets of Baal. "Don't let a single one escape," he commanded.

So they seized them all, and Elijah took them to Kishon Brook and killed them there.

Elijah prays for rain

18:41-45
Jas 5:18

41Then Elijah said to Ahab, "Go and enjoy a good meal! For I hear a mighty rainstorm coming!"

42So Ahab prepared a feast. But Elijah climbed to the top of Mount Carmel and got down on his knees, with his face between his knees, 43and said to his servant, "Go and look out toward the sea."

He did, but returned to Elijah and told him, "I didn't see anything."

Then Elijah told him, "Go again, and again, and again, seven times!"

44Finally, the seventh time, his servant told him, "I saw a little cloud about the size of a man's hand rising from the sea."

Then Elijah shouted, "Hurry to Ahab and tell him to get into his chariot and get down the mountain, or he'll be stopped by the rain!"

45And sure enough, the sky was soon black with clouds, and a heavy wind brought a terrific rainstorm. Ahab left hastily for Jezreel, 46and the Lord gave special strength to Elijah so that he was able to run ahead of Ahab's chariot to the entrance of the city!

PROPHETS— FALSE AND TRUE	False Prophets	True Prophets
	Worked for political purposes to benefit themselves	Worked for spiritual purposes to serve God and the people
	Held positions of great wealth	Owned little or nothing
	Gave false messages	Spoke only true messages
	Spoke only what the people wanted to hear	Spoke only what God told them to say—no matter how unpopular

The false prophets were an obstacle to bringing God's Word to the people. They would bring messages that contradicted the words of the true prophets. They gave "messages" that appealed to the people's sinful natures and comforted their fears. False prophets told people what they wanted to hear. True prophets told God's truth.

18:36, 37 Just as God flashed fire from heaven for Elijah, he will help us accomplish what he commands us to do. The proof may not be as dramatic in our lives as in Elijah's, but God will make resources available to us in creative ways to accomplish his purposes. He will give us the wisdom to raise a family, the courage to take a stand for truth, or the means to provide help for someone in need. Like Elijah, we can have faith that, whatever God commands us to do, he will provide what we need to carry it through.

18:46 Elijah ran the six miles back to the city in order to give Ahab a last chance to turn from his sin before joining Jezebel in Jezreel. His run also insured that the correct story of what happened would reach Jezreel.

Elijah flees for his life

19 When Ahab told Queen Jezebel what Elijah had done, and that he had slaughtered the prophets of Baal, 2she sent this message to Elijah: "You killed my prophets, and now I swear by the gods that I am going to kill you by this time tomorrow night."

3So Elijah fled for his life; he went to Beer-sheba, a city of Judah, and left his servant there. 4Then he went on alone into the wilderness, traveling all day, and sat down under a broom bush and prayed that he might die.

"I've had enough," he told the Lord. "Take away my life. I've got to die sometime, and it might as well be now."

5Then he lay down and slept beneath the broom bush. But as he was sleeping, an angel touched him and told him to get up and eat! 6He looked around and saw some bread baking on hot stones, and a jar of water! So he ate and drank and lay down again.

7Then the angel of the Lord came again and touched him and said, "Get up and eat some more, for there is a long journey ahead of you."

8So he got up and ate and drank, and the food gave him enough strength to travel forty days and forty nights to Mount Horeb, the mountain of God, 9where he lived in a cave.

God speaks to Elijah

But the Lord said to him, "What are you doing here, Elijah?"

10He replied, "I have worked very hard for the Lord God of the heavens; but the people of Israel have broken their covenant with you and torn down your altars and killed your prophets, and only I am left; and now they are trying to kill me, too."

11"Go out and stand before me on the mountain," the Lord told him. And as Elijah stood there the Lord passed by, and a mighty windstorm hit the mountain; it was such a terrible blast that the rocks were torn loose, but the Lord was not in the

19:4 *and it might as well be now,* literally, "I am no better than my fathers."

19:2
2 Kgs 6:31

19:3
Gen 21:31
Amos 7:12

19:4
Num 11:5
Job 3:20,21
Jer 20:14
Jonah 4:3,8

19:8
Ex 3:1; 4:27
24:18; 34:28
Deut 9:9
Mt 4:2

19:10
Rom 11:2,3

19:11
Ex 19:16,19,20
24:12
Ezek 1:4

19:2 Jezebel was enraged about the death of her prophets because they had told her everything *she* wanted to hear, prophesying her future power and glory. Their job was to deify the king and queen and help perpetuate their kingdom. Jezebel was also angry because her supporters had been eliminated and her pride and authority damaged. The money she had invested in these prophets was now lost.

Elijah, who caused the prophets' deaths, was a constant thorn in Jezebel's side because he was always predicting gloom and doom. Because she could not control his actions, she vowed to kill him. As long as God's prophet was around, she could not carry out all the evil she wanted.

19:3, 4 Elijah experienced the depths of fatigue and discouragement just after his two great spiritual victories: the defeat of the prophets of Baal and the answered prayer for rain. Often discouragement sets in after great spiritual experiences, especially those requiring physical effort or producing emotional excitement. To lead him out of depression, God first let Elijah rest and eat. Then God confronted him with the need to return to his mission in life—to be God's prophet. Elijah's battles were not over; there was still work for him to do. When you feel let down after a great spiritual experience, remember that God's purpose for your life is not yet over.

19:8 When Elijah fled to Mount Horeb, he was returning to the sacred place where God met Moses and gave his laws to mankind. Obviously, God gave Elijah special strength to travel this great distance—over 200 miles—without additional food. Like Moses before him and Jesus after him, Elijah fasted for 40 days and 40 nights (Deuteronomy 9:9; Matthew 4:1, 2). Centuries later, Moses, Elijah, and Jesus would be together on a mountaintop (Luke 9:28–36).

19:10 Elijah thought he was the only person left who was still true

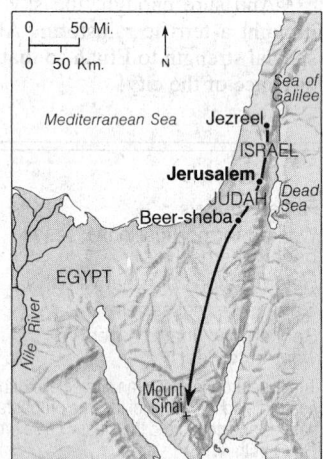

ELIJAH FLEES FROM JEZEBEL
After killing Baal's prophets, Elijah ran from the furious Queen Jezebel. He fled to Beersheba, then into the wilderness, and finally to Mount Horeb (Sinai). There, like Moses centuries earlier, he talked with God.

to God. After experiencing great victory at Mount Carmel, he had to run for his life. His resulting loneliness and discouragement made him feel sorry for himself. Elijah had seen both the king's court and the priesthood become corrupt. In his discouragement, he forgot that others had remained faithful in the midst of the nation's wickedness. When you are tempted to feel you are the only one remaining faithful to a task, don't stop to feel sorry for yourself—self-pity will dilute the good you are doing. Be assured that even if you don't know who they are, others are faithfully obeying God and carrying on their duties.

19:12
Ex 3:2,6
Deut 4:11
Job 4:16

wind. After the wind, there was an earthquake, but the Lord was not in the earthquake. ¹²And after the earthquake, there was a fire, but the Lord was not in the fire. And after the fire, there was the sound of a gentle whisper. ¹³When Elijah heard it, he wrapped his face in his scarf and went out and stood at the entrance of the cave.

And a voice said, "Why are you here, Elijah?"

AHAB

The kings of Israel, both good and evil, had prophets sent by God to advise, confront, and aid them. King David had a faithful friend in God's prophet, Nathan; Ahab could have had an equally faithful friend in Elijah. But while David listened to Nathan, and was willing to repent of his sins, Ahab saw Elijah as his enemy. Why? Because Elijah always brought bad news to Ahab. But Ahab refused to acknowledge that it was his constant disobedience to God and persistent idol worship that brought the evil on his nation. He blamed Elijah for bringing the prophecies of judgment, rather than taking his advice as a prophet of God.

Ahab was trapped by his own choices and he was unwilling to take the right action. As king, he was responsible to God and his prophet Elijah, but he was married to an evil woman who drew him into idol worship. He was a childish man who brooded for days if unable to get his own way. He took his evil wife's advice, listened only to the "prophets" who gave good news, and surrounded himself with people who encouraged him to do whatever he wanted. But the value of advice cannot be judged by the number of people for or against it. Ahab consistently chose to follow the majority opinion—of those who surrounded him—and that led to his death.

It may seem nice to have someone encourage us to do whatever we want, because advice that goes against our wishes is difficult to accept. However, our decisions must be based on the quality of the advice, not the majority opinion of our peers. God encourages us to get advice from wise counselors, but how can we test the advice we receive? Advice that agrees with the principles in God's Word is reliable. We must always separate advice from our own desires, the majority opinion, or whatever seems "best" in our limited perspective, and weigh it against God's commands. He will never lead us to do what he has forbidden in his Word—even in principle. Unlike Ahab, we should trust godly counselors and have the courage to stand against those who would have us do otherwise.

Strengths and accomplishments:
● Seventh king of Israel
● Capable leader and military strategist

Weaknesses and mistakes:
● The most evil king of Israel
● Married Jezebel, a heathen woman, and allowed her to promote Baal worship
● Brooded about not being able to get a piece of land, so his wife had its owner, Naboth, killed
● Was used to getting his own way, and got depressed when he didn't

Lessons from his life:
● The choice of a mate will have a significant effect on life—physically, spiritually, and emotionally
● Selfishness, left unchecked, can lead to great evil

Vital statistics:
● Where: Northern Kingdom of Israel
● Occupation: King
● Relatives: Wife: Jezebel. Father: Omri. Sons: Ahaziah, Jehoram.
● Contemporaries: Elijah, Naboth, Jehu, Ben-hadad, Jehoshaphat

Key verses:
"Ahab . . . was worse than any other king of Israel! And as though that were not enough, he married Jezebel, the daughter of King Ethbaal of the Sidonians, and then began worshiping Baal. First he built a temple and an altar for Baal in Samaria. Then he made other idols and did more to anger the Lord God of Israel than any of the other kings of Israel before him" (1 Kings 16:29–33).

Ahab's story is told in 1 Kings 16:28—22:40. He is also mentioned in 2 Chronicles 18—22; Micah 6:16.

19:11-13 Elijah knew that the gentle whisper was God's voice. He realized that God doesn't reveal himself only in powerful, miraculous ways. To look for God only in something big (rallies, churches, conferences, visible leaders) may be to miss him, because he is often found gently whispering in the quietness of a humbled heart. Are you listening for God? Step back from the noise and activity of your busy life and listen humbly and quietly for his guidance. It may come when you least expect it.

¹⁴He replied again, "I have been working very hard for the Lord God of the armies of heaven, but the people have broken their covenant and have torn down your altars; they have killed every one of your prophets except me; and now they are trying to kill me, too."

¹⁵Then the Lord told him, "Go back by the desert road to Damascus, and when you arrive, anoint Hazael to be king of Syria. ¹⁶Then anoint Jehu (son of Nimshi) to be king of Israel, and anoint Elisha (the son of Shaphat of Abel-meholah) to replace you as my prophet. ¹⁷Anyone who escapes from Hazael shall be killed by Jehu, and those who escape Jehu shall be killed by Elisha! ¹⁸And incidentally, there are 7,000 men in Israel who have never bowed to Baal nor kissed him!"

19:15
2 Kgs 8:8

19:16
2 Kgs 2:9; 9:1

19:17
2 Kgs 8:12,13
9:14; 13:3

19:18
Hos 13:2
Rom 11:4

Elisha follows Elijah

¹⁹So Elijah went and found Elisha who was plowing a field with eleven other teams ahead of him; he was at the end of the line with the last team. Elijah went over to him and threw his coat across his shoulders and walked away again.

19:19
2 Kgs 2:8,13,14

²⁰Elisha left the oxen standing there and ran after Elijah and said to him, "First let me go and say good-bye to my father and mother, and then I'll go with you!"

Elijah replied, "Go on back! Why all the excitement?"

²¹Elisha then returned to his oxen, killed them, and used wood from the plow to build a fire to roast their flesh. He passed around the meat to the other plowmen, and they all had a great feast. Then he went with Elijah, as his assistant.

God gives Israel victory over Syria

20 King Ben-hadad of Syria now mobilized his army and, with thirty-two allied nations and their hordes of chariots and horses, besieged Samaria, the Israeli capital. ², ³He sent this message into the city to King Ahab of Israel: "Your silver and gold are mine, as are your prettiest wives and the best of your children!" ⁴"All right, my lord," Ahab replied. "All that I have is yours!"

20:1
2 Kgs 6:24

20:2
1 Kgs 15:18
2 Chron 16:2

⁵, ⁶Soon Ben-hadad's messengers returned again with another message: "You must not only give me your silver, gold, wives, and children, but about this time

19:19 and walked away again, implied.

19:15, 16 God asked Elijah to anoint three different people. The first was Hazael, as king of Syria. Elijah was to anoint an enemy king because God was going to use Syria as his instrument to punish Israel for its sin. Syria was Israel's *external* punishment.

Israel's *internal* punishment came from Jehu, the next man Elijah was to anoint. As king of Israel, Jehu would destroy those who worshiped the false god Baal (2 Kings 9, 10).

The third person Elijah was to anoint was Elisha, the prophet who would succeed him. Elisha's job was to work in Israel, the Northern Kingdom, and help point the people back to God. The Southern Kingdom at this time was ruled by Jehoshaphat, a king devoted to God.

19:19 The coat was the most important article of clothing a person could own. It was used as protection against the weather, as bedding, as a chair, and as luggage. It could be given as a pledge for a debt or torn into pieces to show grief. Elijah put his coat on Elisha's shoulders to show that he would become Elijah's successor. Later, when the transfer of authority was complete, Elijah left his coat for Elisha (2 Kings 2:11–14).

19:21 By killing his oxen, Elisha made a strong commitment to follow Elijah. Without them, he could not return to his life as a wealthy farmer. This meal was more than a typical feast among farmers. It was an offering of thanks to the Lord who chose Elisha to be his prophet.

20:1ff With two evil and two good kings up to this point, the Southern Kingdom, Judah, wavered between godly and ungodly living. But the Northern Kingdom, Israel, had eight evil kings in succession. To punish both kingdoms for living their own way

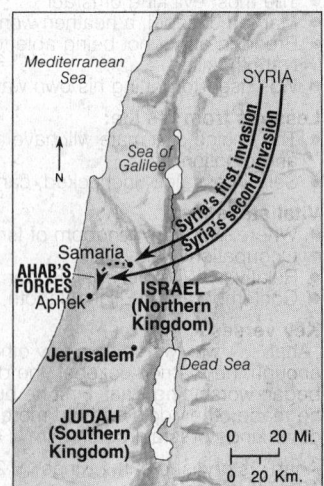

GOD DELIVERS AHAB
Despite Ahab's wickedness, God approached him in love. When Samaria was surrounded by Syrian forces, God miraculously delivered the city. But Ahab refused to give God credit. A year later, the Syrians attacked on the plains near Aphek. Again God gave Ahab victory, but again the king refused to acknowledge God's help.

instead of following God, God allowed other nations to gain strength and become their enemies. Three main enemies threatened Israel and Judah during the next two centuries—Syria, Assyria, and Babylon. Syria, the first to rise to power, presented an immediate threat to King Ahab and Israel.

tomorrow I will send my men to search your palace and the homes of your people, and they will take away whatever they like!"

⁷Then Ahab summoned his advisors. "Look what this man is doing," he complained to them. "He is stirring up trouble despite the fact that I have already told him he could have my wives and children and silver and gold, just as he demanded."

⁸"Don't give him anything more," the elders advised.

⁹So he told the messengers from Ben-hadad, "Tell my lord the king, 'I will give you everything you asked for the first time, but your men may not search the palace and the homes of the people.' " So the messengers returned to Ben-hadad.

20:10
1 Kgs 19:2
2 Kgs 6:31
20:11
Prov 27:1

¹⁰Then the Syrian king sent this message to Ahab: "May the gods do more to me than I am going to do to you if I don't turn Samaria into handfuls of dust!"

¹¹The king of Israel retorted, "Don't count your chickens before they hatch!"

¹²This reply of Ahab's reached Ben-hadad and the other kings as they were drinking in their tents.

"Prepare to attack!" Ben-hadad commanded his officers.

20:13
2 Kgs 6:8-10

¹³Then a prophet came to see King Ahab and gave him this message from the Lord: "Do you see all these enemy forces? I will deliver them all to you today. Then at last you will know that I am the Lord."

¹⁴Ahab asked, "How will he do it?"

And the prophet replied, "The Lord says, 'By the troops from the provinces.' "

"Shall we attack first?" Ahab asked.

"Yes," the prophet answered.

¹⁵So he mustered the troops from the provinces, 232 of them, then the rest of his army of 7,000 men. ¹⁶About noontime, as Ben-hadad and the thirty-two allied kings were still drinking themselves drunk, the first of Ahab's troops marched out of the city.

¹⁷As they approached, Ben-hadad's scouts reported to him, "Some troops are coming!"

¹⁸"Take them alive," Ben-hadad commanded, "whether they have come for truce or for war."

¹⁹By now Ahab's entire army had joined the attack. ²⁰Each one killed a Syrian soldier, and suddenly the entire Syrian army panicked and fled. The Israelis chased them, but King Ben-hadad and a few others escaped on horses. ²¹However, the great bulk of the horses and chariots were captured, and most of the Syrian army was killed in a great slaughter.

²²Then the prophet approached King Ahab and said, "Get ready for another attack by the king of Syria."

²³For after their defeat, Ben-hadad's officers said to him, "The Israeli God is a god of the hills; that is why they won. But we can beat them easily on the plains. ²⁴Only this time replace the kings with generals! ²⁵Recruit another army like the one you lost; give us the same number of horses, chariots, and men, and we will fight against them in the plains; there's not a shadow of a doubt that we will beat them." So King Ben-hadad did as they suggested. ²⁶The following year he called

20:26
1 Sam 4:1; 29:1
2 Kgs 13:17
20:27
Judg 6:5
1 Sam 13:5

up the Syrian army and marched out against Israel again, this time at Aphek. ²⁷Israel then mustered its army, set up supply lines, and moved into the battle; but the Israeli army looked like two little flocks of baby goats in comparison to the vast Syrian forces that filled the countryside!

²⁸Then a prophet went to the king of Israel with this message from the Lord: "Because the Syrians have declared, 'The Lord is a God of the hills and not of the

20:9 *your men may not search the palace and the homes of the people,* literally, "this thing I cannot do."

20:23 Since the days of Joshua, Israel's soldiers had a reputation for being superior fighters in the hills, but ineffective in the open plains and valleys because they did not use chariots in battle. Horse-drawn chariots, useless in hilly terrain and dense forests, could easily run down great numbers of foot soldiers on the plains. What Ben-hadad's officers did not understand was that it was God who made the difference in battle, not the chariots.

plains,' I will help you defeat this vast army, and you shall know that I am indeed the Lord.

29The two armies camped opposite each other for seven days, and on the seventh day the battle began. And the Israelis killed 100,000 Syrian infantrymen that first day. 30The rest fled behind the walls of Aphek, but the wall fell on them and killed another 27,000. Ben-hadad fled into the city and hid in the inner room of one of the houses.

20:30
1 Kgs 22:25
2 Chron 18:24

31"Sir," his officers said to him, "we have heard that the kings of Israel are very merciful. Let us wear sackcloth and put ropes on our heads and go out to King Ahab to see if he will let you live."

20:31
Gen 37:34
1 Kgs 21:27
Esth 4:3

32So they went to the king of Israel and begged, "Your servant Ben-hadad pleads, 'Let me live!' "

"Oh, is he still alive?" the king of Israel asked. "He is my brother!"

33The men were quick to grab this straw of hope and hurried to clinch the matter by exclaiming, "Yes, your brother Ben-hadad!"

"Go and get him," the king of Israel told them. And when Ben-hadad arrived, he invited him up into his chariot!

34Ben-hadad told him, "I will restore the cities my father took from your father, and you may establish trading posts in Damascus, as my father did in Samaria."

20:34
1 Kgs 15:20

A prophet condemns King Ahab

35Meanwhile, the Lord instructed one of the prophets to say to another man, "Strike me with your sword!" But the man refused.

20:35
1 Kgs 13:16,17

36Then the prophet told him, "Because you have not obeyed the voice of the Lord, a lion shall kill you as soon as you leave me." And sure enough, as he turned to go a lion attacked and killed him.

20:36
1 Kgs 13:24

37Then the prophet turned to another man and said, "Strike me with your sword." And he did, wounding him.

38The prophet waited for the king beside the road, having placed a bandage over his eyes to disguise himself.

20:38
2 Sam 14:2,3
1 Kgs 14:2
22:30

39As the king passed by, the prophet called out to him, "Sir, I was in the battle, and a man brought me a prisoner and said, 'Keep this man; if he gets away, you must die, or else pay me $2,000!' 40But while I was busy doing something else, the prisoner disappeared!"

20:39
2 Kgs 10:24

"Well, it's your own fault," the king replied. "You'll have to pay."

41Then the prophet yanked off the bandage from his eyes, and the king recognized him as one of the prophets. 42Then the prophet told him, "The Lord says, 'Because you have spared the man I said must die, now you must die in his place, and your people shall perish instead of his.' "

43So the king of Israel went home to Samaria angry and sullen.

Ahab takes Naboth's vineyard

21 Naboth, a man from Jezreel, had a vineyard on the outskirts of the city near King Ahab's palace. 2One day the king talked to him about selling him this land.

21:1
2 Kgs 9:21

"I want it for a garden," the king explained, "because it's so convenient to the palace." He offered cash or, if Naboth preferred, a piece of better land in trade.

3But Naboth replied, "Not on your life! That land has been in my family for generations."

21:3
Lev 25:23
Num 36:6
Ezek 46:18

4So Ahab went back to the palace angry and sullen. He refused to eat and went to bed with his face to the wall!

20:35, 36 The prophet needed a wound so he would look like an injured soldier and could effectively deliver his prophecy to King Ahab. The other man was killed by a lion because he refused to obey the Lord's instructions through the prophet.

20:41, 42 It is difficult to explain why Ahab let Ben-hadad go, especially after all the trouble Ben-hadad had caused him. God helped Ahab destroy the Syrian army to prove to Ahab and to Syria that he alone was God. But Ahab failed to destroy the king, his greatest enemy. Ben-hadad was under God's judgment to die, and Ahab had no authority to let him live. For this, God told Ahab that he must now die instead. This prophet's message soon came true when Ahab was killed on the battlefield (22:35).

21:7
1 Sam 8:14
21:8
2 Sam 11:14
2 Chron 32:17
Esth 3:12; 8:8
21:10
Ex 22:28
Lev 24:15,16
Mt 26:59
Acts 6:11

⁵"What in the world is the matter?" his wife, Jezebel, asked him. "Why aren't you eating? What has made you so upset and angry?"

⁶"I asked Naboth to sell me his vineyard, or to trade it, and he refused!" Ahab told her.

⁷"Are you the king of Israel or not?" Jezebel demanded. "Get up and eat and don't worry about it. I'll get you Naboth's vineyard!"

⁸So she wrote letters in Ahab's name, sealed them with his seal, and addressed them to the civic leaders of Jezreel, where Naboth lived. ⁹In her letter she commanded: "Call the citizens together for fasting and prayer. Then summon Naboth, ¹⁰and find two scoundrels who will accuse him of cursing God and the king. Then take him out and execute him."

JEZEBEL

The Bible is as honest about the lives of its heroes as it is about those who rejected God. Some found out what God can do with failures when they turned to him. Many, however, neither admitted their failures nor turned to God.

Jezebel ranks as the most evil woman in the Bible. The Scriptures even use her name as an example of people who completely reject God (Revelation 2:20). She, like many other heathen women, married into Israel without acknowledging the God their husbands worshiped. They brought their religions with them. But no one was as determined as Jezebel to make all Israel worship her gods. To the prophet Elijah, she seemed to have succeeded. He felt he was the only one still faithful to God until God told him there were still 7,000 who had not turned from the faith. But Jezebel did succeed in aiding the cause of the eventual downfall of the Northern Kingdom—idolatry. God punished them for their idolatry by having them carried off into captivity.

Jezebel held great power. She not only managed her husband, King Ahab, but she also had 850 assorted pagan priests under her control. She was committed to her gods and to getting what she wanted. She believed that the king had the right and the freedom to possess anything he wanted. When Naboth refused to sell Ahab his vineyard, Jezebel ruthlessly had Naboth killed and took ownership of the land. Jezebel's plan to wipe out worship of God in Israel led to painful consequences. Before she died, Jezebel suffered the loss of her husband in combat and her son at the hand of Jehu, who took the throne by force. She died in the defiant and scornful way she had lived.

When comparing Jezebel and Elijah, we have to admire each one's strength of commitment. The big difference was *to whom* they were committed. Jezebel was committed to herself and her false gods; Elijah was totally committed to the one true God. In the end, God proved Elijah right. To what or to whom are you most committed? How would God evaluate your commitment?

Weaknesses and mistakes:
● Systematically eliminated the representatives of God in Israel
● Promoted and funded Baal worship
● Threatened to have Elijah killed
● Believed kings could rightfully do or have anything they wanted
● Used her strong convictions to get her own way

Lessons from her life:
● It is not enough to be committed or sincere. Where our commitment lies makes a great difference
● Rejecting God always leads to disaster

Vital statistics:
● Where: Sidon, Samaria
● Occupation: Queen of Israel
● Relatives: Husband: Ahab. Father: Ethbaal. Sons: Jehoram and Ahaziah.
● Contemporaries: Elijah, Jehu

Key verse:
"No one else was so completely sold out to the devil as Ahab, for his wife Jezebel encouraged him to do every sort of evil" (1 Kings 21:25).

Jezebel's story is told in 1 Kings 16:31—2 Kings 9:37. She is also mentioned in Revelation 2:20.

21:4 After hearing God's judgment (20:42), Ahab went home to pout. Driven by anger and rebellion against God, he had a fit of rage when Naboth refused to sell his vineyard. The same feelings that led him to a career of power-grabbing drove him to resent Naboth. Rage turned to hatred and led to murder. Naboth in stark contrast to Ahab, wanted to uphold God's laws: it was considered a duty to keep ancestral land in the family. This incident shows the cruel interplay between Ahab and Jezebel, two of the most wicked leaders of Israel.

11The city fathers followed the queen's instructions. 12They called the meeting and put Naboth on trial. 13Then two men who had no conscience accused him of cursing God and the king; and he was dragged outside the city and stoned to death. 14The city officials then sent word to Jezebel that Naboth was dead.

15When Jezebel heard the news, she said to Ahab, "You know the vineyard Naboth wouldn't sell you? Well, you can have it now! He's dead!"

16So Ahab went down to the vineyard to claim it.

17But the Lord said to Elijah, 18"Go to Samaria to meet King Ahab. He will be at Naboth's vineyard, taking possession of it. 19Give him this message from me: 'Isn't killing Naboth bad enough? Must you rob him, too? Because you have done this, dogs shall lick your blood outside the city just as they licked the blood of Naboth!' "

20"So my enemy has found me!" Ahab exclaimed to Elijah.

"Yes," Elijah answered, "I have come to place God's curse upon you because you have sold yourself to the devil. 21The Lord is going to bring great harm to you and sweep you away; he will not let a single one of your male descendants survive! 22He is going to destroy your family as he did the family of King Jeroboam and the family of King Baasha, for you have made him very angry and have led all of Israel into sin. 23The Lord has also told me that the dogs of Jezreel shall tear apart the body of your wife, Jezebel. 24The members of your family who die in the city shall be eaten by dogs and those who die in the country shall be eaten by vultures."

25No one else was so completely sold out to the devil as Ahab, for his wife Jezebel encouraged him to do every sort of evil. 26He was especially guilty because he worshiped idols just as the Amorites did—the people whom the Lord had chased out of the land to make room for the people of Israel. 27When Ahab heard these prophecies, he tore his clothing, put on rags, fasted, slept in sackcloth, and went about in deep humility.

28Then another message came to Elijah: 29"Do you see how Ahab has humbled himself before me? Because he has done this, I will not do what I promised during his lifetime; it will happen to his sons; I will destroy his descendants."

4. Kings of Israel and Judah
Jehoshaphat becomes Ahab's ally

22 For three years there was no war between Syria and Israel. 2But during the third year, while King Jehoshaphat of Judah was visiting King Ahab of Israel, 3Ahab said to his officials, "Do you realize that the Syrians are still occupying our city of Ramoth-gilead? And we're sitting here without doing a thing about it!"

4Then he turned to Jehoshaphat and asked him, "Will you send your army with mine to recover Ramoth-gilead?"

And King Jehoshaphat of Judah replied, "Of course! You and I are brothers; my people are yours to command, and my horses are at your service. 5But," he added, "we should ask the Lord first, to be sure of what he wants us to do."

6So King Ahab summoned his four hundred heathen prophets and asked them, "Shall I attack Ramoth-gilead, or not?"

And they all said, "Yes, go ahead, for God will help you conquer it."

7But Jehoshaphat asked, "Isn't there a prophet of the Lord here? I'd like to ask him, too."

21:19
1 Kgs 22:38
2 Kgs 9:26

21:21
1 Kgs 14:10
2 Kgs 9:8
21:22
1 Kgs 14:16
15:29; 16:3
21:23
2 Kgs 9:10
33,34
21:24
1 Kgs 14:11
16:4-7
21:26
Gen 15:16
Lev 18:25
Judg 6:10
2 Kgs 21:11
21:27
Gen 37:34
2 Kgs 6:26-30
18:37
21:29
1 Kgs 22:38
2 Kgs 9:25,26
2 Chron 12:7
34:27

22:2
1 Kgs 15:24

22:3
Deut 4:43
Josh 20:8
2 Kgs 8:28

22:4
2 Kgs 3:6-8

22:5
Num 27:21
Josh 9:14,15
1 Sam 23:2

22:7
2 Kgs 3:11
2 Chron 18:6,7

21:20 *because you have sold yourself to the devil,* literally, "I have found you because you have sold yourself to that which is evil in the sight of the Lord." **22:6** *Ahab summoned his four hundred heathen prophets,* implied. These were evidently the 400 Asherah priests left alive by Elijah at Carmel, though the 450 prophets of Baal were slain. See 18:19 and 40.

21:19, 23 For the fulfillment of these verses, see 22:38 where dogs licked Ahab's blood, and 2 Kings 9:30—10:28 where Jezebel and the rest of Ahab's family were destroyed.

21:20 Ahab still refused to admit his sin against God. Instead he accused Elijah of being his enemy. When we are blinded by envy and hatred, it is almost impossible to see our own sin.

21:29 Ahab was more wicked than any other king of Israel (16:30; 21:25), but when he repented in deep humility for his sin, God took notice and reduced his punishment. The same Lord who was merciful to Ahab wants to be merciful to you. No matter how evil you have been, it is never too late to humble yourself, turn to God, and to ask for forgiveness.

22:8
1 Kgs 18:17

8"Well, there's one," King Ahab replied, "but I hate him, for he never prophesies anything good. He always has something gloomy to say. His name is Micaiah, the son of Imlah."

"Oh, come now!" Jehoshaphat replied. "Don't talk like that!"

9So King Ahab called to one of his aides, "Go get Micaiah. Hurry!"

10Meanwhile, all the prophets continued prophesying before the two kings, who were dressed in their royal robes and were sitting on thrones placed on the threshing floor near the city gate. 11One of the prophets, Zedekiah (son of Chenaanah), made some iron horns and declared, "The Lord promises that you will push the Syrians around with these horns until they are destroyed."

22:11
2 Chron 18:10

12And all the others agreed. "Go ahead and attack Ramoth-gilead," they said, "for the Lord will cause you to triumph!"

13The messenger who went to get Micaiah told him what the other prophets were saying, and urged him to say the same thing.

22:14
Num 22:18
24:13
2 Chron 18:13
Jer 23:28
Ezek 2:4

14But Micaiah told him, "This I vow, that I will say only what the Lord tells me to!"

15When he arrived, the king asked him, "Micaiah, shall we attack Ramoth-gilead, or not?"

"Why, of course! Go right ahead!" Micaiah told him. "You will have a great victory, for the Lord will cause you to conquer!"

22:17
Num 27:17
1 Kgs 22:36,37
Jer 23:1

16"How many times must I tell you to speak only what the Lord tells you to?" the king demanded.

17Then Micaiah told him, "I saw all Israel scattered upon the mountains as sheep

---

KINGS TO DATE AND THEIR ENEMIES

874
AHAB
Twice defeated
Ben-hadad II
(Syria) and was
later killed in battle
1 Kgs 16:28—22:40
2 Chr 18:1-34

853
AHAZIAH
1 Kgs 22:40—
2 Kgs 1:18
2 Chr 20:35–37

852

I S R A E L

J U D A H

869

910
ASA
Defeated Zerah
(Ethiopia) and
harassed Baasha
1 Kgs 15:8–24
2 Chr 14:1—16:14
Co-regency
872–869

872
JEHOSHAPHAT
Defeated by Ben-
hadad II (Syria),
gained miraculous
victory over Moab
and Ammon, and
crushed a rebellion
by Mesha (Moab)
1 Kgs 22:41–50
2 Chr 17:1—21:1
Co-regency
853–848

853   848
JEHORAM
Lost dominion over
Edom, assaulted
by Philistines and
Arabs
2 Kgs 8:16–24
2 Chr 21:1–20

841

All dates are B.C.
Solid section of the timeline indicates co-regency.
For all the kings of Israel and Judah, see the chart between the books of 1 and 2 Kings.

22:15, 16 Why did Micaiah tell Ahab to attack when he had previously vowed to speak only what God had told him? Perhaps he was speaking sarcastically, making fun of the messages from the heathen prophets by showing that they were telling the king only what he wanted to hear. Somehow, Micaiah's tone of voice let everyone know he was mocking the heathen prophets. When the king confronted him, he predicted that the king would die and the battle would be lost. Although Ahab repented temporarily (21:27), he still maintained the system of false prophets. These false prophets would be instrumental in leading him to his own ruin.

without a shepherd. And the Lord said, 'Their king is dead; send them to their homes.'"

¹⁸Turning to Jehoshaphat, Ahab complained, "Didn't I tell you this would happen? He *never* tells me anything good. It's *always* bad."

¹⁹Then Micaiah said, "Listen to this further word from the Lord. I saw the Lord sitting on his throne, and the armies of heaven stood around him.

²⁰"Then the Lord said, 'Who will entice Ahab to go and die at Ramoth-gilead?'

"Various suggestions were made, ²¹until one angel approached the Lord and said, 'I'll do it!'

²²" 'How?' the Lord asked.

"And he replied, 'I will go as a lying spirit in the mouths of all his prophets.'

"And the Lord said, 'That will do it; you will succeed. Go ahead.'

²³"Don't you see? The Lord has put a lying spirit in the mouths of all these prophets, but the fact of the matter is that the Lord has decreed disaster upon you."

²⁴Then Zedekiah (son of Chenaanah) walked over and slapped Micaiah on the face.

"When did the Spirit of the Lord leave me and speak to you?" he demanded.

²⁵And Micaiah replied, "You will have the answer to your question when you find yourself hiding in an inner room."

²⁶Then King Ahab ordered Micaiah's arrest.

"Take him to Amon, the mayor of the city, and to my son Joash. ²⁷Tell them, 'The king says to put this fellow in jail and feed him with bread and water—and only enough to keep him alive—until I return in peace.'"

²⁸"If you return in peace," Micaiah replied, "it will prove that the Lord has not spoken through me." Then he turned to the people standing nearby and said, "Take note of what I've said."

Ahab dies in battle

²⁹So King Ahab of Israel and King Jehoshaphat of Judah led their armies to Ramoth-gilead.

³⁰Ahab said to Jehoshaphat, "You wear your royal robes, but I'll not wear mine!" So Ahab went into the battle disguised in an ordinary soldier's uniform. ³¹For the king of Syria had commanded his thirty-two chariot captains to fight no one except King Ahab himself. ³², ³³When they saw King Jehoshaphat in his royal robes, they thought, "That's the man we're after." So they wheeled around to attack him. But when Jehoshaphat shouted out to identify himself, they turned back! ³⁴However, someone shot an arrow at random and it struck King Ahab between the joints of his armor.

22:27 *only enough to keep him alive,* literally, "as though the city were under siege." **22:32, 33** *shouted out to identify himself,* implied.

22:19
Isa 6:1
Dan 7:9

22:22
2 Thess 2:11

22:23
Isa 9:14,15
Ezek 14:9
22:24
2 Chron 18:23

22:27
2 Chron 16:10
18:25
Jer 20:2

22:28
Deut 18:22
Isa 44:26

22:30
1 Kgs 14:2
2 Chron 35:22
22:31
2 Chron 18:30

22:19–22 The vision Micaiah saw may not have been a picture of a real incident in heaven, but a parable of what was happening on earth, illustrating that the seductive influence of the false prophets would be part of God's judgment upon Ahab (22:23). Whether or not God sent an angel in disguise, he used the system of false prophets to snare Ahab in his sin. The lying spirit (22:22) symbolized the way of life for these prophets, who told the king only what he wanted to hear.

22:20–22 Does God allow angels to entice people to do evil? To understand evil one must first understand God. (1) God himself is good (Psalm 11:7). (2) God created a good world that fell because of man's sin (Romans 5:12). (3) Someday God will recreate the world and it will be good again (Revelation 21:1). (4) God is stronger than evil (Matthew 13:41; Revelation 19:11–21). (5) God allows evil, and thus he has control over it. While God did not create evil, he offers help to those who wish to overcome it (Matthew 11:28–30). (6) God uses everything—both good and evil—for his good purposes (Romans 8:28).

The Bible shows us a God who hates all evil and will one day do away with it completely and forever (Revelation 20:10–15). God does not entice anyone good to become evil. Those committed to evil, however, may be used by God to sin even more in order to hurry their deserved judgment (Exodus 11:10). We don't need to understand every detail of how God works in order to have perfect confidence in his absolute power over evil and his total goodness toward us.

22:34 Ahab could not escape God's judgment. Ben-hadad sent 32 of his best chariot captains with the sole purpose of killing Ahab. Thinking he could escape, Ahab tried a disguise, but a random shot struck him while the chariots chased the wrong king, Jehoshaphat. It was foolish for Ahab to think he could escape with a disguise. Sometimes people today try to escape reality by disguising themselves—changing jobs, moving to a new town, even changing spouses. Yet when God judges a person, attempted escape is futile.

"Take me out of the battle, for I am badly wounded," he groaned to his chariot driver.

35The battle became more and more intense as the day wore on, and King Ahab went back in, propped up in his chariot with the blood from his wound running down onto the floorboards. Finally, toward evening, he died. 36, 37Just as the sun was going down the cry ran through his troops. "It's all over—return home! The king is dead!"

And his body was taken to Samaria and buried there. 38When his chariot and armor were washed beside the pool of Samaria, where the prostitutes bathed, dogs came and licked the king's blood just as the Lord had said would happen.

22:39
1 Kgs 16:27
22:44
2 Kgs 1:18

39The rest of Ahab's history—including the story of the ivory palace and the cities he built—is written in *The Annals of the Kings of Israel*. 40So Ahab was buried among his ancestors, and Ahaziah his son became the new king of Israel.

Jehoshaphat rules Judah

22:41
1 Chron 3:10
2 Chron 20:31

22:43
1 Kgs 14:23
2 Kgs 12:3

22:45
1 Kgs 22:39
2 Kgs 1:18

22:46
Deut 23:17
1 Kgs 15:12
2 Kgs 23:7

22:47
2 Sam 8:14
2 Kgs 3:9

22:48
1 Kgs 9:26-28
2 Chron 8:17,18

22:50
2 Kgs 8:16
2 Chron 21:1

41Meanwhile, over in Judah, Jehoshaphat the son of Asa had become king during the fourth year of the reign of King Ahab of Israel. 42Jehoshaphat was thirty-five years old when he ascended the throne, and he reigned in Jerusalem for twenty-five years. His mother was Azubah, the daughter of Shilhi. 43He did as his father Asa had done, obeying the Lord in all but one thing: he did not destroy the shrines on the hills, so the people sacrificed and burned incense there. 44He also made peace with Ahab, the king of Israel. 45The rest of the deeds of Jehoshaphat and his heroic achievements and his wars are described in *The Annals of the Kings of Judah*.

46He also closed all the houses of male prostitution that still continued from the days of his father Asa. 47(There was no king in Edom at that time, only a deputy.)

48King Jehoshaphat built great freighters to sail to Ophir for gold; but they never arrived, for they were wrecked at Eziongeber. 49Ahaziah, King Ahab's son and successor, had proposed to Jehoshaphat that his men go too, but Jehoshaphat had refused the offer.

50When King Jehoshaphat died he was buried with his ancestors in Jerusalem, the city of his forefather David; and his son Jehoram took the throne.

Ahaziah rules Israel

22:52
1 Kgs 15:26
16:30

51It was during the seventeenth year of the reign of King Jehoshaphat of Judah that Ahaziah, Ahab's son, began to reign over Israel in Samaria; and he reigned two years. 52, 53But he was not a good king, for he followed in the footsteps of his father and mother and of Jeroboam, who had led Israel into the sin of worshiping idols. So Ahaziah made the Lord God of Israel very angry.

22:35 Just as the prophet had predicted (20:42), Ahab was killed. See Ahab's Profile in chapter 19 for more of Ahab's sad story.

22:41–50 For more details on Jehoshaphat, see the other account of his reign in 2 Chronicles 17—20.

22:43 Just like his ancestors Solomon and Asa, Jehoshaphat followed God, but he didn't destroy the heathen shrines in the hills (2 Chronicles 20:33). It was against God's law to worship idols in the shrines (Numbers 33:52), and at first Jehoshaphat attempted to destroy them (2 Chronicles 17:6). They were so popular, however, that it proved difficult. In spite of Jehoshaphat's many contributions to the spiritual, moral, and material health of his country, he did not succeed in eradicating the hill shrines.

22:52, 53 The book of 1 Kings begins with a united nation under King David, the most devout king in Israel's history. The book ends with a divided kingdom and the death of Ahab, the wickedest king of all. What happened? The people forgot to acknowledge God as their ultimate leader, they appointed human leaders who failed to acknowledge God, and then they conformed to the life-styles of these evil leaders. Occasional wrongdoing gradually turned into wrongdoing as a way of life. Their blatant wickedness could only be met with great judgment from God, who allowed enemy nations to arise and defeat Israel and Judah in battle as punishment for their sins. Failing to acknowledge God as the ultimate leader of our lives is the first step toward ruin.

DIVIDED KINGDOM OF ISRAEL

AHIJAH 934—909

ELIJAH 875—848

930
JEROBOAM
(22 years)
Built a
capital city
(Shechem),
set up two
golden calf-
idols, led the
nation into
sin, allowed
anyone to be
a priest
1 Kgs 11:26—14:20
2 Chr 10:12—13:22

908
BAASHA
(24 years)
Led people
in idol worship
1 Kgs 15:27—16:7
2 Chr 16:1—6

909
NADAB
(2 years)
1 Kgs 15:25—28

885
TIBNI
1 Kgs 16:21, 22

885
ZIMRI
(7 days)
1 Kgs 16:9—20

886
ELAH
(2 years)
Continued
idol worship
1 Kgs 16:6—14

885
OMRI
(12 years)
Built the capital
city of Samaria,
had great military
power, but
continued to lead
Israel into idolatry
1 Kgs 16:15—28

874
AHAB
(22 years)
Married Jezebel
(a non-Jew and
extremely wicked
woman), worshiped
Baal, and suffered
three years of
famine caused
by his consistent
disobedience to
God
1 Kgs 16:28—22:40
2 Chr 18:1—34

CAPITAL: SHECHEM, THEN TIRZAH, THEN SAMARIA
THE NORTHERN KINGDOM OF ISRAEL (TEN TRIBES)

THE SOUTHERN KINGDOM OF JUDAH (TWO TRIBES)
CAPITAL: JERUSALEM

930
REHOBOAM
(17 years)
Built many
fortified cities,
strengthened
the economy
(despite the
tribute paid to
Egypt), followed
God for three
years, but then
set up idols and
shrines to
foreign gods
1 Kgs 11:43—14:31
2 Chr 9:31—12:16

913
ABIJAM
(3 years)
Despite his
wickedness, he
called for God's
help to win the
battle against
Israel
1 Kgs 14:31—15:8
2 Chr 13:1—14:1

910
ASA
(41 years)
Destroyed heathen
altars and rebuilt altar
of God, built fortified
cities, gained much
wealth from plunder of
foreign conquest,
removed the queen-
mother for worshiping
Asteroth, led the people
to worship God with
their hearts, provided
peace on home soil,
was greatly loved, and
given a beautiful funeral
1 Kgs 15:8—24
2 Chr 14:1—16:14

872
JEHOSHAPHAT
(25 years)
Arranged for the
marriage of his son to a
daughter of Ahab (who
made trouble later on),
had a strong military
(kept troops in cities of
Israel his father had
conquered), collected
tribute from the
Philistines, worshiped
the Lord and destroyed
idols, established
education, and
appointed judges and
courts
1 Kgs 22:41—50
2 Chr 17:1—21:1

All dates are B.C. The total years of reign sometimes include years of co-regency.
(See charts, "Kings to Date," throughout 1 and 2 Kings.)

ELISHA 848–797

JONAH
793–753(?)

841
JEHU
(20 years)
Was responsible
for the deaths of
Joram (king of
Judah), Ahaziah
(king of Israel),
Jezebel (wicked
mother of Joram);
destroyed the
priests and
temples of Baal;
but did not
consistently
follow God
2 Kgs 9:1— 10:36
2 Chr 22:7–12

798
**JEHOASH/
JOASH**
(16 years)
Even though he
was evil, he
recognized the
authority of Elisha
as a prophet of
God
2 Kgs
13:10—14:16
2 Chr 25:17–24

793
JEROBOAM II
(41 years)
Very evil but politically
powerful, his nation
enjoyed economic
prosperity and military
peace
2 Kgs 14:16–29

814
JEHOAHAZ
(17 years)
Evil reign included
worship of
Asheroth, usually
called "shameful"
2 Kgs 13:1–9

853
AHAZIAH
(2 years)
Proposed a joint
trade venture with
Judah
1 Kgs 22:40—
2 Kgs 1:18
2 Chr 20:35–37

852
**JEHORAM/
JORAM**
(12 years)
Suffered famine
and war during
most of his reign
2 Kgs 3:1—8:25
2 Chr 22:5–7

853
**JEHORAM/
JORAM**
(8 years)
Married a wicked
daughter of Ahab,
compelled the
people to worship
idols, and killed all
his brothers
2 Kgs 8:16–24
2 Chr 21:1–20

841
**JEHOAHAZ/
AHAZIAH**
(1 year)
Friend of Joram of
Israel
2 Kgs 8:24—9:29
2 Chr 22:1–10

841
**ATHALIAH
(QUEEN)**
(6 years)
Killed all her
grandchildren
except Joash
who was hidden
by his nurse for
six years, and
ravaged the
Temple to furnish
Baal's temple
2 Kgs 11:1–20
2 Chr 22:10—23:21

835
JOASH
(40 years)
Was crowned king
at the age of seven
by Jehoiada (the
High Priest),
promoted peace
and prosperity,
repaired the
Temple and
smashed the altars
to Baal—but after
Jehoiada died,
Joash abandoned
God, and even had
Jehoiada's son
killed
2 Kgs 11:1—12:21
2 Chr 22:10—24:27

796
AMAZIAH
(29 years)
Was basically
good but did not
completely wipe
out idol worship,
organized the
army, took a
census
2 Kgs 14:1–20
2 Chr 25:1–28

792
**UZZIAH/
AZARIAH**
(52 years)
Built a city named
Elath, owned many
farms and
vineyards,
constructed water
reservoirs and
forts, reorganized
the army (so
powerful that his
fame spread to
Egypt), but
violated God's
laws for priestly
function—so God
struck him with
leprosy
2 Kgs 15:1–7
2 Chr 26:1–23

OBADIAH 855–840(?)

JOEL 835–796(?)

HOSEA 753–715

AMOS 760–750

752
SHALLUM
(1 month)
2 Kgs 15:10–15

742
PEKAHIAH
(2 years)
Continued idol
worship
2 Kgs 15:22–26

732
HOSHEA
(9 years)
Suffered heavy
taxation by Assyria
and eventual
conquest—
bringing about
Israelite captivity
and resettlement of
foreigners in Israel
2 Kgs 15:30;
17:1–6

722
END OF THE
NORTHERN
KINGDOM—
Israel taken to
Assyria by
Shalmaneser

753
ZECHARIAH
(6 months)
Encouraged idol
worship
2 Kgs 14:29—15:12

752
MENAHEM
(10 years)
Imposed heavy
taxes and
oppressed his
people
2 Kgs 15:14–22

740
PEKAH
(8 years)
During his reign
many of the
people were taken
captive to Assyria
2 Kgs 15:25–31
2 Chr 28:5–8

ISRAEL

JUDAH

750
JOTHAM
(16 years)
Rebuilt the upper
gate of the
Temple, rebuilt
walls and cities,
but still permitted
idol worship
2 Kgs 15:32–38
2 Chr 27:1–9

735
AHAZ
(16 years)
Sacrificed his own
son to heathen
gods, nailed the
Temple doors shut
2 Kgs 16:1–20
2 Chr 28:1–27

715
HEZEKIAH
(29 years)
Was a devoted follower
of God, reopened
Temple doors, cleansed
the Temple, reinstated
priests and their duties,
organized an orchestra
to aid worship,
destroyed idols
(including the bronze
serpent of Moses
because people had
begun to worship it),
celebrated Passover
and even invited
people who were living
in the North to
participate, constructed
large public
waterworks, was given
15 extra years of life,
foolishly showed
ambassadors the
wealth in the Temple
2 Kgs 18:1—20:21
2 Chr 29:1—32:33

697
MANASSEH
(55 years)
Rebuilt all the
heathen shrines,
sacrificed one of
his own sons,
practiced black
magic, set up an
idol right in the
Temple, murdered
many of his own
people, but
repented during
his Assyrian
captivity
2 Kgs 21:1–18
2 Chr 33:1–20

MICAH 742–687

ISAIAH 740–681

586
END OF THE
SOUTHERN
KINGDOM—carried off
captive to Babylon by
Nebuchadnezzar

642
AMON
(2 years)
2 Kgs 21:19–26
2 Chr 33:21–25

640
JOSIAH
(31 years)
Loved God with all his
heart, repaired the
Temple, found a lost
scroll of the Law (he
promised to obey it, thus
God stayed destruction
for Judah until after his
death), personally
oversaw the major
project of destroying idol
shrines, reinstated the
priests of God,
celebrated Passover
with greater zeal than
had been since
Samuel's day, was
greatly loved by his
people
2 Kgs 22:1—23:30
2 Chr 34:1—35:27

609
JEHOAHAZ
(3 months)
Jailed and taken
to Egypt where
he died
2 Kgs 23:30–34
2 Chr 36:1–4

609
**ELIAKIM/
JEHOIAKIM**
(11 years)
Burned part of
God's Word, was a
puppet king for
Egypt then
Babylon, watched
gold and tools
taken from the
Temple to Babylon,
saw first exile (in
which Daniel was
taken)
2 Kgs 23:34—24:5
2 Chr 36:5–7

598
JEHOIACHIN
(3 months)
Saw next exile to
Babylon
2 Kgs 24:6–16;
25:27–30
2 Chr 36:8–10

597
**MATTANIAH/
ZEDEKIAH**
(11 years)
Saw the Temple
burned and
Jerusalem
destroyed, was
tortured and carried
away in the final
exile to Babylon
2 Kgs 24:17—25:21
2 Chr 36:11–21

HABAKKUK 612–589

NAHUM 663–654

ZEPHANIAH 640–621

HULDA 632

JEREMIAH 627–586

2 KINGS

VITAL STATISTICS

PURPOSE:
To demonstrate the fate that awaits all who refuse to make God their true leader

AUTHOR:
Unknown. Possibly Jeremiah or a group of prophets.

SETTING:
The once-united nation of Israel has been divided into two kingdoms, Israel and Judah, for over a century.

KEY VERSES:
"Again and again the Lord had sent prophets to warn both Israel and Judah to turn from their evil ways; he had warned them to obey his commandments which he had given to their ancestors through these prophets, but Israel wouldn't listen. The people were as stubborn as their ancestors and refused to believe in the Lord their God" (17:13, 14).

KEY PEOPLE:
Elijah, Elisha, Shunemite woman, Naaman, Jezebel, Jehu, Joash, Hezekiah, Sennacherib, Isaiah, Manasseh, Josiah, Jehoiakim, Zedekiah, Nebuchadnezzar

SPECIAL FEATURES:
The 17 prophetic books at the end of the Old Testament give great insights into the time period of 2 Kings.

SPARKLING as it crashes against boulders along its banks, the river swiftly cascades toward the sea. The current grabs, pushes, and tugs at leaves and logs, carrying them along for the ride. Here and there a sportsman is spotted in a kayak or a canoe, going with the flow. Gravity pulls the water, and the river pulls the rest . . . downward. Suddenly, a silver missile breaks the surface and darts upstream, and then another. Oblivious to the swirling opposition, the shining salmon swim against the stream. They must go upstream, and nothing will stop them from reaching their destination.

The current of society's river is flowing fast and furious, pulling downward everything in its way. It would be easy to float along with the current. But God calls us to swim against the flow. It will not be easy, and we may be alone, but it will be the right thing to do.

Second Kings continues the history of Israel, halfway between the death of David and the death of the nation. Israel has been divided (1 Kings 12), and the two kingdoms have begun to slide into idolatry and corruption toward collapse and captivity. Second Kings relates the sordid stories of the 12 kings of the Northern Kingdom (called Israel) and the 16 kings of the Southern Kingdom (called Judah). For 130 years, Israel endures the succession of evil rulers until they are conquered by Shalmaneser of Assyria and led into captivity in 722 B.C. (17:6). Of all the kings in both the north and south, only two—Hezekiah and Josiah—are called "good." Because of their obedience to God and the spiritual revivals during their reigns, Judah stands for an additional 136 years until falling to Nebuchadnezzar and the Babylonians in 586 B.C.

Throughout this dark period, the Bible mentions 30 prophets who proclaim God's message to the people and their leaders. Most notable of these fearless men of God are Elijah and Elisha. As Elijah nears the end of his earthly ministry, Elisha asks for twice the prophetic power as his beloved mentor (2:9). Soon after, Elijah is taken to heaven in a whirlwind (2:11), and Elisha becomes God's spokesman to the Northern Kingdom. Elisha's life is filled with signs, proclamations, warnings, and miracles. Four of the most memorable are the flowing olive oil (4:1–7), the healing of the Shunemite woman's son (4:8–37), the healing of Naaman's leprosy (5:1–27), and the floating axhead (6:1–7).

Even in the midst of terrible situations, God will have his faithful minority, his remnant (19:31). He desires courageous men and women to proclaim his truth.

THE BLUEPRINT

A. THE DIVIDED KINGDOM (1:1—17:41)
1. Elisha's ministry
2. Kings of Israel and Judah
3. Israel is exiled to Assyria

Although Israel had the witness and power of Elisha, the nation turned from God and was exiled to Assyria. Assyria filled the Northern Kingdom with people from other lands. A race developed from the marriage of Jews with these people from other lands—the Samaritans, who were hated by the Jews. There has been no return from this captivity—it was permanent. Such is the end of all who permanently shut God out of their lives.

B. THE SURVIVING KINGDOM
   (18:1—25:30)
   1. Kings of Judah
   2. Judah is exiled to Babylon

The Northern Kingdom was destroyed, and prophets were predicting the same fate for Judah. What more could cause the nation to repent? Hezekiah and Josiah were able to stem the tide of evil. They both repaired the Temple and gathered the people for Passover. Josiah eradicated idolatry from the land, but as soon as these good kings were gone, the people returned again to living their own way instead of God's way. Each individual must believe and live for God in his family, church, and nation.

MEGATHEMES

THEME	EXPLANATION	IMPORTANCE
Elisha	More of Elisha's miracles are recorded than those of anyone else in the Old Testament. The purpose of his ministry was to restore respect for God and his message, and he stood firmly against the evil kings of Israel. By faith, with courage and prayer, he revealed not only God's judgment on sin, but also his mercy, love, and tenderness toward faithful people.	Elisha's mighty miracles showed that God controls not only great armies, but also events in everyday life. When we listen to and obey God, he shows us his power to transform any situation. God's care is not reserved for kings and leaders, but is for all who are willing to follow him. He can perform miracles in our lives.
Idolatry	Every evil king in both Israel and Judah encouraged idolatry. These false gods represented war, cruelty, power, and sex; and the people began to take on their characteristics. Although they had God's Law, priests, and prophets to guide them, the evil kings sought priests and prophets whom they could control and manipulate to their own advantage.	An idol is any idea, ability, possession, or person that we regard more highly than God. We condemn Israel and Judah for foolishly worshiping idols, but we also worship other gods—power, money, physical attractiveness. But behind this "idol" worship is the desire to control our destiny, our pleasure, and other people. Even those who believe in God must resist the lure of these attractive idols.
Evil kings/ good kings	The Northern Kingdom, Israel, had 19 evil kings and no good ones; the Southern Kingdom, Judah, had 12 evil kings, and 8 good ones. Thus, only 20 percent of all the kings followed God. The evil kings were short-sighted. They thought they could control their nations' destinies by importing other religions with their idols, forming alliances with heathen nations, and enriching themselves. The good kings had to spend most of their time undoing the evil done by their predecessors.	Although the evil kings led the people into sin, they were not the only ones responsible for the downfall of their nations. The priests, princes, heads of families, and military leaders all had to cooperate with the proposed evil plans and practices in order for them to be carried out. We cannot discharge our responsibility to obey God by blaming our leaders.
God's patience	As recorded in Deuteronomy, God told his people that if they obeyed him they would live successfully; if they disobeyed, they would be judged and destroyed. God had been patient with the people for hundreds of years. He sent many prophets, including Elisha, to guide them. And he gave ample warning of coming destruction. But even God's patience has limits.	God is patient with us. In his mercy, he gives us many chances to hear his message, to turn from sin, and to believe him. His patience does not mean he is indifferent to how we live, nor does it mean we are free to ignore his warnings. His patience should make us want to come to him now.

Judgment Both kingdoms were destroyed as punishment for their sin. After King Solomon's reign, Israel lasted only 209 years before the Assyrians destroyed it; Judah lasted 345 years before the Babylonians overcame Jerusalem. After repeated warnings to his people, God used these evil nations as instruments for his justice.

The consequences of rejecting God's commands and purpose for our lives are severe. He will not ignore unbelief or rebellion. To avoid the penalty for sin, we must believe in him and accept Christ's sacrificial death on our behalf, or we will be judged also.

KEY PLACES IN 2 KINGS

The history of both Israel and Judah was much affected by the prophet Elisha's ministry. He served Israel for 50 years, fighting the idolatry of its kings and calling its people back to God.

1 **Jericho** Elijah's ministry had come to an end. He touched his cloak to the Jordan River, and he and Elisha crossed on dry land. Elijah was taken by God in a whirlwind, and Elisha returned alone with the cloak. The prophets in Jericho realized that Elisha was Elijah's replacement with Elijah's power (1:1—2:25).

2 **Wilderness of Edom** The king of Moab rebelled against Israel, so the nations of Israel, Judah, and Edom decided to attack from the wilderness of Edom, but ran out of water. The kings consulted Elisha, who said God would send both water and victory (3:1–27).

3 **Shunem** Elisha cared for individuals and their needs. He helped a woman clear a debt by giving her a supply of olive oil to sell. For another family in Shunem, he raised a son from the dead (4:1–37).

4 **Gilgal** Elisha cared for the young prophets in Gilgal—he removed poison from a stew, made a small amount of food feed everyone, and even caused an axhead to float so a student could retrieve it. It was to Elisha that Naaman, a commander in the Syrian army, came to be healed of leprosy (4:38—6:7).

5 **Dothan** Although he cured a Syrian commander's leprosy, Elisha was loyal to Israel. He knew the Syrian army's battle plans and kept Israel's king informed. The Syrian king tracked Elisha down in Dothan and surrounded the city, hoping to kill him. But Elisha prayed that the Syrians would be blinded, then he led the blinded army into Samaria, Israel's capital city (6:8–23).

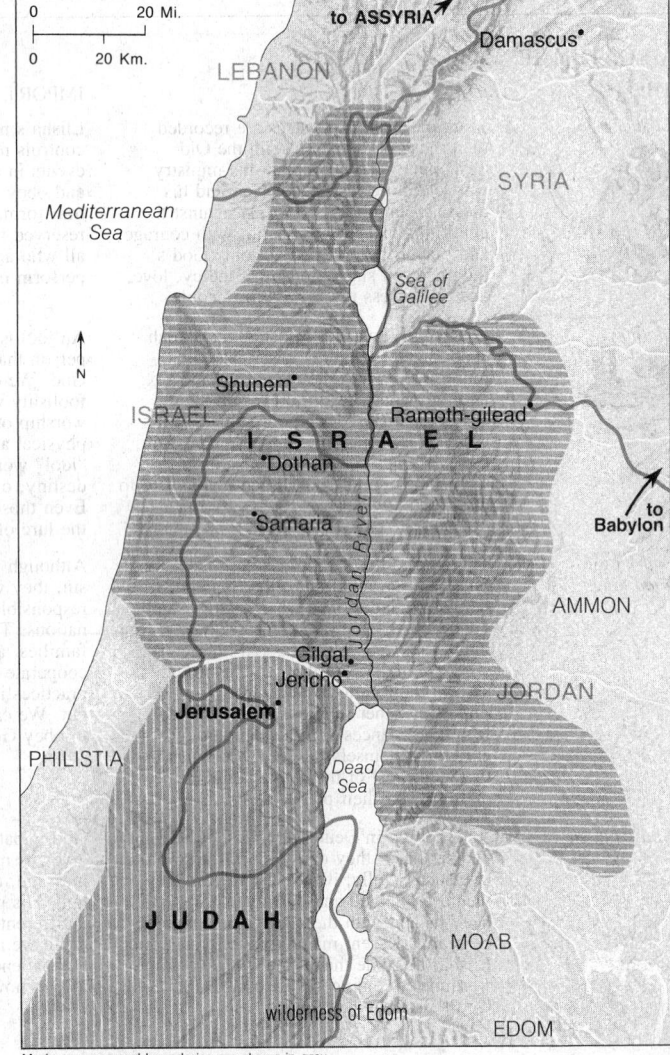

0 — 20 Mi.
0 — 20 Km.

Modern names and boundaries are shown in gray.

to ASSYRIA
Damascus
LEBANON
Mediterranean Sea
Sea of Galilee
SYRIA
N
Shunem
ISRAEL
Ramoth-gilead
I S R A E L
Dothan
Samaria
Jordan River
to Babylon
AMMON
Gilgal
Jericho
JORDAN
Jerusalem
PHILISTIA
Dead Sea
JUDAH
MOAB
wilderness of Edom
EDOM

6 **Samaria** But the Syrians didn't learn their lesson. They later besieged Samaria. Ironically, Israel's king thought it was Elisha's fault, but Elisha said food would be available in abundance the next day. True to Elisha's

word, the Lord caused panic in the Syrian camp, and the enemy ran, leaving their supplies to Samaria's starving people (6:24—7:20).

7 Damascus Despite Elisha's loyalty to Israel, he obeyed God and traveled to Damascus, the capital of Syria. King Ben-hadad was sick, and he sent Hazael to ask Elisha if he would recover. Elisha knew the king would die, and told this to Hazael. But Hazael then murdered Ben-hadad, making himself king. Later, Israel and Judah joined forces to fight this new Syrian threat (8:1—29).

8 Ramoth-gilead As Israel and Judah warred with Syria, Elisha sent a young prophet to Ramoth-gilead to anoint Jehu as Israel's next king. Jehu set out to destroy the wicked dynasties of Israel and Judah, killing Kings Joram and Ahaziah, and wicked Queen Jezebel. He then destroyed King Ahab's family, and all the Baal worshipers in Israel (9:1—11:1).

9 Jerusalem Power-hungry Athaliah became queen of Judah when her son Ahaziah was killed. She had all her grandsons killed except Joash who was hidden by his aunt. Joash was crowned king at the age of seven and overthrew Athaliah. Meanwhile in Samaria, the Syrians continued to harass Israel. Israel's new king met with Elisha and was told that he would be victorious over Syria three times (11:2—13:19).

Following Elisha's death came a series of evil kings in Israel. Their idolatry and rejection of God caused their downfall. The Assyrian Empire captured Samaria and took most of the Israelites into captivity (13:20—17:41). Judah had a short reprieve because of a few good kings who destroyed idols and worshiped God. But many strayed from God. So Jerusalem fell to the next world power, Babylon, and its people were taken captive (18:1—25:30).

A. THE DIVIDED KINGDOM (1:1—17:41)

Elisha begins his ministry to the Northern Kingdom after Elijah is taken away by a chariot of fire. Elisha performs many miracles and calls Israel to return to God, but they persist in their wickedness. Israel is defeated by Assyria and the people of the Northern Kingdom are exiled, never to return. Such is the end of all those who ignore God's warnings and demand their own way in their desire to sin.

King Ahaziah's conflict with Elijah

1:1
2 Sam 8:2
2 Kgs 3:5
1 Chron 18:2

1 After King Ahab's death the nation of Moab declared its independence and refused to pay tribute to Israel any longer.

1:2
1 Kgs 14:3
2 Kgs 8:7

²Israel's new king, Ahaziah, had fallen off the upstairs porch of his palace at Samaria and was seriously injured. He sent messengers to the temple of the god Baal-zebub at Ekron to ask whether he would recover.

1:3
1 Kgs 17:1

³But an angel of the Lord told Elijah the prophet, "Go and meet the messengers and ask them, 'Is it true that there is no God in Israel? Is that why you are going to Baal-zebub, the god of Ekron, to ask whether the king will get well? ⁴, ⁵Because

1:4
2 Kgs 1:16,17

King Ahaziah has done this, the Lord says that he will never leave the bed he is lying on; he will surely die.' "

When Elijah told the messengers this, they returned immediately to the king. "Why have you returned so soon?" he asked them.

⁶"A man came up to us," they said, "and told us to go back to the king and tell him, 'The Lord wants to know why you are asking questions of Baal-zebub, the god of Ekron. Is it because there is no God in Israel? Now, since you have done this, you will not leave the bed you are lying on; you will surely die.' "

⁷"Who was this fellow?" the king demanded. "What did he look like?"

1:8
Mt 3:4
Mk 1:6

⁸"He was a hairy man," they replied, "with a wide leather belt."

"It was Elijah the prophet!" the king exclaimed. ⁹Then he sent an army captain with fifty soldiers to arrest him. They found him sitting on top of a hill. The captain said to him, "O man of God, the king has commanded you to come along with us."

1:3 *Elijah the prophet,* literally, "Elijah the Tishbite."

1:1 Since 1 and 2 Kings were originally one book, 2 Kings continues where 1 Kings ended. The once great nation of Israel is now split in two because the people have forgotten God. The book begins with Elijah, a prophet of God, being carried away to heaven. It ends with the people of Israel and Judah being carried away into captivity. In 1 Kings, the beautiful Temple of God was built. In 2 Kings, it is desecrated and destroyed.

Our world today is strikingly similar to the world described in 2 Kings. National and local governments do not seek God, and countries are tormented by war. Many people follow the false gods of science, materialism, and war. True worship of God is rare upon the earth.

In our chaotic and corrupt world, we can turn to the examples like David, Elijah, and Elisha, who were devoted to God's high

honor and moral law and who brought about renewal and change in their day. More important, we can look to Jesus Christ, the perfect example. For nations to do God's will, they need individuals who will do God's work. If your heart is submitted to God, he can work through you to accomplish the work he has called you to do.

1:2 Baal-zebub was not the same god as Baal, the Canaanite god worshiped by Ahab and Jezebel (1 Kings 16:29–33). Baal-zebub was another popular god whose temple was located in the city of Ekron. Since this god was thought to have the power of prophecy, King Ahaziah sent messengers to Ekron to learn of his fate. Supernatural power and mystery were associated with this god. Ahaziah's action showed the king's disrespect for God.

1:8 For more information on Elijah, see his Profile in 1 Kings 18.

¹⁰But Elijah replied, "If I am a man of God, let fire come down from heaven and destroy you and your fifty men!" Then lightning struck them and killed them all!

¹¹So the king sent another captain with fifty men to demand, "O man of God, the king says that you must come down right away."

¹²Elijah replied, "If I am a man of God, let fire come down from heaven and destroy you and your fifty men." And again the fire from God burned them up.

¹³Once more the king sent fifty men, but this time the captain fell to his knees before Elijah and pleaded with him, "O man of God, please spare my life and the lives of these, your fifty servants. ¹⁴Have mercy on us! Don't destroy us as you did the others."

¹⁵Then the angel of the Lord said to Elijah, "Don't be afraid. Go with him." So Elijah went to the king.

¹⁶"Why did you send messengers to Baal-zebub, the god of Ekron, to ask about your sickness?" Elijah demanded. "Is it because there is no God in Israel to ask? Because you have done this, you shall not leave this bed; you will surely die."

¹⁷So Ahaziah died as the Lord had predicted through Elijah, and his brother Joram became the new king—for Ahaziah did not have a son to succeed him. This occurred in the second year of the reign of King Jehoram (son of Jehoshaphat) of Judah. ¹⁸The rest of the history of Ahaziah's reign is recorded in *The Annals of the Kings of Israel*.

1. Elisha's ministry
God takes Elijah to heaven

2 Now the time came for the Lord to take Elijah to heaven—by means of a whirlwind! Elijah said to Elisha as they left Gilgal, "Stay here, for the Lord has told me to go to Bethel."

But Elisha replied, "I swear to God that I won't leave you!"

So they went on together to Bethel. ³There the young prophets of Bethel Seminary came out to meet them and asked Elisha, "Did you know that the Lord is going to take Elijah away from you today?"

"Quiet!" Elisha snapped. "Of course I know it."

⁴Then Elijah said to Elisha, "Please stay here in Bethel, for the Lord has sent me to Jericho."

But Elisha replied again, "I swear to God that I won't leave you." So they went on together to Jericho.

⁵Then the students at Jericho Seminary came to Elisha and asked him, "Do you know that the Lord is going to take away your master today?"

"Will you please be quiet?" he commanded. "Of course I know it!"

⁶,⁷Then Elijah said to Elisha, "Please stay here, for the Lord has sent me to the Jordan River."

But Elisha replied as before, "I swear to God that I won't leave you."

So they went on together and stood beside the Jordan River as fifty of the young prophets watched from a distance. ⁸Then Elijah folded his cloak together and struck the water with it; and the river divided and they went across on dry ground!

⁹When they arrived on the other side Elijah said to Elisha, "What wish shall I grant you before I am taken away?"

1:10
1 Kgs 18:36
22:28
2 Chron 36:16
Job 1:16
Lk 9:54

1:15
2 Kgs 1:3

1:17
2 Kgs 3:1; 8:16

1:18
2 Kgs 10:34
13:8,12; 14:15

2:1
Gen 5:23,24
1 Kgs 19:16
2 Kgs 2:11
Heb 11:5

2:3
2 Kgs 2:5,7,15

2:4
1 Kgs 16:34
2 Kgs 2:15

2:6
Ruth 1:15-17
2 Sam 15:19-21
2 Kgs 2:1,2

2:8
Ex 14:21
1 Kgs 19:19
Ps 114:5

2:9
1 Kgs 3:5
2 Chron 1:7

1:13–15 Notice how the third captain went to Elijah. Although the first two captains called Elijah "man of God," they were not being genuine. The third captain also called him "man of God," but he humbly begged for mercy. His attitude, which showed respect for God and his power, saved the lives of his men. Effective living begins with a right attitude toward God. Let respect characterize your attitude toward God and others.

1:18 *The Annals of the Kings of Israel* and *The Annals of the Kings of Judah* (8:23) were history books. The inspired writer of 2 Kings selected facts from these books to retell the story of Israel and Judah from God's perspective. God directed the writer's

thoughts and selection process to make sure his message would reach us today.

2:3 At Bethel there was a special school for God's prophets, one of several "prophet schools" started to help stem the tide of spiritual and moral decline that had started under Jeroboam. Most of the schools seem to have been located in Gilgal, Jericho, and Bethel. Those who attended these schools were being trained to be spokesmen for God. These schools were not like schools today, but were a gathering of disciples around a certain leader much like Jesus' disciples gathered around him.

2:9 Elisha asked for a double share of Elijah's prophetic power.

And Elisha replied, "Please grant me twice as much prophetic power as you have had."

10"You have asked a hard thing," Elijah replied. "If you see me when I am taken from you, then you will get your request. But if not, then you won't."

2:11
2 Kgs 2:1; 6:17

11As they were walking along, talking, suddenly a chariot of fire, drawn by horses of fire, appeared and drove between them, separating them, and Elijah was carried by a whirlwind into heaven.

2:12
2 Kgs 13:14

12Elisha saw it and cried out, "My father! My father! The Chariot of Israel and the charioteers!"

As they disappeared from sight he tore his robe. 13, 14Then he picked up Elijah's cloak and returned to the bank of the Jordan River, and struck the water with it.

"Where is the Lord God of Elijah?" he cried out. And the water parted and Elisha went across!

15When the young prophets of Jericho saw what had happened, they exclaimed, "The spirit of Elijah rests upon Elisha!" And they went to meet him and greeted him respectfully.

KINGS TO DATE AND THEIR ENEMIES

	853 AHAZIAH 1 Kgs 22:40— 2 Kgs 1:18 2 Chr 20:35–37	852 JORAM With Judah, defeated Mesha (Moab), and was miraculously delivered from Ben-hadad II (Syria) 2 Kgs 1:17; 3:1—8:25	841

I S R A E L

J U D A H

| 872 JEHOSHAPHAT Defeated by Ben-hadad II (Syria), gained miraculous victory over Moab and Ammon, and crushed a rebellion by Mesha (Moab) 1 Kgs 22:41–50 2 Chr 17:1—20:37 Co-regency 853–848 | 853 JEHORAM Lost dominion over Edom, assaulted by Philistines and Arabs 2 Kgs 8:16–24 2 Chr 21:1–20 | 848 | 841 |

All dates are B.C.
Solid section of the timeline indicates co-regency.
For all the kings of Israel and Judah, see the chart between the books of 1 and 2 Kings.

Deuteronomy 21:17 helps explain Elisha's request. According to custom, the firstborn son received a double share of the father's inheritance (see the note on Genesis 25:31). He was asking to be Elijah's heir, or successor, the one who would continue Elijah's work as leader of the prophets. But the decision to grant Elisha's request was up to God.

2:9 Elisha asked for twice as much power as Elijah had. This was a bold request, but God granted it. Why? Because Elisha's motives

were pure. His main goal was not to be better or more powerful than Elijah, but to accomplish more for God. If our motives are pure, we don't have to be afraid to ask great things from God. When we ask God for great power or ability, we need to examine our desires and get rid of any selfishness we find.

2:14 When Elisha struck the water, it was not out of disrespect to God or Elijah. It was a plea to God to confirm his appointment as Elijah's successor.

16"Sir," they said, "just say the word and fifty of our best athletes will search the wilderness for your master; perhaps the Spirit of the Lord has left him on some mountain or in some ravine."

"No," Elisha said, "don't bother."

17But they kept urging until he was embarrassed, and finally said, "All right, go ahead." Then fifty men searched for three days, but didn't find him.

18Elisha was still at Jericho when they returned. "Didn't I tell you not to go?" he growled.

2:16
1 Kgs 18:12
Ezek 3:14,15
8:3; 11:24
Acts 8:39

Elisha purifies the water

19Now a delegation of the city officials of Jericho visited Elisha. "We have a problem," they told him. "This city is located in beautiful natural surroundings, as you can see; but the water is bad, and causes our women to have miscarriages."

20"Well," he said, "bring me a new bowl filled with salt." So they brought it to him.

21Then he went out to the city well and threw the salt in and declared, "The Lord has healed these waters. They shall no longer cause death or miscarriage."

2:21
Ex 15:25
2 Kgs 4:41

Elisha is mocked

22And sure enough! The water was purified, just as Elisha had said.

23From Jericho he went to Bethel. As he was walking along the road, a gang of young men from the city began mocking and making fun of him because of his bald head. 24He turned around and cursed them in the name of the Lord; and two female bears came out of the woods and tore forty-two of them. 25Then he went to Mount Carmel and finally returned to Samaria.

2:24
Judg 9:20,57
1 Kgs 21:19
2 Kgs 1:10
Jer 28:16

Elisha predicts Israel's victory over Moab

3 Ahab's son Jehoram began his reign over Israel during the eighteenth year of the reign of King Jehoshaphat of Judah; and he reigned twelve years. His capital was Samaria. 2He was a very evil man, but not as wicked as his father and mother had been, for he at least tore down the pillar to Baal that his father had made. 3Nevertheless he still clung to the great sin of Jeroboam (the son of Nebat), who had led the people of Israel into the worship of idols.

4King Mesha of Moab and his people were sheep ranchers. They paid Israel an

3:1
1 Kgs 22:51
2 Kgs 1:17; 8:16
3:2
1 Kgs 16:31,32
2 Kgs 10:26
3:3
1 Kgs 12:28
14:16

2:19 *causes our women to have miscarriages,* implied in vs 21. Literally, "the land is unfruitful."

2:16–18 Elijah was taken to heaven without dying. He is the second person mentioned in Scripture to do so. Enoch was the first (Genesis 5:21–24). The other prophets may not have seen God take Elijah, or they may have had a difficult time believing what they saw. In either case, they wanted to search for Elijah. Finding no physical trace of Elijah would confirm what had happened and strengthen their faith. The only other person taken to heaven in bodily form was Jesus, after his resurrection from the dead (Acts 1:9).

2:16–25 These three incidents were testimonies to Elisha's commission as a prophet of God. They are recorded to demonstrate Elisha's new power and authority as Israel's chief prophet under God's ultimate power and authority.

2:23, 24 The victims of Elisha's curse were not children, but a mob of young men. Because they were from Bethel, the religious center of idolatry in the Northern Kingdom, they were probably warning Elisha not to speak against their immorality as Elijah had done. They were not merely teasing Elisha about his baldness, but showing severe disrespect for Elisha's message and God's power. They may also have mocked him because of their disbelief in the flaming chariot that had taken Elijah. When Elisha cursed them, he did not call out the bears himself. They were sent as a judgment from God.

2:23–25 These young men made fun of God's messenger and paid for it with their lives. Making fun of religious leaders has been

a popular sport through the ages. To take a stand for God is to be different from the world and vulnerable to verbal abuse. When we are cynical and sarcastic toward religious leaders, we are in danger of mocking not just the man, but also his spiritual message. We need to pray for leaders, not laugh at them. True leaders, those who follow God, need to be heard with respect and encouraged in their ministry.

3:1 Although 1:17 states that Jehoram was King of Judah, 3:1 states that Jehoshaphat was Judah's king. As a king grew older, it was common for his son to rule beside him. Jehoshaphat, nearing the end of his reign, appointed his son Jehoram to rule with him. Jehoram (also called Joram) served as co-ruler with Jehoshaphat for five years (853–848 B.C.). (He is mentioned again in 8:16–24.) Thus the kings of Israel and Judah had the same name—Jehoram. Jehoram, king of Israel, was Ahab's son and Ahaziah's brother (1:17). Both Ahab (1 Kings 16:29—22:40) and Ahaziah (1:2–18) served as kings before Jehoram.

3:3 The sins of Israel's kings are often compared to "the great sin of Jeroboam." Jeroboam was the first ruler of the Northern Kingdom of Israel. His great sin was to institute idol worship throughout his kingdom, causing people to turn away from God (1 Kings 12:25–33). By ignoring God and allowing idol worship, Jehoram clung to the great sin of Jeroboam.

3:4 Israel and Judah held some of the most fertile land and strategic positions in the Middle East. It is no wonder that

3:4
2 Sam 8:2
1 Chron 18:2
Ps 60:8
Isa 16:1

3:5
2 Kgs 1:1

annual tribute of 100,000 lambs and the wool of 100,000 rams; 5but after Ahab's death, the king of Moab rebelled against Israel. 6, 7, 8So King Jehoram mustered the Israeli army and sent this message to King Jehoshaphat of Judah:

"The king of Moab has rebelled against me. Will you help me fight him?"

"Of course I will," Jehoshaphat replied. "My people and horses are yours to command. What are your battle plans?"

"We'll attack from the wilderness of Edom," Jehoram replied.

9So their two armies, now joined also by troops from Edom, moved along a roundabout route through the wilderness for seven days; but there was no water for the men or their pack animals.

10"Oh, what shall we do?" the king of Israel cried out. "The Lord has brought us here to let the king of Moab defeat us."

3:11
1 Kgs 19:21
22:7

11But Jehoshaphat, the king of Judah, asked, "Isn't there a prophet of the Lord with us? If so, we can find out what to do!"

"Elisha is here," one of the king of Israel's officers replied. Then he added, "He was Elijah's assistant."

12"Fine," Jehoshaphat said. "He's just the man we want." So the kings of Israel, Judah, and Edom went to consult Elisha.

3:13
1 Kgs 22:6,22

13"I want no part of you," Elisha snarled at King Jehoram of Israel. "Go to the false prophets of your father and mother!"

But King Jehoram replied, "No! For it is the Lord who has called us here to be destroyed by the king of Moab!"

14"I swear by the Lord God that I wouldn't bother with you except for the

3:12 *He's just the man we want,* literally, "the word of the Lord is with him."

MIRACLES OF ELIJAH & ELISHA	Miracle	Found where?	Factors
Baal, the false god worshiped by many Israelites, was the god of rain, fire and farm crops. He also demanded child-sacrifice. Elijah's and Elisha's miracles repeatedly show the power of the true God over the purported realm of Baal, as well as the value God places on the life of a child.	E L I J A H		
	1. Food brought by ravens	1 Kings 17:5,6	Food
	2. Widow's food multiplied	1 Kings 17:12–16	Flour and oil
	3. Widow's son raised to life	1 Kings 17:17–24	Life of a child
	4. Altar and sacrifice consumed	1 Kings 18:16–46	Fire and Water
	5. Ahaziah's soldiers consumed	2 Kings 1:9–14	Fire
	6. Jordan River parted	2 Kings 2:6–8	Water
	7. Transported to heaven	2 Kings 2:11, 12	Fire and wind
	E L I S H A		
	1. Jordan River parted	2 Kings 2:13, 14	Water
	2. Spring purified at Jericho	2 Kings 2:19–22	Water
	3. Widow's oil multiplied	2 Kings 4:1–7	Oil
	4. Dead boy raised to life	2 Kings 4:18–37	Life of a child
	5. Poison in stew purified	2 Kings 4:38–41	Flour
	6. Prophets' food multiplied	2 Kings 4:42–44	Bread and grain
	7. Naaman healed of leprosy	2 Kings 5:1–14	Water
	8. Gehazi became leprous	2 Kings 5:15–27	Words alone
	9. Axhead floated	2 Kings 6:1–7	Water
	10. Syrian army blinded	2 Kings 6:8–23	Elisha's prayer

---

neighboring nations like Moab envied them and constantly attempted to seize the land. Moab lay just southeast of Israel. The country had been under Israel's control for some time due to King Ahab's strong military leadership. When Ahab died, Mesha, the Moabite king, took the opportunity to rebel. While Israel's next king, Ahaziah, did nothing about the revolt, his successor, Jehoram, decided to take action. He joined forces with Jehoshaphat, king of Judah, and went to fight the Moabites. Together, Israel and Judah brought the Moabites to the brink of surrender. But when they saw Moab's king sacrifice his own son (3:27), they returned home in disgust. Moab fought many other battles with both Israel and

Judah. Some of them, in fact, are recorded by Mesha (c. 840 B.C.), who carved his exploits on a plaque called the Moabite Stone (discovered in 1868).

3:11–20 Jehoshaphat's question, "Isn't there a prophet?" shows how true worship and religious experience in both Israel and Judah had declined. In David's day, both the High Priest and the prophets gave the king advice. But most of the priests had left Israel (see the note on 1 Kings 13:33, 34), and God's prophets were seen as messengers of doom (1 Kings 22:18). This miracle predicted by Elisha affirmed God's power and authority and validated Elisha's ministry.

presence of King Jehoshaphat of Judah," Elisha replied. ¹⁵"Now bring me someone to play the lute." And as the lute was played, the message of the Lord came to Elisha:

3:15
1 Sam 10:5
16:23

¹⁶"The Lord says to fill this dry valley with trenches to hold the water he will send. ¹⁷You won't see wind nor rain, but this valley will be filled with water, and you will have plenty for yourselves and for your animals! ¹⁸But this is only the beginning, for the Lord will make you victorious over the army of Moab! ¹⁹You will conquer the best of their cities—even those that are fortified—and ruin all the good land with stones."

²⁰And sure enough, the next day at about the time when the morning sacrifice was offered—look! Water! It was flowing from the direction of Edom, and soon there was water everywhere.

3:20
Ex 29:39

²¹Meanwhile, when the people of Moab heard about the three armies marching against them, they mobilized every man who could fight, old and young, and stationed themselves along their frontier. ²²But early the next morning the sun looked red as it shone across the water!

²³"Blood!" they exclaimed. "The three armies have attacked and killed each other! Let's go and collect the loot!"

3:23
2 Kgs 6:18; 7:6

²⁴But when they arrived at the Israeli camp, the army of Israel rushed out and began killing them; and the army of Moab fled. Then the men of Israel moved forward into the land of Moab, destroying everything as they went. ²⁵They destroyed the cities, threw stones on every good piece of land, stopped up the wells, and felled the fruit trees; finally, only Fort Kir-haraseth was left, but even that finally fell to them.

3:25
Isa 16:7
Jer 48:31,36

²⁶When the king of Moab saw that the battle had been lost, he led 700 of his swordsmen in a last desperate attempt to break through to the king of Edom; but he failed. ²⁷Then he took his oldest son, who was to have been the next king, and to the horror of the Israeli army, killed him and sacrificed him as a burnt offering upon the wall. So the army of Israel turned back in disgust to their own land.

3:27
2 Kgs 16:3
17:17; 21:6
Mic 6:7

Elisha provides oil for a widow

4 One day the wife of one of the seminary students came to Elisha to tell him of her husband's death. He was a man who had loved God, she said. But he had owed some money when he died, and now the creditor was demanding it back. If she didn't pay, he said he would take her two sons as his slaves.

4:1
Lev 25:39,48
Neh 5:2-4
Jer 34:14

3:25 *even that finally fell to them,* literally, "the slingers surrounded and conquered it."

3:15 A lute was a musical instrument resembling a small guitar. In Old Testament times, music often accompanied prophecy (1 Chronicles 25:1).

3:20 The morning sacrifice was one of two sacrifices that the priests were required to offer each day.

4:1ff This chapter records four of Elisha's miracles: providing money for a poverty-stricken widow (4:1–7); healing a boy (4:32–36); purifying poisoned food (4:38–41); and providing food for 100 men (4:42–44). These miracles show God's tenderness and care over those who are faithful to him.

When reading the Old Testament, it is easy to focus on God's harsh judgment of the rebellious and to minimize his tender care for those who love and serve him. To see him at work, providing daily provision for his followers helps us keep his severe justice toward the unrepentant in proper perspective.

4:1 Poor people and debtors were allowed to pay their debts by selling themselves or their children as slaves. God ordered rich people and creditors not to take advantage of these people during their time of extreme need (see Deuteronomy 15:1–18 for an explanation of these practices). This woman's creditor was not acting in the spirit of God's law. Elisha's kind deed demonstrates that compassion goes beyond simply keeping the law.

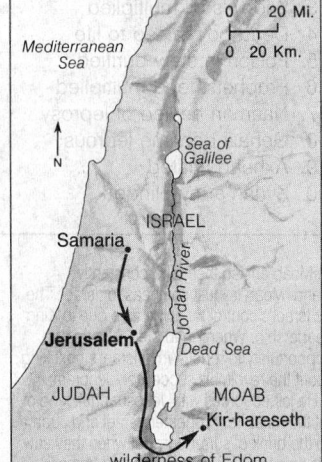

WAR AGAINST MOAB
Moab's king rebelled against Israel. So Jehoram, Israel's king, and Jehoshaphat, Judah's king, attacked Moab. In the parched and rugged wilderness of Edom, the armies ran out of water, but Elisha promised that both water and victory would soon come.

4:2
1 Kgs 17:12

2"What shall I do?" Elisha asked. "How much food do you have in the house?"

"Nothing at all, except a jar of olive oil," she replied.

3"Then borrow many pots and pans from your friends and neighbors!" he instructed. 4"Go into your house with your sons and shut the door behind you. Then pour olive oil from your jar into the pots and pans, setting them aside as they are filled!"

5So she did. Her sons brought the pots and pans to her, and she filled one after another! 6Soon every container was full to the brim!

"Bring me another jar," she said to her sons.

"There aren't any more!" they told her. And then the oil stopped flowing!

7When she told the prophet what had happened, he said to her, "Go and sell the oil and pay your debt, and there will be enough money left for you and your sons to live on!"

Elisha restores a child to life

4:8
1 Sam 28:4
1 Kgs 1:3,4

4:9
Deut 33:1
1 Kgs 13:1
17:18

8One day Elisha went to Shunem. A prominent woman of the city invited him in to eat, and afterwards, whenever he passed that way, he stopped for dinner. 9She said to her husband, "I'm sure this man who stops in from time to time is a holy prophet. 10Let's make a little room for him on the roof; we can put in a bed, a table, a chair, and a lamp, and he will have a place to stay whenever he comes by."

4:11
2 Kgs 4:29
5:20; 8:4

11, 12Once when he was resting in the room he said to his servant Gehazi, "Tell the woman I want to speak to her."

When she came, 13he said to Gehazi, "Tell her that we appreciate her kindness to us. Now ask her what we can do for her. Does she want me to put in a good word for her to the king or to the general of the army?"

"No," she replied, "I am perfectly content."

14"What can we do for her?" he asked Gehazi afterwards.

He suggested, "She doesn't have a son, and her husband is an old man."

4:15
Gen 18:14

15, 16"Call her back again," Elisha told him.

When she returned, he talked to her as she stood in the doorway. "Next year at about this time you shall have a son!"

"O man of God," she exclaimed, "don't lie to me like that!"

17But it was true; the woman soon conceived and had a baby boy the following year, just as Elisha had predicted.

18One day when her child was older, he went out to visit his father, who was

---

THE FAMILY IN SHUNEM
Elisha often stayed with a kind family in Shunem. When the son suddenly died, his mother traveled to Mount Carmel to find Elisha. He returned with her, and raised the boy from the dead. Elisha then went to his home in Gilgal.

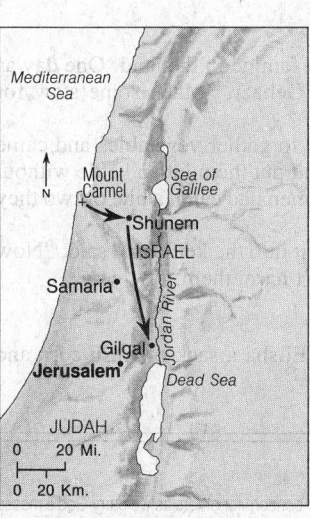

4:6 The woman and her sons collected pots and pans from their neighbors, and they began to pour oil into them from their one small jar. The oil stopped pouring only when they ran out of containers. The number of jars they gathered was an indication of their faith. God's provision was as large as their faith and willingness to obey. Beware of limiting God's blessings by a lack of faith and obedience.

working with the reapers. ¹⁹He complained about a headache, and soon was moaning in pain. His father said to one of the servants, "Carry him home to his mother."

²⁰So he took him home, and his mother held him on her lap; but around noontime he died. ²¹She carried him up to the bed of the prophet and shut the door; ²²then she sent a message to her husband: "Send one of the servants and a donkey so that I can hurry to the prophet and come right back."

²³"Why today?" he asked. "This isn't a religious holiday."

But she said, "It's important. I must go."

²⁴So she saddled the donkey and said to the servant, "Hurry! Don't slow down for my comfort unless I tell you to."

²⁵As she approached Mount Carmel, Elisha saw her in the distance and said to Gehazi, "Look, that woman from Shunem is coming. ²⁶Run and meet her and ask her what the trouble is. See if her husband is all right and if the child is well."

"Yes," she told Gehazi, "everything is fine."

²⁷But when she came to Elisha at the mountain she fell to the ground before him and caught hold of his feet. Gehazi began to push her away, but the prophet said, "Let her alone; something is deeply troubling her and the Lord hasn't told me what it is." **4:27** Mt 28:9

²⁸Then she said, "It was you who said I'd have a son. And I begged you not to lie to me!"

²⁹Then he said to Gehazi, "Quick, take my staff! Don't talk to anyone along the way. Hurry! Lay the staff upon the child's face." **4:29** Ex 4:17; 7:19 14:16

³⁰But the boy's mother said, "I swear to God that I won't go home without you." So Elisha returned with her.

³¹Gehazi went on ahead and laid the staff upon the child's face, but nothing happened. There was no sign of life. He returned to meet Elisha and told him, "The child is still dead."

³²When Elisha arrived, the child was indeed dead, lying there upon the prophet's bed. ³³He went in and shut the door behind him and prayed to the Lord. ³⁴Then he lay upon the child's body, placing his mouth upon the child's mouth, and his eyes upon the child's eyes, and his hands upon the child's hands. And the child's body began to grow warm again! ³⁵Then the prophet went down and walked back and forth in the house a few times; returning upstairs, he stretched himself again upon the child. This time the little boy sneezed seven times and opened his eyes! **4:34** 1 Kgs 17:21

³⁶Then the prophet summoned Gehazi. "Call her!" he said. And when she came in, he said, "Here's your son!"

³⁷She fell to the floor at his feet and then picked up her son and went out. **4:37** Heb 11:35

Elisha makes a poisonous stew edible

³⁸Elisha now returned to Gilgal, but there was a famine in the land. One day as he was teaching the young prophets, he said to Gehazi, "Make some stew for supper for these men." **4:38** 2 Sam 21:1 2 Kgs 8:1

³⁹One of the young men went out into the field to gather vegetables and came back with some wild gourds. He shredded them and put them into a kettle without realizing that they were poisonous. ⁴⁰But after the men had eaten a bite or two they cried out, "Oh, sir, there's poison in this stew!"

⁴¹"Bring me some meal," Elisha said. He threw it into the kettle and said, "Now it's all right! Go ahead and eat!" And then it didn't harm them. **4:41** Ex 15:25 2 Kgs 2:22

Elisha feeds 100 men

⁴²One day a man from Baal-shalishah brought Elisha a sack of fresh corn and

4:42 *a sack of fresh corn*, literally, "fresh grain."

4:32–36 Elisha's prayer and method of healing show God's personal care for hurting people. We must express genuine concern for others as we carry God's message to them. Only then will we faithfully represent our compassionate Father in heaven.

twenty individual loaves of barley bread made from the first grain of his harvest. Elisha told Gehazi to use it to feed the young prophets.

43"What?" Gehazi exclaimed. "Feed one hundred men with only this?"

But Elisha said, "Go ahead, for the Lord says there will be plenty for all, and some will even be left over!"

4:44
Mt 14:16,20

44And sure enough, there was, just as the Lord had said!

The healing of Naaman the leper

5:1
Lk 4:27

5 The king of Syria had high admiration for Naaman, the commander-in-chief of his army, for he had led his troops to many glorious victories. So he was a great hero, but he was a leper. 2Bands of Syrians had invaded the land of Israel and among their captives was a little girl who had been given to Naaman's wife as a maid.

5:2
2 Kgs 6:23

3One day the little girl said to her mistress, "I wish my master would go to see the prophet in Samaria. He would heal him of his leprosy!"

4Naaman told the king what the little girl had said.

5:5
1 Sam 9:8
1 Kgs 13:7
2 Kgs 8:8,9

5"Go and visit the prophet," the king told him. "I will send a letter of introduction for you to carry to the king of Israel."

So Naaman started out, taking gifts of $20,000 in silver, $60,000 in gold, and ten suits of clothing. 6The letter to the king of Israel said: "The man bringing this letter is my servant Naaman; I want you to heal him of his leprosy."

5:7
Gen 30:2; 37:29
1 Sam 2:6

7When the king of Israel read it, he tore his clothes and said, "This man sends me a leper to heal! Am I God, that I can kill and give life? He is only trying to get an excuse to invade us again."

8But when Elisha the prophet heard about the king of Israel's plight, he sent this message to him: "Why are you so upset? Send Naaman to me, and he will learn that there is a true prophet of God here in Israel."

9So Naaman arrived with his horses and chariots and stood at the door of Elisha's home. 10Elisha sent a messenger out to tell him to go and wash in the Jordan River seven times and he would be healed of every trace of his leprosy! 11But Naaman was angry and stalked away.

5:10
Jn 9:7

"Look," he said, "I thought at least he would come out and talk to me! I expected him to wave his hand over the leprosy and call upon the name of the Lord his God, and heal me! 12Aren't the Abana River and Pharpar River of Damascus better than all the rivers of Israel put together? If it's rivers I need, I'll wash at home and get rid of my leprosy." So he went away in a rage.

5:1 Leprosy, much like AIDS today, was one of the most feared diseases of the time. It was extremely contagious and, in many cases, incurable. In its worst forms, leprosy led to death. Many lepers were forced out of the cities into quarantined camps. Since Naaman still held his post, he probably had a mild form of the disease, or perhaps it was still in the early stages. In either case, his career would be tragically shortened by his disease. (For more about leprosy in Bible times, see the note on Leviticus 13:1–3.)

5:2 Syria was Israel's neighbor to the northeast, but the two nations were rarely on friendly terms. Under King David, Syria paid tribute to Israel. In Elisha's day, Syria was growing in power and frequently conducted raids on Israel, trying to frustrate the people and bring about political confusion. Israelite captives were often taken back to Syria after successful raids. Naaman's servant girl was an Israelite, kidnapped from her home and family. Ironically, Naaman's only hope of being cured came from Israel.

5:3, 4 The little girl's faith and Naaman's quest contrast with the stubbornness of Israel's king (5:7). A leader in mighty Syria sought the God of Israel; Israel's own king would not.

5:5 The name of Israel's king is not mentioned in this story. Because the events of 2 Kings 1—8 are mainly about Elisha's

ministry and are not intended to be chronological, we cannot know for sure, but the king was most likely Jehoram (3:1).

5:7 King Ben-hadad of Syria sent Naaman to the king of Israel, thinking the king could order Elisha to cure Naaman. He thought God's gift of healing could be bought. The king of Israel was upset because he knew he had no control over the situation, and he thought the Syrian king was trying to find an excuse to fight. He was completely ignorant of God's power working through Elisha.

5:9–15 Naaman, a great hero, was used to getting respect, and he was outraged when Elisha treated him like an ordinary person. To wash in a great river would be one thing, but the Jordan was small and dirty. To wash in the Jordan, Naaman thought, was beneath a man of his position. But Naaman had to humble himself and obey Elisha's commands in order to be healed.

Obedience to God begins with humility. We must believe that his way is better than our own. We may not always understand his ways of working, but by humbly obeying, we will receive his blessings. We must remember that (1) God's ways are best; (2) God wants our obedience more than anything else; and (3) God can use anything to accomplish his purposes.

13But his officers tried to reason with him and said, "If the prophet had told you to do some great thing, wouldn't you have done it? So you should certainly obey him when he says simply to go and wash and be cured!"

14So Naaman went down to the Jordan River and dipped himself seven times, as the prophet had told him to. And his flesh became as healthy as a little child's, and he was healed! 15Then he and his entire party went back to find the prophet; they stood humbly before him and Naaman said, "I know at last that there is no God in all the world except in Israel; now please accept my gifts."

16But Elisha replied, "I swear by Jehovah my God that I will not accept them."

Naaman urged him to take them, but he absolutely refused. 17"Well," Naaman said, "all right. But please give me two muleloads of earth to take back with me, for from now on I will never again offer any burnt offerings or sacrifices to any other God except the Lord. 18However, may the Lord pardon me this one thing—when my master the king goes into the temple of the god Rimmon to worship there and leans on my arm, may the Lord pardon me when I bow too."

19"All right," Elisha said. So Naaman started home again.

20But Gehazi, Elisha's servant, said to himself, "My master shouldn't have let this fellow get away without taking his gifts. I will chase after him and get something from him."

21So Gehazi caught up with him. When Naaman saw him coming, he jumped down from his chariot and ran to meet him.

"Is everything all right?" he asked.

22"Yes," he said, "but my master has sent me to tell you that two young prophets from the hills of Ephraim have just arrived, and he would like $2,000 in silver and two suits to give to them."

23"Take $4,000," Naaman insisted. He gave him two expensive robes, tied up the money in two bags, and gave them to two of his servants to carry back with Gehazi. 24But when they arrived at the hill where Elisha lived, Gehazi took the bags from the servants and sent the men back. Then he hid the money in his house.

25When he went in to his master, Elisha asked him, "Where have you been, Gehazi?"

"I haven't been anywhere," he replied.

26But Elisha asked him, "Don't you realize that I was there in thought when Naaman stepped down from his chariot to meet you? Is this the time to receive money and clothing and olive farms and vineyards and sheep and oxen and servants? 27Because you have done this, Naaman's leprosy shall be upon you and upon your children and your children's children forever."

5:14
Job 33:23-25
Lk 4:27; 5:13
5:15
Josh 2:9; 9:9
1 Sam 17:46
1 Kgs 18:36
Isa 43:10
5:16
Gen 14:22
2 Kgs 3:14
5:17
Ex 20:24

5:20
2 Kgs 4:11,12,
31,36

5:27
Ex 4:6
Num 12:10

5:17 *two muleloads of earth*, etc. Thus even in a foreign land Naaman could worship God on Israel's soil. **5:24** *at the hill where Elisha lived*, implied.

5:13 Naaman left in a rage because the cure for his disease seemed too simple. He was a hero, and he expected a heroic cure. Full of pride and self-will, he could not accept the simple cure of faith. Sometimes people react to God's offer of forgiveness in the same way. Just to *believe* in Jesus Christ somehow doesn't seem significant enough to bring eternal life. To follow God's advice doesn't seem heroic. What Naaman had to do to have his leprosy washed away is similar to what we must do to have our sin washed away—humbly accept God's mercy. Don't let your reaction to the way of faith keep you from the cure you need the most.

5:16 Elisha refused Naaman's money to show that God's favor cannot be purchased. Our money, like Naaman's, is useless when we face death. No matter how much wealth we accumulate in this life, it will evaporate when we stand before God, our Creator. He will look at our character, not our bank accounts.

5:18, 19 How could Naaman be pardoned for bowing to a heathen idol? Naaman was not asking for permission to worship the god Rimmon, but to do his civil duty, helping the king get down and up as he bowed. Naaman, unlike most of his contemporaries, showed a keen awareness of God's power. Instead of adding God to his nation's collection of idols, he acknowledged that there was only one true God. He did not intend to worship other gods. His asking for pardon in this one area shows the marked contrast between Naaman and the Israelites, who were continually worshiping many idols.

5:20 Gehazi saw a perfect opportunity to get rich by selfishly asking for the reward Elisha had refused. Unfortunately, there were three problems with his plan: (1) he willingly accepted money for what he didn't do; (2) he wrongly implied that money could be exchanged for God's free gift of healing and mercy; (3) he lied and tried to cover up his motives for accepting the money. Although Gehazi had been a helpful servant, personal gain had become more important to him than serving God.

This passage is not teaching that money is evil; instead, it is warning against obtaining it wrongly. True service is motivated by love and devotion to God and seeks no personal gain. As you serve God, check your motives—you can't serve both God and money (Matthew 6:24).

And Gehazi walked from the room a leper, his skin as white as snow.

Elisha makes an axhead float

6:1
2 Kgs 2:3,5,7

6 One day the seminary students came to Elisha and told him, "As you can see, our dormitory is too small. Tell us, as our president, whether we can build a new one down beside the Jordan River, where there are plenty of logs."

"All right," he told them, "go ahead."

3"Please, sir, come with us," someone suggested.

"I will," he said.

4When they arrived at the Jordan, they began cutting down trees; 5but as one of them was chopping, his axhead fell into the river.

6:6
Ex 15:25
2 Kgs 2:21; 4:41

"Oh, sir," he cried, "it was borrowed!"

6"Where did it fall?" the prophet asked. The youth showed him the place, and

ELISHA

Few "replacements" in Scripture were as effective as Elisha, who was Elijah's replacement as God's prophet to Israel. But Elisha had a great example to follow in the prophet Elijah. He remained with Elijah until the last moments of his teacher's life on earth. He was willing to follow and learn in order to gain power to do the work to which God had called him.

Both Elijah and Elisha concentrated their efforts on the particular needs of the people around them. The fiery Elijah confronted and exposed idolatry, helping to create an atmosphere where people could freely and publicly worship God. Elisha then moved in to demonstrate God's powerful, yet caring, nature to all who came to him for help. He spent less time in conflict with evil and more in compassionate care of people. The Bible records 18 encounters between Elisha and needy people.

Elisha saw more *in* life than most people because he recognized that with God there was more *to* life. He knew that all we are and have comes to us from God. The miracles that occurred during Elisha's ministry put people in touch with the personal and all-powerful God. Elijah would have been proud of his replacement's work.

We too have great examples to follow—both people in Scripture and those who have positively influenced our lives. We must resist the tendency to think about the limitations that our family background or environment create for us. Instead, we need to ask God to use us for his purposes—perhaps, like Elijah, to win great conflicts or, like Elisha, to compassionately care for the daily needs of those around us. Ask him to use you as only he can.

Strengths and accomplishments:
- Elijah's successor as a prophet of God
- Had a ministry that lasted over 50 years
- Had a major impact on four nations: Israel, Judah, Moab, and Syria
- Was a man of integrity who did not try to enrich himself at others' expense
- Did many miracles to help those in need

Lessons from his life:
- In God's eyes, one measure of greatness is the willingness to serve the poor as well as the powerful
- An effective replacement not only learns from his master, but also builds upon his master's achievements

Vital statistics:
- Where: From the tribe of Issachar, prophesied to Northern Kingdom
- Occupation: Farmer, prophet
- Relatives: Father: Shaphat
- Contemporaries: Elijah, Ahab, Jezebel, Jehu

Key verse:
"When they arrived on the other side Elijah said to Elisha, 'What wish shall I grant you before I am taken away?' And Elisha replied, 'Please grant me twice as much prophetic power as you have had' " (2 Kings 2:9).

Elisha's story is told in 1 Kings 19:16—2 Kings 13:20. He is also mentioned in Luke 4:27.

6:1–6 The incident of the floating axhead is recorded to show God's care and provison for those who trust him, even in the insignificant events of everyday life. He is always present. Placed between the healing of a Syrian general and the deliverance of Israel's army, this miracle shows Elisha's personal contact with the students who were learning to be prophets. Although he had the respect of kings, Elisha never forgot to care for the faithful. Don't let the importance of your work drive out your concern for human need.

Elisha cut a stick and threw it into the water; and the axhead rose to the surface and floated! ⁷"Grab it," Elisha said to him; and he did.

Elisha captures an army

⁸Once when the king of Syria was at war with Israel, he said to his officers, "We will mobilize our forces at —" (naming the place).

⁹Immediately Elisha warned the king of Israel, "Don't go near —" (naming the same place) "for the Syrians are planning to mobilize their troops there!"

¹⁰The king sent a scout to see if Elisha was right, and sure enough, he had saved him from disaster. This happened several times.

¹¹The king of Syria was puzzled. He called together his officers and demanded, "Which of you is the traitor? Who has been informing the king of Israel about my plans?"

¹²"It's not us, sir," one of the officers replied. "Elisha, the prophet, tells the king of Israel even the words you speak in the privacy of your bedroom!"

¹³"Go and find out where he is, and we'll send troops to seize him," the king exclaimed.

And the report came back, "Elisha is at Dothan."

¹⁴So one night the king of Syria sent a great army with many chariots and horses to surround the city. ¹⁵When the prophet's servant got up early the next morning and went outside, there were troops, horses, and chariots everywhere.

"Alas, my master, what shall we do now?" he cried out to Elisha.

¹⁶"Don't be afraid!" Elisha told him. "For our army is bigger than theirs!"

¹⁷Then Elisha prayed, "Lord, open his eyes and let him see!" And the Lord opened the young man's eyes so that he could see horses of fire and chariots of fire everywhere upon the mountain!

¹⁸As the Syrian army advanced upon them, Elisha prayed, "Lord, please make them blind." And he did.

¹⁹Then Elisha went out and told them, "You've come the wrong way! This isn't the right city! Follow me and I will take you to the man you're looking for." And he led them to Samaria!

²⁰As soon as they arrived Elisha prayed, "Lord, now open their eyes and let them see." And the Lord did, and they discovered that they were in Samaria, the capital city of Israel!

²¹When the king of Israel saw them, he shouted to Elisha, "Oh, sir, shall I kill them? Shall I kill them?"

6:9
1 Kgs 20:13,28

6:13
Gen 37:17

6:14
2 Kgs 1:9

6:16
Ex 14:13
2 Chron 32:7
Ps 3:6; 11:1
Rom 8:31

6:17
2 Kgs 2:11
Ps 34:7
Isa 42:7
Acts 26:18

6:18
Gen 19:11

6:19
1 Kgs 20:1
2 Kgs 3:1

6:21
1 Sam 24:4,19
26:8

6:15 Elisha's servant is not named in this story, but it was probably Gehazi. Chapters 1—8 are not intended to be in chronological order, so this event could have occurred before Gehazi was struck with leprosy (5:27).

6:16, 17 Elisha's servant was no longer afraid when he saw God's mighty army of angels. Faith reveals that God is doing more for his people than we could ever realize through sight alone. When you meet situations that seem insurmountable, remember that spiritual resources are there even if you can't see them. Look through the eyes of faith and let God show you his resources. If you don't see God working in your life, there may be a problem with your spiritual eyesight.

6:21 Elisha told the king not to slaughter the Syrians. The king was not to take credit for what God alone had done.

Mediterranean Sea

SYRIA

N

Sea of Galilee

Dothan • ISRAEL

Samaria •

Jordan River

Jerusalem •

Dead Sea

JUDAH

0   20 Mi.

0   20 Km.

ELISHA AND THE SYRIANS
Elisha knew Syria's battle plans and kept Israel's king informed. The Syrian king tracked down Elisha at Dothan, but Elisha prayed that the Syrian army would be blinded. He then led the blind army into Samaria, Israel's capital city!

6:22
2 Chron 28:8
Rom 12:20

6:23
2 Kgs 5:2

22"Of course not!" Elisha told him. "Do we kill prisoners of war? Give them food and drink and send them home again."

23So the king made a great feast for them, and then sent them home to their king. And after that the Syrian raiders stayed away from the land of Israel.

Elisha predicts the end of a famine

6:24
1 Kgs 20:1

6:25
2 Kgs 7:12

24Later on, however, King Ben-hadad of Syria mustered his entire army and besieged Samaria. 25As a result there was a great famine in the city, and after a long while even a donkey's head sold for fifty dollars and a pint of dove's dung brought three dollars!

6:26
Lev 26:29
Deut 28:53
1 Kgs 21:27
Lam 4:10

26-30One day as the king of Israel was walking along the wall of the city, a woman called to him, "Help, my lord the king!"

"If the Lord doesn't help you, what can I do?" he retorted. "I have neither food nor wine to give you. However, what's the matter?"

She replied, "This woman proposed that we eat my son one day and her son the next. So we boiled my son and ate him, but the next day when I said, 'Kill your son so we can eat him,' she hid him."

When the king heard this he tore his clothes. (The people watching noticed through the rip he tore in them that he was wearing an inner robe made of sackcloth next to his flesh.)

6:31
2 Sam 3:9,10
1 Kgs 2:23,24
19:2

6:32
1 Kgs 18:14
Ezek 8:1; 14:1
20:1

6:33
Isa 8:21

31"May God kill me if I don't execute Elisha this very day," the king vowed.

32Elisha was sitting in his house at a meeting with the elders of Israel when the king sent a messenger to summon him. But before the messenger arrived Elisha said to the elders, "This murderer has sent a man to kill me. When he arrives, shut the door and keep him out, for his master will soon follow him."

33While Elisha was still saying this, the messenger arrived [followed by the king].

"The Lord has caused this mess," the king stormed. "Why should I expect any help from him?"

7:2
Mal 3:10

7 Elisha replied, "The Lord says that by this time tomorrow two gallons of flour or four gallons of barley grain will be sold in the markets of Samaria for a dollar!"

2The officer assisting the king said, "That couldn't happen if the Lord made windows in the sky!"

But Elisha replied, "You will see it happen, but you won't be able to buy any of it!"

6:33 *followed by the king,* implied.

6:23 How long the Syrians stayed away from Israel is not known, but a number of years probably passed before the invasion recorded in 6:24 occurred. The Syrians must have forgotten the time their entire army was supernaturally blinded and sent home.

6:24 This was probably Ben-hadad II, whose father ruled Syria in the days of King Baasha (1 Kings 15:18). Elisha constantly frustrated Ben-hadad II in his attempts to take control of Israel.

6:25 When a city like Samaria faced famine, it was no small matter. Although they grew enough food to feed the people for a specific season, they did not have enough to maintain them in prolonged times of emergency when all supplies were cut off. This famine was so severe that mothers resorted to eating their children (6:26–30). Deuteronomy 28:49–57 predicted that this would happen when the people of Israel rejected God's leadership.

6:31–33 Why did the king blame Elisha for the famine and troubles of the siege? Here are some possible answers. (1) Some commentators say that Elisha must have told the king to trust God for deliverance. The king did this and even wore sackcloth (6:30),

but now the situation seemed hopeless. Apparently the king thought Elisha had given him bad advice and not even God could help them. (2) For years there was conflict between the kings of Israel and the prophets of God. The prophets often predicted gloom because of the kings' evil, so the kings saw them as troublemakers. Thus Israel's king was striking out in frustration at Elisha. (3) The king may have remembered when Elijah helped bring an end to a famine (1 Kings 18:41–46). Knowing Elisha was a man of God, perhaps the king thought he could do any miracle he wanted and was angry that he had not come to Israel's rescue.

7:1, 2 When Elisha prophesied God's deliverance, the king's officer said it couldn't happen. The officer's faith and hope were gone, but God's words came true anyway (7:14–16)! Sometimes we become preoccupied with problems when we should be looking for opportunities. Instead of focusing on the negatives, develop an attitude of expectancy. To say that God *cannot* rescue someone or that a situation is *impossible* demonstrates a lack of faith.

Four lepers discover the abandoned camp

3Now there were four lepers sitting outside the city gates. "Why sit here until we die?" they asked each other. 4"We will starve if we stay here and we will starve if we go back into the city; so we might as well go out and surrender to the Syrian army. If they let us live, so much the better; but if they kill us, we would have died anyway."

5So that evening they went out to the camp of the Syrians, but there was no one there! 6(For the Lord had made the whole Syrian army hear the clatter of speeding chariots and a loud galloping of horses and the sounds of a great army approaching. "The king of Israel has hired the Hittites and Egyptians to attack us," they cried out. 7So they panicked and fled into the night, abandoning their tents, horses, donkeys, and everything else.)

8When the lepers arrived at the edge of the camp they went into one tent after another, eating, drinking wine, and carrying out silver and gold and clothing and hiding it. 9Finally they said to each other, "This isn't right. This is wonderful news, and we aren't sharing it with anyone! Even if we wait until morning, some terrible calamity will certainly fall upon us; come on, let's go back and tell the people at the palace."

10So they went back to the city and told the watchmen what had happened—they had gone out to the Syrian camp and no one was there! The horses and donkeys were tethered and the tents were all in order, but there was not a soul around. 11Then the watchmen shouted the news to those in the palace.

12The king got out of bed and told his officers, "I know what has happened. The Syrians know we are starving, so they have left their camp and have hidden in the fields, thinking that we will be lured out of the city. Then they will attack us and make slaves of us and get in."

13One of his officers replied, "We'd better send out scouts to see. Let them take five of the remaining horses—if something happens to the animals it won't be any greater loss than if they stay here and die with the rest of us!"

14Four chariot-horses were found and the king sent out two charioteers to see where the Syrians had gone. 15They followed a trail of clothing and equipment all the way to the Jordan River—thrown away by the Syrians in their haste. The scouts returned and told the king, 16and the people of Samaria rushed out and plundered the camp of the Syrians. So it was true that two gallons of flour and four gallons of barley were sold that day for one dollar, just as the Lord had said!

17The king appointed his special assistant to control the traffic at the gate, but he was knocked down and trampled and killed as the people rushed out. This is what Elisha had predicted on the previous day when the king had come to arrest him, 18and the prophet had told the king that flour and barley would sell for so little on the following day.

19The king's officer had replied, "That couldn't happen even if the Lord opened the windows of heaven!"

And the prophet had said, "You will see it happen, but you won't be able to buy any of it!"

20And he couldn't, for the people trampled him to death at the gate!

A woman's land is returned

8 Elisha had told the woman whose son he had brought back to life, "Take your family and move to some other country, for the Lord has called down a famine on Israel that will last for seven years."

7:3
Lev 13:45
Num 5:1,2
2 Kgs 5:1
Mt 8:4

7:4
2 Kgs 6:24

7:6
2 Sam 5:24
2 Chron 12:3

7:12
Josh 8:6,7
2 Kgs 6:25

7:17
2 Kgs 7:2

8:1
Gen 41:27
Deut 28:22
Ps 105:16

7:3 According to the Law, lepers were not allowed in the city, but were to depend on charity outside the gate (Leviticus 13:45, 46; Numbers 5:1–4). Because of the famine and the presence of the Syrian army, their situation was desperate.

7:3–10 The lepers discovered the deserted camp and realized their lives had been spared. At first they kept the good news to themselves, forgetting their fellow citizens who were starving in the

city. The Good News about Jesus Christ must be shared too, for no news is more important. We must not forget those who are dying without it. We must not become so preoccupied with our own faith that we neglect sharing it with those around us. Our "wonderful news," like that of the lepers, will not "wait until morning."

8:1–6 This story is probably not in chronological order, because the seven-year famine must have ended before Gehazi was struck

2So the woman took her family and lived in the land of the Philistines for seven years. 3After the famine ended, she returned to the land of Israel and went to see the king about getting back her house and land. 4Just as she came in, the king was talking with Gehazi, Elisha's servant, and saying, "Tell me some stories of the great things Elisha has done." 5And Gehazi was telling the king about the time when Elisha brought a little boy back to life. At that very moment, the mother of the boy walked in!

"Oh, sir!" Gehazi exclaimed. "Here is the woman now, and this is her son—the very one Elisha brought back to life!"

6"Is this true?" the king asked her. And she told him that it was. So he directed one of his officials to see to it that everything she had owned was restored to her, plus the value of any crops that had been harvested during her absence.

Hazael murders King Ben-hadad

7Afterwards Elisha went to Damascus (the capital of Syria), where King Ben-hadad lay sick. Someone told the king that the prophet had come. 8,9When the king heard the news, he said to Hazael, "Take a present to the man of God and tell him to ask the Lord whether I will get well again."

So Hazael took forty camel-loads of the best produce of the land as presents for Elisha and said to him, "Your son Ben-hadad, the king of Syria, has sent me to ask you whether he will recover."

10And Elisha replied, "Tell him, 'Yes.' But the Lord has shown me that he will surely die!"

11Elisha stared at Hazael until he became embarrassed, and then Elisha started crying.

12"What's the matter, sir?" Hazael asked him.

Elisha replied, "I know the terrible things you will do to the people of Israel: you will burn their forts, kill the young men, dash their babies against the rocks, and rip open the bellies of the pregnant women!"

13"Am I a dog?" Hazael asked him. "I would *never* do that sort of thing."

But Elisha replied, "The Lord has shown me that you are going to be the king of Syria."

14When Hazael went back, the king asked him, "What did he tell you?"

And Hazael replied, "He told me that you would recover."

15But the next day Hazael took a blanket and dipped it in water and held it over the king's face until he smothered to death. And Hazael became king instead.

2. Kings of Israel and Judah
Jehoram rules Judah

16King Jehoram, the son of King Jehoshaphat of Judah, began his reign during the fifth year of the reign of King Joram of Israel, the son of Ahab. 17Jehoram was thirty-two years old when he became king, and he reigned in Jerusalem for eight years. 18But he was as wicked as Ahab and the other kings of Israel; he even married one of Ahab's daughters. 19Nevertheless, because God had promised his

8:4
2 Kgs 4:11,12
5:20
8:5
2 Kgs 4:34

8:7
2 Kgs 6:24; 13:3

8:8
1 Kgs 14:3
19:15

8:11
2 Kgs 2:17

8:12
2 Kgs 10:32,33
12:17; 13:3
15:16

8:13
1 Sam 17:43
2 Sam 9:8

8:16
2 Kgs 1:17; 3:1

8:17
2 Chron 21:5

8:19
1 Kgs 11:36

---

with leprosy. This shows Elijah's long-term concern for this widow and contrasts his miraculous public ministry with his private ministry to this family. Elisha's life exemplifies the kind of concern we should have for others.

8:12, 13 Elisha told Hazael he would sin greatly. Hazael protested, "I would *never* do that sort of thing." He did not acknowledge his personal potential for evil. In our "enlightened" society, it is easy to think we are above gross sin and can control our actions. We think that we would never sink so low. Instead, we should take a more biblical and realistic look at ourselves and admit our sinful potential. Then we will ask for God's strength to resist such evil.

8:12–15 Elisha's words about Hazael's treatment of Israel were partially fulfilled in 10:32, 33. Apparently Hazael had known he

would be king because Elijah had told him (1 Kings 19:15). But he was impatient and, instead of waiting for God's timing, took matters into his own hands, killing Ben-hadad. God used Hazael as an instrument of judgment against the disobedient Israelites.

8:18 King Jehoshaphat arranged the marriage between Jehoram, his son, and Athaliah, the daughter of wicked Ahab and Jezebel. Athaliah followed the idolatrous ways of the Northern Kingdom, bringing Baal worship into Judah and starting the Southern Kingdom's decline. When Jehoram died, his son Ahaziah became king. Then, when Ahaziah was killed in battle, Athaliah murdered all her grandsons and made herself queen (11:1–3). Jehoram's marriage may have been politically advantageous, but it was spiritually deadly.

servant David that he would watch over and guide his descendants, he did not destroy Judah.

20During Jehoram's reign, the people in Edom revolted from Judah and appointed their own king. 21King Jehoram tried unsuccessfully to crush the rebellion: he crossed the Jordan River and attacked the city of Zair, but was quickly surrounded by the army of Edom. Under cover of night he broke through their ranks, but his army deserted him and fled. 22So Edom has maintained its independence to this day. Libnah also rebelled at that time.

23The rest of the history of King Jehoram is written in *The Annals of the Kings of Judah.* 24, 25He died and was buried in the royal cemetery in the City of David—the old section of Jerusalem.

Ahaziah rules Judah

Then his son Ahaziah became the new king during the twelfth year of the reign of King Jehoram of Israel, the son of Ahab. 26Ahaziah was twenty-two years old when he began to reign but he reigned only one year, in Jerusalem. His mother was Athaliah, the granddaughter of King Omri of Israel. 27He was an evil king, just as all of King Ahab's descendants were—for he was related to Ahab by marriage.

28He joined King Joram of Israel (son of Ahab) in his war against Hazael, the king of Syria, at Ramoth-gilead. King Joram was wounded in the battle, 29so he went to Jezreel to rest and recover from his wounds. While he was there, King Ahaziah of Judah (son of Jehoram) came to visit him.

Jehu is anointed king of Israel

9 Meanwhile Elisha had summoned one of the young prophets. "Get ready to go to Ramoth-gilead," he told him. "Take this vial of oil with you, 2and find Jehu (the son of Jehoshaphat, the son of Nimshi). Call him into a private room away from his friends, 3and pour the oil over his head. Tell him that the Lord has anointed him to be the king of Israel; then run for your life!"

4So the young prophet did as he was told. When he arrived in Ramoth-gilead, 5he found Jehu sitting around with the other army officers.

8:25 *his son Ahaziah.* Ahaziah is an alternate form of the name Jehoahaz.

8:20
2 Kgs 3:9,26
2 Chron 21:8
8:22
Gen 27:39,40
8:23
1 Kgs 15:23
22:45
2 Kgs 12:19
14:18; 15:6
8:24
1 Kgs 2:10
11:43
2 Chron 21:20
22:1

8:26
2 Kgs 11:1
8:27
1 Kgs 16:30

8:29
2 Kgs 9:14
2 Chron 22:6

9:1
1 Sam 10:1
16:1
1 Kgs 1:39
2 Kgs 8:28
9:2
1 Kgs 19:16
9:3
1 Sam 9:16
2 Chron 22:7

JEHU TAKES OVER ISRAEL
Elisha sent a prophet to Ramoth-gilead to anoint Jehu as Israel's new king. Jehu immediately rode to Jezreel to find and kill King Joram of Israel and King Ahaziah of Judah. Jehu killed Joram; Ahaziah fled toward Beth-haggan where he was wounded. He later died at Meggido. Back in Jezreel, Jehu had Jezebel killed.

8:20–22 Although Judah and Edom shared a common border and a common ancestor (Isaac), the two nations fought continually. Edom had been a vassal of the united kingdom of Israel and then the Southern Kingdom of Judah since the days of David (2 Samuel 8:13, 14). Now Edom rebelled against Jehoram and declared independence. Immediately Jehoram marched out to attack Edom, but his ambush failed. Thus Jehoram lost some of his borderlands as punishment for his failure to honor God.

8:26 Ahaziah was the only remaining son of Jehoram of Judah. Although he was the youngest son, he took the throne because the rest of his brothers had been taken captive in a raid by the Philistines and Arabs (2 Chronicles 21:16, 17). Ahaziah is also referred to as Jehoahaz.

8:26, 27 Ahaziah's mother was Athaliah, daughter of Ahab and Jezebel, former king and queen of Israel. The evil of Ahab and Jezebel spread to Judah through Athaliah.

8:29 Jezreel was the location of the summer palace for the kings of Israel.

9:3 Elijah had prophesied that many people would be killed when Jehu became king (1 Kings 19:16–18). Thus Elisha advised the young prophet to get out of the area as soon as he delivered his message, before the slaughter began. Jehu's actions seem harsh, as he hunted down relatives and friends of Ahab (2 Chronicles 22:8, 9), but unchecked Baal worship was destroying the nation. If Israel was to survive, the followers of Baal had to be eliminated. As a zealous follower of God (at first), Jehu fulfilled the need of the hour—justice.

"I have a message for you, sir," he said.

"For which one of us?" Jehu asked.

"For you," he replied.

9:7
Deut 32:35
1 Kgs 18:3,4
21:15,21
2 Kgs 10:17

9:9
1 Kgs 14:10
15:29; 16:3,11

9:10
1 Kgs 21:23
2 Kgs 9:35,36

6So Jehu left the others and went into the house, and the young man poured the oil over his head and said, "The Lord God of Israel says, 'I anoint you king of the Lord's people, Israel. 7You are to destroy the family of Ahab; you will avenge the murder of my prophets and of all my other people who were killed by Jezebel. 8The entire family of Ahab must be wiped out—every male, no matter who. 9I will destroy the family of Ahab as I destroyed the families of Jeroboam (son of Nebat) and of Baasha (son of Ahijah). 10Dogs shall eat Ahab's wife Jezebel at Jezreel, and no one will bury her.' "

Then he opened the door and ran.

JEHU

Jehu had the basic qualities that could have made him a great success. From a human perspective, in fact, he was a successful king. His family ruled the Northern Kingdom longer than any other. He was used by God as an instrument of punishment to Ahab's evil dynasty, and he fiercely attacked Baal worship. He came close to being God's kind of king, but he recklessly went beyond God's commands and failed to follow through on the obedient actions that began his reign. Within sight of victory, he settled for mediocrity.

Jehu was a man with direction, but without purpose. His kingdom moved, but its destination was unclear. He eliminated one form of idolatry, Baal worship, only to uphold another by continuing to worship the calves Jeroboam had set up. He could have accomplished much for God if he had been obedient to the One who made him king. Even when he was carrying out God's directions, Jehu's style showed he was not fully aware of who was directing him.

As he did with Jehu, God gives each person strengths and abilities that will find their greatest usefulness only under his control. Outside that control, however, they don't accomplish what they could, and often become tools for evil. One way to make sure this does not happen is to consciously tell God of your willingness to be under his control. His presence in your life will cause your natural strengths and abilities to be used to their greatest potential for the greatest good.

Strengths and accomplishments:
- Took the throne from Ahab's family and destroyed his evil influence
- Founded the longest-lived dynasty of the Northern Kingdom
- Was anointed by Elijah and confirmed by Elisha
- Destroyed Baal worship

Weaknesses and mistakes:
- Had a reckless outlook on life that made him bold and prone to error
- Worshiped Jeroboam's calf idols
- Was devoted to God only to the point where it served his own interests

Lessons from his life:
- Fierce commitment needs control because it can result in recklessness
- Obedience involves both action and direction

Vital statistics:
- Where: The Northern Kingdom of Israel
- Occupation: Commander in Jehoram's army, king of Israel
- Relatives: Grandfather: Nimshi. Father: Jehoshaphat. Son: Jehoahaz.
- Contemporaries: Elijah, Elisha, Ahab, Jezebel, Jehoram, Ahaziah

Key verse:
"But Jehu didn't follow the Lord God of Israel with all his heart, for he continued to worship Jeroboam's gold calves that had been the cause of such great sin in Israel" (2 Kings 10:31).

Jehu's story is told in 1 Kings 19:16—2 Kings 10:36. He is also mentioned in 2 Kings 15:12; 2 Chronicles 22:7–9; Hosea 1:4, 5.

9:7 Elisha's statement fulfilled Elijah's prophecy made 20 years earlier: all of Ahab's family would be killed (1 Kings 21:17–24). Jezebel's death, predicted by Elijah, is described in 9:30–37.

9:9 Ahab's dynasty would end as had those of Jeroboam and Baasha. Ahijah had prophesied the end of Jeroboam's dynasty

(1 Kings 14:1–10), and this was fulfilled by King Baasha (1 Kings 15:29). The prophet Jehu—not King Jehu—then told of the end of Baasha's family (1 Kings 16:1–7), and this too was fulfilled (1 Kings 16:11, 12). The end of Ahab's family, therefore, was certain—Elijah had predicted it (1 Kings 21:17–24).

¹¹Jehu went back to his friends and one of them asked him, "What did that crazy fellow want? Is everything all right?"

"You know very well who he was and what he wanted," Jehu replied.

¹²"No, we don't," they said. "Tell us."

So he told them what the man had said and that he had been anointed king of Israel!

¹³They quickly carpeted the bare steps with their coats and blew a trumpet, shouting, "Jehu is king!"

Jehu kills Joram and Ahaziah

¹⁴That is how Jehu (son of Jehoshaphat, son of Nimshi) rebelled against King Joram. (King Joram had been with the army at Ramoth-gilead, defending Israel against the forces of King Hazael of Syria. ¹⁵But he had returned to Jezreel to recover from his wounds.)

"Since you want me to be king," Jehu told the men who were with him, "don't let anyone escape to Jezreel to report what we have done."

¹⁶Then Jehu jumped into a chariot and rode to Jezreel himself to find King Joram, who was lying there wounded. (King Ahaziah of Judah was there too, for he had gone to visit him.) ¹⁷The watchman on the Tower of Jezreel saw Jehu and his company approaching and shouted, "Someone is coming."

"Send out a rider and find out if he is friend or foe," King Joram shouted back. ¹⁸So a soldier rode out to meet Jehu.

"The king wants to know whether you are friend or foe," he demanded. "Do you come in peace?"

Jehu replied, "What do you know about peace? Get behind me!"

The watchman called out to the king that the messenger had met them but was not returning. ¹⁹So the king sent out a second rider. He rode up to them and demanded in the name of the king to know whether their intentions were friendly or not.

Jehu answered, "What do you know about friendliness? Get behind me!"

²⁰"He isn't returning either!" the watchman exclaimed. "It must be Jehu, for he is driving so furiously."

²¹"Quick! Get my chariot ready!" King Joram commanded.

Then he and King Ahaziah of Judah rode out to meet Jehu. They met him at the field of Naboth, ²²and King Joram demanded, "Do you come as a friend, Jehu?"

Jehu replied, "How can there be friendship as long as the evils of your mother Jezebel are all around us?"

²³Then King Joram reined the chariot-horses around and fled, shouting to King Ahaziah, "There is treachery, Ahaziah! Treason!"

²⁴Then Jehu drew his bow with his full strength and shot Joram between the shoulders; and the arrow pierced his heart, and he sank down dead in his chariot.

²⁵Jehu said to Bidkar, his assistant, "Throw him into the field of Naboth, for once when you and I were riding along behind his father Ahab, the Lord revealed this prophecy to me: ²⁶'I will repay him here on Naboth's property for the murder of Naboth and his sons.' So throw him out on Naboth's field, just as the Lord said."

²⁷Meanwhile, King Ahaziah of Judah had fled along the road to Beth-haggan. Jehu rode after him, shouting, "Shoot him, too."

So they shot him in his chariot at the place where the road climbs to Gur, near

9:12
2 Kgs 9:6

9:13
2 Sam 15:10
1 Kgs 1:34,39

9:14
2 Kgs 8:28

9:17
2 Sam 13:34
18:24
Isa 21:6,7

9:21
1 Kgs 21:1

9:22
1 Kgs 16:31
18:19

9:23
2 Kgs 11:14

9:24
1 Kgs 22:34

9:25
1 Kgs 21:1,19

9:27
Josh 17:11
Judg 1:27
2 Chron 22:7

9:18, 19 The riders met Jehu and asked if he came in peace and friendship. But Jehu responded, "What do you know about true peace and friendliness?" These qualities, properly understood, come from God. They are not genuine except when rooted in belief in God and love for him. Jehu knew the men represented a disobedient, wicked king. Don't seek peace and friendship with those who are enemies of the good and the true. Lasting peace and genuine friendship can come only from knowing the God who gave these to us.

9:19 Jehu told the messengers to get behind him so that they could not return to the city and warn the king that his life was in danger. He may also have wanted a clear path when he shot the king.

9:26 King Joram of Israel was wicked like his father and mother, Ahab and Jezebel; therefore his body was thrown into the field that his parents had unlawfully taken. Queen Jezebel had arranged the murder of Naboth, the previous owner, because he would not sell his vineyard—which Ahab wanted for a garden (1 Kings 21:1–24). Little did Ahab know that it would become a burial plot for his evil son.

9:28
2 Kgs 8:25
23:30

9:29
2 Kgs 8:28

Ibleam. He was able to go on as far as Megiddo, but died there. 28His officials took him by chariot to Jerusalem where they buried him in the royal cemetery. 29(Ahaziah's reign over Judah had begun in the twelfth year of the reign of King Joram of Israel.)

Jezebel's terrible death

9:30
Jer 4:30
Ezek 23:40

9:31
1 Kgs 16:9,10

30When Jezebel heard that Jehu had come to Jezreel, she painted her eyelids and fixed her hair and sat at a window. 31When Jehu entered the gate of the palace, she shouted at him, "How are you today, you murderer! You son of a Zimri who murdered his master!"

32He looked up and saw her at the window and shouted, "Who is on my side?" And two or three eunuchs looked out at him.

33"Throw her down!" he yelled.

So they threw her out the window, and her blood spattered against the wall and on the horses; and she was trampled by the horses' hoofs.

9:34
1 Kgs 16:30
21:20

34Then Jehu went into the palace for lunch. Afterwards he said, "Someone go and bury this cursed woman, for she is the daughter of a king."

35But when they went out to bury her, they found only her skull, her feet, and her hands.

9:36
1 Kgs 21:23

36When they returned and told him, he remarked, "That is just what the Lord said would happen. He told Elijah the prophet that dogs would eat her flesh 37and that her body would be scattered like manure upon the field, so that no one could tell whose it was."

Jehu kills Ahab's family

10:1
Judg 8:30; 12:14
1 Kgs 16:24

10 Then Jehu wrote a letter to the city council of Samaria and to the guardians of Ahab's seventy sons—all of whom were living there.

2, 3"Upon receipt of this letter, select the best one of Ahab's sons to be your king, and prepare to fight for his throne. For you have chariots and horses and a fortified city and an armory."

4But they were too frightened to do it. "Two kings couldn't stand against this man! What can we do?" they said.

10:5
Josh 9:8

5So the manager of palace affairs and the city manager, together with the city council and the guardians of Ahab's sons, sent him this message:

"Jehu, we are your servants and will do anything you tell us to. We have decided that you should be our king instead of one of Ahab's sons."

10:6
2 Kgs 9:32

6Jehu responded with this message: "If you are on my side and are going to obey me, bring the heads of your master's sons to me at Jezreel at about this time tomorrow."

10:7
Judg 9:5
2 Kgs 11:1

(These seventy sons of King Ahab were living in the homes of the chief men of the city, where they had been raised since childhood.) 7When the letter arrived, all seventy of them were murdered, and their heads were packed into baskets and presented to Jehu at Jezreel. 8When a messenger told Jehu that the heads of the king's sons had arrived, he said to pile them in two heaps at the entrance of the city gate, and to leave them there until the next morning.

10:9
1 Kgs 8:56
21:19
2 Kgs 9:7

9, 10In the morning he went out and spoke to the crowd that had gathered around them. "You aren't to blame," he told them. "I conspired against my master and killed him, but I didn't kill his sons! The Lord has done that, for everything he says

9:29 *twelfth year,* implied in 8:25. Literally, "eleventh."

9:31 Why did Jezebel call Jehu "son of a Zimri"? Zimri was an army general who, some 40 years earlier, had killed King Elah and then had declared himself king of Israel (1 Kings 16:8–10). Jezebel was accusing Jehu of trying to do the same thing.

9:35 Jezebel's bones were all that remained of her evil life . . . no power, no money, no prestige, no royal finery, no family, no spiritual heritage. In the end, her life of treachery had amounted to

nothing. Power, health, and wealth may make you feel as if you can live forever. But death strips everyone of all external security. The time to set life's course is at the beginning. The end comes soon enough.

10:7 This fulfilled Elijah's prophecy that not one of Ahab's male descendants would survive (1 Kings 21:17–24).

comes true. He declared through his servant Elijah that this would happen to Ahab's descendants."

11Jehu then killed all the rest of the members of the family of Ahab who were in Jezreel, as well as all of his important officials, personal friends, and private chaplains. Finally, no one was left who had been close to him in any way. 12Then he set out for Samaria, and stayed overnight at a shepherd's inn along the way. 13While he was there he met the brothers of King Ahaziah of Judah.

"Who are you?" he asked them.

And they replied, "We are brothers of King Ahaziah. We are going to Samaria to visit the sons of King Ahab and of the Queen Mother, Jezebel."

14"Grab them!" Jehu shouted to his men. And he took them out to the cistern and killed all forty-two of them.

15As he left the inn, he met Jehonadab, the son of Rechab, who was coming to meet him. After they had greeted each other, Jehu said to him, "Are you as loyal to me as I am to you?"

"Yes," Jehonadab replied.

"Then give me your hand," Jehu said, and he helped him into the royal chariot. 16"Now come along with me," Jehu said, "and see how much I have done for the Lord." So Jehonadab rode along with him.

Jehu kills the priests of Baal

17When he arrived in Samaria he butchered all of Ahab's friends and relatives, just as Elijah, speaking for the Lord, had predicted.

Then Jehu called a meeting of all the people of the city and said to them, "Ahab hardly worshiped Baal at all in comparison to the way I am going to! 18, 19Summon all the prophets and priests of Baal, and call together all his worshipers. See to it that every one of them comes, for we worshipers of Baal are going to have a great celebration to praise him. Any of Baal's worshipers who don't come will be put to death."

But Jehu's plan was to exterminate them. 20, 21He sent messengers throughout all Israel summoning those who worshiped Baal; and they all came and filled the temple of Baal from one end to the other. 22He instructed the head of the robing room, "Be sure that every worshiper wears one of the special robes."

23Then Jehu and Jehonadab (son of Rechab) went into the temple to address the people: "Check to be sure that only those who worship Baal are here; don't let anyone in who worships the Lord!"

24As the priests of Baal began offering sacrifices and burnt offerings, Jehu surrounded the building with eighty of his men and told them, "If you let anyone escape, you'll pay for it with your own life."

25As soon as he had finished sacrificing the burnt offering, Jehu went out and told his officers and men, "Go in and kill the whole bunch of them. Don't let a single one escape."

So they slaughtered them all and dragged their bodies outside. Then Jehu's men went into the inner temple, 26dragged out the pillar used for the worship of Baal, and burned it. 27They wrecked the temple and converted it into a public toilet,

10:13 *we are brothers*, literally, "kinsmen."

10:11
1 Kgs 21:22
2 Kgs 9:8; 10:17

10:13
2 Chron 22:8

10:15
2 Kgs 10:23
1 Chron 2:55
Jer 35:6

10:17
2 Kgs 9:8

10:18
1 Kgs 16:31
18:19; 22:6

10:20
1 Kgs 16:32
2 Kgs 11:18

10:24
1 Kgs 20:40

10:25
1 Sam 22:17
1 Kgs 18:40

10:26
1 Kgs 14:23
2 Kgs 3:2

10:11 In his zeal, Jehu went far beyond the Lord's command in this bloodbath. The prophet Hosea later announced punishment upon Jehu's dynasty for this act (Hosea 1:4, 5).

10:15 Jehonadab was a man who, like Jehu, was zealous in following God. Jehonadab, however, demonstrated his zeal by separating himself and his family from the materialistic, idol-worshiping culture. He founded a group called the Rechabites (named after his father Rechab), who strove to keep their lives pure by living apart from society's pressures and temptations. Jeremiah 35 gives us an example of their dedication to God. Because of their dedication, God promised that they would always have descendants who would worship him.

10:24 Israel was supposed to be intolerant of any religion which did not worship the true God. The religions of surrounding nations were evil and corrupt, based on sexual promiscuity, political favors, greed, and materialism. They were designed to destroy life, not uphold it. Israel was God's special nation, chosen to be an example of what was right, true, and fair. But Israel's kings, priests, and elders, contaminated by surrounding pagan beliefs, had become tolerant and apathetic. We are to be completely intolerant of sin and remove it from our lives. It is one thing to be tolerant of others' views, but we should not condone actions that lead people away from God's standards of living.

which it still is today. 28Thus Jehu destroyed every trace of Baal from Israel. 29However, he didn't destroy the gold calves at Bethel and Dan—this was the great sin of Jeroboam (son of Nebat), for it resulted in all Israel sinning.

30Afterwards the Lord said to Jehu, "You have done well in following my instructions to destroy the dynasty of Ahab. Because of this I will cause your son, your grandson, and your great-grandson to be the kings of Israel."

31But Jehu didn't follow the Lord God of Israel with all his heart, for he continued to worship Jeroboam's gold calves that had been the cause of such great sin in Israel.

32, 33At about that time the Lord began to whittle down the size of Israel. King Hazael conquered several sections of the country east of the Jordan River, as well as all of Gilead, Gad, and Reuben; he also conquered parts of Manasseh from the Aroer River in the valley of the Arnon as far as Gilead and Bashan.

34The rest of Jehu's activities are recorded in *The Annals of the Kings of Israel*. 35When Jehu died, he was buried in Samaria; and his son Jehoahaz became the new king. 36In all, Jehu reigned as king of Israel, in Samaria, for twenty-eight years.

Athaliah rules Judah

11 When Athaliah, the mother of King Ahaziah of Judah, learned that her son was dead, she killed all of his children, 2, 3except for his year-old son Joash. Joash was rescued by his Aunt Jehosheba, who was a sister of King Ahaziah (for she was a daughter of King Jehoram, Ahaziah's father). She stole him away from among the rest of the king's children who were waiting to be slain, and hid him and his nurse in a storeroom of the Temple. They lived there for six years while Athaliah reigned as queen.

Young Joash becomes king

4In the seventh year of Queen Athaliah's reign, Jehoiada the priest summoned the officers of the palace guard and the queen's bodyguard. He met them in the Temple, swore them to secrecy, and showed them the king's son.

5Then he gave them their instructions: "A third of those who are on duty on the Sabbath are to guard the palace. 6, 7, 8The other two-thirds shall stand guard at the Temple; surround the king, weapons in hand, and kill anyone who tries to break through. Stay with the king at all times."

9So the officers followed Jehoiada's instructions. They brought to Jehoiada the men who were going off duty on the Sabbath and those who were coming on duty, 10and he armed them from the Temple's supply of spears and shields that had belonged to King David. 11The guards, with weapons ready, stood across the front

Margin references:
10:29 1 Kgs 12:28 13:33,34
10:30 2 Kgs 13:1 15:12
10:31 1 Kgs 12:28,29
10:32 Deut 2:36 2 Kgs 8:12 13:22; 14:25
10:34 2 Kgs 1:18; 13:8 2 Chron 20:34
10:35 2 Kgs 13:1
11:1 2 Kgs 8:26 2 Chron 22:10
11:4 2 Chron 23:1
11:10 2 Sam 8:7 1 Chron 18:7,8 2 Chron 23:9

11:2, 3 *except for his year-old son*, implied.   11:4 *the priest*, implied.

10:28–31 Why did Jehu destroy the idols of Baal but not the calf-idols in Dan and Bethel? Jehu's motives may have been more political than spiritual. (1) If Jehu had destroyed the calf-idols, his people would have traveled to the Temple in Jerusalem, in the rival Southern Kingdom, and worshiped there (which is why Jeroboam set them up in the first place, see 1 Kings 12:25–33). (2) Baal worship was associated with the dynasty of Ahab, so it was politically advantageous to destroy Baal. The golden calves, on the other hand, had a longer history in the Northern Kingdom and were valued by all political factions. (3) Baal worship was anti-God, but the golden calves were thought by many to be visible representations of God himself, even though God's Law stated clearly that such worship was idolatrous (Exodus 20:3–6). Like Jehu, it is easy to denounce the sins of others while tolerating sin in our own lives.

10:30, 31 Jehu did much of what the Lord told him to, but he did not obey him with all his heart. He had become God's *instrument* for carrying out justice, but he had not become God's *servant*. As a result, he gave only lip service to God while he worshiped the golden calves. Check the condition of your heart toward God. We

can be very active in our work for God and still not give the heartfelt obedience he desires.

10:34 King Jehu is mentioned on an ancient stone monument called the Black Obelisk, written by King Shalmaneser III of Assyria. Foreign rulers often recorded their military exploits on stone monuments for everyone to see and remember. Jehu is pictured on the obelisk as kneeling before Shalmaneser III in a gesture of humility. He paid tribute to the Assyrians near the beginning of his reign (841 B.C.) to avoid destruction. The Bible does not record Jehu's dealings with Assyria, a nation soon to become a world power.

11:1 This story is continued from 9:29, where Ahaziah, Athaliah's son, had been killed by Jehu. Athaliah's attempt to kill all of Ahaziah's sons was futile, because God had promised that the Messiah would be born through David's royal descendants (2 Samuel 7).

11:2, 3 Jehosheba was the wife of Jehoiada, the High Priest, so the Temple was both a practical and natural place to hide baby Joash. Athaliah, who loved idolatry, would have had no interest in the Temple.

of the sanctuary, and surrounded the altar, which was near Joash's hideaway.

12Then Jehoiada brought out the young prince and put the crown upon his head and gave him a copy of the Ten Commandments, and anointed him as king. Then everyone clapped and shouted, "Long live the king!

13, 14When Athaliah heard all the noise, she ran into the Temple and saw the new king standing beside the pillar, as was the custom at times of coronation, surrounded by her bodyguard and many trumpeters; and everyone was rejoicing and blowing trumpets.

"Treason! Treason!" she screamed, and began to tear her clothes.

15"Get her out of here," shouted Jehoiada to the officers of the guard. "Don't kill her here in the Temple. But kill anyone who tries to come to her rescue."

16So they dragged her to the palace stables and killed her there.

17Jehoiada made a treaty between the Lord, the king, and the people, that they would be the Lord's people. He also made a contract between the king and the people. 18Everyone went over to the temple of Baal and tore it down, breaking the altars and images and killing Mattan, the priest of Baal, in front of the altar. And Jehoiada set guards at the Temple of the Lord. 19Then he and the officers and the guard and all the people led the king from the Temple, past the guardhouse, and into the palace. And he sat upon the king's throne.

20So everyone was happy, and the city settled back into quietness after Athaliah's death. 21Joash was seven years old when he became king.

Joash rules Judah

12 It was seven years after Jehu had become the king of Israel that Joash became king of Judah. He reigned in Jerusalem for forty years. (His mother was Zibiah, from Beer-sheba.) 2All his life Joash did what was right because Jehoiada the High Priest instructed him. 3Yet even so he didn't destroy the shrines on the hills—the people still sacrificed and burned incense there.

4, 5One day King Joash said to Jehoiada, "The Temple building needs repairing. Whenever anyone brings a contribution to the Lord, whether it is a regular assessment or some special gift, use it to pay for whatever repairs are needed."

6But in the twenty-third year of his reign the Temple was still in disrepair. 7So Joash called for Jehoiada and the other priests and asked them, "Why haven't you done anything about the Temple? Now don't use any more money for your own needs; from now on it must all be spent on getting the Temple into good condition."

8So the priests agreed to set up a special repair fund that would not go through their hands, lest it be diverted to care for their personal needs. 9Jehoiada the priest bored a hole in the lid of a large chest and set it on the right-hand side of the altar at the Temple entrance. The doorkeepers put all of the people's contributions into it. 10Whenever the chest became full, the king's financial secretary and the High Priest counted it, put it into bags, 11, 12and gave it to the construction superinten-

11:12
Ex 31:18
1 Sam 10:24
2 Kgs 12:1

11:13
Gen 37:29
44:13
1 Kgs 1:39,40
2 Chron 23:12

11:17
Josh 24:25
2 Sam 5:3
2 Chron 15:12

11:18
Deut 12:2
1 Kgs 18:40
2 Kgs 10:24

11:21
2 Chron 24:1

12:1
1 Kgs 19:16
2 Chron 24:1

12:2
2 Kgs 14:3

12:3
1 Kgs 14:23
15:14
2 Kgs 14:4
15:34,35

12:4
Ex 35:5-9,22,29
2 Kgs 22:3-6
1 Chron 29:3

12:9
Mk 12:41
Lk 21:1

12:11
2 Kgs 22:5,6
2 Chron 24:11

11:17 The new contract was in fact a new constitution for the people. It was the one set up in the book of Deuteronomy for the righteous rule of the nation. Unfortunately, with Jehoiada's death, the reforms were discontinued.

12:2 God's input yields good output. Joash had a good teacher in Jehoiada, the High Priest. As long as he lived, Jehoiada's faith in God influenced Joash for good. Good intent must be fortified with good content. As long as Joash heeded Jehoida's good instruction, he fulfilled God's plan for his life. All our plans and actions must be guided by God, and his counsel is made clear to us in his Word. Our lives will be productive if we heed God's counsel.

12:2 Joash didn't go far enough in removing sin from the nation, but he did much that was good and right. When we aren't sure if we've gone far enough in correcting our actions, we can ask: (1) Does the Bible expressly prohibit this action? (2) Does this action take me away from loving, worshiping, or serving God?

(3) Does it make me its slave? (4) Is it bringing out the best in me, consistent with God's purpose? (5) Does it benefit other believers?

12:3 The Israelites could only offer sacrifices to God at designated areas, not just anywhere (Deuteronomy 12:13). Making sacrifices on the hilltops copied pagan customs and encouraged other pagan practices to enter into their worship. (For more information on these shrines in the hills see the note on 1 Kings 22:43.)

12:4, 5 The Temple needed repair because it had been damaged and neglected by previous evil leaders, especially Queen Athaliah (2 Chronicles 24:7, 8). The Temple was to be a holy place, set apart to worship God. Thanks to Joash's fund-raising program, it could be restored. The dirt and filth that had collected inside over the years were cleaned out; joints were remortared; heathen idols and other traces of idol worship were removed; and the gold and bronze were polished. The neglected condition of the Temple reveals how far the people had strayed from God.

dents to pay the carpenters, stonemasons, quarrymen, timber dealers, and stone merchants, and to buy the other materials needed to repair the Temple of the Lord. 13, 14It was not used to buy silver cups, gold snuffers, bowls, trumpets, or similar articles, but only for repairs to the building. 15No accounting was required from the construction superintendents, for they were honest and faithful men. 16However, the money that was contributed for guilt offerings and sin offerings was given to the priests for their own use. It was not put into the chest.

17About this time, King Hazael of Syria went to war against Gath and captured it; then he moved on toward Jerusalem to attack it. 18King Joash took all the sacred objects that his ancestors—Jehoshaphat, Jehoram, and Ahaziah, the kings of Judah—had dedicated, along with what he himself had dedicated, and all the gold in the treasuries of the Temple and the palace, and sent it to Hazael. So Hazael called off the attack.

19The rest of the history of Joash is recorded in *The Annals of the Kings of Judah*. 20But his officers plotted against him and assassinated him in his royal residence at Millo on the road to Silla. 21The assassins were Jozachar, the son of Shimeath, and Jehozabad, the son of Shomer—both trusted aides. He was buried in the royal cemetery in Jerusalem, and his son Amaziah became the new king.

Jehoahaz rules Israel

13 Jehoahaz (the son of Jehu) began a seventeen-year reign over Israel during the twenty-third year of the reign of King Joash of Judah. 2But he was an evil king, and he followed the wicked paths of Jeroboam, who had caused Israel to sin. 3So the Lord was very angry with Israel, and he continually allowed King Hazael of Syria and his son Ben-hadad to conquer them. 4But Jehoahaz prayed for the Lord's help, and the Lord listened to him; for the Lord saw how terribly the king of Syria was oppressing Israel. 5So the Lord raised up leaders among the Israelis to rescue them from the tyranny of the Syrians; and then Israel lived in safety again as they had in former days. 6But they continued to sin, following the evil ways of Jeroboam; and they continued to worship the goddess Asherah at Samaria. 7Finally the Lord reduced Jehoahaz's army to fifty mounted troops, ten chariots, and ten thousand infantry; for the king of Syria had destroyed the others as though they were dust beneath his feet.

8The rest of the history of Jehoahaz is recorded in *The Annals of the Kings of Israel*.

Joash rules Israel

9, 10Jehoahaz died and was buried in Samaria, and his son Joash reigned in

12:21 *both trusted aides*, literally, "his servants."

12:13
1 Kgs 7:48,50
12:15
2 Kgs 22:7

12:17
2 Kgs 8:12
10:32,33
12:18
1 Kgs 15:18
2 Kgs 16:8
18:15,16
12:19
2 Kgs 8:23
2 Chron 24:27
12:20
2 Sam 5:9
2 Chron 24:25
12:21
2 Kgs 13:12
2 Chron 25:1

13:1
2 Kgs 10:35
2 Chron 25:17
13:2
1 Kgs 12:28
2 Kgs 10:29
13:3
Judg 2:12-14
2 Kgs 8:8,9
10:32,33; 12:17
13:4
2 Kgs 14:26
2 Chron 33:12
13:5
Judg 2:18,19
Neh 9:27
13:6
2 Kgs 10:29
17:21
13:8
2 Kgs 10:34
13:12; 14:15

12:15 What a contrast between the building superintendents who needed no accounting of their use of the money, and the priests who couldn't be trusted to handle their funds well enough to set some aside for the Temple (12:8). As trained men of God, the Levites should have been responsible and concerned. After all, the Temple was their life's work. Though the priests were not dishonest, they did not have the commitment or energy needed to finish the work. Sometimes God's work is better accomplished by devoted lay people. Don't let your lack of training or position stop you from contributing to God's kingdom. Everyone's energy is needed to carry out God's work.

12:16 To read more about guilt and sin offerings, see Leviticus 4, 5; 6:24—7:10.

12:20 The reasons for the officers' plot against Joash are listed in 2 Chronicles 24:17–26. Joash had begun to worship idols, had killed the prophet Zechariah, and had been conquered by the Syrians. When Joash turned away from God, his life began to unravel. Joash's officers didn't kill him because he turned from God; they killed him because his kingdom was now out of control. In the end he became an evil man and was killed by evil people.

13:4–6 The Lord heard Jehoahaz's prayer for help. God delayed his judgment on Israel when they turned to him for help, but they did not sustain their dependence on God for long. Although there were periodic breaks in their idol worship, there was rarely evidence of genuine faith. It is not enough to say "no" to sin; we must also say "yes" to a life of commitment to God.

13:5 Syria, which lay to the north of Israel, was always an enemy of Israel. This was partly because Israel blocked most of Syria's trade from the south, and Syria cut off most of Israel's from the north. If one nation could conquer the other, all its trade routes would be open and its economy would flourish. Israel and Syria were so busy fighting each other that they didn't notice the rapidly growing strength of the Assyrians to the far north. Soon both nations would be surprised (16:9; 17:6).

13:9, 10 Joash (also called Jehoash) assumed the throne of Israel in 798 B.C. The king of Judah, also named Joash, was nearing the end of his reign. Two kings, both named Joash, one in the south and one in the north, reigned at approximately the same time. While Joash of Judah began as a good king, Joash of Israel was evil.

Samaria for sixteen years. He came to the throne in the thirty-seventh year of the reign of King Joash of Judah. 11But he was an evil man, for, like Jeroboam, he encouraged the people to worship idols and led them into sin. 12The rest of the history of the reign of Joash, including his wars against King Amaziah of Judah, are written in *The Annals of the Kings of Israel.* 13Joash died and was buried in Samaria with the other kings of Israel; and Jeroboam II became the new king.

14When Elisha was in his last illness, King Joash visited him and wept over him. "My father! My father! You are the strength of Israel!" he cried.

15Elisha told him, "Get a bow and some arrows," and he did.

16, 17"Open that eastern window," he instructed.

Then he told the king to put his hand upon the bow, and Elisha laid his own hands upon the king's hands.

"Shoot!" Elisha commanded, and he did.

Then Elisha proclaimed, "This is the Lord's arrow, full of victory over Syria; for you will completely conquer the Syrians at Aphek. 18Now pick up the other arrows and strike them against the floor."

So the king picked them up and struck the floor three times. 19But the prophet was angry with him. "You should have struck the floor five or six times," he exclaimed, "for then you would have beaten Syria until they were entirely destroyed; now you will be victorious only three times."

20, 21So Elisha died and was buried.

In those days bandit gangs of Moabites used to invade the land each spring. Once some men who were burying a friend spied these marauders so they hastily threw his body into the tomb of Elisha. And as soon as the body touched Elisha's bones, the dead man revived and jumped to his feet!

22King Hazael of Syria had oppressed Israel during the entire reign of King Jehoahaz. 23But the Lord was gracious to the people of Israel, and they were not totally destroyed. For God pitied them, and also he was honoring his contract with Abraham, Isaac, and Jacob. And this is still true. 24Then King Hazael of Syria died, and his son Ben-hadad reigned in his place.

25King Joash of Israel (the son of Jehoahaz) was successful on three occasions in reconquering the cities that his father had lost to Ben-hadad.

13:14 *you are the strength of Israel,* literally, "The chariots of Israel and its horsemen!" 13:25 *of Israel,* implied.

Cross-references:
13:11 1 Kgs 12:28; 2 Kgs 10:29; 13:2
13:12 2 Kgs 10:34; 14:8,15,28; 2 Chron 25:17
13:13 2 Kgs 14:24,27; Amos 7:10
13:14 2 Kgs 2:12
13:20 2 Kgs 3:7; 5:2; 24:2
13:22 2 Kgs 8:12; 13:3
13:23 Gen 13:16; 17:2-4; 2 Kgs 14:27
13:24 2 Kgs 8:8,9; 13:3
13:25 2 Kgs 10:32; 14:25

GOD OR IDOLS Why did people continually turn to idols instead of to God?	Idols were:	God is:
	Tangible	Intangible—no physical form
	Morally similar—had human characteristics	Morally dissimilar—had divine characteristics
	Comprehensible	Incomprehensible
	Able to be manipulated	Not able to be manipulated
	Worshiping idols involved:	*Worshiping God involved:*
	Materialism	Sacrifice
	Sexual immorality	Purity and commitment
	Doing whatever a person wanted	Doing what God wants
	Focusing on self	Focusing on others

13:14 Elisha was highly regarded for his prophetic powers and miracles on Israel's behalf. Joash feared Elisha's death because he ascribed the nation's well-being to Elisha rather than to God. Joash's fear reveals his lack of spiritual understanding. At least 43 years had passed since Elisha was last mentioned in Scripture (9:1), where he had anointed Jehu as king (841 B.C.). Joash's reign began in 798 B.C.

13:15-19 When Joash was told to strike the floor with the arrows, he did it only halfheartedly. As a result, Elisha told the king that his victory over Syria would not be complete. Receiving the full

benefits of God's plan for our lives requires full receptiveness of and obedience to God's commands. If we don't follow God's complete instructions, we should not be surprised if his full benefits and blessings are not present.

13:20, 21 Elisha was dead, but his good influence remained, even causing miracles. This demonstrated that Elisha was indeed a prophet of God. It also attested to God's power—no heathen idol ever raised anyone from the dead. This miracle served as one more reminder to Israel that it had rejected God's Word as given through Elisha.

Amaziah rules Judah

14:1
2 Kgs 13:9,10
14:17
2 Chron 25:1

14:3
1 Kgs 11:4; 15:3
2 Kgs 15:3

14:4
1 Kgs 14:23
15:14
2 Kgs 12:3
15:4,34,35
16:4

14:5
2 Kgs 12:20

14:6
Deut 24:16
2 Chron 25:4
Jer 31:30
Ezek 18:4,20

14:7
2 Sam 8:13
1 Chron 18:12
2 Chron 25:11
Isa 16:1

14:8
2 Chron 25:17

14:9
Judg 9:14,15

14 During the second year of the reign of King Joash of Israel, King Amaziah began his reign over Judah. ²Amaziah was twenty-five years old at the time, and he reigned in Jerusalem for twenty-nine years. (His mother was Jeho-addin, a native of Jerusalem.) ³He was a good king in the Lord's sight, though not quite like his ancestor David; but he was as good a king as his father Joash. ⁴However, he didn't destroy the shrines on the hills, so the people still sacrificed and burned incense there.

⁵As soon as he had a firm grip on the kingdom, he killed the men who had assassinated his father; ⁶but he didn't kill their children, for the Lord had commanded through the law of Moses that fathers shall not be killed for their children, nor children for the sins of their fathers: everyone must pay the penalty for his own sins. ⁷Once Amaziah killed ten thousand Edomites in Salt Valley; he also conquered Sela and changed its name to Jokthe-el, as it is called to this day.

⁸One day he sent a message to King Joash of Israel (the son of Jehoahaz and the grandson of Jehu), daring him to mobilize his army and come out and fight.

⁹But King Joash replied, "The thistle of Lebanon demanded of the mighty cedar tree, 'Give your daughter to be a wife for my son.' But just then a wild animal passed by and stepped on the thistle and trod it into the ground! ¹⁰You have destroyed Edom and are very proud about it; but my advice to you is, be content with your glory and stay home! Why provoke disaster for both yourself and Judah?"

KINGS TO DATE AND THEIR ENEMIES

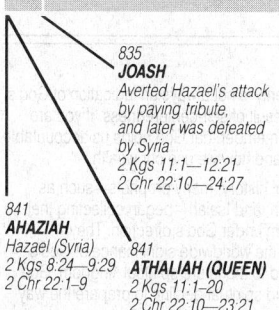

| 841 **JEHU** Lost a large portion of northern Israel to Hazael (Syria) 2 Kgs 9:1—10:36 2 Chr 22:7–12 | 814 **JEHOAHAZ** Continually defeated by Hazael (Syria) 2 Kgs 10:35; 13:1–9 | 798 **JEHOASH** 2 Kgs 13:10—14:16 2 Chr 25:17–24 Co-regency 793–782 | 793 **JEROBOAM II** Recaptured Israel's former territories from Syria and Aram, plundered Judah 2 Kgs 14:16–29 |

I S R A E L

J U D A H

| 835 **JOASH** Averted Hazael's attack by paying tribute, and later was defeated by Syria 2 Kgs 11:1—12:21 2 Chr 22:10—24:27 | 796 **AMAZIAH** Defeated by Jehoash and Jeroboam II (Israel) 2 Kgs 14:1–20 2 Chr 25:1–28 |

841 **AHAZIAH** Hazael (Syria) 2 Kgs 8:24–9:29 2 Chr 22:1–9

841 **ATHALIAH (QUEEN)** 2 Kgs 11:1–20 2 Chr 22:10—23:21

All dates are B.C.
Solid section of the timeline indicates co-regency.
For all the kings of Israel and Judah, see the chart between the books of 1 and 2 Kings.

14:7 Sela was the ancient stronghold of Petra, a city carved into a rock cliff. It was not only a stronghold for Edom, but also a wealthy outpost for trade with India.

14:9, 10 In this parable, Judah is compared to a small thistle. King Ahaziah of Judah had become proud after defeating the Edomites. Now he was trying to pick a fight with Israel because he

was sure his army was stronger. Joash tried to warn Ahaziah not to attack by comparing his army to a thistle and Israel's army to a cedar tree. Ahaziah had overrated his strength; his ambition was greater than his ability. He didn't listen to Joash and was soundly defeated.

¹¹But Amaziah refused to listen, so King Joash of Israel mustered his army. The battle began at Beth-shemesh, one of the cities of Judah, ¹²and Judah was defeated and the army fled home. ¹³King Amaziah was captured, and the army of Israel marched on Jerusalem and broke down its wall from the Gate of Ephraim to the Corner Gate, a distance of about six hundred feet. ¹⁴King Joash took many hostages and all the gold and silver from the Temple and palace treasury, also the gold cups. Then he returned to Samaria.

¹⁵The rest of the history of Joash and his war with King Amaziah of Judah are recorded in *The Annals of the Kings of Israel*. ¹⁶When Joash died, he was buried in Samaria with the other kings of Israel. And his son Jeroboam became the new king.

¹⁷Amaziah lived fifteen years longer than Joash, ¹⁸and the rest of his biography is recorded in *The Annals of the Kings of Judah*. ¹⁹There was a plot against his life in Jerusalem, and he fled to Lachish; but his enemies sent assassins and killed him there. ²⁰His body was returned on horses, and he was buried in the royal cemetery, in the City of David section of Jerusalem.

²¹Then his son Azariah became the new king at the age of sixteen. ²²After his father's death he built Elath and restored it to Judah.

Jeroboam II rules Israel

²³Meanwhile, over in Israel, Jeroboam II had become king during the fifteenth year of the reign of King Amaziah of Judah. Jeroboam's reign lasted forty-one years. ²⁴But he was as evil as Jeroboam I (the son of Nebat), who had led Israel into the sin of worshiping idols. ²⁵Jeroboam II recovered the lost territories of Israel between Hamath and the Dead Sea, just as the Lord God of Israel had predicted through Jonah (son of Amittai) the prophet from Gathhepher. ²⁶For the Lord saw the bitter plight of Israel—she had no one to help her. ²⁷And he had not said that he would blot out the name of Israel, so he used King Jeroboam II to save her.

²⁸The rest of Jeroboam's biography—all that he did, and his great power, and his wars, and how he recovered Damascus and Hamath (which had been captured by Judah)—is recorded in *The Annals of the Kings of Israel*. ²⁹When Jeroboam II died he was buried with the other kings of Israel, and his son Zechariah became the new king of Israel.

Azariah rules Judah

15 New king of Judah: Azariah
Name of his father: Amaziah, the former king
Name of his mother: Jecoliah of Jerusalem

14:11
Josh 19:35-39
1 Sam 6:9
14:13
2 Chron 25:23
Neh 8:16; 12:39
14:15
2 Chron 25:26
14:16
2 Kgs 10:35
14:17
2 Chron 25:25
14:18
2 Kgs 12:19
14:19
2 Kgs 12:20
14:20
2 Kgs 8:24,25
14:21
1 Chron 3:10-14
2 Chron 26:1
Mt 1:9
14:22
2 Kgs 16:6
14:23
2 Kgs 13:13
Hos 1:1
Amos 1:2
14:24
1 Kgs 12:28
2 Kgs 13:2,6
14:25
2 Kgs 13:25
Jonah 1:1
14:26
2 Kgs 13:4
14:27
2 Kgs 13:5,23
14:28
2 Kgs 14:15
15:1
2 Kgs 14:21
15:13,17

14:13 For a city wall to be broken down disgraced the citizens and left them defenseless against future invasions.

14:25 For more information about the prophet Jonah, see the book of Jonah.

14:27 Israel was an evil and immoral nation, and its sins would get even worse. God was not saying that he would never destroy Israel. Instead, he was warning that judgment was certain if Israel didn't turn back to him. In his mercy, however, he gave Israel yet another chance to turn from its evil ways. But the next five kings of Israel didn't respond to God's mercy. They were so evil that God allowed the nation to be destroyed by Assyria.

14:28 Jeroboam had no devotion to God, yet under his warlike policies and skillful administration Israel enjoyed more national power and material prosperity than at any time since the days of Solomon. The prophets Amos and Hosea, however, tell us what was really happening within the kingdom (Hosea 13:4-8; Amos 6:11-13). Jeroboam's administration ignored policies of justice and fairness. As a result, the rich became richer and the poor, poorer. The people became self-centered, relying more on their power, security, and possessions than on God. The poor were so oppressed that it was hard for them to believe that God noticed

their plight. Material prosperity is not always an indication of God's blessing. It can also be a result of self-centeredness. If you are experiencing prosperity, remember that God holds us accountable for how we attain success and how we use our wealth.

14:29 During this period of history, many prophets—such as Hosea, Amos, Jonah, Micah, and Isaiah—began collecting their prophecies and writing them under God's direction. They continued to preach about the worldwide significance of God's work as they looked forward to the future spiritual kingdom. God would use Israel's moral and spiritual decline to prepare the way for the Messiah's coming.

15:1 Azariah was also known as King Uzziah. His story is given in greater detail in 2 Chronicles 26. He is also mentioned in Isaiah 1:1 and 6:1. Before the beginning of Azariah's reign, Israel broke down 200 yards of Jerusalem's walls after defeating Judah and carrying off their king, Amaziah (2 Chronicles 25:23, 24). But during Azariah's 52-year reign, Judah rebuilt the wall, refortified the city with anti-siege weapons, and gained independence from Israel. Azariah's devotion to God helped Judah enjoy peace and prosperity such as it had not experienced since the days of Solomon. During this time, however, Israel declined drastically. It would soon be overthrown.

Length of his reign: 52 years, in Jerusalem
His age at the beginning of his reign: 16 years old
Reigning in Israel at this time: King Jeroboam, who had been the king there for
    27 years.

15:3
2 Kgs 14:3

15:4
Lev 13:46
2 Kgs 12:3; 14:3
2 Chron 26:21

3Azariah was a good king, and he pleased the Lord just as his father Amaziah
had. 4But like his predecessors, he didn't destroy the shrines on the hills where the
people sacrificed and burned incense. 5Because of this the Lord struck him with
leprosy, which lasted until the day of his death; so he lived in a house by himself.

15:6
2 Kgs 14:18
15:36

15:7
2 Kgs 14:20
15:32,33

And his son Jotham was the acting king. 6The rest of the history of Azariah is
recorded in *The Annals of the Kings of Judah*. 7When Azariah died, he was buried
with his ancestors in the City of David, and his son Jotham became king.

Zechariah rules Israel

15:8
2 Kgs 14:29

8New king of Israel: Zechariah
Name of his father: Jeroboam
Length of reign: 6 months
Reigning in Judah at that time: King Azariah, who had been the king there for
    38 years

15:9
2 Kgs 10:29
13:2; 14:24

15:10
Amos 7:9

15:11
2 Kgs 14:28
15:15,21

15:12
2 Kgs 10:30

9But Zechariah was an evil king in the Lord's sight, just like his ancestors. Like
Jeroboam I (the son of Nebat), he encouraged Israel in the sin of worshiping idols.
10Then Shallum (the son of Jabesh) conspired against him and assassinated him at
Ibleam and took the crown himself. 11The rest of the history of Zechariah's reign is
found in *The Annals of the Kings of Israel*. 12(So the Lord's statement to Jehu came
true, that Jehu's son, grandson, and great-grandson would be kings of Israel.)

Shallum rules Israel

15:13
2 Kgs 15:1

13New king of Israel: Shallum
Father's name: Jabesh
Length of reign: 1 month
Reigning in Judah at that time: King Uzziah, who had been the king there for 39
years

15:15
2 Kgs 15:11,21

14One month after Shallum became king, Menahem (the son of Gadi) came to
Samaria from Tirzah and assassinated him and took the throne. 15Additional details
about King Shallum and his conspiracy are recorded in *The Annals of the Kings of
Israel*.

15:16
2 Kgs 8:12

16Menahem destroyed the city of Tappuah and the surrounding countryside, for
its citizens refused to accept him as their king; he killed the entire population and
ripped open the pregnant women.

15:5 *Because of this*, implied. **15:12** *would be kings of Israel*, see 10:30. **15:15** *Shallum and his conspiracy*, see
vs 10.

15:4 Although Azariah accomplished a great deal, he failed to
destroy the heathen shrines in Judah, just as his father Amaziah
and grandfather Joash had failed to do. Azariah imitated the kings
he had heard stories about and watched while growing up.
Although Azariah's father and grandfather were basically good
kings, they were poor models in some important areas. To rise
above the influence of poor models, we must seek better ones.
Christ provides a perfect model. No matter how you were raised or
who influenced your life, you can move beyond those limitations by
taking Christ as your example and consciously trying to live as he
did.

15:5 For ten years Jotham was the co-ruler with his father,
Azariah. A father and a son ruled together for any of the following
reasons: (1) the father was very old and needed help; (2) the
father wanted to train his son in leading the nation; (3) the father
was sick or exiled. There were many co-regents during the period
of the kings—Asa/Jehoshaphat; Jehoshaphat/Jehoram;

Azariah/Jotham; Jehoash/Jeroboam II; Hezekiah/Manasseh.

15:9 Zechariah was an evil king because he encouraged Israel to
sin by worshiping idols. Sin in our own lives is serious, but even
more terrible than sinning ourselves is encouraging others to
disobey God. We are responsible for the way we influence others.
Beware of double sins: ones that not only hurt us, but also hurt
others by encouraging them to sin.

15:10 Zechariah was warned of his impending death and the
subsequent end of Jeroboam's dynasty by the prophet Amos
(Amos 7:9).

15:14 Ancient historical documents say that Menahem was the
commander-in-chief of Jeroboam II's army (see 14:23–29 for an
account of Jeroboam II's reign). After Jeroboam's son was
assassinated (15:8–10), Menahem probably saw himself, and not
Shallum, as the rightful successor to Israel's throne.

Menahem rules Israel

17Name of new king of Israel: Menahem
Length of reign: 10 years, in Samaria
Concurrent with: King Azariah of Judah who had been the king there for 39
  years

18But Menahem was an evil king. He worshiped idols, as King Jeroboam I had
done so long before, and he led the people of Israel into grievous sin. 19, 20Then
King Pul of Assyria invaded the land; but King Menahem bought him off with a gift
of $2,000,000, so he turned around and returned home. Menahem extorted the
money from the rich, assessing each one $2,000 in the form of a special tax. 21The
rest of the history of King Menahem is written in *The Annals of the Kings of Israel*.
22When he died, his son Pekahiah became the new king.

15:18
2 Kgs 14:24

Pekahiah rules Israel

23Name of new king of Israel: Pekahiah
Father's name: King Menahem
Length of reign: 2 years, in Samaria
Concurrent with: King Azariah of Judah, who had been the king there for 50
  years

24But Pekahiah was an evil king, and he continued the idol-worship begun by
Jeroboam I (son of Nebat) who led Israel down that evil trail.
25Then Pekah (son of Remaliah), the commanding general of his army, conspired against him with fifty men from Gilead, and assassinated him in the palace
at Samaria (Argob and Arieh were also slain in the revolt). So Pekah became the
new king. 26The rest of the history of King Pekahiah is recorded in *The Annals of
the Kings of Israel*.

Pekah rules Israel

27New king of Israel: Pekah
Father's name: Remaliah
Length of reign: 20 years, in Samaria
Concurrent with: King Azariah of Judah, who had been the king there for 52
  years

15:27
2 Kgs 15:32
16:5

28Pekah, too, was an evil king, and he continued in the example of Jeroboam I
(son of Nebat), who led all of Israel into the sin of worshiping idols. 29It was during
his reign that King Tiglathpileser led an attack against Israel. He captured the cities
of Ijon, Abel-beth-maacah, Janoah, Kedesh, Hazor, Gilead, Galilee, and all the
land of Naphtali; and he took the people away to Assyria as captives. 30Then
Hoshea (the son of Elah) plotted against Pekah and assassinated him; and he took
the throne for himself.

15:29
2 Kgs 17:6

15:30
2 Kgs 17:4; 18:1

New king of Israel: Hoshea
Concurrent with: Jotham (son of Uzziah) king of Judah, who had been the king
  there for 20 years

15:18 Menahem, like the kings before him, led his people into sin.
What a horrible epitaph for a leader! Leaders profoundly affect the
people they serve. They can either encourage or discourage
devotion to God both by their examples and by the structures they
give their organizations. Good leaders put up no obstacles to faith
in God or to right living.

15:19, 20 When King Pul of Assyria (also called Tiglath-pileser III
in 15:29) took the throne, the Assyrian empire was becoming a

world power, and the nations of Syria, Israel, and Judah were in
decline. This is the first mention of Assyria in 2 Kings. King Pul's
invasion occurred in 743 B.C. Assyria made Israel a vassal, and
Menahem was forced to pay tribute to Assyria. This was the first of
three Assyrian invasions (15:29 and 17:6 tell of the other ones).

15:27 A year after Pekah became king, King Uzziah of Judah
died and Isaiah the prophet had a vision of Israel's future
destruction. See Isaiah 6 for more details on what Isaiah saw.

15:30 Hoshea was Israel's last king.

15:32
2 Kgs 15:7,27
2 Chron 27:1
Mt 1:9

15:34
2 Kgs 12:2,3
14:4; 15:4
2 Chron 26:4
27:1,2

15:36
2 Kgs 15:6
16:19; 20:20

15:37
2 Kgs 16:5
Isa 7:1

15:38
2 Kgs 14:20
15:7; 16:20

16:1
2 Chron 28:1
Mt 1:9

16:2
2 Kgs 14:3

16:3
Lev 18:21
Deut 12:31
2 Kgs 3:27
17:17; 21:6

16:4
Deut 12:2; 14:4

16:5
2 Kgs 15:37
2 Chron 28:5
Isa 7:1

16:6
2 Kgs 14:22
2 Chron 26:2

16:7
2 Kgs 15:29
2 Chron 28:20

16:8
2 Kgs 12:18
18:15

16:9
Isa 7:15,16
Amos 1:3-5

31The rest of the history of Pekah's reign is recorded in *The Annals of the Kings of Israel.*

Jotham rules Judah

32, 33New king of Judah: Jotham
Father's name: King Uzziah
His age when he became king: 25 years old
Duration of his reign: 16 years, in Jerusalem
Mother's name: Jerusha (daughter of Zadok)
Reigning in Israel at this time: Pekah (son of Remaliah), who had been the king there for 2 years

34, 35Generally speaking, Jotham was a good king. Like his father Uzziah, he followed the Lord. But he didn't destroy the shrines on the hills where the people sacrificed and burned incense. It was during King Jotham's reign that the upper gate of the Temple of the Lord was built. 36The rest of Jotham's history is written in *The Annals of the Kings of Judah.* 37In those days the Lord caused King Rezin of Syria and King Pekah of Israel to attack Judah. 38When Jotham died he was buried with the other kings of Judah in the royal cemetery, in the City of David section of Jerusalem. Then his son Ahaz became the new king.

Ahaz rules Judah

16 New king of Judah: Ahaz
Father's name: Jotham
Age: 20 years old
Duration of reign: 16 years, in Jerusalem
Character of his reign: evil
Reigning in Israel at this time: King Pekah (son of Remaliah) who had been the king there for 17 years

2But he did not follow the Lord as his ancestor David had; 3he was as wicked as the kings of Israel. He even killed his own son by offering him as a burnt sacrifice to the gods, following the heathen customs of the nations around Judah—nations which the Lord destroyed when the people of Israel entered the land. 4He also sacrificed and burned incense at the shrines on the hills and at the numerous altars in the groves of trees.

5Then King Rezin of Syria and King Pekah (son of Remaliah) of Israel declared war on Ahaz and besieged Jerusalem; but they did not conquer it. 6However, at that time King Rezin of Syria recovered the city of Elath for Syria; he drove out the Jews and sent Syrians to live there, as they do to this day. 7King Ahaz sent a messenger to King Tiglath-pileser of Assyria, begging him to help him fight the attacking armies of Syria and Israel. 8Ahaz took the silver and gold from the Temple and from the royal vaults and sent it as a payment to the Assyrian king. 9So the Assyrians attacked Damascus, the capital of Syria. They took away the population of the city as captives, resettling them in Kir, and King Rezin of Syria was killed.

16:7 *begging him to . . . fight . . . Syria and Israel,* literally, "saying, 'I am your servant and your son. Come and rescue me.' "

15:34, 35 "Jotham was a good king . . . *but.* " Much good can be said of Jotham and his reign as king of Judah, but he failed in a most critical area: he didn't destroy the shrines to the false gods, although leaving them clearly violated the first commandment (Exodus 20:3). Like Jotham, we may live basically good lives and yet miss doing what is most important. A lifetime of doing good is not enough if we make the crucial mistake of not following God with all our hearts. A true follower of God puts him first.

16:5 Israel and Syria joined forces against Judah because they were under Assyria's control and wanted to rebel. By besieging Jerusalem, Israel and Syria hoped to force Judah to join their revolt, strengthening their western alliance against Assyria. But the plan backfired when King Ahaz of Judah unexpectedly asked Assyria to come to his aid (16:8, 9).

10King Ahaz now went to Damascus to meet with King Tiglath-pileser, and while he was there he noticed an unusual altar in a heathen temple. He jotted down its dimensions and made a sketch and sent it back to Uriah the priest with a detailed description. 11, 12Uriah built one just like it by following these directions and had it ready for the king, who, upon his return from Damascus, inaugurated it with an offering. 13The king presented a burnt offering and a grain offering, poured a drink offering over it, and sprinkled the blood of peace offerings upon it. 14Then he removed the old bronze altar from the front of the Temple (it had stood between the Temple entrance and the new altar), and placed it on the north side of the new altar. 15He instructed Uriah the priest to use the new altar for the sacrifices of burnt offering, the evening grain offering, the king's burnt offering and grain offering, and the offerings of the people, including their drink offerings. The blood from the burnt offerings and sacrifices was also to be sprinkled over the new altar. So the old altar was used only for purposes of divination.

"The old bronze altar," he said, "will be only for my personal use."

16Uriah the priest did as King Ahaz instructed him. 17Then the king dismantled the wheeled stands in the Temple, removed their crosspieces and the water vats they supported, and removed the great tank from the backs of the bronze oxen and placed it upon the stone pavement. 18In deference to the king of Assyria he also removed the festive passageway he had constructed between the palace and the Temple.

19The rest of the history of the reign of King Ahaz is recorded in *The Annals of the Kings of Judah.* 20When Ahaz died he was buried in the royal cemetery, in the City of David sector of Jerusalem, and his son Hezekiah became the new king.

16:10	2 Chron 28:23
	Isa 8:2
16:14	Ex 40:6
	1 Kgs 8:22,23
16:15	Lev 4:14
	Num 28:1,2
16:17	1 Kgs 7:23
16:19	2 Kgs 15:36
	20:20
16:20	2 Kgs 18:1
	2 Chron 28:27
	29:1

3. Israel is exiled to Assyria

Hoshea rules Israel

17 New king of Israel: Hoshea
Father's name: Elah

Length of his reign: 9 years, in Samaria
Character of his reign: evil—but not as bad as some of the other kings of
Israel
Reigning in Judah at this time: King Ahaz, who had been the king there for 12
years
3King Shalmaneser of Assyria attacked and defeated King Hoshea, so Israel had

17:1 2 Kgs 15:30

17:3 2 Kgs 18:9

16:10 *an unusual altar in a heathen temple,* literally, "he saw the altar that was at Damascus." **16:18** The Hebrew is unclear.

16:10 Ahaz went to Damascus to pay tribute money to King Tiglath-pileser. Because the Assyrians had captured Damascus, the capital of Syria (732 B.C.), Ahaz was afraid of a southern sweep. But he was relying more on money than on God to keep the powerful king out of his land, and his plan failed. Although Tiglath-pileser did not conquer Judah, he caused much trouble and Ahaz regretted asking for his help (2 Chronicles 28:20, 21).

16:10–15 Evil King Ahaz copied heathen religious customs, changed the Temple services, and used the Temple altar for his personal benefit. In so doing, he demonstrated a callous disregard for God's commands. We condemn Ahaz for his action, but we do the same thing if we try to mold God's message to fit our personal preferences. We must worship God for who he is, not what we would selfishly like him to be.

16:16–18 Ahaz replaced the Altar of Burnt Offering with a replica of the pagan altar he saw in Damascus. This was extremely serious because God had given specific directions on how the altar should

look and be used (Exodus 27:1–8). Building this new altar was like installing an idol. But because Judah was Assyria's vassal, Ahaz may have been eager to please the Assyrian king. Sadly, Ahaz allowed the king of Assyria to replace God as Judah's leader. No one, no matter how attractive or powerful, should replace God's leadership in our lives.

16:18 Ahaz had become a weak king with a weak and compromising High Priest. Judah's religious system was in shambles. It was now built on heathen customs, and its chief aim was only to please those in power. If we are too quick to copy others in order to please them, we risk making them more important than God in our lives.

17:3 King Shalmaneser was probably Shalmaneser V who became king of Assyria after Tiglath-pileser (727–722 B.C.). He continued to demand heavy tribute from Israel. Israel's King Hoshea decided to rebel against Assyria and join forces with King So of Egypt (17:4). This was not only foolish, but against God's commands. To destroy this conspiracy, Shalmaneser attacked and

17:4
2 Kgs 18:20,21

to pay heavy annual taxes to Assyria. ⁴Then Hoshea conspired against the king of Assyria by asking King So of Egypt to help him shake free of Assyria's power, but this treachery was discovered. At the same time he refused to pay the annual tribute to Assyria. So the king of Assyria put him in prison and in chains for his rebellion. ⁵Now the land of Israel was filled with Assyrian troops for three years besieging

KINGS TO DATE AND THEIR ENEMIES

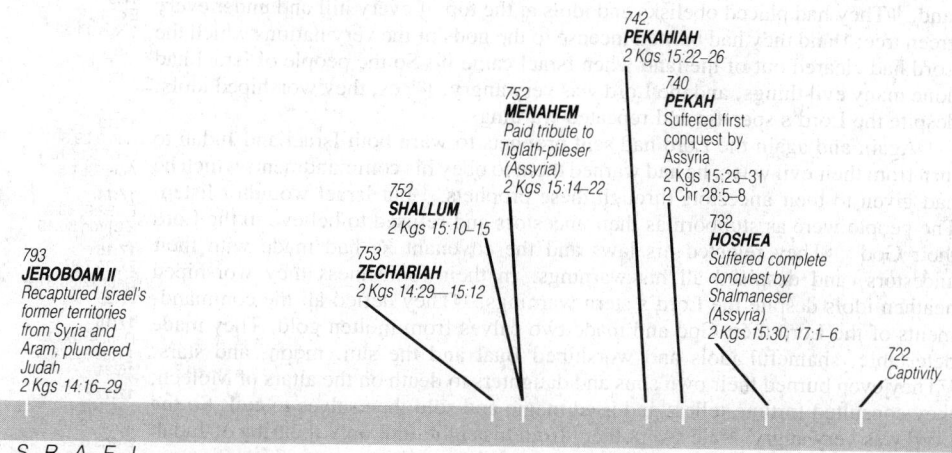

742
PEKAHIAH
2 Kgs 15:22–26

740
PEKAH
Suffered first conquest by Assyria
2 Kgs 15:25–31
2 Chr 28:5–8

752
MENAHEM
Paid tribute to Tiglath-pileser (Assyria)
2 Kgs 15:14–22

752
SHALLUM
2 Kgs 15:10–15

732
HOSHEA
Suffered complete conquest by Shalmaneser (Assyria)
2 Kgs 15:30; 17:1–6

753
ZECHARIAH
2 Kgs 14:29—15:12

793
JEROBOAM II
Recaptured Israel's former territories from Syria and Aram, plundered Judah
2 Kgs 14:16–29

722
Captivity

ISRAEL

JUDAH

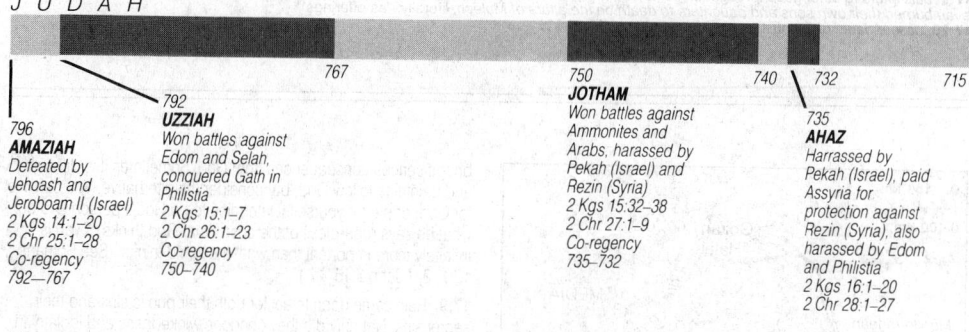

796
AMAZIAH
Defeated by Jehoash and Jeroboam II (Israel)
2 Kgs 14:1–20
2 Chr 25:1–28
Co-regency
792–767

792
UZZIAH
Won battles against Edom and Selah, conquered Gath in Philistia
2 Kgs 15:1–7
2 Chr 26:1–23
Co-regency
750–740

767

750
JOTHAM
Won battles against Ammonites and Arabs, harassed by Pekah (Israel) and Rezin (Syria)
2 Kgs 15:32–38
2 Chr 27:1–9
Co-regency
735–732

740

732

735
AHAZ
Harrassed by Pekah (Israel), paid Assyria for protection against Rezin (Syria), also harassed by Edom and Philistia
2 Kgs 16:1–20
2 Chr 28:1–27

715

All dates are B.C.
Solid section of the timeline indicates co-regency.
For all the kings of Israel and Judah, see the chart between the books of 1 and 2 Kings.

besieged Samaria for three years. But just before Samaria fell, Shalmaneser died. His successor, Sargon II, took credit for capturing the city, destroying the nation of Israel, and carrying away its people.

17:5, 6 This was the third and final invasion of Assyria into Israel. (The first two invasions are recorded in 15:19 and 15:29.) The first wave was merely a warning to Israel—to avoid further attack, pay money and don't rebel. The people should have learned their lesson and returned to God. When they didn't, God allowed Assyria to invade again, this time carrying off some captives from

the northern border. But the people still did not realize that they had caused their own troubles. Thus Assyria invaded for the third and final time, destroying Israel completely, carrying away most of the people, and resettling the land with foreigners.

God was doing what he had said he would do (Deuteronomy 28). He had given Israel ample warning; they knew what would come, but they still ignored God. Israel was now no better than the heathen nations it had destroyed in the days of Joshua. The nation had turned sour and rejected its original purpose—to honor God and be a light to the world.

Samaria, the capital city of Israel. 6Finally, in the ninth year of King Hoshea's reign, Samaria fell and the people of Israel were exiled to Assyria. They were placed in colonies in the city of Halah and along the banks of the Habor River in Gozan, and among the cities of the Medes.

17:6
Deut 28:64
29:28
2 Kgs 18:11
1 Chron 5:26
Hos 13:16

Israel exiled for rejecting God

7This disaster came upon the nation of Israel because the people worshiped other gods, thus sinning against the Lord their God who had brought them safely out of their slavery in Egypt. 8They had followed the evil customs of the nations which the Lord had cast out from before them. 9The people of Israel had also secretly done many things that were wrong, and they had built altars to other gods throughout the land. 10They had placed obelisks and idols at the top of every hill and under every green tree; 11and they had burned incense to the gods of the very nations which the Lord had cleared out of the land when Israel came in. So the people of Israel had done many evil things, and the Lord was very angry. 12Yes, they worshiped idols, despite the Lord's specific and repeated warnings.

17:7
Josh 23:15,16

17:8
Lev 18:3
Deut 18:9
Judg 6:10

17:9
Ex 34:12
1 Kgs 14:23

13Again and again the Lord had sent prophets to warn both Israel and Judah to turn from their evil ways; he had warned them to obey his commandments which he had given to their ancestors through these prophets, 14but Israel wouldn't listen. The people were as stubborn as their ancestors and refused to believe in the Lord their God. 15They rejected his laws and the covenant he had made with their ancestors, and despised all his warnings. In their foolishness they worshiped heathen idols despite the Lord's stern warnings. 16They defied all the commandments of the Lord their God and made two calves from molten gold. They made detestable, shameful idols and worshiped Baal and the sun, moon, and stars. 17They even burned their own sons and daughters to death on the altars of Molech; they consulted fortune-tellers and used magic and sold themselves to evil. So the Lord was very angry. 18He swept them from his sight until only the tribe of Judah remained in the land.

17:13
Neh 9:29,30
Jer 7:5,6; 18:11
Acts 7:51,52

17:14
Ex 32:9; 33:3
2 Chron 36:15

17:15
Ex 24:7,8
Deut 12:30,31
29:25

17:16
Deut 4:16,17
1 Kgs 12:28
16:31

17:17
Lev 19:26
Deut 18:10
2 Kgs 3:27
16:3; 21:6

17:9 *built altars to other gods throughout the land,* literally, "built them high places in all their cities." **17:17** *They even burned their own sons and daughters to death on the altars of Molech,* literally, "as offerings." **17:20** *descendants of Jacob,* literally, "descendants of Israel."

ISRAEL TAKEN CAPTIVE Finally the sins of Israel's people caught up with them. God allowed Assyria to defeat and disperse the people. They were led into captivity, swallowed up by the mighty, evil Assyrian empire. Sin always brings discipline, and the consequences of that sin are sometimes irreversible.

17:7–9 The Lord judged the people of Israel because they copied the evil customs of the surrounding nations, worshiping false gods, accommodating pagan customs, and following their own desires. It [is not] safe to copy the world's customs because godless people [who] live selfishly. And to live for yourself, as Israel learned,

brings serious consequences from God. Sometimes it is difficult and painful to follow God, but consider the alternative. You can live for God, or die for yourself. Determine to be God's person and do what he says regardless of the cost. What God thinks of you is infinitely more important than what the world thinks. (See Romans 12:1, 2; 1 John 2:15–17.)

17:9 Ruin came upon Israel for both their public sins and their secret sins. Not only did they condone wickedness and idolatry in public, but they committed even worse sins in private. Secret sins are often the worst. They are the ones we don't want others to know about, because they are embarrassing or incriminating. Sins done in private are not secret to God, and they have the same terrible results as sins committed in the open.

17:13–15 Israel had forgotten the importance and the benefits of obedience to God's Word. The king and the people were mired in wickedness. Time and again God sent prophets to warn them of how far they had turned away from him and to call them to repentance.

God's patience and mercy are beyond our ability to understand. He will pursue us until we either respond to him or, by our own choice and hardness of heart, make ourselves unreachable. Then God's judgment is swift and sure. The only safe course is to turn to God before our stubbornness puts us out of his reach.

17:17 Witchcraft, fortune-telling, and black magic were expressly forbidden by God (Deuteronomy 18:9–14). Isaiah echoed this law and prophesied of the complete destruction these occult practices would bring to those who participated in them (Isaiah 8:19–22).

17:19
1 Kgs 14:24

17:20
Jer 6:30
Rom 11:1-3

17:21
1 Kgs 11:11,31
12:20
2 Chron
10:16-19
Isa 7:17

17:23
2 Kgs 18:11,12

[19]But even Judah refused to obey the commandments of the Lord their God; they too walked in the same evil paths as Israel had. [20]So the Lord rejected all the descendants of Jacob. He punished them by delivering them to their attackers until they were destroyed. [21]For Israel split off from the kingdom of David and chose Jeroboam I (the son of Nebat) as its king. Then Jeroboam drew Israel away from following the Lord. He made them sin a great sin, [22]and the people of Israel never quit doing the evil things that Jeroboam led them into, [23]until the Lord finally swept them away, just as all his prophets had warned would happen. So Israel was carried off to the land of Assyria where they remain to this day.

Foreigners repopulate Israel

17:24
2 Kgs 18:34

[24]And the king of Assyria transported colonies of people from Babylon, Cuthah, Avva, Hamath, and Sepharvaim and resettled them in the cities of Samaria, replacing the people of Israel. So the Assyrians took over Samaria and the other cities of Israel. [25]But since these Assyrian colonists did not worship the Lord when they first arrived, the Lord sent lions among them to kill some of them.

17:25
1 Kgs 13:24,25
20:36

[26]Then they sent a message to the king of Assyria: "We colonists here in Israel don't know the laws of the god of the land, and he has sent lions among us to destroy us because we have not worshiped him."

[27, 28]The king of Assyria then decreed that one of the exiled priests from Samaria should return to Israel and teach the new residents the laws of the god of the land. So one of them returned to Bethel and taught the colonists from Babylon how to worship the Lord.

17:29
1 Kgs 12:31
13:32

[29]But these foreigners also worshiped their own gods. They placed them in the shrines on the hills near their cities. [30]Those from Babylon worshiped idols of their god Succoth-benoth; those from Cuth worshiped their god Nergal; and the men of Hamath worshiped Ashima. [31]The gods Nibhaz and Tartak were worshiped by the Avvites, and the people from Sephar even burned their own children on the altars of their gods Adrammelech and Anammelech.

17:31
2 Kgs 19:37

17:32
1 Kgs 12:31
13:33

17:34
Gen 32:28
35:10

[32]They also worshiped the Lord, and they appointed from among themselves priests to sacrifice to the Lord on the hilltop altars. [33]But they continued to follow the religious customs of the nations from which they came. [34]And this is still going on among them today—they follow their former practices instead of truly worshiping

---

17:23 Israel was swept away "just as all his *God's* prophets had warned would happen." This short phrase carries profound meaning. Whatever God predicts will come to pass. This, of course, is good news to those who trust and obey him—they can be confident of his promises; but it is bad news to those who ignore or disobey God. Both the promises and warnings God has given in his Word will surely come true.

17:24 Moving the Israelites out and moving foreigners in was Assyria's resettlement policy to prevent revolt. Spreading the captives across Assyria prevented their uniting, and repopulating Israel with foreign captives made it difficult for the remaining Israelites to unite as well. This mixture of peoples resettled in Israel came to be known as "Samaritans." They were despised by the Jews, and they were still looked down upon during the time of Christ (Luke 10:25–37).

17:27–29 The new settlers in Israel worshiped God without giving up their pagan customs. They worshiped God to appease him rather than to please him, treating him as a good luck charm or just another idol to add to their collection. A similar attitude is common today. Many people claim to believe in God while refusing to give up attitudes and actions that God denounces. God cannot be added to the values we already have. He must come first, and his Word must shape all our actions and attitudes.

17:29–31 Israel was conquered because it had lost sight of the only true God and why it was important to follow him. When

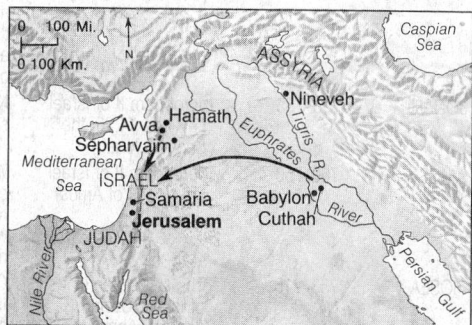

ISRAEL RESETTLED BY FOREIGNERS After the Israelites were deported, foreigners from the Assyrian Empire were sent to resettle the land. This policy helped Assyria keep peace in conquered territories.

conquering the land, they were told to destroy the pagan influences that could lead them away from God. Their failure to do so brought about their ruin. Now they faced an even greater influx of gods from the many heathen peoples moving into the land.

the Lord or obeying the laws he gave to the descendants of Jacob (whose name was later changed to Israel). 35, 36For the Lord had made a contract with them—that they were never to worship or make sacrifices to any heathen gods. They were to worship only the Lord who had brought them out of the land of Egypt with such tremendous miracles and power. 37The descendants of Jacob were to obey all of God's laws and *never* worship other gods.

17:35
Ex 19:5; 24:7
Judg 6:10

17:37
Deut 5:32

WHO WERE

Who?	When? (B.C.)	Ministered during the reign of these kings:	Main message	Significance
AHIJAH	934–909	Jeroboam of Israel (1 Kings 11:29–39)	Said Israel would split in two and stated that God had chosen Jeroboam to lead the ten tribes. Warned that he should remain obedient to God.	We should not take lightly our God-given responsibilities. Jeroboam did, and lost his kingdom.
ELIJAH	875–848	Ahab of Israel (1 Kings 17:1— 2 Kings 2)	In fiery style, urged wicked Ahab to turn back to God. On Mount Carmel, he proved who is the one true God (1 Kings 18).	Even giants of faith can't force sinners to change. But those who remain faithful to God have a great impact for him.
MICAIAH	865–853	Ahab of Israel Jehoshaphat of Judah (1 Kings 22; 2 Chronicles 18)	Ahab would be unsuccessful in fighting the Syrians.	It is foolish to move ahead with plans that are contrary to God's Word.
JEHU	853	Jehoshaphat of Judah (2 Chronicles 19:1–3)	Jehoshaphat should never have allied himself with wicked Ahab.	Partnerships with immoral people can lead us into trouble.
OBADIAH	855–840(?)	Jehoram of Judah (The book of Obadiah)	God would judge the Edomites for taking advantage of God's people.	Pride is one of the most dangerous sins because it causes us to take advantage of others.
ELISHA	848–797	Jehoram, Jehu, Jehoahaz, and Jehoash, all of Israel (2 Kings 2—8; 13:10–21)	Expressed by his actions the importance of helping ordinary people in need.	God is concerned about the everyday needs of his people.
JOEL	835–796(?)	Joash of Judah (The book of Joel)	Because a plague of locusts had come to discipline the nation, he called the people to turn back to God before an even greater judgment occurred.	While God judges all people for their sins, he gives eternal salvation only to those who have turned to him.
JONAH	793–753	Jeroboam II of Israel (2 Kings 14:25; the book of Jonah)	Nineveh, the capital of Assyria, should repent of its sins.	God wants all nations to turn to him. His love reaches out to all peoples.
AMOS	760–750	Jeroboam II of Israel (The book of Amos)	Warned against those who exploited or ignored the needy. (In Amos' day, Israel was an affluent and materialistic society.)	Believing in God is more than a personal matter. God calls all believers to work against injustices in society and to aid those less fortunate.
HOSEA	753–715	The last seven kings of Israel; Uzziah, Jotham, Ahaz, and Hezekiah of Judah (The book of Hosea)	Condemned the people of Israel because they had sinned against God as an adulterous woman sins against her husband.	When we sin, we sever our relationship to God, breaking our commitment to him. While all must answer to God for their sins, those who seek God's forgiveness are spared from eternal judgment.

"Again and again the Lord had sent prophets to warn both Israel and Judah to turn from their evil ways [and] . . . to obey his commandments" (17:13). Who were these prophets? Here are some of those who tried to turn their nations back to God. Predicting the future as revealed by God was just one part of a prophet's job; their main role was to preach God's Word to the

17:38
Deut 4:23
6:10-12
17:39
1 Sam 12:24
17:41
Zeph 1:5
Mt 6:24
Acts 7:42

³⁸For God had said, *"You must never forget the covenant I made with you; never worship other gods.* ³⁹*You must worship only the Lord; he will save you from all your enemies."*

⁴⁰But Israel didn't listen, and the people continued to worship other gods. ⁴¹These colonists from Babylon worshiped the Lord, yes—but they also worshiped their idols. And to this day their descendants do the same thing.

THESE PROPHETS?

Who?	When? (B.C.)	Ministered during the reign of these kings:	Main message	Significance
MICAH	742–687	Jotham, Ahaz, and Hezekiah of Judah (The book of Micah)	Predicted the fall of both the Northern and Southern Kingdoms. This was God's discipline upon the people, actually showing how much he cared for them.	Choosing to live a life apart from God is making a commitment to sin. Sin leads to judgment and death. God alone shows us the way to eternal peace. His discipline often keeps us on the right path.
ISAIAH	740–681	Uzziah, Jotham, Ahaz, Hezekiah, and Manasseh of Judah (The book of Isaiah)	Called the people back to a special relationship with God—although judgment from other nations was inevitable.	Sometimes we must suffer judgment and discipline before we are restored to God.
NAHUM	663–654	Manasseh of Judah (The book of Nahum)	The mighty empire of Assyria that oppressed God's people would soon tumble.	Those who do evil and oppress others will one day meet a bitter end.
ZEPHANIAH	640–621	Josiah of Judah (The book of Zephaniah)	A day will come when God, as Judge, would severely punish all nations; but afterwards, he would show mercy to his people.	We will all be judged for our disobedience to God, but if we remain faithful to him, he will show us mercy.
JEREMIAH	627–586	Josiah, Jehoahaz, Jehoiakim, Jehoiachin, Zedekiah of Judah (The book of Jeremiah)	Repentence would postpone Judah's coming judgment at the hands of Babylon.	Repentance is one of the greatest needs in our world of immorality. God's promises to the faithful shine brightly.
HABAKKUK	612–589	Josiah, Jehoahaz, Jehoiakim, Jehoiachin, Zedekiah of Judah (The book of Habakkuk)	Habakkuk couldn't understand why God seemed to do nothing about the wickedness in society. Then he realized that faith in God alone would one day supply the answer.	Instead of questioning the ways of God, we should realize that he is completely just, and we should have faith that he is in control and that one day evil will be utterly destroyed.
DANIEL	605–536	Prophesied as an exile in Babylon during the reigns of Nebuchadnezzar, Darius the Mede, and Cyrus of Persia (The book of Daniel)	Describes both near and distant future events—throughout all, God is sovereign and triumphant.	We should spend less time wondering when these events will happen and more time learning how we should live *now* so we won't be victims of those events.
EZEKIEL	593–571	Prophesied as an exile in Babylon during the reign of Nebuchadnezzar (The book of Ezekiel)	Sent messages back to Jerusalem urging the people to turn back to God before they were all forced to join him in exile. After Jerusalem fell, Ezekiel urged his fellow exiles to turn back to God so they could eventually return to their homeland.	God disciplines his people to draw them closer to him.

people—warning, instructing, and encouraging them to live as they ought.
   The prophets Haggai, Zechariah, and Malachi were prophets to the people of Judah after they returned from exile. For more information, see the chart in Ezra 5.

B. THE SURVIVING KINGDOM (18:1—25:30)

After seeing their brothers carried away into exile, Judah still lapses into sin. Hezekiah and Josiah begin many reforms, but this is not enough to permanently turn the nation back to God. Judah is defeated by the Babylonians, who exile many of them, but they are not scattered and the land is not repopulated. Sometimes we do not learn from the examples of sin and foolishness around us.

1. Kings of Judah

Hezekiah rules Judah

18 New king of Judah: Hezekiah
Father's name: Ahaz

Length of his reign: 29 years, in Jerusalem
His age at the beginning of his reign: 25 years old
His mother's name: Abi (daughter of Zechariah)
Character of his reign: good (similar to that of his ancestor David)
Reigning in Israel at this time: King Hoshea (son of Elah), who had been the
king there for 3 years

18:1
2 Kgs 15:30
16:20; 20:3
2 Chron 28:27
31:20

⁴He removed the shrines on the hills, broke down the obelisks, knocked down the shameful idols of Asherah, and broke up the bronze serpent that Moses had made, because the people of Israel had begun to worship it by burning incense to it; even though, as King Hezekiah pointed out to them, it was merely a piece of bronze. ⁵He trusted very strongly in the Lord God of Israel. In fact, none of the kings before or after him were as close to God as he was. ⁶For he followed the Lord in everything, and carefully obeyed all of God's commands to Moses. ⁷So the Lord was with him and prospered everything he did. Then he rebelled against the king of Assyria and refused to pay tribute any longer. ⁸He also conquered the Philistines as far distant as Gaza and its suburbs, destroying cities both large and small.

18:4
Num 21:8,9
2 Kgs 12:3
2 Chron 31:1

18:5
2 Kgs 23:25

18:7
Gen 39:2
1 Sam 18:14
2 Chron 15:2
Job 1:10
Dan 6:28

⁹It was during the fourth year of his reign (which was the seventh year of the reign of King Hoshea in Israel) that King Shalmaneser of Assyria attacked Israel and began a siege on the city of Samaria. ¹⁰Three years later (during the sixth year of the reign of King Hezekiah and the ninth year of the reign of King Hoshea of Israel) Samaria fell. ¹¹It was at that time that the king of Assyria transported the Israelis to Assyria and put them in colonies in the city of Halath and along the banks of the Habor River in Gozan, and in the cities of the Medes. ¹²For they had refused to listen to the Lord their God or to do what he wanted them to do. Instead, they had transgressed his covenant and disobeyed all the laws given to them by Moses the servant of the Lord.

18:8
2 Chron 28:18

18:9
2 Kgs 17:3

18:11
2 Kgs 17:6
19:11

18:12
Num 12:7,8
1 Kgs 8:56
2 Kgs 17:7,13
Neh 9:17
Isa 1:20

¹³Later, during the fourteenth year of the reign of King Hezekiah, King Sennach-

18:13
2 Chron 32:1
Isa 36:1

18:4 *King Hezekiah,* implied. **18:8** *destroying cities both large and small,* literally, "from the tower of the watchman to the fortified cities."

18:4 The bronze serpent had been made to cure the Israelites of a deadly plague (Numbers 21:4–9). It demonstrated God's presence and power and reminded the people of his mercy and forgiveness. But it had become an object of worship instead of a reminder of *whom* to worship, so Hezekiah was forced to destroy it. We must be careful that the things we use to aid our worship don't become objects of worship themselves. Most objects of worship are not made to be idols—they become idols by the way people use them.

18:5 In dramatic contrast with his father, Ahaz, Hezekiah followed God more closely and sincerely than any other king of Judah or Israel. This statement refers to the kings after the division of the kingdom and so does not include David, considered the king most devoted to God.

18:7 The nation of Judah was sandwiched between two world powers, Egypt and Assyria. Both wanted to control Judah and Israel because they lay at the vital crossroads of all Middle Eastern trade. The nation who controlled Judah would have a military and economic advantage over its rivals. When Hezekiah became king, Assyria controlled Judah. Acting with great courage, Hezekiah rebelled against this mighty empire to whom his father had

submitted. He placed his faith in God's strength rather than his own, and he obeyed God's commands in spite of the dangers that, from a purely human standpoint, looked insurmountable.

18:9–12 These verses flash back to the days just before Israel's destruction. Hezekiah reigned with his father Ahaz for 14 years (729–715 B.C.), by himself for 18 years (715–697 B.C.), and with his son Manasseh for 11 years (697–686 B.C.), a total of 43 years. The 29 years listed in 18:1 indicate only those years in which Hezekiah had complete control of the kingdom. While Hezekiah was on the throne, the nation of Israel to the north was destroyed (722 B.C.). Knowing Israel's fate probably caused Hezekiah to reform his own nation. (For more on Hezekiah, see 2 Chronicles 29—32 and Isaiah 36—39.)

18:13 This event occurred in 701 B.C., four years after Sennacherib had become Assyria's king. Sennacherib was the son of Sargon II, the king who had deported Israel's people into captivity (see the note on 17:3). To keep Assyria from attacking, the Southern Kingdom paid them tribute annually. But when Sennacherib became king, Hezekiah stopped paying this money, hoping Assyria would ignore him. When Sennacherib and his army

erib of Assyria besieged and captured all the fortified cities of Judah. ¹⁴King Hezekiah sued for peace and sent this message to the king of Assyria at Lachish: "I have done wrong. I will pay whatever tribute you demand if you will only go

HEZEKIAH

The past is an important part of today's actions and tomorrow's plans. The people and kings of Judah had a rich past, filled with God's action, guidance, and commands. But with each passing generation, they also had a growing list of tragedies that occurred when the people forgot that their God, who had cared for them in the past, also cared about the present and the future—and demanded their continued obedience. King Hezekiah was one of the few kings of Judah who was constantly aware of God's acts in the past and his interest in the events of every day. The Bible described him as a king who had a close relationship with God.

As with most reformers, Hezekiah's priorities concentrated on changing the here and now—reforming the people of the present. Judah was filled with visual reminders of their lack of trust in God, and Hezekiah boldly cleaned house. Altars, idols, and pagan temples were destroyed. Even the bronze serpent Moses had made in the desert was not spared because it had ceased to point the people to God and had also become an idol. The Temple in Jerusalem, whose doors had been nailed shut by Hezekiah's own father, was cleaned out and reopened. The Passover was re-instituted as a national holiday, and there was revival in Judah.

Although he had a natural inclination to respond to present problems, Hezekiah's life shows little evidence of concern about the future. He took few actions to preserve the effects of his sweeping reforms. His successful efforts made him proud. His unwise display of wealth to the Babylonian delegation got Judah included on Babylon's "Nations to Conquer" list. When Isaiah informed Hezekiah of the foolishness of his act, the king's answer displayed his persistent lack of foresight—he was thankful that any evil consequences would be delayed until after he died. And the lives of three kings who followed him—Manasseh, Amon, and Josiah—were deeply affected by both Hezekiah's accomplishments *and* his weaknesses.

The past affects your decisions and actions today, and these, in turn, affect the future. There are lessons to learn and errors to avoid repeating. Remember that part of the success of your past will be measured by what you do with it now and how well you use it to prepare for the future.

Strengths and accomplishments:
- King of Judah who instigated civil and religious reforms
- Had a personal, growing relationship with God
- Developed a powerful prayer life
- Noted as the patron of several chapters in the book of Proverbs (see Proverbs 25:1)

Weaknesses and mistakes:
- Showed little interest or wisdom in planning for the future and protecting for others the spiritual heritage he enjoyed
- Rashly showed all his wealth to messengers from Babylon

Lessons from his life:
- Sweeping reforms are short-lived when little action is taken to preserve them for the future
- Past obedience to God does not remove the possibility of present disobedience
- Complete dependence on God yields amazing results

Vital statistics:
- Where: Jerusalem
- Occupation: 15th king of Judah, the Southern Kingdom
- Relatives: Father: Ahaz. Mother: Abi. Son: Manasseh.
- Contemporaries: Isaiah, Hoshea, Micah, Sennacherib

Key verses:
"He trusted very strongly in the Lord God of Israel. In fact, none of the kings before or after him were as close to God as he was. For he followed the Lord in everything, and carefully obeyed all of God's commands to Moses" (2 Kings 18:5, 6).

Hezekiah's story is told in 2 Kings 16:20—20:21; 2 Chronicles 28:27—32:33; Isaiah 36:1—39:8. He is also mentioned in Proverbs 25:1; Isaiah 1:1; Jeremiah 15:4; 26:18, 19; Hosea 1:1; Micah 1:1.

retaliated, Hezekiah realized his mistake and paid the tribute money (18:14), but Sennacherib attacked anyway (18:19ff). Although Sennacherib attacked Judah, he was not as war-hungry as the previous Assyrian kings, preferring to spend most of his time building and beautifying his capital city, Nineveh. With less frequent invasions, Hezekiah was able to institute his many reforms and strengthen the nation.

away." The king of Assyria then demanded a settlement of $1,500,000. 15To **18:15**
gather this amount, King Hezekiah used all the silver stored in the Temple and in   1 Kgs 15:18
the palace treasury. 16He even stripped off the gold from the Temple doors, and   2 Kgs 12:18
from the doorposts he had overlaid with gold, and gave it all to the Assyrian king.

Assyria threatens to conquer Judah
17Nevertheless the king of Assyria sent his field marshal, his chief treasurer, and

HOW DOES ASSYRIA'S HISTORY COMPARE WITH ISRAEL'S HISTORY	Era	Date	Assyria	Israel
	"Prehistory"	B.C. 5000	Pottery found at Jarmo dates back this far	Tablets with pictographic writing found at Kish and Ur prove writing was used before Flood—gives weight to the biblical record of Genesis as valid
		3000	Pottery found at Calah, Assur, Nineveh from this date	Genesis 10:11, 12 names Nimrod as the founder of these cities
	OLD (not all kings listed)	by 2900	There were Sumerians living at Assur and Erech. Thirty kings are listed in an ancient record discovered nearby. Ziggurat temples were being built then.	The Tower of Babel may have been a ziggurat. Genesis 10:10; 11:1–9
		2350	Sargon I of Akkad conquered Sumer and built a capital in Nineveh. This is the first known empire in history.	
		2125	Ur was the seat of the 3rd Dynasty.	Ur was the city of Abraham's forefathers. Genesis 11:26–32
		2025	Ur fell as seat of power.	
		1781	Ishme-dagon was the Assyrian ruler who was contemporary to the famous Hammurabi of Babylon.	Many Assyrian historians suggest that Amraphel of Genesis 14:1 is Hammurabi. If this is true, Abraham knew him.
		1760	Period of lesser importance	The Exodus
	MIDDLE (not all kings listed)	1365	Ashur-uballit I began to regain the empire.	Period of the Judges
		1274 1245	Shalmaneser I—empire builder	
		1115	Tiglath-pileser I—great fortune and power	
		1050		Saul begins his reign over Israel.
		1010		David begins his reign over Israel.
		970		Solomon begins his reign over Israel.
	NEW (complete list of kings after Shalmaneser III)	about 900	Several kings in succession worked to restore Assyria's power.	
		858	Shalmaneser III	Assyrian records say Ahab gave Shalmaneser III 2,000 chariots and over 4,000 men. An Assyrian pillar and obelisk record that Jehu paid tribute to Shalmaneser III.
		824	Shamsi-Adad V	

his chief of staff from Lachish with a great army; and they camped along the highway beside the field where cloth was bleached, near the conduit of the upper pool. 18They demanded that King Hezekiah come out to speak to them, but instead he sent a truce delegation of the following men: Eliakim, his business manager; Shebnah, his secretary; and Joah, his royal historian.

19Then the Assyrian general sent this message to King Hezekiah: "The great King of Assyria says, 'No one can save you from my power! 20, 21You need more

18:18
2 Kgs 19:2
Isa 22:15,16, 20; 36:3

18:20
Isa 30:2,7
Ezek 29:2,6

Era	Date	Assyria	Israel
NEW (continued)	805	Followed by his widow	
	783	Adad-nirari III	
	773	Shalmaneser IV	Israel recaptured some lost territory because Shalmaneser IV was putting pressure on Damascus, Israel's oppressors. 2 Kings 14:23–29
	754	Ashurdan III	Jonah probably preached at Nineveh during Ashurdan III's reign.
	727	Tiglath-pileser III—"Pul"	Menaham paid him tribute. 2 Kings 15:19, 20. Ahaz gave him gifts, asked for military aid, and copied an altar design from him. But Pul double-crossed him. 2 Kings 16:7–18; 2 Chronicles 28:16–21; 1 Chronicles 5:23–26; and Isaiah 7:17–25.
	722	Shalmaneser V	He besieged Samaria, but died just before it was taken. Fall of the Northern Kingdom. 2 Kings 17:3–6.
	705	Sargon II	
	681	Sennacherib	Hezekiah had many dealings with Sennacherib: 2 Kings 18:13, 14 and a bas-relief (an illustration carved in stone) in the palace at Nineveh tell of this conquest. 2 Kings 18:14–16 and Assyrian annals tell of tribute and gifts. 2 Kings 19:35–37 and an Assyrian clay tablet relate that the king could not subdue Hezekiah. An Assyrian king would usually not record a defeat.
	669	Esarhaddon	Deported over 27,000 Israelites. 2 Chronicles 33:11.
		Ashurbanipal—He ruled, but was more interested in the arts and his 22,000 tablet library. He gave power to his sons:	Nahum 1:1–8 and Assyrian annals tell that Nineveh's walls were breached by a flood.
	632	Assur-etel-ilani and	
	628	Sin-sar-iskun—Assyrian records say that Sin-sar-iskun died in a fire.	See also Nahum 3:11–19
	612	Nineveh, Assyria's capital, fell to Nabopolassar of Babylon—the end of the great Assyrian Empire.	

than mere promises of help before rebelling against me. But which of your allies will give you more than words? Egypt? If you lean on Egypt, you will find her to be a stick that breaks beneath your weight and pierces your hand. The Egyptian Pharaoh is totally unreliable! 22And if you say, "We're trusting the Lord to rescue us"—just remember that he is the very one whose hilltop altars you've destroyed. For you require everyone to worship at the altar in Jerusalem!' 23I'll tell you what: Make a bet with my master, the king of Assyria! If you have two thousand men left who can ride horses, we'll furnish the horses! 24And with an army as small as yours, you are no threat to even the least lieutenant in charge of the smallest contingent in my master's army. Even if Egypt supplies you with horses and chariots, it will do no good. 25And do you think we have come here on our own? No! The Lord sent us and told us, 'Go and destroy this nation!' "

26Then Eliakim, Shebnah, and Joah said to them, "Please speak in Aramaic, for we understand it. Don't use Hebrew, for the people standing on the walls will hear you."

18:26
Ezra 4:7
Isa 36:11,12
Dan 2:4

27But the Assyrian general replied, "Has my master sent me to speak only to you and to your master? Hasn't he sent me to the people on the walls too? For they are doomed with you to eat their own excrement and drink their own urine!"

28Then the Assyrian ambassador shouted in Hebrew to the people on the wall, "Listen to the great king of Assyria! 29'Don't let King Hezekiah fool you. He will never be able to save you from my power. 30Don't let him fool you into trusting in the Lord to rescue you. 31, 32Don't listen to King Hezekiah. Surrender! You can live in peace here in your own land until I take you to another land just like this one—with plentiful crops, grain, grapes, olive trees, and honey. All of this instead of death! Don't listen to King Hezekiah when he tries to persuade you that the Lord will deliver you. 33Have any of the gods of the other nations ever delivered their people from the king of Assyria? 34What happened to the gods of Hamath, Arpad, Sepharvaim, Hena, and Ivvah? Did they rescue Samaria? 35What god has ever been able to save any nation from my power? So what makes you think the Lord can save Jerusalem?' "

18:31
Deut 8:7-9

18:33
2 Kgs 19:12
Isa 10:7,9

18:34
2 Kgs 17:24
19:13

36But the people on the wall remained silent, for the king had instructed them to say nothing. 37Then Eliakim (son of Hilkiah) the business manager, and Shebnah the king's secretary, and Joah (son of Asaph) the historian went to King Hezekiah with their clothes torn and told him what the Assyrian general had said.

Isaiah predicts deliverance

19 When King Hezekiah heard their report he tore his clothes and put on sackcloth and went into the Temple to pray. 2Then he told Eliakim, Shebnah, and some of the older priests to clothe themselves in sackcloth and to go to Isaiah (son of Amoz), the prophet, with this message:

19:1
2 Chron 32:20
Isa 37:1

19:2
Isa 1:1

3"King Hezekiah says, 'This is a day of trouble, insult, and dishonor. It is as when a child is ready to be born, but the mother has no strength to deliver it. 4Yet perhaps the Lord your God has heard the Assyrian general defying the living God, and will rebuke him. Oh, pray for the few of us who are left.' "

19:4
2 Kgs 18:35
Isa 1:9

5, 6Isaiah replied, "The Lord says, 'Tell your master not to be troubled by the sneers these Assyrians have made against me.' 7For the king of Assyria will receive bad news from home and will decide to return; and the Lord will see to it that he is killed when he arrives there."

19:5
2 Kgs 18:22

19:7
2 Kgs 19:37

18:24 *with an army as small as yours,* implied.

19:1 Sennacherib, whose armies had captured all the fortified cities of Judah, sent a message to Hezekiah to surrender because resistance was futile. Realizing the situation was hopeless, Hezekiah went to the Temple and prayed. He knew that God specializes in impossible situations. God answered Hezekiah's prayer and delivered Judah by sending an army to attack the Assyrian capital, forcing Sennacherib to leave at once. Prayer should be our first response in any crisis. Our problems are God's opportunities.

19:2 Isaiah the prophet had been working for God since the days of Uzziah—40 years (Isaiah 6:1). Although Assyria was a world power, it could not conquer Judah as long as Isaiah counseled the kings. Isaiah prophesied during the reigns of Uzziah, Jotham, Ahaz, and Hezekiah. Ahaz ignored Isaiah, but Hezekiah listened to his advice. To read his prophecies, see the book of Isaiah.

⁸Then the Assyrian general returned to his king at Libnah (for he received word that he had left Lachish). ⁹Soon afterwards news reached the king that King Tirhakah of Ethiopia was coming to attack him. Before leaving to meet the attack, he sent back this message to King Hezekiah:

¹⁰"Don't be fooled by that god you trust in. Don't believe it when he says that I won't conquer Jerusalem. ¹¹You know perfectly well what the kings of Assyria have done wherever they have gone; they have completely destroyed everything. Why would you be any different? ¹²Have the gods of the other nations delivered them—such nations as Gozan, Haran, Rezeph, and Eden in the land of Telassar? The former kings of Assyria destroyed them all! ¹³What happened to the king of Hamoth and the king of Arpad? What happened to the kings of Sepharvaim, Hena, and Ivvah?"

Hezekiah asks God for help

¹⁴Hezekiah took the letter from the messengers, read it, and went over to the Temple and spread it out before the Lord. ¹⁵Then he prayed this prayer:

"O Lord God of Israel, sitting on your throne high above the angels, you alone are the God of all the kingdoms of the earth. You created the heavens and the earth. ¹⁶Bend low, O Lord, and listen. Open your eyes, O Lord, and see. Listen to this man's defiance of the living God. ¹⁷Lord, it is true that the kings of Assyria have destroyed all those nations, ¹⁸and have burned their idol-gods. But they weren't gods at all; they were destroyed because they were only things that men had made of wood and stone. ¹⁹O Lord our God, we plead with you to save us from his power; then all the kingdoms of the earth will know that you alone are God."

God promises safety for Jerusalem

²⁰Then Isaiah sent this message to Hezekiah: "The Lord God of Israel says, 'I have heard you! ²¹And this is my reply to King Sennacherib: The virgin daughter of Zion isn't afraid of you! The daughter of Jerusalem scorns and mocks at you. ²²Whom have you defied and blasphemed? And toward whom have you felt so cocky? It is the Holy One of Israel!

²³"'You have boasted, "My chariots have conquered the highest mountains, yes, the peaks of Lebanon. I have cut down the tallest cedars and choicest cypress trees and have conquered the farthest borders. ²⁴I have been refreshed at many conquered wells, and I destroyed the strength of Egypt just by walking by!"

²⁵"'Why haven't you realized long before this that it is I, the Lord, who lets you do these things? I decreed your conquest of all those fortified cities! ²⁶So of course the nations you conquered had no power against you! They were like grass shriveling beneath the hot sun, and like grain blighted before it is half grown. ²⁷I know everything about you. I know all your plans and where you are going next; and I also know the evil things you have said about me. ²⁸And because of your arrogance against me I am going to put a hook in your nose and a bridle in your mouth and turn you back on the road by which you came. ²⁹And this is the proof that I will do as I have promised: This year my people will eat the volunteer wheat, and use it as seed for next year's crop; and in the third year they will have a bountiful harvest.

³⁰"'O my people Judah, those of you who have escaped the ravages of the siege

19:15 *angels*, literally, "cherubim."

19:10
2 Kgs 18:5,30

19:12
2 Kgs 17:6
18:33
Isa 37:12

19:13
2 Kgs 17:24
18:34

19:14
Isa 37:14

19:15
Ps 80:1
Isa 37:16,17

19:16
1 Kgs 8:29,30
2 Chron 6:40

19:18
Isa 44:9
Acts 17:29

19:19
1 Sam 17:46
1 Kgs 8:42,43

19:20
2 Kgs 20:5
Ps 65:1,2
Isa 65:24

19:22
Ex 5:2
Isa 5:24
30:10,11
Jer 51:5

19:25
Isa 10:5-7
37:26; 45:5-7
Hab 1:6

19:26
Ps 129:6,7

19:27
Ps 139:1
Jer 23:23,24

19:28
Ps 32:9
Ezek 29:4
Amos 4:2

19:29
Ex 3:12
2 Kgs 20:8
Isa 7:11

19:30
2 Chron 32:22,
23
Isa 1:9

19:15 Although Hezekiah came boldly to God, he did not take him for granted or approach him flippantly. Instead, he acknowledged God's sovereignty and Judah's total dependence upon him. Hezekiah's prayer provides a good model for us. We should not be afraid to approach God with our prayers, but we must come to him with respect for who he is and what he can do.

19:28 God replied to Sennacherib's taunting words (18:19–25), indicting him for arrogance. Sennacherib believed his kingdom had grown because of his own efforts and strength. In reality, said

God, he succeeded only because of what God had allowed and caused. It is arrogance to think we alone are responsible for our achievements. God, as Creator, rules over nations and people.

19:28 The Assyrians treated captives with cruelty. They tortured them for entertainment by blinding them, cutting them, or pulling off strips of their skin until they died. If they wished to make a captive a slave, they would often put a hook in his nose. God was saying that the Assyrians would be treated the way they had treated others.

shall become a great nation again; you shall be rooted deeply in the soil and bear fruit for God. 31A remnant of my people shall become strong in Jerusalem. The Lord is eager to cause this to happen.

32" 'And my command concerning the king of Assyria is that he shall not enter this city. He shall not stand before it with a shield, nor build a ramp against its wall, nor even shoot an arrow into it. 33He shall return by the road he came, 34for I will defend and save this city for the sake of my own name and for the sake of my servant David.' "

35That very night the angel of the Lord killed 185,000 Assyrian troops, and dead bodies were seen all across the landscape in the morning.

36Then King Sennacherib returned to Nineveh; 37and as he was worshiping in the temple of his god Nisroch, his sons Adrammelech and Sharezer killed him. They escaped into eastern Turkey—the land of Ararat—and his son Esarhaddon became the new king.

19:34
1 Kgs 11:12,13
2 Kgs 20:6
Isa 43:25
48:9,11

19:35
2 Chron 32:21
Isa 10:16

19:36
Jonah 1:2
Nah 1:1

19:37
Gen 8:4
Ezra 4:2

Hezekiah's illness

20 Hezekiah now became deathly sick, and Isaiah the prophet went to visit him. "Set your affairs in order and prepare to die," Isaiah told him. "The Lord says you won't recover."

2Hezekiah turned his face to the wall.

3"O Lord," he pleaded, "remember how I've always tried to obey you and to please you in everything I do. . . ." Then he broke down and cried.

4So before Isaiah had left the courtyard, the Lord spoke to him again.

5"Go back to Hezekiah, the leader of my people, and tell him that the Lord God of his ancestor David has heard his prayer and seen his tears. I will heal him, and three days from now he will be out of bed and at the Temple! 6I will add fifteen years to his life and save him and this city from the king of Assyria. And it will all be done for the glory of my own name and for the sake of my servant David."

7Isaiah then instructed Hezekiah to boil some dried figs and to make a paste of them and spread it on the boil. And he recovered!

8Meanwhile, King Hezekiah had said to Isaiah, "Do a miracle to prove to me that the Lord will heal me and that I will be able to go to the Temple again three days from now."

9"All right, the Lord will give you a proof," Isaiah told him. "Do you want the shadow on the sundial to go forward ten points or backward ten points?"

10"The shadow always moves forward," Hezekiah replied; "make it go backward."

11So Isaiah asked the Lord to do this, and he caused the shadow to move ten points backward on the sundial of Ahaz!

20:1
2 Chron 32:24
Isa 38:1

20:3
2 Kgs 18:6
2 Chron 17:3

20:5
2 Kgs 19:20
Ps 39:12

20:6
2 Kgs 19:34

20:7
2 Kgs 2:20; 4:41
Isa 38:21

20:9
Isa 38:7,8
Mt 16:1

20:11
Josh 10:12
2 Chron 32:24,
31

Ambassadors from Babylon visit Hezekiah

12At that time Merodach-baladan (the son of King Baladan of Babylon) sent ambassadors with greetings and a present to Hezekiah, for he had learned of his

---

19:31 As long as a tiny spark remains, a fire can be rekindled and fanned into a roaring blaze. Similarly, if just the smallest remnant of true believers retains the spark of faith, God can rebuild it into a strong nation. And if only a glimmer of faith remains in a heart, God can use it to restore blazing faith in that believer. If you feel that only a spark of faith remains in you, ask God to use it to rekindle a blazing fire of commitment to him.

20:5, 6 Over a 100-year period of Judah's history (732–640 B.C.), Hezekiah was the only faithful king; but what a difference he made! Because of Hezekiah's faith and prayer, God healed him and saved his city from the Assyrians. You can make a difference too, even if your faith puts you in the minority. Faith and prayer, if they are sincere and directed toward the one true God, can bring about change in any situation.

20:11 The sundial of Ahaz is also translated "the steps of Ahaz." Egyptian sundials in this period were sometimes made in the form of miniature staircases so that the shadows moved up and down the steps.

20:12–19 Hezekiah had been a good and faithful king. But when Isaiah asked him what he had shown the ambassadors from Babylon, he replied, "My treasures." From the account in 2 Chronicles 32:31, it appears that Hezekiah's prosperity, success, and deliverance from sickness had made him proud. Rather than giving credit to God for all his blessings, he tried to impress the foreigners. When God helps us, we must not use his blessings to impress others. A testimony of victory can quickly degenerate into vanity and self-congratulations.

20:13
2 Chron 32:27

sickness. [13]Hezekiah welcomed them and showed them all his treasures—the silver, gold, spices, aromatic oils, the armory—everything.

[14]Then Isaiah went to King Hezekiah and asked him, "What did these men want? Where are they from?"

"From far away in Babylon," Hezekiah replied.

[15]"What have they seen in your palace?" Isaiah asked.

And Hezekiah replied, "Everything. I showed them all my treasures."

20:17
2 Kgs 24:13
25:13
Jer 52:17

20:18
2 Kgs 24:12
2 Chron 33:11

[16]Then Isaiah said to Hezekiah, "Listen to the word of the Lord: [17]The time will come when everything in this palace shall be carried to Babylon. All the treasures of your ancestors will be taken—nothing shall be left. [18]Some of your own sons will be taken away and made into eunuchs who will serve in the palace of the king of Babylon."

[19]"All right," Hezekiah replied, "if this is what the Lord wants, it is good." But he was really thinking, "At least there will be peace and security during the remainder of my own life!"

20:20
2 Kgs 16:19
21:17
2 Chron 32:32

20:21
2 Chron 32:33

[20]The rest of the history of Hezekiah and his great deeds—including the pool and conduit he made and how he brought water into the city—are recorded in *The Annals of the Kings of Judah*. [21]When he died, his son Manasseh became the new king.

Manasseh rules Judah

21:1
1 Chron 3:10-14
2 Chron 33:1

21 New king of Judah: Manasseh
His age at beginning of his reign: 12 years
Length of his reign: 55 years, in Jerusalem
Name of his mother: Hephzibah

21:3
Lev 18:25
Deut 12:31
17:2,3
1 Kgs 16:29-31

Character of his reign: evil. He did the same things the nations had done that were thrown out of the land to make room for the people of Israel

[3, 4, 5]He rebuilt the hilltop shrines which his father Hezekiah had destroyed. He built altars for Baal and made a shameful Asherah idol, just as Ahab the king of Israel had done. Heathen altars to the sun god, moon god, and the gods of the stars were placed even in the Temple of the Lord—in the very city and building which the Lord had selected to honor his own name. [6]And he sacrificed one of his sons as a burnt offering on a heathen altar. He practiced black magic and used fortune-telling, and patronized mediums and wizards. So the Lord was very angry, for Manasseh was an evil man, in God's sight. [7]Manasseh even set up a shameful Asherah-idol in the Temple—the very place which the Lord had spoken to David and Solomon about when he said, "I will place my name forever in this Temple, and in Jerusalem—the city I have chosen from among all the cities of the tribes of Israel. [8]If the people of Israel will only follow the instructions I gave them through Moses, I will never again expel them from this land of their fathers."

[9]But the people did not listen to the Lord, and Manasseh enticed them to do even

21:6
Lev 18:21
19:26,31
Deut 18:10
2 Kgs 3:27
16:3; 17:17

21:7
Deut 16:21
1 Kgs 9:3
2 Kgs 23:6

21:8
2 Kgs 18:12
2 Chron 15:2

21:9
2 Chron 36:16
Ezra 9:10
Neh 9:26
Ps 81:11

20:14 Babylon, a city that had rebelled against the Assyrian Empire, was destroyed by Sennacherib in 689 B.C. This story probably occurred shortly before that date. When Sennacherib died in 681 B.C., his son, Esarhaddon, foolishly rebuilt the city of Babylon. Assyria, whose rulers at that time were weak, allowed Babylon plenty of opportunity to become strong. As the Assyrian army marched off to conquer and oppress faraway lands, the city of Babylon grew and expanded into a small nation. After some years, Babylon was strong enough to rebel again. It eventually crushed Assyria (612 B.C.) and became the next world power.

20:19 Hezekiah's statement seems selfish, shortsighted, and proud. However, he knew that his nation would be punished for its sins, so he may have been acknowledging and thanking God for choosing not to destroy Judah during his lifetime.

21:1ff Manasseh followed the example of his grandfather Ahaz more than that of his father. He adopted the wicked practices of

the Babylonians and Canaanites. He did not listen to the words of God's prophets, but willfully led his people into sin. (See his Profile in 2 Chronicles 33 for more information about his life.)

21:6 Manasseh was an evil king, and he angered God with his sin. Listed among his sins are occult practices—black magic, fortune-telling and the use of mediums and wizards. God has specific laws against the occult (Leviticus 19:31; Deuteronomy 18:9-13) because it demonstrates a lack of faith in him, involves sinful actions, and sometimes opens the door to demonic influences. Today, many books, television shows, and games emphasize fortune-telling, seances, and other occult practices. Don't let desire to know the future or the belief that superstition is harmless lead you into condoning occult practices. They are counterfeits of God's power and have as their root a system of beliefs totally opposed to God.

more evil than the surrounding nations had done, even though Jehovah had destroyed those nations for their evil ways when the people of Israel entered the land.

10Then the Lord declared through the prophets,

11"Because King Manasseh has done these evil things and is even more wicked than the Amorites who were in this land long ago, and because he has led the people of Judah into idolatry: 12I will bring such evil upon Jerusalem and Judah that the ears of those who hear about it will tingle with horror. 13I will punish Jerusalem as I did Samaria, and as I did King Ahab of Israel and his descendants. I will wipe away the people of Jerusalem as a man wipes a dish and turns it upside down to dry. 14Then I will reject even those few of my people who are left, and I will hand them over to their enemies. 15For they have done great evil and have angered me ever since I brought their ancestors from Egypt."

16In addition to the idolatry which God hated and into which Manasseh led the people of Judah, he murdered great numbers of innocent people. And Jerusalem was filled from one end to the other with the bodies of his victims.

17The rest of the history of Manasseh's sinful reign is recorded in *The Annals of the Kings of Judah.* 18When he died he was buried in the garden of his palace at Uzza, and his son Amon became the new king.

Amon rules Judah

19, 20Name of the new king of Judah: Amon
His age at the beginning of his reign: 22 years old
Length of his reign: 2 years, in Jerusalem
His mother's name: Meshullemeth (daughter of Haruz, of Jotbah)
Character of his reign: evil

21He did all the evil things his father had done: he worshiped the same idols, 22and turned his back on the Lord God of his ancestors. He refused to listen to God's instructions. 23But his aides conspired against him and killed him in the palace. 24Then a posse of civilians killed all the assassins and placed Amon's son Josiah upon the throne. 25The rest of Amon's biography is recorded in *The Annals of the Kings of Judah*. 26He was buried in a crypt in the garden of Uzza, and his son Josiah became the new king.

Josiah rules Judah

22 New king of Judah: Josiah
His age at the beginning of his reign: 8 years old
Duration of his reign: 31 years in Jerusalem
Name of his mother: Jedidah (daughter of Adaiah of Bozkath)
Character of his reign: good; for he followed in the steps of his ancestor King David, obeying the Lord completely

3, 4In the eighteenth year of his reign, King Josiah sent his secretary Shaphan (son of Azaliah, son of Meshullam) to the Temple to give instruction to Hilkiah, the High Priest:

"Collect the money given to the priests at the door of the Temple when the people come to worship. 5, 6Give this money to the building superintendents so that they can hire carpenters and masons to repair the Temple, and to buy lumber and stone."

21:11
Gen 15:16
1 Kgs 21:26
2 Kgs 21:16
24:3,4

21:12
2 Kgs 22:15,16
Jer 19:3
Mic 3:12

21:16
2 Kgs 24:3,4

21:17
2 Kgs 20:20
21:25
2 Chron 33:18

21:18
2 Kgs 21:26
2 Chron 33:20

21:21
2 Kgs 21:3-5

21:22
Deut 32:15
2 Kgs 22:17

21:23
2 Kgs 12:20
14:19; 15:25

21:25
2 Kgs 21:17
23:28

21:26
2 Kgs 21:18

22:1
Deut 5:32
Josh 1:7
2 Chron 34:1
Jer 1:2
Zeph 1:1

22:3
2 Kgs 12:4,5
2 Chron 34:9

22:5
2 Kgs 12:11,12
Ezra 3:7

21:16 Tradition says that during Manasseh's massive slaughter, Isaiah was sawed in two when trying to hide in a hollow log (see Hebrews 11:37, 38). Other prophets may also have been killed at this time.

22:1, 2 In reading the biblical lists of kings, it is rare to find one who obeyed God completely. Josiah was such a person, and he was only eight years old when he began to reign. For 18 years he reigned obediently; then, when he was 26, he began the reforms based on God's laws. Children are the future leaders of our churches and our world. A person's major work for God may have to wait until he is an adult, but no one is ever too young to take God seriously and obey him. Josiah's early years laid the base for his later task of reforming Judah.

22:7
2 Kgs 12:15
2 Chron 34:13

7(The building superintendents were not required to keep account of their expenditures, for they were honest men.)

Josiah discovers a book of God's Law

22:8
Deut 31:24-26
2 Chron
34:14-16

8One day Hilkiah the High Priest went to Shaphan the secretary and exclaimed, "I have discovered a scroll in the Temple, with God's laws written on it!"

He gave the scroll to Shaphan to read. 9, 10When Shaphan reported to the king about the progress of the repairs at the Temple, he also mentioned the scroll found by Hilkiah. Then Shaphan read it to the king. 11When the king heard what was written in it, he tore his clothes in terror. 12, 13He commanded Hilkiah the priest, and Shaphan, and Asaiah, the king's assistant, and Ahikam (Shaphan's son), and Achbor (Michaiah's son) to ask the Lord, "What shall we do? For we have not been following the instructions of this book: you must be very angry with us, for neither we nor our ancestors have followed your commands."

22:11
Josh 7:6

22:12
Deut 29:24,25
31:17
2 Kgs 25:22
2 Chron 34:20
Jer 26:24

22:14
2 Chron 34:22

14So Hilkiah the priest, and Ahikam, and Achbor, and Shaphan, and Asaiah went to the Mishneh section of Jerusalem to find Huldah the prophetess. (She was the wife of Shallum—son of Tikvah, son of Harhas—who was in charge of the palace tailor shop.) 15, 16She gave them this message from the Lord God of Israel:

22:17
Deut 29:27

22:18
Lev 26:31
Ps 51:17
Isa 51:17

"Tell the man who sent you to me, that I am going to destroy this city and its people, just as I stated in that book you read. 17For the people of Judah have thrown me aside and have worshiped other gods and have made me very angry; and my anger can't be stopped. 18, 19But because you were sorry and concerned and humbled yourself before the Lord when you read the book and its warnings that this land would be cursed and become desolate, and because you have torn your clothing and wept before me in contrition, I will listen to your plea. 20The death of this nation will not occur until after you die—you will not see the evil which I will bring upon this place."

22:20
1 Kgs 21:29

So they took the message to the king.

Josiah destroys idol worship

23:1
2 Kgs 22:8
2 Chron 34:29

23 Then the king sent for the elders and other leaders of Judah and Jerusalem to go to the Temple with him. So all the priests and prophets and the people, small and great, of Jerusalem and Judah gathered there at the Temple so that the king could read to them the entire book of God's laws which had been discovered in the Temple. 3He stood beside the pillar in front of the people, and he and they made a solemn promise to the Lord to obey him at all times and to do everything the book commanded.

23:3
Ex 24:7
2 Kgs 11:17

23:4
2 Kgs 22:3,4

4Then the king instructed Hilkiah the High Priest and the rest of the priests and the guards of the Temple to destroy all the equipment used in the worship of Baal, Asherah, and the sun, moon, and stars. The king had it all burned in the fields of

---

22:8 This scroll may have been the entire Pentateuch (Genesis—Deuteronomy) or just the book of Deuteronomy. Because of the long line of evil kings, the record of God's laws had been lost. Josiah, who was about 26 years old at this time, desired religious reform throughout the nation. When God's Word was found, drastic changes had to be made to bring the kingdom in line with God's commands. Today you have God's Word at your fingertips. How much change must you make in your life in order to bring it into line with God's Word?

22:11ff When Josiah heard the Law, he tore his clothes in terror. He immediately instituted reforms. With just one reading of God's Law, he changed the course of the nation. Today many people own Bibles, but few are affected by the truths found in God's Word. The Word of God should cause us, like Josiah, to take action immediately to reform our lives and bring them into harmony with God's will.

22:14 Huldah was a prophetess, as were Miriam (Exodus 15:20) and Deborah (Judges 4:4). God freely selects his servants to carry out his will—rich or poor, male or female, king or slave (Joel

2:28–30). Huldah was obviously highly regarded by the people of her time.

22:19 When Josiah realized how corrupt his nation had become, he tore his clothes and wept before God. Then God had mercy on him. Josiah used the customs of his day to show his repentance. When we repent today, we are unlikely to tear our clothing, but weeping, fasting, making restitution or apologies (if our sin has involved others) are all acts of repentance which demonstrate our sincerity. The hardest part of repentance is changing the behavior that originally produced the sin.

23:1, 2 For more about the importance and operation of the Temple, see 1 Kings 5—8 and 2 Chronicles 2—7.

23:4–7 When Josiah realized the terrible state of Judah's religious life, he did something about it. It is not enough to say we believe what is right; we must respond with action, doing what faith requires. This is what James was emphasizing when he wrote, "'believing' is useless without *doing* what God wants you to" (James 2:20). This will mean acting differently at home, school, work, or church.

the Kidron Valley outside Jerusalem, and he carried the ashes to Bethel. 5He killed the heathen priests who had been appointed by the previous kings of Judah, for they had burned incense in the shrines on the hills throughout Judah and even in Jerusalem. They had also offered incense to Baal and to the sun, moon, stars, and planets. 6He removed the shameful idol of Asherah from the Temple and took it outside Jerusalem to Kidron Brook; there he burned it and beat it to dust and threw the dust on the graves of the common people. 7He also tore down the houses of male prostitution around the Temple, where the women wove robes for the Asherah-idol.

23:6
2 Kgs 21:7
2 Chron 34:4

23:7
1 Kgs 14:24
15:12; 22:46

8He brought back to Jerusalem the priests of the Lord, who were living in other cities of Judah, and tore down all the shrines on the hills where they had burned incense, even those as far away as Geba and Beersheba. He also destroyed the shrines at the entrance of the palace of Joshua, the former mayor of Jerusalem, located on the left side as one enters the city gate. 9However, these priests did not serve at the altar of the Lord in Jerusalem, even though they ate with the other priests.

23:8
1 Kgs 15:22

23:9
Ezek 44:9-11

10Then the king destroyed the altar of Topheth in the Valley of the Sons of Hinnom, so that no one could ever again use it to burn his son or daughter to death as a sacrifice to Molech. 11He tore down the statues of horses and chariots located near the entrance of the Temple, next to the quarters of Nathan-melech the eunuch. These had been dedicated by former kings of Judah to the sun god. 12Then he tore down the altars which the kings of Judah had built on the palace roof above the Ahaz Room. He also destroyed the altars which Manasseh had built in the two courts of the Temple; he smashed them to bits and scattered the pieces in Kidron Valley.

23:10
Lev 18:21
1 Kgs 11:7
Jer 7:31,32

23:12
2 Kgs 21:3-5
2 Chron 33:4,5
Jer 19:13
Zeph 1:5

13Next he removed the shrines on the hills east of Jerusalem and south of Destruction Mountain. (Solomon had built these shrines for Ashtoreth, the evil goddess of the Sidonians; and for Chemosh, the evil god of Moab; and for Milcom, the evil god of the Ammonites.) 14He smashed the obelisks and cut down the shameful idols of Asherah; then he defiled these places by scattering human bones over them. 15He also tore down the altar and shrine at Bethel which Jeroboam I had made when he led Israel into sin. He crushed the stones to dust and burned the shameful idol of Asherah.

23:13
1 Kgs 11:5
Jer 48:7

23:14
Deut 7:5,25
2 Chron 34:3,4

23:15
1 Kgs 12:28
14:16

16As Josiah was looking around, he noticed several graves in the side of the mountain. He ordered his men to bring out the bones in them and to burn them there upon the altar at Bethel to defile it, just as the Lord's prophet had declared would happen to Jeroboam's altar.

23:16
1 Kgs 13:2,32

17"What is that monument over there?" he asked.

And the men of the city told him, "It is the grave of the prophet who came from Judah and proclaimed that what you have just done would happen here at the altar at Bethel!"

23:17
1 Kgs 13:1,2,30

18So King Josiah replied, "Leave it alone. Don't disturb his bones."

So they didn't burn his bones or those of the prophet from Samaria.

23:18
1 Kgs 13:11,31

19Josiah demolished the shrines on the hills in all of Samaria. They had been built by the various kings of Israel and had made the Lord very angry. But now he crushed them into dust, just as he had done at Bethel. 20He executed the priests of the heathen shrines upon their own altars, and he burned human bones upon the altars to defile them. Finally he returned to Jerusalem.

23:19
2 Kgs 17:19
2 Chron 34:6,7

23:20
2 Kgs 10:26
11:18
2 Chron 34:5

23:9 *these priests,* literally, "the priests of the high places."

23:6 The shameful idol of Asherah was an idol the evil king Manasseh had set up in God's Temple (21:7). Asherah is most often identified as a sea goddess and the mother of several gods, including Baal.

23:13 Destruction Mountain is also called the Mount of Olives. It was called Destruction Mountain in this case because it had become a favorite spot to build heathen shrines, which were

doomed to be destroyed by God. Solomon built a heathen temple and other kings built places of idol worship there. But godly kings such as Hezekiah and Josiah destroyed these heathen worship centers. In New Testament times, Jesus often sat on the Mount of Olives and taught his disciples about serving only God (Matthew 24:3).

23:16-18 The prophecies mentioned in this passage appear in 1 Kings 13:20-32.

23:21
Num 9:2,3
Deut 16:2
2 Chron 35:1

23:22
2 Chron 35:18

23:24
Lev 19:31
Deut 18:10
2 Kgs 21:6; 22:8

21The king then issued orders for his people to observe the Passover ceremonies as recorded by the Lord their God in *The Book of the Covenant*. 22There had not been a Passover celebration like that since the days of the judges of Israel, and there was never another like it in all the years of the kings of Israel and Judah. 23This Passover was in the eighteenth year of the reign of King Josiah, and it was celebrated in Jerusalem.

24Josiah also exterminated the mediums and wizards, and every kind of idol worship, both in Jerusalem and throughout the land. For Josiah wanted to follow all

JOSIAH

Josiah never knew his great-grandfather, Hezekiah, but they were alike in many ways. Both had close, personal relationships with God. Both were passionate reformers, making valiant efforts to lead their people back to God. Both were bright lights of obedience to God among kings with darkened consciences, who seemed bent on outdoing each other in disobedience and evil.

Although Josiah's father and grandfather were exceptionally wicked, his life is an example of God's willingness to provide ongoing guidance to those who set out to be obedient. At a young age, Josiah already understood that there was spiritual sickness in his land. In a sense, Josiah began his search for God by destroying and cleaning up whatever he recognized as not belonging to the worship of the true God. In the process, God's Word was rediscovered. The king's intentions and the power of God's written revelation were brought together.

As the scroll of God's Law was read to Josiah, he was shocked, frightened, and humbled. He realized what a great gap existed between his efforts to lead his people to God and God's expectations for his chosen nation. He was overwhelmed by God's holiness and immediately tried to expose his people to that holiness. The people did respond, but the Bible makes it clear that their renewed worship of God was much more out of respect for Josiah than out of personal understanding of their own guilt before God.

How would you describe your relationship with God? Are your feeble efforts at holiness based more on a desire to "go along" with God like the people of Judah did? Or are you, like Josiah, deeply humbled by God's Word, realizing that great gap between your life and the kind of life God expects, realizing your deep need to be cleansed and renewed by him? Humble obedience pleases God. Good intentions, even reforms, are not enough. You must allow God's Word to truly humble you and change your life.

Strengths and accomplishments:
● King of Judah
● Sought after and was open to God
● Was a reformer like his great-grandfather, Hezekiah
● Cleaned out the Temple and revived obedience to God's laws

Weaknesses and mistakes:
● Became involved in a military conflict that he had been warned against

Lessons from his life:
● God consistently responds to those with repentant and humble hearts
● Even sweeping outward reforms are of little lasting value if there are no changes in people's lives

Vital statistics:
● Where: Jerusalem
● Occupation: 18th king of Judah, the Southern Kingdom
● Relatives: Father: Amon. Mother: Jedidah. Son: Jehoahaz.
● Contemporaries: Jeremiah, Huldah, Hilkiah, Zephaniah

Key verses:
"Why did your father Josiah reign so long? Because he was just and fair in all his dealings. That is why God blessed him. He saw to it that justice and help were given the poor and the needy and all went well for him. This is how a man lives close to God" (Jeremiah 22:15, 16).

Josiah's story is told in 2 Kings 21:24—23:30; 2 Chronicles 33:25—35:26. He is also mentioned in Jeremiah 1—3; 22:11—17.

23:21-23 When Josiah rediscovered the Passover in *The Book of the Covenant,* he ordered everyone to observe the ceremonies exactly as prescribed. This Passover celebration was to have been a yearly holiday celebrated in remembrance of the entire nation's deliverance from slavery in Egypt (Exodus 12), but it had not been kept for many years. As a result, "there had not been a Passover celebration like that since the days of the judges." It is a common misconception that God is against celebration, wanting to take all the fun out of life. In reality, God wants to give us life in its fullness (John 10:10), and those who love him have the most to celebrate.

the laws which were written in the book that Hilkiah the priest had found in the Temple. 25There was no other king who so completely turned to the Lord and followed all the laws of Moses; and no king since the time of Josiah has approached his record of obedience.

26But the Lord still did not hold back his great anger against Judah, caused by the evils of King Manasseh. 27For the Lord had said, "I will destroy Judah just as I have destroyed Israel; and I will discard my chosen city of Jerusalem and the Temple that I said was mine."

28The rest of the biography of Josiah is written in *The Annals of the Kings of Judah*. 29In those days King Neco of Egypt went out to help the king of Assyria at the Euphrates River. Then King Josiah went out with his troops to fight King Neco; but King Neco withstood him at Meggido and killed him. 30His officers took his body back in a chariot from Megiddo to Jerusalem and buried him in the grave he had selected. And his son Jehoahaz was chosen by the nation as its new king.

Jehoahaz rules Judah

31, 32New king of Judah: Jehoahaz
His age when he became king: 23 years old
Length of his reign: 3 months, in Jerusalem
His mother's name: Hamutal (the daughter of Jeremiah of Libnah)
Character of his reign: evil, like the other kings who had preceded him

33Pharaoh-Neco jailed him at Riblah in Hamath to prevent his reigning in Jerusalem, and he levied a tax against Judah totaling $230,000. 34The Egyptian king then chose Eliakim, another of Josiah's sons, to reign in Jerusalem; and he changed his name to Jehoiakim. Then he took King Jehoahaz to Egypt, where he died. 35Jehoiakim taxed the people to get the money that the Pharaoh had demanded.

2. Judah is exiled to Babylon

Jehoiakim rules Judah

36, 37New king of Judah: Jehoiakim
His age when he became king: 25 years old
Length of his reign: 11 years, in Jerusalem
His mother's name: Zebidah (daughter of Pedaiah of Rumah)
Character of his reign: evil, like the other kings who had preceded him

24 During the reign of King Jehoiakim, King Nebuchadnezzar of Babylon attacked Jerusalem. Jehoiakim surrendered and paid him tribute for three

Cross references (margin):

23:25 2 Kgs 18:5

23:26 2 Kgs 21:11 22:15,16

23:27 2 Kgs 17:18 21:13 Ezek 23:32

23:28 2 Kgs 20:20 24:5

23:29 2 Chron 35:20

23:30 2 Chron 36:1

23:31 2 Kgs 21:2 24:18 Jer 22:11

23:33 2 Kgs 23:29 2 Chron 35:20 36:3

23:34 1 Chron 3:15 2 Chron 36:4 Ezek 19:3

23:36 2 Chron 36:5 Jer 1:3; 26:21

24:1 2 Chron 36:6

23:25 Josiah is remembered as Judah's most obedient king. His obedience followed this pattern: (1) he recognized sin; (2) he eliminated sinful practices; and (3) he attacked the causes of sin. This approach for dealing with sin is still effective today. Not only must we remove sinful actions, we must eliminate causes for sin—those structures, systems, and patterns of life that lead us to the door of temptation.

23:25 Both Josiah and Hezekiah (18:5) are praised for their godliness. Hezekiah was said to be greatest in trusting God (faith), while Josiah is said to be greatest in following the Law of God (obedience).

23:29 King (or Pharaoh) Neco of Egypt was marching through Judah to Assyria. Egypt and Assyria had formed an alliance to battle Babylon, which was threatening to become the dominant world power. Josiah may have thought that both nations would turn on him after the battle with Babylon, so he tried to stop Egypt's army from marching through his land. But Josiah was killed, his army was defeated, and the nation of Judah became a vassal of Egypt (609 B.C.). A more detailed account of this story is found in 2 Chronicles 35:20-25.

23:31-33 The people appointed Jehoahaz, one of Josiah's sons, to be Judah's next king. But Neco was not happy with their choice, and he exiled Jehoahaz to Egypt, where he died (23:34). Neco then appointed Jehoiakim, another of Josiah's sons, king of Judah. Jehoiakim was little more than a puppet ruler. In 605 B.C., Egypt was defeated by Babylon. Judah then became a vassal of Babylon (24:1).

23:36, 37 While Josiah followed God, Jehoiakim, his son, was evil. He killed the prophet Uriah (Jeremiah 26:20-23) and was dishonest, greedy, and unjust with the people (Jeremiah 22:13-19). Jehoiakim also rebelled against Babylon, switching his allegiance to Egypt. This proved to be a crucial mistake. Nebuchadnezzar crushed Jehoiakim's rebellion and carried him to Babylon (2 Chronicles 36:6), but he was eventually allowed to return to Jerusalem, where he died. The Bible does not record the cause of his death.

24:1 Babylon became the new world power after overthrowing Assyria in 612 B.C. and defeating Egypt at the Battle of Carchemish in 605 B.C. After defeating Egypt, the Babylonians invaded Judah and brought it under their control. This was the first

24:2
2 Kgs 13:20,21
23:27

24:3
2 Kgs 18:25
21:16; 23:26

24:5
2 Kgs 23:28

24:6
Jer 22:24,25

24:7
Jer 37:5,7; 46:2

24:8
1 Chron 3:16
2 Chron 36:9

years, but then rebelled. 2And the Lord sent bands of Chaldeans, Syrians, Moab-ites, and Ammonites against Judah in order to destroy the nation, just as the Lord had warned through his prophets that he would. 3, 4It is clear that these disasters befell Judah at the direct command of the Lord. He had decided to wipe Judah out of his sight because of the many sins of Manasseh, for he had filled Jerusalem with blood, and the Lord would not pardon it.

5The rest of the history of the life of Jehoiakim is recorded in *The Annals of the Kings of Judah*. 6When he died, his son Jehoiachin became the new king. 7(The Egyptian Pharaoh never returned after that, for the king of Babylon occupied the entire area claimed by Egypt—all of Judah from the Brook of Egypt to the Euphrates River.)

Jehoiachin rules Judah

8, 9New king of Judah, Jehoiachin

His age at the beginning of his reign: 18 years old

Length of his reign: 3 months, in Jerusalem

Name of his mother: Nehushta (daughter of Elnathan, a citizen of Jerusalem)

KINGS TO DATE AND THEIR ENEMIES

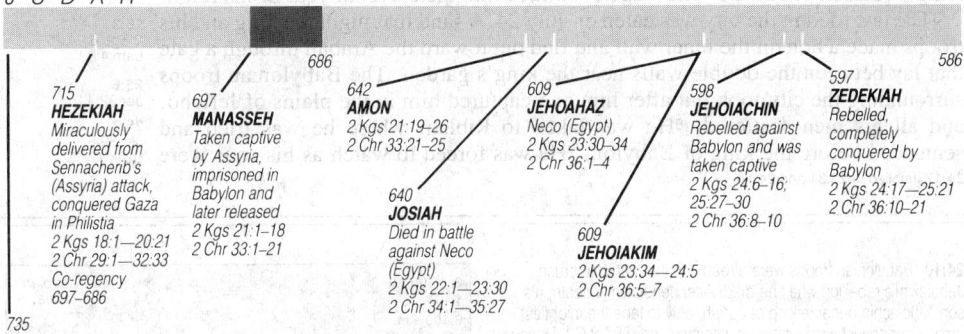

722
Captivity in Assyria

I S R A E L

J U D A H

686   597

715
HEZEKIAH
Miraculously
delivered from
Sennacherib's
(Assyria) attack,
conquered Gaza
in Philistia
2 Kgs 18:1—20:21
2 Chr 29:1—32:33
Co-regency
697–686

697
MANASSEH
Taken captive
by Assyria,
imprisoned in
Babylon and
later released
2 Kgs 21:1–18
2 Chr 33:1–21

642
AMON
2 Kgs 21:19–26
2 Chr 33:21–25

640
JOSIAH
Died in battle
against Neco
(Egypt)
2 Kgs 22:1—23:30
2 Chr 34:1—35:27

609
JEHOAHAZ
Neco (Egypt)
2 Kgs 23:30–34
2 Chr 36:1–4

609
JEHOIAKIM
2 Kgs 23:34—24:5
2 Chr 36:5–7

598
JEHOIACHIN
Rebelled against
Babylon and was
taken captive
2 Kgs 24:6–16;
25:27–30
2 Chr 36:8–10

597
ZEDEKIAH
Rebelled,
completely
conquered by
Babylon
2 Kgs 24:17—25:21
2 Chr 36:10–21

586

735
AHAZ
Harassed by
Pekah (Israel),
paid Assyria for
protection against
Rezin (Syria),
also harassed by
Edom and Philistia
2 Kgs 16:1–20
2 Chr 28:1–27

All dates are B.C.
Solid section of the timeline indicates co-regency.
For all the kings of Israel and Judah, see the chart between the books of 1 and 2 Kings.

---

of three Babylonian invasions of Judah over the next 20 years. The other two invasions occurred in 597 and 586 B.C. With each invasion, captives were taken back to Babylon. Daniel, who wrote the book of Daniel, was one of the captives taken during this first

invasion (605 B.C.; Daniel 1:1, 2).

24:1 For more information on Nebuchadnezzar, see his Profile in Daniel 4.

¹⁰During his reign the armies of King Nebuchadnezzar of Babylon besieged the city of Jerusalem. ¹¹Nebuchadnezzar himself arrived during the siege, ¹²and King Jehoiachin, all of his officials, and the queen mother surrendered to him. The surrender was accepted, and Jehoiachin was imprisoned in Babylon during the eighth year of Nebuchadnezzar's reign.

¹³The Babylonians carried home all the treasures from the Temple and the royal palace; and they cut apart all the gold bowls which King Solomon of Israel had placed in the Temple at the Lord's directions. ¹⁴King Nebuchadnezzar took ten thousand captives from Jerusalem, including all the princes and the best of the soldiers, craftsmen, and smiths. So only the poorest and least skilled people were left in the land. ¹⁵Nebuchadnezzar took King Jehoiachin, his wives and officials, and the queen mother, to Babylon. ¹⁶He also took seven thousand of the best troops and one thousand craftsmen and smiths, all of whom were strong and fit for war. ¹⁷Then the king of Babylon appointed King Jehoiachin's great-uncle, Mattaniah, to be the next king; and he changed his name to Zedekiah.

Zedekiah rules Judah

^{18, 19}New king of Judah: Zedekiah
His age when he became king: 21 years old
Length of his reign: 11 years, in Jerusalem
His mother's name: Hamutal (daughter of Jeremiah of Libnah)
Character of his reign: evil, like that of Jehoiakim

²⁰So the Lord finally, in his anger, destroyed the people of Jerusalem and Judah. But now King Zedekiah rebelled against the king of Babylon.

25 Then King Nebuchadnezzar of Babylon mobilized his entire army and laid siege to Jerusalem, arriving on March 25 of the ninth year of the reign of King Zedekiah of Judah. ²The siege continued into the eleventh year of his reign.

³The last food in the city was eaten on July 24, ^{4, 5}and that night the king and his troops made a hole in the inner wall and fled out toward the Arabah through a gate that lay between the double walls near the king's garden. The Babylonian troops surrounding the city took out after him and captured him in the plains of Jericho, and all his men scattered. ⁶He was taken to Riblah, where he was tried and sentenced before the king of Babylon. ⁷He was forced to watch as his sons were

24:10 2 Kgs 25:2
24:12 2 Chron 36:10 Jer 24:1; 29:1 Ezek 17:12,13
24:13 1 Kgs 7:48 2 Kgs 20:17 25:13 Isa 39:6 Jer 20:5
24:14 2 Kgs 25:12 Jer 24:1; 52:28
24:17 2 Chron 36:10 Jer 37:1; 52:1
24:18 2 Kgs 23:31
24:20 2 Chron 36:13 Jer 27:12 38:17,21,22 39:1
25:1 2 Chron 36:17 Jer 39:1 Ezek 24:2
25:3 2 Kgs 6:24,25 Lam 4:9
25:6 Jer 32:4
25:7 Jer 39:6 Ezek 12:13

24:17 Implied in 23:31 and 24:18.

24:10 Babylonian troops were already on the march to crush Jehoiakim's rebellion when he died. After Jehoiakim's death, his son Jehoiachin became king of Judah, only to face the mightiest army on earth just weeks after he was crowned (597 B.C.). During this second of three invasions, the Babylonians looted the Temple and took most of the leaders, including the king, captive. Then Nebuchadnezzar placed Zedekiah, another son of Josiah, on the throne. The Jews, however, didn't recognize him as their true king as long as Jehoiachin was still alive, even though he was a captive in Babylon.

24:14 The Babylonian policy for taking captives was different from that of the Assyrians, who moved most of the people out and resettled the land with foreigners (see the note on 17:24). The Babylonians took only the strong and skilled, leaving the poor and weak to rule the land, thus elevating them to positions of authority and winning their loyalty. The leaders were taken to Babylonian cities, but they were permitted to live together, find jobs, and become an important part of the society. This policy kept the Jews united and faithful to God throughout the captivity and made it possible for their return in the days of Zerubbabel and Ezra as recorded in the book of Ezra.

25:1 Judah was invaded by the Babylonians three times (24:1; 24:10; 25:1), just as Israel was invaded by the Assyrians three times. Once again, God demonstrated his mercy in the face of

JUDAH EXILED Evil permeated Judah and God's anger flared against his rebellious people. Babylon conquered Assyria and became the new world power. The Babylonian army marched into Jerusalem, burned the Temple, tore down the city's massive walls, and carried off the people into captivity.

deserved judgment by giving the people repeated opportunities to repent.

killed before his eyes; then his eyes were put out and he was bound with chains and taken away to Babylon.

Jerusalem is demolished

8General Nebuzaradan, the captain of the royal bodyguard, arrived at Jerusalem from Babylon on July 22 of the nineteenth year of the reign of King Nebuchadnezzar. 9He burned down the Temple, the palace, and all the other houses of any worth. 10He then supervised the Babylonian army in tearing down the walls of Jerusalem. 11The remainder of the people in the city and the Jewish deserters who had declared their allegiance to the king of Babylon were all taken as exiles to Babylon. 12But the poorest of the people were left to farm the land.

13The Babylonians broke up the bronze pillars of the Temple and the bronze tank and its bases and carried all the bronze to Babylon. 14, 15They also took all the pots, shovels, firepans, snuffers, spoons, and other bronze instruments used for the sacrifices. The gold and silver bowls, with all the rest of the gold and silver, were melted down to bullion. 16It was impossible to estimate the weight of the two pillars and the great tank and its bases—all made for the Temple by King Solomon—because they were so heavy. 17Each pillar was twenty-seven feet high, with an intricate bronze network of pomegranates decorating the 4½-foot capitals at the tops of the pillars.

18The general took Seraiah, the chief priest, his assistant Zephaniah, and the three Temple guards to Babylon as captives. 19A commander of the army of Judah, the chief recruiting officer, five of the king's counselors, and sixty farmers, all of whom were discovered hiding in the city, 20were taken by General Nebuzaradan to the king of Babylon at Riblah, 21where they were put to the sword and died.

So Judah was exiled from its land.

TEMPLE INVADERS	Who?	Reference	What happened
	Shishak, king of Egypt	1 Kings 14:25, 26	Ransacked the Temple, carried away certain treasures
	Asa, king of Judah	1 Kings 15:18, 19	Took Temple treasures and money to buy an alliance with King Ben-hadad of Syria
	Athaliah, queen of Judah	2 Kings 11:13–15 2 Chronicles 24:7, 8	Ravaged the Temple. Later ran into the Temple only to discover that her wicked reign had come to an end.
	Joash, king of Judah	2 Kings 12:18	Took gold and sacred objects from the Temple to stop King Hazael of Syria from attacking
	Joash, king of Israel	2 Kings 14:14	Entered the Temple, taking gold, silver, and gold cups to get back at Amaziah
	Ahaz, king of Judah	2 Kings 16:8–18	Took silver, gold, and various furnishings from the Temple to send sufficient tribute to appease Assyria's king
	Hezekiah, king of Judah	2 Kings 18:13–18	Took all the silver from the Temple and stripped the gold from its doors to persuade Sennacherib, king of Assyria, to call off his attack
	Manasseh, king of Judah	2 Kings 21:1–8	Placed heathen altars in the Temple
	Nebuchadnezzar, king of Babylon	2 Kings 24:13–17 2 Chronicles 36:10 2 Kings 25:1–21 2 Chronicles 36:17–20	Nebuchadnezzar raided the Temple during his second and third invasions of Judah. In his third invasion, he destroyed the Temple and carried away all its treasures.

25:21 Judah, like Israel, was unfaithful to God. So God, as he had warned, allowed Judah to be destroyed and taken away (Deuteronomy 28). The book of Lamentations records the prophet Jeremiah's sorrow at seeing Jerusalem destroyed.

Leadership after the fall of Jerusalem

22Then King Nebuchadnezzar appointed Gedaliah (the son of Ahikam and grandson of Shaphan) as governor over the people left in Judah. 23When the Israeli guerrilla forces learned that the king of Babylon had appointed Gedaliah as governor, some of these underground leaders and their men joined him at Mizpah. These included Ishmael, the son of Nethaniah; Johanan, the son of Kareah; Seraiah, the son of Tanhumeth the Netophathite; and Jaazaniah, son of Maachathite, and their men.

24Gedaliah vowed that if they would give themselves up and submit to the Babylonians, they would be allowed to live in the land and would not be exiled. 25But seven months later, Ishmael, who was a member of the royal line, went to Mizpah with ten men and killed Gedaliah and his court—both the Jews and the Babylonians.

26Then all the men of Judah and the guerrilla leaders fled in panic to Egypt, for they were afraid of what the Babylonians would do to them.

27King Jehoiachin was released from prison on the twenty-seventh day of the last month of the thirty-seventh year of his captivity.

This occurred during the first year of the reign of King Evil-merodach of Babylon. 28He treated Jehoiachin kindly and gave him preferential treatment over all the other kings who were being held as prisoners in Babylon. 29Jehoiachin was given civilian clothing to replace his prison garb, and for as long as he lived, he ate regularly at the king's table. 30The king also gave him a daily cash allowance for the rest of his life.

25:22
Jer 39:14

25:23
Jer 40:7

25:25
Jer 41:1

25:26
Jer 43:5

25:27
Jer 52:31

25:22-30 This story illustrates that the last hope of Israel's gaining back her land was gone—even her guerilla rebels had fled. Judah's earthly kingdom was absolutely demolished, but through prophets like Ezekiel and Daniel, who were also captives, God was able to keep his spiritual kingdom alive in the hearts of many of the exiles.

25:27 King Evil-merodach, the son of Nebuchadnezzar, became king of the Babylonian empire in 583 B.C., 24 years after the beginning of the captivity. He treated Jehoiachin with kindness, even allowing him to eat at his table (25:29). Evil-merodach was later killed in a plot by his brother-in-law, Nergal-sharezer, who succeeded him to the throne.

25:30 The book of 2 Kings opens with Elijah being carried to heaven—the destination awaiting those who follow God. But the book ends with the people of Judah being carried off to foreign lands as humiliated slaves—the result of failing to follow God.

Second Kings is an illustration of what happens when we make anything more important than God, when we make ruinous alliances, when our consciences become desensitized to right and wrong, and when we are no longer able to discern God's purpose for our lives. We may fail, like the people of Judah and Israel, but God's promises do not. He is always there to help us straighten out our lives and start over. And that is just what happens in the book of Ezra. When the people acknowledged their sins, God was ready and willing to help them return to their land and start again.

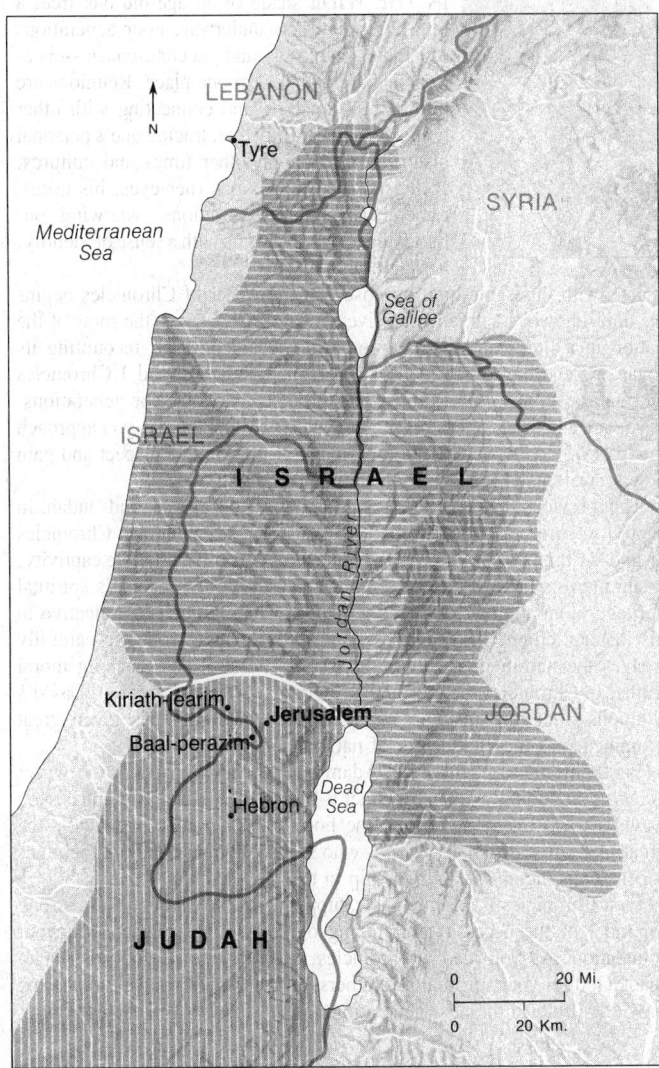

LEBANON

Tyre

Mediterranean
Sea

SYRIA

Sea of
Galilee

ISRAEL

I S R A E L

Jordan River

Kiriath-jearim

Jerusalem

Baal-perazim

JORDAN

Hebron

Dead
Sea

JUDAH

0   20 Mi.

0   20 Km.

Modern names and boundaries are shown in gray.

The genealogies of 1 Chronicles present an overview of
Israel's history. The first nine chapters are filled with
genealogies tracing the lineages of people from the creation
to the exile in Babylon. Saul's death is recorded in chapter
10. Chapter 11 begins the history of David's reign over
Israel.

1 Hebron Although David had been anointed king years
earlier, his reign began when
the leaders of Israel accepted
him as king at Hebron (11:1–3).

2 Jerusalem David set out to
complete the conquest of the
land begun by Joshua. He
attacked Jerusalem, captured it,
and made it his capital
(11:4—12:40).

3 Kiriath-jearim The Ark of the
Covenant, which had been
captured by the Philistines in
battle and returned (1 Samuel
4—6), was in safe-keeping in
Kiriath-jearim. David summoned
all Israel to this city to join in
bringing the Ark to Jerusalem.
Unfortunately, it was not moved
according to God's instructions,
and as a result one man died.
David left the Ark in the home of
Obed-edom until he could
discover how to transport it
correctly (13:1–14).

4 Tyre David did much building
in Jerusalem. King Hiram of
Tyre sent workers and supplies
to help build David's palace.
Cedar, abundant in the
mountains north of Israel, was a
valuable and hardy wood for the
beautiful buildings in Jerusalem
(14:1—17:27).

5 Baal-perazim David was not
very popular with the Philistines
because he had slain Goliath,
one of their greatest warriors
(1 Samuel 17). When David
began to rule over a united
Israel, the Philistines set out to
capture him. But David and his
army attacked the Philistines at
Baal-perazim as they approached Jerusalem. His army defeated
the mighty Philistines twice,
causing all the surrounding
nations to fear David's power
(14:11–17). After this battle,
David moved the Ark to Jerusalem (this time in
accordance with God's instructions for the transportation
of the Ark). There was great celebration as the Ark was
brought into Jerusalem (15:1—17:27). David spent the
remainder of his life making preparations for the building
of the Temple, a central place for the worship of God
(18:1—29:30).

1 CHRONICLES

VITAL STATISTICS

PURPOSE:
To unify God's people, to trace the Davidic line, and to teach that genuine worship ought to be the center of individual and national life

AUTHOR:
Ezra, according to Jewish tradition

TO WHOM WRITTEN:
All Israel

DATE WRITTEN:
Approximately 430 B.C.; recording events which occurred from about 1000–960 B.C.

SETTING:
First Chronicles parallels 2 Samuel and serves as a commentary on it. Written after the exile from a priestly point of view, 1 Chronicles emphasizes the religious history of Judah and Israel.

KEY VERSE:
"David now realized why the Lord had made him king and why he had made his kingdom so great; it was for a special reason—to give joy to God's people" (14:2).

KEY PEOPLE:
David, Solomon

KEY PLACES:
Hebron, Jerusalem, the Temple

IN THE WIDE shade of an age-old oak tree, a family reunion gets underway. Four generations of kids, parents, and second-cousins-once-removed are gathered in one place. Reunions are important—touching and connecting with other branches of the family tree, tracing one's personal history back through other times and cultures, seeing physical reflections (her eyes, his nose), remembering family traditions. Knowing our family history provides us with a sense of identity, heritage, and destiny.

It is with this same high purpose that the writer of Chronicles begins his unifying work with an extensive genealogy. He traces the roots of the nation in a literary family reunion from Adam onward, recounting its royal line and the loving plan of a personal God. We read 1 Chronicles and gain a glimpse of God at work through his people for generations. If you are a believer, these people are your ancestors too. As you approach this part of God's Word, read their names with awe and respect and gain new security and identity in your relationship with God.

The previous book, 2 Kings, ends with both Israel and Judah in captivity, surely a dark age for God's people. Then follows Chronicles (1 and 2 Chronicles were originally one book). Written after the captivity, it summarizes Israel's history, emphasizing the Jewish people's spiritual heritage in an attempt to unify the nation. The chronicler is selective in his history telling. Instead of writing an exhaustive work, he carefully weaves the narrative, highlighting spiritual lessons and teaching moral truths. In Chronicles the Northern Kingdom is virtually ignored, David's triumphs—not his sins—are recalled, and the Temple is given great prominence as the vital center of national life.

First Chronicles begins with Adam and, for nine chapters, the writer gives us a "Who's Who" of Israel's history with special emphasis on David's royal line. The rest of the book tells the story of David—the great man of God, Israel's king—who served God and laid out the plans for the construction of and worship in the Temple.

First Chronicles is an invaluable supplement to 2 Samuel and a strong reminder of the necessity for tracing our roots, thus rediscovering our foundation. As you read 1 Chronicles, trace your own godly heritage, thank God for your spiritual forefathers, and recommit yourself to passing on God's truth to the next generation.

THE BLUEPRINT

A. THE GENEALOGIES OF ISRAEL
(1:1—9:44)
1. Ancestry of the nation
2. The tribes of Israel
3. Returnees from exile in Babylon

The long list of names that follows presents a history of God's work in the world from Adam through Zerubbabel. Some of these names remind us of stories of great faith, and others of tragic failure. About most of the people named, however, we know nothing. But those who died unknown to us are known by God. God will also remember us when we die.

B. THE REIGN OF DAVID (10:1—29:30)
   1. David becomes king over all of Israel
   2. David brings the Ark to Jerusalem
   3. David's military exploits
   4. David arranges for the building of the Temple

David loved the Lord, but in his zeal to demonstrate that love he sometimes pushed ahead without considering all the options. On David's first attempt to bring the Ark into Jerusalem, Uzza was killed. Later, David brought the Ark to Jerusalem in accordance with God's Law. He also wanted to build a temple to replace the Tabernacle, but this time David asked God first and God denied his request. David's greatest contribution to the Temple would not be the construction, but the preparation. Under God's blessing, David began collecting materials and organizing the priests and Levites to work there. We may be unable to see the results of our labors for God in our lifetime, but David's example helps us understand that we serve God so *he* will see *his* results, not so we will see ours.

MEGATHEMES

THEME	EXPLANATION	IMPORTANCE
Israel's history	By retelling Israel's history in the genealogies and the stories of the kings, the writer laid down the true spiritual foundation for the nation. God kept his promises and we are reminded of them in the historical record of his people, leaders, prophets, priests, and kings.	Israel's past formed a reliable basis for reconstructing the nation after the exile. Because God's promises are revealed in the Bible, we can know God and trust him to keep his word. Like Israel, we have no higher goal in life than devoted service to God.
God's people	By listing the names of people in Israel's past, God established Israel's true heritage. They were all one family in Adam, one nation in Abraham, one priesthood under Levi, and one kingdom under David. The national and spiritual unity of the people were important to the rebuilding of the nation.	God is always faithful to his people. He protects them in every generation and provides leaders to guide them. Because God has been at work throughout the centuries, his people can trust him to work in the present. You can rely on his presence today.
David, the king	The story of David's life and his relationship with God showed that he was God's appointed leader. David's devotion to God, the Law, the Temple, true worship, the people, and justice sets the standard for what God's chosen king should be.	Jesus Christ came to earth as a descendant of David. One day he will rule as king over all the earth. His strength and justice will fulfill God's ideal for the king. He is our hope.
True worship	David brought the Ark of the Covenant to the Tabernacle at Jerusalem to restore true worship to the people. God gave the plans for building the Temple, and David organized the priests to make worship central to all Israel.	The Temple stood as the throne of God on earth, the place of true worship. God's true throne is in the hearts of his people. When we acknowledge him as the true king over our lives, true worship takes place.
The priests	God ordained the priests and Levites to guide the people in faithful worship according to his Law. By leading the people in worship according to God's design, the priests and Levites were an important safeguard to Israel's faith.	For true worship to remain central in our lives, God's people need to take a firm stand for the ways of God recorded in the Bible. Today, all believers are priests for one another, and we should encourage each other to faithful worship.

A. THE GENEALOGIES OF ISRAEL (1:1—9:44)

These genealogies are the official family records of the nation of Israel. They give us an overview of the history of God's work from creation through the captivity of his people. These records served to teach the exiles returning from Babylon about their spiritual heritage as a nation and to inspire them to renew their faithfulness to God. Although these lists show the racial heritage of the Jews, they contain the spiritual heritage for every believer. We are a part of the community of faith which has existed from generation to generation since the dawn of man.

1. Ancestry of the nation

Adam's descendants

1 These are the earliest generations of mankind: Adam, Seth, Enosh, Kenan, Mahalalel, Jared, Enoch, Methuselah, Lamech, Noah, **Shem, Ham,** and **Japheth.**

5-9The sons of *Japheth* were: **Gomer,** Magog, Madai, **Javan,** Tubal, Meshech, and Tiras.

The sons of *Gomer:* Ashkenaz, Diphath, and Togarmah.

The sons of *Javan:* Elishah, Tarshish, Kittim, and Rodanim.

The sons of *Ham:* **Cush, Misream, Canaan,** and **Put.**

The sons of *Cush* were: Seba, Havilah, Sabta, Raama, and Sabteca.

The sons of *Raama* were Sheba and Dedan.

10Another of the sons of *Cush* was Nimrod, who became a great hero.

11, 12The clans named after the sons of *Misream* were: the Ludim, the Anamim, the Lehabim, the Naphtuhim, the Pathrusim, the Caphtorim, and the Casluhim (the ancestors of the Philistines).

13-16Among *Canaan's* sons were: Sidon (his firstborn) and Heth.

Canaan was also the ancestor of the Jebusites, Amorites, Girgashites, Hivites, Arkites, Sinites, Arvadites, Zemarites, and Hamathites.

17The sons of *Shem:* Elam, Asshur, **Arpachshad,** Lud, Aram, Uz, Hul, Gether, and Meshech.

18*Arpachshad's* son was **Shelah,** and *Shelah's* son was **Eber.**

19*Eber* had two sons: Peleg (which means "Divided," for it was during his

1:1 Gen 4:25 5:3-32; 10:1 Isa 54:9,10 Ezek 14:14 Mt 24:37 Lk 3:38 Heb 11:7

1:5 Gen 10:2-4,6-8 1 Chron 4:40,42 Ezek 27:13

1:10 Gen 10:8

1:11 Gen 9:22 10:13-18

1:13 Gen 15:19-21

1:17 Gen 10:21,22 11:10 Lk 3:36

1:19 Gen 11:16

1:1-4 *These are the earliest generations of mankind,* implied. *Shem, Ham and Japheth.* The names in bold face type are referred to in the following verse or verses. The use of bold type or italic type does not mean that these persons were more important; it is simply a way of easier identification of ancestors and descendants. **1:5-7** *Japheth.* Italic means that the name has previously appeared in bold face type.

1:1ff This long list of names was compiled after the people of Judah were taken captive to Babylon. As the exiles looked forward to the day when they would return to their homeland, one of their biggest fears was that the records of their heritage would be lost. The Jews placed great importance upon their heritage because each one wanted to be able to prove that he was a descendant of Abraham, the father of the Jewish people. Only then could he enjoy the benefits of the special blessings God promised to Abraham and his descendants (see the notes on Genesis 12:1-3 and 17:2-4 for what these special blessings were). This list reconstructed Judah's and Israel's family tree prior to the captivity and served as proof for those who claimed to be Abraham's descendants. (For more information about why the Bible includes genealogies, read the notes on Genesis 5:1ff, Matthew 1:1, and Luke 3:23-38.)

1:1ff There is more to this long genealogy than meets the eye. It holds importance for us today because it proves the Old Testament claims that Jesus the Messiah would be a descendant of Abraham and David. Two of these claims are recorded in Genesis 12:1-3 and 2 Samuel 7:12, 13.

1:1 This record of names demonstrates that God is interested not only in nations, but also in individuals. Although billions of people have lived since Adam, God knows and remembers the face and name of each person. Each individual is more than a name on a list; he or she is a special person whom God knows and loves. As

we recognize and accept his love, we discover both our uniqueness as individuals and our solidarity with the rest of his family.

1:4 Adam's story and Profile are found in Genesis 1—5. Noah's story and Profile are found in Genesis 6—9.

1:10 Nimrod is also mentioned in Genesis 10:8, 9.

1:11, 12 The Philistines had been Israel's constant enemy from the days of the Judges. King David finally weakened them, and by this time they were no longer a threat. (For more information on the Philistines, see notes on Judges 13:1 and 1 Samuel 4:1.)

1:13—16 Canaan was the ancestor of the Canaanites, who inhabited the Promised Land (also called Canaan) before the Israelites arrived under Joshua's leadership. God helped the Israelites drive out the Canaanites, who were an especially wicked people. The land's name was then changed to Israel. The book of Joshua tells this story.

1:19 At one time, everyone spoke a single language. But some people became proud of their accomplishments and gathered to build a monument to themselves—the tower of Babel. However, the building project was brought to an abrupt conclusion when God caused the people to speak different languages. Without the ability to communicate with one another, the people were unable to be unified. God showed them that their great efforts were useless without him. This story is told in Genesis 11:1-9.

lifetime that the people of the earth were divided into different language groups), and Joktan.

20-23The sons of Joktan: Almodad, Sheleph, Hazarmaveth, Jerah, Hadoram, Uzal, Diklah, Ebal, Abima-el, Sheba, Ophir, Havilah, and Jobab.

1:24
Gen 11:10-26
Lk 3:34

24-27So the son of *Shem* was Arpachshad, the son of Arpachshad was Shelah, the son of Shelah was Eber, the son of Eber was Peleg, the son of Peleg was Reu, the son of Reu was Serug, the son of Serug was Nahor, the son of Nahor was Terah, the son of Terah was Abram (later known as Abraham).

1:28
Gen 16:9-12
17:19; 21:3,9
25:9,10

28-31Abraham's sons were Isaac and Ishmael.

The sons of *Ishmael:* Nabaioth (the oldest), Kedar, Adbeel, Mibsam, Mishma, Dumah, Massa, Hadad, Tema, Jetur, Naphish, and Kedemah.

1:32
Gen 25:1,2

32Abraham also had sons by his concubine Keturah: Zimram, **Jokshan,** Medan, **Midian,** Ishbak, and Shuah.

Jokshan's sons were Sheba and Dedan.

33The sons of *Midian:* Ephah, Epher, Hanoch, Abida, and Eldaah. These were the descendants of Abraham by his concubine Keturah.

1:34
Gen 25:25,26
32:28
Mal 1:2,3
Mt 1:2

34Abraham's son *Isaac* had two sons, Esau and Israel.

35The sons of *Esau:* **Eliphaz, Reuel,** Jeush, Jalam, and Korah.

36The sons of *Eliphaz:* Teman, Omar, Zephi, Gatam, Kenaz, Timna, and Amalek.

1:35
Gen 36:4-12

37The sons of *Reuel:* Nahath, Zerah, Shammah, and Mizzah.

1:38
Gen 36:18-21

38, 39The sons of *Esau* also included **Lotan, Shobal, Zibeon,** Anah, **Dishon, Ezer,** and **Dishan;** and Esau's daughter was named Timna. *Lotan's* sons: Hori and Homam.

40The sons of *Shobal:* Alian, Manahath, Ebal, Shephi, and Onam. *Zibeon's* sons were Aiah and **Anah.**

41*Anah's* son was **Dishon:** The sons of *Dishon:* Hamran, Eshban, Ithran, and Cheran.

42The sons of *Ezer:* Bilhan, Zaavan, and Jaakan. *Dishan's* sons were Uz and Aran.

1:43
Gen 36:31-39

43Here is a list of the names of the kings of Edom who reigned before the kingdom of Israel began:

Bela (the son of Beor), who lived in the city of Dinhabah.

44When Bela died, Jobab the son of Zerah from Bozrah became the new king.

45When Jobab died, Husham from the country of the Temanites became the king.

1:45
Job 2:11

46When Husham died, Hadad the son of Bedad—the one who destroyed the army of Midian in the fields of Moab—became king and ruled from the city of Avith.

47When Hadad died, Samlah from the city of Masrekah came to the throne.

48When Samlah died, Shaul from the river town of Rehoboth became the new king.

49When Shaul died, Baal-hanan the son of Achbor became king.

50When Baal-hanan died, Hadad became king and ruled from the city of Pai (his wife was Mehetabel, the daughter of Matred and granddaughter of Mezahab).

1:38, 39 *Esau,* or "Seir."

1:24-27 "The son of" can also mean "the descendant of." Thus a biblical genealogy may skip several generations. These genealogical lists were not meant to be exhaustive, but to give basic information about the various family lines.

1:24-27 Abraham's story and Profile are found in Genesis 11:26—25:10.

1:28-31 Ishmael's story and Profile are found in Genesis 16—21.

1:34 Israel is another name for Jacob; Jacob's descendants became the nation of Israel. Esau's descendants became the nation of Edom, a constant enemy of Israel. To learn more about the lives of Isaac and his two sons, Jacob and Esau, read their stories and Profiles in Genesis 21—36; 46—49.

1:36 Amalek, Esau's grandson, was the son of his father's

concubine (Genesis 36:12). He was the ancestor of the wicked tribe known as Amalekites, the first people to attack the Israelites on their way to the Promised Land. (For more about the Amalekites, read the note on Exodus 17:8.)

1:43-54 Why are we given information in this genealogy about the descendants of Edom who were Israel's enemies? Esau, ancestor of the Edomites, was Isaac's oldest son and thus a direct descendant of Abraham. As Abraham's first grandson, he deserved a place in the Jewish records. It was through Esau's marriages to heathen women, however, that the nation of Edom began. This genealogy shows the ancestry of enemy nations; they were *not* a part of the direct lineage of David.

51-54At the time of Hadad's death, the kings of Edom were: Chief Timna, Chief Aliah, Chief Jetheth, Chief Oholibamah, Chief Elah, Chief Pinon, Chief Kenaz, Chief Teman, Chief Mibzar, Chief Magdi-el, Chief Iram.

Jacob's descendants

2 The sons of Israel were: Reuben, Simeon, Levi, Judah, Issachar, Zebulun, Dan, Joseph, Benjamin, Naphtali, Gad, Asher.

3Judah had three sons by Bath-shua, a girl from Canaan: **Er,** Onan, and Shelah. But the oldest son, *Er,* was so wicked that the Lord killed him.

4Then Er's widow, Tamar, and her father-in-law, Judah, became the parents of twin sons, **Perez** and **Zerah.** So Judah had five sons.

5The sons of *Perez* were Hezron and Hamul.

6The sons of *Zerah* were: Zimri, **Ethan,** Heman, Calcol, and Dara.

7(Achan, the son of Carmi, was the man who robbed God and was such a troublemaker for his nation.)

8*Ethan's* son was Azariah.

9The sons of *Hezron* were Jerahmeel, Ram, and Chelubai.

10Ram was the father of Amminadab, and Amminadab was the father of Nahshon, a leader of Israel.

11Nahshon was the father of Salma, and Salma was the father of Boaz.

12Boaz was the father of Obed, and Obed was the father of Jesse.

13*Jesse's* first son was Eliab, his second was Abinadab, his third was Shimea, 14his fourth was Nethanel, his fifth was Raddai, 15his sixth was Ozem, and his seventh was David. 16He also had two girls (by the same wife) named **Zeruiah** and **Abigail.**

Zeruiah's sons were Abishai, Joab, and Asahel.

17*Abigail,* whose husband was Jether from the land of Ishmael, had a son named Amasa.

18Caleb (the son of **Hezron**) had two wives, **Azubah** and Jerioth. These are the children of *Azubah:* Jesher, Shobab, and Ardon.

19After Azubah's death, Caleb married Ephrath, who presented him with a son, **Hur.**

20*Hur's* son was **Uri,** and *Uri's* son was Bezalel.

21**Hezron** married Machir's daughter at the age of sixty, and she presented him with a son, **Segub.** (Machir was also the father of Gilead.)

22*Segub* was the father of Jair, who ruled twenty-three cities in the land of Gilead. 23But Geshur and Aram wrested these cities from him and also took Kenath and its sixty surrounding villages.

24Soon after his father *Hezron's* death, Caleb married Ephrathah, his father's widow, and she gave birth to Ashhur, the father of Tekoa.

25These are the sons of **Jerahmeel** (the oldest son of *Hezron*): **Ram** (the oldest), Bunah, Oren, Ozem, and Ahijah.

2:22 *ruled,* literally, "had."

Cross-references (right margin):
2:1 Gen 35:22-26; 46:8-25
Ex 1:1-4
Num 1:2-15
Rev 7:4-8
2:3 Gen 38:2-10
2:4 Gen 38:13-30; 46:8-14
2:7 Josh 7:17; 22:20
2:10 Num 7:12; 10:14
Mt 1:4
Lk 3:32
2:12 Ruth 4:16,17
Mt 1:5
2:13 1 Sam 16:8
2:16 1 Sam 26:5-7
2 Sam 2:13
1 Chron 11:5,6
2:17 2 Sam 17:25; 19:13
1 Kgs 2:5

2:1, 2 The story of Israel's (Jacob's) sons is found in Genesis 29:32—50:26. Profiles of Reuben, Judah, and Joseph are found in the same section.

2:3 This long genealogy not only lists names, but gives us insights into some of the people. Here, almost as an epitaph, the genealogy states that Er "was so wicked that the Lord killed him." Now, centuries later, this is all we know of the man. Each of us is forging a reputation, developing personal qualities by which we will be remembered. How would God summarize your life up to now? Some defiantly claim that how they live is their own business. But Scripture teaches that the way you live today will determine how you will be remembered by others and how you will be judged by God. What you do now *does* matter.

2:12 Boaz was Ruth's husband and an ancestor of both King David and the Messiah. Boaz's Profile is in the book of Ruth.

2:15 David is one of the most well-known people of the Bible. He was certainly not perfect, but he exemplified what it means to seek God first in all areas of life. God called David "a man after my own heart" (Acts 13:22) because his greatest desire was to serve and worship God. David's story is found in 1 Samuel 16:1—1 Kings 2:10 and 1 Chronicles 10:14—29:30. David's Profile is found in 1 Samuel 17.

2:16 Joab's story is found in 2 Samuel 2, 3, 10—20, 24; 1 Kings 1—3; 1 Chronicles 11:4-9; 19—21. His Profile is found in 2 Samuel 19. Abishai's story is found in 1 Samuel 26; 2 Samuel 2, 3, 10, 15—21, 23; 1 Chronicles 18:12; 19. Abishai's Profile is found in 2 Samuel 21.

2:18 This is not the Caleb who spied out the Promised Land with Joshua. Caleb the spy is listed in 4:15.

26*Jerahmeel's* second wife Atarah was the mother of **Onam.**

27The sons of *Ram:* Maaz, Jamin, and Eker.

28*Onam's* sons were **Shammai** and Jada. *Shammai's* sons were **Nadab** and **Abishur.**

29The sons of *Abishur* and his wife Abihail were Ahban and Molid.

30*Nadab's* sons were **Seled** and **Appa-im.** *Seled* died without children, 31but *Appa-im* had a son named **Ishi;** *Ishi's* son was **Sheshan;** and *Sheshan's* son was Ahlai.

32*Shammai's* brother Jada had two sons, **Jether** and **Jonathan.** *Jether* died without children, 33but *Jonathan* had two sons named Peleth and Zaza.

34, 35*Sheshan* had no sons, although he had several daughters. He gave one of his daughters to be the wife of Jarha, his Egyptian servant. And they had a son whom they named **Attai.**

2:36
1 Chron 11:41

36Attai's son was Nathan; Nathan's son was Zabad; 37Zabad's son was Ephlal; Ephlal's son was Obed; 38Obed's son was Jehu; Jehu's son was Azariah; 39Azariah's son was Helez; Helez's son was Ele-asah; 40Ele-asah's son was Sismai; Sismai's son was Shallum; 41Shallum's son was Jekamiah; Jekamiah's son was Elishama.

42The oldest son of **Caleb** (Jerahmeel's brother) was Mesha; he was the father of Ziph, who was father of Mareshah, who was the father of **Hebron.**

43The sons of *Hebron:* Korah, Tappuah, **Rekem,** and **Shema.**

44*Shema* was the father of Raham, who was the father of Jorke-am. *Rekem* was the father of **Shammai.**

45*Shammai's* son was Maon, the father of Bethzur.

46*Caleb's* concubine Ephah bore him **Haran,** Moza, and Gazez; *Haran* had a son named Gazez.

47The sons of Jahdai: Regem, Jotham, Geshan, Pelet, Ephah, and Shaaph.

2:48
Josh 15:17
Judg 1:2

48, 49Another of *Caleb's* concubines, Maacah, bore him Sheber, Tirhanah, Shaaph (the father of Madmannah), and Sheva (the father of Machbenah and of Gibe-a). *Caleb* also had a daughter, whose name was Achsah.

50The sons of Hur (who was the oldest son of *Caleb* and Ephrathah) were **Shobal** (the father of Kiriath-jearim), 51**Salma** (the father of Bethlehem), and Hareph (the father of Beth-gader).

52**Shobal's** sons included **Kiriath-jearim** and Haroeh, the ancestor of half of the Menuhoth tribe.

2:53
1 Chron 4:2

53The families of *Kiriath-jearim* were the Ithrites, the Puthites, the Shumathites, and the Mishraites (from whom descended the Zorathites and Eshtaolites).

2:55
2 Kgs 10:15

54The descendants of Salma were his son Bethlehem, the Netophathites, Atrothbeth-joab, half the Manahathites, and the Zorites; 55they also included the families of the writers living at Jabez—the Tirathites, Shime-athites, and Sucathites. All these are Kenites who descended from Hammath, the founder of the family of Rechab.

David's descendants

3:1
1 Sam 25:42
2 Sam 3:2-5
13:1
1 Chron 2:3
3:2
2 Sam 3:4
13:20; 14:23

3 King David's oldest son was Amnon, who was born to his wife, Ahino-am of Jezreel.

The second was Daniel, whose mother was Abigail from Carmel.

2The third was Absalom, the son of his wife Maacah, who was the daughter of King Talmai of Geshur.

The fourth was Adonijah, the son of Haggith.

3The fifth was Shephatiah, the son of Abital.

The sixth was Ithream, the son of his wife Eglah.

3:4
2 Sam 5:4,5

4These six were born to him in Hebron, where he reigned seven and one-half

2:34, 35 *Sheshan,* apparently a different Sheshan than in vs 31.   **2:50** *Caleb,* implied in 2:24.

3:1 Abigail's story and Profile are found in 1 Samuel 25, 26.   **3:2** Absalom's story and Profile are found in 2 Samuel 13—18.

years. Then he moved the capital to Jerusalem, where he reigned another thirty-three years.

5While he was in Jerusalem, his wife Bathsheba (the daughter of Ammi-el) became the mother of his sons Shime-a, Shobab, Nathan, and **Solomon.**

6, 7, 8David also had nine other sons: Ibhar, Elishama, Eliphelet, Nogah, Nepheg, Japhia, Elishama, Eliada, and Eliphelet.

9(This list does not include the sons of his concubines.) David also had a daughter Tamar.

10-14These are the descendants of King *Solomon:* Rehoboam, Abijah, Asa, Jehoshaphat, Joram, Ahaziah, Joash, Amaziah, Azariah, Jotham, Ahaz, Hezekiah, Manasseh, Amon, Josiah.

15The sons of *Josiah* were: Johanan, **Jehoiakim,** Zedekiah, Shallum.

16The sons of *Jehoiakim:* **Jeconiah,** Zedekiah.

17, 18These are the sons who were born to King *Jeconiah* during the years that he was under house arrest: Shealtiel, Malchiram, **Pedaiah,** Shenazzar, Jekamiah, Hoshama, Nedabiah.

19, 20*Pedaiah* was the father of **Zerubbabel** and Shime-i.

Zerubbabel's children were: Meshullam, **Hananiah,** Hashubah, Ohel, Berechiah, Hasadiah, Jushab-hesed, Shelomith (a daughter).

21, 22*Hananiah's* sons were Pelatiah and Jeshaiah; Jeshaiah's son was Rephaiah; Rephaiah's son was Arnan; Arnan's son was Obadiah; Obadiah's son was Shecaniah. Shecaniah's son was Shemaiah; Shemaiah had six sons, including Hattush, Igal, Bariah, **Neariah,** and Shaphat.

23*Neariah* had three sons: **Eli-o-enai,** Hizkiah, Azrikam.

24*Eli-o-enai* had seven sons: Hodaviah, Eliashib, Pelaiah, Akkub, Johanan, Delaiah, Anani.

2. The tribes of Israel
Judah's descendants

4 These are the sons of Judah: Perez, Hezron, Carmi, Hur, **Shobal.**
2*Shobal's* son Re-aiah was the father of Jahath, the ancestor of Ahumai and Lahad. These were known as the Zorathite clans.

3, 4The descendants of Etam: Jezreel, Ishma, Idbash, Hazzelelponi (his daughter), Penuel (the ancestor of Gedor), Ezer (the ancestor of Hushah), The son of Hur, the oldest son of Ephrathah, who was the father of Bethlehem.

5Ashhur, the father of Tekoa, had two wives—**Helah,** and **Naarah.**

6*Naarah* bore him Ahuzzam, Hepher, Temeni, and Haahashtari; 7and *Helah* bore him Zereth, Izhar, and Ethnan.

8Koz was the father of Anub and Zobebah; he was also the ancestor of the clan named after Aharhel, the son of Harum.

9Jabez was more distinguished than any of his brothers. His mother named him Jabez because she had such a hard time at his birth (Jabez means "Distress"). 10He was the one who prayed to the God of Israel, "Oh, that you would

Cross-references (margin):

3:5
2 Sam 5:14-16
11:3; 12:24
1 Chron 14:4-7

3:10
1 Kgs 11:43
15:1,8,24
22:50
2 Kgs 8:24,25
11:21; 14:1,21
15:30,32,33
16:1; 18:1
21:1,2,19,20
22:1
2 Chron 9:30
13:1; 14:1
17:1; 21:1,17
24:1; 25:1
26:1; 27:1
28:1; 29:1
33:1,20,21
34:1
Mt 1:7-10

3:15
2 Kgs 23:30,34
2 Chron 36:1,4

3:21
Ezra 8:2-14

4:1
Gen 38:29
46:12
Num 26:19-22
Ruth 4:18
1 Chron 2:3
Mt 1:3
Lk 3:33

4:2
1 Chron 2:53

4:3
1 Chron 2:19

4:10
Gen 32:26
Ps 72:17
Eph 1:3

3:5 *Bathsheba,* literally, "Bath-shua." **3:10-14** *Joram,* or "Jehoram." *Azariah,* or "Uzziah." **3:15** *Shallum,* that is, Jehoahaz (see Jer 22:11). **4:9** *Jabez means.* A play on words. *Jabez* sounds like *ozeb,* the Hebrew word meaning "distress."

3:5 Bathsheba's story is found in 2 Samuel 11; 12; 1 Kings 1. Her Profile is in 1 Kings 1. The story of her son, Solomon, who became Israel's third king, is found in 1 Kings 1—11 and 2 Chronicles 2—9. Solomon's Profile is found in 1 Kings 3.

3:9 The tragic story of Tamar, David's daughter, is found in 2 Samuel 13, 14.

3:10-14 Many of King Solomon's descendants ruled the nation of Judah. For Rehoboam's story and Profile see 2 Chronicles 10—12. For Jehoshaphat's story and Profile see 2 Chronicles 17—20. For Azariah's (Uzziah's) story and Profile see 2 Chronicles 26, 27. For Hezekiah's story and Profile see 2 Kings 18—20. For Josiah's story and Profile see 2 Kings 22, 23.

3:15 Jehoiakim's story is found in Jeremiah 22—28, 35, 36. Zedekiah's story is found in Jeremiah 21—39.

3:19, 20 Zerubbabel was the leader of the first group of exiles to return from Babylon. His story and Profile are found in the book of Ezra.

4:10 Jabez is remembered as "the one who prayed." It is significant that he is remembered for a prayer rather than a heroic act. In his prayer, he asked God to (1) bless him, (2) help him in his work, (3) be with him in all he did, and (4) keep him from evil and disaster. Jabez acknowledged God as the true center of his work. When we pray for God's blessing, we should also pray that he will take his rightful position as Lord over all areas of our lives.

WHO'S WHO IN THE BIBLE

Here are some of the people mentioned in this genealogy who are also mentioned elsewhere in the Bible. The writer of 1 Chronicles reproduced a thorough history of Israel in one list of people. Many of the people in this list have exciting stories that can be traced through the Bible. Look up some of the names below that intrigue you. You may be surprised what you discover!

Name	Key life lesson	Story told in:
Adam (1:1)	Our sins have far greater implications than we realize.	Genesis 2, 3
Noah (1:3)	Great rewards come from obeying God.	Genesis 6—9
Abraham (1:28)	Faith alone makes one right in God's eyes.	Genesis 11:26—25:10
Isaac (1:28)	Seeking peace brings true respect.	Genesis 21—35
Esau (1:35)	It is never too late to put away bitterness and forgive.	Genesis 25:19—36:43
Amalek (1:36)	There are evil men and nations who seek to harm God's people.	Exodus 17:8–16
Jacob (2:1)	While our sins may haunt us, God will honor our faith.	Genesis 25:19—50:13
Judah (2:3)	God can change the hearts of even the most wicked people.	Genesis 37—50
Tamar (2:4)	God works his purposes even through sinful events.	Genesis 38
Perez (2:5)	Your background does not matter to God.	Genesis 38:27–30
Boaz (2:12)	Those who are kind to others will receive kindness themselves.	The book of Ruth
Jesse (2:13)	Never take lightly the impact you may have on your children.	1 Samuel 16
David (2:15)	True greatness is having a heart for God.	The books of 1 and 2 Samuel
Joab (2:16)	Those who seek power die with nothing.	2 Samuel 2:13—1 Kings 2:34
Amnon (3:1)	Giving in to lust leads only to tragedy.	2 Samuel 13
Absalom (3:2)	Those seeking to oust a God-appointed leader will have a difficult battle.	2 Samuel 13—18
Adonijah (3:2)	God must determine what is rightfully ours.	1 Kings 1—2
Bath-sheba (3:5)	One wrong act does not disqualify us from accomplishing things for God.	2 Samuel 11, 12; 1 Kings 1, 2
Solomon (3:5)	Man's wisdom is foolishness without God.	1 Kings 1—11
Reuben (5:1)	What is gained from a moment of passion is only perceived; what is lost is real and permanent.	Genesis 35:22; 37; 49:3, 4
Aaron (6:3)	Don't expect God's leaders to be perfect, but don't let them get away with sin either.	Exodus 4—Numbers 20
Nadab (6:3)	Pretending to be God's representative is dangerous business.	Leviticus 10
Eleazar (6:3)	Those who are consistent in their faith are the best models to follow.	Numbers 20:25–29; 26—34; Joshua 24:33
Korah (6:22)	Rebelling against God's leaders is rebelling against God and will always be unsuccessful.	Numbers 16
Joshua (7:27)	Real courage comes from God.	The book of Joshua
Saul (8:33)	Those who say they follow God but don't live like it waste their God-given potential.	1 Samuel 8—31
Jonathan (8:33)	True friends always think of the other person, not just themselves.	1 Samuel 14—31

wonderfully bless me and help me in my work; please be with me in all that I do, and keep me from all evil and disaster!" And God granted him his request.

11, 12The descendants of Recah were:

Chelub (the brother of Shuhah), whose son was Mahir, the father of **Eshton;**
Eshton was the father of Bethrapha, Paseah, and Tehinnah;
Tehinnah was the father of Irnahash.

13The sons of Kenaz were **Othni-el** and **Seraiah.**   4:13
Othni-el's sons were Hathath and **Meonothai;**   Josh 15:17
14*Meonothai* was the father of Ophrah;
Seraiah was the father of Joab, the ancestor of the inhabitants of Craftsman Valley (called that because many craftsmen lived there).

15The sons of Caleb (the son of Jephunneh): Iru, **Elah,** Naam.
The sons of *Elah* included Kenaz.

16Jehallelel's sons were: Ziph, Ziphah, Tiri-a, Asarel.

17Ezrah's sons were: Jether, **Mered,** Epher, Jalon.
Mered married Bithi-ah, an Egyptian princess. She was the mother of Miriam, Shammai, and Ishbah—an ancestor of **Eshtemoa.**

18*Eshtemoa's* wife was a Jewess; she was the mother of Jered, Heber, and Jekuthiel, who were, respectively, the ancestors of the Gedorites, Socoites, and Zanoahites.

19Hodiah's wife was the sister of Naham. One of her sons was the father of Keilah the Garmite, and another was the father of Eshtemoa the Maacathite.

20The sons of Shimon: Amnon, Rinnah, Ben-hanan, Tilon.
The sons of Ishi: Zoheth, Ben-zoheth.

21, 22The sons of Shelah (the son of Judah):

Er (the father of Lecah),
Laadah (the father of Mareshah),
The families of the linen workers who worked at Beth-ashbea,
Jokim,
The clans of Cozeba,
Joash,
Saraph (who was a ruler in Moab before he returned to Lehem).

These names all come from very ancient records.

23These clans were noted for their pottery, gardening, and planting; they all   4:23
worked for the king: Gen 38:5

Simeon's descendants

24The sons of Simeon: Nemu-el, Jamin, Jarib, Zerah, **Shaul.**

25*Shaul's* son was Shallum, his grandson was Mibsam, and his great-grandson was **Mishma.**

26*Mishma's* sons included Hammu-el (the father of Zaccur and grandfather of **Shime-i**).

27*Shime-i* had sixteen sons and six daughters, but none of his brothers had large families—they all had fewer children than was normal in Judah.

28They lived at Beer-sheba, Moladah, Hazar-shual, 29Bilhah, Ezem, Tolad,

---

4:10 Jabez prayed specifically to be protected from evil and disaster. We live in a fallen world where sin abounds, and it is important to ask God to keep us safe from the unavoidable evil that comes our way. But we must also avoid evil motives, desires, and actions that begin within us. Therefore, we must not only seek God's protection from evil, but ask God to keep evil from becoming a part of our thoughts and actions.

4:13 Othni-el was Israel's first judge. He reformed the nation and

brought peace to the land. His story is found in Judges 1:9-15 and 3:5-14.

4:15 Caleb was one of the 12 spies sent into the Promised Land by Moses. Only he and Joshua returned with a positive report. They were the only two among the spies who had faith in God's promise to help the Israelites conquer the land. Caleb's story is told in Numbers 13, 14 and Joshua 14, 15. His Profile is found in Numbers 15.

30Bethuel, Hormah, Ziklag, 31Beth-marcaboth, Hazar-susim, Beth-biri, and Shaa-raim. These cities were under their control until the time of David.

32, 33Their descendants also lived in or near Etam, Ain, Rimmon, Tochen, and Ashan; some were as far away as Baal. (These facts are recorded in their genealogies.)

34-39These are the names of some of the princes of wealthy clans who traveled to the east side of Gedor Valley in search of pasture for their flocks: Meshobab, Jamlech, Joshah, Joel, Jehu, Eli-o-enai, Ja-akobah, Jeshohaiah, Asaiah, Adi-el, Jesimi-el, Benaiah, Ziza (the son of Shiphi, son of Allon, son of Jedaiah, son of Shimri, son of Shemaiah).

40, 41They found good pastures, and everything was quiet and peaceful; but the land belonged to the descendants of Ham.

So during the reign of King Hezekiah of Judah these princes invaded the land and struck down the tents and houses of the descendants of Ham; they killed the inhabitants of the land and took possession of it for themselves.

42Later, five hundred of these invaders from the tribe of Simeon went to Mount Seir. (Their leaders were Pelatiah, Ne-ariah, Rephaiah, and Uzziel—all sons of Ishi.)

43There they destroyed the few surviving members of the tribe of Amalek. And they have lived there ever since.

Reuben's descendants

5 The oldest son of Israel was Reuben, but since he dishonored his father by sleeping with one of his father's wives, his birthright was given to his half brother, Joseph. So the official genealogy doesn't name Reuben as the oldest son.

2Although Joseph received the birthright, yet Judah was a powerful and influential tribe in Israel, and from Judah came a Prince.

3The sons of Reuben, Israel's son, were: Hanoch, Pallu, Hezron, Carmi.

4Joel's descendants were his son Shemaiah, his grandson Gog, and his great-grandson **Shime-i.**

5*Shime-i's* son was Micah; his grandson was Reaiah; and his great-grandson was **Baal.**

6*Baal's* son was Beerah. He was a prince of the tribe of Reuben and was taken into captivity by King Tilgath-pilneser of Assyria.

7, 8His relatives became heads of clans and were included in the official genealogy: Je-iel, Zechariah, Bela (the son of Azaz, grandson of Shema, and great-grandson of **Joel**).

These Reubenites lived in Aroer and as far distant as Mount Nebo and Baal-meon.

9Joel was a cattle man, and he pastured his animals eastward to the edge of the desert and to the Euphrates River, for there were many cattle in the land of Gilead.

10During the reign of King Saul, the men of Reuben defeated the Hagrites in war and moved into their tents on the eastern edge of Gilead.

Gad's descendants

11Across from them, in the land of Bashan, lived the descendants of Gad, who were spread as far as Salecah.

12Joel was the greatest and was followed by Shapham, also Janai and Shaphat.

5:7, 8 *These Reubenites,* implied in 5:1.

Cross-references (margin):

4:40
Judg 18:7-10

4:42
Gen 36:8

4:43
1 Sam 15:7,8
30:16,17

5:1
Gen 29:32
35:22
48:15-22; 49:4
1 Chron 2:1

5:2
Gen 49:8-10
Mic 5:2
Mt 2:6

5:3
Ex 6:14
Num 26:5

5:6
2 Kgs 15:29
16:7
1 Chron 5:26

5:7,8
Num 32:34
Josh 12:2

5:9
Josh 22:8,9

5:10
1 Chron 5:18-21

5:11
Num 32:34-36
Josh 13:11,24

5:1 Reuben's sin of incest was recorded for all future generations to read. The purpose of this epitaph, however, was not to smear Reuben's name, but to show that painful memories aren't the only results of sin. The real consequences of sin are ruined lives. As the oldest son, Reuben was the rightful heir to both a double portion of his father's estate and the leadership of Abraham's descendants, who had grown into a large tribe. But his sin stripped away his rights and privileges and ruined his family. Before you give in to temptation, take a close look at the disastrous consequences sin may have in your life and the lives of others.

5:2 This Prince from the tribe of Judah refers both to King David and his royal line, and to Jesus the Messiah, David's greatest descendant.

13Their relatives, the heads of the seven clans, were Michael, Meshullam, Sheba, Jorai, Jacan, Zia, and Eber.

14The descendants of Buz, in the order of their generations, were: Jahdo, Jeshishai, Michael, Gilead, Jaroah, Huri, Abihail.

15Ahi, the son of Abdi-el and grandson of Guni, was the leader of the clan. 16The clan lived in and around Gilead (in the land of Bashan) and throughout the entire pasture country of Sharon. 17All were included in the official genealogy at the time of King Jotham of Judah and King Jeroboam of Israel.

18There were 44,760 armed, trained, and brave troops in the army of Reuben, Gad, and the half-tribe of Manasseh. 19They declared war on the Hagrites, the Jeturites, the Naphishites, and the Nodabites. 20They cried out to God to help them, and he did, for they trusted in him. So the Hagrites and all their allies were defeated. 21The booty included 50,000 camels, 250,000 sheep, 2,000 donkeys, and 100,000 captives. 22A great number of the enemy also died in the battle, for God was fighting against them. So the Reubenites lived in the territory of the Hagrites until the time of the exile.

5:16
1 Chron 27:29
5:17
2 Kgs 14:16,28
15:5,32,33
5:18
Num 1:3
5:19
Chron 1:31
5:10
5:20
Josh 10:42
2 Chron
14:11-13
Ps 9:10
5:22
Josh 23:10
2 Kgs 17:6
2 Chron 32:8

Manasseh's descendants

23The half-tribe of Manasseh spread through the land from Bashan to Baal-hermon, Senir, and Mount Hermon. They too were very numerous.

24The chiefs of their clans were the following: Epher, Ishi, Eliel, Azri-el, Jeremiah, Hodaviah, Jahdi-el.

Each of these men had a great reputation as a warrior and leader. 25But they were not true to the God of their fathers; instead they worshiped the idols of the people whom God had destroyed. 26So God caused King Pul of Assyria (also known as Tilgath-pilneser III) to invade the land and deport the men of Reuben, Gad, and the half-tribe of Manasseh. They took them to Halah, Habor, Hara, and the Gozan River, where they remain to this day.

5:23
Deut 3:9; 4:48
5:25
Ex 34:15
2 Kgs 17:7
5:26
2 Kgs 15:19,29

Levi's descendants

6 These are the names of the sons of Levi: **Gershom, Kohath, Merari.**
2*Kohath's* sons were: **Amram,** Izhar, Hebron, Uzziel.
3*Amram's* descendants included: **Aaron,** Moses, Miriam.
Aaron's sons were: Nadab, Abihu, Eleazar, Ithamar.
4-15The oldest sons of the successive generations of Aaron were as follows:

6:4-15 *The oldest sons of the successive generations of Aaron were as follows,* implied.

6:1
Gen 46:11
Ex 6:16
Num 3:17
6:3
1 Chron 23:13

5:18–22 The armies of Reuben, Gad, and Manasseh succeeded in battle because they trusted God. Although they had instinct and skill as soldiers, they prayed and sought God's direction. The natural and developed abilities God gives us are meant to be used for him, but they should never replace our dependence on God. When we trust in our own cleverness, skill, and strength rather than in God, we open the door for arrogance. When facing difficult situations, seek God's purpose and ask for his guidance and strength. Psalm 20:7 says, "Some nations boast of armies and of weaponry, but our boast is in the Lord our God."

5:22 The exile mentioned here refers to the captivity of the ten northern tribes of Israel in 722 B.C. These tribes never returned to their homeland. This story is found in 2 Kings 15:29—17:41.

5:24, 25 As warriors and leaders, these men had established excellent reputations for their great skill and leadership qualities. But in God's eyes they failed in the most important quality—putting God first in their lives. If you try to measure up to society's standards for fame and success, you will be in danger of neglecting your true quest—to please and obey God. In the end,

God alone examines our hearts and determines our standing.

6:1ff The tribe of Levi was set apart to serve God in the Tabernacle (Numbers 3, 4), and later in the Temple (1 Chronicles 23—26). Aaron, Levi's descendant (6:3), became Israel's first High Priest. All future priests were required by God to be descendants of Aaron. The rest of the Levites assisted the priests in the various Tabernacle or Temple duties, and assisted the people by teaching them God's Word and encouraging them to obey it.

6:3 The people listed here played major roles in the drama of the exodus. Aaron's story is found in the books of Exodus, Leviticus, and Numbers. His Profile is found in Exodus 32. Moses was one of the greatest prophets and leaders in Israel's history. His story is found in the books of Exodus, Leviticus, Numbers, and Deuteronomy. His Profile is found in Exodus 16. The story of Miriam, Moses' sister, is found in Exodus 2; 15:20, 21; Numbers 12; 20:1. Her Profile is found in Numbers 13. Nadab and Abihu were killed for disobeying God (Leviticus 10). Eleazar became Israel's High Priest after Aaron (Numbers 20:24–28), and Ithamar played an important role in organizing the worship services of the Tabernacle (Numbers 4:28, 33; 7:8).

6:4
1 Chron 9:20

Eleazar, the father of
Phinehas, the father of
Abishua, the father of
Bukki, the father of
Uzzi, the father of
Zerahiah, the father of
Meraioth, the father of
Amariah, the father of
Ahitub, the father of
Zadok, the father of
Ahima-az, the father of
Azariah, the father of
Johanan, the father of
Azariah (the High Priest in Solomon's Temple at Jerusalem), the father of
Amariah, the father of
Ahitub, the father of
Zadok, the father of
Shallum, the father of
Hilkiah, the father of
Azariah, the father of
Seraiah, the father of
Jehozadak (who went into exile when the Lord sent the people of Judah and
   Jerusalem into captivity under Nebuchadnezzar).

¹⁶As previously stated, the sons of Levi were: Gershom, Kohath, Merari.
¹⁷The sons of *Gershom* were: Libni, Shime-i.
¹⁸The sons of *Kohath* were: Amram, Izhar, Hebron, Uzziel.

6:19
1 Chron 23:21

¹⁹, ²⁰, ²¹The sons of *Merari* were: Mahli, Mushi.
The subclans of the Levites were:
In the Gershom clan: Libni, Jahath, Zimmah, Joah, Iddo, Zerah, Jeatherai.
²²,²³,²⁴In the Kohath clan: Amminadab, Korah, Assir, **Elkanah,** Ebiasaph,
Assir, Tahath, Uriel, Uzziah, Shaul.

6:25
1 Sam 1:1

²⁵, ²⁶, ²⁷The subclan of *Elkanah* was further divided into the families of his sons:
Amasai, Ahimoth, Elkanah, Zophai, Nahath, Eliab, Jeroham, Elkanah.

6:28
1 Sam 8:2

²⁸The families of the subclan of Samuel were headed by Samuel's sons: Joel, the
oldest; Abijah, the second.
²⁹, ³⁰The subclans of the clan of Merari were headed by his sons: Mahli, Libni,
Shime-i, Uzzah, Shime-a, Haggiah, Asaiah.

6:31
2 Sam 6:17
1 Chron 15:16,
27; 16:4-6
25:1

³¹King David appointed songleaders and choirs to praise God in the Tabernacle
after he had placed the Ark in it. ³²Then, when Solomon built the Temple at
Jerusalem, the choirs carried on their work there.
³³⁻³⁸These are the names and ancestries of choir leaders: Heman the Cantor was
from the clan of Kohath; his genealogy was traced back through: Joel, Samuel,
Elkanah III, Jeroham, Eliel, Toah, Zuph, Elkanah II, Mahath, Amasai, Elkanah I,

6:16 *As previously stated,* implied in 6:1.   **6:33-38** *ancestries,* implied.

6:28 When Samuel became God's leader and spokesman, Israel
was on the brink of collapse. The last few chapters of the book of
Judges give a vivid picture of the moral decay and the resulting
decline of the nation. But with God's help, Samuel almost
singlehandedly brought the nation from ruin to revival. He unified
the people by showing them that God was their common
denominator and that any nation that focused on him would find
and fulfill its true purpose. For the rest of Samuel's story, and to
see how he set up rules for governing a nation based on spiritual
principles, read the book of 1 Samuel. Samuel's Profile is found in
1 Samuel 8.

6:31 King David did much to bring music into worship. He
established songleaders and choirs to perform regularly at the

Temple (25). As a young man, David was hired for his talent as a
harpist to play for King Saul (1 Samuel 16:15–23). He also wrote
many of the songs found in the book of Psalms.

6:31, 32 The builders and craftsmen had completed the Temple,
and the priests and Levites had been given their responsibilities for
taking care of it. Now it was time for another group of people—the
choirs—to exercise their talents for God. Some of the songleaders'
names are recorded here. You don't have to be an ordained
minister to have an important place in the body of believers.
Builders, craftsmen, worship assistants, choir members, and
songleaders all had significant contributions to make. God has
given you a unique combination of talents. Use them to serve him
in his church.

Joel, Azariah, Zephaniah, Tahath, Assir, Ebiasaph, Korah, Izhar, Kohath, Levi, Israel.

39-43Heman's assistant was his colleague Asaph, whose genealogy was traced back through: Berechiah, Shime-a, Michael, Ba-aseiah, Malchijah, Ethni, Zerah, Adaiah, Ethan, Zimmah, Shime-i, Jahath, Gershom, Levi.

44-47Heman's second assistant was Ethan, a representative from the clan of Merari, who stood on his left. Merari's ancestry was traced back through: Kishi, Abdi, Malluch, Hashabiah, Amaziah, Hilkiah, Amzi, Bani, Shemer, Mahli, Mushi, Merari, Levi.

48Their relatives—all the other Levites—were appointed to various other tasks in the Tabernacle. 49But only Aaron and his descendants were the priests. Their duties included sacrificing burnt offerings and incense, handling all the tasks relating to the inner sanctuary—the Holy of Holies—and the tasks relating to the annual Day of Atonement for Israel. They saw to it that all the details commanded by Moses the servant of God were strictly followed.

6:49
Ex 29:33,34

50-53The descendants of Aaron were: Eleazar, Phinehas, Abishua, Bukki, Uzzi, Zerahiah, Meraioth, Amariah, Ahitub, Zadok, Ahima-az.

6:50
1 Chron 6:4-8

54This is a record of the cities and land assigned by lot to the descendants of Aaron, all of whom were members of the Kohath clan:

6:54
Josh 21:4,10

55, 56, 57Hebron and its surrounding pasturelands in Judah (although the fields and suburbs were given to Caleb the son of Jephunneh), 58, 59and the following Cities of Refuge with their surrounding pasturelands: Libnah, Jattir, Eshtemoa, Hilen, Debir, Ashan, Beth-shemesh.

6:55-57
Josh 14:13
15:13; 21:13,19

6:58
Num 35:6
Deut 4:41; 19:2
Josh 20:2

60Thirteen other cities with surrounding pastures—including Geba, Alemeth, and Anathoth—were given to the priests by the tribe of Benjamin. 61Lots were then drawn to assign land to the remaining descendants of Kohath, and they received ten cities in the territory of the half-tribe of Manasseh.

6:61
Josh 21:5
1 Chron 6:66-70

62The subclans of the Gershom clan received by lot thirteen cities in the Bashan area from the tribes of Issachar, Asher, Naphtali, and Manasseh.

63The subclans of Merari received by lot twelve cities from the tribes of Reuben, Gad, and Zebulun.

6:63
Josh 21:7,34-40
1 Chron 6:77

64, 65Cities and pasturelands were also assigned by lot to the Levites (and then renamed) from the tribes of Judah, Simeon, and Benjamin.

6:64
Josh 21:3,41,42
1 Chron 6:57-60

66-69The tribe of Ephraim gave these Cities of Refuge with the surrounding pasturelands to the subclans of Kohath: Shechem, in Mount Ephraim; Gezer; Jokme-am; Beth-horon; Aijalon; Gath-rimmon.

6:66
Josh 21:20-26
1 Chron 6:61

70The following Cities of Refuge and their pasturelands were given to the subclans of the Kohathites by the half-tribe of Manasseh: Aner, Bile-am.

71Cities of Refuge and pastureland given to the clan of Gershom by the half-tribe of Manasseh were: Golan, in Bashan; Ashtaroth.

6:39-43 *Heman's assistant*, literally, "brother," or "kinsman."

6:49 Aaron and his descendants strictly followed the details of worship commanded by God through Moses. They did not choose only those commands they *wanted* to obey. Note what happened to Uzza when important details in handling the Ark of the Covenant were neglected (1 Chronicles 13:6-10). We should not obey God selectively, choosing those commands we will obey and those we will ignore. God's Word has authority over every aspect of our lives, not just selected portions.

6:49 For more information on priests, see the note on Leviticus 8:1.

6:54 The tribe of Levi was not given a specific area of land as were the other tribes. Instead, the Levites were to be distributed throughout the land in order to aid the people of *every* tribe in their worship of God. Thus the Levites were given cities or farmland within the alloted areas of the other tribes (Joshua 13:14; 21).

6:58 God had told the tribes to designate specific cities as Cities of Refuge once they arrived in the Promised Land (Numbers 35). These cities were to provide refuge for people who had committed unintentional murders. This instruction may have seemed unimportant when it was given—the Israelites hadn't even entered the Promised Land. Sometimes God gives us instructions that do not seem relevant to our lives at the moment. But later we can see the importance of those instructions. The lessons of the Bible should not be discarded because certain details don't seem to be relevant. Obedience to God now may provide a way of escape in the future.

6:61 The Israelites cast lots in order to take the decision-making process out of man's hands and put it into God's hands. Casting lots was like drawing straws or throwing dice. Lots were cast only after seeking God's guidance in prayer. (For more information on casting lots, see the note on Joshua 18:8.)

72The tribe of Issachar gave them Kedesh, Daberath, 73Ramoth, and Anem, and the surrounding pastureland of each.

74The tribe of Asher gave them Abdon, Mashal, 75Hukok, and Rehob, with their pasturelands.

76The tribe of Naphtali gave them Kedesh in Galilee, Hammon, and Kiriathaim with pasturelands.

6:77
1 Chron 6:63

77The tribe of Zebulun gave Rimmono and Tabor to the Merari clan as Cities of Refuge.

78, 79And across the Jordan River, opposite Jericho, the tribe of Reuben gave them Bezer (a desert town), Jahzah, Kedemoth and Mepha-ath, along with their pasturelands.

80The tribe of Gad gave them Ramoth in Gilead, Mahanaim, 81Heshbon, and Jazer, each with their surrounding pasturelands.

Issachar's descendants

7:1
Gen 46:13
Num 26:23

7:2
2 Sam 24:1-9
1 Chron 21:1

7 The sons of Issachar: **Tola,** Puah, Jashub, Shimron. 2The sons of *Tola,* each of whom was the head of a subclan: **Uzzi,** Rephaiah, Jeri-el, Jahmai, Ibsam, Shemuel.

At the time of King David, the total number of men of war from these families totaled 22,600.

3*Uzzi's* son was Izrahiah among whose five sons were Michael, Obadiah, Joel, and Isshiah, all chiefs of subclans. 4Their descendants, at the time of King David, numbered 36,000 troops; for all five of them had several wives and many sons. 5The total number of men available for military service from all the clans of the tribe of Issachar numbered 87,000 stouthearted warriors, all included in the official genealogy.

Benjamin's descendants

7:6
1 Chron 8:1

6The sons of Benjamin were: **Bela, Becher, Jedia-el.**

7The sons of *Bela:* Ezbon, Uzzi, Uzziel, Jerimoth, Iri.

These five mighty warriors were chiefs of subclans and were the leaders of 22,034 troops (all of whom were recorded in the official genealogies).

8The sons of *Becher* were: Zemirah, Joash, Eliezer, Eli-o-enai, Omri, Jeremoth, Abijah, Anathoth, Alemeth.

9At the time of David there were 22,200 mighty warriors among their descendants; and they were led by their clan chiefs.

10The son of *Jedia-el* was **Bilhan.**

The sons of *Bilhan* were: Jeush, Benjamin, Ehud, Chenaanah, Zethan, Tarshish, Ahishahar.

11They were the chiefs of the subclans of *Jedia-el,* and their descendants included 17,200 warriors at the time of King David.

12The sons of Ir were Shuppim and Huppim. Hushim was one of the sons of Aher.

Naphtali's descendants

7:13
Gen 46:23-25
Num 26:49

13The sons of Naphtali (descendants of Jacob's wife Bilhah) were: Jahzi-el, Guni, Jezer, Shallum.

Manasseh's descendants

7:14
Gen 50:23
Num 26:29
Josh 13:31

14The sons of Manasseh, born to his Aramaean concubine, were Asri-el and Machir (who became the father of Gilead).

15It was Machir who found wives for Huppim and Shuppim. Machir's sister was Maacah. Another descendant was Zelophehad, who had only daughters.

16Machir's wife, also named Maacah, bore him a son whom she named Peresh; his brother's name was Sheresh, and he had sons named Ulam and Rakem.

17Ulam's son was Bedan. So these were the sons of Gilead, the grandsons of Machir, and the great-grandsons of Manasseh.

7:13 *Jacob's wife,* implied. **7:15** *Huppim and Shuppim,* see vs 12. *only daughters,* implied. See Numbers 26:33.

18Hammolecheth, Machir's sister, bore Ishhod, Abiezer, and Mahlah. 19The sons of Shemida were Ahian, Shechem, Likhi, and Aniam.

Ephraim's descendants

20, 21The sons of Ephraim: Shuthelah, Bered, Tahath, Eleadah, Tahath, Zabad, Shuthelah, **Ezer, Ele-ad.**

7:20
Num 26:35,36

Ele-ad and *Ezer* attempted to rustle cattle at Gath, but they were killed by the local farmers. 22Their father Ephraim mourned for them a long time, and his brothers tried to comfort him. 23Afterwards, his wife conceived and bore a son whom he called Beriah (meaning "a tragedy") because of what had happened.

24Ephraim's daughter's name was Sheerah. She built Lower and Upper Beth-horon and Uzzen-sheerah.

7:24
Josh 16:3,5

25, 26, 27This is Ephraim's line of descent:

7:25-27
Ex 17:9-14
24:13

Rephah, the father of
Resheph, the father of
Telah, the father of
Tahan, the father of
Ladan, the father of
Ammihud, the father of
Elishama, the father of
Nun, the father of
Joshua.

28They lived in an area bounded on one side by Bethel and its surrounding towns, on the east by Naaran, on the west by Gezer and its villages, and finally by Shechem and its surrounding villages as far as Ayyah and its towns.

29The tribe of Manasseh, descendants of Joseph the son of Israel, controlled the following cities and their surrounding areas: Beth-shean, Taanach, Megiddo, and Dor.

7:29
Josh 17:7-11

Asher's descendants

30The children of Asher: Imnah, Ishvah, Ishvi, **Beriah,** Serah (their sister). 31The sons of *Beriah* were: **Heber,** Malchi-el (the father of Birzaith).

7:30
Gen 46:17
Num 26:44-46

32*Heber's* children were: **Japhlet, Shomer, Hotham,** Shua (their sister). 33*Japhlet's* sons were: Pasach, Bimhal, Ashvath. 34His brother *Shomer's* sons were: Rohgah, Jehubbah, Aram. 35The sons of his brother *Hotham* were: Zophah, Imna, Shelesh, Amal. 36, 37The sons of *Zophah* were: Suah, Harnepher, Shual, Beri, Imrah, Bezer, Hod, Shamma, Shilshah, **Ithran,** Be-era. 38The sons of *Ithran* were: Jephunneh, Pispa, Ara. 39The sons of Ulla were: Arah, Hanniel, Rizia.

40These descendants of Asher were heads of subclans and were all skilled warriors and chiefs. Their descendants in the official genealogy numbered 36,000 men of war.

Benjamin's descendants

8 The sons of Benjamin, according to age, were: **Bela,** the first, Ashbel, the second, Aharah, the third, Nohah, the fourth, Rapha, the fifth.

8:1
Gen 46:21
1 Chron 7:6-12

3, 4, 5The sons of *Bela* were: Addar, Gera, Abihud, Abishua, Naaman, Ahoah, Gera, Shephuphan, Huram.

6, 7The sons of Ehud, chiefs of the subclans living at Geba, were captured in war and exiled to Manahath. They were: Naaman, Ahijah, Gera (also called Heglam), the father of Uzza and Ahihud.

7:34 *Shomer's*, or "Shemer's." **7:35** *Hotham*, literally, "Helem." **7:38** *Ithran*, literally, "Jether."

7:25-27 Joshua was one of Israel's great leaders, leading them into the Promised Land. Joshua's story is told in the book of Joshua. His Profile is found in Joshua 1.

8:8-10 Divorce and polygamy are sometimes recorded in the Old Testament without critical comments. This does not mean that God takes divorce lightly. Malachi 2:15, 16 says, "Keep faith with the

8, 9, 10Shaharaim divorced his wives **Hushim** and Baara, but he had children in the land of Moab by Hodesh, his new wife: Jobab, Zibia, Mesha, Malcam, Jeuz, Sachia, Mirmah.

These sons all became chiefs of subclans.

11His wife *Hushim* had borne him Abitub and **Elpaal.**

12The sons of *Elpaal* were: Eber, Misham, Shemed (who built Ono and Lod and their surrounding villages).

13His other sons were **Beriah** and Shema, chiefs of subclans living in Aijalon; they chased out the inhabitants of Gath.

14*Elpaal's* sons also included: Ahio, **Shashak,** Jeremoth.

15, 16The sons of *Beriah* were: Zebadiah, Arad, Eder, Michael, Ishpah, Joha.

17, 18The sons of *Elpaal* also included: Zebadiah, Meshullam, Hizki, Heber, Ishmerai, Izliah, Jobab.

19, 20, 21The sons of *Shime-i* were: Jakim, Zichri, Zabdi, Eli-enai, Zille-thai, Eliel, Adaiah, Beraiah, Shimrath.

22-25The sons of *Shashak* were: Ishpan, Eber, Eliel, Abdon, Zichri, Hanan, Hananiah, Elam, Anthothijah, Iphdeiah, Penuel.

26, 27The sons of *Jeroham* were: Shamsherai, Shehariah, Athaliah, Jaareshiah, Elijah, Zichri.

28These were the chiefs of the subclans living at Jerusalem.

8:29
1 Chron 9:35-38

29Je-iel, the father of Gibeon, lived at Gibeon; and his wife's name was Maacah.

30, 31, 32His oldest son was named Abdon, followed by: Zur, Kish, Baal, Nadab, Gedor, Ahio, Zecher, Mikloth who was the father of Shimeah.

All of these families lived together near Jerusalem.

8:33
1 Sam 9:1
14:50
1 Chron 9:39-44
8:34
2 Sam 4:4

33Ner was the father of Kish, and Kish was the father of Saul;

Saul's sons included: **Jonathan,** Malchishua, Abinadab, Eshbaal.

34The son of *Jonathan* was Mephibosheth;

The son of Mephibosheth was Micah.

35The sons of Micah: Pithon, Melech, Tarea, Ahaz.

36Ahaz was the father of Jehoaddah, Jehoaddah was the father of: Alemeth, Azmaveth, Zimri. Zimri's son was Moza.

37Moza was the father of Bine-a, whose sons were: Raphah, Eleasah, Azel.

38Azel had six sons: Azrikam, Bocheru, Ishmael, She-ariah, Obadiah, Hanan.

39Azel's brother Eshek had three sons: **Ulam,** the first, Jeush, the second, Eliphelet, the third.

40*Ulam's* sons were prominent warriors who were expert marksmen with their bows. These men had 150 sons and grandsons, and they were all from the tribe of Benjamin.

3. Returnees from exile in Babylon

9:1
1 Kgs 14:19
2 Kgs 1:18

9 The family tree of every person in Israel was carefully recorded in *The Annals of the Kings of Israel.*

8:34 *Mephibosheth,* or "Merib-baal."

---

wife of your youth. For the Lord, the God of Israel, says he hates divorce." Jesus explained that although divorce was allowed, it was not God's will: "Moses did that in recognition of your hard and evil hearts, but it was not what God had originally intended" (Matthew 19:8). Don't assume that God approves of an act because it isn't condemned in every related Scripture reference.

8:33 Saul, Israel's first king, lived an inconsistent life. His story is found in 1 Samuel 9—31, and his Profile is in 1 Samuel 13. Saul's son Jonathan stood in bold contrast to his father. Although he was the rightful heir to the throne, Jonathan realized that David was God's choice to be Israel's next king. Instead of becoming jealous, Jonathan became David's friend and even helped him escape from Saul's attempts at murder. Jonathan's story is told in 1 Samuel 14—31. His Profile is found in 1 Samuel 21.

9:1ff Chronologically, this chapter could be placed at the end of

2 Chronicles because it records the names of the exiles who returned from the Babylonian captivity. The writer of Chronicles includes this chapter here to show his concern for the people of his own day and their need, as a nation, to return to what made them great in the first place—obedience to God.

9:1 The entire nation of Judah suffered the consequences of idol worship. Idol worship is not just bowing down to statues of wood or stone, it is making anything more important than God— possessions, money, reputation, or even a good friend or a worthy charity. Although every person in Judah did not worship idols, the entire nation was carried away into captivity. Everyone was affected by the sin of some. Even if we don't participate in a certain widespread wrongdoing, we will still be affected by those who do. It is not enough to say, "I don't do it." We must speak out against the sins of our society.

Judah was exiled to Babylon because the people worshiped idols.

2The first to return and live again in their former cities were families from the tribes of Israel, and also the priests, the Levites, and the Temple assistants.

3Then some families from the tribes of Judah, Benjamin, Ephraim, and Manasseh arrived in Jerusalem:

4One family was that of Uthai (the son of Ammihud, son of Omri, son of Imri, son of Bani) of the clan of Perez (son of Judah).

5The Shilonites were another family to return, including Asaiah (Shilon's oldest son) and his sons; 6there were also the sons of Zerah, including Jeuel and his relatives: 690 in all.

7,8Among the members of the tribe of Benjamin who returned were these:

Sallu (the son of Meshullam, the son of Hodaviah, the son of Hassenuah);
Ibneiah (the son of Jeroham);
Elah (the son of Uzzi, the son of Michri);
Meshullam (the son of Shephatiah, the son of Reuel, the son of Ibnijah).

9These men were all chiefs of subclans. A total of 956 Benjaminites returned.

10,11The priests who returned were:

Jedaiah, Jehoiarib, Jachin,
Azariah (the son of Hilkiah, son of Meshullam, son of Zadok, son of Meraioth, son of Ahitub). He was the chief custodian of the Temple.

12Another of the returning priests was Adaiah (son of Jeroham, son of Pashhur, son of Malchijah).

Another priest was Maasai (son of Adi-el, son of Jahzerah, son of Meshullam, son of Meshillemith, son of Immer).

13In all, 1,760 priests returned.

14Among the Levites who returned was Shemaiah (son of Hasshub, son of Azrikam, son of Hashabiah, who was a descendant of Merari).

15,16Other Levites who returned included:

Bakbakkar, Heresh, Galal,
Mattaniah (the son of Mica, who was the son of Zichri, who was the son of Asaph).
Obadiah (the son of Shemaiah, son of Galal, son of Jeduthun).
Berechiah (the son of Asa, son of El-kanah, who lived in the area of the Netophathites).

17,18The gatekeepers were Shallum (the chief gatekeeper), Akkub, Talmon, and Ahiman—all Levites. They are still responsible for the eastern royal gate. 19Shallum's ancestry went back through Kore and Ebiasaph to Korah. He and his close relatives the Korahites were in charge of the sacrifices and the protection of the sanctuary, just as their ancestors had supervised and guarded the Tabernacle. 20Phinehas, the son of Eleazar, was the first director of this division in ancient times. And the Lord was with him.

9:2
Ezra 2:43,58
8:20
Neh 11:3-22

9:9
Neh 11:8
9:10
Neh 11:10-14
Jer 20:1

9:14
Neh 11:15-19

9:17
Ezek 46:1,2

9:20
Num 25:7-13

9:2 Only two of the original 12 tribes of Israel returned from exile—Judah and Benjamin (Ezra 1:5).

9:10, 11 When we think of doing God's work, usually preaching, teaching, singing, and other up-front leadership positions come to mind. Azariah, however, was the custodian of the Temple, and he was singled out for special mention. Whatever role you have in God's church, it is important to God.

9:17, 18 Gatekeepers guarded the four main entrances to the Temple and opened the gates each morning for those who wanted to worship. In addition, they did other day-to-day chores to keep the Temple running smoothly—cleaning, preparing the offerings for sacrifice, and accounting for the gifts that were given to the Temple (9:22–32).

Gatekeepers had to be reliable, honest, and trustworthy (9:26). The people in your church who handle the offerings and care for the materials and functions of the building serve in a great tradition and should be honored for their reliability and service.

9:21
1 Chron 26:2,14

9:22
1 Chron 26:1
2 Chron 31:15,
18

9:25
2 Kgs 11:5,7
2 Chron 23:8

9:27
1 Chron
23:30-32

9:29
1 Chron 23:29

9:30
Ex 30:23-25

9:32
Lev 24:5-8

9:33
1 Chron 6:31-47
25:1

9:35
1 Chron 8:29-32

9:39
1 Chron 8:33-38

9:41
1 Chron 8:35-37

²¹At that time Zechariah, the son of Meshelemiah, had been responsible for the protection of the entrance to the Tabernacle. ²²There were 212 doorkeepers in those days. They were chosen from their villages on the basis of their genealogies, and they were appointed by David and Samuel because of their reliability. ²³They and their descendants were in charge of the Lord's Tabernacle. ²⁴They were assigned to each of the four sides: east, west, north, and south. ²⁵And their relatives in the villages were assigned to help them from time to time, for seven days at a time.

²⁶The four head gatekeepers, all Levites, were in an office of great trust, for they were responsible for the rooms and treasuries in the Tabernacle of God. ²⁷Because of their important positions they lived near the Tabernacle, and they opened the gates each morning. ²⁸Some of them were assigned to care for the various vessels used in the sacrifices and worship; they checked them in and out to avoid loss. ²⁹Others were responsible for the furniture, the items in the sanctuary, and the supplies such as fine flour, wine, incense, and spices.

³⁰Other priests prepared the spices and incense.

³¹And Mattithiah (a Levite and the oldest son of Shallum the Korahite) was entrusted with making the flat cakes for grain offerings.

³²Some members of the Kohath clan were in charge of the preparation of the special bread each Sabbath.

³³,³⁴The cantors were all prominent Levites. They lived in Jerusalem at the Temple and were on duty at all hours. They were free from other responsibilities and were selected by their genealogies.

Saul's genealogy

³⁵,³⁶,³⁷Jeiel (whose wife was Maacah) lived in Gibeon. He had many sons, including: Gibeon, Abdon (the oldest), Zur, Kish, Baal, **Ner,** Nadab, Gedor, Ahio, Zechariah, Mikloth.

³⁸Mikloth lived with his son Shime-am in Jerusalem near his relatives.

³⁹Ner was the father of Kish, Kish was the father of Saul, Saul was the father of Jonathan, Malchishua, Abinadab, and Eshbaal.

⁴⁰Jonathan was the father of Mephibosheth;
Mephibosheth was the father of Micah;

⁴¹Micah was the father of Pithon, Melech, Tahre-a, and Ahaz;

⁴²Ahaz was the father of Jarah;
Jarah was the father of Alemeth, Azmaveth, and Zimri;
Zimri was the father of Moza.

⁴³Moza was the father of Bine-a, Rephaiah, Eleasah, and Azel.

⁴⁴Azel had six sons: Azrikam, Bocheru, Ishmael, She-ariah, Obadiah, Hanan.

9:32 *special bread,* literally, "showbread."   **9:35-37** *many,* implied.   **9:40** *Mephibosheth,* or "Merib-baal."

9:22 The doorkeepers were chosen "on the basis of their genealogies." People were not eligible to work in the Temple if they were not on the genealogical records that proved they were Abraham's descendants. If they were on the records, they were then chosen only if they were reliable and trustworthy. We need to follow the principle of choosing officers for our churches who are reliable and exhibit a deep faith and commitment to God (see also 1 Timothy 3:2-7).

9:22-32 The priests and Levites put a great deal of time and care into worship. Not only did they perform rather complicated tasks (described in Leviticus 1—9), they also took care of many pieces of equipment. Everything relating to worship was carefully prepared and maintained so both they and all the people could enter worship with their minds and hearts focused on God.

In our busy world, it is easy to rush into our one-hour-a-week worship services without thinking about worship beforehand. We reflect and worry about the week's problems; we pray about

whatever comes into our minds; and we do not meditate on the words we are singing. But God wants our worship to be conducted "properly in a good and orderly way" (1 Corinthians 14:40). Just as we prepare to meet a business associate or invited guests, we should carefully prepare to meet our King.

9:33, 34 Worship was the primary focus of many of the Israelites whose vocation centered on the house of the Lord. Worship should occupy the core of our lives and not just a few minutes once a week. We too can worship at all hours if we stay aware of God's presence and guidance in all situations and if we maintain an attitude of serving him. Build your whole life around the worship of God rather than making it just another activity in a busy schedule.

B. THE REIGN OF DAVID (10:1—29:30)

David becomes king over all Israel and captures the city of Jerusalem. God promises blessings to him and the nation, but David is not allowed to build the Temple. Instead, he begins to make preparations for its construction. Although stumbling and falling occasionally, David walks step by step with God, sincerely wanting to be obedient. Through David's successes and his failures, we learn the importance of giving our whole heart to God and letting him be the focus of our lives, striving each day to be consistent in our obedience to his will.

1. David becomes king over all of Israel
The death of Saul

10 The Philistines attacked and defeated the Israeli troops, who turned and fled and were slaughtered on the slopes of Mount Gilboa. ²They caught up with Saul and his three sons, Jonathan, Abinadab, and Malchishua, and killed them all. ³Saul had been hard pressed with heavy fighting all around him, when the Philistine archers shot and wounded him.

⁴He cried out to his bodyguard, "Quick, kill me with your sword before these uncircumcised heathen capture and torture me."

But the man was afraid to do it, so Saul took his own sword and fell against its point; and it pierced his body. ⁵Then his bodyguard, seeing that Saul was dead, killed himself in the same way. ⁶So Saul and his three sons died together; the entire family was wiped out in one day.

⁷When the Israelis in the valley below the mountain heard that their troops had been routed and that Saul and his sons were dead, they abandoned their cities and fled. And the Philistines came and lived in them. ⁸When the Philistines went back the next day to strip the bodies of the men killed in action and to gather the booty from the battlefield, they found the bodies of Saul and his sons. ⁹So they stripped off Saul's armor and cut off his head; then they displayed them throughout the nation and celebrated the wonderful news before their idols. ¹⁰They fastened his armor to the walls of the Temple of the Gods and nailed his head to the wall of Dagon's temple.

¹¹But when the people of Jabesh-gilead heard what the Philistines had done to Saul, ¹²their heroic warriors went out to the battlefield and brought back his body and the bodies of his three sons. Then they buried them beneath the oak tree at Jabesh and mourned and fasted for seven days.

¹³Saul died for his disobedience to the Lord and because he had consulted a medium, ¹⁴and did not ask the Lord for guidance. So the Lord killed him and gave the kingdom to David, the son of Jesse.

10:12 *battlefield,* implied. **10:13** *medium.* See 1 Sam 28.

10:1
1 Sam 31:1
10:2
1 Sam 31:2

10:9
1 Sam 31:9

10:13
1 Sam 13:13,14
15:23; 28:7
10:14
1 Sam 15:28
1 Chron 12:23

10:1 The chronology of chapters 1—9 covers Israelite history from creation to the exile in Babylon (586 B.C.). At this point, the narrative goes back to the beginning of Israel's kingdom period, picking up with Israel's first king, Saul. While 1 Chronicles begins with Saul's death, 1 Samuel covers his entire reign as king.

10:10 Dagon, the most important god of the Philistines, was believed to bring rain and provide rich harvests. The Philistines built temples to him when they settled in the grain-producing land of Canaan. In times of drought, people begged Dagon for pity, even to the point of sacrificing their children in his temples. In times of plenty, the temples were used for twisted forms of entertainment, such as the humiliation of captives (Judges 16:23–30). But Dagon, like the other pagan gods, was powerless against the one true God (1 Samuel 5:1–7).

10:11, 12 The actions of the heroic warriors who brought back and buried the bodies of Saul and his sons should encourage us to respect our God-given leaders. David showed respect for Saul's position, even when Saul was doing evil and was his avowed enemy (1 Samuel 26). How easy it is to be critical of those in authority over us, focusing only on their weaknesses. We cannot excuse sin, but we should respect the position of those in authority, whether at work, at church, or in government. 1 Thessalonians

5:12, 13 gives instructions for honoring church leaders. Romans 13:1ff gives instructions for relating to government leaders.

10:13, 14 Saul's disobedience was both active and passive; he not only did wrong, but he *failed to do right.* He actively disobeyed by attempting murder, ignoring God's instructions, and seeking guidance from a witch. He passively disobeyed by neglecting to ask God for guidance as he ran the kingdom. Obedience, too, is both passive and active. It is not enough just to avoid what is wrong, we need to actively pursue what is right.

10:13, 14 Did Saul ever ask God for guidance? In 1 Samuel 28:5, Saul asked for guidance, but this account says he did not. The answer to this apparent contradiction lies in understanding Saul's motives. His frantic requests to God came only when he had tried everything his own way. He never went to God unless there was nowhere else to turn. When he finally asked, God refused to answer. Saul sought God for selfish reasons only, and God rejected him for his constant stubbornness and rebellion.

10:14 Throughout much of Saul's reign, David was forced to hide from him (1 Samuel 19—30). During this time David had opportunities to kill Saul (1 Samuel 24, 26) and to assume the throne that God had promised him (1 Samuel 16:1–13). But David trusted in God's promise that he would be king in God's good

David conquers Jerusalem

11:1
2 Sam 5:1,3,6
11:2
2 Sam 5:2; 7:7

11 Then the leaders of Israel went to David at Hebron and told him, "We are your relatives, 2and even when Saul was king, you were the one who led our armies to battle and brought them safely back again. And the Lord your God has told you, 'You shall be the shepherd of my people Israel. You shall be their king.' "

11:3
1 Sam 16:1,3,
12,13
11:4
Josh 15:8,63
Judg 1:21
11:6
2 Sam 8:16

3So David made a contract with them before the Lord, and they anointed him as king of Israel, just as the Lord had told Samuel. 4Then David and the leaders went to Jerusalem (or Jebus, as it used to be called) where the Jebusites—the original inhabitants of the land—lived. 5, 6But the people of Jebus refused to let them enter the city. So David captured the fortress of Zion, later called the City of David, and said to his men, "The first man to kill a Jebusite shall be made commander-in-chief!" Joab, the son of Zeruiah, was the first, so he became the general of David's army. 7David lived in the fortress and that is why that area of Jerusalem is called the City of David. 8He extended the city out around the fortress while Joab rebuilt the rest of Jerusalem. 9And David became more and more famous and powerful, for the Lord of the heavens was with him.

11:9
2 Sam 3:1

David's bravest warriors

11:10
2 Sam 23:8-39
1 Chron 11:3

10These are the names of some of the bravest of David's warriors (who also encouraged the leaders of Israel to make David their king, as the Lord had said would happen):

11:11
2 Sam 23:8
2 Chron 27:2

11Jashobeam (the son of a man from Hachmon) was the leader of The Top Three—the three greatest heroes among David's men. He once killed 300 men with his spear.

11:12
1 Chron 27:4
11:13
2 Sam 23:11,12

12The second of The Top Three was Eleazar, the son of Dodo, a member of the subclan of Ahoh. 13He was with David in the battle against the Philistines at Pasdammim. The Israeli army was in a barley field and had begun to run away, 14but he held his ground in the middle of the field, and recovered it and slaughtered the Philistines; and the Lord saved them with a great victory.

11:15
1 Chron 14:9
11:16
1 Sam 10:5

15Another time, three of The Thirty went to David while he was hiding in the cave of Adullam. The Philistines were camped in the Valley of Rephaim, 16and David was in the stronghold at the time; an outpost of the Philistines had occupied Bethlehem. 17David wanted a drink from the Bethlehem well beside the gate, and

11:1 *your relatives,* literally, "your bone and flesh."

---

timing. It was not up to David to decide when Saul's reign would end. With this battle, God ended Saul's reign just as he had promised.

10:14 Why does this verse say, "So the Lord killed him," when Saul took his own life (1 Samuel 31:3, 4)? God had rejected Saul because of his stubbornness and rebellion (1 Samuel 15:22, 23) and judged him for his sins (1 Samuel 28:16–19). God arranged a defeat in battle so Saul would die and his kingdom would be taken from his family. If Saul had not taken his own life, the Philistine soldiers would have killed him.

11:1, 2 The details of how David came to power are told more completely in 2 Samuel. Chronicles is emphasizing that *God* brought David to power, although he used the efforts of many people—even some of Saul's own family. God is still sovereign over history, directing events to accomplish his will. Chronicles demonstrates that no matter what men may do to hinder God's work, God still controls all events and works his will in them.

11:3, 4 David was king over Judah for seven-and-a-half years before he captured Jerusalem. When David was finally anointed king over all Israel, 20 years had passed since Samuel had anointed him (1 Samuel 16:1–13). God's promises are worth waiting for.

11:4 David chose Jerusalem for both political and military reasons. Jerusalem was near the center of the kingdom and, because it rested on a tribal border, it was in "neutral" territory. Thus its location decreased tribal jealousies. Jerusalem also sat on

a high ridge, making it difficult to attack. (For more information on the city of Jerusalem, see the note on 2 Samuel 5:6.)

11:9 King David's power and fame increased as a direct result of his consistent trust in God. In contrast, King Saul's power and fame decreased because he wanted all the credit for himself and ignored God (1 Samuel 15:17–26). Those who are concerned about building a name for themselves risk losing the very recognition they crave. Like David, we should be concerned for righteousness, honesty, and excellence, and leave the fame up to God.

11:12–14 Eleazar's action changed the course of a battle. When everyone around him ran, he held his ground and was saved by the Lord. In any struggle, fear can keep us from taking a stand for God and from participating in God's victories. Face your fear head on. If you are grounded in God, victory comes when you hold that ground.

11:15 The Thirty were the most courageous and highest ranking officers of David's army.

11:15–19 These three men risked their lives just to please David. David recognized that their devotion to him was inspired by their devotion to God, so he poured out the water as a drink offering, demonstrating that only God is worthy of such devotion. They gave the water to David and he, in turn, gave it to God. Just as these men gave of themselves to serve David, we should put aside our own interests to serve other Christians (1 John 3:16). When we serve others, we are also serving God.

when he mentioned this to his men, 18, 19these three broke through to the Philistine camp, drew some water from the well, and brought it back to David. But he refused to drink it! Instead he poured it out as an offering to the Lord and said, "God forbid that I should drink it! It is the very blood of these men who risked their lives to get it."

20Abishai, Joab's brother, was commander of The Thirty. He had gained his place among The Thirty by killing 300 men at one time with his spear. 21He was the chief and the most famous of The Thirty, but he was not as great as The Three.

22Benaiah, whose father was a mighty warrior from Kabzeel, killed the two famous giants from Moab. He also killed a lion in a slippery pit when there was snow on the ground. 23Once he killed an Egyptian who was seven and one-half feet tall, whose spear was as thick as a weaver's beam. But Benaiah went up to him with only a club in his hand and pulled the spear away from him and used it to kill him. 24, 25He was nearly as great as The Three, and he was very famous among The Thirty. David made him captain of his bodyguard.

11:22
2 Sam 8:18

26-47Other famous warriors among David's men were:

Asahel (Joab's brother);
Elhanan, the son of Dodo from Bethlehem;
Shammoth from Harod;
Helez from Pelon;
Ira (son of Ikkesh) from Tekoa;
Abi-ezer from Anathoth;
Sibbecai from Hushath;
Ilai from Ahoh;
Maharai from Netophah;
Heled (son of Baanah) from Netophah;
Ithai (son of Ribai) a Benjaminite from Gibe-ah;
Benaiah from Pirathon;
Hurai from near the brooks of Gaash;
Abiel from Arbath;
Azmaveth from Baharum;
Eliahba from Sha-albon;
The sons of Hashem from Gizon;
Jonathan (son of Shagee) from Harar;
Ahiam (son of Sacher) from Harar;
Eliphal (son of Ur);
Hepher from Mecherath;
Ahijah from Pelon;
Hezro from Carmel;
Naarai (son of Ezbai);
Joel (brother of Nathan);
Mibhar (son of Hagri);
Zelek from Ammon;
Naharai from Be-eroth—he was General Joab's armorbearer;
Ira from Ithra;
Gareb from Ithra;
Uriah the Hittite;
Zabad (son of Ahlai);
Adina (son of Shiza) from the tribe of Reuben—he was among the thirty-one leaders of the tribe of Reuben;
Hanan (son of Maacah);
Joshaphat from Mithna;
Uzzia from Ashterath;
Shama and Je-iel (sons of Hotham) from Aroer;
Jedia-el (son of Shimri);
Joha (his brother) from Tiza;

11:22 *giants*, literally, "ariels." The meaning of the term is uncertain. **11:26-47** *sons* (of Hashem), implied in 2 Sam. 23:30.

Eliel from Mahavi;

Jeribai and Joshaviah (sons of Elna-am);

Ithmah from Moab;

Eliel; Obed; Ja-asiel from Mezoba.

Warriors join David

12:1
1 Sam 27:2,3
12:2
Judg 3:15; 20:16

12 These are the names of the famous warriors who joined David at Ziklag while he was hiding from King Saul. ²All of them were expert archers and slingers, and they could use their left hands as readily as their right! Like King Saul, they were all of the tribe of Benjamin.

³⁻⁷Their chief was Ahi-ezer, son of Shemaah from Gibe-ah. The others were:

His brother Joash; Jezi-el and Pelet, sons of Azmaveth; Beracah; Jehu from Anathoth; Ishmaiah from Gibeon (a brave warrior rated as high or higher than The Thirty); Jeremiah; Jahaziel; Johanan; Jozabad from Gederah; Eluzai; Jerimoth; Bealiah; Shemariah; Shephatiah from Haruph; Elkanah, Isshiah, Azarel, Jo-ezer, Jashobe-am—all Korahites; Jo-elah and Zebadiah (sons of Jeroham from Gedor).

12:8
2 Sam 2:18

⁸⁻¹³Great and brave warriors from the tribe of Gad also went to David in the wilderness. They were experts with both shield and spear and were "lion-faced men, swift as deer upon the mountains."

Ezer was the chief;

Obadiah was second in command;

Eliab was third in command;

Mishmannah was fourth in command;

Jeremiah was fifth in command;

Attai was sixth in command;

Eliel was seventh in command;

Johanan was eighth in command;

Elzabad was ninth in command;

Jeremiah was tenth in command;

Machbannai was eleventh in command.

12:14
Deut 32:30
12:15
Josh 3:15; 4:18

¹⁴These men were army officers; the weakest was worth a hundred normal troops, and the greatest was worth a thousand! ¹⁵They crossed the Jordan River during its seasonal flooding and conquered the lowlands on both the east and west banks.

12:1 *King Saul,* literally, "the son of Kish."

12:1 Ziklag was a city in Philistia to which David had escaped to hide from Saul. Achish, the Philistine ruler of the area, was happy to have a famous Israelite warrior defect to his land. He did not know, however, that David was only pretending loyalty. Achish gave the city of Ziklag to David, his family, and his army (1 Samuel 27:5–7). David's whereabouts were not a great secret, and many loyal followers joined him there.

12:1ff David surrounded himself with great warriors, the best of the Israelite army. What qualities made them worthy to be David's warriors and servants? (1) They had practiced long and hard to perfect their skills (with bow, sling, or spear); (2) they were mentally tough and determined (lion-faced); (3) they were physically in shape (swift as deer); and (4) they were dedicated to serving God and David. Weak leaders are easily threatened by competent subordinates, but strong leaders surround themselves with the best. They are not intimidated by able and competent followers.

12:1–7 All the warriors mentioned here were from the tribe of Benjamin. Even members of Saul's own tribe (1 Samuel 9:1, 2)

were deserting him to help David become king of all Israel. It was clear to them that God has chosen David to be Israel's next leader.

12:2 An archer and a slinger each used specific weapons. The sling was unassuming in appearance but deadly in battle. A shallow leather pouch with a cord of leather or goat's hair attached to each side, the sling was whirled around the head and sent a stone to its target. The bow and arrow had been in use for thousands of years. Arrowheads were made of stone, wood, or bone because the Philistines still had a monopoly on metalworking (1 Samuel 13:19, 20). Arrow shafts were made of reed or wood, and bowstrings were made of animal gut.

12:8 While the men of Benjamin were expert archers and slingers, the warriors of Gad were experts with the shield and spear. Israelite spears had wood shafts and spearheads of bone or stone and were often thrown through the air toward their mark. Philistine spears had bronze shafts and iron spearheads, and their shields were made of wood and overlaid with leather. Large shields were often carried by an armor-bearer, whose main task was to protect the warrior.

16Others came to David from Benjamin and Judah. 17David went out to meet them and said, "If you have come to help me, we are friends; but if you have come to betray me to my enemies when I am innocent, then may the God of our fathers see and judge you."

12:16
1 Sam 22:7

18Then the Holy Spirit came upon them, and Amasai, a leader of The Thirty, replied,

12:18
Judg 3:10; 6:34
1 Chron 2:17

"We are yours, David;
We are on your side, son of Jesse.
Peace, peace be unto you,
And peace to all who aid you;
For your God is with you."

So David let them join him, and he made them captains of his army.

19Some men from Manasseh deserted the Israeli army and joined David just as he was going into battle with the Philistines against King Saul. But as it turned out, the Philistine generals refused to let David and his men go with them. After much discussion they sent them back, for they were afraid that David and his men would imperil them by deserting to King Saul.

12:19
1 Sam 29:3,4

20Here is a list of the men from Manasseh who deserted to David as he was en route to Ziklag: Adnah, Jozabad, Jedia-el, Michael, Jozabad, Elihu, Zillethai. Each was a high-ranking officer of Manasseh's troops. 21They were brave and able warriors, and they assisted David when he fought against the Amalek raiders at Ziklag.

12:21
1 Sam 30:1

22More men joined David almost every day until he had a tremendous army—the army of God. 23Here is the registry of recruits who joined David at Hebron. They were all anxious to see David become king instead of Saul, just as the Lord had said would happen.

12:22
Josh 5:13-15
12:23
2 Sam 2:3,4
1 Chron 10:14
11:10

24-37From Judah, 6,800 troops armed with shields and spears.
From the tribe of Simeon, 7,100 outstanding warriors.
From the Levites, 4,600.
From the priests—descendants of Aaron—there were 3,700 troops under the command of Zadok, a young man of unusual courage, and Jehoiada. (He and twenty-two members of his family were officers of the fighting priests.)
From the tribe of Benjamin, the same tribe Saul was from, there were 3,000. (Most of that tribe retained its allegiance to Saul.)
From the tribe of Ephraim, 20,800 mighty warriors, each famous in his respective clan.
From the half-tribe of Manasseh, 18,000 were sent for the express purpose of helping David become king.
From the tribe of Issachar there were 200 leaders of the tribe with their relatives—all men who understood the temper of the times and knew the best course for Israel to take.

12:24
2 Sam 2:8,9
8:17
1 Chron 6:8,53
12:2
Esth 1:13
Ps 12:2

12:21 *Ziklag*, implied.

12:18 How did the Holy Spirit work in Old Testament times? When there was an important job to be done, God chose a person to do it, and the Spirit gave that person the needed power and ability. The Spirit gave Bezalel artistic ability (Exodus 31:1–5), Jephthah military prowess (Judges 11:29), David power to rule (1 Samuel 16:13), and Zechariah an authoritative word of prophecy (2 Chronicles 24:20). Here the Holy Spirit came upon David's warriors. The Spirit came upon individuals in order to accomplish specific goals. Beginning at Pentecost, however, the Spirit came upon all believers (Acts 2:14–21).

12:22 David's army was called the "army of God." These men

were drawn to David by the reputation of his great warriors, the news of their victories, and their desire to see God's will done in making David king. People are often drawn to a great cause and the brave, determined people who support it. As believers, we have the greatest cause—the salvation of mankind. If we are brave, determined, and faithful, others will be drawn to work with us.

12:24–37 In Numbers 1:47–50, God said the Levites were to be exempt from military service. Why then are they listed as part of David's army? Although they were exempt from the draft, here they strongly supported David and volunteered their services to help install him as king.

From the tribe of Zebulun there were 50,000 trained warriors; they were fully armed and totally loyal to David.

From Naphtali there were 1,000 officers and 37,000 troops equipped with shields and spears.

From the tribe of Dan there were 28,600 troops, all of them prepared for war.

From the tribe of Asher, there were 40,000 trained and ready troops.

From the other side of the Jordan River—where the tribes of Reuben and Gad and the half-tribe of Manasseh lived—there were 120,000 troops equipped with every kind of weapon.

12:38
2 Sam 5:1-3
1 Chron 12:33

12:40
1 Sam 25:18

38All these men came in battle array to Hebron with the single purpose of making David the king of Israel. In fact, all of Israel was ready for this change. 39They feasted and drank with David for three days, for preparations had been made for their arrival. 40People from nearby and from as far away as Issachar, Zebulun, and Naphtali brought food on donkeys, camels, mules, and oxen. Vast supplies of flour, fig cakes, raisins, wine, oil, cattle, and sheep were brought to the celebration, for joy had spread throughout the land.

2. David brings the Ark to Jerusalem
Uzza touches the Ark and dies

13 After David had consulted with all of his army officers, 2he addressed the assembled men of Israel as follows:

"Since you think that I should be your king, and since the Lord our God has given his approval, let us send messages to our brothers throughout the land of Israel, including the priests and Levites, inviting them to come and join us. 3And let us bring back the Ark of our God, for we have been neglecting it ever since Saul became king."

13:3
1 Sam 7:I,2
13:5
1 Sam 6:21; 7:1
2 Sam 6:1
1 Kgs 8:65
1 Chron 15:3
13:6
Josh 15:9
2 Kgs 19:15
13:7
1 Sam 7:1

4There was unanimous consent, for everyone agreed with him. 5So David summoned the people of Israel from all across the nation so that they could be present when the Ark of God was brought from Kiriath-jearim.

6Then David and all Israel went to Baalah (i.e., Kiriath-jearim) in Judah to bring back the Ark of the Lord God enthroned above the angels. 7It was taken from the

13:5 *from all across the nation,* literally, "from Shihor—the Brook of Egypt—to the entrance of Hamath." **13:6** *above the angels,* literally "above the cherubim."

12:32 The 200 leaders from Issachar understood the temper of the times and, as a result, their knowledge and judgment provided needed help in making decisions for the nation. For leaders today, it is equally necessary to know what is happening in society in order to plan the best course of action for the church. Knowledge of current events, trends, and needs helps one understand people's thoughts and attitudes. This helps leaders make wise decisions for the church and understand how to make God's message relevant to their lives.

12:38 These troops totaled more than 300,000 men. Their single purpose was to show overwhelming support for David and make him king. God had drawn these men together and had focused their energy on a single purpose. Churches and organizations often dilute their energy by trying to go in too many directions. Instead, they should ask God to narrow their focus to one central purpose—one that will build up the church and glorify God. Churches and other groups should know their purpose as clearly as David's army knew theirs.

12:40 The people were ready for change. They had suffered under Saul's leadership and lack of obedience to God. They were so overjoyed with David's coronation that they contributed lavishly to the celebration. It is right and proper to give generously for celebration and joyous worship. God is the author of joy, and he will join us in our celebrations.

13:1ff The parallel account of moving the Ark (2 Samuel 5, 6) shows that David's building projects were completed *before* he

brought the Ark to Jerusalem. The writer of Chronicles puts the moving of the Ark first because he wanted to highlight David's spiritual accomplishments and relationship to God rather than give an accurate chronological account.

13:1 David took time to consult with all his officers. As king, he had ultimate authority and could have given orders on his own, but he chose to involve others in leadership. Perhaps this is why there was unanimous support for his decisions (13:1-5). When we are in charge, it is tempting to make unilateral decisions, pushing through our own opinions. But effective leaders listen carefully to the opinions of others and they encourage others to participate in making decisions.

13:3 The Ark of God is also called the Ark of the Covenant. It rested in the Holy of Holies, the most holy room in the Temple, and was the most sacred artifact of the Hebrew faith. It was a large box containing the stone tablets on which God had written the Ten Commandments (Exodus 25:10-22). David had already made Jerusalem his political capital (11:4-9). Now he brought the Ark there in hopes of making it the nation's center for worship.

13:3 The Ark of God had been in Kiriath-jearim for many years. The neglect of the Ark symbolized Israel's neglect of God. Bringing the Ark back to the center of Israel's life reflected King David's desire to remind the nation of its true foundation—God. Neglecting those things that remind us of God—the Bible, the church, etc.—will cause us also to neglect God. We must remember to keep God at the center of our lives.

house of Abinadab on a new cart. Uzza and Ahio drove the oxen. 8Then David and all the people danced before the Lord with great enthusiasm, accompanied by singing and by zithers, harps, tambourines, cymbals, and trumpets. 9But as they arrived at the threshing-floor of Chidon, the oxen stumbled and Uzza reached out his hand to steady the Ark. 10Then the anger of the Lord blazed out against Uzza, and killed him because he had touched the Ark. And so he died there before God. 11David was angry at the Lord for what he had done to Uzza, and he named the place "The Outbreak Against Uzza." And it is still called that today.

12Now David was afraid of God and asked, "How shall I ever get the Ark of God home?"

13Finally he decided to take it to the home of Obed-edom the Gittite instead of bringing it to the City of David. 14The Ark remained there with the family of Obed-edom for three months, and the Lord blessed him and his family.

David's good fortune

14 King Hiram of Tyre sent masons and carpenters to help build David's palace and he supplied him with much cedar lumber. 2David now realized why the Lord had made him king and why he had made his kingdom so great; it was for a special reason—to give joy to God's people!

3After David moved to Jerusalem, he married additional wives and became the father of many sons and daughters.

4-7These are the names of the sons born to him in Jerusalem: Shammua, Shobab, Nathan, Solomon, Ibhar, Elishu-a, Elpelet, Nogah, Nepheg, Japhia, Elishama, Beeliada, Eliphelet.

David conquers the Philistines

8When the Philistines heard that David was Israel's new king, they mobilized their forces to capture him. But David learned that they were on the way, so he called together his army. 9The Philistines were raiding the Valley of Rephaim,

13:8
1 Chron 15:16

13:9
2 Sam 6:6

13:10
Lev 10:2
1 Chron 15:13,
15

13:13
2 Chron 25:24
13:14
1 Chron 26:4,5

14:1
2 Sam 5:11

14:4
2 Sam 5:14
1 Chron 3:5-8

14:9
1 Chron 11:15
14:13

13:8 Worship in the Old Testament was more than a sober religious exercise. David's exuberance as he worshiped God with dancing and music is approved in Scripture. Our worship should reflect a healthy balance: sometimes we should be reflective and serious (Exodus 19:14ff), and sometimes we should show enthusiasm and jubilation. Worship, like life, should be balanced. What does your church need—more serious reflection or more joyous celebration?

13:10 Why did Uzza die? He had touched the Ark, and that was an offense that was punishable by death. God had given specific instructions about how the Ark was to be moved and carried (Numbers 4:5–15) and these were neglected here. The Levites were responsible to move the Ark, and it was to be carried on their shoulders with poles through its rings. It was never to be touched. Bringing the Ark on a cart followed the Philistines' example (1 Samuel 6:1–8). Uzza, though sincere in his desire to protect the Ark, had to face the consequences of his sin; and David was reminded that his obedience to God's laws was more important than his enthusiasm.

13:10–14 Uzza died instantly for touching the Ark, but God blessed Obed-edom's home, where the Ark was stored. This demonstrates the two-edged aspect of God's power: he is perfectly loving and perfectly just. Great blessings come to those who obey his commands, but severe judgment comes to those who disobey him. This judgment may come swiftly or over time, but it will come. Sometimes we focus only on the blessings God gives us, while forgetting that when we sin, "it is a fearful thing to fall into the hands of the living God" (Hebrews 10:31). At other times,

however, we concentrate so much on doom that we miss his blessings. Don't fall into a one-sided view of God. Along with God's blessings comes the responsibility to live up to his demands for fairness, honesty, and justice.

13:11 David was angry at both God and himself. He knew he had done something wrong in transporting the Ark, and he was angry that his plans for the joyous return of the Ark had ended in a man's death. But his anger cooled, and he left the Ark in Obed-edom's home until he could consider how to get it to Jerusalem. This allowed him to discover God's instructions for transporting the Ark. The next trip would be carried out according to God's commands.

14:1 King Hiram also sent lumber and craftsmen to help Solomon build the Temple (2 Chronicles 2:1ff).

14:2 God gave David honor and success, but not simply for David's personal gain. David realized that God had blessed him for a special reason—to give joy to God's people! Often we are tempted to use our position or possessions only for our own good. Instead, we must remember that God has placed us where we are and given us all we have so we may bring joy and blessing to others, not just ourselves.

14:3 Accumulating wives and concubines was the custom of the day among Middle Eastern royalty, but it was not God's ideal (Genesis 2:24). David's marriages brought him greater power and influence, but they also caused strife, jealousy, and even murder within his family. (See the chart in 2 Samuel 13 for other consequences of polygamy.)

14:8–16 A map of this battle is in 2 Samuel 5.

¹⁰and David asked the Lord, "If I go out and fight them, will you give me the victory?"

And the Lord replied, "Yes, I will."

¹¹So he attacked them at Baal-perazim and wiped them out. He exulted, "God has used me to sweep away my enemies like water bursting through a dam!" That is why the place has been known as Baal-perazim ever since (meaning, "The Place of Breaking Through").

¹²After the battle the Israelis picked up many idols left by the Philistines, but David ordered them burned.

14:13
1 Chron 14:9

¹³Later the Philistines raided the valley again, ¹⁴and again David asked God what to do.

The Lord replied, "Go around by the mulberry trees and attack from there. ¹⁵When you hear a sound like marching in the tops of the mulberry trees, that is your signal to attack, for God will go before you and destroy the enemy."

14:17
Ex 15:14
Deut 2:25

¹⁶So David did as the Lord commanded him; and he cut down the army of the Philistines all the way from Gibeon to Gezer. ¹⁷David's fame spread everywhere, and the Lord caused all the nations to fear him.

The Levites carry the Ark to Jerusalem

15:1
1 Chron 16:1
17:1
Ps 132:2-5
15:2
Num 4:15
Deut 10:8
15:3
2 Sam 6:12,17
1 Kgs 8:1
1 Chron 13:5
15:1,12
15:4
1 Chron 6:16
12:26

15 David now built several palaces for himself in Jerusalem, and he also built a new Tabernacle to house the Ark of God, ²and issued these instructions: "[When we transfer the Ark to its new home], no one except the Levites may carry it, for God has chosen them for this purpose; they are to minister to him forever."

³Then David summoned all Israel to Jerusalem to celebrate the bringing of the Ark into the new Tabernacle. ⁴⁻¹⁰These were the priests and Levites present:

120 from the clan of Kohath; with Uriel as their leader;
220 from the clan of Merari; with Asaiah as their leader;
130 from the clan of Gershom; with Joel as their leader;
200 from the subclan of Elizaphan; with Shemaiah as their leader;
80 from the subclan of Hebron; with Eliel as their leader;
112 from the subclan of Uzziel; with Amminadab as their leader.

15:11
1 Sam 22:20
1 Kgs 2:26,35
1 Chron 12:28

¹¹Then David called for Zadok and Abiathar, the High Priests, and for the Levite leaders: Uriel, Asaiah, Joel, Shemaiah, Eliel, and Amminadab.

15:12
Ex 19:14,15
2 Chron 35:6

¹²"You are the leaders of the clans of the Levites," he told them. "Now sanctify yourselves with all your brothers so that you may bring the Ark of Jehovah, the God

15:2 *When we transfer the Ark to its new home,* implied.

14:10 Before David went to battle, he talked to God, asking for his presence and guidance. Too often we wait until we are in the midst of trouble before turning to God. By then the consequences of our actions are already unfolding. When do you ask for God's help? Only as a desperate last resort? Instead, go to him first! Like David, you may receive incredible help and avoid serious trouble.

14:12 David's quick and decisive action against idols helped make him great. He was obeying the law that said, "You must break down the heathen altars and shatter the obelisks and cut up the shameful images and burn the idols" (Deuteronomy 7:5). Failing to destroy idols was the greatest weakness of David's successors.

14:12 The soldiers wanted to keep souvenirs from the battle, but David ordered them to burn the idols. The only proper response to sin is to get rid of it completely. You cannot be a follower of God while continuing to hold on to parts of your past life that keep God

from being the center of your thoughts and actions. Destroy whatever takes God's rightful place in your life, and follow him with complete devotion.

14:13–16 In almost every new situation, David prayed for guidance. New developments offer new challenges as well as new risks. We should be open to seeking God's guidance in each new situation because this will help us avoid certain dangers. Don't assume that God's will or way of working in your life will always be the same. If you seek God's leading as circumstances change, you will not see change as a threat but as an opportunity to let God work in new ways.

15:12 The priests sanctified themselves so they would be prepared to carry the Ark. To *sanctify* literally means to *separate.* The priests symbolically separated themselves from sin and evil. This was done by washing themselves and their clothing in a special ceremony (Numbers 8:5–8).

of Israel, to the place I have prepared for it. 13The Lord destroyed us before because we handled the matter improperly—you were not carrying it."

14So the priests and the Levites underwent the ceremonies of sanctification in preparation for bringing home the Ark of Jehovah, the God of Israel. 15Then the Levites carried the Ark on their shoulders with its carrying poles, just as the Lord had instructed Moses.

16King David also ordered the Levite leaders to organize the singers into an orchestra, and they played loudly and joyously upon psaltries, harps, and cymbals. 17Heman (son of Joel), Asaph (son of Berechiah), and Ethan (son of Kushaiah) from the clan of Merari were the heads of the musicians.

18The following men were chosen as their assistants: Zechariah, Ja-aziel, Shemiramoth, Jehiel, Unni, Eliab, Benaiah, Ma-asseiah, Mattithiah, Eliphelehu, Mikneiah, Obed-edom and Je-iel, the doorkeepers.

19Heman, Asaph, and Ethan were chosen to sound the bronze cymbals; 20and Zechariah, Azi-el, Shemiramoth, Jehiel, Unni, Eliab, Ma-aseiah, and Benaiah comprised an octet accompanied by harps. 21Mattithiah, Eliphelehu, Mikneiah, Obed-edom, Je-iel, and Azaziah were the harpists. 22The song leader was Chenaniah, the chief of the Levites, who was selected for his skill. 23Berechiah and Elkanah were guards for the Ark. 24Shebaniah, Joshaphat, Nethanel, Amasai, Zechariah, Benaiah, and Eliezer—all of whom were priests—formed a bugle corps to march at the head of the procession. And Obed-edom and Jehiah guarded the Ark.

25Then David and the elders of Israel and the high officers of the army went with great joy to the home of Obed-edom to take the Ark to Jerusalem. 26And because God didn't destroy the Levites who were carrying the Ark, they sacrificed seven bulls and seven lambs. 27David, the Levites carrying the Ark, the singers, and Chenaniah the song leader were all dressed in linen robes. David also wore a linen ephod. 28So the leaders of Israel took the Ark to Jerusalem with shouts of joy, the blowing of horns and trumpets, the crashing of cymbals, and loud playing on the harps and zithers.

29(But as the Ark arrived in Jerusalem, David's wife Michal, the daughter of King Saul, felt a deep disgust for David as she watched from the window and saw him dancing like a madman.)

15:20 *accompanied by harps,* literally, "set to Alamoth." The meaning of the term is uncertain. **15:21** *were the harpists,* literally, "were to lead with zithers (or harps) set to the Shiminith." The meaning is uncertain.

Marginal cross-references:

15:15 Ex 25:14 / Num 4:5

15:16 1 Chron 13:8 / 25:1

15:17 1 Chron 25:1

15:24 1 Chron 16:6

15:25 2 Sam 6:12,15 / 1 Chron 13:13

15:26 Num 23:1,29

15:13 The incident to which David refers is recorded in 13:8–11 and 2 Samuel 6:1–11. As the Ark was being brought back to Israel on an ox cart, the oxen stumbled. Uzza, trying to steady it with his hand, was killed instantly. The mistake was not in David's desire to move the Ark, but in his method for its return. David either ignored or was unaware of the specific instructions in God's Law about how the Ark was to be moved. Obviously he had now discovered his mistake and was preparing to correct it. This incident was a divine object lesson to all Israel that God governed the king and not the other way around. If David was allowed to handle the Ark of God carelessly, what would that say to the people about their faith?

15:13–15 When David's first attempt to move the Ark failed (1 Chronicles 13:8–14), he learned an important lesson: when God gives specific instructions, it is wise to follow them precisely. This time David saw to it that the Levites carried the Ark (Numbers 4:5–15). We may not fully understand the reasons behind God's instructions, but we can know that his wisdom is complete and his judgment infallible. The way to know God's instructions is to know his Word. But just as children do not understand the reasons for all their parents' instructions until they are adults, we will not understand all of God's instructions in this life. It is far better to obey God first, and then seek to know the reasons.

15:16–25 The great musical procession was designed as a worthy accompaniment to the great occasion. It heightened the excitement, elevated the people's hearts and minds, and focused their attention on the event. It also helped seal it in their memory for years to come. Beginning any task with praise to God can inspire us to give him our best. Develop the practice of giving praise to God, and you will experience greater joy and strength to face any task.

15:22 Chenaniah had developed his musical skills, and this led to greater opportunities for service. Do you have natural skills that could be used in God's service? Let Chenaniah's example inspire you to develop and refine them so that you can offer them as valuable gifts to the Lord.

15:29 David was willing to look foolish in the eyes of some in order to express his thankfulness to God fully and honestly. In contrast, Michal was so disgusted by his undignified actions that she could not rejoice in the Ark's return to Jerusalem. Some godly people may look foolish to us in their heartfelt expressions of worship, but we must accept them. In the same way, we should not be afraid to worship God with whatever expressions seem appropriate.

David gives praise to God

16:1
2 Sam 6:17
1 Kgs 8:5
1 Chron 15:1

16 So they brought the Ark of God into the special tent that David had prepared for it, and the leaders of Israel sacrificed burnt offerings and peace offerings before God. 2At the conclusion of these offerings David blessed the people in the name of the Lord; 3then he gave every person present (men and women alike) a loaf of bread, some wine, and a cake of raisins.

16:4
1 Chron 15:16

4He appointed certain of the Levites to minister before the Ark by giving constant praise and thanks to the Lord God of Israel and by asking for his blessings upon his people. These are the names of those given this assignment: 5Asaph, the leader of this detail, sounded the cymbals. His associates were Zechariah, Je-iel, Shemiramoth, Jehiel, Mattithiah, Eliab, Benaiah, Obededom, and Je-iel; they played the harps and zithers. 6The priests Benaiah and Jahaziel played their trumpets regularly before the Ark.

16:7
2 Sam 22:1

7At that time David began the custom of using choirs in the Tabernacle to sing thanksgiving to the Lord. Asaph was the director of this choral group of priests.

16:8
1 Kgs 8:43
2 Kgs 19:19
Ps 105:1-15

8"Oh, give thanks to the Lord and pray to him," they sang.
"Tell the peoples of the world
About his mighty doings.
9Sing to him; yes, sing his praises
And tell of his marvelous works.
10Glory in his holy name;
Let all rejoice who seek the Lord.
11Seek the Lord; yes, seek his strength
And seek his face untiringly.

16:12
Ps 78:43; 103:2

12, 13O descendants of his servant Abraham,
O chosen sons of Jacob,
Remember his mighty miracles
And his marvelous miracles
And his authority:

16:14
Ps 48:10

14He is the Lord our God!
His authority is seen throughout the earth.
15Remember his covenant forever—
The words he commanded
To a thousand generations:

16:16
Gen 17:2
22:16-18; 26:3

16His agreement with Abraham,
And his oath to Isaac,

16:17
Gen 35:11,12

17And his confirmation to Jacob.
He promised Israel
With an everlasting promise:

16:18
Gen 13:15

18'I will give you the land of Canaan
As your inheritance.'

16:19
Gen 34:30
Deut 7:7

19When Israel was few in number—oh, so few—
And merely strangers in the Promised Land;
20When they wandered from country to country,
From one kingdom to another—

16:3 *every person present*, literally, "to each Israelite."

16:4 Certain Levites were appointed to give *constant* praise and thanks to God. Praise and thanksgiving should be a continuous part of our lives, not expressions reserved only for celebrations. Determine to praise God continuously, and you will find that you won't take his blessings for granted.

16:7-36 Does it ever seem that a simple "thank you" to God is not enough to express your appreciation? Four elements of true thanksgiving are found in the following song: (1) *remembering* what God has done, (2) *telling* others about it, (3) *showing* God's glory to others, and (4) *offering* gifts of self, time, and resources.

Get into the habit of fully expressing your thanks to God.

16:8ff Several parts of this song are parallel to songs in the book of Psalms: 16:8–22 with Psalm 105:1–15; 16:23–33 with Psalm 96; 16:34–36 with Psalm 106:1, 47, 48.

16:15-18 This covenant was given to Abraham (Genesis 15:18–21), and then passed on to Isaac (Genesis 26:24, 25) and Jacob (Genesis 28:13–15). God promised to give the land of Canaan (present-day Israel) to their descendants. He also promised that the Messiah would come from their line.

21God didn't let anyone harm them.
  Even kings were killed who sought to hurt them.
22'Don't harm my chosen people,' he declared.
  'These are my prophets—touch them not.'
23Sing to the Lord, O earth,
  Declare each day that he is the one who saves!
24Show his glory to the nations!
  Tell everyone about his miracles.
25For the Lord is great, and should be highly praised;
  He is to be held in awe above all gods.
26The other so-called gods are demons,
  But the Lord made the heavens.
27Majesty and honor march before him,
  Strength and gladness walk beside him.
28O people of all nations of the earth,
  Ascribe great strength and glory to his name!
29Yes, ascribe to the Lord
  The glory due his name!
  Bring an offering and come before him;
  Worship the Lord when clothed with holiness!
30Tremble before him, all the earth!
  The world stands unmoved.
31Let the heavens be glad, the earth rejoice;
  Let all the nations say, 'It is the Lord who reigns.'
32Let the vast seas roar,
  Let the countryside and everything in it rejoice!
33Let the trees in the woods sing for joy before the Lord,
  For he comes to judge the earth.
34Oh, give thanks to the Lord, for he is good;
  His love and his kindness go on forever.
35Cry out to him, 'Oh, save us, God of our salvation;
  Bring us safely back from among the nations.
  Then we will thank your holy name,
  And triumph in your praise.'
36Blessed be Jehovah, God of Israel,
  Forever and forevermore."

And all the people shouted "Amen!" and praised the Lord.
37David arranged for Asaph and his fellow Levites to minister regularly at the Tabernacle, doing each day whatever needed to be done. 38This group included Obed-edom (the son of Jeduthun), Hosah and sixty-eight of their colleagues as guards.
39Meanwhile the old Tabernacle of the Lord on the hill of Gibeon continued to be active. David left Zadok the priest and his fellow-priests to minister to the Lord there. 40They sacrificed burnt offerings to the Lord each morning and evening upon the altar set aside for that purpose, just as the Lord had commanded Israel. 41David also appointed Heman, Jeduthun, and several others who were chosen by name to give thanks to the Lord for his constant love and mercy. 42They used their trumpets

16:37 *at the Tabernacle,* literally, "before the Ark of the Covenant of the Lord."

Cross references (right margin):
16:21 Gen 12:17; 20:3 Ex 7:15
16:22 Gen 20:7
16:23 Ps 96:1-13
16:25 Ps 89:7 144:3,4
16:26 Lev 19:4 Ps 102:25
16:29 Ps 29:2
16:31 Ps 93:1; 96:10 Isa 44:23; 49:13
16:32 Ps 98:7
16:34 Ps 106:1; 136:1
16:35 Ps 106:47,48
16:36 Deut 27:15 1 Kgs 8:15,56 Neh 8:6 Ps 72:18
16:37 2 Chron 8:14 Ezra 3:4
16:38 1 Chron 13:14 26:10
16:39 1 Kgs 3:4 1 Chron 15:11
16:40 Ex 29:38 Num 28:3,4
16:41 1 Chron 6:33 25:1 2 Chron 5:13
16:42 1 Chron 25:7 2 Chron 7:6 29:27

16:37 Asaph and his fellow Levites ministered in the Temple, doing each day "whatever needed to be done." To carry out God's work is not merely to engage in religious exercises. It includes other necessary tasks. Even if you don't have the opportunity to teach or preach, God can use you in the ministry. What needs to be done? Cleaning, serving, singing, planning, administering? Look for ways to minister each day.

16:39 David brought the Ark to Jerusalem although the Tabernacle was still at Gibeon. His plan was to reunite the Tabernacle and Ark in a new Temple at Jerusalem which would then become Israel's only worship center. The Temple, however, was not built until Solomon's time. In the meantime, Israel had two worship centers and two High Priests (15:11), one at Gibeon and one at Jerusalem.

and cymbals to accompany the singers with loud praises to God. And Jeduthun's sons were appointed as guards.

43At last the celebration ended and the people returned to their homes, and David returned to bless his own household.

God promises blessing to David

17 After David had been living in his new palace for some time he said to Nathan the prophet, "Look! I'm living here in a cedar-paneled home while the Ark of the Covenant of God is out there in a tent!"

2And Nathan replied, "Carry out your plan in every detail, for it is the will of the Lord."

3But that same night God said to Nathan, 4"Go and give my servant David this message: 'You are not to build my temple! 5I've gone from tent to tent as my home from the time I brought Israel out of Egypt. 6In all that time I never suggested to any of the leaders of Israel—the shepherds I appointed to care for my people—that they should build me a cedar-lined temple.'

7"Tell my servant David, 'The Lord of heaven says to you, I took you from being a shepherd and made you the king of my people. 8And I have been with you everywhere you've gone; I have destroyed your enemies, and I will make your name as great as the greatest of the earth. 9And I will give a permanent home to my people Israel, and will plant them in their land. They will not be disturbed again; the wicked nations won't conquer them as they did before, 10when the judges ruled them. I will subdue all of your enemies. And I now declare that I will cause your descendants to be kings of Israel just as you are.

11" 'When your time here on earth is over and you die, I will place one of your sons upon your throne; and I will make his kingdom strong. 12He is the one who shall build me a temple, and I will establish his royal line of descent forever. 13I will be his father, and he shall be my son; I will never remove my mercy and love from him as I did from Saul. 14I will place him over my people and over the kingdom of Israel forever—and his descendants will always be kings.' "

15So Nathan told King David everything the Lord had said.

David's prayer of acceptance

16Then King David went in and sat before the Lord and said, "Who am I, O Lord God, and what is my family that you have given me all this? 17For all the great things you have already done for me are nothing in comparison to what you have promised to do in the future! For now, O Lord God, you are speaking of future generations of my children being kings too! You speak as though I were someone very great. 18What else can I say? You know that I am but a dog, yet you have decided to honor me! 19O Lord, you have given me these wonderful promises just

17:1
2 Sam 7:1,2

17:4
1 Chron 28:3
Acts 7:42

17:5
Ex 40:2,3
2 Sam 7:6

17:6
2 Sam 7:7

17:11
2 Sam 7:12
1 Kgs 2:4; 5:5
8:25

17:13
1 Chron 10:14
Heb 1:5

17:17
2 Sam 7:19

17:19
2 Sam 7:21
Isa 37:35

17:1 David felt guilty that the Ark, the symbol of God's presence, sat in a tent while he lived in a beautiful palace. David's desire was right, but his timing was wrong. God told David *not* to build a Temple (17:3, 4), and David was willing to live by God's timing. If you live in comparative luxury while God's work, house, or servants go lacking, perhaps God wants you to change the situation. Like David, move ahead to correct the imbalance, but be willing to adjust to God's timing.

17:3–14 God did not want a warrior to build his Temple (28:3; 1 Kings 5:3), and David had shed much blood in unifying the nation as God had commanded. So the honor of building the Temple would go to David's son Solomon. David would pass on to Solomon a peaceful and united kingdom, ready to begin work on a beautiful Temple.

17:10 God promised to subdue David's enemies. Chapters 18—20 tell how God kept that promise.

17:12–14 Why, after this eternal promise, were the Israelites eventually taken from the Promised Land into captivity? The promise to David had two parts. The first part was conditional: as

long as David's descendants followed God's laws and honored him, they would continually be on the throne of Israel. The second part was unconditional: a son of David would occupy his throne forever. This was Jesus the Messiah. The first part of the promise was based on the faithful obedience of David's descendants. The second part would come true regardless of the way David's descendants acted.

17:16–27 David prayed by humbling himself (17:16–18), praising God (17:19, 20), recognizing God's blessings (17:21, 22), and accepting God's decisions, promises, and commands (17:23, 24).

17:16–27 David responded to God's answer and promises with deep humility, not resentment. This king who had conquered his enemies and was loved by his people said, "Who am I . . . that you have given me all this?" David recognized that God was the *true* king. God has done just as much for us, and he plans to do even more! Like David, we should humble ourselves and give glory to God, saying, "O Lord, there is no one like you—there is no other God." When God chooses another to implement your ideas, can you respond with such humility?

because you want to be kind to me, because of your own great heart. 20O Lord, there is no one like you—there is no other God. In fact, we have never even heard of another god like you!

21"And what other nation in all the earth is like Israel? You have made a unique nation and have redeemed it from Egypt so that the people could be your people. And you made a great name for yourself when you did glorious miracles in driving out the nations from before your people. 22You have declared that your people Israel belong to you forever, and you have become their God.

23"And now I accept your promise, Lord, that I and my children will always rule this nation. 24And may this bring eternal honor to your name as everyone realizes that you always do what you say. They will exclaim, 'The Lord of heaven is indeed the God of Israel!' And Israel shall always be ruled by my children and their posterity! 25Now I have the courage to pray to you, for you have revealed this to me. 26God himself has promised this good thing to me! 27May this blessing rest upon my children forever, for when you grant a blessing, Lord, it is an eternal blessing!"

17:22
Ex 19:5,6

17:24
2 Sam 7:12,16
1 Kgs 2:4; 8:25

3. David's military exploits
David conquers many enemies

18 David finally subdued the Philistines and conquered Gath and its surrounding towns. 2He also conquered Moab and required its people to send him a large sum of money every year. 3He conquered the dominion of King Hadadezer of Zobah (as far as Hamath) at the time Hadadezer went to tighten his grip along the Euphrates River. 4David captured a thousand of his chariots, seven thousand cavalry, and twenty thousand troops. He crippled all the chariot teams except a hundred that he kept for his own use.

5When the Syrians arrived from Damascus to help King Hadadezer, David killed twenty-two thousand of them; 6then he placed a garrison of his troops in Damascus, the Syrian capital. So the Syrians, too, were forced to send him large amounts of money every year. And the Lord gave David victory everywhere he went. 7He brought the gold shields of King Hadadezer's officers to Jerusalem, 8as well as a great amount of bronze from Hadadezer's cities of Tibhath and Cun. (King Solomon later melted the bronze and used it for the Temple. He molded it into the bronze tank, the pillars, and the instruments used in offering sacrifices on the altar.)

9When King Tou of Hamath learned that King David had destroyed Hadadezer's

18:1
2 Sam 8:1

17:21 David's reference to Israel's exodus from Egypt would have had special significance to the original readers of 1 Chronicles who were either beginning or had just completed a second great exodus back to Israel from captivity in Babylon. Remembering God's promises, mercy, and protection during the first exodus would have encouraged the exiles returning once again to Israel, just as God had promised.

18:2 In 2 Samuel 8:1, 2, it is recorded that David killed two-thirds of Moab. His ancestor, Ruth, was originally from the land of Moab.

18:6, 14 God gave David victory, and David was a just ruler. Although we are not promised victory in every military battle, we see in David's glowing success a hint of what Christ's reign will be like—complete victory and just government. If David's glory was great, how much greater will Christ's glory be. Our confidence is that we can be rightly related to Jesus Christ through faith. One day we will share in his glory as we reign with him.

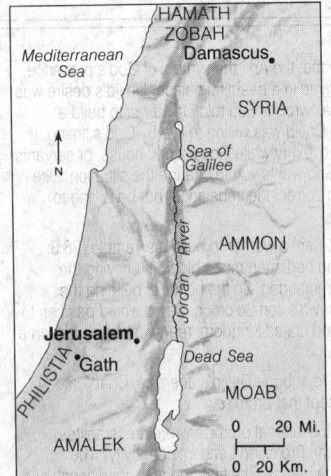

DAVID SUBDUES HIS ENEMIES
David expanded his kingdom as the Lord continued to give him victory. He subdued the Philistines by taking Gath, conquered Moab, won battles as far north as Zobah and Hamath (conquering Syria when they came to help these enemy nations), and subdued the other surrounding nations of Ammon and Amalek.

army, 10he sent his son Hadoram to greet and congratulate King David on his success and to present him with many gifts of gold, silver, and bronze, seeking an alliance. For Hadadezer and Tou had been enemies and there had been many wars between them. 11King David dedicated these gifts to the Lord, as he did the silver and gold he took from the nations of Edom, Moab, Ammon, Amalek, and the Philistines.

12Abishai (son of Zeruiah) then destroyed eighteen thousand Edomites in the Valley of Salt. 13He put garrisons in Edom and forced the Edomites to pay large sums of money annually to David. This is just another example of how the Lord gave David victory after victory. 14David reigned over all of Israel and was a just ruler.

18:15
1 Chron 11:6

15Joab (son of Zeruiah) was commander-in-chief of the army; Jehoshaphat (son of Ahilud) was the historian; 16Zadok (son of Ahitub) and Ahimelech (son of Abiathar) were the head priests; Shavsha was the king's special assistant; 17Benaiah (son of Jehoiada) was in charge of the king's bodyguard—the Cherethites and Pelethites—and David's sons were his chief aides.

David's army fights the Ammonites

19:1
2 Sam 10:1

19 When King Nahash of Ammon died, his son Hanun became the new king. 2, 3Then David declared, "I am going to show friendship to Hanun because of all the kind things his father did for me."

So David sent a message of sympathy to Hanun for the death of his father. But when David's ambassadors arrived, King Hanun's counselors warned him, "Don't fool yourself that David has sent these men to honor your father! They are here to spy out the land so that they can come in and conquer it!"

4So King Hanun insulted King David's ambassadors by shaving their beards and cutting their robes off at the middle to expose their buttocks; then he sent them back to David in shame. 5When David heard what had happened, he sent a message to his embarrassed emissaries, telling them to stay at Jericho until their beards had grown out again. 6When King Hanun realized his mistake he sent $2,000,000 to enlist mercenary troops, chariots, and cavalry from Mesopotamia, Aram-maacah, and Zobah. 7He hired thirty-two thousand chariots, as well as the support of the king of Maacah and his entire army. These forces camped at Medeba where they were joined by the troops King Hanun had recruited from his cities.

19:7
Num 21:30
Josh 13:9,16

8When David learned of this, he sent Joab and the mightiest warriors of Israel. 9The army of Ammon went out to meet them and began the battle at the gates of the city of Medeba. Meanwhile, the mercenary forces were out in the field. 10When Joab realized that the enemy forces were both in front and behind him, he divided

18:16 *special assistant*, literally, "secretary," or "scribe."

18:11 When David received gifts from King Tou, he dedicated them to God, realizing that all had come from him and was to be used for him. What has God given you? Dedicate all your "gifts" and resources to him and use them for his glory.

18:13 All the battles in this chapter show how the Lord gave David victory after victory. Unbelieving men think that victory comes from their own skill plus a little luck. Just as David acknowledged God's role in his success, so should we.

18:17 The Cherethites and Pelethites were probably a group of foreign soldiers who had joined David during his flight from Saul. They remained loyal to David throughout his reign (2 Samuel 15:17, 18) and became part of his bodyguard.

19:1 The land of Ammon bordered Israel to the east. The nation had a sordid beginning—its founding ancestor, Benammi, was conceived through incest between Lot and his daughter (Genesis 19:30–38). The Ammonites, who were constant enemies of Israel, reached their greatest strength in the days of the judges. David was the first military leader of Israel to crush them. They were

unable to cause further trouble for many years.

19:2, 3 Hanun misread David's intentions. Because he was overly suspicious, he brought disaster upon himself. Because of past experiences, it is easy to be overly suspicious of others, questioning every move and second-guessing their motives. But while we should be cautious and wise as we deal with others, we should not assume their every action is ill-intended.

19:4, 5 Jewish men always wore beards. To be forcibly shaven was embarrassing enough, but these men were also left half naked. Hanun's actions humiliated these men and insulted Israel.

19:6 Rather than admit his mistake and seek forgiveness and reconciliation, Hanun spent two million dollars to cover up his error. His cover-up cost him dearly (20:1–3). It often costs more to cover up an error than to admit it honestly. Rather than compound an error through defensiveness, seek forgiveness and reconciliation as soon as you realize your mistake. You will save yourself and others a lot of pain and trouble.

his army and sent one group to engage the Syrians. 11The other group, under the command of his brother Abishai, moved against the Ammonites.

12"If the Syrians are too strong for me, come and help me," Joab told his brother; "and if the Ammonites are too strong for you, I'll come and help you. 13Be courageous and let us act like men to save our people and the cities of our God. And may the Lord do what is best."

14So Joab and his troops attacked the Syrians, and the Syrians turned and fled. 15When the Ammonites, under attack by Abishai's troops, saw that the Syrians were retreating, they fled into the city. Then Joab returned to Jerusalem.

19:14
2 Sam 10:14

16After their defeat, the Syrians summoned additional troops from east of the Euphrates River, led personally by Shophach, King Hadadezer's commander-in-chief. 17, 18When this news reached David, he mobilized all Israel, crossed the Jordan River, and engaged the enemy troops in battle. But the Syrians again fled from David, and he killed seven thousand charioteers and forty thousand of their troops. He also killed Shophach, the commander-in-chief of the Syrian army. 19Then King Hadadezer's troops surrendered to King David and became his subjects. And never again did the Syrians aid the Ammonites in their battles.

19:16
2 Sam 10:15,16

David's army conquers the Ammonites

20 The following spring (spring was the season when wars usually began) Joab led the Israeli army in successful attacks against the cities and villages of the people of Ammon. After destroying them, he laid siege to Rabbah and conquered it. Meanwhile, David had stayed in Jerusalem. 2When David arrived on the scene, he removed the crown from the head of King Milcom of Rabbah and placed it upon his own head. It was made of gold inlaid with gems and weighed seventy-five pounds! David also took great amounts of plunder from the city. 3He drove the people from the city and set them to work with saws, iron picks, and axes, as was his custom with all the conquered Ammonite peoples. Then David and all his army returned to Jerusalem.

20:1
2 Sam 11:1
12:26

20:2
2 Sam 12:29,30

20:3
2 Sam 12:31

David fights the Philistines

4The next war was against the Philistines again, at Gezer. But Sibbecai, a man from Hushath, killed one of the sons of the giant, Sippai, and so the Philistines surrendered. 5During another war with the Philistines, Elhanan (the son of Jair) killed Lahmi, the brother of Goliath the giant; the handle of his spear was like a weaver's beam! 6, 7During another battle, at Gath, a giant with six fingers on each hand and six toes on each foot (his father was also a giant) defied and taunted Israel; but he was killed by David's nephew Jonathan, the son of David's brother Shimea. 8These giants were descendants of the giants of Gath, and they were killed by David and his soldiers.

20:4
2 Sam 21:18

20:5
1 Sam 17:4-7
2 Sam 21:19
1 Chron 11:23

David numbers the men of military age

21 Then Satan brought disaster upon Israel, for he made David decide to take a census.

21:1
2 Sam 24:1

20:2 *Milcom*, implied. See 1 Kgs 11:5. **20:3** *and axes*, literally "he conducted them to the saw." Whether this means that he made them labor with saws or that he sawed them to pieces is uncertain.

20:1 David and Bath-sheba's adultery occurred at this time, while David remained in Jerusalem instead of going to battle (2 Samuel 11—12). This story may have been excluded from 1 Chronicles because the book was written to focus on God's long-term interest in Israel and on the Temple as a symbol of God's presence among them. The story of David and Bath-sheba did not fit this purpose. The story of Absalom's rebellion, which occurred between this chapter and the next, was omitted for the same reason (2 Samuel 15—18).

20:1 Why was spring the season when wars usually began? During the winter, opposing kings plotted and planned future conquests. Then, when the fair weather permitted it, their pent-up

rage and energy broke forth into war. Look for the "springs" in your life, the times when you are most sensitive to the conflicts around you. Then determine to diffuse them by confessing your fear, bitterness, and anger to God, allowing him to heal you.

21:1 David's census brought disaster because, unlike the census taken in the book of Numbers (Numbers 1, 2) which God had ordered, this census was taken so David could take pride in the strength of his army. In determining his military strength, he was beginning to trust more in military power than in God's strength. There is a thin line between confidently relying on God's power and becoming proud because you have been used by God for great purposes.

21:2
1 Chron 27:23, 24

21:3
Deut 1:11

21:5
Num 1:17-19
2 Sam 24:9

21:6
1 Chron 27:24

21:8
2 Sam 12:13

21:9
1 Sam 9:9
2 Sam 24:11
1 Chron 29:29

21:12
2 Sam 24:13

21:13
Ps 51:1
130:4,7

21:15
Ex 32:14
1 Sam 15:11
Jonah 3:10

21:16
1 Kgs 21:27

²"Take a complete census throughout the land and bring me the totals," he told Joab and the other leaders.

³But Joab objected. "If the Lord were to multiply his people a hundred times, would they not all be yours? So why are you asking us to do this? Why must you cause Israel to sin?"

⁴But the king won the argument, and Joab did as he was told; he traveled all through Israel and returned to Jerusalem. ⁵The total population figure which he gave came to 1,100,000 men of military age in Israel and 470,000 in Judah. ⁶But he didn't include the tribes of Levi and Benjamin in his figures because he was so distressed at what the king had made him do.

⁷And God, too, was displeased with the census and punished Israel for it. ⁸But David said to God, "I am the one who has sinned. Please forgive me, for I realize now how wrong I was to do this."

⁹Then the Lord said to Gad, David's personal prophet, 10, 11"Go and tell David, 'The Lord has offered you three choices. Which will you choose? 12You may have three years of famine, or three months of destruction by the enemies of Israel, or three days of deadly plague as the angel of the Lord brings destruction to the land. Think it over and let me know what answer to return to the one who sent me.' "

13"This is a terrible decision to make," David replied, "but let me fall into the hands of the Lord rather than into the power of men, for God's mercies are very great."

¹⁴So the Lord sent a plague upon Israel and 70,000 men died as a result. ¹⁵During the plague God sent an angel to destroy Jerusalem; but then he felt such compassion that he changed his mind and commanded the destroying angel, "Stop! It is enough!" (The angel of the Lord was standing at the time by the threshing-floor of Ornan the Jebusite.) ¹⁶When David saw the angel of the Lord standing between

21:2 *throughout the land,* literally, "from Beer-Sheba to Dan."

21:1 The Bible text says Satan *made* David decide to take a census. Can Satan force people to do wrong things? No, Satan only *tempted* David with the idea, but David *decided to act* on the temptation. Ever since the Garden of Eden, Satan has been tempting people to sin. David's census was not against God's Law, but his motive for the census was wrong—pride in his mighty army while forgetting that his real strength came from God. Even Joab, not known for his high moral ideals, recognized the census as sin. From David's example we learn that an action that may not be wrong in itself can be sinful if we are motivated by greed, arrogance, or selfishness. Often our motives, not our actions, cause the sin. We must constantly weigh our motives before we act.

21:1-3 David fell to Satan's temptation. God provided a way out in Joab's counsel, but David's curiosity was spurred on by arrogance. His faith was in his own strength rather than in God's strength. Pride and curiosity could be our downfall as well. If we feel self-sufficient and put confidence in our strength apart from God, we soon fall to Satan's schemes. In self-sufficiency we lose our security. To escape temptation, examine the inner desires of your heart to understand why the external temptation is so appealing. (See 1 Corinthians 10:13 for more about escaping temptation.)

21:4 Why did 70,000 innocent people die for David's sin? Our society places great emphasis upon the individual. In ancient times, however, the family leaders, tribal leaders, and kings represented the people they led, and all expected to share in their successes as well as their failures and punishments. David deserved punishment for his sin, but his death could have resulted in political chaos and invasion by enemy armies, leaving hundreds of thousands dead. Instead, God graciously spared David's life. He also put a stop to the plague so that most of the people of Jerusalem were spared.

God made us to work together, interdependently. Whether we think it is fair or not, the group usually suffers because of the sins

of its leaders. Similarly, our actions always affect other people whether we want them to or not. We cannot fully know the mind of God in this severe judgment. We don't know where the prophets, the tribal leaders, and the other advisors were during this incident and whether or not they chose to go along with the king. We do know that putting confidence in military might alone is idolatry. Anything that takes God's place is sinful, and sin leads to death.

21:7 With leadership comes responsibility. When David made a mistake, his people were affected. In deciding to take the census, David did not consult God or listen to Joab's advice, and the nation suffered terribly. When faced with important decisions, we should ask for God's direction *first.* He may send his answer in a number of ways, often in the form of advice from others. Although advice that goes against our plans is tough to hear, it may save us from tragic consequences.

21:8 When David realized his sin, he took full responsibility, admitted he was wrong, and asked God to forgive him. Many people want to add God and his blessings to their lives without acknowledging their personal sin and guilt. But confession and repentance must come before receiving forgiveness. Like David, we must take full responsibility for our actions and confess them to God before we can expect him to forgive us and continue his work in our lives.

21:13, 14 Sin has a domino effect; once a sin is committed, a series of consequences follows. God will forgive our sin if we ask him, but the consequences of that sin have already been set in motion. David pleaded for mercy, and God responded by stopping the angel before his mission of death was complete. The consequences of David's sin, however, had already caused severe damage. God will always forgive our sins and will often intervene to make their bitter consequences less severe, but the scars will remain. Thinking through the possible consequences before we act can save us and others much sorrow and suffering.

heaven and earth with his sword drawn, pointing toward Jerusalem, he and the elders of Israel clothed themselves in sackcloth and fell to the ground before the Lord.

17And David said to God, "I am the one who sinned by ordering the census. But what have these sheep done? O Lord my God, destroy me and my family, but do not destroy your people."

21:17
2 Sam 7:8
Ps 74:1

18Then the angel of the Lord told Gad to instruct David to build an altar to the Lord at the threshing-floor of Ornan the Jebusite. 19, 20So David went to see Ornan, who was threshing wheat at the time. Ornan saw the angel as he turned, and his four sons ran and hid. 21Then Ornan saw the king approaching. So he left the threshing-floor and bowed to the ground before King David.

21:18
2 Chron 3:1

22David said to Ornan, "Let me buy this threshing-floor from you at its full price; then I will build an altar to the Lord and the plague will stop."

23"Take it, my lord, and use it as you wish," Ornan said to David. "Take the oxen, too, for burnt offerings; use the threshing instruments for wood for the fire and use the wheat for the grain offering. I give it all to you."

24"No," the king replied, "I will buy it for the full price; I cannot take what is yours and give it to the Lord. I will not offer a burnt offering that has cost me nothing!"

21:24
2 Sam 24:24

25So David paid Ornan $4,300 in gold, 26and built an altar to the Lord there, and sacrificed burnt offerings and peace offerings upon it; and he called out to the Lord, who answered by sending down fire from heaven to burn up the offering on the altar. 27Then the Lord commanded the angel to put back his sword into its sheath; 28and when David saw that the Lord had answered his plea, he sacrificed to him again. 29The Tabernacle and altar made by Moses in the wilderness were on the hill of Gibeon, 30but David didn't have time to go there to plead before the Lord, for he was terrified by the drawn sword of the angel of Jehovah.

21:26
Lev 9:24
Judg 6:21

21:29
1 Kgs 3:4
1 Chron 16:39

4. David arranges for the building of the Temple

David prepares materials for the Temple

22 Then David said, "Right here at Ornan's threshing-floor is the place where I'll build the Temple of the Lord and construct the altar for Israel's burnt offering!"

22:1
2 Sam 24:18
1 Chron 21:18
2 Chron 3:1
6:5,6

2David now drafted all the resident aliens in Israel to prepare blocks of squared stone for the Temple. 3They also manufactured iron into the great quantity of nails needed for the doors in the gates and for the clamps; and they smelted so much bronze that it was too much to weigh. 4The men of Tyre and Sidon brought great rafts of cedar logs to David.

22:2
1 Kgs 5:17,18
9:20,21
2 Chron 2:17

22:4
1 Kgs 5:6

5"Solomon my son is young and tender," David said, "and the Temple of the Lord must be a marvelous structure, famous and glorious throughout the world; so I will begin the preparations for it now."

22:5
1 Kgs 3:7
1 Chron 29:1

22:7
2 Sam 7:2,3
1 Chron 17:1

So David collected the construction materials before his death. 6He now commanded his son Solomon to build a temple for the Lord God of Israel.

22:8
1 Chron 28:3
Acts 7:46

7"I wanted to build it myself," David told him, 8"but the Lord said not to do it.

21:25 *$4,300 in gold,* literally, "six hundred shekels of gold by weight."

21:22-24 When David wanted to buy Ornan's land to build an altar, Ornan generously offered it as a gift. But David refused, saying, "I cannot take what is yours and give it to the Lord." David wanted to offer a sacrifice to God. The word *sacrifice* implies giving something that costs the giver in terms of self, time, or money. Is it costing you anything to serve God, or do you serve comfortably from the excess of what you have? Giving to God what costs you nothing does not demonstrate commitment.

22:1 Out of David's tragic mistake came the purchase of a plot of land that would become the site of God's Temple, the symbol of God's presence among his people. Every time the people went to the Temple they would remember that God is their true King and that everyone, including the king, is human, fallible, and subject to

sin. God can use even our sinful acts for good purposes if we are sorry for them and seek his forgiveness. When we confess our sins, the way is opened for God to work good from a bad situation.

22:5ff David had already chosen Solomon to succeed him as king.

22:7-10 God told David he would not be the one to build the Temple. Instead the task would be left to his son Solomon. David graciously accepted this "no" from God. He was not jealous of the fact that his son would have the honor of building God's Temple, but instead made preparations for Solomon to carry out his task. Similarly, we should take steps now to prepare the way for our children to find and fulfill God's call in their lives. Sooner or later our children will have to make their own decisions, but we can help

'You have killed too many men in great wars,' he told me. 'You have reddened the ground before me with blood: so you are not to build my Temple. 9But I will give you a son,' he told me, 'who will be a man of peace, for I will give him peace with his enemies in the surrounding lands. His name shall be Solomon (meaning "Peaceful"), and I will give peace and quietness to Israel during his reign. 10He shall build my temple, and he shall be as my own son and I will be his father; and I will cause his sons and his descendants to reign over every generation of Israel.'

11"So now, my son, may the Lord be with you and prosper you as you do what he told you to do and build the Temple of the Lord. 12And may the Lord give you the good judgment to follow all his laws when he makes you king of Israel. 13For if you carefully obey the rules and regulations which he gave to Israel through Moses, you will prosper. Be strong and courageous, fearless and enthusiastic!

14"By hard work I have collected several billion dollars worth of gold bullion, millions in silver, and so much iron and bronze that I haven't even weighed it; I have also gathered timber and stone for the walls. This is at least a beginning, something with which to start. 15And you have many skilled stonemasons and carpenters and craftsmen of every kind. 16They are expert gold and silver smiths and bronze and iron workers. So get to work, and may the Lord be with you!"

17Then David ordered all the leaders of Israel to assist his son in this project. 18"The Lord your God is with you," he declared. "He has given you peace with the surrounding nations, for I have conquered them in the name of the Lord and for his people. 19Now try with every fiber of your being to obey the Lord your God, and you will soon be bringing the Ark and the other holy articles of worship into the Temple of the Lord!"

David assigns duties to the Levites

23 By this time David was an old, old man, so he stepped down from the throne and appointed his son Solomon as the new king of Israel. 2He summoned all the political and religious leaders of Israel for the coronation ceremony. 3At this time a census was taken of the men of the tribe of Levi who were thirty years or older. The total came to 38,000.

4, 5"Twenty-four thousand of them will supervise the work at the Temple," David instructed, "six thousand are to be bailiffs and judges, four thousand will be temple guards, and four thousand will praise the Lord with the musical instruments I have made."

6Then David divided them into three main divisions named after the sons of Levi—the Gershom division, the Kohath division and the Merari division.

7Subdivisions of the *Gershom* corps were named after his sons Ladan and Shime-i. 8, 9These subdivisions were still further divided into six groups named after the sons of *Ladan:* Jehiel the leader, Zetham, Joel; and the sons of *Shime-i*—Shelomoth, Haziel, and Haran.

10, 11The subclans of *Shime-i* were named after his four sons: Jahath was greatest,

Marginal cross-references:

22:9
2 Sam 12:24,25
1 Kgs 4:20,25

22:10
2 Sam 12:24,25
1 Chron 17:12

22:11
1 Chron 22:16

22:12
1 Kgs 3:9
2 Chron 1:10

22:13
1 Chron 28:7
Josh 1:6

22:14
1 Chron 22:3
29:4

22:16
1 Chron 22:11

22:18
1 Chron 22:9
23:25

22:19
1 Kgs 8:6,21
1 Chron 28:9
2 Chron 5:7

23:1
1 Chron 28:5
29:22,28

23:3
Num 4:3,48
1 Chron 23:24

23:4
1 Chron 15:16
26:29
Ezra 3:8,9

23:6
1 Chron 6:1

22:14 *several billion dollars worth of gold bullion, and millions in silver,* literally, "a hundred thousand talents of gold" and "a million talents of silver." **23:9** *Shime-i,* probably not the same Shime-i as in vs 7.

---

by supplying them with the proper tools: showing them how to pray, how to study God's Word, the difference between right and wrong, and the importance of church.

22:12, 13 David learned that it takes *total* dedication to please God—obeying with "every fiber of your being" (22:19). This requires both right decisions (good judgment), and right attitudes (strength, courage, and enthusiasm). It isn't enough just to understand what God wants; your heart must be totally dedicated to him. Jesus said, "Anyone who lets himself be distracted from the work I plan for him is not fit for the Kingdom of God" (Luke 9:62). Remove the distractions that pull you away from God, and serve him wholeheartedly.

23:1 For more information on Solomon's coronation and the attempts to seize his throne, see 1 Kings 1, 2.

23:1ff Although David couldn't build the Temple, he could make preparations, and he took that job seriously. He not only gathered funds and materials for God's house, he also planned much of the administration and arranged the worship services. The original readers of Chronicles were rebuilding the Temple, and this information about its procedures would have been invaluable to them. The next five chapters demonstrate that organization is essential for smooth and effective service.

23:3 Why was this census acceptable when the other was not (21)? This census counted only the Levites—those set apart to serve God—and was used to organize the work in the Temple. The census was not based on pride or self-sufficiency as was the previous census of fighting men.

Zizah was next, and Jeush and Beriah were combined into a single subclan because neither had many sons.

12The division of Kohath was subdivided into four groups named after his sons Amram, Izhar, Hebron, and Uzziel.

13*Amram* was the ancestor of Aaron and Moses. Aaron and his sons were set apart for the holy service of sacrificing the people's offerings to the Lord. He served the Lord constantly and pronounced blessings in his name at all times.

14, 15As for Moses, the man of God, his sons Gershom and Eliezer were included with the tribe of Levi. 16*Gershom's* sons were led by Shebuel, 17and *Eliezer's* only son, Rehabiah, was the leader of his clan, for he had many children.

18The sons of *Izhar* were led by Shelomith.

19The sons of *Hebron* were led by Jeriah. Amariah was second in command, Jahaziel was third, and Jekameam was fourth.

20The sons of *Uzziel* were led by Micah, and Isshiah was the second in command.

21The sons of *Merari* were Mahli and Mushi. The sons of *Mahli* were Eleazar and Kish. 22*Eleazar* died without any sons, and his daughters were married to their cousins, the sons of *Kish*. 23*Mushi's* sons were Mahli, Eder, and Jeremoth.

24In the census, all the men of Levi who were twenty years old or older were classified under the names of these clans and subclans; and they were all assigned to the ministry at the Temple. 25For David said, "The Lord God of Israel has given us peace, and he will always live in Jerusalem. 26Now the Levites will no longer need to carry the Tabernacle and its instruments from place to place."

27(This census of the tribe of Levi was one of the last things David did before his death.) 28The work of the Levites was to assist the priests—the descendants of Aaron—in the sacrifices at the Temple; they also did the custodial work and helped perform the ceremonies of purification. 29They provided the Bread of the Presence, the flour for the grain offerings, and the wafers made without yeast (either fried or mixed with olive oil); they also checked all the weights and measures. 30Each morning and evening they stood before the Lord to sing thanks and praise to him. 31They assisted in the special sacrifices of burnt offerings, the Sabbath sacrifices, the new moon celebrations, and at all the festivals. There were always as many Levites present as were required for the occasion. 32And they took care of the Tabernacle and the Temple and assisted the priests in whatever way they were needed.

David divides the priests into groups

24 The priests (the descendants of Aaron) were placed into two divisions named after Aaron's sons, Eleazar and Ithamar.

Nadab and Abihu were also sons of Aaron, but they died before their father did and had no children; so only Eleazar and Ithamar were left to carry on. 3David

23:13
Ex 6:20; 28:1
30:6
Num 3:25-30
26:58,59
23:14
Deut 33:1

23:21
1 Chron 6:19-21

23:24
Num 10:17,21
1 Chron 23:3
23:25
1 Chron 22:18
23:26
Num 4:5,15; 7:9

23:29
Lev 6:20,21
19:35,36; 24:5
1 Kgs 7:48
1 Chron 9:31
23:31
Lev 23:2-4
Isa 1:13,14
23:32
Num 1:53
3:6,38
1 Chron 9:27

24:1
Ex 6:23

24:2
Lev 10:2

23:10, 11 *Zizah,* or "Zina." **23:13** *Aaron and Moses,* literally, "the sons of Amram: Aaron and Moses."

23:14 All that is stated here about Moses is that he was "the man of God." What a profound description of a person! A man or woman of God is one whose life reflects God's presence, priorities, and power.

23:28–32 Priests and Levites had different jobs in and around the Temple. Priests were authorized to perform the sacrifices. Levites were set apart to help the priests. They did the work of elders, deacons, custodians, assistants, musicians, moving men, and repairmen. Both priests and Levites came from the tribe of Levi, but priests also had to be descendants of Aaron, Israel's first High Priest (Exodus 28:1–3). Priests and Levites were supported by Israel's tithes and by revenues from certain cities that had been given to them. Worship in the Temple could not have taken place without the combined efforts of the priests and Levites. Their responsibilities were different, but they were equally important to God's plan. No matter what place of service you have in the church, you are important to its healthy function.

24:1ff The Temple service was highly structured, but this did not hinder the Spirit of God. Rather, it provided an orderly context for worship. (Compare 1 Corinthians 14:40.) Sometimes we feel that planning and structure are unspiritual activities that may hinder spontaneity in worship. But order and structure can free us to respond to God. Order brings glory to God as we experience the joy, freedom, and calm that come when we have wisely prepared in advance.

24:3 This Ahimelech was the son of Abiathar and the grandson of another Ahimelech, one of the priests massacred by Saul (1 Samuel 22:11–18). Abiathar and Zadok were co-High Priests under David: one was at Jerusalem where the Ark of God was kept, and one was at Gibeon serving at the Tabernacle. It appears from this verse and 18:16 that Ahimelech began to assume some of Abiathar's duties as his father grew old.

consulted with Zadok, who represented the Eleazar clan, and with Ahimelech, who represented the Ithamar clan; then he divided Aaron's descendants into many groups to serve at various times. 4*Eleazar's* descendants were divided into sixteen groups and *Ithamar's* into eight (for there was more leadership ability among the descendants of Eleazar).

5All tasks were assigned to the various groups by coin-toss so that there would be no preference, for there were many famous men and high officials of the Temple in each division. 6Shemaiah, a Levite and the son of Nethanel, acted as recording secretary and wrote down the names and assignments in the presence of the king and of these leaders: Zadok the priest, Ahimelech the son of Abiathar, and the heads of the priests and Levites. Two groups from the division of Eleazar and one from the division of Ithamar were assigned to each task.

7-18The work was assigned (by coin-toss) in this order:

First, the group led by Jehoiarib;
Second, the group led by Jedaiah;
Third, the group led by Harim;
Fourth, the group led by Se-orim;
Fifth, the group led by Malchijah;
Sixth, the group led by Mijamin;

24:5 *by coin-toss,* literally, "by lot."

24:6
1 Chron 18:16
24:31

24:7
Neh 12:4
Lk 1:5

DUTIES ASSIGNED IN THE TEMPLE	Administrative Duties	Supervisors	1 Chronicles 23:4, 5
King David charged all these people to do their jobs with every fiber of their being (1 Chronicles 22:17–19). God needs people of every talent—not just prophets and priests—to obey him.		Bailiffs	1 Chronicles 23:4, 5
		Judges	1 Chronicles 23:4, 5
		Public administrators	1 Chronicles 26:29, 30
	Ministerial Duties	Priests	1 Chronicles 24:1
		Prophets	1 Chronicles 25:1
		Assistants for sacrifices	1 Chronicles 23:29–31
		Assistants for purification ceremonies	1 Chronicles 23:27–28
	Service Duties	Bakers of the Bread of the Presence	1 Chronicles 23:29
		Those who checked the weights and measures	1 Chronicles 23:29
		Custodians	1 Chronicles 23:28
	Financial Duties	Those who cared for the treasury	1 Chronicles 26:20
		Those who cared for dedicated items	1 Chronicles 26:26-28
	Artistic Duties	Musicians	1 Chronicles 25:6
		Singers	1 Chronicles 25:7
	Protective Duties	Temple guards	1 Chronicles 23:5
		Guards for the gates and storehouses	1 Chronicles 26:12–18
	Individual Assignments	Recording secretary	1 Chronicles 24:6
		Chaplain to the king	1 Chronicles 25:4
		Private prophet to the king	1 Chronicles 25:2
		Captain of the guard	1 Chronicles 26:1
		Chief officer of the treasury	1 Chronicles 26:23, 24

24:4 Eleazar's descendants were divided into 16 groups (as opposed to Ithamar's eight) for three reasons. (1) Eleazar had received the birthright since his two older brothers, Nadab and Abihu, had been killed (Leviticus 10). The birthright included a double portion of the father's estate. (2) His descendants were greater in number than Ithamar's. (3) His descendants had greater leadership ability.

24:7–18 Each of these 24 groups of priests served two-week shifts each year at the Temple. The rest of the time they served in their hometowns. This system was still in place in Jesus' day (Luke 1:5–9). Zacharias was a member of the Abijah (or Ahijah) division. During his shift at the Temple, an angel appeared to him and predicted that he would have a son, John.

Seventh, the group led by Hakkoz;

Eighth, the group led by Ahijah;

Ninth, the group led by Jeshua;

Tenth, the group led by Shecaniah;

Eleventh, the group led by Eliashib;

Twelfth, the group led by Jakim;

Thirteenth, the group led by Huppah;

Fourteenth, the group led by Jeshebe-ab;

Fifteenth, the group led by Bilgah;

Sixteenth, the group led by Immer;

Seventeenth, the group led by Hezir;

Eighteenth, the group led by Happizzez;

Nineteenth, the group led by Pethahiah;

Twentieth, the group led by Jehezkel;

Twenty-first, the group led by Jachin;

Twenty-second, the group led by Gamul;

Twenty-third, the group led by Delaiah;

Twenty-fourth, the group led by Maaziah.

19Each group carried out the Temple duties as originally assigned by God through their ancestor Aaron.

24:19
1 Chron 9:25

20These were the other descendants of Levi: Amram; his descendant Shuba-el; and Shuba-el's descendant Jehdeiah; 21the Rehabiah group, led by his oldest son Isshiah; 22the Izhar group, consisting of Shelamoth and his descendant Jahath.

23The Hebron group: Jeriah, Hebron's oldest son; Amariah, his second son; Jahaziel, his third son; Jekameam, his fourth son.

24:23
1 Chron 23:19

24, 25The Uzziel group was led by his son Micah and his grandsons Shamir and Isshiah, and by Isshiah's son Zechariah.

26, 27The Merari group was led by his sons: Mahli and Mushi. (Ja-aziah's group, led by his son Beno, included his brothers Shoham, Zaccur, and Ibri.) 28*Mahli's* descendants were Eleazar, who had no sons, 29and Kish, among whose sons was Jerahmeel. 30The sons of *Mushi* were Mahli, Eder, and Jerimoth.

These were the descendants of Levi in their various clans. 31Like the descendants of Aaron, they were assigned to their duties by coin-toss without distinction as to age or rank. It was done in the presence of King David, Zadok, Ahimelech, and the leaders of the priests and the Levites.

24:31
1 Chron 24:5,6

The duties of the musicians

25 David and the officials of the Tabernacle then appointed men to prophesy to the accompaniment of zithers, harps, and cymbals. These men were from the groups of Asaph, Heman, and Jeduthun. Here is a list of their names and their work:

25:1
2 Kgs 3:15
1 Chron 6:33,
39; 15:16

2Under the leadership of Asaph, the king's private prophet, were his sons Zaccur, Joseph, Nethaniah, and Asharelah.

3Under Jeduthun, who led in giving thanks and praising the Lord (while accompanied by the zither), were his six sons: Gedaliah, Zeri, Jeshaiah, Shime-i, Hashabiah, and Mattithiah.

25:3
1 Chron 16:41,
42

4, 5Under the direction of Heman, the king's private chaplain, were his sons: Bukkiah, Mattaniah, Uzziel, Shebuel, Jerimoth, Hananiah, Hanani, Eliathah,

25:4
2 Sam 24:11
1 Chron 21:9

25:1 There is more to prophesying than predicting the future. Prophecy also involves singing God's praises and preaching God's messages (1 Corinthians 14:1). Prophets could be musicians, farmers (Amos 1:1), wives (2 Kings 22:14), or leaders (Deuteronomy 34:10)—anyone who boldly and accurately spoke out for God and tried to bring people back to worshiping him. From a large group of musicians David chose those who showed an unusual ability to tell about God and to encourage others in song.

25:1-7 There were many ways to contribute to the worship in the Tabernacle. Some prophesied (25:1), some led in prayer (25:3), and others played instruments and sang (25:6, 7). God wants all his people to participate in worship. You may not be a master musician, a prophet, or a teacher, but God can use whatever you have to offer. Develop your special gifts to offer in service to God (Romans 12:3-11; 1 Corinthians 12:29-31).

25:6
1 Chron 15:16,
19; 23:5

Geddalti, Romamti-ezer, Joshbekashah, Mallothi, Hothir, and Mahazi-oth. (For God had honored him with fourteen sons and three daughters.) 6, 7Their music ministry included the playing of cymbals, harps, and zithers; all were under the direction of their father as they performed this ministry in the Tabernacle.

Asaph, Jeduthun, and Heman reported directly to the king. They and their families were all trained in singing praises to the Lord; each one—288 of them in all—was a master musician. 8The singers were appointed to their particular term of service by coin-toss, without regard to age or reputation.

25:8
1 Chron 26:13

9-31The first toss indicated Joseph of the Asaph clan;
The second, Gedaliah, along with twelve of his sons and brothers;
The third, Zaccur and twelve of his sons and brothers;
The fourth, Izri and twelve of his sons and brothers;
Fifth, Nethaniah and twelve of his sons and brothers;
Sixth, Bukkiah and twelve of his sons and brothers;
Seventh, Jesharelah and twelve of his sons and brothers;
Eighth, Jeshaiah and twelve of his sons and brothers;
Ninth, Mattaniah and twelve of his sons and brothers;
Tenth, Shime-i and twelve of his sons and brothers;
Eleventh, Azarel and twelve of his sons and brothers;
Twelfth, Hashabiah and twelve of his sons and brothers;
Thirteenth, Shuba-el and twelve of his sons and brothers;
Fourteenth, Mattithiah and twelve of his sons and brothers;
Fifteenth, Jeremoth and twelve of his sons and brothers;
Sixteenth, Hananiah and twelve of his sons and brothers;
Seventeenth, Joshbekasha and twelve of his sons and brothers;
Eighteenth, Hanani and twelve of his sons and brothers;

INSTRUMENTS IN BIBLE TIMES
Paul clearly puts forth the Christian's view that things are not good or bad in and of themselves (see Romans 14 and 1 Corinthians 14:7, 8, 26). The point should always be to worship the Lord or help others by means of the things of this world, including music. Music was created by God and can be returned to him in praise. Does the music you play or listen to have a negative or positive impact upon your relationship with God?

Highlights of musical use in Scripture	References
Jubal is father of all musicians	Genesis 4:21
Miriam and other women sing and dance to praise God	Exodus 15:1–21
The priest is to have bells on his robes	Exodus 28:34, 35
The Ark of the Covenant is accompanied by trumpeters	Numbers 31:6
Jericho fell to the sound of trumpets	Joshua 6:4–20
The King's coronation is accompanied by music	1 Kings 1:39, 40
There were musicians for the King's court	Ecclesiastes 2:8
Saul seemed to lean toward the view of music taken by pagan nations	1 Samuel 10:5–8 1 Samuel 16:14–23
From David's time on, the use of music in worship was much more organized. Music for the Temple became refined.	1 Chronicles 15:16–24 1 Chronicles 16:4–7 2 Chronicles 5:11–14
Everything was to be used by everyone to praise the Lord	Psalm 150

In the New Testament, worship continued in the synagogues until the Christians became unwelcome there, so there was a rich musical heritage already established. The fact that music is mentioned less often in the New Testament does not mean it was less important.

Jesus and the disciples sang a hymn	Matthew 26:30
Paul and Silas sang in jail	Acts 16:25
We are to sing to the Lord as a response to what he has done in our lives	Ephesians 5:19, 20 Colossians 3:16 James 5:13

25:9–31 The singers were divided into 24 groups to match the 24 groups of Levites (24:7–18). This division of labor gave order to the planning of Temple work, promoted excellence by making training easier, gave variety to worship because each group worked a term, and provided opportunities for many to be involved.

Nineteenth, Mallothi and twelve of his sons and brothers;
Twentieth, Eliathah and twelve of his sons and brothers;
Twenty-first, Hothir and twelve of his sons and brothers;
Twenty-second, Giddalti and twelve of his sons and brothers;
Twenty-third, Mahazi-oth and twelve of his sons and brothers;
Twenty-fourth, Romamti-ezer and twelve of his sons and brothers.

The duties of the Temple guards

26 The temple guards were from the Asaph division of the Korah clan. The captain of the guard was Meshelemiah, the son of Kore.

2,3His sergeants were his sons: Zechariah (the oldest), Jedia-el (the second), Zebadiah (the third), Jathni-el (the fourth), Elam (the fifth), Jeho-hanan (the sixth), Elie-ho-enai (the seventh).

4,5The sons of Obed-edom were also appointed as Temple guards: Shemaiah (the oldest), Jehozabad (the second), Joah (the third), Sacar (the fourth), Nethanel (the fifth), Ammi-el (the sixth), Issachar (the seventh), Pe-ullethai (the eighth).

What a blessing God gave him with all those sons!

6,7Shemaiah's sons were all outstanding men, and had positions of great authority in their clan. Their names were: Othni, Repha-el, Obed, Elzabad.

Their brave brothers, Elihu and Semachiah, were also very able men.

8All of these sons and grandsons of Obed-edom—all sixty-two of them—were outstanding men who were particularly well qualified for their work. 9Meshelemiah's eighteen sons and brothers, too, were real leaders. 10Hosah, one of the Merari group, appointed Shimri as the leader among his sons, though he was not the oldest. 11The names of some of his other sons were: Hilkiah, the second; Tebaliah, the third; Zechariah, the fourth.

26:10
1 Chron 16:38

Hosah's sons and brothers numbered thirteen in all.

12The divisions of the Temple guards were named after the leaders. Like the other Levites, they were responsible to minister at the Temple. 13They were assigned guard duty at the various gates without regard to the reputation of their families, for it was all done by coin-toss. 14, 15The responsibility of the east gate went to Shelemiah and his group; of the north gate to his son Zechariah, a man of unusual wisdom; of the south gate to Obed-edom and his group (his sons were given charge of the storehouses); 16of the west gate and the Shallecheth Gate on the upper road, to Shuppim and Hosah. 17Six guards were assigned daily to the east gate, four to the north gate, four to the south gate, and two to each of the storehouses. 18Six guards were assigned each day to the west gate, four to the upper road, and two to the nearby areas. 19The Temple guards were chosen from the clans of Korah and Merari.

26:13
1 Chron 24:5,
31; 25:8

The duties of other officials

20, 21, 22Other Levites, led by Ahijah, were given the care of the gifts brought to the Lord and placed in the Temple treasury. These men of the Ladan subclan from the clan of Gershom included Zetham and Joel, the sons of Jehieli. 23, 24Shebuel, son of Gershom and grandson of Moses, was the chief officer of the treasury. He was in charge of the divisions named after Amram, Izhar, Hebron, and Uzziel.

26:20
1 Chron 26:22,
24

25The line of descendants from Eliezer went through Rehabiah, Jesha-iah, Joram, Zichri, and Shelomoth. 26Shelomoth and his brothers were appointed to

---

26:1 There were 4,000 temple guards (23:4, 5), also called gatekeepers. They were all Levites and did many other jobs as well. Some of their duties included (1) checking out the equipment and utensils used each day and making sure they were returned, (2) storing, ordering, and maintaining the food supplies for the priests and sacrifices, (3) caring for the temple furniture, (4) mixing the incense that was burned daily, (5) accounting for the gifts brought. (For more on gatekeepers, see the note on 9:17, 18.)

26:5 The status of children in society has fluctuated throughout history; sometimes they are highly esteemed, and sometimes abused and cheated. But Scripture shows no such vacillation—children are called a blessing from God and never viewed as a burden (Psalm 127:3–5; Mark 10:13–15).

26:12 The temple guards were called ministers. This indicates that anyone who assists in the Lord's work is a true minister of God.

care for the gifts given to the Lord by King David and the other leaders of the nation such as the officers and generals of the army. 27For these men dedicated their war loot to support the operating expenses of the Temple. 28Shelomoth and his brothers were also responsible for the care of the items dedicated to the Lord by Samuel the prophet, Saul the son of Kish, Abner the son of Ner, Joab the son of Zeruiah, and anyone else of distinction who brought gifts to the Lord.

29Chenaniah and his sons (from the subclan of Izhar) were appointed public administrators and judges. 30Hashabiah and 1,700 of his clansmen from Hebron, all outstanding men, were placed in charge of the territory of Israel west of the Jordan River; they were responsible for the religious affairs and public administration of that area. 31, 32Twenty-seven hundred outstanding men of the clan of the Hebronites, under the supervision of Jerijah, were appointed to control the religious and public affairs of the tribes of Reuben, Gad, and the half-tribe of Manasseh. These men, all of whom had excellent qualifications, were appointed on the basis of their ancestry and ability at Jazer in Gilead in the fortieth year of King David's reign.

Commanders of the army

27 The Israeli army was divided into twelve regiments, each with 24,000 troops, including officers and administrative staff. These units were called up for active duty one month each year. Here is the list of the units and their regimental commanders:

2, 3The commander of the First Division was Jashobeam. He had charge of 24,000 troops who were on duty the first month of each year.

4The commander of the Second Division was Dodai (a descendant of Ahohi). He had charge of 24,000 troops who were on duty the second month of each year. Mikloth was his executive officer.

5, 6The commander of the Third Division was Benaiah. His 24,000 men were on duty the third month of each year. (He was the son of Jehoiada the High Priest, and was the chief of the thirty highest-ranking officers in David's army.) His son Ammizabad succeeded him as division commander.

7The commander of the Fourth Division was Asahel (the brother of Joab), who was later replaced by his son Zebadiah. He had 24,000 men on duty the fourth month of each year.

8The commander of the Fifth Division was Shamuth from Izrah, with 24,000 men on duty the fifth month of each year.

9The commander of the Sixth Division was Ira, the son of Ikkesh from Tekoa; he had 24,000 men on duty the sixth month of each year.

10The commander of the Seventh Division was Helez from Pelona in Ephraim, with 24,000 men on duty the seventh month of each year.

11The commander of the Eighth Division was Sibbecai of the Hushite subclan from Zerah, who had 24,000 men on duty the eighth month of each year.

12The commander of the Ninth Division was Abi-ezer (from Anathoth in the tribe of Benjamin), who commanded 24,000 troops during the ninth month of each year.

13The commander of the Tenth Division was Maharai from Netophah in Zerah, with 24,000 men on duty the tenth month of each year.

14The commander of the Eleventh Division was Benaiah from Pirathon in Ephraim, with 24,000 men on duty during the eleventh month of each year.

15The commander of the Twelfth Division was Heldai from Netophah in the area of Othni-el, who commanded 24,000 men on duty during the twelfth month of each year.

26:28 *anyone else of distinction,* implied.

26:29 1 Chron 23:4
26:30 1 Chron 27:17
26:31 1 Chron 19:11 23:19
27:2 2 Sam 23:8 1 Chron 11:11

26:27 War loot rightfully belonged to the victorious army. These soldiers, however, gave their portion of all the battle spoils to the Temple to express their dedication to God. Like these soldiers, we should think of what we *can* give, rather than what we are obligated to give. Is your giving a matter of rejoicing rather than duty? Give as a response of joy and love for God and others.

Officers of the tribes

16-22The top political officers of the tribes of Israel were as follows:

Over Reuben, Eliezer (son of Zichri);
Over Simeon, Shephatiah (son of Maacah);
Over Levi, Hashabiah (son of Kemuel);
Over the descendants of Aaron, Zadok;
Over Judah, Elihu (a brother of King David);
Over Issachar, Omri (son of Michael);
Over Zebulun, Ishmaiah (son of Obadiah);
Over Naphtali, Jeremoth (son of Azriel);
Over Ephraim, Hoshea (son of Azaziah);
Over the half-tribe of Manasseh, Joel (son of Pedaiah);
Over the other half of Manasseh, in Gilead, Iddo (son of Zechariah);
Over Benjamin, Ja-asiel (son of Abner);
Over Dan, Azarel (son of Jeroham).

23When David took his census he didn't include the twenty-year-olds, or those younger, for the Lord had promised a population explosion for his people. 24Joab began the census, but he never finished it, for the anger of God broke out upon Israel; the final total was never put into the annals of King David.

Administrators of the kingdom

25Azmaveth (son of Adi-el) was the chief financial officer in charge of the palace treasuries, and Jonathan (son of Uzziah) was chief of the regional treasuries throughout the cities, villages, and fortresses of Israel.

26Ezri (son of Chelub) was manager of the laborers on the king's estates. 27And Shime-i from Ramath had the oversight of the king's vineyards; and Zabdi from Shiphma was responsible for his wine production and storage. 28Baal-hanan from Gedera was responsible for the king's olive yards and sycamore trees in the lowlands bordering Philistine territory, while Joash had charge of the supplies of olive oil.

29Shitrai from Sharon was in charge of the cattle on the Plains of Sharon, and Shaphat (son of Adlai) had charge of those in the valleys. 30Obil, from the territory of Ishmael, had charge of the camels, and Jehdeiah from Meronoth had charge of the donkeys. 31The sheep were under the care of Jaziz the Hagrite. These men were King David's overseers.

32The attendant to the king's sons was Jonathan, David's uncle, a wise counselor and an educated man. Jehiel (the son of Hachmoni) was their tutor.

33Ahithophel was the king's official counselor and Hushai the Archite was his personal advisor. 34Ahithophel was assisted by Jehoiada (the son of Benaiah) and by Abiathar. Joab was commander-in-chief of the Israeli army.

David instructs Solomon about the Temple

28 David now summoned all of his officials to Jerusalem—the political leaders, the commanders of the twelve army divisions, the other army officers, those in charge of his property and livestock and all the other men of authority in his kingdom. 2He rose and stood before them and addressed them as follows:

"My brothers and my people! It was my desire to build a temple in which the Ark of the Covenant of the Lord could rest—a place for our God to live in. I have now

27:23 *The Lord had promised a population explosion for his people,* literally, "the Lord had said he would increase Israel like to the stars of heaven." **27:32** *an educated man,* literally, "a scribe." **28:2** *a place for our God to live in,* literally, "a footstool."

Marginal references:

27:16
1 Chron 28:1

27:23
Gen 15:5
Num 1:17-19
2 Sam 24:1

27:24
2 Sam 24:12
1 Chron 21:1

27:28
1 Kgs 10:27
2 Chron 1:15

27:29
1 Chron 5:16

27:31
1 Chron 5:10

27:33
2 Sam 15:12,
32,37

27:34
Kgs 1:7
1 Chron 11:6
27:5

28:1
1 Chron 11:10
23:2; 27:1

28:2
1 Chron 17:1,2
Ps 132:7
Isa 66:1

27:33, 34 When Absalom rebelled against David, Ahithophel betrayed David and joined the rebellion. Hushai pretended loyalty to Absalom, and his advice caused Absalom's downfall (2 Samuel 15:31—17:23).

28:1 The last two chapters of 1 Chronicles present the transition from David to Solomon as king of Israel. The writer of Chronicles doesn't mention Adonijah's conspiracy or David's frailty. Instead, he focuses on the positive—God's plans for Israel and his promise to David's descendants.

28:3
1 Chron 17:4
22:8
Acts 7:46,47

28:4
Gen 49:8
1 Sam 16:1,6
1 Chron 5:2
17:23,27

28:5
1 Chron 3:1
14:3; 22:9,10

28:6
2 Sam 7:13,14

28:7
1 Chron 22:13

28:9
1 Sam 17:7
1 Kgs 8:61
1 Chron 29:17
2 Chron 15:2
Jer 29:13

28:10
1 Chron 22:13

28:11
Ex 25:17,40

28:12
1 Chron 26:20,
28

28:13
1 Chron 23:6
24:1

28:15
Ex 25:31

collected everything that is necessary for the building, 3but God has told me, 'You are not to build my temple, for you are a warrior and have shed much blood.'

4"Nevertheless, the Lord God of Israel has chosen me from among all my father's family to begin a dynasty that will rule Israel forever; he has chosen the tribe of Judah, and from among the families of Judah, my father's family; and from among his sons, the Lord took pleasure in me and has made me king over all Israel. 5And from among my sons—the Lord has given me many children—he has chosen Solomon to succeed me on the throne of his Kingdom of Israel. 6He has told me, 'Your son Solomon shall build my temple; for I have chosen him as my son and I will be his father. 7And if he continues to obey my commandments and instructions as he has until now, I will make his kingdom last forever.' "

8Then David turned to Solomon and said:

"Here before the leaders of Israel, the people of God, and in the sight of our God, I am instructing you to search out every commandment of the Lord so that you may continue to rule this good land and leave it to your children to rule forever. 9Solomon, my son, get to know the God of your fathers. Worship and serve him with a clean heart and a willing mind, for the Lord sees every heart and understands and knows every thought. If you seek him, you will find him; but if you forsake him, he will permanently throw you aside. 10So be very careful, for the Lord has chosen you to build his holy temple. Be strong and do as he commands."

11Then David gave Solomon the blueprint of the Temple and its surroundings—the treasuries, the upstairs rooms, the inside rooms, and the sanctuary for the place of mercy. 12He also gave Solomon his plans for the outer court, the outside rooms, the Temple storage areas, and the treasuries for the gifts dedicated by famous persons. For the Holy Spirit had given David all these plans. 13The king also passed on to Solomon the instructions concerning the work of the various groups of priests and Levites; and he gave specifications for each item in the Temple which was to be used for worship and sacrifice.

14David weighed out enough gold and silver to make these various items, 15as well as the specific amount of gold needed for the lampstands and lamps. He also

28:8 *Then David turned to Solomon and said,* implied.

PRINCIPLES TO LIVE BY

King David gave his son Solomon principles to guide him through life (see 1 Chronicles 28:9, 10). These same ideas are ones that any Christian parent would want to present to a child:

1. Get to know God personally.
2. Learn God's commands and discover what he wants you to do.
3. Worship God with a clean heart.
4. Serve God with a willing mind.
5. Be faithful.
6. Don't become discouraged.

28:5 The kingdom of Israel belonged to God, not to David or anyone else. Israel's king, then, was God's deputy, commissioned to carry out God's will for the nation. Thus God could choose the person he wanted as king without following customary lines of succession. David was not Saul's heir, and Solomon was not David's eldest son, but this did not matter because God appointed them.

28:8 David told Solomon to search out and follow every one of God's commands to insure Israel's prosperity and the continuation of David's descendants upon the throne. It was the solemn duty of the king to study and obey God's laws. The teachings of Scripture are the keys to security, happiness, and justice, but you'll never discover them unless you search God's Word. If God's will is ignored and his teaching neglected, anything we attempt to build, even if it has God's name on it, is headed for collapse. Get to know God's commands through regular Bible study, and obey them every day.

28:9 In 22:18, 19, David told the leaders to obey God with every fiber of their beings. Now he tells Solomon to worship God with a clean heart and willing mind. God demands complete devotion. He sees our hearts, motives, desires, and thoughts. If we desire to know him and love him, he responds with more wisdom and guidance than we could ever imagine.

28:9 Nothing can be hidden from God. He sees and understands everything in our hearts. David found this out the hard way when God sent Nathan to expose David's sins of adultery and murder (2 Samuel 12). David told Solomon to be completely open with God and dedicated to him. It makes no sense to try to hide any thoughts or actions from an all-knowing God. This should cause you joy, not fear, for God knows even the worst things about you and loves you anyway.

28:13 Some of the instructions about the work of the priests and Levites are found in chapters 23, 24.

weighed out enough silver for the silver candlesticks and lamps, each according to its use. 16He weighed out the gold for the table on which the Bread of the Presence would be placed and for the other gold tables, and he weighed the silver for the silver tables. 17Then he weighed out the gold for the solid gold hooks used in handling the sacrificial meat and for the basins, cups, and bowls of gold and silver. 18Finally, he weighed out the refined gold for the altar of incense and for the gold angels whose wings were stretched over the Ark of the Covenant of the Lord.

19"Every part of this blueprint," David told Solomon, "was given to me in writing from the hand of the Lord." 20Then he continued, "Be strong and courageous and get to work. Don't be frightened by the size of the task, for the Lord my God is with you; he will not forsake you. He will see to it that everything is finished correctly. 21And these various groups of priests and Levites will serve in the Temple. Others with skills of every kind will volunteer, and the army and the entire nation are at your command."

<table>
<tr><td>**28:18**
Ex 25:18; 30:1</td></tr>
<tr><td>**28:19**
1 Chron 28:11
12</td></tr>
<tr><td>**28:20**
Josh 1:5
1 Sam 20:13
1 Kgs 1:37
1 Chron 22:13
Heb 13:5</td></tr>
<tr><td>**28:21**
Ex 35:25
36:1,2</td></tr>
</table>

The people bring gifts for the Temple

29 Then King David turned to the entire assembly and said: "My son Solomon, whom God has chosen to be the next king of Israel, is still young and inexperienced, and the work ahead of him is enormous; for the temple he will build is not just another building—it is for the Lord God himself! 2Using every resource at my command, I have gathered as much as I could for building it—enough gold, silver, bronze, iron, wood, and great quantities of onyx, other precious stones, costly jewels, and marble. 3And now, because of my devotion to the Temple of God, I am giving all of my own private treasures to aid in the construction. This is in addition to the building materials I have already collected. 4, 5These personal contributions consist of millions of dollars of gold from Ophir and huge amounts of silver to be used for overlaying the walls of the buildings. It will also be used for the articles made of gold and silver and for the artistic decorations. Now then, who will follow my example? Who will give himself and all that he has to the Lord?"

6, 7Then the clan leaders, the heads of the tribes, the army officers, and the administrative officers of the king pledged huge sums of gold, silver and foreign currency, also 675 tons of bronze; and 3,750 tons of iron. 8They also contributed great amounts of jewelry, which were deposited at the Temple treasury with Jehiel (a descendant of Gershom). 9Everyone was excited and happy for this opportunity of service, and King David was moved with deep joy.

<table>
<tr><td>**29:1**
1 Chron 22:5</td></tr>
<tr><td>**29:2**
1 Chron 22:3</td></tr>
<tr><td>**29:4**
1 Kgs 9:28
1 Chron 22:14</td></tr>
<tr><td>**29:6**
1 Chron 27:1,
25; 28:1</td></tr>
<tr><td>**29:8**
1 Chron 23:8</td></tr>
<tr><td>**29:9**
1 Kgs 8:61
2 Cor 9:7</td></tr>
</table>

David praises God

10While still in the presence of the whole assembly, David expressed his praises to the Lord: "O Lord God of our father Israel, praise your name for ever and ever! 11Yours is the mighty power and glory and victory and majesty. Everything in the heavens and earth is yours, O Lord, and this is your kingdom. We adore you as being in control of everything. 12Riches and honor come from you alone, and you

<table>
<tr><td>**29:11**
Rev 5:13</td></tr>
<tr><td>**29:12**
2 Chron 1:12
20:6</td></tr>
</table>

28:20 David advised Solomon not to be frightened about the size of his task as king and builder of the Temple. Fear can immobilize us. The size of a job, its risks, or the pressure of the situation can cause us to freeze and do nothing. One remedy for fear is found here—don't think about fear; just get to work. Getting started is often the most difficult and frightening part of a job.

29:1 Solomon took the throne in 970 B.C.

29:1 It is possible to be obsessed with a church building to the neglect of the real church, the people of God. But the opposite response, neglecting the church building, is also wrong. David makes this point when he says that the Temple is "not just another building—it is for the Lord God himself!" Although we should avoid wasteful extravagance, we must remember that every church building is a visible witness for God. What does your church building tell the world about God?

29:3–5 David gave all his personal fortune to the Temple. He encouraged others to follow his example, and they willingly did.

Both the Tabernacle (Exodus 35:5—36:7) and the Temple were built from the voluntary gifts of the people. We may not have David's wealth, but we can develop his willingness to give. It is not what we have that counts with God, but our willingness to give of it.

29:6–9 These leaders displayed a right attitude toward their money by giving willingly to God's work. This attitude is described by Paul in 2 Corinthians 9:7: "Every one must make up his own mind as to how much he should give. Don't force anyone to give more than he really wants to, for cheerful givers are the ones God prizes." When we are generous in an attitude of thanksgiving to God, our attitude inspires others. Give generously to God's work.

29:11, 12 David acknowledged God's greatness. Our constantly changing world is controlled by a constant and unchanging God. As we see life come and go, objects fade, materials decay, and friends change, the only thing on which we can truly depend is God's control. His love and purpose for us never change. Only when we understand this can we have real peace and security.

are the Ruler of all mankind; your hand controls power and might, and it is at your discretion that men are made great and given strength. ¹³O our God, we thank you and praise your glorious name, ¹⁴but who am I and who are my people that we should be permitted to give anything to you? Everything we have has come from you, and we only give you what is yours already! ¹⁵For we are here for but a moment, strangers in the land as our fathers were before us; our days on earth are like a shadow, gone so soon, without a trace. ¹⁶O Lord our God, all of this material that we have gathered to build a temple for your holy name comes from you! It all belongs to you! ¹⁷I know, my God, that you test men to see if they are good; for you enjoy good men. I have done all this with good motives, and I have watched your people offer their gifts willingly and joyously.

¹⁸"O Lord God of our fathers: Abraham, Isaac, and Israel! Make your people always want to obey you, and see to it that their love for you never changes. ¹⁹Give my son Solomon a good heart toward God, so that he will want to obey you in the smallest detail, and will look forward eagerly to finishing the building of your temple, for which I have made all of these preparations."

²⁰Then David said to all the people, "Give praise to the Lord your God!" And they did, bowing low before the Lord and the king.

²¹The next day they brought a thousand young bulls, a thousand rams, and a thousand lambs as burnt offerings to the Lord; they also offered drink offerings and many other sacrifices on behalf of all Israel. ²²Then they feasted and drank before the Lord with great joy.

And again they crowned King David's son Solomon as their king. They anointed him before the Lord as their leader, and they anointed Zadok as their priest. ²³So God appointed Solomon to take the throne of his father David; and he prospered greatly, and all Israel obeyed him. ²⁴The national leaders, the army officers, and his brothers all pledged their allegiance to King Solomon. ²⁵And the Lord gave him great popularity with all the people of Israel, and he amassed even greater wealth and honor than his father.

David dies at an old age

²⁶, ²⁷David was king of the land of Israel for forty years; seven of them during his reign in Hebron and thirty-three in Jerusalem. ²⁸He died at an old age, wealthy and honored; and his son Solomon reigned in his place. ²⁹Detailed biographies of King David have been written in the history of Samuel the prophet, the history written by Nathan the prophet, and in the history written by the prophet Gad. ³⁰These accounts tell of his reign and of his might and all that happened to him and to Israel and to the kings of the nearby nations.

29:22 and again, or "and they installed him as co-regent" (with King David).

Cross references (left margin):

29:15
Lev 25:23
Job 14:2,10

29:17
1 Chron 28:9

29:18
1 Kgs 18:36

29:19
1 Chron 28:9
Ps 72:1

29:20
Josh 22:33

29:21
1 Kgs 8:62,63

29:22
1 Kgs 1:33
1 Chron 29:1

29:25
1 Kgs 3:13
2 Chron 1:1,12

29:26
2 Sam 5:4,5
1 Kgs 2:11
1 Chron 18:14

29:28
1 Chron 23:1
Acts 13:36

29:29
1 Sam 9:9; 22:5
2 Sam 7:2

29:15 David contrasts God's everlasting nature with the fleeting lives of his people. Nothing lasts unless it is rooted in God's character. If our most impressive deeds fade as dust before God, where should we place our confidence? Develop an eternal perspective and arrange your priorities accordingly. Is God first in your life?

29:19 A person with a good heart *wants* to obey God. This is what David wished for Solomon—a heart that desired, above all else, to serve God. Do you find it hard to do what God wants, or even harder to want to do it? God can give you a good heart that wants to do his will. If you have believed in Jesus Christ, this is already happening in you. Paul wrote, "For God is at work within you, helping you want to obey him, and then helping you do what he wants" (Philippians 2:13).

29:25 In 29:3-5, we read that David gave his fortune to the Temple. Solomon could have had mixed feelings about his inheritance being given to the Temple project. But apparently he approved of his father's gift. In this verse we see that Solomon amassed an even greater fortune than David had. God blessed Solomon, in part, because of his attitude toward giving to the

Lord's work. An attitude that prizes God's will and work above all else will be rewarded.

29:25 King Solomon surpassed his father's wealth and honor. David's legacy resulted from his vital relationship with the Lord, and he passed his spiritual values on to Solomon. The money and power we leave to our children are not nearly so important as the spiritual legacy that can be passed on. What kind of inheritance will your children receive?

29:30 First Chronicles vividly illustrates the importance of maintaining a relationship with God. The genealogies in chapters 1—9 emphasize the need for a spiritual heritage, whether past or future. The second part of the book details the life of David. Few men or women in the Bible were as close to God as David was. His daily contact with God gave him deep reverence for worship and the desire to build God's Temple. David's life shows us the importance of staying close to God—through studying and obeying his Word and communicating with him daily. Second Chronicles, on the other hand, reveals how quickly our lives can deteriorate (spiritually, mentally, and socially) when we fail to stay in touch with God.

Solomon becomes king 970 B.C.	Temple built 966–959	The kingdom divides 930	Asa becomes king of Judah 910	Jehosha-phat becomes king of Judah 872	Ahab killed in battle 853	Athaliah siezes the throne 841	Uzziah becom king of Judah 792

VITAL STATISTICS

PURPOSE:
To unify the nation around true worship of Jehovah by showing his standard for judging kings. The righteous kings of Judah and the religious revivals under their rule are highlighted, and the sins of the evil kings are exposed.

AUTHOR:
Ezra, according to Jewish tradition

TO WHOM WRITTEN:
All Israel

DATE WRITTEN:
Approximately 430 B.C.; recording events from the beginning of Solomon's reign (970 B.C.) to the beginning of the Babylonian captivity (586 B.C.)

SETTING:
Second Chronicles parallels 1 and 2 Kings and serves as their commentary. Originally 1 and 2 Chronicles were one book. It was written after the exile from a priestly perspective, highlighting the importance of the Temple and the religious revivals in Judah. The Northern Kingdom, Israel, is virtually ignored in this history.

KEY VERSE:
"Then if my people will humble themselves and pray, and search for me, and turn from their wicked ways, I will hear them from heaven and forgive their sins and heal their land" (7:14).

KEY PEOPLE:
Solomon, the queen of Sheba, Rehoboam, Asa, Jehoshaphat, Jehoram, Joash, Uzziah, Ahaz, Hezekiah, Manasseh, Josiah

KEY PLACES:
Jerusalem, the Temple

SPECIAL FEATURES:
Includes a detailed record of the Temple's construction

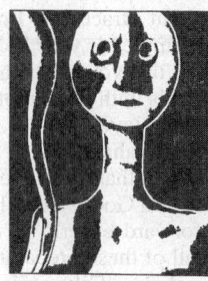

THE slide clicks, and our eyes focus on the image flashed onto the screen in the darkened sanctuary. "This idol," explains the missionary, "is made of stone and is worshiped daily. The natives believe that this will guarantee good crops and healthy children." With condescending smiles, we wonder at their ignorance. How could anyone worship an object? Idols are for the superstitious! Then we return home to *our* idols of wealth, prestige, or self-fulfillment. If we put anything in God's place, we worship it, despite what we profess with our lips.

Our experience parallels Israel's. They were chosen by God to represent him on earth. But too often they forgot the truth and their calling, stumbling blindly after idols as the neighboring nations did. Then prophets, priests, and judgment would push them abruptly back to God, the one true God. Second Chronicles relates this sordid history of Judah's corrupt and idolatrous kings. Here and there a good king arises in Judah, and for a time there is revival, but the downward spiral continues—ending in chaos, destruction, and captivity.

The chronicler writes this volume to bring the nation back to God by reminding them of their past. Only by following God will they prosper! As you read 2 Chronicles you will catch a vivid glimpse of Judah's history (the history of Israel, the Northern Kingdom, is virtually ignored), and you will see the tragic results of idolatry. Learn the lessons of the past: determine to get rid of any idols in your life and to worship God alone.

Second Chronicles continues the history of 1 Chronicles. David's son, Solomon, is inaugurated as king. Solomon builds the magnificent Temple in Jerusalem, thus fulfilling his father's wish and last request (chapters 2—5). Solomon enjoys a peaceful and prosperous reign of 40 years that makes him world famous. After Solomon dies, his son Rehoboam assumes the throne and his immaturity divides the kingdom.

In Judah, there are a few good kings and many evil ones. The writer of Chronicles faithfully records their achievements and failures, noting how each king measures up to God's standard for success. Clearly a good king obeys God's laws, eliminates the places of idol worship, and makes no alliances with other nations. Judah's good kings include Asa, Jehoshaphat, Uzziah, Hezekiah, and Josiah. Of her many evil ones, Ahaz and Manasseh are perhaps the worst. Eventually the nation is conquered and taken captive, and the Temple is destroyed.

The writer's purpose was to reunite the nation around the true worship of God after the captivity. In these pages, he reminds the people of their past. He clearly broadcasts his message through one of the best-known verses in Scripture, "Then if my people will humble themselves and pray, and search for me, and turn from their wicked ways, I will hear them from heaven and forgive their sins and heal their land" (7:14). As you read 2 Chronicles, listen to God's voice and obey him; and receive his redemptive, healing touch.

THE BLUEPRINT

A. THE REIGN OF SOLOMON (1:1—9:31)
1. Solomon asks God for wisdom
2. Solomon builds the Temple
3. Solomon dedicates the Temple
4. Solomon's riches and wisdom

Solomon achieved much in business and government, but most important, he was the man God used to build the glorious Temple. This beautiful building was the religious center of the nation. It symbolized the unity of all the tribes, the presence of God among them, and the nation's high calling. We may achieve great things in life, but we must not neglect any effort that will help nurture God's people or bring others into God's kingdom. It is easy for us to get the wrong perspective on what's really important in life.

B. THE KINGDOM OF JUDAH (10:1—36:23)
1. The nation of Israel splits apart
2. History of apostasy and reform
3. Judah is exiled to Babylon

Throughout the reigns of 20 kings, the nation of Judah wavered between obedience to God and apostasy. The reigning king's response to God determined the spiritual climate of the nation and whether or not God would send judgment upon his people. Our personal history is shaped by our response to God. Just as Judah's failure to repent brought them captivity in Babylon, so the abuse of our high calling by sinful living will ultimately bring us catastrophe and destruction.

MEGATHEMES

THEME	EXPLANATION	IMPORTANCE
Temple	The Temple was the symbol of God's presence and the place set aside for worship and prayer. Built by Solomon from the plans God gave to David, the Temple was the spiritual center of the nation.	As Christians meet together to worship God, they experience the presence of God in a way that no individual believer could. For the dwelling place of God is the people of God. The body of Christ is God's temple.
Peace	As Solomon and his descendants were faithful to God, they experienced victory in battle, success in government, and peace with other nations. Peace was the result of loyalty to God and his Law.	Only God can bring true peace. God is greater than any enemy, army, or national alliance. Just as Israel's faithful response was key to her peace and survival as a nation, so our obedience to God as individuals and as a nation is vital to peace today.
Prayer	After Solomon died, David's kingdom was divided. When a king led the Israelites into idolatry, the nation suffered. When the king and his people prayed to God for deliverance and they turned from their sinful ways, God delivered them.	God still answers prayer today. We have God's promise that if we humble ourselves, seek him, turn from our sin, and pray, God will hear, heal, and forgive us.
Reform	Although idolatry and injustice were common, some kings turned to God and led the people in spiritual revival— renewing their commitment to God and reforming their society. Revival included the destruction of idols, obedience to the Law, and the restoration of the priesthood.	We must constantly commit ourselves to obeying God. We are never secure in what others have done before us. Each generation of believers must rededicate themselves to the task of carrying out God's will in their own lives as well as in society.
National collapse	In 586 B.C. the Babylonians completely destroyed Solomon's beautiful Temple. The formal worship of God was ended. The Israelites had abandoned God. As a result, God brought judgment upon his people and they were carried off into captivity.	Although our disobedience may not be as blatant as Israel's, quite often our commitment to God is insincere and casual. When we forget that all our power, wisdom, and wealth come from God and not ourselves, we are in danger of the same spiritual and moral collapse that Israel experienced.

1 Gibeon David's son Solomon became king of Israel. He summoned the nation's leaders to a ceremony in Gibeon. Here God told Solomon to ask for whatever he desired. Solomon asked for wisdom and knowledge to rule Israel (1:1–12).

2 Jerusalem After the ceremony in Gibeon, Solomon returned to the capital city, Jerusalem. His reign began a golden age for Israel. Solomon implemented the plans for the Temple which had been drawn up by his father David. It was a magnificent construction. It symbolized Solomon's wealth and wisdom which became known worldwide (1:13—9:31).

3 Shechem After Solomon's death, his son Rehoboam was ready to be crowned in Shechem. However, his promise of higher taxes and harder work for the people led to rebellion. Everyone but the tribes of Judah and Benjamin deserted Rehoboam and set up their own kingdom to the north called Israel. Rehoboam returned to Jerusalem as ruler over the Southern Kingdom called Judah (10:1—12:16). The remainder of 2 Chronicles records the history of Judah.

4 Hills of Ephraim Abijah became the next king of Judah, and soon war broke out between Israel and Judah. When the armies of the two nations arrived for battle in the hill country of Ephraim, Israel had twice as many troops as Judah. It looked like Judah's defeat was certain. But they cried out to God, and God gave them victory over Israel. In their

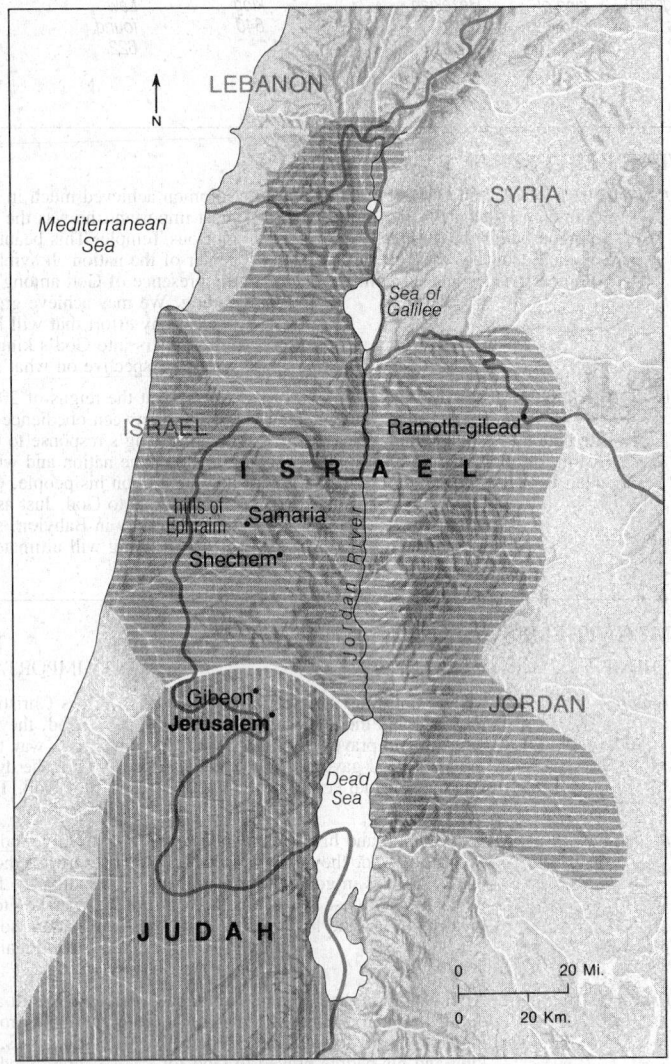

Modern names and boundaries are shown in gray.

Judah had a few godly kings who instituted reforms and brought the people back to God. Israel, however, had a succession of only evil kings (13:1–22).

5 Syria Asa, a godly king, removed every trace of idol worship from Judah and renewed the people's covenant with God in Jerusalem. But King Baasha of Israel built a fortress to control traffic into Judah. Instead of looking to God for guidance, Asa took the silver and gold from the Temple and sent it to the king of Syria requesting his help against King Baasha. As a result, God became angry with Judah (14:1–16:14).

6 Samaria Although Jehoshaphat was a godly king, he allied himself with Israel's most evil king, Ahab. Ahab's capital was in Samaria. Ahab wanted help fighting for Ramoth-gilead. Jehoshaphat wanted advice, but rather than listening to God's prophet who had promised defeat, he joined Ahab in battle (17:1–18:27).

7 Ramoth-gilead The alliance with Israel against Ramoth-

gilead ended in defeat and Ahab's death. Although shaken by his defeat, Jehoshaphat returned to Jerusalem and to God. But his son Jehoram was a wicked king, as was his son, Ahaziah. And history repeated itself. Ahaziah formed an alliance with Israel's King Jehoram (who had the same name as his brother) to do battle with the Syrians at Ramoth-gilead. This led to the death of both kings (18:28—22:9).

8 Jerusalem The rest of Judah's history recorded in 2 Chronicles centers on Jerusalem. Some kings caused Judah to sin by bringing idol worship into their midst. Others cleaned up the idol worship, reopened and restored the Temple and, in the case of Josiah, tried to follow God's laws as they were written by Moses. In spite of the few good influences, a series of evil kings sent Judah into a downward spiral that ended with the Babylonian Empire overrunning the country. The Temple was burned, the walls of the city were broken down, and the people were deported to Babylon.

A. THE REIGN OF SOLOMON (1:1—9:31)

In response to Solomon's request, God gives to Solomon great wisdom. Solomon launches great building programs, including the Temple, his greatest achievement. In the midst of the celebration dedicating the Temple, fire flashes down from heaven and God's glory fills the Temple. God wants to live among his people and to be central in their lives. Today, our bodies are God's temple, the place where God, through his Holy Spirit, lives and reigns.

1. Solomon asks God for wisdom

1:1
1 Kgs 2:12,46
1 Chron 29:25

1:2
Ex 36:8
1 Kgs 3:4
1 Chron 28:1

1:4
1 Chron
15:25-28

1:5
Ex 31:9; 38:1-7
1 Kgs 3:4

1:7
1 Kgs 3:5-14

1:8
1 Chron 28:5

1:9
Gen 13:16
22:17
2 Sam 7:12-16

1:10
2 Sam 5:2

1:12
1 Chron 29:25
2 Chron 9:22

1 King David's son Solomon was now the undisputed ruler of Israel, for the Lord his God had made him a powerful monarch. 2, 3He summoned all the army officers and judges to Gibeon as well as all the political and religious leaders of Israel. He led them up to the hill to the old Tabernacle constructed by Moses, the Lord's assistant, while he was in the wilderness. 4(There was a later Tabernacle in Jerusalem, built by King David for the Ark of God when he removed it from Kiriath-jearim.) 5, 6The bronze altar made by Bezalel (son of Uri, son of Hur) still stood in front of the old Tabernacle, and now Solomon and those he had invited assembled themselves before it, as he sacrificed upon it 1,000 burnt offerings to the Lord.

7That night God appeared to Solomon and told him, "Ask me for anything, and I will give it to you!"

8Solomon replied, "O God, you have been so kind and good to my father David, and now you have given me the kingdom— 9this is all I want! For you have fulfilled your promise to David my father and have made me king over a nation as full of people as the earth is full of dust! 10Now give me wisdom and knowledge to rule them properly, for who is able to govern by himself such a great nation as this one of yours?"

11God replied, "Because your greatest desire is to help your people, and you haven't asked for personal wealth and honor, and you haven't asked me to curse your enemies, and you haven't asked for a long life, but for wisdom and knowledge to properly guide my people— 12yes, I am giving you the wisdom and knowledge you asked for! And I am also giving you such riches, wealth, and honor as no other

1:2, 3 *He summoned all the army officers and judges to Gibeon,* implied. *He led them up the hill to the old Tabernacle.* Moses had built the Tabernacle 500 years before the reign of King Solomon.

1:1 While the book of 1 Chronicles focuses mainly on King David's life, 2 Chronicles focuses on the lives of the rest of the kings of Judah, the Southern Kingdom. Very little is mentioned about Israel, the Northern Kingdom, because (1) Chronicles was written for Judeans who had returned from captivity in Babylon, and (2) Judah represented David's family, from which the Messiah would come. While Israel was in a state of constant turmoil, anarchy, and rebellion against God, Judah at least made sporadic efforts to follow God.

1:1 More details about Solomon's rise to the throne can be read in 1 Kings 1, 2. Solomon's Profile is found in 1 Kings 3.

1:2-5 The Tabernacle Moses built centuries earlier (Exodus 35—40) was still in operation, although it had been moved several times. When Solomon became king, the Tabernacle was located at Gibeon, a town about six miles northwest of Jerusalem. All the Tabernacle furniture was kept at Gibeon except the Ark of God which David had moved to Jerusalem (1 Chronicles 13, 15, 16) because he wanted the Ark, the symbol of God's presence, to reside in the city where he ruled the people. The Tabernacle at Gibeon, however, was still considered Israel's main religious center until Solomon built the Temple in Jerusalem.

1:10 Wisdom is the ability to make good decisions based on proper discernment and judgment. Knowledge, in this verse, refers to the practical know-how necessary for handling everyday matters. Solomon used his wisdom and knowledge not only to build the Temple from his father's plans, but to establish the nation's economic growth.

1:10 God's offer to Solomon stretches the imagination: "Ask me

for anything and I will give it to you" (1:7). But Solomon put the needs of his people first and asked for wisdom rather than riches. He realized that wisdom would be the most valuable asset he could have as king. Later he wrote, "Wisdom is far more valuable than precious jewels. Nothing else compares with it" (Proverbs 3:15). The same wisdom that was given to Solomon is available to you because the same God gives it. How can we acquire wisdom? First, we must ask God, who "is always ready to give a bountiful supply of wisdom" (James 1:5). Second, we must devote ourselves to studying and applying God's Word, the source of divine wisdom. (For more on Solomon's wisdom, read the notes on 1 Kings 3:6–9 and 3:10.)

1:11, 12 Solomon could have had anything, but he asked for wisdom to rule the nation. God approved of the way Solomon ordered his priorities, and he gave him riches, wealth, and honor. Jesus also spoke about priorities. He said that when we put God first, everything we really need will fall into place (Matthew 6:33). This does not guarantee that we will be wealthy and famous like Solomon, but it means that when we wisely put God first, the wisdom he gives us will enable us to live richly rewarding lives.

1:12 Solomon's wealth was impressive. In this specific case, it symbolized God's blessing in his life and served as a reward for seeking God's wisdom. Jesus the Messiah came to fulfill God's promise to David for an eternal kingdom. The spiritual benefits of Jesus' rule are even more impressive than the material benefits of Solomon's. Whereas Solomon's wisdom was limited, and his wealth eventually disappeared, Jesus' wisdom is eternal and his treasures can never be taken away.

king has ever had before you! And there will never again be so great a king in all the world!"

13Solomon then left the Tabernacle, returned down the hill, and went back to Jerusalem to rule Israel. 14He built up a huge force of 1,400 chariots and recruited 12,000 cavalry to guard the cities where the chariots were garaged, though some, of course, were stationed at Jerusalem near the king. 15During Solomon's reign, silver and gold were as plentiful in Jerusalem as rocks on the road! And expensive cedar lumber was used like common sycamore! 16Solomon sent horse-traders to Egypt to purchase entire herds at wholesale prices. 17At that time Egyptian chariots sold for $400 each and horses for $100, delivered at Jerusalem. Many of these were then resold to the kings of the Hittites and Syria.

1:13
2 Chron 1:3
1:14
1 Kgs 4:26
9:19; 10:26-29

2. Solomon builds the Temple
Solomon plans the Temple

2 Solomon now decided that the time had come to build a temple for the Lord and a palace for himself. 2This required a force of 70,000 laborers, 80,000 stone-cutters in the hills, and 3,600 foremen. 3Solomon sent an ambassador to King Hiram at Tyre, requesting shipments of cedar lumber such as Hiram had supplied to David when he was building his palace.

4"I am about to build a temple for the Lord my God," Solomon told Hiram. "It will be a place where I can burn incense and sweet spices before God, and display the special sacrificial bread, and sacrifice burnt offerings each morning and evening, and on the Sabbaths, and at the new moon celebration and other regular festivals of the Lord our God. For God wants Israel always to celebrate these special occasions. 5It is going to be a wonderful temple because he is a great God, greater than any other. 6But who can ever build him a worthy home? Not even the highest heaven would be beautiful enough! And who am I to be allowed to build a temple for God? But it will be a place to worship him.

7"So send me skilled craftsmen—goldsmiths and silversmiths, brass and iron workers; and send me weavers to make purple, crimson, and blue cloth; and skilled

2:1
1 Kgs 5:5
2:2
1 Kgs 5:15,16
2 Chron 2:18
2:3
1 Kgs 5:2-11
1 Chron 14:1
2:4
Ex 25:30
29:38-42; 30:7
Num 28:9,10
2:5
Ex 15:11
1 Chron 16:25
2:6
1 Kgs 8:27
2 Chron 6:18
2:7
Ex 31:3-5
1 Chron 22:15
2 Chron 2:13,14

2:6 *it will be a place to worship him,* literally, "a place to burn incense before him."

2:1 David had asked to build a Temple for God (2 Samuel 7), but God denied his request because David had shed too much blood as a warrior. But God allowed David to make the plans and preparations for the Temple (1 Chronicles 23—26; 28:11-13). David bought the land for the Temple (2 Samuel 24:18-25; 1 Chronicles 22:1), gathered most of the construction materials (1 Chronicles 22:14-16), and received the plans from God (1 Chronicles 28:11, 12). It was Solomon's responsibility to make these plans a reality. His job was made easier by his father's exhaustive preparations. God's work can be forwarded when the older generation paves the way for the younger.

2:4 A celebration is an occasion of joy, and remembering God's goodness to his people was certainly a reason to be joyful. God wanted Israel to celebrate certain occasions regularly because the people were so forgetful, so quick to turn to other gods. In church we use celebrations to recall God's goodness. Because we also have short memories, Christmas, Easter, and other special occasions are designed to help us recall what God has done for all his people. We participate in these celebrations by thanking God for how he has worked in the past. Celebrating with thanksgiving adds vitality to our spiritual lives.

2:4-6, 11, 12 Although King Hiram was one of David's and Solomon's friendly allies, he was the ruler of a nation that worshiped many different gods. Hiram was happy to send materials for the Temple, and both David and Solomon used this occasion to testify about the one true God.

2:7 Why use foreign craftsmen? The Israelites had great knowledge of agriculture, but knew little about metalworking. So they found people who were experts in this area. It is not a sin to

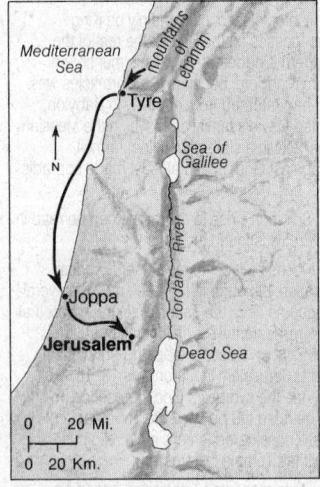

rent secular expertise for God's work. He distributes all natural talents as he chooses, and he often chooses to give skill to non-Christians. When we hire secular contractors to build or repair our church buildings, we are recognizing that God gives gifts liberally. We may also be gaining an opportunity to tell the workers about God.

SHIPPING RESOURCES FOR THE TEMPLE
Solomon asked King Hiram of Tyre to provide supplies and skilled workmen to help build God's Temple in Jerusalem. The plan was to cut the cedar logs in the mountains of Lebanon, float them by sea to Joppa, then bring them inland to Jerusalem by the shortest and easiest route.

engravers to work beside the craftsmen of Judah and Jerusalem who were selected by my father David. 8Also send me cedar trees, fir trees, and algum trees from the Forests of Lebanon, for your men are without equal as lumbermen, and I will send my men to help them. 9An immense amount of lumber will be needed, for the temple I am going to build will be large and incredibly beautiful. 10As to the financial arrangements, I will pay your men 20,000 sacks of crushed wheat, 20,000 barrels of barley, 20,000 barrels of wine, and 20,000 barrels of olive oil."

11King Hiram replied to King Solomon: "It is because the Lord loves his people that he has made you their king! 12Blessed be the Lord God of Israel who made the heavens and the earth and who has given to David such a wise, intelligent, and understanding son to build God's Temple, and a royal palace for himself.

13"I am sending you a master craftsman—my famous Huramabi! He is a brilliant man, 14the son of a Jewish woman from Dan in Israel; his father is from here in Tyre. He is a skillful goldsmith and silversmith, and also does exquisite work with brass and iron, and knows all about stonework, carpentry, and weaving; and he is an expert in the dyeing of purple and blue linen and crimson cloth. He is an engraver besides, and an inventor! He will work with your craftsmen and those appointed by my lord David, your father. 15So send along the wheat, barley, olive oil, and wine you mentioned, 16and we will begin cutting wood from the Lebanon mountains, as much as you need, and bring it to you in log floats across the sea to Joppa, and from there you can take them inland to Jerusalem."

17Solomon now took a census of all foreigners in the country (just as his father David had done) and found that there were 153,600 of them. 18He indentured 70,000 as common laborers, 80,000 as loggers and 3,600 as foremen.

Temple construction begins

3 Finally the actual construction of the Temple began. Its location was in Jerusalem at the top of Mount Moriah, where the Lord had appeared to Solomon's father, King David, and where the threshing-floor of Ornan the Jebusite had been. David had selected it as the site for the Temple. 2The actual construction began on the seventeenth day of April in the fourth year of King Solomon's reign.

3The foundation was ninety feet long and thirty feet wide. 4A covered porch ran along the entire thirty-foot width of the Temple, with the inner walls and ceiling overlaid with pure gold! The roof was 180 feet high.

5The main part of the Temple was paneled with cypress wood, plated with pure gold, and engraved with palm trees and chains. 6Beautiful jewels were inlaid into the walls to add to the beauty; the gold, by the way, was of the best, from Parvaim. 7All the walls, beams, doors, and thresholds throughout the Temple were plated with gold, with angels engraved on the walls.

8Within the Temple, at one end, was the most sacred room—the Holy of Holies—thirty feet square. This too was overlaid with the finest gold, valued at

---

Marginal cross-references (left column):

2:8 2 Chron 9:10,11

2:11 1 Kgs 10:9 2 Chron 9:8

2:12 2 Chron 2:1 Ps 33:6; 102:25

2:14 1 Kgs 7:14

2:15 2 Chron 2:10

2:16 1 Kgs 5:8,9

2:18 1 Chron 22:2 2 Chron 2:2

3:1 1 Kgs 6:1 1 Chron 21:18

3:4 1 Kgs 6:3

3:5 1 Kgs 6:17

3:7 1 Kgs 6:20-22, 29-35

3:8 Ex 26:33 1 Kgs 6:16

2:8, 9 Israel did not have much wood. But Lebanon, a small nation on the seacoast, had some of the finest cedar forests in the Middle East. Lebanon, in turn, imported a great deal of food from Israel. Thus the two kings made a trade agreement that was beneficial to both nations.

2:13 Natural talents are given to all people for God's purposes. We don't know if Huramabi served God (he was half Jewish), but we know he was gifted by God for a task.

2:17, 18 Why would Solomon force foreigners living in Israel to become slaves? These foreigners were descendants of the heathen nations who had not been driven out of the land in Joshua's day (Joshua 9:23–27; Judges 1:21–33; 1 Kings 9:20, 21). Scripture has specific laws about treating slaves fairly (Leviticus 25:39–55), so Solomon would not have treated them harshly as other nations might. They were descendants of evil peoples who were supposed to have been destroyed for their wickedness long

before. Solomon's action was probably not permanent, but only in force during the construction of the Temple.

3:1 Solomon built a permanent Temple on Mount Moriah to replace the movable Tabernacle (now at Gibeon) that had accompanied Israel in the wilderness. Mount Moriah was also the place where God had stopped Abraham from sacrificing Isaac (Genesis 22:1–18). David purchased the land when it was a threshing-floor (see 2 Samuel 24:15–25 and the note on 1 Chronicles 22:1).

3:1ff Why was the Temple decorated so ornately? Although no one can build God a worthy home (2:6), this Temple was going to be the best that humans could design. The care and craftsmanship were acts of worship in themselves. Although a simple chapel is an adequate place to pray and meet God, it is not wrong to want to make a beautiful place of worship.

millions of dollars. ⁹Twenty-six-ounce gold nails were used. The upper rooms were also plated with pure gold.

³:⁹
1 Chron 28:11

¹⁰Within the innermost room, the Holy of Holies, Solomon placed two sculptured statues of angels, and plated them with gold. ¹¹, ¹², ¹³They stood on the floor facing the outer room, with wings stretched wingtip to wingtip across the room, from wall to wall. ¹⁴Across the entrance to this room he placed a veil of blue and crimson finespun linen, decorated with angels.

³:¹⁰
1 Kgs 6:23-28

³:¹⁴
Ex 26:31

¹⁵At the front of the Temple were two pillars 52½ feet high, topped by a 7½-foot capital flaring out to the roof. ¹⁶He made chains and placed them on top of the pillars, with 100 pomegranates attached to the chains. ¹⁷Then he set up the pillars at the front of the Temple, one on the right and the other on the left. And he gave them names: Jachin (the one on the right), and Boaz (the one on the left).

³:¹⁵
1 Kgs 7:15-20

³:¹⁷
1 Kgs 7:21

Huramabi's skillful work

4 He also made a bronze altar thirty feet long, thirty feet wide, and fifteen feet high. ²Then he forged a huge round tank fifteen feet across from rim to rim. The rim stood 7½ feet above the floor, and was forty-five feet around. ³The tank was encircled at its base by two rows of gourd designs, cast as part of the tank. ⁴The tank stood on twelve metal oxen facing outward; three faced north, three faced west, three faced south, and three faced east. ⁵The walls of the tank were five inches thick, flaring out like the cup of a lily. It held 3,000 barrels of water.

⁴:¹
Ex 27:1,2
2 Kgs 16:14

⁴:²
1 Kgs 7:23-26

⁴:⁵
1 Kgs 7:26

⁶He also constructed ten vats for water to wash the offerings, five to the right of the huge tank and five to the left. The priests used the tank, and not the vats, for their own washing.

⁴:⁶
1 Kgs 7:38,40

⁷Carefully following God's instructions, he then cast ten gold lampstands and placed them in the Temple, five against each wall; ⁸he also built ten tables and placed five against each wall on the right and left. And he molded 100 solid gold bowls. ⁹Then he constructed a court for the priests, also the public court, and overlaid the doors of these courts with bronze. ¹⁰The huge tank was in the southeast corner of the outer room of the Temple. ¹¹Huramabi also made the necessary pots, shovels, and basins for use in connection with the sacrifices.

⁴:⁷
1 Kgs 7:49

⁴:⁹
1 Kgs 6:36
⁴:¹⁰
1 Kgs 7:39

So at last he completed the work assigned to him by King Solomon:

¹²⁻¹⁶The construction of the two pillars,
The two flared capitals on the tops of the pillars,
The two sets of chains on the capitals,
The 400 pomegranates hanging from the two sets of chains on the capitals,
The bases for the vats, and the vats themselves,
The huge tank and the twelve oxen under it,
The pots, shovels, and fleshhooks.

⁴:¹²
1 Kgs 7:14; 20,
27-43
2 Chron 2:13

This skillful craftsman, Huramabi, made all of the above-mentioned items for King Solomon, using polished bronze. ¹⁷, ¹⁸The king did the casting at the claybanks of the Jordan valley between Succoth and Zeredah. Great quantities of bronze were used, too heavy to weigh.

⁴:¹⁷
1 Kgs 7:47

¹⁹Solomon commanded that all of the furnishings of the Temple—the utensils, the altar, and the table for the Bread of the Presence must be made of gold; ²⁰also

⁴:²⁰
Ex 25:31-37

3:11-13 *with wings stretched . . . from wall to wall,* literally, "one wing of a cherub, five cubits long." **3:16** *He made chains,* literally, "chains in the Holy of Holies, and . . ."

4:6 Why was everything in the Temple built on such a grand scale? The great size and numbers were necessary in order to accommodate the crowds of thousands that would visit for the feasts, such as the Passover (30:13). The numerous daily sacrifices (5:6) required many priests and a lot of equipment.

4:7 Huramabi followed God's instructions carefully—with spectacular results. When God gives specific instructions, they must be followed to the letter. There is a time to be creative and put forth our own ideas, but not when they add to, alter, or

contradict any specific directions God has already given to us in the Bible. Don't be surprised by poor results in your spiritual life if you are not carefully seeking and following God's instructions.

4:11-16 Vats, tanks, fleshhooks, shovels—these are implements of worship with which we are not familiar. Although the articles we use to aid our worship have changed, the purpose of worship remains the same—to give honor and praise to God. We must never confuse our worship of God with those things we use to help us worship him.

the lamps and lampstands, 21the floral decorations, tongs, 22lamp snuffers, basins, spoons, and firepans—all were made of solid gold. Even the doorway of the Temple, the main door, and the inner doors to the Holy of Holies were overlaid with gold.

5 So the Temple was finally finished. Then Solomon brought in the gifts dedicated to the Lord by his father, King David. They were stored in the Temple treasuries.

3. Solomon dedicates the Temple
The Ark is transferred to the Temple

2Solomon now summoned to Jerusalem all of the leaders of Israel—the heads of

CAREFUL OBEDIENCE	Who?	God's instruction	Disobedience	Result
Solomon and his workers carefully followed God's instructions (4:7). As a result, the Temple work was blessed by God and completed in every detail. Here are a few examples of (1) people in the Bible who did *not* carefully follow one of God's instructions and (2) the resulting consequences. It is not enough to obey God half-heartedly.	Adam and Eve	Don't eat fruit from the Tree of Conscience (Genesis 2:16, 17)	Satan tempted them and they ate (Genesis 3:1–6)	They were banished from the Garden of Eden; pain and death were inflicted on all mankind (Genesis 3:24; Romans 5:12)
	Nadab and Abihu	Fire for the sacrifice must come from the proper source (Leviticus 6:12, 13)	They used unholy fire for their sacrifice (Leviticus 10:1)	They were struck dead (Leviticus 10:2)
	Moses	"Speak to that rock over there and tell it to pour out its water" (Numbers 20:8)	He spoke to the rock, but also struck it with his staff (Numbers 20:11)	He was not allowed to enter the Promised Land (Numbers 20:12)
	Saul	Completely destroy the evil Amalekites (1 Samuel 15:3)	He spared the king and kept some of the booty (1 Samuel 15:8, 9)	God promised to end his reign (1 Samuel 15:16–26)
	Uzzah	Only a priest can touch the sacred Tabernacle furniture (Numbers 4:15)	He touched the Ark of the Covenant (2 Samuel 6:6)	He died instantly (2 Samuel 6:7)
	Uzziah	Only the priests could offer incense in the Temple or Tabernacle sanctuary (Numbers 16:39, 40; 18:7)	He entered the Holy Place in the Temple where only priests were allowed to go (2 Chronicles 26:16–18)	He became a leper (2 Chronicles 26:19)

4:22 All these details about the Temple demonstrated the care Israel gave to acts of worship (see the note on 3:1ff). They also served as a manual to the original readers of 2 Chronicles, those who would build a new Temple on its original site (Ezra 3:8—6:15) after Solomon's Temple was destroyed by the Babylonians (2 Kings 25).

5:1ff Why is there so much emphasis on the Temple in the Old Testament?
(1) *It was a symbol of religious authority.* The Temple was God's way of centralizing worship at Jerusalem in order to insure that correct belief would be kept intact through many generations.
(2) *It was a symbol of God's holiness.* The Temple's beautiful atmosphere inspired respect and awe for God; it was the setting for many of the great visions of the prophets.
(3) *It was a symbol of God's covenant with Israel.* The Temple kept the people focused upon God's Law (the tablets of the Ten Commandments were kept in the Temple), rather than on the exploits of the kings. It was a place where God was especially present to his people.
(4) *It was a symbol of forgiveness.* The Temple's design, furniture, and customs were great object lessons for all the people, reminding them of the seriousness of sin, the penalty which sin incurred, and their need of forgiveness.

(5) *It prepared the people for the Messiah.* In the New Testament, Christ said he came to fulfill the law, not to destroy it. Hebrews 8:1, 2 and 9:11, 12 use Temple customs to explain what Christ did when he died for us.
(6) *It was a testimony to human effort and creativity.* Inspired by the beauty of God's character, people devoted themselves to high achievements in engineering, science, and art in order to praise him.
(7) *It was a place of prayer.* In the Temple, people could spend time in prayer to God.

5:1–3 The Temple took seven years to build. First Kings 6:38 says that the Temple was completed in November of Solomon's eleventh year as king (959 B.C.). Because 5:3 states that the dedication ceremonies were held in October, they must have occurred either one month before or 11 months after the Temple's completion.

5:2 This Tabernacle in the City of David was actually a special tent David had set up to house the Ark of God (2 Samuel 6:17). It was not the original Tabernacle that Moses built in the wilderness. The wilderness Tabernacle still stood at Gibeon (1 Chronicles 16:39).

the tribes and clans—for the ceremony of transferring the Ark from the [Tabernacle in the] City of David, also known as Zion, [to its new home in the Temple]. 3This celebration took place in October at the annual Festival of Tabernacles. 4, 5As the leaders of Israel watched, the Levites lifted the Ark and carried it out of the Tabernacle, along with all the other sacred vessels. 6King Solomon and the others sacrificed sheep and oxen before the Ark in such numbers that no one tried to keep count!

5:2
1 Kgs 8:1-9
2 Chron 1:4

5:4
2 Chron 5:7

7, 8Then the priests carried the Ark into the inner room of the Temple—the Holy of Holies—and placed it beneath the angels' wings; their wings spread over the Ark and its carrying poles. 9These carrying poles were so long that their ends could be seen from the outer room, but not from the outside doorway.

5:9
1 Kgs 8:8,9

The Ark is still there at the time of this writing. 10Nothing was in the Ark except the two stone tablets which Moses had put there at Mount Horeb, when the Lord made a covenant with the people of Israel as they were leaving Egypt.

5:10
Deut 10:2-5
Heb 9:4

11, 12When the priests had undergone the purification rites for themselves, they all took part in the ceremonies without regard to their normal duties. And how the Levites were praising the Lord as the priests came out of the Holy of Holies! The singers were Asaph, Heman, Jeduthun and all their sons and brothers, dressed in finespun linen robes and standing at the east side of the altar. The choir was accompanied by 120 priests who were trumpeters, while others played the cymbals, lyres, and harps. 13, 14The band and chorus united as one to praise and thank the Lord; their selections were interspersed with trumpet obbligatos, the clashing of cymbals, and the loud playing of other musical instruments—all praising and thanking the Lord. Their theme was "He is so good! His lovingkindness lasts forever!"

5:11
1 Chron 13:8
15:16,24
24:1-5; 25:1-4
2 Chron 7:6

5:13
1 Kgs 8:11
1 Chron 16:34,
42
2 Chron 7:3

And at that moment the glory of the Lord, coming as a bright cloud, filled the Temple so that the priests could not continue their work.

Solomon's blessing

6 This is the prayer prayed by Solomon on that occasion:

6:1
1 Kgs 8:12-50

"The Lord has said that he would live in the thick darkness,
But I have made a Temple for you, O Lord, to live in forever!"

3Then the king turned around to the people and they stood to receive his blessing: 4"Blessed be the Lord God of Israel," he said to them, "—the God who talked personally to my father David and has now fulfilled the promise he made to him. For he told him, 5, 6'I have never before, since bringing my people from the land of Egypt, chosen a city anywhere in Israel as the location of my Temple where my name will be glorified; and never before have I chosen a king for my people Israel. But now I have chosen Jerusalem as that city, and David as that king.'

6:5
1 Chron 28:4
2 Chron 12:13

5:3 The Feast of Tabernacles celebrated God's protection of Israel as they wandered in the wilderness. The purpose of this annual festival was to renew Israel's commitment to God and their trust in his guidance and protection. The festival beautifully coincided with the dedication of the Temple. As the people remembered the wanderings in the wilderness, when their ancestors had lived in tents, they were even more thankful for the permanence of this glorious Temple.

5:9 Some books of the Bible were compiled and edited under God's inspiration from other sources. Because 1 and 2 Chronicles cover many centuries, they were compiled from several sources by a single person. The phrase, "the Ark is still there at the time of this writing," was taken from material written before Judah's exile in 586 B.C. Although 1 and 2 Chronicles were compiled after the exile, and after the Temple was destroyed, the writer thought it best to leave this phrase in the narrative.

5:11, 12 The Holy of Holies was the innermost room of the Temple where the Ark, the symbol of God's presence among his people, resided. Ordinarily the room could be entered only once a year by

the High Priest on the Day of Atonement. On this unique occasion, however, several priests had to enter the Holy of Holies in order to carry the Ark to its new resting place. The Levites praised God when these priests emerged from the Holy of Holies because they then knew God had accepted this new home for the Ark (5:14).

5:13 The first service at the Temple began with honoring God and acknowledging his presence and goodness. In the same way, our worship should begin with a recognition of God's love. Praise God first; then you will be prepared to present your needs to him. Recalling God's love and mercy will bring daily worship to life. Psalm 107 is an example of how David recalled God's lovingkindness.

6:3 As the people received Solomon's blessing, they stood; as Solomon prayed, he knelt (6:13). Both standing and kneeling are acts of reverence. Acts of reverence make us feel more worshipful and they let others see that we are honoring God. When you stand and kneel in church or at prayer, don't let these actions become mere forms prescribed by tradition. Instead let them activate your love for God.

6:8
1 Kgs 5:3

6:11
2 Chron 5:7,10

6:12
1 Kgs 8:54
Neh 8:4

6:14
Ex 15:11
Deut 3:24; 7:9
6:15
1 Chron 22:9,10
6:16
1 Kgs 2:4
2 Chron 7:18
6:18
2 Chron 2:6

6:20
Mic 7:18

7"My father David wanted to build this Temple, 8but the Lord said not to. It was good to have the desire, the Lord told him, 9but he was not the one to build it: his son was chosen for that task. 10And now the Lord has done what he promised, for I have become king in my father's place, and I have built the Temple for the Name of the Lord God of Israel, 11and placed the Ark there. And in the Ark is the Covenant between the Lord and his people Israel."

Solomon's prayer of dedication

12, 13As he spoke, Solomon was standing before the people on a platform in the center of the outer court, in front of the altar of the Lord. The platform was made of bronze, 7½ feet square and 4½ feet high. Now, as all the people watched, he knelt down, reached out his arms toward heaven, and prayed this prayer:

14"O Lord God of Israel, there is no God like you in all of heaven and earth. You are the God who keeps his kind promises to all those who obey you, and who are anxious to do your will. 15And you have kept your promise to my father David, as is evident today. 16And now, O God of Israel, carry out your further promise to him that 'your descendants shall always reign over Israel if they will obey my laws as you have.' 17Yes, Lord God of Israel, please fulfill this promise too. 18But will God really live upon the earth with men? Why, even the heaven and the heaven of heavens cannot contain you—how much less this Temple which I have built!

19"How I pray that you will heed my prayers, O Lord my God! Listen to my prayer that I am praying to you now! 20, 21Look down with favor day and night upon this Temple—upon this place where you have said that you would put your name. May you always hear and answer the prayers I will pray to you as I face toward this place. Listen to my prayers and to those of your people Israel when they pray toward this Temple; yes, hear us from heaven, and when you hear, forgive.

22"Whenever someone commits a crime, and is required to swear to his innocence before this altar, 23then hear from heaven and punish him if he is lying, or else declare him innocent.

24"If your people Israel are destroyed before their enemies because they have sinned against you, and if they turn to you and call themselves your people, and pray to you here in this Temple, 25then listen to them from heaven and forgive their sins and give them back this land you gave to their fathers.

26"When the skies are shut and there is no rain because of our sins, and then we pray toward this Temple and claim you as our God, and turn from our sins because you have punished us, 27then listen from heaven and forgive the sins of your people, and teach them what is right; and send rain upon this land which you have given to your people as their own property.

28"If there is a famine in the land, or plagues, or crop disease, or attacks of locusts or caterpillars, or if your people's enemies are in the land besieging our cities—whatever the trouble is— 29listen to every individual's prayer concerning

6:15 *to my father David,* literally, "David your servant."

6:12, 13 It was unusual for a king to kneel before someone else in front of his own people, because kneeling meant submitting to a higher authority. Solomon demonstrated his great love and respect for God by kneeling before him. His action showed that he acknowledged God as the ultimate king and authority, and it encouraged the people to do the same.

6:18 The Temple was a place where the people could worship God. God did not *need* a Temple to live in because not even the highest heaven could contain him. But at the Temple God was present in a special way among his people.

6:18 Solomon marveled that the Temple could contain the power of God and that God would be willing to live on earth among sinful people. We marvel that God, through his Son, Jesus, dwelt among us in human form to reveal his eternal purposes to us. In doing so, God was reaching out to mankind in love. God wants us to reach

back in return and get to know him. Only then will we come to love him with all our hearts. Don't simply marvel at his power, take time to get to know him.

6:19–42 As Solomon led the people in prayer, he asked God to hear their prayers concerning a variety of situations: (1) crime (6:22, 23); (2) enemy attacks (6:24, 25); (3) drought (6:26, 27); (4) famine (6:28–31); (5) the influx of foreigners (6:32, 33); (6) war (6:34, 35); (7) slavery to sin (6:36–39). God is concerned with whatever we face, even the difficult circumstances we bring upon ourselves. He wants us to turn to him in prayer.

6:24 Why would Solomon assume that drought would come as a result of sin? Sin is not necessarily the direct cause of natural disasters today, but this was a special case. God had made a specific agreement with the Israelites that famine could be a consequence of their sins (Deuteronomy 28:23, 24).

his private sorrow, as well as all the public prayers. 30Hear from heaven where you live, and forgive, and give each one whatever he deserves, for you know the hearts of all mankind. 31Then they will reverence you forever, and will continually walk where you tell them to go.

32"And when foreigners hear of your power, and come from distant lands to worship your great name, and to pray toward this Temple, 33hear them from heaven where you live, and do what they request of you. Then all the peoples of the earth will hear of your fame and will reverence you, just as your people Israel do; and they too will know that this Temple I have built is truly yours.

34"If your people go out at your command to fight their enemies, and they pray toward this city of Jerusalem which you have chosen, and this Temple which I have built for your name, 35then hear their prayers from heaven and give them success.

36"If they sin against you (and who has never sinned?) and you become angry with them, and you let their enemies defeat them and take them away as captives to some foreign nation near or far, 37, 38and if in that land of exile they turn to you again, and face toward this land you gave their fathers, and this city and your Temple I have built, and plead with you with all their hearts to forgive them, 39then hear from heaven where you live and help them and forgive your people who have sinned against you.

40"Yes, O my God, be wide awake and attentive to all the prayers made to you in this place. 41And now, O Lord God, arise and enter this resting place of yours where the Ark of your strength has been placed. Let your priests, O Lord God, be clothed with salvation, and let your people rejoice in your kind deeds. 42O Lord God, do not ignore me—do not turn your face away from me, your anointed one. Oh, remember your love for David and your kindness to him."

God's glory fills the Temple

7 As Solomon finished praying, fire flashed down from heaven and burned up the sacrifices! And the glory of the Lord filled the Temple, so that the priests couldn't enter! 3All the people had been watching and now they fell flat on the pavement, and worshiped and thanked the Lord.

"How good he is!" they exclaimed. "He is always so loving and kind."

4, 5Then the king and all the people dedicated the Temple by sacrificing burnt offerings to the Lord. King Solomon's contribution for this purpose was 22,000 oxen and 120,000 sheep. 6The priests were standing at their posts of duty, and the Levites were playing their thanksgiving song, "His Lovingkindness Is Forever," using the musical instruments King David himself had made and had used to praise the Lord. Then, when the priests blew the trumpets, all the people stood again. 7Solomon consecrated the inner court of the Temple for use that day as a place of sacrifice, because there were too many sacrifices for the bronze altar to accommodate.

8For the next seven days, they celebrated the Tabernacle Festival, with large

6:31 where you tell them to go, or, "as long as they are living in this land which you gave to our fathers."

6:30
1 Sam 16:7
1 Chron 28:9

6:36
Job 15:14-16
Jas 3:2
1 Jn 1:8-10

6:40
2 Chron 7:15
Neh 1:6,11
Ps 17:1
6:41
Ps 132:8,9

7:1
1 Kgs 8:54
18:24,38
7:3
2 Chron 5:13
20:21
7:4
1 Kgs 8:62,63
7:6
1 Chron
15:16-21
2 Chron 5:12
7:7
1 Kgs 8:64-66
7:8
1 Kgs 8:65

6:30 Have you ever felt far from God, separated by feelings of failure and personal problems? In his prayer, Solomon underscores the fact that God stands ready to hear us, to forgive our sins, and to restore our relationship to him. God is waiting and listening for our confessions of guilt and willingness to obey him. He is ready to forgive us and restore us to fellowship with him. Don't wait to experience this loving forgiveness.

6:32, 33 A personal testimony is an effective method for convincing people to follow a cause or buy a product. When people see changed lives and watch God's power at work, they will come from far and wide to worship him. Those close to you should be able to see God at work in your life, in your words and in your actions. What kind of testimony do you give?

6:36 The Bible makes it clear that no one is exempt from sin, not even God's appointed kings. Sin is a condition we all share, and

we all should acknowledge it as Solomon did. This truth is also mentioned in Psalm 14:3, Ecclesiastes 7:20, and Romans 3:23.

7:1, 2 God sent fire from heaven to consume the offering and to begin the fire that was to burn continuously under the Altar of Burnt Offering. This symbolized God's presence. God did the same when inaugurating the Tabernacle (Leviticus 9:22-24). This was the real dedication of the Temple, because only the presence of God can make something holy.

7:4, 5 The Temple was dedicated to God, and Solomon and the people prepared to worship him. Dedication means setting apart a place, object, or person for an exclusive purpose. The purpose of this dedication was to set apart the Temple as a place to worship God. Today, our bodies are the temple of God (2 Corinthians 6:16). Solomon's dedication of the Temple is a picture of the way each of us should dedicate our lives for the special purpose God has in store for us.

crowds coming in from all over Israel; they arrived from as far away as Hamath at one end of the country to the brook of Egypt at the other. 9A final religious service was held on the eighth day. 10Then, on October 7, he sent the people home, joyful and happy because the Lord had been so good to David and Solomon and to his people Israel.

7:9
Lev 23:26

God speaks to Solomon

11So Solomon finished building the Temple as well as his own palace. He completed what he had planned to do.

12One night the Lord appeared to Solomon and told him, "I have heard your prayer and have chosen this Temple as the place where I want you to sacrifice to me. 13If I shut up the heavens so that there is no rain, or if I command the locust swarms to eat up all of your crops, or if I send an epidemic among you, 14then if my people will humble themselves and pray, and search for me, and turn from their wicked ways, I will hear them from heaven and forgive their sins and heal their land. 15I will listen, wide awake, to every prayer made in this place. 16For I have chosen this Temple and sanctified it to be my home forever; my eyes and my heart shall always be here.

7:13
2 Chron 6:26-28
7:14
2 Chron 6:37-39

7:15
2 Chron 6:20,40
7:16
2 Chron 7:12
7:18
2 Chron 6:16
7:19
Lev 26:14,33
Deut 28:15
7:20
Deut 28:37
29:28
1 Kgs 14:15
7:21
Deut 29:24,25

17"As for yourself, if you follow me as your father David did, 18then I will see to it that you and your descendants will always be the kings of Israel; 19but if you don't follow me, if you refuse the laws I have given you, and worship idols, 20then I will destroy my people from this land of mine which I have given them, and this Temple shall be destroyed even though I have sanctified it for myself. Instead, I will make it a public horror and disgrace. 21Instead of its being famous, all who pass by will be incredulous.

" 'Why has the Lord done such a terrible thing to this land and to this Temple?' they will ask.

22"And the answer will be, 'Because his people abandoned the Lord God of their fathers, the God who brought them out of the land of Egypt, and they worshiped other gods instead. That is why he has done all this to them.' "

4. Solomon's riches and wisdom
Solomon's building activities

8:1
1 Kgs 9:1-28

8 It was now twenty years since Solomon had become king, and the great building projects of the Lord's Temple and his own royal palace were completed. 2He now turned his energies to rebuilding the cities which King Hiram of Tyre had given to him, and he relocated some of the people of Israel into them. 3It was at this time, too, that Solomon fought against the city of Hamath-zobah and conquered it. 4He built Tadmor in the desert, and built cities in Hamath as supply centers. 5He fortified the cities of upper Beth-horon and lower Beth-horon, both

8:5
1 Chron 7:24
2 Chron 14:7

7:12 Months, maybe years, had passed since Solomon's prayer of dedication (chapter 6). Several other building projects had been completed after the Temple (7:11; 8:1). After all this time God told Solomon that he had heard his prayer. How often do we look for immediate answers to our prayers and, when nothing happens, wonder if God has heard us? God does hear, and we must trust that he will answer at the proper time.

7:14 In chapter 6, Solomon asked God to make provisions for the people when they sinned. God answered with four conditions for forgiveness: (1) humble yourself by admitting your sins, (2) pray to God, asking for forgiveness, (3) search for God continually, and (4) turn from sinful habits. True repentance is more than talk—it is changed behavior. Whether we sin individually, as a group, or as a nation, following these steps will lead to forgiveness.

7:15 When we are in need, there may be no one with whom we can talk, or we may be afraid to share our need with another person. God assures Solomon, however, that he will not lack assistance when he comes to God in humility, seeking help. God promises to listen to every prayer offered in the right attitude.

7:17–22 God plainly set forth certain conditions for Solomon to meet if he wanted the kingdom to continue. If he followed God, Solomon and his descendants would prosper; if he did not, he and the nation would be destroyed. In Deuteronomy 27 and 28, these conditions were outlined before all the people.

But sin is deceptively attractive, and Solomon eventually turned from God and his descendants lost most of his kingdom. Following God brings benefits and rewards. Turning away from him brings suffering, punishment, and ultimately destruction. Today, God's conditions are just as clear as they were in Solomon's day. Will you choose to obey God and live?

7:21, 22 Soon after Solomon's reign, the Temple was ransacked (12:9). It is difficult for us to imagine that such a great and wise king could become corrupted by idols. But even today idols lure us into their traps. When we deliberately bring anything into our lives that rivals God's proper place, we have taken the first step toward moral and spiritual decay.

being supply centers, building their walls and installing barred gates. 6He also built Baalath and other supply centers at this time, and constructed cities where his chariots and horses were kept. He built to his heart's desire in Jerusalem and Lebanon and throughout the entire realm.

7,8He began the practice that still continues of conscripting as slave laborers the Hittites, Amorites, Perizzites, Hivites, and Jebusites—the descendants of those nations which the Israelis had not completely wiped out. 9However, he didn't make slaves of any of the Israeli citizens, but used them as soldiers, officers, charioteers, and cavalrymen; 10also, two hundred fifty of them were government officials who administered all public affairs.

8:7
Gen 15:18-21
1 Kgs 3:1; 7:8

11Solomon now moved his wife (she was Pharaoh's daughter) from the City of David sector of Jerusalem to the new palace he had built for her. For he said, "She must not live in King David's palace, for the Ark of the Lord was there and it is holy ground."

8:11
1 Kgs 3:1; 7:8

12Then Solomon sacrificed burnt offerings to the Lord on the altar he had built in front of the porch of the Temple. 13The number of sacrifices differed from day to day in accordance with the instructions Moses had given; there were extra sacrifices on the Sabbaths, on new moon festivals, and at the three annual festivals—the Passover celebration, the Festival of Weeks, and the Festival of Tabernacles. 14In assigning the priests to their posts of duty he followed the organizational chart prepared by his father David; he also assigned the Levites to their work of praise and of helping the priests in each day's duties; and he assigned the gatekeepers to their gates. 15Solomon did not deviate in any way from David's instructions concerning these matters and concerning the treasury personnel. 16Thus Solomon successfully completed the construction of the Temple.

8:12
2 Chron 4:1
8:13
Ex 23:14-17
29:38-42
Num 28:3
8:14
1 Chron 24:1
25:1; 26:1
Neh 12:24,36

17,18Then he went to the seaport towns of Eziongeber and Eloth, in Edom, to launch a fleet presented to him by King Hiram. These ships, with King Hiram's experienced crews working alongside Solomon's men, went to Ophir and brought back to him several million dollars worth of gold on each trip!

8:17
1 Kgs 9:26
2 Kgs 14:22
2 Chron 9:10,13

The Queen of Sheba

9 When the Queen of Sheba heard of Solomon's fabled wisdom, she came to Jerusalem to test him with hard questions. A very great retinue of aides and servants accompanied her, including camel-loads of spices, gold, and jewels. 2And Solomon answered all her problems. Nothing was hidden from him; he could explain everything to her. 3When she discovered how wise he really was, and how breathtaking the beauty of his palace, 4and how wonderful the food at his tables, and how many servants and aides he had, and when she saw their spectacular

9:1
1 Kgs 10:1-13
Mt 12:42
Lk 11:31

8:11 Solomon married Pharaoh's daughter to secure a military alliance with Egypt. He did not let the woman live in David's palace, however, where the Ark of God had once been kept. This implies that Solomon knew his pagan marriage would not please God. Solomon married many other foreign women, and this was contrary to God's Law (Deuteronomy 7:3, 4). These foreign women worshiped false gods and were certain to contaminate Israel with their beliefs and practices. Eventually his pagan wives caused Solomon's downfall (1 Kings 11:1–11).

8:15 Although Solomon carefully followed God's instructions for building the Temple and offering sacrifices (8:13), he paid no attention to what God's Word said about marriage to heathen women. His sin in marrying a foreign wife (8:11) began his slide away from God. No matter how good or spiritual we are in most areas of life, one unsurrendered area can begin a downfall. Guard carefully *every* area of your life. Don't give sin any foothold.

9:1–8 The Queen of Sheba had heard about Solomon's wisdom, but she was overwhelmed when she saw for herself the fruits of that wisdom. Although Solomon had married Pharaoh's daughter, he still sincerely tried to follow God at this stage in his life. When

people get to know you and begin to ask hard questions, will your responses reflect God? Your life is your most powerful witness; let others see God at work in you.

9:2, 6 Ruling a nation is an awesome task. Solomon realized this when he exclaimed, "Who is able to govern by himself?" (1:10). But God had given him this responsibility, and he also gave Solomon the necessary leadership abilities to carry it out. Following Jesus' example also seems like a difficult task, but God has given you "everything you need for living a truly good life" (2 Peter 1:3). Never despair when you think you do not have the ability to surmount a problem. God will give you all you need to fulfill the responsibilities he has given you. Then, like the Queen of Sheba, others will be amazed at what they see.

9:3, 4 God had promised that Israel would prosper if Solomon followed him as David did (2 Chronicles 7:17). As long as Solomon remained loyal to God, God blessed Israel abundantly. God also honors his promises to us, and his Word is the guarantee. But any good guarantee includes certain conditions. God's promises and blessings are guaranteed as long as we do not break our agreement with him. If we do, the promises no longer apply and may even be used against us in judgment.

uniforms and his stewards in full regalia, and saw the size of the men in his bodyguard, she could scarcely believe it!

⁵Finally she exclaimed to the king, "Everything I heard about you in my own country is true! ⁶I didn't believe it until I got here and saw it with my own eyes. Your wisdom is far greater than I could ever have imagined. ⁷What a privilege for these men of yours to stand here and listen to you talk! ⁸Blessed be the Lord your God! How he must love Israel to give them a just king like you! He wants them to be a great, strong nation forever."

9:8
Deut 7:8
1 Chron 28:5
29:23
2 Chron 2:11

⁹She gave the king a gift of over a million dollars in gold, and great quantities of spices of incomparable quality, and many, many jewels.

9:10
2 Chron 8:18

¹⁰King Hiram's and King Solomon's crews brought gold from Ophir, also sandalwood and jewels. ¹¹The king used the sandalwood to make terraced steps for the Temple and the palace, and to construct harps and lyres for the choir. Never before had there been such beautiful instruments in all the land of Judah.

¹²King Solomon gave the Queen of Sheba gifts of the same value as she had brought to him, plus everything else she asked for! Then she and her retinue returned to their own land.

Solomon's greatness

9:13
1 Kgs 10:14-28

¹³, ¹⁴Solomon received a quarter of a billion dollars worth of gold each year from the kings of Arabia and many other lands that paid annual tribute to him. In addition, there was a trade balance from the exports of his merchants. ¹⁵He used some of the gold to make 200 large shields, each worth $100,000, ¹⁶and 300 smaller shields, each worth $50,000. The king placed these in the Forest of Lebanon Room in his palace. ¹⁷He also made a huge ivory throne overlaid with pure gold. ¹⁸It had six gold steps and a footstool of gold; also gold armrests, each flanked by a gold lion. ¹⁹Gold lions also stood at each side of each step. No other throne in all the world could be compared with it! ²⁰All of King Solomon's cups were solid gold, as were all the furnishings in the Forest of Lebanon Room. Silver was too cheap to count for much in those days!

9:21
2 Chron 20:36,
37
9:22
1 Kgs 3:13
2 Chron 1:12

²¹Every three years the king sent his ships to Tarshish, using sailors supplied by King Hiram, to bring back gold, silver, ivory, apes, and peacocks.

²²So King Solomon was richer and wiser than any other king in all the earth. ²³Kings from every nation came to visit him, and to hear the wisdom God had put into his heart. ²⁴Each brought him annual tribute of silver and gold bowls, clothing, armor, spices, horses, and mules.

9:25
Deut 17:16
1 Kgs 4:26
10:26
2 Chron 1:14
9:26
1 Kgs 4:21,24
9:27
2 Chron 1:15-17

²⁵In addition, Solomon had 4,000 stalls of horses and chariots, and 12,000 cavalrymen stationed in the chariot cities, as well as in Jerusalem to protect the king. ²⁶He ruled over all kings and kingdoms from the Euphrates River to the land of the Philistines and as far away as the border of Egypt. ²⁷He made silver become as plentiful in Jerusalem as stones in the road! And cedar was used as though it were common sycamore.

The death of Solomon

9:28
2 Chron 1:16
9:29
1 Kgs 11:41-43
1 Chron 29:29

²⁸Horses were brought to him from Egypt and other countries.

²⁹The rest of Solomon's biography is written in the history of Nathan the prophet and in the prophecy of Ahijah the Shilonite, and also in the visions of Iddo the seer concerning Jeroboam the son of Nebat.

9:31
1 Kgs 2:10

³⁰So Solomon reigned in Jerusalem over all of Israel for forty years. ³¹Then he died and was buried in Jerusalem, and his son Rehoboam became the new king.

9:8 The Queen of Sheba marveled at Solomon, claiming that God must love his people greatly to give them such a king. The good times are a witness of God's love and faithfulness. But hard times come to believers, too, and our perseverance and continued praise during those times will demonstrate our love and faithfulness to God. Our lives should help others see the loving relationship between God and his people. Good fortune can be a witness of God's love and faithfulness to us; perseverance during

hard times can be a witness of our love and faithfulness to him.

9:11 Sandalwood is a smooth, red-colored wood that accepts a high polish. This beautiful wood was extremely expensive.

9:29 For the rest of Solomon's story, see 1 Kings 10:26—11:43. In his later years, Solomon turned away from God and led the nation into worshiping idols.

B. THE KINGDOM OF JUDAH (10:1—36:23)

After Solomon's death, the northern tribes revolt and we read little more about them in 2 Chronicles. The remainder of 2 Chronicles recounts the alternating periods of apostasy and reform in Judah. In the end, Judah would not turn from its sin, and the tragic result was a 70-year captivity in Babylon. Sin in our lives will also lead to judgment and devastation. Although God's judgment may seem slow, it is nevertheless certain.

1. The nation of Israel splits apart

Rehoboam speaks roughly to the people

10 All the leaders of Israel came to Shechem for Rehoboam's coronation. 2, 3Meanwhile, friends of Jeroboam (son of Nebat) sent word to him of Solomon's death. He was in Egypt at the time, where he had gone to escape from King Solomon. He now quickly returned, and was present at the coronation, and led the people's demands on Rehoboam:

10:1
1 Kgs 12:1-20
10:2
1 Kgs 11:40

4"Your father was a hard master," they said. "Be easier on us than he was, and we will let you be our king!"

5Rehoboam told them to return in three days for his decision. 6He discussed their demand with the old men who had counseled his father Solomon.

"What shall I tell them?" he asked.

7"If you want to be their king," they replied, "you will have to give them a favorable reply and treat them with kindness."

8, 9But he rejected their advice and asked the opinion of the young men who had grown up with him. "What do you fellows think I should do?" he asked. "Shall I be easier on them than my father was?"

10"No!" they replied. "Tell them, 'If you think my father was hard on you, just wait and see what I'll be like!' Tell them, 'My little finger is thicker than my father's loins! 11I am going to be tougher on you, not easier! My father used whips on you, but I'll use scorpions!' "

12So when Jeroboam and the people returned in three days to hear King Rehoboam's decision, 13he spoke roughly to them; for he refused the advice of the old men, 14and followed the counsel of the younger ones.

"My father gave you heavy burdens but I will give you heavier!" he told them. "My father punished you with whips, but I will punish you with scorpions!"

The northern tribes revolt

15So the king turned down the people's demands. (God caused him to do it in order to fulfill his prediction spoken to Jeroboam by Ahijah, the Shilonite.) 16When

10:15
1 Kgs 11:29-39

10:15 *to fulfill his prediction,* see 1 Kgs 11:30, 31.

10:1 The crowning of an Israelite king would normally have taken place in Jerusalem, the capital city. But Rehoboam saw that there was the possibility of trouble in the north; so to maintain his hold on the country, he chose Shechem, a city about 35 miles north of Jerusalem. Shechem was an ancient site for making covenants (Joshua 24:1).

10:1–14 Following bad advice can cause disaster. Rehoboam lost the chance to rule a peaceful, united kingdom because he rejected the advice of Solomon's older counselors, preferring that of his peers. Rehoboam made two errors in seeking advice: (1) he did not give extra consideration to the suggestions of those who knew the situation better than he, and (2) he did not ask God for wisdom to discern which was the better option.

It is easy to follow the advice of our peers because they often feel as we do. But their view may be limited. It is important to listen carefully to those who have more experience than we do and can therefore see the bigger picture.

10:2, 3 Ahijah the prophet had predicted that Israel would split in two and that Jeroboam would become king of the northern section. When Solomon learned of this prophecy, he tried to kill Jeroboam, and Jeroboam was forced to flee to Egypt (1 Kings 11:26–40).

10:14 Rehoboam must have gotten an unbalanced picture of leadership from Solomon. Apparently Rehoboam saw only the difficulty of leading the nation, not the blessings. He mentioned only the harsher aspects of Solomon's rule, and he himself decided to be very harsh toward the people. As you discuss your responsibilities with your children, be sure that you temper words of complaint with words of joy. Otherwise you may sour the attitudes of your children toward those you serve.

10:16–19 In trying to have it all, Rehoboam lost almost everything. Motivated by greed and power, he pressed too hard and divided his kingdom. He didn't need more money or power because he had inherited the richest kingdom in the world. He didn't need more control because the land had peace. His demands were based on selfishness rather than reason or spiritual discernment. Those who insist on having it all often wind up with little or nothing.

10:16–19 Here is the beginning of the divided kingdom. The peaceful united kingdom under Solomon was now divided into two parts: ten of the tribes followed Jeroboam and called their nation Israel, or the Northern Kingdom. The other two tribes, Judah and Benjamin, remained loyal to David's line and accepted Rehoboam's rule. They called their nation Judah, or the Southern Kingdom.

10:16
2 Sam 20:1
2 Chron 10:19

the people realized what the king was saying they turned their backs and deserted him.

"Forget David and his dynasty!" they shouted angrily. "We'll get someone else to be our king. Let Rehoboam rule his own tribe of Judah! Let's go home!" So they did.

17The people of the tribe of Judah, however, remained loyal to Rehoboam.

10:18
1 Kgs 4:6; 5:14

18Afterwards, when King Rehoboam sent Hadoram to draft forced labor from the other tribes of Israel, the people stoned him to death. When this news reached King Rehoboam he jumped into his chariot and fled to Jerusalem. 19And Israel has refused to be ruled by a descendant of David to this day.

Judah is forbidden to reunite the kingdom

11:1
1 Kgs 12:21-24

11 Upon arrival at Jerusalem, Rehoboam mobilized the armies of Judah and Benjamin, 180,000 strong, and declared war against the rest of Israel in an attempt to reunite the kingdom.

11:2
2 Chron 12:5-7,
15

2But the Lord told Shemaiah the prophet,

REHOBOAM

Settling for cheap imitations in exchange for the real thing is a poor way to live. Rehoboam consistently traded away what was real for what was counterfeit. Given wise and unwise counsel by his advisors, he chose to grab for power rather than to take the counsel of those older and wiser than he. Although his position came from God, he chose to abandon God. These unwise decisions made him weaker rather than stronger. As a result, he was invaded by the Egyptians and stripped of the riches he inherited from David and Solomon. To replace them, he had cheap bronze copies made.

Throughout the early part of his reign, Rehoboam fluctuated between obedience to God and going his own way. Godly outward appearances were kept up, but his inward attitudes were evil. Following in the tradition of David and Solomon gave Rehoboam opportunities for greatness. Instead, he ended up with a divided and broken kingdom.

How much of real living have we traded away for the things which do not last? We trade healthy bodies for momentary excitement, personal integrity for fast-fading wealth, honesty for dishonesty, God's wise guidance for our selfish ways. We sin when we willingly give little value to "the real thing" God has already given us.

Our counterfeit lives may fool some people, but they never fool God. Yet in spite of what he sees in us, God offers mercy. Are you a self-managed enterprise, counterfeit at best? Or have you placed yourself in God's care? Do the decisions you must make today need a second consideration in light of Rehoboam's example?

Strengths and accomplishments:
• Third and last king of the united nation of Israel, but only for a short time
• Fortified his kingdom and achieved a measure of popularity

Weaknesses and mistakes:
• Followed unwise advice and divided his kingdom
• Married heathen women like his father Solomon
• Abandoned the worship of God and allowed idolatry to flourish

Lessons from his life:
• Thoughtless decisions often lead to losing what is most valuable in exchange for something of far less value
• Every choice we make has real and long-lasting consequences

Vital statistics:
• Where: Jerusalem
• Occupation: King of the united kingdom of Israel, and later of the Southern Kingdom of Judah
• Relatives: Father: Solomon. Mother: Naamah. Son: Abijah. Wife: Maacah.
• Contemporaries: Jeroboam, Shishak, Shemaiah

Key verse:
"But just when Rehoboam was at the height of his popularity and power he abandoned the Lord, and the people followed him in this sin" (2 Chronicles 12:1).

Rehoboam's story is told in 1 Kings 11:43—14:31 and 2 Chronicles 9:31—13:7. He is also mentioned in Matthew 1:7.

11:1 Rehoboam's foolishness divided his kingdom, and he tried to reunite it with force. True unity, however, cannot be forced—it must be the free response of willing hearts. If you want the loyalty of employees, children, or anyone else in your charge, win their respect through love instead of trying to gain their submission through force.

³"Go and say to King Rehoboam of Judah, Solomon's son, and to the people of Judah and of Benjamin:

⁴" 'The Lord says, Do not fight against your brothers. Go home, for I am behind their rebellion.' " So they obeyed the Lord and refused to fight against Jeroboam.

⁵⁻¹⁰Rehoboam stayed in Jerusalem and fortified these cities of Judah with walls and gates to protect himself: Bethlehem, Etam, Tekoa, Beth-zur, Soco, Adullam, Gath, Mareshah, Ziph, Adoraim, Lachish, Azekah, Zorah, Aijalon, and Hebron.

¹¹He also rebuilt and strengthened the forts, and manned them with companies of soldiers under their officers, and stored them with food, olive oil, and wine. ¹²Shields and spears were placed in armories in every city as a further safety measure. For only Judah and Benjamin remained loyal to him.

Priests and Levites move to Judah

¹³, ¹⁴However, the priests and Levites from the other tribes now abandoned their homes and moved to Judah and Jerusalem, for King Jeroboam had fired them, telling them to stop being priests of the Lord. ¹⁵He had appointed other priests instead who encouraged the people to worship idols instead of God, and to sacrifice to carved statues of goats and calves which he placed on the hills. ¹⁶Laymen, too, from all over Israel began moving to Jerusalem where they could freely worship the Lord God of their fathers, and sacrifice to him. ¹⁷This strengthened the kingdom of Judah, so King Rehoboam survived for three years without difficulty; for during those years there was an earnest effort to obey the Lord as King David and King Solomon had done.

2. History of apostasy and reform
Rehoboam rules Judah

¹⁸Rehoboam married his cousin Mahalath. She was the daughter of David's son Jerimoth and of Abihail, the daughter of David's brother Eliab. ¹⁹Three sons were born from this marriage—Jeush, Shemariah, and Zaham.

²⁰Later he married Maacah, the daughter of Absalom. The children she bore him were Abijah, Attai, Ziza, and Shelomith. ²¹He loved Maacah more than any of his other wives and concubines (he had eighteen wives and sixty concubines—with twenty-eight sons and sixty daughters). ²²Maacah's son Abijah was his favorite, and he intended to make him the next king. ²³He very wisely scattered his other sons in the fortified cities throughout the land of Judah and Benjamin, and gave them large allowances and arranged for them to have several wives apiece.

Egypt conquers Jerusalem

12 But just when Rehoboam was at the height of his popularity and power he abandoned the Lord, and the people followed him in this sin. ²As a result,

11:4   2 Chron 10:15; 28:8-11
11:5   2 Chron 8:2-6; 11:23
11:13   Num 35:2-5; 1 Kgs 12:28-33; 2 Chron 13:9
11:15   1 Kgs 12:31; 13:33
11:16   2 Chron 15:9
11:17   2 Chron 12:1
11:18   1 Sam 16:6
11:21   Deut 17:17
11:22   Deut 21:15-17
12:1   2 Chron 11:17

11:17 *as King David and King Solomon had done*, literally, "they walked in the way of David and Solomon."
11:18 *Rehoboam married his cousin*, implied.

11:4 Why would God support this rebellion? It was part of the nation's punishment for turning away from God (1 Kings 11:11). It may also have been God's way of preserving Rehoboam's smaller kingdom from defeat. In doing so, God preserved David's line and kept intact his plan for the Messiah to be a descendant of David (see 2 Samuel 7:16). When we see division, especially in a church that splits, we wonder what God would have us do. God desires unity, and while we should always work toward reconciliation, we must recognize that only God knows the future. He may allow a division in order to fulfill his greater purposes.

11:13, 14 Before the nation split, the center of worship was in Jerusalem, and people flocked there for the three great annual religious festivals. During the rest of the year, other worship services and rituals were conducted in the tribal territories by priests and Levites who lived throughout the land. They offered sacrifices, taught God's laws, and encouraged the people to continue to follow God and avoid pagan influences.

After the nation split, Jeroboam, the new king of Israel, saw these priests and Levites as a threat to his new government because they retained loyalty to Jerusalem, now the capital of Judah. So he appointed his own priests, effectively banning the Levites from their duties and forcing them to move to the Southern Kingdom. Jeroboam's pagan priests encouraged idol worship. With the absence of spiritual leaders, the new Northern Kingdom was in danger of abandoning God.

11:16 These laymen obeyed God rather than King Jeroboam. By their action, they preserved their integrity and strengthened the Southern Kingdom. In the future, most of the people in the Northern Kingdom would cooperate with the evil designs of the kings, hoping to benefit by going along with their plans. We should not rationalize away God's teachings in order to gain earthly reward.

12:1 During his first three years on the throne Rehoboam made an attempt to obey God, and as a result Judah prospered. But then, at the peak of his popularity and power, he abandoned God

12:3
2 Chron 16:8
Nah 3:9

12:4
2 Chron 11:5-12

12:5
Deut 28:15
2 Chron 11:2
15:2

12:6
Ex 9:27
Dan 9:14

12:7
1 Kgs 21:29
2 Chron
34:25-27
Ps 78:38

12:8
Deut 28:47,48

12:9
1 Kgs 14:26-28
2 Chron 9:15,16

12:12
2 Chron 12:6,7

12:13
1 Kgs 14:21

12:14
2 Chron 19:3

12:15
1 Kgs 14:29
2 Chron 9:29
12:5

12:16
2 Chron 11:20

13:1
1 Kgs 15:1,2,7
2 Chron 11:20

King Shishak of Egypt attacked Jerusalem in the fifth year of King Rehoboam's reign, ³with twelve hundred chariots, sixty thousand cavalrymen and an unnumbered host of infantrymen—Egyptians, Libyans, Sukkiim, and Ethiopians. ⁴He quickly conquered Judah's fortified cities and soon arrived at Jerusalem.

⁵The prophet Shemaiah now met with Rehoboam and the Judean leaders from every part of the nation (they had fled to Jerusalem for safety), and told them, "The Lord says, 'You have forsaken me, so I have forsaken you and abandoned you to Shishak.'"

⁶Then the king and the leaders of Israel confessed their sins and exclaimed, "The Lord is right in doing this to us!"

⁷And when the Lord saw them humble themselves he sent Shemaiah to tell them, "Because you have humbled yourselves, I will not completely destroy you; some will escape. I will not use Shishak to pour out my anger upon Jerusalem. ⁸But you must pay annual tribute to him. Then you will realize how much better it is to serve me than to serve him!"

⁹So King Shishak of Egypt conquered Jerusalem and took away all the treasures of the Temple and of the palace, also all of Solomon's gold shields. ¹⁰King Rehoboam replaced them with bronze shields and committed them to the care of the captain of his bodyguard. ¹¹Whenever the king went to the Temple, the guards would carry them, and afterwards return them to the armory. ¹²When the king humbled himself, the Lord's anger was turned aside and he didn't send total destruction; in fact, even after Shishak's invasion, the economy of Judah remained strong.

¹³King Rehoboam reigned seventeen years in Jerusalem, the city God had chosen as his residence after considering all the other cities of Israel. He had become king at the age of forty-one, and his mother's name was Naamah the Ammonitess. ¹⁴But he was an evil king, for he never did decide really to please the Lord. ¹⁵The complete biography of Rehoboam is recorded in the histories written by Shemaiah the prophet and by Iddo the seer, and in *The Genealogical Register*. There were continual wars between Rehoboam and Jeroboam. ¹⁶When Rehoboam died he was buried in Jerusalem, and his son Abijah became the new king.

Abijah defeats Jeroboam

13 Abijah became the new king of Judah, in Jerusalem, in the eighteenth year of the reign of King Jeroboam of Israel. He lasted three years. His mother's name was Micaiah (daughter of Uriel of Gibeah).

Early in his reign war broke out between Judah and Israel. ³Judah, led by King

---

and the result was destruction. Soon God allowed Judah to be conquered by Egypt. We cannot expect God to protect us if we abandon him, but he loves to intervene on our behalf when we follow him.

12:1 At the height of his popularity and power, Rehoboam abandoned the Lord. What happened? Often it is more difficult to be a believer in good times than in bad. Tough times push us toward God; but easy times can make us feel self-sufficient and self-satisfied. When everything is going right, guard your faith.

12:2 A record of this invasion has been found on an Egyptian stone which says that King Shishak's army penetrated as far north as the Sea of Galilee, in the Northern Kingdom. Egypt was not the world power it had once been, and Shishak wanted to restore his nation to its former greatness. He was not strong enough to conquer both Israel and Judah, but he managed to destroy key cities in Judah in an effort to regain control of the trade routes.

12:6-8 God eased his judgment when Israel's leaders confessed their sins, humbled themselves, and recognized God's justice in punishing them. It's never too late to repent, even in the midst of punishment. Are you struggling alone because sin has severed your fellowship with God? Confession and humility will restore your relationship with him.

12:8 The tribute was the price Judah had to pay for disobeying God. The nation's leaders thought they could succeed in their own strength, but they were wrong. When we rebel against God, we always pay for it. When we leave God out of our lives, we lose more spiritually than we ever gain in worldly goods.

12:10, 11 How ironic that the pure gold of Solomon's Temple was replaced by cheaper bronze. Rehoboam tried to maintain the trappings and appearance of former glory, but he couldn't measure up. When God is no longer central in our lives, maintaining the appearance of a Christian life becomes superficial. Outer beauty must come from inner strength.

12:14 Rehoboam's life was a tragedy because he "never did decide really to please the Lord." God asks us for a firm commitment, and unless we decide to give him our lives, we will drift into evil living and separation from him.

13:1ff In 1 Kings 15:3, Abijah is called a great sinner, but in the Chronicles account only positive things are said about him. For the most part, Abijah was no doubt a wicked king. The writer of Chronicles chose to highlight the little good he did in order to show that he was still under God's covenant promise to David. Because of Abijah's stormy speech to Jeroboam (13:5–12), he was spared the immediate consequences of his sin.

Abijah, fielded 400,000 seasoned warriors against twice as many Israeli troops—strong, courageous men led by King Jeroboam. 4When the army of Judah arrived at Mount Zemaraim, in the hill country of Ephraim, King Abijah shouted to King Jeroboam and the Israeli army:

13:4
Josh 18:22

5"Listen! Don't you realize that the Lord God of Israel swore that David's descendants would always be the kings of Israel? 6Your King Jeroboam is a mere servant of David's son, and was a traitor to his master. 7Then a whole gang of worthless rebels joined him, defying Solomon's son Rehoboam, for he was young and frightened and couldn't stand up to them. 8Do you really think you can defeat the kingdom of the Lord that is led by a descendant of David? Your army is twice as large as mine, but you are cursed with those gold calves you have with you, that Jeroboam made for you—he calls them your gods! 9And you have driven away the priests of the Lord and the Levites, and have appointed heathen priests instead. Just like the people of other lands, you accept as priests anybody who comes along with a young bullock and seven rams for consecration. Anyone at all can be a priest of these no-gods of yours!

13:5
Num 18:19
2 Sam 7:12-16
13:6
1 Kgs 11:26
13:7
2 Chron 12:13
13:8
1 Kgs 12:28
2 Chron 11:15
13:9
Ex 29:29-33
2 Chron 11:14
Jer 2:11; 5:7

10"But as for us, the Lord is our God and we have not forsaken him. Only the descendants of Aaron are our priests, and the Levites alone may help them in their work. 11They burn sacrifices to the Lord every morning and evening—burnt offerings and sweet incense; and they place the Bread of the Presence upon the holy table. The gold lampstand is lighted every night, for we are careful to follow the instructions of the Lord our God; but you have forsaken him. 12So you see, God is with us; he is our Leader. His priests, trumpeting as they go, will lead us into battle against you. O people of Israel, do not fight against the Lord God of your fathers, for you will not succeed!"

13:11
Ex 25:30-39
29:38
Lev 24:5-9
2 Chron 2:4
13:12
Num 10:8,9

13, 14Meanwhile, Jeroboam had secretly sent part of his army around behind the men of Judah to ambush them; so Judah was surrounded, with the enemy before and behind them. Then they cried out to the Lord for mercy, and the priests blew the trumpets. 15, 16The men of Judah began to shout. And as they shouted, God used King Abijah and the men of Judah to turn the tide of battle against King Jeroboam and the army of Israel, 17and they slaughtered 500,000 elite troops of Israel that day.

13:13
Josh 8:4-9
2 Chron 14:11

13:15
2 Chron 16:8

18, 19So Judah, depending upon the Lord God of their fathers, defeated Israel, and chased King Jeroboam's troops, and captured some of his cities—Bethel, Jeshanah, Ephron, and their suburbs. 20King Jeroboam of Israel never regained his power during Abijah's lifetime, and eventually the Lord struck him and he died. 21Meanwhile, King Abijah of Judah became very strong. He married fourteen wives and had twenty-two sons and sixteen daughters. 22His complete biography and speeches are recorded in the prophet Iddo's *History of Judah*.

13:18
2 Chron 14:11

13:20
1 Sam 25:38
1 Kgs 14:20

13:22
2 Chron 9:20
24:27

Asa rules Judah

14 King Abijah was buried in Jerusalem. Then his son Asa became the new king of Judah, and there was peace in the land for the first ten years of his reign, 2for Asa was careful to obey the Lord his God. 3He demolished the heathen altars

14:1
1 Kgs 15:8
14:3
1 Kgs 15:12-14

13:8 Jeroboam's army was cursed because of the gold calves they carried with them. It was as though they had put sin into a physical form so they could haul it around. Consider carefully the things you cherish. If you value anything more than God, it becomes your golden calf and will one day condemn you. Let go of anything that interferes with your relationship with God.

13:9 Abijah criticized Jeroboam's low standards in appointing priests. Anyone is qualified to represent a god that is worthless. To represent the Lord God, however, one must live by his standards, not man's. Those appointed to positions of responsibility in your church should not be selected based on the fact that they volunteer, are influential, or are highly educated. Instead they must demonstrate sound doctrine, dedication to God, and strong spiritual character (1 Timothy 3). Only a holy person can faithfully represent the holy God.

13:18, 19 Although outnumbered by Israel, Judah won this conflict by depending on God's help. Some kings in Judah's history focused on God, but not one Israelite king consistently followed God. All followed Jeroboam's idolatry or served Baal. As a result, Israel experienced God's judgment years before Judah did.

Judah had an advantage—the Temple with its loyal priests and prophets and the sacrifices were kept under the Southern Kingdom's supervision. Many of Judah's kings were good, at least for parts of their reigns. Whenever an idolatrous king reigned, his rule was followed by that of a good king who reformed religious life. Also the idolatrous kings usually served for a much shorter time than the good ones. The result was that true faith in God ran stronger and deeper in Judah than in Israel, but it was still not up to God's standards.

14:1-6 Asa's reign was marked by peace because he was

on the hills, and broke down the obelisks, and chopped down the shameful
Asherim-idols, 4and demanded that the entire nation obey the commandments of
the Lord God of their ancestors. 5Also, he removed the sun-images from the hills,
and the incense altars from every one of Judah's cities. That is why God gave his
kingdom peace. 6This made it possible for him to build walled cities throughout
Judah.

14:5
2 Chron 15:15
34:4,7
14:6
2 Chron 11:5

ASA

God has never accepted the idea that "the ends justify the means." He is just and perfect
in all his ways. People, on the other hand, are far from perfect. That a bond can exist
between a loving and merciful Creator and a resisting and rebellious creation is as great
a miracle as creation itself! As a king, Asa came very close to being good. He traveled a
long way with God before getting off track. His sin was not so much deliberate
disobedience as it was choosing the *easy* way rather than the *right* way.

When the odds seemed impossible in the battle with the Ethiopians, Asa recognized
his need to depend on God. Following that victory, God's promise of peace based on
obedience spurred the king and people to many years of right living. But Asa was to face
a tougher test.

Years of animosity between Asa and Israel's king Baasha took an ugly turn. Baasha,
king of the rival Northern Kingdom, was building a fort that threatened both the peace
and economy of Judah. Asa thought he saw a way out—he bribed King Ben-hadad of
Syria to break his alliance with King Baasha. The plan worked brilliantly, but it wasn't
God's way. When Asa was confronted by God's prophet Hanani, he flew into a rage,
jailed Hanani, and took out his anger on his people. Asa rejected correction and refused
to admit his error to God. His greatest failure was missing what God could have done
with his life if he had been willing to be humble. His pride ruined the health of his reign.
He stubbornly held on to his failure until his death.

Does this attitude sound familiar? Can you identify failures in your life that you have
continued to rationalize rather than admit them to God and accept his forgiveness? The
ends do not justify the means. Such a belief leads to sin and failure. The stubborn refusal
to admit a failure due to sin can become a big problem because it makes you spend time
rationalizing rather than learning from your mistakes and moving on.

Strengths and accomplishments:
- Obeyed God during the first ten years of his reign
- Carried out a partially successful effort to abolish idolatry
- Deposed his idolatrous grandmother Maacah
- Defeated Ethiopia's mighty army

Weaknesses and mistakes:
- Responded with rage when confronted about his sin
- Made alliances with heathen nations and evil people

Lessons from his life:
- God not only reinforces good, he confronts evil
- Efforts to follow God's plans and rules yield positive results
- How well a plan works is no measure of its rightness or approval by God

Vital statistics:
- Where: Jerusalem
- Occupation: King of Judah
- Relatives: Grandmother: Maacah. Father: Abijah. Son: Jehoshaphat.
- Contemporaries: Hanani, Ben-hadad, Zerah, Azariah, Baasha

Key verse:
"For the eyes of the Lord search back and forth across the whole earth, looking for
people whose hearts are perfect toward him, so that he can show his great power in
helping them. What a fool you have been! From now on you shall have wars"
(2 Chronicles 16:9).

Asa's story is told in 1 Kings 15:8—24 and 2 Chronicles 14—16. He is also mentioned
in Jeremiah 41:9; Matthew 1:7.

"careful to obey the Lord his God." This refrain is often repeated in
Chronicles— *obedience* to God leads to *peace* with God and
others. In the case of Judah's kings, obedience to God led to
national peace, just as God had promised centuries earlier. In our
case, obedience may not always bring peace with our enemies,
but it will bring peace with God and complete peace in his future
kingdom. The first steps to peace are steps of obedience to God.

14:3-5 Simply attending worship services is not enough to secure
God's peace. Like Asa, we must also actively remove anything that
is offensive to God. Becoming more active in church attendance or
good works will still leave us in turmoil if we have failed to eliminate
sinful practices from our lives. All believers should continually ask
God to help them remove any such obstacles in their lives.

⁷"Now is the time to do it, while the Lord is blessing us with peace because of our obedience to him," he told his people. "Let us build and fortify cities now, with walls, towers, gates, and bars." So they went ahead with these projects very successfully.

⁸King Asa's Judean army was 300,000 strong, equipped with light shields and spears. His army of Benjaminites numbered 280,000, armed with large shields and bows. Both armies were composed of well-trained, brave men.

⁹, ¹⁰But now he was attacked by an army of 1,000,000 troops from Ethiopia with 300 chariots, under the leadership of General Zerah. They advanced to the city of Mareshah, in the valley of Zephathah, and King Asa sent his troops to battle with them there.

¹¹"O Lord," he cried out to God, "no one else can help us! Here we are, powerless against this mighty army. Oh, help us, Lord our God! For we trust in you alone to rescue us, and in your name we attack this vast horde. Don't let mere men defeat you!"

¹²Then the Lord defeated the Ethiopians, and Asa and the army of Judah triumphed as the Ethiopians fled. ¹³They chased them as far as Gerar, and the entire Ethiopian army was wiped out so that not one man remained; for the Lord and his army destroyed them all. Then the army of Judah carried off vast quantities of plunder. ¹⁴While they were at Gerar they attacked all the cities in that area, and terror from the Lord came upon the residents. As a result, additional vast quantities of plunder were collected from these cities too. ¹⁵They not only plundered the cities, but destroyed the cattle tents and captured great herds of sheep and camels before finally returning to Jerusalem.

Asa rebuilds the altar

15 Then the Spirit of God came upon Azariah (son of Oded), ²and he went out to meet King Asa as he was returning from the battle.

"Listen to me, Asa! Listen, armies of Judah and Benjamin!" he shouted. "The Lord will stay with you as long as you stay with him! Whenever you look for him, you will find him. But if you forsake him, he will forsake you. ³For a long time now, over in Israel, the people haven't worshiped the true God, and have not had a true priest to teach them. They have lived without God's laws. ⁴But whenever

14:7
2 Chron 8:5

14:8
2 Chron 13:3

14:9
2 Chron 11:8
12:2,3; 16:8

14:11
2 Chron 13:14,
18

14:12
2 Chron 13:15
14:13
Gen 10:19

14:14
2 Chron 17:10

15:1
2 Chron 20:14
24:20

15:2
2 Chron 15:4,
15; 20:17

15:3
Lev 10:8-11
1 Kgs 12:28-33
2 Chron 17:9

14:7 Times of peace are not just for resting. They allow us to prepare for times of trouble. King Abijah recognized the period of peace as the right time to build his defenses. He knew that it was too late to prepare defenses at the moment of attack. It is also difficult to withstand spiritual attack unless defenses are prepared beforehand. Decisions about what to do when temptations arise must be made with a cool head in the peace of untroubled moments, long before the heat of temptation is upon us. Build your defenses now before temptation strikes.

14:11 If you are facing battles you feel you can't possibly win, don't give up. In the face of vast hordes of enemy soldiers, Asa prayed for God's help, recognizing his powerlessness against such a mighty army. The secret to victory is first recognizing the futility of unaided human effort and then trusting God to save. His power works best through those who recognize their limitations (2 Corinthians 12:9). It is those who think they can do it all who are in the greatest danger.

15:1, 2 Asa wisely welcomed people who had a close relationship with God, and he listened to their messages. Azariah gave the armies an important warning and encouraged them to stay close to God. Keep in contact with people who are filled with God's Spirit, and you will learn God's counsel. Spend regular time in discussion and prayer with those who can help explain God's message.

15:3 Azariah said that Israel, the Northern Kingdom, no longer worshiped God. Eight kings reigned in Israel during the 41-year rule of Asa, and all eight were evil. Jeroboam, the first ruler of

ASA'S BATTLES
A huge army from Ethiopia under General Zerah advanced toward Mareshah, greatly outnumbering King Asa's army. Asa sent his troops to meet them, and the battle took place in the Valley of Zephathah. Asa prayed to God, and the Ethiopians were defeated and chased as far as Gerar.

Israel, began this wicked trend by setting up idols and expelling God's priests (11:13–15). Azariah used Israel's problems as an example of the evil that would come to Judah if they turned away from God as their northern brothers had.

15:4
Deut 4:29

15:7
Josh 1:7,9

15:8
2 Chron 4:1
8:12; 13:19

15:9
2 Chron 11:16

15:11
2 Chron
14:13-15

15:12
2 Chron 23:16

15:13
Ex 22:20
Deut 13:6-9

15:15
2 Chron 14:7

15:16
Ex 34:13
1 Kgs 15:13-15
2 Chron 14:2-5

16:1
1 Kgs 15:17-22

16:4
Ex 1:11

they have turned again to the Lord God of Israel in their distress, and searched for him, he has helped them. 5In their times of rebellion against God there was no peace. Problems troubled the nation on every hand. Crime was on the increase everywhere. 6There were external wars, and internal fighting of city against city, for God was plaguing them with all sorts of trouble. 7But you men of Judah, keep up the good work and don't get discouraged, for you will be rewarded."

8When King Asa heard this message from God, he took courage and destroyed all the idols in the land of Judah and Benjamin, and in the cities he had captured in the hill country of Ephraim, and he rebuilt the altar of the Lord in front of the Temple.

9Then he summoned all the people of Judah and Benjamin, and the immigrants from Israel (for many had come from the territories of Ephraim, Manasseh, and Simeon, in Israel, when they saw that the Lord God was with King Asa). 10They all came to Jerusalem in June of the fifteenth year of King Asa's reign, 11and sacrificed to the Lord seven hundred oxen and seven thousand sheep—it was part of the plunder they had captured in the battle. 12Then they entered into a contract to worship only the Lord God of their fathers, 13and agreed that anyone who refused to do this must die—whether old or young, man or woman. 14They shouted out their oath of loyalty to God with trumpets blaring and horns sounding. 15All were happy for this covenant with God, for they had entered into it with all their hearts and wills, and wanted him above everything else, and they found him! And he gave them peace throughout the nation.

16King Asa even removed his mother Maacah from being the queen mother because she made an Asherah-idol; he cut down the idol and crushed and burned it at Kidron Brook. 17Over in Israel the idol-temples were not removed. But here in Judah and Benjamin the heart of King Asa was perfect before God throughout his lifetime. 18He brought back into the Temple the silver and gold bowls which he and his father had dedicated to the Lord. 19So there was no more war until the thirty-fifth year of King Asa's reign.

Asa forgets God

16 In the thirty-sixth year of King Asa's reign, King Baasha of Israel declared war on him and built the fortress of Ramah in order to control the road to Judah. 2Asa's response was to take the silver and gold from the Temple and from the palace, and to send it to King Ben-hadad of Syria, at Damascus, with this message:

3"Let us renew the mutual security pact that there was between your father and my father. See, here is silver and gold to induce you to break your alliance with King Baasha of Israel, so that he will leave me alone."

4Ben-hadad agreed to King Asa's request and mobilized his armies to attack Israel. They destroyed the cities of Ijon, Dan, Abel-maim and all of the supply centers in Naphtali. 5As soon as King Baasha of Israel heard what was happening, he discontinued building Ramah and gave up his plan to attack Judah. 6Then King

16:1 *built the fortress,* literally, "high places."

15:7 Azariah encouraged the men of Judah to "keep up the good work . . . for you will be rewarded." This is an inspiration for us too. Recognition and reward are great motivators that have two dimensions: (1) *The temporal dimension.* A life lived by God's standards may result in acclaim here on earth. (2) *The eternal dimension.* But permanent recognition and reward will be given in the next life. Don't be discouraged if you feel your faith in God is going unrewarded here on earth. The best rewards are not in this life, but in the life to come.

15:14, 15 Many people find it difficult to commit themselves to anything. They are tentative, indecisive, and afraid of responsibility. Asa and his people were different—they had undivided hearts and clearly declared themselves for God. Their

oath was punctuated with shouts and trumpet blasts! This decisive and wholehearted commitment pleased God and resulted in peace for the nation. If you want peace in your life, check to see if there is some area where total commitment to God is lacking. Peace comes as a by-product of committing our lives wholeheartedly to God.

15:16 The Ten Commandments tell us to honor our father and mother, and yet Asa removed his mother from the throne. While honoring parents is God's command, maintaining loyalty to God is an even higher priority. Jesus warned that respect for parents should never keep us from following him (Luke 14:26). If you have unbelieving parents, you must respect and honor them, but not allow them to alter your devotion to God.

Asa and the people of Judah went out to Ramah and carried away the building stones and timbers and used them to build Geba and Mizpah instead.

7About that time the prophet Hanani came to King Asa and told him, "Because you have put your trust in the king of Syria instead of in the Lord your God, the army of the king of Syria has escaped from you. 8Don't you remember what happened to the Ethiopians and Libyans and their vast army, with all of their chariots and cavalrymen? But you relied then on the Lord, and he delivered them all into your hand. 9For the eyes of the Lord search back and forth across the whole earth, looking for people whose hearts are perfect toward him, so that he can show his great power in helping them. What a fool you have been! From now on you shall have wars."

10Asa was so angry with the prophet for saying this that he threw him into jail. And Asa oppressed all the people at that time.

11The rest of the biography of Asa is written in *The Annals of the Kings of Israel and Judah.* 12In the thirty-ninth year of his reign, Asa became seriously diseased in his feet but he didn't go to the Lord with the problem, but to the doctors. 13, 14So he died in the forty-first year of his reign, and was buried in his own vault that he had hewn out for himself in Jerusalem. He was laid on a bed perfumed with sweet spices and ointments, and his people made a very great burning of incense for him at his funeral.

16:7
1 Kgs 16:1
2 Chron 14:11
19:2; 32:7,8

16:8
2 Chron 12:3
13:16,18; 14:9

16:9
2 Chron 15:17
Prov 15:3
Zech 4:10

16:11
1 Kgs 15:23,24

16:13
Gen 50:2
2 Chron 21:19
Jn 12:1-7
19:39,40

Jehoshaphat rules Judah

17 Then his son Jehoshaphat became the king and mobilized for war against Israel. 2He placed garrisons in all of the fortified cities of Judah, in various other places throughout the country, and in the cities of Ephraim that his father had conquered.

3The Lord was with Jehoshaphat because he followed in the good footsteps of his father's early years, and did not worship idols. 4He obeyed the commandments of his father's God—quite unlike the people across the border in the land of Israel. 5So the Lord strengthened his position as king of Judah. All the people of Judah cooperated by paying their taxes, so he became very wealthy as well as being very popular. 6He boldly followed the paths of God—even knocking down the heathen altars on the hills, and destroying the Asherim idols.

7, 8, 9In the third year of his reign he began a nationwide religious education program. He sent out top government officials as teachers in all the cities of Judah. These men included Ben-hail, Obadiah, Zechariah, Nethanel, and Micaiah. He also used the Levites for this purpose, including Shemaiah, Nethaniah, Zebadiah, Asahel, Shemiramoth, Jehonathan, Adonijah, Tobijah, and Tobadonijah; also the priests, Elishama and Jehoram. They took copies of *The Book of the Law of the Lord* to all the cities of Judah, to teach the Scriptures to the people.

17:1
1 Kgs 15:24

17:2
2 Chron 11:5
15:8

17:4
1 Kgs 12:28

17:5
2 Chron 18:1

17:6
2 Chron 15:17

17:7
Deut 6:4-9
2 Chron 15:3
19:8; 35:3

16:7–10 Judah and Israel never learned! Although God had delivered them even when they were outnumbered (13:3ff; 14:9ff), they repeatedly sought help from heathen nations rather than from God. That Asa sought help from Syria was evidence of an inward spiritual decline. With help from God alone, Asa had defeated Egypt in open battle. But his confidence in God had slipped, and now he sought only a human solution to his problem. When confronted by the prophet Hanani, Asa threw him in jail, revealing the true condition of his heart. It is not sin to use human means to solve our problems, but it is sin to trust them more than God, to think they are better than God's ways, or to leave God completely out of the problem-solving process.

16:10 Asa was angry with Hanani's message, so he threw the prophet in jail. God's truth will not always be welcomed with open arms, especially when it reveals people's sins. But we must speak and live by God's truth, regardless of the consequences.

16:12 The criticism of Asa's visit to the doctors was not a general indictment of medicine. Asa's problem was that he completely ignored God's help. The medicine practiced at this time was a mixture of superstition and folk remedies. We should certainly avoid any pseudo medical treatment derived from occult sources. Asa's experience should also encourage us to follow the New Testament practice of receiving prayer for our sickness (James 5:14) as we seek responsible medical help.

17:7–9 The people of Judah were biblically illiterate. They had never taken time to listen to and discuss God's Word and understand how it could change their lives. Jehoshaphat realized that knowing God's Word was the first step to getting people to live as they should, so he initiated a nationwide religious education program. He reversed the religious decline that occurred at the end of Asa's reign by putting God first in the people's minds and instilling in them a sense of commitment and mission. Because of this action, the nation began to follow God. Churches and schools today need solid Christian education programs. Exposure to good Bible teaching through Sunday school, church, Bible study, and personal and family devotions is essential for living as God intended.

17:10
2 Chron 14:14

17:11
2 Chron 9:14
26:8

17:16
Judg 5:2; 9
1 Chron 29:9

17:19
2 Chron 17:2

¹⁰Then the fear of the Lord fell upon all the surrounding kingdoms so that none of them declared war on King Jehoshaphat.

¹¹Even some of the Philistines brought him presents and annual tribute, and the Arabs donated 7,700 rams and 7,700 male goats. ¹²So Jehoshaphat became very strong, and built fortresses and supply cities throughout Judah.

¹³His public works program was also extensive, and he had a huge army stationed at Jerusalem, his capital. ¹⁴, ¹⁵Three hundred thousand Judean troops were there under General Adnah. Next in command was Jeho-hanan with an army of 280,000 men. ¹⁶Next was Amasiah (son of Zichri), a man of unusual piety, with 200,000 troops. ¹⁷Benjamin supplied 200,000 men equipped with bows and shields under the command of Eliada, a great general. ¹⁸His second in command was Jehozabad, with 180,000 trained men. ¹⁹These were the troops in Jerusalem in addition to those placed by the king in the fortified cities throughout the nation.

JEHOSHAPHAT

Are children more likely to learn from their parents' mistakes or simply repeat them? In the lives of the people in the Bible, we find that the effects of parental examples are powerful and long-lasting. For much of his life, Jehoshaphat seems to have been a son who learned from his father Asa's mistakes and followed his positive actions. But on several occasions, his decisions reveal the negative aspects of his father's example.

When the challenges were obvious, like the need for religious education of the people or the threat of war with a vast army, Jehoshaphat turned to God for guidance and made the right choices. His dependence on God was consistent when the odds were clearly against him. It was in depending on God for the day-to-day plans and actions that Jehoshaphat was weak. He allowed his son to marry Athaliah, the daughter of the wicked Ahab and Jezebel of Israel, who did her best to be as evil as her parents. Jehoshaphat was almost killed when, without asking God, he made an alliance with Ahab. Later, he got involved in an unwise shipbuilding venture with Ahab's son, Ahaziah—a venture that was shipwrecked by God.

God's faithfulness when the issues are clear and the enemy is overwhelming is more than enough reason to seek his guidance when the issues are unclear and the enemy is unseen. Jehoshaphat knew this, yet he made little use of that knowledge.

We repeat Jehoshaphat's error when we relegate God to the background in the "easy" decisions of life. Then, when things get out of hand, we want him to get us out of the mess we got ourselves into. God wants us to give him not only the major decisions, but also our daily lives—the things we are most often fooled into believing we can control. Perhaps there is nothing major facing you today. Have you paused long enough to give your day to God anyway?

Strengths and accomplishments:
• A bold follower of God, he reminded the people of the early years of his father, Asa
• Carried out a national program of religious education
• Had many military victories
• Developed an extensive legal structure throughout the kingdom

Weaknesses and mistakes:
• Failed to recognize the long-term results of his decisions
• Did not completely destroy idolatry in the land
• Became entangled with evil King Ahab through alliances
• Allowed his son Jehoram to marry Athaliah, Ahab's daughter
• Became Ahaziah's business partner in an ill-fated shipping venture

Vital statistics:
• Where: Jerusalem
• Occupation: King of Judah
• Relatives: Father: Asa. Mother: Azubah. Son: Jehoram. Daughter-in-law: Athaliah.
• Contemporaries: Ahab, Jezebel, Micaiah, Ahaziah, Jehu

Key verses:
"He was a good king, just as his father Asa was. He continually tried to follow the Lord, with the exception that he did not destroy the idol shrines on the hills, nor had the people as yet really decided to follow the God of their ancestors" (2 Chronicles 20:32, 33).

Jehoshaphat's story is told in 1 Kings 15:24—22:50 and 2 Chronicles 17:1—21:1. He is also mentioned in 2 Kings 3:1–14 and Joel 3:2, 12.

Jehoshaphat joins forces with Ahab

18 But rich, popular King Jehoshaphat of Judah made a marriage alliance [for his son] with [the daughter of] King Ahab of Israel. ²A few years later he went down to Samaria to visit King Ahab, and King Ahab gave a great party for him and his aides, butchering great numbers of sheep and oxen for the feast. Then he asked King Jehoshaphat to join forces with him against Ramoth-gilead.

18:1
2 Chron: 17:5

18:2
1 Kgs 22:2-35

18:1 *for his son,* implied. *the daughter of,* implied in 21:6.

BIBLE

The Persecuted	The Persecutors	Why the Persecution	Result	Reference
Isaac	The Philistines	God was blessing Isaac	The Philistines could not subdue Isaac, so they made peace with him	Genesis 26:12–33
Moses	Israelites	The Israelites wanted water	God provided water, thanks to Moses' prayer	Exodus 17:1–7
David	Saul and others	David was becoming a powerful leader, threatening Saul's position as king	David endured the persecution and became king	1 Samuel 20—27 Psalms 31:13; 59:1–4
Priests of Nob	Saul and Doeg	Saul and Doeg thought the priests helped David escape	85 priests were killed	1 Samuel 22
Prophets	Jezebel	Jezebel didn't like to have her evil ways pointed out	Many prophets were killed	1 Kings 18:3, 4
Elijah	Ahab and Jezebel	Elijah confronted their sins	Elijah had to flee for his life	1 Kings 18:10—19:2
Micaiah	Ahab	Ahab thought Micaiah was stirring up trouble rather than prophecying from God	Micaiah was thrown into prison	2 Chronicles 18:12–26
Elisha	A king of Israel	The king thought Elisha had caused the famine	Elisha ignored the threatened persecution and prophesied the famine's end	2 Kings 6:31
Hanani	Asa	Hanani criticized Asa for trusting in Syria's help more than in God's help	Hanani was thrown in jail	2 Chronicles 16:7–10
Zechariah	Joash	Zechariah confronted the people of Judah for disregarding God's Word	Zechariah was executed	2 Chronicles 24:20–22
Uriah	Jehoiakim	Uriah confronted Jehoiakim about his evil ways	Uriah was butchered to death	Jeremiah 26:20–23
Jeremiah	Zedekiah	Zedekiah thought Jeremiah was a traitor for prophesying Jerusalem's fall	Jeremiah was thrown in prison, then into a muddy cistern	Jeremiah 37:1—38:13
Shadrach, Meshach, Abednego	Nebuchadnezzar	The three men refused to bow down to anyone but God	They were thrown into a fiery furnace, but God miraculously saved them	Daniel 3

18:1ff Although Jehoshaphat was deeply committed to God, he arranged for his son to marry Athaliah, the daughter of wicked King Ahab of Israel, and then made a military alliance with him. Jehoshaphat's popularity and power made him attractive to the cunning and opportunistic Ahab. This alliance had three devastating consequences: (1) Jehoshaphat incurred God's wrath (19:2); (2) When Jehoshaphat died and Athaliah became queen, she seized the throne and almost destroyed all of David's descendants (22:10ff); (3) Athaliah brought the evil practices of

Israel into Judah, which eventually led to the nation's downfall.
When believers in leadership positions become allied with unbelievers, values can be compromised and spiritual awareness dulled. Scripture often warns against teaming up with unbelievers (2 Corinthians 6:14). (See the note on 20:37 for more on alliances.)

18:3–5 Evil kings did not like God's prophets bringing messages of doom (18:17; Jeremiah 5:13). Many, therefore, hired prophets who told them only what they wanted to hear (Isaiah 30:10, 11; Jeremiah 14:13–16; 23:16, 21, 30–36). The Bible calls these men

3, 4, 5"Why, of course!" King Jehoshaphat replied. "I'm with you all the way. My troops are at your command! However, let's check with the Lord first."

So King Ahab summoned 400 of his heathen prophets and asked them, "Shall we go to war with Ramoth-gilead or not?"

And they replied, "Go ahead, for God will give you a great victory!"

6, 7But Jehoshaphat wasn't satisfied. "Isn't there some prophet of the Lord around here too?" he asked. "I'd like to ask him the same question."

PERSECUTIONS

The Persecuted	The Persecutors	Why the Persecution	Result	Reference
Daniel	National leaders	Daniel was praying	Daniel was thrown into a den of lions, but God miraculously saved him	Daniel 6
Job	Satan	Satan wanted to prove that pain and suffering would make a person abandon God	Job remained faithful to God and was restored	Job 1:8–13; 2:3–8
John the Baptist	Herod and Herodias	John confronted King Herod's adultery	John was beheaded	Matthew 14:3–13
Jesus	Religious leaders	Jesus exposed their sinful motives	Jesus was crucified, but rose again from the dead to show his authority over all evil	Mark 7:1–16; Luke 22:63—24:7
Peter and John	Religious leaders	Peter and John preached that Jesus was God's Son and the only way to salvation	They were thrown into prison, but later released	Acts 4:1–31
Stephen	Religious leaders	Stephen exposed their guilt in crucifying Jesus	Stephen was stoned to death	Acts 6—7
The Church	Paul and others	The Christians preached Jesus as the Messiah	Believers faced death, prison, torture, exile	Acts 8:1–3; 9:1–9
James	Herod Agrippa I	To please the Jewish leaders	James was executed	Acts 12:1–2
Peter	Herod Agrippa I	To please the Jewish leaders	Peter was thrown into prison	Acts 12:3–17
Paul	Jews, city officials	Paul preached about Jesus and confronted those who made money by manipulating others	Paul was stoned; thrown into prison	Acts 14:19; 16:16ff
Timothy	Unknown	Unknown	Timothy was thrown into prison	Hebrews 13:23
John	Probably the Romans	John told others about Jesus	John was sent into exile on a remote island	Revelation 1:9

Micaiah, like thousands of believers before and after him, was persecuted for his faith. The chart shows that persecution comes from a variety of people and is given in a variety of ways. Sometimes God protects us from it, sometimes he doesn't. But as long as we remain faithful to God *alone*, we must expect persecution (see also Luke 6:22; 2 Corinthians 6:4–10; 2 Timothy 2:9–12; Revelation 2:10). God also seems to have a special reward for those who endure such persecution (Revelation 6:9–11; 20:4).

false prophets because they extolled the greatness of the king and predicted victory regardless of the true situation.

18:3-5 Wicked Ahab asked Jehoshaphat to join forces with him in battle (18:2). Before making that commitment, Jehoshaphat rightly sought God's advice. However, when God gave his answer through the prophet Micaiah (18:16), Jehoshaphat ignored it (18:28). It does us no good to seek God's advice if we ignore it when it is given. Real love for God is shown not by merely asking for direction, but by following that direction once it is given.

18:5–15 When you want to please or impress someone, it is

tempting to lie to make yourself look good. Ahab's 400 prophets did just that, telling Ahab only what he wanted to hear. They were then rewarded for making Ahab happy. Micaiah, however, told the truth and got arrested (18:25). Obeying God doesn't always protect us from evil consequences. Obedience may, in fact, provoke them. But it is better to suffer from man's displeasure than from God's wrath (Matthew 10:28). If you are ridiculed for being honest, remember that this can be a sign that you are indeed doing what is right in God's eyes (Matthew 5:10–12; Romans 8:17, 35–39).

"Well," Ahab told him, "there is one, but I hate him, for he never prophesies anything but evil! His name is Micaiah (son of Imlah)."

"Oh, come now, don't talk like that!" Jehoshaphat exclaimed. "Let's hear what he has to say."

8So the king of Israel called one of his aides. "Quick! Go and get Micaiah (son of Imlah)," he ordered.

9The two kings were sitting on thrones in full regalia at an open place near the Samaria gate, and all the "prophets" were prophesying before them. 10One of them, Zedekiah (son of Chenaanah), made some iron horns for the occasion and proclaimed, "The Lord says you will gore the Syrians to death with these!"

11And all the others agreed. "Yes," they chorused, "go up to Ramoth-gilead and prosper, for the Lord will cause you to conquer."

12The man who went to get Micaiah told him what was happening, and what all the prophets were saying—that the war would end in triumph for the king.

"I hope you will agree with them and give the king a favorable reading," the man ventured.

13But Micaiah replied, "I vow by God that whatever God says is what I will say."   **18:13**
14When he arrived before the king, the king asked him, "Micaiah, shall we go to   Num 22:18-20, 35
war against Ramoth-gilead or not?"

And Micaiah replied, "Sure, go ahead! It will be a glorious victory!"

15"Look here," the king said sharply, "how many times must I tell you to speak nothing except what the Lord tells you to?"

16Then Micaiah told him, "In my vision I saw all Israel scattered upon the   **18:16**
mountain as sheep without a shepherd. And the Lord said, 'Their master has been   Num 27:17
killed. Send them home.' "   Ezek 34:5-8
   Mt 9:36

17"Didn't I tell you?" the king of Israel exclaimed to Jehoshaphat. "He does it every time. He *never* prophesies *anything* but evil against me."

18"Listen to what else the Lord has told me," Micaiah continued. "I saw him   **18:18**
upon his throne surrounded by vast throngs of angels.   Isa 6:1-5
   Dan 7:9,10

19, 20"And the Lord said, 'Who can get King Ahab to go to battle against Ramoth-gilead and be killed there?'

"There were many suggestions, but finally a spirit stepped forward before the Lord and said, 'I can do it!'

" 'How?' the Lord asked him.

21"He replied, 'I will be a lying spirit in the mouths of all of the king's prophets!'

" 'It will work,' the Lord said; 'go and do it.'

22"So you see, the Lord has put a lying spirit in the mouths of these prophets of

---

18:22 God used the seductive influence of these false prophets to judge Ahab. These prophets, supported by Ahab, snared him in his sin. Because he listened to them instead of God, he was killed in battle. The lying spirit is a picture of the prophets' entire way of life—telling the king only what he wanted to hear, not what he needed to hear.

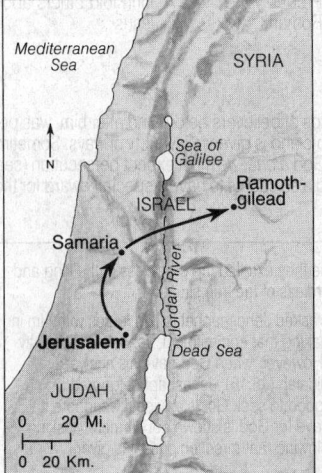

BATTLE WITH SYRIA
King Jehoshaphat made an alliance with evil King Ahab of Israel. Together they decided to attack Ramoth-gilead and rout the Syrians who had occupied the city. But Jehoshaphat first wanted to seek the advice of a prophet. Ahab's prophets predicted victory; but Micaiah predicted defeat. The two kings were defeated and Ahab was killed.

yours, when actually he has determined just the opposite of what they are telling you!"

²³Then Zedekiah (son of Chenaanah) walked up to Micaiah and slapped him across the face. "You liar!" he yelled. "When did the Spirit of the Lord leave me and enter you?"

²⁴"You'll find out soon enough," Micaiah replied, "—when you are hiding in an inner room!"

18:25
2 Chron 18:8
34:8

18:26
2 Chron 16:10

18:27
Mic 1:2

²⁵"Arrest this man and take him back to Governor Amon and to my son Joash," the king of Israel ordered. ²⁶"Tell them, 'The king says to put this fellow in prison and feed him with bread and water until I return safely from the battle!' "

²⁷Micaiah replied, "If you return safely, the Lord has not spoken through me." Then, turning to those around them, he remarked, "Take note of what I have said."

Ahab dies in battle

²⁸So the king of Israel and the king of Judah led their armies to Ramoth-gilead.

²⁹The king of Israel said to Jehoshaphat, "I'll disguise myself so that no one will recognize me, but you put on your royal robes!" So that is what they did.

³⁰Now the king of Syria had issued these instructions to his charioteers: "Ignore everyone but the king of Israel!"

18:31
2 Chron 13:14,
15

³¹So when the Syrian charioteers saw King Jehoshaphat of Judah in his royal robes, they went for him, supposing that he was the man they were after. But Jehoshaphat cried out to the Lord to save him, and the Lord made the charioteers see their mistake and leave him. ³²For as soon as they realized he was not the king of Israel, they stopped chasing him. ³³But one of the Syrian soldiers shot an arrow haphazardly at the Israeli troops, and it struck the king of Israel at the opening where the lower armor and the breastplate meet. "Get me out of here," he groaned to the driver of his chariot, "for I am badly wounded." ³⁴The battle grew hotter and hotter all that day, and King Ahab went back in, propped up in his chariot, to fight the Syrians, but just as the sun sank into the western skies, he died.

A prophet rebukes Jehoshaphat

19:2
1 Kgs 16:1
2 Chron 18:1,3
20:34; 24:18

19:3
2 Chron 12:12,
14; 17:6

19 As King Jehoshaphat of Judah returned home, uninjured, ²the prophet Jehu (son of Hanani) went out to meet him.

"Should you be helping the wicked, and loving those who hate the Lord?" he asked him. "Because of what you have done, God's wrath is upon you. ³But there are some good things about you, in that you got rid of the shame-idols throughout the land, and you have tried to be faithful to God."

Jehoshaphat appoints judges

19:4
Deut 16:18-20

19:6
Lev 19:15
Deut 1:17

⁴So Jehoshaphat made no more trips to Israel after that, but remained quietly at Jerusalem. Later he went out again among the people, traveling from Beer-sheba to the hill country of Ephraim to encourage them to worship the God of their ancestors. ⁵He appointed judges throughout the nation in all the larger cities, ⁶and instructed them:

18:31 Jehoshaphat's troubles began when he joined forces with evil King Ahab. Almost at once he found himself the target for soldiers who mistakenly identified him as Ahab. He could have accepted this fate, because he richly deserved it, but instead he cried out to God, who miraculously saved him. When we sin and the inevitable consequences follow, we may be tempted to give up. "I chose to sin," we may think; "It's my fault and I must accept the consequences." While we may deserve what comes to us, that is no reason to avoid calling on God for help. Had Jehoshaphat given up, he may have died. No matter how greatly you have sinned, you can still call upon God.

18:33 Micaiah prophesied death for King Ahab (18:16, 27), so Ahab disguised himself to fool the enemy. Apparently the disguise

worked, but that didn't change the prophecy. A random Syrian arrow found a crack in his armor and killed him. God's will is always fulfilled despite the defenses people try to erect. God can use anything, even an error, to bring his will to pass. This is good news for God's followers, because we can trust him to work his plans and keep his promises no matter what the circumstances.

19:5-10 Jehoshaphat delegated some of the responsibilities for ruling and judging the people, but he warned his appointees that they were accountable to God for the standards they used to judge others. Jehoshaphat's advice is helpful for all leaders: (1) allow God to help you be just (19:6); (2) be impartial (19:7); (3) be honest (19:9); (4) act only out of fear of God, not men (19:9).

"Watch your step—I have not appointed you—God has; and he will stand beside you and help you give justice in each case that comes before you. 7Be very much afraid to give any other decision than what God tells you to. For there must be no injustice among God's judges, no partiality, no taking of bribes."

8Jehoshaphat set up courts in Jerusalem, too, with the Levites and priests and clan leaders and judges. 9These were his instructions to them: "You are to act always in the fear of God, with honest hearts. 10Whenever a case is referred to you by the judges out in the provinces, whether murder cases or other violations of the laws and ordinances of God, you are to clarify the evidence for them and help them to decide justly, lest the wrath of God come down upon you and them; if you do this, you will discharge your responsibility."

11Then he appointed Amariah, the High Priest, to be the court of final appeal in cases involving violation of sacred affairs; and Zebadiah (son of Ishmael), a ruler in Judah, as the court of final appeal in all civil cases; with the Levites as their assistants. "Be fearless in your stand for truth and honesty. And may God use you to defend the innocent," was his final word to them.

Jehoshaphat defeats Moab and Ammon

20 Later on, the armies of the kings of Moab, Ammon, and of the Meunites declared war on Jehoshaphat and the people of Judah. 2Word reached Jehoshaphat that "a vast army is marching against you from beyond the Dead Sea, from Syria. It is already at Hazazon-tamar" (also called Engedi). 3Jehoshaphat was badly shaken by this news and determined to beg for help from the Lord; so he announced that all the people of Judah should go without food for a time, in penitence and intercession before God. 4People from all across the nation came to Jerusalem to plead unitedly with him. 5Jehoshaphat stood among them as they gathered at the new court of the Temple, and prayed this prayer:

6"O Lord God of our fathers—the only God in all the heavens, the Ruler of all the kingdoms of the earth—you are so powerful, so mighty. Who can stand against you? 7O our God, didn't you drive out the heathen who lived in this land when your people arrived? And didn't you give this land forever to the descendants of your friend Abraham? 8Your people settled here and built this Temple for you, 9truly believing that in a time like this—whenever we are faced with any calamity such as war, disease, or famine—we can stand here before this Temple and before you—for you are here in this Temple—and cry out to you to save us; and that you will hear us and rescue us.

10"And now see what the armies of Ammon, Moab, and Mount Seir are doing. You wouldn't let our ancestors invade those nations when Israel left Egypt, so we went around and didn't destroy them. 11Now see how they reward us! For they have come to throw us out of your land which you have given us. 12O our God, won't you stop them? We have no way to protect ourselves against this mighty army. We don't know what to do, but we are looking to you."

13As the people from every part of Judah stood before the Lord with their little

19:7
Gen 18:25
Deut 10:17,18
32:4

19:8
2 Chron 17:8,9

19:10
Deut 17:8
2 Chron 19:2

19:11
1 Chron 28:20
2 Chron 19:8

20:2
Gen 14:7

20:3
1 Sam 7:6
2 Chron 19:3
Ezra 8:21

20:6
Deut 4:39
1 Chron 29:11

20:7
Isa 41:8

20:9
2 Chron 6:20,
28-30

20:10
Num 20:17-21
2 Chron 20:1,22

20:12
Judg 11:27
Ps 25:15
121:1,2

19:8 Jehoshaphat appointed priests and Levites to help in administering civil laws. In some of today's circles, it is fashionable to believe that Christians should have nothing to do with politics or government. But it is obvious that the best kind of leader is one who always acts with reverence for God. In the same way, Moses chose men who were capable, faithful, and honest to help him judge disputes among the people (Exodus 18:21). Effective leaders get the job done; faithful leaders make sure the job is done in God's way with God's timing. They will be careful to instill God's wisdom in future leaders and build God's values into the entire community.

20:3 When the nation was faced with disaster, Jehoshaphat called upon the people to get serious with God by going without food for a designated time. By separating themselves from the daily routine of food preparation and eating, they could devote that extra time to considering their sin and praying to God for help. Hunger pangs would reinforce their feelings of penitence and remind them of their weakness and their dependence upon God. Fasting is still helpful today as we seek God's will in special situations.

20:6ff Jehoshaphat's prayer had several interesting ingredients: (1) He committed the situation to God, acknowledging that only God could save the nation. (2) He sought God's favor because his people were God's people. (3) He acknowledged God's sovereignty over the current situation. (4) He praised God's glory and took comfort in his promises. (5) He professed complete dependence on God, not himself, for deliverance. To be God's kind of leader today, follow Jehoshaphat's example—focus entirely on God rather than yourself.

20:14
2 Chron 15:1
24:20

20:15
Ex 14:13
1 Sam 17:47
2 Chron 32:7,8

20:17
Ex 14:13
2 Chron 15:2

20:19
2 Chron 7:3

20:20
Isa 7:9

20:21
1 Chron 16:29,
34
Ps 29:2

20:22
2 Chron 13:13
20:10

20:23
Judg 7:22
1 Sam 14:20

20:29
2 Chron 14:6,7
15:15

20:30
1 Kgs 22:41-43

20:31
2 Chron 17:6

20:33
2 Chron 17:6
19:3

ones, wives, and children, 14the Spirit of the Lord came upon one of the men standing there—Jahaziel (son of Zechariah, son of Benaiah, son of Je-iel, son of Mattaniah the Levite, who was one of the sons of Asaph).

15"Listen to me, all you people of Judah and Jerusalem, and you, O king Jehoshaphat!" he exclaimed. "The Lord says, 'Don't be afraid! Don't be paralyzed by this mighty army! For the battle is not yours, but God's! 16Tomorrow, go down and attack them! You will find them coming up the slopes of Ziz at the end of the valley that opens into the wilderness of Jeruel. 17But you will not need to fight! Take your places; stand quietly and see the incredible rescue operation God will perform for you, O people of Judah and Jerusalem! Don't be afraid or discouraged! Go out there tomorrow, for the Lord is with you!' "

18Then King Jehoshaphat fell to the ground with his face to the earth, and all the people of Judah and the people of Jerusalem did the same, worshiping the Lord. 19Then the Levites of the Kohath clan and the Korah clan stood to praise the Lord God of Israel with songs of praise that rang out strong and clear.

20Early the next morning the army of Judah went out into the wilderness of Tekoa. On the way Jehoshaphat stopped and called them to attention. "Listen to me, O people of Judah and Jerusalem," he said. "Believe in the Lord your God, and you shall have success! Believe his prophets, and everything will be all right!"

21After consultation with the leaders of the people, he determined that there should be a choir leading the march, clothed in sanctified garments and singing the song "His Lovingkindness Is Forever" as they walked along praising and thanking the Lord! 22And at the moment they began to sing and to praise, the Lord caused the armies of Ammon, Moab, and Mount Seir to begin fighting among themselves, and they destroyed each other! 23For the Ammonites and Moabites turned against their allies from Mount Seir and killed every one of them. And when they had finished that job, they turned against each other! 24So, when the army of Judah arrived at the watchtower that looks out over the wilderness, as far as they could look there were dead bodies lying on the ground—not a single one of the enemy had escaped. 25King Jehoshaphat and his people went out to plunder the bodies and came away loaded with money, garments, and jewels stripped from the corpses—so much that it took them three days to cart it all away! 26On the fourth day they gathered in the Valley of Blessing, as it is called today, and how they praised the Lord!

27Then they returned to Jerusalem, with Jehoshaphat leading them, full of joy that the Lord had given them this marvelous rescue from their enemies. 28They marched into Jerusalem accompanied by a band of harps, lyres, and trumpets and proceeded to the Temple. 29And as had happened before, when the surrounding kingdoms heard that the Lord himself had fought against the enemies of Israel, the fear of God fell upon them. 30So Jehoshaphat's kingdom was quiet, for his God had given him rest.

Summary of Jehoshaphat's reign

31A thumbnail sketch of King Jehoshaphat: He became king of Judah when he was thirty-five years old, and reigned twenty-five years, in Jerusalem. His mother's name was Azubah, the daughter of Shilhi. 32He was a good king, just as his father Asa was. He continually tried to follow the Lord, 33with the exception that he did not destroy the idol shrines on the hills, nor had the people as yet really decided to follow the God of their ancestors.

20:15 As the enemy bore down on Judah, God spoke through Jahaziel: "Don't be afraid. The battle is not yours, but God's." We may not fight an enemy army, but every day we battle temptation, pressure, and "wicked spirits in the spirit world" (Ephesians 6:12) who want us to rebel against God. We must remember that, as believers, we have God's Spirit in us. If we ask for God's help when we face struggles, God will fight for us. And God always triumphs.
How do we let God fight for us? (1) By realizing the battle is not ours, but God's; (2) by recognizing human limitations and allowing

God's strength and power to work through our fears and weaknesses; (3) by making sure our battle is for God and not our selfish desires; (4) by asking God for help in our daily battles.

20:33 This verse says that Jehoshaphat did not destroy the corrupt idol shrines while 17:6 and 19:3 say he destroyed them. Jehoshaphat destroyed most of the Baal and Asherah idols, but he did not succeed in wiping out the corrupt religions practiced at the hilltop shrines.

³⁴The details of Jehoshaphat's reign from first to last are written in the history of Jehu the son of Hanani, which is inserted in *The Annals of the Kings of Israel.* ³⁵But at the close of his life, Jehoshaphat, king of Judah, went into partnership with Ahaziah, king of Israel, who was a very wicked man. ³⁶They made ships in Ezion-geber to sail to Tarshish. ³⁷Then Eliezer, son of Dodavahu from Mareshah, prophesied against Jehoshaphat, telling him, "Because you have allied yourself with King Ahaziah, the Lord has destroyed your work." So the ships met disaster and never arrived at Tarshish.

20:34
1 Kgs 16:1,7
2 Chron 19:2

20:35
1 Kgs 22:48,49

20:36
2 Chron 9:21

Jehoram rules Judah

21 When Jehoshaphat died, he was buried in the cemetery of the kings in Jerusalem, and his son Jehoram became the new ruler of Judah. ²His brothers—other sons of Jehoshaphat—were Azariah, Jehiel, Zechariah, Azariah, Michael, and Shephatiah. ^{3, 4}Their father had given each of them valuable gifts of money and jewels, also the ownership of some of the fortified cities of Judah. However, he gave the kingship to Jehoram because he was the oldest. But when Jehoram had become solidly established as king, he killed all of his brothers and many other leaders of Israel. ⁵He was thirty-two years old when he began to reign, and he reigned eight years, in Jerusalem. ⁶But he was as wicked as the kings who were over in Israel. Yes, as wicked as Ahab, for Jehoram had married one of the daughters of Ahab, and his whole life was one constant binge of doing evil. ⁷However, the Lord was unwilling to end the dynasty of David, for he had made a covenant with David always to have one of his descendants upon the throne.

⁸At that time the king of Edom revolted, declaring his independence of Judah. ⁹Jehoram attacked him with his full army and with all of his chariots, marching by night, and almost managed to subdue him. ¹⁰But to this day Edom has been successful in throwing off the yoke of Judah. Libnah revolted too, because Jehoram had turned away from the Lord God of his fathers. ¹¹What's more, Jehoram constructed idol shrines in the mountains of Judah, and led the people of Jerusalem in worshiping idols; in fact, he compelled his people to worship them.

¹²Then Elijah the prophet wrote him this letter: "The Lord God of your ancestor David says that because you have not followed in the good ways of your father Jehoshaphat, nor the good ways of King Asa, ¹³but you have been as evil as the

21:1
1 Kgs 22:50

21:3
2 Kgs 8:17-22
2 Chron 11:5

21:6
1 Kgs 12:28-30
2 Chron 18:1

21:7
2 Sam 7:12-17
1 Kgs 11:13

21:8
2 Chron 20:22,
23; 21:10

21:11
Lev 20:5
1 Kgs 11:7

21:12
2 Chron 14:2-5
17:3,4

21:13
1 Kgs 16:31-33
2 Chron 21:4,6

21:9 *Jehoram attacked him . . . and almost,* literally, "Jehoram . . . struck down the Edomites . . . Nevertheless Edom . . . revolted. . . ."

20:37 Jehoshaphat met disaster when he joined forces with wicked King Ahaziah. He did not learn from his disastrous alliance with Ahab (18:28–34) or from his father's alliance with Syria (16:2–9). The partnership stood on unequal footing because one man served God and the other worshiped idols. We court disaster when we enter into partnership with unbelievers because the very foundation of our lives differs (2 Corinthians 6:14–18). While one serves the Lord, the other does not recognize God's authority. Inevitably, the one who serves God is faced with the temptation to compromise values. When that happens, spiritual disaster results.
Before entering into partnerships ask: (1) What are my motives? (2) What problems am I avoiding by seeking this partnership? (3) Is this partnership the best solution, or is it only a quick solution to my problem? (4) Have I prayed or asked others to pray for guidance? (5) Are my partner and I really working toward the same goals? (6) Am I willing to settle for less of this world's goods in order to do God's will?

21:6 Jehoram, the new king of Judah, married Athaliah, one of the daughters of King Ahab of Israel. She became the mother of Judah's next king, Ahaziah (22:2). Athaliah's mother was Jezebel, the most wicked woman Israel had ever known. Jehoram's marriage to Athaliah was Judah's downfall, for Athaliah brought her mother's wicked influence into Judah, causing the nation to forget God and turn to Baal worship (22:3).

21:7 God promised that a descendant of David would always sit on the throne (2 Samuel 7:8–16). What happened to this promise when the nation was destroyed and carried away? There were two parts to God's promise: (1) In the physical sense, as long as there was an actual throne in Judah, a descendant of David would sit upon it. But this part of the promise was conditional upon the obedience of these kings. When they disobeyed, God was not bound to continue David's temporal line. (2) In the spiritual sense, this promise was completely fulfilled in the coming of Jesus the Messiah, a descendant of David, who will sit on the throne of David forever.

21:8–11 Jehoram's reign was marked by sin and cruelty. He married a woman who worshiped idols; he killed his six brothers; he allowed and even promoted idol worship. Yet he was not killed in battle or by treachery—he died by a lingering and painful disease (21:18, 19). Just because punishment is not immediate or dramatic does not mean God is indifferent to our sin. We cannot ignore God's laws and think we are immune from the consequences of our sin. There can be no healing or deliverance for the rebel against God until one's relationship with God is made right.

21:12 Chronicles mentions Elijah only here, but much more about this great prophet can be found in 1 Kings 17:1—2 Kings 2:11. Elijah's Profile is found in 1 Kings 18.

kings over in Israel, and have made the people of Jerusalem and Judah worship idols just as in the times of King Ahab, and because you have killed your brothers who were better than you, [14]now the Lord will destroy your nation with a great plague. You, your children, your wives, and all that you have will be struck down. [15]You will be stricken with an intestinal disease and your bowels will rot away."

21:15
2 Chron 21:18, 19

[16]Then the Lord stirred up the Philistines and the Arabs living next to the Ethiopians to attack Jehoram. [17]They marched against Judah, broke across the border, and carried away everything of value in the king's palace, including his sons and his wives; only his youngest son, Jehoahaz, escaped.

21:16
2 Chron 17:11
22:1; 33:11

21:17
2 Chron 25:23

[18]It was after this that Jehovah struck him down with the incurable bowel disease. [19]In the process of time, at the end of two years, his intestines came out and he died in terrible suffering. (The customary pomp and ceremony was omitted at his funeral.) [20]He was thirty-two years old when he began to reign and he reigned in Jerusalem eight years, and died unmourned. He was buried in Jerusalem, but not in the royal cemetery.

21:18
2 Chron 21:15

21:19
2 Chron 16:14

21:20
2 Chron 24:25
28:27
Jer 22:18,28

Ahaziah rules Judah

22:1
2 Kgs 8:24-29
2 Chron 21:16

22 Then the people of Jerusalem chose Ahaziah, his youngest son, as their new king (for the marauding bands of Arabs had killed his older sons). [2]Ahaziah was twenty-two years old when he began to reign, and he reigned one year, in Jerusalem. His mother's name was Athaliah, granddaughter of Omri. [3]He, too, walked in the evil ways of Ahab, for his mother encouraged him in doing wrong. [4]Yes, he was as evil as Ahab, for Ahab's family became his advisors after his father's death, and they led him on to ruin.

22:2
2 Chron 21:6

[5]Following their evil advice, Ahaziah made an alliance with King Joram of Israel (the son of Ahab), who was at war with King Hazael of Syria at Ramoth-gilead. Ahaziah led his army there to join the battle. King Joram of Israel was wounded, [6]and returned to Jezreel to recover. Ahaziah went to visit him, [7]but this turned out to be a fatal mistake; for God had decided to punish Ahaziah for his alliance with Jehoram. It was during this visit that Ahaziah went out with Joram to challenge Jehu (son of Nimshi), whom the Lord had appointed to end the dynasty of Ahab.

22:7
2 Kgs 9:6,7,21
2 Chron 10:15

[8]While Jehu was hunting down and killing the family and friends of Ahab, he met King Ahaziah's nephews, the princes of Judah, and killed them. [9]As he and his men were searching for Ahaziah, they found him hiding in the city of Samaria, and brought him to Jehu, who killed him. Even so, Ahaziah was given a royal burial because he was the grandson of King Jehoshaphat—a man who enthusiastically served the Lord.

22:8
2 Kgs 10:11-14

22:9
2 Kgs 9:27,28
2 Chron 17:4

Athaliah rules Judah

22:10
2 Kgs 11:1-3

None of his sons, however, except for Joash, lived to succeed him as king, [10]for their grandmother Athaliah killed them when she heard the news of her son Ahaziah's death.

[11]Joash was rescued by his Aunt Jehoshabeath, who was King Ahaziah's sister, and was hidden away in a storage room in the Temple. She was a daughter of King Jehoram, and the wife of Jehoiada the priest. [12]Joash remained hidden in the Temple for six years while Athaliah reigned as queen. He was cared for by his nurse and by his aunt and uncle.

22:1 *Ahaziah*, also called "Jehoahaz." **22:2** *was twenty-two years old*, some manuscripts read "forty-two years old"; but see 2 Kgs 8:26. **22:11** *who was King Ahaziah's sister*, literally, "the king's daughter," i.e., King Jehoram's daughter, vs 11.

22:4, 5 Although it is good to seek advice, we must also carefully weigh what is said. Ahaziah had advisors, but they were wicked and led him to ruin. When you seek advice, listen carefully and use God's Word to "test everything that is said to be sure it is true" (1 Thessalonians 5:21).

22:7 Jehu's Profile and a more complete story of his reign are found in 2 Kings 9:1—10:36.

Young Joash becomes king

23 In the seventh year of the reign of Queen Athaliah, Jehoiada the priest got up his courage and took some of the army officers into his confidence: Azariah (son of Jeroham), Ishmael (son of Jehohanan), Azariah (son of Obed), Maaseiah (son of Adaiah), and Elishaphat (son of Zichri). 2, 3These men traveled out across the nation secretly, to tell the Levites and clan leaders about his plans and to summon them to Jerusalem. On arrival they swore allegiance to the young king, who was still in hiding at the Temple.

23:1
2 Kgs 11:4-20

23:2
2 Chron 21:7

"At last the time has come for the king's son to reign!" Jehoiada exclaimed. "The Lord's promise—that a descendant of King David shall be our king—will be true again. 4This is how we'll proceed: A third of you priests and Levites who come off duty on the Sabbath will stay at the entrance as guards. 5, 6Another third will go over to the palace, and a third will be at the Lower Gate. Everyone else must stay in the outer courts of the Temple, as required by God's laws. For only the priests and Levites on duty may enter the Temple itself, for they are sanctified. 7You Levites, form a bodyguard for the king, weapons in hand, and kill any unauthorized person entering the Temple. Stay right beside the king."

23:4
1 Chron 9:25
23:6
1 Chron 23:28-32
Ex 25:16,21
1 Sam 10:24

8So all the arrangements were made. Each of the three leaders led a third of the priests arriving for duty that Sabbath, and a third of those whose week's work was done and were going off duty—for Jehoiada the chief priest didn't release them to go home. 9Then Jehoiada issued spears and shields to all the army officers. These had once belonged to King David and were stored in the Temple. 10These officers, fully armed, formed a line from one side to the other in front of the Temple and around the altar in the outer court. 11Then they brought out the little prince and placed the crown upon his head and handed him a copy of the law of God, and proclaimed him king.

A great shout went up, "Long live the king!" as Jehoiada and his sons anointed him.

12When Queen Athaliah heard all the noise and commotion, and the shouts of praise to the king, she rushed over to the Temple to see what was going on—and there stood the king by his pillar at the entrance, with the army officers and the trumpeters surrounding him, and people from all over the land rejoicing and blowing trumpets, and the singers singing, accompanied by an orchestra leading the people in a great psalm of praise.

Athaliah ripped her clothes and screamed, "Treason! Treason!"

13, 14"Take her out and kill her," Jehoiada the priest shouted to the army officers. "Don't do it here at the Temple. And kill anyone who tries to help her."

15, 16, 17So the crowd opened up for them to take her out and they killed her at the palace stables.

23:15
Deut 13:6-9
1 Kgs 18:40
2 Chron 22:10

Then Jehoiada made a solemn contract that he and the king and the people would be the Lord's. And all the people rushed over to the temple of Baal and knocked it down, and broke up the altars and knocked down the idols, and killed Mattan the priest of Baal before his altar. 18Jehoiada now appointed the Levite priests as guards, and to sacrifice the burnt offering to the Lord as prescribed in the law of Moses. He made the identical assignments of the Levite clans that King David had.

23:18
1 Chron 9:22
23:6,25-31
2 Chron 5:5

23:1 After seven years of rule by Athaliah, the queen mother, Jehoida the priest finally got up his courage and took action to get rid of the idolatrous ruler. To confront the king (or queen) with the demands of God's Law was supposed to be the role of every priest in every generation. Tragically, few priests took this duty seriously, and thus few made a difference in the nation.

23:1 Although it could have cost him his life, this priest gathered up his courage and did what was right, restoring the Temple worship and anointing the new king. There are times when we must take action to correct a wrong or to speak out for what is right. When such a situation arises, gather up your courage and take action.

23:12 Queen Athaliah thought she had it made. After assuming the throne, she killed all potential heirs to it—so she thought. But even the best plans for evil go sour. When the truth was revealed, she was overthrown immediately. It is much safer to live according to the truth, even if it means that you will not obtain everything you want.

23:15–17 Athaliah's life ended as her mother Jezebel's had—by execution. Her life of idolatry and treachery was cut short by God's judgment of her sin. By this time Judah had slipped so far away from God that Baal was worshiped in Jerusalem.

23:18 Jehoida restored the Temple procedures and its worship services according to David's original plans, recorded in 1 Chronicles 24, 25.

They sang with joy as they worked. ¹⁹The guards at the Temple gates kept out everything that was not consecrated and all unauthorized personnel.

²⁰Then the army officers, nobles, governors, and all the people escorted the king from the Temple, wending their way from the Upper Gate to the palace, and seated the king upon his throne. ²¹So all the people of the land rejoiced, and the city was quiet and peaceful because Queen Athaliah was dead.

Joash repairs the Temple

24:1
2 Kgs 11:21

24 Joash was seven years old when he became king, and he reigned forty years, in Jerusalem. His mother's name was Zibiah, from Beer-sheba. ²Joash tried

JOASH

All parents want their children to make the right decisions. But to do this, children must first learn to make *their own* decisions. Making bad ones helps them learn to make good ones. If parents make all the decisions for their children, they leave their children without the skills for wise decision-making when they are on their own. This problem seriously affected King Joash. He had great advice, but he never grew up. He became so dependent on what he was told that his effectiveness was limited to the quality of his advisors.

When Joash was one year old, his grandmother Athaliah decided to slaughter all her descendants in a desperate bid for power. Joash was the only survivor, rescued and hidden by his aunt and uncle, Jehosheba and Jehoiada. Jehoiada's work as a priest made it possible to keep Joash hidden in the Temple for six years. At that point, Jehoiada arranged for the overthrow of Athaliah and the crowning of Joash. For many years following, Jehoiada made most of the kingdom's decisions for Joash. When the old priest died, he was buried in the cemetery of kings as a tribute to his role.

But after Jehoiada's death, Joash didn't know what to do. He listened to counsel that carried him into evil. Within a short time he even ordered the death of Jehoiada's son Zechariah. After a few months, Joash's army had been soundly defeated by the Syrians. Jerusalem was saved only because Joash stripped the Temple of its treasures as a bribe. Finally, the king's own officials assassinated him. In contrast to Jehoiada, Joash was not buried among the kings; he is not even listed in Christ's genealogy in the New Testament.

As dependent as Joash was on Jehoiada, there is little evidence that he ever established a real dependence on the God Jehoiada obeyed. Like many children, Joash's knowledge of God was second-hand. It was a start, but the king needed his own relationship with God that would outlast and overrule the changes in the advice he received.

It would be easy to criticize Joash's failure were it not for the fact that we often fall into the same traps. How often have we acted on poor advice without considering God's Word?

Strengths and accomplishments:
• Carried out extensive repairs on the Temple
• Was faithful to God as long as Jehoiada was alive

Weaknesses and mistakes:
• Allowed idolatry to continue among his people
• Used the Temple treasures to bribe King Hazael of Syria
• Killed Jehoiada's son Zechariah
• Allowed his advisors to lead the people away from God

Lessons from his life:
• A good and hopeful start can be ruined by an evil end
• Even the best counsel is ineffective if it does not help us make wise decisions
• As helpful or hurtful as others may be, we are individually responsible for what we do

Vital statistics:
• Where: Jerusalem
• Occupation: King of Judah
• Relatives: Father: Ahaziah. Mother: Zibiah. Grandmother: Athaliah. Aunt: Jehosheba. Uncle: Jehoiada. Son: Amaziah. Cousin: Zechariah.
• Contemporaries: Jehu, Hazael

Key verses:
"But after his death the leaders of Judah came to King Joash and induced him to abandon the Temple of the God of their ancestors, and to worship shame-idols instead! So the wrath of God came down upon Judah and Jerusalem again" (2 Chronicles 24:17, 18).

Joash's story is told in 2 Kings 11:1—14:23 and 2 Chronicles 22:11—25:25.

hard to please the Lord all during the lifetime of Jehoiada the priest. ³Jehoiada arranged two marriages for him, and he had sons and daughters.

⁴Later on, Joash decided to repair and recondition the Temple. ⁵He summoned the priests and Levites and gave them these instructions:

"Go to all the cities of Judah and collect offerings for the building fund, so that we can maintain the Temple in good repair. Get at it right away. Don't delay." But the Levites took their time.

⁶So the king called for Jehoiada, the High Priest, and asked him, "Why haven't you demanded that the Levites go out and collect the Temple taxes from the cities of Judah, and from Jerusalem? The tax law enacted by Moses the servant of the Lord must be enforced so that the Temple can be repaired."

⁷,⁸(The followers of wicked Athaliah had ravaged the Temple, and everything dedicated to the worship of God had been removed to the temple of Baalim.) So now the king instructed that a chest be made and set outside the Temple gate. ⁹Then a proclamation was sent to all the cities of Judah and throughout Jerusalem telling the people to bring to the Lord the tax that Moses the servant of God had assessed upon Israel. ¹⁰And all the leaders and the people were glad, and brought the money and placed it in the chest until it was full.

¹¹Then the Levites carried the chest to the king's accounting office where the recording secretary and the representative of the High Priest counted the money, and took the chest back to the Temple again. This went on day after day, and money continued to pour in. ¹²The king and Jehoiada gave the money to the building superintendents, who hired masons and carpenters to restore the Temple; and to foundrymen who made articles of iron and brass. ¹³So the work went forward, and finally the Temple was in much better condition than before. ¹⁴When all was finished, the remaining money was brought to the king and Jehoiada, and it was agreed to use it for making the gold and silver spoons and bowls used for incense, and for making the instruments used in the sacrifices and offerings.

Burnt offerings were sacrificed continually during the lifetime of Jehoiada the priest. ¹⁵He lived to a very old age, finally dying at 130. ¹⁶He was buried in the City of David among the kings, because he had done so much good for Israel, for God, and for the Temple.

God judges Joash

¹⁷,¹⁸But after his death the leaders of Judah came to King Joash and induced him to abandon the Temple of the God of their ancestors, and to worship shame-idols instead! So the wrath of God came down upon Judah and Jerusalem again. ¹⁹God sent prophets to bring them back to the Lord, but the people wouldn't listen.

²⁰Then the Spirit of God came upon Zechariah, Jehoiada's son. He called a meeting of all the people. Standing before them upon a platform, he said to them, "God wants to know why you are disobeying his commandments. For when you

24:4
2 Chron 24:7

24:6
Ex 30:12-16

24:9
2 Chron 24:6
36:22

24:16
2 Chron 21:20

24:17
Ex 34:12-14
Josh 22:20
2 Chron 24:4
24:19
Jer 7:25
24:20
Num 14:41
2 Chron 20:14

24:5 The Levites took their time carrying out the king's order, even though he told them not to delay. A tax for keeping the Temple in order was not just the king's order, but God's command (Exodus 30:11–16). The Levites, therefore, were not only disregarding the king, but disregarding God. When it comes to following God's commands, slow obedience may be little better than disobedience.

24:10 Evidently the Levites weren't convinced that the people would want to contribute to the rebuilding of the Temple (24:5), but the people were glad to give of what they had for this project. Don't underestimate people's desire to be faithful to God. When challenged to do great things for God, they will often respond willingly.

24:17, 18 If everything went so well in Judah when the people worshiped God, why did they turn away from him? Prosperity is both a blessing and a curse. While it can be a sign of God's blessing to those who follow him, it carries with it the potential for

moral and spiritual decline. Prosperous people are tempted to become self-sufficient and proud—to take God for granted. In our prosperity, we must not lose sight of the fact that God is the source of our blessings.

24:18–20 When King Joash and the nation of Judah abandoned God, God sent Zechariah to call them to repentance. Before dispensing judgment and punishment, God gave them another chance. In the same way, God does not abandon us or lash out in revenge when we sin. Instead, he aggressively pursues us through his Word, his Spirit in us, the words of others, and sometimes discipline. This is not intended to destroy us, but to urge us to return to him. When you are away from God, he is pursuing you. Stop and listen. Allow him to point out your sin so you can repent and follow him again.

24:19 God sent many prophets to King Joash and the people to warn them that they were headed for destruction. Joel may have been one of these prophets. Read the book of Joel for more information about the political and spiritual climate of the times.

do, everything you try fails. You have forsaken the Lord, and now he has forsaken you."

24:22
Mt 23:34,35

21Then the leaders plotted to kill Zechariah, and finally King Joash himself ordered him executed in the court of the Temple. 22That was how King Joash repaid Jehoiada for his love and loyalty—by killing his son. Zechariah's last words as he died were, "Lord, see what they are doing and pay them back."

24:23
Gen 9:5

23A few months later the Syrian army arrived and conquered Judah and Jerusalem, killing all the leaders of the nation and sending back great quantities of booty to the king of Damascus.

24:24
2 Kgs 12:17
2 Chron 16:7,8

24It was a great triumph for the tiny Syrian army, but the Lord let the great army of Judah be conquered by them because they had forsaken the Lord God of their ancestors. In that way God executed judgment upon Joash.

24:25
2 Kgs 12:20,21

25When the Syrians left—leaving Joash severely wounded—his own officials decided to kill him for murdering the son of Jehoiada the priest. They assassinated him as he lay in bed, and buried him in the City of David, but not in the cemetery of the kings. 26The conspirators were Zabad, whose mother was Shime-ath, a woman from Ammon; and Jehozabad, whose mother was Shimrith, a woman from Moab.

24:27
2 Chron 13:22
24:12

27If you want to read about the sons of Joash, and the curses laid upon Joash, and about the restoration of the Temple, see *The Annals of the Kings*.

When Joash died, his son Amaziah became the new king.

Amaziah rules Judah

25:1
2 Kgs 14:1-6

25 Amaziah was twenty-five years old when he became king, and he reigned twenty-nine years, in Jerusalem. His mother's name was Jeho-addan, a native of Jerusalem. 2He did what was right, but sometimes resented it! 3When he was well established as the new king, he executed the men who had assassinated his father.

25:4
Deut 24:16

4However, he didn't kill their children but followed the command of the Lord written in the law of Moses, that the fathers shall not die for the children's sins, nor the children for the father's sins. No, everyone must pay for his own sins.

25:5
Num 1:3
2 Chron 26:13

5, 6Another thing Amaziah did was to organize the army, assigning leaders to each clan from Judah and Benjamin. Then he took a census and found that he had an army of 300,000 men twenty years old and older, all trained and highly skilled in the use of spear and sword. He also paid $200,000 to hire 100,000 experienced mercenaries from Israel.

25:7
2 Kgs 4:9
25:8
2 Chron 14:11
20:6

7But a prophet arrived with this message from the Lord: "Sir, do not hire troops from Israel, for the Lord is not with them. 8If you let them go with your troops to battle, you will be defeated no matter how well you fight; for God has power to help or to frustrate."

9"But the money!" Amaziah whined. "What shall I do about that?"

And the prophet replied, "The Lord is able to give you much more than this!"

25:11
2 Kgs 14:7

10So Amaziah sent them home again to Ephraim, which made them very angry and insulted. 11Then Amaziah took courage and led his army to the Valley of Salt, and there killed 10,000 men from Seir. 12Another 10,000 were taken alive to the top of a cliff and thrown over, so that they were crushed upon the rocks below.

13Meanwhile, the army of Israel that had been sent home raided several of the cities of Judah in the vicinity of Beth-horon, toward Samaria, killing 3,000 people and carrying off great quantities of booty.

24:22 Zechariah asked God to pay the people back for their sins. He was not seeking revenge, but pleading for justice. When we feel like despairing over the wickedness around us, we can rest assured that in the end God will restore complete justice to the earth.

25:2 Amaziah did what was right on the outside, but inside he often resented what he had to do. His obedience was at best halfhearted. When the prophet promised God's deliverance, Amaziah first complained about the money that had been lost (25:9). He valued military success more than God's will. We must

search our own hearts and root out any resistance to obeying God. Grudging obedience is not true obedience.

25:9, 10 Amaziah made a financial agreement with wicked Israelite soldiers, offering to pay them to fight for him (25:6). But before they went to battle, Amaziah sent them home with their pay after the prophet's warning. Although it cost him plenty, he wisely realized that the money was not worth the ruin the alliance could cause. How would you have chosen? Money must never stand in the way of making right decisions. The Lord's blessing is priceless, worth more than any amount of money.

14When King Amaziah returned from this slaughter of the Edomites, he brought with him idols taken from the people of Seir, and set them up as gods, and bowed before them, and burned incense to them! 15This made the Lord very angry and he sent a prophet to demand, "Why have you worshiped gods who couldn't even save their own people from you?"

16"Since when have I asked your advice?" the king retorted. "Be quiet now, before I have you killed."

The prophet left with this parting warning: "I know that God has determined to destroy you because you have worshiped these idols, and have not accepted my counsel."

17King Amaziah of Judah now took the advice of his counselors and declared war on King Joash of Israel (son of Jehoahaz, grandson of Jehu).

18King Joash replied with this parable: "Out in the Lebanon mountains a thistle demanded of a cedar tree, 'Give your daughter in marriage to my son.' Just then a wild animal came by and stepped on the thistle, crushing it! 19You are very proud about your conquest of Edom, but my advice is to stay home and don't meddle with me, lest you and all Judah get badly hurt."

20But Amaziah wouldn't listen, for God was arranging to destroy him for worshiping the gods of Edom. 21The armies met at Beth-shemesh, in Judah, 22and Judah was defeated, and its army fled home. 23King Joash of Israel captured the defeated King Amaziah of Judah and took him as a prisoner to Jerusalem. Then King Joash ordered two hundred yards of the walls of Jerusalem dismantled, from the gate of Ephraim to the Corner Gate. 24He carried off all the treasures and gold bowls from the Temple, as well as the treasures from the palace; and he took hostages, including Obed-edom, and returned to Samaria.

25However, King Amaziah of Judah lived on for fifteen years after the death of King Joash of Israel. 26The complete biography of King Amaziah is written in *The Annals of the Kings of Judah and Israel.* 27This account includes a report of Amaziah's turning away from God, and how his people conspired against him in Jerusalem, and how he fled to Lachish—but they went after him and killed him there. 28And they brought him back on horses to Jerusalem and buried him in the royal cemetery.

Uzziah rules Judah

26 The people of Judah now crowned sixteen-year-old Uzziah as their new king. 2After his father's death, he rebuilt the city of Eloth and restored it to Judah. 3In all, he reigned fifty-two years, in Jerusalem. His mother's name was Jecoliah, from Jerusalem. 4He followed in the footsteps of his father Amaziah, and was, in general, a good king in the Lord's sight.

5While Zechariah was alive Uzziah was always eager to please God. Zechariah was a man who had special revelations from God. And as long as the king followed the paths of God, he prospered, for God blessed him.

6He declared war on the Philistines and captured the city of Gath and broke down its walls, also those of Jabneh and Ashdod. Then he built new cities in the Ashdod area and in other parts of the Philistine country. 7God helped him not only with his

25:14
2 Chron 28:23

25:15
2 Chron 25:11, 12

25:17
2 Kgs 14:8-14

25:18
Judg 9:8-15

25:19
2 Chron 26:16
32:25

25:24
1 Chron 26:15

25:25
2 Kgs 14:17-22

26:1
2 Kgs 15:2,3

26:5
2 Chron 15:2

26:6
Isa 14:29
26:7
2 Chron 21:16

25:14 After the victory, Amaziah returned and burned incense to idols. We are very susceptible to sin after great victories. It is then that we feel confident. We let our defenses down, and Satan attacks with all sorts of temptations. When you win, watch out. After the mountain peaks come the valleys.

25:15 Amaziah made a foolish mistake by worshiping the gods of the nation he had just conquered. Impressed by the accomplishments of the Edomites, he worshiped their idols! How foolish to serve the gods of a defeated enemy. We make the same mistake as Amaziah when we run after money, power, or recognition—false gods that are symbols of our society, but that Jesus, the suffering servant, conquered at the cross. By recognizing the emptiness of worldly pursuits, we can free

ourselves from the desire to follow them.

25:15 The Lord became angry when the king brought idols back to Judah. The more we love someone, the more anger and hurt we feel when that person rejects us. The Lord became angry because he loved Amaziah and the nation of Judah. He had just saved them from their enemies, and now they were thanking other gods. Love without anger is mere sentimentality. We should be thankful that God, who loves us very much, cares deeply when we reject him.

25:18 In this parable, Judah is the small thistle and Israel's army is the cedar tree. Ahaziah was proud after defeating Edom. He wanted to defeat Israel, but Joash warned him not to attack. Ahaziah had more ambition than ability, and he paid for it when he was soundly defeated.

wars against the Philistines but also in his battles with the Arabs of Gurbaal and in his wars with the Meunites. ⁸The Ammonites paid annual tribute to him, and his fame spread even to Egypt, for he was very powerful.

⁹He built fortified towers in Jerusalem at the Corner Gate, and the Valley Gate, and at the turning of the wall. ¹⁰He also constructed forts in the Negeb, and made many water reservoirs, for he had great herds of cattle out in the valleys and on the plains. He was a man who loved the soil and had many farms and vineyards, both on the hillsides and in the fertile valleys.

¹¹He organized his army into regiments to which men were drafted under quotas set by Je-iel, the secretary of the army, and his assistant, Ma-aseiah. The commander-in-chief was General Hananiah. ¹²Twenty-six hundred brave clan leaders commanded these regiments. ¹³The army consisted of 307,500 men, all elite troops. ¹⁴Uzziah issued to them shields, spears, helmets, coats of mail, bows, and slingstones. ¹⁵And he produced engines of war manufactured in Jerusalem, invented by brilliant men to shoot arrows and huge stones from the towers and battlements. So he became very famous, for the Lord helped him wonderfully until he was very powerful.

26:8
2 Chron 17:11

26:9
2 Chron 25:23
Neh 3:13
21:13,15
26:10
Gen 26:18-21

26:13
2 Chron 25:5

UZZIAH

We are never closer to failure than during our greatest successes. The failure to recognize God's part in our achievements makes them no better than failures. Uzziah was a remarkably successful king. His achievements brought him fame. He was successful in war and peace, in planning and execution, in building and planting.

Uzziah overestimated his own importance in bringing about the great achievements he experienced. He did so many things well that a consuming pride gradually invaded his life like the leprous disease that finally destroyed his body. In trying to act as a priest, he took on a role that God did not mean for him to have. He had forgotten not only how much God had given him, but also that God had certain roles for others that he needed to respect.

Uzziah's pride was rooted in his lack of thankfulness. We have no examples of this king ever showing appreciation to God for the marvelous gifts he had received. Our accomplishments may not compare with Uzziah's, but we still owe a debt of thanksgiving to God for our very lives. If God is not getting the credit for your successes, shouldn't you start looking at your life differently?

Strengths and accomplishments:
- Pleased God during his early years as king
- Successful warrior and city-builder
- Skillful in organizing and delegating
- Reigned for 52 years

Weaknesses and mistakes:
- Developed a prideful attitude due to his great success
- Tried to perform the priest's duties, in direct disobedience to God
- Failed to remove many of the symbols of idolatry in the land

Lessons from his life:
- Lack of thankfulness to God can lead to pride
- Even successful people must acknowledge the role God has for others in their lives

Vital statistics:
- Where: Jerusalem
- Occupation: King of Judah
- Relatives: Father: Amaziah. Mother: Jecoliah. Son: Jotham.
- Contemporaries: Isaiah, Amos, Hosea, Jeroboam, Zechariah, Azariah

Key verses:
"And he produced engines of war manufactured in Jerusalem, invented by brilliant men to shoot arrows and huge stones from the towers and battlements. So he became very famous, for the Lord helped him wonderfully until he was very powerful. But at that point he became proud—and corrupt. He sinned against the Lord his God by entering the forbidden sanctuary of the Temple and personally burning incense upon the altar" (2 Chronicles 26:15, 16).

Uzziah's story is told in 2 Kings 15:1–7 and 2 Chronicles 26:1–23. He is also mentioned in Isaiah 1:1; 6:1; 7:1; Hosea 1:1; Amos 1:1; Zechariah 14:5.

Uzziah becomes a leper

16But at that point he became proud—and corrupt. He sinned against the Lord his God by entering the forbidden sanctuary of the Temple and personally burning incense upon the altar. 17, 18Azariah the High Priest went in after him with eighty other priests, all brave men, and demanded that he get out.

"It is not for you, Uzziah, to burn incense," they declared. "That is the work of the priests alone, the sons of Aaron who are consecrated to this work. Get out, for you have trespassed, and the Lord is not going to honor you for this!"

19Uzziah was furious, and refused to set down the incense burner he was holding. But look! Suddenly—leprosy appeared in his forehead! 20When Azariah and the others saw it, they rushed him out; in fact, he himself was as anxious to get out as they were to get him out, because the Lord had struck him.

21So King Uzziah was a leper until the day of his death and lived in isolation, cut off from his people and from the Temple. His son Jotham became vice-regent, in charge of the king's affairs and of the judging of the people of the land.

22The other details of Uzziah's reign from first to last are recorded by the prophet Isaiah (son of Amoz). 23When Uzziah died, he was buried in the royal cemetery even though he was a leper, and his son Jotham became the new king.

26:16
Deut 32:15
1 Kgs 13:1-4
2 Chron 25:19

26:17
Ex 30:7,8
Num 16:39,40
1 Chron 6:10
2 Chron 19:2

26:19
2 Kgs 5:25-27

26:21
Lev 13:46
2 Kgs 15:5-7

26:22
Isa 1:1

26:23
2 Chron 21:20
28:27

Jotham rules Judah

27 Jotham was twenty-five years old at the time he became king, and he reigned sixteen years, in Jerusalem. His mother was Jerushah, daughter of Zadok. 2He followed the generally good example of his father Uzziah—who had, however, sinned by invading the Temple—but even so his people became very corrupt.

3He built the Upper Gate of the Temple, and also did extensive rebuilding of the walls on the hill where the Temple was situated. 4And he built cities in the hill country of Judah, and erected fortresses and towers on the wooded hills.

5His war against the Ammonites was successful, so that for the next three years he received from them an annual tribute of $200,000 in silver, 10,000 sacks of wheat, and 10,000 sacks of barley. 6King Jotham became powerful because he was careful to follow the path of the Lord his God.

7The remainder of his history, including his wars and other activities, is written in *The Annals of the Kings of Israel and Judah.* 8In summary, then, he was twenty-five years old when he began to reign and he reigned sixteen years, in Jerusalem. 9When he died, he was buried in Jerusalem, and his son Ahaz became the new king.

27:1
2 Kgs 15:33-35

27:2
2 Chron 26:16

27:3
2 Chron 33:14
Neh 3:26

27:4
2 Chron 11:5

27:6
2 Chron 26:5

27:7
2 Kgs 15:36

27:8
2 Chron 27:1

Ahaz rules Judah

28 Ahaz was twenty years old when he became king and he reigned sixteen years, in Jerusalem. But he was an evil king, unlike his ancestor King David. 2For he followed the example of the kings over in Israel and worshiped the idols of Baal. 3He even went out to the Valley of Hinnom, and it was not just to burn incense to the idols, for he even sacrificed his own children in the fire, just like the heathen nations that were thrown out of the land by the Lord to make room for Israel. 4Yes, he sacrificed and burned incense at the idol shrines on the hills and under every green tree.

28:1
2 Kgs 16:2-4

28:2
Ex 34:17
2 Chron 22:3

28:3
Lev 18:21
Josh 15:8
2 Chron 33:2,6

26:15, 16 After God gave Uzziah great blessings and power, he became proud and corrupt. It is true that "pride goes before destruction" (Proverbs 16:18). If God has given you wealth, influence, popularity, and power, be thankful and be careful. God hates pride. Check your attitudes and remember to give God the credit for what you have. Use your gifts in ways that please him.

26:17, 20 When people have power, they often think they can live above the law. But even rulers are subject to God, as Uzziah discovered. No matter what your position in society, God expects you to honor, worship, and obey him.

26:21 For much of his life, Uzziah was "a good king in the Lord's sight" (26:4). But Uzziah turned away from God and died a leper.

He is remembered more for his arrogant act and subsequent punishment than for his great reforms. God requires continuous obedience. Spurts of obedience are not enough. Only those who "endure to the end" will be rewarded (Mark 13:13). Be remembered for your consistent faith; otherwise you, too, may become more famous for the punishment you received than for the faith you lived by.

26:23 This was the year that God called Isaiah to be a prophet (Isaiah 6:1).

27:2 Jotham was generally a good king (27:6), but his people became corrupt. Those you lead will not always follow your example, but that should not affect the way you live for God. This sinfulness of Jotham's kingdom is vividly portrayed in Isaiah 1—5.

28:5
2 Chron 24:24

28:6
2 Kgs 16:5

28:8
Deut 28:25,41

28:9
2 Chron 25:15
Ezra 9:6
Isa 47:6
Rev 18:5

28:10
2 Chron 28:8

28:15
Deut 34:3
2 Kgs 6:22
2 Chron 28:12
Prov 25:21,22

28:16
2 Kgs 16:7

28:17
Ezek 16:57

28:20
1 Chron 5:26
28:21
2 Kgs 16:8,9
28:23
2 Chron 25:14
Jer 44:17,18

28:24
2 Kgs 16:17
2 Chron 29:7
30:14; 33:3-5

⁵That is why the Lord God allowed the king of Syria to defeat him and deport large numbers of his people to Damascus. The armies from Israel also slaughtered great numbers of his troops. ⁶On a single day, Pekah, the son of Remaliah, killed 120,000 of his bravest soldiers because they had turned away from the Lord God of their fathers. ⁷Then Zichri, a great warrior from Ephraim, killed the king's son Ma-aseiah, and the king's administrator Azrikam, and the king's second-in-command Elkanah. ⁸The armies from Israel also captured 200,000 Judean women and children, and tremendous amounts of booty which they took to Samaria.

⁹But Oded, a prophet of the Lord, was there in Samaria and he went out to meet the returning army.

"Look!" he exclaimed. "The Lord God of your fathers was angry with Judah and let you capture them, but you have butchered them without mercy, and all heaven is disturbed. ¹⁰And now are you going to make slaves of these people from Judah and Jerusalem? What about your own sins against the Lord your God? ¹¹Listen to me and return these relatives of yours to their homes, for now the fierce anger of the Lord is upon *you*."

¹²Some of the top leaders of Ephraim also added their opposition. These men were Azariah the son of Johanan, Berechiah the son of Meshillemoth, Jehizkiah the son of Shallum, and Amasa the son of Hadlai.

¹³"You must not bring the captives here!" they declared. "If you do, the Lord will be angry, and this sin will be added to our many others. We are in enough trouble with God as it is."

¹⁴So the army officers turned over the captives and booty to the political leaders to decide what to do. ¹⁵Then the four men already mentioned distributed captured stores of clothing to the women and children who needed it, and gave them shoes, food, and wine, and put those who were sick and old on donkeys, and took them back to their families in Jericho, the City of Palm Trees. Then their escorts returned to Samaria.

¹⁶About that time King Ahaz of Judah asked the king of Assyria to be his ally in his war against the armies of Edom. For Edom was invading Judah and capturing many people as slaves. ¹⁷, ¹⁸Meanwhile, the Philistines had invaded the lowland cities and the Negeb and had already captured Beth-shemesh, Aijalon, Gederoth, Soco, Timnah, and Gimzo with their surrounding villages, and were living there. ¹⁹For the Lord brought Judah very low on account of the evil deeds of King Ahaz of Israel, for he had destroyed the spiritual fiber of Judah and had been faithless to the Lord. ²⁰But when Tilgath-pilneser, king of Assyria, arrived, he caused trouble for King Ahaz instead of helping him. ²¹So even though Ahaz had given him the Temple gold and the palace treasures, it did no good.

²²In this time of deep trial, King Ahaz collapsed spiritually. ²³He sacrificed to the gods of the people of Damascus who had defeated him, for he felt that since these gods had helped the kings of Syria, they would help him too if he sacrificed to them. But instead, they were his ruin, and that of all his people. ²⁴The king took the gold bowls from the Temple and slashed them to pieces, and nailed the door of the Temple shut so that no one could worship there, and made altars to the heathen gods in every corner of Jerusalem. ²⁵And he did the same in every city of Judah, thus angering the Lord God of his fathers.

28:1ff During Ahaz's reign the Northern Kingdom of Israel was conquered by the Assyrians and carried into captivity (2 Kings 17). Chronicles mentions very little about the Northern Kingdom because the writer was focusing on David's descendants from whom the Messiah would one day come.

28:3 Imagine the monstrous evil of a religion that offers young children as sacrifices. God allowed the nation to be conquered in response to Ahaz's evil practices. Even today the practice hasn't abated. The sacrifice of children to the harsh gods of convenience, economy, and whim continues in sterile medical facilities in numbers that would astound the wicked Ahaz. If we are to allow children to come to Christ (Matthew 19:14), we must first allow them to come into the world.

28:19 King Ahaz ruled two tribes, Judah and Benjamin. Although the Northern Kingdom (Israel) had split off from them, Judah and Benjamin were two of the original 12 tribes of Israel. Thus Ahaz is called a king of Israel.

28:22 Difficulties and struggles can devastate people, or they can stimulate growth and maturity. For King Ahaz, deep trials led to spiritual collapse. This need not be so in our lives. When facing problems or tragedy, we must remember that rough times give us a chance to grow (James 1:2–4). When you are facing trials, don't turn away from God; turn *to* him.

26The other details of his life and activities are recorded in *The Annals of the Kings of Judah and Israel*. 27When King Ahaz died, he was buried in Jerusalem but not in the royal tombs, and his son Hezekiah became the new king.

28:26
2 Kgs 16:19,20
28:27
2 Chron 24:25

Hezekiah reopens the Temple

29 Hezekiah was twenty-five years old when he became the king of Judah, and he reigned twenty-nine years, in Jerusalem. His mother's name was Abijah, the daughter of Zechariah. 2His reign was generally good in the Lord's sight, just as his ancestor David's had been.

29:1
2 Kgs 18:1-3
29:2
2 Chron 28:1
34:2

3In the very first month of the first year of his reign, he reopened the doors of the Temple and repaired them. 4, 5He summoned the priests and Levites to meet him at the open space east of the Temple, and addressed them thus:

29:3
2 Chron 28:24
29:7

"Listen to me, you Levites. Sanctify yourselves and sanctify the Temple of the Lord God of your ancestors—clean all the debris from the holy place. 6For our fathers have committed a deep sin before the Lord our God; they abandoned the Lord and his Temple and turned their backs on it. 7The doors have been shut tight, the perpetual flame has been put out, and the incense and burnt offerings have not been offered. 8Therefore the wrath of the Lord has been upon Judah and Jerusalem. He has caused us to be objects of horror, amazement, and contempt, as you see us today. 9Our fathers have been killed in war, and our sons and daughters and wives are in captivity because of this.

29:5
2 Chron 29:15,
34; 35:6
29:6
Ezek 8:16
29:8
Deut 28:25
2 Chron 24:18
28:5
Jer 25:9,18
29:9
2 Chron 28:5-8,
17

10"But now I want to make a covenant with the Lord God of Israel so that his fierce anger will turn away from us. 11My children, don't neglect your duties any longer, for the Lord has chosen you to minister to him and to burn incense."

29:10
2 Chron 23:16
29:11
Num 3:6; 8:6

12, 13, 14Then the Levites went into action:

29:12
Num 3:19,20
2 Chron 31:13

From the Kohath clan, Mahath (son of Amasai) and Joel (son of Azariah);
From the Merari clan, Kish (son of Abdi) and Azariah (son of Jehallelel);
From the Gershon clan, Joah (son of Zimmah) and Eden (son of Joah).
From the Elizaphan clan, Shimri and Jeuel;
From the Asaph clan, Zechariah and Mattaniah;
From the Hemanite clan, Jehuel and Shime-i;
From the Jeduthun clan, Shemaiah and Uzziel.

15They in turn summoned their fellow Levites and sanctified themselves, and began to clean up and sanctify the Temple, as the king (who was speaking for the Lord) had commanded them. 16The priests cleaned up the inner room of the Temple, and brought out into the court all the filth and decay they found there. The Levites then carted it out to the brook Kidron. 17This all began on the first day of April, and by the eighth day they had reached the outer court, which took eight days to clean up, so the entire job was completed in sixteen days.

29:15
1 Chron 23:28
2 Chron 29:5
30:12
29:16
2 Chron 15:16

18Then they went back to the palace and reported to King Hezekiah, "We have completed the cleansing of the Temple and of the altar of burnt offerings and of its accessories, also the table of the Bread of the Presence and its equipment. 19What's more, we have recovered and sanctified all the utensils thrown away by King Ahaz when he closed the Temple. They are beside the altar of the Lord."

29:19
2 Chron 28:24

20Early the next morning, King Hezekiah went to the Temple with the city officials, 21taking seven young bulls, seven rams, seven lambs, and seven male goats for a sin offering for the nation and for the Temple.

29:21
Lev 4:3-14

29:1 Hezekiah's Profile is found in 2 Kings 18.

29:11 The Levites, chosen by God to serve in the Temple, had been kept from their duties by Ahaz's wickedness (28:24). But Hezekiah called them back into service, saying, "Don't neglect your duties any longer, for the Lord has chosen you to minister."

We may not have to face a wicked king, but pressures or responsibilities can render us inactive and ineffective. When you have been given the responsibility to minister, don't neglect your duty. If your Christian service has been rendered inactive, whether by choice or by force, look for the opportunities (and listen to the "Hezekiahs") God will send your way to help you resume your responsibilities. Then, like the Levites, be ready for action (29:12).

29:21 Throughout the Old Testament, the sacrifice was God's appointed way of approaching him and restoring a right relationship with him. The sin offering made by Hezekiah was one such sacrifice, given to ask God's forgiveness for unintentional sins. (For more information on why God required sacrifices and how they were carried out, see the notes in Leviticus 1.)

29:22
Lev 4:18

29:23
Lev 4:15

29:24
Lev 4:26

He instructed the priests, the sons of Aaron, to sacrifice them on the altar of the Lord. 22So they killed the young bulls, and the priests took the blood and sprinkled it on the altar, and they killed the rams and sprinkled their blood upon the altar, and did the same with the lambs. 23The male goats for the sin offering were then brought before the king and his officials, who laid their hands upon them. 24Then the priests killed the animals and made a sin offering with their blood upon the altar, to make atonement for all Israel as the king had commanded—for the king had specified that the burnt offering and sin offering must be sacrificed for the entire nation.

29:25
2 Sam 7:2
24:11
1 Chron 25:6
2 Chron 5:12
8:14

29:27
2 Chron 23:18

25, 26He organized Levites at the Temple into an orchestral group, using cymbals, psalteries, and harps. This was in accordance with the directions of David and the prophets Gad and Nathan—who had received their instructions from the Lord. The priests formed a trumpet corps. 27Then Hezekiah ordered the burnt offering to be placed upon the altar, and as the sacrifice began, the instruments of music began to play the songs of the Lord, accompanied by the trumpets. 28Throughout the entire ceremony everyone worshiped the Lord as the singers sang and the trumpets blew.

29:29
2 Chron 20:18

29Afterwards the king and his aides bowed low before the Lord in worship. 30Then King Hezekiah ordered the Levites to sing before the Lord some of the psalms of David and of the prophet Asaph, which they gladly did, and bowed their heads and worshiped.

29:31
Ex 35:5,22

31"The consecration ceremony is now ended," Hezekiah said. "Now bring your sacrifices and thank offerings." So the people from every part of the nation brought their sacrifices and thank offerings, and those who wished to, brought burnt offerings too. 32, 33In all, there were 70 young bulls for burnt offerings, 100 rams, and 200 lambs. In addition, 600 oxen and 3,000 sheep were brought as holy gifts.

29:34
2 Chron 35:11

34But there were too few priests to prepare the burnt offerings, so their brothers the Levites helped them until the work was finished—and until more priests had reported to work—for the Levites were much more ready to sanctify themselves

GREET REVIVALS IN THE BIBLE	Leader	Reference	How the People Responded
The Bible records several great revivals where people in great numbers turned to God and gave up their sinful ways of living. Each revival was characterized by a *leader* who recognized his nation's spiritual dryness. And in each case, the leader *took action,* and was not afraid to make his desires known to the people.	Moses	Exodus 32, 33	Accepted God's laws and built the Tabernacle
	Samuel	1 Samuel 7:1–13	Promised to make God first in their lives by destroying their idols
	David	2 Samuel 6	Brought the Ark of the Covenant to Jerusalem; praised God with singing and musical instruments
	Jehoshaphat	2 Chronicles 20	Decided to trust in God alone to help them, and their discouragement turned to joy
	Hezekiah	2 Chronicles 29—31	Purified the Temple; got rid of idols; brought tithes to God's house
	Josiah	2 Chronicles 34, 35	Made a commitment to obey God's Word and remove sinful influences from their lives
	Ezra	Ezra 9, 10 Haggai 1	Stopped associating with those who caused them to compromise their faith; renewed their commitment to God's Word
	Nehemiah (with Ezra)	Nehemiah 8—10	Fasted, confessed their sins, read God's Word publicly, and promised in writing to again serve God wholeheartedly

29:22 The blood sprinkled upon the altar represented the innocence of the sacrificed animal taking the place of the guilt of the person making the offering. The animal died so the sinner could live. This ritual looked forward to the day when Jesus Christ, God's perfect Son, would sacrifice his innocent life on the cross in order that sinful and guilty mankind might be spared the punishment they deserve (Hebrews 10:1–14).

29:31 A thank (or peace) offering was given as an expression of gratitude toward God. It symbolized restored peace and fellowship with God.

29:34 It is ironic that the assistants were more prepared than their leaders, but we sometimes see "volunteers" in the church today with more zeal to serve the Lord than "professional" Christian workers.

than the priests were. 35There was an abundance of burnt offerings, and the usual drink offering with each, and many peace offerings. So it was that the Temple was restored to service, and the sacrifices offered again. 36And Hezekiah and all the people were very happy because of what God had accomplished so quickly.

Hezekiah reinstates the Passover

30 King Hezekiah now sent letters throughout all of Israel, Judah, Ephraim, and Manasseh, inviting everyone to come to the Temple at Jerusalem for the annual Passover celebration. 2, 3The king, his aides, and all the assembly of Jerusalem had voted to celebrate the Passover in May this time, rather than at the normal time in April, because not enough priests were sanctified at the earlier date, and there wasn't enough time to get notices out. 4The king and his advisors were in complete agreement in this matter, 5so they sent a Passover proclamation throughout Israel, from Dan to Beer-sheba, inviting everyone. They had not kept it in great numbers as prescribed.

6"Come back to the Lord God of Abraham, Isaac, and Israel," the king's letter said, "so that he will return to us who have escaped from the power of the kings of Assyria. 7Do not be like your fathers and brothers who sinned against the Lord God of their fathers and were destroyed. 8Do not be stubborn, as they were, but yield yourselves to the Lord and come to his Temple which he has sanctified forever, and worship the Lord your God so that his fierce anger will turn away from you. 9For if you turn to the Lord again, your brothers and your children will be treated mercifully by their captors, and they will be able to return to this land. For the Lord your God is full of kindness and mercy and will not continue to turn away his face from you if you return to him."

10So the messengers went from city to city throughout Ephraim and Manasseh and as far as Zebulun. But for the most part they were received with laughter and scorn! 11However, some from the tribes of Asher, Manasseh, and Zebulun turned to God and came to Jerusalem. 12But in Judah the entire nation felt a strong, God-given desire to obey the Lord's direction as commanded by the king and his officers. 13And so it was that a very large crowd assembled at Jerusalem in the month of May for the Passover celebration. 14They set to work and destroyed the heathen altars in Jerusalem, and knocked down all the incense altars, and threw them into Kidron Brook.

29:35
Num 15:5-10
2 Chron 29:32

30:2
Num 9:10,11
2 Chron 30:13, 15

30:5
Judg 20:1

30:6
2 Chron 28:20

30:7
2 Chron 29:8
Ezek 20:13

30:8
Ex 3:29
2 Chron 29:10

30:9
Ex 34:6,7
Deut 30:2
Mic 7:18

30:10
2 Chron 36:16

30:11
2 Chron 30: 18, 21,35

30:13
2 Chron 30:2
30:14
2 Chron 28:24
29:16

30:5 *They had not kept it in great numbers as prescribed,* or, "The Passover had not been celebrated by the northern tribes of Israel for a long time; only a faithful few had been doing it in the proper way."

30:1 The Passover celebration commemorated the time that God spared the lives of Israel's firstborn sons in Egypt. God had promised to send a plague to kill all the firstborn sons except in those homes where the blood of a slain lamb had been painted on the doorposts. The Israelites obeyed, and when the Angel of the Lord saw the blood, he "passed over" the house and did not harm anyone in it (Exodus 12:23). After this plague, Pharaoh freed the Israelites from slavery. This celebration was to be a yearly reminder of how God delivered his people. The careful preparations, both in the Temple and for the feast, show that this was not a temporary or impulsive revival, but a deep-seated change of heart and life.

30:2, 3 God's Law had a provision that, under certain circumstances, the Passover could be celebrated one month later (Numbers 9:10, 11).

30:6-9 Hezekiah was a king dedicated to God and to the spiritual life of the nation. He sent letters throughout Judah and Israel urging everyone to return to God. He told them not to be stubborn, but to yield themselves to the Lord. We, too, must temper our stubborn selfishness by putting God first in our lives, acknowledging that he knows what is best for us, and living his way.

30:10 The Northern Kingdom of Israel had recently been conquered by Assyria, and most of the people had been carried away to foreign lands. Hezekiah sent letters to the few people who remained, inviting them to come to the Passover (30:1), but they responded with laughter and scorn. Those who serve the Lord may face mockery when they try to promote spiritual renewal and growth. Are you prepared to handle ridicule for your faith? When it comes your way, do not waver. Stand strong in your faith, as Hezekiah did, and God will honor you.

30:11 In most places, Hezekiah's messengers were scorned when they invited people to the Passover, but some accepted the invitation. Our efforts to tell others about God often meet with similar reactions. Many people will not accept the invitation to accept Christ. But this must not stop us from reaching out. If you know and understand that rejection of the gospel is common, it can help you guard against feelings of personal rejection. Remember that the Holy Spirit convicts and convinces. Our task is to invite others to consider God's actions, his claims, and his promises.

30:14 Just as the priests had cleansed the Temple (29:4, 5), so the people cleansed the city of heathen idols and then cleansed themselves to prepare for worship (30:17–19). Even the good kings of Judah found it difficult to get rid of the heathen idols and altars on the high places (2 Kings 14:4; 2 Chronicles 20:33). Finally Hezekiah, with the help of his people, completed this task.

30:15 The people were so zealous to bring gifts and offerings to

30:15
2 Chron 29:34
30:2,3
30:16
2 Chron 35:10,
15

30:17
Ex 12:43-49
Num 9:10
2 Chron 19:3
29:34; 30:11,25

30:21
Ex 12:15; 13:6

30:22
Ezra 10:11

30:23
1 Kgs 8:65

30:24
2 Chron 29:34
30:3; 35:7,8
30:25
2 Chron 30:11,
18
30:26
2 Chron 7:8-10
30:27
Num 6:23
Deut 26:15
2 Chron 23:18
Ps 68:5

31:1
2 Kgs 18:4

31:2
1 Chron
23:28-31; 24:1
31:3
Num 28:1-29,40
2 Chron 35:7
31:4
Num 18:8

15On the first day of May the people killed their Passover lambs. Then the priests and Levites became ashamed of themselves for not taking a more active part, so they sanctified themselves and brought burnt offerings into the Temple. 16They stood at their posts as instructed by the law of Moses the man of God; and the priests sprinkled the blood received from the Levites.

17, 18, 19Since many of the people arriving from Ephraim, Manasseh, Issachar, and Zebulun were ceremonially impure because they had not undergone the purification rites, the Levites killed their Passover lambs for them, to sanctify them. Then King Hezekiah prayed for them and they were permitted to eat the Passover anyway, even though this was contrary to God's rules. But Hezekiah said, "May the good Lord pardon everyone who determines to follow the Lord God of his fathers, even though he is not properly sanctified for the ceremony." 20And the Lord listened to Hezekiah's prayer and did not destroy them.

21So the people of Israel celebrated the Passover at Jerusalem for seven days with great joy.

Meanwhile the Levites and priests praised the Lord with music and cymbals day after day. 22(King Hezekiah spoke very appreciatively to the Levites of their excellent music.)

So, for seven days the observance continued, and peace offerings were sacrificed, and the people confessed their sins to the Lord God of their fathers. 23The enthusiasm continued, so it was unanimously decided to continue the observance for another seven days. 24King Hezekiah gave the people 1,000 young bulls for offerings, and 7,000 sheep; and the princes donated 1,000 young bulls and 10,000 sheep. And at this time another large group of priests stepped forward and sanctified themselves.

25Then the people of Judah, together with the priests, the Levites, the foreign residents, and the visitors from Israel, were filled with deep joy. 26For Jerusalem hadn't seen a celebration like this one since the days of King David's son Solomon. 27Then the priests and Levites stood and blessed the people, and the Lord heard their prayers from his holy temple in heaven.

Hezekiah restores worship

31 Afterwards a massive campaign against idol worship was begun. Those who were at Jerusalem for the Passover went out to the cities of Judah, Benjamin, Ephraim, and Manasseh and tore down the idol altars, the obelisks, shameimages, and other heathen centers of worship. Then the people who had come to the Passover from the northern tribes returned again to their own homes.

2Hezekiah now organized the priests and Levites into service corps to offer the burnt offerings and peace offerings, and to worship and give thanks and praise to the Lord. 3He also made a personal contribution of animals for the daily morning and evening burnt offerings, as well as for the weekly Sabbath and monthly new moon festivals, and for the other annual feasts as required in the law of God.

4In addition, he required the people in Jerusalem to bring their tithes to the priests

---

the Temple that the priests and Levites were ashamed they did not share the same enthusiasm. The zeal of the common man's faith motivated the ministers to take action. The devoted faith of laypersons today should motivate professional church staff to rekindle their enthusiasm for God's work. Laypersons should never be shut out of church government or decision-making. The church needs their good examples of faith.

30:26 It had been more than 200 years since there had been such a celebration in Jerusalem.

31:1ff Why was idol worship so bad? The Israelites had access to the one true God, but they constantly fell into worshiping lifeless idols made of wood or stone. They put aside worshiping the Creator in order to worship his creation. We are just as guilty when God no longer holds first place in our lives. When we think more about wealth, prestige, or material possessions than about God,

we are actually worshiping them as idols. Because of idol worship, the people of Judah were sent into captivity in foreign lands (36:14–17). We may not be sent into captivity, but discipline awaits all those who put earthly objects above spiritual priorities.

31:2-21 The priests had not been supported by the government during the evil kings reigns. Hezekiah organized the priests and the work of the Temple resumed according to a plan originally set up by King David (1 Chronicles 23:6–23; 24:3–19).

31:4-6 Hezekiah reinstated the practice of tithing—giving the first portion of one's income to the priests and Levites so they could be free to serve God and minister to the people. The people responded immediately with their first crops. Does God receive the first portion of your income? Generosity makes our giving delightful to God (2 Corinthians 8, 9). How different the church would be today if all believers consistently followed this pattern.

and Levites, so that they wouldn't need other employment but could apply themselves fully to their duties as required in the law of God. 5, 6The people responded
immediately and generously with the first of their crops and grain, new wine, olive
oil, money, and everything else—a tithe of all they owned, as required by law to be
given to the Lord their God. Everything was laid out in great piles. The people who
had moved to Judah from the northern tribes and the people of Judah living in the
provinces also brought in the tithes of their cattle and sheep, and brought a tithe of
the dedicated things to give to the Lord and piled them up in great heaps. 7, 8The
first of these tithes arrived in June, and the piles continued to grow until October.
When Hezekiah and his officials came and saw these huge piles, how they blessed
the Lord and praised his people!

9"Where did all this come from?" Hezekiah asked the priests and Levites.
10And Azariah the High Priest from the clan of Zadok replied, "These are tithes!
We have been eating from these stores of food for many weeks, but all this is left
over, for the Lord has blessed his people."

11Hezekiah decided to prepare storerooms in the Temple. 12, 13All the dedicated
supplies were brought into the Lord's house. Conaniah, the Levite, was put in
charge, assisted by his brother Shime-i and the following aides: Jehiel, Azaziah,
Nahath, Asahel, Jerimoth, Jozabad, Eliel, Ismachiah, Mahath, Benaiah.
These appointments were made by King Hezekiah and Azariah the High Priest.

14, 15Kore (son of Imnah, the Levite), who was the gatekeeper at the East Gate,
was put in charge of distributing the offerings to the priests. His faithful assistants
were Eden, Miniamin, Jeshua, Shemaiah, Amariah, and Shecaniah. They distributed the gifts to the clans of priests in their cities, dividing it to young and old alike.
16However, the priests on duty at the Temple and their families were supplied
directly from there, so they were not included in this distribution. 17, 18The priests
were listed in the genealogical register by clans, and the Levites twenty years old
and older were listed under the names of their work corps. A regular food allotment
was given to all families of properly registered priests, for they had no other source
of income because their time and energies were devoted to the service of the
Temple. 19One of the priests was appointed in each of the cities of the priests to
issue food and other supplies to all priests in the area, and to all registered Levites.
20In this way King Hezekiah handled the distribution throughout all Judah, doing
what was just and fair in the sight of the Lord his God. 21He worked very hard to
encourage respect for the Temple, the law, and godly living, and was very
successful.

Assyria invades Judah

32 Some time later, after this good work of King Hezekiah, King Sennacherib
of Assyria invaded Judah and laid siege to the fortified cities, planning to

31:16 *and their families,* literally, "males from three years old and upward."

Margin references
31:5 Lev 27:30 / Deut 14:28 / Neh 13:12
31:10 1 Chron 6:8,9 / Mal 3:10
31:11 1 Kgs 6:5,8
31:12 2 Chron 31:10
31:14 Josh 21:9-19 / 2 Chron 29:12
31:17 1 Chron 23:24
31:19 2 Chron 31:12-15
31:20 2 Kgs 20:3; 22:2
32:1 Isa 36:1—37:38

31:20, 21 Hezekiah led the people of Judah in spiritual renewal.
His actions serve as a model of renewal for us: (1) begin by
remembering God's past faithfulness (30:2, 3); (2) keep going
despite ridicule (30:10); (3) aggressively seek to remove evil
influences from your life (30:14; 31:1); (4) confess your sin to God
(30:22); (5) be open to spontaneity in worship (30:23);
(6) contribute generously to God's work (31:4-8).

32:1 Assyria was a great empire by Hezekiah's time, controlling
most of the Middle East. From a small strip of land located in
present-day Iran and Iraq, it began to establish its power under
Ashurnasirpal II (883–859 B.C.) and his son Shalmaneser III
(859–824). Under Tiglath-pileser III (745–727), Assyria's
boundaries extended to the borders of Israel, making it one of the
largest empires in ancient history. Shalmaneser V destroyed the
Northern Kingdom in 722, and his grandson, Sennacherib
(705–681), tried to bring Judah, the Southern Kingdom, under his
control. Less than a century later, Assyria would lie in ruins (612).

(For more information on Assyria and its kings, see the chart in
2 Kings 18.)

32:1 Forcing nations to pay tribute was an excellent way for these
foreign kings to build their income base. Often the Assyrian king
would get an oath of allegiance from a country which required
them to pay taxes in the form of livestock, wine, battle equipment
(horses, chariots, weapons), gold, silver, and anything else that
pleased the invading king. Captives cost a king money, so they
were taken only in cases of extreme rebellion or to repopulate
cities that had been destroyed.

32:1ff When King Hezekiah was confronted with the frightening
prospect of an Assyrian invasion, he made two important
decisions. He did everything he could to deal with the situation,
and he trusted God for the outcome. That is exactly what we must
do when faced with difficult or frightening situations. Do everything
you possibly can to solve the problem or improve the situation. As
you do this, commit it to God in prayer and trust him for the
solution.

place them under tribute. 2When it was clear that Sennacherib was intending to attack Jerusalem, 3Hezekiah summoned his princes and officers for a council of war, and it was decided to plug the springs outside the city. 4They organized a huge work crew to block them, and to cut off the brook running through the fields. "Why should the king of Assyria come and find water?" they asked.

5Then Hezekiah further strengthened his defenses by repairing the wall wherever it was broken down and by adding to the fortifications, and constructing a second wall outside it. He also reinforced Fort Millo in the City of David, and manufactured large numbers of weapons and shields. 6He recruited an army and appointed officers and summoned them to the plains before the city, and encouraged them with this address:

7"Be strong, be brave, and do not be afraid of the king of Assyria or his mighty army, for there is someone with us who is far greater than he is! 8He has a great army, but they are all mere men, while we have the Lord our God to fight our battles for us!" This greatly encouraged them.

9Then King Sennacherib of Assyria, while still besieging the city of Lachish, sent ambassadors with this message to King Hezekiah and the citizens of Jerusalem:

10"King Sennacherib of Assyria asks, 'Do you think you can survive my siege of Jerusalem? 11King Hezekiah is trying to persuade you to commit suicide by staying there—to die by famine and thirst—while he promises that "the Lord our God will deliver us from the king of Assyria"! 12Don't you realize that Hezekiah is the very person who destroyed all the idols, and commanded Judah and Jerusalem to use only the one altar at the Temple, and to burn incense upon it alone? 13Don't you realize that I and the other kings of Assyria before me have never yet failed to conquer a nation we attacked? The gods of those nations weren't able to do a thing to save their lands! 14Name just one time when anyone, anywhere, was able to resist us successfully. What makes you think your God can do any better? 15Don't let Hezekiah fool you! Don't believe him. I say it again—no god of any nation has ever yet been able to rescue his people from me or my ancestors; how much less your God!'" 16Thus the ambassador mocked the Lord God and God's servant Hezekiah, heaping up insults.

17King Sennacherib also sent letters scorning the Lord God of Israel.

"The gods of all the other nations failed to save their people from my hand, and the God of Hezekiah will fail, too," he wrote.

18The messengers who brought the letters shouted threats in the Jewish language to the people gathered on the walls of the city, trying to frighten and dishearten

Cross-references (left margin)

32:3
2 Kgs 20:20

32:4
2 Chron 32:30

32:5
1 Kgs 9:24
2 Kgs 25:4
2 Chron 25:23

32:6
2 Chron 30:22

32:7
2 Kgs 6:16
1 Chron 22:13

32:8
2 Chron 20:17
Jer 17:5

32:12
2 Chron 31:1

32:14
Isa 10:9-11

32:17
2 Chron 32:14

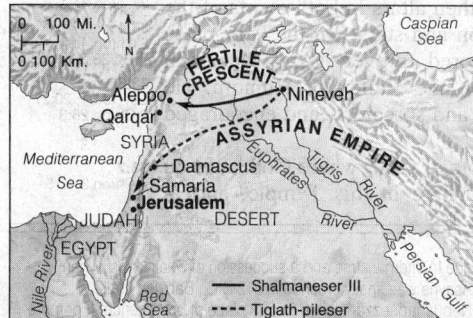

THE ASSYRIAN EMPIRE The mighty Assyrian Empire extended from the Persian Gulf, across the Fertile Crescent, and south to Egypt. Shalmaneser III extended the Empire toward the Mediterranean Sea by conquering cities as far west as Qarqar. Tiglath-pileser extended the Empire south into Syria, Israel, Judah, and Philistia. It was Shalmaneser V who destroyed Samaria, Israel's capital.

32:3, 4 Natural springs were some of Jerusalem's major sources of water. Cities had to be built near springs that were reliable sources of water. In a brilliant military move, Hezekiah plugged the springs outside the city and channeled the water through an underground tunnel (32:30); therefore, Jerusalem would have water even through a long seige. Hezekiah's tunnel has been discovered along with an inscription describing how it was built: two groups of workers started digging underground, one in Jerusalem and one at the Gihon Spring, and they met in the middle.

32:7, 8 Hezekiah could see with "eyes of faith." The number of his opponents meant nothing as long as he was on the Lord's side. Victory is "not by might, nor by power, but by my Spirit, says the Lord Almighty" (Zechariah 4:6). Hezekiah could confidently encourage his men because he had no doubt about where he stood with God. Are you on the Lord's side? You may never face an enemy army, but the battles you face every day can be won with God's strength.

them. 19These messengers talked about the God of Jerusalem just as though he were one of the heathen gods—a handmade idol!

20Then King Hezekiah and Isaiah the prophet (son of Amoz) cried out in prayer to God in heaven, 21and the Lord sent an angel who destroyed the Assyrian army with all its officers and generals! So Sennacherib returned home in deep shame to his own land. And when he arrived at the temple of his god, some of his own sons killed him there. 22That is how the Lord saved Hezekiah and the people of Jerusalem. And now there was peace at last throughout his realm.

23From then on King Hezekiah became immensely respected among the surrounding nations, and many gifts for the Lord arrived at Jerusalem, with valuable presents for King Hezekiah, too.

32:23
2 Sam 8:10

24But about that time Hezekiah became deathly sick, and he prayed to the Lord, and the Lord replied with a miracle. 25However, Hezekiah didn't respond with true thanksgiving and praise, for he had become proud, and so the anger of God was upon him and upon Judah and Jerusalem. 26But finally Hezekiah and the residents of Jerusalem humbled themselves, so the wrath of the Lord did not fall upon them during Hezekiah's lifetime.

32:24
2 Kgs 20:1-11
Isa 38:1-8
32:25
2 Chron 24:18
26:16
32:26
Jer 26:18,19

27So Hezekiah became very wealthy and was highly honored. He had to construct special treasury buildings for his silver, gold, precious stones, and spices, and for his shields and gold bowls. 28, 29He also built many storehouses for his grain, new wine, and olive oil, with many stalls for his animals, and folds for the great flocks of sheep and goats he purchased; and he acquired many towns, for God had given him great wealth. 30He dammed up the Upper Spring of Gihon and brought the water down through an aqueduct to the west side of the City of David sector in Jerusalem. He prospered in everything he did.

32:30
1 Kgs 1:33
2 Kgs 20:20

31However, when ambassadors arrived from Babylon to find out about the miracle of his being healed, God left him to himself in order to test him and to see what he was really like.

32:31
2 Kgs 20:12
2 Chron 32:24
Isa 38:7; 8; 39:1

32The rest of the story of Hezekiah and all of the good things he did are written in *The Book of Isaiah* (the prophet, the son of Amoz), and in *The Annals of the Kings of Judah and Israel*. 33When Hezekiah died he was buried in the royal hillside cemetery among the other kings, and all Judah and Jerusalem honored him at his death. Then his son Manasseh became the new king.

Manasseh rules Judah

33 Manasseh was only twelve years old when he became king, and he reigned fifty-five years, in Jerusalem. 2But it was an evil reign, for he encouraged his people to worship the idols of the heathen nations destroyed by the Lord when the people of Israel entered the land. 3He rebuilt the heathen altars his father Hezekiah had destroyed—the altars of Baal, and of the shame-images, and of the sun, moon, and stars. 4, 5He even constructed heathen altars in both courts of the Temple of the Lord, for worshiping the sun, moon and stars—in the very place where the Lord had said that he would be honored forever. 6And Manasseh sacrificed his own children as burnt offerings in the Valley of Hinnom. He consulted spirit-mediums, too, and fortune-tellers and sorcerers, and encouraged every sort of evil, making the Lord very angry.

33:1
2 Kgs 21:1-9
33:2
2 Chron 28:3
33:3
Deut 16:21
2 Kgs 23:5,6
2 Chron 31:1
33:4
2 Chron 4:9
7:16; 28:24
33:6
Lev 19:31; 20:27
2 Chron 28:3

7Think of it! He placed an idol in the very Temple of God, where God had told David and his son Solomon, "I will be honored here in this Temple, and in

33:7
2 Chron 3:4,15

32:31 A test can bring out a person's true character. God tested Hezekiah to see what he was really like. In times of success, most of us can live good lives. But pressure, trouble, or pain quickly removes our thin veneer of goodness unless our strengths run deep into our inner being. What are you like under pressure or when everything is going wrong? Those who are consistently faithful don't have to worry what pressure may reveal about them.

32:31 Babylon was slowly and quietly rising to become a world power. At the same time, the Assyrian Empire was slowly declining due to internal strife and a succession of weak kings. When Assyria was finally crushed in 612 B.C., Babylon under Nebuchadnezzar moved into its place of prominence. (For more information on Babylon, see the note on 2 Kings 20:14.)

32:31 Why did God leave Hezekiah to himself? After Hezekiah was healed of his sickness, he apparently developed a prideful attitude. When envoys came to inquire about his miraculous healing, God stepped back to see how Hezekiah would respond. Unfortunately, Hezekiah's actions revealed his pride. He pointed to his own accomplishments rather than to God.

33:8
2 Sam 7:10

Jerusalem—the city I have chosen to be honored forever above all the other cities of Israel. 8And if you will only obey my commands—all the laws and instructions given to you by Moses—I won't ever again exile Israel from this land which I gave your ancestors."

9But Manasseh encouraged the people of Judah and Jerusalem to do even more evil than the nations the Lord destroyed when Israel entered the land. 10Warnings from the Lord were ignored by both Manasseh and his people. 11So God sent the Assyrian armies, and they seized him with hooks and bound him with bronze chains and carted him away to Babylon. 12Then at last he came to his senses and cried out humbly to God for help. 13And the Lord listened, and answered his plea by returning him to Jerusalem and to his kingdom! At that point Manasseh finally realized that the Lord was really God!

33:11
Deut 28:36
2 Chron 36:6

33:12
2 Chron 32:26

33:13
Ezra 8:23
Dan 4:32

33:14
1 Kgs 1:33
Neh 3:3

14It was after this that he rebuilt the outer wall of the City of David and the wall from west of the Spring of Gihon in the Kidron Valley, and then to the Fish Gate, and around Citadel Hill, where it was built very high. And he stationed his army generals in all of the fortified cities of Judah. 15He also removed the foreign gods from the hills and took his idol from the Temple and tore down the altars he had built on the mountain where the Temple stood, and the altars that were in

33:15
2 Chron 33:3-7

MANASSEH

Even a brief outline of King Manasseh's evil sickens us and we wonder how God could ever forgive him. Not only did he intentionally offend God by desecrating Solomon's Temple with idols, but he also worshiped pagan gods and even sacrificed his children to them! Child sacrifice is a vile act of pagan idolatry, an act against both God and people. Such blatant sins require severe correction.

God showed justice to Manasseh in warning and punishing him. He showed mercy in responding to Manasseh's heartfelt repentance by forgiving and restoring him. Given the nature of Manasseh's rebellion, we are not surprised by God's punishment—defeat and exile at the hands of the Assyrians. But Manasseh's repentance and God's forgiveness are unexpected. Manasseh's life was changed. He was given a new start.

How far has God gone to get your attention? Have you ever, like Manasseh, come to your senses and cried out to God for help? Only your repentance and a prayer for a new attitude stand between you and God's complete forgiveness.

Strengths and accomplishments:
• Despite bitter consequences for his sins, he learned from them
• Humbly repented of his sins before God

Weaknesses and mistakes:
• Challenged God's authority and was defeated
• Reversed many of the positive effects of his father Hezekiah's rule
• Sacrificed his children to idols

Lessons from his life:
• God will go a long way to get someone's attention
• Forgiveness is limited not by the amount of sin, but by our willingness to repent

Vital statistics:
• Where: Jerusalem
• Occupation: King of Judah
• Relatives: Father: Hezekiah. Mother: Hephzibah. Son: Amon.

Key verses:
"Then at last he came to his senses and cried out humbly to God for help. And the Lord listened, and answered his plea by returning him to Jerusalem and to his kingdom! At that point Manasseh finally realized that the Lord was really God!" (2 Chronicles 33:12, 13).

Manasseh's story is told in 2 Kings 21:1–18 and 2 Chronicles 32:33—33:20. He is also mentioned in Jeremiah 15:4.

33:11 Between 652 and 648 B.C., the city of Babylon rebelled against Assyria. The rebellion was crushed, but Assyria may have suspected that Manasseh supported it. That may explain why Manasseh was taken to Babylon for trial rather than to the Assyrian capital of Nineveh.

33:12, 13 In a list of corrupt kings, Manasseh would rank near the top. His life is a catalog of evil deeds including idol worship,

sacrificing his own children, and Temple desecration. Eventually, however, he realized his sins and cried out to God for forgiveness. And God listened. If God can forgive Manasseh, surely he can forgive anyone. Are you burdened by overpowering guilt? Do you doubt that anyone could forgive what you have done? Take heart—until death, no one is beyond God's forgiveness.

Jerusalem, and dumped them outside the city. [16]Then he rebuilt the altar of the Lord and offered sacrifices upon it—peace offerings and thanksgiving offerings—and demanded that the people of Judah worship the Lord God of Israel. [17]However, the people still sacrificed upon the altars on the hills, but only to the Lord their God.

[18]The rest of Manasseh's deeds, and his prayer to God, and God's reply through the prophets—this is all written in *The Annals of the Kings of Israel*. [19]His prayer, and the way God answered, and a frank account of his sins and errors, including a list of the locations where he built idols on the hills and set up shame-idols and graven images (this of course was before the great change in his attitude) is recorded in *The Annals of the Prophets*.

Amon rules Judah

[20, 21]When Manasseh died he was buried beneath his own palace, and his son Amon became the new king. Amon was twenty-two years old when he began to reign in Jerusalem, but he lasted for only two years. [22]It was an evil reign like the early years of his father Manasseh; for Amon sacrificed to all the idols just as his father had. [23]But he didn't change as his father did; instead he sinned more and more. [24]At last his own officers assassinated him in his palace. [25]But some public-spirited citizens killed all of those who assassinated him, and declared his son Josiah to be the new king.

Josiah rules Judah

34 Josiah was only eight years old when he became king. He reigned thirty-one years, in Jerusalem. [2]His was a good reign, as he carefully followed the good example of his ancestor King David. [3]For when he was sixteen years old, in the eighth year of his reign, he began to search for the God of his ancestor David; and four years later he began to clean up Judah and Jerusalem, destroying the heathen altars and the shame-idols on the hills. [4]He went out personally to watch as the altars of Baal were knocked apart, the obelisks above the altars chopped down, and the shame-idols ground into dust and scattered over the graves of those who had sacrificed to them. [5]Then he burned the bones of the heathen priests upon their own altars, feeling that this action would clear the people of Judah and Jerusalem from the guilt of their sin of idol-worship.

[6]Then he went to the cities of Manasseh, Ephraim, and Simeon, even to distant Naphtali, and did the same thing there. [7]He broke down the heathen altars, ground to powder the shame-idols, and chopped down the obelisks. He did this everywhere throughout the whole land of Israel before returning to Jerusalem.

[8]During the eighteenth year of his reign, after he had purged the land and cleaned up the situation at the Temple, he appointed Shaphan (son of Azaliah) and Maaseiah, governor of Jerusalem, and Joah (son of Joahaz), the city treasurer, to repair the Temple. [9]They set up a collection system for gifts for the Temple. The money was collected at the Temple gates by the Levites on guard duty there. Gifts were brought by the people coming from Manasseh, Ephraim, and other parts of the remnant of Israel, as well as from the people of Jerusalem. The money was taken to Hilkiah the High Priest for accounting, [10, 11]and then used by the Levites to pay the carpenters and stonemasons, and to purchase building materials—stone building blocks, timber, lumber, and beams. He now rebuilt what earlier kings of Judah had torn down.

33:17
2 Chron 32:12

33:18
2 Chron 33:10, 12,13

33:19
2 Chron 33:3,13

33:20
2 Kgs 21:19-24

33:22
2 Chron 33:2-7

33:23
2 Chron 33:12, 19

33:24
2 Chron 25:27

34:1
2 Kgs 22:1,2

34:2
2 Chron 29:2

34:3
2 Chron 33:22

34:4
Ex 32:20
2 Kgs 23:4,5

34:5
2 Kgs 23:20

34:6
2 Kgs 23:15,19

34:7
Chron 31:1

34:8
2 Kgs 22:3-20
2 Chron 18:25

34:9
2 Chron 30:10, 18; 35:8

33:17 Although the people worshiped God alone, they worshiped him in the wrong way. God had told them to make their sacrifices only in certain places (Deuteronomy 12:13, 14). This kept them from changing their way of worship and protected them against the dangerous influence of pagan religious practices. Unfortunately, the people continued to use these places of worship, not realizing that (1) they were adopting practices which God opposed, and (2) these places were against God's Law. We must take care that subtle secular influences do not distort our worship practices.

34:1 Josiah's Profile is found in 2 Kings 23.

34:3 In Josiah's day, boys were considered men at age 12. By 16, Josiah understood the responsibility of his office. Even at this young age, he showed greater wisdom than many of the older kings who came before him, because he had decided to seek the Lord God and his wisdom. Clearly, wisdom from God is not the exclusive possession of the old. Young people may also be wise enough to fill spiritual leadership positions. Paul counseled Timothy, "Don't let anyone think little of you because you are young" (1 Timothy 4:12). If God has given you wisdom and spiritual insight, use it in his service regardless of your age.

34:12
1 Chron 25:1

34:13
2 Chron 8:10
Neh 4:10

12The workmen were energetic under the leadership of Jahath and Obadiah, Levites of the subclan of Merari. Zechariah and Meshullam, of the subclan of Kohath, were the building superintendents. The Levites who were skilled musicians played background music while the work progressed. 13Other Levites superintended the unskilled laborers who carried in the materials to the workmen. Still others assisted as accountants, supervisors, and carriers.

God's Law is discovered in the Temple

34:14
2 Chron 34:9

14One day when Hilkiah, the High Priest, was at the Temple recording the money collected at the gates, he found an old scroll which turned out to be the laws of God as given to Moses!

15, 16"Look!" Hilkiah exclaimed to Shaphan, the king's secretary. "See what I have found in the Temple! These are the laws of God!" Hilkiah gave the scroll to Shaphan, and Shaphan took it to the king, along with his report that there was good progress being made in the reconstruction of the Temple.

17"The money chests have been opened and counted, and the money has been put into the hand of the overseers and workmen," he said to the king.

34:19
Josh 7:6

18Then he mentioned the scroll, and how Hilkiah had discovered it. So he read it to the king. 19When the king heard what these laws required of God's people, he ripped his clothing in despair, 20and summoned Hilkiah, Ahikam (son of Shaphan), Abdon (son of Micah), Shaphan the treasurer, and Asaiah, the king's personal aide.

34:21
2 Chron 29:8

21"Go to the Temple and plead with the Lord for me!" the king told them. "Pray for all the remnant of Israel and Judah! For this scroll says that the reason the Lord's great anger has been poured out upon us is that our ancestors have not obeyed these laws that are written here."

22So the men went to Huldah the prophetess, the wife of Shallum (son of Tokhath, son of Hasrah). (Shallum was the king's tailor, living in the second ward.) When they told her of the king's trouble, 23she replied, "The Lord God of Israel says, Tell the man who sent you,

34:24
Deut 28:15-68
2 Chron 36:14-20

34:25
2 Chron 33:3

24" 'Yes, the Lord will destroy this city and its people. All the curses written in the scroll will come true. 25For my people have forsaken me and have worshiped heathen gods, and I am very angry with them for their deeds. Therefore, my unquenchable wrath is poured out upon this place.'

34:27
2 Chron 12:7
32:26

26"But the Lord also says this to the king of Judah who sent you to ask me about this: Tell him, the Lord God of Israel says, 27'Because you are sorry and have humbled yourself before God when you heard my words against this city and its people, and have ripped your clothing in despair and wept before me—I have heard you, says the Lord, 28and I will not send the promised evil upon this city and its people until after your death.' " So they brought back to the king this word from the Lord. 29Then the king summoned all the elders of Judah and Jerusalem, 30and the priests and Levites and all the people great and small, to accompany him to the Temple. There the king read the scroll to them—the covenant of God that was found in the Temple. 31As the king stood before them, he made a pledge to the Lord to follow his commandments with all his heart and soul, and to do what was written

34:29
2 Kgs 23:1-3
34:30
Neh 8:1-3
34:31
2 Chron 23:16
29:10

34:15, 16 The laws of God that Hilkiah found were probably the book of Deuteronomy, which had been lost during the reigns of the evil kings. Now that it was found, Josiah realized that drastic changes had to be made in order to bring the nation back in line with God's commands.

34:19 It is human nature to treat sin lightly—to make excuses, blame somebody else, or minimize the harm done. Not so with godly Josiah. He was so appalled at the people's neglect of the Law that he tore his clothing to express his grief. True understanding of our sins should lead to sincere sorrow, helping us to "turn away from sin and seek eternal life" (2 Corinthians 7:10). Are you always excusing your sin, blaming others, and pretending

that it's not so bad? God does not take sin lightly, and he wants us to respond as Josiah did.

34:31 When Josiah read the scroll that Hilkiah discovered (34:14), he responded with repentance and humility and promised to follow God's commandments as written on the scroll. The Bible is God's Word to us, "full of living power" (Hebrews 4:12), but we cannot know what God wants us to do if we do not read it. And even reading God's Word is not enough; we must be willing to do what it says. There is not much difference between the scroll hidden in the Temple and the Bible hidden on the bookshelf. An unread Bible is just as useless as a lost one.

in the scroll. 32And he required everyone in Jerusalem and Benjamin to subscribe to this pact with God, and all of them did.

33So Josiah removed all idols from the areas occupied by the Jews, and required all of them to worship Jehovah their God. And throughout the remainder of his lifetime they continued serving Jehovah, the God of their ancestors.

34:33
2 Chron 34:3-7

Josiah proclaims a celebration of the Passover

35 Then Josiah announced that the Passover would be celebrated on the first day of April, in Jerusalem. The Passover lambs were slain that evening. 2He also reestablished the priests in their duties, and encouraged them to begin their work at the Temple again. 3He issued this order to the sanctified Levites, the religious teachers in Israel:

35:1
Ex 12:6
Num 9:3
2 Kgs 23:21

35:2
2 Chron 29:11

"Since the Ark is now in Solomon's Temple and you don't need to carry it back and forth upon your shoulders, spend your time ministering to the Lord and to his people. 4, 5Form yourselves into the traditional service corps of your ancestors, as first organized by King David of Israel and by his son Solomon. Each corps will assist particular clans of the people who bring in their offerings to the Temple. 6Kill the Passover lambs and sanctify yourselves and prepare to assist the people who come. Follow all of the instructions of the Lord through Moses."

35:3
1 Chron 23:26
2 Chron 17:8,9
Neh 8:7

35:4
1 Chron 9:10-13
2 Chron 8:14

35:6
2 Chron 29:5
35:1

7Then the king contributed 30,000 lambs and young goats for the people's Passover offerings, and 3,000 young bulls. 8The king's officials made willing contributions to the priests and Levites. Hilkiah, Zechariah, and Jehiel, the overseers of the Temple, gave the priests 2,600 sheep and goats, and 300 oxen as Passover offerings. 9The Levite leaders—Conaniah, Shemaiah, and Nethanel, and his brothers Hashabiah, Je-iel, and Jozabad—gave 5,000 sheep and goats and 500 oxen to the Levites for their Passover offerings.

35:8
2 Chron 31:13

35:9
2 Chron 31:12

10When everything was organized, and the priests were standing in their places, and the Levites were formed into service corps as the king had instructed, 11then the Levites killed the Passover lambs and presented the blood to the priests, who sprinkled it upon the altar as the Levites removed the skins. 12They piled up the carcasses for each tribe to present its own burnt sacrifices to the Lord, as it is written in the law of Moses. They did the same with the oxen. 13Then, as directed by the laws of Moses, they roasted the Passover lambs and boiled the holy offerings in pots, kettles, and pans, and hurried them out to the people to eat. 14Afterwards the Levites prepared a meal for themselves and for the priests, for they had been busy from morning till night offering the fat of the burnt offerings.

35:10
2 Chron 35:5

35:11
2 Chron 29:22
35:1,6

35:13
Ex 12:8,9
Lev 6:25

15The singers (the sons of Asaph) were in their places, following directions issued centuries earlier by King David, Asaph, Heman, and Jeduthun the king's prophet. The gatekeepers guarded the gates, and didn't need to leave their posts of duty, for their meals were brought to them by their Levite brothers. 16The entire Passover ceremony was completed in that one day. All the burnt offerings were sacrificed upon the altar of the Lord, as Josiah had instructed.

35:15
1 Chron 25:1
26:12-19

17Everyone present in Jerusalem took part in the Passover observance, and this was followed by the Feast of Unleavened Bread for the next seven days. 18Never since the time of Samuel the prophet had there been such a Passover—not one of the kings of Israel could vie with King Josiah in this respect, involving so many of the priests, Levites, and people from Jerusalem and from all parts of Judah, and from over in Israel. 19This all happened in the eighteenth year of the reign of Josiah.

35:17
2 Chron 30:21

35:18
2 Kgs 23:21,22
2 Chron 30:5

35:3 In Moses' day, one of the duties of the Levites was to carry the Ark of the Covenant whenever Israel traveled. This was no longer necessary because the Ark was now permanently housed in the Temple. Josiah was simply making the Levites aware of the duties God had assigned to them through David when the Temple was first being planned (1 Chronicles 24).

35:15 The Temple gatekeepers, who were all Levites, guarded the four main entrances to the Temple and opened the gates each morning. They also did other day-to-day chores such as cleaning and preparing the offerings for sacrifice and accounting for the

gifts given to the Temple. (For more on gatekeepers, see 1 Chronicles 26:1ff.)

35:17 The Feast of Unleavened Bread was a seven-day celebration beginning the day after Passover. Like Passover, it commemorated the Exodus from Egypt. For seven days the people ate bread without yeast just as their ancestors did while leaving Egypt because it could be made quickly in preparation for their swift departure (Exodus 12:14-20). This feast reminded the people that they had left slavery behind and had come to the land God promised them.

Josiah dies in battle

35:20
2 Kgs 23:29,30
Isa 10:9
Jer 46:2

20Afterwards King Neco of Egypt led his army at Carchemish on the Euphrates River, and Josiah declared war on him.

21But King Neco sent ambassadors to Josiah with this message: "I don't want a fight with you, O king of Judah! I have come only to fight the king of Assyria! Leave me alone! God has told me to hurry! Don't meddle with God or he will destroy you, for he is with me."

35:22
Judg 5:19
2 Chron 18:29
35:21

22But Josiah refused to turn back. Instead he led his army into the battle at the Valley of Megiddo. (He laid aside his royal robes so that the enemy wouldn't recognize him.) Josiah refused to believe that Neco's message was from God. 23The enemy archers struck King Josiah with their arrows and fatally wounded him.

"Take me out of the battle," he exclaimed to his aides.

24, 25So they lifted him out of his chariot and placed him in his second chariot and brought him back to Jerusalem where he died. He was buried there, in the royal cemetery. And all Judah and Jerusalem, including even Jeremiah the prophet, mourned for him, as did the Temple choirs. To this day they still sing sad songs about his death, for these songs of sorrow were recorded among the official lamentations.

35:25
Jer 22:10-13
Lam 4:20
Zech 12:11

26The other activities of Josiah, and his good deeds, and how he followed the laws of the Lord, 27all are written in *The Annals of the Kings of Israel and Judah.*

3. Judah is exiled to Babylon
Jehoahaz rules Judah

36:1
Jer 22:11

36:2
2 Kgs 23:30-34

36 Josiah's son Jehoahaz was selected as the new king. 2He was twenty-three years old when he began to reign, but lasted only three months. 3Then he was deposed by the king of Egypt, who demanded an annual tribute from Judah of $230,000.

Jehoiakim rules Judah

36:4
Jer 22:10,12

36:5
Jer 22:13-19

4The king of Egypt now appointed Eliakim, the brother of Jehoahaz, as the new king of Judah. (Eliakim's name was changed to Jehoiakim.) Jehoahaz was taken to Egypt as a prisoner. 5Jehoiakim was twenty-five years old when he became king,

---

THE BATTLE AT CARCHEMISH A world war was brewing in 609 B.C. when Pharaoh Neco of Egypt set out for the city of Carchemish to join the Assyrians in an attempt to defeat the Babylonians, who were rising to great power. Neco marched his armies through Judah, where King Josiah tried to stop him at Megiddo, but was killed. The battle began at Carchemish in 605 B.C. and the Egyptians and Assyrians were soundly defeated, chased to Hamath and defeated again. Babylon was now the new world power.

35:20 This event occurred in 609 B.C. Nineveh, the Assyrian capital, had been destroyed three years earlier by the Babylonians. The defeated Assyrians regrouped at Haran and Carchemish, but Babylon sent its army to destroy them once and for all. Pharaoh Neco, who wanted to make Egypt a world power, was worried about Babylon's growing strength, so he marched his army north through Judah to help the Assyrians at Carchemish. But King Josiah of Judah tried to prevent Neco from passing through his land on his way to Carchemish. Josiah was killed, and Judah became subject to Egypt. Neco went on to Carchemish and held off the Babylonians for four years; but in 605 he was soundly defeated and Babylon moved into the spotlight as the dominant world power.

35:21-23 Josiah ignored Neco's message because of who Neco was—king of a heathen nation. The mistaken assumption that Neco could not be part of God's larger plan cost Josiah his life. A message from God may come in unexpected ways. Don't let prejudice or false assumptions blind you to God's message.

and he reigned eleven years, in Jerusalem; but his reign was an evil one. 6Finally Nebuchadnezzar king of Babylon conquered Jerusalem, and took away the king in chains to Babylon. 7Nebuchadnezzar also took some of the gold bowls and other items from the Temple, placing them in his own temple in Babylon. 8The rest of the deeds of Jehoiakim, and all the evil he did, are written in *The Annals of the Kings of Judah;* and his son Jehoiachin became the new king.

36:6
2 Kgs 24:1
2 Chron 33:11
Jer 22:19,20

36:7
2 Kgs 24:13

36:8
2 Kgs 24:5

Jehoiachin rules Judah

9Jehoiachin was eighteen years old when he ascended the throne. But he lasted only three months and ten days, and it was an evil reign as far as the Lord was concerned. 10The following spring he was summoned to Babylon by King Nebuchadnezzar. Many treasures from the Temple were taken away to Babylon at that time, and King Nebuchadnezzar appointed Jehoiachin's brother Zedekiah as the new king of Judah and Jerusalem.

36:9
2 Kgs 24:8-17

36:10
2 Sam 11:1
Jer 37:1

Zedekiah rules Judah

11Zedekiah was twenty-one years old when he became king and he reigned eleven years, in Jerusalem. 12His reign, too, was evil so far as the Lord was concerned, for he refused to take the counsel of Jeremiah the prophet, who gave him messages from the Lord. 13He rebelled against King Nebuchadnezzar, even though he had taken an oath of loyalty. Zedekiah was a hard and stubborn man so far as obeying the Lord God of Israel was concerned, for he refused to follow him.

14All the important people of the nation, including the High Priests, worshiped the heathen idols of the surrounding nations, thus polluting the Temple of the Lord in Jerusalem. 15Jehovah the God of their fathers sent his prophets again and again to warn them, for he had compassion on his people and on his Temple. 16But the people mocked these messengers of God and despised their words, scoffing at the prophets until the anger of the Lord could no longer be restrained, and there was no longer any remedy.

36:11
2 Kgs 24:18-20
Jer 52:1

36:12
Jer 21:3-7

36:13
2 Chron 30:8
Jer 52:3
Ezek 17:15

36:15
Jer 7:13; 25:3

36:16
2 Chron 30:10
Ezra 5:12
Prov 1:24-32
Jer 5:12,13

The Babylonian army destroys the Temple

17Then the Lord brought the king of Babylon against them and killed their young men, even going after them right into the Temple, and had no pity upon them, killing even young girls and old men. The Lord used the king of Babylon to destroy them completely. 18He also took home with him all the items, great and small, used in the Temple, and treasures from both the Temple and the palace, and took with him all the royal princes. 19Then his army burned the Temple and broke down the walls of Jerusalem and burned all the palaces and destroyed all the valuable Temple

36:17
2 Kgs 25:1-7

36:18
2 Chron 36:7,10

36:19
2 Kgs 25:9
Jer 52:13

36:9 *eighteen.* Some manuscripts read "eight years old."

EXILE TO BABYLON Despite Judah's few good kings and timely reforms, the people never truly changed. Their evil continued and finally God used the Babylonian Empire, under Nebuchadnezzar, to conquer Judah, destroy Jerusalem, and take the people captive to Babylon.

36:6 Nebuchadnezzar was the son of the founder of the new Babylonian Empire. In 605 B.C., the year he became king, Nebuchadnezzar won the battle of Carchemish which crushed Assyria (see the note on 35:20). (For more information about Nebuchadnezzar, read his Profile in Daniel 4.)

36:16 God warned Judah about its sin and continually restored the people to his favor, only to have them turn away. Eventually the situation was beyond remedy. Beware of harboring sin in your heart. The day will come when remedy is no longer possible and God's judgment replaces his mercy. Sin often repeated, but never repented of, invites disaster.

36:20
2 Kgs 25:11
Jer 27:7

36:21
Lev 25:4; 26:33
Jer 29:10

36:22
Ezra 1:1-3
Isa 44:28
Jer 25:12
29:10

utensils. 20Those who survived were taken away to Babylon as slaves to the king and his sons until the kingdom of Persia conquered Babylon.

21Thus the word of the Lord spoken through Jeremiah came true, that the land must rest for seventy years to make up for the years when the people refused to observe the Sabbath.

22, 23But in the first year of King Cyrus of Persia, the Lord stirred up the spirit of Cyrus to make this proclamation throughout his kingdom, putting it into writing:

"All the kingdoms of the earth have been given to me by the Lord God of heaven, and he has instructed me to build him a Temple in Jerusalem, in the land of Judah. All among you who are the Lord's people, return to Israel for this task, and the Lord be with you."

This also fulfilled the prediction of Jeremiah the prophet.

36:21 Leviticus 26:27–45 strikingly predicts the captivity, telling how God's people would be torn from their land for disobeying him. One of the laws they ignored stated that one year in every seven the land should lie fallow, resting from producing crops (Exodus 23:10, 11). The 70-year captivity allowed the land to rest, making up for all the years the Israelites did not observe this law. We know that God keeps all his promises—not only his promises of blessing, but also his promises of judgment.

36:22, 23 Cyrus made this proclamation 48 years after the Temple was destroyed (36:18, 19), the year after he conquered Babylon. The Book of Ezra tells the story of this proclamation and the return of the exiles to Judah.

36:22, 23 Second Chronicles focuses on the rise and fall of the

worship of God as symbolized by the Jerusalem Temple. The Temple had been planned by David and built by Solomon, who put on the greatest dedication service the world had ever seen. Worship in the Temple was superbly organized.

But under several evil kings, the Temple was defiled and worship degraded to the point where idols were revered more highly than God. Finally, the Temple itself was destroyed by King Nebuchadnezzar of Babylon (36:19). The kings were gone, the Temple destroyed, the people removed. The nation was stripped to its very foundation. But fortunately there was a greater foundation—God himself. When everything in life seems stripped away from us, we too still have God—his Word, his presence, and his promises.

EZRA

VITAL STATISTICS

PURPOSE:
To show God's faithfulness and the way he kept his promise to restore his people to their land

AUTHOR:
Not stated, but probably Ezra

DATE WRITTEN:
Around 450 B.C., recording events from about 538–450 B.C. (omitting 516–458 B.C.). Possibly begun earlier in Babylon and finished in Jerusalem.

SETTING:
Ezra follows 2 Chronicles as a history of the Jewish people, recording their return to the Land after the captivity

KEY VERSES:
"And some of the heathen people who had been relocated in Judah turned from their immoral customs and joined the Israelis in worshiping the Lord God. They, with the entire nation, ate the Passover feast and celebrated the Feast of Unleavened Bread for seven days. There was great joy throughout the land because the Lord had caused the king of Assyria to be generous to Israel and to assist in the construction of the Temple" (6:21, 22).

KEY PEOPLE:
Cyrus, Zerubbabel, Haggai, Zechariah, Darius, Artaxerxes I, Ezra

KEY PLACES:
Babylon, Jerusalem

SPECIAL FEATURES:
Ezra and Nehemiah were one book in the Hebrew Bible and, with Esther, comprise the post-captivity historical books. The post-captivity prophetic books are Haggai, Zechariah, and Malachi. Haggai and Zechariah should be studied with Ezra since they prophesied during the period of the reconstruction.

NAME the truly great men and women of your lifetime. Celebrities including politicians, war heroes, sports figures, and maybe your parents and special friends would come to mind. You remember them because of certain acts or character qualities. Now, name some biblical heroes—figures etched into your life through countless sermons and Sunday school lessons. This list undoubtedly includes many who served God faithfully and courageously. Does your list include Ezra? Far from being well-known, this unheralded man of God deserves to be mentioned in any discussion of greatness.

Ezra was a priest, a scribe, and a great leader. His name means "help," and his whole life was dedicated to serving God and God's people. Tradition says Ezra wrote most of 1 and 2 Chronicles, Ezra, Nehemiah, and Psalm 119, and that he led the council of 120 men who formed the Old Testament canon. He centers the narrative of the book of Ezra around God and his promise that the Jews would return to their land, as promised by Jeremiah (see the note on 1:1). This message formed the core of Ezra's life. The last half of the book gives a very personal glimpse of Ezra. His knowledge of Scripture and his God-given wisdom were so obvious to the king that he appointed Ezra to lead the second emigration to Jerusalem, to teach the people God's Word, and to administer national life (7:14–26).

Ezra not only knew God's Word, he believed and obeyed it. Upon learning of the Israelites' sins of intermarriage and idolatry, Ezra fell in humility before God and prayed for the nation (9:1–15). Their disobedience touched him deeply (10:1). His response helped lead the people back to God.

Read Ezra, the book, and remember Ezra, the man—a humble, obedient helper. Commit yourself to serving God as he did, with your whole life.

Second Chronicles ends with Cyrus, king of Persia, asking for volunteers to return to Jerusalem to build "the house of the Lord." Ezra continues this account (1:1–3 is identical to 2 Chronicles 36:22, 23) as two caravans of God's people return to Jerusalem. Zerubbabel, the leader of the first trip, is joined by over 42,360 pilgrims who journey homeward (chapter 2). After arriving, they begin to build the altar and the Temple foundations (chapter 3). But opposition arises from the local inhabitants, and a campaign of accusations and rumors temporarily halts the project (chapter 4). During this time, the prophets Haggai and Zechariah encourage the people (chapter 5). Finally, Darius decrees that the work should proceed unhindered (chapter 6).

After a 58-year gap, Ezra leads a group of Jews from Persia. Armed with decrees and authority from Artaxerxes I, Ezra's task is to administer the affairs of the land (chapters 7, 8). Upon arriving, Ezra learns of intermarriage between God's people and their pagan neighbors. He weeps and prays for the nation (chapter 9). Ezra's example of humble confession leads to national revival (chapter 10). Ezra, a man of God and a true hero, was a model for Israel, and he is a fitting model for us.

Darius becomes king of Persia 522	Temple work resumed/ messages of Haggai, Zechariah 520	Temple completed 516	Ezra comes to Jerusalem 458	Nehemiah comes to Jerusalem 445

THE BLUEPRINT

A. THE RETURN LED BY ZERUBBABEL
   (1:1—6:22)
   1. The first group of exiles returns to the Land
   2. The people rebuild the Temple

Finally given the chance to return to their homeland, the people started to rebuild the Temple, only to be stopped by opposition from their enemies. God's work in the world is not without opposition. We must not get discouraged and quit, as the returning people did at first, but continue on boldly in the face of difficulties, as they did later with the encouragement from the prophets.

B. THE RETURN LED BY EZRA
   (7:1—10:44)
   1. The second group of exiles returns to the Land
   2. Ezra opposes intermarriage

Ezra returned to Jerusalem almost 80 years after Zerubbabel, only to discover that the people had married heathen spouses. This polluted the religious purity of the people and endangered the future of the nation. Believers today must be careful not to threaten their walk with God by taking on the practices of unbelievers.

MEGATHEMES

THEME	EXPLANATION	IMPORTANCE
The Jews return	By returning to the land of Israel from Babylon, the Jews showed their faith in God's promise to restore them as a people. They returned not only to their homeland, but also to the place where their forefathers had promised to follow God.	God shows his mercy to every generation. He compassionately restores his people. No matter how difficult our present "captivity," we are never far from his love and mercy. He restores us when we return to him.
Rededication	In 536 B.C., Zerubbabel led the people in rebuilding the altar and laying the Temple foundation. They reinstated daily sacrifices and annual festivals, and rededicated themselves to a new spiritual worship of God.	In rededicating the altar, the people were recommitting themselves to God and his service. To grow spiritually, our commitment must be reviewed and renewed often. As we rededicate ourselves to God, our lives become altars to him.
Opposition	Opposition came soon after the altar was built and the Temple foundation laid. Enemies of the Jews used deceit to hinder the building for over six years. Finally, there was a decree to stop the building altogether. This opposition severely tested their wavering faith.	There will always be adversaries who oppose God's work. The life of faith is never easy. But God can overrule all opposition to his service. When we face opposition, we must not falter or withdraw, but keep active and patient.
God's Word	When the people returned to the Land, they were also returning to the influence of God's Word. The prophets Haggai and Zechariah helped encourage them while Ezra's preaching of Scripture built them up. God's Word gave them what they needed to do God's work.	We also need the encouragement and direction of God's Word. We must make it the basis for our faith and actions to finish God's work and fulfill our obligations. We must never waver in our commitment to hear and obey his Word.
Faith and action	The urging of Israel's leaders motivated the people to complete the Temple. Over the years, they had intermarried with idol-worshipers and adopted their pagan practices. Their faith, tested and revived, also led them to remove these sins from their lives.	Faith led them to complete the Temple and to remove sin from their society. As we trust God with our hearts and minds, we must also act by completing our daily activities.

A. THE RETURN LED BY ZERUBBABEL (1:1—6:22)

After 70 years in exile, the captives from Judah were allowed to return to their homeland. Nearly 50,000 people made this journey. Upon arrival they began to rebuild the Temple, but became discouraged by opposition. After encouragement from Haggai and Zechariah, they returned to the task and completed the Temple. The message of the prophets still speaks to us today, encouraging us to continue building up God's church.

1. The first group of exiles returns to the Land

King Cyrus releases captive Jews

1 During the first year of the reign of King Cyrus of Persia, the Lord fulfilled Jeremiah's prophecy by giving King Cyrus the desire to send this proclamation throughout his empire (he also put it into the permanent records of the realm): ²"Cyrus, king of Persia, hereby announces that Jehovah, the God of heaven who gave me my vast empire, has now given me the responsibility of building him a Temple in Jerusalem, in the land of Judah. ³All Jews throughout the kingdom may now return to Jerusalem to rebuild this Temple of Jehovah, who is the God of Israel and of Jerusalem. May his blessings rest upon you. ⁴Those Jews who do not go should contribute toward the expenses of those who do, and also supply them with clothing, transportation, supplies for the journey, and a freewill offering for the Temple."

⁵Then God gave a great desire to the leaders of the tribes of Judah and Benjamin, and to the priests and Levites, to return to Jerusalem at once to rebuild the Temple. ⁶And all the Jewish exiles who chose to remain in Persia gave them whatever assistance they could, as well as gifts for the Temple.

⁷King Cyrus himself donated the gold bowls and other valuable items which King Nebuchadnezzar had taken from the Temple at Jerusalem and had placed in the temple of his own gods. ⁸He instructed Mithredath, the treasurer of Persia, to present these gifts to Shesh-bazzar, the leader of the exiles returning to Judah.

⁹,¹⁰The items Cyrus donated included: 1,000 gold trays, 1,000 silver trays, 29 censers, 30 bowls of solid gold, 2,410 silver bowls (of various designs), 1,000 miscellaneous items. ¹¹In all there were 5,469 gold and silver items turned over to Shesh-bazzar to take back to Jerusalem.

1:1
2 Chron 36:22, 23
Ezra 5:13-17
6:3-5
Jer 25:12-14
29:10
1:2
Ezra 3:1,2
Isa 44:28
45:1-13

1:5
2 Chron 36:22

1:7
2 Kgs 24:13
25:13-16
2 Chron 36:7-18
Ezra 1:9-11; 6:5
1:8
Ezra 1:11
5:14-16
1:9
Ezra 1:7
1:11
Ezra 1:8

The exiles who returned with Zerubbabel

2 Here is the list of the Jewish exiles who now returned to Jerusalem and to the other cities of Judah, from which their parents had been deported to Babylon by King Nebuchadnezzar.

2:1
2 Kgs 24:14-16
25:11
2 Chron 36:20

1:4 *Those Jews,* implied. also in vs 6. **2:1** *their parents,* implied.

1:1 The book of Ezra opens in 538 B.C., 48 years after Nebuchadnezzar destroyed Jerusalem, defeated the Southern Kingdom of Judah, and carried the Jews away to Babylon as captives (2 Kings 25; 2 Chronicles 36). Nebuchadnezzar died in 562, and because his successor was not strong, Babylon was overthrown by Persia in 539, just prior to the events recorded in this book. Both the Babylonians and the Persians had a relaxed policy toward their captives, allowing them to own land and homes and to take ordinary jobs. Many of the Jews like Daniel, Mordecai, and Esther rose to prominent positions within the nation. King Cyrus of Persia went a step further: he allowed many groups of exiles, including the Jews, to return to their homelands. By doing this, he hoped to win their loyalty and thus provide buffer zones around the borders of his empire.

1:1 Cyrus, King of Persia (559–530 B.C.), had already begun his rise to power in the Near East by unifying the Medes and Persians into a strong empire. As he conquered cities, he treated the inhabitants with mercy. Although not a servant of God, Cyrus was used by God to return the Jews to their homeland. Cyrus may have been shown the prophecy of Isaiah 44:28—45:6, written over a century earlier, which predicted that Cyrus himself would help the Jews return to Jerusalem. Daniel, a prominent government official (Daniel 5:29; 6:28), would have been familiar with the prophecy.

The book of Daniel has more to say about Cyrus.

1:1 Jeremiah prophesied that the Jews would remain in captivity for 70 years (Jeremiah 25:11; 29:10). The 70-year period has been calculated two different ways: (1) from the first captivity in 605 B.C. (2 Kings 24:1) until the altar was rebuilt by the returned exiles in 536 (Ezra 3:1–6), or (2) from the destruction of the Temple in 586 until the exiles finished rebuilding it in 516. Many scholars prefer the second approach because the Temple was the focus and heartbeat of the nation. Without it, the Jews did not consider themselves reestablished as a nation.

1:2 Cyrus was not a Jew, but God worked through him to return the exiled Jews to their homeland. Cyrus gave the decree allowing their return and gave them protection, money, and the Temple vessels taken by Nebuchadnezzar. When we face difficult situations and feel surrounded, outnumbered, overpowered, or outclassed, we must remember that God's power is not limited to our resources. He is able to use anyone to bring about his will.

1:4–6 This decree provided that the Jews would work together to accomplish the huge task of rebuilding the Temple. Some did the actual building, while others operated the supply lines. Significant ventures require teamwork, with some people in the forefront and others providing support. Each function is vital to accomplishing the task.

2:2
Neh 7:7

²The leaders were: Zerubbabel, Jeshua, Nehemiah, Seraiah, Re-el-aiah, Mordecai, Bilshan, Mispar, Bigvai, Rehum, Baanah.

Here is a census of those who returned (listed by subclans):

2:3
1 Chron 9:1-44
Neh 7:8-38

3-35From the subclan of Parosh, 2,172;
From the subclan of Shephatiah, 372;

PROPHECIES FULFILLED BY THE RETURN OF ISRAEL FROM EXILE

Reference	Prophecy	Approximate Date of the Prophecy	Fulfillment Date	Significance
Isaiah 44:28	Cyrus would be used by God to guarantee the return of a remnant. Jerusalem would be rebuilt and the Temple restored.	688 B.C.	539 B.C.	As God named Cyrus even before he was born, God knows what will happen—he is in control.
Jeremiah 25:12	Babylon would be punished for destroying Jerusalem and exiling God's people.	605 B.C.	539 B.C.	Babylon was conquered by Cyrus the Great. God may seem to allow evil to go unpunished, but consequences for wrongdoing are inevitable. God will punish evil.
Jeremiah 29:10	The people would spend 70 years in Babylon, then God would bring them back to their homeland.	594 B.C.	537 B.C.	The 70 years of captivity passed (see the note on 1:1), and God provided the opportunity for Zerubbabel to lead the first group of captives home. God's plans may allow for hardship, but his desire is for our good.
Daniel 5:17–30	God had judged the Babylonian Empire. It would be given to the Medes and the Persians, forming a new world power.	539 B.C.	539 B.C.	Belshazzar was killed and Babylon was conquered the same night. God's judgment is accurate and swift. God knows the point of no return in each of our lives. Until then he allows the freedom for us to repent and seek his forgiveness.

God, through his faithful prophets, predicted that the people of Judah would be taken into captivity because of their sinfulness. But he also predicted that they would return to Jerusalem and rebuild the city, the Temple, and the nation.

1:5 Cyrus was king over the entire region that had once been Assyria and Babylon. Assyria had deported the Israelites from the Northern Kingdom (Israel) in 722 B.C. Babylon had taken Israelites captive from the Southern Kingdom (Judah) in 586 B.C. Cyrus' proclamation of freedom, therefore, went to all the original 12 tribes, but only Judah and Benjamin responded and returned to rebuild God's Temple. The ten tribes of the Northern Kingdom had been so fractured and dispersed by Assyria, and so much time had elapsed since their captivity, that many were unsure of their real heritage and unwilling to share in the vision of rebuilding the Temple.

1:5 God "gave a great desire" to the leaders to return to Jerusalem and rebuild the Temple. Major changes begin on the inside as God works on our attitudes, beliefs, and desires. These inner changes lead to faithful actions. After 48 years of captivity, the arrogant Jewish nation had been humbled. When the people's attitudes and desires changed, God ended the disciplining of his people and gave them another opportunity to go home and try again. Paul reminds us that "God is at work within you, helping you want to obey him, and then helping you do what he wants" (Philippians 2:13). Doing God's will begins with your desires. Are you willing to be humble, to be open to his opportunities, and to move at his direction? Ask God to give you the desire to follow him more closely.

1:6 Many Jews chose to remain in Persia rather than to return to their homeland. The journey back to Jerusalem was difficult, dangerous, and expensive, lasting over four months. Jerusalem and the surrounding countryside were in ruins, so travel conditions were poor. The people living in the area were hostile.

Persian records indicate that many Jews in Persia had accumulated great wealth. Returning to Jerusalem would have meant giving up everything they had and starting over. Many people couldn't bring themselves to do that; they preferred wealth and security to the sacrifice that God's work would require. Their priorities were upside down (Mark 4:18, 19). Believers today must beware of any comfort, security, or material possessions that prevent them from doing what God wants.

1:7 When King Nebuchadnezzar ransacked the Temple, he took many of the valuable Temple artifacts with him. What he did not take, he burned (2 Chronicles 36:18, 19). Most of these items were made of solid gold (1 Kings 7:48–50), and Cyrus kindly returned them to the Jews for the Temple they would soon rebuild.

1:8 Shesh-bazzar was either the Babylonian name for Zerubbabel, one of the Jewish leaders during the first return (2:2; 3:8; 4:3), or he was a government official with responsibility for the returning party. The reasons Shesh-bazzar may be identified with Zerubbabel are: (1) both were called governors (5:14; Haggai 1:1); (2) both were called leaders of the returning exiles (1:8; 2:2); (3) both laid the Temple foundation (3:8; 5:16); and (4) Jews in exile were often given Babylonian names (see Daniel 1:7 where Daniel and his companions were given new names).

2:2 This is a different Nehemiah from the one who rebuilt Jerusalem's walls 80 years later, and the Mordecai listed here is not the one who appears in the book of Esther.

2:3–35 These people were from the tribes of Judah and Benjamin (1:5). Subclans could be families, cities, or territories.

From the subclan of Arah, 775;
From the subclan of Pahath-moab (the descendants of Jeshua and Joab), 2,812;
From the subclan of Elam, 1,254;
From the subclan of Zattu, 945;
From the subclan of Zaccai, 760;
From the subclan of Bani, 642;
From the subclan of Bebai, 623;
From the subclan of Azgad, 1,222;
From the subclan of Adonikam, 666;
From the subclan of Bigvai, 2,056;
From the subclan of Adin, 454;
From the subclan of Ater (the descendants of Hezekiah), 98;
From the subclan of Bezai, 323;
From the subclan of Jorah, 112;
From the subclan of Hashum, 223;
From the subclan of Gibbar, 95;
From the subclan of Bethlehem, 123;
From the subclan of Netophah, 56;
From the subclan of Anathoth, 128;
From the subclan of Azmaveth, 42;
From the subclans of Kiriatharim, Chephirah, and Be-eroth, 743;
From the subclans of Ramah and Geba, 621;
From the subclan of Michmas, 122;
From the subclans of Bethel and Ai, 223;
From the subclan of Nebo, 52;
From the subclan of Magbish, 156;
From the subclan of Elam, 1,254;
From the subclan of Harim, 320;
From the subclans of Lod, Hadid, and Ono, 725;
From the subclan of Jericho, 345;
From the subclan of Senaah, 3,630.

36-39Here are the statistics concerning the returning priests:

2:36
1 Chron 9:10,
11; 24:7-18
Neh 7:39-42

From the families of Jedaiah of the subclan of Jeshua, 973;
From the subclan of Immer, 1,052;
From the subclan of Pashhur, 1,247;
From the subclan of Harim, 1,017.

40, 41, 42Here are the statistics concerning the Levites who returned:

2:40
Neh 7:43-45

From the families of Jeshua and Kedmi-el of the subclan of Hodaviah, 74;
The choir members from the clan of Asaph, 128;
From the descendants of the gatekeepers (the families of Shallum, Ater,
   Talmon, Akkub, Hatita, and Shobai), 139.

43-54The following families of the Temple assistants were represented: Ziha,
Hasupha, Tabbaoth, Keros, Siaha, Padon, Lebanah, Hagabah, Akkub, Hagab,
Shamlai, Hanan, Giddel, Gahar, Re-aiah, Rezin, Nekoda, Gazzam, Uzza, Paseah,
Besai, Asnah, Me-unim, Nephisim, Bakbuk, Hakupha, Harhur, Bazluth, Mehida,
Harsha, Barkos, Sisera, Temah, Neziah, Hatipha.

2:43
Neh 7:46-56

55, 56, 57Those who made the trip also included the descendants of King Solomon's officials: Sotai, Hassophereth, Peruda, Jaalah, Darkon, Giddel, Shephatiah,
Hattil, Pochereth-hazzebaim, Ami.

2:55
Neh 7:57-59

58The Temple assistants and the descendants of Solomon's officers numbered
392.

59Another group returned to Jerusalem at this time from the Persian cities of
Telmelah, Tel-harsha, Cherub, Addan, and Immer. However, they had lost their
genealogies and could not prove that they were really Israelites. 60This group
included the subclans of Delaiah, Tobiah, and Nekoda—a total of 652.

2:59
Neh 7:61,63-65

2:60
Neh 7:62

2:61
2 Sam 17:27

2:62
Ex 28:30
Lev 21:21-23
Num 3:10
16:39,40
Ezra 2:59

2:64
Neh 7:66,67

2:68
Neh 7:70-72

61Three subclans of priests—Habaiah, Hakkoz, and Barzillai (he married one of the daughters of Barzillai the Gileadite and took her family name)—also returned to Jerusalem. 62, 63But they too had lost their genealogies, so the leaders refused to allow them to continue as priests; they would not even allow them to eat the priests' share of food from the sacrifices until the Urim and Thummim could be consulted, to find out from God whether they actually were descendants of priests or not.

64, 65So a total of 42,360 persons returned to Judah; in addition to 7,337 slaves and 200 choir members, both men and women. 66, 67They took with them 736 horses, 245 mules, 435 camels, and 6,720 donkeys.

68Some of the leaders were able to give generously toward the rebuilding of the Temple, 69and each gave as much as he could. The total value of their gifts amounted to $300,000 of gold, $170,000 of silver, and 100 robes for the priests.

THE RETURN FROM EXILE	Year	Number of People Returned	Persian King	Jewish Leader	Main Accomplishment
	537 B.C.	50,000	Cyrus	Zerubbabel	They rebuilt the Temple, but only after a 20-year struggle. The work was halted for several years, but was finally completed.
	458 B.C.	2,000 men and their families	Artaxerxes	Ezra	Ezra confronted the spiritual disobedience of the people and they repented and established worship at the Temple. But the wall of Jerusalem remained in ruins.
	445 B.C.	Small group	Artaxerxes	Nehemiah	The city was rebuilt and a spiritual awakening followed. But the people still struggled with ongoing disobedience.

Babylon, the once-mighty nation that had destroyed Jerusalem and carried the people of Judah into captivity, had itself become a defeated nation. Persia was the new world power and under its new foreign policy, captured peoples were allowed to return to their homelands. The people of Judah and Israel returned to their land in three successive waves.

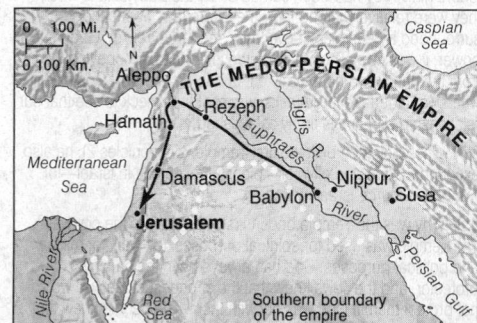

THE JOURNEY HOME The vast Medo-Persian Empire included all the area on this map and more. A group of exiles began the long trip back to their homeland. Many exiles, however, preferred the comfort and security they had in Persia to the dangerous trip back to Jerusalem, and so they decided to stay in Persia.

2:59 Genealogies were very important to the Hebrew people. If they could not prove they had descended from Abraham, they were not considered true Jews and were excluded from some special privileges. For example, only descendants of Levi (Abraham's great-grandson) could serve in the Temple.

2:62, 63 The Urim and Thummim were two objects, probably shaped like flat stones, originally carried in the garment worn by the High Priest. They were used to determine God's will in important matters. (See the note on 1 Samuel 10:20.)

2:68, 69 As the Temple reconstruction progressed, everyone contributed. Everyone's effort and cooperation were required, and the people gave as much as they could. Often we limit our giving to ten percent of our income. The Bible, however, emphasizes that we should give from the heart all that we are able (2 Corinthians 8:12; 9:6). Let the amount of your gift be decided by God's call to give generously, not by the amount of your leftovers.

2:69 The money given was enough to start rebuilding the Temple. The people put what resources they had to their best use. They were enthusiastic and sincere, but this Temple would never match the splendor of Solomon's. The money David gathered to start the building of Solomon's Temple was a thousand times more (1 Chronicles 22:14). Some people wept as they remembered the glorious Temple that had been destroyed (3:12).

70So the priests and Levites and some of the common people settled in Jerusalem and its nearby villages; and the singers, the gatekeepers, the Temple workers, and the rest of the people returned to the other cities of Judah from which they had come.

2:70
Neh 7:73

2. The people rebuild the Temple
The leaders rebuild the altar

3 During the month of September everyone who had returned to Judah came to Jerusalem from their homes in the other towns. Then Jeshua (son of Jozadak) with his fellow priests, and Zerubbabel (son of Shealtiel) and his clan, rebuilt the altar of the God of Israel; and sacrificed burnt offerings upon it, as instructed in the laws of Moses, the man of God. 3The altar was rebuilt on its old site, and it was used immediately to sacrifice morning and evening burnt offerings to the Lord; for the people were fearful of attack.

3:1
Lev 1:1-17
6:8-13
Deut 12:4-7
1 Chron 3:17-20
Ezra 2:2
Neh 12:1,8
Hag 1:1
Zech 3:1
4:6-10; 6:10,11

4And they celebrated the Feast of Tabernacles as prescribed in the laws of Moses, sacrificing the burnt offerings specified for each day of the feast. 5They also offered the special sacrifices required for the Sabbaths, the new moon celebrations, and the other regular annual feasts of the Lord. Voluntary offerings of the people were also sacrificed. 6It was on the fifteenth day of September that the priests began sacrificing the burnt offerings to the Lord. (This was before they began building the foundation of the Temple.)

3:3
Ex 29:38-42
Num 28:1-8
3:4
Lev 23:34-36
Num 8:14-17
3:5
Ex 29:42
Lev 1:3
Num 28:11-14
29:39
Deut 12:6,17

7Then they hired masons and carpenters, and bought cedar logs from the people of Tyre and Sidon, paying for them with food, wine, and olive oil. The logs were brought down from the Lebanon mountains and floated along the coast of the Mediterranean Sea to Joppa, for King Cyrus had included this provision in his grant.

3:7
1 Kgs 5:9-11
2 Chron 2:10-16

The people begin to rebuild the Temple

8The actual construction of the Temple began in June of the second year of their arrival at Jerusalem. The work force was made up of all those who had returned, and they were under the direction of Zerubbabel (son of Shealtiel), Jeshua (son of Jozadak), and their fellow priests and the Levites. The Levites who were twenty

3:8
Num 4:3
1 Chron
23:24-32

3:6 *fifteenth day of September,* literally, "the first day of the seventh month" of the Hebrew calender.

3:2, 3 The Jews set up the altar as one of their first official acts. It symbolized God's presence and protection. It also demonstrated their commitment to serve God alone. Zerubbabel sacrificed burnt offerings as the laws of Moses instructed (Leviticus 1—7). The sacrifices were essential because they demonstrated that the people were seeking God's guidance, were rededicating themselves to living as he commanded, and were daily coming to him for forgiveness of sin.

3:3 The Jews were afraid that they were going to be attacked by the surrounding people—a mixed group whose ancestors had been conquered by the Assyrians. Foreigners had been forced to resettle in the Northern Kingdom of Israel after Israel was defeated and her people taken captive in 722 B.C. (4:1, 2). This resettlement procedure was a common tactic of the Assyrians to prevent strong nationalistic uprisings by conquered peoples (see 4:10). Some of the resettled people in Israel had migrated south near Jerusalem, and they thought the returning exiles threatened their claim on the land.

3:4 The Feast of Tabernacles lasted for seven days. During this time the people lived in temporary dwellings (tents, booths, lean-tos) just as their ancestors had done years before as they journeyed through the wilderness on their way to the Promised Land. The feast reminded the people of God's past protection and guidance in the wilderness and of his continued love for them. The Feast of Tabernacles (the Festival of Shelters) is described in detail in Leviticus 23:33–36.

3:5 Almost immediately after arriving in the new land, the returning exiles built an altar. The people began worshiping God through sacrifices even before the Temple foundations were laid. After many years in captivity, they had learned their lesson—they knew that God does not offer special protection to people who ignore him. They had been carried off by the Babylonians when they were relatively strong; now they were few, weak, and surrounded by enemies. If ever they needed to rely on God's power, it was now. They realized the importance of obeying God from the heart, and not merely out of habit. If we want God's help when we undertake large tasks, we must first check to see that our relationship with him is firmly established.

3:7 When Solomon built the first Temple (2 Chronicles 2), he also exchanged food and olive oil—plentiful resources in Israel—for wood, a resource Israel lacked.

3:8 Why was the Temple begun first, even before the city wall? The Temple was used for spiritual purposes; the wall, for military and political purposes. God had always been the nation's protector, and the Jews knew that the strongest stone wall would not protect them if God was not with them. The people knew that putting their spiritual lives in order was a far higher priority than assuring the national defense.

3:8 It took from September (3:1) to June just to *prepare* to build the Temple. During this time, the altar was built, materials were ordered and collected, and workers were hired. The exiles took some time to make plans because the project was important to them. Preparation may not feel heroic or spiritual, but it is vital to any project meant to be done well.

years old or older were appointed to supervise the workmen. 9The supervision of the entire project was given to Jeshua, Kadmi-el, Henadad, and their sons and relatives, all of whom were Levites.

3:10
1 Chron
28:11-13,19

10When the builders completed the foundation of the Temple, the priests put on their official robes and blew their trumpets; and the descendants of Asaph crashed their cymbals to praise the Lord in the manner ordained by King David. 11They sang rounds of praise and thanks to God, singing this song: "He is good, and his love and mercy toward Israel will last forever." Then all the people gave a great shout, praising God because the foundation of the Temple had been laid.

3:11
1 Chron 16:34,
41; 29:20
Neh 12:24
Ps 24:7-10
103:17; 106:1
Isa 12:6

3:12
Hag 2:3

12But many of the priests and Levites and other leaders—the old men who remembered Solomon's beautiful Temple—wept aloud, while others were shouting for joy! 13So the shouting and the weeping mingled together in a loud commotion that could be heard from far away!

Enemies oppose the rebuilding

4 When the enemies of Judah and Benjamin heard that the exiles had returned and were rebuilding the Temple, 2they approached Zerubbabel and the other leaders and suggested, "Let us work with you, for we are just as interested in your God as you are; we have sacrificed to him ever since King Esar-haddon of Assyria brought us here."

4:2
2 Kgs 19:37
Ezra 4:7-10
Neh 4:1-13

3But Zerubbabel and Jeshua and the other Jewish leaders replied, "No, you may have no part in this work. The Temple of the God of Israel must be built by the Israelis, just as King Cyrus has commanded."

4:3
Ezra 1:1-4
6:3-5
Neh 2:20

4, 5Then the local residents tried to discourage and frighten them by sending agents to tell lies about them to King Cyrus. This went on during his entire reign and lasted until King Darius took the throne.

4:4
Ezra 4:24; 5:5-7
Neh 12:22
Hag 1:1,14,15

3:10, 11 David had given clear instructions concerning the use of music and choirs for the worship services in the Temple (1 Chronicles 16, 25).

3:10, 11 Completing the foundation for the Temple required great effort on the part of all involved. But no one tried to get praise for himself and his own hard work. Instead, everyone praised God for what had been done. All good gifts come from God—talents, abilities, strength, and leadership—and God gives us both the desire and the power to use our gifts for him. Rather than seeking praise for ourselves, we should thank God for what has been done in and through us!

3:11 The Bible records many songs and musical events. For a list of such events, see the chart in Exodus 15.

3:12 Fifty years after its destruction, the Temple was being rebuilt (536 B.C.). Some of the older people remembered Solomon's Temple and were filled with emotion because the new Temple would not be as glorious as the first one. But the beauty of the building is not nearly so important to God as the attitudes of the builders and worshipers. God cares more about what we *are* than what we accomplish. Our world is always changing, and magnificent accomplishments decay and disappear. Do not be concerned if it seems as if your work for God is not so great as what others have done. Your relationship with him is more important.

3:12 Since the new Temple was built on the foundation of Solomon's Temple, the two structures apparently were not that different in size, but the old Temple was far more elaborate and ornate, and it was surrounded by many buildings and a vast courtyard. Both Temples were constructed of imported cedar wood, but Solomon's was decorated with vast amounts of gold and precious stones. Solomon's Temple took over seven years to build; Zerubbabel's took about four years. Solomon's Temple was at the hub of a thriving city; Zerubbabel's was in the midst of ruins. No wonder the people wept.

3:13 The celebration after laying the Temple foundation was

marked by contrasts of emotion—weeping and shouting. Both were legitimate. God's work among us can stimulate us both to rejoice over the goodness of his grace and to mourn over our sins that have required him to intervene. When we come into the presence of Almighty God, we should not be surprised if we feel full of joy and thanksgiving, yet at the same time are soberly aware of our unworthiness.

4:1 The enemies of Judah and Benjamin were people who had been relocated in the Northern Kingdom when Assyria conquered Israel (see 2 Kings 17 and the note on 3:3). In an attempt to infiltrate and disrupt the project, these people offered to help the Jews rebuild the Temple. They wanted to keep a close eye on what the Jews were doing. They were hoping to keep Jerusalem from becoming strong again. The Jews, however, saw through their ploy. Such a partnership with unbelievers would have tempted God's people to compromise their goals.

4:1–6 Believers can expect opposition as they do God's work (2 Timothy 3:12). Unbelievers and evil spiritual forces are always working against God and his people. The opposition may involve offers of alliance (4:2), attempts to discourage and intimidate (4:4, 5), or unjust accusations (4:6). If you learn to expect this opposition, you won't be halted by it. Move ahead with the work God has planned for you, and trust him to show you the way to overcome the obstacles.

4:2 These enemies claimed to worship the same God as Zerubbabel and the rest of the Jews. In one sense, this was true; they worshiped God along with a host of other gods (see 2 Kings 17:27–29, 32–34, 41). But in God's eyes, this was not worship—it was sin and rebellion. True worship involves devotion to God alone (Exodus 20:3–5). To these foreigners, God was just another idol to be added to their collection. Their real motive was not to worship God but to disrupt the Temple project. Believers today must beware of those who claim to be Christians but whose actions clearly reveal they are seeking only their own best interests.

King Artaxerxes stops the work

6And afterwards, when King Ahasuerus began to reign, they wrote him a letter of accusation against the people of Judah and Jerusalem, 7and did the same thing during the reign of Artaxerxes. Bishlam, Mithredath, and Tabe-el and their associates wrote a letter to him in the Aramaic language, and it was translated to him. 8, 9Others who participated were Governor Rehum, Shimshai (a scribe), several judges and other local leaders, the Persians, the Babylonians, the men of Erech and Susa, 10and men from several other nations. (They had been taken from their own lands by the great and noble Osnappar and relocated in Jerusalem, Samaria, and throughout the neighboring lands west of the Euphrates River.)

11Here is the text of the letter they sent to King Artaxerxes:

"Sir: Greetings from your loyal subjects west of the Euphrates River. 12Please be informed that the Jews sent to Jerusalem from Babylon are rebuilding this historically rebellious and evil city; they have already rebuilt its walls and have repaired the foundations of the Temple. 13But we wish you to know that if this city is rebuilt, it will be much to your disadvantage, for the Jews will then refuse to pay their taxes to you.

14"Since we are grateful to you as our patron, and we do not want to see you taken advantage of and dishonored in this way, we have decided to send you this information. 15We suggest that you search the ancient records to discover what a rebellious city this has been in the past; in fact, it was destroyed because of its long history of sedition against the kings and countries who attempted to control it. 16We wish to declare that if this city is rebuilt and the walls finished, you might as well forget about this part of your empire beyond the Euphrates, for it will be lost to you."

17Then the king made this reply to Governor Rehum and Shimshai the scribe, and to their companions living in Samaria and throughout the area west of the Euphrates River:

18"Gentlemen: Greetings! The letter you sent has been translated and read to me. 19I have ordered a search made of the records and have indeed found that Jerusalem has in times past been a hotbed of insurrection against many kings; in fact, rebellion and sedition are normal there! 20I find, moreover, that there have been some very great kings in Jerusalem who have ruled the entire land beyond the Euphrates River and have received vast tribute, custom, and toll. 21Therefore, I command that these

4:6
Esth 1:1
2:1,12-14
Dan 9:1

4:7
2 Kgs 18:26
Ezra 4:11,23
7:1-21
Neh 1:1; 5:14
Isa 36:11
Dan 2:4

4:8
Ezra 5:6; 6:13

4:12
Ezra 5:3
Neh 1:3
Dan 9:25

4:13
Ezra 4:20; 7:24
Neh 5:4

4:20
1 Kgs 4:21,24
1 Chron 18:3,4,
6,13; 19:19
2 Chron 17:11
Ezra 4:13

Name	Date of Reign	Relationship to Israel	
Cyrus	559–530 B.C.	Conquered Babylon. Established a policy of returning exiles to their homelands. Sent Zerubbabel to Jerusalem, financed his project, and returned the gold and silver articles that Nebuchadnezzar had taken from the Temple. He probably knew Daniel.	**THE PERSIAN KINGS OF EZRA'S DAY**
Darius	522–486 B.C.	Stopped construction of the Temple in Jerusalem.	
Ahasuerus (Xerxes)	486–465 B.C.	Was Esther's husband. Allowed the Jews to protect themselves against Haman's attempt to eliminate their people.	
Artaxerxes	465–424 B.C.	Had Nehemiah as his cupbearer. Allowed both Ezra and Nehemiah to return to Jerusalem.	

4:6 This letter sent to King Ahasuerus may have been inscribed on a clay tablet, a fragment of pottery, or sheets of parchment.

4:6-23 In these verses, Ezra summarizes the entire story of the opposition to building the Temple, the walls, and other important buildings in Jerusalem. Chronologically, 4:6 fits between chapters 6 and 7; 4:7-23 refers to the events between Ezra 7 and Nehemiah 1. Ezra grouped them here to highlight the persistent opposition to God's people over the years, and God's ability to overcome it.

4:10 Osnappar was another name for Ashurbanipal (669–626 B.C.), the Assyrian king who completed the relocation of Israelite

captives. He was the last of the strong Assyrian kings, and after his death the nation quickly declined. It was conquered in 612.

4:19, 20 Artaxerxes called Jerusalem a "hotbed of insurrection against many kings." By reading the historical records, he learned that mighty kings had come from Jerusalem, and he may have feared that another would arise if the city were rebuilt. Solomon had ruled a huge empire (1 Kings 4:21), and Jerusalem's kings had rebelled against mighty powers—for example, Zedekiah rebelled against Nebuchadnezzar despite his oath of loyalty (2 Chronicles 36:13). Artaxerxes did not want to aid the rebuilding of a rebellious city and nation.

ZERUBBABEL

Sometimes God's ownership of a project is only recognized after *our* best efforts have failed. It is dangerous to think of God as responsible for the insignificant details while we take charge of the larger aspects of a project. Instead, it is God who is in control and we only play a part in his overall plan. When God gives us important jobs to do, it isn't because he needs our help. Zerubbabel learned this lesson.

God's people had been exiled in Babylon for many years. Many had settled into comfortable life-styles there and wanted to stay. There were, however, almost 60,000 who had not forgotten Judah. When Babylon was defeated in 539 B.C., the Persian ruler, Cyrus, allowed the Jews to return to Jerusalem and rebuild their Temple. Zerubbabel led the first and largest group back to the Promised Land.

Zerubbabel's leadership was by right and recognition. Not only was he a descendant of David, he also had personal leadership qualities. When the people arrived in Judah, they were given time to establish living quarters, and then were called to begin the work. They began not by laying the city walls or government buildings, but by rebuilding the altar, worshiping God together, and celebrating a feast. Under Zerubbabel's leadership, they established a spiritual foundation for their building efforts.

The Temple foundation was then quickly completed followed by another round of celebration. But soon, two problems arose. A few old men remembered Solomon's glorious Temple and were saddened at how much smaller and less glorious this one was. Also, some enemies of the Jews tried to infiltrate the work force and stop the building with political pressure. Fear caused the work to grind to a halt. The people went to their homes and 16 years passed.

We do not know what Zerubbabel did during this time. His discouragement, following those first months of excitement and accomplishment, must have been deep. Those feelings eventually hardened into hopelessness. So God sent the prophets Haggai and Zechariah to be Zerubbabel's encouraging companions. They confronted the people's reluctance and comforted their fears. The work began once again with renewed energy and was completed in four years.

Zerubbabel, like many of us, knew how to start well but found it hard to keep going. His successes depended on the quality of encouragement he received. Zerubbabel let discouragement get the better of him. But when he let God take control, the work was finished. God is always in control. We must not let circumstances or lack of encouragement slow us from doing the tasks God has given us.

Strengths and accomplishments:
• Led the first group of Jewish exiles back to Jerusalem from Babylon
• Completed the rebuilding of God's Temple
• Demonstrated wisdom in the help he accepted and refused
• Started his building project with worship as the focal point

Weaknesses and mistakes:
• Needed constant encouragement
• Allowed problems and resistance to stop the rebuilding work

Lessons from his life:
• A leader needs to provide not only the initial motivation for a project, but the continued encouragement necessary to keep the project going
• A leader must find his/her own dependable source of encouragement
• God's faithfulness is shown in the way he preserved David's line

Vital statistics:
• Where: Babylon, Jerusalem
• Occupation: Recognized leader of the exiles
• Relatives: Father: Shealtiel. Grandfather: Jehoiachin.
• Contemporaries: Cyrus, Darius, Zechariah, Haggai

Key verses:
"This is God's message to Zerubbabel: 'Not by might, nor by power, but by my Spirit, says the Lord Almighty—you will succeed because of my Spirit, though you are few and weak.' Therefore, no mountain, however high, can stand before Zerubbabel! For it will flatten out before him! And Zerubbabel will finish building this Temple with mighty shouts of thanksgiving for God's mercy, declaring that all was done by grace alone" (Zechariah 4:6, 7).

Zerubbabel's story is told in Ezra 2:2—5:2. He is also mentioned in 1 Chronicles 3:19; Nehemiah 7:7; 12:1, 47; Haggai 1:1, 12, 13; 2:4, 21, 23; Zechariah 4:6–10; Matthew 1:12, 13; Luke 3:27.

men must stop their work until I have investigated the matter more thoroughly. 22Do not delay, for we must not permit the situation to get out of control!"

23When this letter from King Artaxerxes was read to Rehum and Shimshai, they hurried to Jerusalem and forced the Jews to stop building. 24So the work ended until the second year of the reign of King Darius of Persia.

4:24
Neh 6:3,9
Hag 1:14,15

The rebuilding continues

5 But there were prophets in Jerusalem and Judah at that time—Haggai, and Zechariah (the son of Iddo)—who brought messages from the God of Israel to Zerubbabel (son of Shealtiel) and Jeshua (son of Jozadak), encouraging them to begin building again! So they did and the prophets helped them.

5:1
Ezra 3:2; 6:14
Hag 1:1
Zech 1:1

3But Tattenai, the governor of the lands west of the Euphrates, and Shethar-bozenai, and their companions soon arrived in Jerusalem and demanded, "Who gave you permission to rebuild this Temple and finish these walls?"

5:3
Ezra 5:6,9,17
6:6,13

4They also asked for a list of the names of all the men who were working on the Temple. 5But because the Lord was overseeing the entire situation, our enemies did not force us to stop building, but let us continue while King Darius looked into the matter and returned his decision.

5:4
Ezra 5:10

5:5
Ezra 4:4; 6:1
7:6,12; 8:22
Ps 33:18
1 Pet 3:12

Enemies inform King Darius

6Following is the letter which Governors Tattenai and Shethar-bozenai, and the other officials sent to King Darius:

5:6
Ezra 4:11,23

7"To King Darius:

"Greetings!

8"We wish to inform you that we went to the construction site of the Temple of the great God of Judah. It is being built with huge stones, and timber is being laid in the city walls. The work is going forward with great energy and success. 9We asked the leaders, 'Who has given you permission to do this?' 10And we demanded their names so that we could notify you. 11Their answer was, 'We are the servants of the God of heaven and earth and we are rebuilding the Temple that was constructed here many centuries ago by a great king of Israel. 12But afterwards our ancestors angered the God of heaven, and he abandoned them and let King Nebuchadnezzar destroy this Temple and exile the people to Babylonia.'

5:10
Ezra 5:4

5:11
1 Kgs 6:1-38
2 Chron 3:1—
5:14

5:12
2 Kgs 24:2,10
25:1,8-11
2 Chron 36:6-20

13"But they insist that King Cyrus of Babylon, during the first year of his reign, issued a decree that the Temple should be rebuilt, 14and they say King Cyrus returned the gold and silver bowls which Nebuchadnezzar had taken from the Temple in Jerusalem and had placed in the temple of Babylon. They say these items were delivered into the safekeeping of a man named Shesh-bazzar, whom King

5:13
2 Chron 36:22
23
Ezra 1:1-8
6:3-5

5:14
Ezra 1:7,8,11
5:16; 6:3-5

4:24 Ezra resumes his chronological account here. It may have been ten years since the Israelites had worked on the Temple. It did not begin again until 520 B.C., the second year of King Darius' reign (5:1ff).

5:1 More details about the work and messages of Haggai and Zechariah are found in the books of the Bible which bear their names.

5:1, 2 God sometimes sends prophets to encourage and strengthen his people. To accomplish this, Haggai and Zechariah not only preached, but also got involved in the labor. In the church today, God appoints prophetic voices to help us with our work (Ephesians 4:11–13). Their ministry should have the same effect upon us as Haggai's and Zechariah's had on Israel. "One who prophesies, preaching the messages of God, is helping others grow in the Lord, encouraging and comforting them" (1 Corinthians 14:3). In turn, we should encourage those who bring God's words to us.

5:5 The non-Jews who lived nearby attempted to hinder the construction of the Temple. But while the legal debate went on, and the decision was under appeal, the Jews continued to rebuild. When we are doing God's work, others may try to delay, confuse,

or frustrate us, but we can proceed confidently. God will accomplish his purposes in our world, no matter who disagrees.

5:11 While rebuilding the Temple, the workers were confronted by the Babylon-appointed governor, demanding to know who gave permission for their construction project (5:3). This could have been intimidating, but, as we learn from the letter, they boldly replied, "We are the servants of the God of heaven and earth."

It is not always easy to speak up for our faith in an unbelieving world, but we must. The way to deal with pressure and intimidation is to recognize that we are workers for God. Our allegiance is to him first, people second. When we contemplate the reactions and criticisms of hostile people, we can become paralyzed with fear; if we make a policy of offending no one or pleasing everyone, our effectiveness will be stopped. God is our leader, and his rewards are most important. So don't be intimidated. Let others know by your actions and words whom you serve first.

5:13–17 Cyrus is called king of Persia in 1:1 and king of Babylon in 5:13. Because Persia had just conquered Babylon, Cyrus was king of both nations. Babylon is more important to this story because it was the location of the Hebrews' 70-year captivity. The Babylon in 5:17 may refer to the city of Babylon which was the capital of the province of Babylon.

Cyrus appointed as governor of Judah. [15]The king instructed him to return the bowls to Jerusalem and to let the Temple of God be built there as before. [16]So Shesh-bazzar came and laid the foundations of the Temple at Jerusalem; and the people have been working on it ever since, though it is not yet completed. [17]We request that you search in the royal library of Babylon to discover whether King Cyrus ever made such a decree; and then let us know your pleasure in this matter."

5:17
Ezra 6:1,2

King Darius approves the rebuilding

6:1
Ezra 5:17

6 So King Darius issued orders that a search be made in the Babylonian archives, where documents were stored.

6:2
Esth 1:1,13-15
10:2
Jer 25:25

[2]Eventually the record was found in the palace at Ecbatana, in the province of Media. This is what it said:

6:3
Ezra 1:2-4

[3]"In this first year of the reign of King Cyrus, a decree has been sent out concerning the Temple of God at Jerusalem where the Jews offer sacrifices. It is to be rebuilt, and the foundations are to be strongly laid. The height will be ninety feet and the width will be ninety feet. [4]There will be three layers of huge stones in the foundation, topped with a layer of new timber. All expenses will be paid by the king. [5]And the gold and silver bowls which were taken from the Temple of God by Nebuchadnezzar shall be taken back to Jerusalem and put into the Temple as they were before."

6:5
1 Kgs 6:36

[6]So King Darius II sent this message to Governor Shethar-bozenai, and the other officials west of the Euphrates:

"Do not disturb the construction of the Temple. Let it be rebuilt on its former site, [7]and don't molest the governor of Judah and the other leaders in their work. [8]Moreover, I decree that you are to pay the full construction costs without delay from my taxes collected in your territory. [9]Give the priests in Jerusalem young bulls, rams, and lambs for burnt offerings to the God of heaven; and give them wheat, wine, salt, and olive oil each day without fail. [10]Then they will be able to offer acceptable sacrifices to the God of heaven, and to pray for me and my sons. [11]Anyone who attempts to change this message in any way shall have the beams

6:11
Ezra 7:26
Dan 2:5; 3:29

6:6 *King Darius sent this message,* implied.

THE POST-EXILIC PROPHETS
God used these men to confront and comfort his people after their return to their homeland from exile in Babylon.

Who?	When?	Ministered to These Contemporary Leaders	Main Message	Significance
Haggai	520 B.C.	Zerubbabel Joshua	● Encouraged the leaders and the people to continue rebuilding the Temple, which God would bless ● Challenged the people's careless worship, which God would not bless	Disobedience and careless obedience of God's commands lead to judgment.
Zechariah	520 B.C.	Zerubbabel Joshua	● Emphasized God's command to rebuild his Temple ● Gave the people another look at God's plan to bless the world through Israel and her coming king—the Messiah (9:9, 10)	Encouragement for today's effort sometimes requires that we remember God has a plan and purpose for tomorrow. Meanwhile, the challenge is to live for him today.
Malachi	430 B.C.	The priests are the only leaders mentioned	● Confronted the people and priests with God's promises of judgment on those who reject him and God's blessing on those who live as he desires	God expects our obedience to him to affect our attitude toward him and our treatment of one another.

6:1, 2 Many clay and papyrus documents recording various transactions and historical data have been discovered in this area (near present-day Syria). A great library and archives with thousands of such records have been discovered at Ebla in Syria.

pulled from his house and built into a gallows on which he will be hanged; and his house shall be reduced to a pile of rubble. 12The God who has chosen the city of Jerusalem will destroy any king and any nation that alters this commandment and destroys this Temple. I, Darius, have issued this decree; let it be obeyed with all diligence."

6:12
Deut 12:4,5,11
1 Kgs 9:2,3

The Temple is completed and dedicated

13Governors Tattenai and Shethar-bozenai, and their companions complied at once with the command of King Darius.

14So the Jewish leaders continued in their work, and they were greatly encouraged by the preaching of the prophets Haggai and Zechariah (son of Iddo). The Temple was finally finished, as had been commanded by God and decreed by Cyrus, Darius, and Artaxerxes, the kings of Persia. 15The completion date was February 18 in the sixth year of the reign of King Darius II.

6:14
Ezra 1:1; 5:1
6:12
7:1,7-9,11
Zech 4:9

16The Temple was then dedicated with great joy by the priests, the Levites, and all the people. 17During the dedication celebration 100 young bulls, 200 rams, and 400 lambs were sacrificed; and twelve male goats were presented as a sin offering for the twelve tribes of Israel. 18Then the priests and Levites were divided into their various service corps, to do the work of God as instructed in the laws of Moses.

6:16
Ezra 3:11,12
6:21,22

6:18
2 Chron 35:4,5

The Passover is celebrated

19The Passover was celebrated on the first day of April. 20For by that time many of the priests and Levites had consecrated themselves. 21, 22And some of the heathen people who had been relocated in Judah turned from their immoral customs and joined the Israelis in worshiping the Lord God. They, with the entire nation, ate the Passover feast and celebrated the Feast of Unleavened Bread for seven days. There was great joy throughout the land because the Lord had caused the king of Assyria to be generous to Israel and to assist in the construction of the Temple.

6:19
Ex 12:6

6:20
2 Chron 29:34
30:15-17

6:21
Ex 19:10,14
Num 9:6,7,
10-14
Ezra 9:1-15

B. THE RETURN LED BY EZRA (7:1—10:44)

Ezra returned to the Land with a second group of exiles, 80 years after Zerubbabel. Ezra found the Temple rebuilt, but the lives of the people in shambles. Intermarriage with foreigners opposed to God threatened the spiritual future of the nation. So Ezra prayed for guidance and then followed through with action. Christians today must also strive to keep their lives pure, refusing to let the sinful allurements of the world around them compromise their life-style.

1. The second group of exiles returns to the Land

Ezra's background

7 Here is the genealogy of Ezra, who traveled from Babylon to Jerusalem during the reign of King Artaxerxes of Persia:

7:1
Ezra 7:12,21
8:1—10:44
Neh 2:1; 8:1-18

Ezra was the son of Seriah;
Seriah was the son of Azariah;
Azariah was the son of Hilkiah;
Hilkiah was the son of Shallum;
Shallum was the son of Zadok;
Zadok was the son of Ahitub;
Ahitub was the son of Amariah;

6:11 *hanged*, literally, impaled. 6:15 *February 18*, literally "the third day of the month of Adar." 6:19 *first day of April*, literally, "the fourteenth day of the first month" of the Hebrew calendar. 7:1 *to Jerusalem*, implied.

6:14 Ezra carefully pointed out that rebuilding the Temple was decreed first by God and then by the kings, who were his instruments. How wonderful that God's work was carried on and the opposition of powerful forces was stopped by a clause in a legal document. God's will is supreme over all in authority over nations, all historical events, and all hostile forces. If we trust in his power and love, we will not be deterred by any opposition.

6:15 The Temple was completed in 516 B.C.

6:18 Feasting and celebration were in order at the great Temple

dedication. But the priests and Levites were organized into groups in order to "do the work of God as instructed in the laws of Moses." There is a time to celebrate, but there is also a time to work. Both, in their time, are proper and necessary when worshiping and serving God; and God is evident in both.

7:1 There is a gap of almost 60 years between the events of chapters six and seven. The story in the book of Esther occurred during this time, in the reign of Ahasuerus, also called Xerxes the Great, who ruled from 486-465 B.C. Artaxerxes, his son, became king in 465, and Ezra returned to Jerusalem in 458.

Amariah was the son of Meraioth;
Meraioth was the son of Zerahiah;
Zerahiah was the son of Uzzi;
Uzzi was the son of Bukki;
Bukki was the son of Abishu-a;
Abishu-a was the son of Phinehas;
Phinehas was the son of Eleazar;
Eleazar was the son of Aaron, the chief priest.

7:6
Ezra 7:10,21,25
Neh 8:9,13

7:7
1 Chron 6:31,48,
49
Ezra 2:40-58
Neh 7:39-60
7:10
Ezra 7:6

6As a Jewish religious leader, Ezra was well versed in Jehovah's laws which Moses had given to the people of Israel. He asked to be allowed to return to Jerusalem, and the king granted his request; for the Lord his God was blessing him. 7, 8, 9Many ordinary people as well as priests, Levites, singers, gatekeepers, and Temple workers traveled with him. They left Babylon in the middle of March in the seventh year of the reign of Artaxerxes and arrived at Jerusalem in the month of August; for the Lord gave them a good trip. 10This was because Ezra had determined to study and obey the laws of the Lord and to become a Bible teacher, teaching those laws to the people of Israel.

Ezra's letter from King Artaxerxes

7:11
Ezra 4:11; 5:6

7:12
Ezek 26:7
Dan 2:37,47

11King Artaxerxes presented this letter to Ezra the priest, the student of God's commands:
12"From: Artaxerxes, the king of kings.
"To: Ezra, the priest, the teacher of the laws of the God of heaven.

THE MEDO-PERSIAN EMPIRE
The Medo-Persian Empire included the lands of Media and Persia, much of the area shown on this map and more. The Jewish exiles were concentrated in the area around Nippur in the Babylonian province. The decree by King Cyrus which allowed the Israelites to return to their homeland and rebuild the Temple was discovered in the palace at Ecbatana.

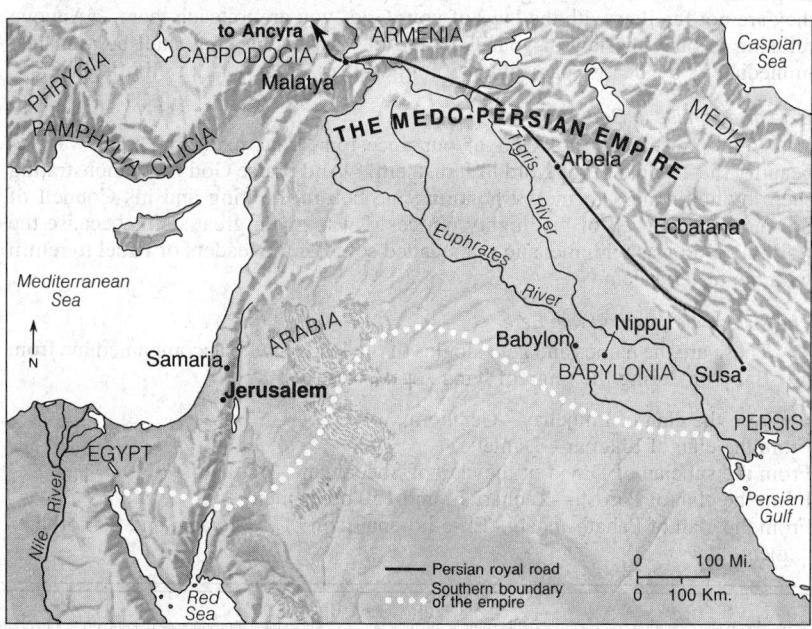

7:6 Eighty years after the first exiles returned to Jerusalem (2:1), Ezra himself returned. This was his first trip, and it took four months. The Temple had been standing for about 58 years. Up to this point in the narrative, Ezra had remained in Babylon, probably compiling a record of the events that had taken place.

Why did he have to ask the king if he could return? Ezra wanted to lead many Jews back to Jerusalem, and he needed a decree from the king stating that any Jew who wanted to return could do so. This decree would be like a passport in case they ran into opposition along the way. The king's generous decree showed that

God was blessing Ezra (7:6, 28) and that Ezra was a prominent man in Artaxerxes' kingdom. He was willing to give up his position to return to his homeland and teach the Israelites God's laws.

7:6–10 Ezra demonstrates how a gifted Bible teacher can move God's people forward. He was effective because he was a well-versed student of God's laws and because he was determined to obey those laws. He taught through both his speaking and his example. Like Ezra, we should determine both to study and to obey God's Word.

13"I decree that any Jew in my realm, including the priests and Levites, may return to Jerusalem with you. 14I and my Council of Seven hereby instruct you to take a copy of God's laws to Judah and Jerusalem and to send back a report of the religious progress being made there. 15We also commission you to take with you to Jerusalem the silver and gold which we are presenting as an offering to the God of Israel.

16"Moreover, you are to collect voluntary Temple offerings of silver and gold from the Jews and their priests in all of the provinces of Babylon. 17These funds are to be used primarily for the purchase of oxen, rams, lambs, grain offerings, and drink offerings, all of which will be offered upon the altar of your Temple when you arrive in Jerusalem. 18The money that is left over may be used in whatever way you and your brothers feel is the will of your God. 19And take with you the gold bowls and other items we are giving you for the Temple of your God at Jerusalem. 20If you run short of money for the construction of the Temple or for any similar needs, you may requisition funds from the royal treasury.

21"I, Artaxerxes the king, send this decree to all the treasurers in the provinces west of the Euphrates River: 'You are to give Ezra whatever he requests of you (for he is a priest and teacher of the laws of the God of heaven), 22up to $200,000 in silver; 1,225 bushels of wheat; 990 gallons of wine; any amount of salt; 23and whatever else the God of heaven demands for his Temple; for why should we risk God's wrath against the king and his sons? 24I also decree that no priest, Levite, choir member, gatekeeper, Temple attendant, or other worker in the Temple shall be required to pay taxes of any kind.'

25"And you, Ezra, are to use the wisdom God has given you to select and appoint judges and other officials to govern all the people west of the Euphrates River; if they are not familiar with the laws of your God, you are to teach them. 26Anyone refusing to obey the law of your God and the law of the king shall be punished immediately by death, banishment, confiscation of goods, or imprisonment."

Ezra gives praise to God

27Well, praise the Lord God of our ancestors, who made the king want to beautify the Temple of the Lord in Jerusalem! 28And praise God for demonstrating such lovingkindness to me by honoring me before the king and his Council of Seven and before all of his mighty princes! I was given great status because the Lord my God was with me; and I persuaded some of the leaders of Israel to return with me to Jerusalem.

The exiles who returned with Ezra

8 These are the names and genealogies of the leaders who accompanied me from Babylon during the reign of King Artaxerxes:

2-14From the clan of Phinehas—Gershom;
From the clan of Ithamar—Daniel;
From the subclan of David of the clan of Shecaniah—Hattush;
From the clan of Parosh—Zechariah, and 150 other men;
From the clan of Pahath-moab—Eli-e-ho-enai (son of Zerahiah), and 200 other men;

Marginal cross-references:

7:14 Ezra 7:28; Esth 1:14
7:16 Deut 16:10; Ezra 1:4,6; 8:28
7:17 Ex 30:9; Lev 23:13; Num 6:15; Deut 12:4-11
7:24 Gen 47:26
7:25 Ex 18:21-25; Deut 16:18; Ezra 7:6,10
7:26 Ezra 6:11; Ps 52:5
7:28 Ezra 7:14
8:1 Ezra 2:2-35,62, 63; 7:1-5

7:14 When Nebuchadnezzar destroyed the Temple, he took a vast amount of booty that may have included a copy of the Book of the Law (2 Chronicles 36:18). It is also possible that this book was brought by the Jews into exile and was confiscated and read by their conquerors. Foreign leaders who worshiped many gods liked to have records of the gods of other nations for both military and political reasons.

7:24 Why did Artaxerxes exempt Temple workers from paying taxes? He recognized that the priests and Levites filled an important role in society as spiritual leaders, so he freed them of tax burdens. While the Bible does not teach tax-exemption for religious employees, Artaxerxes, a pagan king, recognized and supported the principle of keeping worldly burdens off the shoulders of spiritual workers. Today that responsibility is given to churches.

7:27, 28 Ezra praised God for all he had done for him and through him. Ezra had honored God throughout his life, and God chose to honor him. Ezra could have assumed that his own greatness and charisma had won over the king and his princes, but he gave the credit to God. We, too, should be grateful when things work out well for us, refusing to let our pride make us think we did it in our own power.

7:28 The speaker here is Ezra. He writes in the first person for the remainder of the book.

From the clan of Shecaniah—the son of Jahaziel, and 300 other men;
From the clan of Adin—Ebed (son of Jonathan), and 50 other men;
From the clan of Elam—Jeshaiah (son of Athaliah), and 70 other men;
From the clan of Shephatiah—Zebadiah (son of Michael), and 80 other men;
From the clan of Joab—Obadiah (son of Jehiel), and 218 other men;
From the clan of Bani—Shelomith (son of Josiphiah), and 160 other men;
From the clan of Bebai—Zechariah (son of Bebai), and 28 other men;
From the clan of Azgad—Johanan (son of Hakkatan), and 110 other men;
From the clan of Adonikam—Eliphelet, Jeuel, Shemaiah, and 60 other men
    (they arrived at a later time);
From the clan of Bigvai—Uthai, Zaccur, and 70 other men.

It is not personal achievement, but personal commitment to live for God that is important. Achievements are simply used as examples of what God can do through someone's life. The most effective leaders spoken of in the Bible had little awareness of the impact their lives had on others. They were too busy obeying God to keep track of their successes. Ezra fits that description.

About 80 years after the rebuilding of the Temple under Zerubbabel, Ezra returned to Judah with about 2,000 men and their families. He was given a letter from King Artaxerxes instructing him to carry out a program of religious education. Along with the letter came significant power. But long before Ezra's mission began, God had shaped him with three important controls for the power he was to be given. First, as a scribe, he dedicated himself to carefully studying God's Word. Second, he intended to personally apply and obey the commands he discovered in God's Word. Third, he was committed to teaching others both God's Word and its application to life.

Knowing Ezra's priorities, it is not surprising to note his actions when he arrived in Jerusalem. The people had disobeyed God's command not to marry women of foreign nations. On a cold and rainy day, Ezra addressed the people and made it clear they had sinned. Because of the sins of many, all were under God's condemnation. Confession, repentance, and action were needed. The people admitted their sin and devised a plan to deal with the problem.

This initial effort on Ezra's part set the stage for what Nehemiah would later accomplish. Ezra carried on his ministry under Nehemiah, and the two were used by God to start a spiritual movement that swept the nation following the rebuilding of Jerusalem.

Ezra achieved great things in life, but he had significant impact because he had the right starting place for his actions and his life: God's Word. He studied it seriously and applied it faithfully. He taught others what he learned. He is, therefore, a great model for anyone who wants to live for God.

Strengths and accomplishments:
- Committed to study, follow, and teach God's Word
- Led the second group of exiles from Babylon to Jerusalem
- May have written 1 and 2 Chronicles
- Concerned about keeping the details of God's commands
- Sent by King Artaxerxes to Jerusalem to evaluate the situation, set up a religious education system, and return with a firsthand report
- Worked alongside Nehemiah during the last spiritual awakening in the Old Testament

Lessons from his life:
- A person's willingness to know and practice God's Word will have a direct effect on how God uses his/her life
- The starting place for serving God is a personal commitment to serve him today, even before knowing what that service will be

Vital statistics:
- Where: Babylon, Jerusalem
- Occupation: Scribe among the exiles in Babylon, king's envoy, teacher
- Relatives: Father: Seriah
- Contemporaries: Nehemiah, Artaxerxes

Key verse:
"This was because Ezra had determined to study and obey the laws of the Lord and to become a Bible teacher, teaching those laws to the people of Israel" (Ezra 7:10).

Ezra's story is told in Ezra 7:1—10:16 and Nehemiah 8:1—12:36.

Ezra returns to Jerusalem

15We assembled at the Ahava River and camped there for three days while I went over the lists of the people and the priests who had arrived; and I found that not one Levite had volunteered! 16So I sent for Eliezer, Ari-el, Shemaiah, Elnathan, Jarib, Elnathan, Nathan, Zechariah, and Meshullam, the Levite leaders; I also sent for Joiarib and Elnathan, who were very wise men. 17I sent them to Iddo, the leader of the Jews at Casiphia, to ask him and his brothers and the Temple attendants to send us priests for the Temple of God at Jerusalem. 18And God was good! He sent us an outstanding man named Sherebiah, along with eighteen of his sons and brothers; he was a very astute man and a descendant of Mahli, the son of Levi and grandson of Israel. 19God also sent Hashabiah; and Jeshaiah (the son of Merari), with twenty of his sons and brothers; 20and 220 Temple attendants. (The Temple attendants were assistants to the Levites—a job classification of Temple employees first instituted by King David.) These 220 men were all listed by name.

21Then I declared a fast while we were at the Ahava River so that we would humble ourselves before our God; and we prayed that he would give us a good journey and protect us, our children, and our goods as we traveled. 22For I was ashamed to ask the king for soldiers and cavalry to accompany us and protect us from the enemies along the way. After all, we had told the king that our God would protect all those who worshiped him, and that disaster could come only to those who had forsaken him! 23So we fasted and begged God to take care of us. And he did.

24I appointed twelve leaders of the priests—Sherebiah, Hashabiah, and ten other priests— 25to be in charge of transporting the silver, gold, the gold bowls, and the other items which the king and his council and the leaders and people of Israel had presented to the Temple of God. 26, 27I weighed the money as I gave it to them and found it to total $1,300,000 in silver; $200,000 in silver utensils; many millions in gold; and twenty gold bowls worth a total of $100,000. There were also two beautiful pieces of brass which were as precious as gold. 28I consecrated these men to the Lord, and then consecrated the treasures—the equipment and money and bowls which had been given as free-will offerings to the Lord God of our fathers.

8:15
Ezra 8:21,31

8:17
Ezra 2:43-54
8:20
Neh 7:46-56

8:20
Ezra 8:17

8:21
Lev 23:32
2 Chron 7:14
20:3
Ezra 8:15,31
Ps 37:11
Jonah 3:5
8:22
2 Chron 15:2
Ezra 7:6

8:28
Lev 21:6-8
Ezra 7:16
Isa 52:11

8:15 Ezra's progress back to Jerusalem was halted while he waited to recruit Levites. God had called these men to a special service, and yet they were unwilling to volunteer when their services were needed. God has gifted each of us with abilities so we can make a contribution to his Kingdom work (Romans 12:4–8). Don't wait to be recruited, but look for opportunities to volunteer. Don't hinder God's work by holding back. "God has given each of you some special abilities; be sure to use them to help each other" (1 Peter 4:10).

8:21 Ezra and the people traveled approximately 900 miles on foot. The trip took them through dangerous and difficult territory and lasted about four months. They prayed that God would protect them and give them a good journey. Our journeys today may not be as difficult and dangerous as Ezra's, but we should feel free to ask God for guidance and protection.

8:21-23 Before making all the physical preparations for the journey, Ezra made spiritual preparations. Their prayers and fasting prepared them spiritually by showing their dependence on God for protection, their faith that God was in control, and their affirmation that they were not strong enough to make the trip without him. When we take time to put God first in any endeavor, we are preparing well for whatever lies ahead.

8:23 Ezra knew God's promises to protect his people, but he didn't take them for granted. He also knew that God's blessings are appropriated through prayer; so Ezra and the people humbled themselves by fasting and prayer. And their prayers were answered. Fasting humbled them because going without food reminded them of their complete dependence on God's provision. Fasting also gave them extra time to pray and meditate on God.
Too often we pray glibly and superficially. Serious prayer, by

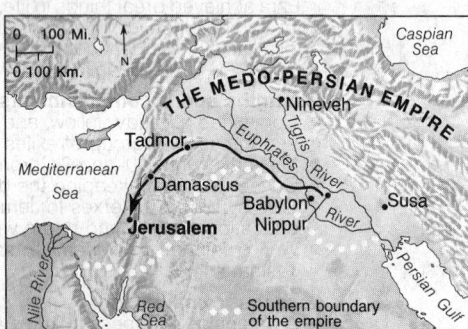

EZRA'S JOURNEY Ezra led a second group of exiles back to Judah and Jerusalem about 80 years after the first group. He traveled the dangerous route without military escort (8:22); but the people prayed and, under Ezra's godly leadership, arrived safely in Jerusalem after several months.

contrast, requires concerted effort. It puts us in touch with God's will and can really change us. Without this kind of prayer, we reduce God to a quick-service pharmacy with painkillers for our every ailment, rather than a God with whom we want to share a relationship.

8:28, 29 Every object used in Temple service was set apart for God; they were considered holy treasures to be guarded with special care. Stewardship is taking special care of whatever God has entrusted to you. Special care means considering these things

29"Guard these treasures well!" I told them; "present them without a penny lost to the priests and the Levite leaders and the elders of Israel at Jerusalem, where they are to be placed in the treasury of the Temple."

8:31
Ezra 7:15,21

30So the priests and the Levites accepted the responsibility of taking it to God's Temple in Jerusalem. 31We broke camp at the Ahava River at the end of March and started off to Jerusalem; and God protected us and saved us from enemies and bandits along the way. 32So at last we arrived safely at Jerusalem.

33On the fourth day after our arrival the silver, gold, and other valuables were weighed in the Temple by Meremoth (the son of Uriah the priest), Eleazar (son of Phinehas), Jozabad (son of Jeshua), and Noadiah (son of Binnui)—all of whom were Levites. 34A receipt was given for each item, and the weight of the gold and silver was noted.

8:36
Ezra 5:3,6

35Then everyone in our party sacrificed burnt offerings to the God of Israel—twelve oxen for the nation of Israel; ninety-six rams; seventy-seven lambs; and twelve goats as a sin offering. 36The king's decrees were delivered to his lieutenants and the governors of all the provinces west of the Euphrates River, and of course they then cooperated in the rebuilding of the Temple of God.

2. Ezra opposes intermarriage

Ezra prays before the people

9:1
Ex 23:23
Lev 18:3,24-30
Deut 12:30,31
18:9; 20:17,18

9:2
Ex 34:16
Deut 7:3-6
Ezra 10:16-44
Neh 13:23,24

9 But then the Jewish leaders came to tell me that many of the Jewish people and even some of the priests and Levites had taken up the horrible customs of the heathen people who lived in the land—the Canaanites, Hittites, Perizzites, Jebusites, Ammonites, Moabites, Egyptians, and Amorites. 2The men of Israel had married heathen girls from these heathen nations, and had taken them as wives for their sons. So the holy people of God were being polluted by these mixed marriages, and the political leaders were some of the worst offenders.

9:3
Josh 7:6
2 Kgs 18:37
19:1
Neh 1:4
Job 2:12,13

3When I heard this, I tore my clothing and pulled hair from my head and beard and sat down utterly baffled. 4Then many who feared the God of Israel because of this sin of his people came and sat with me until the time of the evening burnt offering.

9:4
Ex 29:38,39

9:6
2 Chron 28:9

5Finally I stood before the Lord in great embarrassment; then I fell to my knees and lifted my hands to the Lord, 6and cried out, "O my God, I am ashamed; I blush to lift up my face to you, for our sins are piled higher than our heads and our guilt is as boundless as the heavens. 7Our whole history has been one of sin; that is why we and our kings and our priests were slain by the heathen kings—we were captured, robbed, and disgraced, just as we are today. 8But now we have been

9:7
2 Kgs 24:1-4
2 Chron
36:16-20

8:31 *end of March,* or, "the twelfth day of the first month" of the Hebrew calendar.

---

as being *from* God and *for* him. What has God entrusted to your care?

9:1, 2 Since the time of the judges, Israelite men had married heathen women and then adopted their religious practices (Judges 3:5–7). Even Israel's great King Solomon was guilty of this sin (1 Kings 11:1–8). Although this practice was forbidden in God's Law (Exodus 34:11–16; Deuteronomy 7:1–4), it happened in Ezra's day and again only a generation after him (Nehemiah 13:23–27). Opposition to mixed marriage was not racial prejudice, because Jews and non-Jews of this area were of the same semitic background. The reasons were strictly spiritual. One who married a heathen spouse was inclined to adopt that person's heathen practices. If the Israelites were insensitive enough to disobey God in something as important as marriage, they couldn't be strong enough to stand firm against their spouses' idolatry. Until the Israelites finally stopped this practice, idolatry remained a constant problem.

9:2 Some Israelites had married heathen spouses and lost track of God's purpose for them. The New Testament says that believers should not marry unbelievers (2 Corinthians 6:14). Such marriages cannot have unity in the most important issue in life—commitment and obedience to God. Because marriage involves two people

becoming one, faith may become an issue, and one spouse may have to compromise beliefs for the sake of unity. Don't allow emotion or passion to blind you to the ultimate importance of marrying someone with whom you can truly be united.

9:5–15 After learning about the sins of the people, Ezra fell to his knees in prayer. His heartfelt prayer provides a good perspective on sin. He recognized: (1) that sin is serious (9:6); (2) that no one sins without affecting others (9:7); (3) that he was not sinless, although he didn't have a heathen wife (9:10ff); (4) that God's love and mercy had spared the nation when they did nothing to deserve it (9:8, 9, 15). It is easy to view sin lightly in a world that sees sin as inconsequential, but we should view sin as seriously as Ezra did.

9:5–15 Ezra's prayer confessed the sins of his people. Although he had not sinned in the way his people had, he identified with their sins. With weeping, he expressed shame for sin, fear of the consequences, and desire that the people would come to their senses and repent. His prayer moved the people to tears (10:1). Ezra demonstrated the need for a holy community around the rebuilt Temple. We need a holy community in our local churches too. Even in the midst of our worst sins, we can turn to God with prayers of repentance.

given a moment of peace, for you have permitted a few of us to return to Jerusalem from our exile. You have given us a moment of joy and new life in our slavery. ⁹For we were slaves, but in your love and mercy you did not abandon us to slavery; instead you caused the kings of Persia to be favorable to us. They have even given us their assistance in rebuilding the Temple of our God and in giving us Jerusalem as a walled city in Judah.

¹⁰"And now, O God, what can we say after all of this? For once again we have abandoned you and broken your laws! ¹¹The prophets warned us that the land we would possess was totally defiled by the horrible practices of the people living there. From one end to the other it is filled with corruption. ¹²You told us not to let our daughters marry their sons, and not to let our sons marry their daughters, and not to help those nations in any way. You warned us that only if we followed this rule could we become a prosperous nation and forever leave that prosperity to our children as an inheritance. ¹³And now, even after our punishment in exile because of our wickedness (and we have been punished far less than we deserved), and even though you have let some of us return, ¹⁴we have broken your commandments again and intermarried with people who do these awful things. Surely your anger will destroy us now until not even this little remnant escapes. ¹⁵O Lord God of Israel, you are a just God; what hope can we have if you give us justice as we stand here before you in our wickedness?"

The people confess their sin

10 As I lay on the ground in front of the Temple, weeping and praying and making this confession, a large crowd of men, women, and children gathered around and cried with me.

²Then Shecaniah (the son of Jehiel of the clan of Elam) said to me, "We acknowledge our sin against our God, for we have married these heathen women. But there is hope for Israel in spite of this. ³For we agree before our God to divorce our heathen wives and to send them away with our children; we will follow your commands, and the commands of the others who fear our God. We will obey the laws of God. ⁴Take courage and tell us how to proceed in setting things straight, and we will fully cooperate."

⁵So I stood up and demanded that the leaders of the priests and the Levites and all the people of Israel swear that they would do as Shecaniah had said; and they all agreed. ⁶Then I went into the room of Jehohanan in the Temple and refused all food and drink; for I was mourning because of the sin of the returned exiles.

⁷, ⁸Then a proclamation was made throughout Judah and Jerusalem that everyone should appear at Jerusalem within three days and that the leaders and elders had decided that anyone who refused to come would be disinherited and excommunicated from Israel. ⁹Within three days, on the fifth day of December, all the men of Judah and Benjamin had arrived and were sitting in the open space before the Temple; and they were trembling because of the seriousness of the matter and

9:8 2 Kgs 19:4,30, 31 / Isa 1:9 / Jer 44:14
9:9 Ex 1:11-14 / Neh 9:36,37 / Ps 106:45,46 / Ezek 11:16
9:12 Deut 7:3 / Josh 1:6-9 / 23:12,13 / Ezra 9:2
9:14 Num 16:21,22, 45,46 / Deut 9:7,8,13, 14 / Ezra 9:2
9:15 Neh 9:33,34 / Job 9:2,3 / Ps 130:3 / Dan 9:7-11 / Rom 3:19; 10:3
10:2 Ezra 10:11
10:3 Deut 7:2,3 / 24:1; 29:12 / Josh 1:17,18 / Mt 5:32
10:4 Josh 1:6-9 / 1 Chron 28:10
10:5 Ezra 10:3 / Neh 5:12; 13:25
10:6 Deut 9:18
10:9 1 Sam 12:17,18 / Jer 10:10,13

10:9 *fifth day of December,* literally, "the twentieth day of the ninth month" of the Hebrew calendar.

9:15 Ezra asked, "What hope can we have if you [God] give us justice?" Often we cry out for justice when we feel abused and unfairly treated. In those moments, we forget the reality of our sin and the righteous judgment we deserve. How fortunate we are that God gives us mercy and grace rather than only justice. The next time you ask God for fair and just treatment, pause to think what would happen if God gave you what you really deserve.

10:3 Why were the people commanded to divorce their wives and leave their children? Although the measure was extreme, intermarriage with heathens was strictly forbidden (Deuteronomy 7:3, 4). This could be compared today to a Christian marrying a devil worshiper. However, 10:16-19 seem to indicate that those women who had become true worshipers of God would not be forced to leave.
Ezra's strong act, though very difficult for many, was necessary to preserve Israel as a nation committed to God. The exiles of the

Northern Kingdom of Israel had lost both their spiritual and physical identity through intermarriage. Their heathen spouses had caused the people to worship idols. Ezra did not want this to happen to the exiles of the Southern Kingdom of Judah.

10:3, 4, 11 Following Ezra's earnest prayer, the people admitted their sin to God. Then they asked for direction in restoring their relationship with God. True repentance does not end with words of confession; it must lead to corrected behavior and changed attitudes. When you sin and are truly sorry, confess this to God, ask his forgiveness, and accept his grace and mercy. Then, as an act of thankfulness for your forgiveness, change your ways.

10:8 To be disinherited meant losing one's legal right to own land. This was to insure that no pagan children would inherit Israel's land. Excommunication meant being excluded from the assembly and not being allowed to worship in the Temple. The Jews considered this a horrible punishment.

because of the heavy rainfall. ¹⁰Then I, Ezra the priest, arose and addressed them: "You have sinned, for you have married heathen women; now we are even more deeply under God's condemnation than we were before. ¹¹Confess your sin to the Lord God of your fathers and do what he demands: separate yourselves from the heathen people about you and from these women."

10:11
Ezra 10:2
Neh 13:3
2 Cor 6:17

¹²Then all the men spoke up and said, "We will do what you have said. ¹³But this isn't something that can be done in a day or two, for there are many of us involved in this sinful affair. And it is raining so hard that we can't stay out here much longer. ¹⁴Let our leaders arrange trials for us. Everyone who has a heathen wife will come at the scheduled time with the elders and judges of his city; then each case will be decided and the situation will be cleared up and the fierce wrath of our God will be turned away from us."

10:14
Num 25:4
Deut 13:17
2 Chron 29:10
Ezra 9:14

¹⁵Only Jonathan (son of Asahel), Jahzeiah (son of Tikvah), Meshullam, and Shabbethai the Levite opposed this course of action.

The men who married heathen wives

¹⁶⁻¹⁹So this was the plan that was followed: Some of the clan leaders and I were designated as judges; we began our work on December 15, and finished by March 15.

Following is the list of priests who had married heathen wives (they vowed to divorce their wives and acknowledged their guilt by offering rams as sacrifices): Ma-aseiah, Eliezer, Jarib, Gedaliah.

²⁰The sons of Immer: Hanani, Zebadiah.

²¹The sons of Harim: Ma-aseiah, Elijah, Shemaiah, Jehiel, Uzziah.

²²The sons of Pashhur: Eli-o-enai, Ma-aseiah, Ishmael, Nethanel, Jozabad, Elasah.

²³The Levites who were guilty: Jozabad, Shime-i, Kelaiah (also called Kelita), Petha-haiah, Judah, Eliezer.

²⁴Of the singers, there was Eliashib. Of the gatekeepers, Shallum, Telem, and Uri.

²⁵Here is the list of ordinary citizens who were declared guilty: From the clan of Parosh: Ramiah, Izziah, Malchijah, Mijamin, Eleazar, Hashabiah, Benaiah.

²⁶From the clan of Elam: Mattaniah, Zechariah, Jehiel, Abdi, Jeremoth, Elijah.

²⁷From the clan of Zattu: Eli-o-enai, Eliashib, Mattaniah, Jeremoth, Zabad, Aziza.

²⁸From the clan of Bebai: Jeho-hanan, Hananiah, Zabbai, Athlai.

²⁹From the clan of Bani: Meshullam, Malluch, Adaiah, Jashub, Sheal, Jeremoth.

³⁰From the clan of Pahath-moab: Adna, Chelal, Benaiah, Ma-aseiah, Mattaniah, Bezalel, Binnui, Manasseh.

³¹, ³²From the clan of Harim: Eliezer, Isshijah, Malchijah, Shemaiah, Shime-on, Benjamin, Malluch, Shemariah.

³³From the clan of Hashum: Mattenai, Mattattah, Zabad, Eliphelet, Jeremai, Manasseh, Shime-i.

³⁴⁻⁴²From the clan of Bani: Ma-adai, Amram, Uel, Banaiah, Bedeiah, Cheluhi, Vaniah, Meremoth, Eliashib, Mattaniah, Mattenai, Jaasu, Bani, Binnui, Shime-i, Shelemiah, Nathan, Adaiah, Machnadebai, Shashai, Sharai, Azarel, Shelemiah, Shemariah, Shallum, Amariah, Joseph.

⁴³From the clan of Nebo: Je-iel, Mattithiah, Zabad, Zebina, Jaddai, Joel, Benaiah.

⁴⁴Each of these men had heathen wives, and many had children by these wives.

10:44 The book of Ezra opens with God's Temple in ruins and the people of Judah captive in Babylon. Ezra tells of the return of God's people, the rebuilding of the Temple, and the restoration of the sacrificial worship system. Similarly, God is able to restore and rebuild the lives of people today. No one is so far away from God that he or she cannot be restored. Repentance is all that is required. No matter how far we have strayed, or how long it has been since we have worshiped God, he is able to restore our relationship to him and rebuild our lives.

NEHEMIAH

VITAL STATISTICS

PURPOSE:
Nehemiah is the last of the Old Testament historical books. It records the history of the third return to Jerusalem after captivity, telling how the walls were rebuilt and the people renewed in their faith.

AUTHOR:
Much of the book is written in the first person, suggesting Nehemiah as the author. Nehemiah probably wrote the book with Ezra serving as editor.

DATE WRITTEN:
Approximately 445–432 B.C.

SETTING:
Zerubbabel led the first return to Jerusalem in 537 B.C. In 458, Ezra led the second return. Finally, in 445, Nehemiah returned with the third group of exiles to rebuild the city walls.

KEY VERSES:
"The wall was finally finished in early September—just fifty-two days after we had begun! When our enemies and the surrounding nations heard about it, they were frightened and humiliated, and they realized that the work had been done with the help of our God" (6:15, 16).

KEY PEOPLE:
Nehemiah, Ezra, Sanballat, Tobiah

KEY PLACE:
Jerusalem

SPECIAL FEATURES:
The book shows the fulfillment of the prophecies of Zechariah and Daniel concerning the rebuilding of Jerusalem's walls.

IT'S EASY to analyze, scrutinize, and talk about all the problems in the world. Gripers, complainers, self-proclaimed prophets, and "armchair quarterbacks" abound. But we really need people who will not only discuss a situation, but *do* something about it!

Nehemiah saw a problem and was distressed. Instead of wallowing in self-pity and grief, he took action. Nehemiah knew that God wanted him to motivate the Jews to rebuild Jerusalem's walls, so he left a responsible position in the Persian government to do what God wanted. Nehemiah knew God could use his talents to get the job done. From the moment he arrived in Jerusalem, everyone knew who was in charge. He organized, managed, supervised, encouraged, met opposition, confronted injustice, and kept going until the walls were built. Nehemiah was a man of action.

As the story begins, Nehemiah is talking with fellow Jews who report that the walls and gates of Jerusalem are in disrepair. This is disturbing news, and rebuilding those walls becomes Nehemiah's burden. At the appropriate time, Nehemiah asks King Artaxerxes for permission to go to Jerusalem to rebuild its fallen walls. The king approves.

Armed with royal letters, Nehemiah travels to Jerusalem. He organizes the people into groups and assigns them to specific sections of the wall (chapter 3). The construction project is not without opposition, however. Sanballat, Tobiah, and others try to halt the work with insults, ridicule, threats, and sabotage. Some of the workers become fearful; others become weary. In each case, Nehemiah employs a strategy to frustrate the enemies—prayer, encouragement, guard duty, consolidation (chapter 4). But a different problem arises—an internal one. Rich Jews are profiteering off the plight of their working countrymen. Hearing of their oppression and greed, Nehemiah confronts the extortioners face to face (chapter 5). With the walls almost complete, Sanballat, Tobiah, and company try one last time to stop Nehemiah. But Nehemiah stands firm, and the wall is finished in just 52 days. What a tremendous monument to God's love and faithfulness. Enemies and friends alike knew that God had helped (chapter 6).

After building the walls, Nehemiah continues to organize the people, taking a census and appointing gatekeepers, Levites, and other officials (chapter 7). Ezra leads the city in worship and Bible instruction (chapters 8, 9). This leads to a reaffirmation of faith and religious revival as the people promise to serve God faithfully (chapters 10, 11).

Nehemiah closes with the listing of the clans and their leaders, the dedication of the new wall of Jerusalem, and the purging of sin from the land (chapters 12, 13). As you read this book, be like Nehemiah, and be willing to *do* whatever God asks.

THE BLUEPRINT

A. REBUILDING THE WALL (1:1—7:73)
  1. Nehemiah returns to Jerusalem
  2. Nehemiah leads the people

Nehemiah's life is an example of leadership and organization. Giving up a comfortable and wealthy position in Persia, he returned to the fractured homeland of his ancestors and rallied the people to rebuild Jerusalem's wall. In the face of opposition, he used wise defense measures to care for the people and to keep the project moving. To accomplish things for the sake of God's kingdom, we must pray, persevere, and sacrifice, as Nehemiah did.

B. REFORMING THE PEOPLE (8:1—13:31)
  1. Ezra renews the covenant
  2. Nehemiah establishes policies

After the wall was rebuilt, Ezra read the Law to the people, bringing about national repentance. Nehemiah and Ezra were very different people, yet God used them both to lead the nation. God uses each person in a unique way to accomplish his purposes.

MEGATHEMES

THEME	EXPLANATION	IMPORTANCE
Vision	Although the Jews completed the Temple in 516 B.C., the city walls remained in shambles for the next 70 years. These walls represented power, protection, and beauty to the city of Jerusalem. They were also desperately needed to protect the Temple from attack and to insure the continuity of worship. God put the desire to rebuild the walls in Nehemiah's heart, giving him a vision for the work.	Does God have a vision for us? Are there "walls" that need to be built today? God still wants his people to be united and trained to do his work. As we recognize deep needs in our world, God can give us the vision and desire to "build."
Prayer	Both Nehemiah and Ezra responded to problems with prayer. When Nehemiah began his work, he recognized the problem, immediately prayed, and then acted on the problem.	Prayer is still God's mighty force in solving problems today. Prayer and action go hand in hand. Through prayer, God guides our preparation, teamwork, and diligent efforts to carry out his will.
Leadership	Nehemiah demonstrated excellent leadership. He was spiritually ready to heed God's call. He used careful planning, teamwork, problem solving, and courage to get the work done. Although he had tremendous faith, he never avoided the extra work necessary for good leadership.	Being God's leader is not just gaining recognition, holding a position, or being the boss. It requires planning, hard work, courage, and perseverance. Positive expectations are never a substitute for doing the difficult work. And in order to lead others, you need to listen for God's direction in your own life.
Problems	After the work began, Nehemiah faced scorn, slander, and threats from enemies, as well as fear, conflict, and discouragement from his own workers. Although these problems were difficult, they did not stop Nehemiah from finishing the work.	When difficulties come, there is a tendency for conflict and discouragement to set in. We must recognize that there are no triumphs without troubles. When problems arise, we must face them squarely and press on to complete God's work.
Repentance/ Revival	Although God had enabled them to build the wall, the work wasn't complete until the people rebuilt their lives spiritually. Ezra instructed the people in God's Word. As they listened, they recognized the sin in their lives, admitted it, and took steps to remove it.	Recognizing and admitting sin is not enough; revival must result in reform or it is merely the expression of enthusiasm. God does not want halfhearted measures. We must not only remove sin from our lives, but ask God to move into the center of all we do.

A. REBUILDING THE WALL (1:1—7:73)

Despite the fact that the returned exiles had been in Jerusalem for many years, the walls of the city remained unrepaired, leaving its people defenseless and vulnerable. Upon hearing this news, Nehemiah seeks permission from the Persian king to go to Jerusalem. Arriving in Jerusalem, he mobilizes the people to begin rebuilding the wall. Faced with opposition, both from without and from within, Nehemiah perseveres until the project is complete, and the city resettled. Seemingly impossible tasks can be accomplished when God is helping those who honor him and when their efforts are united.

1. Nehemiah returns to Jerusalem

Nehemiah receives tragic news about Jerusalem

1 The autobiography of *Nehemiah, the son of Hecaliah:*

In December of the twentieth year of the reign of King Artaxerxes of Persia, when I was at the palace at Shushan, ²one of my fellow Jews named Hanani came to visit me with some men who had arrived from Judah. I took the opportunity to inquire about how things were going in Jerusalem.

"How are they getting along?" I asked. "—the Jews who returned to Jerusalem from their exile here?"

³"Well," they replied, "things are not good; the wall of Jerusalem is still torn down, and the gates are burned."

Nehemiah prays for the people of Israel

⁴When I heard this, I sat down and cried. In fact, I refused to eat for several days, for I spent the time in prayer to the God of heaven.

⁵"O Lord God," I cried out; "O great and awesome God who keeps his promises and is so loving and kind to those who love and obey him! Hear my prayer! 6, ⁷Listen carefully to what I say! Look down and see me praying night and day for your people Israel. I confess that we have sinned against you; yes, I and my people have committed the horrible sin of not obeying the commandments you gave us through your servant Moses. ⁸Oh, please remember what you told Moses! You said,

" '*If you sin, I will scatter you among the nations;* ⁹*but if you return to me and*

1:1 *King Artaxerxes of Persia,* implied.

1:1
Neh 2:1; 10:1
Esth 1:2
Zech 7:1
1:2
Neh 7:2

1:3
Neh 2:3,17

1:4
Ezra 9:3; 10:1
Dan 9:3

1:6
Deut 28:14,15
Ezra 10:1
Ps 32:5
Dan 9:8,17-20
1:8
Lev 26:33
1:9
Deut 12:5
30:2-4
Jer 29:11-14

1:1 Nehemiah wasn't the first of the exiles to return to Jerusalem. Zerubbabel had led the first group back in 537 B.C., more than 90 years earlier (Ezra 1, 2). Ezra followed with a second group in 458 B.C. (Ezra 7), and now Nehemiah was ready to lead the third major return to Jerusalem (445 B.C.). When he arrived after a three-month journey, he saw the completed Temple and became acquainted with others who had returned to their homeland.

But Nehemiah also found a disorganized group of people and a defenseless city with no walls to protect it. Before the exile, Israel had its own language, king, army, and identity. Now it had none of these. What the Jews lacked most was leadership; there was no one to show them where to start and what direction to take as they tried to rebuild their city. As soon as Nehemiah arrived he began a "back to the basics" program. He helped care for the people's physical needs by setting up a fair system of government and rebuilding Jerusalem's walls. He also cared for their spiritual needs by rebuilding broken lives. Nehemiah is a model of committed, God-honoring leadership, and his book contains many lessons that still apply today.

1:2-4 Nehemiah was concerned about Jerusalem because it was the Jews' Holy City. As Judah's capital city, it represented Jewish national identity, and it was blessed with God's special presence in the Temple. Jewish history was connected with the city from the time of Abraham's gifts to Melchizedek, king of Salem (Genesis 14:17-20), to the days when Solomon built the glorious Temple (1 Kings 7:51) and throughout the history of the kings. Nehemiah loved his homeland even though he had lived his whole life in Babylon. He wanted to return to Jerusalem to reunite the Jews and to remove the shame of Jerusalem's broken-down walls. This

would bring glory to God and restore the reality and power of God's presence among his people.

1:4 Nehemiah broke down and cried when he heard that Jerusalem's walls still had not been rebuilt. Why did this upset him? Walls mean little in most present-day cities, but in Nehemiah's day they were essential. They offered safety from raids and symbolized strength and peace. Nehemiah was also upset for his people, the Jews, who had been stifled by a previous edict that kept them from rebuilding their walls (Ezra 4:6–23).

1:4 Nehemiah was deeply grieved about the condition of Jerusalem, but he didn't just brood about it. After his initial grief, he poured his heart out to God (1:5–11) and looked for ways to improve the situation. He poured all his resources of knowledge, experience, and organization into determining what should be done. When tragic news comes to you, first pray. Then seek ways to move beyond grief to specific action that offers help to those who need it.

1:5 Nehemiah fasted and prayed for several days, expressing his sorrow for Israel's sin and his desire that Jerusalem again come alive with the worship of the one true God. Nehemiah demonstrates the elements of effective prayer: (1) praise, (2) thanksgiving, (3) repentance, (4) specific request, and (5) commitment.

Heartfelt prayers like Nehemiah's can help clarify (1) any problem you may be facing, (2) God's great power to help you, and (3) the job you have to do. By the end of his prayer time, Nehemiah knew what action he had to take (1:11). When God's leaders are people of prayer, difficult decisions can be made in proper perspective, and appropriate action can follow.

obey my laws, even though you are exiled to the farthest corners of the universe, I will bring you back to Jerusalem. For Jerusalem is the place in which I have chosen to live.'

1:10
Ex 32:11
Deut 9:29

10"We are your servants, the people you rescued by your great power. 11O Lord, please hear my prayer! Heed the prayers of those of us who delight to honor you. Please help me now as I go in and ask the king for a great favor—put it into his heart to be kind to me." (I was the king's cupbearer.)

1:11
Gen 40:21
Neh 2:1

The king permits Nehemiah to return

2:1
Neh 1:11

2 One day in April, four months later, as I was serving the king his wine he asked me, "Why so sad? You aren't sick, are you? You look like a man with deep troubles." (For until then I had always been cheerful when I was with him.) I was badly frightened, 3but I replied, "Sir, why shouldn't I be sad? For the city where my ancestors are buried is in ruins, and the gates have been burned down."

2:3
Neh 1:3

2:3 *Sir*, literally, "Let the king live forever."

HOW NEHEMIAH USED PRAYER

Reference	Occasion	Summary of his Prayer	What Prayer Accomplished	Our Prayers
1:4–11	After receiving the bad news about the state of Jerusalem's walls	Recognized God's holiness. Asked for a hearing. Confessed sin. Asked for specific help in approaching the king	Included God in Nehemiah's plans and concerns. Prepared Nehemiah's heart and gave God room to work	How often do you pour out your heart to God? How often do you give him a specific request to answer?
2:4	During his conversation with the king	"Here's where you can help, God!"	Put the expected results in God's hands	Giving God credit for what happens before it happens keeps us from taking more credit than we should.
4:4, 5	After being taunted and ridiculed by Tobiah and Sanballat	"They're mocking you, God. You decide what to do with them."	Expressed anger to God, but Nehemiah did not take matters into his own hands	We are prone to do exactly the opposite—take matters into our own hands and not tell God how we feel.
4:9	After threats of attack by enemies	"We are in your hands, God. We'll keep our weapons handy in case you want us to use them."	Trusted God and took necessary precautions	Trusting God does not mean we do nothing. Action does not mean we do not trust.
6:9	Responding to threats	"Oh Lord God, please strengthen me!"	Showed Nehemiah's reliance on God for emotional and mental stability	How often do you ask God for help when under pressure?
13:29	Reflecting on the actions of his enemies	Asked God to deal with the enemies and their evil plans	Took away the compulsion to get revenge, and entrusted justice to God	When did you last settle a desire for revenge by turning the matter over to God?
5:19; 13:14, 22, 31	Reflecting on his own efforts to serve God	"Remember me, God."	Kept clear in Nehemiah's mind his own motives for action	How many of your actions today will be done with the purpose of pleasing God?

1:11 Nehemiah was in a unique position to speak to the king. He was the trusted cupbearer who ensured the safety and quality of the king's food and drink. Nehemiah was concerned, prayerful, and prepared as he looked for the right opportunity to tell the king about God's people. Each of us is unique and capable of serving no matter what our position. Just as Nehemiah used his place as the king's trusted servant to intercede for his people, we can use our present positions to serve God.

2:2 Nehemiah was frightened when the king noticed his sad appearance. It was dangerous to show sorrow before the king,

who could execute anyone who displeased him by doing so. Anyone wearing mourning clothes could not even enter the palace (Esther 4:2).

2:3 Nehemiah wasn't ashamed to admit his fear, but he refused to allow fear to stop him from doing what God had called him to do. When we allow our fears to rule our lives, we make them more powerful than God. Is there a task God wants you to do, but fear is holding you back? God is greater than all our fears. To recognize your fear is the first step in committing it to God. Realize that if God has called you to a task, he will help you accomplish it.

4"Well, what should be done?" the king asked.

With a quick prayer to the God of heaven, I replied, "If it please Your Majesty and if you look upon me with your royal favor, send me to Judah to rebuild the city of my fathers!"

5, 6The king replied, with the queen sitting beside him, "How long will you be gone? When will you return?"

So it was agreed! And I set a time for my departure!

7Then I added this to my request: "If it please the king, give me letters to the governors west of the Euphrates River instructing them to let me travel through their countries on my way to Judah; 8also a letter to Asaph, the manager of the king's forest, instructing him to give me timber for the beams and for the gates of the fortress near the Temple, and for the city walls, and for a house for myself."

And the king granted these requests, for God was being gracious to me.

9When I arrived in the provinces west of the Euphrates River, I delivered the king's letters to the governors there. (The king, I should add, had sent along army officers and troops to protect me!) 10But when Sanballat (the Horonite) and Tobiah (an Ammonite who was a government official) heard of my arrival, they were very angry that anyone was interested in helping Israel.

2:7
Ezra 6:6; 7:21
8:36
Neh 2:9

2:8
Neh 7:2
Eccles 2:5,6

2:9
Ezra 8:22
Neh 2:7

2:10
Neh 2:19
4:1-3; 6:1

2. Nehemiah leads the people
Nehemiah secretly inspects the wall

11, 12Three days after my arrival at Jerusalem I stole out during the night, taking

---

2:4 With little time to think, Nehemiah quickly prayed to God. Eight times in this book we read that he offered a spontaneous prayer (2:4; 4:4, 5, 9; 5:19; 6:14; 13:14, 22, 29). Nehemiah prayed at any time, even while talking with others. He knew that God is always in charge, is always present, and hears and answers every prayer. He could confidently pray to God throughout the day because he had established an intimate relationship with him during times of extended prayer (1:4–7). If we want to be confident about our brief prayers, we need to take time to cultivate a strong relationship with God through times of in-depth prayer.

2:5, 6 The king asked Nehemiah how long he would be gone. The Bible does not record Nehemiah's immediate answer, but he ended up staying in Jerusalem 12 years (5:14; 13:6).

2:7, 8 After his prayer, Nehemiah asked the king for permission to go to Judah. As soon as he got a positive answer, he began asking for additional help. Sometimes when we have needs, we hesitate to ask the right people for help because we are afraid to approach them. Not Nehemiah! He went directly to the person who could help him the most. Don't be reluctant to ask those who are most able to help. They may be more interested and approachable than you think. God's answers to prayer may come as a result of our asking others.

2:9, 10, 19 When Nehemiah arrived in Judah, he was greeted with opposition. Opposition to the rebuilding of Jerusalem had been going on for 90 years by those who settled in the area when the Jews were taken captive. In every generation there are those who hate God's people and try to block God's purpose. When you attempt to do God's work, some will oppose you; some will even hope you fail. If you expect opposition, you can be prepared rather than surprised (1 John 3:13). Knowing that God is behind your task is the best incentive to move ahead in the face of opposition.

2:10 Why were Sanballat and Tobiah, government officials of nearby Samaria, so concerned about the arrival of Nehemiah and his small band of exiles? There are several possible reasons: (1) When Zerubbabel first returned with his group (Ezra 1, 2), his refusal to accept help from the Samaritans had caused bad relations. (2) Nehemiah was no ordinary exile, he was the king's personal advisor and cupbearer, arriving in Jerusalem with the king's approval to build and fortify the city. If anyone could rebuild Jerusalem, he could. A rebuilt Jerusalem was a threat to the

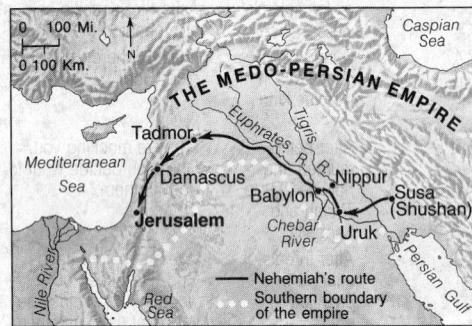

NEHEMIAH GOES TO JERUSALEM Nehemiah worked in Shushan as a personal assistant for the king of the vast Medo-Persian Empire. When he heard that the rebuilding projects in Jerusalem were progressing slowly, he asked the king if he could go there to help his people complete the task of rebuilding their city's walls. The king agreed to let him go; so he left as soon as possible, traveling along much the same route Ezra had taken.

authority of the Samaritan officials who had been in charge of the land since Judah's exile. (3) These people were the third group to return from exile. The increasing number of people in Jerusalem made Sanballat and Tobiah nervous. They did not want returned exiles taking control of the land and threatening their secure position.

2:11–17 Nehemiah arrived quietly in Jerusalem and spent several days carefully observing and assessing the damage to the walls. Following this time of thoughtful consideration, he confidently presented his plan. Nehemiah demonstrated an excellent approach to problem solving. He got firsthand information and carefully considered the situation. Then he presented a realistic strategy. Before jumping into a project, follow Nehemiah's example and plan ahead. Check your information to make sure your ideas will work—be realistic. Then you will be able to present your plan with confidence.

only a few men with me; for I hadn't told a soul about the plans for Jerusalem which God had put into my heart. I was mounted on my donkey and the others were on foot, 13and we went out through the Valley Gate toward the Jackal's Well and over to the Dung Gate to see the broken walls and burned gates. 14, 15Then we went to the Fountain Gate and to the King's Pool, but my donkey couldn't get through the rubble. So we circled the city, and I followed the brook, inspecting the wall, and entered again at the Valley Gate.

16The city officials did not know I had been out there, or why, for as yet I had said nothing to anyone about my plans—not to the political or religious leaders, or even to those who would be doing the work.

Nehemiah calls the people to begin rebuilding

17But now I told them, "You know full well the tragedy of our city; it lies in ruins and its gates are burned. Let us rebuild the wall of Jerusalem and rid ourselves of this disgrace!"

18Then I told them about the desire God had put into my heart, and of my conversation with the king, and the plan to which he had agreed.

They replied at once, "Good! Let's rebuild the wall!" And so the work began.

19But when Sanballat and Tobiah and Geshem the Arab heard of our plan, they scoffed and said, "What are you doing, rebelling against the king like this?"

20But I replied, "The God of heaven will help us, and we, his servants, will rebuild this wall; but you may have no part in this affair."

The builders of the city wall

3 Then Eliashib the High Priest and the other priests rebuilt the wall as far as the Tower of the Hundred and the Tower of Hananel; then they rebuilt the Sheep Gate, hung its doors, and dedicated it. 2Men from the city of Jericho worked next to them, and beyond them was the work crew led by Zaccur (son of Imri).

3The Fish Gate was built by the sons of Hassenaah; they did the whole thing—cut the beams, hung the doors, and made the bolts and bars. 4Meremoth (son of Uriah, son of Hakkoz) repaired the next section of wall, and beyond him were Meshullam

2:13
Neh 1:3; 2:15
3:13; 12:31

2:14
2 Kgs 20:20
2 Chron 32:30
Neh 2:13; 3:15

2:17
Neh 1:3; 2:14

2:19
Neh 2:10; 6:6

2:20
Ezra 4:3

3:1
Neh 3:20,32
12:39; 13:28
Jer 31:38

3:2
Neh 7:36

3:3
Neh 12:39

2:16 Nehemiah kept his mission a secret and surveyed the walls by moonlight to avoid unhealthy gossip about his arrival and to prevent enemies from being alerted to his plans. Only after planning carefully would he be ready to go public with his mission from God. A premature announcement could have caused rivalry among the Jews as to the best way to begin. In this case, Nehemiah didn't need tedious planning sessions, he needed one plan that brought quick action.

2:17, 18 Spiritual renewal often begins with one person's vision. Nehemiah had a vision, and he shared it with enthusiasm, inspiring Jerusalem's leaders to rebuild the walls.

We frequently underestimate people and don't challenge them with our dreams for God's work in the world. When God plants an idea in your mind to accomplish something for him, share it with others and trust the Holy Spirit to impress them with similar thoughts. Don't see yourself as the only one through whom God is working. Often God uses one person to express the vision and others to turn it into reality. When you encourage and inspire others, you put teamwork into action to accomplish God's goals.

2:19 Sanballat and Tobiah labeled the rebuilding of Jerusalem's walls a rebellious act, probably threatening to report the builders as traitors. These enemies also ridiculed Nehemiah, saying the walls could never be rebuilt because the damage was too extensive. Nehemiah did not tell them he already had permission from the king to rebuild. Instead, he simply said he had God's approval—that was enough.

3:1 The High Priest is the first person mentioned who pitched in and helped with the work. Spiritual leaders must not lead only by word, but by action. The Sheep Gate was the gate used to bring sheep into the city to the Temple for sacrifices. Nehemiah had the priests repair this gate and section of the wall, respecting the priests' area of interest and at the same time emphasizing the priority of worship.

3:1ff All the citizens of Jerusalem did their part on the huge job of rebuilding the city wall. Similarly, the work of the church requires every member's effort in order for the body of Christ to function effectively (1 Corinthians 12:27). The body needs you! Are you doing your part? Find a place to serve God and start contributing whatever is needed (time, talent, money, etc.).

3:1ff Jerusalem was a large city, and because many roads converged there, it required many gates. The wall on each side of these heavy wooden gates was taller and thicker so soldiers could stand guard to defend them against attack. Sometimes two stone towers guarded the gate. In times of peace, the city gates were hubs of activity—city council was held there, and shopkeepers set up their wares along the entrance. Building the city walls and gates was not only a military priority, but also a boost for trade and commerce.

3:3 One of the main roads through Jerusalem entered the city through the Fish Gate (2 Chronicles 33:14). The fish market was near the gate, and merchants from Tyre, the Sea of Galilee, and other fishing areas entered this gate to sell their goods.

(son of Berechiah, son of Meshezabel) and Zadok (son of Baana). 5Next were the
men from Tekoa, but their leaders were lazy and didn't help.

3:5
Neh 3:27

6The Old Gate was repaired by Joiada (son of Paseah) and Meshullam (son of
Besodeiah). They laid the beams, set up the doors, and installed the bolts and bars.
7Next to them were Melatiah from Gibeon; Jadon from Meronoth; and men from
Gibeon and Mizpah, who were citizens of the province. 8Uzziel (son of Harhaiah)
was a goldsmith by trade, but he too worked on the wall. Beyond him was
Hananiah, a manufacturer of perfumes. Repairs were not needed from there to the
Broad Wall.

3:6
Neh 12:39

3:8
Neh 3:31

9Rephaiah (son of Hur), the mayor of half of Jerusalem, was next down the wall
from them. 10Jedaiah (son of Harumaph) repaired the wall beside his own house,
and next to him was Hattush (son of Hashabneiah). 11Then came Malchijah (son of
Harim) and Hasshub (son of Pahath-moab), who repaired the Furnace Tower in
addition to a section of the wall. 12Shallum (son of Hallohesh) and his daughters
repaired the next section. He was the mayor of the other half of Jerusalem.

3:9
Neh 3:12,17

3:11
Neh 12:38

3:12
Neh 3:9

13The people from Zanoah, led by Hanun, built the Valley Gate, hung the doors,
and installed the bolts and bars; then they repaired the 1,500 feet of wall to the
Dung Gate.

3:13
Neh 2:13

14The Dung Gate was repaired by Malchijah (son of Rechab), the mayor of the
Beth-haccherem area; and after building it, he hung the doors and installed the bolts
and bars.

3:14
Neh 2:13; 3:13

15Shallum (son of Colhozeh), the mayor of the Mizpah district, repaired the
Fountain Gate. He rebuilt it, roofed it, hung its doors, and installed its locks and
bars. Then he repaired the wall from the Pool of Siloam to the king's garden and the
stairs that descend from the City of David section of Jerusalem. 16Next to him was
Nehemiah (son of Azbuk), the mayor of half the Bethzur district; he built as far as
the royal cemetery, the water reservoir, and the old Officers' Club building. 17Next

3:15
2 Kgs 25:4,5
Neh 2:14; 12:37

3:16
1 Kgs 14:28
2 Kgs 20:20
2 Chron 12:10,
11; 16:14
Neh 2:14

3:16 *the old Officers' Club building,* literally, "the house of the mighty men."

3:5 The leaders of Tekoa were lazy and wouldn't help. These men
were the only ones who did not support the building project in
Jerusalem. Every group, even every church, will have those who
think they are too wise or important to work hard. Gentle
encouragement doesn't seem to help. Sometimes the best policy is
to ignore them. They may think they are getting away with
something, but their inactivity will be remembered by all who
worked hard.

3:12 Even Shallum's daughters helped with the difficult work of
repairing the city walls. Rebuilding Jerusalem's walls was a matter
of national emergency for the Jews, not just a civic beautification
project. Nearly everyone was dedicated to the task and willing to
work at it.

3:14 The Dung or Refuse Gate was the gate through which the
people carried their garbage to be burned in the Valley of Hinnom.

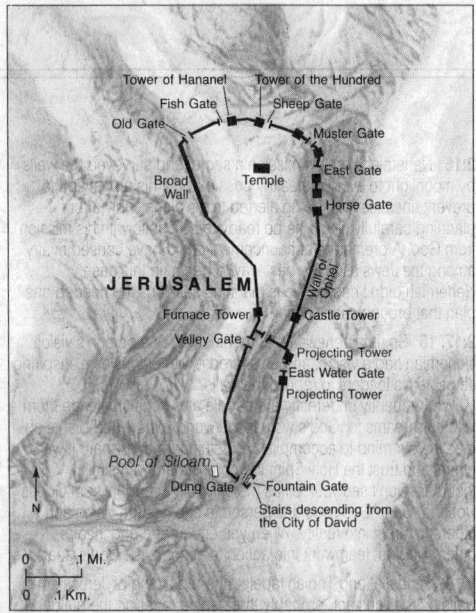

THE RESTORATION OF THE CITY WALLS Nehemiah
takes us on a counter-clockwise tour around Jerusalem
(beginning with the Sheep Gate). He describes for us each
section, gate, and tower on the wall and who worked to
rebuild it.

was a group of Levites working under the supervision of Rehum (son of Bani). Then came Hashabiah, the mayor of half the Keilah district, who supervised the building of the wall in his own district. 18Next down the line were his clan brothers led by Bavvai (son of Henadad), the mayor of the other half of the Keilah district.

19Next to them the workers were led by Ezer (son of Jeshua), the mayor of another part of Mizpah; they also worked on the section of wall across from the Armory, where the wall turns. 20Next to him was Baruch (son of Zabbai), who built from the turn in the wall to the home of Eliashib the High Priest. 21Meremoth (son of Uriah, son of Hakkoz) built a section of the wall extending from a point opposite the door of Eliashib's house to the side of the house.

22Then came the priests from the plains outside the city. 23Benjamin, Hasshub, and Azariah (son of Ma-aseiah, son of Ananiah) repaired the sections next to their own houses. 24Next was Binnui (son of Henadad), who built the portion of the wall from Azariah's house to the corner. 25Palal (son of Uzai) carried on the work from the corner to the foundations of the upper tower of the king's castle beside the prison yard. Next was Pedaiah (son of Parosh).

26The Temple attendants living in Ophel repaired the wall as far as the East Water Gate and the Projecting Tower. 27Then came the Tekoites, who repaired the section opposite the Castle Tower and over to the wall of Ophel. 28The priests repaired the wall beyond the Horse Gate, each one doing the section immediately opposite his own house.

29Zadok (son of Immer) also rebuilt the wall next to his own house, and beyond him was Shemaiah (son of Shecaniah), the gatekeeper of the East Gate. 30Next was Hananiah (son of Shelemiah); Hanun (the sixth son of Zalaph); and Meshullam (son of Berechiah), who built next to his own house. 31Malchijah, one of the goldsmiths, repaired as far as the Temple attendants' and merchants' Guild Hall, opposite the Muster Gate; then to the upper room at the corner. 32The other goldsmiths and merchants completed the wall from that corner to the Sheep Gate.

Enemies oppose rebuilding the wall

4 Sanballat was very angry when he learned that we were rebuilding the wall. He flew into a rage, and insulted and mocked us and laughed at us, and so did his friends and the Samaritan army officers. "What does this bunch of poor, feeble Jews think they are doing?" he scoffed. "Do they think they can build the wall in a day if they offer enough sacrifices? And look at those charred stones they are pulling out of the rubbish and using again!"

3Tobiah, who was standing beside him, remarked, "If even a fox walked along the top of their wall, it would collapse!

3:22 *from the plains outside the city,* implied.

3:19
Neh 3:16
2 Chron 26:9
3:20
Neh 3:1

3:22
Neh 12:28

3:25
Jer 32:2

3:26
Neh 3:27; 7:46
8:1,3; 11:21
12:37
3:27
Neh 3:5,26
3:28
2 Kgs 11:16
2 Chron 23:15
Jer 31:40
3:29
Jer 19:2
3:31
Neh 3:1,8
3:32
Neh 3:1; 12:39

4:1
Ezra 4:9,10
Neh 2:10

4:3
Neh 2:10; 4:1

3:28 Each priest also repaired the wall opposite his own house, in addition to other sections. If each person was responsible for the part of the wall behind his own house, (1) he would be more motivated to build it quickly and properly, (2) he wouldn't waste time commuting to more distant parts of the wall, (3) he would defend his own home if the wall were attacked, and (4) he would be able to make the building a family effort. Nehemiah blended self-interest with the group's objectives, helping everyone to feel that the wall project was his own. If you are part of a group working on a large project, make sure each person sees the importance and meaning of the job he has to do. This will insure high-quality work and personal satisfaction.

4:1 Sanballat was governor of Samaria, the region just north of Judea where Jerusalem was located. Sanballat may have hoped to become governor of Judea as well, but Nehemiah's arrival spoiled his plans. (For his other reasons for opposing Nehemiah, see the note on 2:10.) Sanballat tried to scare Nehemiah away or at least discourage him by bluffs (6:5–9), scorn (6:6), and even threats (6:7–19). He also formed a military alliance against Nehemiah (4:7–9) and used his political clout to promote his own purposes (6:14–19).

4:1, 2 The word Samaritan is used for the first time in the Bible in the book of Nehemiah. Almost 300 years earlier the Northern Kingdom of Israel had been conquered and most of the people carried away as captives (722 B.C.). King Sargon of Assyria repopulated Israel with captives from other lands. These captives eventually intermarried with the few Jews who remained in the land to form a mixed race of people who became known as Samaritans. Those who returned to Jerusalem and the southern region of Judea during the days of Ezra and Nehemiah would have nothing to do with these people because they were racially impure. Relations between these peoples grew progressively worse, and 400 years later the Jews and Samaritans hated each other (Luke 10:33; John 4:9).

4:1–5 Ridicule can cut deeply, causing discouragement and despair. Sanballat and Tobiah used ridicule to try to dissuade the Jews from building the wall. Instead of trading insults, however, Nehemiah prayed and the work continued. When you are mocked for your faith or criticized for doing what you know is right, refuse to respond in the same way or to become discouraged. Telling God how you feel will open your heart and mind to receive his strength to carry on.

4Then I prayed, "Hear us, O Lord God, for we are being mocked. May their scoffing fall back upon their own heads, and may they themselves become captives in a foreign land! 5Do not ignore their sin. Do not blot it out, for they have despised you in despising us who are building your wall."

6At last the wall was completed to half its original height around the entire city—for the workers worked hard.

7But when Sanballat and Tobiah and the Arabians, Ammonites, and Ashdodites heard that the work was going right ahead and that the breaks in the wall were being repaired, they became furious. 8They plotted to lead an army against Jerusalem to bring about riots and confusion. 9But we prayed to our God and guarded the city day and night to protect ourselves.

4:9
Neh 4:11

10Then some of the leaders began complaining that the workmen were becoming tired; and there was so much rubble to be removed that we could never get it done by ourselves. 11Meanwhile, our enemies were planning to swoop down upon us and kill us, thus ending our work. 12And whenever the workers who lived in the nearby cities went home for a visit, our enemies tried to talk them out of returning to Jerusalem. 13So I placed armed guards from each family in the cleared spaces behind the walls.

4:13
Neh 4:9,17,18

14Then as I looked over the situation, I called together the leaders and the people and said to them, "Don't be afraid! Remember the Lord who is great and glorious; fight for your friends, your families, and your homes!"

4:14
Num 14:9
Deut 1:29,30
2 Sam 10:12

15Our enemies learned that we knew of their plot, and that God had exposed and frustrated their plan. Now we all returned to our work on the wall; 16but from then on, only half worked while the other half stood guard behind them. 17And the masons and laborers worked with weapons within easy reach beside them, 18or with swords belted to their sides. The trumpeter stayed with me to sound the alarm.

19"The work is so spread out," I explained to them, "and we are separated so widely from each other, that when you hear the trumpet blow you must rush to where I am; and God will fight for us."

4:19
Ex 14:14
Deut 1:30
Josh 23:10

20, 21We worked early and late, from sunrise to sunset; and half the men were always on guard. 22I told everyone living outside the walls to move into Jerusalem so that their servants could go on guard duty as well as work during the day. 23During this period none of us—I, nor my brothers, nor the servants, nor the guards who were with me—ever took off our clothes except for washing. And we carried our weapons with us at all times.

4:23 *except for washing,* or "even when we went for water," or "not even at night." The meaning of the Hebrew text is uncertain.

4:6 The work of rebuilding the wall progressed well because the people had set their hearts and minds on accomplishing the task. They did not lose heart or give up, but they persevered in the work. If God has called you to a task, determine to complete it, even if you face opposition or discouragement. The rewards of work well done will be worth the effort.

4:9 Nehemiah constantly combined prayer with preparation. His people trusted God, and at the same time kept vigilant watch over what had been entrusted to them. Too often we are tempted to pray without looking for the role God wants us to have in our projects. We show God we are serious when we combine prayer with thought, preparation, and effort.

4:10–14 Accomplishing any large task is tiring. There are always pressures that foster discouragement—the task seems impossible, it can never be finished, or too many things are working against you. The only cure for fatigue and discouragement is focusing on God's purposes. Nehemiah reminded the workers of their calling, their goal, and of God's protection. If you are overwhelmed by an assignment, tired and discouraged, remember God's purpose for your life and the special purpose of the project.

4:16 The workers were spread out along the wall, so Nehemiah devised a plan of defense that would unite and protect his people. Half the men worked while the other half stood guard behind them. Christians need to help one another in the same way. As we work, we can become so afraid of approaching danger that we can't get anything done. When we look out for each other, we are free to put forth our best efforts, confident that others are ready to offer help when needed. Team members need to be united for mutual support and defense. Don't cut yourself off from others, but join together for mutual benefit. You need other people as much as they need you. No one of us alone is as strong as all of us together.

4:18, 19 To further relieve the anxieties of the people, Nehemiah set up a communication system. The man who sounded the trumpet stayed with Nehemiah, and the people knew what to do if they heard it. We have no record that the trumpet was used, but simply knowing it would issue a warning when needed was reassuring. The promise of open, immediate communication helped the group accomplish their task.

Nehemiah defends the poor

5:1
Lev 25:35
Deut 15:7

5 About this time there was a great outcry of protest from parents against some of the rich Jews who were profiteering on them. 2, 3, 4What was happening was that families who ran out of money for food had to sell their children or mortgage their fields, vineyards, and homes to these rich men; and some couldn't even do that, for they already had borrowed to the limit to pay their taxes.

5:5
Lev 25:39
2 Kgs 4:1

5"We are their brothers, and our children are just like theirs," the people protested. "Yet we must sell our children into slavery to get enough money to live. We have already sold some of our daughters, and we are helpless to redeem them, for our fields, too, are mortgaged to these men."

God is in the business of working through his people to accomplish seemingly impossible tasks. God often shapes certain people with personality characteristics, experiences, and training that prepare them for his purpose. And usually the person had no idea what God had in store for him. Nehemiah was prepared and positioned by God to be used to accomplish one of the Bible's "impossible" tasks.

Nehemiah was a common man in a unique position. He was secure and successful as cupbearer to the Persian king Artaxerxes. Nehemiah had little power, but he had great influence. He was trusted by the king. He was also a man of God, concerned about the fate of Jerusalem.

Ninety years earlier, Zerubbabel had managed to rebuild God's Temple. Ten years had passed since Ezra had returned to Jerusalem and helped the people with their spiritual needs. Now Nehemiah was needed. Jerusalem's wall was still in ruins, and the news broke his heart. As he talked to God, a plan began to take form in Nehemiah's mind about his own role in the rebuilding of the city walls. He willingly left the security of his home and job in Persia to follow God on an "impossible" mission. And the rest is history.

From beginning to end, Nehemiah prayed for God's help. He never hesitated to ask God to remember him, closing his autobiography with these words: "Remember me, my God, with your kindness." Throughout the "impossible" task, Nehemiah displayed unusual leadership. The wall around Jerusalem was rebuilt in record time, despite resistance. Even Israel's enemies had to grudgingly and fearfully admit that God was with these builders. Not only that, but God worked through Nehemiah to bring about a spiritual awakening among the people of Judah.

You may not have Nehemiah's unique abilities or feel that you are in a position where you can do anything for God, but there are two ways you can become useful to God. First, be a person who *talks* to God. Welcome him into your thoughts and share yourself with him—your concerns, feelings, and dreams. Second, be a person who *walks* with God. Put what you learn from his Word into action. God may have an "impossible" mission that he wants to do through you.

Strengths and accomplishments:
• A man of character, persistence, and prayer
• Brilliant planner, organizer, and motivator
• Under his leadership, the wall around Jerusalem was rebuilt in 52 days
• As political leader, led the nation to religious reform and spiritual awakening
• Was calm under opposition
• Was capable of being bluntly honest with his people when they were sinning

Lessons from his life:
• The first step in any venture is to pray
• People under God's direction can accomplish impossible tasks
• There are two parts to real service for God: talking with him, and walking with him

Vital statistics:
• Where: Babylon, Jerusalem
• Occupation: King's cupbearer, city builder, governor of Judah
• Relatives: Father: Hecaliah
• Contemporaries: Ezra, Artaxerxes, Tobiah, Sanballat

Key verse:
"Then I told them about the desire God had put into my heart, and of my conversation with the king, and the plan to which he had agreed. They replied at once, 'Good! Let's rebuild the wall!' And so the work began" (Nehemiah 2:18).

Nehemiah's story is told in the book of Nehemiah.

5:1 Who were these rich Jews? They were either (1) Jews who had become wealthy in exile and brought this wealth with them to Jerusalem, or (2) descendants of Jews who had arrived almost a century earlier during the first return under Zerubbabel (Ezra 1, 2) and had established lucrative businesses.

⁶I was very angry when I heard this; ⁷so after thinking about it I spoke out against these rich government officials.

"What is this you are doing?" I demanded. "How dare you demand a mortgage as a condition for helping another Israelite?"

Then I called a public trial to deal with them.

⁸At the trial I shouted at them, "The rest of us are doing all we can to *help* our Jewish brothers who have returned from exile as slaves in distant lands, but you are forcing them right back into slavery again. How often must we redeem them?"

And they had nothing to say in their own defense.

⁹Then I pressed further. "What you are doing is very evil," I exclaimed. "Should you not walk in the fear of our God? Don't we have enough enemies among the nations around us who are trying to destroy us? ¹⁰The rest of us are lending money and grain to our fellow-Jews without any interest. I beg you, gentlemen, stop this business of usury. ¹¹Restore their fields, vineyards, oliveyards, and homes to them this very day and drop your claims against them."

¹²So they agreed to do it and said that they would assist their brothers without requiring them to mortgage their lands and sell them their children. Then I summoned the priests and made these men formally vow to carry out their promises. ¹³And I invoked the curse of God upon any of them who refused.

"May God destroy your homes and livelihood if you fail to keep this promise," I declared.

And all the people shouted, "Amen," and praised the Lord. And the rich men did as they had promised.

¹⁴I would like to mention that for the entire twelve years that I was governor of Judah—from the twentieth until the thirty-second year of the reign of King Artaxerxes—my aides and I accepted no salaries or other assistance from the people of Israel. ¹⁵This was quite a contrast to the former governors who had demanded food and wine and $100 a day in cash, and had put the population at the mercy of their aides, who tyrannized them; but I obeyed God and did not act that way. ¹⁶I stayed at work on the wall and refused to speculate in land; I also required my officials to spend time on the wall. ¹⁷All this despite the fact that I regularly fed 150 Jewish officials at my table, besides visitors from other countries! ¹⁸The provisions required for each day were one ox, six fat sheep, and a large number of domestic fowls; and we needed a huge supply of all kinds of wines every ten days. Yet I refused to make a special levy against the people, for they were already having a difficult time. ¹⁹O my God, please keep in mind all that I've done for these people and bless me for it.

5:13 *I invoked the curse of God upon any of them who refused,* literally, "then I shook out the lap of my gown...."

5:7
Ex 22:25
Lev 25:36

5:8
Lev 25:48

5:10
Neh 5:7
Ezek 18:13

5:12
Ezra 10:5
Neh 10:31

5:14
Neh 1:1; 13:6

5:15
Neh 5:9

5:17
1 Kgs 18:19
5:18
1 Kgs 4:22,23
2 Thess 3:8

5:19
Neh 13:14,22,31

5:9-11 Many of the returned exiles were suffering at the hands of corrupt government officials. These leaders would lend large sums of money; then, when the debtors missed a payment, they would take over their fields. Left with no means of income, the debtors were forced to sell their children into slavery, a common practice of this time. Nehemiah was angry with these officials who were taking advantage of their own people in order to enrich themselves.

5:9-11 God's concern for the poor is revealed in almost every book of the Bible. Here, Nehemiah insists that fairness to the poor and oppressed is central to following God. The way we help those in need ought to mirror God's love and concern.

5:10 Nehemiah told the rich Jews to stop charging interest on their loans to their needy brothers. In contrast to the values of this world, God says that caring for one another is more important than personal gain. When a Christian brother or sister suffers, we all suffer (1 Corinthians 12:26). We should help needy fellow believers, not exploit them. The Jerusalem church was praised for working together to eliminate poverty (Acts 4:34, 35). Remember,

"If you give to the poor, your needs will be supplied" (Proverbs 28:27). Make it a practice to help those in need around you.

5:13 This curse was a symbolic act. Nehemiah "shook out the lap of his gown" and pronounced that anyone who broke the vow would likewise be "shaken out," losing all he had.

5:14, 15 This comment by Nehemiah was a parenthetical statement, comparing his 12 years as governor with the unjust proceedings in the land before he arrived.

5:16 Nehemiah led the entire construction project, but he also worked on the wall alongside the others. He was not a bureaucrat in a well-guarded office, but a leader who got involved in the day-to-day work. He did not use his position to take advantage of his people. A good leader keeps in touch with the work to be done. Those who lead best lead through what they *do* as well as what they say.

6:1ff Sanballat and Tobiah were desperate. The wall was almost complete, and their efforts to stop its construction were failing. So they tried a new approach, centering their attacks on Nehemiah's

Continued opposition to rebuilding the wall

6 When Sanballat, Tobiah, Geshem the Arab, and the rest of our enemies found out that we had almost completed the rebuilding of the wall—though we had not yet hung all the doors of the gates— ²they sent me a message asking me to meet them in one of the villages in the Plain of Ono. But I realized they were plotting to kill me, ³so I replied by sending back this message to them:

"I am doing a great work! Why should I stop to come and visit with you?"

⁴Four times they sent the same message, and each time I gave the same reply. ⁵, ⁶The fifth time, Sanballat's servant came with an open letter in his hand and this is what it said:

"Geshem tells me that everywhere he goes he hears that the Jews are planning to rebel, and that is why you are building the wall. He claims you plan to be their king—that is what is being said. ⁷He also reports that you have appointed prophets to campaign for you at Jerusalem by saying, 'Look! Nehemiah is just the man we need!'

"You can be very sure that I am going to pass along these interesting comments to King Artaxerxes! I suggest that you come and talk it over with me—for that is the only way you can save yourself!"

⁸My reply was, "You know you are lying. There isn't one bit of truth to the whole story. ⁹You're just trying to scare us into stopping our work." (O Lord God, please strengthen me!)

¹⁰A few days later I went to visit Shemaiah (son of Delaiah, who was the son of Mehetabel), for he said he was receiving a message from God.

"Let us hide in the Temple and bolt the door," he exclaimed, "for they are coming tonight to kill you."

¹¹But I replied, "Should I, the governor, run away from danger? And if I go into the Temple, not being a priest, I would forfeit my life. No, I won't do it!"

¹²,¹³Then I realized that God had not spoken to him, but Tobiah and Sanballat had hired him to scare me and make me sin by fleeing to the Temple; and then they would be able to accuse me.

¹⁴"O my God," I prayed, "don't forget all the evil of Tobiah, Sanballat, Noadiah the prophetess, and all the other prophets who have tried to discourage me."

The workers complete the wall

¹⁵The wall was finally finished in early September—just fifty-two days after we had begun!

6:15 *September,* or, "twenty-fifth day of the month Elul."

Margin references:

6:2
1 Chron 8:12

6:5
Neh 2:19

6:12
Neh 6:6

6:14
Ezek 13:17
Joel 2:28

6:15
Neh 4:1,2

---

character. They attacked him personally with rumors (6:6), deceit (6:10–13), and false reports (6:17). Personal attacks hurt, and when the criticism is unjustified, it is easy to despair. When you are doing God's work, you may receive attacks on your character. Follow Nehemiah's example by trusting God to accomplish a task and by overlooking unjustified abuse.

6:7 During these days, prophets such as Malachi proclaimed the coming of the Messiah (Malachi 3:1–3). Sanballat, with his usual flair for stirring up trouble, tried to turn Nehemiah's people against him by implying that Nehemiah wanted to set himself up as the Messiah. He also tried to turn the local officials against Nehemiah by threatening to report to the king of Persia that Nehemiah was starting a revolt. The fact that Sanballat had an open, or unsealed, letter delivered to Nehemiah shows that he wanted to make sure the letter's contents were made public. But Sanballat's accusations were untrue and did not divert Nehemiah from his task.

6:10 The priest gave Nehemiah what was supposed to be a message from God, warning him of danger and telling him to hide in the Temple. Nehemiah wisely tested the message, exposing it as another trick of the enemy. People may misuse God's name by saying they know God's will when they have other motives. Examine self-proclaimed "messengers from God" to see if they

stand up to the test of being consistent with what is revealed in God's Word.

6:10–13 When Nehemiah was attacked personally, he refused to give in to fear and flee to the Temple. According to God's Law, it would have been wrong for Nehemiah to go into the Temple to hide because he wasn't a priest (Numbers 18:22). If he had run for his life, he would have undermined the courage he was trying to instill in the people. Leaders are targets for attacks. Make it a practice to pray for those in authority (1 Timothy 2:2). Pray that they will stand against personal attacks and temptation. They need God-given courage to overcome fear.

6:15 Daniel, who was among the first group of captives taken from Jerusalem to Babylon (605 B.C.), predicted the rebuilding of the city walls (Daniel 9:25). Here his prophecy comes true. He, like Nehemiah, was a Jew who held a prominent position in the kingdom where they had been exiled (Daniel 5:29—6:3).

6:15 They said it couldn't be done. The job was too big, and the problems were too great. But God's men and women, joined together for special tasks, can solve huge problems and accomplish great goals. Don't let the size of a task or the length of time needed to accomplish it keep you from doing it. With God's help, it can be done.

16When our enemies and the surrounding nations heard about it, they were frightened and humiliated, and they realized that the work had been done with the help of our God. 17During those fifty-two days many letters went back and forth between Tobiah and the wealthy politicians of Judah. 18For many in Judah had sworn allegiance to him because his father-in-law was Shecaniah (son of Arah) and because his son Jehohanan was married to the daughter of Meshullam (son of Berechiah). 19They all told me what a wonderful man Tobiah was, and then they told him everything I had said; and Tobiah sent many threatening letters to frighten me.

6:16
Neh 2:10; 4:1,7

Nehemiah gives instructions for guarding the wall

7 After the wall was finished and we had hung the doors in the gates and had appointed the gatekeepers, singers, and Levites, 2I gave the responsibility of governing Jerusalem to my brother Hanani and to Hananiah, the commander of the fortress—a very faithful man who revered God more than most people do. 3I issued instructions to them not to open the Jerusalem gates until well after sunrise, and to close and lock them while the guards were still on duty. I also directed that the guards be residents of Jerusalem, and that they must be on duty at regular times, and that each homeowner who lived near the wall must guard the section of wall next to his own home. 4For the city was large, but the population was small; and only a few houses were scattered throughout the city.

7:2
Neh 1:2; 10:23

Nehemiah registers the people

5Then the Lord told me to call together all the leaders of the city, along with the ordinary citizens, for registration. For I had found the record of the genealogies of those who had returned to Judah before, and this is what was written in it:

6"The following is a list of the names of the Jews who returned to Judah after being exiled by King Nebuchadnezzar of Babylon.

7:6
Ezra 2:1-70

7"Their leaders were: Zerubbabel, Jeshua, Nehemiah, Azariah, Ra-amiah, Nahamani, Mordecai, Bilshan, Mispereth, Bigvai, Nehum, Baanah.

7:7
Ezra 2:2

"The others who returned at that time were:

8-38From the subclan of Parosh, 2,172;
From the subclan of Shephatiah, 372;
From the subclan of Arah, 652;
From the families of Jeshua and Joab of the subclan of Pahath-moab, 2,818;
From the subclan of Elam, 1,254;
From the subclan of Zattu, 845;
From the subclan of Zaccai, 760;
From the subclan of Binnui, 648;
From the subclan of Bebai, 628;
From the subclan of Azgad, 2,322;
From the subclan of Adonikam, 667;
From the subclan of Bigvai, 2,067;
From the subclan of Adin, 655;

7:8
Ezra 2:3-35

7:2 Faithfulness and reverence were the key character traits that qualified these men to govern Jerusalem. Faithful people can be trusted to carry out their work; reverent people can be expected to do so in line with God's priorities. These men had both qualities. If you are in a position of selecting leaders, look for faithfulness and reverence as two of the most important qualifications. Although other qualities may seem more impressive, faithfulness and reverence pass the test of time.

7:3 City gates were usually opened at sunrise, enabling merchants to enter and set up their tent-stores while most of the citizens were awakening. Nehemiah didn't want Jerusalem to be caught unprepared by an enemy attack, so he ordered the gates

closed until well after sunrise when the people were sure to be awake and alert.

7:3, 4 The wall was complete, but the work was not finished. Nehemiah assigned each family the task of protecting the section of wall next to their home. It is tempting to relax our guard and rest on past accomplishments after we have completed a large task. But we must continue to serve and to take care of all that God has entrusted to us. Following through after a project is completed is as vital as doing the project itself.

7:5ff Nehemiah says he found the record of the genealogies. Because Nehemiah's genealogy is almost identical to Ezra's (Ezra 2), most likely Ezra's list was stored in the Temple archives, and Nehemiah used it as his source.

From the family of Hezekiah of the subclan of Ater, 98;
From the subclan of Hashum, 328;
From the subclan of Bezai, 324;
From the subclan of Hariph, 112;
From the subclan of Gibeon, 95;
From the subclans of Bethlehem and Netophah, 188;
From the subclan of Anathoth, 128;
From the subclan of Beth-azmaveth, 42;
From the subclans of Kiriath-jearim, Chephirah, and Be-eroth, 743;
From the subclans of Ramah and Geba, 621;
From the subclan of Michmas, 122;
From the subclans of Bethel and Ai, 123;
From the subclan of Nebo, 52;
From the subclan of Elam, 1,254;
From the subclan of Harim, 320;
From the subclan of Jericho, 345;
From the subclans of Lod, Hadid, and Ono, 721;
From the subclan of Senaah, 3,930.

7:39
Ezra 2:36-39

39-42"Here are the statistics concerning the returning priests:

From the family of Jeshua of the subclan of Jedaiah, 973;
From the subclan of Immer, 1,052;
From the subclan of Pashhur, 1,247;
From the subclan of Harim, 1,017.

7:43
Ezra 2:40-42

43, 44, 45"Here are the statistics concerning the Levites:

From the family of Kadmi-el of the subclan of Hodevah of the clan of Jeshua, 74;
The choir members from the clan of Asaph, 148;
From the clans of Shallum, (all of whom were gatekeepers), 138.

7:46
Ezra 2:43-54

46-56"Of the Temple assistants, the following subclans were represented: Ziha, Hasupha, Tabbaoth, Keros, Sia, Padon, Lebana, Hagaba, Shalmai, Hanan, Giddel, Gahar, Re-aiah, Rezin, Nekoda, Gazzam, Uzza, Paseah, Besai, Asnah, Me-unim, Nephushesim, Bakbuk, Hakupha, Harhur, Bazlith, Mehida, Harsha, Barkos, Sisera, Temah, Neziah, Hatipha.

7:57
Ezra 2:55-57

57, 58, 59"Following is a list of the descendants of Solomon's officials who returned to Judah: Sotai, Sophereth, Perida, Jaala, Darkon, Giddel, Shephatiah, Hattil, Pochereth-hazzebaim, Amon.

7:60
Ezra 2:58

60"In all, the Temple assistants and the descendants of Solomon's officers numbered 392."

7:61
Ezra 2:59,60

61Another group returned to Jerusalem at that time from the Persian cities of Telmelah, Tel-harsha, Cherub, Addon, and Immer. But they had lost their genealogies and could not prove their Jewish ancestry; 62these were the subclans of Delaiah, Tobiah, and Nekoda—a total of 642.

7:63
Ezra 2:61

7:64
Ezra 2:62,63

63There were also several subclans of priests named after Habaiah, Hakkoz, and Barzillai (he married one of the daughters of Barzillai the Gileadite and took her family name), 64, 65whose genealogies had been lost. So they were not allowed to continue as priests or even to receive the priests' share of food from the sacrifices until the Urim and Thummim had been consulted to find out from God whether or not they actually were descendants of priests.

7:61 Genealogies were greatly valued by the Jews. It was vitally important for a Jew to be able to prove that he or she was a descendant of Abraham and was, therefore, part of God's people (Genesis 12:1-3; 15; Exodus 19:5, 6; Deuteronomy 11:22-28). A lost genealogy put one's status as a Jew at risk.

7:64, 65 The Urim and Thummim were means of learning God's will (Exodus 28:30, 31). It is not clear whether these were the originals which had survived the destruction of Jerusalem or whether they were new.

66There was a total of 42,360 citizens who returned to Judah at that time; 67also, 7,337 slaves and 245 choir members, both men and women. 68, 69They took with them 736 horses, 245 mules, 435 camels, and 6,720 donkeys.

7:66
Ezra 2:64-67

70Some of their leaders gave gifts for the work. The governor gave $5,000 in gold, 50 gold bowls, and 530 sets of clothing for the priests. 71The other leaders gave a total of $100,000 in gold and $77,000 in silver; 72and the common people gave $100,000 in gold, $70,000 in silver, and sixty-seven sets of clothing for the priests.

7:70
Ezra 2:68,69

73The priests, the Levites, the gatekeepers, the choir members, the Temple attendants, and the rest of the people now returned home to their own towns and villages throughout Judah. But during the month of September, they came back to Jerusalem.

7:73
Ezra 2:70

B. REFORMING THE PEOPLE (8:1—13:31)

When Nehemiah arrived in Jerusalem he found more than just broken walls, he found broken lives. In response, Nehemiah gathers the people together to hear Ezra read God's Law. The people repent and promise to change their lives by obeying God's words. No matter where we live, backsliding is an ever-present danger. We must constantly check our behavior against God's standards in the Bible so that we do not slide back into sinful ways of living.

1. Ezra renews the covenant

Ezra reads the Law

8 Now, in mid-September, all the people assembled at the plaza in front of the Water Gate and requested Ezra, their religious leader, to read to them the law of God which he had given to Moses.

8:1
2 Chron 34:15
Ezra 7:6
Neh 3:26

So Ezra the priest brought out to them the scroll of Moses' laws. He stood on a wooden stand made especially for the occasion so that everyone could see him as he read. He faced the square in front of the Water Gate, and read from early morning until noon. Everyone stood up as he opened the scroll. And all who were old enough to understand paid close attention. To his right stood Mattithiah, Shema, Anaiah, Uriah, Hilkiah, and Ma-aseiah. To his left were Pedaiah, Misha-el, Malchijah, Hashum, Hash-baddenah, Zechariah, and Meshullam.

6Then Ezra blessed the Lord, the great God, and all the people said, "Amen," and lifted their hands toward heaven; then they bowed and worshiped the Lord with their faces toward the ground.

8:6
Gen 14:22
Ex 4:31
2 Chron 20:18
Neh 5:13
1 Tim 2:8

7, 8As Ezra read from the scroll, Jeshua, Bani, Sherebiah, Jamin, Akkub, Shabbethai, Hodiah, Ma-aseiah, Kelita, Azariah, Jozabad, Hanan, Pelaiah, and the Levites went among the people and explained the meaning of the passage that was being read. 9All the people began sobbing when they heard the commands of the law.

8:7
Lev 10:11
Deut 33:10

8:9
Deut 12:7,12
Neh 8:2

Then Ezra the priest, and I as governor, and the Levites who were assisting me,

8:7, 8 *the Levites went among the people,* literally, "while the people remained in their places."

8:1 This is the first mention of Ezra in this book. He had arrived in Jerusalem from Babylon over 13 years before Nehemiah (458 B.C., see Ezra 7:6–9).

8:1 Ezra and Nehemiah were contemporaries (8:9), although Ezra was probably much older. Nehemiah was the governor (the political leader), and Ezra was the Chief Priest (the religious leader). No doubt the Jews would have liked to set up the kingdom again as in the days of David, but this would have signaled rebellion against the king of Persia to whom they were subject. The best alternative was having Nehemiah as governor over Jerusalem and Ezra serving in the Temple as priest.

8:1–5 The people paid close attention to Ezra as he read God's Word, and their lives were changed. Because we hear the Bible so often, we can become dulled to its words and immune to its teachings. Instead, we should *listen carefully* to every verse and ask the Holy Spirit to help us answer the question, "How does this apply to *my* life?"

8:9 Ezra, not Nehemiah, was the religious leader. It is significant that Nehemiah was a layman, not a member of the religious establishment or a prophet. He was motivated by his relationship with God, and he devoted his life to doing God's will in a secular world. Such people are crucial to God's work in all aspects of life.

8:9, 10 The people wept openly when they heard God's laws and realized how far they were from obeying them. But Ezra told them they should be filled with joy because they had the opportunity to listen and *understand* God's words (8:12). Then he told them to celebrate and to give gifts to those in need.

Celebration is not to be self-centered. Ezra connected celebration with giving. This gave those in need an opportunity to celebrate as well. Often when we celebrate and give to others (even when we don't feel like it), we are strengthened spiritually and filled with joy. Enter into celebrations that honor God, and allow him to fill you with his joy.

said to them, "Don't cry on such a day as this! For today is a sacred day before the Lord your God— 10it is a time to celebrate with a hearty meal, and to send presents to those in need, for the joy of the Lord is your strength. You must not be dejected and sad!"

11And the Levites, too, quieted the people, telling them, "That's right! Don't weep! For this is a day of holy joy, not of sadness."

12So the people went away to eat a festive meal and to send presents; it was a time of great and joyful celebration because they could hear and understand God's words.

13The next day the clan leaders and the priests and Levites met with Ezra to go over the law in greater detail. 14As they studied it, they noted that Jehovah had told Moses that the people of Israel should live in tents during the Festival of Tabernacles to be held that month. 15He had said also that a proclamation should be made throughout the cities of the land, especially in Jerusalem, telling the people to go to the hills to get branches from olive, myrtle, palm, and fig trees and to make huts in which to live for the duration of the feast.

16So the people went out and cut branches and used them to build huts on the roofs of their houses, or in their courtyards, or in the court of the Temple, or on the plaza beside the Water Gate, or at the Ephraim Gate Plaza. 17They lived in these huts for the seven days of the feast, and everyone was filled with joy! (This procedure had not been carried out since the days of Joshua.) 18Ezra read from the scroll on each of the seven days of the feast, and on the eighth day there was a solemn closing service as required by the laws of Moses.

Ezra leads the people in confession

9 On October 10 the people returned for another observance; this time they fasted and clothed themselves with sackcloth and sprinkled dirt in their hair. And the Israelis separated themselves from all foreigners. 3The laws of God were read aloud to them for two or three hours, and for several more hours they took turns confessing their own sins and those of their ancestors. And everyone worshiped the Lord their God. 4Some of the Levites were on the platform praising the Lord God with songs of joy. These men were Jeshua, Kadmi-el, Bani, Shebaniah, Bunni, Sherebiah, Bani, and Chenani.

5Then the Levite leaders called out to the people, "Stand up and praise the Lord your God, for he lives from everlasting to everlasting. Praise his glorious name! It is far greater than we can think or say."

The leaders in this part of the service were Jeshua, Kadmi-el, Bani, Hashabneiah, Sherebiah, Hodiah, Shebaniah, and Pethahiah.

6Then Ezra prayed, "You alone are God. You have made the skies and the heavens, the earth and the seas, and everything in them. You preserve it all; and all the angels of heaven worship you.

9:1 *On October 10,* literally, "the twenty-fourth day" of the Hebrew month.

Cross-references (margin):

8:10
Deut 26:11-13
Esth 9:19,22
Ps 28:6-8

8:12
Neh 8:7,8,10
Rom 7:7

8:14
Lev 23:34,40,42

8:16
2 Kgs 14:13
Neh 8:1; 12:39
Jer 32:29

8:17
2 Chron 7:8
8:13; 30:21

8:18
Lev 23:36
Num 29:35
Deut 31:11

9:1
1 Sam 4:12
Ezra 8:23; 10:11
Neh 8:9
Job 2:12

9:6
Gen 1:1
Deut 6:4
2 Kgs 19:15
Ps 103:21
148:2-4
Col 1:17

8:13ff After Ezra read God's laws to the people, they studied them further and then acted upon them. A careful reading of Scripture always calls for a response to these questions: What should I *do* with this knowledge? How should my life change? We must *do* something about what we have learned if it is to have real significance for our lives.

8:14–17 During the seven-day Feast of Tabernacles, the people lived in huts made of branches. This practice was instituted as a reminder of their rescue from Egypt and the time spent in shelters in the wilderness (Leviticus 23:43). They were to think about God's protection and guidance during their years of wandering and the fact that God would still protect and guide them if they obeyed him. This was a time to remember their origins, where they came from. It is helpful to remember our beginnings in order to appreciate where we are today. Think back on your life to see where God has led you. Then thank God for his continuing work in your life.

9:3 The Hebrews practiced open confession, admitting their sins to one another. Reading and studying God's Word precedes confession (8:18; 9:3) because God can show us through his Word where we are sinning. Honest confession precedes true worship because we cannot have a right relationship with God if we are protecting certain sins in our lives.

9:6–38 Many prayers and speeches in the Bible include a long summary of Israel's history, because individuals did not have their own copies of the Bible as we do today. This summary of God's past works reminded the people of their great heritage and God's promises.

It is essential to remember our history as well, to avoid repeating our mistakes so that we can serve God better. Reviewing our past helps us understand how to improve our behavior. It shows us if there is a pattern to our spiritual growth. Learn from past experiences so that you will become the kind of person God wants you to be.

7"You are the Lord God who chose Abram and brought him from Ur of the
Chaldeans and renamed him Abraham. 8When he was faithful to you, you made a
contract with him to forever give him and his descendants the land of the Canaanites, Hittites, Amorites, Perizzites, Jebusites, and Girgashites; and now you have
done what you promised, for you are always true to your word.

9"You saw the troubles and sorrows of our ancestors in Egypt, and you heard
their cries from beside the Red Sea. 10You displayed great miracles against Pharaoh
and his people, for you knew how brutally the Egyptians were treating them; you
have a glorious reputation because of those never-to-be-forgotten deeds. 11You
divided the sea for your people so they could go through on dry land! And then you
destroyed their enemies in the depths of the sea; they sank like stones beneath the
mighty waters. 12You led our ancestors by a pillar of cloud during the day and a
pillar of fire at night so that they could find their way.

13"You came down upon Mount Sinai and spoke with them from heaven and
gave them good laws and true commandments, 14including the laws about the holy
Sabbath; and you commanded them, through Moses your servant, to obey them all.

15"You gave them bread from heaven when they were hungry and water from the
rock when they were thirsty. You commanded them to go in and conquer the land
you had sworn to give them; 16but our ancestors were a proud and stubborn lot, and
they refused to listen to your commandments.

17"They refused to obey and didn't pay any attention to the miracles you did for
them; instead, they rebelled and appointed a leader to take them back into slavery
in Egypt! But you are a God of forgiveness, always ready to pardon, gracious and
merciful, slow to become angry, and full of love and mercy; you didn't abandon
them, 18even though they made a calf-idol and proclaimed, 'This is our God! He
brought us out of Egypt!' They sinned in so many ways, 19but in your great mercy
you didn't abandon them to die in the wilderness! The pillar of cloud led them
forward day by day, and the pillar of fire showed them the way through the night.
20You sent your good Spirit to instruct them, and you did not stop giving them
bread from heaven or water for their thirst. 21For forty years you sustained them in
the wilderness; they lacked nothing in all that time. Their clothes didn't wear out
and their feet didn't swell!

22"Then you helped them conquer great kingdoms and many nations, and you
placed your people in every corner of the land; they completely took over the land
of King Sihon of Heshbon and King Og of Bashan. 23You caused a population
explosion among the Israelis and brought them into the land you had promised to
their ancestors. 24You subdued whole nations before them—even the kings and the
people of the Canaanites were powerless! 25Your people captured fortified cities
and fertile land; they took over houses full of good things, with cisterns and
vineyards and oliveyards and many, many fruit trees; so they ate and were full and
enjoyed themselves in all your blessings.

26"But despite all this they were disobedient and rebelled against you. They
threw away your law, killed the prophets who told them to return to you, and they
did many other terrible things. 27So you gave them to their enemies. But in their
time of trouble they cried to you and you heard them from heaven, and in great
mercy you sent them saviors who delivered them from their enemies. 28But when
all was going well, your people turned to sin again, and once more you let their
enemies conquer them. Yet whenever your people returned to you and cried to you
for help, once more you listened from heaven, and in your wonderful mercy

9:7 Gen 11:31; 12:1; 15:7; 17:5
9:8 Gen 12:1-3; 15:18-21; 17:2-8; Josh 21:43-45
9:9 Ex 5:2; 7:8-14; 14:10-12
9:10 Ex 5:2
9:11 Ex 14:21; 15:1,5,10
9:12 Ex 13:21,22; 14:19,20
9:13 Ex 19:11,18-20; Ps 19:7-9
9:14 Ex 16:23; 20:8
9:15 Ex 16:4,14,15; 17:6; Num 20:7-13; Deut 1:8; Josh 1:2-4
9:16 Deut 31:27; Neh 9:10,29
9:17 Num 14:4
9:18 Ex 32:4-8,31
9:19 Neh 9:12
9:20 Num 11:17; Neh 9:15,30; Isa 63:11-14
9:21 Ex 16:35; Deut 2:7
9:22 Num 21:21-35; Deut 2:26-36; 3:1-17
9:24 Josh 18:1
9:25 Deut 3:5; 6:11
9:26 Judg 2:11; 2 Chron 36:16; Ezek 16:15-21
9:27 Judg 2:16; 1 Sam 12:10,11; 2 Kgs 13:5

9:17-21 God's patience is amazing! In spite of our repeated failings, he is always ready to pardon (9:17), and his Spirit is always ready to instruct us (9:20). Realizing the extent of God's forgiveness should help us to forgive those who fail us, even "seventy times seven" if necessary (Matthew 18:21, 22).

9:28-31 Israel was devastated by times of intense rebellion and sin. Yet when the people repented and returned to God, he delivered them. God puts no limit on the number of times we can come to him to obtain mercy, but we must *come* in order to obtain it, recognizing our need and asking him for help. This miracle of grace should inspire us to say, "What a gracious and merciful God you are!" If there is a recurring problem or difficulty in your life, continue to ask God for help, and be willing and ready to make changes in your attitude and behavior that will correct that difficulty.

9:29
Lev 18:5
Neh 9:26-30
Zech 7:11
9:30
Neh 9:20
9:31
Neh 9:17
Jer 4:27

9:32
2 Kgs 15:19,29
17:3
Isa 7:17,18

9:33
Gen 18:25
Jer 12:1

9:35
Deut 8:7-10
32:12-15

9:36
Deut 28:48

9:38
1 Kgs 21:8
Neh 10:1,29

delivered them! 29You punished them in order to turn them toward your laws; but even though they should have obeyed them, they were proud and wouldn't listen, and continued to sin. 30You were patient with them for many years. You sent your prophets to warn them about their sins, but still they wouldn't listen. So once again you allowed the heathen nations to conquer them. 31But in your great mercy you did not destroy them completely or abandon them forever. What a gracious and merciful God you are!

32"And now, O great and awesome God, you who keep your promises of love and kindness—do not let all the hardships we have gone through become as nothing to you. Great trouble has come upon us and upon our kings and princes and priests and prophets and ancestors from the days when the kings of Assyria first triumphed over us until now. 33Every time you punished us you were being perfectly fair; we have sinned so greatly that you gave us only what we deserved. 34Our kings, princes, priests, and ancestors didn't obey your laws or listen to your warnings. 35They did not worship you despite the wonderful things you did for them and the great goodness you showered upon them. You gave them a large, fat land, but they refused to turn from their wickedness.

36"So now we are slaves here in the land of plenty which you gave to our ancestors! Slaves among all this abundance! 37The lush yield of this land passes into the hands of the kings whom you have allowed to conquer us because of our sins. They have power over our bodies and our cattle, and we serve them at their pleasure and are in great misery. 38Because of all this, we again promise to serve

9:29 *even though they should have obeyed them,* literally, "by the observance of which a man shall live."

GOING HOME: TWO GREAT JOURNEYS OF ISRAEL	What about the Journeys?	The Exodus	The Return from Exile
	Where were they?	Egypt (430 years)	Babylon (70 years)
	How many?	About 1 million	60,000
	How long did the journey take them?	40 years and 2 attempts	100 years and 3 journeys
	Who led them?	Moses/Aaron/Joshua	Zerubbabel/Ezra/ Nehemiah
	What was their purpose?	To reclaim the Promised Land	To rebuild the Temple and city of Jerusalem
	What obstacles did they face?	Red Sea/Desert/Enemies	Ruins/Limited Resources/ Enemies
	What failures did they experience?	Complaining/Disobedience/ Retreat—all of which turned a journey of a few weeks into a 40-year epic	Fear/Discouragement/ Apathy—all of which turned a project of a few months into one which required a century to complete
	What successes did they have?	Eventually entered the Promised Land	Eventually rebuilt Jerusalem's Temple and wall
	What lessons did they learn?	God will build his nation. God is both faithful and just. God will accomplish great acts to make his promises come true.	God will preserve his nation. God will continue to have a chosen people, a home for them, and a plan to offer himself to mankind.

9:35, 36 Sometimes the very blessings God has showered on us make us forget him. We are often tempted to rely on wealth for security rather than on God. As you see what happened to the Israelites, look at your own life. Do your blessings make you thankful to God, or do they make you feel independent of God?

9:36 The Israelites were in the strange position of being slaves in their own land, having to turn over a part of their resources each year to a foreign king. How ironic, since God had given the land to them.

9:38 This covenant, or promise, between the people and God, had six provisions. They agreed to: (1) not marry heathens (10:30), (2) observe the Sabbath (10:31), (3) observe every seventh year as a Sabbath year (10:31), (4) pay a Temple tax (10:32, 33), (5) supply wood for the burnt offerings in the Temple (10:34), and (6) give dues to the Temple (10:35–38). After years of decadence and exile, the people once again began to take seriously their responsibility to God, pledging to follow him and his laws.

the Lord! And we and our princes and Levites and priests put our names to this covenant."

The people agree to obey

10 I, Nehemiah the governor, signed the covenant. The others who signed it were: Zedekiah, Seraiah, Azariah, Jeremiah, Pashhur, Amariah, Malchijah, Hattush, Shebaniah, Malluch, Harim, Meremoth, Obadiah, Daniel, Ginnethon, Baruch, Meshullam, Abijah, Mija-min, Ma-aziah, Bilgai, Shemaiah. (All those listed above were priests.)

9-13These were the Levites who signed: Jeshua (son of Azaniah), Binnui (son of Henadad), Kadmi-el, Shebaniah, Hodiah, Kelita, Pelaiah, Hanan, Mica, Rehob, Hashabiah, Zaccur, Sherebiah, Shebaniah, Hodiah, Bani, Beninu.

14-27The political leaders who signed: Parosh, Pahath-moab, Elam, Zattu, Bani, Bunni, Azgad, Bebai, Adonijah, Bigvai, Adin, Ater, Hezekiah, Azzur, Hodiah, Hashum, Bezai, Hariph, Anathoth, Nebai, Magpiash, Meshullam, Hezir, Meshez-abel, Zadok, Jaddu-a, Pelatiah, Hanan, Anaiah, Hoshea, Hananiah, Hasshub, Hallohesh, Pilha, Shobek, Rehum, Hashabnah, Ma-aseiah, Ahiah, Hanan, Anan, Malluch, Harim, Baanah.

28These men signed on behalf of the entire nation—for the common people; the priests; the Levites; the gatekeepers; the choir members; the Temple servants; and all the rest who, with their wives and sons and daughters who were old enough to understand, had separated themselves from the heathen people of the land in order to serve God. 29For we all heartily agreed to this oath and vowed to accept the curse of God unless we obeyed God's laws as issued by his servant Moses.

30We also agreed not to let our daughters marry non-Jewish men and not to let our sons marry non-Jewish girls.

31We further agreed that if the heathen people in the land should bring any grain or other produce to be sold on the Sabbath or on any other holy day, we would refuse to buy it. And we agreed not to do any work every seventh year and to forgive and cancel the debts of our brother Jews.

32We also agreed to charge ourselves annually with a Temple tax so that there would be enough money to care for the Temple of our God; 33for we needed supplies of the special Bread of the Presence, as well as grain offerings and burnt offerings for the Sabbaths, the new moon feasts, and the annual feasts. We also needed to purchase the other items necessary for the work of the Temple and for the atonement of Israel.

34Then we tossed a coin to determine when—at regular times each year—the families of the priests, Levites, and leaders should supply the wood for the burnt offerings at the Temple as required in the law.

35We also agreed always to bring the first part of every crop to the Temple—whether it be a ground crop or from our fruit and olive trees.

36We agreed to give to God our oldest sons and the firstborn of all our cattle,

10:34 Then we tossed a coin, literally, "cast lots," a form of dice.

10:1	Neh 1:1; 9:38 12:26
10:9	Neh 3:19; 7:43 8:7; 9:4
10:28	Neh 9:2
10:29	Neh 5:12
10:30	Ex 34:16 Deut 7:3 Ezra 9:1-3, 12-14; 10:10-12
10:31	Ex 23:10 Lev 25:1-7 Deut 15:1,2 Neh 13:15-22
10:32	Ex 30:11-16 Mt 17:24
10:33	Ex 20:8-11 Lev 1:1-17 2:1-16; 6:8-23 23:1-44; 24:5 Num 10:10 28:11-15 Deut 16:1-17 Ezra 3:5
10:34	Neh 11:1; 13:31
10:35	Ex 23:19 Lev 23:17

10:28ff The wall was completed, and the covenant God made with his people in the days of Moses was restored (Deuteronomy 8). In this covenant are principles which are important for us today. Our relationship with God goes far beyond church attendance and regular devotions. It should affect our relationships (10:30), our time (10:31), and our material resources (10:32-40). When you chose to follow God, you made a promise to serve him in this way. The Israelites had fallen away from the original commitment they had made to follow God. We must be careful not to do the same.

10:30 If God's chosen people were going to witness for him in a heathen world, they needed united, God-fearing families. They also needed to avoid any enticements to worship the idols of the people who lived around them. This was why God prohibited marriage between Israelites and the heathen inhabitants who lived in the land (Deuteronomy 7:3, 4). But Israelites and heathens often

intermarried anyway, and the results were disastrous for the families and for the nation. Time after time, marrying foreigners led God's people into idolatry (1 Kings 11:1-11). Whenever the nation turned its back on God, it also lost its prosperity and influence for good.

10:31 God recognized that the lure of money would conflict with the need for a day of rest, so trade was forbidden inside the city on the Sabbath. By deciding to honor God first, the Israelites would be refusing to make money their god. Our culture often makes us choose between convenience and profit on the one hand, and setting God first on the other. Look at your work and worship habits: is God really first?

10:32 The Temple had been rebuilt under Zerubbabel's leadership about 70 years earlier (Ezra 6:14, 15).

10:36 This practice was instituted at the time of the Exodus from

10:37
Lev 27:30

herds, and flocks, just as the law requires; we presented them to the priests who minister in the Temple of our God. 37They stored the produce in the Temple of our God—the best of our grain crops, and other contributions, the first of our fruit, and the first of the new wine and olive oil. And we promised to bring to the Levites a tenth of everything our land produced, for the Levites were responsible to collect

10:38
Neh 13:12,13
1 Chron 9:26
2 Chron 31:11,
12

the tithes in all our rural towns. 38A priest—a descendant of Aaron—would be with the Levites as they received these tithes, and a tenth of all that was collected as tithes was delivered to the Temple and placed in the storage areas. 39The people and the Levites were required by law to bring these offerings of grain, new wine, and olive oil to the Temple and place them in the sacred containers for use by the ministering priests, the gatekeepers, and the choir singers.

So we agreed together not to neglect the Temple of our God.

2. Nehemiah establishes policies
The people occupy the restored city

11:1
Neh 7:4; 11:18

11 The Israeli officials were living in Jerusalem, the Holy City, at this time; but now a tenth of the people from the other cities and towns of Judah and Benjamin were selected by lot to live there too. 2Some who moved to Jerusalem at this time were volunteers, and they were highly honored.

11:3
1 Chron 9:2-34
Ezra 2:43-57
8:2-14
Neh 7:57-59
11:20

3Following is a list of the names of the provincial officials who came to Jerusalem (though most of the leaders, the priests, the Levites, the Temple assistants, and the descendants of Solomon's servants continued to live in their own homes in the various cities of Judah).

4, 5, 6Leaders from the tribe of Judah:

Athaiah (son of Uzziah, son of Zechariah, son of Amariah, son of Shephatiah, son of Mahalalel, a descendant of Perez);
Ma-aseiah (son of Baruch, son of Col-hozeh, son of Hazaiah, son of Adaiah, son of Joiarib, son of Zechariah, son of the Shilonite).
These were the 468 stalwart descendants of Perez who lived in Jerusalem.

7, 8, 9Leaders from the tribe of Benjamin:

Sallu (son of Meshullam, son of Joed, son of Pedaiah, son of Kolaiah, son of Ma-aseiah, son of Ithi-el, son of Jeshaiah).
The 968 descendants of Gabbai and Sallai. Their chief was Joel, son of Zichri, who was assisted by Judah, son of Hassenu-ah.

10-14Leaders from among the priests:

Jedaiah (son of Joiarib);
Jachin;
Seraiah (son of Hilkiah, son of Meshullam, son of Zadok, son of Meraioth, son of Ahitub the chief priest).

In all, there were 822 priests doing the work at the Temple under the leadership of these men. And there were 242 priests under the leadership of Adaiah (son of

---

Egypt. The people needed to relearn the importance of dedicating the firstfruits of their yield to God. Nehemiah was simply reinstating this practice from the early days of the nation (Exodus 13:1, 2; Numbers 3:40–51).

11:1 The exiles who returned were few in number compared to Jerusalem's population in the days of the kings, and because the walls had been rebuilt on their original foundations, the city seemed sparsely populated. Nehemiah asked one-tenth of the people from the outlying areas to move inside the city walls to keep large areas of the city from being vacant. Apparently these people did not want to move into the city. Only a few people volunteered

(11:1, 2), and Nehemiah cast lots to determine who among the remaining people would have to move.

Many of them may not have wanted to live in the city because (1) non-Jews attached a stigma to Jerusalem residents, often excluding them from trade because of their religious beliefs; (2) moving into the city meant rebuilding their homes and reestablishing their businesses, a major investment of time and money; (3) living in Jerusalem required stricter obedience to God's Word because of greater social pressure and proximity to the Temple.

Jeroham, son of Pelaliah, son of Amzi, son of Zechariah, son of Pashhur, son of Malchijah).

There were also 128 stalwart men under the leadership of Amashsai (son of Azarel, son of Ahzai, son of Meshillemoth, son of Immer); who was assisted by Zabdiel (son of Haggedolim).

15, 16, 17Levite leaders:

11:15
1 Chron
26:29-32

Shemaiah (son of Hasshub, son of Azrikam, son of Hashabiah, son of Bunni);
Shabbethai and Jozabad, who were in charge of the work outside the Temple;
Mattaniah (son of Mica, son of Zabdi, son of Asaph) was the one who began the thanksgiving services with prayer;
Bakbukiah and Abda (son of Shammua, son of Galal, son of Jeduthun) were his assistants.

18In all, there were 284 Levites in Jerusalem.

11:18
Neh 11:3

19There were also 172 gatekeepers, led by Akkub, Talmon, and others of their clan. 20The other priests, Levites, and people lived wherever their family inheritance was located. 21However, the Temple workers (whose leaders were Ziha and Gishpa) all lived in Ophel.

11:19
2 Chron 27:3
33:14
Neh 3:26,27

22, 23The supervisor of the Levites in Jerusalem and of those serving at the Temple was Uzzi (son of Bani, son of Hashabiah, son of Mattaniah, son of Mica), a descendant of Asaph, whose clan became the Tabernacle singers. He was appointed by King David, who also set the pay scale of the singers.

11:22
1 Chron 9:33
25:1-6
Ezra 3:10; 6:8
7:20
Neh 11:17
12:46

24Pethahiah (son of Meshezabel, a descendant of Zerah, a son of Judah) assisted in all matters of public administration.

25-30Some of the towns where the people of Judah lived were: Kiriath-arba, Dibon, Jekabzeel (and their surrounding villages), Jeshua, Moladah, Beth-pelet, Hazar-shual, Beer-sheba (and its surrounding villages), Ziklag, Meconah and its villages, En-rimmon, Zorah, Jarmuth, Zanoah, Adullam (and their surrounding villages), Lachish and its nearby fields, Azekah and its towns.

11:25
Josh 13:9,17
14:15; 15:31
1 Sam 27:6

So the people spread from Beer-sheba to the valley of Hinnom.

31-35The people of the tribe of Benjamin lived at: Geba, Michmash, Aija, Bethel (and its surrounding villages), Anathoth, Nob, Ananiah, Hazor, Ramah, Gittaim, Hadid, Zeboim, Neballat, Lod, Ono (the Valley of the Craftsmen).

11:31
Gen 28:19
Josh 18:13
1 Chron 4:14
8:12
Neh 6:2

36Some of the Levites who lived in Judah were sent to live with the tribe of Benjamin.

The priests and Levites

12 Here is a list of the priests who accompanied Zerubbabel (son of Shealtiel) and Jeshua: Seraiah, Jeremiah, Ezra, Amariah, Malluch, Hattush, Shecaniah, Rehum, Meremoth, Iddo, Ginnethoi, Abijah, Mijamin, Ma-adiah, Bilgah, Shemaiah, Joiarib, Jedaiah, Sallu, Amok, Hilkiah, Jedaiah.

12:1
Ezra 2:36-39
Neh 7:39-42

8The Levites who went with them were: Jeshua, Binnui, Kadmi-el, Sherebiah, Judah, Mattaniah—who was the one in charge of the thanksgiving service.

9Bakbukiah and Unno, their fellow clansmen, helped them during the service.

10, 11Jeshua was the father of Joiakim;
Joiakim was the father of Eliashib;
Eliashib was the father of Joiada;
Joiada was the father of Jonathan;
Jonathan was the father of Jaddu-a.

12:10
Ezra 2:2; 7:1-5
Neh 7:7

12-21The following were the clan leaders of the priests who served under the High Priest Joiakim:

Meraiah, leader of the Seraiah clan;
Hananiah, leader of the Jeremiah clan;
Meshullam, leader of the Ezra clan;

11:22, 23 He was appointed by King David, literally, "There was a commandment from the king concerning them."

Jehohanan, leader of the Amariah clan;
Jonathan, leader of the Malluchi clan;
Joseph, leader of the Shebaniah clan;
Adna, leader of the Harim clan;
Helkai, leader of the Meraioth clan;
Zechariah, leader of the Iddo clan;
Meshullam, leader of the Ginnethon clan;
Zichri, leader of the Abijah clan;
Piltai, leader of the Moadiah and Miniamin clans;
Shammu-a, leader of the Bilgah clan;
Jehonathan, leader of the Shemaiah clan;
Mattenai, leader of the Joiarib clan;
Uzzi, leader of the Jedaiah clan;
Kallai, leader of the Sallai clan;
Eber, leader of the Amok clan;
Hashabiah, leader of the Hilkiah clan;
Nethanel, leader of the Jedaiah clan.

12:22
1 Chron 9:1-44
Ezra 4:5,24
5:5; 6:1-15
8:2-14

12:23
Josh 10:13
1 Sam 10:25
1 Chron 29:29
Esth 6:1; 9:32
Jer 32:12

22A genealogical record of the heads of the clans of the priests and Levites was compiled during the reign of King Darius of Persia, in the days of Eliashib, Joiada, Johanan, and Jaddu-a—all of whom were Levites. 23In *The Book of the Chronicles* the Levite names were recorded down to the days of Johanan, the son of Eliashib.

24These were the chiefs of the Levites at that time: Hashabiah, Sherebiah, and Jeshua (son of Kadmi-el). Their fellow-clansmen helped them during the ceremonies of praise and thanksgiving, just as commanded by David, the man of God.

12:24
Neh 11:15

12:25
1 Chron 26:15

12:26
Neh 1:1; 10:1

25The gatekeepers who had charge of the collection centers at the gates were: Mattaniah, Bakbukiah, Obadiah, Meshullam, Talmon, Akkub. 26These were the men who were active in the time of Joiakim (son of Jeshua, son of Jozadak), and when I was the governor, and when Ezra was the priest and teacher of religion.

The dedication of the city wall

12:27
1 Chron 15:16,
28
Ezra 3:10,11

12:28
1 Chron 2:54
9:16

27During the dedication of the new Jerusalem wall, all the Levites throughout the land came to Jerusalem to assist in the ceremonies and to take part in the joyous occasion with their thanksgiving, cymbals, psaltries, and harps. 28The choir members also came to Jerusalem from the surrounding villages and from the villages of the Netophathites; 29they also came from Bethgilgal and the area of Geba and Azmaveth, for the singers had built their own villages as suburbs of Jerusalem. 30The priests and Levites first dedicated themselves, then the people, the gates, and the wall.

12:30
Ezra 10:11
Neh 10:28
13:22,30

12:31
Neh 2:13
3:13,14

31, 32I led the Judean leaders to the top of the wall and divided them into two long lines to walk in opposite directions along the top of the wall, giving thanks as they went. The group which went to the right toward the Dung Gate consisted of half of the leaders of Judah, 33including Hoshaiah, Azariah, Ezra, Meshullam, 34Judah, Benjamin, Shemaiah, and Jeremiah.

12:35
Neh 12:28

12:37
2 Sam 5:7-9
Neh 2:14
3:15,26
8:1,3,16

12:38
Neh 3:8,11

12:39
2 Kgs 14:13
Neh 3:1,3,6,25,
31,32; 8:16
Jer 31:38

35, 36The priests who played the trumpets were Zechariah (son of Jonathan, son of Shemaiah, son of Mattaniah, son of Micaiah, son of Zaccur, son of Asaph), Shemaiah, Azarel, Milalai, Gilalai, Maai, Nethanel, Judah, and Hanani. (They used the original musical instruments of King David.) Ezra the priest led this procession. 37When they arrived at the Fountain Gate they went straight ahead and climbed the stairs which go up beside the castle to the old City of David; then they went to the Water Gate on the east.

38The other group, of which I was a member, went around the other way to meet them. We walked from the Tower of Furnaces to the Broad Wall, 39then from the

---

12:35, 36 How could the priests have used King David's original musical intruments? David had instituted music into worship in the Temple, and so his instruments had probably been stored there. Although Nebuchadnezzar destroyed the Temple, he took many Temple items back to Babylon with him (2 Chronicles 36:18). These were most likely preserved in Babylon and given back to the Israelites by Cyrus when they returned to their land (Ezra 1:7–11).

Ephraim Gate to the Old Gate, passed the Fish Gate and the Tower of Hananel, and went on to the gate of the Tower of the Hundred; then we continued on to the Sheep Gate and stopped at the Prison Gate.

40, 41Both choirs then proceeded to the Temple. Those with me were joined by the trumpet-playing priests—Eliakim, Ma-aseiah, Miniamin, Micaiah, Eli-o-enai, Zechariah, and Hananiah, 42and by the singers—Ma-aseiah, Shemaiah, Eleazar, Uzzi, Jehohanan, Malchijah, Elam and Ezer.

They sang loudly and clearly under the direction of Jezrahiah the choirmaster.

43Many sacrifices were offered on that joyous day, for God had given us cause for great joy. The women and children rejoiced too, and the joy of the people of Jerusalem was heard far away!

Arrangements made for supporting Levites

44On that day men were appointed to be in charge of the treasuries, the wave offerings, the tithes, and first-of-the-harvest offerings, and to collect these from the farms as decreed by the laws of Moses. These offerings were assigned to the priests and Levites, for the people of Judah appreciated the priests and Levites and their ministry. 45They also appreciated the work of the singers and gatekeepers, who assisted them in worshiping God and performing the purification ceremonies as required by the laws of David and his son Solomon. 46(It was in the days of David and Asaph that the custom began of having choir directors to lead the choirs in hymns of praise and thanks to God.) 47So now, in the days of Zerubbabel and Nehemiah, the people brought a daily supply of food for the members of the choir, the gatekeepers, and the Levites. The Levites, in turn, gave a portion of what they received to the priests.

12:44
Ex 29:26-28
Lev 7:29-34
23:20; 27:30-33
Deut 26:3-10
Neh 10:35-39
Neh 13:5,12,13
12:45
1 Chron 25:1-8
26:1-32
12:46
1 Chron 25:1,7
26:1
2 Chron 29:30
Neh 11:23
12:47
Num 18:21-29

Foreigners are expelled

13 On that same day, as the laws of Moses were being read, the people found a statement which said that the Ammonites and Moabites should never be permitted to worship at the Temple. 2For they had not been friendly to the people of Israel. Instead, they had hired Balaam to curse them—although God turned the curse into a blessing. 3When this rule was read, all the foreigners were immediately expelled from the assembly.

4Before this had happened, Eliashib the priest, who had been appointed as custodian of the Temple storerooms and who was also a good friend of Tobiah, 5had converted a storage room into a beautiful guest room for Tobiah. The room had previously been used for storing the grain offerings, frankincense, bowls, and tithes of grain, new wine, and olive oil. Moses had decreed that these offerings belonged to the priests, Levites, the members of the choir, and the gatekeepers. 6I was not in Jerusalem at the time, for I had returned to Babylon in the thirty-second year of the reign of King Artaxerxes (though I later received his

13:1
Deut 23:3-5
Neh 13:23
13:2
Num 22:3-11
13:3
Ezra 10:11
Neh 9:2; 10:28
13:4
Neh 6:17-19
12:44
13:5
Neh 2:10
6:1,17,18; 13:7
13:6
Ezra 4:11
7:1,11,12,21
Neh 1:1; 5:14

12:47 to the priests, literally, "to the descendants of Aaron the priest."

12:44–47 The dedication of the city wall was characterized by joy, praise, and singing (12:24, 27–29, 35, 36, 40–42). Nehemiah repeatedly mentioned King David, who began the custom of using choirs in worship. In David's day, Israel was a vigorous, God-fearing nation. These exiles who had returned wanted their rebuilt Jerusalem to be the hub of a renewed nation, strengthened by God; therefore, they dedicated themselves and their city to God.

13:1 This statement is in Deuteronomy 23:3–5.

13:3 "All the foreigners" refers to the Moabites and Ammonites, two nations who were bitter enemies of Israel (13:1). God's Law clearly stated that these two peoples should never be allowed into the Temple (Deuteronomy 23:3–5). This had nothing to do with racial prejudice because God clearly loved all people, including foreigners (Deuteronomy 10:18). He allowed foreigners to make sacrifices (Numbers 15:15, 16), and he desires all nations to know

and love him (Isaiah 42:6). But while God wants all to come to him, he warns believers to stay away from those bent on evil (Hosea 7:8). The relationships established between the Jews and the heathens had caused their captivity in the first place. In their celebration and rededication, they had to show they were serious about following God's Law.

13:5–7 Nehemiah had to return to Babylon in 433 B.C., 12 years after he had arrived in Jerusalem. He was either recalled by King Artaxerxes, or he was fulfilling an agreement to return. It is not known how long he remained in Babylon, but when he returned to Jerusalem (13:7) he found that one of his major opponents in rebuilding the wall, Tobiah, had been given his own room at the Temple. Eliashib, the priest, had married Tobiah's daughter, so Eliashib used his influence to get this special room for his father-in-law. Chapters 2, 4, and 6 tell about Tobiah's opposition to Nehemiah and Nehemiah's appropriate action.

13:7
Neh 13:5

permission to go back again to Jerusalem). ⁷When I arrived back in Jerusalem and learned of this evil deed of Eliashib—that he had prepared a guest room in the Temple for Tobiah— ⁸I was very upset and threw out all of his belongings from the room. ⁹Then I demanded that the room be thoroughly cleaned, and I brought back the Temple bowls, the grain offerings, and frankincense.

13:9
2 Chron 29:5,
15-19

The people support the Levites once again

13:10
Neh 12:28,29

¹⁰I also learned that the Levites had not been given what was due them, so they and the choir singers who were supposed to conduct the worship services had returned to their farms. ¹¹I immediately confronted the leaders and demanded, "Why has the Temple been forsaken?" Then I called all the Levites back again and restored them to their proper duties. ¹²And once more all the people of Judah began bringing their tithes of grain, new wine, and olive oil to the Temple treasury.

13:12
Neh 10:37
12:44

13:13
Neh 7:2

¹³I put Shelemiah the priest, Zadok the scribe, and Pedaiah the Levite in charge of the administration of the storehouses; and I appointed Hanan (son of Zaccur, son of Mattaniah) as their assistant. These men had an excellent reputation, and their job was to make an honest distribution to their fellow-Levites.

¹⁴O my God, remember this good deed and do not forget all that I have done for the Temple.

Nehemiah halts the work on the Sabbath

13:15
Ex 20:8-11
34:21
Neh 13:21

¹⁵One day I was on a farm and saw some men treading winepresses on the Sabbath, hauling in sheaves, and loading their donkeys with wine, grapes, figs, and all sorts of produce which they took that day into Jerusalem. So I opposed them publicly. ¹⁶There were also some men from Tyre bringing in fish and all sorts of wares and selling them on the Sabbath to the people of Jerusalem.

¹⁷Then I asked the leaders of Judah, "Why are you profaning the Sabbath? ¹⁸Wasn't it enough that your fathers did this sort of thing and brought the present evil days upon us and upon our city? And now you are bringing more wrath upon the people of Israel by permitting the Sabbath to be desecrated in this way."

13:19
Lev 23:32

¹⁹So from then on I commanded that the gates of the city be shut as darkness fell on Friday evenings and not be opened until the Sabbath had ended; and I sent some of my servants to guard the gates so that no merchandise could be brought in on the Sabbath day. ²⁰The merchants and tradesmen camped outside Jerusalem once or twice, ²¹but I spoke sharply to them and said, "What are you doing out here, camping around the wall? If you do this again, I will arrest you." And that was the last time they came on the Sabbath.

13:22
1 Chron 15:12
Neh 12:30

²²Then I commanded the Levites to purify themselves and to guard the gates in order to preserve the sanctity of the Sabbath. Remember this good deed, O my God! Have compassion upon me in accordance with your great goodness.

Nehemiah opposes marriage to heathens

13:23
Neh 10:30

13:24
Ezra 4:7; 9:2

²³About the same time I realized that some of the Jews had married women from Ashdod, Ammon, and Moab, ²⁴and that many of their children spoke in the language of Ashdod and couldn't speak the language of Judah at all. ²⁵So I

13:10 Because the Levites were no longer supported, they had returned to their farms to fend for themselves, neglecting their Temple duties and the spiritual welfare of the people. Spiritual workers deserve their pay, and their support ought to be enough to care for their needs. They shouldn't have to suffer (or leave) because some of their own people, who claim to be believers, don't adequately assess and meet the needs of their ministers.

13:17 God had commanded Israel not to work on the Sabbath, but to rest in remembrance of creation and the Exodus (Exodus 20:8-11; Deuteronomy 5:12-15). The Sabbath rest, lasting from sunset Friday to sunset Saturday, was to be honored and observed by all Jews, servants, visiting foreigners, and even farm animals. Jerusalem's busy Sabbath trade directly violated God's Law, so

Nehemiah commanded that the city gates be shut and traders be sent home every Friday afternoon as the Sabbath hours approached.

13:25 Nehemiah was filled with righteous indignation at the blatant way the Jews were breaking God's laws and disregarding the covenant they had previously reaffirmed (10:30). The people had promised not to allow their children to marry heathens. But during Nehemiah's absence, the people had been intermarrying, breaking their solemn covenant with God. Nehemiah's severe treatment of these people shows the contrast between his great faithfulness to God and the people's neglect, disobedience, and disloyalty.

confronted these parents and cursed them and punched a few of them and knocked them around and pulled out their hair; and they vowed before God that they would not let their children intermarry with non-Jews.

13:25
Deut 25:2
Neh 10:29,30
13:11,17,

26"Wasn't this exactly King Solomon's problem?" I demanded. "There was no king who could compare with him, and God loved him and made him the king over all Israel; but even so he was led into idolatry by foreign women. 27Do you think that we will let you get away with this sinful deed?"

13:26
1 Kgs 11:1-8

28One of the sons of Jehoiada (the son of Eliashib the High Priest) was a son-in-law of Sanballat the Horonite, so I chased him out of the Temple. 29Remember them, O my God, for they have defiled the priesthood and the promises and vows of the priests and Levites. 30So I purged out the foreigners, and assigned tasks to the priests and Levites, making certain that each knew his work. 31They supplied wood for the altar at the proper times and cared for the sacrifices and the first offerings of every harvest. Remember me, my God, with your kindness.

13:28
Num 25:13
Neh 2:10,19

13:30
Neh 10:30
13:31
Neh 10:34
13:14,22

13:26 Nehemiah used Solomon's example to teach his people about the mistakes of the past. If one of the greatest kings of Israel fell because of the influence of unbelievers, others could too. Nehemiah saw this principle in Solomon's example: your gifts and strengths won't be of much benefit if you fail to deal with your weaknesses. Although he was a great king, Solomon's marriages to foreign women brought tragedy to the whole kingdom. A tendency to sin must be recognized and dealt with swiftly; otherwise, it may overpower you and bring you down. One of the strongest reasons for reading the Bible is to learn from the mistakes of God's people.

13:31 Nehemiah's life story provides many principles of effective leadership that are still valid today. (1) *Have a clear purpose; and*

keep evaluating it in light of God's will. Nothing prevented Nehemiah from staying on track. (2) *Be straightforward and honest.* Everyone knew exactly what Nehemiah needed, and he spoke the truth even when it made his goal harder to achieve. (3) *Live above reproach.* The accusations against Nehemiah were empty and false. (4) *Be a person of constant prayer, deriving power and wisdom from your contact with God.* Everything Nehemiah did glorified God.

Leadership appears glamorous at times, but it is often lonely, thankless, and filled with pressures to compromise values and standards. Nehemiah was able to accomplish a huge task against incredible odds because he learned that there is no success without risk of failure, no reward without hard work, no opportunity without criticism, and no true leadership without trust in God.

ESTHER

DRAMA, power, romance, intrigue—this is the stuff of which best-selling novels are made. The writer weaves into the narrative of Esther the profound interplay of God's sovereignty and human will. God prepared the place and the opportunity, and Esther and Mordecai chose to act for him. As you read Esther, determine to be God's servant in your place and time.

The book of Esther begins with Queen Vashti refusing to obey an order from her husband, King Ahasuerus. She is subsequently banished, and the search begins for a new queen. The king sends out a decree to gather together all the beautiful women in the Empire and bring them into the royal harem. Esther, a young Jewish woman, is one of those chosen to be in the royal harem. King Ahasuerus is so pleased with Esther that he makes her his queen.

Meanwhile, Mordecai, Esther's older cousin, becomes a government official and, during his tenure, foils an assassination plot. But the ambitious and self-serving Haman is appointed Prime Minister—second in command in the Empire. When Mordecai refuses to bow in reverence to him, Haman becomes furious and determines to destroy Mordecai and all the Jews along with him.

To accomplish his vengeful deed, Haman deceives the king and persuades him to issue an edict condemning the Jews to death. Mordecai tells Queen Esther about this edict, and she determines to risk her life to save her people. Esther asks King Ahasuerus and Haman to be her guests at a banquet. During the feast, the king asks Esther what she really wants and promises to give her anything. Esther simply invites both men to another banquet the next day.

That night, unable to sleep, the king flips through some records in the royal archives and reads of the assassination plot which Mordecai thwarted. Surprised to learn that Mordecai had never been rewarded for this deed, the king asks Haman what should be done to properly thank a hero. Haman thinks the king must be talking about him, and so he describes a lavish reward. The king agrees, but to Haman's shock and utter humiliation, he learns that Mordecai is the person to be so honored.

During the second banquet, the king again asks Esther what she desires. She replies that someone has plotted to destroy her and her people, and she names Haman as the culprit. Immediately the king sentences Haman to die on the gallows which he had built for Mordecai.

In the final act of this true-life drama, Mordecai is appointed as Prime Minister, and the Jews are guaranteed protection throughout the land. To celebrate this historic occasion, the Feast of Purim is established.

Because of Queen Esther's courageous act, a whole nation is saved. Seeing her God-given opportunity, she seized it! Her life made a difference. Read Esther and watch for God at work in *your* life. Perhaps he has prepared you to act in "such a time as this" (4:14).

VITAL STATISTICS

PURPOSE:
To demonstrate God's sovereignty and his loving care for his people

AUTHOR:
Unknown. Possibly Mordecai (9:29). Some have suggested Ezra or Nehemiah because of the similarity of the writing style.

DATE WRITTEN:
Approximately 483–471 B.C. (Esther became queen in 479)

SETTING:
Although Esther follows Nehemiah in the Bible, its events are about 30 years prior to those recorded in Nehemiah. The story is set in the Persian Empire, and most of the action takes place in the king's palace in Shushan (Susa), the Persian capital.

KEY VERSE:
"If you keep quiet at a time like this, God will deliver the Jews from some other source, but you and your relatives will die; what's more, who can say but that God has brought you into the palace for just such a time as this?" (4:14).

KEY PEOPLE:
Esther, Mordecai, King Ahasuerus (Xerxes I), Haman

KEY PLACE:
The king's palace in Susa, Persia

SPECIAL FEATURES:
Esther is one of only two books named for women (Ruth is the other). The book is unusual in that, in the original version, no name, title, or pronoun for God appears in it (see the note on 4:14). This caused some church fathers to question its inclusion in the canon. But God's presence is clear throughout the book.

THE BLUEPRINT

1. Esther becomes queen (1:1—2:23)
2. The Jews are threatened (3:1—4:17)
3. Esther intercedes for the Jews
   (5:1—8:17)
4. The Jews are delivered (9:1—10:3)

The book of Esther is an example of God's divine guidance and care over our lives. God's sovereignty and power are seen throughout this book. Although we may question certain circumstances in our lives, we must have faith that God is in control, working through both the pleasant and difficult times so that we can serve him effectively.

MEGATHEMES

THEME	EXPLANATION	IMPORTANCE
God's sovereignty	The book of Esther tells of the circumstances that were essential to the survival of God's people in Persia. These "circumstances" were not the result of chance, but of God's grand design. God is sovereign over every area of life.	With God in charge, we can take courage. He can guide us through the circumstances we face in our lives. We should expect God to display his power in carrying out his will. As we unite our life's purposes to God's purpose, we benefit from his sovereign care.
Racial hatred	The Jews in Persia had been a minority since their deportation from Judah 100 years earlier. Haman was a descendant of King Agag, an enemy of the Jews. Lust for power and pride drove Haman to hate Mordecai, Esther's uncle. Haman convinced the king to kill all the Jews.	Racial hatred is always sinful. We must never condone it in any form. Every person on earth has intrinsic worth because God created mankind in his image. Therefore, God's people must stand against racism whenever and wherever it occurs.
Deliverance	On February 28th, the Jews celebrate the Feast of Purim which symbolizes God's deliverance. "Purim" means dice, such as those used by Haman to set the date for the extermination of all Jews from Persia. But God overruled, using Queen Esther to intercede on behalf of the Jews.	Because God is in control of history, he is never frustrated by any turn of events or action of man. He is able to save us from the evil of this world and deliver us from sin and death. Because we trust God, we are not to fear what men may do to us; instead, we are to be confident in God's control.
Action	Faced with death, Esther and Mordecai set aside their own fear and took action. Esther risked her life by asking King Ahasuerus to save the Jews. They were not paralyzed by fear.	When outnumbered and powerless, it is natural for us to feel helpless. Esther and Mordecai resisted this temptation and acted with courage. It is not enough to know that God is in control, we must act with self-sacrifice and courage to follow God's guidance.
Wisdom	The Jews were a minority in a world hostile to them. It took great wisdom for Mordecai to survive. Serving as a faithful official of the king, Mordecai took steps to understand and work with the Persian law. Yet he did not compromise his integrity.	It takes great wisdom to survive in a non-believing world. In a setting which is for the most part hostile to Christianity, we can demonstrate wisdom by giving respect to what is true and good and by humbly standing against what is wrong.

1. Esther becomes queen
Queen Vashti is deposed

1 It was the third year of the reign of King Ahasuerus, emperor of vast Media-Persia, with its 127 provinces stretching from India to Ethiopia. This was the year of the great celebration at Shushan Palace, to which the emperor invited all his

1:1
Ezra 1:2; 4:6
Neh 1:1
Dan 5:28; 8:2

1:1 Esther's story begins in 483 B.C., 103 years after Nebuchadnezzar had taken the Jews into captivity (2 Kings 25), 55 years after Zerubbabel led the first group of exiles back to Jerusalem (Ezra 1, 2), and 25 years before Ezra led the second group to Jerusalem (Ezra 7). Esther lived in the kingdom of Persia, formerly called Babylon (which fell in 539 B.C.). Esther's parents must have been among those exiles who chose not to return to Jerusalem, even though Cyrus, the king at the time, had issued a decree allowing them to do so. The Jewish exiles had great freedom in Persia, and many remained because they had

established successful businesses or were fearful of the dangerous journey back to their homeland.

1:1 Ahasuerus, also called Xerxes the Great, was Persia's fifth king (486–465 B.C.). He was proud and impulsive, as we see from the events in chapter 1. His winter palace was in Susa, where he held the banquet described in 1:3–7. Persian kings often held great banquets before going to war. In 481, Ahasuerus launched an attack against Greece. After his fleet won a great victory at Thermopolae, he was defeated at Salamis in 480, and had to return to Persia. In 479, Esther became queen.

governors, aides, and army officers, bringing them in from every part of Media-Persia for the occasion. 4The celebration lasted six months, a tremendous display of the wealth and glory of his empire.

1:5
Esth 7:7,8

5When it was all over, the king gave a special party for the palace servants and officials—janitors and cabinet officials alike—for seven days of revelry, held in the courtyard of the palace garden. 6The decorations were green, white, and blue, fastened with purple ribbons tied to silver rings imbedded in marble pillars. Gold and silver benches stood on pavements of black, red, white, and yellow marble.

1:7
Esth 2:18

7Drinks were served in gold goblets of many designs, and there was an abundance of royal wine, for the king was feeling very generous. 8The only restriction on the drinking was that no one should be compelled to take more than he wanted, but those who wished could have as much as they pleased. For the king had instructed his officers to let everyone decide this matter for himself.

1:9
Esth 1:11,12,
16-19; 2:1,4

9Queen Vashti gave a party for the women of the palace at the same time.

1:10
Judg 16:25
Esth 2:21
6:2
Dan 1:3-5,18,
19

10On the final day, when the king was feeling high, half drunk from wine, he told the seven eunuchs who were his personal aides—Mehuman, Biztha, Harbona, Bigtha, Abagtha, Zethar, and Carkas— 11to bring Queen Vashti to him with the royal crown upon her head so that all the men could gaze upon her beauty—for she

1:6 *fastened with purple ribbons,* literally, "fastened with cords of fine linen and purple thread."

THE WORLD OF ESTHER'S DAY
Esther lived in the capital of the vast Medo-Persian Empire, which incorporated the provinces of Media and Persia, as well as the previous empires of Assyria and Babylon. Esther, a Jewess, was chosen by King Ahasuerus to be his queen. The story of how she saved her people takes place in the palace in Susa (Shushan).

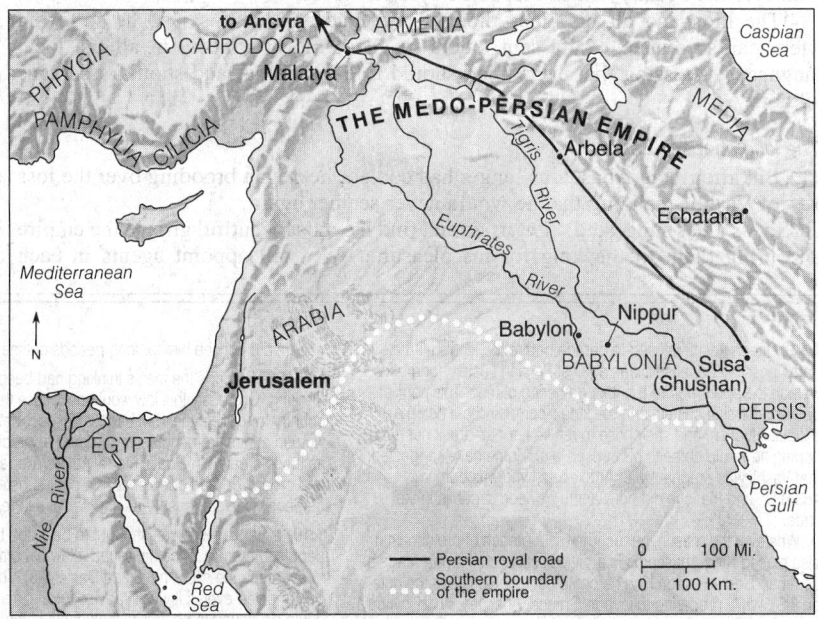

1:4 The celebration lasted six months because its real purpose was to plan the battle strategy for invading Greece and to demonstrate that the king had sufficient wealth to carry it out. Waging war was not for survival; it was a means of acquiring more wealth, territory, and power.

1:5–7 Persia was a world power, and the king, as the center of that power, was one of the wealthiest people in the world. Persian kings loved to flaunt their wealth, even wearing precious gemstones in their beards. Jewelry was a sign of rank for Persian men. Persian soldiers even wore great amounts of gold jewelry into battle.

1:9 Ancient Greek documents call Ahasuerus' wife Amestris, believed to be a Greek form of Vashti. Vashti was deposed in 484/483 B.C., but she is mentioned again in ancient records as the queen mother during the reign of her son, Artaxerxes, who succeeded Ahasuerus. Toward the end of Ahasuerus' reign, either Queen Esther died or Vashti was able, through her son, to regain the influence she had lost.

1:10 Some advisors and cabinet officials were castrated in order to prevent them from having children and then rebelling and trying to establish a dynasty of their own. A castrated official was called a eunuch.

1:10, 11 Ahasuerus made a rash, half-drunk decision, based purely on feelings. His self-restraint and practical wisdom were weakened by too much wine, and he later regretted his decision (2:1). Poor decisions are made when clear thinking is not involved. Base your decisions on careful thinking, not on the spur of the moment.

was a very beautiful woman. 12But when they conveyed the emperor's order to Queen Vashti, she refused to come. The king was furious 13, 14, 15but first consulted his lawyers, for he did nothing without their advice. They were men of wisdom who knew the temper of the times as well as Persian law and justice, and the king trusted their judgment. These men were Carshena, Shethar, Admatha, Tarshish, Meres, Marsena, and Memucan—seven high officials of Media-Persia. They were his personal friends as well as being the chief officers of the government.

"What shall we do about this situation?" he asked them. "What penalty does the law provide for a queen who refuses to obey the king's orders, properly sent through his aides?"

16Memucan answered for the others, "Queen Vashti has wronged not only the king but every official and citizen of your empire. 17For women everywhere will begin to disobey their husbands when they learn what Queen Vashti has done. 18And before this day is out, the wife of every one of us officials throughout your empire will hear what the queen did and will start talking to us husbands the same way, and there will be contempt and anger throughout your realm. 19We suggest that, subject to your agreement, you issue a royal edict, a law of the Medes and Persians that can never be changed, that Queen Vashti be forever banished from your presence and that you choose another queen more worthy than she. 20When this decree is published throughout your great kingdom, husbands everywhere, whatever their rank, will be respected by their wives!"

21The king and all his aides thought this made good sense, so he followed Memucan's counsel, 22and sent letters to all of his provinces, in all the local languages, stressing that every man should rule his home, and should assert his authority.

The king chooses Esther

2 But after King Ahasuerus' anger had cooled, he began brooding over the loss of Vashti, realizing that he would never see her again.

2So his aides suggested, "Let us go and find the most beautiful girls in the empire and bring them to the king for his pleasure. 3We will appoint agents in each

Cross-references:
1:13 Ezra 7:14; Esth 1:16
1:16 Esth 1:9; 13
1:19 Esth 8:8; Dan 6:8-15,17
1:20 Eph 5:33; Col 3:18; 1 Pet 3:1-7
1:21 Esth 1:13,16
1:22 Esth 3:12; 8:9,10
2:1 Esth 1:9
2:3 Esth 1:1-3; 2:9,15

1:12 Queen Vashti refused to parade before the king's all-male party, possibly because it was against Persian custom for a woman to appear before a public gathering of men. This conflict between Persian custom and the king's command put her in a difficult situation, and she chose to refuse her half-drunk husband, hoping he would come to his senses later. Some have suggested that Vashti was pregnant with Artaxerxes, who was born in 483 B.C., and that she did not want to be seen in public in that state.

Whatever the reason, her action was a breach of protocol that also placed King Ahasuerus in a difficult situation. Having made a command, as a Persian king he could not reverse it (see the note on 8:8). While preparing to invade Greece, Ahasuerus had invited important officials from all over his land to see his power, wealth, and authority. If it was perceived that he did not have authority over his own wife, his military credibility would be damaged—and military leadership was the greatest criterion of success for an ancient king. In addition, King Ahasuerus was accustomed to getting what he wanted.

1:13-15 Ahasuerus, like most rulers past and present, kept a handful of advisors whom he consulted on almost all matters. Often a king's success rose or fell on the wisdom of these men. Daniel was such an advisor under kings Darius and Cyrus (Daniel 6:28) and perhaps also under the next three Persian kings.

1:15 Oriental kings often did not have close personal relationships with their wives. Ahasuerus demonstrates this because (1) he had a harem (2:3); (2) he showed no respect for Vashti's personhood (1:13-15); (3) Esther, when she became

queen, did not see him for long periods of time (4:11).

1:16-21 Perhaps the men's thinking had been clouded by drinking. Obviously this law would not cause the women of the country to respect their husbands. Respect between men and women comes from mutual regard and appreciation for each other as those created in God's image, not from legal pronouncements and orders. Forced obedience is a poor substitute for the love and respect wives and husbands should have for each other.

1:19 A Persian king was thought to be a god by many of his people; therefore, once he issued a law or command, it stood forever (see the note on 8:8 and Daniel 6:8). The law could never be canceled even if it was ill-advised; but if necessary, a new law could be issued to neutralize the effects of the old law.

1:20, 21 One way to rule is to issue edicts that force people to comply. King Ahasuerus and his advisors responded this way. But in Matthew 20:25, 26, Jesus reminds us that this is how the heathen act, lording it over everyone. As believers, we are to act differently. God offers his free gift of salvation to all (Titus 2:11), and he tells us to treat each other with respect and love (1 Corinthians 13).

2:3, 14 Persian kings collected not only vast amounts of jewelry, but also great numbers of women. These young virgins were taken from their homes and required to live in a separate building near the palace, called a harem. Their sole purpose was to serve the king and to await his call for sexual pleasure. They rarely saw the king, and their lives were restricted and boring. If rejected, Esther would be one of many girls the king had seen once and forgotten. But Esther's presence and beauty pleased the king enough that

province to select young lovelies for the royal harem. Hegai, the eunuch in charge, will see that they are given beauty treatments, ⁴and after that, the girl who pleases you most shall be the queen instead of Vashti."

This suggestion naturally pleased the king very much, and he put the plan into immediate effect.

⁵Now there was a certain Jew at the palace named Mordecai (son of Jair, son of Shime-i, son of Kish, a Benjaminite). ⁶He had been captured when Jerusalem was destroyed by King Nebuchadnezzar, and had been exiled to Babylon along with King Jeconiah of Judah and many others. ⁷This man had a beautiful and lovely young cousin, Hadassah (also called Esther), whose father and mother were dead, and whom he had adopted into his family and raised as his own daughter. ⁸So now, as a result of the king's decree, Esther was brought to the king's harem at Shushan Palace, along with many other young girls. ⁹Hegai, who was responsible for the harem, was very much impressed with her, and did his best to make her happy; he ordered a special menu for her, favored her for the beauty treatments, gave her seven girls from the palace as her maids, and gave her the most luxurious apartment in the harem. ¹⁰Esther hadn't told anyone that she was a Jewess, for Mordecai had said not to. ¹¹He came daily to the court of the harem to ask about Esther and to find out what was happening to her.

¹², ¹³, ¹⁴The instructions concerning these girls were that before being taken to the king's bed, each would be given six months of beauty treatments with oil of myrrh, followed by six months with special perfumes and ointments. Then, as each girl's turn came for spending the night with King Ahasuerus, she was given her choice of clothing or jewelry she wished, to enhance her beauty. She was taken to the king's apartment in the evening and the next morning returned to the second harem where the king's wives lived. There she was under the care of Shaashgaz, another of the king's eunuchs, and lived there the rest of her life, never seeing the king again unless he had especially enjoyed her, and called for her by name.

¹⁵When it was Esther's turn to go to the king, she accepted the advice of Hegai, the eunuch in charge of the harem, dressing according to his instructions. And all the other girls exclaimed with delight when they saw her. ¹⁶So Esther was taken to the palace of the king in January of the seventh year of his reign. ¹⁷Well, the king loved Esther more than any of the other girls. He was so delighted with her that he set the royal crown on her head and declared her queen instead of Vashti. ¹⁸To celebrate the occasion, he threw another party for all his officials and servants, giving generous gifts to everyone and making grants to the provinces in the form of remission of taxes.

¹⁹Later, the king demanded a second bevy of beautiful girls. By that time Mordecai had become a government official.

2:5 Esth 3:2-6; 10:3
2:6 2 Kgs 24:14,15 2 Chron 36:17-20
2:7 Dan 1:6,7
2:10 Esth 2:20
2:17 Esth 1:11 Zech 6:10,11
2:18 Esth 1:5-8

2:7 *his own daughter,* showing that Mordecai had adopted his cousin as his daughter. **2:15** *Esther's,* literally, "Esther, the daughter of Abihail, who was Mordecai's uncle, who had adopted her." **2:19** *a second bevy of beautiful girls,* or "When Esther and the other girls had been transferred to the second harem."

---

she was crowned queen in place of Vashti. The queen held a more influential position than a concubine, and she was given more freedom and authority than others in the harem. But even as queen, Esther had few rights—especially since she had been chosen to replace a woman who had become too assertive.

2:5, 6 Mordecai was a Jew. The Jews had multiplied since being exiled over 100 years earlier. They had been given great freedom and were allowed to run their own businesses and hold positions in government (2:19; Daniel 6:3).

2:6 The Bible says that Mordecai was carried into exile when Jerusalem was destroyed. If this was so, Mordecai would have been over 100 years old at the time of this story. This conflict can be resolved by understanding that the word "he," referring to Mordecai, can also mean "the family of Mordecai." It is likely that Mordecai's parents, grandparents, or even great-grandparents were carried into captivity rather than Mordecai himself.

2:6 Jeconiah is also called Jehoiachin in 2 Kings 24:8–17.

2:10 With virtually no rights and little access to the king, it was better for Esther not to reveal her identity. While boldness in stating our identity as God's people is our responsibility, at times a good strategy is to keep quiet until we have won the right to be heard. This is especially true when dealing with those in authority over us. But we can always let them see the difference God makes in our lives.

2:17 God placed Esther on the throne even before the Jews faced the possibility of complete destruction (3:5ff), so that when trouble came, a person would already be in the position to help. If you are changing jobs, position, or location and can't see God's purpose in your situation, understand that God may be placing you in a position where you will be able to help when the need arises.

2:19 Ahasuerus ordered a second group of girls, not to continue his search for a queen, but simply for his own selfish pleasure.

20Esther still hadn't told anyone she was a Jewess, for she was still following Mordecai's orders, just as she had in his home.

21One day, as Mordecai was on duty at the palace, two of the king's eunuchs, Bigthan and Teresh—who were guards at the palace gate—became angry at the king and plotted to assassinate him. 22Mordecai heard about it and passed on the information to Queen Esther, who told the king, crediting Mordecai with the information. 23An investigation was made, the two men found guilty, and impaled alive. This was all duly recorded in the book of the history of King Ahasuerus' reign.

2:20
Esth 2:10

2:21
Esth 1:10; 6:2

2:22
Esth 6:1,2

2:23
Ezra 6:11
Esth 5:14
6:1,2; 7:10

2. The Jews are threatened
Haman plans to exterminate the Jews

3 Soon afterwards King Ahasuerus appointed Haman (son of Hammedatha the Agagite), as prime minister. He was the most powerful official in the empire next to the king himself. 2Now all the king's officials bowed before him in deep reverence whenever he passed by, for so the king had commanded. But Mordecai refused to bow.

3, 4"Why are you disobeying the king's commandment?" the others demanded day after day, but he still refused. Finally they spoke to Haman about it, to see whether Mordecai could get away with it because of his being a Jew, which was the excuse he had given them. 5, 6Haman was furious, but decided not to lay hands on Mordecai alone, but to move against all of Mordecai's people, the Jews, and destroy all of them throughout the whole kingdom of Ahasuerus.

7The most propitious time for this action was determined by throwing dice. This was done in April of the twelfth year of the reign of Ahasuerus, and February of the following year was the date indicated.

8Haman now approached the king about the matter. "There is a certain race of people scattered through all the provinces of your kingdom," he began, "and their laws are different from those of any other nation, and they refuse to obey the king's laws; therefore, it is not in the king's interest to let them live. 9If it please the king, issue a decree that they be destroyed, and I will pay $20,000,000 into the royal treasury for the expenses involved in this purge."

10The king agreed, confirming his decision by removing his ring from his finger

3:1
Num 24:3-9
1 Sam 15:8,
31-33
Esth 3:10; 5:11
7:6; 8:2
9:24,25; 10:3
Dan 6:2

3:2
Esth 5:9

3:7
Esth 9:24-26
Prov 16:33
Ezek 21:21,22
Mt 27:35

3:8
Acts 16:20,21

3:9
Esth 4:7

3:10
Esth 8:2,9,10

2:23 *impaled alive,* literally, "hanged on a tree." Possibly the meaning is that they were crucified. **3:10** *to Haman,* literally, "Haman, son of Hammedatha the Agagite."

2:23 A common form of punishment in Esther's day was to be impaled on a sharpened stake and left to die.

3:2 Mordecai's faith was based on conviction. He did not first take a poll to determine the safest or most popular course of action; he had the courage to stand alone. Doing what is right is not always popular. Those who do right will be in the minority, but to obey God is more important than to obey people (Acts 5:29).

3:2-4 Mordecai refused to bow to Haman. Jews did bow to government authorities, at times, as a sign of respect (Genesis 23:7; 1 Samuel 24:8). But in Persia, kings and their chief officials were considered divine. Mordecai was not about to kneel before wicked Haman and, by his act, acknowledge him as a god. Daniel's three friends had the same convictions (Daniel 3). Our worship must be reserved for God alone. We should never let any person take the place of God. When people demand loyalties or duties from you that do not honor God, don't give in. It may be time to take a stand.

3:5, 6 Haman enjoyed the power of his position, and he was enraged when Mordecai did not respond with the expected reverential bow. Haman's anger was not just toward Mordecai, but toward what Mordecai stood for—the Jews' dedication to God as the only authority worthy of reverence. Haman's attitude was prejudicial, hating a group of people because of a difference in belief or culture. Prejudice grows out of personal pride—considering yourself better than others. In the end, Haman was punished for his

arrogant attitude (7:9, 10). God will harshly judge those who are prejudiced or who have a prideful attitude toward others (Proverbs 18:12; Isaiah 23:8, 9; 1 Timothy 3:6).

3:5, 6 Why did Haman want to destroy all Jews just because of one man's action? As second in command in the Empire (3:1), Haman loved his power and authority and the reverence shown him. The Jews, however, looked to God as their final authority, not to any man. Haman realized that the only way to fulfill his prideful desires was to kill all those who looked to a higher authority than himself and the king. His quest for personal power led him to an all-consuming racial hatred.

3:7 Haman threw dice (or cast lots) to determine the best day to carry out his decree. Little did he know that he was playing into the hands of God, for the day of death was set for almost a year away, giving Esther time to make her plea to the king. The Persian word for dice, or lots, is *purim,* which became the name for the holiday celebrated by the Jews when they were delivered, instead of killed, on the day appointed by Haman.

3:9 Haman must have hoped to acquire this tremendous sum of money by plundering the homes and businesses of the Jews who would be killed through his decree.

3:10, 12 Officials in the ancient world used signet rings as personal signatures. The ring's surface had a raised imprint made of metal, wood, or bone; Ahasuerus' was probably made of silver or gold. Each individual had his own imprint. Letters were sealed

and giving it to Haman, telling him, 11"Keep the money, but go ahead and do as you like with these people—whatever you think best."

3:12
1 Kgs 21:8
Esth 1:22
8:8-10

12Two or three weeks later, Haman called in the king's secretaries and dictated letters to the governors and officials throughout the empire, to each province in its own languages and dialects; these letters were signed in the name of King Ahasuerus and sealed with his ring.

3:13
Esth 1:1,2
8:9-11,14
9:2,7-10,17
Isa 10:5,6

13They were then sent by messengers into all the provinces of the empire, decreeing that the Jews—young and old, women and children—must all be killed

3:12 *two or three weeks later,* literally, "Then, on the thirteenth day of the first month."

MORDECAI

Following Jerusalem's last stand against Nebuchadnezzar, Mordecai's family was deported to Babylon. He was probably born in Shushan and inherited an official position among the Jewish captives that kept him around the palace even after the Babylonians had been conquered by the Persians. At one time, when he overheard plans to assassinate King Ahasuerus, he reported the plot and saved the king's life.

Mordecai's life was filled with challenges that he turned into opportunities. When his aunt and uncle died, he adopted Esther, their daughter and his young cousin, probably because his own parents were dead and he felt responsible for her. Later, when she was drafted into Ahasuerus' harem and chosen to be queen, Mordecai continued to advise her. Shortly after this, he found himself in conflict with Ahasuerus' recently appointed Prime Minister, Haman. Although willing to serve the king, Mordecai refused to worship the king's representative, Haman. Haman was furious with Mordecai. So he planned to have Mordecai and all the Jews killed. His plan became a law of the Medes and Persians, and it looked as though the Jews were doomed.

But Mordecai, willing to be God's servant where he was, responded by contacting Esther and telling her that one reason God had allowed her to be queen might well be to save her people from this threat. But God had also placed *him* in the right place years earlier. God revealed to the king through his reading in the archives that Mordecai had once saved his life, and the king realized that he had never thanked Mordecai. The great honor then given to Mordecai ruined Haman's plan to hang him on the gallows. God had woven an effective counter-strategy against which Haman's plan could not stand.

Later, Mordecai instituted the Jewish Feast of Purim. He had a lengthy career of service to the king on behalf of the Jews. In Mordecai's life, God blended both character and circumstances to accomplish great things. He has not changed the way he works. God is using the situations you face each day to weave a pattern of godliness into your character. Pause and ask God to help you respond appropriately to the situations you find yourself in today.

Strengths and accomplishments:
• Exposed an assassination plot against the king
• Cared enough to adopt his cousin
• Refused to bow to anyone except God
• Took Haman's place as Prime Minister

Lessons from his life:
• The opportunities we have are more important than the ones we wish we had
• We can trust God to weave together the events of life for our best, even though we may not be able to see the overall pattern
• The rewards for doing right are sometimes delayed, but they are guaranteed by God himself

Vital statistics:
• Where: Shushan, one of several capital cities in Persia
• Occupation: Jewish official who became Prime Minister under Ahasuerus
• Relatives: Adopted daughter: Esther. Father: Jair.
• Contemporaries: Ahasuerus, Haman

Key verse:
"Mordecai the Jew was the Prime Minister, with authority next to that of King Ahasuerus himself. He was, of course, very great among the Jews, and respected by all his countrymen because he did his best for his people, and was a friend at court for all of them" (Esther 10:3).

Mordecai's story is told in the book of Esther.

---

by the ring pressed into soft wax, and official documents were certified by using the royal signet. By giving Haman his signet ring, Ahasuerus gave him his personal signature and with it the authority to do whatever he wished. Little did the king realize that his own signature would sign the death warrant for his wife, Esther.

3:13 Haman's death decree was against all Jews in the Persian Empire; this included Israel. If his decree had been carried out, all of God's chosen people could have been exterminated and God's plan to send his son to earth as a Jew could have been ruined. But God's plans cannot be stopped (Job 42:2).

on the 28th day of February of the following year, and their property given to those who killed them. 14"A copy of this edict," the letter stated, "must be proclaimed as law in every province, and made known to all your people, so that they will be ready to do their duty on the appointed day." 15The edict went out by the king's speediest couriers, after being first proclaimed in the city of Shushan. Then the king and Haman sat down for a drinking spree as the city fell into confusion and panic.

3:14
Esth 4:8
8:13,14

3:15
Esth 1:1-3

Mordecai asks Esther to help

4 When Mordecai learned what had been done, he tore his clothes and put on sackcloth and ashes, and went out into the city, crying with a loud and bitter wail. 2Then he stood outside the gate of the palace, for no one was permitted to enter in mourning clothes. 3And throughout all the provinces there was great mourning among the Jews, fasting, weeping, and despair at the king's decree; and many lay in sackcloth and ashes.

4:1
Gen 27:34
2 Sam 1:11
13:19
Isa 15:4
Ezek 27:30
Jonah 3:4-9
Mic 1:8

4When Esther's maids and eunuchs came and told her about Mordecai, she was deeply distressed and sent clothing to him to replace the sackcloth, but he refused it. 5Then Esther sent for Hathach, one of the king's eunuchs who had been appointed as her attendant, and told him to go out to Mordecai and find out what the trouble was, and why he was acting like that. 6So Hathach went out to the city square, and found Mordecai just outside the palace gates, 7and heard the whole story from him; and about the $20,000,000 Haman had promised to pay into the king's treasury for the destruction of the Jews. 8Mordecai also gave Hathach a copy of the king's decree dooming all Jews, and told him to show it to Esther and to tell her what was happening, and that she should go to the king to plead for her people. 9So Hathach returned to Esther with Mordecai's message. 10Esther told Hathach to go back and say to Mordecai,

4:7
Esth 3:9

4:8
Esth 3:14
8:13,14

11"All the world knows that anyone, whether man or woman, who goes into the king's inner court without his summons is doomed to die unless the king holds out his gold scepter; and the king has not called for me to come to him in more than a month."

4:11
Esth 5:1,2; 8:4

12So Hathach gave Esther's message to Mordecai.

13This was Mordecai's reply to Esther: "Do you think you will escape there in the palace, when all other Jews are killed? 14If you keep quiet at a time like this, God will deliver the Jews from some other source, but you and your relatives will die; what's more, who can say but that God has brought you into the palace for just such a time as this?"

4:11—5:2 Esther risked her life by coming before the king. Her courageous act is a model for us to follow in approaching a difficult or dangerous task. We should: (1) *Calculate the cost.* Esther realized her life was at stake. (2) *Set priorities.* She believed that the safety of the Jewish race was more important than her life. (3) *Prepare.* She gathered support and fasted. (4) *Determine our course of action and move ahead boldly.* She didn't think too long about it, allowing the interlude to lessen her commitment to what she had to do.

Do you have to face a hostile audience, confront a friend on a delicate subject, or talk to your family about changes to be made? Rather than dreading difficult situations or putting them off, take action with confidence by following Esther's inspiring example.

4:13 Although Esther was the queen and shared some of the king's power and wealth, her position did not mean she didn't need God's protection and wisdom. No human is secure in his own strength in any political system. It is foolish to believe that wealth or position can make us impervious to danger.

4:13–17 Esther and Mordecai believed that God would deliver his people, but they didn't just sit around and wait. They took action. Although God is sovereign, he works through people. That is why we must *do* his will, not just watch and pray. Many people believe

God's promises, but they hesitate to get involved. Esther, however, determined to see the king, and Mordecai carried out her instructions. Don't wait for others to do for you what you can do. *Get involved* and enjoy the results of sharing in God's purposes for mankind.

4:13, 14 After the decree to kill the Jews was given, Mordecai and Esther could have despaired, decided to save only themselves, or just waited for God's intervention. Instead, they saw that God had placed them in their positions for a purpose, so they seized the moment and acted. When it is within our reach to save others, we must do so. In a life-threatening situation, don't withdraw, behave selfishly, wallow in despair, or wait for God to fix everything. Instead, ask God for his direction and *act!* God may have placed you where you are for such a time as this.

4:14 In the ancient manuscripts, God is not specifically mentioned in the book of Esther. The literal translation of "God will deliver the Jews from some other source" is "deliverance will arise from another source." God is named in this translation, however, because it is obvious that Mordecai was referring to him. While the book of Esther does not mention God directly, it is filled with his presence. Esther and Mordecai believed in God's care, and, because they acted at the right time, God used them to save his people.

4:16
2 Chron 20:3
Joel 2:2-17
Jonah 3:4-9

15Then Esther said to tell Mordecai:

16"Go and gather together all the Jews of Shushan and fast for me; do not eat or drink for three days, night or day; and I and my maids will do the same; and then, though it is strictly forbidden, I will go in to see the king; and if I perish, I perish."

17So Mordecai did as Esther told him to.

3. Esther intercedes for the Jews
Esther appears before the king

5:1
Esth 4:11

5 Three days later Esther put on her royal robes and entered the inner court just beyond the royal hall of the palace, where the king was sitting upon his royal

5:2
Esth 4:11; 8:4

throne. 2And when he saw Queen Esther standing there in the inner court, he welcomed her, holding out the golden scepter to her. So Esther approached and touched its tip.

5:3
1 Kgs 2:20
Esth 5:6; 7:2
9:12
Mt 20:20-22
Lk 18:41

3Then the king asked her, "What do you wish, Queen Esther? What is your request? I will give it to you, even if it is half the kingdom!"

4And Esther replied, "If it please Your Majesty, I want you and Haman to come to a banquet I have prepared for you today."

5:5
Esth 6:14

5The king turned to his aides. "Tell Haman to hurry!" he said. So the king and Haman came to Esther's banquet.

6During the wine course the king said to Esther, "Now tell me what you really want, and I will give it to you, even if it is half of the kingdom!"

GOD BEHIND THE SCENES IN ESTHER
Although God's name is not mentioned in the Hebrew text of Esther, he makes himself known in these ways:

Divine Incidents
The book of Esther is filled with divine interventions:

Indirect References		
4:14	In the Hebrew text God's existence and his power over the affairs of men are assumed. (Because of this, the Living Bible includes God's name.)
4:16	Fasting was a distinct spiritual activity usually connected with prayer.
9:22	"The Jews were saved" raises the question, "Who saved them?"
2:17	Esther, a Jew in exile, becomes queen
2:21, 22	Mordecai overhears a death plot and saves the king's life
6:1	Ahasuerus can't sleep, decides to read a history book
6:2	Ahasuerus reads the exact page needed for the moment, reminding him of an unpaid reward to Mordecai
7:9, 10	Haman's plan is exactly reversed—the intended victims are the victors

Why was God's name hidden in the book of Esther? There were many gods in the Middle East and Persian Empire. Usually, their names were mentioned in official documents in order to control the peoples who worshiped those particular gods. The Jews were unique in being the people of one God. A story about them was naturally a story about God, for even the name "Jew" carried with it the connotation of one who worshiped Jehovah.

4:16 By calling for a fast, Esther was asking the Jews to pray for God's help on her dangerous mission. An important function of a community of believers is mutual support in difficult times. When you are experiencing struggles, turn to fellow believers for support by sharing your trials with them and gaining strength from the bond you share. And when others need your support, give it willingly.

4:16 *Save your own skin* and *Watch out for number one* are mottoes that reflect the world's selfish outlook on life. Esther's attitude stands in sharp contrast to this. She knew what she had to do and that it could cost her life. And yet she responded, "If I perish, I perish." We should have the same commitment to do what is right despite the possible consequences. Faith is doing what

God wants and trusting him to work out the results. Do you try to save your own skin by remaining silent rather than standing up for what is right? Commit yourself to do what God wants and trust him for the outcome.

4:17—5:1 God was in control, yet Mordecai and Esther had to decide to act. We cannot understand how both can be true at the same time, and yet they are. Possibly it is because God chooses to work through those *willing* to act for him. We should pray as if all depended on God and act as if all depended on us. We should avoid two extremes: doing nothing and feeling that we must do it all.

7, 8Esther replied, "My request, my deepest wish, is that if Your Majesty loves me, and wants to grant my request, that you come again with Haman tomorrow to the banquet I shall prepare for you. And tomorrow I will explain what this is all about."

Haman becomes furious with Mordecai

9What a happy man was Haman as he left the banquet! But when he saw Mordecai there at the gate, not standing up or trembling before him, he was furious. 10However, he restrained himself and went on home and gathered together his friends and Zeresh his wife, 11and boasted to them about his wealth, and his many children, and promotions the king had given him, and how he had become the greatest man in the kingdom next to the king himself.

12Then he delivered his punch line: "Yes, and Esther the queen invited only me and the king himself to the banquet she prepared for us; and tomorrow we are invited again! 13But yet," he added, "all this is nothing when I see Mordecai the Jew just sitting there in front of the king's gate, refusing to bow to me."

14"Well," suggested Zeresh his wife and all his friends, "get ready a 75-foot-high gallows, and in the morning ask the king to let you hang Mordecai on it; and when this is done you can go on your merry way with the king to the banquet." This pleased Haman immensely and he ordered the gallows built.

5:9
Esth 3:2

5:10
Esth 5:14; 6:13

5:14
Esth 5:10; 7:9

The king honors Mordecai

6 That night the king had trouble sleeping and decided to read awhile. He ordered the historical records of his kingdom from the library, and in them he came across the item telling how Mordecai had exposed the plot of Bigthana and Teresh, two of the king's eunuchs, watchmen at the palace gates, who had plotted to assassinate him.

3"What reward did we ever give Mordecai for this?" the king asked.

His courtiers replied, "Nothing!"

4"Who is on duty in the outer court?" the king inquired. Now, as it happened, Haman had just arrived in the outer court of the palace to ask the king to hang Mordecai from the gallows he was building.

5So the courtiers replied to the king, "Haman is out there."

"Bring him in," the king ordered. 6So Haman came in and the king said to him, "What should I do to honor a man who truly pleases me?"

Haman thought to himself, "Whom would he want to honor more than me?" 7, 8So he replied, "Bring out some of the royal robes the king himself has worn, and the king's own horse, and the royal crown, 9and instruct one of the king's most noble princes to robe the man and to lead him through the streets on the king's own horse, shouting before him, 'This is the way the king honors those who truly please him!' "

6:1
Esth 2:21-23

6:7
1 Kgs 1:33
Zech 9:9

6:9
Gen 41:43
1 Kgs 1:34

5:9 Hatred and bitterness are like weeds with long roots that grow in the heart and corrupt all of life. Haman was so consumed with hatred toward Mordecai that he could not even enjoy the honor of being invited to Esther's party. Scripture warns us to "watch out that no bitterness takes root among you, for as it springs up it causes deep trouble, hurting many in their spiritual lives" (Hebrews 12:15). Don't let hatred and its resulting bitterness build in your heart. Like Haman, you will find it backfiring against you (see 6:13; 7:9, 10). If the mere mention of someone's name provokes you to anger, confess your bitterness as sin. Ignoring bitterness, hiding it from others, or making superficial changes in behavior is not enough. If bitterness isn't completely removed, it will grow back, making matters worse.

5:14 Haman's family and friends, who were as arrogant as he, suggested that the gallows be 75 feet high, built on the city wall or some prominent building. They wanted to make sure that all the

people of the city saw Mordecai's death and would be reminded of the consequences of disobeying Haman. Ironically, these high gallows allowed everyone to see Haman's death.

6:1, 2 When he couldn't sleep, King Ahasuerus may have fought sleeplessness through women, food, and music. But this night he decided to read. He had many choices of subjects, but he chose to read from the archives and discovered Mordecai's good deed. This seems coincidental, but God is *always* at work. God has been working quietly and patiently throughout your life. Many of the events that have worked together for good are more than mere coincidence; they are the result of God's involvement in the lives of his people.

6:7–9 Haman had wealth, but he craved something even his money couldn't buy—respect. He could buy the trappings of success and power, but his lust for popularity had become an obsession. Don't let your desire for approval, applause, and popularity drive you to immoral actions.

¹⁰"Excellent!" the king said to Haman. "Hurry and take these robes and my horse, and do just as you have said—to Mordecai the Jew, who works at the Chancellery. Follow every detail you have suggested."

¹¹So Haman took the robes and put them on Mordecai and mounted him on the king's own steed, and led him through the streets of the city, shouting, "This is the way the king honors those he delights in."

6:12
2 Sam 15:30
Esth 7:8
Jer 14:3
6:13
Esth 5:10,14

¹²Afterwards Mordecai returned to his job, but Haman hurried home utterly humiliated. ¹³When Haman told Zeresh his wife and all his friends what had happened, they said, "If Mordecai is a Jew, you will never succeed in your plans against him; to continue to oppose him will be fatal."

We treasure security, even though we know that security in this life carries no guarantees—possessions can be destroyed, beauty fades, relationships can be broken, death is inevitable. Real security, then, must be found beyond this life. Only when our security rests on God and his unchanging nature can we face the challenges that life is sure to bring our way.

Esther's beauty and character won King Ahasuerus' heart, and he made her his queen. Even in her favored position, however, she would risk her life by attempting to see the king when he had not requested her presence. Although she was queen, she was still not secure. But, cautiously and courageously, Esther decided to risk her life by approaching the king on behalf of her people. There was no guarantee that the king would even see her.

She made her plans carefully. The Jews were asked to fast and pray with her before she went to the king. Then on the chosen day she went before him, and he *did* ask her to come forward and speak. But instead of issuing her request directly, she invited him and Haman to a banquet. He was astute enough to realize she had something on her mind, yet she conveyed the importance of the matter by insisting on a second banquet.

In the meantime, God was working behind the scenes. He caused Ahasuerus to read the historical records of the kingdom late one night, and discovered that Mordecai had once saved his life. Ahasuerus lost no time in honoring Mordecai for that act. During the second banquet, Esther told the king of Haman's plot against the Jews, and he was doomed. There is grim justice in Haman's death on the gallows he had built for Mordecai. Esther's risk confirmed that God was the source of her security.

How much of your security lies in your possessions, position, or reputation? God has not placed you in your present position for your own benefit. He put you there *to serve him.* As in Esther's case, this may involve risking your security. Are you willing to let God be your ultimate security?

Strengths and accomplishments:
● Her beauty and character won the heart of Persia's king
● She combined courage with careful planning
● She was open to advice and willing to act
● She was more concerned for others than for her own security

Lessons from her life:
● Serving God often demands that we risk our own security
● God has a purpose for the situations in which he places us
● Courage, while often vital, does not replace careful planning

Vital statistics:
● Where: Persian Empire
● Occupation: Ahasuerus' wife, queen of Persia
● Relatives: Cousin: Mordecai. Husband: Ahasuerus. Father: Abihail.

Key verse:
"Go and gather together all the Jews of Shushan and fast for me; do not eat or drink for three days, night or day; and I and my maids will do the same; and then, though it is strictly forbidden, I will go in to see the king; and if I perish, I perish" (Esther 4:16).

Esther's story is told in the book of Esther.

6:10-13 Mordecai had uncovered a plot to assassinate Ahasuerus and thus saved the king's life (2:21-23). Although his good deed was recorded in the history books, Mordecai had gone unrewarded. But God was saving Mordecai's reward for the right time. Just as Haman was about to hang Mordecai unjustly, the king was ready to give the reward, and Mordecai's life was spared. Although God promises to reward our good works, we sometimes feel our "payoff" is too far away and we easily become dis-

couraged. Be patient. God steps in when it will do the most good.

6:12 Just the night before (5:9-14), Haman had bragged about his position and the honor he was about to receive. Now he was humiliated and soon to be marked for death (7:8-10). How quickly the course of life can change. Because we cannot predict what will happen, it is best to avoid bragging (James 4:13-16). God is displeased with this kind of self-confidence and self-reliance.

¹⁴While they were still discussing it with him, the king's messengers arrived to conduct Haman quickly to the banquet Esther had prepared.

6:14
Esth 5:5-8

The king hangs Haman

7 So the king and Haman came to Esther's banquet. ²Again, during the wine course, the king asked her, "What is your petition, Queen Esther? What do you wish? Whatever it is, I will give it to you, even if it is half of my kingdom!"

7:2
Esth 5:3,6
7:3-6

³And at last Queen Esther replied, "If I have won your favor, O king, and if it please Your Majesty, save my life and the lives of my people. ⁴For I and my people have been sold to those who will destroy us. We are doomed to destruction and slaughter. If we were only to be sold as slaves, perhaps I could remain quiet, though even then there would be incalculable damage to the king that no amount of money could begin to cover."

7:3
Esth 5:7,8; 8:5
7:4
Deut 28:68
Esth 3:9,13
4:7,8; 8:6

⁵"What are you talking about?" King Ahasuerus demanded. "Who would dare touch you?"

⁶Esther replied, "This wicked Haman is our enemy."

Then Haman grew pale with fright before the king and queen. ⁷The king jumped to his feet and went out into the palace garden as Haman stood up to plead for his life to Queen Esther, for he knew that he was doomed. ⁸In despair he fell upon the couch where Queen Esther was reclining, just as the king returned from the palace garden.

7:6
Esth 8:1

"Will he even rape the queen right here in the palace, before my very eyes?" the king roared. Instantly the death veil was placed over Haman's face.

⁹Then Harbona, one of the king's aides, said, "Sir, Haman has just ordered a 75-foot gallows constructed, to hang Mordecai, the man who saved the king from assassination! It stands in Haman's courtyard."

7:9
Esth 5:14

"Hang Haman on it," the king ordered.

¹⁰So they did, and the king's wrath was pacified.

7:10
Esth 8:7
9:24,25
Ps 7:16; 94:23

The king makes a decree for the Jews

8 On that same day King Ahasuerus gave the estate of Haman, the Jews' enemy, to Queen Esther. Then Mordecai was brought before the king, for Esther had told the king that he was her cousin and foster father. ²The king took off his ring—which he had taken back from Haman—and gave it to Mordecai [appointing him Prime Minister]; and Esther appointed Mordecai to be in charge of Haman's estate.

8:1
Esth 7:6
8:2
Esth 3:10
8:4
Esth 4:11; 5:2

³And now once more Esther came before the king, falling down at his feet and begging him with tears to stop Haman's plot against the Jews. ⁴And again the king held out the golden scepter to Esther. So she arose and stood before him, ⁵and said, "If it please Your Majesty, and if you love me, send out a decree reversing Haman's order to destroy the Jews throughout the king's provinces. ⁶For how can I endure it, to see my people butchered and destroyed?"

8:5
Esth 1:22
5:7,8; 7:3
8:9,10
8:6
Esth 3:13; 7:4
8:7
Esth 7:10; 8:1

⁷Then King Ahasuerus said to Queen Esther and Mordecai the Jew, "I have given Esther the palace of Haman and he has been hanged upon the gallows because he tried to destroy you. ⁸Now go ahead and send a message to the Jews, telling them

8:8
Esth 1:19
3:2,12
8:2,9,10,14
Dan 6:8-15,17

8:1 *he was her cousin and foster father,* literally, "had made known how they were related." **8:2** *appointing him Prime Minister,* implied.

7:6–10 Haman's hatred and evil plotting turned against him as his true intentions were discovered. He was hanged on the gallows he had built for someone else. Proverbs 26:27 says that a man who sets a trap for others will fall into it himself. What happened to Haman shows the often violent results of setting any kind of trap for others.

7:8 A veil was placed over the face of anyone condemned to death, because a Persian king refused to look upon the face of a condemned man.

8:1–7 While we should not expect earthly rewards for being faithful to God, they often come. Esther and Mordecai were faithful, even to the point of risking their lives to save others. When they were willing to give up everything, God gave them a reward in proportion to their all-out commitment.

8:8 Haman's message had been sealed with the king's ring and could not be reversed, even by the king. It was part of the famed "law of the Medes and Persians." Now the king gave permission for whatever other decree Mordecai could devise that would offset the first, without actually canceling it.

8:12 This was the day set by Haman for the extermination of the Jews.

whatever you want to in the king's name, and seal it with the king's ring, so that it can never be reversed."

8:9
Esth 1:1,2,22
3:12; 8:8

9, 10Immediately the king's secretaries were called in—it was now the 23rd day of the month of July—and they wrote as Mordecai dictated—a decree to the Jews and to the officials, governors, and princes of all the provinces from India to Ethiopia, 127 in all: the decree was translated into the languages and dialects of all the people of the kingdom. Mordecai wrote in the name of King Ahasuerus and sealed the message with the king's ring and sent the letters by swift carriers—riders on camels, mules, and young dromedaries used in the king's service. 11This decree gave the Jews everywhere permission to unite in the defense of their lives and their families, to destroy all the forces opposed to them, and to take their property. 12The day chosen for this throughout all the provinces of King Ahasuerus was the 28th day of February! 13It further stated that a copy of this decree, which must be recognized everywhere as law, must be broadcast to all the people so that the Jews would be ready and prepared to overcome their enemies. 14So the mail went out

8:11
Esth 9:2

8:12
Esth 3:13
9:1,17

8:13
Esth 3:14; 4:8

HAMAN

The most arrogant people are often those who must measure their self-worth by the power or influence they think they have over others. Haman was an extremely arrogant leader. He recognized the king as his superior, but could not accept anyone as an equal. When one man, Mordecai, refused to bow in submission to him, Haman wanted to destroy him. He became consumed with hatred for Mordecai and, in turn, for all the Jewish people. Mordecai's dedication to God and his refusal to give homage to any human person challenged Haman's self-centered religion. Haman saw the Jews as a threat to his power, and he decided to kill them all.

God was preparing Haman's downfall and the protection of his people long before Haman had become Prime Minister under King Ahasuerus. Esther, a Jewess, became queen, and Mordecai's role in exposing an assassination plot had made the king indebted to him. Not only was Haman prevented from killing Mordecai, he also had to suffer the humiliation of publicly honoring him. Within hours, Haman died on the gallows he had built to hang Mordecai and his plan to wipe out the Jews was thwarted. In contrast to Esther, who risked everything for God and won, Haman risked everything for an evil purpose and lost.

Our initial response to the story about Haman is to say that he got what he deserved. But the Bible leads us to ask deeper questions, "How much of Haman is in me?" "Do I desire to control others?" "Am I threatened when others don't appreciate me as I think they should?" "Do I want revenge when my pride is attacked?" Confess these attitudes to God and ask him to replace them with an attitude of forgiveness. Otherwise, God's justice will settle the matter.

Accomplishment:
• Achieved great power, second in command to Persia's King Ahasuerus

Weaknesses and mistakes:
• The desire to control others and receive honor was his highest goal
• Was blinded by arrogance and self-importance
• Planned to murder Mordecai and built a gallows for him
• Orchestrated the plan to slaughter God's people throughout the Empire

Lessons from his life:
• Hatred will be punished
• God has an amazing record for making evil plans backfire on the planners
• Pride and self-importance will be punished
• An insatiable thirst for power and prestige is self-destructive

Vital statistics:
• Where: Sushan, the capital of Persia
• Occupation: Prime Minister
• Relative: Wife: Zeresh
• Contemporaries: Ahasuerus, Mordecai, Esther

Key verses:
"Haman was furious, but decided not to lay hands on Mordecai alone, but to move against all of Mordecai's people, the Jews, and destroy all of them throughout the whole kingdom of Ahasuerus" (Esther 3:5, 6).

Haman's story is told in the book of Esther.

swiftly, carried by the king's couriers and speeded by the king's commandment. The same decree was also issued at Shushan Palace.

15Then Mordecai put on the royal robes of blue and white and the great crown of gold, with an outer cloak of fine linen and purple, and went out from the presence of the king through the city streets filled with shouting people. 16And the Jews had joy and gladness, and were honored everywhere. 17And in every city and province, as the king's decree arrived, the Jews were filled with joy and had a great celebration and declared a holiday. And many of the people of the land pretended to be Jews, for they feared what the Jews might do to them.

8:15
Esth 1:6; 5:1
6:8,11
Lk 16:19

8:17
Esth 9:19-31
Zech 8:20-23

4. The Jews are delivered
The Jews triumph over their enemies

9 So on the 28th day of February, the day the two decrees of the king were to be put into effect—the day the Jews' enemies had hoped to vanquish them, though it turned out quite to the contrary—the Jews gathered in their cities throughout all the king's provinces to defend themselves against any who might try to harm them; but no one tried, for they were greatly feared. 3And all the rulers of the provinces—the governors, officials, and aides—helped the Jews for fear of Mordecai; 4for Mordecai was a mighty name in the king's palace and his fame was known throughout all the provinces, for he had become more and more powerful.

5But the Jews went ahead on that appointed day and slaughtered their enemies. 6They even killed 500 men in Shushan. 7–10They also killed the ten sons of Haman (son of Hammedatha), the Jews' enemy—Parshandatha, Dalphon, Aspatha, Poratha, Adalia, Aridatha, Parmashta, Arisai, Aridai, and Vaizatha.

But they did not try to take Haman's property.

11Late that evening, when the king was informed of the number of those slain in Shushan, 12he called for Queen Esther. "The Jews have killed 500 men in Shushan alone," he exclaimed, "and also Haman's ten sons. If they have done that here, I wonder what has happened in the rest of the provinces! But now, what more do you want? It will be granted to you. Tell me and I will do it."

13And Esther said, "If it please Your Majesty, let the Jews who are here at Shushan do again tomorrow as they have done today, and let Haman's ten sons be hanged upon the gallows."

14So the king agreed, and the decree was announced at Shushan, and they hung up the bodies of Haman's ten sons. 15Then the Jews at Shushan gathered together the next day also and killed 300 more men, though again they took no property.

9:1
Esth 3:13
8:11,12; 9:17

9:3
Esth 8:17

9:5
Esth 3:13
9:6-16

9:7
Esth 9:12,13,
24,25

The Feast of Purim is inaugurated

16Meanwhile, the other Jews throughout the king's provinces had gathered together and stood for their lives and destroyed all their enemies, killing 75,000 of those who hated them; but they did not take their goods. 17Throughout the provinces this was done on the 28th day of February, and the next day they rested, celebrating their victory with feasting and gladness. 18But the Jews at Shushan went on killing their enemies the second day also, and rested the next day, with feasting and gladness. 19And so it is that the Jews in the unwalled villages

9:17
Esth 3:13; 8:12
9:1

9:19
Neh 8:10
Esth 8:17
9:20-31

8:15–17 Everyone wants to be a hero and receive praise, honor, and wealth. But few are willing to pay the price. Mordecai served the government faithfully for years, bore Haman's hatred and oppression, and risked his life for his people. The price to be paid by God's heroes is long-term commitment. Are you ready or willing to pay the price?

9:5–16 Haman had decreed that on February 28, anyone could kill the Jews and take their property. Mordecai's decree could not reverse Haman's because no law signed by the king could be repealed. Instead, Mordecai had the king sign a new law giving Jews the right to fight back. When the dreaded day arrived, there was much fighting, but the Jews killed only those who wanted to kill them, and they did not take their enemies' possessions even

though they could have (8:11; 9:10, 16). There were no additional riots after the two-day slaughter, so obviously selfish gain or revenge were not primary motives of the Jews. They simply wanted to defend themselves and their families from those who hated them.

9:19–22 People tend to have short memories when it comes to God's faithfulness. To help counter this, Mordecai wrote down these events and encouraged an annual holiday to commemorate the historic day of Purim. Celebrations of feasting, gladness, and gift-giving are important ways to remember God's specific acts. Today we celebrate holidays commemorating great events like the birth and resurrection of Jesus Christ. Don't let the celebration or the exchanging of gifts hide the meaning of these great events.

throughout Israel to this day have an annual celebration on the second day, when they rejoice and send gifts to each other.

20Mordecai wrote a history of all these events, and sent letters to the Jews near and far, throughout all the king's provinces, 21encouraging them to declare an annual holiday on the last two days of the month, 22to celebrate with feasting, gladness, and the giving of gifts these historic days when the Jews were saved from their enemies, when their sorrow was turned to gladness and their mourning into happiness.

23So the Jews adopted Mordecai's suggestion and began this annual custom, 24, 25as a reminder of the time when Haman (son of Hammedatha the Agagite), the enemy of all the Jews, had plotted to destroy them at the time determined by a throw of the dice; and to remind them that when the matter came before the king, he issued a decree causing Haman's plot to boomerang, and he and his sons were hanged on the gallows. 26That is why this celebration is called "Purim," because the word for "throwing dice" in Persian is "pur." 27All the Jews throughout the realm agreed to inaugurate this tradition and to pass it on to their descendants and to all who became Jews; they declared they would never fail to celebrate these two

9:24
Esth 3:1,7
7:9,10; 8:7
9:12,13

9:26
Esth 3:7

9:27
Esth 9:20,21

HOW GOD WORKS IN THE WORLD	God's will	What God wants done—He works through ...		
	God's action	♥Natural order	♥Miracles	♥Providence
		♥God set into action through creation a normal working of his universe. He also revealed his expectations of man through his Word and man's conscience.	♥God breaks into the natural order to respond to the expressed needs of people.	♥God overrules the natural order to accomplish an act which people may or may not have requested.
	Examples from Esther	♥God gave Esther natural beauty.	♥God allowed Esther to speak to the king.	♥God allowed Mordecai to overhear a plot.
		♠Esther planned a way to save her people.	♠The people prayed and fasted.	♠Mordecai trusted God to accomplish what was impossible in human terms.
	Man's will	What man wants done—He either ...		
		♠Plans	♠Prays	♠Trusts & Obeys
	Action we can take	♠Can make plans based on the order and dependability of God's creation. Know and obey his words.	♠Can ask God to intervene in certain affairs while realizing that our knowledge and perspective are limited.	♠Can trust that God is in control even when the circumstances may not seem to indicate that he is.
		or ...		
	Mistakes we can make	♥Disobeys	♥Demands	♥Despairs
		♥Can violate the natural order, disobey God's commands.	♥Can assume that we understand what is needed and expect God to agree and answer our prayers that way.	♥Can assume God doesn't answer prayer or respond to our needs and live as though there is nothing but the natural order.

days at the appointed time each year. 28It would be an annual event from generation to generation, celebrated by every family throughout the countryside and cities of the empire, so that the memory of what had happened would never perish from the Jewish race.

29, 30, 31Meanwhile, Queen Esther (daughter of Abihail and later adopted by Mordecai the Jew) had written a letter throwing her full support behind Mordecai's letter inaugurating his annual Feast of Purim. In addition, letters were sent to all the Jews throughout the 127 provinces of the kingdom of Ahasuerus with messages of good will, and encouragement to confirm these two days annually as the Feast of Purim, decreed by both Mordecai the Jew and by Queen Esther; indeed, the Jews themselves had decided upon this tradition as a remembrance of the time of their national fasting and prayer. 32So the commandment of Esther confirmed these dates and it was recorded as law.

Mordecai is given great authority

10 King Ahasuerus not only laid tribute upon the mainland, but even on the islands of the sea. 2His great deeds, and also the full account of the greatness of Mordecai and the honors given him by the king, are written in *The Book of the Chronicles of the Kings of Media and Persia*. 3Mordecai the Jew was the Prime Minister, with authority next to that of King Ahasuerus himself. He was, of course, very great among the Jews, and respected by all his countrymen because he did his best for his people, and was a friend at court for all of them.

9:28
Esth 9:23

9:29
Esth 1:1,2
8:9,10
9:23,26-28

10:2
Esth 2:23; 6:1

10:3
Gen 41:43,44
Esth 5:11; 8:2
Dan 6:2

9:29–31 Among Jews, women were expected to be quiet, to serve in the home, and to stay on the fringe of religious and political life. But Esther was a Jewish woman who broke through the cultural norms, stepping outside her expected role to risk her life to help God's people. Whatever your place in life, God can use you. Be open, available, and ready, because God may use you to do what others are afraid even to consider.

10:3 Mordecai enjoyed a good reputation among the Jews because he was still their friend when he rose to a place of power. Corruption and abuse of authority often characterize those in power. But power used to lift the fallen and ease the burden of the oppressed is power used well. Those people whom God places in positions of power or political influence must not turn their backs on those in need.

10:3 There are no archeological records of Mordecai's being Prime Minister, but during this time there is a strange gap in

ancient Persian records. The records indicate that another man became Prime Minister in 465 B.C., about seven years after Mordecai was first appointed. One tablet has been discovered naming Mardukaya as an official in the early years of Ahasuerus' reign; some believe this was Mordecai.

10:3 In the book of Esther, we clearly see God at work in the lives of individuals and in the affairs of a nation. Even when it looks as if the world is in the hands of evil men, God is still in control, protecting those who are his. Although we may not understand everything happening around us, we must trust in God's protection and retain our integrity by doing what we know is right. Esther, who risked her life appearing before the king, became a heroine. Mordecai, who was on "death row" (so to speak), rose to become the Prime Minister of the nation. No matter how hopeless our condition, or how much we would like to give up, we need not despair. God is in control of our world.

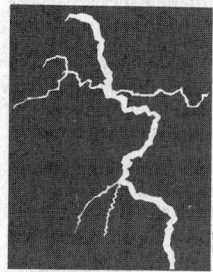

TREES are wrenched from the earth, telephone poles snap like toothpicks, walls collapse, and water engulfs the land. Only solid foundations can survive the unbridled fury of a hurricane. But those foundations can be used for rebuilding after the storm.

For any building, the foundation is critical. It must be deep enough and solid enough to withstand the structural stresses placed upon it. Lives are like buildings: the quality of the foundation determines the ability to cope with difficulties. Too often, inferior materials are used and, when tests come, lives crumble.

The book of Job is a gripping drama of riches-to-rags-to-riches, a theological treatise about suffering and divine sovereignty, and a picture of faith that endures. Job was tested. But his life was built on God, and he endured. As you read Job, analyze your life and make sure that God is your foundation.

Job is a prosperous farmer living in the land of Uz. He has thousands of sheep, camels, and other livestock, a large family, and a lot of servants. Suddenly Satan, the Accuser, comes before God claiming that Job trusts God only because he is wealthy and everything is going well for him. And so the testing of Job's faith begins.

Satan is allowed to destroy Job's children, servants, livestock, herdsmen, and home; but Job continues to trust in God. Next Satan attacks Job physically, covering him with painful boils. Job's wife tells him to curse God and die (2:9), but Job suffers in silence.

Three of Job's friends, Eliphaz, Bildad, and Zophar, come to visit him. At first they silently grieve with Job. But when they begin to talk about the reasons for Job's tragedies, they tell him that sin caused his suffering. He should confess his sins and turn back to God. But Job maintains his innocence.

Unable to convince Job of his sin, the three men fall silent (32:1). At this point, another voice—the young Elihu—enters the debate. But his argument is similar to that of the three older men, so no one bothers to answer him.

Finally, God speaks out of a mighty whirlwind. Confronted with the great power and majesty of God, Job falls in humble reverence before God—speechless. God rebukes Job's friends, and the drama ends with Job restored to happiness and wealth.

It is easy to think that we have all the answers. In reality, only God knows exactly why things happen as they do, and we must submit to him as our Sovereign. As you read this book, emulate Job and decide to trust God no matter what happens.

VITAL STATISTICS

PURPOSE:
To demonstrate God's sovereignty and the meaning of true faith. It addresses the question, "Why do the righteous suffer?"

AUTHOR:
Possibly Job. Some have suggested Moses, Solomon, or Elihu.

DATE WRITTEN:
Unknown. Records events which probably occurred during the time of the patriarchs, approximately 2000–1800 B.C.

SETTING:
The land of Uz, probably located northeast of Palestine, near desert land between Damascus and the Euphrates River

KEY VERSE:
" 'Well, have you noticed my servant Job?' the Lord asked. 'He is the finest man in all the earth—a good man who fears God and turns away from all evil. And he has kept his faith in me despite the fact that you persuaded me to let you harm him without any cause' " (2:3).

KEY PEOPLE:
Job, Eliphaz the Temanite, Bildad the Shuhite, Zophar the Naamathite, Elihu the Buzite

SPECIAL FEATURES:
Job is the first of the poetic books in the Hebrew Bible. Many believe this to be the oldest book in the Bible. The book gives us insights into the work of Satan. Ezekiel 14:14, 20 and James 5:11 mention Job as an historical character.

THE BLUEPRINT

A. JOB IS TESTED (1:1—2:13)

Job, a wealthy and upright man, loses his possessions, his children, and his health. Job did not understand why he was suffering. Why does God allow his children to suffer? Although there is an explanation, we may not know it while we are here on earth. In the meantime, we must always be ready for testing in our lives.

B. THREE FRIENDS ANSWER JOB (3:1—31:40)
1. First round of discussion
2. Second round of discussion
3. Third round of discussion

Job's friends wrongly assumed that suffering always came as a result of sin. With this in mind, they tried to persuade Job to repent of his sin. Because the three friends were wrong, we know that suffering is not always a direct result of personal sin. When we experience severe suffering, it may not be our fault, so we don't have to add to our pain by feeling guilty that some hidden sin is causing our trouble.

C. A YOUNG MAN ANSWERS JOB (32:1—37:24)

A young man named Elihu, who has been listening to the entire conversation, criticizes the three friends for being unable to answer Job. He says that although Job was a good man, he had allowed himself to become proud, and God was punishing him in order to humble him. This answer was partially true because suffering does purify our faith. But God is beyond our comprehension and we cannot know why he allows each instance of suffering to come into our lives. Our part is to simply remain faithful.

D. GOD ANSWERS JOB (38:1—41:34)

God himself finally answers Job. God is in control of the world and only he understands why the good are allowed to suffer. This only becomes clear to us when we see God for who he is. We must courageously accept what God allows to happen in our lives and remain firmly committed to him.

E. JOB IS RESTORED (42:1–17)

Job finally learned that when nothing else was left, he had God, and that was enough. Through suffering, we learn that God is enough for our lives and our future. We must love God regardless of whether he allows blessing or suffering to come to us. Testing is difficult, but the result is often a deeper relationship with God. Those who endure the testing of their faith will experience God's great rewards in the end.

MEGATHEMES

THEME	EXPLANATION	IMPORTANCE
Suffering	Through no fault of his own, Job lost his wealth, children, and health. Even his friends were convinced that Job had brought this suffering upon himself. For Job, the greatest trial was not the pain or the loss; it was not being able to understand why God allowed him to suffer.	Suffering can be, but is not always, a penalty for sin. In the same way, prosperity is not always a reward for being good. Those who love God are not exempt from trouble. Although we may not be able to understand fully the pain we experience, it can lead us to rediscover God.
Satan's attacks	Satan attempted to drive a wedge between Job and God by getting Job to believe that God's governing of the world was not just and good. Satan had to ask God for permission to take Job's wealth, children, and health away. Satan was limited to what God allowed.	We must learn to recognize and not fear Satan's attacks because Satan cannot exceed the limits that God sets. Don't let any experience drive a wedge between you and God. Although you can't control how Satan may attack, you can always choose how you will respond when it happens.
God's goodness	God is all-wise and all-powerful. His will is perfect, yet he doesn't always act in ways that we understand. Job's suffering didn't make sense because everyone believed good people were supposed to prosper. When Job was at the point of despair, God spoke to him, showing him his great power and wisdom.	Although God is present everywhere, at times he may seem far away. This may cause us to feel alone and to doubt his care for us. We should serve God for who he is, not what we feel. He is never insensitive to our suffering. Because God is sufficient, we must hold on to him.

Pride

Job's friends were certain that they were correct in their judgment of him. God rebuked them for their pride and arrogance. Man's wisdom is always partial and temporary, so undue pride in our own conclusions is sin.

We must be careful not to judge others who are suffering. We may be demonstrating the sin of pride. We must be cautious in maintaining the certainty of our own conclusions about how God treats us. When we congratulate ourselves for being right, we become proud.

Trusting

God alone knew the purpose behind Job's suffering, and yet he never explained it to Job. In spite of this, Job never gave up on God—even in the midst of suffering. He never placed his hope in his experience, his wisdom, his friends, or his wealth. Job focused on God.

Job showed the kind of trust we are to have. When everything is stripped away, we are to recognize that God is all we ever really had. We should not demand that God explain everything. God gives us himself, but not all the details of his plans. We must remember that this life, with all its pain, is not our final destiny.

A. JOB IS TESTED (1:1—2:13)

Job is portrayed as a wealthy man of upright character who loves God. Yet God allows Satan to destroy his flocks, his possessions, his children, and his health. Job refuses to give up on God, even though he does not understand why this is happening to him. We, too, must trust God when we do not understand the difficulties we face.

Job's character

1:1
Gen 6:9; 17:1
22:12
Ex 18:21
Job 28:28
29:25; 42:12
Jer 25:20
Ezek 14:14
Lam 4:21
Jas 5:11

1:2
Job 42:13

1:5
Job 8:4; 42:8

1 There lived in the land of Uz a man named Job—a good man who feared God and stayed away from evil. 2, 3He had a large family of seven sons and three daughters, and was immensely wealthy, for he owned 7,000 sheep, 3,000 camels, 500 teams of oxen, 500 female donkeys, and employed many servants. He was, in fact, the richest cattleman in that entire area.

4Every year when Job's sons had birthdays, they invited their brothers and sisters to their homes for a celebration. On these occasions they would eat and drink with great merriment. 5When these birthday parties ended—and sometimes they lasted several days—Job would summon his children to him and sanctify them, getting up early in the morning and offering a burnt offering for each of them. For Job said, "Perhaps my sons have sinned and turned away from God in their hearts." This was Job's regular practice.

1:1 *a good man*, literally, "upright." 1:2, 3 *was immensely wealthy*, implied. 1:5 *turned away from God*, literally, "have cursed God."

1:1 When reading the book of Job, we have information which the characters of the story do not. Job, the main character of the book, loses all he has through no fault of his own. As he struggles to understand why all this is happening to him, it becomes clear that he is not meant to know the reasons. He would have to face life with the answers and explanations held back. Only then would his faith fully develop. We must experience life as Job did—one day at a time and without complete answers to all of life's questions. Will we, like Job, trust God no matter what? Or will we give in to the temptation to say that God doesn't really care?

1:1ff As we see calamity and suffering in the book of Job, we must remember that we live in a fallen world where good behavior is not always rewarded and bad behavior is not always punished. When we see a notorious criminal prospering or an innocent child in pain, we say, "That's wrong." And it is. Sin has twisted justice and made our world unpredictable and ugly.

The book of Job shows a good man suffering for no apparent reason. Sadly, our world is like that. But Job's story does not end in despair. Through Job's life we can see that faith in God is justified even when our situations look hopeless. Faith based on rewards or prosperity is hollow. To be unshakable, faith must be built on the confidence that God's ultimate purpose will come to pass.

1:1 Job was called a good man because he feared God; he respected, worshiped, and obeyed him. He was also called good because he stayed away from evil. He did not allow sin to creep into his life or temptation to overcome him. Being a good person is

more than obeying God's laws. It requires all the above characteristics. In light of these, can you be called a good person?

1:1 The location of the land of Uz is uncertain. We only know that Uz had plentiful pastures and crops (1:2, 3, 14, 15), was located near a wilderness (1:19), and was close enough to the Sabeans and Chaldeans to be raided (1:14–17). Uz is also mentioned in Jeremiah 25:19, 20. Most scholars believe Uz was located near Canaan (Israel), where those to whom God first revealed himself (the Jews) lived. Job probably knew about God because he knew God's people.

1:5 It is not known for sure, but Job probably lived during the days of the patriarchs (Abraham, Isaac, Jacob) before God gave his Law or appointed priests to be religious leaders. During Job's day, the father was the family's religious leader. Because there were no priests to instruct him in God's laws, Job acted as the priest and offered sacrifices to God to ask for forgiveness for sins he and his family had committed. Job did this out of conviction and love for God, not just because it was his role as head of the house. Do we carry out our spiritual duties because they are expected, or spontaneously from a heart of devotion?

1:5 Job showed deep concern for the spiritual welfare of his children. Fearful that they might have sinned unknowingly, he offered sacrifices for them as part of their birthday celebrations. Parents today can show the same concern by praying for their children. Regular prayer means "sacrificing" some time each day to plead with God to help them lead lives pleasing to him.

God permits Satan to destroy Job's wealth

⁶One day as the angels came to present themselves before the Lord, Satan, the Accuser, came with them.

⁷"Where have you come from?" the Lord asked Satan.

And Satan replied, "From Earth, where I've been watching everything that's going on."

⁸Then the Lord asked Satan, "Have you noticed my servant Job? He is the finest man in all the earth—a good man who fears God and will have nothing to do with evil."

⁹"Why shouldn't he, when you pay him so well?" Satan scoffed. ¹⁰"You have always protected him and his home and his property from all harm. You have prospered everything he does—look how rich he is! No wonder he 'worships' you! ¹¹But just take away his wealth, and you'll see him curse you to your face!"

¹²,¹³And the Lord replied to Satan, "You may do anything you like with his wealth, but don't harm him physically."

So Satan went away; and sure enough, not long afterwards when Job's sons and daughters were dining at the oldest brother's house, tragedy struck.

¹⁴,¹⁵A messenger rushed to Job's home with this news: "Your oxen were plowing, with the donkeys feeding beside them, when the Sabeans raided us, drove away the animals and killed all the farmhands except me. I am the only one left." ¹⁶While this messenger was still speaking, another arrived with more bad news:

1:6 *the angels,* literally, "the sons of God." **1:8** *a good man,* implied.

1:7
1 Pet 5:8

1:8
Num 12:7
Josh 1:2,7
Job 7:8

1:10
Job 29:2-6
31:25
Prov 10:22

1:11
Job 2:5; 19:21

1:14
Gen 25:3
Job 1:16-19
6:19

1:16
Gen 19:24
Lev 10:2
Num 11:1-3

1:6 The Bible speaks of other heavenly councils where God and the angels plan their activities on earth and where angels are required to give account of themselves (1 Kings 22:19–23). Because God is Creator of all angels—both good and bad—he has complete power and authority over them.

1:6, 7 Satan was originally an angel of God, but became corrupt through his own pride. Satan has been evil since his rebellion against God (1 John 3:8). Satan is God's enemy. He tries to hinder God's work in people, but he is limited by God's power and can do only what he is permitted to do (Luke 22:31, 32; 1 Timothy 1:19, 20; 2 Timothy 2:23–26). Satan is called the Adversary or Accuser because he actively looks for people to attack with temptation (1 Peter 5:8, 9) and because he wants to make people hate God. He does this through lies and deception (Genesis 3:1–6). Job, a righteous man who had been greatly blessed, was a perfect target for Satan. Any person who is committed to God can expect Satan's attacks. Satan, who hates God, hates God's people as well.

1:6–13 From this conversation, we learn a great deal about Satan. (1) He is accountable to God. All angelic beings, good and evil, are compelled to give an account of themselves before God (1:6). (2) His thoughts are open to God (1:7). God knew Satan was intent on attacking Job. (3) Satan can only be at one place at a time (1:6, 7). His demons aid him in his work, but as a created being he is limited. (4) Satan cannot see into our minds or foretell the future (1:9–11). If he could, he would have known that Job would not break under pressure. (5) Because Satan can do nothing without God's permission (1:12), God's people can overcome his attacks through God's power. (6) God always puts limitations on what Satan can do (1:12; 2:6). Satan's response to the Lord's question (1:7) tells us that Satan is real and active on earth. Knowing this about Satan should cause us to remain close to the One who is greater than Satan—God himself.

1:7ff Some people suggest that this dialogue was made up by the author of this book. Could this conversation between God and Satan really have happened? Other Bible passages tell us that Satan does indeed have access to God (see Revelation 12:10). He even went into God's presence to make accusations against Joshua, the High Priest (Zechariah 3:1, 2). If this conversation didn't take place, then the reasons for Job's suffering become meaningless and the book of Job is reduced to fiction rather than fact.

1:8 God called Job his servant. This was a great honor which placed Job in the same company as Moses and David, whom he also called servants (Numbers 12:7, 8; 2 Samuel 7:5). Those who are servants of God serve him with their whole lives—they are faithful to him in all they do.

1:8, 12 Job was a model of trust and obedience to God; therefore, God permitted Satan to attack him in an especially harsh manner. Although God loves us, faith and obedience to him do not shelter us from life's calamities. Setbacks, tragedies, and sorrows strike Christian and non-Christian homes alike. But in the midst of these trials, God expects us to express our faith to the world. How do you respond to your troubles? Do you ask God, "Why me?" or do you say, "Use me!"?

1:9 Satan could not deny that Job was a righteous man; so he attacked Job's motives, saying he was righteous only because he had no reason to turn against God. Ever since he had started following God everything had gone well for him. Satan wanted to prove that Job worshiped God, not out of love, but because God paid him well.

Satan's statement to God is an accurate analysis of why many people trust God. They are fair-weather believers, following God only when everything is going well or for what they can get. Adversity destroys this counterfeit faith. But adversity strengthens real faith by causing believers to dig their roots deeper into God in order to withstand the storms. How deep does your faith go? Put the roots of your faith down deep into God so that you can withstand any storm you may face.

1:12, 13 This conversation between God and Satan teaches us an important fact about God—he is fully aware of every attempt by Satan to bring suffering and difficulty upon us. While he may allow us to suffer for a reason beyond our understanding, he is never caught by surprise by our troubles and is always compassionate toward our situation.

1:16 "The fire of God" may be a poetic Hebrew phrase to describe lightning. In Job's case, the fire was sent by Satan. The messenger only thought it was from God.

"The fire of God has fallen from heaven and burned up your sheep and all the herdsmen, and I alone have escaped to tell you."

1:17
Gen 11:28,31

17Before this man finished, still another messenger rushed in: "Three bands of Chaldeans have driven off your camels and killed your servants, and I alone have escaped to tell you."

18As he was still speaking, another arrived to say, "Your sons and daughters were feasting in their oldest brother's home, 19when suddenly a mighty wind swept in from the desert, and engulfed the house so that the roof fell in on them and all are dead; and I alone escaped to tell you."

1:20
Gen 37:29,34
Josh 7:6
Ezra 9:3

1:21
1 Sam 2:7,8
Job 2:10
Eccles 5:15
1 Tim 6:7

20Then Job stood up and tore his robe in grief and fell down upon the ground before God. 21"I came naked from my mother's womb," he said, "and I shall have nothing when I die. The Lord gave me everything I had, and they were his to take away. Blessed be the name of the Lord."

1:22
Job 2:10

22In all of this, Job did not sin or revile God.

God permits Satan to destroy Job's health

2:1
Job 1:6-8
Isa 6:1,2

2 Now the angels came again to present themselves before the Lord, and Satan with them.

2"Where have you come from?" the Lord asked Satan.

"From Earth, where I've been watching everything that's going on," Satan replied.

3"Well, have you noticed my servant Job?" the Lord asked. "He is the finest man in all the earth—a good man who fears God and turns away from all evil. And he has kept his faith in me despite the fact that you persuaded me to let you harm him without any cause."

2:4
Job 1:11
19:20,21

4, 5"Skin for skin," Satan replied. "A man will give anything to save his life. Touch his body with sickness and he will curse you to your face!"

1:20 *tore his robe in grief,* literally, "tore his robe and shaved his head." **2:1** *the angels,* literally, "the sons of God."

THE SOURCES OF SUFFERING

Sources	Who is Responsible	Who is Affected	Needed Response
My sin	I am	Myself and others	Repentance and confession to God
Others' sin	Person who sinned and others who allowed the sin	Probably many people, including those who sinned	Active resistance to the sinful behavior, while accepting the sinner
Avoidable physical (or, natural) disaster	Persons who ignore the facts or refuse to take precautions	Most of those exposed to the cause	Prevent them if possible, be prepared if they can't be prevented
Unavoidable physical (or, natural) disaster	God, Satan	Most of those present	Ongoing trust in God's faithfulness

When suffering or troubles happen, do they always come from Satan? In Job's story, his series of tragedies did come from Satan, but this is not always the case. The chart above demonstrates the four main causes of suffering. Any one of these or a combination of them may create suffering. If knowing why we are suffering will teach us to avoid the cause, then the causes are worth knowing. However, it is most important to know how to respond during suffering.

1:20–22 Job did not hide his overwhelming grief. This emotional display did not mean he had lost his faith in God; instead, it showed that he was human and that he loved his family. God created our emotions, and it is not sinful to express them as Job did. If you have experienced a deep loss, a disappointment, or a heartbreak, admit your feelings to yourself and others, and grieve.

1:20–22 Job lost his possessions and family in this first of Satan's tests, but he reacted rightly toward God by acknowledging God's sovereign authority over everything God had given him. Job passed the test and proved that people can love God for who he is, not for what he gives.

2:3–6 Can Satan persuade God to change his plans? At first God

said he did not want Job harmed physically, but now he is going to allow it. Satan is unable to persuade God to go against his character: God is completely and eternally good. But God was willing to go along with Satan's plan because God knew the eventual outcome of Job's story.

2:4, 5 "Skin for skin" was Satan's comment concerning Job's response to the loss of his family. Satan still held to his opinion that Job was faithful only because of God's blessings. Satan believed that Job was selfishly untouched by the loss of his family. Satan's next step, therefore, was to inflict physical suffering upon Job to prove his original accusation (1:9).

6"Do with him as you please," the Lord replied; "only spare his life."

7So Satan went out from the presence of the Lord and struck Job with a terrible case of boils from head to foot. 8Then Job took a broken piece of pottery to scrape himself, and sat among the ashes.

9His wife said to him, "Are you still trying to be godly when God has done all this to you? Curse him and die."

10But he replied, "You talk like some heathen woman. What? Shall we receive only pleasant things from the hand of God and never anything unpleasant?" So in all this Job said nothing wrong.

Job's friends gather

11When three of Job's friends heard of all the tragedy that had befallen him, they got in touch with each other and traveled from their homes to comfort and console him. Their names were Eliphaz the Temanite, Bildad the Shuhite, and Zophar the Naamathite. 12Job was so changed that they could scarcely recognize him. Wailing loudly in despair, they tore their robes and threw dust into the air and put earth on their heads to demonstrate their sorrow. 13Then they sat upon the ground with him silently for seven days and nights, no one speaking a word; for they saw that his suffering was too great for words.

Side references:
2:7 Deut 28:35 / Job 7:5; 13:28
2:8 Job 42:6 / Jer 6:26 / Jonah 3:6 / Mt 11:21
2:10 Job 1:21,22 / Mt 12:34-37 / Jas 3:2
2:12 Josh 7:6 / Job 1:20 / Lam 2:10 / Rev 18:19
2:13 Ezek 3:15

B. THREE FRIENDS ANSWER JOB (3:1—31:40)

Job agonizes over his situation. His three friends explain that he must be suffering because of some terrible sin he committed. They try to persuade Job to repent of his sin. When Job argues that he has not sinned enough to deserve such suffering, his friends respond with even harsher accusations. While there are elements of truth in the speeches of Job's three friends, they are based on wrong assumptions. We must be careful what we assume to be true in the lives of others. We cannot assume that suffering is their own fault or a result of their sin.

1. First round of discussion

Job curses his birth

3 At last Job spoke, and cursed the day of his birth.

2,3"Let the day of my birth be cursed," he said, "and the night when I was conceived. 4Let that day be forever forgotten. Let it be lost even to God, shrouded

3:2 Jer 20:14-18

3:4 *day be forever forgotten,* literally, "a day of darkness."

2:6 Again Satan had to seek permission from God to inflict pain upon Job. God limits Satan, and he did not allow him to destroy Job.

2:7 At times believers may actually suffer more than unbelievers because those who follow God may become Satan's special targets. Believers, therefore, may have to endure hardship, persecution, or testing. This was the case with Job. We must be prepared for Satan's attacks. When we suffer, we must not conclude that God has abandoned us (he did not abandon Job). Consistent faith is the way to defeat Satan.

2:9 Why was Job's wife spared when the rest of his family was killed? It is possible that her very presence caused him even more suffering because of her chiding or due to her own sorrow over all they had lost.

2:10 Many people think that believing in God protects them from trouble, so when calamity comes, they question God's goodness and justice. But the message of Job is that you should not give up on God just because bad things happen. Faith in God does not guarantee personal prosperity, and lack of faith does not guarantee troubles in this life. If this were so, people would believe in God simply to get rich. God is capable of rescuing us from suffering, but he may also allow suffering to come for reasons we cannot understand. Job shows here a perspective broader than his own personal comfort. If we always know why we suffer, our faith will have no room to grow.

2:11 Eliphaz, Bildad, and Zophar were not only Job's friends, they were also known for their wisdom. In the end, however, their wisdom was shown to be narrow-minded and incomplete.

2:11 Upon learning of Job's difficulties, three of his friends came to comfort and console him. Later we learn that their words of comfort were not helpful—but at least they came. While God rebuked them for what they said (42:7), he did not rebuke them for what they did—making the effort to come to someone who was in need. Unfortunately, when they came, they did a poor job of comforting Job because they were proud of their own advice and insensitive to Job's needs. When someone is in need, go to him, but be sensitive in how you comfort him.

2:13 Why did the friends arrive and then just sit quietly? According to Jewish tradition, people who come to comfort someone in mourning are not to speak until the mourner speaks. Often the best response to another person's suffering is silence. Job's friends realized that his pain was too deep to be healed with mere words, so they said nothing. (If only they had continued to just sit quietly!) Often, we feel we must say something spiritual and insightful to a hurting friend. Perhaps what he or she needs most is just our presence, showing that we care. Pat answers and trite quotations say much less than empathetic silence and loving companionship.

3:1ff Job's response to his second test—physical affliction—was in stark contrast to his attitude after the first test (1:20–22). Job still did not curse God, but he cursed the day of his birth. He felt it would be better never to be born than to be forsaken by God. Job was struggling emotionally, physically, and spiritually; his misery was pervasive and deep.

in eternal darkness. ⁵Yes, let the darkness claim it for its own, and may a black cloud overshadow it. ⁶May it be blotted off the calendar, never again to be counted among the days of the month of that year. ⁷Let that night be bleak and joyless. ⁸Let those who are experts at cursing curse it. ⁹Let the stars of the night disappear. Let it long for light, but never see it, never see the morning light. ¹⁰Curse it for its failure to shut my mother's womb, for letting me be born to come to all this trouble.

3:8
Job 41:25
3:9
Job 41:18

3:8 *Let those who are experts at cursing curse it,* literally, "Let them who can curse the sea, who know how to rouse the sea monster, curse it."

Children never tire of asking "why?" Yet the question produces a bitter taste the older we get. Children wonder about everything; adults wonder about suffering. We notice that the world seems to run by a system of cause and effect, yet there are some effects for which we can't find a clear cause, and some causes that don't lead to the expected effects. We would expect Job's wealth and family to give him a very happy life and, for awhile, it does. But the loss and pain that he experienced shocks us. The first two chapters of his story are more than we can bear. To those so quick to ask "Why?" at the smallest misfortune, Job's faithfulness seems incredible. But even Job had something to learn. We can learn with him.

Our age of "instant" everything has caused us to lose the ability to wait. We expect to learn patience instantly and in our hurry, we miss the contradiction. Of all that we want now, relief from pain is at the top of our list. We want an instant cure for everything from toothaches to heartbreaks.

Although some pains have been cured, we still live in a world where many people suffer. Job was not expecting instant answers for the intense emotional and physical pain he endured. But in the end, what broke Job's patience was not the suffering—rather, it was not knowing *why* he suffered.

When Job expressed his frustration, his friends were ready with their answers. They believed that the law of cause and effect applied to all people's experiences. Their view of life boiled down to: good things happen to good people and bad things happen to bad people. Because of this, they felt their role was to help Job admit to the bad thing he had done which was causing his suffering.

Job actually looked at life almost the same way as his friends. What he couldn't understand was why he was suffering so much when he was sure he had done nothing to deserve such punishment. The last friend, Elihu, did offer another explanation for the pain by pointing out that God might be allowing it to purify Job. But this was only partly helpful. When God finally spoke, he didn't offer Job an answer. Instead, he drove home the point that it is better to know God than to know answers.

Often we suffer consequences for bad decisions and actions. Job's willingness to repent and confess known wrongs is a good guideline for us. Sometimes suffering shapes us for special service to others. Sometimes suffering is an attack by Satan on our lives. And sometimes we don't know why we suffer. At those times, are we willing to trust God in spite of unanswered questions?

Strengths and accomplishments:
• Was a man of faith, patience, and endurance
• Was known as a generous and caring person
• Was very wealthy

Weakness and Mistake:
• Allowed his suffering to overwhelm him and make him question God

Lessons from his life:
• Knowing God is better than knowing answers
• God is not arbitrary or uncaring
• Pain is not always punishment

Vital statistics:
• Where: Land of Uz
• Occupation: Wealthy land and livestock owner
• Relatives: Wife and first ten children not named. Daughters from the second set of children: Jemima, Kezia, Keren.
• Contemporaries: Eliphaz, Bildad, Zophar, Elihu

Key verses:
"For examples of patience in suffering, look at the Lord's prophets. We know how happy they are now because they stayed true to him then, even though they suffered greatly for it. Job is an example of a man who continued to trust the Lord in sorrow; from his experiences we can see how the Lord's plan finally ended in good, for he is full of tenderness and mercy" (James 5:10, 11).

Job's story is told in the book of Job. He is also referred to in Ezekiel 14:14, 20 and James 5:11.

11"Why didn't I die at birth? 12Why did the midwife let me live? Why did she nurse me at her breasts? 13For if only I had died at birth, then I would be quiet now, asleep and at rest, 14, 15along with prime ministers and kings with all their pomp, and wealthy princes whose castles are full of rich treasures. 16Oh, to have been still-born!—to have never breathed or seen the light. 17For there in death the wicked cease from troubling, and there the weary are at rest. 18There even prisoners are at ease, with no brutal jailer to curse them. 19Both rich and poor alike are there, and the slave is free at last from his master.

20, 21"Oh, why should light and life be given to those in misery and bitterness, who long for death, and it won't come; who search for death as others search for food or money? 22What blessed relief when at last they die! 23Why is a man allowed to be born if God is only going to give him a hopeless life of uselessness and frustration? 24I cannot eat for sighing; my groans pour out like water. 25What I always feared has happened to me. 26I was not fat and lazy, yet trouble struck me down."

4 *A reply to Job from Eliphaz the Temanite:*
2"Will you let me say a word? For who could keep from speaking out? 3, 4In the past you have told many a troubled soul to trust in God and have encouraged those who are weak or falling, or lie crushed upon the ground or are tempted to despair. 5But now, when trouble strikes, you faint and are broken.

6"At such a time as this should not trust in God still be your confidence? Shouldn't you believe that God will care for those who are good? 7, 8Stop and think! Have you ever known a truly good and innocent person who was punished? Experience teaches that it is those who sow sin and trouble who harvest the same. 9They die beneath the hand of God. 10Though they are fierce as young lions, they shall all be broken and destroyed. 11Like aged, helpless lions they shall starve, and all their children shall be scattered.

12"This truth was given me in secret, as though whispered in my ear. 13It came

3:11 Job 10:18,19
3:13 Job 3:13-19
6:8,9
14:10-15
19:25-27
Eccles 6:3-5
3:23 Job 19:6,8,12
Ps 88:8
3:24 Job 6:7; 33:20
Ps 42:4
Isa 59:11
3:25 Job 9:28; 30:15
3:26 Job 7:13,14
4:3 Job 29:21,25
4:6 Prov 3:26; 14:26
4:7,8 Job 8:20
Ps 37:25
Prov 22:8
Gal 6:7
4:9 Job 15:30
2 Thess 2:8
4:11 Job 5:4; 29:17
Jer 4:7
Hos 11:10
4:12 Job 33:15-18

4:3, 4 *in the past,* implied. *you have told many a troubled soul to trust in God,* literally, "you have instructed many."
4:6 *God will care for those who are good?* Literally, "the integrity of your ways, your hope."

3:11 Job was experiencing extreme physical pain as well as grief over the loss of his family and possessions. He can't be blamed for wishing he were dead. Job's grief placed him at the crossroads of his faith, shattering many misconceptions about God (he promises to make you rich, always keeps you from trouble, or protects your loved ones). At his deepest point of despair, Job was driven back to the basics of his faith in God. He only had two choices: (1) he could curse God and give up, or (2) he could trust God and draw strength from him to continue.

3:23-26 Job had been careful not to worship material possessions but to worship only God. Now he was overwhelmed by calamities that mocked all his caution, and he complained about trials that came despite his right living. All the principles by which he had lived were crumbling, and Job began to lose his perspective. Trials and grief, whether temporary or enduring, do not destroy the real purpose of life (Ecclesiastes 3:11). Life is not given merely for happiness and personal fulfillment, but primarily to give glory and honor to God. The worth and meaning of life is not based on what we feel, but on the one reality no one can take away—God's love for us. Don't mistakenly believe that if God truly loves you, he will not allow you to suffer. In fact, the opposite may be true. There is no relationship between the level of your suffering and the measure of God's love (Romans 8:38, 39).

4:1ff Eliphaz claimed to be a man of great knowledge (4:12; 5:27); everything he said was based on his personal experience (4:8; 5:27). He argued that suffering is a direct result of sin, and that if Job would only confess his sin, his suffering would end. Eliphaz saw suffering as God's punishment which should be welcomed in order to bring a person back to God. In some cases, of course, this may be true (Galatians 6:7, 8), but it was not true with Job. Although Eliphaz had many good and true comments, he

made three wrong assumptions: (1) a good and innocent person never suffers; (2) those who suffer are being punished for their past sins; and (3) Job, because he was suffering, had done something wrong in God's eyes. (For more information about Eliphaz, see the chart in chapter 25.)

4:7, 8 Part of what Eliphaz said is true, and part is false. It is true that those who promote sin and trouble will eventually be punished; it is false that anyone who is good and innocent will never suffer. All the material recorded and quoted in the Bible is there by God's choice. Some is there as a record of what people said and did, but not as an example to follow. The sins, the defeats, the evil thoughts and misconceptions about God are all part of God's divinely inspired Word, but that does not mean we are to follow these wrong examples just because they are in the Bible. The Bible gives us teachings and examples of what we *should* do as well as what we *should not* do. Eliphaz's comments are an example of what we should try to avoid—the tendency to make false assumptions about others based on our own experiences.

4:13 Eliphaz's vision could have been simply a dream, or it may have been a supernatural vision. Although Eliphaz claimed his vision was divinely inspired, it is doubtful that it came from God because God criticized Eliphaz for misrepresenting him (42:7). Whatever the vision's source, it is summarized in 4:17. On the surface, this statement is completely true—a mere man cannot compare to God and should not try to question God's motives and actions. Eliphaz, however, took this thought and expounded on it later expressing his own opinions. His conclusion (5:8) shows a very limited view of the reason Job was suffering. It is easy for teachers, counselors, and well-meaning friends to begin with a portion of God's truth but end with man-made wisdom.

in a nighttime vision as others slept. ¹⁴Suddenly, fear gripped me; I trembled and shook with terror, ¹⁵as a spirit passed before my face—my hair stood up on end. ¹⁶I felt the spirit's presence, but couldn't see it standing there. Then out of the dreadful silence came this voice:

4:17
Gen 18:25
Job 9:2; 25:4
35:10; 36:3

¹⁷" 'Is mere man more just than God? More pure than his Creator?'

4:18
Gen 2:7; 3:19
Job 15:15; 22:16
Isa 6:2,3

18, 19"If God cannot trust his own messengers (for even angels make mistakes), how much less men made of dust, who are crushed to death as easily as moths! ²⁰They are alive in the morning, but by evening they are dead, gone forever with hardly a thought from anyone. ²¹Their candle of life is snuffed out. They die and no one cares.

4:20
Job 14:2,20

4:21
Job 8:22; 36:12

5:2
Prov 12:16; 27:3

5 "They cry for help but no one listens; they turn to their gods, but none gives them aid. ²They die in helpless frustration, overcome by their own anger. ³Those who turn from God may be successful for the moment, but then comes sudden disaster. ⁴Their children are cheated, with no one to defend them. ⁵Their harvests are stolen and their wealth slakes the thirst of many others, not themselves! ⁶Misery comes upon them to punish them for sowing seeds of sin. ⁷Mankind heads for sin and misery as predictably as flames shoot upwards from a fire.

5:3
Job 24:18; 31:30

5:5
Job 18:8-10

5:7
Job 14:1
Eccl 5:15-17

ADVICE FROM FRIENDS	Overwhelmed by suffering, Job was not comforted, but condemned by his friends. Each of their views represents a well-known way to understand suffering. God proves each explanation given by Job's friends has less than the whole answer.

Who they were	Where they spoke	How they helped	How they explained Job's pain	Their advice to Job	Job's response	God's response to Job's friends
Eliphaz the Temanite	Job 4, 5, 15, 22	They sat in silence with Job for seven days (2:11–13)	Job is suffering because he has sinned	"Go to God and confess your sins to him." (5:8)	"Stop assuming my guilt, for I am righteous." (6:29)	God rebukes Job's friends (42:7)
Bildad the Shuhite	Job 8, 18, 25		Job won't admit he sinned, so he's still suffering	"How long will you go on like this?" (8:2)	"I will say to God, . . . tell me why you are doing it." (10:2)	
Zophar the Naamathite	Job 11, 20		Job's sin deserves even more suffering than he's experienced	"Get rid of your sins." (11:13, 14)	"I know that I am righteous." (13:18)	
Elihu the Buzite	Job 32—37		God is using suffering to mold and train Job	"Keep silence and I will teach you wisdom." (33:33)	No response	God does not directly address Elihu.
God	Job 38—41	Confronted Job with the need to be content without knowing why he was suffering	Did not explain the reason for the pain	"Do you still want to argue with the Almighty?" (40:2)	"I was talking about things I knew nothing about." (42:3)	

4:18, 19 Do angels really make mistakes? Remember that Eliphaz was speaking, not God, so we must be careful about building our knowledge of the spiritual world from Eliphaz's opinions. In addition, the word translated "mistakes" is used only here, and its meaning is unclear. We could save Eliphaz's credibility by saying he meant fallen angels, but this passage is not meant to teach about angels. What Eliphaz was saying is that sinful human beings

are far beneath God and the angels. Eliphaz was right about God's greatness, but he did not understand God's greater purposes concerning suffering.

5:7 The Bible teaches that everyone has a natural tendency to sin, and Eliphaz supports this view. Those who follow God, however, can decide to resist sin. Eliphaz implied that he had done well at resisting sin while Job had not. This was far from the truth.

8"My advice to you is this: Go to God and confess your sins to him. 9For he does wonderful miracles, marvels without number. 10He sends the rain upon the earth to water the fields, 11and gives prosperity to the poor and humble, and takes sufferers to safety.

12"He frustrates the plans of crafty men. 13They are caught in their own traps; he thwarts their schemes. 14They grope like blind men in the daylight; they see no better in the daytime than at night.

15"God saves the fatherless and the poor from the grasp of these oppressors. 16And so at last the poor have hope, and the fangs of the wicked are broken.

17"How enviable the man whom God corrects! Oh, do not despise the chastening of the Lord when you sin. 18For though he wounds, he binds and heals again. 19He will deliver you again and again, so that no evil can touch you.

20"He will keep you from death in famine, and from the power of the sword in time of war.

21"You will be safe from slander; no need to fear the future.

22"You shall laugh at war and famine; wild animals will leave you alone. 23Dangerous animals will be at peace with you.

24"You need not worry about your home while you are gone; nothing shall be stolen from your barns.

25"Your sons shall become important men; your descendants shall be as numerous as grass! 26You shall live a long, good life; like standing grain, you'll not be harvested until it's time! 27I have found from experience that all of this is true. For your own good, listen to my counsel."

6 Job's reply:
2"Oh, that my sadness and troubles were weighed. 3For they are heavier than the sand of a thousand seashores. That is why I spoke so rashly. 4For the Lord has struck me down with his arrows; he has sent his poisoned arrows deep within my heart. All God's terrors are arrayed against me. 5, 6, 7When wild donkeys bray, it is because their grass is gone; oxen do not low when they have food; a man complains when there is no salt in his food. And how tasteless is the uncooked white of an egg—my appetite is gone when I look at it; I gag at the thought of eating it!

8, 9"Oh, that God would grant the thing I long for most—to die beneath his hand, and be freed from his painful grip. 10This, at least, gives me comfort despite all the

5:9
Job 9:10
37:14,16; 42:3
5:10
Job 36:27-29
37:6
Ps 65:9-11
Amos 4:7
5:11
Job 22:29; 36:7
5:14
Deut 28:29
Prov 4:19
5:17
Ps 94:12
Prov 3:1
Heb 12:5-11
5:18
Deut 32:39
Isa 30:26
Hos 6:1
5:20
Ps 33:19
144:10
Prov 10:3
5:23
Isa 11:6-9
65:25
5:26
Gen 15:15
Job 42:17
Prov 9:11; 10:27
6:2
Job 31:6
6:3
Job 23:2
6:4
Job 16:13
21:20; 30:15
Ps 38:2
6:8
Num 11:15
1 Kgs 19:4
Job 7:16; 9:21
10:1

5:8 Go to God and confess your sins to him, literally, "I would seek God, and to God would I commit my cause."

5:8 All three of Job's friends made the mistake of assuming that Job had committed some great sin which caused his suffering. Neither they nor Job knew of Satan's conversation with God (1:6—2:8). It is human nature to blame people for their own troubles, but Job's story makes it clear that blame cannot always be attached to those whom trouble strikes.

5:13 Paul later quoted part of this verse (1 Corinthians 3:19)—the only time Job is clearly quoted in the New Testament. Although God rebuked Eliphaz for being wrong in his advice to Job (42:7), not all he said was in error. The part Paul quoted was correct—men are often caught in their own traps. This illustrates how Scripture must be used to explain and comment on itself. We must be familiar with the entire scope of God's Word to properly understand the difficult portions of it.

5:17 Eliphaz was correct—it is a blessing to be disciplined by God when we do wrong. His advice, however, did not apply to Job. As we know from the beginning of the book, Job's suffering was not a result of some great sin. We sometimes give people excellent advice only to learn that it does not apply to them and is therefore not very helpful. All those who offer counsel from God's Word should take care to thoroughly understand a person's situation before giving advice.

5:17—26 Eliphaz's words in 5:17, 18 show a view of discipline that has been almost forgotten today: pain can help us grow. These are good words to remember when we face hardship and loss.

Because Job did not understand why he suffered, his faith in God had a chance to grow. On the other hand, we must not make Eliphaz's mistake recorded in 5:19–26. God does not eliminate all hardship when we are following him closely, and good behavior is not always rewarded by prosperity.

6:1ff Job's reply to Eliphaz has three key points: (1) you are giving me all this advice without being sympathetic to my situation, (2) your criticisms are not based on fact but only on your own experience, and (3) you still have not answered my basic question, "Why am I suffering like this?" Although Job could not understand why he was going through this extreme suffering, until he found an answer, he was determined to remain true to God (6:10).

6:6, 7 Job said that Eliphaz's advice was like the disgusting white of an uncooked egg. When we are going through severe trials, ill-advised counsel is as distasteful as slimy food. We may listen politely, but inside we feel like gagging. Be slow to give advice to those who are hurting. They often need compassion more than they need advice.

6:8, 9 In his grief, Job wanted to give in, to be freed from his discomfort, and to die. But God did not grant Job's request. He had a greater plan for him. Our tendency, like Job's, is to want to give up and get out when the going gets rough. To trust God in the good times is commendable, but to trust him during the difficult times tests us to our limits and exercises our faith. In your struggles, large or small, trust that God is in control (Romans 8:28).

pain—that I have not denied the words of the holy God. ¹¹Oh, why does my strength sustain me? How can I be patient till I die? ¹²Am I unfeeling, like stone? Is my flesh made of brass? ¹³For I am utterly helpless, without any hope.

¹⁴"One should be kind to a fainting friend, but you have accused me without the slightest fear of God. ¹⁵⁻¹⁸My brother, you have proved as unreliable as a brook; it floods when there is ice and snow, but in hot weather, disappears. The caravans turn aside to be refreshed, but there is nothing there to drink, and so they perish. ¹⁹, ²⁰, ²¹When caravans from Tema and from Sheba stop for water there, their hopes are dashed. And so my hopes in you are dashed—you turn away from me in terror and refuse to help. ²²But why? Have I ever asked you for one slightest thing? Have I begged you for a present? ²³Have I ever asked your help? ²⁴All I want is a reasonable answer—then I will keep quiet. Tell me, what have I done wrong?

²⁵, ²⁶"It is wonderful to speak the truth, but your criticisms are not based on fact. Are you going to condemn me just because I impulsively cried out in desperation? ²⁷That would be like injuring a helpless orphan, or selling a friend. ²⁸Look at me! Would I lie to your face? ²⁹Stop assuming my guilt, for I am righteous. Don't be so unjust. ³⁰Don't I know the difference between right and wrong? Would I not admit it if I had sinned?

7 "How mankind must struggle. A man's life is long and hard, like that of a slave. ²How he longs for the day to end. How he grinds on to the end of the week and his wages. ³And so to me also have been allotted months of frustration, these long and weary nights. ⁴When I go to bed I think, 'Oh, that it were morning,' and then I toss till dawn.

⁵"My skin is filled with worms and blackness. My flesh breaks open, full of pus. ⁶My life drags by—day after hopeless day. ⁷My life is but a breath, and nothing good is left. ⁸You see me now, but not for long. Soon you'll look upon me dead. ⁹As a cloud disperses and vanishes, so those who die shall go away forever— ¹⁰gone forever from their family and their home—never to be seen again. ¹¹Ah, let me express my anguish. Let me be free to speak out of the bitterness of my soul.

¹²"O God, am I some monster, that you never let me alone? ¹³, ¹⁴Even when I try to forget my misery in sleep, you terrify with nightmares. ¹⁵I would rather die of strangulation than go on and on like this. ¹⁶I hate my life. Oh, let me alone for these few remaining days. ¹⁷What is mere man that you should spend your time persecuting him? ¹⁸Must you be his inquisitor every morning, and test him every moment of the day? ¹⁹Why won't you let me alone—even long enough to spit?

²⁰"Has my sin harmed you, O God, Watcher of mankind? Why have you made me your target, and made my life so heavy a burden to me? ²¹Why not just pardon my sin and take it all away? For all too soon I'll lie down in the dust and die, and when you look for me, I shall be gone."

8 *Bildad the Shuhite replies to Job:*
²"How long will you go on like this, Job, blowing words around like wind?

6:19
Gen 25:15
Job 1:15
Isa 21:14
Jer 14:3

6:25
Job 8:2; 15:2
16:3
Mt 12:37

6:27
Job 22:9; 24:9
Joel 3:3
Nah 3:10
2 Pet 2:3

6:29
Job 13:18
27:5,6; 42:1-6

6:30
Job 12:11
Heb 5:14

7:1
Lev 25:50
Deut 15:18
Mt 20:1-15

7:4
Deut 28:67
Job 7:13,14
Isa 54:11

7:5
Ps 38:5-7

7:7
Job 7:16; 9:25

7:9
Ps 39:13

7:13
Ps 6:6; 77:4

7:16
Job 6:9; 7:7
9:21; 10:1

7:17
Job 22:2
Heb 2:6

7:19
Ps 6:3

7:20
Job 35:3,6

7:21
Job 10:9,14

6:29, 30 Job called himself a righteous man, not because he was sinless, but because he had a right relationship with God. He was not guilty of the sins his friends accused him of (see Job 31 for his summary of the kind of life he had led). *Righteousness* is not the same as *sinlessness* (Romans 3:23). No one but Jesus Christ has ever been sinless—free from all wrong thoughts and actions. Even Job needed to make some changes in his attitude toward God, as we will see by the end of the book. Nevertheless, Job was righteous (1:8). He carefully obeyed God to the best of his ability in all aspects of his life.

7:11 Job felt deep anguish and bitterness, and he spoke honestly to God about it to let out his frustrations. If we express our feelings to God, we can deal with them without exploding in harsh words and actions, possibly hurting ourselves and others. The next time strong emotions threaten to overwhelm you, express them openly

to God in prayer. This will help you gain an eternal perspective on the situation, giving you greater ability to deal with it constructively.

7:12 Job stopped talking to Eliphaz and spoke directly to God. Although Job had lived a righteous life, he was beginning to doubt the value of living in such a way. By doing this, he was coming dangerously close to suggesting that God didn't care about him and was not being fair. God later reproved Job for this attitude (38:2). Our suffering, like Job's, may not be the result of our sin, but we must be careful not to sin as a result of our suffering.

8:1ff Bildad was upset that Job still claimed innocence while questioning God's justice. The basis of Bildad's argument (the justice of God) was correct, but his idea of God's justice was not. Bildad's argument went like this: God could not be unjust, and God would not punish a just man; therefore Job must be unjust. Bildad felt there were no exceptions to his theory.

3Does God twist justice? 4If your children sinned against him, and he punished them, 5and you begged Almighty God for them— 6if you were pure and good, he would hear your prayer, and answer you, and bless you with a happy home. 7And though you started with little, you would end with much.

8"Read the history books and see— 9for we were born but yesterday and know so little; our days here on earth are as transient as shadows. 10But the wisdom of the past will teach you. The experience of others will speak to you, reminding you that 11, 12, 13those who forget God have no hope. They are like rushes without any mire to grow in; or grass without water to keep it alive. Suddenly it begins to wither, even before it is cut. 14A man without God is trusting in a spider's web. Everything he counts on will collapse. 15If he counts on his home for security, it won't last. 16At dawn he seems so strong and virile, like a green plant; his branches spread across the garden. 17His roots are in the stream, down among the stones. 18But when he disappears, he isn't even missed! 19That is all he can look forward to! And others spring up from the earth to replace him!

20"But look! God will not cast away a good man, nor prosper evildoers. 21He will yet fill your mouth with laughter and your lips with shouts of joy. 22Those who hate you shall be clothed with shame, and the wicked destroyed."

9 Job's reply:

2"Yes, I know all that. You're not telling me anything new. But how can a man be truly good in the eyes of God? 3If God decides to argue with him, can a man answer even one question of a thousand he asks? 4For God is so wise and so mighty. Who has ever opposed him successfully?

5"Suddenly he moves the mountains, overturning them in his anger. 6He shakes the earth to its foundations. 7The sun won't rise, the stars won't shine, if he commands it so! 8Only he has stretched the heavens out and stalked along the seas. 9He made the Bear, Orion and the Pleiades, and the constellations of the southern Zodiac.

10"He does incredible miracles, too many to count. 11He passes by, invisible; he moves along, but I don't see him go. 12When he sends death to snatch a man away, who can stop him? Who dares to ask him, 'What are you doing?'

13"And God does not abate his anger. The pride of man collapses before him. 14And who am I that I should try to argue with Almighty God, or even reason with him? 15Even if I were sinless I wouldn't say a word. I would only plead for mercy. 16And even if my prayers were answered I could scarce believe that he had heard my cry. 17For he is the one who destroys, and multiplies my wounds without a cause. 18He will not let me breathe, but fills me with bitter sorrows. 19He alone is strong and just.

20"But I? Am I righteous? My own mouth says no. Even if I were perfect, God would prove me wicked. 21And even if I am utterly innocent, I dare not think of it. I despise what I am. 22Innocent or evil, it is all the same to him, for he destroys both kinds. 23He will laugh when calamity crushes the innocent. 24The whole earth is in the hands of the wicked. God blinds the eyes of the judges and lets them be unfair. If not he, then who?

9:12 to snatch a man away, literally, "he seizes."   **9:13** The pride of man, or, "the helpers of Rahab."

8:4	Job 1:15-19
8:5	Job 5:17-27
8:6	Job 22:27
8:7	Job 42:12
8:8	Deut 4:32; 32:7
8:11	Isa 19:5-7
8:15	Job 27:18 Ps 49:11
8:16	Ps 37:35; 80:11
8:21	Ps 126:1,2
8:22	Ps 132:18
9:2	Job 4:17; 25:4
9:3	Job 10:2; 40:2
9:5	Job 26:6-14
9:6	Isa 2:19; 13:13
9:7	Job 38:12-15
9:8	Gen 1:1 Ps 77:19; 104:2
9:9	Job 38:31,32
9:11	Job 23:8,9
9:12	Job 10:7
9:15	Job 8:5; 10:15
9:17	Job 16:12,14
9:18	Job 27:2
9:22	Eccles 9:2
9:24	Job 12:6,17 16:11 Dan 4:17 5:18-21

8:14, 15 Bildad wrongly assumed that Job was trusting in something other than God for security, so he pointed out that such supports will collapse. One of man's basic needs is security, and people will do almost anything to feel secure. Eventually, however, our money, possessions, knowledge, and relationships will fail or be gone. Only God can give lasting security. What have you trusted for your security? How lasting is it? If you have a secure foundation with God, then feelings of insecurity cannot uproot you.

9:1ff Bildad said nothing new to Job (9:2). Job knew that the wicked ultimately perish, but this confused him. Why, then, was he perishing? Job didn't think his life warranted such suffering, so he wanted to present his case before God (9:35). He recognized, however, that arguing with God would be futile and unproductive (9:4). Job didn't claim to be perfect (7:20, 21; 9:20), but he did claim to be good and faithful (6:29, 30). While Job showed impatience toward God, he did not reject or curse God.

9:20, 21 Job was saying, "In spite of my good life, God is determined to condemn me." As his suffering continued, he became more impatient. Although Job remained loyal to God, he made statements he would later regret.

9:25
2 Sam 1:23
Job 39:29
Isa 18:2
Hab 1:8

9:28
Job 3:25; 7:21
10:14

9:29
Ps 37:33
Jer 2:35

9:30
Job 31:7
Jer 2:22
Rom 10:3
1 Jn 1:8

9:32
1 Sam 2:25
Rom 9:20

10:1
Job 7:11,16
Isa 38:15,17

10:2
Job 9:29
Ps 139:23,24

10:3
Job 9:22-24
10:8; 19:6
21:16; 22:18

10:4-7
1 Sam 16:7
Job 9:12; 36:26

10:8
Job 9:22
Ps 119:73
Isa 43:7

10:9
Job 4:19; 7:21

10:12
Job 33:4

10:13
Job 7:20,21
9:28; 23:13

10:15
Job 6:29

10:16
Job 5:9

10:17
Job 7:1; 16:8

10:18
Job 3:11-13

10:20
Job 7:19; 14:1

11:2
Job 8:2; 15:2

11:3
Job 17:2; 21:3

25"My life passes swiftly away, filled with tragedy. 26My years disappear like swift ships, like the eagle that swoops upon its prey.

27"If I decided to forget my complaints against God, to end my sadness and be cheerful, 28then he would pour even greater sorrows upon me. For I know that you will not hold me innocent, O God, 29but will condemn me. So what's the use of trying? 30Even if I were to wash myself with purest water and cleanse my hands with lye to make them utterly clean, 31even so you would plunge me into the ditch and mud; and even my clothing would be less filthy than you consider me to be!

32, 33"And I cannot defend myself, for you are no mere man as I am. If you were, then we could discuss it fairly, but there is no umpire between us, no middle man, no mediator to bring us together. 34Oh, let him stop beating me, so that I need no longer live in terror of his punishment. 35Then I could speak without fear to him, and tell him boldly that I am not guilty.

10 "I am weary of living. Let me complain freely. I will speak in my sorrow and bitterness. 2I will say to God, 'Don't just condemn me—tell me *why* you are doing it. 3Does it really seem right to you to oppress and despise me, a man you have made; and to send joy and prosperity to the wicked? 4-7Are you unjust like men? Is your life so short that you must hound me for sins you know full well I've not committed? Is it because you know no one can save me from your hand?

8" 'You have made me, and yet you destroy me. 9Oh, please remember that I'm made of dust—will you change me back again to dust so soon? 10You have already poured me from bottle to bottle like milk, and curdled me like cheese. 11You gave me skin and flesh and knit together bones and sinews. 12You gave me life and were so kind and loving to me, and I was preserved by your care.

13, 14" 'Yet all the time your real motive in making me was to destroy me if I sinned; and to refuse to forgive my iniquity. 15Just the slightest wickedness, and I am done for. And if I'm good, that doesn't count. I am filled with frustration. 16If I start to get up off the ground, you leap upon me like a lion and quickly finish me off. 17Again and again you witness against me and pour out an ever-increasing volume of wrath upon me and bring fresh armies against me.

18" 'Why then did you even let me be born? Why didn't you let me die at birth? 19Then I would have been spared this miserable existence. I would have gone directly from the womb to the grave. 20, 21Can't you see how little time I have left? Oh, let me alone that I may have a little moment of comfort before I leave for the land of darkness and the shadow of death, never to return— 22a land as dark as midnight, a land of the shadow of death where only confusion reigns, and where the brightest light is dark as midnight.' "

11 *Zophar the Naamathite replies to Job:*
2"Shouldn't someone stem this torrent of words? Is a man proved right by all this talk? 3Should I remain silent while you boast? When you mock God,

10:4-7 *Are you unjust,* literally, "Have you the eyes of flesh?"

10:1 When we face baffling affliction, a human response is to feel sorry for ourselves. Our pain lures us toward self-pity. At this point we are only one step from self-righteousness, where we keep track of life's injustices and say, "Look what happened to me; how unfair it is!" This comes close to saying God is unfair. Remember that life's trials, whether allowed by God or sent by God, can be the means for development and refinement. When facing trials, ask, "What can I learn and how can I grow?" rather than "Who did this to me and how can I get out of it?"

10:13, 14 In frustration, Job jumped to the false conclusion that God was out to get him. Wrong assumptions lead to wrong conclusions. We dare not take the limited experiences of our lives and jump to conclusions about life in general. If you find yourself not trusting God, remember that you don't have all the facts. The truth is that God wants only the very best for your life. Many people

endure great pain, but ultimately good will be produced. When you're struggling, don't assume the worst.

10:20–22 Job is expressing the view of death common in Old Testament times, that the dead went to a joyless, dark place called Sheol. There was no punishment or reward in Sheol, and no escape from it. (See the note on 19:26 for a broader picture of Job's view of death.)

11:1ff Zophar was the third of Job's friends to speak, and the least courteous. Full of anger, he lashed out at Job, saying Job deserved more punishment, not less. Zophar takes the same position as Eliphaz (Job 4, 5) and Bildad (Job 8)—that Job was suffering because of sin—but his speech was by far the most arrogant. Zophar was the kind of person who had an answer for everything; he was totally insensitive to Job's unique situation. (For more on Zophar, see the chart in Job 5.)

shouldn't someone make you ashamed? 4You claim you are pure in the eyes of
God! 5Oh, that God would speak and tell you what he thinks! 6Oh, that he would
make you truly see yourself, for he knows everything you've done. Listen! God is
doubtless punishing you far less than you deserve!

7"Do you know the mind and purposes of God? Will long searching make them
known to you? Are you qualified to judge the Almighty? 8He is as faultless as
heaven is high—but who are you? His mind is fathomless—what can you know in
comparison? 9His Spirit is broader than the earth and wider than the sea. 10If he
rushes in and makes an arrest, and calls the court to order, who is going to stop
him? 11For he knows perfectly all the faults and sins of mankind; he sees all sin
without searching.

12"Mere man is as likely to be wise, as a wild donkey's colt is likely to be born
a man!

13, 14"Before you turn to God and stretch out your hands to him, get rid of your
sins and leave all iniquity behind you. 15Only then, without the spots of sin to defile
you, can you walk steadily forward to God without fear. 16Only then can you forget
your misery. It will all be in the past. 17And your life will be cloudless; any
darkness will be as bright as morning!

18"You will have courage because you will have hope. You will take your time,
and rest in safety. 19You will lie down unafraid and many will look to you for help.
20But the wicked shall find no way to escape; their only hope is death."

12 *Job's reply:*
2"Yes, I realize you know everything! All wisdom will die with you!
3Well, I know a few things myself—you are no better than I am. And who doesn't
know these things you've been saying? 4I, the man who begged God for help, and
God answered him, have become a laughingstock to my neighbors. Yes, I, a
righteous man, am now the man they scoff at. 5Meanwhile, the rich mock those in
trouble and are quick to despise all those in need. 6For robbers prosper. Go ahead
and provoke God—it makes no difference! He will supply your every need anyway!

7, 8, 9"Who doesn't know that the Lord does things like that? Ask the dumbest
beast—he knows that it is so; ask the birds—they will tell you; or let the earth teach
you, or the fish of the sea. 10For the soul of every living thing is in the hand of God,
and the breath of all mankind. 11Just as my mouth can taste good food, so my mind
tastes truth when I hear it. 12And as you say, older men like me are wise. They
understand. 13But true wisdom and power are God's. He alone knows what we
should do; he understands.

14"And how great is his might! What he destroys can't be rebuilt. When he closes
in on a man, there is no escape. 15He withholds the rain, and the earth becomes a
desert; he sends the storms, and floods the ground. 16Yes, with him is strength and
wisdom. Deceivers and deceived are both his slaves.

17"He makes fools of counselors and judges. 18He reduces kings to slaves and
frees their servants. 19Priests are led away as slaves. He overthrows the mighty.
20He takes away the voice of orators, and the insight of the elders. 21He pours
contempt upon princes, and weakens the strong. 22He floods the darkness with
light, even the dark shadow of death. 23He raises up a nation and then destroys it.
12:12 *older men like me,* implied.

11:4 Job 6:10
11:6 Job 22:5
11:7 Job 33:12,13 36:26; 37:5
11:8 Job 22:12; 38:17
11:11 Job 24:23 34:21-23
11:12 Ps 62:9
11:13 Ps 78:8; 88:9
11:15 Ps 27:3; 46:2
11:17 Ps 37:6
11:19 Lev 26:6
11:20 Job 6:9; 34:22
12:2 Job 16:1,2 17:10
12:4 Job 6:29; 17:6 30:1,9,10
12:6 Job 9:24; 21:9
12:11 Job 34:3
12:12 Job 32:7
12:14 Job 19:10; 37:7
12:16 Job 13:7,9
12:19 Job 34:24-28
12:20 Job 32:9
12:21 Job 12:18; 34:19
12:22 Dan 2:22 1 Cor 4:5
12:23 Isa 9:3 Zech 10:8

11:11 Zophar incorrectly assumed that Job was hiding secret
faults and sins. Although his assumption was wrong, he explained
quite accurately that God knows and sees everything. We are often
tempted by the thought, "No one will ever know!" Perhaps we can
hide some sin from others, but we can do *nothing* without God
knowing about it. Because our very thoughts are known to God, of
course he will notice our sins. Job understood this as well as
Zophar did, but it didn't apply to his current dilemma.

12:1ff Job answered Zophar's argument with great sarcasm: "I
did not know you had a hotline to God and knew all his ways." Job
went on to say that his three friends didn't need to explain God to
him—they were saying nothing he didn't already know (12:7–9;
13:1, 2). Job continued to maintain that his friends had completely
misunderstood the reason for his suffering (13:7). Job did not know
it either, but he was certain that his friends' reasons were both
narrow-minded and incorrect (13:8–12). Once again Job appealed
to God to give him an answer (13:3).

12:24
Dan 4:16,33
Hos 7:11

He makes it great, and then reduces it to nothing. 24, 25He takes away the understanding of presidents and kings, and leaves them wandering, lost and groping, without a guiding light.

13:2
Job 12:3

13:3
Job 13:22; 23:4
Jer 12:1,2

13:4
Ps 119:69
Jer 23:32
Hos 5:13

13:5
Job 21:5

13:7
Job 27:4

13:10
Job 32:21

13:11
Job 31:23

13:12
Job 15:3

13:15
Job 7:6; 27:5

13:16
Job 34:21-23

13:18
Job 9:21; 23:4

13:19
Job 7:21

13:21
Job 9:34
Ps 39:10

13:22
Job 14:15

13:24
Job 19:11; 33:10

13:25
Job 11:18

13:26
Job 9:18

13:27
Job 2:7

14:1
Job 5:7

14:2
Job 8:9

14:4
Job 15:14; 25:4

14:5
Job 21:21

13 "Look, I have seen many instances such as you describe. I understand what you are saying. 2I know as much as you do. I'm not stupid. 3Oh, how I long to speak directly to the Almighty. I want to talk this over with God himself. 4For you are misinterpreting the whole thing. You are doctors who don't know what they are doing. 5Oh, please be quiet! That would be your highest wisdom.

6"Listen to me now, to my reasons for what I think, and to my pleadings. 7"Must you go on 'speaking for God' when he never once has said the things that you are putting in his mouth? 8Does God want your help if you are going to twist the truth for him? 9Be careful that he doesn't find out what you are doing! Or do you think you can fool God as well as men? 10No, you will be in serious trouble with him if you use lies to try to help him out. 11Doesn't his majesty strike terror to your heart? How can you do this thing? 12These tremendous statements you have made have about as much value as ashes. Your defense of God is as fragile as a clay vase!

13"Be silent now and let me alone, that I may speak—and I am willing to face the consequences. 14Yes, I will take my life in my hand and say what I really think. 15God may kill me for saying this—in fact, I expect him to. Nevertheless I am going to argue my case with him. 16This at least will be in my favor, that I am not godless, to be rejected instantly from his presence. 17Listen closely to what I am about to say. Hear me out.

18"This is my case: *I know that I am righteous.* 19Who can argue with me over this? If you could prove me wrong I would stop defending myself and die.

20"O God, there are two things I beg you not to do to me; only then will I be able to face you. 21Don't abandon me. And don't terrify me with your awesome presence. 22Call to me to come—how quickly I will answer! Or let me speak to you, and you reply. 23Tell me, what have I done wrong? Help me! Point out my sin to me. 24Why do you turn away from me? Why hand me over to my enemy? 25Would you blame a leaf that is blown about by the wind? Will you chase dry, useless straws?

26"You write bitter things against me and bring up all the follies of my youth. 27, 28You send me to prison and shut me in on every side. I am like a fallen, rotten tree, like a moth-eaten coat.

14 "How frail is man, how few his days, how full of trouble! 2He blossoms for a moment like a flower—and withers; as the shadow of a passing cloud, he quickly disappears. 3Must you be so harsh with frail men, and demand an accounting from them? 4How can you demand purity in one born impure? 5You have set mankind so brief a span of life—months is all you give him! Not one bit longer may he live. 6So give him a little rest, won't you? Turn away your angry gaze and let him have a few moments of relief before he dies.

13:15 Or, "Though he slay me, yet will I trust in him. I will argue my case before him."

12:24, 25 Job affirms that no leader has any real wisdom apart from God. No research or report can outweigh God's opinion. When we look for guidance for our lives, we must recognize that God's wisdom is superior to any the world has to offer.

13:4 Job compared his three friends to doctors who did not know what they were doing. They were like eye surgeons trying to perform open-heart surgery. Many of their ideas about God were true, but they did not apply to Job's situation. They were right to say that God is just. They were right to say God punishes sin. But they were wrong to assume that Job's suffering was a just punishment for his sin. They took a true principle and applied it wrongly, ignoring the vast differences in human circumstances. We must be careful and compassionate in how we apply biblical insights to the lives of others.

13:21-24 Job was especially upset because God was silent, giving no reasons for his suffering. Job misinterpreted God's silence as rejection, and once again he said that it was not his suffering that bothered him as much as this apparent rejection (13:21, 22). If God had given reasons, however, Job's faith would probably not have been stretched and strengthened.

14:1ff Life is brief and full of trouble, Job laments in his closing remarks. Sickness, loneliness, disappointment, and death cause him to say that life is not fair. Still, he clings to the one truth that also gives hope to us—resurrection (14:14, 15). God's solution to an unfair world is to guarantee life with him forever. No matter how unfair your present world seems, God offers the hope of being in his presence eternally.

7"For there is hope for a tree—if it's cut down it sprouts again, and grows tender, new branches. 8, 9Though its roots have grown old in the earth, and its stump decays, it may sprout and bud again at the touch of water, like a new seedling. 10But when a man dies and is buried, where does his spirit go? 11, 12As water evaporates from a lake, as a river disappears in drought, so a man lies down for the last time, and does not rise again until the heavens are no more; he shall not awaken, nor be roused from his sleep. 13Oh, that you would hide me with the dead, and forget me there until your anger ends; but mark your calendar to think of me again!

14"If a man dies, shall he live again? This thought gives me hope, so that in all my anguish I eagerly await sweet death! 15You would call and I would come, and you would reward all I do. 16But now, instead, you give me so few steps upon the stage of life, and notice every mistake I make. 17You bundle them all together as evidence against me.

18, 19"Mountains wear away and disappear. Water grinds the stones to sand. Torrents tear away the soil. So every hope of man is worn away. 20, 21Always you are against him, and then he passes off the scene. You make him old and wrinkled, then send him away. He never knows it if his sons are honored; or they may fail and face disaster, but he knows it not. 22For him there is only sorrow and pain."

2. Second round of discussion

15 *The answer of Eliphaz the Temanite:*

2"You are supposed to be a wise man, and yet you give us all this foolish talk. You are nothing but a windbag. 3It isn't right to speak so foolishly. What good do such words do? 4, 5Have you no fear of God? No reverence for him? Your sins are telling your mouth what to say! Your words are based on clever deception, 6but why should I condemn you? Your own mouth does!

7, 8"Are you the wisest man alive? Were you born before the hills were made? Have you heard the secret counsel of God? Are you called into his counsel room? Do you have a monopoly on wisdom? 9What do you know more than we do? What do you understand that we don't? 10On our side are aged men much older than your father! 11Is God's comfort too little for you? Is his gentleness too rough?

12"What is this you are doing, getting carried away by your anger, with flashing eyes? 13And you turn against God and say all these evil things against him. 14What man in all the earth can be as pure and righteous as you claim to be? 15Why, God doesn't even trust the angels! Even the heavens can't be absolutely pure compared with him! 16How much less someone like you, who is corrupt and sinful, drinking in sin as a sponge soaks up water!

17, 18, 19"Listen, and I will answer you from my own experience, confirmed by the experience of wise men who have been told this same thing from their fathers—our ancestors to whom alone the land was given—and they have passed this wisdom to us:

20"A wicked man is always in trouble throughout his life. 21He is surrounded by

14:10
Job 13:19
14:11
Job 3:13
Isa 19:5
14:13
Isa 26:20

14:16
Job 10:6; 31:4
34:21
14:17
Deut 32:32-34
14:18
Job 7:6
14:20
Job 20:7; 34:20

15:2
Job 6:26

15:4
Job 5:12,13
15:6
Job 9:20

15:7
Job 38:4,21

15:9
Job 12:3; 13:2
15:10
Job 12:12
15:11
Job 6:10
15:12
Job 36:13
15:14
Job 14:4
15:15
Job 4:18; 25:5
15:16
Job 34:7
15:17
Job 8:8; 20:4
15:21
Job 18:11
20:21,25

14:7–22 The Old Testament does not say much about the resurrection of the dead. This is not surprising, because Jesus had not yet conquered death. Job's pessimism about death is understandable. What is remarkable is his budding hope. If only God would hide him with the dead and then bring him out again! If only he could die and live again! When we must endure suffering, we have an advantage over Job. We know that the dead will rise. We have hope based on revealed truth.

14:22 Job's profound speech in this chapter illustrates a great truth: to have a right set of doctrines is not enough. To know what to believe is not all that is required to live rightly. Truth untested by life's experiences may become static and stagnant. Suffering can bring a dynamic quality to life. Just as drought drives the roots of a tree deeper to find water, so suffering can drive us beyond

superficial acceptance of truth to dependence on God for hope and life.

15:1ff With the first round of talks concluded, each friend, in the same order, pressed the argument further. Again Job answered each argument (Job 15—31). This time Eliphaz was ruder, more intense, and more threatening, but he said nothing new. (See his first speech in Job 4, 5.) He began by calling Job foolish and arrogant; then he restated his opinion that Job must be a great sinner. According to Eliphaz, the experience and wisdom of their ancestors were more valuable than Job's individual thoughts. Eliphaz assumed that his words were as true as God's. It is not difficult to spot his arrogance.

15:15, 16 Eliphaz was repeating his argument that the moral integrity of all creation is far below God's. (See the note on 4:18, 19.)

15:22
Job 15:30
19:29; 27:14

15:25
Job 36:9

15:27
Job 3:14
Ps 73:7; 119:70

15:29
Job 27:16,17

15:30
Job 4:9; 5:14
22:20

15:31
Isa 59:4

15:34
Job 8:13,22

15:35
Ps 7:14
Isa 59:4

16:2
Job 13:4; 21:34

16:3
Job 6:26

16:4
Ps 22:7; 109:25

16:6
Job 9:27,28

16:7
Job 7:3
19:13-15

16:8
Job 10:17; 19:20

16:9
Job 13:24; 33:10

16:10
Job 30:12

16:12
Job 7:20; 9:17

16:13
Job 6:4; 19:12

16:14
Job 9:17

16:15
Job 30:19

16:16
Job 16:20; 24:17

16:17
Job 27:4

16:19
Job 19:25-27
31:2

16:22
Job 3:13

terrors, and if there are good days they will soon be gone. 22He dares not go out into the darkness, lest he be murdered. 23, 24He wanders around begging for food. He lives in fear, distress, and anguish. His enemies conquer him as a king defeats his foes. 25, 26Armed with his tin shield, he clenches his fist against God, defying the Almighty, stubbornly assaulting him.

27, 28"This wicked man is fat and rich, and has lived in conquered cities after killing off its citizens. 29But he will not continue to be rich, or to extend his possessions. 30No, darkness shall overtake him forever; the breath of God shall destroy him; the flames shall burn up all he has.

31"Let him no longer trust in foolish riches; let him no longer deceive himself, for the money he trusts in will be his only reward. 32Before he dies, all this futility will become evident to him. For all he counted on will disappear, 33and fall to the ground like a withered grape. How little will come of his hopes! 34For the godless are barren: they can produce nothing truly good. God's fire consumes them with all their possessions. 35The only thing they can 'conceive' is sin, and their hearts give birth only to wickedness."

16 *Job's reply:*

2"I have heard all this before. What miserable comforters all of you are. 3Won't you ever stop your flow of foolish words? What have I said that makes you speak so endlessly? 4But perhaps I'd sermonize the same as you—if you were I and I were you. I would spout off my criticisms against you and shake my head at you. 5But no! I would speak in such a way that it would help you. I would try to take away your grief.

6"But now my grief remains no matter how I defend myself; nor does it help if I refuse to speak. 7For God has ground me down, and taken away my family. 8O God, you have turned me to skin and bones—as a proof, they say, of my sins. 9God hates me and angrily tears at my flesh; he has gnashed upon me with his teeth, and watched to snuff out any sign of life. 10These 'comforters' have gaping jaws to swallow me; they slap my cheek. My enemies gather themselves against me. 11And God has delivered me over to sinners, into the hands of the wicked.

12"I was living quietly until he broke me apart. He has taken me by the neck and dashed me to pieces, then hung me up as his target. 13His archers surround me, letting fly their arrows, so that the ground is wet from my blood. 14Again and again he attacks me, running upon me like a giant. 15Here I sit in sackcloth; and have laid all hope in the dust. 16My eyes are red with weeping and on my eyelids is the shadow of death.

17"Yet I am innocent, and my prayer is pure. 18O earth, do not conceal my blood. Let it protest on my behalf.

19"Yet even now the Witness to my innocence is there in heaven; my Advocate is there on high. 20My friends scoff at me, but I pour out my tears to God, 21pleading that he will listen as a man would listen to his neighbor. 22For all too soon I must go down that road from which I shall never return.

15:31 *trust in foolish riches,* literally, "trust in vanity." **15:33** *fall to the ground like a withered grape,* literally, "shall cast off his flower as the olive tree."

16:1ff Job's friends were supposed to be comforting him in his grief. Instead they condemned him for causing his own suffering. Job began his reply to Eliphaz by calling him and his friends "miserable comforters." Job's words reveal several ways to become a better comforter to those in pain: (1) don't talk just for the sake of talking; (2) don't sermonize by giving pat answers; (3) don't criticize; (4) put yourself in the other person's place; and (5) offer help and encouragement. Try Job's suggestions, knowing that they are given by one who needed great comfort. The best comforters are those who know something about personal suffering.

16:7 First Job's children died, then his friends condemned him,

and now he felt that God had deserted him. No wonder he wanted to die! But God still had something important to reveal to him and to us through his experiences.

16:19 Job was afraid that God hated him. Yet he appealed directly to God (his witness and advocate) and to God's knowledge of his innocence. A witness is one who has seen what has happened, and an advocate is one who speaks up to protect another. By using these terms, Job showed he had cast all his hope for any fair defense upon God. In the New Testament we learn that Jesus Christ witnesses on our behalf (Hebrews 7:25; 1 John 2:1); therefore, we have nothing to fear.

17 "I am sick and near to death; the grave is ready to receive me. 2I am surrounded by mockers. I see them everywhere. 3, 4Will no one anywhere confirm my innocence? But you, O God, have kept them back from understanding this. Oh, do not let them triumph. 5If they accept bribes to denounce their friends, their children shall go blind.

6"He has made me a mockery among the people; they spit in my face. 7My eyes are dim with weeping and I am but a shadow of my former self. 8Fair-minded men are astonished when they see me.

"Yet, finally, the innocent shall come out on top, above the godless; 9the righteous shall move onward and forward; those with pure hearts shall become stronger and stronger.

10"As for you—all of you please go away; for I do not find a wise man among you. 11My good days are in the past. My hopes have disappeared. My heart's desires are broken. 12They say that night is day and day is night; how they pervert the truth!

13, 14"If I die, I go out into darkness, and call the grave my father, and the worm my mother and my sister. 15Where then is my hope? Can anyone find any? 16No, my hope will go down with me to the grave. We shall rest together in the dust!"

18 *The further reply of Bildad the Shuhite:*
2"Who are you trying to fool? Speak some sense if you want us to answer! 3Have we become like animals to you, stupid and dumb? 4Just because you tear your clothes in anger, is this going to start an earthquake? Shall we all go and hide?

5"The truth remains that if you do not prosper, it is because you are wicked. And your bright flame shall be put out. 6There will be darkness in every home where there is wickedness.

7"The confident stride of the wicked man will be shortened; he will realize his failing strength. 8, 9He walks into traps, and robbers will ambush him. 10There is a booby-trap in every path he takes. 11He has good cause for fear—his enemy is close behind him!

12"His vigor is depleted by hunger; calamity stands ready to pounce upon him. 13His skin is eaten by disease. Death shall devour him. 14The wealth he trusted in shall reject him, and he shall be brought down to the King of Terrors. 15His home shall disappear beneath a fiery barrage of brimstone. 16He shall die from the roots up, and all his branches will be lopped off.

17"All memory of his existence will perish from the earth; no one will remember him. 18He will be driven out from the kingdom of light into darkness, and chased out of the world. 19He will have neither son nor grandson left, nor any other relatives. 20Old and young alike will be horrified by his fate. 21Yes, that is what happens to sinners, to those rejecting God."

17:2
Job 12:4
17:3
Job 12:20
17:5
Job 11:20
17:6
Job 30:10
17:8
Job 22:19
17:9
Job 22:30
17:10
Job 12:2
17:11
Job 7:6
17:13
Job 3:13; 21:26
25:6
17:15
Job 7:6
17:16
Job 3:17; 21:33

18:3
Ps 73:22
18:5
Job 21:17
18:6
Job 12:25
18:8
Job 22:10
18:11
Job 15:21; 18:18
18:14
Job 8:22; 15:21
27:18
18:16
Job 15:30,32
18:17
Job 24:20
18:18
Job 5:14
27:21-23
18:19
Job 27:14,15
18:20
Jer 50:27
Obad 12
Lk 19:42,44

17:10 Job's three friends had a reputation for being wise, but Job said that none of them had shown wisdom. God backed up Job's claim in 42:7, where he condemned these men for their false portrayal of him. Obviously these men had a faulty view of wisdom. They assumed that because they were prosperous and successful, God must have been pleased with the way they were living and thinking. Job, however, told his friends that they were starting with the wrong idea. Earthly success and prosperity are not proof of faith in God. Likewise, trouble and affliction do not prove faithlessness. The truly wise man knows that wisdom comes from God alone, not from human successes or failures. And the truly wise man never forsakes God. In the end, God proved that Job was wiser than any of his friends.

17:15 Job gave up hope of any future restoration of wealth and family, and he wrapped himself in thoughts of death and the rest from grief and pain it promised. The rewards about which Job's friends spoke were all related to this present life. They were silent about the possibility of life after death. We must be careful to avoid

viewing life only in terms of this present world, because God promises the faithful a never-ending future.

18:1ff Bildad thought he knew how the universe should be run, and he saw Job's life as an illustration of the consequences of sin. He rejected Job's side of the story because it did not fit in with his outlook on life. It is easy to condemn Bildad because his errors are obvious; unfortunately, however, we often act the same way when our ideas are threatened.

18:14 The "King of Terrors" is a figure of speech referring to death. Bildad viewed death as a great devourer (18:13), but the Bible teaches that God has the power to devour even death (Psalm 49:15; 1 Corinthians 15:55, 56).

18:21 Bildad's second speech was really no different from his first except that it was more harsh, as was Eliphaz's. When we face difficulties, pain, and suffering, we can expect well-meaning "Bildads" to come along, quoting proverbs and giving advice and not really listening to us or identifying with our pain. Rather than seeking to understand, they give unhelpful, trite answers. When receiving this useless advice, listen politely. Then in order to sort

19:5
Ps 35:26; 38:16

19:6
Job 16:11

19:7
Job 30:20,24

19:8
Job 3:23; 30:26

19:10
Job 7:6; 12:14

19:11
Job 13:24; 16:9

19:12
Job 16:13

19:13
Job 16:7,20

19:19
Ps 38:11; 55:13

19:20
Job 33:21

19:21
Job 1:11

19:22
Ps 16:11; 69:26

19:23
Isa 30:8

19:25
Job 16:19
Isa 43:14
Jer 50:34

19:26
Ps 17:15
Mt 5:8
1 Cor 13:12
1 Jn 3:2

19 *The reply of Job:*

2"How long are you going to trouble me, and try to break me with your words? 3Ten times now you have declared I am a sinner. Why aren't you ashamed to deal with me so harshly? 4And if indeed I was wrong, you have yet to prove it. 5You think yourselves so great? Then prove my guilt!

6"The fact of the matter is that God has overthrown me and caught me in his net. 7I scream for help and no one hears me. I shriek, but get no justice. 8God has blocked my path and turned my light to darkness. 9He has stripped me of my glory and removed the crown from my head. 10He has broken me down on every side, and I am done for. He has destroyed all hope. 11His fury burns against me; he counts me as an enemy. 12He sends his troops to surround my tent.

13"He has sent away my brothers, and my friends. 14My relatives have failed me; my friends have all forsaken me. 15Those living in my home, even my servants, regard me as a stranger. I am like a foreigner to them. 16I call my servant, but he doesn't come; I even beg him! 17My own wife and brothers refuse to recognize me. 18Even young children despise me. When I stand to speak, they mock.

19"My best friends abhor me. Those I loved have turned against me. 20I am skin and bones and have escaped death by the skin of my teeth.

21"Oh, my friends, pity me, for the angry hand of God has touched me. 22Why must you persecute me as God does? Why aren't you satisfied with my anguish? 23, 24Oh, that I could write my plea with an iron pen in the rock forever.

25"But as for me, I know that my Redeemer lives, and that he will stand upon the earth at last. 26And I know that after this body has decayed, this body shall see God! 27Then he will be on *my* side! Yes, I shall see him, not as a stranger, but as a friend! What a glorious hope!

28"How dare you go on persecuting me, as though I were proven guilty? 29I warn you, you yourselves are in danger of punishment for your attitude."

20 *The speech of Zophar the Naamathite:*

20:3
Job 19:3

20:5
Job 8:12,13
Ps 37:35,36

2"I hasten to reply, for I have the answer for you. 3You have tried to make me feel ashamed of myself for calling you a sinner, but my spirit won't let me stop.

4"Don't you realize that ever since man was first placed upon the earth, 5the triumph of the wicked has been short-lived, and the joy of the godless but for a

19:26 *this body shall see God,* or, "then even without my flesh I shall see God."

---

out the helpful advice from the empty words, talk to God about what was said. When giving advice, avoid empty words and stock answers. It is more important to convey care and support than to worry about saying the right thing.

19:3–5 It is easy to point out someone else's faults or sins. Job's friends accused him of sin to make him feel guilty, not to encourage or correct him. If we feel we must admonish someone, we should be sure we are confronting that person because we love him, not because we are annoyed, inconvenienced, or seeking to blame him.

19:6 Job felt that God was treating him as an enemy when, in fact, God was his friend and thought highly of him (1:8; 2:3). In the midst of difficulty, Job pointed at the wrong person. It was Satan, not God, who was Job's enemy. Most Israelites believed that both good and evil came from God; they also thought people were responsible for their own destinies. But the evil power loose in this world accounts for much of the suffering we experience.

19:25–27 At the heart of the book of Job comes his ringing affirmation of confidence: "I know that my Redeemer lives." In ancient Israel a redeemer was a family member who bought a slave's way to freedom or who took care of a widow (see the note in Ruth 3:1). What tremendous faith Job had, especially in light of the fact that he was unaware of the conference between God and

Satan. Job thought that God had brought all these disasters upon him! Faced with death and decay, Job still expected to see God—and he expected to do so in his body. When the book of Job was written, Israel did not have a well-developed doctrine of the resurrection. Although Job struggled with the idea that God was presently against him, he firmly believed that in the end God would be on his side. This belief was so strong that Job became one of the first to talk about the resurrection of the body (see also Psalm 16:10; Isaiah 26:19; Daniel 12:2, 13).

19:26 While some Bible translations say, "Then even without my flesh I shall see God," this does not fit well with 19:27, where Job says that he will see God with his own eyes. Most translators today agree that the better translation is "in my flesh I shall see God." In Job's situation, it seemed unlikely that he would, in his flesh, see God. And that's just the point of Job's faith! He was confident that God's justice would triumph, even if it would take a miracle like resurrection to accomplish this.

20:1ff Zophar's speech again revealed his false assumption, because he based his arguments purely on the idea that Job was an evil hypocrite. Zophar said that while Job had it good for a while, he didn't live righteously, so God took his wealth from him. According to Zophar, Job's calamities *proved* his wickedness.

moment? 6Though the godless be proud as the heavens, and walk with his nose in the air, 7yet he shall perish forever, cast away like his own dung. Those who knew him will wonder where he is gone. 8He will fade like a dream. 9Neither his friends nor his family will ever see him again.

10"His children shall beg from the poor, their hard labor shall repay his debts. 11Though still a young man, his bones shall lie in the dust.

12"He enjoyed the taste of his wickedness, letting it melt in his mouth, 13sipping it slowly, lest it disappear.

14"But suddenly the food he has eaten turns sour within him. 15He will vomit the plunder he gorged. God won't let him keep it down. 16It is like poison and death to him. 17He shall not enjoy the goods he stole; they will not be butter and honey to him after all. 18His labors shall not be rewarded; wealth will give him no joy. 19For he has oppressed the poor and foreclosed their homes; he will never recover. 20Though he was always greedy, now he has nothing; of all the things he dreamed of—none remain. 21Because he stole at every opportunity, his prosperity shall not continue.

22"He shall run into trouble at the peak of his powers; all the wicked shall destroy him. 23Just as he is about to fill his belly, God will rain down wrath upon him. 24He will be chased and struck down. 25The arrow is pulled from his body—and the glittering point comes out from his gall. The terrors of death are upon him.

26"His treasures will be lost in deepest darkness. A raging fire will devour his goods, consuming all he has left. 27The heavens will reveal his sins, and the earth will give testimony against him. 28His wealth will disappear beneath the wrath of God. 29This is what awaits the wicked man, for God prepares it for him."

21 *Job's reply:*
2, 3"Listen to me; let me speak, and afterwards, mock on.

4"I am complaining about God, not man; no wonder my spirit is so troubled. 5Look at me in horror, and lay your hand upon your mouth. 6Even I am frightened when I see myself. Horror takes hold upon me and I shudder.

7"The truth is that the wicked live on to a good old age, and become great and powerful. 8They live to see their children grow to maturity around them, and their grandchildren, too. 9Their homes are safe from every fear, and God does not punish them. 10Their cattle are productive, 11they have many happy children, 12, 13they spend their time singing and dancing. They are wealthy and need deny themselves nothing; they are prosperous to the end. 14All this despite the fact that they ordered God away and wanted no part of him and his ways.

15" 'Who is Almighty God?' they scoff. 'Why should we obey him? What good will it do us?'

16"Look, everything the wicked touch has turned to gold! But I refuse even to deal with people like that. 17Yet the wicked get away with it every time. They never have trouble, and God skips them when he distributes his sorrows and anger. 18Are they driven before the wind like straw? Are they carried away by the storm? Not at all!

19" 'Well,' you say, 'at least God will punish their children!' But I say that God should punish the man who sins, not his children! Let him feel the penalty himself. 20Yes, let him be destroyed for his iniquity. Let him drink deeply of the anger of the

21:4 *I am complaining about God,* implied.

20:6
Isa 14:13,14
20:7
Job 4:20; 7:10
8:18; 14:20
20:9
Job 7:8,10
8:18
20:10
Job 5:4
27:16,17
20:11
Job 13:26
20:12
Job 15:16
20:19
Job 24:2-4; 35:9
20:21
Job 15:29
20:22
Job 5:5; 15:21
20:25
Job 16:13
18:11,14
20:26
Job 15:30; 18:18
20:27
Deut 31:28
20:28
Deut 28:31
Job 21:30
20:29
Job 27:13
31:2,3

21:2
Job 11:3; 17:2
21:4
Job 6:11; 7:11
21:6
Ps 55:5
21:7
Ps 73:3
21:8
Ps 17:14
21:9
Job 12:6
21:12
Job 36:11
21:14
Job 22:17
21:15
Job 22:17; 34:9
21:17
Job 18:5,6
21:18
Job 13:25
Ps 1:4; 35:5
21:19
Ex 20:5
Mt 23:31-35

20:6, 7 Although Zophar was wrong in directing this tirade against Job, he was correct in talking about the final end of evil people. At first, sin seems enjoyable and attractive. Lying, stealing, or oppressing others often brings temporary gain to those who practice these sins. Some even live a long time with ill-gotten gain. But in the end, God's justice will prevail. What Zophar missed is that judgment for these sins may not come in the lifetime of the sinner. Punishment may be deferred until the last judgment, when sinners will be eternally cut off from God. We should not be impressed with the success and power of evil people. God's judgment on them is certain.

21:1ff Job refuted Zophar's idea that evil people never experience wealth and happiness, pointing out that in the real world the wicked do indeed prosper. God does as he wills to individuals (21:22–25), and people cannot use their circumstances to measure their own goodness or God's—they are not necessarily related. Success to Job's friends was based on outward performance; success to God, however, is in a person's heart.

21:22
Job 36:22

21:23
Job 20:11

21:26
Job 3:13; 24:20

21:28
Job 1:3
Ps 37:36
52:5,6

21:30
Job 20:29

21:33
Job 3:19,22
17:16; 24:24

21:34
Job 16:2; 42:7

22:2
Job 35:7

22:4
Job 14:3

22:5
Job 11:6; 15:5

22:6
Ex 22:26

22:7
Job 31:31

22:8
Job 9:24; 12:19

22:9
Job 6:27
24:3,21

22:10
Job 15:21; 18:8

22:12
Job 11:7-9

22:14
Job 26:9

22:15
Job 14:19

22:17
Job 21:14,15

22:18
Job 12:6; 21:16

22:20
Job 15:30

22:22
Job 6:10; 23:12

Almighty. 21For when he is dead, then he will never again be able to enjoy his family.

22"But who can rebuke God, the supreme Judge? 23, 24He destroys those who are healthy, wealthy, fat, and prosperous; 25God also destroys those in deep and grinding poverty who have never known anything good. 26Both alike are buried in the same dust, both eaten by the same worms.

27"I know what you are going to say— 28you will tell me of rich and wicked men who came to disaster because of their sins. 29But I reply, Ask anyone who has been around and he can tell you the truth, 30, 31, 32that the evil man is usually spared in the day of calamity, and allowed to escape. No one rebukes him openly. No one repays him for what he has done. And an honor guard keeps watch at his grave. 33A great funeral procession precedes and follows him as the soft earth covers him. 34How can you comfort me when your whole premise is so wrong?"

3. Third round of discussion

22 *Another address from Eliphaz:*

2"Is mere man of any worth to God? Even the wisest is of value only to himself! 3Is it any pleasure to the Almighty if you are righteous? Would it be any gain to him if you were perfect? 4Is it because you are good that he is punishing you? 5Not at all! It is because of your wickedness! Your sins are endless!

6"For instance, you must have refused to loan money to needy friends unless they gave you all their clothing as a pledge—yes, you must have stripped them to the bone. 7You must have refused water to the thirsty, and bread to the starving. 8But no doubt you gave men of importance anything they wanted, and let the wealthy live wherever they chose. 9You sent widows away without helping them, and broke the arms of orphans. 10, 11That is why you are now surrounded by traps and sudden fears, and darkness and waves of horror.

12"God is so great—higher than the heavens, higher than the stars. 13But you reply, 'That is why he can't see what I am doing! How can he judge through the thick darkness? 14For thick clouds swirl about him so that he cannot see us. He is way up there, walking on the vault of heaven.'

15, 16"Don't you realize that those treading the ancient paths of sin are snatched away in youth, and the foundations of their lives washed out forever? 17For they said to God, 'Go away, God! What can you do for us?' 18(God forbid that I should say a thing like that.) Yet they forgot that he had filled their homes with good things. 19And now the righteous shall see them destroyed; the innocent shall laugh the wicked to scorn. 20'See,' they will say, 'the last of our enemies have been destroyed in the fire.'

21"Quit quarreling with God! Agree with him and you will have peace at last! His favor will surround you if you will only admit that you were wrong. 22Listen to his

---

21:22 In the midst of Job's confusion about his suffering, he asked, "But who can rebuke God, the supreme Judge?" Even if your personal struggles seem as great and difficult as Job's, your response indicates your current attitude toward God. Rather than becoming angry with God, continue to trust him, no matter what your circumstances may be. Although it is sometimes difficult to see, God *is* in control.

21:29–32 If wicked people become wealthy despite their sin, why should we try to be good? The wicked may *seem* to get away with sin, but there is a higher Judge and a future judgment (Revelation 20:11–15). The final settlement of justice will not come in this life, but in the next. What is important is how a person views God through prosperity or poverty, not the prosperity or poverty itself.

22:1ff This is Eliphaz's third and final speech to Job. When he first spoke to Job (Job 4, 5), he commended Job's good works and gently suggested that Job might need to repent of some sin. While he said nothing new in this speech, he did get more specific. He couldn't shake his belief that suffering is God's punishment for evil deeds, so he suggested several possible sins that Job might have

committed. Eliphaz wasn't trying to destroy Job; at the end of his speech he promised that Job would receive peace and restoration if he would only admit his sin and repent.

22:12–14 Eliphaz declared that Job's view of God was too small, and he criticized Job for thinking that God was too far removed from earth to care about him. And, he said, if Job knew of God's intense, personal interest in him, he wouldn't dare take his sins so lightly. Eliphaz had a point—some people do take sin lightly because they think God is far away and doesn't notice all we do. But his point did not apply to Job.

22:21–30 Several times Job's friends showed a partial knowledge of God's truth and character, but they had trouble accurately applying this truth to life. Such was the case with Eliphaz, who gave a beautiful summary of repentance. He was correct in saying that we must ask for God's forgiveness when we sin, but his statement did not apply to Job who had already sought God's forgiveness (7:20, 21; 9:20; 13:23) and had lived closely in touch with God all along.

instructions and store them in your heart. 23If you return to God and put right all the wrong in your home, then you will be restored. 24If you give up your lust for money, and throw your gold away, 25then the Almighty himself shall be your treasure; he will be your precious silver!

26"Then you will delight yourself in the Lord, and look up to God. 27You will pray to him, and he will hear you, and you will fulfill all your promises to him. 28Whatever you wish will happen! And the light of heaven will shine upon the road ahead of you. 29If you are attacked and knocked down, you will know that there is someone who will lift you up again. Yes, he will save the humble, 30and help even sinners by your pure hands."

22:23
Job 8:5; 11:14

22:24
Job 31:24,25

22:26
Job 27:10

22:27
Job 33:26; 34:28

22:28
Job 11:17

22:29
Job 5:11

23 The reply of Job:

2"My complaint today is still a bitter one, and my punishment far more severe than my fault deserves. 3Oh, that I knew where to find God—that I could go to his throne and talk with him there. 4, 5I would tell him all about my side of this argument, and listen to his reply, and understand what he wants. 6Would he merely overpower me with his greatness? No, he would listen with sympathy. 7Fair and honest men could reason with him, and be acquitted by my Judge.

8"But I search in vain. I seek him here, I seek him there, and cannot find him. 9I seek him in his workshop in the North, but cannot find him there; nor can I find him in the South; there, too, he hides himself. 10But he knows every detail of what is happening to me; and when he has examined me, he will pronounce me completely innocent—as pure as solid gold!

11"I have stayed in God's paths, following his steps. I have not turned aside. 12I have not refused his commandments but have enjoyed them more than my daily food. 13Nevertheless, his mind concerning me remains unchanged, and who can turn him from his purposes? Whatever he wants to do, he does. 14So he will do to me all he has planned, and there is more ahead.

15"No wonder I am so terrified in his presence. When I think of it, terror grips me. 16, 17God has given me a fainting heart; he, the Almighty, has terrified me with darkness all around me, thick, impenetrable darkness everywhere.

23:2
Job 6:2,3; 7:11

23:4
Job 13:18
Isa 43:26

23:6
Job 9:4
2 Cor 12:9,10

23:7
Job 13:3,16

23:8
Job 9:11

23:10
Job 7:18
Ps 7:9; 11:5

23:11
Job 31:7
Ps 17:5; 44:18
1 Thess 2:10

23:12
Job 6:10

23:16
Deut 20:3
Job 10:18,19

24 "Why doesn't God open the court and listen to my case? Why must the godly wait for him in vain? 2For a crime wave has engulfed us—landmarks are moved, flocks of sheep are stolen, 3and even the donkeys of the poor and fatherless are taken. Poor widows must surrender the little they have as a pledge to get a loan. 4The needy are kicked aside; they must get out of the way. 5Like the wild donkeys in the desert, the poor must spend all their time just getting barely enough to keep

24:3
Ex 22:26

24:4
Job 29:16; 30:25

24:5
Job 39:5-8

23:14 and there is more ahead, literally, "and many such things are with him."

23:1—24:25 Job continued his questioning, saying that his suffering would be more bearable if only he knew why it was happening. If there was sin for which he could repent, he would! He knew about the wicked and the fact that they would be punished; he knew God could vindicate him if he so chose. In all his examples of the wicked in the world, his overriding desire was for God to clear his name, prove his righteousness, and explain why he was chosen to receive all this calamity. Job tried to make his friends see that questions about God, life, and justice are not as simple as they assumed.

23:9 This verse can also be translated, "When I look to the left or right (north or south), I can't find God." Job was not saying that God lives in any one place, but that he appeared to be avoiding him. In 23:10, however, he expressed confidence that God knew every detail about his situation and would come to his rescue.

23:10 In Job 22, Eliphaz tried to condemn Job by identifying some secret sin which he may have committed. We are always likely to have hidden sin in our lives, sin we don't even know about, especially when God's standards are so high and our performance so imperfect. If we are true believers, however, all of our sins are

forgiven because of what Christ did on the cross in our behalf (Romans 5:1; 8:1). The Bible also teaches that even if our mind should condemn us, God is greater than our mind (1 John 3:17–24; see the textual note on 1 John 3:20). His forgiveness and cleansing are sufficient; they overrule our mind's nagging doubts. The Holy Spirit in us is our proof that we are innocent in God's eyes even though we may feel guilty. If we, like Job, are truly seeking God, we can stand up to the accusations of others as well as our own nagging doubts. If God has forgiven and accepted us, we are forgiven indeed.

23:14 Job wavered back and forth, first proclaiming loyalty to God and then calling God his enemy. His friends' words and his own suspicions were undermining his confidence in God. When affliction comes, it is natural to blame God and to think that our suffering must be divine punishment. But we must not assume that God is being hostile toward us. His purposes go deeper than our ability to grasp all that is really happening. While this sounds like a pat answer, it is the same answer God gave Job in chapters 38—41. We shouldn't demand to know why certain calamities befall us. Often we cannot or are not meant to know until later.

soul and body together. They are sent into the desert to search for food for their children. ⁶They eat what they find that grows wild, and must even glean the vineyards of the wicked. ⁷All night they lie naked in the cold, without clothing or covering. ⁸They are wet with the showers of the mountains and live in caves for want of a home.

⁹"The wicked snatch fatherless children from their mother's breasts, and take a poor man's baby as a pledge before they will loan him any money or grain. ¹⁰That is why they must go about naked, without clothing, and are forced to carry food while they are starving. ¹¹They are forced to press out the olive oil without tasting it, and to tread out the grape juice as they suffer from thirst. ¹²The bones of the dying cry from the city; the wounded cry for help; yet God does not respond to their moaning.

¹³"The wicked rebel against the light and are not acquainted with the right and the good. ¹⁴, ¹⁵They are murderers who rise in the early dawn to kill the poor and needy; at night they are thieves and adulterers, waiting for the twilight 'when no one will see me,' they say. They mask their faces so no one will know them. ¹⁶They break into houses at night and sleep in the daytime—they are not acquainted with the light. ¹⁷The black night is their morning; they ally themselves with the terrors of the darkness.

¹⁸"But how quickly they disappear from the face of the earth. Everything they own is cursed. They leave no property for their children. ¹⁹Death consumes sinners as drought and heat consume snow. ²⁰Even the sinner's own mother shall forget him. Worms shall feed sweetly on him. No one will remember him any more. For wicked men are broken like a tree in the storm. ²¹For they have taken advantage of the childless who have no protecting sons. They refuse to help the needy widows. ²², ²³"Yet sometimes it seems as though God preserves the rich by his power, and restores them to life when anyone else would die. God gives them confidence and strength, and helps them in many ways. ²⁴But though they are very great now, yet in a moment they shall be gone like all others, cut off like heads of grain. ²⁵Can anyone claim otherwise? Who can prove me a liar and claim that I am wrong?"

25 The further reply of Bildad the Shuhite:
²"God is powerful and dreadful. He enforces peace in heaven. ³Who is able to number his hosts of angels? And his light shines down on all the earth. ⁴How can mere man stand before God and claim to be righteous? Who in all the earth can boast that he is clean? ⁵God is so glorious that even the moon and stars are less than nothing as compared to him. ⁶How much less is man, who is but a worm in his sight?"

26 Job's reply:
²"What wonderful helpers you all are! And how you have encouraged me
24:22, 23 *Yet sometimes,* implied.

24:8
Lam 4:5
Heb 11:38
24:9
Job 6:27
24:12
Job 9:23,24
Mal 2:17
Rom 2:4,5
24:14
Ps 10:8
Prov 7:9
Mic 2:1
24:16
Ex 22:2
Mt 6:19
24:17
Ps 91:5
24:18
Job 5:3
22:11,16; 27:20
24:19
Job 6:16,17
21:13
24:20
Job 18:17
19:10; 21:26
Prov 10:7
Isa 49:15
Dan 4:14
24:21
Job 22:9
24:22
Job 9:4,10:4
11:11; 12:6
24:24
Job 14:21
Ps 37:10
24:25
Job 6:28; 27:4

25:2
Job 9:4; 16:19
31:2; 36:5
37:23
25:4
Job 4:17; 9:2
25:5
Job 15:15; 31:26

24:18–21 Job suddenly seemed to be arguing on his friends' side. For this reason, some commentators think one of Job's friends said these words. But we shouldn't expect Job to present a unified argument. He was confused. He was not arguing that God rewards the wicked and punishes the righteous; he was simply asserting that in his case, a righteous man was suffering.

25:1ff Bildad's final reply was weak. It avoided Job's examples of the prosperity of the wicked. Instead of attempting to refute Job, Bildad accused Job of pride because he was claiming that his suffering was not the result of sin. Job never claimed to be without sin, but only that his sin could not have caused his present trouble.

25:6 It is important to understand that Bildad, not God, was calling man a worm. Human beings are created in God's image (Genesis 1:26, 27). Psalm 8:5 says that man is "only a little lower than the angels." Bildad may have simply been using a poetic description to contrast our worth to the worth and power of God.

26:1ff Job has the distinction of giving the longest speech in the book—six chapters—weaving together pictures of God's mystery and power in a beautiful poem of trust. Beginning by brushing off Bildad's latest reply as irrelevant (Job 25), Job then tells Bildad and his friends that they could not possibly know everything about God. Wisdom does not originate from this life or from the human mind—it comes from God (28:27, 28). Job then defends his upright and honest life. While admitting that he was not perfect, Job maintains that his motives were right.

26:2–4 With great sarcasm, Job attacked his friends' comments. Their theological explanations failed to bring any relief, because they were unable to turn their knowledge into helpful counsel. When dealing with people, it is more important to love and understand them than to analyze them or give advice. Compassion produces greater results than criticism or blame.

in my great need! 3How you have enlightened my stupidity! What wise things you have said! 4How did you ever think of all these brilliant comments?

5, 6"The dead stand naked, trembling before God in the place where they go. 7God stretches out heaven over empty space, and hangs the earth upon nothing. 8He wraps the rain in his thick clouds and the clouds are not split by the weight. 9He shrouds his throne with his clouds. 10He sets a boundary for the ocean, yes, and a boundary for the day and for the night. 11The pillars of heaven tremble at his rebuke. 12And by his power the sea grows calm; he is skilled at crushing its pride! 13The heavens are made beautiful by his Spirit; he pierces the swiftly gliding serpent.

14"These are some of the minor things he does, merely a whisper of his power. Who then can withstand his thunder?"

27 Job's final defense:

2"I vow by the living God, who has taken away my rights, even the Almighty God who has embittered my soul, 3that as long as I live, while I have breath from God, 4my lips shall speak no evil, my tongue shall speak no lies. 5I will never, never agree that you are right; until I die I will vow my innocence. 6I am *not* a sinner—I repeat it again and again. My conscience is clear for as long as I live. 7Those who declare otherwise are my wicked enemies. They are evil men.

8"But what hope has the godless when God cuts him off and takes away his life? 9Will God listen to his cry when trouble comes upon him? 10For he does not delight himself in the Almighty or pay any attention to God except in times of crisis.

11"I will teach you about God— 12but really, I don't need to, for you yourselves know as much about him as I do; yet you are saying all these useless things to me.

13"This is the fate awaiting the wicked from the hand of the Almighty: 14If he has a multitude of children, it is so that they will die in war, or starve to death. 15Those who survive shall be brought down to the grave by disease and plague, with no one to mourn them, not even their wives.

16"The evil man may accumulate money like dust, with closets jammed full of clothing— 17yes, he may order them made by his tailor, but the innocent shall wear that clothing, and shall divide his silver among them. 18Every house built by the wicked is as fragile as a spider web, as full of cracks as a leafy booth!

19"He goes to bed rich, but wakes up to find that all his wealth is gone. 20Terror overwhelms him, and he is blown away in the storms of the night. 21The east wind carries him away, and he is gone. It sweeps him into eternity. 22For God shall hurl at him unsparingly. He longs to flee from God. 23Everyone will cheer at his death, and boo him into eternity.

28 "Men know how to mine silver and refine gold, 2to dig iron from the earth and melt copper from stone. 3, 4Men know how to put light into darkness so that a mine shaft can be sunk into the earth, and the earth searched and its deep secrets explored. Into the black rock, shadowed by death, men descend on ropes, swinging back and forth.

5"Men know how to obtain food from the surface of the earth, while underneath there is fire.

6"They know how to find sapphires and gold dust— 7treasures that no bird of prey can see, no eagle's eye observe— 8for they are deep within the mines. No wild animal has ever walked upon those treasures; no lion has set his paw there. 9Men

26:13 *The heavens are made beautiful by his Spirit, or "the bars of heaven are afraid of him." See vs 11.*

Cross references (right margin):

26:5 Job 3:13
26:7 Job 9:8
26:8 Job 37:11
26:9 Job 22:14 Ps 97:2; 105:39
26:10 Job 38:1-11,19, 20,24
26:13 Job 9:8
26:14 Job 36:29 37:4,5
27:1 Job 13:12; 29:1
27:2 Job 9:18; 16:11
27:3 Job 32:8; 33:4
27:4 Job 6:28; 33:3
27:6 Job 2:3; 13:18
27:8 Job 8:13; 11:20
27:9 Job 35:12,13
27:10 Job 22:26,27
27:13 Job 20:29
27:17 Job 20:18-21
27:18 Job 8:15
27:19 Job 7:8,21
27:20 Job 15:21; 20:8
27:21 Job 7:10; 21:18
27:22 Job 11:20

27:6 In the midst of all the accusations, Job was able to declare, "My conscience is clear." Only right living before God can bring a clear conscience, and how important Job's record became as he was being accused. Like Job, we can't claim sinless lives, but we *can* claim forgiven lives. When we confess our sins to God, we are forgiven and can live our lives with clear consciences (1 John 1:9).

27:13–23 Job agreed with his friends that the end of the wicked will be disaster, but he did not agree that *he* was wicked and deserving of punishment. Most of the punishments Job listed never happened to him, and he certainly never longed to "flee from God." So he wasn't including himself as one of the wicked. On the contrary, he continually pleaded for God to come and vindicate him.

know how to tear apart flinty rocks and how to overturn the roots of mountains. ¹⁰They drill tunnels in the rocks and lay bare precious stones. ¹¹They dam up streams of water and pan the gold.

¹²"But though men can do all these things, they don't know where to find wisdom and understanding. ¹³They not only don't know how to get it, but, in fact, it is not to be found among the living.

¹⁴" 'It's not here,' the oceans say; and the seas reply, 'Nor is it here.'

¹⁵"It cannot be bought for gold or silver, ¹⁶nor for all the gold of Ophir or precious onyx stones or sapphires. ¹⁷Wisdom is far more valuable than gold and glass. It cannot be bought for jewels mounted in fine gold. ¹⁸Coral or crystal is worthless in trying to get it; its price is far above rubies. ¹⁹Topaz from Ethiopia cannot purchase it, nor even the purest gold.

²⁰"Then where can we get it? Where can it be found? ²¹For it is hid from the eyes of all mankind; even the sharp-eyed birds in the sky cannot discover it.

²²"But Destruction and Death speak of knowing something about it! ²³, ²⁴And God surely knows where it is to be found, for he looks throughout the whole earth, under all the heavens. ²⁵He makes the winds blow and sets the boundaries of the oceans. ²⁶He makes the laws of the rain and a path for the lightning. ²⁷He knows where wisdom is and declares it to all who will listen. He established it and examined it thoroughly. ²⁸And this is what he says to all mankind: 'Look, to fear the Lord is true wisdom; to forsake evil is real understanding.' "

29 *Job continues:*
²"Oh, for the years gone by when God took care of me, ³when he lighted the way before me and I walked safely through the darkness; ⁴yes, in my early

28:11 *They dam up streams of waters and pan the gold,* literally, "He brings forth to the light things that are hidden."

28:12
Job 28:23,28

28:17
Prov 8:10; 16:16

28:18
Prov 8:11

28:19
Prov 8:19

28:22
Job 26:6

28:23
Ps 11:4
33:13,14
Prov 8:22-36
15:3

28:25
Job 12:15
38:8-11
Ps 135:7

28:26
Job 37:3,6,11,
12; 38:25

28:28
Ps 111:10
Prov 1:7; 9:10

29:3
Job 11:17

WHERE CAN WISDOM BE FOUND? Job and his friends differed in their ideas of how men become wise.	Person	His source of wisdom	Attitude toward God
	Eliphaz	Wisdom is learned by observing and experiencing life. He based his advice to Job on his confident, firsthand knowledge (4:7, 8; 5:27).	"I have personally observed how God works and have figured him out."
	Bildad	Wisdom is inherited from the past. Trustworthy knowledge is secondhand. He based his advice to Job on traditional proverbs and sayings which he frequently quoted (8:8, 9; 18:5–21).	"Those who have gone before us figured God out and all we have to do is use that knowledge."
	Zophar	Wisdom belongs to the wise. He based his advice on his wisdom which had no other source than himself (11:6; 20:1–29).	"The wise know what God is like, but there aren't many of us around."
	Job	God is the source of wisdom and the first step toward wisdom is to fear God (28:27, 28).	"God reveals his wisdom to those who humbly trust him."

28:12 People can perform all kinds of technological wonders. They can find stars invisible to the eye, they visit space, they can store volumes of information on a microchip. But even the greatest scientists, on their own, are at a loss to discover wisdom for their daily lives. Only God can show them where to look to find wisdom because he is the source of wisdom (28:27). True wisdom is having God's perspective on life. As the Creator of life, only he knows what is best for his creation. It is fruitless for us to try to become wise merely through our own observations and efforts, because God alone sees the greater purpose for his world.

28:13 Job stated that wisdom cannot be found among the living. It is natural for people who do not understand the importance of God's Word to seek wisdom here on earth. They look to philosophers and other leaders to give them direction for living. Yet Job said, "It is not here." No leader or group of leaders can

produce enough knowledge or insight to explain the totality of human experience. The ultimate interpretation of life, of who we are and where we are going, must come from outside and above our mortal life. When looking for guidance, seek to know God's wisdom as made clear in the Bible. To be lifted above and beyond the boundaries of life, we must know and trust the Lord of life.

28:16 Gold from Ophir was considered the finest gold available. Ophir was probably located in Africa or along the Arabian coast. Wherever it was, it was a good distance from Israel, for it took King Solomon's ships three years to make the voyage (1 Kings 10:22).

28:28 To "fear the Lord" is a key theme in the wisdom literature of the Bible (Job through the Song of Solomon). It means to have respect and reverence for God and to feel in awe of his majesty and power. This is the starting point to finding real wisdom (see Proverbs 1:7–9).

years, when the friendship of God was felt in my home; 5when the Almighty was still with me and my children were around me; 6when my projects prospered, and even the rock poured out streams of olive oil to me!

7"Those were the days when I went out to the city gate and took my place among the honored elders. 8The young saw me and stepped aside, and even the aged rose and stood up in respect at my coming. 9The princes stood in silence and laid their hands upon their mouths. 10The highest officials of the city stood in quietness. 11All rejoiced in what I said. All who saw me spoke well of me.

12"For I, as an honest judge, helped the poor in their need, and the fatherless who had no one to help them. 13I helped those who were ready to perish and they blessed me. And I caused the widows' hearts to sing for joy. 14All I did was just and honest, for righteousness was my clothing! 15I served as eyes for the blind and feet for the lame. 16I was as a father to the poor, and saw to it that even strangers received a fair trial. 17I knocked out the fangs of the godless oppressors and made them drop their victims.

18"I thought, 'Surely I shall die quietly in my nest after a long, good life.' 19For everything I did prospered; the dew lay all night upon my fields and watered them. 20Fresh honors were constantly given me, and my abilities were constantly refreshed and renewed. 21Everyone listened to me and valued my advice, and were silent until I spoke. 22And after I spoke, they spoke no more, for my counsel satisfied them. 23They longed for me to speak as those in drought-time long for rain. They waited eagerly with open mouths. 24When they were discouraged, I smiled and that encouraged them, and lightened their spirits. 25I told them what they should do, and corrected them as their chief, or as a king instructs his army, and as one who comforts those who mourn.

30 "But now those younger than I deride me—young men whose fathers are less than my dogs. 2Oh, they have strong backs all right, but they are useless, stupid fools. 3They are gaunt with famine and have been cast out into deserts and the wastelands, desolate and gloomy. 4They eat roots and leaves, 5having been driven from civilization. Men shouted after them as after thieves. 6So now they live in frightening ravines, and in caves, and among the rocks. 7They sound like animals among the bushes, huddling together for shelter beneath the nettles. 8These sons of theirs have also turned out to be fools, yes, children of no name, outcasts of civilization.

9"And now I have become the subject of their ribald song! I am a joke among *them!* 10*They* despise me and won't come near me, and don't mind spitting in my face. 11For God has placed my life in jeopardy. These young men, having humbled me, now cast off all restraint before me. 12This rabble trip me and lay traps in my path. 13They block my road and do everything they can to hasten my calamity, knowing full well that I have no one to help me. 14They come at me from all directions. They rush upon me when I am down.

15"I live in terror now. They hold me in contempt and my prosperity has vanished as a cloud before a strong wind. 16My heart is broken. Depression haunts my days. 17My weary nights are filled with pain as though something were relentlessly

29:12 *For I, as an honest judge,* implied in vs 7.

29:6
Deut 32:13
Ps 81:16

29:9
Job 21:5

29:11
Job 4:3,4

29:12
Job 24:4,9
31:17,21; 34:28

29:13
Job 31:19
Isa 27:13

29:14
Job 27:5,6
Ps 132:9

29:16
Prov 29:7
Eph 5:1
Jas 1:27

29:17
Ps 3:7
Prov 30:14

29:19
Jer 17:8
Hos 14:5

29:20
Gen 49:24
Ps 18:34

29:21
Job 4:3
32:11,12

29:25
Job 1:3; 4:4
16:5; 31:37
Isa 61:1-3

30:1
Job 12:4
Isa 3:5

30:9
Job 12:4; 17:6
Ps 35:15,16
69:12

30:10
Isa 50:6
Mt 26:67

30:11
Ruth 1:21
Ps 32:9; 88:7

30:12
Ps 140:4,5
Isa 3:5

30:15
Job 3:25; 7:9
Ps 55:3-5

30:16
Ps 22:14

29:7 Job was walking a fine line between bragging about past accomplishments and recalling good deeds in order to answer the charges against him. Job's one weakness throughout his conversations is that he came dangerously close to pride. Pride is especially deceptive when we are doing right. It separates us from God by making us think we're better than we really are. Then comes the tendency to trust our own opinions, which leads to other kinds of sin. While it is not wrong to recount past deeds, it is far better to recount God's blessings to us. This will help to keep us from inadvertently falling into pride.

29:12 In Job's day, a judge served as both a city councilman and a magistrate, helping to manage the community and settle

disputes. In most cases, this was not a full-time position but a part-time post held on the basis of one's respect and standing in the area. Job was a judge (see 29:7–17).

30:1ff To suffer extreme loss, as Job did, was humiliating. But to face abuse at the hands of younger men added insult to injury. Job had lost his family, possessions, and health, his position and good name. He was not even respected for suffering bravely. Unfortunately, younger people sometimes laugh at and take advantage of older people and those who are limited in some way. Instead, they should realize that all our physical abilities and attributes are short-lived and that all people are equally loved by God.

30:19
Ps 69:2,14

30:20
Job 19:7

30:21
Job 16:9,14

30:22
Job 9:17; 27:21

30:23
Job 9:22; 10:8

30:24
Job 19:7

30:26
Job 19:8

30:28
Job 19:7

30:30
Job 2:7

31:1
Gen 6:2
2 Sam 11:2-4
Mt 5:28

31:4
Job 14:16
28:24; 34:21
Prov 5:21

31:6
Prov 16:11
Isa 26:7

31:7
Lev 26:16
Job 9:30; 23:11
Mic 6:15

31:10
Deut 28:30
Jer 8:10
Hos 4:13,14

31:11
Lev 20:10
Deut 22:24

31:12
Job 15:30

31:13
Deut 24:14,15

31:15
Job 10:3

31:16
Ex 22:22-24
Job 20:19

31:17
Job 22:7,9

31:19
Job 22:6; 24:4

31:23
Job 13:11

31:24
Job 22:24
Mk 10:24

31:30
Job 5:3

gnawing at my bones. 18All night long I toss and turn, and my garments bind about me. 19God has thrown me into the mud. I have become as dust and ashes.

20"I cry to you, O God, but you don't answer me. I stand before you and you don't bother to look. 21You have become cruel toward me, and persecute me with great power and effect. 22You throw me into the whirlwind and dissolve me in the storm. 23And I know that your purpose for me is death. 24I expected my fall to be broken, just as one who falls stretches out his hand or cries for help in his calamity.

25"And did I not weep for those in trouble? Wasn't I deeply grieved for the needy? 26I therefore looked for good to come. Evil came instead. I waited for the light. Darkness came. 27My heart is troubled and restless. Waves of affliction have come upon me. 28, 29I am black, but not from sunburn. I stand up and cry to the assembly for help. [But I might as well save my breath,] for I am considered a brother to jackals and a companion to ostriches. 30My skin is black and peeling. My bones burn with fever. 31The voice of joy and gladness has turned to mourning.

31 "I made a covenant with my eyes not to look with lust upon a girl. 2, 3I know full well that Almighty God above sends calamity on those who do. 4He sees everything I do, and every step I take.

5"If I have lied and deceived— 6but God knows that I am innocent— 7, 8or if I have stepped off God's pathway, or if my heart has lusted for what my eyes have seen, or if I am guilty of any other sin, then let someone else reap the crops I have sown and let all that I have planted be rooted out.

9"Or if I have longed for another man's wife, 10then may I die, and may my wife be in another man's home, and someone else become her husband. 11For lust is a shameful sin, a crime that should be punished. 12It is a devastating fire that destroys to hell, and would root out all I have planted.

13"If I have been unfair to my servants, 14how could I face God? What could I say when he questioned me about it? 15For God made me, and made my servant too. He created us both.

16"If I have hurt the poor or caused widows to weep, 17or refused food to hungry orphans— 18(but we have always cared for orphans in our home, treating them as our own children)— 19, 20or if I have seen anyone freezing and not given him clothing, or fleece from my sheep to keep him warm, 21or if I have taken advantage of an orphan because I thought I could get away with it— 22if I have done any of these things, then let my arm be torn from its socket! Let my shoulder be wrenched out of place! 23Rather that than face the judgment sent by God; that I dread more than anything else. For if the majesty of God opposes me, what hope is there?

24"If I have put my trust in money, 25if my happiness depends on wealth, 26or if I have looked at the sun shining in the skies, or the moon walking down her silver pathway, 27and my heart has been secretly enticed, and I have worshiped them by kissing my hand to them, 28this, too, must be punished by the judges. For if I had done such things, it would mean that I denied the God of heaven.

29"If I have rejoiced at harm to an enemy— 30(but actually I have never cursed anyone nor asked for revenge)— 31or if any of my servants have ever gone hungry— 32(actually I have never turned away even a stranger but have opened my doors to all)— 33or if, like Adam, I have tried to hide my sins, 34fearing the crowd

30:28, 29 *But I might as well save my breath,* implied.

31:1–4 Job talked about lust in order to prove a point. He had not only avoided committing a great sin (like adultery); he had not even taken the first step toward that sin (looking at a woman with greedy desire). In chapter 29, Job reviewed his good deeds. Here in chapter 31 he listed sins he had not done—in his heart (31:1–12), against his neighbors (31:13–23), and against God (31:24–34).

31:24–28 In these verses, Job says that depending on wealth for happiness is idolatry and denying the God of heaven. We excuse our society's obsession with money and possessions as a

necessary evil or "the way it works" in the modern world. But every society in every age has valued the power and prestige that money brings. True believers must purge themselves of the deep-seated desire for more power, prestige, and possessions.

31:33, 34 Job declared that he did not try to hide his sin as Adam did (Genesis 3). Adam did not have a crowd watching him, but he tried to hide from God. The fear that our sins will be discovered leads us to patterns of deception. We cover up with lies so that we will appear good to others. But we cannot hide from God. Acknowledge your sins and free yourself to receive forgiveness and a new life.

and its contempt, so that I refused to acknowledge my sin and do not go out of my way to help others— 35(oh, that there were someone who would listen to me and try to see my side of this argument. Look, I will sign my signature to my defense; now let the Almighty show me that I am wrong; let *him* approve the indictments made against me by my enemies. 36I would treasure it like a crown. 37Then I would tell him exactly what I have done and why, presenting my defense as one he listens to).

38, 39"Or if my land accuses me because I stole the fruit it bears, or if I have murdered its owners to get their land for myself, 40then let thistles grow on that land instead of wheat, and weeds instead of barley."

Job's words are ended.

C. A YOUNG MAN ANSWERS JOB (32:1—37:24)
Young Elihu rebukes the three friends for being unable to give Job a reasonable answer for why he was suffering. But he only gives a partial answer to Job's question by saying that man cannot understand all that God allows, but must trust him. This was the best answer that man could give, yet it was incomplete. Often the best human answers are incomplete because we do not have all the facts.

32 The three men refused to reply further to Job because he kept insisting on his innocence.

2Then Elihu (son of Barachel, the Buzite, of the Clan of Ram) became angry because Job refused to admit he had sinned and to acknowledge that God had just cause for punishing him. 3But he was also angry with Job's three friends because they had been unable to answer Job's arguments and yet had condemned him. 4Elihu had waited until now to speak because the others were older than he.

5But when he saw that they had no further reply, he spoke out angrily, 6and said, "I am young and you are old, so I held back and did not dare to tell you what I think, 7for those who are older are said to be wiser; 8, 9but it is not mere age that makes men wise. Rather, it is the spirit in a man, the breath of the Almighty which makes him intelligent. 10So listen to me awhile and let me express my opinion.

11, 12"I have waited all this time, listening very carefully to your arguments, but not one of them has convinced Job that he is a sinner, or has proved that he is. 13And don't give me that line about 'only God can convince the sinner of his sin.' 14If Job had been arguing with me, I would not answer with that kind of logic!

15"You sit there baffled, with no further replies. 16Shall I then continue to wait when you are silent? 17No, I will give my answer too. 18For I am pent up and full of words, and the spirit within me urges me on. 19I am like a wine cask without a vent! My words are ready to burst out! 20I must speak to find relief, so let me give my answers. 21, 22Don't insist that I be cautious lest I insult someone, and don't make me flatter anyone. Let me be frank, lest God should strike me dead.

33 "Please listen, Job, to what I have to say. 2I have begun to speak; now let me continue. 3I will speak the truth with all sincerity. 4For the Spirit of God has

31:35
Job 19:7; 27:7
30:20,24,28
35:14
Ps 26:1

31:38
1 Kgs 21:19
Job 24:2,6,
10-12
Hab 2:11
Jas 5:4

31:40
Isa 5:6
Zeph 2:9

32:1
Job 10:7; 13:18
31:6; 33:9

32:6
Job 15:10
Rom 13:7
1 Tim 5:1
Tit 2:6

32:8
Job 33:4; 38:36
Prov 2:6

32:11
Prov 18:17

32:16
Prov 17:28
Amos 5:13

32:21
Lev 19:15
Job 13:8,10
34:19
Prov 24:23

33:3
Job 6:28; 27:4
36:4

32:1 If Job was really a good man, his three friends would have to drop their theory that suffering is always God's punishment for evil actions. Instead of considering another viewpoint, however, they cut off the discussion. They were convinced that Job had some hidden fault or sin, so there was no point in talking if Job would not confess his sin. But Job knew that he had lived rightly before God and others (chapter 29) and had avoided wrong thoughts and actions (chapter 31). He wasn't about to invent a sin to satisfy his friends!

32:2ff When Eliphaz, Bildad, and Zophar had nothing more to say, Elihu became the fourth person to speak to Job. This was the first and only time he spoke. Apparently he was a bystander and much younger than the others (32:6, 7), but he introduced a new viewpoint. While Job's three friends said he was suffering from some past sins, Elihu said Job's suffering would not go away until he realized his *present* sin. Job wasn't suffering because of sin, he

was sinning because of suffering. Elihu pointed out that Job's attitude had become arrogant as he tried to defend his innocence. Elihu also said that suffering is not meant to punish us as much as it is meant to correct and restore us, to keep us on the right path.

There is much truth in Elihu's speech. He was urging Job to look at his suffering from a different perspective and with a greater purpose in mind. While his speech is on a higher spiritual plateau than the others, Elihu still wrongly assumed that a correct response to suffering always brings prosperity (33:23–30) and that suffering is always in some way connected to sin (34:11).

32:7–9 It is not enough to recognize a great truth; it must be lived out in your life. Elihu recognized the truth that God was the only source of real wisdom, but he did not use God's wisdom to help Job. While he recognized where wisdom came from, he did not seek to acquire it. Becoming wise is an ongoing, lifelong pursuit. Don't be content just to know about wisdom; make it part of your life.

made me, and the breath of the Almighty gives me life. 5Don't hesitate to answer me if you can.

6"Look, I am the one you were wishing for, someone to stand between you and God and to be both his representative and yours. 7You need not be frightened of me. I am not some person of renown to make you nervous and afraid. I, too, am made of common clay.

8"You have said it in my hearing, yes, you've said it again and again— 9'I am pure, I am innocent; I have not sinned.' 10You say God is using a fine-toothed comb to try to find a single fault, and so to count you as his enemy. 11'And he puts my feet in the stocks,' you say, 'and watches every move I make.'

12"All right, here is my reply: In this very thing, you have sinned by speaking of God that way. For God is greater than man. 13Why should you fight against him just because he does not give account to you of what he does?

14"For God speaks again and again, 15in dreams, in visions of the night when deep sleep falls on men as they lie on their beds. 16He opens their ears in times like that, and gives them wisdom and instruction, 17, 18causing them to change their minds, and keeping them from pride, and warning them of the penalties of sin, and keeping them from falling into some trap.

19"Or, God sends sickness and pain, even though no bone is broken, 20so that a man loses all taste and appetite for food and doesn't care for even the daintiest dessert. 21He becomes thin, mere skin and bones, 22and draws near to death. 23, 24"But if a messenger from heaven is there to intercede for him as a friend, to show him what is right, then God pities him and says, 'Set him free. Do not make him die, for I have found a substitute.' 25Then his body will become as healthy as a child's, firm and youthful again. 26And when he prays to God, God will hear and answer and receive him with joy, and return him to his duties. 27And he will declare to his friends, 'I sinned, but God let me go. 28He did not let me die. I will go on living in the realm of light.'

29"Yes, God often does these things for man— 30brings back his soul from the pit, so that he may live in the light of the living. 31Mark this well, O Job. Listen to me, and let me say more. 32But if you have anything to say at this point, go ahead. I want to hear it, for I am anxious to justify you. 33But if not, then listen to me. Keep silence and I will teach you wisdom!"

34 Elihu continued:

2"Listen to me, you wise men. 3We can choose the sounds we want to listen to; we can choose the taste we want in food, 4and we should choose to follow what is right. But first of all we must define among ourselves what is good. 5For Job has said, 'I am innocent, but God says I'm not. 6I am called a liar, even though I am innocent. I am horribly punished, even though I have not sinned.'

7, 8"Who else is as arrogant as Job? He must have spent much time with evil men, 9for he said, 'Why waste time trying to please God?'

10"Listen to me, you with understanding. Surely everyone knows that God

33:23, 24 then God pities him and says, or, "and if the Angel says."

Cross references (left margin):

33:9
Job 7:21; 9:21
10:7,14

33:10
Job 13:23,24
16:17

33:11
Job 13:27

33:13
Job 40:2
Isa 45:9

33:14
Job 40:5
Ps 62:11

33:15
Job 4:12-17

33:16
Job 36:10,15

33:17
Job 15:22

33:19
Job 30:17

33:20
Job 3:24; 6:7
Ps 107:18

33:21
Job 16:8; 19:20
Ps 22:17

33:23
Job 36:18
Ps 49:7
Isa 38:17

33:26
Job 22:26,27
34:28

33:27
2 Sam 12:13
Lk 15:21
Rom 6:21

33:28
Job 22:28

33:29
Eph 1:11
Phil 2:13

34:3
1 Cor 2:15
Heb 5:14

34:7
Ps 50:18

34:9
Job 21:15; 35:3
Mal 3:14

34:10
Ps 92:15

33:13 Being informed brings a sense of security. It's natural to want to know what's happening in our lives. Job wanted to know what was going on, why he was suffering. In previous chapters, we sense his frustration. Elihu claimed to have the answer for Job's biggest question, "Why doesn't God tell me what is happening?" Elihu told Job that God was trying to answer him, but he was not listening. Elihu misjudged God on this point. If God were to answer all our questions, we would not be adequately tested. What if God had said, "Job, Satan's going to test you and afflict you, but in the end you'll be healed and get everything back"? Job's greatest test was not the pain and suffering, but that he did not know why it happened. Our greatest test may be that we must trust God's goodness even though we don't understand why our lives are going a certain way. We must learn to trust *God* who is good and not in the goodness of life.

33:14-24 Elihu's point was that God had spoken again and again. He spoke in dreams and visions (33:15-18), through suffering (33:19-22), and by messengers (or mediating angels) who take men's sacrifices to God (33:23, 24). Job already knew that. Elihu accused Job of not listening to God, which, of course, was not true.

34:10-15 God doesn't sin and is never unjust, Elihu claimed. Throughout this book, Eliphaz, Bildad, Zophar, and Elihu all have elements of truth in their speeches. Unfortunately, the nuggets of truth are buried under layers of false assumptions and conclusions. Although we might have a wealth of Bible knowledge and life experiences, we must make sure that our conclusions are consistent with all of God's Word, not just parts of it.

doesn't sin! [11]Rather, he punishes the sinners. [12]There is no truer statement than this: *God is never wicked or unjust.* [13]He alone has authority over the earth and dispenses justice for the world. [14]If God were to withdraw his Spirit, [15]all life would disappear and mankind would turn again to dust.

[16]"Listen now and try to understand. [17]Could God govern if he hated justice? Are you going to condemn the Almighty Judge? [18]Are you going to condemn this God who says to kings and nobles, 'You are wicked and unjust'? [19]For he doesn't care how great a man may be, and doesn't pay any more attention to the rich than to the poor. He made them all. [20]In a moment they die, and at midnight great and small shall suddenly pass away, removed by no human hand.

[21]"For God carefully watches the goings on of all mankind; he sees them all. [22]No darkness is thick enough to hide evil men from his eyes, [23]so there is no need to wait for some great crime before a man is called before God in judgment. [24]Without making a big issue over it, God simply shatters the greatest of men, and puts others in their places. [25]He watches what they do and in a single night he overturns them, destroying them, [26]or openly strikes them down as wicked men. [27]For they turned aside from following him, [28]causing the cry of the poor to come to the attention of God. Yes, he hears the cries of those being oppressed. [29, 30]Yet when he chooses not to speak, who can criticize? Again, he may prevent a vile man from ruling, thus saving a nation from ruin, and he can depose an entire nation just as easily.

[31]"Why don't people exclaim to their God, 'We have sinned, but we will stop'? [32]Or, 'We know not what evil we have done; only tell us, and we will cease at once.'

[33]"Must God tailor his justice to your demands? Must he change the order of the universe to suit your whims? The answer must be obvious even to you! [34, 35]Anyone even half bright will agree with me that you, Job, are speaking like a fool. [36]You should be given the maximum penalty for the wicked way you have talked about God. [37]For now you have added rebellion, arrogance and blasphemy to your other sins."

35 *Elihu continued:*

[2, 3]"Do you think it is right for you to claim, 'I haven't sinned, but I'm no better off before God than if I had'?

[4]"I will answer you, and all your friends too. [5]Look up there into the sky, high above you. [6]If you sin, does that shake the heavens and knock God from his throne? Even if you sin again and again, what effect will it have upon him? [7]Or if you are good, is this some great gift to him? [8]Your sins may hurt another man, or your good deeds may profit him. [9, 10]The oppressed may shriek beneath their wrongs and groan beneath the power of the rich; yet none of them cry to God, asking, 'Where is God my Maker who gives songs in the night, [11]and makes us a little wiser than the animals and birds?'

[12]"But when anyone does cry out this question to him, he never replies by instant punishment of the tyrants. [13]But it is false to say he doesn't hear those cries; [14, 15]and it is even more false to say that he doesn't see what is going on. He *does* bring about justice at last, if you will only wait. But do you cry out against him because he does not instantly respond in anger? [16]Job, you have spoken like a fool."

36 *Elihu continued:*

[2]"Let me go on and I will show you the truth of what I am saying. For I

35:12 *instant punishment of the tyrants,* or, "because of man's base pride."

34:14
Ps 104:29

34:15
Gen 3:19; 7:21
Job 9:22; 10:9
Ps 90:3-10

34:17
Job 40:8

34:19
Deut 10:17
Acts 10:34
Rom 2:11
Eph 6:9
1 Pet 1:17

34:20
Ex 12:29
Job 12:19; 36:20

34:21
Prov 52:1; 15:3
Amos 9:8

34:22
Ps 139:11,12
Amos 9:2,3
Heb 4:13

34:24
Job 12:19

34:26
Ps 9:5; 11:5
Isa 66:24

34:27
1 Sam 15:11
Zeph 1:6
Lk 17:31,32

34:28
Ex 22:23
Job 22:27; 35:9

34:29
Job 5:15; 20:5

34:31
Dan 9:17-14

34:36
Ps 17:3; 26:2

35:2
Job 27:2

35:5
Ps 8:3,4

35:6
Job 7:20

35:7
Job 22:2,3

35:9
Job 27:10; 36:13

35:11
Job 36:33

35:13
Job 27:9

35:14
Job 31:35
Ps 37:5,6

35:16
Job 34:35; 38:2

35:1ff Sometimes we wonder if faithfulness to our convictions really does any good at all. Elihu spoke to this very point. His conclusion was, "Just because God fails to intervene immediately in every situation doesn't mean he is unconcerned. In the broad scope of time God does execute justice." We have his promise on that. Don't lose hope. Wait upon God. Your right living and faith will not go unnoticed.

36:3
Job 8:3; 37:23
Dan 9:7,14

36:4
Job 33:3; 37:16

36:5
Ps 22:24; 69:33
1 Cor 1:24-28

36:6
Job 5:15; 8:22
34:26

36:7
Job 5:11
Ps 33:18; 34:15
113:8

36:9
Job 15:25

36:10
Job 33:16; 36:21

36:12
Job 4:21; 15:22

36:17
Job 22:5,10,11

36:18
Job 33:24; 34:33

36:20
Job 34:20,25

36:21
Ps 31:6; 66:18

36:22
Job 35:11
Jer 31:33

36:23
Job 8:3

36:26
Job 11:7-9
Ps 90:2

36:27
Job 5:10
37:6,11

36:29
Job 26:14

36:31
Job 37:11,13,16

36:32
Job 37:11,12,15

have not finished defending God! 3I will give you many illustrations of the righteousness of my Maker. 4I am telling you the honest truth, for I am a man of well-rounded knowledge.

5"God is almighty and yet does not despise anyone! And he is perfect in his understanding. 6He does not reward the wicked with his blessings, but gives them their full share of punishment. 7He does not ignore the good men but honors them by placing them upon eternal, kingly thrones. 8If troubles come upon them, and they are enslaved and afflicted, 9then he takes the trouble to point out to them the reason, what they have done that is wrong, or how they have behaved proudly. 10He helps them hear his instruction to turn away from their sin.

11"If they listen and obey him, then they will be blessed with prosperity throughout their lives. 12If they won't listen to him, they shall perish in battle and die because of their lack of good sense. 13But the godless reap his anger. They do not even return to him when he punishes them. 14They die young after lives of dissipation and depravity. 15He delivers by distress! This makes them listen to him!

16"How he wanted to lure you away from danger into a wide and pleasant valley and to prosper you there. 17But you are too preoccupied with your imagined grievances against others. 18Watch out! Don't let your anger at others lead you into scoffing at God! Don't let your suffering embitter you at the only one who can deliver you. 19Do you really think that if you shout loudly enough against God, he will be ashamed and repent? Will this put an end to your chastisement?

20"Do not desire the nighttime, with its opportunities for crime. 21Turn back from evil, for it was to prevent you from getting into a life of evil that God sent this suffering.

22"Look, God is all-powerful. Who is a teacher like him? 23Who can say that what he does is absurd or evil? 24Instead, glorify him for his mighty works for which he is so famous. 25Everyone has seen these things from a distance.

26"God is so great that we cannot begin to know him. No one can begin to understand eternity. 27He draws up the water vapor and then distills it into rain, 28which the skies pour down. 29Can anyone really understand the spreading of the clouds, and the thunders within? 30See how he spreads the lightning around him, and blankets the tops of the mountains. 31By his fantastic powers in nature he punishes or blesses the people, giving them food in abundance. 32He fills his hands

HOW SUFFERING AFFECTS US	Suffering is helpful when:	Suffering is harmful when:
	We turn to God for understanding, endurance, and deliverance	We become hardened and reject God
	We ask important questions we might not take time to think about in our normal routine	We refuse to ask any questions and miss any lessons that might be good for us
	We are prepared by it to identify with and comfort others who suffer	We allow it to make us self-centered and selfish
	We are open to be helped by others who are obeying God	We withdraw from the help others can give
	We are ready to learn from a trustworthy God	We reject the fact that God can bring good out of calamity
	We realize we can identify with what Christ suffered on the cross for us	We accuse God of being unjust and perhaps lead others to reject him
	We are sensitized to the amount of suffering in the world	We refuse to be open to any changes in our lives

36:26 One theme in the poetic literature of the Bible is that God is incomprehensible; we cannot know him completely. This does not mean that we cannot have any knowledge about him, for the Bible is full of details about who God is, how we can know him, and how we can have an eternal relationship with him. What it means is that we can never know enough to answer all of life's questions (Ecclesiastes 3:11), to predict our own future, or to manipulate God for our own ends. Life always has more questions than answers, and we must constantly go to God for fresh insights into life's dilemmas. (See 37:19–24.)

with lightning bolts. He hurls each at its target. 33We feel his presence in the thunder. Even the cattle know when a storm is coming.

37 "My heart trembles at this. 2Listen, listen to the thunder of his voice. 3It rolls across the heavens and his lightning flashes out in every direction. 4Afterwards comes the roaring of the thunder—the tremendous voice of his majesty. 5His voice is glorious in the thunder. We cannot comprehend the greatness of his power. 6For he directs the snow, the showers, and storm to fall upon the earth. 7Man's work stops at such a time, so that all men everywhere may recognize his power. 8The wild animals hide in the rocks or in their dens.

9"From the south comes the rain; from the north, the cold. 10God blows upon the rivers, and even the widest torrents freeze. 11He loads the clouds with moisture and they send forth his lightning. 12The lightning bolts are directed by his hand, and do whatever he commands throughout the earth. 13He sends the storms as punishment, or, in his lovingkindness, to encourage.

14"Listen, O Job, stop and consider the wonderful miracles of God. 15Do you know how God controls all nature, and causes the lightning to flash forth from the clouds? 16, 17Do you understand the balancing of the clouds with wonderful perfection and skill? Do you know why you become warm when the south wind is blowing and everything is still? 18Can you spread out the gigantic mirror of the skies as he does?

19, 20"You who think you know so much, teach the rest of us how we should approach God. For we are too dull to know! With your wisdom, would we then dare to approach him? Well, does a man wish to be swallowed alive? 21For as we cannot look at the sun for its brightness when the winds have cleared away the clouds, 22neither can we gaze at the terrible majesty of God breaking forth upon us from heaven, clothed in dazzling splendor. 23We cannot imagine the power of the Almighty, and yet he is so just and merciful that he does not destroy us. 24No wonder men everywhere fear him! For he is not impressed by the world's wisest men!"

D. GOD ANSWERS JOB (38:1—41:34)

Instead of answering Job's question directly, God asks Job a series of questions which no human could possibly answer. Job responds by recognizing that God's ways are best. During difficult times, we, too, must humbly remember our position before the eternal, holy, incomprehensible God.

38 Then the Lord answered Job from the whirlwind: 2"Why are you using your ignorance to deny my providence? 3Now get ready to fight, for I am going to demand some answers from you, and you must reply.

4"Where were you when I laid the foundations of the earth? Tell me, if you know so much. 5Do you know how its dimensions were determined, and who did the

37:13 *He sends the storms,* implied.   37:19, 20 *You who think you know so much,* implied.

Cross-references (right margin):

36:33 Job 37:2
37:2 Job 36:33; 34:26
37:5 Job 5:9; 26:14 Rom 11:33
37:6 Job 36:27; 38:22
37:7 Job 12:14
37:8 Job 38:40
37:9 Job 9:9
37:10 Job 38:29 Ps 147:17
37:11 Job 36:27,29
37:12 Job 36:32 Ps 148:8 Isa 14:21; 27:6
37:16 Job 36:4
37:18 Gen 1:6-8 Job 9:8,9 Ps 104:2 Isa 45:12
37:23 Isa 63:9 Rom 11:13
37:24 Job 5:13 1 Cor 1:26
38:1 Job 40:6
38:2 Job 35:16; 42:3
38:3 Job 40:7; 42:4
38:4 Job 15:7

37:14 Nothing can compare to God. His power and presence are awesome, and when he speaks, we must listen. Too often we presume to speak for God (as did Job's friends), to put words in his mouth, to take him for granted, or to interpret his silence to mean that he is absent or unconcerned. But God cares. He is in control, and he will speak. Be ready to hear his voice—in the Bible, in your life through the Holy Spirit, and in circumstances and relationships.

37:21-24 Elihu concludes his speech with the tremendous truth that faith in God is far more important than Job's desire for an explanation for his suffering. He came so close to helping Job but then went down the wrong path. Significantly, it is here that God himself breaks into the discussion to draw the right conclusions from this important truth (38:1ff).

37:23 Elihu stressed God's sovereignty over all of nature as a

reminder of his sovereignty over our lives. God is in control—he directs, preserves, and maintains his created order. Although we can't see it, God is divinely governing the moral and political affairs of people as well. By spending time observing the majestic and intricate parts of God's creation, we can be reminded of his power in every aspect of our lives.

38:1ff From a whirlwind or mighty storm, God spoke. Surprisingly, he didn't answer any of Job's questions; Job's questions were not the heart of the issue. Instead, God used Job's ignorance of the earth's natural order to reveal his ignorance of God's moral order. If Job did not understand the workings of God's physical creation, how could he possibly understand God's mind and character? There is no standard or criterion higher than God himself by which to judge. God himself is the standard. Our only option is to submit to his authority and care.

38:6
Job 1:6; 26:7

38:10
Gen 1:9
Ps 33:7
Prov 8:29
Jer 5:22

38:13
Job 37:3
34:25,26

38:15
Job 5:14
Ps 10:15; 37:17

38:16
Gen 7:11; 8:2
Prov 8:24,28
Jer 51:36

38:17
Job 28:24; 34:22

38:20
Job 26:10

38:21
Job 15:7

38:22
Ex 9:18
Job 37:6
Isa 30:30
Ezek 13:11,13

38:24
Job 26:10

38:25
Job 36:27

38:28
Job 36:27,28

38:29
Job 37:10

38:31
Job 9:9

surveying? 6, 7What supports its foundations, and who laid its cornerstone, as the morning stars sang together and all the angels shouted for joy?

8, 9"Who decreed the boundaries of the seas when they gushed from the depths? Who clothed them with clouds and thick darkness, 10and barred them by limiting their shores, 11and said, 'Thus far and no farther shall you come, and here shall your proud waves stop!'?

12"Have you ever once commanded the morning to appear, and caused the dawn to rise in the east? 13Have you ever told the daylight to spread to the ends of the earth, to end the night's wickedness? 14Have you ever robed the dawn in red, 15and disturbed the haunts of wicked men and stopped the arm raised to strike?

16"Have you explored the springs from which the seas come, or walked in the sources of their depths? 17, 18Has the location of the gates of Death been revealed to you? Do you realize the extent of the earth? Tell me about it if you know! 19Where does the light come from, and how do you get there? Or tell me about the darkness. Where does it come from? 20Can you find its boundaries, or go to its source? 21But of course you know all this! For you were born before it was all created, and you are so very experienced!

22, 23"Have you visited the treasuries of the snow, or seen where hail is made and stored? For I have reserved it for the time when I will need it in war. 24Where is the path to the distribution point of light? Where is the home of the east wind? 25, 26, 27Who dug the valleys for the torrents of rain? Who laid out the path for the lightning, causing the rain to fall upon the barren deserts, so that the parched and barren ground is satisfied with water, and tender grass springs up?

28"Has the rain a father? Where does dew come from? 29Who is the mother of the ice and frost? 30For the water changes and turns to ice, as hard as rock.

31"Can you hold back the stars? Can you restrain Orion or Pleiades? 32Can you ensure the proper sequence of the seasons, or guide the constellation of the Bear

GOD SPEAKS
On various occasions in the Old Testament, God chose to communicate audibly with individuals. God will always find a way to make contact with those who want to know him. Some of those occasions are listed here.

Whom he spoke to	What he said	Reference
Adam and Eve	Confronted them about sin	Genesis 3:8–13
Noah	Gave him directions about building the ark	Genesis 6:8–22; 7:1; 8:15–17
Abraham	Commanded him to follow God's leading and promised to bless him	Genesis 12:1–9
	Tested his obedience by commanding him to sacrifice his son	Genesis 22:1–14
Jacob	Permitted him to go to Egypt	Genesis 46:1–4
Moses	Sent him to lead the people out of Egypt	Exodus 3:1–10
	Gave him the Ten Commandments	Exodus 19:1—20:20
Moses, Aaron, Miriam	Pronounced judgment on a family argument	Numbers 12:1–15
Joshua	Promised to be with him as he was with Moses	Joshua 1:1–9
Samuel	Chose him to be his spokesman	1 Samuel 3:1–18
Isaiah	Sent him to the people with his message	Isaiah 6:1–13
Jeremiah	Encouraged him to be his prophet	Jeremiah 1:4–10
Ezekiel	Sent him to Israel to warn them of coming judgment	Ezekiel 2:1–8

38:22-35 God stated that he has all the forces of nature at his command and can unleash or restrain them at will. No one completely understands such common occurrences as rain or snow, and no one can command them—only God who created them has that power. God's point was that if Job could not explain such common events in nature, how could he possibly explain or question God? And if nature is not ordered the way we might have thought, God's moral purposes may not be what we imagine either.

38:22, 23 God said he was reserving the treasuries of snow and hail for times of war. God used hail to help Joshua and the Israelites win a battle (Joshua 10:11). Just as armies keep weapons in the armory, God has all the forces of nature in his control; sometimes he uses them to confound those opposed to him or his people.

with her satellites across the heavens? 33Do you know the laws of the universe and how the heavens influence the earth? 34Can you shout to the clouds and make it rain? 35Can you make lightning appear and cause it to strike as you direct it? 36"Who gives intuition and instinct? 37, 38Who is wise enough to number all the clouds? Who can tilt the water jars of heaven, when everything is dust and clods? 39, 40Can you stalk prey like a lioness, to satisfy the young lions' appetites as they lie in their dens, or lie in wait in the jungle? 41Who provides for the ravens when their young cry out to God as they try to struggle up from their nest in hunger?

39 "Do you know how mountain goats give birth? Have you ever seen them giving birth to their young? 2, 3Do you know how many months of pregnancy they have before they bow themselves to give birth to their young, and carry their burden no longer? 4Their young grow up in the open field, then leave their parents and return to them no more.

5"Who makes the wild donkeys wild? 6I have placed them in the wilderness and given them salt plains to live in. 7For they hate the noise of the city and want no drivers shouting at them! 8The mountain ranges are their pastureland; there they search for every blade of grass.

9"Will the wild ox be your happy servant? Will he stay beside your feeding crib? 10Can you use a wild ox to plow with? Will he pull the harrow for you? 11Because he is so strong, will you trust him? Will you let him decide where to work? 12Can you send him out to bring in the grain from the threshing-floor?

13"The ostrich flaps her wings grandly, but has no true motherly love. 14She lays her eggs on top of the earth, to warm them in the dust. 15She forgets that someone may step on them and crush them, or the wild animals destroy them. 16She ignores her young as though they weren't her own, and is unconcerned though they die, 17for God has deprived her of wisdom. 18But whenever she jumps up to run, she passes the swiftest horse with its rider.

19"Have you given the horse strength, or clothed his neck with a quivering mane? 20Have you made him able to leap forward like a locust? His majestic snorting is something to hear! 21, 22, 23He paws the earth and rejoices in his strength, and when he goes to war, he is unafraid and does not run away though the arrows rattle against him, or the flashing spear and javelin. 24Fiercely he paws the ground and rushes forward into battle when the trumpet blows. 25At the sound of the bugle he shouts, 'Aha!' He smells the battle when far away. He rejoices at the shouts of battle and the roar of the captain's commands.

38:36 *Who gives intuition and instinct?* Or, "Who has put wisdom in the inward parts, and given understanding to the mind?"

38:34
Job 22:11
38:35
Job 36:32; 37:3
38:36
Job 32:8
Eccles 2:26
38:39
Job 37:8
38:41
Mt 6:26

39:1
Deut 14:5
Ps 29:9

39:5
Job 6:5; 11:12
24:5
Dan 5:21
Hos 8:9
39:6
Job 24:5
Jer 2:24
39:9
Num 23:22
Deut 33:17
Ps 92:10
Isa 1:3

39:16
Lam 4:3

39:20
Jer 8:16
Joel 2:5
39:21
Prov 21:31
Jer 8:6

GOD'S JUSTICE

Wrong view	Correct view
LAW OF FAIRNESS	GOD
GOD	JUSTICE

There is a law of fairness or justice that is higher and more absolute than God. It is binding even for God. God must act in response to that law in order to be fair. Our response is to appeal to that law.	God himself is the standard of justice. Although he has the power to do whatever he wants, he uses his power according to his own moral perfection. Thus, whatever he does is fair, even if we don't understand it. Our response is to appeal directly to him.

39:1ff God asked Job several questions about the animal kingdom in order to demonstrate how limited Job's knowledge really was. God was not seeking answers from Job. Instead, he was getting Job to recognize and submit to God's power and sovereignty. Only then would he be able to hear what God was really saying to him.

39:27
Jer 49:16
39:29
Job 9:26
39:30
Ezek 39:17-19
Mt 24:28

26"Do you know how a hawk soars and spreads her wings to the south? 27Is it at your command that the eagle rises high upon the cliffs to make her nest? 28She lives upon the cliffs, making her home in her mountain fortress. 29From there she spies her prey, from a very great distance. 30Her nestlings gulp down blood, for she goes wherever the slain are."

40:2
Job 9:3; 10:2
13:3; 23:4
31:35; 33:13
40:4
Job 21:5; 29:9
40:5
Job 9:3,15
40:6
Job 38:1
40:7
Job 38:3; 42:4
40:8
Job 10:3,7
13:18; 27:2,6
40:9
Job 37:5
Ps 39:3-9
Isa 45:9
40:11
Isa 2:12; 42:25
Dan 4:37
Nah 1:6,8
40:12
Isa 13:11; 63:3
40:13
Isa 2:10-12
Jn 11:44
40:15
Job 40:19
40:19
Job 41:33
Ps 7:12
Isa 27:1

40 *The Lord went on:*
2"Do you still want to argue with the Almighty? Or will you yield? Do you—God's critic—have the answers?"
3*Then Job replied to God:*
4"I am nothing—how could I ever find the answers? I lay my hand upon my mouth in silence. 5I have said too much already."
6*Then the Lord spoke to Job again from the whirlwind:*
7"Stand up like a man and brace yourself for battle. Let me ask you a question, and give me the answer. 8Are you going to discredit my justice and condemn me, so that you can say you are right? 9Are you as strong as God, and can you shout as loudly as he? 10All right then, put on your robes of state, your majesty and splendor. 11Give vent to your anger. Let it overflow against the proud. 12Humiliate the haughty with a glance; tread down the wicked where they stand. 13Knock them into the dust, stone-faced in death. 14If you can do that, then I'll agree with you that your own strength can save you.

15"Take a look at the hippopotamus! I made him, too, just as I made you! He eats grass like an ox. 16See his powerful loins and the muscles of his belly. 17His tail is as straight as a cedar. The sinews of his thighs are tightly knit together. 18His vertebrae lie straight as a tube of brass. His ribs are like iron bars. 19How ferocious he is among all of God's creation, so let whoever hopes to master him bring a sharp sword! 20The mountains offer their best food to him—the other wild animals on which he preys. 21He lies down under the lotus plants, hidden by the reeds, 22covered by their shade among the willows there beside the stream. 23He is not disturbed by raging rivers, not even when the swelling Jordan rushes down upon him. 24No one can catch him off guard or put a ring in his nose and lead him away.

41:1
Job 3:8

41 "Can you catch a crocodile with a hook and line? Or put a noose around his tongue? 2Can you tie him with a rope through the nose, or pierce his jaw with

40:15 *the hippopotamus,* literally, "behemoth." **41:1** *a crocodile,* literally, "leviathan."

FOUR VIEWS OF SUFFERING	*Satan's view*	People believe in God only when they are prospering and not suffering. This is wrong.
	The view of Job's three friends	Suffering is God's judgment for sin. This is not always true.
	Elihu's view	Suffering is God's way to teach, discipline, and refine. This is true, but an incomplete explanation.
	God's view	Suffering causes us to trust God for who he is, not what he does.

40:1-6 Throughout his time of suffering, Job longed to have an opportunity to plead his innocence before God. Now God appeared to Job and gave him that opportunity. But Job decided to remain quiet because it was no longer necessary for him to speak. God had shown Job that, as a limited human being, he had neither the ability to judge the God who created the universe nor the right to ask why. God's actions do not depend on ours. He will do what he knows is best, regardless of what we think is fair. It is important to note, however, that God came to Job, demonstrating his love and care for him.

40:2-5 How do you argue with Almighty God? Do you demand answers when things don't go your way, you lose a job, someone

close to you is ill or dies, finances are tight, you fail, or unexpected changes occur? The next time you are tempted to complain to God, consider how much he loves you and remember Job's reaction when he had his chance to speak. Are you worse off than Job or more righteous than he? Give God a chance to reveal his greater purposes for you, but remember that they may unfold over the course of your life and not at any given moment.

40:15 The behemoth (see the textual note on 40:15) was a large land animal, possibly an elephant or hippopotamus.

41:1 The leviathan (see the textual note on 41:1) was probably a large sea animal.

a spike? 3Will he beg you to desist or try to flatter you from your intentions? 4Will he agree to let you make him your slave for life? 5Can you make a pet of him like a bird, or give him to your little girls to play with? 6Do fishing partners sell him to the fishmongers? 7Will his hide be hurt by darts, or his head with a harpoon?

8"If you lay your hands upon him, you will long remember the battle that ensues, and you will never try it again! 9No, it's useless to try to capture him. It is frightening even to think about it! 10No one dares to stir *him* up, let alone try to conquer him. And if no one can stand before *him,* who can stand before *me?* 11I owe no one anything. Everything under the heaven is mine.

12"I should mention, too, the tremendous strength in his limbs, and throughout his enormous frame. 13Who can penetrate his hide, or who dares come within reach of his jaws? 14For his teeth are terrible. 15, 16, 17His overlapping scales are his pride, making a tight seal, so no air can get between them, and nothing can penetrate.

18"When he sneezes, the sunlight sparkles like lightning across the vapor droplets. His eyes glow like sparks. 19Fire leaps from his mouth. 20Smoke flows from his nostrils, like steam from a boiling pot that is fired by dry rushes. 21Yes, his breath would kindle coals—flames leap from his mouth.

22"The tremendous strength in his neck strikes terror wherever he goes. 23His flesh is hard and firm, not soft and fat. 24His heart is hard as rock, just like a millstone. 25When he stands up, the strongest are afraid. Terror grips them. 26No sword can stop him, nor spear nor dart nor pointed shaft. 27, 28Iron is nothing but straw to him, and brass is rotten wood. Arrows cannot make him flee. Slingstones are as ineffective as straw. 29Clubs do no good, and he laughs at the javelins hurled at him. 30His belly is covered with scales as sharp as shards; they tear up the ground as he drags through the mud.

31, 32"He makes the water boil with his commotion. He churns the depths. He leaves a shining wake of froth behind him. One would think the sea was made of frost! 33There is nothing else so fearless anywhere on earth. 34Of all the beasts, he is the proudest—monarch of all that he sees."

41:8
1 Kgs 20:11
2 Kgs 10:4
Lk 14:31,33

41:10
Job 3:8

41:11
Ex 19:5
Deut 10:14
Ps 24:1; 50:12
1 Cor 10:26

41:18
Job 3:9

41:33
Job 40:19

41:34
Job 28:8
Ezek 29:3

E. JOB IS RESTORED (42:1–17)
In response to God's speech, Job humbles himself. God rebukes the three friends for adding to Job's suffering by their false assumptions and critical attitudes. Job's material possessions and family are restored, and he receives even greater blessings than he had before. Those who persist in trusting God will be rewarded.

42 *Then Job replied to God:*
2"I know that you can do anything and that no one can stop you. 3You ask

JOB AND JESUS	Subject	Reference in Job	How Jesus is the Answer
The book of Job is intimately tied to the New Testament because Job's questions and problems are answered perfectly in Jesus Christ.	Someone must help us approach God	9:32, 33	1 Timothy 2:5
	Is there life after death?	14:14	John 11:25
	There is one in heaven working on our behalf	16:19	Hebrews 9:24
	There is one who can save us from judgment	19:25	Hebrews 7:24, 25
	Where do we find God?	23:3–5	John 14:9
	What is important in life?	40:4, 5	Matthew 16:26; John 3:16

41:11 When facing a crisis, it is easy to question God. God told Job, however, that he owes no one an explanation for his actions. He is sovereign. We often look for answers, but faith requires that we live as we should despite our unanswered questions. Remember that God knows your situation and loves you. Continue to trust him, even though you do not understand why your life is going the way it is.

42:1ff Throughout the book, Job's friends had asked him to admit his sin and ask for forgiveness, and eventually Job did indeed repent. Ironically, Job's repentance was not the kind called for by

his friends. He did not ask for forgiveness for secret sins, but for questioning God's sovereignty and justice. Job repented of his attitude and acknowledged God's great power and perfect justice. We sin when we angrily ask, "If God is in control, how could he let this happen?" Since we are locked into time, unable to see beyond today, we cannot know the reasons for everything that happens. Thus we must often choose between anger and trust. Will you trust God with your unanswered questions?

42:2, 3 Job openly and honestly faced God and admitted that he was the one who had been foolish. Are you using what you can't

who it is who has so foolishly denied your providence. It is I. I was talking about things I knew nothing about and did not understand, things far too wonderful for me.

⁴"[You said,] 'Listen and I will speak! Let me put the questions to you! See if you can answer them!'

⁵"[But now I say,] 'I had heard about you before, but now I have seen you, ⁶and I loathe myself and repent in dust and ashes.' "

⁷*After the Lord had finished speaking with Job, he said to Eliphaz the Temanite:*
"I am angry with you and with your two friends, for you have not been right in what you have said about me, as my servant Job was. ⁸Now take seven young bulls and seven rams and go to my servant Job and offer a burnt offering for yourselves; and my servant Job will pray for you, and I will accept his prayer on your behalf, and won't destroy you as I should because of your sin, your failure to speak rightly concerning my servant Job."

⁹So Eliphaz the Temanite, and Bildad the Shuhite, and Zophar the Naamathite did as the Lord commanded them, and the Lord accepted Job's prayer on their behalf.

God blesses Job more than before

¹⁰Then, when Job prayed for his friends, the Lord restored his wealth and happiness! In fact, the Lord gave him twice as much as before! ¹¹Then all of his brothers, sisters, and former friends arrived and feasted with him in his home, consoling him for all his sorrow, and comforting him because of all the trials the Lord had brought upon him. And each of them brought him a gift of money, and a gold ring.

42:4 *You said,* implied.   **42:5** *But now I say,* implied.

42:4
Gen 18:27,
30-32
Job 38:3; 40:7

42:5
Job 26:14
Isa 6:5
Jn 1:18; 12:41

42:7
Job 40:3-5

42:8
Job 1:5; 22:30

42:10
Ps 14:7; 85:1-3
126:1-6

42:11
Job 2:11; 19:13

WHEN WE SUFFER	Questions	Our response
Here are six questions to ask ourselves when we suffer; and what to do if the answer is "yes."	Am I being punished by God for sin?	Confess known sin.
	Is Satan attacking me as I try to survive as a Christian?	Call on God for strength.
	Am I being prepared for a special service, learning to be compassionate to those who suffer?	Resist self-pity. Ask God to open up doors of opportunity and help you discover others who suffer as you do.
	Am I specifically selected for testing, like Job?	Accept help from the body of believers. Trust God to work his purpose through you.
	Is my suffering a result of natural consequences, for which I am not directly responsible?	Recognize that in a sinful world, both good and evil people will suffer. But the good person has a promise from God that his suffering will one day come to an end.
	Is my suffering due to some unknown reason?	Don't draw inward from the pain. Proclaim your faith in God, know that he cares, and wait patiently for his aid.

---

understand as an excuse for your lack of trust? Admit to God that you don't even have enough faith to trust him. True faith begins in such humility.

42:7, 8 God made it clear that Job's friends were wrong. The fact that God did not mention any specific sins of Job shows that God confirmed Job's godly life. Job's friends had made the error of assuming Job's suffering was caused by some great sin. They were judging Job without knowing what God was doing. We must be careful to avoid making judgments about a person, because God may be working in ways we know nothing about.

42:8-10 After receiving much criticism, Job was still able to pray for his three friends. It is difficult to forgive someone who has accused you of wrongdoing, but Job did. Are you praying for those who have wronged you? Can you forgive them? Follow the actions of Job, whom God called a good man, and pray for those who have wronged you.

42:10, 11 Would the message of Job change if God had not restored to him his former blessings? No. God is still sovereign. Jesus said that anyone who gives up something for the Kingdom of God will be repaid (Luke 18:29, 30). Our restoration may or may not be the same kind as Job's, which was both spiritual and material. Our complete restoration may not be in this life—but it will happen. God loves us and he is just. He will not only restore whatever we have lost unjustly, but will give us more than we can imagine as we live with him in eternity. Cling tightly to your faith through all your trials, and you too will be rewarded by God, if not now, in the life to come.

12So the Lord blessed Job at the end of his life more than at the beginning. For now he had 14,000 sheep, 6,000 camels, 1,000 teams of oxen, and 1,000 female donkeys.

13, 14God also gave him seven more sons and three more daughters. These were the names of his daughters: Jemima, Kezia, Keren.

15And in all the land there were no other girls as lovely as the daughters of Job; and their father put them into his will along with their brothers.

16Job lived 140 years after that, living to see his grandchildren and great-grandchildren too. 17Then at last he died, an old, old man, after living a long, good life.

42:12
Job 1:3,10
Prov 10:22
1 Tim 6:17

42:13
Job 1:2
Ps 107:41

42:17
Gen 15:15; 25:8
Job 5:26
Prov 3:16

42:13, 14 *gave him seven more sons and three more daughters,* making a total of twenty children, ten of whom were in heaven. *Keren,* literally "Keren-happuch."

42:17 Job's question is timeless; "Why do believers experience troubles and suffering?" Through a long debate, Job's "wise" friends were unable to answer the question, just as people are unable to answer it today. Job's friends made a serious error for which God rebuked them. They assumed that trouble comes only because people are bad. We see the same error today in those who assert that sickness and lack of material blessing are a sign of unconfessed sin and lack of faith. The truth is that no one is truly good except God, but on a relative scale some people are better than others. In our fallen world bad things happen to "good" and bad people alike.

Bad things do not happen because God doesn't notice, doesn't care, is unjust, or is not powerful enough to protect us. Bad things happen because we live in a fallen world, a world where both believers and unbelievers are hit with the tragic consequences of sin. God is allowing evil for a time, although he often turns it around for our good (Romans 8:28). We may have no answers as to why God allows evil, but we can be sure he is all-powerful and knows what he is doing. The next time you face trials and dilemmas, look to God for strength. Only then will you find a God who is waiting to show his love and compassion to you. If you can trust him regardless of your situation, you will win the victory and eliminate one of Satan's greatest footholds in your life. If God is your foundation, you can never lose everything.

CLICHÉS are a way of life. They keep us from having to reveal our true selves. Rather than being a vehicle for expressing true feelings, such empty words often cover up the real person. But genuine relationships are built on honest communication, where we share with others who we really are. It is only when honest feelings are shared that real people can be known, loved, and helped at the deepest levels.

Often, patterns of superficial communication spill over into our talks with God. We easily slide through well-worn lines recited for decades, or we quickly toss a cliché or two at God and call it prayer. There is no doubt that God hears and understands these feeble attempts, but by limiting the depth of our communication, we become shallow in our relationship with God. But he knows us, and he wants to have genuine communication with us.

At the center of the Bible is the book of Psalms. This great collection of songs and prayers expresses the heart and soul of humanity. In them, the whole range of human experiences is expressed. There are no clichés in this book. Instead, David and the other writers honestly pour out their true feelings, reflecting a dynamic, powerful, and life-changing friendship with God. The psalmists confess their sins, express their doubts and fears, ask God for help in times of trouble, and they praise and worship him.

As you read the book of Psalms, you will hear believers crying out to God from the depths of despair, and you will hear them singing to him in the heights of celebration. But whether despairing or rejoicing, you will always hear them sharing honest feelings with their God. Because of the honesty expressed by the psalmists, men and women throughout history have come, again and again, to the book of Psalms for comfort during times of struggle and distress. And with the psalmists, they have risen from the depths of despair to new heights of joy and praise as they also discovered the power of God's everlasting love and forgiveness. Let the honesty of the psalmists guide you into a more deep and genuine relationship with God.

VITAL STATISTICS

PURPOSE:
To provide poetry for the expression of praise, worship, and confession to God

AUTHORS:
David wrote 73 psalms; Asaph wrote 12; the sons of Korah wrote nine; Solomon wrote two; Heman (with the sons of Korah), Ethan, and Moses each wrote one; and 51 psalms are anonymous. The New Testament ascribes two of the anonymous psalms (Psalms 2 and 95) to David (see Acts 4:25; Hebrews 4:7).

DATE WRITTEN:
Between the time of Moses (around 1440 B.C.) and the Babylonian captivity (586 B.C.)

SETTING:
For the most part, the psalms were not intended to be narrations of historical events. However, they often parallel events in history, such as David's flight from Saul and his sin with Bath-sheba.

KEY VERSE:
"Let everything alive give praises to the Lord! *You* praise him! Hallelujah!" (150:6).

KEY PERSON:
David

KEY PLACE:
God's Holy Temple

THE BLUEPRINT

A. THE FIRST BOOK OF PSALMS
(1:1—41:13)

While the psalms are not organized by topic, it is helpful to compare the dominant themes in each section of the psalms to the five books of Moses. This first collection of psalms, mainly written by David, is similar to the book of Genesis. Just as Genesis tells how mankind was created, fell into sin, and was then promised redemption, many of these psalms discuss humans as blessed, fallen, and redeemed by God.

B. THE SECOND BOOK OF PSALMS
(42:1—72:20)

This collection of psalms, mainly written by David and the sons of Korah, is similar to the book of Exodus. Just as Exodus describes the nation of Israel, many of these psalms describe the nation as ruined and then recovered. As God rescued the nation of Israel, he also rescues us. We do not have to work out solutions first, but we can go to God with our problems and ask him to help.

C. THE THIRD BOOK OF PSALMS
(73:1—89:52)

This collection of psalms, mainly written by Asaph, is similar to the book of Leviticus. Just as Leviticus discusses the Tabernacle and God's holiness, many of these psalms discuss the Temple and God's enthronement. Because God is almighty, we can turn to him for deliverance. These psalms praise God because he is holy, and his perfect holiness deserves our worship and reverence.

D. THE FOURTH BOOK OF PSALMS
(90:1—106:48)

This collection of psalms, mainly written by unknown authors, is similar to the book of Numbers. Just as Numbers discusses the relationship of the nation of Israel to surrounding nations, these psalms often mention the relationship of God's overruling kingdom to the other nations. Since we are citizens of the Kingdom of God, we can keep the events and troubles of earth in their proper perspective.

E. THE FIFTH BOOK OF PSALMS
(107:1—150:6)

This collection of psalms, mainly written by David, is similar to the book of Deuteronomy. Just as Deuteronomy was concerned with God and his Word, these psalms are anthems of praise and thanksgiving for God and his Word. Most of the psalms were originally set to music and used in worship. We can use these psalms today as they were used in the past, as a hymnbook of praise and worship. This is a book which ought to make our hearts sing.

MEGATHEMES

THEME	EXPLANATION	IMPORTANCE
Praise	Psalms are songs of praise to God as our Creator, Sustainer, and Redeemer. Praise is recognizing, appreciating, and expressing God's greatness.	Focusing our thoughts on God moves us to praise him. The more we know him, the more we can appreciate what he has done for us.
God's power	God is all-powerful; and he always acts at the right time. He is sovereign over every situation. God's power is shown by the ways he reveals himself in creation, history, and his Word.	When we feel powerless, God can help us. His strength can overcome the despair of any pain or trial. We can always pray that he will deliver, protect, and sustain us.
Forgiveness	Many psalms are intense prayers asking God for forgiveness. God forgives us when we confess our sin and turn from it.	Because God forgives us, we can pray to him honestly and directly. When we receive his forgiveness, we move from alienation to intimacy, from guilt to love.
Thankfulness	We are grateful to God for his personal concern, help, and mercy. Not only does he protect, guide, and forgive us, but his creation provides everything we need.	When we realize how we benefit from knowing God, we can fully express our thanks to him. By thanking him often, we develop spontaneity in our prayer life.
Trust	God is faithful and just. When we put our trust in him, he quiets our hearts. Because he has been faithful throughout history, we can trust him in times of trouble.	People can be unfair and friends may desert us. But we can trust God. Knowing God intimately drives away doubt, fear, and loneliness.

A. THE FIRST BOOK OF PSALMS (1:1—41:13)

In this book, the psalmists praise God for his justice, express confidence in God's compassion, recount the depravity of man, plead for vindication, ask God to deliver them from their enemies, speak of the blessedness of the forgiven sinner, and portray God as a shepherd. We should worship God with the same sense of adoration found in these psalms.

Theme: Life's two roads. The life of the faithful person is contrasted with the life of the faithless person.
Author: Anonymous

1 Oh, the joys of those who do not follow evil men's advice, who do not hang around with sinners, scoffing at the things of God: 2But they delight in doing

1:1 Ps 17:4; 26:5

1:1 God doesn't judge people on the basis of race, sex, or national origin. He judges them on the basis of their faith in him and their response to his revealed will. Those who diligently try to obey God's will are like healthy, fruit-bearing trees with strong roots (Jeremiah 17:5–8) and God promises to watch over them. God's wisdom guides their lives. In contrast, those who don't obey God

1:3
Jer 17:7,8
Ezek 47:12

1:4
Job 21:18
Ps 35:5
Isa 17:13

1:6
Neh 1:7
Jn 10:14
2 Tim 2:19

everything God wants them to, and day and night are always meditating on his laws and thinking about ways to follow him more closely.

³They are like trees along a river bank bearing luscious fruit each season without fail. Their leaves shall never wither, and all they do shall prosper.

⁴But for sinners, what a different story! They blow away like chaff before the wind. ⁵They are not safe on Judgment Day; they shall not stand among the godly.

⁶For the Lord watches over all the plans and paths of godly men, but the paths of the godless lead to doom.

REASONS TO	When you want . . .	Read . . .
READ PSALMS	to find comfort	Psalm 23
	to meet God intimately	Psalm 103
	to learn a new prayer	Psalm 136
	to learn a new song	Psalm 92
	to learn more about God	Psalm 24
	to understand yourself more clearly	Psalm 8
	to know how to come to God each day	Psalm 5
	to be forgiven for your sins	Psalm 51
	to feel worthwhile	Psalm 139
	to understand why you should read the Bible	Psalm 119
	to give praise to God	Psalm 145
	to know that God is in control	Psalm 146
	to give thanks to God	Psalm 136
	to please God	Psalm 15
	to know why you should worship God	Psalm 104

God's Word was written to be studied, understood, and applied, and the book of Psalms lends itself most directly to application. We understand Psalms best when we "stand under" them and allow them to flow over us like a rain shower. We may turn to Psalms looking for something, but sooner or later we will meet Someone. As we read and memorize the psalms, we will gradually discover how much they are already part of us. They put into words our deepest hurts, longings, thoughts, and prayers. They gently push us toward being what God designed us to be—people loving and living for him.

---

have meaningless lives which blow away like dust.

There are only two paths of life from which to choose—God's way of obedience or the way of rebellion and destruction. By choosing your pathway, you choose your eternity.

1:1 The writer began his psalm extolling the joys of being a godly person—one who obeys God and refuses to listen to those who discredit or ridicule him. Our friends and associates can have a profound influence on us, often in very subtle ways. If we insist on friendships with those who scoff at what God considers important, we may be drawn into sin and become indifferent to God's will. This attitude is the same as scoffing. Do your friends build up your faith or do they tear it down? The influence of true friends should draw you closer to God.

1:1 The psalmist focused on the age-old question of joy (or happiness). In this verse he tells us what to avoid—the company of scoffing sinners. In the next verse he tells us what not to avoid—the company of the God of all joy and his Word. The shadowy influence of scoffing sinners separates us from the radiance of God's joyful presence, as a dark ominous cloud separates us from the joyful presence of the morning sun.

1:2 You can learn how to follow God by meditating on his laws. Meditating means spending time reading and thinking about God's Word and how you should change so you're living as God wants. Knowing and meditating on God's Word are the first steps towards applying it to your everyday life. If you want to follow God more closely, you must know what he says.

1:2 These "laws" on which we are to meditate include all of Scripture: the first five books of Moses, the prophets, and the other writings. The more we know of the whole scope of God's Word, the

more resources we will have for our daily decisions.

1:2 There is a most simple bit of wisdom in these two verses—the more we bask in the radiant joy of God's presence and his Word, the more we cultivate the spirit of joy within us. On the other hand, the more we allow the dark influences of scoffing sinners to overshadow us, the more we separate ourselves from the very source of great joy. If you want despair, spend time with scoffing sinners; but if you want joy, you will find it only in the presence of God and his Word.

1:3 When Scripture promises, "everything you do shall prosper," it does not mean immunity from failure or difficulties. Nor is it a guarantee of health, wealth, and happiness. What Scripture means by prosperity is this: when God's wisdom is applied to our lives, the fruit it bears in us will be good and receive God's approval. As a tree soaks up water and bears luscious fruit, we also are to soak up God's Word, producing actions and attitudes that honor God. True prosperity is found by knowing the true value of God's Word!

1:4 Chaff is the outer shell (or husk) that must be removed to get at the valuable kernels of grain inside. Chaff was removed by a process called threshing and winnowing. After the plants were cut, they were crushed, then the pieces were thrown into the air. Chaff is very light and is carried away by even the slightest wind, while the good grain falls back to the earth. Chaff is a symbol of a faithless life that drifts along without direction. Good grain is a symbol of a faithful life that can be used by God.

1:5 Although evil people may get the upper hand at times, God assures us that a day is coming when their sins will be punished (see Matthew 25:31–46; Revelation 6:16, 17; 20:11–15 for other references to God's judgment).

Theme: God's ultimate rule. A psalm written to celebrate the coronation of of an Israelite king, but also written for the coronation of Christ, the eternal King.
Author: David (see Acts 4:25, 26)

2 What fools the nations are to rage against the Lord! How strange that men should try to outwit God! ²For a summit conference of the nations has been called to plot against the Lord and his Messiah, Christ the King. ³"Come, let us break his chains," they say, "and free ourselves from all this slavery to God."

⁴But God in heaven merely laughs! He is amused by all their puny plans. ⁵And then in fierce fury he rebukes them and fills them with fear.

⁶For the Lord declares, "This is the King of my choice, and I have enthroned him in Jerusalem, my holy city."

⁷His chosen one replies, "I will reveal the everlasting purposes of God, for the Lord has said to me, 'You are my Son. This is your Coronation Day. Today I am giving you your glory.'" ⁸"Only ask, and I will give you all the nations of the world. ⁹Rule them with an iron rod; smash them like clay pots!"

¹⁰O kings and rulers of the earth, listen while there is time. ¹¹Serve the Lord with reverent fear; rejoice with trembling. ¹²Fall down before his Son and kiss his feet before his anger is roused and you perish. I am warning you—his wrath will soon begin. But oh, the joys of those who put their trust in him!

2:1
Acts 4:25,26
2:4
Ps 37:12,13
59:8
2:6
Ps 3:4; 45:6
48:1,2
2:7
Acts 13:32,33
Heb 1:5,6; 5:5
2:9
Ps 28:5; 110:5,6
Rev 2:27; 12:5
19:15
2:11
Ps 5:7; 32:8
119:119,120
Heb 12:28
2:12
Ps 5:11
34:8,22
Jn 5:23
Rom 9:33

Theme: Confidently trusting God for protection and peace
Author: David

3 *A Psalm of David, when he fled from Absalom his son.*
O Lord, so many are against me. So many seek to harm me. I have so many enemies. ²So many say that God will never help me. ³But Lord, you are my shield,

3:1
2 Sam 15:12
Ps 69:4

2:1 *What fools the nations are,* literally, "Why do the heathen rage?" *How strange that men should try to outwit God,* literally, "meditate a vain thing." **2:2** *his Messiah, Christ the King,* literally, "his anointed." **2:6** *for the Lord declares,* implied. *Jerusalem, my holy city,* literally, "Upon Zion, my holy mountain." **2:7** *His chosen one replies,* implied. *This is your Coronation Day,* literally, "this day have I begotten thee." **2:12** *Fall down before his Son and kiss his feet,* implied.

2:1ff Several psalms are called *messianic* because of their prophetic descriptions of Jesus the Messiah (Christ)—his life, death, resurrection, and future reign. David, the author of this psalm, was also a prophet (Acts 2:30) because this psalm describes the rebellion of the nations and the coming of Christ to establish his eternal reign. Much of the psalm is referred to in the New Testament (see Acts 4:25, 26; 13:33; Hebrews 1:5, 6; 5:5; Revelation 2:26, 27; 12:5; 19:15).

2:1ff David may have written these words in the midst of a rebellion by some of the surrounding heathen nations. Chosen and anointed by God, David knew that God would fulfill his promise to bring the Messiah into the world through his bloodline (2 Samuel 7:16; 1 Chronicles 17:11, 12).

2:3 People often think they will be free if they can get away from God. Yet we all inevitably serve somebody or something, whether a human king, the wishes of friends, or our own selfish desires. Just as a fish is not free when it leaves the water and a tree is not free when it leaves the soil, we are not free when we leave the Lord. The one sure route to freedom is wholeheartedly serving God the Creator. He can set you free to be who he created you to be.

2:4 God laughs, not at the nations, but at their confused thoughts about power. It is the kind of laughter which a father has with his preschool son who boasts of outrunning his father or conquering him in a wrestling match. The father knows the boundaries of power of his little boy, and God knows the boundaries of power of the nations. If you must choose to put your confidence in God or the nations, choose God!

2:4 God is all-powerful. He created the world, and knew about the empires of the earth long before they came into being (Daniel 2:26-45). But power causes nations and leaders to rage against God and they even try to outwit him. Our world has many leaders who boast of their power, who rant and rave against God and his

people, who promise to take over and form their own empire. But God laughs because any power they have comes from him, and he can also take it from them. We need not fear the boasts of the tyrant because he is in God's hands.

2:5-12 David's praise of the Messiah's coronation was prophetic. The rule of Christ described here began after his crucifixion and resurrection, and will be fulfilled when he comes to set up his kingdom on earth.

2:11, 12 To "kiss his feet" refers to full surrender and submission to the king. Christ is not only God's chosen king, but he also must be king in our hearts and lives. To be ready for his coming, we must submit to his leadership each day.

3:1, 2 David felt like he was in the minority. There may have been as many as 10,000 soldiers surrounding him at this time (3:6). Not only did David's enemies view life differently, they actively sought to harm him. As king, David could have trusted his army to defeat Absalom, but he depended upon God's mercy instead (3:4). Therefore, he was at peace with whatever outcome occurred, knowing that God's great purposes would prevail. We can overcome fear when we cry out to God for his mercy in our darkest hour.

3:1-3 King David was not sitting on his throne in a place of power, but was running for his life from his rebellious son Absalom and a host of traitors. When circumstances go against us, it is easy to think that God also is against us. But David reminds us that the opposite is true. When everything seems to go against us, God is the only one who is for us. If life seems against you, don't blame God—seek him!

3:3 Sometimes life offers little hope, and when hope is gone, only despair remains. When facing problems, trials, suffering, and death, we may feel like giving up. David ran from his beloved son who threatened to kill him, knowing there was no hope *except* in God. When we feel like there is no hope, when life has

3:4
Ps 34:4; 99:9

3:5
Lev 26:6
Prov 3:24-26

3:6
Ps 23:4; 27:3

3:8
Isa 43:11

my glory, and my only hope. You alone can lift my head, now bowed in shame. 4I cried out to the Lord, and he heard me from his Temple in Jerusalem. 5Then I lay down and slept in peace and woke up safely, for the Lord was watching over me. 6And now, although ten thousand enemies surround me on every side, I am not afraid. 7I will cry to him, "Arise, O Lord! Save me, O my God!" And he will slap them in the face, insulting them and breaking off their teeth.

8For salvation comes from God. What joys he gives to all his people.

3:3 *now bowed in shame,* implied.   3:4 *from his Temple in Jerusalem,* literally, "from his holy mountain."
3:7 *insulting them and breaking off their teeth,* implied.

PSALMS FROM DAVID'S LIFE	Event in David's life	Reference	Psalm	What David learned about God
Of the more than 70 psalms attributed to David, at least 14 of them are connected with specific events in his life. From them we see an outline of a growing relationship with God. They are listed here, roughly in chronological order.	When Saul sent troops to David's home to capture him	1 Samuel 19	59	"You are my high tower of safety, my God of mercy."
	While running from Saul	1 Samuel 21	34	"I will praise the Lord no matter what happens."
	While running from Saul	1 Samuel 21	56	"But when I am afraid, I will put my confidence in you."
	While hiding in the cave of Adullam	1 Samuel 22	142	"You are my only place of refuge. Only you can keep me safe."
	After learning Doeg had murdered 85 priests and their families	1 Samuel 22	52	"But God will strike you down . . . See what happens to those who despise God."
	When the people of Ziph tried to betray him	1 Samuel 23	54	"But God is my helper."
	While hiding in a cave	1 Samuel 24	57	"I will hide beneath the shadow of your wings until this storm is past."
	While hiding in the wilderness of Judea	1 Samuel 24	63	"I follow close behind you, protected by your strong right arm."
	When Saul's pursuit was over	2 Samuel 22	18	"Lord, how merciful you are to those who are merciful. And you do not punish those who run from evil."
	After being confronted about his adultery with Bath-sheba	2 Samuel 12	51	"It is a broken spirit you want— remorse and penitence. A broken and a contrite heart, O God, you will not ignore."
	During Absalom's rebellion	2 Samuel 15	3	"Salvation comes from God."
	During Absalom's rebellion	2 Samuel 15	7	"For you, the righteous God, look deep within the hearts of men and examine all their motives and their thoughts."

disappointed us to the point of despair, we also have only *one* hope. But God is all the hope we need because he promises to be a shield to protect us. When we focus our thoughts on God, our hope is restored.

3:4 Why did David mention the Temple when it wasn't built until his son Solomon's reign? Other translations say "holy mountain" or "holy hill." David laid the plans for the Temple and knew where it would be constructed—on a threshing floor on Mount Moriah in Jerusalem (1 Chronicles 22:1). David knew God could not be confined to any space, but he wrote poetically, expressing confidence that God would hear him when he prayed.

3:5 Sleep does not come easily in the midst of a crisis. David could have had sleepless nights when his son Absalom rebelled and gathered an army to kill him. But he slept peacefully, even in

the midst of the rebellion. What made the difference? David cried out to the Lord and the Lord heard him. The assurance of answered prayer brings peace. It is easier to sleep well when we accept with full assurance that God is in control of circumstances. If you are lying awake at night worrying about circumstances you can't change, ask God to get involved. Then go to sleep!

3:7 This description of God's anger may seem unusual, but it reveals David's desire for justice against his persecutors. David himself was slapped and insulted, and here he simply asked for equal treatment for his enemies. He does this, not out of personal revenge, but for the sake of God's justice. Verse 8 shows the humility behind David's words—he realized that without God there would be no solution to the unfair success experienced by the wicked.

Theme: Rejoicing in God's protection and peace. We can place our confidence in God because he will listen when we call on him.
Author: David

4 O God, you have declared me perfect in your eyes; you have always cared for me in my distress; now hear me as I call again. Have mercy on me. Hear my prayer.

4:1
Ps 3:4; 17:6
18:6,18,19

2The Lord God asks, "Sons of men, will you forever turn my glory into shame by worshiping these silly idols, when every claim that's made for them is false?"

4:2
Ps 3:3
69:7-10,19

3Mark this well: The Lord has set apart the redeemed for himself. Therefore he will listen to me and answer when I call to him.

4:3
Ps 6:8,9; 17:6
31:23; 50:5

4Stand before the Lord in awe, and do not sin against him. Lie quietly upon your bed in silent meditation. 5Put your trust in the Lord, and offer him pleasing sacrifices.

4:4
Ps 33:8; 77:6

4:5
Ps 37:3,5
50:14; 51:19

6Many say that God will never help us. Prove them wrong, O Lord, by letting the light of your face shine down upon us. 7Yes, the gladness you have given me is far greater than their joys at harvest time as they gaze at their bountiful crops. 8I will lie down in peace and sleep, for though I am alone, O Lord, you will keep me safe.

4:7
Ps 97:11,12
119:14

4:8
Ps 3:5; 16:9

Theme: The lies of enemies. God is able to defend us from lies spoken against us.
Author: David

5 O Lord, hear me praying; listen to my plea, O God my King, for I will never pray to anyone but you. 3Each morning I will look to you in heaven and lay my requests before you, praying earnestly.

5:1
Ps 54:2; 84:3

5:3
Ps 88:13; 130:5

4I know you get no pleasure from wickedness and cannot tolerate the slightest sin. 5Therefore proud sinners will not survive your searching gaze, for how you hate their evil deeds. 6You will destroy them for their lies; how you abhor all murder and deception.

5:4
Ps 11:5; 34:16

5:5
Ps 1:5; 11:5

5:6
Ps 52:4,5

7But as for me, I will come into your Temple protected by your mercy and your love; I will worship you with deepest awe.

5:7
Ps 69:13

8Lord, lead me as you promised me you would; otherwise my enemies will conquer me. Tell me clearly what to do, which way to turn. 9For they cannot speak one truthful word. Their hearts are filled to the brim with wickedness. Their suggestions are full of the stench of sin and death. Their tongues are filled with flatteries to gain their wicked ends. 10O God, hold them responsible. Catch them in

5:8
Ps 27:11

5:9
Rom 3:13

5:10
Ps 9:16; 36:12

4:1 *O God, you have declared me perfect in your eyes,* literally, "God of my righteousness." **4:4** *Stand before the Lord in awe,* literally, "Be ye angry." **4:6** *Prove them wrong,* implied.

4:1ff This psalm may have been written as David was asking his enemies to reconsider their support of Absalom. It was probably written shortly after Psalm 3.

4:2 Idol worship was a recurring problem for Israel throughout its history. The Israelites had entered a land filled with idols and had not destroyed them as God had commanded; therefore, idols continued to be a temptation for them (Judges 2:1–3). Worshiping idols of wood and stone mocked God, the Creator of wood and stone. Worshiping money or status also mocks God, the Creator of wealth and worth. We worship idols today when we trust the creation to meet our needs more than the Creator himself.

4:3 David knew that God heard his prayers and would answer him. We too can know that God listens and answers when we call on him. Sometimes we think God will not hear us because we have fallen short of his high standards for holy living. But God listens to us because we have been forgiven. When you feel that your prayers are "bouncing off the ceiling," remember that as a believer you have been set apart by God and that he loves you. He hears and answers (although his answers may not be what we expect). Look at your problems in the light of God's power instead of looking at God in the light of your problems.

4:5 Worship in David's day included animal sacrifices by the priests in the Tabernacle. The animal's blood "covered" (was a remedy for) the sins of the one who offered the animal. There were specific rules for offering sacrifices, but more important to God

than ceremony was the offerer's attitude of submission and obedience (1 Samuel 15:22, 23). Today, a pleasing sacrifice to God is still the same—he wants our obedience and our praise before our gifts (Hebrews 13:15). Offer him the sacrifice of total obedience and heartfelt praise.

4:7 Two kinds of joy are contrasted here—inward joy that comes from knowing and trusting God, and happiness that comes as a result of pleasant circumstances. Inward joy is steady as long as we trust God; happiness is unpredictable. Inward joy defeats discouragement; happiness covers it up. Inward joy is lasting; happiness is temporary.

5:1–3 The secret of a close relationship with God is to pray to him earnestly *each morning.* Regular communication is fundamental to any friendship and is certainly necessary for a strong relationship with God. We need to communicate with him daily. Do you have a regular time to pray and read God's Word?

5:4 It is impossible to sin just "a little bit" because God cannot tolerate even the smallest sin. As we grow in our spiritual lives, our sensitivity to sin increases. What is your reaction to sin in your life? Are you insensitive, unconcerned, disappointed, or comfortable? As God makes us aware of sin, we must develop an attitude of intolerance toward it and a willingness to change. All believers should strive to be more tolerant of people but less tolerant of the sin in others and in themselves.

5:10 When David was in trouble because of lies against him, he

5:11
Ps 2:12; 12:7
33:1; 64:10
Isa 65:13

5:12
Ps 29:11
32:7,10

their own traps; let them fall beneath the weight of their own transgressions, for they rebel against you.

¹¹But make everyone rejoice who puts his trust in you. Keep them shouting for joy because you are defending them. Fill all who love you with your happiness. ¹²For you bless the godly man, O Lord; you protect him with your shield of love.

Theme: Deliverance in trouble. God is able to rescue us.
Author: David

6:1
Ps 2:5; 38:1

6:2
Ps 22:14

6:3
Ps 88:3; 90:13

6:5
Ps 30:9

6:6
Ps 42:3; 69:3

6:7
Ps 31:9

6:10
Ps 71:24; 73:19

6 No, Lord! Don't punish me in the heat of your anger. ²Pity me, O Lord, for I am weak. Heal me, for my body is sick, ³and I am upset and disturbed. My mind is filled with apprehension and with gloom. Oh, restore me soon.

⁴Come, O Lord, and make me well. In your kindness save me. ⁵For if I die I cannot give you glory by praising you before my friends. ⁶I am worn out with pain; every night my pillow is wet with tears. ⁷My eyes are growing old and dim with grief because of all my enemies.

⁸Go, leave me now, you men of evil deeds, for the Lord has heard my weeping ⁹and my pleading. He will answer all my prayers. ¹⁰All my enemies shall be suddenly dishonored, terror-stricken, and disgraced. God will turn them back in shame.

Theme: A request for justice against those who make slanderous comments. God is the perfect judge and will punish those who persecute the innocent.
Author: David

7:1
Ps 11:1

7:2
Ps 17:12; 57:4

7:3
1 Sam 24:11

7:4
1 Sam 26:9

7:6
Ps 3:7; 35:23

7:7
Ps 18:20; 35:24

7 I am depending on you, O Lord my God, to save me from my persecutors. ²Don't let them pounce upon me as a lion would and maul me and drag me away with no one to rescue me. ³It would be different, Lord, if I were doing evil things— ⁴if I were paying back evil for good or unjustly attacking those I dislike. ⁵Then it would be right for you to let my enemies destroy me, crush me to the ground, and trample my life in the dust.

⁶But Lord! Arise in anger against the anger of my enemies. Awake! Demand justice for me, Lord! ⁷, ⁸Gather all peoples before you; sit high above them, judging their sins. But justify me publicly; establish my honor and truth before them all. ⁹End all wickedness, O Lord, and bless all who truly worship God; for you, the

6:5 *For if I die I cannot give you glory by praising you before my friends,* literally, "In the grave, who shall give you thanks?" Isaiah 57:1, 2 may indicate that Old Testament saints believed in a conscious and pleasant hereafter for those who love God.   **7:9** *God,* literally, "the just."

---

prayed, confident that God's love would not only console him, but defend (5:11) and shield (5:12) him. We often make the mistake of thinking of love only in terms of gentleness. But God's love is stronger than any evil we might face.

6:1ff This is the first of seven "penitential" psalms in which the writer humbly realizes his predicament (usually the result of sin), expresses sorrow over it, and demonstrates a fresh commitment to remain close to God. We don't know the cause of David's pain, but whatever the cause, he sought God for the antidote.

6:1-3 David accepted God's punishment, but begged God not to punish in anger. Jeremiah also asked God to correct him gently and not in anger (Jeremiah 10:23, 24). David recognized that if God treated him with justice alone and not with mercy, he would be wiped out by God's wrath. Often we want God to show mercy to us and justice to everyone else. In God's kindness, he often forgives us instead of giving us what we deserve.

6:6 Pouring out his heart with tears, David was completely honest with God. We can be honest with God, even if we are filled with anger and despair, because he knows us thoroughly and wants the very best for us. Anger and despair often result in rash outward acts or turning inward which can lead to depression. Because we trust in our all-powerful God, we don't have to be victims of circumstance or be weighed down by the guilt of sin. Be honest with God and he will help you turn your attention from yourself to his wonderful presence.

6:8-10 David's feelings shifted from fear to confidence. To defend ourselves against the lies and propaganda of our enemies, our best preparation is to be saturated with the knowledge of God and filled with his presence. Our daily study of his Word, our prayers, our worship, and our confidence in his presence will keep us strong.

7:1-6 Have you ever been falsely accused or badly hurt and wanted revenge? David wrote this psalm in response to the slanderous accusations of those who claimed that he was trying to kill King Saul and seize the throne (1 Samuel 24:9-11). Instead of taking matters into his own hands and striking back, David cried out to God for justice. The proper response to slander is prayer, not revenge, because God says, "Justice belongs to me; I will repay them" (Deuteronomy 32:35, 36; Hebrews 10:30). Instead of striking back, ask God to take your case, bring justice, and restore your reputation.

7:9 Nothing is hidden from God—this can be either terrifying or comforting. Our thoughts are an open book to him. Because he knows even our motives, we have no place to hide, no way to pretend that we can get away with sin. But that very knowledge also gives us great comfort. We don't have to impress God or put up a front. Instead, we can trust God to help us work through our particular weaknesses in order to serve him as he had planned. If we truly seek to follow him, our effort will be rewarded.

righteous God, look deep within the hearts of men and examine all their motives and their thoughts.

10God is my shield; he will defend me. He saves those whose hearts and lives are true and right.

11God is a judge who is perfectly fair, and he is angry with the wicked every day. 12Unless they repent, he will sharpen his sword and slay them.

He has bent and strung his bow 13and fitted it with deadly arrows made from shafts of fire.

14The wicked man conceives an evil plot, labors with its dark details, and brings to birth his treachery and lies; 15let him fall into his own trap. 16May the violence he plans for others boomerang upon himself; let him die.

17Oh, how grateful and thankful I am to the Lord because he is so good. I will sing praise to the name of the Lord who is above all lords.

7:10
Ps 18:2,30
97:10,11

7:11
Deut 32:41

7:12
Ps 64:7

7:13
Ps 18:14; 45:5
64:7

7:14
Job 15:35

7:15
Job 4:7,8

7:17
Ps 9:2
66:1,2,4
71:15,16

Theme: The greatness of God assures the worth of mankind. God, the all-powerful Creator, cares for his most valuable creation—people.
Author: David

8 O Lord our God, the majesty and glory of your name fills all the earth and overflows the heavens. 2You have taught the little children to praise you perfectly. May their example shame and silence your enemies!

3When I look up into the night skies and see the work of your fingers—the moon and the stars you have made— 4I cannot understand how you can bother with mere puny man, to pay any attention to him!

5And yet you have made him only a little lower than the angels, and placed a crown of glory and honor upon his head.

6You have put him in charge of everything you made; everything is put under his authority: 7all sheep and oxen, and wild animals too, 8the birds and fish, and all the life in the sea. 9O Jehovah, our Lord, the majesty and glory of your name fills the earth.

8:1
Ps 57:5,11
66:2; 113:4
148:13

8:2
Mt 21:16

8:3
Ps 89:11; 136:9

8:4
Job 7:17
Ps 144:3
Heb 2:6-8

8:5
Ps 21:5; 82:6

8:6
Gen 1:26,28

7:10 *He saves those whose hearts and lives are true and right,* literally, "the upright in heart." **8:5** *only a little lower than the angels,* or, "only a little lower than God!"

7:11 When evil gets the upper hand, life seems unfair. We know that God's justice will ultimately prevail, but we also know that not all of God's justice is reserved for the future. He is angry with the wicked every day and often punishes them and rescues the innocent in *this* life.

7:14–16 When allowed to run its course, evil destroys itself. Violent people become victims of violence, and liars are victims of the deceit of others (9:15, 16). But in the process, innocent people are hurt. Sometimes God intervenes and stops evildoers in their tracks in order to protect his followers. At other times, for reasons known only to him, God allows evil to continue even though innocent people may be hurt. It is during these times that we, like David, must ask God to protect us. Remember that God will execute final justice, even if it is not during our earthly lives.

7:17 During a time of great evil and injustice, David was grateful that God is fair and just (see also 7:11). When we wonder if anyone is honest or fair, we can be assured that God will continue to bring justice and fairness where we involve him in our activities. If you ever feel you are not being treated fairly, ask the one who is always fair and just to be with you, then thank him for his presence (see Isaiah 42:1–6).

8:1ff Portions of this psalm are quoted in the New Testament as applying to Christ (1 Corinthians 15:27; Hebrews 2:6–8). Jesus became a man who was a little lower than the angels (8:5) and he will raise all who belong to him above the angels when he comes

to reign over the new heavens and new earth. Jesus is the only man who perfectly reflected God's image (Galatians 2:20; Colossians 1:15).

8:2 Children are able to trust and praise God without doubts or reservations. As we get older, we find this more and more difficult to do. Ask God to give you a childlikeness, removing those barriers to having a closer walk with him.

8:3–5 When we look at the marvels of creation, we wonder how God could be concerned for people who constantly disappoint him. Yet God created us only a little lower than himself (see the textual note on 8:5). The next time you question your worth as a person or feel down about yourself, remember that God considers you to be highly valuable. We have great worth because we bear the stamp of the Creator. (See Genesis 1:26, 27 for the extent of worth God places on all people.) Because God has already declared how valuable we are to him, we can be set free from feelings of worthlessness.

8:3, 4 To respect God's majesty, we must see ourselves in the light of his greatness. When we look at creation, we often feel small by comparison. Humility means proper respect for God, not self-deprecation.

8:6 God gave mankind tremendous authority—to be in charge of the whole earth. But with great authority comes great responsibility. If we own a pet, we have the authority to do with it as we wish, but we also have the responsibility to feed and care for it in health and sickness. How do you treat God's creation? Use your resources wisely because God holds you accountable for your stewardship.

Theme: God never ignores our cries for help.
Author: David, probably written after a victory over the Philistines

9 O Lord, I will praise you with all my heart, and tell everyone about the marvelous things you do. ²I will be glad, yes, filled with joy because of you. I will sing your praises, O Lord God above all gods.

³My enemies will fall back and perish in your presence; ⁴you have vindicated me; you have endorsed my work, declaring from your throne that it is good. ⁵You have rebuked the nations and destroyed the wicked, blotting out their names forever and ever. ⁶O enemies of mine, you are doomed forever. The Lord will destroy your cities; even the memory of them will disappear.

7, 8But the Lord lives on forever; he sits upon his throne to judge justly the nations of the world. ⁹All who are oppressed may come to him. He is a refuge for them in their times of trouble. ¹⁰All those who know your mercy, Lord, will count on you for help. For you have never yet forsaken those who trust in you.

¹¹Oh, sing out your praises to the God who lives in Jerusalem. Tell the world about his unforgettable deeds. ¹²He who avenges murder has an open ear to those who cry to him for justice. He does not ignore the prayers of men in trouble when they call to him for help.

¹³And now, O Lord, have mercy on me; see how I suffer at the hands of those who hate me. Lord, snatch me back from the jaws of death. ¹⁴Save me, so that I can praise you publicly before all the people at Jerusalem's gates and rejoice that you have rescued me.

¹⁵The nations fall into the pitfalls they have dug for others; the trap they set has snapped on them. ¹⁶The Lord is famous for the way he punishes the wicked in their own snares!

¹⁷The wicked shall be sent away to hell; this is the fate of all the nations forgetting the Lord. ¹⁸For the needs of the needy shall not be ignored forever; the hopes of the poor shall not always be crushed.

¹⁹O Lord, arise and judge and punish the nations; don't let them defy you! ²⁰Make them tremble in fear; put the nations in their place until at last they know they are but puny men.

9:2 *O Lord God above all gods,* literally, "O Most High." **9:4** *you have endorsed my work, declaring from your throne that it is good,* literally, "You sit on the throne, judging righteously." **9:11** *in Jerusalem,* literally, "in Zion." **9:14** *at Jerusalem's gates,* literally, "in the gates of the daughter of Zion." **9:16** The Hebrew text adds at the end of the verse: "Higgaion. Selah." The meanings of these words are not known.

9:1ff Praise is expressing back to God our appreciation and understanding of his worth. It is saying "thank you" for each aspect of his divine nature. Our inward attitude becomes outward expression. In so doing, we help ourselves by expanding our vision of who he is.

9:1, 2 One of the natural results of praising God is witnessing. When we know God is wonderful, we naturally want to tell others and have them praise God with us.

9:4 God is our vindicator (one who clears us from criticism and justifies us before others). In this life, we may face many injustices: (1) we may be falsely accused and misunderstood by friends and enemies; (2) we may not truly be appreciated by others for the love we show; (3) the true value of our work and service may not duly be rewarded; (4) our ideas may be ignored. But God is to be praised, for he sees and remembers all the good we do; and it is up to him to decide the timing and the appropriateness of our rewards. If we do not trust him to vindicate us, then we are susceptible to hatred and self-pity. If we do trust him, we can experience God's peace and be free from the worry of how others perceive us and treat us.

9:10 God will never forsake those who trust in him. To forsake someone is to abandon that person. God's promise does not mean that if we trust in him we will never experience loss or suffering; it means that God himself will never leave us.

9:11 God does not live only in Jerusalem—he is everywhere all the time. The focal point of Israelite worship, however, was Jerusalem and its beautiful Temple. God was present in the Tabernacle (Exodus 25:8, 9) and in the Temple built by Solomon (2 Chronicles 7:16). From this central place of worship, the Jews were to tell the world about the one true God.

9:14 All of us want God to help us when we are in trouble, but often for different reasons. Some want God's help so that they will be successful and other people will like them. Others want God's help so that they will be comfortable and feel good about themselves. David, however, wanted help from God so that justice would be restored to Israel and so that he could show others the power of God. When you call to God for help, consider your motive. Is it to save yourself pain and embarrassment or to bring God glory and honor?

9:15, 16 For the boomerang effect of evil, see the note on 7:14–16.

9:18 The world may ignore the plight of the needy, crushing any earthly hope they may have. But God, the champion of the weak and needy, promises that this will not be the case forever. The wicked nations who forget the Lord and refuse to help their people will be judged by God. He knows our needs, he knows our tendency to despair, and he has given us the promise that he himself will care for us (see also 9:9, 12). Even when others forget us, he will remember.

Theme: Why do the wicked succeed? Although God may seem to be hidden at times, we can be assured that he is aware of every injustice.
Author: Anonymous, but probably David. Many ancient manuscripts combine Psalms 9 and 10, and Psalm 9 was written by David

10 Lord, why are you standing aloof and far away? Why do you hide when I need you the most?

2Come and deal with all these proud and wicked men who viciously persecute the poor. Pour upon these men the evil they planned for others! 3For these men brag of all their evil lusts; they revile God and congratulate those the Lord abhors, whose only goal in life is money.

4These wicked men, so proud and haughty, seem to think that God is dead. They wouldn't think of looking for him! 5Yet there is success in everything they do, and their enemies fall before them. They do not see your punishment awaiting them. 6They boast that neither God nor man can ever keep them down—somehow they'll find a way!

7Their mouths are full of profanity and lies and fraud. They are always boasting of their evil plans. 8They lurk in dark alleys of the city and murder passersby. 9Like lions they crouch silently, waiting to pounce upon the poor. Like hunters they catch their victims in their traps. 10The unfortunate are overwhelmed by their superior strength and fall beneath their blows. 11"God isn't watching," they say to themselves; "he'll never know!"

12O Lord, arise! O God, crush them! Don't forget the poor or anyone else in need. 13Why do you let the wicked get away with this contempt for God? For they think that God will never call them to account. 14Lord, you see what they are doing. You have noted each evil act. You know what trouble and grief they have caused. Now punish them. O Lord, the poor man trusts himself to you; you are known as the helper of the helpless. 15Break the arms of these wicked men. Go after them until the last of them is destroyed.

16The Lord is King forever and forever. Those who follow other gods shall be swept from his land.

17Lord, you know the hopes of humble people. Surely you will hear their cries and comfort their hearts by helping them. 18You will be with the orphans and all who are oppressed, so that mere earthly man will terrify them no longer.

10:1 Ps 13:1; 22:1
10:2 Ps 7:15; 9:16 73:6,8
10:3 Ps 49:6; 94:3,4
10:4 Ps 14:1; 36:1,2
10:5 Ps 28:5; 52:7
10:6 Ps 30:6,7
10:7 Ps 59:12; 73:8 140:3 Rom 3:14
10:8 Ps 11:2; 94:6,7
10:9 Ps 17:12; 59:3
10:11 Ps 10:4
10:12 Ps 9:12; 17:7
10:14 Ps 9:12 22:9-11; 37:5
10:15 Ps 37:17 140:11
10:16 Ps 29:10
10:17 Ps 9:18; 34:15
10:18 Ps 9:9; 74:21 146:9

Theme: God's rule provides stability in the midst of panic.
Because we can trust him, we can face our problems.
Author: David

11 How dare you tell me, "Flee to the mountains for safety," when I am trusting in the Lord?

11:1 Ps 56:10,11

10:4 *that God is dead,* literally, "that there is no God." **11:1** *Flee,* literally, "Flee as a bird."

10:1 To the psalmist, God seemed far away. "Why do you hide when I need you the most?" he asked God. But even though he had honest doubts, he did not stop praying or assume that God no longer cared. He was not complaining, but simply asking God to hurry to his aid. It is during those times when we feel most alone or oppressed that we need to keep praying, telling God about our troubles.

10:4–6 Some people succeed in everything they do, and they brag that no one, not even God, can keep them down. We may wonder why God allows these people to amass great wealth while they despise him as they do. But why are we upset when the wicked prosper? Are we angry about the damage they are doing, or just jealous of their success? To answer these questions we must gain the right perspective on wickedness and wealth. The wicked will surely be punished (10:5) because God hates their evil deeds (7:11). Wealth is only temporary and is not a sign of God's approval on a person's life; nor is lack of it a sign of God's disapproval. Don't let wealth or lack of it become your obsession.

10:11 There is an incompatibility between blind arrogance and the presence of God in our hearts. The proud person depends on

himself rather than on God. This causes God's guiding influences to leave his life. When God's presence is welcome, there is no room for pride because he makes us aware of our true selves.

10:12–18 This is the victim's prayer. When evil people are predators and we are their prey, we must remember to trust God for our help. God calls all people to account for their attitudes, so be sure your heart is right toward him.

10:14 God sees and takes note of each evil deed, hears our cries, and comforts our hearts (10:17). Sometimes our questions are left unanswered (10:13), but God's presence is always with us. We can face the wicked because we do not face them alone. God is by our side.

11:1–4 David was forced to flee for safety several times during his life. Being God's anointed king did not make him immune to injustice and hatred from others. This psalm may have been written when David was being hunted by King Saul (1 Samuel 18—31), or during the days of Absalom's rebellion (2 Samuel 15—18). In both instances, David did flee, but not as if all was lost because he knew God was in control. While David wisely avoided trouble, he did not fearfully run away from his troubles.

11:2
Ps 7:12; 64:3,4

11:3
Ps 82:5

11:4
Ps 34:15,16

11:5
Ps 5:5; 34:19

11:7
Ps 7:9-11

2For the wicked have strung their bows, drawn their arrows tight against the bowstrings, and aimed from ambush at the people of God. 3"Law and order have collapsed," we are told. "What can the righteous do but flee?"

4But the Lord is still in his holy temple; he still rules from heaven. He closely watches everything that happens here on earth. 5He puts the righteous and the wicked to the test; he hates those loving violence. 6He will rain down fire and brimstone on the wicked and scorch them with his burning wind.

7For God is good, and he loves goodness; the godly shall see his face.

Theme: The proud and lying words of men versus the true and pure words of God. A call for protection against those who try to manipulate us.
Author: David

12:2
Ps 28:3; 41:6

12:3
Ps 73:8,9

12:5
Ps 3:7; 9:9
34:6; 35:10

12:6
Ps 19:8-10
119:140

12:7
Ps 37:28; 97:10

12:8
Ps 55:10,11

12 Lord! Help! Godly men are fast disappearing. Where in all the world can dependable men be found? 2Everyone deceives and flatters and lies. There is no sincerity left.

3, 4But the Lord will not deal gently with people who act like that; he will destroy those proud liars who say, "We will lie to our hearts' content. Our lips are our own; who can stop us?"

5The Lord replies, "I will arise and defend the oppressed, the poor, the needy. I will rescue them as they have longed for me to do." 6The Lord's promise is sure. He speaks no careless word; all he says is purest truth, like silver seven times refined. 7O Lord, we know that you will forever preserve your own from the reach of evil men, 8although they prowl on every side and vileness is praised throughout the land.

Theme: Praying for relief from despair. We must continue to trust God even when he doesn't answer us immediately.
Author: David

13:1
Ps 44:24; 89:46

13:2
Ps 42:4,5,9

13:4
Ps 25:2; 38:16

13 How long will you forget me, Lord? Forever? How long will you look the other way when I am in need? 2How long must I be hiding daily anguish in my heart? How long shall my enemy have the upper hand?

3Answer me, O Lord my God; give me light in my darkness lest I die. 4Don't let my enemies say, "We have conquered him!" Don't let them gloat that I am down.

11:3 *Law and order have collapsed,* literally, "If the foundations have been torn down." **11:7** *For God is good, and he loves goodness; the godly shall see his face* or, "His face shines down in mercy and joy upon the good."

11:1-4 David's faith stood in dramatic contrast to the fear of his advisors. Faith in God keeps us from losing hope and helps us resist fear. David's advisors were afraid because they saw only frightening circumstances. David was comforted and optimistic because he knew God was greater than anything his enemies could bring against him (7:10; 16:1; 31:2, 3).

11:4 When law and order collapse and we wish we could hide, remember that God is still in control. Nothing happens without his knowledge and permission. When you feel like running away—run to God. He will restore justice and goodness on the earth in his good time.

11:5 God does not preserve believers from difficult circumstances, but puts both the righteous and the wicked to the test. For some, God's tests become a refining fire, while for others, they become an incinerator for destruction. Don't ignore or defy the tests and challenges that come your way in life.

12:1 Living for God in a deceitful world can be a difficult and lonely battle. At one time the great prophet Elijah felt so lonely he wanted to die. But God told him that there were 7,000 other faithful men (1 Kings 19:4, 14, 18). We are never alone in our battle against evil. When you feel alone, seek out other believers from whom you can gain strength and support.

12:2-4 We may be tempted to believe that lies are relatively harmless, even "useful" at times. But deceit, flattery, boasting, and lies are not overlooked by God. Each of these sins originate from a bad attitude that is eventually expressed in our speech. The tongue can be our greatest enemy because, though small, it can do great damage (James 3:5). Be careful how you use yours.

12:6 Sincerity and truth are extremely valuable because they are so rare. Many people are deceivers, liars, flatterers; they think they will get what they want by deception. As a king, David certainly faced his share of such people who hoped to win his favor and gain advancement through the use of flattery. When we feel as though sincerity and truth have nearly gone out of existence, we have one hope—the Word of God. God's words *are* as pure as refined silver. So listen carefully when he speaks.

13:1 Sometimes all we need to do is talk over a problem with a friend to help put it in perspective. In this psalm, the phrase "how long" occurs four times in the first two verses, indicating the depth of David's distress. David expressed his feelings to God and found strength. By the end of his prayer, he was able to express hope and trust in God. Prayer is one way we can express our feelings and talk our problems out with God. He helps us have the right perspective, leading to peace (Habakkuk 3:17-19).

5But I will always trust in you and in your mercy and shall rejoice in your **13:5**
salvation. 6I will sing to the Lord because he has blessed me so richly. Ps 52:8

Theme: Only the fool denies God. How foolish it must seem to God
when people say there is no God.
Author: David

14 That man is a fool who says to himself, "There is no God!" Anyone who **14:1**
talks like that is warped and evil and cannot really be a good person at all. Ps 10:4; 53:1
Rom 3:10-12

2The Lord looks down from heaven on all mankind to see if there are any who are **14:2**
wise, who want to please God. 3But no, all have strayed away; all are rotten with Ps 33:13-15
102:19
sin. Not one is good, not one! 4They eat my people like bread and wouldn't think **14:3**
of praying! Don't they really know any better? Ps 58:3; 143:2

5Terror shall grip them, for God is with those who love him. 6He is the refuge of **14:6**
the poor and humble when evildoers are oppressing them. 7Oh, that the time of Ps 9:9; 40:17
their rescue were already here, that God would come from Zion now to save his **14:7**
Ps 53:6; 85:1,2
people. What gladness when the Lord has rescued Israel! Job 42:10

Theme: Guidelines for living a blameless life
Author: David

15 Lord, who may go and find refuge and shelter in your tabernacle up on your **15:1**
holy hill? Ps 24:3; 27:5,6

2Anyone who leads a blameless life and is truly sincere. 3Anyone who refuses to **15:2**
Ps 24:4
slander others, does not listen to gossip, never harms his neighbor, 4speaks out **15:3**
against sin, criticizes those committing it, commends the faithful followers of the Ps 28:3
Lord, keeps a promise even if it ruins him, 5does not crush his debtors with high **15:5**
Ex 22:25; 23:8

13:5 David frequently claimed that God was slow to act on his behalf. We often feel this same impatience. It seems that evil and suffering go unchecked, and we wonder when God is going to stop them. David affirmed that he would continue to trust God no matter how long he had to wait for God's justice to be realized. When you feel impatient, remember David's steadfast faith in God's unfailing mercy.

13:5, 6 David was a faithful man, but he felt the pressure of his problems as much as anyone. His response to pressure, however, stands in stark contrast to the people described in Psalm 11 who wanted to give up. David held on to his faith. In the midst of despair, it is much harder to hold on than to give up. But if you give up on God, you give in to a life of despair.

14:1 A fool is not someone who is stupid or uneducated, but a person who rejects God. By rejecting God, the fool rejects the one who made the moral and spiritual laws that make life just and good. A fool is indeed "warped and evil" because to deny God's existence allows wickedness to prevail. The apostle Paul quotes these verses in Romans 3:10–12 as he mourns the lack of singleheartedness toward God and thus the rampant spread of evil. The wise, however, not only believe there is a God, but also strive to please him. To believe there is a God but refuse to please him is also foolish. Don't be a fool of either sort.

14:1–3 The true atheist is either foolish or wicked—foolish because he ignores the evidence that God exists, or wicked because he refuses to live by God's truths. The fool mentioned here is someone who is aggressively perverse in his actions. To speak in direct defiance of God is utterly foolish according to the Bible.

14:3 No one but God is perfect—all of us stand guilty before him (see Romans 3:23). You may be better at certain skills than someone else, but that is irrelevant. When you compare yourself to God's standard (what he wants you to be), you will recognize your sin. Only then can you turn away from it and turn to God.

14:3, 4 This statement is true of all human beings, and David applies it specifically to his enemies, the godless and fierce people who "eat my people like bread." "All have strayed away; . . . not

one is good." By contrast, David said, "You have . . . seen that I am good" (17:3).

There is a clear distinction between those who worship God and those who refuse to worship God. David worshiped God, and under his leadership Israel obeyed God and prospered. Several hundred years later, however, Israel had forgotten God. It was difficult to distinguish between God's followers and those who worshiped idols. When Isaiah called Israel to repentance, he, like David, spoke of people who had strayed away (Isaiah 53:6). But Isaiah was talking about the Israelites themselves. Paul quoted Psalm 14 in Romans 3:10–12. He made the image of straying sheep even more general. The whole human race—Jew and Gentile alike—has strayed from God.

14:5ff If God is with those who love him, then those who attack God's followers may be attacking God. To attack God is utterly futile (see 2:4, 5, 10–12). Thus, while we may feel we are losing the battle, there can be absolutely no doubt that our ultimate victory is in God.

15:1ff God calls his people to live holy lives and, in this psalm, gives us ten standards by which we can determine how we are doing. We live in the midst of evil people whose standards and morals are eroding. Our standards for living do not come from our evil society, but from God. Other standards for conduct are found in Isaiah 33:15; 56:1; Micah 6:8; Habakkuk 2:4; and Mark 12:29–31.

15:1 The tabernacle and holy hill are interchangeable words describing the focal point of Israelite worship—the dwelling place of God. In Hebrew poetry the repetition is found more in the thought, than in the sound or rhythm.

15:3, 4 Words are powerful and they reflect on you and your relationship with God. Perhaps nothing so identifies Christians as their ability to control their speech—refusing to slander, ignoring gossip, speaking out against sin, and guiding the faithful. Watch out for what you say. (See James 3:1–12 for more on the importance of controlling your tongue.)

15:5 Some people are so obsessed with money that they will change their God-given standards and lifestyle to get it. If money is

interest rates, and refuses to testify against the innocent despite the bribes offered him—such a man shall stand firm forever.

Theme: The joys and benefits of a life lived in companionship with God. We enjoy these benefits now and eternally.
Author: David

16 Save me, O God, because I have come to you for refuge. ²I said to him, "You are my Lord; I have no other help but yours." ³I want the company of the godly men and women in the land; they are the true nobility. ⁴Those choosing other gods shall all be filled with sorrow; I will not offer the sacrifices they do or even speak the names of their gods.

⁵The Lord himself is my inheritance, my prize. He is my food and drink, my highest joy! He guards all that is mine. ⁶He sees that I am given pleasant brooks and meadows as my share! What a wonderful inheritance! ⁷I will bless the Lord who counsels me; he gives me wisdom in the night. He tells me what to do.

⁸I am always thinking of the Lord; and because he is so near, I never need to stumble or to fall.

16:6 *He sees that I am given pleasant brooks and meadows as my share,* literally, "The boundary lines are fallen unto me in pleasant places."

16:1
Ps 7:1; 17:8

16:3
Ps 101:6
119:63

16:4
Ps 32:10
106:37,38

16:6
Ps 78:55

16:7
Ps 73:24; 77:6

16:8
Ps 27:8; 73:23
110:5; 123:1,2

TROUBLES AND COMPLAINTS IN PSALMS

We can relate to the psalms because they express our feelings. We all face troubles, as did the psalm writers hundreds of years ago, and we often respond as they did. In Psalm 3, David told God how he felt about the odds against him. But within three verses, the king realized that God's presence and care made the odds meaningless. This experience is repeated in many of the psalms. Usually, the hope and confidence in God outweigh the fear and suffering; sometimes they do not. Still, the psalm writers consistently poured out their thoughts and emotions to God. When they felt abandoned by God, they told him so. When they were impatient with how slowly God seemed to be answering their prayers, they also told him so. Because they recognized the difference between themselves and God, they were free to be men and to be honest with their Creator. That is why so many of the dark psalms end in the light. The psalmists started by expressing their feelings and ended up remembering to whom they were speaking.

Although we have much in common with the psalmists, we may differ in two ways: we might not tell God what we are really thinking and feeling; and therefore we also might not recognize, even faintly, who is listening to our prayers!

Notice this pattern as you read Psalms, and put the psalmists' insight to the test. You may well find that your awareness and appreciation of God will grow as you are honest with him. (See Psalms 3, 6, 13, 31, 37, 64, 77, 102, 121, 142.)

---

a controlling force in your life, it must be curbed or it will harm others and destroy your relationship with God.

15:5 As we grow in our relationship with our Redeemer, we develop a desire to live by his standards. Our eternal relationship with him is intimately tied to how we live out that relationship by reflecting his standards in our lives daily.

16:1 David cried out for God to be his refuge. We, like David, want to be saved *from* threatening enemies. But that is not enough. We want also to be saved *to* something or someone—a refuge. Our ultimate safety is in God, our refuge.

16:3 At one time or another, we have tried to impress friends by "name-dropping." If we have personally known a famous person, for example, we may casually mention this fact to others. Truly noble people are not necessarily famous, but they live as God desires. Seek the company of those who can build you up spiritually, those who are committed to God and have the right perspective on life.

16:7, 8 It is human nature to make our own plans and *then* ask

God to bless them. Instead, we should seek God's will first. By constantly thinking about the Lord and his way of living, we will gain insights that will help us make right decisions and live the way God desires.

16:8 God does not exempt believers from the day-to-day circumstances of life. Believers and unbelievers alike experience pain, trouble, and failure at times (Matthew 5:45). David was talking about the unique sense of security felt by believers. Unbelievers have a sense of hopelessness about life and confusion over their true purpose on earth. Those who seek after God, however, can move ahead confidently with what they know is right and important in God's eyes.

16:8–11 This psalm is often called a messianic psalm because it is quoted in the New Testament as referring to the resurrection of Jesus Christ. Both Peter and Paul quoted from this psalm when speaking of Christ's bodily resurrection (see Acts 2:25–28, 31; 13:35–37).

9Heart, body, and soul are filled with joy. 10For you will not leave me among the dead; you will not allow your beloved one to rot in the grave. 11You have let me experience the joys of life and the exquisite pleasures of your own eternal presence.

16:10
Ps 49:15; 86:13
Acts 2:27; 13:35

Theme: A plea for justice in the face of false accusations and persecution. David urges us to realize the true goal of life—to know God—and the true reward of life—to one day see God.
Author: David, written while he was being persecuted by Saul

17 I am pleading for your help, O Lord; for I have been honest and have done what is right, and you must listen to my earnest cry! 2Publicly acquit me, Lord, for you are always fair. 3You have tested me and seen that I am good. You have come even in the night and found nothing amiss and know that I have told the truth. 4I have followed your commands and have not gone along with cruel and evil men. 5My feet have not slipped from your paths.

6Why am I praying like this? Because I know you will answer me, O God! Yes, listen as I pray. 7Show me your strong love in wonderful ways, O Savior of all those seeking your help against their foes. 8Protect me as you would the pupil of your eye; hide me in the shadow of your wings as you hover over me.

9My enemies encircle me with murder in their eyes. 10They are pitiless and arrogant. Listen to their boasting. 11They close in upon me and are ready to throw me to the ground. 12They are like lions eager to tear me apart, like young lions hiding and waiting their chance.

13, 14Lord, arise and stand against them. Push them back! Come and save me from these men of the world whose only concern is earthly gain—these men whom you have filled with your treasures so that their children and grandchildren are rich and prosperous.

15But as for me, my contentment is not in wealth but in seeing you and knowing all is well between us. And when I awake in heaven, I will be fully satisfied, for I will see you face to face.

17:1
Ps 61:1; 88:2
142:6
17:2
Ps 98:8,9
99:4; 103:6
17:3
Ps 26:1,2
17:4
Ps 10:5-11
119:9,101
17:5
Ps 18:36
37:30,31; 44:18
17:8
Deut 32:10
Ruth 2:12
Ps 36:7; 91:1,4
17:10
1 Sam 2:3
Ps 31:18
73:7,8
17:12
Ps 7:2; 10:9
17:13
Ps 22:20; 49:6
73:3-7
17:15
Ps 4:6,7
16:11; 140:13

Theme: Gratitude for deliverance and victory. The only sure way to be delivered from surrounding evil is to call upon God for help and strength.
Author: David

18 *This song of David was written at a time when the Lord had delivered him from his many enemies, including Saul.*
Lord, how I love you! For you have done such tremendous things for me.

18:1
Ps 59:17

16:9 David found the secret to joy. True joy is far deeper than happiness; joy can be felt even in the midst of and in spite of one's deepest troubles. Happiness is temporary because it is based on external circumstances, but joy is lasting because it is based on God's presence within us. As you contemplate his daily presence, you will find contentment. Don't base your life on circumstances, but on God.

16:10 David stated confidently that God will not leave his loved ones in the grave or among the dead. Many people fear death because they cannot control it and do not understand it. As believers, we can be assured that God will not forget us after we die. He will bring us to life again to live with him forever. This provides *real* security. For other passages about resurrection, see Job 19:25, 26; Isaiah 26:19; Daniel 12:2, 13; Mark 13:27; 1 Corinthians 15:12-58; 1 Thessalonians 4:13-18; Revelation 20:11—21:4.

17:3 Was David saying that he was sinless? David's claim was not a proud assumption of purity, it was an understanding of his relationship with God. In 14:3, David said, "All are rotten with sin." He realized that he had indeed committed sin, as all people do, but his relationship with God was one of close fellowship and constant repentance and forgiveness. His goodness, therefore, came from seeking to know God intimately. By contrast, the fools (14:1-3) are wicked because they have rejected God and thus have not repented or received God's forgiveness.

17:8 The "shadow of your wings" is a figure of speech

symbolizing God's protection. He guards us just as a mother bird protects her young by covering them with her wings. Moses used this same metaphor in Deuteronomy 32:11.

17:8 David called on God to value him as much as one would value his eyes, and to let that measure of value also be a measure of protection. We must not conclude that we have somehow missed God's protection if we experience troubles. God's protection has far greater purposes than avoiding pain; it is to make us better servants for him. God protects us by seeing us through circumstances, not by helping us escape them.

17:13-15 We deceive ourselves when we measure our happiness or contentment in life by the amount of wealth we possess. When we put riches at the top of our value system, the comforts of today overshadow the eternal value of our relationship with God. We think we will be happy or content when we get riches, only to discover that they bring nothing but transient pleasure. The true measurement of happiness or contentment is an eternal one. You will find true happiness if you put eternal riches above earthly riches.

17:15 David believed in life after death. There are several verses in the Old Testament that support the view that "awake" refers to hope in the resurrection. Some of these are Job 19:25-27; Psalms 11:7; 49:15; 73:23; 139:17, 18; Isaiah 26:19; and Daniel 12:2, 13.

18:1ff This psalm is almost a duplicate of 2 Samuel 22. It may have been written toward the end of David's life when there was peace. God is praised for his glorious works and constant blessings.

18:2
1 Sam 2:2
Ps 28:1; 19:14
59:9,11; 71:3
75:10; 144:2

18:3
Ps 34:6; 96:4

18:4
Ps 69:1,2
116:3, 124:2-5

18:6
Ps 3:4; 34:15

18:7
Ps 114:4,6,7

18:9
Ex 20:21
Ps 97:2; 144:5

18:10
Ps 80:1; 99:1

18:12
Ps 104:1,2

18:13
Ps 29:3
104:7,8

18:14
Judg 4:15
Ps 144:6

18:15
Ex 15:8
Ps 106:9

18:18
Ps 16:8; 59:16

18:19
Ps 31:8; 37:23
41:1,11; 118:5

18:20
Ps 7:8; 24:4

18:21
Ps 37:34
119:33,102,103

18:25
Ps 62:12

18:27
Ps 72:12; 101:5
Prov 6:16-19

18:28
Ps 27:1

18:29
Ps 118:10-12
2 Cor 12:9

18:30
Ps 12:6; 19:7

2The Lord is my fort where I can enter and be safe; no one can follow me in and slay me. He is a rugged mountain where I hide; he is my Savior, a rock where none can reach me, and a tower of safety. He is my shield. He is like the strong horn of a mighty fighting bull. 3All I need to do is cry to him—oh, praise the Lord—and I am saved from all my enemies!

4Death bound me with chains, and the floods of ungodliness mounted a massive attack against me. 5Trapped and helpless, I struggled against the ropes that drew me on to death.

6In my distress I screamed to the Lord for his help. And he heard me from heaven; my cry reached his ears. 7Then the earth rocked and reeled, and mountains shook and trembled. How they quaked! For he was angry. 8Fierce flames leaped from his mouth, setting fire to the earth; smoke blew from his nostrils. 9He bent the heavens down and came to my defense; thick darkness was beneath his feet. 10Mounted on a mighty angel, he sped swiftly to my aid with wings of wind. 11He enshrouded himself with darkness, veiling his approach with dense clouds dark as murky waters. 12Suddenly the brilliance of his presence broke through the clouds with lightning and a mighty storm of hail.

13The Lord thundered in the heavens; the God above all gods has spoken—oh, the hailstones; oh, the fire! 14He flashed his fearful arrows of lightning and routed all my enemies. See how they run! 15Then at your command, O Lord, the sea receded from the shore. At the blast of your breath the depths were laid bare.

16He reached down from heaven and took me and drew me out of my great trials. He rescued me from deep waters. 17He delivered me from my strong enemy, from those who hated me—I who was helpless in their hands.

18On the day when I was weakest, they attacked. But the Lord held me steady. 19He led me to a place of safety, for he delights in me.

20The Lord rewarded me for doing right and being pure. 21For I have followed his commands and have not sinned by turning back from following him. 22I kept close watch on all his laws; I did not refuse a single one. 23I did my best to keep them all, holding myself back from doing wrong. 24And so the Lord has paid me with his blessings, for I have done what is right, and I am pure of heart. This he knows, for he watches my every step.

25Lord, how merciful you are to those who are merciful. And you do not punish those who run from evil. 26You give blessings to the pure but pain to those who leave your paths. 27You deliver the humble but condemn the proud and haughty ones. 28You have turned on my light! The Lord my God has made my darkness turn to light. 29Now in your strength I can scale any wall, attack any troop. 30What a God he is! How perfect in every way! All his promises prove true. He

18:6 *from heaven,* literally, "out of his temple." **18:8** *setting fire to the earth,* literally, "coals were kindled by it." **18:9** *He bent the heavens down and came to my defense,* implied. **18:10** *a mighty angel,* literally, "a cherub." **18:12** *lightning,* literally, "coals of fire." **18:25** *And you do not punish those who run from evil,* literally, "with the upright you show yourself upright."

18:2, 3 God's protection of his people is limitless and can take many forms. David characterized God's care with six military symbols. God is like: (1) a *fort* or place of safety where the enemy can't follow, (2) a *rugged mountain* full of hiding places, (3) a *rock* that can't be penetrated by any who would harm us, (4) a *tower* high above our enemies, (5) a *shield* that comes between us and harm, and (6) a *horn* to scare the enemy away or to warn us if he comes too close. If you need protection, look to God.

18:10 Cherubim are divine beings that may be one of several ranks of angels. One of their functions was to serve as guardians. These "mighty angels" guarded the entrances to both the Tree of Life (Genesis 3:24) and the Holy of Holies (Exodus 26:31–33). Their images were part of the Ark of the Covenant (Exodus 25:18–22). They are also described as carrying God's throne (Ezekiel 1).

18:13 "The God above all gods" is an important designation for David to make. Heathen idol worship was deeply rooted in the land, and each region had its own deity. But these images of wood and stone were powerless. David was placing the Lord alone in a superior category.

18:16 Our troubles, like deep waters, threaten to drown us. David, helpless and weak, knew that God alone had rescued him from his enemies during times when he was defenseless. How often we wish that God would quickly rescue us out of our troubles. Remember that God can deliver us or help us remain steady as we go through troubles (18:18). Either way, his protection is best for us. When you feel drowned by troubles, ask God to help you, hold you steady, and protect you. In his care, you are never helpless.

18:30 Many say belief in God is a crutch for weak people who cannot make it on their own. God is indeed a shield to protect us when we *are* too weak to face certain trials by ourselves. He strengthens, protects, and guides us in order to send us back into an evil world to fight for him.

is a shield for everyone who hides behind him. ³¹For who is God except our Lord? Who but he is as a rock?

³²He fills me with strength and protects me wherever I go. ³³He gives me the surefootedness of a mountain goat upon the crags. He leads me safely along the top of the cliffs. ³⁴He prepares me for battle and gives me strength to draw an iron bow!

³⁵You have given me your salvation as my shield. Your right hand, O Lord, supports me; your gentleness has made me great. ³⁶You have made wide steps beneath my feet so that I need never slip. ³⁷I chased my enemies; I caught up with them and did not turn back until all were conquered. ³⁸I pinned them to the ground; all were helpless before me. I placed my feet upon their necks. ³⁹For you have armed me with strong armor for the battle. My enemies quail before me and fall defeated at my feet. ⁴⁰You made them turn and run; I destroyed all who hated me. ⁴¹They shouted for help but no one dared to rescue them; they cried to the Lord, but he refused to answer them. ⁴²So I crushed them fine as dust and cast them to the wind. I threw them away like sweepings from the floor. ⁴³, ⁴⁴, ⁴⁵You gave me victory in every battle. The nations came and served me. Even those I didn't know before come now and bow before me. Foreigners who have never seen me submit instantly. They come trembling from their strongholds.

⁴⁶God is alive! Praise him who is the great rock of protection. ⁴⁷He is the God who pays back those who harm me and subdues the nations before me.

⁴⁸He rescues me from my enemies; he holds me safely out of their reach and saves me from these powerful opponents. ⁴⁹For this, O Lord, I will praise you among the nations. ⁵⁰Many times you have miraculously rescued me, the king you appointed. You have been loving and kind to me and will be to my descendants.

18:31
Deut 32:31,39
Ps 62:2; 86:8-10
18:33
Hab 3:19
18:35
Ps 33:20,63:8
119:117
18:36
Ps 31:8; 66:9
18:37
Ps 44:5
18:38
Ps 36:12; 47:3
18:40
Ps 94:23; 21:12
18:41
Ps 50:22
18:43
2 Sam 3:1
Ps 89:27
Isa 55:5
Mic 7:17
18:47
Ps 47:3
94:1,2; 144:2
18:48
Ps 3:7; 27:5,6
18:49
Ps 108:1
Rom 15:9
18:50
Ps 21:1; 28:8
89:4

Theme: Both God's creation and his Word reveal his greatness.
Author: David

19 The heavens are telling the glory of God; they are a marvelous display of his craftsmanship. ²Day and night they keep on telling about God. ³, ⁴Without a sound or word, silent in the skies, their message reaches out to all the world. The sun lives in the heavens where God placed it ⁵and moves out across the skies as radiant as a bridegroom going to his wedding, or as joyous as an athlete looking

19:1
1 Gen 1:6-8
Rom 1:20
19:2
Ps 74:16

18:34 *an iron bow*, literally, "a bow of bronze." **19:5** *as radiant as a bridegroom*, literally, "is like a bridegroom." *going to his wedding*, implied. Literally, "going forth from his chamber."

18:32–34 God promises to give us strength for life-building challenges and protection from life-threatening troubles. But he doesn't promise to eliminate our troubles. If God promised no rough roads, no mountains to climb, and no battles, we would not grow. But with these life-building challenges, he sends strength to overcome. If he left us alone with life-threatening troubles, we would not survive. But God sends his protection. We need his protection to survive life's impossible threats and his strength to grow as we respond to life's challenging circumstances.

18:35 David offers an interesting twist to the concept of greatness, saying that God's gentleness made him great. Our society believes that greatness is attained through a combination of opportunity, talent, and aggressiveness. But true greatness comes from living according to God's laws and standards and recognizing that all we have comes from the gentleness of God's mercy.

18:40–42 David was a man characterized by mercy. He spared the lives of Saul (1 Samuel 24:1–8), Nabal (1 Samuel 25:21–35), and Shime-i (2 Samuel 16:5–12) and showed great kindness to Mephibosheth (2 Samuel 9). But here David asked God to destroy his enemies. David, however, was simply asking God to give the wicked the punishment they deserved.

18:43–45 David's great power had indeed become legendary. God gave him victory in every battle. The book of 2 Samuel records victories over the Jebusites (5:6–10), the Philistines (5:17–25; 8:1, 2), Hadadezer of Zobah (8:3, 4), the Syrians (8:5, 6;

10), the Edomites (8:13, 14), and the Ammonites (12:26–31). In addition, the king of Tyre sent supplies and workmen to help David build his palace (5:11). But David did not attribute his victories to himself. He fully realized that the purpose of his position was to bless God's people (1 Chronicles 14:2).

19:1ff David's steps of meditation take him from creation, through God's Word, through his own sinfulness, to salvation. As God reveals himself through nature (19:1–6), we learn about his glory and our finiteness. As God reveals himself through Scripture (19:7–11), we learn about his holiness and our sinfulness. As God reveals himself through daily experiences (19:12–14), we learn about his gracious forgiveness and our salvation.

19:1–6 We are surrounded by fantastic displays of God's craftsmanship—the heavens give dramatic evidence of his existence, his power, his love, his care. To say that the universe happened by chance is absurd—its intricacy and dependability give proof of a personally involved Creator. As you look at God's craftsmanship in nature and the heavens, thank him for such magnificent beauty and the truth it reveals about the Creator.

19:3, 4 The apostle Paul referred to this psalm when he explained that everyone knows about God because his existence and power are proclaimed by nature (Romans 1:19, 20). This does not cancel the need for missions because the message of God's salvation must still be told to the ends of the earth. However, people everywhere should already believe in a loving Creator by just looking at the evidence of nature around them. The saddest and most hopeless people are those who say there is no God.

19:6 Ps 113:3
19:7 Ps 36:9
19:9 Ps 119:138,142
19:10 Ps 119:127
19:11 Ps 17:4
19:12 Ps 51:1,2
19:13 Ps 25:11; 32:2

forward to a race! 6The sun crosses the heavens from end to end, and nothing can hide from its heat.

7,8God's laws are perfect. They protect us, make us wise, and give us joy and light. 9God's laws are pure, eternal, just. 10They are more desirable than gold. They are sweeter than honey dripping from a honeycomb. 11For they warn us away from harm and give success to those who obey them.

12But how can I ever know what sins are lurking in my heart? Cleanse me from these hidden faults. 13And keep me from deliberate wrongs; help me to stop doing them. Only then can I be free of guilt and innocent of some great crime.

14May my spoken words and unspoken thoughts be pleasing even to you, O Lord my Rock and my Redeemer.

Theme: A prayer for victory in battle. Such a prayer can help us prepare for any great challenge. David knew that trust should be placed in the Lord more than in human power.
Author: David. The events in 2 Samuel 10 may have prompted this prayer.

20:1 Ps 46:7,11
20:2 Ps 3:4; 110:2 119:28
20:3 Ps 51:19 Acts 10:4
20:4 1 Sam 1:17 Ps 21:2; 145:19
20:5 Ps 9:14; 60:4
20:7 Ps 33:16,17

20 In your day of trouble, may the Lord be with you! May the God of Jacob keep you from all harm. 2May he send you aid from his sanctuary in Zion. 3May he remember with pleasure the gifts you have given him, your sacrifices and burnt offerings. 4May he grant you your heart's desire and fulfill all your plans. 5May there be shouts of joy when we hear the news of your victory, flags flying with praise to God for all that he has done for you. May he answer all your prayers!

6"God save the king"—I know he does! He hears me from highest heaven and sends great victories. 7Some nations boast of armies and of weaponry, but our boast is in the Lord our God. 8Those nations will collapse and perish; we will arise to stand firm and sure!

9Give victory to our king, O Lord; oh, hear our prayer.

Theme: Praising God after victory in battle. When God answers our prayers for victory, we must quickly and openly thank him for his help.
Author: David

21:1 Ps 59:16,17
21:2 Ps 37:4
21:4 Ps 61:6; 91:16 133:3
21:5 Ps 8:5; 96:6

21 How the king rejoices in your strength, O Lord! How he exults in your salvation. 2For you have given him his heart's desire, everything he asks you for!

3You welcomed him to the throne with success and prosperity. You set a royal crown of solid gold upon his head. 4He asked for a long, good life, and you have granted his request; the days of his life stretch on and on forever. 5You have given him fame and honor. You have clothed him with splendor and majesty. 6You have

19:9 *God's laws are pure, eternal, just,* or, "The rules governing the worship of the Lord are pure and need never be changed."

19:7-11 When we think of the Law, we often think of something that keeps us from having fun. But here we see the opposite—laws that free us, protect us, make us wise, and bring joy and light. That's because God's laws are guidelines and lights on our path, rather than chains on our hands and feet. They point at harm and warn us, then point at success and guide us.

19:12, 13 Guilt plagues many Christians. They worry that they have committed a sin unknowingly, done something good with selfish intentions, failed to put their whole heart into a task, or neglected something they should have done. Guilt can play an important role in bringing us to Christ and in keeping us behaving properly, but it should not cripple us or make us fearful. God's forgiveness is full and complete—even for those sins of which we are unaware.

19:12-14 David distinguished between "hidden faults" and "deliberate wrongs." Hidden faults are sins committed unknowingly or in ignorance of God's laws. Deliberate wrongs are sins committed in defiant rebellion against God. David asked forgiveness for both and realized that even his dreadful sins of murder and adultery (2 Samuel 11, 12) were covered by God's mercy. David also recognized that not only his words and actions,

but even his thoughts, must be pleasing to God.

20:2 Zion is another name for the city of Jerusalem, where David kept the Ark of the Covenant and where Solomon built the great Temple for God. God himself chose Zion to represent his presence upon the earth (Psalm 132:13).

20:6-8 As long as there have been armies and weapons, nations have boasted of their power, but such power does not last. Throughout history, empires and kingdoms have risen to great power only to vanish in the dust. David, however, knew that the true might of his nation was not in weaponry but in worship; not in fire-power, but in God's power. Since God alone can preserve a nation or an individual, be sure your confidence is in God, who gives eternal victory. Whom do you trust?

21:1-6 David described all that he had as gifts from God. "You have given him his heart's desire" (21:2). "You welcomed him to the throne" (21:3). "You have granted his request" for long life (21:4). "You have given him" fame, honor, splendor, majesty (21:5). "You have endowed him" with happiness and joy (21:6). We too must look upon all we have—position, family, wealth, talent—as gifts from God.

endowed him with eternal happiness. You have given him the unquenchable joy of your presence. 7And because the king trusts in the Lord, he will never stumble, never fall; for he depends upon the steadfast love of the God who is above all gods.

8Your hand, O Lord, will find your enemies, all who hate you. 9, 10When you appear, they will be destroyed in the fierce fire of your presence. The Lord will destroy them and their children. 11For these men plot against you, Lord, but they cannot possibly succeed. 12They will turn and flee when they see your arrows aimed straight at them.

13Accept our praise, O Lord, for all your glorious power. We will write songs to celebrate your mighty acts!

21:7
Ps 112:6; 125:1

21:9
Ps 37:28
Mal 4:1

21:11
Ps 2:1-3

21:12
Ps 7:12,13
18:40

21:13
Ps 59:16; 81:1

Theme: A prayer that carries us from great suffering to great joy. Despite apparent rejection by his friends and God, David believed that God would lead him out of despair. He looked forward to that future day when God would rule over the entire earth.
Author: David

22 My God, my God, why have you forsaken me? Why do you refuse to help me or even to listen to my groans? 2Day and night I keep on weeping, crying for your help, but there is no reply— 3, 4for *you are holy.*

The praises of our fathers surrounded your throne; they trusted you and you delivered them. 5You heard their cries for help and saved them; they were never disappointed when they sought your aid.

6But I am a worm, not a man, scorned and despised by my own people and by all mankind. 7Everyone who sees me mocks and sneers and shrugs. 8"Is this the one who rolled his burden on the Lord?" they laugh. "Is this the one who claims the Lord delights in him? We'll believe it when we see God rescue him!"

9, 10, 11Lord, how you have helped me before! You took me safely from my mother's womb and brought me through the years of infancy. I have depended upon you since birth; you have always been my God. Don't leave me now, for trouble is near and no one else can possibly help.

12I am surrounded by fearsome enemies, strong as the giant bulls from Bashan. 13They come at me with open jaws, like roaring lions attacking their prey. 14My strength has drained away like water, and all my bones are out of joint. My heart melts like wax; 15my strength has dried up like sun-baked clay; my tongue sticks to my mouth, for you have laid me in the dust of death. 16The enemy, this gang of evil men, circles me like a pack of dogs; they have pierced my hands and feet. 17I can count every bone in my body. See these men of evil gloat and stare; 18they divide my clothes among themselves by a toss of the dice.

22:1
Mt 27:46
Mk 15:34

22:2
Ps 42:3; 88:1

22:3
Ps 99:9; 78:53
107:6; 148:14

22:6
Job 25:6
Ps 31:11
Isa 41:14

22:7
Isa 53:3
Mt 27:39
Mk 15:29,30

22:9
Ps 71:5,6,12
72:12
Isa 46:3; 49:1

22:13
Job 16:10
Ps 17:12

22:15
Ps 38:10
104:29

22:16
Mt 27:35
Jn 20:25

22:18
Lk 23:34
Jn 19:23,24

22:9-11 *Lord, how you have helped me before,* implied.

21:7 David was not saying that we won't ever stumble when we trust in God, but that as long as we trust God our favor with him cannot be shaken. He will never leave or desert us.

21:7 A good leader trusts God and depends upon his steadfast love. Too often our leaders trust in their own cleverness and strength, or in the "god" of military power. But God is above all these gods. If you aspire to leadership, keep the Lord God at the center of your life and depend on him.

21:7 One of the most prized treasures of life is security—the sure knowlege that life's foundations will not be shaken in the midst of life's struggles. David had struggled with enemy forces and had won a great victory, not because he was confident in his own uncertain power, but because he trusted in God's unfailing love.

21:11 When you see people getting away with evil, remember that they will not succeed forever. Their power is only temporary and God's very presence would send them scattering in a moment. God, when he so desires, will intervene for his people and give the wicked the judgment they deserve.

22:1 David gave an amazingly accurate description of the suffering the Messiah would endure hundreds of years later. David was obviously enduring some great trial, but through his suffering he, like the Messiah to come, gained victory. Jesus, the Messiah,

quoted this verse while hanging on the cross carrying our burden of sin (Matthew 27:46). It was not a complaint, but an appeal to God.

22:6 When others despise us and heap scorn upon us, they treat us as less than human, with the same disdain as we would treat a worm. After much degradation, we, like King David, could begin to have low self-esteem. When we feel the sting of rejection, we must keep in mind the hope and victory God promises to us (22:22ff).

22:9-11 God's loving concern does not begin on the day we are born and conclude on the day we die, but reaches back to those days when we were unborn, and reaches ahead along the unending path of eternity. The only sure help for our lives comes from a God whose concern for us reaches beyond our earthly existence.

22:12 The land of Bashan, located east of the Sea of Galilee, was known for its strong and fat cattle (Amos 4:1). Because of its grainfields, it was often called the breadbasket of Palestine.

22:18 It is a great insult to human dignity to rob a person of everything, even his clothing, leaving him naked and destitute. Jesus the Messiah would suffer this humiliating experience on the cross (Matthew 27:35). Most of us will never know the shame and suffering of being penniless and naked in a public place, as many

22:19
Ps 70:5

22:20
Ps 35:17; 37:14

22:21
Ps 34:4; 118:5
120:1

22:22
Heb 2:12

22:23
135:19,20

22:24
Ps 27:9; 31:22
Heb 5:7

22:25
Ps 35:18
40:9,10

22:26
Ps 40:16; 69:32

¹⁹O Lord, don't stay away. O God my Strength, hurry to my aid. ²⁰Rescue me from death; spare my precious life from all these evil men. ²¹Save me from these lions' jaws and from the horns of these wild oxen. Yes, God will answer me and rescue me.

²²I will praise you to all my brothers; I will stand up before the congregation and testify of the wonderful things you have done. ²³"Praise the Lord, each one of you who fears him," I will say. "Each of you must fear and reverence his name. Let all Israel sing his praises, ²⁴for he has not despised my cries of deep despair; he has not turned and walked away. When I cried to him, he heard and came."

²⁵Yes, I will stand and praise you before all the people. I will publicly fulfill my vows in the presence of all who reverence your name.

²⁶The poor shall eat and be satisfied; all who seek the Lord shall find him and shall praise his name. Their hearts shall rejoice with everlasting joy. ²⁷The whole earth shall see it and return to the Lord; the people of every nation shall worship him.

22:20 *Rescue me from death; spare my precious life from all these evil men,* literally, "Deliver my soul from the sword, my only one from the power of the dog!" **22:23** *Each of you,* literally, "all you sons of Jacob." **22:25** *praise you,* literally, "praise from you." **22:26** *The poor,* literally, "the afflicted."

CHRIST IN THE PSALMS

Both the Jewish and Christian faiths have long believed that many psalms referred as much to the promised Messiah as they did to events at the time. Because the Messiah was to be a descendant of David, it was expected that many of the royal psalms would apply to him. Christians noted how many of the passages seemed to describe in detail events from Christ's life and death. Jesus himself frequently quoted from Psalms. Almost everything that happened at the crucifixion and most of Jesus' words during his final hours came directly from Psalms.

The following is a list of the main references in Psalms pertaining to Christ.

Reference in Psalms	Reference to Christ	Fulfillment in the New Testament
2:7	The Messiah will be God's Son	Hebrews 1:5, 6
16:8–10	He will rise from the dead	Luke 24:5–7
22:1–21	He will be crucified	Matthew 26, 27
22:18	Soldiers gamble for his clothing	Matthew 27:35; John 19:23, 24
22:15	He thirsts while on the cross	John 19:28
22:22	He will speak of his Father	Hebrews 2:12
34:20	His bones would not be broken	John 19:36, 37
40:6–8	He came to do God's will	Hebrews 10:5–7
41:9	One close to him would betray him	Luke 22:48
45:6, 7	His Kingdom will last forever	Hebrews 1:8, 9
68:18	He ascended into heaven	Ephesians 4:8–10
69:9	He is zealous for God	John 2:17
69:21	He was offered gall and vinegar for his thirst on the cross	Matthew 27:48
89:3, 4, 35, 36	He will be a descendant of David	Luke 1:31–33
96:13	He will return to judge the world	1 Thessalonians 1:10
102:25–28	His words are eternal	Matthew 24:35
110:1	He is David's son and God's Son	Matthew 22:44
110:4	He is the eternal priest-king	Hebrews 6:20
118:22	He is rejected by many but accepted by God	1 Peter 2:7, 8

---

of the Jews did during the Nazi holocaust. But most of us at some time will feel equally exposed and naked when some sin, secret or not-so-secret, is uncovered. At that time, we will need to cry out with the psalmist, "O God my Strength, hurry to my aid" (22:19).

22:21, 22 The psalmist's private deliverance deserved a public testimony. God does many wonderful things for us in the quiet moments of our lives, and we must be prepared to offer public praise for them.

28For the Lord is King and rules the nations. 29Both proud and humble together, all who are mortal—born to die—shall worship him. 30Our children too shall serve him, for they shall hear from us about the wonders of the Lord; 31generations yet unborn shall hear of all the miracles he did for us.

22:28
Ps 47:6,7,8
22:30
Ps 102:18,28

Theme: God is seen as a caring shepherd and a dependable guide. We must follow God and obey his commands. He is our only hope for eternal life and security.
Author: David

23 Because the Lord is my Shepherd, I have everything I need! 2,3He lets me rest in the meadow grass and leads me beside the quiet streams. He gives me new strength. He helps me do what honors him the most. 4Even when walking through the dark valley of death I will not be afraid, for you are close beside me, guarding, guiding all the way.

5You provide delicious food for me in the presence of my enemies. You have welcomed me as your guest; blessings overflow!

6Your goodness and unfailing kindness shall be with me all of my life, and afterwards I will live with you forever in your home.

23:1
Jn 10:11
1 Pet 2:25
23:2
Ps 5:8; 46:4
23:4
Ps 27:1; 107:14
23:5
Ps 16:5; 92:10
23:6
Ps 25:6,7,10

Theme: Everything belongs to God—the glorious eternal king.
Let us worship him and welcome his glorious reign.
Author: David

24 The earth belongs to God! Everything in all the world is his! 2He is the one who pushed the oceans back to let dry land appear.

3Who may climb the mountain of the Lord and enter where he lives? Who may stand before the Lord? 4Only those with pure hands and hearts, who do not practice dishonesty and lying. 5They will receive God's own goodness as their blessing

24:1
Ps 89:11
1 Cor 10:26
24:3
Ps 15:1; 65:4
24:5
Deut 11:26,27

23:4 *for you are close beside me, guarding, guiding all the way,* literally, "Your rod and your staff comfort me."
23:5 *You have welcomed me as your guest,* literally, "You have anointed my head with oil, my cup runs over."
24:2 *He is the one who pushed the oceans back to let dry land appear,* literally, "He has founded it upon the seas."
24:5 *God's own goodness,* literally, "righteousness," right standing with God.

22:30, 31 If we want future generations to know about God's wonders and miracles, we must teach them to our children. If we want our children to serve the Lord, they must hear about him from us. It is not enough to rely on the church or "those with more authority" to provide all their Christian education. The lessons of Scripture must be reinforced in the home.

22:30, 31 Unborn generations of tomorrow are depending on our faithfulness today. As we teach our children today about the Lord, so they will teach their children and their children's children tomorrow. If we fail to tell our children about the Lord, we may well be breaking the chain of God's influence in generations to come.

23:1 In describing the Lord as a shepherd, David wrote out of his own experience because he had spent his early years caring for sheep (1 Samuel 16:10, 11). Sheep are completely dependent on the shepherd for provision, guidance, and protection. The New Testament calls Jesus the Good Shepherd (John 10:11); the great Shepherd (Hebrews 13:20, 21); and the Head Shepherd (1 Peter 5:4). As the Lord is the Good Shepherd, so we are his sheep—not dumb, frightened, passive animals, but obedient followers wise enough to follow one who will lead us in the right places and in right ways. This psalm is not to focus on the animal-like qualities of sheep, but the discipleship qualities of those who follow. When you recognize the Good Shepherd, follow him!

23:2, 3 When we allow God our Shepherd to guide us, we have contentment. When we choose to sin, however, we are choosing to go our own way and we cannot blame God for the environment in which we find ourselves. Our Shepherd knows the "meadow grass" and "quiet streams" that will restore us. We will reach these places only by following him obediently. Rebelling against the Shepherd's leading is actually rebelling against our own best interests for the future. We must remember this the next time we are tempted to go our own way rather than the Shepherd's way.

23:4 Death casts the most frightening shadow of all over our lives because we are the most helpless in its presence. We can struggle with many other enemies—pain, suffering, disease, injury—but we cannot wrestle with death. It has the final word. Only one person can walk with us through death's dark valley and bring us through safely to the other side—the God of life, our Shepherd. With the time of our death uncertain, we should follow this Shepherd with an eternal confidence.

23:6 In Middle Eastern culture, hosts were expected to protect their guests at all cost. God offers the protection of a host even when we stand in the midst of enemies. In the final scene of this psalm, we see that believers will dwell with God. God, the perfect Shepherd and Host, promises to guide and protect us through life to bring us into his home forever.

24:1ff This psalm could have been written to celebrate the moving of the Ark of the Covenant from Obed-edom's house to Jerusalem (2 Samuel 6:10–12). Tradition says this psalm was sung on the first day of each week in the Temple services. Verses 1–6 tell who is worthy to join in such a celebration of worship.

24:1 The writer exclaims that "the earth belongs to God"; therefore, all of us are stewards, or caretakers. We are committed to the proper management of this world and its resources, but we are not to become devoted to these things because they will all pass away (1 John 2:17).

24:4 How greatly God values honesty! Dishonesty comes easily, especially when complete truthfulness could cost us something, make us uncomfortable, or put us in an unfavorable light. Without honest communication, relationships are hindered. Without honesty, a relationship with God is impossible. If we lie to others, we begin to deceive ourselves. God cannot hear us or speak to us if we are building a wall of self-deception.

24:8
Ex 15:3,6
Ps 76:3-6

24:9
Zech 9:9
Mt 21:5

24:10
Josh 5:14

from him, planted in their lives by God himself, their Savior. ⁶These are the ones who are allowed to stand before the Lord and worship the God of Jacob.

⁷Open up, O ancient gates, and let the King of Glory in. ⁸Who is this King of Glory? The Lord, strong and mighty, invincible in battle. ⁹Yes, open wide the gates and let the King of Glory in.

¹⁰Who is this King of Glory? The Commander of all of heaven's armies!

Theme: A prayer for defense, guidance, and pardon. As we trust in God, he grants these same requests for us.
Author: David

25:3
Ps 37:9; 40:1

25:4
Ps 5:8; 86:11

25:5
Ps 24:5; 40:1

25:6
Ps 51:1

25:8
Ps 86:5

25 To you, O Lord, I pray. ²Don't fail me, Lord, for I am trusting you. Don't let my enemies succeed. Don't give them victory over me. ³None of those who have faith in God will ever be disgraced for trusting him. But all who harm the innocent shall be defeated.

⁴Show me the path where I should go, O Lord; point out the right road for me to walk. ⁵Lead me; teach me; for you are the God who gives me salvation. I have no hope except in you. ⁶, ⁷Overlook my youthful sins, O Lord! Look at me instead through eyes of mercy and forgiveness, through eyes of everlasting love and kindness.

⁸The Lord is good and glad to teach the proper path to all who go astray; ⁹he will

---

PSALMS TO LEARN AND LOVE

Almost everybody, whether religious or not, has heard Psalm 23 because it is quoted so frequently. Many other psalms are also familiar because they are quoted in music, in literature, or in the words of the worship service.

The psalms we know and love are the ones that come into our minds when we need them. They inspire us, comfort us, correct us just when we need a word from the Lord. If you want to begin memorizing psalms, start with some of these favorites. Memorize the whole psalm or just the verses that speak most directly to you. Or read the psalm aloud several times a day until it is part of you.

Psalms to bring us into God's Presence	29; 95:1–7a; 96; 100
Psalms about goodness	1; 19; 24; 133; 136; 139
Psalms of praise	8; 97; 103; 107; 113; 145; 150
Psalms of repentance and forgiveness	32:1–5; 51; 103
Psalms for times of trouble	3; 14; 22; 37:1–11; 42; 46; 53; 116:1–7
Psalms of confidence and trust	23; 40:1–4; 91; 119:11; 121; 127

24:7–10 This psalm, often set to music, was probably used in corporate worship. It may have been re-enacted many times at the Temple. The people outside would call out to the Temple gates to open up and let the King of Glory in. From inside, the priests or another group would ask, "Who is this King of Glory?" Outside, the people responded in unison, "The Lord, invincible in battle," proclaiming his great power and might. This would have been an important lesson for children who may have been participating. The exchange was then repeated (24:9, 10) and the Temple gates swung open, symbolizing the people's desire to have God's presence among them.

24:7 Who is the King of Glory? The King of glory, identified also as the Commander of heaven's armies, is the Messiah himself, eternal, holy, and mighty (Revelation 19:11–21). This psalm is not only a battle cry for the church, it also looks forward to Christ's future entry into the new Jerusalem to reign forever.

25:2 Seventy-two psalms—almost half the book—speak about enemies. Enemies are those who not only oppose us, but also oppose God's way of living. Enemies can also be temptations—money, success, prestige, lust. And our greatest enemy is Satan. David asked God to keep his enemies from overcoming him because they opposed what God stood for. If his enemies succeeded, David feared that many would think that living for God was futile. David knew that God would triumph, but he didn't want his enemies' success to be an obstacle to the faith of others.

25:4 David expressed his desire for guidance. How do we receive God's guidance? The first step is to want to be guided and to realize that God's guidance is found mainly in his Word, the Bible. Psalm 119 tells of the endless knowledge found in God's Word. By reading it and constantly learning from it, we will gain the wisdom to perceive God's direction for our lives (Hebrews 5:14).

25:5–7 These verses suggest that David may have written this psalm toward the end of his life. Despite his youthful sins, he had a close relationship with God because he was forgiven. David realized, as we must, that God is unlimited, all-conquering, and has unrestrained authority over all of creation and over each individual. Therefore, he is the only source of salvation, hope, and true peace through the forgiveness of sins.

25:8–11 We are bombarded today with unlimited appeals to "go my way." TV advertising alone places hundreds of options before us, in addition to appeals made by political parties, cults, false religions, and dozens of other groups. Numerous organizations, including Christian organizations, seek to motivate us to "support the cause." Add to that the dozens of decisions we must make concerning our jobs, our families, our money, our society, and we become desperate for someone to show us the right way. If you find yourself pulled in several directions, remember that the Lord "will teach the ways that are right and best to those who humbly turn to him" (25:9).

teach the ways that are right and best to those who humbly turn to him. ¹⁰And when we obey him, every path he guides us on is fragrant with his lovingkindness and his truth.

¹¹But Lord, my sins! How many they are. Oh, pardon them for the honor of your name.

¹²Where is the man who fears the Lord? God will teach him how to choose the best.

¹³He shall live within God's circle of blessing, and his children shall inherit the earth.

¹⁴Friendship with God is reserved for those who reverence him. With them alone he shares the secrets of his promises.

¹⁵My eyes are ever looking to the Lord for help, for he alone can rescue me. ¹⁶Come, Lord, and show me your mercy, for I am helpless, overwhelmed, in deep distress; ¹⁷my problems go from bad to worse. Oh, save me from them all! ¹⁸See my sorrows; feel my pain; forgive my sins. ¹⁹See how many enemies I have and how viciously they hate me! ²⁰Save me from them! Deliver my life from their power! Oh, let it never be said that I trusted you in vain!

²¹Assign me Godliness and Integrity as my bodyguards, for I expect you to protect me ²²and to ransom Israel from all her troubles.

25:10	Ps 40:11; 103:17,18
25:11	Ps 79:9
25:12	Ps 31:19
25:13	Ps 37:11; 69:36; Prov 19:23
25:14	Prov 3:32
25:15	Ps 31:4; 123:2
25:16	Ps 69:16
25:17	Ps 40:12; 107:6
25:18	Ps 31:7; 103:3
25:19	Ps 3:1; 9:13
25:20	Ps 25:2; 86:2
25:21	Ps 25:3

Theme: Declaring loyalty to God. If we are genuinely committed to God, we can stand up to opposition and cross-examination.
Author: David, possibly written during the days of Absalom's rebellion

26 Dismiss all the charges against me, Lord, for I have tried to keep your laws and have trusted you without wavering. ²Cross-examine me, O Lord, and see that this is so; test my motives and affections too. ³For I have taken your lovingkindness and your truth as my ideals. ⁴I do not have fellowship with tricky, two-faced men; they are false and hypocritical. ⁵I hate the sinners' hangouts and refuse to enter them. ⁶I wash my hands to prove my innocence and come before your altar, ⁷singing a song of thanksgiving and telling about your miracles.

⁸Lord, I love your home, this shrine where the brilliant, dazzling splendor of your presence lives.

⁹, ¹⁰Don't treat me as a common sinner or murderer who plots against the innocent and demands bribes.

¹¹No, I am not like that, O Lord; I try to walk a straight and narrow path of doing what is right; therefore in mercy save me.

¹²I publicly praise the Lord for keeping me from slipping and falling.

26:1	Ps 7:8; 13:5
26:2	Ps 7:9; 139:23
26:3	Ps 1:2; 48:9
26:5	Ps 1:1; 31:6
26:6	Ps 43:3,4
26:7	Ps 9:1
26:8	Ps 27:4
26:11	Ps 26:1; 44:26
26:12	Ps 22:22; 40:2

25:12 To fear the Lord is to recognize him for who he is: holy, almighty, righteous, pure, all-knowing, all-powerful, and all-wise. Seeing God in this light, we see ourselves for who we are: sinful, weak, frail, and needy. When you recognize God for who he is and yourself for who you are, you will fall at his feet where he will teach you how to choose the best—his ways.

25:14 God offers intimate and lasting friendship to those who reverence him, who hold him in highest honor. What relationship could ever compare with having the Lord of all creation for a friend? Your everlasting friendship with God will grow as you reverence him.

25:16, 17 Life's problems always seem to go from bad to worse. God is the only one who can reverse this downward spiral. He can take our problems and turn them into glorious victories. There is one necessary requirement—we, the psalmist, must cry out, "Come, Lord, and show me your mercy." When you are willing to do that, the worst can become something wonderful. But the next step is yours, for God has already made his offer.

25:21 If ever we needed two powerful forces to see us along life's way, they are godliness and integrity. The psalmist asks for these to be his bodyguards, to protect him step by step. Godliness protects us from fighting life's battles alone and seeking entrance into God's eternal home on our own merit. It causes us to depend

upon God for his help. Integrity—trying to be what we say we are—keeps us from claiming to be godly while living as if we do not know him. Godliness says "this is the Shepherd's way," and integrity says, "I will walk consistently in it."

26:1–3 David was not claiming to be sinless—that is impossible for any human being. But he was consistently in fellowship with God, clearing his record when he sinned by asking for forgiveness. And he pleaded with God to clear his name of the false charges laid against him by his enemies. We also can ask God to cross-examine us so we stay in close fellowship with him, trusting him to forgive our sins according to his mercy.

26:5 Should we stay away from unbelievers? No. Although there are some places Christians should avoid, Jesus demonstrated that we must go among unbelievers to help them. But there is a difference between being *with* them and being *one of* them. Trying to be one of them harms our witness for God. Ask about the places you enjoy, "If I come here often, will I become less obedient to God in outlook or action?" If the answer is yes, carefully monitor how often you go there and what effect it has on you.

26:8 The "shrine" is either the Tabernacle in Gibeon (the same one constructed in the days of Moses), or the temporary dwelling David built to house the Ark of the Covenant (2 Samuel 6:17). David exclaimed how he loved to worship God at this place. The

Theme: God offers help for today and hope for the future. Unwavering confidence in God is our antidote for fear and loneliness.
Author: David

27:1
Ps 18:28
118:6,14

27:3
Ps 3:6,7

27:4
Ps 23:6; 26:8

27:5
Ps 17:8; 31:20

27:6
Ps 13:6; 107:22

27:7
Ps 13:3; 37:12

27:8
Ps 105:4

27:9
Ps 6:1; 40:17
69:17; 94:14

27:10
Isa 40:11; 49:15

27:11
Ps 5:8; 25:4
86:11

27:12
Ps 35:11
Jer 11:19

27:13
Ps 116:9; 142:5

27:14
Ps 31:24; 37:34

27 The Lord is my light and my salvation; he protects me from danger—whom shall I fear? ²When evil men come to destroy me, they will stumble and fall! ³Yes, though a mighty army marches against me, my heart shall know no fear! I am confident that God will save me.

⁴The one thing I want from God, the thing I seek most of all, is the privilege of meditating in his Temple, living in his presence every day of my life, delighting in his incomparable perfections and glory. ⁵There I'll be when troubles come. He will hide me. He will set me on a high rock ⁶out of reach of all my enemies. Then I will bring him sacrifices and sing his praises with much joy.

⁷Listen to my pleading, Lord! Be merciful and send the help I need.

⁸My heart has heard you say, "Come and talk with me, O my people." And my heart responds, "Lord, I am coming."

⁹Oh, do not hide yourself when I am trying to find you. Do not angrily reject your servant. You have been my help in all my trials before; don't leave me now. Don't forsake me, O God of my salvation. ¹⁰For if my father and mother should abandon me, you would welcome and comfort me.

¹¹Tell me what to do, O Lord, and make it plain because I am surrounded by waiting enemies. ¹²Don't let them get me, Lord! Don't let me fall into their hands! For they accuse me of things I never did, and all the while are plotting cruelty. ¹³I am expecting the Lord to rescue me again, so that once again I will see his goodness to me here in the land of the living.

¹⁴Don't be impatient. Wait for the Lord, and he will come and save you! Be brave, stouthearted and courageous. Yes, wait and he will help you.

Theme: Prayer when surrounded by trouble or wickedness. God is our only real source of safety. Prayer is our best help when trials come our way because it keeps us in communion with God.
Author: David

28:1
Ps 18:2; 35:22

28:2
Ps 141:2

28 I plead with you to help me, Lord, for you are my Rock of safety. If you refuse to answer me, I might as well give up and die. ²Lord, I lift my hands to heaven and implore your help. Oh, listen to my cry.

28:2 *to heaven,* literally, "Your innermost shrine," i.e., the Holy of Holies within the Tabernacle.

---

goal of all believers should be to worship God with the same love and reverence as David did.

26:12 This verse can also be translated, "My feet stand on level ground." David was not saying that God always prevents us from slipping or falling into sin (although often he does). Instead, David was saying that as long as he trusted in God, he could stand on the firm foundation of God's Word and have a godly perspective on life.

26:12 Too often we complain about our problems publicly and only praise God in private. How much better it would be to complain privately and praise God publicly.

27:1 Fear is a dark shadow that envelops us and ultimately imprisons us within ourselves. Each of us has been a prisoner of fear at one time or another—fear of rejection, misunderstanding, uncertainty, sickness, or even death. But fear can be conquered by the bright liberating light of the Lord who brings salvation. If you want to dispel the darkness of fear in your life, remember with the psalmist that "the Lord is my light and my salvation."

27:4 "His Temple" can also be translated "house of the Lord." David could be referring to the Tabernacle in Gibeon, the sanctuary he had put up to house the Ark of the Covenant, or to the Temple that his son Solomon was to build. David probably had the Temple in mind because he made many of the plans for it (1 Chronicles 22). But David may also have used the word Temple to mean "the presence of the Lord." His greatest desire was to live in God's presence each day of his life. Sadly, this is not the

greatest desire of many who claim to be believers. But those who can live daily in God's presence now will be able to do so forever.

27:5 We often run to God when we are experiencing difficulties. But David sought God's guiding presence *every day.* When troubles came his way, he was *already* in God's presence and prepared to handle any test. Believers can call to God for help at any time, but how shortsighted to call on God only after trouble has come. Many of our problems could be avoided or handled far more easily by relying on God's help and direction.

27:13 The "land of the living" simply means this life. David was obviously going through a trial, but he was confident that in this present life, God would see him through it.

27:14 David knew from experience what it meant to wait for the Lord. He had been anointed king at age 16, but didn't become king until he was 30. During the interim, he was chased through the wilderness by jealous King Saul. Later, after becoming king, he was chased by his rebellious son Absalom. David had to wait on God for the fulfillment of his promise to reign.

Waiting on God is not easy. Often it seems that he isn't answering our prayers or doesn't understand the urgency of our situation. That kind of thinking implies that God is not in control or is not fair. But God is worth waiting for. Isaiah 40:27–31 calls us to wait because often God uses waiting to refresh, renew, and teach us. Make good use of your waiting times by discovering what God may be trying to teach you in them.

3Don't punish me with all the wicked ones who speak so sweetly to their neighbors while planning to murder them. 4Give them the punishment they so richly deserve! Measure it out to them in proportion to their wickedness; pay them back for all their evil deeds. 5They care nothing for God or what he has done or what he has made; therefore God will dismantle them like old buildings, never to be rebuilt again.

6Oh, praise the Lord, for he has listened to my pleadings! 7He is my strength, my shield from every danger. I trusted in him, and he helped me. Joy rises in my heart until I burst out in songs of praise to him. 8The Lord protects his people and gives victory to his anointed king.

9Defend your people, Lord; defend and bless your chosen ones. Lead them like a shepherd and carry them forever in your arms.

28:3
Ps 26:9,10
55:21; 62:4
28:4
Ps 62:12
2 Tim 4:14
Rev 18:6
28:6
Ps 116:1
28:7
Ps 13:5,6
16:9; 40:3
59:17
28:9
Deut 9:29; 32:9
Ps 33:12; 80:1
Isa 40:11

Theme: God reveals his great power in nature. We can trust God to give us both the peace and the strength to weather the storms of life.
Author: David

29 Praise the Lord, you angels of his; praise his glory and his strength. 2Praise him for his majestic glory, the glory of his name. Come before him clothed in sacred garments.

3The voice of the Lord echoes from the clouds. The God of glory thunders through the skies. 4So powerful is his voice; so full of majesty. 5, 6It breaks down the cedars. It splits the giant trees of Lebanon. It shakes Mount Lebanon and Mount Sirion. They leap and skip before him like young calves! 7The voice of the Lord thunders through the lightning. 8It resounds through the deserts and shakes the wilderness of Kadesh. 9The voice of the Lord spins and topples the mighty oaks. It strips the forests bare. They whirl and sway beneath the blast. But in his temple all are praising, "Glory, glory to the Lord."

10At the Flood, the Lord showed his control of all creation. Now he continues to unveil his power. 11He will give his people strength. He will bless them with peace.

29:1
Ps 96:7-9
29:2
Ps 110:3
29:4
Ps 104:3
29:5
Ps 104:16
29:8
Num 13:26
29:9
Ps 26:8
29:10
Gen 6:17
29:11
Ps 37:11; 68:35

Theme: A celebration of God's deliverance. Earthly security is uncertain, but God is always faithful.
Author: David

30 I will praise you, Lord, for you have saved me from my enemies. You refuse to let them triumph over me. 2O Lord my God, I pleaded with you, and you gave me my health again. 3You brought me back from the brink of the grave, from death itself, and here I am alive!

4Oh, sing to him, you saints of his; give thanks to his holy name. 5His anger lasts a moment; his favor lasts for life! Weeping may go on all night, but in the morning there is joy.

30:1
Ps 25:2
35:19,24
118:28; 145:1
30:2
Ps 6:2; 88:13
30:4
Ps 97:12; 149:1

29:9 *spins and topples the mighty oaks,* or, "makes the hinds to calve."

28:3-5 It's easy to pretend friendship. Wicked people often masquerade in goodness, pretending kindness or friendship in order to gain their own ends. David, in his royal position, may have met many who pretended friendship only to meet their own goals. David knew that God would punish them accordingly, but he prayed that their punishment would come swiftly. True believers live honest lives before God and others.

28:7 In the sports world there is a phrase: "A good offense is the best defense." In the spiritual battle around us, God is our strength and shield. He is our defense against all that would harm us. If we trust in him, he will certainly defend us from the vicious attacks of our enemies.

29:5, 6 The cedars of Lebanon were indeed "giant trees." They could grow to 120 feet tall and 30 feet in circumference. A voice that could split the cedars of Lebanon would be a truly powerful voice—the voice of God.

29:10 The Flood mentioned here is the same Hebrew word for the great Flood that covered the earth in Noah's day. The story of the Flood is recorded in Genesis 6—9.

29:10, 11 Throughout history, God has revealed his power through mighty miracles over nature, such as the great Flood (Genesis 6—9). He promises to continue to reveal his power. Paul urged us to understand how great God's power is (Ephesians 1:18-23). The same power that raised Christ from the dead is available to all who believe. When you feel weak and limited, remember that God can give you strength. The power that controls creation and raises the dead is available to you.

30:1ff David may have written this psalm when he dedicated Araunah's threshing floor, and after God stopped the great plague he had used to discipline him (2 Samuel 24:18-25). The serious illness mentioned in 30:2, 3 may refer to an illness David experienced or to the plague itself.

30:5 Like a shot given by a doctor, the discomfort of God's anger is momentary, but the good effects go on for a long time. Let God's anger be a brief discomfort that helps you repent and turn from sin.

30:6
Ps 10:6; 104:29
143:7

30:9
Ps 6:5

30:10
Ps 4:1; 27:7,9

30:11
Ps 6:8
Jer 31:4,13

30:12
Ps 44:8; 57:8
108:1

31:1
Ps 25:2; 71:1-3
143:1

31:2
Ps 71:3; 86:1
102:2

31:3
Ps 18:2; 23:2,3

31:4
Ps 25:15

31:5
Lk 23:46
Acts 7:59

31:9
Ps 6:7; 32:3
38:3,4; 39:11
63:1; 69:17
102:1,3,4

31:11
Ps 38:11
88:8,18
Isa 53:4

31:12
Ps 88:5

31:13
Ps 41:7
Jer 20:10
Mt 27:1

31:14
Ps 140:6; 143:9

6, 7In my prosperity I said, "This is forever; nothing can stop me now! The Lord has shown me his favor. He has made me steady as a mountain." Then, Lord, you turned your face away from me and cut off your river of blessings. Suddenly my courage was gone; I was terrified and panic-stricken. 8I cried to you, O Lord; oh, how I pled: 9"What will you gain, O Lord, from killing me? How can I praise you then to all my friends? How can my dust in the grave speak out and tell the world about your faithfulness? 10Hear me, Lord; oh, have pity and help me." 11Then he turned my sorrow into joy! He took away my clothes of mourning and clothed me with joy 12so that I might sing glad praises to the Lord instead of lying in silence in the grave. O Lord my God, I will keep on thanking you forever!

Theme: In times of stress, depending upon God requires complete commitment.
Author: David, although some say Jeremiah

31 Lord, I trust in you alone. Don't let my enemies defeat me. Rescue me because you are the God who always does what is right. 2Answer quickly when I cry to you; bend low and hear my whispered plea. Be for me a great Rock of safety from my foes. 3Yes, you are my Rock and my fortress; honor your name by leading me out of this peril. 4Pull me from the trap my enemies have set for me. For you alone are strong enough. 5, 6Into your hand I commit my spirit.

You have rescued me, O God who keeps his promises. I worship only you; how you hate all those who worship idols, those imitation gods. 7I am radiant with joy because of your mercy, for you have listened to my troubles and have seen the crisis in my soul. 8You have not handed me over to my enemy, but have given me open ground in which to maneuver.

9, 10O Lord, have mercy on me in my anguish. My eyes are red from weeping; my health is broken from sorrow. I am pining away with grief; my years are shortened, drained away because of sadness. My sins have sapped my strength; I stoop with sorrow and with shame. 11I am scorned by all my enemies and even more by my neighbors and friends. They dread meeting me and look the other way when I go by. 12I am forgotten like a dead man, like a broken and discarded pot. 13I heard the lies about me, the slanders of my enemies. Everywhere I looked I was afraid, for they were plotting against my life.

14, 15But I am trusting you, O Lord. I said, "You alone are my God; my times are in your hands. Rescue me from those who hunt me down relentlessly. 16Let your

30:6, 7 *cut off your river of blessings,* implied. **31:2** *hear my whispered plea,* implied. **31:4** *For you alone are strong enough,* literally, "For you are my refuge." **31:9, 10** *My sins have sapped my strength; I stoop with sorrow and shame,* literally, "Even my bones are rotting away."

30:6, 7 Prosperity had made David feel invincible. Although he knew his riches and power had come from God, they had gone to his head, making him proud. Wealth, power, and fame have an intoxicating effect on people, making them feel self-reliant, self-secure, and independent of God. But this is a false security that is easily shattered. Don't be trapped by the false security of prosperity. Depend on God for your security and you won't be shaken when worldly possessions disappear.

31:1, 3 David called upon God to rescue him. He wanted God to stop those who were unjustly causing trouble. Therefore, David made his request based upon what he knew of God's character—that God was just and loving.

31:1-6 We say we have faith in God, but do we really trust him? David's words, "Into your hand I commit my spirit," convey his complete trust in God. Jesus used this phrase as he was dying on the cross—showing his absolute dependence on God the Father (Luke 23:46). Stephen repeated these words as he was being stoned to death (Acts 7:59), confident that in death, he was simply passing from God's earthly care to God's eternal care. We should commit our possessions, our families, and our vocations to God. But first and foremost, we should commit ourselves completely to God.

31:5, 6 Why did David suddenly bring up the subject of idol worship? He wanted to contrast his total devotion to God with the diluted worship offered by many Israelites. Heathen religious rituals were never completely banished from Israel and Judah, despite the efforts of David and a few other kings. Obviously a person who bowed to idols could not put his spirit in God's hands. When we put today's idols (wealth, material possessions, success) first in our lives, we cannot expect God's Spirit to guide us.

31:8 In David's day, armies needed wide open spaces in which to conduct their military maneuvers. David praised God for the open spaces which gave his troops and chariots the freedom to move within God's protective boundaries. If you feel restrained by God's protective boundaries, remember that God has given us much freedom, far more than we need to move within those boundaries. He also gives you freedom to move beyond his boundaries, but outside them you are on your own. That freedom comes with a very high price.

31:9-13 David described the helplessness and hopelessness we feel when we are hated or rejected. But adversity is easier to accept when we recognize our true relationship with the sovereign God (31:14-18). Although our enemies may seem to have the upper hand, they are ultimately the helpless and hopeless ones (31:23). Those who know God will be victorious in the end (31:22).

31:14, 15 In saying, "my times are in your hands," David was simply expressing his belief that all of life's circumstances are under God's control.

favor shine again upon your servant; save me just because you are so kind! 17Don't disgrace me, Lord, by not replying when I call to you for aid. But let the wicked be shamed by what they trust in; let them lie silently in their graves, 18their lying lips quieted at last—the lips of these arrogant men who are accusing honest men of evil deeds."

19Oh, how great is your goodness to those who publicly declare that you will rescue them. For you have stored up great blessings for those who trust and reverence you.

20Hide your loved ones in the shelter of your presence, safe beneath your hand, safe from all conspiring men. 21Blessed is the Lord, for he has shown me that his never-failing love protects me like the walls of a fort! 22I spoke too hastily when I said, "The Lord has deserted me," for you listened to my plea and answered me.

23Oh, love the Lord, all of you who are his people; for the Lord protects those who are loyal to him, but harshly punishes all who haughtily reject him. 24So cheer up! Take courage if you are depending on the Lord.

Theme: Forgiveness brings true happiness. Only when we ask God to forgive our sins will he give us real happiness and relief from guilt.
Author: David

32 What happiness for those whose guilt has been forgiven! What joys when sins are covered over! What relief for those who have confessed their sins and God has cleared their record.

3There was a time when I wouldn't admit what a sinner I was. But my dishonesty made me miserable and filled my days with frustration. 4All day and all night your hand was heavy on me. My strength evaporated like water on a sunny day 5until I finally admitted all my sins to you and stopped trying to hide them. I said to myself, "I will confess them to the Lord." And you forgave me! All my guilt is gone.

6Now I say that each believer should confess his sins to God when he is aware of them, while there is time to be forgiven. Judgment will not touch him if he does. 7You are my hiding place from every storm of life; you even keep me from getting into trouble! You surround me with songs of victory. 8I will instruct you (says the Lord) and guide you along the best pathway for your life; I will advise you and watch your progress. 9Don't be like a senseless horse or mule that has to have a bit in its mouth to keep it in line!

10Many sorrows come to the wicked, but abiding love surrounds those who trust in the Lord. 11So rejoice in him, all those who are his, and shout for joy, all those who try to obey him.

32:3 *when I wouldn't admit what a sinner I was,* literally, "when I kept silence." 32:6 *Judgment will not touch him,* literally, "When the great waters overflow they shall not reach him." 32:11 *all those who are his,* literally, "you righteous." *all those who try to obey him,* literally, "all who are upright in heart."

31:17
1 Sam 2:9
Ps 25:2,3,20
31:18
1 Sam 2:3
Ps 94:4; 120:2

31:20
Ps 27:5; 31:13
31:21
Ps 17:7; 28:7
31:22
Ps 66:19
116:11,12
145:19
Lam 3:54-56
31:23
Deut 32:40,41
Ps 37:28
31:24
Ps 27:14

32:1
Ps 85:2
Rom 4:7,8
32:3
Ps 31:10; 39:2
32:4
Ps 22:15; 39:10
32:5
Lev 26:40
Job 31:33
Ps 38:18
1 Jn 1:9
32:6
Ps 69:13
Isa 43:2
32:7
Ex 15:1
Ps 31:20; 40:3
121:7
32:8
Ps 25:8
33:18,19
32:10
Ps 16:4

32:1ff This psalm is a sequel to Psalm 51. Here David expresses the joy of forgiveness. God had forgiven him for the sins he had committed against Bath-sheba and Uriah (2 Samuel 11,12). This is another of the penitential (repentance) psalms where the writer confesses his sin to God.

32:1, 2 God *wants* to forgive sinners. Forgiveness has always been part of his loving nature. He announced this to Moses (Exodus 34:7); he revealed it to David; and he dramatically showed it to the world through Jesus Christ. These verses speak of several actions which express God's forgiveness: removing guilt, covering sin, clearing the sinner's record, and pointing the sinner in the right direction. Paul quoted these verses in Romans 4:7, 8 and showed that this joyous experience of forgiveness comes through faith in Christ.

32:5 Confession is much more than saying you're sorry for your

sins. It involves a commitment to follow God and a sincere desire to seek God's guidance in your life.

32:6 When you have hurt someone, it is freeing to receive his forgiveness. When God forgives us, he clears the record of our wrongs and takes away our guilt. Experiencing God's forgiveness, however, is contingent upon our confession. When we confess our sins, we must also make a commitment to change our behavior. A person planning to return to that sin is not sincere in his confession.

32:8, 9 God describes some people as being "stubborn as mules." Rather than letting God guide them step by step, God must use discipline and punishment (like a bit in a mule's mouth) to keep them useful for him. God longs to guide us with love rather than punishment. He offers to guide us along the *best* pathway for our lives. Accept the advice written in God's Word so you won't need to be forced into usefulness.

Theme: Because God is Creator, Lord, Savior, and Deliverer, he is worthy of our trust and praise. Because he is faithful and his Word is dependable, we can rejoice and sing, giving thanks and praise.
Author: Anonymous

33:1
Ps 32:11; 147:1
33:2
Ps 92:3
33:3
Ps 98:1
Rev 5:9
33:4
Ps 19:8
33:5
Ps 11:7; 119:64
33:6
Gen 1:6,7
Ps 148:5
Heb 11:3
33:7
Ex 15:8
33:8
Ps 67:7; 96:9
33:9
Gen 1:3
Ps 148:5
33:10
Gen 11:8
Isa 8:9,10
33:12
Ex 19:5
Ps 144:15
33:16
Ps 44:6; 147:10
33:18
Ps 34:15; 37:19

33 Let all the joys of the godly well up in praise to the Lord, for it is right to praise him. 2Play joyous melodies of praise upon the lyre and on the harp. 3Compose new songs of praise to him, accompanied skillfully on the harp; sing joyfully.

4For all God's words are right, and everything he does is worthy of our trust. 5He loves whatever is just and good; the earth is filled with his tender love. 6He merely spoke, and the heavens were formed, and all the galaxies of stars. 7He made the oceans, pouring them into his vast reservoirs.

8Let everyone in all the world—men, women and children—fear the Lord and stand in awe of him. 9For when he but spoke, the world began! It appeared at his command! 10And with a breath he can scatter the plans of all the nations who oppose him, 11but his own plan stands forever. His intentions are the same for every generation.

12Blessed is the nation whose God is the Lord, whose people he has chosen as his own. 13, 14, 15The Lord gazes down upon mankind from heaven where he lives. He has made their hearts and closely watches everything they do.

16, 17The best-equipped army cannot save a king—for great strength is not enough to save anyone. A war horse is a poor risk for winning victories—it is strong but it cannot save.

18, 19But the eyes of the Lord are watching over those who fear him, who rely upon his steady love. He will keep them from death even in times of famine! 20We depend upon the Lord alone to save us. Only he can help us; he protects us like a shield. 21No wonder we are happy in the Lord! For we are trusting him. We trust his

---

CONFESSION, REPENTANCE, AND FORGIVENESS IN PSALMS

Over the centuries, many believers, overcome by an awareness of their own sins, have found in the words of the penitential (confession) psalms a ray of hope. The psalmists shared with God both the depth of their sorrow and repentance, as well as the height of joy at being forgiven. They rejoiced in the knowledge that God would respond to confession and repentance with complete forgiveness. We, who live on the other side of the cross of Christ, can rejoice even more because we understand more. God has shown us that he is willing to forgive because his judgment on sin was satisfied by Christ's death on the cross.

As you read these psalms, note the pattern followed by the psalmists in responding to God: (1) they recognized their sinfulness and tendency to do wrong; (2) they realized that sin was rebellion against God himself; (3) they admitted their sins to God; (4) they trusted in God's willingness to forgive; and (5) they accepted his forgiveness. Use these psalms as a reminder of how easy it is to drift away from God and fall into sin, and what is needed to reestablish that fellowship.

Selected psalms that emphasize these themes are 6, 14, 31, 32, 38, 41, 51, 102, 130, 143.

33:2, 3 Because David was an accomplished harpist (1 Samuel 16:15–23), he frequently spoke about musical instruments throughout his psalms. He undoubtedly composed music for many of the psalms, and he commissioned music for Temple worship (1 Chronicles 25).

33:4 A person's words are measured by the quality of his or her character. If your friends trust what you say, it is because they trust you. If you trust what God says, it is because you trust him to be the God he claims to be. If you doubt his words, you doubt the integrity of God himself. If you believe God is truly God, then believe what he says!

33:4 All God's words are true and trustworthy. The Bible is reliable because, unlike people, God does not lie, forget, change his words, or leave his promises unfulfilled. We can trust the Bible because it contains the words of a holy, trustworthy, and unchangeable God.

33:6–9 God is not just the coordinator of natural forces, he

is the Lord of creation, the almighty God.

33:11 God's plan stands forever! Are you frustrated by inconsistencies you see in others, or even in yourself? God is completely trustworthy—his intentions never change. There is a promise that good and perfect gifts come to us from the Creator who never changes (James 1:17). When you wonder if there is anyone in whom you can trust, remember that God is completely consistent.

33:18, 19 This is not a promise that all believers will escape starvation or violent death. Thousands of Christian saints have been beaten to death, whipped, fed to lions, or executed (Romans 8:35, 36; Hebrews 11:32–40). God can (and often miraculously does) deliver his followers from pain and death, though sometimes (for purposes known only to him) he chooses not to. In the midst of these harsh realities, we must focus on the wise judgments of God. David was pleading for God's watchful care and protection. In times of crisis, we can do the same.

holy name. ²²Yes, Lord, let your constant love surround us, for our hopes are in you alone.

Theme: God pays attention to those who call on him. Whether God offers escape from trouble or help in times of trouble, we can be certain that he always hears and acts on behalf of those who love him.

Author: David, after pretending to be insane in order to escape from King Achish (1 Samuel 21:10–15)

34 I will praise the Lord no matter what happens. I will constantly speak of his glories and grace. ²I will boast of all his kindness to me. Let all who are discouraged take heart. ³Let us praise the Lord together, and exalt his name.

⁴For I cried to him and he answered me! He freed me from all my fears. ⁵Others too were radiant at what he did for them. Theirs was no downcast look of rejection! ⁶This poor man cried to the Lord—and the Lord heard him and saved him out of his troubles. ⁷For the Angel of the Lord guards and rescues all who reverence him.

⁸Oh, put God to the test and see how kind he is! See for yourself the way his mercies shower down on all who trust in him. ⁹If you belong to the Lord, reverence him; for everyone who does this has everything he needs. ¹⁰Even strong young lions sometimes go hungry, but those of us who reverence the Lord will never lack any good thing.

¹¹Sons and daughters, come and listen and let me teach you the importance of trusting and fearing the Lord. ¹²Do you want a long, good life? ¹³Then watch your tongue! Keep your lips from lying. ¹⁴Turn from all known sin and spend your time in doing good. Try to live in peace with everyone; work hard at it.

¹⁵For the eyes of the Lord are intently watching all who live good lives, and he gives attention when they cry to him. ¹⁶But the Lord has made up his mind to wipe out even the memory of evil men from the earth. ¹⁷Yes, the Lord hears the good man when he calls to him for help, and saves him out of all his troubles.

¹⁸The Lord is close to those whose hearts are breaking; he rescues those who are

34:1
Ps 71:6
34:2
Jer 9:24
34:3
Lk 1:46
34:4
Mt 7:7
34:7
Ps 91:14
34:8
Ps 23:1
1 Pet 2:3
34:9
Ps 23:1; 31:23
34:10
Ps 84:11
34:12
1 Pet 3:10-12
34:13
Jas 1:26
34:14
Rom 14:18,19
Heb 12:14
34:16
Ps 9:6; 109:15
34:18
Isa 57:15

34:1 *I will constantly speak of his glories and grace,* literally, "His praise shall continually be in my mouth."

34:1ff God promises great blessings to his people, but many of these blessings are conditional. He will free us from fear (34:4), deliver us from trouble (34:6), guard us (34:7), show us kindness (34:8), supply our needs (34:9), listen when we talk to him (34:15), help us through our troubles (34:19), and redeem us (34:22), *IF we* cry out to him (34:4, 6, 17), reverence him (34:7, 10), trust him (34:8), fear him (34:11), watch our tongues and keep from lying (34:13), turn from sin, do good, and seek peace (34:14), have humble hearts (34:18), and serve him (34:22).

34:8 "Put God to the test" can also be translated, "Taste and see that the Lord is good." This does not mean, "Check out God's credentials," instead it is a warm invitation, "Try this; I know you'll like it." When we take that first step of obedience in following God, we cannot help but discover that he is good and kind. We begin the Christian life with a misunderstanding of God and right living. It is only by experience that we see how good he actually is.

34:9 You believe you belong to the Lord, but do you know how to reverence him? To show reverence means to show deep respect and honor to another. True reverence is not faking respect; it is accompanied by a humble attitude and genuine worship. True reverence was shown by Abraham (Genesis 17:2–4); Moses (Exodus 3:5, 6); and the Israelites (Exodus 19:16–24). Their reactions to God's presence varied, but all demonstrated reverence for him.

34:9, 10 "Those of us who reverence the Lord will never lack any good thing." At first, we may question the truth of this statement because we lack many "good" things. This is not a blanket promise that all Christians will be rich. Instead, this is David's observation of God's goodness—all those who call upon God in their need will be answered, sometimes in unexpected ways.

Remember, our deepest needs are spiritual. While many Christians have more than enough spiritual nourishment to live a

life for God, many others face unbearable poverty and hardship. David was saying that to have God is to have all that one needs. God is enough.

If you feel you don't have everything you need, ask: (1) Is this really a need? (2) Is this really good for me? (3) Is this the best time for me to have what I desire? Even if you answer yes to all three questions, God may allow you to go without to help you grow more dependent on him. We may need to learn that we need *him* more than those things.

34:10–14 The Bible often connects reverence (trusting and fearing God) with obedience. "Fear God and obey his commandments" (Ecclesiastes 12:13); "Anyone who doesn't obey me doesn't love me" (John 14:24). David defined reverence as: don't lie, turn from sin, do good, promote peace. Reverence is much more than sitting quietly in church. It includes the way we live in obedience to God.

34:11–14 David encouraged others to trust and fear God, and to exemplify faith, truth, obedience, and goodness in their lives. He feared God and for the most part he chose the way of goodness and peace. David even treated some of his worst enemies with kindness (see 1 Samuel 24:1–8; 26:5–23). Peter quoted these verses as a strategy for living in a non-Christian environment (1 Peter 3:10–12).

34:14 Somehow we think that peace should come to us with no effort. But David explained that we are to work hard at living in peace with everyone. Paul echoed this thought in Romans 12:18. A person who wants peace cannot be argumentative and contentious. Since peaceful relationships come from our efforts at peacemaking, work hard at living in peace with others each day.

34:18, 19 We often wish that we could escape troubles—the pain of grief, loss, sorrow, failure, or even the small daily frustrations that constantly wear us down. God promises to be our source of power,

34:19
Ps 71:20
2 Tim 3:11,12

34:21
Ps 94:23

34:22
1 Kgs 1:29
Ps 71:23

35:1
Ps 56:1,2
Isa 49:25

35:4
Ps 40:14
70:2,3

35:5
Ps 1:4; 83:13
Isa 29:5

35:6
Ps 73:18
Jer 23:12

35:7
Ps 69:4; 109:3

35:8
Ps 9:15
Isa 47:11
1 Thess 5:3

35:9
Isa 61:10
Lk 1:47

35:10
Ex 15:11,12
Ps 18:17; 37:14

35:11
Ps 27:12

35:12
Ps 38:20
Jn 10:32

35:13
Job 30:25
Jer 18:20

35:17
Ps 13:1
22:20,21

35:18
Ps 22:23,25

35:19
Ps 13:4
38:16,19; 69:4

35:21
Ps 22:13; 40:15

humbly sorry for their sins. 19The good man does not escape all troubles—he has them too. But the Lord helps him in each and every one. 20Not one of his bones is broken.

21Calamity will surely overtake the wicked; heavy penalties are meted out to those who hate the good. 22But as for those who serve the Lord, he will redeem them; everyone who takes refuge in him will be freely pardoned.

Theme: A prayer to God for help against those who try to inflict injury for no reason. When our enemies are unjust and lie about us, even when we do good to them, we can appeal to God who is always just.
Author: David, probably written when he was being hunted by Saul (1 Samuel 24)

35 O Lord, fight those fighting me; declare war on them for their attacks on me. 2Put on your armor, take your shield and protect me by standing in front. 3Lift your spear in my defense, for my pursuers are getting very close. Let me hear you say that you will save me from them. 4Dishonor those who are trying to kill me. Turn them back and confuse them. 5Blow them away like chaff in the wind—wind sent by the Angel of the Lord. 6Make their path dark and slippery before them, with the Angel of the Lord pursuing them. 7For though I did them no wrong, yet they laid a trap for me and dug a pitfall in my path. 8Let them be overtaken by sudden ruin, caught in their own net, and destroyed.

9But I will rejoice in the Lord. He shall rescue me! 10From the bottom of my heart praise rises to him. Where is his equal in all of heaven and earth? Who else protects the weak and helpless from the strong, and the poor and needy from those who would rob them?

11These evil men swear to a lie. They accuse me of things I have never even heard about. 12I do them good, but they return me harm. I am sinking down to death. 13When they were ill, I mourned before the Lord in sackcloth, asking him to make them well; I refused to eat; I prayed for them with utmost earnestness, but God did not listen. 14I went about sadly as though it were my mother, friend or brother who was sick and nearing death. 15But now that I am in trouble they are glad; they come together in meetings filled with slander against me—I didn't even know some of those who were there. 16For they gather with the worthless fellows of the town and spend their time cursing me.

17Lord, how long will you stand there, doing nothing? Act now and rescue me, for I have but one life and these young lions are out to get it. 18Save me, and I will thank you publicly before the entire congregation, before the largest crowd I can find.

19Don't give victory to those who fight me without any reason! Don't let them rejoice at my fall—let them die. 20They don't talk of peace and doing good, but of plots against innocent men who are minding their own business. 21They shout that they have seen *me* doing wrong! "Aha!" they say. "With our own eyes we saw him do it." 22Lord, you know all about it. Don't stay silent! Don't desert me now!

35:19 *Don't let them rejoice,* literally, "wink with the eye."

---

courage, and wisdom to help us through our problems. Sometimes he chooses to deliver us from those problems. When trouble strikes, don't get frustrated with God. Instead, thank him for being by your side.

34:20 This is a prophecy about Christ when he was crucified on the cross. Although it was the Roman custom to break the legs of the victim to speed his death, not one of Jesus' bones was broken (John 19:32–37). Aside from the prophetic meaning, David was making a plea for God's protection in the midst of crisis.

35:1ff This is one of the "imprecatory" (justice) psalms that calls upon God to deal with enemies. These psalms sound extremely harsh, but there are several things to keep in mind when reading them. (1) David was fleeing from men who were unjustly seeking to kill him. As God's anointed king over a nation which had been called to annihilate the evil people of the land, this was difficult for David to understand. (2) David's call for justice was sincere; it was

not a cover for vengeance. He truly wanted to seek God's perfect ideal for a nation. (3) David did not say *he* would take vengeance, but gave the matter to God. These are merely his "suggestions." (4) These psalms use hyperbole. They were meant to motivate others to take a strong stand against sin and evil.

Cruelty is far removed from many people's experience, but is a daily reality to others. God promises to help the persecuted and bring judgment on unrepentant sinners. When we pray for justice to be done, we are praying as David did. When Christ returns, the wicked will be punished.

35:21–23 David cried out to God to defend him when he was unjustly accused. If you are unjustly accused, your natural reaction may be to lash out in revenge or to give a detailed defense of your every move. Ask God to fight the battle for you. He will clear your name in the eyes of those who really matter.

23Rise up, O Lord my God; vindicate me. 24Declare me "not guilty," for you are just. Don't let my enemies rejoice over me in my troubles. 25Don't let them say, "Aha! Our dearest wish against him will soon be fulfilled!" and, "At last we have him!" 26Shame them; let these who boast against me and who rejoice at my troubles be themselves overcome by misfortune that strips them bare of everything they own. Bare them to dishonor. 27But give great joy to all who wish me well. Let them shout with delight, "Great is the Lord who enjoys helping his child!" 28And I will tell everyone how great and good you are; I will praise you all day long.

35:24
Ps 9:4; 43:1
35:25
Ps 56:1
35:26
Ps 38:16; 40:14
35:27
Ps 40:16; 70:4
35:28
Ps 51:14,15

Theme: God's faithfulness, justice, and love are contrasted with the sinful hearts of men and women. In spite of our fallen condition, God pours out his love on those who know him.
Author: David

36 Sin lurks deep in the hearts of the wicked, forever urging them on to evil deeds. They have no fear of God to hold them back. 2Instead, in their conceit, they think they can hide their evil deeds and not get caught. 3Everything they say is crooked and deceitful; they are no longer wise and good. 4They lie awake at night to hatch their evil plots, instead of planning how to keep away from wrong.

5Your steadfast love, O Lord, is as great as all the heavens. Your faithfulness reaches beyond the clouds. 6Your justice is as solid as God's mountains. Your decisions are as full of wisdom as the oceans are with water. You are concerned for men and animals alike. 7How precious is your constant love, O God! All humanity takes refuge in the shadow of your wings. 8You feed them with blessings from your own table and let them drink from your rivers of delight.

9For you are the Fountain of life; our light is from your Light. 10Pour out your unfailing love on those who know you! Never stop giving your blessings to those who long to do your will.

11Don't let these proud men trample me. Don't let their wicked hands push me around. 12Look! They have fallen. They are thrown down and will not rise again.

36:1
Rom 3:18
36:3
Ps 10:7
36:5
Ps 57:10
103:11; 108:4
36:6
Job 11:8
Ps 104:14,15
145:16,17
Rom 11:33
36:7
Ruth 2:12
Ps 91:4
139:17,18
36:8
Ps 46:4
Isa 25:6
Rev 22:1
36:9
1 Pet 2:9
36:12
Ps 140:10

Theme: Trust in the Lord and wait patiently for him to act. This psalm vividly contrasts the wicked person with the upright.
Author: David

37 Never envy the wicked! 2Soon they fade away like grass and disappear. 3Trust in the Lord instead. Be kind and good to others; then you will live safely here in the land and prosper, feeding in safety.

4Be delighted with the Lord. Then he will give you all your heart's desires. 5Commit everything you do to the Lord. Trust him to help you do it and he will.

37:3
Deut 30:20
37:4
Ps 145:19
37:5
Ps 55:22

35:24 *Declare me "not guilty," for you are just,* literally, "Judge me according to your righteousness." **35:27** *child,* literally, "servant." **36:6** *You are concerned,* literally, "You preserve." **36:10** *your blessings,* literally, "your righteousness."

36:1 Because the wicked have no fear of God, nothing restrains them from sinning. They plunge ahead as if nothing will happen to them. But God is just and is only delaying their punishment. This knowledge should restrain us from sinning. Let the fear of God do its work in you to keep you from sin. As you discover that God is loving, don't ignore his justice.

36:5–8 In contrast to evil men and their wicked plots that end in failure, God is loving, faithful, just, and wise. His love is greater than the heavens; his faithfulness reaches past the clouds; his justice is as solid as a mountain; and his decisions as full of wisdom as the oceans with water. We need not fear evil people because we know God loves us, judges evil, and will care for us throughout eternity.

36:9 This metaphor for God—"Fountain of Life"—gives us a sense of fresh, cleansing water that does indeed give life to the spiritually thirsty. This same picture is used in Jeremiah 2:13, where God is called the "Fountain of Life-giving Water." Jesus spoke of himself as living water that could quench "thirst" forever and give eternal life (John 4:14).

37:1 We should never envy the wicked, even though some may be extremely popular or excessively rich. No matter how much they have, it will fade and vanish like grass that withers and dies. Those who follow God live in a different manner than the wicked, and in the end, have far greater treasures in heaven. What the unbeliever gets lasts a lifetime, if he is lucky. What you get from following God lasts forever.

37:4, 5 David calls us to take delight in the Lord and to commit everything we have and do to him. But how do we do this? To delight in someone means to experience great pleasure and joy in his or her presence. This happens only when we know that person well. To *commit* ourselves to the Lord means entrusting everything—our lives, families, jobs, possessions—to his control and guidance. Thus, to *delight* in the Lord we must know him. Knowledge of his great love for us will indeed give us delight. To commit ourselves to the Lord means to trust him (37:5), believing that he can care for us better than we can ourselves. We should be willing to wait (37:7) for him to work out what is best for us.

37:6
Isa 58:8,10
Mic 7:9

37:7
Ps 40:1; 62:5
Jer 12:1

37:8
Eph 4:31
Col 3:8

37:9
Ps 25:13

37:10
Job 24:24

37:11
Mt 5:3,5

37:12
Job 18:20
Ps 2:4; 31:13

37:14
Ps 11:2; 35:10

37:15
Ps 9:16; 46:9

37:16
Prov 15:16; 16:8

37:17
Ps 10:15

37:19
Job 5:20
Ps 33:18,19

37:20
Ps 68:2; 73:27

37:22
Prov 3:33

37:23
Ps 40:2; 147:11

37:24
Ps 145:14

37:25
Isa 41:17
Heb 13:5

37:26
Ps 147:13

37:27
Ps 34:14

37:28
Ps 11:7; 30:23

37:32
Ps 10:8; 37:14

37:33
Ps 37:22

37:34
Ps 27:14; 37:9

⁶Your innocence will be clear to everyone. He will vindicate you with the blazing light of justice shining down as from the noonday sun.

⁷Rest in the Lord; wait patiently for him to act. Don't be envious of evil men who prosper.

⁸Stop your anger! Turn off your wrath. Don't fret and worry—it only leads to harm. ⁹For the wicked shall be destroyed, but those who trust the Lord shall be given every blessing. ¹⁰Only a little while and the wicked shall disappear. You will look for them in vain. ¹¹But all who humble themselves before the Lord shall be given every blessing, and shall have wonderful peace.

¹², ¹³The Lord is laughing at those who plot against the godly, for he knows their judgment day is coming. ¹⁴Evil men take aim to slay the poor; they are ready to butcher those who do right. ¹⁵But their swords will be plunged into their own hearts and all their weapons will be broken.

¹⁶It is better to have little and be godly than to own an evil man's wealth; ¹⁷for the strength of evil men shall be broken, but the Lord takes care of those he has forgiven.

¹⁸Day by day the Lord observes the good deeds done by godly men, and gives them eternal rewards. ¹⁹He cares for them when times are hard; even in famine, they will have enough. ²⁰But evil men shall perish. These enemies of God will wither like grass, and disappear like smoke. ²¹Evil men borrow and "cannot pay it back"! But the good man returns what he owes with some extra besides. ²²Those blessed by the Lord shall inherit the earth, but those cursed by him shall die.

²³The steps of good men are directed by the Lord. He delights in each step they take. ²⁴If they fall it isn't fatal, for the Lord holds them with his hand.

²⁵I have been young and now I am old. And in all my years I have never seen the Lord forsake a man who loves him; nor have I seen the children of the godly go hungry. ²⁶Instead, the godly are able to be generous with their gifts and loans to others, and their children are a blessing.

²⁷So if you want an eternal home, leave your evil, low-down ways and live good lives. ²⁸For the Lord loves justice and fairness; he will never abandon his people. They will be kept safe forever; but all who love wickedness shall perish.

²⁹The godly shall be firmly planted in the land, and live there forever. ³⁰, ³¹The godly man is a good counselor because he is just and fair and knows right from wrong.

³²Evil men spy on the godly, waiting for an excuse to accuse them and then demanding their death. ³³But the Lord will not let these evil men succeed, nor let the godly be condemned when they are brought before the judge.

³⁴Don't be impatient for the Lord to act! Keep traveling steadily along his

37:17 *those he has forgiven,* literally, "the righteous." **37:18** *Day by day the Lord observes the good deeds done by godly men,* literally, "knows the days of the upright."

37:8, 9 Anger and worry are two of the most destructive emotions. They reveal a lack of faith that God is in control. We should not fret and worry; instead, we should trust in the Lord. When you dwell on your problems, you will become anxious and angry. But if you concentrate on God and his goodness, you will find peace. Where do you focus your attention?

37:11, 34, 37 It is difficult to wait patiently for God to act when we want change right away. But God promises that if we submit to his timing, he will honor us. Peter said "If you will humble yourselves under the mighty hand of God, in his good time he will lift you up" (1 Peter 5:6). Be patient, steadily doing the work God has given you to do, and allow God to choose the best time to change your circumstances.

37:21 You can tell a lot about a person's character by the way he handles money. The wicked person steals under the guise of "borrowing." The good person pays back with extra. The wicked person, therefore, focuses on himself while the good person focuses on others.

37:23, 24 A good person is one who follows God, trusts him, and tries to do his will. God watches over and directs every step that person takes. If you would like to have God direct your way, then follow and trust him.

37:25 Since children starve today, as they did in David's time, what did he mean? The children of the godly do not go hungry because other believers help out in their time of need. In David's day, Israel obeyed God's laws which dealt with treating the poor fairly and mercifully. As long as Israel was obedient, there was enough food for everyone. When Israel forgot God, the rich took care only of themselves and the poor suffered (Amos 2:6, 7).

When we see a Christian brother or sister suffering today, we can respond in one of three ways. (1) We can say, as Job's friends did, that the afflicted person brought this on himself. (2) We can say that this is a test to help the poor develop more patience and trust in God. (3) We can help the person in need. David would only approve of the last option. Although many governments today have their own laws for helping those in need, this is no excuse for ignoring the poor and needy within our reach.

pathway and in due season he will honor you with every blessing, and you will see the wicked destroyed. 35, 36I myself have seen it happen: a proud and evil man, towering like a cedar of Lebanon, but when I looked again, he was gone! I searched but could not find him! 37But the good man—what a different story! For the good man—the blameless, the upright, the man of peace—he has a wonderful future ahead of him. For him there is a happy ending. 38But evil men shall be destroyed, and their posterity shall be cut off.

39The Lord saves the godly! He is their salvation and their refuge when trouble comes. 40Because they trust in him, he helps them and delivers them from the plots of evil men.

37:37
Ps 7:10
Isa 57:1,2
37:38
Ps 1:4; 73:18
37:39
Ps 3:8; 9:9
62:1
37:40
Ps 22:3,4
34:22
Dan 3:17; 6:23

Theme: Sorrow for sin brings hope. God alone is the true source of healing and protection for those who confess their sins to him.
Author: David

38 O Lord, don't punish me while you are angry! 2Your arrows have struck deep; your blows are crushing me. 3, 4Because of your anger my body is sick, my health is broken beneath my sins. They are like a flood, higher than my head; they are a burden too heavy to bear. 5, 6My wounds are festering and full of pus. Because of my sins I am bent and racked with pain. My days are filled with anguish. 7My loins burn with inflammation and my whole body is diseased. 8I am exhausted and crushed; I groan in despair.

9Lord, you know how I long for my health once more. You hear my every sigh. 10My heart beats wildly, my strength fails, and I am going blind. 11My loved ones and friends stay away, fearing my disease. Even my own family stands at a distance.

12Meanwhile my enemies are trying to kill me. They plot my ruin and spend all their waking hours planning treachery. 13, 14But I am deaf to all their threats; I am silent before them as a man who cannot speak. I have nothing to say. 15For I am waiting for you, O Lord my God. Come and protect me. 16Put an end to their arrogance, these who gloat when I am cast down!

17How constantly I find myself upon the verge of sin; this source of sorrow always stares me in the face. 18I confess my sins; I am sorry for what I have done. 19But my enemies persecute with vigor, and continue to hate me—though I have done nothing against them to deserve it. 20They repay me evil for good and hate me for standing for the right.

21Don't leave me, Lord; don't go away! 22Come quickly! Help me, O my Savior.

38:1
Ps 6:1
38:2
Ps 32:4
38:3
Ps 6:2
31:9,10; 40:12
Isa 1:5,6
38:5
Ps 42:9; 69:5
38:7
Ps 102:3,4
38:8
Job 3:24
Ps 22:1
38:9
Ps 6:6; 10:17
38:12
Ps 35:20; 54:3
38:15
Ps 17:6; 37:9
38:16
Ps 13:4; 35:26
38:18
2 Cor 7:9,10
38:20
Ps 35:12
1 Jn 3:12
38:21
Ps 22:19; 35:22

37:34 with every blessing, literally, "to possess the land." **38:7** My loins burn with inflammation, implied. **38:8** in despair, or, "because of the pains in my heart." **38:17** How constantly I find myself upon the verge of sin, literally, "I am ready to fall."

38:1ff This is called a penitential psalm because David expressed true repentance for his sin (38:18). He stated that he suffered guilt from sin that led to health problems (38:1–8) and that his sin separated him from God and others causing extreme loneliness (38:9–14). He then confessed his sin and repented (38:15–22).

38:1 As a child might cry to his father, so David cried to God. David was not saying, "Don't punish me," but "Don't punish me while you are angry." He acknowledged that he deserved to be punished, but asked that God temper his discipline with mercy. Like responsible children, we are free to ask for mercy, but should not deny that we deserve punishment.

38:2–4 David saw his anguish as judgment from God for his sins. Although God does not always send physical illness to punish us for sin, this verse and others in Scripture (Acts 12:21–23; 1 Corinthians 11:30–32) indicate that he did so in certain circumstances. Our sin can have physical or mental side-effects that can cause even greater suffering. Sometimes God has to punish his children in order to bring them back to himself

(Hebrews 12:5–11). When we repent of our sin, God promises to forgive us, although he does not promise to undo sin's direct consequences.

38:13, 14 One of the most difficult tasks in life is to be silent when others tear us down, because we want to protect our reputation. We find it difficult to do nothing while something so precious to us is being assaulted. But we can trust God to protect even our reputation, so we do not have to defend it ourselves. If David had responded with a loud voice, it may have been to lash back in revenge or justify his position. Jesus was silent before his accusers (Luke 23:9, 10), so he could leave his case in God's hands (1 Peter 2:21–24). That is a good place to leave our case too!

38:17 In David's confession of sin, he acknowledged that he was constantly on the verge of sin. No matter how hard we try to follow God, we are sinners by nature and we often sin. It is difficult to escape situations where we are tempted. We stand on the verge of sin as if we are walking along the edge of a cliff and could fall at any moment. Those who think they are beyond sin are sure to fall. Therefore, the first step toward avoiding sin is to acknowledge our tendency to sin. Only then will we be ready to say "no."

Theme: Apart from God, life is fleeting and empty. This is an appeal for God's mercy because life is so brief.
Author: David

39:1
Ps 34:13; 141:3

39:2
Ps 38:13-16

39:4
Ps 78:39; 90:12

39:5
Job 14:2
Ps 49:10; 62:9
89:47; 144:4

39:8
Ps 51:9; 79:4,9

39:9
2 Sam 16:10
Job 2:10

39:10
Job 9:34
Ps 32:4

39:11
Job 13:27,28
Ps 90:7

39:12
2 Chron 29:15
Heb 11:13

39:13
Job 10:20; 14:6

39 I said to myself, I'm going to quit complaining! I'll keep quiet, especially when the ungodly are around me. 2, 3But as I stood there silently the turmoil within me grew to the bursting point. The more I mused, the hotter the fires inside. Then at last I spoke, and pled with God: 4Lord, help me to realize how brief my time on earth will be. Help me to know that I am here for but a moment more. 5, 6My life is no longer than my hand! My whole lifetime is but a moment to you. Proud man! Frail as breath! A shadow! And all his busy rushing ends in nothing. He heaps up riches for someone else to spend. 7And so, Lord, my only hope is in you.

8Save me from being overpowered by my sins, for even fools will mock me then.

9Lord, I am speechless before you. I will not open my mouth to speak one word of complaint, for my punishment is from you.

10Lord, don't hit me anymore—I am exhausted beneath your hand. 11When you punish a man for his sins, he is destroyed, for he is as fragile as a moth-infested cloth; yes, man is frail as breath.

12Hear my prayer, O Lord; listen to my cry! Don't sit back, unmindful of my tears. For I am your guest. I am a traveler passing through the earth, as all my fathers were.

13Spare me, Lord! Let me recover and be filled with happiness again before my death.

Theme: Doing God's will sometimes means waiting patiently. While we wait, we can love God, serve others, and tell others about him.
Author: David

40:1
Ps 27:14; 34:15

40:2
Ps 27:5; 69:1,2

40:3
Ps 32:7; 64:9

40:4
Job 37:24
Ps 84:12

40:5
Job 5:9
Ps 136:4
139:17,18

40 I waited patiently for God to help me; then he listened and heard my cry. 2He lifted me out of the pit of despair, out from the bog and the mire, and set my feet on a hard, firm path and steadied me as I walked along. 3He has given me a new song to sing, of praises to our God. Now many will hear of the glorious things he did for me, and stand in awe before the Lord, and put their trust in him. 4Many blessings are given to those who trust the Lord, and have no confidence in those who are proud, or who trust in idols.

5O Lord my God, many and many a time you have done great miracles for us and we are ever in your thoughts. Who else can do such glorious things? No one else can be compared with you. There isn't time to tell of all your wonderful deeds.

39:9 *for my punishment is from you,* literally, "for you have done it."

39:1-3 We all have complaints about job, money, or situations in life. David certainly had reason to complain. He was the anointed king of Israel, but had to wait many years before taking the throne. Then one of his sons tried to kill him and become king instead. But David chose not to complain about his problems to others, but instead took his complaints directly to God. This does not mean we should present a false front before other people. But complaining before others may make them think that God cannot take care of us. It may also look like we blame God for our troubles. Instead, like David, we should take our complaints directly to God.

39:4 Life is short no matter how long we live. If there is something important we want to do, we must not put it off for a better day. Ask yourself, "If I only had six months to live, what would I do?" Tell someone that you love him or her? Deal with an undisciplined area in your life? Tell someone about Jesus? Since life is short, don't neglect what is truly important.

39:5, 6 The brevity of life is a theme throughout the books of Psalms, Proverbs, and Ecclesiastes. Christ also spoke about it (Luke 12:20). It is ironic that people spend so much time securing their lives on earth and spend little or no thought on where they will spend eternity. David realized that amassing riches and busily

accomplishing worldly tasks would make no difference in eternity. Few people understand that their only hope is in the Lord. (For other verses on the brevity of life, see Ecclesiastes 2:18 and James 4:14.)

39:10 What did David mean when he asked God to stop hitting him? This is a metaphor of the discipline a parent should give to a disobedient child. It may also be a picture of the difficulties David was facing that caused him to feel like he was being struck. Just as a loving father carefully disciplines his children, so God corrects us (Hebrews 12:5-9).

39:12 We are guests on earth—travelers passing through—our real home is in heaven with God. This perspective should change the way we live. How temporary our lives are! But while our time here is short, the effects of what we do can be eternal. One well-worn saying states: "Only one life will soon be past, only what's done for Christ will last."

40:1-4 Waiting for God to help us is not easy, but David received four benefits from waiting on God: (1) God *lifted* him out of his despair, (2) God *set* his feet on firm ground, (3) God *steadied* his walk, and (4) God *gave* him a new purpose. Often blessings cannot be received unless we go through the trial of waiting.

⁶It isn't sacrifices and offerings which you really want from your people. Burnt animals bring no special joy to your heart. But you have accepted the offer of my life-long service. ⁷Then I said, "See, I have come, just as all the prophets foretold. ⁸And I delight to do your will, my God, for your law is written upon my heart!"

⁹I have told everyone the Good News that you forgive people's sins. I have not been timid about it, as you well know, O Lord. ¹⁰I have not kept this Good News hidden in my heart, but have proclaimed your lovingkindness and truth to all the congregation.

¹¹O Lord, don't hold back your tender mercies from me! My only hope is in your love and faithfulness. ¹²Otherwise I perish, for problems far too big for me to solve are piled higher than my head. Meanwhile my sins, too many to count, have all caught up with me and I am ashamed to look up. My heart quails within me.

¹³Please, Lord, rescue me! Quick! Come and help me! ¹⁴, ¹⁵Confuse them! Turn them around and send them sprawling—all these who are trying to destroy me. Disgrace these scoffers with their utter failure!

¹⁶But may the joy of the Lord be given to everyone who loves him and his salvation. May they constantly exclaim, "How great God is!"

¹⁷I am poor and weak, yet the Lord is thinking about me right now! O my God, you are my helper. You are my Savior; come quickly, and save me. Please don't delay!

40:6
1 Sam 15:22
Jer 7:22,23
Mic 6:6-8
Heb 10:5-7
40:8
Ps 37:31
2 Cor 3:3
Jn 4:34
Rom 7:22
40:9
Ps 22:25
119:13
40:10
Ps 89:1
Acts 20:20,27
40:11
Ps 43:3; 61:7
40:12
Ps 18:5; 38:4
73:26; 116:3
40:13
Ps 22:19; 71:12
40:14
Ps 35:4,26
70:2,3
40:16
Ps 35:27; 70:4

Theme: A prayer for God's mercy when feeling sick or abandoned. When we're sick or when everyone deserts us, God remains at our side.
Author: David

41 God blesses those who are kind to the poor. He helps them out of their troubles. ²He protects them and keeps them alive; he publicly honors them and destroys the power of their enemies. ³He nurses them when they are sick, and soothes their pains and worries.

⁴"O Lord," I prayed, "be kind and heal me, for I have confessed my sins." ⁵But my enemies say, "May he soon die and be forgotten!" ⁶They act so friendly when they come to visit me while I am sick; but all the time they hate me and are glad that I am lying there upon my bed of pain. And when they leave, they laugh and mock. ⁷They whisper together about what they will do when I am dead. ⁸"It's fatal, whatever it is," they say. "He'll never get out of that bed!"

⁹Even my best friend has turned against me—a man I completely trusted; how often we ate together. ¹⁰Lord, don't you desert me! Be gracious, Lord, and make me well again so I can pay them back! ¹¹I know you are pleased with me because

41:1
Ps 37:19
82:3,4
41:2
Ps 27:12
37:22,28
41:4
Ps 5:4; 6:2
41:5
Ps 38:12
41:6
Ps 12:2
41:9
Job 19:19
Ps 55:12,13,20
Jer 20:10
Jn 13:18
41:10
Ps 3:3

40:6 *But you have accepted the offer of my lifelong service,* literally, "my ears you have dug." **40:9** *the Good News that you forgive people's sins,* literally, "your righteousness." Also in vs 10. **41:3** *He nurses them when they are sick, and soothes their pains and worries,* literally, "You make all his bed in his sickness."

40:6 Continuous devotion to God is life's choicest accomplishment. The religious ritual of David's day involved sacrificing animals in the Tabernacle. Today we often make rituals of going to church, taking communion, or singing hymns. These activities are empty if our reasons for doing them are selfish. God doesn't want these sacrifices and offerings without an attitude of devotion to him. The prophet Samuel had told King Saul, "Obedience is far better than sacrifice" (1 Samuel 15:22). Make sure you give God the obedience and lifelong service he desires from you.

40:8 Jesus quoted this verse as referring to himself (John 4:34). He did indeed come as the prophets foretold, proclaiming the Good News of God's righteousness and forgiveness of sins. Verses 6–8 are also referred to in Hebrews 10:5–10 as applying to Jesus.

40:9, 10 The Good News from God is that he forgives our sins, and David boldly shared this Good News to those around him. When we feel the impact of this on our lives, we cannot keep it hidden, but will want to tell other people what God has done for us. If God's Good News has changed your life, don't be timid. Since it

is natural to share a good bargain with others or recommend a skillful doctor, then we should also feel natural sharing what God has done for us.

40:17 The leader of your country probably does not know you by name, let alone think about you. But the King of all creation, the Ruler of the universe is thinking about you right now. Allow this truth to buoy your self-esteem. If God always has us in his thoughts, perhaps we could do more to keep him in our thoughts.

41:1 The Bible often speaks of God's care for the poor and his blessing on those who share this concern. God does not want the poor to suffer. God wants our generosity to reflect his own free giving; as he has blessed us, we should bless others.

41:9 "Best friend" can also be translated "close friend." This verse is viewed in the New Testament as a prophecy of Christ's betrayal (John 13:18). Judas, one of Jesus' 12 disciples, had spent three years learning from Jesus, traveling and eating with him (Mark 3:14–19). While Judas was not Jesus' closest friend, he was trusted with the disciples' money. Eventually, Judas betrayed Jesus (Matthew 26:14–16, 20–25).

41:12
Ps 18:32; 21:6
37:17

41:13
Ps 72:18,19
106:48

you haven't let my enemies triumph over me. 12You have preserved me because I was honest; you have admitted me forever to your presence.

13Bless the Lord, the God of Israel, who exists from everlasting ages past—and on into everlasting eternity ahead. Amen and amen!

B. THE SECOND BOOK OF PSALMS (42:1—72:20)
These psalms include a prayer for rescue, a call to worship, a confession of sin, an encouragement to trust God, a psalm for those hurt by friends, a prayer for those who have been slandered, and a missionary psalm. These psalms can help us retain a sense of wonder in our worship.

Theme: A thirst for God. When you feel lonely or depressed meditate on God's kindness and love.
Author: The sons of Korah, who were Temple musicians and assistants

42:1
Ps 63:1

42:2
Ps 43:4; 84:2
143:6
Jer 10:10
Rom 9:26

42:3
Ps 79:10; 80:5
Joel 2:17

42:4
Job 30:16
Ps 62:8; 71:14
Isa 30:29
Lam 3:24
Mt 26:38

42:6
Ps 61:2

42:7
Ps 88:7
Jonah 2:3

42:8
Ps 16:7; 57:3
77:6; 149:4,5
Job 35:10

42:9
Ps 17:9; 18:2
38:6

42 As the deer pants for water, so I long for you, O God. 2I thirst for God, the living God. Where can I find him to come and stand before him? 3Day and night I weep for his help, and all the while my enemies taunt me. "Where is this God of yours?" they scoff.

4, 5Take courage, my soul! Do you remember those times (but how could you ever forget them!) when you led a great procession to the Temple on festival days, singing with joy, praising the Lord? Why then be downcast? Why be discouraged and sad? Hope in God! I shall yet praise him again. Yes, I shall again praise him for his help.

6Yet I am standing here depressed and gloomy, but I will meditate upon your kindness in this lovely land where the Jordan River flows and where Mount Hermon and Mount Mizar stand. 7All your waves and billows have gone over me, and floods of sorrow pour upon me like a thundering cataract.

8Yet day by day the Lord also pours out his steadfast love upon me, and through the night I sing his songs and pray to God who gives me life.

9"O God my Rock," I cry, "why have you forsaken me? Why must I suffer these attacks from my enemies?" 10Their taunts pierce me like a fatal wound; again and again they scoff, "Where is that God of yours?" 11But O my soul, don't be discouraged. Don't be upset. Expect God to act! For I know that I shall again have plenty of reason to praise him for all that he will do. He is my help! He is my God!

42:5 *for his help,* literally, "for the help of his countenance." **42:7** *floods of sorrow pour upon me like a thundering cataract,* literally, "deep calls to deep at the noise of your waterfalls."

41:13 Psalms is divided into five "books," and each one ends with a doxology or an expression of praise to God. The first book of the psalms takes us on a journey through suffering, sorrow, and great joy. It teaches us much about God's eternal love and care for us and how we should trust him even in the day-to-day experiences of life.

42:1ff Psalms 42—49 were written by the sons of Korah. Korah was a Levite who led a rebellion against Moses (Numbers 16:1–35). He was killed, but his descendants remained faithful to God and continued to serve God in the Temple. David appointed men from the clan of Korah to serve as choir leaders (1 Chronicles 6:31–38), and they continued to be Temple musicians for hundreds of years (2 Chronicles 20:18, 19).

42:1ff There may come times in life when after thirsting for God, weeping for his help, and enduring ridicule, he still remains silent (42:1–3). Such times often lead to depression and discouragement, but the psalmist discovered a remedy. He remembered God's great blessings on his life (42:4, 5); he realized that although God seemed silent, he was there and would once again receive praise (42:4, 5); he gazed upon God's beautiful creation that proclaims his love (42:6). The psalmist had felt billows of sorrow, but he realized that he was never adrift from God's steadfast love (42:7, 8). Finally he faithfully *expected* God to act (42:11). When

you cannot seem to find God, use this remedy and you will, once again, find reason to praise him.

42:1, 2 As the life of a deer depends upon water, our lives depend upon God. Those who seek him and long to understand him find never-ending life. Feeling separated from God, this psalmist wouldn't rest until his relationship with God had been restored because he knew that his life depended on it.

42:4, 5 The writer of this psalm was discouraged because he was exiled to a place far from Jerusalem and could not worship in the Temple. Because he remembers the joyous parades he led to the Temple on festival days, he must have been a national leader or Temple official. During these God-given holidays, the nation was to remember all that God had done for them. Many of these festivals are explained in the chart in Leviticus 23.

42:6 Depression is one of the most common emotional ailments. One antidote for depression is to meditate on the record of God's goodness to his people. This will take your mind off the present situation and give hope that it will improve. It focuses your thoughts on God's ability to help you rather than your inability to help yourself. When you feel depressed, take advantage of this psalm's anti-depressant. Read the Bible's accounts of God's goodness and meditate on them.

Theme: Hope in a time of discouragement. In the face of discouragement, our only hope is in God.
Author: The sons of Korah (Temple assistants). Psalms 42 and 43 are one psalm in many Hebrew manuscripts.

43 O God, defend me from the charges of these merciless, deceitful men. 2For you are God, my only place of refuge. Why have you tossed me aside? Why must I mourn at the oppression of my enemies?

3Oh, send out your light and your truth—let them lead me. Let them lead me to your Temple on your holy mountain, Zion. 4There I will go to the altar of God my exceeding joy, and praise him with my harp. O God—my God! 5O my soul, why be so gloomy and discouraged? Trust in God! I shall again praise him for his wondrous help; he will make me smile again, *for he is my God!*

43:1
1 Sam 24:15
Ps 26:1; 35:24

43:2
Ps 28:7; 42:9
44:9

43:3
Ps 36:9
42:4,5; 84:1

43:4
Ps 26:6; 33:2

Theme: A plea for victory by the battle-weary and defeated. When it seems that God has let you down, don't despair. Instead, remember God's past deliverance and be confident that he will restore you.
Author: The sons of Korah (Temple assistants)

44 O God, we have heard of the glorious miracles you did in the days of long ago. Our forefathers have told us how you drove the heathen nations from this land and gave it all to us, spreading Israel from one end of the country to the other. 3They did not conquer by their own strength and skill, but by your mighty power and because you smiled upon them and favored them.

4You are my King and my God. Decree victories for your people. 5For it is only by your power and through your name that we tread down our enemies; 6I do not trust my weapons. They could never save me. 7Only you can give us the victory over those who hate us.

8My constant boast is God. I can never thank you enough! 9And yet for a time, O Lord, you have tossed us aside in dishonor, and have not helped us in our battles. 10You have actually fought against us and defeated us before our foes. Our enemies have invaded our land and pillaged the countryside. 11You have treated us like sheep in a slaughter pen, and scattered us among the nations. 12You sold us for a pittance. You valued us at nothing at all. 13The neighboring nations laugh and mock at us because of all the evil you have sent. 14You have made the word "Jew" a byword of contempt and shame among the nations, disliked by all. 15, 16I am constantly despised, mocked, taunted and cursed by my vengeful enemies.

17And all this has happened, Lord, despite our loyalty to you. We have not violated your covenant. 18Our hearts have not deserted you! We have not left your path by a single step. 19If we had, we could understand your punishing us in the barren wilderness and sending us into darkness and death. 20If we had turned away from worshiping our God, and were worshiping idols, 21would God not know it? Yes, he knows the secrets of every heart. 22But that is not our case. For we are

44:1
Ps 78:2,3,12,
55; 80:8

44:3
Deut 4:37
Ps 77:15

44:5
Ps 60:12

44:7
Ps 53:5; 136:24

44:8
Ps 30:12; 34:2

44:9
Ps 43:2; 60:10
74:1

44:10
Lev 26:33
Josh 7:8,12
Ps 89:42

44:14
Ps 17:6; 109:25

44:17
Ps 119:61,83,
109,141,153,
176

44:18
Ps 119:51,157

44:19
Ps 51:8; 94:5

44:20
Ps 78:11; 81:9

43:5 *he will make me smile again,* literally, "he is the help of my countenance."

43:3 Zion is another name for Jerusalem. David made this city Israel's capital. The Temple was built in Jerusalem on a hill often called the holy mountain because it was the place for the people to meet God in worship and prayer.

43:3, 4 The psalmist asked God to send his light and truth to guide him to the Temple where he would meet God. God's truth (see 1 John 2:27) provides the right path to follow, and God's light (see 1 John 1:5) provides the clear vision to follow it. If you feel surrounded by darkness and uncertainty, follow God's light and truth back to him.

44:1ff This psalm may have been sung at an occasion like the one in 2 Chronicles 20:18, 19 where the faithful King Jehoshaphat was surrounded by enemies and the Levites sang to the Lord before the battle.

44:1-3 "Driving heathen nations from the land" refers to the conquest of Canaan (the Promised Land) described in the book of Joshua. God gave the land to Israel and they were to enter and drive out anyone who was wicked and determined to oppose God.

Israel was told to settle the land and be a witness to the world of God's power and love. Surrounded by enemies, the psalmist remembered what God had done for his people and took heart. We can have this same confidence in God when we feel attacked.

44:22 Israel had been defeated despite their faith (44:17) and obedience (44:18) to God. The psalmist could not understand why God allowed this to happen, but he did not give up hope of discovering the answer (44:17–22). Although he felt his suffering was undeserved, he revealed the real reason for suffering in this verse. He suffered because he was *serving God.* Paul quoted the psalmist's complaint (Romans 8:36) to show that we must always be ready to face death for the cause of Christ. Thus, our suffering may not be a punishment, but a battle scar to demonstrate our loyalty.

44:22–26 The writer cried to God to save his people by his constant love—they "are like sheep awaiting slaughter." Nothing can separate us from God's love, not even death (Romans 8:36–39). When you fear for your life, ask God for deliverance and

44:22
Isa 53:7
Rom 8:36

44:23
Ps 7:6; 77:7
78:65

44:24
Ps 42:9; 88:14

facing death threats constantly because of serving you! We are like sheep awaiting slaughter.

23Waken! Rouse yourself! Don't sleep, O Lord! Are we cast off forever? 24Why do you look the other way? Why do you ignore our sorrows and oppression? 25We lie face downward in the dust. 26Rise up, O Lord, and come and help us. Save us by your constant love.

Theme: A poem to the king (possibly Solomon) on the occasion of his wedding. While this psalm was written for an historic occasion, it is also seen as a prophecy about Christ and his bride, the church, who will praise him throughout all generations.
Author: The sons of Korah (Temple assistants)

45:1
Ezra 7:6

45 My heart is overflowing with a beautiful thought! I will write a lovely poem to the King, for I am as full of words as the speediest writer pouring out his story.

45:2
Ps 21:6
Lk 4:22

2You are the fairest of all;
  Your words are filled with grace;
  God himself is blessing you forever.

45:3
Isa 9:6

3Arm yourself, O Mighty One,
  So glorious, so majestic!

45:4
Rev 6:2

4And in your majesty
  Go on to victory,
  Defending truth, humility, and justice.
  Go forth to awe-inspiring deeds!

45:5
Ps 120:4
Isa 5:28

5Your arrows are sharp
  In your enemies' hearts;
  They fall before you.

45:6
Ps 93:2; 98:8,9
Heb 1:8,9

6Your throne, O God, endures forever.
  Justice is your royal scepter.

45:7
Ps 11:7; 21:6
33:5

7You love what is good
  And hate what is wrong.
  Therefore God, your God,

45:8
Song 1:3
4:13,14

Has given you more gladness
  Than anyone else.

45:9
1 Kgs 2:19; 9:28
Song 6:8
Isa 13:12

8Your robes are perfumed with myrrh, aloes and cassia. In your palaces of inlaid ivory, lovely music is being played for your enjoyment. 9Kings' daughters are among your concubines. Standing beside you is the queen, wearing jewelry of finest gold from Ophir.

45:10
Deut 21:13
Isa 54:5
Eph 5:33
1 Pet 3:6

10, 11"I advise you, O daughter, not to fret about your parents in your homeland far away. Your royal husband delights in your beauty. Reverence him, for he is your lord. 12The people of Tyre, the richest people of our day, will shower you with gifts and entreat your favors."

45:12
Ps 22:29
72:10,11

45:13
Isa 61:10

13The bride, a princess, waits within her chamber, robed in beautiful clothing

45:9 *concubines,* literally, "honorable women." **45:13** *The bride,* literally, "The king's daughter."

remember that even physical death cannot separate you from him.

44:23–25 The psalmist's words suggest that he did not believe God had left him; instead, he urged God to hurry to help him, wondering why God seemed to be asleep. A New Testament parallel is in Mark 4:35–41, when Jesus fell asleep in the boat during the storm. It was not that Jesus was unconcerned, but that he had a lesson to teach his followers.

45:1ff This is called a "messianic" psalm because it prophetically describes the Messiah's future relationship to the church, his body of believers. Verse 2 expresses God's abundant blessing on his Messiah; 45:6–8 find their true fulfillment in Christ (Hebrews 1:8, 9). The church is described as Christ's bride in Revelation 19.

45:1ff In this royal wedding song, the bridegroom is a man who has everything—power, position, wealth, and now a beautiful bride. But the tribute to the king is not because of these things, but

because the king pleases God. He defends truth, humility, and justice, loves good and hates evil, and for this has earned the praise of many nations. True royalty is not characterized by the robes worn or thrones occupied, but by a faithful obedience to the most royal of all, the King of kings. We have been called to be a "royal priesthood, a holy nation," and we honor that royalty by honoring our Lord the King who gave it to us.

45:8 Myrrh is a fragrant gum from certain trees in Arabia generally used in perfumes. Aloe, a spice, may have come from sandalwood, a close-grained and fragrant wood often used for storage boxes or chests (see also Proverbs 7:14–17; Song of Solomon 4:13, 14). Cassia grows as a thistle; its sweet fragrance comes from the roots of the plant.

45:13–17 In this beautiful poetry we have a picture of Christ's bride, the church, pictured with the richest blessings.

woven with gold. ¹⁴Lovely she is, led beside her maids of honor to the king! ¹⁵What a joyful, glad procession as they enter in the palace gates! ¹⁶"Your sons will some day be kings like their father. They shall sit on thrones around the world!

45:14
Song 1:4
Ezek 16:9-13

¹⁷"I will cause your name to be honored in all generations; the nations of the earth will praise you forever."

45:17
Ps 138:4
Mal 1:11

Theme: God is always there to help, providing refuge, security, and peace. God's power is complete and his ultimate victory is certain. He will not fail to rescue those who love him.
Author: The sons of Korah (Temple assistants)

46 God is our refuge and strength, a tested help in times of trouble. ²And so we need not fear even if the world blows up, and the mountains crumble into the sea. ³Let the oceans roar and foam; let the mountains tremble!

46:1
Ps 9:9; 14:6
62:7,8; 145:18

⁴There is a river of joy flowing through the City of our God—the sacred home of the God above all gods. ⁵God himself is living in that City; therefore it stands unmoved despite the turmoil everywhere. He will not delay his help. ⁶The nations rant and rave in anger—but when God speaks, the earth melts in submission and kingdoms totter to ruin.

46:4
Ps 87:3
Isa 60:14
Rev 3:12; 22:1

46:5
Isa 12:6; 41:14
Ezek 43:7

⁷The Commander of the armies of heaven is here among us. He, the God of Jacob, has come to rescue us.

46:6
Ps 2:1

⁸Come, see the glorious things that our God does, how he brings ruin upon the world, ⁹and causes wars to end throughout the earth, breaking and burning every weapon. ¹⁰"Stand silent! Know that I am God! I will be honored by every nation in the world!

46:7
Num 14:9
Ps 9:9

46:8
Ps 66:5

46:9
Isa 2:4; 9:5

¹¹The Commander of the heavenly armies is here among *us!* He, the God of Jacob, has come to rescue *us!*

46:10
Ps 100:3

Theme: God is still king of the world. All nations of the earth will eventually recognize his Lordship.
Author: The sons of Korah (Temple assistants)

47 Come, everyone, and clap for joy! Shout triumphant praises to the Lord! ²For the Lord, the God above all gods, is awesome beyond words; he is the great King of all the earth. ³He subdues the nations before us, ⁴and will personally select his choicest blessings for his Jewish people—the very best for those he loves.

47:2
Deut 7:21

47:4
1 Pet 1:4

⁵God has ascended with a mighty shout, with trumpets blaring. ⁶, ⁷Sing out your praises to our God, our King. Yes, sing your highest praises to our King, the King of all the earth. Sing thoughtful praises! ⁸He reigns above the nations, sitting on his holy throne. ⁹The Gentile rulers of the world have joined with us in praising

47:5
Ps 68:18,25,33

47:6
Ps 68:4; 89:18

47:8
1 Chron 16:31

45:14 *Lovely,* literally, "embroidered work." **47:4** *his Jewish people,* literally, "the pride of Jacob." **47:9** *praising . . . praising,* implied.

46—48 Psalms 46—48 are hymns of praise, celebrating deliverance from some great foe. Psalm 46 may have been written when the Assyrian army invaded the land and surrounded Jerusalem (2 Kings 18:13—19:37).

46:1–3 The fear of mountains or cities suddenly crumbling into the sea by a nuclear blast haunts many people today. But the psalmist says that even if the world ends, "We need not fear!" Even in the face of utter destruction, he expressed a quiet confidence in God's ability to save him. It seems impossible to face the end of the world without fear, but the Bible is clear—God is our refuge even in the face of total destruction. He is not merely a temporary retreat; he is our eternal refuge and can provide strength even in the face of global destruction.

46:4, 5 Many great cities have rivers flowing through them, sustaining people's lives and becoming the center of trade. Jerusalem had no river, but it had God who, like a river, sustained the people's lives and was the center of their attention. As long as God lived among the people, the city was invincible. But when the people abandoned him, God left them, and Jerusalem fell to the Babylonian army.

46:10 War and destruction are inevitable, but so is God's final

victory. At that time, all will stand silent before Almighty God. How proper, then, for us to stand silent now in reverent quiet to honor him and his power and majesty. Take time each day to be silent and to exalt God.

47:1ff This psalm was written about the same event as Psalm 46—the Assyrian invasion of Judah by Sennacherib (2 Kings 18:13—19:37).

47:2 The Lord God is awesome beyond words, but this didn't keep Bible writers from trying to describe him. And it shouldn't keep us from praising him either. We can't describe God completely, but we can tell others what he has done for us. Don't let the indescribable greatness of God prevent you from telling others what you know about him.

47:9 The word translated "Gentile" is a Hebrew word that literally means "the nations." In other words, a Gentile was anyone who was not a Jew and did not worship Jehovah as the only God. But Gentiles could come to believe in God (Acts 13:26) because God wants all people to come to him (Romans 16:25–27; Galatians 3:14).

47:9 Abraham was the father of the Israelite nation. The one true God was sometimes called "the God of Abraham" (Exodus 3:6;

47:9
Ps 72:11
Isa 49:7,23

48:1
1 Chron 16:25
Ps 87:1; 96:4
145:3
Zech 8:3

48:2
Ps 50:2
Lam 2:15
Mt 5:35

48:3
Ps 46:7

48:6
Isa 13:8

48:8
Ps 87:5

48:9
Ps 26:3; 40:10

48:10
Josh 7:9
Mal 1:11

48:11
Ps 97:8

48:13
Ps 78:5-7

him—praising the God of Abraham—for the battle shields of all the armies of the world are his trophies. He is highly honored everywhere.

Theme: God's presence is our joy, security, and salvation. God is praised as the defender of Jerusalem, the holy city of the Jews. He is also our defender and guide forever.
Author: The sons of Korah (Temple assistants)

48 How great is the Lord! How much we should praise him. He lives upon Mount Zion in Jerusalem. 2What a glorious sight! See Mount Zion rising north of the city high above the plains for all to see—Mount Zion, joy of all the earth, the residence of the great King.

3God himself is the defender of Jerusalem. 4The kings of the earth have arrived together to inspect the city. 5They marvel at the sight and hurry home again, 6afraid of what they have seen; they are filled with panic like a woman in travail! 7For God destroys the mightiest warships with a breath of wind. 8We have heard of the city's glory—the city of our God, the Commander of the armies of heaven. And now we see it for ourselves! God has established Jerusalem forever.

9Lord, here in your Temple we meditate upon your kindness and your love. 10Your name is known throughout the earth, O God. You are praised everywhere for the salvation you have scattered throughout the world. 11O Jerusalem, rejoice! O people of Judah, rejoice! For God will see to it that you are finally treated fairly. 12Go, inspect the city! Walk around and count her many towers! 13Note her walls and tour her palaces, so that you can tell your children.

14For this great God is our God forever and ever. He will be our guide until we die.

48:2 *north of the city*, literally, "on the sides of the north." **48:3** *God himself is the defender of Jerusalem*, literally, "God has made himself known in her palaces for a high tower." **48:10** *You are praised everywhere for the salvation*, literally, "Your right hand is filled with righteousness." **48:11** *O Jerusalem*, literally, "Mount Zion."

PSALMS THAT HAVE INSPIRED HYMNS		
Psalm 23	The King of Love My Shepherd Is	
	My Shepherd Shall Supply My Need	
	The Lord Is My Shepherd	
Psalm 46	A Mighty Fortress Is Our God	
Psalm 61	Hiding in Thee (O Safe to the Rock That Is Higher Than I . . .)	
Psalm 87	Glorious Things of Thee Are Spoken	
Psalm 90	O God, Our Help in Ages Past	
Psalm 100	All People That on Earth Do Dwell	
	Before Jehovah's Aweful Throne	
Psalm 103	Praise to the Lord, the Almighty	
Psalm 104	O Worship the King, All Glorious Above	
Psalm 126	Bringing in the Sheaves	

1 Kings 18:36). In a spiritual sense, however, God's promises to Abraham apply to all who believe in God (Romans 4:11, 12).

48:2 Why is Jerusalem "the residence of the great King"? Because the Temple was located in Jerusalem, the city was seen as the center of God's presence in the world. In eternity, however, the Bible pictures Jerusalem as the place to which believers will flock in the "last days" (Isaiah 2:2ff) and as the spiritual home of all believers where God will live among them (Revelation 21:2, 3).

48:8 Since Jerusalem has been destroyed several times since this psalm was written, the phrase, "God has established Jerusalem forever" may refer prophetically to the new Jerusalem where God will live with all believers (Revelation 21).

48:11 The people of Judah were from Israel's largest tribe which settled in the southern part of Canaan where Jerusalem was located (Joshua 15:1–12). King David was from Judah and made Jerusalem his capital and center of the nation's worship. Jesus was a descendant of the tribe of Judah. The psalmist was saying

that the day would come when God would bring justice to the land and his people would get the respect they deserved.

48:12, 13 After an enemy army had unsuccessfully besieged Jerusalem, it was common for the people to make a tour of the city, inspecting its defenses and praising God for the protection it had offered. In times of great joy or after God has brought us through some great trial, we ought to inspect our defenses to make sure that the foundations of God, his Word, and the body of believers remain strong (Ephesians 2:20–22).

48:14 We often pray for God's guidance as we struggle with decisions. What we need is both guidance and a guide—a map that gives us landmarks and directions and a constant companion who has an intimate knowledge of the way and will make sure we interpret the map correctly. The Bible will be such a map, and God will be the constant companion and guide. As you make your way through life, lean upon both the map and the Guide.

Theme: Trusting in worldly possessions is futile. You cannot take possessions with you when you die, and they cannot buy forgiveness from sin.
Author: The sons of Korah (Temple assistants)

49 Listen, everyone! High and low, rich and poor, all around the world—listen to my words, 3for they are wise and filled with insight.

4I will tell in song accompanied by harps the answer to one of life's most perplexing problems:

5*There is no need to fear when times of trouble come*, even though surrounded by enemies! 6They trust in their wealth and boast about how rich they are, 7yet not one of them, though rich as kings, can ransom his own brother from the penalty of sin! For God's forgiveness does not come that way. 8, 9For a soul is far too precious to be ransomed by mere earthly wealth. There is not enough of it in all the earth to buy eternal life for just one soul, to keep it out of hell.

10Rich man! Proud man! Wise man! You must die like all the rest! You have no greater lease on life than foolish, stupid men. You must leave your wealth to others. 11You name your estates after yourselves as though your lands could be forever yours, and you could live on them eternally. 12But man with all his pomp must die like any animal. 13Such is the folly of these men, though after they die they will be quoted as having great wisdom.

14Death is the shepherd of all mankind. And "in the morning" those who are evil will be the slaves of those who are good. For the power of their wealth is gone when they die; they cannot take it with them.

15But as for me, God will redeem my soul from the power of death, for he will receive me. 16So do not be dismayed when evil men grow rich and build their lovely homes. 17For when they die they carry nothing with them! Their honors will not follow them. 18Though a man calls himself happy all through his life—and the world loudly applauds success— 19yet in the end he dies like everyone else, and enters eternal darkness.

20For man with all his pomp must die like any animal.

49:1
Ps 78:1
49:3
Ps 39:30
119:130
49:4
2 Kgs 3:15
Ps 78:23
49:5
Ps 23:4; 27:1
49:6
Ps 52:7
Mark 10:24
49:7
Job 36:18
Mt 25:8,9
49:8
Ps 16:10; 89:48
Mt 16:26
49:10
Ps 39:6
Lk 12:20,21
49:11
Deut 3:14
49:14
Ps 9:17
Rev 2:26
49:15
Ps 16:10,11
49:16
Ps 37:7
49:17
Ps 17:14
1 Tim 6:7
49:18
Ps 10:3

Theme: The contrast between true and false faith. God desires sincere thanks, trust, and praise.
Author: Asaph, one of David's chief musicians

50 The mighty God, the Lord, has summoned all mankind from east to west! 2God's glory-light shines from the beautiful Temple on Mount Zion. 3He comes with the noise of thunder, surrounded by devastating fire; a great storm rages round about him. 4He has come to judge his people. To heaven and earth he shouts, 5"Gather together my own people who by their sacrifice upon my altar have

50:1
Ps 113:3
50:2
Ps 48:2; 80:1
50:3
Ps 18:12,13

49:7 *For God's forgiveness does not come that way,* implied in text. **49:8, 9** *to keep it out of hell,* literally, "so that he should not see the Pit." **49:14** *For the power of their wealth is gone when they die,* literally, "Their beauty shall be for Sheol to consume." **49:20** *with all his pomp,* literally, "but without insight." It is uncertain whether this phrase was part of the original text. **50:2** *from the beautiful Temple,* literally, "Out of Zion, the perfection of beauty." **50:3** *comes with the noise of thunder,* literally, "comes, and does not keep silence." **50:5** *who by their sacrifice upon my altar have promised to obey,* literally, "who made a covenant with me by sacrifice."

49:1ff The futility of worldliness—riches, pride, fame—resounds from this psalm. Comparable in form to the book of Ecclesiastes, this psalm is one of the few written more to instruct than to give praise.

49:8, 9, 15 In the slave market of the ancient world, a slave had to be redeemed or ransomed (someone paid the price) in order to go free. In Mark 10:45, Ephesians 1:7, and Hebrews 9:12, we learn that Jesus paid such a price so that we could be set free from slavery to sin in order to begin living a new life with him.

There is no way for a person to buy eternal life with God. God alone can redeem a soul. If you are counting on wealth and physical comforts to keep you happy, understand that you will never have enough wealth to keep yourself from hell.

49:10–14 The rich and poor have one thing in common—when they die, they leave all they own here on earth. At the moment of death (and all of us will face that moment), both rich and poor are naked and empty-handed before God. The only riches we have at that time are those we have already invested in our eternal

heritage. At the time of death, each of us will wish we had invested less on earth, where we must leave it, and more in heaven, where we will retain it forever. This is a good time to check up on your investments and see where you have invested the most. Then do something about it!

50:1ff This psalm begins as though God is finally ready to judge the evil people on earth. But surprisingly, God's great fury is leveled against his own people (or at least those who claim to be his). God's judgment must begin with his own people (1 Peter 4:17).

50:1ff God judges people for treating him lightly. First he speaks to the superficially religious people who bring their sacrifices but are only going through the motions (50:1–15). They do not honor God with true praise and thankfulness. Second, he chides evil, hard-hearted people for their religious words coming from lying mouths and immoral lives (50:16–22). To the superficially religious he says, "Trust me completely." To the evil people he says, "This is your last chance and then I will punish."

50:6
Ps 96:13; 97:6

50:9
Ps 69:31

50:10
Ps 104:24

50:13
Hos 6:6

50:14
Deut 23:21
Hos 14:2
Rom 12:1
Heb 13:15

50:16
Isa 29:13

50:17
Rom 2:21,22

50:18
1 Tim 5:22

50:19
Ps 10:7; 36:3

50:20
Mt 10:21

50:21
Ps 90:8

50:23
Ps 91:16

promised to obey me." 6God will judge them with complete fairness, for all heaven declares that he is just.

7O my people, listen! For I am your God. Listen! Here are my charges against you: 8I have no complaint about the sacrifices you bring to my altar, for you bring them regularly. 9But it isn't sacrificial bullocks and goats that I really want from you. 10, 11For all the animals of field and forest are mine! The cattle on a thousand hills! And all the birds upon the mountains! 12If I were hungry, I would not mention it to you—for all the world is mine, and everything in it. 13No, I don't need your sacrifices of flesh and blood. 14, 15What I want from you is your true thanks; I want your promises fulfilled. *I want you to trust me in your times of trouble, so I can rescue you, and you can give me glory.*

16But God says to evil men: Recite my laws no longer, and stop claiming my promises, 17for you have refused my discipline, disregarding my laws. 18You see a thief and help him, and spend your time with evil and immoral men. 19You curse and lie, and vile language streams from your mouths. 20You slander your own brother. 21I remained silent—you thought I didn't care—but now your time of punishment has come, and I list all the above charges against you. 22This is the last chance for all of you who have forgotten God, before I tear you apart—and no one can help you then.

23But true praise is a worthy sacrifice; this really honors me. Those who walk my paths will receive salvation from the Lord.

Theme: David's plea for mercy, forgiveness, and cleansing.
God wants our hearts to be right with him.
Author: David

51 *Written after Nathan the prophet had come to inform David of God's judgment against him because of his adultery with Bath-sheba, and his murder of Uriah, her husband.*
O loving and kind God, have mercy. Have pity upon me and take away the awful stain of my transgressions. 2Oh, wash me, cleanse me from this guilt. Let me be pure again. 3For I admit my shameful deed—it haunts me day and night. 4It is against you and you alone I sinned, and did this terrible thing. You saw it all, and your sentence against me is just. 5But I was born a sinner, yes, from the moment my mother conceived me. 6You deserve honesty from the heart; yes, utter sincerity and truthfulness. Oh, give me this wisdom.

7Sprinkle me with the cleansing blood and I shall be clean again. Wash me and I shall be whiter than snow. 8And after you have punished me, give me back my joy

51:2
Jer 33:8
Acts 22:16
Heb 9:13,14
1 Jn 1:7,9

51:4
Rom 3:4

51:5
Job 14:4
Eph 2:3

51:7
Ex 12:22
Isa 1:18

50:5–9 God's perfect justice demands that sin be judged by death; but a person could offer an animal to God as a substitute for himself, symbolizing the person's faith in the merciful, forgiving God. However, the people were offering their sacrifices and forgetting their significance! The very act of sacrifice showed that they had once agreed to follow God wholeheartedly. But now their hearts were not in it. We may fall into the same pattern when we participate in "religious activities," tithe, or attend church out of habit or conformity rather than out of heartfelt love and obedience.

50:16–22 Some people glibly recite God's laws, but are filled with deceit and evil. They claim his promises, but refuse to obey his laws. This is sin, and God will judge people for it. We too are hypocrites when we do not live what we believe. To let this inconsistency remain shows we are not true followers of God.

50:21 At times God seems silent. This silence does not mean he doesn't care, but that he is withholding deserved punishment, giving time for people to repent (2 Peter 3:9). But his silence is not forever—a time of punishment will come.

51:1–7 David was truly sorry for his adultery with Bath-sheba and for murdering her husband to cover it up. He knew his actions had hurt many people. But because David repented of those sins, God mercifully forgave him. No sin is too great to be forgiven! Do you feel that you could never come close to God because you have

done something terrible? God can and will forgive you of any sin. While God forgives us, however, he does not erase the natural consequences of our sin—David's life and family were never the same as a result of his sin (see 2 Samuel 12:1–23).

51:4 Although David sinned with Bath-sheba, he said he had sinned against God. When someone steals, murders, or slanders, it is against someone else—a victim. According to the world's standards, sex between two "consenting adults" is acceptable because nobody *do*get hurt. But people *do* get hurt—in David's case, a baby died and a man was murdered. All sin hurts us and others, and ultimately it offends God because sin in any form is a rebellion against God's way of living. When tempted to do wrong, remembering that you will be sinning against God may help you stay on the right track.

51:7 The "cleansing blood" refers to a ceremony where blood from a sacrificed animal was sprinkled on the priests to prepare them to serve God (Exodus 29:19–21). Other translations say, "Purge me with hyssop." Hyssop branches were used by the Israelites to place the blood of a lamb on the doorposts of their homes to keep them safe from the angel of death (Exodus 12:22; Hebrews 9:18–22). By this act the Israelites showed their faith and secured their release from slavery in Egypt. This verse, therefore, calls for cleansing from sin and readiness to serve the Lord.

again. 9Don't keep looking at my sins—erase them from your sight. 10Create in me a new, clean heart, O God, filled with clean thoughts and right desires. 11Don't toss me aside, banished forever from your presence. Don't take your Holy Spirit from me. 12Restore to me again the joy of your salvation, and make me willing to obey you. 13Then I will teach your ways to other sinners, and they—guilty like me—will repent and return to you. 14, 15Don't sentence me to death. O my God, you alone can rescue me. Then I will sing of your forgiveness, for my lips will be unsealed—oh, how I will praise you.

16You don't want penance; if you did, how gladly I would do it! You aren't interested in offerings burned before you on the altar. 17It is a broken spirit you want—remorse and penitence. A broken and a contrite heart, O God, you will not ignore.

18And Lord, don't punish Israel for my sins—help your people and protect Jerusalem.

19And when my heart is right, then you will rejoice in the good that I do and in the bullocks I bring to sacrifice upon your altar.

51:9
Jer 16:17

51:10
Mt 5:8
Acts 15:9
Eph 2:10

51:11
Eph 4:30

51:13
Ps 22:27

51:14
2 Sam 12:9
Ps 9:14; 25:5
71:15

51:16
1 Sam 15:22
Ps 40:6

51:17
Ps 34:18

51:19
Ps 4:5
66:13,15

Theme: God will judge the evildoer. Our anger must not block our confidence in God's ability to defeat evil.
Author: David

52 *Written by David to protest against his enemy Doeg (1 Samuel 22), who later slaughtered eighty-five priests and their families.*
You call yourself a *hero*, do you? You *boast* about this evil deed of yours against God's people. 2You are sharp as a tack in plotting your evil tricks. 3How you love wickedness—far more than good! And lying more than truth! 4You love to slander—you love to say anything that will do harm, O man with the lying tongue.

5But God will strike you down and pull you from your home, and drag you away from the land of the living. 6The followers of God will see it happen. They will watch in awe. Then they will laugh and say, 7"See what happens to those who despise God and trust in their wealth, and become ever more bold in their wickedness."

8But I am like a sheltered olive tree protected by the Lord himself. I trust in the mercy of God forever and ever. 9O Lord, I will praise you forever and ever for your punishment. And I will wait for your mercies—for everyone knows what a merciful God you are.

52:2
Ps 5:9; 57:4
59:7

52:3
Ps 36:4; 58:3
Jer 9:5

52:4
Ps 120:3

52:5
Prov 2:22
Ps 27:13
Isa 22:18,19

52:6
Job 22:19
Ps 37:34

52:8
Ps 13:5; 128:3
Jer 11:16

51:14, 15 *forgiveness,* literally, "righteousness." **51:16** *penance,* literally, "a sacrifice." **51:18** *and protect Jerusalem,* literally, "Do good in your good pleasure unto Zion; build the walls of Jerusalem." **51:19** *And when my heart is right,* implied. *then you will rejoice in the good that I do,* literally, "then you will delight in the sacrifice of righteousness." **52:7** *become ever more bold in their wickedness,* literally, "strengthened himself in his wickedness." **52:9** *for your punishment,* literally, "because you have done it."

51:10 Because we are born as sinners (51:5), our natural inclination is to please ourselves rather than God. David followed that inclination when he took another man's wife. We also follow it when we sin in any way, acting according to our own selfish desires. Like David, we must ask God to cleanse us from within (51:7), clearing our hearts and minds for new thoughts and desires. Right conduct can come only from a clean heart and mind. Ask God to create in you a clean heart and mind.

51:12 Do you ever feel stagnant in your faith, like you are just going through the motions? Has sin driven a wedge between you and God, making him seem distant? David felt this way. He had sinned with Bath-sheba and had just been confronted by Nathan the prophet. In his prayer to God he cried, "Restore to me again the joy of your salvation." God wants us to be close to him and to experience his full and complete life. But sin that remains unconfessed makes such intimacy impossible. Confess your sin to God. You may still have to face the consequences, as David did, but God will give back the joy of your relationship with him.

51:13 When God forgives our sin and restores us to a relationship

with him, we want to reach out to others who need this forgiveness and reconciliation. The more you have felt God's forgiveness in your life, the more you desire to tell others about it.

51:17 God wants a broken and contrite heart. In Isaiah 1:12, 13, the Lord says, "Who wants your sacrifices when you have no sorrow for your sins?" You can never please God by outward actions—no matter how good—if your inward heart attitude is not right. Do you have an attitude of remorse for sin?

52:1 Doeg thought he was a great hero—even boasting about his deed. In reality, his deed was evil, an offense to God. It is easy to mistake "accomplishment" with goodness. Just because something is done well or thoroughly doesn't mean it is good (for example, someone may be a great gambler or a skillful liar). Measure all you do by the rule of God's Word, not by how proficiently you do it.

52:8 With God by his side, David compared himself to a sheltered olive tree. Not only is an olive tree one of the longest living trees, but a sheltered tree has even greater longevity. David was contrasting God's eternal protection of the godly with the sudden destruction of the wicked (52:5–7).

Theme: All have sinned. Because of sin, no person can find God on his own. Only God can save us.
Author: David

53:1
Ps 14:1-4

53:2
Ps 33:13-15

53:3
Rom 3:10,12

53:4
Jer 4:22

53:5
Lev 26:17,36
Ps 44:7
Prov 28:1
Jer 6:30; 8:1,2
Ezek 6:5

53:6
Ps 14:7

53 Only a fool would say to himself, "There is no God." And why does he say it? Because of his wicked heart, his dark and evil deeds. His life is corroded with sin.

²God looks down from heaven, searching among all mankind to see if there is a single one who does right and really seeks for God. ³But all have turned their backs on him; they are filthy with sin—corrupt and rotten through and through. Not one is good, not one! ⁴How can this be? Can't they understand anything? For they devour my people like bread and refuse to come to God. ⁵But soon unheard-of terror will fall on them. God will scatter the bones of these, your enemies. They are doomed, for God has rejected them.

⁶Oh, that God would come from Zion now and save Israel! Only when the Lord himself restores them can they ever be really happy again.

Theme: A call for God to overcome enemies. God is our helper, even in times of hurt and betrayal.
Author: David

54:1
2 Chron 20:6
Ps 20:1

54:3
1 Sam 20:1
Ps 36:1; 40:14
86:14; 140:1,4

54:4
Ps 37:17,24,40

54:6
Ps 50:14

54:7
Ps 34:6; 59:10

54 *Written by David at the time the men of Ziph tried to betray him to Saul.* Come with great power, O God, and save me! Defend me with your might! ²Oh, listen to my prayer. ³For violent men have risen against me—ruthless men who care nothing for God are seeking my life.

⁴But God is my helper. He is a friend of mine! ⁵He will cause the evil deeds of my enemies to boomerang upon them. Do as you promised and put an end to these wicked men, O God. ⁶Gladly I bring my sacrifices to you; I will praise your name, O Lord, for it is good.

⁷God has rescued me from all my trouble, and triumphed over my enemies.

Theme: Expressing deep dismay over the treachery of a close friend. When friends hurt us, the burden is too difficult to carry alone.
Author: David

55:1
Ps 27:9; 61:1

55:2
1 Sam 1:16
Ps 77:3; 86:6,7
Isa 38:14

55:3
2 Sam 16:7,8
Ps 17:9; 71:11

55:4
Ps 116:3

55:6
Job 3:13

55 Listen to my prayer, O God; don't hide yourself when I cry to you. ²Hear me, Lord! Listen to me! For I groan and weep beneath my burden of woe.

³My enemies shout against me and threaten me with death. They surround me with terror and plot to kill me. Their fury and hatred rise to engulf me. ⁴My heart is in anguish within me. Stark fear overpowers me. ⁵Trembling and horror overwhelm me. ⁶Oh, for wings like a dove, to fly away and rest! ⁷I would fly to the far-off deserts and stay there. ⁸I would flee to some refuge from all this storm.

⁹O Lord, make these enemies begin to quarrel among themselves—destroy them with their own violence and strife. ¹⁰Though they patrol their walls night and day against invaders, their real problem is internal—wickedness and dishonesty are

53:1 *And why does he say it?* Implied. **54:1** *great power,* literally, "your name." **54:4** *He is a friend of mine,* literally, "The Lord is of them that uphold my soul." **55:9** *destroy them with their own violence and strife,* literally, "for I have seen violence and strife in the city."

53:1 Echoing the message of Psalm 14, David proclaimed that "Only a fool would say to himself, 'There is no God' " (see also Romans 3:10). People may say there is no God in order to cover their sin, to have an excuse to continue in sin, and/or to ignore the Judge in order to avoid the judgment. A "fool" is not necessarily lacking intelligence; many atheists and unbelievers are highly learned. Fools are people who reject God.

54:3, 4 Many of David's psalms follow the pattern found in these two verses—a transition from prayer to praise. He was not afraid to come to God and express his true feelings and needs. Because he did so, his spirit was lifted, and he could not help but praise God, his helper, protector, and friend.

54:5 David said that God causes the evil deeds of his enemies to return upon their own heads. Proverbs 26:27 says that those who set a trap will get caught in it themselves. What we have intended

for others may blow up in our own faces. To be honest before God and others is safer in the long run.

55:1ff This psalm was most likely written during the time of Absalom's rebellion and Ahithophel's betrayal (2 Samuel 15—17). Some say 55:12–14 are messianic because they also describe Judas' betrayal of Christ (Matthew 26:14–16, 20–25).

55:6–8 Even those who are especially close to God, like David was, have moments when they want to get away from it all and escape the problems and pressures of life.

55:10 The people described here were looking for trouble outside their city, watching carefully for attacks from invaders. But the real problem was internal. The people themselves were corrupt. Although we defend ourselves against these external pressures, we often fail to see that our own sins cause many of our troubles.

entrenched in the heart of the city. [11]There is murder and robbery there, and cheating in the markets and wherever you look.

55:11
Ps 5:9; 10:7

[12]It was not an enemy who taunted me—then I could have borne it; I could have hidden and escaped. [13]But it was you, a man like myself, my companion and my friend. [14]What fellowship we had, what wonderful discussions as we walked together to the Temple of the Lord on holy days.

55:13
Ps 41:9

[15]Let death seize them and cut them down in their prime, for there is sin in their homes, and they are polluted to the depths of their souls.

55:16
Ps 57:2,3

55:17
Ps 5:3; 88:13
141:2

[16]But I will call upon the Lord to save me—and he will. [17]I will pray morning, noon, and night, pleading aloud with God; and he will hear and answer. [18]Though the tide of battle runs strongly against me, for so many are fighting me, yet he will rescue me. [19]God himself—God from everlasting ages past—will answer them! For they refuse to fear him or even honor his commands.

55:18
Ps 103:4

55:19
Ps 36:1; 90:2
93:2

[20]This friend of mine betrayed me—I who was at peace with him. He broke his promises. [21]His words were oily smooth, but in his heart was war. His words were sweet, but underneath were daggers.

55:20
Ps 7:3,4; 89:34

55:21
Ps 12:2; 28:3

[22]Give your burdens to the Lord. He will carry them. He will not permit the godly to slip or fall. [23]He will send my enemies to the pit of destruction. Murderers and liars will not live out half their days. But I am trusting you to save me.

55:22
Ps 37:5; 112:6

55:23
Ps 5:6; 56:3,4
73:18

Theme: Trusting in God's care in the midst of fear. When all seems dark, one truth still shines bright: when God is for us, those against us will never succeed.
Author: David

56

Lord, have mercy on me; all day long the enemy troops press in. So many are proud to fight against me; how they long to conquer me.

56:1
Ps 17:9
35:1,25

[3, 4]But when I am afraid, I will put my confidence in you. Yes, I will trust the promises of God. And since I am trusting him, what can mere man do to me? [5]They are always twisting what I say. All their thoughts are how to harm me. [6]They meet together to perfect their plans; they hide beside the trail, listening for my steps, waiting to kill me. [7]They expect to get away with it. Don't let them, Lord. In anger cast them to the ground.

56:3
Ps 11:1
56:10,11

56:5
Ps 41:7
2 Pet 3:15,16

56:6
Ps 17:11; 59:3

[8]You have seen me tossing and turning through the night. You have collected all my tears and preserved them in your bottle! You have recorded every one in your book.

56:7
Ps 36:12; 55:23

56:8
Ps 39:12; 139:3

[9]The very day I call for help, the tide of battle turns. My enemies flee! This one thing I *know: God is for me!* [10, 11]I am trusting God—oh, praise his promises! I am not afraid of anything mere man can do to me! Yes, praise his promises. [12]I will surely do what I have promised, Lord, and thank you for your help. [13]For you have

56:9
Ps 41:11; 118:6

56:13
Ps 33:19; 86:13

55:12-14 Nothing hurts as much as a wound from a "friend." Real friends, however, stick by you in times of trouble and bring healing, love, acceptance, and understanding. There will be times when friends lovingly confront us, and their motives will be to help. What kind of friend are you? Don't betray those whom you love.

55:17 Praying morning, noon, and night is certainly an excellent way to keep in contact with God and maintain correct priorities throughout every day. Daniel followed this pattern (Daniel 6:10), as did Peter (Acts 10:9, 10). The prayers of God's people are the ultimate weapon against the overwhelming evil in the world.

55:22 In our relationship with God, it's easy to continue to carry our own burdens. He wants to carry our burdens, but often we continue to bear them even when we say we are trusting in him. The same strength that carries you can also carry your burdens.

56:1ff This was probably written on the same occasion as Psalm 34, when David fled from Saul to Philistine territory, but then had to pretend insanity before King Achish when some officials grew suspicious of him (1 Samuel 21:10-15).

56:3, 4 How much harm can people do to us? They can inflict

pain, suffering, and death. But no person can rob us of our souls or our future beyond this life. How much harm can we do to ourselves? The worst thing we can do is to turn away from God and lose our bodies, souls, and future beyond this life. Jesus said, "Don't be afraid of those who can kill only your bodies—but can't touch your souls!" (Matthew 10:28). We should fear God, who controls this life and the next.

56:8 Even in our deepest sorrow, God cares! Jesus reminded us further of how much God understands us—he knows even the number of hairs on our heads (Matthew 10:30). Often we waver between faith and fear. When you feel so discouraged that you are sure no one understands, remember that God knows every problem and sees every tear.

56:9-11 Fear can cause physical problems and paralyze us from action. What could be more fearful than being surrounded by an enemy who is pressing in from all sides! Faced with this situation, David suggested several antidotes for fear: (1) remember that God is with you, (2) trust him, and (3) praise him for fulfilling his promises. When faced with persecution, insecurity, or insurmountable odds, use these to overcome your fear.

saved me from death and my feet from slipping, so that I can walk before the Lord in the land of the living.

Theme: God's faithful help and love in times of trouble. When we face trials, God will quiet our hearts and give us confidence.
Author: David

57 O God, have pity, for I am trusting you! I will hide beneath the shadow of your wings until this storm is past. ²I will cry to the God of heaven who does such wonders for me. ³He will send down help from heaven to save me, because of his love and his faithfulness. He will rescue me from these liars who are so intent upon destroying me. ⁴I am surrounded by fierce lions—hotheads whose teeth are sharp as spears and arrows. Their tongues are like swords. ⁵Lord, be exalted above the highest heavens! Show your glory high above the earth. ⁶My enemies have set a trap for me. Frantic fear grips me. They have dug a pitfall in my path. But look! They themselves have fallen into it!

⁷O God, my heart is quiet and confident. No wonder I can sing your praises! ⁸Rouse yourself, my soul! Arise, O harp and lyre! Let us greet the dawn with song! ⁹I will thank you publicly throughout the land. I will sing your praises among the nations. ¹⁰Your kindness and love are as vast as the heavens. Your faithfulness is higher than the skies.

¹¹Yes, be exalted, O God, above the heavens. May your glory shine throughout the earth.

Theme: A prayer for God's justice. When no justice can be found, rejoice in knowing that justice will triumph because there is a God who will judge with complete fairness.
Author: David, at a time when men in authority were twisting justice

58 Justice? You high and mighty politicians don't even know the meaning of the word! Fairness? Which of you has any left? Not one! All your dealings are crooked: you give "justice" in exchange for bribes. ³These men are born sinners, lying from their earliest words! ⁴, ⁵They are poisonous as deadly snakes, cobras that close their ears to the most expert of charmers.

⁶O God, break off their fangs. Tear out the teeth of these young lions, Lord. ⁷Let them disappear like water into thirsty ground. Make their weapons useless in their hands. ⁸Let them be as snails that dissolve into slime; and as those who die at birth, who never see the sun. ⁹God will sweep away both old and young. He will destroy them more quickly than a cooking pot can feel the blazing fire of thorns beneath it.

¹⁰The godly shall rejoice in the triumph of right; they shall walk the blood-

58:1, 2 *All your dealings are crooked: you give "justice" in exchange for bribes*, literally, "you deal out the violence of your hands in the land." **58:7** *Make their weapons useless in their hands*, or, "Let them be trodden down and wither like grass." **58:10** *in the triumph of right*, literally, "when he sees the vengeance."

Cross-references (left margin):

57:1
Ruth 2:12
Ps 36:7; 91:4
57:2
Ps 138:8
57:3
Ps 18:16; 25:10
56:2; 144:5,7
57:4
Ps 58:6; 64:3
57:5
Ps 108:5
57:6
Ps 10:9; 35:7
Prov 26:27
57:7
Ps 108:1-5
112:7
57:8
Ps 150:3
57:10
Ps 36:5

58:1
Ps 82:2; 94:20
58:3
Ps 53:3
58:4
Ps 81:11; 140:3
58:6
Ps 3:7
58:7
Ps 64:3
58:9
Job 27:21
58:10
Ps 32:11; 64:10
68:22,23; 91:8

57:1ff This psalm was probably written when David was hiding in a cave from Saul (see 1 Samuel 22—24).

57:3 When we think of faithfulness, we may recall a friend or a spouse. Embodied in this concept is knowing that no matter how unloveable we may act, the faithful one still accepts and loves us. At a deeper level is the loyalty to keep promises—whether they be promises of support or the vows of marriage. God's faithfulness includes these aspects, but he completes them to perfection—something we as humans are unable to do. He loves us (in spite of our constant bent toward sin) and keeps all the promises he has made to us, even when we break our promises to him.

57:4 At times, we may be surrounded by people who gossip about us or criticize us. Verbal cruelty can damage us as badly as physical abuse. Rather than throwing back more unacceptable talk, we, like David, can quietly talk with God about the problem.

57:7 David's quiet confidence in God contrasted sharply with his enemies' loud lying and boasting. When confronted with verbal attacks, the best defense is simply to be quiet and praise God,

realizing that our confidence is in his kindness, love, and faithfulness (57:10). In times of great suffering, don't turn inward to self-pity or outward to revenge, but upward to God.

58:1ff This is called an "imprecatory" psalm because it is a cry for justice so intense that it seems, at first glance, to be a call for revenge. (For more about imprecatory psalms, see the note on Psalm 35:1ff.)

58:1ff The Old Testament is filled with references about justice and it is a key topic in the Psalms. Unfortunately, many judges and rulers in ancient times took justice into their own hands. They had complete authority with no accountability, and had the power to make their own laws. When earth's judges are corrupt, there is little hope of justice in this life. But God loves justice, and those who obey him will see perfect justice in eternity.

58:6—9 David pronounced seven curses on the men in authority who abused the judicial system. The number seven represented completion or perfection. Thus a sevenfold curse showed David's desire for complete destruction of these wicked men.

stained fields of slaughtered, wicked men. ¹¹Then at last everyone will know that good is rewarded, and that there is a God who judges justly here on earth.

58:11
Ps 9:8; 18:20
Lk 6:23,35

Theme: Prayer and praise for God's saving help.
God's constant love is our place of safety in a wicked world.
Author: David

59 *Written by David at the time King Saul set guards at his home to capture and kill him. (1 Samuel 19:11)*

O my God, save me from my enemies. Protect me from these who have come to destroy me. ²Preserve me from these criminals, these murderers. ³They lurk in ambush for my life. Strong men are out there waiting. And not, O Lord, because I've done them wrong. ⁴Yet they prepare to kill me. Lord, waken! See what is happening! Help me! ⁵(And O Jehovah, God of heaven's armies, God of Israel, arise and punish the heathen nations surrounding us.) Do not spare these evil, treacherous men. ⁶At evening they come to spy, slinking around like dogs that prowl the city. ⁷I hear them shouting insults and cursing God, for "No one will hear us," they think. ⁸Lord, laugh at them! (And scoff at these surrounding nations too.)

⁹O God my Strength! I will sing your praises, for you are my place of safety. ¹⁰My God is changeless in his love for me and he will come and help me. He will let me see my wish come true upon my enemies. ¹¹Don't kill them—for my people soon forget such lessons—but stagger them with your power and bring them to their knees. Bring them to the dust, O Lord our shield. ¹², ¹³They are proud, cursing liars. Angrily destroy them. Wipe them out. (And let the nations find out too that God rules in Israel and will reign throughout the world.) ¹⁴, ¹⁵Let these evil men slink back at evening, and prowl the city all night before they are satisfied, howling like dogs and searching for food.

¹⁶But as for me, I will sing each morning about your power and mercy. For you have been my high tower of refuge, a place of safety in the day of my distress. ¹⁷O my Strength, to you I sing my praises; for you are my high tower of safety, my God of mercy.

59:1
Ps 20:1; 143:9
59:2
Ps 14:4; 28:3
94:16; 139:19
59:3
Ps 7:3,4; 56:6
69:4
59:4
Ps 35:19,23
59:5
Ps 9:5; 84:8
59:7
Job 22:13
Ps 10:11; 73:11
94:47
59:8
Ps 2:4; 37:13
59:9
Ps 9:9
59:10
Ps 54:7
59:11
Ps 106:27
144:6
59:12
Ps 10:7; 83:18
59:16
Ps 21:13; 46:1
101:1
59:17
Ps 59:9,10

Theme: Real help comes from God alone. When a situation seems out of control, we can trust God to do mighty things.
Author: David, when Israel was away at war with Syria in the north, and Edom invaded Judah from the south (2 Samuel 8)

60 *Written by David at the time he was at war with Syria, with the outcome still uncertain; this was when Joab, captain of his forces, slaughtered 12,000 men of Edom in the Valley of Salt.*

O God, you have rejected us and broken our defenses; you have become angry and deserted us. Lord, restore us again to your favor. ²You have caused this nation to tremble in fear; you have torn it apart. Lord, heal it now, for it is shaken to its depths. ³You have been very hard on us and made us reel beneath your blows.

⁴, ⁵But you have given us a banner to rally to; all who love truth will rally to it;

60:1
Ps 44:9; 79:5
80:3
60:2
2 Chron 7:14
Ps 18:7
60:3
Ps 66:12
60:4
Ps 11:12; 13:2

60:4, 5 *all who love truth will rally to it,* literally, "that it may be displayed because of the truth."

58:11 Of all people, our national leaders should be just and fair. When they are unjust and unfair, people suffer. The rich get richer, the poor get poorer, politicians wrest power from the people, the nation deteriorates, and God is ignored. When right triumphs at last, "the godly shall rejoice" (58:10). Be assured that there is a day of accountability and God will judge fairly. Be careful that you never side with injustice lest you find yourself standing before an angry Judge.

59:7, 8 Vile men curse God as if he cannot hear and will not respond. But God listens patiently until that day when those curses will fall back in judgment like stones from heaven. Evil people live their lives as if God cannot see and will not punish. But God watches patiently until that day when their deeds rise up to accuse them. We who are believers must be careful that we do not follow the same foolish practices as evil people. We must remember

that God hears and sees everything we do.

59:10 David was hunted by those whose love had turned to jealousy, and this was driving them to murder him. Trusted friends, and even his son, turned against him. What changeable love! But David knew that God's love for him was *changeless.* God's love for all who trust him is also changeless. When the love of others fails or disappoints us, we can rest in God's changeless love.

60:1ff This psalm gives us information about David's reign not found in the books of 1 and 2 Samuel or 1 and 2 Chronicles. Although the setting of the psalm is found in 2 Samuel 8, that passage makes no reference to the fact that David's forces met stiff resistance (60:1–3) and apparently even a temporary defeat (60:9, 10). The truth is that the closer we get to God, the stronger the enemy attacks us because we become a threat to their evil and selfish way of living.

60:6
Gen 33:17
49:10
Josh 13:31; 17:7
Ps 89:35

60:8
2 Sam 8:1,2,14

60:9
Ps 44:9

60:11
Ps 146:3

60:12
Num 24:15-19
Ps 44:5; 118:16

then you can deliver your beloved people. Use your strong right arm to rescue us. 6, 7God has promised to help us. He has vowed it by his holiness! No wonder I exult! "Shechem, Succoth, Gilead, Manasseh—still are mine!" he says. "Judah shall continue to produce kings, and Ephraim great warriors. 8Moab shall become my lowly servant, and Edom my slave. And I will shout in triumph over the Philistines."

9, 10Who will bring me in triumph into Edom's strong cities? God will! He who cast us off! He who abandoned us to our foes! 11Yes, Lord, help us against our enemies, for man's help is useless.

12With God's help we shall do mighty things, for he will trample down our foes.

Theme: Prayer for security and assurance. Wherever we are, we can trust that God will be there to answer our cries for help.
Author: David, written when he was forced to escape during the days of Absalom's rebellion (2 Samuel 15—18), or after he had narrowly escaped one of Saul's efforts to kill him while hiding in the wilderness

61:1
Ps 64:1; 86:6

61:2
Ps 18:2; 77:3

61:3
Ps 62:7

61:4
Ps 17:8; 23:6
27:4; 91:4

61:5
Ps 56:12; 86:11

61:7
Ps 40:11; 41:12

61:8
Ps 30:4; 65:1

61 O God, listen to me! Hear my prayer! 2For wherever I am, though far away at the ends of the earth, I will cry to you for help. When my heart is faint and overwhelmed, lead me to the mighty, towering Rock of safety. 3For you are my refuge, a high tower where my enemies can never reach me. 4I shall live forever in your tabernacle; oh, to be safe beneath the shelter of your wings! 5For you have heard my vows, O God, to praise you every day, and you have given me the blessings you reserve for those who reverence your name.

6You will give me added years of life, as rich and full as those of many generations, all packed into one. 7And I shall live before the Lord forever. Oh, send your lovingkindness and truth to guard and watch over me, 8and I will praise your name continually, fulfilling my vow of praising you each day.

Theme: Placing all hope in God. Knowing that God is in control allows us to wait patiently for him to rescue us. True relief does not come when the problem is resolved because more problems are on the way! True relief comes from an enduring hope in God's ultimate salvation. Only then will all trials be resolved.
Author: David, written during the days of Absalom's rebellion (2 Samuel 15—18)

62:1
Ps 33:20; 37:39

62:2
Ps 59:17; 89:26

62:3
Ps 28:3; 55:21

62:7
Ps 46:1

62 I stand silently before the Lord, waiting for him to rescue me. For salvation comes from him alone. 2Yes, he alone is my Rock, my rescuer, defense and fortress. Why then should I be tense with fear when troubles come?

3, 4But what is this? They pick on me at a time when my throne is tottering; they plot my death and use lies and deceit to try to force me from the throne. They are so friendly to my face while cursing in their hearts!

5But I stand silently before the Lord, waiting for him to rescue me. For salvation comes from him alone. 6Yes, he alone is my Rock, my rescuer, defense and fortress—why then should I be tense with fear when troubles come?

7My protection and success come from God alone. He is my refuge, a Rock

61:5 *to praise,* implied in vs 8.　**61:6** *me,* literally, "to the days of the king."　**62:3, 4** *when my throne,* implied.
62:7 *success,* literally, "glory."

60:4, 5 God loves truth and the people who belong to God will rally to truth like soldiers to their flag. The apostle John wrote, "the Holy Spirit . . . shall guide you into all truth" (John 16:13). Let the truth of God's Word stir you to action and rally you to his cause.

60:6–10 God said the cities of Israel were still his and he knew the future of each of the nations. When the world seems out of control, we must remind ourselves that God owns the cities and he knows the future of every nation. God is in control.

60:8 David mentioned the enemy nations that surrounded Israel. Moab lay directly to the east, Edom to the south, and Philistia to the west. At the time this psalm was written, David was fighting Syria to the north. Although he was literally surrounded by enemies, David believed that God would help him triumph.

61:1 David must have been far from home when he wrote this psalm. Fortunately, God is not limited to any geographic location.

Among people and surroundings that are unknown, God never changes. His presence is always with us.

61:5 David continually praised God through both the good and difficult times of his life. He made a commitment to praise God every day which showed his reverence for God. Do you find something to praise God for each day? As you do, you will find your heart elevated from daily distractions to lasting confidence.

61:7 Here David compared the lasting security of living forever with God to the present feelings of uncertainty in his strange surroundings (61:1, 2).

62:3–6 Prayer can release our tensions in times of emotional stress. Trusting God to be our Rock, rescuer, defense, and fortress (62:2) changes our entire outlook on life. No longer are we held captive by hurtful treatment from friends or relatives, but are released to follow an unchanging God, our Rock and fortress.

where no enemy can reach me. 8O my people, trust him all the time. Pour out your longings before him, for he can help! 9The greatest of men, or the lowest—both alike are nothing in his sight. They weigh less than air on scales.

62:8
Lam 2:19

62:9
Isa 40:15

10, 11Don't become rich by extortion and robbery; if your riches increase, don't be proud. 12God has said it many times, that power belongs to him; (and also, O Lord, steadfast love belongs to you). He rewards each one of us according to what our works deserve.

62:10
Mk 10:24
1 Tim 6:10

Theme: A desire for God's presence, provision, and protection. No matter where we are, our desire should be for God because only he satisfies fully.
Author: David

63

A Psalm of David when he was hiding in the wilderness of Judea.

O God, my God! How I search for you! How I thirst for you in this parched and weary land where there is no water. How I long to find you! 2How I wish I could go into your sanctuary to see your strength and glory, 3for your love and kindness are better to me than life itself. How I praise you! 4I will bless you as long as I live, lifting up my hands to you in prayer. 5At last I shall be fully satisfied; I will praise you with great joy.

63:1
Ps 42:2; 84:2

63:2
Ps 27:4

63:3
Ps 69:16

63:4
Ps 28:2; 104:33

6I lie awake at night thinking of you— 7of how much you have helped me—and how I rejoice through the night beneath the protecting shadow of your wings. 8I follow close behind you, protected by your strong right arm. 9But those plotting to destroy me shall go down to the depths of hell. 10They are doomed to die by the sword, to become the food of jackals. 11But I will rejoice in God. All who trust in him exult, while liars shall be silenced.

63:5
Ps 36:8; 71:23

63:6
Ps 4:4; 16:7

63:8
Ps 18:35

63:9
Ps 40:14

Theme: A complaint against conspiracy. When others conspire against us, we can ask God for protection because he knows everything.
Author: David

64

Lord, listen to my complaint: Oh, preserve my life from the conspiracy of these wicked men, these gangs of criminals. 3They cut me down with sharpened tongues; they aim their bitter words like arrows straight at my heart. 4They shoot from ambush at the innocent. Suddenly the deed is done, yet they are not afraid. 5They encourage each other to do evil. They meet in secret to set their traps. "He will never notice them here," they say. 6They keep a sharp lookout for opportunities of crime. They spend long hours with all their endless evil thoughts and plans.

64:1
Ps 56:6; 59:2

64:3
Ps 140:3

64:4
Ps 10:8; 11:2

64:5
Ps 140:5

64:6
Ps 49:11

7But God himself will shoot them down. Suddenly his arrow will pierce them. 8They will stagger backward, destroyed by those they spoke against. All who see it happening will scoff at them. 9Then everyone shall stand in awe and confess the

64:7
Ps 7:12,13

64:8
Ps 9:3

63:11 *I*, literally, "the king." **64:6** *They spend long hours with all their endless evil thoughts and plans,* literally, "And the inward thought and the heart of everyone is deep."

62:9-12 When we weigh people on the scales of importance, certain things such as wealth, honor, power, or prestige add immeasurably to a person's importance in our eyes. But God cancels out all of these things so that all people are weighed equally in his eyes. What, then, can tilt the scales when God weighs us? The work we do for him (62:12). Wealth, honor, power, or prestige add nothing to our "weight" in God's eyes, but the faithful work we do for him has eternal value.

63:1ff Psalms 61, 62, and 63 were probably written when David was seeking refuge during Absalom's rebellion (2 Samuel 15—18).

63:1-5 Hiding from his enemies in the barren wilderness of Judea, David was intensely lonely. He longed for a friend he could trust to ease his loneliness. No wonder he cried out, "O God, my God! How I search for you! How I thirst for you," as he sought lasting satisfaction. If you are lonely or thirst for something lasting in your life, remember David's prayer. God alone can satisfy our deepest longings!

63:6 A cure for sleepless nights is to turn our thoughts to God. There are many reasons we can't sleep—illness, stress, worry—but sleepless nights can be turned into quiet times of reflection and worship. Use them to review how God has guided and helped you.

64:1ff Evil can come in the form of a conspiracy or an ambush (64:1, 4) because Satan wants to catch us unprepared. He tempts us in our weakest areas when we least expect it. But God himself will shoot down our enemies (64:7), whether they be physical or spiritual. Wickedness may seem widespread and affect us in many ways, but the final victory already belongs to God and those who trust and believe in him.

64:1, 2 We may believe that God wants to hear only certain requests from us. While it is true that we should offer praise, confession, and respectful petitions, it is true also that God is willing to listen to *anything* we want to tell him. David expressed himself honestly, asking God to listen to all his complaints. God will always listen attentively and will fully understand us.

64:10
Ps 11:1; 32:11

65:1
Ps 86:9; 116:18
65:3
Ps 38:4; 40:12
Heb 9:14
65:4
Ps 33:12; 36:8
65:5
Ps 45:4; 48:10
65:6
Ps 93:1; 95:4
65:7
Ps 89:9
Isa 17:12,13
65:8
Ps 139:9,10
65:9
Ps 46:4
104:13,14,24
65:11
Job 38:26,27
65:13
Ps 98:8; 144:13
Isa 30:23; 55:12

66:3
Ps 18:44; 47:2
66:4
Ps 22:27; 67:4
66:5
Ps 46:8
66:6
Ex 14:21
66:7
Ps 11:4; 145:13
66:9
Ps 30:3
66:10
Ps 17:3

greatness of the miracles of God; at last they will realize what amazing things he does. 10And the godly shall rejoice in the Lord, and trust and praise him.

Theme: God provides abundantly. We can be thankful to God for his many blessings.
Author: David

65 O God in Zion, we wait before you in silent praise, and thus fulfill our vow. And because you answer prayer, all mankind will come to you with their requests. 3Though sins fill our hearts, you forgive them all. 4How greatly to be envied are those you have chosen to come and live with you within the holy tabernacle courts! What joys await us among all the good things there. 5With dread deeds and awesome power you will defend us from our enemies, O God who saves us. You are the only hope of all mankind throughout the world and far away upon the sea.

6He formed the mountains by his mighty strength. 7He quiets the raging oceans and all the world's clamor. 8In the farthest corners of the earth the glorious acts of God shall startle everyone. The dawn and sunset shout for joy! 9He waters the earth to make it fertile. The rivers of God will not run dry! He prepares the earth for his people and sends them rich harvests of grain. 10He waters the furrows with abundant rain. Showers soften the earth, melting the clods and causing seeds to sprout across the land. 11, 12Then he crowns it all with green, lush pastures in the wilderness; hillsides blossom with joy. 13The pastures are filled with flocks of sheep, and the valleys are carpeted with grain. All the world shouts with joy, and sings.

Theme: God answers prayer. Individually and as a body of believers, we should praise and worship God.
Author: Anonymous, written after a great victory in battle

66 Sing to the Lord, all the earth! 2Sing of his glorious name! Tell the world how wonderful he is.

3How awe-inspiring are your deeds, O God! How great your power! No wonder your enemies surrender! 4All the earth shall worship you and sing of your glories. 5Come, see the glorious things God has done. What marvelous miracles happen to his people! 6He made a dry road through the sea for them. They went across on foot. What excitement and joy there was that day!

7Because of his great power he rules forever. He watches every movement of the nations. O rebel lands, he will deflate your pride.

8Let everyone bless God and sing his praises, 9for he holds our lives in his hands. And he holds our feet to the path. 10You have purified us with fire, O Lord, like silver in a crucible. 11You captured us in your net and laid great burdens on our

65:5 *will defend us from our enemies,* literally, "will answer in righteousness." **66:10** *You have purified us with fire,* implied.

65:1, 2 In Old Testament times, vows were taken seriously and fulfilled completely. No one had to make a vow, but once made, it was binding (Deuteronomy 23:21–23). The vow being fulfilled here is of silent praise to God for his answers to prayer.

65:3 Although sins fill our hearts, God will forgive them all if we ask sincerely. Do you feel as though God could never forgive you, that your sins are too many, or that some of them are too great? The good news is that God can and will forgive them all. Nobody is beyond redemption, and nobody is so full of sin that he cannot be made clean.

65:4 Access to God, the joy of living in the Tabernacle courts, was a great honor. God had chosen a special group of Israelites, the tribe of Levi, to serve as ministers in the Tabernacle (Numbers 3:5–51). They were the only ones who could enter the sacred rooms where God's presence resided. Because of Jesus' death on the cross, all believers today have personal access to God's presence everywhere and any time. We gain this access into God's presence by believing in Christ's death and resurrection.

65:6–13 This harvest psalm glorifies God the Creator as reflected in the beauty of nature. Nature helps us understand something of God's character. The Jews believed that God's care of nature was a sign of his love and provision for them. Nature shows God's generosity—giving us more than we need or deserve. Reflecting on such abundant generosity should produce grateful and generous hearts in us.

66:5–7 The writer was referring to the famous story when God rescued the Israelites by parting the Red Sea. God saved the Israelites then, and he continues to save his people today.

66:10–12 Just as fire refines silver in the smelting process, trials refine our character. They bring a new and deeper wisdom to our lives, helping us to discern truth from falsehood and equipping us with the discipline to carry out what we know is right. Above all, these trials help us realize that life is a gift from God to be cherished, not a right to be taken for granted.

backs. 12You sent troops to ride across our broken bodies. We went through fire and flood. But in the end, you brought us into wealth and great abundance.

66:12
Ps 18:19

13Now I have come to your Temple with burnt offerings to pay my vows. 14For when I was in trouble I promised you many offerings. 15That is why I am bringing you these fat male goats, rams and calves. The smoke of their sacrifice shall rise before you.

66:13
Ps 22:25
66:15
Num 6:14
Ps 51:19

16Come and hear, all of you who reverence the Lord, and I will tell you what he did for me: 17For I cried to him for help, with praises ready on my tongue. 18He would not have listened if I had not confessed my sins. 19But he listened! He heard my prayer! He paid attention to it!

66:16
Ps 34:11
66:18
Ps 18:41
66:19
Ps 116:1,2

20Blessed be God who didn't turn away when I was praying, and didn't refuse me his kindness and love.

66:20
Ps 22:24; 68:35

Theme: Joy comes from spreading the news about God around the world.
Author: Anonymous, probably written for one of the harvest festivals

67 O God, in mercy bless us; let your face beam with joy as you look down at us.

67:1
Num 6:25
Ps 4:6
80:3,7,19

2Send us around the world with the news of your saving power and your eternal plan for all mankind. 3How everyone throughout the earth will praise the Lord! 4How glad the nations will be, singing for joy because you are their King and will give true justice to their people! 5Praise God, O world! May all the peoples of the earth give thanks to you. 6, 7For the earth has yielded abundant harvests. God, even our own God, will bless us. And peoples from remotest lands will worship him.

67:3
Ps 66:4
67:4
Ps 96:10,13
67:6
Lev 26:4
Ps 22:27

Theme: Remembering God's glory and power. Times and cultures change, but God is always majestically present as protector and provider.
Author: David

68 Arise, O God, and scatter all your enemies! Chase them away! 2Drive them off like smoke before the wind; melt them like wax in fire! So let the wicked perish at the presence of God.

68:1
Num 10:35
68:2
Ps 37:20
Isa 9:18

3But may the godly man exult. May he rejoice and be merry. 4Sing praises to the Lord! Raise your voice in song to him who rides upon the clouds! Jehovah is his name—oh, rejoice in his presence. 5He is a father to the fatherless; he gives justice to the widows, for he is holy. 6He gives families to the lonely, and releases

68:4
Ps 40:3; 68:33
68:5
Deut 10:18

66:12 *You sent troops to ride across our broken bodies,* literally, "You caused men to ride over our heads."
67:4 *are their King,* literally, "govern the nations." 68:4 *clouds,* or, "deserts." 68:5 *for he is holy,* literally, "in his holy habitation."

66:14, 15 People sometimes make bargains with God, saying, "If you heal me (or get me out of this mess), I'll obey you for the rest of my life." However, soon after they recover, the vow is often forgotten and the old lifestyle resumes. This writer made a promise to God, but he remembered the promise and paid his vow. God always keeps his promises, and wants us to follow his example. Be careful to follow through on whatever you promise to do.

66:16–20 The writer cried to God for help, offering praise while confessing his sins. Confession acknowledges our sin; praise acknowledges God's gracious forgiveness; and crying out to God in prayer acknowledges that we trust God to forgive our sins. No believer's life is complete without daily confession, praise, and prayer.

66:18 We must constantly confess our sins because we continue to do wrong. But confession can only be constant if we are listening to God and are sensitive to our sins. David confessed his sin and prayed, "Cleanse me from these hidden faults. And keep me from deliberate wrongs" (Psalm 19:12, 13). If we *refuse* to repent, if we harbor and cherish certain sins, then a wall is placed between us and God. We may not be able to confess *every* sin we have ever committed, but our attitude toward life should be one of confession and obedience.

67:2 Could the psalmist have looked across the years to see the

gospel go throughout the earth? This psalm surely speaks of the fulfillment of the Great Commission (Matthew 28:18–20), when Jesus commanded that the message of God's Good News be taken to all nations. Count yourself among that great crowd of believers worldwide who know the Savior, praise him for his Good News, and share that gospel until there is an abundant harvest.

68:1ff This psalm begins just like Moses' song in Numbers 10:33–35 as the Israelites followed the Ark. It was written in a similar setting, perhaps when David led a joyous procession that brought the Ark from the house of Obed-edom to Jerusalem (2 Samuel 6:11–15).

68:3–6 With shouts of praise and the sound of trumpets, David and his people took the holy Ark toward Mount Zion. It was a time to sing praises to the Lord, whose presence brings great joy. Only in him is there hope for the orphans, widows, prisoners, and all others who are lonely. If you are among the ranks of the lonely or disadvantaged, join King David in praise and discover great joy as you invite him to be with you.

68:4–6 David praised God for his protection and provision. When we see God's true majesty, our response should be to praise him. This song was a song of faith, since many of these benefits had not yet come true in David's time. It is a song of faith for us as well. We must continue to trust God because, in time, he will fulfill all his promises.

prisoners from jail, singing with joy! But for rebels there is famine and distress.

68:7
Ex 13:21

7O God, when you led your people through the wilderness, 8the earth trembled and the heavens shook. Mount Sinai quailed before you—the God of Israel.

68:8
Ex 19:18

9, 10You sent abundant rain upon your land, O God, to refresh it in its weariness! There your people lived, for you gave them this home when they were destitute.

68:9
Deut 11:11

11, 12, 13The Lord speaks. The enemy flees. The women at home cry out the happy news: "The armies that came to destroy us have fled!" Now all the women of Israel are dividing the booty. See them sparkle with jewels of silver and gold, covered all over as wings cover doves! 14God scattered their enemies like snowflakes melting in the forests of Zalmon.

68:11
Ex 15:20

68:15
Deut 12:4,5

15, 16O mighty mountains in Bashan! O splendid many-peaked ranges! Well may you look with envy at Mount Zion, the mount where God has chosen to live forever. 17Surrounded by unnumbered chariots, the Lord moves on from Mount Sinai and comes to his holy temple high upon Mount Zion. 18He ascends the heights, leading many captives in his train. He receives gifts for men, even those who once were rebels. God will live among us here.

68:17
Deut 33:2

68:18
Eph 4:8
1 Tim 1:13

68:19
Ps 55:22; 65:5
Isa 46:4

19What a glorious Lord! He who daily bears our burdens also gives us our salvation.

68:20
Ps 56:13

20He frees us! He rescues us from death. 21But he will crush his enemies, for they refuse to leave their guilty, stubborn ways. 22The Lord says, "Come," to all his people's enemies; they are hiding on Mount Hermon's highest slopes and deep within the sea! 23His people must destroy them. Cover your feet with their blood; dogs will eat them.

68:21
Ps 110:6
Heb 3:13

68:22
Amos 9:1-3

68:23
1 Kgs 21:19
Ps 58:10
Jer 15:3

24The procession of God my King moves onward to the sanctuary— 25singers in front, musicians behind, girls playing the timbrels in between. 26Let all the people of Israel praise the Lord, who is Israel's fountain. 27The little tribe of Benjamin leads the way. The princes and elders of Judah, and the princes of Zebulun and Naphtali are right behind. 28Summon your might; display your strength, O God, for you have done such mighty things for us.

68:25
Ex 15:20
1 Chron 13:8

68:26
Deut 33:28
Ps 22:22,23

68:28
Ps 29:11; 44:4

68:29
Ps 72:10

29The kings of the earth are bringing their gifts to your temple in Jerusalem. 30Rebuke our enemies, O Lord. Bring them—submissive, tax in hand. Scatter all who delight in war. 31Egypt will send gifts of precious metals. Ethiopia will stretch out her hands to God in adoration. 32Sing to the Lord, O kingdoms of the earth—sing praises to the Lord, 33to him who rides upon the ancient heavens, whose mighty voice thunders from the sky.

68:30
Ps 89:10

68:32
Ps 102:21,22

68:33
Deut 10:14
Ps 18:10; 29:4

68:35
Deut 10:17
Ps 29:11; 47:2

34Power belongs to God! His majesty shines down on Israel; his strength is mighty in the heavens. 35What awe we feel, kneeling here before him in the

68:11-13 *at home,* literally, "among the sheepfolds." **68:22** *to all his people's enemies,* literally, "I will bring back from Bashan." **68:27** *are right behind,* implied. **68:30** *submissive, tax in hand,* literally, "everyone submitting himself with pieces of silver." An alternate rendering of vs 30 could be, "Trample upon those who lust after the tribute of smaller nations, and who delight in aggressive wars."

68:8 Mount Sinai had a prominent role in Israelite history. It was at Mount Sinai that God met Moses and commissioned him to lead Israel out of Egypt (Exodus 3:1–10). It was to Mount Sinai that the nation of Israel returned and received God's laws (Exodus 19:1–3), and God's presence made the entire mountain quake (Exodus 19:18). This sacred mountain served to remind the people of God's words and promises.

68:15, 16 Bashan, the land northeast of Israel, was the home of mighty mountains, including Mount Hermon, the tallest and most awesome mountain in the region. God's choice of Mount Zion, a foothill by comparison, for the site of the Temple led the psalmist to write poetically of the envy of the mountains of Bashan.

68:17 This picture of the Lord moving from Mount Sinai to Mount Zion probably describes the moving of the Ark of the Covenant into Jerusalem. This psalm celebrates the final stages of a journey which began at Mount Sinai with the construction of the Ark and finally ended appropriately at Mount Zion, the chosen dwelling place of God among his people.

68:18 This verse is quoted in Ephesians 4:8 as referring to the ministry of the ascended Christ. It celebrates his victory over evil.

68:19–21 God frees his people and crushes his enemies. Salvation is freedom from sin and death. Those who refuse to turn to God will be crushed by sin and death. They will be trapped by the sin they loved and destroyed by the death they feared. How much better it is for those who love God and fear the consequences of sin.

68:19–21 Each day, we must deal with our share of earthly burdens. As we face these burdens, the Lord is there to help us bear them. Each morning, praise God for the strength he will send you today. It is as sure as the sunrise.

68:34, 35 We should feel an overwhelming sense of awe as we kneel before the Lord in his sanctuary. Surrounding us are countless signs of his wonderful power. Shining down upon us are countless signs of his majesty. Unlimited power and unspeakable majesty leave us breathless in his presence. When you catch your breath, praise the Lord!

sanctuary. The God of Israel gives strength and mighty power to his people. Blessed be God!

Theme: A cry of distress in a sea of trouble. We may have to suffer severely for our devotion to God, but that should cause us to look forward with joy to the day when evil and injustice will be gone forever.
Author: David

69 Save me, O my God. The floods have risen. Deeper and deeper I sink in the mire; the waters rise around me. 3I have wept until I am exhausted; my throat is dry and hoarse; my eyes are swollen with weeping, waiting for my God to act. 4I cannot even count all those who hate me without cause. They are influential men, these who plot to kill me though I am innocent. They demand that I be punished for what I didn't do.

5O God, you know so well how stupid I am, and you know all my sins. 6O Lord God of the armies of heaven, don't let me be a stumbling block to those who trust in you. O God of Israel, don't let me cause them to be confused, 7though I am mocked and cursed and shamed for your sake. 8Even my own brothers pretend they don't know me! 9My zeal for God and his work burns hot within me. And because I advocate your cause, your enemies insult me even as they insult you. 10How they scoff and mock me when I mourn and fast before the Lord! 11How they talk about me when I wear sackcloth to show my humiliation and sorrow for my sins! 12I am the talk of the town and the song of the drunkards. 13But I keep right on praying to you, Lord. For now is the time—you are bending down to hear! You are ready with a plentiful supply of love and kindness. Now answer my prayer and rescue me as you promised. 14Pull me out of this mire. Don't let me sink in. Rescue me from those who hate me, and from these deep waters I am in.

15Don't let the floods overwhelm me, or the ocean swallow me; save me from the pit that threatens me. 16O Jehovah, answer my prayers, for your lovingkindness is wonderful; your mercy is so plentiful, so tender and so kind. 17Don't hide from me, for I am in deep trouble. Quick! Come and save me. 18Come, Lord, and rescue me. Ransom me from all my enemies. 19You know how they talk about me, and how they so shamefully dishonor me. You see them all and know what each has said.

20Their contempt has broken my heart; my spirit is heavy within me. If even one would show some pity, if even one would comfort me! 21For food they gave me gall; for my awful thirst they offered vinegar. 22Let their joys turn to ashes and their peace disappear; 23let darkness, blindness and great feebleness be theirs. 24Pour out your fury upon them; consume them with the fierceness of your anger. 25Let their homes be desolate and abandoned. 26For they persecute the one you have smitten, and scoff at the pain of the one you have pierced. 27Pile their sins high and do not overlook them. 28Let these men be blotted from the list of the living; do not give them the joys of life with the righteous.

69:3	Ps 6:6 119:82,123
69:4	Ps 35:11; 59:3 Jn 15:25
69:5	Ps 44:21
69:6	2 Sam 12:14
69:8	Ps 31:11; 38:11
69:9	Jn 2:17
69:12	Job 30:9
69:13	Ps 32:6
69:14	Ps 144:7
69:15	Ps 124:4,5
69:18	Ps 49:15 119:134
69:19	Ps 22:6,7 Isa 53:3
69:21	Mt 27:48 Jn 19:29
69:25	Lk 13:35 Acts 1:20
69:26	2 Chron 28:9 Isa 53:4
69:28	Ex 32:33 Lk 10:20 Rev 3:5; 13:8 20:15

69:9 *his work,* literally, "for your house." **69:13** *and rescue me as you promised,* literally, "in the truth of your salvation." **69:17** *me,* literally, "your servant." **69:22** *their joys,* literally, "their table." **69:28** *Let these men be blotted from the list of the living,* or, "Let them be blotted out of the book of life."

69:1ff This is one of the psalms most quoted in the New Testament, and is often applied to the ministry and suffering of Jesus. Verse 4, like John 15:25, speaks of Jesus' many enemies. The experience of being mocked by his brothers (69:8) is expressed in John 7:5. Verse 9 portrays David's zeal for God; Christ showed great zeal when he threw the moneychangers out of the Temple (John 2:14–17). Paul quoted part of 69:9 in Romans 15:3. Christ's great suffering is portrayed in 69:20, 21 (Matthew 27:24; Mark 15:23; Luke 23:36; John 19:28–30). Verses 22 through 28 are quoted in Romans 11:9, 10; and Peter applied 69:25 to Judas (Acts 1:20).

69:3 David wept until he was physically exhausted, with a dry throat and swollen eyes. He wept until he could weep no more, yet he still trusted God to save him. When devastated by death or tragedy, we need not collapse or despair because we can turn to God and ask him to save us and help us. The tears will still come, but we will not be crying in vain.

69:5–7 Although we want to do God's will, we still make mistakes. But, like David, we should pray that our foolish mistakes will not cause others to stumble. We too need to ask God to protect others who look up to us from being harmed by our mistakes and sins. Are you genuinely concerned about those who may copy your lifestyle?

69:13 What problems David faced! He was scoffed at, mocked, insulted, humiliated, and the object of city-wide gossip. But still he prayed. When we are completely beaten down, we are tempted to turn from God, to give up, and to quit trusting him. When your situation seems hopeless or when you just don't care anymore, determine that no matter how bad things become you will continue to pray. God will hear your prayer and he will rescue you. When others reject us, we need God most. Don't turn from your most faithful friend.

69:30
Ps 28:7

69:31
Ps 50:13,14

69:32
Ps 22:26; 34:2

69:34
Ps 148:1-13

69:35
Ps 147:2

69:36
Ps 25:13; 27:29

29But rescue me, O God, from my poverty and pain. 30Then I will praise God with my singing! My thanks will be his praise— 31that will please him more than sacrificing a bullock or an ox. 32The humble shall see their God at work for them. No wonder they will be so glad! All who seek for God shall live in joy. 33For Jehovah hears the cries of his needy ones, and does not look the other way.

34Praise him, all heaven and earth! Praise him, all the seas and everything in them! 35For God will save Jerusalem; he rebuilds the cities of Judah. His people shall live in them and not be dispossessed. 36Their children shall inherit the land; all who love his name shall live there safely.

Theme: An urgent prayer for help. It can be your prayer when you're short on time and long on need.
Author: David

70:1
Ps 40:13-17

70:5
Ps 141:1

70 Rescue me, O God! Lord, hurry to my aid! 2, 3They are after my life, and delight in hurting me. Confuse them! Shame them! Stop them! Don't let them keep on mocking me! 4But fill the followers of God with joy. Let those who love your salvation exclaim, "What a wonderful God he is!" 5But I am in deep trouble. Rush to my aid, for only you can help and save me. O Lord, don't delay.

Theme: God's constant help—from childhood to old age. Our lives are a testimony of what God has done for us.
Author: Anonymous

71:1
Ps 31:1-3

71:3
Deut 33:27
Ps 18:2; 44:4

71:5
Ps 22:9-11; 39:7
Jer 17:7,13,17

71:6
Ps 22:9,10

71:9
Ps 92:14

71:10
Mt 27:1

71:11
Ps 3:2; 7:2

71:12
Ps 22:9-11

71:13
Ps 35:4,26

71:15
Ps 35:28; 40:5

71:16
Ps 106:2

71 Lord, you are my refuge! Don't let me down! 2Save me from my enemies, for you are just! Rescue me! Bend down your ear and listen to my plea and save me. 3Be to me a great protecting Rock, where I am always welcome, safe from all attacks. For you have issued the order to save me. 4Rescue me, O God, from these unjust and cruel men. 5O Lord, you alone are my hope; I've trusted you from childhood. 6Yes, you have been with me from birth and have helped me constantly—no wonder I am always praising you! 7My success—at which so many stand amazed—is because you are my mighty protector. 8All day long I'll praise and honor you, O God, for all that you have done for me.

9And now, in my old age, don't set me aside. Don't forsake me now when my strength is failing. 10My enemies are whispering, 11"God has forsaken him! Now we can get him. There is no one to help him now!" 12O God, don't stay away! Come quickly! Help! 13Destroy them! Cover them with failure and disgrace—these enemies of mine.

14I will keep on expecting you to help me. I praise you more and more. 15I cannot count the times when you have faithfully rescued me from danger. I will tell everyone how good you are, and of your constant, daily care. 16I walk in the strength of the Lord God. I tell everyone that you alone are just and good. 17O God,

69:35 *Jerusalem,* literally, "Zion."

69:32 Most people want lasting joy and will try almost anything to obtain it, from scrambling for more money to being involved in sexual escapades. The only genuine source of happiness is God, and we receive lasting joy only by seeking him. How are you trying to find happiness? Seek God and live as he says you should (Matthew 6:33, 34), and true joy will soon follow.

70:1–5 When others disappoint us, we feel empty, as though a vital part of ourselves has been stolen. When others break the trust we have placed in them, they break us and leave us like cracked, dry cisterns. At those dry, empty moments, we must join the psalmist in begging God to rush to our aid. He alone can fill the empty, dry cisterns of our lives with his joy (70:4). With the psalmist we cry out, "O Lord, don't delay."

70:4 This short psalm was David's plea for God to rush to his aid. Yet even in this moment of panic, praise was not forgotten. Praise is important because it helps us remember who God is. Often our prayers are filled with requests for ourselves and others, and we forget to thank God for what he has done and to worship him for

who he is. Don't take God for granted and treat him as a vending machine. Even in the midst of his fear, David praised God.

71:1ff The psalmist was old and saw his life as a testimony of all God had done for him (71:9, 18). Remembering God's lifetime of blessing will help you see the consistency of his grace throughout the years, help you trust him for the future, and help motivate you to share with others the benefits of following God.

71:6, 7 God helps us constantly. He is the reason we succeed at anything in life. He is worthy of our praise and thanks. To take all the credit for our success is dishonest and robs God of the glory due to him.

71:14 As we face the sunset years, we recognize that God has been our constant help in the past. As physical powers wain, we need God even more, and we realize he is still our constant help. We must never despair, but keep on expecting his help no matter how severe our limitations. Hope in him helps us to keep going, to keep serving him.

you have helped me from my earliest childhood—and I have constantly testified to
others of the wonderful things you do. ¹⁸And now that I am old and gray, don't
forsake me. Give me time to tell this new generation (and their children too) about
all your mighty miracles. ¹⁹Your power and goodness, Lord, reach to the highest
heavens. You have done such wonderful things. Where is there another God like
you? ²⁰You have let me sink down deep in desperate problems. But you will bring
me back to life again, up from the depths of the earth. ²¹You will give me greater
honor than before, and turn again and comfort me.

²²I will praise you with music, telling of your faithfulness to all your promises,
O Holy One of Israel. ²³I will shout and sing your praises for redeeming me. ²⁴I
will talk to others all day long about your justice and your goodness. For all who
tried to hurt me have been disgraced and dishonored.

71:18
Ps 22:31
78:4,6

71:19
Deut 3:24
Ps 35:10; 57:10
Lk 1:49

71:20
Ps 23:4; 60:3
119:25
Hos 6:2

71:22
Ps 33:2; 89:18
147:7

71:23
Ps 5:11; 103:4

Theme: The perfect king. In this psalm, a king asks God to help his son rule the nation justly and
wisely. It looks forward to the endless reign of the Messiah, who alone can rule with perfect
justice and whose citizens will enjoy perfect peace.
Author: Solomon

72 O God, help the king to judge as you would, and help his son to walk in
godliness. ²Help him to give justice to your people, even to the poor. ³May
the mountains and hills flourish in prosperity because of his good reign. ⁴Help him
to defend the poor and needy and to crush their oppressors. ⁵May the poor and
needy revere you constantly, as long as sun and moon continue in the skies! Yes,
forever!

⁶May the reign of this son of mine be as gentle and fruitful as the springtime rains
upon the grass—like showers that water the earth! ⁷May all good men flourish in
his reign, with abundance of peace to the end of time.

⁸Let him reign from sea to sea, and from the Euphrates River to the ends of the
earth. ⁹The desert nomads shall bow before him; his enemies shall fall face
downward in the dust. ¹⁰Kings along the Mediterranean coast—the kings of
Tarshish and the islands—and those from Sheba and from Seba—all will bring
their gifts. ¹¹Yes, kings from everywhere! All will bow before him! All will serve
him!

¹²He will take care of the helpless and poor when they cry to him; for they have
no one else to defend them. ¹³He feels pity for the weak and needy, and will rescue
them. ¹⁴He will save them from oppression and from violence, for their lives are
precious to him.

¹⁵And he shall live; and to him will be given the gold of Sheba, and there will be
constant praise for him. His people will bless him all day long. ¹⁶Bless us with
abundant crops throughout the land, even on the highland plains; may there be fruit
like that of Lebanon; may the cities be as full of people as the fields are of grass.

¹⁷His name will be honored forever; it will continue as the sun; and all will be
blessed in him; all nations will praise him.

¹⁸Blessed be Jehovah God, the God of Israel, who only does wonderful things!

72:1
1 Kgs 3:9
Ps 24:5

72:2
Ps 82:3
Isa 9:7; 11:2-5

72:3
Isa 9:5,6
Mic 4:3,4
Zech 9:10

72:5
Ps 89:36,37

72:6
Deut 32:2
Ps 65:10
Hos 6:3

72:8
Ex 23:31
Zech 9:10

72:9
Isa 49:23
Mic 7:17

72:10
Ps 45:12; 68:29
Isa 42:4,10
60:6

72:11
Ps 86:9; 138:4
Isa 49:23

72:12
Job 29:12

72:17
Ps 89:36

72:18
Ex 15:11

72:6 *this son of mine.* The reference seems to look beyond Solomon's son to Jesus the Messiah. **72:15** *there will*
be constant praise for him, literally, "men shall pray for him continually." *His people,* implied. Literally, "they" or "he."

71:18 Solomon wrote that the glory of old people is their
experience (Proverbs 20:29). A person is never too old to serve
God, never too old to pray. Though age may stop us from certain
physical activities, it need not end our desire to tell others
(especially children) about all we have seen God do in the many
years we've lived.

72:1, 2 What qualities do we want most in our rulers? God desires
all who rule under him to walk in godliness (72:1), and to be just
toward their people. As you think of world leaders today, think how
the world would change if they would commit themselves to these
two qualities. Perhaps we should commit ourselves to pray that
they will (see 1 Timothy 2:2).

72:12–14 God cares for the helpless and poor because they are
precious to him. If God feels so strongly about the poor and loves
them so deeply, how can we ignore their plight? Examine what you
are doing to reach out with God's love to the poor, weak, and
needy in the world. Are you ignoring their plight?

72:17 Solomon, David's son, reigned in Israel's golden age. He
built the magnificent Temple and the land rested in peace. The
reference to the "son" in 72:6 looks beyond Solomon's son to
Jesus the Messiah. His kingdom, which is "to the ends of the earth"
(72:8), is greater than any human empire and it will arrive when
Christ returns to reign forever (Revelation 11:15). The name of
Jesus is the only name that has the power to bless all people and
is worthy of complete praise.

72:19
Num 14:20,21
Neh 9:5

¹⁹Blessed be his glorious name forever! Let the whole earth be filled with his glory. Amen, and amen!

²⁰(This ends the psalms of David, son of Jesse.)

C. THE THIRD BOOK OF PSALMS (73:1—89:52)

These psalms celebrate the sovereignty of God, God's hand in history, God's faithfulness, and God's covenant with David. These psalms remind us that our worship of the almighty God should be continual.

Theme: The temporary prosperity of the wicked and the lasting rewards of the righteous. We should live holy lives and trust God for our future rewards.
Author: Asaph, a leader of one of the Temple choirs (see 1 Chronicles 25:1)

73:1
Ps 24:3,4
51:10
Mt 5:8

73:2
Ps 94:18

73:3
Ps 37:1,7

73:5
Job 21:9,10

73:6
Ps 109:18

73:7
Job 15:27,28

73:8
Ps 1:1; 17:10
Jude 16

73:11
Job 22:13

73:12
Ps 49:6
Ezek 23:42

73:13
Job 21:15; 34:9

73:14
Ps 38:5,6

73:16
Eccles 8:16,17

73:17
Ps 27:4; 77:13

73:19
Num 16:21
Isa 47:11

73:22
Eccles 3:18

73:24
Ps 32:8; 48:14

73:26
Ps 16:5; 38:10

73:27
Ex 34:15

73 How good God is to Israel—to those whose hearts are pure. ²But as for me, I came *so* close to the edge of the cliff! My feet were slipping and I was almost gone. ³For I was envious of the prosperity of the proud and wicked. ⁴Yes, all through life their road is smooth! They grow sleek and fat. ⁵They aren't always in trouble and plagued with problems like everyone else, ⁶so their pride sparkles like a jeweled necklace, and their clothing is woven of cruelty! ⁷These fat cats have everything their hearts could ever wish for! ⁸They scoff at God and threaten his people. How proudly they speak! ⁹They boast against the very heavens, and their words strut through the earth.

¹⁰And so God's people are dismayed and confused, and drink it all in. ¹¹"Does God realize what is going on?" they ask. ¹²"Look at these men of arrogance; they never have to lift a finger—theirs is a life of ease; and all the time their riches multiply."

¹³Have I been wasting my time? Why take the trouble to be pure? ¹⁴All I get out of it is trouble and woe—every day and all day long! ¹⁵If I had really said that, I would have been a traitor to your people. ¹⁶Yet it is so hard to explain it—this prosperity of those who hate the Lord. ¹⁷Then one day I went into God's sanctuary to meditate, and thought about the future of these evil men. ¹⁸What a slippery path they are on—suddenly God will send them sliding over the edge of the cliff and down to their destruction: ¹⁹an instant end to all their happiness, an eternity of terror. ²⁰Their present life is only a dream! They will awaken to the truth as one awakens from a dream of things that never really were!

²¹When I saw this, what turmoil filled my heart! ²²I saw myself so stupid and so ignorant; I must seem like an animal to you, O God. ²³But even so, you love me! You are holding my right hand! ²⁴You will keep on guiding me all my life with your wisdom and counsel; and afterwards receive me into the glories of heaven! ²⁵Whom have I in heaven but you? And I desire no one on earth as much as you! ²⁶My health fails; my spirits droop, yet God remains! He is the strength of my heart; he is mine forever!

²⁷But those refusing to worship God will perish, for he destroys those serving other gods.

73:4 *all through life their road is smooth,* or, "they never have any pains."   **73:24** *receive me into the glories of heaven,* or, "you will bring me unto honor."

72:20 Book 2 ends with "Amen, and amen," as did Psalm 41 which closed Book 1. This last verse does not mean that David wrote this psalm, but that he wrote most of the psalms in Book 2.

73:1ff Until Asaph entered God's sanctuary, he could not understand the justice of allowing the wicked to thrive while the righteous endured hardship. But when he saw that one day justice would be done, he acknowledged the wisdom of God.

73:1-20 Two strong themes wind their way through these verses: (1) the wicked prosper, leaving faithful people wondering why they bother to be good, and (2) the wealth of the wicked looks so inviting that faithful people may wish they could trade places. But these two themes come to unexpected ends, for the wealth of the wicked suddenly stops at that great gulf separating this life and the next, and the rewards for the good suddenly take on eternal value.

What seemed like wealth is now waste, and what seemed worthless now lasts forever. Don't be tempted, as Asaph was, to wish you could trade places with evil people to get their wealth. One day they will wish they could trade places with you and have your eternal wealth.

73:20 Asaph realized that the rich who put their hope, joy, and confidence in their wealth are living in a dream. A dream exists only in the mind of the dreamer. Don't let your life's goals be as unreal as a dream and awaken too late to the fact that you missed the reality of God's truth. Happiness and hope can be a reality, but only when they are based on God, not on riches. Because true reality is in God, we should get as close to him as we can in order to be realistic about life.

28But as for me, I get as close to him as I can! I have chosen him and I will tell everyone about the wonderful ways he rescues me.

73:28
Ps 40:5

Theme: A plea for God to help his people defend his cause and remember his promises. When we feel devastated or forgotten, we can plead to God for help, knowing that he hears.
Author: Asaph (or one of his descendants, since many believe this to be written after Jerusalem's fall in 586 B.C.)

74 O God, why have you cast us away forever? Why is your anger hot against us—the sheep of your own pasture? 2Remember that we are your people—the ones you chose in ancient times from slavery and made the choicest of your possessions. You chose Jerusalem as your home on earth!

3Walk through the awful ruins of the city, and see what the enemy has done to your sanctuary. 4There they shouted their battle cry and erected their idols to flaunt their victory. 5, 6Everything lies in shambles like a forest chopped to the ground. They came with their axes and sledgehammers and smashed and chopped the carved paneling, 7and set the sanctuary on fire, and razed it to the ground—your sanctuary, Lord. 8"Let's wipe out every trace of God," they said, and went through the entire country burning down the assembly places where we worshiped you.

9, 10There is nothing left to show that we are your people. The prophets are gone, and who can say when it all will end? How long, O God, will you allow our enemies to dishonor your name? Will you let them get away with this forever? 11Why do you delay? Why hold back your power? Unleash your fist and give them a final blow.

12God is my King from ages past; you have been actively helping me everywhere throughout the land. 13, 14You divided the Red Sea with your strength; you crushed the sea-god's heads! You gave him to the desert tribes to eat! 15At your command the springs burst forth to give your people water; and then you dried a path for them across the ever-flowing Jordan. 16Day and night alike belong to you; you made the starlight and the sun. 17All nature is within your hands; you make the summer and the winter too. 18Lord, see how these enemies scoff at you. O Jehovah, an arrogant nation has blasphemed your name.

19O Lord, save me! Protect your turtledove from the hawks. Save your beloved people from these beasts. 20Remember your promise! For the land is full of darkness and cruel men. 21O Lord, don't let your downtrodden people be constantly insulted. Give cause for these poor and needy ones to praise your name! 22Arise, O God, and state your case against our enemies. Remember the insults these rebels have hurled against you all day long. 23Don't overlook the cursing of these enemies of yours; it grows louder and louder.

74:1
Deut 29:20
Ps 44:9; 89:46
74:2
Deut 32:6,9
Ps 68:16
74:3
Ps 79:1
Isa 61:4
74:5
1 Kgs 6:18,29,
32,35
Jer 46:22
74:7
2 Kgs 25:9
74:9
Lev 24:16
Ps 78:43; 79:12
74:11
Ps 59:13
74:12
Ps 44:4
74:13
Ex 14:21
74:15
Ex 14:21,22
17:5,6
74:16
Gen 1:14-18
Ps 136:7,8
74:17
Gen 8:22
74:18
Deut 32:6
74:20
Gen 17:7
Ps 106:45
74:21
Ps 35:10
Isa 41:17
74:22
Ps 43:1

Theme: Because God is the final judge, the tables will be turned upon the wicked. When arrogant people threaten our security, we can be confident that God will ultimately overrule and destroy them.
Author: Asaph

75 How we thank you, Lord! Your mighty miracles give proof that you care. 2"Yes," the Lord replies, "and when I am ready, I will punish the wicked!

75:1
Ps 44:1; 71:17

74:2 *Jerusalem*, literally, "Mount Zion."   74:19 *the hawks*, literally, "the wild beasts."

74:1, 2 God's hot anger against Israel had grown during the many years of their sin and idolatry. His patience endured for generations, but at last was set aside for judgment. If you fall into sin and quickly seek God's forgiveness, his mercy may come quickly and his anger may leave quickly. But if you practice sin against him for a long time, don't be surprised if his patience gives way to anger.

74:8 When enemy armies defeated Israel, they sacked Jerusalem, trying to wipe out every trace of God. This has often been the response of people who hate God. Today many are trying to erase all traces of God from traditions in our society and subjects taught in our schools. Do what you can to help maintain a Christian influence, but don't become discouraged when others

appear to make great strides in eliminating all traces of God, for they cannot eliminate his presence in the lives of believers.

74:11–18 From our perspective, God sometimes seems to be slow to intervene on our behalf. But what might appear slow to us is good timing from God's perspective. It's easy to become impatient for God to act, but never give up waiting on him. When God is silent and we are deep in anguish, follow the method in this psalm. Review the great acts of God throughout biblical history and review what he has done in your life. This will restore the perspective that God is at work not only in history, but in your life as well.

75:2 Children have difficulty grasping the concept of time. "It's not time yet," is not a reason they easily understand. They only

75:3
1 Sam 2:8
Ps 46:6

3Though the earth shakes and all its people live in turmoil, yet its pillars are firm, for I have set them in place!"

75:6
1 Sam 2:7
Ps 113:6-8

4I warned the proud to cease their arrogance! I told the wicked to lower their insolent gaze, 5and to stop being stubborn and proud. 6, 7For promotion and power come from nowhere on earth, but only from God. He promotes one and deposes another. 8In Jehovah's hand there is a cup of pale and sparkling wine. It is his judgment, poured out upon the wicked of the earth. They must drain that cup to the dregs.

75:8
Ps 11:6

75:9
Ps 40:10

75:10
Ps 89:17
148:14

9But as for me, I shall forever declare the praises of the God of Jacob. 10"I will cut off the strength of evil men," says the Lord, "and increase the power of good men in their place."

Theme: A call for God to punish evildoers. Even man's angry revolt will be used by God to bring glory to himself.
Author: Asaph

76:2
Ps 48:2,3
132:13; 135:21

76 God's reputation is very great in Judah and in Israel. 2His home is in Jerusalem. He lives upon Mount Zion. 3There he breaks the weapons of our enemies.

76:3
Ps 46:9

76:5
Isa 10:12

4The everlasting mountains cannot compare with you in glory! 5The mightiest of our enemies are conquered. They lie before us in the sleep of death; not one can lift a hand against us. 6When you rebuked them, God of Jacob, steeds and riders fell. 7No wonder you are greatly feared! Who can stand before an angry God? 8You pronounce sentence on them from heaven; the earth trembles and stands silently before you. 9You stand up to punish the evil-doers and to defend the meek of the earth. 10Man's futile wrath will bring you glory. You will use it as an ornament!

76:6
Ex 15:1,21
Ps 78:53

76:7
Ps 89:7
Nah 1:6
Rev 6:17

76:8
1 Chron 16:30

76:9
Ps 9:7-9; 72:4

11Fulfill all your vows that you have made to Jehovah your God. Let everyone bring him presents. He should be reverenced and feared, 12for he cuts down princes and does awesome things to the kings of the earth.

Theme: We are comforted through the hard times by remembering God's help in the past. Recalling God's miracles and previous works can give us courage to continue.
Author: Asaph

77:2
Job 11:13
Ps 50:15; 88:9
Isa 26:9

77 I cry to the Lord; I call and call to him. Oh, that he would listen. 2I am in deep trouble and I need his help so much. All night long I pray, lifting my hands to heaven, pleading. There can be no joy for me until he acts. 3I think of God and moan, overwhelmed with longing for his help. 4I cannot sleep until you act. I am too distressed even to pray!

77:3
Ps 43:5; 61:2
142:2,3

77:5
Ps 143:5

5I keep thinking of the good old days of the past, long since ended. 6Then my nights were filled with joyous songs. I search my soul and meditate upon the difference now. 7Has the Lord rejected me forever? Will he never again be

77:6
Ps 42:8

75:4 *lower their insolent gaze*, literally, "lift not up the horn." **75:10** *says the Lord*, implied.

---

comprehend the present. As limited human beings, we can't comprehend God's perspective in one view. We want everything now, not recognizing that God's timing is better for us. When God is ready, he will do what needs to be done, not what we would like him to do. We may be impatient as children, but it is clear that God's timing is perfect, so we should accept it.

75:8 The judgment of God is coming against the wicked. God will pour out his fury on his enemies and they will be forced to drink it. Drinking the cup of God's judgment is a picture used frequently in Scripture (Isaiah 51:17, 22; Jeremiah 25:15; 49:12; Habakkuk 2:16; Revelation 14:10; 16:19; 18:6). It gives the impression of taking a dose of one's own medicine. To drink the dregs means to suffer complete punishment.

76:1ff This psalm praises God for his awesome power, and was most likely written to celebrate the defeat of Sennacherib's army after he invaded Judah (see 2 Kings 18:13-37).

76:10 How can someone's wrath bring glory to God? Hostility to God and his people gives God the opportunity to do great deeds.

For example, the Pharaoh of Egypt refused to free the Hebrew slaves (Exodus 5:1, 2), but this allowed God to work mighty miracles for his people (Exodus 11:9). God turns the tables on evildoers and brings glory to himself from the foolishness of those who deny him or revolt against him (see Psalm 14:1).

76:11 Because God is so great and powerful, he should be reverenced and feared. Those who take God lightly now will be dealt with severely in the day of wrath. Those who revere him now will find his favor.

77:1-12 Asaph cried out to God for courage during a time of deep distress. His plea was, "I need help." But in 77:13-20, the "I" is gone. As Asaph expressed his requests to God, his focus changed from thinking of himself to worshiping God, "You are the God of miracles and wonders" (77:14). As we pray to God, he lifts us from looking at ourselves to looking to him.

77:4-9 The source of Asaph's distress (77:4) was his doubt (77:7-9). Only after he put aside his doubts about God's holiness and care for him (77:13, 14) did he eliminate his distress (77:20).

favorable? 8Is his lovingkindness gone forever? Has his promise failed? 9Has he
forgotten to be kind to one so undeserving? Has he slammed the door in anger on
his love? 10And I said: This is my fate, that the blessings of God have changed to
hate. 11I recall the many miracles he did for me so long ago. 12Those wonderful
deeds are constantly in my thoughts. I cannot stop thinking about them.

13O God, your ways are holy. Where is there any other as mighty as you? 14You
are the God of miracles and wonders! You still demonstrate your awesome power.

15You have redeemed us who are the sons of Jacob and of Joseph by your might.
16When the Red Sea saw you, how it feared! It trembled to its depths! 17The clouds
poured down their rain, the thunder rolled and crackled in the sky. Your lightning
flashed. 18There was thunder in the whirlwind; the lightning lighted up the world!
The earth trembled and shook.

19Your road led by a pathway through the sea—a pathway no one knew was
there! 20You led your people along that road like a flock of sheep, with Moses and
Aaron as their shepherds.

Theme: Lessons from history. Asaph retells the history of the Jewish nation from the time of
slavery in Egypt to David's reign. It was told over and over to each generation so they would not
forget God and make the same mistakes as their ancestors.
Author: Asaph

78 O my people, listen to my teaching. Open your ears to what I am saying.
2, 3For I will show you lessons from our history, stories handed down to us
from former generations. 4I will reveal these truths to you so that you can describe
these glorious deeds of Jehovah to your children, and tell them about the mighty
miracles he did. 5For he gave his laws to Israel, and commanded our fathers to
teach them to their children, 6so that they in turn could teach their children too.
Thus his laws pass down from generation to generation. 7In this way each generation has been able to obey his laws and to set its hope anew on God and not forget
his glorious miracles. 8Thus they did not need to be as their fathers
were—stubborn, rebellious, unfaithful, refusing to give their hearts to God.

9The people of Ephraim, though fully armed, turned their backs and fled when
the day of battle came, 10because they didn't obey his laws. They refused to follow
his ways. 11, 12And they forgot about the wonderful miracles God had done for
them, and for their fathers in Egypt. 13For he divided the sea before them and led
them through! The water stood banked up along both sides of them! 14In the
daytime he led them by a cloud, and at night by a pillar of fire. 15He split open the
rocks in the wilderness to give them plenty of water, as though gushing from a
spring. 16Streams poured from the rock, flowing like a river!

17Yet they kept on with their rebellion, sinning against the God who is above all

77:10 *that the blessings of God have changed to hate,* literally, "that the right hand of the Most High has changed."

77:8	Ps 89:49
77:9	Ps 25:6
77:10	Ps 31:22
77:13	Ex 15:11
77:15	Ex 6:6
77:16	Ex 14:21
77:17	Ps 68:33
77:18	Judg 5:4
77:20	Ex 13:21
	Ps 78:52
78:2	Mt 13:34,35
78:4	Deut 11:19
78:5	Deut 6:4-9
78:6	Deut 11:19
78:7	Deut 4:2,9
	Josh 22:5
78:9	Ex 32:9
78:10	2 Kgs 18:12
78:13	Ex 14:21; 15:18
78:14	Ex 13:21
78:15	Ex 17:5,6
78:16	Num 20:8,10,11

77:11, 12 Memories of God's goodness and faithfulness
sustained Israel through their difficulties. They knew that God was
capable and trustworthy. When you meet new trials, review the
good things God has done in your life and this will strengthen your
faith.

77:16 The miraculous parting of the Red Sea is mentioned many
times in the Old Testament (Joshua 24:6; Nehemiah 9:9; Psalms
74:13, 14; 106:9; 136:13). Shortly after leaving Egypt, the Israelites
found themselves trapped against the Red Sea with Pharaoh's
army ready to capture them. God parted the sea and led the entire
nation across on dry land. The story of this incredible miracle was
handed down from generation to generation, reminding the
Israelites of God's power, protection, and love.

78:1ff The people of Israel rebelled and refused to give their
hearts to God (78:8); forgot about God's miracles (78:11, 12);
selfishly complained (78:18); made empty promises to repent
(78:37); and were ungrateful (78:42). This is recorded in God's
Word so we can avoid the same errors.

78:5 God commanded that the stories of his mighty acts in
Israel's history and his laws be passed on from parents to children.
This shows the purpose and importance of religious education—to
help each generation obey God and set their hope on him. It is
important to keep children from repeating the same mistakes as
their ancestors. What are you doing to pass on the history of God's
work in the world to the next generation?

78:9, 10 Ephraim was the prominent tribe of Israel from the days
of Moses to Saul's time. The Tabernacle was set up in its territory.
There is no other biblical record of Ephraim's soldiers fleeing in
battle, so this is probably a metaphor referring to Ephraim's failure
to provide strong leadership during those years. When David
became king, the tribe of Judah gained prominence. Because of
David's faith and obedience, God chose Jerusalem in Judah to be
the place for the new Temple and rejected Ephraim (78:67),
causing tension between the two tribes. This psalm may have been
written because of that tension in order to demonstrate once again
why God chose Judah. God often chooses to work through those
who are most faithful to him.

78:18
Num 11:4,5
1 Cor 10:9,10

78:19
Ex 16:3
Num 21:5

78:21
Num 11:1

78:22
Heb 3:18

78:24
Ex 16:4
Jn 6:30,31

78:26
Num 11:31

78:27
Ex 16:13
Ps 105:40

78:29
Num 11:19,20

78:31
Num 11:33,34

78:32
Num 14:10,11

78:33
Num 14:29,34,
35

78:35
Deut 9:26; 32:4

78:38
Ex 34:5,6
Num 14:19

78:42
Judg 8:34

78:43
Ex 7:3

78:44
Ex 7:20
Ps 105:29

78:45
Ex 8:6,24
Ps 105:30,31

78:46
Ex 10:14

78:47
Ex 9:23
Ps 105:32

78:48
Ex 9:19

78:49
Ex 15:7

78:51
Ex 12:29,30
Ps 105:36

78:52
Ps 77:20

78:53
Ex 14:19,20,
27,28

78:54
Ex 15:17

78:55
Josh 23:4,5

78:58
Lev 26:1
Deut 32:16,21

78:59
Lev 26:30
Deut 32:19

78:60
1 Sam 4:11

78:61
1 Sam 4:17

gods. 18They murmured and complained, demanding other food than God was giving them. 19, 20They even spoke against God himself. "Why can't he give us decent food as well as water?" they grumbled. 21Jehovah heard them and was angry; the fire of his wrath burned against Israel, 22because they didn't believe in God or trust in him to care for them, 23even though he commanded the skies to open—he opened the windows of heaven— 24and rained down manna for their food. He gave them bread from heaven! 25They ate angels' food! He gave them all they could hold.

26And he led forth the east wind and guided the south wind by his mighty power. 27He rained down birds as thick as dust, clouds of them like sands along the shore! 28He caused the birds to fall to the ground among the tents. 29The people ate their fill. He gave them what they asked for. 30But they had hardly finished eating, and the meat was yet in their mouths, 31when the anger of the Lord rose against them and killed the finest of Israel's young men. 32Yet even so the people kept on sinning and refused to believe in miracles. 33So he cut their lives short and gave them years of terror and disaster.

34Then at last, when he had ruined them, they walked awhile behind him; how earnestly they turned around and followed him! 35Then they remembered that God was their Rock—that their Savior was the God above all gods. 36But it was only with their words they followed him, not with their hearts; 37their hearts were far away. They did not keep their promises. 38Yet he was merciful and forgave their sins and didn't destroy them all. Many and many a time he held back his anger. 39For he remembered that they were merely mortal men, gone in a moment like a breath of wind.

40Oh, how often they rebelled against him in those desert years and grieved his heart. 41Again and again they turned away and tempted God to kill them, and limited the Holy One of Israel from giving them his blessings. 42They forgot his power and love, and how he had rescued them from their enemies; 43they forgot the plagues he sent upon the Egyptians in Tanis— 44how he turned their rivers into blood, so that no one could drink, 45and how he sent vast swarms of flies to fill the land, and how the frogs had covered all of Egypt!

46He gave their crops to caterpillars. Their harvest was consumed by locusts. 47He destroyed their grapevines and their sycamores with hail. 48Their cattle died in the fields, mortally wounded by huge hailstones from heaven. Their sheep were killed by lightning. 49He loosed on them the fierceness of his anger, sending sorrow and trouble. He dispatched against them a band of destroying angels. 50He gave free course to his anger and did not spare the Egyptians' lives, but handed them over to plagues and sickness. 51Then he killed the eldest son in each Egyptian family—he who was the beginning of its strength and joy.

52But he led forth his own people like a flock, guiding them safely through the wilderness. 53He kept them safe, so they were not afraid. But the Sea closed in upon their enemies and overwhelmed them. 54He brought them to the border of his land of blessing, to this land of hills he made for them. 55He drove out the nations occupying the land, and gave each tribe of Israel its apportioned place as its home.

56Yet though he did all this for them, they still rebelled against the God above all gods, and refused to follow his commands. 57They turned back from entering the Promised Land and disobeyed as their fathers had. Like a crooked arrow, they missed the target of God's will. 58They made him angry by erecting idols and altars to other gods.

59When God saw their deeds, his wrath was strong and he despised his people. 60Then he abandoned his Tabernacle at Shiloh, where he had lived among mankind, 61and allowed his Ark to be captured; he surrendered his glory into enemy

78:43 *Tanis,* literally, "the plains of Zoan." **78:51,** *the eldest son,* literally, "all the firstborn."

78:36, 37 Over and over the children of Israel said they would follow God, but then they turned away from him. The problem was that they followed God with words and not with their hearts, thus their repentance was empty. Talk is cheap. God wants our lives to back up our spiritual claims and promises—he wants us to be true believers, he wants our whole selves.

hands. 62He caused his people to be butchered because his anger was intense. 63Their young men were killed by fire and their girls died before they were old enough to sing their wedding songs. 64The priests were slaughtered and their widows died before they could even begin their lament. 65Then the Lord rose up as though awakening from sleep, and like a mighty man aroused by wine, 66he routed his enemies and drove them back and sent them to eternal shame. 67But he rejected Joseph's family, the tribe of Ephraim, 68and chose the tribe of Judah—and Mount Zion which he loved. 69There he built his towering temple, solid and enduring as the heavens and the earth. 70He chose his servant David, taking him from feeding sheep, 71, 72and from following the ewes with lambs; God presented David to his people as their shepherd and he cared for them with a true heart and skillful hands.

78:62
Judg 20:21
1 Sam 4:10
78:63
Num 11:1
Jer 7:34; 16:9
78:64
1 Sam 22:18
78:69
1 Kgs 6:1-38
78:70
1 Sam 16:10-12
78:71
2 Sam 5:2; 7:8
1 Kgs 9:4
1 Chron 11:2

Theme: When outraged by injustice, cry out to God, not against him. In times of disaster, our mood may be anger, but our trust must remain in God.
Author: Asaph (or one of his descendants), probably written after the Babylonians had leveled Jerusalem (see 2 Kings 25)

79 O God, your land has been conquered by the heathen nations. Your Temple is defiled and Jerusalem is a heap of ruins. 2The bodies of your people lie exposed—food for birds and animals. 3The enemy has butchered the entire population of Jerusalem; blood has flowed like water. No one is left even to bury them. 4The nations all around us scoff. They heap contempt on us.

5O Jehovah, how long will you be angry with us? Forever? Will your jealousy burn till every hope is gone? 6Pour out your wrath upon the godless nations, not on us! And on kingdoms that refuse to pray, that will not call upon your name! 7For they have destroyed your people Israel, invading every home. 8Oh, do not hold us guilty for our former sins! Let your tenderhearted mercies meet our needs, for we are brought low to the dust. 9Help us, God of our salvation! Help us for the honor of your name. Oh, save us and forgive our sins. 10Why should the heathen nations be allowed to scoff, "Where is their God?" Publicly avenge this slaughter of your people! 11Listen to the sighing of the prisoners and those condemned to die. Demonstrate the greatness of your power by saving them. 12O Lord, take sevenfold vengeance on these nations scorning you.

13Then we your people, the sheep of your pasture, will thank you forever and forever, praising your greatness from generation to generation.

79:1
Ps 74:2-7
Jer 26:18
Lam 1:10
79:2
Deut 28:26
Jer 7:33; 16:4
79:3
Jer 14:16
79:6
Jer 10:25
79:7
Ps 53:4
79:8
Ps 106:6; 142:6
Isa 26:5; 64:9
79:9
Chron 14:11
Jer 14:7
79:10
Ps 115:2
79:12
Gen 4:15

Theme: A prayer for revival and restoration after experiencing destruction. God is our only hope for salvation.
Author: Asaph (or one of his descendants), probably written after the Northern Kingdom of Israel was defeated and its people deported to Assyria

80 O Shepherd of Israel who leads Israel like a flock; O God enthroned above the Guardian Angels, bend down your ear and listen as I plead. Display your power and radiant glory. 2Let Ephraim, Benjamin and Manasseh see you rouse yourself and use your mighty power to rescue us.

80:1
Ex 25:22
Ps 23:1; 77:20
80:2
Ps 35:23

78:70–72 With love and skill, David the shepherd boy cared for his flocks. As Israel's king, David cared for his people the same way—with skillful hands and a true heart. Skill and integrity are basic requirements for effective leadership. Those without skill are ineffective. Those without high moral character lead people astray or become easily corrupted. In your pursuit to become more highly skilled, don't neglect integrity.

78:71, 72 Although David had been on the throne when this psalm was written, he is called a shepherd and not a king. Shepherding, a common profession in biblical times, was a highly responsible job. The flocks were completely dependent upon shepherds for guidance, provision, and protection. David had spent his early years as a shepherd (1 Samuel 16:10, 11). This was a training ground for the future responsibilities God had in store for him. When he was ready, God took him from caring for sheep to caring for Israel, God's people. Don't treat your present situation

lightly or irresponsibly; it may be God's training ground for your future.

79:6 According to the Old Testament, God's wrath and judgment often fell on entire nations because of the sins of people within that nation. Here, Asaph pled for judgment on kingdoms who refused to acknowledge God's authority. Ironically, Asaph's own nation of Judah was being judged by God for refusing to do this very thing (2 Chronicles 36:14–20). These were people who had sworn allegiance to God, but were now rejecting him. This made their judgment even worse.

79:10 Can we expect God to care for us so others won't scoff at our beliefs? In the end, God will bring himself glory (Psalm 76:10), but in the meantime, we must endure suffering with patience and allow God to purify us through it. For reasons that we do not know, the heathen are allowed to scoff at believers. We should be prepared for criticism, jokes, and unkind remarks because God does not place us beyond the attacks of scoffers.

80:3
Num 6:24-26
Ps 31:16; 60:1

80:4
Ps 79:5; 84:8

80:6
Ps 44:13

80:8
2 Chron 20:7
Ps 44:2
Isa 5:2,7
Jer 2:21; 11:17
Ezek 17:6,23
Amos 9:15

80:9
Ex 23:28
Isa 5:2
Hos 14:5

80:11
Ps 72:8

80:12
Ps 89:40
Isa 5:5

80:13
Jer 5:6

80:16
2 Chron 36:19
Jer 52:13

80:17
Ps 89:21

³Turn us again to yourself, O God. Look down on us in joy and love; only then shall we be saved.

⁴O Jehovah, God of heaven's armies, how long will you be angry and reject our prayers? ⁵You have fed us with sorrow and tears, ⁶and have made us the scorn of the neighboring nations. They laugh among themselves.

⁷Turn us again to yourself, O God of Hosts. Look down on us in joy and love; only then shall we be saved. ⁸You brought us from Egypt as though we were a tender vine and drove away the heathen from your land and planted us. ⁹You cleared the ground and tilled the soil and we took root and filled the land. ¹⁰The mountains were covered with our shadow; we were like the mighty cedar trees, ¹¹covering the entire land from the Mediterranean Sea to the Euphrates River. ¹²But now you have broken down our walls, leaving us without protection. ¹³The boar from the forest roots around us, and the wild animals feed on us.

¹⁴Come back, we beg of you, O God of the armies of heaven, and bless us. Look down from heaven and see our plight and care for this your vine! ¹⁵Protect what you yourself have planted, this son you have raised for yourself. ¹⁶For we are chopped and burned by our enemies. May they perish at your frown. ¹⁷Strengthen the man you love, the son of your choice, ¹⁸and we will never forsake you again. Revive us to trust in you.

¹⁹Turn us again to yourself, O God of the armies of heaven. Look down on us, your face aglow with joy and love—only then shall we be saved.

80:3 *Look down on us in joy and love,* literally, "Cause your face to shine upon us." **80:7** *in joy and love,* literally, "Cause your face to shine upon us." **80:10** *the mighty cedar trees,* literally, "the cedars of God." **80:17** *the man you love,* literally, "the man of your right hand." *the son of your choice,* literally, "the son of man you made strong for yourself."

PRAYER IN THE BOOK OF PSALMS

Prayer is human communication with God. Psalms could be described as a collection of song-prayers. Probably the most striking feature of these prayers is their unedited honesty. The words often express our own feelings—feelings which we would prefer no one, much less God, ever knew. Making these psalms our prayers can teach us a great deal about how God wants us to communicate with him. Too often we give God a watered-down version of our feelings, hoping we won't offend him or make him curious about our motives. As we use the psalms to express our feelings, we learn that honesty, openness, and sincerity are valuable to God.

Following are several types of prayers with examples from Psalms. Note that the psalm writers communicated with God in a variety of ways for a variety of reasons. Each of us is invited to communicate with God. Using the psalms will enrich your personal prayer life.

Prayers of:	Psalms:
Praise to God	100, 113, 117
Thanksgiving by a community	67, 75, 136
Thanksgiving by an individual	18, 30, 32
Request by the community	79, 80, 123
Request by an individual	3, 55, 86
Sorrow by the community	44, 74, 137
Sorrow by an individual	5, 6, 120
Anger	35, 109, 140
Confession	6, 32, 51
Faith	11, 16, 23

80:3, 7, 19 Three times the writer calls on God to "turn us again to yourself." Repentance involves humbling ourselves and turning to God to receive his forgiveness and restoration. As we turn to God, he helps us to see ourselves more clearly, including our sin. And as we see our sin, the process of repentance must be repeated over and over again.

80:15, 17 The "son" is probably not the Messiah, but Israel, whom God calls elsewhere his "eldest son" (Exodus 4:22). The psalmist is making a plea that God would restore his mercy to Israel, the people whom he had chosen to bring his message into the world.

Theme: A holiday hymn. This hymn celebrates the Exodus from Egypt—God's goodness versus Israel's waywardness. God is our deliverer in spite of our wanderings.
Author: Asaph, probably written to be used during the Feast of Tabernacles

81

The Lord makes us strong! Sing praises! Sing to Israel's God! ²Sing, accompanied by drums; pluck the sweet lyre and harp. ³Sound the trumpet! Come to the joyous celebrations at full moon, new moon and all the other holidays. ⁴For God has given us these times of joy; they are scheduled in the laws of Israel. ⁵He gave them as reminders of his war against Egypt where we were slaves on foreign soil.

I heard an unknown voice that said, ⁶"Now I will relieve your shoulder of its burden; I will free your hands from their heavy tasks." ⁷He said, "You cried to me in trouble and I saved you; I answered from Mount Sinai where the thunder hides. I tested your faith at Meribah, when you complained there was no water. ⁸Listen to me, O my people, while I give you stern warnings. O Israel, if you will only listen! ⁹*You must never worship any other god,* nor ever have an idol in your home. ¹⁰For it was I, Jehovah your God, who brought you out of the land of Egypt. Only test me! Open your mouth wide and see if I won't fill it. You will receive every blessing you can use!

¹¹"But no, my people won't listen. Israel doesn't want me around. ¹²So I am letting them go their blind and stubborn way, living according to their own desires.

¹³"But oh, that my people would listen to me! Oh, that Israel would follow me, walking in my paths! ¹⁴How quickly then I would subdue her enemies! How soon my hands would be upon her foes! ¹⁵Those who hate the Lord would cringe before him; their desolation would last forever. ¹⁶But he would feed you with the choicest foods. He would satisfy you with honey for the taking."

81:1 Ps 46:1; 59:16 66:1; 95:1,2
81:2 Ps 108:2; 144:9 149:3
81:3 Lev 23:24 Num 10:10
81:5 Ex 11:4
81:7 Ex 2:23; 17:5-7 19:19 Ps 50:15; 95:8
81:9 Ex 20:3 Isa 43:12
81:10 Ex 20:2 Ps 78:25; 103:5
81:11 Ex 32:1
81:12 Rom 1:24,26
81:13 Deut 5:29 Isa 48:18 Jer 7:23
81:16 Deut 32:13,14

Theme: A fair judge. God will judge the wicked who have unfairly treated others.
Author: Asaph

82

God stands up to open heaven's court. He pronounces judgment on the judges. ²How long will you judges refuse to listen to the evidence? How long will you shower special favors on the wicked? ³Give fair judgment to the poor man, the afflicted, the fatherless, the destitute. ⁴Rescue the poor and helpless from the grasp of evil men. ⁵But you are so foolish and so ignorant! Because you are in darkness, all the foundations of society are shaken to the core. ⁶I have called you all "gods" and "sons of the Most High." ⁷But in death you are mere men. You will fall as any prince—for all must die.

⁸Stand up, O God, and judge the earth. For all of it belongs to you. All nations are in your hands.

82:1 Ps 58:11 Isa 3:13
82:2 Deut 1:17
82:3 Deut 24:17
82:6 Jn 10:34-36
82:7 Ps 49:12; 83:11
82:8 Ps 2:8; 12:5 Rev 11:15

81:7 *from Mount Sinai,* implied. Literally, "in the hiding place of thunder." **81:9** *nor ever have an idol in your home,* literally, "There shall no foreign god be in you." **81:10** *Only test me,* implied. **81:16** *honey for the taking,* literally, "honey out of the rock." **82:1** *He pronounces judgment on the judges,* implied in vss 2-4, 6. Literally, "He judges among the gods." **82:5** *of society,* literally, "of the earth."

81:2–4 Music and worship go hand in hand. King David instituted music for the Temple worship services (1 Chronicles 16:7). Worship involves the whole person, and music helps focus worship by lifting one's thoughts and emotions to God. Through music we can reflect upon our sins as well as celebrate God's greatness.

81:4, 5 Israel's holidays reminded the nation of God's great miracles. It was a time of rejoicing and a time to renew one's strength for life's daily struggles. At Christmas, do your thoughts revolve around presents for the most part? Is Easter only a warm anticipation of spring, and Thanksgiving only a good meal? Remember the spiritual origins of these special days, and use

them as opportunities to worship God for his goodness to you, your family, and your nation.

81:11, 12 God let the Israelites go on blindly, stubbornly, and selfishly, when they should have been obeying and pursuing God's desires. God sometimes lets us continue in our stubbornness to bring us to our senses. He does not keep us from rebelling because he knows we will learn the consequences of sin.

82:6 This psalm calls the judges of Israel "gods" and "sons of the Most High." They were called "gods" because they represented God in executing judgment. In John 10:34-36, Jesus used this passage to defend his claims to be God. His argument was as follows: if God would call mere men "gods," why was it blasphemous for him, the Son of God, to declare himself equal with God?

Theme: Combatting God's enemies. This psalm is a prayer for God to do whatever it takes to convince the world that he is indeed God. Someday all will recognize and admit that God is in charge.
Author: Asaph (or one of his descendants)

83 O God, don't sit idly by, silent and inactive when we pray. Answer us! Deliver us!

2Don't you hear the tumult and commotion of your enemies? Don't you see what they are doing, these proud men who hate the Lord? 3They are full of craftiness and plot against your people, laying plans to slay your precious ones. 4"Come," they say, "and let us wipe out Israel as a nation—we will destroy the very memory of her existence." 5This was their unanimous decision at their summit conference—they signed a treaty to ally themselves against Almighty God— 6these Ishmaelites and Edomites and Moabites and Hagrites; 7people from the lands of Gebal, Ammon, Amalek, Philistia and Tyre; 8Assyria has joined them too, and is allied with the descendants of Lot.

9Do to them as once you did to Midian, or as you did to Sisera and Jabin at the river Kishon, 10and as you did to your enemies at Endor, whose decaying corpses fertilized the soil. 11Make their mighty nobles die as Oreb did, and Zeeb; let all their princes die like Zebah and Zalmunna, 12who said, "Let us seize for our own use these pasturelands of God!"

13O my God, blow them away like dust; like chaff before the wind— 14as a forest fire that roars across a mountain. 15Chase them with your fiery storms, tempests and tornados. 16Utterly disgrace them until they recognize your power and name, O Lord. 17Make them failures in everything they do; let them be ashamed and terrified 18until they learn that you alone, Jehovah, are the God above all gods in supreme charge of all the earth.

Theme: God's living presence is our greatest joy. His radiant presence helps us grow in strength, grace, and glory.
Author: The sons of Korah

84 How lovely is your Temple, O Lord of the armies of heaven.
2I long, yes, faint with longing to be able to enter your courtyard and come near to the Living God. 3Even the sparrows and swallows are welcome to come and nest among your altars and there have their young, O Lord of heaven's armies, my King and my God! 4How happy are those who can live in your Temple, singing your praises.

5Happy are those who are strong in the Lord, who want above all else to follow your steps. 6When they walk through the Valley of Weeping it will become a place

83:2
Ps 2:1
83:3
Ps 31:20
83:4
Esth 3:5,6
83:5
Ps 2:2
83:6
Gen 25:12-16
2 Chron 20:1,10
83:7
2 Chron 20:10
1 Sam 4:1; 15:2
Ezek 27:2,3,9
83:9
Judg 4:22,23
83:11
Judg 7:25; 8:21
83:12
2 Chron 20:11
83:14
Isa 9:18
83:15
Ps 58:9
83:16
Ps 109:29
83:18
Isa 45:21

84:1
Ps 27:5
84:2
Ps 42:1,2; 63:1
84:3
Ps 43:4
84:4
Ps 65:4
84:6
Ps 107:35

83:5–8 This alliance against God may refer to the gathering of certain kings to fight against Jehoshaphat and the people of Judah (2 Chronicles 20). The psalm's author is called Asaph, but this is an inclusive term meaning Asaph or one of his descendants. "One of the sons of Asaph" named Jahaziel prophesied victory for Judah in the battle against Jehoshaphat (2 Chronicles 20:13–17). The psalmist says the alliance against Judah is really against God. Thus Jahaziel exclaimed, "The battle is not yours, but God's" (2 Chronicles 20:15). Because God is in supreme charge of all the earth (83:18), the enemies of Israel were considered God's enemies.

83:8–11 The "descendants of Lot" refers to the Moabites and Ammonites (Genesis 19:36–38). (For the story of Oreb and Zeeb, see Judges 7:25; for Zebah and Zalmunna, see Judges 8:21.)

83:13–18 The rulers of the nations exercise great power, changing the course of history and its peoples. Surrounding Judah were heathen nations that sought its downfall. Asaph prayed that God would blow his hot breath of judgment upon them until, in their defeat, they recognized that the Lord is above all rulers of the earth. Sometimes we must be dragged in the dust before we will look up and see the Lord; we must be defeated before we can have the ultimate victory. Wouldn't it be better to seek the Lord in

times of prosperity than to wait until his judgment is upon us?

84:1, 4 The writer longed to step outside the bustling world and meet God inside his holy Temple. We can meet God anywhere at any time, but we know that going into a church building helps us step aside from the busy mainstream of life into a place where we can quietly meditate and pray. We find joy, not in the beautiful building, but in the praying, singing, teaching, preaching, and fellowship that take place there.

84:5–7 The pilgrimage to the Temple passed through the barren Valley of Weeping (or Baca). No specific valley has been identified, and it may have been symbolic of the times of struggles and tears through which people must pass on their way to meet God. Growing strong in God's presence is often preceded by our pilgrimage through barren places in our lives. If you are walking through your own Valley of Weeping today, be sure you are on your pilgrimage toward God, not away from him.

84:6 The Valley of Weeping is probably not an actual place; it is symbolic of a dry valley miraculously turned into fertile land by rains. The person who loves to spend time in God's presence will view adverse circumstances as opportunities to experience God's faithfulness and blessing anew.

of springs where pools of blessing and refreshment collect after rains! 7They will grow constantly in strength and each of them is invited to meet with the Lord in Zion.

8O Jehovah, God of the heavenly armies, hear my prayer! Listen, God of Israel. 9O God, our Defender and our Shield, have mercy on the one you have anointed as your king.

10A single day spent in your Temple is better than a thousand anywhere else! I would rather be a doorman of the Temple of my God than live in palaces of wickedness. 11For Jehovah God is our Light and our Protector. He gives us grace and glory. No good thing will he withhold from those who walk along his paths. 12O Lord of the armies of heaven, blessed are those who trust in you.

84:7
Deut 16:16
2 Chron 3:18
Isa 40:31
84:8
Ps 59:5; 81:1
84:9
Gen 15:1
2 Sam 19:21
Ps 115:9-11
84:10
1 Chron 23:5
Ps 27:4
84:11
Ps 34:10
Isa 60:19,20

Theme: From reverence to restoration. Reverence leads to forgiveness, restoring our love and joy for God.
Author: The sons of Korah

85 Lord, you have poured out amazing blessings on this land! You have restored the fortunes of Israel, 2and forgiven the sins of your people—yes, covered over each one, 3so that all your wrath, your blazing anger, is now ended.

4Now bring us back to loving you, O Lord, so that your anger will never need rise against us again. 5(Or will you be always angry—on and on to distant generations?) 6Oh, revive us! Then your people can rejoice in you again. 7Pour out your love and kindness on us, Lord, and grant us your salvation.

8I am listening carefully to all the Lord is saying—for he speaks peace to his people, his saints, if they will only stop their sinning. 9Surely his salvation is near to those who reverence him; our land will be filled with his glory.

10Mercy and truth have met together. Grim justice and peace have kissed! 11Truth rises from the earth and righteousness smiles down from heaven.

12Yes, the Lord pours down his blessings on the land and it yields its bountiful crops. 13Justice goes before him to make a pathway for his steps.

85:1
Jer 30:18
Ezek 39:25
Joel 3:1
85:2
Num 14:19
Jer 31:34
Ps 32:1
85:3
Ex 32:12
Ps 78:38
85:8
Ps 29:11; 78:57
85:9
Ps 34:18; 84:11
85:10
Ps 89:4
85:11
Isa 45:8

Theme: Devoted trust in times of deep trouble
Author: David

86 Bend down and hear my prayer, O Lord, and answer me, for I am deep in trouble.

2Protect me from death, for I try to follow all your laws. Save me, for I am serving you and trusting you. 3Be merciful, O Lord, for I am looking up to you in constant hope. 4Give me happiness, O Lord, for I worship only you. 5O Lord, you are so good and kind, so ready to forgive; so full of mercy for all who ask your aid.

6Listen closely to my prayer, O God. Hear my urgent cry. 7I will call to you whenever trouble strikes, and you will help me.

8Where among the heathen gods is there a god like you? Where are their miracles? 9All the nations—and you made each one—will come and bow before

86:2
Ps 4:3; 25:20
86:4
Ps 25:1
86:5
Ps 103:8; 130:4
86:7
Ps 50:14,15
86:8
Ex 15:11
86:9
Isa 66:23

84:9 *your king,* literally, "your anointed." **84:10** *palaces,* literally, "tents." **84:11** *walk along his paths,* literally, "walk uprightly." **85:1** *restored the fortunes of Israel,* literally, "brought back the captivity." **85:4** *Now bring us back to loving you,* or, "Turn to us." **85:10** *justice,* literally, "righteousness." **85:13** *make a pathway for his steps,* or, "set us in the way of his steps."

84:11 This verse does not promise that God will give us everything we think is good, but that he will not withhold what is permanently good. He will give us the means to walk along his paths, but we must do the walking. When we obey him, he will not hold anything back that will help us continue to live for him.

85:6, 7 The psalmist was asking God to revive his people. God is capable of reviving both churches and individuals. He can pour out his love on us, bringing us back to loving you. If you need renewal in your church, family, or your personal spiritual life, ask God to give you a fresh touch of his love and kindness.

85:10, 11 These characteristics—mercy, truth, justice, and

peace—are not opponents who have made a truce, but co-laborers who have joined hands in working together. They are the outflowing of righteousness on the earth.

86:8-10 The God of the Bible is unique! He is alive and able to work mighty miracles for those who love him. All man-created deities are powerless before him because they are merely inventions of the mind, not living beings. The Lord alone is "worthy to receive the glory and the honor and the power" (Revelation 4:11). While people around the world believe in many heathen deities, you never have to fear that God is only one among many, or that you may be worshiping the wrong God. The Lord alone is God.

86:10
Deut 32:39
Isa 44:6,8
Mk 12:29
1 Cor 8:4

86:11
Ps 25:5
Jer 32:39

86:12
Ps 111:1

86:14
Ps 54:3

86:17
Ps 112:10
118:13; 119:122

you, Lord, and praise your great and holy name. ¹⁰For you are great, and do great miracles. You alone are God.

¹¹Tell me where you want me to go and I will go there. May every fiber of my being unite in reverence to your name. ¹²With all my heart I will praise you. I will give glory to your name forever, ¹³for you love me so much! You are constantly so kind! You have rescued me from deepest hell.

¹⁴O God, proud and insolent men defy me; violent, godless men are trying to kill me. ¹⁵But you are merciful and gentle, Lord, slow in getting angry, full of constant lovingkindness and of truth; ¹⁶so look down in pity and grant strength to your servant and save me. ¹⁷Send me a sign of your favor. When those who hate me see it they will lose face because you help and comfort me.

Theme: Jerusalem, where all believers will one day gather
Author: The sons of Korah (Temple assistants)

87:1
Ps 78:68,69
Isa 28:16

87:3
Ps 46:4; 48:8

87:4
Ps 45:12; 68:31
Isa 19:23-25

87:6
Isa 4:2-4

87:7
Ps 30:11; 36:9

87 High on his holy mountain stands Jerusalem, the city of God, the city he loves more than any other!

³O city of God, what wondrous tales are told of you! ⁴Nowadays when I mention among my friends the names of Egypt and Babylonia, Philistia and Tyre, or even distant Ethiopia, someone boasts that he was born in one or another of those countries. ⁵But someday the highest honor will be to be a native of Jerusalem! For the God above all gods will personally bless this city. ⁶When he registers her citizens he will place a checkmark beside the names of those who were born here. ⁷And in the festivals they'll sing, "All my heart is in Jerusalem."

Theme: When there is no relief in sight. God understands even our deepest misery.
Author: Heman, one of the sons of Korah (possibly the same man mentioned in 1 Chronicles 15:19; 16:41; 25:4, 5 as the king's prophet)

88:1
Ps 22:2; 24:5
Lk 18:7

88:3
Ps 107:18
116:3

88:5
Ps 31:12
Isa 53:8

88:6
Ps 32:4; 42:7
69:15; 143:3
Lam 3:55

88:8
Job 19:19; 30:10
Ps 31:11

88:9
Job 11:13
Ps 6:7; 22:2

88:10
Ps 6:5

88:13
Ps 5:3; 119:147

88:14
Ps 13:1

88:17
Ps 22:12,16

88 O Jehovah, God of my salvation, I have wept before you day and night. ²Now hear my prayers; oh, listen to my cry, ³for my life is full of troubles, and death draws near. ⁴They say my life is ebbing out—a hopeless case. ⁵They have left me here to die, like those slain on battlefields, from whom your mercies are removed.

⁶You have thrust me down to the darkest depths. ⁷Your wrath lies heavy on me; wave after wave engulfs me. ⁸You have made my friends to loathe me, and they have gone away. I am in a trap with no way out. ⁹My eyes grow dim with weeping. Each day I beg your help; O Lord, I reach my pleading hands to you for mercy.

¹⁰Soon it will be too late! Of what use are your miracles when I am in the grave? How can I praise you then? ¹¹Can those in the grave declare your lovingkindness? Can they proclaim your faithfulness? ¹²Can the darkness speak of your miracles? Can anyone in the Land of Forgetfulness talk about your help?

¹³O Lord, I plead for my life and will keep on pleading day by day. ¹⁴O Jehovah, why have you thrown my life away? Why are you turning your face from me, and looking the other way?

¹⁵From my youth I have been sickly and ready to die. I stand helpless before your terrors. ¹⁶Your fierce wrath has overwhelmed me. Your terrors have cut me off. ¹⁷They flow around me all day long. ¹⁸Lover, friend, acquaintance—all are gone. There is only darkness everywhere.

87:1 *Jerusalem,* literally, "Zion."

86:11, 12 Wholehearted reverence means appreciating God and honoring him in all areas of life. We need to show our loyalty to him in every part of our lives, not just in going to church. If we reverence God with our whole heart, then our work, relationships, use of money, and desires will be in keeping with his will.

87:1ff Jerusalem and its Temple are here symbolized as the future community of all believers. This psalm looks ahead to the Holy City of God described in Revelation 21:10–27. The honor of living there will be granted to all those whose names are recorded

in the Lamb's Book of Life (Revelation 21:27).

88:1ff Have you ever felt as if you have hit the bottom? The psalmist is so low he even despairs of life itself. Although everything was bad and getting worse, he was able to tell it all to God. This is one of the few psalms that gives no answer or hope. Don't think that you must always be cheerful and positive. Grief and depression take time to heal. No matter how low we feel, we can always take our problems to God and express our anguish to him.

Theme: God's promise to preserve David's descendants. God's promise is fulfilled in Jesus Christ, who will reign for eternity. The love and kindness promised to David is ours in Christ.
Author: Ethan (a Levite leader and possibly one of the head musicians in the Temple, 1 Chronicles 15:17, 19), or one of his descendants

89 Forever and ever I will sing about the tender kindness of the Lord! Young and old shall hear about your blessings. ²Your love and kindness are forever; your truth is as enduring as the heavens.

89:1
Ps 40:10; 59:16
89:2
Ps 36:5

³, ⁴The Lord God says, "I have made a solemn agreement with my chosen servant David. I have taken an oath to establish his descendants as kings forever on his throne, from now until eternity!"

89:3
2 Sam 7:16
Ps 132:11
Isa 9:7
Lk 1:31-33

⁵All heaven shall praise your miracles, O Lord; myriads of angels will praise you for your faithfulness. ⁶For who in all of heaven can be compared with God? What mightiest angel is anything like him? ⁷The highest of angelic powers stand in dread and awe of him. Who is as revered as he by those surrounding him? ⁸O Jehovah, Commander of the heavenly armies, where is there any other Mighty One like you? Faithfulness is your very character.

89:6
Ps 29:1; 96:4
89:7
Ps 47:2; 96:4
89:8
Ps 35:10

⁹You rule the oceans when their waves arise in fearful storms; you speak, and they lie still. ¹⁰You have cut haughty Egypt to pieces. Your enemies are scattered by your awesome power. ¹¹The heavens are yours, the world, everything—for you created them all. ¹²You created north and south! Mount Tabor and Mount Hermon rejoice to be signed by your name as their maker! ¹³Strong is your arm! Strong is your hand! Your right hand is lifted high in glorious strength.

89:9
Ps 65:7; 107:29
89:10
Ps 18:14
89:11
Gen 1:1
Ps 24:1

¹⁴, ¹⁵Your throne is founded on two strong pillars—the one is Justice and the other Righteousness. Mercy and Truth walk before you as your attendants. Blessed are those who hear the joyful blast of the trumpet, for they shall walk in the light of your presence. ¹⁶They rejoice all day long in your wonderful reputation and in your perfect righteousness. ¹⁷You are their strength. What glory! Our power is based on your favor! ¹⁸Yes, our protection is from the Lord himself and he, the Holy One of Israel, has given us our king.

89:14
Ps 97:2; 98:6
89:17
Ps 44:3; 75:10
148:14
89:19
2 Sam 17:10
1 Kgs 11:34
89:20
1 Sam 16:13
Acts 13:22

¹⁹In a vision you spoke to your prophet and said, "I have chosen a splendid young man from the common people to be the king— ²⁰he is my servant David! I have anointed him with my holy oil. ²¹I will steady him and make him strong. ²²His enemies shall not outwit him, nor shall the wicked overpower him. ²³I will beat down his adversaries before him, and destroy those who hate him. ²⁴I will protect and bless him constantly and surround him with my love; he will be great because of me. ²⁵He will hold sway from the Euphrates River to the Mediterranean Sea. ²⁶And he will cry to me, 'You are my Father, my God, and my Rock of Salvation.'

89:22
2 Sam 7:10,11
89:23
2 Sam 7:9
89:26
2 Sam 7:14
1 Chron 22:10
89:27
Ps 2:7; 72:11
Rev 19:1,5,16

²⁷"I will treat him as my firstborn son, and make him the mightiest king in all the earth. ²⁸I will love him forever, and be kind to him always; my covenant with him will never end. ²⁹He will always have an heir; his throne will be as endless as the days of heaven. ³⁰, ³¹, ³²If his children forsake my laws and don't obey them, then I will punish them, ³³but I will never completely take away my lovingkindness

89:29
1 Kgs 2:4
Isa 9:7
Jer 33:17
89:30
2 Sam 7:14
89:33
2 Sam 7:15

89:3, 4 *The Lord says,* implied. **89:5** *myriads of angels,* literally, "the assembly of the holy ones." **89:6** *mightiest angel,* literally, "the sons of the mighty." **89:7** *angelic powers,* literally, "the assembly of the holy ones." **89:10** *Egypt,* literally, "Rahab."

89:1ff This psalm was written to describe the glorious reign of King David. God had promised to make David the mightiest king on earth and to keep his descendants on the throne forever (2 Samuel 7:8–16). Because Jerusalem was destroyed and kings no longer reign there, these verses can only look forward prophetically to the future reign of Jesus Christ, David's descendant. Verse 27 is a prophecy concerning David's never-ending dynasty, which will be consummated in Christ's future reign over the world (see Revelation 22:5).

89:5 In the courts of heaven, a myriad of angels praise the Lord. This scene is one of majesty and grandeur to show that God is beyond compare. His power and purity place him high above nature and angels. (See Deuteronomy 33:2; Luke 2:13; and Hebrews 12:22 for more about angels.)

89:14, 15 God's throne is pictured with pillars of Justice and Righteousness and attended by Mercy and Truth. These describe fundamental aspects of the way God deals with people. As God's ambassadors, we should deal with people similarly. Make sure your actions flow out of justice, righteousness, mercy, and truth because any unfair, unloving, or dishonest action cannot come from God.

89:17 "Our power is based on your favor" means that when we are full of sin we are weak and powerless, inadequate for even the simplest spiritual tasks. But when we are filled with God's Spirit, his power flows through us and we can accomplish things for him beyond our expectations.

89:19 The prophet mentioned here may be Samuel, who anointed David as king of Israel (1 Samuel 16:1–13), or Nathan who was a prophet to Israel when David became king (2 Samuel 7:4–17).

89:34
Num 23:19
Jer 33:20,21

89:38
1 Chron 28:9

89:39
Ps 78:59
Lam 2:7; 5:16

89:40
Ps 80:12
Lam 2:2,5

89:42
Ps 13:2; 80:6

89:43
Ps 44:10

89:44
Ezek 28:7

89:45
Ps 44:15,16

89:46
Ps 13:1; 79:5

89:47
Job 7:7; 14:1
Ps 39:5; 6
Eccles 1:2; 2:11

89:48
Ps 22:29
Heb 11:5

from them, nor let my promise fail. 34No, I will not break my covenant; I will not take back one word of what I said. 35, 36For I have sworn to David (and a holy God can never lie), that his dynasty will go on forever, and his throne will continue to the end of time. 37It shall be eternal as the moon, my faithful witness in the sky!"

38Then why cast me off, rejected? Why be so angry with the one you chose as king? 39Have you renounced your covenant with him? For you have thrown his crown in the dust. 40You have broken down the walls protecting him and laid in ruins every fort defending him. 41Everyone who comes along has robbed him while his neighbors mock. 42You have strengthened his enemies against him and made them rejoice. 43You have struck down his sword and refused to help him in battle. 44You have ended his splendor and overturned his throne. 45You have made him old before his time and publicly disgraced him.

46O Jehovah, how long will this go on? Will you hide yourself from me forever? How long will your wrath burn like fire? 47Oh, remember how short you have made man's lifespan. Is it an empty, futile life you give the sons of men? 48No man can live forever. All will die. Who can rescue his life from the power of the grave?

49Lord, where is the love you used to have for me? Where is your kindness that you promised to David with a faithful pledge? 50Lord, see how all the people are despising me. 51Your enemies joke about me, the one you anointed as their king.

52And yet—blessed be the Lord forever! Amen and amen!

D. THE FOURTH BOOK OF PSALMS (90:1—106:48)

These psalms include a prayer of Moses, a psalm about oppressors, and a psalm praising God as our king. These psalms remind us that we should remember our place and be submissive before the almighty God.

Theme: God's eternal nature is contrasted with man's frailty. Our time on earth is limited and we are to use it wisely, not living for the moment, but with our eternal home in mind. This psalm is often used in funerals.

Author: Moses, making this the oldest of the psalms. (For more information on Moses, see his Profile in Exodus 16.)

90:1
Deut 33:27
Ezek 11:16

90:2
Gen 1:1
Ps 102:24,
25,27

90:4
Ps 39:5
2 Pet 3:8

90:5
Job 14:2; 20:8
Mt 6:30

90:9
Ps 78:33

90:10
Ps 78:39
Eccles 12:2-7

90 A prayer of Moses, the man of God.

Lord, through all the generations you have been our home! 2Before the mountains were created, before the earth was formed, you are God without beginning or end.

3You speak, and man turns back to dust. 4A thousand years are but as yesterday to you! They are like a single hour! 5, 6We glide along the tides of time as swiftly as a racing river, and vanish as quickly as a dream. We are like grass that is green in the morning but mowed down and withered before the evening shadows fall. 7We die beneath your anger; we are overwhelmed by your wrath. 8You spread out our sins before you—our secret sins—and see them all. 9No wonder the years are long and heavy here beneath your wrath. All our days are filled with sighing.

10Seventy years are given us! And some may even live to eighty. But even the best of these years are often emptiness and pain; soon they disappear, and we are

89:35, 36 *his throne will continue to the end of time,* literally, "his throne as the sun before me." **90:4** *They are like a single hour,* literally, "as a watch in the night."

89:34-37 In light of Israel's continual disobedience throughout history, this is an amazing promise. God promised that David's descendants would always sit on the throne (89:29), but that if the people disobeyed, they would be punished (89:30-32). And yet, even through their disobedience and punishment, God would never fail to keep his promises (89:33). Israel *did* disobey, evil ran rampant, the nation was divided, exile came—but through it all, a remnant of God's people remained faithful. Centuries later, the Messiah arrived, the eternal king from David's line, just as God had promised. All that God promises, he fulfills. He will not take back even one word of what he says. God can also be trusted to save us as he promised he would (Hebrews 6:13-18). God is completely reliable.

90:4 Moses reminds us that a thousand years are like a day to the Lord. God is not limited by time. It's easy to get discouraged when years pass and the world doesn't get better. Since we cannot see into the future, we sometimes wonder if God is able to see the future. But don't make the mistake of assuming that God has the same limitations as we do. God is completely unrestricted by time.

90:8 God knows all our sins as if they were spread out before him, even the secret ones. We don't need to cover up our sins before him because we can talk openly and honestly with him. God is not shocked by what we confess; he already knows it. But while he knows all that terrible information about us, God loves us and wants to forgive us. This should encourage rather than frighten us.

gone. 11Who can realize the terrors of your anger? Which of us can fear you as he should?

12Teach us to number our days and recognize how few they are; help us to spend them as we should.

13O Jehovah, come and bless us! How long will you delay? Turn away your anger from us. 14Satisfy us in our earliest youth with your lovingkindness, giving us constant joy to the end of our lives. 15Give us gladness in proportion to our former misery! Replace the evil years with good. 16Let us see your miracles again; let our children see glorious things, the kind you used to do, 17and let the Lord our God favor us and give us success. May he give permanence to all we do.

Theme: God's protection in the midst of danger. God doesn't promise a world free from danger, but he does promise his help whenever we face danger.
Author: Anonymous

91 We live within the shadow of the Almighty, sheltered by the God who is above all gods.

2This I declare, that he alone is my refuge, my place of safety; he is my God, and I am trusting him. 3For he rescues you from every trap, and protects you from the fatal plague. 4He will shield you with his wings! They will shelter you. His faithful promises are your armor. 5Now you don't need to be afraid of the dark any more, nor fear the dangers of the day; 6nor dread the plagues of darkness, nor disasters in the morning.

7Though a thousand fall at my side, though ten thousand are dying around me, the evil will not touch me. 8I will see how the wicked are punished but I will not share it. 9For Jehovah is my refuge! I choose the God above all gods to shelter me. 10How then can evil overtake me or any plague come near? 11For he orders his angels to protect you wherever you go. 12They will steady you with their hands to keep you from stumbling against the rocks on the trail. 13You can safely meet a lion or step on poisonous snakes, yes, even trample them beneath your feet!

14For the Lord says, "Because he loves me, I will rescue him; I will make him great because he trusts in my name. 15When he calls on me I will answer; I will be with him in trouble, and rescue him and honor him. 16I will satisfy him with a full life and give him my salvation."

Theme: Be thankful and faithful every day.
This psalm was used in Temple services on the Sabbath.
Author: Anonymous

92 *A song to sing on the Lord's Day.*
It is good to say, "Thank you" to the Lord, to sing praises to the God who is above all gods.

2Every morning tell him, "Thank you for your kindness," and every evening rejoice in all his faithfulness. 3Sing his praises, accompanied by music from the harp and lute and lyre. 4You have done so much for me, O Lord. No wonder I am glad! I sing for joy.

5O Lord, what miracles you do! And how deep are your thoughts! 6Unthinking

Cross references (right margin):
90:11 Ps 76:7
90:12 Ps 39:4
90:13 Deut 32:36
90:14 Ps 36:8; 103:5 / Jer 31:14
90:15 Ps 31:10; 86:4
90:16 Ps 44:1
91:1 Isa 25:4; 32:2
91:2 Ps 18:2; 142:5 / Jer 16:19
91:3 2 Chron 20:9 / Ps 124:7
91:4 Ps 35:2; 57:1 / 63:7 / Isa 51:1-6
91:5 Job 5:19-23 / Ps 23:4
91:11 Ps 34:7 / Mt 4:6 / Lk 4:9-11
91:13 Judg 14:6 / Lk 10:19
91:15 1 Sam 2:30
92:3 1 Sam 10:5 / 1 Chron 13:8 / Neh 12:27
92:5 Ps 36:6; 40:5 / 139:17 / Rom 11:33

90:14 *earliest,* literally, "early." **91:6** *in the morning,* literally, "at noonday." **91:16** *with a full life,* literally, "with long life." **92:1** *on the Lord's Day,* literally, "for the Sabbath day."

90:12 It is easy to forget how short life really is. Realizing that life is short helps us use the little time we have more wisely. It helps us concentrate on using our lives for eternal good, not just for the pleasure of the moment. Take time to number your days by asking, "What do I want to see happen in my life before I die? What small step could you take toward that purpose today?"

91:5, 6 God is a refuge, a shelter when we are afraid. The writer's faith in God as Protector would carry him through all the dangers and fears of life. This should be a picture of our trust—trading all our fears for faith in him, no matter what kind of fear it may be.

91:11 One of the functions of angels is to watch over believers (Hebrews 1:14). There are examples of guardian angels in

Scripture (1 Kings 19:5; Daniel 6:22; Matthew 18:10; Luke 16:22; Acts 12:7), although there is no indication that one angel is assigned to each believer. Angels can also be God's messengers (Matthew 2:13; Acts 27:23, 24). Angels are not visible, except on special occasions (Numbers 22:31; Luke 2:9).

92:1, 2 During the Thanksgiving holiday, we focus on our blessings and express our gratitude to God for them. But thanks should be on our lips daily. We can never say thank you enough to parents, friends, leaders, and especially, to God. When thanksgiving becomes an integral part of your life, you will find that your attitude toward life will change. You will become more positive, gracious, loving, and humble.

92:7
Ps 37:38

92:9
Ps 37:20; 68:1

92:10
Ps 23:5; 45:7
75:10

92:14
Jn 15:2

92:15
Rom 9:14

93:1
Isa 51:9

93:3
Ps 98:7,8

93:4
Ps 65:7

94:1
Deut 32:35
Isa 35:4
Rom 12:19

94:6
Job 22:13
Isa 10:2

94:9
Ex 4:11
Prov 20:12

94:11
1 Cor 3:20

94:12
Deut 8:5
Ps 9:15
Heb 12:5,6

94:14
Rom 11:2

94:15
Isa 42:3
Mic 7:9

94:16
Num 10:35

people do not understand them! No fool can comprehend this: 7that although the wicked flourish like weeds, there is only eternal destruction ahead of them. 8But the Lord continues forever, exalted in the heavens, 9while his enemies—all evil-doers—shall be scattered.

10But you have made me as strong as a wild bull. How refreshed I am by your blessings! 11I have heard the doom of my enemies announced and seen them destroyed. 12But the godly shall flourish like palm trees, and grow tall as the cedars of Lebanon. 13For they are transplanted into the Lord's own garden, and are under his personal care. 14Even in old age they will still produce fruit and be vital and green. 15This honors the Lord, and exhibits his faithful care. He is my shelter. There is nothing but goodness in him!

Theme: God's unchanging and almighty nature. His creation reminds us of his great power.
Author: Anonymous

93 Jehovah is King! He is robed in majesty and strength. The world is his throne.

2O Lord, you have reigned from prehistoric times, from the everlasting past. 3The mighty oceans thunder your praise. 4You are mightier than all the breakers pounding on the seashores of the world! 5Your royal decrees cannot be changed. Holiness is forever the keynote of your reign.

Theme: God will keep his people from the severe punishment awaiting the wicked. Since God is holy and just, we can be certain that the wicked will not prevail.
Author: Anonymous

94 Lord God, to whom vengeance belongs, let your glory shine out. Arise and judge the earth; sentence the proud to the penalties they deserve. 3Lord, how long shall the wicked be allowed to triumph and exult? 4Hear their insolence! See their arrogance! How these men of evil boast! 5See them oppressing your people, O Lord, afflicting those you love. 6, 7They murder widows, immigrants, and orphans, for "The Lord isn't looking," they say, "and besides, he doesn't care." 8Fools! 9Is God deaf and blind—he who makes ears and eyes? 10He punishes the nations—won't he also punish you? He knows everything—doesn't he also know what you are doing?

11The Lord is fully aware of how limited and futile the thoughts of mankind are, 12, 13so he helps us by punishing us. This makes us follow his paths, and gives us respite from our enemies while God traps them and destroys them. 14The Lord will not forsake his people, for they are his prize. 15Judgment will again be just and all the upright will rejoice.

16Who will protect me from the wicked? Who will be my shield? 17I would have died unless the Lord had helped me. 18I screamed, "I'm slipping, Lord!" and he was kind and saved me.

92:10 *by your blessings,* literally, "anointed with fresh oil." **93:1** *The world is his throne,* literally, "The world is established . . . your throne is established." **94:6, 7** *he,* literally, "the God of Jacob."

92:12, 13 Palm trees are known for their long life. To flourish like palm trees means to stand tall and to live long. The cedars of Lebanon grew to 120 feet in height and up to 30 feet in circumference; thus, they were solid, strong, and unmoveable. The psalmist saw believers as upright, strong, and unmoved by the winds of circumstance.

92:14 Honoring God is not limited to young people who are still blessed with physical strength and vitality. Even in old age, devoted believers can produce spiritual fruit. There are many faithful older people who have much to share and teach from a lifetime of living with God. Seek out an elderly friend or relative to tell you about life experiences with the Lord and challenge you to new heights of spiritual living.

93:1ff Jewish tradition claims that the next seven psalms (93–99) anticipate some of the works of the Messiah. Psalm 93 is said to

have been used in post-captivity Temple services and may have been written during Sennacherib's invasion (2 Kings 18,19).

93:5 The key to God's eternal reign is his holiness. God will never do anything that is not holy and, ultimately, he will not allow anything that is not holy to remain. This demonstrates to us the danger of using unholy means to reach a holy goal, for God says, "You must be holy because I, the Lord your God, am holy" (Leviticus 19:1, 2).

94:8–13 At times, God must punish us to help us. This is similar to a loving parent disciplining his child; the punishment is not very enjoyable to the child, but is essential to teach him right from wrong. The Bible says that "being punished isn't enjoyable. . . . But afterwards we can see the result, a quiet growth in grace and character" (Hebrews 12:11). When you feel God's hand of correction, accept it as proof of his love.

¹⁹Lord, when doubts fill my mind, when my heart is in turmoil, quiet me and give me renewed hope and cheer. ²⁰Will you permit a corrupt government to rule under your protection—a government permitting wrong to defeat right? ²¹, ²²Do you approve of those who condemn the innocent to death? No! The Lord my God is my fortress—the mighty Rock where I can hide. ²³God has made the sins of evil men to boomerang upon them! He will destroy them by their own plans. Jehovah our God will cut them off.

94:19
Isa 57:18,66:13
94:20
Ps 58:2
94:21
Ex 23:7
Mt 27:4
94:23
Ps 140:9,11

Theme: An invitation to worship God
Author: David

95 Oh, come, let us sing to the Lord! Give a joyous shout in honor of the Rock of our salvation!

²Come before him with thankful hearts. Let us sing him psalms of praise. ³For the Lord is a great God, the great King of all gods. ⁴He controls the formation of the depths of the earth and the mightiest mountains; all are his. ⁵He made the sea and formed the land; they too are his. ⁶Come, kneel before the Lord our Maker, ⁷for he is our God. We are his sheep and he is our Shepherd. Oh, that you would hear him calling you today and come to him!

⁸Don't harden your hearts as Israel did in the wilderness at Meribah and Massah. ⁹For there your fathers doubted me, though they had seen so many of my miracles before. My patience was severely tried by their complaints. ¹⁰"For forty years I watched them in disgust," the Lord God says. "They were a nation whose thoughts and heart were far away from me. They refused to accept my laws. ¹¹Therefore in mighty wrath I swore that they would never enter the Promised Land, the place of rest I planned for them."

95:4
Ps 135:5,6
95:5
Gen 1:9,10
95:7
Heb 3:7-11,15
4:7
95:8
Num 20:13
Deut 6:16
95:9
Num 14:22
95:10
Acts 7:36; 13:18
Heb 3:17
95:11
Deut 1:35
Heb 4:3,5

Theme: How to praise God. We can sing about him, tell others about him, worship him, give him glory, bring offerings to him, and live holy lives.
Author: Probably David because this psalm closely resembles David's hymn of praise in 1 Chronicles 16:23–36

96 Sing a new song to the Lord! Sing it everywhere around the world! ²Sing out his praises! Bless his name. Each day tell someone that he saves.

³Publish his glorious acts throughout the earth. Tell everyone about the amazing things he does. ⁴For the Lord is great beyond description, and greatly to be praised. Worship only him among the gods! ⁵For the gods of other nations are merely idols, but our God made the heavens! ⁶Honor and majesty surround him; strength and beauty are in his Temple.

⁷O nations of the world, confess that God alone is glorious and strong. ⁸Give him the glory he deserves! Bring your offering and come to worship him. ⁹Worship the Lord with the beauty of holy lives. Let the earth tremble before him. ¹⁰Tell the nations that Jehovah reigns! He rules the world. His power can never be overthrown. He will judge all nations fairly.

¹¹Let the heavens be glad, the earth rejoice; let the vastness of the roaring seas

96:3
Ps 145:12
96:5
1 Chron 16:26
Isa 42:5
96:8
Ps 115:1
96:9
1 Chron 16:29
2 Chron 20:21
96:10
Ps 58:11; 67:4
96:11
Isa 49:13

95:3 King of, literally, "King above." **95:8** in the wilderness, see Exodus 17:7. **96:8** come to worship him, literally, "enter his courts." **96:9** with the beauty of holy lives, or, "in the priestly robes."

94:19 We have all experienced times when doubts fill our minds. The psalmist saw evil people prospering and oppressing others (94:3-7), corrupt governments (94:20), condemnation of the innocent (94:21, 22)—much like we see in our world today. But because we know that God will not allow evil to continue forever, we must trust his timing and be responsible for our own obedience.

95:8 A hardened heart is as useless as a hardened lump of clay or a hardened loaf of bread. Nothing can restore it and make it useful. David warns against hardening our hearts as Israel did in the wilderness by continuing to resist God's will (Exodus 17:7). They were so convinced that God couldn't deliver them that they simply lost their faith in him. When someone's heart becomes hardened, that person is so stubbornly set in his ways that he

cannot turn to God. This does not happen all at once; it is the result of a series of choices to disregard God's will. If you resist God long enough, he may cast you aside like hardened bread, useless and worthless.

95:11 What keeps us from God's ultimate blessings? Unthankful hearts (95:2), not listening (95:7), hardening our hearts (95:8), doubt (95:9). In Hebrews 4:5–11, we are encouraged not to harden our hearts, but to reject the glamour of sin and anything that would lead us away from God.

96:1–4 If we believe God is great, we cannot help but tell others about him. God has chosen to use us to "publish his glorious acts throughout the earth." Praise for our great God overflows from his creation and should overflow from our lips. How well are you doing at telling others about God's greatness?

96:12
Isa 35:1; 44:23
55:12,13

demonstrate his glory. 12Praise him for the growing fields, for they display his greatness. Let the trees of the forest rustle with praise. 13For the Lord is coming to judge the earth; he will judge the nations fairly and with truth!

Theme: God, our awesome Conqueror, is righteous and just.
Author: Anonymous

97:2
Ex 19:9
Deut 4:11

97:3
Heb 12:29

97:5
Josh 3:11
Amos 9:5

97:7
Jer 10:14
Heb 1:6

97:8
Ex 18:11
Zeph 3:14

97:10
Dan 3:28
Rom 12:9

97 Jehovah is King! Let all the earth rejoice! Tell the farthest islands to be glad. 2Clouds and darkness surround him. Righteousness and justice are the foundation of his throne. 3Fire goes forth before him and burns up all his foes. 4His lightning flashes out across the world. The earth sees and trembles. 5The mountains melt like wax before the Lord of all the earth. 6The heavens declare his perfect righteousness; every nation sees his glory.

7Let those who worship idols be disgraced—all who brag about their worthless gods—for every god must bow to him! 8, 9Jerusalem and all the cities of Judah have heard of your justice, Lord, and are glad that you reign in majesty over the entire earth and are far greater than these other gods.

10The Lord loves those who hate evil; he protects the lives of his people, and rescues them from the wicked. 11Light is sown for the godly and joy for the good. 12May all who are godly be happy in the Lord and crown him, our holy God.

Theme: A song of joy and victory. Because God is victorious over evil, all those who follow him will be victorious with him when he judges the earth.
Author: Anonymous

98:1
Ex 15:6
Isa 52:10

98:2
Lk 1:54,72
Rom 3:25

98:6
Num 10:10
2 Chron 15:14

98:7
Ps 24:1

98 Sing a new song to the Lord telling about his mighty deeds! For he has won a mighty victory by his power and holiness. 2, 3He has announced this victory and revealed it to every nation by fulfilling his promise to be kind to Israel. The whole earth has seen God's salvation of his people. 4That is why the earth breaks out in praise to God, and sings for utter joy!

5Sing your praise accompanied by music from the harp. 6Let the cornets and trumpets shout! Make a joyful symphony before the Lord, the King! 7Let the sea in all its vastness roar with praise! Let the earth and all those living on it shout, "Glory to the Lord."

97:12 *crown him,* literally, "give glory to his holy name."

JUSTICE IN THE BOOK OF PSALMS

Justice is a major theme in Psalms. The psalmists praise God because he is just; they plead for him to intervene and bring justice where there is oppression and wickedness; they condemn the wicked who trust in their wealth; they extol the righteous who are just toward their neighbors.

Justice in Psalms is more than honesty. It is active intervention on behalf of the helpless, especially the poor. The psalmists do not merely wish the poor could be given what they need, but they plead with God to destroy those nations that are subverting justice and oppressing God's people.

Here are some examples of psalms that speak about justice. As you read them, ask yourself, "Who is my neighbor? Does my lifestyle—my work, my play, my buying habits, my giving—help or hurt people who have less than I do? What one thing could I do this week to help a helpless person?"

Selected psalms that emphasize this theme are 7, 9, 15, 37, 50, 72, 75, 82, 94, 145.

97:2 The clouds and darkness that surround God symbolize his unapproachable holiness and the inability of people to find him.

97:7 Although God reveals himself and his love through nature and the Bible, there are many who decide to ignore or reject him and pursue goals they believe are more important. The Bible makes it clear that these people are idol-worshipers because they give their highest loyalty to something else.

97:10 A sincere desire to please God will result in an alignment of your desires with God's desires. You will love what God loves and hate what God hates. Here we read that God loves those who hate evil. If you do not despise the actions of people who take advantage of others, if you admire people who only look out for

themselves, or if you envy those who get ahead using any means to accomplish their ends, then your primary desire in life is not to please God. Learn to love God's ways and hate evil in every form—not only the obvious sins but the "socially acceptable" ones as well.

98:1ff This is a psalm of praise anticipating the coming of Jesus. Jesus came to save all men from their sins (98:2, 3), and is coming again to judge the earth (98:8, 9). God is both perfectly loving and perfectly just. He is merciful when he punishes, and he overlooks no sin when he loves. Praise him for his promise to save you and to return again.

8, 9Let the waves clap their hands in glee, and the hills sing out their songs of joy **98:9**
before the Lord, for he is coming to judge the world with perfect justice. Isa 55:12

Theme: Praise for God's fairness and holiness. Because God is perfectly just and fair, we can trust him completely.
Author: Anonymous

99 Jehovah is King! Let the nations tremble! He is enthroned between the **99:1**
Guardian Angels. Let the whole earth shake. Ex 25:22
1 Sam 4:4

2Jehovah sits in majesty in Zion, supreme above all rulers of the earth. 3Let them **99:3**
reverence your great and holy name. Deut 28:58
Josh 24:19

4This mighty King is determined to give justice. Fairness is the touchstone of 1 Sam 2:2
everything he does. He gives justice throughout Israel. 5Exalt the Lord our holy **99:4**
God! Bow low before his feet. Ps 17:2

6When Moses and Aaron and Samuel, his prophet, cried to him for help, he **99:6**
answered them. 7He spoke to them from the pillar of cloud and they followed his Ex 15:25
1 Sam 7:9
instructions. 8O Jehovah our God! You answered them and forgave their sins, yet **99:7**
punished them when they went wrong. Ex 33:9
Num 12:5

9Exalt the Lord our God, and worship at his holy mountain in Jerusalem, for he **99:8**
is holy. Num 14:20

Theme: An invitation to enter joyfully into God's presence. His faithfulness extends to our generation and beyond.
Author: Anonymous

100 Shout with joy before the Lord, O earth! 2Obey him gladly; come before **100:2**
him, singing with joy. Deut 12:11,12
28:47

3Try to realize what this means—the Lord is God! He made us—we are his **100:3**
people, the sheep of his pasture. 1 Kgs 18:39
Isa 40:11
Ezek 34:30,31
4Go through his open gates with great thanksgiving; enter his courts with praise. Mk 14:27
Give thanks to him and bless his name. 5For the Lord is always good. He is always Jn 10:11
loving and kind, and his faithfulness goes on and on to each succeeding generation. **100:5**
Ps 25:8

Theme: A prayer for help to live a holy life. To live with integrity, both our efforts and God's help are necessary.
Author: David

101 I will sing about your lovingkindness and your justice, Lord. I will sing **101:1**
your praises! Ps 145:7

99:1 "Guardian Angels" is also translated "cherubim." Cherubim are divine beings that are one of several ranks of angels. (For more on angels, see the note on 91:11.)

99:3 Everyone, even kings and rulers, should reverence God's great and holy name because his name symbolizes his nature, his personage, and his reputation. But the name of God is used so often in vulgar conversation that we have lost sight of its holiness. How easy it is to treat God lightly in everyday life. If you claim him as your father, live worthy of the family name. Reverence God's name by both your *words* and your *life*.

99:5 God's holiness is terribly frightening for sinners, but a wonderful comfort for believers. God is morally perfect and is set apart from people and sin. He has no weaknesses or shortcomings. For sinners, this is frightening because all their inadequacies and evil are exposed by the light of his holiness. God cannot tolerate, ignore, or excuse sin. For believers, God's holiness gives comfort because, as we worship him, we are lifted from the mire of sin. As we believe in him, we are made holy.

99:6 The Bible records several instances where Moses, Aaron, and Samuel cried out to God for help (Exodus 15:25; 17:4; Numbers 11:11–15; 12:13; 14:13ff; 1 Samuel 7:5, 9; 15:11).

100:2 Some employees work reluctantly, complaining as they go. Others cheerfully give their best all day long. We are to be like the

faithful employees who serve with gladness. To brood and complain is only a waste of energy. Are you glad to obey the Lord?

100:3 God is our Creator; we did not create ourselves. Many people live as though they are the creator and center of their own little world. This mindset leads to a greedy possessiveness and, if everything should be taken away, a loss of hope itself. But when we realize that God created us and gives us all we have, we will want to give to others as God gave to us (Ephesians 2:10). Then, if all is lost, we still have God and all he gives us.

100:4 God is the Creator of all; thus he alone is worthy of being worshiped. What is your attitude toward worship? Do you willingly and joyfully come into God's presence or are you just going through the motions, reluctantly going to church? This psalm tells us to remember God's goodness and faithfulness, and then to worship with thanksgiving and praise!

101:1ff David may have written this psalm early in his reign as he set down the standards he wanted to follow. He knew that if he was to walk a blameless path he would need God's help (101:2). We can walk this blameless path if we avoid: (1) low and vulgar activities (101:3), (2) crooked deals (101:3), (3) selfishness (101:4), (4) evil (101:4), (5) gossip and slander (101:5), (6) conceit and pride (101:5). While avoiding the wrongs listed above, we must also let God's Word show us how to live rightly.

2I will try to walk a blameless path, but how I need your help, especially in my own home, where I long to act as I should.

3Help me to refuse the low and vulgar things; help me to abhor all crooked deals of every kind, to have no part in them. 4I will reject all selfishness and stay away from every evil. 5I will not tolerate anyone who secretly slanders his neighbors; I will not permit conceit and pride. 6I will make the godly of the land my heroes, and invite them to my home. Only those who are truly good shall be my servants. 7But I will not allow those who deceive and lie to stay in my house. 8My daily task will be to ferret out criminals and free the city of God from their grip.

Theme: The cure for distress. Because God is living, eternal, and unchanging, we can trust him to help his people in this generation just as he helped his people in past generations.
Author: Anonymous

102 *A prayer when overwhelmed with trouble.*
Lord, hear my prayer! Listen to my plea!

2Don't turn away from me in this time of my distress. Bend down your ear and give me speedy answers, 3, 4for my days disappear like smoke. My health is broken and my heart is sick; it is trampled like grass and is withered. My food is tasteless, and I have lost my appetite. 5I am reduced to skin and bones because of all my groaning and despair. 6I am like a vulture in a far-off wilderness, or like an owl alone in the desert. 7I lie awake, lonely as a solitary sparrow on the roof.

8My enemies taunt me day after day and curse at me. 9, 10I eat ashes instead of bread. My tears run down into my drink because of your anger against me, because of your wrath. For you have rejected me and thrown me out. 11My life is passing swiftly as the evening shadows. I am withering like grass, 12while you, Lord, are a famous King forever. Your fame will endure to every generation.

13I know that you will come and have mercy on Jerusalem—and now is the time to pity her—the time you promised help. 14For your people love every stone in her walls and feel sympathy for every grain of dust in her streets. 15Now let the nations and their rulers tremble before the Lord, before his glory. 16For Jehovah will rebuild Jerusalem! He will appear in his glory!

17He will listen to the prayers of the destitute, for he is never too busy to heed their requests. 18I am recording this so that future generations will also praise the Lord for all that he has done. And a people that shall be created shall praise the Lord. 19Tell them that God looked down from his temple in heaven, 20and heard the groans of his people in slavery—they were children of death—and released them, 21, 22so that multitudes would stream to the Temple in Jerusalem to praise him, and his praises were sung throughout the city; and many rulers throughout the earth came to worship him.

23He has cut me down in middle life, shortening my days. 24But I cried to him, "O God, you live forever and forever! Don't let me die half through my years! 25In

Cross references (left margin):

101:3 Deut 15:9
101:4 Prov 11:20
101:5 Prov 6:16-19
101:8 Ps 46:4; 75:10
102:1 Ex 2:23; 1 Sam 9:16
102:3 Ezra 10:6; Job 30:30; Jas 4:14
102:5 Lam 4:8
102:8 2 Sam 16:5; Isa 65:15; Lk 23:11; Acts 26:11
102:12 Ex 3:15; Lam 5:19
102:13 Isa 60:10; Zech 1:12
102:15 1 Kgs 8:41,42
102:16 Isa 60:1,2
102:17 Neh 1:6
102:18 Deut 31:19; 1 Cor 10:11
102:19 Deut 26:15
102:21 Isa 49:22; 23; Zech 8:20-23
102:24 Isa 38:10
102:25 Gen 1:1; Heb 1:10-12

101:2 Close relationships have much potential for conflict. Our homes can be difficult places in which to live godly lives. Our families usually see us at our worst because we relax and let down our mask of good behavior. Often we do not treat our family members with the same respect and kindness we show to friends and business associates. David must have experienced this difficulty as he cried to God for help. Since we should want to treat those who are closest to us well, and since we want our lives to be Christian examples for them, pray that God will help you live a blameless life at home.

101:6 David set different standards for heroes than most. He said that he would make the "godly of the land" his heroes. Our heroes, those we set up in our minds as models to emulate, have a profound influence on our lives. Choose your heroes with care.

102:1-11 We have the freedom to go directly to God with our laments, our distresses, our complaints. We don't need to cover our real feelings or bring ourselves to a certain point of maturity first. No matter how low we feel, we can turn to God.

102:3, 4 When we face sickness and despair, not only our food, but our lives become tasteless. In these times, God alone is our comfort and strength. Even when we are too weak to fight, we can lean on him. It is often through our weaknesses that God's greatest strength is made available.

102:16-22 Christ's future reign on earth will encompass two events mentioned in these verses. Jerusalem will be restored and the entire world will worship God (Revelation 11:15; 21:1-27).

102:25-27 The writer of this psalm felt rejected and cast aside because of his great troubles (102:9, 10). Problems and heartaches can overwhelm us and cause us to feel that God has forgotten us. But God our Creator is eternally with us and will keep all his promises, even though we may feel alone. Hebrews 1:10-12 quotes these verses to show that Jesus Christ, God's Son, was also present and active at the creation of the world.

ages past you laid the foundations of the earth, and made the heavens with your hands! 26They shall perish, but you go on forever. They will grow old, like worn-out clothing, and you will change them like a man putting on a new shirt and throwing away the old one! 27But you yourself never grow old. You are forever, and your years never end.

28"But our families will continue; generation after generation will be preserved by your protection."

102:26
Mt 24:35
2 Pet 3:10
Rev 20:11

102:27
Mal 3:6
Jas 1:17

Theme: God's great love for us. What God does for us tells us what he is really like.
Author: David

103

I bless the holy name of God with all my heart. 2Yes, I will bless the Lord and not forget the glorious things he does for me.

3He forgives all my sins. He heals me. 4He ransoms me from hell. He surrounds me with lovingkindness and tender mercies. 5He fills my life with good things! My youth is renewed like the eagle's! 6He gives justice to all who are treated unfairly. 7He revealed his will and nature to Moses and the people of Israel.

8He is merciful and tender toward those who don't deserve it; he is slow to get angry and full of kindness and love. 9He never bears a grudge, nor remains angry forever. 10He has not punished us as we deserve for all our sins, 11for his mercy toward those who fear and honor him is as great as the height of the heavens above the earth. 12He has removed our sins as far away from us as the east is from the west. 13He is like a father to us, tender and sympathetic to those who reverence him. 14For he knows we are but dust, 15and that our days are few and brief, like grass, like flowers, 16blown by the wind and gone forever.

17, 18But the lovingkindness of the Lord is from everlasting to everlasting, to those who reverence him; his salvation is to children's children of those who are faithful to his covenant and remember to obey him!

19The Lord has made the heavens his throne; from there he rules over everything there is. 20Bless the Lord, you mighty angels of his who carry out his orders, listening for each of his commands. 21Yes, bless the Lord, you armies of his angels who serve him constantly.

22Let everything everywhere bless the Lord. And how I bless him too!

103:3
Ex 34:7
Jer 30:17

103:4
Ps 49:15

103:5
Isa 40:31

103:7
Ex 33:13

103:8
Num 14:18
Neh 1:3; 9:17
Joel 2:13
Jonah 4:2

103:10
Lam 3:22

103:12
Isa 38:17
Heb 9:26

103:13
Mal 3:17

103:14
Gen 3:19
Eccles 12:7

103:15
Jas 1:10,11
1 Pet 1:24

103:20
Mt 6:10
Heb 1:14

Theme: Appreciating God through his creation. He not only creates, but maintains his creation. The Lord's care is the source of our joy.
Author: Anonymous

104

I bless the Lord: O Lord my God, how great you are! You are robed with honor and with majesty and light! You stretched out the starry curtain of the heavens, 3and hollowed out the surface of the earth to form the seas. The clouds

104:1
Dan 7:9

104:3
Amos 9:6

103:1ff David's praise focused on God's glorious acts. It is easy to complain about life, but David's list gives us plenty for which to praise God—his love, forgiveness, salvation, kindness, mercy, justice, patience, tenderness—we receive all of these without deserving any of them. No matter how difficult your life's journey, you can always count your blessings—past, present, and future. When you feel like you have nothing for which to praise God, read David's list.

103:1, 22 All nature, armies of angels, everything everywhere is to bless the Lord! To bless God is to praise him, remembering all he has done for us (103:2), reverencing him and obeying his commands (103:17, 18), and serving him constantly (103:21). Is your life a blessing to the Lord?

103:7 God's Law was given first to Moses and the people of Israel. God's Law presents a clear picture of who God is and how he wants us to live. Review the Ten Commandments and God's other laws in the Old Testament, asking him to show you his nature and will through them.

103:12 East and west can never meet. This is a symbolic portrait of God's forgiveness—when he forgives our sin, he separates it from us and doesn't even remember it. We need never wallow in the forgiven past, for God forgives and forgets. We tend to dredge up the ugly past, but God will not do this for he has wiped our record clean. If we are to follow God, we must model his forgiveness. When we forgive another, we must also forget the sin. Otherwise, we have not truly forgiven.

104:1ff This psalm is a poetic summary of God's creation of the world as found in Genesis 1. What God created each day is mentioned by the psalmist as a reason to praise God. On day one, God created light (Genesis 1:3; Psalm 104:1, 2); day two, sky and water (Genesis 1:6; Psalm 104:1–4); day three, land and vegetation (Genesis 1:9–13; Psalm 104:6–18); day four, the sun, moon, and stars (Genesis 1:14–16; Psalm 104:19–23); day five, fish and birds (Genesis 1:20–23; Psalm 104:25, 26); and on day six, animals, man, and food to sustain them (Genesis 1:24–31; Psalm 104:21–24, 27–30). God's act of creation deserves the praise of all people.

104:4
2 Kgs 2:11; 6:17
Heb 1:7

104:5
Job 38:4

104:6
Gen 1:2

104:7
Ps 18:15; 29:3

104:10
Isa 41:18

104:12
Mt 8:20

104:14
Gen 1:29
Job 28:5

104:15
Judg 9:13
19:5,8
Prov 31:6
Eccles 10:19
Lk 7:46

104:18
Lev 11:5
Prov 30:26

104:19
Gen 1:14

104:20
Isa 45:7; 56:9

104:22
Job 37:8

104:23
Gen 3:19

104:24
Jer 10:12; 51:15

104:26
Job 41:1

104:27
Ps 136:25

104:29
Gen 3:19

are his chariots. He rides upon the wings of the wind. 4The angels are his messengers—his servants of fire!

5You bound the world together so that it would never fall apart. 6You clothed the earth with floods of waters covering up the mountains. 7, 8You spoke, and at the sound of your shout the water collected into its vast ocean beds, and mountains rose and valleys sank to the levels you decreed. 9And then you set a boundary for the seas, so that they would never again cover the earth.

10He placed springs in the valleys, and streams that gush from the mountains. 11They give water for all the animals to drink. There the wild donkeys quench their thirst, 12and the birds nest beside the streams and sing among the branches of the trees. 13He sends rain upon the mountains and fills the earth with fruit. 14The tender grass grows up at his command to feed the cattle, and there are fruit trees, vegetables and grain for man to cultivate, 15and wine to make him glad, and olive oil as lotion for his skin, and bread to give him strength. 16The Lord planted the cedars of Lebanon. They are tall and flourishing. 17There the birds make their nests, the storks in the firs. 18High in the mountains are pastures for the wild goats, and rock-badgers burrow in among the rocks and find protection there.

19He assigned the moon to mark the months, and the sun to mark the days. 20He sends the night and darkness, when all the forest folk come out. 21Then the young lions roar for their food, but they are dependent on the Lord. 22At dawn they slink back into their dens to rest, 23and men go off to work until the evening shadows fall again. 24O Lord, what a variety you have made! And in wisdom you have made them all! The earth is full of your riches.

25There before me lies the mighty ocean, teeming with life of every kind, both great and small. 26And look! See the ships! And over there, the whale you made to play in the sea. 27Every one of these depends on you to give them daily food. 28You supply it, and they gather it. You open wide your hand to feed them and they are satisfied with all your bountiful provision.

29But if you turn away from them, then all is lost. And when you gather up their breath, they die and turn again to dust.

104:4 *angels,* literally, "spirits."

HOW GOD IS DESCRIBED IN PSALMS

Most of the psalms speak to God or about God. Because they were composed in a variety of situations, various facets of God's character are mentioned. Here is a sample of God's characteristics as understood and experienced by the psalm writers. As you read these psalms, ask yourself if this is the God you know.

God is . . .	References
All-knowing and ever-present	Psalm 139
Beautiful and desirable	Psalms 27, 36, 45
Creator	Psalms 8, 104, 148
Good and generous	Psalms 34, 81, 107
Great and sovereign	Psalms 33, 89, 96
Holy	Psalms 66, 99, 145
Loving and faithful	Psalms 23, 42, 51
Merciful and forgiving	Psalms 32, 111, 130
Powerful	Psalms 76, 89, 93
Willing to reveal his will, law, and direction	Psalms 1, 19, 119
Righteous and just	Psalms 71, 97, 113
Spirit	Psalms 104, 139, 143

104:5 The world runs like a beautifully crafted machine. God himself holds it together. The same power that holds the world together also binds us together as believers.

104:24 Creation is filled with stunning variety, revealing the rich creativity, goodness, and wisdom of our loving God. As you observe your natural surroundings, thank God for his creativity. Take a fresh look at people, seeing each one as God's unique

creation, each with his or her own special talents, abilities, and gifts.

104:29 Psalm 105 expresses god's sovereignty in history; this psalm tells of his sovereignty over all creation. God has supreme, unlimited power over the entire universe. He creates; he preserves; he governs. As we understand God's power, we realize that he is sufficient to handle our lives.

30Then you send your Spirit, and new life is born to replenish all the living of the earth. 31Praise God forever! How he must rejoice in all his work! 32The earth trembles at his glance; the mountains burst into flame at his touch.

33I will sing to the Lord as long as I live. I will praise God to my last breath! 34May he be pleased by all these thoughts about him, for he is the source of all my joy. 35Let all sinners perish—all who refuse to praise him. But I will praise him. Hallelujah!

104:30
Ezek 37:9

104:31
Gen 1:31

104:32
Ex 19:18
Judg 5:5

104:35
Ps 37:10

Theme: God's mighty deeds in bringing Israel to the Promised Land. Remembering his miracles encourages us to keep living close to him.
Author: David

105 Thank the Lord for all the glorious things he does; proclaim them to the nations. 2Sing his praises and tell everyone about his miracles. 3Glory in the Lord; O worshipers of God, rejoice.

4Search for him and for his strength, and keep on searching!

5, 6Think of the mighty deeds he did for us, his chosen ones—descendants of God's servant Abraham, and of Jacob. Remember how he destroyed our enemies. 7He is the Lord our God. His goodness is seen everywhere throughout the land. 8, 9Though a thousand generations pass he never forgets his promise, his covenant with Abraham and Isaac, 10, 11and confirmed with Jacob. This is his never-ending treaty with the people of Israel: *"I will give you the land of Canaan as your inheritance."* 12He said this when they were but few in number, very few, and were only visitors in Canaan. 13Later they were dispersed among the nations, and were driven from one kingdom to another; 14but through it all he would not let one thing be done to them apart from his decision. He destroyed many a king who tried! 15"Touch not these chosen ones of mine," he warned, "and do not hurt my prophets."

16He called for a famine on the land of Canaan, cutting off its food supply. 17Then he sent Joseph as a slave to Egypt to save his people from starvation. 18There in prison they hurt his feet with fetters, and placed his neck in an iron collar, 19until God's time finally came—how God tested his patience! 20Then the king sent for him and set him free. 21He was put in charge of all the king's possessions. 22At his pleasure he could imprison the king's aides and teach the king's advisors.

23Then Jacob (Israel) arrived in Egypt and lived there with his sons. 24In the years that followed, the people of Israel multiplied explosively, until they were a greater nation than their rulers. 25At that point God turned the Egyptians against the Israelis; they hated and enslaved them.

26But God sent Moses as his representative, and Aaron with him, 27to call down miracles of terror upon the land of Egypt. 28They followed his instructions and he sent thick darkness through the land, 29and turned the nation's water into blood, poisoning the fish. 30Then frogs invaded in enormous numbers; they were found even in the king's private rooms. 31When Moses spoke, the flies and other insects swarmed in vast clouds from one end of Egypt to the other. 32Instead of rain he sent

105:1
1 Chron 16:8-22, 34

105:2
Ps 98:5

105:4
Ps 27:8

105:5
1 Chron 16:13

105:7
Isa 26:9

105:8
Gen 22:16-18
Deut 7:9
Lk 1:72
Gal 3:17

105:10
Gen 28:13-15
Josh 23:4

105:12
Gen 34:30
Heb 11:9

105:14
Gen 12:17
20:7; 35:5

105:16
Lev 26:26
Isa 3:1
Ezek 4:16

105:17
Gen 37:28,36
Acts 7:9

105:19
Ps 66:10

105:20
Gen 41:14

105:24
Ex 1:7,9

105:25
Acts 7:19

105:26
Ex 3:10

105:27
Ex 8:10
Ps 78:43-51

104:30 born, literally, "created." **105:7** *His goodness*, literally, "His judgments." **105:14** *he would not let one thing be done to them apart from his decision*, literally, "He suffered no man to do them wrong." **105:28** *they*, implied.

104:30 Many people today are arrogant enough to think they don't need God. But our every breath depends on the Spirit he has breathed into us (Genesis 2:7; 3:19; Job 33:4; 34:14, 15; Daniel 5:23). Not only do we depend on God for our very lives, we must also desire to learn more of his plans for us each day.

105:1ff The first 15 verses of this psalm are also found in 1 Chronicles 16:7–22 where David brought the Ark of the Covenant to Jerusalem. Three other psalms are also hymns recounting Israel's history—78, 106, and 136.

105:4 If God seems far away, persist in your search for him. God rewards those who sincerely look for him (Hebrews 11:6). Jesus promised "seek, and you will find" (Matthew 7:7). David suggested

a valuable way to search out God—become familiar with the way he has helped his people in the past. The Bible records the history of God's people. In searching its pages we will discover a loving God who is waiting for us to find him.

105:5, 6 The nation Israel, the people through whom God revealed his laws to mankind, is descended from Abraham. God chose Abraham and promised that his descendants would live in the land of Canaan (now called Israel), and that his descendants would be too numerous to count (Genesis 17:6–8). Abraham's son was Isaac; Isaac's son was Jacob. These three men are considered the patriarchs or founders of Israel. God blessed them because of their faith (see Hebrews 11:8–21).

down murderous hail, and lightning flashes overwhelmed the nation. 33Their grape vines and fig trees were ruined; all the trees lay broken on the ground. 34He spoke, and hordes of locusts came, 35and ate up everything green, destroying all the crops. 36Then he killed the oldest child in each Egyptian home, their pride and joy— 37and brought his people safely out from Egypt, loaded with silver and gold; there were no sick and feeble folk among them then. 38Egypt was glad when they were gone, for the dread of them was great.

39He spread out a cloud above them to shield them from the burning sun, and gave them a pillar of flame at night to give them light. 40They asked for meat and he sent them quail, and gave them manna—bread from heaven. 41He opened up a rock, and water gushed out to form a river through the dry and barren land; 42for he remembered his sacred promises to Abraham his servant.

43So he brought his chosen ones singing into the Promised Land. 44He gave them the lands of the Gentiles, complete with their growing crops; they ate what others planted. 45This was done to make them faithful and obedient to his laws. Hallelujah!

Theme: A song of national repentance as the people return from captivity. God patiently delivers us, in spite of our forgetfulness and self-willed rebellion.
Author: Anonymous

106 Hallelujah! Thank you, Lord! How good you are! Your love for us continues on forever. 2Who can ever list the glorious miracles of God? Who can ever praise him half enough?

3Happiness comes to those who are fair to others and are always just and good.

4Remember me too, O Lord, while you are blessing and saving your people. 5Let me share in your chosen ones' prosperity and rejoice in all their joys, and receive the glory you give to them.

6Both we and our fathers have sinned so much. 7They weren't impressed by the wonder of your miracles in Egypt, and soon forgot your many acts of kindness to them. Instead they rebelled against you at the Red Sea. 8Even so you saved them—to defend the honor of your name and demonstrate your power to all the world. 9You commanded the Red Sea to divide, forming a dry road across its bottom. Yes, as dry as any desert! 10Thus you rescued them from their enemies. 11Then the water returned and covered the road and drowned their foes; not one survived.

12Then at last his people believed him. Then they finally sang his praise.

Side references

105:36 Ex 12:30
105:39 Neh 9:12 / Isa 4:5
105:40 Num 11:31 / Jn 6:31
105:41 1 Cor 10:4
105:43 Ex 15:1
105:44 Josh 13:7
105:45 Deut 4:40
106:1 1 Chron 16:34
106:3 Ps 15:2
106:4 Ps 44:3
106:5 Ps 1:3
106:6 2 Chron 30:7 / Ezra 9:7 / Neh 1:7 / Zech 1:4
106:7 Judg 3:7
106:8 Ezek 20:9
106:9 Ex 14:21 / Isa 63:11-13
106:11 Ex 15:5

HISTORY IN THE BOOK OF PSALMS

For the original hearers, the historical psalms were vivid reminders of God's past acts in behalf of Israel. These history songs were written for passing on important lessons to succeeding generations. They celebrated the many promises God had made and faithfully kept; they also recounted the faithlessness of the people.

We cannot read this ancient history without reflecting on how consistently God's people failed to learn from the past. They repeatedly turned from fresh examples of God's faithfulness and forgiveness only to plunge back into sin. God can use these psalms to remind us how often we do exactly the same thing: having every reason to live for God, we choose instead to live for everything but God. If we paid more attention to "his story" we wouldn't make so many mistakes in our own stories.

Selected historical psalms include: 68, 78, 95, 105, 106, 111, 114, 135, 136, 149.

105:45 Each morning, God helps us prepare for the unknown path that lies ahead by providing in his Word a record of his past dealings with people. When we learn about God through the pages of his Word, we learn how to be faithful and obedient, and the future is not as uncertain as it seems at times. We need not fear tomorrow when we know more about the God who will be with us tomorrow.

106:1ff While Psalm 105 is a summary of God's faithfulness throughout history, Psalm 106 is a summary of man's sinfulness throughout history. Psalm 105 covers events up to the Exodus from Egypt (Exodus 5—14), and Psalm 106 covers events from the

Exodus up to what appears to be the Babylonian captivity (2 Kings 25).

106:2 If we ever stopped to list all the miracles in the Bible, we would be astounded. They cover every aspect of life. The more we think about what God has done, the more we can appreciate the miracles he has done in our lives—birth, personality development, loving friends and family, specific guidance, healing, salvation . . . the list goes on and on. If you think you have never seen a miracle, look closer—you will see God's power and loving intervention on your behalf. God still performs great miracles!

13Yet how quickly they forgot again! They wouldn't wait for him to act, 14but demanded better food, testing God's patience to the breaking point. 15So he gave them their demands, but sent them leanness in their souls. 16They were envious of Moses; yes, and Aaron, too, the man anointed by God as his priest. 17Because of this the earth opened and swallowed Dathan, Abiram and his friends; 18and fire fell from heaven to consume these wicked men. 19, 20For they preferred a statue of an ox that eats grass, to the glorious presence of God himself. 21, 22Thus they despised their Savior who had done such mighty miracles in Egypt and at the Sea. 23So the Lord declared he would destroy them. But Moses, his chosen one, stepped into the breach between the people and their God and begged him to turn from his wrath, and not destroy them.

24They refused to enter the Promised Land, for they wouldn't believe his solemn oath to care for them. 25Instead, they pouted in their tents and mourned and despised his command. 26Therefore he swore that he would kill them in the wilderness 27and send their children away to distant lands as exiles. 28Then our fathers joined the worshipers of Baal at Peor and even offered sacrifices to the dead! 29With all these things they angered him—and so a plague broke out upon them 30and continued until Phineas executed those whose sins had caused the plague to start. 31(For this good deed Phineas will be remembered forever.)

32At Meribah, too, Israel angered God, causing Moses serious trouble, 33for he became angry and spoke foolishly.

34Nor did Israel destroy the nations in the land as God had told them to, 35but mingled in among the heathen and learned their evil ways, 36sacrificing to their idols, and were led away from God. 37, 38They even sacrificed their little children to the demons—the idols of Canaan—shedding innocent blood and polluting the land with murder. 39Their evil deeds defiled them, for their love of idols was adultery in the sight of God. 40That is why Jehovah's anger burned against his people, and he abhorred them. 41, 42That is why he let the heathen nations crush them. They were ruled by those who hated them and oppressed by their enemies.

43Again and again he delivered them from their slavery, but they continued to rebel against him, and were finally destroyed by their sin. 44Yet, even so, he listened to their cries and heeded their distress; 45he remembered his promises to them and relented because of his great love, 46and caused even their enemies who captured them to pity them.

47O Lord God, save us! Regather us from the nations so we can thank your holy name and rejoice and praise you.

106:14 *demanded better food,* literally, "lusted exceedingly." **106:15** God *sent them leanness in their souls,* or, "but sent a plague to punish them." **106:16** *the man anointed,* literally, "the holy one of Jehovah." **106:28** *to the dead,* or, "to lifeless idols."

106:14 Num 11:4	
106:15 Ps 78:29-31	
106:17 Num 16:32	
106:19 Acts 7:41 Rom 1:23	
106:21 Deut 10:21	
106:23 Ex 32:10-14	
106:24 Jer 3:19	
106:26 Heb 3:11	
106:28 Hos 9:10	
106:30 Num 25:7-13	
106:32 Ps 78:40	
106:34 Judg 1:21,27-36	
106:37 Num 35:33 2 Kgs 17:17	
106:39 Hos 4:12	
106:40 Judg 2:12-14	
106:41 Neh 9:27	
106:43 Judg 6:6 Ps 81:12	
106:45 Lev 26:42	
106:46 2 Chron 30:9 Ezra 9:9	
106:47 Ps 147:2	

106:13-15 In the wilderness, Israel was so intent on getting the food and water *they* wanted that they became blind to what God wanted. They were more concerned about immediate physical gratification than lasting spiritual satisfaction. They did not want what was best for them, and they refused to trust in God's care and provision (Numbers 11:18–33).

If you complain enough, God may give you what you ask for, even if it is not the best for you. If you're not getting what you want, perhaps God knows it is not in your best interest. Trust in his care and provision.

106:34-39 Israel constantly turned from their Provider and Protector. How, after the great miracles they saw, could they turn from God and worship the idols of the land? We also have seen God's great miracles, but sometimes find ourselves enticed by the world's gods—power, convenience, fame, sex, and pleasure. As Israel forgot God, so we are susceptible to forgetting him and being defiled by an evil world. Remember all that God has done for you so you won't be drawn away from him by the world's "pleasures."

106:40-42 Why does God allow his people to be disciplined by

pagan forces more evil than they? The tool he uses to discipline his followers is not as important as the discipline itself. When we have turned or drifted away from God, we should not be surprised that he disciplines us. We do not choose his methods of discipline, nor should we complain about them. Our job is to get the message and return to him.

106:40-42 God allowed trouble to come to the Israelites in order to help them. Our troubles can be helpful because they (1) humble us, (2) wean us from the allurements of the world and drive us back to God, (3) quicken our prayers, (4) allow us to experience more of God's faithfulness, (5) make us more dependent upon God, (6) encourage us to submit to God's purpose for our lives, and (7) make us more compassionate to others in trouble.

106:44-46 This is a beautiful picture of God being gracious toward his people who deserved only judgment. Fortunately, God's faithfulness to us is not limited by our faithfulness to him. God was gracious to us in sending his Son to die for our sin. If he did this while we were yet sinners, how much more gracious will he be now that we are his children?

107:1 This psalm speaks of four different types of people in

48Blessed be the Lord, the God of Israel, from everlasting to everlasting. Let all the people say, "Amen!" Hallelujah!

E. THE FIFTH BOOK OF PSALMS (107:1—150:6)

These psalms praise God's works, recount the blessings of righteous living, thank God for deliverance, and praise God for his wonderful Word. These psalms remind us that the most perfect sacrifice we can offer to God is a faithful and obedient life.

Theme: Thankfulness to God should constantly be on the lips of those whom he has saved. This psalm was written to celebrate the Jews' return from their exile in Babylon.
Author: Anonymous

107:2
Isa 35:9,10
107:3
Neh 1:9
Ezek 20:34
107:4
Josh 5:6
107:7
Jer 31:9
107:9
Mt 5:6
Lk 1:53
107:10
Mic 7:8
Lk 1:79
107:11
Num 15:31
107:12
Ps 22:11
107:14
Acts 12:7
107:16
Isa 45:1,2
107:17
Isa 65:6,7
Ezek 24:23
107:18
Job 33:19-22
Ps 9:13
107:20
2 Kgs 20:5
Mt 8:8
107:22
Lev 7:12
Ps 73:28
107:25
Ps 93:3,4
107:29
Mt 8:26
Lk 8:24
107:32
Ps 22:22; 25
Isa 25:1
107:34
Gen 19:24,25
107:35
Isa 35:6,7
41:18
107:37
2 Kgs 19:29
Amos 9:14
107:38
Gen 12:2
Ex 1:7

107 Say "Thank you" to the Lord for being so good, for always being so loving and kind. 2Has the Lord redeemed you? Then speak out! Tell others he has saved you from your enemies.

3He brought the exiles back from the farthest corners of the earth. 4They were wandering homeless in the desert, 5hungry and thirsty and faint. 6"Lord, help!" they cried, and he did! 7He led them straight to safety and a place to live. 8Oh, that these men would praise the Lord for his loving-kindness, and for all of his wonderful deeds! 9For he satisfies the thirsty soul and fills the hungry soul with good.

10Who are these who sit in darkness, in the shadow of death, crushed by misery and slavery? 11They rebelled against the Lord, scorning him who is the God above all gods. 12That is why he broke them with hard labor; they fell and none could help them rise again. 13Then they cried to the Lord in their troubles, and he rescued them! 14He led them from the darkness and shadow of death and snapped their chains. 15Oh, that these men would praise the Lord for his lovingkindness and for all of his wonderful deeds! 16For he broke down their prison gates of brass and cut apart their iron bars.

17Others, the fools, were ill because of their sinful ways. 18Their appetites were gone and death was near. 19Then they cried to the Lord in their troubles, and he helped them and delivered them. 20He spoke, and they were healed—snatched from the door of death. 21Oh, that these men would praise the Lord for his lovingkindness and for all of his wonderful deeds! 22Let them tell him "Thank you" as their sacrifice, and sing about his glorious deeds.

23And then there are the sailors sailing the seven seas, plying the trade routes of the world. 24They, too, observe the power of God in action. 25He calls to the storm winds; the waves rise high. 26Their ships are tossed to the heavens and sink again to the depths; the sailors cringe in terror. 27They reel and stagger like drunkards and are at their wit's end. 28Then they cry to the Lord in their trouble, and he saves them. 29He calms the storm and stills the waves. 30What a blessing is that stillness, as he brings them safely into harbor! 31Oh, that these men would praise the Lord for his lovingkindness and for all of his wonderful deeds! 32Let them praise him publicly before the congregation, and before the leaders of the nation.

33He dries up rivers, 34and turns the good land of the wicked into deserts of salt. 35Again, he turns deserts into fertile, watered valleys. 36He brings the hungry to settle there and build their cities, 37to sow their fields and plant their vineyards, and reap their bumper crops! 38How he blesses them! They raise big families there, and many cattle.

39But others become poor through oppression, trouble and sorrow. 40For God pours contempt upon the haughty and causes princes to wander among ruins; 41but

---

distress and how God rescues them: the wanderer (107:3-6), the prisoners (107:10-16), the foolish caught in their troubles (107:17-20), and the storm-tossed (107:23-30). No matter how extreme our calamity, God is able to break through to help us. He is loving and kind to those who are distressed.

107:2 God has done so much for us, and we have so much for which to thank him (see Psalm 103). He wants us to proclaim to everyone all that he has done. This verse is not as much a man-

date to witness as it is a declaration of the fact that those who truly live in God's presence will not be able to keep this glorious experience to themselves (see also Acts 1:8; 2 Corinthians 5:18-20).

107:28–32 Sometimes we feel as though all is hopeless. But trouble can lead us to depend on God as we cry to him for help. When he saves us, we will praise him for the good he has done. Then we understand that God can bring good out of troubles because our afflictions strengthen our faith.

he rescues the poor who are godly and gives them many children and much prosperity. ⁴²Good men everywhere will see it and be glad, while evil men are stricken silent.

⁴³Listen, if you are wise, to what I am saying. Think about the lovingkindness of the Lord!

107:42
Job 22:19
Rom 3:19

107:43
Hos 14:9

Theme: Victory in God's strength. With God's help, we can do more than we think.
Author: David

108 O God, my heart is ready to praise you! I will sing and rejoice before you. ²Wake up, O harp and lyre! We will meet the dawn with song. ³I will praise you everywhere around the world, in every nation. ⁴For your lovingkindness is great beyond measure, high as the heavens. Your faithfulness reaches the skies. ⁵His glory is far more vast than the heavens. It towers above the earth. ⁶Hear the cry of your beloved child—come with mighty power and rescue me.

⁷God has given sacred promises; no wonder I exult! He has promised to give us all the land of Shechem, and also Succoth Valley. ⁸"Gilead is mine to give to you," he says, "and Manasseh as well; the land of Ephraim is the helmet on my head. Judah is my scepter. ⁹But Moab and Edom are despised; and I will shout in triumph over the Philistines."

¹⁰Who but God can give me strength to conquer these fortified cities? Who else can lead me into Edom?

¹¹Lord, have you thrown us away? Have you deserted our army? ¹²Oh, help us fight against our enemies, for men are useless allies. ¹³But with the help of God we shall do mighty acts of valor. For he treads down our foes.

108:1
Ps 57:7-11

108:11
Ps 44:9

Theme: Righteous indignation against liars and slanderers.
We can tell God our true feelings and desires.
Author: David

109 O God of my praise, don't stand silent and aloof ²while the wicked slander me and tell their lies. ³They have no reason to hate and fight me, yet they do! ⁴I love them, but even while I am praying for them, they are trying to destroy me. ⁵They return evil for good, and hatred for love.

⁶Show him how it feels! Let lies be told about him, and bring him to court before an unfair judge. ⁷When his case is called for judgment, let him be pronounced guilty. Count his prayers as sins. ⁸Let his years be few and brief; let others step forward to replace him. ⁹, ¹⁰May his children become fatherless and his wife a widow; may they be evicted from the ruins of their home. ¹¹May creditors seize his entire estate and strangers take all he has earned. ¹², ¹³Let no one be kind to him; let

109:5
Mt 5:44

109:6
Zech 3:1

109:8
Acts 1:20

109:9
Ex 22:24

109:11
Isa 1:7

109:12
Isa 9:17

108:9 *But Moab and Edom are despised,* literally, "Moab is my washbasin; upon Edom I cast my shoe."
109:6 *Show him how it feels,* implied.

107:43 Those who have never truly suffered may not appreciate God as much as those who have matured under hardship. Those who have seen God work in times of distress have a deeper insight into his lovingkindness. If you have experienced great trials, you have the potential for great praise.

108:1ff The conclusions from two previous psalms have been put together to make this psalm. The first five verses are quoted from Psalm 57:7–11, and the next eight verses (108:6–13) are from Psalm 60:4–12.

108:7 God's Word is sacred because God is holy. What he says, he will do because his Word and his person are inseparable. To violate his own Word would cause him to cease to be God.

108:9 Moab, Edom, and Philistia were Israel's enemies to the east, south, and west respectively. They were enemies because they despised the Israelites and Israel's God.

108:13 Do our prayers end with requests just to make it through stressful situations? David prayed not just for rescue, but for victory. With God's help we can claim more than just survival, we

can claim victory! Look for ways God can use your distress as an opportunity to show his mighty power.

109:1–4 David endured many false accusations (1 Samuel 22:7–13; 2 Samuel 15:3, 4), as did Christ centuries later (Matthew 26:59–61; 27:39–44). David's prayer for his enemies is echoed in Jesus' prayer for those who nailed him to the cross (Luke 23:34). Also, 109:8 is quoted in Acts 1:20 as fulfillment of Judas' death.

109:4 David was angry at being attacked by evil people who slandered him and lied. Yet he said he loved his enemies and prayed for them. While we must hate evil and work to overcome it, we must love everyone, including those who do evil, because God loves them. We are called to hate the sin, but love the person. Only through prayer for our enemies will we find the strength to follow David's example.

109:6–20 This is another of the imprecatory psalms, a call for God to judge the wicked. (For an explanation of imprecatory psalms, see the note on Psalm 35:1ff.) David was not taking vengeance into his own hands, but was asking that God be swift in his promised judgment of evil people. David's words depict the eventual doom of all God's enemies.

109:14
Neh 4:5
Isa 65:6,7

109:15
Jer 16:17

109:16
Ps 37:32

109:17
Mt 7:2

109:18
Ps 73:6

109:19
Ezek 7:27

109:20
Isa 3:11
2 Tim 4:14

109:21
Ps 25:11
Ezek 36:22

109:22
Ps 40:17
Prov 18:14

109:24
Heb 12:12

109:28
2 Sam 16:11,12

109:29
Job 8:22
Ps 35:26

109:31
Ps 16:8; 37:33

no one pity his fatherless children. May they die. May his family name be blotted out in a single generation. 14Punish the sins of his father and mother. Don't overlook them. 15Think constantly about the evil things he has done, and cut off his name from the memory of man.

16For he refused all kindness to others, and persecuted those in need, and hounded brokenhearted ones to death. 17He loved to curse others; now you curse him. He never blessed others; now don't you bless him. 18Cursing is as much a part of him as his clothing, or as the water he drinks, or the rich food he eats.

19Now may those curses return and cling to him like his clothing or his belt. 20This is the Lord's punishment upon my enemies who tell lies about me and threaten me with death.

21But as for me, O Lord, deal with me as your child, as one who bears your name! Because you are so kind, O Lord, deliver me.

22,23I am slipping down the hill to death; I am shaken off from life as easily as a man brushes a grasshopper from his arm. 24My knees are weak from fasting and I am skin and bones. 25I am a symbol of failure to all mankind; when they see me they shake their heads.

26Help me, O Lord my God! Save me because you are loving and kind. 27Do it publicly, so all will see that you yourself have done it. 28Then let them curse me if they like—I won't mind that if you are blessing me! For then all their efforts to destroy me will fail, and I shall go right on rejoicing!

29Make them fail in everything they do. Clothe them with disgrace. 30But I will give repeated thanks to the Lord, praising him to everyone. 31For he stands beside the poor and hungry to save them from their enemies.

Theme: The credentials for the Messiah. Jesus is the Messiah.
Author: David

110:1
Mt 22:44
Lk 20:42,43
Acts 2:34,35
Heb 1:13

110:2
Ps 45:6
Dan 7:13,14

110:3
Ps 96:9

110:4
Heb 6:20; 7:21

110:5
Rev 6:17

110 Jehovah said to my Lord the Messiah, "Rule as my regent—I will subdue your enemies and make them bow low before you."

2Jehovah has established your throne in Jerusalem to rule over your enemies. 3In that day of your power your people shall come to you willingly, dressed in holy altar robes. And your strength shall be renewed day by day like morning dew. 4Jehovah has taken oath, and will not rescind his vow, that you are a priest forever like Melchizedek. 5God stands beside you to protect you. He will strike down many kings in the day of his anger. 6He will punish the nations, and fill them with their dead. He will crush many heads. 7But he himself shall be refreshed from springs along the way.

Theme: All that God does is good. Reverence for God is the beginning of wisdom.
Author: Anonymous

111:1
Ps 92:5; 138:1

111:3
Ps 96:6; 145:5

111 Hallelujah! I want to express publicly before his people my heartfelt thanks to God for his mighty miracles. All who are thankful should ponder them with me. 3For his miracles demonstrate his honor, majesty, and eternal goodness.

110:2 Jehovah has established your throne, literally, "The Lord will send forth the rod of your strength out of Zion." in Jerusalem, literally, "from Zion." **110:3** holy altar robes, literally, "in holy array." **110:4** like, literally, "after the manner of."

109:21 A name is more than a label, it is a representation of character and reputation. Foul deeds exhibit foul character, taint our reputation, and hurt our name. The world will praise or ridicule the name we represent according to how we act.

110:1 This is one of the most-quoted psalms in the New Testament because of its clear references to the Messiah. In Matthew 22:41–45, Jesus recited the words of this verse in reference to himself. Verses 1 and 6 look forward to Christ's final and total destruction of the wicked (Revelation 6—9); 110:2 prophesies Christ's reign on the earth (Revelation 20:1–7); 110:3, 4 tell of Christ's priestly work for his people (Hebrews 5—7); and 110:5, 6 look forward to the final battle on earth when Christ will overcome the forces of evil (Revelation 19:11–21).

110:1–7 Many people have a vague belief in God, but refuse to accept Jesus as anything more than a great human teacher. But the Bible does not allow that option. This psalm shows God's promise of sending the Messiah. The New Testament clearly shows that Jesus is God's Son, the Messiah. You can't straddle the fence, calling Jesus "just a good teacher," because the Bible clearly calls him the Messiah.

110:4 For more about Melchizedek, see his Profile in Genesis 15. To be a priest like Melchizedek means that Christ will never abuse his divine position and that his reign will be forever.

111—118 Psalms 111—118 are called hallelujah psalms. "Hallelujah" means "praise the Lord" and expresses the uplifting and optimistic tone of these songs.

4Who can forget the wonders he performs—deeds of mercy and of grace? 5He gives food to those who trust him; he never forgets his promises. 6He has shown his great power to his people by giving them the land of Israel, though it was the home of many nations living there. 7All he does is just and good, and all his laws are right, 8for they are formed from truth and goodness, and stand firm forever. 9He has paid a full ransom for his people; now they are always free to come to Jehovah (what a holy, awe-inspiring name that is).

10How can men be wise? The only way to begin is by reverence for God. For growth in wisdom comes from obeying his laws. Praise his name forever.

Theme: The advantages of having faith in God. God guards the minds and actions of those who follow his commands.
Author: Anonymous

112 Praise the Lord! For all who fear God and trust in him are blessed beyond expression. Yes, happy is the man who delights in doing his commands.

2His children shall be honored everywhere, for good men's sons have a special heritage. 3He himself shall be wealthy, and his good deeds will never be forgotten. 4When darkness overtakes him, light will come bursting in. He is kind and merciful— 5and all goes well for the generous man who conducts his business fairly.

6Such a man will not be overthrown by evil circumstances. God's constant care of him will make a deep impression on all who see it. 7He does not fear bad news, nor live in dread of what may happen. For he is settled in his mind that Jehovah will take care of him. 8That is why he is not afraid, but can calmly face his foes. 9He gives generously to those in need. His deeds will never be forgotten. He shall have influence and honor.

10Evil-minded men will be infuriated when they see all this; they will gnash their teeth in anger and slink away, their hopes thwarted.

Theme: The scope of God's care. God's great mercy is demonstrated by his concern for the poor and the oppressed.
Author: Anonymous

113 Hallelujah! O servants of Jehovah, praise his name. 2Blessed is his name forever and forever. 3Praise him from sunrise to sunset! 4For he is high above the nations; his glory is far greater than the heavens.

5Who can be compared with God enthroned on high? 6Far below him are the heavens and the earth; he stoops to look, 7and lifts the poor from the dirt, and the hungry from the garbage dump, 8and sets them among princes! 9He gives children to the childless wife, so that she becomes a happy mother.

Hallelujah! Praise the Lord.

112:9 *His deeds will never be forgotten,* literally, "his righteousness endures forever."

Cross references:

111:4 Ps 86:15; 103:8
111:5 Mt 6:31-33
111:8 Isa 40:8; Mt 5:18
111:9 Lk 1:68
111:10 Prov 1:7,9; 3:4,5; 9:10

112:2 Ps 25:13
112:3 Prov 3:16,17; 8:18
112:4 Job 11:17; Ps 97:11
112:6 Ps 15:5; 55:22
112:7 Ps 56:4
112:8 Ps 56:10,11
112:9 2 Cor 9:9; Ps 148:14
112:10 Mt 8:12; Lk 13:28

113:4 Ps 8:1; 97:9
113:5 Ps 89:6; 103:19
113:6 Ps 11:4; Isa 57:15
113:7 1 Sam 2:8

111:9 A ransom is paid for someone who is being held hostage. Mankind was being held hostage by sin, but Jesus paid the price to free us—giving his life as a perfect sacrifice. Before Jesus offered himself as a sacrifice for sin, people were not permitted into God's presence (the Holy of Holies); now, all believers can freely approach God's throne through prayer and have the presence of the Holy Spirit in their lives.

111:10 The only way to become truly wise is to reverence God. This same thought is expressed in Proverbs 1:7-9. Too often people want to skip this step, thinking they can become wise by life experience and academic knowledge alone. But if God is not acknowledged as the source of wisdom, then the foundation for making wise decisions cannot be laid, and we are doomed to mistakes and foolish choices. Always remember that the foundation for growing in wisdom is to recognize that God is the source of wisdom and that obeying his laws is the path to wisdom.

112:1 Many blessings are available to us—honor, prosperity,

security, freedom from fear (112:2-9)—if we *fear* the Lord, *trust* in him, and *delight* in obeying his commands. If you expect God's blessings, you must first reverence him, believe in his promises, and gladly obey him.

112:7, 8 We all want to live without fear; our heroes are fearless people who take on all dangers and overcome them. The psalmist teaches us that *fear* of God can lead to a *fearless* life. To fear God means to respect and reverence him as the almighty Lord. When we trust God completely to take care of us, we will find that our other fears—even of death itself—will subside.

113:5-9 In God's eyes, a person's value has no relationship to his or her wealth or position on the social ladder. Many people who have excelled in God's work began in poverty or humble beginnings. God supercedes the social orders of this world, often choosing his future leaders and ambassadors from among the social outcasts. Do you treat the unwanted in society as though they have value? Demonstrate by your actions that all people are valuable and useful in God's eyes.

Theme: The mighty God who delivered Israel from Egypt. We can celebrate God's great work in our lives.
Author: Anonymous

114 Long ago when the Israelis escaped from Egypt, from that land of foreign tongue, 2then the lands of Judah and of Israel became God's new home and kingdom.

3The Red Sea saw them coming and quickly broke apart before them. The Jordan River opened up a path for them to cross. 4The mountains skipped like rams, the little hills like lambs! 5What's wrong, Red Sea, that made you cut yourself in two? What happened, Jordan River, to your waters? Why were they held back? 6Why, mountains, did you skip like rams? Why, little hills, like lambs?

7Tremble, O earth, at the presence of the Lord, the God of Jacob. 8For he caused gushing streams to burst from flinty rock.

Theme: God is alive. He is thinking about us and caring for us, and we should put him first in our lives.
Author: Anonymous

115 Glorify your name, not ours, O Lord! Cause everyone to praise your lovingkindness and your truth. 2Why let the nations say, "Their God is dead!"

3For he is in the heavens, and does as he wishes. 4Their gods are merely manmade things of silver and of gold. 5They can't talk or see, despite their eyes and mouths! 6Nor can they hear, nor smell, 7nor use their hands or feet! Nor speak! 8And those who make and worship them are just as foolish as their idols are.

9O Israel, trust the Lord! He is your helper. He is your shield. 10O priests of Aaron, trust the Lord! He is your helper; he is your shield. 11All of you, his people, trust in him. He is your helper; he is your shield.

12Jehovah is constantly thinking about us and he will surely bless us. He will bless the people of Israel and the priests of Aaron, 13and all, both great and small, who reverence him.

14May the Lord richly bless both you and your children. 15Yes, Jehovah who made heaven and earth will personally bless you! 16The heavens belong to the Lord, but he has given the earth to all mankind.

115:2 *Their God is dead*, literally, "Where is their God?"

Side references: 114:1 Ex 13:3 · 114:2 Ex 29:45,46 · 114:3 Ex 14:21 · 114:4 Ps 29:5,6 · 114:5 Hab 3:8 · 114:8 Ex 17:5,6 Deut 8:15 · 115:1 Ps 29:2 Isa 48:11 Ezek 36:22,32 · 115:3 Ps 103:19 Dan 4:35 · 115:4 2 Kgs 19:18 Ps 115:4-8 135:15-18 Jer 10:25 · 115:9 Ps 33:20; 62:8 · 115:11 Ps 103:11 135:20 · 115:12 Ps 98:3 128:1,4 · 115:15 Gen 1:1; 14:19

114:7 Even with our great technology, the seas, rivers, and mountains still present us with formidable challenges. But to God, who controls nature, they are nothing. When observing the power of an ocean wave or the majesty of a mountain peak, think of God's greatness and glory, which are far more awesome than the natural wonders you can see. To tremble at God's presence means recognizing God's complete power and authority, and our frailty by comparison.

115—118 Psalms 115—118 are traditionally sung at the Passover meal, commemorating Israel's escape from slavery in Egypt (Exodus 11, 12).

115:1 The psalmist asked that God's name alone be glorified. Too often we ask God to glorify his name *with* ours. For example, we may pray for help to do a good job so that our work will be noticed. Or we may ask that a presentation go well so we will get applause. There is nothing wrong with looking good or impressing others; the problem comes when we want to look good no matter what happens to God's reputation in the process. Your glory should be a by-product of seeking God's glory.

115:1, 2 This may have been written at the time when God was allowing the heathen nations to punish his people for their idolatry. Since God's people suffered, the heathen taunted them and said their God was dead. Nothing has changed. People too often think God is dead because his people appear weak or wounded. The psalmist's people were being refined for God's purposes and God

was very much alive and in control of the refining process. God is presiding over our refinement too.

115:4-8 When the psalms were written, many people in Israel worshiped idols—statues of wood, stone, or metal. They took pride in what they could see and had contempt for what they couldn't see. Today, we still put more value in tangible objects (position, money, home, clothing, possessions) than in intangible results (spiritual growth, salvation, giving to those in need, spending time with loved ones). Those who give their whole lives to obtaining these tangible objects are as foolish and empty as the idols themselves. (For more on the foolishness of idols, see Isaiah 44:9-20.)

115:8 These gods are powerless to do anything because God is in control of the universe, and those who worship them become just as powerless as their gods. The gods of wealth and power, though they seem powerful, are just as powerless. They can't guarantee immunity from death and they can't give eternal life.

115:12 "Jehovah is constantly thinking about us" says the psalm writer. What a fantastic truth! There are many times when we feel isolated, alone, and abandoned, even by God. In reality, he sees, understands, and is thinking about us. When depressed by problems or struggling with self-worth, be encouraged that God keeps you in his thoughts. If he thinks about you, surely his help is near.

¹⁷The dead cannot sing praises to Jehovah here on earth, ¹⁸but we can! We praise him forever! Hallelujah! Praise the Lord!

115:17
Ps 6:5; 31:17

Theme: Praise for being saved from certain death. Worship is a thankful response and not a repayment for what God has done.
Author: Anonymous

116 I love the Lord because he hears my prayers and answers them. ²Because he bends down and listens, I will pray as long as I breathe!

³Death stared me in the face—I was frightened and sad. ⁴Then I cried, "Lord, save me!" ⁵How kind he is! How good he is! So merciful, this God of ours! ⁶The Lord protects the simple and the childlike; I was facing death and then he saved me. ⁷Now I can relax. For the Lord has done this wonderful miracle for me. ⁸He has saved me from death, my eyes from tears, my feet from stumbling. ⁹I shall live! Yes, in his presence—here on earth!

¹⁰, ¹¹In my discouragement I thought, "They are lying when they say I will recover." ¹²But now what can I offer Jehovah for all he has done for me? ¹³I will bring him an offering of wine and praise his name for saving me. ¹⁴I will publicly bring him the sacrifice I vowed I would. ¹⁵His loved ones are very precious to him and he does not lightly let them die.

¹⁶O Lord, you have freed me from my bonds and I will serve you forever. ¹⁷I will worship you and offer you a sacrifice of thanksgiving. ¹⁸, ¹⁹Here in the courts of the Temple in Jerusalem, before all the people, I will pay everything I vowed to the Lord. Praise the Lord.

116:1
Ps 18:1; 66:19
116:2
Ps 17:6; 31:2
116:3
Ps 18:4-6
116:5
Ex 34:6
116:6
Ps 142:6
Prov 1:4
116:7
Ps 13:6
Mt 11:29
116:8
Ps 49:15
116:12
2 Chron 32:25
1 Thess 3:9
116:14
Ps 22:25; 50:14
116:15
Ps 72:14

Theme: Another reason for praise—God's love for the whole world.
We should praise God for his unlimited love.
Author: Anonymous

117 Praise the Lord, all nations everywhere. Praise him, all the peoples of the earth. ²For he loves us very dearly, and his truth endures. Praise the Lord.

117:1
Rom 15:11

Theme: Confidence in God's eternal love. God's love is unchanging in the midst of changing situations. This gives us security.
Author: Anonymous

118 Oh, thank the Lord, for he's so good! His lovingkindness is forever. ²Let the congregation of Israel praise him with these same words: "His lovingkindness is forever." ³And let the priests of Aaron chant, "His lovingkindness is forever." ⁴Let the Gentile converts chant, "His lovingkindness is forever."

⁵In my distress I prayed to the Lord and he answered me and rescued me. ⁶He is for me! How can I be afraid? What can mere man do to me? ⁷The Lord is on my side, he will help me. Let those who hate me beware.

⁸It is better to trust the Lord than to put confidence in men. ⁹It is better to take refuge in him than in the mightiest king!

118:1
Ps 136
118:5
Ps 18:19
118:6
Job 19:27
Heb 13:6
118:7
Ps 54:7
118:8
2 Chron 32:7,8
Isa 57:13

115:17 *The dead cannot sing praises to Jehovah here on earth,* implied. **116:10, 11** *In my discouragement I thought, "They are lying when they say I will recover."* Literally, "I said in my alarm, all men are liars." **116:13** *an offering of wine,* literally, "the cup of salvation," i.e., the thank offering of wine for saving me. **116:15** *His loved ones are very precious to him and he does not lightly let them die,* literally, "Precious in the sight of the Lord is the death of his saints." See context for the validity of the paraphrase.

116:1, 2 God is not so far away that you cannot reach him. He "bends down and listens" to your prayers. This writer's love for the Lord had grown because he had experienced answers to his prayers. If you are discouraged, remember that God is near, listening carefully to every prayer and answering each prayer in order to give you his best.

116:15 Eventually everyone must die. When someone we love is nearing death, we may become embittered and feel hopeless. But the phrase, "he does not lightly let them die," means that they (as believers) are precious to God and he carefully chooses the time when they are to be called into his presence. Let this truth provide comfort when you've lost a loved one.

117:1, 2 Psalm 117 is not only the shortest chapter in the Bible,

but the middle chapter. Paul quotes from it in Romans 15:11 to show that God's salvation is for *all* people, not just the Jews.

117:1, 2 Have you ever said, "I can't think of anything God has done for me. How can I praise him?" This psalm gives two reasons for praising God: "He loves us very much" and "His truth endures." If he did nothing else for us our whole lives, he would still be worthy of our highest praise.

118:8 Pilots put confidence in their planes. Commuters place confidence in trains, cars, or buses. Each day we must put our confidence in something or someone. If you are willing to trust a plane or car to get you to your destination, are you willing to trust God to guide you here on earth and to your eternal destination? Do you trust him more than any human being? If not, why not?

118:12
Deut 1:44

118:14
Ex 15:2
Isa 12:2

118:15
Lk 1:51

118:18
Jer 31:18
1 Cor 11:32
2 Cor 6:9

118:19
Isa 26:2

118:22
Mt 21:42
Mk 12:10,11
Lk 20:17
Acts 4:11
1 Pet 2:7

118:25
Ps 122:6,7

118:26
Mt 21:9
Mk 11:9
Lk 13:35
Jn 12:13

118:27
Isa 25:1
1 Pet 2:9

¹⁰Though all the nations of the world attack me, I will march out behind his banner and destroy them. ¹¹Yes, they surround and attack me; but with his flag flying above me I will cut them off. ¹²They swarm around me like bees; they blaze against me like a roaring flame. Yet beneath his flag I shall destroy them. ¹³You did your best to kill me, O my enemy, but the Lord helped me. ¹⁴He is my strength and song in the heat of battle, and now he has given me the victory. ¹⁵, ¹⁶Songs of joy at the news of our rescue are sung in the homes of the godly. The strong arm of the Lord has done glorious things! ¹⁷I shall not die, but live to tell of all his deeds. ¹⁸The Lord has punished me, but not handed me over to death.

¹⁹Open the gates of the Temple—I will go in and give him my thanks. ²⁰Those gates are the way into the presence of the Lord, and the godly enter there. ²¹O Lord, thank you so much for answering my prayer and saving me.

²²The stone rejected by the builders has now become the capstone of the arch! ²³This is the Lord's doing, and it is marvelous to see! ²⁴This is the day the Lord has made. We will rejoice and be glad in it. ²⁵O Lord, please help us. Save us. Give us success. ²⁶Blessed is the one who is coming, the one sent by the Lord. We bless you from the Temple.

²⁷, ²⁸Jehovah God is our light. I present to him my sacrifice upon the altar, for you are my God, and I shall give you this thanks and this praise. ²⁹Oh, give thanks to the Lord, for he is so good! For his lovingkindness is forever.

Theme: God's Word is true and wonderful. Stay true to God and his Word no matter how bad the world becomes. Obedience to God's laws is the only way to achieve real happiness.
Author: Anonymous, some suggest Ezra the priest

119:1
Prov 11:20; 13:6

119:2
Deut 4:29
10:12; 11:13
30:2

119:4
Deut 4:13

119:9
1 Kgs 8:25
2 Chron 6:16

119 Happy are all who perfectly follow the laws of God. ²Happy are all who search for God, and always do his will, ³rejecting compromise with evil, and walking only in his paths. ⁴You have given us your laws to obey— ⁵oh, how I want to follow them consistently. ⁶Then I will not be disgraced, for I will have a clean record.

⁷After you have corrected me I will thank you by living as I should! ⁸I *will* obey! Oh, don't forsake me and let me slip back into sin again.

⁹How can a young man stay pure? By reading your Word and following its rules. ¹⁰I have tried my best to find you—don't let me wander off from your instructions. ¹¹I have thought much about your words, and stored them in my heart so that they would hold me back from sin.

118:19 *the gates of the Temple,* literally, "the gates of righteousness." **118:22** *the capstone of the arch,* literally, "the head of the corner." **118:26** *the one sent by the Lord,* literally, "in the name of the Lord." **119:7** *After you have corrected me,* literally, "when I learn [have experienced] your righteous judgments." **119:8** *Oh, don't forsake me and let me slip back into sin again,* literally, "Oh, forsake me not utterly."

118:22, 23 Jesus referred to this verse when he spoke of being rejected by his own people (Matthew 21:42; Mark 12:10, 11; Luke 20:17). Although he was rejected, Jesus is now the "chief cornerstone," the most important part of the church (Acts 4:11; Ephesians 2:20; 1 Peter 2:6, 7).

118:24 There are days when the last thing we want to do is rejoice. Our mood is down, our situation out of hand, our sorrow or guilt overwhelming. We can relate to the writers of the psalms who often felt this way. But no matter how low the psalmists got, they were always honest with God about how they felt. And as they talked to God, their prayers ended in praise. When you don't feel like rejoicing, tell God how you truly feel. You will find that God will give you a reason to rejoice.

119:1ff This is both the longest psalm and the longest chapter in the Bible. It may have been written by Ezra after the Temple had been rebuilt (Ezra 6:14, 15) as a repetitive meditation on the beauty of God's Word and how it helps us stay pure and grow in faith. This psalm has 22 carefully constructed sections each corresponding to a different letter in the Hebrew alphabet and each verse beginning with the letter of its section. Almost every verse mentions God's Word. Such repetition was common in the Hebrew culture—people did not have personal copies of the

Scriptures to read as we do, so among the common people, God's Word was memorized and passed along orally. The structure of this psalm allowed for easy memorization.

119:7 Loving parents discipline their children to teach them how to live properly. At times, our heavenly Father must correct us through loving discipline. When you are corrected by God, thank him for loving you enough to get involved directly in your life. Then resolve to obey God when temptation strikes again.

119:9 We are drowning in a sea of impurity. Everywhere we look, we find temptation to lead impure lives. The psalmist asked a question that troubles us all: how do we stay pure in an impure environment? We cannot do this on our own, but must have counsel and strength more dynamic than the tempting influences around us. Where can we find that measure of strength and wisdom? The psalmist rises up triumphantly with the answer—by reading God's Word and doing what it says.

119:11 Storing God's Word in our hearts and minds is a deterrent to sin. This alone should inspire us to want to memorize Scripture. But memorization alone will not keep us from sin; we must also put God's Word to work in our lives.

12Blessed Lord, teach me your rules. 13I have recited your laws, 14and rejoiced in them more than in riches. 15I will meditate upon them and give them my full respect. 16I will delight in them and not forget them.

17Bless me with life so that I can continue to obey you. 18Open my eyes to see wonderful things in your Word. 19I am but a pilgrim here on earth: how I need a map—and your commands are my chart and guide. 20I long for your instructions more than I can tell.

21You rebuke those cursed proud ones who refuse your commands— 22don't let them scorn me for obeying you. 23For even princes sit and talk against me, but I will continue in your plans. 24Your laws are both my light and my counselors.

25I am completely discouraged—I lie in the dust. Revive me by your Word. 26I told you my plans and you replied. Now give me your instructions. 27Make me understand what you want; for then I shall see your miracles.

28I weep with grief; my heart is heavy with sorrow; encourage and cheer me with your words. 29, 30Keep me far from every wrong; help me, undeserving as I am, to obey your laws, for I have chosen to do right. 31I cling to your commands and follow them as closely as I can. Lord, don't let me make a mess of things. 32If you will only help me to want your will, then I will follow your laws even more closely.

33, 34Just tell me what to do and I will do it, Lord. As long as I live I'll wholeheartedly obey. 35Make me walk along the right paths for I know how delightful they really are.

36Help me to prefer obedience to making money! 37Turn me away from wanting any other plan than yours. Revive my heart toward you. 38Reassure me that your promises are for me, for I trust and revere you.

39How I dread being mocked for obeying, for your laws are right and good. 40, 41, 42I long to obey them! Therefore in fairness renew my life, for this was your promise—yes, Lord, to save me! Now spare me by your kindness and your love. Then I will have an answer for those who taunt me, for I trust your promises.

43May I never forget your words; for they are my only hope. 44, 45, 46Therefore I will keep on obeying you forever and forever, free within the limits of your laws. I will speak to kings about their value, and they will listen with interest and respect.

47How I love your laws! How I enjoy your commands! 48"Come, come to me," I call to them, for I love them and will let them fill my life.

49, 50Never forget your promises to me your servant, for they are my only hope. They give me strength in all my troubles; how they refresh and revive me! 51Proud

119:13
Ps 40:9
119:15
Isa 58:2

119:19
1 Chron 29:15
Heb 11:13

119:21
Deut 27:26
Ps 37:22

119:25
Ps 44:25

119:28
Ps 22:14
1 Pet 5:10
119:31
Deut 11:22

119:33
1 Chron 22:12
Ezek 44:24

119:35
Ps 25:4; 112:1
119:36
Lk 12:15
Heb 13:5
119:37
Ps 71:20
Isa 33:15
119:38
2 Sam 7:25
119:40
Ps 102:39

119:44
Acts 26:1,2

119:49
Job 6:10
Rom 15:14

119:51
Job 23:11
Jer 20:7

119:17 *Bless me with life,* literally, "deal bountifully that I may live." **119:37** *from wanting any other plan than yours,* literally, "from beholding vanity."

119:12–18 Most of us chafe under rules, for we think they restrict us from doing what we want. At first glance, then, it may seem strange to hear the psalmist talk of rejoicing in God's laws more than in riches (119:14). But God's laws were given to free us to be all he wants us to be. They restrict us from doing those things that will cripple us and keep us from being our best. God's laws are guidelines to help us follow in his path and not wander onto paths that would lead to destruction.

119:19 Almost any long trip requires a map or guide. As we travel through life, the Bible should be our road map, pointing out safe routes, obstacles to avoid, and our final destination. We must recognize ourselves as "pilgrims," travelers here on earth who need to study God's "map" to learn the way. If we ignore the map, we will wander aimlessly through life and risk missing our real destination.

119:25 How can God's Word revive us? Our world is full of evil; God's Word revives us with the promise of victory over evil. Our world says we are worthless without certain looks or possessions; God's Word gives us value by telling us that God created us and loves us. Our world is full of discouragement; God's Word encourages us. Our world has no real, lasting answers; God's Word gives satisfying, eternal answers. Read it and be revived.

119:32 Our lives are cluttered with rule books, but the authors never come with us to help us follow the rules. But God does. That is the uniqueness of our Bible. God not only provides the rules and guidelines, but comes with us personally each day to help us live according to those rules. Of course, we must invite him to do this. Do you?

119:36 Money—it's all some people think about. It can ease labor, buy certain comforts, and offer some security. Money has become so important to some people that they will do almost anything to get it. But far more valuable than wealth is obedience to God, for it is a heavenly treasure rather than an earthly one (Luke 12:33). We should do what God wants regardless of the financial implications. Make the psalmist's prayer your own, asking God to help you prefer obedience to making money; it's in your own best interest in the long run.

119:44–46 The psalmist talks about being "free within the limits of God's laws." Ironically, obeying God's laws frees us to be what God designed us to be. By seeking God's salvation and forgiveness, we have freedom from sin and the resulting oppressive guilt. By living God's way, we have freedom to fulfill God's plan for us.

119:52
Ps 103:18

119:53
Ex 32:19
Neh 13:25

119:55
Ps 42:8; 63:6
92:2
Isa 26:9
Acts 16:25

119:57
Ps 16:5

119:58
Ps 41:4

119:59
Mk 14:72
Lk 15:17

119:61
Ps 140:5

119:63
Ps 101:6

119:64
Ps 33:5

119:66
Phil 1:9

119:67
Jer 31:18,19
Heb 12:5-11

119:68
Deut 30:5
Ps 86:5; 125:4

119:70
Isa 6:10
Jer 5:28

119:71
Prov 8:10,11,19

119:73
Job 31:15
Ps 139:15,16

119:74
Ps 35:27

119:75
Heb 12:10

119:82
Isa 38:14
Lam 2:11

119:83
Job 30:30

119:84
Ps 39:4
Rev 6:10

119:85
Ps 35:19; 57:6
Jer 18:22

119:89
Isa 40:8
Mt 24:35
1 Pet 1:25

119:90
Ps 89:1,2
104:2-4; 148:6
Jer 31:35

119:95
Ps 40:14
Isa 32:7

119:98
Deut 4:6

men hold me in contempt for obedience to God, but I stand unmoved. 52From my earliest youth I have tried to obey you; your Word has been my comfort.

53I am very angry with those who spurn your commands. 54For these laws of yours have been my source of joy and singing through all these years of my earthly pilgrimage. 55I obey them even at night and keep my thoughts, O Lord, on you. 56What a blessing this has been to me—to constantly obey.

57Jehovah is mine! And I promise to obey! 58With all my heart I want your blessings. Be merciful just as you promised. 59, 60I thought about the wrong direction in which I was headed, and turned around and came running back to you. 61Evil men have tried to drag me into sin, but I am firmly anchored to your laws.

62At midnight I will rise to give my thanks to you for your good laws. 63Anyone is my brother who fears and trusts the Lord and obeys him. 64O Lord, the earth is full of your lovingkindness! Teach me your good paths.

65Lord, I am overflowing with your blessings, just as you promised. 66Now teach me good judgment as well as knowledge. For your laws are my guide. 67I used to wander off until you punished me; now I closely follow all you say. 68You are good and do only good; make me follow your lead.

69Proud men have made up lies about me, but the truth is that I obey your laws with all my heart. 70Their minds are dull and stupid, but I have sense enough to follow you.

71, 72The punishment you gave me was the best thing that could have happened to me, for it taught me to pay attention to your laws. They are more valuable to me than millions in silver and gold!

73You made my body, Lord; now give me sense to heed your laws. 74All those who fear and trust in you will welcome me because I too am trusting in your Word.

75, 76, 77I know, O Lord, that your decisions are right and that your punishment was right and did me good. Now let your lovingkindness comfort me, just as you promised. Surround me with your tender mercies, that I may live. For your law is my delight.

78Let the proud be disgraced, for they have cut me down with all their lies. But I will concentrate my thoughts upon your laws.

79Let all others join me, who trust and fear you, and we will discuss your laws. 80Help me to love your every wish; then I will never have to be ashamed of myself.

81I faint for your salvation; but I expect your help, for you have promised it. 82My eyes are straining to see your promises come true. When will you comfort me with your help? 83I am shriveled like a wineskin in the smoke, exhausted with waiting. But still I cling to your laws and obey them. 84How long must I wait before you punish those who persecute me? 85, 86These proud men who hate your truth and laws have dug deep pits for me to fall in. Their lies have brought me into deep trouble. Help me, for you love only truth. 87They had almost finished me off, yet I refused to yield and disobey your laws. 88In your kindness, spare my life; then I can continue to obey you.

89Forever, O Lord, your Word stands firm in heaven. 90, 91Your faithfulness extends to every generation, like the earth you created; it endures by your decree, for everything serves your plans.

92I would have despaired and perished unless your laws had been my deepest delight. 93I will never lay aside your laws, for you have used them to restore my joy and health. 94I am yours! Save me! For I have tried to live according to your desires. 95Though the wicked hide along the way to kill me, I will quietly keep my mind upon your promises.

96Nothing is perfect except your words. 97Oh, how I love them. I think about them all day long. 98They make me wiser than my enemies, because they are my

---

119:61 Like a ship tossed by the waves at sea, pressures of life push and pull at us, moving us to try anything to survive, even if it's wrong. The only sure way to stay afloat amidst such temptation is to be anchored firmly in God's Word. If you feel like you're drifting, anchor your life in God's Word.

119:96–104 God's Word makes us wise—wiser than our enemies, wiser than any teachers who ignore it. True wisdom is not amassing knowledge, but *applying* knowledge in a life-changing way. Wisdom comes from allowing what God teaches to make a difference in our lives.

constant guide. 99Yes, wiser than my teachers, for I am ever thinking of your rules.
100They make me even wiser than the aged.

101I have refused to walk the paths of evil for I will remain obedient to your
Word. 102, 103No, I haven't turned away from what you taught me; your words are
sweeter than honey. 104And since only your rules can give me wisdom and
understanding, no wonder I hate every false teaching.

105Your words are a flashlight to light the path ahead of me, and keep me from
stumbling. 106I've said it once and I'll say it again and again: I will obey these
wonderful laws of yours.

107I am close to death at the hands of my enemies; oh, give me back my life
again, just as you promised me. 108Accept my grateful thanks and teach me your
desires. 109My life hangs in the balance, but I will not give up obedience to your
laws. 110The wicked have set their traps for me along your path, but I will not turn
aside. 111Your laws are my joyous treasure forever. 112I am determined to obey you
until I die.

113I hate those who are undecided whether or not to obey you; but my choice is
clear—I love your law. 114You are my refuge and my shield, and your promises are
my only source of hope. 115Begone, you evil-minded men. Don't try to stop me
from obeying God's commands. 116Lord, you promised to let me live! Never let it
be said that God failed me. 117Hold me safe above the heads of all my enemies; then
I can continue to obey your laws.

118But you have rejected all who reject your laws. They are only fooling
themselves. 119The wicked are the scum you skim off and throw away; no wonder
I love to obey your laws! 120I tremble in fear of you; I fear your punishments.

121Don't leave me to the mercy of my enemies, for I have done what is right; I've
been perfectly fair. 122Commit yourself to bless me! Don't let the proud oppress
me! 123My eyes grow dim with longing for you to fulfill your wonderful promise to
rescue me. 124Lord, deal with me in lovingkindness, and teach me, your servant, to
obey; 125for I am your servant; therefore give me common sense to apply your rules
to everything I do.

126Lord, it is time for you to act. For these evil men have violated your laws,
127while I love your commandments more than the finest gold. 128Every law of God
is right, whatever it concerns. I hate every other way.

129Your laws are wonderful; no wonder I obey them. 130As your plan unfolds,
even the simple can understand it. 131No wonder I wait expectantly for each of your
commands.

132Come and have mercy on me as is your way with those who love you.
133Guide me with your laws so that I will not be overcome by evil. 134Rescue me
from the oppression of evil men; then I can obey you. 135Look down in love upon
me and teach me all your laws. 136I weep because your laws are disobeyed.

137O Lord, you are just and your punishments are fair. 138Your demands are just
and right. 139I am indignant and angry because of the way my enemies have
disregarded your laws. 140I have thoroughly tested your promises and that is why I
love them so much. 141I am worthless and despised, but I don't despise your laws.

142Your justice is eternal for your laws are perfectly fair. 143In my distress and
anguish, your commandments comfort me. 144Your laws are always fair; help me
to understand them and I shall live.

119:100
Job 32:7-9

119:102
Deut 17:20
Josh 23:6
Ps 19:10
Prov 24:13,14

119:108
Hos 14:2
Heb 13:15

119:110
Ps 91:3; 140:5

119:111
Deut 33:4

119:113
1 Kgs 18:21
Jas 1:8; 4:8

119:114
Ps 31:20; 61:4

119:115
Ps 6:8; 139:19
Mt 7:23

119:116
Ps 25:2,20
31:1,17
Rom 5:5; 9:33
Phil 1:20

119:117
Ps 12:5
Prov 29:25

119:119
Isa 1:22,25
Ezek 22:18,19

119:120
Job 4:14
Hab 3:16

119:121
2 Sam 8:15
Job 29:14

119:124
Ps 51:1; 106:45
109:26

119:126
Jer 18:23
Ezek 31:11

119:128
Ps 19:8

119:133
Ps 19:13

119:134
Ps 142:6

119:135
Num 6:25
Ps 67:1

119:136
Jer 9:1,18
14:17
Lam 3:48

119:137
Ezra 9:15
Jer 12:1
Dan 9:7,14

119:139
Ps 69:9

119:144
Ps 19:9

119:105 A walk in the woods at night makes it obvious that a light is necessary to prevent one from tripping over tree roots or falling in holes. In this life, we walk through a dark forest of evil in a world that has turned its back on God. But the Bible can be our light to show us the way ahead so we won't stumble as we walk. It reveals the entangling roots of false values and philosophies. Study the Bible so you can see your way clear enough to stay on the right path.

119:113 When it comes to obeying God, there is no middle ground; you must take a stand. Either you are obeying him or you are not. Either you are doing what he wants or you are doing what you want. Choose to obey God and say with the psalmist, "I love your law."

119:125 Faith comes alive at the points where we apply Scripture to our lives. With the psalmist, we need the common sense and the desire to apply Scripture where we need help. The Bible is like medicine—it goes to work only when you apply it to the infected areas. As you read the Bible, be on the alert for lessons, commands, or examples that you can apply to your life situation.

119:151
Ps 34:18
Isa 50:8

119:154
Ps 35:1
Mic 7:9

119:156
2 Sam 24:14

119:158
Ps 139:21
Isa 24:16

119:161
1 Sam 26:18

119:162
1 Sam 30:16
Isa 9:3

119:163
Ps 31:6
Prov 13:5

119:165
Prov 3:23
1 Jn 2:10

119:166
Gen 49:18

119:168
Ps 139:3
Prov 5:21

119:169
Ps 18:6

119:170
Ps 22:20; 31:2
140:6

119:171
Isa 2:3
Mic 4:2

119:173
Josh 24:22
Lk 10:42

119:175
Isa 55:3

119:176
Isa 53:6
Lk 15:4

145I am praying with great earnestness; answer me, O Lord, and I will obey your laws. 146"Save me," I cry, "for I am obeying." 147Early in the morning, before the sun is up, I am praying and pointing out how much I trust in you. 148I stay awake through the night to think about your promises. 149Because you are so loving and kind, listen to me and make me well again.

150Here come these lawless men to attack me; 151but you are near, O Lord; all your commandments are based on truth. 152I have known from earliest days that your will will never changes.

153Look down upon my sorrows and rescue me, for I am obeying your commands. 154Yes, rescue me and give me back my life again just as you have promised. 155The wicked are far from salvation for they do not care for your laws. 156Lord, how great is your mercy; oh, give me back my life again.

157My enemies are so many. They try to make me disobey, but I have not swerved from your will. 158I loathed these traitors because they care nothing for your laws. 159Lord, see how much I really love your demands. Now give me back my life and health because you are so kind. 160There is utter truth in all your laws; your decrees are eternal.

161Great men have persecuted me, though they have no reason to, but I stand in awe of only your words. 162I rejoice in your laws like one who finds a great treasure. 163How I hate all falsehood but how I love your laws. 164I will praise you seven times a day because of your wonderful laws.

165Those who love your laws have great peace of heart and mind and do not stumble. 166I long for your salvation, Lord, and so I have obeyed your laws. 167I have looked for your commandments and I love them very much; 168yes, I have searched for them. You know this because everything I do is known to you.

169O Lord, listen to my prayers; give me the common sense you promised. 170Hear my prayers; rescue me as you said you would. 171I praise you for letting me learn your laws. 172I will sing about their wonder, for each of them is just. 173Stand ready to help me because I have chosen to follow your will. 174O Lord, I have longed for your salvation, and your law is my delight. 175If you will let me live, I will praise you; let your laws assist me.

176I have wandered away like a lost sheep; come and find me for I have not turned away from your commandments.

Theme: A prayer for deliverance from false accusers. All believers must live with the tension of being in the world but not belonging to it.
Author: Anonymous, many suggest Hezekiah

120:1ff
Ps 18:6; 66:14
102:2

120:4
Ps 45:15

120:5
Jer 2:10; 49:28

120 In my troubles I pled with God to help me and he did! 2Deliver me, O Lord, from liars. 3O lying tongue, what shall be your fate? 4You shall be pierced with sharp arrows and burned with glowing coals. 5, 6My troubles pile high among these haters of the Lord, these men of Meshech and Kedar. I am tired of being here among these men who hate peace. 7I am for peace, but they are for war, and my voice goes unheeded in their councils.

119:159 This is not a demand for physical healing, but it carries the request, "Revive me." (See the note on 119:25 for how God's Word can revive us.)

119:160 One of God's characteristics is truthfulness. He embodies perfect truth, and therefore, his Word cannot lie; it is true and dependable for guidance and help (see John 10:34–38). The Bible is completely true and trustworthy.

119:165 Modern society longs for peace of mind. Here is clear-cut instruction on how to realize this in our lives. If we love God and obey his laws, we will have "great peace of heart and mind."

120—134 Psalms 120—134 are called "Pilgrim Psalms" or "Songs of Ascent." They were sung by those who journeyed to the Temple for the annual festivals. Each psalm is a "step" along the journey. Psalm 120 begins the journey in a distant land in hostile

surroundings; Psalm 122 pictures the pilgrims arriving in Jerusalem; and the rest of the psalms move toward the Temple and the various characteristics of God associated with it.

120:5, 6 Meshech was a nation far to the north of Israel; Kedar a nation to the southeast. Both were known for being warlike and barbarian. Because the psalmist couldn't have been in both places at once, he was probably referring to these nations as a way of saying that he felt far from home and surrounded by heathen people.

120:7 Peacemaking is not popular among many because it is more human to "fight for what is right." The glory of battle is the hope of winning, but someone must be a loser. The glory of peacemaking is that it may actually produce two winners. Peacemaking is God's way, so we should carefully and prayerfully attempt to be peacemakers.

Theme: We can depend upon God for help. Pilgrims must travel through lonely country to their destination; they are protected, not by anything created, but by the Creator of everything.
Author: Anonymous, many suggest Hezekiah

121 Shall I look to the mountain gods for help? 2No! My help is from Jehovah who made the mountains! And the heavens too! 3, 4He will never let me stumble, slip or fall. For he is always watching, never sleeping.

5Jehovah himself is caring for you! He is your defender. 6He protects you day and night. 7He keeps you from all evil, and preserves your life. 8He keeps his eye upon you as you come and go, and always guards you.

121:3
Ps 66:9
121:5
Ps 91:4
121:6
Rev 7:16
121:7
Ps 91:10-12

Theme: Stepping into the presence of God. What Jerusalem was for the Israelites, the church is to the believer.
Author: David

122 I was glad for the suggestion of going to Jerusalem, to the Temple of the Lord. 2, 3Now we are standing here inside the crowded city. 4All Israel—Jehovah's people—have come to worship as the law requires, to thank and praise the Lord. 5Look! There are the judges holding court beside the city gates, deciding all the people's arguments.

6Pray for the peace of Jerusalem. May all who love this city prosper. 7O Jerusalem, may there be peace within your walls and prosperity in your palaces. 8This I ask for the sake of all my brothers and my friends who live here; 9and may there be peace as a protection to the Temple of the Lord.

122:1
Isa 2:3
Zech 8:21
122:5
Deut 17:8
2 Chron 19:8
122:6
Ps 102:14
122:7
Isa 62:6
122:8
Ps 133:1

Theme: Look to God for mercy. We are encouraged to be attentive to God's leading.
Author: Anonymous, many suggest Hezekiah

123 O God enthroned in heaven, I lift my eyes to you. 2We look to Jehovah our God for his mercy and kindness just as a servant keeps his eyes upon his master or a slave girl watches her mistress for the slightest signal.

3, 4Have mercy on us, Lord, have mercy. For we have had our fill of contempt and of the scoffing of the rich and proud.

123:1
Ps 11:4; 141:8
123:2
Mal 1:6
123:3
Neh 4:4
Ps 4:1; 51:1
79:4; 119:22

Theme: God delivers us from those who seek to destroy us. God is on the side of those who seek him.
Author: David, probably written after his defeat of the Philistines (2 Samuel 5:17–25)

124 If the Lord had not been on our side (let all Israel admit it), if the Lord had not been on our side, 2, 3we would have been swallowed alive by our enemies, destroyed by their anger. 4, 5We would have drowned beneath the flood of these men's fury and pride.

6Blessed be Jehovah who has not let them devour us. 7We have escaped with our

124:2
Ps 56:1; 138:7
124:4
Ps 18:16; 69:2
124:7
Ps 91:3; 141:10

121:5 He is your defender, literally, "your shade at your right hand."

121:1ff This is the children's prayer expressing assurance and hope in God's protection day and night. We never outgrow our need for God's untiring watch over our lives.

122:1 Going to God's house can be a chore or a delight. For the psalmist, it was a delight. As a pilgrim to one of the three great religious feasts, he was excited to worship with God's people in God's house. We may find worship a chore if we have sin in our lives or if our love for God has cooled. But if we are close to God and enjoy his presence, we will hunger to worship and praise him. Our attitude toward God will determine our view of worship.

122:5 In Bible times, the elders in a city sat to hear cases and administer justice at the city gate (Ruth 4:1, 2). Sometimes the king himself would sit at the gate to meet his subjects and make legal decisions (2 Samuel 19:8-10). Speeches and prophecies were also made at the city gate (Nehemiah 8:1; Jeremiah 17:19, 20).

122:6-9 The psalmist was not praying for his own peace and prosperity, but for his fellow citizens of Jerusalem. This is

intercessory prayer, prayer on the behalf of others. Such prayer is unselfish in its motive. Too often we pray for our own needs and desires when we should be interceding for others. Will you intercede for someone in need today?

122:6-9 The peace sought in these verses is much more than the mere absence of conflict. It also suggests completeness, health, justice, prosperity, and protection. Real peace comes from faith in God because he alone embodies all the characteristics of peace. To find real peace you must find God.

123:1ff The psalmist lifted his eyes to God, waiting and watching for him to send his mercy. The more he waited, the more he cried out to God because he knew that the evil and proud offered no help—they had only contempt for God.

124:7, 8 Do you ever feel trapped by overwhelming odds? David compared this feeling to that of a bird outwitted and snared by a hunter. With God, there is always a way out because he is the Creator of all that exists. No problem is beyond his ability to solve,

lives as a bird from a hunter's snare. The snare is broken and we are free! 8Our help is from the Lord who made heaven and earth.

Theme: God is our Protector.
The mountains around Jerusalem symbolize God's protection for his people.
Author: Anonymous, many suggest Hezekiah

125:1
Ps 46:5

125:3
1 Sam 24:10
Prov 22:8
Isa 14:5

125:5
Gal 6:16

125 Those who trust in the Lord are steady as Mount Zion, unmoved by any circumstance.

2Just as the mountains surround and protect Jerusalem, so the Lord surrounds and protects his people. 3For the wicked shall not rule the godly, lest the godly be forced to do wrong. 4O Lord, do good to those who are good, whose hearts are right with the Lord; 5but lead evil men to execution. And let Israel have quietness and peace.

Theme: God does great things. His power not only releases us from sin's captive hold, but brings us back to him.
Author: Anonymous, probably written to celebrate the exiles' return from captivity (Ezra 1)

126:1
Jer 29:14

126 When Jehovah brought back his exiles to Jerusalem, it was like a dream! 2How we laughed and sang for joy. And the other nations said, "What amazing things the Lord has done for them."

126:4
Isa 35:6; 43:19

126:5
Ps 80:5
Gal 6:9

3Yes, glorious things! What wonder! What joy! 4May we be refreshed as by streams in the desert.

5Those who sow tears shall reap joy. 6Yes, they go out weeping, carrying seed for sowing, and return singing, carrying their sheaves.

Theme: Life without God is senseless. All of life's work—building a home, establishing a career, and raising a family—must have God as the foundation.
Author: Solomon

127:1
Ps 78:69

127:2
Gen 3:17
Job 11:18,19
Eccles 5:12

127 Unless the Lord builds a house, the builders' work is useless. Unless the Lord protects a city, sentries do no good. 2It is senseless for you to work so hard from early morning until late at night, fearing you will starve to death; for God wants his loved ones to get their proper rest.

127:3
Deut 28:4

3Children are a gift from God; they are his reward. 4Children born to a young man are like sharp arrows to defend him.

5Happy is the man who has his quiver full of them. That man shall have the help he needs when arguing with his enemies.

126:4 *May we be refreshed,* literally, "Restore our fortunes, Lord." **127:5** *when arguing with his enemies,* literally, "when they speak with their enemies in the gate."

no circumstance is too difficult for him. We can turn to the Creator for help in our time of need, for he is on our side. God will provide a way out, we need only trust him and look for it.

125:1 Have you ever known someone whose lifestyle changed as often as the weather because they were drawn to every new fad and idea? That kind of person is inconsistent, and therefore unreliable and insecure. The secret to consistency is to trust in God because he never changes and will keep us steady and secure.

125:3 Although the psalmist wrote, "the wicked shall not rule the godly," this did often happen in Israel's history. But he expressed what will ultimately happen when God executes his final judgment. The sinfulness of people often ruins God's ideal on earth, but that doesn't mean God has lost control. Evil prevails only as long as God allows.

126:5, 6 God's capacity for restoring life is beyond our understanding. Forests burn down and are able to grow back. Broken bones heal. Even grief is not a permanent condition. Our tears can be seeds that will grow into a harvest of joy because God is able to bring good out of tragedy. When burdened by sorrow, know that your times of grief will end soon and that you will again find joy. We must be patient as we wait. God's great harvest of joy is coming!

127:1 Families establish homes and sentries guard a city, but both of these activities are futile unless God is with them. A family without God can never experience the spiritual bond God brings to relationships. A city without God will crumble from evil and corruption on the inside. Don't make the mistake of leaving God out of your life—if you do, it will be lived in vain. Make God your highest priority and let him do the building.

127:2 God is not against human effort. Hard work honors God (Proverbs 31:10–29). But working to the exclusion of rest or neglecting family may be a cover-up for an inability to trust God to provide for our needs. We all need adequate rest and times of spiritual refreshment. On the other hand, this verse is not an excuse to be lazy (Proverbs 18:9). Be careful to maintain a balance: work hard while trusting God, and also rest while trusting him.

127:3–5 Children are too often seen as liabilities rather than assets. But the Bible calls children "a gift from God," a reward. We can also learn valuable lessons from their inquisitive minds and trusting spirits. Those who view children as a distraction or nuisance should instead see them as an opportunity to shape the future. We dare not treat them as an inconvenience when God values them so highly.

Theme: God, the true head of the home. This is called the marriage prayer because it was often sung at Israelite marriages. God will reward your devotion to him with inner peace.
Author: Anonymous, many suggest Hezekiah

128 Blessings on all who reverence and trust the Lord—on all who obey him! ²Their reward shall be prosperity and happiness. ³Your wife shall be contented in your home. And look at all those children! There they sit around the dinner table as vigorous and healthy as young olive trees. ⁴That is God's reward to those who reverence and trust him.

⁵May the Lord continually bless you with heaven's blessings as well as with human joys. ⁶May you live to enjoy your grandchildren! And may God bless Israel!

128:2
Eccles 8:12
128:3
Ps 52:8
128:5
Ps 122:9; 134:3
128:6
Gen 48:11

Theme: Confidence in the midst of persecution. God will bring us through the tough times.
Author: Anonymous, many suggest Hezekiah

129 Persecuted from my earliest youth (Israel is speaking), ²and faced with never-ending discrimination—but not destroyed! My enemies have never been able to finish me off!

³,⁴Though my back is cut to ribbons with their whips, the Lord is good. For he has snapped the chains that evil men had bound me with.

⁵May all who hate the Jews be brought to ignominious defeat. ⁶,⁷May they be as grass in shallow soil, turning sere and yellow when half grown, ignored by the reaper, despised by the binder. ⁸And may those passing by refuse to bless them by saying, "Jehovah's blessings be upon you; we bless you in Jehovah's name."

129:1
Ex 1:11
Jer 22:21
Hos 2:15; 11:1
129:2
Jer 15:20
Mt 16:17
2 Cor 4:8,9
129:5
Ps 71:13
129:6
2 Kgs 19:26

Theme: Assurance of the Lord's forgiveness.
God will surely forgive us if we confess our sins to him.
Author: Anonymous, many suggest Hezekiah

130 O Lord, from the depths of despair I cry for your help: ²"Hear me! Answer! Help me!"

³,⁴Lord, if you keep in mind our sins then who can ever get an answer to his prayers? But you forgive! What an awesome thing this is! ⁵That is why I wait expectantly, trusting God to help, for he has promised. ⁶I long for him more than sentinels long for the dawn.

⁷O Israel, hope in the Lord; for he is loving and kind, and comes to us with armloads of salvation. ⁸He himself shall ransom Israel from her slavery to sin.

130:1
Ps 42:7; 69:2
130:3
Neh 9:17
130:5
Isa 8:17
130:7
Ps 103:4
130:8
Lk 1:68

Theme: Trust and contentment. Quiet trust in God is the basis for our contentment.
Author: David

131 Lord, I am not proud and haughty. I don't think myself better than others. I don't pretend to "know it all." ²I am quiet now before the Lord, just as a child who is weaned from the breast. Yes, my begging has been stilled.

³O Israel, you too should quietly trust in the Lord—now, and always.

131:1
Rom 12:16
131:2
Ps 62:1

128:3, 4 The psalmist wrote that a good family life is a reward for following God. The values outlined in God's Word include love, service, honesty, integrity, prayer, and these help rather than destroy relationships and are vital to home life. All families have problems. Instead of trying to escape from our families, we must learn to confront our problems. Is your home life heavenly or hectic? Reading and obeying God's Word is a good place to start to make your family all that it can be.

129:2 The people of Israel were persecuted from their earliest days, but never destroyed completely. The same is true for the church. Christians have faced times of severe persecution, but the church has never been destroyed. As Jesus said to Peter, "Upon this rock I will build my church; and all the powers of hell shall not prevail against it" (Matthew 16:18). When you face persecution and discrimination, take courage—the church will never be destroyed.

129:3, 4 This verse foreshadows Jesus' unjust punishment before his death. He endured the horrible lashes from the whip of his tormentors, which indeed cut his back to ribbons (John 19:1).

130:1, 2 In the depths of despair, the psalmist cried out to God,

"Hear me! Help me!" Despair makes us feel isolated and distant from God, but this is precisely when we need God most. Despair over sin should not lead to self-pity, causing us to think more about ourselves than God. Instead, it should lead to confession, and then, to God's mercy, forgiveness, and redemption. When we feel overwhelmed by a problem, feeling sorry for ourselves will only increase hopeless feelings; but crying out to God turns our attention to the only one who can really help.

130:3, 4 Holding a grudge is like building a wall between you and another person, and it is nearly impossible to talk openly while holding a grudge. God never holds a grudge; when he forgives, he forgives completely, tearing down any wall between us and him. Therefore, we can talk to him about anything. When you pray, realize that God is holding nothing against you. The lines of communication are completely open.

131:1 Pride results from overvaluing ourselves and undervaluing others. It leads to restlessness because it makes us dissatisfied with what we have and concerned about what everyone else is doing. Haughtiness keeps us always hungering for more attention

Theme: Honor God and he will honor you. The psalmist reflects upon that great day when the Ark of the Covenant was brought to Jerusalem and praises God for his promise to perpetuate David's line.
Author: Anonymous

132:2
1 Kgs 8:17
1 Chron 22:7
Acts 7:46
Isa 49:26

132:6
Gen 35:19
1 Sam 7:1

132:7
1 Chron 28:2
Ps 5:7; 99:5

132:8
Num 10:35
2 Chron 6:41
Ps 78:61

132:9
Job 29:14
Ps 149:5

132:11
2 Sam 7:12-16
2 Chron 6:16

132:12
Lk 1:32
Acts 2:30

132:13
Ps 78:68

132:14
Mt 23:21

132:15
Ps 107:9

132 Lord, do you remember that time when my heart was so filled with turmoil? 2–5I couldn't rest, I couldn't sleep, thinking how I ought to build a permanent home for the Ark of the Lord, a Temple for the mighty one of Israel. Then I vowed that I would do it; I made a solemn promise to the Lord.

6First the Ark was in Ephrathah, then in the distant countryside of Jaar. 7But now it will be settled in the Temple, in God's permanent home here on earth. That is where we will go to worship him. 8Arise, O Lord, and enter your Temple with the Ark, the symbol of your power.

9We will clothe the priests in white, the symbol of all purity. May our nation shout for joy.

10Do not reject your servant David—the king you chose for your people. 11For you promised me that my son would sit on my throne and succeed me. And surely you will never go back on a promise! 12You also promised that if my descendants will obey the terms of your contract with me, then the dynasty of David shall never end.

13O Lord, you have chosen Jerusalem as your home: 14"This is my permanent home where I shall live," you said, "for I have always wanted it this way. 15I will make this city prosperous and satisfy her poor with food. 16I will clothe her priests with salvation; her saints shall shout for joy. 17David's power shall grow, for I have decreed for him a mighty Son. 18I'll clothe his enemies with shame, but he shall be a glorious King."

Theme: The joy of harmonious relationships
Author: David

133:2
Ex 30:25,30
Lev 8:12

133:3
Deut 4:48; 28:8

133 How wonderful it is, how pleasant, when brothers live in harmony! 2For harmony is as precious as the fragrant anointing oil that was poured over Aaron's head, and ran down onto his beard, and onto the border of his robe. 3Harmony is as refreshing as the dew on Mount Hermon, on the mountains of

132:1 *my heart,* literally, "David's soul." **132:2-5** *the Ark of the Lord,* implied. **132:6** *First the Ark was in Ephrathah,* literally, "Lo, we heard of it in Ephrathah." **132:7** *That is where we will go to worship him,* literally, "We will go into his tabernacles; we will worship at his footstool." **132:13** *Jerusalem,* literally, "Zion." **132:17** *a mighty Son,* literally, "a progeny."

---

and adoration. By contrast, humility puts others first and allows us to be content with God's leading in our lives. Such contentment gives us security so that we no longer have to prove ourselves to others. Let humility and trust affect your life's perspective and give you the strength and freedom to serve God and others.

132:2–5 The Ark of the Covenant was the symbol of God's presence among his people (Exodus 25:10–22). When David became king, he built a beautiful palace, but was troubled that the Ark remained in a tent (2 Samuel 6:17; 7:1–17). This so bothered David that he couldn't sleep until he corrected the situation. He began to lay the plans for the Temple in which the Ark would be housed. We must live close enough to God so that we will be restless until God's will is accomplished through us.

132:12 This promise that David's descendants would be on the throne forever is found in 2 Samuel 7:8–29. This promise had two parts: (1) David's descendants would perpetually rule over Israel as long as they followed God, and (2) David's royal line would never end. The first part was conditional and when the people rebelled against God, the nation was defeated and no kings have sat on a throne in Jerusalem since. The second part of the promise is unconditional and was fulfilled in Jesus Christ, a descendant of David, who reigns forever.

132:17, 18 These verses state that the mighty Son of David will be a glorious king. David's son, Solomon, was indeed a glorious king

(1 Kings 3:10–14); but these verses look ahead even further to another descendant of David, Jesus the Messiah (Matthew 1:17). The power, might, and glory of the Messiah will last forever.

133:1–3 David stated that harmony is pleasant, precious, and refreshing. Unfortunately, harmony does not abound in the church as it should. People disagree and cause division over unimportant issues. Some seem to delight in causing tension by discrediting others. Harmony is important because: (1) it makes us a positive example to the world and helps draw others to us; (2) it helps us function as a body of believers as God meant us to, giving us a foretaste of heaven; (3) it is renewing and revitalizing because there is less tension to sap our energy.

Living in harmony does not mean we will agree on everything; there will be many opinions just as there are many notes in a harmonious chord of music. But we agree on our purpose in life—to work together for God. Our outward expression of unity should reveal our inward unity of purpose.

133:2 The anointing oil was used by Moses to anoint Aaron as the first High Priest of Israel (Exodus 29:7), and to dedicate all the priests into God's service. Brotherly unity, like the anointing oil, shows that we are dedicated to serve God wholeheartedly.

133:3 Mount Hermon is the tallest mountain in Palestine, located northeast of the Sea of Galilee.

Israel. And God has pronounced this eternal blessing on Jerusalem, even life forevermore.

Theme: Worship God and experience the joy of his blessings
Author: Anonymous, some suggest Hezekiah

134 Oh, bless the Lord, you who serve him as watchmen in the Temple every night. 2Lift your hands in holiness and bless the Lord.
3The Lord bless you from Zion—the Lord who made heaven and earth.

134:1
Deut 10:8
1 Chron 9:33
2 Chron 29:11

Theme: A hymn of praise. This psalm contrasts the greatness of God with the vanity of idols. The heathen worship idols while God's people worship the living God.
Author: Anonymous

135 Hallelujah! 2Yes, let his people praise him as they stand in his Temple courts. 3Praise the Lord because he is so good; sing to his wonderful name. 4For the Lord has chosen Israel as his personal possession.

5I know the greatness of the Lord—that he is greater far than any other god. 6He does whatever pleases him throughout all of heaven and earth, and in the deepest seas. 7He makes mists rise throughout the earth and sends the lightning to bring down the rain; and sends the winds from his treasuries. 8He destroyed the eldest child in each Egyptian home, along with the firstborn of the flocks. 9He did great miracles in Egypt before Pharaoh and all his people. 10He smote great nations, slaying mighty kings— 11Sihon, king of Amorites; and Og, the king of Bashan; and the kings of Canaan— 12and gave their land as an eternal gift to his people Israel.

13O Jehovah, your name endures forever; your fame is known to every generation. 14For Jehovah will vindicate his people, and have compassion on his servants.

15The heathen worship idols of gold and silver, made by men— 16idols with speechless mouths and sightless eyes 17and ears that cannot hear; they cannot even breathe. 18Those who make them become like them! And so do all who trust in them!

19O Israel, bless Jehovah! High priests of Aaron, bless his name. 20O Levite priests, bless the Lord Jehovah! Oh, bless his name, all of you who trust and reverence him. 21All people of Jerusalem, praise the Lord, for he lives here in Jerusalem. Hallelujah!

135:2
Ps 116:19
135:3
Ps 68:4; 100:5
135:4
Ex 19:5
Deut 7:6; 10:15
1 Pet 2:9
135:5
Ps 48:1; 97:9
135:7
Job 38:25,26
Jer 51:16
Zech 10:1
135:9
Deut 6:22
135:10
Ps 136:17-21
135:11
Num 21:33-35
Josh 12:7-24
135:13
Ex 3:15
135:14
Deut 32:36
Ps 106:45
135:15
Ps 115:4-8

Theme: The never-ending story of God's love.
God deserves our praise because his endless love never fails.
Author: Anonymous

136 Oh, give thanks to the Lord, for he is good; his lovingkindness continues forever.

2Give thanks to the God of gods, for his lovingkindness continues forever. 3Give thanks to the Lord of lords, for his lovingkindness continues forever. 4Praise him who alone does mighty miracles, for his lovingkindness continues forever. 5Praise him who made the heavens, for his lovingkindness continues forever. 6Praise him who planted the water within the earth, for his lovingkindness continues forever.

136:1
1 Chron 16:41
2 Chron 20:21
136:2
Deut 10:17
136:4
Ps 72:18
136:6
Ps 24:2

133:3 *Jerusalem,* literally, "Zion." **135:21** *All people of Jerusalem, praise the Lord,* literally, "the Lord be blessed from Zion." **136:6** *who planted the water within the earth,* or, "who separated the earth from the oceans."

134:1-3 Why is an entire psalm aimed directly at a very small group—the Temple's watchmen? As the last of the "psalms of ascent" (Psalms 120—134), the worshipers have ascended the hill where the Temple sits and see the guards who protect it day and night. They view the guards' work as an act of praise to God, done reverently and responsibly. Make your job or your responsibility in the church an act of praise by doing it with reverence to God. Honor him by the quality of your work and the attitude of service you bring to it.

134:3 Zion is another name for Jerusalem.

135:4 God claims and accepts all those who love and obey him (see 1 Peter 2:9).

135:18 In subtle, imperceptible ways we become like the gods we worship. It is also true, however, that if the true God is your God, you will become more like him as you worship him. What are your goals? What takes priority in your life? Choose carefully, because you will take on the characteristics of whatever you worship.

136:1ff Repeated throughout this psalm is the phrase, "for his lovingkindness continues forever." This psalm may have been a responsive reading, the congregation saying these words in unison after each sentence. The repetition made this important lesson sink in. "Lovingkindness" is a translation of a Hebrew word that envelops the aspects of love, kindness, mercy, and faithfulness. We never have to worry that God will run out of love because his lovingkindness flows from a well that will never run dry.

136:7
Ps 74:16
136:8
Gen 1:16
136:10
Ex 12:29
Ps 78:51
136:11
Ex 12:51; 13:3
Deut 9:29
Ps 44:3
Jer 32:17,21
136:13
Ex 14:21
Ps 78:13
136:14
Ps 106:9
136:16
Ex 13:18
Deut 8:15
136:17
Ps 135:10-12
136:22
Ps 105:6
Isa 41:8; 45:4
136:23
Ps 9:12; 106:45
136:24
Judg 6:9
136:25
Ps 104:27
136:26
2 Chron 36:23
Ezra 5:11

7Praise him who made the heavenly lights, for his lovingkindness continues forever: 8the sun to rule the day, for his lovingkindness continues forever; 9and the moon and stars at night, for his lovingkindness continues forever. 10Praise the God who smote the firstborn of Egypt, for his lovingkindness to Israel continues forever.

11, 12He brought them out with mighty power and upraised fist to strike their enemies, for his lovingkindness to Israel continues forever. 13Praise the Lord who opened the Red Sea to make a path before them, for his lovingkindness continues forever, 14and led them safely through, for his lovingkindness continues forever— 15but drowned Pharaoh's army in the sea, for his lovingkindness to Israel continues forever.

16Praise him who led his people through the wilderness, for his lovingkindness continues forever. 17Praise him who saved his people from the power of mighty kings, for his lovingkindness continues forever, 18and killed famous kings who were their enemies, for his lovingkindness to Israel continues forever: 19Sihon, king of Amorites—for God's lovingkindness to Israel continues forever— 20and Og, king of Bashan—for his lovingkindness to Israel continues forever. 21God gave the land of these kings to Israel as a gift forever, for his lovingkindness to Israel continues forever; 22yes, a permanent gift to his servant Israel, for his lovingkindness continues forever.

23He remembered our utter weakness, for his lovingkindness continues forever. 24And saved us from our foes, for his lovingkindness continues forever.

25He gives food to every living thing, for his lovingkindness continues forever. 26Oh, give thanks to the God of heaven, for his lovingkindness continues forever.

Theme: A person in exile weeps over the bitterness of captivity. In times of sorrow, it is difficult to imagine singing joyful songs again.
Author: Anonymous

137:1
Neh 1:4
Ezek 1:1,3
137:2
Ezek 26:13
137:3
2 Chron 29:27
Neh 12:46
137:7
Jer 49:7-22
Ezek 25:12-14
137:8
Isa 13:1-22
47:1-15
Jer 50:1-46
51:1-64

137 Weeping, we sat beside the rivers of Babylon thinking of Jerusalem. 2We have put away our lyres, hanging them upon the branches of the willow trees, 3, 4for how can we sing? Yet our captors, our tormentors, demand that we sing for them the happy songs of Zion! 5, 6If I forget you, O Jerusalem, let my right hand forget its skill upon the harp. If I fail to love her more than my highest joy, let me never sing again.

7O Jehovah, do not forget what these Edomites did on that day when the armies of Babylon captured Jerusalem. "Raze her to the ground!" they yelled. 8O Babylon, evil beast, you shall be destroyed. Blessed is the man who destroys you as you have destroyed us. 9Blessed is the man who takes your babies and smashes them against the rocks!

Theme: Thanksgiving for answered prayer. God works out his plans for our lives and will bring us through the difficulties we face.
Author: David

138:2
Ps 5:7
Isa 42:21

138 Lord, with all my heart I thank you. I will sing your praises before the armies of angels. 2I face your Temple as I worship, giving thanks to you for all your lovingkindness and your faithfulness, for your promises are backed by

136:10 *to Israel,* implied here and in verses 12, 15, 18, 19, 20, 21. **137:9** *Blessed is the man who takes your babies and smashes them against the rocks!* Perhaps this could be paraphrased, "Blessed is he who invades and sacks your city." **138:1** *before the armies of angels,* or, "before the gods." The same Hebrew word is used here as in Ps 8:5. **138:2** *for your promises are backed by all the honor of your name,* literally, "You have exalted your Word above all your name."

137:7 The Edomites were blood brothers of the Israelites, both nations descending from Isaac and his father Abraham. Although Israel shared its southern border with Edom, there was bitter hatred between the two nations. The Edomites did not come to help when the city of Jerusalem was besieged by the Babylonian army. In fact, they rejoiced when the city was destroyed (Jeremiah 49:7–22; Joel 3:19; Obadiah 1:1–20).

137:8 Babylon was destroyed in 539 B.C.

138:1 Thanksgiving should be an integral part of our lives. This theme is woven throughout the psalms. As we thank God for material and spiritual blessings, we should also thank him for answered prayer. Remember when you asked God for protection, strength, comfort, patience, love, or other special needs and he supplied them? Beware of taking God's provision and answered prayer for granted.

all the honor of your name. ³When I pray, you answer me, and encourage me by giving me the strength I need.

⁴Every king in all the earth shall give you thanks, O Lord, for all of them shall hear your voice. ⁵Yes, they shall sing about Jehovah's glorious ways, for his glory is very great. ⁶Yet though he is so great, he respects the humble, but proud men must keep their distance. ⁷Though I am surrounded by troubles, you will bring me safely through them. You will clench your fist against my angry enemies! Your power will save me. ⁸The Lord will work out his plans for my life—for your lovingkindness, Lord, continues forever. Don't abandon me—for you made me.

138:4
Ps 102:15

138:6
Ps 101:5
113:4-7

138:7
Ex 15:12
Ezra 9:8,9
Ps 20:6; 23:4

138:8
Job 10:3
Ps 27:9; 71:9

Theme: God is all-seeing, all-knowing, all-holy, all-present. God knows us, God is with us, and his greatest gift is to allow us to know him.
Author: David

139 O Lord, you have examined my heart and know everything about me. ²You know when I sit or stand. When far away you know my every thought. ³You chart the path ahead of me, and tell me where to stop and rest. Every moment, you know where I am. ⁴You know what I am going to say before I even say it. ⁵You both precede and follow me, and place your hand of blessing on my head.

139:1
Ps 44:21

139:2
Ps 94:11

139:3
Job 14:16

139:4
Heb 4:13

⁶This is too glorious, too wonderful to believe! ⁷I can *never* be lost to your Spirit! I can *never* get away from my God! ⁸If I go up to heaven, you are there; if I go down to the place of the dead, you are there. ⁹If I ride the morning winds to the farthest oceans, ¹⁰even there your hand will guide me, your strength will support me. ¹¹If I try to hide in the darkness, the night becomes light around me. ¹²For even darkness cannot hide from God; to you the night shines as bright as day. Darkness and light are both alike to you.

139:7
Jer 23:24

139:8
Prov 15:11
Amos 9:2-4

139:10
Ps 23:2,3

139:11
Job 22:13

139:12
Job 34:22
1 Jn 1:5

¹³You made all the delicate, inner parts of my body, and knit them together in my mother's womb. ¹⁴Thank you for making me so wonderfully complex! It is amazing to think about. Your workmanship is marvelous—and how well I know it. ¹⁵You were there while I was being formed in utter seclusion! ¹⁶You saw me before I was born and scheduled each day of my life before I began to breathe. Every day was recorded in your Book!

139:13
Ps 119:73

139:15
Job 10:8-10
Eccles 11:5

139:16
Job 14:5
Ps 56:8

¹⁷,¹⁸How precious it is, Lord, to realize that you are thinking about me constantly! I can't even count how many times a day your thoughts turn towards me. And when I waken in the morning, you are still thinking of me!

¹⁹Surely you will slay the wicked, Lord! Away, bloodthirsty men! Begone! ²⁰They blaspheme your name and stand in arrogance against you—how silly can they be? ²¹O Lord, shouldn't I hate those who hate you? Shouldn't I be grieved with them? ²²Yes, I hate them, for your enemies are my enemies too.

139:19
Isa 11:4

139:20
Ex 20:7
Deut 5:11

139:17, 18 *I can't even count how many times a day your thoughts turn towards me,* literally, "how precious are your thoughts to me."

138:8 Each of us dreams and makes plans for our future. We work hard to see those dreams and plans come true. But to truly make the most of life, we must include God's plans in our plans. He alone knows what is best for us. As you make plans and dream dreams, talk with God about them.

139:1–5 Sometimes we don't let people get to know us completely because we are afraid they will discover something about us they won't like. But God already knows everything about us and still accepts and loves us. God cares about us so much that he numbers the hairs on our heads (Matthew 10:30). He is with us through every situation, in every trial—protecting, loving, guiding. He knows us completely.

139:7 God is omnipresent—he is present everywhere. Because this is so, you can never be lost to his Spirit. This is good news to those who know and love God because no matter what we do or where we go, we can never be far from God's comforting presence.

139:13–15 God's character goes into the creation of every

person. When you feel worthless or even begin to hate yourself, remember that God's Spirit is ready and willing to work within you to make your character all God meant it to be. God thinks of you constantly (139:17, 18). We should have as much respect for ourselves as our Maker has for us.

139:17, 18 When someone you love is thinking about you all the time, it comforts you. God is concerned to keep us from failing and to catch us if we fall. If he thinks about us this much, shouldn't we find time to think about him each day?

139:21–24 David's hatred of his enemies came from his zeal for God. David regarded his enemies as God's enemies, so his hatred was a desire for God's righteous justice and not for personal vengeance. Is it all right to be angry at people who hate God? Yes, but we must remember that it is God who will deal with them, not us. If we truly love God then we will be deeply hurt if someone hates him. David asked God to scrutinize his heart and mind and point out any wrong motives that may have been behind his strong words. But while we seek justice against evil, we must also pray

139:23
Ps 26:2

²³Search me, O God, and know my heart; test my thoughts. ²⁴Point out anything you find in me that makes you sad, and lead me along the path of everlasting life.

Theme: Prayer for protection against those who slander or threaten you. Deliverance begins with concentrating on our future life with God.
Author: David

140:2
Ps 56:6
Prov 6:14
Isa 59:4

140:3
Rom 3:13
Jas 3:8

140:5
Job 18:9
Ps 35:7; 57:6

140:6
Esth 9:25
Ps 112:10

140:10
Ps 11:6
Mt 3:10

140:11
Ps 34:21
1 Kgs 8:45,49

140 O Lord, deliver me from evil men. Preserve me from the violent, ²who plot and stir up trouble all day long. ³Their words sting like poisonous snakes. ⁴Keep me out of their power. Preserve me from their violence, for they are plotting against me. ⁵These proud men have set a trap to catch me, a noose to yank me up and leave me dangling in the air; they wait in ambush with a net to throw over and hold me helpless in its meshes.

6, 7, 8O Jehovah, my Lord and Savior, my God and my shield—hear me as I pray! Don't let these wicked men succeed; don't let them prosper and be proud. ⁹Let their plots boomerang! Let them be destroyed by the very evil they have planned for me. ¹⁰Let burning coals fall down upon their heads, or throw them into the fire, or into deep pits from which they can't escape.

¹¹Don't let liars prosper here in our land; quickly punish them. ¹²But the Lord will surely help those they persecute; he will maintain the rights of the poor. ¹³Surely the godly are thanking you, for they shall live in your presence.

ANGER AND VENGEANCE IN THE BOOK OF PSALMS

Several psalms shock those familiar with New Testament teachings. The psalmists didn't hesitate to demand God's justice and make vivid suggestions on how he might carry it out. Apparently, no subject was unsuitable for discussion with God, but our tendency is to avoid the subjects of anger and vengeance in the psalms.

To understand the words of anger and vengeance, we need to understand several things:

(1) The judgments asked for are to be carried out by God, and are written out of intense personal and national suffering. The people are unable or unwilling to take vengeance themselves and are asking God to intervene. Because few of us have suffered intense cruelty on a personal or national level, we find it difficult to grasp these outbursts.

(2) These writers were intimately aware of God's justice. Some of their words are efforts to vividly imagine what God might allow to happen to those who had harmed his people.

(3) If we dared to write down our thoughts while unjustly attacked or suffering cruelty, we might be shocked at our own bold desire for vengeance. We would be surprised at how much we have in common with these men of old. The psalmists did not have Jesus' command to pray for one's enemies, but they did point to the right place to start. We are challenged to return good for evil, but until we respond to this challenge, we will not know how much we need God's help in order to forgive others.

(4) There is a helpful parallel between the psalms of anger and the psalms of vengeance. The "angry" psalms are intense and graphic, but they are directed at God. He is boldly told how disappointing it is when he turns his back on his people or acts too slowly. But while these thoughts and feelings were sincerely expressed, we know from the psalms themselves that these passing feelings were followed by renewed confidence in God's faithfulness. It is reasonable to expect the same of the "vengeance" psalms. We read, for example, David's angry outburst against Saul's pursuit in Psalm 59, yet we know that David never took personal vengeance on Saul. The psalmists freely spoke their minds to God, having confidence that he could sort out what was meant and what was felt. Pray with that same confidence—God can be trusted with your heart.

Selected psalms that emphasize these themes are 10, 23, 28, 35, 59, 69, 109, 137, 139, 140.

---

that God's enemies will turn to him before he judges them (see Matthew 5:44).

139:23, 24 David asked God to search for sin and point it out, even to the level of testing his thoughts. This is exploratory surgery for sin. How are we to recognize sin unless God points it out? Then when God shows us, we can repent and be forgiven. Make this verse your prayer. If you ask the Lord to search your thoughts and to reveal sin in your life, you will be on "the path of everlasting life."

140:12 To whom can the poor turn when they are persecuted? They lack the money to get professional help; they may be unable to defend themselves. But there is always someone on their side—the Lord will stand by them and ultimately bring about justice. This should be a comfort for us all. No matter what our situation may be, the Lord is with us. But it should also call us to responsibility. We as God's people are required to defend the rights of the powerless.

Theme: A prayer for help when facing temptation. David asks God to protect him and to give him wisdom in accepting criticism. Be open to honest criticism—God may be speaking to you through others.
Author: David

141 Quick, Lord, answer me—for I have prayed. Listen when I cry to you for help! 2Regard my prayer as my evening sacrifice and as incense wafting up to you.

3Help me, Lord, to keep my mouth shut and my lips sealed. 4Take away my lust for evil things; don't let me want to be with sinners, doing what they do, sharing their delicacies. 5Let the godly smite me! It will be a kindness! If they reprove me, it is medicine! Don't let me refuse it. But I am in constant prayer against the wicked and their deeds. 6, 7When their leaders are condemned, and their bones are strewn across the ground, then these men will finally listen to me and know that I am trying to help them.

8I look to you for help, O Lord God. You are my refuge. Don't let them slay me. 9Keep me out of their traps. 10Let them fall into their own snares, while I escape.

141:2
Ex 29:41; 30:8
Dan 9:21
Rev 5:8; 8:3,4

141:3
Ps 39:1
Prov 13:3; 21:23

141:4
Ps 119:36
Prov 23:6
Mal 3:15

141:5
Ps 23:5; 35:14
Prov 19:25; 27:6
Gal 6:1

141:9
Ps 91:3

Theme: A prayer when overwhelmed and desperate. When we feel cornered by our enemies, only God can keep us safe.
Author: David

142 How I plead with God, how I implore his mercy, pouring out my troubles before him. 3For I am overwhelmed and desperate, and you alone know which way I ought to turn to miss the traps my enemies have set for me. 4(There's one—just over there to the right!) No one gives me a passing thought. No one will help me; no one cares a bit what happens to me. 5Then I prayed to Jehovah. "Lord," I pled, "you are my only place of refuge. Only you can keep me safe.

6"Hear my cry, for I am very low. Rescue me from my persecutors, for they are too strong for me. 7Bring me out of prison, so that I can thank you. The godly will rejoice with me for all your help."

142:1
Ps 30:8

142:4
Ps 88:8,18
Jer 30:17

142:5
Ps 91:2,9

142:6
Ps 18:17; 79:8

142:7
Ps 13:6

Theme: A prayer in the midst of hopelessness and depression. Our prayers should fit into what we know is consistent with God's character and plans.
Author: David

143 Hear my prayer, O Lord; answer my plea, because you are faithful to your promises. 2Don't bring me to trial! For as compared with you, no one is perfect.

3My enemies chased and caught me. They have knocked me to the ground. They force me to live in the darkness like those in the grave. 4I am losing all hope; I am paralyzed with fear.

5I remember the glorious miracles you did in days of long ago. 6I reach out for you. I thirst for you as parched land thirsts for rain. 7Come quickly, Lord, and

143:2
1 Kgs 8:46
Job 14:3; 22:4

143:3
Lam 3:6

143:5
Ps 77:5,10,11

143:6
Ps 63:1

143:7
Ps 69:17; 88:4

141:6, 7 When their leaders are condemned, and their bones are strewn across the ground, literally, "As when one plows and cleaves the earth, our bones are scattered at the mouth of Sheol." **143:1** answer my plea, because you are faithful to your promises, literally, "answer me in faithfulness and righteousness."

141:3 James wrote that "the tongue is a small thing, but what enormous damage it can do" (James 3:5). On the average, a person opens his mouth approximately 700 times a day to speak. David wisely asked God to help him keep his mouth shut—sometimes even as he underwent persecution. Jesus himself was silent before his accusers (Matthew 26:63). Knowing the power of the tongue, we would do well to ask God to guard what we say so that our words will bring honor to his name.

141:4 Evil acts begin with evil desires. It isn't enough to ask God to keep you away from temptation, make you stronger, or change your circumstances. You must ask him to change your desires.

141:5 Nobody really likes criticism, but everybody can benefit from it when it is given wisely and taken humbly. David suggested how to accept criticism: (1) don't refuse it, (2) consider it a kindness, (3) consider the source (God's people often have sound advice and insight), and (4) keep your mouth shut (don't fight

back). Putting these suggestions into practice will help you control how you react to criticism and how to make it productive rather than destructive, no matter how it was originally intended.

142:4, 5 Have you ever felt that no one cared what happened to you? David had good reason to feel that way and wrote, "Then I prayed." Through prayer we can pull out of our tailspin and be reminded that God cares for us deeply.

142:7 This psalm was probably written when David was hiding from Saul in caves like the ones at Adullam (1 Samuel 22) or Engedi (1 Samuel 24). These may have seemed like prisons to him because of the confinement.

143:7 David was losing hope, caught in a deep depression that was paralyzing him with fear. At times, we feel caught in depression that deepens and we are unable to pull ourselves out. At those times, we can come to the Lord and, like David, express our true feelings. Then he will help us as we remember his miracles

143:8
Ps 32:8

143:9
Ps 59:1

143:10
Neh 9:20
Ps 23:3; 119:12

143:12
Ps 52:5; 116:16

answer me, for my depression deepens; don't turn away from me or I shall die. 8Let me see your kindness to me in the morning, for I am trusting you. Show me where to walk, for my prayer is sincere. 9Save me from my enemies. O Lord, I run to you to hide me. 10Help me to do your will, for you are my God. Lead me in good paths, for your Spirit is good.

11Lord, saving me will bring glory to your name. Bring me out of all this trouble because you are true to your promises. 12And because you are loving and kind to me, cut off all my enemies and destroy those who are trying to harm me; for I am your servant.

Theme: Rejoicing in God's care. Whether in times of prosperity or adversity, happy are those whose God is the Lord.
Author: David

144:1
Ps 18:2

144:2
Ps 84:9

144:3
Ps 8:4

144:4
Job 8:9; 14:2
Ps 39:11
109:23

144:5
Ex 19:18
Ps 18:9
Isa 64:1

144:6
Hab 3:11
Zech 9:14

144:7
Ps 18:44
69:1,14

144:8
Deut 32:40
Ps 12:2; 41:6
Isa 44:20

144:9
Ps 40:3

144:10
2 Sam 18:7
Ps 140:7

144:12
2 Kgs 25:10,11
Ps 33:12; 60:2
92:12-14; 128:3
Song 4:4; 7:4
Prov 3:9; 10
Isa 24:11
Jer 14:2
Amos 5:3

144 Bless the Lord who is my immovable Rock. He gives me strength and skill in battle. 2He is always kind and loving to me; he is my fortress, my tower of strength and safety, my deliverer. He stands before me as a shield. He subdues my people under me.

3O Lord, what is man that you even notice him? Why bother at all with the human race? 4For man is but a breath; his days are like a passing shadow.

5Bend down the heavens, Lord, and come. The mountains smoke beneath your touch.

6Let loose your lightning bolts, your arrows, Lord, upon your enemies, and scatter them.

7Reach down from heaven and rescue me; deliver me from deep waters, from the power of my enemies. 8Their mouths are filled with lies; they swear to the truth of what is false.

9I will sing you a new song, O God, with a ten-stringed harp. 10For you grant victory to kings! You are the one who will rescue your servant David from the fatal sword. 11Save me! Deliver me from these enemies, these liars, these treacherous men.

12-15Here is my description of a truly happy land where Jehovah is God:

Sons vigorous and tall as growing plants.
Daughters of graceful beauty like the pillars of a palace wall.
Barns full to the brim with crops of every kind.
Sheep by the thousands out in our fields.
Oxen loaded down with produce.
No enemy attacking the walls, but peace everywhere.
No crime in our streets.
Yes, happy are those whose God is Jehovah.

Theme: A time will come when all people will join together in recognizing and worshiping God. Because God is full of love, he satisfies all who trust in him.
Author: David

145:3
Rom 11:33

145:4
Isa 38:19

145:6
Deut 10:21; 32:3

145 I will praise you, my God and King, and bless your name each day and forever.

3Great is Jehovah! Greatly praise him! His greatness is beyond discovery! 4Let each generation tell its children what glorious things he does. 5I will meditate about your glory, splendor, majesty and miracles. 6Your awe-inspiring deeds shall be on

144:3 *Why bother at all with the human race?* literally, "or the son of man that you take account of him?"
144:12-15 *Here is my description of,* implied.

(143:5), reach out to him (143:6), trust him (143:8), and decide to do his will (143:10).

143:10 David's prayer was for strength to do God's will, not for strength to do his own will. A prayer for guidance is self-centered if it doesn't recognize God's power to redirect our lives. Asking God to restructure our priorities awakens our minds and stirs our wills.

144:3, 4 Life is short. David reminded us that it "is but a breath"

and our "days are like a passing shadow." James said that the length of our lives "is as uncertain as the morning fog—now you see it; soon it is gone" (James 4:14). Because life is short, we should live for God while we have the time. Don't waste your life by giving yourself to an inferior purpose that has no lasting value. Live for God who alone can make your life worthwhile, purposeful, and meaningful.

every tongue; I will proclaim your greatness. 7Everyone will tell about how good you are, and sing about your righteousness.

8Jehovah is kind and merciful, slow to get angry, full of love. 9He is good to everyone, and his compassion is intertwined with everything he does. 10All living things shall thank you, Lord, and your people will bless you. 11They will talk together about the glory of your kingdom and mention examples of your power. 12They will tell about your miracles and about the majesty and glory of your reign. 13For your kingdom never ends. You rule generation after generation.

14The Lord lifts the fallen and those bent beneath their loads. 15The eyes of all mankind look up to you for help; you give them their food as they need it. 16You constantly satisfy the hunger and thirst of every living thing.

17The Lord is fair in everything he does, and full of kindness. 18He is close to all who call on him sincerely. 19He fulfills the desires of those who reverence and trust him; he hears their cries for help and rescues them. 20He protects all those who love him, but destroys the wicked.

21I will praise the Lord and call on all men everywhere to bless his holy name forever and forever.

145:7
Ps 51:14
Isa 63:7
145:8
Ex 34:6
145:9
Ps 100:5
Nah 1:7
Mt 19:17
Mk 10:18
145:12
Ps 105:1
Isa 2:10,19,21
145:13
2 Pet 1:11
145:15
Ps 104:27
145:18
Deut 4:7
145:19
Ps 10:17
145:20
Ps 31:23; 37:38

Theme: The help of man versus the help of God. Help from man is temporal and unstable, but help from God is lasting and complete.
Author: Anonymous

146 Praise the Lord! Yes, really praise him! 2I will praise him as long as I live, yes, even with my dying breath.

3Don't look to men for help; their greatest leaders fail; 4for every man must die. His breathing stops, life ends, and in a moment all he planned for himself is ended. 5But happy is the man who has the God of Jacob as his helper, whose hope is in the Lord his God— 6the God who made both earth and heaven, the seas and everything in them. He is the God who keeps every promise, 7and gives justice to the poor and oppressed, and food to the hungry. He frees the prisoners, 8and opens the eyes of the blind; he lifts the burdens from those bent down beneath their loads. For the Lord loves good men. 9He protects the immigrants, and cares for the orphans and widows. But he turns topsy-turvy the plans of the wicked.

10The Lord will reign forever. O Jerusalem, your God is King in every generation! Hallelujah! Praise the Lord!

146:2
Ps 63:4; 104:33
146:3
Ps 60:11
146:6
Acts 14:15
146:7
Ps 68:6
146:8
Mt 9:30
Jn 9:7
146:9
Ex 22:21
Lev 19:34
Deut 10:18
146:10
Ps 10:16

Theme: What gives God joy. Although God created everything, his greatest joy comes from our genuine worship and trust.
Author: Anonymous, written when the exiles returned to Jerusalem

147 Hallelujah! Yes, praise the Lord! How good it is to sing his praises! How delightful, and how right!

2He is rebuilding Jerusalem and bringing back the exiles. 3He heals the broken-hearted, binding up their wounds. 4He counts the stars and calls them all by name.

147:2
Isa 11:12; 56:8
Ezek 39:28
147:4
Gen 15:5
Isa 40:26

146:10 *O Jerusalem,* literally, "Zion."

145:14 Sometimes our burdens seem more than we can bear and we wonder how we can go on. The psalmist stands at this bleak intersection of life's road and points toward the Lord, the great burden-bearer. God is able to bear our unbearable burdens because he: (1) is great beyond discovery (145:3); (2) does glorious things across many generations (145:4); (3) is full of glory, splendor, majesty, and miracles (145:5); (4) does awe-inspiring deeds (145:6); (5) is righteous (145:7); (6) is kind, merciful, patient, and loving (145:8); (7) reaches out to us with compassion (145:9); (8) rules over an unending kingdom (145:13); (9) is our source of food, water, and help (145:15, 16); (10) is fair in all his dealings and full of kindness (145:17); (11) remains close to those who call on him (145:18); (12) listens to our cries and sends his protection (145:19, 20). If you are bending under a burden and feel that you are about to fall, turn to God for help. He is ready to bear your burden.

146—150 These last five psalms overflow with praise. Each begins with "hallelujah" or "praise the Lord." They show us where, why, and how to praise God. What does praise do? (1) Praise takes our minds off our problems and shortcomings, and focuses them on God. (2) Praise takes us from individual meditation to corporate worship. (3) Praise causes us to consider and appreciate God's character. (4) Praise takes our perspective from the earthly to the heavenly.

146:9 God's plans seem topsy-turvy to our society. Jesus turned society's values upside-down when he proclaimed that "many who are first now will be last then" (Matthew 19:30); "anyone who loses his life for me shall find it again" (Matthew 16:25); and "many who are considered least here shall be greatest there" (Mark 10:31). Don't be surprised when others don't understand your Christian values, but don't give in to theirs. Instead be like the early Christians who turned their world "upside down" (Acts 17:6).

5How great he is! His power is absolute! His understanding is unlimited. 6The Lord supports the humble, but brings the wicked into the dust.

7Sing out your thanks to him; sing praises to our God, accompanied by harps. 8He covers the heavens with clouds, sends down the showers and makes the green grass grow in mountain pastures. 9He feeds the wild animals and the young ravens cry to him for food. 10The speed of a horse is nothing to him. How puny in his sight is the strength of a man. 11But his joy is in those who reverence him, those who expect him to be loving and kind.

12Praise him, O Jerusalem! Praise your God, O Zion! 13For he has fortified your gates against all enemies, and blessed your children. 14He sends peace across your nation, and fills your barns with plenty of the finest wheat. 15He sends his orders to the world. How swiftly his word flies. 16He sends the snow in all its lovely whiteness, and scatters the frost upon the ground, 17and hurls the hail upon the earth. Who can stand before his freezing cold? 18But then he calls for warmer weather, and the spring winds blow and all the river ice is broken. 19He has made known his laws and ceremonies of worship to Israel— 20something he has not done with any other nation; they have not known his commands.

Hallelujah! Yes, praise the Lord!

Theme: Let all creation praise and worship the Lord.
Author: Anonymous

148 Praise the Lord, O heavens! Praise him from the skies! 2Praise him, all his angels, all the armies of heaven. 3Praise him, sun and moon, and all you twinkling stars. 4Praise him, skies above. Praise him, vapors high above the clouds.

5Let everything he has made give praise to him. For he issued his command, and they came into being; 6he established them forever and forever. His orders will never be revoked.

7And praise him down here on earth, you creatures of the ocean depths. 8Let fire and hail, snow, rain, wind and weather, all obey. 9Let the mountains and hills, the fruit trees and cedars, 10the wild animals and cattle, the snakes and birds, 11the kings and all the people with their rulers and their judges, 12young men and

---

**PRAISE IN
THE BOOK
OF PSALMS**

Most of the psalms are prayers, and most of the prayers include praise to God. Praise expresses admiration, appreciation, and thanks. Praise in the book of Psalms is often directed to God, and just as often the praise is shared with others. Considering all that God has done and does for us, what could be more natural than outbursts of heartfelt praise?

As you read Psalms, note the praise given to God, not only for what he does—his creation, his blessings, his forgiveness—but also for who he is—loving, just, faithful, forgiving, patient. Note also those times when the praise of God is shared with others, and they too are encouraged to praise him. In what ways have you recently praised God or told others all that he has done for you?

Selected psalms that emphasize this theme are 8, 19, 30, 65, 84, 96, 100, 136, 145, 150.

147:5 Sometimes we feel as if we don't understand ourselves— what we want, how we feel, what's wrong with us, or what we should do about it. But God's understanding is unlimited and therefore he understands us fully. If you feel troubled and don't understand yourself, remember that God understands you perfectly. Take your mind off yourself and focus it on God. Strive to become more and more like him. The more you learn about God and his ways, the better you will understand yourself.

147:10, 11 We spend much of our lives trying to sharpen our skills or increase our strength. There is nothing wrong with doing so and, in fact, each can be used to glorify God. But when we use our skills or strength with no regard for God, they are indeed worth little. It is out *trust* that God desires. When he has that, he will use our skills and strength in ways far greater than we can imagine.

147:19, 20 The nation of Israel was special to God because to its people God brought his laws, and through its people he sent his Son, Jesus Christ. Now any individual who follows God is just as special to him. In fact, the Bible says that the real nation of Israel is not a specific people or geographic place, but the community of all who believe in and obey God (see Romans 2:29).

148:5 All creation is like a majestic symphony or a great choir comprised of many harmonious parts which together offer up songs of praise. Each part (independent, yet part of the whole) is caught up and carried along in the swelling tides of praise. This is a picture of how we as believers should praise God—individually, yet part of the great choir of believers worldwide. Are you singing your part well in the worldwide choir of praise?

maidens, old men and children— 13all praise the Lord together. For he alone is worthy. His glory is far greater than all of earth and heaven. 14He has made his people strong, honoring his godly ones—the people of Israel, the people closest to him.

Hallelujah! Yes, praise the Lord!

148:13
Ps 8:1; 113:4
Rev 5:12

148:14
Deut 10:21
1 Sam 2:1
Eph 2:17

Theme: A victory celebration. We have the assurance that God truly enjoys his people.
Author: Anonymous

149

Hallelujah! Yes, praise the Lord! Sing him a new song. Sing his praises, all his people.

2O Israel, rejoice in your Maker. O people of Jerusalem, exult in your King. 3Praise his name with dancing, accompanied by drums and lyre.

4, 5For Jehovah enjoys his people; he will save the humble. Let his people rejoice in this honor. Let them sing for joy as they lie upon their beds.

6, 7Adore him, O his people! And take a double-edged sword to execute his punishment upon the nations. 8Bind their kings and leaders with iron chains, 9and execute their sentences.

He is the glory of his people. Hallelujah! Praise him!

149:1
Ps 33:3; 89:5

149:2
Judg 8:23
Ps 47:6

149:3
Ex 15:20

149:4
Ps 35:27

149:6
Ps 66:17

149:8
Nah 3:10

Theme: A closing hymn of praise. God's creation praises him everywhere in every way. We should join this rejoicing song of praise.
Author: Anonymous

150

Hallelujah! Yes, praise the Lord!

Praise him in his Temple, and in the heavens he made with mighty power. 2Praise him for his mighty works. Praise his unequaled greatness. 3Praise him with the trumpet and with lute and harp. 4Praise him with the drums and dancing. Praise him with stringed instruments and horns. 5Praise him with the cymbals, yes, loud clanging cymbals.

6Let everything alive give praises to the Lord! *You* praise him! Hallelujah!

150:1 *in the heavens he made with mighty power,* literally, "in the firmament of his power."

150:1
Ps 19:1; 73:17
102:19

150:2
Deut 3:24

150:3
Ps 98:6

149:3–5 Although the Bible invites us to praise God, we often aren't sure how to go about it. Here, several ways are suggested—with your voice, in music, in your actions. God enjoys his people. We should enjoy praising him as well.

149:6, 7 The double-edged sword symbolizes the completeness of judgment that will be executed by the Messiah when he returns to punish all evildoers (Revelation 1:16).

150:3–5 Music and song were an integral part of Old Testament worship. King David introduced music into the Tabernacle and Temple services (1 Chronicles 16:4–7). The music must have been loud and joyous as evidenced by the list of instruments as well as the presence of choirs and songleaders. Music was also important in New Testament worship (Ephesians 5:19; Colossians 3:16).

150:6 How could the message be more clear? The writer was

telling the individual listeners to praise God. What a fitting way to end this book of praise—with a direct encouragement for *you* to praise God too. Remember to praise him every day!

150:6 In a way, the book of Psalms parallels our spiritual journey through life. It begins by presenting the reader with two roads—the way to life and the way to death. The godly person chooses the way to life, but still faces both blessings and troubles, joy and grief, successes and obstacles. But throughout it all, God is at his side, guiding, encouraging, comforting, caring. As the godly person's life draws to an end, it becomes increasingly clear that he or she has chosen the right road. Knowing this will cause him or her to praise God for leading in the right direction and for the assurance of soon entering the perfect world God has in store for those who have faithfully followed him.

WHERE TO GET HELP IN THE BOOK OF PSALMS

When you feel . . .

Afraid, 3, 4, 27, 46, 49, 56, 91, 118
Alone, 9, 10, 12, 13, 27, 40, 43
"Burned out", 6, 63
Cheated, 41
Confused, 10, 12, 73
Depressed, 27, 34, 42, 43, 88, 143
Distressed, 13, 25, 31, 40, 107
Elated, 19, 96
Guilty, 19, 32, 38, 51
Hateful, 11
Impatient, 13, 27, 37, 40
Insecure, 3, 5, 12, 91
Insulted, 41, 70
Jealous, 37
Like Quitting, 29, 43, 145
Lost, 23, 139

Overwhelmed, 25, 69, 142
Penitent/Sorry, 32, 51, 66
Proud, 14, 30, 49
Purposeless, 14, 25, 39, 49, 90
Sad, 13
Self-confident, 24
Tense, 4
Thankful, 118, 136, 138
Threatened, 3, 11, 17
Tired/Weak, 6, 13, 18, 28, 29, 40, 86
Trapped, 7, 17, 42, 88, 142
Unimportant, 8, 90, 139
Vengeful, 3, 7, 109
Worried, 37
Worshipful, 8, 19, 27, 29, 150

When you're facing . . .

Atheists, 10, 14, 19, 52, 53, 115
Competition, 133
Criticism, 35, 56, 120
Danger, 11
Death, 6, 71, 90
Decisions, 1, 119
Discrimination, 54
Doubts, 34, 37, 94
Evil people, 10, 35, 36, 49, 52, 109, 140
Enemies, 3, 25, 35, 41, 56, 59
Handicap/Illness, 6, 139
Heresy, 14
Hypocrisy, 26, 28, 40, 50

Lies, 5, 12, 120
Old Age, 71, 92
Persecution, 1, 3, 7, 56
Poverty, 9, 10, 12
Punishment, 6, 38, 39
Slander/Insults, 7, 15, 35, 43, 120
Slaughter, 6, 46, 83
Sorrow, 23, 34
Success, 18, 112, 127, 128
Temptation, 38, 141
Troubles, 34, 55, 86, 102, 142, 145
Verbal Cruelty, 35, 120

When you want . . .

Acceptance, 139
Answers, 4, 17
Confidence, 46, 71
Courage, 11, 42
Fellowship with God, 5, 16, 25, 27, 37, 133
Forgiveness, 32, 38, 40, 51, 69, 86, 103, 130
Friendship, 16
Godliness, 15, 25
Guidance, 1, 5, 15, 19, 25, 32, 48
Healing, 6, 41
Hope, 16, 17, 18, 23, 27
Humility, 19, 147
Illumination, 19
Integrity, 24, 25
Joy, 9, 16, 28, 126

Justice, 2, 7, 14, 26, 37, 49, 58, 82
Knowledge, 2, 8, 18, 19, 25, 29, 97, 103
Leadership, 72
Miracles, 60, 111
Money, 15, 16, 17, 49
Peace, 3, 4
Perspective, 2, 11
Prayer, 5, 17, 27, 61
Protection, 3, 4, 7, 16, 17, 18, 23, 27, 31, 91, 121, 125
Provision, 23
Rest, 23, 27
Salvation, 26, 37, 49, 126
Stability, 11, 33, 46
Vindication, 9, 14, 28, 35, 109
Wisdom, 1, 16, 19, 64, 111

PROVERBS

VITAL STATISTICS

PURPOSE:
To teach people how to be understanding, just, and fair in everything they do, to make the simple-minded wise, to warn young men about some problems they will face, and to help the wise become good leaders (see 1:2–6)—in short, to apply divine wisdom to daily life and to provide moral instruction

AUTHOR:
Solomon wrote most of this book, with Agur and Lemuel contributing some of the later sections

DATE WRITTEN:
Solomon wrote and compiled most of these proverbs early in his reign

SETTING:
This is a book of wise sayings, a textbook for teaching people how to live godly lives through the repetition of wise thoughts

KEY VERSE:
"How does a man become wise? The first step is to trust and reverence the Lord! Only fools refuse to be taught" (1:7).

SPECIAL FEATURES:
The book uses varied *literary forms:* poems, brief parables, pointed questions, and couplets. Other *literary devices* include antithesis, comparison, and personification.

FROM friendly advice to impassioned speeches and from dusty volumes to daily tabloids, messages are sent and received with each sender trying to impart knowledge and wisdom. The desire to learn and understand is woven into the very nature of human beings. We analyze, conceptualize, theorize, discuss, and debate everything from science to the supernatural. We build schools, institutes, and universities where learned professors can teach us about the world and about life.

Knowledge is good, but there is a vast difference between *knowledge* (having the facts), and *wisdom* (applying those facts to life). We may amass knowledge, but without wisdom, our knowledge is useless. We must learn how to *live* out what we know.

Solomon, the wisest man who ever lived, left us a legacy of written wisdom in three volumes—Proverbs, Ecclesiastes, and the Song of Solomon. In these books, under the inspiration of the Holy Spirit, he gives practical insights and guidelines for life.

In the first of these three volumes, Solomon passes on his practical advice in the form of proverbs. A proverb is a short, concise sentence which conveys moral truth. The book of Proverbs is a collection of these wise statements. The main theme of Proverbs, as we might expect, is the nature of true wisdom. "How does a man become wise?" Solomon writes, "The first step is to trust and reverence the Lord" (1:7). He then proceeds to give hundreds of practical examples of how to live according to godly wisdom.

Proverbs covers a wide range of topics, including youth and discipline, family life, self-control and resisting temptation, business matters, words and the tongue, knowing God, marriage, seeking the truth, wealth and poverty, immorality, and, of course, wisdom. These proverbs are short poems (usually in couplet form), containing a holy mixture of common sense and timely warnings. Although they are not meant to teach doctrine, a person who follows their advice will walk closely with God. The word "proverb" comes from a Hebrew word which means "to rule or to govern," and these sayings, reminders, and admonitions provide profound advice for governing our lives.

As you read Proverbs, understand that knowing God is the key to wisdom. Listen to the thoughts and lessons from the world's wisest man, and apply these truths to your life. Don't just read these proverbs, act on them!

THE BLUEPRINT

A. WISDOM FOR YOUNG MEN (1:1—9:18)

Solomon instructed the young men of his day like a father giving advice to his son. While many of these proverbs are directed toward young men, the principles supporting them are helpful to all believers, male and female, young and old. Anyone beginning their journey to discover more of wisdom will benefit greatly from these wise sayings. As Solomon said, "I want to make the simple-minded wise! I want to warn young men about some problems they will face" (1:4).

B. WISDOM FOR ALL PEOPLE (10:1—24:34)

Solomon wanted to impart wisdom to all people, regardless of their age, sex, or position in society. These short wise sayings give us practical wisdom for daily living. We should study them diligently and integrate them into our lives. Solomon wanted to "teach his people how to live—how to act in every circumstance, for he wanted them to be understanding, just and fair in everything they did" (1:2, 3).

C. WISDOM FOR THE LEADERS (25:1—31:31)

In addition to the proverbs which Solomon collected, the men of Hezekiah collected many proverbs that Solomon and others wrote. While most of these are general in nature, many are directed specifically to the king and those who dealt with the king. These are particularly useful for those who are leaders or aspire to be leaders. As Solomon said, "I want those already wise to become the wiser and become leaders by exploring the depths of meaning in these nuggets of truth" (1:5, 6).

MEGATHEMES

THEME	EXPLANATION	IMPORTANCE
Wisdom	God wants his people to be wise. Two kinds of people portray two contrasting paths of life. The fool is the wicked, stubborn person who hates or ignores God. The wise person seeks to know and love God.	When we choose God's way, he grants us wisdom. His Word, the Bible, leads us to live rightly, have right relationships, and make right decisions.
Relationships	Proverbs gives us advice for developing our personal relationships with friends, our family, and at work. In every relationship, we must show love, dedication, and high moral standards.	To relate to people, we need consistency, tact, and discipline to use the wisdom God gives us. If we don't treat others according to the wisdom God gives, our relationships will suffer.
Speech	What we say shows our real attitude toward others. How we talk reveals what we're really like. Our speech is a test of how wise we have become.	To be wise in our speech we need to use self-control. Our words should be honest and well-chosen.
Work	God controls the final outcome of all we do. We are accountable to carry out our work with diligence and discipline, not laziness.	Because God evaluates how we live, we should work purposefully. We must never be lax or self-satisfied in using our skills.
Success	Although people work very hard for money and fame, God views success as having a good reputation, moral character, and the spiritual devotion to obey him.	A successful relationship with God counts for eternity. Everything else is perishable. All our resources, time, and talents come from God. We should strive to use them wisely.

A. WISDOM FOR YOUNG MEN (1:1—9:18)

Proverbs begins with a clear statement of its purpose—to impart wisdom for godly living. The first few chapters are Solomon's fatherly advice to young men. Although most of the material in this section is directed toward young men, all who seek wisdom will greatly benefit from these wise words. This is where one can discover the source of wisdom, the value of wisdom, and the benefits of wisdom.

The purpose of Proverbs

1 These are the proverbs of King Solomon of Israel, David's son: ²He wrote them to teach his people how to live—how to act in every circumstance, ³for he wanted them to be understanding, just and fair in everything they did. ⁴"I want to make the simple-minded wise!" he said. "I want to warn young men about some problems they will face. ⁵, ⁶I want those already wise to become the wiser and become leaders by exploring the depths of meaning in these nuggets of truth."

1:1
1 Kgs 4:32
Prov 25:1

1:2
Prov 4:5; 7:4

1:3
Prov 2:9; 19:20

1:4
Prov 8:4; 9:4

Wisdom keeps a young man from disaster

⁷, ⁸, ⁹How does a man become wise? The first step is to trust and reverence the Lord!

Only fools refuse to be taught. Listen to your father and mother. What you learn from them will stand you in good stead; it will gain you many honors.

¹⁰If young toughs tell you, "Come and join us"—turn your back on them! ¹¹"We'll hide and rob and kill," they say. ¹²"Good or bad, we'll treat them all alike. ¹³And the loot we'll get! All kinds of stuff! ¹⁴Come on, throw in your lot with us; we'll split with you in equal shares."

¹⁵Don't do it, son! Stay far from men like that, ¹⁶for crime is their way of life, and murder is their specialty. ¹⁷When a bird sees a trap being set, it stays away, ¹⁸but not these men; they trap themselves! They lay a booby trap for their own lives. ¹⁹Such is the fate of all who live by violence and murder. They will die a violent death.

1:7
Prov 9:10; 15:33

1:8,9
Prov 6:20

1:10
Ps 1:1

1:11
Prov 7:21; 13:20

1:15
Ps 1:1; 26:4
2 Cor 6:17

1:16
Prov 4:16

1:18
Prov 5:22; 9:17

1:19
Prov 15:27
28:25

The voice of wisdom

²⁰Wisdom shouts in the streets for a hearing. ²¹She calls out to the crowds along

1:7-9 *many honors,* literally, "a fair garland and adornment." **1:19** *all who live by violence and murder,* literally, "all who are greedy of gain."

1:1 What the book of Psalms is to devotional life, the book of Proverbs is to everyday life. Proverbs gives practical suggestions for effective living. This book is not just a collection of homey sayings; it contains deep spiritual insights drawn from experience. A *proverb* is a short, wise, easy-to-learn saying that calls a person to action. It doesn't argue about basic spiritual and moral beliefs; it assumes we already hold them. The book of Proverbs focuses on God—his character, works, and blessings, and how we can live in close relationship to him.

1:1 Solomon, the third king of Israel, son of the great King David, reigned during Israel's Golden Age. When God granted him one wish, he asked for wisdom (1 Kings 3:5–14). God was pleased with this request, and he not only made Solomon wise, but also gave him great riches, power, and peace. Solomon built the glorious Temple in Jerusalem (1 Kings 6) and wrote most of the book of Proverbs. His profile is found in 1 Kings 3.

1:7–9 In this age of information, knowledge is plentiful, but wisdom is scarce. Wisdom means far more than simply knowing a lot. It is a basic attitude that affects every aspect of life. The first step to wisdom is to trust and respect God. Faith in God should be the foundation for your understanding of the world, your attitudes, and your actions. Trust in God and he will make you truly wise.

1:7–9 Our actions speak louder than our words. This is especially true in the home. Children learn values, morals, and priorities by observing their parents act and react every day. If parents exhibit a deep reverence for and dependence on God, the children will catch these attitudes. Show reverence for God by living rightly

before your children. Teach them right living by giving worship an important place in your family life and by reading the Bible together.

1:9 One of the most annoying types of people is a know-it-all, a person who has a dogmatic opinion about everything and who is closed to anything new. Solomon calls this kind of person a fool. Don't be a know-it-all. Instead, be open to the advice of others, especially those who know you well and can give valuable insight and counsel. Learn how to learn from others. Remember, only God knows it all.

1:10–19 Sin is attractive because it offers a quick route to prosperity and makes us feel like "one of the crowd." When we go along with others and refuse to listen to the truth, our own appetites become our masters, and we'll do anything to satisfy them. But sin, even when attractive, is deadly. We must learn to make choices, not on the basis of flashy appeal or short-range pleasure, but in view of the long-range effects. Sometimes this means steering clear of people who want to draw us into activities that we know are wrong. We can't be friendly with sin and expect our lives to remain unaffected. Turn and run—this is not cowardly; it is extremely brave.

1:20 The picture of wisdom shouting in the streets is a personification—a literary device to make wisdom come alive for us. Wisdom is not a separate being, it is the mind of God revealed. By reading about Jesus Christ's earthly ministry in the gospel narratives, we can see wisdom in action. In order to understand how we can become wise, we can listen to wisdom calling and instructing us in the book of Proverbs.

Main Street, and to the judges in their courts, and to everyone in all the land: 22"You simpletons!" she cries. "How long will you go on being fools? How long will you scoff at wisdom and fight the facts? 23Come here and listen to me! I'll pour out the spirit of wisdom upon you, and make you wise. 24I have called you so often but still you won't come. I have pleaded, but all in vain. 25For you have spurned my counsel and reproof. 26Some day you'll be in trouble, and I'll laugh! Mock me, will you?—I'll mock you! 27When a storm of terror surrounds you, and when you are engulfed by anguish and distress, 28then I will not answer your cry for help. It will be too late though you search for me ever so anxiously.

29"For you closed your eyes to the facts and did not choose to reverence and trust the Lord, 30and you turned your back on me, spurning my advice. 31That is why you must eat the bitter fruit of having your own way, and experience the full terrors of the pathway you have chosen. 32For you turned away from me—to death; your own complacency will kill you. Fools! 33But all who listen to me shall live in peace and safety, unafraid."

Wisdom is from God

2 Every young man who listens to me and obeys my instructions will be given wisdom and good sense. 3, 4, 5Yes, if you want better insight and discernment, and are searching for them as you would for lost money or hidden treasure, then wisdom will be given you, and knowledge of God himself; you will soon learn the importance of reverence for the Lord and of trusting him.

6For the Lord grants wisdom! His every word is a treasure of knowledge and understanding. 7, 8He grants good sense to the godly—his saints. He is their shield, protecting them and guarding their pathway. 9He shows how to distinguish right from wrong, how to find the right decision every time. 10For wisdom and truth will enter the very center of your being, filling your life with joy. 11, 12, 13You will be given the sense to stay away from evil men who want you to be their partners in crime—men who turn from God's ways to walk down dark and evil paths, 14and exult in doing wrong, for they thoroughly enjoy their sins. 15Everything they do is crooked and wrong.

1:22
Prov 9:4; 14:15
1:24
Prov 15:32
Isa 65:12; 66:4
1:25
2 Chron 36:16
1:27
Prov 3:25; 10:25
1:28
Job 27:9
Ezek 8:18
1:31
Job 4:8
Prov 5:22; 22:8
1:33
Prov 3:24-26
2:1
Prov 3:1; 4:10
2:3
Mt 13:44
2:6
Jas 1:5
2:9
Prov 1:2-6
2:10
Prov 14:33
2:11
Prov 4:19; 6:12
2:14
Prov 10:23

UNDERSTAND-ING PROVERBS Most often, proverbs are written in the form of couplets. These are constructed in three ways:

Type	Description	Key Word(s)	Examples
Contrasting	Meaning and application come from the difference or contrast between the two statements of the proverb	"but"	10:6; 15:25, 27
Comparing	Meaning and application come from the similarities or comparison between the two statements of the proverb	"like" "better/than"	10:26; 15:16, 17; 25:25
Complimenting	Meaning and application come from the way the second statement compliments the first	"and"	10:24; 15:3, 23

1:22 In the book of Proverbs, a fool is not someone with a *mental* deficiency but someone with a *character* deficiency. He is not dumb or stupid, he is unable to tell right from wrong or good from bad.

1:23–28 To hear wisdom's advice, we must be willing to listen. We cannot let pride stand in our way. Pride is thinking more highly of our own wisdom and desires than of God's. If we think we know better than God, we have fallen into foolish pride. When we feel we have no need of God's direction, we are ignoring the bridge that connects us to him—humility.

2:3–6 Wisdom is both a God-given gift and an energetic search. Wisdom's starting point is God and his revealed Word, the "treasure of knowledge and understanding" (2:6). In that sense, it is his gift to us. But he gives it only to those who earnestly seek it. The pathway to wisdom is strenuous. When we are on it, we discover that true wisdom is God's and that we cannot create it by our own efforts. But because God's wisdom is hidden from the

rebellious and foolish, it takes effort to find it and use it.

2:3–5 These verses highlight two ways we respond to God, ways that correspond to two basic aspects of his nature. First, we have reverence and awe for him. At the same time, we have confidence and trust in him. Our reverence for God recognizes his transcendence—his perfection and power over his created world. Our confidence and trust are our responses to his immanence—his everyday presence in our lives.

2:9, 10 Wisdom comes through a constant process of growth. First, we must trust and honor God. Second, we must realize that the Bible reveals God's wisdom to us. Third, we must make a lifelong series of right choices. Fourth, when we make sinful or mistaken choices, we must learn from our errors. People don't develop all aspects of wisdom at once. For example, some people have more insight than discretion; others have more knowledge than common sense. But we can pray for all aspects of wisdom and seek to develop them in our lives.

16, 17Only wisdom from the Lord can save a man from the flattery of prostitutes; these girls have abandoned their husbands and flouted the laws of God. 18Their houses lie along the road to death and hell. 19The men who enter them are doomed. None of these men will ever be the same again.

20Follow the steps of the godly instead, and stay on the right path, 21for only good men enjoy life to the full; 22evil men lose the good things they might have had, and they themselves shall be destroyed.

Wisdom is extremely valuable

3 My son, never forget the things I've taught you. If you want a long and satisfying life, closely follow my instructions. 3Never tire of loyalty and kindness. Hold these virtues tightly. Write them deep within your heart. 4, 5If you want favor with both God and man, and a reputation for good judgment and common sense, then trust the Lord completely; don't ever trust yourself. 6In

2:19 *None of these men will ever be the same again,* literally, "never return to the ways of life." **2:21** *enjoy life to the full,* literally, "shall dwell in the land." **2:22** *lose the good things they might have had,* literally, "shall be cut off from the land."

2:16
Prov 6:24; 23:27

2:20
Prov 13:20

2:21
Prov 10:30

2:22
Deut 28:63

3:1
Ps 119:93
Prov 9:11; 10:27

3:3
Prov 6:21; 7:3

3:4
Prov 8:35; 22:19

The Person	Their Role	Reference	How they practiced wisdom	
Joseph	Wise leader	Acts 7:10	Prepared for a major drought. Helped rule Egypt.	**PEOPLE CALLED "WISE" IN THE BIBLE**
Moses	Wise leader	Acts 7:20–22	Learned all the Egyptian wisdom, then graduated to God's lessons in wisdom to lead Israel out of Egypt.	The special description "wise" is used for 12
Bezalel	Wise artist	Exodus 31:1–5	Designed and supervised the construction of the Tabernacle and its utensils in the wilderness.	significant people in the Bible. They can be helpful models in our
Joshua	Wise leader	Deuteronomy 34:9	Learned by observing Moses, obeyed God, led the people into the Promised Land.	own pursuit of wisdom.
David	Wise leader	2 Samuel 14:20	Never let his failures keep him from the source of wisdom—reverence for God.	
Abigail	Wise wife	1 Samuel 25:3, 32	Managed her household well in spite of an alcoholic husband.	
Solomon	Wise leader	1 Kings 3:5–14; 4:29–34	Knew what to do even though he often failed to put his own wisdom into action.	
Daniel	Wise counselor	Daniel 5:11, 12	Known as a man in touch with God. A solver of complex problems with God's help	
Wise men	Wise learners	Matthew 2:1–10	Not only received special knowledge of God's visit to earth, but checked it out personally.	
Stephen	Wise leader	Acts 6:8–10	Organized the distribution of food to the Grecian widows. Preached the gospel to the Jews.	
Paul	Wise messenger	2 Peter 3:15, 16	Spent his life communicating God's love to all who would listen.	
Christ	Wise youth Wise Savior Wisdom of God	Luke 2:40, 52 1 Corinthians 1:20–25	Not only lived a perfect life, but died on the cross to save us and make God's wise plan of eternal life available to us.	

2:16, 17 Two of the most difficult sins to resist are pride and sexual immorality. Pride says, "I deserve it"; sexual desire says "I need it." In combination, their appeal is deadly. In fact, says Solomon, only by relying on God's strength can we overcome them. Pride appeals to the empty head, sexual enticement to the empty heart. By looking to God, we can fill our heads with his wisdom and our hearts with his love. Don't be fooled—remember what God says about who you are and what you were meant to be. Ask him for strength to resist these temptations.

3:3 Two important character qualities are loyalty and kindness. Both of these involve actions as well as attitudes. A loyal person not only feels love; he also acts responsibly and faithfully. A kind person not only cares for others in his heart; he also helps them.

Thoughts and words are not enough—our lives reveal whether we are truly loyal and kind. Do your actions measure up to your attitudes?

3:4, 5 When we have an important decision to make, we sometimes feel that we can't trust anyone—not even God. But God knows what is best for us. He is a better judge of what we want than even we are! We must trust him completely in every choice we make. This does not mean we cannot study the options and make intelligent decisions, or that we should have no confidence in our ability. It means, however, that we must not be wise in our own eyes. We should always be willing to listen to and be corrected by others. Bring your decisions to God in prayer; use the Bible as your guide; and then do what is right.

3:7
Job 1:1; 28:28
Prov 4:21; 8:13
16:6
3:9
Ex 23:19
Prov 11:24
19:17
Joel 2:24
Mal 3:10
3:11
Deut 8:5
Job 5:17
Ps 94:12
Prov 13:24
Heb 12:5,6
3:13
Job 28:17
Prov 8:10,34
16:16

everything you do, put God first, and he will direct you and crown your efforts with success.

7, 8Don't be conceited, sure of your own wisdom. Instead, trust and reverence the Lord, and turn your back on evil; when you do that, then you will be given renewed health and vitality.

9, 10Honor the Lord by giving him the first part of all your income, and he will fill your barns with wheat and barley and overflow your wine vats with the finest wines.

11, 12Young man, do not resent it when God chastens and corrects you, for his punishment is proof of his love. Just as a father punishes a son he delights in to make him better, so the Lord corrects you.

13, 14, 15The man who knows right from wrong and has good judgment and common sense is happier than the man who is immensely rich! For such wisdom is far more valuable than precious jewels. Nothing else compares with it. 16, 17Wisdom

3:13-15 *The man who knows right from wrong,* literally, "The man that finds wisdom."

WISDOM: APPLIED TRUTH	Reference	The Person who has Wisdom	Benefits of Wisdom
The book of Proverbs tells us about people who have wisdom and enjoy its benefits.	Proverbs 3, 4 A father's instructions	Is loyal Is kind Trusts in the Lord Puts God first Turns back on evil Knows right from wrong Listens and learns Does what is right	Long, satisfying life Favor with God and people Reputation for good judgment Success Health, vitality Riches, honor, pleasure, peace Protection
	Proverbs 8, 9 Wisdom speaks	Knows where to find knowledge and understanding Hates pride, arrogance, corruption, and deceit Respects and fears God Gives good advice and has common sense Loves correction and is teachable Knows God	Riches, honor Justice Righteousness Life God's approval Constant learning Understanding

3:6 To succeed, said Solomon, we must put God first in our lives. About a thousand years later, Jesus emphasized this same truth (Matthew 6:33). Look at your values and priorities. What is important to you? Where is God on that list? Keep him in first place in everything you do; then he will crown your efforts with success because you will be working to accomplish his purposes. For example, when it comes to money, putting God first means considering what his portion of your income should be before making any further financial decisions (3:9, 10).

3:9, 10 Many people give God their leftovers. If they can afford to donate anything, they do so. Many of those people are sincere and contribute willingly, but their attitude is nonetheless backward. It is better to give God the first part of our income. This demonstrates that God, not possessions, has first place in our lives and that our resources belong to him (we are only managers of God's resources). Giving to God first helps us conquer greed, helps us properly manage God's resources, and opens us to God's special blessings.

3:11, 12 The word for punishment in this chapter is also translated "discipline"—to teach and to train. Discipline sounds negative to many people, because some disciplinarians are not loving. God, however, is the source of all love. He doesn't punish us because

he enjoys inflicting pain but because he is deeply concerned about our development. He knows that in order to become morally strong and good, we must learn the difference between right and wrong. His loving discipline enables us to do this.

3:11, 12 It's difficult to know when God has been disciplining us until we look back on the situation later. Not all bad things that happen to us come directly from God, of course. But if we are in rebellion against God, refusing to repent when he has identified some sin in our lives, we can safely assume that God is using guilt, crises, or bad experiences to encourage us to turn to him. Sometimes, however, difficult times come when there is no flagrant sin in our lives. Our response then should be patience, integrity, and trust that God will show us what to do.

3:13–15 How do people become successful in their family life, in business, or in athletics? By hard work and consistent discipline. The Christian life is much the same. Some people think it is too much work, but achieving anything worthwhile takes hard work. Being a Christian is not a shortcut to an easy life. When you search for wisdom, working hard at applying it and living as God asks, you discover that no worldly success can compare with the joy of the Christian life.

gives: A long, good life, riches, honor, pleasure, peace. 18Wisdom is a tree of life to those who eat her fruit; happy is the man who keeps on eating it.

19The Lord's wisdom founded the earth; his understanding established all the universe and space. 20The deep fountains of the earth were broken open by his knowledge, and the skies poured down rain.

21Have two goals: wisdom—that is, knowing and doing right—and common sense. Don't let them slip away, 22for they fill you with living energy, and bring you honor and respect. 23They keep you safe from defeat and disaster and from stumbling off the trail. 24, 25, 26With them on guard you can sleep without fear; you need not be afraid of disaster or the plots of wicked men, for the Lord is with you; he protects you.

27, 28Don't withhold repayment of your debts. Don't say "some other time," if you can pay now. 29Don't plot against your neighbor; he is trusting you. 30Don't get into needless fights. 31Don't envy violent men. Don't copy their ways. 32For such men are an abomination to the Lord, but he gives his friendship to the godly.

33The curse of God is on the wicked, but his blessing is on the upright. 34The Lord mocks at mockers, but helps the humble. 35The wise are promoted to honor, but fools are promoted to shame!

Wisdom can be learned

4 Young men, listen to me as you would to your father. Listen, and grow wise, for I speak the truth—don't turn away. 3For I, too, was once a son, tenderly loved by my mother as an only child, and the companion of my father. 4He told me never to forget his words. "If you follow them," he said, "you will have a long and happy life. 5Learn to be wise," he said, "and develop good judgment and common sense! I cannot overemphasize this point." 6Cling to wisdom—she will protect you. Love her—she will guard you.

7Getting wisdom is the most important thing you can do! And with your wisdom, develop common sense and good judgment. 8, 9If you exalt wisdom, she will exalt you. Hold her fast and she will lead you to great honor; she will place a beautiful

Side references:

3:16 Prov 16:7; 22:4

3:18 Prov 11:30

3:21 Prov 4:21; 9:11

3:23 Ps 37:23; 91:11 Prov 4:12; 10:9

3:29 Ps 35:20; 55:20 Prov 14:22

3:30 Prov 18:6; 26:17 Rom 12:18

3:31 Ps 37:11; 73:3 Prov 23:17

3:32 Prov 6:16; 11:20

3:34 Jas 4:6

4:1 Prov 1:8; 5:1 6:20

4:4 Prov 3:1; 4:10 9:11

4:6 Prov 2:16; 3:26 8:14,17 2 Thess 2:10

4:7 Ps 119:104 Prov 18:15 23:23

3:22 bring you honor and respect, literally, "be an ornament to your neck."   **4:5** I cannot overemphasize this point, literally, "Forget not nor turn from the words of my mouth."

3:16, 17 Proverbs has many strong statements about the benefits of wisdom, which include long life, wealth, honor, and peace. If these aren't happening to you, does that mean you are short on wisdom? Not necessarily. Instead of guarantees, these statements are general principles to make us think. In a perfect world, wise behavior would always lead to these benefits. Even in our troubled world, living wisely usually results in obvious blessings—but not always. Sometimes sin intervenes, and the blessings must be delayed until Jesus returns to establish his eternal kingdom. Whether or not we see immediate benefits we must "know these things are true by believing, not by seeing" (2 Corinthians 5:7). We can be sure that wisdom ultimately leads to blessing.

3:21 What is the difference between wisdom and common sense? Common sense is the ability God gives to all people to think and make correct choices. Wisdom, however, he gives only to those who follow him. Wisdom includes common sense, but goes beyond it. It also includes the knowledge that comes from instruction, training, and discipline; the understanding that comes through insight, discretion, and discernment; and the insight that results from knowing and applying God's truths.

3:27, 28 It is easy to get into debt and hard to get out of it. Unfortunately, debt owed to a friend can destroy trust and divide even the best of friends. Be as eager to repay your loans as you were to get them, and pay them back ahead of schedule, if possible.

3:30 This verse implies that there is a time for fighting. Injustice must be combated, sin resisted, and evil confronted wherever it

appears. But don't waste time and energy on needless fights, arguing about trivial matters or personal inconvenience. Save your energy for the real battles against sin and God's enemies.

4:3, 4 One of the greatest responsibilities of parents is to encourage their children to become wise. Here Solomon tells how his father, David, encouraged him to seek after wisdom (see 1 Kings 2 and 1 Chronicles 28 for David's full charge to his son). This encouragement may have prompted Solomon to ask God for wisdom above everything else (1 Kings 3:9). Wisdom can be passed on from parents to children, from generation to generation. Ultimately, of course, all wisdom comes from God. Parents can only urge their children to turn to him for wisdom. If your parents never taught you in this way, God's Word can function as a loving and compassionate father to you. You can learn from the Scriptures and then begin a new chain of wisdom as you raise your own children.

4:5–7 If you want wisdom, you must decide to go after it. It takes resolve—a determination not to abandon the search once you begin no matter how difficult the road may become. This is not a once-in-a-lifetime step, but a daily process of choosing between two paths—the wicked (4:14–17) and the good (4:18, 19).

4:7 David taught Solomon as a young boy that seeking God's wisdom was the most important thing he could do. Solomon learned the lesson well. When God appeared to the new king to grant him any request, Solomon chose wisdom above all else (1 Kings 3:9). We should also make God's wisdom our first choice. We don't have to wait for God to appear to us. We can boldly ask him for wisdom today through prayer.

crown upon your head. 10My son, listen to me and do as I say, and you will have a long, good life.

4:12
Ps 37:23; 91:11

11I would have you learn this great fact: that a life of doing right is the wisest life there is. 12If you live that kind of life, you'll not limp or stumble as you run. 13Carry out my instructions; don't forget them, for they will lead you to real living.

4:13
Jn 6:63

4:14
Ps 1:1

14Don't do as the wicked do. 15Avoid their haunts—turn away, go somewhere else, 16for evil men can't sleep until they've done their evil deed for the day. They can't rest unless they cause someone to stumble and fall. 17They eat and drink wickedness and violence!

4:16
Ps 36:4
Mic 2:1

4:19
Jn 1:4,5

18But the good man walks along in the ever-brightening light of God's favor; the dawn gives way to morning splendor, 19while the evil man gropes and stumbles in the dark.

4:23
Lk 6:45

4:24
Job 11:14

20Listen, son of mine, to what I say. Listen carefully. 21Keep these thoughts ever in mind; let them penetrate deep within your heart, 22for they will mean real life for you, and radiant health.

4:25
Job 31:1
Mt 6:22

4:26
Prov 5:21; 15:3
Eph 5:15
Heb 12:13

23Above all else, guard your affections. For they influence everything else in your life. 24Spurn the careless kiss of a prostitute. Stay far from her. 25Look straight ahead; don't even turn your head to look. 26Watch your step. Stick to the path and be safe. 27Don't sidetrack; pull back your foot from danger.

4:27
Deut 5:32; 28:14

Warning against sexual sin

5:3
Ps 55:21
Prov 5:20; 7:5

5 Listen to me, my son! I know what I am saying; *listen!* 2Watch yourself, lest you be indiscreet and betray some vital information. 3For the lips of a prostitute are as sweet as honey, and smooth flattery is her stock in trade. 4But afterwards only a bitter conscience is left to you, sharp as a double-edged sword. 5She leads you down to death and hell. 6For she does not know the path to life. She staggers down a crooked trail, and doesn't even realize where it leads.

5:4
Eccles 7:26

5:6
Prov 3:23
2 Pet 2:14

7Young men, listen to me, and never forget what I'm about to say: 8Run from her! Don't go near her house, 9lest you fall to her temptation and lose your honor, and give the remainder of your life to the cruel and merciless; 10lest strangers obtain your wealth, and you become a slave of foreigners. 11Lest afterwards you groan in anguish and in shame, when syphilis consumes your body, 12and you say, "Oh, if only I had listened! If only I had not demanded my own way! 13Oh, why wouldn't

5:8
Prov 7:25; 9:14
2 Tim 2:22

5:11
Prov 3:35; 9:13

5:13
Lk 15:18

4:24 *Spurn the careless kiss of a prostitute,* implied; literally, "Put away from you a wayward mouth." **5:3** *of a prostitute,* or "of another man's wife." **5:4** *But afterwards only a bitter conscience is left you,* literally, "But in the end she is bitter as wormwood." **5:9** *and give the remainder of your life to the cruel and merciless.* Perhaps the reference is to blackmail, or to fear of vengeance from the wronged husband. **5:11** *syphilis,* literally, "disease."

STRATEGY FOR EFFECTIVE LIVING	Begins with	God's Wisdom	Respecting and appreciating who God is. Reverence and awe in recognizing the almighty God.
	Requires	Moral Application	Trusting in God and his Word. Allowing his Word to speak to us personally. Willing to obey.
	Requires	Practical Application	Acting on God's direction in daily devotions.
	Results in	Effective Living	Experiencing what God does with our obedience.

4:23-27 Our affections—our feelings of love and desire—dictate to a great extent how we live, because we always find time to do what we enjoy. Solomon tells us to guard our affections, making sure we concentrate on those desires that will keep us on the right path. Make sure your affections are pushing you in the right direction. Put boundaries on your desires: don't go after everything you see. Look straight ahead: keep your eyes fixed on your goal.

5:3 Why does Proverbs include so many warnings against prostitutes? First, a prostitute's charm is used as an example of any temptation to do wrong or to leave the pursuit of wisdom.

Second, sexual immorality of any kind was and still is extremely dangerous. It destroys family life. It eats away at one's ability to love. It degrades human beings and turns them into objects. It can lead to disease. It can result in unwanted children. These are some of the reasons that sexual immorality is against God's Law.

5:13 When temptation strikes, it is too late to ask for advice. When desire is fully activated, people don't want advice—they want satisfaction. The best time to learn the dangers and foolishness of going after prostitutes is long before the temptation comes. Resistance is easier if the decision has already been made.

I take advice? Why was I so stupid? ¹⁴For now I must face public disgrace."

¹⁵Drink from your own well, my son—be faithful and true to your wife. ¹⁶Why should you beget children with women of the street? ¹⁷Why share your children with those outside your home? ¹⁸Be happy, yes, rejoice in the wife of your youth. ¹⁹Let her breasts and tender embrace satisfy you. Let her love alone fill you with delight. ²⁰Why delight yourself with prostitutes, embracing what isn't yours? ²¹*For God is closely watching you,* and he weighs carefully everything you do.

²²The wicked man is doomed by his own sins; they are ropes that catch and hold him. ²³He shall die because he will not listen to the truth; he has let himself be led away into incredible folly.

Warning against foolish actions

6 Son, if you endorse a note for someone you hardly know, guaranteeing his debt, you are in serious trouble. ²You may have trapped yourself by your agreement. ³Quick! Get out of it if you possibly can! Swallow your pride; don't let embarrassment stand in the way. Go and beg to have your name erased. ⁴Don't put it off. Do it now. Don't rest until you do. ⁵If you can get out of this trap you have saved yourself like a deer that escapes from a hunter, or a bird from the net.

⁶Take a lesson from the ants, you lazy fellow. Learn from their ways and be wise! ⁷For though they have no king to make them work, ⁸yet they labor hard all summer, gathering food for the winter. ⁹But you—all you do is sleep. When will you wake up? ¹⁰"Let me sleep a little longer!" Sure, just a little more! ¹¹And as you sleep, poverty creeps upon you like a robber and destroys you; want attacks you in full armor.

¹², ¹³Let me describe for you a worthless and a wicked man; first, he is a constant liar; he signals his true intentions to his friends with eyes and feet and fingers. ¹⁴He is always thinking up new schemes to swindle people. He stirs up trouble everywhere. ¹⁵But he will be destroyed suddenly, broken beyond hope of healing.

¹⁶⁻¹⁹For there are six things the Lord hates—no, seven: haughtiness, lying, murdering, plotting evil, eagerness to do wrong, a false witness, sowing discord among brothers.

Warning against adultery

²⁰Young man, obey your father and your mother. ²¹Take to heart all of their advice; keep in mind everything they tell you. ²²Every day and all night long their counsel will lead you and save you from harm; when you wake up in the morning, let their instructions guide you into the new day. ²³For their advice is a beam of

5:19 *Let her breasts and tender embrace,* literally, "as a loving hind and a pleasant doe."

Cross references (right margin):

5:15 Eccles 9:9; Song 4:15
5:18 Eccles 9:9; Mal 2:14
5:19 Song 4:5; 7:3
5:21 Job 14:16
5:22 Num 32:23
6:1 Prov 17:18; 22:26; 27:13
6:6 Prov 10:26; 13:4,30;24,25
6:10 Prov 24:33,34
6:11 Prov 23:19
6:12 Prov 4:27; 8:13; 10:27; 16:27
6:14 Prov 10:32; 17:11
6:16-19 Gen 6:5; Prov 1:16; 6:14; 19:5,9; 21:4; 24:2; 28:17; 30:21; Isa 1:15
6:20 Prov 1:7
6:23 Ps 119:105; Prov 13:9

5:15 "Drink from your own well" is a picture of faithfulness in marriage. In desert lands, water is precious, and a well is a family's most important possession. In Old Testament times, it was considered a crime to steal water from someone else's well, just as it was a crime to have intercourse with another man's wife.

5:15-21 In contrast to much of what we read, see, and hear today, this passage urges couples to look to each other for lifelong satisfaction and companionship. Many temptations entice husbands and wives to desert each other for excitement and pleasures to be found elsewhere, when marriage becomes dull. But God designed marriage and sanctified it, and only within this covenant relationship can we find real love and fulfillment. Don't let God's best for you be wasted on the illusion of greener pastures elsewhere. Instead, rejoice with your spouse as you give yourselves to God and to each other.

5:18-20 God does not intend faithfulness in marriage to be boring, lifeless, pleasureless, and dull. Sex is a gift which God gives to married people for their mutual enjoyment. Real happiness comes when we decide to find pleasure in the relationship God has given or will give us, and to commit ourselves to making it pleasurable for the one God gives us to love.

5:19 See the Song of Solomon 4:5, 12, 15 for parallels to this frank expression of the joys of sexual pleasure in marriage.

6:1-5 These verses are not against generosity, but against overextending one's financial resources and acting in irresponsible ways that could lead to poverty. It is important to maintain a balance between generosity and good stewardship. God wants us to help the needy, but he does not promise to cover the costs of every unwise commitment we make. It is equally important to act responsibly so that our own families do not suffer want.

6:6-11 Those last few moments of sleep are delicious—we savor them as we resist beginning another workday. Proverbs warns against giving in to this temptation. This does not mean we should never rest: God gave the Jews the Sabbath, a weekly day of rest and restoration. But we should not rest when we should be working. If laziness turns us from our responsibilities, poverty will soon bar us from the legitimate rest we should enjoy.

6:20-24 It is natural and good for children, as they grow toward adulthood, to strive to become independent of their parents. Young adults, however, should take care not to turn a deaf ear to their parents—to reject their advice just when they may need it most. If you are struggling with a decision or looking for insight, check with your parents or other older adults who know you well. Their extra years of experience may have given them the wisdom you seek.

light directed into the dark corners of your mind to warn you of danger and to give you a good life. 24Their counsel will keep you far away from prostitutes with all their flatteries, and unfaithful wives of other men.

25Don't lust for their beauty. Don't let their coyness seduce you. 26For a prostitute will bring a man to poverty, and an adulteress may cost him his very life. 27Can a man hold fire against his chest and not be burned? 28Can he walk on hot coals and not blister his feet? 29So it is with the man who commits adultery with another's wife. He shall not go unpunished for this sin. 30Excuses might even be found for a thief, if he steals when he is starving! 31But even so, he is fined seven times as much as he stole, though it may mean selling everything in his house to pay it back.

32But the man who commits adultery is an utter fool, for he destroys his own soul. 33Wounds and constant disgrace are his lot, 34for the woman's husband will be furious in his jealousy, and he will have no mercy on you in his day of vengeance. 35You won't be able to buy him off no matter what you offer.

Wisdom guards against immorality

7 Follow my advice, my son; always keep it in mind and stick to it. 2Obey me and live! Guard my words as your most precious possession. 3Write them down, and also keep them deep within your heart. 4Love wisdom like a sweetheart; make her a beloved member of your family. 5Let her hold you back from affairs with other women—from listening to their flattery.

6I was looking out the window of my house one day, 7and saw a simple-minded lad, a young man lacking common sense, 8, 9walking at twilight down the street to the house of this wayward girl, a prostitute. 10She approached him, saucy and pert, and dressed seductively. 11, 12She was the brash, coarse type, seen often in the streets and markets, soliciting at every corner for men to be her lovers.

13She put her arms around him and kissed him, and with a saucy look she said, "I was just coming to look for you and here you are! 14-17Come home with me and I'll fix you a wonderful dinner, and after that—well, my bed is spread with lovely, colored sheets of finest linen imported from Egypt, perfumed with myrrh, aloes

7:3 *Write them down,* literally, "Bind them upon your fingers." **7:14-17** *I'll fix you a wonderful dinner,* literally, "Sacrifices of peace offerings were due from me; this day have I paid my vows." If she meant this literally, she was telling him that she had plenty of food on hand, left from her sacrifice at the Temple.

THINGS GOD HATES The book of Proverbs notes 14 types of people and actions that God hates. Let these be a guideline of what we are *not* to be and do!		
	Violent people	Proverbs 3:32
	Haughtiness	Proverbs 6:16–19
	Lying	
	Murdering	
	Plotting evil	
	Eagerness to do wrong	
	A false witness	
	Sowing discord among brothers	
	Those who don't keep their promises	Proverbs 12:22
	The gifts of the wicked	Proverbs 15:8
	The deeds of the wicked	Proverbs 15:9, 10
	The thoughts of the wicked	Proverbs 15:26
	Pride	Proverbs 16:5
	Those who say bad is good and good is bad	Proverbs 17:15

6:25–35 Some people argue that it is all right to break God's law against sexual sin if nobody gets hurt. In truth, somebody always gets hurt. Spouses are devastated. Children are scarred. The partners themselves, even if they escape disease and unwanted pregnancy, lose their ability to fulfill commitments, to trust, and to be entirely open with another person. God's laws are not arbitrary. They do not forbid good, clean fun; rather, they warn us against destroying ourselves through unwise actions.

7:6–23 The person who has no purpose in life is simple-minded

(7:7). Without aim or direction, an empty life is vulnerable to many temptations. Even though the young man in this passage doesn't know where he is going, the seductress knows where she wants him. Notice her strategies: she is dressed to allure men (7:10); her approach is bold (7:13); she invites him over to her place (7:14); she answers his every objection (7:19, 20); she flatteres him (7:21); she traps him (7:23). To combat temptation, make sure your life is full of God's Word and wisdom (7:3, 4). Recognize the strategies of temptation, and run away from them—fast.

and cinnamon. 18Come on, let's take our fill of love until morning, 19for my husband is away on a long trip. 20He has taken a wallet full of money with him, and won't return for several days."

7:16
Ps 45:8
Prov 31:22
Ezek 27:7

21So she seduced him with her pretty speech, her coaxing and her wheedling, until he yielded to her. He couldn't resist her flattery. 22He followed her as an ox going to the butcher, or as a stag that is trapped, 23waiting to be killed with an arrow through its heart. He was as a bird flying into a snare, not knowing the fate awaiting it there.

7:21
Prov 5:3; 6:24

7:23
Prov 1:17
Eccles 9:12

24Listen to me, young men, and not only listen but obey; 25don't let your desires get out of hand; don't let yourself think about her. Don't go near her; stay away from where she walks, lest she tempt you and seduce you. 26For she has been the ruin of multitudes—a vast host of men have been her victims. 27If you want to find the road to hell, look for her house.

7:24
Prov 4:1; 5:7

7:25
Prov 4:23; 5:8

7:27
Prov 2:18; 5:5

Wisdom gives good advice

8 Can't you hear the voice of wisdom? She is standing at the city gates and at every fork in the road, and at the door of every house. Listen to what she says: 4, 5"Listen, men!" she calls. "How foolish and naive you are! Let me give you understanding. O foolish ones, let me show you common sense! 6, 7Listen to me! For I have important information for you. Everything I say is right and true, for I hate lies and every kind of deception. 8My advice is wholesome and good. There is nothing of evil in it. 9My words are plain and clear to anyone with half a mind—if it is only open! 10My instruction is far more valuable than silver or gold."

8:1
Job 19:7

8:4
Ps 19:7

8:9
Ps 25:12

8:10
Ps 119:72,127

11For the value of wisdom is far above rubies; nothing can be compared with it. 12Wisdom and good judgment live together, for wisdom knows where to discover knowledge and understanding. 13If anyone respects and fears God, he will hate evil. For wisdom hates pride, arrogance, corruption and deceit of every kind.

8:11
Prov 3:14,15
16:16; 20:15

8:13
Isa 13:11

14, 15, 16"I, Wisdom, give good advice and common sense. Because of my strength, kings reign in power, and rulers make just laws. 17I love all who love me. Those who search for me shall surely find me. 18Unending riches, honor, justice and righteousness are mine to distribute. 19My gifts are better than the purest gold or sterling silver! 20My paths are those of justice and right. 21Those who love and follow me are indeed wealthy. I fill their treasuries. 22The Lord formed me in the beginning, before he created anything else. 23From ages past, I am. I existed before the earth began. 24I lived before the oceans were created, before the springs bubbled forth their waters onto the earth; 25before the mountains and the hills were made. 26Yes, I was born before God made the earth and fields, and the first handfuls of soil.

8:14
Isa 1:26
Rom 13:1

8:17
1 Sam 2:30
Jn 14:21

8:18
Ps 112:3
Mt 6:33

8:20
Ps 23:3; 25:4
Isa 2:3

8:22
Job 28:27
Ps 104:24
Jn 1:1

8:23
Jn 17:5,24

27, 28, 29"I was there when he established the heavens and formed the great springs in the depths of the oceans. I was there when he set the limits of the seas and gave them his instructions not to spread beyond their boundaries. I was there when he made the blueprint for the earth and oceans. 30I was the craftsman at his side. I was his constant delight, rejoicing always in his presence. 31And how happy I was with

8:24
Gen 1:9
Job 38:16

8:27
Job 26:10; 38:6
Ps 33:6; 104:5

8:22 The reference here is to Wisdom. If this verse refers to Christ, this alternate translation is possible from the Hebrew text: "The Lord possessed me at the beginning of his work."

7:25 There are definite steps you can take to avoid sexual sins. First, guard your mind. Don't read books, look at pictures, or encourage fantasies that stimulate the wrong desires. Second, keep away from settings and friends that tempt you to sin. Third, don't think only of the moment—focus on the future. Today's thrill may lead to tomorrow's ruin.

8:1ff Wisdom is portrayed as a woman who guides us (8:1–13) and makes us succeed (8:14–21). Wisdom was present at the creation and works with the Creator (8:22–31). God approves of those who listen to wisdom's counsel (8:32–35). Those who ignore wisdom love death (8:36). Wisdom should affect every aspect of

our entire lives, from beginning to end. Be sure to open all corners of your life to God's direction and guidance.

8:13 The more a person respects and fears God, the more he or she will hate evil. Love for God and love for sin cannot coexist. Harboring secret sins means that you are tolerating evil within yourself. Make a clean break with sin and commit yourself completely to God.

8:22–31 God says wisdom is primary and fundamental. It is the foundation on which all life is built. Paul and John may have alluded to some of Solomon's statements about wisdom to describe Christ's presence at the creation of the world (Colossians 1:15–17; 2:3; Revelation 3:14).

8:32
Prov 5:7; 29:18

8:34
Ps 27:4
Prov 1:21; 2:3

8:35
Jn 17:3

8:36
Prov 15:32

9:1
Eph 2:20
Heb 3:5,6
1 Pet 2:5

9:3
Mt 22:3

9:6
Prov 3:22; 4:22
9:11; 16:22

9:9
Prov 1:5; 25:12

9:10
Job 28:28
Ps 111:10

9:12
Job 22:2
Ezek 18:4
Gal 6:5

9:17
Prov 20:17
30:20

10:1
Prov 15:20

what he created—his wide world and all his family of mankind! 32And so, young men, listen to me, for how happy are all who follow my instructions.

33"Listen to my counsel—oh, don't refuse it—and be wise. 34Happy is the man who is so anxious to be with me that he watches for me daily at my gates, or waits for me outside my home! 35For whoever finds me finds life and wins approval from the Lord. 36But the one who misses me has injured himself irreparably. Those who refuse me show that they love death."

Wisdom is its own reward

9 Wisdom has built a palace supported on seven pillars, 2and has prepared a great banquet, and mixed the wines, 3and sent out her maidens inviting all to come. She calls from the busiest intersections in the city, 4"Come, you simple ones without good judgment; 5come to wisdom's banquet and drink the wines that I have mixed. 6Leave behind your foolishness and begin to live; learn how to be wise."

7,8If you rebuke a mocker, you will only get a smart retort; yes, he will snarl at you. So don't bother with him; he will only hate you for trying to help him. But a wise man, when rebuked, will love you all the more. 9Teach a wise man, and he will be the wiser; teach a good man, and he will learn more. 10*For the reverence and fear of God are basic to all wisdom. Knowing God results in every other kind of understanding.* 11"I, Wisdom, will make the hours of your day more profitable and the years of your life more fruitful." 12Wisdom is its own reward, and if you scorn her, you hurt only yourself.

13A prostitute is loud and brash, and never has enough of lust and shame. 14She sits at the door of her house or stands at the street corners of the city, 15whispering to men going by, and to those minding their own business. 16"Come home with me," she urges simpletons. 17"Stolen melons are the sweetest; stolen apples taste the best!" 18But they don't realize that her former guests are now citizens of hell.

B. WISDOM FOR ALL PEOPLE (10:1—24:34)

These short couplets are what we commonly recognize as proverbs. They cover a wide range of topics. The first section was written by Solomon. The next two sections were written by others, but collected by Solomon. These sayings give people practical wisdom for godly living at every stage of life.

Proverbs of Solomon

10 Happy is the man with a level-headed son; sad the mother of a rebel. 2Ill-gotten gain brings no lasting happiness; right living does.

9:17 *Stolen melons,* literally, "stolen water." *stolen apples,* literally, "stolen food."

9:1ff Wisdom and foolishness are portrayed in this chapter as rival young women, each preparing a feast and inviting people to it. But wisdom is a responsible woman of character, while foolishness is a prostitute serving stolen food. Wisdom appeals first to the mind; foolishness to the senses. It is easier to excite the senses, but the joys of foolishness are temporary. By contrast, the satisfaction which wisdom brings lasts forever.

9:1 The seven pillars are figurative; they do not represent seven principles of wisdom. In the Bible, the number seven represents completeness and perfection. This verse poetically states that wisdom lacks nothing—it is complete and perfect.

9:1-3 The banquet described in this chapter has some interesting parallels to the banquet Jesus described in one of his parables (Luke 14:15–24). Many may intend to go, but they never make it because they get sidetracked by everything else that seems important at the time. Don't let anything else become more important than your search for God.

9:7-10 Are you a mocker or a wise person? You can tell by the way you respond to criticism. Instead of tossing back a quick put-down or clever retort when rebuked, listen to what is being

said. Learn from your critics; this is the path to wisdom. Wisdom begins with knowing God. He gives insight into living because he created life. To know God is not just to know the facts about him, but to stand in awe of him and have a relationship with him. Do you really want to be wise? Get to know God better and better. (See James 1:5; 2 Peter 1:2 for more on how to become wise.)

9:17 There is something hypnotic and intoxicating about wickedness. One sin leads us to want more; sinful behavior seems more exciting than the "boring" Christian life. That is why many people put aside all thought of Wisdom's sumptuous banquet (9:1–6) in order to eat the stolen food of Foolishness, the harlot. Don't be deceived—sin is dangerous. Before reaching for forbidden fruit, take a look at what happens to those who eat it.

10:2 Some people bring unhappiness on themselves by choosing wrong living. For example, craving satisfaction, they may have an affair that destroys their chances of ever achieving happiness. God's principles for right living bring lasting happiness, because they guide us into long-term right behavior in spite of our ever-changing feelings.

³The Lord will not let a good man starve to death, nor will he let the wicked man's riches continue forever.

⁴Lazy men are soon poor; hard workers get rich.

⁵A wise youth makes hay while the sun shines, but what a shame to see a lad who sleeps away his hour of opportunity.

⁶The good man is covered with blessings from head to foot, but an evil man inwardly curses his luck.

⁷We all have happy memories of good men gone to their reward, but the names of wicked men stink after them.

⁸The wise man is glad to be instructed, but a self-sufficient fool falls flat on his face.

⁹A good man has firm footing, but a crook will slip and fall.

¹⁰Winking at sin leads to sorrow; bold reproof leads to peace.

¹¹There is living truth in what a good man says, but the mouth of the evil man is filled with curses.

¹²Hatred stirs old quarrels, but love overlooks insults.

¹³Men with common sense are admired as counselors; those without it are beaten as servants.

¹⁴A wise man holds his tongue. Only a fool blurts out everything he knows; that only leads to sorrow and trouble.

¹⁵The rich man's wealth is his only strength. The poor man's poverty is his only curse.

¹⁶The good man's earnings advance the cause of righteousness. The evil man squanders his on sin.

¹⁷Anyone willing to be corrected is on the pathway to life. Anyone refusing has lost his chance.

¹⁸To hide hatred is to be a liar; to slander is to be a fool.

¹⁹Don't talk so much. You keep putting your foot in your mouth. Be sensible and turn off the flow!

²⁰When a good man speaks, he is worth listening to, but the words of fools are a dime a dozen.

²¹A godly man gives good advice, but a rebel is destroyed by lack of common sense.

²²The Lord's blessing is our greatest wealth. All our work adds nothing to it!

10:3	Ps 34:9,10 37:25 Mt 6:33
10:4	Prov 6:6
10:6	Prov 9:11; 28:20
10:7	Ps 9:5,6 109:13; 112:6
10:8	Mt 7:24
10:9	Ps 23:4 Prov 3:23; 26:27 Isa 33:15,16 Mt 10:26
10:10	Prov 6:13
10:11	Ps 37:20 Prov 13:14 18:4; 20:5
10:12	Prov 17:9 1 Cor 13:4-7
10:14	Prov 13:3; 18:7 Jas 3:2,5
10:15	Prov 18:11; 19:7
10:17	Prov 6:23; 12:1 22:17
10:18	Prov 26:24
10:19	Job 11:2 Prov 18:21
10:21	Prov 12:18; 15:4 Hos 4:6
10:22	Gen 24:35 26:12 Deut 8:18

10:6 *an evil man inwardly curses his luck,* literally, "but the mouth of the wicked conceals violence." **10:13** *admired,* implied. **10:15** *only . . . only,* implied. **10:22** *All our work adds nothing to it,* or, "and he adds no sorrow therewith."

10:3 Proverbs is full of verses contrasting the good man with the wicked. These statements are not intended to apply universally to all people in every situation. Some good people do starve. Rather, they are intended to communicate the general truth that the life of the person who seeks God fares better in the long run than the life of the wicked person, which leads to ruin. These statements are not ironclad promises, but general truths. In addition, a proverb like this assumes a just government that cares for the poor and needy—the kind of government Israel was intended to have (see Deuteronomy 24:17-22). A corrupt government often thwarts the plans of good men and women.

10:4, 5 Every day has 24 hours filled with opportunities to grow, serve, and be productive. It is so easy to waste time, letting life slip from our grasp. Instead, refuse to be a lazy person, sleeping or frittering away the hours meant for productive work. See time as God's gift, and seize the opportunities to live for him.

10:10 Sin is serious not just because of what it does to us and to others, but because it is personal rebellion against God. He does not take sin lightly, and we dare not either. If there is an area in your life that you have been withholding from God's control, end your rebellion. If you have minimized and rationalized disobedience, put aside your excuses. Don't wink at sin. Boldly confront it and confess it to God, because sin is serious business.

10:16 God supplies some people with the personal and financial

abilities to respond to the needs of others. If these people all realized why God has blessed them, and if they all used their resources to do God's will, hunger and poverty would be wiped out. God is not opposed to wealth. He expects us to work hard so that we can be a blessing to others. But wealth is a blessing only if we use it in the way God intended.

10:18 By hating another person you may become a liar or a fool. If you try to conceal your hate, you end up lying. If you slander the other person, you are a fool. The only way out is to admit your hateful feelings to God. Ask him to change your heart, to help you love instead of hate.

10:20 A lot of poor advice is worth less than a little good advice. It is easy to get opinions from people who will tell us only what they think will please us, but such advice is not helpful. Instead we should look for those who will speak the truth, even when it hurts. Think about the people to whom you go for advice. What do you expect to hear from them?

10:22 This proverb is in sharp contrast to our society which measures personal worth by how much a person owns. Our relationship to God is our most valuable possession. This blessing is not reserved for the rich; it is for all who call upon the name of the Lord. Neither is it something for which we must work hard; our efforts can add nothing to what God freely offers. Those who spend their lives enjoying only material wealth will never

10:23
Prov 2:14; 15:21

10:24
Job 15:21
Prov 1:27; 15:8

10:25
Ps 15:1-5; 125:1

10:27
Ps 55:23
Prov 14:27

10:28
Job 11:20

10:30
Ps 37:25; 125:1
Prov 2:22

10:31
Ps 37:30

10:32
Prov 6:12
Eccles 12:10

11:1
Deut 25:13-16

11:2
Prov 16:18

11:3
Prov 13:6; 21:7
22:12

11:4
Ezek 7:19
1 Tim 4:8; 6:7

11:6
Ps 7:15,16
9:15

11:8
Ps 22:8
51:14,15

23A fool's fun is being bad; a wise man's fun is being wise!

24The wicked man's fears will all come true, and so will the good man's hopes.

25Disaster strikes like a cyclone and the wicked are whirled away. But the good man has a strong anchor.

26A lazy fellow is a pain to his employers—like smoke in their eyes or vinegar that sets the teeth on edge.

27Reverence for God adds hours to each day; so how can the wicked expect a long, good life?

28The hope of good men is eternal happiness; the hopes of evil men are all in vain.

29God protects the upright but destroys the wicked.

30The good shall never lose God's blessings, but the wicked shall lose everything.

31The good man gives wise advice, but the liar's counsel is shunned.

32The upright speak what is helpful; the wicked speak rebellion.

11 The Lord hates cheating and delights in honesty.

2Proud men end in shame, but the meek become wise.

3A good man is guided by his honesty; the evil man is destroyed by his dishonesty.

4Your riches won't help you on Judgment Day; only righteousness counts then.

5Good people are directed by their honesty; the wicked shall fall beneath their load of sins.

6The good man's goodness delivers him; the evil man's treachery is his undoing.

7When an evil man dies, his hopes all perish, for they are based upon this earthly life.

8God rescues good men from danger while letting the wicked fall into it.

9Evil words destroy. Godly skill rebuilds.

10:27 *adds hours to each day,* literally, "prolongs days." **11:9** *Evil words destroy. Godly skill rebuilds,* or, "When a godless man slanders his neighbor, the charges won't stick because everyone knows his reputation."

GOD'S ADVICE ABOUT MONEY

Proverbs gives some practical instruction on the use of money, although sometimes it is advice we would rather not hear. It's more comfortable to continue in our habits than to learn how to use money more wisely. The advice includes:

Advance the cause of righteousness with money; don't squander it	10:16
Be generous	11:24, 25; 22:9
Place people's needs ahead of profit	11:26
Be cautious of countersigning for another	17:18; 22:26, 27
Don't accept bribes	17:23
Help the poor	19:17; 21:13; 22:9
Save for the future	21:20
Be careful about borrowing	22:7

Other verses to study include: 11:15; 20:16; 25:14; 27:13

---

experience the true happiness that comes from enjoying God.

10:24 Those who do not believe in God usually fear death, and with good reason. By contrast, believers hope for eternal life and God's salvation, and their hopes will be rewarded. This verse offers a choice: you can have either your fears or your hopes come true. You make that choice by rejecting God or accepting God.

11:4 *Judgment Day* refers to death or to the time when God settles accounts with all people. On Judgment Day, each of us will stand alone, accountable for all our deeds. At that time, no amount of riches or shrewdness will buy reconciliation with God. Only our love and obedience for God will count.

11:8 This verse, like 10:3, contrasts two paths in life, but is not

intended to apply universally to all people in all circumstances. It does not mean God's people will never have problems or struggles. If a person follows God's wisdom, however, God can rescue him from danger, whereas a wicked person will fall into his own traps. Even if a good person suffers, he can be sure he will ultimately be rescued from eternal death.

11:9 Words can be used either as weapons or tools, hurting relationships or building them up. Sadly, it is often easier to destroy than to build, and most people have experienced more destructive words than words which build up. Every person you meet today is either a demolition site or a construction opportunity. Your words will make a difference. Will they be weapons for destruction or tools for construction?

¹⁰The whole city celebrates a good man's success—and also the godless man's death.

¹¹The good influence of godly citizens causes a city to prosper, but the moral decay of the wicked drives it downhill.

¹²To quarrel with a neighbor is foolish; a man with good sense holds his tongue.

¹³A gossip goes around spreading rumors, while a trustworthy man tries to quiet them.

¹⁴Without wise leadership, a nation is in trouble; but with good counselors there is safety.

¹⁵Be sure you know a person well before you vouch for his credit! Better refuse than suffer later.

¹⁶Honor goes to kind and gracious women, mere money to cruel men.

¹⁷Your own soul is nourished when you are kind; it is destroyed when you are cruel.

¹⁸The evil man gets rich for the moment, but the good man's reward lasts forever.

¹⁹The good man finds life; the evil man, death.

²⁰The Lord hates the stubborn but delights in those who are good.

²¹You can be very sure the evil man will not go unpunished forever. And you can also be very sure God will rescue the children of the godly.

²²A beautiful woman lacking discretion and modesty is like a fine gold ring in a pig's snout.

²³The good man can look forward to happiness, while the wicked can expect only wrath.

²⁴, ²⁵It is possible to give away and become richer! It is also possible to hold on too tightly and lose everything. Yes, the liberal man shall be rich! By watering others, he waters himself.

²⁶People curse the man who holds his grain for higher prices, but they bless the man who sells it to them in their time of need.

²⁷If you search for good you will find God's favor; if you search for evil you will find his curse.

²⁸Trust in your money and down you go! Trust in God and flourish as a tree!

²⁹The fool who provokes his family to anger and resentment will finally have nothing worthwhile left. He shall be the servant of a wiser man.

³⁰Godly men are growing a tree that bears life-giving fruit, and all who win souls are wise.

³¹Even the godly shall be rewarded here on earth; how much more the wicked!

11:16 *mere*, implied. 11:30 *all who win souls are wise*, or, "he that is wise wins souls."

11:10
Prov 28:28

11:12
Prov 10:14
13:3; 18:7

11:13
Prov 19:11
20:19
1 Tim 5:13

11:14
Prov 15:22
20:18; 24:6

11:15
Prov 6:1; 27:13

11:17
Mt 5:7; 25:34-36

11:18
Hos 10:12

11:19
Prov 10:16
19:23; 21:16
Rom 6:23

11:20
Ps 75:5
Prov 13:6; 21:29

11:22
Ezek 16:15
1 Pet 3:3

11:23
Rom 2:8,9

11:24
Prov 3:9,10
Mt 5:7
2 Cor 9:6,7

11:26
Gen 41:56,57
Amos 8:4

11:27
Prov 17:11

11:28
Ps 1:2,3; 92:12
Jer 17:7,8
Mk 10:24,25
1 Tim 6:17

11:29
Prov 14:19
15:27

11:30
Jas 5:20

11:14 A good leader needs and uses wise counselors. One person's perspective and understanding is severely limited; he or she may not have all the facts or may be blinded by bias, wrong impressions, or emotions. To be a wise leader at home, at church, or at work, seek the counsel of others and be open to their advice. Then, after considering all the facts, make your decision.

11:19 Why does the good man find life? He finds life because wisdom makes the hours of the day more profitable and the years more fruitful (9:11). He lives life more fully each day. He also finds life because people usually live longer when they live right—proper diet, exercise, and rest. In addition, those who find eternal life need not fear death (John 11:25), whereas the evil person not only finds eternal death, but also misses out on real life on earth.

11:22 Physical attractiveness without inner strength soon wears thin. We are to seek those qualities that help us make wise decisions, not just those that make us look good.

11:24, 25 These two verses present a paradox: that we become richer by being generous. The world says to hold on to as much as possible, but God blesses those who give freely of their possessions, time, and energy. When we give, God supplies us

with more so that we can give more. In addition, giving helps us gain a right perspective on our possessions. We realize they were never really ours to begin with, but were given to us by God to be used to help others. What then do we gain by giving? Freedom from enslavement to our possessions, the joy of helping others, and God's blessings.

11:29 One of the greatest resources God gives us is the family. The family provides acceptance, encouragement, exhortation, and counsel. Rejecting one's family—whether through anger or through an exaggerated desire for independence—is foolish. When you put distance between your family and yourself, you cut yourself off from all they provide. In your family, strive for healing and understanding.

11:30 A wise person is a model of a meaningful life. His sense of purpose attracts others who want to know how they too can find meaning. Gaining wisdom yourself, then, can be the first step in leading people to God. Why is it so important to lead people to God? Because it keeps us in touch with God while it offers others eternal life.

11:31 Contrary to popular opinion, no one sins and gets away with it. The faithful are rewarded for their faith. The wicked are

12:1
Prov 25:12
12:3
Ps 15:1-5
12:4
Prov 14:1
19:13; 21:9
27:15; 31:10
1 Cor 11:7
12:5
Prov 16:23
Mt 12:34; 15:18
12:6
Ps 12:5; 35:11
Prov 14:3; 31:8
12:7
Isa 3:10,11
Mt 7:24-27
12:9
Lk 14:11
12:11
Prov 9:6; 14:24
12:12
Prov 1:18,19
11:24,25; 21:10

12 To learn, you must want to be taught. To refuse reproof is stupid. ²The Lord blesses good men and condemns the wicked.

³Wickedness never brings real success; only the godly have that.

⁴A worthy wife is her husband's joy and crown; the other kind corrodes his strength and tears down everything he does.

⁵A good man's mind is filled with honest thoughts; an evil man's mind is crammed with lies.

⁶The wicked accuse; the godly defend.

⁷The wicked shall perish; the godly shall stand.

⁸Everyone admires a man with good sense, but a man with a warped mind is despised.

⁹It is better to get your hands dirty—and eat, than to be too proud to work—and starve.

¹⁰A good man is concerned for the welfare of his animals, but even the kindness of godless men is cruel.

¹¹Hard work means prosperity; only a fool idles away his time.

¹²Crooks are jealous of each other's loot, while good men long to help each other.

12:9 *and eat,* implied. **12:11** *Hard work means prosperity,* literally, "He who tills his ground shall have his fill of bread."

TEACHING AND LEARNING

Good teaching comes from good learning—and Proverbs has more to say to students than to teachers. Proverbs is concerned with the learning of wisdom. The book makes it clear that there are no good alternatives to learning wisdom. We are either becoming wise learners, or refusing to learn and becoming foolish failures. Proverbs encourages us to make the right choice.

Wise Learners	Proverb(s)	Foolish Failures
Gladly receive instruction and criticism	10:8; 23:12; 25:12	Ignore instruction
Desire to be taught	12:1	Refuse reproof
Listen to others	12:15; 21:11; 24:6	Think they need no advice
Ask for advice	12:26; 13:14; 19:20; 25:11	Plunge ahead
Accept parents' discipline	13:1	Mock parents
Choose whom to listen to	14:7; 15:7; 17:16; 19:27; 20:5; 29:1	Don't learn from mistakes
Receive life	10:17	Lose opportunities
Receive fame	13:18	End in poverty and disgrace
Profit from constructive criticism	15:31, 32; 29:1	Self-destruct by refusing criticism
Find life-long wisdom	19:20	Refuse to heed the advice of others

Advice to teachers:
Make your advice refreshing and encouraging (13:14)
Make learning a joy for your learners (15:2; 16:21)
Give wise advice—right words at the right time (15:23; 18:20)

---

punished for their sins. Don't think for a moment that "it won't matter" or "nobody will know" or "we won't get caught" (see also 1 Peter 4:18).

12:1 You can go to school for years and learn nothing. But if you want to be taught, there is no end to what you can learn. Part of wanting to be taught is being willing to accept correction and to learn from the wisdom of others. A person who refuses criticism has a problem with pride. Such a person is unlikely to learn much.

12:3 If real success comes only to those who follow God, what kind of success does wickedness bring? We all know people who

cheat and pass the course or get a larger tax refund—is this not success? And what about the person who ignores his family commitments and mistreats his workers but gets ahead in business? These apparent successes are only temporary. They are bought at the expense of character. Cheaters grow more and more dishonest, and those who hurt others become callous and cruel. In the long run, evil behavior does not lead to success; it leads only to more evil. Real success does not compromise personal integrity. If you are not a success by God's standards, you have not achieved true success.

13Lies will get any man into trouble, but honesty is its own defense.

14Telling the truth gives a man great satisfaction, and hard work returns many blessings to him.

15A fool thinks he needs no advice, but a wise man listens to others.

16A fool is quick-tempered; a wise man stays cool when insulted.

17A good man is known by his truthfulness; a false man by deceit and lies.

18Some people like to make cutting remarks, but the words of the wise soothe and heal.

19Truth stands the test of time; lies are soon exposed.

20Deceit fills hearts that are plotting for evil; joy fills hearts that are planning for good!

21No real harm befalls the good, but there is constant trouble for the wicked.

22God delights in those who keep their promises, and abhors those who don't.

23A wise man doesn't display his knowledge, but a fool displays his foolishness.

24Work hard and become a leader; be lazy and never succeed.

25Anxious hearts are very heavy but a word of encouragement does wonders!

26The good man asks advice from friends; the wicked plunge ahead—and fall.

27A lazy man won't even dress the game he gets while hunting, but the diligent man makes good use of everything he finds.

28The path of the godly leads to life. So why fear death?

13 A wise youth accepts his father's rebuke; a young mocker doesn't.
2The good man wins his case by careful argument; the evil-minded only wants to fight.

3Self-control means controlling the tongue! A quick retort can ruin everything.

4Lazy people want much but get little, while the diligent are prospering.

5A good man hates lies; wicked men lie constantly and come to shame.

6A man's goodness helps him all through life, while evil men are being destroyed by their wickedness.

13:5 *wicked men lie constantly,* implied.

12:13
Prov 25:18
12:14
Prov 24:12
Isa 3:10
12:15
Prov 14:12
16:2; 21:2
12:16
Prov 19:11
29:11
12:18
Prov 8:6,7; 15:4
12:19
Job 20:5
Prov 19:9
12:20
Prov 2:10
26:24-26
12:22
Isa 19:21
12:25
Prov 15:13
17:22
12:26
Prov 18:15

13:3
Prov 18:7, 21
20:19; 21:23
Jas 3:2
13:4
Prov 12:11,24
14:11; 22:29
13:5
Prov 3:35
13:6
Ps 15:3

12:13 Honesty is its own defense because the facts will always support what the honest person says. Dishonest people need a defense. They need to twist the facts to support the claims they are making. But for someone who always tells the truth, the facts—plain and unvarnished—give an unshakable defense. If you find you always have to defend your actions to yourself and to others, maybe your honesty is less than it should be.

12:16 When someone insults you, it is natural to insult in return. But this solves nothing and only encourages trouble. Instead, "keep your cool" and answer slowly and quietly. Your positive response will achieve positive results.

12:19 Truth is both timeless and timely; it applies today and always. Because it is connected with God's changeless character, it is also changeless. Think for a moment about the centuries that have passed since these proverbs were written. Consider the countless hours that have been spent carefully studying every sentence of Scripture. The Bible has withstood the test of time. Because God is its source of truth, you can trust its guidance.

12:21 This is another general, but not universal, truth. Although bad things do happen to good people, they are able to see opportunities in their problems and move ahead. The wicked, without God's wisdom, are unequipped to handle their problems. (See the notes on 3:16, 17; 10:3; 11:8 for more about general truths that are not intended as universal statements.)

12:22 How many people do you know whose promises you can depend on completely? Probably not many. *Who* makes a promise is just as important as *what* promise is made. Two people may both say, "Let's have lunch. I'll call you." One means, "It would be nice to see you again sometime." The other means, "I want to see you again, and I'll arrange it." You know which promise will be kept, because you know the people. A person with good intentions

makes promises. A person with good character keeps them. Be a person in whom God delights—a person who keeps promises.

12:23 There is a quiet confidence about skillful people. Insecure or uncertain people feel the need to prove themselves, but skillful people don't have to prove anything. They know they are good, so they can get on with their work. Beware of the trap of showing off. If you are modest, people may think a little less of you at first, but they will respect you more later.

12:27 Waste has become a way of life for many who live in a land of plenty. But waste is a sign of laziness. People are unwilling to look for creative uses for leftovers, so they discard them instead. Waste is poor stewardship. Reject this lazy life-style and commit yourself to diligence. Make good use of everything God has given you.

12:28 For many, death is a darkened door at the end of their lives, a passageway to an unknown and feared destiny. But for God's people, death is a bright doorway to a new and better life. So why do we fear death? Is it because of the pain we expect, the separation from loved ones, the surprise of it? God can help us deal with those fears. He has shown us that death is just another step in the continuing eternal life we began when we started to follow him. Death is not final; it is the first step into eternity.

13:3 You have not mastered self-control if you do not control what you say. Words can cut and destroy. James recognized this truth when he stated, "The tongue is a small thing, but what enormous damage it can do" (James 3:5). If you wish to be self-controlled, begin with your tongue. If you can control this small but powerful member, you can control the rest of your body.

13:6 Every choice for good sets into motion other opportunities for good. Evil choices follow the same pattern, but in the opposite direction. Each choice you make in obedience to God's Word will

13:7
Lk 12:20,21
Jas 2:5

13:9
Job 18:5; 29:3
Prov 4:18; 24:20

13:10
Prov 12:15
17:14; 19:20

13:13
2 Chron 36:16
Prov 1:25,30

13:14
Prov 8:8

13:15
Ps 111:10
Prov 3:4; 8:35

13:16
Prov 16:1,9
27:1

13:17
Prov 26:6

13:18
Prov 23:12

13:20
Prov 2:20

13:21
Ps 32:10
Isa 3:10; 47:11

13:22
Ezra 9:12
Ps 37:25
Prov 28:8

⁷Some rich people are poor, and some poor people have great wealth!

⁸Being kidnapped and held for ransom never worries the poor man!

⁹The good man's life is full of light. The sinner's road is dark and gloomy.

¹⁰Pride leads to arguments; be humble, take advice and become wise.

¹¹Wealth from gambling quickly disappears; wealth from hard work grows.

¹²Hope deferred makes the heart sick; but when dreams come true at last, there is life and joy.

¹³Despise God's Word and find yourself in trouble. Obey it and succeed.

¹⁴The advice of a wise man refreshes like water from a mountain spring. Those accepting it become aware of the pitfalls on ahead.

¹⁵A man with good sense is appreciated. A treacherous man must walk a rocky road.

¹⁶A wise man thinks ahead; a fool doesn't, and even brags about it!

¹⁷An unreliable messenger can cause a lot of trouble. Reliable communication permits progress.

¹⁸If you refuse criticism you will end in poverty and disgrace; if you accept criticism you are on the road to fame.

¹⁹It is pleasant to see plans develop. That is why fools refuse to give them up even when they are wrong.

²⁰Be with wise men and become wise. Be with evil men and become evil.

²¹Curses chase sinners, while blessings chase the righteous!

²²When a good man dies, he leaves an inheritance to his grandchildren; but when a sinner dies, his wealth is stored up for the godly.

²³A poor man's farm may have good soil, but injustice robs him of its riches.

13:12 *but when dreams come true at last, there is life and joy,* literally, "it is a tree of life."

---

bring a greater sense of order to your life, while each choice made in disobedience will bring confusion and destruction. The choices you make will shape your character, which will in turn determine your eternal destiny.

13:7, 8 Some rich people are poor because they are spiritually bankrupt, while some poor people are rich in contentment and satisfaction. Money brings opportunities and power, but it also has many negative side effects. A full life is better than a life full of money.

13:10 "I was wrong" or "I need help" are difficult phrases to utter because they require humility. Pride is an ingredient in every quarrel. It stirs up conflict and divides people. Humility, by contrast, heals. Guard against pride. If you find yourself constantly arguing, examine your life for pride. Be open to the advice of others, ask for help when you need it, and be willing to admit your mistakes.

13:13 God created us, knows us, and loves us. It only makes sense, then, to listen to his instructions and do what he says. The Bible is his unfailing word to us. It is like an owner's manual to a car. If you obey God's instructions, you will "run right" and find his kind of success. If you ignore them, you are doomed to breakdowns, accidents, and failure.

13:14 When most people need advice, they go to their friends first, because friends accept them and usually agree with them. But that is why they may not be able to help them with difficult problems. Our friends are so much like us that they may not have any answers we haven't already heard. Instead, we should seek out older and wiser people to advise us. Wise people have experienced a lot of life—and succeeded. They are not afraid to tell the truth. Who are the wise, godly people who can warn you of the pitfalls ahead?

13:16 Being spontaneous can be fun, but it is not the best way to approach every situation. There is a place for planning and self-discipline, especially when you have goals you want to reach.

Some people think planning is too restrictive. In reality, it can set a person free to enjoy life and to be productive. Take time to set goals, to plan your course of action, and to set priorities before you launch into action.

13:17 In Solomon's day, kings had to rely on messengers for information about their country. Messengers had to be trustworthy. Inaccurate information could even lead to bloodshed. Reliable communication is still vital. If the message received is different from the message sent, marriages, businesses, and diplomatic relations can all break down. It is important to choose your words well and to avoid taking action until you clearly understand what the other person means.

13:19 When you set your heart on something, you may lose your ability to assess it objectively. Your desire blinds your judgment, and you proceed with an unwise relationship, a wasteful purchase, or a poorly conceived plan in spite of objections from others. Faithfulness is a virtue, but stubbornness is not. If your plans cause you to use people and love things rather than using things and loving people, give them up immediately.

13:20 The old saying, "A rotten apple spoils the barrel" is often applied to friendships, and with good reason. Our friends and associates affect us, sometimes profoundly. Be careful whom you choose as your closest friends. Spend time with people you'd be glad to be like—because you and your friends will surely grow to resemble each other.

13:23 The poor are often victims of an unjust society. This proverb does not take poverty lightly or wink at injustice; it simply describes what often occurs. We should do what we can to fight injustice of every sort. Since our efforts will always seem inadequate, however, it is comforting to know that in the end God's justice will prevail.

24If you refuse to discipline your son, it proves you don't love him; for if you love him you will be prompt to punish him.

25The good man eats to live, while the evil man lives to eat.

14 A wise woman builds her house, while a foolish woman tears hers down by her own efforts.

2To do right honors God; to sin is to despise him.

3A rebel's foolish talk should prick his own pride! But the wise man's speech is respected.

4An empty stable stays clean—but there is no income from an empty stable.

5A truthful witness never lies; a false witness always lies.

6A mocker never finds the wisdom he claims he is looking for, yet it comes easily to the man with common sense.

7If you are looking for advice, stay away from fools.

8The wise man looks ahead. The fool attempts to fool himself and won't face facts.

9The common bond of rebels is their guilt. The common bond of godly people is good will.

10Only the person involved can know his own bitterness or joy—no one else can really share it.

11The work of the wicked will perish; the work of the godly will flourish.

12Before every man there lies a wide and pleasant road that seems right but ends in death.

13Laughter cannot mask a heavy heart. When the laughter ends, the grief remains.

14The backslider gets bored with himself; the godly man's life is exciting.

15Only a simpleton believes everything he's told! A prudent man understands the need for proof.

16A wise man is cautious and avoids danger; a fool plunges ahead with great confidence.

17A short-tempered man is a fool. He hates the man who is patient.

18The simpleton is crowned with folly; the wise man is crowned with knowledge.

13:24
Prov 19:18
22:15; 23:13
Heb 12:6

14:1
Prov 12:4; 21:9
27:15; 31:10
14:2
Ps 92:15
14:3
Prov 24:7,9
26:9
14:5
Prov 14:25; 19:9
14:6
Prov 9:7,8
15:12,14
14:7
Prov 9:6; 23:9
14:8
Prov 1:22; 10:8
12:15; 18:2
28:26
14:11
Prov 12:7,11
13:11; 22:29
14:12
Prov 16:25
Rom 6:21
14:13
Eccles 2:1
14:14
Prov 1:31
12:14,21
14:16
Prov 22:3; 27:12
14:17
Prov 12:16
14:29; 19:19
22:24,25
14:18
Prov 3:35
14:24; 16:22

13:25 *while the evil man lives to eat*, literally, "but the wicked never get enough." **14:9** *The common bond of rebels is their guilt*, or, "Fools make a mock at sin." The Hebrew is obscure.

13:24 It is not easy for a loving parent to discipline a child, but it is necessary. The greatest responsibility God gives parents is the nurture and guidance of their children. Lack of discipline puts a parent's love in question because it shows a lack of concern for the character development of their children. Disciplining children averts long-range disaster. Without correction, children often grow up with no clear understanding of right and wrong and with little direction to their lives. Don't be afraid to discipline your children. It is an act of love. Remember, however, that your efforts cannot make your children wise; they can only encourage your children to seek God's wisdom above all else!

14:4 It is good to be clean, but it is better to be useful. The only way to have a perfect stable is to keep all the animals out. The only way to keep your life in perfect order is to keep it free of other people. But if the stable is empty, it is useless; and if you live only for yourself, your life loses its meaning. Instead of sitting on the sidelines, we should serve others, share the faith, and work for justice. Is your life clean, but empty? Or does it give evidence of your serving God wholeheartedly? Be involved and productive.

14:6 We all know mockers, people who scoff at every word of instruction or advice. They never find wisdom, because they don't seek it seriously. Wisdom comes easily only to those who pay attention to experienced people and to God. If the wisdom you need does not come easily to you, perhaps your attitude is the barrier.

14:8 We can fool ourselves by refusing to admit our wrongs and face the consequences of our actions. Like children we close our eyes and wish the problem would go away. Instead, wisely look ahead with your eyes wide open. Then you will be ready to act.

14:9 How rarely we find good will around us today. Angry drivers scowl at each other in the streets. People fight to be first in line. Disgruntled employers and employees both demand their rights. But the common bond of God's people should be good will. Those with good will think the best of others and assume that others have good motives and intend to do what is right. When someone crosses you, and you feel your blood pressure rising, ask yourself, "How can I show good will to this person?"

14:12 The wide and pleasant road seems to offer many options and require few sacrifices. Easy choices, however, should make us take a second look at the options. Is this solution attractive because it allows me to be lazy? Because it doesn't ask me to change my life-style? Because it requires no moral restraints? The right choice often requires hard work and self-sacrifice. Don't be trapped by apparent shortcuts.

14:14 When God slips from first place in our lives, everything else loses its meaning. Life seems to be no more than the tiresome process of making money to spend on food, clothing, and shelter—just getting through the day so we can do the same thing again tomorrow. But when God has first priority, life becomes an adventure. Even our routine projects take on meaning and promise because they hold a greater purpose. If you are bored with life, check your relationship with God. Your boredom could be a signal that your priorities have shifted.

14:20
Prov 19:4,7
14:21
Ps 41:1
Prov 19:17; 28:8

14:23
Prov 20:13; 28:19
14:24
Prov 14:18
16:22

14:26
Ps 34:7
Prov 3:7,8,
24-26; 18:10
19:23

19Evil men shall bow before the godly.

20, 21Even his own neighbors despise the poor man, while the rich have many "friends." But to despise the poor is to sin. Blessed are those who help them.

22Those who plot evil shall wander away and be lost, but those who plan good shall be granted mercy and quietness.

23Work brings profit; talk brings poverty!

24Wise men are praised for their wisdom; fools are despised for their folly.

25A witness who tells the truth saves good men from being sentenced to death, but a false witness is a traitor.

26Reverence for God gives a man deep strength; his children have a place of refuge and security.

27Reverence for the Lord is a fountain of life; its waters keep a man from death.

WISDOM AND FOOLISHNESS The wise and the foolish are often contrasted in Proverbs. The characteristics, reputation, and results of each are worth knowing if wisdom is our goal.		*The Wise*	*The Foolish*	
	Characteristics	Give good advice	Destroyed by lack of wisdom	10:21
		Enjoy wisdom	Enjoy foolishness	10:23
		Work hard	Too proud to work	12:9
		Receptive to wisdom	Mock wisdom	14:6
		Cautious with reason	Gullible	14:15
		Respect wisdom	Deaf to wisdom	14:33
			Avoid wisdom	15:12
		Hungry for truth	Feed on "trash"	15:14
		Value wisdom above riches		16:16
		Enjoy life	Miss life	16:22
		Respond to correction	Harden under correction	17:10
		Pursue wisdom	Pursue illusive dreams	17:24
		Express deep thoughts		18:4
			Blame failure on God	19:3
		Profit from correction	Avert reproof to others	19:25
		Pursue good advice		20:5
			Are proud, haughty, arrogant	21:24
			Despise advice	23:9
			Make truth useless	26:7
			Misapply truth	26:9
			Repeat their foolishness	26:11
		Trust God's wisdom	Trust in themselves	28:26
		Control anger	Shout in anger	29:11
	Reputation	Admired as counselors	Beaten as servants	10:13
		Rewarded with more knowledge	Seen as fools	14:18
			Cause tension, fighting, and quarrels	22:10
			Have no honor	26:1
		Keep peace	Start fights	29:8
		Praised for their wisdom	Despised for their folly	14:24
		Stay on right pathways	Enjoy folly and go wrong way	15:21
			Lash out when discovered in folly	17:12
			Get into fights; their words endanger them	18:6, 7
		Their wisdom conquers others' strength		21:22
		Avoid rebellion	Walk a rough road as rebels	22:5
		Have wisdom mightier than strength		24:5
			Cannot handle wisdom; will never be chosen as counselors	24:7
			Must be guided by hardship	26:3
			Weighed down by frustrations	27:3
			Persist in foolishness	27:22

28A growing population is a king's glory; a dwindling nation is his doom.
29A wise man controls his temper. He knows that anger causes mistakes.
30A relaxed attitude lengthens a man's life; jealousy rots it away.
31Anyone who oppresses the poor is insulting God who made them. To help the poor is to honor God.
32The godly have a refuge when they die, but the wicked are crushed by their sins.
33Wisdom is enshrined in the hearts of men of common sense, but it must shout loudly before fools will hear it.
34Godliness exalts a nation, but sin is a reproach to any people.
35A king rejoices in servants who know what they are doing; he is angry with those who cause trouble.

14:28
1 Kgs 4:20
14:29
Prov 16:32
19:11; 29:11
Jas 1:19
14:31
Ps 12:5
Prov 14:21
17:5; 22:2,16
Eccles 5:8
14:33
Prov 1:20; 8:4
14:34
Deut 4:6
28:1,15

15 A gentle answer turns away wrath, but harsh words cause quarrels.
2A wise teacher makes learning a joy; a rebellious teacher spouts foolishness.
3The Lord is watching everywhere and keeps his eye on both the evil and the good.
4Gentle words cause life and health; griping brings discouragement.
5Only a fool despises his father's advice; a wise son considers each suggestion.
6There is treasure in being good, but trouble dogs the wicked.
7Only the good can give good advice. Rebels can't.
8The Lord hates the gifts of the wicked, but delights in the prayers of his people.
9, 10The Lord despises the deeds of the wicked, but loves those who try to be good. If they stop trying, the Lord will punish them; if they rebel against that punishment, they will die.
11The depths of hell are open to God's knowledge. How much more the hearts of all mankind!
12A mocker stays away from wise men because he hates to be scolded.
13A happy face means a glad heart; a sad face means a breaking heart.
14A wise man is hungry for truth, while the mocker feeds on trash.
15When a man is gloomy, everything seems to go wrong; when he is cheerful, everything seems right!

15:1
Judg 8:1-3
1 Sam 25:10-13
Prov 25:10,15
15:3
1 Chron 29:17
Heb 4:13
15:5
1 Sam 2:25
Prov 10:1; 13:1
23:22
15:8
Prov 15:29
21:27
Isa 1:11
15:9,10
Ps 1:6; 146:8,9
Prov 4:18
15:11
Job 26:6
Ps 139:1
15:13
Prov 17:22
Eccles 8:1
15:14
Prov 18:15

14:29 Anger can be like a fire out of control. It can burn us and everything in its path. Anger divides people. It pushes us into hasty decisions that only cause bitterness and guilt. Yet anger, in itself, is not wrong. Anger is a legitimate reaction to injustice and sin. When you feel yourself getting angry, look for the cause. Are you reacting to an evil situation or action that you are going to set right? Or are you responding selfishly to a personal insult? Pray that God will help you control your anger, channeling legitimate anger into effective action and conquering selfish anger through humility and repentance.

14:31 God has a special attitude toward the poor. He insists that those who have material goods should be generous with those who are needy. As Creator, he takes mistreatment of the poor personally. Providing for the poor is not just a suggestion in the Bible; it is a command that may require a change of attitude on your part (see Leviticus 23:22; Deuteronomy 15:7, 8; Psalm 113:5–9; Psalm 146:5–9; Isaiah 58:7; Mark 10:21; 2 Corinthians 9:9; James 2:1–9).

15:1 Have you ever tried to argue in a whisper? It is equally hard to argue with someone who insists on answering softly. On the other hand, a rising voice almost always triggers an angry response. If the most important goal is to win the argument, then you had better warm up your vocal cords. But if your goal is to seek peace, then a consistently quiet response is your best choice.

15:3 At times it seems that God has let evil run rampant in the world. We wonder if he even notices it. But God sees it

clearly—both the evil actions and the evil intentions lying behind them (15:11). He is not just a disinterested observer. He cares and is active in our world. One day he will wipe out evil and punish the evildoers, just as he will establish the good and reward those who do his will.

15:11 Because God is good, many Old Testament people thought hell was hidden from God's sight. In reality, however, nothing is hidden from God. If he can see beyond death, how much more can he know our present wrong motivations and thoughts? How foolish we are when we try to hide our motives and intentions from God!

15:14 What we feed our minds is just as important as what we feed our bodies. The kinds of books we read, the people we talk with, the music we listen to, and the films we watch are all part of our mental diet. What you feed your mind influences your total health and well-being. Thus, a strong desire for discovering truth is a mark of wisdom.

15:15 Our attitudes color our whole personality. We cannot always choose what happens to us, but we can choose our attitude toward each situation. The secret to a good attitude is filling our minds with good things—thoughts that are true, pure, and lovely; thoughts that dwell on the good things in life (Philippians 4:8). This was Paul's secret as he faced imprisonment, and it can be ours as we face the struggles of daily living. Look at your attitudes, and then examine what you allow to enter your mind and what you choose to dwell on. You may need to make some changes.

15:16
Prov 16:8; 28:6

15:17
Prov 17:1

15:18
Prov 14:29
16:28; 26:21

15:19
Prov 22:13

15:20
Prov 10:1; 29:3
30:17

15:22
Prov 11:14; 24:6

15:23
Prov 12:14
24:26; 25:11

15:25
Ps 68:5; 146:9
Prov 14:11

15:27
Ex 23:8
Prov 20:21
28:16

15:28
Prov 10:19,32
13:16; 16:23

15:31
Prov 8:33
13:18; 15:5
23:12

15:33
Prov 1:7

16:1
Prov 16:9
19:21; 20:24

16:3
Prov 3:6

16:4
Isa 43:7; 54:16

16:5
Prov 6:16,17

16Better a little with reverence for God, than great treasure and trouble with it.
17It is better to eat soup with someone you love than steak with someone you hate.
18A quick-tempered man starts fights; a cool-tempered man tries to stop them.
19A lazy fellow has trouble all through life; the good man's path is easy!
20A sensible son gladdens his father. A rebellious son saddens his mother.
21If a man enjoys folly, something is wrong! The sensible stay on the pathways of right.
22Plans go wrong with too few counselors; many counselors bring success.
23Everyone enjoys giving good advice, and how wonderful it is to be able to say the right thing at the right time!
24The road of the godly leads upward, leaving hell behind.
25The Lord destroys the possessions of the proud but cares for widows.
26The Lord hates the thoughts of the wicked but delights in kind words.
27Dishonest money brings grief to all the family, but hating bribes brings happiness.
28A good man thinks before he speaks; the evil man pours out his evil words without a thought.
29The Lord is far from the wicked, but he hears the prayers of the righteous.
30Pleasant sights and good reports give happiness and health.
31, 32If you profit from constructive criticism you will be elected to the wise men's hall of fame. But to reject criticism is to harm yourself and your own best interests.
33Humility and reverence for the Lord will make you both wise and honored.

16 We can make our plans, but the final outcome is in God's hands.
2We can always "prove" that we are right, but is the Lord convinced?
3Commit your work to the Lord, then it will succeed.
4The Lord has made everything for his own purposes—even the wicked, for punishment.
5Pride disgusts the Lord. Take my word for it—*proud men shall be punished*.
6Iniquity is atoned for by mercy and truth; evil is avoided by reverence for God.

15:20 *saddens his mother*, literally, "despises his mother." **15:26** *but delights in kind words*, literally, "but kind words are pure." **15:27** *brings happiness*, literally, "you will live."

15:17–19 The "good man's life" doesn't always seem easy (15:19), but look at the alternatives. Hatred (15:17), bad temper (15:18), and laziness (15:19) cause problems that the good man does not have to face. By comparison, his life is a smooth, level road because it is built on a solid foundation.

15:22 Those with tunnel vision, people who are locked into one way of thinking, are likely to miss the right road because they have closed their minds to any new options. We need the help of those who can enlarge our vision and broaden our perspective. Seek out the advice of those who know you and have a wealth of experience. Build a network of counselors. Then be open to new ideas and be willing to weigh their suggestions carefully.

15:28 The good man thinks before he speaks because he wants to say what he knows in the best possible way. The evil man doesn't wait to speak because he doesn't care about the effects of his words. It is important to have something to say, but it is equally important to say it well. Do you carefully plan your words, or do you pour out your thoughts without concern for their impact?

16:1 If the final outcome is in God's hands anyway, why make plans? In doing God's will, there must be partnership between our efforts and God's control. He wants us to use our minds, to seek the advice of others, and to plan. Nevertheless, the results are in his hands. Planning, then, helps us do things God's way. As you live for him, ask for his guidance.

16:2 People can rationalize anything if they have no standards for judging right and wrong. It is important to ask two questions before moving ahead in a questionable area: (1) Is this plan in harmony with God's truth? (2) Will it work under real-life conditions?

16:3 There are different ways to fail to commit our work to the Lord. Some commit their work only superficially. They say the project is being done for the Lord, but in reality they are doing it for themselves. Others tend to give God temporary control of their interests, only to take control back the moment things stop going the way they expect. Still others commit their task fully to the Lord, then put forth no effort themselves. They wonder why they do not experience success. We must maintain a delicate balance: trusting God as if everything depended on him, while working as if everything depended on us. Think of a specific effort in which you are involved right now. Have you committed it to the Lord?

16:4 This verse doesn't mean that God created some people to be wicked, but rather that God uses even the activities of wicked people to fulfill his good purposes. God is infinite and we are finite. No matter how great our intellects, we will never be able to understand him completely. But we can accept by faith that he is all-powerful, all-loving, and all-good. We can believe that he is not the cause of evil (James 1:13, 17). And we can trust that there are no loose ends in his system of judgment. Evil is a temporary condition in the universe. One day God will destroy it. In the meantime, he uses even evil intentions for his good purposes (see Genesis 50:20).

16:5 Pride is the inner voice that whispers, "I want to do it my way." It is resisting God's leadership in your life and believing that you are able to live without his help. Whenever you find it difficult to humble yourself, you are being pulled by pride.

7When a man is trying to please God, God makes even his worst enemies to be at peace with him.

8A little, gained honestly, is better than great wealth gotten by dishonest means.

9We should make plans—counting on God to direct us.

10God will help the king to judge the people fairly; there need be no mistakes.

11The Lord demands fairness in every business deal. He established this principle.

12It is a horrible thing for a king to do evil. His right to rule depends upon his fairness.

13The king rejoices when his people are truthful and fair.

14The anger of the king is a messenger of death and a wise man will appease it.

15Many favors are showered on those who please the king.

16How much better is wisdom than gold, and understanding than silver!

17The path of the godly leads away from evil; he who follows that path is safe.

18Pride goes before destruction and haughtiness before a fall.

19Better poor and humble than proud and rich.

20God blesses those who obey him; happy the man who puts his trust in the Lord.

21The wise man is known by his common sense, and a pleasant teacher is the best.

22Wisdom is a fountain of life to those possessing it, but a fool's burden is his folly.

23From a wise mind comes careful and persuasive speech.

24Kind words are like honey—enjoyable and healthful.

25Before every man there lies a wide and pleasant road he thinks is right, but it ends in death.

26Hunger is good—if it makes you work to satisfy it!

27Idle hands are the devil's workshop; idle lips are his mouthpiece.

28An evil man sows strife; gossip separates the best of friends.

29Wickedness loves company—and leads others into sin.

30The wicked man stares into space with pursed lips, deep in thought, planning his evil deeds.

31White hair is a crown of glory and is seen most among the godly.

32It is better to be slow-tempered than famous; it is better to have self-control than to control an army.

33We toss the coin, but it is the Lord who controls its decision.

16:7	2 Chron 17:10 / Prov 29:25
16:8	Prov 15:16; 21:6 / 1 Tim 6:8
16:9	Ps 37:23 / Prov 16:1 / 19:21; 20:24
16:10	1 Kgs 3:28
16:12	Prov 14:34 / 25:5; 29:14
16:13	Prov 22:11
16:14	Prov 19:12; 20:2 / Dan 3:13
16:16	Ps 119:127
16:18	Jer 49:16
16:20	Ps 2:12; 34:8 / Jer 17:7
16:22	Prov 3:22 / 14:18,24,27
16:23	Ps 37:30 / Prov 12:5 / 15:18,28
16:24	Prov 4:22 / 17:22; 24:13
16:27	Jas 3:6
16:28	Prov 6:14,19 / 18:8; 26:20
16:31	Mt 5:36
16:32	Prov 14:29 / 15:18; 19:11

16:11 *The Lord demands fairness in every business deal,* literally, "A just balance and scales are the Lord's; all the weights in the bag are his work." **16:12** *His right to rule depends upon his fairness,* literally, "for the throne is established by righteousness." **16:27** *Idle hands are the devil's workshop; idle lips are his mouthpiece,* literally, "A worthless man devises mischief; and in his lips there is a scorching fire." **16:29** *Wickedness loves company—and leads others into sin,* or, "An evil man deceives his neighbor and leads him into loss."

16:7 We want other people to like us, and sometimes we will do almost anything to win their approval. But God tells us to put our energy into trying to please him instead. Such behavior will usually make us attractive to those around us, even our enemies. But even if it doesn't, we haven't lost anything. We are still pleasing God, the only one who truly matters.

16:11 Whether we buy or sell, make a product or offer a service, we know what is fair and what is unfair. Sometimes we feel pressure to be unfair in order to advance ourselves or gain more profit. But if we want to obey God, there is no middle ground: God demands fairness in every business transaction. No amount of rationalizing can cover for an unfair business practice. Fairness is not always easy, but it is what God demands. Ask him for discernment and strength to be consistently fair.

16:18 Proud people take little account of their weaknesses and do not anticipate stumbling blocks. They think they are above the frailties of common people. In this state of mind they are easily tripped up. Ironically, proud people seldom realize that pride is their problem, although everyone around them is well aware of it. Ask someone you trust whether your attitudes are prideful. He or she may help you avoid a fall.

16:22 For centuries people sought a fountain of youth, a spring which they thought would give eternal life and vitality. It was never found. But God's wisdom is a fountain of life that can make a person happy, healthy, and alive forever. How? When we live by God's Word he washes away the deadly effects of sin (see Titus 3:4–8), and the hope of eternal life with him gives us a joyful perspective on our present life. The fountain of youth was only a dream, but the fountain of life is reality. The choice is yours. You can be enlightened by God's wisdom, or you can be dragged down by the weight of your own foolishness.

16:27 It is amazing how much trouble people get into when they have nothing to do. Idleness is used by the devil to lead people into wickedness. It is hard to refuse temptations when you are doing nothing. Keep busy. Do something constructive so your idle time doesn't become destructive. Idle hands are the devil's workshop, and his workshop is most productive when you are not.

16:31 The Hebrews believed that a long life was a sign of God's blessing; therefore, white hair and old age were good. While young people glory in their strength, old people can rejoice in their years of experience and practical wisdom. Rather than white hair being a sign of disgrace to be covered over, it is their crown of glory.

17 A dry crust eaten in peace is better than steak every day along with argument and strife.

²A wise slave will rule his master's wicked sons and share their estate.

³Silver and gold are purified by fire, but God purifies hearts.

⁴The wicked enjoy fellowship with others who are wicked; liars enjoy liars.

⁵Mocking the poor is mocking the God who made them. He will punish those who rejoice at others' misfortunes.

⁶An old man's grandchildren are his crowning glory. A child's glory is his father.

⁷Truth from a rebel or lies from a king are both unexpected.

⁸A bribe works like magic. Whoever uses it will prosper!

⁹Love forgets mistakes; nagging about them parts the best of friends.

¹⁰A rebuke to a man of common sense is more effective than a hundred lashes on the back of a rebel.

¹¹The wicked live for rebellion; they shall be severely punished.

¹²It is safer to meet a bear robbed of her cubs than a fool caught in his folly.

16:33 *toss the coin,* literally, "cast dice into the lap." **17:8** This is a fact, but not to be encouraged! **17:11** *they shall be severely punished,* literally, "a stern (ruthless) messenger will be sent against him."

HOW GOD IS DESCRIBED IN PROVERBS

Proverbs is a book about wise living. It often focuses on a person's response and attitude toward God, who is the source of wisdom. And a number of proverbs point out aspects of God's character. Knowing God helps us on the way to wisdom.

God . . .		
is aware of all that happens	15:3	
knows all people	15:11; 16:2; 21:2	
is the maker of all things	16:4; 21:30	
controls all things	16:33	
is a strong fortress	18:10	
rescues good people from danger	11:8, 21	
rewards the godly	11:31	
blesses good people, condemns the wicked	12:2	
delights in our prayers	15:8, 29	
loves those who obey him	11:27; 15:9, 10; 16:20; 22:12	
cares for poor, sick, and widows	15:25; 22:22, 23	
purifies hearts	17:3	
hates evil	17:5; 21:27; 28:9	

Our Response should be . . .		
to reverence God	10:27; 14:26, 27; 15:16; 16:6; 19:23; 28:14	
to obey God's Word	13:13; 19:16	
to please God	16:7; 20:12; 21:3	
to trust God	22:17–19; 29:25	

17:3 It takes intense heat to purify gold and silver. Similarly, it often takes the heat of trials for the Christian to be purified. Through trials, God shows us what is in us and clears out anything that gets in the way of complete trust in him. Peter says, "If your faith remains strong after being tried in the test tube of fiery trials, it will bring you much praise" (1 Peter 1:7). So when tough times come your way, realize that God wishes to use them to refine your faith and purify your heart.

17:5 Few acts are as cruel as mocking those who are less fortunate, but many people do it because it makes them feel good to be better off or more successful than someone else. Mocking the poor is mocking the God who made them. We also mock God when we mock the weak, or those who are different, or anyone who is an easy target. When you catch yourself putting down others just

for fun, stop. If you don't, you will drag yourself down and anger God.

17:8 This verse is not condoning bribery, but is making an observation about the way things operate in the world. Bribes may get people what they want, but the Bible clearly condemns using them (Exodus 23:8; Psalm 58:1, 2; Proverbs 17:23; Habakkuk 1:1–4; Matthew 28:11–15).

17:9 Forgetting mistakes is necessary to any relationship. It is tempting, especially in an argument, to bring up all the mistakes the other person has ever made. Love, however, keeps its mouth shut—difficult though that may be. Try never to bring anything into an argument that is unrelated to the topic being discussed. As we grow to be like Christ, we will acquire God's ability to forget the confessed mistakes of the past.

¹³If you repay evil for good, a curse is upon your home.
¹⁴It is hard to stop a quarrel once it starts, so don't let it begin.
¹⁵The Lord despises those who say that bad is good, and good is bad.
¹⁶It is senseless to pay tuition to educate a rebel who has no heart for truth.
¹⁷A true friend is always loyal, and a brother is born to help in time of need.
¹⁸It is poor judgment to countersign another's note, to become responsible for his debts.
¹⁹Sinners love to fight; boasting is looking for trouble.
²⁰An evil man is suspicious of everyone and tumbles into constant trouble.
²¹It's no fun to be a rebel's father.
²²A cheerful heart does good like medicine, but a broken spirit makes one sick.
²³It is wrong to accept a bribe to twist justice.
²⁴Wisdom is the main pursuit of sensible men, but a fool's goals are at the ends of the earth!
²⁵A rebellious son is a grief to his father and a bitter blow to his mother.
²⁶How short-sighted to fine the godly for being good! And to punish nobles for being honest!
²⁷, ²⁸The man of few words and settled mind is wise; therefore, even a fool is thought to be wise when he is silent. It pays him to keep his mouth shut.

18 The selfish man quarrels against every sound principle of conduct by demanding his own way.
²A rebel doesn't care about the facts. All he wants to do is yell.
³Sin brings disgrace.
⁴A wise man's words express deep streams of thought.
⁵It is wrong for a judge to favor the wicked and condemn the innocent.
⁶, ⁷A fool gets into constant fights. His mouth is his undoing! His words endanger him.
⁸What dainty morsels rumors are. They are eaten with great relish!
⁹A lazy man is brother to the saboteur.
¹⁰The Lord is a strong fortress. The godly run to him and are safe.
¹¹The rich man thinks of his wealth as an impregnable defense, a high wall of safety. What a dreamer!
¹²Pride ends in destruction; humility ends in honor.
¹³What a shame—yes, how stupid!—to decide before knowing the facts!

17:13	Prov 13:21
17:14	Prov 20:3; 25:8
17:15	Prov 24:24
17:17	Prov 18:24
17:18	Prov 6:1; 11:15
17:19	Prov 13:2; 29:22,23
17:21	Prov 10:1; 17:25; 19:13
17:22	Prov 15:13
17:23	Ex 23:8
17:25	Prov 10:1
17:27	Prov 10:19; Jas 1:19
18:5	Prov 17:15; 24:23
18:6	Prov 10:14; 13:3
18:8	Lev 19:16; Prov 11:13
18:10	2 Sam 22:2; Ps 61:3; 91:2; Prov 29:25
18:11	Prov 10:15
18:12	Prov 11:2; 16:18; 29:23
18:13	Prov 20:25; Jn 7:51

17:14 *It is hard to stop a quarrel once it starts,* literally, "as when one lets out water." **17:16** *no heart for truth,* literally, "no heart." **17:20** *is suspicious of everyone,* or "does not prosper." **18:2** *yell,* literally, "express his opinion." **18:10** *The Lord,* literally, "The name of the Lord."

17:17 What kind of friend are you? There is a vast difference between knowing someone well and being a true friend. The greatest evidence of genuine friendship is loyalty (see 1 Corinthians 13:7)—being available to help in times of distress or personal struggles. Too many people are fair-weather friends. They stick around when the friendship helps them, and leave when they're not getting anything out of the relationship. Think of your friends and assess your loyalty to them. Be the kind of true friend the Bible encourages.

17:24 While there is something to be said for having big dreams, this proverb points out the folly of chasing fantasies. How much better to align your goals with God's, being the kind of person he wants you to be! Such goals (wisdom, honesty, patience, love) may not seem exciting, but they will determine your eternal future. Take time to think about your dreams and goals, and make sure they cover the really important areas of life.

17:27, 28 This proverb highlights several benefits of silence: (1) it is the best policy if you have nothing worthwhile to say; (2) it allows you the opportunity to listen and learn; and (3) it gives you something in common with those who are wiser. Make sure to use times of silence for thinking and listening so that when you do speak, you will have something important to say.

18:1 Our society values assertiveness, and at times, it is a needed characteristic. But assertiveness can become selfishness if it is not tempered by love. God's people prefer others before themselves; they are humble and seek to serve rather than be served. When we insist on our own way, we call it assertiveness. But when God weighs our actions, he may call them selfish. Doing things "your way" may in fact be a good course of action, but only if it considers the rights and concerns of others. The line between selfishness and assertiveness is often the line between "others" and "myself."

18:8 It is as hard to refuse to listen to a rumor as it is to turn down a delicious dessert. Taking just one morsel of either one creates a taste for more. You can resist rumors the same way a determined dieter resists candy—never even open the box. If you don't take the first bite of gossip, you can't take the second and the third.

18:11 Money cannot provide safety—there are too many ways for it to lose its power. The government may cease to back it; thieves may steal it; inflation may rob it of all value. But God never loses his power. He is always dependable. Where do you place your hope for safety—on uncertain wealth or on God who is always faithful?

18:13, 15, 17 In these concise statements, the writer gives three

18:15
Prov 12:26
15:14; 23:23

18:16
Gen 32:20
1 Sam 25:27
Prov 17:8

18:18
Prov 16:33

18:19
2 Cor 6:3

18:21
Prov 13:3
Mt 12:37

18:22
Prov 12:4
19:14; 31:10-31

18:23
2 Chron 10:13
Prov 19:7
Jas 2:3

18:24
Prov 14:20
19:4,6

19:1
Prov 11:18; 13:7

14A man's courage can sustain his broken body, but when courage dies, what hope is left?

15The intelligent man is always open to new ideas. In fact, he looks for them.

16A gift does wonders; it will bring you before men of importance!

17Any story sounds true until someone tells the other side and sets the record straight.

18A coin toss ends arguments and settles disputes between powerful opponents.

19It is harder to win back the friendship of an offended brother than to capture a fortified city. His anger shuts you out like iron bars.

20Ability to give wise advice satisfies like a good meal!

21Those who love to talk will suffer the consequences. Men have died for saying the wrong thing!

22The man who finds a wife finds a good thing; she is a blessing to him from the Lord.

23The poor man pleads and the rich man answers with insults.

24There are "friends" who pretend to be friends, but there is a friend who sticks closer than a brother.

19

Better be poor and honest than rich and dishonest.
2It is dangerous and sinful to rush into the unknown.

18:14 *courage,* literally, "spirit." **18:18** *a coin toss,* literally, "the lot." **18:19** The Hebrew of this verse is not clear. **19:1** *rich,* literally, "a fool."

HUMILITY AND PRIDE	Results of . . .	Humility	Pride	
Proverbs is direct and forceful in rejecting pride. The proud attitude heads the list of seven things God hates (6:16). The harmful results of pride are constantly contrasted with humility and its benefits.		Leads to wisdom	Ends in shame	11:2
		Takes advice and becomes wise	Leads to arguments	13:10
		Has reverence for the Lord; makes one both wise and honored		15:33
			Disgusts the Lord and leads to punishment	16:5
			Leads to destruction	16:18
		Brings true contentment	May lead to riches but. . .	16:19
		Ends in honor	Ends in destruction	18:12
			Worse than being foolish	26:12
		Ends in honor	Ends in a fall	29:23

basic principles for making sound decisions: (1) get the facts before deciding; (2) be open to new ideas; (3) make sure you hear both sides of the story before judging. All three principles center around seeking additional information. This is hard work, but the only alternative is to become like the person who says, "My mind is made up; don't confuse me with facts."

18:22 When you announce marriage plans, don't expect praise from the world. A lot of people nowadays view a permanent tie to one spouse as a loss of freedom. But today's emphasis on individual freedom is misguided. Strong marriages produce strong children, and healthy families are the backbone of healthy nations. God created marriage, and he pronounced it good.

18:23 This verse is not telling us to insult the poor; it is simply recording an unfortunate fact of life. It is wrong for rich people to treat the less fortunate with contempt and arrogance, and God will judge such actions severely (see 14:31).

18:24 Loneliness is rampant. Many people today feel cut off and alienated from others. Being in a crowd just makes people more aware of their isolation. Lonely people don't need to hear "Have a nice day." They need friends who will stick close, listen, care, and offer help when it is needed—in good times and bad. It is better to have one such friend than dozens of superficial acquaintances.

Instead of wishing you could find a true friend, seek to become one yourself. There are people who need your friendship. Ask God to reveal them to you, and then take on the challenge of being a true friend.

19:1 Honesty is far more valuable than wealth, but most people don't act as if they believe this. They are so afraid of being short of money that they will pay any price to have more—cheating on their taxes, stealing from stores or employers, withholding tithes, refusing to give. But when we know and love God, we realize that honesty is a greater treasure than money in the bank. A lower standard of living—or even poverty—is a small price to pay for personal integrity. Do your actions show that you value integrity more than wealth? What changes do you need to make in order to get your priorities straight?

19:2 In spite of the dangers, we often rush into the unknown. Many people marry without knowing what to expect of their partner or of married life. Others try illicit sex or drugs without considering the consequences. Some plunge into jobs without evaluating whether they are suitable to that line of work. Don't rush into the unknown. Be sure you understand what you're getting into and where you want to go before you take the first step.

³A man may ruin his chances by his own foolishness and then blame it on the Lord!

⁴A wealthy man has many "friends"; the poor man has none left.

⁵Punish false witnesses. Track down liars.

⁶Many beg favors from a man who is generous; everyone is his friend!

⁷A poor man's own brothers turn away from him in embarrassment; how much more his friends! He calls after them, but they are gone.

⁸He who loves wisdom loves his own best interest and will be a success.

⁹A false witness shall be punished and a liar shall be caught.

¹⁰It doesn't seem right for a fool to succeed or for a slave to rule over princes!

¹¹A wise man restrains his anger and overlooks insults. This is to his credit.

¹²The king's anger is as dangerous as a lion's. But his approval is as refreshing as the dew on grass.

¹³A rebellious son is a calamity to his father, and a nagging wife annoys like constant dripping.

¹⁴A father can give his sons homes and riches, but only the Lord can give them understanding wives.

¹⁵A lazy man sleeps soundly—and he goes hungry!

¹⁶Keep the commandments and keep your life; despising them means death.

¹⁷When you help the poor you are lending to the Lord—and he pays wonderful interest on your loan!

¹⁸Discipline your son in his early years while there is hope. If you don't you will ruin his life.

¹⁹A short-tempered man must bear his own penalty; you can't do much to help him. If you try once you must try a dozen times!

²⁰Get all the advice you can and be wise the rest of your life.

²¹Man proposes, but God disposes.

19:7 *turn away from him in embarrassment,* literally, "despise him."

19:3	Isa 8:21
19:5	Ex 23:1 / Prov 19:9
19:7	Prov 4:20; 18:23
19:8	Prov 16:20 / 8:35,36
19:10	Prov 26:1
19:11	Prov 14:29 / Col 4:6
19:12	Prov 16:14,15
19:13	Prov 12:4 / 15:20; 17:25 / 21:9,19
19:15	Prov 6:9; 16:26 / 24:33
19:16	Prov 16:17
19:17	Deut 15:7 / Prov 14:31 / 28:27
19:18	Prov 13:24 / Heb 12:6
19:19	Prov 12:16 / 14:17; 15:18

HOW TO SUCCEED IN GOD'S EYES Proverbs notes two significant by-products of wise living: success and good reputation. Several verses also point out what causes failure and poor reputation.

Qualities that promote success and a good reputation:

Goodness	10:7
Hating lies	13:5
Commiting all work to the Lord	16:3
Speaking few words; having a settled mind	17:27, 28
Loving wisdom	19:8
Kindness	19:22
Goodness, love, kindness	21:21
Humility and respect for the Lord	22:4
Godliness	28:12
Willingness to admit mistakes, confess, and forsake sin	28:13

Qualities that prevent success and cause a bad reputation:

Wickedness	10:7; 12:3; 28:12
Treachery	11:6
Constant lying	13:5
Hatred	26:24–26
Praising oneself	27:2
Refusing to admit mistakes	28:13

Other verses dealing with one's reputation are: 11:10, 16; 14:3; 19:10; 22:1; 23:17, 18; 24:13, 14; 25:27

19:8 Is it good to love your own best interest? Yes, when your soul is at stake! This proverb does not refer to the self-centered person who loves and protects his or her selfish interests and will do anything to serve them. Instead it speaks to those people who seek to live sensibly out of concern for their lives and eternal souls.

19:16 The commandments we are told to keep are those found in God's Word—both the Ten Commandments (Exodus 20) and other passages of instruction. To obey what God teaches in the Bible is self-preserving. To disobey is self-destructive.

19:17 In this proverb God identifies with the poor as Jesus does in Matthew 25:31–46. As our Creator, God values all of us, whether we are poor or rich. When we help the poor, we show honor both to the Creator and to his creation. God accepts our help as if we had offered it directly to him.

19:23
Ps 25:13
Prov 14:27; 22:3
1 Tim 4:8

19:25
Prov 9:7,8
19:29; 21:11

19:26
Prov 20:20

19:29
Prov 9:12
19:9,25; 26:3

20:1
Prov 31:4

20:2
Prov 16:14

22Kindness makes a man attractive. And it is better to be poor than dishonest. 23Reverence for God gives life, happiness, and protection from harm. 24Some men are so lazy they won't even feed themselves! 25Punish a mocker and others will learn from his example. Reprove a wise man and he will be the wiser. 26A son who mistreats his father or mother is a public disgrace. 27Stop listening to teaching that contradicts what you know is right. 28A worthless witness cares nothing for truth—he enjoys his sinning too much. 29Mockers and rebels shall be severely punished.

20 Wine gives false courage; hard liquor leads to brawls; what fools men are to let it master them, making them reel drunkenly down the street! 2The king's fury is like that of a roaring lion; to rouse his anger is to risk your life.

HONESTY AND DISHONESTY

Proverbs tells us plainly that God despises all forms of dishonesty. Not only does God hate dishonesty, but we are told that it works against us— others no longer trust us, and we cannot even enjoy our dishonest gains. It is wiser to be honest because "honesty is its own defense" (12:13).

Others' Opinion

People know good men for their honesty and evil men for their dishonesty.	12:17
Leaders rejoice when their people are truthful and fair.	16:13
People appreciate truth more than flattery.	28:23

Quality of life

Good men are filled with honesty; evil men are filled with lies.	12:5
Truthful witnesses never lie; false witnesses always lie.	14:5
Truthful witnesses save good men; false witnesses are traitors.	14:25
Honest gain, even if small, is better than dishonest gain.	16:8
Better to be poor and honest than rich and dishonest.	19:1
It is a wonderful heritage to have an honest father.	20:7
Better to be poor and honest than rich and a cheater.	28:6

Short-term results

Ill-gotten gain brings no lasting happiness; right living does.	10:2
Good people are directed by honesty; the wicked shall fall under their sins.	11:5
Lies get people into trouble; honesty is its own defense.	12:13
Dishonest money brings grief; hating bribes brings happiness.	15:27
Ill-gotten gain cannot be fully enjoyed.	20:17
Leaders will have long reigns if they hate dishonesty and bribes.	28:16

Long-term results

A good man is guided by honesty; an evil man is destroyed by dishonesty.	11:3
Truth stands the test of time; lies are soon exposed.	12:19
Getting rich quickly is not a blessing in the end.	20:21
Dishonest gain doesn't last.	21:6
Good men are rescued from harm; cheaters will be destroyed.	28:18

God's Opinion

God hates cheating and delights in honesty.	11:1
God delights in those who keep their promises; he abhors those who don't.	12:22
God demands fairness in business.	16:11
God despises every kind of cheating.	20:10
God loathes all cheating and dishonesty.	20:23
God is more pleased with justice and fairness than gifts.	21:3

19:22 You can't do much with the body you were born with—you can trim it and paint it, but it still looks pretty much like the original. However, you can do a lot about what is on the inside. You can be as attractive as you want to be inwardly. You can have kindness, for example, in any amount you choose. You may not be able to control your looks, but you can control the attractiveness of your character.

19:23 Those who trust God are spared much harm because of their habits, their life-style, and sometimes through God's direct intervention. Nevertheless, reverence does not always protect us from harm in this life; bad things still happen to people who love

God. This verse is not a universal promise, but a general guideline. It describes what would happen if this world were sinless, and what will happen in the new earth, when faithful believers will be under God's protection forever. (See the note on Proverbs 3:16, 17 for more about this concept.)

19:25 There is a great difference between the person who learns from criticism and the person who refuses to accept correction. How we respond to criticism determines whether or not we grow in wisdom. The next time someone criticizes you, make a point of listening carefully to all that is said. You might learn something.

3It is an honor for a man to stay out of a fight. Only fools insist on quarreling.

4If you won't plow in the cold, you won't eat at the harvest.

5Though good advice lies deep within a counselor's heart, the wise man will draw it out.

6Most people will tell you what loyal friends they are, but are they telling the truth?

7It is a wonderful heritage to have an honest father.

8A king sitting as judge weighs all the evidence carefully, distinguishing the true from false.

9Who can ever say, "I have cleansed my heart; I am sinless"?

10The Lord despises every kind of cheating.

11The character of even a child can be known by the way he acts—whether what he does is pure and right.

12If you have good eyesight and good hearing, thank God who gave them to you.

13If you love sleep, you will end in poverty. Stay awake, work hard, and there will be plenty to eat!

14"Utterly worthless!" says the buyer as he haggles over the price. But afterwards he brags about his bargain!

15Good sense is far more valuable than gold or precious jewels.

16It is risky to make loans to strangers!

17Some men enjoy cheating, but the cake they buy with such ill-gotten gain will turn to gravel in their mouths.

18Don't go ahead with your plans without the advice of others; don't go to war until they agree.

19Don't tell your secrets to a gossip unless you want them broadcast to the world.

20God puts out the light of the man who curses his father or mother.

21Quick wealth is not a blessing in the end.

22Don't repay evil for evil. Wait for the Lord to handle the matter.

23The Lord loathes all cheating and dishonesty.

24Since the Lord is directing our steps, why try to understand everything that happens along the way?

25It is foolish and rash to make a promise to the Lord before counting the cost.

26A wise king stamps out crime by severe punishment.

27A man's conscience is the Lord's searchlight exposing his hidden motives.

20:3
Prov 14:29
16:32; 19:11
20:6
Prov 25:14
Mt 6:2
20:7
Ps 37:26; 112:2
20:8
Prov 16:12
18:13; 23:23
20:9
2 Chron 6:36
20:10
Prov 11:1; 20:23
20:11
Mt 7:16
Prov 21:8
20:13
Prov 6:9,10
19:15; 24:32,33
20:16
Ex 22:26
Prov 6:1-5
20:18
Prov 11:14
Lk 14:31
20:19
Prov 11:13
20:20
Ex 21:17
Lev 20:9
Prov 19:26
20:21
Prov 15:27
28:16
20:22
Prov 17:23
24:28,29
Mt 5:39
Rom 12:17
20:23
Prov 11:1; 20:10
20:24
Gen 50:20
1 Kgs 12:15
Ps 37:23

20:10 *every kind of cheating,* literally, "diverse weights and diverse measures." **20:12** *thank,* implied. **20:19** *Don't tell your secrets to a gossip,* literally, "company not with him." **20:23** *all cheating and dishonesty,* literally, "diverse weights . . . false scales." **20:27** *conscience,* literally, "spirit."

20:3 A man who is truly confident of his strength does not need to parade it. A truly brave man does not look for chances to prove his bravery. A resourceful man can find a way out of a fight. A man of endurance can take abuse without retaliating. Insignificant men find it impossible to stay out of fights. Men of character can. What kind of person are you?

20:4 You've heard similar warnings: if you don't study, you'll fail the test; if you don't save, you won't have money when you need it. God wants us to anticipate future needs and prepare for them. We can't expect him to come to our rescue when we cause our own problems through lack of planning. He provides for us, but he also expects us to be responsible.

20:9 No one is without sin. As soon as we confess our sin and repent, sinful thoughts and actions begin to creep back into our lives. We all need ongoing cleansing, moment by moment. Thank God he provides it by his mercy when we ask for it. Make confession and repentance a regular part of your talks with God. Rely on him moment by moment for the cleansing you need.

20:23 Dishonesty is a difficult sin to avoid. It is easy to cheat if we think no one else is looking. But dishonesty affects the very core of a person. It makes him untrustworthy and untrusting. It eventually makes him unable to know himself or relate to others. Don't take dishonesty lightly. Even the smallest portion of dishonesty contains enough of the poison of deceit to kill your spiritual life. If there is

any unconfessed dishonesty in your life, tell God about it now.

20:24 We are often confused by the events in our lives. Many things we will never understand; others will fall into place in years to come as we look back and see how God was working. This proverb counsels us not to worry if we don't understand everything as it happens. Instead, we should trust that God knows what he's doing, even if his design is not clear to us. See Psalm 37:23 for a reassuring promise of God's involvement in our lives.

20:25 God takes vows seriously and requires that they be carried out (Deuteronomy 23:21-23). We often have good intentions when making a vow because we want to show God that we are determined to please him. Jesus, however, says it is better not to make a promise to God because he knows how difficult they are to keep (Matthew 5:33-36). If you still feel it is important to make a vow, make sure that you weigh the consequences of breaking that vow. Jephthah (Judges 11) made a rash promise to sacrifice the first thing he saw on his return home. As it happened, he saw his daughter first. It is better not to make promises than to make them and then later want to change them. It is better still to make promises, counting the cost beforehand, and then to fulfill them. (For a list of other Bible people who made rash vows, see the chart in Judges 11.)

20:27 God has given each of us a conscience to tell us right from wrong. Without it, we would be unaware of the harm caused by

20:28
Prov 29:14
20:29
Prov 16:31

21:1
Ezra 6:21,22
Prov 16:1,9
21:2
Prov 16:2
Lk 16:15
21:3
Ps 50:8,9
Prov 15:8
21:4
Prov 6:17; 30:13
Lk 11:34

21:9
Prov 19:13
21:19

21:11
Prov 9:9; 15:14
19:25

21:13
Prov 24:11,12
Mt 18:30-34
Lk 16:19-31
1 Jn 3:17
21:17
Prov 23:19-21
21:18
Prov 11:8
Isa 43:3,4
21:19
Prov 19:13; 21:9
21:20
Prov 8:21
21:21
Prov 2:10,21
3:16; 11:19
21:22
2 Sam 5:6-9
Prov 24:5
Eccles 9:15
21:23
Prov 13:3
Jas 3:2

28If a king is kind, honest and fair, his kingdom stands secure.
29The glory of young men is their strength; of old men, their experience.
30Punishment that hurts chases evil from the heart.

21 Just as water is turned into irrigation ditches, so the Lord directs the king's thoughts. He turns them wherever he wants to.
2We can justify our every deed but God looks at our motives.
3God is more pleased when we are just and fair than when we give him gifts.
4Pride, lust, and evil actions are all sin.
5Steady plodding brings prosperity; hasty speculation brings poverty.
6Dishonest gain will never last, so why take the risk?
7Because the wicked are unfair, their violence boomerangs and destroys them.
8A man is known by his actions. An evil man lives an evil life; a good man lives a godly life.
9It is better to live in the corner of an attic than with a crabby woman in a lovely home.
10An evil man loves to harm others; being a good neighbor is out of his line.
11The wise man learns by listening; the simpleton can learn only by seeing scorners punished.
12God, the Righteous One, knows what is going on in the homes of the wicked, and will bring the wicked to judgment.
13He who shuts his ears to the cries of the poor will be ignored in his own time of need.
14An angry man is silenced by giving him a gift!
15A good man loves justice, but it is a calamity to evil-doers.
16The man who strays away from common sense will end up dead!
17A man who loves pleasure becomes poor; wine and luxury are not the way to riches!
18The wicked will finally lose; the righteous will finally win.
19Better to live in the desert than with a quarrelsome, complaining woman.
20The wise man saves for the future, but the foolish man spends whatever he gets.
21The man who tries to be good, loving and kind finds life, righteousness and honor.
22The wise man conquers the strong man and levels his defenses.
23Keep your mouth closed and you'll stay out of trouble.

20:29 *their experience,* literally, "the hoary head." **21:4** *evil actions,* literally, "the tillage of the wicked." **21:8** *A man is known by his actions,* implied. **21:18** *The wicked will finally lose; the righteous will finally win,* literally "the wicked is a ransom for the righteous." **21:20** *The wise man saves for the future,* literally, "There is precious treasure and oil in the dwelling of the wise."

certain actions, and we would not know how to do good either. The conscience is a light exposing hidden motives. Because our consciences are not perfect, we need the additional light of God's Word (see Psalm 119:105). The best way to stay on God's path is to use both lights at once—our conscience exposing our motives, and the Bible directing our steps.

21:1 In Solomon's day, kings possessed absolute authority and were often considered gods. This proverb shows that God, not earthly rulers, has ultimate authority over world politics. Although they may not have realized it, the earth's most powerful kings have always been under God's control. (See Isaiah 10:5–8 for an example of a king who was used for God's purposes.)

21:2 People can find an excuse for doing almost anything, but God looks behind the excuse to the motives. We often have to make difficult choices in areas of life where the right action is difficult to discern. We can help ourselves make such decisions by trying to identify our motives first, and then asking, "Would God be pleased with my real reasons for doing this?" God is not pleased when we do good deeds only to receive something back.

21:3 Offerings are not bribes to make God overlook our character

faults. If our personal and business dealings are not on the level, no amount of generosity in the offering plate will make up for it.

21:5 Faithful completion of mundane tasks is a great accomplishment. Such work is patiently carried out according to a plan. Diligence does not come naturally to most people. It is a result of strong character. Don't look for quick and easy answers. Be a faithful and diligent servant of God.

21:11, 12 It is usually better to learn from the mistakes of others than from our own. We can do this through listening to their advice and through watching what happens to them—through keeping our mouths shut and our eyes open. Take counsel from others instead of plunging ahead and learning the hard way.

21:20 Easy credit has many people living on the edge of bankruptcy. The desire to keep up and accumulate more, pushes them to spend every penny they earn, and they stretch their credit to the limit. But anyone who spends all he has is spending more than he can afford. A wise man puts money aside for when he may have less. God approves of foresight and restraint. God's people need to examine their life-styles to see whether their spending is God-pleasing or merely self-pleasing.

24Mockers are proud, haughty and arrogant.

25, 26The lazy man longs for many things but his hands refuse to work. He is greedy to get, while the godly love to give!

27God loathes the gifts of evil men, especially if they are trying to bribe him!

28No one believes a liar, but everyone respects the words of an honest man.

29An evil man is stubborn, but a godly man will reconsider.

30No one, regardless of how shrewd or well-advised he is, can stand against the Lord.

31Go ahead and prepare for the conflict, but victory comes from God.

21:24
Ps 1:1
Prov 13:1; 14:6

21:25
Ps 37:26; 112:5
Prov 10:4; 12:24

21:30
Isa 8:9; 14:27
Acts 5:38,39

21:31
Isa 31:1-3
1 Cor 15:57

21:29 *An evil man is stubborn, but a godly man will reconsider,* or "The wicked man is brazen; the godly man is thoughtful." **21:31** *Go ahead and prepare for the conflict,* literally, "The horse is prepared against the day of battle."

RIGHTEOUSNESS

		Righteous	Wicked	References
Proverbs often compares the lifestyles of the wicked and the righteous, and makes a strong case for living by God's pattern. The advantages of righteous living and the disadvantages of wicked living are pointed out. The kind of person we decide to be will affect every area of our lives.	Outlook on life	Hopeful	Fearful	10:24
		Concerned about the welfare of God's creation	Even their kindness is cruel	12:10
		Concerned for justice	Don't care about justice	28:5
	Response to life	Covered with blessings	Curse their luck	10:6
			Plan evil deeds	16:30
		Willing to reconsider and change plans	Stubborn, refuse to compromise	21:29
		Persevere against evil	Try to trip and cheat the righteous	24:15, 16
		Will pray for enemies	Try to kill the godly	29:10
	How they are seen by others	Help others	Take advantage of others	12:12
		Appreciated	Walk a rocky road	13:15
			Lead others into sin	16:29
			Enjoy fellowship with other wicked people	17:4
		Live godly lives	Live evil lives	21:8
		Are not to enjoy the company of godless men	Spend their days plotting violence and cheating	24:1, 2
		Others are glad for their success	Others are sad at their success	28:12
		Care for the poor	Don't care about the poor	29:7
		Hate evil people's evil	Hate good people's goodness	29:27
	Quality of life	Have a strong anchor	Face disaster	10:25
		Their goodness delivers them	Their treachery is their undoing	11:6
		No real harm befalls them	Face constant trouble	12:21

21:27 How do people try to bribe God? Often they go to church, tithe, or volunteer, not because of their love and devotion to God, but because they hope God will bless them in return. But God has made it very clear that he desires obedience and love more than religious ritual (see 1 Samuel 15:22). God does not want our sacrifices of time, energy, and money alone; he wants our hearts—our complete love and devotion. We may be able to bribe people (21:14), but we cannot bribe God.

21:31 All our preparation is useless without God, but even with God's help we still must do our part and prepare. His control of the outcome does not negate our responsibilities. God may want you to produce a great book, but you must learn to write. God may want to use you in foreign missions, but you must learn the language. God will accomplish his purposes, but maybe not through us if we can't do our part by being well prepared.

22

22:2
Prov 14:31
29:13

22:3
Prov 14:15

22:4
Prov 3:16; 4:4

22:5
Prov 13:9,15

22:6
Ps 78:4
Eph 6:4

22:7
Prov 22:15

If you must choose, take a good name rather than great riches; for to be held in loving esteem is better than silver and gold.

²The rich and the poor are alike before the Lord who made them all.

³A prudent man foresees the difficulties ahead and prepares for them; the simpleton goes blindly on and suffers the consequences.

⁴True humility and respect for the Lord lead a man to riches, honor and long life.

⁵The rebel walks a thorny, treacherous road; the man who values his soul will stay away.

⁶Teach a child to choose the right path, and when he is older he will remain upon it.

⁷Just as the rich rule the poor, so the borrower is servant to the lender.

AND WICKEDNESS

		Righteous	Wicked	References
Quality of life (cont.)		Have treasure for their goodness	Are dogged by trouble	15:6
		Their path leads away from evil		16:17
			Suspicious of everyone and tumble into constant trouble	17:20
		Are bold as lions	Are fearful constantly	28:1
		Rescued from harm	Will be destroyed	28:18
Short-term results		Have firm footing	Will slip and fall	10:9
		Their goodness helps them through life	They are destroyed by their wickedness	13:6
		Chased by blessings	Chased by curses	13:21
		Have a common bond of good will	Have a common bond of guilt	14:9
Long-term results		God protects them	God destroys them	10:29
		Life is full of light	Life is dark and gloomy	13:9
			Will be punished for rebellion	17:11
		Will finally win	Will finally lose	21:18
Eternal expectations		Never lose God's blessings	Shall lose everything	10:30
		Reward lasts forever	Riches last for only a moment	11:18
		Find life	Find death	11:19
		Look forward to happiness	Can expect only God's wrath	11:23
		Shall stand	Shall perish	12:7
		Have a refuge when they die	Will be crushed by their sins	14:32
God's opinion of them		Delights in the good	Hates the stubborn	11:20
		Evil men shall bow to them	They shall bow to the righteous ones	14:19

22:4 This is a general observation that would have been especially applicable to an obedient Israelite living in Solomon's God-fearing kingdom. Nevertheless, some have been martyrs at a young age, and some have given away all their wealth for the sake of God's kingdom. The book of Proverbs describes life the way it should be. It does not dwell on the exceptions.

22:6 Many parents want to make all the choices for their child, but this hurts him in the long run. When parents teach a child how to

make decisions, they don't have to watch every step he takes. They know he will remain on the right path because he has made the choice himself.

22:7 This doesn't mean you should never borrow. It warns you, however, never to take on a loan without carefully examining your ability to repay it. A loan you can handle is enabling; a loan you can't handle is enslaving. The borrower must realize that until the loan is repaid, he is a servant to the one that made it.

⁸The unjust tyrant will reap disaster and his reign of terror shall end.

⁹Happy is the generous man, the one who feeds the poor.

¹⁰Throw out the mocker, and you will be rid of tension, fighting and quarrels.

¹¹He who values grace and truth is the king's friend.

¹²The Lord preserves the upright but ruins the plans of the wicked.

¹³The lazy man is full of excuses. "I can't go to work!" he says. "If I go outside I might meet a lion in the street and be killed!

¹⁴A prostitute is a dangerous trap; those cursed of God are caught in it.

¹⁵A youngster's heart is filled with rebellion, but punishment will drive it out of him.

¹⁶He who gains by oppressing the poor or by bribing the rich shall end in poverty.

22:8
Prov 24:16
22:9
2 Cor 9:6
22:11
Prov 14:35
16:15; 22:29
Mt 5:8
22:14
Prov 5:3; 23:26
22:15
Prov 13:24
22:16
Job 20:19
Prov 14:31; 28:3

Proverbs of the wise

¹⁷,¹⁸,¹⁹Listen to this wise advice; follow it closely, for it will do you good, and you can pass it on to others: *Trust in the Lord.*

²⁰,²¹In the past, haven't I been right? Then believe what I am telling you now, and share it with others.

²²,²³Don't rob the poor and sick! For the Lord is their defender. If you injure them he will punish you.

²⁴,²⁵Keep away from angry, short-tempered men, lest you learn to be like them and endanger your soul.

²⁶,²⁷Unless you have the extra cash on hand, don't countersign a note. Why risk everything you own? They'll even take your bed!

²⁸Do not move the ancient boundary marks. That is stealing.

²⁹Do you know a hard-working man? He shall be successful and stand before kings!

22:17
Prov 1:7; 2:1,2
22:24
Prov 1:15; 14:7
29:22
22:26
Ex 22:26
Prov 6:1-5
20:16
22:28
Deut 19:14
27:17
Prov 23:10,11
22:29
Prov 27:18

23 When dining with a rich man, be on your guard and don't stuff yourself, though it all tastes so good; for he is trying to bribe you, and no good is going to come of his invitation.

⁴,⁵Don't weary yourself trying to get rich. Why waste your time? For riches can disappear as though they had the wings of a bird!

⁶,⁷,⁸Don't associate with evil men; don't long for their favors and gifts. Their kindness is a trick; they want to use you as their pawn. The delicious food they serve will turn sour in your stomach and you will vomit it, and have to take back your words of appreciation for their "kindness."

⁹Don't waste your breath on a rebel. He will despise the wisest advice.

23:1
Ps 141:4
Prov 23:6
Eccles 7:7
Dan 1:5
23:4
Prov 15:27
27:23,24; 28:20
Mt 6:19
1 Tim 6:17
23:6
Prov 1:15; 4:14
23:9
Prov 14:7; 24:7

22:12 *the plans,* literally, "the words." **22:28** *That is stealing,* implied, see 23:10, 11. **23:1** *a rich man,* literally, "a ruler."

22:8 Sometimes God intervenes and directly destroys tyrants. More often, he uses other rulers to overthrow them or their own oppressed people to rebel against them. This proverb is a message of hope to people who must live and work under unjust authoritarian leaders. It is also a warning to those who enjoy ruling with an iron hand. If you are in a position of authority at church, work, or home, remember what happens to tyrants. Leadership through kindness is more effective and longer lasting than leadership by force.

22:12 It takes discipline, determination, and hard work to live God's way, but God protects and rewards those who make the commitment to follow him. The wicked may seem to have an easier time of it, but in the long run their plans fail and their lives amount to nothing. Don't resist God and expect lasting success.

22:15 Young children often do foolish and dangerous things simply because they don't understand the consequences. Punishment can also be translated "discipline" or "training." Just as God trains and corrects us to make us better, so parents must discipline their children to make them learn the difference between right and wrong. Read how God corrects us in Proverbs 3:11, 12.

22:24, 25 People tend to become like those around them. Even the negative characteristics sometimes rub off. The Bible exhorts us to be cautious in our choice of companions. Choose companions with characteristics you would like to develop in your own life.

22:28 In Joshua 13—21, the land was divided and the boundaries marked out for each tribe. Moses had already warned the people that when they reached the Promised Land they shouldn't cheat their neighbors by moving a marker stone to give themselves more land and their neighbors less (Deuteronomy 19:14; 27:17). Gerrymandering—changing political boundaries so that one group of voters benefits and another loses—is a modern form of moving boundary markers.

23:4, 5 We have all heard of people who have won millions of dollars and then lost it all. Even the average person can spend an inheritance—or a paycheck—with lightning speed and have little to show for it. Don't spend your time chasing fleeting earthly treasures. Instead store up treasures in heaven, for such treasures will never be lost. (To learn how to do this, see Luke 12:33, 34.)

23:10
Deut 19:14
27:17
Jer 22:3
Zech 7:10

23:12
Prov 2:2; 5:1
22:17

23:13
Prov 13:24
19:18; 29:15
1 Cor 5:5

23:15
Prov 4:1; 10:1
15:20; 27:11

23:17
Ps 19:11; 37:1
73:3
Prov 24:1,14,19

23:19
Prov 20:1; 23:29

23:22
Prov 13:1; 15:5
Deut 21:18

23:23
Prov 4:7; 15:14
18:15
Mt 13:44

23:24
Prov 10:1; 23:15

23:26
Prov 6:26; 22:14
Eccles 7:26

23:29
Prov 20:1; 23:19
Isa 5:11,22

23:32
Ps 140:3

24:1
Ps 1:1; 37:3
Prov 1:15

24:5
Prov 21:22

24:6
Prov 11:14

24:7
Prov 14:6

24:8
Prov 6:14; 14:22

10, 11Don't steal the land of defenseless orphans by moving their ancient boundary marks, for their Redeemer is strong; he himself will accuse you.

12Don't refuse to accept criticism; get all the help you can.

13, 14Don't fail to correct your children; discipline won't hurt them! They won't die if you use a stick on them! Punishment will keep them out of hell.

15, 16My son, how I will rejoice if you become a man of common sense. Yes, my heart will thrill to your thoughtful, wise words.

17, 18Don't envy evil men but continue to reverence the Lord all the time, for surely you have a wonderful future ahead of you. There is hope for you yet!

19, 20, 21O my son, be wise and stay in God's paths; don't carouse with drunkards and gluttons, for they are on their way to poverty. And remember that too much sleep clothes a man with rags. 22Listen to your father's advice and don't despise an old mother's experience. 23Get the facts at any price, and hold on tightly to all the good sense you can get. 24, 25The father of a godly man has cause for joy—what pleasure a wise son is! So give your parents joy!

26, 27, 28O my son, trust my advice—stay away from prostitutes. For a prostitute is a deep and narrow grave. Like a robber, she waits for her victims as one after another become unfaithful to their wives.

29, 30Whose heart is filled with anguish and sorrow? Who is always fighting and quarreling? Who is the man with bloodshot eyes and many wounds? It is the one who spends long hours in the taverns, trying out new mixtures. 31Don't let the sparkle and the smooth taste of strong wine deceive you. 32For in the end it bites like a poisonous serpent; it stings like an adder. 33You will see hallucinations and have delirium tremens, and you will say foolish, silly things that would embarrass you no end when sober. 34You will stagger like a sailor tossed at sea, clinging to a swaying mast. 35And afterwards you will say, "I didn't even know it when they beat me up. . . . Let's go and have another drink!"

24 Don't envy godless men; don't even enjoy their company. 2For they spend their days plotting violence and cheating.

3, 4Any enterprise is built by wise planning, becomes strong through common sense, and profits wonderfully by keeping abreast of the facts.

5A wise man is mightier than a strong man. Wisdom is mightier than strength.

6Don't go to war without wise guidance; there is safety in many counselors.

7Wisdom is too much for a rebel. He'll not be chosen as a counselor!

8To plan evil is as wrong as doing it.

9The rebel's schemes are sinful, and the mocker is the scourge of all mankind.

23:12 *help,* literally, "knowledge."

23:10, 11 The term *redeemer* referred to someone who had to buy back a family member who had fallen into slavery or to accept the obligation to marry the widow of a family member (Ruth 3:12, 13). God is also called a Redeemer, delivering his people from their slavery to sin (Exodus 6:6; Job 19:25). (For an explanation of ancient boundary markers, see the note on Proverbs 22:28.)

23:12 The world is full of people who think they know everything. They don't want to be instructed, and they think it shows weakness to learn from others. They are wrong. Listening to others is a sign of wisdom, not weakness. Refusing to learn from others can be a great mistake. It can cause a person who could have been successful to fall flat on his face.

23:29, 30 The soothing comfort of alcohol is only temporary. Real relief comes from dealing with the cause of the anguish and sorrow and turning to God for peace. Don't lose yourself in alcohol; find yourself in God.

24:5 The athlete who thinks—who assesses the situation and plans strategies—has an advantage over a physically stronger but unthinking opponent. And wisdom, not muscle, is certainly what

has put man in charge of the animal kingdom. We exercise regularly and eat well to build our strength; do we take equal pains to develop wisdom? Since wisdom is mightier than strength, it pays to work on it.

24:6 In any major decision concerning college, marriage, career, children, etc., it doesn't show weakness to ask for advice. It shows foolishness not to ask for it. Find good advisers before making any big decision.

24:8 Planning evil can be as wrong as doing it, because what you think determines what you will do. Jesus made this clear when he said that lust makes a man guilty of adultery (Matthew 5:27, 28). God wants pure lives, free from sin; and planning evil spoils the purity even if the evil action has not yet been committed. Should you say, "Then I might as well go ahead and do it, because I've already planned it"? No. You may be just as guilty before God as if you'd committed the act, but you have not yet damaged other people. Stop in your tracks and ask God to forgive you and put you on a different path.

10You are a poor specimen if you can't stand the pressure of adversity.

11, 12Rescue those who are unjustly sentenced to death; don't stand back and let them die. Don't try to disclaim responsibility by saying you didn't know about it. For God, who knows all hearts, knows yours, and he knows you knew! And he will reward everyone according to his deeds.

13, 14My son, honey whets the appetite, and so does wisdom! When you enjoy becoming wise, there is hope for you! A bright future lies ahead!

15, 16O evil man, leave the upright man alone, and quit trying to cheat him out of his rights. Don't you know that this good man, though you trip him up seven times, will each time rise again? But one calamity is enough to lay you low.

17Do not rejoice when your enemy meets trouble. Let there be no gladness when he falls— 18for the Lord may be displeased with you and stop punishing him!

19, 20Don't envy the wicked. Don't covet his riches. For the evil man has no future; his light will be snuffed out.

21, 22My son, watch your step before the Lord and the king, and don't associate with radicals. For you will go down with them to sudden disaster, and who knows where it all will end?

More proverbs of the wise

23It is wrong to sentence the poor, and let the rich go free. 24He who says to the wicked, "You are innocent," shall be cursed by many people of many nations; 25but blessings shall be showered on those who rebuke sin fearlessly.

26It is an honor to receive a frank reply.

27Develop your business first before building your house.

28, 29Don't testify spitefully against an innocent neighbor. Why lie about him? Don't say, "Now I can pay him back for all his meanness to me!"

30, 31I walked by the field of a certain lazy fellow and saw that it was overgrown with thorns, and covered with weeds; and its walls were broken down. 32, 33Then, as I looked, I learned this lesson:

"A little extra sleep,
A little more slumber,
A little folding of the hands to rest"

34means that poverty will break in upon you suddenly like a robber, and violently like a bandit.

C. WISDOM FOR THE LEADERS (25:1—31:31)
These proverbs were collected by Hezekiah's aides. The first section was written by Solomon, and the next two sections were written by others. While we all can learn from these proverbs, many were originally directed toward the king or those who dealt with the king. These are particularly helpful for those who are leaders or aspire to become leaders. The book ends with a description of a truly good wife, who is an example of godly wisdom.

More proverbs by Solomon

25 These proverbs of Solomon were discovered and copied by the aides of King Hezekiah of Judah:

25:1 *These proverbs of Solomon.* 1 Kgs 4:32. *King Hezekiah.* Hezekiah lived 200 years after Solomon.

Cross-references (right margin):

24:10 Job 4:5; Heb 12:3
24:11 1 Sam 16:7; Ps 82:4; Eccles 5:8
24:13 Ps 19:10; Prov 25:16
24:15 Job 5:19; Ps 10:9-12; Prov 6:15; 14:32; 24:21,22
24:17 Ps 35:15; Rom 11:18-21
24:19 Job 15:31; Prov 13:9; 24:1
24:21 Prov 24:15,16; Rom 13:4
24:23 Prov 18:5; 28:21
24:26 Job 6:25; Prov 15:23; 25:12; 27:5
24:28 Prov 20:22; 25:18; Mt 5:39; Rom 12:17
24:30 Job 4:8; Prov 6:6; Isa 5:6,7
24:32 Prov 6:10; 12:24; 23:21
25:1 Prov 1:1

24:10 Adversity can be useful. It shows you who you really are, what kind of character you have developed. In addition, it helps you grow stronger. When Jeremiah questioned God because of the adversity he faced, the Lord asked how he ever expected to face big challenges if the little ones wearied him (Jeremiah 12:5). Don't complain about your problems. The adversity you face today is training you to be strong for the more difficult situations you will face in the future.

24:17, 18 King David, Solomon's father, refused to gloat over the death of his lifelong enemy Saul (see 2 Samuel 1). On the other hand, the nation of Edom gloated over Israel's defeat and was punished by God for this (Obadiah 1:12). To gloat over others' misfortune is to make yourself the avenger and to put yourself in the place of God, who alone is the real judge of all the earth (see Deuteronomy 32:35).

24:27 We should do things in their proper order. If a farmer builds his house in the spring, he misses the planting season and goes a year without food. If a businessman invests his money in a house while his business is struggling to grow, he may lose both. It is possible to work hard and still lose everything, if the work is done in the wrong sequence.

25:1 King Hezekiah's story is told in 2 Kings 18—20; 2 Chronicles

25:2
Deut 29:29
Ezra 6:1
Rom 11:33

25:4
Prov 20:8
Ezek 22:18
Mal 3:2,3

25:6
Ps 131:1
Prov 25:27; 27:2
Mt 12:39
Lk 14:7

25:8
Prov 17:14; 18:6
Mt 5:25

25:11
Prov 15:23

25:12
Prov 15:31
26:23

25:15
Prov 15:1
Eccles 10:4

25:16
Prov 25:27

25:18
Ps 57:4
Prov 12:18
24:28
Jer 9:8

25:19
Job 6:15

25:20
Prov 27:14

25:21
Ex 23:4
2 Kgs 6:22
2 Chron 28:15
Mt 5:44; 6:6
Rom 12:20

25:23
Prov 13:3; 26:20

25:24
Prov 19:13
21:9; 27:15

25:25
2 Cor 7:7
1 Thess 3:5-8

25:26
Ezek 34:18

2, 3It is God's privilege to conceal things, and the king's privilege to discover and invent. You cannot understand the height of heaven, the size of the earth, or all that goes on in the king's mind!

4, 5When you remove dross from silver, you have sterling ready for the silversmith. When you remove corrupt men from the king's court, his reign will be just and fair.

6, 7Don't demand an audience with the king as though you were some powerful prince. It is better to wait for an invitation rather than to be sent back to the end of the line, publicly disgraced!

8, 9, 10Don't be hot-headed and rush to court! You may start something you can't finish and go down before your neighbor in shameful defeat. So discuss the matter with him privately. Don't tell anyone else, lest he accuse you of slander and you can't withdraw what you said.

11Timely advice is as lovely as gold apples in a silver basket.

12It is a badge of honor to accept valid criticism.

13A faithful employee is as refreshing as a cool day in the hot summertime.

14One who doesn't give the gift he promised is like a cloud blowing over a desert without dropping any rain.

15Be patient and you will finally win, for a soft tongue can break hard bones.

16Do you like honey? Don't eat too much of it, or it will make you sick!

17Don't visit your neighbor too often, or you will outwear your welcome!

18Telling lies about someone is as harmful as hitting him with an axe, or wounding him with a sword, or shooting him with a sharp arrow.

19Putting confidence in an unreliable man is like chewing with a sore tooth, or trying to run on a broken foot.

20Being happy-go-lucky around a person whose heart is heavy is as bad as stealing his jacket in cold weather, or rubbing salt in his wounds.

21, 22If your enemy is hungry, give him food! If he is thirsty, give him something to drink! This will make him feel ashamed of himself, and God will reward you.

23As surely as a wind from the north brings cold, just as surely a retort causes anger!

24It is better to live in a corner of an attic than in a beautiful home with a cranky, quarrelsome woman.

25Good news from far away is like cold water to the thirsty.

26If a godly man compromises with the wicked, it is like polluting a fountain or muddying a spring.

25:13 *a cool day,* literally, "snow." **25:20** *rubbing salt in his wounds,* literally, "like vinegar upon soda." **25:23** *cold,* literally, "rain."

29—32; and Isaiah 36—39. He was one of the few kings of Judah who honored the Lord. By contrast, his father Ahaz actually nailed the Temple door shut. Hezekiah restored the Temple, destroyed idol worship centers, and earned the respect of surrounding nations, many of whom brought gifts to God because of Hezekiah. It is not surprising that he had these proverbs copied and read, for "He worked very hard to encourage respect for the Temple, the law, and godly living, and was very successful" (2 Chronicles 31:21).

25:13 It is often difficult to find people you can really trust. A faithful employee is punctual, responsible, honest, and hardworking. An invaluable employee helps take some of the pressure off his or her employer. Find out what your employer needs from you to make his own job easier, and do it.

25:14 Most churches, missions organizations, and Christian groups depend on the gifts of people to keep their ministries going. But many who promise to give, fail to come through. The Bible is very clear about the effect this has on those involved in the ministry. If you pledge to give, make every effort to do so.

25:18 Lying is vicious. Its effects can be as permanent as those of a stab wound. The next time you are tempted to pass on a bit of gossip, imagine yourself striking the victim of your remarks with an axe. This image may shock you into silence.

25:23 It is hard to keep your mouth shut when someone speaks rudely to you, but answering back is a sure step into a full-scale argument. Plan ahead of time to avoid defensive retorts. Either speak softly or say nothing at all. If you control your tongue, you may be able to prevent an angry explosion.

25:26 "Compromise" here means setting aside your standards of right and wrong, allowing the wicked to muddy up your life. This is ugly to those who are counting on your high moral standards.

25:27 Dwelling on the honors you deserve can only be harmful. It can make you bitter, discouraged, or angry, and it will not bring you the honors you think should be yours. Pining for what you should have had may make you miss some honors you could be earning.

²⁷Just as it is harmful to eat too much honey, so also it is bad for men to think about all the honors they deserve!

²⁸A man without self-control is as defenseless as a city with broken-down walls.

26

Honor doesn't go with fools any more than snow with summertime or rain with harvest time!

²An undeserved curse has no effect. Its intended victim will be no more harmed by it than by a sparrow or swallow flitting through the sky.

³Guide a horse with a whip, a donkey with a bridle, and a rebel with a rod to his back!

^{4, 5}When arguing with a rebel, don't use foolish arguments as he does, or you will become as foolish as he is! Prick his conceit with silly replies!

⁶To trust a rebel to convey a message is as foolish as cutting off your feet and drinking poison!

⁷In the mouth of a fool a proverb becomes as useless as a paralyzed leg. ⁸Honoring a rebel will backfire like a stone tied to a slingshot!

⁹A rebel will misapply an illustration so that its point will no more be felt than a thorn in the hand of a drunkard.

¹⁰The master may get better work from an untrained apprentice than from a skilled rebel!

¹¹As a dog returns to its vomit, so a fool repeats his folly.

¹²There is one thing worse than a fool, and that is a man who is conceited.

¹³The lazy man won't go out and work. "There might be a lion outside!" he says. ¹⁴He sticks to his bed like a door to its hinges! ¹⁵He is too tired even to lift his food from his dish to his mouth! ¹⁶Yet in his own opinion he is smarter than seven wise men.

¹⁷Yanking a dog's ears is no more foolish than interfering in an argument that isn't any of your business.

^{18, 19}A man who is caught lying to his neighbor and says, "I was just fooling," is like a madman throwing around firebrands, arrows and death!

²⁰Fire goes out for lack of fuel, and tensions disappear when gossip stops.

²¹A quarrelsome man starts fights as easily as a match sets fire to paper. ²²Gossip is a dainty morsel eaten with great relish.

²³Pretty words may hide a wicked heart, just as a pretty glaze covers a common clay pot.

^{24, 25, 26}A man with hate in his heart may sound pleasant enough, but don't believe him; for he is cursing you in his heart. Though he pretends to be so kind, his hatred will finally come to light for all to see.

26:4, 5 *Prick his conceit with silly replies,* implied. Literally, "Reply to a fool as his folly requires." **26:21** *as easily as a match,* literally, "like hot embers to coals and wood to fire."

25:27	Prov 25:16
26:1	1 Sam 12:17 / Prov 26:8
26:2	Num 23:8 / 2 Sam 16:12 / Ps 109:28
26:3	Ps 32:9 / Prov 10:13
26:4	Prov 23:9; 29:8
26:6	Prov 13:17 / 25:13
26:7	Ps 50:16,17 / Prov 17:7
26:11	Ex 8:15 / 2 Pet 2:22
26:12	Prov 3:7; 28:11
26:13	Prov 15:19
26:14	Prov 6:9; 19:15
26:15	Prov 12:27 / Eccles 4:5
26:17	Prov 3:30; 18:6
26:18	Prov 24:12,28
26:20	Prov 16:28 / Jas 3:6
26:21	Prov 10:12 / 15:18; 29:22
26:22	Prov 18:8; 20:19
26:23	Mt 23:28 / Lk 11:39
26:24	Prov 12:20

25:28 Even though city walls restricted the inhabitants' movements, people were happy to have them. Without walls, they would have been vulnerable to attack by any passing group of marauders. Self-control limits us, to be sure, but it is necessary. An out-of-control life is open to all sorts of enemy attack. Think of self-control as a wall for defense and protection.

26:7 Some people don't learn much from reading these proverbs. Only those who want to be wise have the receptive attitude needed to make the most of them.

26:8 Sometimes when someone in a group causes discord or dissension, the leader tries to make him loyal and productive by giving him a place of privilege or responsibility. This doesn't always work. The dissenter's new power may be just what he needs to destroy the group.

26:9 One way to avoid learning is to refuse to see where an illustration touches your life. Instead of taking its point to heart, a rebel will apply it to his church, his employer, his spouse, or whoever he is rebelling against. The next time you find yourself saying, "So-and-so should really pay attention to that," stop and ask yourself—"Is there a message in it for me?"

26:13–16 If a person is not willing to work, he can find endless excuses to avoid it. But laziness is more dangerous than a prowling lion. The less you do, the less you want to do, and the more useless you become. To overcome laziness, take a few small steps toward change. Set a concrete, realistic goal. Figure out the steps needed to reach it. Pray for strength and persistence. And follow those steps. To keep your excuses from making you useless, stop making useless excuses.

26:17 Yanking a dog's ears is a good way to get bitten, and interfering in arguments is a good way to get hurt. Many times both arguers will turn on the person who interferes. It is best simply to keep out of arguments that are none of your business. If you must become involved, try to wait until the arguers have stopped fighting and cooled off a bit. Then maybe you can help them mend their differences and their relationship.

26:20 Talking about every little irritation only keeps the fires of anger going. Refusing to discuss them cuts the fuel line and makes the fires die out. Does someone continually irritate you? Try cutting off the gossip, and see if your irritation dies from lack of fuel.

26:27
Ps 7:15
26:28
Prov 6:24

27:1
Mt 6:34
Lk 12:19,20
Jas 4:13-16
27:2
Prov 25:27
2 Cor 10:12,18
27:4
Prov 6:34
27:5
Prov 24:26
25:12; 28:23
27:6
Ps 141:5
Mt 26:49
27:8
1 Sam 26:19
Prov 21:16
Heb 11:13
27:10
1 Kgs 12:6
2 Chron 10:6
Prov 17:17
27:11
Prov 10:1; 23:15
27:12
Prov 22:3
27:13
Prov 6:1-5
27:14
Prov 26:18,19
27:15
Prov 19:13
21:9; 25:24

²⁷The man who sets a trap for others will get caught in it himself. Roll a boulder down on someone, and it will roll back and crush you.

²⁸Flattery is a form of hatred and wounds cruelly.

27 Don't brag about your plans for tomorrow—wait and see what happens. ²Don't praise yourself; let others do it!

³A rebel's frustrations are heavier than sand and rocks.

⁴Jealousy is more dangerous and cruel than anger.

⁵Open rebuke is better than hidden love!

⁶Wounds from a friend are better than kisses from an enemy!

⁷Even honey seems tasteless to a man who is full; but if he is hungry, he'll eat anything!

⁸A man who strays from home is like a bird that wanders from its nest.

⁹Friendly suggestions are as pleasant as perfume.

¹⁰Never abandon a friend—either yours or your father's. Then you won't need to go to a distant relative for help in your time of need.

¹¹My son, how happy I will be if you turn out to be sensible! It will be a public honor to me.

¹²A sensible man watches for problems ahead and prepares to meet them. The simpleton never looks, and suffers the consequences.

¹³The world's poorest credit risk is the man who agrees to pay a stranger's debts.

¹⁴If you shout a pleasant greeting to a friend too early in the morning, he will count it as a curse!

¹⁵A constant dripping on a rainy day and a cranky woman are much alike! ¹⁶You can no more stop her complaints than you can stop the wind or hold onto anything with oil-slick hands.

¹⁷A friendly discussion is as stimulating as the sparks that fly when iron strikes iron.

THE FOUR TONGUES	*The Controlled Tongue*	Those with this speech pattern think before speaking, know when silence is best, and give wise advice.	10:14, 19; 11:12, 13; 12:16; 13:3; 15:1, 4, 28; 16:23; 17:14, 27, 28; 18:4; 21:23; 24:26; 26:17
What we say probably affects more people than any other action we take. It is not surprising, then, to find that Proverbs gives special attention to words and how they are used. Four common speech patterns are described in Proverbs. The first two should be copied, while the last two should be avoided.	*The Caring Tongue*	Those with this speech pattern speak truthfully while seeking to encourage.	10:32; 12:18, 25; 15:23, 26; 16:24; 25:15; 27:9
	The Conniving Tongue	Those with this speech pattern are filled with wrong motives, gossip, slander, and twist truth.	6:12–14; 8:13; 16:28; 18:8; 25:18; 26:4, 5, 20–28
	The Careless Tongue	Those with this speech pattern are filled with lies, curses, quick-tempered words—which can lead to rebellion and destruction.	10:18, 32; 11:9; 12:16, 18; 15:4; 17:9, 14, 19; 18:21; 20:19; 25:23

Other verses about our speech include: 10:11, 20, 31; 12:6, 17–19; 13:2; 14:3; 19:5, 28; 25:11; 27:2, 5, 14, 17; 29:9

27:6 Who would prefer a friend's cut to an enemy's kiss? Anyone who considers the source. A friend who has your best interests at heart may have to give you unpleasant advice at times, but you know it is for your own good. An enemy, by contrast, may whisper sweet words and happily send you on your way to ruin. A friend's advice, no matter how painful, is much better than an enemy's kiss.

27:15, 16 Nagging, a steady stream of unwanted advice, is a form of torture. People nag because they think they're not getting through, but nagging hinders communication more than it helps. When tempted to engage in this destructive habit, stop and examine your motives. Are you more concerned about

yourself—getting your way, being right—than about the person you are pretending to help? If you are truly concerned about other people, is there a more effective way to get through to them? Surprise them with words of love, and see what happens.

27:17 A meeting of minds can help people see their ideas with new clarity, refine them, and shape them into brilliant insights. This requires discussion partners who can challenge each other and stimulate thought—people who focus on the idea without involving their egos in the discussion, people who know how to attack the thought and not the thinker. Two friends who bring their ideas together can help each other become sharper.

¹⁸A workman may eat from the orchard he tends; anyone should be rewarded who protects another's interests.

¹⁹A mirror reflects a man's face, but what he is really like is shown by the kind of friends he chooses.

²⁰Ambition and death are alike in this: neither is ever satisfied.

²¹The purity of silver and gold can be tested in a crucible, but a man is tested by his reaction to men's praise.

²²You can't separate a rebel from his foolishness though you crush him to powder.

²³, ²⁴Riches can disappear fast. And the king's crown doesn't stay in his family forever—so watch your business interests closely. Know the state of your flocks and your herds; ²⁵, ²⁶, ²⁷then there will be lamb's wool enough for clothing, and goat's milk enough for food for all your household after the hay is harvested, and the new crop appears, and the mountain grasses are gathered in.

28 The wicked flee when no one is chasing them! But the godly are bold as lions!

²When there is moral rot within a nation, its government topples easily; but with honest, sensible leaders there is stability.

³When a poor man oppresses those even poorer, he is like an unexpected flood sweeping away their last hope.

⁴To complain about the law is to praise wickedness. To obey the law is to fight evil.

⁵Evil men don't understand the importance of justice, but those who follow the Lord are much concerned about it.

⁶Better to be poor and honest than rich and a cheater.

⁷Young men who are wise obey the law; a son who is a member of a lawless gang is a shame to his father.

⁸Income from exploiting the poor will end up in the hands of someone who pities them.

⁹God doesn't listen to the prayers of those who flout the law.

¹⁰A curse on those who lead astray the godly. But men who encourage the upright to do good shall be given a worthwhile reward.

¹¹Rich men are conceited, but their real poverty is evident to the poor.

¹²When the godly are successful, everyone is glad. When the wicked succeed, everyone is sad.

¹³A man who refuses to admit his mistakes can never be successful. But if he confesses and forsakes them, he gets another chance.

27:20 *Ambition,* literally, "A man's eyes." Possibly the reference is to lust. **27:23, 24** *business,* implied.

Cross references (right margin):

27:18
Lk 12:42
2 Tim 2:6

27:20
Prov 30:15
Eccles 1:8-11
Hab 2:5

27:21
1 Sam 18:7,8
2 Sam 14:25
Ps 12:6
Prov 17:3
Zech 13:9
Lk 6:26

27:22
Prov 23:35
26:11
Jer 5:3

27:23
Job 19:9

28:1
Ps 27:1,2

28:2
1 Kgs 16:8-28
2 Kgs 15:8-15
Hos 7:7; 8:4

28:4
Rom 1:32

28:5
Ps 92:6,7
Prov 2:9; 21:15

28:6
Prov 12:9

28:7
Prov 2:1
23:25,26; 29:3

28:8
Ex 22:25
Deut 23:19,20

28:9
Ps 66:18; 109:7
Prov 15:8

28:10
Prov 26:27
Mt 5:19; 18:6

28:11
Prov 18:23
25:27; 26:12

28:13
Ps 32:1-11
1 Jn 1:6-9

27:18 With all the problems and concerns a leader has, it can be easy to overlook the very people who most deserve attention—faithful employees or volunteers. The people who stand behind you, who work hard and help you get the job done, deserve to share in your success. Be sure that in all your worrying, planning, and organizing, you don't forget the people who are helping you the most.

27:21 How does praise affect you? Do you work to get it? Do you work harder after you've gotten it? Do you do whatever you must to earn it? Your attitude toward praise tells a lot about your character. People of high integrity are not swayed by praise. They are attuned to their inner convictions, and they do what they should whether or not they are praised for it.

28:2 One person's selfishness quickly affects others. A selfish employee who steals from his company impairs its efficiency. A selfish driver who drinks before taking the wheel makes the state highways unsafe. A selfish spouse who has an adulterous affair often breaks up several families. When enough people live for themselves with little concern for how their actions affect others, the resulting moral rot can topple an entire nation. Are you part of the problem . . . or the solution?

28:5 Because justice is part of God's character, a person who follows God treats others with justice. The beginning of justice is concern for what is happening to others. A Christian cannot be indifferent to human suffering, because God isn't. And we certainly must not contribute to human suffering through selfish business practices or unfair government policies. Be sure you are more concerned for justice than you are for the bottom line.

28:9 God does not listen to our prayers if we intend to go back to our sin as soon as we get off our knees. If we want to forsake our sin and follow him, however, he willingly listens—no matter how bad our sin has been. What closes his ears is not the depth of our sin, but our secret intention to do it again.

28:11 Through dependence on God in their struggles, the poor develop a richness of spirit that no amount of wealth can provide. The rich man can lose all his material wealth, while no one can take away the poor man's character. Don't be jealous of the rich; money may be all they will ever have.

28:13 It is hard to learn from a mistake you don't acknowledge making. And what good is a mistake if it can't teach you

14Blessed is the man who reveres God, but the man who doesn't care is headed for serious trouble.

15A wicked ruler is as dangerous to the poor as a lion or bear attacking them.

16Only a stupid prince will oppress his people, but a king will have a long reign if he hates dishonesty and bribes.

17A murderer's conscience will drive him into hell. Don't stop him!

18Good men will be rescued from harm, but cheaters will be destroyed.

19Hard work brings prosperity; playing around brings poverty.

20The man who wants to do right will get a rich reward. But the man who wants to get rich quick will quickly fail.

21Giving preferred treatment to rich people is a clear case of selling one's soul for a piece of bread.

22Trying to get rich quick is evil and leads to poverty.

**THE CHARAC-
TERISTICS OF
DILIGENCE AND
LAZINESS**
Proverbs makes
it clear that
diligence—being
willing to work
hard and do
one's best at any
job given to him
or her—is a vital
part of wise living.
We work hard
not to become
rich, famous, or
admired (although
those may be by-
products), but to
serve God with
our very best
during our lives.

The Diligent	The Lazy	References
Get rich	Are soon poor	10:4
Hard work is wise	Laziness causes one to sleep away opportunities	10:5
	Are a pain to their employers	10:26
Hard work gives prosperity	Only fools idle away the time	12:11
Hard work returns blessings		12:14
Become leaders	Never succeed	12:24
Make good use of everything they find	Waste good opportunities	12:27
Prosper	Want much but get little	13:4
Bring profit	Experience poverty	14:23
Have an easy path	Have trouble all through life	15:19
	Have idle hands, which are the devil's workshop	16:27
	Become saboteurs	18:9
	Sleep soundly and go hungry	19:15
	Are so lazy they won't feed themselves	19:24
Work even when inconvenient in order to reap the reward		20:4
Stay awake, work hard	Love sleep and end in poverty	20:13
Are steady plodders, reaping prosperity	Make hasty speculations, leading to poverty	21:5
	Love pleasure and become poor	21:17
Love to give	Desire things but refuse to work for them	21:25, 26
	Are full of excuses for not working	22:13
Will be successful and stand before kings		22:29
	Sleep too much which leads to poverty	24:30–34
	Refuse to work but think themselves wise	26:13–16
Reap prosperity through hard work	Experience poverty because of laziness	28:19

---

something? To learn from an error you need to admit it, analyze it, and make adjustments so that it doesn't happen again. Everybody makes mistakes, but only fools repeat them.

28:13 Something in each of us strongly resists admitting we are wrong. That is why we admire people who openly and graciously admit their mistakes. These people have a strong self-image. They do not always have to be right to feel good about themselves. Be willing to reconsider—to admit you are wrong and to change

your plans when it is necessary.

28:17 A sinner's conscience will drive him either into the hell of guilt and on to repentance, or into hell itself because of a refusal to repent. It is no act of kindness to try to make him feel better; the more guilt he feels, the more likely he is to turn to God and repent. If we interfere with the natural consequences of his act, we may make it easier for him to continue in sin.

²³In the end, people appreciate frankness more than flattery.

²⁴A man who robs his parents and says, "What's wrong with that?" is no better than a murderer.

²⁵Greed causes fighting; trusting God leads to prosperity.

²⁶A man is a fool to trust himself! But those who use God's wisdom are safe.

²⁷If you give to the poor, your needs will be supplied! But a curse upon those who close their eyes to poverty.

²⁸When the wicked prosper, good men go away; when the wicked meet disaster, good men return.

28:23
Ps 141:5
Prov 29:5,6
Mt 18:15

28:24
Prov 19:26

28:26
Job 28:28
Prov 3:5

28:27
Prov 11:24
19:17

29 The man who is often reproved but refuses to accept criticism will suddenly be broken and never have another chance.

²With good men in authority, the people rejoice; but with the wicked in power, they groan.

³A wise son makes his father happy, but a lad who hangs around with prostitutes disgraces him.

⁴A just king gives stability to his nation, but one who demands bribes destroys it.

^{5, 6}Flattery is a trap; evil men are caught in it, but good men stay away and sing for joy.

⁷The good man knows the poor man's rights; the godless don't care.

⁸Fools start fights everywhere while wise men try to keep peace.

⁹There's no use arguing with a fool. He only rages and scoffs, and tempers flare.

¹⁰The godly pray for those who long to kill them.

¹¹A rebel shouts in anger; a wise man holds his temper in and cools it.

¹²A wicked ruler will have wicked aides on his staff.

¹³Rich and poor are alike in this: each depends on God for light.

¹⁴A king who is fair to the poor shall have a long reign.

¹⁵Scolding and spanking a child helps him to learn. Left to himself, he brings shame to his mother.

¹⁶When rulers are wicked, their people are too; but good men will live to see the tyrant's downfall.

¹⁷Discipline your son and he will give you happiness and peace of mind.

¹⁸Where there is ignorance of God, crime runs wild; but what a wonderful thing it is for a nation to know and keep his laws.

29:1
Prov 1:24,25
13:18; 15:31,32

29:2
Esth 8:15,16
Prov 11:10

29:3
Prov 6:26; 10:1
Lk 15:13

29:4
Prov 8:15

29:5
Ps 5:9
Prov 28:23

29:7
Ps 41:1

29:8
Prov 13:2; 17:19
Jas 3:13-18

29:11
Prov 14:17,29

29:13
Job 3:19

29:14
Ps 72:4
Prov 16:12; 29:4

29:16
Ps 37:34-38

29:18
Ex 32:25
Ps 1:1,2; 74:9

28:26 For many people, the rugged individualist is a hero. We admire the bold, self-directed men and women who know what they want and fight for it. They are self-reliant, neither giving nor asking advice. What a contrast to God's way. A person can't know the future and can't predict the consequences of his choices with certainty. The totally self-reliant person is self-condemned by self-proclaimed independence, but the wise person is protected by dependence on God.

28:27 God wants us to identify with the needy, not ignore them. The second part of this proverb could be restated, "A blessing on those who open their eyes to human need." If we help others when they are in trouble, they will be open to do whatever they can to return the favor (see Proverbs 11:24, 25). Paul promises that God will supply all our needs (Philippians 4:19); he does this through other people. What can you do today to help God supply someone's need?

29:1 Making the same mistake over and over is an invitation to disaster. Someday you will have to face the consequences of your refusal to learn. If your mistake is refusing God's invitations or rejecting his commands, the consequences will be especially serious. In the end, God may have to turn you away.

29:5, 6 We all want to be liked, so we are all vulnerable to flattery. But flattery can be a dangerous trap. To avoid falling into it, be realistic about yourself. Set goals and work toward them, and you will know when you deserve praise and when you need rebuke. This knowledge can make you immune to flattery and protect you from being manipulated by the people who use it.

29:10 Proverbs is full of short characterizations that, put together, give us a picture of what it means to be a godly ("God-like") person. This one parallels Jesus' counsel to pray for our enemies (Matthew 5:44). Few acts are harder to do; that is why godliness is rare. Measured by this standard, are you like God?

29:15 As parents, we weary of disciplining our children. It seems that all we do is nag, scold, and punish. When you're tempted to give up and let them do what they want, or when you wonder if you've ruined every chance for a loving relationship with them, remember—kind, firm discipline helps them learn, and learning makes them wise. Consistent, loving discipline will ultimately teach them to discipline themselves.

29:16 In any organization—whether a church, a business, a family, or a government—the climate comes from the top. The people become like their leaders. What kind of climate are you setting for the people you lead?

29:18 These proverbs were written under a monarchy. If the king was law-abiding, the people tended to follow suit. In a democracy, the people themselves are the leaders. When they turn to a standard higher than themselves and keep God's moral laws, the nation becomes strong. When everyone does whatever seems "right in his own eyes" (Judges 17:6), the nation becomes weak and can no longer effectively protect its citizens. Don't be ashamed of your high moral standards—they are making your country a better place.

29:20
Prov 26:12
29:22
Prov 22:24
29:23
Prov 15:33; 22:4
Dan 4:30
29:24
Prov 1:10,11
29:25
Prov 16:7
29:27
Mt 10:22; 24:9
2 Cor 6:14-18

[19]Sometimes mere words are not enough—discipline is needed. For the words may not be heeded.

[20]There is more hope for a fool than for a man of quick temper.

[21]Pamper a servant from childhood, and he will expect you to treat him as a son!

[22]A hot-tempered man starts fights and gets into all kinds of trouble.

[23]Pride ends in a fall, while humility brings honor.

[24]A man who assists a thief must really hate himself! For he knows the consequence but does it anyway.

[25]Fear of man is a dangerous trap, but to trust in God means safety.

[26]Do you want justice? Don't fawn on the judge, but ask the Lord for it!

[27]The good hate the badness of the wicked. The wicked hate the goodness of the good.

Wise sayings of Agur

30:2
Job 42:3-6
30:4
Job 26:8
Ps 24:2; 68:18
Isa 45:18
30:5
Ps 3:3; 12:6
18:30; 84:11
30:6
Deut 4:2; 12:32
Rev 22:18

30 *These are the messages of Agur, son of Jakeh addressed to Ithiel and Ucal:* [2]I am tired out, O God, and ready to die. I am too stupid even to call myself a human being! [3]I cannot understand man, let alone God. [4]Who else but God goes back and forth to heaven? Who else holds the wind in his fists, and wraps up the oceans in his cloak? Who but God has created the world? If there is any other, what is his name—and his Son's name—if you know it?

[5]Every word of God proves true. He defends all who come to him for protection. [6]Do not add to his words, lest he rebuke you, and you be found a liar.

[7]O God, I beg two favors from you before I die: [8]First, help me never to tell a lie.

29:19 *Sometimes,* literally, "for a servant." **30:3** *I cannot understand man,* literally, "I have not learned wisdom."

LEADERSHIP
Since many of the proverbs came from King Solomon, it is natural to expect some of his interest to be directed toward leadership.

Qualities of good leadership	References
Hard work	12:24
Reliable communication	13:17
Don't penalize people for good behavior or reward evil people	17:26
Know the facts before making decisions	18:13
Open to new ideas	18:15
Listen to both sides of the story	18:17
Wise planning and common sense	24:3, 4
Can stand under adversity	24:10
Stands well under praise	27:21

Benefits of good leadership	
Safety	11:14
Strength, profitable to all	24:3
The people rejoice	29:2

What happens without good leadership	
People have only pain	25:19
Honoring the wrong people backfires	26:8
A wicked ruler is dangerous	28:15
A wicked ruler has wicked aides	29:12
When rulers are wicked, so are the people	29:16

Other verses to study: 24:27; 25:13; 26:6, 10; 27:18

29:25 Fear of man can hamper everything you try to do. In extreme forms, it can make you afraid to leave your home. By contrast, fear of God—respect, reverence, and trust—is liberating. Why fear people who can do no eternal harm? Instead, fear God who can turn the harm intended by others into good for those who trust him.

30:1 The origin of these sayings is not clear. Nothing is known about Agur except that he was a wise teacher from Massa, the kingdom under Lemuel (see the note on Proverbs 31:1).

30:2-4 Since God is infinite, certain aspects of his nature will always remain a mystery. Compare these questions with the questions God asked Job (Job 38—41).

30:7-9 Having too much money can be dangerous, but so can having too little. Being poor can, in fact, be hazardous to spiritual as well as physical health. On the other hand, being rich is not the answer. As Jesus pointed out, rich people have trouble getting into God's kingdom (Matthew 19:23, 24). Like Paul, we can learn "how to live on almost nothing or with everything" (Philippians 4:12), but our lives have a better chance of being more effective if we have neither too much nor too little money.

Second, give me neither poverty nor riches! Give me just enough to satisfy my needs! 9For if I grow rich, I may become content without God. And if I am too poor, I may steal, and thus insult God's holy name.

30:9
Deut 8:12; 31:20
Neh 9:25
Hos 13:6

10Never falsely accuse a man to his employer, lest he curse you for your sin.

30:10
Eccles 7:21

11, 12There are those who curse their father and mother, and feel themselves faultless despite their many sins. 13, 14They are proud beyond description, arrogant, disdainful. They devour the poor with teeth as sharp as knives!

30:11
Ex 21:17
Prov 20:20

15, 16There are two things never satisfied, like a leech forever craving more: no, three things! no, four! Hell, the barren womb, a barren desert, fire.

30:13
Job 29:17
Ps 57:4
Lk 18:11

17A man who mocks his father and despises his mother shall have his eye plucked out by ravens and eaten by vultures.

30:15
Gen 30:1,2
Prov 27:20

18, 19There are three things too wonderful for me to understand—no, four!

30:17
Gen 9:22
Prov 19:26
20:20

How an eagle glides through the sky.
How a serpent crawls upon a rock.
How a ship finds its way across the heaving ocean.
The growth of love between a man and a girl.

30:18
Job 39:27; 42:3
Ps 139:6

20There is another thing too: how a prostitute can sin and then say, "What's wrong with that?"

30:20
Prov 7:13

21, 22, 23There are three things that make the earth tremble—no, four it cannot stand:

30:21
1 Sam 25:25
Ps 14:1
Prov 17:7,21

A slave who becomes a king.
A rebel who prospers.
A bitter woman when she finally marries.
A servant girl who marries her mistress' husband.

24-28There are four things that are small but unusually wise:

30:24
Lev 11:5
Job 12:7-9
Ps 104:18
Prov 6:6-8
Joel 1:6

Ants: they aren't strong, but store up food for the winter.
Cliff badgers: delicate little animals who protect themselves by living among the rocks.
The locusts: though they have no leader, they stay together in swarms.
The lizards: they are easy to catch and kill, yet are found even in king's palaces!

29, 30, 31There are three stately monarchs in the earth—no, four:

30:29
Mic 5:8
Prov 20:2

The lion, king of the animals. He won't turn aside for anyone.
The peacock.
The male goat.
A king as he leads his army.

32If you have been a fool by being proud or plotting evil, don't brag about it—cover your mouth with your hand in shame.

30:32
Job 21:5; 40:4
Prov 17:27,28
Mic 7:16

33As the churning of cream yields butter, and a blow to the nose causes bleeding, so anger causes quarrels.

30:33
Prov 15:18
16:28; 26:21
29:22

30:18, 19 *The growth of love between a man and a girl,* literally, "the way of a man with a maid." Some linguists believe the meaning is, "why a girl will let herself be seduced." 30:21-23 *marries her mistress' husband,* literally, "who succeeds her mistress."

30:15ff "Two things . . . no, three things! no, four!" This is a poetic way of saying the list is not complete. The writer of these proverbs is observing the world with delighted interest. Verses 15–30 are an invitation to look from the perspective of a keen observer. There are many lessons we can learn from nature.

30:24–28 Ants can teach us about preparation; badgers about

wise building; locusts about cooperation and order; and lizards about fearlessness.

31:1 Nothing is known about Lemuel except that he was a king who received wise teachings from his mother. His name means "devoted to God." The kingdom of Massa, home of both Lemuel and Agur (the author of the proverbs in chapter 30), is also

Wise sayings of Lemuel

31 *These are the wise sayings of King Lemuel of Massa, taught to him at his mother's knee:*

31:3
Prov 5:9; 7:26

²O my son, whom I have dedicated to the Lord, ³do not spend your time with women—the royal pathway to destruction.

31:4
Prov 20:1
Eccles 10:16,17

⁴And it is not for kings, O Lemuel, to drink wine and whiskey. ⁵For if they drink they may forget their duties and be unable to give justice to those who are oppressed. ⁶, ⁷Hard liquor is for sick men at the brink of death, and wine for those in deep depression. Let them drink to forget their poverty and misery.

31:5
Deut 16:19
Prov 17:15

31:8
Job 29:12-17

⁸You should defend those who cannot help themselves. ⁹Yes, speak up for the poor and helpless, and see that they get justice.

A truly good wife

31:10
Ruth 3:11
Prov 8:11; 12:4

¹⁰If you can find a truly good wife, she is worth more than precious gems! ¹¹Her husband can trust her, and she will richly satisfy his needs. ¹²She will not hinder him, but help him all her life. ¹³She finds wool and flax and busily spins it. ¹⁴She buys imported foods, brought by ship from distant ports. ¹⁵She gets up before dawn to prepare breakfast for her household, and plans the day's work for her servant girls. ¹⁶She goes out to inspect a field, and buys it; with her own hands she plants a vineyard. ¹⁷She is energetic, a hard worker, ¹⁸and watches for bargains. She works far into the night!

31:11
1 Pet 3:1,2

31:13
Gen 18:6
24:18-20

31:19
Deut 15:11
Job 31:16
Prov 22:9
Rom 12:13

¹⁹, ²⁰She sews for the poor, and generously helps those in need. ²¹She has no fear of winter for her household, for she has made warm clothes for all of them. ²²She also upholsters with finest tapestry; her own clothing is beautifully made—a purple gown of pure linen. ²³Her husband is well known, for he sits in the council chamber with the other civic leaders. ²⁴She makes belted linen garments to sell to the merchants.

31:22
Ps 45:13,14
Ezek 16:9,10
1 Pet 3:3

31:23
Job 29:7

31:25
Prov 14:26

²⁵She is a woman of strength and dignity, and has no fear of old age. ²⁶When she speaks, her words are wise, and kindness is the rule for everything she says. ²⁷She watches carefully all that goes on throughout her household, and is never lazy. ²⁸Her children stand and bless her; so does her husband. He praises her with these words: ²⁹"There are many fine women in the world, but you are the best of them all!"

31:26
Prov 11:16

31:27
Prov 6:6-11

31:30
Prov 1:7; 8:13

³⁰Charm can be deceptive and beauty doesn't last, but a woman who fears and reverences God shall be greatly praised. ³¹Praise her for the many fine things she does. These good deeds of hers shall bring her honor and recognition from people of importance.

31:31
Ps 128:2,3

31:1 *King Lemuel of Massa,* or, *"of King Lemuel the oracle."* **31:31** *These good deeds of hers shall bring her honor and recognition from people of importance,* literally, *"Give her the fruit of her hands; and let her works praise her in the gates."*

---

unknown. It may be the same as one of the twelve tribes of Ishmael listed in Genesis 25:14. If this is the case, then Lemuel and Agur were not Jews, but Arabs who chose to worship the one true God.

31:4–7 Drunkenness might be understandable among unbelievers who are on the brink of death, but it is inexcusable for national leaders. Alcohol clouds the mind and can lead to injustice and poor decisions. Leaders have better things to do than anesthetize themselves with alcohol.

31:10–31 Proverbs has a lot to say about women. How fitting that the book ends with a picture of "the best of them all"—a woman of strong character, great wisdom, many skills, and great compassion.

Some people have the mistaken idea that the ideal woman in the Bible is retiring, servile, and entirely domestic. Not so! This woman is an excellent wife and mother. She is also a manufacturer, importer, manager, realtor, farmer, seamstress, upholsterer, and merchant. Her strength and dignity do not come from her amazing achievements, however. They are a result of her reverence for God. In our society where physical appearance counts for so much, it may surprise us to realize that her

appearance is never mentioned. Her attractiveness comes entirely from her character.

The woman described in this chapter has outstanding abilities. Her family's social position is high. In fact, she may not be one woman at all—she may be a composite portrait of ideal womanhood. Do not see her as a model to imitate in every detail; your days are not long enough to do everything she does! See her instead as an inspiration to be all you can be. We can't be just like her, but we can learn from her industry, integrity, and resourcefulness.

31:31 The book of Proverbs begins with the command to trust and reverence the Lord (1:7) and ends with the picture of a woman who fulfills this command. Her qualities are mentioned throughout the book: hard work, fear of God, respect for spouse, foresight, encouragement, care for others, concern for the poor, wisdom in handling money. These qualities, when coupled with fear of God, lead to enjoyment, success, honor, and worth. Proverbs is very practical for our day because it shows us how to become wise, make good decisions, and live according to God's ideal.

VITAL STATISTICS

PURPOSE:
To spare future generations the bitterness of learning through their own experience that life is meaningless apart from God

AUTHOR:
Solomon, although no passages mention him by name

TO WHOM WRITTEN:
Solomon's subjects in particular, and all people in general

DATE WRITTEN:
Probably around 935 B.C., late in Solomon's life

SETTING:
Solomon looks back on his life, much of which was lived apart from God

KEY VERSE:
"Here is my final conclusion: fear God and obey his commandments, for this is the entire duty of man" (12:13).

EMPTY, futile, and hollow are words which capture the feelings of disappointment and disillusionment. This is the life experience of many. They strive to find the "good life"—filled with possessions, power, and pleasure—only to find life empty and meaningless. Such disappointment ends in despair.

Almost 3,000 years ago, Solomon spoke of this human dilemma; but the insights and applications of his message are relevant in our century. Ecclesiastes, Solomon's written sermon, is an analysis of life's experiences and a critical essay about its meaning. In this profound book, Solomon takes us on a mental journey through his life, and he explains how everything he tried, tested, or tasted was useless (2:11), irrational (2:17), pointless (4:8), foolish (4:16), and empty (6:12)—an exercise in futility. And remember, these words are from one who "had it all"—tremendous power, wisdom, and wealth. After this biographical tour, Solomon makes his triumphant conclusion, "Fear God and obey his commandments, for this is the entire duty of man. For God will judge us for everything we do, including every hidden thing, good or bad" (12:13, 14).

When Solomon became king, he asked God for wisdom (2 Chronicles 1:7–12), and he became the wisest man in the world (1 Kings 4:29–34). He studied, taught, judged, and wrote. Kings and leaders from other nations came to Jerusalem to learn from him. But with all of his practical insight on life, Solomon failed to heed his own advice, and his life began its downward spiral. Near the end of his life, he looked back with an attitude of humility and repentance. He took stock of the world as he had experienced it, hoping to spare his readers the bitterness of learning through personal experience that everything apart from God is empty, hollow, and meaningless.

Although the tone of Ecclesiastes is negative and pessimistic, we must not conclude that the only chapter worth reading and applying is the last where he draws his conclusions. In reality, the entire book is filled with practical wisdom (how to accomplish things in the world and stay out of trouble) and spiritual wisdom (how to find and know eternal values). Solomon had a very honest approach to life. All of his remarks relating to the futility of life are there for a purpose—to lead people to seek true happiness in God alone. He was not trying to destroy all hope, but direct our hopes to the only One who can truly fulfill them. Solomon affirms the value of knowledge, relationships, work, and pleasure; but only *in their proper place*. All of these temporal things in life must be seen in light of the eternal.

Read Ecclesiastes and learn about life. Hear the stern warnings and dire predictions, and commit yourself to honor your Creator now (12:1).

THE BLUEPRINT

1. Solomon's personal experience
   (1:1—2:26)
2. Solomon's general observations
   (3:1—5:20)
3. Solomon's practical counsel
   (6:1—8:15)
4. Solomon's final conclusion
   (8:16—12:14)

Ecclesiastes shows the paths in life that lead to emptiness and helps us discover true purpose in life. Such wisdom can spare us from the emptiness that results from a life without God. Solomon teaches that meaning in life is not found in knowledge, money, pleasure, work, or popularity. True satisfaction comes from knowing that what we are doing is part of God's purpose for our lives. This is a book which can help free us from our scramble for power, approval, and money, and draw us closer to God.

MEGATHEMES

THEME	EXPLANATION	IMPORTANCE
Searching	Solomon searched for satisfaction almost like it was a scientific experiment. He discovered that life without God was a long and fruitless search for enjoyment, meaning, and fulfillment. True happiness is not in our power to accumulate or attain because we always desire more than we can have. There are circumstances beyond our control which can snatch away our possessions or attainments.	People are still searching. Yet the more they try to get, the more they realize how little they really have. No pleasure or happiness is possible without God. Above everything we should strive to know and love God.
Emptiness	Solomon shows how empty it is to pursue this life's pleasures rather than a relationship with an eternal God. The search for pleasure, wealth, and success is ultimately disappointing. Nothing in the world can satisfy our longing, restless hearts.	The cure for emptiness is to center on God. Fear God throughout your life and fill your life with serving God and others rather than selfish pleasures.
Work	Solomon tried to shake people's confidence in their own efforts, abilities, and wisdom, and direct them to faith in God as the only sound basis for living. Without God, there is no lasting reward or benefit in hard work.	Work done with the wrong attitude leaves us empty. Work accepted as an assignment from God can be seen as a gift. Examine what you expect from your efforts. God gives you abilities and opportunities to work so you can use your time well.
Death	The certainty of death makes all merely human achievements futile. God has a plan for human destiny that goes beyond life and death. The reality of aging and dying reminds us of the end to come when God will judge each person's life.	Because life is short, we need wisdom which is greater than this world can offer. We need the words of God. If we listen to him, his wisdom spares us the bitterness of futile human experience.
Wisdom	Human wisdom doesn't contain all the answers. Knowledge and education have their limits. To understand life, we need the wisdom that can be found only in God's word to us—the Bible.	When we realize that God will evaluate all we do, we should learn to live wisely, remembering that he is present each day, and obeying his guidelines for living. We can only have God's wisdom when we find God.

1. Solomon's personal experience

Everything is futile

1 The author: Solomon of Jerusalem, King David's son, "The Preacher."
²In my opinion, nothing is worthwhile; everything is futile. ³⁻⁷For what does a man get for all his hard work?

Generations come and go but it makes no difference. The sun rises and sets and hurries around to rise again. The wind blows south and north, here and there, twisting back and forth, getting nowhere. The rivers run into the sea but the sea is never full, and the water returns again to the rivers, and flows again to the sea . . . ⁸⁻¹¹everything is unutterably weary and tiresome. No matter how much we see, we are never satisfied; no matter how much we hear, we are not content.

History merely repeats itself. Nothing is truly new; it has all been done or said before. What can you point to that is new? How do you know it didn't exist long ages ago? We don't remember what happened in those former times, and in the future generations no one will remember what we have done back here.

The king finds wisdom meaningless

¹²⁻¹⁵I, the Preacher, was king of Israel, living in Jerusalem. And I applied myself to search for understanding about everything in the universe. I discovered that the lot of man, which God has dealt to him, is not a happy one. It is all foolishness, chasing the wind. What is wrong cannot be righted; it is water over the dam; and there is no use thinking of what might have been.

¹⁶, ¹⁷, ¹⁸I said to myself, "Look, I am better educated than any of the kings before me in Jerusalem. I have greater wisdom and knowledge." So I worked hard to be

1:1 *Solomon,* implied. Literally, "the words of the Preacher, the son (or descendant) of David, King of Jerusalem."
1:3-7 *it makes no difference,* literally, "but the earth remains forever." *getting nowhere,* implied. **1:16-18** *So I worked hard to be wise instead of foolish,* or, "I sought to learn about composure and madness."

Marginal references:
1:1 Eccles 1:12
1:2 Ps 39:5,6 62:9; 144:4 Rom 8:20
1:3 Ps 19:4-6 Eccles 2:11 3:9; 5:16
1:6 Eccles 11:5
1:8 Prov 27:20 Eccles 4:8 6:10; 9:5
1:11 Eccles 2:16; 9:5
1:12 Eccles 7:27
1:13 Eccles 1:17 3:10,11; 7:25
1:14 Eccles 2:11
1:16 Eccles 12:12

1:1 The author, probably Solomon, referred to himself as *The Preacher,* meaning "one who gathers or assembles." He was both assembling people to hear a message and gathering wise sayings (proverbs). Solomon, one person in the Bible who had everything (wisdom, power, riches, honor, reputation, God's favor), was the one who discussed the ultimate emptiness of all that this world has to offer. He tried to destroy people's confidence in their own efforts, abilities, and righteousness, and direct them to faith in God as the only reason for living.

1:1–11 Solomon had a purpose in writing skeptically and pessimistically. Near the end of his life he looked back over everything he had done, and most of it seemed futile. A common belief was that only good people prospered and that only the wicked suffered, but that hadn't proven true in his experience. Solomon wrote this book after he had tried everything and achieved much, only to find that nothing apart from God made him happy. He wanted his readers to avoid these same senseless pursuits. If we try to find meaning in our accomplishments rather than in God, we will never be satisfied, and everything we pursue will become wearying and tiresome.

1:2 Solomon's kingdom, Israel, was in its Golden Age, but Solomon wanted the people to see that success and prosperity can disappear like a vapor of breath on a cold day (Psalm 103:14–16; Isaiah 40:6–8; James 4:14). All human accomplishments will one day disappear, and we must keep this in mind in order to live wisely. If we don't, we can become either proud and self-sufficient when we succeed or sorely disappointed when we fail. Solomon's goal was to show that earthly possessions and accomplishments are ultimately futile. Only the pursuit of God brings real satisfaction. We should include him in all we say, think, and do.

1:8–11 Many people feel restless and dissatisfied. They wonder (1) If I am in God's will, why am I so dissatisfied? (2) What is the meaning of life? (3) When I look back on it all, will I be happy with my accomplishments? (4) Why do I feel burned out, disillusioned,

dry? (5) What is to become of me? Solomon tests our faith, challenging us to find true and lasting meaning in God alone. As you take a hard look at your life, as Solomon did his, you will see how important serving God is over all other options. Perhaps God is asking you to rethink your purpose and direction in life as Solomon did in Ecclesiastes.

1:12–15 Life's experiences are not always happy. But the world tells us to demand happiness, do all we can to attain it, and make personal satisfaction our chief goal. Solomon, writing about his own life, discovered that his wealth, power, position, wives, and accomplishments did not make him happy. Happiness is an elusive goal because people and circumstances change quickly. True and lasting happiness, however, comes from pleasing God. Thus, happiness cannot be achieved; it can only be received through a right relationship with God, because only God knows what is really best for us. If you are chasing after happiness, you will never find it. If you are seeking after God, you will find endless joy.

1:16–18 After writing that everything is futile (1:2–11), Solomon recorded that even his great wisdom could not offer the satisfaction he was seeking. Wisdom, in itself, brought grief rather than satisfaction. Knowledge is simply a tool for living life better, not the end for which we were created.

1:16–18 The more you understand, the more pain and difficulty you experience. For example, the more you know, the more imperfection you see around you; and the more you observe, the more evil becomes evident. As you set out with Solomon to find the meaning of life, you must be ready to feel more, think more, question more, hurt more, and do more. Are you ready to pay the price for wisdom?

1:16–18 Solomon highlights two kinds of wisdom in the book of Ecclesiastes: (1) human knowledge, reasoning, or philosophy, and (2) the wisdom that comes from God. In these verses Solomon is talking about human knowledge. When human knowledge ignores God, it only highlights our problems because it can't provide answers that need an eternal perspective and solution.

wise instead of foolish—but now I realize that even this was like chasing the wind. For the more my wisdom, the more my grief; to increase knowledge only increases distress.

The king finds pleasures meaningless

2 I said to myself, "Come now, be merry; enjoy yourself to the full." But I found that this, too, was futile. For it is silly to be laughing all the time; what good does it do?

3So, after a lot of thinking, I decided to try the road of drink, while still holding steadily to my course of seeking wisdom.

Next I changed my course again and followed the path of folly, so that I could experience the only happiness most men have throughout their lives.

4, 5, 6Then I tried to find fulfillment by inaugurating a great public works program: homes, vineyards, gardens, parks and orchards for myself, and reservoirs to hold the water to irrigate my plantations.

7, 8Next I bought slaves, both men and women, and others were born within my household. I also bred great herds and flocks, more than any of the kings before me. I collected silver and gold as taxes from many kings and provinces.

In the cultural arts, I organized men's and women's choirs and orchestras. And then there were my many beautiful concubines.

9So I became greater than any of the kings in Jerusalem before me, and with it all I remained clear-eyed, so that I could evaluate all these things. 10Anything I wanted, I took, and did not restrain myself from any joy. I even found great pleasure in hard work. This pleasure was, indeed, my only reward for all my labors.

The king finds work meaningless

11But as I looked at everything I had tried, it was all so useless, a chasing of the wind, and there was nothing really worthwhile anywhere.

12Now I began a study of the comparative virtues of wisdom and folly, and anyone else would come to the same conclusion I did— 13, 14that wisdom is of more value than foolishness, just as light is better than darkness; for the wise man sees, while the fool is blind. And yet I noticed that there was one thing that happened to wise and foolish alike— 15just as the fool will die, so will I. So of what value is all my wisdom? Then I realized that even wisdom is futile. 16For the wise and fool

2:1
Prov 14:13
Eccles 7:4,6
8:15

2:3
Prov 20:1
23:29-35
Eccles 1:17
6:12; 8:15
12:13

2:4
1 Kgs 7:1-12
Song 8:10,11

2:5
Song 4:16; 5:1

2:6
Neh 2:14
3:15,16

2:7
1 Kgs 4:23
9:28
10:10,14,21

2:9
1 Chron 29:25
Eccles 1:16

2:10
Eccles 3:22
5:18; 6:2; 9:9

2:11
Eccles 5:16

2:12
Eccles 7:25

2:13
Eccles 3:19
7:2,11,12,19

2:15
Eccles 6:8,11

2:1ff Solomon conducted his search for life's meaning as an experiment. He first tried pursuing pleasure. He began grand public works programs, bought slaves, had many wives and concubines, set his mind on complex matters, became extremely wealthy, organized musical groups and supported the arts. But none of these gave him the satisfaction he was seeking. Some of the pleasures Solomon sought were wrong and some were worthy, but even the worthy pursuits were futile when he pursued them as an end in themselves. We must look beyond our activities to the reasons we do them. Is your goal in life to search for meaning, or to search for God who gives meaning?

2:4-6 Solomon had built a huge home, a Temple, a kingdom, a family (see 1 Kings 3—11). In the course of history, it would all be ruined. In Psalm 127 Solomon states, "Unless the Lord builds a house, the builders' work is useless. Unless the Lord protects a city, sentries do no good." These verses are part of his testimony to what happens to a kingdom or family that forgets God. As you examine your projects or goals, what is your starting point, your motivation? Without God as your foundation, all you have lived for will one day be useless to you.

2:11 Solomon summarized all his attempts at finding life's meaning as "chasing of the wind." We feel the wind as it passes, but we can't catch hold of it, or keep it. In all our accomplishments, even the big ones, our good feelings are only temporary. Security and self-worth are not found in these accomplishments, but far

beyond them in the love of God. Think about what you consider worthwhile in your life—where you place your time, energy, and money. Will you one day look back and decide that these, too, were a "chasing of the wind"?

2:13-16 Solomon concluded that even if life is futile, it is still better to be wise than foolish, to live with good judgment than spend your life in ignorance. Seeking wisdom has definite advantages in this life. The wise man, however, will die like anyone else. This thought caused Solomon to say that wisdom, while beneficial in this life, is ultimately futile. Because knowledge has its limits, the most important knowledge is found in knowing the infinite God.

2:16 Solomon realized that wisdom alone cannot guarantee eternal life. Wisdom, riches, and fitness matter very little after death—and everyone must die. We must not build our lives on perishable pursuits, but on the solid foundation of God. Then even if everything we have is taken away, we still have God, who is all we really need anyway. This is the point of the book of Job (see the introduction to Job).

2:16-19 Is death the ultimate equalizer of all people, no matter what they attained in life? While this appears to be true from an earthly perspective, God makes it clear (as Solomon later points out in 12:14) that what we do here has a great impact upon where we will spend our eternal life.

both die, and in the days to come both will be long forgotten. 17So now I hate life because it is all so irrational; all is foolishness, chasing the wind.

2:17
Num 11:15
Eccles 4:2

18And I am disgusted about this, that I must leave the fruits of all my hard work to others. 19And who can tell whether my son will be a wise man or a fool? And yet all I have will be given to him—how discouraging!

2:18
Ps 39:6; 49:10
Eccles 2:11
1 Cor 3:10

20-23So I turned in despair from hard work as the answer to my search for satisfaction. For though I spend my life searching for wisdom, knowledge, and skill, I must leave all of it to someone who hasn't done a day's work in his life; he inherits all my efforts, free of charge. This is not only foolish, but unfair. So what does a man get for all his hard work? Days full of sorrow and grief, and restless, bitter nights. It is all utterly ridiculous.

2:20
Job 5:7; 14:1
Ps 127:2
Eccles 1:18
5:17

Pleasure is from the hand of God

24, 25, 26So I decided that there was nothing better for a man to do than to enjoy his food and drink, and his job. Then I realized that even this pleasure is from the hand of God. For who can eat or enjoy apart from him? For God gives those who please him wisdom, knowledge, and joy; but if a sinner becomes wealthy, God takes the wealth away from him and gives it to those who please him. So here, too, we see an example of foolishly chasing the wind.

2:24
Prov 2:6; 13:22
Eccles 2:3
3:12,13,22
5:18; 6:12
8:15; 9:7
1 Tim 6:17

2. Solomon's general observations

A right time for everything

3 There is a right time for everything:

2A time to be born; a time to die;
  A time to plant; a time to harvest;
3A time to kill; a time to heal;
  A time to destroy; a time to rebuild;
4A time to cry; a time to laugh;
  A time to grieve; a time to dance;
5A time for scattering stones; a time for gathering stones;
  A time to hug; a time not to hug;
6A time to find; a time to lose;
  A time for keeping; a time for throwing away;
7A time to tear; a time to repair;
  A time to be quiet; a time to speak up;
8A time for loving; a time for hating;
  A time for war; a time for peace.

3:2
Gen 17:21
1 Sam 2:5
Job 7:1
Ps 52:5
Heb 9:27

3:4
Ex 15:20
Ps 126:2
Rom 12:15

3:7
Amos 5:13

3:8
Ps 101:3
Prov 5

2:17 As king, Solomon had everything a person could want, but here he says he hates his life. What happened? His marvelous accomplishments left him sour because he pursued them as a means to personal satisfaction. Personal satisfaction, by itself, is empty because we are alone in the enjoyment we receive. What is your attitude about what you do? If your goals are based on making only you feel satisfied, you will find yourself empty, seeking one thing after another, as Solomon did. If your goal is to serve God and others, then you will experience a full life, one that won't leave you sour.

2:18-23 Solomon continued to show that work bears no lasting fruit for those who work solely to earn money and gain possessions. Not only will everything be left behind at death, but it may be left to those who have done nothing to earn it. In addition, it may not be well cared for, and all that was gained could be lost. (Solomon's son who inherited the throne, it turned out, was often foolish—see 1 Kings 12.) Hard work done with proper motives (caring for your family, serving God) is not wrong. We must survive, and more important, we are responsible for the physical and spiritual well-being of those under our care. Their eternal

well-being may depend partly on us. But the fruit of hard work done to glorify only yourself will be passed on to those who may later lose or spoil it all. Such toil often leads to grief, while serving God leads to everlasting joy. Do you know the real reason you are working so hard?

2:24–26 Is Solomon recommending we make life a big, irresponsible party? No, he is encouraging us to take pleasure in what we're doing now and to enjoy life because it comes from God's hand. True enjoyment in life comes only as we follow God's guidelines for living. Those who really know how to enjoy life are the ones who take life each day as a gift from God, thanking him for it and serving him in it.

3:1—5:20 Solomon's point in this section is that God has a plan for all people. Thus, he provides cycles of life and work for us to do. But there are many problems we face that seem to contradict God's plan. These should not be barriers to believing in him, but rather opportunities to discover that, without God, life's problems offer no lasting solutions!

3:1–8 Timing is important. All the experiences listed in these verses are appropriate at certain times. The secret to peace with God is to discover, accept, and appreciate God's perfect timing.

9What does one really get from hard work?

10I have thought about this in connection with all the various kinds of work God has given to mankind. 11Everything is appropriate in its own time. But though God has planted eternity in the hearts of men, even so, many cannot see the whole scope of God's work from beginning to end. 12So I conclude that, first, there is nothing better for a man than to be happy and to enjoy himself as long as he can; 13and second, that he should eat and drink and enjoy the fruits of his labors, for these are gifts from God.

14And I know this, that whatever God does is final—nothing can be added or taken from it; God's purpose in this is that man should fear the all-powerful God.

15Whatever is, has been long ago; and whatever is going to be has been before; God brings to pass again what was in the distant past and disappeared.

16Moreover, I notice that throughout the earth justice is giving way to crime and even the police courts are corrupt. 17I said to myself, "In due season God will judge everything man does, both good and bad."

18And then I realized that God is letting the world go on its sinful way so that he can test mankind, and so that men themselves will see that they are no better than beasts. 19For men and animals both breathe the same air, and both die. So mankind has no real advantage over the beasts; what an absurdity! 20All go to one place—the dust from which they came and to which they must return. 21For who can prove that the spirit of man goes upward and the spirit of animals goes downward into dust? 22So I saw that there is nothing better for men than that they should be happy in their work, for that is what they are here for, and no one can bring them back to life to enjoy what will be in the future, so let them enjoy it now.

Oppression and sadness in life

4 Next I observed all the oppression and sadness throughout the earth—the tears of the oppressed, and no one helping them, while on the side of their oppressors were powerful allies. 2So I felt that the dead were better off than the living.

3:14 *God's purpose in this is that man should fear the all-powerful God,* implied. **3:15** *God brings to pass again what was in the distant past and disappeared,* literally, "God seeks what has been driven away."

3:8 When is there a time for hating? We shouldn't hate evil people, but we should hate what they do. We should also hate it when people are mistreated, when children are starving, and when God is being dishonored. In addition, we must hate sin in our lives (Psalm 5:5).

3:9–13 Your ability to enjoy your work depends to a large extent upon your attitude. Work becomes toil when you lose the sense of purpose God intended for it. We can enjoy our work if we (1) remember that God has given us work to do and he has equipped us for particular tasks (3:10), and (2) realize that the fruit of our labor is a gift from him (3:13). See your work as a way to serve God.

3:11 We can never be completely satisfied with earthly pleasures and pursuits because God created us in his image and has "planted eternity" in us. This means that (1) we have a spiritual thirst, (2) we have eternal value, and (3) nothing but the eternal God can truly satisfy us.

3:12 The ability to enjoy life is one of God's most excellent gifts to us, although we can abuse it. God wants us to enjoy life. When we have the proper view of God, we discover that real pleasure is not found in what we accumulate, but in enjoying whatever we have as gifts from God.

3:14 What is the purpose of life? It is that we should fear the all-powerful God. Fear does not mean to cringe in terror, but to respect, revere, and stand in awe of God because of who he is. Purpose in life starts with *whom* we know, not what we know or how good we are. It is impossible to fulfill your God-given purpose

unless you fear God and give him first place in your life.

3:16ff Solomon reflects on several apparent contradictions concerning God's control of the world: (1) there is unfairness where there should be justice (3:16, 17); (2) people created in God's image die just like the animals (3:18–21); (3) no one helps the oppressed (4:1–3); (4) so many people are motivated by envy and jealousy (4:4–6); (5) people are lonely (4:7–12); (6) recognition for accomplishments is temporary (4:13–16). It is easy to use such contradictions as excuses not to believe in God. But Solomon used them to show how we can honestly look at life's problems yet still keep our faith in God. This life is not all there is, yet even in this life we should not pass judgment on God because we don't know everything. God's plan is for us to live forever with him. So live with eternal values in view, realizing that all contradictions will one day be cleared up by the Creator himself (12:14).

3:17 Solomon asked how God's plan can be perfect when there is so much injustice and oppression in the world (4:1). He concluded that God does not ignore injustice, but will bring it to an end at his appointed time (12:13, 14).

3:19–22 Our bodies can't live forever in their present state. In that sense, mankind and animals are alike. But Solomon acknowledged that God has given man the hope of eternity (3:11), making us different from animals. Because man has eternity planted in his heart, he has a unique purpose in God's overall plan. Yet, we cannot discover God's purpose for our lives by our own efforts, but only through building a relationship with him and seeking his guidance. Are you now using your life as God would have you do? Do you see it as a gift from him?

3And most fortunate of all are those who have never been born, and have never seen all the evil and crime throughout the earth.

4Then I observed that the basic motive for success is the driving force of envy and jealousy! But this, too, is foolishness, chasing the wind. 5, 6The fool won't work and almost starves, but feels that it is better to be lazy and barely get by, than to work hard when, in the long run, it is all so futile.

7I also observed another piece of foolishness around the earth. 8This is the case of a man who is quite alone, without a son or brother, yet he works hard to keep gaining more riches, and to whom will he leave it all? And why is he giving up so much now? It is all so pointless and depressing.

The blessings of companionship

9Two can accomplish more than twice as much as one, for the results can be much better. 10If one falls, the other pulls him up; but if a man falls when he is alone, he's in trouble.

11Also, on a cold night, two under the same blanket gain warmth from each other, but how can one be warm alone? 12And one standing alone can be attacked and defeated, but two can stand back-to-back and conquer; three is even better, for a triple-braided cord is not easily broken.

Success does not last

13It is better to be a poor but wise youth than to be an old and foolish king who refuses all advice. 14Such a lad could come from prison and succeed. He might even become king, though born in poverty. 15Everyone is eager to help a youth like that, even to help him usurp the throne. 16He can become the leader of millions of people, and be very popular. But, then, the younger generation grows up around him and rejects him! So again, it is all foolishness, chasing the wind.

Have respect for God

5 As you enter the Temple, keep your ears open and your mouth shut! Don't be a fool who doesn't even realize it is sinful to make rash promises to God, for he is in heaven and you are only here on earth, so let your words be few. Just as being too busy gives you nightmares, so being a fool makes you a blabbermouth. 4So when you talk to God and vow to him that you will do something, don't delay in doing it, for God has no pleasure in fools. Keep your promise to him. 5It is far better not to say you'll do something than to say you will and then not do it. 6, 7In that case, your mouth is making you sin. Don't try to defend yourself by telling the messenger from God that it was all a mistake [to make the vow]. That would make God very angry; and he might destroy your prosperity. Dreaming instead of doing is foolishness, and there is ruin in a flood of empty words; fear God instead.

8If you see some poor man being oppressed by the rich, with miscarriage of justice anywhere throughout the land, don't be surprised! For every official is

5:6, 7 *to make the vow,* implied. *he might,* implied.

4:3
Eccles 6:3

4:4
Eccles 1:14
2:21

4:5
Prov 6:10
15:16,17; 16:8
24:33

4:8
Prov 27:20
Eccles 1:8
2:21; 5:10

4:11
1 Kgs 1:1

4:13
Eccles 7:19
9:15

4:14
Gen 41:14,
41-43

4:16
Eccles 1:14

5:1
1 Sam 15:22
Prov 15:8; 21:27
Eccles 10:14

5:4
Ps 50:14
66:13,14; 76:11

5:5
Prov 20:25

5:6
Num 15:25
Eccles 3:14
7:18; 8:12,13
12:13

5:8
Ps 12:5
Eccles 4:1

4:4–6 Some people are lazy while others are workaholics. The lazy person, seeing the futility of dashing about for success, folds his hands and hurts both himself and those who depend on him. The workaholic is driven by envy, greed, and a constant desire to stay ahead of everyone else. Both extremes are foolish and irresponsible. The antidote for both is to work hard but with moderation. Take time to enjoy the other gifts God has given, and realize that it is God who gives out the assignments and the rewards, not us.

4:9–12 There are advantages to cooperating with others. Life is not designed for isolation, but companionship; not for loneliness, but for intimacy. Some people prefer isolation because they feel they cannot trust anyone. But we are not here on earth to serve ourselves, but to serve God and others. Don't isolate yourself from others and "go it alone." Seek companions; be a team member.

4:13–16 Popularity and prestige are poor goals for a life's work.

Although many seek them, they are shadows without substance. They can change quickly, and they are easily forgotten.

4:15–5:1 When we "enter the Temple" (5:1) we should go with the attitude of being open and ready to listen to God, not to dictate to him what we think he should do.

5:4, 5 Solomon warns his readers about making foolish promises to God. In Israelite culture, making vows was a serious matter. Vows were voluntary but, once made, unbreakable (Deuteronomy 23:21–23). It is foolish to make a vow you cannot keep or to play games with God by only partially fulfilling your vow (Proverbs 20:25). It's better not to vow than to make a promise to God and break it. It's better still to make a good promise and keep it. (See the note on Matthew 5:33ff.)

5:10, 11 We always want more than we have. Solomon observed that those who love money and seek it obsessively never find the happiness it promises. Wealth also attracts freeloaders and thieves

under orders from higher up, and the higher officials look up to their superiors. And so the matter is lost in red tape and bureaucracy. 9And over them all is the king. Oh, for a king who is devoted to his country! Only he can bring order from this chaos.

10He who loves money shall never have enough. The foolishness of thinking that wealth brings happiness! 11The more you have, the more you spend, right up to the limits of your income, so what is the advantage of wealth—except perhaps to watch it as it runs through your fingers! 12The man who works hard sleeps well whether he eats little or much, but the rich must worry and suffer insomnia.

13, 14There is another serious problem I have seen everywhere—savings are put into risky investments that turn sour, and soon there is nothing left to pass on to one's son. 15The man who speculates is soon back to where he began—with nothing. 16This, as I said, is a very serious problem, for all his hard work has been for nothing; he has been working for the wind. It is all swept away. 17All the rest of his life he is under a cloud—gloomy, discouraged, frustrated, and angry.

To enjoy life is a gift from God

18Well, one thing, at least, is good: It is for a man to eat well, drink a good glass of wine, accept his position in life, and enjoy his work whatever his job may be, for however long the Lord may let him live. 19, 20And, of course, it is very good if a man has received wealth from the Lord, and the good health to enjoy it. To enjoy your work and to accept your lot in life—that is indeed a gift from God. The person who does that will not need to look back with sorrow on his past, for God gives him joy.

3. Solomon's practical counsel
The king finds life meaningless

6 Yes, but there is a very serious evil which I have seen everywhere— 2God has given to some men very great wealth and honor, so that they can have everything they want but he doesn't give them the health to enjoy it, and they die and others get it all! This is absurd, a hollow mockery, and a serious fault.

3Even if a man has a hundred sons and as many daughters and lives to be very old, but leaves so little money at his death that his children can't even give him a decent burial—I say that he would be better off born dead. 4For though his birth would then be futile and end in darkness, without even a name, 5never seeing the sun or even knowing its existence, yet that is better than to be an old, unhappy man. 6Though a man lives a thousand years twice over, but doesn't find contentment—well, what's the use?

7, 8Wise men and fools alike spend their lives scratching for food, and never seem to get enough. Both have the same problem, yet the poor man who is wise lives a far better life. 9A bird in the hand is worth two in the bush; mere dreaming of nice things is foolish; it's chasing the wind.

10All things are decided by fate; it was known long ago what each man would be. So there's no use arguing with God about your destiny.

11The more words you speak, the less they mean, so why bother to speak at all?

5:8 the matter is lost in red tape and bureaucracy, literally, "and there are yet higher ones over them."

5:10
Eccles 2:10,11
5:11
Eccles 2:9
5:12
Prov 3:24
5:13
Eccles 6:2
5:15
Job 1:21
Ps 49:17
5:16
Prov 11:29
Eccles 1:3
2:11; 3:9
5:17
Eccles 2:23

5:18
Eccles 2:10,24
9:7
5:19
2 Chron 1:12
Eccles 3:13; 6:2
5:20
Deut 28:8-12
Isa 64:5

6:1
Eccles 5:13
6:2
1 Kgs 3:13
Ps 17:14; 73:7
6:3
Job 3:16
Eccles 4:3
6:6
Eccles 2:14
6:7
Prov 16:26
6:8
Eccles 2:15
6:9
Prov 30:15,16
Eccles 1:14
11:9
6:10
Prov 21:30
Eccles 1:9; 3:15
6:11
Hos 12:1

---

who want it, causes sleeplessness and fear, and ultimately ends in loss because it must be left behind (Mark 10:23-25; Luke 12:16-21). No matter how much you earn, if you try to create happiness by accumulating wealth, you will never have enough. Money in itself is not wrong, but loving money leads to all sorts of sin. Whatever financial situation you are in, don't depend on money to make you happy. Instead, use what you have for the Lord.

5:19, 20 God wants us to view what we have (be it much or little) with the right perspective—our possessions are a gift from God. They are a reason to rejoice, but not the source of joy, since every good thing comes from God. We should focus more on the giver than the gift. We can be content with what we have when we realize that with God we have everything we need.

6:1—8:15 In this section Solomon shows that having the right

attitude about God can help us deal with present injustices. Prosperity is not always good and adversity is not always bad. But God is always good, and if we live as he wants us to, we will experience contentment.

6:1-6 Many people work hard to prolong life and improve their physical condition (better diet, proper exercise, excellent health care). Yet people don't spend nearly as much time or effort on their spiritual health. How shortsighted it is to work hard to extend this life and not work equally hard to secure eternal life.

6:10 In this verse, fate is best understood as "God's providence." God is in control over our lives, even though at times it may not seem like it. As created beings, how foolish it is for us to argue with our Creator, who knows us completely and can see the future.

12In these few days of our empty lifetimes, who can say how one's days can best be spent? Who can know what will prove best for the future after he is gone? For who knows the future?

6:12
Lam 3:24-27
Mic 6:8

Wise advice for living

7 A good reputation is more valuable than the most expensive perfume. The day one dies is better than the day he is born! 2It is better to spend your time at funerals than at festivals. For you are going to die and it is a good thing to think about it while there is still time. 3Sorrow is better than laughter, for sadness has a refining influence on us. 4Yes, a wise man thinks much of death, while the fool thinks only of having a good time now.

7:1
Eccles 4:2; 7:8
7:2
Eccles 2:16
3:19,20; 9:2,3
7:3
Eccles 2:2

5It is better to be criticized by a wise man than to be praised by a fool! 6For a fool's compliment is as quickly gone as paper in fire, and it is silly to be impressed by it.

7:5
Eccles 9:17
7:6
Eccles 2:2

7The wise man is turned into a fool by a bribe; it destroys his understanding.

7:7
Eccles 4:1; 5:8

8Finishing is better than starting! Patience is better than pride! 9Don't be quick-tempered—that is being a fool.

7:8
Eccles 7:1

10Don't long for "the good old days," for you don't know whether they were any better than these!

7:9
Prov 14:17

11To be wise is as good as being rich; in fact, it is better. 12You can get anything by either wisdom or money, but being wise has many advantages.

7:12
Eccles 9:18

13See the way God does things and fall into line. Don't fight the facts of nature. Who can straighten what he has made crooked? 14Enjoy prosperity whenever you can, and when hard times strike, realize that God gives one as well as the other—so that everyone will realize that nothing is certain in this life.

7:13
Eccles 1:15
3:11; 8:17
7:14
Eccles 3:22
9:7; 11:9

15, 16, 17In this silly life I have seen everything, including the fact that some of the good die young and some of the wicked live on and on. So don't be too good or too

7:15
Eccles 6:12
8:12-14; 9:9

7:13 *Don't fight the facts of nature,* implied.

6:12 Solomon is stating the profound truth that we do not know what the future holds, but we know who holds the future. He ends with a rhetorical question—the answer to which is God! No human knows the future, so each day must be lived for its own value. Solomon is arguing against the notion that man can take charge of his own destiny. In all our plans we should look up to God, not just ahead to the future.

7:1-4 This seems to contradict Solomon's previous advice to eat, drink, and be merry—to enjoy what God has given. We are to enjoy what we have while we can, but realize that adversity also strikes. Adversity reminds us that life is short, teaches us to live wisely, and refines our character. Christianity and Judaism see value in suffering and sorrow. Eastern religions seek to escape it, the Greeks and Romans despised it, but Christians and Jews see it as a refining fire. Most would agree that we learn more about God from difficult times than from happy times. Do you try to avoid sorrow and suffering at all costs? See sorrow and struggles as great opportunities to learn from God.

7:2, 4 Many people avoid thinking about death, refuse to face it, and are reluctant to attend funerals. Solomon is not encouraging us to think morbidly, but knows that it is helpful at times to think about death. It reminds us that there is still time for change, time to examine the direction of our lives, and time to confess our sins and find forgiveness from God. Because everyone will eventually die, it makes sense to plan ahead to experience God's mercy rather than his justice.

7:5, 6 Have you ever been paid a compliment, knowing it was inappropriate and merely an attempt to flatter you? Some people would rather feel good than know the truth. Pleasant compliments are too often valued above helpful information (Proverbs 27:6). Solomon reminds us that it is far better to face honest criticism than to wallow in the compliments of fools.

7:7 Money talks, and it can confuse those who would otherwise judge fairly. We hear about bribes given to judges, police officers, and witnesses. Bribes are given to hurt those who tell the truth and help those who oppose it. The person who takes a bribe is indeed a fool, no matter how wise he thought he was before. Some say that everyone has his price, but those who are truly wise cannot be bought at any price.

7:8, 9 To finish what we start takes hard work, wise guidance, and self-discipline. Anyone with vision can start a big project. But vision without wisdom often results in unfinished projects and goals.

7:10 The "good old days" are easy to talk about, but they may never have existed. Sometimes we remember only the good things about the past, forgetting that those days also had problems. Instead of living in the past, decide to live for today. Live in such a way that you will look back on today as one of the "good old days."

7:14 God allows both adversity and prosperity to come to all. He blends them in our lives in such a way that we can't predict the future or count on human wisdom and power. In prosperous times, we love to give ourselves the credit. Then in adversity, we tend to blame God without thanking him for the good that comes out of it. When life appears certain and controllable, don't let pride make you too comfortable or God may allow adversity to drive you back to him. When life seems uncertain and uncontrollable, don't despair—God is in control and will bring good results out of tough times.

7:15-17 How can someone be too good or too wise? This is a warning against extremism. Solomon was saying that some people are excessively wise or righteous *in their own eyes.* They are so rigid or narrow in their views that they lose their sensitivity to the true reason for being good—to honor God. Solomon may be taking to task the wisdom teachers of the day, who often mechanically and coldly applied their teachings to others (Job's three friends did this in the book of Job). Balance is important. God created us to be whole people, not extremists whose specific viewpoints become more important than the larger picture.

wise! Why destroy yourself? On the other hand, don't be too wicked either—don't be a fool! Why should you die before your time?

7:18
Prov 4:25-27
Eccles 3:14
5:7; 8:12,13

18Tackle every task that comes along, and if you fear God you can expect his blessing.

7:20
1 Kgs 8:46
2 Chron 6:36
Ps 143:2

19A wise man is stronger than the mayors of ten big cities! 20And there is not a single man in all the earth who is always good and never sins.

21, 22Don't eavesdrop! You may hear your servant cursing you! For you know how often you yourself curse others!

7:24
Deut 30:11-14
Job 11:7; 37:23
Rom 11:33

23I have tried my best to be wise. I declared, "I *will* be wise," but it didn't work. 24Wisdom is far away, and very difficult to find. 25I searched everywhere, determined to find wisdom and the reason for things, and to prove to myself the wickedness of folly, and that foolishness is madness.

7:25
Eccles 1:7
10:13
Jer 12:1,2

26A prostitute is more bitter than death. May it please God that you escape from her, but sinners don't evade her snares.

7:26
Prov 5:4
6:23,24; 7:23
22:14

27, 28This is my conclusion, says the Preacher. Step by step I came to this result after researching in every direction: One tenth of one percent of the men I interviewed could be said to be wise, but not one woman!

7:28
1 Kgs 11:3

7:29
Gen 1:27

29And I found that though God has made men upright, each has turned away to follow his own downward road.

8:1
Deut 28:50

8 How wonderful to be wise, to understand things, to be able to analyze them and interpret them. Wisdom lights up a man's face, softening its hardness.

8:2
Eccles 10:4

2, 3Obey the king as you have vowed to do. Don't always be trying to get out of doing your duty, even when it's unpleasant. For the king punishes those who disobey. 4The king's command is backed by great power, and no one can withstand it or question it. 5Those who obey him will not be punished. The wise man will find a time and a way to do what he says. 6, 7Yes, there is a time and a way for everything, though man's trouble lies heavy upon him; for how can he avoid what he doesn't know is going to happen?

8:4
Prov 19:12; 20:2

8:5
Eccles 10:2
12:14

8:6
Eccles 3:1,17,
22; 6:12; 7:14

8:8
Eccles 8:13

8No one can hold back his spirit from departing; no one has the power to prevent his day of death, for there is no discharge from that obligation and that dark battle. Certainly a man's wickedness is not going to help him then.

Those who fear God are better off

8:9
Eccles 1:11
2:16; 4:1,16
5:8; 9:5,15

9, 10I have thought deeply about all that goes on here in the world, where people have the power of injuring each other. I have seen wicked men buried and as their friends returned from the cemetery, having forgotten all the dead man's evil deeds, these men were praised in the very city where they had committed their many crimes! How odd! 11Because God does not punish sinners instantly, people feel it is safe to do wrong. 12But though a man sins a hundred times and still lives, I know

8:12
1 Kgs 2:5-9
Prov 1:33
Eccles 7:15

7:26 *A prostitute is more bitter than death,* literally, "the woman whose heart is snares and nets."

7:23-25 Solomon, the wisest man in the world, confessed how difficult it had been to act and think wisely. He emphasized that no matter how much we know, there are always mysteries we will never understand. So thinking you have enough wisdom is a sure sign that you don't.

7:27, 28 Did Solomon think women were not capable of having wisdom? No, because in the book of Proverbs he personified wisdom as a beautiful woman. The point of Solomon's statement is not that he couldn't find a wise woman, but that hardly anyone, man or woman, is wise before God (less than one tenth of one percent). In his search, he found that wisdom was almost as scarce among men as among women, even though men were given a religious education program in his culture and women were not. In effect, the verse is saying, "I have found only one in a thousand people who is wise in God's eyes. No, I have found fewer than that!"

8:1 Wisdom is the ability to see life from God's perspective and then to know the best course of action to take. Most would agree

that wisdom is a valuable asset, but how can we acquire it? In Proverbs 9:10, we learn that we can begin to find wisdom through reverence and fear of God. Wisdom, therefore, is a result of knowing and trusting God, not the way to find God. Knowing God will lead to understanding and to sharing this knowledge with others.

8:11 If God doesn't punish us immediately, we must not assume that he doesn't care or that sin has no consequences. But how much easier it is to sin when we don't feel the consequences at once. When a young child does something wrong and it is not discovered, how much easier it will be for him to do it again. But God knows every wrong we commit, and one day we will have to answer for everything we have done (12:14).

8:12–14 Solomon's presentation, though pessimistic, nevertheless shows that life is ultimately better with God. His presence does not shield us from all trouble, but it guarantees us that we will have his power with which to meet adversity. Both our eternal destiny and our present trials are in his hands.

very well that those who fear God will be better off, 13unlike the wicked, who will not live long, good lives—their days shall pass away as quickly as shadows because they don't fear God.

8:13
Eccles 6:12; 8:8
Isa 3:11

14There is a strange thing happening here upon the earth: Providence seems to treat some good men as though they were wicked, and some wicked men as though they were good. This is all very vexing and troublesome!

8:14
Job 21:7
Ps 73:3,12
Eccles 2:14
7:15

Happiness in work comes from God

15Then I decided to spend my time having fun, because I felt that there was nothing better in all the earth than that a man should eat, drink, and be merry, with the hope that this happiness would stick with him in all the hard work which God gives to mankind everywhere.

8:15
Eccles 2:24
3:12,13; 5:18
1 Tim 6:17

4. Solomon's final conclusion
Everyone has a common destiny

16, 17In my search for wisdom I observed all that was going on everywhere across the earth—ceaseless activity, day and night. (Of course, only God can see everything, and even the wisest man who says he knows everything, doesn't!)

8:16
Eccles 1:13,14
3:11
Isa 40:28

9 This, too, I carefully explored—that godly and wise men are in God's will; no one knows whether he will favor them or not. All is chance! 2, 3The same providence confronts everyone, whether good or bad, religious or irreligious, profane or godly. It seems so unfair, that one fate comes to all. That is why men are not more careful to be good, but instead choose their own mad course, for they have no hope—there is nothing but death ahead anyway.

9:1
1 Sam 2:9
Ps 37:5,6
Prov 16:3
Eccles 9:6
10:14

9:2
Job 9:22
Eccles 2:14
3:19; 6:6; 7:2

4There is hope only for the living. "It is better to be a live dog than a dead lion!" 5For the living at least know that they will die! But the dead know nothing; they don't even have their memories. 6Whatever they did in their lifetimes—loving, hating, envying—is long gone, and they have no part in anything here on earth any more. 7So go ahead, eat, drink, and be merry, for it makes no difference to God! 8Wear fine clothes—with a dash of cologne! 9Live happily with the woman you love through the fleeting days of life, for the wife God gives you is your best reward down here for all your earthly toil. 10Whatever you do, do well, for in death, where you are going, there is no working or planning, or knowing, or understanding.

9:5
Job 7:8-10
Ps 88:12
Eccles 1:11
2:16; 8:10

9:6
Eccles 2:10
3:22

9:7
Eccles 2:24

9:8
Ps 23:5

11Again I looked throughout the earth and saw that the swiftest person does not always win the race, nor the strongest man the battle, and that wise men are often poor, and skillful men are not necessarily famous; but it is all by chance, by happening to be at the right place at the right time. 12A man never knows when he is going to run into bad luck. He is like a fish caught in a net, or a bird caught in a snare.

9:10
Job 21:13
Eccles 9:5; 11:6

9:11
1 Sam 6:9
2 Chron 20:15
Ps 76:5

13Here is another thing that has made a deep impression on me as I have watched human affairs: 14There was a small city with only a few people living in it, and a

9:12
Eccles 8:7

8:16, 17 Even if he had access to all the world's wisdom, the wisest man would know very little. There are always more questions than answers to life. But the unknown should not cast a shadow over our joy, faith, or work because we know that someone greater is in control and that we can put our trust in him. Are you letting what you don't know about the future destroy the joy God wants to give you today?

9:5, 10 When Solomon says the dead know nothing, and there is no working, planning, knowing, or understanding in death, he is not contrasting life with afterlife, but life with death. Once you die, you can't change what you have done or suddenly plan to become a better person. Resurrection to a new life after death was a vague concept for Old Testament believers. It was only made clear after Jesus rose from the dead.

9:7–10 Considering the uncertainties of the future and the certainty of death, Solomon recommends enjoying life as God's gift. He may have been criticizing those who put off all present pleasures in order to accumulate wealth, much like those who get caught up in today's rat race. Solomon asks, "What is your wealth really worth anyway?" It is important to enjoy God's gifts while we are able, because the future is so uncertain.

9:9 Solomon also wrote a proverb about marriage. "The man who finds a wife finds a good thing; she is a blessing to him from the Lord" (Proverbs 18:22). How sad to be married and not appreciate and enjoy this great blessing God has given you.

9:11 It isn't difficult to think of cases where the swiftest or the strongest don't win, the wise remain poor, and the skillful are unknown for their talents. Some see such examples and call life unfair, and they are right. Mankind has twisted life, making it what God did not intend. Solomon is trying to reduce our expectations of this imperfect world. The book of Proverbs emphasizes how things ought to work if everyone is living fairly; Ecclesiastes tells us what often happens in our less than perfect world. We must keep our perspective by remembering that we live in a fallen world.

9:15
Eccles 8:10

9:16
Eccles 7:12,19
9:17
Eccles 7:5
10:12
9:18
Eccles 9:16

great king came with his army and besieged it. 15There was in the city a wise man, very poor, and he knew what to do to save the city, and so it was rescued. But afterwards no one thought any more about him. 16Then I realized that though wisdom is better than strength, nevertheless, if the wise man is poor, he will be despised, and what he says will not be appreciated. 17But even so, the quiet words of a wise man are better than the shout of a king of fools. 18Wisdom is better than weapons of war, but one rotten apple can spoil a barrelful.

Behave wisely

10:1
Ex 30:25
10:3
Prov 13:16; 18:2

10:4
1 Sam 25:24-33
Prov 25:15
Eccles 8:3

10:6
Prov 28:12; 29:2
10:7
Prov 19:10
30:22
10:8
Ps 7:15
Prov 26:27

10 Dead flies will cause even a bottle of perfume to stink! Yes, a small mistake can outweigh much wisdom and honor. 2A wise man's heart leads him to do right, and a fool's heart leads him to do evil. 3You can identify a fool just by the way he walks down the street!

4If the boss is angry with you, don't quit! A quiet spirit will quiet his bad temper.

5There is another evil I have seen as I have watched the world go by, a sad situation concerning kings and rulers: 6For I have seen foolish men given great authority, and rich men not given their rightful place of dignity! 7I have even seen servants riding, while princes walk like servants!

8, 9Dig a well—and fall into it! Demolish an old wall—and be bitten by a snake! When working in a quarry, stones will fall and crush you! There is risk in each stroke of your axe!

10A dull axe requires great strength; be wise and sharpen the blade.

11When the horse is stolen, it is too late to lock the barn.

10:12
Prov 10:14,32
22:11
Eccles 7:25

10:14
Prov 15:2
Eccles 3:22
5:3; 6:12; 7:14
8:7

10:16
2 Chron 13:7
Prov 20:1,2
10:18
Prov 24:30-34
10:19
Ps 104:15
Eccles 2:3; 7:12

12, 13It is pleasant to listen to wise words, but a fool's speech brings him to ruin. Since he begins with a foolish premise, his conclusion is sheer madness. 14A fool knows all about the future and tells everyone in detail! But who can really know what is going to happen? 15A fool is so upset by a little work that he has no strength for the simplest matter.

16, 17Woe to the land whose king is a child and whose leaders are already drunk in the morning. Happy the land whose king is a nobleman, and whose leaders work hard before they feast and drink, and then only to strengthen themselves for the tasks ahead! 18Laziness lets the roof leak, and soon the rafters begin to rot. 19A party gives laughter, and wine gives happiness, and money gives everything! 20Never curse the king, not even in your thoughts; nor the rich man, either; for a little bird will tell them what you've said.

Generosity will be repaid

11 Give generously, for your gifts will return to you later. 2Divide your gifts among many, for in the days ahead you yourself may need much help.

10:11 *it is too late to lock the barn,* literally, "If the serpent bites before it is charmed, there is no advantage to the charmer." **10:15** *for the simplest matter,* literally, "for a trip to the city." **11:2** *Divide your gifts among many,* literally, "Give a portion to seven, yes, even to eight."

9:15–18 Our society honors wealth, attractiveness, and success above wisdom. It is sad to see people strive to look important in man's eyes while ruining their relationship with God.

10:5–9 By describing these circumstances that aren't fair or don't make sense, Solomon is saying that wisdom alone can't bring justice. Solomon continues to build to his conclusion that everything we have (from wisdom to riches) is nothing without God. And what little we have, when God is using it, becomes all we could ever want.

10:10 Trying to do anything without the necessary skills or tools is like chopping with a dull axe. If your tool is dull, you sharpen it to do a better job. Similarly, if you lack skills, you should sharpen them through training and practice. In each situation, sharpening the axe means recognizing where a problem exists, acquiring or honing the skills (or tools) to do the job better, and then going out and doing it. Find the areas of your life where your "axe" is dull, and sharpen your skills so you can be more effective for God's work.

10:16–19 When the Hebrews had immature and irresponsible leaders, their nation fell. The books of 1 and 2 Kings describe the decline of the kingdoms when the leaders were concerned only about themselves. Verse 18 pinpoints the basic problem of these selfish leaders—laziness.

10:19 Government leaders, businesses, families, even churches get trapped into thinking money is the answer to every problem. We throw money at our problems, but just as the thrill of liquor is only temporary, the soothing effect of the last purchase soon wears off and we have to buy more. Scripture recognizes that money is necessary for survival, but it warns against the love of money (see Matthew 6:24; 1 Timothy 6:10; Hebrews 13:5). Money is dangerous because it deceives us into thinking that wealth is the easiest way to get everything we want. The love of money is sinful because we trust it, rather than God, to solve our problems. Those who pursue its empty promises one day discover that they have nothing, because they are spiritually bankrupt.

3When the clouds are heavy, the rains come down; when a tree falls, whether south or north, the die is cast, for there it lies. 4If you wait for perfect conditions, you will never get anything done. 5God's ways are as mysterious as the pathway of the wind, and as the manner in which a human spirit is infused into the little body of a baby while it is yet in its mother's womb. 6Keep on sowing your seed, for you never know which will grow—perhaps it all will.

11:5
Ps 139:13-16
Eccles 1:15
3:10; 8:17
Jn 3:8

11:6
Eccles 9:10

Enjoy life fully

7It is a wonderful thing to be alive! 8If a person lives to be very old, let him rejoice in every day of life, but let him also remember that eternity is far longer, and that everything down here is futile in comparison.

11:7
Eccles 6:5; 7:11

11:8
Eccles 9:7; 12:1

9Young man, it's wonderful to be young! Enjoy every minute of it! Do all you want to; take in everything, but realize that you must account to God for everything you do. 10So banish grief and pain, but remember that youth, with a whole life before it, can make serious mistakes.

11:9
Job 31:7
Eccles 2:10
3:17; 12:4

Remember your Creator now

12 Don't let the excitement of being young cause you to forget about your Creator. Honor him in your youth before the evil years come—when you'll no longer enjoy living. 2It will be too late then to try to remember him, when the sun and light and moon and stars are dim to your old eyes, and there is no silver lining left among your clouds. 3For there will come a time when your limbs will tremble with age, and your strong legs will become weak, and your teeth will be too few to do their work, and there will be blindness, too. 4Then let your lips be tightly closed while eating, when your teeth are gone! And you will waken at dawn with the first note of the birds; but you yourself will be deaf and tuneless, with quavering voice. 5You will be afraid of heights and of falling—a white-haired, withered old man, dragging himself along: without sexual desire, standing at death's door, and nearing his everlasting home as the mourners go along the streets.

12:1
2 Sam 19:35
Ps 63:6; 119:55
Eccles 11:8

12:2
Ezek 32:7,8
Joel 3:5

12:3
1 Sam 3:2
Ps 35:14; 38:6

12:4
2 Sam 19:35
Rev 18:22

12:5
Job 17:13
Zech 4:2,3

6Yes, remember your Creator now while you are young, before the silver cord of life snaps, and the gold bowl is broken, and the pitcher is broken at the fountain, and the wheel is broken at the cistern; 7and the dust returns to the earth as it was, and the spirit returns to God who gave it. 8All is futile, says the Preacher; utterly futile.

12:7
Gen 3:19
Ps 104:29
Eccles 3:20,21

12:8
Eccles 1:2

11:4 *you will never get anything done,* literally, "He that observeth the wind shall not sow and he that regardeth the clouds shall not reap."

11:3–5 Solomon's pessimistic writing is designed to teach us *not* to embrace a materialistic life-style. Solomon shoots down most common beliefs about life. He attacks these false philosophies so that we may escape the bitterness he experienced. Solomon does not support a despairing attitude. Just because life is uncertain does not mean we should do nothing. We are to face life's opportunities with God-directed activities.

11:4 Waiting for perfect conditions will mean inactivity. This practical insight is especially applicable to our spiritual life. If we wait for the perfect time and place for personal Bible reading, we will never begin. If we wait for a perfect church, we will never join. If we wait for the perfect ministry, we will never serve. Take steps now to grow spiritually. Don't wait for conditions that will never exist.

11:7, 8 Solomon is no dreary pessimist in 11:7—12:14. He encourages us to rejoice in every day but to remember that eternity is far longer than a person's life span. Psalm 90:12 says, "Teach us to number our days and recognize how few they are; help us to spend them as we should." The wise person does not just think about the moment and its impact; he takes the long-range view from eternity. Approach your decisions from an eternal perspective—consider their impact ten years from now and forever. Live with the attitude that although this life is short, we can live with God forever.

11:10 We often hear people say, "It doesn't matter." But many of your choices will be irreversible—they will stay with you for a lifetime. What you do when you're young *does* matter. Enjoy life now, but don't do anything physically, morally, or spiritually that will prevent you from enjoying life when you are old.

12:1 A life without God produces a bitter, lonely, and hopeless old person. A life centered around God is fulfilling; it makes the "evil years"—when disabilities, sicknesses, and handicaps could cause barriers to enjoying life—satisfying because of the hope of eternal life. Being young is exciting. But the excitement of youth can become a barrier to closeness with God because those things that most young people live for (sports, sex, popularity) become increasingly unimportant with old age. Make your strength available to God when it is still yours—during your youthful years. Don't waste it on evil or meaningless activities that become bad habits and make you callous. Seek God now.

12:6–8 The silver cord, golden bowl, pitcher, and wheel symbolize how fragile life is. How easily death comes to us; how swiftly and unexpectedly we can return to the dust from which we came. Therefore, we should not act as if nothing could harm us.

12:7–11 Stripped of God's Spirit, our bodies return to dust. Stripped of God's purpose, our work is in vain. Stripped of God's love, our service is futile. We must put God first over all we do and in all we do, because without him we have nothing. Knowing that life is futile without God motivates the wise person to find God.

Fear God and obey his commandments

12:9
1 Kgs 4:32
Prov 10:1; 25:1

9But then, because the Preacher was wise, he went on teaching the people all he knew; and he collected proverbs and classified them. 10For the Preacher was not only a wise man, but a good teacher; he not only taught what he knew to the people, but taught them in an interesting manner. 11The wise man's words are like goads

12:11
Eccles 7:5
10:12
Isa 22:23

that spur to action. They nail down important truths. Students are wise who master what their teachers tell them.

12:12
1 Kgs 4:32,33

12But, my son, be warned: there is no end of opinions ready to be expressed. Studying them can go on forever, and become very exhausting!

12:13
Eccles 3:14

13Here is my final conclusion: fear God and obey his commandments, for this is

12:14
Mt 10:26
Rom 2:16

the entire duty of man. 14For God will judge us for everything we do, including every hidden thing, good or bad.

12:11 A goad (also called an ox goad) was a sharp metal tip attached to a handle; it was used to keep oxen or cattle moving. Like a goad, a wise word or important truth might be unpleasant when first applied, but it will keep us moving in God's direction.

12:11, 12 The last sentence of 12:11, "Students are wise who master what their teachers tell them," is also translated "They are given by one shepherd," meaning God himself (see also Psalm 23:1; 80:1; Isaiah 40:11; Jeremiah 31:10). Solomon is saying that the words of this book are inspired by God. There are endless opinions about life and philosophies about how we should live, and they could be read and studied forever. It is not wrong to study them, but spend the majority of your time feeding on the truth of God's Word. Wisdom should lead to action. Wise students of the Bible will understand and do what they are taught. Because our time on earth is so short, we should use it to "nail down important truths," for they affect this life and eternity.

12:13, 14 Solomon presents his antidotes for the two main ailments presented in this book. Those who lack purpose and direction in life should respect God and follow his principles for living. Those who think life is unfair should remember that God will review every person's life to determine how he or she has

responded to him. Have you committed your life to him, both present and future? Does your life measure up to his standards?

12:13, 14 The book of Ecclesiastes cannot be interpreted correctly without reading these final verses. No matter what the mysteries and apparent contradictions of life, you must work toward the single purpose of knowing God.

In Ecclesiastes, Solomon shows us that we should enjoy life, but this does not exempt us from obeying God's commands. We should search for purpose and meaning in life, but they cannot be found in human endeavors. We should acknowledge the evil, foolishness, and injustice in life, yet maintain a positive attitude and strong faith in God.

All people will have to stand before God and be judged for what they did in this life. We will not be able to use life's inconsistencies as an excuse for failing to live properly. To live properly, we need to (1) recognize that human effort apart from God is futile; (2) put God first—now; (3) receive everything good as a gift from God; (4) realize that God will judge both evil and good, and (5) know that God will judge the quality of every person's life. How strange that people spend their lives striving for the very enjoyment that God gives freely, as a gift.

VITAL STATISTICS

PURPOSE:
To tell of the love between a bridegroom (King Solomon) and his bride, to affirm the sanctity of marriage, and to picture God's love for his people

AUTHOR:
Solomon

DATE WRITTEN:
Probably early in Solomon's reign

SETTING:
Israel—the Shulamite woman's garden and the king's palace

KEY VERSE:
"I am my beloved's and my beloved is mine. He pastures his flock among the lilies!" (6:3).

KEY PEOPLE:
King Solomon, the Shulamite woman, and the young women of Jerusalem

SATURATED with stories of sexual escapades and extra-marital affairs, the message communicated by today's media is that immorality means freedom, perversion is natural, and commitment is old-fashioned. Sex, which was created by God and pronounced good, has been twisted, exploited, and turned into an illicit, casual, and self-gratifying activity. Love has turned into lust, giving into getting, and lasting commitment into "no strings attached."

But Scripture contains numerous guidelines concerning sexual expression and warnings against violating those guidelines. In reality, sexual intercourse, the physical and emotional union of a man and a woman, should be a holy means of celebrating love, producing children, and experiencing pleasure, protected by the commitment of marriage. The Song of Solomon is an intimate story of a man and a woman, of their love, courtship, and marriage.

The Song of Solomon is a moving, dramatic story, featuring the love dialogue between a simple Jewish maiden (the Shulamite woman) and her lover (King Solomon). The book describes in detail their feelings for each other and their longings to be together. Throughout the dialogue, sex and marriage are put in their proper, God-given perspective.

There has been much debate over the meaning of this song. Some say that it is an allegory of God's love for Israel and/or for the church. Others say it is a literal story about married love. But in reality, it is both—an historical story with two layers of meaning. On one level we learn about love, marriage, and sex; and on the other level, we see God's overwhelming love for his people. As you read the Song of Solomon, remember that you are loved by God, and commit yourself to seeing life, sex, and marriage from his point of view.

THE BLUEPRINT

1. The wedding day (1:1—2:7)
2. Memories of courtship (2:8—3:5)
3. Memories of engagement (3:6—5:1)
4. A troubling dream (5:2—6:3)
5. Praising the bride's beauty (6:4—7:9)
6. The bride's tender appeal (7:10—8:4)
7. The power of love (8:5—14)

The Song of Solomon is a wedding song honoring marriage. The most explicit statements on sex in the Bible can be found in this book. It has often been criticized through the centuries because of its sensuous language. The purity and sacredness of love represented here, however, are greatly needed in our day where distorted attitudes about love and marriage are commonplace. God created sex and intimacy, and it is holy and good when enjoyed within the bounds of marriage. A husband and wife honor God when they love and enjoy each other.

MEGATHEMES

THEME	EXPLANATION	IMPORTANCE
Sex	Sex is God's gift to his creatures. He endorses sex, but restricts its expression to those committed to each other in marriage.	God wants sex to be motivated by love and commitment, not lust. It is for mutual pleasure, not selfish enjoyment.

Love	As the relationship developed, the beauty and wonder of a romance unfolded between Solomon and his bride. The intense power of love affected the hearts, minds, and bodies of the two lovers.	Because love is such a powerful expression of feeling and commitment between two people, it is not to be regarded casually. We are not to manipulate others into loving us, and love should not be prematurely encouraged in a relationship.
Commitment	The power of love requires more than the language of feeling to protect it. Sexual expression is such an integral part of our selfhood that we need the boundary of marriage to safeguard our love. Marriage is the celebration of daily commitment to each other.	While romance keeps a marriage interesting, commitment keeps romance from dwindling away. The decision to commit yourself to your spouse alone *begins* at the marriage altar. It must be maintained day by day.
Beauty	The two lovers praise the beauty they see in each other. The language they use shows the spontaneity and mystery of love. Our praise should not be limited to physical beauty; beautiful personality and moral purity should also be praised.	Our love for our spouse makes him or her appear beautiful. It is the inner qualities that keep love alive. Don't just look for physical attractiveness in a spouse. Look for the qualities that don't fade with time—spiritual commitment, integrity, sensitivity, and sincerity.
Problems	Over time, feelings of loneliness, indifference, and isolation came between Solomon and his bride. During those times, love grew cold and barriers were raised.	Through careful communication, lovers can be reconciled, commitment can be renewed and romance refreshed. Don't let walls come between you and your partner. Take care of problems while they are still small.

1. The wedding day

1:1
1 Kgs 4:32
1:2
Song 4:10
1:3
Song 4:10
1:4
Song 2:3-5

1 *This song of songs, more wonderful than any other, was composed by King Solomon:*

The Girl: 2"Kiss me again and again, for your love is sweeter than wine. 3How fragrant your cologne, and how great your name! No wonder all the young girls love you! 4Take me with you; come, let's run!"

1:2 *The Girl.* The headings identifying the speakers are conjectures and are not in the original text.

1:1 King Solomon frequently visited the various parts of his kingdom. One day, as he visited some royal vineyards in the north, his royal entourage came by surprise upon a beautiful peasant woman tending the vines. Embarrassed, she ran from them. But Solomon could not forget her. Later, disguised as a shepherd, he returned to the vineyards and won her love. He revealed his true identity and asked her to return to Jerusalem with him and become his queen. Solomon and his bride are being married in the palace as this book begins.

The Song of Solomon is a series of seven poems, not necessarily in chronological order, which reflect upon the first meeting of Solomon and the peasant woman, their engagement, their wedding, their wedding night, and the growth of their marriage after the wedding.

1:1 Solomon, a son of King David, became king and was chosen by God to build the Temple in Jerusalem. God gave him extraordinary wisdom. Much of his reign was characterized by wisdom and reverence for God, although toward the end of his life he became proud and turned from God. Read about Solomon in

1 Kings 1—11 and 1 Chronicles 28:8—2 Chronicles 9:31. Solomon wrote more than 3,000 proverbs (see the book of Proverbs) and over 1,000 songs, one of which is this book. His profile is found in 1 Kings 3.

1:1 There are four characters in this book: the girl, King Solomon, the young women of Jerusalem (3:6), and the girl's brothers (8:8). The girl who caught Solomon's attention was from Shulam (thought by many to be Shunem), a farming community about 60 miles north of Jerusalem. Her tanned skin indicates that she worked outside in the vineyards (1:6)—thus she may not have been from the upper class. The women of Jerusalem were either those in Solomon's harem or those who worked in the palace. In either case, the girl had to live and work with these women in her new surroundings.

1:1-4 This vivid description of a love relationship begins with a picture of love itself. Love is "sweet, fragrant, happy, and better than wine." We can enjoy love. God created it as a gift to us and a treat for all our senses.

The Girl: "The king has brought me into his palace. How happy we will be! Your love is better than wine. No wonder all the young girls love you!"

The Girl: 5"I am dark but beautiful, O girls of Jerusalem, tanned as the dark tents of Kedar."

King Solomon: "But lovely as the silken tents of Solomon!"

The Girl: 6"Don't look down on me, you city girls, just because my complexion is so dark—the sun has tanned me. My brothers were angry with me and sent me out into the sun to tend the vineyards, but see what it has done to me!"

The Girl: 7"Tell me, O one I love, where are you leading your flock today? Where will you be at noon? For I will come and join you there instead of wandering like a vagabond among the flocks of your companions."

King Solomon: 8"If you don't know, O most beautiful woman in all the world, follow the trail of my flock to the shepherds' tents, and there feed your sheep and their lambs. 9What a lovely filly you are, my love! 10How lovely your cheeks are, with your hair falling down upon them! How stately your neck with that long string of jewels. 11We shall make you gold earrings and silver beads."

The Girl: 12"The king lies on his bed, enchanted by the fragrance of my perfume. 13My beloved one is a sachet of myrrh lying between my breasts."

King Solomon: 14"My beloved is a bouquet of flowers in the gardens of Engedi. 15How beautiful you are, my love, how beautiful! Your eyes are soft as doves'. 16What a lovely, pleasant thing you are, lying here upon the grass, 17shaded by the cedar trees and firs."

2   *The Girl:* "I am the rose of Sharon, the lily of the valley."

    King Solomon: 2"Yes, a lily among thorns, so is my beloved as compared with any other girls."

The Girl: 3"My lover is an apple tree, the finest in the orchard as compared with any of the other youths. I am seated in his much-desired shade and his fruit is lovely to eat. 4He brings me to the banquet hall and everyone can see how much he loves me. 5Oh, feed me with your love—your 'raisins' and your 'apples'—for I am utterly lovesick. 6His left hand is under my head and with his right hand he embraces me. 7O girls of Jerusalem, I adjure you by the gazelles and deer in the park, that you do not awaken my lover. Let him sleep!"

2. Memories of courtship

The Girl: 8"Ah, I hear him—my beloved! Here he comes, leaping upon the

---

1:6 *you city girls,* implied in vs 5. *sent me out into the sun,* implied. *see what it has done to me,* literally, "but my own vineyards are neglected." **1:9** *What a lovely filly you are,* literally, "I compare you to my mare harnessed to Pharaoh's chariot." **1:10** *with your hair,* literally, "ornaments."

1:5 Kedar was a nomadic community in northern Arabia. It was known for its tents made from black goat hair.

1:6 The vineyard mentioned here was apparently owned by Solomon (because he came to visit it) and leased to the girl's stepbrothers (also translated "mother's sons"), who made her work among the vines in the hot sun. When she was brought to Jerusalem, the young girl was embarrassed about her tanned complexion because the girls in the city had fair, delicate skin which was considered much more beautiful. But Solomon loved her dark skin.

1:7 The girl felt insecure at being different from the women of Jerusalem (1:6) and at being alone while her lover was away (1:7). She longed for the security of his presence. The basis of true love is commitment, and in a relationship where there is genuine love, there is never any fear of deceit, manipulation, or exploitation.

1:14 Engedi was an oasis hidden at the base of rugged limestone cliffs west of the Dead Sea. It was known for its fruitful palm trees and fragrant balsam oil. The terrain surrounding Engedi was some of the most desolate in Palestine and it was in the midst of an extremely hot desert climate. A flower at Engedi would have

appeared all the more beautiful because of its stark surroundings; thus, Solomon was complimenting his bride's beauty and comparing her favorably with the women she feared.

2:1 The rose of Sharon and lily of the valley are flowers commonly found in Israel. Perhaps the girl was saying, "I'm not so special; I'm just an ordinary flower," to which Solomon replied, "Oh no, you are extraordinary—a lily among thorns." Solomon used the language of love. There is nothing more vital than encouraging and appreciating the person you love. Be sure to tell your spouse "I love you" every day and show that love by your actions.

2:7 This verse can be more literally translated, "O girls of Jerusalem, I adjure you . . . that you stir not up nor awaken love until it please." Feelings of love can create intimacy that overpower reason. Young people are too often in a hurry to develop an intimate relationship based on their strong feelings. But feelings aren't enough to support a lasting relationship. This verse encourages us not to force romance lest the feelings of love grow faster than the commitment needed to make love last. Patiently wait for feelings of love and commitment to develop together.

2:8—3:5 In this section Solomon's bride (the girl), reflects on her

---

Marginal cross-references:

1:5 Ps 90:17 / Song 2:7,14 / 4:3; 6:4
1:6 Song 8:11
1:7 Ps 18:1 / Song 3:1-4 / 8:13
1:8 Song 5:9; 6:1
1:9 2 Chron 1:16,17 / Isa 31:1
1:10 Song 5:13
1:12 Song 4:13,14
1:14 1 Sam 23:29 / Song 4:13
1:15 Song 1:16 / 2:10,13; 4:1
1:17 2 Chron 3:5
2:3 Song 1:13,16 / 8:5
2:4 Ps 63:2-5 / Song 1:4; 5:1
2:6 Prov 4:8 / Song 8:3
2:7 Song 3:5; 5:8 / 8:14

mountains and bounding over the hills. 9My beloved is like a gazelle or young deer. Look, there he is behind the wall, now looking in at the windows.

10"My beloved said to me, 'Rise up, my love, my fair one, and come away. 11For the winter is past, the rain is over and gone. 12The flowers are springing up and the time of the singing of birds has come. Yes, spring is here. 13The leaves are coming out and the grape vines are in blossom. How delicious they smell! Arise, my love, my fair one, and come away.'

14"My dove is hiding behind some rocks, behind an outcrop of the cliff. Call to me and let me hear your lovely voice and see your handsome face.

15"The little foxes are ruining the vineyards. Catch them, for the grapes are all in blossom.

16"My beloved is mine and I am his. He is feeding among the lilies! 17Before the dawn comes and the shadows flee away, come to me, my beloved, and be like a gazelle or a young stag on the mountains of spices."

3 *The Girl:* "One night my lover was missing from my bed. I got up to look for him but couldn't find him. 2I went out into the streets of the city and the roads to seek him, but I searched in vain. 3The police stopped me and I said to them, 'Have you seen him anywhere, this one I love so much?' 4It was only a little while afterwards that I found him and held him and would not let him go until I had brought him into my childhood home, into my mother's old bedroom. 5I adjure you, O women of Jerusalem, by the gazelles and deer of the park, not to awake my lover. Let him sleep."

3. Memories of engagement

The Young Women of Jerusalem: 6"Who is this sweeping in from the deserts like a cloud of smoke along the ground, smelling of myrrh and frankincense and every other spice that can be bought? 7Look, it is the chariot of Solomon with sixty of the mightiest men of his army surrounding it. 8They are all skilled swordsmen and experienced bodyguards. Each one has his sword upon his thigh to defend his king against any onslaught in the night. 9For King Solomon made himself a chariot from the wood of Lebanon. 10Its posts are silver, its canopy gold, the seat is purple; and the back is inlaid with these words: 'With love from the girls of Jerusalem!' "

The Girl: 11"Go out and see King Solomon, O young women of Zion; see the

2:12 *spring is here,* literally, "the voice of the turtledove is heard in our land." **2:13** *the leaves are coming out,* literally, "The fig tree puts forth its figs." **3:7** *it is the chariot,* literally, "litter."

---

courtship with Solomon, remembering the first day they met (2:8-14). She recalls one of her dreams about their being together (3:1-4).

2:15 Some believe this verse was spoken by the girl's brothers (see the note on 1:6). Just when the girl and Solomon were enjoying each other's company, the brothers told her that foxes had gotten into the vineyard and she must leave and tend to the problem.

"The little foxes" are an example of the kinds of problems that can disturb or destroy a relationship. The girl wanted anything that could potentially cause problems between her and Solomon to be removed. It is often the "little foxes" that cause the biggest problems in marriage. These irritations must not be minimized or ignored, but identified so that, together, the couple can deal with them.

2:16 Solomon (the beloved) had left the girl for a while, but their commitment to each other kept their relationship strong. It is wonderful to belong to another and have someone belong to you, but belonging to each other is not the same as possessing each other. Togetherness doesn't require us to spend all our time in each other's company. In your love relationship, remember to allow your partner some room. Be willing to release your partner for his or her work or Christian service. Loving someone is like holding

sand: close your hand tightly and you lose some; leave your hand open and all the sand remains.

3:1-4 Most scholars agree that in these verses, the girl was recalling a dream in which she became so concerned about her lover's whereabouts that she arose in the middle of the night to search for him. When you love someone, you will do all you can to ensure the safety of that person and care for his or her needs, even at a cost to your personal comfort. This shows up most often in small actions—walking upstairs to get someone you love a glass of water, leaving work early to attend some function your child is involved in, or sacrificing your personal comfort to tend to the needs of the ones you love.

3:6—5:1 Here the scene changes. Some believe that the wedding procession is described in 3:6-11, the wedding night in 4:1—5:1, and the consummation of the marriage in 4:16—5:1. Another possible explanation is that the period of Solomon's engagement to the girl is being remembered. In the previous section (2:8—3:5), Solomon and the girl fell in love. In this section, Solomon returns to the girl in all his royal splendor (3:6-11), expresses his great love for her (4:1-5), and then proposes (4:7-15). The girl accepts (4:16), and Solomon responds to her acceptance (5:1).

crown with which his mother crowned him on his wedding day, his day of gladness."

4 *King Solomon:* "How beautiful you are, my love, how beautiful! Your eyes are those of doves. Your hair falls across your face like flocks of goats that frisk across the slopes of Gilead. ²Your teeth are white as sheep's wool, newly shorn and washed; perfectly matched, without one missing. ³Your lips are like a thread of scarlet—and how beautiful your mouth. Your cheeks are matched loveliness behind your locks. ⁴Your neck is stately as the tower of David, jeweled with a thousand heroes' shields. ⁵Your breasts are like twin fawns of a gazelle, feeding among the lilies. ⁶Until the morning dawns and the shadows flee away, I will go to the mountain of myrrh and to the hill of frankincense. ⁷You are so beautiful, my love, in every part of you.

⁸"Come with me from Lebanon, my bride. We will look down from the summit of the mountain, from the top of Mount Hermon, where the lions have their dens, and panthers prowl. ⁹You have ravished my heart, my lovely one, my bride; I am overcome by one glance of your eyes, by a single bead of your necklace. ¹⁰How sweet is your love, my darling, my bride. How much better it is than mere wine. The perfume of your love is more fragrant than all the richest spices. ¹¹Your lips, my dear, are made of honey. Yes, honey and cream are under your tongue, and the scent of your garments is like the scent of the mountains and cedars of Lebanon.

¹²"My darling bride is like a private garden, a spring that no one else can have, a fountain of my own. ¹³, ¹⁴You are like a lovely orchard bearing precious fruit, with the rarest of perfumes; nard and saffron, calamus and cinnamon, and perfume from every other incense tree, as well as myrrh and aloes, and every other lovely spice. ¹⁵You are a garden fountain, a well of living water, refreshing as the streams from the Lebanon mountains."

The Girl: ¹⁶"Come, north wind, awaken; come, south wind, blow upon my garden and waft its lovely perfume to my beloved. Let him come into his garden and eat its choicest fruits."

5 *King Solomon:* "I am here in my garden, my darling, my bride! I gather my myrrh with my spices and eat my honeycomb with my honey. I drink my wine with my milk."

The Young Women of Jerusalem: "Oh, lover and beloved, eat and drink! Yes, drink deeply!"

4. A troubling dream

The Girl: ²"One night as I was sleeping, my heart awakened in a dream. I heard the

4:1
Ps 45:11
Song 1:15
Ezek 16:14
Mic 7:14
4:3
Prov 10:13,20,
21; 16:21-24
Song 5:13,16
4:4
Song 7:4
4:5
Song 2:16
6:2,3; 7:3
4:8
1 Kgs 4:33
2 Kgs 5:12
1 Chron 5:23
Song 5:1
4:9
Ezek 16:11
4:11
Song 7:9
4:12
Gen 29:3
Prov 5:15-18
4:13
Ps 45:8
Song 1:12; 3:6
4:6
4:15
Zech 14:8
4:16
Song 1:13; 2:3
4:13
2 Cor 9:10-15
2 Pet 3:18
5:1
Prov 9:5
Song 1:13; 4:9
6:2
Isa 55:1
Jn 3:29

4:3 *matched loveliness,* literally, "like halves of a pomegranate." *behind your locks,* literally, "behind your veil."
4:4 *your neck is stately,* implied. **4:8** *top of Mount Hermon,* literally, "Depart from the peak of Amana, from the peak of Senir and Hermon." **4:13, 14** *You are like a lovely orchard bearing precious fruit,* literally, "Your shoots are an orchard of pomegranates. . . ."

4:1–7 We feel like awkward onlookers when we read this intensely private and intimate exchange. In the ecstasy of their love, the lovers praise each other using beautiful imagery. Their words may seem strange to readers from a different culture, but their intense feelings of love and admiration are universal. Communicating love and expressing admiration in both words and actions can enhance every marriage.

4:12 In comparing his bride to a private garden, Solomon was praising her virginity. Virginity, considered old fashioned by many in today's culture, has always been God's plan for unmarried people—and with good reason. Sex without marriage is cheap. It cannot compare with the joy of giving yourself completely to the one who is totally committed to you.

4:15 Solomon's bride was as refreshing to him as a mountain stream. Could your spouse say the same about you? Sometimes

the familiarity that comes with marriage causes us to forget the overwhelming feelings of love and refreshment we shared at the beginning. Many marriages could use a course in "refreshing." Do you refresh your spouse, or are you a burden of complaints, sorrows, and problems? Partners in marriage should continually work at refreshing each other through such small things as an encouraging word, an unexpected gift, a change of pace, a surprise call or note, or even by withholding a discussion of some problem until the proper time. Your spouse needs you to be a haven of refreshment because the rest of the world usually isn't.

5:2ff This new section tells how the couple's marriage grew and matured in spite of problems. Some time had passed since the wedding, and the girl felt as though some indifference had developed in their relationship. She had become cool to his advances, and by the time she changed her mind and responded

voice of my beloved; he was knocking at my bedroom door. 'Open to me, my darling, my lover, my lovely dove,' he said, 'for I have been out in the night and am covered with dew.'

³"But I said, 'I have disrobed. Shall I get dressed again? I have washed my feet, and should I get them soiled?'

⁴"My beloved tried to unlatch the door and my heart was thrilled within me. ⁵I jumped up to open it and my hands dripped with perfume, my fingers with lovely myrrh as I pulled back the bolt. ⁶I opened to my beloved, but he was gone. My heart stopped. I searched for him but couldn't find him anywhere. I called to him, but there was no reply. ⁷The guards found me and struck and wounded me. The watchman on the wall tore off my veil. ⁸I adjure you, O women of Jerusalem, if you find my beloved one, tell him that I am sick with love."

The Young Women of Jerusalem: ⁹"O woman of rare beauty, what is it about your loved one that is better than any other, that you command us this?"

The Girl: ¹⁰"My beloved one is tanned and handsome, better than ten thousand others! ¹¹His head is purest gold, and he has wavy, raven hair. ¹²His eyes are like doves beside the water brooks, deep and quiet. ¹³His cheeks are like sweetly scented beds of spices. His lips are perfumed lilies, his breath like myrrh. ¹⁴His arms are round bars of gold set with topaz; his body is bright ivory encrusted with jewels. ¹⁵His legs are as pillars of marble set in sockets of finest gold, like cedars of Lebanon; none can rival him. ¹⁶His mouth is altogether sweet, lovable in every way. Such, O women of Jerusalem, is my beloved, my friend."

6 *The Young Women of Jerusalem:* "O rarest of beautiful women, where has your loved one gone? We will help you find him."

The Girl: ²"He has gone down to his garden, to his spice beds, to pasture his flock and to gather the lilies. ³I am my beloved's and my beloved is mine. He pastures his flock among the lilies!"

5. Praising the bride's beauty

King Soloman: ⁴"O my beloved, you are as beautiful as the lovely land of Tirzah, yes, beautiful as Jerusalem, and how you capture my heart. ⁵Look the other way, for your eyes have overcome me! Your hair, as it falls across your face, is like a flock of goats frisking down the slopes of Gilead. ⁶Your teeth are white as freshly washed ewes, perfectly matched and not one missing. ⁷Your cheeks are matched loveliness behind your hair. ⁸I have sixty other wives, all queens, and eighty concubines, and unnumbered virgins available to me; ⁹but you, my dove, my

6:4 *how you capture my heart,* literally, "You are . . . terrible as an army with banners." **6:7** *Your cheeks are matched loveliness,* literally, "like the halves of a pomegranate."

---

to him, he had left. Her self-centeredness and impatience, though brief, caused separation. But she quickly moved to correct the problem by searching out her husband (5:8ff).

5:2–7 It is inevitable that, with the passing of time and the growth of familiarity, a marriage will start to lose its initial sparkle. Glances and touches no longer produce the same emotional response. Conflicts and pressures creep in, causing you to lose your tenderness toward your spouse. The world is not a haven for lovers; in fact, external stress often works against the marriage relationship. But spouses can learn to be havens for each other. If a decline in intimacy and passion does occur, remember that they can be renewed and regenerated. Take time to remember those first thrills, the excitement of sex, your spouse's strengths, and the commitment you made. When you focus on the positives, reconciliation and renewal can result.

5:7 The girl was alone outside during the night. In Old Testament times, she would have been looked upon as a criminal or a prostitute and treated as such. This image symbolizes the pain she felt at being separated from her lover.

5:16 The girl calls Solomon her "friend." In a healthy marriage,

lovers are also good friends. Too often people are driven into marriage by the exciting feelings of love before they take the time to develop a deep friendship that includes listening, sharing, and showing understanding for the other's likes and dislikes. Friendship takes time, but it makes a love relationship much deeper and far more satisfying.

6:3 The girl said that she and her beloved belonged to each other—they had given themselves to each other unreservedly. No matter how close we may be to our parents or our best friends, it is only in marriage that the complete union of mind, heart, and body is realized.

6:4 Tirzah was a city about 35 miles northeast of Jerusalem. Its name means "pleasure" or "beauty." King Jeroboam made Tirzah the first capital of the divided Northern Kingdom (1 Kings 14:17).

6:8, 9 Solomon did indeed have many wives and concubines (1 Kings 11:3). Polygamy, though not condoned, was common in Old Testament days. Solomon says his love for this woman has not diminished since their wedding night, even though he has many other women available to him.

Cross references: 5:3 Gen 19:2; 5:5 Song 5:13; 5:6 Prov 1:28, Song 3:1; 5:2, 6:1; 5:7 Song 3:3; 5:8 Song 2:7; 3:5; 5:9 Song 6:1; 5:10 1 Sam 16:12, Ps 45:2; 5:12 Song 1:15; 4:1; 5:13 Song 2:1; 5:5, 6:2; 5:15 1 Kgs 4:33, Song 7:4; 5:16 2 Sam 1:23, Song 7:9; 6:2 Song 1:7; 2:1, 4:16; 5:1,13; 6:3 Song 2:16; 4:5, 7:10; 6:4 1 Kgs 14:17, Song 6:10; 6:8 1 Kgs 11:3, Song 1:3; 6:9 Song 2:14; 5:2

perfect one, are the only one among them all, without an equal! The women of Jerusalem were delighted when they saw you and even the queens and concubines praise you. 10'Who is this,' they ask, 'arising as the dawn, fair as the moon, pure as the sun, so utterly captivating?' "

The Girl: 11"I went down into the orchard of nuts and out to the valley to see the springtime there, to see whether the grape vines were budding or the pomegranates were blossoming yet. 12Before I realized it I was stricken with terrible homesickness and wanted to be back among my own people."

The Young Women of Jerusalem: 13"Return, return to us, O maid of Shulam. Come back, come back, that we may see you once again."

The Girl: "Why should you seek a mere Shulammite?"

King Solomon: "Because you dance so beautifully."

7   *King Solomon:* "How beautiful your tripping feet, O queenly maiden. Your rounded thighs are like jewels, the work of the most skilled of craftsmen. 2Your navel is lovely as a goblet filled with wine. Your waist is like a heap of wheat set about with lilies. 3Your two breasts are like two fawns, yes, lovely twins. 4Your neck is stately as an ivory tower, your eyes as limpid pools in Heshbon by the gate of Bath-rabbim. Your nose is shapely like the tower of Lebanon overlooking Damascus.

5"As Mount Carmel crowns the mountains, so your hair is your crown. The king is held captive in your queenly tresses.

6"Oh, how delightful you are; how pleasant, O love, for utter delight! 7You are tall and slim like a palm tree, and your breasts are like its clusters of dates. 8I said, I will climb up into the palm tree and take hold of its branches. Now may your breasts be like grape clusters, and the scent of your breath like apples, 9and your kisses as exciting as the best of wine, smooth and sweet, causing the lips of those who are asleep to speak."

6. The bride's tender appeal

The Girl: 10"I am my beloved's and I am the one he desires. 11Come, my beloved, let us go out into the fields and stay in the villages. 12Let us get up early and go out to the vineyards and see whether the vines have budded and whether the blossoms have opened and whether the pomegranates are in flower. And there I will give you my love. 13There the mandrakes give forth their fragrance and the rarest fruits are at our doors, the new as well as old, for I have stored them up for my beloved."

8   *The Girl:* "Oh, if only you were my brother; then I could kiss you no matter who was watching, and no one would laugh at me. 2I would bring you to my childhood home, and there you would teach me. I would give you spiced wine to drink, sweet pomegranate wine. 3His left hand would be under my head and his right hand would embrace me. 4I adjure you, O women of Jerusalem, not to awaken him until he please."

Cross-references (margin):

6:10 Job 31:26; Song 6:4; Mt 17:2; Rev 1:16
6:11 Song 4:13; 7:12
6:13 Gen 32:2; Judg 21:21; 2 Sam 17:24
7:1ff Ps 45:13
7:3 Song 4:5
7:4 Num 21:26; Song 4:4
7:5 Isa 35:2
7:8 Song 2:5
7:9 Prov 23:31; Song 5:16
7:10 Ps 45:11; Song 2:16; 6:3
7:13 Gen 30:14; Song 2:3; 4:13,16
8:2 Song 3:4
8:3 Song 2:6
8:4 Song 2:7; 3:5

6:10 *so utterly captivating,* literally, "terrible as an army with banners." **6:12** *among my own people,* literally, "the chariots of my princely people." Another possible reading is, "terrible desire to sit beside my beloved in his chariot." **6:13** *you dance so beautifully,* literally, "as upon a dance before two armies." **7:2** *your waist,* literally, "belly." **7:3** *lovely twins,* literally, "twins of a gazelle." **7:4** *Your nose is shapely,* implied. **8:2** *my childhood home,* literally, "my mother's house."

7:10–13 As a marriage matures, there should be more love and freedom between marriage partners. Here the girl takes the initiative in lovemaking. Many cultures have stereotypes of the roles which men and women play in lovemaking, but the security of true love gives both marriage partners the freedom to initiate acts of love.

7:13 Mandrakes were a somewhat rare plant often thought to increase fertility. Mandrakes are also mentioned in Genesis 30:14–17.

8:1 In the ancient Near East, it was improper to show public affection except between family members. The girl is wishing she could freely show her lover affection even in public.

7. The power of love

8:5
Song 2:3; 3:6

The Young Women of Jerusalem: 5"Who is this coming up from the desert, leaning on her beloved?"

King Solomon: "Under the apple tree where your mother gave birth to you in her travail, there I awakened your love."

8:6
Prov 6:34
Isa 49:16
Jer 22:24
Hag 2:23

The Girl: 6"Seal me in your heart with permanent betrothal, for love is strong as death and jealousy is as cruel as Sheol. It flashes fire, the very flame of Jehovah. 7Many waters cannot quench the flame of love, neither can the floods drown it. If a man tried to buy it with everything he owned, he couldn't do it."

8:8
Ezek 16:7

The Girl's Brothers: 8"We have a little sister too young for breasts. What shall we do if someone asks to marry her?"

8:9
1 Kgs 6:15

King Solomon: 9"If she has no breasts we will build upon her a battlement of silver, and if she is a door we will enclose her with cedar boards."

The Girl: 10"I am slim, tall, and full-breasted and I have found favor in my lover's

8:11
Eccles 2:4
Song 1:6; 8:12
Isa 7:23
Mt 21:33

eyes. 11Solomon had a vineyard at Baal-hamon which he rented out to some farmers there, the rent being one thousand pieces of silver from each. 12But as for my own vineyard, you, O Solomon, shall have my thousand pieces of silver and I will give two hundred pieces to those who care for it.

8:13
Song 1:7

13O my beloved, living in the gardens, how wonderful that your companions

8:14
Song 2:7,9,17
4:6

may listen to your voice; let me hear it too. 14Come quickly, my beloved, and be like a gazelle or young deer upon the mountains of spices."

8:9 *if she has no breasts,* literally, "if she be a wall." *build upon her a battlement of silver . . . enclose her with cedar boards,* the meaning is obscure. **8:10** *tall,* literally, "I am as a wall." *full-breasted,* literally, "My breasts are as towers."

8:6, 7 In this final description of their love, the girl includes some of its significant characteristics (see also 1 Corinthians 13). Love is as strong as death; it cannot be killed by time or disaster; and it cannot be bought for any price, because it is freely given. Love is priceless, and even the richest king cannot buy it. It must be accepted as a gift from God and then shared within the guidelines God provides. Accept the love of your spouse as God's gift and strive to make it a reflection of the perfect love that comes from God himself.

8:8, 9 The girl is reflecting on the days when she was younger and under the care of her brothers, who wondered how to help her prepare for marriage. They decided that if she was like a wall, standing firm against sexual temptation, they would praise her. But if she was like a door, open to immorality, they would take steps to guard her from doing something foolish. In 8:10, she testifies that she has been like a wall, and thus has found favor in Solomon's eyes.

8:11, 12 The girl gives a picture of total submission to her beloved, saying, "You are the owner of my vineyard." In other words, everything she has is his. There is no private property in marriage, for each partner freely gives all to the other.

8:14 The love between Solomon and his bride did not diminish in intensity since their wedding night. The lovers relied on each other and kept no secrets from each other. Devotion and commitment were the keys to their relationship, just as they are in our relationships to our spouses and to God. The faithfulness of our marital love should reflect God's perfect faithfulness to us.

Paul shows how marriage represents Christ's relationship to his church (Ephesians 5:25–32), and John pictures the Second Coming as a great marriage feast for Christ and his bride, his faithful followers (Revelation 19:7, 8; 21:1, 2). Medieval theologians thought the Song of Solomon was an allegory showing Christ's love for his church. It makes even better sense to say that it is a love poem about a real human love relationship, and that all loving, committed marriages reflect God's love.

ISAIAH

VITAL STATISTICS

PURPOSE:
To call the nation of Judah back to God and to tell of God's salvation through the Messiah

AUTHOR:
The prophet Isaiah, son of Amoz

DATE WRITTEN:
The events of chapters 1—39 occurred during Isaiah's ministry, so they were probably written about 700 B.C. Chapters 40—66, however, may have been written near the end of his life, about 681 B.C.

SETTING:
Isaiah is speaking and writing mainly in Jerusalem

KEY VERSE:
"But he was wounded and bruised for *our* sins. He was beaten that we might have peace; he was lashed—and we were healed!" (53:5).

KEY PEOPLE:
Isaiah, his two sons Shear-jashub and Maher-shalal-hash-baz

SPECIAL FEATURES:
The book of Isaiah contains both prose and poetry and uses personification (attributing personal qualities to divine beings or inanimate objects). Also, many of the prophecies in Isaiah contain predictions that foretell a soon-to-occur event and a distant future event at the same time.

SLOWLY he rose, and the crowd fell silent. Those at the back leaned forward, straining to hear. The atmosphere was electric. He spoke, and his carefully chosen words flew like swift arrows, and found their mark. The great man, a spokesman for God, was warning . . . and condemning. The crowd became restless—shifting positions, clenching fists, and murmuring. Some agreed with his message, nodding their heads and weeping softly. But most were angry, and they began to shout back insults and threats. Such was the life of a prophet.

The "office" of prophet was instituted during the days of Samuel, the last of the judges. Prophets stood with the priests as God's special representatives. The role of the prophet was to speak for God, confronting the people and their leaders with God's commands and promises. Because of this confrontational stance and the continuing tendency of people to disobey God, true prophets usually were not very popular. Although their message often went unheeded, they faithfully and forcefully proclaimed the truth.

The book of Isaiah is the first of the writings of the Prophets in the Bible; and Isaiah, the author, is generally considered to be the greatest prophet. He was reared in an aristocratic home and married to a prophetess. In the beginning of his ministry he was well-liked. But, like most prophets, he soon became unpopular because his messages were so difficult to hear. He called the people to turn from their lives of sin and warned them of God's judgment and punishment. Isaiah had an active ministry for 60 years before he was executed during Manasseh's reign (according to tradition). As God's special messenger to Judah, Isaiah prophesied during the reigns of several of its rulers, and many of those messages are recorded in his book: Uzziah and Jotham, chapters 1—6; Ahaz, chapters 7—14; and Hezekiah, chapters 15—39.

The first half of the book of Isaiah (chapters 1—39) contains scathing denunciations and pronouncements as he calls Judah, Israel, and the surrounding nations to repent of their sins. However, the last 27 chapters (40–66) are filled with consolation and hope as Isaiah unfolds God's promise of future blessings through his Messiah.

As you read Isaiah, imagine this strong and courageous man of God, fearlessly proclaiming God's Word, and listen to his message in relation to your own life—*return, repent, and be renewed.* Then trust in God's *redemption* through Christ and *rejoice.* Your Savior has come, and he's coming again!

nnach- Manasseh   Isaiah's   Josiah
b   becomes   ministry   becomes
rounds king of   ends   king of
usalem Judah   681   Judah
        697   640

THE BLUEPRINT

A. WORDS OF JUDGMENT (1:1—39:8)
1. The sins of Israel and Judah
2. Judgment against heathen nations
3. God's purpose in judgment
4. Jerusalem's true and false hopes
5. Events during the reign of Hezekiah

The 39 chapters in the first half of Isaiah generally carry the message of judgment for sin. Isaiah brings the message of judgment to Judah, Israel, and the surrounding heathen nations. Judah had a form of godliness, but in their hearts they were corrupt. Isaiah's warnings were intended to purify the people by helping them understand God's true nature and message. However, they ignored the repeated warnings that Isaiah brought. We need not repeat their error; rather, we should heed the prophetic voice.

B. WORDS OF COMFORT (40:1—66:24)
1. Israel's release from captivity
2. The future Redeemer
3. The future kingdom

The 27 chapters in the second half of Isaiah generally bring a message of forgiveness, comfort, and hope. This message of hope looks forward to the coming of the Messiah. Isaiah speaks more about the Messiah than any other Old Testament prophet. He describes the Messiah as both a suffering servant and a sovereign Lord. The fact that the Messiah was to be both a suffering servant and a sovereign Lord could not be understood clearly until New Testament times. Based on what Jesus Christ has done, God freely offers forgiveness to all who turn to him in faith. This is God's message of comfort to us because those who heed it find eternal peace and fellowship with him.

MEGATHEMES

THEME	EXPLANATION	IMPORTANCE
Holiness	God is highly exalted above all his creatures. His moral perfection stands in contrast to evil people and nations. God is perfect and sinless in all his motives and actions, so he is in perfect control of his power, judgment, love, and mercy. His holy nature is our yardstick for morality.	Because God is without sin, he alone can help us with our sin. It is only right that we regard him as supreme in power and moral perfection. We must never treat God as common or ordinary. He alone deserves our devotion.
Punishment	Because God is holy, he requires his people to treat others justly. He promised to punish Israel, Judah, and other nations for faithless immorality and idolatry. True faith had degenerated into national pride and empty religious rituals.	We must trust in God alone and fulfill his commands. We cannot forsake justice nor give in to selfishness. If we harden our hearts against his message, punishment will surely come to us.
Salvation	Because God's judgment is coming, we need a Savior. No man or nation can be saved without God's help. Christ's perfect sacrifice for our sins is foretold and portrayed in Isaiah. All who trust God can be freed from their sin and restored to him.	Christ died to save us from our sin. We need his help. He is willing to save all those who turn from their sin and come to him. Salvation is from God alone.
Messiah	God will send the Messiah to save his people. He will set up his own kingdom as the faithful Prince of Peace who rules with righteousness. He would come as sovereign Lord, but he would do so as a servant who died to take away sins.	Our trust must be in the Messiah, not in ourselves or in any nation or power. There is no hope unless we believe in him. Trust Christ fully and let him rule in your life as your sovereign Lord.
Hope	God promises comfort, deliverance, and restoration in his future kingdom. The Messiah will rule over his faithful followers in the age to come. Hope is possible because Christ is coming.	We can be refreshed since there is compassion for those who repent. No matter how bleak our current situation or how evil the world is, we must continue to be God's faithful people who hope for his return.

A. WORDS OF JUDGMENT (1:1—39:8)

Isaiah begins by bringing a message of divine judgment for both Israel and Judah. Although the advance of the Assyrians poses a problem for Judah, God foretells the destruction of Assyria and other evil surrounding nations through the prophet Isaiah. This section ends with the Assyrian invasion being held off, demonstrating the clear unfolding of God's plan and promises for the nation at this time.

1. The sins of Israel and Judah

Messages to a rebellious people

1 *These are the messages that came to Isaiah, son of Amoz, in the visions he saw during the reigns of King Uzziah, King Jotham, King Ahaz and King Hezekiah—all kings of Judah. In these messages God showed him what was going to happen to Judah and Jerusalem in the days ahead.*

2Listen, O heaven and earth, to what the Lord is saying:

The children I raised and cared for so long and tenderly have turned against me. 3Even the animals—the donkey and the ox—know their owner and appreciate his care for them, but not my people Israel. No matter what I do for them, they still don't care. 4Oh, what a sinful nation they are! They walk bent-backed beneath their load of guilt. Their fathers before them were evil too. Born to be bad, they have turned their backs upon the Lord, and have despised the Holy One of Israel. They have cut themselves off from my help.

5, 6Oh, my people, haven't you had enough of punishment? Why will you force me to whip you again and again? Must you forever rebel? From head to foot you are sick and weak and faint, covered with bruises and welts and infected wounds, unanointed and unbound. 7Your country lies in ruins; your cities are burned; while you watch, foreigners are destroying and plundering everything they see. 8You stand there helpless and abandoned like a watchman's shanty in the field when the harvest time is over—or when the crop is stripped and robbed.

9*If the Lord Almighty had not stepped in to save a few of us, we would have been wiped out as Sodom and Gomorrah were.* 10An apt comparison! Listen, you leaders of Israel, you men of Sodom and Gomorrah, as I call you now. Listen to the Lord. Hear what he is telling you! 11I am sick of your sacrifices. Don't bring me any more

1:1
2 Kgs 15:1,13
18:1
Isa 2:1; 40:9

1:2
Deut 32:1
Jer 3:22
Isa 65:2
Mic 1:2

1:3
Jer 8:7

1:4
Song 2:7,9,17
4:6
Isa 5:24

1:5
Ps 38:3

1:7
Lev 26:33
Jer 44:6

1:9
Isa 10:20-22
11:11,16
Rom 9:29

1:10
Ezek 16:46

1:11
Jer 6:20
Mal 1:10

1:10 *An apt comparison*, implied.

1:1 Isaiah was a prophet while the nation of Israel was divided into two kingdoms—Israel in the north, and Judah in the south. The Northern Kingdom, Israel, had sinned greatly against God, and Judah was headed in the same direction—perverting justice, oppressing the poor, turning from God to idols, and looking for military aid from heathen nations rather than from God. Isaiah came primarily as a prophet to Judah, but his message was also for Israel. In fact, Isaiah lived to see the destruction and captivity of the Northern Kingdom in 722 B.C. Thus, his ministry began as one of warning.

1:2 Isaiah had a vision of what God wanted him to communicate to the people because he was receptive to God's messages—he was mentally, morally, and spiritually tuned-in to God. He was, therefore, guided by the Holy Spirit in such a way as to convey God's exact thinking to the people. If we are ready to listen to God, we will hear his messages through his Word, other believers, and the Holy Spirit.

1:2-4 The people of Judah were sinning greatly and did not even care. God brought charges against them through Isaiah because they had forgotten God and had broken their contract with him (Deuteronomy 28). By breaking the contract they were bringing God's punishment upon themselves. God gave them prosperity and they didn't serve him; he sent them warnings and they refused to listen; now he would bring the fire of his judgment.

1:4-9 As long as the people of Judah continued to sin, they cut themselves off from God's help and isolated themselves. Has sin ever made you feel lonely and separated from God? Remember, God does not abandon you—it is your sin that cuts you off from

him. The only sure cure for this kind of loneliness is to restore a meaningful relationship with God by confessing your sin, obeying his instructions, and communicating regularly with him (see Psalm 140:13; Isaiah 1:16-19; 1 John 1:9).

1:7 Was this destruction taking place at that time? Judah was attacked many times during Isaiah's lifetime. This verse could be a picture of the results of these invasions or a prediction of the coming invasion of Israel by Assyria. Most likely it pointed to Babylon's future invasion of Judah in 586 B.C.

1:9 Sodom and Gomorrah were two cities that God destroyed for their great wickedness (Genesis 19:1-25). They are mentioned elsewhere in the Bible as examples of God's judgment against sin (Jeremiah 50:40; Ezekiel 16:46-63; Matthew 11:23, 24; Jude 1:7).

1:10 To hear what God wanted to say to Judah, the people had to listen. When we can't understand God's message, perhaps we are not listening carefully or do not expect him to speak to us.

1:10-15 God was not revoking the system of sacrifices he had initiated with Moses. Instead, he was calling for sincere hearts of faith. The leaders were carefully making the traditional sacrifices at holy celebrations, but they were still unfaithful to God in their hearts. Sacrifices were to be an outward sign of their inward faith in God, but the outward signs were empty when no inward faith existed. Why, then, did they continue to offer sacrifices? Like many people today, they had come to place more faith in the rituals of their religion than in the God they worshiped. Examine your own religious practices: do they spring from your faith in the living God? The outward expression is meaningless if the inward faith is missing (see Deuteronomy 10:12-16; 1 Samuel 15:22, 23; Psalm 51:16-19).

of them. I don't want your fat rams; I don't want to see the blood from your offerings. 12, 13Who wants your sacrifices when you have no sorrow for your sins? The incense you bring me is a stench in my nostrils. Your holy celebrations of the new moon and the Sabbath, and your special days for fasting—even your most pious meetings—all are frauds! I want nothing more to do with them. 14I hate them all; I can't stand the sight of them. 15From now on, when you pray with your hands stretched out to heaven, I won't look or listen. Even though you make many prayers, I will not hear, for your hands are those of murderers; they are covered with the blood of your innocent victims.

16Oh, wash yourselves! Be clean! Let me no longer see you doing all these wicked things; quit your evil ways. 17Learn to do good, to be fair and to help the poor, the fatherless, and widows.

18Come, let's talk this over! says the Lord; no matter how deep the stain of your sins, I can take it out and make you as clean as freshly fallen snow. Even if you are stained as red as crimson, I can make you white as wool! 19If you will only let me help you, if you will only obey, then I will make you rich! 20But if you keep on turning your backs and refusing to listen to me, you will be killed by your enemies; I, the Lord, have spoken.

21Jerusalem, once my faithful wife! And now a prostitute! Running after other gods! Once "The City of Fair Play," but now a gang of murderers. 22Once like sterling silver; now mixed with worthless alloy! Once so pure, but now diluted like watered-down wine! 23Your leaders are rebels, companions of thieves; all of them take bribes and won't defend the widows and orphans. 24Therefore the Lord, the Mighty One of Israel, says: I will pour out my anger on you, my enemies! 25I myself will melt you in a smelting pot, and skim off your slag.

26And afterwards I will give you good judges and wise counselors like those you used to have. Then your city shall again be called "The City of Justice," and "The Faithful Town." 27Those who return to the Lord, who are just and good, shall be redeemed.

28(But all sinners shall utterly perish, for they refuse to come to me.) 29Shame will cover you, and you will blush to think of all those times you sacrificed to idols in your groves of "sacred" oaks. 30You will perish like a withered tree or a garden

1:12
1 Chron 23:31
Jer 7:9,10

1:15
Isa 59:2
Mic 3:4

1:16
Ps 26:6
Isa 52:11
Jer 25:5

1:17
Jer 22:3

1:18
Ps 51:7
Isa 43:26; 44:22
Rev 7:14

1:19
Deut 30:15,16

1:23
Ex 23:8
Jer 5:28
Ezek 22:7
Mic 7:3

1:25
Ezek 22:19-22
Mal 3:3

1:26
Isa 33:5
Zech 8:3

1:28
Ps 9:5
2 Thess 1:8,9

ISAIAH served as a prophet to Judah from 740–681 B.C.	*Climate of the times*	Society was in a great upheaval. Under King Ahaz and King Manasseh the people reverted to idolatry and there was even child sacrifice.
	Main message	Although judgment from other nations was inevitable, the people could still have a special relationship with God.
	Importance of message	Sometimes we must suffer judgment and discipline before we are restored to God.
	Contemporary prophets	Hosea (753–715) Micah (742–687)

1:12, 13 Although the people did not feel sorry for their sins, they continued to offer sacrifices for forgiveness. Gifts and sacrifices mean nothing to God when they come from a corrupt heart. God wants us to remove sin from our lives first; after that, we may offer our "sacrifices" of time, money, or energy.

1:18 A deep stain is virtually impossible to remove from clothing, and the stain of sin seems equally permanent. But God can remove the stain of sin from our lives just as he promised to do for the Israelites. We don't have to go through life permanently soiled. Through prayer we can be assured that Christ has forgiven our worst sins and removed our most indelible stains (Psalm 51:1–7).

1:21, 22 God compares his relationship with his people to marriage. The people had turned from the worship of the true God to worshiping idols. Idolatry, outward or inward, is spiritual adultery, breaking our commitment to God in order to love something else. Jesus described the people of his day as adulterous, even though they were religiously strict. The church is the bride of Christ (Revelation 19:7); are we an impure bride or a faithful one?

1:25 God promised to refine his people as metal in a smelting pot. This process involves melting the metal and skimming off the impure slag so that the worker can see his own image in the liquid metal. We must be willing to submit to God, allowing him to remove our sin or imperfection until we reflect his image.

1:26 Isaiah often speaks with both the present and the future in mind. When he says *the day is coming, those days,* or *one day* his prophecies do not necessarily apply to one event, but may apply to a series of present and future events. The *last days* refers to the final days when God will establish a new heaven and a new earth.

1:29 Throughout history, the oak tree has been a symbol of strength. Ezekiel mentions that groves of oak trees were used as places for idol worship (Ezekiel 6:13).

without water. ³¹The strongest among you will disappear like burning straw; your evil deeds are the spark that sets the straw on fire, and no one will be able to put it out.

1:31
Isa 33:11-14
Mt 3:12

Walk in the light of the Lord

2 This is another message to Isaiah from the Lord concerning Judah and Jerusalem:

²In the last days Jerusalem and the Temple of the Lord will become the world's greatest attraction, and people from many lands will flow there to worship the Lord.

2:2
Isa 66:20
Mic 4:1,2

³"Come," everyone will say, "let us go up the mountain of the Lord, to the Temple of the God of Israel; there he will teach us his laws, and we will obey them." For in those days the world will be ruled from Jerusalem. ⁴The Lord will settle international disputes; all the nations will convert their weapons of war into implements of peace. Then at the last all wars will stop and all military training will end. ⁵O Israel, come, let us walk in the light of the Lord, and be obedient to his laws!

2:3
Isa 51:4,5

2:4
Isa 11:6-9
Hos 2:18
Joel 3:10
Zech 9:10

2:5
Isa 60:1,2,
19,20
1 Jn 1:5,7

⁶The Lord has rejected you because you welcome foreigners from the East who practice magic and communicate with evil spirits, as the Philistines do.

2:6
2 Kgs 1:2

⁷Israel has vast treasures of silver and gold, and great numbers of horses and chariots ⁸and idols—the land is full of them! They are man-made, and yet you *worship* them! ⁹Small and great, all bow before them; God will not forgive you for this sin.

2:8
Ps 115:4-8
Isa 44:17

¹⁰Crawl into the caves in the rocks and hide in terror from his glorious majesty, ¹¹for the day is coming when your proud looks will be brought low; the Lord alone will be exalted. ¹²On that day the Lord Almighty will move against the proud and haughty and bring them to the dust. ¹³All the tall cedars of Lebanon and all the mighty oaks of Bashan shall bend low, ¹⁴and all the high mountains and hills, ¹⁵and every high tower and wall, ¹⁶and all the proud ocean ships and trim harbor craft—*all* shall be crushed before the Lord that day. ¹⁷All the glory of mankind will bow low; the pride of men will lie in the dust, and the Lord alone will be exalted. ¹⁸And all idols will be utterly abolished and destroyed.

2:10
Rev 6:15,16

2:11
Isa 13:11

2:12
Job 40:11,12
Mal 4:1

2:13
Isa 10:33,34
Zech 11:2

2:16
Isa 23:1,14

2:18
Isa 21:9
Mic 1:7

¹⁹When the Lord stands up from his throne to shake up the earth, his enemies will crawl with fear into the holes in the rocks and into the caves because of the glory of his majesty. ²⁰Then at last they will abandon their gold and silver idols to the moles and bats, ²¹and crawl into the caverns to hide among the jagged rocks at the tops of the cliffs to try to get away from the terror of the Lord and the glory of his majesty

2:19
Ps 18:7
Hag 2:6,7

2:20
Isa 30:22

2:2 *will become the world's greatest attraction,* literally, "shall be established as the highest of the mountains."
2:4 *will convert their weapons of war into implements of peace,* literally, "beat their swords into plowshares and their spears into pruning hooks." **2:5** *and be obedient to his laws,* implied.

1:31 A spark set to straw ignites a quick, devouring fire. God compares strong men whose evil deeds devour them to burning straw. Our lives can be destroyed quickly by a small but deadly spark of evil. What potential "fire hazards" do you need to remove?

2:2 For more on the significance of the Temple, see the note on 2 Chronicles 5:1ff. In the last days, the Temple will be attractive not for its architecture, but because of God's presence there.

2:2-4 God gave Isaiah the gift of seeing the future. Here God showed Isaiah what would eventually happen to Jerusalem. Revelation 21 depicts the glorious fulfillment of this prophecy in the new earth, where only those whose names are written in God's book will be allowed to enter. God made a covenant (promise) with his people and will never break it. This prophecy gives people hope for the future.

2:5 We are told here of a wonderful future of peace, when we will be taught God's laws and will obey them. We know that one day God will remove all sin that causes war, conflict, and disruption. Yet we do not need to wait to obey God. In 2:5, we are encouraged along with Judah to obey God now. He has given us his Word for

direction and guidance in order to obey him now. Some benefits of obedience we will receive only in the future. But we may enjoy some benefits now as we apply God's Word to our lives.

2:6 The Philistines worshiped Dagon, Ashtoreth, and Baal-zebub. During the more sinful periods of their history, the people of Israel worshiped these heathen gods along with Jehovah, and even gave them Hebrew names.

2:8, 9 Idol worship was serious because it destroyed the people's relationship with God. Under the reign of evil kings, idol worship flourished in both Israel and Judah. A few good kings in Judah stopped it during their reigns. Idol worship is bad because (1) it insults God when we worship something he created rather than worshiping him; (2) it distracts us from God by destroying the relationship of trust we have with him; (3) it causes us to rely on our own efforts rather than on God (see Deuteronomy 27:15).

2:12 "That day" is the day of judgment, the time when God will judge both evil and good. That day will come, and we will want a proper relationship with God when it does.

2:19 See Revelation 6:15-17 for a description of the fear of God's enemies in the day of his wrath.

2:22
Ps 8:4; 144:3,4
Jer 17:5

3:1
Ezek 4:16
3:2
Isa 9:14,15
3:4
Eccles 10:16
3:5
Jer 9:3-8
Mic 7:3-6

3:7
Ezek 34:4

3:8
Isa 65:3,5
3:9
Gen 13:13
Prov 8:36

3:10
Deut 28:1-14
3:11
Deut 28:15-68

3:13
Hos 4:1
Mic 6:2

3:14
Job 24:9,14
Ps 10:9; 14:4
Ezek 18:12
Jas 2:6
3:15
Ps 94:5

when he rises to terrify the earth. 22Puny man! Frail as his breath! Don't ever put your trust in him!

Isaiah warns of judgment on Judah

3 The Lord will cut off Jerusalem's and Judah's food and water supplies 2and kill her leaders; he will destroy her armies, judges, prophets, elders, 3army officers, businessmen, lawyers, magicians and politicians. 4Israel's kings will be like babies, ruling childishly. 5And the worst sort of anarchy will prevail—everyone stepping on someone else, neighbors fighting neighbors, youths revolting against authority, criminals sneering at honorable men.

6In those days a man will say to his brother, "You have some extra clothing, so you be our king and take care of this mess."

7"No!" he will reply. "I cannot be of any help! I have no extra food or clothes. Don't get me involved!"

8Israel's civil government will be in utter ruin because the Jews have spoken out against their Lord and will not worship him; they offend his glory. 9The very look on their faces gives them away and shows their guilt. And they boast that their sin is equal to the sin of Sodom; they are not even ashamed. What a catastrophe! They have doomed themselves.

10But all is well for the godly man. Tell him, "What a reward you are going to get!" 11But say to the wicked, "Your doom is sure. You too shall get your just deserts. Your well-earned punishment is on the way."

12O my people! Can't you see what fools your rulers are? Weak as women! Foolish as little children playing king. True leaders? No, misleaders! Leading you down the garden path to destruction.

13The Lord stands up! He is the great Prosecuting Attorney presenting his case against his people! 14First to feel his wrath will be the elders and the princes, for they have defrauded the poor. They have filled their barns with grain extorted from the helpless peasants.

15"How dare you grind my people in the dust like that?" the Lord Almighty will demand of them.

16Next, he will judge the haughty Jewish women, who mince along, noses in the air, tinkling bracelets on their ankles, with wanton eyes that rove among the crowds

---

2:22 People are "puny" compared to God. They are undependable, sinful, and mortal. Often we trust human beings with our lives and our futures instead of trusting the all-knowing God. Beware of people who want you to trust them instead of God. Remember that only God is completely reliable, because only God loves us with an eternal love (Psalm 100:5).

3:1–3 Jerusalem besieged, her leaders destroyed—this unhappy picture would soon become a reality. The people's disobedience brought great afflictions and destruction, as God had warned (Deuteronomy 28).

3:5–9 People lose a vital ability when they can no longer see their own sinfulness. The results are broken relationships, authority out of control, blindness to the needy, and, worst of all, forgetfulness toward God. Spiritual blindness is a matter of life and death, not merely an inconvenience.

3:9–11 Sin is self-destructive. In today's world, sinful living often appears glamorous, exciting, and clever. But sin is wrong regardless of how society perceives it because in the long run sin will destroy us and make us miserable. Thus, God is trying to protect us by warning us about our sins. Those who are proud of their sins will receive the punishment from God they deserve. They have rejected God's path to life (see Psalm 1), and the only alternative is the path to destruction.

3:10, 11 Eventually the faithful will receive God's reward and the wicked will receive his punishment. It is disheartening to see the wicked prospering while we seem defeated as we follow God's plan. Yet we must hold on and take heart! God will bring about

justice in the end, and we will receive his reward if we have been faithful.

3:14 The elders and princes were responsible for helping people, but instead they defrauded the poor. Because they were unjust leaders, Isaiah said they would be the first to receive God's wrath. Leaders will be held accountable for how they lead. If you are in a position of leadership, you must lead according to God's just commands. Corruption will bring God's wrath, especially if others follow your example.

3:14 Why is justice so important to God? (1) Justice is part of God's nature; it is the way he runs the universe. (2) Even as sinners, we all want justice for ourselves. (3) When government and church leaders are unjust, the poor and powerless suffer. (4) God holds the poor in high regard. They are the ones most likely to turn to him for help and comfort. Injustice, then, attacks God's children. Because we follow a just God, we must uphold justice.

3:16–26 The women of Judah had placed their emphasis on clothing and jewelry rather than on God. They dressed to be noticed, to gain approval, and to be fashionable. Instead of being concerned about the oppression around them (3:14, 15), they were self-serving and self-centered. Those who abuse their possessions will end up with nothing. These verses are not an indictment against clothing and jewelry, but a judgment on those who use them lavishly while blind to the needs of others. When God blesses you, don't flaunt your wealth. Use what you have to help others.

to catch the glances of the men. 17The Lord will send a plague of scabs to ornament
their heads! He will expose their nakedness for all to see. 18No longer shall they
tinkle with self-assurance as they walk. For the Lord will strip away their artful
beauty and their ornaments, 19their necklaces and bracelets and veils of shimmer-
ing gauze. 20Gone shall be their scarves and ankle chains, headbands, earrings, and
perfumes; 21their rings and jewels, 22and party clothes and negligees and capes
and ornate combs and purses; 23their mirrors, lovely lingerie, beautiful dresses and
veils. 24Instead of smelling of sweet perfume, they'll stink; for sashes they'll use
ropes; their well-set hair will all fall out; they'll wear sacks instead of robes.

3:24
Esth 2:12
Isa 15:3
1 Pet 3:3

All their beauty will be gone; all that will be left to them is shame and disgrace.
25, 26Their husbands shall die in battle; the women, ravaged, shall sit crying on the
ground.

3:25
Isa 65:12
Lam 2:10

God's holy people will be cleansed

4 At that time so few men will be left alive that seven women will fight over each
of them and say, "Let us all marry you! We will furnish our own food and
clothing; only let us be called by your name so that we won't be mocked as old
maids."

4:1
Isa 54:4

2, 3, 4Those whose names are written down to escape the destruction of Jerusalem
will be washed and rinsed of all their moral filth by the horrors and the fire. They
will be God's holy people. And the land will produce for them its lushest bounty
and its richest fruit. 5Then the Lord will provide shade on all Jerusalem—over
every home and all its public grounds—a canopy of smoke and cloud throughout
the day, and clouds of fire at night, covering the Glorious Land, 6protecting it from
daytime heat and from rains and storms.

4:2-4
Ex 32:32
Ps 72:16
Isa 28:6; 62:12
Joel 2:32
Obad 17
Lk 10:20

4:5
Num 9:15-23

4:6
Ps 27:5
Isa 32:1,2

God's people are his vineyard

5 Now I will sing a song about his vineyard to the one I love. *My Beloved has a
vineyard on a very fertile hill. 2He plowed it and took out all the rocks and
planted his vineyard with the choicest vines. He built a watchtower and cut a
winepress in the rocks. Then he waited for the harvest, but the grapes that grew
were wild and sour and not at all the sweet ones he expected.*

5:1
Ps 80:8
Jer 12:10

5:2
Jer 2:21
Mk 11:13

3Now, men of Jerusalem and Judah, you have heard the case! You be the judges!
4What more could I have done? Why did my vineyard give me wild grapes instead
of sweet? 5I will tear down the fences and let my vineyard go to pasture to be
trampled by cattle and sheep. 6I won't prune it or hoe it, but let it be overgrown with
briars and thorns. I will command the clouds not to rain on it any more.

5:4
Jer 7:25,26
Mt 23:37

5:5
Lam 1:15
Lk 21:24
Rev 11:2

7I have given you the story of God's people. They are the vineyard that I spoke
about. Israel and Judah are his pleasant acreage! He expected them to yield a crop
of justice, but found bloodshed instead. He expected righteousness, but the cries of
deep oppression met his ears. 8You buy up property so others have no place to live.
Your homes are built on great estates so you can be alone in the midst of the earth!
9But the Lord Almighty has sworn your awful fate—with my own ears I heard him
say, "Many a beautiful home will lie deserted, their owners killed or gone." 10An

5:6
Jer 14:1-22
25:11

5:8
Jer 22:13-17
Mic 2:2

5:9
Mt 23:38

5:10
Hag 1:6; 2:16

4:2-4 *its richest fruit.* Literally, "In that day the branch of the Lord will be beautiful and glorious." The phrase "branch
of the Lord" refers to God's people, or it may be a prophecy of the coming Messiah.

4:2-4 In the midst of the tribulation predicted by Isaiah, some
people will be protected by God's loving grace. Those protected
will become God's people when Messiah rules the earth (Jeremiah
23:5, 6; Zechariah 3:8). Their distinctive mark will be their holiness,
not wealth or prestige. This holiness comes from a sincere desire
to obey God and from wholehearted devotion to him. Things will
not always continue as they are now. God will put an end to all evil,
and his faithful followers will share in his glorious reign.

5:1-7 The lesson of the vineyard shows that God's chosen nation
was "to bear fruit"—to carry out his work, to uphold justice. It did
bear fruit, but the fruit was sour and wild. This passage uses plays

on words: the Hebrew words for *justice* and *bloodshed* sound very
much alike, as do those for *righteousness* and *cry.* Jesus said, "the
way to identify a tree or a person is by the kind of fruit produced"
(Matthew 7:20). Have you examined your own "fruit" lately? Is it
sweet or sour?

5:8-25 God condemns six sins: (1) exploiting others (5:8-10);
(2) being drunk (5:11-17); (3) blaspheming (5:18, 19);
(4) confusing moral standards (5:20); (5) being conceited (5:21);
and (6) perverting justice (5:22-25). Because of these sins, God
punished Israel with destruction by Assyria (5:26-30). A similar
fate was awaiting Judah if they didn't turn from these sins.

acre of vineyard will not produce a gallon of juice! Ten bushels of seed will yield a one-bushel crop!

5:11
Prov 23:29,30
Isa 28:1,3,7,8

5:12
Ps 28:5

5:13
Hos 4:6

11Woe to you who get up early in the morning to go on long drinking bouts that last till late at night—woe to you drunken bums. 12You furnish lovely music at your grand parties; the orchestras are superb! But for the Lord you have no thought or care. 13Therefore I will send you into exile far away because you neither know nor care that I have done so much for you. Your great and honored men will starve, and the common people will die of thirst.

5:16
Isa 33:5,10

5:17
Zeph 2:6

5:18
Jer 23:10-14

5:19
2 Pet 3:3,4

14Hell is licking its chops in anticipation of this delicious morsel, Jerusalem. Her great and small shall be swallowed up, and all her drunken throngs. 15In that day the haughty shall be brought down to the dust; the proud shall be humbled; 16but the Lord Almighty is exalted above all, for he alone is holy, just and good. 17In those days flocks will feed among the ruins. Lambs and calves and kids will pasture there!

5:20
Job 17:12
Prov 17:15

5:21
Prov 3:7
Rom 12:16
1 Cor 3:18-20

18Woe to those who drag their sins behind them like a bullock on a rope. 19They even mock the Holy One of Israel and dare the Lord to punish them. "Hurry up and punish us, O Lord," they say. "We want to see what you can do!" 20They say that what is right is wrong, and what is wrong is right; that black is white and white is black; bitter is sweet and sweet is bitter.

5:22
Isa 56:12
Hab 2:15

5:23
Mic 3:11
Jas 5:6

5:24
Isa 30:12

5:25
2 Kgs 22:17
Isa 9:12,17,21
10:4; 66:15

21Woe to those who are wise and shrewd in their own eyes! 22Woe to those who are "heroes" when it comes to drinking, and boast about the liquor they can hold. 23They take bribes to pervert justice, letting the wicked go free and putting innocent men in jail. 24Therefore God will deal with them and burn them. They will disappear like straw on fire. Their roots will rot and their flowers wither, for they have thrown away the laws of God and despised the Word of the Holy One of Israel. 25That is why the anger of the Lord is hot against his people; that is why he has reached out his hand to smash them. The hills will tremble, and the rotting bodies of his people will be thrown as refuse in the streets. But even so, his anger is not ended; his hand is heavy on them still.

5:26
Isa 13:2,3

5:27
Joel 2:7,8

5:28
Jer 4:13

5:29
Isa 42:22
Zeph 3:3

5:30
Jer 4:23-28
6:23
Joel 2:10

26He will send a signal to the nations far away, whistling to those at the ends of the earth, and they will come racing toward Jerusalem. 27They never weary, never stumble, never stop; their belts are tight, their bootstraps strong; they run without stopping for rest or for sleep. 28Their arrows are sharp; their bows are bent; sparks fly from their horses' hoofs, and the wheels of their chariots spin like the wind. 29They roar like lions and pounce upon the prey. They seize my people and carry them off into captivity with none to rescue them. 30They growl over their victims

5:18 *like a bullock on a rope,* or *"with cords of falsehood."*   **5:19** *and dare the Lord to punish them,* implied.

5:11-13 These men spent many hours drinking, but Isaiah predicted that many would eventually die of thirst. Ironically, our pleasures—if they do not have God's blessing—may eventually destroy us. Leaving God out of our lives allows sin to come into them. God wants us to enjoy life (1 Corinthians 10:26) but to avoid those activities that could lead us away from him.

5:13 This took place when Israel was exiled to Assyria and Judah to Babylon. Where once there were parties with food and music, there would be hunger, thirst, and death. These people brought judgment on themselves. Turning away from God exposes us to judgment.

5:13 The nation's heroes—the great and honored men—would suffer the same humiliation as the common people. Why? Because they lived by their own values rather than God's. Many of today's heroes in TV, movies, and books are idolized because of their ability to live as they please. Are your heroes those who defy God, or those who defy the world in order to serve God?

5:18-20 Some people drag their sins around with them. But their sins become a burden that wears them out. Are you dragging around a cartload of sins that you refuse to give up? Before you find yourself worn out and useless, turn to the One who promises to take away your burden of sin (see Matthew 11:28-30).

5:20 When people do not carefully observe the distinction between right and wrong, destruction soon follows. It is easy for people to say, "No one can decide for anyone else what is really right or wrong." They may think getting drunk can't hurt them, extramarital sex isn't really wrong, or money doesn't really control them. But when we make excuses for our actions, we break down the distinction between right and wrong. If we do not take God's Word, the Bible, as our standard, soon all of life's moral choices appear fuzzy. Without God, we are headed for a breakdown and much suffering.

5:24 The people suffered because they threw out God's laws. It is sad to see so many people today searching for meaning in life while tossing aside God's Word. We can avoid the error of Israel and Judah by making the Bible a high priority in our lives.

5:26-30 This passage describes what God would do if the people disobeyed him (Deuteronomy 28). Assyria began to torment Israel during the reign of Ahaz (735-715 B.C.). This powerful aggressor destroyed the Northern Kingdom in 722 B.C. and scattered the people throughout its own empire. Sin has consequences. Although they may not be immediate, they will come.

like the roaring of the sea. Over all Israel lies a pall of darkness and sorrow and the heavens are black.

God commissions Isaiah

6 The year King Uzziah died I saw the Lord! He was sitting on a lofty throne, and the Temple was filled with his glory. ²Hovering about him were mighty, six-winged angels of fire. With two of their wings they covered their faces; with two others they covered their feet, and with two they flew. ³In a great antiphonal chorus they sang, "Holy, holy, holy is the Lord Almighty; the whole earth is filled with his glory." ⁴Such singing it was! It shook the Temple to its foundations, and suddenly the entire sanctuary was filled with smoke.

⁵Then I said, "My doom is sealed, for I am a foul-mouthed sinner, a member of a sinful, foul-mouthed race; and I have looked upon the King, the Lord of heaven's armies."

⁶Then one of the mighty angels flew over to the altar and with a pair of tongs picked out a burning coal. ⁷He touched my lips with it and said, "Now you are pronounced 'Not guilty' because this coal has touched your lips. Your sins are all forgiven."

⁸Then I heard the Lord asking, "Whom shall I send as a messenger to my people? Who will go?"

And I said, "Lord, I'll go! Send *me*."

⁹And he said, "Yes, go. But tell my people this: 'Though you hear my words repeatedly, you won't understand them. Though you watch and watch as I perform my miracles, still you won't know what they mean.' ¹⁰Dull their understanding, close their ears and shut their eyes. I don't want them to see or to hear or to understand, or to turn to me to heal them."

¹¹Then I said, "Lord, how long will it be before they are ready to listen?"

And he replied, "Not until their cities are destroyed—without a person left—and

6:1
Jn 12:41

6:2
Rev 4:8

6:3
Ps 72:19

6:5
Lk 5:8
Jer 9:3-8

6:7
Isa 40:2
Jer 1:9
Jn 1:7

6:8
Mt 13:14
Lk 8:10
Acts 26:19
Rom 11:8

6:10
Jer 5:21

6:11
Lev 26:31
Mic 3:12

6:1 The year of King Uzziah's death was approximately 740 B.C. He died of leprosy for trying to take over the High Priest's duties (2 Chronicles 26:20, 21). although he was generally a good king and his reign was long and prosperous, many of his people were turning away from God.

6:1ff Isaiah's vision was his call to be God's messenger to his people. Isaiah was given a difficult mission. He had to tell people who believed they were blessed by God that God was going to destroy them because of their disobedience.

6:1ff Isaiah's lofty view of God in 6:1-4 gives us a sense of God's greatness, mystery, and power. His recognition of his sinfulness before God encourages us to confess our sin. His picture of forgiveness reminds us that we, too, are forgiven. When we recognize how great our God is, how sinful we are, and the extent of his forgiveness, we are energized to do his work. How does your concept of the greatness of God measure up to Isaiah's?

6:2, 3 The seraphs are an order of angelic beings created by God. This is the only place in the Bible where seraphs are mentioned. Here they functioned as God's agents in commissioning Isaiah. Isaiah could understand them when they spoke to him and when they praised God. Because they hovered around God's throne, they may have been heavenly attendants. They were awe-inspiring and powerful creatures—their singing shook the Temple!

6:3 The lofty throne, the attending angels, and the threefold *holy* all stress God's holiness. In a time when moral and spiritual laxity had reached its peak, it was important to see God in his holiness. Holiness means morally perfect, pure, and set apart from all sin. We need to rediscover God's holiness.

6:5-8 Listening to the praise of the angels, Isaiah realized he was common and unclean before God, with no hope of measuring up to God's standard of holiness. When his lips were touched with a

burning coal, however, he was told his sins were forgiven. It wasn't the coal that cleansed him, but God. In response he submitted himself entirely to God's service. No matter how difficult his task would be, he said, "I'll go! Send me!" The painful cleansing process was necessary before Isaiah could fulfill the task to which God was calling him. Before we accept God's call to speak for him to those around us, we must be cleansed as Isaiah was. Letting God purify us may be painful, but we must be purified so that we can truly represent God, who is pure and holy.

6:8 The more clearly Isaiah saw God (6:5), the more aware he became of his own powerlessness and inadequacy both in terms of moral purity and capability to deliver God's message on his own. The more we know God, the more we will see how impossible it is to do anything of lasting value without him.

6:9-13 God told Isaiah that the people would not listen to his message because their hearts had hardened beyond repentance. God's patience with their chronic rebellion was finally exhausted, and his judgment was to abandon them to their rebellion and hardness of heart. Why did God send Isaiah if he knew the people wouldn't listen? Although the nation itself would not repent and would reap judgment, some individuals would listen. In 6:13 God explains his plan for a remnant. Even in judgment God is merciful. We can gain encouragement from God's promise to preserve his people. If we are faithful to him we can be sure of his mercy.

6:11-13 When would the people listen? Only after they had come to the end and had nowhere to turn but to God. This would happen when the land was destroyed by invading armies and the people taken into captivity. The remnant refers either to those who remained in the land after the captivity, or those who returned from Babylon to rebuild the land. Both were about a tenth of the total population. When will we listen to God? Must we, like Judah, go through calamities with nowhere left to turn before we will listen to God's words? Consider what God may be telling you, and obey him before there is no time left.

6:12
Jer 4:29

6:13
Job 14:7

the whole country is an utter wasteland, 12and they are all taken away as slaves to other countries far away, and all the land of Israel lies deserted! 13Yet a tenth—a remnant—will survive; and though Israel is invaded again and again and destroyed, yet Israel will be like a tree cut down, whose stump still lives to grow again."

Immanuel—God with us

7:1
2 Kgs 16:1

7 During the reign of Ahaz (the son of Jotham and grandson of Uzziah), Jerusalem was attacked by King Rezin of Syria and King Pekah of Israel (the son of Remaliah). But it was not taken; the city stood. 2However, when the news came to the royal court, "Syria is allied with Israel against us!" the hearts of the king and his people trembled with fear as the trees of a forest shake in a storm.

7:1 *the son of Remaliah.* "The usurper, the son of Remaliah" is implied.

ISAIAH

Trees and prophets share at least one important characteristic—both are planted for the future. Yet seedlings are often overlooked and prophets often ignored. Isaiah is one of the best examples of this. The people of his time could have been rescued by his words. Instead, they refused to believe him. With the passing of centuries, however, Isaiah's words have cast a shadow on all of history.

Isaiah was active as a prophet during the reigns of five kings, but he did not set out to be a prophet. By the time King Uzziah died, Isaiah was established as a scribe in the royal palace in Jerusalem. It was a respectable career, but God had other plans for his servant. Isaiah's account of God's call leaves little doubt about what motivated the prophet for the next half-century. His vision of God was unforgettable.

The encounter with God permanently affected Isaiah's character. He reflected the God he represented. Isaiah's messages—some comforting, some confronting—are so distinct that some have guessed they came from different authors. Isaiah's testimony is that the messages came from the only One capable of being perfect in justice as well as in mercy—God himself.

When he called Isaiah as a prophet, God did not encourage him with predictions of great success. God told Isaiah that the people would not listen. But he was to speak and write his messages anyway because eventually some *would* listen. God compared his people to a tree that would have to be cut down so that a new tree could grow from the old roots (Isaiah 6:13).

We, who are part of that future, can see how many of the promises God gave through Isaiah have been fulfilled in Jesus Christ. We also gain the hope of knowing that God is active in all of history, including our own.

Strengths and accomplishments:
- Considered the greatest Old Testament prophet
- Quoted at least 50 times in the New Testament
- Had powerful messages of both judgment and hope
- Carried out a consistent ministry even though there was little positive response from his listeners
- His ministry spanned the reigns of five kings of Judah

Lessons from his life:
- God's help is needed in order to effectively confront sin while comforting people
- One result of experiencing forgiveness is the desire to share that forgiveness with others
- God is purely and perfectly holy, just, and loving

Vital statistics:
- Where: Jerusalem
- Occupations: Scribe, prophet
- Relatives: Father: Amoz. Sons: Shear-jashub, Maher-shalal-hash-baz.
- Contemporaries: Uzziah, Jotham, Ahaz, Hezekiah, Manasseh, Micah

Key verse:
"Then I heard the Lord asking, 'Whom shall I send as a messenger to my people? Who will go?' And I said, 'Lord, I'll go! Send *me*'" (Isaiah 6:8).

Isaiah's story is told in 2 Kings 19:2—20:19. He is also mentioned in 2 Chronicles 26:22; 32:20, 32; Matthew 3:3; 8:17; 12:17–21; John 12:38; Romans 10:16, 20.

7:1 The year was 734 B.C. Ahaz, king of Judah in Jerusalem, was about to be attacked by an alliance of the Northern Kingdom of Israel and Syria. He was frightened by the possible end of his reign and by the invading armies who killed many people or took them as captives (2 Chronicles 28:5–21). But, as Isaiah predicted, the kingdom of Judah did not come to an end at this time.

³Then the Lord said to Isaiah, "Go out to meet King Ahaz, you and Shear-jashub, your son. You will find him at the end of the aqueduct which leads from Gihon Spring to the upper reservoir, near the road that leads down to the bleaching field. ⁴Tell him to quit worrying. Tell him he needn't be frightened by the fierce anger of those two has-beens, Rezin and Pekah. ⁵Yes, the kings of Syria and Israel are coming against you.

7:4
Ex 14:13
Isa 10:24; 35:4
Lam 3:26

"They say, ⁶'We will invade Judah and throw her people into panic. Then we'll fight our way into Jerusalem and install the son of Tabeel as their king.'

⁷"But the Lord God says, This plan will not succeed, ⁸for Damascus will remain the capital of Syria alone, and King Rezin's kingdom will not increase its boundaries. And within sixty-five years Ephraim, too, will be crushed and broken. ⁹Samaria is the capital of Ephraim alone and King Pekah's power will not increase. You don't believe me? If you want me to protect you, you must learn to believe what I say."

7:7
Ps 2:4-6
7:8
Isa 17:1-3
7:9
2 Chron 20:20
Isa 30:12-14

¹⁰Not long after this, the Lord sent this further message to King Ahaz: ¹¹"Ask me for a sign, Ahaz, to prove that I will indeed crush your enemies as I have said. Ask anything you like, in heaven or on earth."

7:11
2 Kgs 19:29
Isa 37:30

⊗ ¹²But the king refused. "No," he said, "I'll not bother the Lord with anything like that." ¹³Then Isaiah said, O House of David, you aren't satisfied to exhaust *my* patience; you exhaust the Lord's as well! ¹⁴All right then, the Lord himself will choose the sign—a child shall be born to a virgin! And she shall call him Immanuel (meaning, "God is with us"). ¹⁵, ¹⁶By the time this child is weaned and knows right from wrong, the two kings you fear so much—the kings of Israel and Syria—will both be dead.

7:14
Isa 8:8,10
Mt 1:23
7:15
Isa 8:4; 17:3

¹⁷But later on, the Lord will bring a terrible curse on you and on your nation and your family. There will be terror, such as has not been known since the division of Solomon's empire into Israel and Judah—the mighty king of Assyria will come with his great army! ¹⁸At that time the Lord will whistle for the army of Upper Egypt, and of Assyria too, to swarm down upon you like flies and destroy you, like bees to sting and to kill. ¹⁹They will come in vast hordes, spreading across the whole land, even into the desolate valleys and caves and thorny parts, as well as to

7:17
1 Kgs 12:16,17
Isa 10:5,6

7:19
Jer 16:16

7:11 *Ask anything you like, in heaven or on earth,* literally, "let it be deep as Sheol or high as heaven." **7:14** *a child shall be born to a virgin.* The controversial Hebrew word used here sometimes means "virgin" and sometimes "young woman." Its immediate use here refers to Isaiah's young wife and her newborn son (8:1-4). This, of course, was not a virgin birth. God's sign was that before this child was old enough to talk (vs 4) the two invading kings would be destroyed. However, the Gospel of Matthew (1:23) tells us that there was a further fulfillment of this prophecy, in that a virgin (Mary) conceived and bore a son, Immanuel, the Christ. We have therefore properly used this higher meaning, "virgin," in vs 14, as otherwise the Matthew account loses its significance. **7:15, 16** *By the time this child is weaned,* literally, "For before this child shall know (is old enough) to refuse evil and to choose the good . . . and (is old enough to) eat curds and honey." *the kings of Israel and Syria,* implied. *will both be dead,* or, "the lands will be deserted (of their kings)." **7:17** *But later on,* implied. **7:18** *will whistle for the army of Upper Egypt,* literally, "sources of the streams of Egypt" refers to Upper Egypt where the powerful 25th Ethiopian Dynasty would soon arise.

7:3 "Shear-jashub" means "a remnant will return." God told Isaiah to give his son this name as a reminder of his plan for mercy. From the beginning of God's judgment he planned to restore a remnant of his people. Shear-jashub was a reminder to the people of God's faithfulness to them.

7:3 This bleaching field was a well-known place where clothing or newly woven cloth was laid in the sun to dry and whiten (see 36:2). The Gihon Spring, located to the east of Jerusalem, was the main source of water for the holy city. This was also the spring that emptied into Hezekiah's famous water tunnel (2 Chronicles 32:30).

7:4—8:15 Isaiah predicts the break-up of Israel's alliance with Syria (7:4–17). Because of this alliance, Israel would be destroyed (8:1–4). Assyria would be the instrument God would use to destroy them (8:5–8); but God would not let Assyria destroy Judah (8:9–15). They would be spared because they were trying to follow God.

7:8 Ahaz, one of Judah's worst kings, refused God's help and instead tried to buy aid from the Assyrians, paying for it with gold from the Temple. When the Assyrians came, they brought further trouble instead of help. In 722 B.C., Samaria, the capital of

"Ephraim" (another name for Israel, the Northern Kingdom), fell to the Assyrian armies, ending the Northern Kingdom.

7:12 Ahaz appeared righteous by saying he would not test God with a sign ("I'll not bother the Lord with anything like that"). In fact, God had told him to ask, but Ahaz didn't really want to know what God would say. Often we use some excuse, such as not wanting to bother God, to keep us from communicating with him. Don't let anything keep you from hearing and obeying God.

7:14–16 See the textual notes on 7:14 and 7:15, 16.

7:18 Egypt and Assyria did not at this time devastate Judah. Hezekiah followed Ahaz as king, and he honored God, thus God held back his hand of judgment. Two more evil kings reigned before Josiah, of whom it was said no other king turned so completely to the Lord (2 Kings 23:25). However, Judah's doom had been sealed by the extreme evil of Josiah's father. During Josiah's reign, Egypt marched against the Assyrians. Josiah then declared war on Egypt, though God told him not to. After he was killed (2 Chronicles 35:20–27), only weak kings reigned in Judah. The Egyptians carried off Josiah's son after three months. The next king, Jehoiakim, was taken by Nebuchadnezzar to Babylon. Egypt and Assyria had dealt death blows to Judah.

7:20
Isa 24:1
Ezek 5:1-4

all your fertile acres. 20In that day the Lord will take this "razor"—these Assyrians you have hired to save you—and use it on you to shave off everything you have: your land, your crops, your people.

7:21
Jer 39:10

21, 22When they finally stop plundering, the whole nation will be a pastureland; whole flocks and herds will be destroyed, and a farmer will be fortunate to have a cow and two sheep left. But the abundant pastureland will yield plenty of milk, and everyone left will live on curds and wild honey. 23At that time the lush vineyards will become patches of briars. 24All the land will be one vast thornfield, a hunting ground overrun by wildlife. 25No one will go to the fertile hillsides where once the gardens grew, for thorns will cover them; cattle, sheep and goats will graze there.

Isaiah predicts the invasion by Assyria

8:1
Hab 2:2

8 Again the Lord sent me a message: "Make a large signboard and write on it the birth announcement of the son I am going to give you. Use capital letters! His name will be Maher-shalal-hash-baz, which means 'Your enemies will soon be destroyed.' " 2I asked Uriah the priest and Zechariah the son of Jeberechiah, both known as honest men, to watch me as I wrote so they could testify that I had written it [before the child was even on the way]. 3Then I had sexual intercourse with my wife and she conceived, and bore me a son, and the Lord said, "Call him Maher-shalal-hash-baz. 4This name prophesies that within a couple of years, before this child is even old enough to say 'Daddy' or 'Mommy,' the king of Assyria will invade both Damascus and Samaria and carry away their riches."

8:2
2 Kgs 16:10,11,
15,16

5Then the Lord spoke to me again and said:

8:6
Isa 30:12

6"Since the people of Jerusalem are planning to refuse my gentle care and are enthusiastic about asking King Rezin and King Pekah to come and aid them,

8:7
Isa 7:14
17:12,13
Amos 8:8; 9:5

7, 8therefore I will overwhelm my people with Euphrates' mighty flood; the king of Assyria and all his mighty armies will rage against them. This flood will overflow all its channels and sweep into your land of Judah, O Immanuel, submerging it from end to end."

8:9
Dan 2:34,35
Rom 8:31

9, 10Do your worst, O Syria and Israel, our enemies, but you will not succeed—you will be shattered. Listen to me, all you enemies of ours: Prepare for war against us—and perish! Yes! Perish! Call your councils of war, develop your strategies, prepare your plans of attacking us, and perish! For God is with us.

8:11
Ezek 2:8

11The Lord has said in strongest terms: Do not under any circumstances go along with the plans of Judah to surrender to Syria and Israel. 12Don't let people call you a traitor for staying true to God. Don't you panic as so many of your neighbors are doing when they think of Syria and Israel attacking you. 13Don't fear anything except the Lord of the armies of heaven! If you fear him, you need fear nothing else. 14, 15He will be your safety; but Israel and Judah have refused his care and thereby stumbled against the Rock of their salvation and lie fallen and crushed

8:12
1 Pet 3:13-15

8:14
Isa 25:4
Ezek 11:16
Lk 2:34
Rom 9:32,33
1 Pet 2:8

8:1 *Your enemies will soon be destroyed,* literally, "plundering and despoiling (will) come quickly." **8:2** *before the child was even on the way,* implied. **8:6** *are planning to refuse my gentle care,* literally means "have refused the waters of Shiloah that go softly." **8:9, 10** *O Syria and Israel,* literally, "O peoples." *our enemies,* implied. *For God is with us,* or, "Immanuel."

7:20 Hiring Assyria to save them would be Israel's downfall (2 Kings 16:7, 8). The "shaving" of Israel's hair was symbolic of total humiliation. Numbers 6:9 explains that after being defiled, a person who had been set apart for the Lord had to shave his head as part of the cleansing process. Shaving bodily hair was an embarrassment—an exposure of nakedness. For a Hebrew man, having his beard shaved was humiliating.

7:21-25 Rich farmland would be trampled until it became pastureland fit only for grazing. No longer would it be a land "flowing with milk and honey" (Exodus 3:8), symbols of agricultural abundance, but a land with only curds and wild honey.

8:1-4 These verses predict the fall of Israel and Syria, two of Judah's strongest enemies. Syria fell to Assyria in 732 B.C., and Israel followed in 722 B.C. Isaiah put his message on a large sign in a public place with writing that all could read. God was eager for all his people to be warned.

8:6, 14, 15 Because Judah rejected God's gentle care, choosing instead to seek help from other nations, God would punish them. We see two distinct attributes of God—his love and his wrath. To ignore his love and guidance results in sin and invites his wrath. We must recognize the consequences of our choices. God seeks to protect us from bad choices, but he still gives us the freedom to make them.

8:7, 8 The heart of the Assyrian Empire was between the Tigris and Euphrates rivers. The flood from the Euphrates is a poetic way of describing the overwhelming force of the Assyrian army.

8:12 Isaiah, along with most of the prophets, was viewed as a traitor because he did not support Judah's national policies. He called the people to commit themselves first to God, and then to the king. He even predicted the overthrow of the government.

beneath it: God's presence among them has endangered them! 16Write down all these things I am going to do, says the Lord, and seal it up for the future. Entrust it to some godly man to pass on down to godly men of future generations.

8:16
Isa 50:4
Dan 12:4

17I will wait for the Lord to help us, though he is hiding now. My only hope is in him. 18I and the children God has given me have symbolic names that reveal the plans of the Lord of heaven's armies for his people: Isaiah means "Jehovah will save (his people)," Shear-jashub means "A remnant shall return," and Maher-shalal-hash-baz means "Your enemies will soon be destroyed." 19So why are you trying to find out the future by consulting witches and mediums? Don't listen to their whisperings and mutterings. Can the living find out the future from the dead? Why not ask your God?

8:17
Deut 31:17
Isa 30:18; 54:8
Hab 2:3
8:18
Heb 2:13
8:19
Lev 20:6
2 Kgs 21:6

20"Check these witches' words against the Word of God!" he says. "If their messages are different than mine, it is because I have not sent them; for they have no light or truth in them. 21My people will be led away captive, stumbling, weary and hungry. And because they are hungry they will rave and shake their fists at heaven and curse their King and their God. 22Wherever they look there will be trouble and anguish and dark despair. And they will be thrust out into the darkness."

8:22
Jer 13:16
Amos 5:18,20
Zeph 1:14,15

A prophecy about the coming Messiah

9 Nevertheless, that time of darkness and despair shall not go on forever. Though soon the land of Zebulun and Naphtali will be under God's contempt and judgment, yet in the future these very lands, Galilee and Northern Transjordan, where lies the road to the sea, will be filled with glory. 2The people who walk in darkness shall see a great Light—a Light that will shine on all those who live in the land of the shadow of death. 3For Israel will again be great, filled with joy like that of reapers when the harvest time has come, and like that of men dividing up the plunder they have won. 4For God will break the chains that bind his people and the whip that scourges them, just as he did when he destroyed the vast host of the Midianites by Gideon's little band. 5In that glorious day of peace there will no longer be the issuing of battle gear; no more the blood-stained uniforms of war; all such will be burned.

9:2
Mt 4:15,16
9:3
Isa 26:15
35:10; 66:10
9:4
Isa 49:26

6For unto us a Child is born; unto us a Son is given; and the government shall be upon his shoulder. These will be his royal titles: "Wonderful," "Counselor," "The Mighty God," "The Everlasting Father," "The Prince of Peace." 7His ever-expanding, peaceful government will never end. He will rule with perfect fairness and justice from the throne of his father David. He will bring true justice and peace to all the nations of the world. This is going to happen because the Lord of heaven's armies has dedicated himself to do it!

9:6
Deut 10:17
Neh 9:32
Isa 26:3,12
Mt 28:18
Lk 2:11
1 Cor 15:25
9:7
Dan 2:44
Lk 1:32,33

8:16 Because some people faithfully passed on these words from generation to generation, we have the book of Isaiah today. Each of us needs to accept the responsibility to pass on God's Word to our children and grandchildren, encouraging them to love the Bible, read it, and learn from it. Then they will faithfully pass it on to their children and grandchildren.

8:17 Isaiah decided to wait for God's help, "though he [God] is hiding now." Many of the prophecies God gave through the prophets would not come true for 700 years; others still haven't been fulfilled. Are you willing to accept the Lord's timing?

8:19 The people consulted witches and mediums who tried to seek answers from dead people, instead of consulting the living God. God alone knows the future, for he alone has already been there. Only God is eternal.

8:21 After rejecting God's plan for them, the people of Judah would blame God for their trials. People continually blame God for their self-induced problems. How do you respond to the unpleasant results of your own sin? Where do you fix the blame? Instead of blaming God, seek ways to grow through your failures.

8:22 Those who consult the forces of darkness will be led onto paths of darkness. The darkness is not necessarily hell; it may mean despair, judgment, trouble, or anguish (see 9:1).

9:1-7 This Deliverer is the Messiah, Jesus. Matthew quotes these verses in describing Christ's ministry (Matthew 4:15, 16). The territories of Zebulun and Naphtali are the Northern Kingdom as a whole. These were also the territories in which Jesus grew up and often ministered; this is why they would be "filled with glory."

9:1 In our despair, we fear that our sorrows and troubles will never end. But we can take comfort in this certainty: although the Lord may not take us around our troubles, he will lead us safely through them. Like Judah, we must follow him if we are to be led safely through.

9:2-6 In a time of great darkness, God promised to send a Light who would shine on everyone living in the shadow of death. He is both "Mighty God" (all-powerful) and "Counselor" (all-loving). This message of hope was fulfilled in the birth of Christ and the establishment of his eternal kingdom. He came to deliver all people from their slavery to sin.

9:2 The apostle John also refered to Jesus as the "Light" (John 1:9).

9:8
Mal 1:4

9:11
Ps 79:7
Jer 10:25

9:13
Jer 5:3
Hos 7:10
9:16
Mt 15:14

9:17
Isa 32:6
Amos 8:13
Mt 12:34
9:18
Mal 4:1

9:19
Joel 2:3
Mic 7:2,6
9:21
Isa 11:13

8, 9, 10The Lord has spoken out against that braggart Israel who says that though our land lies in ruins now, we will rebuild it better than before. The sycamore trees are cut down, but we will replace them with cedars! 11, 12The Lord's reply to your bragging is to bring your enemies against you—the Syrians on the east and the Philistines on the west. With bared fangs they will devour Israel. And even then the Lord's anger against you will not be satisfied—his fist will still be poised to smash you. 13For after all this punishment you will not repent and turn to him, the Lord of heaven's armies. 14, 15Therefore the Lord, in one day, will destroy the leaders of Israel and the lying prophets. 16For the leaders of his people have led them down the paths of ruin.

17That is why the Lord has no joy in their young men, and no mercy upon even the widows and orphans, for they are all filthy-mouthed, wicked liars. That is why his anger is not yet satisfied, but his fist is still poised to smash them all. 18He will burn up all this wickedness, these thorns and briars; and the flames will consume the forests, too, and send a vast cloud of smoke billowing up from their burning. 19, 20The land is blackened by that fire, by the wrath of the Lord of heaven's armies. The people are fuel for the fire. Each fights against his brother to steal his food, but will never have enough. Finally they will even eat their own children! 21Manasseh against Ephraim and Ephraim against Manasseh—and both against Judah. Yet even after all of this, God's anger is not yet satisfied. His hand is still heavy upon them, to crush them.

God will punish Assyria

10:1
Ps 94:20
Isa 59:13,14

10:3
Isa 13:6
Lk 19:43,44

10:4
Isa 34:3; 66:16

10:5
Isa 13:5
Jer 51:20

10:7
Gen 50:20
Mic 4:11,12
Acts 2:23,24

10 Woe to unjust judges and to those who issue unfair laws, says the Lord, 2so that there is no justice for the poor, the widows and orphans. Yes, it is true that they even rob the widows and fatherless children.

3Oh, what will you do when I visit you in that day when I send desolation upon you from a distant land? To whom will you turn then for your help? Where will your treasures be safe? 4I will not help you; you will stumble along as prisoners or lie among the slain. And even then my anger will not be satisfied, but my fist will still be poised to strike you. 5, 6Assyria is the whip of my anger; his military strength is my weapon upon this godless nation, doomed and damned; he will enslave them and plunder them and trample them like dirt beneath his feet. 7But the king of Assyria will not know that it is I who sent him. He will merely think he is

9:11, 12 *your enemies*, or, "Rezin's enemies," in some ancient versions.

NAMES FOR MESSIAH
Isaiah uses five names to describe the Messiah. These names have special meaning to us.

Wonderful	• He is exceptional, distinguished, and without peer.
Counselor	• He gives the right advice.
The Mighty God	• He is God himself.
The Everlasting Father	• He is timeless; he is God our Father.
The Prince of Peace	• His government is one of justice and peace.

9:8–10 Israel is called a braggart for saying, in essence, "We've faced a temporary setback, but *by our own strength* we will rebuild our city." Even though God made Israel a nation and gave them the land they occupied, the people put their trust in themselves rather than in him. Too often we take pride in our accomplishments, forgetting that it is God who has given us every ability we have. We even become proud of our unique status as Christians. God is not pleased with *any* pride or trust in ourselves because it cuts off our contact with him.

9:21 Ephraim and Manasseh were tribes in the Northern Kingdom descended from Joseph's two sons. They fought a civil war because of their selfishness and wickedness (2 Chronicles 28).

10:1 God will judge crooked judges and those who make unfair laws. Those who oppress others will be oppressed themselves. It is not enough to live in a land founded on justice; each individual must deal justly with the poor and the powerless. Don't pass your responsibility off to your nation or even your church. You are accountable to God for what you do.

10:7 Although Assyria did not know it was part of God's plan, God used this nation to judge his people. God accomplishes his plans in history despite people or nations who reject him. He did not merely set the world in motion and let it go! Because our all-powerful, sovereign God is still in control today, we have security even in a rapidly changing world.

attacking my people as part of his plan to conquer the world. ⁸He will declare that every one of his princes will soon be a king, ruling a conquered land.

⁹"We will destroy Calno just as we did Carchemish," he will say, "and Hamath will go down before us as Arpad did; and we will destroy Samaria just as we did Damascus. ¹⁰Yes, we have finished off many a kingdom whose idols were far greater than those in Jerusalem and Samaria, ¹¹so when we have defeated Samaria and her idols we will destroy Jerusalem with hers."

10:10
2 Kgs 19:17,18

¹²After the Lord has used the king of Assyria to accomplish his purpose, then he will turn upon the Assyrians and punish them too—for they are proud and haughty men.

10:12
Jer 50:18

¹³They boast, "We in our own power and wisdom have won these wars. We are great and wise. By our own strength we broke down the walls and destroyed the people and carried off their treasures. ¹⁴In our greatness we have robbed their nests of riches and gathered up kingdoms as a farmer gathers eggs, and no one can move a finger or open his mouth to peep against us!"

10:13
2 Kgs 19:22-24
Isa 37:24-27
Dan 4:30

¹⁵But the Lord says, "Shall the axe boast greater power than the man who uses it? Is the saw greater than the man who saws? Can a rod strike unless a hand is moving it? Can a cane walk by itself?"

10:15
Isa 29:16

¹⁶Because of all your evil boasting, O king of Assyria, the Lord of Hosts will send a plague among your proud troops, and strike them down. ¹⁷God, the Light and Holy One of Israel, will be the fire and flame that will destroy them. In a single night he will burn these thorns and briars, the Assyrians who destroyed the land of Israel. ¹⁸Assyria's vast army is like a glorious forest, yet it will be destroyed. The Lord will destroy them, soul and body, as when a sick man wastes away. ¹⁹Only a few from all that mighty army will be left; so few a child could count them!

10:17
Isa 27:4; 30:33
31:9; 33:12
37:23
Jer 4:4

10:19
Isa 21:17

²⁰Then at last, those left in Israel and in Judah will trust the Lord, the Holy One of Israel, instead of fearing the Assyrians. ²¹A remnant of them will return to the mighty God. ²²But though Israel be now as many as the sands along the shore, yet only a few of them will be left to return at that time; God has rightly decided to destroy his people. ²³Yes, it has already been decided by the Lord God to consume them.

10:20
Isa 17:7,8

10:22
Isa 28:22
Rom 9:27,28

²⁴Therefore the Lord God says, "O my people in Jerusalem, don't be afraid of the Assyrians when they oppress you just as the Egyptians did long ago. ²⁵It will not last very long; in a little while my anger against you will end, and then it will rise against them to destroy them."

10:24
Ex 5:14-16

10:25
Isa 17:14

²⁶The Lord Almighty will send his angel to slay them in a mighty slaughter like the time when Gideon triumphed over Midian at the rock of Oreb or the time God

10:26
Ex 14:16,27
Judg 7:25
Isa 37:36-38

10:17 *land of Israel*, see 2 Kings 19:35 and Isaiah 37:36.

10:9 Assured of great victories that would enlarge his empire, the king of Assyria gave an arrogant speech. Already Assyria had conquered several cities. Little did the king know that he was under the mightier hand of God.

10:10 Samaria and Jerusalem were filled with idols which were of no use against the Assyrian military machine. Only the God of the universe could and would do that, but not until he had used the Assyrians for his purposes.

10:12 The predicted punishment of the Assyrians soon took place. In 701 B.C., 185,000 Assyrian soldiers were slain by an angel (37:36, 37). Later, the Assyrian Empire fell to Babylon, never to rise again as a world power.

10:12 The Assyrians were haughty. Proud of the victories God permitted, they thought they had accomplished them in their own power. Our perspective can become distorted by our accomplishments if we fail to recognize God working his purposes through us. When we think we are strong enough for anything, we are bound to fail because pride has blinded us to the reality that God is ultimately in control.

10:15 No instrument or tool accomplishes its purposes without a

greater power. The Assyrians were a tool in God's hands, but they failed to recognize it. When a tool boasts of greater powers than the one who uses it, it is in danger of being discarded. We are useful only to the extent that we allow God to use us.

10:17 Assyria's downfall came in 612 B.C. when Nineveh, the capital city, was destroyed. Assyria had been God's instrument of judgment against Israel, but it too would be judged for its wickedness. No one escapes God's judgment against sin, not even the most powerful nations (Psalm 2).

10:20, 21 Once Assyria's army was destroyed, a small remnant of the people of Israel would stop fearing Assyria and start trusting God. This remnant would be but a fraction of Israel's total population (see Ezra 2:64, 65 for the small number who returned to Judah).

10:20, 21 Those who remained faithful to God despite the horrors of the invasion are called the remnant. The key to being a part of the remnant was *faith*. Being a descendant of Abraham, living in the Promised Land, having trusted God at one time—none of these were good enough. Are you relying on your Christian heritage, the rituals of worship, or past experience to put you in a right relationship with God? The key to being set apart by God is faith in him.

10:27
Isa 14:25

drowned the Egyptian armies in the sea. 27On that day God will end the bondage of his people. He will break the slave-yoke off their necks, and destroy it as decreed.

28, 29Look, the mighty armies of Assyria are coming! Now they are at Aiath, now at Migron; they are storing some of their equipment at Michmash and crossing over the pass; they are staying overnight at Geba. Fear strikes the city of Ramah; all the people of Gibeah—the city of Saul—are running for their lives. 30Well may you scream in terror, O people of Gallim. Shout out a warning to Laish, for the mighty army comes. O poor Anathoth, what a fate is yours! 31There go the people of

10:32
Isa 19:16
Zech 2:9

Madmenah, all fleeing, and the citizens of Gebim are preparing to run. 32But the enemy stops at Nob for the remainder of that day. He shakes his fist at Jerusalem on Mount Zion.

10:33
Isa 37:24
Ezek 31:2,3
Amos 2:9

33Then, look, look! The Lord, the Lord of the armies of heaven, is chopping down the mighty tree! He is destroying all of that vast army, great and small alike, both officers and men. 34He, the Mighty One, will cut down the enemy as a woodsman's axe cuts down the forest trees in Lebanon.

A new branch from Jesse

11:1
Jer 23:5
Zech 6:12
Rev 5:5

11 The royal line of David will be cut off, chopped down like a tree; but from the stump will grow a Shoot—yes, a new Branch from the old root. 2And the Spirit of the Lord shall rest upon him, the Spirit of wisdom, understanding, counsel

11:2
Isa 61:1
Jn 1:32
Eph 1:17

and might; the Spirit of knowledge and of the fear of the Lord. 3His delight will be obedience to the Lord. He will not judge by appearance, false evidence, or hearsay,

11:3
Jn 2:24,25

4but will defend the poor and the exploited. He will rule against the wicked who oppress them. 5For he will be clothed with fairness and with truth.

11:4
Isa 30:28
2 Thess 2:8

6In that day the wolf and the lamb will lie down together, and the leopard and goats will be at peace. Calves and fat cattle will be safe among lions, and a little

11:6
Isa 65:25

child shall lead them all. 7The cows will graze among bears; cubs and calves will lie down together, and lions will eat grass like the cows. 8Babies will crawl safely among poisonous snakes, and a little child who puts his hand in a nest of deadly

11:9
Isa 45:6
Ezek 34:25
Hos 2:18
Hab 2:14

adders will pull it out unharmed. 9Nothing will hurt or destroy in all my holy mountain, for as the waters fill the sea, so shall the earth be full of the knowledge of the Lord.

11:10
Lk 2:32
Jn 3:14,15
Rom 15:12

10In that day he who created the royal dynasty of David will be a banner of salvation to all the world. The nations will rally to him, for the land where he lives will be a glorious place. 11At that time the Lord will bring back a remnant of his

11:11
Isa 60:9
Zech 10:10

people for second time, returning them to the land of Israel from Assyria, Upper and Lower Egypt, Ethiopia, Elam, Babylonia, Hamath and all the distant coastal lands. 12He will raise a flag among the nations for them to rally to; he will gather

11:12
Zeph 3:10

the scattered Israelites from the ends of the earth. 13Then, at last, the jealousy

11:13
Ezek 37:16,
17,22

between Israel and Judah will end; they will not fight each other any more. 14Together they will fly against the nations possessing their land on the east and on

10:27 *as decreed,* literally, "because of ointment." Some see here a reference to the Messiah, the Anointed One.
11:10 *royal dynasty of David,* literally, "the Root of Jesse." Possibly the meaning is, "the Heir of David's royal line."

11:1-9 Assyria would be like a tree cut down at the height of its power (10:33, 34), never to rise again. Judah (the royal line of David) would be like a tree chopped down to a stump. But from that stump a new shoot would grow—the Messiah. He would be greater than the original tree and would bear much fruit.

11:3-5 How we long for fair treatment from others, but do we give it? We hate those who base their judgments on appearance, false evidence, or hearsay. But we are quick to judge others using those standards. Only Christ can be the perfectly fair judge, and only as he governs our hearts can we learn to be as fair in our treatment of others as we expect others to be toward us.

11:5 Judah had become corrupt, and now it was surrounded by hostile foreign powers. That is why peace, fairness, and justice were the primary needs of the common people. Those who possess much dare not neglect those who are denied the opportunities of obtaining justice.

11:6-16 A golden age is yet to come. Such perfect tranquility is possible only when Christ reigns over the earth.

11:8 It is incredible to think of hostile animals living at peace. It is even more incredible for hostile people to live at peace with one another. Only in Christ can hostilities be laid to rest as true love prevails.

11:11 When will this remnant of God's people be returned to their land? Old Testament prophecy often applies both to the near future and the distant future. Judah would soon be exiled to Babylon and a remnant would return to Jerusalem in 539 B.C. at Cyrus' decree. In the ages to come, however, God's people would be dispersed throughout the world but ultimately regathered when Christ comes to reign over the earth.

11:14 Edom, Moab, and Ammon were three countries bordering Israel. They were the nations who rejoiced when Israel was defeated and took their land.

the west, uniting forces to destroy them, and they will occupy the nations of Edom and Moab and Ammon.

¹⁵The Lord will dry a path through the Red Sea, and wave his hand over the Euphrates, sending a mighty wind to divide it into seven streams that can easily be crossed. ¹⁶He will make a highway from Assyria for the remnant there, just as he did for all of Israel long ago when they returned from Egypt.

11:15
Isa 51:10

11:16
Ex 14:26-29
Isa 19:23

Singing God's praise

12 On that day you will say, "Praise the Lord! He was angry with me, but now he comforts me. ²See, God has come to save me! I will trust and not be afraid, for the Lord is my strength and song; he is my salvation. ³Oh, the joy of drinking deeply from the Fountain of Salvation!"

12:1
Isa 40:1

12:2
Ps 118:14
Isa 26:3; 62:11

⁴In that wonderful day you will say, "Thank the Lord! Praise his name! Tell the world about his wondrous love. How mighty he is!" ⁵Sing to the Lord, for he has done wonderful things. Make known his praise around the world. ⁶Let all the people of Jerusalem shout his praise with joy. For great and mighty is the Holy One of Israel, who lives among you.

12:5
Ps 98:1
Isa 44:23

12:6
Isa 54:1
Zeph 3:14,15-17

2. Judgment against heathen nations
Prophecy against Babylon

13 This is the vision God showed Isaiah (son of Amoz) concerning Babylon's doom.

²See the flags waving as their enemy attacks. Shout to them, O Israel, and wave them on as they march against Babylon to destroy the palaces of the rich and mighty. ³I, the Lord, have set apart these armies for this task; I have called those rejoicing in their strength to do this work, to satisfy my anger. ⁴Hear the tumult on the mountains! Listen as the armies march! It is the tumult and the shout of many nations. The Lord Almighty has brought them here, ⁵from countries far away. They are his weapons against you, O Babylon. They carry his anger with them and will destroy your whole land.

13:2
Isa 45:1-3

13:4
Isa 5:30

13:5
Isa 5:26

13:6
Isa 34:2,8
Ezek 30:3
Amos 5:18

⁶Scream in terror, for the Lord's time has come, the time for the Almighty to crush you. ⁷Your arms lie paralyzed with fear; the strongest hearts melt, ⁸and are afraid. Fear grips you with terrible pangs, like those of a woman in labor. You look at one another, helpless, as the flames of the burning city reflect upon your pallid faces. ⁹For see, the day of the Lord is coming, the terrible day of his wrath and fierce anger. The land shall be destroyed, and all the sinners with it. ¹⁰The heavens will be black above them. No light will shine from stars or sun or moon.

13:7
Ezek 21:7

13:8
Isa 21:3; 26:17

13:9
Isa 66:15,16

13:10
Mt 24:29

¹¹And I will punish the world for its evil, the wicked for their sin; I will crush the arrogance of the proud man and the haughtiness of the rich. ¹²Few will live when I have finished up my work.

Men will be as scarce as gold—of greater value than the gold of Ophir. ¹³For I will shake the heavens in my wrath and fierce anger, and the earth will move from its place in the skies.

13:11
Dan 5:22,23

13:12
Isa 6:11,12

13:13
Hag 2:6

13:14
1 Kgs 22:17
Mt 9:36

¹⁴The armies of Babylon will run until exhausted, fleeing back to their own land

11:15 *the Red Sea,* literally, "the Sea of Egypt." *the Euphrates,* literally, "the River." **12:4** *Tell the world about his wondrous love,* literally, "Proclaim his doings among the nations."

11:15, 16 Isaiah is talking about a new or second Exodus when God brings his scattered people back to Israel and the Messiah comes to rule the world. The Lord dried up the Red Sea so the Israelites could walk through it on their way to the Promised Land (Exodus 14). He dried up the Jordan River so the nation could cross into the land (Joshua 3). God will again provide a way of return for his people.

12:1ff This chapter is a hymn of praise—another graphic description of the people's joy when Jesus Christ comes to reign over the earth. Even now we need to express our gratitude to God—thanking him, praising him, and telling others about him.

From the depths of our gratitude, we must praise him. In our overflowing praise, we must share him with others.

13:1ff Chapters 1—6 tell of judgment against Judah. Chapters 7—12 speak of judgment against Israel. Chapters 13—23 are about the judgment on other nations. Chapter 13 concerns Babylon. Long before Babylon became a world power and threatened Israel, Isaiah spoke of its condemnation. Babylon was the rallying point of rebellion against God after the flood (Genesis 11). Revelation 17 and 18 use Babylon as a symbol of God's enemies. Isaiah is trying to tell the people not to fear other nations, but to fear God alone. And he lets them know that their greatest enemy will receive from God the punishment they deserve.

13:15
Jer 51:3,4
13:16
Ps 137:8,9
Hos 10:14
13:17
Jer 51:11
13:18
2 Chron 36:17
13:19
Gen 19:24
Rev 18:11-16,19
13:20
Jer 51:37-43
13:21
Isa 34:11-15
Zeph 2:14
Isa 32:14; 34:13

14:1
Ps 102:13
Isa 41:8,9
49:13,15
Zech 2:11,12
14:2
Isa 45:14
Dan 7:18,27
14:3
Ezra 9:8,9
Jer 30:10
14:6
Isa 47:6
14:7
Ps 98:1-9

14:10
Ezek 32:21

14:12
Lk 10:18
Rev 9:1
14:13
Ezek 28:2

like deer chased by dogs, wandering like sheep deserted by their shepherd. 15Those who don't run will be butchered. 16Their little children will be dashed to death against the pavement right before their eyes; their homes will be sacked, and their wives raped by the attacking hordes. 17For I will stir up the Medes against Babylon, and no amount of silver or gold will buy them off. 18The attacking armies will have no mercy on the young people of Babylon or the babies or the children.

19And so Babylon, the most glorious of kingdoms, the flower of Chaldean culture, will be as utterly destroyed as Sodom and Gomorrah were when God sent fire from heaven; 20Babylon will never rise again. Generation after generation will come and go, but the land will never again be lived in. The nomads will not even camp there. The shepherds won't let their sheep stay overnight. 21The wild animals of the desert will make it their home. The houses will be haunted by howling creatures. Ostriches will live there, and the demons will come there to dance. 22Hyenas and jackals will den within the palaces. Babylon's days are numbered; her time of doom will soon be here.

God promises compassion on Israel

14 But the Lord will have mercy on the Israelis; they are still his special ones. He will bring them back to settle once again in the land of Israel. And many nationalities will come and join them there and be their loyal allies. 2The nations of the world will help them to return, and those coming to live in their land will serve them. Those enslaving Israel will be enslaved—Israel shall rule her enemies!

3In that wonderful day when the Lord gives his people rest from sorrow and fear, from slavery and chains, 4you will jeer at the king of Babylon and say, "You bully, you! At last you have what was coming to you! 5For the Lord has crushed your wicked power, and broken your evil rule." 6You persecuted my people with unceasing blows of rage and held the nations in your angry grip. You were unrestrained in tyranny. 7But at last the whole earth is at rest and is quiet! All the world begins to sing! 8Even the trees of the woods—the fir trees and cedars of Lebanon—sing out this joyous song: "Your power is broken; no one will bother us now; at last we have peace."

9The denizens of hell crowd to meet you as you enter their domain. World leaders and earth's mightiest kings, long dead, are there to see you. 10With one voice they all cry out, "Now you are as weak as we are!" 11Your might and power are gone; they are buried with you. All the pleasant music in your palace has ceased; now maggots are your sheet, worms your blanket!

12How you are fallen from heaven, O Lucifer, son of the morning! How you are cut down to the ground—mighty though you were against the nations of the world. 13For you said to yourself, "I will ascend to heaven and rule the angels. I will take

14:13 *the angels,* literally, "the stars of God." *I will preside on the Mount of Assembly far away in the north,* literally, "I will sit upon the mount of the congregation in the sides of the north" (Ps 48:2); or, "on the slopes of Mount Saphon."

13:20 Even before Babylon became a world power, Isaiah prophesied that, though it would shine for a while, its destruction would be so complete that the land would never again be inhabited. Babylon, in present-day Iraq, still lies in utter ruin.

14:1 God destroyed Babylon to rescue and restore the remnant of his people (i.e., those who remained faithful to him). His patience with his rebellious people followed several steps: (1) Because his chosen people rebelled and sinned against him, God had to use others, even heathen nations, to punish them. (2) But these nations were themselves wicked, and God punished them as well. (3) Because God promised to bless Israel, and God does not break promises, he will restore Israel. (4) God makes Israel an essential ingredient in his work of blessing the Gentile nations.

14:2 A prominent theme in Isaiah is that non-Israelites would join the returning Israelites (56:6, 7; 60:10; 61:5).

14:4–11 These verses could have both present and future significance in reference to Babylon. The historical city and empire would be permanently destroyed. Babylon has also been used as

a picture of all those who oppose God. Thus, in the end times, all who oppose God will be destroyed and all evil removed from the earth forever.

14:5, 6 Power is transient. God permitted Babylon to have temporary power for a purpose—to chastise his wayward people. When the purpose ended, so did the power. Beware of placing confidence in human power, for one day it will fade no matter how secure it appears.

14:12–14 There are several interpretations of these verses. (1) Lucifer is another name for Satan, because the person here is too powerful to be any human king. (2) This could be Sennacherib or Nebuchadnezzar, kings with supreme power. Their people looked upon them as gods. These kings desired to rule the world. (3) This could refer to both Satan and a great human king, probably Nebuchadnezzar since Babylon is pictured as the seat of evil in Revelation 17, 18. Pride was Satan's sin as well as Babylon's. Common to all three viewpoints is the truth that pride is against God and will result in judgment.

the highest throne. I will preside on the Mount of Assembly far away in the north. [14]I will climb to the highest heavens and be like the Most High." [15]But instead, you will be brought down to the pit of hell, down to its lowest depths. [16]Everyone there will stare at you and ask, "Can this be the one who shook the earth and the kingdoms of the world? [17]Can this be the one who destroyed the world and made it into a shambles and demolished its greatest cities and had no mercy on his prisoners?"

[18]The kings of the nations lie in stately glory in their graves, [19]but your body is thrown out like a broken branch; it lies in an open grave, covered with the dead bodies of those slain in battle. It lies as a carcass in the road, trampled and mangled by horses' hoofs. [20]No monument will be given you, for you have destroyed your nation and slain your people. Your son will not succeed you as the king. [21]Slay the children of this sinner. Do not let them rise and conquer the land nor rebuild the cities of the world.

[22]I, myself, have risen against him, says the Lord of heaven's armies, and will cut off his children and his children's children from ever sitting on his throne. [23]I will make Babylon into a desolate land of porcupines, full of swamps and marshes. I will sweep the land with the broom of destruction, says the Lord of the armies of heaven. [24]He has taken an oath to do it! For this is his purpose and plan. [25]I have decided to break the Assyrian army when they are in Israel and to crush them on my mountains; my people shall no longer be their slaves. [26]This is my plan for the whole earth—I will do it by my mighty power that reaches everywhere around the world. [27]The Lord, the God of battle, has spoken—who can change his plans? When his hand moves, who can stop him?

Prophecy against Philistia

[28]This is the message that came to me the year King Ahaz died: [29]Don't rejoice, Philistines, that the king who smote you is dead. That rod is broken, yes; but his son will be a greater scourge to you than his father ever was! From the snake will be born an adder, a fiery serpent to destroy you! [30]I will shepherd the poor of my people; they shall graze in my pasture! The needy shall lie down in peace. But as for you—I will wipe you out with famine and the sword. [31]Weep, Philistine cities—you are doomed. All your nation is doomed. For a perfectly trained army is coming down from the north against you. [32]What then shall we tell the reporters? Tell them that the Lord has founded Jerusalem and is determined that the poor of his people will find a refuge within her walls.

Prophecy against Moab

15 Here is God's message to Moab: In one night your cities of Ar and Kir will be destroyed. [2]Your people in Dibon go mourning to their temples to weep for the fate of Nebo and Medeba; they shave their heads in sorrow and cut off their beards. [3]They wear sackcloth through the streets, and from every home comes the sound of weeping. [4]The cries from the cities of Heshbon and Elealeh are heard far away, even in Jahaz. The bravest warriors of Moab cry in utter terror.

[5]My heart weeps for Moab! His people flee to Zoar and Eglath. Weeping, they climb the upward road to Luhith, and their crying will be heard all along the road to Horonaim. [6]Even Nimrim River is desolate! The grassy banks are dried up and the tender plants are gone. [7]The desperate refugees take only the possessions they can carry, and flee across the Brook of Willows. [8]The whole land of Moab is a land of weeping, from one end to the other. [9]The stream near Dibon will run red with

---

14:14
2 Thess 2:4

14:19
Isa 5:25

14:21
Ex 20:5
Isa 13:16

14:24
Job 23:13
Isa 46:11
14:25
Isa 9:4
Nah 1:13
14:27
Isa 43:13
Dan 4:31,35

14:28
2 Kgs 16:20

14:30
Isa 8:21; 11:4

14:31
Isa 3:26
Jer 1:14
14:32
Isa 25:4

15:2
Jer 48:37
15:3
Isa 22:4
Jer 48:38
Jonah 3:6-8
15:5
Jer 31:5
15:6
Jer 48:34
Joel 1:10-12
15:7
Jer 48:36
15:9
2 Kgs 17:25
Jer 50:17

14:24–27 This prophecy came true as Isaiah predicted (see 2 Kings 19 and Isaiah 37:21–38).

14:28–30 Isaiah received this message from the Lord in 715 B.C., the year that King Ahaz of Judah died. "The king who smote you" (14:29) was not Ahaz but Shalmaneser V of Assyria. The trained army was the soldiers of Sargon of Assyria.

15:1 Moab was east of the Dead Sea. The Moabites were descendants of Lot through his incestuous relationship with his older daughter (Genesis 19:31–38). Moab had always been Israel's enemy. They oppressed Israel and invaded their land (Judges 3:12–14), fought against Saul (1 Samuel 14:47), and fought against David (2 Samuel 8:2, 11, 12). Moab would be punished for its harsh treatment of Israel.

blood, but I am not through with Dibon yet! Lions will hunt down the survivors, both those who escape and those who remain.

God rebukes Moab for its pride

16 Moab's refugees at Sela send lambs as a token of alliance with the king of Judah. 2The women of Moab are left at the fords of the Arnon River like homeless birds. 3[The ambassadors, who accompany the gift to Jerusalem] plead for advice and help. "Give us sanctuary. Protect us. Do not turn us over to our foes. 4, 5Let our outcasts stay among you; hide them from our enemies! God will reward you for your kindness to us. If you let Moab's fugitives settle among you, then, when the terror is past, God will establish David's throne forever, and on that throne he will place a just and righteous King."

6Is this proud Moab, concerning which we heard so much? His arrogance and insolence are all gone now! 7Therefore all Moab weeps. Yes, Moab, you will mourn for stricken Kir-hareseth, 8and for the abandoned farms of Heshbon and the vineyards at Sibmah. The enemy war-lords have cut down the best of the grape vines; their armies spread out as far as Jazer in the deserts, and even down to the sea. 9So I wail and lament for Jazer and the vineyards of Sibmah. My tears shall flow for Heshbon and Elealeh, for destruction has come upon their summer fruits and harvests. 10Gone now is the gladness, gone the joy of harvest. The happy singing in the vineyards will be heard no more; the treading out of the grapes in the wine presses has ceased forever. I have ended all their harvest joys.

11I will weep, weep, weep, for Moab; and my sorrow for Kir-haresh will be very great. 12The people of Moab will pray in anguish to their idols at the tops of the hills, but it will do no good; they will cry to their gods in their idol temples, but none will come to save them. 13, 14All this concerning Moab has been said before; but now the Lord says that within three years, without fail, the glory of Moab shall be ended, and few of all its people will be left alive.

Prophecy against Syria

17 This is God's message to Damascus, capital of Syria:
Look, Damascus is gone! It is no longer a city—it has become a heap of ruins! 2The cities of Aroer are deserted. Sheep pasture there, lying quiet and unafraid, with no one to chase them away. 3The strength of Israel and the power of Damascus will end, and the remnant of Syria shall be destroyed. For as Israel's glory departed, so theirs, too, will disappear, declares the Lord Almighty. 4Yes, the glory of Israel will be very dim when poverty stalks the land. 5Israel will be as abandoned as the harvested grain fields in the Valley of Rephaim. 6Oh, a very few of her people will be left, just as a few stray olives are left on the trees when the harvest is ended, two or three in the highest branches, four or five out on the tips of the limbs. That is how it will be in Damascus and Israel—stripped bare of people except for a few of the poor who remain.

16:3 *The ambassadors, who accompany the gift to Jerusalem,* implied.

16:1ff Attacked by the Assyrians, Moabite refugees would flee to Sela, which lay in the country of Edom to the south. Desperate Moabite women would send a tribute of lambs to Jerusalem asking for Judah's protection. Jerusalem would be a safe refuge for a while. Isaiah advised Judah to accept these refugees as a sign of compassion in the enemy's time of devastation.

16:10 The treading of grapes (squeezing the juice from grapes by mashing them with bare feet) climaxed during the harvest season, a time of great joy in the vineyards. But the joy of harvest would soon be ended, because they ignored God and rebelled against him.

16:12, 13 When the people of Moab experienced God's wrath, they sought their own idols and gods. Nothing happened, however, because there was no one there to save them. We seek

our own ways of escape in order to get through our daily troubles. The effect is the same: none will come to save us. Our hope lies in God, the only one who can hear and help.

16:13, 14 Tiglath-pileser III invaded Moab in 732 B.C.; Sennacherib invaded Moab the same year that he invaded Judah, 701 B.C. The earlier event occurred three years after Isaiah's prediction, marking Isaiah as a true prophet. In these events, the people of Israel saw prophecy fulfilled before their eyes.

17:1ff Israel and Syria made an alliance to fight against Assyria. But Tiglath-pileser III captured Damascus, the capital of Syria, in 732 B.C. and annexed the northern part of Israel to the Assyrian Empire. Ahaz, king of Judah, then paid tribute to Tiglath-pileser III when he visited the Assyrian king in Damascus.

7Then at last they will think of God their Creator and have respect for the Holy One of Israel. 8They will no longer ask their idols for help in that day, neither will they worship what their hands have made! They will no longer have respect for the images of Ashtaroth and the sun-idols.

17:7
Isa 10:20
Hos 6:1

17:8
Ex 34:13
Isa 27:9; 30:22

9Their largest cities will be as deserted as the distant wooded hills and mountain tops and become like the abandoned cities of the Amorites, deserted when the Israelites approached (so long ago). 10Why? Because you have turned from the God who can save you—the Rock who can hide you; therefore, even though you plant a wonderful, rare crop of greatest value, 11and though it grows so well that it will blossom on the very morning that you plant it, yet you will never harvest it—your only harvest will be a pile of grief and incurable pain.

17:10
Deut 32:4,18,
30,31
Isa 30:29; 62:11

17:11
Hos 10:13

17:12
Jer 6:23

17:13
Ps 1:4
Isa 29:5

12Look, see the armies thundering toward God's land. 13But though they roar like breakers rolling upon a beach, God will silence them. They will flee, scattered like chaff by the wind, like whirling dust before a storm. 14In the evening Israel waits in terror, but by dawn her enemies are dead. This is the just reward of those who plunder and destroy the people of God.

17:14
2 Kgs 19:35
Isa 41:11,12

Prophecy against Ethiopia

18 Ah, land beyond the upper reaches of the Nile, where winged sailboats glide along the river! 2Land that sends ambassadors in fast boats down the Nile! Let swift messengers return to you, O strong and supple nation feared far and wide, a conquering, destroying nation whose land the upper Nile divides. And this is the message sent to you:

3When I raise my battle flag upon the mountain, let all the world take notice! When I blow the trumpet, listen! 4For the Lord has told me this: Let your mighty army now advance against the land of Israel. God will watch quietly from his Temple in Jerusalem—serene as on a pleasant summer day or a lovely autumn morning during harvest time. 5But before you have begun the attack, and while your plans are ripening like grapes, he will cut you off as though with pruning shears. He will snip the spreading tendrils. 6Your mighty army will be left dead on the field for the mountain birds and wild animals to eat; the vultures will tear bodies all summer, and the wild animals will gnaw bones all winter. 7But the time will come when that strong and mighty nation, a terror to all both far and near, that conquering, destroying nation whose land the rivers divide, will bring gifts to the Lord Almighty in Jerusalem, where he has placed his name.

18:3
Ps 49:1
Mic 1:2

18:5
Ezek 17:6-10

18:6
Isa 56:9
Ezek 39:17-20

18:7
Zech 14:16,17

Prophecy against Egypt

19 This is God's message concerning Egypt: Look, the Lord is coming against Egypt, riding on a swift cloud; the idols of Egypt tremble; the hearts of the

19:1
Josh 2:11
Jer 43:12

17:9 so long ago, implied.   18:1 upper reaches of the Nile, literally, "land beyond the rivers of Ethiopia."
18:2 whose land the upper Nile divides, literally, "whose land the rivers divide."   18:4 of Israel, implied.

17:7-11 God's message to Damascus is one of complete destruction. The Assyrians had turned from the God who could save them, depending instead on their idols and their own strength. No matter how successful they were, God's judgment was sure. Often we depend on the trappings of success (expensive cars, clothes, homes) to give us fulfillment. But God says we will reap grief and pain if we have depended on temporal things to give us eternal security. If we don't want the same treatment Damascus received, we must turn from these false allurements and trust in God.

17:8 Ashtoreth (or Asherah) was a goddess of love and fertility, often considered the female counterpart of Baal. Queen Jezebel may have brought the worship of Ashtoreth into the land (see 1 Kings 18:19). The cult encouraged immoral sexual practices and attracted many people. The Bible warns against worshiping Ashtoreth (Judges 2:12–14; 10:6–8; 1 Samuel 7:3), and King Manasseh was condemned for putting up an idol to her in the Temple (2 Kings 21:7). Unlike heathen gods, our God does not try to attract the greatest number of people, but instead seeks the greatest good for all people.

18:1ff This prophecy was probably given in the days of Hezekiah (2 Kings 19, 20). The land beyond the upper reaches of the Nile River was Ethiopia, located directly south of Egypt (the Nile flows north). The Ethiopian king had heard that Assyria's great army was marching south toward them. He sent messengers up the Nile asking the surrounding nations to form an alliance. Judah was also asked, but Isaiah told the messenger to return home because Judah needed only God's help to repel the Assyrians. Isaiah prophesied that Assyria would be destroyed at the proper time.

18:3 This is the call to all nations to watch for the signal of the fall of Assyria. Ethiopia had been summoning other nations to join an alliance against Assyria. God would stop Assyria in its attempt to overtake the world.

19:1 Egypt, the nation where Israel was enslaved for 400 years (Exodus 1), was a symbol of hatred for the people of Israel. Yet, Judah was considering an alliance with Egypt against Assyria. But

19:2
Judg 7:22
Mt 10:21,36
19:3
Isa 8:19

19:4
Isa 20:4
Ezek 29:19
19:5
Ezek 30:12
19:6
Ex 7:18

19:11
Gen 41:38,39
1 Kgs 4:30
Acts 7:22
19:12
Rom 9:17
19:13
Jer 46:14,19

19:14
Isa 3:12

19:16
Jer 51:30
Heb 10:31
19:17
Dan 4:35

19:19
Gen 28:18
Josh 22:10,
26,27
19:20
Isa 43:3,11
45:15,21; 49:25

Egyptians melt with fear. 2I will set them to fighting against each other—brother against brother, neighbor against neighbor, city against city, province against province. 3Her wise counselors are all at their wits' ends to know what to do; they plead with their idols for wisdom, and call upon mediums, wizards and witches to show them what to do.

4I will hand over Egypt to a hard, cruel master, to a vicious king, says the Lord Almighty. 5And the waters of the Nile will fail to rise and flood the fields; the ditches will be parched and dry, 6their channels fouled with rotting reeds. 7All green things along the river bank will wither and blow away. All crops will perish; everything will die. 8The fishermen will weep for lack of work; those who fish with hooks and those who use the nets will all be unemployed. 9The weavers will have no flax or cotton, for the crops will fail. 10Great men and small—all will be crushed and broken.

11What fools the counselors of Zoan are! Their best counsel to the king of Egypt is utterly stupid and wrong. Will they still boast of their wisdom? Will they dare tell Pharaoh about the long line of wise men they have come from? 12What has happened to your "wise counselors," O Pharaoh? Where has their wisdom gone? If they are wise, let them tell you what the Lord is going to do to Egypt. 13The "wise men" from Zoan are also fools, and those from Memphis are utterly deluded. They are the best you can find, but they have ruined Egypt with their foolish counsel. 14The Lord has sent a spirit of foolishness on them, so that all their suggestions are wrong; they make Egypt stagger like a sick drunkard. 15Egypt cannot be saved by anything or anybody—no one can show her the way.

16In that day the Egyptians will be as weak as women, cowering in fear beneath the upraised fist of God. 17Just to speak the name of Israel will strike deep terror in their hearts, for the Lord Almighty has laid his plans against them.

18At that time five of the cities of Egypt will follow the Lord Almighty and will begin to speak the Hebrew language. One of these will be Heliopolis, "The City of the Sun." 19And there will be an altar to the Lord in the heart of Egypt in those days, and a monument to the Lord at its border. 20This will be for a sign of loyalty to the Lord Almighty; then when they cry to the Lord for help against those who oppress them, he will send them a Savior—and he shall deliver them.

19:18 *the Hebrew language*, literally, "the language of Canaan."

**ALLIANCES
TODAY**

Government	We rely on government legislation to protect the moral decisions we want made, but legislation cannot change people's hearts.
Science	We enjoy the benefits of science and technology. We look to scientific predictions and analysis before we look to the Bible.
Education	We act as though education and degrees can guarantee our future and success without considering what God plans for our future.
Medical care	We regard medicine as the way to prolong life and preserve its quality—quite apart from faith and moral living.
Financial systems	We place our faith in financial "security"—making as much money as we can for ourselves—forgetting that, while being wise with our money, we must trust God for our needs.

Isaiah warned Judah not to ally with Egypt. He knew that trust in any nation or any military might was futile. Their only hope was to trust in God. Although we don't consciously put our hope for deliverance in political alliances in quite the same way, we often put our hope in other forces.

Isaiah warned against this alliance because God would destroy Assyria in his time.

19:14, 15 Egypt was noted for its wisdom, but God had sent a spirit of foolishness to the "wise men" of Egypt. True wisdom can come only from God. We must ask him for wisdom in our lives, or we will also be uncertain and misdirected. Are you confused about something in your life now? Ask God for wisdom in dealing with it.

19:19, 23 After Egypt's chastening, it would turn from idols and

worship the one true God. Even more amazing is Isaiah's prophecy that the two chief oppressors of Israel, Egypt and Assyria, would unite in worship. This prophecy will come true "in that day," the future day of Christ's reign.

19:20 When Egypt calls to God for help, he will send a Savior to deliver them. Our Savior, Jesus Christ, is available to all who call upon him. We can pray and receive his saving power too!

²¹In that day the Lord will make himself known to the Egyptians. Yes, they will know the Lord and give their sacrifices and offerings to him; they will make promises to God and keep them. ²²The Lord will smite Egypt and then restore her! For the Egyptians will turn to the Lord and he will listen to their plea and heal them.

²³In that day Egypt and Iraq will be connected by a highway, and the Egyptians and the Iraqi will move freely back and forth between their lands, and they shall worship the same God. ²⁴And Israel will be their ally; the three will be together, and Israel will be a blessing to them. ²⁵For the Lord will bless Egypt and Iraq because of their friendship with Israel. He will say, "Blessed be Egypt, my people; blessed be Iraq, the land I have made; blessed be Israel, my inheritance!"

19:21
Isa 56:7

19:22
Deut 32:39
Isa 27:13
Heb 12:11

19:23
Isa11:16

19:25
Hos 2:23

The barefoot prophet

20 In the year when Sargon, king of Assyria, sent the commander-in-chief of his army against the Philistine city of Ashdod and captured it, ²the Lord told Isaiah, the son of Amoz, to take off his clothing, including his shoes, and to walk around naked and barefoot. And Isaiah did as he was told.

³Then the Lord said, My servant Isaiah, who has been walking naked and barefoot for the last three years, is a symbol of the terrible troubles I will bring upon Egypt and Ethiopia. ⁴For the king of Assyria will take away the Egyptians and Ethiopians as prisoners, making them walk naked and barefoot, both young and old, their buttocks uncovered, to the shame of Egypt. ⁵, ⁶Then how dismayed the Philistines will be, who counted on "Ethiopia's power" and their "glorious ally," Egypt! And they will say, "If this can happen to Egypt, what chance have we?"

20:2
1 Sam 19:24
Mic 1:8

20:3
Isa 8:18; 43:3

20:4
Isa 19:4; 47:2,3

20:5
Isa 31:3
Jer 9:23,24

Prophecy against Babylon

21 This is God's message concerning Babylon:
Disaster is roaring down upon you from the terrible desert, like a whirlwind sweeping from the Negeb. ²I see an awesome vision: oh, the horror of it all! God is telling me what he is going to do. I see you plundered and destroyed. Elamites and Medes will take part in the siege. Babylon will fall, and the groaning of all the nations she enslaved will end. ³My stomach constricts and burns with pain; sharp pangs of horror are upon me, like the pangs of a woman giving birth to a child. I faint when I hear what God is planning; I am terrified, blinded with dismay. ⁴My mind reels; my heart races; I am gripped by awful fear. All rest at night—so pleasant once—is gone; I lie awake, trembling.

⁵Look! They are preparing a great banquet! They load the tables with food; they pull up their chairs to eat. . . . Quick, quick, grab your shields and prepare for battle! You are being attacked!

⁶, ⁷Meanwhile (in my vision) the Lord had told me, "Put a watchman on the city

21:1
Isa 13:20-22
Jer 51:41
Zech 9:14

21:3
Ps 48:6
1 Thess 5:3

21:4
Deut 28:67

21:5
Jer 51:39,57

19:23 *Iraq,* literally, "Assyria." **19:25** *because of their friendship,* implied. **20:5, 6** *Philistines,* literally, "inhabitants of the coastland." **21:1** *Babylon,* implied in v 9. **21:6, 7** *in my vision,* implied. *riders in pairs on donkeys and camels,* literally, "When he sees a troop, horsemen in pairs, riders on asses, riders on camels." Possibly the meaning is that the asses and camels were paired for the attack.

19:22 Egypt is but one Gentile nation who will bow before the Lord. (Philippians 2:10, 11 says *every* knee shall bow, every tongue shall confess that Jesus Christ is Lord.) So we shouldn't be surprised that Egyptians and Assyrians are part of the "every." Each of us is part of that "every" too. We may bow now in devotion, or later in shameful submission.

19:23–25 In Jesus Christ, former enemies may unite in love. In Christ, people and nations that are poles apart politically will bow at his feet as brothers and sisters because he breaks down every barrier that threatens relationships.

20:1 Sargon II was king of Assyria from 722–705 B.C., and this event happened in 711 B.C. Isaiah graphically reminds Judah that they should not count on foreign alliances to protect them.

20:2 God's command to Isaiah was to walk about naked for three years, a humiliating experience. God was using Isaiah to demonstrate the humiliation that Egypt and Ethiopia would

experience at the hands of Assyria. But the message was really for Judah: "Don't put your trust in foreign governments or you will experience this kind of shame and humiliation from your captors."

20:3 God asked Isaiah to do something that seemed shameful and illogical. There may be times when we are asked to obey God in ways we don't understand at present. We must obey God in complete faith, for he will never ask us to do something wrong.

21:1ff Some say this prophecy was fulfilled at Babylon's fall in 539 B.C. (see Daniel 5). But others say this was a prophecy of Babylon's revolt against Assyria around 700 B.C.

21:5 If the prophecy refers to the fall of Babylon in 539 B.C., this refers to the feast in Daniel 5.

21:6, 7 Watchmen often appear in prophetic visions of destruction. They are the first to see trouble coming. The vision of the riders in pairs could represent the Medes and Persians attacking Babylon in 539 B.C.

wall to shout out what he sees. When he sees riders in pairs on donkeys and camels, tell him, 'This is it!' "

8, 9So I put the watchman on the wall, and at last he shouted, "Sir, day after day and night after night I have been here at my post. Now at last—look! Here come riders in pairs!"

Then I heard a Voice shout out, "Babylon is fallen, is fallen; and all the idols of Babylon lie broken on the ground."

10O my people, threshed and winnowed, I have told you all that the Lord Almighty, the God of Israel, has said.

Prophecy against Edom

11This is God's message to Edom:

Someone from among you keeps calling, calling to me: "Watchman, what of the night? Watchman, what of the night? How much time is left?" 12The watchman replies, "Your judgment day is dawning now. Turn again to God, so that I can give you better news. Seek for him, then come and ask again!"

Prophecy against Arabia

13This is God's message concerning Arabia:

O caravans from Dedan, you will hide in the deserts of Arabia. 14O people of Tema, bring food and water to these weary fugitives! 15They have fled from drawn swords and sharp arrows and the terrors of war! 16"But a long year from now," says the Lord, "the great power of their enemy, the mighty tribe of Kedar, will end. 17Only a few of its stalwart archers will survive." The Lord, the God of Israel, has spoken.

Prophecy about Jerusalem

22 This is God's message concerning Jerusalem:

What is happening? Where is everyone going? Why are they running to the rooftops? What are they looking at? 2The whole city is in terrible uproar. What's the trouble in this busy, happy city? Bodies! Lying everywhere, slain by plague and not by sword. 3All your leaders flee; they surrender without resistance. The people slip away but they are captured, too. 4Let me alone to weep. Don't try to comfort me—let me cry for my people as I watch them being destroyed. 5Oh, what a day of crushing trouble! What a day of confusion and terror from the Lord God of heaven's armies! The walls of Jerusalem are breached and the cry of death

Side references:

21:8
Isa 13:19
46:1,2
Jer 50:2
Hab 2:1
Rev 14:8

21:10
Jer 51:33

21:11
Gen 32:3

21:15
Isa 13:14,15

21:17
Isa 10:19

22:1
Jer 21:13

22:2
Isa 23:7
Jer 14:18

22:4
Jer 9:1

22:5
Isa 37:3
Lam 2:2

21:11 Edom, literally, "Dumah." **21:16** But a long year from now. The Dead Sea manuscript reads, "within three years, according to the year of a hireling," like 16:14. the great power of their enemy. implied. **22:1** Jerusalem, literally, "The Valley of Vision." **22:2** happy city and slain by plague, implied.

21:8, 9 Babylon was not only a great and powerful city, but also filled with horrible sin. Babylon was, and it remains, a symbol of all that stands against God. Despite all its glory and power, Babylon would be destroyed with all its idols.

21:10 Threshing and winnowing were two steps in the farming process in ancient Israel. The heads of wheat (often used to symbolize Israel) were first trampled to break open the seeds and expose the valued grain inside. The seeds were then thrown into the air, and the worthless chaff blew away while the grain fell back to the ground. Israel would experience this same kind of process—the worthless, sinful, rebellious people would be taken away, but God would keep the good "grain" to replenish Israel.

21:11, 12 Everyone wants to hear the good news that all troubles are over and prosperity lies ahead. The watchman tells how to get that good news—turn to God, and seek him with all your heart. Without God, the news of world events and the world's future is anything but good. Without God, our personal future is bad news.

21:12 Edom had been a constant enemy of God's people. They rejoiced when Israel fell to the Assyrians, and this sealed Edom's doom. Obadiah foretells, in great detail, the destruction of Edom.

21:13 The places listed here are all in Arabia. They are border

cities that controlled the trade routes through the land. Nabonidus, king of Babylon, would attack Arabia and make the people his servants. He set up court in Tema, leaving Belshazzar in Babylon as regent. This is Isaiah's prediction of disaster. Judah kept trying to make alliances with Arabia against Nabonidus, but Isaiah warned the people against such an alliance and urged them to trust in God alone.

22:1-13 Jerusalem would be attacked unless God's people returned to him. Instead they used every means of protection possible except asking God for help. They wanted to trust in their ingenuity, weapons, and even their pagan neighbors (see 2 Chronicles 32 and 36 for sieges of Jerusalem).

22:4 Isaiah had warned his people; but they did not repent, so they would experience God's judgment. Because of his care for them, Isaiah was hurt by their punishment and mourned deeply for them. Sometimes people we care for ignore our attempts to help, so they suffer the very things from which we wanted to spare them. At times like that we grieve because of our concern. God expects us to be involved with others, and this may sometimes cause us to suffer with them.

echoes from the mountainsides. 6, 7Elamites are the archers; Syrians drive the **22:6**
chariots; the men of Kir hold up the shields. They fill your choicest valleys and Isa 21:2
crowd against your gates.

8God has removed his protecting care. You run to the armory for your weapons!
9, 10, 11You inspect the walls of Jerusalem to see what needs repair! You check over **22:9**
the houses and tear some down for stone for fixing walls. Between the city walls, 2 Kgs 25:4
you build a reservoir for water from the lower pool! But all your feverish plans will
not avail, for you never ask for help from God, who lets this come upon you. He is
the one who planned it long ago. 12The Lord God called you to repent, to weep and **22:12**
mourn and shave your heads in sorrow for your sins, and to wear clothes made of Isa 32:11
sackcloth to show your remorse. 13But instead, you sing and dance and play, and **22:13**
feast and drink. "Let us eat, drink, and be merry," you say: "What's the difference, Isa 5:11,22
for tomorrow we die." 14The Lord Almighty has revealed to me that this sin will 1 Cor 15:32
never be forgiven you until the day you die.

15, 16Furthermore, the same Lord God of the armies of heaven has told me this: **22:15**
Go and say to Shebna, the palace administrator: "And who do you think you are, 2 Chron 16:14
building this beautiful sepulchre in the rock for yourself? 17For the Lord who Mt 27:60
allowed you to be clothed so gorgeously will hurl you away, sending you into
captivity, O strong man! 18He will wad you up in his hands like a ball and toss you
away into a distant, barren land; there you will die, O glorious one—you who
disgrace your nation!

19"Yes, I will drive you out of office," says the Lord, "and pull you down from **22:19**
your high position. 20And then I will call my servant Eliakim, the son of Hilkiah, Ezek 17:24
to replace you. 21He shall have your uniform and title and authority, and he will be **22:20**
a father to the people of Jerusalem and all Judah. 22I will give him responsibility Isa 36:3
over all my people; whatever he says will be done; none will be able to stop him. **22:21**
23, 24I will make of him a strong and steady peg to support my people; they will load Gen 45:8
him with responsibility, and he will be an honor to his family name." 25But the **22:23**
Lord will pull out that other peg that seems to be so firmly fastened to the wall! It Job 36:7
will come out and fall to the ground, and everything it supports will fall with it, for Zech 10:4
the Lord has spoken. **22:25**
Esth 9:24,25
Isa 46:11

Prophecy against Tyre

23 This is God's message to Tyre: **23:1**
Weep, O ships of Tyre, returning home from distant lands! Weep for your Ezek 26:1-28
harbor, for it is gone! The rumors that you heard in Cyprus are all true. 2, 3Deathly **23:2**
Ezek 27:3-23

23:1 *Tyre.* Tyre was originally a colony of the mother-city, Sidon. Also in vs 4.

22:6, 7 Elamites, Syrians, and men of Kir were all under Assyrian
rule. The entire Assyrian army, including its vassals, joined in the
attack against Jerusalem.

22:8–11 The leaders did what they could to prepare for war: they
got weapons, inspected the walls, and built a water reservoir. But
all their work was pointless because they never asked God for
help. Too often we turn to things which, though good in
themselves, really won't give us the help we need. We must get the
weapons and inspect the walls, but God must guide the work.

22:13 National danger should be a call to national repentance.
But when these people were threatened, they decided to enjoy
what they had instead of gathering together in repentance. When
the people saw the Assyrians, they should have repented, realizing
their sin, the prophet's warnings, and their helplessness. Attacked
on every side (22:8), they could have repented (22:12), but they
chose to feast instead. The root problem was that Judah did not
trust God's power or his promises (see 56:12; 1 Corinthians 15:32).
When you face difficulties, turn to God.

22:13, 14 The people said, "Let us eat, drink, and be merry"
because they had given up hope. Today, we see people giving up
hope as well. There are two common responses to hopelessness:
despair and self-indulgence. But this life is not all there is, so we

are not to act as if we have no hope. The proper response is to turn
to God and trust in his promise of a perfect and just future in the
new world he will create.

22:15–25 Shebna, a high court official, was materialistic, like the
rest of Jerusalem who wanted to "eat, drink, and be merry" (22:13).
He may have been in the group favoring an alliance with
foreigners, thus ignoring Isaiah's advice. Shebna is the "peg" that
will be pulled out of the wall, and everything (his riches, his glory)
will fall with it (22:25). The other peg, the good one, is Eliakim,
chosen to replace Shebna. He had a godly influence on the
people, but even his strength could not keep Jerusalem from
falling because the people refused to repent (see 2 Kings 18:18ff).

22:20–24 Eliakim would be a responsible leader, supporting his
followers. Good leaders build up others, not themselves. To do
this, they must depend on the Lord.

23:1ff Isaiah's prophecies against other nations began in the east
with Babylon (chapter 13) and ended in the west with Tyre in
Phoenicia. Tyre was one of the most famous cities of the ancient
world, a major trading center with a large seaport. It was a wealthy
city and very evil. Tyre was rebuked by Jeremiah (Jeremiah 25:22;
47:4), Ezekiel (Ezekiel 26—28), Joel (Joel 3:4–8), Amos (Amos 1:9,
10), and Zechariah (Zechariah 9:3, 4). This is another warning
against political alliances with unstable neighbors.

silence is everywhere. Stillness reigns where once your hustling port was full of ships from Sidon, bringing merchandise from far across the ocean, from Egypt and along the Nile. You were the merchandise mart of the world. 4Be ashamed, O Sidon, stronghold of the sea. For you are childless now! 5When Egypt hears the news, there will be great sorrow. 6Flee to Tarshish, men of Tyre, weeping as you go. 7This silent ruin is all that's left of your once joyous land. What a history was yours! Think of all the colonists you sent to distant lands!

8Who has brought this disaster on Tyre, empire builder and top trader of the world? 9The Commander of the armies of heaven has done it to destroy your pride and show his contempt for all the greatness of mankind. 10Sail on, O ships of Tarshish, for your harbor is gone. 11The Lord holds out his hand over the seas; he shakes the kingdoms of the earth; he has spoken out against this great merchant city, to destroy its strength.

12He says, "Never again, O dishonored virgin, daughter of Sidon, will you rejoice, will you be strong. Even if you flee to Cyprus, you will find no rest."

13It will be the Babylonians, not the Assyrians, who consign Tyre to the wild beasts. They will lay siege to it, raze its palaces and make it a heap of ruins. 14Wail, you ships that ply the oceans, for your home port is destroyed!

15, 16For seventy years Tyre will be forgotten. Then, in the days of another king, the city will come back to life again; she will sing sweet songs as a harlot sings who, long absent from her lovers, walks the streets to look for them again and is remembered. 17Yes, after seventy years, the Lord will revive Tyre, but she will be no different than she was before; she will return again to all her evil ways around the world. 18Yet [the distant time will come when] her businesses will give their profits to the Lord! They will not be hoarded but used for good food and fine clothes for the priests of the Lord!

3. God's purpose in judgment
God's judgment on the land

24 Look! The Lord is overturning the land of Judah and making it a vast wasteland of destruction. See how he is emptying out all its people and scattering them over the face of the earth. 2Priests and people, servants and masters, slave girls and mistresses, buyers and sellers, lenders and borrowers, bankers and debtors—none will be spared. 3The land will be completely emptied and looted. The Lord has spoken. 4, 5The land suffers for the sins of its people. The earth languishes, the crops wither, the skies refuse their rain. The land is defiled by crime; the people have twisted the laws of God and broken his everlasting commands. 6Therefore the curse of God is upon them; they are left desolate, destroyed by the drought. Few will be left alive.

7All the joys of life will go: the grape harvest will fail, the wine will be gone, the

23:18 *the distant time will come,* implied.

23:4
Gen 10:15,19
Jer 47:4

23:5
Josh 2:9-11

23:7
Isa 32:13

23:9
Isa 5:13
Dan 4:37

23:11
Isa 50:2
Zech 9:3,4

23:12
Rev 18:22

23:13
Isa 13:21

23:15
Jer 25:11

24:2
Lev 25:36,37
Deut 23:19,20

24:4
Gen 3:17
Num 35:33

24:6
Isa 34:5
Zech 5:3,4

24:7
Joel 1:10,12

23:5 Why would Egypt be sad when Tyre fell? Egypt depended on Tyre's shipping expertise to promote and carry their products around the world. Egypt would lose an important trading partner with the fall of Tyre.

23:9 God destroyed Tyre because he hated its people's pride. Pride separates people from God, and he will not tolerate it. We must examine our lives and remember that all true accomplishment comes from God, our Creator. We have no reason for pride in ourselves.

23:13 Assyria invaded Tyre in 705 B.C. and again in 681–669 B.C. This message is astounding, however, because it prophesies that the Babylonians, not yet a world power, will destroy Tyre. They did so in 572 B.C., a century after Isaiah made this prophecy.

23:15, 16 Some scholars believe this is a literal 70 years; some say it is symbolic of a long period of time. If it is literal, this may have occurred between 700–630 B.C. during the Assyrian captivity of Israel, or it may have been during the 70-year captivity of the Jews in Babylon (605–536 B.C.). During the 70 years the Jews

would forget about Tyre, but when they returned from captivity they would once again trade with Tyre (see Ezekiel 29:17–20).

24—27 These four chapters are often called "Isaiah's Apocalypse." They discuss God's judgment on the entire world for its sin. Isaiah's prophecies were first directed to Judah, then to Israel, then to the surrounding nations, and finally to the whole world. These chapters describe the last days when God will judge the whole world, when good will finally and permanently conquer evil.

24:4, 5 The people not only suffered from their sins; even the land suffered with bad crops and crime. Today we see the results of sin in our own land—pollution, crime, poverty. Sin affects every aspect of society so extensively that even those faithful to God suffer. We cannot blame God for these conditions, because human sin has brought them about. The more we who are believers renounce sin and share God's Word with others, the more we slow our society's deterioration. We must not give up: sin is rampant, but we can make a difference.

merrymakers will sigh and mourn. 8The melodious chords of the harp and timbrel
are heard no more; the happy days are ended. 9No more are the joys of wine and
song; strong drink turns bitter in the mouth.

10The city lies in chaos; every home and shop is locked up tight to keep out
looters. 11Mobs form in the streets, crying for wine; joy has reached its lowest ebb;
gladness has been banished from the land. 12The city is left in ruins; its gates are
battered down. 13Throughout the land the story is the same—only a remnant is left.

14But all who are left will shout and sing for joy; those in the west will praise the
majesty of God, 15, 16and those in the east will respond with praise. Hear them
singing to the Lord from the ends of the earth, singing glory to the Righteous One!

But my heart is heavy with grief, for evil still prevails and treachery is everywhere. 17Terror and the captivity of hell are still your lot, O men of the world.
18When you flee in terror you will fall into a pit, and if you escape from the pit you
will step into a trap, for destruction falls from the heavens upon you; the world is
shaken beneath you. 19The earth has broken down in utter collapse; everything is
lost, abandoned and confused. 20The world staggers like a drunkard; it shakes like
a tent in a storm. It falls and will not rise again, for the sins of the earth are very
great.

21On that day the Lord will punish the fallen angels in the heavens, and the proud
rulers of the nations on earth. 22They will be rounded up like prisoners and
imprisoned in a dungeon until they are tried and condemned. 23Then the Lord of
heaven's armies will mount his throne in Zion and rule gloriously in Jerusalem, in
the sight of all the elders of his people. Such glory there will be that all the
brightness of the sun and moon will seem to fade away.

Praise to the Lord

25 O Lord, I will honor and praise your name, for you are my God; you do such
wonderful things! You planned them long ago, and now you have accomplished them, just as you said! 2You turn mighty cities into heaps of ruins. The
strongest forts are turned to rubble. Beautiful palaces in distant lands disappear and
will never be rebuilt. 3Therefore strong nations will shake with fear before you;
ruthless nations will obey and glorify your name.

4But to the poor, O Lord, you are a refuge from the storm, a shadow from the
heat, a shelter from merciless men who are like a driving rain that melts down an
earthen wall. 5As a hot, dry land is cooled by clouds, you will cool the pride of
ruthless nations. 6Here on Mount Zion in Jerusalem, the Lord Almighty will spread
a wondrous feast for everyone around the world—a delicious feast of good food,
with clear, well-aged wine and choice beef. 7At that time he will remove the cloud
of gloom, the pall of death that hangs over the earth; 8he will swallow up death

24:8
Jer 16:9
24:9
Isa 5:11,22
24:10
Gen 1:2
24:11
Isa 32:13
24:12
Isa 45:2
24:13
Isa 17:6
24:14
Isa 12:6; 52:8
24:15
Isa 42:4,10,12
Jer 5:1
24:18
Gen 7:10-12
Ps 46:2
24:19
Num 16:31,32
24:20
Isa 19:14; 43:27
24:21
Ps 76:12
24:22
Isa 10:4
24:23
Mic 4:7
Rev 21:23

25:1
Ex 15:2
Ps 40:5
Eph 1:11
25:2
Isa 17:1
25:4
Isa 32:2
25:5
Jer 51:54-56
25:8
Ps 69:9
Isa 65:19
1 Cor 15:54
1 Pet 4:14
Rev 21:4

24:13 throughout the land, or possibly, "throughout the nations of the world."

24:14–16 The believers who are left behind after God judges
Judah will sing to the glory of the Righteous One. Isaiah was heavy
with grief because of his world's condition. We too can become
depressed by the evil all around us. At those times we need to
hold on to God's promises for the future and look forward to
singing praises to him when he restores heaven and earth.

24:21 "Fallen angels" refers to spiritual forces which are opposed
to God. Nobody, not even the fallen angels, will escape due
punishment.

25:1 Isaiah gave honor and praise to God because he realized
that God completes his plans as promised. God also fulfills his
promises to you. Think of the prayers he has answered, and praise
him for his goodness and faithfulness.

25:4 The poor suffered because the rich oppressed them. But
God is concerned for the poor and is a refuge for them. When we
are disadvantaged or oppressed, we can turn to God for comfort
and help. Jesus states in Luke 6:20 that the Kingdom of God
belongs to the poor.

25:6 Here is a marvelous prophecy of the Gentiles joining the
Jews at God's feast to celebrate the overthrow of evil and the
reality of eternity with God. It shows that God intended his saving
message to go out to the whole world, not just to the Jews. During
the feast, God will end death forever (25:7, 8). The people who
participate in this great feast will be those who have been living by
faith, and are now being rewarded. That is why they say, "This is
our God, in whom we trust, for whom we waited. Now at last he is
here" (25:9).

25:8 When the Lord speaks, he does what he says. It is
comforting to know that God's plans and activities are closely tied
to his Word. When we pray according to God's will (as expressed
in the Bible) and claim his promises (as recorded in the Bible), he
hears us and answers our requests.

25:8 The first part of this verse is quoted in the New Testament to
describe Christ's victory over death (1 Corinthians 15:54). God's
ultimate victory is seen when death, our ultimate enemy, is
defeated (see also Hosea 13:14). The second part of this verse is
quoted in Revelation 21:4, which describes the glorious scene of
God's presence with his people.

forever. The Lord God will wipe away all tears and take away forever all insults and mockery against his land and people. The Lord has spoken—he will surely do it!

9In that day the people will proclaim, "This is our God, in whom we trust, for whom we waited. Now at last he is here." What a day of rejoicing! 10For the Lord's good hand will rest upon Jerusalem, and Moab will be crushed as straw beneath his feet and left to rot. 11God will push them down just as a swimmer pushes down the water with his hands. He will end their pride and all their evil works. 12The high walls of Moab will be demolished and brought to dust.

The people sing to God

26 Listen to them singing! In that day the whole land of Judah will sing this song:

"Our city is strong! We are surrounded by the walls of his salvation!" 2Open the gates to everyone, for all may enter in who love the Lord. 3He will keep in perfect peace all those who trust in him, whose thoughts turn often to the Lord! 4Trust in the Lord God always, for in the Lord Jehovah is your everlasting strength. 5He humbles the proud and brings the haughty city to the dust; its walls come crashing down. 6He presents it to the poor and needy for their use.

7But for good men the path is not uphill and rough! God does not give them a rough and treacherous path, but smooths the road before them. 8O Lord, we love to do your will! Our hearts' desire is to glorify your name. 9All night long I search for you; earnestly I seek for God; for only when you come in judgment on the earth to punish it will people turn away from wickedness and do what is right.

10Your kindness to the wicked doesn't make them good; they keep on doing wrong and take no notice of your majesty. 11They do not listen when you threaten; they will not look to see your upraised fist. Show them how much you love your people. Perhaps then they will be ashamed! Yes, let them be burned up by the fire reserved for your enemies.

12Lord, grant us peace; for all we have and are has come from you. 13O Lord our God, once we worshiped other gods; but now we worship you alone. 14Those we served before are dead and gone; never again will they return. You came against them and destroyed them, and they are long forgotten. 15O praise the Lord! He has made our nation very great. He has widened the boundaries of our land!

16Lord, in their distress they sought for you. When your punishment was on them, they poured forth a whispered prayer. 17How we missed your presence, Lord! We suffered as a woman giving birth, who cries and writhes in pain. 18We too have writhed in agony, but all to no avail. No deliverance has come from all our efforts. 19Yet we have this assurance: Those who belong to God shall live again.

25:9
Isa 30:18
35:1,2,10; 40:9

25:11
Isa 16:6

25:12
Isa 26:5

26:1
Isa 12:1; 31:9
60:18

26:2
Isa 45:25

26:3
Isa 57:19

26:4
Isa 50:10

26:6
Isa 29:19

26:7
Ps 25:4,5
Isa 42:16

26:8
Isa 12:4

25:9
Ps 63:1; 77:2
Hos 5:15

26:10
Isa 22:12,13
Jn 5:37,38

26:13
Isa 2:8

26:14
Hab 2:19

26:15
Isa 54:2

26:16
Hos 5:15

26:17
Jn 16:21

26:18
Isa 33:11

26:19
Ezek 37:1-14
Dan 12:2
Eph 5:14

25:10 Moab was a symbol of all who oppose God and are rebellious to the end.

26:1ff People will praise God on the day of the Lord when Christ establishes his kingdom (see chapter 12). God revealed the words of this hymn to Isaiah, which he presents here. Once more, God revealed the future to Isaiah.

26:2 Isaiah portrays Judah opening the gates of salvation to all who love the Lord. This was accomplished through Christ. Now all who love God are welcome to dwell together as his people. Because God wants to reach all people with his love, we must not exclude anyone who wants to have fellowship with him.

26:3 We can never avoid strife in the world around us, but with God we can know perfect peace even in the midst of turmoil. Supported by God's unchanging love and mighty power, we are not shaken by the surrounding chaos (see Philippians 4:7).

26:7, 8 At times it doesn't seem smooth and easy to do God's will, but we are never alone when we face tough times. God is there to help us through difficulties, comfort us, and lead us.

26:10 Even wicked people receive God's benefits, but that doesn't teach them to be good. Sometimes God's judgment teaches us more than God's good gifts. If you have been enriched by God's goodness, have you learned to respond to him with your grateful devotion?

26:16–19 The people realize the pain of being away from God's presence, and yet they are assured that they will live again. God turned his back on Israel when they disobeyed, but a small number never lost hope and continued to seek him. No matter how difficult times may be, we have hope when we keep our trust in him. Can you wait patiently for God to act?

26:19 Some people say there is no life after death. Others believe that there is, but it is not physical life. But Isaiah tells us that our bodies shall rise again. According to 1 Corinthians 15:50–53, all the dead believers will arise with new incorruptible bodies—bodies like Jesus had when he was resurrected (see Philippians 3:21). Isaiah 26:19 is not the only Old Testament verse to speak about the resurrection; see also Job 19:26; Psalm 16:10; Daniel 12:2, 13.

Their bodies shall rise again! Those who dwell in the dust shall awake and sing for joy! For God's light of life will fall like dew upon them!

20Go home, my people, and lock the doors! Hide for a little while until the Lord's wrath against your enemies has passed. 21Look! The Lord is coming from the heavens to punish the people of the earth for their sins. The earth will no longer hide the murderers. The guilty will be found.

26:20
Ps 30:5
26:21
Job 16:18
Mic 1:3

The Lord will deliver Israel

27 In that day the Lord will take his terrible, swift sword and punish leviathan, the swiftly moving serpent, the coiling, writhing serpent, the dragon of the sea.

27:1
Job 3:8
Ps 74:14

2In that day [of Israel's freedom] let this anthem be their song:

3Israel is my vineyard; I, the Lord, will tend the fruitful vines; every day I'll water them, and day and night I'll watch to keep all enemies away. 4, 5My anger against Israel is gone. If I find thorns and briars bothering her, I will burn them up, unless these enemies of mine surrender and beg for peace and my protection. 6The time will come when Israel will take root and bud and blossom and fill the whole earth with her fruit!

27:3
Jn 10:28
27:4
2 Sam 23:6
Isa 33:12
Rom 5:1
27:6
Isa 35:1,2

7, 8Has God punished Israel as much as he has punished her enemies? No, for he has devastated her enemies, while he has punished Israel but a little, exiling her far from her own land as though blown away in a storm from the east. 9And why did God do it? It was to purge away her sins, to rid her of all her idol altars and her idols. They will never be worshiped again. 10Her walled cities will be silent and empty, houses abandoned, streets grown up with grass, cows grazing through the city munching on twigs and branches.

27:7
Isa 10:12,17
Hos 13:15
27:9
Dan 11:35
Isa 17:8

11My people are like the dead branches of a tree, broken off and used to burn beneath the pots. They are a foolish nation, a witless, stupid people, for they turn away from God. Therefore, he who made them will not have pity on them or show them his mercy. 12Yet the time will come when the Lord will gather them together one by one like handpicked grain, selecting them here and there from his great threshing floor that reaches all the way from the Euphrates River to the Egyptian boundary. 13In that day the great trumpet will be blown, and many about to perish among their enemies, Assyria and Egypt, will be rescued and brought back to Jerusalem to worship the Lord in his holy mountain.

27:11
Deut 32:18,28
Isa 43:1,7
27:12
Deut 30:3,4
Isa 11:11
27:13
Zech 14:16
Mt 24:31
Rev 11:15

4. Jerusalem's true and false hopes

Prophecy against Samaria

28 Woe to the city of Samaria, surrounded by her rich valley—Samaria, the pride and delight of the drunkards of Israel! Woe to her fading beauty, the

27:2 of Israel's freedom, implied.   **27:3** Israel, implied. Also in vs 4.   **27:7** devastated her enemies, implied.
27:9 purge away, literally, "atone for."

26:21 When God comes to judge the earth, the guilty will find no place to hide. Jesus said that secret plots will become public information, because his truth, like a light shining in a dark corner, will reveal them (Matthew 10:26). Instead of trying to hide your shameful thoughts and actions from God, confess them to him and receive his forgiveness.

27:1 That day is a reference to the end of the evil world as we know it. In some ancient literature, the dragon (leviathan) was the enemy of God's created order. Thus Isaiah is comparing God's slaughter of the wicked to the conquering of a great enemy. Although evil is a powerful foe, God will crush it and abolish it from the earth forever.

27:3-6 The trampled vineyard of chapter 5 is restored in God's new earth. God will protect and care for the vineyard, his people. It will no longer produce worthless fruit, but will produce enough good fruit for the whole world. Gentiles will come to know God through Israel.

27:11 Isaiah compares the state of Israel's spiritual life with dead

branches that are broken off and used as fuel. Trees in Scripture often represent spiritual life. The trunk is the channel of strength from God; the branches are the people who serve him. Tree branches sometimes waver and blow in the wind. Like Israel, they may dry up from internal rottenness and become useless for anything except building a fire. What kind of branch are you? If you are withering spiritually, check to see if you are firmly rooted in God.

27:12 God's purpose in judging the earth is not vengeance, but purging. He wants to correct us and bring us back to him. God does not punish us for our sin just to make us suffer, but to make the faithful better equipped for fruitful service.

28:1 Samaria was the capital of the Northern Kingdom of Israel, and the seat of a line of evil kings. When Israel split into two kingdoms after Solomon's reign, Jerusalem ended up in the Southern Kingdom. Leaders in the Northern Kingdom, wishing to stay entirely separate from their relatives to the south, set up idols to keep the people from going to the Temple in Jerusalem to

28:2
Isa 8:7; 30:28
Nah 1:8

28:4
Hos 9:10
Nah 3:12

28:5
Isa 41:16

28:6
2 Chron 32:6-8

28:7
Hab 2:15,16

28:8
Jer 48:26

28:9
Heb 5:12,13

28:11
Isa 33:19
1 Cor 14:21

28:12
Jer 6:16
Mt 11:28,29

28:13
Mt 21:44

28:15
Isa 28:18

28:16
Ps 118:22
Mt 21:42
Acts 4:11
Eph 2:20

28:17
Isa 61:8
Amos 7:7-9

28:21
2 Sam 5:20
Lk 19:41-44

crowning glory of a nation of men lying drunk in the streets! 2For the Lord will send a mighty army (the Assyrians) against you; like a mighty hailstorm he will burst upon you and dash you to the ground. 3The proud city of Samaria—yes, the joy and delight of the drunkards of Israel—will be hurled to the ground and trampled beneath the enemies' feet. 4Once glorious, her fading beauty surrounded by a fertile valley will suddenly be gone, greedily snatched away as an early fig is hungrily snatched and gobbled up!

5Then at last the Lord Almighty himself will be their crowning glory, the diadem of beauty to his people who are left. 6He will give a longing for justice to your judges and great courage to your soldiers who are battling to the last before your gates. 7But Jerusalem is now led by drunks! Her priests and prophets reel and stagger, making stupid errors and mistakes. 8Their tables are covered with vomit; filth is everywhere.

9"Who does Isaiah think he is," the people say, "to speak to us like this! Are we little children, barely old enough to talk? 10He tells us everything over and over again, a line at a time and in such simple words!"

11But they won't listen; the only language they can understand is punishment! So God will punish them by sending against them foreigners who speak strange gibberish! Only then will they listen to him! 12They could have rest in their own land if they would obey him, if they were kind and good. He told them that, but they wouldn't listen to him. 13So the Lord will spell it out for them again, repeating it over and over in simple words whenever he can; yet over this simple, straightforward message they will stumble and fall and be broken, trapped and captured.

14Therefore hear the word of the Lord, you scoffing rulers in Jerusalem:

15You have struck a bargain with Death, you say, and sold yourselves to the devil in exchange for his protection against the Assyrians. "They can never touch us," you say, "for we are under the care of one who will deceive and fool them."

16But the Lord God says, See, I am placing a Foundation Stone in Zion—a firm, tested, precious Cornerstone that is safe to build on. He who believes need never run away again. 17I will take the line and plummet of justice to check the foundation wall you built; it looks so fine, but it is so weak a storm of hail will knock it down! The enemy will come like a flood and sweep it away, and you will be drowned. 18I will cancel your agreement of compromise with Death and the devil, so when the terrible enemy floods in, you will be trampled into the ground. 19Again and again that flood will come and carry you off, until at last the unmixed horror of the truth of my warnings will finally dawn on you.

20The bed you have made is far too short to lie on; the blankets are too narrow to cover you. 21The Lord will come suddenly and in anger, as at Mount Perazim and Gibeon, to do a strange, unusual thing—to destroy his own people! 22So scoff no more, lest your punishment be made even greater, for the Lord God has plainly told me that he is determined to crush you.

28:15 *and sold yourselves to the devil,* literally, "Sheol," "the underworld."

---

worship. Thus Samaria led the people into idolatry. Isaiah gave this message to Judah to encourage them to repent before being punished as Samaria would be punished only a few years later.

28:13 God used repetition and simple words to get his messages through to the people. Do you find that God has to teach you the same lessons over and over again? The simplicity of God's message can be a stumbling block for some (28:9, 10), leading them to think it must have little value. We must not be too proud to heed God's simple message.

28:15 Judah was afraid of the Assyrians. Instead of trusting God, the Judeans turned to other sources for security. God accused them of bargaining with death. This passage probably refers to Hezekiah's alliance with Pharaoh Tirhakah against Assyria. God would cancel this agreement—Egypt would be of no help when

Assyria attacked. Is it worth selling out what you believe in for temporary protection against an enemy? If you want lasting protection, turn to the only one able to deliver you from *eternal* death—God.

28:16 If you're building anything, you need a firm base. Isaiah speaks of a *Foundation Stone,* a *Cornerstone,* that will be laid in Zion. This Cornerstone is the Messiah, the Foundation on whom we build our lives. Is your life built on the flimsy base of your own successes or dreams? Or is it set on a firm Foundation (see Psalm 118:22; 1 Peter 2:8)?

28:21 God fought on Joshua's side at Gibeon (Joshua 10:1–14) and on David's side at Perazim (2 Samuel 5:20). But now he would fight *against* Israel, his own people, in these same places.

23, 24Listen to me, listen as I plead: Does a farmer always plow and never sow? Is he forever harrowing the soil and never planting it? 25Does he not finally plant his many kinds of grain, each in its own section of his land? 26He knows just what to do, for God has made him see and understand. 27He doesn't thresh all grains the same. A sledge is never used on dill, but it is beaten with a stick. A threshing wheel is never rolled on cummin, but it is beaten softly with a flail. 28Bread grain is easily crushed, so he doesn't keep on pounding it. 29The Lord Almighty is a wonderful teacher and gives the farmer wisdom.

28:27
Amos 1:3

28:29
Rom 11:33

Prophecy against Jerusalem

29 Woe to Jerusalem, the city of David. Year after year you make your many offerings, 2but I will send heavy judgment upon you and there will be weeping and sorrow. For Jerusalem shall become as her name "Ariel" means—an altar covered with blood. 3I will be your enemy. I will surround Jerusalem and lay siege against it, and build forts around it to destroy it. 4Your voice will whisper like a ghost from the earth where you lie buried.

29:1
2 Sam 5:9

29:2
Lam 2:5

29:3
Lk 19:43,44

5But suddenly your ruthless enemies will be driven away like chaff before the wind. 6In an instant, I, the Lord of Hosts, will come upon them with thunder, earthquake, whirlwind and fire. 7And all the nations fighting Jerusalem will vanish like a dream! 8As a hungry man dreams of eating, but is still hungry, and as a thirsty man dreams of drinking, but is still faint from thirst when he wakes up, so your enemies will dream of victorious conquest, but all to no avail.

29:5
Isa 17:14
41:15,16
1 Thess 5:3

29:6
Lk 21:11
Rev 11:13,19

29:7
Zech 12:9

9You are amazed, incredulous? You don't believe it? Then go ahead and be blind if you must! You are stupid—and not from drinking, either! Stagger, and not from wine! 10For the Lord has poured out upon you a spirit of deep sleep. He has closed the eyes of your prophets and seers, 11so all of these future events are a sealed book to them. When you give it to one who can read, he says, "I can't, for it's sealed." 12When you give it to another, he says, "Sorry, I can't read."

29:8
Isa 54:17

29:10
Rom 11:8
2 Thess 2:9-12

29:11
Dan 12:4

13And so the Lord says, "Since these people say they are mine but they do not obey me, and since their worship amounts to mere words learned by rote, 14therefore I will take awesome vengeance on these hypocrites, and make their wisest counselors as fools."

29:13
Ezek 33:31
Mk 7:6,7

29:14
Isa 44:25
1 Cor 1:19

15Woe to those who try to hide their plans from God, who try to keep him in the dark concerning what they do! "God can't see us," they say to themselves. "He doesn't know what is going on!" 16How stupid can they be! Isn't he, the Potter, greater than you, the jars he makes? Will you say to him, "He didn't make us"? Does a machine call its inventor dumb?

29:15
Ps 10:11,13
Isa 47:10

29:16
Isa 45:9
Rom 9:19-21

17Soon—and it will not be very long—the wilderness of Lebanon will be a fruitful field again, a lush and fertile forest. 18In that day the deaf will hear the words of a book, and out of their gloom and darkness the blind will see my plans. 19The meek will be filled with fresh joy from the Lord, and the poor shall exult in the Holy One of Israel. 20Bullies will vanish and scoffers will cease, and all those plotting evil will be killed— 21the violent man who fights at the drop of a hat, the

29:18
Isa 32:3

29:19
Isa 14:30,32
Mt 5:5
Jas 2:5

29:21
Amos 5:10,12

29:1 to Jerusalem, literally, "to Ariel."

28:23-28 The farmer uses special tools to plant and harvest tender herbs so he will not destroy them. He takes into account how fragile they are. In the same way God will never allow us to be tempted or to suffer more than we can bear. He takes all our individual circumstances and weaknesses into account. We should follow his example when we deal with others. Different people require different treatment. Be sensitive to the needs of those around you and the special treatment they may need.

29:13, 14 The people claimed to belong to God, but they were disobedient and merely went through the motions; therefore, God would bring vengeance upon them. Religion had become routine instead of real. Isaiah condemns the people for being hypocrites (29:13). Jesus quoted this verse (Matthew 15:8; Mark 7:6, 7) when he spoke to the Pharisees, the religious leaders of his day. We are

all capable of hypocrisy. Often we slip into routine forms of worship which mean nothing to us. If we want to be called God's people, we must be obedient and worship him honestly and sincerely.

29:15, 16 Thinking God couldn't see them and didn't know what was happening, the people of Jerusalem tried to hide their plans from him. How strange that so many people think they can hide from God. In Psalm 139 we learn that God has examined us and knows everything about us. Would you be embarrassed if your best friends knew your personal thoughts? Remember that God knows all of them.

29:17-24 The world described here, under Christ's rule, will be far different from the one we live in today. There will be no more violence or gloom. This new world will be characterized by joy and praise to God.

man who waits in hiding to beat up the judge who sentenced him, and the men who use any excuse to be unfair.

22That is why the Lord who redeemed Abraham says: My people will no longer pale with fear, or be ashamed. 23For when they see the surging birth rate and the expanding economy, then they will fear and rejoice in my name, and praise the Holy One of Israel, and stand in awe of him. 24Those in error will believe the truth, and complainers will be willing to be taught!

Prophecy against rebels

30 Woe to my rebellious children, says the Lord; you ask advice from everyone but me, and decide to do what I don't want you to do. You yoke yourselves with unbelievers, thus piling up your sins. 2For without consulting me you have gone down to Egypt to find aid and have put your trust in Pharaoh for his protection. 3But in trusting Pharaoh, you will be disappointed, humiliated and disgraced, for he can't deliver on his promises to save you. 4For though his power extends to Zoan and Hanes, 5yet it will all turn out to your shame—he won't help one little bit!

6See them moving slowly across the terrible desert to Egypt—donkeys and camels laden down with treasure to pay for Egypt's aid. On through the badlands they go, where lions and swift venomous snakes live—and Egypt will give you nothing in return! 7For Egypt's promises are worthless! "The Reluctant Dragon," I call her!

8Now go and write down this word of mine concerning Egypt, so that it will stand until the end of time, forever and forever, as an indictment of Israel's unbelief. 9For if you don't write it, they will claim I never warned them. "Oh, no," they'll say, "you never told us that!"

For they are stubborn rebels. 10, 11They tell my prophets, "Shut up—we don't want any more of your reports!" Or they say, "Don't tell us the truth; tell us nice things; tell us lies. Forget all this gloom; we've heard more than enough about your 'Holy One of Israel' and all he says."

12This is the reply of the Holy One of Israel:

Because you despise what I tell you and trust instead in frauds and lies and won't repent, 13therefore calamity will come upon you suddenly, as upon a bulging wall that bursts and falls; in one moment it comes crashing down. 14God will smash you like a broken dish; he will not act sparingly. Not a piece will be left large enough to use for carrying coals from the hearth, or a little water from the well. 15For the Lord God, the Holy One of Israel, says: Only in returning to me and waiting for me

29:22
Isa 41:8

29:24
Isa 30:21; 41:20

30:1
Isa 8:11,12

30:2
Isa 8:19; 31:1

30:3
Isa 36:6
Jer 42:18,22

30:5
Isa 31:3
Jer 2:36

30:6
Deut 8:15

30:7
Isa 51:9

30:10
1 Kgs 22:8,13
Jer 6:14
Ezek 13:7
Amos 2:12
2 Tim 4:3,4

30:12
Isa 5:24; 59:13

30:14
Ps 2:9
Jer 19:10,11
30:15
Isa 28:12; 32:17

29:23 the surging birth rate and the expanding economy, literally, "when he sees his children, the work of my hands, in his midst." **30:7** The Reluctant Dragon, literally, "Rahab who sits still."

30:1 The people of Judah sought advice from everyone but God. When we are driven by fear, we tend to search everywhere for comfort, advice, and relief, hoping to find an easy way out of our troubles. Instead, we should consult with God. Although he gives emergency help in times of crisis, he prefers to be our Guide throughout our lives. By reading his Word and actively seeking to do his will, we can maintain contact that provides stability no matter what the crisis.

30:1-5 God was not happy with his people because they sought power and protection from other kings and nations. He warned them that these alliances, though inviting, would only prove harmful in the long run. Enamored with power or prestige, we also may have sought direction and guidance from sources that are not pleasing to God. Ask God to help you choose what is best and wisest.

30:2ff King Hezekiah had been seeking a defensive alliance with Egypt against Sennacherib of Assyria (see 2 Kings 18:21).

30:7 The dragon is also called Rahab, an ancient Canaanite name for a mythological sea monster. In time, Rahab became

another name for Egypt. "Rahab who sits still" means that Egypt was doing nothing to help Judah in any way (see also 51:9).

30:10, 11 Some people in Israel sought refuge in Egypt. Comfortably settled there, they wanted to hear only good news. They did not welcome the truth from God's prophets. Often the truth makes us uncomfortable. We prefer lies when they make us feel more secure. But Jesus said the truth will set us free (John 8:32). It is much better to face reality than to live a lie. Don't be comfortable with something that makes you feel good but is not true.

30:15 God warned Judah that turning to Egypt and other nations could not save them. Only God could do that. They must wait for him in quietness and confidence. No amount of fast talking or hasty activity could speed up God's grand design. Salvation comes from God alone. Because he has saved us, we can trust him and be peacefully confident that he will give us strength to face difficulties in our lives.

30:15 "In quietness . . . is your strength" means that we have nothing to say but "thank you" to God, who alone is our help.

will you be saved; in quietness and confidence is your strength; but you'll have none of this.

16"No," you say. "We will get our help from Egypt; they will give us swift horses for riding to battle." But the only swiftness you are going to see is the swiftness of your enemies chasing you! 17One of them will chase a thousand of you! Five of them will scatter you until not two of you are left together. You will be like lonely trees on the distant mountain tops. 18Yet the Lord still waits for you to come to him, so he can show you his love; he will conquer you to bless you, just as he said. For the Lord is faithful to his promises. Blessed are all those who wait for him to help them.

19O my people in Jerusalem, you shall weep no more, for he will surely be gracious to you at the sound of your cry. He will answer you. 20Though he give you the bread of adversity and water of affliction, yet he will be with you to teach you—with your own eyes you will see your Teacher. 21And if you leave God's paths and go astray, you will hear a Voice behind you say, "No, this is the way; walk here." 22And you will destroy all your silver idols and gold images and cast them out like filthy things you hate to touch. "Ugh!" you'll say to them. "Be gone!"

23Then God will bless you with rain at planting time and with wonderful harvests and with ample pastures for your cows. 24The oxen and young donkeys that till the ground will eat grain, its chaff blown away by the wind. 25In that day when God steps in to destroy your enemies, he will give you streams of water flowing down each mountain and every hill. 26The moon will be as bright as the sun, and the sunlight brighter than seven days! So it will be when the Lord begins to heal his people and to cure the wounds he gave them.

27See, the Lord comes from afar, aflame with wrath, surrounded by thick rising smoke. His lips are filled with fury; his words consume like fire. 28His wrath pours out like floods upon them all, to sweep them all away. He will sift out the proud nations and bridle them and lead them off to their doom.

29But the people of God will sing a song of solemn joy, like songs in the night when holy feasts are held; his people will have gladness of heart, as when a flutist leads a pilgrim band to Jerusalem to the Mountain of the Lord, the Rock of Israel. 30And the Lord shall cause his majestic voice to be heard and shall crush down his mighty arm upon his enemies with angry indignation and with devouring flames and tornados and terrible storms and huge hailstones. 31The voice of the Lord shall punish the Assyrians, who had been his rod of punishment. 32And when the Lord smites them, his people will rejoice with music and song. 33The funeral pyre has long been ready, prepared for Molech, the Assyrian god; it is piled high with wood. The breath of the Lord, like fire from a volcano, will set it all on fire.

The futility of trusting in Egypt

31 Woe to those who run to Egypt for help, trusting their mighty cavalry and chariots instead of looking to the Holy One of Israel and consulting him. 2In his wisdom, he will send great evil on his people and will not change his mind. He will rise against them for the evil they have done, and crush their allies too. 3For these Egyptians are mere men, not God! Their horses are puny flesh, not mighty spirits! When the Lord clenches his fist against them, they will stumble and fall among those they are trying to help. All will fail together.

4, 5But the Lord has told me this: When a lion, even a young one, kills a sheep,

30:16
Isa 31:1,3

30:17
Deut 32:30

30:18
Isa 25:9
2 Pet 3:9,15

30:19
Isa 25:8; 65:24
30:20
Ps 80:5
30:21
Isa 35:8,9
30:22
Ex 32:2,4
30:23
Ps 65:9-13
30:24
Mt 3:12
30:25
Isa 41:18
30:26
Isa 33:24
Hos 6:1,2
30:27
Isa 66:15
30:28
2 Kgs 19:28
Isa 8:7,8

30:32
1 Sam 18:6
Jer 31:4
30:33
Gen 19:24
Isa 34:9

31:1
Isa 10:17
Hos 11:9
Hab 1:12

31:2
Num 23:19
Jer 44:29
Rom 16:27
31:3
Jer 15:6
Ezek 28:9

30:20 The Lord gave his people the bread of adversity and the water of affliction, but he promised to be with them, teach them, and guide them during hard times. God demands a lot from us, and many times following him can be painful; but he does this out of his love for us. Next time you go through a difficult time, try to appreciate the experience and grow from it, learning what God wants to teach you. God may be showing you his love by patiently walking with you through adversity.

30:21 If the people of Jerusalem left God's path, he would correct

them. He will do the same for us. But when we hear his voice of correction, we must be willing to follow it!

31:1 It was wrong for Judah to look to these other nations for help. (1) They were trusting in man instead of God. Judah sought protection from those who had far less power than God. (2) They were serving their own interests instead of God's, and thus they did not even consult him. (3) They did not want to pay the price of looking to God and repenting of their sinful ways. Where we seek help is where we place our trust for the future. If the help does not come, the trust is broken.

he pays no attention to the shepherd's shouts and noise. He goes right on and eats. In such manner the Lord will come and fight upon Mount Zion. He will not be frightened away! He, the Lord Almighty, will hover over Jerusalem as birds hover round their nests, and he will defend the city and deliver it.

⁶Therefore, O my people, though you are such wicked rebels, come, return to God. ⁷I know the glorious day will come when every one of you will throw away his gold idols and silver images—which in your sinfulness you have made. ⁸And the Assyrians will be destroyed, but not by swords of men. The "sword of God" will smite them. They will panic and flee, and the strong young Assyrians will be taken away as slaves. ⁹Even their generals will quake with terror and flee when they see the battle flags of Israel, says the Lord. For the flame of God burns brightly in Jerusalem.

Prophecy of peace for Israel

32 Look, a righteous King is coming, with honest princes! ²He will shelter Israel from the storm and wind. He will refresh her as a river in the desert and as the cooling shadow of a mighty rock within a hot and weary land. ³Then at last the eyes of Israel will open wide to God; his people will listen to his voice. ⁴Even the hotheads among them will be full of sense and understanding, and those who stammer in uncertainty will speak out plainly.

⁵In those days the ungodly, the atheists, will not be heroes! Wealthy cheaters will not be spoken of as generous, outstanding men! ⁶Everyone will recognize an evil man when he sees him, and hypocrites will fool no one at all. Their lies about God and their cheating of the hungry will be plain for all to see. ⁷The smooth tricks of evil men will be exposed, as will all the lies they use to oppress the poor in the courts. ⁸But good men will be generous to others and will be blessed of God for all they do.

⁹Listen, you women who loll around in lazy ease; listen to me and I will tell you your reward: ¹⁰In a short time—in just a little more than a year—suddenly you'll care, O careless ones. For the crops of fruit will fail; the harvest will not take place. ¹¹Tremble, O women of ease; throw off your unconcern. Strip off your pretty clothes—wear sackcloth for your grief. ¹²Beat your breasts in sorrow for those bountiful farms of yours that will soon be gone, and for those fruitful vines of other years. ¹³For your lands will thrive with thorns and briars; your joyous homes and happy cities will be gone. ¹⁴Palaces and mansions will all be deserted, the crowded cities empty. Wild herds of donkeys and goats will graze upon the mountains where the watchtowers are, ¹⁵until at last the Spirit is poured down on us from heaven. Then once again enormous crops will come. ¹⁶Then justice will rule through all the land, ¹⁷and out of justice, peace. Quietness and confidence will reign forevermore.

¹⁸My people will live in safety, quietly at home, ¹⁹but the Assyrians will be

32:19 *but the Assyrians,* implied.

31:6
Isa 55:7
Jer 3:10,14,22
31:8
Isa 10:12; 14:2

31:9
Isa 13:2

32:1
Jer 23:5
Ezek 37:24
Zech 9:9
32:2
Isa 25:4; 35:6
32:4
Isa 29:24

32:6
Isa 10:2
59:7,13
32:7
Isa 5:23
Jer 5:26-28
Mic 7:3
32:8
2 Cor 9:6-11
32:9
Isa 47:8
32:10
Isa 5:5,6
32:13
Isa 5:5,6,10,17
32:14
Isa 24:12
32:15
Ps 107:35
Isa 11:2
Joel 2:28
32:16
Isa 33:5
32:17
Isa 2:4
Jas 3:18
32:18
Hos 2:18-23

31:7 Someday these people would throw their idols away, recognizing that they are nothing but wood or stone. Idols such as money, fame, or success are seductive. Instead of contributing to our spiritual development, they rob us of our thoughts, time, energy, and devotion to God. At first they seem exciting and promise to "take our places," but in the end we will find that we have become their slaves. We need to recognize their worthlessness now, before they rob us of our freedom.

32:1 Judah was hungry for a strong king who would rule effectively. This desire will be fulfilled when Christ reigns. Evil will be banished, and the king will be powerful and just. In the immediate future, Judah would be destroyed and taken into captivity. But one day, God's Son, the King unlike any other king, will reign in righteousness and wisdom.

32:5, 6 When the righteous King comes, people's motives will become transparent. Those who have opposed God's standards of living will be unable to maintain their deception. In the blazing light of the holy Savior, sin cannot disguise itself and appear good.

Christ's revealing light shines into the darkest corners of our hearts, showing sin clearly for what it is. When King Jesus reigns in your heart, there is no place for sin, no matter how well-hidden you think it is.

32:9–13 The people turned their backs on God and concentrated on their own best interests. This warning is not just to the women of Israel, but to all who sit back in their thoughtless ease, enjoying crops, clothes, land, and cities while an enemy approaches. Wealth and luxury bring false security, lulling us into thinking all is well when disaster is around the corner. By abandoning God's purpose for our lives, we also abandon his help.

32:15–17 God acts from above to change man's condition here on earth. Only when God's Spirit is among us can we achieve true peace and prosperity (Ezekiel 36:27; Galatians 5:22, 23). This will happen in the end times. We can also have God's Spirit with us now, for he is available to all believers through Christ (John 15:26). But the outpouring mentioned here happens when the worldwide Kingdom of God is established for all eternity.

destroyed and their cities laid low. ²⁰And God will greatly bless his people. | **32:20** Isa 30:23

Wherever they plant, bountiful crops will spring up, and their flocks and herds will graze in green pastures.

The Lord is judge

33 Woe to you, Assyrians, who have destroyed everything around you but have never felt destruction for yourselves. You expect others to respect their promises to you, while you betray them! Now you, too, will be betrayed and destroyed. | **33:1** Jer 25:12-14 Hab 2:8

²But to us, O Lord, be merciful, for we have waited for you. Be our strength each day and our salvation in the time of trouble. ³The enemy runs at the sound of your voice. When you stand up, the nations flee. ⁴Just as locusts strip the fields and vines, so Jerusalem will strip the fallen army of Assyria! | **33:2** Isa 25:9; 40:10 **33:3** Jer 25:30,31

⁵The Lord is very great, and lives in heaven. He will make Jerusalem the home of justice and goodness and righteousness. ⁶An abundance of salvation is stored up for Judah in a safe place, along with wisdom and knowledge and reverence for God. | **33:5** Ps 97:9 **33:6** Ps 112:1-3 Isa 51:6

⁷But now your ambassadors weep in bitter disappointment, for Assyria has refused their cry for peace. ⁸Your roads lie in ruins; travelers detour on back roads. The Assyrians have broken their peace pact and care nothing for the promises they made in the presence of witnesses—they have no respect for anyone. ⁹All the land of Israel is in trouble; Lebanon has been destroyed; Sharon has become a wilderness; Bashan and Carmel are plundered. | **33:9** Isa 10:34; 24:4 35:2

¹⁰But the Lord says, I will stand up and show my power and might. ¹¹You Assyrians will gain nothing by all your efforts. Your own breath will turn to fire and kill you. ¹²Your armies will be burned to lime, like thorns cut down and tossed in the fire. | **33:10** Ps 12:5 Isa 2:19 **33:11** Isa 26:18

¹³Listen to what I have done, O nations far away! And you that are near, acknowledge my might! ¹⁴The sinners among my people shake with fear. "Which one of us," they cry, "can live here in the presence of this all-consuming, Everlasting Fire?" ¹⁵I will tell you who can live here: All who are honest and fair, who reject making profit by fraud, who hold back their hands from taking bribes, who refuse to listen to those who plot murder, who shut their eyes to all enticement to do wrong. ¹⁶Such as these shall dwell on high. The rocks of the mountains will be their fortress of safety; food will be supplied to them and they will have all the water they need. | **33:12** 2 Sam 23:6,7 Isa 10:17 **33:13** Isa 49:1 **33:14** Isa 1:28; 30:27 Heb 12:29 **33:15** Ps 24:3,4 Isa 58:6-11 **33:16** Isa 49:10

¹⁷Your eyes will see the King in his beauty, and the highlands of heaven far away. ¹⁸Your mind will think back to this time of terror when the Assyrian officers outside your walls are counting your towers and estimating how much they will get from your fallen city. ¹⁹But soon they will all be gone. These fierce, violent people, with a strange, jabbering language you can't understand, will disappear. | **33:17** Isa 6:5 **33:19** Deut 28:49,50

33:1 *Assyrians*, implied.

33:1 The Assyrians continually broke their promises, but demanded that others keep theirs. It is easy to put ourselves in the same selfish position, demanding our rights while violating the rights of others. Broken promises shatter trust and destroy relationships. Determine to make no promises you can't keep; equally important, ask forgiveness for past promises you have broken. Exercise the same fairness with others that you demand for yourself.

33:2 These are the words of the righteous remnant who were waiting for God to deliver them from their oppression.

33:4 See 2 Kings 19:20–37 for a description of this victory over Assyria.

33:5 When Christ's kingdom is established, Jerusalem will be the home of righteousness and justice because the Messiah reigns there. As a light to the world, the new Jerusalem will be the Holy City (Revelation 21:2).

33:6 "An abundance of salvation is stored up." In preparation for famine, war, or siege, provisions were stockpiled to be released when conditions required. If Judah would change the direction of its life, its attitudes, and its actions, God would release his overflowing abundance of salvation. God has more than we need, but he supplies according to our need and our willingness to receive of his abundance.

33:8 The Assyrians broke their peace pact (2 Kings 18:14–17).

33:14–16 These sinners realized that they could not live in the presence of the Holy God, for he is like a fire that consumes evil. Only those whose faith produces honesty and fairness can live with God. We are given examples of how to demonstrate our honesty and fairness: we can reject fraud and bribes, refuse to plot wrong actions, and resist temptation. If we are fair and honest in our relationships, we will be able to dwell with God, and he will supply our needs.

33:20
Ps 46:5
33:21
Isa 48:18
33:22
Isa 49:25,26
Zech 9:9
33:24
Mic 7:18,19
1 Jn 1:7-9

20Instead you will see Jerusalem at peace, a place where God is worshiped, a city quiet and unmoved. 21The glorious Lord will be to us as a wide river of protection, and no enemy can cross. 22For the Lord is our Judge, our Lawgiver and our King; he will care for us and save us. 23The enemies' sails hang loose on broken masts with useless tackle. Their treasure will be divided by the people of God; even the lame will win their share. 24The people of Israel will no longer say, "We are sick and helpless," for the Lord will forgive them their sins and bless them.

God will destroy his enemies

34:1
Deut 32:1

34 Come here and listen, O nations of the earth; let the world and everything in it hear my words. 2For the Lord is enraged against the nations; his fury is against their armies. He will utterly destroy them and deliver them to slaughter.

34:3
Ezek 35:6
34:4
Joel 2:31
Mt 24:29
2 Pet 3:10
Rev 6:12-14

3Their dead will be left unburied, and the stench of rotting bodies will fill the land, and the mountains will flow with their blood. 4At that time the heavens above will melt away and disappear just like a rolled-up scroll, and the stars will fall as leaves, as ripe fruit from the trees.

34:5
Isa 24:6
34:6
Isa 63:1

5And when my sword has finished its work in the heavens, then watch, for it will fall upon Edom, the people I have doomed. 6The sword of the Lord is sated with blood; it is gorged with flesh as though used for slaying lambs and goats for sacrifice. For the Lord will slay a great sacrifice in Edom and make a mighty slaughter there. 7The strongest will perish, young boys and veterans too. The land will be soaked with blood, and the soil made rich with fat. 8For it is the day of

34:8
Isa 13:6; 63:4

vengeance, the year of recompense for what Edom has done to Israel. 9The streams of Edom will be filled with burning pitch, and the ground will be covered with fire.

34:10
Isa 1:31
Ezek 29:11
Mal 1:3,4
Rev 14:11; 19:3
34:11
Lam 2:8
34:13
Jer 9:11; 10:22
34:14
Isa 13:21

10This judgment on Edom will never end. Its smoke will rise up forever. The land will lie deserted from generation to generation; no one will live there anymore. 11There the hawks and porcupines will live, and owls and ravens. For God will observe that land and find it worthy of destruction. He will test its nobles and find them worthy of death. 12It will be called "The Land of Nothing," and its princes soon will all be gone. 13Thorns will overrun the palaces, and nettles will grow in its forts, and it will become the haunt of jackals and a home for ostriches. 14The wild animals of the desert will mingle there with wolves and hyenas. Their howls will fill the night. There the night-monsters will scream at each other, and the demons will come there to rest. 15There the owl will make her nest and lay her eggs and hatch her young and nestle them beneath her wings, and the kites will come, each one with its mate.

34:16
Isa 40:5

16Search the Book of the Lord and see all that he will do; not one detail will he miss; not one kite will be there without a mate, for the Lord has said it, and his Spirit will make it all come true. 17He has surveyed and subdivided the land and deeded it to those doleful creatures; they shall possess it forever, from generation to generation.

Streams in the desert

35:1
Isa 41:18,19
51:3; 55:12,13

35 Even the wilderness and desert will rejoice in those days; the desert will blossom with flowers. 2Yes, there will be an abundance of flowers and

---

34:5 Edom and Israel shared a common ancestry. The Israelites were descended from Jacob; the Edomites from Jacob's twin brother, Esau. Edom was always Israel's bitter enemy. The destruction of Edom mentioned here is a picture of the ultimate end of all who oppose God and his people.

34:16 Isaiah validated his prophecies with the phrase "Book of the Lord." Prophecy predicts and history reveals what has been in God's mind for all time.

35:1ff In chapters 1—35, Isaiah delivered a message of judgment on all nations, including Israel and Judah, for rejecting God. Although there have been glimpses of relief and restoration for the remnant of faithful believers, the climate of wrath, fury, judgment, and destruction has prevailed. Now Isaiah breaks through with a

vision of beauty and encouragement. God is just as complete in his mercy as he is severe in his judgment. God's complete moral perfection is revealed by his hatred of all sin, and this leads to judgment. This same moral perfection is revealed in his love for all he has created. This leads to mercy for those who have been less than perfect but who have sincerely loved and obeyed him.

35:1ff This chapter is a beautiful picture of the final Kingdom in which God will establish his justice and destroy all evil. This is the world the faithful can anticipate after the judgment, when creation itself will rejoice in God. Chapter 34 spoke of tribulation—a time when God will judge all people for their actions. Chapter 35 pictures the days after judgment, when life will be peaceful at last.

singing and joy! The deserts will become as green as the Lebanon mountains, as lovely as Mount Carmel's pastures and Sharon's meadows; for the Lord will display his glory there, the excellency of our God.

3With this news bring cheer to all discouraged ones. 4Encourage those who are afraid. Tell them, "Be strong, fear not, for your God is coming to destroy your enemies. He is coming to save you." 5And when he comes, he will open the eyes of the blind, and unstop the ears of the deaf. 6The lame man will leap up like a deer, and those who could not speak will shout and sing! Springs will burst forth in the wilderness, and streams in the desert. 7The parched ground will become a pool, with springs of water in the thirsty land. Where desert jackals lived, there will be reeds and rushes!

8And a main road will go through that once-deserted land; it will be named "The Holy Highway." No evil-hearted men may walk upon it. God will walk there with you; even the most stupid cannot miss the way. 9No lion will lurk along its course, nor will there be any other dangers; only the redeemed will travel there. 10These, the ransomed of the Lord, will go home along that road to Zion, singing the songs of everlasting joy. For them all sorrow and all sighing will be gone forever; only joy and gladness will be there.

35:3 Job 4:3,4

35:4 Ps 145:19 Isa 63:4

35:5 Jn 9:6,7

35:6 Lk 11:14 Jn 7:38 Acts 3:7,8

35:7 Mt 7:13,14

35:9 Isa 51:10

35:10 Rev 21:4

5. Events during the reign of Hezekiah

Assyria threatens Judah

36 So in the fourteenth year of King Hezekiah's reign, Sennacherib, king of Assyria, came to fight against the walled cities of Judah and conquered them. 2Then he sent his personal representative with a great army from Lachish to confer with King Hezekiah in Jerusalem. He camped near the outlet of the upper pool, along the road going past the field where cloth is bleached.

3Then Eliakim, Hilkiah's son, who was the prime minister of Israel, and Shebna, the king's scribe, and Joah (Asaph's son), the royal secretary, formed a truce team and went out of the city to meet with him. 4The Assyrian ambassador told them to go and say to Hezekiah, "The mighty king of Assyria says you are a fool to think that the king of Egypt will help you. 5What are the Pharaoh's promises worth? Mere words won't substitute for strength, yet you rely on him for help, and have rebelled against me! 6Egypt is a dangerous ally. She is a sharpened stick that will pierce your hand if you lean on it. That is the experience of everyone who has ever looked to her for help. 7But perhaps you say, 'We are trusting in the Lord our God!' Oh? Isn't he the one your king insulted, tearing down his temples and altars in the hills and making everyone in Judah worship only at the altars here in Jerusalem? 8, 9My master, the king of Assyria, wants to make a little bet with you!—that you don't have 2,000 men left in your entire army! If you do, he will give you 2,000 horses for them to ride on! With that tiny army, how can you think of proceeding against even the smallest and worst contingent of my master's troops? For you'll

36:2 2 Kgs 18:17— 20:11 2 Chron 32:9-24

36:4 2 Kgs 18:19

36:5 2 Kgs 18:7

36:6 Ps 146:3 Ezek 29:6,7

36:7 Deut 12:2-5 2 Kgs 18:4,5

36:8 Isa 30:2-5,7 31:3

35:8-10 The "Holy Highway" is the way from the desert of suffering to the blessings of the new life. It is found only by following God. Only the redeemed will travel God's "Holy Highway"; they will be protected from wicked travelers and harmful animals. God is preparing a way for his people to travel to his home, and he will walk with us. God never stops at pointing the way for us to go; he is always beside us as we go.

36:1 The next four chapters form a transition between the first and second parts of the book and lay the foundation for chapters 40—66. These chapters coincide with the time of King Hezekiah's reign (2 Kings 18, 19).

36:4 Chapter 19 describes Isaiah's warning to Judah not to ally itself with Egypt in the face of Assyria's impending attack. Sennacherib of Assyria taunts Judah for trusting in Egypt. Even the Assyrians knew that Egypt could not help Judah.

36:5 Hezekiah put great trust in Pharaoh's promise to help Israel against the Assyrians, but promises are only as good as the

credibility of the person making them. It was Pharaoh's word against God's. How quickly we organize our lives around human advice while we neglect God's eternal promises. When you are confronted with a choice between God's Word and someone else's, whom will you believe?

36:7 The team from Assyria claimed that Hezekiah insulted God by tearing down his altars in the hills and making the people worship only in Jerusalem. But Hezekiah's reform sought to eliminate idol worship (which occured mainly in the hills) so that the people worshiped only the true God. Either the Assyrians didn't know about the religion of the true God, or they wanted to deceive the people into thinking they had angered a powerful god.

In the same way, Satan tries to confuse or deceive us. People don't necessarily need to be sinful to be ineffective for God; they need only be confused about what God wants. To avoid Satan's deceit, study God's Word carefully and regularly. When you know what God says, you will not fall for Satan's lies.

36:10
1 Kgs 13:18

36:11
Ezra 4:7
Dan 2:4

36:13
2 Chron 32:18

36:14
Isa 37:10

36:16
Zech 3:10

get no help from Egypt. ¹⁰What's more, do you think I have come here without the Lord's telling me to take this land? The Lord said to me, 'Go and destroy it!' "

¹¹Then Eliakim and Shebna and Joah said to him, "Please talk to us in Aramaic for we understand it quite well. Don't speak in Hebrew, for the people on the wall will hear."

¹²But he replied, "My master wants everyone in Jerusalem to hear this, not just you. He wants them to know that if you don't surrender, this city will be put under siege until everyone is so hungry and thirsty that he will eat his own dung and drink his own urine."

¹³Then he shouted in Hebrew to the Jews listening on the wall, "Hear the words of the great king, the king of Assyria:

¹⁴"Don't let Hezekiah fool you—nothing he can do will save you. ¹⁵Don't let him talk you into trusting in the Lord by telling you the Lord won't let you be conquered by the king of Assyria. ¹⁶Don't listen to Hezekiah, for here is the king of Assyria's offer to you: Give me a present as a token of surrender; open the gates and come out, and I will let you each have your own farm and garden and water, ¹⁷until I can arrange to take you to a country very similar to this one—a country where there are bountiful harvests of grain and grapes, a land of plenty. ¹⁸Don't let Hezekiah deprive you of all this by saying the Lord will deliver you from my

**ASSYRIA
ADVANCES**
As Sennacherib beautified his capital city, Nineveh, Hezekiah withheld tribute and prepared for battle. The Assyrians advanced toward their rebellious western border, attacking swiftly down the Mediterranean coast. From Lachish, Sennacherib threatened to take Jerusalem, but Isaiah knew his threats would die with him on his return to Nineveh.

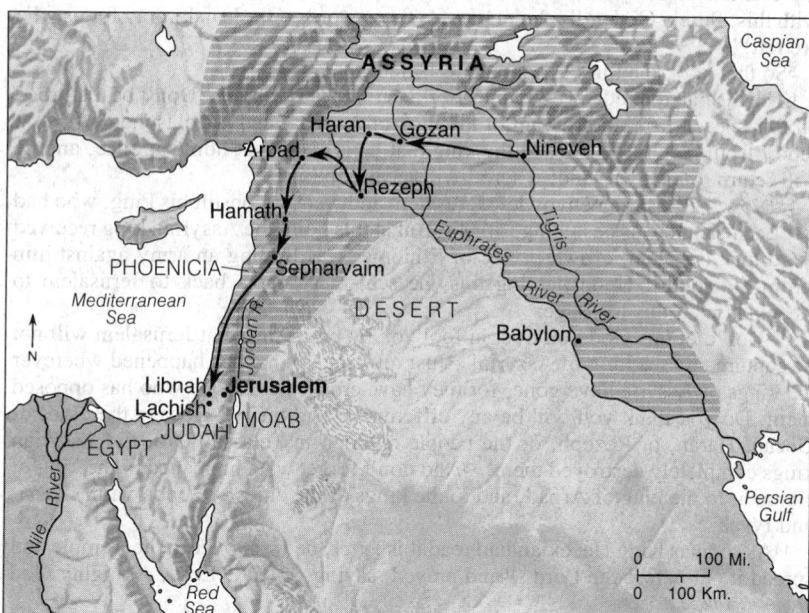

36:10 Sennacherib continued his demoralization campaign by trying to convince the people of Judah that God had turned against them. The Assyrians hoped to convince the people of Judah to surrender without fighting. But Isaiah had already said that the Assyrians *would not* destroy Jerusalem, so the people did not need to be afraid of them (10:24–27; 29:5–8).

36:11 Aramaic was an international language at this time. See also Isaiah 22:15–25 for Isaiah's prophecies concerning Eliakim and Shebna.

36:17 Sennacherib tried yet another ploy to demoralize the people. He appealed to the starving city under siege by offering to take them to a land with plenty of food if they surrendered. The Assyrian policy for dealing with conquered nations was to resettle the inhabitants and then to move their own people into the recently conquered area. This provided manpower for their armies and prevented revolts in conquered territories.

armies. Have any other nation's gods ever gained victory over the armies of the king of Assyria? 19Don't you remember what I did to Hamath and Arpad? Did their gods save them? And what about Sepharvaim and Samaria? Where are their gods now? 20Of all the gods of these lands, which one has ever delivered their people from my power? Name just one! And do you think this God of yours can deliver Jerusalem from me? Don't be ridiculous!"

21But the people were silent and answered not a word, for Hezekiah had told them to say nothing in reply. 22Then Eliakim (son of Hilkiah), the prime minister, and Shebna, the royal scribe, and Joah (son of Asaph), the royal secretary, went back to Hezekiah with clothes ripped to shreds as a sign of their despair and told him all that had happened.

God will deliver Jerusalem

37 When King Hezekiah heard the results of the meeting, he tore his robes and wound himself in coarse cloth used for making sacks, as a sign of humility and mourning, and went over to the Temple to pray. 2Meanwhile he sent Eliakim his prime minister, and Shebna his royal scribe, and the older priests—all dressed in sackcloth—to Isaiah the prophet, son of Amoz. 3They brought him this message from Hezekiah:

"This is a day of trouble and frustration and blasphemy; it is a serious time, as when a woman is in heavy labor trying to give birth, and the child does not come. 4But perhaps the Lord your God heard the blasphemy of the king of Assyria's representative as he scoffed at the Living God. Surely God won't let him get away with this. Surely God will rebuke him for those words. Oh, Isaiah, pray for us who are left!"

5So they took the king's message to Isaiah.

6Then Isaiah replied, "Tell King Hezekiah that the Lord says, Don't be disturbed by this speech from the servant of the king of Assyria, and his blasphemy. 7For a report from Assyria will reach the king that he is needed at home at once, and he will return to his own land, where I will have him killed."

8, 9Now the Assyrian envoy left Jerusalem and went to consult his king, who had left Lachish and was besieging Libnah. But at this point the Assyrian king received word that Tirhakah, crown prince of Ethiopia, was leading an army against him [from the south]. Upon hearing this, he sent messengers back to Jerusalem to Hezekiah with this message:

10"Don't let this God you trust in fool you by promising that Jerusalem will not be captured by the king of Assyria! 11Just remember what has happened wherever the kings of Assyria have gone, for they have crushed everyone who has opposed them. Do you think you will be any different? 12Did their gods save the cities of Gozan, Haran, or Rezeph, or the people of Eden in Telassar? No, the Assyrian kings completely destroyed them! 13And don't forget what happened to the king of Hamath, to the king of Arpad, and to the kings of the cities of Sepharvaim, Hena, and Ivvah."

14As soon as King Hezekiah had read this letter, he went over to the Temple and spread it out before the Lord, 15and prayed, saying, 16, 17"O Lord, Almighty God

37:8, 9 *from the south,* implied.

36:19
2 Kgs 17:6
Isa 10:9-11
37:13
Jer 49:23

36:20
1 Kgs 20:23,28

37:1
2 Kgs 19:1-37

37:3
Isa 22:5
26:17,18

37:4
Isa 1:9
10:20-22

37:6
Isa 7:4; 35:4

37:8
Isa 20:5

37:11
Isa 10:9-11

37:12
Gen 11:31
2 Kgs 17:6

37:16
Ex 25:22
Ps 17:6; 74:22
80:1; 86:10
Jer 10:12

36:19, 20 Sennacherib said that the gods of the other cities he had conquered had not been able to save their people, so how could the God of Jerusalem save them? Jehovah was the God of Samaria and it fell. But Jehovah was the God of Samaria in name only, because the people were not worshiping him. That is why prophets foretold the fall of Samaria. But the people in Jerusalem were at this time actively worshiping God, and he would rescue them from the Assyrian army.

37:3 Judah is compared to a woman trying to give birth to a child who does not come. Too weak to help herself, she wishes for death to end her pain. When the situation seemed hopeless, Hezekiah

didn't give up. Instead, he asked the prophet Isaiah to pray that God would help them.

37:4 Hezekiah did exactly what Isaiah had been calling the people to do (chapters 1—35). He turned to God and watched him come to Judah's aid. Turning to God means believing that God is there and that he is able to help us.

37:8-10 Although the answer to Hezekiah's prayer was already in motion because Ethiopia was poised to attack, Hezekiah did not know it. He persisted in prayer and faith even though he could not see the answer coming. When we pray, we must have faith that God has already prepared the best answer. Our task is to ask in faith and wait.

of Israel enthroned between the Guardian Angels, *you alone* are God of all the kingdoms of the earth. You alone made heaven and earth. Listen as I plead; see me as I pray. Look at this letter from King Sennacherib, for he has mocked the Living God. 18It is true, O Lord, that the kings of Assyria have destroyed all those nations, just as the letter says, 19and thrown their gods into the fire; for they weren't gods at all, but merely idols, carved by men from wood and stone. Of course the Assyrians could destroy them. 20O Lord our God, save us so that all the kingdoms of the earth will know that you are God, and you alone."

God will destroy Sennacherib

21Then Isaiah, the son of Amoz, sent this message to King Hezekiah: "The Lord God of Israel says, This is my answer to your prayer against Sennacherib, Assyria's king.

22"The Lord says to him: My people—the helpless virgin daughter of Zion—laughs at you and scoffs and shakes her head at you in scorn. 23Who is it you scoffed against and mocked? Whom did you revile? At whom did you direct your violence and pride? It was against the Holy One of Israel! 24You have sent your messengers to mock the Lord. You boast, 'I came with my mighty army against the nations of the west. I cut down the tallest cedars and choicest cypress trees. I conquered their highest mountains and destroyed their thickest forests.'

25"You boast of wells you've dug in many a conquered land, and Egypt with all its armies is no obstacle to you! 26But do you not yet know that it was I who decided all this long ago? That it was I who gave you all this power from ancient times? I have caused all this to happen as I planned—that you should crush walled cities into ruined heaps. 27That's why their people had so little power, and were such easy prey for you. They were as helpless as the grass, as tender plants you trample down beneath your feet, as grass upon the housetops, burnt yellow by the sun. 28But I know you well—your comings and goings and all you do—and the way you have raged against me. 29Because of your anger against the Lord—and I heard it all!—I have put a hook in your nose and a bit in your mouth and led you back to your own land by the same road you came."

30Then God said to Hezekiah, "Here is the proof that I am the one who is delivering this city from the king of Assyria: This year he will abandon his siege. Although it is too late now to plant your crops, and you will have only volunteer grain this fall, still it will give you enough seed for a small harvest next year, and two years from now you will be living in luxury again. 31And you who are left in Judah will take root again in your own soil and flourish and multiply. 32For a remnant shall go out from Jerusalem to repopulate the land; the power of the Lord Almighty will cause all this to come to pass.

33"As for the king of Assyria, his armies shall not enter Jerusalem, nor shoot their arrows there, nor march outside its gates, nor build up an earthen bank against its walls. 34He will return to his own country by the road he came on, and will not enter this city, says the Lord. 35For my own honor I will defend it, and in memory of my servant David."

36That night the Angel of the Lord went out to the camp of the Assyrians and killed 185,000 soldiers; when the living wakened the next morning, all these lay dead before them. 37Then Sennacherib, king of Assyria, returned to his own country, to Nineveh. 38And one day while he was worshiping in the temple of

37:30 *This year,* implied. *two years from now you will be living in luxury again.* The third harvest from then would yield a bumper crop.

Cross references (margin):

37:19 Isa 17:8; 26:14

37:20 1 Kgs 18:36,37 Isa 33:22 Ezek 36:23

37:22 Lam 2:13 Zeph 3:14

37:23 Isa 5:15,21 Ezek 39:7 Hab 1:12

37:24 Isa 14:8

37:26 Isa 25:2 Acts 2:23 4:27,28

37:27 Ps 129:6 Isa 40:7

37:28 Ps 139:1

37:29 Isa 30:28 Ezek 38:4

37:30 Lev 25:5,11

37:31 Isa 10:20; 27:6

37:32 2 Kgs 19:31

37:35 2 Kgs 20:6 Isa 48:9,11

37:36 2 Kgs 19:35 Isa 10:12,33,34

37:37 Gen 10:11 Jonah 3:3 Zeph 2:13

37:29 This was a common torture the Assyrians used on their captives. They were often led away with hooks in their noses or bits in their mouths as signs of humiliation.

37:30 Volunteer grain grows by itself, springing up from fallen seeds of the previous year's crop.

37:35 God would defend Jerusalem for his honor and in David's

memory. Assyria had insulted God. They would not be his instrument to punish Jerusalem. What Jerusalem could not possibly do, God would do for them. God is prepared to do the impossible if we trust him enough to ask.

37:38 The death of Sennacherib was prophesied by Isaiah in 10:12, 33, 34 and in 37:7. His death is recorded in 2 Kings 19.

Nisroch his god, his sons Adrammelech and Sharezer killed him with their swords; then they escaped into the land of Ararat, and Esar-haddon his son became king.

37:38
Gen 8:4

Hezekiah receives 15 extra years

38 It was just before all this that Hezekiah became deathly sick and Isaiah the prophet (Amoz' son) went to visit him and gave him this message from the Lord:

38:1
2 Kgs 20:1-6

"Set your affairs in order, for you are going to die; you will not recover from this illness."

2When Hezekiah heard this, he turned his face to the wall and prayed:

3"O Lord, don't you remember how true I've been to you and how I've always tried to obey you in everything you said?" Then he broke down with great sobs.

38:3
2 Kgs 18:5,6
Neh 13:14
Ps 6:6-8

4So the Lord sent another message to Isaiah:

5"Go and tell Hezekiah that the Lord God of your forefather David hears you praying and sees your tears and will let you live fifteen more years. 6He will deliver you and this city from the king of Assyria. I will defend you, says the Lord, 7and here is my guarantee: 8I will send the sun backwards ten degrees as measured on Ahaz' sundial!"

38:5
2 Kgs 18:2,13
38:6
Isa 31:5
38:7
Isa 7:11,14
38:8
2 Kgs 20:9-11

So the sun retraced ten degrees that it had gone down!

9When King Hezekiah was well again, he wrote this poem about his experience:

10"My life is but half done and I must leave it all. I am robbed of my normal years, and now I must enter the gates of Sheol. 11Never again will I see the Lord in the land of the living. Never again will I see my friends in this world. 12My life is blown away like a shepherd's tent; it is cut short as when a weaver stops his working at the loom. In one short day my life hangs by a thread.

38:10
Ps 102:24
38:11
Ps 27:13
38:12
Job 4:20
2 Cor 5:1

13"All night I moaned; it was like being torn apart by lions. 14Delirious, I chattered like a swallow and mourned like a dove; my eyes grew weary of looking up for help. 'O God,' I cried, 'I am in trouble—help me.' 15But what can I say? For he himself has sent this sickness. All my sleep has fled because of my soul's bitterness. 16O Lord, your discipline is good and leads to life and health. Oh, heal me and make me live!

38:14
Ps 119:123
Ezek 7:16
38:15
Job 7:11
38:16
Ps 39:13
119:71,75

17"Yes, now I see it all—it was good for me to undergo this bitterness, for you have lovingly delivered me from death; you have forgiven all my sins. 18For dead men cannot praise you. They cannot be filled with hope and joy. 19The living, only the living, can praise you as I do today. One generation makes known your faithfulness to the next. 20Think of it! The Lord healed me! Every day of my life from now on I will sing my songs of praise in the Temple, accompanied by the orchestra."

38:17
Isa 43:25
Jer 31:34
Jonah 2:6
38:18
Ps 6:5
38:19
Ps 78:5-7
119:175
38:20
Ps 33:1-3
116:17-19
146:2

21(For Isaiah had told Hezekiah's servants, "Make an ointment of figs and spread it over the boil, and he will get well again."

22And then Hezekiah had asked, "What sign will the Lord give me to prove that he will heal me?")

38:1ff The events of chapters 38 and 39 happened before those of chapters 36 and 37.

38:1–5 When Isaiah went to Hezekiah who was extremely ill and told him of his impending death, Hezekiah immediately turned to God. God responded to his prayer, allowing Hezekiah to live another 15 years. In response to fervent prayer, God may change the course of our lives too. Never hesitate to ask God for radical changes if you will honor him with those changes.

38:1–5 According to 2 Chronicles 32:24–26, Hezekiah had a problem with pride even after this double miracle of healing and deliverance. Eventually he and his subjects humbled themselves, and God's judgment was put off for several more generations.

38:16–18 Hezekiah realized that his prayer brought deliverance and forgiveness. His words "dead men cannot praise you" may reveal that he was unaware of the blessedness of the future life for

those who trust in God (57:1, 2), or they may simply mean that dead bodies cannot praise God. In either case, Hezekiah knew God had spared his life, and in his poem he praises him. Hezekiah recognized the good that came from his bitter experience. The next time you pass through a bitter experience, pray that God will bring good from it.

38:19 Hezekiah speaks of the significance of passing the joy of the Lord from generation to generation. The heritage of our faith has come to us because of faithful men and women who have carried God's message throughout the centuries. Do you share with your children or other young people the excitement of your relationship with God?

39:1ff Merodach-baladan, a Babylonian prince, was planning a revolt against Assyria and was forming an alliance. He probably hoped to convince Hezekiah to join this alliance against Assyria. Hezekiah, feeling friendly toward this nation that was also an

Messengers from Babylon

39:1
2 Kgs 20:12-19

39 Soon afterwards, the king of Babylon (Merodach-baladan, the son of Bala-dan) sent Hezekiah a present and his best wishes, for he had heard that Hezekiah had been very sick and now was well again. ²Hezekiah appreciated this

39:2
2 Kgs 18:15,16
2 Chron 32:25,
31

and took the envoys from Babylon on a tour of the palace, showing them his treasure house full of silver, gold, spices and perfumes. He took them into his jewel rooms, too, and opened to them all his treasures—everything.

39:3
Jer 5:15

³Then Isaiah the prophet came to the king and said, "What did they say? Where are they from?"

"From far away in Babylon," Hezekiah replied.

⁴"How much have they seen?" asked Isaiah.

And Hezekiah replied, "I showed them everything I own, all my priceless treasures."

⁵Then Isaiah said to him, "Listen to this message from the Lord Almighty:

39:6
2 Kgs 24:13
Jer 20:5

⁶"The time is coming when everything you have—all the treasures stored up by your fathers—will be carried off to Babylon. Nothing will be left. ⁷And some of your own sons will become slaves, yes, eunuchs, in the palace of the king of Babylon."

39:8
2 Chron 34:28

⁸"All right," Hezekiah replied. "Whatever the Lord says is good. At least there will be peace during my lifetime!"

B. WORDS OF COMFORT (40:1—66:24)

Isaiah now speaks of events which will occur after the captivity. This includes the decree by Cyrus to release the remnant captives and allow them to return to Jerusalem after he conquered Babylon. But Isaiah also foretells the coming of the Suffering Servant, Jesus Christ, and describes his life and death with incredible detail. Isaiah also speaks about the coming of the new heavens and earth, when God's people will be completely restored. Since all believers will participate in this new world to come, we can have confident hope in the future.

1. Israel's release from captivity

God will feed his flock

40:2
Isa 53:5,6,11
Zech 9:12

40:3
Mal 3:1
Mt 3:3

40 Comfort, yes, comfort my people, says your God. ²Speak tenderly to Jerusalem and tell her that her sad days are gone. Her sins are pardoned, and I have punished her in full for all her sins.

³Listen! I hear the voice of someone shouting, "Make a road for the Lord through

39:1 *Merodach-baladan . . . sent Hezekiah a present and his best wishes.* Merodach-baladan was at this time planning a revolt in the east against Sennacherib, so he was especially interested in Hezekiah's activities in the west.

---

enemy of Assyria, showed the Babylonian envoys his assets. But Isaiah warned the king not to trust Babylon. Someday they would turn on Judah and devour Jerusalem's wealth.

39:4-7 What was so wrong about showing these Babylonians around? Hezekiah failed to see that the Babylonians would become his next threat, and they, not the Assyrians, would conquer his city. When Isaiah told him Babylon would someday carry it all away, this was an amazing prophecy because Babylon was struggling for independence under Assyria. Hezekiah's self-satisfied display of his earthly wealth brought its own consequences (2 Kings 25; Daniel 1:1, 2). His response (39:8) may seem a bit brash, but he simply was expressing gratitude for the blessing from God that peace would reign during his lifetime and that God's judgment would not be more severe.

39:8 Hezekiah, one of Judah's most faithful kings, worked hard throughout his reign to stamp out idol worship and to purify the worship of the true God at the Jerusalem Temple. Nevertheless, he knew his kingdom was not pure. Powerful undercurrents of evil invited destruction, and only God's miraculous interventions preserved Judah from its enemies. Here Hezekiah expressed gratefulness that God was preserving peace during his reign. As soon as Hezekiah died, evil burst forth under the leadership of Manasseh, Hezekiah's son, who actually rebuilt the centers of idolatry his father had destroyed.

40:1ff The book of Isaiah makes a dramatic shift at this point. The following chapters discuss the majesty of God, who is coming to rule the earth and judge all people. He will reunite Israel and Judah and restore them to glory. Instead of warning the people of impending judgment, Isaiah now comforts them. This foretells the end of time when "Babylon"—the future evil world system—will be destroyed and the persecution of God's people will end.

40:1 God's people still had 100 years of trouble before Jerusalem would fall, then 70 years of exile. So God tells Isaiah to speak tenderly and to comfort Jerusalem.

The seeds of comfort may take root in the soil of adversity. When your life seems to be falling apart, ask God to comfort you. You may not escape adversity, but you may find God's comfort in the midst of it. Sometimes, however, the only comfort we have is in the knowledge that someday we will be with God. Appreciate the comfort and encouragement found in his Word, his presence, and his people.

40:3-5 Preparing a straight, smooth road means removing obstacles or rolling out the red carpet for the coming of the Lord. The desert is a picture of life's trials and sufferings. We are not immune to these, but our faith need not be hindered by them. Isaiah told people to prepare to see God work. John the Baptist used these words as he challenged the people to prepare for the coming Messiah (Matthew 3:3).

the wilderness; make him a straight, smooth road through the desert. ⁴Fill the
valleys; level the hills; straighten out the crooked paths and smooth off the rough
spots in the road. ⁵The glory of the Lord will be seen by all mankind together." The
Lord has spoken—it shall be.

⁶The voice says, "Shout!"

"What shall I shout?" I asked.

"Shout that man is like the grass that dies away, and all his beauty fades like
dying flowers. ⁷The grass withers, the flower fades beneath the breath of God. And
so it is with fragile man. ⁸The grass withers, the flowers fade, but the Word of our
God shall stand forever."

⁹O Crier of Good News, shout to Jerusalem from the mountain tops! Shout
louder—don't be afraid—tell the cities of Judah, "Your God is coming!" ¹⁰Yes, the
Lord God is coming with mighty power; he will rule with awesome strength. See,
his reward is with him, to each as he has done. ⑴¹He will feed his flock like a
shepherd; he will carry the lambs in his arms and gently lead the ewes with young.

¹²Who else has held the oceans in his hands and measured off the heavens with
his ruler? Who else knows the weight of all the earth and weighs the mountains and
the hills? ¹³Who can advise the Spirit of the Lord or be his teacher or give him
counsel? ¹⁴Has he ever needed anyone's advice? Did he need instruction as to what
is right and best? ¹⁵No, for all the peoples of the world are nothing in comparison
with him—they are but a drop in the bucket, dust on the scales. He picks up the
islands as though they had no weight at all. ¹⁶All of Lebanon's forests do not
contain sufficient fuel to consume a sacrifice large enough to honor him, nor are all
its animals enough to offer to our God. ¹⁷All the nations are as nothing to him; in
his eyes they are less than nothing—mere emptiness and froth.

¹⁸How can we describe God? With what can we compare him? ¹⁹With an idol?
An idol, made from a mold, overlaid with gold, and with silver chains around its
neck? ²⁰The man too poor to buy expensive gods like that will find a tree free from
rot and hire a man to carve a face on it, and that's his god—a god that cannot even
move!

²¹Are you so ignorant? Are you so deaf to the words of God—the words he gave
before the world began? Have you never heard nor understood? ²²It is God who sits
above the circle of the earth. (The people below must seem to him like grasshoppers!) He is the one who stretches out the heavens like a curtain and makes his tent
from them. ²³He dooms the great men of the world and brings them all to naught.
²⁴They hardly get started, barely take root, when he blows on them and their work
withers and the wind carries them off like straw.

²⁵"With whom will you compare me? Who is my equal?" asks the Holy One.
²⁶Look up into the heavens! Who created all these stars? As a shepherd leads his
sheep, calling each by its pet name, and counts them to see that none are lost or
strayed, so God does with stars and planets!

²⁷O Jacob, O Israel, how can you say that the Lord doesn't see your troubles and
isn't being fair? ²⁸Don't you yet understand? Don't you know by now that the
everlasting God, the Creator of the farthest parts of the earth, never grows faint or
weary? No one can fathom the depths of his understanding. ²⁹He gives power to the

40:26 *As a shepherd leads his sheep,* implied.

40:4	Ezek 17:24
40:5	Hab 2:14
40:6	Job 14:2
40:7	Jas 1:10,11
40:8	Mt 5:18
40:10	Isa 59:16, Rev 22:12
40:11	Ezek 34:12-14, 23,31, Jn 10:11,14-16
40:12	Isa 48:13
40:13	Rom 11:34
40:14	Col 2:3
40:15	Isa 17:13
40:17	Isa 29:7
40:18	Ex 8:10, Isa 46:5, Mic 7:18
40:19	Ps 115:4-8, Hab 2:18,19
40:20	Isa 46:7
40:21	Isa 51:13, Rom 1:19
40:22	Ps 104:2
40:23	Ps 107:40, Jer 25:18-27
40:24	Isa 17:13
40:26	Ps 147:4, Isa 42:5
40:27	Job 34:5,6, Isa 54:8
40:28	Ps 90:2; 147:5
40:29	Jer 31:25

40:6-8 People are compared here to grass and flowers that fade
away. Our lives are mortal, but God's Word is eternal and unfailing.
Public opinion changes and is unreliable, but God's Word is
constant. Only in God's eternal Word will we find lasting solutions
to our problems and needs.

40:11 God is often pictured as a shepherd, gently caring for and
guiding his flock. He is powerful and mighty (40:10), yet careful
and gentle. He is called a Shepherd (Psalm 23); the Good
Shepherd (John 10:11, 14); the Great Shepherd (Hebrews 13:20);
and the Head Shepherd (1 Peter 5:4). Note that the shepherd is
caring for the most powerless members of that society: children
and pregnant (or nursing) women. This reinforces the prophetic

theme that the truly powerful nation is not the one with a strong
military, but rather the one that relies on God's caring strength.

40:12-31 Isaiah describes God's power to create, his provision,
and his presence to help. God is almighty and all-powerful; but
even so, he cares for each of us personally. No person or thing
can be compared to God (40:25). We describe God as best we
can with our limited knowledge and language, but we only limit our
understanding of him and his power when we compare him to what
we experience on earth. What is your concept of God, especially
as revealed in his Son, Jesus Christ? Don't limit his work in your life
by underestimating him.

40:29-31 Even the strongest people get tired at times, but God's

40:30
Jer 9:21

40:31
2 Cor 4:8-10,16
Heb 12:3

tired and worn out, and strength to the weak. ³⁰Even the youths shall be exhausted, and the young men will all give up. ³¹But they that wait upon the Lord shall renew their strength. They shall mount up with wings like eagles; they shall run and not be weary; they shall walk and not faint.

God will help Israel

41:1
Hab 2:20

41 Listen in silence before me, O lands beyond the sea. Bring your strongest arguments. Come now and speak. The court is ready for your case.

41:2
2 Chron 36:23
Isa 46:11

²Who has stirred up this one from the east, whom victory meets at every step? Who, indeed, but the Lord? God has given him victory over many nations and permitted him to trample kings underfoot and to put entire armies to the sword. ³He

41:4
Isa 44:7; 48:12
Rev 1:8,17,18

chases them away and goes on safely, though the paths he treads are new. ⁴Who has done such mighty deeds, directing the affairs of generations of mankind as they march by? It is I, the Lord, the First and Last; I alone am he.

41:5
Josh 5:1
Ezek 26:15,16

⁵The lands beyond the sea watch in fear and wait for word of Cyrus' new campaigns. Remote lands tremble and mobilize for war. ⁶, ⁷The craftsmen encour-

41:6
Joel 3:9-11

age each other as they rush to make new idols to protect them. The carver hurries

41:8
Isa 51:2
Jas 2:23

the goldsmith, and the molder helps at the anvil. "Good," they say. "It's coming along fine. Now we can solder on the arms." Carefully they join the parts together, and then fasten the thing in place so it won't fall over!

41:9
Deut 7:6
Isa 11:11

⁸But as for you, O Israel, you are mine, my chosen ones; for you are Abraham's family, and he was my friend. ⁹I have called you back from the ends of the earth

41:10
Deut 31:6
Ps 89:13
Rom 8:31

and said that you must serve but me alone, for I have chosen you and will not throw you away. ¹⁰Fear not, for I am with you. Do not be dismayed. I am your God. I will strengthen you; I will help you; I will uphold you with my victorious right hand.

41:11
Isa 29:5,7,8

¹¹See, all your angry enemies lie confused and shattered. Anyone opposing you

41:12
Job 20:7-9

will die. ¹²You will look for them in vain—they will all be gone. ¹³I am holding you

41:13
Isa 45:1

by your right hand—I, the Lord your God—and I say to you, Don't be afraid; I am

41:14
Isa 43:14

here to help you. ¹⁴Despised though you are, fear not, O Israel; for I will help you. I am the Lord, your Redeemer; I am the Holy One of Israel. ¹⁵You shall be a new

41:15
Mic 4:13

and sharp-toothed threshing instrument to tear all enemies apart, making chaff of

41:16
Isa 35:10

mountains. ¹⁶You shall toss them in the air; the wind shall blow them all away; whirlwinds shall scatter them. And the joy of the Lord shall fill you full; you shall

41:17
Isa 30:19
42:16; 44:3

glory in the God of Israel.

41:18
Ps 107:35
Isa 30:25

¹⁷When the poor and needy seek water and there is none and their tongues are parched from thirst, then I will answer when they cry to me. I, Israel's God, will not ever forsake them. ¹⁸I will open up rivers for them on high plateaus! I will give

41:5 Cyrus', implied from 45:1.　**41:10** with my victorious right hand, or, "with the right hand of my righteousness."

---

power and strength never diminish. He is never too tired or too busy to help and listen. His strength is our source of strength. When you feel all of life crushing you and you cannot go another step, remember that you can call upon God to renew your strength.

40:31 We all need regular times to listen to God. Waiting on the Lord is expecting his promised strength to help us rise above life's distractions and difficulties. Listening to God helps us to be prepared for when he speaks to us, to be patient when he asks us to wait, and to expect him to fulfill the promises found in his Word.

41:1ff This "one from the east" is Cyrus II of Persia, who would be king within a century and a half (he is also mentioned in 44:28). God promised to protect Israel and care for them even against pagan nations. God is in control of all world empires and politics.

41:4 Each generation gets caught up in its own problems, but God's plan embraces all generations. When your great-grandparents lived, God worked personally in the lives of his people. When your great-grandchildren live, God will still work personally in the lives of his people. He is the only One who sees as clearly a hundred years from now as he saw a hundred years ago. When you are concerned about the future, talk with God, who

knows the generations of the future as well as he knows the generations of the past.

41:8 God calls Israel his own because of his wonderful friendship with Abraham. He had chosen Israel, and they had the assurance that God would be with them. God considers us friends when we give ourselves to him as he gives himself to us. When we are God's friends, we know he is always there when we need him. Do you consider God your friend? Are you as devoted to him as he is to you?

41:8–10 God chose Israel through Abraham because he wanted to, not because the people deserved it (Deuteronomy 7:6–8; 9:4–6). Although God chose the Israelites to represent him to the world, they failed and sinned; so God punished them and sent them into captivity. Now all believers are God's chosen people, and all share the responsibility of representing him to the world. God will one day bring all his faithful people together. We need not fear because (1) God's presence is with us ("I am with you"), (2) God has established a relationship with us ("I am your God"), and (3) God's assurance of strength, help, and victory over sin and death is certain.

them fountains of water in the valleys! In the deserts will be pools of water, and rivers fed by springs shall flow across the dry, parched ground. ¹⁹I will plant trees—cedars, myrtle, olive trees, the cypress, fir and pine—on barren land. ²⁰Everyone will see this miracle and understand that it is God who did it, Israel's Holy One.

²¹Can your idols make such claims as these? Let them come and show what they can do! says God, the King of Israel. ²²Let them try to tell us what occurred in years gone by, or what the future holds. ²³Yes, that's it! If you are gods, tell what will happen in the days ahead! Or do some mighty miracle that makes us stare, amazed. ²⁴But no! You are less than nothing, and can do nothing at all. Anyone who chooses you needs to have his head examined!

²⁵But I have stirred up (Cyrus) from the north and east; he will come against the nations and call on my name, and I will give him victory over kings and princes. He will tread them as a potter tramples clay.

²⁶Who but I have told you this would happen? Who else predicted this, making you admit that he was right? No one else! None other said one word! ²⁷I was the first to tell Jerusalem, "Look! Look! Help is on the way!" ²⁸Not one of your idols told you this. Not one gave any answer when I asked. ²⁹See, they are all foolish, worthless things; your idols are all as empty as the wind.

God's chosen one

42 See my servant, whom I uphold; my Chosen One, in whom I delight. I have put my Spirit upon him; he will reveal justice to the nations of the world. ²He will be gentle—he will not shout nor quarrel in the streets. ³He will not break the bruised reed, nor quench the dimly burning flame. He will encourage the faint-hearted, those tempted to despair. He will see full justice given to all who have been wronged. ⁴He won't be satisfied until truth and righteousness prevail throughout the earth, nor until even distant lands beyond the seas have put their trust in him.

⁵The Lord God who created the heavens and stretched them out and created the earth and everything in it, and gives life and breath and spirit to everyone in all the world, he is the one who says [to his Servant, the Messiah],

⁶"I the Lord have called you to demonstrate my righteousness. I will guard and support you, for I have given you to my people as the personal confirmation of my covenant with them. You shall also be a light to guide the nations unto me. ⁷You will open the eyes of the blind, and release those who sit in prison darkness and despair. ⁸I am the Lord! That is my name, and I will not give my glory to anyone else; I will not share my praise with carved idols. ⁹Everything I prophesied came

42:4 *He won't be satisfied,* literally, "He will not burn dimly or be bruised until. . . ." **42:5** *to his Servant, the Messiah,* implied. **42:6** *I have given you to my people as the personal confirmation of my covenant with them,* or, "You will be my convenant with all the people. . . ."

Cross references

41:19 Isa 55:13
41:20 Job 12:7-9
41:22 Isa 43:9; 45:21
41:23 Jer 10:5 Jn 13:19
41:24 1 Cor 8:4
41:25 Jer 50:3 Mic 7:10
41:26 Isa 44:7
41:27 Isa 40:9
41:28 Isa 63:5
41:29 Jer 5:13
42:1 Isa 11:2; 53:11 Mt 3:17 12:18-21
42:3 Ps 72:2,4
42:4 Isa 24:15; 66:19
42:5 Job 33:4 Ps 104:2 Isa 45:18
42:6 Jer 23:5,6 Lk 2:32
42:7 Isa 35:5; 61:1
42:8 Ex 3:15; 20:3-5

41:21-24 Israel was surrounded by many nations whose gods supposedly had special powers, such as raising crops and providing victories in war. These gods, however, often failed to deliver. A god with limited power or no power at all is not really a god. When we are tempted to put our trust in something other than the living God—money, perhaps, or military power—we should stop and ask some serious questions. Will it deliver? Will it unfailingly provide what I am looking for? God delivers. When he makes a promise, he keeps it. He is the only completely trustworthy God.

42:1-17 Sometimes called the "Servant Song," these verses are about the Servant-Messiah, not the servant Cyrus (as in chapter 41). Israel and the Messiah are both often called *servant.* Israel, as God's servant, was to help bring the world to a knowledge of God. The Messiah, Jesus would fulfill this task and show God himself to the world.

42:1-4a These verses were quoted in Matthew 12:18–21 with reference to Christ, the Chosen One. The Chosen One reveals a character of gentleness, encouragement, justice, and truth. When

you feel broken and bruised, or burned out in your spiritual life, God won't step on you or toss you aside as useless, but he will gently pick you up. God's loving attributes are desperately needed by mankind today. We can show such sensitivity through God's Spirit to people around us, reflecting God's goodness and honesty to them.

42:6 What is righteousness? It is having right actions, right attitudes, and right relationships—all based on our right standing with God. When he forgives us, takes away our sin, and restores us as his children, he not only gives us his righteousness, but he also empowers us to demonstrate it to others.

42:6, 7 Part of Christ's mission on earth was to demonstrate God's righteousness and to be a light to the nations. Through Christ, all people have the opportunity to share in his mission. God calls us to be servants of his Son, demonstrating God's righteousness and bringing his light. What a rare privilege to help the Messiah fulfill his mission! But we must seek his righteousness before we demonstrate it to others, and let his light shine in us before we can be lights ourselves.

true, and now I will prophesy again. I will tell you the future before it happens."

42:10
Ps 33:3

¹⁰Sing a new song to the Lord; sing his praises, all you who live in earth's remotest corners! Sing, O sea! Sing, all you who live in distant lands beyond the sea! ¹¹Join in the chorus, you desert cities—Kedar and Sela! And you, too, dwellers in the mountain tops. ¹²Let the western coastlands glorify the Lord and sing his mighty power.

42:13
Isa 59:17
66:14-16
42:15
Ezek 38:19,20
Nah 1:4-6
42:16
Ps 94:14
Isa 40:4
Lk 1:78,79
Eph 5:8
42:17
Ps 97:7
Isa 44:9,11

¹³The Lord will be a mighty warrior, full of fury toward his foes. He will give a great shout and prevail. ¹⁴Long has he been silent; he has restrained himself. But now he will give full vent to his wrath; he will groan and cry like a woman delivering her child. ¹⁵He will level the mountains and hills and blight their greenery. He will dry up the rivers and pools. ¹⁶He will bring blind Israel along a path they have not seen before. He will make the darkness bright before them and smooth and straighten out the road ahead. He will not forsake them. ¹⁷But those who trust in idols and call them gods will be greatly disappointed; they will be turned away.

Blind and deaf toward God

42:18
Isa 35:5
42:19
Isa 44:26
42:20
Jer 6:10

¹⁸Oh, how blind and deaf you are towards God! Why won't you listen? Why won't you see? ¹⁹Who in all the world is as blind as my own people, who are designed to be my messengers of truth? Who is so blind as my "dedicated one," the "servant of the Lord"? ²⁰You see and understand what is right but won't heed nor do it; you hear but you won't listen.

42:22
Isa 24:18

²¹The Lord has magnified his law and made it truly glorious. Through it he had planned to show the world that he is righteous. ²²But what a sight his people are—these who were to demonstrate to all the world the glory of his law; for they are robbed, enslaved, imprisoned, trapped, fair game for all, with no one to protect them. ²³Won't even one of you apply these lessons from the past and see the ruin

42:24
Isa 10:5; 48:18
42:25
Isa 5:25

that awaits you up ahead? ²⁴Who let Israel be robbed and hurt? Did not the Lord? It is the Lord they sinned against, for they would not go where he sent them nor listen to his laws. ²⁵That is why God poured out such fury and wrath on his people and destroyed them in battle. Yet, though set on fire and burned, they will not understand the reason why—that it is God, wanting them to repent.

There is no other Savior

43:1
Isa 44:2,21,22,
23,24; 45:3,4
43:2
Deut 31:6,8
Isa 8:7,8
Dan 3:25,27
43:4
Isa 63:9

43 But now the Lord who created you, O Israel, says, Don't be afraid, for I have ransomed you; I have called you by name; you are mine. ²When you go through deep waters and great trouble, I will be with you. When you go through rivers of difficulty, you will not drown! When you walk through the fire of oppression, you will not be burned up—the flames will not consume you. ³For I am the Lord your God, your Savior, the Holy One of Israel. I gave Egypt and Ethiopia and Seba [to Cyrus] in exchange for your freedom, as your ransom. ⁴Others died

42:19 *as my own people,* literally, "as my servant." 42:22 *these who were to demonstrate to all the world the glory of his law,* implied in previous verse. 42:25 *wanting them to repent,* implied. 43:3 *to Cyrus,* implied.

42:10 Look at all the Lord will do to us and through us (42:6–9). Majestic works prompt majestic responses. Do you really appreciate the good that God does to you and through you? If so, you ought to burst forth in songs of praise.

42:19, 20 How could Israel and Judah be God's servants and yet be so blind? How could they be so close to God and see so little? Yet do we not fail in the same way? Sometimes limited blindness—seeing but not understanding, or knowing what is right but not doing it—can be worse than not seeing at all.

42:23 We may condemn our predecessors for their failures, but we are twice as guilty if we repeat the same actions after they are recognized as failures. Often we are so ready to direct God's message at others that we can't see how it touches our own lives. Make sure you are willing to take your own advice as you teach or lead.

43:1ff Chapter 42 ends with God's sorrow over the spiritual decay

of his people. In chapter 43, God tells the people that despite their spiritual failure, he will show them mercy, bring them back from captivity, and restore them. He would give them an outpouring of love, not an outpouring of wrath. Then the world would know that God alone had done this.

43:1–4 God created Israel and made her special to him. He ransomed her and called her by his name. We are special to God, and he calls us by his name! When we bear his wonderful name, we must never do anything that would bring shame to it.

43:2 Going through rivers of difficulty will either cause you to drown or force you to grow stronger. If you go in your own strength, you are more likely to drown. If you invite the Lord to go with you, he will protect you.

43:3 God gave other nations to Cyrus in exchange for returning the Jews to their homeland. Egypt, Ethiopia, and parts of Arabia had attacked Persia, and Cyrus defeated them.

that you might live; I traded their lives for yours because you are precious to me and honored, and I love you.

5Don't be afraid, for I am with you. I will gather you from east and west, 6from north and south. I will bring my sons and daughters back to Israel from the farthest corners of the earth. 7All who claim me as their God will come, for I have made them for my glory; I created them. 8Bring them back to me—blind as they are and deaf when I call (although they see and hear!).

9Gather the nations together! Which of all their idols ever has foretold such things? Which can predict a single day ahead? Where are the witnesses of anything they said? If there are no witnesses, then they must confess that only God can prophesy.

10But I have witnesses, O Israel, says the Lord! You are my witnesses and my servants, chosen to know and to believe me and to understand that I alone am God. There is no other God; there never was and never will be. 11I am the Lord, and there is no other Savior. 12Whenever you have thrown away your idols, I have shown you my power. With one word I have saved you. You have seen me do it; you are my witnesses that it is true. 13From eternity to eternity I am God. No one can oppose what I do.

The promise of victory

14The Lord, your Redeemer, the Holy One of Israel, says:

For your sakes I will send an invading army against Babylon that will walk in, almost unscathed. The boasts of the Babylonians will turn to cries of fear. 15I am the Lord, your Holy One, Israel's Creator and King. 16I am the Lord, who opened a way through the waters, making a path right through the sea. 17I called forth the mighty army of Egypt with all its chariots and horses, to lie beneath the waves, dead, their lives snuffed out like candlewicks.

18But forget all that—it is nothing compared to what I'm going to do! 19For I'm going to do a brand new thing. See, I have already begun! Don't you see it? I will make a road through the wilderness of the world for my people to go home, and create rivers for them in the desert! 20The wild animals in the fields will thank me, the jackals and ostriches too, for giving them water in the wilderness, yes, springs in the desert, so that my people, my chosen ones, can be refreshed. 21I have made Israel for myself, and these my people will some day honor me before the world.

22But O my people, you won't ask my help; you have grown tired of me! 23You have not brought me the lambs for burnt offerings; you have not honored me with sacrifices. Yet my requests for offerings and incense have been very few! I have not treated you as slaves. 24You have brought me no sweet-smelling incense nor pleased me with the sacrificial fat. No, you have presented me only with sins, and wearied me with all your faults.

25I, yes, I alone am he who blots away your sins for my own sake and will never

43:5
Isa 49:12
Jer 30:10,11

43:6
Ps 107:3
2 Cor 6:17,18

43:7
Ps 100:3
Isa 46:13
Eph 2:10

43:8
Ezek 12:2

43:11
Hos 13:4

43:12
Ps 81:9

43:13
Job 9:12
Ps 90:2

43:14
Isa 41:14

43:15
Isa 44:6

43:16
Ex 14:21,22
Josh 3:15,16
Ps 77:19

43:17
Ps 76:5,6

43:18
Jer 16:14

43:19
Deut 8:15
2 Cor 5:17

43:20
Isa 41:17,18

43:22
Mic 6:3

43:23
Ex 30:34
Mal 1:6-8

43:24
Jer 6:20
Mal 2:17

43:25
Isa 55:7
Jer 31:34
Ezek 36:22

43:5, 6 Isaiah is speaking primarily of Israel's return from Babylon. But there is a broader meaning: all Israel will be regathered when Christ comes to rule in peace over the earth.

43:10, 11 Israel's task was to be a witness, telling the world who God is and what he has done. Believers today share the responsibility of being God's witnesses. Do people know what God is like through your words and example? They cannot see God directly, but they can see him reflected in you.

43:14 This was fulfilled when the Medo-Persian army dammed up the Euphrates river and virtually walked in and took the city of Babylon.

43:15–21 The Israelites would be oppressed again, as they had been as slaves in Egypt before the Exodus. They would cry to God, and again he would hear and deliver them. A new exodus would take place through a new wilderness. The past miracles were nothing compared to what God would do for his people.

43:22–24 A sacrifice required both giving up a valuable animal and pleading with God for forgiveness. But the people presented God with sins instead of sacrifices. Can you imagine bringing the best of your sins to God's altar? This ironic picture shows the depths to which Israel had sunk. What do you present to God—your sins, or a plea for his forgiveness?

43:22–24 Sin separates the sinner from God. God, however, does not want to be separated from his people, so he instituted the sacrificial system in which sins were symbolically transferred to animals and then destroyed. The people of Judah chose to ignore God's provision for sins, and thus they were in danger of losing his protection. Do you try to "go it on your own," or do you accept God's provision of forgiveness through Christ's sacrifice?

43:25 How tempting it is to remind someone of a past offense! But when God forgives our sins he totally forgets them. We never have to fear that he will remind us of them later. Because God does this for us, we need to do this for others.

43:27
Isa 51:2

43:28
Lam 2:2,6
Ezek 5:15

44:1
Jer 30:10

44:3
Isa 61:9
Joel 2:28

44:6
Isa 41:21
45:5,6,21
Rev 1:8,17

44:8
Deut 4:35,39
Isa 30:29

44:9
Ps 97:7

44:10
Jer 10:5
Hab 2:18
Acts 19:26

44:13
Ps 115:5-7
Isa 41:7

44:15
2 Chron 25:14

44:17
1 Kgs 18:26,28
Isa 45:20

44:18
Ps 81:12
Isa 6:9,10
29:10
Jer 10:8,14

44:19
Deut 27:15

think of them again. 26Oh, remind me of this promise of forgiveness, for we must talk about your sins. Plead your case for my forgiving you. 27From the very first your ancestors sinned against me—all your forebears transgressed my law. 28That is why I have deposed your priests and destroyed Israel, leaving her to shame.

The idols are false gods

44 Listen to me, O my servant Israel, O my chosen ones: 2The Lord who made you, who will help you, says, O servant of mine, don't be afraid. O Jerusalem, my chosen ones, don't be afraid. 3For I will give you abundant water for your thirst and for your parched fields. And I will pour out my Spirit and my blessings on your children. 4They shall thrive like watered grass, like willows on a river bank. 5"I am the Lord's," they'll proudly say, or, "I am a Jew," and tattoo upon their hands the name of God or the honored name of Israel.

6The Lord, the King of Israel, says—yes, it is Israel's Redeemer, the Lord Almighty, who says it—I am the First and Last; there is no other God. 7Who else can tell you what is going to happen in the days ahead? Let them tell you if they can, and prove their power. Let them do as I have done since ancient times. 8Don't, don't be afraid. Haven't I proclaimed from ages past [that I would save you]? You are my witnesses—is there any other God? No! None that I know about! There is no other Rock!

9What fools they are who manufacture idols for their gods. Their hopes remain unanswered. They themselves are witnesses that this is so, for their idols neither see nor know. No wonder those who worship them are so ashamed. 10Who but a fool would make his own god—an idol that can help him not one whit! 11All that worship these will stand before the Lord in shame, along with all these carpenters—mere men—who claim that they have made a god. Together they will stand in terror. 12The metalsmith stands at his forge to make an axe, pounding on it with all his might. He grows hungry and thirsty, weak and faint. 13Then the woodcarver takes the axe and uses it to make an idol. He measures and marks out a block of wood and carves the figure of a man. Now he has a wonderful idol that can't so much as move from where it is placed. 14He cuts down cedars, he selects the cypress and the oak, he plants the ash in the forest to be nourished by the rain. 15And after his care, he uses part of the wood to make a fire to warm himself and bake his bread, and then—he really does—he takes the rest of it and makes himself a god—a god for men to worship! An idol to fall down before and praise! 16Part of the tree he burns to roast his meat and to keep him warm and fed and well content, 17and with what's left he makes his god: a carved idol! He falls down before it and worships it and prays to it. "Deliver me," he says. "You are my god!"

18Such stupidity and ignorance! God has shut their eyes so that they cannot see, and closed their minds from understanding. 19The man never stops to think or figure out, "Why, it's just a block of wood! I've burned it for heat and used it to bake my bread and roast my meat. How can the rest of it be a god? Should I fall

44:5 *proudly,* implied. **44:8** *that I would save you,* implied.

TODAY'S IDOLATRY

Isaiah tells us, "What fools they are who manufacture idols for their gods. Their hopes remain unanswered" (44:9). We think of idols as statues of wood or stone, but in reality an idol is anything natural that is given sacred value and power. If your answer to any of the following questions is anything or anyone other than God, you may need to check out who or what you are ultimately worshiping.

- Who created me?
- Whom do I ultimately trust?
- Whom do I look to for ultimate truth?
- Whom do I look to for security and happiness?
- Who is in charge of my future?

44:5 The time will come when Israel will be proud of belonging to God and even display their relationship to him with tattoos. If we are truly God's, we should be unashamed and delighted to let everyone know about our relationship with him.

44:9-20 Here Isaiah describes how people make their own gods. How absurd to make a god from the same tree that gives firewood. Do we make our own gods—money, fame, or power? If we make a god, we cannot expect it to empower our lives.

down before a chunk of wood?" 20The poor, deluded fool feeds on ashes; he is trusting what can never give him any help at all. Yet he cannot bring himself to ask, "Is this thing, this idol that I'm holding in my hand, a lie?"

21Pay attention, Israel, for you are my servant; I made you, and I will not forget to help you. 22I've blotted out your sins; they are gone like morning mist at noon! Oh, return to me, for I have paid the price to set you free.

23Sing, O heavens, for the Lord has done this wondrous thing. Shout, O earth; break forth into song, O mountains and forests, yes, and every tree; for the Lord redeemed Jacob and is glorified in Israel! 24The Lord, your Redeemer who made you, says, All things were made by me; I alone stretched out the heavens. By myself I made the earth and everything in it.

25I am the one who shows what liars all false prophets are, by causing something else to happen than the things they say. I make wise men give opposite advice to what they should, and make them into fools. 26But what my prophets say, I do; when they say Jerusalem will be delivered and the cities of Judah lived in once again—it shall be done! 27When I speak to the rivers and say, "Be dry!" they shall be dry. 28When I say of Cyrus, "He is my shepherd," he will certainly do as I say; and Jerusalem will be rebuilt and the Temple restored, for I have spoken it.

Jehovah is the one true God

45 This is Jehovah's message to Cyrus, God's anointed, whom he has chosen to conquer many lands. God shall empower his right hand and he shall crush the strength of mighty kings. God shall open the gates of Babylon to him; the gates shall not be shut against him any more. 2I will go before you, Cyrus, and level the mountains and smash down the city gates of brass and iron bars. 3And I will give you treasures hidden in the darkness, secret riches; and you will know that I am doing this—I, the Lord, the God of Israel, the one who calls you by your name.

4And why have I named you for this work? For the sake of Jacob, my servant—Israel, my chosen. I called you by name when you didn't know me. 5I am Jehovah; there is no other God. I will strengthen you and send you out to victory even though you don't know me, 6and all the world from east to west will know there is no other God. I am Jehovah and there is no one else. I alone am God. 7I form the light and make the dark. I send good times and bad. I, Jehovah, am he who does these things. 8Open up, O heavens. Let the skies pour out their righteousness. Let salvation and righteousness sprout up together from the earth. I, Jehovah, created them.

9Woe to the man who fights with his Creator. Does the pot argue with its maker? Does the clay dispute with him who forms it, saying, "Stop, you're doing it wrong!" or the pot exclaim, "How clumsy can you be!"? 10Woe to the baby just being born who squalls to his father and mother, "Why have you produced me? Can't you do anything right at all?"

44:20 Ps 102:9
Hos 4:12

44:22 Ps 51:1,9
Isa 55:7
Acts 3:19
1 Pet 1:18,19

44:23 Ps 69:34
98:7,8

44:24 Isa 40:22

44:25 1 Cor 1:20,27

44:26 Jer 32:15,44

44:27 Isa 50:2

44:28 2 Chron 36:22, 23
Isa 14:32

45:1 Ps 73:23
Jer 51:11,20,24

45:2 Isa 40:4
Jer 51:30

45:3 Isa 49:1

45:4 Isa 43:1
Acts 17:23

45:6 Mal 1:11

45:7 Ps 104:20
Amos 3:6

45:8 Ps 72:6; 85:11
Isa 61:11

45:9 Rom 9:20,21

44:22 God said that we should serve our Creator (17:7; 40:28; 43:15; 45:9). Idolaters do the opposite—serving or worshiping what they have made, rather than the One who made them. Our Creator paid the price to set us free from our sins against him. No idol, however, ever created anybody, and no idol can redeem us from our sins.

44:25, 26 God himself is the standard for all teachings, so we can always trust his Word as absolute truth. In his Word we have a completely accurate "ruler" against which we can measure all other teachings. If you are unsure about a teaching, test it against God's Word. False prophets were false because they gave advice opposite to God's advice.

44:28 Isaiah who lived from about 740–681 B.C., called Cyrus by name almost 150 years before he ruled (559–530 B.C.)! Later historians said that Cyrus read this prophecy and was so moved that he carried it out. Isaiah had also predicted that Jerusalem would fall more than 100 years before it happened (586 B.C.) and that the Temple would be rebuilt about 200 years before it

happened. It is clear that these prophecies came from a God who knows the future.

45:1-8 This is the only place in the Bible where a Gentile ruler is called "anointed." God is the power over all powers, and he anoints whom he chooses for his special tasks. Cyrus' kingdom spread across 2,000 miles (the largest of any empire then known), including the territories of both the Assyrian and the Babylonian empires. Why did God anoint Cyrus? Because God had a special task for him to do for Israel. Cyrus would allow God's city, Jerusalem, to be rebuilt, and he would set the exiles free without expecting anything in return. Few kings of Israel or Judah had done as much for God's people as Cyrus would.

45:7 God tells us that he sends the good times and the bad. Our lives are sprinkled with both types of experiences, and both are needed for us to grow spiritually. When good times come, thank God and use your prosperity for him. When bad times come, don't resent them, but ask what you can learn from this refining experience to make you a better servant of God.

45:11
Ezek 39:7

45:12
Neh 9:6
Jer 27:5

45:13
2 Chron 36:22,
23
Isa 52:3

45:14
Isa 14:1,2
49:23
1 Cor 14:25

45:16
Isa 44:11

45:17
Isa 51:6

45:18
Gen 1:2,26
Ps 115:16
Isa 42:5

45:19
2 Chron 15:2
Isa 43:12
Jer 29:13,14

45:20
Isa 44:18,19
46:6,7
Jer 10:5

45:21
Isa 43:3,11
44:7

45:22
Num 21:8,9
Isa 52:10
Mic 7:7

45:23
Rom 14:11

45:25
Isa 53:11

46:1
Isa 21:9
Jer 43:12,13
51:44

46:3
Isa 10:21,22

46:5
Isa 40:18,25

46:6
Isa 44:12-17

46:7
Isa 40:20
Jer 10:5

11Jehovah, the Holy One of Israel, Israel's Creator, says: What right have you to question what I do? Who are you to command me concerning the work of my hands? 12I have made the earth and created man upon it. With my hands I have stretched out the heavens and commanded all the vast myriads of stars. 13I have raised up Cyrus to fulfill my righteous purpose, and I will direct all his paths. He shall restore my city and free my captive people—and not for a reward!

14Jehovah says: The Egyptians, Ethiopians and Sabeans shall be subject to you. They shall come to you with all their merchandise and it shall all be yours. They shall follow you as prisoners in chains, and fall down on their knees before you and say, "The only God there is, is your God!"

15Truly, O God of Israel, Savior, you work in strange, mysterious ways. 16All who worship idols shall be disappointed and ashamed. 17But Israel shall be saved by Jehovah with eternal salvation; they shall never be disappointed in their God through all eternity. 18For Jehovah created the heavens and earth and put everything in place, and he made the world to be lived in, not to be an empty chaos. I am Jehovah, he says, and there is no other! 19I publicly proclaim bold promises; I do not whisper obscurities in some dark corner so that no one can know what I mean. And I didn't tell Israel to ask me for what I didn't plan to give! No, for I, Jehovah, speak only truth and righteousness.

20Gather together and come, you nations that escape from Cyrus' hand. What fools they are who carry around the wooden idols and pray to gods that cannot save! 21Consult together, argue your case and state your proofs that idol-worship pays! Who but God has said that these things concerning Cyrus would come true? What idol ever told you they would happen? For there is no other God but me—a just God and a Savior—no, not one! 22Let all the world look to me for salvation! For I am God; there is no other. 23I have sworn by myself and I will never go back on my word, for it is true—that every knee in all the world shall bow to me, and every tongue shall swear allegiance to my name.

24"In Jehovah is all my righteousness and strength," the people shall declare. And all who were angry with him shall come to him and be ashamed. 25In Jehovah all the generations of Israel shall be justified, triumphant.

The false gods of Babylon

46 The idols of Babylon, Bel and Nebo, are being hauled away on ox carts! But look! The beasts are stumbling! The cart is turning over! The gods are falling out onto the ground! Is that the best that they can do? If they cannot even save themselves from such a fall, how can they save their worshipers from Cyrus?

3"Listen to me, all Israel who are left; I have created you and cared for you since you were born. 4I will be your God through all your lifetime, yes, even when your hair is white with age. I made you and I will care for you. I will carry you along and be your Savior.

5"With what in all of heaven and earth do I compare? Whom can you find who equals me? 6Will you compare me with an idol made lavishly with silver and with gold? They hire a goldsmith to take your wealth and make a god from it! Then they fall down and worship it! 7They carry it around on their shoulders, and when they

45:13 *I have raised up Cyrus,* literally, "I have raised up him...." The reference probably is also to Christ in the more distant future, as well as to Cyrus.

45:17 Until this time, Israel had heard of temporal salvation—God would save them from their enemies. Now Isaiah tells of eternal salvation with God.

45:18, 19 God's promises are public, and their fulfillment is sure. So why do we ever doubt him? We never have to be uncertain when we have a God of truth and righteousness.

45:22 Salvation is for everyone, not just the Israelites. Many times it seems as though Israel had an inside track on salvation. But God makes it clear that his people are *all* those who follow him. Israel was to be the means through which the whole world would come to know God. Jesus, the Messiah, fulfilled Israel's role and gave all

people the opportunity to follow God. (See also Romans 11:11; Galatians 3:28; Ephesians 3:6; Philippians 2:10.)

46:1–4 Cyrus would carry out God's judgment against Babylon. Bel (Marduk) was the chief deity of the Babylonians; Nebo (Nabu) was the god of the royal family. These "gods," however, needed men to carry them around and could not even save themselves from falling from a cart! They had no power at all. In contrast to gods who helplessly fall off carts and must be hauled around by men, our God created us and cares for us. His love is so enduring that he will care for us throughout our lifetime and even through death.

set it down it stays there, for it cannot move! And when someone prays to it there is no answer, for it cannot get him out of his trouble.

8"Don't forget this, O guilty ones. 9And don't forget the many times I clearly told you what was going to happen in the future. For I am God—I only—and there is no other like me 10who can tell you what is going to happen. All I say will come to pass, for I do whatever I wish. 11I will call that swift bird of prey from the east—that man Cyrus from far away. And he will come and do my bidding. I have said I would do it and I will. 12Listen to me, you stubborn, evil men! 13For I am offering you my deliverance; not in the distant future, but right now! I am ready to save you, and I will restore Jerusalem, and Israel, who is my glory.

46:9
Isa 41:26,27
42:9
46:10
Acts 5:39
46:11
Num 23:19
46:12
Zech 7:11,12
46:13
Isa 51:5; 61:3

A prophecy of doom for Babylon

47 "O Babylon, the unconquered, come sit in the dust; for your days of glory, pomp and honor are ended. O daughter of Chaldea, never again will you be the lovely princess, tender and delicate. 2Take heavy millstones and grind the corn; remove your veil; strip off your robe; expose yourself to public view. 3You shall be in nakedness and shame. I will take vengeance upon you and will not repent."

47:1
Jer 48:18

47:2
Gen 24:65
1 Cor 11:5
47:3
Isa 63:4

4So speaks our Redeemer, who will save Israel from Babylon's mighty power; the Lord Almighty is his name, the Holy One of Israel.

5Sit in darkness and silence, O Babylon; never again will you be called "The Queen of Kingdoms." 6For I was angry with my people Israel and began to punish them a little by letting them fall into your hands, O Babylon. But you showed them no mercy. You have made even the old folks carry heavy burdens. 7You thought your reign would never end, Queen Kingdom of the world. You didn't care a whit about my people or think about the fate of those who do them harm.

47:5
Lam 2:10
Dan 2:37
47:6
Deut 28:50
Zech 1:15

8O pleasure-mad kingdom, living at ease, bragging as the greatest in the world—listen to the sentence of my court upon your sins. You say, "I alone am God! I'll never be a widow; I'll never lose my children." 9Well, those two things shall come upon you in one moment, in full measure in one day: widowhood and the loss of your children, despite all your witchcraft and magic.

47:8
Isa 22:13
32:9,11
Rev 18:7
47:9
Isa 13:16
1 Thess 5:2,3
Rev 18:8,10,23

10You felt secure in all your wickedness. "No one sees me," you said. Your "wisdom" and "knowledge" have caused you to turn away from me and claim that you yourself are Jehovah. 11That is why disaster shall overtake you suddenly—so suddenly that you won't know where it comes from. And there will be no atonement then to cleanse away your sins.

47:10
Ps 52:7
Isa 5:21
Ezek 8:12
47:11
Jer 51:8,43

12Call out the demon hordes you've worshiped all these years. Call on them to help you strike deep terror into many hearts again. 13You have advisors by the ton—your astrologers and stargazers, who try to tell you what the future holds. 14But they are as useless as dried grass burning in the fire. They cannot even deliver themselves! You'll get no help from them at all. Theirs is no fire to sit beside to

47:13
Isa 8:19
47:14
Jer 51:30,32,58
Nah 1:10

47:2 *remove your veil.* In ancient Babylonia (and in many eastern lands today) only harlots were permitted to go without veils.

46:13 Much of the book of Isaiah speaks of a future deliverance when we will all live with God in perfect peace. God offers not only this future hope, but also help for our present needs.

47:1ff Isaiah predicted the fall of Babylon more than 150 years before it happened. At this time, Babylon had not yet emerged as the mightiest force on earth. When that occurred, they destroyed Judah and Jerusalem. But the Babylonians, Judah's captors, would become captives themselves in 539 B.C. God, the Redeemer, not Babylon, has the ultimate power. He used Babylon to punish his sinful people; he would use Medo-Persia to destroy Babylon and free his people.

47:8, 9 Caught up in the pursuit of power and pleasure, Babylon believed in its own greatness and claimed to be the *only* power on earth. Babylon felt completely secure. Nebuchadnezzar, its king, called himself "god," but the true God taught him a powerful lesson by taking everything away from him (Daniel 4:27-37). Our society

is addicted to pleasure and power, but these can quickly pass away. Look at your own life and ask yourself how you can be more responsible with the talents and possessions God has given you. How can you use your life for God's honor rather than for your own?

47:10 The wealth that comes from wickedness gives a false sense of security. Knowledge can also deceive people into feeling that they don't need others. In times of plenty we may think we don't even need God. Yet our wisdom and wealth will never give us what God can give. Remind yourself to rely on his wisdom for true wealth.

47:12-15 The people of Babylon sought advice and help from astrologers, stargazers, and childhood friends. But like the idols of wood or gold, they could not even deliver themselves. Why rely on those who are powerless? The helpless cannot help us. If you want help, find it in God, who has proven his power in creation and in history.

make you warm! 15And all your friends of childhood days shall slip away and disappear, unable to help.

There is no peace for the wicked

48 Hear me, my people: you swear allegiance to the Lord without meaning a word of it, when you boast of living in the Holy City and brag about depending on the God of Israel. 3Time and again I told you what was going to happen in the future. My words were scarcely spoken when suddenly I did just what I said. 4I knew how hard and obstinate you are. Your necks are as unbending as iron; you are as hardheaded as brass. 5That is why I told you ahead of time what I was going to do, so that you could never say, "My idol did it; my carved image commanded it to happen!" 6You have heard my predictions and seen them fulfilled, but you refuse to agree it is so. Now I will tell you new things I haven't mentioned before, secrets you haven't heard.

7Then you can't say, "We knew that all the time!"

8Yes, I'll tell you things entirely new, for I know so well what traitors you are, rebels from earliest childhood, rotten through and through. 9Yet for my own sake and for the honor of my name I will hold back my anger and not wipe you out. 10I refined you in the furnace of affliction, but found no silver there. You are worthless, with nothing good in you at all. 11Yet for my own sake—yes, *for my own sake*—I will save you from my anger and not destroy you lest the heathen say their gods have conquered me. I will not let them have my glory.

12Listen to me, my people, my chosen ones! I alone am God. I am the First; I am the Last. 13It was my hand that laid the foundations of the earth; the palm of my right hand spread out the heavens above; I spoke and they came into being.

14Come, all of you, and listen. Among all your idols, which one has ever told you this: "The Lord loves Cyrus. He will use him to put an end to the empire of Babylonia. He will utterly rout the armies of the Chaldeans"? 15But I am saying it. I have called Cyrus; I have sent him on this errand and I will prosper him.

48:1 Isa 45:23; 52:1 Rom 2:17
48:3 Josh 21:45 Isa 42:9
48:4 Ezek 2:4
48:5 Jer 44:15-18
48:6 Isa 43:19
48:8 Deut 9:7,24 Ps 58:3
48:9 Ps 103:8-10
48:10 1 Kgs 8:51 Ezek 22:18-22
48:11 Deut 32:26,27 Ps 106:8 Isa 42:8
48:12 Deut 32:39
48:13 Ps 102:25
48:14 Jer 50:21-29
48:15 Isa 41:2; 45:1,2

MAJOR IDOLS MENTIONED IN THE BIBLE	Name	Where they were worshiped	What they stood for	What the worship included
	Bel (Marduk)	Babylon	Weather, War, Sun god	Prostitution, child sacrifice
	Nebo (Son of Marduk)	Babylon	Learning, astronomy, science	
	Ashtoreth (Asherah)	Canaan	Goddess of love, childbirth, and fertility	Prostitution
	Chemosh	Moab		Child sacrifice
	Molech	Ammon	National god	Child sacrifice
	Baal	Canaan	Rain, harvest, symbolized strength and fertility	Prostitution
	Dagon	Philistia	Harvest, grain, success in farming	Child sacrifice

48:1 The Israelites felt confident because they lived in Jerusalem, the city with God's Temple. They depended on their heritage, their city, and their Temple—but this was false security because they did not depend on God. Do you feel secure because you go to church or live in a certain country? Heritage, buildings, or nations cannot give us a relationship with God; we must truly depend on him personally, with all our hearts and minds.

48:9–11 When God refined Israel in the furnace of affliction, he said, "I can find no silver; you are worthless." There was nothing in Israel's actions, attitudes, or accomplishments to compel God to love and to save them. But for his own sake, to show who he is and

what he can do, he saved them. God does not save us because we are good, but because he loves us and because of his forgiving nature.

48:14, 15 When Isaiah proclaimed, "The Lord loves Cyrus," this must have shocked his audience. How could the Lord love a pagan king, an enemy? But it was Cyrus whom God would use to free his people from their captivity in Babylon. Cyrus' errand was to set Israel free by conquering Babylon, then to decree that all Jews could return to their homeland. Who but a prophet of God could tell such an inconceivable but true story almost 200 years before it happened?

16Come closer and listen. I have always told you plainly what would happen, so that you could clearly understand. And now the Lord God and his Spirit have sent me (with this message):

48:16
Isa 45:19

17The Lord, your Redeemer, the Holy One of Israel, says, I am the Lord your God, who punishes you for your own good and leads you along the paths that you should follow.

48:17
Ps 32:8
Isa 41:14

18Oh, that you had listened to my laws! Then you would have had peace flowing like a gentle river, and great waves of righteousness. 19Then you would have become as numerous as the sands along the seashores of the world, too many to count, and there would have been no need for your destruction.

48:18
Deut 5:29
Ps 119:165
Amos 5:24
48:19
Gen 12:17

20Yet even now, be free from your captivity! Leave Babylon, singing as you go; shout to the ends of the earth that the Lord has redeemed his servants, the Jews. 21They were not thirsty when he led them through the deserts; he divided the rock, and water gushed out for them to drink. 22But there is no peace, says the Lord, for the wicked.

48:20
Isa 52:9
Jer 31:10
48:21
Ps 78:15,16
Mt 1:20,21

2. The future Redeemer

God's servant will be a light

49 Listen to me, all of you in far-off lands: The Lord called me before my birth. From within the womb he called me by my name. 2God will make my words of judgment sharp as swords. He has hidden me in the shadow of his hand; I am like a sharp arrow in his quiver.

49:2
Isa 51:16
Heb 4:12
Rev 1:16

3He said to me: "You are my Servant, a Prince of Power with God, and you shall bring me glory."

4I replied, "But my work for them seems all in vain; I have spent my strength for them without response. Yet I leave it all with God for my reward."

5"And now," said the Lord—the Lord who formed me from my mother's womb to serve him who commissioned me to restore to him his people Israel, who has given me the strength to perform this task and honored me for doing it!— 6"you shall do more than restore Israel to me. I will make you a Light to the nations of the world to bring my salvation to them too."

49:5
Isa 12:2
49:6
Ps 37:28
Acts 13:47
26:23

7The Lord, the Redeemer and Holy One of Israel, says to the one who is despised, rejected by mankind, and kept beneath the heel of the world's rulers: "Kings shall stand at attention when you pass by; princes shall bow low because the Lord has chosen you; he, the faithful Lord, the Holy One of Israel, chooses you."

49:7
Ps 22:6-8
Isa 53:3

The Lord will comfort his people

8, 9The Lord says, "Your request has come at a favorable time. I will keep you from harm and give you as a token and pledge to Israel, proof that I will reestablish the land of Israel and reassign it to its own people again. Through you I am saying to the prisoners of darkness, 'Come out! I am giving you your freedom!' They will be my sheep, grazing in green pastures and on the grassy hills. 10They shall neither hunger nor thirst; the searing sun and scorching desert winds will not reach them

49:8
Ps 69:13
Isa 26:3; 42:7
44:26
Lk 4:18
2 Cor 6:2
49:10
Ps 23:2
Rev 7:16

49:3 *a Prince of Power,* or, "Israel."

48:16 God's message has been told plainly and clearly, not in secret. We have a tendency to complicate God's message as we add to it. When God talks through his messenger, whomever he has chosen, our job is to listen. The closer we come to God, the better we can listen to what he says.

48:17, 18 Like a loving parent, God punishes us or corrects us for our own good. We should listen to him, because peace of mind and heart comes to us as we obey his Word. Disobedience invites punishment and threatens the peace of mind and heart we want so much.

48:20 Do you see the captives leaving Babylon many years later? No wonder they are singing, as their ancestors sang after they crossed the Red Sea, free from Egypt's slavery at last! What is holding you captive? Be free! The Lord has redeemed his servants

from the slavery of sin. When you let him free you from your captivity, you will feel like singing.

48:22 There is no peace for the wicked. Many people cry out for comfort, security, and relief, but they haven't taken the first steps to remove the sin in their lives and open channels to God. They have not sought to repent and trust in him. If you want true peace, seek God first. Then you will have it.

49:1–7 Before the Servant, the Messiah, was born, God had chosen him to bring the light of the gospel (the message of salvation) to the world (see Acts 13:47). Christ offered salvation to all nations, and the apostle Paul began the missionary movement to take this gospel to the ends of the earth. Missionary work today continues Jesus' Great Commission (Matthew 28:18–20), taking the light of the gospel to all nations.

any more. For the Lord in his mercy will lead them beside the cool waters. 11And I will make my mountains into level paths for them; the highways shall be raised above the valleys. 12See, my people shall return from far away, from north and west and south."

49:13
Isa 54:7,8,10
Rev 12:12

13Sing for joy, O heavens; shout, O earth. Break forth with song, O mountains, for the Lord has comforted his people, and will have compassion upon them in their sorrow.

14Yet they say, "My Lord deserted us; he has forgotten us."

49:16
Song 8:6

15"Never! Can a mother forget her little child and not have love for her own son? Yet even if that should be, I will not forget you. 16See, I have tattooed your name upon my palm and ever before me is a picture of Jerusalem's walls in ruins. 17Soon

49:18
Isa 45:23

your rebuilders shall come and chase away all those destroying you. 18Look and see, for the Lord has vowed that all your enemies shall come and be your slaves. They will be as jewels to display, as bridal ornaments.

49:19
Ps 56:1,2
Isa 1:7
Zech 10:10

19"Even the most desolate parts of your abandoned land shall soon be crowded with your people, and your enemies who enslaved you shall be far away. 20The generations born in exile shall return and say, 'We need more room! It's crowded

49:20
Isa 54:1-3

here!' 21Then you will think to yourself, 'Who has given me all these? For most of

49:21
Lam 1:1

my children were killed and the rest were carried away into exile, leaving me here alone. Who bore these? Who raised them for me?' "

49:22
Isa 11:10,12
14:2

22The Lord God says, "See, I will give a signal to the Gentiles and they shall carry your little sons back to you in their arms, and your daughters on their

49:23
Ps 25:3; 72:9
Isa 60:14,16

shoulders. 23Kings and queens shall serve you; they shall care for all your needs. They shall bow to the earth before you, and lick the dust from off your feet; then you shall know I am the Lord. Those who wait for me shall never be ashamed."

49:25
Jer 50:33,34

24Who can snatch the prey from the hands of a mighty man? Who can demand that a tyrant let his captives go? 25But the Lord says, "Even the captives of the most

49:26
Isa 14:4
Ezek 39:7

mighty and most terrible shall all be freed; for I will fight those who fight you, and I will save your children. 26I will feed your enemies with their own flesh and they shall be drunk with rivers of their own blood. All the world shall know that I, the Lord, am your Savior and Redeemer, the Mighty One of Israel."

God's servant obeys

50:1
Deut 32:30
Isa 59:2
Jer 3:8

50 The Lord asks, Did I sell you to my creditors? Is that why you aren't here? Is your mother gone because I divorced her and sent her away? No, you went away as captives because of your sins. And your mother, too, was taken in payment

50:2
Gen 18:14
Ex 14:21
Josh 3:16

for your sins. 2Was I too weak to save you? Is that why the house is silent and empty when I come home? Have I no longer power to deliver? No, that is not the reason! For I can rebuke the sea and make it dry! I can turn the rivers into deserts,

50:3
Rev 6:12

covered with dying fish. 3I am the one who sends the darkness out across the skies.

50:4
Ps 5:3
Jer 31:25

4The Lord God has given me his words of wisdom so that I may know what I should say to all these weary ones. Morning by morning he wakens me and opens my understanding to his will. 5The Lord God has spoken to me and I have listened;

50:5
Mt 26:39
Heb 5:8

I do not rebel nor turn away. 6I give my back to the whip, and my cheeks to those

50:6
Mk 15:19

who pull out the beard. I do not hide from shame—they spit in my face.

50:7
Ezek 3:8,9

7Because the Lord God helps me, I will not be dismayed; therefore, I have set my face like flint to do his will, and I know that I will triumph. 8He who gives me justice is near. Who will dare to fight against me now? Where are my enemies? Let

---

49:14, 15 The people of Israel felt that God had deserted them in Babylon; but Isaiah points out that God would never leave them, as a mother would not leave her little child. When we feel that God has deserted us, we must ask if we have deserted God.

49:24, 25 God would prove to the world that he is God by doing the impossible—causing a captor to set his captives free, and even helping them leave. He had done this before at the Exodus and would do it again when the exiles returned to Israel. Never should we doubt that God will fulfill his promises.

50:2 God promised to fight for Israel, but Israel sold itself into sin. Israel had caused its own problems. The people of Israel forgot God and trusted in other countries to help them. God did not reject Israel, but Israel rejected God.

50:6-11 This is a picture of the ultimate Servant, the Messiah. The prophet speaks for God, but the Messiah reveals God perfectly (Hebrews 1:1, 2).

them appear! 9See, the Lord God is for me! Who shall declare me guilty? All my **50:9** Isa 54:17
enemies shall be destroyed like old clothes eaten up by moths!

10Who among you fears the Lord and obeys his Servant? If such men walk in **50:10** Eph 5:8
darkness, without one ray of light, let them trust the Lord, let them rely upon their
God. 11But see here, you who live in your own light, and warm yourselves from **50:11** Isa 65:13-15
your own fires and not from God's; you will live among sorrows.

The people must fear God

51 Listen to me, all who hope for deliverance, who seek the Lord! Consider the **51:1** Gen 12:1 17:15-17 Heb 11:11,12
quarry from which you were mined, the rock from which you were cut! Yes,
think about your ancestors Abraham and Sarah, from whom you came. You worry
at being so small and few, but Abraham was only *one* when I called him. But when
I blessed him, he became a great nation. 3And the Lord will bless Israel again, and **51:3** Gen 2:8 Isa 41:19
make her deserts blossom; her barren wilderness will become as beautiful as the
Garden of Eden. Joy and gladness will be found there, thanksgiving and lovely
songs.

4Listen to me, my people; listen, O Israel, for I will see that right prevails. 5My **51:4** Ps 78:1 Isa 42:4
mercy and justice are coming soon; your salvation is on the way. I will rule the
nations; they shall wait for me and long for me to come. 6Look high in the skies and **51:5** Isa 46:13
watch the earth beneath, for the skies shall disappear like smoke, the earth shall **51:6** Ps 102:25,26 2 Pet 3:10
wear out like a garment, and the people of the earth shall die like flies. But my
salvation lasts forever; my righteous rule will never die nor end.

7Listen to me, you who know the right from wrong and cherish my laws in your **51:7** Ps 37:30,31 Mt 5:11 Acts 5:40,41
hearts: don't be afraid of people's scorn or their slanderous talk. 8For the moth shall
destroy them like garments; the worm shall eat them like wool; but my justice and **51:8** Isa 14:11
mercy shall last forever, and my salvation from generation to generation.

9Awake, O Lord! Rise up and robe yourself with strength. Rouse yourself as in **51:9** Deut 4:34
the days of old when you slew Egypt, the dragon of the Nile. 10Are you not the
same today, the mighty God who dried up the sea, making a path right through it **51:10** Ex 14:21,22 Isa 63:11,12
for your ransomed ones? 11The time will come when God's redeemed will all come
home again. They shall come with singing to Jerusalem, filled with joy and **51:11** Isa 61:7 Rev 21:4
everlasting gladness; sorrow and mourning will all disappear.

12I, even I, am he who comforts you and gives you all this joy. So what right **51:12** Ps 118:6
have you to fear mere mortal men, who wither like the grass and disappear? 13And **51:13** Deut 8:11 Job 9:8
yet you have no fear of God, your Maker—you have forgotten him, the one who
spread the stars throughout the skies and made the earth. Will you be in constant
dread of men's oppression, and fear their anger all day long? 14Soon, soon you **51:14** Isa 49:10
slaves shall be released; dungeon, starvation and death are not your fate. 15For I am **51:15** Ps 107:25
the Lord your God, the Lord Almighty, who dried a path for you right through the
sea, between the roaring waves. 16And I have put my words in your mouth and **51:16** Ex 33:22 Deut 18:18
hidden you safe within my hand. I planted the stars in place and molded all the
earth. I am the one who says to Israel, "You are mine."

51:9 Egypt, the dragon, literally, "Rahab, the dragon."

50:10, 11 If we warm ourselves "from our own fires and not from God's" we become self-sufficient, and the result of self-sufficiency is sorrow. When we place confidence in our own intelligence, appearance, or accomplishments, we risk deep sorrow later when these strengths fade.

51:1, 2 The faithful remnant felt alone because they were few. But God reminded them of their ancestors, the source of their spiritual heritage—Abraham and Sarah. Abraham was only one person, but much came from his faithfulness. If the faithful few would remain faithful, even more could come from them. If we Christians, even a faithful few, remain faithful, think what God can do through us!

51:7 Isaiah encouraged those who serve God to discern right from wrong and follow God's laws. He also gave them hope when they faced people's scorn or slander because of their faith. We need not fear when people ridicule us for our faith, because God is

with us and truth will prevail. If people make fun of you or dislike you because you believe in God, remember that they are not against you personally, but against God. He will deal with them; you should concentrate on loving and obeying him.

51:10 God performed many powerful miracles in founding Israel, perhaps none were more exciting than the parting of the Red Sea (Exodus 14). Our God is the very God who made a path through the sea. His methods may change, but his love and care do not.

51:12–16 Jerusalem feared Assyria, but not God. It had reason to fear Assyria for the harm it wanted to do, but it should also have realized that God's power is much greater than Assyria's. Assyria was interested in making the people captives; God was interested in setting them free. The people had misplaced their fear and their love. Jerusalem should have feared God's power and loved his mercy and grace.

51:17
Jer 25:15

51:18
Ps 142:4

51:20
Isa 66:15
Jer 14:16

51:22
Jer 50:34

51:23
Jer 25:15-17
26,28

17Wake up, wake up, Jerusalem! You have drunk enough from the cup of the fury of the Lord. You have drunk to the dregs the cup of terror and squeezed out the last drops. 18Not one of her sons is left alive to help or tell her what to do. 19These two things have been your lot: desolation and destruction. Yes, famine and the sword. And who is left to sympathize? Who is left to comfort you? 20For your sons have fainted and lie in the streets, helpless as wild goats caught in a net. The Lord has poured out his fury and rebuke upon them. 21But listen now to this, afflicted ones—full of troubles and in a stupor (but not from being drunk)— 22this is what the Lord says, the Lord your God who cares for his people: "See, I take from your hands the terrible cup; you shall drink no more of my fury; it is gone at last. 23But I will put that terrible cup into the hands of those who tormented you and trampled your souls to the dust and walked upon your backs."

The Lord will bring his people home

52:1
Ex 28:2,40
Neh 11:1
Isa 48:2; 61:10

52:3
Ps 44:12
Isa 63:4

52:5
Ezek 36:20,23

52 Wake up, wake up, Jerusalem, and clothe yourselves with strength [from God]. Put on your beautiful clothes, O Zion, Holy City; for sinners—those who turn from God—will no longer enter your gates. 2Rise from the dust, Jerusalem; take off the slave bands from your neck, O captive daughter of Zion. 3For the Lord says, When I sold you into exile I asked no fee from your oppressors; now I can take you back again and owe them not a cent! 4My people were tyrannized without cause by Egypt and Assyria, and I delivered them.

5And now, what is this? asks the Lord. Why are my people enslaved again, and oppressed without excuse? Those who rule them shout in exultation, and my name is constantly blasphemed, day by day. 6Therefore I will reveal my name to my people and they shall know the power in that name. Then at last they will recognize that it is I, yes, I, who speaks to them.

52:7
Ps 93:1
Rom 10:15

52:8
Isa 62:6

52:9
Ps 98:4
Isa 61:4

52:10
Ps 98:1-3
Lk 3:6

52:11
Isa 1:16
2 Cor 6:17

52:12
Ex 12:11,33
14:19,20
Isa 26:7

7How beautiful upon the mountains are the feet of those who bring the happy news of peace and salvation, the news that the God of Israel reigns. 8The watchmen shout and sing with joy, for right before their eyes they see the Lord God bring his people home again. 9Let the ruins of Jerusalem break into joyous song, for the Lord has comforted his people; he has redeemed Jerusalem. 10The Lord has bared his holy arm before the eyes of all the nations; the ends of the earth shall see the salvation of our God.

11Go now, leave your bonds and slavery. Put Babylon and all it represents far behind you—it is unclean to you. You are the holy people of the Lord; purify yourselves, all you who carry home the vessels of the Lord. 12You shall not leave in haste, running for your lives; for the Lord will go ahead of you, and he, the God of Israel, will protect you from behind.

God's servant will be despised

52:13
Phil 2:9

52:14
Ps 22:6,7
Rom 15:21

13See, my Servant shall prosper; he shall be highly exalted. 14, 15Yet many shall be amazed when they see him—yes, even far-off foreign nations and their kings; they shall stand dumbfounded, speechless in his presence. For they shall see and understand what they had not been told before. They shall see my Servant beaten and bloodied, so disfigured one would scarcely know it was a person standing there. So shall he cleanse many nations.

52:1 *from God,* implied. **52:15** *So shall he cleanse many nations,* or, "So shall he startle many nations." The meaning of the Hebrew word is uncertain.

51:17—52:10 Jerusalem was God's holy city, the city with God's Temple. But the people of Judah experienced desolation instead of prosperity, destruction instead of liberty. Because of their sins, the people suffered. But God promised to restore Jerusalem as a holy city where sinners cannot enter. God reigns. He is in control.

52:12 The people did not leave in fearful haste because Cyrus, God's anointed (45:1), decreed that the Jewish exiles could return

safely to Jerusalem (Ezra 1:1–4). They had the king's approval, his guaranteed protection. God was protecting them.

52:13 The Servant of the Lord, as the term is used here, is the Messiah, our Lord Jesus. He would be highly exalted because of his sacrifice, described in chapter 53.

52:14, 15 This Servant, Christ, will be "beaten and bloodied"; but through his suffering, he will cleanse the nations (1 Peter 1:2).

53

But, oh, how few believe it! Who will listen? To whom will God reveal his saving power? [2]In God's eyes he was like a tender green shoot, sprouting from a root in dry and sterile ground. But in our eyes there was no attractiveness at all, nothing to make us want him. [3]We despised him and rejected him—a man of sorrows, acquainted with bitterest grief. We turned our backs on him and looked the other way when he went by. He was despised and we didn't care.

[4]Yet it was *our* grief he bore, *our* sorrows that weighed him down. And we thought his troubles were a punishment from God, for his *own* sins! [5]But he was wounded and bruised for *our* sins. He was beaten that we might have peace; he was lashed—and we were healed! [6]*We*—every one of us—have strayed away like sheep! *We*, who left God's paths to follow our own. Yet God laid on *him* the guilt and sins of every one of us!

[7]He was oppressed and he was afflicted, yet he never said a word. He was brought as a lamb to the slaughter; and as a sheep before her shearers is dumb, so he stood silent before the ones condemning him. [8]From prison and trial they led him away to his death. But who among the people of that day realized it was their sins that he was dying for—that he was suffering their punishment? [9]He was buried like a criminal, but in a rich man's grave; but he had done no wrong, and had never spoken an evil word.

[10]But it was the Lord's good plan to bruise him and fill him with grief. However when his soul has been made an offering for sin, then he shall have a multitude of children, many heirs. He shall live again and God's program shall prosper in his hands. [11]And when he sees all that is accomplished by the anguish of his soul, he shall be satisfied; and because of what he has experienced, my righteous Servant shall make many to be counted righteous before God, for he shall bear all their sins. [12]Therefore I will give him the honors of one who is mighty and great, because he has poured out his soul unto death. He was counted as a sinner, and he bore the sins of many, and he pled with God for sinners.

53:1
Jn 12:38
Rom 10:16

53:2
Isa 11:1

53:3
Ps 22:6
Lk 18:31-33

53:4
Mt 8:17
Jn 19:7

53:5
1 Cor 15:3
Heb 5:8; 9:28
1 Pet 2:24,25

53:7
Mt 27:12-14
Lk 23:9
Acts 8:32,33

53:9
Mt 27:57-60
1 Pet 2:22

53:10
Ps 22:30
Jn 1:29

53:11
Jn 10:14-18
Rom 5:18,19

53:12
Mt 26:38,39,42
Lk 22:37
2 Cor 5:21
Phil 2:9-11

Israel will be rebuilt

54

Sing, O childless woman! Break out into loud and joyful song, Jerusalem, for she who was abandoned has more blessings now than she whose husband stayed! [2]Enlarge your house; build on additions; spread out your home! [3]For you

54:1
Isa 62:4
Gal 4:27

53:2 *In God's eyes,* literally, "before him." **53:10** *He shall live again,* literally, "He shall prolong his days." **54:1** *Jerusalem,* implied. *blessings,* literally, "children."

53:1ff This chapter speaks of the Messiah, Jesus, who would suffer for the sins of all people. Such a prophecy is astounding! Who would believe that God would choose to save the world through a humble, suffering Servant rather than a glorious king? The idea is contrary to humanistic pride and worldly ways. But God often works in ways we don't expect. The Messiah's strength is shown by humility, suffering, and mercy.

53:2 There was nothing in the physical appearance of this Servant that was attractive. But even though Jesus was not physically attractive, he brought salvation and healing. Are you attracted most by outer appearance or by inner character?

53:3 This man of sorrows was rejected by those around him, and he is still rejected by many today. Some reject him by standing against him. Others ignore him and his great gift of forgiveness. Do you reject him, ignore him, or accept him?

53:4, 5 How could an Old Testament person understand the idea of Christ dying for our sins—actually taking our sins as his own? The sacrifices suggested this idea, but it is one thing to kill a lamb, but something quite different to think of God's Chosen Servant as that Lamb. But God was pulling aside the curtain of time to let the people of Isaiah's day look ahead to the suffering of the future Messiah and the resulting forgiveness made available to all of mankind.

53:6 Isaiah speaks of Israel straying from God and likens them to wandering sheep. Yet God will send the Messiah to bring them

back into the fold. We have the hindsight to see and know the identity of the promised Messiah, who has come and died for our sins. But if we can see all that Jesus did and still reject him, we have a much greater sin than that of the ancient Israelites, who could not see what we have seen. Have you given your life to Jesus Christ, the "Good Shepherd" (John 10:11–16), or are you still like a wandering sheep?

53:7–12 In the Old Testament, people offered animals as sacrifices for their sins. Here, the sinless Servant of the Lord offers himself for our sins. He is the Lamb (53:7) offered for the sins of all people (John 1:29; Revelation 5:6–14). The Messiah suffered for our sakes, bearing our sins to make us acceptable to God. What can we say to such love? How will we respond to him?

53:11 "Make many to be counted righteous" tells of the enormous family of believers who will become righteous, not by their own works, but by the Messiah's great work on the cross. They are counted righteous because they have claimed Christ, the Righteous One, as their Savior and Lord (see Romans 5:18; 2 Corinthians 5:21). Their life of sin is stripped away, and they are clothed with Christ's goodness.

54:1 To be childless at that time was a woman's great shame, a disgrace. Families depended on children for survival, especially when the parents became elderly. Israel was unfruitful, like a childless woman, but God would permit her to have many children and change her mourning into singing.

54:3
Gen 28:14
Isa 14:1,2

54:5
Hos 2:19

54:6
Isa 62:4

54:7
Isa 11:12

54:8
Isa 49:10,13
60:10

54:9
Gen 9:9-11
Ezek 39:29

54:10
2 Sam 23:5
Ps 89:34
102:25,26

54:11
Isa 28:16

54:13
Isa 66:12
Jer 31:34

54:14
Isa 9:4,7

54:15
Isa 41:11-16

54:17
Isa 29:8

will soon be bursting at the seams! And your descendants will possess the cities left behind during the exile, and rule the nations that took their lands.

4Fear not; you will no longer live in shame. The shame of your youth and the sorrows of widowhood will be remembered no more, 5for your Creator will be your "husband." The Lord Almighty is his name; he is your Redeemer, the Holy One of Israel, the God of all the earth. 6For the Lord has called you back from your grief—a young wife abandoned by her husband. 7For a brief moment I abandoned you. But with great compassion I will take you back. 8In a moment of anger I turned my face a little while; but with everlasting love I will have pity on you, says the Lord, your Redeemer.

9Just as in the time of Noah I swore that I would never again permit the waters of a flood to cover the earth and destroy its life, so now I swear that I will never again pour out my anger on you. 10For the mountains may depart and the hills disappear, but my kindness shall not leave you. My promise of peace for you will never be broken, says the Lord who has mercy upon you.

11O my afflicted people, tempest-tossed and troubled, I will rebuild you on a foundation of sapphires and make the walls of your houses from precious jewels. 12I will make your towers of sparkling agate, and your gates and walls of shining gems. 13And all your citizens shall be taught by me, and their prosperity shall be great. 14You will live under a government that is just and fair. Your enemies will stay far away; you will live in peace. Terror shall not come near. 15If any nation comes to fight you, it will not be sent by me to punish you. Therefore it will be routed, for I am on your side. 16I have created the smith who blows the coals beneath the forge and makes the weapons of destruction. And I have created the armies that destroy. 17But in that coming day, no weapon turned against you shall succeed, and you will have justice against every courtroom lie. This is the heritage of the servants of the Lord. This is the blessing I have given you, says the Lord.

Blessings for those who seek him

55:1
Ps 63:1
Mt 10:8
Jn 4:14

55:2
Ps 22:26
Eccles 6:2

55:3
Acts 13:34
Rom 10:5

55:5
Zech 8:22

55:6
Ps 32:6
2 Cor 6:1,2

55:7
Isa 1:16; 44:22

55 Say there! Is anyone thirsty? Come and drink—even if you have no money! Come, take your choice of wine and milk—it's all free! 2Why spend your money on food that doesn't give you strength? Why pay for groceries that do you no good? Listen and I'll tell you where to get good food that fattens up the soul!

3Come to me with your ears wide open. Listen, for the life of your soul is at stake. I am ready to make an everlasting covenant with you, to give you all the unfailing mercies and love that I had for King David. 4He proved my power by conquering foreign nations. 5You also will command the nations and they will come running to obey, not because of your own power or virtue but because I, the Lord your God, have glorified you.

6Seek the Lord while you can find him. Call upon him now while he is near. 7Let men cast off their wicked deeds; let them banish from their minds the very thought

54:15 *for I am on your side,* literally, "because of you."   **55:4** *foreign nations,* implied.

54:6–8 God says that he has abandoned Israel for a brief time, so she is like a young wife abandoned by her husband. But he still calls Israel his own. The God we serve is holy, and he cannot tolerate sin. When Israel blatantly sinned, God in his anger chose to punish her. Sin separates us from God and brings us pain and suffering. But if we confess our sin and repent, God forgives us. Have you ever been separated from a loved one and then experienced joy when that person returned? You can experience the same joy when you repent and return to God.

54:9, 10 God made a promise to Noah that he never broke (Genesis 9:8–17). Likewise, God promised Israel that the time would come when he would cease to rebuke her, would restore her wealth, and would personally teach her children.

55:1–6 Food costs money, lasts only a short time, and meets only physical needs. But God offers us *free* nourishment that feeds our soul. How do we get it? We come (55:1), listen (55:3), seek, and call upon God (55:6). God's salvation is freely offered, but to

nourish our souls, we must eagerly receive it. We will starve spiritually without this food as surely as we will starve physically without our daily bread.

55:3 God's covenant with King David promised a permanent homeland for the Israelites, no threat from heathen nations, and no wars (2 Samuel 7:10, 11). But Israel did not fulfill its part of the covenant by obeying God and staying away from idols. Even so, God was ready to renew his covenant again. He is a forgiving God!

55:6 Isaiah tells us to call upon the Lord while he is near. God is not planning to move away from us, but we often move far from him or erect a barrier between ourselves and him. Don't wait until you have drifted away from God to seek him. Later in life turning to him may be far more difficult. Or God may come to judge the earth before you decide to seek him. Do it now while you can, before it is too late.

of doing wrong! Let them turn to the Lord that he may have mercy upon them, and to our God, for he will abundantly pardon! 8This plan of mine is not what you would work out, neither are my thoughts the same as yours! 9For just as the heavens are higher than the earth, so are my ways higher than yours, and my thoughts than yours.

10As the rain and snow come down from heaven and stay upon the ground to water the earth, and cause the grain to grow and to produce seed for the farmer and bread for the hungry, 11so also is my Word. I send it out and it always produces fruit. It shall accomplish all I want it to, and prosper everywhere I send it. 12You will live in joy and peace. The mountains and hills, the trees of the field—all the world around you—will rejoice. 13Where once were thorns, fir trees will grow; where briars grew, the myrtle trees will sprout up. This miracle will make the Lord's name very great and be an everlasting sign [of God's power and love].

Blessings for the Gentiles

56 Be just and fair to all, the Lord God says. Do what's right and good, for I am coming soon to rescue you. 2Blessed is the man who refuses to work during my Sabbath days of rest, but honors them; and blessed is the man who checks himself from doing wrong.

3And my blessings are for Gentiles, too, when they accept the Lord; don't let them think that I will make them second-class citizens. And this is for the eunuchs too. They can be as much mine as anyone. 4For I say this to the eunuchs who keep my Sabbaths holy and choose the things that please me, and obey my laws: 5I will give them—in my house, within my walls—a name far greater than the honor they would receive from having sons and daughters. For the name that I will give them is an everlasting one; it will never disappear.

6As for the Gentiles, the outsiders who join the people of the Lord and serve him and love his name, and are his servants and don't desecrate the Sabbath, and have accepted his covenant and promises, 7I will bring them also to my holy mountain of Jerusalem, and make them full of joy within my House of Prayer.

I will accept their sacrifices and offerings, for my Temple shall be called "A House of Prayer for All People"! 8For the Lord God who brings back the outcasts of Israel says, I will bring others too besides my people Israel.

9Come, wild animals of the field; come, tear apart the sheep; come, wild animals of the forest, devour my people. 10For the leaders of my people—the Lord's watchmen, his shepherds—are all blind to every danger. They are featherbrained and give no warning when danger comes. They love to lie there, love to sleep, to dream. 11And they are as greedy as dogs, never satisfied; they are stupid shepherds who only look after their own interest, each trying to get as much as he can for himself from every possible source.

12"Come," they say. "We'll get some wine and have a party; let's all get drunk. This is really living; let it go on and on, and tomorrow will be even better!"

55:13 of God's power and love, implied.   **56:9** devour my people, implied.

Cross references (right margin):
55:8 Isa 65:2
55:9 Ps 103:11
55:10 2 Cor 9:10
55:11 Isa 46:10
55:12 1 Chron 16:33 / Jer 29:11
55:13 Jer 33:9
56:1 Ps 85:9 / Isa 1:17
56:2 Ex 31:13-17 / Ps 119:1,2 / Ezek 20:12,20
56:3 Acts 8:27,37
56:5 Isa 2:2,3; 26:1 / 62:2
56:7 Isa 65:25 / Mic 4:1,2 / Mk 11:17 / Rom 12:1 / Heb 13:15
56:8 Jn 10:16
56:9 Jer 12:9
56:10 Jer 14:13,14 / Ezek 3:17
56:11 Jer 22:17 / Mic 3:5,11
56:12 Lk 12:19,20

55:8, 9 The people of Israel were foolish to act as if their thoughts were God's thoughts. His knowledge and wisdom are far greater than man's. We are foolish to try to fit God into our mold—to make his plans and purposes conform to ours. Instead, we must strive to fit into his plans.

56:2 God commanded his people to rest and honor him on the Sabbath (Exodus 20:8, 9). He wants us to serve him every day, but he wants us to make one day special when we rest and focus our thoughts on him. For the Israelites, this special day was the Sabbath (Saturday). A few Christians set Saturday aside as this special day, but most accept Sunday as the "Lord's Day," a day of rest and honor to God.

56:3 Isaiah clearly proclaims the radical message that God's blessings are for all people, even Gentiles and eunuchs, who were often not even considered as citizens in Israel. Whatever your race, social position, work, or financial situation, God's blessings are as much for you as for anyone else.

56:7 Jesus quoted this verse when he threw the moneychangers out of the Temple (Mark 11:17). See the note on Mark 11:15–17.

56:9-11 The leaders of Israel were blind to every danger. Apathetic about their people's needs, they were more concerned about satisfying their own greed. Leadership's special privileges can cause the leader either to sacrifice for the good of his people or to sacrifice his people for his own greed. If you are in a leadership position, use it for the good of your people.

The godly shall rest in peace

57 The good men perish; the godly die before their time and no one seems to care or wonder why. No one seems to realize that God is taking them away from evil days ahead. 2For the godly who die shall rest in peace.

3But you—come here, you witches' sons, you offspring of adulterers and harlots! 4Who is it you mock, making faces and sticking out your tongues? You children of sinners and liars! 5You worship your idols with great zeal beneath the shade of every tree, and slay your children as human sacrifices down in the valleys, under overhanging rocks. 6Your gods are the smooth stones in the valleys. You worship them and they, not I, are your inheritance. Does all this make me happy? 7, 8You have committed adultery on the tops of the mountains, for you worship idols there, deserting me. Behind closed doors you set your idols up and worship someone other than me. This is adultery, for you are giving these idols your love, instead of loving me. 9You have taken pleasant incense and perfume to Molech as your gift. You have traveled far, even to hell itself, to find new gods to love. 10You grew weary in your search, but you never gave up. You strengthened yourself and went on. 11Why were you more afraid of them than of me? How is it that you gave not even a second thought to me? Is it because I've been too gentle, that you have no fear of me?

12And then there is your "righteousness" and your "good works"—none of which will save you. 13Let's see if the whole collection of your idols can help you when you cry to them to save you! They are so weak that the wind can carry them off! A breath can puff them away. But he who trusts in me shall possess the land and inherit my Holy Mountain. 14I will say, Rebuild the road! Clear away the rocks and stones. Prepare a glorious highway for my people's return from captivity.

15The high and lofty one who inhabits eternity, the Holy One, says this: I live in that high and holy place where those with contrite, humble spirits dwell; and I refresh the humble and give new courage to those with repentant hearts. 16For I will not fight against you forever, nor always show my wrath; if I did, all mankind would perish—the very souls that I have made. 17I was angry and smote these greedy men. But they went right on sinning, doing everything their evil hearts desired. 18I have seen what they do, but I will heal them anyway! I will lead them and comfort them, helping them to mourn and to confess their sins. 19Peace, peace to them, both near and far, for I will heal them all. 20But those who still reject me are like the restless sea, which is never still, but always churns up mire and dirt. 21There is no peace, says my God, for them!

An admonition to share with the needy

58 Shout with the voice of a trumpet blast; tell my people of their sins! 2Yet they act so pious! They come to the Temple every day and are so delighted to hear the reading of my laws—just as though they would obey them—just as though they don't despise the commandments of their God! How anxious they are to worship correctly; oh, how they love the Temple services!

3"We have fasted before you," they say. "Why aren't you impressed? Why don't you see our sacrifices? Why don't you hear our prayers? We have done much

57:20 *But those who still reject me*, literally, "the wicked."

Cross-references (margin):

57:1 2 Kgs 22:19,20 Ps 12:1
57:2 Isa 26:7
57:5 Ps 106:37,38 Jer 2:20; 7:31
57:6 Jer 5:9,29; 7:18 Hab 2:19
57:7 Ezek 16:16,28
57:9 Ezek 23:16,40
57:10 Jer 2:25
57:11 Prov 29:25 Jer 2:32
57:12 Mic 3:1-4
57:13 Ps 37:3,9 Jer 30:14
57:14 Isa 62:10
57:15 Deut 33:27 Ps 34:18 Isa 66:1
57:16 Mic 7:18
57:17 Isa 1:4
57:18 Isa 53:5; 61:1-3
57:19 Isa 26:12 Eph 2:17
57:20 Job 18:5-14
57:21 Isa 48:22
58:2 Isa 29:13 Jer 7:9,10 Titus 1:16
58:3 Zech 7:5,6 Lk 18:12

57:7, 8 Marriage is an exclusive relationship in which a man and woman become one. Adultery breaks this beautiful bond of unity. When the people turned from God and gave their love to idols, God said they were committing adultery—breaking their exclusive commitment to God. How could people give their love to worthless wood and stone instead of the God who made them and loved them so very much?

57:12 Isaiah warned these people that their righteousness and good works would not save them any more than their weak, worthless idols. We cannot gain our salvation through good works because our best works are not good enough to outweigh our sins. Salvation is a gift from God.

57:15-21 Verses 1–14 speak of pride and lust; verses 15–21 tell how God relates to those who are humble and repentant. The high and holy God came down to our level to save us because it is impossible for us to go up to his level to save ourselves (see 2 Chronicles 6:18; Psalm 51:17; Philippians 2).

58:1ff True worship was more than religious ritual, going to the Temple every day, and listening to Scripture readings. These people missed the point of a living, vital relationship with God. He doesn't want us fasting or acting pious when we have unforgiven sin in our hearts and perform sinful practices with our hands. More important even than correct worship and doctrine is genuine compassion for the poor, the helpless, and the oppressed.

penance, and you don't even notice it!" I'll tell you why! Because you are living in evil pleasure even while you are fasting, and you keep right on oppressing your workers. 4Look, what good is fasting when you keep on fighting and quarreling? This kind of fasting will never get you anywhere with me. 5Is this what I want—this doing of penance and bowing like reeds in the wind and putting on sackcloth and covering yourselves with ashes? Is this what you call fasting?

58:4
1 Kgs 21:9,10

6No, the kind of fast I want is that you stop oppressing those who work for you and treat them fairly and give them what they earn. 7I want you to share your food with the hungry and bring right into your own homes those who are helpless, poor and destitute. Clothe those who are cold and don't hide from relatives who need your help.

58:6
Neh 5:10-12
58:7
Deut 22:1-4
Ezek 18:7,16
Lk 3:11
Heb 13:2

8If you do these things, God will shed his own glorious light upon you. He will heal you; your godliness will lead you forward, and goodness will be a shield before you, and the glory of the Lord will protect you from behind. 9Then, when you call, the Lord will answer. "Yes, I am here," he will quickly reply. All you need to do is to stop oppressing the weak, and to stop making false accusations and spreading vicious rumors!

58:8
Ps 85:13
Jer 30:17

10Feed the hungry! Help those in trouble! Then your light will shine out from the darkness, and the darkness around you shall be as bright as day. 11And the Lord will guide you continually, and satisfy you with all good things, and keep you healthy too; and you will be like a well-watered garden, like an ever-flowing spring. 12Your sons will rebuild the long-deserted ruins of your cities, and you will be known as "The People Who Rebuild Their Walls and Cities."

58:10
Deut 15:7
58:11
Ps 107:9
Song 4:15
Jn 4:14
58:12
Ezek 36:10
Amos 9:11

13If you keep the Sabbath holy, not having your own fun and business on that day, but enjoying the Sabbath and speaking of it with delight as the Lord's holy day, and honoring the Lord in what you do, not following your own desires and pleasure, nor talking idly— 14then the Lord will be your delight, and I will see to it that you ride high, and get your full share of the blessings I promised to Jacob, your father. The Lord has spoken.

58:13
Ps 84:2,10
Jer 17:21-27
58:14
Deut 32:13

Warnings against sin

59 Listen now! The Lord isn't too weak to save you. And he isn't getting deaf! He can hear you when you call! 2But the trouble is that your sins have cut you off from God. Because of sin he has turned his face away from you and will not listen anymore. 3For your hands are those of murderers and your fingers are filthy with sin. You lie and grumble and oppose the good. 4No one cares about being fair and true. Your lawsuits are based on lies; you spend your time plotting evil deeds and doing them. 5You spend your time and energy in spinning evil plans which end up in deadly actions. 6You cheat and shortchange everyone. Everything you do is filled with sin; violence is your trademark. 7Your feet run to do evil and rush to murder; your thoughts are only of sinning, and wherever you go you leave behind a trail of misery and death. 8You don't know what true peace is, nor what it means to be just and good; you continually do wrong and those who follow you won't experience any peace, either.

59:1
Jer 32:17
Ezek 8:18
59:2
Isa 1:15
59:3
Jer 2:30,34
Hos 4:2
59:4
Ps 7:14
59:6
Jer 6:7
59:7
Prov 1:16
Mk 7:21,22
Rom 3:15-17

9It is because of all this evil that you aren't finding God's blessings; that's why

59:9
Isa 5:30

58:6–12 We cannot be saved by works of service without faith, but our faith lacks sincerity if it doesn't reach out to others. Fasting can be beneficial spiritually and physically, but at its best it helps only the person doing it. God says he wants our service to go beyond our own personal growth to acts of kindness, charity, justice, and generosity. Pleasing God is more than what we don't eat or don't do; it is what we do for him and for others.

58:13, 14 The day of rest should not be honored merely because Sabbath-keeping is a commandment, but because it is best for us and because it honors God. Keeping the Sabbath honors God, our Creator, who also rested on the seventh day (Genesis 2:3). It also unifies our family and sets priorities for them. Our day of rest

refreshes us spiritually and physically—providing time when we can gather together for worship and when we can reflect on God without the stress of our everyday lives.

59:1–12 Sin offends our holy God. Because God is holy, he cannot ignore, excuse, or tolerate sin as though it didn't matter. Sin cuts people off from him, forming a wall to isolate God from the people he loves. No wonder this long list of wretched sins makes God angry and forces him to look the other way. People who die with their sin unforgiven separate themselves eternally from God. God wants them to live with him forever, but he cannot take them into his holy presence unless their sin is removed. Wouldn't you be angry to see people you love cut themselves off from you and condemn themselves to eternal separation from you?

he doesn't punish those who injure you. No wonder you are in darkness when you expected light. No wonder you are walking in the gloom. 10No wonder you grope like blind men and stumble along in broad daylight, yes, even at brightest noontime, as though it were the darkest night! No wonder you are like corpses when compared with vigorous young men! 11You roar like hungry bears; you moan with mournful cries like doves. You look for God to keep you, but he doesn't. He has turned away. 12For your sins keep piling up before the righteous God, and testify against you.

Yes, we know what sinners we are. 13We know our disobedience; we have denied the Lord our God. We know what rebels we are and how unfair we are, for we carefully plan our lies. 14Our courts oppose the righteous man; fairness is unknown. Truth falls dead in the streets, and justice is outlawed.

15Yes, truth is gone, and anyone who tries a better life is soon attacked. The Lord saw all the evil and was displeased to find no steps taken against sin. 16He saw no one was helping you, and wondered that no one intervened. Therefore he himself stepped in to save you through his mighty power and justice. 17He put on righteousness as armor, and the helmet of salvation on his head. He clothed himself with robes of vengeance and of godly fury. 18He will repay his enemies for their evil deeds—fury for his foes in distant lands. 19Then at last they will reverence and glorify the name of God from west to east. For he will come like a flood-tide driven by Jehovah's breath. 20He will come as a Redeemer to those in Zion who have turned away from sin.

21"As for me, this is my promise to them," says the Lord: "My Holy Spirit shall not leave them, and they shall want the good and hate the wrong—they and their children and their children's children forever."

3. The future kingdom
Promises of glory for God's people

60 Arise, my people! Let your light shine for all the nations to see! For the glory of the Lord is streaming from you. 2Darkness as black as night shall cover all the peoples of the earth, but the glory of the Lord will shine from you. 3All nations will come to your light; mighty kings will come to see the glory of the Lord upon you.

4Lift up your eyes and see! For your sons and daughters are coming home to you from distant lands. 5Your eyes will shine with joy, your hearts will thrill, for merchants from around the world will flow to you, bringing you the wealth of many lands. 6Vast droves of camels will converge upon you, dromedaries from Midian and Sheba and Ephah, too, bringing gold and incense to add to the praise of God. 7The flocks of Kedar shall be given you, and the rams of Nabaioth for my altars, and I will glorify my glorious Temple in that day.

8And who are these who fly like a cloud to Israel, like doves to their nests? 9I have reserved the ships of many lands, the very best, to bring the sons of Israel

60:9 *the very best,* literally, "the ships of Tarshish."

59:10
Deut 28:29
Lam 3:6

59:11
Ezek 7:16

59:12
Ezra 9:6
Hos 5:5

59:13
Mt 10:33

59:14
Hab 1:4

59:15
Isa 1:21-23
5:23

59:16
Ezek 22:30

59:17
Eph 6:14

59:19
Isa 30:28

59:20
Ezek 18:30,31
Acts 2:38
Rom 11:26,27

59:21
Isa 44:3
Jer 31:31-34

60:1
Eph 5:14

60:2
Col 1:13

60:3
Isa 2:3

60:5
Ps 34:5
Isa 61:6

60:6
Ps 72:10

60:9
Isa 49:22

59:15 Because of Israel's willful, persistent rebellion (chapters 56—59), God declared her unable to take action against her sins. Sin fills the vacuum left when God's truth no longer fills our lives. Only God can save us.

59:16, 17 God would rescue the nation from enemy armies (Assyria and Babylon). He would also rescue his people from sin. Because this is an impossible task for any human, God himself, the Messiah, would personally step in to help (Romans 11:26, 27). Whether we sin once or many times, our sin separates us from God and will continue to separate us until God forgives it (see Jeremiah 5:1).

59:21 When the Holy Spirit dwells within his people, they change. Their former desires no longer entice them; now their chief aim is to please God. We who are Christians today are the heirs of this

prophecy; we are given discernment between right and wrong because the Holy Spirit dwells within us (John 14:26; Philippians 2:13; Hebrews 5:14).

60:1–3 God's light will shine on Israel, who will radiate his light to the nations, dispelling the darkness of the surrounding world. God's light alone can dispel the darkness around us. We don't have any light apart from him.

60:6, 7 The places mentioned belonged to obscure tribes in the Arabian desert hundreds of miles from Israel. All people would come to Jerusalem because God would be living there and they would be attracted to his light. Don't be discouraged when you look around and see so few people turning to God; one day people throughout the earth will recognize him as the one true God.

home again from far away, bringing their wealth with them. For the Holy One of Israel, known around the world, has glorified you in the eyes of all.

[10] Foreigners will come and build your cities. Presidents and kings will send you aid. For though I destroyed you in my anger, I will have mercy on you through my grace. [11] Your gates will stay wide open around the clock to receive the wealth of many lands. The kings of the world will cater to you. [12] For the nations refusing to be your allies will perish; they shall be destroyed. [13] The glory of Lebanon will be yours—the forests of firs and pines, and box trees—to beautify my sanctuary. My Temple will be glorious.

[14] The sons of anti-Semites will come and bow before you! They will kiss your feet! They will call Jerusalem "The City of the Lord" and "The Glorious Mountain of the Holy One of Israel."

[15] Though once despised and hated and rebuffed by all, you will be beautiful forever, a joy for all the generations of the world, for I will make you so. [16] Powerful kings and mighty nations shall provide you with the choicest of their goods to satisfy your every need, and you will know at last and really understand that I, the Lord, am your Savior and Redeemer, the Mighty One of Israel. [17] I will exchange your brass for gold, your iron for silver, your wood for brass, your stones for iron. Peace and righteousness shall be your taskmasters! [18] Violence will disappear out of your land—all war will end. Your walls will be "Salvation" and your gates "Praise."

[19] No longer will you need the sun or moon to give you light, for the Lord your God will be your everlasting light, and he will be your glory. [20] Your sun shall never set; the moon shall not go down—for the Lord will be your everlasting light; your days of mourning all will end. [21] All your people will be good. They will possess their land forever, for I will plant them there with my own hands; this will bring me glory. [22] The smallest family shall multiply into a clan; the tiny group shall be a mighty nation. I, the Lord, will bring it all to pass when it is time.

Good news for those who suffer

61 The Spirit of the Lord God is upon me, because the Lord has anointed me to bring good news to the suffering and afflicted. He has sent me to comfort the brokenhearted, to announce liberty to captives and to open the eyes of the blind. [2] He has sent me to tell those who mourn that the time of God's favor to them has come, and the day of his wrath to their enemies. [3] To all who mourn in Israel he will give: Beauty for ashes; joy instead of mourning; praise instead of heaviness.

For God has planted them like strong and graceful oaks for his own glory.

[4] And they shall rebuild the ancient ruins, repairing cities long ago destroyed, reviving them though they have lain there many generations. [5] Foreigners shall be your servants; they shall feed your flocks and plow your fields and tend your vineyards. [6] You shall be called priests of the Lord, ministers of our God. You shall be fed with the treasures of the nations and shall glory in their riches. [7] Instead of shame and dishonor, you shall have a double portion of prosperity and everlasting joy.

[8] For I, the Lord, love justice; I hate robbery and wrong. I will faithfully reward

60:12 *For the nations refusing to be your allies,* literally, "that will not serve you."

60:10 Isa 49:23
60:11 Isa 26:2
60:12 Zech 14:17
60:13 Ps 132:7
60:14 Isa 1:26; 14:1,2 Rev 3:9
60:15 Isa 65:18 Jer 30:17
60:16 Isa 43:3,11 63:16
60:18 Isa 26:1
60:19 Isa 9:2 Zech 2:5 Rev 21:23
60:20 Rev 21:4
60:21 Ps 37:22 Isa 45:24,25
60:22 Isa 51:2
61:1 Isa 49:9 Lk 4:18,19
61:2 Mt 5:4
61:3 Ps 23:5 Jer 17:7,8
61:4 Ezek 36:33 Amos 9:14
61:5 Isa 14:2
61:6 Isa 66:21
61:7 Zech 9:12
61:8 Gen 17:7 Isa 5:16

60:19, 20 See Revelation 21:23, 24 where this beautiful reality is also promised.

60:22 As we read these promises, we long for their fulfillment. But we must patiently wait for God's timing. He is in control of history, and he weaves together all our lives into his plan.

61:1, 2 Jesus quoted these words in Luke 4:18–21. As he read to the people in the synagogue, he stopped in the middle of 61:2 after the words, "the time of God's favor has come." Closing the book, he said, "These scriptures came true today" (Luke 4:21). The rest of 61:2, "and the day of his wrath to their enemies," will come true when Jesus returns to earth again. We are now under God's favor; his wrath is yet to come.

61:6 Under the Old Covenant, God ordained the priests of Israel to stand between him and his people. They brought God's Word to the people, and the people's needs and sins to God. Under the New Covenant, all believers are priests before God, reading God's Word and seeking to understand it, confessing their sins directly to God and ministering to others.

61:8 We suffer for many reasons—our own mistakes, someone else's mistakes, injustice. When we suffer for our own mistakes, we get what we deserve. When we suffer because of others or injustice, God is angry. God in his mercy says that his people have suffered enough. God will reward those who suffer because of injustice. He will settle all accounts.

my people for their suffering and make an everlasting covenant with them. 9Their descendants shall be known and honored among the nations; all shall realize that they are a people God has blessed.

61:10
Isa 51:3; 52:1

10Let me tell you how happy God has made me! For he has clothed me with garments of salvation and draped about me the robe of righteousness. I am like a bridegroom in his wedding suit or a bride with her jewels. 11The Lord will show the nations of the world his justice; all will praise him. His righteousness shall be like a budding tree, or like a garden in early spring, full of young plants springing up everywhere.

Isaiah prays for Jerusalem

62:1
Isa 46:13

62 Because I love Zion, because my heart yearns for Jerusalem, I will not cease to pray for her or to cry out to God on her behalf until she shines forth in his righteousness and is glorious in his salvation. 2The nations shall see your righteousness. Kings shall be blinded by your glory; and God will confer on you a new name. 3He will hold you aloft in his hands for all to see—a splendid crown for the King of kings. 4Never again shall you be called "The God-forsaken Land" or the "Land that God Forgot." Your new name will be "The Land of God's Delight" and "The Bride," for the Lord delights in you and will claim you as his own. 5Your children will care for you, O Jerusalem, with joy like that of a young man who marries a virgin; and God will rejoice over you as a bridegroom with his bride.

62:2
Isa 56:5

62:3
Zech 9:16
1 Thess 2:19

62:4
Isa 54:6,7
Jer 32:41
Zeph 3:17,18

6, 7O Jerusalem, I have set intercessors on your walls who shall cry to God all day and all night for the fulfillment of his promises. Take no rest, all you who pray, and give God no rest until he establishes Jerusalem and makes her respected and admired throughout the earth. 8The Lord has sworn to Jerusalem with all his integrity: "I will never again give you to your enemies; never again shall foreign soldiers come and take away your grain and wine. 9You raised it; you shall keep it, praising God. Within the Temple courts you yourselves shall drink the wine you pressed.

62:6
Jer 14:21
Ezek 33:7
Zeph 3:19,20
Lk 18:1-8

62:8
Lev 26:16
Deut 28:31,33

62:9
Isa 65:13,21-23

10"Go out! Go out! Prepare the roadway for my people to return! Build the roads, pull out the boulders, raise the flag of Israel."

11See, the Lord has sent his messengers to every land and said, "Tell my people, I, the Lord your God, am coming to save you and will bring you many gifts." 12And they shall be called "The Holy People" and "The Lord's Redeemed," and Jerusalem shall be called "The Land of Desire" and the "The City God Has Blessed."

62:11
Isa 49:6
Zech 9:9

62:12
Deut 7:6
1 Pet 2:9

God's judgment and lovingkindness

63:1
Jer 49:13
Zeph 3:17

63 Who is this who comes from Edom, from the city of Bozrah, with his magnificent garments of crimson? Who is this in royal robes, marching in the greatness of his strength?

"It is I, the Lord, announcing your salvation; I, the Lord, the one who is mighty to save!"

63:2
Rev 19:13,15

63:3
Isa 22:5
Mic 7:10

2"Why are your clothes so red, as from treading out the grapes?"

3"I have trodden the winepress alone. No one was there to help me. In my wrath I have trodden my enemies like grapes. In my fury I trampled my foes. It is their

62:6, 7 *intercessors,* literally, "watchmen."

61:10 "Me" could refer to the Messiah, the person anointed with the Spirit of the Lord (61:1), or to Zion (62:1), which symbolizes God's people. The imagery of the bridegroom is often used in Scripture to depict the Messiah (see Matthew 9:15), while the imagery of the bride is used to depict God's people (see Revelation 19:6-8).

62:1-7 Isaiah's zeal for his country and his desire to see the work of salvation completed caused him to pray without ceasing, hoping that Israel would be saved. We should have Isaiah's zeal to see God's will done. This is what we mean when we pray, "thy kingdom come, thy will be done on earth as it is in heaven." It is good to keep praying persistently for others.

62:12 The people of Jerusalem will have new names—"The Holy People," and "The Lord's Redeemed." Believers today also have new names—Christians. In 1 Peter 2:5, we are called "his holy priests."

63:1-4 Edom was a constant enemy to Israel despite its common ancestry in Isaac (Genesis 25:23). Edom rejoiced at any trouble Israel faced. The watchman on the wall of Jerusalem, seeing Edom approaching, fears that the Edomite king in his crimson robe is leading an attack. But it turns out to be the Lord, in blood-stained clothes, who has trampled and destroyed Edom. (For other prophecies against Edom see Amos 1:11; Obadiah 1:10, 11; Malachi 1:2-4.)

blood you see upon my clothes. 4For the time has come for me to avenge my
people, to redeem them from the hands of their oppressors. 5I looked but no one
came to help them; I was amazed and appalled. So I executed vengeance alone;
unaided, I meted out judgment. 6I crushed the heathen nations in my anger and
made them stagger and fall to the ground."

7I will tell of the lovingkindnesses of God. I will praise him for all he has done;
I will rejoice in his great goodness to Israel, which he has granted in accordance
with his mercy and love. 8He said, "They are my very own; surely they will not be
false again." And he became their Savior. 9In all their affliction he was afflicted,
and he personally saved them. In his love and pity he redeemed them and lifted
them up and carried them through all the years.

10But they rebelled against him and grieved his Holy Spirit. That is why he
became their enemy and personally fought against them. 11Then they remembered
those days of old when Moses, God's servant, led his people out of Egypt and they
cried out, "Where is the one who brought Israel through the sea, with Moses as
their shepherd? Where is the God who sent his Holy Spirit to be among his people?
12Where is he whose mighty power divided the sea before them when Moses lifted
up his hand, and established his reputation forever? 13Who led them through the
bottom of the sea? Like fine stallions racing through the desert, they never
stumbled. 14Like cattle grazing in the valleys, so the Spirit of the Lord gave them
rest. Thus he gave himself a magnificent reputation."

15O Lord, look down from heaven and see us from your holy, glorious home;
where is the love for us you used to show—your power, your mercy and your
compassion? Where are they now? 16Surely you are still our Father! Even if
Abraham and Jacob would disown us, still you would be our Father, our Redeemer
from ages past. 17O Lord, why have you hardened our hearts and made us sin and
turn against you? Return and help us, for we who belong to you need you so. 18How
briefly we possessed Jerusalem! And now our enemies have destroyed her.
19O God, why do you treat us as though we weren't your people, as though we were
a heathen nation that never called you "Lord"?

The Lord is the potter

64 Oh, that you would burst forth from the skies and come down! How the
mountains would quake in your presence! 2The consuming fire of your glory
would burn down the forests and boil the oceans dry. The nations would tremble
before you; then your enemies would learn the reason for your fame! 3So it was
before when you came down, for you did awesome things beyond our highest
expectations, and how the mountains quaked! 4For since the world began no one
has seen or heard of such a God as ours, who works for those who wait for him!
5You welcome those who cheerfully do good, who follow godly ways.

But we are not godly; we are constant sinners and have been all our lives.
Therefore your wrath is heavy on us. How can such as we be saved? 6We are all
infected and impure with sin. When we put on our prized robes of righteousness we
find they are but filthy rags. Like autumn leaves we fade, wither and fall. And our

63:4
Jer 51:6

63:7
1 Kgs 8:66
Ps 25:6,7; 86:5
Eph 2:4
63:8
Ex 6:7
63:9
Ex 23:20-23
Judg 10:16
63:10
Ps 78:40
Eph 4:30
63:11
Num 11:17,
25,29
Isa 51:9,10
63:12
Ex 6:6
14:21,22
63:13
Jer 31:9
63:14
Josh 21:44
63:15
Ps 80:14; 123:1
Jer 31:20
63:16
Isa 41:8
63:17
Isa 29:13,14
63:18
Ps 74:3-7
63:19
Lam 3:43-45

64:1
Ex 19:18
Judg 5:5
Nah 1:5
64:2
Ps 99:1
64:3
Ps 65:5
64:4
Isa 40:31
1 Cor 2:9

64:6
Ps 90:5,6
Isa 1:30; 48:1

63:9 *he personally saved them,* or, "The Angel of his Presence saved them out of their affliction." **63:17** *for we who belong to you need you so,* literally, "for your servants' sake." **64:6** *filthy rags,* literally, "filthy as a menstruating woman's rags."

63:15–19 The faithful remnant asks God for two favors: show
compassion to them (63:15–19), and punish their enemies
(64:1–7). Before making these requests, these people recited the
Lord's past favors, reminding him of his compassion in former days
(63:7–14).

64:1–6 God's glory is so intense it is like a consuming fire that
burns everything in its path. If we are so impure, how can we be
saved? Only by God's mercy. The Israelites had experienced
God's glory at Mount Sinai (Exodus 19:16–19). When God met with
Moses there was a thunderstorm, smoke, and an earthquake. If
God were to meet us today, his glory would overwhelm us,
especially when we look at our "filthy rags" (64:6).

64:6 Sin makes us unclean so that we cannot approach God
(Leviticus 13:45; Ezekiel 36:17) any more than a beggar in rotten
rags could dine at a king's table. Our best efforts are still infected
with sin. Our only hope, therefore, is to find the One, Jesus Christ,
who can cleanse us and bring us into God's presence (read
Romans 3).

This passage can easily be misunderstood. It doesn't mean
God will reject us if we come to him in faith. It means that if we
come to him demanding acceptance on the basis of our "good"
conduct, God will point out that our goodness is nothing compared
to his infinite goodness. This message is primarily for the
unrepentant, not the true follower of God.

64:7
Deut 31:18
Isa 1:15

64:8
Ps 100:3
Isa 45:9

64:9
Ps 79:13
Mic 7:18

64:11
Ps 74:5-7

64:12
Ps 83:1

sins, like the wind, sweep us away. 7Yet no one calls upon your name or pleads with you for mercy. Therefore you have turned away from us and turned us over to our sins.

8And yet, O Lord, you are our Father. We are the clay and you are the Potter. We are all formed by your hand. 9Oh, be not so angry with us, Lord, nor forever remember our sins. Oh, look and see that we are all your people.

10Your holy cities are destroyed; Jerusalem is a desolate wilderness. 11Our holy, beautiful Temple where our fathers praised you is burned down, and all the things of beauty are destroyed. 12After all of this, must you still refuse to help us, Lord? Will you stand silent and still punish us?

The new heavens and the new earth

65:1
Hos 1:10

65:2
Ps 81:11,12
Rom 10:21

65:3
Job 2:5

65:4
Lev 11:7

65:5
Mt 9:11

65:6
Ps 50:3,21
Isa 42:14

65:7
Jer 13:25
Ezek 20:27,28
Hos 2:13

65:9
Amos 9:11-15

65:10
Josh 7:24
Isa 33:9

65 The Lord says, People who never before inquired about me are now seeking me out. Nations who never before searched for me are finding me.

2But my own people—though I have been spreading out my arms to welcome them all day long—have rebelled; they follow their own evil paths and thoughts. 3All day long they insult me to my face by worshiping idols in many gardens and burning incense on the rooftops of their homes. 4At night they go out among the graves and caves to worship evil spirits, and they eat pork and other forbidden foods. 5Yet they say to one another, "Don't come too close, you'll defile me! For I am holier than you!" They stifle me. Day in and day out they infuriate me.

6See, here is my decree all written out before me: *I will not stand silent; I will repay. Yes, I will repay them*— 7not only for their own sins but for those of their fathers too, says the Lord, for they also burned incense on the mountains and insulted me upon the hills. I will pay them back in full.

8But I will not destroy them all, says the Lord; for just as good grapes are found among a cluster of bad ones (and someone will say, "Don't throw them all away—there are some good grapes there!") so I will not destroy all Israel, for I have true servants there. 9I will preserve a remnant of my people to possess the land of Israel; those I select will inherit it and serve me there. 10As for my people who

---

THE SPIRIT IN ISAIAH

Reference	Main Teaching
11:2	The Spirit of the Lord brings wisdom, understanding, knowledge, and the fear of God.
32:15	The Spirit of the Lord brings blessings.
34:16	The Spirit of the Lord carries out God's Word.
40:13	The Spirit of the Lord is the Master Counselor.
42:1	The Messiah, God's Servant, will be given the Spirit.
44:3–5	Through the Spirit, God's true children will thrive.
48:16	The Spirit of the Lord sent Isaiah to prophesy.
61:1	God's servants (Isaiah and then Jesus) were anointed by the Spirit to proclaim the Good News.
63:10, 11	The Spirit of the Lord was grieved because of God's people.
63:14	The Spirit of the Lord gives rest.

65:1 Israel considered itself to be the only people of God, but the time would come when other nations would seek him. Paul mentions Isaiah's statement in Romans 10:20 and points out that these other nations were the Gentiles. God's people today are those who accept Jesus as Savior and Lord, whether they are Jews or Gentiles. The gospel is for every person. Do not ignore or reject anyone when you share the gospel. You may be surprised at how many are sincerely searching for God.

65:3–5 God said these people directly disobeyed his laws when they worshiped idols (Exodus 20:1–6), consulted dead and evil spirits (Leviticus 19:26), and ate forbidden foods (Leviticus 11). But they were so perverse that they still thought they were holier than others. Jesus called such people hypocrites (Matthew 23:13–36).

65:6 God said he would repay the people for their sins. Judgment is not our job but his, because he alone is just. Who else knows our hearts and minds? Who else knows what is a completely fair reward or punishment?

65:8, 9 God will always preserve a faithful remnant of his people. No matter how bad the world is, there are always a few who remain loyal to him. Jesus made this point in Matthew 13:36–43.

65:10 The plains of Sharon are in the western part of Israel. The Valley of Achor is in the east near Jericho. The Valley of Achor was also called the Valley of Calamity because Achan was executed there for hiding forbidden spoils of battle (Joshua 7:10–26). Even in this valley there will be peace: the coming restoration will be complete.

have sought me, the plains of Sharon shall again be filled with flocks, and the valley of Achor shall be a place to pasture herds.

¹¹But because the rest of you have forsaken the Lord and his Temple and worship gods of "Fate" and "Destiny," ¹²therefore I will "destine" you to the sword, and your "fate" shall be a dark one; for when I called, you didn't answer; when I spoke, you wouldn't listen. You deliberately sinned before my very eyes, choosing to do what you know I despise. ¹³Therefore the Lord God says, You shall starve, but my servants shall eat; you shall be thirsty while they drink; you shall be sad and ashamed, but they shall rejoice. ¹⁴You shall cry in sorrow and vexation and despair, while they sing for joy. ¹⁵Your name shall be a curse word among my people, for the Lord God will slay you and call his true servants by another name.

¹⁶And yet, the days will come when all who invoke a blessing or take an oath shall swear by the God of Truth; for I will put aside my anger and forget the evil that you did. ¹⁷For see, I am creating new heavens and a new earth—so wonderful that no one will even think about the old ones anymore. ¹⁸Be glad; rejoice forever in my creation. Look! I will recreate Jerusalem as a place of happiness, and her people shall be a joy! ¹⁹And I will rejoice in Jerusalem, and in my people; and the voice of weeping and crying shall not be heard there any more.

²⁰No longer will babies die when only a few days old; no longer will men be considered old at 100! Only sinners will die that young! ²¹, ²²In those days, when a man builds a house, he will keep on living in it—it will not be destroyed by invading armies as in the past. My people will plant vineyards and eat the fruit themselves—their enemies will not confiscate it. For my people will live as long as trees and will long enjoy their hard-won gains. ²³Their harvests will not be eaten by their enemies; their children will not be born to be cannon fodder. For they are the children of those the Lord has blessed; and their children, too, shall be blessed. ²⁴I will answer them before they even call to me. While they are still talking to me about their needs, I will go ahead and answer their prayers! ²⁵The wolf and lamb shall feed together, the lion shall eat straw as the ox does, and poisonous snakes shall strike no more! In those days nothing and no one shall be hurt or destroyed in all my Holy Mountain, says the Lord.

The world will see God's goodness

66 Heaven is my throne and the earth is my footstool: What Temple can you build for me as good as that? ²My hand has made both earth and skies, and they are mine. Yet I will look with pity on the man who has a humble and a contrite heart, who trembles at my word.

³But those who choose their own ways, delighting in their sins, are cursed. God will not accept their offerings. When such men sacrifice an ox on the altar of God, it is no more acceptable to him than human sacrifice. If they sacrifice a lamb, or bring an offering of grain, it is as loathsome to God as putting a dog or the blood of a swine on his altar! When they burn incense to him, he counts it the same as though they blessed an idol. ⁴I will send great troubles upon them—all the things they feared, for when I called them, they refused to answer, and when I spoke to them, they would not hear. Instead, they did wrong before my eyes, and chose what they knew I despised.

65:11	Isa 1:4,28
65:12	2 Chron 36:15, 16 Prov 1:24
65:13	Isa 5:13
65:14	Mt 8:12 Lk 13:28
65:15	Jer 24:9
65:16	Isa 45:23
65:17	2 Pet 3:13
65:18	Ps 98 Isa 35:10
65:19	Jer 32:41
65:20	Eccles 8:12,13
65:21	Deut 32:46,47 Ps 92:12-14 Amos 9:14
65:23	Isa 61:9
65:24	Ps 91:15 Dan 10:12
65:25	Gen 3:14 Isa 11:6,9
66:1	Ps 11:4 Mt 5:34,35 Jn 4:20,21 Acts 7:48-50
66:2	Ps 34:18 Lk 18:13,14
66:4	Prov 1:31,32 10:24 Jer 7:13,30

65:16 *the days will come,* implied. **65:25** *snakes shall strike no more,* literally, "dust (i.e., not men!) shall be the serpent's food."

65:16–25 Here we have a pictorial description of the new heaven and the new earth. They are eternal, and in them safety, peace, and plenty will be available to all (see also 66:22, 23; 2 Peter 3:13; Revelation 21:1).

66:1 Even the beautiful Temple in Jerusalem was woefully inadequate for a God who is present everywhere. God cannot be confined to any human structure (see 2 Chronicles 6:18; Acts 7:49, 50). This chapter is a fitting climax to the book. God will lift up the humble, judge all people, destroy the wicked, bring all believers together, and establish a new heaven and a new earth.

66:2, 3 These are key verses in Isaiah, and a fitting conclusion. Two ways of living are contrasted: that of the humble person who has a profound reverence for God's messages and their application to life, and that of those who choose their own way of living. God shows mercy to the humble, but he curses the proud and self-sufficient (see Luke 1:51–53). Our society urges us to be assertive and to affirm ourselves. We need to be careful that our freedom and right to choose don't lead us away from God's pathway to eternal life.

66:5
Ps 38:20
Mt 5:10-12
Jn 9:34

66:6
Joel 3:7

66:9
Isa 37:3

66:10
Ps 122:6
Rom 15:10
66:12
Isa 48:18; 60:5

66:14
Prov 3:8
Zech 10:7

66:16
Ezek 38:22

66:17
Lev 11:7

66:19
1 Chron 16:24
Isa 42:12

66:20
Isa 2:2; 43:5,6
49:22; 52:11
60:4

66:21
Isa 61:6
1 Pet 2:5,9

66:22
Jn 10:27-29
2 Pet 3:13

66:23
Isa: 27:13

66:24
Isa,1:31
Dan 12:2

5Hear the words of God, all you who fear him, and tremble at his words: Your brethren hate you and cast you out for being loyal to my name. "Glory to God," they scoff. "Be happy in the Lord!" But they shall be put to shame.

6What is all the commotion in the city? What is that terrible noise from the Temple? It is the voice of the Lord taking vengeance upon his enemies.

7, 8Who has heard or seen anything as strange as this? For in one day, suddenly, a nation, Israel, shall be born, even before the birth pains come. In a moment, just as Israel's anguish starts, the baby is born; the nation begins. 9Shall I bring to the point of birth and then not deliver? asks the Lord your God. No! Never!

10Rejoice with Jerusalem; be glad with her, all you who love her, you who mourned for her. 11Delight in Jerusalem; drink deep of her glory even as an infant at a mother's generous breasts. 12Prosperity shall overflow Jerusalem like a river, says the Lord, for I will send it; the riches of the Gentiles will flow to her. Her children shall be nursed at her breasts, carried on her hips and dandled on her knees. 13I will comfort you there as a little one is comforted by its mother. 14When you see Jerusalem, your heart will rejoice; vigorous health will be yours. All the world will see the good hand of God upon his people, and his wrath upon his enemies.

15For see, the Lord will come with fire and with swift chariots of doom to pour out the fury of his anger and his hot rebuke with flames of fire. 16For the Lord will punish the world by fire and by his sword, and the slain of the Lord shall be many! 17Those who worship idols that are hidden behind a tree in the garden, feasting there on pork and mouse and all forbidden meat—they will come to an evil end, says Jehovah. 18I see full well what they are doing; I know what they are thinking, so I will gather together all nations and people against Jerusalem, where they shall see my glory. 19I will perform a mighty miracle against them, and I will send those who escape, as missionaries to the nations—to Tarshish, Put, Lud, Meshech, Rosh, Tubal, Javan, and to the lands beyond the sea that have not heard my fame nor seen my glory. There they shall declare my glory to the Gentiles. 20And they shall bring back all your brethren from every nation as a gift to the Lord, transporting them gently on horses and in chariots, and in litters, and on mules and camels, to my holy mountain, to Jerusalem, says the Lord. It will be like offerings flowing into the Temple of the Lord at harvest time, carried in vessels consecrated to the Lord. 21And I will appoint some of those returning to be my priests and Levites, says the Lord.

22As surely as my new heavens and earth shall remain, so surely shall you always be my people, with a name that shall never disappear. 23All mankind shall come to worship me from week to week and month to month. 24And they shall go out and look at the dead bodies of those who have rebelled against me, for their worm shall never die; their fire shall not be quenched, and they shall be a disgusting sight to all mankind.

66:19 *I will send those who escape.* It is not clear from the Hebrew whether "those who escape" means survivors of the armies of the nations, or survivors of the Jews in Israel. The context seems to favor the former. Put and Lud were in North Africa; Meshech, Rosh, and Tubal were in Asia Minor and Armenia. **66:20** *transporting them gently,* implied.

66:7–9 God will not leave his work of national restoration unfinished. In this image of birth, God shows that he will accomplish what he promised. It is as unstoppable as the birth of a baby. When all the pain is over, the joy begins.

66:15–17 This is a vivid picture of the great judgment that will come at Christ's Second Coming (2 Thessalonians 1:7–9).

66:22, 23 God has something new and wonderful planned. No matter what or where this Jerusalem is, God's Servant, the Messiah, lays its foundation and makes this glorious future possible.

66:22–24 Isaiah brings his book to a close with great drama. For the faithless there is a sobering portrayal of judgment. For the faithful, there is a glorious picture of rich reward—"surely shall you always be my people, with a name that shall never disappear." The contrast is so striking that it would seem that everyone would want to be God's follower. But we are often just as foolish and reluctant to change as the Israelites. We are just as negligent in feeding the poor, working for justice, and obeying God's Word. Make sure you are among those who will be richly blessed.

JEREMIAH

VITAL STATISTICS

PURPOSE:
To urge God's people to turn from their sins and to turn back to God

AUTHOR:
Jeremiah

TO WHOM WRITTEN:
Judah (the Southern Kingdom) and its capital city, Jerusalem

DATE WRITTEN:
During Jeremiah's ministry, approximately 627–586 B.C.

SETTING:
Jeremiah ministered during the reigns of Judah's last five kings—Josiah, Jehoahaz, Jehoiakim, Jehoiachin, and Zedekiah. The nation was sliding quickly toward destruction and was eventually conquered by Babylon in 586 B.C. (see 2 Kings 21—25). The prophet Zephaniah preceded Jeremiah, and Habakkuk was his contemporary.

KEY VERSE:
"Your own wickedness will punish you. You will see what an evil, bitter thing it is to rebel against the Lord your God, fearlessly forsaking him, says the Lord Almighty" (2:19).

KEY PEOPLE:
Judah's kings (listed above), Baruch, Ebed-melech, King Nebuchadnezzar, the Rechabites

KEY PLACES:
Anathoth, Jerusalem, Ramah, Egypt

SPECIAL FEATURES:
The book of Jeremiah is a combination of history, poetry, and biography. Jeremiah often used symbolism to communicate his message.

WHAT is success? Most definitions include references to achieving goals and acquiring wealth, prestige, favor, and power. "Successful" people enjoy the good life—financially and emotionally secure, surrounded by admirers, and enjoying the fruits of their labors. They are leaders, opinion makers, trend-setters. Their example is emulated; their accomplishments are noticed. They know who they are and where they are going, and they stride confidently to meet their goals.

By these standards, Jeremiah was a miserable failure. For 40 years he served as God's spokesman to Judah; but when Jeremiah spoke, nobody listened. Consistently and passionately he urged them to act, but nobody moved. And he certainly did not attain material success. He was poor and underwent severe deprivation to deliver his prophecies. He was thrown into prison (chapter 37) and into a well (chapter 38), and he was taken to Egypt against his will (chapter 43). He was rejected by his neighbors (11:19–21), his family (12:6), the false priests and prophets (20:1, 2), friends (20:10), his audience (26:8), and the kings (36:23). Throughout his life, Jeremiah stood alone, declaring God's messages of doom, announcing the new covenant, and weeping over the fate of his beloved country. In the eyes of the world, Jeremiah was not a success.

But in God's eyes, Jeremiah was one of the most successful people in all of history. Success, as measured by God, involves obedience and faithfulness. Regardless of opposition and personal cost, Jeremiah courageously and faithfully proclaimed the Word of God. He was obedient to his calling. Jeremiah's book begins with his call to be a prophet. The next 38 chapters are prophecies about Israel (the nation united) and Judah (the Southern Kingdom). Chapters 2—20 are general and undated, and chapters 21—39 are particular and dated. The basic theme of Jeremiah's message is simple: "Repent and turn to God or he will punish." But then, because the people reject this warning, Jeremiah moves to predicting specifically the destruction of Jerusalem. This terrible event is described in chapter 39. Chapters 40—44 describe events following Jerusalem's fall. The book concludes with prophecies concerning a variety of nations (chapters 45—52).

As you read Jeremiah, feel with him as he agonizes over the message he must deliver, pray with him for those who refuse to respond to the truth, and watch his example of faith and courage. Then commit yourself to being successful in God's eyes.

ah falls;
salem destroyed;
miah's ministry ends

First
exiles
return
to Judah
537

THE BLUEPRINT

A. GOD'S JUDGMENT ON JUDAH
   (1:1—45:5)
   1. God calls Jeremiah
   2. Jeremiah condemns Judah for her sins
   3. Jeremiah prophesies destruction
   4. Jeremiah accuses Judah's leaders
   5. Restoration is promised
   6. God's promised judgment arrives

Jeremiah confronts many people with their sins: kings, false prophets, those at the temples, and those at the gates. A lack of response made Jeremiah wonder if he was doing any good at all. He often felt discouraged and sometimes bitter. To bring such gloomy messages to these people was a burdensome task. We too have a responsibility to bring this news to a fallen world: those who continue in their sinful ways are eternally doomed. Although we may feel discouraged at the lack of response, we must press on to tell others about the consequences of sin and the hope that God offers. Telling people only what they want to hear isn't remaining faithful to God's message.

B. GOD'S JUDGMENT ON THE NATIONS
   (46:1—52:34)
   1. Prophecies about foreign nations
   2. Details about the fall of Jerusalem

Jeremiah lived to see many of his prophecies come true—most notably the fall of Jerusalem. The fulfillment of this and other prophecies against the foreign nations came as a result of sin. Sin, when unconfessed, will bring a full judgment from God in order to curb evil and bring people to God.

MEGATHEMES

THEME	EXPLANATION	IMPORTANCE
Sin	King Josiah's reformation failed because the people's repentance was shallow. They continued in their selfishness and worship of idols. All the leaders rejected God's law and will for the people. Jeremiah lists all their sins, predicts God's judgment, and begs for repentance.	Judah's deterioration and disaster came from their callous disregard and disobedience of God. When we ignore sin and refuse to listen to God's warning, we invite disaster.
Punishment	Because of sin, Jerusalem was destroyed, the Temple was ruined, and the people were captured and carried off to Babylon. The people were responsible for their destruction and captivity because they refused to listen to God's message.	Unconfessed sin brings God's full punishment. It is useless to blame anyone else for our sin—we are accountable to God before anyone else. We must answer to him for how we live.
God is Lord of all	God is the righteous Creator. He is accountable to no one. He wisely and lovingly directs all creation to fulfill his plans, and he brings events to pass according to his timetable. He is Lord over all the world.	Because of God's majestic power and love, our only duty is to submit to his authority. By following his plans, not our own, we can have a loving relationship with him and serve him with our whole hearts.
New hearts	Jeremiah predicted that after the destruction of the nation, God would send a new Shepherd, the Messiah. He would lead them into a new future, a new covenant, and a new day of hope. He would accomplish this by changing their sinful hearts into hearts of love for God.	God still restores his people by renewing their hearts. His love can transform the problems created by sin. We can have hope for a new heart by loving God, trusting Christ to save us, and repenting of our sin.
Faithful service	Jeremiah served God faithfully for 40 years. During that time the people ignored, rejected, and persecuted him. Jeremiah's preaching was unsuccessful by human standards, yet he did not fail in his task. He remained faithful to God.	People's acceptance or rejection of us is not the measure of our success. God's approval alone should be our standard for service. We must bring God's message to others even when we are rejected. We must do God's work even if it means suffering for it.

A. GOD'S JUDGMENT ON JUDAH (1:1—45:5)

Jeremiah was called by God to be a prophet to Judah (the Southern Kingdom). He faithfully confronted the leaders and the people with their sin, prophesied both their 70-year captivity in Babylon and their eventual return from exile. After surviving the fall of Jerusalem, Jeremiah was forcefully taken to Egypt. Yet Jeremiah remained faithful in spite of Jerusalem's destruction. Years of obedience had made him strong and courageous. May we be able to stand through difficult times as did Jeremiah.

1. God calls Jeremiah

1 These are God's messages to Jeremiah the priest (the son of Hilkiah) who lived in the town of Anathoth in the land of Benjamin. The first of these messages came to him in the thirteenth year of the reign of Amon's son Josiah, king of Judah. ³Others came during the reign of Josiah's son Jehoiakim, king of Judah, and at various other times until July of the eleventh year of the reign of Josiah's son Zedekiah, king of Judah, when Jerusalem was captured and the people were taken away as slaves.

⁴The Lord said to me, ⁵"I knew you before you were formed within your mother's womb; before you were born I sanctified you and appointed you as my spokesman to the world."

⁶"O Lord God," I said, "I can't do that! I'm far too young! I'm only a youth!"

⁷"Don't say that," he replied, "for you will go wherever I send you and speak whatever I tell you to. ⁸And don't be afraid of the people, for I, the Lord, will be with you and see you through."

⁹Then he touched my mouth and said, "See, I have put my words in your mouth! ¹⁰Today your work begins, to warn the nations and the kingdoms of the world. In accord with my words spoken through your mouth I will tear down some and destroy them, and plant others and nurture them and make them strong and great."

¹¹Then the Lord said to me, "Look, Jeremiah! What do you see?"

And I replied, "I see a whip made from the branch of an almond tree."

¹²And the Lord replied, "That's right, and it means that I will surely carry out my threats of punishment."

1:1
1 Kgs 13:2
2 Kgs 21:24
2 Chron 36:12
Ezra 1:1
Jer 3:6; 36:2
Dan 9:2
1:3
2 Kgs 23:34
Jer 25:1; 39:2
1:5
Ps 139:15,16
Isa 49:1,5
Jer 25:15-26
1:6
Ex 4:10
1:7
Ezek 2:3,4
1:8
Ezek 2:6
1:9
Ex 4:11-16
Deut 18:18
1:10
Isa 44:26-28
Jer 24:6; 31:28
1:11
Jer 24:3
Amos 7:8
1:12
Deut 32:35

1:12 *I will surely carry out my threats of punishment.* There is a word play here between *shaqedh* (almond) in vs 11 and *shoqedh* (watching) in vs 12: "For I am watching over my word to perform it."

1:1, 2 The united kingdom of Israel had split into rival northern and southern kingdoms. The Northern Kingdom was called Israel; the Southern, Judah. Jeremiah lived and prophesied during the reigns of the last five kings of Judah. This was a chaotic time politically, morally, and spiritually. As Babylon, Egypt, and Assyria battled for world supremacy, Judah found herself caught in the middle of the triangle. Although Jeremiah prophesied for 40 years, he never saw his people repent.

1:2, 3 God spoke many times to Jeremiah over many years, but Jeremiah's job was to determine what God wanted him to do each day. So it is with us—God has given us his Word, with many messages. But as we search the Scriptures, we must keep asking, "What do you want me to do for you *today?*"

1:4 God knew you, as he knew Jeremiah, long before you were born or even conceived. He knew you, thought about you, and planned for you. When you feel discouraged or inadequate, remember that God has always thought of you as valuable and has had a purpose in mind for you.

1:5 Each Christian has a purpose in life, but some are appointed or anointed by God for a specific kind of work. Samson (Judges 13:3-5), David (1 Samuel 16:1), John the Baptist (Luke 1:15), and Paul (Galatians 1:15, 16) were each called to do a particular job for God. Whatever work you do should be done for the glory of God. If God gives you a specific task, accept it cheerfully and do it with excellence. If God has not given you a specific assignment, then seek to fulfill the mission common to all believers—love, obey, and serve God—until such time as his guidance becomes more clear.

1:6–8 Often people struggle with new challenges because they lack self-confidence. They feel they have inadequate ability,

training, or experience. Jeremiah thought he was too young and inexperienced to be God's spokesman to the world. But God promised to be with him. We must never allow feelings of inadequacy to keep us from obeying God's call. He will *always* be with us. When you find yourself avoiding something you know you should do, be careful not to use lack of self-confidence as an excuse. If God gives you a job to do, he will provide all you need to do it.

1:7–10 God's message to Jeremiah was like his message to Moses: the God who made our mouths can provide the words he wants us to speak (Exodus 3:10—4:12).

1:8 God promised to see Jeremiah through trouble, not to keep trouble from coming. God did not insulate him from jailings, deportation, or insults. God does not keep us from encountering life's storms, but he will see us through them. In fact, he walks through these storms with us.

1:10 Jeremiah's work was to warn not only the Jews, but all the nations of the world about God's judgment on sin. Don't forget in reading the Old Testament that, while God was consistently working through the people of Judah and Israel, his plan was to communicate to every nation and person. We are included in Jeremiah's message of judgment and hope, and as believers, we are to share God's desire to reach the whole world for him.

1:11–14 The vision of the almond branch reveals the beginning of God's judgment, for the almond tree is among the first to blossom in the spring. God sees the sins of Judah and the nations, and will carry out swift and certain judgment (as the whip symbolizes). The boiling pot tipping southward and spilling over Judah is filled with God's scalding judgment through Babylon, against Jeremiah's people.

1:13
Zech 4:2

13Then the Lord asked me, "What do you see now?"

And I replied, "I see a pot of boiling water, tipping southward, spilling over Judah."

1:14
Isa 41:25
Jer 4:6; 10:22

14"Yes," he said, "for terror from the north will boil out upon all the people of this land. 15I am calling the armies of the kingdoms of the north to come to Jerusalem and set their thrones at the gates of the city and all along its walls, and in all the other cities of Judah. 16This is the way I will punish my people for deserting me and for worshiping other gods—yes, idols they themselves have made! 17Get up and dress and go out and tell them whatever I tell you to say. Don't be afraid of them, or else I will make a fool of you in front of them. 18For see, today I have made you impervious to their attacks. They cannot harm you. You are strong like a fortified city that cannot be captured, like an iron pillar and heavy gates of brass. All the kings of Judah and its officers and priests and people will not be able to prevail against you. 19They will try, but they will fail. For I am with you," says the Lord. "I will deliver you."

1:15
Isa 22:7
Jer 25:9

1:16
Isa 2:8; 37:19
Jer 7:9; 10:3-5
19:4

1:17
Ezek 3:16-18

1:19
Jer 20:11

2. Jeremiah condemns Judah for her sins
Israel turns away from God

2:2
Isa 58:1
Ezek 16:8

2 Again the Lord spoke to me and said: 2Go and shout this in Jerusalem's streets: The Lord says, I remember how eager you were to please me as a young bride long ago and how you loved me and followed me even through the barren deserts. 3In those days Israel was a holy people, the first of my children. All who harmed them were counted deeply guilty, and great evil fell on anyone who touched them.

2:3
Ex 19:5,6
Deut 7:6; 14:2
Isa 41:11
Jer 30:16

4, 5O Israel, says the Lord, why did your fathers desert me? What sin did they find in me that turned them away and changed them into fools who worship idols?

2:4
2 Kgs 17:15
Mic 6:3

1:13 *spilling over Judah,* implied.   2:3 *the first of my children,* literally, "the firstfruits of his harvest."

JEREMIAH
served as a
prophet to Judah
from 627 B.C.
until the exile in
586 B.C.

Climate of the times	• Society was deteriorating economically, politically, spiritually. • Wars and captivity. • God's Word was outlawed.
Main message	Repentance from sin would postpone Judah's coming judgment at the hands of Babylon.
Importance of message	Repentance is one of the greatest needs in our immoral world. God's promises to the faithful shine brightly by bringing hope for tomorrow and strength for today.
Contemporary Prophets	Habakkuk (612–589) Zephaniah (640–621)

1:14-19 The problems we face may not seem as ominous as Jeremiah's problems, but they are critical to us and may overwhelm us! God's promise to Jeremiah and to us is that nothing will defeat us completely; he will help us through the most agonizing problems. Live with the assurance that God will be with you and see you through.

1:16 The people of Judah sinned greatly by continuing to worship idols. God had commanded them specifically against this (Exodus 20:3, 4) because idolatry places trust in creation rather than the Creator. Many "idols" entice us to turn away from God. Material possessions, dreams for the future, approval of others, and vocational goals compete for our total commitment. Striving after these at the expense of our commitment to God puts our heart where Judah's was—and God severely punished Judah.

2:1–3:5 In this section, the marriage analogy sharply contrasts God's love for his people with their love for other gods and reveals Judah's faithlessness. Jeremiah condemns Judah for seeking security in changeable things rather than the unchangeable God. We may be tempted to seek security from possessions, people, or our own abilities, but these will fail us. There is no lasting security apart from our eternal God.

2:2 We appreciate a friend who remains true to his commitment, and we are disappointed with someone who fails to keep a promise. God was pleased when his people obeyed initially, but he became angry with them when they refused to keep their commitment. Temptations distract us from our original commitment to God. Think about your original commitment to obey God, and ask yourself if you are remaining true.

2:3 The phrase *first of my children* is also translated *the firstfruits of his harvest.* As the first portion of the harvest was set apart for God (Deuteronomy 26:1–11), so was Israel in years gone by. In those years, Israel was as eager to please God as if she were his young bride, a holy, committed people—this was in stark contrast with the people of Jeremiah's time.

2:4–8 Jeremiah knew Israel's history well (the united nation of Israel included both Israel and Judah). The prophets recited history to the people for several reasons: (1) to remind them of God's faithfulness; (2) to make sure the people wouldn't forget; (3) to emphasize God's love for them; and (4) to remind them that there was a time when they were close to God. We should learn from history the successes and failures of others so we can build on the successes and avoid repeating the failures.

⁶They ignore the fact that it was I, the Lord, who brought them safely out of Egypt and led them through the barren wilderness, a land of deserts and rocks, of drought and death, where no one lives or even travels. ⁷And I brought them into a fruitful land, to eat of its bounty and goodness, but they made it into a land of sin and corruption and turned my inheritance into an evil thing. ⁸Even their priests cared nothing for the Lord, and their judges ignored me; their rulers turned against me, and their prophets worshiped Baal and wasted their time on nonsense.

⁹But I will not give you up—I will plead for you to return to me, and will keep on pleading; yes, even with your children's children in the years to come!

¹⁰, ¹¹Look around you and see if you can find another nation anywhere that has traded in its old gods for new ones—even though their gods are nothing. Send to the west to the island of Cyprus; send to the east to the deserts of Kedar. See if anyone there has ever heard so strange a thing as this. And yet my people have given up their glorious God for silly idols! ¹²The heavens are shocked at such a thing and shrink back in horror and dismay. ¹³For my people have done two evil things: They have forsaken me, the Fountain of Life-giving Water; and they have built for themselves broken cisterns that can't hold water!

¹⁴Why has Israel become a nation of slaves? Why is she captured and led far away?

¹⁵I see great armies marching on Jerusalem with mighty shouts to destroy her and leave her cities in ruins, burned and desolate. ¹⁶I see the armies of Egypt rising against her, marching from their cities of Memphis and Tahpanhes to utterly destroy Israel's glory and power. ¹⁷And you have brought this on yourselves by rebelling against the Lord your God when he wanted to lead you and show you the way!

¹⁸What have you gained by your alliances with Egypt and with Assyria? ¹⁹Your own wickedness will punish you. You will see what an evil, bitter thing it is to rebel against the Lord your God, fearlessly forsaking him, says the Lord Almighty. ²⁰Long ago you shook off my yoke and broke away from my ties. Defiant, you would not obey me. On every hill and under every tree you've bowed low before idols.

²¹How could this happen? How could this be? For when I planted you, I chose my seed so carefully—the very best. Why have you become this degenerate race of evil men? ²²No amount of soap or lye can make you clean. You are stained with guilt that cannot ever be washed away. I see it always before me, the Lord God says. ²³You say it isn't so, that you haven't worshiped idols? How can you say a thing like that? Go and look in any valley in the land! Face the awful sins that you have done, O restless female camel, seeking for a male! ²⁴You are a wild donkey, sniffing the wind at mating time. (Who can restrain your lust?) Any jack wanting you need not search, for you come running to him! ²⁵Why don't you turn from all

2:6
Deut 8:15; 32:10

2:7
Deut 8:7-9
11:10-12
Jer 3:2; 16:18

2:8
Jer 10:21; 23:13
Hab 2:18
Mal 2:6,7

2:10
Ps 106:20
120:5
Isa 23:12; 37:19
Jer 16:20; 49:28
Rom 1:23

2:13
Ps 36:9
Jer 17:13
Jn 4:14

2:15
Jer 4:7

2:16
Jer 44:1
Hos 9:6

2:17
Deut 32:10
Jer 4:18

2:19
Ps 36:1
Isa 3:9
Jer 3:8; 5:24
Hos 11:7
Amos 8:10

2:20
Deut 12:2
Isa 57:5
Jer 32:6; 17:2

2:21
Ex 15:17
Ps 80:8
Isa 5:2,4

2:22
Jer 4:14

2:23
Prov 30:12
Jer 7:31

2:25
Deut 32:16
Jer 18:12

2:15 *I see great armies marching on Jerusalem with mighty shouts,* literally, "The lions have roared against him."

2:9 God's love persists, even when we don't deserve it. Why? God knows how much we will lose if we fail to respond to his love—eternity is a long, long time without him.

2:13 Who would set aside a sparkling fresh spring of water for a cistern, a pit that collected rain water? God told the Israelites that was what they were doing when they turned from him, the Fountain of Life-giving Water, to idols. Not only that, the cisterns they chose were broken and empty. The people had built religious systems to store truth in, but they were worthless. Why should we cling to the broken promises of unstable "cisterns" (money, power, religious sytems, or whatever transient thing we are putting in place of God), when God promises to constantly refresh us with himself, the Life-giving Water?

2:16, 17 Jeremiah could be speaking of Pharaoh Shishak's previous invasion of Judah in 925 B.C., or he may have been predicting Pharaoh Neco's invasion in 607 B.C. when King Josiah

of Judah would be killed (2 Kings 23:29, 30). His point is that the people brought this on themselves by rebelling against God.

2:22 The stain of sin is more than skin deep. Israel had stains that could not be washed out, even with the strongest cleansers. Spiritual cleansing must reach deep into the heart—and this is a job that God alone can do. We cannot ignore the stain of sin and hope it will go away. Your sin has caused a deep stain that God can and will remove if you are willing to let him cleanse you (Isaiah 1:18).

2:23-27 The people are compared to animals who search for mates in mating season. Unrestrained, they rush for power, money, alliances with foreign powers, and other gods. The idols did not seek the people; the people sought the idols and then ran wildly after them. Then they became so comfortable in their sin that they could not think of giving it up. Their only shame was in getting caught. If we desire something so much that we'll do anything to get it, this is a sign that we are out of tune with God.

this weary running after other gods? But you say, "Don't waste your breath. I've fallen in love with these strangers and I can't stop loving them now!"

26, 27Like a thief, the only shame that Israel knows is getting caught. Kings, princes, priests and prophets—all are alike in this. They call a carved-up wooden post their father, and for their mother they have an idol chiseled out from stone. Yet in time of trouble they cry to me to save them! 28Why don't you call on these gods you have made? When danger comes, let *them* go out and save you if they can! For you have as many gods as there are cities in Judah. 29Don't come to me—you are all rebels, says the Lord. 30I have punished your children but it did them no good; they still will not obey. And you yourselves have killed my prophets as a lion kills its prey.

31O my people, listen to the words of God: Have I been unjust to Israel? Have I been to them a land of darkness and of evil? Why then do my people say, "At last we are free from God; we won't have anything to do with him again!" 32How can you disown your God like that? Can a girl forget her jewels? What bride will seek to hide her wedding dress? Yet for years on end my people have forgotten me—the most precious of their treasures.

33How you plot and scheme to win your lovers. The most experienced harlot could learn a lot from you! 34Your clothing is stained with the blood of the innocent and the poor. Brazenly you murder without a cause. 35And yet you say, "I haven't done a thing to anger God. I'm sure he isn't angry!" I will punish you severely because you say, "I haven't sinned!"

36First here, then there, you flit about, going from one ally to another for their help; but it's all no good—your new friends in Egypt will forsake you as Assyria did before. 37You will be left in despair, and cover your face with your hands, for the Lord has rejected the ones that you trust. You will not succeed despite their aid.

3 There is a law that if a man divorces a woman who then remarries, he is not to take her back again, for she has become corrupted. But though you have left me and married many lovers, yet I have invited you to come to me again, the Lord

2:32 *How can you disown your God like that?* Implied. *The most precious of their treasures,* implied. 2:35 *he isn't angry,* implied.

Cross-references (left margin):

2:26
Isa 26:16

2:28
Deut 32:37
2 Kgs 17:30,31
Isa 45:20
Jer 11:12,13

2:29
Dan 9:11

2:30
Neh 9:26
Isa 1:5
Jer 5:3; 7:28
26:20-24

2:31
Deut 32:15

2:32
Isa 17:10
Jer 3:21
Hos 8:14

2:34
2 Kgs 21:16
Jer 7:6; 19:4

2:35
Jer 25:31

2:36
2 Chron 28:16,
20,21
Hos 12:1
1 Jn 1:8,10

2:37
Jer 37:7-10

3:1
Deut 24:4
Ezek 16:26,
28,29

THE KINGS OF JEREMIAH'S LIFETIME	King	Story of his reign	Dates of his reign	Character of reign	Jeremiah's message to the King
	Josiah	2 Kings 22:1—23:30	640–609 B.C.	Mostly good	3:6–25; 47:1–7
	Jehoahaz	2 Kings 23:31–33	609 B.C.	Evil	22:11, 12
	Jehoiakim	2 Kings 23:34—24:7	609–598 B.C.	Evil	22:13–23; 25:1–38; 26:1–24; 27:1–11; 35:1–19; 36:1–32
	Jehoiachin	2 Kings 24:8–17	598–597 B.C.	Evil	13:18–27 22:24–30
	Zedekiah	2 Kings 24:18—25:26	597–586 B.C.	Evil	21:1–14; 24:8–10; 27:12–22; 32:1–5; 34:1–22; 37:1–21; 38:1–28; 51:59–64

2:30 Being a prophet in those days was risky business. Prophets had to criticize the policies of evil kings, and this made them appear to be traitors. The kings hated the prophets for standing against their policies, and the people often hated them for preaching against their idolatrous life-styles. (See Acts 7:52.)

2:31, 32 Forgetting can be dangerous, whether it is intentional or an oversight. Israel forgot God by focusing its affections on the allurements of the world. The more we focus on the pleasures of the world, the easier it becomes to forget God's care, his love, his dependability, his guidance, and most of all, God himself. What pleases you most? Have you been forgetting God lately?

2:36 God is not against alliances or working partnerships, but he is against people trusting others for the help that should come from

him. This was the problem in Jeremiah's time. After the days of David and Solomon, Israel fell apart because the leaders turned to other nations and gods instead of the true God. They played power politics, thinking that their strong neighbors could protect them. But Judah would soon learn that its alliance with Egypt would be just as disappointing as its former alliance with Assyria (2 Kings 16:7–9; Isaiah 7:13–25).

3:1 This law, found in Deuteronomy 24:1–4, says that a divorced woman who remarries can never be reunited with her first husband. Judah "divorced" God and "married" other gods. God had every right to permanently disown his wayward people, but in his mercy he was willing to take them back again.

says. ²Is there a single spot in all the land where you haven't been defiled by your adulteries—your worshiping these other gods? You sit like a prostitute beside the road waiting for a client! You sit alone like a Bedouin in the desert. You have polluted the land with your vile prostitution. ³That is why even the springtime rains have failed. For you are a prostitute, and completely unashamed. ⁴,⁵And yet you say to me, "O Father, you have always been my Friend; surely you won't be angry about such a little thing! Surely you will just forget it?" So you talk, and keep right on doing all the evil that you can.

Israel is like a faithless wife

⁶This message from the Lord came to me during the reign of King Josiah: Have you seen what Israel does? Like a wanton wife who gives herself to other men at every chance, so Israel has worshiped other gods on every hill, beneath every shady tree. ⁷I thought that someday she would return to me and once again be mine; but she didn't come back. And her faithless sister Judah saw the continued rebellion of Israel. ⁸Yet she paid no attention, even though she saw that I divorced faithless Israel. But now Judah too has left me and given herself to prostitution, for she has gone to other gods to worship them. ⁹She treated it all so lightly—to her it was nothing at all that she should worship idols made of wood and stone. And so the land was greatly polluted and defiled. ¹⁰Then, afterwards, this faithless one "returned" to me, but her "sorrow" was only faked, the Lord God says. ¹¹In fact, faithless Israel is less guilty than treacherous Judah!

¹²Therefore go and say to Israel, O Israel, my sinful people, come home to me again, for I am merciful; I will not be forever angry with you. ¹³Only acknowledge your guilt; admit that you rebelled against the Lord your God and committed adultery against him by worshiping idols under every tree; confess that you refused to follow me. ¹⁴O sinful children, come home, for I am your Master and I will bring you again to the land of Israel—one from here and two from there, wherever you are scattered. ¹⁵And I will give you leaders after my own heart, who will guide you with wisdom and understanding.

3:2 *your worshiping these other gods,* implied.

3:2
Deut 12:2
Jer 2:7,20
Ezek 16:25

3:3
Jer 6:15; 14:3-6

3:6
Jer 17:2
Ezek 23:4-10

3:8
Isa 50:1
Ezek 16:46,47
23:11

3:9
Isa 57:6
Jer 2:7,27

3:10
Jer 12:2

3:11
Ezek 16:51

3:12
Ps 86:15
Jer 31:20; 33:26

3:13
Deut 12:2
30:1-3
Jer 14:20

3:14
Jer 50:4,5
Hos 2:19

3:15
Jer 23:4
Acts 20:28

3:3 The words *corrupted, defiled,* and *polluted* reveal a serious problem that has gradually spread until it affects everything. In this situation, even nature has been affected by a drought, which God permitted to bring the people to their senses. Sin brings drastic consequences once it gains a foothold in our lives. Lies lead to more lies and hatred to more hatred. Jeremiah reminded his people repeatedly that sin must not go on unchecked.

3:4, 5 Notice how the people of Israel played down their sin. When we know we've done something wrong, we want to downplay the error by saying "It wasn't that bad!" thereby relieving some of the guilt we feel. As we play down our sinfulness, we naturally shy away from making changes, and so we keep on sinning. But if we view every wrong attitude and action as a serious offense to God, we will begin to understand what living for God is all about. Is there any sin in your life that you've written off as too small to worry about? God says that we must confess every sin, and in confessing it, turn from it.

3:6—6:30 The Northern Kingdom, Israel, had fallen to Assyria and its people had been taken into captivity. The tragic lesson of their fall should have caused the Southern Kingdom, Judah, to return to God, but it paid no attention. Jeremiah urges Judah to return to God to avoid certain disaster. This message came between 627–621 B.C. during Josiah's reign. Although Josiah obeyed God's commands, his example apparently did not influence the people. If the people refused to repent, God said he would destroy the nation because of the evils of King Manasseh (2 Kings 23:25–27).

3:11–13 Israel was not even trying to look as if it were obeying God, but Judah maintained the appearance of right faith without a true heart. Believing the right doctrines without heart-commitment

is like offering sacrifices without true repentance. Judah's false repentance brought Jeremiah's words of condemnation. To live without faith is hopeless; to express sorrow without change is treacherous. Being sorry for sin is not enough. Repentance demands a change of mind and heart which results in changed behavior.

3:12–18 The Northern Kingdom, Israel, was in captivity, punished for their sins. The people of Judah looked down on these northern neighbors for their blatant heresy and degraded morals. Even so, Jeremiah promised the remnant of Israel God's blessings if they would still turn to him. Judah, still secure, should have turned to God after seeing the destruction of Israel. But they refused, so Jeremiah startled them by telling them about God's promise to Israel's remnant if they would repent.

3:15 God promised to give his people leaders who would follow him, filled with wisdom and understanding. God saw Israel's lack of direction, so he promised to provide the right kind of leadership for them. We look to and trust our leaders for guidance and direction. But if they do not follow God, they will lead us astray. Pray for godly leaders in our nations, communities, and churches, leaders who will be good examples and bring God's wisdom to his people.

3:16, 17 In the days of David and Solomon's reign over a united Israel, the people had a beautiful Temple where they worshiped God. The Temple housed the Ark of the Covenant, the symbol of God's presence with the people. The Ark held the tablets of the Ten Commandments (see Exodus 25:10–22). Those days with the Ark won't be missed in the future kingdom, because God's presence by the Holy Spirit will be there personally among his people.

3:16
Isa 65:17

3:17
Jer 12:15,16
16:19; 17:12
Ezek 43:7

3:18
Isa 60:9
Jer 16:14,15
31:8; 50:4,5
Hos 1:11

3:19
Isa 63:16

3:21
Isa 15:2
Jer 2:32

3:22
Hos 6:1; 14:4

16Then, when your land is once more filled with people, says the Lord, you will no longer wish for "the good old days of long ago" when you possessed the Ark of God's covenant. Those days will not be missed or even thought about, and the Ark will not be reconstructed, 17for the Lord himself will be among you, and the whole city of Jerusalem will be known as the throne of the Lord, and all nations will come to him there and no longer stubbornly follow their evil desires. 18At that time the people of Judah and of Israel will return together from their exile in the north, to the land I gave their fathers as an inheritance forever. 19And I thought how wonderful it would be for you to be here among my children. I planned to give you part of this beautiful land, the finest in the world. I looked forward to your calling me "Father," and thought that you would never turn away from me again. 20But you have betrayed me; you have gone off and given yourself to a host of foreign gods; you have been like a faithless wife who leaves her husband.

21I hear voices high upon the windswept mountains, crying, crying. It is the sons of Israel who have turned their backs on God and wandered far away. 22O my

---

Endurance is not a common quality. Many people lack the long-term commitment, care, and willingness that are vital to sticking with a task despite all odds. But Jeremiah was a prophet who endured.

Jeremiah's call by God teaches how intimately God knows us. He valued us before anyone else knew we would exist. He cared for us while we were in our mother's womb. He planned our lives while our bodies were still being formed. He values us more highly than we value ourselves.

Jeremiah had to depend on God's love as he developed endurance. His audiences were usually antagonistic or apathetic to his messages. He was ignored; his life was often threatened. He saw both the excitement of a spiritual awakening and the sorrow of a national return to idolatry. With the exception of the good King Josiah, Jeremiah watched king after king ignore his warnings and lead the people away from God. He saw fellow prophets murdered. He himself was severely persecuted. Finally, he watched the defeat of Judah at the hands of the Babylonians.

Jeremiah responded to all this with God's Word and human tears. He felt firsthand God's love for his people and the people's rejection of that love. But even when he was angry with God and tempted to give up, Jeremiah knew he had to keep going. God had called him to endure. He expressed intense feelings but he also saw beyond the feelings to the God who was soon to execute justice, but who afterward would administer mercy.

It may be easy for us to identify with Jeremiah's frustrations and discouragement, but we need to realize that this prophet's life is also an encouragement to faithfulness.

Strengths and accomplishments:
● Wrote two Old Testament books, Jeremiah and Lamentations
● Ministered during the reigns of the last five kings of Judah
● Was a catalyst for the great spiritual reformation under Josiah
● Acted as God's faithful messenger in spite of many attempts on his life
● Was so deeply sorrowful for the fallen condition of Israel that he earned the title "weeping prophet"

Lessons from his life:
● The majority opinion is not necessarily God's will
● Although punishment for sin is severe, there is hope in God's mercy
● God will not accept empty or insincere worship
● Serving God does not guarantee earthly security

Vital statistics:
● Where: Anathoth
● Occupation: Prophet
● Relatives: Father: Hilkiah
● Contemporaries: Josiah, Jehoahaz, Jehoiakim, Jehoiachin, Zedekiah, Baruch

Key verses:
" 'O Lord God,' I said, 'I can't do that! I'm far too young! I'm only a youth!' 'Don't say that,' he replied, 'for you will go wherever I send you and speak whatever I tell you to. And don't be afraid of the people, for I, the Lord, will be with you and see you through' " (Jeremiah 1:6–8).

Jeremiah's story is told in the book of Jeremiah. He is also mentioned in Ezra 1:1; Daniel 9:2; Matthew 2:17; 16:14; 27:9. See also 2 Chronicles 34, 35 for the story of the spiritual revival under Josiah.

rebellious children, come back to me again and I will heal you from your sins. And they reply, Yes, we will come, for you are the Lord our God. ²³We are weary of worshiping idols on the hills and of having orgies on the mountains. It is all a farce. Only in the Lord our God can Israel ever find her help and her salvation. ²⁴From our childhood we have seen everything our fathers had—flocks and herds and sons and daughters—squandered on priests and idols. ²⁵We lie in shame and in dishonor, for we and our fathers have sinned from childhood against the Lord our God; we have not obeyed him.

3:23
Ps 3:8; 121:1,2
Jer 17:14

3:25
Jer 22:21
Ezra 9:7

Destruction rolls over the land

4 O Israel, if you will truly return to me and absolutely discard your idols, ²and if you will swear by me alone, the living God, and begin to live good, honest, clean lives, then you will be a testimony to the nations of the world and they will come to me and glorify my name.

³The Lord is saying to the men of Judah and Jerusalem, Plow up the hardness of your hearts; otherwise the good seed will be wasted among the thorns. ⁴Cleanse your minds and hearts, not just your bodies, or else my anger will burn you to a crisp because of all your sins. And no one will be able to put the fire out.

⁵Shout to Jerusalem and to all Judea, telling them to sound the alarm throughout the land. "Run for your lives! Flee to the fortified cities!" ⁶Send a signal from Jerusalem: "Flee now, don't delay!" For I the Lord am bringing vast destruction on you from the north. ⁷A lion—a destroyer of nations—stalks from his lair; and he is headed for your land. Your cities will lie in ruin without inhabitant. ⁸Put on clothes of mourning and weep with broken hearts, for the fierce anger of the Lord has not stopped yet. ⁹In that day, says the Lord, the king and the princes will tremble in fear; and the priests and the prophets will be stricken with horror.

¹⁰(Then I said, "But Lord, the people have been deceived by what you said, for you promised great blessings on Jerusalem. Yet the sword is even now poised to strike them dead!")

¹¹, ¹²At that time he will send a burning wind from the desert upon them—not in little gusts but in a roaring blast—and he will pronounce their doom. ¹³The enemy shall roll down upon us like a storm wind; his chariots are like a whirlwind; his steeds are swifter than eagles. Woe, woe upon us, for we are doomed.

¹⁴O Jerusalem, cleanse your hearts while there is time. You can yet be saved by casting out your evil thoughts. ¹⁵From Dan and from Mount Ephraim your doom has been announced. ¹⁶Warn the other nations that the enemy is coming from a distant land and they shout against Jerusalem and the cities of Judah. ¹⁷They surround Jerusalem like shepherds moving in on some wild animal! For my people have rebelled against me, says the Lord. ¹⁸Your ways have brought this down upon you; it is a bitter dose of your own medicine, striking deep within your hearts.

¹⁹My heart, my heart—I writhe in pain; my heart pounds within me. I cannot be

4:1
Jer 7:3,7; 35:15
Joel 2:12

4:2
Deut 10:20
Isa 65:16
Jer 9:24
1 Cor 1:31

4:3
Hos 10:12
Mt 13:7,22

4:4
Deut 10:16
Isa 30:27
Jer 9:25,26
Mk 9:43,48
Rom 2:28,29

4:5
Josh 10:20
Jer 6:1

4:6
Jer 1:14,15
6:1,22

4:7
Isa 1:7; 6:11
Jer 2:15; 5:6
25:9,38

4:8
Isa 5:25; 10:4
Jer 6:26

4:9
Jer 48:41

4:13
Isa 66:15
Lam 4:19

4:14
Isa 1:16
Jer 13:27

4:16
Ezek 21:22

4:17
2 Kgs 25:1

4:19
Isa 21:3; 22:4

4:4 *Cleanse your minds and hearts,* literally, "Circumcise yourselves . . . remove the foreskin of your hearts."

3:23–25 Jeremiah predicted a day when the nation would be reunited, true worship would be reinstated, and sin would be seen for what it is. Our world glorifies the thrill that comes from wealth, competition, and sexual sin. It is sad that so few see sin as it really is—a farce. Most people can't see this until they are destroyed by the sin they pursue. The advantage of believing God's Word is that we don't have to learn by experience the destructive results of sin.

4:3, 4 Jeremiah told the people to break up the hardness of their hearts as a plow breaks up rocky soil. Good kings like Josiah had tried to turn the people back to God, but the people had continued to worship their idols in secret. Their hearts had become hardened to God's Word. Jeremiah said the people needed to remove the sin that hardened their hearts before the good seed of God's Word could take root. Likewise we must remove our heart-hardening sin if we expect God's Word to take root and grow in our lives.

4:6, 7 The destruction from the north would come from Babylon

when Nabopolasser and Nebuchadnezzar II attacked (see 2 Chronicles 36).

4:10 Jeremiah, moved by God's words, expressed his deep sorrow to God. Jeremiah was intercessor for the people. They had false expectations because of the past promises of blessings, their blindness to their own sin, and the false prophets who kept telling them that all was well.

4:15 Doom was announced first from Dan and Mount Ephraim because they were located at the northern border of Israel and thus would be the first to see the approaching armies as they attacked from the north. No one would be able to stop the armies because they came as punishment for the people's sin.

4:19–31 Jeremiah was overcome by the sure devastation of the coming judgment. This judgment would continue until the people turned from their sin and listened to God. Although this prophecy refers to the future destruction by Babylon, it could also describe

still because I have heard, O my soul, the blast of the enemies' trumpets and the enemies' battle cries. 20Wave upon wave of destruction rolls over the land, until it lies in utter ruin; suddenly, in a moment, every house is crushed. 21How long must this go on? How long must I see war and death surrounding me?

22"Until my people leave their foolishness, for they refuse to listen to me; they are dull, retarded children who have no understanding. They are smart enough at doing wrong, but for doing right they have no talent, none at all."

23I looked down upon their land and as far as I could see in all directions everything was ruins. And all the heavens were dark. 24I looked at the mountains and saw that they trembled and shook. 25I looked, and mankind was gone and the birds of the heavens had fled.

26The fertile valleys were wilderness and all the cities were broken down before the presence of the Lord, and crushed by his fierce anger. 27The Lord's decree of desolation covers all the land.

"Yet," he says, "there will be a little remnant of my people left. 28The earth shall mourn, the heavens shall be draped with black, because of my decree against my people, but I have made up my mind and I will not change it."

29All the cities flee in terror at the noise of marching armies coming near. The people hide in the bushes and flee to the mountains. All the cities are abandoned—all have fled in terror. 30Why do you put on your most beautiful clothing and jewelry and brighten your eyes with mascara? It will do you no good! Your allies despise you and will kill you.

31I have heard great crying like that of a woman giving birth to her first child; it is the cry of my people gasping for breath, pleading for help, prostrate before their murderers.

No respect for God

5 Run up and down through every street in all Jerusalem; search high and low and see if you can find even one person who is fair and honest! Search every square, and if you find just one, I'll not destroy the city! 2Even under oath, they all lie. 3O Lord, you are looking for faithfulness. You have tried to get them to be honest, for you have punished them, but they won't change! You have destroyed them but they refuse to turn from their sins. They are determined, with faces hard as rock, not to repent.

4Then I said, "But what can we expect from the poor and ignorant? They don't know the ways of God. How can they obey him?"

5I will go now to their leaders, the men of importance, and speak to them, for they know the ways of the Lord and the judgment that follows sin. But they too had utterly rejected their God.

6So I will send upon them the wild fury of the "lion from the forest"; the "desert wolves" shall pounce upon them, and a "leopard" shall lurk around their cities so that all who go out shall be torn apart. For their sins are very many; their rebellion against me is great.

Cross references

4:20
Jer 10:20
Ezek 7:26

4:22
Jer 5:21; 10:8
13:23
Rom 16:19

4:23
Isa 24:19

4:24
Isa 5:25
Ezek 38:20

4:25
Jer 9:10; 12:4
Zeph 1:3

4:27
Jer 5:10,18
12:11,12
30:11; 46:28

4:28
Num 23:19
Isa 5:30; 50:3
Jer 23:20; 30:24
Hos 4:3
Joel 2:30,31

4:29
Isa 2:19-21
Jer 16:16

4:30
2 Kgs 9:30
Jer 22:20,22
Ezek 23:9,10,22

4:31
Jer 13:21
Lam 1:17

5:1
Gen 18:26,32
2 Chron 16:9

5:2
Tit 1:16

5:3
Jer 7:26,28
8:5; 19:15
Ezek 3:8
Zeph 3:2

5:4
Isa 27:11
Jer 4:22
Hos 4:6

5:5
Jer 2:20
Mic 3:1

5:6
Jer 30:14,15
Hos 13:7
Hab 1:8

---

the judgment of all sinners at the end of the world.

4:22 Judah was talented at doing wrong and lacked the will and ability to do right. Right living is more than simply avoiding sin. It requires decision and discipline. We must develop skills in right living because our behavior attracts attention to our God. We should pursue excellence in Christian living with as much effort as we pursue excellence at work.

4:27 God warned that destruction was certain. But he promised that a remnant would remain faithful to him and would be spared, even though the nation would be wiped out. God is committed to preserving those who are faithful to him. Jerusalem was the capital city and center of worship for Judah, but God told Jeremiah there might not be *one* fair and honest person in the entire city. God was willing to spare the city if one such person could be found (he made a similar statement about Sodom, see Genesis 18:32). Have

you ever thought how significant your testimony may be in your city or community? You may represent the only witness for God to many people. Are you faithful to that witness?

5:3 Nothing but truth is acceptable to God. When we pray, sing, speak, or serve, nothing closes the door of God's acceptance more than hypocrisy, lying, or pretense. If we come to God pretending to be something we're not, God sees through us and will refuse to listen.

5:4, 5 Even those who knew God's laws and understood his words of judgment had rejected him. They were supposed to teach and guide the people but instead they led them into sin. Jeremiah observed the poor and ignorant—those who were uninformed of God's ways—and realized they were not learning God's laws from their teachers. Thus, God's search in Jerusalem was complete—there were no true followers in any level of society.

7How can I pardon you? For even your children have turned away, and worship gods that are not gods at all. I fed my people until they were fully satisfied, and their thanks was to commit adultery wholesale and to gang up at the city's brothels. 8They are well-fed, lusty stallions, each neighing for his neighbor's mate. 9Shall I not punish them for this? Shall I not send my vengeance on such a nation as this? 10Go down the rows of the vineyards and destroy them! But leave a scattered few to live. Strip the branches from each vine, for they are not the Lord's.

11For the people of Israel and Judah are full of treachery against me, says the Lord. 12They have lied and said, "He won't bother us! No evil will come upon us! There will be neither famine nor war! 13God's prophets," they say, "are windbags full of words with no divine authority. Their claims of doom will fall upon themselves, not us!"

14Therefore this is what the Lord God of Hosts says to his prophets: Because of talk like this I'll take your words and prophecies and turn them into raging fire and burn up these people like kindling wood. 15See, I will bring a distant nation against you, O Israel, says the Lord—a mighty nation, an ancient nation whose language you don't understand. 16Their weapons are deadly; the men are all mighty. 17And they shall eat your harvest and your children's bread, and your flocks of sheep and herds of cattle, yes, and your grapes and figs; and they shall sack your walled cities that you think are safe.

18But I will not completely blot you out. So says the Lord.

19And when your people ask, "Why is it that the Lord is doing this to us?" then you shall say, "You rejected him and gave yourselves to other gods while in your land; now you must be slaves to foreigners in their lands."

20Make this announcement to Judah and to Israel:

21Listen, O foolish, senseless people—you with the eyes that do not see and the ears that do not listen— 22have you no respect at all for me? the Lord God asks. How can it be that you don't even tremble in my presence? I set the shorelines of the world by perpetual decrees, so that the oceans, though they toss and roar, can never pass those bounds. Isn't such a God to be feared and worshiped?

23, 24But my people have rebellious hearts; they have turned against me and gone off into idolatry. Though I am the one who gives them rain each year in spring and fall and sends the harvest times, yet they have no respect or fear for me. 25And so I have taken away these wondrous blessings from them. This sin has robbed them of all of these good things.

26Among my people are wicked men who lurk for victims like a hunter hiding in a blind. They set their traps for men. 27Like a coop full of chickens their homes are full of evil plots. And the result? Now they are great and rich, 28and well fed and well groomed, and there is no limit to their wicked deeds. They refuse justice to

5:7
Deut 32:21
Jer 2:11
Gal 4:8

5:8
Jer 29:23
Ezek 22:11

5:10
Jer 4:27

5:11
Jer 3:6,7

5:12
2 Chron 36:16
Jer 43:1-4

5:13
Jer 14:13,15

5:14
Jer 23:29

5:15
Deut 28:49
Isa 5:26; 28:11

5:16
Isa 5:28,13:18

5:17
Lev 26:16
Deut 28:31,33
Jer 8:16
Hos 8:14

5:19
Deut 29:24-26
28:48
1 Kgs 9:8,9
Jer 16:10-13

5:21
Isa 43:8
Ezek 12:2
Mt 13:14

5:22
Deut 28:58
Job 38:8-11
Jer 10:7

5:23
Gen 8:22
Ps 78:8; 147:8
Joel 2:23
Mt 5:45

5:25
Jer 2:17; 4:18

5:26
Ps 10:9
Jer 18:22

5:28
Deut 32:15
Isa 1:23
Jer 7:6; 22:3
Zech 7:10

5:7 God held these people responsible for the sins of their children because the children had followed their parents' example. The sin of leading others astray by our example, especially our children, is one for which God will hold us accountable.

5:13 The people refused God's message by saying: (1) that it could never come true, (2) that the prophets did not really have authority, and (3) that the punishments would fall on others. This refusal was not because the prophets failed to do their job but because the people failed to listen. The prophet and his people both have responsibilities—the prophet to faithfully proclaim God's message, and the people to apply it to their lives.

5:15 Babylon was indeed an ancient nation. The old Babylonian Empire lasted from about 1900 B.C. to 1550 B.C., and earlier kingdoms had been on her soil as early as 3000 B.C. Babylon in Jeremiah's day would shortly rebel against Assyrian domination, form its own army, conquer Assyria, and become the next dominant world power.

5:21 Have you ever listened to someone talk, only to realize that you haven't heard a word they said? Jeremiah told the people their

eyes and ears did them no good because they refused to see or hear God's message. The people of Judah and Israel were foolishly deaf when God promised blessings for obedience and destruction for disobedience. When God speaks through his Word or his messengers, we harm ourselves if we fail to listen. God's message will never change us unless we listen to it.

5:22-24 What is your attitude when you come into God's presence? We should come with awe and respect, for God sets the boundaries of the roaring seas and establishes the rains and harvests. God had to strip away all those things that Israel had grown to respect more than he. Without them, the people could once again reverence God. Don't wait until God removes the objects of your reverence and respect before you think of him as you should.

5:28, 29 Justice to orphans and care for the poor are key marks of nations and people who please God. Wicked men in Israel treated the defenseless unjustly, which displeased God greatly. Some of these defenseless ones—orphans, the poor, the lonely—are within your reach. What action can you take to help one of them?

5:30
Jer 23:14
Hos 6:10

5:31
Jer 14:14
Mic 2:11

orphans and the rights of the poor. 29Should I sit back and act as though nothing is going on? the Lord God asks. Shouldn't I punish a nation such as this?

30A horrible thing has happened in this land— 31the priests are ruled by false prophets, and my people like it so! But your doom is certain.

Jerusalem's last warning

6:1
Jer 1:14; 4:6

6:2
Deut 28:56

6:3
2 Kgs 25:1
Jer 4:17
Lk 19:43

6:5
Isa 32:14
Jer 52:13

6:6
Deut 20:19,20

6:7
Jer 30:12,13
Ezek 7:11,23
Jas 3:10-12

6:8
Jer 7:28; 17:23
Hos 9:12

6:9
Jer 8:3,16:16
49:9
Obad 5,6

6:11
Job 32:18,19
Jer 7:20; 9:21
15:6

6:12
Deut 28:30
Jer 8:10; 38:22

6:13
Isa 56:11; 57:17
Jer 22:17
Mic 3:5,11

6:14
Jer 8:11,12
Ezek 13:10

6:15
Jer 3:3; 8:12

6:16
Jer 18:15; 31:21
Mt 11:29

6:17
Isa 21:11; 58:1
Jer 25:4
Ezek 3:17

6:18
Prov 1:31
Isa 1:2
Jer 8:9; 22:29

6 Run, people of Benjamin, run for your lives! Flee from Jerusalem! Sound the alarm in Tekoa; send up a smoke signal at Beth-haccherem; warn everyone that a powerful army is on the way from the north, coming to destroy this nation! 2Helpless as a girl, you are beautiful and delicate—and doomed. 3Evil shepherds shall surround you. They shall set up camp around the city, and divide your pastures for their flocks. 4See them prepare for battle. At noon it has begun. All afternoon it rages, until the evening shadows fall. 5"Come," they say. "Let us attack by night and destroy her palaces!"

6For the Lord Almighty has said to them, Cut down her trees for battering rams; smash down the walls of Jerusalem. This is the city to be punished, for she is vile through and through. 7She spouts evil like a fountain! Her streets echo with the sounds of violence; her sickness and wounds are ever before me.

8This is your last warning, O Jerusalem. If you don't listen, I will empty the land. 9Disaster on disaster shall befall you. Even the few who remain in Israel shall be gleaned again, the Lord Almighty has said; for as a grape-gatherer checks each vine to pick what he has missed, so the remnant of my people shall be destroyed again. 10But who will listen when I warn them? Their ears are closed and they refuse to hear. The word of God has angered them; they don't want it at all.

11For all this I am full of the wrath of God against them. I am weary of holding it in. I will pour it out over Jerusalem, even upon the children playing in the streets, upon the gatherings of young men, and on husbands and wives and grandparents. 12Their enemies shall live in their homes and take their fields and wives. For I will punish the people of this land, the Lord has said. 13They are swindlers and liars, from the least of them right to the top! Yes, even my prophets and priests! 14You can't heal a wound by saying it's not there! Yet the priests and prophets give assurances of peace when all is war. 15Were my people ashamed when they worshiped idols? No, not at all—they didn't even blush. Therefore they shall lie among the slain. They shall die beneath my anger.

16Yet the Lord pleads with you still: Ask where the good road is, the godly paths you used to walk in, in the days of long ago. Travel there, and you will find rest for your souls. But you reply, "No, that is not the road we want!" 17I set watchmen over you who warned you: "Listen for the sound of the trumpet! It will let you know when trouble comes." But you said, "No! We won't pay any attention!"

18, 19This, then, is my decree against my people: (Listen to it, distant lands; listen to it, O my people in Jerusalem; listen to it, all the earth!) I will bring evil upon this people; it will be the fruit of their own sin, because they will not listen to me. They

---

5:31 At this time, the religious climate was chaotic. The priests, God's ministers, were leading by their own authority, not by the truth of God's Word. Many prophets were telling lies and half truths, not messages from God. The people had turned from truth (God's Word) and heard only what they wanted to hear. No wonder Jeremiah's words had little effect.

6:1 Jeremiah warned his own tribe of Benjamin, north of Jerusalem. He advised them to flee, not to the security of the great walled city of Jerusalem, but to Tekoa, a town about 12 miles south of Jerusalem. The warning smoke signal was lit at Beth-haccherem, halfway between Jerusalem and Bethlehem.

6:3 The evil shepherds were the leaders of Babylon's armies, and their "flocks" were the armies of soldiers.

6:9 The remnant mentioned here is not to be confused with the righteous remnant. This remnant is those left after the first wave of destruction. Like a grape-gatherer, Babylon wouldn't be satisfied

until every person was taken. Babylon invaded Judah three times until they destroyed the nation and its Temple completely (2 Kings 24, 25).

6:10 The people became angry and wanted no part of God's commands. Living for God did not appear very exciting. As in Jeremiah's day, people today dislike God's demand for disciplined living. As unsettling as people's responses might be, we must continue to share God's Word. Our responsibility is to present God's Word—their responsibility is to accept it. We must not let what people want to hear set the standard for what we say.

6:14 "Ignore it and maybe it will go away!" Sound familiar? This was Israel's response to Jeremiah's warnings. But denying the truth never changes it; what God says always happens. Sin is never removed by denying its existence. We must confess to God that we have sinned and ask him to forgive us.

reject my law. 20There is no use now in burning sweet incense from Sheba before me! Keep your expensive perfumes! I cannot accept your offerings; they have no sweet fragrance for me. 21I will make an obstacle course of the pathway of my people; fathers and sons shall be frustrated; neighbors and friends shall collapse together. 22The Lord God says, See the armies marching from the north—a great nation is rising against you. 23They are a cruel, merciless people, fully armed, mounted for war. The noise of their army is like a roaring sea.

24We have heard the fame of their armies and we are weak with fright. Fright and pain have gripped us like that of women in travail. 25Don't go out to the fields! Don't travel the roads! For the enemy is everywhere, ready to kill; we are terrorized at every turn.

26O Jerusalem, pride of my people, put on mourning clothes and sit in ashes and weep bitterly as for an only son. For suddenly the destroying armies will be upon you.

27Jeremiah, I have made you an assayer of metals, that you may test this my people and determine their value. Listen to what they are saying and watch what they are doing. 28Are they not the worst of rebels, full of evil talk against the Lord? They are insolent as brass, hard and cruel as iron. 29The bellows blow fiercely; the refining fire grows hotter, but it can never cleanse them, for there is no pureness in them to bring out. Why continue the process longer? All is dross. No matter how hot the fire, they continue in their wicked ways. 30I must label them "Impure, Rejected Silver," and I have discarded them.

The people indulge in false worship

7 Then the Lord said to Jeremiah:
2Go over to the entrance of the Temple of the Lord and give this message to the people: O Judah, listen to this message from God. Listen to it, all of you who worship here. 3The Lord, the God of Israel says: Even yet, if you quit your evil ways I will let you stay in your own land. 4But don't be fooled by those who lie to you and say that since the Temple of the Lord is here, God will never let Jerusalem be destroyed. 5You may remain under these conditions only: If you stop your wicked thoughts and deeds, and are fair to others, 6and stop exploiting orphans, widows and foreigners. And stop your murdering. And stop worshiping idols as you do now to your hurt. 7Then, and only then, will I let you stay in this land that I gave to your fathers to keep forever.

8You think that because the Temple is here, you will never suffer? Don't fool yourselves! 9Do you really think that you can steal, murder, commit adultery, lie, and worship Baal and all of those new gods of yours, 10and then come here and

6:20
Ps 40:6; 50:7-9
Isa 1:11; 60:6
66:3
Amos 5:21

6:21
Isa 8:14
9:14-17
Jer 9:21,22

6:22
Jer 1:15; 10:22

6:23
Isa 5:30
Jer 4:29; 50:42

6:24
Isa 28:19
Jer 4:19-21

6:25
Jer 12:12; 14:18

6:26
Jer 4:8
Amos 8:10
Mic 1:10

6:27
Jer 1:18; 15:20

6:28
Ezek 22:18

6:30
Ps 119:119
Isa 1:22

7:2
Jer 17:19

7:3
Jer 4:1; 18:11
26:13

7:4
Mic 3:11

7:5
Isa 1:19
Jer 21:12; 22:3

7:6
Ex 22:21-24
Deut 6:14,15
Jer 5:28; 13:10

7:7
Deut 4:40

7:9
Jer 11:13,17

6:27-30 Metal is purified by fire. As it is heated, impurities are burned away and only the pure metal remains. As God tested the people of Judah, however, he could find no purity in their lives. They continued in their sinful ways. Do you see impurities in your life that should be burned away? Confess these to God and allow him to purify you as he sees fit. Take time right now to reflect on the areas of your life that he has already refined; then thank him for what he is doing.

7:1—10:25 As this section opens, God sends Jeremiah to the Temple gates to confront the false belief that God will not let harm come to the Temple and those who live near it. Jeremiah rebukes the people for their empty religion, idolatry, and the shameless behavior of the people and their leaders. Judah, he says, is ripe for judgment and exile. This came to pass during the reign of Jehoiakim, a puppet of Egypt. The nation, in shock over the death of Josiah, was going through a spiritual reversal that removed much of the good Josiah had done. The themes of this section are false religion, idolatry, and hypocrisy. Jeremiah was almost put to death for this sermon, but he was saved by the princes.

7:2 The entrance of the Temple was the perfect place to confront people about their biggest problem—hypocrisy. The people believed that the presence of the Temple in their city would protect them and that their religious ritual would save them. God may let Judah fall, but he would never let his Temple be destroyed, they thought. But Jeremiah proclaimed that the Temple and its rituals were worthless if the people's hearts were not right with God.

7:8 The people followed a worship ritual but maintained a sinful lifestyle. It was religion without personal commitment to God. We can easily fall into this snare. Church attendance, sharing communion, teaching Sunday school, singing in the choir—all are empty exercises unless we are truly doing them for God. It is good to do these things, not because we ought to do them for the church, but because we want to do them for God.

7:8-11 There are several parallels between how the people of Judah viewed their Temple and how many today view their churches. (1) *They didn't take the Temple home with them.* We go to beautiful churches well-prepared for worship, but we don't usually take the presence of God with us through the week. (2) *The image of the Temple became more important than the substance of faith.* The image of going to church and belonging to a group can become more important than the substance of a life changed for God. (3) *The people used their Temple as a hideout.* Many use religious affiliation as a mental crutch, thinking it will protect them from evil and problems.

stand before me in my Temple and chant, "We are saved!"—only to go right back to all these evil things again? 11Is my Temple but a den of robbers in your eyes? For I see all the evil going on in there.

12Go to Shiloh, the city I first honored with my name, and see what I did to her because of all the wickedness of my people Israel. 13, 14And now, says the Lord, I will do the same thing here because of all this evil you have done. Again and again I spoke to you about it, rising up early and calling, but you refused to hear or answer. Yes, I will destroy this Temple, as I did in Shiloh—this Temple called by my name, which you trust for help, and this place I gave to you and to your fathers. 15And I will send you into exile, just as I did your brothers, the people of Ephraim.

16Pray no more for these people, Jeremiah. Neither weep for them nor pray nor beg that I should help them, for I will not listen. 17Don't you see what they are doing throughout the cities of Judah and in the streets of Jerusalem? 18No wonder my anger is great! Watch how the children gather wood and the fathers build fires, and the women knead dough and make cakes to offer to "The Queen of Heaven" and to their other idol-gods! 19Am I the one that they are hurting? asks the Lord. Most of all they hurt themselves, to their own shame. 20So the Lord God says, I will pour out my anger, yes, my fury on this place—people, animals, trees and plants will be consumed by the unquenchable fire of my anger.

21The Lord, the God of Israel says, Away with your offerings and sacrifices! 22It wasn't offerings and sacrifices I wanted from your fathers when I led them out of Egypt. That was not the point of my command. 23But what I told them was: *Obey* me and I will be your God and you shall be my people; only do as I say and all shall be well!

24But they wouldn't listen; they kept on doing whatever they wanted to, following their own stubborn, evil thoughts. They went backward instead of forward. 25Ever since the day your fathers left Egypt until now, I have kept on sending them my prophets, day after day. 26But they wouldn't listen to them or even try to hear. They are hard and stubborn and rebellious—worse even than their fathers were.

27Tell them everything that I will do to them, but don't expect them to listen. Cry out your warnings, but don't expect them to respond. 28Say to them: This is the nation that refuses to obey the Lord its God, and refuses to be taught. She continues to live a lie.

29O Jerusalem, shave your head in shame and weep alone upon the mountains; for the Lord has rejected and forsaken this people of his wrath. 30For the people of Judah have sinned before my very eyes, says the Lord. They have set up their idols right in my own Temple, polluting it. 31They have built the altar called Topheth in the Valley of Ben-Hinnom, and there they burn to death their little sons and daughters as sacrifices to their gods—a deed so horrible I've never even thought of it, let alone commanded it to be done. 32The time is coming, says the Lord, when

---

7:11
Isa 56:7
Jer 29:23
Mt 21:13
Mk 11:17
Lk 19:46

7:12
Josh 18:1,10
Jer 26:6

7:13
1 Kgs 9:7
Jer 4:1,2
18:11; 26:13

7:15
Deut 6:14,15
2 Kgs 17:23

7:16
Deut 4:40
Jer 11:14; 15:1

7:18
Deut 32:16
Jer 11:17; 44:17

7:21
Isa 1:11
Jer 6:20; 14:12
Hos 8:13
Amos 5:21

7:22
1 Sam 15:22
Ps 51:16
Hos 6:6

7:23
Isa 3:10
Jer 11:4; 38:20

7:24
Jer 11:8
Ezek 20:8,13,
16,21

7:26
Jer 16:12; 17:23
Mt 23:32

7:27
Isa 65:12
Jer 26:2

7:28
Jer 11:10

7:29
Isa 15:2; 22:12
Jer 6:30; 14:19

7:30
2 Kgs 21:4
2 Chron 33:4,
5,7
Jer 32:34

7:31
2 Kgs 16:17
Jer 19:5

7:11, 12 Jesus used these words in cleansing the Temple (Mark 11:17; Luke 19:46). This passage applied to the evil in the Temple in his day as well as in Jeremiah's. God's Tabernacle had been at Shiloh, but Shiloh apparently had been abandoned. If God did not preserve Shiloh because the Tabernacle was there, why would he preserve Jerusalem with its Temple?

7:15 Ephraim is another name for Israel, the Northern Kingdom, which had been taken into captivity by Assyria in 722 B.C.

7:18 The Queen of Heaven was a name for Ishtar, the Mesopotamian goddess of love and war. After the fall of Jerusalem, the refugees from Judah who fled to Egypt continued to worship her (chapter 44). A papyrus dating from the 5th century B.C., found at Hermopolis in Egypt, mentions the Queen of Heaven among the gods honored by the Jewish community living there.

7:19 This verse answers the question, "Who gets hurt when we turn away from God?" We do! Separating ourselves from God is like keeping a green plant away from sunlight or water, or cutting off its food supply. God is our only source of spiritual strength. Cut yourself off from that source, and you cut off life itself.

7:21-23 God had set up a system of sacrifices to encourage the people to obey him (see the book of Leviticus). He required the people to make these sacrifices, not because the sacrifices themselves pleased him, but because they caused the people to recognize their sin and refocus on living for God. They faithfully made the sacrifices but forgot the reason they were offering them, and thus they disobeyed God. Jeremiah reminded the people that acting out religious rituals is meaningless if one is not prepared to obey God in all areas of life.

7:25 From the time of David to the end of the Old Testament period, God sent many prophets to Israel and Judah. No matter how bad the circumstances, God always had a prophet to speak against their lethargic spiritual attitudes.

7:31 The altar called Topheth (meaning "fireplace") was set up in the Hinnom Valley, the valley where debris and rubbish from the city was thrown away. This altar was used to worship Molech—a god who required child sacrifice (2 Kings 21:6). Where the people had slain their children in sinful idol worship, they themselves would be slain.

that valley's name will be changed from "Topheth," or the "Valley of Ben-Hinnom," to the "Valley of Slaughter"; for there will be so many slain to bury that there won't be room enough for all the graves and they will dump the bodies in that valley.

33The bodies of my people shall be food for the birds and animals, and no one shall be left to scare them away. 34I will end the happy singing and laughter in the streets of Jerusalem and in the cities of Judah, and the joyous voices of the bridegrooms and brides. For the land shall lie in desolation.

8 Then, says the Lord, the enemy shall break open the graves of the kings of Judah and of the princes and priests and prophets and people, 2and dig out their bones and spread them out on the ground before the sun and moon and stars—the gods of my people!—whom they have loved and worshiped. Their bones shall not be gathered up again nor buried but shall be scattered like dung upon the ground. 3And those of this evil nation who are still left alive shall long to die, rather than live where I will scatter them, says the Lord Almighty.

The people are deceived by false teachers

4, 5Once again give them this message from the Lord: When a person falls, he jumps up again; when he is on the wrong road and discovers his mistake, he goes back to the fork where he made the wrong turn. But these people keep on along their evil path, even though I warn them. 6I listen to their conversation and what do I hear? Is anyone sorry for sin? Does anyone say, "What a terrible thing I have done?" No, all are rushing pell-mell down the path of sin as swiftly as a horse rushing to the battle! 7The stork knows the time of her migration, as does the turtledove, and the crane, and the swallow. They all return at God's appointed time each year; but not my people! They don't accept the laws of God.

8How can you say, "We understand his laws," when your teachers have twisted them up to mean a thing I never said? 9These wise teachers of yours will be shamed by exile for this sin, for they have rejected the word of the Lord. Are they then so wise? 10I will give their wives and their farms to others; for all of them, great and small, prophet and priest, have one purpose in mind—to get what isn't theirs. 11They give useless medicine for my people's grievous wounds, for they assure them all is well when that isn't so at all! 12Are they ashamed because they worship idols? No, not in the least; they don't even know how to blush! That is why I will see to it that they lie among the fallen. I will visit them with death. 13Their figs and grapes will disappear, their fruit trees will die, and all the good things I prepared for them will soon be gone.

14Then the people will say, "Why should we wait here to die? Come, let us go to the walled cities and perish there. For the Lord our God has decreed our doom and given us a cup of poison to drink because of all our sins. 15We expected peace, but no peace came; we looked for health but there was only terror."

16The noise of war resounds from the northern border. The whole land trembles at the approach of the terrible army, for the enemy is coming, and is devouring the land and everything in it—the cities and people alike. 17For I will send these enemy

7:33
Deut 28:26
Ps 79:2
Jer 12:9

7:34
Isa 1:7; 24:7
Jer 4:27; 16:9
Ezek 26:13
Hos 2:11

8:2
2 Kgs 23:5
Jer 22:19; 36:30
Zeph 1:5
Acts 7:42

8:3
Deut 30:1,4
Job 3:21,22
Jonah 4:3
Rev 9:6

8:4
Jer 7:24,27; 9:6
Mic 7:8

8:6
Job 39:21-25
Mal 3:16

8:7
Prov 6:6-8
Isa 1:3

8:8
Jer 4:22
Rom 1:22; 2:17

8:9
Jer 6:15
1 Cor 1:27

8:10
Deut 28:30
Isa 56:11
Jer 6:12,13

8:11
Jer 6:14
14:13,14
Lam 2:14
Ezek 13:10

8:12
Deut 32:35
Isa 3:9; 9:14
Jer 6:15
Zeph 3:5

8:13
Mt 21:19

8:14
Deut 29:18
Ps 69:21
Jer 3:25; 4:5
9:15; 14:20

8:15
Jer 14:19

8:16 The noise of war resounds from the northern border, literally, "The snorting of their war horses can be heard all the way from Dan in the north."

8:1 The threat that the graves of Judah's people would be opened was horrible to a people that highly honored the dead and believed it the highest insult to open graves. This would be an ironic punishment for idol worshipers—their bodies would be laid out before the sun, moon, and stars—the gods they thought could save them.

8:4-6 When a person falls or realizes he is headed in the wrong direction, it only makes sense to get up or get directions. But as God watched the nation, he saw people living sinful lives by

choice, deceiving themselves that there would be no consequences. They had lost perspective concerning God's will for their lives and were trying to minimize their sin. Are there some indicators that you're heading in a wrong direction? What are you doing to get back on the right path?

8:11 The prophets and priests were giving "useless medicine," false assurances rather than correction. How can we correct a fault or turn from a sin if our leaders tell us all is well? Beware of people who are always agreeable. At best, they give you no help; at worst, they may be trying to manipulate you.

troops among you like poisonous snakes which you cannot charm. No matter what you do, they will bite you and you shall die.

8:19
Deut 32:21
Ps 31:6
Isa 13:4,5
Jer 9:16

18My grief is beyond healing; my heart is broken. 19Listen to the weeping of my people all across the land.

"Where is the Lord?" they ask. "Has God deserted us?"

"Oh, why have they angered me with their carved idols and strange evil rites?" the Lord replies.

8:21
Jer 4:19; 9:1
14:17

20"The harvest is finished; the summer is over and we are not saved."

8:22
Gen 37:25
Jer 30:13; 46:11

21I weep for the hurt of my people; I stand amazed, silent, dumb with grief. 22Is there no medicine in Gilead? Is there no physician there? Why doesn't God do something? Why doesn't he help?

Jeremiah weeps for the people

9:1
Jer 8:18; 13:17

9 Oh, that my eyes were a fountain of tears; I would weep forever; I would sob day and night for the slain of my people! 2Oh, that I could go away and forget them and live in some wayside shack in the desert, for they are all adulterous, treacherous men.

9:3
Ps 64:3
Isa 59:4
Hos 4:1

3"They bend their tongues like bows to shoot their arrows of untruth. They care nothing for right and go from bad to worse; they care nothing for me," says the Lord.

9:4
Gen 27:35
Jer 12:6

4Beware of your neighbor! Beware of your brother! All take advantage of one another and spread their slanderous lies. 5With practiced tongues they fool and defraud each other; they wear themselves out with all their sinning.

9:6
Jer 5:27; 11:10

6"They pile evil upon evil, lie upon lie, and utterly refuse to come to me," says the Lord.

9:7
Isa 1:25
Mal 3:3

7Therefore the Lord Almighty says this: "See, I will melt them in a crucible of affliction. I will refine them and test them like metal. What else can I do with them?

9:8
Ps 28:3
Jer 5:26

8For their tongues aim lies like poisoned spears. They speak cleverly to their neighbors while planning to kill them. 9Should not I punish them for such things as this?" asks the Lord. "Shall not my soul be avenged on such a nation as this?"

9:9
Isa 1:24
Jer 5:9,29

9:10
Jer 4:24,25
Ezek 29:11
Hos 4:3

10Sobbing and weeping, I point to their mountains and pastures, for now they are desolate, without a living soul. Gone is the lowing of cattle, gone the birds and wild animals. All have fled.

9:11
Isa 25:2; 34:13
Jer 26:9

11"And I will turn Jerusalem into heaps of ruined houses where only jackals have their dens. The cities of Judah shall be ghost towns, with no one living in them."

9:12
Jer 23:10,16
Hos 14:9

12Who is wise enough to understand all this? Where is the Lord's messenger to explain it? Why is the land a wilderness so that no one dares even to travel through?

9:13
2 Chron 7:19,20
Ps 89:30
Jer 5:19; 22:9

13"Because," the Lord replies, "my people have forsaken my commandments and not obeyed my laws. 14Instead they have done whatever they pleased and worshiped the idols of Baal, as their fathers told them to. 15Therefore this is what the Lord, the God of Israel, says: Look! I will feed them with bitterness and give them poison to drink. 16I will scatter them around the world, to be strangers in distant lands; and even there the sword of destruction shall chase them until I have utterly destroyed them.

9:14
Jer 2:8; 7:24
Rom 1:21-24
1 Pet 1:18

9:15
Jer 8:14; 23:15

9:16
Deut 28:64
Jer 13:24; 44:27
Ezek 5:2,12

17, 18"The Lord Almighty says: Send for the mourners! Quick! Begin your crying! Let the tears flow from your eyes. 19Hear Jerusalem weeping in despair. 'We are ruined! Disaster has befallen us! We must leave our land and homes!' "

9:17
Isa 22:4
Jer 9:1; 14:17

9:19
7:15,29; 15:1

20Listen to the words of God, O women who wail. Teach your daughters to wail

---

8:18, 19 These verses provide a vivid picture of Jeremiah's emotion as he watches his people reject God. He responds with anguish to a world dying in sin. We watch that same world still dying in sin, still rejecting God. But how often is our heart broken for our lost friends and neighbors, our lost world? Only when we have Jeremiah's kind of concern will we be moved to help. We must begin by asking God to break our hearts for the world he loves.

8:22 Although the people's spiritual sickness was still very deep,

it could be cured. But the people refused the medicine. God could heal their self-inflicted wounds, but he would not force his healing on them.

9:1-4 Jeremiah felt conflicting emotions concerning his people. He was angered by their sin, but he had compassion too. He was set apart from them by his work for God, but he was also one of them. Jesus had similar feelings when he stood before Jerusalem, the city that would reject him (Matthew 23:37).

and your neighbors too. ²¹For death has crept in through your windows into your homes. He has killed off the flower of your youth. Children no longer play in the streets; the young men gather no more in the squares.

²²Tell them this, says the Lord: Bodies shall be scattered across the fields like manure, like sheaves after the mower, and no one will bury them.

²³The Lord says: Let not the wise man bask in his wisdom, nor the mighty man in his might, nor the rich man in his riches. ²⁴Let them boast in this alone: That they truly know me, and understand that I am the Lord of justice and of righteousness whose love is steadfast; and that I love to be this way.

²⁵,²⁶A time is coming, says the Lord, when I will punish all those who are circumcised in body but not in spirit—the Egyptians, Edomites, Ammonites, Moabites, Arabs, and yes, even you people of Judah. For all these pagan nations also circumcise themselves. Unless you circumcise your hearts by loving me, your circumcision is only a heathen rite like theirs, and nothing more.

The Lord is the God of creation

10 Hear the word of the Lord, O Israel:
²,³Don't act like the people who make horoscopes and try to read their fate and future in the stars! Don't be frightened by predictions such as theirs, for it is all a pack of lies. Their ways are futile and foolish. They cut down a tree and carve an idol, ⁴and decorate it with gold and silver and fasten it securely in place with hammer and nails, so that it won't fall over, ⁵and there stands their god like a helpless scarecrow in a garden! It cannot speak, and it must be carried, for it cannot walk. Don't be afraid of such a god for it can neither harm nor help, nor do you any good.

⁶O Lord, there is no other god like you. For you are great and your name is full of power. ⁷Who would not fear you, O King of nations? (And that title belongs to you alone!) Among all the wise men of the earth and in all the kingdoms of the world there isn't anyone like you.

⁸The wisest of men who worship idols are altogether stupid and foolish. ⁹They bring beaten sheets of silver from Tarshish and gold from Uphaz, and give them to skillful goldsmiths who make their idols; then they clothe these gods in royal purple robes that expert tailors make.

¹⁰But the Lord is the only true God, the living God, the everlasting King. The whole earth shall tremble at his anger; the world shall hide before his displeasure.

¹¹Say this to those who worship other gods: Your so-called gods, who have not made the heavens and earth, shall vanish from the earth, ¹²but our God formed the earth by his power and wisdom, and by his intelligence he hung the stars in space and stretched out the heavens. ¹³It is his voice that echoes in the thunder of the storm clouds. He causes mist to rise upon the earth; he sends the lightning and brings the rain, and from his treasuries he brings the wind.

¹⁴But foolish men without knowledge of God bow before their idols. It is a shameful business that these men are in, for what they make are frauds, gods without life or power in them. ¹⁵All are worthless, silly; they will be crushed when their makers perish. ¹⁶But the God of Jacob is not like these foolish idols. He is the

9:21
2 Chron 36:17
Jer 6:11; 18:21

9:22
Isa 5:25
Jer 8:2; 16:4

9:23
1 Kgs 20:10,11
Ezek 28:3-7

9:24
Ex 34:6,7
Isa 61:8
Mic 7:18
1 Cor 1:31
2 Cor 10:17
Gal 6:14

9:25
Jer 4:4
Ezek 44:7
Rom 2:8,9,
28,29

10:2
Lev 18:3
Isa 44:9-20
47:12-14

10:4
Isa 40:19; 41:7

10:5
Isa 41:23,24
46:1,7

10:6
Deut 33:26
Ps 48:1; 96:4
Isa 12:6
Jer 10:16

10:7
Ps 22:28
Dan 2:27,28
1 Cor 1:19,20

10:10
Ps 10:16; 29:10
76:7
Isa 65:16

10:11
Ps 96:5
Isa 2:18

10:12
Job 9:8; 38:4-7
Isa 40:22; 45:18
Jer 51:15

10:13
Job 36:27-29
Ps 29:3-9; 135:7

10:15
Isa 41:24
Jer 8:12; 14:22

10:16
Deut 32:9
Isa 45:7
Jer 31:35
32:18; 51:19

9:23, 24 People tend to admire three qualities in others: beauty, power, and riches. But God puts a higher priority on knowing him personally and living a life that reflects his justice, righteousness, and love. What do you want people to admire most about you?

9:25, 26 Circumcision went back to the time of Abraham. For the people of Israel it was a symbol of their covenant relationship to God (Genesis 17:9–14). Circumcision was practiced by heathen nations as well, but not as the sign of a covenant with God. By Jeremiah's time, the Israelites had forgotten the spiritual significance of circumcision even though they continued to do it.

10:2, 3 Everyone would like to know the future. Decisions would be easier, failures avoided, and success assured. The people of

Judah wanted to know the future too, and they tried to discern it in horoscopes. Jeremiah's response applies today: God made the stars that people consult. No one will discover the future in made-up charts of God's stars. But God, who promises to guide you, knows your future and will be with you all the way. He may not reveal your future to you, but he will walk with you as the future unfolds. Don't trust the stars; trust the One who made the stars.

10:8 God divides people here into the truly wise and the truly foolish. Those who put their trust in a chunk of wood, even though it is carved well and clothed beautifully, are foolish. The simplest person who worships God is wiser than the wisest person who worships the worthless idol, for this person has discerned who is truly God and who is not. In what or whom do you place your trust?

Creator of all, and Israel is his chosen nation. The Lord Almighty is his name.

17Pack your bags, he says. Get ready now to leave; the siege will soon begin. 18For suddenly I'll fling you from this land and pour great troubles down; at last you shall feel my wrath.

19*Desperate is my wound. My grief is great. My sickness is incurable, but I must bear it.* 20*My home is gone; my children have been taken away and I will never see them again. There is no one left to help me rebuild my home.* 21The shepherds of my people have lost their senses; they no longer follow God nor ask his will. Therefore they perish and their flocks are scattered. 22Listen! Hear the terrible sound of great armies coming from the north. The cities of Judah shall become dens of jackals.

23O Lord, I know it is not within the power of man to map his life and plan his course— 24so you correct me, Lord; but please be gentle. Don't do it in your anger, for I would die. 25Pour out your fury on the nations who don't obey the Lord, for they have destroyed Israel and made a wasteland of this entire country.

3. Jeremiah prophesies destruction
Remember the covenant

11 Then the Lord spoke to Jeremiah once again and said: Remind the men of Judah and all the people of Jerusalem that I made a contract with their fathers—and cursed is the man who does not heed it! 4For I told them at the time I brought them out of slavery in Egypt that if they would obey me and do whatever I commanded them, then they and all their children would be mine and I would be their God. 5And now, Israel, obey me, says the Lord, so that I can do for you the wonderful things I swore I would if you obeyed. I want to give you a land that "flows with milk and honey," as it is today. Then I replied, "So be it, Lord!"

6Then the Lord said: Broadcast this message in Jerusalem's streets—go from city to city throughout the land and say, Remember this agreement that your fathers made with God, and do all the things they promised him they would. 7For I solemnly said to your fathers when I brought them out of Egypt—and have kept on saying it over and over again until this day: Obey my every command! 8But your fathers didn't do it. They wouldn't even listen. Each followed his own stubborn will and his proud heart. Because they refused to obey, I did to them all the evils stated in the contract.

9Again the Lord spoke to me and said: I have discovered a conspiracy against me among the men of Judah and Jerusalem. 10They have returned to the sins of their fathers, refusing to listen to me and worshiping idols. The agreement I made with their fathers is broken and canceled. 11Therefore, the Lord says, I am going to bring calamity down upon them and they shall not escape. Though they cry for mercy, I will not listen to their pleas. 12Then they will pray to their idols and burn incense before them, but that cannot save them from their time of anguish and despair. 13O my people, you have as many gods as there are cities, and your altars of shame (your altars to burn incense to Baal) are along every street in Jerusalem.

10:21 The shepherds of the nation are the evil leaders who are responsible for the calamity. The flocks are the people of Judah. When the leaders should have been guiding the people to God, they were leading them astray.

10:23, 24 God's ability to plan our lives well is infinitely beyond our ability. Sometimes we are afraid of God's power and God's plans, because we know his power would easily crush us if he used it against us. He does not do this, however, when we come to him for guidance. Be unafraid to let God correct your plans. He will give you wisdom if you are willing.

11:1—13:27 This section concerns the broken covenant, a rebuke for those who returned to idols after King Josiah's reform. Jeremiah's rebuke prompted a threat against his life by his own

countrymen. As Jeremiah suffered, he pondered the prosperity of the wicked. As he brought these words to a close, he used a rotten linen belt and clay wine pots as object lessons of God's coming judgment (see the note on 13:1–11).

11:1–8 God tells Jeremiah to remind the people of their past history—specifically what God had done for them as a result of their obedience or disobedience to his Word. Obedience to God's Word was like finding the single safe passageway through treacherous water. Disobedience brought ultimate disaster. We have the freedom to obey and find the refuge God has waiting for us; we also have the freedom to sail any other direction into disaster. The choice is yours.

¹⁴Therefore, Jeremiah, pray no longer for this people, neither weep nor plead for them; for I will not listen to them when they are finally desperate enough to beg me for help. ¹⁵What right do my beloved people have to come any more to my Temple? For you have been unfaithful and worshiped other gods. Can promises and sacrifices now avert your doom and give you life and joy again? ¹⁶The Lord used to call you his green olive tree, beautiful to see and full of good fruit; but now he has sent the fury of your enemies to burn you up and leave you broken and charred. ¹⁷It is because of the wickedness of Israel and Judah in offering incense to Baal that the Lord Almighty who planted the tree has ordered it destroyed.

¹⁸Then the Lord told me all about their plans and showed me their evil plots. ¹⁹I had been as unsuspecting as a lamb or ox on the way to slaughter. I didn't know that they were planning to kill me! "Let's destroy this man and all his messages," they said. "Let's kill him so that his name will be forever forgotten."

²⁰O Lord Almighty, you are just. See the hearts and motives of these men. Repay them for all that they have planned! I look to you for justice.

²¹,²²And the Lord replied, The men of the city of Anathoth shall be punished for planning to kill you. They will tell you not to prophesy in God's name on pain of death. And so their young men shall die in battle; their boys and girls shall starve. ²³Not one of these plotters of Anathoth shall survive, for I will bring a great disaster upon them. Their time has come.

Jeremiah complains to God

12 O Lord, you always give me justice when I bring a case before you to decide. Now let me bring you this complaint: Why are the wicked so prosperous? Why are evil men so happy? ²You plant them. They take root and their business grows. Their profits multiply, and they are rich. They say, "Thank God!" But in their hearts they give no credit to you. ³But as for me—Lord, you know my heart—you know how much it longs for you. (And I am poor, O Lord!) Lord, drag them off like helpless sheep to the slaughter. Judge them, O God!

⁴How long must this land of yours put up with all their goings on? Even the grass of the field groans and weeps over their wicked deeds! The wild animals and birds have moved away, leaving the land deserted. Yet the people say, "God won't bring judgment on us. We're perfectly safe!"

⁵The Lord replied to me: If racing with mere men—these men of Anathoth—has wearied you, how will you race against horses, against the king, his court and all his evil priests? If you stumble and fall on open ground, what will you do in Jordan's jungles? ⁶Even your own brothers, your own family, have turned against

12:3 *I am poor*, implied. 12:5 *these men of Anathoth . . . against the king, his court and all his evil priests,* implied.

11:14
Ps 66:18
Jer 7:16; 14:11
Hos 5:6

11:16
Ps 52:8; 83:2
Isa 27:11
Jer 21:14

11:17
Jer 2:21; 32:29

11:18
1 Sam 23:11,12
2 Kgs 6:9,10
Ezek 8:6

11:19
Ps 52:5; 83:4
109:13

11:20
Ps 7:9
Jer 17:10; 20:12

11:21
2 Chron 36:17
Jer 1:1; 12:5,6
18:21; 20:10
26:8; 38:4

11:23
Jer 6:9; 23:12
Hos 9:7
Mic 7:4

12:1
Ezra 9:15
Job 13:3
Jer 5:27,28
11:20
Hab 1:4

12:2
Isa 29:13
Ezek 17:5-10
33:31
Tit 1:16

12:3
Ps 7:9; 139:1-4
Jer 11:20

12:4
Jer 5:31
Hos 4:3
Joel 1:10-17

12:6
Gen 37:4-11
Ps 69:8
Prov 26:25

11:14 At first glance this verse is shocking—God tells Jeremiah not to pray, and says he won't listen to the people if they pray. A time comes when God must be just. Sin brings its own bitter reward. If the people were unrepentant and continued in their sin, neither Jeremiah's prayers nor those of the people would prevent God's judgment. Their only hope was repentance—sorrow for sin, turning from it, and turning to God. How can we keep praying for God's blessings in our lives if we haven't committed our lives to him? His blessings come when we are committed to him, not when we selfishly hang on to our sinful ways.

11:18–23 To Jeremiah's surprise, the people of Anathoth, his hometown, were plotting to kill him. They wanted to silence his message for several reasons: (1) economic—this would hurt the business of the idol-makers; (2) religious—the message of doom and gloom made the people feel guilty; (3) political—he openly rebuked their hypocritical politics; and (4) personal—the people hated him for showing them they were wrong. Jeremiah had two options: run and hide, or call on God. Jeremiah called, and God answered. Like Jeremiah, we can either run and hide when we face threats because of our faithfulness to God, or we can call on

God for help. Hiding compromises our message; calling on God lets him reinforce it.

12:1–6 Many have asked, "Why do the wicked prosper?" (See, for example. Job 21:4-21; Habakkuk 1:12-17.) Jeremiah knows that God's ultimate justice will come, but he is impatient because he wants justice to come quickly. God doesn't give a doctrinal answer; instead he gives a challenge—if Jeremiah can't handle this, how will he handle the injustices ahead? It is natural for us to demand fair play and cry for justice against those who take advantage of others. But when we call for justice, we must realize that we ourselves would be in big trouble if God gave each of us what we truly deserve.

12:5, 6 Life was extremely difficult for Jeremiah despite his love for and obedience to God. When he called to God for relief, God's reply in effect was, "If you think this is bad, how are you going to cope when it gets really tough?"

Not all of God's answers to prayer are nice or easy to cope with. Any Christian who has experienced war, grief, or a serious illness knows this. But we are to be committed to God even when the going gets tough and when his answers to our prayers don't bring immediate relief.

you. They have plotted to call for a mob to lynch you. Don't trust them, no matter how pleasantly they speak. Don't believe them.

God abandons his faithless people

7Then the Lord said: I have abandoned my people, my inheritance; I have surrendered my dearest ones to their enemies. 8My people have roared at me like a lion of the forest, so I have treated them as though I hated them. 9My people have fallen. I will bring upon them swarms of vultures and wild animals to pick the flesh from their corpses.

10Many foreign rulers have ravaged my vineyard, trampling down the vines, and turning all its beauty into barren wilderness. 11They have made it desolate; I hear its mournful cry. The whole land is desolate and no one cares. 12Destroying armies plunder the land; the sword of the Lord devours from one end of the nation to the other; nothing shall escape. 13My people have sown wheat but reaped thorns; they have worked hard but it does them no good. They shall harvest a crop of shame, for the fierce anger of the Lord is upon them.

14And now the Lord says this to the evil nations, the nations surrounding the land God gave his people Israel: See, I will force you from your land just as Judah will be forced from hers; 15but afterwards I will return and have compassion on all of you, and will bring you home to your own land again, each man to his inheritance. 16And if these heathen nations quickly learn my people's ways and claim me as their God instead of Baal (whom they taught my people to worship), then they shall be strong among my people. 17But any nation refusing to obey me will be expelled again and finished, says the Lord.

The people threatened with captivity

13 The Lord said to me, Go and buy a linen loincloth and wear it, but don't wash it—don't put it in water at all. 2So I bought the loincloth and put it on. 3Then the Lord's message came to me again. This time he said, 4Take the loincloth out to the Euphrates River and hide it in a hole in the rocks.

5So I did; I hid it as the Lord had told me to. 6Then, a long time afterwards, the Lord said: Go out to the river again and get the loincloth. 7And I did; I dug it out of the hole where I had hidden it. But now it was mildewed and falling apart. It was utterly useless!

8, 9Then the Lord said: This illustrates the way that I will rot the pride of Judah and Jerusalem. 10This evil nation refuses to listen to me, and follows its own evil desires and worships idols; therefore it shall become as this loincloth—good for nothing. 11Even as a loincloth clings to a man's loins, so I made Judah and Israel to cling to me, says the Lord. They were my people, an honor to my name. But then they turned away.

12Tell them this: The Lord God of Israel says, All your wine jugs will be full of wine. And they will reply, Of course, you don't need to tell us how prosperous we will be! 13Then tell them: That's not what I mean. I mean that I will fill everyone living in this land with helpless bewilderment—from the king sitting on David's throne, and the priests and the prophets right on down to all the people. 14And I will smash fathers and sons against each other, says the Lord. I will not let pity nor mercy spare them from utter destruction.

13:12 *Of course, you don't need to tell us how prosperous we will be,* literally, "that every bottle will be filled with wine." **13:13** *That's not what I mean,* implied.

Cross references (margin)

12:7
Jer 7:29; 11:15
Hos 11:1-4

12:8
Amos 6:8

12:9
Jer 7:33,15:3

12:10
Ps 80:8-16
Isa 5:1-7

12:11
Jer 4:20,27

12:13
Jer 4:26; 17:10
25:37,38

12:14
Jer 2:3; 49:1
50:11,12
Zech 2:8

12:15
Isa 11:11-16
Jer 49:6,39

12:16
Isa 49:6
Jer 16:19

12:17
Ps 2:8-12
Isa 60:12

13:1
Jer 13:11

13:2
Isa 20:2

13:4
Jer 51:63

13:5
Ex 39:42,43
40:16

13:8
Lev 26:19
Isa 2:10-17
23:9

13:11
Ex 19:5,6
Deut 32:10,11
Ps 81:11
Isa 43:21
Jer 7:24; 33:9

13:13
Ps 60:3; 75:8
Jer 25:27

13:14
Isa 27:11
Jer 6:21; 16:5
19:9-11

12:14–17 God speaks to the nations surrounding Judah with a message that contains both judgment and hope. They will be punished by the same enemy that punishes Judah, and like Judah they will be deported from their homelands. If they repent and turn to God, they will be permitted to return. The nations that led Judah into idolatry may share Judah's true God—but only if they repent. The same offer is made to us—if we repent and turn to God, we will share in the same God who makes these promises.

13:1–11 Actions speak louder than words. Jeremiah often used vivid object lessons to arouse the people's curiosity and get his point across. This lesson of the loincloth illustrated Judah's destiny. Although the people had once been close to God, their pride had made them useless. A proud person may look important, but God says his pride makes him good for nothing. Pride rots our hearts until we lose our usefulness to God.

15Oh, that you were not so proud and stubborn! Then you would listen to the Lord, for he has spoken. 16Give glory to the Lord your God before it is too late, before he causes deep, impenetrable darkness to fall upon you so that you stumble and fall upon the dark mountains; then, when you look for light, you will find only terrible darkness. 17Do you still refuse to listen? Then in loneliness my breaking heart shall mourn because of your pride. My eyes will overflow with tears because the Lord's flock shall be carried away as slaves.

18Say to the king and queen-mother, Come down from your thrones and sit in the dust, for your glorious crowns are removed from your heads. They are no longer yours. 19The cities of the Negeb to the south of Jerusalem have closed their gates against the enemy. They must defend themselves, for Jerusalem cannot help; and all Judah shall be taken away as slaves. 20See the armies marching from the north! Where is your flock, Jerusalem, your beautiful flock I gave you to take care of? 21How will you feel when I set your allies over you as your rulers? You will writhe in pain like a woman having a child. 22And if you ask yourself, Why is all this happening to me? It is because of the grossness of your sins; that is why you have been raped and destroyed by the invading army.

23Can the Ethiopian change the color of his skin? or a leopard take away his spots? Nor can you who are so used to doing evil now start being good. 24, 25Because you have put me out of your mind and put your trust in false gods, I will scatter you as chaff is scattered by the fierce winds off the desert. This then is your allotment, that which is due you, which I have measured out especially for you. 26I myself will expose you to utter shame. 27I am keenly aware of your apostasy, your faithlessness to me, and your abominable idol worship in the fields and on the hills. Woe upon you, O Jerusalem! How long before you will be pure?

God pronounces doom for Jerusalem

14 This message came to Jeremiah from the Lord, explaining why he was holding back the rain:

2Judah mourns; business has ground to a halt; all the people prostrate themselves to the earth and a great cry rises from Jerusalem. 3The nobles send servants for water from the wells, but the wells are dry. The servants return, baffled and desperate, and cover their heads in grief. 4The ground is parched and cracked for lack of rain; the farmers are afraid. 5The deer deserts her fawn because there is no grass. 6The wild donkeys stand upon the bare hills panting like thirsty jackals. They strain their eyes looking for grass to eat, but there is none to be found.

7O Lord, we have sinned against you grievously, yet help us for the sake of your own reputation! 8O Hope of Israel, our Savior in times of trouble, why are you as a stranger to us, as one passing through the land who is merely stopping for the night? 9Are you also baffled? Are you helpless to save us? O Lord, you are right here among us, and we carry your name; we are known as your people. O Lord, don't desert us now!

10But the Lord replies: You have loved to wander far from me and have not tried to follow in my paths. Now I will no longer accept you as my people; now I will remember all the evil you have done, and punish your sins.

13:16
Ps 96:8
Isa 5:30,59:9
Amos 5:18
13:17
Jer 9:1; 23:1,2
Mal 2:2
Lk 19:41,42
13:18
2 Kgs 24:12,15
13:20
Jer 1:15; 6:22
13:17; 23:2
Hab 1:6
13:21
Isa 13:8
Jer 4:31; 38:22
13:22
Jer 2:17-19
9:2-9
13:23
Prov 27:22
Jer 4:22
Mt 19:24
13:24
Lev 26:33
Ps 9:17
Jer 2:32; 9:16
18:17
Ezek 5:2,12
13:26
Lam 1:8
13:27
Prov 1:22
Jer 2:20; 5:7,8
11:15

14:2
Jer 11:11
Zech 7:13
14:3
2 Sam 15:30
1 Kgs 18:5
14:4
Joel 1:11,19,20
14:6
Job 39:5,6
14:7
Isa 59:12
Hos 5:5
14:8
Ps 9:9
Isa 43:3; 63:8
Jer 17:13
14:9
Num 11:23
Ps 46:5
Isa 50:2; 63:19
Jer 8:19; 15:16
14:10
Ps 119:101
Jer 2:25
44:21-23

13:19 *for Jerusalem cannot help,* literally, "the cities are closed and none can open them." Perhaps the meaning is that they are permanently abandoned. **13:20** *Jerusalem,* implied.

13:15 While it is good to respect our country and our church, our loyalties always carry a hidden danger—pride. When is pride harmful? When it causes us (1) to look down on others; (2) to be selfish with our resources; (3) to force our solutions on others' problems; (4) to think God is blessing us because of our own merits; (5) to be content with our plans rather than seeking God's plans.

13:18 The king is Jehoiachin, and the queen-mother, Nehashta. The king's father, Jehoiakim, had surrendered to Nebuchadnezzar but later rebelled. During Jehoiachin's reign, Nebuchadnezzar's

armies besieged Jerusalem, and both Jehoiachin and Nehashta surrendered. Jehoiachin was sent to Babylon and imprisoned (2 Kings 24:8-12). Jeremiah's prophecy came true.

14:1—15:21 This section opens with God sending a drought on Judah and refusing to answer their prayers for rain. It continues with Jeremiah's description of judgment to come.

14:1ff Drought was a judgment with devastating consequences. As usual, when their backs were to the wall, the people cried out to God. But God rejected their plea because they did not repent; they merely wanted his rescue. Not even Jeremiah's prayers would help. Their only hope was to turn to God.

¹¹The Lord told me again: Don't ask me any more to bless this people. Don't pray for them any more. ¹²When they fast, I will not pay any attention; when they present their offerings and sacrifices to me, I will not accept them. What I will give them in return is war and famine and disease.

¹³Then I said, O Lord God, their prophets are telling them that all is well—that no war or famine will come. They tell the people you will surely send them peace, that you will bless them.

¹⁴Then the Lord said: The prophets are telling lies in my name. I didn't send them or tell them to speak or give them any message. They prophesy of visions and revelations they have never seen nor heard; they speak foolishness concocted out of their own lying hearts. ¹⁵Therefore, the Lord says, I will punish these lying prophets who have spoken in my name though I did not send them, who say no war shall come nor famine. By war and famine they themselves shall die! ¹⁶And the people to whom they prophesy—their bodies shall be thrown out into the streets of Jerusalem, victims of famine and war; there shall be no one to bury them. Husbands, wives, sons and daughters—all will be gone. For I will pour out terrible punishment upon them for their sins.

¹⁷Therefore, tell them this: Night and day my eyes shall overflow with tears; I cannot stop my crying, for my people have been run through with a sword and lie mortally wounded on the ground. ¹⁸If I go out in the fields, there lie the bodies of those the sword has killed; and if I walk in the streets, there lie those dead from starvation and disease. And yet the prophets and priests alike have made it their business to travel through the whole country, reassuring everyone that all is well, speaking of things they know nothing about.

¹⁹"O Lord," the people will cry, "have you completely rejected Judah? Do you abhor Jerusalem? Even after punishment, will there be no peace? We thought, Now at last he will heal us and bind our wounds. But no peace has come and there is only trouble and terror everywhere. ²⁰O Lord, we confess our wickedness, and that of our fathers too. ²¹Do not hate us, Lord, for the sake of your own name. Do not disgrace yourself and the throne of your glory by forsaking your promise to bless us! ²²What heathen god can give us rain? Who but you alone, O Lord our God, can do such things as this? Therefore we will wait for you to help us."

Jerusalem is persecuted

15 Then the Lord said to me, Even if Moses and Samuel stood before me pleading for these people, even then I wouldn't help them—away with them! Get them out of my sight! ²And if they say to you, But where can we go? tell them the Lord says: Those who are destined for death, to death; those who must die by the sword, to the sword; those doomed to starvation, to famine; and those for captivity, to captivity. ³I will appoint over them four kinds of destroyers, says the Lord—the sword to kill, the dogs to tear, and the vultures and wild animals to finish

---

14:11, 12 Israel had stretched God's patience. Their false repentance and empty rituals had continued long enough, and now God turned deaf ears to their cries. For a third time, God told Jeremiah not to pray for the people. Why not let the idols answer their prayers? If you are putting something ahead of God when all is going well, will you be content to trust in this false god when you are in trouble?

14:14 What made the people listen to the false prophets? They said what the people wanted to hear. False teachers have always been willing to earn fame and money by giving people what they want to hear, but false teachers lead people away from God. If we encourage them, we are as guilty as they are.

14:17 Was this Jeremiah or God crying? Actually it was both. Jeremiah was so in tune with God that he expressed God's great compassion and sorrow for his chosen people in his own tears. This was a symbol the people could understand.

14:19–22 Interceding for the people, Jeremiah asks God, "If they do repent, will you help them?" But God refuses (15:1) because

the people are insincere, wicked, and stubborn. They know he wants to bless them, and they know what they need to do to receive that blessing. They want God to do his part, but they do not want to do theirs. It's easy to express sorrow for wrong actions, especially when we want something, but we must be willing to turn away from those wrong actions.

15:1 Moses and Samuel were two of God's greatest prophets. Like Jeremiah, both interceded between God and the people (Exodus 17:11; 32:11; Numbers 14:13; 1 Samuel 7:9; 12:17; Psalm 99:6). Intercession is often effective. In this case, however, the people were so wicked and stubborn that God knew they would not turn to him.

15:3, 4 The goal of these destroyers is to destroy the living and consume the dead. This would happen because of Manasseh's evil reign and the people's sin (2 Kings 21:1–16; 23:26; 24:3), and the destruction would be total. The people may have argued that they should not be responsible for Manasseh's sins, but they continued what Manasseh began.

up what's left. 4Because of the wicked things Manasseh, son of Hezekiah, king of Judah, did in Jerusalem, I will punish you so severely that your fate will horrify the peoples of the world.

5Who will feel sorry for you, Jerusalem? Who will weep for you? Who will even bother to ask how you are? 6You have forsaken me and turned your backs upon me. Therefore I will clench my fists against you to destroy you. I am tired of always giving you another chance. 7I will sift you at the gates of your cities and take from you all that you hold dear, and I will destroy my own people because they refuse to turn back to me from all their evil ways. 8There shall be countless widows; at noon time I will bring death to the young men and sorrow to their mothers. I will cause anguish and terror to fall upon them suddenly. 9The mother of seven sickens and faints, for all her sons are dead. Her sun is gone down while it is yet day. She sits childless now, disgraced, for all her children have been killed.

10Then Jeremiah said, "What sadness is mine, my mother; oh, that I had died at birth. For I am hated everywhere I go. I am neither a creditor soon to foreclose nor a debtor refusing to pay—yet they all curse me. 11Well, let them curse! Lord, you know how I have pled with you on their behalf—how I have begged you to spare these enemies of mine."

12, 13Can a man break bars of northern iron or bronze? This people's stubborn will can't be broken either. So, because of all your sins against me, I will deliver your wealth and treasures as loot to the enemy. 14I will have your enemies take you as slaves to a land where you have never been before, for my anger burns like fire, and it shall consume you.

15Then Jeremiah replied, "Lord, you know it is for your sake that I am suffering. They are persecuting me because I have proclaimed your word to them. Don't let them kill me! Rescue me from their clutches, and give them what they deserve! 16Your words are what sustain me; they are food to my hungry soul. They bring joy to my sorrowing heart and delight me. How proud I am to bear your name, O Lord. 17, 18I have not joined the people in their merry feasts. I sit alone beneath the hand of God. I burst with indignation at their sins. Yet you have failed me in my time of need! You have let them keep right on with all their persecutions. Will they never stop hurting me? Your help is as uncertain as a seasonal mountain brook— sometimes a flood, sometimes as dry as a bone."

19The Lord replied: "Stop this foolishness and talk some sense! Only if you return to trusting me will I let you continue as my spokesman. You are to influence *them,* not let them influence *you!* 20They will fight against you like a besieging army against a high city wall. But they will not conquer you for I am with you to protect and deliver you, says the Lord. 21Yes, I will certainly deliver you from these wicked men and rescue you from their ruthless hands."

A prophecy of disaster

16 On yet another occasion God spoke to me, and said:

2You must not marry and have children here. 3For the children born in this city, and their mothers and fathers, 4shall die from terrible diseases. No one shall mourn for them or bury them, but their bodies shall lie on the ground to rot and fertilize the soil. They shall die from war and famine, and their bodies shall be picked apart by vultures and wild animals. 5Do not mourn or weep for them, for I

Cross references (right column)

15:4
2 Kgs 23:26,27
24:3,4
Jer 24:9; 29:18

15:5
Ps 69:20
Jer 13:14

15:6
Isa 1:4
Jer 6:11
7:16,24
Zeph 1:4

15:7
Jer 18:21; 51:2
Hos 9:12-16

15:8
Isa 3:25,26; 4:1

15:9
1 Sam 2:5
Isa 47:9
Amos 8:9

15:10
Deut 23:19
Job 3:3
Jer 1:18,19
20:7,8,14

15:11
Isa 41:10

15:12
Jer 17:3; 20:5

15:14
Deut 28:64
Jer 16:13; 17:4

15:15
Ps 69:7-9
Jer 20:8

15:16
Job 23:12
Ps 119:103
Jer 14:9

15:17
Job 6:15,20
Ps 102:7
Jer 13:17; 16:8
30:12,15
2 Cor 6:17

15:19
Ezek 44:23

15:20
Jer 1:8,18,19
Ps 46:7
Isa 41:10
Ezek 3:9

15:21
Isa 49:26
Jer 39:11,12

16:4
Ps 79:2
Isa 18:6
Jer 15:2,3

16:5
Ps 25:6
Isa 27:11
Jer 12:12
Ezek 24:16-23

15:17-21 Jeremiah accused God of not helping him when he really needed it. Jeremiah had taken his eyes off God's purposes and was feeling sorry for himself. He was angry, hurt, and afraid. In response, God didn't get angry at Jeremiah; he answered by reorienting Jeremiah's priorities—"You are to influence them, not let them influence you!" There are three important lessons in this passage: (1) in prayer we can reveal our deepest thoughts to God; (2) God expects us to trust no matter what; and (3) we are here to influence others for God.

16:1—17:18 This section begins by showing Jeremiah's loneliness. He is a social outcast because of his harsh messages

and his celibate lifestyle. He must not marry, have children, or take part in funerals or times of joy. The section concludes with another appeal to avoid judgment by turning to God. The people did not heed Jeremiah's words, however, and the first wave of destruction came almost immediately, in 605 B.C. (2 Kings 24:8–12). The second wave came in 597 B.C., and Judah was completely destroyed in 586 B.C.

16:5 In Jeremiah's culture, it was unthinkable not to show grief publicly. The absence of mourning showed the people how complete their devastation would be. So many people would die that it would be impossible to have mourning rituals for all of them.

16:6
Deut 14:1
Ezek 9:6

16:8
Eccles 7:2-4
Isa 22:12-14
Jer 15:17

16:9
Jer 7:34; 25:10
Hos 2:11

16:10
Deut 29:24,25
1 Kgs 9:8,9
Jer 5:19; 13:22

16:11
Neh 9:26-29
Ps 106:35-41
1 Pet 4:3

16:12
Jer 7:24; 9:14
Mark 7:21

16:13
Deut 4:26,27
Jer 5:19; 15:14

16:14
Deut 15:15
Ps 106:47
Isa 11:11-16
Jer 23:7,8
Hos 3:4,5

16:16
Isa 2:21
Amos 4:2,9:1-3
Hab 1:14,15

16:17
Ps 90:8
Jer 23:24; 32:19
Lk 12:2
1 Cor 4:5
Heb 4:13

16:18
Num 35:34
Jer 2:7; 3:9
Rev 18:6

16:19
Isa 25:4
Jer 3:17; 4:2

16:20
Ps 115:4-8
Jer 5:7
Hos 8:4-6

16:21
Isa 43:3
Amos 5:8

17:1
Prov 3:3; 7:3
2 Cor 3:3

have removed my protection and my peace from them—taken away my loving-kindness and my mercies. 6Both great and small shall die in this land, unburied and unmourned, and their friends shall not cut themselves nor shave their heads as signs of sorrow (as is their heathen custom). 7No one shall comfort the mourners with a meal, or send them a cup of wine expressing grief for their parents' death.

8As a sign to them of these sad days ahead, don't you join them any more in their feasts and parties—don't even eat a meal with them. 9For the Lord Almighty, the God of Israel, says: In your own lifetime, before your very eyes, I will end all laughter in this land—the happy songs, the marriage feasts, the songs of bridegrooms and of brides.

10And when you tell the people all these things and they ask, "Why has the Lord decreed such terrible things against us? What have we done to merit such treatment? What is our sin against the Lord our God?" 11tell them the Lord's reply is this: Because your fathers forsook me. They worshiped other gods and served them; they did not keep my laws, 12*and you have been worse than your fathers were!* You follow evil to your hearts' content and refuse to listen to me. 13Therefore I will throw you out of this land and chase you into a foreign land where neither you nor your fathers have been before, and there you can go ahead and worship your idols all you like—and I will grant you no favors!

14, 15But there will come a glorious day, says the Lord, when the whole topic of conversation will be that God is bringing his people home from a nation in the north, and from many other lands where he had scattered them. You will look back no longer to the time when I rescued you from your slavery in Egypt. That mighty miracle will scarcely be mentioned any more. Yes, I will bring you back again, says the Lord, to this same land I gave your fathers.

16Now I am sending for many fishermen to fish you from the deeps where you are hiding from my wrath. I am sending for hunters to chase you down like deer in the forests or mountain goats on inaccessible crags. Wherever you run to escape my judgment, I will find you and punish you. 17For I am closely watching you and I see every sin. You cannot hope to hide from me.

18And I will punish you doubly for all your sins because you have defiled my land with your detestable idols, and filled it up with all your evil deeds.

19O Lord, my Strength and Fortress, my Refuge in the day of trouble, nations from around the world will come to you saying, "Our fathers have been foolish, for they have worshiped worthless idols! 20Can men make God? The gods they made are not real gods at all." 21And when they come in that spirit, I will show them my power and might and make them understand at last that I alone am God.

Jeremiah warns the people

17 My people sin as though commanded to, as though their evil were laws chiseled with an iron pen or diamond point upon their stony hearts or on the

16:8 *As a sign to them of these sad days ahead,* implied.   **16:21** *I will show them,* literally, "Therefore, behold, I will cause them to know."

16:14, 15 The book of Exodus records God's miraculous rescue of his people from Egyptian slavery (Exodus 1—15). The people's return from exile would be so momentous that it would overshadow even the Exodus from Egypt.

16:17 Small children think that if they can't see you, then you can't see them. The people of Israel may have wished that hiding from God was as simple as closing their eyes. Although they closed their eyes to their sinful ways, their sins certainly weren't hidden from God. He who sees all cannot be deceived. Do you have a sinful attitude or action that you hope God won't notice?—he knows about it. To acknowledge that he knows about our sins is the first step toward repentance.

16:19 In this prayer, Jeremiah approaches God with three descriptive names: strength, refuge, and fortress. Each gives a slightly different glimpse of how Jeremiah experienced God's presence, and each is a picture of security. Let God be your

strength when you feel weak, your refuge when you need to retreat from life's pressures, and your fortress when enemies come against you.

16:20 God will be number one in your life or not in your life at all. To put God in second place is to make someone or something greater than the Creator of all the universe. How can the created ever be greater than the Creator?

16:21 The order of events in this verse is significant. Notice that the nation must first come with the right attitude. Then God would show them his power, and finally he would make them understand that he alone is God. Sometimes people reverse this process—they want to understand God and see his power before they are willing to open themselves to him. Reversing this process keeps us from knowing God; he makes himself known to people with open hearts.

corners of their altars. 2, 3Their youths do not forget to sin, worshiping idols beneath each tree, high in the mountains or in the open country down below. And so I will give all your treasures to your enemies as the price that you must pay for all your sins. 4And the wonderful heritage I reserved for you will slip out of your hand, and I will send you away as slaves to your enemies in distant lands. For you have kindled a fire of my anger that shall burn forever.

5The Lord says: Cursed is the man who puts his trust in mortal man and turns his heart away from God. 6He is like a stunted shrub in the desert, with no hope for the future; he lives on the salt-encrusted plains in the barren wilderness; good times pass him by forever.

7But blessed is the man who trusts in the Lord and has made the Lord his hope and confidence. 8He is like a tree planted along a riverbank, with its roots reaching deep into the water—a tree not bothered by the heat nor worried by long months of drought. Its leaves stay green and it goes right on producing all its luscious fruit.

9The heart is the most deceitful thing there is, and desperately wicked. No one can really know how bad it is! 10Only the Lord knows! He searches all hearts and examines deepest motives so he can give to each person his right reward, according to his deeds—how he has lived.

11Like a bird that fills her nest with young she has not hatched and which will soon desert her and fly away, so is the man who gets his wealth by unjust means. Sooner or later he will lose his riches and at the end of his life become a poor old fool.

12But our refuge is your throne, eternal, high and glorious. 13O Lord, the Hope of Israel, all who turn away from you shall be disgraced and shamed; they are registered for earth and not for glory, for they have forsaken the Lord, the Fountain of living waters. 14Lord, you alone can heal me, you alone can save, and my praises are for you alone.

15Men scoff at me and say, "What is this word of the Lord you keep talking about? If these threats of yours are really from God, why don't they come true?"

16Lord, I don't want the people crushed by terrible calamity. The plan is yours, not mine. It is *your* message I've given them, not my own. *I* don't want them doomed! 17Lord, don't desert me now! You alone are my hope. 18Bring confusion and trouble on all who persecute me, but give me peace. Yes, bring double destruction upon them!

God will burn the city gates

19Then the Lord said to me, Go and stand in the gates of Jerusalem, first at the gate where the king goes out, and then at each of the other gates, 20and say to all the people: Hear the word of the Lord, kings of Judah and all the people of this nation, and all you citizens of Jerusalem. 21, 22The Lord says: Take warning and live; do no unnecessary work on the Sabbath day but make it a holy day. I gave this commandment to your fathers, 23but they didn't listen or obey. They stubbornly refused to pay attention and be taught.

17:21, 22 *unnecessary,* implied.

17:2
Ex 34:13
Isa 39:4-6
Jer 3:6; 15:13
20:5

17:4
Deut 28:48
Isa 5:25
Jer 7:20; 12:7
15:14

17:5
Ps 146:3
Isa 30:1; 31:3
Ezek 29:6,7

17:6
Deut 29:23
Jer 48:6

17:7
Ps 34:8; 40:4
84:12

17:8
Ps 1:3; 92:12-14

17:9
Eccles 9:3
Mt 13:15
Mk 2:17
Rom 1:21

17:10
1 Sam 16:7
Jer 11:20
Rom 8:27

17:12
Jer 14:21

17:13
Jer 14:8

17:14
Deut 10:21
Ps 54:1
Jer 33:6

17:15
Isa 5:19
Amos 5:18

17:17
Jer 16:19
Nah 1:7

17:18
Ps 35:4,26
Jer 20:11

17:21
Ex 16:23-29
Num 15:32-36
Neh 13:15-21
Isa 56:2; 58:13
Ezek 20:12
Mk 4:24
Jn 5:9-12

17:23
Jer 7:26; 19:15

17:5-8 Two kinds of people are contrasted here: the wicked and the righteous. The wicked, specifically Judah, trust false gods and military alliances instead of God, and thus are barren and unfruitful. The righteous place their confidence in God, so they flourish like trees planted by water. In times of trouble, the wicked are already impoverished and spiritually weak, so they have no strength to draw on. But the righteous have abundant strength, not only for their own needs, but even for those of others. Are you satisfied with being unfruitful, or do you, like a well-watered tree, have strength for the time of crisis and even some to share?

17:9, 10 God makes it clear why we sin—it is a matter of the heart: our hearts have been inclined toward sin from the time we were born. But we can still choose whether or not to continue in sin. Either we can yield to a specific temptation, or we can ask

God to help us resist temptation when it comes.

17:11 There is a right way and a wrong way to do any task. Jeremiah says that the man who becomes wealthy through deceit will end up foolish and poor. Whether at work, school, or play, we should strive to be honest in all our dealings. Getting a promotion, passing an exam, or gaining prestige through deceit will never bring God's blessing or lasting happiness.

17:19-27 The people were using the Sabbath, their day of rest (Exodus 20:8-11), to work. They considered making money more important than keeping God's law. If they would repent and put God first in their lives, God promised them honor among the nations. Over a century later, when Nehemiah led the exiles who were returning to Jerusalem, one of his most important reforms was to reinstitute the Sabbath (Nehemiah 13:15-22).

17:24
Ex 15:26
20:8-11
Deut 11:13
Ezek 20:20

17:25
2 Sam 7:16
Ps 132:13,14
Jer 22:4
Lk 1:32

17:26
Ps 107:22
Jer 33:11

17:27
Jer 39:8
Ezek 20:47
Amos 2:5

18:2
Jer 19:1,2

18:6
Isa 45:9; 64:8
Rom 9:21

18:7
Jer 1:10

18:8
Jer 7:3-7
Ezek 18:21

18:9
Jer 31:28
Amos 9:11-15

18:10
1 Sam 2:30
Jer 7:24-28
Ezek 33:18

24But if you obey me, says the Lord, and refuse to work on the Sabbath day and keep it separate, special and holy, 25then this nation shall continue forever. There shall always be descendants of David sitting on the throne here in Jerusalem; there shall always be kings and princes riding in pomp and splendor among the people, and this city shall remain forever. 26And from all around Jerusalem and from the cities of Judah and Benjamin, and from the Negeb and from the lowlands west of Judah, the people shall come with their burnt offerings and grain offerings and incense, bringing their sacrifices to praise the Lord in his Temple.

27But if you will not listen to me, if you refuse to keep the Sabbath holy, if on the Sabbath you bring in loads of merchandise through these gates of Jerusalem, just as on other days, then I will set fire to these gates. The fire shall spread to the palaces and utterly destroy them, and no one shall be able to put out the raging flames.

The people try to silence Jeremiah

18 Here is another message to Jeremiah from the Lord: 2Go down to the shop where clay pots and jars are made and I will talk to you there. 3I did as he told me, and found the potter working at his wheel. 4But the jar that he was forming didn't turn out as he wished, so he kneaded it into a lump and started again.

5Then the Lord said:

6O Israel, can't I do to you as this potter has done to his clay? As the clay is in the potter's hand, so are you in my hand. 7Whenever I announce that a certain nation or kingdom is to be taken up and destroyed, 8then if that nation renounces its evil ways, I will not destroy it as I had planned. 9And if I announce that I will make a certain nation strong and great, 10but then that nation changes its mind and turns to evil and refuses to obey me, then I too will change my mind and not bless that nation as I had said I would.

GOD'S OBJECT LESSONS IN JEREMIAH	Reference	Object Lesson	Significance
	1:11, 12	Whip from the almond tree	God will carry out his threats of punishment.
	1:13	Pot of boiling water tipping southward	God will punish Judah.
	13:1–11	A ruined belt	Because the people refused to listen to God they had become useless, good for nothing, like a ruined belt (or loincloth).
	18:1–17	Potter's clay	God could destroy his sinful people if he so desired. This is a warning to them to repent before he is forced to bring judgment.
	19:1–12	Broken clay jars	God would smash Judah just as Jeremiah smashed the clay jars.
	24:1–10	Two baskets of figs	Good figs represent God's remnant. Bad figs are the people left behind.
	27:2–11	Yoke	Any nation who refused to submit to Babylon's yoke of control would be punished.
	43:8–13	Large stones	The stones marked the place where Nebuchadnezzar would set his throne when God allowed him to conquer Egypt.
	51:59–64	Book sunk in the river	Babylon would sink to rise no more.

18, 19 The parables in these chapters, probably written during the early years of Jehoiakim's reign, illustrate God's sovereignty over the nation. God has power over the clay (Judah), and he continues to work with it to make it a useful vessel. But Judah must soon repent or the clay will harden the wrong way. Then it will be worth nothing, and it will be broken and destroyed.

18:6 As the potter molded or shaped a clay pot on the potter's wheel, defects often appeared. The potter had power over the clay, to allow the defects or to reshape the pot. Likewise, God had power to reshape the nation to conform to his purposes. When we repent, God begins reshaping us into valuable vessels.

¹¹Therefore go and warn all Judah and Jerusalem, saying: Hear the word of the Lord. I am planning evil against you now instead of good; turn back from your evil paths and do what is right.

¹²But they replied, "Don't waste your breath. We have no intention whatever of doing what God says. We will continue to live as we want to, free from any restraint, full of stubbornness and wickedness!"

¹³Then the Lord said: Even among the heathen, no one has ever heard of such a thing! My people have done something too horrible to understand. ¹⁴The snow never melts high up in the Lebanon mountains. The cold, flowing streams from the crags of Mount Hermon never run dry. ¹⁵These can be counted on. But not my people! For they have deserted me and turned to foolish idols. They have turned away from the ancient highways of good, and walk the muddy paths of sin. ¹⁶Therefore their land shall become desolate, so that all who pass by will gasp and shake their heads in amazement at its utter desolation. ¹⁷I will scatter my people before their enemies as the east wind scatters dust; and in all their trouble I will turn my back on them and refuse to notice their distress.

¹⁸Then the people said, "Come, let's get rid of Jeremiah. We have our own priests and wise men and prophets—we don't need his advice. Let's silence him that he may speak no more against us, nor bother us again."

¹⁹*O Lord, help me! See what they are planning to do to me!* ²⁰Should they repay evil for good? They have set a trap to kill me, yet I spoke well of them to you and tried to defend them from your anger. ²¹Now, Lord, let their children starve to death and let the sword pour out their blood! Let their wives be widows and be bereft of all their children! Let their men die in epidemics and their youths die in battle! ²²Let screaming be heard from their homes as troops of soldiers come suddenly upon them, for they have dug a pit for me to fall in, and they have hidden traps along my path. ²³Lord, you know all their murderous plots against me. Don't forgive them, don't blot out their sin, but let them perish before you; deal with them in your anger.

God will shatter Jerusalem

19 The Lord said, Buy a clay jar and take it out into the valley of Ben-Hinnom by the east gate of the city. Take some of the elders of the people and some of the older priests with you, and speak to them whatever words I give you.

³Then the Lord spoke to them and said: Listen to the word of the Lord, kings of Judah and citizens of Jerusalem! The Lord Almighty, the God of Israel, says, I will bring terrible evil upon this place, so terrible that the ears of those who hear it will prickle. ⁴For Israel has forsaken me and turned this valley into a place of shame and wickedness. The people burn incense to idols—idols that neither this generation nor their forefathers nor the kings of Judah have worshiped before—and they have filled this place with the blood of innocent children. ⁵They have built high altars to Baal and there they burn their sons in sacrifice—a thing I never commanded them nor even thought of!

⁶The day is coming, says the Lord, when this valley shall no longer be called "Topheth" or "Ben-Hinnom Valley," but "The Valley of Slaughter." ⁷For I will upset the battle plans of Judah and Jerusalem and I will let invading armies kill you here and leave your dead bodies for vultures and wild animals to feed upon. ⁸And I will wipe Jerusalem off the earth, so that everyone going by will gasp with astonishment at all that I have done to her. ⁹I will see to it that your enemies lay

18:11
2 Kgs 17:13
Isa 1:16-19
Jer 4:6; 11:11
Acts 28:20

18:12
Deut 29:19
Jer 2:25; 16:12

18:13
Jer 2:10,11
23:14
Hos 6:10

18:15
Isa 62:10
Jer 2:32; 6:16
7:9; 44:17

18:16
Jer 25:9; 48:27
50:13
Ezek 33:28,29

18:17
Jer 13:24

18:18
Ps 52:2
Jer 2:8; 5:13
8:8; 11:19
18:11; 20:10

18:20
Ps 35:7; 57:6
Jer 5:26

18:21
Ps 109:9-20
Jer 9:21; 11:22
14:16

18:22
Ps 140:5
Jer 6:26

18:23
Jer 6:15,21
7:20; 17:4

19:1
Num 11:16
Josh 15:8
Jer 7:31,32

19:4
2 Kgs 21:6,16
Isa 65:11
Jer 2:34; 7:6,9
11:13; 17:13
Dan 11:31

19:5
2 Kgs 7:17
Ps 106:37,38
Jer 32:35

19:7
Ps 33:10,11
79:2,3
Isa 28:17,18

19:8
1 Kgs 9:8
2 Chron 7:21
Jer 18:16

19:9
Deut 28:53,55
Ezek 5:10
Lam 4:10

18:18 Jeremiah's words and actions challenged the people's social and moral behavior. He wasn't afraid to give unpopular criticism. The people could either obey him or silence him. They chose the latter. They did not think they needed Jeremiah; their false prophets told them what they wanted to hear.

19:1-6 This valley was the garbage dump of Jerusalem and the place where children were sacrificed to the god Molech. It is also mentioned in 7:31, 32.

19:7-14 The horrible carnage that Jeremiah predicted happened twice, during the Babylonian invasion under Nebuchadnezzar in 586 B.C. and in A.D. 70 when Titus destroyed Jerusalem. During the Babylonian siege, food became so scarce that people became cannibals, even eating their own children. (See Leviticus 26:29; Deuteronomy 28:53-57 for prophecies concerning this, and see 2 Kings 6:28, 29; Lamentations 2:20; 4:10 for accounts of actual occurrences.)

siege to the city until all food is gone, and those trapped inside begin to eat their own children and friends.

¹⁰And now, Jeremiah, as these men watch, smash the jar you brought with you, ¹¹and say to them, This is the message to you from the Lord Almighty: As this jar lies shattered, so I will shatter the people of Jerusalem; and as this jar cannot be mended, neither can they. The slaughter shall be so great that there won't be room enough for decent burial anywhere, and their bodies shall be heaped in this valley. ¹²And as it will be in this valley, so it will be in Jerusalem. For I will fill Jerusalem with dead bodies too. ¹³And I will defile all the homes in Jerusalem, including the palace of the kings of Judah—wherever incense has been burned upon the roofs to your stargods, and libations poured out to them.

¹⁴As Jeremiah returned from Topheth where he had delivered this message, he stopped in front of the Temple of the Lord and said to all the people, ¹⁵The Lord Almighty, the God of Israel, says: I will bring upon this city and her surrounding towns all the evil I have promised, because you have stubbornly refused to listen to the Lord.

Jeremiah is put in stocks

20 Now when Pashhur (son of Immer), the priest in charge of the Temple of the Lord, heard what Jeremiah was saying, ²he arrested Jeremiah and had him whipped and put in the stocks at Benjamin Gate near the Temple. ³He left him there all night.

The next day when Pashhur finally released him, Jeremiah said, "Pashhur, the Lord has changed your name. He says from now on to call you 'The Man Who Lives in Terror.' ⁴For the Lord will send terror on you and all your friends, and you will see them die by the swords of their enemies. I will hand over Judah to the king of Babylon, says the Lord, and he shall take away these people as slaves to Babylon and kill them. ⁵And I will let your enemies loot Jerusalem. All the famed treasures of the city, with the precious jewels and gold and silver of your kings, shall be carried off to Babylon. ⁶And as for you, Pashhur, you and all your family and household shall become slaves in Babylon and die there—you and those to whom you lied when you prophesied that everything would be all right."

⁷Then I said, O Lord, you deceived me when you promised me your help. I have to give them your messages because you are stronger than I am, but now I am the laughingstock of the city, mocked by all. ⁸You have never once let me speak a word of kindness to them; always it is disaster and horror and destruction. No wonder they scoff and mock and make my name a household joke. ⁹And I can't quit! For if I say I'll never again mention the Lord—never more speak in his name—then his word in my heart is like fire that burns in my bones, and I can't hold it in any longer. ¹⁰Yet on every side I hear their whispered threats, and am afraid. "We will report," they say. Even those who were my friends are watching me, waiting for a fatal slip. "He will trap himself," they say, "and then we will get our revenge on him."

¹¹But the Lord stands beside me like a great warrior, and before him, the Mighty, Terrible One, they shall stumble. They cannot defeat me; they shall be shamed and thoroughly humiliated, and they shall have a stigma upon them forever. ¹²O Lord

19:11
Ps 2:9
Isa 30:14
Jer 7:32
Rev 2:27

19:13
Deut 4:19
2 Kgs 17:16
Jer 8:2,32:29
52:13
Ezek 20:28
Zeph 1:5

19:14
Jer 26:2

19:15
Neh 9:17,29
Jer 7:26; 17:23

20:1
1 Chron 24:14
Ezra 2:37,38

20:2
1 Kgs 22:27
2 Chron 16:10
Jer 1:19; 37:13
Zech 14:10

20:4
Jer 29:21
39:6,7
Ezek 26:21

20:5
2 Kgs 20:17
2 Chron 36:10
Jer 15:13; 17:3
27:21,22

20:6
Jer 14:14,15
Lam 2:14

20:7
Ps 22:7
Lam 3:14
Ezek 3:14
Mic 3:8

20:9
Ps 39:3
Jer 4:19
Acts 4:20

20:10
1 Kgs 19:2
22:27
Neh 6:6-13
Ps 41:9

20:11
Deut 32:35,36
Jer 1:8,15:20

20:12
Ps 7:9; 17:3
139:23
Jer 11:20; 17:10

20:1ff This event took place during the reign of Jehoiakim of Judah. Jeremiah preached at the Valley of Hinnom, the center of idolatry in the city. He also preached in the Temple, which should have been the center of true worship. Both places attracted many people; both were places of false worship.

20:1-3 Pashhur heard Jeremiah's words and, because of his guilt, locked Jeremiah up instead of taking his message to heart and acting upon it. The truth sometimes stings, but our reaction to the truth shows what we are made of. We can deny the changes and destroy evidence of our misdeeds, or we can take the truth humbly to heart and let it change us. Pashhur may have thought he was a strong leader, but he was really a coward.

20:4-6 This prophecy of destruction came true in three waves of invasion by Babylon. The first wave happened within the year (605 B.C.). Pashhur was probably exiled to Babylon during the second wave in 597 B.C. when King Jehoiachin was taken captive. The third invasion occurred in 586 B.C.

20:7-18 Jeremiah cries out in despair mixed with praise, unburdening his heart to God. He has faithfully proclaimed God's Word and has received nothing in return but persecution and sorrow. Yet when he withheld God's Word for a while, it became fire in his bones until he could withhold it no longer. When God's living Word becomes "fire in your bones," you also will feel compelled to share it with others, whatever the results.

Almighty, who knows those who are righteous and examines the deepest thoughts of hearts and minds, let me see your vengeance on them. For I have committed my cause to you. 13Therefore I will sing out in thanks to the Lord! Praise him! For he has delivered me, poor and needy, from my oppressors.

14Yet, cursed be the day that I was born! 15Cursed be the man who brought my father the news that a son was born. 16Let that messenger be destroyed like the cities of old which God overthrew without mercy. Terrify him all day long with battle shouts, 17because he did not kill me at my birth! Oh, that I had died within my mother's womb, that it had been my grave! 18Why was I ever born? For my life has been but trouble and sorrow and shame.

4. Jeremiah accuses Judah's leaders

God refuses the king's request

21 Then King Zedekiah sent Pashhur (son of Malchiah) and Zephaniah the priest (son of Ma-aseiah) to Jeremiah, and begged, "Ask the Lord to help us, for Nebuchadnezzar, king of Babylon, has declared war on us! 2Perhaps the Lord will be gracious to us and do a mighty miracle as in olden times and force Nebuchadnezzar to withdraw his forces."

3, 4Jeremiah replied, "Go back to King Zedekiah and tell him the Lord God of Israel says, I will make all your weapons useless against the king of Babylon and the Chaldeans besieging you. In fact, I will bring your enemies right into the heart of this city, 5and I myself will fight against you, for I am very angry. 6And I will send a terrible plague on this city, and both men and animals shall die. 7And finally I will deliver King Zedekiah himself and all the remnant left in the city into the hands of King Nebuchadnezzar of Babylon, to slaughter them without pity or mercy.

8"Tell these people, the Lord says: Take your choice of life or death! 9Stay here in Jerusalem and die—slaughtered by your enemies, killed by starvation and disease—or go out and surrender to the Chaldean army and live. 10For I have set my face against this city; I will be its enemy and not its friend, says the Lord. It shall be captured by the king of Babylon and he shall reduce it to ashes.

11"And to the king of Judah, the Lord says: 12I am ready to judge you because of all the evil you are doing. Quick! Give justice to these you judge! Begin doing what is right before my burning fury flashes out upon you like a fire no man can quench. 13I will fight against this city of Jerusalem, which boasts, 'We are safe; no one can touch us here!' 14And I myself will destroy you for your sinfulness, says the Lord. I will light a fire in the forests that will burn up everything in its path."

God decrees judgment on evil kings

22 Then the Lord said to me: Go over and speak directly to the king of Judah and say, 2Listen to this message from God, O king of Judah, sitting on David's throne; and let your servants and your people listen too.

20:13
Ps 34:6; 69:33
Jer 15:21

20:14
Job 3:3-6

20:17
Job 3:10,11,16
10:18,19

20:18
Job 3:20; 14:1
Ps 102:3
Jer 15:10
1 Cor 4:9-13

21:1
2 Kgs 25:18-21
Jer 29:25,29

21:2
2 Kgs 25:1,2
Ps 44:1-4

21:3
Jer 32:5; 33:5
37:8-10
38:17,18; 39:3
Lam 2:5,7
Zech 14:2

21:5
Isa 5:25; 63:10
Jer 6:12

21:7
2 Chron 36:17
Jer 13:14
Ezek 7:9
Hab 1:6-10

21:9
Jer 38:2; 39:18

21:10
2 Chron 36:19
Jer 32:28,29
39:8; 44:11,27
52:13

21:12
Isa 1:17
Jer 4:5
Ezek 20:47,48
Zech 7:9,10

21:14
2 Chron 36:19
Jer 52:13

22:2
Isa 9:7
Jer 17:25
Lk 1:32

21:1 Chapters 21—28 are Jeremiah's messages concerning Nebuchadnezzar's attacks on Jerusalem between 588 and 586 B.C. (see also 2 Kings 25). King Zedekiah decided to rebel against Nebuchadnezzar, and the nobles advised allying with Egypt. Jeremiah pronounced judgment on the kings (21:1—23:8) and false prophets (23:9–40) for leading the people astray.

21:1, 2 King Zedekiah probably referred to God's deliverance of Jerusalem from Sennacherib, king of Assyria, in the days of Hezekiah (Isaiah 36—37). But Zedekiah's hopes were dashed. He was Judah's last ruler before the exile of 597 B.C.

21:1, 2 Pashhur's abuse had driven Jeremiah to the point of despondency and depression, but now Pashhur comes to the prophet for help. God still had important work for Jeremiah to do. In living out our faith, we may find that rejection, disappointment, or hard work has brought us to the point of despondency. But we are still needed. God has important work for us to do.

21:1–14 Jeremiah had foretold Jerusalem's destruction. The city's leaders had denied his word and mocked his announcements. In desperation, King Zedekiah turned to God for help, but without acknowledging God's warnings or admitting his sin. Too often we expect God to help us in our time of trouble even though we have ignored him in our time of prosperity. But God wants a lasting relationship. Are you trying to build a lasting friendship with God or are you merely using him occasionally to escape trouble? What would you think of your family or friends if they thought of you only as a temporary resource?

22:1ff Chapters 22—25 are not in chronological order. In 21:9 God says it is too late for repentance. In 22:4 God says there is still time to change. The events of this chapter occurred before those of chapter 21. This message was probably given during the reign of Jehoiakim (22:13), who reigned about ten years before Zedekiah.

22:3
Ex 22:21-24
Ps 72:4
Jer 7:6; 19:4
21:12; 22:17

22:5
Amos 6:8
Heb 6:13

22:6
Isa 6:11
Jer 7:34

22:7
Isa 10:3-6,
33,34
Jer 4:6,7

22:8
Deut 29:24-26
1 Kgs 9:8,9
2 Chron 7:20,22
Jer 16:10

22:9
2 Chron 34:25
Jer 11:3

22:12
2 Kgs 23:34

22:13
Jer 17:11
Hab 2:9

22:14
Isa 5:8,9
Hab 1:4

22:15
2 Kgs 23:25
Jer 21:12; 42:6

22:16
Ps 72:1-4,12,13
Jer 9:24

22:17
Jer 6:13; 8:10
Lk 12:15-20

22:19
Jer 36:30

22:20
Deut 32:49

22:22
Jer 30:14

3The Lord says: Be fair-minded. Do what is right! Help those in need of justice! Quit your evil deeds! Protect the rights of aliens and immigrants, orphans and widows; stop murdering the innocent! 4If you put an end to all these terrible deeds you are doing, then I will deliver this nation and once more give kings to sit on David's throne, and there shall be prosperity for all.

5But if you refuse to pay attention to this warning, I swear by my own name, says the Lord, that this palace shall become a shambles. 6For this is the Lord's message concerning the palace: You are as beloved to me as fruitful Gilead and the green forests of Lebanon; but I will destroy you and leave you deserted and uninhabited. 7I will call for a wrecking crew to bring out its tools to dismantle you. They will tear out all of your fine cedar beams and throw them on the fire. 8Men from many nations will pass by the ruins of this city and say to one another, "Why did the Lord do it? Why did he destroy such a great city?" 9And the answer will be, "Because the people living here forgot the Lord their God and violated his agreement with them, for they worshiped idols."

10Don't weep for the dead! Instead weep for the captives led away! For they will never return to see their native land again. 11For the Lord says this about Jehoahaz who succeeded his father King Josiah, and was taken away as a captive: 12He shall die in a distant land and never again see his own country.

13And woe to you, King Jehoiakim, for you are building your great palace with forced labor. By not paying wages you are building injustice into its walls and oppression into its doorframes and ceilings. 14You say, "I will build a magnificent palace with huge rooms and many windows, paneled throughout with fragrant cedar and painted a lovely red." 15But a beautiful palace does not make a great king! Why did your father Josiah reign so long? Because he was just and fair in all his dealings. That is why God blessed him. 16He saw to it that justice and help were given the poor and the needy and all went well for him. This is how a man lives close to God. 17But you! You are full of selfish greed and all dishonesty! You murder the innocent, oppress the poor and reign with ruthlessness.

18Therefore this is God's decree of punishment against King Jehoiakim, who succeeded his father Josiah on the throne: His family will not weep for him when he dies. His subjects will not even care that he is dead. 19He shall be buried like a dead donkey—dragged out of Jerusalem and thrown on the garbage dump beyond the gate! 20Weep, for your allies are gone. Search for them in Lebanon; shout for them at Bashan; seek them at the fording points of Jordan. See, they are all destroyed. Not one is left to help you! 21When you were prosperous I warned you, but you replied, "Don't bother me." Since childhood you have been that way—you just won't listen! 22And now all your allies have disappeared with a puff of wind; all your friends are taken off as slaves. Surely at last you will see your wickedness and be ashamed. 23It's very nice to live graciously in a beautiful palace among the cedars of Lebanon, but soon you will cry and groan in anguish—anguish as of a woman in labor.

22:13 *King Jehoiakim,* implied. See vs 18. He was chosen by the Egyptians to replace Jehoahaz, whom they took back to Egypt with them. He ruled from 609-598 B.C.

22:3 God gave the king the basis for rebuilding the nation—turn from evil and do right. Doing right is more than simply believing all the right doctrines about God. It is living obediently to God. Good works do not save us, but they display our faith (James 2:17-26).

22:10-12 Good King Josiah had died at the battle of Megiddo; his son Jehoahaz reigned for three brief months in 609 B.C. before being taken away to Egypt by Pharaoh Neco. He would be the first ruler to die in exile. The people were told not to waste their tears on the death of Josiah, but to cry for the king (Jehoahaz) who was taken into exile and would never return.

22:15, 16 God passed judgment on King Jehoiakim. His father, King Josiah, had been one of Judah's great kings, but Jehoiakim was evil. Josiah had been faithful with his responsibility to teach his son and model right living, but Jehoiakim had been unfaithful with

his responsibility to imitate his father. God's judgment was on unfaithful Jehoiakim. He could not claim his father's blessings when he had not followed his father's God. We may inherit our parents' money but we cannot inherit their faith or blessings. A great heritage, a good education, or a beautiful home doesn't guarantee a strong character. We must choose our own relationship with God.

22:21 Jehoiakim had been hardheaded and hardhearted since childhood. God warned him, but he refused to listen. His prosperity always took a higher priority than his relationship with God. If you ever find yourself so comfortable that you don't have time for God, stop and ask which is more important—the comforts of this life or a close relationship with God.

24, 25And as for you, Coniah, son of Jehoiakim king of Judah—even if you were the signet ring on my right hand, I would pull you off and give you to those who seek to kill you, of whom you are so desperately afraid—to Nebuchadnezzar, king of Babylon, and his mighty army. 26I will throw you and your mother out of this country, and you shall die in a foreign land. 27You will never again return to the land of your desire. 28This man Coniah is like a discarded, broken dish. He and his children will be exiled to distant lands.

29O earth, earth, earth! Hear the word of the Lord! 30The Lord says:

Record this man Coniah as childless, for none of his children shall ever sit upon the throne of David or rule in Judah. His life will amount to nothing.

A righteous king will come

23 The Lord declares:

I will send disaster upon the leaders of my people—the shepherds of my sheep—for they have destroyed and scattered the very ones they were to care for. 2Instead of leading my flock to safety, you have deserted them and driven them to destruction. And now I will pour out judgment upon you for the evil you have done to them. 3And I will gather together the remnant of my flock from wherever I have sent them, and bring them back into their own fold, and they shall be fruitful and increase. 4And I will appoint responsible shepherds to care for them, and they shall not need to be afraid again; all of them shall be accounted for continually. 5, 6For the time is coming, says the Lord, when I will place a righteous Branch upon King David's throne. He shall be a King who shall rule with wisdom and justice and cause righteousness to prevail everywhere throughout the earth. And this is his name: *The Lord Our Righteousness*. At that time Judah will be saved and Israel will live in peace.

7In that day people will no longer say when taking an oath, "As the Lord lives who rescued the people of Israel from the land of Egypt," 8but they will say, "As the Lord lives who brought the Jews back to their own land of Israel from the countries to which he had exiled them."

Warning against false prophets

9My heart is broken for the false prophets, full of deceit. I awake with fear and stagger as a drunkard does from wine, because of the awful fate awaiting them, for God has decreed holy words of judgment against them. 10For the land is full of adultery and the curse of God is on it. The land itself is mourning—the pastures are dried up—for the prophets do evil and their power is used wrongly. 11And the priests are like the prophets, all ungodly, wicked men. I have seen their despicable acts right here in my own Temple, says the Lord. 12Therefore their paths will be

22:24
2 Kgs 24:15,16
Jer 21:7
34:20,21
Hag 2:23

22:28
Jer 15:1
Hos 8:8

22:29
Jer 6:19
Mic 1:2

22:30
Jer 36:30
Mt 1:12

23:1
Isa 56:9-12
Jer 10:21; 50:6
Ezek 13:3; 34:2
Zech 11:17

23:2
Ex 32:34
Jer 44:22

23:3
Isa 11:11-16
Jer 31:7,8

23:4
Jer 3:15; 31:10
Jn 6:39; 10:28
1 Pet 1:5

23:5
Isa 9:6; 11:1-5
53:2
Jer 33:15,16
Zech 3:8
6:12,13
Mt 1:21-23
Rom 3:21,22
1 Cor 1:30

23:7
Isa 43:18,19
Jer 16:14,15

23:10
Ps 107:34
Jer 5:7,8; 9:10

23:11
Jer 6:13
7:9-10; 8:10

23:12
Isa 8:22
Jer 13:16
Jn 12:35

22:30 *none of his children shall ever sit upon the throne of David or rule in Judah.* This man Coniah's grandson, Zerubbabel, was briefly governor, but not king. **23:5, 6** *throughout the earth,* or, "throughout the land."
23:9 *because of the awful fate awaiting them,* implied.

22:24, 25 Coniah may be an abbreviation for Jeconiah (another name for Jehoiachin). A signet ring was extremely valuable because a king used it to authenticate valuable documents. Jehoiachin's sins spoiled his usefulness to God. Even if he was God's own signet ring, God would depose him because of his sins (see 24:1).

22:30 Zedekiah reigned after Jehoiachin but died before him (52:10, 11). Jehoiachin (Coniah) was the last living Judean king, and his line died with him (1 Chronicles 3:15–20). Although Jehoiachin's grandson, Zerubbabel, ruled after the return from exile (Ezra 2:2), he was only a governor, not a king.

23:1–4 After his indictment of Israel's civil leaders, Jeremiah lashed out at the religious leaders. Those leaders who were responsible to lead Israel in God's path were the ones responsible for Israel's present plight, and so God had decreed harsh judgment against them. Leaders are held responsible for those entrusted to their care. Whom has God placed in your care?

Remember that you are accountable to God for those you lead.

23:5, 6 Jeremiah contrasted the present corrupt kings and priests with the coming Messiah, perfect King and perfect Priest. This spiritual King would come from David's line to reign over Israel.

23:9–14 How did the nation become so corrupt? A major factor was false prophecy. The false prophets had a large, enthusiastic audience and were very popular because they made the people believe that all was well. By contrast, Jeremiah's message from God was unpopular because it showed the people how bad they were.

There are four warning signs of false prophets—characteristics we need to watch for even today. (1) They may appear to live according to religious principles, but they do not speak God's message. (2) They water down God's message in order to make it more palatable. (3) They encourage their listeners, often subtly, to disobey God. (4) They tend to be arrogant and self-serving, appealing to the desires of their audience instead of being true to God's Word.

23:13
1 Kgs 18:18-21
Jer 2:8

23:14
Isa 1:9,10
Jer 5:30,32
Ezek 13:22,23
Mt 11:24

23:15
Deut 29:18
Jer 8:14; 9:15

23:16
Jer 14:14
Ezek 13:2,3,6
Mt 7:15
2 Cor 11:13-15
Gal 1:8,9
1 Jn 4:1

23:17
Jer 5:12; 8:11
Amos 9:10
Mic 2:11; 3:11

23:19
Jer 30:23
Amos 1:14

23:20
Isa 55:11
Jer 30:24
Zech 1:5,6

23:22
Jer 35:15
Zech 1:4
1 Thess 1:9,10

23:23
Ps 139:1-10

23:24
Job 22:13,14
Ps 139:7-12
Isa 29:15,16

23:25
Jer 8:6; 29:8

23:26
1 Tim 4:1,2

23:27
Deut 13:1-3
Judg 3:12
8:33,34

23:28
1 Cor 3:12,13

23:29
Jer 5:14; 20:9
2 Cor 10:4,5

23:30
Ezek 13:8

23:33
Nah 1:1
Hab 1:1
Zech 9:1

23:34
Zech 13:3

23:35
Jer 33:3; 42:4

23:36
2 Kgs 19:4
Jer 10:10
2 Pet 3:16

dark and slippery; they will be chased down dark and treacherous trails, and fall. For I will bring evil upon them and see to it, when their time has come, that they pay their penalty in full for all their sins.

13I knew the prophets of Samaria were unbelievably evil, for they prophesied by Baal and led my people Israel into sin; 14but the prophets of Jerusalem are even worse! The things they do are horrible; they commit adultery and love dishonesty. They encourage and compliment those who are doing evil, instead of turning them back from their sins. These prophets are as thoroughly depraved as the men of Sodom and Gomorrah were.

15Therefore the Lord Almighty says: I will feed them with bitterness and give them poison to drink. For it is because of them that wickedness fills this land. 16This is my warning to my people, says the Lord Almighty. Don't listen to these false prophets when they prophesy to you, filling you with futile hopes. They are making up everything they say. They do not speak for me! 17They keep saying to these rebels who despise me, "Don't worry! All is well"; and to those who live the way they want to, "The Lord has said you shall have peace!"

18But can you name even one of these prophets who lives close enough to God to hear what he is saying? Has even one of them cared enough to listen? 19See, the Lord is sending a furious whirlwind to sweep away these wicked men. 20The terrible anger of the Lord will not abate until it has carried out the full penalty he decrees against them. Later, when Jerusalem has fallen, you will see what I mean.

21I have not sent these prophets, yet they claim to speak for me; I gave them no message, yet they say their words are mine. 22If they were mine, they would try to turn my people from their evil ways. 23Am I a God who is only in one place and cannot see what they are doing? 24Can anyone hide from me? Am I not everywhere in all of heaven and earth?

25"Listen to the dream I had from God last night," they say. And then they proceed to lie in my name. 26How long will this continue? If they are "prophets," they are prophets of deceit, inventing everything they say. 27By telling these false dreams they are trying to get my people to forget me in the same way as their fathers did, who turned away to the idols of Baal. 28Let these false prophets tell their dreams and let my true messengers faithfully proclaim my every word. There is a difference between chaff and wheat! 29Does not my word burn like fire? asks the Lord. Is it not like a mighty hammer that smashed the rock to pieces? 30, 31So I stand against these "prophets" who get their messages from each other—these smooth-tongued prophets who say, "This message is from God!" 32Their made-up dreams are flagrant lies that lead my people into sin. I did not send them and they have no message at all for my people, says the Lord.

33When one of the people or one of their "prophets" or priests asks you, "Well, Jeremiah, what is the sad news from the Lord today?" you shall reply, "What sad news? You are the sad news, for the Lord has cast you away!" 34And as for the false prophets and priests and people who joke about "today's sad news from God," I will punish them and their families for saying this. 35You can ask each other, "What is God's message? What is he saying?" 36But stop using this term, "God's sad news." For what is sad is you and your lying. You are twisting my words and inventing "messages from God" that I didn't speak. 37You may respectfully ask

23:20 *Later, when Jerusalem has fallen,* literally, "in the latter days."

23:14 Sodom and Gomorrah were sinful cities destroyed by God (Genesis 19:23, 24).

23:28 True prophets and false prophets are as different as chaff and wheat. Worthless chaff blows away with the wind, while wheat remains to nourish many. To share God's Word is a great responsibility, because the way we present it and live it will encourage people either to accept it or reject it. Whether we speak from a pulpit, teach in a class, or share with friends, we are entrusted with accurately communicating and living out God's Word. As you share God's Word with friends and neighbors, they will look for its

effectiveness in your life. Unless it has changed you, why should they let it change them? If you don't live it, don't preach it!

23:33 People mocked Jeremiah and God because it seemed that Jeremiah brought nothing but sad news. But this sad news was the truth. If they accepted it, they would have to repent and turn to God. Because they did not want to do this, they rejected Jeremiah's message. Have you ever rejected a message or made fun of it because it would require you to change your ways? Before dismissing someone who brings "sad news," look carefully at your motives.

Jeremiah, "What is the Lord's message? What has he said to you?" 38, 39But if you
ask him about "today's sad news from God," when I have warned you not to mock
like that, then I, the Lord God, will unburden myself of the burden you are to me.
I will cast you out of my presence, you and this city I gave to you and your fathers.
40And I will bring reproach upon you and your name shall be infamous through the
ages.

23:38
Jer 7:14,15
Ezek 8:18

23:40
Jer 20:11
Ezek 5:14,15

Jeremiah's vision of the figs

24 After Nebuchadnezzar, king of Babylon, had captured and enslaved Jeconiah (son of Jehoiakim), king of Judah, and exiled him to Babylon along
with the princes of Judah and the skilled tradesmen—the carpenters and
blacksmiths—the Lord gave me this vision. 2I saw two baskets of figs placed in
front of the Temple in Jerusalem. In one basket there were fresh, just-ripened figs,
but in the other the figs were spoiled and moldy—too rotten to eat. 3Then the Lord
said to me, "What do you see, Jeremiah?"

I replied, "Figs, some very good and some very bad."

4, 5Then the Lord said: "The good figs represent the exiles sent to Babylon. I have
done it for their good. 6I will see that they are well treated and I will bring them
back here again. I will help them and not hurt them; I will plant them and not pull
them up. 7I will give them hearts that respond to me. They shall be my people and
I will be their God, for they shall return to me with great joy.

8"But the rotten figs represent Zedekiah, king of Judah, his officials and all the
others of Jerusalem left here in this land; those too who live in Egypt. I will treat
them like spoiled figs, too bad to use. 9I will make them repulsive to every nation
of the earth, and they shall be mocked and taunted and cursed wherever I compel
them to go. 10And I will send massacre and famine and disease among them until
they are destroyed from the land of Israel, which I gave to them and to their
fathers."

24:1
2 Kgs 24:10-16
2 Chron 36:10
Jer 27:19-21

24:4
Nah 1:7
Zech 13:9

24:6
Jer 29:10; 31:4
32:37,41; 33:7
Ezek 11:17

24:7
Jer 31:33; 32:40
Zech 8:8
Heb 8:10

24:8
Jer 29:17; 39:5
44:26-30
Ezek 12:13

24:9
1 Kgs 9:7
Ps 44:13,14
Isa 65:15
Jer 15:4; 29:18
34:17

24:10
Isa 51:19
Jer 27:8
Ezek 5:12-17

Jeremiah prophesies captivity

25 This message for all the people of Judah came from the Lord to Jeremiah
during the fourth year of the reign of King Jehoiakim of Judah (son of
Josiah). This was the year Nebuchadnezzar, king of Babylon, began his reign.
2, 3For the past twenty-three years, Jeremiah said, from the thirteenth year of the
reign of Josiah (son of Amon) king of Judah, until now, God has been sending me
his messages. I have faithfully passed them on to you, but you haven't listened.
4Again and again down through the years, God has sent you his prophets, but you
have refused to hear. 5Each time the message was this: Turn from the evil road you
are traveling and from the evil things you are doing. Only then can you continue to

25:1
2 Kgs 24:1,2
Jer 36:1; 46:2

25:2
Jer 1:2
7:25,26
11:7,8; 26:5
36:2,3

25:5
Gen 17:8-10
Isa 55:6,7
Jer 4:1; 7:7
35:15

23:38, 39 *will unburden myself of the burden,* literally, either, "the *burden* of the Lord," or, "the *message* of the Lord."
This is a Hebrew pun.

24:1 This happened in 597 B.C. Jeconiah (also known as
Jehoiachin) was taken to Babylon and Zedekiah became king.
Princes were exiled to keep them from exerting power and starting
a rebellion. Skilled tradesmen were taken because they were
valuable for Babylon's building program. Jeremiah foretold this
event in 22:24, 25.

24:2-10 The good figs represented the exiles to Babylon—not
because they themselves were good, but because their hearts
would respond to God. So he would preserve them and bring them
back to the land. The bad figs represented those who remained in
Judah or ran away to Egypt. The people believed they would be
blessed if they remained in the land, but the opposite was true, for
God would use the captivity to refine the exiles. We may assume
we are blessed when life goes well and cursed when it does not.
But trouble is a blessing when it makes us stronger, and prosperity
is a curse if it entices us away from God. If you are facing trouble,
ask God to help you grow stronger for him. If things are going your
way, ask God to help you use your prosperity faithfully for him.

24:6 The exiles in Babylon were treated well. Although they were
moved to a foreign land, their captivity was not enslavement. The
people could function in business and own homes. Some, like
Daniel, even held high positions (see Daniel 2:48).

25:1 Jeremiah gave this message in 605 B.C., the year
Nebuchadnezzar came to power. From verse 2 we learn that the
beginning of Jeremiah's ministry was in 627 B.C. He predicted the
70 years of captivity a full 20 years before it began.

25:2-6 Imagine preaching the same message for 23 years and
continually being rejected! Jeremiah faced this; but because he
had committed his life to God, he continued to proclaim the
message—"turn from your evil ways." Regardless of the people's
response, Jeremiah did not give up. God never stops loving us,
even when we reject him. We can thank God that he won't give up
on us; and like Jeremiah, we can commit ourselves to never giving
him up. No matter how people respond when you tell them about
God, remain faithful to God's high call and continue to witness for
him.

live here in this land which the Lord gave to you and to your ancestors forever. 6*Don't anger me by worshiping idols; but if you are true to me, then I'll not harm you.* 7But you won't listen; you have gone ahead and made me furious with your idols. So you have brought upon yourselves all the evil that has come your way.

8, 9And now the Lord God says, Because you have not listened to me, I will gather together all the armies of the north under Nebuchadnezzar, king of Babylon (I have appointed him as my deputy), and I will bring them all against this land and its people and against the other nations near you, and I will utterly destroy you and make you a byword of contempt forever. 10I will take away your joy, your gladness and your wedding feasts; your businesses shall fail and all your homes shall lie in silent darkness. 11This entire land shall become a desolate wasteland; all the world will be shocked at the disaster that befalls you. Israel and her neighboring lands shall serve the king of Babylon for seventy years.

12Then, after these years of slavery are ended, I will punish the king of Babylon and his people for their sins; I will make the land of Chaldea an everlasting waste. 13I will bring upon them all the terrors I have promised in this book—all the penalties announced by Jeremiah against the nations. 14For many nations and great kings shall enslave the Chaldeans, just as they enslaved my people; I will punish them in proportion to their treatment of my people.

The cup of God's wrath

15For the Lord God said to me: "Take from my hand this wine cup filled to the brim with my fury, and make all the nations to whom I send you drink from it. 16They shall drink from it and reel, crazed by the death blows I rain upon them."

17So I took the cup of fury from the Lord and made all the nations drink from it—every nation God had sent me to; 18I went to Jerusalem and to the cities of Judah, and their kings and princes drank of the cup so that from that day until this they have been desolate, hated and cursed, just as they are today. 19, 20I went to Egypt, and Pharaoh and his servants, the princes and the people—they too drank from that terrible cup, along with all the foreign population living in his land. So did all the kings of the land of Uz and the kings of the Philistine cities: Ashkelon, Gaza, Ekron, and what remains of Ashdod, 21and I visited the nations of Edom, Moab and Ammon; 22and all the kings of Tyre and Sidon, and the kings of the regions across the sea; 23Dedan and Tema and Buz, and the other heathen there; 24and all the kings of Arabia and of the nomadic tribes of the desert; 25and all the kings of Zimri, Elam and Media; 26and all the kings of the northern countries, far and near, one after the other; and all the kingdoms of the world. And finally, the king of Babylon himself drank from this cup of God's wrath.

27Tell them, "The Lord of heaven's armies, the God of Israel, says, Drink from this cup of my wrath until you are drunk and vomit and fall and rise no more, for I am sending terrible wars upon you." 28And if they refuse to accept the cup, tell them, "The Lord of heaven's armies says you *must* drink it! You cannot escape! 29I have begun to punish my own people, so should you go free? No, you shall not evade punishment. I will call for war against all the peoples of the earth."

30Therefore prophesy against them. Tell them the Lord will shout against his own from his holy temple in heaven, and against all those living on the earth. He will shout as the harvesters do who tread the juice from the grapes. 31That cry of judgment will reach the farthest ends of the earth, for the Lord has a case against all the nations—all mankind. He will slaughter all the wicked. 32See, declares the Lord Almighty, the punishment shall go from nation to nation—a great whirlwind of wrath shall rise against the farthest corners of the earth. 33On that day those the

Cross-references (margin)

25:6 Deut 6:14; 8:19 2 Kgs 17:35

25:7 2 Kgs 17:17 21:15 Jer 7:19 32:30-33

25:8 Jer 27:6; 43:10

25:10 Isa 24:8-11 Jer 16:9 Ezek 26:13

25:11 Dan 9:2 Zech 7:5

25:12 Ezra 1:1 Isa 13:14 Jer 29:10, 50,51

25:13 Jer 36:4,29,32

25:14 Jer 27:7

25:15 Jer 51:7

25:17 Jer 1:10

25:19 Jer 46:2-28 Lam 4:21

25:21 Jer 48:1-47 49:1-22 Amos 1:13-15 2:1-3

25:22 Jer 47:4 Zech 9:2-4

25:23 Jer 49:7,8

25:25 Jer 49:34

25:26 Jer 50:9; 51:41

25:29 Prov 11:31 1 Pet 4:17

25:30 Joel 2:11 Amos 1:2

25:31 Isa 66:16

25:32 Isa 30:30 34:2,3

25:33 Isa 5:25 Jer 16:4 Ezek 39:4,7

25:12 This event is further described in Daniel 5. The troops of Cyrus the Great entered Babylon in 539 B.C. and killed Belshazzar, the last Babylonian ruler.

25:15-38 Judah would not be the only nation to drink the cup of God's wrath. Jeremiah listed other wicked nations who would experience God's wrath at the hand of Babylon. Finally, Babylon itself would suffer the same fate because of its sin.

Lord has slain shall fill the earth from one end to the other. No one shall mourn for them nor gather up the bodies to bury them; they shall fertilize the earth.

34Weep and moan, O evil shepherds; let the leaders of mankind beat their heads upon the stones, for their time has come to be slaughtered and scattered; they shall fall like fragile women. 35And you will find no place to hide, no way to escape.

36Listen to the frantic cries of the shepherds and to the leaders shouting in despair, for the Lord has spoiled their pastures. 37People now living undisturbed will be cut down by the fierceness of the anger of the Lord. 38He has left his lair like a lion seeking prey; their land has been laid waste by warring armies—because of the fierce anger of the Lord.

Jeremiah narrowly escapes death

26 This message came to Jeremiah from the Lord during the first year of the reign of Jehoiakim (son of Josiah), king of Judah:

2Stand out in front of the Temple of the Lord and make an announcement to all the people who have come there to worship from many parts of Judah. Give them the entire message; don't leave out one word of all I have for them to hear. 3For perhaps they will listen and turn from their evil ways, and then I can withhold all the punishment I am ready to pour out upon them because of their evil deeds. 4Tell them the Lord says: If you will not listen to me and obey the laws I have given you, 5and if you will not listen to my servants, the prophets—for I sent them again and again to warn you, but you would not listen to them— 6then I will destroy this Temple as I destroyed the Tabernacle at Shiloh, and I will make Jerusalem a curse word in every nation of the earth.

7, 8When Jeremiah had finished his message, saying everything the Lord had told him to, the priests and false prophets and all the people in the Temple mobbed him, shouting, "Kill him! Kill him! 9What right do you have to say the Lord will destroy this Temple like the one at Shiloh?" they yelled. "What do you mean—Jerusalem destroyed and not one survivor?"

10When the high officials of Judah heard what was going on, they rushed over from the palace and sat down at the door of the Temple to hold court. 11Then the priests and the false prophets presented their accusations to the officials and the people. "This man should die!" they said. "You have heard with your own ears what a traitor he is, for he has prophesied against this city."

12Then Jeremiah spoke in his defense. "The Lord sent me," he said, "to prophesy against this Temple and this city. He gave me every word of all that I have spoken. 13But if you stop your sinning and begin obeying the Lord your God, he will cancel all the punishment he has announced against you. 14As for me, I am helpless and in your power—do with me as you think best. 15But there is one thing sure, if you kill me, you will be killing an innocent man and the responsibility will lie upon you and upon this city and upon every person living in it; for it is absolutely true that the Lord sent me to speak every word that you have heard from me."

16Then the officials and people said to the priests and false prophets, "This man

25:34
Isa 34:7
Jer 50:27

25:38
Jer 4:7; 5:6
Hos 5:14
13:7,8

26:2
Deut 4:2
Jer 7:2; 19:14
42:4
Acts 20:20,27

26:3
Isa 1:16-19
Jer 36:3-7

26:4
Lev 26:14
1 Kgs 9:6
Isa 1:20
Jer 17:27; 22:5
44:10,23

26:5
Ezra 9:11
Jer 25:4

26:6
Ps 78:60,61
Jer 7:12,14
25:8

26:7
Jer 5:31; 11:19
Lam 4:13,14
Mic 3:11
Mt 23:34,35

26:10
Acts 21:31,32

26:11
Jer 18:23; 38:4
Mt 26:66
Acts 6:11-14

26:13
Jer 7:3,5; 18:11

26:15
Num 35:33

26:16
Jer 36:19,25
38:7,13
Acts 5:34-39
23:9,29; 25:25
26:31

26:1 This chapter follows chapter 25 in chronological order; its events take place in 609–608 B.C. Jehoiakim was a materialistic and self-centered king who persecuted and murdered innocent people (36:22–32).

26:2 God reminded Jeremiah that he wanted his entire message given—"Don't leave out one word!" Jeremiah may have been tempted to leave out the parts that would turn his audience against him, would sound too harsh (the "sad news" he had been accused of giving, 23:33–40), or would make him sound like a traitor. But by God's command, he was not to delete parts of God's message to suit himself, his audience, or the circumstances in which he found himself. Like Jeremiah, we must never ignore important parts of God's Word to please anyone.

26:2–9 When Jeremiah said that Jerusalem, the city of God,

would become a curse word and the Temple would be destroyed (26:6), the priests and false prophets were infuriated. The Temple was important to them because the people's reverence for it brought them power. By saying that the Temple would be destroyed, Jeremiah undermined their authority.

26:11 Jeremiah was branded a traitor because he recommended surrender to Babylon (as God commanded, 27:5–8), while the "courageous" people advocated a foreign alliance to fight Babylon and retain their independence.

26:16, 17, 24 Jeremiah's life was in serious danger, but God used officials and wise men to protect the prophet. God spared Jeremiah because his work for God was not done. Believers, even some of God's prophets, are permitted to die painful deaths. God does not promise to keep every follower from suffering. But he promises to be with us in the midst of trials.

does not deserve the death sentence, for he has spoken to us in the name of the Lord our God."

17Then some of the wise old men stood and spoke to all the people standing around and said:

26:18
Mic 1:1

18"The decision is right; for back in the days when Micah the Morasthite prophesied in the days of King Hezekiah of Judah, he told the people that God said: 'This hill shall be plowed like an open field and this city of Jerusalem razed into heaps of stone, and a forest shall grow at the top where the great Temple now stands!' 19But did King Hezekiah and the people kill him for saying this? No, they turned from their wickedness and worshiped the Lord and begged the Lord to have mercy upon them; and the Lord held back the terrible punishment he had pronounced against them. If we kill Jeremiah for giving us the messages of God, who knows what God will do to us!"

26:19
2 Chron 29:6-11; 32:26
Isa 37:1,15-20

26:21
1 Kgs 19:2-4
2 Chron 16:10
Jer 36:26
Mt 10:23,28

20Another true prophet of the Lord, Uriah (son of Shemaiah) from Kiriathjearim, was also denouncing the city and the nation at the same time as Jeremiah was. 21But when King Jehoiakim and the army officers and officials heard what he was saying, the king sent to kill him. Uriah heard about it and fled to Egypt. 22Then King Jehoiakim sent Elnathan (son of Achbor) to Egypt along with several other men to capture Uriah. 23They took him prisoner and brought him back to King Jehoiakim, who butchered him with a sword and had him buried in an unmarked grave.

26:22
Jer 36:12

26:23
Jer 2:30

26:24
2 Kgs 22:12-14
Jer 1:18,19
39:14; 40:5,6

24But Ahikam (son of Shaphan), the royal secretary, stood with Jeremiah and persuaded the court not to turn him over to the mob to kill him.

Jeremiah urges submission to Babylon

27 This message came to Jeremiah from the Lord at the beginning of the reign of Jehoiakim (son of Josiah), king of Judah:

27:2
Jer 28:10,13

2Make a yoke and fasten it on your neck with leather thongs as you would strap a yoke on a plow-ox. 3Then send messages to the kings of Edom, Moab, Ammon, Tyre and Sidon, through their ambassadors in Jerusalem, 4saying, Tell your masters that the Lord, the God of Israel, sends you this message:

27:3
Jer 25:21,22

27:5
Jer 10:12
32:17; 51:15

5"By my great power I have made the earth and all mankind and every animal; and I give these things of mine to anyone I want to. 6So now I have given all your countries to King Nebuchadnezzar of Babylon, who is my deputy. And I have handed over to him all your cattle for his use. 7All the nations shall serve him and his son and his grandson until his time is up, and then many nations and great kings shall conquer Babylon and make him their slave. 8Submit to him and serve him—put your neck under Babylon's yoke! I will punish any nation refusing to be his slave; I will send war, famine and disease upon that nation until he has conquered it.

27:6
Jer 21:7; 22:25
28:14; 43:10
Ezek 29:18-20

27:7
Isa 14:4-6
Jer 25:12; 44:30

27:8
Jer 24:10
29:17; 42:15,16
Ezek 14:21
17:19-21

9"Do not listen to your false prophets, fortune-tellers, dreamers, mediums and magicians who say the king of Babylon will not enslave you. 10For they are all liars, and if you follow their advice and refuse to submit to the king of Babylon, I will drive you out of your land and send you far away to perish. 11But the people of

27:9
Deut 18:10
Isa 8:19

27:11
Jer 21:9; 38:2
40:9-12

26:24 *the royal secretary,* implied. See 2 Kgs 22:12. **27:1** *reign of Jehoiakim.* Some versions read "Zedekiah."

26:17–19 The wise men remembered the words of the prophet Micah (Micah 3:12), similar to the words Jeremiah spoke. When Micah called the people to repent, they did not kill him but turned from their wickedness. Although the people did not kill Jeremiah because of this story, they missed the main point—that the application of the story was for them. They spared Jeremiah, but they did not spare themselves by repenting of their sins. As you recall a great story of the Bible, ask how it can be applied to your life.

27:1ff The year was 597 B.C., and Nebuchadnezzar had already invaded Judah once and taken many captives. Jeremiah wore a yoke (a wooden frame used to fasten a team of animals to a plow) as a symbol of bondage. This was an object lesson, telling the people they should put themselves under Babylon's yoke or be destroyed.

27:5, 6 God punished the people of Israel in an unusual way, by appointing a sinful foreign ruler to be his deputy. Nebuchadnezzar was not used to proclaim God's Word, but to fulfill God's promise of judgment on sin. Because God is in control of all events, he uses whomever he wants. God may use unexpected people or circumstances to correct you. Be ready to accept his unusual instruments or circumstances for your improvement.

27:9–11 The false prophets told the people what they wanted to hear, even though they knew it was not true. The people in Jeremiah's day needed a true friend like Jeremiah, who brought God's painful, corrective word. A true friend speaks the truth no matter how much it hurts to hear. Seek friends who speak truthfully, even though their correction is painful. Someone who flatters you by telling you lies is not a true friend.

any nation submitting to the king of Babylon will be permitted to stay in their own country and farm the land as usual."

¹²Jeremiah repeated all these prophecies to Zedekiah, king of Judah. "If you want to live, submit to the king of Babylon," he said. ¹³"Why do you insist on dying—you and your people? Why should you choose war and famine and disease, which the Lord has promised to every nation that will not submit to Babylon's king? ¹⁴Don't listen to the false prophets who keep telling you the king of Babylon will not conquer you, for they are liars. ¹⁵I have not sent them, says the Lord, and they are telling you lies in my name. If you insist on heeding them, I must drive you from this land to die—you and all these 'prophets' too."

¹⁶I spoke again and again to the priests and all the people and told them: "The Lord says, Don't listen to your prophets who are telling you that soon the gold dishes taken from the Temple will be returned from Babylon. It is all a lie. ¹⁷Don't listen to them. Surrender to the king of Babylon and live, for otherwise this whole city will be destroyed. ¹⁸If they are really God's prophets, then let them pray to the Lord Almighty that the gold dishes still here in the Temple, left from before; and that those in the palace of the king of Judah and in the palaces in Jerusalem will not be carried away with you to Babylon!

¹⁹, ²⁰, ²¹"For the Lord Almighty says, The pillars of bronze standing before the Temple, and the great bronze basin in the Temple court, and the metal stands and all the other ceremonial articles left here by Nebuchadnezzar, king of Babylon, when he exiled all the important people of Judah and Jerusalem to Babylon, along with Jeconiah (son of Jehoiakim), king of Judah, ²²will all yet be carried away to Babylon and will stay there until I send for them. Then I will bring them all back to Jerusalem again."

Jeremiah rebukes a false prophet

28 On a December day in that same year—the fourth year of the reign of Zedekiah, king of Judah—Hananiah (son of Azzur), a false prophet from Gibeon, addressed me publicly in the Temple while all the priests and people listened. He said:

²"The Lord of Hosts, the God of Israel, declares: I have removed the yoke of the king of Babylon from your necks. ³Within two years I will bring back all the Temple treasures that Nebuchadnezzar carried off to Babylon, ⁴and I will bring back King Jeconiah, son of Jehoiakim, king of Judah, and all the other captives exiled to Babylon, says the Lord. I will surely remove the yoke put on your necks by the king of Babylon."

⁵Then Jeremiah said to Hananiah, in front of all the priests and people, ⁶"Amen! May your prophecies come true! I hope the Lord will do everything you say and bring back from Babylon the treasures of this Temple, with all our loved ones. ⁷But listen now to the solemn words I speak to you in the presence of all these people. ⁸The ancient prophets who preceded you and me spoke against many nations, always warning of *war, famine* and *plague*. ⁹So a prophet who foretells *peace* has

28:4 *Jeconiah,* or "Jehoiachin," as he is also called.

Cross references (right margin)

27:13
Jer 38:23
Ezek 18:31

27:14
2 Chron 11:13-15
Ezek 13:22

27:15
2 Chron 25:16
Jer 23:21,25
29:9

27:16
2 Kgs 24:13
2 Chron 36:7,10
Jer 28:3

27:18
1 Kgs 18:24

27:19
1 Kgs 7:15
2 Kgs 25:13,17
Jer 22:28; 24:1
52:17-23

27:22
Ezra 5:13-15
7:9
Jer 29:10; 32:5
34:2,3

28:1
Jer 27:12

28:3
2 Chron 36:10
Jer 27:16
Dan 1:2

28:4
2 Kgs 25:27
Jer 22:10; 27:8

28:5
Ps 41:13
Jer 11:5; 17:16

28:7
1 Kgs 22:28

28:8
1 Kgs 14:15
17:1; 22:17
Isa 5:5-7
Joel 1:20
Amos 1:2
Nah 1:2

28:9
Deut 18:22

27:12 Zedekiah was in a tough spot. Jeremiah called upon him to surrender to Nebuchadnezzar, while many of the other leaders wanted him to form an alliance and fight. It would be disgraceful for a king to surrender, and he would look like a coward. This was a great opportunity for the false prophets, who kept saying that the Babylonians would not defeat the great city of Jerusalem and that God would never allow the magnificent, holy Temple to be destroyed.

27:19–21 Nebuchadnezzar invaded Judah in 597 B.C. for the second time, taking away many important people living in Jerusalem—including Ezekiel and Daniel. Although these men were captives, they had a profound impact on the exiles and

leaders in Babylon. Jeremiah predicted that more people and even the large, precious objects in the Temple would be taken. This happened in 586 B.C. during the third and last invasion from Babylon.

28:8–17 Jeremiah spoke the truth, but it was unpopular; Hananiah spoke lies, but his deceitful words brought false hope and comfort to the people. God had already outlined the marks of a true prophet (Deuteronomy 13; 18:9–22): a true prophet's predictions always come true and his words never contradict previous revelation. Jeremiah's predictions were already coming true, from Hananiah's death to the Babylonian invasions. But the people still preferred to listen to comforting lies rather than painful truth.

28:10
1 Kgs 22:11,24
Jer 27:2

28:11
Jer 14:15; 27:10

28:12
Jer 1:2

28:13
Ps 107:16

28:14
Deut 28:48
Jer 25:11
27:6,8

28:15
Jer 29:31
Ezek 13:2,3,22
22:28
Lam 2:14

28:16
Gen 7:4
Deut 6:15; 13:5
1 Kgs 13:34
Jer 20:6; 29:32

the burden of proof on him to prove that God has really sent him. Only when his message comes true can it be known that he really is from God."

10Then Hananiah, the false prophet, took the yoke off Jeremiah's neck and broke it. 11And Hananiah said again to the crowd that had gathered, "The Lord has promised that within two years he will release all the nations now in slavery to King Nebuchadnezzar of Babylon." At that point Jeremiah walked out.

12Soon afterwards, the Lord gave this message to Jeremiah:

13Go and tell Hananiah that the Lord says, You have broken a wooden yoke but these people have yokes of iron on their necks. 14The Lord, the God of Israel, says: I have put a yoke of iron on the necks of all these nations, forcing them into slavery to Nebuchadnezzar, king of Babylon. And nothing will change this decree, for I have even given him all your flocks and herds.

15Then Jeremiah said to Hananiah, the false prophet, "Listen, Hananiah, the Lord has not sent you, and the people are believing your lies. 16Therefore the Lord says you must die. This very year your life will end because you have rebelled against the Lord."

17And sure enough, two months later Hananiah died.

Jeremiah warns the people against false prophets

29:1
2 Kgs 24:12
Jer 22:24-28
24:1; 27:20

29:6
Jer 16:1-4

29:7
Ezra 6:10
Dan 4:27
1 Tim 2:1,2

29:8
Jer 14:14
23:21,25,27

29:9
Jer 27:15; 29:31

29:10
2 Chron 36:21-23
Jer 24:6,7
Dan 9:2

29:11
Isa 40:9-11
Jer 23:5,6
30:9,10,18-22
Hos 2:15

29:12
Jer 33:3

29:13
Jer 24:7

29:14
Deut 30:1-10
Isa 43:5,6
Jer 12:15
16:14,15; 30:3

29 After Jeconiah the king, and the queen-mother, and the court officials, and the tribal officers and craftsmen had been deported to Babylon by Nebuchadnezzar, Jeremiah wrote them a letter from Jerusalem, addressing it to the Jewish elders and priests and prophets, and to all the people. 3He sent the letter with Elasah (son of Shaphan) and Gemariah (son of Hilkiah) when they went to Babylon as King Zedekiah's ambassadors to Nebuchadnezzar. And this is what the letter said:

4The Lord Almighty, the God of Israel, sends this message to all the captives he has exiled to Babylon from Jerusalem:

5Build homes and plan to stay; plant vineyards, for you will be there many years. 6Marry and have children, and then find mates for them and have many grandchildren. Multiply! Don't dwindle away! 7And work for the peace and prosperity of Babylon. Pray for her, for if Babylon has peace, so will you.

8The Lord Almighty, the God of Israel, says: Don't let the false prophets and mediums who are there among you fool you. Don't listen to the dreams that they invent, 9for they prophesy lies in my name. I have not sent them, says the Lord. 10The truth is this: You will be in Babylon for seventy years. But then I will come and do for you all the good things I have promised, and bring you home again. 11For I know the plans I have for you, says the Lord. They are plans for good and not for evil, to give you a future and a hope. 12In those days when you pray, I will listen. 13You will find me when you seek me, if you look for me in earnest. 14Yes, says the Lord, I will be found by you, and I will end your slavery and restore your fortunes, and gather you out of the nations where I sent you and bring you back home again to your own land.

29:4-7 Jeremiah wrote to the captives in Babylon, instructing them to move ahead with their lives and to pray for the heathen nation that enslaved them. Life cannot grind to a halt during troubled times. In an unpleasant or distressing situation, we must adjust and keep moving. You may find it difficult to pray for those in authority if they are evil, but that is when your prayers are most needed (1 Timothy 2:1, 2). When you enter times of trouble or sudden change, pray diligently and move ahead, doing whatever you can rather than giving up because of uncertainty.

29:10 Scholars differ on the exact dates of this 70 years in Babylon. Some say it refers to the years 605-535 B.C., from the first deportation to Babylon to the arrival of the first exiles back in Jerusalem after Cyrus' freedom decree. Others point to the years 586-516 B.C., from the last deportation to Babylon and the destruction of the Temple until its rebuilding. A third possibility is

that 70 years is an approximate number meaning a lifetime.

29:11 We're all encouraged by a leader who stirs us to move ahead, someone who believes we can do the task he has given and who will be with us all the way. God is that kind of leader. He knows the future, and his plans for us are good and full of hope. As long as the God who knows the future provides our agenda and goes with us as we fulfill his mission, we can have boundless hope. This does not mean we will be spared pain, suffering, or hardship, but that God will see us through to a glorious conclusion.

29:12-14 God did not forget his people, even though they were captive in Babylon. He planned to give them a new beginning with a new purpose—to turn them into new people. In times of deep trouble, it may seem that God has forgotten you. But he may be preparing you, as he did the people of Judah, for a new beginning with God at the center.

15But now, because you accept the false prophets among you and say the Lord has sent them, 16, 17I will send war, famine and plague upon the people left here in Jerusalem—on your relatives who were not exiled to Babylon, and on the king who sits on David's throne—and make them like rotting figs, too bad to eat. 18And I will scatter them around the world. And in every nation where I place them they will be cursed and hissed and mocked, 19for they refuse to listen to me though I spoke to them again and again through my prophets.

20Therefore listen to the word of God, all you Jewish captives over there in Babylon. 21The Lord Almighty, the God of Israel, says this about your false prophets, Ahab (son of Kolaiah) and Zedekiah (son of Ma-aseiah), who are declaring lies to you in my name: Look, I am turning them over to Nebuchadnezzar to execute publicly. 22Their fate shall become proverbial of all evil, so that whenever anyone wants to curse someone he will say, "The Lord make you like Zedekiah and Ahab whom the king of Babylon burned alive!" 23For these men have done a terrible thing among my people. They have committed adultery with their neighbors' wives and have lied in my name. I know, for I have seen everything they do, says the Lord. 24And say this to Shemaiah the dreamer:

25The Lord, the God of Israel, says: You have written a letter to Zephaniah (son of Ma-aseiah) the priest, and sent copies to all the other priests and to everyone in Jerusalem. 26And in this letter you have said to Zephaniah, "The Lord has appointed you to replace Jehoiada as priest in Jerusalem. And it is your responsibility to arrest any madman who claims to be a prophet, and to put him in the stocks and collar. 27Why haven't you done something about this false prophet Jeremiah of Anathoth? 28For he has written to us here in Babylon saying that our captivity will be long, and that we should build permanent homes and plan to stay many years, that we should plant fruit trees, for we will be here to eat the fruit from them for a long time to come."

29Zephaniah took the letter over to Jeremiah and read it to him! 30Then the Lord gave this message to Jeremiah:

31Send an open letter to all the exiles in Babylon and tell them this: The Lord says that because Shemaiah the Nehelamite has "prophesied" to you when I didn't send him, and has fooled you into believing his lies, 32I will punish him and his family. None of his descendants shall see the good I have waiting for my people, for he has taught you to rebel against the Lord.

5. Restoration is promised
Restoration will follow punishment

30 This is another of the Lord's messages to Jeremiah: 2The Lord God of Israel says, Write down for the record all that I have said to you. 3For the time is coming when I will restore the fortunes of my people, Israel and Judah, and I will bring them home to this land that I gave to their fathers; they shall possess it and live here again.

4And write this also concerning Israel and Judah:

5"Where shall we find peace?" they cry. "There is only fear and trembling. 6Do men give birth? Then why do they stand there, ashen-faced, hands pressed against their sides like women in labor?"

7Alas, in all history when has there ever been a time of terror such as in that coming day? It is a time of trouble for my people—for Jacob—such as they have

29:16
Jer 24:3,8-10

29:18
Isa 65:15
Jer 25:9; 42:18
Lam 2:15,16

29:19
Jer 6:19; 26:5

29:20
Jer 24:5
Ezek 11:9

29:21
Jer 14:14,15
Lam 2:14

29:22
Isa 65:15

29:23
2 Sam 13:12
Prov 5:21
Jer 5:8; 7:11

29:25
2 Kgs 25:18
Jer 21:1; 37:3

29:26
Deut 13:1-5
Jer 20:1,2
Hos 9:7
Zech 13:1-5
Jn 10:20
Acts 16:24
26:24,25
2 Cor 5:13

29:27
Jer 1:1

29:31
Jer 14:14,15
28:15
Ezek 13:8,16,
22,23

29:32
Deut 13:5
1 Sam 2:30-34
Jer 22:30
28:16; 36:31

30:2
Jer 25:13
36:4,28,32

30:3
Jer 3:18; 16:15
23:7,8; 25:13
29:10; 30:18
36:4,28

30:6
Jer 4:31; 6:24
22:23

30:7
Isa 2:12
Jer 2:27; 50:19

29:24 *Shemaiah the dreamer,* literally, "the Nehelamite." Nehelem was Shemaiah's home town, the name of which means "Dreamer." This seems to be another of the frequent puns in the prophetic books.

29:21 These false prophets, Ahab and Zedekiah, should not be confused with the kings who had the same names. Their family connections clearly identify them.

29:25-29 To discredit Jeremiah, Shemaiah accused him of false prophecy. Although Jeremiah's message was true and his words from God, the people hated him because he chastised them. But Jeremiah's truth from God offered temporary correction and

long-range benefit. The lies of false teachers offered temporary comfort and long-range punishment.

30:1ff Chapters 30 and 31 show that Jeremiah spoke of hope as well as trouble and gloom. The people will one day be restored to their land, and God will make a new contract with them to replace the one they broke. Where once they sinned and disobeyed, they will one day repent and obey.

30:8
Isa 9:4
Ezek 34:27

30:9
Ezek 34:23,24
37:24
Hos 3:5
Lk 1:69
Acts 2:30
13:23,24

30:10
Isa 35:9; 43:5
44:2
Jer 23:3; 29:14
46:27,28
Mic 4:4

30:11
Jer 1:8,19
4:27; 5:10,18
10:24; 46:28

30:13
Jer 14:19; 46:11

30:14
Jer 22:20,22

30:16
Isa 14:2
Jer 2:3; 10:25

30:17
Ps 107:20
Isa 56:8
Jer 8:22
33:6,24

30:18
1 Chron 29:1,19
Ps 48:3; 122:7
Jer 31:38-40

30:19
Isa 12:1; 51:3
55:5; 60:9
Jer 17:26; 33:11

30:20
Isa 54:14

30:21
Ex 3:5
Num 16:5

30:22
Ex 6:7
Jer 32:38
Hos 2:23
Zech 13:9

30:23
Jer 23:19,20

31:1
Rom 11:26-28

31:2
Ex 33:14

never known before. Yet God will rescue them! 8For on that day, says the Lord Almighty, I will break the yoke from their necks and snap their chains, and foreigners shall no longer be their masters! 9For they shall serve the Lord their God, and David their King, whom I will raise up for them, says the Lord.

10So don't be afraid, O Jacob my servant; don't be dismayed, O Israel; for I will bring you home again from distant lands, and your children from their exile. They shall have rest and quiet in their own land, and no one shall make them afraid. 11For I am with you and I will save you, says the Lord. Even if I utterly destroy the nations where I scatter you, I will not exterminate you; I will punish you, yes—you will not go unpunished.

12For your sin is an incurable bruise, a terrible wound. 13There is no one to help you or to bind up your wound and no medicine does any good. 14All your lovers have left you and don't care anything about you any more; for I have wounded you cruelly, as though I were your enemy; mercilessly, as though I were an implacable foe; for your sins are so many, your guilt is so great.

15Why do you protest your punishment? Your sin is so scandalous that your sorrow should never end! It is because your guilt is great that I have had to punish you so much.

16But in that coming day, all who are destroying you shall be destroyed, and all your enemies shall be slaves. Those who rob you shall be robbed; and those attacking you shall be attacked. 17I will give you back your health again and heal your wounds. Now you are called "The Outcast" and "Jerusalem, the Place Nobody Wants."

18But, says the Lord, when I bring you home again from your captivity and restore your fortunes, Jerusalem will be rebuilt upon her ruins; the palace will be reconstructed as it was before. 19The cities will be filled with joy and great thanksgiving, and I will multiply my people and make of them a great and honored nation. 20Their children shall prosper as in David's reign; their nations shall be established before me, and I will punish anyone who hurts them. 21They will have their own ruler again. He will not be a foreigner. And I will invite him to be a priest at my altars, and he shall approach me, for who would dare to come unless invited. 22And you shall be my people and I will be your God.

23Suddenly the devastating whirlwind of the Lord roars with fury; it shall burst upon the heads of the wicked. 24The Lord will not call off the fierceness of his wrath until it has finished all the terrible destruction he has planned. Later on you will understand what I am telling you.

God promises to rebuild the nation

31 At that time, says the Lord, all the families of Israel shall recognize me as the Lord; they shall act like my people. 2I will care for them as I did those who escaped from Egypt, to whom I showed my mercies in the wilderness, when Israel

30:9 *David their King.* The Messiah, David's greater Son, whom God has raised up for them. **30:24** *Later on,* literally, "in the latter days."

30:8, 9 Like Isaiah, Jeremiah associates events of the near future and those of the distant future. Reading these prophecies is like looking at several mountain peaks in a range. From a distance they look as though they are next to each other, when actually they are miles apart. Jeremiah presents near and distant events as if they will all happen soon. He sees the exile, but he sees also the future day when Christ will reign forever. The reference to David is not to King David, but to his famous descendant, the Messiah (Luke 1:69).

30:12, 13, 17 The medical language here conveys the idea that sin is terminal. It cannot be cured by being good or being religious. Beware of putting your confidence in useless cures while your sin spreads and causes you pain. God alone can cure the disease of sin, but you must be willing to let him do it.

30:15 Israel protested its punishment, even though the sin that caused it was scandalous. But punishment is an opportunity for

growth, because it makes us aware of sin's consequences. The people should have asked how they could profit from their mistakes. Remember this the next time you are corrected.

30:18 This prophecy that Jerusalem would be rebuilt was not completely fulfilled by the work of Ezra, Nehemiah, and Zerubbabel. The city was indeed rebuilt after the captivity, but the final restoration will occur when all believers are gathered in Christ's Kingdom. This will include buildings (30:18), people (30:19), rulers (30:21), and a region (30:22).

30:21 This verse refers to the restoration after the Babylonian captivity (the rulers of the Maccabean period were both priests and kings), as well as to the final restoration under Christ.

31:1 This promise is to all the families of Israel, not only to the tribe of Judah. The restoration will include all people who trust God.

sought for rest. ³For long ago the Lord had said to Israel: I have loved you, O my people, with an everlasting love; with loving-kindness I have drawn you to me. ⁴I will rebuild your nation, O virgin of Israel. You will again be happy and dance merrily with the timbrels. ⁵Again you will plant your vineyards upon the mountains of Samaria and eat from your own gardens there.

⁶The day shall come when watchmen on the hills of Ephraim will call out and say, "Arise, and let us go up to Zion to the Lord our God." ⁷For the Lord says, Sing with joy for all that I will do for Israel, the greatest of the nations! Shout out with praise and joy: "The Lord has saved his people, the remnant of Israel." ⁸For I will bring them from the north and from earth's farthest ends, not forgetting their blind and lame, young mothers with their little ones, those ready to give birth. It will be a great company who comes. ⁹Tears of joy shall stream down their faces, and I will lead them home with great care. They shall walk beside the quiet streams and not stumble. For I am a Father to Israel, and Ephraim is my oldest child.

¹⁰Listen to this message from the Lord, you nations of the world, and publish it abroad: The Lord who scattered his people will gather them back together again and watch over them as a shepherd does his flock. ¹¹He will save Israel from those who are too strong for them! ¹²They shall come home and sing songs of joy upon the hills of Zion, and shall be radiant over the goodness of the Lord—the good crops, the wheat and the wine and the oil, and the healthy flocks and herds. Their life shall be like a watered garden, and all their sorrows shall be gone. ¹³The young girls will dance for joy, and men folk—old and young—will take their part in all the fun; for I will turn their mourning into joy and I will comfort them and make them rejoice, for their captivity with all its sorrows will be behind them. ¹⁴I will feast the priests with the abundance of offerings brought to them at the Temple; I will satisfy my people with my bounty, says the Lord.

¹⁵The Lord spoke to me again, saying: In Ramah there is bitter weeping—Rachel weeping for her children and cannot be comforted, for they are gone. ¹⁶But the Lord says: Don't cry any longer, for I have heard your prayers and you will see them again; they will come back to you from the distant land of the enemy. ¹⁷There is hope for your future, says the Lord, and your children will come again to their own land.

¹⁸I have heard Ephraim's groans: "You have punished me greatly; but I needed it all, as a calf must be trained for the yoke. Turn me again to you and restore me, for you alone are the Lord, my God. ¹⁹I turned away from God but I was sorry afterwards. I kicked myself for my stupidity. I was thoroughly ashamed of all I did in younger days."

²⁰And the Lord replies: Ephraim is still my son, my darling child. I had to punish him, but I still love him. I long for him and surely will have mercy on him.

²¹As you travel into exile, set up road signs pointing back to Israel. Mark your pathway well. For you shall return again, O virgin Israel, to your cities here. ²²How long will you vacillate, O wayward daughter? For the Lord will cause something new and different to happen—Israel will search for God.

²³The Lord, the God of Israel, says: When I bring them back again they shall say in Judah and her cities, "The Lord bless you, O center of righteousness, O holy hill!" ²⁴And city dwellers and farmers and shepherds alike shall live together in

31:3
Deut 4:37; 7:8
Ps 25:6

31:4
Isa 30:32
Jer 24:6; 33:7

31:5
Ps 107:37
Isa 65:21
Ezek 28:26

31:7
Ps 14:7; 28:9
Isa 37:31; 61:9
Jer 20:13; 23:3

31:8
Deut 30:64
Isa 40:11; 43:6
Ezek 34:16
Mic 4:6

31:9
Isa 49:10; 63:13

31:10
Isa 40:11; 66:19

31:12
Isa 2:2; 35:10
58:11; 60:20
65:19
Hos 2:22
Joel 3:18
Mic 4:1
Jn 16:22

31:13
Ps 30:11
Isa 51:11; 61:3
Zech 8:4,5

31:14
Jer 50:19

31:15
Ps 77:2
Jer 10:20

31:16
Isa 25:8; 30:19
Jer 30:3
Ezek 11:17

31:17
Jer 29:11

31:18
Job 5:17
Ps 80:3,7,19
94:12
Jer 17:14
Hos 4:16

31:19
Ezek 36:31
Lk 18:13

31:20
Isa 55:7
Hos 11:8; 14:4

31:21
Isa 48:20; 52:11

31:23
Ps 48:1; 87:1
Isa 1:26

31:24
Ezek 36:10
Zech 8:4-8

31:16 *for I have heard your prayers,* literally, "for your work shall be rewarded." **31:22** *Israel will search for God,* literally, "a woman shall court a suitor," or, "a woman shall encompass a man."

31:3 God reaches toward his people with lovingkindness—kindness motivated by a deep love. He is eager to do the best for them if they will only let him. After many words of warning about sin, this reminder of God's magnificent love is a fresh breath. We may often think of God with dread or fear, but if we look carefully we can see him lovingly drawing us toward himself.

31:15 Rachel, Jacob's favorite wife, was the symbolic mother of the northern tribes, who were taken away by the Assyrians as slaves. Rachel is pictured crying for the exiles at Ramah, a staging

point of deportation. This verse is quoted in Matthew 2:18 to describe the sadness of the mothers of Bethlehem as their children were killed. The weeping was great in both cases.

31:18–20 Ephraim was one of the major tribes of the Northern Kingdom. Although the Northern Kingdom had sunk into the most degrading sins, God still loved the people. A remnant would turn to God, repenting of their sins, and God would forgive. God still loves you, despite what you have done. He will forgive you if you turn back to him.

31:27
Ezek 36:9-11
Hos 2:23

31:28
Dan 9:14

31:29
Ezek 18:2
Lam 5:7

31:30
Deut 24:16
Isa 3:11
Ezek 18:4,20

31:31
Ezek 37:26
Lk 22:20
1 Cor 11:25
Heb 8:8-12

31:32
Deut 1:31; 5:2,3
Isa 63:12

31:33
Heb 10:16,17

31:34
Isa 11:9; 43:25
Jer 50:20
Mic 7:18
1 Thess 4:9
1 Jn 2:27

31:35
Gen 1:14-18

31:36
Isa 54:9,10
Jer 33:20-26
Amos 9:8,9

31:37
Rom 11:2-5,
26,27

31:38
2 Chron 26:9
Neh 3:1; 12:39
Zech 14:10

31:40
2 Kgs 23:6
Joel 3:17
Zech 14:20

32:1
2 Kgs 25:1,2
Jer 39:1,2

32:3
Jer 21:4-7
26:8,9; 34:2,3

32:4
2 Kgs 25:4-7
Jer 37:17

32:5
Ezek 12:12,13

peace and happiness. 25For I have given rest to the weary and joy to all the sorrowing.

26(Then Jeremiah wakened. "Such sleep is very sweet!" he said.)

27The Lord says: The time will come when I will greatly increase the population and multiply the number of cattle here in Israel. 28In the past I painstakingly destroyed the nation but now I will carefully build it up. 29The people shall no longer quote this proverb—"Children pay for their fathers' sins." 30For everyone shall die for his own sins—the person eating sour grapes is the one whose teeth are set on edge.

31The day will come, says the Lord, when I will make a new contract with the people of Israel and Judah. 32It won't be like the one I made with their fathers when I took them by the hand to bring them out of the land of Egypt—a contract they broke, forcing me to reject them, says the Lord. 33But this is the new contract I will make with them: I will inscribe my laws upon their hearts, so that they shall want to honor me; then they shall truly be my people and I will be their God. 34At that time it will no longer be necessary to admonish one another to know the Lord. For everyone, both great and small, shall really know me then, says the Lord, and I will forgive and forget their sins.

35The Lord who gives us sunlight in the daytime and the moon and stars to light the night, and who stirs the sea to make the roaring waves—his name is Lord Almighty—says this:

36I am as likely to reject my people Israel as I am to do away with these laws of nature! 37Not until the heavens can be measured and the foundations of the earth explored, will I consider casting them away forever for their sins!

38, 39For the time is coming, says the Lord, when all Jerusalem shall be rebuilt for the Lord, from the Tower of Hananel at the northeast corner, to the Corner Gate at the northwest; and from the Hill of Gareb at the southwest, across to Goah on the southeast. 40And the entire city including the graveyard and ash dump in the valley shall be holy to the Lord, and so shall all the fields out to the brook of Kidron, and from there to the Horse Gate on the east side of the city; it shall never again be captured or destroyed.

Jeremiah buys land in Judah

32 The following message came to Jeremiah from the Lord in the tenth year of the reign of Zedekiah, king of Judah (which was the eighteenth year of Nebuchadnezzar's reign). 2At this time Jeremiah was imprisoned in the dungeon beneath the palace, while the Babylonian army was besieging Jerusalem. 3King Zedekiah had put him there for continuing to prophesy that the city would be conquered by the king of Babylon, 4and that King Zedekiah would be caught and taken as a prisoner before the king of Babylon for trial and sentencing.

5"He shall take you to Babylon and imprison you there for many years until you

31:29 *Children pay for their fathers' sins,* literally, "The fathers eat the sour grapes and the children's teeth are set on edge." **31:32** *a contract they broke, forcing me to reject them.* Some versions read, "a covenant they broke, even though I cared for them as a husband does his wife." See Heb 8:9b. **31:33** *upon their hearts,* i.e., rather than upon tablets of stone, as were the Ten Commandments. *so that they shall want to honor me.* In Jeremiah 17:1 their sin was inscribed on their hearts, so that they wanted above all to disobey. This change seems to describe an experience very much like, if not the same as, the new birth. **31:38, 39** *northeast corner . . . northwest . . . southwest . . . southeast,* implied. **32:2** *in the dungeon beneath,* literally, "in the court of the prison in the palace."

31:29, 30 The people tried to blame God's judgment on the sins of their fathers. One person's sin does indeed affect other people, but all people are still held personally accountable for the sin in their own lives (Deuteronomy 24:16; Ezekiel 18:2-4).

31:33 The old covenant, broken by the people, would be replaced by a new covenant. The foundation of this new covenant is Christ (Hebrews 8:6). It is revolutionary, involving not only Israel and Judah, but even the Gentiles. It offers a unique personal relationship with God himself, with his laws inscribed on hearts instead of on stone. Jeremiah looked forward to the day when Jesus would come to establish this covenant. But for us today, this covenant is here. We have the wonderful opportunity to make a

fresh start and establish a permanent, personal relationship with God.

31:36, 37 God has the power to do away with the laws of nature or his people. But he will do neither. This is not a prediction, but a promise. It is God's way of saying he will not reject Israel any more than he will do away with nature's laws. Neither will happen!

32:1-12 God told Jeremiah to buy a field outside Jerusalem. The city had been under siege for a year, and Jeremiah bought land that the soldiers occupied—certainly a poor investment. In addition, Jeremiah was a prisoner in the palace courtyard at the time. But Jeremiah was showing the people his faith in God's promises to return his people and rebuild Jerusalem.

die. Why fight the facts? You can't win! Surrender now!" Jeremiah had told him again and again.

6,7Then this message from the Lord came to Jeremiah: Your cousin Hanamel (son of Shallum) will soon arrive to ask you to buy the farm he owns in Anathoth, for by law you have a chance to buy before it is offered to anyone else. 8So Hanamel came, as the Lord had said he would, and visited me in the prison. "Buy my field in Anathoth, in the land of Benjamin," he said, "for the law gives you the first right to purchase it." Then I knew for sure that the message I had heard was really from the Lord.

9So I bought the field, paying Hanamel seventeen pieces of silver. 10I signed and sealed the deed of purchase before witnesses, and weighed out the silver and paid him. 11Then I took the sealed deed containing the terms and conditions, and also the unsealed copy, 12and publicly, in the presence of my cousin Hanamel and the witnesses who had signed the deed, and as the prison guards watched, I handed the papers to Baruch (son of Neriah, who was the son of Mahseiah). 13And I said to him as they all listened:

14"The Lord, God of Israel, says: Take both this sealed deed and the copy and put them into a pottery jar to preserve them for a long time. 15For the Lord, God of Israel, says, In the future these papers will be valuable. Someday people will again own property here in this country and will be buying and selling houses and vineyards and fields."

16Then after I had given the papers to Baruch I prayed:

17"O Lord God! You have made the heavens and earth by your great power; nothing is too hard for you! 18You are loving and kind to thousands, yet children suffer for their fathers' sins; you are the great and mighty God, the Lord Almighty. 19You have all wisdom and do great and mighty miracles; for your eyes are open to all the ways of men, and you reward everyone according to his life and deeds. 20You have done incredible things in the land of Egypt—things still remembered to this day. And you have continued to do great miracles in Israel and all around the world. You have made your name very great, as it is today.

21"You brought Israel out of Egypt with mighty miracles and great power and terror. 22You gave Israel this land that you promised their fathers long ago—a wonderful land that 'flows with milk and honey.' 23Our fathers came and conquered it and lived in it, but they refused to obey you or to follow your laws; they have hardly done one thing you told them to. That is why you have sent all this terrible evil upon them. 24See how the siege mounds have been built against the city walls, and the Babylonians shall conquer the city by sword, famine and disease. Everything has happened just as you said—as you determined it should! 25And yet you say to buy the field—paying good money for it before these witnesses—even though the city will belong to our enemies."

26Then this message came to Jeremiah:

27I am the Lord, the God of all mankind; is there anything too hard for me? 28Yes, I will give this city to the Babylonians and to Nebuchadnezzar, king of Babylon; he shall conquer it. 29And the Babylonians outside the walls shall come in and set fire to the city and burn down all these houses where the roofs have been used to offer incense to Baal, and to pour out libations to other gods, causing my fury to rise! 30For Israel and Judah have done nothing but wrong since their earliest days; they have infuriated me with all their evil deeds. 31From the time this city was built until now it has done nothing but anger me; so I am determined to be rid of it.

32The sins of Israel and Judah—the sins of the people, of their kings, officers, priests and prophets—stir me up. 33They have turned their backs upon me and

32:15 *In the future these papers will be valuable,* implied.

32:6
Lev 25:25
Ruth 4:3,4

32:8
1 Sam 9:16,17

32:10
Ruth 4:1,9
Isa 8:1,2

32:15
Amos 9:14,15
Zech 3:10

32:16
Gen 32:9-12
Jer 12:1
Phil 4:6,7

32:17
Gen 18:14
2 Kgs 19:15
Isa 40:26-29
Jer 27:5

32:18
Ex 34:6,7
Deut 7:9,10
1 Kgs 16:1-3
Jer 10:16
20:11; 31:35
Mt 23:32-36

32:19
Isa 28:29
Jer 17:10
21:14; 23:24
Mt 16:27
Jn 5:29

32:20
Ps 78:43
105:27
Isa 63:12,14
Dan 9:15

32:21
Deut 4:34; 26:8
1 Chron 17:21

32:22
Ex 13:5
Deut 1:8
Ps 105:9-11
Jer 11:5

32:23
Ezra 9:7
Ps 44:2,3
78:54,55
Jer 2:7; 44:10
Lam 1:18
Dan 9:11,12

32:24
Josh 23:15,16
Ezek 14:21
Zech 1:6

32:28
Jer 19:7-12

32:29
2 Chron 36:19
Jer 19:13
21:10; 39:8
44:17-19,25

32:31
1 Kgs 11:7,8
2 Kgs 21:4-7,
15; 23:27
Jer 5:9-11
Mt 23:37

32:32
Jer 2:26

32:33
2 Chron 36:15,
Jer 25:3; 26:5

32:6–12 Trust doesn't come easy. It wasn't easy for Jeremiah to publicly buy land already captured by the enemy. But he trusted God. It wasn't easy for David to think he would become king, even after he was anointed. But he trusted God (1 Samuel 16—31). It wasn't easy for Moses to believe he and his people would escape Egypt, even after God spoke to him from a burning bush. But he trusted God (Exodus 3:1—4:20). It isn't easy for us to believe God can transform our lives when we see the mess we've made. But we must trust God. He who worked in the lives of biblical heroes is the same God who offers to work in our lives, if we will let him do it.

refused to return; day after day, year after year, I taught them right from wrong, but they would not listen or obey. 34They have even defiled my own Temple by worshiping their abominable idols there. 35And they have built high altars to Baal in the Valley of Hinnom. There they have burnt their children as sacrifices to Molech—something I never commanded, and cannot imagine suggesting. What an incredible evil, causing Judah to sin so greatly!

36Now therefore the Lord God of Israel says concerning this city that it will fall to the king of Babylon through warfare, famine and disease, 37but I will bring my people back again from all the countries where in my fury I will scatter them. I will bring them back to this very city, and make them live in peace and safety. 38And they shall be my people and I will be their God. 39And I will give them one heart and mind to worship me forever, for their own good and for the good of all their descendants.

40And I will make an everlasting covenant with them, promising never again to desert them, but only to do them good. I will put a desire into their hearts to worship me, and they shall never leave me. 41I will rejoice to do them good and will replant them in this land, with great joy. 42Just as I have sent all these terrors and evils upon them, so will I do all the good I have promised them.

43Fields will again be bought and sold in this land, now ravaged by the Babylonians, where men and animals alike have disappeared. 44Yes, fields shall once again be bought and sold—deeds signed and sealed and witnessed—in the country of Benjamin and here in Jerusalem, in the cities of Judah and in the hill country, in the Philistine plain and in the Negeb too, for some day I will restore prosperity to them.

God promises peace and prosperity

33 While Jeremiah was still in jail, the Lord sent him this second message: 2The Lord, the Maker of heaven and earth—Jehovah is his name—says this:

3Ask me and I will tell you some remarkable secrets about what is going to happen here. 4For though you have torn down the houses of this city, and the king's palace too, for materials to strengthen the walls against the siege weapons of the enemy, 5yet the Babylonians will enter, and the men of this city are already as good as dead, for I have determined to destroy them in my furious anger. I have abandoned them because of all their wickedness, and I will not pity them when they cry for help.

6Nevertheless the time will come when I will heal Jerusalem's damage and give her prosperity and peace. 7I will rebuild the cities of both Judah and Israel and restore their fortunes. 8And I will cleanse away all their sins against me, and pardon them. 9Then this city will be an honor to me, and it will give me joy and be a source of praise and glory to me before all the nations of the earth! The people of the world will see the good I do for my people and will tremble with awe!

10, 11The Lord declares that the happy voices of bridegrooms and of brides, and the joyous song of those bringing thanksgiving offerings to the Lord will be heard again in this doomed land. The people will sing: "Praise the Lord! For he is good and his mercy endures forever!" For I will make this land happier and more prosperous than it has ever been before. 12This land—though every man and animal and city is doomed—will once more see shepherds leading sheep and lambs. 13Once again their flocks will prosper in the mountain villages and in the cities east of the Philistine plain, in all the cities of the Negeb, in the land of Benjamin, in the vicinity of Jerusalem and in all the cities of Judah. 14Yes, the day will come, says the Lord, when I will do for Israel and Judah all the good I promised them.

32:35
Lev 18:21
20:2-5
2 Chron 28:2,3
33:6
Acts 7:43

32:37
Deut 30:3
Isa 11:11-16
Jer 23:6
Ezek 11:17
34:25,28
Amos 9:14,15
Hos 1:11
Zech 14:11

32:39
Deut 11:18-21
Ezek 37:25
Jn 17:21
Acts 4:32

32:40
Isa 55:3

32:41
Deut 30:9
Isa 65:19
Jer 31:28
Amos 9:15

32:42
Jer 31:28
Zech 8:14,15

32:43
Ezek 37:11-14

33:2
Ex 3:15

33:3
Ps 50:15
Isa 48:6; 55:6,7

33:4
Isa 32:13,14

33:5
Jer 21:10

33:6
Isa 66:12
Jer 17:14
Gal 5:22,23

33:7
Ps 85:1
Jer 30:18
Amos 9:14,15

33:8
Ps 51:2
Jer 50:20
Heb 9:11-16

33:9
Ps 40:3
Isa 62:2,4
Jer 16:19; 24:6
Hos 3:5

33:10
Isa 35:10

33:12
Ezek 34:12-14
Zeph 2:6,7

33:14
Hag 2:6-9

32:36–42 God uses his power to accomplish *his* purposes through *his* people. Faith is not "God giving me power to be all I want to be," but "God giving me power to be all he wants me to be." The people of Israel had to learn that trusting God means radically realigning one's purposes and desires toward God. That is our lesson too.

33:1ff God would restore Jerusalem, not because the people cried, but because it was part of his ultimate plan. The Babylonian disaster did not change God's purposes for his people. Although Jerusalem would be destroyed, it would be restored (both after the 70-year captivity and in the end times when the Messiah will rule). God's justice is always tempered by his mercy.

15At that time I will bring to the throne the true Son of David, and he shall rule justly. 16In that day the people of Judah and Jerusalem shall live in safety and their motto will be, "The Lord is our righteousness!" 17For the Lord declares that from then on, David shall forever have an heir sitting on the throne of Israel. 18And there shall always be Levites to offer burnt offerings and meal offerings and sacrifices to the Lord.

19Then this message came to Jeremiah from the Lord:

20, 21If you can break my covenant with the day and with the night so that day and night don't come on their usual schedule, only then will my covenant with David, my servant, be broken so that he shall not have a son to reign upon his throne; and my covenant with the Levite priests, my ministers, is non-cancelable. 22And as the stars cannot be counted nor the sand upon the seashores measured, so the descendants of David my servant and the line of the Levites who minister to me will be multiplied.

23The Lord spoke to Jeremiah again and said:

24Have you heard what people are saying?—that the Lord chose Judah and Israel and then abandoned them! They are sneering and saying that Israel isn't worthy to be counted as a nation. 25, 26But this is the Lord's reply: I would no more reject my people than I would change my laws of night and day, of earth and sky. I will never abandon the Jews, or David my servant, or change the plan that his Child will someday rule these descendants of Abraham, Isaac and Jacob. Instead I will restore their prosperity and have mercy on them.

6. God's promised judgment arrives

Zedekiah will be exiled to Babylon

34 This is the message that came to Jeremiah from the Lord when Nebuchadnezzar, king of Babylon, and all his armies from all the kingdoms he ruled, came and fought against Jerusalem and the cities of Judah:

2Go tell Zedekiah, king of Judah, that the Lord says this: I will give this city to the king of Babylon and he shall burn it. 3You shall not escape; you shall be captured and taken before the king of Babylon and he shall pronounce sentence against you and you shall be exiled to Babylon. 4But listen to this, O Zedekiah, king of Judah: God says you won't be killed in war and carnage, 5but that you will die quietly among your people, and they will burn incense in your memory, just as they did for your fathers. They will weep for you and say, "Alas, our king is dead!" This I have decreed, says the Lord.

6So Jeremiah delivered the message to King Zedekiah. 7At this time the Babylo-

Cross references (right margin)

33:15
Ps 72:1-5
Isa 11:1-5

33:16
Isa 45:24,25
Jer 23:6
2 Cor 5:21
Phil 3:9

33:17
1 Kgs 2:4
Ps 89:29-37

33:18
Deut 18:1
Ezek 44:15
Heb 13:15

33:20
2 Sam 23:5
2 Chron 21:7
Ps 104:19-23
Isa 54:9

33:22
Gen 22:17

33:24
Neh 4:2-4
Ps 44:13,14
Isa 11:13
Jer 3:7,8,10,18
Ezek 36:2

33:25
Gen 49:10
Ezek 39:25
Hos 2:23

34:1
Jer 1:15
Dan 2:37,38

34:2
2 Chron 36:11, 12
Jer 37:1-4

34:3
2 Kgs 25:4-7
Jer 21:7

34:5
2 Chron 16:14

34:7
Josh 10:3,10
2 Kgs 14:19
2 Chron 11:5-10

33:15, 16 These verses refer to both the first and second comings of Christ. At his first coming he would set up his reign in the hearts of believers; at his second coming he will execute justice and righteousness throughout the whole earth. Christ is "the true vine from the root of David," the man after God's own heart.

33:18 As Christ fulfills the role of King, he also fulfills the role of Priest, maintaining constant fellowship with God and mediating for the people. This verse does not mean that actual priests will perform sacrifices, for they will no longer be necessary (Hebrews 7:11). Now that Christ is our High Priest, all believers are priests of God, and we can come before him personally.

33:22 The promise of countless descendants was also given to Abraham (Genesis 15:5; 22:17). Not only is God remembering his promises to the nation's forefathers, he is also giving an even greater promise during the nation's darkest hour.

34:1 This chapter describes the fulfillment of many of Jeremiah's predictions. In the book of Jeremiah, many prophecies are both given and quickly fulfilled.

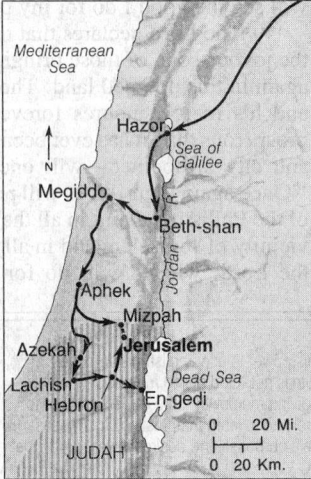

BABYLON ATTACKS JUDAH

Zedekiah incurred Babylon's wrath in allying with Egypt and not surrendering as God told him through Jeremiah. Nebuchadnezzar attacked Judah for the third and final time, moving systematically until all its cities fell. Jerusalem withstood siege for several months but was burned, as Jeremiah predicted.

nian army was besieging Jerusalem, Lachish and Azekah—the only walled cities of Judah still standing.

God proclaims freedom for slaves

34:8
Lev 25:39-46
Neh 5:1-13

34:9
Gen 14:13

34:11
Ps 78:34-36
Hos 6:4

34:13
Deut 5:2,3,27
Jer 31:32

34:14
Ex 21:2
1 Kgs 9:22
2 Kgs 17:13,14

34:15
Neh 10:29

34:16
Ex 20:7
1 Sam 15:11
Ezek 18:24

34:17
Lev 26:34,35
Deut 28:25,64
Mt 7:2

34:18
Gen 15:10
Hos 6:7
Mic 7:1-5

34:20
1 Sam 17:46
Jer 19:7

34:21
2 Kgs 25:18-21
Ezek 17:16

34:22
Jer 44:22

8This is the message that came to Jeremiah from the Lord after King Zedekiah of Judah had freed all the slaves in Jerusalem— 9(for King Zedekiah had ordered everyone to free his Hebrew slaves, both men and women. He had said that no Jew should be the master of another Jew for all were brothers. 10The princes and all the people had obeyed the king's command and freed their slaves, but the action was only temporary. 11They changed their minds and made their servants slaves again. 12That is why the Lord gave the following message to Jerusalem.)

13The Lord, the God of Israel, says:

I made a covenant with your fathers long ago when I brought them from their slavery in Egypt. 14I told them that every Hebrew slave must be freed after serving six years. But this was not done. 15Recently you began doing what was right, as I commanded you, and freed your slaves. You had solemnly promised me in my Temple that you would do it. 16But now you refuse and have defiled my name by shrugging off your oath and have made them slaves again.

17Therefore, says the Lord, because you will not listen to me and release them, I will release you to the power of death by war and famine and disease. And I will scatter you over all the world as exiles. 18, 19Because you have refused the terms of our contract I will cut you apart just as you cut apart the calf when you walked between its halves to solemnize your vows. Yes, I will butcher you, whether you are princes, court officials, priests or people—for you have broken your oath. 20I will give you to your enemies and they shall kill you. I will feed your dead bodies to the vultures and wild animals. 21And I will surrender Zedekiah, king of Judah, and his officials to the army of the king of Babylon, though he has departed from the city for a little while. 22I will summon the Babylonian armies back again and they will fight against it and capture this city and burn it. And I will see to it that the cities of Judah are completely destroyed and left desolate without a living soul.

The Rechabites demonstrate obedience

35:1
2 Kgs 23:34-36
Dan 1:1

35:2
1 Kgs 6:5,6,8
1 Chron 2:55

35:5
2 Cor 2:9

35:6
Lev 10:9
Num 6:2-4
2 Kgs 10:15,23
1 Chron 2:55
Lk 1:15

35 This is the message the Lord gave Jeremiah when Jehoiakim (son of Josiah) was the king of Judah:

2Go to the settlement where the families of the Rechabites live and invite them to the Temple. Take them into one of the inner rooms and offer them a drink of wine.

3So I went over to see Ja-azaniah (son of Jeremiah, who was the son of Habazziniah), and brought him and all his brothers and sons—representing all the Rechab families— 4to the Temple, into the room assigned for the use of the sons of Hanan the prophet (the son of Igdaliah). This room was located next to the one used by the palace official, directly above the room of Ma-aseiah (son of Shallum), who was the temple doorman. 5I set cups and jugs of wine before them and invited them to have a drink, 6but they refused.

35:1 *when Jehoiakim . . . was the king of Judah.* This is apparently an early message of Jeremiah, and is not here in its chronological order with the other messages.

34:8 Babylon had laid siege to Jerusalem and the city was about to fall. Zedekiah finally decided to listen to Jeremiah and to try to appease God—so he freed the slaves. He thought he could win God's favor with a kind act; but what he needed was a change of heart. The people had been disobeying God's law from the beginning (Exodus 21:2-11; Leviticus 25:39-55; Deuteronomy 15:12-18). When the siege was temporarily lifted, the people became bold and returned to their sins.

34:15, 16 The people of Israel had a hard time keeping their promises to God. In the Temple, they would solemnly promise to obey God, but back in their homes and at work they wouldn't do it. God expressed his great displeasure. If you want to please him, make sure you keep your promises. God wants promises lived out, not just piously made.

34:18, 19 Cutting a calf in two and walking between the halves was a customary way to ratify a contract (Genesis 15:9-17). This action symbolized the judgment on anyone who broke the contract. God was saying, "You have broken the contract you made with me, so you know the judgment awaiting you!"

35:1ff The Rechabites' code of conduct resembled that of the Nazirites, who took a special vow of dedication to God (Numbers 6). For 200 years, they had obeyed their ancestors' vow to abstain from wine. While the rest of the nation was breaking its covenant with God, these people were steadfast in their commitment. "Why can't the rest of the people remain as committed to their covenant with me as the Rechabites are to their vow?" God was saying.

35:6 Jehonadab, son of Rechab, had joined Jehu in purging Israel of Baal worship (2 Kings 10:15-31).

"No," they said. "We don't drink, for Jonadab our father (son of Rechab) commanded that none of us should ever drink, neither we nor our children forever. 7He also told us not to build houses or plant crops or vineyards and not to own farms, but always to live in tents; and that if we obeyed we would live long, good lives in our own land. 8And we have obeyed him in all these things. We have never had a drink of wine since then, nor our wives or our sons or daughters either. 9We haven't built houses or owned farms or planted crops. 10We have lived in tents and have fully obeyed everything that Jonadab our father commanded us. 11But when Nebuchadnezzar, king of Babylon, arrived in this country, we were afraid and decided to move to Jerusalem. That's why we are here."

12Then the Lord gave this message to Jeremiah:

13The Lord, the God of Israel, says: Go and say to Judah and Jerusalem, Won't you learn a lesson from the families of Rechab? 14They don't drink, because their father told them not to. But I have spoken to you again and again and you won't listen or obey. 15I have sent you prophet after prophet to tell you to turn back from your wicked ways and to stop worshiping other gods and that if you obeyed, then I would let you live in peace here in the land I gave to you and your fathers. But you wouldn't listen or obey. 16The families of Rechab have obeyed their father completely, but you have refused to listen to me. 17Therefore the Lord Almighty, the God of Israel, says: Because you refuse to listen or answer when I call, I will send upon Judah and Jerusalem all the evil I have ever threatened.

18, 19Then Jeremiah turned to the Rechabites and said: "The Lord, the God of Israel, says that because you have obeyed your father in every respect, he shall always have descendants who will worship me."

Baruch reads God's messages

36 In the fourth year of the reign of King Jehoiakim of Judah (son of Josiah) the Lord gave this message to Jeremiah:

2"Get a scroll and write down all my messages against Israel, Judah and the other nations. Begin with the first message back in the days of Josiah, and write down every one of them. 3Perhaps when the people of Judah see in writing all the terrible things I will do to them, they will repent. And then I can forgive them."

4So Jeremiah sent for Baruch (son of Neriah), and as Jeremiah dictated, Baruch wrote down all the prophecies.

5When all was finished, Jeremiah said to Baruch, "Since I am a prisoner here, 6you read the scroll in the Temple on the next Day of Fasting, for on that day people will be there from all over Judah. 7Perhaps even yet they will turn from their evil ways and ask the Lord to forgive them before it is too late, even though these curses of God have been pronounced upon them."

8Baruch did as Jeremiah told him to, and read all these messages to the people at the Temple. 9This occurred on the Day of Fasting held in December of the fifth year of the reign of King Jehoiakim (son of Josiah). People came from all over Judah to attend the services at the Temple that day. 10Baruch went to the office of Gemariah

35:7
Ex 20:12
1 Chron 16:19
Heb 11:9

35:8
Prov 4:1,2,10
6:20
Col 3:20

35:9
Ps 37:16
1 Tim 6:6

35:11
2 Kgs 24:1,2
Dan 1:1,2

35:13
Isa 28:9-12

35:14
2 Chron 36:15
Isa 30:9

35:15
Deut 6:14
Jer 29:19
Ezek 18:30-32
Acts 26:20

35:16
Mal 1:6

35:17
Prov 1:24,25
Mic 3:12
Lk 13:34,35
Rom 10:21

35:18
Ex 20:12
Jer 15:19
Eph 6:1-3

36:1
Jer 25:1-3; 45:1

36:2
Jer 1:2,3,5,9,
10; 25:9-29
Zech 5:1,2

36:3
Isa 55:7
Jer 18:8,11
Mk 4:12
Acts 3:19

36:4
Jer 32:12
Ezek 2:9

36:5
Jer 32:2

36:6
Zech 8:19

36:7
1 Kgs 8:33
2 Kgs 22:13
Jer 26:3

36:10
Jer 26:10

35:13–17 There is a vivid contrast between the Rechabites and the other Israelites: (1) The Rechabites kept their vows to a fallible human leader; Israel broke their covenant with their infallible divine Leader. (2) Jonadab told his family one time not to drink and they didn't; God commanded Israel constantly to turn from sin and they refused. (3) The Rechabites obeyed laws that dealt with temporal issues; Israel refused to obey God's laws that dealt with eternal issues. (4) The Rechabites had obeyed for hundreds of years; Israel had disobeyed for hundreds of years. (5) The Rechabites would be rewarded; Israel would be punished. We often are willing to observe customs merely for the sake of tradition; how much more should we obey God's Word because it is eternal.

36:1ff This happened in the summer of 605 B.C., shortly after Nebuchadnezzar's victory over the Egyptian army at Carchemish,

before the events recorded in chapters 34 and 35.

36:2-4 Most people in ancient times could neither read nor write, so those who could were extremely valuable. They held positions of great importance and were well respected for their knowledge. Writing was often done on vellum or papyrus sheets that were sewn or glued together and stored in long rolls called scrolls. After the exile, scribes became teachers of the Law. In New Testament times, the scribes formed a powerful political party.

36:9 Days of fasting (when people abstained from eating food to show their humility and repentance) were often called at times of national emergency. Babylon was destroying city after city and closing in on Jerusalem. As the people came to the Temple, Baruch told them how to avert the coming tragedy. But they refused to listen.

the Scribe (son of Shaphan) to read the scroll. (This room was just off the upper assembly hall of the Temple, near the door of the New Gate.)

11When Micaiah (son of Gemariah, son of Shaphan) heard the messages from God, 12he went down to the palace to the conference room where the administrative officials were meeting. Elishama (the scribe) was there, as well as Delaiah (son of Shamaiah), Elnathan (son of Achbor), Gemariah (son of Shaphan), Zedekiah (son of Hananiah), and all the others with similar responsibilities. 13When Micaiah told them about the messages Baruch was reading to the people, 14, 15the officials sent Jehudi (son of Nethaniah, son of Shelemiah, son of Cushi) to ask Baruch to come and read the messages to them too, and Baruch did.

16By the time he finished they were badly frightened. "We must tell the king," they said. 17"But first, tell us how you got these messages. Did Jeremiah himself dictate them to you?" 18So Baruch explained that Jeremiah had dictated them to him word by word, and he had written them down in ink upon the scroll. 19"You and Jeremiah both hide," the officials said to Baruch. "Don't tell a soul where you are!" 20Then the officials hid the scroll in the room of Elishama the scribe and went to tell the king.

21The king sent Jehudi to get the scroll. Jehudi brought it from Elishama the scribe and read it to the king as all his officials stood by. 22The king was in a winterized part of the palace at the time, sitting in front of a fireplace, for it was December, and cold. 23And whenever Jehudi finished reading three or four columns, the king would take his knife, and slit off the section and throw it into the fire, until the whole scroll was destroyed. 24, 25And no one protested except Elnathan, Delaiah and Gemariah. They pled with the king not to burn the scroll, but he wouldn't listen to them. Not another of the king's officials showed any signs of fear or anger at what he had done.

26Then the king commanded Jerahmeel (a member of the royal family) and Seraiah (son of Azri-el) and Shelemiah (son of Abdeel) to arrest Baruch and Jeremiah. But the Lord hid them!

27After the king had burned the scroll, the Lord said to Jeremiah:

28Get another scroll and write everything again just as you did before, 29and say this to the king: "The Lord says, You burned the scroll because it said the king of Babylon would destroy this country and everything in it. 30And now the Lord adds this concerning you, Jehoiakim, king of Judah: He shall have no one to sit upon the throne of David. His dead body shall be thrown out to the hot sun and frosty nights, 31and I will punish him and his family and his officials because of their sins. I will pour out upon them all the evil I promised—upon them and upon all the people of Judah and Jerusalem, for they wouldn't listen to my warnings."

32Then Jeremiah took another scroll and dictated again to Baruch all he had written before, only this time the Lord added a lot more!

Jeremiah is put in prison

37 Nebuchadnezzar, King of Babylon, did not appoint Coniah (King Jehoiakim's son) to be the new king of Judah. Instead he chose Zedekiah (son of

36:22 *sitting in front of a fireplace*, more literally, "a large brazier in which a fire was burning." 36:26 *a member of the royal family*, i.e., "a son of the king."

36:24, 25 Only three leaders protested this evil act of burning God's Word. This shows how complacent and insensitive to God the people had become.

36:27-32 God told Jeremiah to write his words on a scroll. Because he was not allowed to go to the Temple, Jeremiah asked his scribe, Baruch, to whom he had dictated the scroll, to read it to the people gathered there. Baruch then read it to the officials, and finally Jehudi read it to the king himself. Although the king burned the scroll, he could not destroy God's Word. Today many people try to put God's Word aside or say that it contains errors and therefore cannot be trusted. People may reject God's Word, but they cannot destroy it. God's Word will stand forever (Psalm 119:89).

36:30 Jehoiakim's son, Jehoiachin, was king for three months before he was taken into captivity, but this did not qualify as "sitting on the throne of David"—an expression that implied permanence. Jehoiachin did not secure a dynasty. Zedekiah, the next ruler, was Jehoiachin's uncle. Thus the line of human kings who had descended from David was finished, but in less than 600 years the eternal King would come.

37:1ff The people of Jerusalem assassinated King Jehoiakim and appointed his son Coniah (Jehoiachin) king, but he was taken captive to Babylon three months later. Nebuchadnezzar then appointed Zedekiah as his vassal in Israel.

Cross references (left margin):

36:12 Jer 26:22

36:13 2 Kgs 22:9,10

36:16 Amos 7:10,11 / Acts 24:25

36:18 Jer 43:2,3

36:19 1 Kgs 17:3; 18:4 / Jer 26:20-24

36:21 2 Kgs 22:9,10 / 2 Chron 34:18 / Ezek 2:4,5

36:22 Amos 3:15

36:23 Prov 1:29,30 / Isa 5:18,19 / 28:14,22

36:24 2 Kgs 19:1,2 / Ps 36:1 / Isa 26:10,11 / Acts 5:34-39

36:26 1 Kgs 19:1-3, 10,14 / Jer 15:20,21

36:28 Jer 28:13,14 / 44:28 / Zech 1:5,6

36:29 Deut 29:19 / Isa 30:10,11 / 45:9 / Jer 25:8-11 / 26:9

36:30 2 Kgs 24:12-15 / Jer 22:30

36:31 Deut 28:15-19 / Prov 29:1 / Jer 19:15

36:32 Ex 34:1

37:1 2 Chron 36:9,10 / Jer 22:24,28

Josiah). ²But neither King Zedekiah nor his officials nor the people who were left in the land listened to what the Lord said through Jeremiah. ³Nevertheless, King Zedekiah sent Jehucal (son of Shelemiah) and Zephaniah the priest (son of Maaseiah) to ask Jeremiah to pray for them. ⁴(Jeremiah had not been imprisoned yet, so he could go and come as he pleased.)

⁵When the army of Pharaoh Hophra of Egypt appeared at the southern border of Judah to relieve the besieged city of Jerusalem, the Babylonian army withdrew from Jerusalem to fight the Egyptians.

⁶Then the Lord sent this message to Jeremiah:

⁷"The Lord, the God of Israel, says: Tell the king of Judah, who sent you to ask me what is going to happen, that Pharaoh's army, though it came here to help you, is about to return in flight to Egypt! The Babylonians shall defeat them and send them scurrying home. ⁸These Babylonians shall capture this city and burn it to the ground. ⁹Don't fool yourselves that the Babylonians are gone for good. They aren't! ¹⁰Even if you destroyed the entire Babylonian army until there was only a handful of survivors and they lay wounded in their tents, yet they would stagger out and defeat you and put this city to the torch!"

¹¹When the Babylonian army set out from Jerusalem to engage Pharaoh's army in battle, ¹²Jeremiah started to leave the city to go to the land of Benjamin, to see the property he had bought. ¹³But as he was walking through the Benjamin Gate, a sentry arrested him as a traitor, claiming he was defecting to the Babylonians. The guard making the arrest was Irijah (son of Shelemiah, grandson of Hananiah).

¹⁴"That's not true," Jeremiah said. "I have no intention whatever of doing any such thing!"

But Irijah wouldn't listen; he took Jeremiah before the city officials. ¹⁵, ¹⁶They were incensed with Jeremiah and had him flogged and put into the dungeon under the house of Jonathan the scribe, which had been converted into a prison. Jeremiah was kept there for several days, ¹⁷but eventually King Zedekiah sent for him to come to the palace secretly. The king asked him if there was any recent message from the Lord. "Yes," said Jeremiah, "there is! You shall be defeated by the king of Babylon!"

¹⁸Then Jeremiah broached the subject of his imprisonment. "What have I ever done to deserve this?" he asked the king. "What crime have I committed? Tell me what I have done against you or your officials or the people? ¹⁹Where are those prophets now who told you that the king of Babylon would not come? ²⁰Listen, O my lord the king: I beg you, don't send me back to that dungeon, for I'll die there."

²¹Then King Zedekiah commanded that Jeremiah not be returned to the dungeon, but be placed in the palace prison instead, and that he be given a small loaf of fresh bread every day as long as there was any left in the city. So Jeremiah was kept in the palace prison.

Jeremiah is rescued

38 But when Shephatiah (son of Mattan) and Gedaliah (son of Pashhur) and Jucal (son of Shelemiah) and Pashhur (son of Malchiah) heard what Jeremiah had been telling the people— ²that everyone remaining in Jerusalem would die by sword, starvation or disease, but anyone surrendering to the Babylonians

37:2
2 Kgs 24:18-20
2 Chron 36:12
Prov 29:12
37:3
Jer 2:26,27
21:1,2; 52:24
37:5
Ezek 17:15,16
37:7
Isa 30:1-3
31:1-3
Jer 21:1,2
Ezek 17:17
37:8
Jer 34:22
37:9
Jer 29:8
Obad 3
Eph 5:6
37:10
Lev 26:36-38
Isa 30:17
Joel 2:11
37:12
Jer 32:8
37:13
Jer 18:18; 20:10
Zech 14:10
Acts 24:5-9,13
37:14
Ps 27:12
Jer 40:4-6
Mt 5:11,12
37:15
Jer 18:23; 38:6
Mt 21:35
Acts 5:18
37:17
Jer 21:7
38:14-16,24-27
Ezek 12:12,13
17:19-21
37:18
1 Sam 24:9
26:18
Jn 10:32
Acts 25:8,10,11
37:19
Deut 32:37,38
37:20
Jer 38:26
37:21
Job 5:20
Ps 33:18,19
Isa 33:16
Jer 52:6
38:1
Jer 21:8
38:2
Jer 21:9; 42:17

37:12 *he had bought, see chapter 32:6-15.* **37:21** *in the palace prison, literally, "the court of the guard."*

37:2, 3 King Zedekiah and his officials did not want to listen to Jeremiah's words, but they wanted the blessings of his prayers. They wanted a superficial religion that wouldn't cost anything. But God is not pleased with those who come to him only for what they can get rather than seeking to establish or deepen a relationship with him. We would not accept that kind of relationship with someone else, and we shouldn't expect God to accept it from us.

37:5 When Nebuchadnezzar besieged Jerusalem in 589 B.C., Pharaoh Hophra marched against him at Zedekiah's invitation.

Jerusalem looked to Egypt for help in spite of Jeremiah's warnings. But the Egyptians were no help, for as soon as the Babylonians turned on them, they retreated. Jeremiah's warnings had been correct.

37:17 Zedekiah teetered between surrender and resistance. Too frightened and weak to exercise authority, he asked Jeremiah to come secretly to the palace, perhaps hoping for some better news from God. Zedekiah was desperate; he wanted to hear God's Word, but he feared the political ramifications of being caught talking to Jeremiah.

38:3
Jer 21:10
32:3-5

38:4
1 Kgs 18:17,18
Jer 26:11
Amos 7:10
Acts 16:20,21

38:5
1 Sam 15:24
29:9

38:6
Ps 40:2
69:1,2,14
Jer 37:15,16
Zech 9:11

38:8
Job 29:7

38:9
Jer 37:21

38:13
Jer 37:21
39:14,15

38:14
1 Kgs 22:16
Jer 21:1,2
37:17

38:15
Jer 42:2-5,20
Lk 22:67,68

38:17
2 Kgs 25:27-30
Ps 80:7,14
Jer 21:8-10
27:12,17

38:18
2 Kgs 25:4-10
Jer 27:8; 37:8

38:19
Isa 51:12,13
57:11
Jer 39:9
Jn 12:42

38:20
Isa 55:3
Jer 7:23
11:4,8; 26:13

38:21
Jer 6:12; 8:10
43:6

would live, 3and that the city of Jerusalem would surely be captured by the king of Babylon— 4they went to the king and said: "Sir, this fellow must die. That kind of talk will undermine the morale of the few soldiers we have left, and of all the people too. This man is a traitor."

5So King Zedekiah agreed. "All right," he said. "Do as you like—I can't stop you."

6They took Jeremiah from his cell and lowered him by ropes into an empty cistern in the prison yard. (It belonged to Malchiah, a member of the royal family.) There was no water in it, but there was a thick layer of mire at the bottom, and Jeremiah sank down into it.

7When Ebed-melech the Ethiopian, an important palace official, heard that Jeremiah was in the cistern, 8he rushed out to the Gate of Benjamin where the king was holding court.

9"My lord the king," he said, "these men have done a very evil thing in putting Jeremiah into the cistern. He will die of hunger, for almost all the bread in the city is gone."

10Then the king commanded Ebed-melech to take thirty men with him and pull Jeremiah out before he died. 11So Ebed-melech took thirty men and went to a palace depot for discarded supplies where used clothing was kept. There he found some old rags and discarded garments which he took to the cistern and lowered to Jeremiah on a rope. 12Ebed-melech called down to Jeremiah, "Use these rags under your armpits to protect you from the ropes." Then, when Jeremiah was ready, 13they pulled him out and returned him to the palace prison, where he remained.

14One day King Zedekiah sent for Jeremiah to meet him at the side entrance of the Temple.

"I want to ask you something," the king said, "and don't try to hide the truth."

15Jeremiah said, "If I tell you the truth, you will kill me. And you won't listen to me anyway."

16So King Zedekiah swore before Almighty God his Creator that he would not kill Jeremiah or give him to the men who were after his life.

17Then Jeremiah said to Zedekiah, "The Almighty Lord, the God of Israel, says: If you will surrender to Babylon, you and your family shall live and the city will not be burned. 18If you refuse to surrender, this city shall be set afire by the Babylonian army and you will not escape."

19"But I am afraid to surrender," the king said, "for the Babylonians will hand me over to the Jews who have defected to them, and who knows what they will do to me?"

20Jeremiah replied, "You won't get into their hands if only you will obey the Lord; your life will be spared and all will go well for you. 21, 22But if you refuse to surrender, the Lord has said that all the women left in your palace will be brought out and given to the officers of the Babylonian army; and these women will taunt

---

38:4 No wonder Judah was in turmoil: the king agreed with everybody. He listened to Jeremiah (37:21); then he agreed Jeremiah should be killed (38:5); and finally he rescued Jeremiah (38:10). Jeremiah was not popular; his words undermined the morale of the army and the people. Zedekiah couldn't decide between public opinion and God's word.

38:6 Officials put Jeremiah in an empty cistern to kill him. A cistern was a large hole in the ground lined with rocks to collect rain water. The bottom would have been dark, damp, and, in this case, full of mud. Jeremiah could drown, die of exposure, or starve to death in the cistern.

38:6 Judah's leaders persecuted Jeremiah repeatedly for faithfully proclaiming God's messages. For 40 years of faithful ministry, he received no acclaim, no love, no popular following. He was beaten, jailed, threatened, and even forced to leave his homeland. Only the heathen Babylonians showed him any respect. God does not guarantee that his servants will escape persecution, even when they are faithful. But God does promise that he will be

with them and will give them strength to endure (2 Corinthians 1:3-7). As you minister to others, recognize that your service is for God and not just for human approval. God's rewards are often not in this life.

38:7, 8 The Gate of Benjamin was one of Jerusalem's city gates where legal matters were handled. A palace official, Ebed-melech, had access to the king. When he heard of Jeremiah's plight, he went immediately to deal with the injustice.

38:9–13 Ebed-melech feared God more than man. He alone among the palace officials stood up against the murder plot. His obedience could have cost him his life. Because he obeyed, however, he was spared when Jerusalem fell (39:15–18). You can either go along with the crowd or speak up for God. When someone is treated unkindly or unjustly, for example, reach out to that person with God's love. You may be the only one who does. And, when you're being treated unkindly yourself, be sure to thank God when he sends an "Ebed-melech" your way.

you with bitterness. 'Fine friends you have,' they'll say, 'those Egyptians. They have betrayed you and left you to your fate!' 23All your wives and children will be led out to the Babylonians, and you will not escape. You will be seized by the king of Babylon, and this city will be burned."

38:23
2 Kgs 25:7
Jer 39:6; 41:10

24Then Zedekiah said to Jeremiah, "On pain of death, don't tell anyone you told me this! 25And if my officials hear that I talked with you and they threaten you with death unless you tell them what we discussed, 26just say that you begged me not to send you back to the dungeon in Jonathan's house, for you would die there."

38:26
Jer 37:15,16,20

27And sure enough, it wasn't long before all the city officials came to Jeremiah and asked him why the king had called for him. So he said what the king had told him to, and they left without finding out the truth, for the conversation had not been overheard by anyone. 28And Jeremiah remained confined to the prison yard until the day Jerusalem was captured.

38:27
1 Sam 10:15,
16; 16:2-5

38:28
Ps 23:4
Jer 37:20,21
39:13,14

Nebuchadnezzar captures Jerusalem

39 It was in January of the ninth year of the reign of King Zedekiah of Judah, that King Nebuchadnezzar and all his army came against Jerusalem again and besieged it. 2Two years later, in the month of July, they breached the wall, and the city fell, 3and all the officers of the Babylonian army came in and sat in triumph at the middle gate. Nergal-sharezer was there, and Samgar-nebo and Sarsechim and Nergal-sharezer the king's chief assistant, and many others.

39:1
2 Kgs 25:1-12

39:3
Jer 21:3,4

39:4
2 Kgs 25:4
Isa 30:15,16
Jer 52:7
Amos 2:14

4When King Zedekiah and his soldiers realized that the city was lost, they fled during the night, going out through the gate between the two walls back of the palace garden and across the fields toward the Jordan valley. 5But the Babylonians chased the king and caught him on the plains of Jericho and brought him to Nebuchadnezzar, king of Babylon who was at Riblah, in the land of Hamath, where he pronounced judgment upon him. 6The king of Babylon made Zedekiah watch as they killed his children and all the nobles of Judah. 7Then he gouged out Zedekiah's eyes and bound him in chains to send him away to Babylon as a slave.

39:5
Jer 32:4,5; 52:9
Lam 4:20; 52:8

39:6
Jer 24:8-10
34:18-21; 52:10

39:7
2 Kgs 25:7
Jer 52:11
Ezek 12:13

8Meanwhile the army burned Jerusalem, including the palace, and tore down the walls of the city. 9Then Nebuzaradan, the captain of the guard, and his men sent the remnant of the population and all those who had defected to him to Babylon. 10But throughout the land of Judah he left a few people, the very poor, and gave them fields and vineyards.

39:8
2 Kgs 25:9,10
Neh 1:3

39:9
2 Kgs 25:11,20
Jer 52:12-16,26

39:10
2 Kgs 25:12

11, 12Meanwhile King Nebuchadnezzar had told Nebuzaradan to find Jeremiah. "See that he isn't hurt," he said. "Look after him well and give him anything he wants." 13So Nebuzaradan, the captain of the guard, and Nebushazban, the chief of the eunuchs, and Nergal-sharezer, the king's advisor, and all the officials took steps to do as the king had commanded. 14They sent soldiers to bring Jeremiah out of the prison, and put him into the care of Gedaliah (son of Ahikam, son of

39:11
Job 5:15,16
Prov 16:7; 21:1
Jer 1:8
15:20,21

39:14
2 Kgs 22:12,14
Jer 26:24
40:1-6

38:27 The officials wanted accurate information, but not God's truth. They wanted to use this information against God, his prophet, and the king. But Jeremiah told the officials only what the king ordered him to say. We must not withhold God's truth from others, but we should withhold information that will be used to bring evil to God's people.

39:1ff This chapter includes a concise account of the capture of Jerusalem and the release of Jeremiah and Ebed-melech. These events authenticated Jeremiah's prophecies. (See also 2 Kings 25; 2 Chronicles 36.)

39:1 Zedekiah, son of King Josiah and last king of Judah, ruled 11 years, from 597 to 586 B.C. Zedekiah's two older brothers, Jehoahaz and Jehoiakim, and his nephew Coniah (also called Jehoiachin) ruled before him. When Coniah was exiled to Babylon, Nebuchadnezzar made 21-year-old Mattaniah the king, changing his name to Zedekiah. Zedekiah rebelled against Nebuchadnezzar, who captured him, killed his sons before him, and then blinded him and took him back to Babylon where he later died (see

2 Kings 24; 2 Chronicles 36; and Jeremiah 52).

39:10 Babylon had a shrewd foreign policy toward conquered lands. They deported the rich and powerful, leaving only the very poor in charge, thus making them grateful to their conquerors. This policy assured that conquered populations would be too loyal and too weak to revolt.

39:11, 12 God had promised to see Jeremiah through his trouble (1:8). The superstitious Babylonians, who highly respected magicians and fortune tellers, treated Jeremiah as a seer. Because he had been imprisoned by his own people, they assumed he was a traitor and on their side. They undoubtedly knew he had counseled cooperation with Babylon and predicted a Babylonian victory. So the Babylonians freed Jeremiah and protected him.

39:14 What a difference between Jeremiah's fate and Zedekiah's. Jeremiah was freed, Zedekiah imprisoned. Jeremiah was saved by his faith, Zedekiah destroyed by his fear. Jeremiah was treated with respect, Zedekiah treated with contempt. Jeremiah was concerned for the people, Zedekiah concerned for himself.

Shaphan), to take him back to his home. And Jeremiah lived there among his people who were left in the land.

15The Lord gave the following message to Jeremiah before the Babylonians arrived, while he was still in prison:

16"Send this word to Ebed-melech the Ethiopian: The Lord, the God of Israel, says: I will do to this city everything I threatened; I will destroy it before your eyes, 17but I will deliver you. You shall not be killed by those you fear so much. 18As a reward for trusting me, I will preserve your life and keep you safe."

Jeremiah stays in the occupied land

40 Nebuzaradan, captain of the guard, took Jeremiah to Ramah along with all the exiled people of Jerusalem and Judah who were being sent to Babylon, but then released him.

2,3The captain called for Jeremiah and said, "The Lord your God has brought this disaster on this land, just as he said he would. For these people have sinned against the Lord. That is why it happened. 4Now I am going to take off your chains and let you go. If you want to come with me to Babylon, fine; I will see that you are well cared for. But if you don't want to come, don't. The world is before you—go where you like. 5If you decide to stay, then return to Gedaliah, who has been appointed as governor of Judah by the king of Babylon, and stay with the remnant he rules. But it's up to you; go where you like."

Then Nebuzaradan gave Jeremiah some food and money and let him go. 6So Jeremiah returned to Gedaliah and lived in Judah with the people left in the land.

7Now when the leaders of the Jewish guerrilla bands in the countryside heard that the king of Babylon had appointed Gedaliah as governor over the poor of the land who were left behind, and had not exiled everyone to Babylon, 8they came to see Gedaliah at Mizpah, where his headquarters were. These are the names of the leaders who came: Ishmael (son of Nethaniah), Johanan and Jonathan (sons of Kareah), Seraiah (son of Tanhumeth), the sons of Ephai (the Netophathite), Jezaniah (son of a Ma-acathite), and their men. 9And Gedaliah assured them that it would be safe to surrender to the Babylonians.

"Stay here and serve the king of Babylon," he said, "and all will go well for you. 10As for me, I will stay at Mizpah and intercede for you with the Babylonians who will come here to oversee my administration. Settle in any city you wish and live off the land. Harvest the grapes and summer fruits and olives and store them away."

11When the Jews in Moab and among the Ammonites and in Edom and the other nearby countries heard that a few people were still left in Judah, and that the king of Babylon had not taken them all away, and that Gedaliah was the governor, 12they all began to return to Judah from the many places to which they had fled. They stopped at Mizpah to discuss their plans with Gedaliah and then went out to the deserted farms and gathered a great harvest of wine grapes and other crops.

13,14But soon afterwards Johanan (son of Kareah) and the other guerrilla leaders came to Mizpah to warn Gedaliah that Baalis, king of the Ammonites, had sent Ishmael (son of Nethaniah) to assassinate him. But Gedaliah wouldn't believe

---

39:17, 18 Ebed-melech risked his life to save God's prophet Jeremiah. When Babylon conquered Jerusalem, God protected Ebed-melech from the Babylonians. God has special rewards for his faithful people.

40—45 These six chapters cover events following Jerusalem's fall to Babylon.

40:2, 3 The Babylonian captain, who did not know God, acknowledged that God had given the Babylonians victory. It is strange when people recognize that God exists and does miracles, but still they do not personally accept him. Knowing God is more than knowing about him. Be sure you know him personally.

40:4 Jeremiah was free to go anywhere. In Babylon he would

have had great comfort and power. In Judah, he would continue to face hardship. In Babylon, he would have been favored by the Babylonians, but hated by the Judean exiles. In Judah he would remain poor and unwanted, but the Judean remnant would know he was not a traitor. He returned to Judah.

40:13, 14 Gedaliah, appointed governor of Judah, foolishly ignored the warnings of assassination. Ishmael, in the line of David, may have been angry that he had been passed over for leadership. This is similar to the political structure that Ezra and Nehemiah faced when they returned to rebuild the Temple and the city.

them. 15Then Johanan had a private conference with Gedaliah. Johanan volunteered to kill Ishmael secretly.

"Why should we let him come and murder you?" Johanan asked. "What will happen then to the Jews who have returned? Why should this remnant be scattered and lost?"

16But Gedaliah said, "I forbid you to do any such thing, for you are lying about Ishmael."

40:15
1 Sam 26:8
2 Sam 21:17
Jer 42:1,2

40:16
Mt 10:16

Governor Gedaliah is assassinated

41 But in October, Ishmael (son of Nethaniah, son of Elishama), who was a member of the royal family and one of the king's top officials, arrived in Mizpah, accompanied by ten men. Gedaliah invited them to dinner. 2While they were eating, Ishmael and the ten men in league with him suddenly jumped up, pulled out their swords and killed Gedaliah. 3Then they went out and slaughtered all the Jewish officials and Babylonian soldiers who were in Mizpah with Gedaliah.

4The next day, before the outside world knew what had happened, 5eighty men approached Mizpah from Shechem, Shiloh and Samaria, to worship at the Temple of the Lord. They had shaved off their beards, torn their clothes and cut themselves, and were bringing offerings and incense. 6Ishmael went out from the city to meet them, crying as he went. When he faced them he said, "Oh, come and see what has happened to Gedaliah!"

7Then, when they were all inside the city, Ishmael and his men killed all but ten of them and threw their bodies into a cistern. 8The ten had talked Ishmael into letting them go by promising to bring him their treasures of wheat, barley, oil and honey they had hidden away. 9The cistern where Ishmael dumped the bodies of the men he murdered was the large one constructed by King Asa when he fortified Mizpah to protect himself against Baasha, king of Israel.

10Ishmael made captives of the king's daughters and of the people who had been left under Gedaliah's care in Mizpah by Nebuzaradan, captain of the guard. Soon after he took them with him when he headed toward the country of the Ammonites.

11But when Johanan (son of Kareah) and the rest of the guerrilla leaders heard what Ishmael had done, 12they took all their men and set out to stop him. They caught up with him at the pool near Gibeon. 13, 14The people with Ishmael shouted for joy when they saw Johanan and his men, and ran to meet them.

15Meanwhile Ishmael escaped with eight of his men into the land of the Ammonites.

16, 17Then Johanan and his men went to the village of Geruth Chimham, near Bethlehem, taking with them all those they had rescued—soldiers, women, children and eunuchs, to prepare to leave for Egypt. 18For they were afraid of what the Babylonians would do when the news reached them that Ishmael had killed Gedaliah the governor, for he had been chosen and appointed by the Babylonian emperor.

41:1
2 Kgs 25:25
Jer 39:14
40:5,6,8,13,14

41:2
2 Sam 3:27
20:8-10
Ps 41:9; 109:5
Jn 13:18

41:5
Deut 14:1
Josh 18:1
1 Kgs 16:24
Ps 78:60
Jer 16:6

41:6
Jer 50:4

41:7
Isa 59:7
Ezek 22:27
33:24,26

41:9
1 Sam 13:6
1 Kgs 15:17-22
2 Chron 16:1-6
Heb 11:37,38

41:10
Jer 40:11,12
43:6

41:11
Jer 40:7,8
13-16

41:12
2 Sam 2:13

41:15
Prov 28:17

41:16
2 Sam 19:37,
38,40
Jer 42:8,14
43:4-7

41:18
Isa 57:11
Lk 12:4,5

God warns against going to Egypt

42 Then Johanan and the army captains and all the people, great and small, came to Jeremiah 2and said, "Please pray for us to the Lord your God, for as you know so well, we are only a tiny remnant of what we were before. 3Beg the Lord your God to show us what to do and where to go."

4"All right," Jeremiah replied. "I will ask him and I will tell you what he says. I will hide nothing from you."

42:1
Jer 40:8,12,13

42:2
Deut 28:62
Isa 1:9

42:4
Ps 40:10
Jer 23:28

41:9 he fortified Mizpah to protect himself against Baasha, king of Israel. See 1 Kgs 15:22. Fifty-three cisterns have been uncovered by excavators at the site of ancient Mizpah.

41:4–9 The 80 men came from three cities of the Northern Kingdom to worship in Jerusalem. Ishmael probably killed them for the money and food they were carrying. Without a king, with no law, and no loyalty to God, Judah was subjected to complete anarchy.

41:16, 17 Johanan and his group were already on their way to Egypt, headed south from Gibeon, stopping first at Chimham, near Bethlehem. Their visit to Jeremiah (42:1–6) was deceptive, as Jeremiah later told them (42:20).

42:5
Jer 43:2
Mic 1:2

42:6
Ex 24:7
Deut 5:29
Jer 7:23

42:7
Ps 27:14

42:10
Jer 31:28
Hos 11:8
Joel 2:13

42:11
Ps 46:7,11
Isa 43:5
Jer 41:18
Rom 8:31

42:12
Ps 106:45,46
Prov 16:7

42:13
Isa 31:1
Jer 41:16,17

42:15
Jer 44:12

42:16
Jer 44:13,27

42:17
Jer 44:13,14,28

42:18
2 Chron
36:16-19
Jer 29:18,19
39:1-9

42:19
Deut 17:16
Ezek 2:5

42:20
Ezek 14:3

42:21
Deut 11:26
Ezek 2:7

42:22
Jer 43:11

5Then they said to Jeremiah, "May the curse of God be on us if we refuse to obey whatever he says we should do! 6Whether we like it or not, we will obey the Lord our God, to whom we send you with our plea. For if we obey him, everything will turn out well for us."

7Ten days later the Lord gave his reply to Jeremiah. 8So he called for Johanan and the captains of his forces, and for all the people, great and small, 9and said to them: "You sent me to the Lord, the God of Israel, with your request, and this is his reply:

10"Stay here in this land. If you do, I will bless you and no one will harm you. For I am sorry for all the punishment I have had to give to you. 11Don't fear the king of Babylon any more, for I am with you to save you and to deliver you from his hand. 12And I will be merciful to you by making him kind so that he will not kill you or make slaves of you but will let you stay here in your land.

13, 14"But if you refuse to obey the Lord and say, 'We will not stay here,'—and insist on going to Egypt where you think you will be free from war and hunger and alarms, 15then this is what the Lord replies, O remnant of Judah: The Lord Almighty, the God of Israel, says: If you insist on going to Egypt, 16the war and famine you fear will follow close behind you and you will perish there. 17That is the fate awaiting every one of you who insists on going to live in Egypt. Yes, you will die from sword, famine and disease. None of you will escape from the evil I will bring upon you there.

18"For the Lord, the God of Israel, says: Just as my anger and fury were poured out upon the people of Jerusalem, so it will be poured out on you when you enter Egypt. You will be received with disgust and with hatred—you will be cursed and reviled. And you will never again see your own land. 19For the Lord has said: O remnant of Judah, do not go to Egypt!"

Jeremiah concluded: "Never forget the warning I have given you today. 20If you go, it will be at the cost of your lives. For you were deceitful when you sent me to pray for you and said, 'Just tell us what God says and we will do it!' 21And today I have told you exactly what he said, but you will not obey any more now than you did the other times. 22Therefore know for a certainty that you will die by sword, famine and disease in Egypt, where you insist on going."

The people refuse to believe

43:2
Jer 5:12,13
36:4,10,32
38:4; 42:5

43 When Jeremiah had finished giving this message from God to all the people, 2, 3Azariah (son of Hoshaiah) and Johanan (son of Kareah) and all the other proud men, said to Jeremiah, "You lie! The Lord our God hasn't told you to tell us not to go to Egypt! Baruch (son of Neriah) has plotted against us and told you to say this so that we will stay here and be killed by the Babylonians or carried off to Babylon as slaves."

43:4
Jer 42:5,6,
10-12

43:5
Jer 40:11,12

43:6
Jer 40:7

4So Johanan and all the guerrilla leaders and all the people refused to obey the Lord and stay in Judah. 5All of them, including all those who had returned from the nearby countries where they had fled, now started off for Egypt with Johanan and the other captains in command. 6In the crowd were men, women and children, the king's daughters and all those whom Nebuzaradan, the captain of the guard, had left with Gedaliah. They even forced Jeremiah and Baruch to go with them too.

42:5, 6 Johanan and his associates spoke their own curse; Jeremiah merely elaborated on it. It was a tragic mistake to ask for God's guidance with no intention of following it. Be sure never to ask God for something if you know in your heart that you do not want it. It is better not to pray than to pray deceptively. God cannot be deceived.

43:1–3 Johanan and his tiny band had come to Jeremiah for God's approval of their plan, not for his direction. This is a recurring problem for most of us—seeking God's approval of our desires rather than asking him for guidance. It's not good to make plans unless we are willing to have God change them, and it is not

good to pray unless we are willing to accept God's answer.

43:6 Afraid to obey, the people headed for Egypt, even forcing Jeremiah to go with them. (They thought that perhaps God would spare them if Jeremiah was with them.) Jeremiah had served as a prophet for 40 years, many of his words had already come true, and he had turned down an offer to live comfortably in Babylon, returning instead to his beloved people. But the people still rejected Jeremiah's advice. The response of our audience is not necessarily a measure of our success. Jeremiah was doing all God asked, but he had been called to minister to a very stubborn audience.

7And so they arrived in Egypt at the city of Tahpanhes, for they would not obey the Lord.

8Then at Tahpanhes, the Lord spoke to Jeremiah again and said:

9"Call together the men of Judah and, as they watch you, bury large rocks between the pavement stones at the entrance of Pharaoh's palace here in Tahpanhes, 10and tell the men of Judah this: The Lord Almighty, the God of Israel, says: I will surely bring Nebuchadnezzar, king of Babylon, here to Egypt, for he is my servant. I will set his throne upon these stones that I have hidden. He shall spread his royal canopy over them. 11And when he comes he shall destroy the land of Egypt, killing all those I want killed, and capturing those I want captured, and many shall die of plague. 12He will set fire to the temples of the gods of Egypt and burn the idols and carry off the people as his captives. And he shall plunder the land of Egypt as a shepherd picks fleas from his cloak! And he himself shall leave unharmed. 13And he shall break down the obelisks standing in the city of Heliopolis, and burn down the temples of the gods of Egypt."

God's judgment because of idolatry

44 This is the message God gave to Jeremiah concerning all the Jews who were living in the north of Egypt in the cities of Migdol, Tahpanhes and Memphis, and throughout southern Egypt as well:

2,3The Lord Almighty, the God of Israel, says: You saw what I did to Jerusalem and to all the cities of Judah. Because of all their wickedness they lie in heaps and ashes, without a living soul. For my anger rose high against them for worshiping other gods—"gods" that neither they nor you nor any of your fathers have ever known.

4I sent my servants, the prophets, to protest over and over again and to plead with them not to do this horrible thing I hate, 5but they wouldn't listen and wouldn't turn back from their wicked ways; they have kept right on with their sacrifices to these "gods." 6And so my fury and anger boiled over and fell as fire upon the cities of Judah and into the streets of Jerusalem, and there is desolation until this day.

7And now the Lord, the Lord Almighty, the God of Israel, asks you: Why are you destroying yourselves?—not a man, woman or child among you who has come here from Judah, not even the babies in arms. 8For you are rousing my anger with the idols you have made and worshiped here in Egypt, burning incense to them, and causing me to destroy you completely and to make you a curse and a stench in the nostrils of all the nations of the earth. 9Have

43:8
Ps 139:7
Jer 44:1; 46:14
Ezek 30:18
2 Tim 2:9

43:10
Ps 18:11
Jer 25:8,9,11
27:6; 46:13

43:11
Isa 19:1-25
44:13

43:12
Jer 46:25
Ezek 29:19
30:13

44:2
Isa 6:11
Jer 6:11
Mic 3:12

44:3
Deut 32:17
Jer 32:30-32

44:4
Jer 32:34,35
35:15
Ezek 8:10
Zech 7:7

44:6
Isa 51:17-20
Jer 7:17,34

44:7
Jer 9:21
Ezek 33:11

44:8
1 Kgs 9:7,8
2 Kgs 17:15-17
2 Chron 7:19,20
Jer 11:12,17
1 Cor 10:21,22

44:9
Jer 7:9,10
17,18

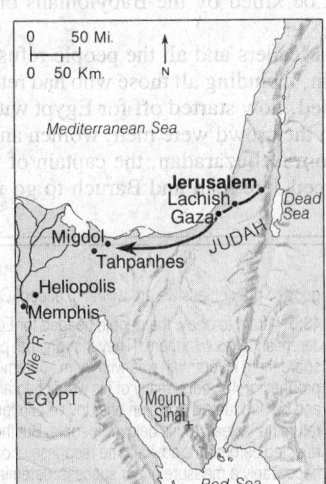

ESCAPE TO EGYPT
With Judah in turmoil after the murder of Gedaliah, the people turned to Jeremiah for guidance. Jeremiah had God's answer, "stay in the land." But the leaders disobeyed and went to Egypt, taking Jeremiah with them. In Egypt, Jeremiah told them they were not safe.

Map labels: Mediterranean Sea; Jerusalem; Lachish; Gaza; Dead Sea; Migdol; Tahpanhes; JUDAH; Heliopolis; Memphis; Nile R.; EGYPT; Mount Sinai; Red Sea; 0 50 Mi.; 0 50 Km.; N

43:11 Nebuchadnezzar invaded Egypt in 568–567 B.C. Like Judah, Egypt rebelled against him and was quickly crushed. So much for the great empire on which Judah had constantly placed her hopes!

44:1 This message, given in 580 B.C. while Jeremiah was in Egypt against his will, reminded the people that their sins had brought destruction on their land. Jeremiah told them they would never return to Judah because the escape to Egypt had been against God's advice (42:9ff). But the people refused to learn any lessons from all the destruction their sins had caused.

44:7 "Why are you destroying yourselves?" These people cursed themselves (42:5, 6) yet still refused to listen to God's clear directions. They feared the Babylonians, who would have been kind to them, and destroyed themselves. Self-destruction, whether through foolish decisions, dangerous habits, or blatant disobedience to God, is worse than destruction by an enemy. There is no honor whatsoever in self-destruction.

44:9, 10 When we forget a lesson or refuse to learn it, we risk repeating our mistakes. The people of Judah struggled with this same matter; to forget their former sins was to repeat them. To fail to learn from failure is to assure future failure. Your past is your school of experience. Let your past mistakes point you to God's way.

you forgotten the sins of your fathers, and the sins of the kings and queens of Judah, and your own sins, and the sins of your wives in Judah and Jerusalem? 10And even until this very hour there has been no apology; no one has wanted to return to me, or follow the laws I gave you and your fathers before you.

11Therefore the Lord, the God of Israel, says: There is fury in my face and I will destroy every one of you! 12I will take this remnant of Judah that insisted on coming here to Egypt and I will consume them. They shall fall here in Egypt, killed by famine and sword; all shall die, from the least important to the greatest. They shall be despised and loathed, cursed and hated. 13I will punish them in Egypt just as I punished them in Jerusalem, by sword, famine and disease. 14Not one of them shall escape from my wrath except those who repent of their coming and escape from the others by returning again to their own land.

15Then all the women present and all the men who knew that their wives had burned incense to idols (it was a great crowd of all the Jews in southern Egypt) answered Jeremiah:

16"We will not listen to your false 'Messages from God'! 17We will do whatever we want to. We will burn incense to the 'Queen of Heaven' and sacrifice to her just as much as we like—just as we and our fathers before us, and our kings and princes have always done in the cities of Judah and in the streets of Jerusalem; for in those days we had plenty to eat and we were well off and happy! 18But ever since we quit burning incense to the 'Queen of Heaven' and stopped worshiping her we have been in great trouble and have been destroyed by sword and famine."

19"And," the women added, "do you suppose that we were worshiping the 'Queen of Heaven' and pouring out our libations to her and making cakes for her with her image on them, without our husbands knowing it and helping us? Of course not!"

20Then Jeremiah said to all of them, men and women alike, who had given him that answer:

21"Do you think the Lord didn't know that you and your fathers and your kings and princes and all the people were burning incense to idols in the cities of Judah and in the streets of Jerusalem? 22It was because he could no longer bear all the evil things you were doing that he made your land desolate, an incredible ruin, cursed, without an inhabitant, as it is today. 23The very reason all these terrible things have befallen you is because you have burned incense and sinned against the Lord and refused to obey him."

24Then Jeremiah said to them all, including the women: "Listen to the word of the Lord, all you citizens of Judah who are here in Egypt! 25The Lord, the God of Israel, says: Both you and your wives have said that you will never give up your devotion and sacrifices to the 'Queen of Heaven,' and you have proved it by your actions. Then go ahead and carry out your promises and vows to her! 26But listen to the word of the Lord, all you Jews who are living in the land of Egypt: I have sworn by my great name, says the Lord, that it will do you no good to seek my help and blessing any more, saying, 'O Lord our God, help us!' 27For I will watch over you, but *not* for good! I will see to it that evil befalls you, and you shall be destroyed by war and famine until all of you are dead.

28"Only those who return to Judah (it will be but a tiny remnant) shall escape my wrath, but all who refuse to go back—who insist on living in Egypt—shall find out

44:17 *Queen of Heaven.* See note to 7:18.

44:10
Jer 6:15; 8:12

44:11
Lev 26:17
Jer 21:10

44:12
Isa 65:15
Jer 42:15-18,22

44:13
Jer 24:10

44:14
Isa 10:20
Rom 9:27

44:15
Jer 5:1-5

44:16
Jer 8:6; 13:10

44:17
Ex 16:3
2 Kgs 17:16
Jer 7:18
Phil 3:19

44:18
Num 11:5,6
Mal 3:13-15

44:19
Num 30:6,7

44:21
Jer 11:13; 14:10
Ezek 8:10,11
16:24
Hos 7:2

44:22
Isa 7:13
Jer 4:4
25:11,18,38
30:14

44:23
1 Kgs 9:9
Jer 7:13-15
40:3
Dan 9:11,12

44:24
Jer 43:7

44:25
Ezek 20:39
Jas 1:14,15

44:26
Deut 32:40
Ps 50:16,17
Heb 6:13,18

44:27
Jer 1:10

44:28
Isa 14:27
46:9,10
Zech 1:5,6

44:14 Only those who repented of going to Egypt and returned to their own land would escape judgment. God wanted both a change of attitude and action. God always offers a way of escape—even when we get ourselves in so deep it doesn't look like there is any way out. And the steps are always the same: (1) admitting we have rebelled against God, (2) forsaking our sinful direction, and (3) seeking to live as God instructs in his Word.

44:16–18 The farther we drift from God, the more confused our thinking becomes. Whatever spiritual life was left in the Israelites when they went to Egypt was lost as they sank into the depths of idolatry. (For more information on the "Queen of Heaven," see the note on 7:18.) The escape to Egypt had brought a change in their pagan worship habits, and they blamed their troubles on their neglect of their idols. But idol worship had started all their problems in the first place. They refused to recognize the true source of their problems—departure from God's leading. When calamity forces you to examine your life, take a close look at God's instructions for you.

44:28 After Jeremiah's forced move to Egypt, there is no further word about his life.

who tells the truth, I or they! 29And this is the proof I give you that all I have threatened will happen to you, and that I will punish you here: 30I will turn Pharaoh Hophra, king of Egypt, over to those who seek his life, just as I turned Zedekiah, king of Judah, over to Nebuchadnezzar, king of Babylon."

44:29
Isa 40:8
Mt 24:15,16,32
44:30
2 Kgs 25:4-7
Jer 46:25

An admonition to Baruch

45 This is the message Jeremiah gave to Baruch in the fourth year of the reign of King Jehoiakim (son of Josiah), after Baruch had written down all God's messages as Jeremiah was dictating them to him:

45:1
Jer 25:1
36:4,18,32

2O Baruch, the Lord God of Israel says this to you:

3You have said, Woe is me! Don't I have troubles enough already? And now the Lord has added more! I am weary of my own sighing and I find no rest. 4But tell Baruch this, The Lord says: I will destroy this nation that I built; I will wipe out what I established. 5Are you seeking great things for yourself? Don't do it! For though I will bring great evil upon all these people, I will protect you wherever you go, as your reward.

45:3
Ps 6:6
2 Cor 4:1,16
Gal 6:9
45:5
Isa 66:16
Mt 6:25; 31,32
Rom 12:16

B. GOD'S JUDGMENT ON THE NATIONS (46:1—52:34)

All of Jeremiah's prophecies against foreign nations have been grouped together. Many of the people in these nations assumed that they were free from judgment and punishment for their sin. Following these prophecies is an historical appendix recounting the fall of Jerusalem. Just as Jerusalem received its punishment, these nations were certain to receive theirs as well. Those today who think that judgment will never touch them are forewarned.

1. Prophecies about foreign nations
The Egyptians

46 Here are the messages given to Jeremiah concerning foreign nations. 2This message as given against Egypt at the occasion of the battle of Carchemish when Pharaoh Necho, king of Egypt, and his army were defeated beside the Euphrates River by Nebuchadnezzar, king of Babylon, in the fourth year of the reign of Jehoiakim (son of Josiah), king of Judah:

46:1
Jer 1:10
Ezek 29-32

46:2
2 Kgs 23:29
2 Chron 35:20

3Buckle on your armor, you Egyptians and advance to battle! 4Harness the horses and prepare to mount them—don your helmets, sharpen your spears, put on your armor. 5But look! The Egyptian army flees in terror; the mightiest of its soldiers run without a backward glance. Yes, terror shall surround them on every side, says the Lord. 6The swift will not escape, nor the mightiest of warriors. In the north, by the river Euphrates, they have stumbled and fallen.

46:3
Joel 3:9
46:4
Ezek 21:9-11
46:5
Isa 42:17
Jer 6:25; 49:29
Ezek 39:18

7What is this mighty army, rising like the Nile at flood time, overflowing all the land? 8It is the Egyptian army, boasting that it will cover the earth like a flood, destroying every foe. 9Then come, O horses and chariots and mighty soldiers of Egypt! Come, all of you from Cush and Put and Lud who handle the shield and bend the bow! 10For this is the day of the Lord, the Lord Almighty, a day of vengeance upon his enemies. The sword shall devour until it is sated, yes, drunk with your blood, for the Lord, the Lord Almighty will receive a sacrifice today in

46:6
Isa 30:16
Dan 11:18
46:8
Isa 10:13
46:9
Nah 3:9
46:10
Isa 31:8; 34:6
Zeph 1:7

44:30 Pharaoh Hophra ruled Egypt from 588 to 568 B.C. and was killed by Amasis, one of his generals, who was then crowned in his place.

45:1ff The event relating to this chapter is recorded in 36:1–8. The chapter was written in 605–604 B.C. Baruch was the scribe who recorded Jeremiah's scroll.

45:5 Baruch had long been serving this unpopular prophet, writing his book of struggles and judgments, and now he was upset. God told Baruch to take his eyes off himself and whatever rewards he thought he deserved. If he did this, God would protect him. It is easy to lose the joy of serving our God when we take our eyes off him. The more we look away from God's purposes toward our own sacrifices, the more frustrated we become. As you serve God, beware of focusing on what you are giving up. When this

happens, ask God's forgiveness; then fix your eyes on him rather than on yourself.

46:1 In this chapter, we gain several insights about God and his plan for this world. (1) Although God chose Israel for a special purpose, he loves all people and wants all to come to him. (2) God is holy and will not tolerate sin. (3) God's judgments are not based on prejudice and a desire for revenge, but on fairness and justice. (4) God does not delight in judgment, but in salvation. (5) God is impartial—he judges everyone by the same standard.

46:2 At the Battle of Carchemish in 605 B.C., Babylon and Egypt, the two major world powers after Assyria's fall, clashed. The Babylonians entered the city by surprise and defeated Egypt. This battle, which established Babylon as the next world leader, was Nebuchadnezzar's first victory, establishing him in his new position as king of the Empire.

46:11
Jer 8:22; 30:13
Ezek 30:21-26
Nah 3:19

46:12
Jer 2:36
Nah 3:8-10

46:14
Jer 44:1
Nah 2:13

46:15
Ps 18:39
68:1,2

46:16
Jer 51:9

46:17
Ex 15:9,10
1 Kgs 20:10,11
Isa 19:11-16

46:18
1 Kgs 18:42
Ps 89:12
Jer 48:15

46:19
Isa 20:4
Ezek 30:13

46:20
Isa 34:7
Jer 48:44
Obad 13

46:22
Isa 10:34

46:25
Isa 20:5,6
Jer 43:12,13
Ezek 30:13-16

46:26
Jer 44:30
Ezek 29:8-14
32:11

46:27
Isa 41:13,14
Jer 23:3,4

46:28
Ps 46:7
Isa 43:2
Jer 10:24
Amos 9:8,9

47:1
Jer 25:17,20

47:2
Isa 14:31

47:3
Jer 8:16

47:4
Isa 14:31

47:5
Jer 25:19,20
Amos 1:7,8
Zeph 2:4,7; 9:5

the north country beside the river Euphrates! 11Go up to Gilead for medicine, O virgin daughter of Egypt! Yet there is no cure for your wounds. Though you have used many medicines, there is no healing for you. 12The nations have heard of your shame. The earth is filled with your cry of despair and defeat; your mightiest soldiers will stumble across each other and fall together.

13Then God gave Jeremiah this message concerning the coming of Nebuchadnezzar, king of Babylon, to attack Egypt:

14Shout it out in Egypt; publish it in the cities of Migdol, Memphis and Tahpanhes! Mobilize for battle, for the sword of destruction shall devour all around you. 15Why has Apis, your bull god, fled in terror? Because the Lord knocked him down before your enemies. 16Vast multitudes fall in heaps. (Then the remnant of the Jews will say, "Come, let us return again to Judah where we were born and get away from all this slaughter here!")

17Rename Pharaoh Hophra and call him "The Man with No Power But with Plenty of Noise!"

18As I live, says the King, the Lord of Hosts, one is coming against Egypt who is as tall as Mount Tabor or Mount Carmel by the sea! 19Pack up; get ready to leave for exile, you citizens of Egypt, for the city of Memphis shall be utterly destroyed, and left without a soul alive. 20, 21Egypt is sleek as a heifer, but a gadfly sends her running—a gadfly from the north! Even her famed mercenaries have become like frightened calves. They turn and run, for it is the day of great calamity for Egypt, a time of great punishment. 22, 23Silent as a serpent gliding away, Egypt flees; the invading army marches in. The numberless soldiers cut down your people like woodsmen who clear a forest of its trees. 24Egypt is as helpless as a girl before these men from the north.

25The Lord, the God of Israel, says: I will punish Amon, god of Thebes, and all the other gods of Egypt. I will punish Pharaoh too, and all who trust in him. 26I will deliver them into the hands of those who want them killed—into the hands of Nebuchadnezzar, king of Babylon, and his army. But afterwards the land shall recover from the ravages of war.

27But don't you be afraid, O my people who return to your own land, don't be dismayed; for I will save you from far away and bring your children from a distant land. Yes, Israel shall return and be at rest and nothing shall make her afraid. 28Fear not, O Jacob, my servant, says the Lord, for I am with you. I will destroy all the nations to which I have exiled you, but I will not destroy you. I will punish you, but only enough to correct you.

The Philistines

47 This is God's message to Jeremiah concerning the Philistines of Gaza, before the city was captured by the Egyptian army.

2The Lord says: A flood is coming from the north to overflow the land of the Philistines; it will destroy their cities and everything in them. Strong men will scream in terror and all the land will weep. 3Hear the clattering hoofs and rumbling wheels as the chariots go rushing by; fathers flee without a backward glance at their helpless children, 4for the time has come when all the Philistines and their allies from Tyre and Sidon will be destroyed. For the Lord is destroying the Philistines, those colonists from Caphtor. 5The cities of Gaza and Ashkelon will be razed to the

47:1 *before the city was captured.* In 609 B.C., the year King Josiah died.

46:17 In 589 B.C. when Nebuchadnezzar beseiged Jerusalem, Pharaoh Hophra marched against him at King Zedekiah's invitation. But when the Babylonians stood up to the Egyptians, Hophra and his troops retreated. Jeremiah had prophesied that Hophra would be killed by his enemies (44:30). This was fulfilled nearly 20 years later when Hophra's co-regent Amasis led a revolt.

46:28 God punished his people in order to bring them back to himself, and he punishes us to correct and purify us. No one welcomes punishment, but we should all welcome its results: correction and purity.

47:1 Located on the coastal plain next to Judah, Philistia had always been a thorn in Israel's side. The two nations battled constantly. Other prophets who spoke against Philistia include: Isaiah (14:28–32); Ezekiel (25:15–17); Amos (1:6–8); and Zephaniah (2:4–7).

47:5 The Anakim were called giants in Deuteronomy 2:10. Seeing these people in the Promised Land made the Israelites afraid to enter it the first time (Deuteronomy 1:28).

ground and lie in ruins. O descendants of the Anakim, how you will lament and mourn!

6O sword of the Lord, when will you be at rest again? Go back into your scabbard; rest and be still! 7But how can it be still when the Lord has sent it on an errand? For the city of Ashkelon and those living along the sea must be destroyed.

47:6
Jer 12:12
47:7
Mic 6:9

The Moabites

48 This is the message of the Lord of Hosts, the God of Israel, against Moab: Woe to the city of Nebo, for it shall lie in ruins. The city of Kiriathaim and its forts are overwhelmed and captured. 2, 3, 4No one will ever brag about Moab any more, for there is a plot against her life. In Heshbon, plans have been completed to destroy her. "Come," they say, "we will cut her off from being a nation." In Madmen all is silent. And then the roar of battle will surge against Horonaim, for all Moab is being destroyed. Her crying will be heard as far away as Zoar. 5Her refugees will climb the hills of Luhith, weeping bitterly, while cries of terror rise from the city below. 6Flee for your lives; hide in the wilderness! 7For you trusted in your wealth and skill; therefore you shall perish. Your god Chemosh, with his priests and princes, shall be taken away to distant lands!

8All the villages and cities, whether they be on the plateaus or in the valleys, shall be destroyed, for the Lord has said it. 9Oh, for wings for Moab that she could fly away, for her cities shall be left without a living soul. 10Cursed be those withholding their swords from your blood, refusing to do the work that God has given them!

11From her earliest history Moab has lived there undisturbed from all invasions. She is like wine that has not been poured from flask to flask, and is fragrant and smooth. But now she shall have the pouring out of exile! 12The time is coming soon, the Lord has said, when he will send troublemakers to spill her out from jar to jar and then shatter the jars! 13Then at last Moab shall be ashamed of her idol Chemosh, as Israel was of her calf-idol at Bethel.

14Do you remember that boast of yours: "We are heroes, mighty men of war"? 15But now Moab is to be destroyed; her destroyer is on the way; her choicest youth are doomed to slaughter, says the King, the Lord Almighty. 16Calamity is coming fast to Moab.

17O friends of Moab, weep for her and cry! See how the strong, the beautiful is shattered! 18Come down from your glory and sit in the dust, O people of Dibon, for those destroying Moab shall shatter Dibon too, and tear down all her towers. 19Those in Aroer stand anxiously beside the road to watch, and shout to those who flee from Moab, "What has happened there?"

20And they reply, "Moab lies in ruins; weep and wail. Tell it by the banks of the Arnon, that Moab is destroyed."

21All the cities of the tableland lie in ruins too, for God's judgment has been poured out upon them all—on Holon and Jahzah and Mepha-ath, 22and Dibon and Nebo and Beth-diblathaim, 23and Kiria-thaim and Beth-gamul and Beth-meon, 24and Keri-oth and Bozrah—and all the cities of the land of Moab, far and near.

25The strength of Moab is ended—her horns are cut off; her arms are broken. 26Let her stagger and fall like a drunkard, for she has rebelled against the Lord. Moab shall wallow in her vomit, scorned by all. 27For you scorned Israel and robbed her, and were happy at her fall.

28O people of Moab, flee from your cities and live in the caves like doves that nest in the clefts of the rocks. 29We have all heard of the pride of Moab, for it is very great. We know your loftiness, your arrogance and your haughty heart. 30I know

48:1
Num 32:37,38
Ezek 25:9,10
48:2
Isa 15:4,5
16:13,14
48:5
Isa 15:5
48:7
Num 21:29
Jer 9:23
48:8
Josh 13:10,
17,21
48:9
Isa 16:2
48:10
1 Kgs 20:42
Jer 47:6,7
48:11
Zech 1:15
48:13
1 Kgs 12:29
Isa 45:16
Hos 10:6
48:14
Ps 33:16,17
Isa 10:13-16
48:18
Josh 13:9,17
Isa 47:1
48:19
Josh 12:2
48:20
Num 21:13
Isa 16:7
48:21
Josh 13:18
Isa 15:4
48:23
Josh 13:19
48:24
Amos 2:2
48:25
Ps 10:15; 75:10
Zech 1:19-21
48:26
Jer 25:15,27
48:27
Lam 2:15-17
Zeph 2:8
48:28
Ps 55:6
Song 2:14
Isa 2:19
48:29
Ps 138:6
Isa 16:6
Zeph 2:8

48:1 The Moabites were descendants of Lot through an incestuous relationship with one of his daughters (Genesis 19:30-37). They led the Israelites into idolatry (Numbers 25:1-3) and joined the bands of raiders Nebuchadnezzar sent into Judah in 602 B.C. They were later destroyed by Babylon.

48:13 After Israel divided into northern and southern kingdoms, the Northern Kingdom set up calf-idols in Bethel and Dan to keep people from going to worship in Jerusalem, capital of the Southern Kingdom (1 Kings 12:28—13:10).

her insolence, the Lord has said, but her boasts are false—her helplessness is great. ³¹Yes, I wail for Moab, my heart is broken for the men of Kir-heres.

³²O men of Sibmah, rich in vineyards, I weep for you even more than for Jazer. For the destroyer has cut off your spreading tendrils and harvested your grapes and summer fruits. He has plucked you bare! ³³Joy and gladness are gone from fruitful Moab. The presses yield no wine; no one treads the grapes with shouts of joy. There is shouting, yes, but not the shouting of joy. ³⁴Instead the awful cries of terror and pain rise from all over the land—from Heshbon clear across to Elealeh and to Jahaz; from Zoar to Horonaim and to Eglath-she-lishiyah. The pastures of Nimrim are deserted now.

³⁵For the Lord says: I have put a stop to Moab's worshiping false gods and burning incense to idols. ³⁶Sad sings my heart for Moab and Kir-heres, for all their wealth has disappeared. ³⁷They shave their heads and beards in anguish, and slash their hands and put on clothes of sackcloth. ³⁸Crying and sorrow will be in every Moabite home and on the streets; for I have smashed and shattered Moab like an old, unwanted bottle. ³⁹How it is broken! Hear the wails! See the shame of Moab! For she is a sign of horror and of scoffing to her neighbors now.

⁴⁰A vulture circles ominously above the land of Moab, says the Lord. ⁴¹Her cities are fallen; her strongholds are seized. The hearts of her mightiest warriors fail with fear like women in the pains of giving birth. ⁴²Moab shall no longer be a nation, for she has boasted against the Lord. ⁴³Fear and traps and treachery shall be your lot, O Moab, says the Lord. ⁴⁴He who flees shall fall in a trap and he who escapes from the trap shall run into a snare. I will see to it that you do not get away, for the time of your judgment has come. ⁴⁵They flee to Heshbon, unable to go farther. But a fire comes from Heshbon—Sihon's ancestral home—and devours the land from end to end with all its rebellious people.

⁴⁶Woe to you, O Moab; the people of the god Chemosh are destroyed, and your sons and daughters are taken away as slaves. ⁴⁷But in the latter days, says the Lord, I will reestablish Moab. (Here the prophecy concerning Moab ends.)

The Ammonites

49 What is this you are doing? Why are you living in the cities of the Jews? Aren't there Jews enough to fill them up? Didn't they inherit them from me? Why then have you, who worship Milcom, taken over Gad and all its cities? ²I will punish you for this, the Lord declares, by destroying your city of Rabbah. It shall become a desolate heap, and the neighboring towns shall be burned. Then Israel shall come and take back her land from you again. She shall dispossess those who dispossessed her, says the Lord.

³Cry out, O Heshbon, for Ai is destroyed! Weep, daughter of Rabbah! Put on garments of mourning; weep and wail, hiding in the hedges, for your god Milcom shall be exiled along with his princes and priests. ⁴You are proud of your fertile valleys, but they will soon be ruined. O wicked daughter, you trusted in your wealth and thought no one could ever harm you. ⁵But see, I will bring terror upon you, says the Lord, the Lord Almighty. For all your neighbors shall drive you from your land and none shall help your exiles as they flee. ⁶But afterward I will restore the fortunes of the Ammonites, says the Lord.

The Edomites

⁷The Lord says: Where are all your wise men of days gone by? Is there not one

48:31
Isa 15:5
16:7,11

48:32
Isa 16:8,9

48:33
Isa 16:10

48:34
Gen 13:10
Isa 15:4-6

48:36
Isa 16:11

48:37
Isa 15:2,3

48:38
Jer 25:34

48:40
Jer 49:22

48:41
Jer 30:6; 49:22

48:42
Ps 83:4
Jer 48:26

48:43
Isa 24:17
Lam 3:47

48:44
1 Kgs 19:17
Amos 5:19

48:45
Num 21:27-30
Ps 135:10,11

48:46
Num 21:27-30

48:47
Jer 12:14-17

49:1
1 Kgs 11:5
Ezek 25:2

49:2
2 Sam 11:1
Isa 14:2
Ezek 21:28

49:3
Josh 7:2-5
8:1-29
Jer 48:2

49:4
Ps 62:10,11
Ezek 28:4,5
1 Tim 6:17

49:5
Jer 16:16
Lam 4:15

49:6
Jer 48:47; 49:39

48:31 Kir-heres was a stronghold city in Moab. God's compassion reaches to all creation, even to his enemies.

49:1 The Ammonites were descendants of Lot through an incestuous relationship with one of his daughters (as were the Moabites; see Genesis 19:30–38). They were condemned for stealing land from God's people and for their worship of the idol Molech, to whom they made child-sacrifices.

49:7 The Israelites descended from Jacob and the Edomites from

his twin brother, Esau. So Israel and Edom both descended from Isaac, the father of Jacob and Esau. There was constant conflict between these nations, and Edom rejoiced at the fall of Jerusalem (Obadiah). Teman, a town in the northern part of Edom, was known for its wisdom and was the hometown of Eliphaz, one of Job's friends (Job 2:11). But even the wisdom of Teman could not save Edom from God's wrath.

left in all of Teman? 8Flee to the remotest parts of the desert, O people of Dedan; for when I punish Edom, I will punish you! 9, 10Those who gather grapes leave a few for the poor, and even thieves don't take everything, but I will strip bare the land of Esau, and there will be no place to hide. Her children, her brothers, her neighbors—all will be destroyed—and she herself will perish too. 11(But I will preserve your fatherless children who remain, and let your widows depend upon me.)

12The Lord says to Edom: If the innocent must suffer, how much more must you! You shall not go unpunished! You must drink this cup of judgment! 13For I have sworn by my own name, says the Lord, that Bozrah shall become heaps of ruins, cursed and mocked; and her cities shall be eternal wastes.

14I have heard this message from the Lord:

He has sent a messenger to call the nations to form a coalition against Edom and destroy her. 15I will make her weak among the nations and despised by all, says the Lord. 16You have been fooled by your fame and your pride, living there in the mountains of Petra, in the clefts of the rocks. But though you live among the peaks with the eagles, I will bring you down, says the Lord.

17The fate of Edom will be horrible; all who go by will be appalled, and gasp at the sight. 18Your cities will become as silent as Sodom and Gomorrah and their neighboring towns, says the Lord. No one will live there anymore. 19I will send against them one who will come like a lion from the wilds of Jordan stalking the sheep in the fold. Suddenly Edom shall be destroyed, and I will appoint over the Edomites the person of my choice. For who is like me and who can call me to account? 20What shepherd can defy me? Take note: The Lord will certainly do this to Edom and also the people of Teman—even little children will be dragged away as slaves! It will be a shocking thing to see.

21The earth shakes with the noise of Edom's fall; the cry of the people is heard as far away as the Red Sea. 22The one who will come will fly as swift as a vulture and will spread his wings against Bozrah. Then the courage of the mightiest warriors will disappear like that of women in labor.

Damascus

23The cities of Hamath and Arpad are stricken with fear, for they have heard the news of their doom. Their hearts are troubled like a wild sea in a raging storm. 24Damascus has become feeble and all her people turn to flee. Fear, anguish and sorrow have gripped her as they do women in labor. 25O famous city, city of joy, how you are forsaken now! 26Your young men lie dead in the streets; your entire army shall be destroyed in one day, says the Lord Almighty. 27And I will start a fire at the edge of Damascus that shall burn up the palaces of Benhadad.

Kedar and Hazor

28This prophecy is about Kedar and the kingdoms of Hazor, which are going to be destroyed by Nebuchadnezzar, king of Babylon, for the Lord will send him to destroy them. 29Their flocks and their tents will be captured, says the Lord, with all their household goods. Their camels will be taken away, and all around will be the shouts of panic, "We are surrounded and doomed!" 30Flee for your lives, says the Lord. Go deep into the deserts, O people of Hazor, for Nebuchadnezzar, king of Babylon, has plotted against you and is preparing to destroy you.

49:8
Isa 21:13
Jer 25:23

49:9
Isa 17:14
Jer 13:26
Obad 5

49:11
Ps 68:5
Zech 7:10

49:12
Jer 25:15,28,29
1 Pet 4:17

49:13
Isa 34:6,9-15

49:14
Jer 50:14
Obad 1-4

49:15
Lk 1:51

49:16
Isa 14:13-15
Amos 9:2

49:17
Jer 51:37
Ezek 35:7

49:18
Gen 19:24,25

49:19
Isa 46:9
Jer 50:44

49:20
Isa 14:24,27
Jer 50:45

49:21
Jer 50:46

49:22
Isa 13:8
Jer 48:40,41

49:23
Ex 15:15
Isa 10:9; 57:20
Jer 39:5
Amos 6:2

49:25
Jer 51:41

49:27
1 Kgs 15:18-20
Amos 1:3-5

49:28
Isa 21:16,17

49:30
Jer 25:8,9,24
27:6

49:8 Dedan was a flourishing caravan city. God tells its inhabitants to flee to the desert or they will also be destroyed. Teman and Dedan were at opposite ends of the country, so this shows the completeness of God's destruction of Edom.

49:16 Edom was destroyed because of her pride. Pride destroys individuals as well as nations. It makes us think we can take care of ourselves without God's help. Even serving God and others can lead us into pride. Take inventory of your life and service for God,

asking God to point out and remove any pride you may have.

49:23-26 Damascus was the capital of Syria, north of Israel. This city was defeated by both Assyria and Babylon. Nebuchadnezzar attacked Damascus in 605 B.C. and defeated it (Amos 1:4, 5). It is difficult to attribute the defeat of the army to a particular event, but God utterly destroyed Syria.

49:28 Kedar and Hazor were nomadic tribes east of Israel and south of Syria, in the desert. In 599 B.C. Nebuchadnezzar destroyed them.

49:31
Judg 18:7
Isa 47:8

49:32
Jer 9:25,26
25:23

49:33
Isa 13:20-22
Zeph 2:9,13-15

49:34
Gen 10:22
2 Kgs 24:17,18
Isa 11:11
Dan 8:2

49:36
Ezek 5:10
Rev 7:1

49:37
Jer 6:19; 30:24

³¹"Go," said the Lord to King Nebuchadnezzar. "Attack those wealthy Bedouin tribes living alone in the desert without a care in the world, boasting that they are self-sufficient—that they need neither walls nor gates. ³²Their camels and cattle shall all be yours, and I will scatter these heathen to the winds. From all directions I will bring calamity upon them."

³³Hazor shall be a home for wild animals of the desert. No one shall ever live there again. It shall be desolate forever.

Elam

³⁴God's message against Elam came to Jeremiah in the beginning of the reign of Zedekiah, king of Judah:

³⁵The Lord says: I will destroy the army of Elam, ³⁶and I will scatter the people of Elam to the four winds; they shall be exiled to countries throughout the world. ³⁷My fierce anger will bring great evil upon Elam, says the Lord, and I will cause her enemies to wipe her out. ³⁸And I will set my throne in Elam, says the Lord. I will destroy her king and princes. ³⁹But in the latter days I will bring the people back, says the Lord.

Babylon

50 This is the message from the Lord against Babylon and the Chaldeans, spoken by Jeremiah the prophet:

50:2
Isa 46:1
Jer 51:31

50:3
Zeph 1:3

50:4
Isa 11:12,13
Ezra 3:12,13
Hos 1:11
Jer 31:9

50:5
Isa 55:3
Jer 6:16; 32:40

50:6
Isa 53:6
Jer 13:16
Ezek 34:15,16
Mt 9:36

50:7
Jer 17:13

50:10
Jer 51:24,35

50:12
Jer 22:6

50:13
Jer 18:16

50:14
Hab 2:8,17

²Tell all the world that Babylon will be destroyed; her god Marduk will be utterly disgraced! ³For a nation shall come down upon her from the north with such destruction that no one shall live in her again; all shall be gone—both men and animals shall flee.

⁴Then the people of Israel and Judah shall join together, weeping and seeking the Lord their God. ⁵They shall ask the way to Zion and start back home again. "Come," they will say, "let us be united to the Lord with an eternal pledge that will never be broken again."

⁶My people have been lost sheep. Their shepherds led them astray and then turned them loose in the mountains. They lost their way and didn't remember how to get back to the fold. ⁷All who found them devoured them and said, "We are permitted to attack them freely, for they have sinned against the Lord, the God of justice, the hope of their fathers."

⁸But now, flee from Babylon, the land of the Chaldeans; lead my people home again, ⁹for see, I am raising up an army of great nations from the north and I will bring them against Babylon to attack her, and she shall be destroyed. The enemies' arrows go straight to the mark; they do not miss! ¹⁰And Babylon shall be sacked until everyone is sated with loot, says the Lord.

¹¹Though you were glad, O Chaldeans, plunderers of my people, and are fat as cows that feed in lush pastures, and neigh like stallions, ¹²yet your mother shall be overwhelmed with shame, for you shall become the least of the nations—a wilderness, a dry and desert land. ¹³Because of the anger of the Lord, Babylon shall become deserted wasteland, and all who pass by shall be appalled and shall mock at her for all her wounds.

¹⁴Yes, prepare to fight with Babylon, all you nations round about; let the archers

49:32 *these heathen,* literally, "those who cut the corners of their hair."

49:34 Elam lay east of Babylon and was attacked by Nebuchadnezzar in 597 B.C. Later it became the nucleus of the Persian Empire (Daniel 8:2) and the residence of Darius.

49:38 The throne represents God's judgment and sovereignty. He would preside over Elam's destruction. He is the King over all kings, including Elam's.

50:1ff Babylon is another name for the nation of the Chaldeans. At the height of its power, this empire seemed immovable. But when Babylon had finished serving God's purpose of punishing Judah for her sins, it would be punished and crushed for its own.

Babylon was destroyed in 539 B.C. by the Medo-Persians (Daniel 5:30, 31). Babylon is also used in Scripture as a symbol of all evil. This message can thus apply to the end times when God wipes out all evil, once and for all.

50:3 The nation from the north was Medo-Persia, an alliance of Media and Persia which would become the next world power. Cyrus took the city of Babylon by surprise and brought the nation to its knees in 539 B.C. (Daniel 5:30, 31). The complete destruction of the city was accomplished by later Persian kings.

shoot at her; spare no arrows, for she has sinned against the Lord. ¹⁵Shout against her from every side. Look! She surrenders! Her walls have fallen. The Lord has taken vengeance. Do to her as she has done! ¹⁶Let the farm hands all depart. Let them rush back to their own lands as the enemies advance.

¹⁷The Israelites are like sheep the lions chase. First the king of Assyria ate them up; then Nebuchadnezzar, the king of Babylon, crunched their bones. ¹⁸Therefore the Lord, the God of Israel, says: Now I will punish the king of Babylon and his land as I punished the king of Assyria. ¹⁹And I will bring Israel home again to her own land, to feed in the fields of Carmel and Bashan and to be happy once more on Mount Ephraim and Mount Gilead. ²⁰In those days, says the Lord, no sin shall be found in Israel or in Judah, for I will pardon the remnant I preserve.

²¹Go up, O my warriors, against the land of Merathaim and against the people of Pekod. Yes, march against Babylon, the land of rebels, a land that I will judge! Annihilate them, as I have commanded you. ²²Let there be the shout of battle in the land, a shout of great destruction. ²³Babylon, the mightiest hammer in all the earth, lies broken and shattered. Babylon is desolate among the nations! ²⁴O Babylon, I have set a trap for you and you are caught, for you have fought against the Lord.

²⁵The Lord has opened his armory and brought out weapons to explode his wrath upon his enemies. The terror that befalls Babylon will be the work of the Lord God. ²⁶Yes, come against her from distant lands; break open her granaries; knock down her walls and houses into heaps of ruins and utterly destroy her; let nothing be left. ²⁷Not even her cattle—woe to them, too! Kill them all! For the time has come for Babylon to be devastated.

²⁸But my people will flee; they will escape back to their own country to tell how the Lord their God has broken forth in fury upon those who destroyed his Temple.

²⁹Send out a call for archers to come to Babylon; surround the city so that none can escape. Do to her as she has done to others, for she has haughtily defied the Lord, the Holy One of Israel. ³⁰Her young men will fall in the streets and die; her warriors will all be killed. ³¹For see, I am against you, O people so proud; and now your day of reckoning has come. ³²Land of pride, you will stumble and fall and no one will raise you up, for the Lord will light a fire in the cities of Babylon that will burn everything around them.

³³The Lord says: The people of Israel and Judah have been wronged. Their captors hold them and refuse to let them go. ³⁴But their Redeemer is strong. His name is the Lord Almighty. He will plead for them and see that they are freed to live again in quietness in Israel.

As for the people of Babylon—there is no rest for them! ³⁵The sword of destruction shall smite the Chaldeans, says the Lord. It shall smite the people of Babylon—her princes and wise men too. ³⁶All her wise counselors shall become fools! Panic shall seize her mightiest warriors! ³⁷War shall devour her horses and chariots, and her allies from other lands shall become as weak as women. Her treasures shall all be robbed; ³⁸even her water supply will fail. And why? Because the whole land is full of images, and the people are madly in love with their idols.

³⁹Therefore this city of Babylon shall become inhabited by ostriches and jackals; it shall be a home for the wild animals of the desert. Never again shall it be lived in by human beings; it shall lie desolate forever. ⁴⁰The Lord declares that he will destroy Babylon just as he destroyed Sodom and Gomorrah and their neighboring towns. No one has lived in them since, and no one will live again in Babylon.

50:15	Ps 137:8
50:16	Jer 46:16
50:17	2 Kgs 18:9-13 24:1,10-12 Jer 4:7
50:18	Isa 10:12 Nah 1:1 3:7,18,19
50:19	Jer 31:10
50:20	Jer 31:34 Mic 7:19
50:22	Jer 4:19-21
50:23	Jer 51:20-24
50:24	Job 9:4; 40:2,9 Jer 48:43
50:25	Isa 13:4,5
50:26	Isa 14:23
50:27	Ps 37:13 Ezek 7:7
50:28	Ps 149:6-9 Isa 48:20 Lam 1:10
50:29	Ex 10:3 Ps 137:8
50:30	Jer 18:21
50:31	Nah 2:13
50:32	Isa 10:12-15 Jer 21:14
50:33	Isa 14:17
50:34	Isa 14:3-7 43:14 Mic 7:9
50:35	Jer 47:6
50:36	Isa 44:25
50:37	Ps 20:7,8 Jer 25:19,20 48:41
50:39	Isa 13:20
50:40	Lk 17:28-30 2 Pet 2:6 Jude 7

50:17-20 God would punish wicked Babylon as he punished Assyria for what they had done to Israel. Assyria was crushed by Babylon, over which it had once ruled. Babylon in turn would be crushed by Medo-Persia, which it then ruled. These verses also look to the time when the Messiah will rule and Israel will be fully restored. No sin will then be found in Israel because those who sought God will be forgiven.

50:21 Merathaim was located in southern Babylonia; Pekod was in eastern Babylonia.

50:32 Babylon, along with several other nations, is called a "land of pride." Pride comes from feeling self-sufficient, or believing that we don't need God. The proud nation or person, however, will eventually fail due to refusing to recognize God as the ultimate power. Getting rid of pride is not easy, but we can admit it and ask God to forgive us and help us struggle against it. The best antidote to pride is to focus your attention on the greatness and goodness of God.

50:39 Babylon remains a wasteland to this day. See Isaiah 13:22.

50:41
Isa 13:2-5

50:42
Isa 13:17,18
Hab 1:8

50:43
Jer 30:6

50:44
Num 16:5
Job 41:10
Isa 46:9

50:46
Jer 10:10
Ezek 26:18

51:1
Jer 4:11,12

51:2
Jer 15:7
Mt 3:12

51:5
Isa 54:7,8
Jer 33:24-26

51:6
Num 16:26

51:7
Jer 25:15
Rev 14:8; 18:3

51:9
Jer 46:16

51:10
Isa 40:2
Mic 7:9

51:11
Joel 3:9,10

51:12
Jer 4:28

51:13
Hab 2:9-11

51:14
Nah 3:15

51:15
Ps 146:5,6
Jer 10:12-16
Rom 1:20

51:16
Job 37:2-5
Ps 18:13; 135:7
Jonah 1:4

51:17
Ps 73:22
Isa 44:18-20
Hab 2:18,19

⁴¹See them coming! A great army from the north! It is accompanied by many kings called by God from many lands. ⁴²They are fully armed for slaughter; they are cruel and show no mercy; their battle cry roars like the surf against the shoreline. O Babylon, they ride against you fully ready for the battle.

⁴³When the king of Babylon received the dispatch, his hands fell helpless at his sides; pangs of terror gripped him like the pangs of a woman in labor.

⁴⁴*I will send against them an invader who will come upon them suddenly, like a lion from the jungles of Jordan that leaps upon the grazing sheep. I will put her defenders to flight and appoint over them whomsoever I please. For who is like me? What ruler can oppose my will? Who can call me to account?* ⁴⁵*Listen to the plan of the Lord against Babylon, the land of the Chaldeans. For even little children shall be dragged away as slaves; oh, the horror; oh, the terror.* ⁴⁶The whole earth shall shake at Babylon's fall, and her cry of despair shall be heard around the world.

Jeremiah predicts the fall of Babylon

51 The Lord says: I will stir up a destroyer against Babylon, against that whole land of the Chaldeans, and destroy it. ²Winnowers shall come and winnow her and blow her away; they shall come from every side to rise against her in her day of trouble. ³The arrows of the enemy shall strike down the bowmen of Babylon and pierce her warriors in their coats of mail. No one shall be spared; both young and old alike shall be destroyed. ⁴They shall fall down slain in the land of the Chaldeans, slashed to death in her streets. ⁵For the Lord Almighty has not forsaken Israel and Judah. He is still their God, but the land of the Chaldeans is filled with sin against the Holy One of Israel.

⁶Flee from Babylon! Save yourselves! Don't get trapped! If you stay, you will be destroyed when God takes his vengeance on all of Babylon's sins. ⁷Babylon has been as a gold cup in the Lord's hands, a cup from which he made the whole earth drink and go mad. ⁸But now, suddenly Babylon too has fallen. Weep for her; give her medicine; perhaps she can yet be healed. ⁹We would help her if we could, but nothing can save her now. Let her go. Abandon her and return to your own land, for God is judging her from heaven. ¹⁰The Lord has vindicated us. Come, let us declare in Jerusalem all the Lord our God has done.

¹¹Sharpen the arrows! Lift up the shields! For the Lord has stirred up the spirit of the kings of the Medes to march on Babylon and destroy her. This is his vengeance on those who wronged his people and desecrated his Temple. ¹²Prepare your defenses, Babylon! Set many watchmen on your walls; send out an ambush, for the Lord will do all he has said he would concerning Babylon. ¹³O wealthy port, great center of commerce, your end has come; the thread of your life is cut. ¹⁴The Lord Almighty has taken this vow, and sworn to it in his own name: Your cities shall be filled with enemies, like fields filled with locusts in a plague, and they shall lift to the skies their mighty shouts of victory.

¹⁵God made the earth by his power and wisdom. He stretched out the heavens by his understanding. ¹⁶When he speaks there is thunder in the heavens and he causes the vapors to rise around the world; he brings the lightning with the rain and the winds from his treasuries. ¹⁷Compared to him, all men are stupid beasts. They have no wisdom—none at all! The silversmith is dulled by the images he makes, for in

51:5 *the land of the Chaldeans,* implied.

50:44-46 The invader was Cyrus, who attacked Babylon by surprise and overthrew it. The world was shocked that its greatest empire was overthrown so quickly. No amount of earthly power can last forever.

51:2 Winnowers worked to separate the wheat from the chaff. When they threw the mixture into the air, the wind blew away the worthless chaff while the wheat settled to the ground. Babylon would be blown away like chaff in the wind. (See also Matthew 3:12 where John the Baptist says Jesus will separate the wheat from the chaff.)

51:11 Cyrus, king of Persia, had allied with Babylon to defeat Nineveh (capital of the Assyrian Empire) in 612 B.C. Then the Medes joined Persia to defeat Babylon (539 B.C.).

51:17-19 It is foolish to trust in man-made images rather than God. It is easy to think that things we see and touch will bring us more security than God. But things rust, rot, and decay. God is eternal. Why put your trust in something that will disappear within a few years?

making them he lies; for he calls them gods, when there is not a breath of life in them at all! 18Idols are nothing! They are lies! And the time is coming when God will come and see, and shall destroy them all. 19But the God of Israel is no idol! For he made everything there is, and Israel is his nation; the Lord Almighty is his name.

51:19 Jer 10:16

20Cyrus is God's battleaxe and sword. I will use you, says the Lord, to break nations in pieces and to destroy many kingdoms. 21With you I will crush armies, destroying the horse and his rider, the chariot and the charioteer— 22yes, and the civilians too, both old and young, young men and maidens, 23shepherds and flocks, farmers and oxen, captains and rulers; 24before your eyes I will repay Babylon and all the Chaldeans for all the evil they have done to my people, says the Lord.

51:20 Mic 4:12,13
51:21 Ex 15:1 Isa 43:17
51:22 Isa 13:15,16,18 Rev 8:8

25For see, I am against you, O mighty mountain, Babylon, destroyer of the earth! I will lift my hand against you and roll you down from your heights and leave you, a burnt-out mountain. 26You shall be desolate forever; even your stones shall never be used for building again. You shall be completely wiped out.

51:25 Rev 8:8
51:26 Isa 13:19-22

27Signal many nations to mobilize for war on Babylon. Sound the battle cry; bring out the armies of Ararat, Minni, and Ashkenaz. Appoint a leader; bring a multitude of horses! 28Bring against her the armies of the kings of the Medes and their generals, and the armies of all the countries they rule.

51:27 Gen 8:4; 10:3 2 Kgs 19:37 Isa 13:2-5

29Babylon trembles and writhes in pain, for all that the Lord has planned against her stands unchanged. Babylon will be left desolate without a living soul. 30Her mightiest soldiers no longer fight; they stay in their barracks. Their courage is gone; they have become as women. The invaders have burned the houses and broken down the city gates. 31Messengers from every side come running to the king to tell him all is lost! 32All the escape routes are blocked; the fortifications are burning and the army is in panic.

51:29 Jer 10:10 Amos 8:8
51:30 Isa 13:7,8; 45:1

33For the Lord, the God of Israel, says: Babylon is like the wheat upon a threshing floor; in just a little while the flailing will begin.

51:33 Isa 21:10 Joel 3:13

34, 35The Jews in Babylon say, "Nebuchadnezzar, king of Babylon, has eaten and crushed us and emptied out our strength; he has swallowed us like a great monster and filled his belly with our riches and cast us out of our own country. May Babylon be repaid for all she did to us! May she be paid in full for all our blood she spilled!"

51:34 Job 20:15 Ps 137:8 Isa 24:1-3

36And the Lord replies: I will be your lawyer; I will plead your case; I will avenge you. I will dry up her river, her water supply, 37and Babylon shall become a heap of ruins, haunted by jackals, a land horrible to see, incredible, without a living soul. 38In their drunken feasts, the men of Babylon roar like lions. 39And while they lie inflamed with all their wine, I will prepare a different kind of feast for them, and make them drink until they fall unconscious to the floor, to sleep forever, never to waken again, says the Lord. 40I will bring them like lambs to the slaughter, like rams and goats.

51:36 Ps 140:12 Rom 12:19
51:39 Ps 76:5 Jer 25:27

41How Babylon is fallen—great Babylon, lauded by all the earth! The world can scarcely believe its eyes at Babylon's fall! 42The sea has risen upon Babylon; she is covered by its waves. 43Her cities lie in ruins—she is a dry wilderness where no one lives nor even travelers pass by. 44And I will punish Bel, the god of Babylon, and pull from his mouth what he has taken. The nations shall no longer come and worship him; the wall of Babylon has fallen.

51:43 Isa 13:20
51:44 Isa 2:2 Ezra 1:7
51:45 Gen 19:12-16 Isa 48:20 Acts 2:40

45O my people, flee from Babylon; save yourselves from the fierce anger of the Lord. 46But don't panic when you hear the first rumor of approaching forces. For

51:46 Isa 19:2

51:20 *Cyrus*, literally, "You are . . ." Cyrus was used of God to conquer Babylon. See also Isa 44:28; 45:1.
51:26 *You shall be desolate forever.* This complete destruction of the city of Babylon was accomplished by later Persian kings. Jeremiah here sees the long-range picture of the city's history, and does not confine himself to Cyrus.

51:33 Grain was threshed on a threshing floor, where sheaves were brought from the field. The stalks of grain were distributed on the floor, a large level section of hard ground. There the grain was crushed to separate the kernels from the stalk. Flailing was beating the grain with a wooden tool. Sometimes a wooden sledge was pulled over the grain by animals to break the kernels loose.

Babylon would soon be trampled and flailed as God judged her for her sins.

51:36 This verse may refer to an event accomplished by Cyrus, who took Babylon by surprise by diverting the river far upstream and walking in on the dry riverbed. More likely it is saying that Babylon will be deprived of life-giving water. Unlike Jerusalem, Babylon will not be restored.

rumors will keep coming year by year. Then there will be a time of civil war as the governors of Babylon fight against each other. 47For the time is surely coming when I will punish this great city and all her idols; her dead shall lie in the streets. 48Heaven and earth shall rejoice, for out of the north shall come destroying armies against Babylon, says the Lord. 49Just as Babylon killed the people of Israel, so must she be killed. 50Go, you who escaped the sword! Don't stand and watch—flee while you can! Remember the Lord and return to Jerusalem far away!

51 *"We are ashamed because the Temple of the Lord has been defiled by foreigners from Babylon."*

52Yes, says the Lord. But the time is coming for the destruction of the idols of Babylon. All through the land will be heard the groans of the wounded. 53Though Babylon be as powerful as heaven, though she increase her strength immeasurably, she shall die, says the Lord.

54Listen! Hear the cry of great destruction out of Babylon, the land the Chaldeans rule! 55For the Lord is destroying Babylon; her mighty voice is stilled as the waves roar in upon her. 56Destroying armies come and slay her mighty men; all her weapons break in hands, for the Lord God gives just punishment and is giving Babylon all her due. 57I will make drunk her princes, wise men, rulers, captains, warriors. They shall sleep and not wake up again! So says the King, the Lord Almighty. 58For the wide walls of Babylon shall be leveled to the ground and her high gates shall be burned; the builders from many lands have worked in vain—their work shall be destroyed by fire!

59During the fourth year of Zedekiah's reign, this message came to Jeremiah to give to Seraiah (son of Neriah, son of Mahseiah), concerning Seraiah's capture and exile to Babylon along with Zedekiah, king of Judah. (Seraiah was quartermaster of Zedekiah's army.) 60Jeremiah wrote on a scroll all the terrible things God had scheduled against Babylon—all the words written above— 61, 62and gave the scroll to Seraiah and said to him, "When you get to Babylon, read what I have written and say, 'Lord, you have said that you will destroy Babylon so that not a living creature will remain, and it will be abandoned forever.' 63Then, when you have finished reading the scroll, tie a rock to it and throw it into the Euphrates River, 64and say, 'So shall Babylon sink, never more to rise, because of the evil I am bringing upon her.'" (This ends Jeremiah's messages.)

2. Details about the fall of Jerusalem *(Events told about in chapter 39)*

52 Zedekiah was twenty-one years old when he became king, and he reigned eleven years in Jerusalem. His mother's name was Hamutal (daughter of Jeremiah of Libnah). 2But he was a wicked king, just as Jehoiakim had been. 3Things became so bad at last that the Lord, in his anger, saw to it that Zedekiah rebelled against the king of Babylon until he and the people of Israel were ejected from the Lord's presence in Jerusalem and Judah, and were taken away as captives to Babylon.

4In the ninth year of Zedekiah's reign, on the tenth day of the tenth month, Nebuchadnezzar, king of Babylon, came with all his army against Jerusalem and built forts around it, 5and laid siege to the city for two years. 6Then finally, on the ninth day of the fourth month, when the famine in the city was very serious, with the last of the food entirely gone, 7the people in the city tore a hole in the city wall

51:47
Isa 21:9; 46:1,2

51:48
Isa 44:23

51:51
Lam 1:10

51:53
Job 20:6,7

51:55
Ps 69:2

51:56
Ps 76:3; 94:1,2

51:57
Ps 76:5,6

51:58
Isa 45:1,2
Hab 2:13

51:62
Isa 13:19-22
Ezek 35:9

51:63
Rev 18:21

51:64
Nah 1:8,9

52:1
2 Kgs 8:22
24:18-20

52:2
Jer 36:30,31

52:3
2 Chron 36:13

52:4
2 Kgs 25:1-7
Jer 39:1

52:6
Jer 38:9

52:7
Jer 39:2,4-7

51:59 *concerning Seraiah's capture.* This event occurred six years after this prophecy.

51:51 The people were paralyzed with guilt over their past. The Babylonian armies had desecrated the Temple and the people were ashamed to return to Jerusalem. But God told them to return to the city, for he would destroy Babylon for its sins.

51:59 Jeremiah could not visit Babylon, so he sent the message with Seraiah, the officer who cared for the comforts of the army. Seriah was probably Baruch's brother (32:12).

51:60–64 In this last of Jeremiah's messages, we find again the twin themes of God's sovereignty and his judgment. Babylon has been allowed to oppress the people of Israel, but now Babylon

itself will be judged. Although God brings good out of evil, he does not allow evil to remain unpunished. The wicked may succeed for a while, but resist the temptation to follow them or you may share in their judgment.

52:1ff This chapter provides more detail about the destruction of Jerusalem recorded in chapter 39 (similar material is found in 2 Kings 24:18—25:21). This appendix shows that Jeremiah's prophecies concerning the destruction of Jerusalem and the Babylonian captivity happened just as he predicted. For more information on Zedekiah, see the note on 39:1.

and all the soldiers fled from the city during the night, going out by the gate between the two walls near the king's gardens (for the city was surrounded by the Chaldeans), and made a dash for it across the fields, toward Arabah.

8But the Chaldean soldiers chased them and caught King Zedekiah in some fields near Jericho—for all his army was scattered from him. 9They brought him to the king of Babylon who was staying in the city of Riblah in the kingdom of Hamath, and there judgment was passed upon him. 10He made Zedekiah watch while his sons and all the princes of Judah were killed before his eyes, 11and then his eyes were gouged out and he was taken in chains to Babylon and put in prison for the rest of his life.

12On the tenth day of the fifth month during the nineteenth year of the reign of Nebuchadnezzar, king of Babylon, Nebuzaradan, captain of the guard, arrived in Jerusalem, 13and burned the Temple and the palace and all the larger homes, 14and set the Chaldean army to work tearing down the walls of the city. 15Then he took to Babylon, as captives, some of the poorest of the people—along with those who survived the city's destruction, and those who had deserted Zedekiah and had come over to the Babylonian army, and the tradesmen who were left. 16But he left some of the poorest people to care for the crops as vinedressers and plowmen.

17The Babylonians dismantled the two large bronze pillars that stood at the entrance of the Temple, and the bronze laver and bronze bulls on which it stood, and carted them off to Babylon. 18And he took along all the bronze pots and kettles, and ash shovels used at the altar, and the snuffers, spoons, bowls, and all the other items used in the Temple. 19He also took the firepans and the solid gold and silver candlesticks and cups and bowls.

20The weight of the two enormous pillars and the laver and twelve bulls was tremendous. They had no way of estimating it. (They had been made in the days of King Solomon.) 21For the pillars were each twenty-seven feet high and eighteen feet in circumference, hollow, with three-inch walls. 22The top 7½ feet of each column had bronze carvings, a network of bronze pomegranates. 23There were ninety-six pomegranates on the sides, and on the network round about there were a hundred more.

24, 25The captain of the guard took along with him, as his prisoners, Seraiah the chief priest, and Zephaniah his assistant, the three chief Temple guards, one of the commanding officers of the army, seven of the king's special counselors discovered in the city, and the secretary of the general-in-chief of the Jewish army (who was in charge of recruitment) and sixty other men of importance found hiding. 26He took them to the king of Babylon at Riblah, 27where the king killed them all.

So it was that Judah's exile was accomplished.

28The number of captives taken to Babylon in the seventh year of Nebuchadnezzar's reign was 3,023. 29Then, eleven years later, he took 832 more; 30five years after that he sent Nebuzaradan, his captain of the guard, and took 745—a total of 4,600 captives in all.

31On February 25, of the 37th year of the imprisonment in Babylon of Jehoiachin, king of Judah, Evil-merodach, who became king of Babylon that year, was kind to King Jehoiachin and brought him out of prison, 32and spoke pleasantly to him and gave him preference over all the other kings in Babylon, 33and gave him new clothes and fed him from the king's kitchen as long as he lived. 34And he was given a regular allowance to cover his daily needs until the day of his death.

52:8
Jer 21:7; 38:23

52:9
2 Kgs 25:6
Jer 39:5

52:10
Jer 39:6

52:11
Ezek 12:13

52:12
2 Kgs 25:8-21

52:13
2 Chron 36:19
Ps 74:6-8
Jer 39:8

52:14
2 Kgs 25:10

52:17
1 Kgs 7:15-36

52:18
1 Kgs 7:40,45

52:20
1 Kgs 7:47

52:22
1 Kgs 7:20,42

52:24
2 Kgs 25:18
Ezra 7:1
Esth 1:14

52:27
Jer 13:19
Mic 4:10

52:28
2 Kgs 24:2,3,
12-16

52:31
2 Kgs 25:27-30
Ps 3:3

52:33
2 Sam 9:7,13

52:12 This is August 17, 587 or 586 B.C., depending on whether Nebuchadnezzar's first year was when he ascended the throne or at the beginning of his first full year as king.

52:31 Babylon's kings showed kindness to Jehoiachin. In 560 B.C. he was released from prison and allowed to eat with the king. God continued to show kindness to the descendants of King David, even in exile.

52:34 In the world's eyes, Jeremiah looked totally unsuccessful. He had no money, family, or friends. He prophesied the destruction of the nation, the capital city, and the Temple, but the political and religious leaders would not accept or follow his advice. No group of people liked him or listened to him. Yet as we look back, we see that he successfully completed the work God gave him to do. Success must never be measured by prosperity, fame, or fortune, for these are temporal measures. King Zedekiah, for example, lost everything by pursuing selfish goods. God measures our success with the yardsticks of obedience, faithfulness, and righteousness. If you are faithfully doing the work God gives you, you are successful in his eyes.

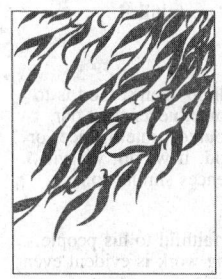

TEARS are defined simply as "drops of salty fluid flowing from the eyes." They can be caused by irritation or laughter but are usually associated with weeping, sorrow, and grief. When we cry, friends wonder what's wrong and try to console us. Babies cry for food, children at the loss of a pet, and adults when confronted with trauma and death.

Jeremiah is called the "weeping prophet." His tears flowed from a broken heart. As God's spokesman, he knew what lay ahead for Judah, his country, and for Jerusalem, the capital and "city of God." God's judgment would fall and destruction would come. And Jeremiah wept. His tears were not self-centered, mourning over personal suffering or loss. He wept because the people had rejected their God—the God who had made them, loved them, and sought repeatedly to bless them. His heart was broken because he knew that the selfishness and sinfulness of the people would bring them much suffering and an extended exile. Jeremiah's tears were tears of empathy and sympathy. His heart was broken with those things that break God's heart.

Jeremiah's two books focus on one event—the destruction of Jerusalem. The book of Jeremiah predicts it, and Lamentations looks back on it. Known as the book of tears, Lamentations is a dirge, a funeral song written for the fallen city of Jerusalem.

What makes a person cry says a lot about that person—whether he or she is self-centered or God-centered. The book of Lamentations allows us to see what made Jeremiah sorrowful. As one of God's choice servants, he stands alone in the depth of his emotions, his care for the people, his love for the nation, and his devotion to God.

What causes your tears? Do you weep because your selfish pride has been wounded, or because the people around you sin against and reject the God who loves them dearly? Do you weep because you have lost something that gives you pleasure, or because people all around you will suffer for their sinfulness? Our world is filled with injustice, poverty, war, and rebellion against God, all of which should move us to tears and to action. Read Lamentations and learn what it means to grieve with God.

VITAL STATISTICS

PURPOSE:
To teach people that to disobey God is to invite disaster and to show that God suffers when his people suffer

AUTHOR:
Jeremiah

DATE WRITTEN:
Soon after the fall of Jerusalem in 586 B.C.

SETTING:
Jerusalem had been destroyed by Babylon and her people killed, tortured, or taken captive.

KEY VERSE:
"I have cried until the tears no longer come; my heart is broken, my spirit poured out, as I see what has happened to my people; little children and tiny babies are fainting and dying in the streets" (2:11).

KEY PEOPLE:
Jeremiah, the people of Jerusalem

KEY PLACE:
Jerusalem

SPECIAL FEATURES:
Three strands of Hebrew thought meet in Lamentations—prophecy, ritual, and wisdom. Lamentations is written in the rhythm and style of ancient Jewish funeral songs or chants. It contains five poems corresponding to the five chapters (see the note on 3:1ff).

THE BLUEPRINT

1. Jeremiah mourns for Jerusalem (1:1–22)
2. God's anger at sin (2:1–22)
3. Hope in the midst of affliction (3:1–66)
4. God's anger is satisfied (4:1–22)
5. Jeremiah pleads for restoration (5:1–22)

Jeremiah grieves deeply because of the destruction of Jerusalem and the devastation of his nation. But in the middle of the book, in the depths of his grief, there shines a ray of hope. God's compassion is ever-present. His faithfulness is great. Jeremiah realizes that it is only the Lord's mercy that has prevented total annihilation. This book shows us the serious consequences of human sin and how we can still have hope in the midst of tragedy because God is able to turn it around for good. We see the timeless importance of prayer and confession of sin. We will all face tragedy in our lives. But in the midst of our afflictions, there is hope in God.

MEGATHEMES

THEME	EXPLANATION	IMPORTANCE
Destruction of Jerusalem	Lamentations is a sad funeral song for the great capital city of the Jews. The Temple has been destroyed, the king is gone, and the people are in exile. God had warned that he would destroy them if they abandoned him. Now, afterwards, the people realize their condition and confess their sin.	God's warnings are fulfilled. He does what he says he will do. His punishment for sin is certain. Only by confessing and renouncing our sin can we turn to him for deliverance. How much better to do so before his warnings are fulfilled.
Sin's consequences	God was angry at the prolonged rebellion by his people. Sin is the cause of their misery and destruction is the result of their sin. The destruction of the nation shows the vanity of human glory and pride.	To continue in rebellion against God is to invite disaster. We must never trust our own leadership, resources, intelligence, or power more than God. If we do, we will experience consequences similar to Jerusalem's.
God's mercy	God's compassion was at work even when the Israelites were experiencing the affliction of their Babylonian conquerors. Although the people had been unfaithful, God's faithfulness was great. He used this affliction to bring his people back to him.	God will always be faithful to his people. His merciful, refining work is evident even in affliction. At those times, we must pray for forgiveness and then turn to him for deliverance.
Hope	God's mercy in sparing some of the people offers hope for better days. One day, the people will be restored to a true and fervent relationship with God.	Only God can deliver us from sin. Without him there is no comfort or hope for the future. Because of Christ's death for us and his promise to return, we have a bright hope for tomorrow.

1. Jeremiah mourns for Jerusalem

1 Jerusalem's streets, once thronged with people, are silent now. Like a widow broken with grief, she sits alone in her mourning. She, once queen of nations, is now a slave.

1:1
Isa 22:2
Jer 31:7; 40:9

²She sobs through the night; tears run down her cheeks. Among all her lovers, there is none to help her. All her friends are now her enemies.

1:2
Jer 2:25
22:20-22
Mic 7:5

³Why is Judah led away, a slave? Because of all the wrong she did to others, making them her slaves. Now she sits in exile far away. There is no rest, for those she persecuted have turned and conquered her.

1:3
Lev 26:39
Deut 28:64-67
2 Kgs 25:4,5

⁴The roads to Zion mourn, no longer filled with joyous throngs who come to celebrate the Temple feasts; the city gates are silent, her priests groan, her virgins have been dragged away. Bitterly she weeps.

1:4
Jer 9:11; 10:22
Lam 2:6,7
Joel 1:8-13

⁵Her enemies prosper, for the Lord has punished Jerusalem for all her many sins; her young children are captured and taken far away as slaves.

1:5
Ps 90:7,8
Ezek 8:17,18
9:9,10

⁶All her beauty and her majesty are gone; her princes are like starving deer that search for pasture—helpless game too weak to keep on running from their foes.

1:6
Ps 132:13
Jer 13:18

⁷And now in the midst of all Jerusalem's sadness she remembers happy bygone days. She thinks of all the precious joys she had before her mocking enemy struck her down—and there was no one to give her aid.

1:7
Jer 37:7
Lam 4:17

1:1 This is the prophet Jeremiah's song of sorrow for Jerusalem's destruction. The nation of Judah had been utterly defeated, the Temple destroyed, and captives had been taken away to Babylon. Jeremiah's tears were for the suffering and humiliation of the people, but they went even deeper. He cried because God had rejected the people for their rebellious ways. Each year this book was read aloud to remind all the Jews that their great city fell because of their stubborn sinfulness.

1:2 The term *lovers* refers to nations such as Egypt to whom Judah kept turning for help. As the Babylonians closed in on Jerusalem, the nation of Judah turned away from God and sought help and protection from other nations instead.

1:8
Isa 59:2-13
Lam 1:15

1:9
Ps 74:23
Isa 3:8
Jer 13:17,18

1:10
Ps 74:4-8
Isa 64:10,11
Jer 51:51

1:11
1 Sam 30:12
Jer 15:19

1:12
Isa 13:13
Jer 4:8; 18:16
48:27

1:13
Job 19:6; 30:30
Ps 22:14
Jer 44:6
Hab 3:16

1:14
Prov 5:22
Isa 47:6
Jer 32:3,5
Ezek 25:4,7

1:15
Isa 41:2
Jer 13:24; 37:10

1:16
Ps 69:20
Eccles 4:1
Lam 1:2

1:17
2 Kgs 24:2-4
Isa 1:15
Jer 4:31

1:18
Deut 28:32,41
1 Sam 12:14,15
Ps 119:75
Jer 12:1

1:19
Job 19:13-19
Jer 14:15
Lam 1:2; 2:20

1:20
Isa 16:11
Jer 4:19

1:21
Ps 35:15
Isa 14:5,6; 47:6
Jer 30:16

1:22
Neh 4:4,5
Ps 137:7,8

8For Jerusalem sinned so horribly; therefore she is tossed away like dirty rags. All who honored her despise her now, for they have seen her stripped naked and humiliated. She groans and hides her face.

9She indulged herself in immorality, and refused to face the fact that punishment was sure to come. Now she lies in the gutter with no one left to lift her out. "O Lord," she cries, "see my plight. The enemy has triumphed."

10Her enemies have plundered her completely, taking everything precious she owns. She has seen foreign nations violate her sacred Temple—foreigners you had forbidden even to enter.

11Her people groan and cry for bread; they have sold all they have for food to give a little strength. "Look, O Lord," she prays, "and see how I'm despised."

12Is it nothing to you, all you who pass by? Look and see if there is any sorrow like my sorrow, because of all the Lord has done to me in the day of his fierce wrath.

13He has sent fire from heaven that burns within my bones; he has placed a pitfall in my path and turned me back. He has left me sick and desolate the whole day through.

14He wove my sins into ropes to hitch me to a yoke of slavery. He sapped my strength and gave me to my enemies; I am helpless in their hands.

15The Lord has trampled all my mighty men. A great army has come at his command to crush the noblest youth. The Lord has trampled his beloved city as grapes in a winepress.

16For all these things I weep; tears flow down my cheeks. My Comforter is far away—he who alone could help me. My children have no future; we are a conquered land.

17Jerusalem pleads for help but no one comforts her. For the Lord has spoken: "Let her neighbors be her foes! Let her be thrown out like filthy rags!"

18And the Lord is right, for we rebelled. And yet, O people everywhere, behold and see my anguish and despair, for my sons and daughters are taken far away as slaves to distant lands.

19I begged my allies for their help. False hope—they could not help at all. Nor could my priests and elders—they were starving in the streets while searching through the garbage dumps for bread.

20*See, O Lord, my anguish;* my heart is broken and my soul despairs, for I have terribly rebelled. In the streets the sword awaits me; at home, disease and death.

21*Hear my groans!* And there is no one anywhere to help. All my enemies have heard my troubles and they are glad to see what you have done. And yet, O Lord, the time will surely come—for you have promised it—when you will do to them as you have done to me.

22Look also on their sins, O Lord, and punish them as you have punished me, for my sighs are many and my heart is faint.

1:19 *allies,* literally, "lovers," which probably refers to Egypt.

1:9 The warning was loud and clear: "If you play with fire, you will get burned." Jerusalem foolishly took a chance and lost, refusing to believe that immoral living brings God's punishment. The ultimate consequence of sin is punishment (Romans 6:23). We can choose to ignore God's warnings, but as sure as judgment came upon Jerusalem, so it will come upon those who defy God. Are you listening to God's Word? Are you obeying it? Obedience is a sure sign of your love for him.

1:14 At first, sin seems to offer freedom. But the liberty to do anything we want gradually becomes a desire to do everything. Then we become captive to sin. Freedom from sin's captivity comes only from God. He gives us the freedom, not to do anything we want, but to do what he knows is best for us. Strange as it may seem, true freedom comes in obeying God—following his guidance so that we can receive his best.

1:16 God is the Comforter, but because of Israel's sins he had to turn away from them and become their Judge.

1:19 Jerusalem's allies could not come to her aid because, like Jerusalem, they failed to seek God. Though these allies appeared strong, they were actually weak because God was not with them. Dependable assistance can come only from an ally whose power is from God. When you seek wise counsel, go to Christians who get their wisdom from the all-knowing God.

1:22 Babylon, although sinful, was God's instrument of judgment on Judah and its capital, Jerusalem. The people of Jerusalem pleaded for God to punish sinful Babylon as he had punished them. God would do this, for he had already passed judgment on Babylon (see Jeremiah 50:1-27).

2. God's anger at sin

2 A cloud of anger from the Lord has overcast Jerusalem; the fairest city of Israel lies in the dust of the earth, cast from the heights of heaven at his command. In his day of awesome fury he has shown no mercy even to his Temple.

²The Lord without mercy has destroyed every home in Israel. In his wrath he has broken every fortress, every wall. He has brought the kingdom to dust, with all its rulers.

³All the strength of Israel vanishes beneath his wrath. He has withdrawn his protection as the enemy attacks. God burns across the land of Israel like a raging fire.

⁴He bends his bow against his people as though he were an enemy. His strength is used against them to kill their finest youth. His fury is poured out like fire upon them.

⁵Yes, the Lord has vanquished Israel like an enemy. He has destroyed her forts and palaces. Sorrows and tears are his portion for Jerusalem.

⁶He has violently broken down his Temple as though it were a booth of leaves and branches in a garden! No longer can the people celebrate their holy feasts and Sabbaths. Kings and priests together fall before his wrath.

⁷The Lord has rejected his own altar, for he despises the false "worship" of his people; he has given their palaces to their enemies, who carouse in the Temple as Israel used to do on days of holy feasts!

⁸The Lord determined to destroy Jerusalem. He laid out an unalterable line of destruction. Therefore the ramparts and walls fell down before him.

⁹Jerusalem's gates are useless. All their locks and bars are broken, for he has crushed them. Her kings and princes are enslaved in far-off lands, without a temple, without a divine law to govern them, or prophetic vision to guide them.

¹⁰The elders of Jerusalem sit upon the ground in silence, clothed in sackcloth; they throw dust upon their heads in sorrow and despair. The virgins of Jerusalem hang their heads in shame.

¹¹I have cried until the tears no longer come; my heart is broken, my spirit poured out, as I see what has happened to my people; little children and tiny babies are fainting and dying in the streets.

¹²"Mama, Mama, we want food," they cry, and then collapse upon their mothers' shrunken breasts. Their lives ebb away like those wounded in battle.

¹³In all the world has there ever been such sorrow? O Jerusalem, what can I compare your anguish to? How can I comfort you? For your wound is deep as the sea. Who can heal you?

¹⁴Your "prophets" have said so many foolish things, false to the core. They have

2:1	Ps 99:5; 132:7
	Isa 64:11
	Ezek 28:14-16
2:2	Ps 21:9
	89:39,40
	Lam 3:43
2:3	Ps 75:5,10
	Isa 42:25
	Jer 21:14
2:4	Job 6:4; 16:13
	Jer 7:20
2:5	Jer 52:13
	Lam 2:2
2:6	Lam 1:4
	Zeph 3:18
2:7	Ps 74:3-8
	Isa 64:11
	Ezek 7:20-22
2:8	2 Kgs 21:13
	Isa 34:11
	Amos 7:7-9
2:9	Neh 1:3
	Jer 23:16
2:10	Job 2:13
	Isa 3:26
	Amos 8:3
	Jonah 3:6-8
2:11	Job 16:13
	Jer 4:19
	Lam 2:19
2:12	Job 30:16
	Ps 42:4
2:13	Lam 1:12
2:14	Ezek 22:25,28
	23:36
	Mic 3:8

2:1 *Temple,* literally, "footstool."

2:1ff While chapter 1 described Jerusalem's desolation and called for God's revenge on his enemies, chapter 2 calls for God's people to repent if they expect mercy from him. The people must turn from their sins; they must sincerely mourn over their wrongs against God. The people had much to cry about. Because of their stubborn rebellion against God, they had brought great suffering to all, especially to the innocent. Was this suffering God's fault? No, it was the fault of the wayward people. Sinful people brought destruction on themselves, but tragically, sin's consequences affected everyone—good and evil alike.

2:6 King Solomon's Temple in Jerusalem represented God's presence with the people (1 Kings 8:1-11). The Temple was the central place of worship. Its destruction symbolized God's rejection of his people—that he no longer lived among them.

2:7 Our place of worship is not so important to God as our pattern of worship. A church may be beautiful, but if its people don't sincerely follow God, it decays from within. The people of Judah, despite their beautiful Temple, had rejected in their daily lives what they proclaimed by their worship rituals. Thus their worship turned into a mocking lie. When you worship, are you saying words you

don't really mean? Do you pray for help you don't really believe will come? Do you express love for God you don't really have? Earnestly seek God and catch a fresh vision of his love and care. Then worship him wholeheartedly.

2:9 Four powerful symbols and sources of security are lost: the protection of the *city;* the regularity of *Temple worship;* the guidance of *God's law;* and the vision of his *prophets.* With those four factors present, the people were lulled into a false sense of security and felt comfortable with their sins. But now that they are removed, the people are confronted with the choice of repenting and returning to God or continuing on this path of suffering. Don't substitute symbols, even good ones, for the reality of a living, personal relationship with God himself.

2:11 Jeremiah's tears were sincere and full of compassion. Sorrow does not mean we lack faith or strength. There is nothing wrong with crying—Jesus himself felt sorrow and even wept (John 11:35). How do we react to the tearing down of our society and the moral degradation around us? This may not be as obvious as an invading enemy army, but the destruction is just as certain. We too should be deeply moved when we see moral decay around us.

not tried to hold you back from slavery by pointing out your sins. They lied and said that all was well.

¹⁵All who pass by scoff and shake their heads and say, "Is this the city called 'Most Beautiful in All the World,' and 'Joy of All the Earth'?"

¹⁶All your enemies deride you. They hiss and grind their teeth and say, "We have destroyed her at last! Long have we waited for this hour and it is finally here! With our own eyes we've seen her fall."

¹⁷But it is the Lord who did it, just as he had warned. He has fulfilled the promises of doom he made so long ago. He has destroyed Jerusalem without mercy and caused her enemies to rejoice over her and boast of their power.

¹⁸Then the people wept before the Lord. O walls of Jerusalem, let tears fall down upon you like a river; give yourselves no rest from weeping day or night.

¹⁹Rise in the night and cry to your God. Pour out your hearts like water to the Lord; lift up your hands to him; plead for your children as they faint with hunger in the streets.

²⁰*O Lord, think! These are your own people to whom you are doing this.* Shall mothers eat their little children, those they bounced upon their knees? Shall priests and prophets die within the Temple of the Lord?

²¹See them lying in the streets—old and young, boys and girls, killed by the enemies' swords. You have killed them, Lord, in your anger; you have killed them without mercy.

²²You have deliberately called for this destruction; in the day of your anger none escaped or remained. All my little children lie dead upon the streets before the enemy.

3. Hope in the midst of affliction

3 I am the man who has seen the afflictions that come from the rod of God's wrath. ²He has brought me into deepest darkness, shutting out all light. ³He has turned against me. Day and night his hand is heavy on me. ⁴He has made me old and has broken my bones.

⁵He has built forts against me and surrounded me with anguish and distress. ⁶He buried me in dark places, like those long dead. ⁷He has walled me in; I cannot escape; he has fastened me with heavy chains. ⁸And though I cry and shout, he will not hear my prayers! ⁹He has shut me into a place of high, smooth walls; he has filled my path with detours.

¹⁰He lurks like a bear, like a lion, waiting to attack me. ¹¹He has dragged me into the underbrush and torn me with his claws, and left me bleeding and desolate. ¹²He has bent his bow and aimed it squarely at me, ¹³and sent his arrows deep within my heart.

¹⁴My own people laugh at me; all day long they sing their ribald songs. ¹⁵He has filled me with bitterness, and given me a cup of deepest sorrows to drink. ¹⁶He has made me eat gravel and broken my teeth; he has rolled me in ashes and dirt. ¹⁷O Lord, all peace and all prosperity have long since gone, for you have

3:9 *He has shut me into a place of high, smooth walls,* literally, "He has walled up my ways with hewn stone."

Cross references (left margin):

2:15
Job 27:23
Ps 48:2; 50:2
Jer 18:16

2:16
Ps 56:2
Lam 3:46
Obad 12-15

2:17
Deut 28:43,44
Ps 89:42
Lam 1:5

2:18
Ps 119:145
Lam 2:8
Hos 7:14
Hab 2:11

2:19
1 Sam 1:15
Ps 42:3,4
Isa 51:20

2:20
Ex 32:11
Deut 9:26
Ps 78:64
Jer 23:11,12
Lam 4:13,16

2:21
2 Chron 36:17
Jer 6:11

2:22
Ps 31:13
Isa 24:17,18
Jer 16:2-4

3:2
Jer 4:23

3:4
Jer 50:17

3:5
Job 19:8
Ps 69:21
Jer 23:15

3:6
Ps 88:5,6

3:7
Jer 40:4

3:8
Ps 22:2

3:11
Job 16:12,13
Hos 6:1

3:14
Lam 3:63

3:17
Isa 59:11
Jer 12:12

2:14 False prophets were everywhere in Jeremiah's day. While Jeremiah warned the people of coming destruction and lengthy captivity, the false prophets said all was well and the people need not fear. All of Jeremiah's words came true because he was a true prophet of God (Jeremiah 14:14-16).

2:19 Jerusalem's suffering and sin should have brought her to the Lord, weeping for forgiveness. Only when sin breaks our hearts can God come to our rescue. Just feeling sorry for our sins does not bring forgiveness, but if we cry out to God, he will forgive us.

2:21, 22 This horrible scene could have been avoided. Jeremiah had warned the people for years that this would happen, and it broke his heart to see it fulfilled. We are always shocked when we hear of tragedy striking the innocent. But often innocent bystanders are victims of judgment. Sin has a way of causing

great sorrow and devastation to many.

3:1ff In Jeremiah's darkest moment, his hope was strengthened with two assurances: (1) God had been faithful and would continue to be faithful, and (2) the captives were alive. Jeremiah saw both God's judgment and God's mercy. In the time of judgment, Jeremiah could still cling to God's mercy just as, in times of prosperity, he had warned of his judgment.

3:1ff In the original Hebrew, the chapters in Lamentations are acrostic poems. Each verse in each chapter begins with a successive letter of the Hebrew alphabet. Chapter 3 has 66 verses rather than 22 because it is a triple acrostic: the first three verses begin with the equivalent of "A," the next three with "B," and so on. This was a typical form for Hebrew poetry. Other examples of acrostics are Psalm 119, Psalm 145, and Proverbs 31.

taken them away. I have forgotten what enjoyment is. 18All hope is gone; my strength has turned to water, for the Lord has left me. 19Oh, remember the bitterness and suffering you have dealt to me! 20For I can never forget these awful years; always my soul will live in utter shame.

21*Yet there is one ray of hope:* 22*his compassion never ends.* It is only the Lord's mercies that have kept us from complete destruction. 23Great is his faithfulness; his lovingkindness begins afresh each day. 24My soul claims the Lord as my inheritance; therefore I will hope in him. 25The Lord is wonderfully good to those who wait for him, to those who seek for him. 26It is good both to hope and wait quietly for the salvation of the Lord.

27It is good for a young man to be under discipline, 28for it causes him to sit apart in silence beneath the Lord's demands, 29to lie face downward in the dust; then at last there is hope for him. 30Let him turn the other cheek to those who strike him, and accept their awful insults, 31for the Lord will not abandon him forever. 32Although God gives him grief, yet he will show compassion too, according to the greatness of his lovingkindness. 33For he does not enjoy afflicting men and causing sorrow.

34, 35, 36But you have trampled and crushed beneath your feet the lowly of the world, and deprived men of their God-given rights, and refused them justice. No wonder the Lord has had to deal with you! 37For who can act against you without the Lord's permission? 38It is the Lord who helps one and harms another.

39Why then should we, mere humans as we are, murmur and complain when punished for our sins? 40Let us examine ourselves instead, and repent and turn again to the Lord. 41Let us lift our hearts and hands to him in heaven, 42for we have sinned; we have rebelled against the Lord, and he has not forgotten it.

43You have engulfed us by your anger, Lord, and slain us without mercy. 44You have veiled yourself as with a cloud so that our prayers do not reach through. 45You have made us as refuse and garbage among the nations. 46All our enemies have spoken out against us. 47We are filled with fear, for we are trapped and desolate, destroyed.

48, 49My eyes flow day and night with never-ending streams of tears because of the destruction of my people. 50Oh, that the Lord might look down from heaven and respond to my cry! 51My heart is breaking over what is happening to the young girls of Jerusalem.

52My enemies, whom I have never harmed, chased me as though I were a bird. 53They threw me in a well and capped it with a rock. 54The water flowed above my head. I thought, This is the end! 55But I called upon your name, O Lord, from deep within the well, 56and you heard me! You listened to my pleading; you heard my weeping! 57Yes, you came at my despairing cry and told me not to fear.

58O Lord, you are my lawyer! Plead my case! For you have redeemed my life. 59You have seen the wrong they did to me; be my Judge, to prove me right. 60You have seen the plots my foes have laid against me. 61You have heard the vile names they have called me, 62and all they say about me and their whispered plans. 63See how they laugh and sing with glee, preparing my doom.

3:18
Job 17:15
Ezek 37:11
3:20
Ps 42:5,6,11
43:5
3:22
Ps 78:38
Jer 3:12
Mal 3:6
3:24
Ps 73:26
3:25
Isa 25:9; 26:9
3:30
Job 16:10
Isa 50:6
Mt 5:39
3:31
Isa 54:7-10
3:36
Jer 22:3
Hab 1:13
3:38
Job 2:10
Jer 32:42
3:39
Mic 7:2
Heb 12:5,6
3:40
Ps 119:59
139:23,24
2 Cor 13:5
3:42
Neh 9:26
Jer 14:20
3:47
Isa 24:17,18
Jer 48:43,44
3:50
Isa 63:15
3:54
Jonah 2:3-5
3:56
Job 34:28
Ps 55:1; 116:12
3:57
Josh 1:6
Isa 41:10,14
3:58
Ps 34:22
Jer 50:34; 51:36
3:62
Ezek 36:3

3:21 Jeremiah saw one ray of hope in all the sin and sorrow surrounding him: *God's compassion never ends.* Compassion is love in action. God willingly responds with help when we ask. Perhaps there is some sin in your life that you thought God would not forgive. God's compassion is greater than any sin, and he promises forgiveness.

3:23 Jeremiah knew about God's faithfulness. God had promised that punishment would follow disobedience, and it did. But God also promised future restoration and blessing, and Jeremiah knew that God would keep that promise also. Trusting in God's faithfulness day by day makes us confident in his great promises for the future.

3:27-33 True learning involves several important factors: (1) reflective silence on what God wants, (2) repentant humility,

(3) self-control in the face of adversity, and (4) confident patience, depending on the Teacher to bring about the loving lesson in our lives. God has several long-term and short-term lessons for you right now. Are you doing your homework?

3:39-42 Parents discipline children to produce right behavior. God disciplined Israel to produce right living and worship. We must not complain about discipline but learn from it, trusting God and being willing to change. We must allow God's correction to bring about the kind of behavior in our lives that pleases him.

3:52-57 At one point in his ministry, Jeremiah was thrown into an empty cistern and left to die in the mire at the bottom (Jeremiah 38:6-13). But God rescued him. Jeremiah used this experience as a picture of the nation sinking into sin. If they turned to God, he would rescue them.

3:64
Jer 51:24

3:65
Deut 2:30

64O Lord, repay them well for all the evil they have done. 65Harden their hearts and curse them, Lord. 66Go after them in fierce pursuit and wipe them off the earth, beneath the heavens of the Lord.

4. God's anger is satisfied

4:1
2 Kgs 25:9,10

4:2
Isa 30:14
Jer 19:1,11

4:6
Gen 19:25
Jer 20:16
Ezek 16:48

4:8
Ps 102:5
Lam 5:10

4:9
Lev 26:39

4:10
Deut 28:53-55
2 Kgs 6:26-30

4:11
Deut 32:22

4:12
Jer 21:13

4:13
Jer 2:30; 26:8,9

4:14
Deut 28:28,29
Isa 29:10
56:10; 59:9,10

4:15
Lev 13:45,46
Jer 45:5

4:16
Isa 9:14-16
Jer 52:24-27

4:17
Jer 37:7
Lam 1:7
Ezek 29:16

4:19
Deut 28:49
Jer 4:13

4:20
Jer 39:5
Ezek 12:12,13
Dan 4:12

4 How the finest gold has lost its luster! For the inlaid Temple walls are scattered in the streets! 2The cream of our youth—the finest of the gold—are treated as earthenware pots. 3, 4Even the jackals feed their young, but not my people, Israel. They are like cruel desert ostriches, heedless of their babies' cries. The children's tongues stick to the roofs of their mouths for thirst, for there is not a drop of water left. Babies cry for bread but no one can give them any. 5Those who used to eat fastidiously are begging in the streets for anything at all. Those brought up in palaces now scratch in garbage pits for food. 6For the sin of my people is greater than that of Sodom, where utter disaster struck in a moment without the hand of man.

7Our princes were lean and tanned, the finest specimens of men; 8but now their faces are as black as soot. No one can recognize them. Their skin sticks to their bones; it is dry and hard and withered. 9Those killed by the sword are far better off than those who die of slow starvation. 10Tenderhearted women have cooked and eaten their own children; thus they survived the siege.

11But now at last the anger of the Lord is satisfied; his fiercest anger has been poured out. He started a fire in Jerusalem that burned it down to its foundations. 12Not a king in all the earth—no one in all the world—would have believed an enemy could enter through Jerusalem's gates! 13Yet God permitted it because of the sins of her prophets and priests, who defiled the city by shedding innocent blood. 14Now these same men are blindly staggering through the streets, covered with blood, defiling everything they touch.

15"Get away!" the people shout at them. "You are defiled!" They flee to distant lands and wander there among the foreigners; but none will let them stay. 16The Lord himself has dealt with them; he no longer helps them, for they persecuted the priests and elders who stayed true to God.

17We look for our allies to come and save us, but we look in vain. The nation we expected most to help us makes no move at all.

18We can't go into the streets without danger to our lives. Our end is near—our days are numbered. We are doomed. 19Our enemies are swifter than the eagles; if we flee to the mountains they find us. If we hide in the wilderness, they are waiting for us there. 20Our king—the life of our life, the Lord's anointed—was captured in

4:1 *inlaid.* Implied. **4:7** *Our princes were lean and tanned,* literally, "were purer than snow, whiter than milk, more ruddy than rubies, polished like sapphires." **4:17** *allies,* probably the reference is to Egypt.

4:1ff This chapter contrasts the situation before the siege of Jerusalem with the situation after the siege. The sights and sounds of prosperity were gone because of the people's sin. This chapter warns us not to assume that when life is going well, it will always stay that way. We must be careful not to glory in our prosperity and fall into spiritual bankruptcy.

4:1-10 When a city was under siege, the city wall—built for protection—sealed the people inside. They could not get out to the fields to get food and water because the enemy was camped around the city. As food ran out in the city, the people watched their enemies harvest and eat the food in the fields. The siege was a test of wills to see who could outlast the other. Jerusalem was under siege for two years. Life became so harsh that people even ate their own children, and dead bodies were left to rot in the streets. All hope was gone.

4:6 Sodom, destroyed by fire from heaven because of its wickedness (Genesis 18:20—19:29), became a symbol of God's ultimate judgment. Yet the sin of Jerusalem was even greater than the sin of Sodom!

4:13-15 To be defiled meant to be unfit to enter the Temple or to

worship before God. The priests and prophets should have been the most careful to maintain ceremonial purity so they could continue to perform their duties before God. But many priests and prophets did evil and were defiled. As the nation's leaders, their example led the people into sin and caused the ultimate downfall of the nation and its capital city, Jerusalem.

4:17 Judah asked Egypt to help them fight the Babylonian army. Egypt gave Judah false hope—they started to help, but then retreated (Jeremiah 37:5-7). Jeremiah warned Judah not to ally itself with Egypt. He told the leaders to rely on God, but they refused to listen.

4:20 This king, Zedekiah, though God's anointed king, had little spiritual depth and leadership power. Instead of putting his faith in God and listening to God's true prophet, Jeremiah, he listened to the false prophets. To make matters worse, the people chose to follow and trust in their king (2 Chronicles 36:11-23). They chose the path of false confidence and complacency, wanting to feel secure rather than follow the directives which God was giving to his people through Jeremiah. But the object of their confidence—King Zedekiah—was captured.

their snares. Yes, even our mighty king, about whom we had boasted that under his protection we could hold our own against any nation on earth!

²¹Do you rejoice, O people of Edom, in the land of Uz? But you too will feel the awful anger of the Lord. ²²Israel's exile for her sins will end at last, but Edom's never.

4:21
Isa 34:7
Amos 1:11

4:22
Isa 40:2
Jer 49:10

5. Jeremiah pleads for restoration

5 O Lord, remember all that has befallen us; see what sorrows we must bear! ²Our homes, our nation, now are filled with foreigners. ³We are orphans—our fathers dead, our mothers widowed. ⁴We must even pay for water to drink; our fuel is sold to us at the highest of prices. ⁵We bow our necks beneath the victors' feet; unending work is now our lot. ⁶We beg for bread from Egypt, and Assyria too.

⁷Our fathers sinned but died before the hand of judgment fell. We have borne the blow that they deserved!

⁸Our former servants have become our masters; there is no one left to save us. ⁹We went into the wilderness to hunt for food, risking death from enemies. ¹⁰Our skin was black from famine. ¹¹They rape the women of Jerusalem and the girls in Judah's cities. ¹²Our princes are hanged by their thumbs. Even aged men are treated with contempt. ¹³They take away the young men to grind their grain and the little children stagger beneath their heavy loads.

¹⁴The old men sit no longer in the city gates; the young no longer dance and sing. ¹⁵The joy of our hearts has ended; our dance has turned to death. ¹⁶Our glory is gone. The crown is fallen from our head. Woe upon us for our sins. ¹⁷Our hearts are faint and weary; our eyes grow dim. ¹⁸Jerusalem and the Temple of the Lord are desolate, deserted by all but wild animals lurking in the ruins.

¹⁹O Lord, forever you remain the same! Your throne continues from generation to generation. ²⁰Why do you forget us forever? Why do you forsake us for so long? ²¹Turn us around and bring us back to you again! That is our only hope! Give us back the joys we used to have! ²²*Or have you utterly rejected us? Are you angry with us still?*

5:15 *to death,* literally, "to mourning."

5:2
Isa 1:7
Hos 8:7,8

5:3
Jer 15:8; 18:21

5:4
Isa 3:1

5:7
Jer 14:20; 16:12

5:9
Jer 40:9-12

5:11
Isa 13:16
Zech 14:2

5:12
Isa 47:6
Lam 4:16

5:14
Isa 24:8
Jer 7:34

5:15
Jer 25:10

5:17
Job 17:7
Ps 6:7

5:19
Ps 45:6

5:20
Ps 13:1; 44:24

5:21
Jer 31:18

4:21, 22 Edom was Judah's archenemy, even though they had a common ancestor, Isaac (see Genesis 25:19–26; 36:1). Edom actively aided Babylon in the siege of Jerusalem. As a reward, Nebuchadnezzar gave the outlying lands of Judah to Edom. Jeremiah said that Edom would be judged for her treachery against her brothers. (See also Jeremiah 49:7–22; Ezekiel 25:12–14; Amos 9:12; Obadiah 1:1–21.)

5:1ff After expressing the full extent of one's grief, the true believer should turn to God in prayer. Here Jeremiah prayed for mercy for his people. At the end of his prayer he asked, "Are you angry with us still?" God would not stay angry with them forever—

as it says in Micah 7:18, "You cannot stay angry with your people, for you love to be merciful."

5:22 A high calling flouted by low living results in deep suffering. Lamentations gives us a portrait of the bitter suffering the people of Jerusalem experienced when sin caught up with them and God turned his back on them. Every material goal they had lived for collapsed. But although God turned away from them because of their sin, he did not abandon them—that was their great hope. Despite their sinful past, God would restore them if they returned to him. There is no hope except in the Lord. Thus, our grief should turn us toward him, not away from him.

EZEKIEL

BY conditioning a dog with rewards and punishments, you can teach him to obey. As every parent knows, however, children are not so easily taught. People have wills and must *choose* to follow the instructions of their parents and leaders. Discipline is a necessary part of teaching children to obey those in authority. Boys and girls should know the consequences of disobedience, and that they are responsible for the choices they make.

Ezekiel was a man who chose to obey God. Although he was a priest (1:3), he served as a Jewish "street preacher" in Babylon for 22 years, telling everyone about God's judgment and salvation, and calling them to repentance and obedience. And Ezekiel *lived* what he preached. During his ministry God told him to illustrate his messages with dramatic object lessons. Some of these acts included (1) lying on his side for 390 days during which he could eat only one eight-ounce meal a day cooked over manure, (2) shaving his head and beard, and (3) showing no sorrow when his wife died. Ezekiel did what God asked—he obeyed and faithfully proclaimed God's Word.

God may not ask you to do anything quite so dramatic or difficult; but if he did, would you obey?

The book of Ezekiel chronicles the prophet's life and ministry. Beginning with his call as a prophet and commissioning as a "watchman for Israel" (chapters 1—3), Ezekiel immediately begins to preach and demonstrate God's truth, as he predicts the approaching siege and destruction of Jerusalem (chapters 4—24). This devastation would be God's judgment for the people's idolatry. Ezekiel challenges them to turn from their wicked ways. In the next section, he speaks to the surrounding nations, prophesying that God will judge them for their sins as well (chapters 25—32). The book concludes with a message of hope, as Ezekiel proclaims the faithfulness of God and foretells the future blessings for God's people (chapters 33—48).

As you read this exciting record of God's message, watch Ezekiel fearlessly preach the Word of God to the exiled Jews in the streets of Babylon, hear the timeless truth of God's love and power, and think about the responsibility to trust God which each individual bears, and about the inevitability of God's judgment against idolatry, rebellion, and indifference. Commit yourself to obey God, whatever, wherever, and whenever he asks.

VITAL STATISTICS

PURPOSE:
To announce God's judgment on Israel and other nations and to foretell the eventual salvation for God's people

AUTHOR:
Ezekiel—the son of Buzi, a Zadokite priest

TO WHOM WRITTEN:
The Jews in captivity in Babylon and God's people everywhere

DATE WRITTEN:
Approximately 571 B.C.

SETTING:
Ezekiel was a younger contemporary of Jeremiah. While Jeremiah ministered to the people still in Judah, Ezekiel prophesied to those already exiled in Babylon after the defeat of Jehoiachin. He was among the captives taken there in 597 B.C.

KEY VERSES:
"For I will bring you back home again to the land of Israel. Then it will be as though I had sprinkled clean water on you, for you will be clean—your filthiness will be washed away, your idol worship gone. And I will give you a new heart—I will give you new and right desires—and put a new spirit within you. I will take out your stony hearts of sin and give you new hearts of love" (36:24–26).

KEY PEOPLE:
Ezekiel, Israel's leaders, Ezekiel's wife, Nebuchadnezzar, the "Prince"

KEY PLACES:
Jerusalem, Babylon, and Egypt

THE BLUEPRINT

A. MESSAGES OF DOOM (1:1—24:27)
1. Ezekiel's call and commission
2. Visions of sin and judgment
3. Punishment is certain

While Jeremiah was prophesying in Jerusalem that the city would soon fall to the Babylonians, Ezekiel was giving the same message to the captives who were already in Babylon. Like those in Jerusalem, the captives stubbornly believed that Jerusalem would not fall and that they would soon return to their land. Ezekiel warned them that punishment was certain because of their sins and that God was purifying his people. God will always punish sin, whether we believe it or not.

B. MESSAGES AGAINST FOREIGN NATIONS (25:1—32:32)

Ezekiel condemns the sinful actions of seven nations. The people in these nations were saying that God was obviously too weak to defend his people and the city of Jerusalem. But God was allowing them to be defeated in order to punish them for their sins. These heathen nations, however, would face a similar fate and then they would know that God is all-powerful. Those who dare to mock God today will also face a terrible fate.

C. MESSAGES OF HOPE (33:1—48:35)
1. Restoring the people of God
2. Restoring the worship of God

After the fall of Jerusalem, Ezekiel delivered messages of future restoration and hope for the people. God is holy, but Jerusalem and the Temple had become defiled. The nation had to be cleansed through 70 years of captivity. Ezekiel gives a vivid picture of the unchangeable holiness of God. We too must gain a personal vision of the glory of God, a fresh sense of his greatness as we face the struggles of daily life.

MEGATHEMES

THEME	EXPLANATION	IMPORTANCE
God's holiness	Ezekiel had a vision that revealed God's absolute moral perfection. God was spiritually and morally superior to Israel's corrupt and compromising society. Ezekiel wrote to let the people know that God was also present in Babylon, not just in Jerusalem.	Because God is morally perfect, he can help us live above our tendency to compromise with this world. When we focus on his greatness, he gives us the power to overcome sin and to reflect his holiness.
Sin	Israel had sinned, and God's punishment came. The fall of Jerusalem and the Babylonian exile were used by God to correct the rebels and draw them back from their sinful way of life. Ezekiel warned them that not only was the nation responsible for sin, but each individual was also accountable to God.	We cannot excuse ourselves from our responsibilities before God. We are accountable to God for our choices. Rather than neglect sin, we must recognize sin for what it is—rebellion against God—and choose to follow him instead.
Restoration	Ezekiel consoles the people by telling them that the day will come when God will restore those who turn from sin. God will be their King and Shepherd. He will give his people a new heart to worship him, and he will establish a new government and a new Temple.	The certainty of future restoration encourages believers in times of trial. But we must be faithful to God because we love him, not merely for what he can do for us. Is our faith in *him* or merely in our future benefits?
Leaders	Ezekiel condemned the shepherds (unfaithful priests and leaders) who led the people astray. By contrast, he served as a caring shepherd and a watchful sentry to warn the people about their sin. One day God's perfect Shepherd, the Messiah, will lead his people.	Jesus is our perfect leader. If we truly want him to lead us, our devotion must be more than talk. If we are given the responsibility of leading others, we must take care of them even if it means sacrificing personal pleasure, happiness, time, or money. We are responsible for those we lead.
Worship	An angel gave Ezekiel a vision of the Temple in great detail. God's holy presence had departed from Israel and the Temple because of sin. The building of a future temple portrays the return of God's presence. God will cleanse his people and restore true worship.	All of God's promises will be fulfilled under the rule of the Messiah. The faithful followers will be restored to perfect fellowship with God and with one another. To be prepared for this time, we must focus on God. We do this through regular worship. Through worship we learn about God's holiness and the changes we must make in how we live.

A. MESSAGES OF DOOM (1:1—24:27)

Ezekiel prophesied to the exiles in Babylon. He had to dispel the false hope that Israel's captivity would be short, explain the reasons for the severe judgments on their nation, and bring a message of future hope. Although the people did not respond positively, they heard the messages and knew the truth. God's people were not without explanation and direction, and neither are we.

1. Ezekiel's call and commission

A vision of living beings

1:1
Ezek 40:2

1:4
Ezek 13:11,13
1:5
Ezek 10:15-17, 20
Rev 4:6-8; 6:6
1:6
Ezek 10:14,21
1:7
Rev 1:15; 2:18
1:8
Ezek 10:8,21

1 *Ezekiel was a priest (the son of Buzi) who lived with the Jewish exiles beside the Chebar Canal in Babylon.*

One day late in June, when I was thirty years old, the heavens were suddenly opened to me and I saw visions from God. ⁴I saw, in this vision, a great storm coming toward me from the north, driving before it a huge cloud glowing with fire, with a mass of fire inside that flashed continually; and in the fire there was something that shone like polished brass.

⁵Then from the center of the cloud, four strange forms appeared that looked like men, ⁶except that each had four faces and two pairs of wings! ⁷Their legs were like those of men, but their feet were cloven like calves' feet, and shone like burnished brass. ⁸And beneath each of their wings I could see human hands.

1:1-3 *when I was thirty years old,* literally, "in the thirtieth year."

1:1 Ezekiel, born and raised in the land of Judah, was preparing to become a priest in God's Temple when the Babylonians attacked in 597 B.C. and carried him away along with 10,000 other captives (2 Kings 24:10–14). The nation was on the brink of complete destruction. Five years later, when Ezekiel was 30 (the normal age for becoming a priest), God called him to be a prophet. During the first six years that Ezekiel ministered in Babylon, Jeremiah was preaching to the Jews still in Judah, and Daniel was serving in Nebuchadnezzar's court.

1:1 Why did the Jewish exiles in Babylon need a prophet? God wanted Ezekiel to (1) help the exiles see why they had been taken captive, (2) dispel the false hope that captivity was going to be short, (3) bring a new message of hope, and (4) call the people to a new awareness of their dependency upon God.

1:1ff Ezekiel's latest dated message from God (29:17) was given in 571 B.C. He was taken captive during the second Babylonian invasion of Judah in 597 B.C. The Babylonians invaded Judah a third and final time in 586 B.C., completely destroying Jerusalem, burning the Temple, and deporting the rest of the people (see 2 Kings 25). Ezekiel dates all of his messages from the year he was taken captive (597). His first prophecy to the exiles occurred four years after he arrived in the land of Babylon (593 B.C.).

1:1–3 God communicated to Ezekiel in visions. A vision is a miraculous revelation of God's truth. These visions seem strange to us because they are *apocalyptic.* This means that Ezekiel saw symbolic pictures that graphically convey an idea. Daniel and John were others in the Bible who used apocalyptic imagery. The people in exile had lost their perspective of God's purpose and presence, and Ezekiel came to them with a vision from God to warn them of sin's consequences before it was too late.

1:3 The name "Ezekiel" means "God is strong" or "God makes strong." In a very real sense, this sums up the basic message of the book—that in spite of the captivity, God's sovereign strength continues and will be seen in the judgment of his enemies and the restoration of his true people.

1:4ff This is Ezekiel's first vision where God calls him to be a prophet. Nothing in his previous experience had prepared him for such a display of God's presence and power. The storm from the north was a symbol of the great armies of Babylon approaching Jerusalem, God's instrument of judgment upon the nation of Judah. In the midst of the storm cloud shone a brilliant light from which came four living beings sent by God. They showed Ezekiel that Jerusalem's coming destruction was God's punishment of

Judah for her sins. The Babylonian attack was certainly a physical disaster, but the four living beings dramatically portrayed the truth that it was also a spiritual judgment. (These living beings are also seen in Revelation 4:6, 7.)

Ezekiel was far away from the Temple in Jerusalem, the physical symbol of God's presence, when he received this vision. Through this vision he learned that God is present everywhere, and his activities in heaven are shaping the events on earth.

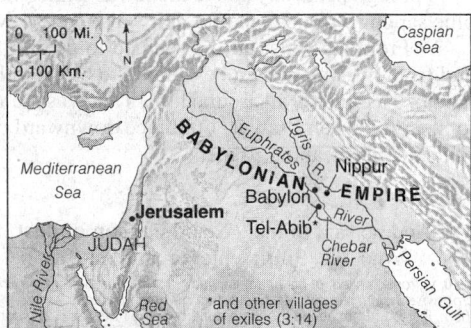

EXILE IN BABYLON Ezekiel worked for God right where he was—among the exiles in various colonies near the Chebar River in Babylonia. Jerusalem and its Temple lay over 500 miles away, but Ezekiel helped the people understand that although they were far from home, they did not need to be far from God.

1:5 Each of the four living beings had four faces, symbolizing God's perfect nature. Some believe that the lion represented strength; the ox, diligent service; the man, intelligence; and the eagle, divinity. Others see these as the most majestic of God's creatures, and that they therefore represent God's whole creation. The early church fathers saw a connection between these beings and the four Gospels: the lion with Matthew, presenting Christ as the Lion of Judah; the ox with Mark, portraying Christ as the Servant; the man with Luke, portraying Christ as the perfect Man; the eagle with John, portraying Christ as the Son of God, high and divine. The vision of John in Revelation chapter four parallels this vision of Ezekiel.

9The four living beings were joined wing to wing, and they flew straight forward without turning. 10Each had the face of a man [in front], with a lion's face on the right side [of his head], and the face of an ox on the left side, and the face of an eagle at the back! 11Each had two pairs of wings spreading out from the middle of his back. One pair stretched out to attach to the wings of the living beings on each side, and the other pair covered his body. 12Wherever their spirit went they went, going straight forward without turning.

13Going up and down among them were other forms that glowed like bright coals of fire or brilliant torches, and it was from these the lightning flashed. 14The living beings darted to and fro, swift as lightning.

15As I stared at all of this, I saw four wheels on the ground beneath them, one wheel belonging to each. 16The wheels looked as if they were made of polished amber and each wheel was constructed with a second wheel crosswise inside. 17They could go in any of the four directions without having to face around. 18The four wheels had rims and spokes, and the rims were filled with eyes around their edges.

19, 20, 21When the four living beings flew forward, the wheels moved forward with them. When they flew upwards, the wheels went up too. When the living beings stopped, the wheels stopped. For the spirit of the four living beings was in the wheels; so wherever their spirit went, the wheels and the living beings went there too.

22The sky spreading out above them looked as though it were made of crystal; it was inexpressibly beautiful.

23The wings of each stretched straight out to touch the others' wings, and each had two wings covering his body. 24And as they flew, their wings roared like waves against the shore, or like the voice of God, or like the shouting of a mighty army. When they stopped they let down their wings. 25And every time they stopped, there came a voice from the crystal sky above them.

26For high in the sky above them was what looked like a throne made of beautiful blue sapphire stones, and upon it sat someone who appeared to be a Man.

27, 28From his waist up, he seemed to be all glowing bronze, dazzling like fire; and from his waist down he seemed to be entirely flame, and there was a glowing halo like a rainbow all around him. That was the way the glory of the Lord appeared to me. And when I saw it, I fell face downward on the ground, and heard the voice of someone speaking to me:

God calls Ezekiel

2 And he said to me: "Stand up, son of dust, and I will talk to you." 2And the Spirit entered into me as he spoke, and set me on my feet.

1:10 *in front,* implied. *of his head,* implied. **1:12** *Wherever their spirit,* literally, "the spirit." **1:16** *a second wheel crosswise inside,* literally, "a wheel within a wheel," perhaps as in a gyroscope. **1:25** *from the crystal sky above them,* literally, "from above the firmament, over their heads." **2:1** *son of dust,* or "son of man.". . . and so also eighty-seven times throughout the book of Ezekiel. The connotation is "mortal man." In Daniel 7:13, the corresponding Aramaic expression is used for the Messiah as representative of the human race of which he is the head.

1:9
Ezek 10:22
1:10
Ezek 10:14
Rev 4:7
1:11
Isa 6:2
Ezek 10:16,19
1:13
Ps 104:4
Dan 10:5,6
Rev 4:5
1:14
Zech 4:10
Mt 24:27
1:16
Ezek 10:9-13
1:18
Prov 15:3
Ezek 10:9-13
Zech 4:10
Rev 4:6,8
1:19
Ezek 10:16, 17,19
1:22
Ex 24:10
Job 37:22
Ezek 10:1
Rev 4:6; 22:1
1:24
Ezek 10:5; 43:2
Dan 10:6
Rev 1:15; 19:6
1:26
Ex 24:10
Isa 6:1; 54:11
Ezek 10:1
24:10; 43:6
Dan 7:9
Rev 1:13
1:27
Gen 9:13
Ezek 3:23; 8:2
2 Thess 1:7
Rev 1:17; 4:3
10:1
2:2
Ezek 3:24
Dan 8:18

1:16–18 The wheel within a wheel probably pictures two wheels, one facing north-south and the other facing east-west, demonstrating the ability to move anywhere. This symbol shows that God is present everywhere and is able to see all things (1:18).

1:26 This Man revealed God's holiness and prepared Ezekiel for what God was about to tell him. This Man represented God himself on the throne. In a similar way, Christ revealed God in human form and prepared us for his message of salvation, not in a vision, but in real life.

1:27, 28 The four living beings and the four wheels are powerful pictures of judgment, yet the rainbow over the throne symbolizes God's never-ending faithfulness to his people. Just as God sent a rainbow to Noah to symbolize his promise never again to destroy the earth by a flood (Genesis 9:8–17), so this rainbow symbolizes his promise to preserve those who remain faithful to him. The

purpose of God's judgment is to correct us and, ultimately, to allow perfect peace and righteousness to reign on the earth forever.

1:27, 28 A bright light, a dazzling fire—that is what the glory of the Lord looked like to Ezekiel. He fell to the ground, overwhelmed by the holiness of God and his own sinfulness and insignificance. Eventually every person will fall before God, either out of reverence and awe for his mercy or out of fear for his judgment. Based on the way you are living today, how will you respond?

2:1 The immortal God addressed mortal man by calling him "son of dust" (or "son of man"), emphasizing the distance between them. It is amazing that God chooses to work his divine will on earth through finite, imperfect beings. We are made from dust, yet God chooses to place within us his life and breath.

2:2 We can only imagine what it was like for Ezekiel to experience this vision. Certainly there was much he did not understand, but he

2:3
Dan 9:5-13
2:5
Ezek 3:11,27
Mt 10:12-15
Lk 10:10,11
Jn 15:22
Acts 13:46
2:6
2 Sam 23:6,7
Isa 51:12
Jer 1:8
Ezek 3:9
2:7
Ezek 3:17
2:8
1 Tim 4:14-16
Rev 10:9
2:9
Dan 5:5; 10:10
Rev 5:1-5; 8:13
10:8-11

³"Son of dust," he said, "I am sending you to the nation of Israel, to a nation rebelling against me. They and their fathers have kept on sinning against me until this very hour. ⁴For they are a hardhearted, stiff-necked people. But I am sending you to give them my messages—the messages of the Lord God. ⁵And whether they listen or not (for remember, they are rebels), they will at least know they have had a prophet among them.

⁶"Son of dust, don't be afraid of them; don't be frightened even though their threats are sharp and barbed and sting like scorpions. Don't be dismayed by their dark scowls. For remember, they are rebels! ⁷You must give them my messages whether they listen or not (but they won't, for they are utter rebels). ⁸Listen, son of dust, to what I say to you. Don't you be a rebel too! Open your mouth and eat what I give you."

⁹, ¹⁰Then I looked and saw a hand holding out to me a scroll, with writing on both sides. He unrolled it, and I saw that it was full of warnings and sorrows and pronouncements of doom.

God appoints Ezekiel to be a watchman

3:2
Jer 25:17
Acts 26:19

3 And he said to me: "Son of dust, eat what I am giving you—eat this scroll! Then go and give its message to the people of Israel." ²So I took the scroll.

2:7 but they won't, implied.

EZEKIEL served as a prophet to the exiles in Babylon from 593–571 B.C.

Climate of the times	● Ezekiel and his people are taken to Babylon as captives.
	● The Jews become foreigners in a strange land ruled by an authoritarian government.
Main message	Because of the people's sins, God allowed the nation of Judah to be destroyed. But there was still hope—God promised to restore the land to those who remained faithful to him.
Importance of message	God never forgets those who faithfully seek to obey him. They have a glorious future ahead.
Contemporary Prophets	Daniel (605–536)
	Habakkuk (612–589)
	Jeremiah (627–586)

---

knew that each part had significance because it came from God. When God saw Ezekiel's open and obedient attitude, he filled him with his Spirit and gave him power for the job ahead. God doesn't expect us to understand everything about him, but to be willing and obedient servants, faithful to what we know is true and right.

2:3–5 In business, success is often measured by consumer demand. Ezekiel, however, was to give God's message to the people "whether they listen or not." The measure of Ezekiel's success would not be how well the people responded to his messages, but how well he obeyed God and thus fulfilled God's purpose for him. Isaiah and Jeremiah also prophesied with little positive response (see Isaiah 6:9–12; Jeremiah 1:17–19). God's truth is not dependent on human response. God will not judge us for how well others respond to our faith, but for how faithful we have been. What God accomplishes *through* us is important, yet we should also be concerned about what he accomplishes *in* us.

2:4, 5 God called the people hardhearted and stiff-necked because they refused to admit their sin. Obstinacy and rebellion (2:7, 8) were the primary characteristics of the nation. Even when their wrongdoing was made clear, they ignored the truth or assumed that conditions would improve. Is God pointing at sin in your life? Don't be stubborn—confess your sin and begin to live for God. By obeying him now we will be ready for God's review of our lives.

2:6–8 Ezekiel was given the difficult responsibility of presenting God's message to the ungrateful and abusive. Sometimes we are also called to be an example or share our faith with people who may be unkind to us. Just as the Lord told Ezekiel not to give up, he tells us not give up and join the rebels, but rather to tell the Good News "when it is convenient and when it is not" (2 Timothy 4:2).

2:6–10 Three times God told Ezekiel not to be afraid or dismayed. When God's Spirit is within us, we can lay aside our fears of rejection or ridicule. God's strength is powerful enough to help us live for him even under the heaviest criticism.

2:9, 10 A scroll was an ancient book made of one long page (up to 30 feet) and rolled up simultaneously from both ends. Normally, scrolls had writing on only one side. But in this case, the warnings overflowed to the scroll's other side, showing the full measure of judgment about to come down upon Judah.

3:1–3 In his vision, Ezekiel ate God's message and found this spiritual food not only good for him, but also sweet as honey (see Revelation 10:8–10 for a similar use of this image). If you "digest" God's Word, you will find that not only does it make you stronger in your faith, but its wisdom sweetens your life. You need to feed yourself spiritually just as you do physically. This means doing more than simply giving God's message a casual glance (like looking through a bakery window). It means making the Word part of your life.

3"Eat it all," he said. And when I ate it, it tasted sweet as honey.

4Then he said: "Son of dust, I am sending you to the people of Israel with my messages. 5I am not sending you to some far-off foreign land where you can't understand the language— 6no, not to tribes with strange, difficult tongues. (If I did, they would listen!) 7I am sending you to the people of Israel, and they won't listen to you any more than they listen to me! For the whole lot of them are hard, impudent and stubborn. 8But see, I have made you hard and stubborn too—as tough as they are. 9I have made your forehead as hard as rock. So don't be afraid of them, or fear their sullen, angry looks, even though they are such rebels."

10Then he added: "Son of dust, let all my words sink deep into your own heart first; listen to them carefully for yourself. 11Then, afterward, go to your people in exile, and whether or not they will listen, tell them: This is what the Lord God says!"

12Then the Spirit lifted me up and the glory of the Lord began to move away, accompanied by the sound of a great earthquake. 13It was the noise of the wings of the living beings as they touched against each other, and the sound of their wheels beside them.

14, 15The Spirit lifted me up and took me away to Tel Abib, another colony of Jewish exiles beside the Chebar River. I went in bitterness and anger, but the hand of the Lord was strong upon me. And I sat among them, overwhelmed, for seven days.

16At the end of the seven days, the Lord said to me:

17"Son of dust, I have appointed you as a watchman for Israel; whenever I send my people a warning, pass it on to them at once. 18If you refuse to warn the wicked when I want you to tell them, you are under the penalty of death, therefore repent and save your life—they will die in their sins, but I will punish you. I will demand your blood for theirs. 19But if you warn them and they keep on sinning, and refuse to repent, they will die in their sins, but you are blameless—you have done all you could. 20And if a good man becomes bad, and you refuse to warn him of the

3:3
Ps 19:10
119:102,103
Jer 6:11; 15:16
Rev 10:9,10

3:5
Ps 81:5
Jonah 1:2; 3:2-4
Acts 26:17,18

3:6
Isa 28:11

3:7
Ezek 2:4
Lk 10:16
Jn 5:40-47

3:8
Jer 1:18

3:10
Ezek 2:8
Lk 8:15
1 Thess 2:13

3:11
Ezek 2:5,7

3:12
Ezek 8:3
Acts 2:2; 8:39

3:13
Ezek 1:15,24
10:5,16,17

3:14
Ezek 8:1

3:17
Isa 52:8; 58:1
Ezek 33:7-9

3:18
Ezek 33:6,8

3:19
Ezek 33:3,9

3:20
Ezek 18:24

3:12 *accompanied by the sound of a great earthquake,* literally, "I heard behind me the sound of a great earthquake."
3:14, 15 *I went in bitterness and anger,* literally, "I went in the heat of my spirit"—not necessarily anger, but indicated here by this reaction.

3:8, 9 Belief in God is not a crutch for those too weak to stand on their own. God makes his followers strong enough to stand against anything or anyone, including those who hate what is right. Just as God gave Ezekiel tough love and tough faith, he wants to give you the stability, perseverance, and insight you need to live up to the great task he has given you. Give yourself over to God's conditioning, and let him get your life in shape.

3:10, 11 Ezekiel was to let God's message sink deep into his heart before preaching it to others. God's message must sink deep into your heart and show in your actions before you can effectively help others understand and apply it.

3:14, 15 Ezekiel was angry, not at God, but at the sins and attitudes of the people. His extraordinary vision had ended, and now he had to begin the tedious job of prophesying among his people, who seemingly cared little about God's messages. Before the exile, the people had heard Jeremiah, but they would not listen. Now Ezekiel had to give a similar message, and he expected to be rejected as well. But both the living creatures and the rumbling wheels were on his side. He had nothing to fear because God was with him. Despite the probable outcome, Ezekiel obeyed God. In our spiritual walk, there will be times of great joy when we feel close to God, and there will be times when sins, struggles, or everyday tasks overwhelm us. Like Ezekiel, we should obey God even when we don't feel like it. Don't let feelings hinder obedience.

3:14, 15 Ezekiel sat quietly among the people for seven days. This was the customary period of mourning for the dead (Genesis 50:10; 1 Samuel 31:13; Job 2:13). Ezekiel was mourning for those who were spiritually dead.

3:17, 18 A watchman stood on the city wall and warned the people of approaching danger. Ezekiel's role was to be a spiritual watchman, warning the people of coming judgment. Just as a watchman on the wall would pay with his life if he failed to warn the city of approaching enemies, some think that Ezekiel would be punished by death if he refused to warn the people that judgment was coming because of their sins. Others believe it simply means that God would hold Ezekiel responsible for those lost.

3:18 God had already told Ezekiel that the people would not listen, so why should he bother to tell them God's message? God didn't want the people to say they hadn't been warned. Ezekiel's job was to obey God. We are responsible to tell others about God's judgment and his message of salvation, but we are not held responsible for how they respond. But if we refuse to tell others what we know, God will judge us. We must remember this illustration when we are tempted to remain silent among those who don't believe.

3:18-21 The word *save* can also be translated "deliver" or "rescue"; thus it is clear that God is talking about physical death, not eternal punishment. If the people back in Judah continued in their sins, they and their land and cities would be destroyed by Nebuchadnezzar's armies. If, on the other hand, they turned to God, they would be spared. God would hold Ezekiel responsible for his fellow Jews if he failed to warn them of the consequences of their sins. All people are individually responsible to God, but believers have a special responsibility to tell unbelievers the consequences of wrong living. If we fail to do this, God will hold us responsible for what happens in their lives. This should motivate us to begin sharing our faith with others—by both word and deed—and avoid living callous, unconcerned lives.

consequences, and the Lord destroys him, his previous good deeds won't help him—he shall die in his sin. But I will hold you responsible for his death, and punish you. 21But if you warn him and he repents, he shall live and you have saved your own life too."

22I was helpless in the hand of God, and when he said to me, "Go out into the valley and I will talk to you there"— 23I arose and went, and oh, I saw the glory of the Lord there, just as in my first vision! And I fell to the ground on my face.

24Then the Spirit entered into me and set me on my feet. He talked to me and

3:21
Acts 20:31

3:22
Acts 9:6

3:23
Ezek 1:28; 8:4
Acts 7:55

3:24
Ezek 2:2

EZEKIEL

Although Ezekiel's visions and prophecies were clear and vivid, very little is known about the prophet's personal life. He was among the thousands of young men deported from Judah to Babylon when King Jehoiakim surrendered. Until those tragic days, Ezekiel was being trained for the priesthood. But during the exile in Babylon, God called Ezekiel to be his prophet during one of Israel's darkest times.

Ezekiel experienced the same kind of shocking encounter with God that Isaiah had reported 150 years earlier. Like Isaiah, Ezekiel was never the same after his personal encounter with God. Although God's messages through both these prophets had many points in common, the conditions in which they lived were very different. Isaiah warned of the coming storm; Ezekiel spoke in the midst of the storm of national defeat that devastated his people. He announced that even Jerusalem would not escape destruction. In addition, during this time Ezekiel had to endure the pain of his wife's death.

God's description of Ezekiel as a watchman on the walls of the city captures the personal nature of his ministry. A watchman's job was dangerous. If he failed at his post, he and the entire city might be destroyed. His own safety depended on the quality of his work. The importance of each person's accountability before God was a central part of Ezekiel's message. He taught the exiles that God expected personal obedience and worship from each of them.

As in Ezekiel's day, it is easy for us today to forget that God has a personal interest in each one of us. We may feel insignificant in the middle of world events or that our own lives are out of control. But knowing that God is ultimately in control, that he cares, and that he is willing to be known by us can bring a new sense of purpose to our lives. How do you measure your worth? Are you valuable because of your achievements and potential, or because God, your Creator and Designer, declares you valuable?

Strengths and accomplishments:
- Was a priest by training, a prophet by God's call
- Received vivid visions and delivered powerful messages
- Served as God's messenger during Israel's captivity in Babylon
- God shaped his character to fit his mission—a tough and stalwart man to reach a hard and stubborn people (3:8)

Lessons from his life:
- Even the repeated failures of his people will not prevent God's plan for the world from being fulfilled
- It is each person's response to God that determines his or her eternal destiny
- In seemingly hopeless situations God still has people through whom he can work

Vital statistics:
- Where: Babylon
- Occupation: Prophet to the captives in Babylon
- Relatives: Father: Buzi. Wife: Unknown.
- Contemporaries: Jehoiachin, Jeremiah, Jehoiakim, Nebuchadnezzar

Key verses:
"Then he added: 'Son of dust, let all my words sink deep into your own heart first; listen to them carefully for yourself. Then, afterward, go to your people in exile, and whether or not they will listen, tell them: This is what the Lord God says!' " (3:10, 11).

Ezekiel's story is told in the book of Ezekiel.

3:22 Ezekiel recognized his helplessness before God. Sometimes our prosperity, popularity, or physical strength blind us to our spiritual helplessness. But nothing we do on our own can accomplish much for God. Only when God is in control of our wills can we accomplish great tasks for him. The first step to being God's person is to admit your helplessness, then you can begin to see what God can really do in your life.

3:24 Ezekiel is called "son of dust" (see the note on 2:1) to show his frail humanity in contrast to God's power. Whenever Ezekiel saw God for who he really is, he fell down in respect and submission and did whatever God asked. Then God's Spirit empowered him (see 2:2, 3:12). Although we may not have a task like Ezekiel's, we have the same Spirit of power.

3:24-27 This strange command shows that Ezekiel was allowed to speak only when God had a message for the people. The people knew that whatever Ezekiel said was God's message.

said: "Go, imprison yourself in your house, 25and I will paralyze you so you can't leave; 26and I will make your tongue stick to the roof of your mouth so that you can't reprove them; for they are rebels. 27But whenever I give you a message, then I will loosen your tongue and let you speak, and you shall say to them: The Lord God says, Let anyone listen who wants to, and let anyone refuse who wants to, for they are rebels.

2. Visions of sin and judgment

A symbol of the coming siege

4 "And now, son of dust, take a large brick and lay it before you and draw a map of the city of Jerusalem on it. Draw a picture of siege mounds being built against the city, and enemy camps around it, and battering rams surrounding the walls. 3And put an iron plate between you and the city, like a wall of iron. Demonstrate how an enemy army will capture Jerusalem!

"There is special meaning in each detail of what I have told you to do. For it is a warning to the people of Israel.

4, 5"Now lie on your left side for 390 days, to show that Israel will be punished for 390 years by captivity and doom. Each day you lie there represents a year of punishment ahead for Israel. 6Afterwards, turn over and lie on your right side for forty days, to signify the years of Judah's punishment. Each day will represent one year.

7"Meanwhile continue your demonstration of the siege of Jerusalem; lie there with your arm bared [to signify great strength and power in the attack against her]. This will prophesy her doom. 8And I will paralyze you so that you can't turn over from one side to the other until you have completed all the days of your siege.

9"During the first 390 days eat bread made of flour mixed from wheat, barley, beans, lentils, and spelt. Mix the various kinds of flour together in a jar. 10You are to ration this out to yourself at the rate of eight ounces at a time, one meal a day. 11And use one quart of water a day; don't use more than that. 12Each day take flour from the barrel and prepare it as you would barley cakes. While all the people are watching, bake it over a fire, using dried human dung as fuel, and eat it. 13For the Lord declares, Israel shall eat defiled bread in the Gentile lands to which I exile them!"

14Then I said, "O Lord God, must I be defiled by using dung? For I have never been defiled before in all my life. From the time I was a child until now I have never eaten any animal that died of sickness or that I found injured or dead; and I have never eaten any of the kinds of animals our law forbids."

15Then the Lord said, "All right, you may use cow dung instead of human dung." 16Then he told me, "Son of dust, bread will be tightly rationed in Jerusalem. It

3:25
Ezek 4:8
Hos 4:17
3:26
Amos 8:11,12
3:27
Ezek 33:22

4:1
Isa 20:2
Jer 6:6; 13:1
19:1
Ezek 21:22
4:3
Isa 8:18; 20:3
Jer 39:1,2
Ezek 12:6,11
24:24-27
4:4
Num 14:34
4:6
Dan 9:24-26
26:11,12
Rev 11:2,3
4:7
Ezek 21:2
4:8
Ezek 3:25
4:9
Ex 9:32
Isa 28:25
4:10
Ezek 45:12
4:12
Isa 36:12
4:13
Dan 1:8
Hos 9:3
4:14
Lev 17:15; 22:8
Deut 14:3-5
Isa 66:17
Ezek 20:49
Acts 10:14
4:16
Lev 26:26
Isa 3:1
Lam 5:4
Ezek 5:16
12:18,19; 14:13

3:25 *will paralyze you*, literally, "lay bands upon you." **4:4, 5** *for 390 days.* Some versions read, "190 days." **4:7** *to signify great strength and power in the attack against her*, implied. **4:8** *I will paralyze you*, literally, "I will lay bands upon you." **4:14** *the kinds of animals our law forbids.* See Leviticus 11 for the dietary laws Ezekiel refers to here.

4:1ff Ezekiel enacted the coming siege and fall of Jerusalem before it actually happened. God gave Ezekiel specific instructions about what to say and how to say it. Each detail had a special meaning. Often we ignore or disregard the smaller details of God's Word, thinking he probably doesn't care. Like Ezekiel, we should want to obey God completely, even in the details.

4:4-8 Ezekiel's unusual actions symbolically portrayed the fate of Jerusalem. The amount of food he was allowed to eat was the normal ration provided to those living in a city under siege by enemy armies. The food cooked over cow dung was a symbol of Judah's spiritual uncleanness. Ezekiel was not allowed to move, symbolizing the fact that the people of Jerusalem would be imprisoned within the walls of the city. Certainly many people came to view these spectacles and, in the process, heard Ezekiel's occasional speeches (3:27). We know that Ezekiel did not have to lie on his side all day, because 4:9-17 tells of other tasks God

asked him to do during this time. How many of us would be willing to so dramatically portray the sins of our nation? We need to pray for greater boldness in our witness.

4:6 Whether the 390 days and 40 days refer to Judah's past sin or future punishment is unclear because the phrase "years of Judah's punishment" can also be translated "years of Judah's sin." If it refers to the past, it probably means from the time Solomon turned from God until the time Judah would fall to Babylon. Regardless, the intensity of Babylon's final attack would correspond to the many years Judah had sinned against God.

4:12-14 Ezekiel asked God not to make him use human dung for fuel because it violated the laws for purity (Leviticus 21, 22; Deuteronomy 23:12-14). To use dung for fuel would paint a dramatic picture of ruin. If nothing was left in the city that could be burned, it would be impossible to continue to follow the ceremonial laws for purity. The people would have been especially shocked to see Ezekiel, a priest, cooking food this way.

will be weighed out with great care and eaten fearfully. And the water will be portioned out in driblets, and the people will drink it with dismay. 17I will cause the people to lack both bread and water, and to look at one another in frantic terror, and to waste away beneath their punishment.

4:17
Ezek 24:23
33:10

Jerusalem will be a public example

5 "Son of dust, take a sharp sword and use it as a barber's razor to shave your head and beard; use balances to weigh the hair into three equal parts. 2Place a third of it at the center of your map of Jerusalem. After your siege, burn it there. Scatter another third across your map and slash at it with a knife. Scatter the last third to the wind, for I will chase my people with the sword. 3Keep just a bit of the hair and tie it up in your robe; 4then take a few hairs out and throw them into the fire, for a fire shall come from this remnant and destroy all Israel."

5, 6, 7The Lord God says, "This illustrates what will happen to Jerusalem, for she has turned away from my laws and has been even more wicked than the nations surrounding her." 8Therefore the Lord God says, I, even I, am against you and will punish you publicly while all the nations watch. 9Because of the terrible sins you have committed, I will punish you more terribly than I have ever done before or ever will again. 10Fathers will eat their own sons, and sons will eat their fathers; and those who survive will be scattered into all the world.

11"For I promise you: Because you have defiled my Temple with idols and evil sacrifices, therefore I will not spare you nor pity you at all. 12One-third of you will die from famine and disease; one-third will be slaughtered by the enemy; and one-third I will scatter to the winds, sending the sword of the enemy chasing after you. 13Then at last my anger will be appeased. And all Israel will know that what I threaten, I do.

5:1
Lev 21:5
Ezek 44:20
Dan 5:27
5:2
Lev 26:33
Jer 39:1,2
Ezek 4:1-8
5:3
2 Kgs 25:15
Jer 39:10
5:5
2 Kgs 17:8-20
Ezek 4:1
16:47,48,51
5:8
Jer 24:9
Ezek 5:15; 15:7
Zech 14:2
5:9
Dan 9:12
Mt 24:21
5:11
Jer 7:9-11
Ezek 8:5,6,
16,18
5:12
Ezek 6:11,12
12:14; 15:2

EZEKIEL'S ACTS OF OBEDIENCE	2:1	Stood and received God's message
	3:24–27	Imprisoned himself in his house
	3:27	Faithfully proclaimed God's message
	4:1ff	Drew a map of the city of Jerusalem on a large stone
	4:4, 5	Lay on his left side for 390 days
	4:6	Lay on his right side for 40 days
	4:9–17	Followed specific cooking instructions
	5:1–4	Shaved his head and beard
	12:2–7	Left home to demonstrate exile
	13:1ff	Spoke against false prophets
	19:1ff	Sang a death dirge
	21:2	Prophesied against Israel and the Temple
	21:19–23	Made a map
	24:16, 17	Could not mourn his wife's death

5:1–4 Shaving one's head was a sign of mourning, humiliation, and repentance. Ezekiel was directed to shave his head and beard, and then to divide the hair into three parts. Along with verbal prophecies, God asked Ezekiel to use visual images to command the people's attention and to burn an indelible impression on their minds. Just as Ezekiel used creative means to communicate his message to the exiles, we can creatively communicate the Good News about God to a lost generation.

5:3, 4 The tiny bit of hair Ezekiel put in his robe symbolized the small remnant of faithful people God would preserve. But even some from this remnant would be judged and destroyed because their faith was not genuine (5:4). Where will you stand in the coming judgment? Matthew 7:22, 23 warns that many who believe they are safe are not.

5:11 It was a serious sin to pollute the Temple, God's dwelling place, by worshiping idols and practicing evil within its very walls.

In the New Testament, we learn that God now makes his home *within* those who are his. Our bodies are his temple (see 1 Corinthians 6:19). We pollute the temple of God today by allowing gossip, bitterness, love of money, lies, or any other wrong actions or attitudes to be a part of our lives. Nothing should be allowed to pollute God's dwelling place.

5:13 Have you ever seen someone try to discipline a child by saying, "If you do that one more time . . ."? If the parent doesn't follow through, the child learns not to listen. Empty threats backfire. God was going to punish the Israelites for their blatant sins, and he wanted them to know that he would do what he said. The people learned the hard way that God always follows through on his word. Too many people ignore God's warnings to punish sin, treating them as empty threats. But God says, "What I threaten, I will do." Don't make the mistake of thinking that God doesn't really mean what he says.

14"So I will make a public example of you before all the surrounding nations and before everyone traveling past the ruins of your land. 15You will become a laughingstock to the world and an awesome example to everyone, for all to see what happens when the Lord turns against an entire nation in furious rebuke. I, the Lord, have spoken it!

16"I will shower you with deadly arrows of famine to destroy you. The famine will become more and more serious until every bit of bread is gone. 17And not only famine will come, but wild animals will attack you and kill you and your families; disease and war will stalk your land, and the sword of the enemy will slay you; I, the Lord, have spoken it!"

Ezekiel prophesies against the mountains

6 Again a message came from the Lord:

2"Son of dust, look over toward the mountains of Israel and prophesy against them. 3Say to them, O mountains of Israel, hear the message of the Lord God against you and against the rivers and valleys. I, even I the Lord, will bring war upon you to destroy your idols. 4–7All your cities will be smashed and burned, and the idol altars abandoned. Your gods will be shattered; the bones of their worshipers will lie scattered among the altars. Then at last you will know I am the Lord.

8"But I will let a few of my people escape—to be scattered among the nations of the world. 9Then when they are exiled among the nations, they will remember me, for I will take away their adulterous hearts—their love of idols—and I will blind their lecherous eyes that long for other gods. Then at last they will loathe themselves for all this wickedness. 10They will realize that I alone am God, and that I wasn't fooling when I told them that all this would happen to them.

11"The Lord God says: Raise your hands in horror and shake your head with deep remorse and say, Alas for all the evil we have done! For you are going to perish from war and famine and disease. 12Disease will strike down those in exile; war will destroy those in the land of Israel; and any who remain will die by famine and siege. So at last I will expend my fury on you. 13When your slain lie scattered among your idols and altars on every hill and mountain and under every green tree and great oak where they offered incense to their gods—you will realize that I alone am God. 14I will crush you and make your cities desolate from the wilderness in the south to Riblah in the north. Then you will know I am the Lord."

God will pour out his anger

7 This further message came to me from God:

2"Tell Israel, Wherever you look—east, west, north or south—your land is

6:11 *Raise your hands in horror and shake your head,* literally, "Clap your hands and stamp your feet."

5:14
Ps 74:3-10
79:1-4
Ezek 22:4

5:15
Isa 66:15,16
Jer 22:8,9
Ezek 25:17
1 Cor 10:11

5:16
Deut 32:23,24

5:17
Ezek 14:21

6:2
Ezek 36:1

6:3
Ezek 36:4

6:4
2 Chron 14:5
Isa 27:9
Ezek 6:6
Mic 1:7

6:8
Jer 44:14,28
Ezek 7:16; 14:22

6:9
Deut 30:2
Isa 7:13; 43:24
Ezek 20:43
Hos 11:8

6:11
Ezek 5:12; 7:15
9:4; 25:6

6:12
Lam 4:11,12
Ezek 5:13

6:13
1 Kgs 14:23
2 Kgs 16:4
Isa 57:5-7
Ezek 20:27,28

6:14
Ezek 14:13

7:2
Ezek 11:13
Amos 8:2,10

5:14, 15 Just like Judah, our sins will one day be exposed in plain sight. Our lives can be ruined just as visibly as Jerusalem's walls tumbled. Sins rot us from the inside out, and, in God's timing, they will all be exposed! Don't deceive yourself by thinking you can hide your sin.

5:16, 17 Prophets often used this threefold description of judgment upon Jerusalem—sword, famine, and disease—as a way of saying that the destruction would be complete. The sword meant death in battle, famine came when enemies besieged a city, and disease was always a danger during famine. Don't make the mistake of underestimating the extent of God's judgment. If you ignore the biblical warnings and approach God only on the basis of your works, eternal judgment awaits you.

6:1ff This is the beginning of a two-part message. Remember that Ezekiel could speak only when giving messages from God. The message in chapter six is that Judah's idolatry will surely call down God's judgment. The message in chapter seven describes the nature of that judgment—utter destruction of their country. They were punished because the nature of their sins laid them wide

open to invasion. Nevertheless, God in his mercy saved a remnant.

6:8–10 A ray of light appears in this prophecy of darkness—God would spare a remnant of people, but only after they had learned some hard lessons. God sometimes has to "break a heart" in order to bring a person to true repentance. The people needed new attitudes, but they wouldn't change until God broke their hearts with humiliation, pain, suffering, and defeat. Does your heart long for God enough to change those areas displeasing him? Or will God have to "break" you?

6:14 The phrase "then you will know I am the Lord" occurs 70 times in the book of Ezekiel. The purpose of all God's punishment was not revenge, but to impress upon the people the truth that the Lord is the only true and living God. Many people in Ezekiel's day were worshiping man-made idols and calling them gods. Today, money, sex, and power have become idols for many. Punishment will come upon all who put other things ahead of God. It is easy in our secular world to forget that the Lord alone is God, the supreme authority and the only source of eternal love and life. Remember that God may be using the difficulties of your life to remind you that he alone is God.

7:4
Ezek 11:21

7:5
2 Kgs 21:12,13

7:7
Ezek 12:23-25, 28

7:8
Ezek 9:8; 14:19
33:20; 36:19

7:10
Isa 10:5; 59:6-8

7:12
Isa 5:13,14
Ezek 6:11,12
1 Cor 7:29-31
Jas 5:8,9

7:13
Lev 25:24-28,31

7:14
Num 10:9
Jer 4:5

7:15
Jer 14:18
Ezek 6:11,12

7:16
Isa 38:14; 59:11
Ezek 6:8; 14:22
Nah 2:7

7:17
Isa 13:7
Ezek 21:7; 22:14
Heb 12:12

7:18
Job 21:6
Isa 15:3
Ezek 27:31
Amos 8:10

7:19
Prov 11:4
Isa 2:20; 30:22
Zeph 1:8

7:21
2 Kgs 24:13
Ps 74:2-8
Jer 7:30

7:22
Ezek 39:23,24

7:23
Ezek 8:17; 9:9

7:24
Ezek 21:31
28:7; 33:28

7:26
Ezek 21:7
22:26; 26:16

finished. ³No hope remains, for I will loose my anger on you for your worshiping of idols. ⁴I will turn my eyes away and show no pity; I will repay you in full, and you shall know I am the Lord."

⁵, ⁶The Lord God says: "With one blow after another I will finish you. The end has come; your final doom is waiting. ⁷O Israel, the day of your damnation dawns; the time has come; the day of trouble nears. It is a day of shouts of anguish, not shouts of joy! ⁸, ⁹Soon I will pour out my fury and let it finish its work of punishing you for all your evil deeds. I will not spare nor pity you, and you will know that I, the Lord, am doing it. ¹⁰, ¹¹The day of judgment has come; the morning dawns, for your wickedness and pride have run their course and reached their climax—none of these rich and wicked men of pride shall live. All your boasting will die away, and no one will be left to bewail your fate.

¹²"Yes, the time has come; the day draws near. There will be nothing to buy or sell, for the wrath of God is on the land. ¹³And even if a merchant lives, his business will be gone, for God has spoken against all the people of Israel; all will be destroyed. Not one of those whose lives are filled with sin will recover.

¹⁴"The trumpets shout to Israel's army, 'Mobilize!' but no one listens, for my wrath is on them all. ¹⁵If you go outside the walls, there stands the enemy to kill you. If you stay inside, famine and disease will devour you. ¹⁶Any who escape will be lonely as mourning doves hiding on the mountains, each weeping for his sins. ¹⁷All hands shall be feeble, and all knees as weak as water. ¹⁸You shall clothe yourselves with sackcloth, and horror and shame shall cover you; you shall shave your heads in sorrow and remorse.

¹⁹"Throw away your money! Toss it out like worthless rubbish, for it will have no value in that day of wrath. It will neither satisfy nor feed you, for your love of money is the reason for your sin. ²⁰I gave you gold to use in decorating the Temple, and you used it instead to make idols! Therefore I will take it all away from you. ²¹I will give it to foreigners and to wicked men as booty. They shall defile my Temple. ²²I will not look when they defile it, nor will I stop them. Like robbers, they will loot the treasures and leave the Temple in ruins.

²³"Prepare chains for my people, for the land is full of bloody crimes. Jerusalem is filled with violence, so I will enslave her people. ²⁴I will crush your pride by bringing to Jerusalem the worst of the nations to occupy your homes, break down your fortifications you are so proud of, and defile your Temple. ²⁵For the time has come for the cutting off of Israel. You will sue for peace, but you won't get it. ²⁶, ²⁷Calamity upon calamity will befall you; woe upon woe, disaster upon disaster! You will long for a prophet to guide you, but the priests and elders and the kings and princes will stand helpless, weeping in despair. The people will tremble with fear, for I will do to them the evil they have done, and give them all their just deserts. They shall learn that I am the Lord."

7:10, 11 In chapter seven, Ezekiel predicts the complete destruction of Judah. The wicked and proud will finally get what they deserve. If it seems that God ignores the evil and proud of our day, be assured that another day of judgment will come, just as it came for the people of Judah. God is waiting patiently for sinners to repent (see 2 Peter 3:9), but when his judgment comes, "none of these rich and wicked men of pride shall live." What you decide about God now will determine your fate then.

7:12, 13 The nation of Judah trusted in its prosperity instead of in God. So God planned to destroy the basis of their prosperity. Whenever we begin to trust in jobs, the economy, a political system, or military might for our security, we put God in the back seat.

7:19 Money has a strange power to lead people into sin. Paul said the love of money is the first step to sin (1 Timothy 6:10). How ironic that we use wealth—a gift of God—to buy things that separate us from him. How tragic it is that we spend so much time looking for ways to satisfy ourselves with money, and so little time looking for God, the true source of satisfaction.

7:20 God gave the people gold to decorate the Temple, but they used it to make idols. The resources God gives us should be used to do his work and carry out his will, but too often we consume them to satisfy our own desires. Those who abuse God's gifts or use resources for selfish purposes are guilty of idolatry.

7:24 The people of Jerusalem took great pride in their houses and fortifications. The Temple itself was a source of pride (see 24:20, 21). This pride would be crushed when the evil and godless Babylonians destroyed Jerusalem's buildings. If you are going through a humiliating experience, it is possible that God is using that experience to weed out pride in your life.

7:26, 27 Too often, we fail to see that we deserve the same treatment as Judah. If we saw what we deserve because of our sins, we too would tremble. But God's mercy protects us from the punishment due to us for our sinful actions. If we realized that our "just deserts" are punishment and death, we would respond to God's mercy with grateful obedience. The people of Judah didn't respond in this way, and they got what they truly deserved.

The sins of the people

8 Then, late in August of the sixth year of King Jehoiachin's captivity, as I was talking with the elders of Judah in my home, the power of the Lord God fell upon me. 2I saw what appeared to be a Man; from his waist down, he was made of fire; from his waist up, he was all amber-colored brightness. 3He put out what seemed to be a hand and took me by the hair. And the Spirit lifted me up into the sky and seemed to transport me to Jerusalem, to the entrance of the north gate, where the large idol was that had made the Lord so angry. 4Suddenly the glory of the God of Israel was there, just as I had seen it before in the valley.

5He said to me, "Son of dust, look toward the north." So I looked and, sure enough, north of the altar gate, in the entrance, stood the idol.

6And he said: "Son of dust, do you see what they are doing? Do you see what great sins the people of Israel are doing here, to push me from my Temple? But come, and I will show you greater sins than these!"

7Then he brought me to the door of the Temple court, where I could see an opening in the wall.

8"Now dig into the wall," he said. I did, and uncovered a door to a hidden room. 9"Go in," he said, "and see the wickedness going on in there!"

10So I went in. The walls were covered with pictures of all kinds of snakes, lizards and hideous creatures, besides all the various idols worshiped by the people of Israel. 11Seventy elders of Israel were standing there along with Ja-azaniah (son of Shaphan) worshiping the pictures. Each of them held a censer of burning incense, so there was a thick cloud of smoke above their heads.

12Then the Lord said to me: "Son of dust, have you seen what the elders of Israel are doing in their minds? For they say, 'The Lord doesn't see us; he has gone away!'" 13Then he added, "Come, and I will show you greater sins than these!"

14He brought me to the north gate of the Temple, and there sat women weeping for Tammuz, their god.

15"Have you seen this?" he asked. "But I will show you greater evils than these!"

16Then he brought me into the inner court of the Temple and there at the door, between the porch and the bronze altar, were about twenty-five men standing with their backs to the Temple of the Lord, facing east, worshiping the sun!

17"Have you seen this?" he asked. "Is it nothing to the people of Judah that they commit these terrible sins, leading the whole nation into idolatry, thumbing their noses at me and arousing my fury against them? 18Therefore I will deal with them in fury. I will neither pity nor spare. And though they scream for mercy, I will not listen."

The death of idolaters

9 Then he thundered, "Call those to whom I have given the city! Tell them to bring their weapons with them!"

8:1 *the sixth year of King Jehoiachin's captivity,* implied.

Cross-references (margin):

8:2 Ezek 1:4,27,28
8:3 Jer 7:30; Ezek 3:12; 11:1; Dan 5:5
8:4 Ezek 1:27,28
8:5 Ps 78:58; Jer 3:2; 7:30; 32:34; Ezek 8:3; Zech 5:5
8:6 2 Kgs 23:4,5; Ezek 5:11; 8:9,17
8:8 Job 34:22; Isa 29:15
8:10 Ex 20:4; Isa 29:15
8:11 Num 11:16,25; 16:17,35; Jer 19:1; Lk 10:1
8:12 Ezek 9:9
8:14 Ezek 44:4; 46:9
8:16 Deut 4:19; 17:3; 2 Chron 29:6; Job 31:26-28; Jer 2:27; 44:17; Ezek 23:39
8:17 Jer 7:18,19; Ezek 7:10,11, 23; 9:9; Amos 3:10; Mic 2:2
8:18 Isa 1:15; Jer 11:11; Mic 3:4; Zech 7:13

8:1ff This prophecy is dated 592 B.C. The message of chapters 8—11 is directed specifically toward Jerusalem and its leaders. In chapter eight Ezekiel is taken in spirit from Babylon to the Temple in Jerusalem to see the great wickedness being practiced there. Both the people and their religious leaders are thoroughly corrupt. While Ezekiel's first vision showed that judgment was from God, this vision shows the reason for judgment.

8:2 This Man could have been an angel or a manifestation of God himself. In Ezekiel's previous vision, such a man was pictured as God on his throne (1:26-28). Ezekiel was careful to say that this Being *appeared* to be a man. God was making himself visible to Ezekiel in a recognizable form.

8:5 This could be referring to Asherah, the Canaanite goddess of fertility whose character encouraged sexual immorality and self-gratification. King Manasseh had placed such an idol in the Temple (2 Kings 21:7). King Josiah burned it (2 Kings 23:6), but there were many other idols around.

8:6ff In scene after scene, God reveals to Ezekiel the extent to which the people have embraced idolatry and wickedness. God's Spirit works with us in a similar way, revealing sin that lurks in our lives. How comfortable would you feel if God held an open house in your life today?

8:14 Tammuz was the Babylonian god of spring. The followers of this cult believed that the green vegetation shriveled and died in the hot summer because Tammuz had died and descended into the underworld. Thus, the worshipers wept and mourned his death. In the springtime, when the new vegetation appeared, they rejoiced believing he had come back to life. God was showing Ezekiel that many people were no longer worshiping the *true* God of life and vegetation. We must also be careful not to spend so much time thinking about created things that we lose sight of the Creator.

9:1ff This chapter presents a picture of coming judgment. Now that Ezekiel has seen how corrupt Jerusalem had become, God

9:2
Ezek 10:2

9:3
Ezek 10:4
11:22,23

9:4
Ex 12:7,13
Ps 119:53,136
2 Cor 1:22
2 Tim 2:19
Rev 7:2,3

9:6
Ex 12:23
2 Chron 36:17
Ezek 5:11
8:11,12
Rev 9:4

9:7
Ezek 7:20-22

9:8
1 Chron 21:16
Ezek 11:13
Amos 7:2-6

9:9
2 Kgs 21:16
Ps 10:11; 94:7
Isa 29:15
Ezek 7:23; 8:12
22:2,3,29
Mic 3:1-3; 7:3

9:10
Isa 65:6
Ezek 7:4; 24:14
Hos 9:7

10:1
Ex 24:10
Ezek 1:22,26
Rev 4:2,3

²Six men appeared at his call, coming from the upper north gate, each one with his sword. One of them wore linen clothing and carried a writer's case strapped to his side. They all went into the Temple and stood beside the bronze altar. ³And the glory of the God of Israel rose from between the Guardian Angels where it had rested and stood above the entrance to the Temple.

And the Lord called to the man with the writer's case, ⁴and said to him, "Walk through the streets of Jerusalem and put a mark on the foreheads of the men who weep and sigh because of all the sins they see around them."

⁵Then I heard the Lord tell the other men: "Follow him through the city and kill everyone whose forehead isn't marked. Spare not nor pity them— ⁶kill them all—old and young, girls, women and little children; but don't touch anyone with the mark. And begin right here at the Temple." And so they began by killing the seventy elders.

⁷And he said, "Defile the Temple! Fill its courts with the bodies of those you kill! Go!" And they went out through the city and did as they were told.

⁸While they were fulfilling their orders, I was alone. I fell to the ground on my face and cried out: "O Lord God! Will your fury against Jerusalem wipe out everyone left in Israel?"

⁹But he said to me, "The sins of the people of Israel and Judah are very great and all the land is full of murder and injustice, for they say, 'The Lord doesn't see it! He has gone away!' ¹⁰And so I will not spare them nor have any pity on them, and I will fully repay them for all that they have done."

¹¹Just then the man in linen clothing, carrying the writer's case, reported back and said, "I have finished the work you gave me to do."

Burning coals are scattered over Jerusalem

10 Suddenly a throne of beautiful blue sapphire appeared in the sky above the heads of the Guardian Angels.

²Then the Lord spoke to the man in linen clothing and said: "Go in between the

9:3 *above the entrance,* literally, "above the threshold of . . ." **10:1** *blue sapphire,* literally, "lapis lazuli." *Guardian Angels,* literally, "cherubim."

---

calls six men to slaughter the wicked of the city. Then he calls one man to spare the small minority who have been faithful. This judgment was ordered by God himself (9:5-7).

9:2 The writer's case was a common object in Ezekiel's day. It was a long narrow board with a groove to hold the reed brush used to write on parchment, papyrus, or dried clay. The board had hollowed out areas that held cakes of black and red ink which had to be moistened before use. Some other translations say that the man with the writer's case was an addition to the other six men.

9:3 The Guardian Angels are called "cherubim" in many translations. Cherubim are an order of angelic beings created to glorify God. They are associated with God's absolute holiness and moral perfection. God placed cherubim at the entrance of Eden to keep Adam and Eve out after they sinned (Genesis 3:24). Representations of cherubim were used to decorate the Tabernacle and Temple. The lid of the Ark of the Covenant was adorned with two gold cherubim (Exodus 37:6-9). The cherubim seen by Ezekiel left the Temple along with the glory of God. Ezekiel then recognized them as the divine beings he had seen in his first vision (see chapter one).

9:3 What is God's glory? It is the manifestation of God's character—his ultimate power, transcendence, and moral perfection. He is completely above man and his limitations. Yet he reveals himself to people so that they can worship and follow him.

9:4, 5 The man with the writer's case was to put a mark on those who were faithful to God. Their faithfulness was determined by their sensitivity to and sorrow over sin. Those with the mark were spared when the six men began to destroy the wicked people. During the Exodus, the Israelites put a mark of blood on their door to save them from the angel of death. In the final days, God will mark the

foreheads of those destined for salvation (Revelation 7:3). God's promise to preserve his people is not forgotten in the midst of judgment.

9:6 The spiritual leaders (elders) of Israel blatantly promoted their idolatrous beliefs, and the people abandoned God and followed their leaders. Spiritual leaders are especially accountable to God because they are entrusted with the task of teaching the truth (see James 3:1, 2). When they pervert the truth, they can lead countless people away from God and even cause a nation to fall. It is not surprising, then, that when God began to judge the nation, he started at the Temple and worked outward (see 1 Peter 4:17). How sad that in the Temple, the one place where truth should have been found, the teaching was far from the truth.

9:9, 10 The people said that the Lord had gone away and wouldn't see their sin. People have many convenient explanations to make it easier to sin: "It doesn't matter," "Everybody's doing it," or "Nobody will ever know." Do you find yourself making excuses for sin? Rationalizing sin makes it easier to commit it, but it does not influence God's promise to punish it.

10:1ff In chapters 8—11, God's glory is graphically presented as departing from the Temple. In 8:4, his glory is over the northern gate. It then moved to the door (9:3), then to the south side of the Temple (10:3), to the eastern gate (10:18, 19; 11:1), and finally to the mountain east of the Temple (11:23), probably the Mount of Olives. Due to the nation's sins, God's glory had departed.

10:2 God's perfect holiness (10:1) demands judgment for sin. The glowing coals scattered over the city represent the purging of sin. For Jerusalem, this meant the destruction of all the people who blatantly sinned and refused to repent. Shortly after this prophecy, the Babylonians destroyed Jerusalem by fire (2 Chronicles 36:19).

whirling wheels beneath the Guardian Angels, and take a handful of glowing coals and scatter them over the city."

He did so while I watched. 3The Guardian Angels were standing at the south end of the Temple when the man went in. And the cloud of glory filled the inner court. 4Then the glory of the Lord rose from above the Guardian Angels and went over to the door of the Temple. The Temple was filled with the cloud of glory, and the court of the Temple was filled with the brightness of the glory of the Lord. 5And the sound of the wings of the Guardian Angels was as the voice of Almighty God when he speaks and could be heard clear out in the outer court.

6When the Lord told the man in linen clothing to go between the Guardian Angels and take some burning coals from between the wheels, the man went in and stood beside one of the wheels, 7, 8and one of the Guardian Angels reached out his hand (for each of the mighty angels had, beneath his wings, what looked like human hands) and took some live coals from the flames between the Angels and put them into the hands of the man in linen clothes, who took them and went out.

9-13Each of the four Guardian Angels had a wheel beside him—"The Whirl-Wheels," as I heard them called, for each one had a second wheel crosswise within—sparkling like chrysolite, giving off a greenish-yellow glow. Because of the construction of these wheels, the Angels could go straight forward in each of four directions; they did not turn when they changed direction but could go in any of the four ways their faces looked. Each of the four wheels was covered with eyes, including the rims and spokes. 14Each of the four Guardian Angels had four faces—the first was that of an ox; the second, a man's; the third, a lion's; and the fourth, an eagle's.

15, 16These were the same beings I had seen beside the Chebar Canal, and when they rose into the air the wheels rose with them, and stayed beside them as they flew. 17When the Guardian Angels stood still, so did the wheels, for the spirit of the Guardian Angels was in the wheels.

18Then the glory of the Lord moved from the door of the Temple and stood above the Guardian Angels. 19And as I watched, the Guardian Angels flew with their wheels beside them to the east gate of the Temple. And the glory of the God of Israel was above them.

20These were the living beings I had seen beneath the God of Israel beside the Chebar Canal. I knew they were the same, 21for each had four faces and four wings, with what looked like human hands under their wings. 22Their faces too were identical to the faces of those I had seen at the Canal, and they traveled straight ahead, just as the others did.

God will regather Israel

11 Then the Spirit lifted me and brought me over to the east gate of the Temple, where I saw twenty-five of the most prominent men of the city, including two officers, Ja-azaniah (son of Azzur) and Pelatiah (son of Benaiah).

Then the Spirit said to me, "Son of dust, these are the men who are responsible for all of the wicked counsel being given out in this city. 3For they say to the people, 'It is time to rebuild Jerusalem, for our city is an iron shield and will protect us from all harm.' 4Therefore, son of dust, prophesy against them loudly and clearly."

5Then the Spirit of the Lord came upon me and told me to say: "The Lord says

10:3 Ezek 8:3,16

10:4 Ex 40:34,35 Isa 6:1-4 Ezek 1:27,28 9:3; 11:22,23

10:5 Job 40:9 Ezek 1:24 Rev 10:3

10:7 Ezek 1:8

10:9 Ezek 1:16,17 Rev 21:18-20

10:14 1 Kgs 7:27-30, 36 Ezek 1:6,10 10:21 Rev 4:7

10:15 Ezek 1:3-6, 19-21

10:17 Ezek 1:12

10:18 Ps 18:10

10:20 Ezek 1:5,26 10:15

10:21 Ezek 1:6,8 10:14; 41:18-20

10:22 Ezek 1:10,12

11:1 1 Kgs 18:12 2 Kgs 2:16 Isa 30:1 Jer 5:5 Ezek 8:3; 43:5 Mic 2:1

11:3 Jer 1:13 Ezek 24:3,6 2 Pet 3:4

11:4 Ezek 3:4,17

10:9-13 Because of the construction of these wheels, implied. **10:14** ox, literally, "cherub's face." See 1:10. **10:17** for the spirit of the Guardian Angels was in the wheels. That is, the wheel was a living part of the bodies of the cherubim. Hence it could not be separated from the cherubim. **11:3** for our city is an iron shield and will protect us from all harm, literally, "this city the caldron and we the flesh."

11:1-4 God was abandoning his altar and Temple (chapters 9—11); his judgment was now complete as he left Jerusalem. The city gate was where merchants and politicians conducted business, so the 25 men may have represented the rulers of the nation. Because of their leadership positions, they were responsible for leading the people astray. They had wrongly said that Jerusalem was secure from another attack by the Babylonians.

11:5 God knew everything about the Israelites, even their thoughts. And he knows everything about us, even the sins we have only imagined. How ironic that we worry about people noticing how we look or what we do, but we don't care what God thinks—and he sees everything. Trying to hide our thoughts and actions from God is futile. The only effective way to deal with sin is to confess it and ask God to help you overcome it.

11:6
Ezek 7:23
22:2-6,9,12,27

11:7
2 Kgs 25:18-22
Jer 52:24-27

11:9
Rom 13:4

11:10
Num 34:8,9
Josh 13:5

11:12
Lev 26:40
Deut 12:30,31
2 Kgs 16:3-12
Ezek 8:10,14,
16; 18:8,9

11:13
Ezek 9:8

11:15
Jer 24:1-5
Ezek 33:24

11:17
Isa 11:11-16
Hos 1:10,11
Amos 9:14,15

11:18
Ezek 5:11; 37:23

11:19
Deut 30:6
2 Kgs 22:19
Jer 24:7; 32:39
Ezek 36:26
2 Cor 3:3

11:20
Ezek 36:27
Hos 2:23

11:21
Jer 16:18

11:22
Ezek 10:19

11:23
Ezek 8:4

11:24
Ezek 8:3; 37:1
2 Cor 12:2-4
Acts 10:16

11:25
Ezek 2:7

to the people of Israel: Is that what you are saying? Yes, I know it is, for I know everything you think—every thought that comes into your minds. 6You have murdered endlessly and filled your streets with the dead.

7"Therefore the Lord God says: You think this city is an iron shield? No, it isn't! It will not protect you. Your slain will lie within it, but you will be dragged out and slaughtered. 8I will expose you to the war you have so greatly feared, says the Lord God, 9and I will take you from Jerusalem and hand you over to foreigners who will carry out my judgments against you. 10You will be slaughtered all the way to the borders of Israel, and you will know I am the Lord. 11No, this city will not be an iron shield for you, and you safe within. I will chase you even to the borders of Israel, 12and you will know I am the Lord—you who have not obeyed me, but rather have copied the nations all around you."

13While I was still speaking and telling them this, Pelatiah (son of Benaiah) suddenly died. Then I fell to the ground on my face and cried out: "O Lord God, are you going to kill everyone in all Israel?"

14Again a message came from the Lord:

15"Son of dust, the remnant left in Jerusalem are saying about your brother exiles: 'It is because they were so wicked that the Lord has deported them. Now the Lord has given us their land!'

16"But tell the exiles that the Lord God says: Although I have scattered you in the countries of the world, yet I will be a sanctuary to you for the time that you are there, 17and I will gather you back from the nations where you are scattered and give you the land of Israel again. 18And when you return you will remove every trace of all this idol worship. 19I will give you one heart and a new spirit; I will take from you your hearts of stone and give you tender hearts of love for God, 20so that you can obey my laws and be my people, and I will be your God. 21But as for those now in Jerusalem, who long for idols, I will repay them fully for their sins," the Lord God says.

22Then the Guardian Angels lifted their wings and rose into the air with their wheels beside them, and the glory of the God of Israel stood above them. 23Then the glory of the Lord rose from over the city and stood above the mountain on the east side.

24Afterwards the Spirit of God carried me back again to Babylon, to the Jews in exile there. And so ended the vision of my visit to Jerusalem. 25And I told the exiles everything the Lord had shown me.

11:7 *but you will be dragged out and slaughtered,* literally, "Your slain . . . are the flesh and this is the caldron; but you will be brought out from it." **11:21** *as for those now in Jerusalem,* implied.

11:7 Some translations use the word *caldron* rather than *iron shield.* The city leaders thought Jerusalem was safe, like meat cooking in a pot. But Ezekiel said that the pot's contents would be poured out over the cooking fire, illustrating how precarious Jerusalem's position really was.

11:12 From the time they entered the Promised Land, the Israelites were warned not to copy the customs and religious practices of other nations. Disobeying this command and following heathen customs instead of God's laws always got them into trouble. Today, believers are still tempted to copy the ways of the world. But we must get our standards of right and wrong from God, not from the popular trends of society.

11:14ff God promised the exiles in Babylon that he would continue to be with them even though they had left Jerusalem. This was a major concern to the Jews because they believed God was present primarily in the Temple. But God assured them that he would continue to be their God and give them his Spirit regardless of where they were. In the midst of Ezekiel's burning message of judgment stands a cool oasis—God's promise to restore the faithful few to their homeland. His arms are now open to receive those who will repent of their sins.

11:15-21 God's messages through Ezekiel are full of irony. Here he says that the Jews in captivity are the faithful ones, and those in Jerusalem are the sinful and wicked ones. This was the opposite of the people's perception. Appearances can be deceiving. God will evaluate your life by your faith and obedience, not by your apparent earthly success and blessings. We cannot accurately judge the lives of others.

11:16 God is a "sanctuary" for the righteous remnant. Those idolatrous people now worshiping in the Temple (11:15) would find no true "sanctuary" but those now in exile were already protected by God. Likewise, our external circumstances are not truly indicative of our stand with God. It is faithfulness, not status, which determines true "sanctuary."

11:23 God's glory left Jerusalem and stood above a mountain on the east side of Jerusalem—almost certainly the Mount of Olives. Ezekiel 43:1-4 implies that God will return the same way he left, when he comes back to earth to set up his perfect kingdom.

3. Punishment is certain
Ezekiel demonstrates the exile

12 Again a message came to me from the Lord: 2"Son of dust," he said, "you live among rebels who could know the truth if they wanted to, but they don't want to; they could hear me if they would listen, but they won't, 3for they are rebels. So now put on a demonstration, to show them what being exiled will be like. Pack whatever you can carry on your back and leave your home—go somewhere else. Go in the daylight so they can see, for perhaps even yet they will consider what this means, even though they are such rebels. 4Bring your baggage outside your house during the daylight so they can watch. Then leave the house at night, just as captives do when they begin their long march to distant lands. 5Dig a tunnel through the city wall while they are observing and carry your possessions out through the hole. 6As they watch, lift your pack to your shoulders and walk away into the night; muffle your face and don't gaze around. All this is a sign to the people of Israel of the evil that will come upon Jerusalem."

7So I did as I was told. I brought my pack outside in the daylight—all I could take into exile—and in the evening I dug through the wall with my hands. I went out into the darkness with my pack on my shoulder while the people looked on. 8The next morning this message came to me from the Lord:

9"Son of dust, these rebels, the people of Israel, have asked what all this means. 10Tell them the Lord God says it is a message to King Zedekiah in Jerusalem and to all the people of Israel. 11Explain that what you did was a demonstration of what is going to happen to them, for they shall be driven out of their homes and sent away into exile.

12"Even King Zedekiah shall go out at night through a hole in the wall, taking only what he can carry with him, with muffled face, for he won't be able to see. 13I will capture him in my net and bring him to Babylon, the land of the Chaldeans; but he shall not see it, and he shall die there. 14I will scatter his servants and guards to the four winds and send the sword after them. 15And when I scatter them among the nations, then they shall know I am the Lord. 16But I will spare a few of them from death by war and famine and disease. I will save them to confess to the nations how wicked they have been, and they shall know I am the Lord."

17Then this message came to me from the Lord:

18"Son of dust, tremble as you eat your meals; ration out your water as though it were your last, 19and say to the people, the Lord God says that the people of Israel and Jerusalem shall ration their food with utmost care and sip their tiny portions of water in utter despair because of all their sins. 20Your cities shall be destroyed and your farmlands deserted, and you shall know I am the Lord."

21Again a message came to me from the Lord:

22"Son of dust, what is that proverb they quote in Israel—'The days as they pass make liars out of every prophet.' 23The Lord God says, I will put an end to this proverb and they will soon stop saying it. Give them this one instead: 'The time has come for all these prophecies to be fulfilled.'

24"Then you will see what becomes of all the false predictions of safety and security for Jerusalem. 25For I am the Lord! What I threaten always happens. There

12:2
Deut 29:4
Isa 6:9,10
Jer 5:21
Ezek 2:6-8
Mt 13:13,14
Jn 9:39-41

12:3
Deut 5:29
Ps 18:13
Jer 26:3
Lk 20:13
2 Tim 2:25

12:4
2 Kgs 25:4
Jer 39:4; 52:7

12:6
Isa 20:3
Ezek 4:3

12:7
Ezek 24:18

12:9
Ezek 2:5-8
17:12; 24:19

12:10
2 Kgs 9:25
Isa 13:1; 14:28

12:11
Jer 15:2,28-30

12:12
2 Kgs 25:4
Jer 39:4; 52:7

12:13
Isa 24:17
Jer 39:7
Hos 7:12

12:14
Ezek 5:2; 17:21

12:16
Deut 29:24-28
1 Kgs 9:6-9
Jer 22:8,9

12:19
Isa 6:11
Mic 7:13
Zech 7:14

12:20
Isa 7:23,24
Jer 25:9
Dan 9:17

12:22
Jer 5:12
Amos 6:3
2 Pet 3:3,4

12:24
1 Kgs 22:11-13
Prov 26:28
Jer 14:13-16
Zech 13:2-4

12:25
Num 14:28-34

12:10 *King Zedekiah*, literally, "to the prince in Jerusalem." **12:12** *for he won't be able to see*, literally, "that he may not see the land with his eyes." Apparently a reference to the fact that his eyes were put out before he was taken to Babylon, Jer 52:11. Also in vs 13.

12:1ff Ezekiel played the role of a captive being led away to exile, portraying what was about to happen to King Zedekiah and the people remaining in Jerusalem. The exiles knew exactly what Ezekiel was doing because only six years before they had made similar preparations as they left Jerusalem for Babylon. This was to show the people that they should not trust the king or the capital city to save them from the Babylonian army—only God could do that. And the exiles who hoped for an early return from exile would be disappointed. Ezekiel's graphic demonstration was proven correct to the last detail.

12:10-12 Zedekiah, Judah's last king (597–586 B.C.), was reigning in Jerusalem when Ezekiel gave these messages. Ezekiel showed the people what would happen to Zedekiah. Jerusalem would be attacked again, and Zedekiah would join the exiles already in Babylon (2 Kings 25:3–7). Zedekiah would be unable to see because Nebuchadnezzar would have his eyes gouged out (Jeremiah 52:10, 11).

12:21-28 These two short messages were warnings that God's words would come true— *soon!* . Less than six years later, Jerusalem was destroyed. Judgment comes swiftly and no one dares assume there is plenty of time left to get right with God.

will be no more delays, O rebels of Israel! I will do it in your own lifetime!" says the Lord God.

²⁶Then this message came:

12:27
Dan 10:14

²⁷"Son of dust, the people of Israel say, 'His visions won't come true for a long, long time.' ²⁸Therefore say to them: 'The Lord God says, All delay has ended! I will do it now!' "

Judgment against false prophets

13 Then this message came to me:

13:2
Isa 9:15
56:9-12
Jer 37:19
Zech 11:15
2 Pet 2:1-3

²,³"Son of dust, prophesy against the false prophets of Israel who are inventing their own visions and claiming to have messages from me when I have never told them anything at all. Woe upon them!

⁴"O Israel, these 'prophets' of yours are as useless as foxes for rebuilding your walls! ⁵O evil prophets, what have you ever done to strengthen the walls of Israel

13:5
Ps 106:23
Isa 58:12
Eph 6:13,14
Rev: 16:14

against her enemies—by strengthening Israel in the Lord? ⁶Instead you have lied when you said, 'My message is from God!' God did not send you. And yet you

13:6
Prov 14:15
Jer 28:15; 29:8
Mk 13:22,23
2 Thess 2:11

expect him to fulfill your prophecies. ⁷Can you deny that you have claimed to see 'visions' you never saw, and that you have said, 'This message is from God,' when I never spoke to you at all?

13:8
Nah 2:13

⁸"Therefore the Lord God says: I will destroy you for these 'visions' and lies. ⁹My hand shall be against you, and you shall be cut off from among the leaders of Israel; I will blot out your names and you will never see your own country again.

13:9
Ex 32:32,33
Ezra 2:59-63
Ps 69:28
Jer 20:3-6
Dan 12:1
Phil 4:3

And you shall know I am the Lord. ¹⁰For these evil men deceive my people by saying, 'God will send peace,' when that is not my plan at all! My people build a flimsy wall and these prophets praise them for it—and cover it with whitewash!

13:10
Jer 8:11; 50:6
1 Tim 4:1
2 Tim 3:13

¹¹"Tell these evil builders that their wall will fall. A heavy rainstorm will undermine it; great hailstones and mighty winds will knock it down. ¹²And when the wall falls, the people will cry out, 'Why didn't you tell us that it wasn't good enough? Why did you whitewash it and cover up its faults?' ¹³Yes, it will surely

13:13
Ex 9:24,25
Ps 18:12,13
Rev 11:19
16:21

fall. The Lord God says: I will sweep it away with a storm of indignation and with a great flood of anger and with hailstones of wrath. ¹⁴I will break down your whitewashed wall, and it will fall on you and crush you, and you shall know I am

13:14
Mic 1:6
1 Cor 3:11-15

the Lord. ¹⁵Then at last my wrath against the wall will be completed; and concerning those who praised it, I will say: The wall and its builders both are gone. ¹⁶For

13:16
Isa 57:21

they were lying prophets, claiming Jerusalem will have peace when there is no peace, says the Lord God.

13:17
Judg 4:4
2 Kgs 22:14
Lk 2:36
Acts 21:9
Rev 2:20

¹⁷"Son of dust, speak out against the women prophets too who pretend the Lord has given them his messages. ¹⁸Tell them the Lord God says: Woe to these women who are damning the souls of my people, of both young and old alike, by tying magic charms on their wrists and furnishing them with magic veils and selling them

13:19
Jer 23:14,17

indulgences. They refuse to even offer help unless they get a profit from it. ¹⁹For the sake of a few paltry handfuls of barley or a piece of bread will you turn away my people from me? You have led those to death who should not die! And you have promised life to those who should not live, by lying to my people—and how they love it!

²⁰"And so the Lord says: I will crush you because you hunt my people's souls with all your magic charms. I will tear off the charms and set my people free like

13:21
Ps 91:3; 124:7

birds from cages. ²¹I will tear off the magic veils and save my people from you;

13:18 *unless they get a profit from it,* literally, "Will you hunt the souls of my people and save your own souls alive?"

13:1ff This warning was directed against false prophets whose messages were not from God, but were lies intended to win popularity by saying whatever made the people happy. False prophets did not care about the truth as Ezekiel did. They lulled people into a false sense of security, making Ezekiel's job even more difficult. Beware of leaders who are willing to bend the truth in their quest for popularity and power.

13:2, 3 The false prophets had a large following because they

comforted the people and approved of their actions even while they were sinning. Lies are often attractive, and liars may have large followings. Today, for example, some leaders assure us that God wants everyone to have health and material success. This is comforting, but is it true? God's own Son did not have an easy life on earth. Make sure the messages you believe are consistent with what God teaches in his Word.

they will no longer be your victims, and you shall know I am the Lord. 22Your lies have discouraged the righteous, when I didn't want it so. And you have encouraged the wicked by promising life, though they continue in their sins. 23But you will lie no more; no longer will you talk of seeing 'visions' that you never saw, nor practice your magic, for I will deliver my people out of your hands by destroying you, and you shall know I am the Lord."

Idolatry is condemned

14 Then some of the elders of Israel visited me, to ask me for a message from the Lord, 2and this is the message that came to me to give to them:

3"Son of dust, these men worship idols in their hearts—should I let them ask me anything? 4Tell them, the Lord God says: I the Lord will personally deal with anyone in Israel who worships idols and then comes to ask my help. 5For I will punish the minds and hearts of those who turn from me to idols.

6, 7"Therefore warn them that the Lord God says: Repent and destroy your idols, and stop worshiping them in your hearts. I the Lord will personally punish everyone, whether people of Israel or the foreigners living among you, who rejects me for idols, and then comes to a prophet to ask for my help and advice. 8I will turn upon him and make a terrible example of him, destroying him; and you shall know I am the Lord. 9And if one of the false prophets gives him a message anyway, it is a lie. His prophecy will not come true, and I will stand against that 'prophet' and destroy him from among my people Israel. 10False prophets and hypocrites—evil people who say they want my words—all will be punished for their sins, 11so that the people of Israel will learn not to desert me and not to be polluted any longer with sin, but to be my people and I their God. So says the Lord."

12Then this message of the Lord came to me:

13"Son of dust, when the people of this land sin against me, then I will crush them with my fist and break off their food supply and send famine to destroy both man and beast. 14If Noah, Daniel and Job were here today, they alone would be saved by their righteousness, and I would destroy the remainder of Israel, says the Lord God.

15"When I send an invasion of dangerous wild animals into the land to devastate the land, 16even if these three men were here, the Lord God swears that it would do no good—it would not save the people from their doom. Those three only would be saved, but the land would be devastated.

17"Or when I bring war against that land and tell the armies of the enemy to come and destroy everything, 18even if these three men were in the land, the Lord God declares that they alone would be saved.

19"And when I pour out my fury by sending an epidemic of disease into the land, and the plague kills man and beast alike, 20though Noah, Daniel and Job were living there, the Lord God says that only they would be saved, because of their righteousness.

21"And the Lord says: Four great punishments await Jerusalem to destroy all life: war, famine, ferocious beasts, plague. 22If there are survivors and they come here to join you as exiles in Babylon, you will see with your own eyes how wicked they

13:22
Amos 5:12
2 Pet 2:18,19
13:23
Mic 3:6
Zech 13:3

14:1
2 Kgs 6:32

14:3
Isa 1:15
Zeph 1:3
14:4
1 Kgs 21:20-24
2 Kgs 1:16
Isa 66:4
14:5
Deut 32:14,15
Jer 2:11
Hos 10:2
Zech 7:12
14:6
1 Sam 7:3
Neh 1:9
Isa 30:22
55:6,7
14:8
Isa 65:15
Jer 24:9
Rom 11:22
14:9
Jer 6:14,15
14:11
Deut 13:11
19:20
Isa 9:16
Ezek 44:10,15
14:13
Ezek 15:8; 20:27
14:14
Gen 6:8
8:20,21
Job 1:1,5
Dan 10:11
Heb 11:7
14:16
Gen 19:29
Acts 27:24

14:19
Jer 14:12
Ezek 5:12

14:21
Amos 4:6-10
Rev 6:4-8
14:22
Ezek 36:20

14:3 God condemned the elders for worshiping idols in their hearts. On the outside, they appeared to worship God. They made regular visits to the Temple where they offered sacrifices, but they were not sincere. It is easy for us to criticize the Israelites for worshiping idols when they so clearly needed God. But we have idols in our hearts when we put anything above God, whether it is reputation, acceptance, wealth, or sensual pleasure. When we make anything more important than God, we are guilty of idolatry. True allegiance comes from the heart.

14:6-11 The nation of Judah, though eager to accept the messages of false prophets, considered the presence of a few godly men in the nation an insurance policy against disaster. But merely having godly people around doesn't help. We must

remember that the godliness of our pastor or friends will not protect us from the consequences of our own sins. Each person is responsible for his or her own relationship with God. How are you living?

14:14 Noah, Daniel, and Job were great men in Hebrew history, renowned for their relationships with God and their wisdom (see Genesis 6:8–10; Daniel 6:22; Job 1:1). Daniel had been taken into captivity during Babylon's first invasion of Judah in 605 B.C., eight years before Ezekiel was taken captive. At the time of Ezekiel's message, Daniel occupied a high government position in Babylon (see Daniel 1). But even these great men of God could not have saved the people of Judah, because God had already passed judgment on the nation's great evil.

are, and you will know it was right for me to destroy Jerusalem. 23You will agree, when you meet them, that it is not without cause that all these things are being done to Israel."

Jerusalem is a useless vine

15 Then this message came to me from the Lord: 2"Son of dust, what good are vines from the forest? Are they as useful as trees? Are they even as valuable as a single branch? 3No, for vines can't be used even for making pegs to hang up pots and pans! 4All they are good for is fuel—and even so, they burn but poorly! 5, 6So they are useless both before and after being put in the fire!

"This is what I mean, the Lord God says: The people of Jerusalem are like the vines of the forest—useless before being burned and certainly useless afterwards! 7And I will set myself against them to see to it that if they escape from one fire, they will fall into another; and then you shall know I am the Lord. 8And I will make the land desolate because they worship idols," says the Lord God.

Israel's loathsome sins

16 Then again a message came to me from the Lord. 2"Son of dust," he said, "speak to Jerusalem about her loathsome sins. 3Tell her, the Lord God says: You are no better than the people of Canaan—your father must have been an Amorite and your mother a Hittite! 4When you were born, no one cared for you. When I first saw you, your umbilical cord was uncut, and you had been neither washed nor rubbed with salt nor clothed. 5No one had the slightest interest in you; no one pitied you or cared for you. On that day when you were born, you were dumped out into a field and left to die, unwanted.

6, 7"But I came by and saw you there, covered with your own blood, and I said, 'Live! Thrive like a plant in the field!' And you did! You grew up and became tall, slender and supple, a jewel among jewels. And when you reached the age of maidenhood your breasts were full-formed and your pubic hair had grown; yet you were naked.

8"Later, when I passed by and saw you again, you were old enough for marriage; and I wrapped my cloak around you to legally declare my marriage vow. I signed a covenant with you, and you became mine. 9, 10Then, when the marriage had taken place, I gave you beautiful clothes of linens and silk, embroidered, and sandals made of dolphin hide. 11I gave you lovely ornaments, bracelets and beautiful necklaces, 12a ring for your nose and two more for your ears, and a lovely tiara for your head. 13And so you were made beautiful with gold and silver, and your clothes were silk and linen and beautifully embroidered. You ate the finest foods and became more beautiful than ever. You looked like a queen, and so you were! 14Your reputation was great among the nations for your beauty; it was perfect because of all the gifts I gave you, says the Lord God.

15:2
Ps 80:8-16
Isa 5:1-7
Hos 10:1
Jn 15:1-6

15:4
Isa 27:11
Heb 6:8

15:7
Lev 26:17
1 Kgs 19:17
Amos 5:19
9:1-4

16:2
Isa 58:1
Hos 8:1

16:5
Deut 32:10
Isa 49:15
Jer 9:21,22
22:19

16:6
Ex 1:7
Deut 1:10
Ps 105:10-15

16:8
Gen 22:16-18
Ex 24:7,8
Deut 4:31
Hos 2:18-20

16:9
Ex 26:36
Ezek 26:16
27:7,16

16:11
Gen 24:22,47
Isa 3:18,19

16:12
Jer 13:18

16:13
Deut 32:13,14
Ps 45:13,14

16:14
Deut 4:6-8,
32-38
1 Kgs 10:1,24
Ps 50:2

15:1ff The messages given to Ezekiel in chapters 15—17 provided further evidence that God was going to destroy Jerusalem. The first message was about a vine, useless at first and even more useless after being burned. The people of Jerusalem were useless to God because of their idol worship, and so they would be destroyed and their cities burned. Isaiah also compared the nation of Israel to a vine (see Isaiah 5:1–10). Have you also become "useless" to God? Each of us must take a spiritual inventory of our true worthiness to stand before God.

16:1ff This message reminds Jerusalem of her former despised status among the Canaanite nations. Using the imagery of a young maiden growing to mature womanhood, God reminded her that he raised her from a lowly state to great glory as his bride. However, she betrayed God's trust and prostituted herself among the pagan nations who had formerly mistreated her. This same history has

been repeated in our time, as formerly orthodox denominations have denied their historical stance, and "Christian" nations have denied the very God who established them.

16:3 *Canaan* was the ancient name of the territory taken over by the children of Israel. The Bible often uses this name to refer to all the corrupt heathen nations of the region. The Hittites and Amorites, two Canaanite nations, were known for their wickedness. But now God says his people are no better than the Canaanites.

16:8-14 God chose Israel to be the channel through whom he would communicate his message of salvation to the entire world. He gave Israel special privileges and trained them to do his work. But these resources and advantages became her source of pride and vanity. We must remember that it is God who made us what we are. To use our gifts and opportunities only for our own selfish pursuits is both dangerous and foolish.

15"But you thought you could get along without me—you trusted in your beauty instead; and you gave yourself as a prostitute to every man who came along. Your beauty was his for the asking. 16You used the lovely things I gave you for making idol shrines and to decorate your bed of prostitution. Unbelievable! There has never been anything like it before! 17You took the very jewels and gold and silver ornaments I gave to you and made statues of men and worshiped them, which is adultery against me. 18You used the beautifully embroidered clothes I gave you—to cover your idols! And used my oil and incense to worship *them!* 19You set before them—imagine it—the fine flour and oil and honey I gave you; you used it as a lovely sacrifice to *them!* 20And you took my sons and daughters you had borne to me, and sacrificed them to your gods; and they are gone. Wasn't it enough that you should be a prostitute? 21Must you also slay my children by sacrificing them to idols?

22"And in all these years of adultery and sin you have not thought of those days long ago when you were naked and covered with blood.

23"And then, in addition to all your other wickedness—woe, woe upon you, says the Lord God— 24you built a spacious brothel for your lovers, and idol altars on every street, 25and there you offered your beauty to every man who came by, in an endless stream of prostitution. 26And you added lustful Egypt to your prostitutions by your alliance with her. My anger is great.

27"Therefore I have crushed you with my fist; I have reduced your boundaries and delivered you into the hands of those who hate you—the Philistines—and even they are ashamed of you.

28"You have committed adultery with the Assyrians too [by making them your allies and worshiping their gods]; it seems that you can never find enough new gods. After your adultery there, you still weren't satisfied, 29so you worshiped the gods of that great merchant land of Babylon—and you still weren't satisfied. 30What a filthy heart you have, says the Lord God, to do such things as these; you are a brazen prostitute, 31building your idol altars, your brothels, on every street. You have been worse than a prostitute, so eager for sin that you have not even charged for your love! 32Yes, you are an adulterous wife who lives with other men instead of her own husband. 33, 34Prostitutes charge for their services—men pay with many gifts. But not you, you give *them* gifts, bribing them to come to you! So you are different from other prostitutes. But you had to pay them, for no one wanted you.

35"O prostitute, hear the word of the Lord:

36"The Lord God says: Because I see your filthy sins, your adultery with your lovers—your worshiping of idols—and the slaying of your children as sacrifices to your gods, 37this is what I am going to do: I will gather together all your allies—these lovers of yours you have sinned with, both those you loved and those you hated—and I will make you naked before them, that they may see you. 38I will punish you as a murderess is punished and as a woman breaking wedlock living with other men. 39I will give you to your lovers—these many nations—to destroy, and they will knock down your brothels and idol altars, and strip you and take your beautiful jewels and leave you naked and ashamed. 40, 41They will burn your homes, punishing you before the eyes of many women. And I will see to it that you

16:28 *by making them your allies and worshiping their gods,* implied.

16:15
Ezek 27:3

16:17
Ex 32:3,4
Hos 2:13; 10:1

16:20
Ex 13:2,12
Ps 106:37,38
Jer 7:31
16:21
2 Kgs 17:17
21:6

16:24
2 Kgs 21:3-7
23:5-7
Ps 78:58
Isa 57:5-7
16:26
Jer 7:18,19
16:27
Isa 9:12

16:28
Judg 10:6
2 Kgs 16:7-18
2 Chron
28:16-23
Hos 10:6
16:30
Prov 7:11-13
9:13
Isa 3:9
Rev 17:1-6
16:31
Isa 52:3
Hos 12:11
16:33
Hos 8:9,10
Joel 3:3
Lk 15:30

16:36
Jer 19:5
Ezek 20:31
23:37
16:37
Isa 47:3
Nah 3:5,6
16:38
Ps 79:3,5
Zeph 1:17
Rev 16:6
16:40
2 Kgs 25:9
Jer 39:8

16:15 Don't confuse maturity with independence from God. This was what happened to the people of Jerusalem. God cared for her and loved her, only to have her turn away to other nations and their false gods. This is a picture of spiritual adultery (called apostasy—turning from the one true God). Don't turn away from the one who truly loves you. Real maturity is recognizing that God is all you need to make life worthwhile.

16:20, 21 Child sacrifice had been practiced by the Canaanites long before Israel invaded their land. But it was strictly forbidden

by God (Leviticus 20:1–3). By Ezekiel's time, however, the people were openly sacrificing their own children (2 Kings 16:3; 21:6). Jeremiah confirmed that this was a common practice (Jeremiah 7:31; 32:35). Because of such vile acts among the people and priesthood, the Temple became unfit for God to inhabit. When he left the Temple, he was no longer Judah's guide and protector.

16:27 The actions of the Jews were so disgusting that even those who worshiped other gods, including their great enemy the Philistines, would be ashamed to behave that way.

stop your adulteries with other gods and end your payments to your allies for their love.

42"Then at last my fury against you will die away; my jealousy against you will end, and I will be quiet and not be angry with you anymore. 43But first, because you have not remembered your youth, but have angered me by all these evil things you do, I will fully repay you for all of your sins, says the Lord. For you are thankless in addition to all your other faults.

44" 'Like mother, like daughter'—that is what everyone will say of you. 45For your mother loathed her husband and her children, and you do too. And you are exactly like your sisters, for they despised their husbands and their children. Truly, your mother must have been a Hittite and your father an Amorite.

46"Your older sister is Samaria, living with her daughters north of you; your younger sister is Sodom and her daughters, in the south. 47You have not merely sinned as they do—no, that was nothing to you; in a very short time you far surpassed them.

48"As I live, the Lord God says, Sodom and her daughters have never been as wicked as you and your daughters. 49Your sister Sodom's sins were pride and laziness and too much food, while the poor and needy suffered outside her door. 50She insolently worshiped many idols as I watched. Therefore I crushed her.

51"Even Samaria has not committed half your sins. You have worshiped idols far more than your sisters have; they seem almost righteous in comparison with you! 52Don't be surprised then by the lighter punishment they get. For your sins are so awful that in comparison with you, your sisters seem innocent! 53(But someday I will restore the fortunes of Sodom and Samaria again, and those of Judah too.) 54Your terrible punishment will be a consolation to them, for it will be greater than theirs.

55"Yes, your sisters, Sodom and Samaria, and all their people will be restored again, and Judah too will prosper in that day. 56In your proud days you held Sodom in unspeakable contempt. 57But now your greater wickedness has been exposed to all the world, and you are the one who is scorned—by Edom and all her neighbors and by all the Philistines. 58This is part of your punishment for all your sins, says the Lord.

59, 60"For the Lord God says: I will repay you for your broken promises. You lightly broke your solemn vows to me, yet I will keep the pledge I made to you when you were young. I will establish an everlasting covenant with you forever, 61and you will remember with shame all the evil you have done; and you will be overcome by my favor when I take your sisters, Samaria and Sodom, and make them your daughters, for you to rule over. You will know you don't deserve this gracious act, for you did not keep my covenant. 62I will reaffirm my covenant with you, and you will know I am the Lord. 63Despite all you have done, I will be kind to you again; you will cover your mouth in silence and in shame when I forgive you all that you have done, says the Lord God."

16:42
2 Sam 24:25
Isa 40:1,2
54:9,10

16:43
Ps 78:42
Isa 63:10

16:45
Isa 1:4
Zech 11:8

16:46
Gen 13:11-13
Deut 32:32
Jer 3:8-1 1

16:47
1 Kgs 16:31
2 Kgs 21:9
Jn 15:21,22
1 Cor 5:1

16:48
Mt 11:23,24

16:49
Gen 13:10
Ps 138:6
Isa 22:13
Lk 12:16-20

16:50
Gen 19:24,25

16:51
Jer 3:8-11
Mt 12:41,42
Rom 3:9-20

16:53
Isa 19:24,25

16:54
Jer 2:26

16:57
2 Kgs 16:5-7
2 Chron 28:5,6,
18-23
Hos 2:10; 7:1

16:59
Isa 24:5
Jer 32:38-41

16:62
Jer 24:7

16:63
Ezra 9:6
Ps 39:9
Dan 9:7,8
Rom 3:19

16:44-50 The city of Sodom, a symbol of total corruption, was completely destroyed by God for its wickedness (Genesis 19:24, 25). Samaria, the capital of what had been the Northern Kingdom (Israel), was despised and rejected by the Jews in Judah. To be called a "sister" was bad enough, but to be called *worse* than Samaria meant that Judah's sins were an unspeakable abomination and that her doom was inevitable. The reason she was considered "worse" was not that her sins were worse, but that she knew better. In that light, we who live in an age where God's message is made clear to us through the Bible are "worse" than Judah if we continue in sin! (See also Matthew 11:20-24.)

16:49 It is easy to point our finger at Sodom, especially for its terrible sexual sins. Ezekiel reminded Judah, however, that Sodom was destroyed because of pride, laziness, gluttony, and ignoring the needy within her reach. If we do not commit such horrible sins as adultery, homosexuality, stealing, and murder, we may think we

are living upright lives. But what about sins like pride, laziness, gluttony, and ignoring the needy (see Revelation 3:14-22)? These sins may not be as openly shocking as the others, but they are just as deserving of punishment.

16:55 The phrase *in that day* refers to the future restoration of Judah, when Christ comes to reign over his eternal kingdom.

16:59-63 Although the people had broken their promises and did not deserve anything but punishment, God would not break his promises. If the people turned back to him, he would again forgive them and guarantee their eternal life with him. This promise was put into effect when Jesus paid for the sins of all mankind by his death on the cross (Hebrews 10:8-10). No one is beyond redemption. Although we don't deserve anything but punishment for our sins, God's arms are still outstretched. He will not break his promise to give us salvation and forgiveness if we repent and turn to him.

The riddle of the great eagle

17 Then this message came to me from the Lord:

2"Son of dust, give this riddle to the people of Israel:

3, 4"A great eagle with broad wings full of many-colored feathers came to Lebanon and plucked off the shoot at the top of the tallest cedar tree and carried it into a city filled with merchants. 5There he planted it in fertile ground beside a broad river, where it would grow as quickly as a willow tree. 6It took root and grew and became a low but spreading vine that turned toward the eagle and produced strong branches and luxuriant leaves. 7But when another great, broad-winged, full-feathered eagle came along, this tree sent its roots and branches out toward him instead, 8even though it was already in good soil with plenty of water to become a splendid vine, producing leaves and fruit.

9"The Lord God asks: Shall I let this tree grow and prosper? No! I will pull it out, roots and all! I will cut off its branches and let its leaves wither and die. It will pull out easily enough—it won't take a big crew or a lot of equipment to do that. 10Though the vine began so well, will it thrive? No, it will wither away completely when the east wind touches it, dying in the same choice soil where it had grown so well."

11Then this message came to me from the Lord:

12, 13"Ask these rebels of Israel: Don't you understand what this riddle of the eagles means? I will tell you. Nebuchadnezzar, king of Babylon [the first of the two eagles], came to Jerusalem and took away her king and princes [her topmost buds and shoots] and brought them to Babylon. Nebuchadnezzar made a covenant with a member of the royal family [Zedekiah], and made him take an oath of loyalty. He took a seedling and planted it in fertile ground beside a broad river and he exiled the top men of Israel's government, 14so that Israel would not be strong again and revolt. But by keeping her promises, Israel could be respected and maintain her identity.

15"Nevertheless, Zedekiah rebelled against Babylon, sending ambassadors to Egypt to seek for a great army and many horses to fight against Nebuchadnezzar. But will Israel prosper after breaking all her promises like that? Will she succeed? 16No! For as I live, says the Lord, the king of Israel shall die. (Nebuchadnezzar will pull out the tree, roots and all!) Zedekiah shall die in Babylon, where the king lives who gave him his power, and whose covenant he despised and broke. 17Pharaoh and all his mighty army shall fail to help Israel when the king of Babylon lays siege to Jerusalem again and slaughters many lives. 18For the king of Israel broke his promise after swearing to obey; therefore he shall not escape.

19"The Lord God says: As I live, surely I will punish him for despising the solemn oath he made in my name. 20I will throw my net over him and he shall be captured in my snare, and I will bring him to Babylon and deal with him there for this treason against me. 21And all the best soldiers of Israel will be killed by the sword, and those remaining in the city will be scattered to the four winds. Then you will know that I, the Lord, have spoken these words.

22, 23"The Lord God says: I will take a tender sprout from the top of a tall cedar, and I will plant it on the top of Israel's highest mountain. It shall become a noble

17:2 Ezek 20:49; 24:3

17:3 Jer 48:40 Dan 4:22

17:5 Deut 8:7-9 Isa 44:4 Jer 37:1

17:7 Ezek 31:4

17:10 Ezek 19:12-14 Hos 13:15 Mt 21:19

17:12 2 Kgs 24:10-17 2 Chron 36:13 Jer 22:24-28

17:14 Jer 27:12-17 38:17

17:15 Deut 29:12-15 2 Kgs 24:20 2 Chron 36:13 Jer 38:18,23

17:16 Jer 52:11 Hos 10:4

17:17 Isa 36:6 Jer 37:7

17:18 1 Chron 29:24 2 Chron 30:8

17:21 2 Kgs 25:5,11 Jer 48:44 Amos 9:1-10

17:22 Ps 72:16; 80:15 Isa 27:6 Zech 3:8 4:12-14

17:5 *planted it,* literally, "planted the seed of the land."   **17:12, 13** *the first of the two eagles . . . her topmost buds and shoots . . . Zedekiah,* implied. So also in vs 16.

17:1 The first eagle in this chapter represents King Nebuchadnezzar of Babylon (see 17:12), who appointed or "planted" Zedekiah as king in Jerusalem. Zedekiah rebelled against this arrangement and tried to ally with Egypt, the second eagle, to battle against Babylon. This took place while Ezekiel, miles away in Babylon, was describing these events. Jeremiah, a prophet in Judah, was also warning Zedekiah not to form this alliance (Jeremiah 2:36, 37). Although miles apart, the prophets had the same message because both spoke for God. God still directs his chosen spokesmen to speak his truth all around the world.

17:10 This east wind was the hot, dry wind blowing off the desert, a wind that could wither a flourishing crop in seconds. The hot wind of Nebuchadnezzar's armies was about to overcome the nation of Judah.

17:22, 23 Ezekiel's prophecy of judgment ends in hope. When the people put their hope in foreign alliances, they were disappointed. Only God could give them true hope. God said he would plant a tender twig, the Messiah, whose kingdom would grow and become a shelter for all who come to him (see Isaiah 11:1). This prophecy was fulfilled at the coming of Jesus Christ.

cedar, bringing forth branches and bearing seed. Animals of every sort will gather under it; its branches will shelter every kind of bird. 24And everyone shall know that it is I, the Lord, who cuts down the high trees and exalts the low, that I make the green tree wither and the dead tree grow. I, the Lord, have said that I would do it, and I will."

Each person is responsible for his own sin

18 Then the Lord's message came to me again.

2"Why do people use this proverb about the land of Israel: The children are punished for their fathers' sins? 3As I live, says the Lord God, you will not use this proverb any more in Israel, 4for all souls are mine to judge—fathers and sons alike—and my rule is this: It is for a man's own sins that he will die.

5"But if a man is just and does what is lawful and right, 6and has not gone out to the mountains to feast before the idols of Israel and worship them, and does not commit adultery, nor lie with any woman during the time of her menstruation, 7and is a merciful creditor, not holding on to the items given to him in pledge by poor debtors, and is no robber, but gives food to the hungry and clothes to those in need, 8and grants loans without interest, and stays away from sin, and is honest and fair when judging others, 9and obeys my laws—that man is just, says the Lord, and he shall surely live.

10"But if that man has a son who is a robber or murderer and who fulfills none of his responsibilities, 11who refuses to obey the laws of God, but worships idols on the mountains and commits adultery, 12and oppresses the poor and helpless, and robs his debtors by refusing to let them redeem what they have given him in pledge, and loves idols and worships them, 13and loans out his money at interest—shall that man live? No! He shall surely die, and it is his own fault.

14"But if this sinful man has, in turn, a son who sees all his father's wickedness, so that he fears God and decides against that kind of life, 15and doesn't go up on the mountains to feast before the idols and worship them, and does not commit adultery, 16and is fair to those who borrow from him and doesn't rob them, but feeds the hungry and clothes the needy, 17and helps the poor and does not loan money at interest, and obeys my laws—he shall not die because of his father's sins; he shall surely live. 18But his father shall die for his own sins because he is cruel and robs and does wrong.

19" 'What?' you ask. 'Doesn't the son pay for his father's sins?' No! For if the son does what is right and keeps my laws, he shall surely live. 20The one who sins is the one who dies. The son shall not be punished for his father's sins, nor the father for his son's. The righteous person will be rewarded for his own goodness and the wicked person for his wickedness. 21But if a wicked person turns away from all his sins and begins to obey my laws and do what is just and right, he shall surely live and not die. 22All his past sins will be forgotten, and he shall live because of his goodness.

23"Do you think I like to see the wicked die? asks the Lord. Of course not! I only

18:2 *The children are punished for their fathers' sins?* Literally, "The fathers have eaten sour grapes and the children's teeth are set on edge." **18:8** *without interest,* or, "without any usury." **18:13** *at interest,* or, "at usurious interest."

18:1ff Some of the people of Judah believed they were being punished for the sins of their ancestors, not their own. Here Ezekiel flatly refutes that misconception. Although we often suffer from the effects of sins committed by those who came before us, God does not punish us for someone else's sins; and we can't use their mistakes as an excuse for our sins. Each person is accountable to God for his or her actions. The people of Judah thought that because of their righteous ancestors (18:5-9) they would live. God told them that they would not; they were the evil sons of righteous parents and, as such, would die (18:10-13). If, however, they returned to God, they would live (18:14-18).

18:14-18 Family traditions were very important to the Jews, but God made it clear that people should not follow a tradition of sin.

Although your family is a powerful influence in your life, your actions are not determined by them. You can choose not to follow a pattern of sin. Even if you come from a sinful family, if you choose to believe in God and obey him, you will be saved. It is far better to begin a new spiritual heritage than to hold on to traditions of sin.

18:23 God is a God of love, but he is also a God of perfect justice. His perfect love causes him to be merciful to those who recognize their sin and turn back to him, but he cannot wink at those who willfully sin. Wicked people die both physically and spiritually. God takes no joy in their deaths; he would prefer they turn to him and have eternal life. Likewise, we should not rejoice in the misfortunes of nonbelievers. Instead, we should do all in our power to bring them to faith.

Side references: 17:24 Isa 37:12,13; 55:12; Amos 9:11; 1 Cor 1:27,28 / 18:2 Jer 31:29; Mt 23:36; Rom 9:20 / 18:4 Num 16:22; 27:16; Isa 57:16; Zech 12:1; Rom 6:23 / 18:6 Deut 4:19; Mt 5:28; 1 Cor 6:9-11; 10:20 / 18:7 Lev 19:13; 1 Sam 12:3,4; Mt 25:35-40; Lk 3:11 / 18:8 Ex 22:25; Zech 8:16 / 18:9 Hab 2:4; Rom 1:17 / 18:12 2 Kgs 21:11; Hos 12:7; Amos 4:1 / 18:14 2 Chron 29:6-10; 34:21; Prov 17:21; Mt 23:32 / 18:16 Job 31:16; Ps 41:1 / 18:19 Zech 1:3-6 / 18:20 Deut 24:16; 1 Kgs 14:13; Isa 53:11; Mt 16:27; Rom 2:6-9 / 18:22 Ps 18:20-24; Mic 7:19 / 18:23 Ps 147:11; 2 Pet 3:9

want him to turn from his wicked ways and live. 24However, if a righteous person turns to sinning and acts like any other sinner, should he be allowed to live? No, of course not. All his previous goodness will be forgotten and he shall die for his sins.

18:24
1 Sam 15:11
Prov 21:16
Gal 3:3,4

25"Yet you say: The Lord isn't being fair! Listen to me, O people of Israel. Am I the one who is unfair, or is it you? 26When a good man turns away from being good and begins sinning and dies in his sins, he dies for the evil he has done. 27And if a wicked person turns away from his wickedness and obeys the law, and does right, he shall save his soul, 28for he has thought it over and decided to turn from his sins and live a good life. He shall surely live—he shall not die.

18:25
Gen 18:25
Deut 32:4
Zeph 3:5
Mal 3:13-15

29"And yet the people of Israel keep saying: 'The Lord is unfair!' O people of Israel, it is you who are unfair, not I. 30I will judge each of you, O Israel, and punish or reward each according to your own actions. Oh, turn from your sins while there is yet time. 31Put them behind you and receive a new heart and a new spirit. For why will you die, O Israel? 32I do not enjoy seeing you die, the Lord God says. Turn, turn and live!

18:30
Ezek 14:6; 33:11
Hos 12:6

18:31
Ps 51:10
Jer 32:39
Acts 3:19
Rom 8:13
Jas 4:8

A death dirge for Israel's leaders

19 "Sing this death dirge for the leaders of Israel: 2What a woman your mother was—like a lioness! Her children were like lion's cubs! 3One of her cubs [King Jehoahaz] grew into a strong young lion, and learned to catch prey and became a man-eater. 4Then the nations called out their hunters and trapped him in a pit and brought him in chains to Egypt.

19:1
2 Kgs 25:5-7
2 Chron 36:3-10
Jer 22:10-12,
28-30

19:3
2 Kgs 23:31-34
2 Chron 36:1-4

5"When Israel, the mother lion, saw that all her hopes for him were gone, she took another of her cubs [King Jehoiachin] and taught him to be 'king of the beasts.' 6He became a leader among the lions and learned to catch prey, and he too became a man-eater. 7He demolished the palaces of the surrounding nations and ruined their cities; their farms were desolated, their crops destroyed; everyone in the land shook with terror when they heard him roar. 8Then the armies of the nations surrounded him, coming from every side, and trapped him in a pit and captured him. 9They prodded him into a cage and brought him before the king of Babylon. He was held in captivity so that his voice could never again be heard upon the mountains of Israel.

19:5
2 Kgs 24:8-12
2 Chron 36:9,10

19:9
2 Kgs 24:15

10"Your mother was like a vine beside an irrigation ditch, with lush, green foliage because of all the water. 11Its strongest branch became a ruler's scepter and it was very great, towering above the others and noticed from far away. 12But the vine was uprooted in fury and thrown down to the ground. Its branches were broken and withered by a strong wind from the east; the fruit was destroyed by fire. 13Now the vine is planted in the wilderness where the ground is hard and dry. 14It is decaying from within; no strong branch remains. The fulfillment of this sad prophecy has already begun, and there is more ahead."

19:10
Ps 80:8-11

19:12
Hos 13:15
Mt 3:10
Jn 15:6

19:13
2 Kgs 24:12-16

A reminder of rebellion

20 Late in July, six years after King Jeconiah was captured, some of the elders of Israel came to ask instructions from the Lord, and sat before me awaiting his reply.

20:1
Ezek 8:1,11,12

2Then the Lord gave me this message:

19:3 *King Jehoahaz,* implied.   **19:14** *It is decaying from within,* literally, "A fire is gone out of its branches and devoured its fruit."   **20:1** *six years after King Jeconiah was captured,* literally, "in the seventh year of Jeconiah's captivity."

18:25 A typical childish response to punishment is to say, "That isn't fair!" In reality, God is fair, but *we* have broken the rules. It is not God who must live up to our ideas of fairness; instead, we must live up to his. Don't spend your time looking for the loopholes in God's law, decide instead to work toward living up to God's standards.

19:1ff Ezekiel used illustrations to communicate many of his messages. With the picture of the lioness and her cubs, he raised the curiosity of his listeners. The lioness symbolized the nation of Judah, and the two cubs were two of her kings. The first cub was

King Jehoahaz, who was taken captive to Egypt in 609 B.C. by Pharaoh Neco. The second cub was either King Jehoiachin, who had already been taken into captivity (2 Kings 24:8ff), or King Zedekiah, who soon would be. This illustration showed that for Judah, there was no hope for a quick return from exile, and no escape from the approaching Babylonian armies.

19:11, 12 Not even the political and military might of Judah's kings could save her. Like branches of a vine, they would be cut off and uprooted by "a strong wind from the east"—the Babylonian army.

³"Son of dust, say to the elders of Israel: The Lord God says: How dare you come to ask my help? I swear that I will tell you nothing. ⁴Judge them, son of dust; condemn them; tell them of all the sins of this nation from the times of their fathers until now. ⁵, ⁶Tell them the Lord God says: When I chose Israel and revealed myself to her in Egypt, I swore to her and her descendants that I would bring them out of Egypt to a land I had discovered and explored for them—a good land, flowing as it were with milk and honey, the best of all lands anywhere.

⁷"Then I said to them: Get rid of every idol; do not defile yourselves with the Egyptian gods, for I am the Lord your God. ⁸But they rebelled against me and would not listen. They didn't get rid of their idols, nor forsake the gods of Egypt. Then I thought, I will pour out my fury upon them and fulfill my anger against them while they are still in Egypt.

⁹, ¹⁰"But I didn't do it, for I acted to protect the honor of my name, lest the Egyptians laugh at Israel's God who couldn't keep them back from harm. So I brought my people out of Egypt right before the Egyptians' eyes, and led them into the wilderness. ¹¹There I gave them my laws so they could live by keeping them. If anyone keeps them, he shall live. ¹²And I gave them the Sabbath—a day of rest every seventh day—as a symbol between them and me, to remind them that it is I, the Lord, who sanctifies them, that they are truly my people.

¹³"But Israel rebelled against me. There in the wilderness they refused my laws. They would not obey my rules even though obeying them means life. And they misused my Sabbaths. Then I thought, I will pour out my fury upon them and utterly consume them in the desert.

¹⁴"But again I refrained in order to protect the honor of my name, lest the nations who saw me bring them out of Egypt would say that it was because I couldn't care for them that I destroyed them. ¹⁵But I swore to them in the wilderness that I would not bring them into the land I had given them, a land full of milk and honey, the choicest spot on earth, ¹⁶because they laughed at my laws, ignored my wishes, and violated my Sabbaths—their hearts were with their idols! ¹⁷Nevertheless, I spared them. I didn't finish them off in the wilderness.

¹⁸"Then I spoke to their children and said: Don't follow your fathers' footsteps. Don't defile yourselves with their idols, ¹⁹for I am the Lord your God. Follow my laws; keep my ordinances; ²⁰hallow my Sabbaths; for they are a symbol of the contract between us to help you remember that I am the Lord your God.

²¹"But their children too rebelled against me. They refused my laws—the laws that, if a person keeps them, he shall live. And they defiled my Sabbaths. So then I said: Now at last I will pour out my fury upon you in the wilderness.

²²"Nevertheless, again I withdrew my judgment against them to protect my name among the nations who had seen my power in bringing them out of Egypt. ²³, ²⁴But I took a solemn oath against them while they were in the wilderness that I would scatter them, dispersing them to the ends of the earth because they did not obey my laws but scorned them and violated my Sabbaths and longed for their fathers' idols. ²⁵I let them adopt customs and laws which were worthless. Through the keeping of them they could not attain life. ²⁶In the hope that they would draw back in horror, and know that I alone am God, I let them pollute themselves with the very gifts I gave them. They burnt their firstborn children as offerings to their gods!

20:25 *let them adopt,* literally, "gave them." *Through the keeping of them they could not attain life,* literally, "ordinances by which they could not have life." Doubtless, the reference is to the pagan customs of vss 18 and 26. In contrast, see vs 11.

Cross-references:

20:4 Ezek 16:2; 22:2

20:5 Ezek 6:2-9; 33:3
Deut 7:6; 14:2
Jer 33:24
Mk 13:20

20:7 Deut 29:16,18

20:8 Isa 63:10

20:9 Ex 32:11-14
Num 14:13
Deut 9:28
32:26,27

20:11 Ex 20:1-23,33
Lev 18:5
Neh 9:13,14

20:13 Num 14:11
Isa 56:6

20:16 Ezek 11:21
14:3-7

20:17 Jer 4:27; 5:18
Nah 1:8,9

20:18 Deut 4:3,4
Ps 78:6,8

20:19 Ex 6:7; 20:2

20:21 Num 25:1-3

20:22 Job 13:21
Ps 78:38
Isa 48:9-11

20:23 Deut 28:64-68
32:26,27
Jer 15:4

20:25 Ps 81:12
Rom 1:21-25,28
2 Thess 2:9-11

20:26 Rom 11:8

20:1ff Here Ezekiel gives a panoramic view of Israel's history of rebellion. The emphasis is upon God's attempts to bring the nation back to himself and upon Israel's responsibility for the judgments she has experienced and is about to encounter.

20:12 The Sabbath, instituted by God at creation, was entrusted to Israel as a sign that God had created and redeemed them (Exodus 20:8–11; Deuteronomy 5:12–15). It was a gift from a loving God, not a difficult obligation, but they repeatedly desecrated the Sabbath and ignored their God.

20:23, 24 At the very beginning of Israel's history, God clearly warned the people about the consequences of disobedience (Leviticus 26:23–26). When the people disobeyed, God let them experience those devastating consequences to make them aware of the seriousness of their sins. If we choose to live for ourselves alone, apart from God, we can expect similar destructive consequences. If we understand that even suffering may be a way for God to call us, our misfortunes may bring us to our senses before it is too late.

27, 28"Son of dust, tell them that the Lord God says: Your fathers continued to blaspheme and betray me when I brought them into the land I promised them, for they offered sacrifices and incense on every high hill and under every tree! They roused my fury as they offered up their sacrifices to those 'gods.' They brought their perfumes and incense and poured out their drink offerings to them! 29I said to them: 'What is this place of sacrifice where you go?' And so it is still called 'The Place of Sacrifice'—that is how it got its name.

30"The Lord God wants to know whether you are going to pollute yourselves just as your fathers did, and keep on worshiping idols? 31For when you offer gifts to them and give your little sons to be burned to ashes as you do even today, shall I listen to you or help you, Israel? As I live, the Lord God says, I will not give you any message, though you have come to me to ask.

32"What you have in mind will not be done—to be like the nations all around you, serving gods of wood and stone. 33I will rule you with an iron fist and in great anger and with power. 34With might and fury I will bring you out from the lands where you are scattered, 35, 36and will bring you into my desert judgment hall. I will judge you there, and get rid of the rebels, just as I did in the wilderness after I brought you out of Egypt. 37I will count you carefully and let only a small quota return. 38And the others—the rebels and all those who sin against me—I will purge from among you. They shall not enter Israel, but I will bring them out of the countries where they are in exile. And when that happens, you will know I am the Lord.

39"O Israel, the Lord God says: If you insist on worshiping your idols, go right ahead, but then don't bring your gifts to me as well! Such desecration of my holy name must stop!

40"For at Jerusalem in my holy mountain, says the Lord, all Israel shall worship me. There I will accept you, and require you to bring me your offerings and the finest of your gifts. 41You will be to me as an offering of perfumed incense when I bring you back from exile, and the nations will see the great change in your hearts. 42Then, when I have brought you home to the land I promised your fathers, you will know I am the Lord. 43Then you will look back at all your sins and loathe yourselves because of the evil you have done. 44And when I have honored my name by blessing you despite your wickedness, then, O Israel, you will know I am the Lord."

45Then this message came to me from the Lord:

46"Son of dust, look toward Jerusalem and speak out against it and the forest lands of the Negeb. 47Prophesy to it and say: Hear the word of the Lord. I will set you on fire, O forest, and every tree will die, green and dry alike. The terrible flames will not be quenched and they will scorch the world. 48And all the world will see that I, the Lord, have set the fire. It shall not be put out."

49Then I said, "O Lord God, they say of me, 'He only talks in riddles!'"

20:29 *place of sacrifice*, literally, "bamah"—a hilltop area where sacrifices were made to the gods. **20:35, 36** *desert judgment hall*, literally, "the wilderness of the people," meaning the Syro-Arabian deserts, peopled by nomadic tribes.

20:27
1 Kgs 14:23

20:30
Judg 2:19
20:31
Ps 106:37-39

20:34
Lam 2:4
20:35
Deut 32:10
1 Cor 10:5-10
20:38
Ps 95:11
Ezek 34:17-22
Heb 4:3

20:39
Isa 1:12-15

20:40
Ezek 43:12,27
20:41
Isa 27:12,13
Amos 9:14

20:43
Zech 12:10-14
Lk 18:13
2 Cor 7:11

20:46
Jer 13:19
20:47
Isa 9:18
20:48
Jer 17:27

20:49
Mt 13:12,13
Jn 16:25

20:30 Water containing contaminants, even in small amounts, is polluted. Likewise, our lives are polluted when we accept the contaminants—immoral values—of this world. If we love money, we become greedy. If we lust, we become sexually immoral. Remaining pure in a polluted world is difficult, to say the least. But a heart filled with God's Holy Spirit leaves little room for pollution (see Titus 1:15, 16).

20:35, 36 God chose to purify his people by forcing them to wander in the wilderness until an entire generation died (Numbers 14:26-35). Here he promises to purge the nation again as they cross the vast wilderness to their captivity in Babylon. Only those who faithfully follow God will be able to return to their land. The purpose of this purging is restoration and redemption.

20:39 The Israelites were worshiping idols and sacrificing to God at the same time! Often we think that some religion is better than

none at all. While persisting in a life of sin, we may think, "Well, at least I go to church. God will be pleased with this effort." But God wants all of our lives, not just part. No amount of religious ritual or personal sacrifice can make up for continuing sinful practices.

20:49 Ezekiel was exasperated and discouraged. Many Israelites complained that he spoke only in riddles, so they refused to listen. No matter how important our work or how significant our ministry, we will have moments of discouragement. Apparently God did not answer Ezekiel's plea; instead, he gave Ezekiel another message to proclaim. What has been discouraging you? Have you felt like giving up? Instead, continue doing what God has told you to do. He promises to reward the faithful (Mark 13:13). God's cure for discouragement is often another assignment.

21:1ff The short message in 20:45-49 introduces the four messages in chapter 21 about the judgments that would come

Babylon will attack Judah

21 Then this message came to me from the Lord: 2"Son of dust, face toward Jerusalem and prophesy against Israel and against my Temple! 3For the Lord says: I am against you, Israel. I will unsheath my sword and destroy your people, good and bad alike— 4I will not spare even the righteous. I will make a clean sweep throughout the land from the Negeb to your northern borders. 5All the world shall know that it is I, the Lord. His sword is in his hand, and it will not return to its sheath again until its work is finished.

6"Sigh and groan before the people, son of dust, in your bitter anguish; sigh with grief and broken heart. 7When they ask you why, tell them: Because of the fearsome news that God has given me. When it comes true, the boldest heart will melt with fear; all strength will disappear. Every spirit will faint; strong knees will tremble and become as weak as water. And the Lord God says: Your doom is on the way; my judgments will be fulfilled!"

8Then again this message came to me from God:

9, 10, 11"Son of dust, tell them this: A sword is being sharpened and polished for terrible slaughter. Now will you laugh? For those far stronger than you have perished beneath its power. It is ready now to hand to the executioner. 12Son of dust, with sobbing, beat upon your thigh, for that sword shall slay my people and all their leaders. All alike shall die. 13It will put them all to the test—and what chance do they have? the Lord God asks.

14"Prophesy to them in this way: Clap your hands vigorously, then take a sword and brandish it twice, thrice, to symbolize the great massacre they face! 15Let their hearts melt with terror, for a sword glitters at every gate; it flashes like lightning; it is razor-edged for slaughter. 16O sword, slash to the right and slash to the left, wherever you will, wherever you want. 17And you have prophesied with clapping hands that I, the Lord, will smite Jerusalem and satisfy my fury."

18Then this message came to me. The Lord said:

19, 20"Son of dust, make a map and on it trace two routes for the king of Babylon to follow—one to Jerusalem and the other to Rabbah in Trans-Jordan. And put a signpost at the fork in the road from Babylon. 21For the king of Babylon stands at a fork, uncertain whether to attack Jerusalem or Rabbah. He will call his magicians to use divination; they will cast lots by shaking arrows from the quiver; they will sacrifice to idols and inspect the liver of their sacrifice. 22They will decide to turn toward Jerusalem! With battering rams they will go against the gates, shouting for the kill; they will build siege towers and make a hill against the walls to reach the top. 23Jerusalem won't understand this treachery; how could the diviners make this terrible mistake? For Babylon is Judah's ally and has sworn to defend Jerusalem! But (the king of Babylon) will think only of the times the people rebelled. He will attack and defeat them.

24"The Lord God says: Again and again your guilt cries out against you, for your sins are open and unashamed. Wherever you go, whatever you do, all is filled with sin. And now the time of punishment has come.

25"O King Zedekiah, evil prince of Israel, your final day of reckoning is here. 26Take off your jeweled crown, the Lord God says. The old order changes. Now the poor are exalted, and the rich brought very low. 27I will overturn, overturn,

21:3
Isa 57:1
Jer 21:13
Nah 2:13; 3:5

21:4
Jer 12:12
Ezek 7:2

21:5
1 Sam 3:12
Neh 1:9

21:7
Isa 13:7
Ezek 7:26

21:9
Ps 110:5,6
Isa 34:5,6

21:12
Joel 1:13

21:15
Josh 2:11
2 Sam 17:10
Jer 17:27

21:17
Ezek 5:13

21:19
Deut 3:11
Amos 1:14

21:21
Prov 16:33; 21:1
Hos 4:12
Zech 10:2

21:22
Ezek 4:2; 26:9

21:23
Num 5:15
Ezek 17:16,18

21:25
Ps 37:13
Ezek 7:2-7

21:26
Ps 75:7
Jer 13:18

21:27
Ps 2:6
Jer 23:56
Hag 2:21,22

21:2 *against my Temple*, literally, "against the sanctuaries." **21:19, 20** *Rabbah in Trans-Jordan*, literally, "Rabbah of the Ammonites." **21:21** *inspect the liver.* A very common type of divination by which ancients thought they could obtain information from the gods. **21:25** *O King Zedekiah*, implied.

---

upon Jerusalem. The city would be destroyed because it was defiled. According to Jewish law, defiled objects were to be passed through fire in order to purify them (see Numbers 31:22, 23; Psalm 66:10; Proverbs 17:3). God's judgment is designed to purify; destruction is often a necessary part of that process.

21:19-23 In 589 B.C., the nations of Judah and Ammon made a peace treaty, conspiring against Babylon. Ezekiel gave this message to the exiles who had heard the news and were again filled with hope of returning to their homeland. Ezekiel said that

Babylon's king would march his armies into the region to stop the rebellion. Traveling from the north, he would stop at a fork in the road, one leading to Rabbah, the capital of Ammon, and the other leading to Jerusalem, the capital of Judah. He had to decide which city to destroy. Just as Ezekiel predicted, King Nebuchadnezzar went to Jerusalem and besieged it.

21:27 Instead of using exclamation points for emphasis, the Hebrew language used repetition. The repetition of *overturn* shows the certainty of the end of the old order—the world as it is now.

overturn the kingdom, so that even the new order that emerges will not succeed until the Man appears who has a right to it. And I will give it all to him.

28"Son of dust, prophesy to the Ammonites too, for they mocked my people in their woe. Tell them this:

"Against you also my glittering sword is drawn from its sheath; it is sharpened and polished and flashed like lightning. 29Your magicians and false prophets have told you lies of safety and success—that your gods will save you from the king of Babylon. Thus they have caused your death along with all the other wicked, for when the day of final reckoning has come you will be wounded unto death. 30Shall I return my sword to its sheath before I deal with you? No, I will destroy you in your own country where you were born. 31I will pour out my fury upon you and blow upon the fire of my wrath until it becomes a roaring conflagration, and I will deliver you into the hands of cruel men skilled in destruction. 32You are the fuel for the fire; your blood will be spilled in your own country and you will be utterly wiped out, your memory lost in history. For I, the Lord, have spoken it."

21:28 Jer 12:12 / Zeph 2:8-10
21:29 Jer 27:9 / Ezek 13:6-9
21:30 Jer 47:6,7 / Ezek 25:5
21:31 Ps 18:15 / Nah 1:6 / Hab 1:6,10
21:32 Mal 4:1 / Mt 3:10

God lists Jerusalem's sins

22 Now another message came from the Lord. He said:

2"Son of dust, indict Jerusalem as the City of Murder. Publicly denounce her terrible deeds. 3City of Murder, doomed and damned—City of Idols, filthy and foul— 4you are guilty both of murder and idolatry. Now comes your day of doom. You have reached the limit of your years. I will make you a laughingstock and a reproach to all the nations of the world. 5Near and far they will mock you, a city of infamous rebels.

6"Every leader in Israel who lives within your walls is bent on murder. 7Fathers and mothers are contemptuously ignored; immigrants and visitors are forced to pay you for your 'protection'; orphans and widows are wronged and oppressed. 8The things of God are all despised; my Sabbaths are ignored. 9Prisoners are falsely accused and sent to their death. Every mountain top is filled with idols; lewdness is everywhere. 10There are men who commit adultery with their fathers' wives and lie with menstruous women. 11Adultery with a neighbor's wife, a daughter-in-law, a half sister—this is common. 12Hired murderers, loan racketeers and extortioners are everywhere. You never even think of me and my commands, the Lord God says.

13"But now I snap my fingers and call a halt to your dishonest gain and bloodshed. 14How strong and courageous will you be then, in my day of reckoning? For I, the Lord, have spoken, and I will do all that I have said. 15I will scatter you throughout the world and burn out the wickedness within you. 16You will be dishonored among the nations, and you shall know I am the Lord."

17Then the Lord said this:

18, 19, 20"Son of dust, the people of Israel are the worthless slag left when silver is smelted. They are the dross, compounded from the brass, the tin, the iron and the lead. Therefore the Lord God says: Because you are worthless dross, I will bring you to my crucible in Jerusalem, to smelt you with the heat of my wrath. 21I will

22:3 Ezek 23:37,45
22:4 2 Kgs 21:16 / Ps 44:13,14 / Ezek 5:14,15 / Dan 9:16
22:6 Isa 1:23 / Mic 3:1-3,9-11
22:7 Ex 22:22; 23:9 / Deut 27:19 / Prov 22:22,23
22:9 Judg 20:6 / Hos 4:2,10,14
22:10 Lev 18:8,19 / Deut 27:20-23 / 1 Cor 5:1
22:11 Lev 18:15 / 2 Sam 13:14
22:12 Lev 19:13; 25:36 / Deut 27:25 / Ps 106:21
22:13 Num 24:10 / Prov 28:8 / Isa 33:15 / Amos 2:6-8
22:15 Deut 4:27
22:16 Ezek 6:4-7

22:10 *There are men who commit adultery with their father's wives and lie with menstruous women,* or, "You degrade yourselves through homosexual practices and through lying with women in their time of menstruation."

21:28 The Ammonites and Israelites were usually at odds with each other. God told the Israelites not to ally with foreign nations, but Judah and Ammon allied in 589 B.C. God first judged Judah; now he judges Ammon, not for allying with Judah, but for watching Judah's destruction with delight.

22:1 Chapter 22 explains why Jerusalem's judgment would come (22:2–16), how it would come (22:17–22), and who would be judged by it (22:23–31).

22:6–13 The leaders were especially responsible for the moral climate of the nation because they had been chosen by God to lead. The same is true today (see James 3:1, 2). Unfortunately, many of the sins mentioned here have been committed in recent years by Christian leaders. We are living in a time of unprecedented attacks by Satan. It is vital that we uphold our leaders in prayer; and it is vital for leaders to seek accountability and help in their spiritual walk.

22:17–22 Precious metals are refined with intense heat to remove the impurities. When heated, the slag (impurities) rises to the top of the molten metal and is skimmed off and thrown away. The purpose of the invasion of Jerusalem was to refine the people, but the refining process showed that the people of the city, like worthless slag, had nothing good in them.

22:26 The priests were supposed to keep God's worship pure and teach the people right living. But God had become

blow the fire of my wrath upon you, 22and you will melt like silver in fierce heat, and you will know that I, the Lord, have poured my wrath upon you."

23Again the message of the Lord came to me, saying:

24"Son of dust, say to the people of Israel: In the day of my indignation you shall be like an uncleared wilderness, or a desert without rain. 25Your 'prophets' have plotted against you like lions stalking prey. They devour many lives; they seize treasures and extort wealth; they multiply the widows in the land. 26Your priests have violated my laws and defiled my Temple and my holiness. To them the things of God are no more important than any daily task. They have not taught my people the difference between right and wrong, and they disregard my Sabbaths, so my holy name is greatly defiled among them. 27Your leaders are like wolves, who tear apart their victims, and they destroy lives for profit. 28Your 'prophets' describe false visions and speak false messages they claim are from God, when he hasn't spoken one word to them at all. Thus they repair the walls with whitewash! 29Even the common people oppress and rob the poor and needy and cruelly extort from aliens.

30"I looked in vain for anyone who would build again the wall of righteousness that guards the land, who could stand in the gap and defend you from my just attacks, but I found not one. 31And so the Lord God says: I will pour out my anger upon you; I will consume you with the fire of my wrath. I have heaped upon you the full penalty for all your sins."

A parable of adultery

23 The Lord's message came to me again, saying:

2, 3"Son of dust, there were two sisters who as young girls became prostitutes in Egypt.

4, 5"The older girl was named Oholah; her sister was Oholibah. (I am speaking of Samaria and Jerusalem!) I married them, and they bore me sons and daughters. But then Oholah turned to other gods instead of me, and gave her love to the Assyrians, her neighbors, 6for they were all attractive young men, captains and commanders, in handsome blue, dashing about on their horses. 7And so she sinned with them—the choicest men of Assyria—worshiping their idols, defiling herself. 8For when she left Egypt, she did not leave her spirit of prostitution behind, but was still as lewd as in her youth, when the Egyptians poured out their lusts upon her and robbed her of her virginity.

9"And so I delivered her into the evil clutches of the Assyrians whose gods she loved so much. 10They stripped her and killed her and took away her children as their slaves. Her name was known to every woman in the land as a sinner who had received what she deserved.

11"But when Oholibah (Jerusalem) saw what had happened to her sister she went

---

commonplace to them, they ignored the Sabbath, and they refused to teach the people. They no longer carried out their God-given duties (Leviticus 10:10, 11; Ezekiel 44:23). When doing God's work becomes no more important than any mundane task, we are no longer giving God the reverence he deserves.

22:28-30 The wall spoken of here is not made of stones, but of faithful people united in their efforts to resist evil. This "wall of righteousness" is in disrepair because there was no one who could lead the people back to God. The feeble attempts to repair it—through religious rituals or messages based on opinion rather than God's Word—were as worthless as whitewash, which only covers up problems. What the people really needed was to rebuild their lives! When we give the appearance of loving God without living his way, we are covering up sins which could eventually damage our lives beyond repair. Don't use religion as a whitewash; repair your life by living out the principles of God's Word.

23:1ff Ezekiel continues his discussion of the reasons for God's judgment upon the nation by telling a further allegory. He compared the Northern and Southern Kingdoms to two sisters

giving themselves to adultery. The proud citizens of Jerusalem had long scorned their sister city of Samaria, thinking that they were superior. But God called both of these cities filthy whores—a shock to the people of Jerusalem who thought that they were righteous. Just as the imagery of this message was shocking and distasteful to the people, so our sins are repugnant to God.

23:4-6 Oholah (meaning, "her tent"), the Northern Kingdom of Israel, was lured away from God by the dashing Assyrians—their handsome clothes and powerful positions. The people coveted youth, strength, power, wealth, and pleasure—the same qualities people think will bring happiness today. But the charming Assyrians drew Israel away from God.

23:11ff Oholibah (meaning, "my tent is in her") is now shown to be worse because she did not learn from the judgment upon her sister, but continued in her lust for the Assyrians and Babylonians. Therefore, her judgment was equally certain. Just as Oholibah was privileged and should have known better, so we are privileged because we know about Christ.

right ahead in the same way, and sinned even more than her sister. ¹²She fawned over her Assyrian neighbors, those handsome young men on fine steeds, those army officers in handsome uniforms—all of them desirable. ¹³I saw the way she was going, following right along behind her older sister.

¹⁴, ¹⁵"She was in fact more debased than Samaria, for she fell in love with pictures she saw painted on a wall! They were pictures of Babylonian military officers, outfitted in striking red uniforms, with handsome belts, and flowing turbans on their heads. ¹⁶When she saw these paintings she longed to give herself to the men pictured, so she sent messengers to Chaldea to invite them to come to her. ¹⁷And they came and committed adultery with her, defiling her in the bed of love, but afterward she hated them and broke off all relations with them.

¹⁸"And I despised her just as I despised her sister, because she flaunted herself before them and gave herself to their lust. ¹⁹, ²⁰But that didn't bother her. She turned to even greater prostitution, sinning with the lustful men she remembered from her youth when she was a prostitute in Egypt. ²¹And thus you celebrated those former days when as a young girl you gave your virginity to those from Egypt.

²²"And now the Lord God says that he will raise against you, O Oholibah (Jerusalem), those very nations from which you turned away, disgusted. ²³For the Babylonians will come, and all the Chaldeans from Pekod and Shoa and Koa; and all the Assyrians with them—handsome young men of high rank, riding their steeds. ²⁴They will come against you from the north with chariots and wagons and a great army fully prepared for attack. They will surround you on every side with armored men and I will let them at you, to do with you as they wish. ²⁵And I will send my jealousy against you and deal furiously with you, and cut off your nose and ears; your survivors will be killed; your children will be taken away as slaves, and everything left will be burned. ²⁶They will strip you of your beautiful clothes and jewels.

²⁷"And so I will put a stop to your lewdness and prostitution brought from the land of Egypt; you will no more long for Egypt and her gods. ²⁸For the Lord God says: I will surely deliver you over to your enemies, to those you loathe. ²⁹They will deal with you in hatred, and rob you of all you own, leaving you naked and bare. And the shame of your prostitution shall be exposed to all the world.

³⁰"You brought all this upon yourself by worshiping the gods of other nations, defiling yourself with all their idols. ³¹You have followed in your sister's footsteps, so I will punish you with the same terrors that destroyed her. ³²Yes, the terrors that fell upon her will fall upon you—and the cup from which she drank was full and large. And all the world will mock you for your woe. ³³You will reel like a drunkard beneath the awful blows of sorrow and distress, just as your sister Samaria did. ³⁴In deep anguish you will drain that cup of terror to the very bottom and will lick the inside to get every drop. For I have spoken, says the Lord. ³⁵Because you have forgotten me and turned your backs upon me, therefore you must bear the consequence of all your sin.

³⁶"Son of dust, you must accuse Jerusalem and Samaria of all their awful deeds. ³⁷For they have committed both adultery and murder; they have worshiped idols and murdered my children whom they bore to me, burning them as sacrifices on their altars. ³⁸On the same day they defiled my Temple and ignored my Sabbaths, ³⁹for when they had murdered their children in front of their idols, then even that

23:13
Hos 12:1,2

23:14
Ezek 8:10

23:16
Prov 6:25
Mt 5:28
2 Pet 2:14

23:17
2 Kgs 24:17

23:18
Deut 32:19
Ps 78:59
106:40
Jer 8:12

23:20
Ezek 17:15

23:21
Jer 3:9

23:22
Isa 10:5,6
Hab 1:6-10

23:23
Gen 25:18
2 Kgs 20:14-17
Job 1:17

23:24
Jer 39:5,6

23:26
Isa 3:16-24

23:28
Jer 21:7-10

23:29
Deut 28:48
2 Sam 13:15

23:31
1 Kgs 21:8-14
2 Kgs 21:13
Dan 9:12

23:32
Ps 60:3
Ezek 5:14,15

23:33
Jer 25:15,16,27

23:34
Ps 75:8
Isa 51:17

23:35
1 Kgs 14:9
Neh 9:26
Hos 13:6

23:36
Isa 58:1
Jer 1:10
Mt 23:13-35

23:38
2 Kgs 21:4,7
Neh 13:17,18
Jer 17:27

23:39
Jer 7:9-11

23:12 This "fawning" (excessively trying to please) probably refers to Ahaz paying protection money to Tiglath-pileser III (2 Kings 16:7, 8).

23:16 This invitation to Chaldea (Babylon) was given by Hezekiah to the envoys from Babylon (Isaiah 38, 39).

23:17 At first, Judah made an alliance with Babylon (Chaldea), but then changed her mind. During the reigns of the last two Judean kings, Jehoiakim and Zedekiah, she looked to Egypt for help. Judah's faithlessness (her alliances with godless nations)

cost her the only real protection she ever had—God.

23:22-26 This predicts the last attack on Jerusalem, which would destroy the city and bring to Babylon the third wave of captives in 586 B.C. (2 Kings 25; Jeremiah 52). The first attack came in 605 B.C., the second in 597 B.C.

23:39 The Israelites went so far as to sacrifice their own children to idols and then sacrifice to the Lord the same day. This made a mockery of worship. We cannot praise God and willfully sin at the same time. That would be like celebrating one's wedding anniversary and then going to bed with a neighbor.

same day they actually came into my Temple to worship! That is how much regard they have for me!

40"You even sent away to distant lands for priests to come with other gods for you to serve, and they have come and been welcomed! You bathed yourself, painted your eyelids, and put on your finest jewels for them. 41You sat together on a beautifully embroidered bed and put my incense and my oil upon a table spread before you. 42From your apartment came the sound of many men carousing—lewd men and drunkards from the wilderness, who put bracelets on your wrists and beautiful crowns upon your head. 43Will they commit adultery with these who have become old harlot hags? 44Yet that is what they did. They went in to them—to Samaria and Jerusalem, these shameless harlots—with all the zest of lustful men who visit prostitutes. 45But just persons everywhere will judge them for what they really are—adulteresses and murderers. They will mete out to them the sentences the law demands.

46"The Lord God says: Bring an army against them and hand them out to be crushed and despised. 47For their enemies will stone them and kill them with swords; they will butcher their sons and daughters and burn their homes. 48Thus will I make lewdness and idolatry to cease from the land. My judgment will be a lesson against idolatry for all to see. 49For you will be fully repaid for all your harlotry, your worshiping of idols. You will suffer the full penalty, and you will know that I alone am God."

The parable of the cooking pot

24 One day late in December of the ninth year (of King Jehoiachin's captivity), another message came to me from the Lord.

2"Son of dust," he said, "write down this date, for today the king of Babylon has attacked Jerusalem. 3And now give this parable to these rebels, Israel; tell them the Lord God says: Put a pot of water on the fire to boil. 4Fill it with choicest mutton, the rump and shoulder and all the most tender cuts. 5Use only the best sheep from the flock, and heap fuel on the fire beneath the pot. Boil the meat well, until the flesh falls off the bones.

6"For the Lord God says: Woe to Jerusalem, City of Murderers; you are a pot that is pitted with rust and with wickedness. So take out the meat chunk by chunk in whatever order it comes—for none is better than any other. 7For her wickedness is evident to all—she boldly murders, leaving blood upon the rocks in open view for all to see; she does not even try to cover it. 8And I have left it there, uncovered, to shout to me against her and arouse my wrath and vengeance.

9"Woe to Jerusalem, City of Murderers. I will pile on the fuel beneath her. 10Heap on the wood; let the fire roar and the pot boil. Cook the meat well and then empty the pot and burn the bones. 11Now set it empty on the coals to scorch away the rust and corruption. 12But all for naught—it all remains despite the hottest fire. 13It is the rust and corruption of your filthy lewdness, of worshiping your idols. And now, because I wanted to cleanse you and you refused, remain filthy until my fury has accomplished all its terrors upon you! 14I, the Lord, have spoken it; it shall come to pass and I will do it."

24:6 *for none is better than any other,* literally, "no lot has fallen upon it."

Cross references (left margin):

23:40
2 Kgs 9:30
20:13-15
Ezek 16:13-16

23:41
Esth 1:6
Jer 44:17

23:42
Gen 24:30
Amos 6:3-6

23:43
Ezra 9:7

23:47
Jer 24:9; 29:18

23:49
Isa 59:18
Ezek 9:10

24:2
2 Kgs 25:1
Jer 39:1; 52:4
Hab 2:2,3

24:3
Jer 1:13,14

24:4
Mic 3:2,3

24:5
Jer 52:10; 24-27

24:6
2 Kgs 24:3,4
Rev 11:7,8
17:6; 18:24

24:7
Lev 17:13
Deut 12:16

24:8
Isa 26:21
Jer 22:8,9

24:9
Lk 13:34,35
Rev 14:20
16:6,19

24:12
Jer 6:28-30
Dan 9:13,14

24:13
Ezek 8:18
Rom 2:8,9

24:1–14 Ezekiel gave this illustration in 588 B.C., three years after the first of the previous messages (see 20:1, 2). The people in Judah thought they were the choice meat because they hadn't been taken into captivity in 597 when the Babylonians last invaded the land. Ezekiel used this illustration before (chapter 11) to show that though the people thought they were safe and secure inside the pot, this pot would actually be the place of their destruction. This message was given to the exiles in Babylon the very day that the Babylonians attacked Jerusalem (24:2), beginning a siege that lasted over two years and resulted in the city's destruction.

24:6–13 The city of Jerusalem was like a pot that was so encrusted with the filth of sin that it would not come clean, even in the hottest fire. God wanted to cleanse the lives of those who lived in Jerusalem, and he wants to cleanse people's lives today. Sometimes he tries to purify our lives through difficulties and troublesome circumstances. When you face tough times, allow the sin to be burned from your life. Look at your problems as an opportunity for your faith to grow. Above all, do not allow sin to so dominate your life that God's judgment must fall (see 1 Corinthians 11:29, 30).

¹⁵Again a message came to me from the Lord, saying:

¹⁶"Son of dust, I am going to take away your lovely wife. Suddenly, she will die. Yet you must show no sorrow. Do not weep; let there be no tears. ¹⁷You may sigh, but only quietly. Let there be no wailing at her grave; don't bare your head nor feet, and don't accept the food brought to you by consoling friends."

¹⁸I proclaimed this to the people in the morning, and in the evening my wife died. The next morning I did all the Lord had told me to.

¹⁹Then the people said: "What does all this mean? What are you trying to tell us?"

^{20, 21}And I answered, "The Lord told me to say to the people of Israel: I will destroy my lovely, beautiful Temple, the strength of your nation. And your sons and daughters in Judea will be slaughtered by the sword. ²²And you will do as I have done; you may not mourn in public or console yourself by eating the food brought to you by sympathetic friends. ²³Your head and feet shall not be bared; you shall not mourn or weep. But you will sorrow to one another for your sins, and mourn privately for all the evil you have done. ²⁴Ezekiel is an example to you, the Lord God says. You will do as he has done. And when that time comes, then you will know I am the Lord."

²⁵"Son of dust, on the day I finish taking from them in Jerusalem the joy of their hearts and their glory and joys—their wives and their sons and their daughters— ²⁶on that day a refugee from Jerusalem will start on a journey to come to you in Babylon to tell you what has happened. ²⁷And on the day of his arrival, your voice will suddenly return to you so that you can talk with him; and you will be a symbol for these people and they shall know I am the Lord."

B. MESSAGES AGAINST FOREIGN NATIONS (25:1—32:32)

These messages were given concerning seven nations which surrounded Judah. The Ammonites were judged because of their joy over the profaning of the Temple, the Moabites because they scorned Judah as special people, the Edomites because of their special hatred of the Jews, and the Philistines because of their vengeance. All these nations would soon realize that God is supreme. Nations today are also under limits imposed by God.

A prophecy against Ammon

25 Then the Lord's message came to me again. He said:

²"Son of dust, look toward the land of Ammon and prophesy against its people. ³Tell them: Listen to what the Lord God says. Because you scoffed when my Temple was destroyed, and mocked Israel in her anguish, and laughed at Judah when she was marched away captive, ⁴therefore I will let the Bedouins from the desert to the east of you overrun your land. They will set up their encampments

24:16
Job 23:2
Song 7:10
Jer 22:10
24:17
Lev 21:10-12
2 Sam 15:30
Jer 16:7
24:20
Ps 27:4; 84:1
Jer 16:3,4
Dan 11:31
24:24
Ezek 4:3
Lk 11:29,30
Jn 13:19; 14:29
24:25
Ps 48:2; 122:1-9
Jer 7:4; 11:22
24:26
1 Sam 4:12
Job 1:15-19
Ezek 33:21,22
24:27
Ex 6:11,12
Ps 51:15
Eph 6:19
25:3
Ps 70:2,3
Ezek 21:28
26:2; 36:2
25:4
Deut 28:33,51
Judg 6:3,33

24:15-18 God told Ezekiel that his wife would die and he was not to grieve for her. Ezekiel obeyed God fully, even as Hosea did when he was told to marry an unfaithful woman (Hosea 1:2, 3). In both cases, these unusual events were intended as symbolic acts to picture God's relationship with his people. Obedience to God can carry a high cost. The only thing more excruciating than losing your spouse and not being allowed to grieve would be to lose eternal life because you did not obey God. Ezekiel always obeyed God wholeheartedly. Our lives should show the same wholehearted obedience. Such obedience begins by doing all that God commands us to do in the Scriptures, even when we don't feel like it. Are you willing to serve God as completely as Ezekiel did?

24:20-24 Ezekiel was not allowed to mourn for his dead wife in order to show his fellow exiles that they were not to mourn over Jerusalem when it was destroyed. Any personal sorrow felt would soon be eclipsed by national sorrow over the horror of the city's total destruction. The individuals would mourn for their sins which caused the city's destruction.

24:27 For some time Ezekiel had not been allowed to speak except when God gave him a message to deliver to the people

(3:25-27). This restriction would soon end, when Jerusalem was destroyed and all Ezekiel's prophecies about Judah and Jerusalem had come true (33:21, 22).

24:27 God gave these messages to Ezekiel so the people would know that he is the Lord. How would they know this? (1) The judgments God pronounced on Jerusalem (chapters 1—24) were all about to come true; (2) the judgments God pronounced on the other nations (chapters 25—32) would all come true; and (3) the remnant of faithful people God promised to preserve were still present.

25:1ff Chapters 25—32 are God's word concerning the seven nations surrounding Judah. The judgments in these chapters are not simply the vengeful statements of Jews against their enemies; they are God's judgments on nations who failed to acknowledge the one true God and fulfill the good purposes God intended for them. The Ammonites were judged because of their joy over the desecration of the Temple (25:1-7), the Moabites because they found pleasure in Judah's wickedness (25:8-11), the Edomites because of their racial hatred for the Jews (25:12-14), and the Philistines because they sought revenge against Judah for past battle victories (25:15-17).

among you. They will harvest all your fruit and steal your dairy cattle. 5And I will turn the city of Rabbah into a pasture for camels and all the country of the Ammonites into a waste land where flocks of sheep can graze. Then you will know I am the Lord.

6"For the Lord God says: Because you clapped and stamped and cheered with glee at the destruction of my people, 7therefore I will lay my hand heavily upon you, delivering you to many nations for devastation. I will cut you off from being a nation any more. I will destroy you; then you shall know I am the Lord.

A prophecy against Moab

8"And the Lord God says: Because the Moabites have said that Judah is no better off than any other nation, 9, 10therefore I will open up the eastern flank of Moab, wiping out her frontier cities, the glory of the nation—Beth-jeshimoth, Baal-meon and Kiriathaim. And Bedouin tribes from the desert to the east will pour in upon her, just as they will upon Ammon. And Moab will no longer be counted among the nations. 11Thus I will bring down my judgment upon the Moabites, and they shall know I am the Lord.

A prophecy against Edom

12"And the Lord God says: Because the people of Edom have sinned so greatly by avenging themselves upon the people of Judah, 13I will smash Edom with my fist and wipe out her people, her cattle and her flocks. The sword will destroy everything from Teman to Dedan. 14By the hand of my people, Israel, this shall be done. They will carry out my furious vengeance.

A prophecy against Philistia

15"And the Lord God says: Because the Philistines have acted against Judah out of revenge and long-standing hatred, 16I will shake my fist over the land of the Philistines, and I will wipe out the Cherithites and utterly destroy those along the sea coast. 17I will execute terrible vengeance upon them to rebuke them for what they have done. And when all this happens, then they shall know I am the Lord."

A prophecy against Tyre

26 Another message came to me from the Lord on the first day of the month, in the eleventh year (after King Jehoiachin was taken away to captivity). 2"Son of dust, Tyre has rejoiced over the fall of Jerusalem, saying, 'Ha! She who

26:2 *the course of the Jordan River,* literally, "the gate of the peoples."

JUDAH'S ENEMIES
Ammon, Moab, Edom, and Philistia, although once allied to Judah against Babylon, had abandoned Judah and rejoiced to see its ruin. But these nations were as sinful as Judah and would also feel the sting of God's judgment.

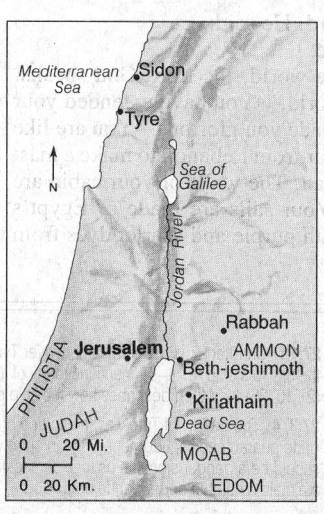

25:13 The Edomites were blood brothers of the Jews, both nations being descended from Isaac (Genesis 25:19-26). Edom shared its northern border with Israel, and the two nations were always at odds. The Edomites hated Israel so much that they rejoiced when Jerusalem, Israel's capital, was destroyed. Teman was the northernmost city in Edom; Dedan, the southernmost. Thus, Ezekiel was saying that the entire country would be destroyed. Similarly, those who rejoice at the fall of Christian leaders today had better re-examine their own actions, for God's judgment may fall upon them as well.

26:1, 2 This message came to Ezekiel in 586 B.C. Chapters 26 and 27 are a prophecy against Tyre, the capital of Phoenicia just north of Israel. Part of the city was on the coastline, and part was on a beautiful island. Tyre rejoiced when Jerusalem fell, because Tyre and Judah always competed for the lucrative trade which came through their lands from Egypt in the south and Mesopotamia to the north. Tyre dominated the sea trading routes while Judah dominated the caravan routes. Now that Judah was defeated, Tyre thought it had all the trade routes to itself. But this gloating didn't last long. In 585 B.C., Nebuchadnezzar attacked the city of Tyre. It took him 13 years to capture the city because its back side lay on the sea and fresh supplies could be shipped in daily.

controlled the lucrative north-south trade routes along the coast and along the course of the Jordan River has been broken, and I have fallen heir! Because she has been laid waste, I shall become wealthy!'

3"Therefore the Lord God says: I stand against you, Tyre, and I will bring nations against you like ocean waves. 4They will destroy the walls of Tyre and tear down her towers. I will scrape away her soil and make her a bare rock! 5Her island shall become uninhabited, a place for fishermen to spread their nets, for I have spoken it, says the Lord God. Tyre shall become the prey of many nations, 6and her mainland city shall perish by the sword. Then they shall know I am the Lord.

7"For the Lord God says: I will bring Nebuchadnezzar, king of Babylon—the king of kings from the north—against Tyre with a great army and cavalry and chariots. 8First he will destroy your suburbs; then he will attack your mainland city by building a siege wall and raising a roof of shields against it. 9He will set up battering rams against your walls and with sledge hammers demolish your forts. 10The hoofs of his cavalry will choke the city with dust, and your walls will shake as the horses gallop through your broken gates, pulling chariots behind them. 11Horsemen will occupy every street in the city; they will butcher your people, and your famous, huge pillars will topple.

12"They will plunder all your riches and merchandise and break down your walls. They will destroy your lovely homes and dump your stones and timber and even your dust into the sea. 13I will stop the music of your songs. No more will there be the sound of harps among you. 14I will make your island a bare rock, a place for fishermen to spread their nets. You will never be rebuilt, for I, the Lord, have spoken it. So says the Lord. 15The whole country will shake with your fall; the wounded will scream as the slaughter goes on.

16"Then all the seaport rulers shall come down from their thrones and lay aside their robes and beautiful garments and sit on the ground shaking with fear at what they have seen. 17And they shall wail for you, singing this dirge: 'O mighty island city, with your naval power that terrorized the mainland, how you have vanished from the seas! 18How the islands tremble at your fall! They watch dismayed.'

19"For the Lord God says: I will destroy Tyre to the ground. You will sink beneath the terrible waves of enemy attack. Great seas shall swallow you. 20I will send you to the pit of hell to lie there with those of long ago. Your city will lie in ruins, dead, like the bodies of those in the underworld who entered long ago the nether world of the dead. Never again will you be inhabited or be given beauty here in the land of those who live. 21I will bring you to a dreadful end; no search will be enough to find you, says the Lord."

The greatness of Tyre

27 Then this message came to me from the Lord. He said: 2"Son of dust, sing this sad dirge for Tyre:

3"O mighty seaport city, merchant center of the world, the Lord God speaks. You say, 'I am the most beautiful city in all the world.' 4You have extended your boundaries out into the sea; your architects have made you glorious. 5You are like a ship built of finest fir from Senir. They took a cedar from Lebanon to make a mast for you. 6They made your oars from oaks of Bashan. The walls of your cabin are of cypress from the southern coast of Cyprus. 7Your sails are made of Egypt's finest linens; you stand beneath awnings bright with purple and scarlet dyes from eastern Cyprus.

26:3
Jer 50:42; 51:42
Lk 21:25
26:4
Isa 23:11
Amos 1:10
26:6
Jer 47:4; 49:2
26:7
Dan 2:37,47
Nah 2:3,4
26:8
Jer 6:6; 32:24
26:10
Jer 39:3
26:11
Isa 5:28; 26:5
Hab 1:8
26:12
2 Chron 32:27
Isa 23:8,18
Dan 11:8
Amos 5:11
26:13
Isa 24:8,9
Amos 6:5
Jas 5:1-5
Rev 18:22,23
26:14
Deut 13:16
Isa 14:27
26:15
Jer 49:21
Heb 12:26,27
26:16
Ps 35:26
Jonah 3:6
26:17
Isa 14:12
Jer 48:39; 50:23
Mic 2:4
26:18
Isa 23:5-7,
10-15
26:19
Isa 8:7,8
Dan 9:26; 11:40
Rev 17:15
26:20
Ps 88:6
Jonah 2:2,6
Zech 2:8

27:2
Jer 7:20
27:5
Isa 14:8
27:6
Num 21:33
Jer 22:20
27:7
Ex 25:4
1 Kgs 10:28
Jer 10:9

26:14 After a 13-year siege, Nebuchadnezzar could not conquer the part of Tyre located on the island; thus certain aspects of the description in 26:12, 14 exceed the actual damage done to Tyre by Nebuchadnezzar and predicted what would happen to the island settlement later during the conquests of Alexander the Great. Alexander threw the rubble of the mainland city into the sea until it made a bridge to the island. Today the island city is still a pile of rubble, a testimony to God's judgment.

27:1ff Chapter 27 is a funeral lament over Tyre's fall. It compares the city to a ship (27:1–9), mentions many of its trading partners (27:10–25), and then describes how the ship sank (27:26–36).

27:3, 4 The beauty of Tyre was the source of its pride, and its pride guaranteed its judgment. Pride in our own accomplishments should be a danger signal to us (see James 4:13–17). We must maintain a humble dependence upon God.

27:8
Gen 10:18
1 Kgs 9:27
1 Chron 1:16

27:10
Ezek 38:5

27:13
Gen 10:2,3
1 Chron 1:5,7
Isa 66:19
Dan 8:21; 10:20
Rev 18:13

27:14
1 Kgs 10:22

27:16
Ezek 16:13,18

27:17
Judg 11:33
1 Kgs 5:9
Ezra 3:7
Acts 12:20

27:18
Gen 14:15
Ezek 47:16-18

27:21
Gen 25:13
Isa 21:13; 60:7
Gal 4:25

27:22
Gen 10:7; 43:11
1 Kgs 10:2
Ezek 38:13

27:23
2 Kgs 19:12
Isa 37:12
Amos 1:5; 6:2

27:26
Ps 48:7
Jer 18:17
Acts 27:14,41
Rev 17:15

27:29
Rev 18:17-19

27:30
1 Sam 4:12
2 Sam 1:2
Isa 23:1-6
Jonah 3:6
Mic 1:10

27:31
Isa 16:9
Ezek 7:18

27:32
Lam 2:13
Rev 18:18

27:34
Zech 9:3,4

27:36
Ps 37:10,36
Jer 49:17
Zeph 2:15

28:2
2 Thess 2:4

8"Your sailors come from Sidon and Arvad; your helmsmen are skilled men from Zemer. 9Wise old craftsmen from Gebal do the calking. Ships come from every land with all their goods to barter for your trade.

10"Your army includes men from far-off Paras, Lud and Put. They serve you—it is a feather in your cap to have their shields hang upon your walls; it is the ultimate of honor. 11Men from Arvad and from Helech are the sentinels upon your walls; your towers are manned by men from Gamad. Their shields hang row on row upon the walls, perfecting your glory.

12"From Tarshish come all kinds of riches to your markets—silver, iron, tin and lead. 13Merchants from Javan, Tubal and Meshech bring slaves and bronze dishes, 14while from Togarmah come chariot horses, steeds and mules.

15"Merchants come to you from Rhodes, and many coastlands are your captive markets, giving payment in ebony and ivory. 16Edom sends her traders to buy your many wares. They bring emeralds, purple dyes, embroidery, fine linen, and jewelry of coral and agate. 17Judah and the cities in what was once the kingdom of Israel send merchants with wheat from Minnith and Pannag, and with honey, oil and balm. 18Damascus comes. She brings wines from Helbon, and white Syrian wool to trade for all the rich variety of goods you make. 19Vedan and Javan bring Arabian yarn, wrought iron, cassia and calamus, 20while Dedan brings expensive saddlecloths for riding.

21"The Arabians, and Kedar's wealthy merchant princes bring you lambs and rams and goats. 22The merchants of Sheba and Raamah come with all kinds of spices, jewels and gold. 23Haran and Canneh, Eden, Asshur and Chilmad all send their wares. 24They bring choice fabrics to trade—blue cloth, embroidery and many-colored carpets bound with cords and made secure. 25The ships of Tarshish are your ocean caravans; your island warehouse is filled to the brim!

26"But now your statesmen bring your ship of state into a hurricane! Your mighty vessel flounders in the heavy eastern gale, and you are wrecked in the heart of the seas! 27Everything is lost. Your riches and wares, your sailors and pilots, your shipwrights and merchants and soldiers and all the people sink into the sea on the day of your vast ruin.

28"The surrounding cities quake at the sound as your pilots scream with fright. 29All your sailors out at sea come to land and watch upon the mainland shore, 30weeping bitterly and casting dust upon their heads and wallowing in ashes. 31They shave their heads in grief and put on sackcloth and weep for you with bitterness of heart and deep mourning.

32"And this is the song of their sorrow: 'Where in all the world was there ever such a wondrous city as Tyre, destroyed in the midst of the sea? 33Your merchandise satisfied the desires of many nations. Kings at the ends of the earth rejoiced in the riches you sent them. 34Now you lie broken beneath the sea; all your merchandise and all your crew have perished with you. 35All who live along the coastlands watch, incredulous. Their kings are horribly afraid and look on with twisted faces. 36The merchants of the nations shake their heads, for your fate is dreadful; you have forever perished.' "

The king of Tyre is condemned

28 Here is another message given to me from the Lord:

2, 3"Son of dust, say to the prince of Tyre: The Lord God says: You are so

27:10 *Paras, Lud and Put.* These were three cities of ancient North Africa. **27:11** *Helech,* a region in ancient Cilicia known from Assyrian records as Hilakku. **27:13, 14** *Javan, Tubal and Meshech . . . from Togarmah.* Regions of Asia Minor, now in Turkey. **27:17** *with wheat from Minnith and Pannag,* or, "with wheat, minnith and pannag." If these were commodities, their identification is uncertain. **27:19** *Vedan and Javan bring Arabian yarn,* or, probably better, "They exchanged wine from Uzal for your wares." The text here is uncertain. **27:26** *Your mighty vessel flounders in the heavy eastern gale,* i.e., Nebuchadnezzar of Babylonia.

28:1ff Previously Ezekiel prophesied against the nation and city of Tyre (chapters 26, 27). Now he focuses his prophecy on Tyre's leader. The chief sin of Tyre's king was pride, believing himself to be a god. But Ezekiel made a broader application, speaking about the real king of Tyre, Satan, whom the people were following.

28:2, 3 Daniel, an important official in Nebuchadnezzar's kingdom (14:14), was already renowned for his wisdom. Daniel proclaimed that all his wisdom came from God (Daniel 2:20–23). The king of Tyre thought that he himself *was* a god.

proud you think you are God, sitting on the throne of a god on your island home in the midst of the seas. But you are only a man, and not a god, though you boast yourself to be like God. You are wiser than Daniel, for no secret is hidden from you. ⁴You have used your wisdom and understanding to get great wealth—gold and silver and many treasures. ⁵Yes, your wisdom has made you very rich and very proud.

⁶"Therefore the Lord God says: Because you claim that you are as wise as God, ⁷an enemy army, the terror of the nations, shall suddenly draw their swords against your marvelous wisdom and defile your splendor! ⁸They will bring you to the pit of hell and you shall die as those pierced with many wounds, there on your island in the heart of the seas. ⁹Then will you boast as a god? At least to these invaders you will be no god, but merely man! ¹⁰You will die like an outcast at the hands of foreigners. For I have spoken it, the Lord God says."

¹¹Then this further message came to me from the Lord:

¹²"Son of dust, weep for the king of Tyre. Tell him, the Lord God says: You were the perfection of wisdom and beauty. ¹³You were in Eden, the garden of God; your clothing was bejeweled with every precious stone—ruby, topaz, diamond, chrysolite, onyx, jasper, sapphire, carbuncle, and emerald—all in beautiful settings of finest gold. They were given to you on the day you were created. ¹⁴I appointed you to be the anointed Guardian Angel. You had access to the holy mountain of God. You walked among the stones of fire.

¹⁵"You were perfect in all you did from the day you were created until that time when wrong was found in you. ¹⁶Your great wealth filled you with internal turmoil and you sinned. Therefore, I cast you out of the mountain of God like a common sinner. I destroyed you, O Guardian Angel, from the midst of the stones of fire. ¹⁷Your heart was filled with pride because of all your beauty; you corrupted your wisdom for the sake of your splendor. Therefore I have cast you down to the ground and exposed you helpless before the curious gaze of kings. ¹⁸You defiled your holiness with lust for gain; therefore I brought forth fire from your own actions and let it burn you to ashes upon the earth in the sight of all those watching you. ¹⁹All who know you are appalled at your fate; you are an example of horror; you are destroyed forever."

²⁰Then another message came to me from the Lord:

²¹"Son of dust, look toward the city of Sidon and prophesy against it. Say to it: ²²"The Lord God says: I am your enemy, O Sidon, and I will reveal my power over you. When I destroy you and show forth my holiness upon you then all who see shall know I am the Lord. ²³I will send an epidemic of disease and an army to destroy; the wounded shall be slain in your streets by troops on every side. Then you will know I am the Lord. ²⁴No longer shall you and Israel's other neighbor nations prick and tear at Israel like thorns and briars, though they formerly despised her and treated her with great contempt.

²⁵"The people of Israel will once more live in their own land, the land I gave their

28:3
Dan 2:20-23
28:4
Prov 18:11
23:4,5
Zech 9:2-4
28:5
Job 31:24,25
Ps 52:7
Hos 12:7,8
28:6
Ex 9:17
1 Cor 10:22
Jas 1:11
28:7
Dan 7:7
Hab 1:6-8
28:10
1 Sam 17:26,36
Acts 7:51
Phil 3:3
28:13
Gen 2:8
Ex 28:17-20
39:10-21
Isa 51:3
54:11,12
28:14
Ex 25:17-20
Ezek 20:40
Dan 2:37,38
5:18-23
Rev 18:16
28:15
Isa 14:12
Rom 7:9
28:16
Ezek 8:17
Hab 2:8,17
28:17
Isa 19:11
Jer 8:9
28:18
Amos 1:9,10
Mal 4:3
28:19
Jer 51:64
Rev 18:21
28:21
Gen 10:15-19
Isa 23:2-4,12
Jer 25:22; 27:3
Joel 3:4-8
28:24
Num 33:35
Josh 23:13
28:25
Ps 106:47
Isa 11:12,13
Jer 23:8

28:14 *You walked among the stones of fire.* Probably a symbol of the angels.   **28:16** *O Guardian Angel, from the midst of the stones of fire,* or, "and the guardian cherub drove you out from the midst of the stones of fire."
28:18 *with lust for gain,* literally, "in the unrighteousness of your trade." *I brought forth fire from your own actions,* literally, "I brought fire from the midst of you."

28:6-10 The enemy army that attacked Tyre was the Babylonian army under Nebuchadnezzar. This attack occurred in 573 or 572 B.C. Jesus spoke of Tyre in Matthew 11:22.

28:12-19 Some of the phrases in this passage which describe the human king of Tyre may describe Satan. Great care must be taken to interpret these verses with discernment. It is clear that, at times, Ezekiel describes this king in terms that could not apply to a mere man. This king had been in the garden of Eden (28:13), had been a guardian angel (28:14), and had access to the holy mountain of God (28:14) but he was cast down from the mountain (28:16, 17). Ezekiel, therefore, may have been pronouncing judgment not only on the king of Tyre, but on Satan, who had motivated the king to sin.

28:20, 21 Sidon was another famous seaport, located a few miles north of Tyre. God charged this city with contempt for his people. Sidon's economy was bound to Tyre's, so when Tyre fell to Nebuchadnezzar, Sidon was doomed to follow.

28:24-26 This promise that God's people will live in complete safety has yet to be fulfilled. While many were allowed to return from exile under Zerubbabel, Ezra, and Nehemiah; and although the political nation is restored today, the inhabitants do not yet live in complete safety (28:26). Therefore, this promise will have its ultimate fulfillment when Christ sets up his eternal Kingdom. Then all people who have been faithful to God will dwell together in harmony and complete safety.

father Jacob. For I will gather them back again from distant lands where I have scattered them and I will show the nations of the world my holiness among my people. 26They will live safely in Israel, and build their homes and plant their vineyards. When I punish all the bordering nations that treated them with such contempt, then they shall know I am the Lord their God."

A prophecy against Egypt

29 Late in December of the tenth year (of the imprisonment of King Jehoia-chin), this message came to me from the Lord:

2"Son of dust, face toward Egypt and prophesy against Pharaoh her king and all her people. 3Tell them that the Lord God says: I am your enemy, Pharaoh, king of Egypt—mighty dragon lying in the middle of your rivers. For you have said, 'The Nile is mine; I have made it for myself!' 4I will put hooks into your jaws and drag you out onto the land with fish sticking to your scales. 5And I will leave you and all the fish stranded in the desert to die, and you won't be buried, for I have given you as food to the wild animals and birds.

6"Because of the way your might collapsed when Israel called on you for aid [instead of trusting me], all of you shall know I am the Lord. 7Israel leaned on you but, like a cracked staff, you snapped beneath her hand and wrenched her shoulder out of joint and made her stagger with the pain. 8Therefore the Lord God says: I will bring an army against you, O Egypt, and destroy both men and herds. 9The land of Egypt shall become a desolate wasteland, and the Egyptians will know that I, the Lord, have done it.

10"Because you said: 'The Nile is mine! I made it!' therefore I am against you and your river and I will utterly destroy the land of Egypt, from Migdol to Syene, as far south as the border of Ethiopia. 11For forty years not a soul will pass that way, neither men nor animals. It will be completely uninhabited. 12I will make Egypt desolate, surrounded by desolate nations, and her cities will lie as wastelands for forty years. I will exile the Egyptians to other lands.

13"But the Lord God says that at the end of the forty years he will bring the Egyptians home again from the nations to which they will be banished. 14And I will restore the fortunes of Egypt and bring her people back to the land of Pathros in southern Egypt where they were born, but she will be an unimportant, minor kingdom. 15She will be the lowliest of all the nations; never again will she raise herself above the other nations; never again will Egypt be great enough for that.

16"Israel will no longer expect any help from Egypt. Whenever she thinks of asking for it, then she will remember her sin in seeking it before. Then Israel will know that I alone am God."

28:26
Jer 32:15,43,44
Amos 9:13,14

29:2
Isa 19:1-17
Jer 43:8-13
46:2-16
Joel 3:19

29:3
Ps 74:13
Isa 27:1

29:4
2 Kgs 19:28
Isa 37:29
Ezek 38:4

29:5
Jer 7:33; 34:20

29:6
Isa 36:6
Jer 2:36

29:7
Prov 25:19
Jer 37:5-11
Ezek 17:15-17

29:9
Prov 18:12
29:23

29:11
Jer 43:11,12
Dan 9:2

29:12
Jer 25:15-19
27:6-11

29:14
Isa 11:11
Jer 44:1

29:15
Dan 11:42,43
Nah 3:8,9
Zech 10:11

29:16
Isa 30:1-3; 64:9
Hos 5:13; 8:13
9:9

29:1ff There are seven prophecies in chapters 29—32, all dealing with judgment on Egypt. This is the first prophecy which was probably given by Ezekiel in 587 B.C. Hezekiah, Jehoiakim, and Zedekiah (kings of Judah) had all sought help from Egypt despite God's warnings.

There are three key reasons for this prophecy: (1) Egypt was an ancient enemy of the Jews, having once enslaved them for 400 years; (2) Egypt worshiped many gods; (3) Egypt's wealth and power made her seem like a good ally. Egypt offered to help Judah only because of the benefits she hoped to receive from such an alliance. When the Egyptians didn't get what they hoped for, they bailed out of their agreement without regard to any promises they had made.

29:2ff Egypt had great artistic treasures, a flourishing civilization, and world-renowned military power. Unfortunately, it was also cruel, idolatrous, and had slaves. And for those sins God condemned Egypt. At the battle of Carchemish in 605 B.C., Babylon crushed Egypt along with Assyria, its rivals for the position of world ruler.

29:10 The Nile was Egypt's pride and joy, a life-giving river

cutting through the middle of the desert. Rather than thanking God, however, Egypt declared, "The Nile is mine!" We do the same when we say "This house is mine; I built it," or "I have brought myself to the place where I am today," or "I have built this church, business, or reputation, from the ground up." These statements reveal our pride. We sometimes take for granted what God has given us, thinking we have made it ourselves. Of course, we have put forth a lot of hard effort, but God supplied the resources, gave us the abilities, and provided us with the opportunities to make it happen. Instead of claiming our own greatness, as the Egyptians did, we should proclaim God's greatness and give him the credit.

29:11-15 This 40-year period of desolation in Egypt is hard to pinpoint. Nebuchadnezzar attacked Egypt around 572 B.C. and carried many people off to Babylon, while others fled for safety to surrounding nations. Approximately 33 years later, Cyrus, king of the Persian Empire, conquered Babylon and allowed the nations which Babylon had conquered to return to their homelands. Assuming a seven-year regrouping and travel period, this 40-year time span is feasible. Since that time, Egypt has never returned to its previous dominance as a world power.

17In the twenty-seventh year of King Jehoiachin's captivity, around the middle of March, this message came to me from the Lord:

18"Son of dust, the army of King Nebuchadnezzar of Babylon fought hard against Tyre. The soldiers' heads were bald (from carrying heavy basketfuls of earth); their shoulders were raw and blistered (from burdens of stones for the siege). And Nebuchadnezzar received no compensation and could not pay the army for all this work. 19Therefore, the Lord God says, I will give the land of Egypt to Nebuchadnezzar, king of Babylon, and he will carry off her wealth, plundering everything she has, for his army. 20Yes, I have given him the land of Egypt for his salary, because he was working for me during those thirteen years at Tyre, says the Lord. 21And the day will come when I will cause the ancient glory of Israel to revive, and then at last her words will be respected, and Egypt shall know I am the Lord."

Egypt faces doom

30 Another message from the Lord!

2, 3"Son of dust, prophesy and say: The Lord God says, Weep, for the terrible day is almost here; the day of the Lord; a day of clouds and gloom; a day of despair for the nations! 4A sword shall fall on Egypt; the slain shall cover the ground. Her wealth is taken away, her foundations destroyed. The land of Cush has been ravished. 5For Cush and Put and Lud, Arabia and Libya and all the countries leagued with them shall perish in that war.

6"For the Lord says: All Egypt's allies shall fall, and the pride of her power shall end. From Migdol to Syene they shall perish by the sword. 7She shall be desolate, surrounded by desolate nations, and her cities shall be in ruins, surrounded by other ruined cities. 8And they will know I am the Lord when I have set Egypt on fire and destroyed her allies. 9At that time I will send swift messengers to bring panic to the Ethiopians; great terror shall befall them at that time of Egypt's doom. This will all come true.

10"For the Lord God says: Nebuchadnezzar, king of Babylon, will destroy the multitudes of Egypt. 11He and his armies—the terror of the nations—are sent to demolish the land. They shall war against Egypt and cover the ground with the slain. 12I will dry up the Nile and sell the whole land to wicked men. I will destroy Egypt and everything in it, using foreigners to do it. I, the Lord, have spoken it.

13"And I will smash the idols of Egypt and the images at Memphis, and there will be no king in Egypt; anarchy shall reign!

14"The cities of Pathros [along the upper Nile], and Zoan and Thebes shall lie in ruins by my hand. 15And I will pour out my fury upon Pelusium, the strongest fortress of Egypt, and I will stamp out the people of Thebes. 16Yes, I will set fire to Egypt, Pelusium will be racked with pain, Thebes will be torn apart, Memphis will be in daily terror. 17The young men of Heliopolis and Bubastis shall die by the sword and the women will be taken away as slaves. 18When I come to break the power of Egypt it will be a dark day for Tehaphnehes too; a dark cloud will cover her, and her daughters will be taken away as captives. 19And so I will greatly punish Egypt and they shall know I am the Lord."

29:17 King Jehoiachin's captivity, implied. **30:14** along the upper Nile, implied.

Cross references

29:17
Ezek 24:1; 30:20

29:18
Jer 25:9; 27:6
Ezek 26:7-12

29:19
Jer 43:10-13
Ezek 30:10-12
29:20
Isa 10:6,7
45:1-3
29:21
1 Sam 2:10
Ps 92:10
Amos 3:7,8
Lk 21:15

30:2
Isa 13:6; 65:14
Joel 1:5,11,
13,15
Jas 5:1

30:5
Isa 18:1; 20:4
Jer 25:20,24
Nah 3:8,9

30:6
Isa 20:3-6

30:8
Ps 58:11
Amos 1:4,7,
10-14
Nah 1:5,6

30:9
Isa 23:6
Jer 49:21
Zech 11:2,3

30:12
Ezek 29:3,9

30:13
Isa 2:18
Jer 44:1; 46:14
Hos 9:6

30:14
Ps 78:12,43
Isa 19:11,13
Nah 3:8

30:17
Gen 41:45

30:18
Lev 26:13
Jer 43:8-13
46:20-26

30:19
Num 33:4
Ps 9:16
Ezek 5:8,15

29:17, 18 This prophecy was given in 571 B.C. and is actually the latest prophecy in Ezekiel. Nebuchadnezzar had finally conquered Tyre after a long and costly 13-year siege (587-574 B.C.). He had not counted on such an expense, so he went south and conquered Egypt to make up for all he had lost in taking Tyre. Ezekiel placed this prophecy here to describe who would bring this punishment to Egypt. God was using Nebuchadnezzar, an evil man, as an instrument of his judgment on Tyre, Judah, and Egypt—evil nations themselves. When Babylon didn't recognize God's help, he judged them too.

30:1-19 This is a prophecy against Egypt and her allies. Because of the pride and idolatry of the Egyptians, they would be brought down.

30:12 Egypt's pharaohs claimed they had made the Nile—the river on which the entire nation depended. If God dried up the Nile, the nation would be doomed.

30:13-19 The list of cities to be destroyed shows the breadth of the destruction; the drying up of the Nile (30:12) shows its depth. Egypt would be completely incapacitated. This should have given a clear message to Judah not to trust Egypt for help against the Babylonians.

20A year later, around the middle of March of the eleventh year of King Jehoiachin's captivity, this message came to me: 21"Son of dust, I have broken the arm of Pharaoh, king of Egypt, and it has not been set nor put into a cast to make it strong enough to hold a sword again. 22For, the Lord God says, I am against Pharaoh, king of Egypt, and I will break both his arms—the strong one and the one that was broken before, and I will make his sword clatter to the ground. 23And I will banish the Egyptians to many lands. 24And I will strengthen the arms of the king of Babylon and place my sword in his hand. But I will break the arms of Pharaoh, king of Egypt, and he shall groan before the king of Babylon as one who has been wounded unto death. 25I will strengthen the hands of the king of Babylon, while the arms of Pharaoh fall useless to his sides. Yes, when I place my sword into the hand of the king of Babylon, and he swings it over the land of Egypt, Egypt shall know I am the Lord. 26I will scatter the Egyptians among the nations; then they shall know I am the Lord."

Egypt's pride

31 In mid-May of the eleventh year of King Jehoiachin's captivity, this message came to me from the Lord:

2, 3"Son of dust, tell Pharaoh, king of Egypt, and all his people: You are as Assyria was—a great and mighty nation—like a cedar of Lebanon, full of thick branches and forest shade, with its head high up among the clouds. 4Its roots went deep into the moist earth. It grew luxuriantly and gave streamlets of water to all the trees around. 5It towered above all the other trees. It prospered and grew long thick branches because of all the water at its roots. 6The birds nested in its branches, and in its shade the flocks and herds gave birth to young. All the great nations of the world lived beneath its shadow. 7It was strong and beautiful, for its roots went deep to water. 8This tree was taller than any other in the garden of God; no cypress had branches equal to it; none had boughs to compare; none equaled it in beauty. 9Because of the magnificence that I gave it, it was the envy of all the other trees of Eden.

10"But Egypt has become proud and arrogant, the Lord God says. Therefore because she has set herself so high above the others, reaching to the clouds, 11I will deliver her into the hands of a mighty nation, to destroy her as her wickedness deserves. I, myself, will cut her down. 12A foreign army (from Babylon)—the terror of the nations—will invade her land and cut her down and leave her fallen on the ground. Her branches will be scattered across the mountains and valleys and rivers of the land. All those who live beneath her shade will go away and leave her lying there. 13The birds will pluck off her twigs and the wild animals will lie among her branches; 14let no other nation exult with pride for its own prosperity, though it be higher than the clouds, for all are doomed and they will land in hell, along with all the proud men of the world.

31:1 *the eleventh year of King Jehoiachin's captivity,* implied. It was the year 587 B.C., the year Jerusalem fell.
31:10 *But Egypt,* implied.

30:20, 21 This message came in 587 B.C., while Jerusalem was under attack from Babylon. Judah had rebelled against Babylon and made an alliance with Egypt in spite of God's warnings (Jeremiah 2:36, 37). Pharaoh Hophrah made a half-hearted attempt to help Jerusalem; but when Nebuchadnezzar's army turned on him, he fled back to Egypt (Jeremiah 37:5–7). This defeat is what Ezekiel meant when he said God would break the arm of Pharaoh.

30:21–26 This prophecy was given to Ezekiel in 587 B.C. God destroyed Egypt's military superiority and gave it to Babylon. God allows nations to rise to power to accomplish a particular purpose, often beyond our immediate understanding. When you read about armies and wars, don't despair. Remember that God is sovereign and in charge of everything, even military might. Besides praying for your military and government leaders, pray that God's greater purposes be carried out and that his will be done "on earth

just as it is in heaven" (see Matthew 6:10).

31:1ff This message was given in 587 B.C. Ezekiel compared Egypt to Assyria, calling Assyria a great cedar tree. The Egyptians were to look at the fall of the mighty nation of Assyria (whose demise they had seen) as an example of what would happen to them. Just like Assyria, Egypt took pride in her strength and beauty; this would be her downfall. She would crash like a mighty tree and be sent to the place of the dead. There is no permanence apart from God, even for a great society with magnificent culture and military power.

31:2–9 A strong nation will often protect the weaker nations around it. Similarly, the fall of a strong nation may endanger the weaker ones.

31:9 "All the other trees of Eden" may refer to all the other nations of the world who were jealous of Assyria's power and grandeur.

15"The Lord God says: When she fell I made the oceans mourn for her and restrained their tides. I clothed Lebanon in black and caused the trees of Lebanon to weep. 16I made the nations shake with fear at the sound of her fall, for I threw her down to hell with all the others like her. And all the other proud trees of Eden, the choicest and the best of Lebanon, the ones whose roots went deep into the water, are comforted to find her there with them in hell. 17Her allies too are all destroyed and perish with her. They went down with her to the nether world—those nations that had lived beneath her shade.

18"O Egypt, you are great and glorious among the trees of Eden—the nations of the world. And you will be brought down to the pit of hell with all these other nations. You will be among the nations you despise, killed by the sword. This is the fate of Pharaoh and all his teeming masses, says the Lord."

All of Israel's enemies will perish

32 In mid-February of the twelfth year of King Jehoiachin's captivity, this message came to me from the Lord:

2"Son of dust, mourn for Pharaoh, king of Egypt, and say to him: You think of yourself as a strong young lion among the nations, but you are merely a crocodile along the banks of the Nile, making bubbles and muddying the stream.

3"The Lord God says: I will send a great army to catch you with my net. I will haul you out, 4and leave you stranded on the land to die. And all the birds of the heavens will light upon you and the wild animals of the whole earth will devour you until they are glutted and full. 5And I will cover the hills with your flesh and fill the valleys with your bones. 6And I will drench the earth with your gushing blood, filling the ravines to the tops of the mountains. 7I will blot you out, and I will veil the heavens and darken the stars. I will cover the sun with a cloud, and the moon shall not give you her light. 8Yes, darkness will be everywhere across your land—even the bright stars will be dark above you.

9"And when I destroy you, grief will be in many hearts among the distant nations you have never seen. 10Yes, terror shall strike in many lands, and their kings shall be terribly afraid because of all I do to you. They shall shudder with terror when I brandish my sword before them. They shall greatly tremble for their lives on the day of your fall.

11"For the Lord God says: The sword of the king of Babylon shall come upon you. 12I will destroy you with Babylon's mighty army—the terror of the nations. It will smash the pride of Egypt and all her people; all will perish. 13I will destroy all your flocks and herds that graze beside the streams, and neither man nor animal will disturb those waters any more. 14Therefore the waters of Egypt will be as clear and flow as smoothly as olive oil, the Lord God says. 15And when I destroy Egypt and wipe out everything she has, then she shall know that I, the Lord, have done it. 16Yes, cry for the sorrows of Egypt. Let all the nations weep for her and for her people, says the Lord."

17Two weeks later, another message came to me from the Lord. He said: 18"Son of dust, weep for the people of Egypt and for the other mighty nations. Send them down to the nether world among the denizens of death. 19What nation is as beautiful as you, O Egypt? Yet your doom is the pit; you will be laid beside the people you despise. 20The Egyptians will die with the multitudes slain by the

31:15
Nah 2:8-10
Rev 18:9-11,16,
19
31:16
Isa 14:8
Hag 2:7
Heb 12:26,27
Rev 18:9
31:17
Ps 9:17
Dan 4:11,12
Nah 3:17
31:18
Ps 52:7
Jer 9:25,26
Mt 13:19

32:2
Jer 46:7,8
Nah 2:11-13

32:4
1 Sam 17:44-46
Isa 34:2-7
Jer 8:2
32:6
Ex 7:17
Isa 34:3,7
Rev 14:20; 16:6
32:7
Ex 10:21-23
Prov 13:9
Amos 8:9
32:8
Gen 1:14
32:9
Ex 15:14-16
Jer 25:15-26
Rev 18:10-15

32:15
Ex 7:5; 14:4,18
Ps 83:17,18
Ezek 8:7
32:16
2 Sam 3:33,34
2 Chron 35:25
Jer 9:17
32:18
Jer 1:10
Hos 6:5
32:19
Jer 9:25,26
32:20
Ps 28:3
Prov 24:11
Jer 22:19

31:15 *restrained their tides,* literally, "the great waters were held back."   **32:2** *crocodile,* or, "sea serpent."
32:9 *when I destroy you,* or, "when I carry you captive among the nations."   **32:17** *Two weeks later,* literally, "In the
twelfth year, on the fifteenth day of the month."

32:1 This prophecy was given in 585 B.C., two months after the news of Jerusalem's fall reached the exiles in Babylon. Ezekiel prophesied numerous judgments upon many wicked nations. These judgments served a positive purpose: they showed that evil forces are continually being overcome and that one day God will overthrow all evil, making the world the perfect place he intended. They also serve as warnings that only God is sovereign. Even the

mightiest rulers, like Pharaoh, will fall before God.

32:18 The Hebrews believed in an existence beyond the grave for all people, good and bad. Ezekiel's message assumed that the evil nations had already been sent there and Egypt would soon follow. The Egyptians had a preoccupation with the afterlife (the pyramids were built solely to ensure the Pharaohs' comfort in the next life). This message should remind us that such human attempts are foolish. God alone controls the future and life after death.

sword, for the sword is drawn against the land of Egypt. She will be drawn down to judgment. 21The mighty warriors in the nether world will welcome her as she arrives with all her friends, to lie there beside the nations she despised, all victims of the sword.

22"The princes of Assyria lie there surrounded by the graves of all her people, those the sword has slain. 23Their graves are in the depths of hell, surrounded by their allies. All these mighty men who once struck terror into the hearts of everyone are now dead at the hands of their foes.

24"Great kings of Elam lie there with their people. They scourged the nations while they lived, and now they lie undone in hell; their fate is the same as that of ordinary men. 25They have a resting place among the slain, surrounded by the graves of all their people. Yes, they terrorized the nations while they lived, but now they lie in shame in the pit, slain by the sword.

26"The princes of Meshech and Tubal are there, surrounded by the graves of all their armies—all of them idolaters—who once struck terror to the hearts of all; now they lie dead. 27They are buried in a common grave, and not as the fallen lords who are buried in great honor with their weapons beside them, with their shields covering them and their swords beneath their heads. They were a terror to all while they lived. 28Now you will lie crushed and broken among the idolaters, among those who are slain by the sword.

29"Edom is there with her kings and her princes; mighty as they were, they too lie among the others whom the sword has slain, with the idolaters who have gone down to the pit. 30All the princes of the north are there, and the Sidonians, all slain. Once a terror, now they lie in shame; they lie in ignominy with all the other slain who go down to the pit.

31"When Pharaoh arrives, he will be comforted to find that he is not alone in having all his army slain, says the Lord God. 32For I have caused my terror to fall upon all the living. And Pharaoh and his army shall lie among the idolaters who are slain by the sword."

C. MESSAGES OF HOPE (33:1—48:35)

This begins a new direction in Ezekiel's prophecies. Ezekiel is reminded that he is the nation's watchman. Before Jerusalem's fall, he told the people of their punishment and dispersion. Now he is to proclaim the hope of restoration, but even this message does not improve the people's response. They listen to him with curiosity and then live as they please. Today we have the Good News of forgiveness, but how easy it is to ignore the message and continue to live sinful lives.

1. Restoring the people of God

God reminds Ezekiel that he is a watchman

33 Once again a message came to me from the Lord. He said: 2"Son of dust, tell your people: When I bring an army against a country,

32:27 *and their swords beneath their heads,* literally, "their iniquity (iniquities) upon their bones."

Cross-references (side margin)

32:21
Isa 14:9-12
Lk 16:23,24

32:22
Ps 83:8-10
Isa 37:36-38
Nah 1:7-12

32:24
Gen 10:22
Job 28:13
Ps 52:5
Jer 49:32-39

32:25
Ps 139:8

32:26
Gen 10:2
Isa 66:19

32:27
Prov 14:32
Isa 14:18,19
Jn 8:24

32:29
Isa 34:5-15
Jer 49:7-22
Ezek 25:13

32:30
Jer 1:15; 25:26
Ezek 28:21-23
38:15

32:31
Lam 2:13
Ezek 31:16

33:2
Jer 12:12

32:24 "Undone in hell" can also be translated "uncircumcised in death." There is no spiritual hope outside of God's covenant. Even if these people were physically circumcised, they were not spiritually circumcised—they did not have pure hearts set apart to worship God alone.

32:26 Meshech and Tubal were located in the eastern region of Asia Minor, now eastern and central Turkey. In chapters 38 and 39 they are described as Gog's allies and are included among the evil nations who will be judged for fighting against God's people.

32:32 After reading Ezekiel's prophecies against all these foreign nations, we may wonder if he was blindly loyal to his own nation. But Ezekiel spoke only when God gave him a message (3:27). Besides, God's prophets pronounced judgment on God's sinful people just as much as on God's enemies. But if Babylon was God's enemy, why isn't it mentioned in Ezekiel's judgments? Perhaps because (1) God wanted to foster a spirit of cooperation between the exiles and Babylon in order to preserve his people; (2) God was still using Babylon to refine his own people; (3) God

wanted to use Daniel, a powerful official in Babylon, to draw the Babylonians to him.

33:1ff This chapter sets forth a new direction for Ezekiel's prophecies. Up to this point, Ezekiel has pronounced judgment upon Judah (chapter 1—24) and the surrounding evil nations (chapters 25—32) for their sins. Now that Jerusalem has fallen, he turns from messages of doom and judgment to messages of comfort, hope, and future restoration for God's people (chapters 33—48). God previously appointed Ezekiel to be a watchman warning the nation of coming judgment (see 3:17-21). Here God appoints him to be a watchman again, but this time to preach a message of hope. There are still warning sections (33:23-29; 34:1-10; 36:1-7), but these are part of the larger picture of hope. God would not forsake his promise to restore his blessings to those who were faithful to him. We must pay attention to both aspects of Ezekiel's message: warning and promise. The hope is given only to the righteous "remnant" in our churches who remain true to God.

and the people of that land choose a watchman, 3and when he sees the army coming, and blows the alarm to warn them, 4then anyone who hears the alarm and refuses to heed it—well, if he dies the fault is his own. 5For he heard the warning and wouldn't listen; the fault is his. If he had heeded the warning, he would have saved his life. 6But if the watchman sees the enemy coming and doesn't sound the alarm and warn the people, he is responsible for their deaths. They will die in their sins, but I will charge the watchman with their deaths.

7"So with you, son of dust. I have appointed you as a watchman for the people of Israel; therefore listen to what I say and warn them for me. 8When I say to the wicked, 'O wicked man, you will die!' and you don't tell him what I say, so that he does not repent—that wicked person will die in his sins, but I will hold you responsible for his death. 9But if you warn him to repent and he doesn't, he will die in his sin, and you will not be responsible.

10"O people of Israel, you are saying: 'Our sins are heavy upon us; we pine away with guilt. How can we live?' 11Tell them: As I live, says the Lord God, I have no pleasure in the death of the wicked; *I desire that the wicked turn from his evil ways and live*. Turn, turn from your wickedness, for why will you die, O Israel? 12For the good works of a righteous man will not save him if he turns to sin; and the sins of an evil man will not destroy him if he repents and turns from his sins.

13"I have said the good man will live. But if he sins, expecting his past goodness to save him, then none of his good deeds will be remembered. I will destroy him for his sins. 14And when I tell the wicked he will die and then he turns from his sins and does what is fair and right— 15if he gives back the borrower's pledge and returns what he has stolen and walks along the paths of right, not doing evil—he shall surely live. He shall not die. 16None of his past sins shall be brought up against him, for he has turned to the good and shall surely live.

17"And yet your people are saying the Lord isn't fair. The trouble is *they* aren't fair. 18For again I say, when the good man turns to evil, he shall die. 19But if the wicked turns from his wickedness and does what's fair and just, he shall live. 20Yet you are saying the Lord isn't fair. But I will judge each of you in accordance with his deeds."

Those in Judah will not possess the land

21In the eleventh year of our exile, late in December, one of those who escaped from Jerusalem arrived to tell me, "The city has fallen!" 22Now the hand of the Lord had been upon me the previous evening, and he had healed me so that I could speak again by the time the man arrived.

23Then this message came to me:

24"Son of dust, the scattered remnants of Judah living among the ruined cities keep saying, 'Abraham was only one man and yet he got possession of the whole country! We are many, so we should certainly be able to get it back!' 25But the Lord God says: You are powerless, for you do evil! You eat meat with the blood; you worship idols, and murder. Do you suppose I'll let you have the land? 26Murderers! Idolators! Adulterers! Should you possess the land?

33:21 *In the eleventh year.* Some manuscripts read, "In the twelfth year."

Cross-references (right margin):

33:3 Neh 4:18-20
33:4 Ezek 18:13
33:5 Ex 9:19-21,25
33:6 Ezek 3:18,20
33:7 Isa 62:6,7; Jer 26:2
33:8 Ezek 18:4,13,18-20; Acts 20:26,27
33:9 Ezek 3:19,21; Acts 13:40-46; Gal 5:19-21
33:10 Ezek 24:23
33:11 1 Tim 2:4; 2 Pet 3:9
33:12 Ezek 3:20; Mt 21:28-31
33:13 Ezek 18:26; 2 Pet 2:20,21
33:14 Ezek 18:27
33:15 Lev 6:4,5
33:16 Isa 1:18; 43:25; Ezek 18:22; Rom 5:16,21; 1 Jn 2:1-3
33:17 Ezek 18:24-29
33:21 Jer 39:1,2; Ezek 24:1,2,26
33:22 Ezek 3:26,27
33:24 Isa 51:1,2; Rom 4:12; 9:7
33:25 Lev 17:10-14; Deut 12:16,23; Jer 7:9,10
33:26 Mic 2:1,2

33:10-12 The exiles were discouraged by their past sins. They felt heavy guilt for living in rebellion against God for so many years. This is an important turning point—elsewhere in Ezekiel the people had refused to face their sins. Therefore, God assured them of forgiveness if they repented. God *wants* everyone to turn to him. He looks at what we are and will become, not what we have been. God gives every person the opportunity to turn to him, so take it. Sincerely try to follow him, and ask him to forgive you when you fail.

33:13 Past good deeds will not save a person who decides to turn to a life of sin. Some people think they have done enough good deeds to overshadow the wrong things they don't want to give up. But it's useless to try to be good in some areas and bad in others. God wants wholehearted love and obedience.

33:14-16 While good deeds will not save us, our salvation must lead to righteous action (see Ephesians 2:10; James 2:14-17). This includes restitution for past sins (as exemplified in the story of Zacchaeus, see Luke 19:1-10). We are expected by God to make restitution for the wrongs we have committed.

33:21, 22 Near the beginning of his ministry, Ezekiel was unable to speak except to give specific messages from God (3:26, 27). Now that his prophecies have come true and the false prophets have been exposed, Ezekiel is again able to talk freely. No longer needing to prove himself, he is free to offer God's message of restoration and hope.

33:27
Isa 2:19
Jer 15:2-4
Ezek 5:12-14

33:28
Jer 44:22
Ezek 6:14; 36:34
Mic 7:13

33:29
Ezek 23:33,35

33:30
Ezek 14:3; 29:13

33:31
Ps 78:36,37
Isa 29:13
Mt 13:22
Lk 12:15
Jas 2:14-16
1 Jn 3:18

33:32
Mk 6:20

33:33
Ezek 2:5; 33:29

27"Tell them: The Lord God says: As I live, surely those living in the ruins shall die by the sword. Those living in the open fields shall be eaten by wild animals, and those in the forts and caves shall die of disease. 28I will desolate the land and her pride, and her power shall come to an end. And the mountain villages of Israel shall be so ruined that no one will even travel through them. 29When I have ruined the land because of their sins, then they shall know I am the Lord.

30"Son of dust, your people are whispering behind your back. They talk about you in their houses and whisper about you at the doors, saying, 'Come on, let's have some fun! Let's go hear him tell us what the Lord is saying!' 31So they come as though they are sincere and sit before you listening. But they have no intention of doing what I tell them to; they talk very sweetly about loving the Lord, but with their hearts they are loving their money. 32You are very entertaining to them, like someone who sings lovely songs with a beautiful voice or plays well on an instrument. They hear what you say but don't pay any attention to it! 33But when all these terrible things happen to them—as they will—then they will know a prophet has been among them."

Israel is God's flock

34:2
Jer 10:21; 23:1
Mic 3:1-3
Jn 10:11
21:15-17

34:3
Isa 56:11
Zech 11:5,16

34:4
Mt 9:36
18:12,13
1 Pet 5:3

34:5
Jer 10:21; 23:2
Zech 10:2

34:6
1 Pet 2:25

34 Then this message came to me from the Lord:
2"Son of dust, prophesy against the shepherds, the leaders of Israel, and say to them: The Lord God says to you: Woe to the shepherds who feed themselves instead of their flocks. Shouldn't shepherds feed the sheep? 3You eat the best food and wear the finest clothes, but you let your flocks starve. 4You haven't taken care of the weak nor tended the sick nor bound up the broken bones nor gone looking for those who have wandered away and are lost. Instead you have ruled them with force and cruelty. 5So they were scattered, without a shepherd. They have become a prey to every animal that comes along. 6My sheep wandered through the mountains and hills and over the face of the earth, and there was no one to search for them or care about them.

7"Therefore, O shepherds, hear the word of the Lord:

33:30 *Come on, let's have some fun! Let's go hear him tell us what the Lord is saying!* Literally, "Come and let us hear what the word is that comes from the Lord!"

BAD SHEPHERDS VS. GOOD SHEPHERDS	Bad Shepherds	Good Shepherds
	Feed themselves	Feed their flock
	Worry about their own health	Tend for the weak and sick, search for the lost
	Rule with force and cruelty	Rule with love
	Abandon and scatter the sheep	Gather and protect the sheep
	Keep the best for themselves	Give their best to the sheep

33:30–32 The people refused to act upon Ezekiel's message. When people mock your witness for Christ or fail to act upon advice which you give, don't give up. You are not witnessing for their sake's alone, but out of faithfulness to God. You cannot make them accept your message; you can only be faithful in delivering it.

33:31 In your heart, do you really love God? These people gave the appearance of following God, but they loved their money more. Many today also give the outward impression of being religious while remaining inwardly greedy. Jesus warned that we cannot love God and money at the same time (Matthew 6:24). It's easy to say "I surrender all" when we don't have much. It's when we start gaining a lot that it becomes difficult to avoid loving it.

33:32 Many people see church as entertainment. They enjoy the music, the people, and the activities; but they don't take the messages to heart. Have you reduced church services to the level of entertainment, or does your worship truly have an impact on your life?

34:1ff Ezekiel called the exiles the nation of Israel, referring to all Jews in captivity from both the Northern and Southern Kingdoms. Ezekiel criticized Israel's leaders for taking care of themselves

rather than taking care of their people. He outlined their sins (34:1–6) and pronounced judgment upon them (34:7–10). Then he promised that a true Shepherd (the Messiah) would come who would take care of the people as the other leaders were supposed to do (34:11–31). The fate of the present shepherds, the work of the new Shepherd, and the future of the sheep are all seen in this beautiful message.

34:2 Ezekiel prophesied against the religious leaders of Israel who took care of themselves while neglecting and even abusing their people. Jeremiah accused these leaders of this same neglect (Jeremiah 23:1–4). Leaders in the church today must not fall into the trap of spending time and money to promote themselves when they should use resources to provide for the needs of those they serve. To avoid this, leaders must stay close to their flocks.

34:4–6 God would judge the religious leaders because they were caught up in their own concerns and were neglecting their service to others. Spiritual leaders must be careful not to pursue self-development at the expense of broken, scattered people. When we give too much attention to our own needs, we may push God aside and abandon those who depend upon us.

8"As I live, says the Lord God, you abandoned my flock, leaving them to be
attacked and destroyed, and you were no real shepherds at all, for you didn't search
for them. You fed yourselves and let them starve; 9, 10therefore I am against the
shepherds, and I will hold them responsible for what has happened to my flock. I
will take away their right to feed the flock—and take away their right to eat. I will
save my flock from being taken for their food.

11"For the Lord God says: I will search and find my sheep. 12I will be like a
shepherd looking for his flock. I will find my sheep and rescue them from all the
places they were scattered in that dark and cloudy day. 13And I will bring them back
from among the people and nations where they were, back home to their own land
of Israel, and I will feed them upon the mountains of Israel and by the rivers where
the land is fertile and good. 14Yes, I will give them good pasture on the high hills
of Israel. There they will lie down in peace and feed in luscious mountain pastures.
15, 16I myself will be the Shepherd of my sheep, and cause them to lie down in
peace, the Lord God says. I will seek my lost ones, those who strayed away, and
bring them safely home again. I will put splints and bandages upon their broken
limbs and heal the sick. And I will destroy the powerful, fat shepherds; I will feed
them, yes—feed them punishment!

17"And as for you, O my flock—my people—the Lord God says, I will judge
you and separate good from bad, sheep from goats.

18"Is it a small thing to you, O evil shepherds, that you not only keep the best of
the pastures for yourselves, but trample down the rest? That you take the best water
for yourselves, and muddy the rest with your feet? 19All that's left for my flock is
what you've trampled down; all they have to drink is water that you've fouled.

20"Therefore the Lord God says: I will surely judge between these fat shepherds
and their scrawny sheep. 21For these shepherds push and butt and crowd my sick
and hungry flock until they're scattered far away. 22So I myself will save my flock;
no more will they be picked on and destroyed. And I will notice which is plump and
which is thin, and why!

23"And I will set one Shepherd over all my people, even my Servant, David. He
shall feed them and be a Shepherd to them.

24"And I, the Lord, will be their God, and my Servant David shall be a Prince
among my people. I, the Lord, have spoken it.

25"I will make a peace pact with them, and drive away the dangerous animals
from the land so that my people can safely camp in the wildest places and sleep
safely in the woods. 26I will make my people and their homes around my hill a
blessing. And there shall be showers, showers of blessing, for I will not shut off the
rains but send them in their seasons. 27Their fruit trees and fields will yield bumper
crops, and everyone will live in safety. When I have broken off their chains of
slavery and delivered them from those who profiteered at their expense, they shall
know I am the Lord. 28No more will other nations conquer them nor wild animals
attack. They shall live in safety and no one shall make them afraid.

29"And I will raise up a notable Vine [the Messiah], in Israel so that my people
will never again go hungry nor be shamed by heathen conquest. 30In this way they
will know that I, the Lord their God, am with them, and that they, the people of

34:8
1 Sam 2:29,30
Ps 72:12-14
Zech 10:3
Acts 20:29

34:11
Ezek 11:17
Mt 13:11,12
Jn 10:16

34:12
Jer 23:3; 31:10
Ezek 30:3
Lk 19:10

34:13
Isa 30:25
Ps 23:1-3
Ezek 36:29,30

34:14
Isa 49:26
Mt 18:11
Lk 5:32
Jn 10:9

34:16
Isa 10:16; 49:26

34:17
Ezek 20:38
Zech 10:3
Mal 4:1
Mt 25:32

34:18
Num 16:9,13
Mt 23:13,14
Lk 11:52

34:21
Lk 13:14-16

34:22
Ps 72:12-14
Jer 23:2,3
Zech 11:7-9

34:23
Isa 40:11
Jer 23:4-6; 30:9
Jn 10:11
Heb 13:20

34:24
Jer 30:9
Ezek 37:24,25

34:25
Isa 11:6-9
Ezek 37:26

34:26
Gen 12:2
Deut 28:12
Isa 32:15; 44:3
Zech 8:13
Mal 3:10

34:27
Isa 52:2,3
Jn 15:5-8

34:29
Isa 53:2; 60:21
Ezek 36:6,15,29
Zech 3:8; 6:12

34:30
Ezek 36:28

34:29 *And I will raise up a notable Vine (the Messiah)*, literally, "a plant of renown"; so perhaps the meaning is, "I will give them bumper crops." Either translation is permissible, but the word for "plant" is in the singular.

34:9, 10 Those shepherds who failed their flock were to be removed from office. Christian leaders must heed this warning and care for their flock or total failure will be the result (see 1 Corinthians 9:24-27). It is not enough merely to keep a congregation satisfied. We must strengthen, exhort, and edify God's people, or God may remove us from our ministries.

34:11-16 God will sovereignly take over as pastor of the scattered flock. When our leaders fail us, we must not despair, but turn to God for help. He is still in control and can turn even this tragic situation to produce good for the kingdom (Romans 8:28).

34:18-20 A bad shepherd is not only selfish but destructive. A minister who muddies the waters for others by raising unnecessary doubts, teaching false ideas, and acting sinfully is destroying his flock's spiritual nourishment.

34:23-25 In contrast to the present incompetent and ineffective shepherds (leaders) of God's people (34:1-6), God will send a perfect Shepherd, the Messiah, who will take care of every need his people have and set up a kingdom of perfect peace and justice (see Psalm 23; Jeremiah 23:5, 6; John 10:11; Hebrews 13:20, 21; Revelation 21).

34:31
Ps 100:2
Jn 10:11

Israel, are my people, says the Lord God. 31You are my flock, the sheep of my pasture. You are my men and I am your God, so says the Lord."

Edom will be wiped out

35:2
Gen 36:6-8
Ezek 25:12

35 Again a message came from the Lord. He said:
  2"Son of dust, face toward Mount Seir and prophesy against the people saying:

35:3
Jer 49:13,17,18
Ezek 25:13

  3"The Lord God says: I am against you and I will smash you with my fist and utterly destroy you. 4, 5Because you hate my people Israel, I will demolish your

35:4
Ps 137:7
Ezek 6:6
Amos 1:11
Mal 1:2-4

cities and make you desolate, and then you shall know I am the Lord. You butchered my people when they were helpless, when I had punished them for all their sins. 6As I live, the Lord God says, since you enjoy blood so much, I will give

35:8
Isa 34:5,6
Ezek 31:12
32:4,5

you a blood bath—your turn has come! 7I will utterly wipe out the people of Mount Seir, killing off all those who try to escape and all those who return. 8I will fill your

35:9
Jer 49:13
Ezek 25:13

mountains with the dead—your hills, your valleys and your rivers will be filled with those the sword has killed. 9Never again will you revive. You will be abandoned forever; your cities will never be rebuilt. Then you shall know I am the

35:10
Ps 48:1-3
Ezek 36:2,5

Lord.
  10"For you said, 'Both Israel and Judah shall be mine. We will take possession

35:11
Ps 9:16; 137:7
Ezek 25:14

of them. What do we care that God is there!' 11Therefore as I live, the Lord God says, I will pay back your angry deeds with mine—I will punish you for all your

35:12
Ezek 36:2

acts of envy and of hate. And I will honor my name in Israel by what I do to you. 12And you shall know that I have heard each evil word you spoke against the Lord,

35:13
Isa 10:13,14
Ezek 36:3

saying, 'His people are helpless; they are food for us to eat!' 13Saying that, you boasted great words against the Lord. And I have heard them all!

35:14
Isa 44:23,49:13

  14"The whole world will rejoice when I make you desolate. 15You rejoiced at Israel's fearful fate. Now I will rejoice at yours! You will be wiped out, O people

35:15
Isa 34:5,6

of Mount Seir and all who live in Edom! And then you will know I am the Lord!

God promises that good times will return

36:1
Ezek 6:2,3
37:22

36 "Son of dust, prophesy to Israel's mountains. Tell them: Listen to this message from the Lord.

36:2
Deut 32:13
Ps 78:69
Isa 58:14
Ezek 35:10

  2"Your enemies have sneered at you and claimed your ancient heights as theirs, 3and destroyed you on every side and sent you away as slaves to many lands. You are mocked and slandered. 4Therefore, O mountains of Israel, hear the word of the

36:3
Jer 2:15; 51:34
Ezek 35:13

Lord God. He says to the hills and mountains, dales and valleys, and to the ruined farms and the long-deserted cities, destroyed and mocked by heathen nations all

36:4
Ezek 34:28

around: 5My anger is afire against these nations, especially Edom, for grabbing my land with relish, in utter contempt for me, to take it for themselves.

36:5
Isa 66:15,16
Ezek 35:15

  6"Therefore prophesy and say to the hills and mountains, dales and valleys of Israel: The Lord God says, I am full of fury because you suffered shame before the surrounding nations. 7Therefore I have sworn with hand held high, that those

36:8
Ezek 17:22,23
34:26-29

nations are going to have their turn of being covered with shame, 8but for Israel, good times will return. There will be heavy crops of fruit to prepare for my people's return—and they will be coming home again soon! 9See, I am for you, and I will

---

35:1ff Ezekiel gave another prophecy against Edom (also called Seir); his first prophecy against Edom is found in 25:12–14. In this prophecy, Ezekiel is probably using Edom to represent *all* the nations opposed to God's people. Chapter 36 says that Israel will be restored, while this chapter says that Edom (God's enemies) will be removed.

35:2 Edom offered to help destroy Jerusalem and rejoiced when the city fell. Edom's long-standing hostility against God's people resulted in God's judgment.

35:8 Ezekiel prophesied not only against the people of Edom, but also against their mountains and land. Mountains, symbols of strength and power, represent the pride of these people who thought they could get away with evil. Does such worldly pride

typify the nation in which you live? If so, it is in danger of divine wrath similar to that experienced by Edom.

36:1ff In this chapter, Ezekiel said that Israel would be restored as a nation and would return to its own land. To the exiles in Babylon, this seemed impossible. This message again emphasizes God's sovereignty and trustworthiness. He would first judge the nations used to punish Israel (36:1–7) and then restore his people (36:8–15).

36:8 The "heavy crops of fruit" are in contrast with the desolation earlier prophesied for Israel. Only through *God's* restoration would this be possible. God's restoration was intended to show that he is the Lord (36:11).

come and help you as you prepare the ground and sow your crops. ¹⁰I will greatly increase your population throughout all Israel, and the ruined cities will be rebuilt and filled with people. ¹¹Not only the people, but your flocks and herds will also greatly multiply. O mountains of Israel, again you will be filled with homes. I will do even more for you than I did before. Then you shall know I am the Lord. ¹²My people will walk upon you once again, and you will belong to them again; and you will no longer be a place for burning their children on idol altars.

¹³"The Lord God says: Now the other nations taunt you, saying, 'Israel is a land that devours her people!' ¹⁴But they will not say this any more. Your birth rate will rise and your infant mortality rate will drop off sharply, says the Lord. ¹⁵No longer will those heathen nations sneer, for you will no longer be a nation of sinners, the Lord God says."

¹⁶Then this further word came to me from the Lord:

¹⁷"Son of dust, when the people of Israel were living in their own country, they defiled it by their evil deeds; to me their worship was as foul as filthy rags. ¹⁸They polluted the land with murder and with the worshiping of idols, so I poured out my fury upon them. ¹⁹And I exiled them to many lands; that is how I punished them for the evil way they lived. ²⁰But when they were scattered out among the nations, then they were a blight upon my holy name because the nations said, 'These are the people of God and he couldn't protect them from harm!' ²¹I am concerned about my reputation that was ruined by my people throughout the world.

²²"Therefore say to the people of Israel: The Lord God says, I am bringing you back again, but not because you deserve it; I am doing it to protect my holy name which you tarnished among the nations. ²³I will honor my great name that you defiled, and the people of the world shall know I am the Lord. I will be honored before their eyes by delivering you from exile among them. ²⁴For I will bring you back home again to the land of Israel.

²⁵"Then it will be as though I had sprinkled clean water on you, for you will be clean—your filthiness will be washed away, your idol worship gone. ²⁶And I will give you a new heart—I will give you new and right desires—and put a new spirit within you. I will take out your stony hearts of sin and give you new hearts of love. ²⁷And I will put my Spirit within you so that you will obey my laws and do whatever I command.

²⁸"And you shall live in Israel, the land which I gave your fathers long ago. And you shall be my people and I will be your God. ²⁹I will cleanse away your sins. I will abolish crop failures and famine. ³⁰I will give you huge harvests from your fruit trees and fields, and never again will the surrounding nations be able to scoff at your land for its famines. ³¹Then you will remember your past sins and loathe yourselves for all the evils you did. ³²But always remember this: It is not for your own sakes that I will do this, but for mine. O my people Israel, be utterly ashamed of all that you have done!

³³"The Lord God says: When I cleanse you from your sins, I will bring you home again to Israel, and rebuild the ruins. ³⁴Acreage will be cultivated again that

36:10 Isa 27:6 49:17-22 Jer 31:27,28 Ezek 37:21,22
36:11 Jer 30:18 Ezek 16:55
36:12 Jer 32:44 Ezek 34:13,14 47:14
36:15 Isa 54:4 Jer 18:15 Ezek 22:4; 34:29
36:17 Jer 2:7
36:18 2 Chron 34:21 Lam 2:4; 4:11 Ezek 22:18-20
36:19 Ezek 22:15 Rom 2:6 Rev 20:12-15
36:20 Isa 52:5 Ezek 12:16 Rom 2:24
36:21 Ezek 20:44
36:22 Deut 9:5-7
36:24 Deut 30:3-5 Isa 43:5,6 Ezek 34:13
36:25 Jn 3:5 Tit 3:5,6 Heb 10:22
36:26 Ps 51:10 Ezek 11:19 2 Cor 5:17
36:27 Ezek 11:20
36:28 Ezek 14:11 37:23,27 2 Cor 6:16-18
36:29 Ezek 34:27,29
36:30 Deut 29:23-28
36:31 Ezek 6:9 16:61-63; 20:43
36:32 Dan 9:18,19

36:17 *as filthy rags*, literally, "as a menstruous cloth." **36:23** *by delivering you from exile among them*, implied. **36:26** *hearts of love*, literally, "hearts of flesh," in contrast to "hearts of stone."

36:21 Why did God want to protect his reputation? God was concerned about the salvation not only of his people, but also of the whole world. To allow his people to remain in sin and be permanently destroyed by their enemies would lead other nations to conclude that their heathen gods were victorious (Isaiah 48:11). God will not share his glory with false gods—he alone is the one true God. The people had the responsibility to represent God properly to the rest of the world. Believers today have that same responsibility. Do you represent God properly?

36:25-27 God promised to restore Israel not only physically, but spiritually, giving them a new heart for following him. To accomplish this, God would put his Spirit within them (see 11:19, 20; Psalm 51:7-11). Again the new covenant is promised (16:61-63; 34:23-25), ultimately to be fulfilled in Christ. No matter

how impure your life is right now, God offers you a fresh start. You can have your sins washed away, receive a new heart for God, and have his Spirit within you—if you accept God's promise. Why try to patch up your old life when you can have a new one?

36:32 God said his people should be ashamed of their sins. The people had become so callous that they had lost all sensitivity to sin. First they had to "remember" (36:31) their sins, then despise them, and finally repent of them (see James 4:8, 9). As we examine our lives, we may find that we too have lost our sensitivity to certain sins. But if we measure ourselves against God's standards of right living, we will be ashamed of them. The first step toward a relationship with God is to recognize sin for what it is, feel sorry for displeasing God, and ask his forgiveness. This will remove the barrier between us and him.

through the years of exile lay empty as a barren wilderness; all who passed by were shocked to see the extent of ruin in your land. 35But when I bring you back they will say, 'This God-forsaken land has become like Eden's garden! The ruined cities are rebuilt and walled and filled with people!' 36Then the nations all around—all those still left—will know that I, the Lord, rebuilt the ruins and planted lush crops in the wilderness. For I, the Lord, have promised it, and I will do it.

37, 38"The Lord God says: I am ready to hear Israel's prayers for these blessings, and to grant them their requests. Let them but ask and I will multiply them like the flocks that fill Jerusalem's streets at time of sacrifice. The ruined cities will be crowded once more, and everyone will know I am the Lord."

The valley of dried bones

37 The power of the Lord was upon me and I was carried away by the Spirit of the Lord to a valley full of old, dry bones that were scattered everywhere across the ground. He led me around among them, 3and then he said to me:

"Son of dust, can these bones become people again?"

I replied, "Lord, you alone know the answer to that."

4Then he told me to speak to the bones and say: "O dry bones, listen to the words of God, 5for the Lord God says, See! I am going to make you live and breathe again! 6I will replace the flesh and muscles on you and cover you with skin. I will put breath into you, and you shall live and know I am the Lord."

7So I spoke these words from God, just as he told me to; and suddenly there was a rattling noise from all across the valley, and the bones of each body came together and attached to each other as they used to be. 8Then, as I watched, the muscles and flesh formed over the bones, and skin covered them, but the bodies had no breath. 9Then he told me to call to the wind and say: "The Lord God says: Come from the four winds, O Spirit, and breathe upon these slain bodies, that they may live again." 10So I spoke to the winds as he commanded me and the bodies began breathing; they lived, and stood up—a very great army.

11Then he told me what the vision meant: "These bones," he said, "represent all the people of Israel. They say: 'We have become a heap of dried-out bones—all hope is gone.' 12But tell them, the Lord God says: My people, I will open your graves of exile and cause you to rise again and return to the land of Israel. 13And, then at last, O my people, you will know I am the Lord. 14I will put my Spirit into you, and you shall live and return home again to your own land. Then you will know that I, the Lord, have done just what I promised you."

Cross references (margin):

36:35
Isa 51:3
Joel 2:3

36:36
Hos 14:4-7
Mic 7:15-17
Mt 24:35

36:37
1 Kgs 8:62,63
2 Chron 35:7-9
Zech 11:17
Jn 10:9,16

37:1
Jer 7:32—8:2
Ezek 33:22; 40:1

37:3
Jn 6:5,6
Rom 4:17

37:4
Num 20:8
Isa 42:18
Jer 22:29

37:5
Ps 104:29,30
Jn 20:22

37:6
Joel 2:27

37:9
Ps 104:30
Hos 13:14

37:10
Rev 11:11

37:11
Num 17:12,13
Ps 141:7
Isa 49:14

37:12
Deut 32:39
Isa 26:19
Ezek 36:24
Amos 9:14,15

37:14
Ezek 11:19
36:27
Joel 2:28,29

OLD AND NEW COVENANTS

Old Covenant	New Covenant
Placed upon stone	Placed upon people's hearts
Based on the law	Based on desire to love and serve God
Must be taught	Known by all
Legal relationship with God	Personal relationship with God

36:37, 38 God said that if the people asked, he would come to their aid. We cannot expect his mercy, however, until we have sought new hearts from him (36:26). We can be thankful that his invitation is open to all.

37:1ff This vision illustrates the promise of chapter 36—new life and a nation restored, both physically and spiritually. The dry bones are a picture of the Jews in captivity—scattered and dead. The two sticks (37:15-17) represent the reunion of the entire nation of Israel which had divided into Northern and Southern Kingdoms after Solomon. The scattered exiles of both Israel and Judah would be released from the "graves" of captivity and one day regathered in their homeland, with the Messiah as their leader. This vision has yet to be fulfilled. Ezekiel probably felt he was speaking to the

dead as he preached to the exiles because they rarely responded to his message. But these bones responded! And just as God brought life to the dead bones, he would bring life again to his spiritually dead people.

37:5 The dry bones represented the people's spiritually dead condition. Your church may seem like a heap of dried-up bones to you, spiritually dead with no hope of vitality. But just as God promised to restore his nation, he can restore any church, no matter how dry or dead it may be. Rather than give up, pray for renewal, for God can restore it to life. The hope and prayer of every church should be that God will put his Spirit into it (37:14). In fact, God is at work calling his people back to himself, bringing new life into dead churches.

The kingdom will be reunited

15Again a message from the Lord came to me, saying:

16"Take a stick and carve on it these words: 'This stick represents Judah and her allied tribes.' Then take another stick and carve these words on it: 'This stick represents all the other tribes of Israel.' 17Now hold them together in your hand as one stick. 18, 19, 20Tell these people (holding the sticks so they can see what you are doing), the Lord God says: I will take the tribes of Israel and join them to Judah and make them one stick in my hand.

21"For the Lord God says: I am gathering the people of Israel from among the nations, and bringing them home from around the world to their own land, 22to unify them into one nation. One king shall be king of them all; no longer shall they be divided into two nations. 23They shall stop polluting themselves with idols and their other sins, for I will save them from all this foulness. Then they shall truly be my people and I their God.

24"And David, my Servant—the Messiah—shall be their King, their only Shepherd; and they shall obey my laws and all my wishes. 25They shall live in the land of Israel where their fathers lived, the land I gave my servant Jacob. They and their children after them shall live there, and their grandchildren, for all generations. And my Servant David, their Messiah, shall be their Prince forever. 26And I will make a covenant of peace with them, an everlasting pact. I will bless them and multiply them and put my Temple among them forever. 27And I will make my home among them. Yes, I will be their God and they shall be my people. 28And when my Temple remains among them forever, then the nations will know that I, the Lord, have chosen Israel as my very own."

A prophecy against Gog

38 Here is another message to me from the Lord:

2, 3"Son of dust, face northward toward the land of Magog, and prophesy against Gog king of Meshech and Tubal. Tell him that the Lord God says: I am against you, Gog. 4I will put hooks into your jaws and pull you to your doom. I will mobilize your troops and armored cavalry, and make you a mighty host, all fully armed. 5Peras, Cush and Put shall join you too with all their weaponry, 6and so shall Gomer and all his hordes and the armies of Togarmah from the distant north, as well as many others. 7Be prepared! Stay mobilized. You are their leader, Gog!

8"A long time from now you will be called to action. In distant years you will swoop down onto the land of Israel, that will be lying in peace after the return of its people from many lands. 9You and all your allies—a vast and awesome army—will roll down upon them like a storm and cover the land like a cloud. 10For at that time an evil thought will have come to your mind. 11You will have said, 'Israel is an unprotected land of unwalled villages! I will march against her and destroy these people living in such confidence! 12I will go to those once-desolate cities that are now filled with people again—those who have returned from all the nations—and I will capture vast amounts of loot and many slaves. For the people are rich with cattle now, and the whole earth revolves around them!'

37:16
1 Kgs 12:16-20
37:17
Isa 11:13; 50:4
37:18
Ezek 20:49
24:19
37:21
Ezek 39:27
37:22
Ezek 34:23,24
37:23
Ezek 11:18
36:25
Zech 13:1,2
14:21
37:24
Isa 40:11
Ezek 34:23,24
37:25
Isa 11:1
37:26
Isa 55:3
Ezek 43:7
Heb 13:20,21
37:27
Lev 26:11,12
Jn 1:14
2 Cor 6:16
37:28
Ezek 20:12
36:23

38:2
Ezek 39:1,9
Rev 20:8,9
38:4
Isa 43:17
Ezek 39:2
Dan 11:40
38:5
Gen 10:6,7
Ezek 27:10
38:6
Gen 10:2,3
Ezek 27:14
38:8
Ezek 34:13
Amos 9:14,15
38:9
Isa 5:28
Jer 4:13
Dan 11:40
Joel 2:2
38:12
Ezek 29:19

37:24, 25 The Messiah is often called David because he is David's descendant. David was a good king, but the Messiah would be the perfect king (Revelation 17:14; 19:16; 21:1ff).

37:26, 27 God's promise here goes beyond the physical and geographical restoration of Israel. He promises to breathe new spiritual life into his people so that their hearts and attitudes will be right with him. This same process is described throughout God's Word as the cleansing of our hearts by God's Spirit (Titus 3:4–6; 1 John 2:27).

37:26–28 The Temple symbolized God's rule on earth and his rule in the heart of every person who seeks to obey him. Ezekiel describes the Temple in detail in chapters 40–48.

38:1ff In chapter 37, Ezekiel revealed how Israel (God's people) would be restored to their land from many parts of the world. Once Israel became strong, a confederacy of nations from the north would attack, led by Gog (mentioned also in Revelation 20:8). Their purpose would be to destroy God's kingdom. Gog's allies came from the mountainous area southeast of the Black Sea and southwest of the Caspian Sea (currently in central Turkey), as well as from the area that is present-day Iran, Ethiopia, Libya, and possibly the Soviet Union. Gog could be a person, but from the context Gog could also be a symbol of all evil in the world. Whether symbolic or literal, he represents the aggregate military might of all the forces opposed to God. Many say that the battle Ezekiel described will occur at the end of human history, but there are nevertheless many differences between the events described here and those in Revelation 20.

13"But Sheba and Dedan and the merchant princes of Tarshish with whom she trades will ask, 'Who are you to rob them of silver and gold and drive away their cattle and seize their goods and make them poor?'

14"The Lord God says to Gog: When my people are living in peace in their land, then you will rouse yourself. 15, 16You will come from all over the north with your vast host of cavalry and cover the land like a cloud. This will happen in the distant future—in the latter years of history. I will bring you against my land, and my holiness will be vindicated in your terrible destruction before their eyes, so that all the nations will know that I am God.

17"The Lord God says: You are the one I spoke of long ago through the prophets of Israel, saying that after many years had passed, I would bring you against my people. 18But when you come to destroy the land of Israel, my fury will rise! 19For in my jealousy and blazing wrath, I promise a mighty shaking in the land of Israel on that day. 20All living things shall quake in terror at my presence; mountains shall be thrown down; cliffs shall tumble; walls shall crumble to the earth. 21I will summon every kind of terror against you, says the Lord God, and you will fight against yourselves in mortal combat! 22I will fight you with sword, disease, torrential floods, great hailstones, fire and brimstone! 23Thus will I show my greatness and bring honor upon my name, and all the nations of the world will hear what I have done, and know that I am God!

God's holiness will be vindicated

39 "Son of dust, prophesy this also against Gog. Tell him:
I stand against you, Gog, leader of Meshech and Tubal. 2I will turn you and drive you toward the mountains of Israel, bringing you from the distant north. And I will destroy 85 percent of your army in the mountains. 3I will knock your weapons from your hands and leave you helpless. 4You and all your vast armies will die upon the mountains. I will give you to the vultures and wild animals to devour you. 5You will never reach the cities—you will fall upon the open fields; for I have spoken, the Lord God says. 6And I will rain down fire on Magog and on all your allies who live safely on the coasts, and they shall know I am the Lord.

7"Thus I will make known my holy name among my people Israel; I will not let it be mocked at anymore. And the nations too shall know I am the Lord, the Holy One of Israel. 8That day of judgment will come; everything will happen just as I have declared it.

9"The people of the cities of Israel will go out and pick up your shields and bucklers, bows and arrows, javelins and spears, to use for fuel—enough to last them seven years. 10For seven years they will need nothing else for their fires. They won't cut wood from the fields or forests, for these weapons will give them all they need. They will use the possessions of those who abused them.

11"And I will make a vast graveyard for Gog and his armies in the Valley of the Travelers, east of the Dead Sea. It will block the path of the travelers. There Gog and all his armies will be buried. And they will change the name of the place to 'The Valley of Gog's Army.' 12It will take seven months for the people of Israel to bury the bodies. 13Everyone in Israel will help, for it will be a glorious victory for Israel on that day when I demonstrate my glory, says the Lord. 14At the end of the

38:15, 16 *in the latter years of history,* implied. Literally, "in the latter days," an expression which does not, in Hebrew usage, necessarily mean "the end times." **39:2** *I will destroy 85 percent,* literally, "leave one-sixth of you."

38:13 Sheba and Dedan, great trading centers in Arabia, would say to God's people, "Who are you to usurp our position as the world's trade leaders?" Tarshish was the leading trade center in the west; many believe it was in Spain.

39:1ff The story of the battle continues. The defeat of the evil forces will be final and complete; they will be completely destroyed by divine intervention. Because of this victory, God's name will be known throughout the world. The nations will understand that he alone is in charge of human history. God's love for his people will be clearly shown as he restores them to their homeland.

39:12-16 Two themes are intertwined: God's total victory over his enemies, and the need to purify the land to make it holy. After the final battle, teams will be used to give proper burial to the bodies of the dead enemies in order for the land to be cleansed. Yet there will be so many that the carrion birds will be called to the "feast" in order to help dispose of the corpses (39:17-20). The message for us is an exciting one: with God on our side, we are assured of ultimate victory over any foe, for God will fight on our behalf (see also Zephaniah 3:14-17; Romans 8:37).

seven months, they will appoint men to search the land systematically for any skeletons left and bury them, so that the land will be cleansed. 15, 16Whenever anyone sees some bones, he will put up a marker beside them so that the buriers will see them and take them to the Valley of Gog's Army to bury them. A city named 'Multitude' is there! And so the land will finally be cleansed.

17"And now, son of dust, call all the birds and animals and say to them: Gather together for a mighty sacrificial feast. Come from far and near to the mountains of Israel. Come, eat the flesh and drink the blood! 18Eat the flesh of mighty men and drink the blood of princes—they are the rams, the lambs, the goats and the fat young bulls of Bashan for my feast! 19Gorge yourselves with flesh until you are glutted, drink blood until you are drunk; this is the sacrificial feast I have prepared for you. 20Feast at my banquet table—feast on horses, riders and valiant warriors, says the Lord God. 21Thus I will demonstrate my glory among the nations; all shall see the punishment of Gog and know that I have done it.

22"And from that time onward, the people of Israel will know I am the Lord their God. 23And the nations will know why Israel was sent away to exile—it was punishment for sin, for they acted in treachery against their God. Therefore I turned my face away from them and let their enemies destroy them. 24I turned my face away and punished them in proportion to the vileness of their sins.

25"But now, the Lord God says, I will end the captivity of my people and have mercy upon them and restore their fortunes, for I am concerned about my reputation! 26Their time of treachery and shame will all be in the past; they will be home again, in peace and safety in their own land, with no one bothering them or making them afraid. 27I will bring them home from the lands of their enemies—and my glory shall be evident to all the nations when I do it. Through them I will vindicate my holiness before the nations. 28Then my people will know I am the Lord their God—responsible for sending them away to exile, and responsible for bringing them home. I will leave none of them remaining among the nations. 29And I will never hide my face from them again, for I will pour out my Spirit upon them, says the Lord God."

2. Restoring the worship of God

The new Temple

40 Early in April of the twenty-fifth year of our exile—the fourteenth year after Jerusalem was captured—the hand of the Lord was upon me, 2and in a vision he took me to the land of Israel and set me down on a high mountain where I saw

39:17
Isa 34:6,7
Jer 46:10
Zeph 1:7
Rev 19:17,18

39:18
Deut 32:14
Ps 22:12

39:20
Ps 75:5,6
Ezek 38:4
Hag 2:22

39:21
Ex 9:16; 14:4
Ezek 38:16,23

39:23
Isa 59:2
Jer 22:8,9
Ezek 36:18,19

39:24
2 Kgs 17:7
Jer 2:17,19
4:18
Ezek 36:19

39:25
Jer 33:7
Ezek 34:13
36:10

39:26
Ezek 34:25-28
Dan 9:16

39:27
Ezek 28:25,26
37:21

39:28
Deut 30:3,4
Neh 1:8-10
Rom 9:6-8
11:1-7

39:29
Ezek 37:14
Joel 2:28
Acts 2:17

40:1
2 Kgs 25:1-7
Jer 39:1-9

39:29 Both in this prophecy and in Joel 2:28, 29, God promises to pour out his Spirit on mankind. The early church believed this began to be fulfilled at Pentecost, when God's Holy Spirit came to dwell in all believers (Acts 2:17).

40:1ff This vision of the Temple has been interpreted in three main ways: (1) Zerubbabel's Temple, built after the return from exile; (2) a literal Temple yet to come; (3) a symbolic Temple representing the restoration of Israel. Whether the Temple is literal or symbolic, it seems clear that this is a vision of God's final perfect kingdom. This gave hope to the people of Ezekiel's time who had just seen their nation and its Temple destroyed with no hope of rebuilding it in the near future. The details of this vision gave the people more hope that what Ezekiel saw had come from God and would surely come to pass in the future.

40:1ff One argument against the view that Ezekiel's Temple is a literal building of the future is that sacrifices are mentioned. If the sacrifices were to be reinstituted in the last days, then Christ's once-and-for-all sacrifice would be meaningless. The New Testament makes it clear that Christ died once for the sins of all mankind (Romans 6:10; Hebrews 9:12; 10:10). Our sins have been removed, no further sacrifice is needed.

In Ezekiel's day, however, the only kind of worship the people knew was the kind that revolved around the sacrifices and ceremonies described in Exodus through Deuteronomy. Ezekiel had to explain the new order of worship in terms the people would understand. The next nine chapters tell how the Temple is the focal point of everything, which shows that the ideal relationship with God is one where all of life centers on him.

40:1ff Ezekiel explained God's dwelling place in words and images which the people could understand. God wanted them to see the great splendor he had planned for those who lived faithful lives and would live with him forever. The Temple is a symbol of the perfect sacrifice of Jesus Christ; it was never built, but was a vision intended to typify God's perfect plans for his people. Don't let the details obscure the point of this vision—one day all those who have been faithful to God will enjoy eternal life with him. Let the majesty of this vision lift you and teach you about the God you worship and serve.

40:1—43:27 This vision came to Ezekiel in 573 B.C. Chapters 40—43 give the Temple's measurements and then describe how it is filled with God's glory. Because Ezekiel was a priest, he would have been familiar with the furnishings and ceremonies of

40:3
Dan 10:5,6
Zech 2:1,2
Rev 11:1; 21:15

40:4
Jer 26:2
Ezek 43:10; 44:5
40:5
Ezek 42:20

40:6
Ezek 8:16; 11:1
43:1

40:7
1 Kgs 6:5-10
2 Chron 31:11
Jer 35:4

40:14
Ex 27:9
1 Chron 28:6
Ps 100:4
Isa 62:4
Ezek 42:1
40:16
1 Kgs 6:4
Ezek 41:26
1 Cor 13:12

40:17
1 Chron 9:26
2 Chron 31:11
Ezek 46:21
Rev 11:2

40:18
Ezek 46:1,2

40:22
1 Kgs 6:29-35
7:36
2 Chron 3:5
Rev 7:9

40:23
Ex 27:9-18
38:9-12

40:24
Ezek 46:9

what appeared to be a city opposite me. ³Going nearer, I saw a man whose face shone like bronze, standing beside the Temple gate, holding in his hand a measuring tape and a measuring stick.

⁴He said to me: "Son of dust, watch and listen and take to heart everything I show you, for you have been brought here so I can show you many things; and then you are to return to the people of Israel to tell them all you have seen." ⁵The man began to measure the wall around the outside of the Temple area with his measuring stick, which was 10½ feet long. He told me, "This wall is 10½ feet high and 10½ feet wide." ⁶Then he took me over to the passageway that goes through the eastern wall. We climbed the seven steps into the entrance and he measured the entry hall of the passage; it was 10½ feet wide.

⁷⁻¹²Walking on through the passageway I saw that there were three guardrooms on each side; each of these rooms was 10½ feet square, with a distance of 8¾ feet along the wall between them. In front of these rooms was a low barrier eighteen inches high and eighteen inches wide. Beyond the guardrooms was a 10½-foot doorway opening into a 14-foot hall with 3½-foot columns. Beyond this hall, at the inner end of the passageway was a vestibule 22¾ feet wide and 17½ feet long.

¹³Then he measured the entire outside width of the passageway, measuring across the roof from the outside doors of the guardrooms; this distance was 43¾ feet. ¹⁴Then he estimated the pillars on each side of the porch to be about 100 feet high. ¹⁵The full length of the entrance passage was 87½ feet from one end to the other. ¹⁶There were windows that narrowed inward through the walls along both sides of the passageway and along the guardroom walls. The windows were also in the exit and in the entrance halls. The pillars were decorated with palm tree decorations.

¹⁷And so we passed through the passageway to the court inside. A stone pavement ran around the inside of the walls, and thirty rooms were built against the walls, opening onto this pavement. ¹⁸This was called "the lower pavement." It extended out from the walls into the court the same distance as the passageway did.

¹⁹Then he measured across to the wall on the other side of this court (which was called "the outer court" of the Temple) and found that the distance was 175 feet. ²⁰As I followed, he left the eastern passageway and went over to the passage through the northern wall and measured it. ²¹Here too there were three guardrooms on each side, and all the measurements were the same as for the east passageway—87½ feet long and 43¾ feet from side to side across the top of the guardrooms. ²²There were windows, an entry hall and the palm tree decorations just the same as on the east side. And there were seven steps leading up to the doorway to the entry hall inside.

²³Here at the north entry, just as at the east, if one walked through the passageway into the court, and straight across it, he came to an inner wall and a passageway through it to an inner court. The distance between the two passageways was 175 feet. ²⁴Then he took me around to the south gate and measured the various sections of its passageway and found they were just the same as in the others. ²⁵It had windows along the walls as the others did, and an entry hall. And like the others, it was 87½ feet long and 43¾ feet wide. ²⁶It too had a stairway of seven steps leading up to it, and there were palm tree decorations along the walls. ²⁷And here again, if one walked through the passageway into the court and straight across it, he came to the inner wall and a passageway through it to the inner court. And the distance between the passageways was 175 feet.

²⁸Then he took me over to the inner wall and its south passageway. He measured this passageway and found that it had the same measurements as the passageways

40:3 *standing beside the Temple gate,* implied.   **40:7-12** *eighteen inches wide,* or, an eighteen-inch pillar in front of (or between) the guardrooms, projecting out into the hallway.   **40:19** *which was called "the outer court" of the Temple,* implied.   **40:28** Some manuscripts add to this verse: "And the arches around it were 37½ feet by 8¾ feet broad."

Solomon's Temple. As in Revelation 11:1–6, the command to "measure" defines the areas of God's special control. Once again the sovereignty of God is stressed.

40:3 Who is this man? He is obviously not a human being, so he is probably an angel. Some say he may be Christ, because through him we have access to God.

of the outer wall. ²⁹, ³⁰Its guardrooms, pillars and entrance and exit hall were identical to all the others, and so were the windows along its walls and entry. And, like the others, it was 87½ feet long by 43¾ feet wide. ³¹The only difference was that it had eight steps leading up to it instead of seven. It had palm tree decorations on the pillars, just as the others.

³²Then he took me along the court to the eastern entrance of the inner wall, and measured it. It too had the same measurements as the others. ³³Its guardrooms, pillars and entrance hall were the same size as those of the other passageways, and there were windows along the walls and in the entry hall; and it was 87½ feet long by 43¾ feet wide. ³⁴Its entry hall faced the outer court and there were palm tree decorations on its columns, but there were eight steps instead of seven going up to the entrance.

³⁵Then he took me around to the north gate of the inner wall, and the measurements there were just like the others: ³⁶The guardrooms, pillars and entry hall of this passageway were the same as the others, with a length of 87½ feet and a width of 43¾ feet. ³⁷Its entry hall faced toward the outer court, and it had palm tree decorations on the walls of each side of the passageway, and there were eight steps leading up to the entrance.

³⁸But a door led from its entry hall into a side room where the flesh of the sacrifices was washed before being taken to the altar; ³⁹on each side of the entry hall of the passageway there were two tables where the animals for sacrifice were slaughtered for the burnt offerings, sin offerings and guilt offerings to be presented in the Temple. ⁴⁰Outside the entry hall, on each side of the stairs going up to the north entrance, there were two more tables. ⁴¹So, in all, there were eight tables, four inside and four outside, where the sacrifices were cut up and prepared. ⁴²There were also four stone tables where the butchering knives and other implements were laid. These tables were about 2⅝ feet square and 1¾ feet high. ⁴³There were hooks, three or four inches long, fastened along the walls of the entry hall, and on the tables the flesh of the offering was to be laid.

⁴⁴In the inner court, there were two one-room buildings, one beside the northern entrance, facing south, and one beside the southern entrance, facing north.

⁴⁵And he said to me: "The building beside the inner northern gate is for the priests who supervise the maintenance. ⁴⁶The building beside the inner southern entrance is for the priests in charge of the altar—the descendants of Zadok—for they alone of all the Levites may come near to the Lord to minister to him."

⁴⁷Then he measured the inner court [in front of the Temple] and found it to be 175 feet square, and there was an altar in the court, standing in front of the Temple. ⁴⁸, ⁴⁹Then he brought me to the entrance hall of the Temple. Ten steps led up to it from the inner court. Its walls extended up on either side to form two pillars, each of them 8¾ feet thick. The entrance was 24½ feet wide with 5¼-foot walls. Thus the entry hall was 35 feet wide and 19¼ feet long.

The Holy of Holies

41 Afterward he brought me into the nave, the large main room of the Temple, and measured the pillars that formed its doorway. They were 10½ feet square. ²The entrance hall was 17½ feet wide and 8¾ feet deep. The nave itself was seventy feet long by thirty-five feet.

³Then he went into the inner room at the end of the nave and measured the columns at the entrance and found them to be 3½ feet thick; its doorway was 10½ feet wide, with a hallway 12¼ feet deep behind it. ⁴The inner room was thirty-five feet square. "This," he told me, "is the Most Holy Place."

40:30 Verse 30, omitted in the Septuagint and several other of the ancient manuscripts, reads, "There were vestibules round about, and they were 37½ feet long and 8¾ feet broad." **40:47** *in front of the Temple,* implied.

40:38, 39 The washing of the sacrifices was done according to the standards of preparation established in Leviticus 1:6–9. This washing was part of the process of presenting an acceptable sacrifice to God.

41:4 The Most Holy Place was the innermost room in the Temple (Exodus 26:33, 34). This was where the Ark of the Covenant was kept and where God's glory was said to dwell. It was entered only once a year by the High Priest, who performed a ceremony to

40:35
Ezek 44:4; 47:2

40:38
1 Kgs 6:8
1 Chron 28:12
Ezek 41:10
42:13
Neh 13:5,9

40:39
Lev 1:2-17
4:2,3; 5:6; 6:6
7:1,2
Ezek 46:2

40:42
Ex 20:25

40:44
1 Chron 6:31,
32; 16:41-43
25:1-7

40:45
Lev 8:35
Num 3:27-32
18:5
1 Chron 9:23
Mal 2:4-7

40:46
1 Kgs 2:35
Ezek 43:19
48:11

40:48
1 Kgs 6:3
2 Chron 3:17
Jer 52:17-23
Rev 3:12

41:1
Ezek 40:2,3,17
Zech 6:12,13
Eph 2:20-22
Rev 11:1,2
21:3,15

41:2
1 Kgs 6:2,17

41:4
Ex 26:33,34
Heb 9:3-8

41:5
1 Kgs 6:5
41:6
1 Kgs 6:6,10

41:7
1 Kgs 6:8

41:8
Ezek 40:5
Rev 21:16

41:10
Ezek 40:17

41:12
Ezek 42:1
Rev 21:27
22:14,15
41:13
Ezek 40:47
41:15
1 Kgs 6:4,15
Isa 6:4
Zech 3:7
41:17
1 Kgs 6:29,32
2 Chron 3:5
Ezek 10:18
41:19
Ezek 1:10; 10:14

41:21
1 Kgs 6:33
41:22
Ex 25:23,30
30:1-3,8
Ezek 44:16
Mal 1:7,12
Rev 8:3
41:23
1 Kgs 6:31-35
41:24
1 Kgs 6:34
41:26
Ezek 40:7-12

42:1
Ezek 40:2,3,17
41:9,12-15
42:2
Ezek 41:13
42:3
Ezek 40:17
41:10
42:4
Ezek 46:19

42:6
1 Kgs 6:8
Ezek 41:6
42:7
Ezek 41:13,14

42:9
Ezek 44:5; 46:19

⁵Then he measured the wall of the Temple and found that it was 10½ feet thick, with a row of rooms along the outside. Each room was seven feet wide. ⁶These rooms were in three tiers, one above the other, with thirty rooms in each tier. The whole structure was supported by girders and not attached to the Temple wall for support. ⁷Each tier was wider than the one below it, corresponding to the narrowing of the Temple wall as it rose higher. A stairway at the side of the Temple led up from floor to floor.

⁸I noticed that the Temple was built on a terrace and that the bottom row of rooms extended out 10½ feet onto the terrace. ⁹The outer wall of these rooms was 8¾ feet thick, leaving a free space of 8¾ feet out to the edge of the terrace, the same on both sides.

¹⁰Thirty-five feet away from the terrace, on both sides of the Temple, was another row of rooms down in the inner court. ¹¹Two doors opened from the tiers of rooms to the terrace yard, which was 8¾ feet wide; one door faced north and the other south.

¹²A large building stood on the west, facing the Temple yard, measuring 122½ feet wide by 157½ feet long. Its walls were 8¾ feet thick. ¹³Then he measured the Temple and its immediately surrounding yards. The area was 175 feet square. ¹⁴The inner court at the east of the Temple was also 175 feet wide, ¹⁵, ¹⁶and so was the building west of the Temple, including its two walls.

The nave of the Temple and the Holy of Holies and the entry hall were paneled, and all three had recessed windows. The inner walls of the Temple were paneled with wood above and below the windows. ¹⁷, ¹⁸The space above the door leading into the Holy of Holies was also paneled. The walls were decorated with carvings of Guardian Angels, each with two faces, and of palm trees alternating with the Guardian Angels. ¹⁹, ²⁰One face—that of a man—looked toward the palm tree on one side, and the other face—that of a young lion—looked toward the palm tree on the other side. And so it was, all around the inner wall of the Temple.

²¹There were square doorposts at the doors of the nave, and in front of the Holy of Holies was what appeared to be an altar, but it was made of wood. ²²This altar was 3½ feet square, and 5¼ feet high; its corners, base and sides were all of wood. "This," he told me, "is the Table of the Lord."

²³Both the nave and the Holy of Holies had double doors, ²⁴each with two swinging sections. ²⁵The doors leading into the nave were decorated with cherubim and palm trees, just as on the walls. And there was a wooden canopy over the entry hall. ²⁶There were recessed windows and carved palm trees on both sides of the entry hall, the hallways beside the Temple, and on the canopy over the entrance.

Rooms for the priests

42 Then he led me out of the Temple, back into the inner court to the rooms north of the Temple yard, and to another building. ²This group of structures was 175 feet long by 87½ feet wide. ³The rows of rooms behind this building were the inner wall of the court. The rooms were in three tiers, overlooking the outer court on one side, and having a 35-foot strip of inner court on the other. ⁴A 17½-foot walk ran between the building and the tiers of rooms, extending the entire length, with the doors of the building facing north. ⁵The upper two tiers of rooms were not as wide as the lower one, because the upper tiers had wider walkways beside them. ⁶And since the building was not built with girders as those in the outer court were, the upper stories were set back from the ground floor.

⁷, ⁸The north tiers, next to the outer court, were 87½ feet long—only half as long as the inner wing that faced the Temple court, which was 175 feet long. But a wall extended from the end of the shorter wing, parallel to the longer wing. ⁹, ¹⁰And there was an entrance from the outer court to these rooms from the east. On the

41:22 *the Table of the Lord,* literally, "the table which is before the Lord."

---

atone for the nation's sins. God's holiness is a central theme throughout both the Old and New Testaments.

41:22 The altar could be either the table of showbread (Exodus 25:30) or the altar of incense (Exodus 30:1-3).

opposite side of the Temple a similar building composed of two units of tiers was on the south side of the inner court, between the Temple and the outer court, arranged the same as the other. ¹¹There was a walk between the two wings of the building, the same as in the other building across the court—the same length and width and the same exits and doors—they were identical units. ¹²And there was a door from the outer court at the east.

¹³Then he told me: "These north and south tiers of rooms facing the Temple yard are holy; there the priests who offer up the sacrifices to the Lord shall eat of the most holy offerings and store them—the cereal offerings, sin offerings, and guilt offerings, for these rooms are holy. ¹⁴When the priests leave the Holy Place—the nave of the Temple—they must change their clothes before going out to the outer court. The special robes in which they have been ministering must first be removed, for these robes are holy. They must put on other clothes before entering the parts of the building open to the public."

¹⁵When he had finished making these measurements, he led me out through the east passageway to measure the entire Temple area. ¹⁶⁻²⁰He found that it was in the form of a square, 875 feet long on each side, with a wall all around it to separate the restricted area from the public places.

Sacrifices in the Temple

43 Afterward he brought me out again to the passageway through the outer wall leading to the east. ²And suddenly the glory of the God of Israel appeared from the east. The sound of his coming was like the roar of rushing waters and the whole landscape lighted up with his glory. ³It was just as I had seen it in the other visions, first by the Chebar Canal, and then later at Jerusalem when he came to destroy the city. And I fell down before him with my face in the dust. ⁴And the glory of the Lord came into the Temple through the eastern passageway.

⁵Then the Spirit took me up and brought me into the inner court; and the glory of the Lord filled the Temple. ⁶And I heard the Lord speaking to me from within the Temple (the man who had been measuring was still standing beside me).

⁷And the Lord said to me:

"Son of dust, this is the place of my throne, and my footstool, where I shall remain, living among the people of Israel forever. They and their kings will not defile my holy name any longer through the adulterous worship of other gods or by worshiping the totem poles erected by their kings. ⁸They built their idol temples beside mine, with only a wall between, and worshiped their idols. Because they sullied my holy name by such wickedness, I consumed them in my anger. ⁹Now let them put away their idols and the totem poles erected by their kings, and I will live among them forever.

¹⁰"Son of dust, describe the Temple I have shown you to the people of Israel. Tell them its appearance and its plan so they will be ashamed of all their sins. ¹¹And if they are truly ashamed of what they have done, then explain to them the details of its construction—its doors and entrances—and everything about it. Write out all the directions and the rules for them to keep. ¹²And this is the basic law of the

42:13
Lev 6:25,29
7:6; 10:13-17
Num 18:9,10

42:14
Ex 29:4-9
Isa 61:10
Ezek 22:26
Zech 3:4,5

42:16
Ezek 40:3,5
45:2
Zech 2:5
Rev 11:1,2

43:1
Ezek 10:19
40:6; 44:1; 46:1

43:2
Isa 6:3
Ezek 10:4,18,
19; 11:23
Hab 2:14; 3:3

43:3
Ezek 1:4,27,28

43:4
Ezek 44:2

43:5
1 Kgs 8:10,11
Hag 2:7-9

43:6
Ezek 1:26; 40:3

43:7
Ezek 6:4-7
37:26-28

43:8
2 Kgs 21:4-7
Ezek 8:3

43:9
Ezek 18:30,31

43:10
Ezek 40:4

43:11
Ezek 11:20
36:27; 44:5

43:12
Ezek 40:2

42:12 *from the outer court,* implied. **42:16-20** *to separate the restricted area from the public places,* literally, "between the holy and the common." **43:3** *at Jerusalem,* implied. **43:9** *totem poles,* literally, "stellae."

42:14 The holy robes may symbolize the importance of having a holy heart when approaching God.

42:16-20 The perfect symmetry of the Temple may represent the order and harmony in God's kingdom.

43:1ff This is the culmination of chapters 40—42, for God's glory returns to the Temple. It reverses the negative cast of the book and concludes all the passages dealing with the blessings reserved for the restored remnant. All true believers should long for that moment when God's name will finally be glorified once and for all.

43:2 In Ezekiel 11:23, God's glory stopped over the Mount of

Olives, to the east of Jerusalem, before leaving the city. This prophecy states that his glory would also return from the east.

43:2-4 Just as it was completely devastating when God's glory departed (11:23), so it was overwhelming beyond expression when Ezekiel saw God's glory return.

43:12 The basic law of God's Temple was holiness. In all he does, God is holy. There is no trace of evil or sin in him. Just as God is holy, so we are to be holy (Leviticus 19:1, 2; 1 Peter 1:15, 16). People are holy when they are devoted to God and separated from sin. If we do not understand the basic concept of holiness, we will never progress very far in our Christian lives.

43:13
Ex 27:1-8
2 Chron 4:1

43:14
Ezek 45:19

43:15
Ex 27:2
Lev 9:9
1 Kgs 1:49,50
Ps 118:27

43:16
Ex 27:1; 38:1,2
Ezra 3:3

43:17
Neh 9:4
Ezek 40:6

43:18
Ex 40:29
Lev 1:5,11
Heb 9:21,22

43:19
1 Kgs 2:35
Ezek 40:46
44:15
Heb 7:27

43:20
Lev 8:15; 9:9

43:21
Ex 29:14
Lev 4:11,12
Heb 13:11

43:22
Ex 29:15-18
Lev 8:18-21

43:23
Ex 29:1

43:24
Lev 2:13
Num 18:19
Num 18:19
Mk 9:49,50
Col 4:6

43:25
Ex 29:35-37
Lev 8:33,35

43:27
Lev 3:1; 9:1
Ezek 20:40
Hos 8:13
1 Pet 2:5

44:1
Ezek 40:6

44:2
Ezek 43:4

44:3
Ex 24:9-11
Deut 12:7,17,18
Ezek 37:25
Zech 6:12,13

44:4
Isa 6:3,4
Ezek 1:28; 3:23
Hag 2:7

44:5
Ezek 40:4
43:10,11

Temple: *Holiness!* The entire top of the hill where the Temple is built is *holy*. Yes, this is the primary law concerning it.

13"And these are the measurements of the altar: The base is twenty-one inches high, with a nine-inch rim around its edge, and it extends twenty-one inches beyond the altar on all sides. 14The first stage of the altar is a stone platform 3½ feet high. This platform is twenty-one inches narrower than the base block on all sides. Rising from this is a narrower platform, twenty-one inches narrower on all sides, and seven feet high. 15From it a still narrower platform rises seven feet, and this is the top of the altar, with four horns projecting twenty-one inches up from the corners. 16This top platform of the altar is twenty-one feet square. 17The platform beneath it is 24½ feet square with a 10½-inch curb around the edges. The entire platform extends out from the top twenty-one inches on all sides. On the east side are steps to climb the altar."

18And he said to me:

"Son of dust, the Lord God says: These are the measurements of the altar to be made in the future, when it is erected for the burning of offerings and the sprinkling of blood upon it. 19At that time the Zadok family of the Levite tribe, who are my ministers, are to be given a bullock for a sin offering. 20You shall take some of its blood and smear it on the four horns of the altar and on the four corners of the top platform and in the curb around it. This will cleanse and make atonement for the altar. 21Then take the bullock for the sin offering and burn it at the appointed place outside the Temple area.

22"The second day, sacrifice a young male goat without any defects—without sickness, deformities, cuts or scars—for a sin offering. Thus the altar shall be cleansed, as it was by the bullock. 23When you have finished this cleansing ceremony, offer another perfect bullock and a perfect ram from the flock. 24Present them before the Lord, and the priests shall sprinkle salt upon them as a burnt offering.

25"Every day for seven days a male goat, a bullock and a ram from the flock shall be sacrificed as a sin offering. None are to have any defects or unhealthiness of any kind. 26Do this each day for seven days to cleanse and make atonement for the altar, thus consecrating it. 27On the eighth day, and on each day afterward, the priests will sacrifice on the altar the burnt offerings and thank offerings of the people, and I will accept you, says the Lord God."

Requirements for the priests

44 Then the Lord brought me back to the outer wall's eastern passageway, but it was closed. 2And he said to me:

"This gate shall remain closed; it shall never be opened. No man shall pass through it; for the Lord, the God of Israel, entered here and so it shall remain shut. 3Only the prince—because he is the prince—may sit inside the passageway to feast there before the Lord. But he shall go and come only through the entry hall of the passage."

4Then he brought me through the north passageway to the front of the Temple. I looked and saw that the glory of the Lord filled the Temple of the Lord, and I fell to the ground with my face in the dust.

5And the Lord said to me:

"Son of dust, notice carefully; use your eyes and ears. Listen to all I tell you

---

43:18–27 This vision was simultaneously flashing back to Mount Sinai and forward to Mount Calvary. When the people returned from exile, they would seek forgiveness through the sacrificial system instituted in Moses' day. Today, Christ's death has made the forgiveness of our sins possible, making us acceptable to God (Hebrews 9:9–15). God stands ready to forgive those who come to him in faith.

44:2 Why was this east gate to remain closed? Several reasons have been suggested. (1) This was the gate through which God entered the Temple, and no one else could walk where God had

(43:2); (2) the closed gate indicated that God would never again leave the Temple; (3) it would prevent people from worshiping the sun from within the Temple grounds (8:16).

44:3 Although Christ is called a Prince (37:25), some say this prince is probably not Christ, because he offers a sacrifice to God (46:4). They say he is a princely ruler of the city, but he is distinguished from other princes because he will be just and fair (see 45:8). Another view is that this is indeed a picture of Christ offering a sacrifice to God himself.

about the laws and rules of the Temple of the Lord. Note carefully who may be admitted to the Temple, and who is to be excluded from it. 6And say to these rebels, the people of Israel, The Lord God says: O Israel, you have sinned greatly, 7by letting the uncircumcised into my sanctuary—those who have no heart for God—when you offer me my food, the fat and the blood. Thus you have broken my covenant in addition to all your other sins. 8You have not kept the laws I gave you concerning these holy affairs, for you have hired foreigners to take charge of my sanctuary.

9"The Lord God says: No foreigner of all the many among you shall enter my sanctuary if he has not been circumcised and does not love the Lord. 10And the men of the tribe of Levi who abandoned me when Israel strayed away from God to idols must be punished for their unfaithfulness. 11They may be Temple guards and gatemen; they may slay the animals brought for burnt offerings and be present to help the people. 12But because they encouraged the people to worship other gods, causing Israel to fall into deep sin, I have raised my hand and taken oath, says the Lord God, that they must be punished. 13They shall not come near me to minister as priests; they may not touch any of my holy things, for they must bear their shame for all the sins they have committed. 14They are the Temple caretakers, to do maintenance work and to assist the people in a general way.

15"However, the sons of Zadok, of the tribe of Levi, continued as my priests in the Temple when Israel abandoned me for idols. These men shall be my ministers; they shall stand before me to offer the fat and blood of the sacrifices, says the Lord God. 16They shall enter my sanctuary and come to my Table to minister to me; they shall fulfill my requirements.

17"They must wear only linen clothing when they enter the passageway to the inner court, for they must wear no wool while on duty in the inner court or in the Temple. 18They must wear linen turbans and linen trousers; they must not wear anything that would cause them to perspire. 19When they return to the outer court, they must take off the clothes they wear while ministering to me, leaving them in the sacred chambers, and put on other clothes lest they harm the people by touching them with this clothing.

20"They must not let their hair grow too long, nor shave it off. Regular, moderate haircuts are all they are allowed. 21No priest may drink wine before coming to the inner court. 22He may marry only a Jewish maiden, or the widow of a priest; he may not marry a divorced woman.

23"He shall teach my people the difference between what is holy and what is secular, what is right and what is wrong.

24"They will serve as judges to resolve any disagreements among my people. Their decisions must be based upon my laws. And the priests themselves shall obey my rules and regulations at all the sacred festivals, and they shall see to it that the Sabbath is kept a sacred day.

25"A priest must not defile himself by being in the presence of a dead person, unless it is his father, mother, child, brother or unmarried sister. In such cases it is all right. 26But afterward he must wait seven days before he is cleansed and able to perform his Temple duties again. 27The first day he returns to work and enters the inner court and the sanctuary, he must offer a sin offering for himself, the Lord God says.

28"As to property, they shall not own any, for I am their heritage! That is enough!

44:23 between what is holy and what is secular, what is right and what is wrong, literally, "between what is ritually clean and ritually unclean." **44:28** That is enough! Implied.

44:6
Ezek 2:5-7; 3:9
1 Pet 4:3
44:7
Gen 17:14
Ex 12:43-49
Jer 4:4; 9:26
Heb 8:9
44:8
Num 18:7
Acts 7:53
1 Tim 6:13
44:10
Num 18:23
2 Kgs 23:8,9
Ezek 22:26
44:11
Num 3:5-37
4:1-33; 16:8,9
44:12
2 Kgs 16:10-16
Ezek 14:3,4
Hos 4:6,5:1
44:13
Num 18:3
2 Kgs 23:9
Ezek 16:61,63
44:14
Num 18:4,6
Ezek 40:45
44:15
Jer 33:18-22
Ezek 48:11
Zech 3:7
44:16
Ezek 41-22
44:17
Ex 28:39-43
39:27-29
44:18
Ex 28:40,42
44:19
Lev 16:23,24
Ezek 42:14
Mt 23:17-19
44:20
Lev 21:5
44:21
Lev 10:8,9
44:22
Lev 21:7,13-15
44:23
Lev 10:10
Deut 33:10
Ezek 22:26
44:24
2 Chron 19:8-10
Ezek 20:12,20
44:25
Lev 21:1-3
44:26
Num 19:13-19
Heb 9:13,14
44:27
Num 6:9-11
44:28
1 Pet 5:2-4

44:15 Zadok's descendants are mentioned because the priests in Zadok's line remained faithful to God, while others became corrupt. Zadok supported God's choice of Solomon to succeed David, and was therefore appointed High Priest during his reign (1 Kings 1:32–35; 2:27, 35). His descendants were considered the true priestly line throughout the intertestamental period.

44:20-31 These laws were originally given to God's people in the wilderness. They are recorded in the books of Exodus and Leviticus.

44:23 Teaching people the difference between right and wrong is one of the responsibilities of ministers (see also Leviticus 10:8–11; Philippians 1:10). Ministers are God's representatives and spokesmen. Encourage your minister to speak out on moral issues.

44:29
Lev 27:21,28
Num 18:9,14,15
Josh 13:14
44:30
Num 18:12
Neh 10:35-37
44:31
Lev 22:8
Ezek 4:14

29"Their food shall be the gifts and sacrifices brought to the Temple by the people—the cereal offerings, the sin offerings and the guilt offerings. Whatever anyone gives to the Lord shall be the priests'. 30The first of the first-ripe fruits and all the gifts for the Lord shall go to the priests. The first samples of each harvest of grain shall be donated to the priests too, so that the Lord will bless your homes. 31Priests may never eat meat from any bird or animal that dies a natural death or that dies after being attacked by other animals.

The Lord's portion of land

45:1
Josh 13:7; 14:2
Ps 16:5,6
Ezek 47:21
48:8,9
45:2
Ezek 42:16-20
45:3
Ezek 48:10
45:4
Num 16:5
Ezek 40:45
44:13,14
48:10,11
45:5
Ezek 48:12-14
45:6
Ezek 48:15,16
45:7
Ezek 46:16-18
48:21,22
45:8
Isa 11:3-5
Jer 23:5,6
Ezek 22:27
45:9
Jer 6:7; 22:3
Nah 5:1-5
Zech 8:16
45:10
Lev 19:35,36
Deut 25:13-15
Prov 11:1; 16:11
Mic 6:10,11
45:12
Ex 30:13
Lev 27:25
Num 3:47
45:15
Lev 1:4; 6:30
Dan 9:24
45:17
Lev 23:1-44
1 Kgs 8:62-64
Ezek 43:27
46:4-12
45:18
Ex 12:2
Heb 9:14
45:19
Lev 16:18-20
Ezek 43:20
45:20
Rom 16:18,19
Heb 5:2

45 "When you divide the land among the tribes of Israel, you shall first give a section of it to the Lord as his holy portion. This piece shall be 8⅓ miles long and 6⅔ miles wide. It shall all be holy 8⅓ ground.

2"A section of this land, 875 feet square, shall be designated for the Temple. An additional 87½-foot strip all around is to be left empty. 3The Temple shall be built within the area which is 8⅓ miles long and 3⅓ miles wide. 4All this section shall be 3⅓ miles wide. 4All this section shall be holy land; it will be used by the priests, who minister in the sanctuary, for their homes and for my Temple.

5"The strip next to it, 8⅓ miles long and 3⅓ miles wide, shall be the residence area for the Levites who work at the Temple. 6Adjacent to the holy lands will be a section 8⅓ miles by 1⅔ miles for a city open to everyone in Israel.

7"Two special sections of land shall be set apart for the prince—one on each side of the holy lands and city; it is contiguous with them in length, and its eastern and western boundaries are the same as those of the tribal sections. 8This shall be his allotment. My princes shall no longer oppress and rob my people, but shall assign all the remainder of the land to the people, giving a portion to each tribe. 9For the Sovereign Lord says to the rulers: Quit robbing and cheating my people out of their land, and expelling them from their homes. Always be fair and honest.

10"You must use honest scales, honest bushels, honest gallons. 11A homer [about five bushels] shall be your standard unit of measurement for both liquid and dry measure. Smaller units shall be the ephah [about one half bushel] for dry measure, and the bath [about seventeen quarts] for liquid. 12The unit of weight shall be the silver shekel [about half an ounce]; it must always be exchanged for twenty gerahs, no less; five shekels shall be valued at five shekels, no less; and ten shekels at ten shekels! Fifty shekels shall always equal one mina.

13"This is the tax you must give to the prince: a bushel of wheat or barley for every sixty you reap; 14and one percent of your olive oil; 15from each 200 sheep in all your flocks in Israel, give him one sheep. These are the meal offerings, burnt offerings and thank offerings to make atonement for those who bring them, says the Lord God. 16All the people of Israel shall bring their offerings to the prince.

17"The prince shall be required to furnish the people with sacrifices for public worship—sin offerings, burnt offerings, meal offerings, drink offerings and thank offerings—to make reconciliation for the people of Israel. This shall be done at the time of the religious feasts, the new moon ceremonies, the Sabbaths and all other similar occasions.

18"The Lord God says: On each New Year's Day sacrifice a young bull with no blemishes, to purify the Temple. 19The priest shall take some of the blood of this sin offering and put it on the door posts of the Temple and upon the four corners of the base of the altar and upon the walls at the entry of the inner court. 20Do this also

45:12 *fifty shekels,* or, sixty shekels, the manuscripts are unclear. **45:18** *On each New Year's Day,* literally, "on the first day of the first month. The first month of the Hebrew year corresponded approximately to March 15—April 15 of our calendar.

45:1–7 The land allotted to the Temple and the prince was in the center of the nation. God is central to life. He must be our first priority.

45:9–11 Greed and extortion were two of the major social sins of the nation during this time (see Amos 5:7–13). In the new economy there would be plenty of land for the "princes" (45:7, 8) and no longer any basis for greed. Therefore, the princes and the people

are commanded to be fair and honest, especially when they do business. Consider the ways you measure goods, money, or services. If you are paid for an hour of work, be sure you work for a full hour. If you sell a bushel of apples, make sure it is a full bushel. God is completely trustworthy and his followers should be too.

45:17 The conditions and regulations for these offerings are described in detail in Leviticus 1—7.

on the seventh day of that month for anyone who has sinned through error or ignorance, and so the Temple will be cleansed.

21"On the fourteenth day of the same month, you shall celebrate the Passover. It will be a seven-day feast. Only bread without yeast shall be eaten during those days. 22On the day of Passover the prince shall provide a young bull for a sin offering for himself and all the people of Israel. 23On each of the seven days of the feast he shall prepare a burnt offering to the Lord. This daily offering will consist of seven young bulls and seven rams without blemish. A male goat shall also be given each day for a sin offering. 24And the prince shall provide one half bushel of grain with each bullock and ram for a meal offering, and three quarts of olive oil.

25"Early in October, during each of the seven days of the annual festival of shelters, he shall provide these same sacrifices for the sin offering, burnt offering, meal offering and oil offering.

Special offerings in the Temple

46 "The Lord God says, the inner wall's eastern entrance shall be closed during the six work days but open on the Sabbath and on the days of the new moon celebrations. 2The prince shall enter the outside entry hall of the passageway and proceed to the inner wall at the other end while the priest offers his burnt offering and peace offering. He shall worship inside the passageway and then return back to the entrance, which shall not be closed until evening. 3The people shall worship the Lord in front of this passageway on the Sabbaths and on the days of the new moon celebrations.

4"The burnt offering which the prince sacrifices to the Lord on the Sabbath days shall be six lambs and a ram, all unblemished. 5He shall present a meal offering of one half bushel of flour to go with the ram, and whatever amount he is willing for, to go with each lamb. And he shall bring three quarts of olive oil for each half bushel of flour. 6At the new moon celebration, he shall bring one young bull, in perfect condition; six lambs and one ram, all without any blemish. 7With the young bull, he must bring one half bushel of flour for a meal offering. With the ram, he must bring one half bushel of flour. With the lamb, he is to bring whatever he is willing to give. With each half bushel of grain he is to bring three quarts of olive oil.

8"The prince shall go in at the entry hall of the passageway and out the same way; 9but when the people come in through the north passageway to sacrifice during the religious feasts, they must go out through the south passageway. Those coming in from the south must go out by the north. They must never go out the same way they come in, but must always use the opposite passageway. 10The prince shall enter and leave with the common people on these occasions.

11"To summarize: At the special feasts and sacred festivals the meal offering shall be one half bushel with the young bull; one half bushel with the ram; as much as the prince is willing to give with each lamb; and three quarts of oil with each half bushel of grain. 12Whenever the prince offers an extra burnt offering or peace offering to be sacrificed to the Lord, the inner eastern gate shall be opened up for him to enter and he shall offer his sacrifices just as on the Sabbaths. Then he shall turn around and go out, and the passage shall be shut behind him.

13"Each morning a yearling lamb must be sacrificed as a burnt offering to the Lord. 14, 15And there must be a meal offering each morning—five pounds of flour with one quart of oil with which to mix it. This is a permanent ordinance—the

46:7 *bushel,* literally, "one ephah."

45:21
Ex 1:24
Lev 23:5-8
Num 9:2,3
28:16,17

45:22
Lev 4:14
2 Cor 5:21

45:23
Lev 23:8
Num 28:16-25
Heb 10:8-12

45:24
Num 28:12-15
Ezek 46:5-7

45:25
Lev 23:33-36
Num 29:12-38

46:1
Ex 20:9,10
Isa 66:23
Ezek 44:1,2

46:2
Ezek 44:3
Jn 10:1-3

46:3
Lk 1:10
Jn 10:9
Heb 10:19-22

46:4
Ezek 45:17

46:5
Ezek 45:24

46:7
Deut 16:17

46:8
Ezek 44:1-3
Col 1:18

46:9
Ex 23:14-17
Deut 16:16
Ps 84:7
Heb 10:38
2 Pet 2:20,21

46:10
2 Chron 6:3; 7:4
Ps 42:4

46:11
Ezek 45:17

46:12
Lev 23:38
2 Chron 29:31
Ezek 44:3; 45:17

46:13
Ex 29:38
Num 28:3,4
Isa 50:4
Dan 8:11-13

46:14
Ex 29:42
Num 28:5,6

45:21 The Passover was an annual seven-day feast instituted by God so that his people would remember when he brought them out of slavery in Egypt. On that first Passover night, the Angel of Death passed over the homes marked by lamb's blood; he struck only the unmarked homes (see Exodus 11, 12).

45:25 This annual feast celebrated in October is called the Feast of Tabernacles (or Festival of Shelters). It commemorates God's

protection of his people as they traveled through the wilderness from Egypt to the Promised Land (see Leviticus 23:33–43; Deuteronomy 16:13–17).

46:1–15 Ezekiel continues to describe various aspects of daily worship. While allowing for diversity in worship, God prescribed order and continuity. This continuity gave a healthy rhythm to the spiritual life of his people.

lamb, the grain offering and the olive oil shall be provided every morning for the daily sacrifice.

16"The Sovereign Lord says: If the prince gives a gift of land to one of his sons, it will belong to him forever. 17But if he gives a gift of land to one of his servants, the servant may keep it only until the Year of Release (every seventh year) when he is set free; then the land returns to the prince. Only gifts to his sons are permanent. 18And the prince may never take anyone's property by force. If he gives property to his sons, it must be from his own land, for I don't want my people losing their property and having to move away."

19, 20After that, using the door through the wall at the side of the main passage-way, he led me through the entrance to the block of sacred chambers that faced north. There, at the extreme west end of these rooms, I saw a place where, my guide told me, the priests boil the meat of the trespass offering and sin offering and bake the flour of the flour offerings into bread. They do it here to avoid the necessity of carrying the sacrifices through the outer court, in case they harm the people.

21, 22Then he brought me out to the outer court again and led me to each of the four corners of the court. I saw that in each corner there was a room 70 feet long by 52½ feet wide, enclosed by walls. 23Around the inside of these walls there ran a line of brick boiling vats, with ovens underneath. 24He said these rooms were where the Temple assistants—the Levites—boil the sacrifices the people offer.

The river of healing

47 Then he brought me back to the door of the Temple. I saw a stream flowing eastward from beneath the Temple and passing to the right of the altar, that is, on its south side. 2Then he brought me outside the wall through the north passageway and around to the eastern entrance, where I saw the stream flowing along on the south side [of the eastern passageway]. 3Measuring as he went, he took me 1,500 feet east along the stream and told me to go across. At that point the water was up to my ankles. 4He measured off another 1,500 feet and told me to cross again. This time the water was up to my knees. 5Fifteen hundred feet after that it was up to my waist. Another 1,500 feet and it had become a river so deep I wouldn't be able to get across unless I were to swim. It was too deep to cross on foot.

6He told me to keep in mind what I had seen, then led me back along the bank. 7And now, to my surprise, many trees were growing on both sides of the river!

8He told me: "This river flows east through the desert and the Jordan Valley to the Dead Sea, where it will heal the salty waters and make them fresh and pure. 9Everything touching the water of this river shall live. Fish will abound in the Dead Sea, for its waters will be healed. Wherever this water flows, everything will live. 10Fishermen will stand along the shores of the Dead Sea, fishing all the way from En-gedi to En-eglaim. The shores will be filled with nets drying in the sun. Fish of every kind will fill the Dead Sea just as they do the Mediterranean! 11But the marshes and swamps will not be healed; they will still be salty. 12All kinds of fruit trees will grow along the river banks. The leaves will never turn brown and fall, and there will always be fruit. There will be a new crop every month—without fail! For they are watered by the river flowing from the Temple. The fruit will be for food and the leaves for medicine.

The boundaries of the nation

13"The Lord God says: Here are the instructions for dividing the land to the twelve tribes of Israel: The tribe of Joseph (Ephraim and Manasseh) shall be given

47:2 *through the north passageway.* The eastern passageway was closed. *of the eastern passageway,* implied. **47:7** *to my surprise,* implied. **47:13** *Ephraim and Manasseh,* implied.

46:17
Lev 25:10
Mt 25:14-29
Lk 19:25,26
Gal 4:30,31

46:18
Isa 11:3,4
Ezek 45:8
Mic 2:1,2

46:19
Lev 2:4-7
2 Chron 35:13
Ezek 42:9; 44:19

46:24
Lev 44:10,11
1 Pet 5:2

47:1
Ps 46:4
Joel 2:13
Zech 13:1
Rev 22:1,17

47:2
Ezek 44:1-4

47:3
Ezek 40:3
Zech 2:1
Rev 11:1; 21:15

47:5
Isa 11:9
Hab 2:14

47:6
Ezek 40:4; 44:5

47:7
Isa 60:21; 61:3
Rev 22:2

47:8
Isa 35:6,7
41:17-19; 44:3
Jer 31:9

47:9
Zech 2:11
8:21-23
Jn 4:14
7:37,38
Rev 21:6

47:10
Ps 104:25
Lk 5:5-9

47:12
Gen 2:9
Jer 17:8
Rev 22:2

47:13
Num 34:1-13

47:1–12 This river (or stream) is similar to the river mentioned in Revelation 22:1, 2, both of which are associated with the river of life in the Garden of Eden (see Genesis 2:10). The river symbolizes life from God and the blessings that flow from his throne. It is a gentle, safe, deep river, which expands as it flows.

two sections. ¹⁴Otherwise, each tribe will have an equal share. I promised with hand raised in oath of truth to give the land to your fathers, and you shall inherit it now.

¹⁵"The northern boundary will run from the Mediterranean toward Hethlon, then on through Labweh to Zedad; ¹⁶then to Berothah and Sibraim, which are on the border between Damascus and Hamath, and finally to Hazer-hatticon, on the border of Hauran. ¹⁷So the northern border will be from the Mediterranean to Hazar-enon, on the border with Hamath to the north and Damascus to the south.

¹⁸"The eastern border will run south from Hazar-enon to Mount Hauran, where it will bend westward to the Jordan at the southern tip of the Sea of Galilee, and down along the Jordan River separating Israel from Gilead, past the Dead Sea to Tamar.

¹⁹"The southern border will go west from Tamar to the springs at Meribath-kadesh and then follow the course of the Brook of Egypt (Wadi el-Arish) to the Mediterranean.

²⁰"On the west side, the Mediterranean itself will be your boundary, from the southern boundary to the point where the northern boundary begins.

²¹"Divide the land within these boundaries among the tribes of Israel. ²²Distribute the land as an inheritance for yourselves and for the foreigners who live among you with their families. All children born in the land—whether or not their parents are foreigners—are to be considered citizens and have the same rights your own children have. ²³All these immigrants are to be given land according to the tribe where they now live.

The land divided among the tribes

48 "Here is the list of the tribes and the territory each is to get. For Dan: From the northwest boundary at the Mediterranean, across to Hethlon, then to Labweh, and then on to Hazar-enon on the border between Damascus to the south and Hamath to the north. Those are the eastern and western limits of the land. ²Asher's territory lies south of Dan's and has the same east and west boundaries. ³Naphtali's land lies south of Asher's, with the same boundary lines on the east and the west. ⁴Then comes Manasseh, south of Naphtali, with the same eastern and western boundary lines. ⁵, ⁶, ⁷Next, to the south, is Ephraim, and then Reuben and then Judah, all with the same boundaries on the east and the west.

⁸"South of Judah is the land set aside for the Temple. It has the same eastern and western boundaries as the tribal units, with the Temple in the center. ⁹This Temple area will be 8⅓ miles long and 6⅔ miles wide.

¹⁰"A strip of land measuring 8⅓ miles long by 3⅓ miles wide, north to south, surrounds the Temple. ¹¹It is for the priests, that is, the sons of Zadok who obeyed me and didn't go into sin when the people of Israel and the rest of their tribe of Levi did. ¹²It is their special portion when the land is distributed, the most sacred land of all. Next to it lies the area where the other Levites will live. ¹³It will be of the same size and shape as the first. Together they measure 8⅓ miles by 6⅔ miles. ¹⁴None of this special land shall ever be sold or traded or used by others, for it belongs to the Lord; it is holy.

¹⁵"The strip of land 8⅓ miles long by 1⅔ miles wide, south of the Temple section, is for public use—homes, pasture and parks, with a city in the center. ¹⁶The city itself is to be 1½ miles square. ¹⁷Open land for pastures shall surround the city for approximately a tenth of a mile. ¹⁸Outside the city, stretching east and west for three miles alongside the holy grounds, is garden area belonging to the city, for public use. ¹⁹It is open to anyone working in the city, no matter where he comes from in Israel.

²⁰"The entire area—including sacred lands and city lands—is 8⅓ miles square.

²¹,²²"The land on both sides of this area, extending clear out to the eastern and western boundaries of Israel, shall belong to the prince. This land, lying between the sections alloted to Judah and Benjamin, is 8⅓ miles square on each side of the sacred and city lands.

47:15 *Labweh.* The present village on this site is so named. It was originally called Lebo-Hamath. **48:17** *for approximately a tenth of a mile,* literally, "437½ feet" in every direction.

47:14
Gen 12:7
Deut 1:8
Ezek 20:5,6

47:15
Num 34:7-9
Ezek 48:1

47:16
Num 13:21
1 Kgs 8:65
Amos 6:14
Zech 9:2

47:17
Num 34:9
Ezek 48:1

47:18
Gen 13:10,11
Num 34:10-12
Judg 10:8
Job 40:23

47:19
Num 34:3-5
Deut 32:51
Isa 27:12

47:20
Num 34:6

47:22
Isa 14:1; 56:6,7
Acts 11:18
Rom 10:12
Eph 2:12-14
Col 3:11

48:1
Ex 1:1
Josh 19:40-48
2 Sam 24:2
1 Kgs 12:28,29

48:2
Gen 30:12,13
Josh 19:24-31

48:3
Gen 30:7,8
Josh 19:32-39

48:4
Gen 30:22-24
41:51
48:5,14-20
Josh 13:29-31
17:1-11

48:5
Josh 13:15-23
15:1-63
16:5-10
17:8-10,14-18
19:9

48:8
Ezek 45:1-6
Zech 2:11,12
2 Cor 6:16
Rev 21:3,22

48:10
Ezek 44:28; 45:4

48:11
Ezek 44:10-15

48:14
Lev 25:32-34
Mal 3:8-10

48:15
Ezek 42:20; 45:6

48:16
Rev 21:16

48:21
Ezek 34:24; 45:7

48:23
Josh 18:21-28
48:24
Gen 49:5-7
Josh 19:1-9
48:25
Gen 30:14-18
Josh 19:17-23
48:26
Gen 30:19,20
Josh 19:10-16
48:27
Gen 30:10,11

23"The sections given to the remaining tribes are as follows: Benjamin's section extends across the entire country of Israel, from its eastern border clear across to the western border. 24South of Benjamin's area lies that of Simeon, also extending out to these same eastern and western borders. 25Next is Issachar, with the same boundaries. 26Then comes Zebulun, also extending all the way across. 27, 28Then Gad, with the same borders on east and west, while its south border runs from Tamar to the Spring at Meribath-kadesh, and then follows the Brook of Egypt (Wadi el-Arish) to the Mediterranean. 29These are the allotments to be made to each tribe, says the Lord God.

The city gates

48:30
Rev 21:12,13

30, 31"Each city gate will be named in honor of one of the tribes of Israel. On the north side, with its 1½-mile wall, there will be three gates, one named for Reuben, one for Judah and one for Levi. 32On the east side, with its 1½-mile wall, the gates will be named for Joseph, Benjamin and Dan. 33The south wall, also the same

48:35
Isa 12:6; 24:23
Jer 23:6
Joel 3:21
Zech 2:10
Rev 21:3; 22:3

length, will have the gates of Simeon, Issachar and Zebulun; 34on the 1½ miles of the west side, they will be named for Gad, Asher and Naphtali.

35"The entire circumference of the city is six miles. And the name of the city will be 'The City of God.' "

48:35 *The City of God,* literally, "Jehovah-Shammah," "The Lord is there."

48:1ff The division of the land shows that in God's kingdom there is a place for all who believe in and obey the one true God (see John 14:1-6).

48:35 The book of Ezekiel begins by describing the holiness of God, which Israel had despised and ignored. As a result, God's presence departed from the Temple, the city, and the people. The book ends with a detailed vision of the new Temple, the new city, and the new people—all demonstrating God's holiness. The pressures of everyday life can persuade us to focus on the here and now and thus forget God. That is why worship is so important; it takes our eyes off our current worries, gives us a glimpse of God's holiness, and allows us to look toward his future kingdom. God's presence makes everything glorious, and worship brings us into his presence.

DANIEL

VITAL STATISTICS

PURPOSE:
To give an historical account of the faithful Jews who lived in captivity and to show how God is in control of heaven and earth, directing the forces of nature, the destiny of nations, and the care of his people

AUTHOR:
Daniel

TO WHOM WRITTEN:
The other captives in Babylon and God's people everywhere

DATE WRITTEN:
Approximately 535 B.C., recording events which occurred from about 605–535 B.C.

SETTING:
Daniel had been taken captive and deported to Babylon by Nebuchadnezzar in 605 B.C. There he served in the government for about 60 years during the reigns of Nebuchadnezzar, Belshazzar, Darius, and Cyrus.

KEY VERSE:
"He [God] reveals profound mysteries beyond man's understanding. He knows all hidden things, for he is light, and darkness is no obstacle to him" (2:22).

KEY PEOPLE:
Daniel, Nebuchadnezzar, Shadrach, Meshach, Abednego, Belshazzar, Darius

KEY PLACES:
Nebuchadnezzar's palace, the fiery furnace, Belshazzar's banquet, the den of lions

SPECIAL FEATURES:
Daniel's apocalyptic visions (chapters 8—12) give a glimpse of God's plan for the ages, including a direct prediction of the Messiah.

AN EARTHQUAKE shakes the foundation of our security; a tornado blows away a lifetime of mementoes; an assassin's bullet changes national history; a drunk driver claims an innocent victim; a divorce shatters a home. International and personal tragedies make our world seem a fearful place, overflowing with evil and seemingly out of control. And the litany of bombings, coups, murders, and natural disasters could cause us to think that God is absent or impotent. "Where is God?" we cry, engulfed by sorrow and despair.

Twenty-five centuries ago, Daniel could have despaired. Daniel and thousands of his countrymen were deported to a foreign land after Judah was conquered. Daniel found himself facing an egocentric despot and surrounded by idolaters. Instead of giving in or giving up, this courageous young man held fast to his faith in his God. Daniel knew that despite the circumstances, God was sovereign and was working out his plan for nations and individuals. The book of Daniel centers around this profound truth—the sovereignty of God.

After a brief account of Nebuchadnezzar's siege and defeat of Jerusalem, the scene quickly shifts to Daniel and his three friends, Hananiah, Mishael, and Azariah (Shadrach, Meshach, and Abednego). These men held prominent positions within the Babylonian government. Daniel, in particular, held such a position because of his ability to interpret the king's dreams which tell of God's unfolding plan (chapters 2 and 4). Sandwiched between the dreams is the fascinating account of Daniel's three friends and the furnace (chapter 3). Because they refused to bow down to a golden idol, they were condemned to a fiery death. But God intervened and spared their lives.

Belshazzar ruled Babylon after Nebuchadnezzar, and chapter 5 tells of his encounter with God's message written on a wall. Daniel, who was summoned to interpret the message, predicted Babylon's fall to the Medes and Persians. This prediction came true that very night, and Darius the Mede conquered the Babylonian kingdom.

Daniel became one of Darius' most trusted advisers. His privileged position angered other administrators who plotted his death by convincing the king to outlaw prayer. In spite of the law, Daniel continued to pray to his sovereign Lord. As a result, he was condemned to die in a den of hungry lions. Again, God intervened and saved Daniel, shutting the mouths of the lions (chapter 6).

The book concludes with a series of visions which Daniel had during the reigns of Belshazzar (chapters 7, 8), Darius (chapter 9), and Cyrus (chapters 10—12). These dreams dramatically outline God's future plans, beginning with Babylon and continuing to the end of the age. They give a preview of God's redemption and have been called the key to all biblical prophecy.

God is sovereign. He was in control in Babylon, and he has been moving in history, controlling the destinies of people ever since. And he is here now! Despite news reports or personal stress, we can be confident that God is in control. As you read Daniel, watch God work and find your security in his sovereignty.

Nebuchad-nezzar dies 562	Daniel's first vision 553		Babylon overthrown; Daniel thrown to lions 539	First exiles return to Judah 537	Daniel's ministry ends 536

THE BLUEPRINT

A. DANIEL'S LIFE (1:1—6:28)

Daniel and his three friends chose not to eat the king's food. They did not bow down to the king's idol even under penalty of death. Daniel continued to pray even though he knew he might be noticed and sentenced to death. Daniel and his three friends are inspiring examples of living a faithful life in a sinful world. When we face trials, we can expect God to remain present with us through our trials. God grant us the same courage to refuse to fold under the pressure of our sinful world.

B. DANIEL'S VISIONS (7:1—12:13)

These visions gave the captives added confidence that God is in control of history. They were to wait patiently and in faith and not to worship the gods of Babylon or accept their way of life. God still rules over human activities. Evil will be overcome, so we should wait patiently and not give in to the temptations and pressures of the sinful way of life around us.

MEGATHEMES

THEME	EXPLANATION	IMPORTANCE
God is in control	God is all-knowing, and he is in charge of world events. God overrules and removes rebellious leaders who defy him. God will overcome evil; no one is exempt. But he will deliver the faithful who follow him.	Although nations vie for world control now, one day Christ's Kingdom will replace and surpass the kingdoms of this world. Our faith is sure because our future is secure in Christ. We must have courage and put our faith in God who controls everything.
Purpose in life	Daniel and his three friends are examples of dedication and commitment. They determined to serve God regardless of the consequences. They did not give in to pressures from an ungodly society because they had a clear purpose in life.	It is wise to make trusting and obeying God alone our true purpose in life. This will give us direction and peace in spite of the circumstances or consequences. We should disobey anyone who asks us to disobey God. Our first allegiance must be to God.
Perseverance	Daniel served in a foreign land that was hostile to God for 70 years, yet he did not compromise his faith in God. He was truthful, persistent in prayer, and disinterested in power for personal glory.	In order to fulfill your life's purpose, you need staying power. Don't let your Christian distinctives become blurred. Be relentless in your prayers, stay firm in your integrity, and be content to serve God wherever he puts you.
God's faithfulness	God was faithful in Daniel's life. He delivered him from prison, from a den of lions, and from enemies who hated him. God cares for his people and deals patiently with them.	We can trust God to be with us through any trial because he promises to be there. Because he has been faithful to us, we should remain faithful to him.

A. DANIEL'S LIFE (1:1—6:28)

While Ezekiel was ministering to the captives in Babylon, Daniel was drafted as a counselor to King Nebuchadnezzar. With God's help, Daniel interpreted two of the king's dreams, Daniel's three friends were rescued from certain death in the fiery furnace, and Daniel was rescued from a lions' den. Daniel's life is a picture of the triumph of faith. May God grant us this type of faith to live courageously each day.

Daniel becomes the king's counselor

1 Three years after King Jehoiakim began to rule in Judah, Babylon's King Nebuchadnezzar attacked Jerusalem with his armies, and the Lord gave him victory over Jehoiakim. When he returned to Babylon, he took along some of the sacred cups from the Temple of God, and placed them in the treasury of his god in the land of Shinar.

3, 4Then he ordered Ashpenaz, who was in charge of his palace personnel, to select some of the Jewish youths brought back as captives—young men of the royal family and nobility of Judah—and to teach them the Chaldean language and literature. "Pick strong, healthy, good-looking lads," he said; "those who have read widely in many fields, are well informed, alert and sensible, and have enough poise to look good around the palace."

5The king assigned them the best of food and wine from his own kitchen during their three-year training period, planning to make them his counselors when they graduated.

6Daniel, Hananiah, Misha-el, and Azariah were four of the young men chosen, all from the tribe of Judah. 7However, their superintendent gave them Babylonian names, as follows:

Daniel was called Belteshazzar;
Hananiah was called Shadrach;
Misha-el was called Meshach;
Azariah was called Abednego.

8But Daniel made up his mind not to eat the food and wine given to them by the

1:1
Gen 10:10
2 Kgs 24:1,2,13
2 Chron 36:5-7
Jer 25:1
52:12,28-30
Dan 2:37,38
5:2
Zech 5:11

1:3
2 Kgs 24:14
Isa 39:7
Dan 5:7,11,30
9:1

1:5
1 Sam 16:22
Dan 1:19

1:6
Ezek 14:14,20
28:3
Mt 24:15

1:7
Dan 2:49
3:12-30; 4:8

1:8
Lev 11:47
Deut 32:38
Ezek 4:13,14
Hos 9:3

1:9
Ezra 7:27,28
Neh 1:11
Ps 106:46
Prov 16:7

1:8 *not to eat the food and wine given to them by the king,* literally, "determined . . . that he would not defile himself." The defilement was probably in eating pork or other foods outlawed in Lev 11 and Deut 14:3-21.

1:1, 2 Daniel was born during the middle of Josiah's reign (2 Kings 22, 23) and grew up during the king's reforms. During this time he probably heard Jeremiah, a prophet he quoted in 9:2. In 609 B.C., Josiah was killed in a battle against Egypt, and within four years, Judah had returned to its evil ways.

In 605 B.C. Nebuchadnezzar became king of Babylon. In September of that year, he swept into Palestine and surrounded Jerusalem, making Judah his vassal state. To demonstrate his dominance, he took many of Jerusalem's wisest men and most beautiful women to Babylon as captives. Daniel was among this group.

1:1, 2 Nebuchadnezzar, the supreme leader of Babylon, was feared throughout the world. When he swept into a country, defeat was certain. After a victory, the Babylonians usually took the most valuable people back to Babylon and left the poor behind to take whatever land they wanted and live peacefully there. This system fostered great loyalty from conquered lands and ensured a steady supply of wise and talented people for Babylon's civil service.

1:3, 4 The language of Chaldea (Babylon) was Aramaic. Babylon's academic program would have included mathematics, astronomy, and history with a strong dose of alchemy and magic.

1:7 Nebuchadnezzar changed the names of Daniel and his friends because he wanted to make them Babylonian—in their own eyes and in the eyes of the Babylonian people. New names would help them assimilate into the culture. Daniel, which means "God is my judge" in Hebrew, was changed to Belteshazzar, which means "he whom Bel favors." Bel was a Babylonian god. This was the king's attempt to change the religious loyalty of these young men from Judah's God to Babylon's god.

TAKEN TO BABYLON Daniel, as a captive of Babylonian soldiers, faced a long and difficult march to a new land. The 500-mile trek, under harsh conditions, certainly tested his faith in God.

1:8 Daniel chose not to eat this food because the meat was probably pork or some other food forbidden in Leviticus (see Leviticus 11), it was not prepared according to Jewish law, and it had probably been sacrificed to idols. Although Daniel was in a culture that did not follow God's laws, he still obeyed them himself.

1:8 It is easier to resist temptation if you have thought through your convictions well before the temptation arises. Daniel and his friends made their decision to be faithful to the laws of their religion before they were faced with the king's delicacies, so they did not

king. He asked the superintendent for permission to eat other things instead. 9Now as it happened, God had given the superintendent a special appreciation for Daniel, and sympathy for his predicament. 10But he was alarmed by Daniel's suggestion.

"I'm afraid you will become pale and thin compared with the other youths your age," he said, "and then the king will behead me for neglecting my responsibilities."

11Daniel talked it over with the steward who was appointed by the superintendent to look after Daniel, Hananiah, Misha-el, and Azariah, 12and suggested a ten-day diet of only vegetables and water; 13then, at the end of this trial period the steward could see how they looked in comparison with the other fellows who ate the king's rich food, and decide whether or not to let them continue their diet.

14The steward finally agreed to the test. 15Well, at the end of the ten days, Daniel and his three friends looked healthier and better nourished than the youths who had been eating the food supplied by the king! 16So after that the steward fed them only vegetables and water, without the rich foods and wines!

17God gave these four youths great ability to learn and they soon mastered all the literature and science of the time, and God gave to Daniel special ability in understanding the meanings of dreams and visions.

18, 19When the three-year training period was completed, the superintendent brought all the young men to the king for oral exams, as he had been ordered to do. King Nebuchadnezzar had long talks with each of them, and none of them impressed him as much as Daniel, Hananiah, Misha-el, and Azariah. So they were put on his regular staff of advisors. 20And in all matters requiring information and balanced judgment, the king found these young men's advice ten times better than that of all the skilled magicians and wise astrologers in his realm.

21Daniel held this appointment as the king's counselor until the first year of the reign of King Cyrus.

1:8 *He asked the superintendent for permission to eat other things instead,* literally, "He asked . . . to allow him not to defile himself."

Marginal references (left column):

1:12
1:15
Ex 23:25
Prov 10:22

1:15
Ex 23:25
Prov 10:22

1:17
1 Kgs 3:12,28
Job 32:8
Dan 1:20; 2:21
7:1; 8:1

1:19
Gen 41:46
1 Kgs 17:1
Prov 22:29
Jer 15:1
Dan 1:5

1:20
Num 14:22
Isa 19:3
Dan 1:17; 2:2
4:18; 5:7

1:21
Dan 6:28; 10:1

DANIEL served as a prophet to the exiles in Babylon from 605–536 B.C.	Climate of the times	The people of Judah were captives in a strange land, feeling hopeless.
	Main message	God is sovereign over all of human history, past, present, and future.
	Importance of message	We should spend less time wondering when future events will happen and more time learning how we should live now.
	Contemporary prophets	Jeremiah (627–586)
		Habakkuk (612–589)
		Ezekiel (593–571)

---

hesitate to stick with their convictions. Sometimes we get into trouble because we have not previously decided where to draw the line. Before such situations arise, decide on your commitments. Then when temptation comes, you will be ready.

1:12 The Babylonians were trying to change the *thinking* of these Jews by giving them a Chaldean education, their *loyalty* by changing their names, and their *life-style* by changing their diet. Without compromising, Daniel found a way to live by God's standards in a culture that did not honor God. Wisely choosing to negotiate rather than to rebel, he suggested an experimental ten-day diet. As God's people, we may adjust to our culture as long as we do not compromise our convictions.

1:17 Daniel and his friends learned all they could about their new culture so they could do their work with excellence. But while they learned, they maintained steadfast allegiance to God. Culture need

not be God's enemy. If it does not violate his commands, it can aid in accomplishing his purpose. We who follow God are free to be competent leaders in our culture, but we are required to put our allegiance to God first.

1:20 The king's advisors were masters at communicating their message so that it sounded authoritative—as if it came directly from their gods. In addition to knowledge, however, Daniel and the other Jewish young men had insight, which was a gift from God.

1:21 One of the first captives taken to Babylon, Daniel lived to see the first exiles return to Jerusalem in 538 B.C. Throughout this time he honored God, and God honored him. While serving as a counselor to the kings of Babylon, Daniel was God's spokesman to the Babylonian Empire. Babylon was a wicked nation, but it would have been much worse without Daniel's influence.

Daniel interprets the king's dream

2 One night in the second year of his reign, Nebuchadnezzar had a terrifying nightmare, and awoke trembling with fear. And to make matters worse, he couldn't remember his dream! He immediately called in all his magicians, incantationists, sorcerers, and astrologers, and demanded that they tell him what his dream had been.

"I've had a terrible nightmare," he said as they stood before him, "and I can't remember what it was. Tell me, for I fear some tragedy awaits me."

4Then the astrologers (speaking in Aramaic) said to the king, "Sir, tell us the dream and then we can tell you what it means."

5But the king replied, "I tell you, the dream is gone—I can't remember it. And if you won't tell me what it was and what it means, I'll have you torn limb from limb and your houses made into heaps of rubble! 6But I will give you many wonderful gifts and honors if you tell me what the dream was and what it means. So, begin!"

7They said again, "How can we tell you what the dream means unless you tell us what it was?"

8, 9The king retorted, "I can see your trick! You're trying to stall for time until the calamity befalls me that the dream foretells. But if you don't tell me the dream, you certainly can't expect me to believe your interpretation!"

10The astrologers replied to the king, "There isn't a man alive who can tell others what they have dreamed! And there isn't a king in all the world who would ask such a thing! 11This is an impossible thing the king requires. No one except the gods can tell you your dream, and they are not here to help."

12Upon hearing this, the king was furious, and sent out orders to execute all the wise men of Babylon. 13And Daniel and his companions were rounded up with the others to be killed.

14But when Ari-och, the chief executioner, came to kill them, Daniel handled the situation with great wisdom by asking, 15"Why is the king so angry? What is the matter?"

Then Ari-och told him all that had happened.

16So Daniel went in to see the king. "Give me a little time," he said, "and I will tell you the dream and what it means."

17Then he went home and told Hananiah, Misha-el, and Azariah, his companions. 18They asked the God of heaven to show them his mercy by telling them the secret, so they would not die with the others. 19And that night in a vision God told Daniel what the king had dreamed.

Then Daniel praised the God of heaven, 20saying, "Blessed be the name of God

2:1
Gen 40:5-8
41:1
Job 33:15-17
Dan 2:3; 4:5
6:18

2:4
Ezra 4:7
Isa 36:11

2:5
Deut 13:16
Ezra 6:11
Dan 2:12; 3:29

2:6
Dan 2:48
5:7,16,29

2:7
Dan 2:26; 4:8
5:12

2:8
Isa 41:23
Dan 3:15

2:11
Gen 41:39
Ex 29:45
1 Kgs 8:27
Isa 57:15
Dan 5:11

2:12
Ps 76:10
Dan 2:5; 3:13

2:18
Gen 18:28
Esth 4:15
Ps 50:15
Isa 37:4
Ezek 36:27
Dan 2:23

2:19
Num 12:6
2 Kgs 6:8-12
Job 33:15,16
Dan 7:2,7

2:20
1 Chron 29:11,
12
Job 12:13
Ps 103:1,2
Dan 2:21-23
Mt 6:13

2:1-5 Dreams were considered messages from the gods, and the wise men were expected to interpret them. Usually they could give some sort of interpretation as long as they knew what the dream was about. This time, however, Nebuchadnezzar demanded to be told the dream because he could not remember it. God sent a series of dreams to Nebuchadnezzar with prophetic messages which could be revealed and understood only by a servant of God. Other people who received dreams from God included Jacob (Genesis 28:10–15), Joseph (Genesis 37:5–20), Pharaoh (Genesis 40, 41), Solomon (1 Kings 3:5–15), and Joseph (Matthew 1:20–24).

2:11 *Impossible* is a hopeless word. The Chaldeans told the king it was impossible to know the dreams of another person. But Daniel was able to give the answer because God was working through him. In daily life, we face many apparently impossible situations that would be hopeless if we had to handle them with limited human strength alone. But God specializes in the impossible.

2:11 The Chaldeans said that the gods were not there to help. Of course they weren't—they didn't even exist! This exposed the limitations of the astrologers and wise men. They could invent interpretations, but they could not correctly explain the meaning of Nebuchadnezzar's dream. Although his request was

unreasonable, Nebuchadnezzar was furious when his advisors couldn't fulfill it. He was probably already suspicious of them because of his previous experience with them.

2:16–18 Daniel was at a crisis point. Imagine going to see the powerful, temperamental king who had just angrily ordered your death! Daniel did not shrink back in fear, however, but confidently believed God would tell him all the king wanted to know. When the king gave Daniel time to find the answer, Daniel found his three friends and they prayed. When you find yourself in a tight spot, share your needs with trusted friends who also believe in God's power. Prayer is more effective than panic. Panic confirms your hopelessness, prayer confirms your hope in God. Daniel's trust in God saved himself, his three friends, and all the wise men.

2:20 After Daniel asked God to reveal Nebuchadnezzar's dream to him, he saw a vision of the dream. His prayer was answered. Before rushing to Ari-och, he took time to give God credit for all wisdom and power, thanking him for answering his request. How do you feel when your prayers are answered? Excited, surprised, relieved? There are times when we seek God in prayer and, after having been answered, dash off in our excitement, forgetting to give God credit for the answer. Match your persistence in prayer with humble thanksgiving when your requests are answered.

2:21
1 Sam 2:7,8
1 Kgs 3:9,10
4:29
Jas 1:5

2:22
Gen 37:5-9
Job 12:22; 26:6
Isa 45:7
Dan 2:19,28
1 Jn 1:5

2:23
Ex 3:15
Ps 21:2,4
Dan 2:21

2:25
Dan 1:6; 5:13
6:13

2:27
Dan 2:2,10,11
5:7,8

forever and ever, for he alone has all wisdom and all power. 21World events are under his control. He removes kings and sets others on their thrones. He gives wise men their wisdom, and scholars their intelligence. 22He reveals profound mysteries beyond man's understanding. He knows all hidden things, for he is light, and darkness is no obstacle to him. 23I thank and praise you, O God of my fathers, for you have given me wisdom and glowing health, and now, even this vision of the king's dream, and the understanding of what it means."

24Then Daniel went in to see Ari-och, who had been ordered to execute the wise men of Babylon, and said, "Don't kill them. Take me to the king and I will tell him what he wants to know."

25Then Ari-och hurried Daniel in to the king and said, "I've found one of the Jewish captives who will tell you your dream!"

26The king said to Daniel, "Is this true? Can you tell me what my dream was and what it means?"

27Daniel replied, "No wise man, astrologer, magician, or wizard can tell the king

---

DANIEL

Daniel's early life demonstrates that there is more to being young than making mistakes. No characteristic wins the respect of adults more quickly than wisdom in the words and actions of a young person. Daniel and his friends had been taken from their homes in Judah and exiled. Their futures were in doubt, but they all had personal traits that qualified them for jobs as servants in the king's palace. They took advantage of the opportunity without letting the opportunity take advantage of them.

Our first hint of Daniel's greatness comes in his quiet refusal to give up his convictions. He had applied God's Word to his own life, and he resisted changing the habits he had formed from that application. Both his physical and spiritual diets were an important part of his relationship with God. He ate carefully and lived prayerfully. One of the benefits of being in training for royal service was eating food from the king's table. Daniel tactfully chose a simpler menu and proved it was a healthy choice. As with Daniel, mealtimes are obvious and regular tests of our efforts to control our appetites.

While Daniel limited his food intake, he indulged in prayer. He was able to communicate with God because he made it a habit. He put into practice his convictions, even when that meant being thrown into a den of hungry lions. His life proved he made the right choice.

Do you hold so strongly to your faith in God that whatever happens, you will do what God says? Such conviction keeps you a step ahead of temptation; such conviction gives you wisdom and stability in changing circumstances. Prayerfully live out your convictions in everyday life and trust God for the results.

Strengths and accomplishments:
• Although young when deported, remained true to his faith
• Served as a counselor to two Babylonian kings and two Medo-Persian kings
• Was a man of prayer and a statesman with the gift of prophecy
• Survived the lions' den

Lessons from his life:
• Quiet convictions often earn long-term respect
• Don't wait until you are in a tough situation to learn about prayer
• God can use people wherever they are

Vital statistics:
• Where: Judah and the courts of both Babylon and Persia
• Occupation: A captive from Israel who became a counselor of kings
• Contemporaries: Hananiah, Misha-el, Azariah, Nebuchadnezzar, Belshazzar, Darius, Cyrus

Key verse:
"Call for this man, Daniel—or Belteshazzar, as the king called him—for his mind is filled with divine knowledge and understanding. He can interpret dreams, explain riddles, and solve knotty problems. He will tell you what the writing means" (5:12).

Daniel's story is told in the book of Daniel. He is also mentioned in Matthew 24:15.

2:21 When we see evil leaders who live long and good leaders who die young, we may wonder if God controls world events. Daniel saw evil rulers with almost limitless power, but he knew and proclaimed that God controls everything that happens. The world is moving according to God's purposes and toward his specified ends. Let this knowledge give you confidence and peace no

matter what may happen in your life.

2:27-30 Before Daniel told the king anything else, he gave credit to God, explaining that he did not know the dream through his own wisdom but only because God revealed it. How easily we take credit for what God does through us! This robs God of the honor which is due him.

such things, 28but there is a God in heaven who reveals secrets, and he has told you in your dream what will happen in the future. This was your dream:

2:28
Gen 40:8; 41:16
Isa 41:21
Dan 2:22,45
Hos 3:5

29"You dreamed of coming events. He who reveals secrets was speaking to you. 30(But remember, it's not because I am wiser than any living person that I know this secret of your dream, for God showed it to me for your benefit.)

2:30
Gen 41:16
Ps 139:2
Isa 43:3
Dan 1:17
Acts 3:12
1 Cor 3:21-23

31"O king, you saw a huge and powerful statue of a man, shining brilliantly, frightening and terrible. 32The head of the statue was made of purest gold, its chest and arms were of silver, its belly and thighs of brass, 33its legs of iron, its feet part iron and part clay. 34But as you watched, a Rock was cut from the mountainside by supernatural means. It came hurtling toward the statue and crushed the feet of iron and clay, smashing them to bits. 35Then the whole statue collapsed into a heap of iron, clay, brass, silver, and gold; its pieces were crushed as small as chaff, and the wind blew them all away. But the Rock that knocked the statue down became a great mountain that covered the whole earth.

2:34
Dan 8:25
Zech 4:6

2:35
Ps 1:4
Isa 17:13
Hos 13:3

36"That was the dream; now for its meaning:

37"Your Majesty, you are a king over many kings, for the God of heaven has given you your kingdom, power, strength and glory. 38You rule the farthest provinces, and even animals and birds are under your control, as God decreed. You are that head of gold.

2:37
1 Kgs 4:24
Ezra 7:12
Isa 10:8; 47:5
Jer 27:6,7
Ezek 26:7
Hos 8:10
Rev 1:5; 17:14

39"But after your kingdom has come to an end, another world power will arise to take your place. This empire will be inferior to yours. And after that kingdom has fallen, yet a third great power—represented by the bronze belly of the statue—will rise to rule the world. 40Following it, the fourth kingdom will be strong as iron—smashing, bruising, and conquering. 41, 42The feet and toes you saw—part iron and part clay—show that later on, this kingdom will be divided. Some parts of it will be as strong as iron, and some as weak as clay. 43This mixture of iron with clay also shows that these kingdoms will try to strengthen themselves by forming alliances with each other through intermarriage of their rulers; but this will not succeed, for iron and clay don't mix.

2:38
Ps 50:10

2:44
Gen 49:10
Ps 2:9; 21:8,9
145:13
Isa 9:6,7
Ezek 37:25
Mic 4:7

44"During the reigns of those kings, the God of heaven will set up a kingdom that will never be destroyed; no one will ever conquer it. It will shatter all these kingdoms into nothingness, but it shall stand forever, indestructible. 45That is the meaning of the Rock cut from the mountain without human hands—the Rock that crushed to powder all the iron and brass, the clay, the silver, and the gold.

2:45
Gen 41:28,32
Deut 10:17
2 Sam 7:22
Dan 2:29
Rev 1:19; 4:1

"Thus the great God has shown what will happen in the future, and this interpretation of your dream is as sure and certain as my description of it."

2:46
Lev 26:31
Dan 3:5,7
Acts 10:25
Rev 19:10; 22:8

46Then Nebuchadnezzar fell to the ground before Daniel and worshiped him, and commanded his people to offer sacrifices and burn sweet incense before him.

2:47
Deut 10:17
Dan 3:15; 4:25
Amos 3:7

47"Truly, O Daniel," the king said, "your God is the God of gods, Ruler of kings, the Revealer of mysteries, because he has told you this secret."

48Then the king made Daniel very great; he gave him many valuable gifts, and appointed him to be ruler over the whole province of Babylon, as well as chief over all his wise men.

2:48
Gen 41:39-43
Dan 2:6
3:1,12,30; 5:16

49Then, at Daniel's request, the king appointed Shadrach, Meshach, and Abed-

2:49
Esth 2:19,21
Dan 3:12-30
Amos 5:15

2:34 *a Rock was cut from the mountainside,* implied.

2:31ff The head of gold represented Nebuchadnezzar, ruler of the Babylonian Empire. The silver chest and two arms represented the Medo-Persian Empire, which conquered Babylon in 539 B.C. The belly and thighs of bronze were Greece and Macedonia under Alexander the Great, who conquered the Medo-Persian Empire in 334–330 B.C. The legs of iron represented Rome, which conquered the Greeks in 63 B.C. The feet and toes of clay and iron represented the break-up of the Roman Empire, when the territory Rome ruled divided into a mixture of strong and weak nations. The type of metal in each part represented the strength of the political power it represented. The Rock cut from the mountain depicted God's Kingdom which would be ruled eternally by the Messiah, the King of kings.

2:47 Nebuchadnezzar honored Daniel and Daniel's God. If Daniel had taken the credit himself, the king would have honored only Daniel. Because Daniel gave God the credit, the king honored both of them. Part of our mission in this world is to show nonbelievers what God is like. We can do that by giving God credit for the great things he does in our lives. Our acts of love and compassion may impress people, but if we give God credit for our actions, they will want to know more about him. Give thanks to God for what he is doing in and through you.

2:49 After being named ruler over the whole province of Babylon and chief over the wise men, Daniel requested that his companions, Shadrach, Meshach, and Abednego, be appointed

nego as Daniel's assistants, to be in charge of all the affairs of the province of Babylon; Daniel served as chief magistrate in the king's court.

Four men in the fiery furnace

3 King Nebuchadnezzar made a gold statue ninety feet high and nine feet wide and set it up on the Plain of Dura, in the province of Babylon; 2then he sent messages to all the princes, governors, captains, judges, treasurers, counselors, sheriffs, and rulers of all the provinces of his empire, to come to the dedication of his statue. 3When they had all arrived and were standing before the monument, 4a herald shouted out, "O people of all nations and languages, this is the king's command:

3:1
Isa 46:6
Jer 16:20
Dan 2:31
Hab 2:19
3:2
Dan 3:3,27
6:1-7
3:4
Dan 3:7; 4:1

Shadrach/Meshach/Abednego

Friendships make life enjoyable and difficult times bearable. They are tested and strengthened by hardships. Such was the relationship between three young Jewish men deported to Babylon along with Daniel. Shadrach, Meshach, and Abednego help us think about the real meaning of friendship. As much as these friends meant to each other, they never allowed their friendship to usurp God's place in their lives—not even in the face of death.

Together they silently defied King Nebuchadnezzar's order to bow to and worship the idol he had made of himself. They shared a courageous act, while others, eager to get rid of them, told the king that the three Jews were being disloyal. While this was not true, Nebuchadnezzar could not spare them without shaming himself.

This was the moment of truth. Death was about to end their friendship. A small compromise would have allowed them to live and go on enjoying each other, serving God, and serving their people while in this foreign land. But they were wise enough to see that compromise would have poisoned the very conviction that bound them so closely—each had a higher allegiance to God. So they did not hesitate to place their lives in the hands of God. The rest was victory!

When we leave God out of our most important relationships, we tend to expect those relationships to meet needs in us that only God can meet. Friends are helpful, but they cannot meet our deepest spiritual needs. Leaving God out of our relationships indicates how unimportant he really is in our own lives. Our relationship with God should be important enough to touch our other relationships—especially our closest friendships.

Strengths and accomplishments:
• Stood with Daniel against eating food from the king's table
• Shared a friendship that stood the tests of hardship, success, wealth, and possible death
• Unwilling to compromise their convictions even in the face of death
• Survived the fiery furnace

Lessons from their lives:
• There is great strength in real friendship
• It is important to stand with others with whom we share convictions
• God can be trusted even when we can't predict the outcome

Vital statistics:
• Where: Babylon
• Occupations: King's servants and counselors
• Contemporaries: Daniel, Nebuchadnezzar

Key verses:
"Shadrach, Meshach, and Abednego replied, 'O Nebuchadnezzar, we are not worried about what will happen to us. If we are thrown into the flaming furnace, our God is able to deliver us; and he will deliver us out of your hand, Your Majesty. But if he doesn't, please understand, sir, that even then we will never under any circumstance serve your gods or worship the gold statue you have erected' " (3:16–18).

The story of Shadrach (Hananiah), Meshach (Misha-el), and Abednego (Azariah) is told in the book of Daniel.

his assistants. Daniel knew he could not handle such an enormous responsibility without capable assistants, so he chose the best men he knew—his three Hebrew companions. A competent leader never does all the work alone; he knows how to delegate and supervise. Moses, Israel's greatest leader, shared the burden of administration with dozens of assistants. (See his story in Exodus 18:13-27.)

3:1 In Babylon's religious culture, statues were frequently worshiped. Nebuchadnezzar hoped to use this statue as a strategy to unite the nation and solidify his power. This gold image may have been inspired by his dream. Instead of having only a head of gold, however, it was gold from head to toe: Nebuchadnezzar wanted his kingdom to last forever. When he made the statue, he showed that he did not understand the God behind the dream.

5"When the band strikes up, you are to fall flat on the ground to worship King Nebuchadnezzar's gold statue; 6anyone who refuses to obey will immediately be thrown into a flaming furnace."

7So when the band began to play, everyone—whatever his nation, language, or religion—fell to the ground and worshiped the statue.

8But some officials went to the king and accused some of the Jews of refusing to worship!

9"Your Majesty," they said to him, 10"you made a law that everyone must fall down and worship the gold statue when the band begins to play, 11and that anyone who refuses will be thrown into a flaming furnace. 12But there are some Jews out there—Shadrach, Meshach, and Abednego, whom you have put in charge of Babylonian affairs—who have defied you, refusing to serve your gods or to worship the gold statue you set up."

13Then Nebuchadnezzar, in a terrible rage, ordered Shadrach, Meshach, and Abednego to be brought in before him.

14"Is it true, O Shadrach, Meshach, and Abednego," he demanded, "that you are refusing to serve my gods or to worship the gold statue I set up? 15I'll give you one more chance. When the music plays, if you fall down and worship the statue, all will be well. But if you refuse, you will be thrown into a flaming furnace within the hour. And what god can deliver you out of my hands then?"

16Shadrach, Meshach, and Abednego replied, "O Nebuchadnezzar, we are not worried about what will happen to us. 17If we are thrown into the flaming furnace, our God is able to deliver us; and he will deliver us out of your hand, Your Majesty. 18But if he doesn't, please understand, sir, that even then we will never under any circumstance serve your gods or worship the gold statue you have erected." 19Then Nebuchadnezzar was filled with fury and his face became dark with anger at Shadrach, Meshach, and Abednego. He commanded that the furnace be heated up seven times hotter than usual, 20and called for some of the strongest men of his army to bind Shadrach, Meshach, and Abednego, and throw them into the fire.

21So they bound them tight with ropes and threw them into the furnace, fully clothed. 22And because the king, in his anger, had demanded such a hot fire in the furnace, the flames leaped out and killed the soldiers as they threw them in! 23So Shadrach, Meshach, and Abednego fell down bound into the roaring flames.

24But suddenly, as he was watching, Nebuchadnezzar jumped up in amazement and exclaimed to his advisors, "Didn't we throw three men into the furnace?"

"Yes," they said, "we did, Your Majesty."

3:5 *When the band,* literally, "the cornet, flute, harp, sackbut, psaltry, dulcimer, and every other sort of instrument." So also in vss 7 and 10.   **3:7** *whatever his nation, language, or religion,* implied.

Cross references (right margin):

3:5 Dan 3:7,10

3:6 Dan 3:11,15, 21; 6:7 Mt 13:42 Rev 9:2; 14:11

3:8 Ezra 4:12-16 Esth 3:8,9 Dan 6:12,13

3:10 Esth 3:12-14 Dan 3:4-6

3:13 Dan 2:12; 3:19

3:14 Ex 21:13,14 Isa 46:1 Dan 3:1; 4:8

3:15 Ex 5:2 Isa 36:18-20 Dan 2:47

3:16 Dan 1:7; 3:12

3:17 1 Sam 17:37 Ps 27:1,2 Isa 26:3,4 Jer 1:8

3:18 Josh 24:15 1 Kgs 19:14 Dan 3:28 Lk 12:3-9 Rev 12:11

3:19 Lev 26:18-28 Dan 3:13

3:22 Dan 2:15

3:6 This flaming furnace was not a small oven for cooking dinner or heating a house. It was a huge industrial furnace that could have been used for baking bricks or smelting metals. The temperatures were hot enough to assure that no one could survive its heat. The roaring flames could be seen leaping from its top opening, and a fiery blast killed the soldiers who went up to the furnace door (3:22).

3:12 Why didn't the three men just bow to the image and tell God that they didn't mean it? They had determined never to worship another god, and they courageously took their stand. As a result, they were condemned and led away to be executed. They did not know whether they would be delivered from the fire; all they knew was that they would not bow to an idol. Are you ready to take a stand for God no matter what? When you stand for God, you will stand out. It may be painful, and it may not always have a happy ending. Be prepared to say, "If he delivers me, or if he doesn't, I will serve only God."

3:15 The three men had one more chance. Here are eight excuses they could have used to bow to the statue and save their lives: (1) We will bow down but not actually *worship* the idol. (2) We won't become idol worshipers, but will do this one time, then ask God for forgiveness. (3) The king has absolute power and we must obey him. God will understand. (4) The king appointed us—we owe this to him. (5) This is a foreign land so God will excuse us for following the customs of the land. (6) Our ancestors set up idols in God's Temple! This isn't half as bad! (7) We're not hurting anybody. (8) If we get ourselves killed and some heathens take our high positions, they won't help our people in exile!

Although all these excuses sound sensible at first, they are dangerous. To bow down to the image would violate God's command in Exodus 20:3, "You may worship no other god than me." It would also erase their testimony for God forever. Never again could they talk about the power of their God above all other gods. What excuses do you use for not standing up for him?

3:16-18 Shadrach, Meshach, and Abednego were pressured to deny God, but they chose to be faithful to him no matter what happened! They trusted God to deliver them, but they were determined to be faithful regardless of the consequences. If God always rescued those who are true to him, Christians would not need faith. Their religion would be a great insurance policy, and there would be lines of selfish people ready to sign up. We should be faithful to God whether he intervenes on our behalf or not. Our eternal reward is worth any suffering we may have to endure first.

3:25
Ps 91:3-9
Jer 1:8,19

3:26
Deut 4:20
1 Kgs 8:51
Dan 3:17; 4:2

3:27
Dan 3:21
Heb 11:34

3:28
Ps 34:7,8
Isa 37:36
Dan 3:25; 6:22
Acts 5:19; 12:7

3:29
Ezra 6:11
Dan 3:12,15

3:30
Dan 2:49; 3:12

4:3
Deut 4:34
Isa 25:1
Dan 2:44; 4:34
6:26

4:4
Isa 47:7,8
Zeph 1:12

4:5
Job 7:13,14
Dan 4:10,13

4:7
Isa 44:25
Jer 27:9,10
Dan 2:7

4:8
Num 11:17
Isa 63:11
Dan 1:7; 4:9,18

4:12
Jer 27:6,7
Ezek 31:7

4:13
Deut 33:2
Dan 8:13

4:14
Jer 51:5,6
Ezek 31:10-14
Rev 10:3; 18:2

25"Well, look!" Nebuchadnezzar shouted. "I see *four* men, unbound, walking around in the fire, and they aren't even hurt by the flames! And the fourth looks like a god!"

26Then Nebuchadnezzar came as close as he could to the open door of the flaming furnace and yelled: "Shadrach, Meshach, and Abednego, servants of the Most High God! Come out! Come here!" So they stepped out of the fire.

27Then the princes, governors, captains, and counselors crowded around them and saw that the fire hadn't touched them—not a hair of their heads was singed; their coats were unscorched, and they didn't even smell of smoke!

28Then Nebuchadnezzar said, "Blessed be the God of Shadrach, Meshach, and Abednego, for he sent his angel to deliver his trusting servants when they defied the king's commandment, and were willing to die rather than serve or worship any god except their own. 29Therefore, I make this decree, that any person of any nation, language, or religion who speaks a word against the God of Shadrach, Meshach, and Abednego shall be torn limb from limb and his house knocked into a heap of rubble. For no other God can do what this one does."

30Then the king gave promotions to Shadrach, Meshach, and Abednego, so that they prospered greatly there in the province of Babylon.

The king dreams about a tree

4 This is the proclamation of Nebuchadnezzar the king, which he sent to people of every language in every nation of the world:

Greetings: 2I want you all to know about the strange thing that the Most High God did to me. 3It was incredible—a mighty miracle! And now I know for sure that his kingdom is everlasting; he reigns forever and ever.

4I, Nebuchadnezzar, was living in peace and prosperity, 5when one night I had a dream that greatly frightened me. 6I called in all the wise men of Babylon to tell me the meaning of my dream, 7but when they came—the magicians, astrologers, fortunetellers, and wizards—and I told them the dream, they couldn't interpret it. 8At last Daniel came in—the man I named Belteshazzar after my god—the man in whom is the spirit of the holy gods, and I told him the dream.

9"O Belteshazzar, master magician," I said, "I know that the spirit of the holy gods is in you and no mystery is too great for you to solve. Tell me what my dream means:

10, 11"I saw a very tall tree out in a field, growing higher and higher into the sky until it could be seen by everyone in all the world. 12Its leaves were fresh and green, and its branches were weighted down with fruit, enough for everyone to eat. Wild animals rested beneath its shade and birds sheltered in its branches, and all the world was fed from it. 13Then as I lay there dreaming, I saw one of God's angels coming down from heaven.

14"He shouted, 'Cut down the tree; lop off its branches; shake off its leaves, and scatter its fruit. Get the animals out from under it and the birds from its branches,

3:25 Literally, "looks like a son of the gods." **3:29** *of any nation, language, or religion,* implied. **4:13** *one of God's angels,* literally, "a watcher, a holy one."

3:25 It was obvious to those watching that this fourth person was not human. We cannot be certain who the fourth man was. It could have been an angel or a pre-incarnate appearance of Christ. In either case, God sent a heavenly visitor to accompany these faithful men during their time of great trial.

3:27 These young men were completely untouched by the fire and heat. No scorch mark was found on them, and they didn't even smell of smoke! Only the rope that bound them had been burned. No human can bind us if God wants us to be free. The power available to us is the same that delivered Shadrach, Meshach, and Abednego and raised Christ from the dead (Ephesians 1:19, 20). Trust God in the midst of every trial. There are eternal reasons for temporary trials; we can be thankful that our destiny is in God's hands, not man's.

3:28, 29 Nebuchadnezzar was not making a commitment here to

serve Daniel's God alone. Instead, he acknowledged that God is powerful, and he commanded his people not to speak against him. He didn't say the people should throw away all the other gods, but that they should add this one to the list.

3:30 Where was Daniel in this story? The Bible doesn't say, but there are several possibilities. (1) He may have been on official business in another part of the kingdom. (2) He may have been present, but because he was a ruler, the officials didn't accuse him of not bowing down to the idol. (3) He could have been in the capital city handling the administration while Nebuchadnezzar was away. (4) He could have been considered exempt from bowing to the idol because of his reputation for interpreting dreams through his God. Whether Daniel was there or not, we can be sure that he would not have bowed to the idol.

15but leave its stump and roots in the ground, banded with a chain of iron and brass, surrounded by the tender grass. Let the dews of heaven drench him and let him eat grass with the wild animals! 16For seven years let him have the mind of an animal instead of a man. 17For this has been decreed by the Watchers, demanded by the Holy Ones. The purpose of this decree is that all the world may understand that the Most High dominates the kingdoms of the world, and gives them to anyone he wants to, even the lowliest of men!'

18"O Belteshazzar, that was my dream; now tell me what it means. For no one else can help me; all the wisest men of my kingdom have failed me. But you can tell me, for the spirit of the holy gods is in you."

19Then Daniel sat there stunned and silent for an hour, aghast at the meaning of the dream. Finally the king said to him: "Belteshazzar, don't be afraid to tell me what it means."

Daniel replied: "Oh, that the events foreshadowed in this dream would happen to your enemies, my lord, and not to you! 20For the tree you saw growing so tall, reaching high into the heavens for all the world to see, 21with its fresh green leaves, loaded with fruit for all to eat, the wild animals living in its shade, with its branches full of birds— 22that tree, Your Majesty, is you. For you have grown strong and great; your greatness reaches up to heaven, and your rule to the ends of the earth.

23"Then you saw God's angel coming down from heaven and saying, 'Cut down the tree and destroy it, but leave the stump and the roots in the earth surrounded by tender grass, banded with a chain of iron and brass. Let him be wet with the dew of heaven. For seven years let him eat grass with the animals of the field.'

24"Your Majesty, the Most High God has decreed—and it will surely happen— 25that your people will chase you from your palace, and you will live in the fields like an animal, eating grass like a cow, your back wet with dew from heaven. For seven years this will be your life, until you learn that the Most High God dominates the kingdoms of men, and gives power to anyone he chooses. 26But the stump and the roots were left in the ground! This means that you will get your kingdom back again, when you have learned that heaven rules.

27"O King Nebuchadnezzar, listen to me—stop sinning; do what you know is right; be merciful to the poor. Perhaps even yet God will spare you."

28But all these things happened to Nebuchadnezzar. 29Twelve months after this dream, he was strolling on the roof of the royal palace in Babylon, 30and saying, "I, by my own mighty power, have built this beautiful city as my royal residence, and as the capital of my empire."

31While he was still speaking these words, a voice called down from heaven, "O King Nebuchadnezzar, this message is for you: You are no longer ruler of this kingdom. 32You will be forced out of the palace to live with the animals in the fields, and to eat grass like the cows for seven years until you finally realize that God parcels out the kingdoms of men and gives them to anyone he chooses."

33That very same hour this prophecy was fulfilled. Nebuchadnezzar was chased from his palace and ate grass like the cows, and his body was wet with dew; his hair grew as long as eagles' feathers, and his nails were like birds' claws.

4:19 *Then Daniel,* literally, "Daniel, whose name was Belteshazzar." 4:23 *God's angel,* literally, "a holy watcher."

4:15 Job 14:7-9
4:16 1 Chron 29:30 / Isa 6:10 / Dan 4:23-25 / 7:25 / Heb 1:11
4:17 Ex 9:16 / 1 Sam 2:8 / Ps 9:16 / Dan 4:25; 11:21
4:18 Gen 41:8 / 1 Kgs 14:2,3 / Dan 4:7; 5:8
4:19 1 Sam 3:17 / 2 Sam 18:32 / 1 Kgs 18:7 / Dan 7:15,28 / 8:27
4:22 Jer 27:6,7 / Dan 2:37,38
4:25 Job 40:11,12 / Ps 75:7; 107:40 / Jer 27:5 / Dan 4:17,33 / 5:21
4:26 Dan 4:31
4:27 Gen 41:33-37 / 2 Sam 12:7 / 1 Kgs 21:29 / Ps 41:1-3 / 119:46 / Prov 28:13 / Isa 55:6,7 / Jonah 3:9
4:28 Num 23:19 / Zech 1:6
4:29 2 Pet 3:9
4:30 Hab 2:4
4:33 Dan 4:25; 5:21

4:17 Babylonians believed in *Watchers,* spiritual beings who watch over the universe. Nebuchadnezzar explained that these messengers were announcing what would happen to him and why.

4:19 When Daniel understood Nebuchadnezzar's dream, he was stunned. How could he be so deeply grieved at the fate of Nebuchadnezzar—the king who was responsible for the destruction of his home and nation? Daniel had forgiven him, and so God was able to use Daniel. Very often when we have been wronged by someone, we find it difficult to forget the past. We may even be glad if that person suffers. Forgiving people means putting the past behind us. Can you love someone who has hurt you? Ask God to help you forgive, forget, and love. God may use you in an extraordinary way in that person's life!

4:19 Although the entire world thought Nebuchadnezzar was a mighty (even divine) king, God demonstrated that he was an ordinary man. God humiliated Nebuchadnezzar to show that he, not Nebuchadnezzar, was Lord of the nations.

4:28 Ancient kings tried to avoid mentioning their weaknesses or defeats in their monuments and official records. From Nebuchadnezzar's records, however, we can infer that for a time during his 43-year reign he did not rule. In the scriptural account Nebuchadnezzar's pride and punishment are explained.

4:29, 30 Daniel pleaded with Nebuchadnezzar to change his ways, and God gave him 12 months in which to do it. Unfortunately, there was no repentance in the heart of this king, and so the dream was fulfilled.

4:34
Jer 10:10
Dan 4:2
5:18,21

4:35
Job 42:2
Isa 43:13
Dan 6:27
Acts 4:28

4:36
Dan 4:22,34
2 Cor 4:17

³⁴"At the end of seven years I, Nebuchadnezzar, looked up to heaven, and my sanity returned, and I praised and worshiped the Most High God and honored him who lives forever, whose rule is everlasting, his kingdom evermore. ³⁵All the people of the earth are nothing when compared to him; he does whatever he thinks best among the angels of heaven, as well as here on earth. No one can stop him or challenge him, saying, 'What do you mean by doing these things?' ³⁶When my mind returned to me, so did my honor and glory and kingdom. My counselors and officers came back to me and I was reestablished as head of my kingdom, with even greater honor than before.

4:34 *At the end of seven years,* literally, "At the end of the days."

NEBUCHADNEZZAR

Nebuchadnezzar was one world leader who decided he could get more cooperation from the people he conquered by letting them keep their gods. Their lands he took, their riches he looted, their lives he controlled, but he allowed them to worship their idols, sometimes even worshiping them himself. Nebuchadnezzar's plan worked well, with one glaring exception. When he conquered the little nation of Judah, he met a God who demanded *exclusive* worship—not just his share among many gods. In a sense, Nebuchadnezzar had always been able to rule the gods. This new God was different; this God dared to claim that he had made Nebuchadnezzar all that he was. One of the great conquerors in history was himself conquered by his Creator.

The Bible allows us to note the ways in which God worked on Nebuchadnezzar. God allowed him victories, but he was accomplishing God's purposes. God allowed him to deport the best young Jewish leaders as his palace servants, while placing close to him a young man named Daniel who would change the king's life. God allowed Nebuchadnezzar to attempt to kill three of his servants to teach the king that he did not really have power over life and death. God warned him of the dangers in his pride, then allowed Nebuchadnezzar to live through seven years of mental illness before restoring him to the throne. God showed the king who was really in control!

These lessons are clear to us today because of our place in history. When our attention shifts to our own lives, we find ourselves unable to see how God is working today. But we do have the advantage of God's Word as our guide for today's challenges. We are commanded to obey God; we are also commanded to trust him. Trusting him covers those times when we are not sure about the outcome. God has entrusted us with this day; have we trusted him with our lives?

Strengths and accomplishments:
- Greatest of the Babylonian kings
- Known as a builder of cities
- Described in the Bible as one of the foreign rulers God used for his purposes

Weaknesses and mistakes:
- Thought of himself as a god and was persuaded to build a statue of himself that all were to worship
- Became extremely proud, which led to a bout of mental illness
- Tended to forget the demonstrations of God's power he had witnessed

Lessons from his life:
- History records the actions of God's willing servants and those who were his unwitting tools
- A leader's greatness is affected by the quality of his counselors
- Uncontrolled pride is self-destructive

Vital statistics:
- Where: Babylon
- Occupation: King
- Relatives: Father: Nabopolassar. Son: Evil-Merodach. Grandson: Belshazzar.
- Contemporaries: Jeremiah, Ezekiel, Daniel, Jehoiakim, Jehoiachin

Key verse:
" 'Now, I, Nebuchadnezzar, praise and glorify and honor the King of Heaven, the Judge of all, whose every act is right and good; for he is able to take those who walk proudly and push them into the dust!' " (4:37).

Nebuchadnezzar's story is told in 2 Kings 24, 25; 2 Chronicles 36; Jeremiah 21—52; Daniel 1—4.

4:34 Nebuchadnezzar's pilgrimage with God is one of the themes of this book. In 2:47, he acknowledged that God revealed dreams to Daniel. In 3:28, 29 he praised the God who delivered the three Hebrews. Despite Nebuchadnezzar's recognition that God exists and works great miracles, in 4:30 we see that he still did not acknowledge God as his own ruler. We may recognize that God exists and does wonderful miracles, but God is not going to shape our lives until we acknowledge him as Lord.

37"Now, I, Nebuchadnezzar, praise and glorify and honor the King of Heaven, the Judge of all, whose every act is right and good; for he is able to take those who walk proudly and push them into the dust!"

4:37
Ex 18:11
1 Sam 2:3
Mt 11:25

Daniel interprets the writing on the wall

5 Belshazzar the king invited a thousand of his officers to a great feast where the wine flowed freely. 2, 3, 4While Belshazzar was drinking he was reminded of the gold and silver cups taken long before from the Temple in Jerusalem during Nebuchadnezzar's reign, and brought to Babylon. Belshazzar ordered that these sacred cups be brought in to the feast, and when they arrived he and his princes, wives, and concubines drank toasts from them to their idols made of gold and silver, brass and iron, wood and stone.

5:1
Esth 1:3
Isa 22:12-14
5:2
2 Kgs 24:13
2 Chron 36:10,
18
Ezra 1:7-11
Jer 27:7
Dan 1:2; 3:1
Hab 2:19

5Suddenly, as they were drinking from these cups, they saw the fingers of a man's hand writing on the plaster of the wall opposite the lampstand. The king himself saw the fingers as they wrote. 6His face blanched with fear, and such terror gripped him that his knees knocked together and his legs gave way beneath him.

5:6
Ps 69:23
Dan 7:28
Nah 2:10

7"Bring the magicians and astrologers!" he screamed. "Bring the Chaldeans! Whoever reads that writing on the wall, and tells me what it means, will be dressed in purple robes of royal honor with a gold chain around his neck, and become the third ruler in the kingdom!"

5:7
Gen 41:42-44
Isa 44:25
Ezek 16:11
Dan 5:11,16,
29; 6:2,3

8But when they came, none of them could understand the writing or tell him what it meant.

9The king grew more and more hysterical; his face reflected the terror he felt, and his officers too were shaken. 10But when the queen-mother heard what was happening, she rushed to the banquet hall and said to Belshazzar, "Calm yourself, Your Majesty, don't be so pale and frightened over this. 11For there is a man in your kingdom who has within him the spirit of the holy gods. In the days of your father this man was found to be as full of wisdom and understanding as though he were himself a god. And in the reign of King Nebuchadnezzar, he was made chief of all the magicians, astrologers, Chaldeans and soothsayers of Babylon. 12Call for this man, Daniel—or Belteshazzar, as the king called him—for his mind is filled with divine knowledge and understanding. He can interpret dreams, explain riddles, and solve knotty problems. He will tell you what the writing means."

5:9
Job 18:11-14
Ps 18:14
Isa 21:2-4
Jer 6:24
Dan 5:6
Mt 2:3
5:10
Dan 3:9; 6:6
5:11
Gen 41:11-15
2 Sam 14:17
Dan 2:47
4:8,9; 5:14
Acts 16:16
5:12
Dan 5:14; 6:3

13So Daniel was rushed in to see the king. The king asked him, "Are you the Daniel brought from Israel as a captive by King Nebuchadnezzar? 14I have heard that you have the spirit of the gods within you and that you are filled with enlightenment and wisdom. 15My wise men and astrologers have tried to read that writing on the wall, and tell me what it means, but they can't. 16I am told you can solve all kinds of mysteries. If you can tell me the meaning of those words, I will clothe you in purple robes, with a gold chain around your neck, and make you the third ruler in the kingdom."

5:13
Dan 1:1; 2:25
5:15
Isa 47:12
Dan 5:8

17Daniel answered, "Keep your gifts, or give them to someone else, but I will tell

5:17
2 Kgs 5:16

5:11 And in the reign of King Nebuchadnezzar, literally, "King Nebuchadnezzar your father"—the Aramaic word for "father" can also mean "predecessor," in this instance, fifth removed.

5:1 Sixty-six years have elapsed since chapter 1, which tells of Nebuchadnezzar's strike against Jerusalem in 605 B.C. Nebuchadnezzar died in 562 B.C. after a reign of 43 years. His son, Awel-Marduk (Evil-Merodach), ruled from 562–560 B.C.; his brother-in-law Neriglissar reigned four years from 560–556 B.C. After a two-month reign by Labashi-Marduk in 556 B.C., the Babylonian Empire continued from 556–539 B.C. under the command of Nabonidus. Belshazzar was the son of Nabonidus. He co-reigned with his father from 553–539 B.C.

5:1 Archeologists have recently discovered Belshazzar's name on several documents. He ruled with his father, Nabonidus, staying home to administer the affairs of the kingdom while his father tried to reopen trade routes taken over by Cyrus and the Persians. Belshazzar was in charge when Cyrus captured Babylon.

5:7 Belshazzar served as co-regent with his father Nabonidus. Thus, Nabonidus was first ruler and his son Belshazzar, the second. The person who could read the writing would be given third place.

5:8 Although the writing on the wall was only three words in Aramaic, a language understood by Babylonians, the people could not determine its prophetic significance. God gave Daniel alone the ability to interpret the message of doom to Babylon.

5:10 This queen mother was either Nabonidus' wife or the wife of one of his predecessors, possibly even of Nebuchadnezzar. She was not Belshazzar's wife, for his wives were with him in the banquet hall.

5:17 The king offered Daniel beautiful gifts and great power if he

5:18
Deut 32:8
Dan 2:37
4:2,17; 5:21

5:19
Prov 16:14
Dan 2:12; 3:6
11:3

5:20
Ex 9:17
Prov 16:5,18
Isa 14:13-15
Jer 13:18
Dan 4:30
Lk 18:14

5:21
Ex 9:14-16
Ezek 17:24

5:22
Ex 10:3
2 Chron 33:23
36:12
Acts 4:8-13

5:23
2 Kgs 14:10
Job 12:10
Jer 50:29
Dan 5:3,4
Hab 2:18,19
1 Cor 8:4

5:26
Job 14:14
Isa 13:6,17
Jer 25:11
Acts 15:18

5:28
Isa 21:2; 45:1,2
Dan 5:31; 6:28

5:30
Isa 21:4-9
Jer 51:11,31,
39,57

6:2
Ezra 4:22
Esth 7:4
Dan 2:48,49
5:16,29
Mt 18:23

6:3
Gen 41:40
Eccles 2:13
Dan 5:12

you what the writing means. [18]Your Majesty, the Most High God gave Nebuchadnezzar, who long ago preceded you, a kingdom and majesty and glory and honor. [19]He gave him such majesty that all the nations of the world trembled before him in fear. He killed any who offended him, and spared any he liked. At his whim they rose or fell. [20]But when his heart and mind were hardened in pride, God removed him from his royal throne and took away his glory, [21]and he was chased out of his palace into the fields. His thoughts and feelings became those of an animal, and he lived among the wild donkeys; he ate grass like the cows and his body was wet with the dew of heaven, until at last he knew that the Most High overrules the kingdoms of men, and that he appoints anyone he desires to reign over them.

[22]"And you, his successor, O Belshazzar—you knew all this, yet you have not been humble. [23]For you have defied the Lord of Heaven, and brought here these cups from his Temple; and you and your officers and wives and concubines have been drinking wine from them while praising gods of silver, gold, brass, iron, wood, and stone—gods that neither see nor hear, nor know anything at all. But you have not praised the God who gives you the breath of life and controls your destiny! [24, 25]And so God sent those fingers to write this message: 'Mene,' 'Mene,' 'Tekel,' 'Parsin.'

[26]"This is what it means:

"Mene means 'numbered'—God has numbered the days of your reign, and they are ended.

[27]"Tekel means 'weighed'—you have been weighed in God's balances and have failed the test.

[28]"Parsin means 'divided'—your kingdom will be divided and given to the Medes and Persians."

[29]Then at Belshazzar's command, Daniel was robed in purple, and a gold chain was hung around his neck, and he was proclaimed third ruler in the kingdom.

[30]That very night Belshazzar, the Chaldean king, was killed, [31]and Darius the Mede entered the city and began reigning at the age of sixty-two.

Daniel in the lion's den

6 Darius divided the kingdom into 120 provinces, each under a governor. [2]The governors were accountable to three presidents (Daniel was one of them) so the king could administer the kingdom efficiently.

[3]Daniel soon proved himself more capable than all the other presidents and governors, for he had great ability, and the king began to think of placing him over the entire empire as his administrative officer.

[4]This made the other presidents and governors very jealous, and they began

---

would explain the writing, but Daniel turned him down. He was not showing disrespect in refusing the gifts, but he knew they would be short-lived and he wanted to show that he was giving an unbiased interpretation to the king.

5:22 Belshazzar knew Babylonian history, and so he knew how God had humbled Nebuchadnezzar. Nevertheless, his banquet was a rebellious challenge to God's authority. No one who understands that God is the Creator of the universe would be foolish enough to challenge him.

5:27 The handwriting on the wall was for Belshazzar. Although Belshazzar had power and wealth, his kingdom was totally corrupt and he could not withstand the judgment of God. God's time of judgment comes for all people. Turn away from your sin now. Ask God to forgive you, and begin to live by his standards of justice.

5:28 The Medes and Persians joined forces to overthrow Babylon. This event began the second phase of Nebuchadnezzar's dream in chapter 2—the silver chest and arms.

5:31 Darius and his soldiers entered Babylon by diverting the river that ran through the city, then walking in on the dry river bed.

5:31 This Darius is not to be confused with Darius I, mentioned in

Ezra, Haggai, and Zechariah, or Darius II (the Persian), mentioned in Nehemiah. Darius the Mede is named only in the book of Daniel. Other records name no king between Belshazzar and Cyrus. Thus, Darius may have been (1) appointed by Cyrus to rule over Babylon as a province of Persia, (2) another name for Cyrus himself or for his son, Cambyses, or (3) a descendant of Ahasuerus who is usually called Xerxes I.

6:1-3 At this time, Daniel was in his eighties and one of Darius' top three administrators. He was working with those who did not believe in his God, but he worked more efficiently and capably than all the rest. Thus, he attracted the attention of the pagan king and earned a place of respect. One of the best ways to influence non-Christian employers is to work hard. How do you represent God to your employer?

6:4, 5 The jealous officials couldn't find anything about Daniel's life to criticize, so they attacked his religion. If you face jealous critics because of your faith, be glad they're criticizing that part of your life—perhaps they had to focus on your religion as a last resort! Respond by continuing to believe and live as you should. Then remember that God is in control, fighting this battle for you.

searching for some fault in the way Daniel was handling his affairs so that they could complain to the king about him. But they couldn't find anything to criticize! He was faithful and honest, and made no mistakes. 5So they concluded, "Our only chance is his religion!"

6They decided to go to the king and say, "King Darius, live forever! 7We presidents, governors, counselors and deputies have unanimously decided that you should make a law, irrevocable under any circumstance, that for the next thirty days anyone who asks a favor of God or man—except from you, Your Majesty—shall be thrown to the lions. 8Your Majesty, we request your signature on this law; sign it so that it cannot be canceled or changed; it will be a 'law of the Medes and Persians' that cannot be revoked."

9So King Darius signed the law.

10But though Daniel knew about it, he went home and knelt down as usual in his upstairs bedroom, with its windows open toward Jerusalem, and prayed three times a day, just as he always had, giving thanks to his God.

11Then the men thronged to Daniel's house and found him praying there, asking favors of his God. 12They rushed back to the king and reminded him about his law. "Haven't you signed a decree," they demanded, "that permits no petitions to any God or man—except you—for thirty days? And anyone disobeying will be thrown to the lions?"

"Yes," the king replied, "it is 'a law of the Medes and Persians,' that cannot be altered or revoked."

13Then they told the king, "That fellow Daniel, one of the Jewish captives, is paying no attention to you or your law. He is asking favors of his God three times a day."

14Hearing this, the king was very angry with himself for signing the law, and determined to save Daniel. He spent the rest of the day trying to think of some way to get Daniel out of this predicament.

15In the evening the men came again to the king and said, "Your Majesty, there is nothing you can do. You signed the law and it cannot be changed."

16So at last the king gave the order for Daniel's arrest, and he was taken to the den of lions. The king said to him, "May your God, whom you worship continually, deliver you." And then they threw him in. 17A stone was brought and placed over the mouth of the den; and the king sealed it with his own signet ring, and that of his government, so that no one could rescue Daniel from the lions.

18Then the king returned to his palace and went to bed without dinner. He refused his usual entertainment and didn't sleep all night. 19Very early the next morning he hurried out to the lions' den, 20and called out in anguish, "O Daniel, servant of the Living God, was your God, whom you worship continually, able to deliver you from the lions?"

21Then he heard a voice! "Your Majesty, live forever!" It was Daniel! 22"My God has sent his angel," he said, "to shut the lions' mouths so that they can't touch me; for I am innocent before God, nor, sir, have I wronged you."

23The king was beside himself with joy and ordered Daniel lifted from the den. And not a scratch was found on him, because he believed in his God.

24Then the king issued a command to bring the men who had accused Daniel, and

6:5
1 Sam 24:17
Jn 19:6,7
Acts 24:13-16

6:7
Ps 62:4; 64:2-6
Dan 6:16
Mt 12:14

6:8
Esth 3:12; 8:10
Isa 10:1
Dan 6:12,13
Mt 24:35

6:9
Ps 62:9,10
118:9

6:10
1 Kgs 8:48,49
2 Chron 6:38
Ps 34:1
Dan 9:4-19
Col 3:17
1 Thess 5:17,18

6:11
Ps 37:32,33
Dan 6:6

6:12
Esth 1:19
Dan 3:8-12; 6:8

6:13
Esth 3:8
Dan 3:12
Acts 5:29; 17:7

6:14
Mk 6:26

6:15
Esth 8:8
Ps 94:20,21
Dan 6:8,12

6:16
Job 5:19
Ps 37:39,40
Jer 38:5
Dan 6:20

6:17
Lam 3:53
Mt 27:66
Acts 12:4

6:18
2 Sam 12:16,17
Rev 18:22

6:20
Jer 32:17
Dan 3:17
Hos 12:6

6:22
Num 20:16
Ps 91:11-13
Acts 12:11
2 Tim 4:17
Heb 11:33

6:23
Ps 118:8
Isa 26:3
Dan 3:17,28

6:24
Deut 19:18,19
Prov 11:8
Isa 38:13

6:8, 9 In Babylon, the king's word *was* the law. In the Medo-Persian Empire, however, when a law was made, even the king couldn't change it. Darius was an effective government administrator, but he had a fatal flaw—pride. By appealing to his pride, the men talked him into signing a law effectively making himself a god for 30 days. This law could not be broken—not even by an important official like Daniel. Another example of the irrevocable nature of the laws of the Medes and Persians appears in Esther 8:8.

6:10 Although Daniel knew about the law against praying, he still prayed three times a day, "as he always had." Daniel had a disciplined prayer life. Our prayers are usually interrupted not by threats, but simply by the pressure of our schedules. Don't let threats or pressures cut into your prayer time. Pray regularly, no matter what.

6:17 Lions roamed the countryside and forests in Mesopotamia, and the ancient people had great respect for them. Some kings hunted lions for sport. The Persians captured lions, keeping them in large parks where they were fed and attended. Lions were also used for executing people.

6:24 In accordance with Persian custom, this cruel punishment was transferred to those who had conspired against the king by flattering him into an unjust action. The king's great anger resulted in the execution of the criminals and their families.

throw them into the den along with their children and wives, and the lions leaped upon them and tore them apart before they even hit the bottom of the den.

6:25
Ezra 1:1,2
Ps 93:1,2
Dan 3:29; 4:1
6:20
Hos 1:10
1 Pet 1:2

25, 26Afterward King Darius wrote this message addressed to everyone in his empire:

"Greetings! I decree that everyone shall tremble and fear before the God of Daniel in every part of my kingdom. For his God is the living, unchanging God whose kingdom shall never be destroyed and whose power shall never end. 27He delivers his people, preserving them from harm; he does great miracles in heaven and earth; it is he who delivered Daniel from the power of the lions."

28So Daniel prospered in the reign of Darius, and in the reign of Cyrus the Persian.

B. DANIEL'S VISIONS (7:1—12:13)

Daniel had many dreams and visions which he did not understand. He dreamed of four beasts which represented four kingdoms of the world, and of a ram and goat, which depicted two of those kingdoms in greater detail. Daniel's visions reveal that the Messiah will be the Ruler of a spiritual kingdom that will overpower and overshadow all other earthly kingdoms. We should interpret all of history in light of God's eternal kingdom.

Daniel dreams of four beasts

7:1
Num 12:6
Job 33:14-16
Dan 1:7
2:1,26-28
4:5-9
Jer 36:4
Joel 2:28

7 One night during the first year of Belshazzar's reign over the Babylonian empire, Daniel had a dream and he wrote it down. This is his description of what he saw:

7:2
Rev 7:1

2In my dream I saw a great storm on a mighty ocean, with strong winds blowing from every direction. 3Then four huge animals came up out of the water, each different from the other. 4The first was like a lion, but it had eagle's wings! And as

7:3
Rev 13:1

I watched, its wings were pulled off so that it could no longer fly, and it was left standing on the ground, on two feet, like a man; and a man's mind was given to it.

KINGS DANIEL SERVED	Name	Empire	Story told in	Memorable event
	Nebuchadnezzar	Babylon	chapters 1—4	Shadrach, Meshach, and Abednego thrown into fiery furnace; Nebuchadnezzar went mad for 7 years
	Belshazzar	Babylon	chapters 5, 7, 8	Daniel read the writing on the wall that signaled the end of the Babylonian Empire
	Darius	Medo-Persia	chapters 6, 9	Daniel thrown into a lions' den
	Cyrus	Medo-Persia	chapters 10—12	The exiles return to their homeland in Judah and their capital city, Jerusalem

6:25–27 Nebuchadnezzar believed in God because of the faithfulness of Daniel and his friends. Now Darius was also convinced of God's power because Daniel was faithful and God delivered him. Although Daniel was captive in a strange land, his devotion to God was a testimony to powerful rulers. If you find yourself in new surroundings, take the opportunity to testify about God's power in your life. Be faithful to God so he can use you to reach others.

7:1 Chronologically, this chapter takes place before chapter five. At this time, Belshazzar had just been given a position of authority (553 B.C.) and Daniel was probably in his late sixties. Chapter seven begins the second division of the book of Daniel. The first six chapters present history; the last six chapters are prophecies about the future.

7:1ff Daniel had a vision of four animals, each representing a world empire. This was similar to Nebuchadnezzar's dream in chapter two. Nebuchadnezzar's dream covered the political aspects of the empires; Daniel's dream depicted their moral aspects. These nations, who would reign over Israel, were evil and

cruel; but Daniel also saw God's future kingdom arrive and conquer them all.

7:4–7 The lion with eagle's wings represents Babylon with her swift conquests (statues of winged lions have been recovered from Babylon's ruins). The bear who ravaged the lion is Medo-Persia. The three ribs in its mouth represent the conquests of three major enemies. The leopard is Greece. Its wings show the swiftness of Alexander the Great's campaign as he conquered much of the civilized world in four years. The leopard's four heads are the four divisions of the Greek Empire after Alexander's death.

The fourth beast was not a world power which Daniel recognized; it represents Rome and the end times. Many Bible scholars believe that the horns correspond to ten kings who will reign shortly before God sets up his never-ending kingdom (Revelation 17:12). These ten kings had still not come to power at the time of John's vision recorded in the book of Revelation. The little horn is a future human ruler or the Antichrist (2 Thessalonians 2:3, 4).

5The second animal looked like a bear with its paw raised, ready to strike. It held three ribs between its teeth, and I heard a voice saying to it, "Get up! Devour many people!" 6The third of these strange animals looked like a leopard, but on its back it had wings like those of birds, and it had four heads! And great power was given to it over all mankind.

7Then, as I watched in my dream, a fourth animal rose up out of the ocean, too dreadful to describe and incredibly strong. It devoured some of its victims by tearing them apart with its huge iron teeth, and others it crushed beneath its feet. It was far more brutal and vicious than any of the other animals, and it had ten horns.

7:7
Rev 12:3; 13:1

8As I was looking at the horns, suddenly another small horn appeared among them, and three of the first ones were yanked out, roots and all, to give it room; this little horn had a man's eyes and a bragging mouth.

9I watched as thrones were put in place and the Ancient of Days—the Almighty God—sat down to judge. His clothing was as white as snow, his hair like whitest wool. He sat upon a fiery throne brought in on flaming wheels, and 10a river of fire flowed from before him. Millions of angels ministered to him and hundreds of millions of people stood before him, waiting to be judged. Then the court began its session and The Books were opened.

7:9
Ezek 1:13
10:2,6
Mic 5:2
Mk 9:3
Rev 1:14
7:10
Ps 50:3; 97:3
Isa 30:27
Dan 7:22,26
12:1
Mt 25:31
Rev 5:11
20:11-15

11As I watched, the brutal fourth animal was killed and its body handed over to be burned because of its arrogance against Almighty God, and the boasting of its little horn. 12As for the other three animals, their kingdoms were taken from them, but they were allowed to live a short time longer.

7:11
Rev 19:20
20:10

13Next I saw the arrival of a Man—or so he seemed to be—brought there on clouds from heaven; he approached the Ancient of Days and was presented to him. 14He was given the ruling power and glory over all the nations of the world, so that all people of every language must obey him. His power is eternal—it will never end; his government shall never fall.

7:14
Ps 2:6-8; 72:17
102:22
Dan 7:27
Eph 1:20-22
Heb 12:28
Rev 1:6

15I was confused and disturbed by all I had seen [Daniel wrote in his report], 16so I approached one of those standing beside the throne and asked him the meaning of all these things, and he explained them to me.

7:15
Dan 4:19; 7:28

17"These four huge animals," he said, "represent four kings who will someday rule the earth. 18But in the end the people of the Most High God shall rule the governments of the world forever and forever."

7:16
Dan 8:13-16
10:5,6,11,12
Zech 1:8-11
Rev 5:5
7:13,14

19Then I asked about the fourth animal, the one so brutal and shocking, with its iron teeth and brass claws that tore men apart and that stamped others to death with its feet. 20I asked, too, about the ten horns and the little horn that came up afterward and destroyed three of the others—the horn with the eyes, and the loud, bragging mouth, the one which was stronger than the others. 21For I had seen this horn warring against God's people and winning, 22until the Ancient of Days came and opened his court and vindicated his people, giving them worldwide powers of government.

7:18
Dan 7:22,25,27
2 Tim 2:11,12
Rev 2:26,27
20:4
7:21
Rev 13:7
7:22
Dan 7:10
1 Cor 6:2,3

23"This fourth animal," he told me, "is the fourth world power that will rule the earth. It will be more brutal than any of the others; it will devour the whole world, destroying everything before it. 24His ten horns are ten kings that will rise out of his empire; then another king will arise, more brutal than the other ten, and will destroy

7:12 *a short time longer*, literally, "for a season and a time."

7:9 Here the prophecy shifts to the end times. This judgment scene is similar to one seen by the apostle John (Revelation 1:14, 15). God, who assigns power to kingdoms, will himself judge those kingdoms in the end.

7:10 Daniel saw God judging millions of people as they stood before him. We all must stand before Almighty God and give an account of our lives. If your life were judged by God today, what would he say about it? How would he measure it against his Word? As we look toward God's judgment, we should ask what we would like him to see at that time. Then we should live that way today!

7:13, 14 This Man is the Messiah. Jesus used this verse to refer

to himself (Luke 21:27; John 1:51).

7:15 If you feel as Daniel did about these prophecies—disturbed and confused—recognize with him that their full meaning has not been revealed. The full implications of these prophecies will not be known until God reveals them to his people.

7:24 The ten horns, or ten kings, are again mentioned in Revelation 17:12. There were also ten toes in Nebuchadnezzar's vision (2:41, 42). There are many theories concerning the identity of these ten kings. We are reminded in Revelation 17:12–14 that these kings will war against Christ, but as the King of kings, he will conquer them. The other king mentioned is the future Antichrist of 2 Thessalonians 2:3, 4.

7:25
Dan 4:2; 11:36
12:7,14
Rev 12:14
13:6,7

7:26
Rev 17:14; 19:2

7:27
Isa 60:12
Dan 2:44; 4:34
7:14,18,22
Rev 11:1; 20:4

8:2
Gen 10:22; 14:1

8:4
Deut 33:17
1 Kgs 22:11
Ezek 34:21
Mic 5:8

8:8
2 Chron 26:16
Dan 5:20; 7:2
Rev 7:1

8:9
Dan 8:23
11:16,41

8:10
Jer 48:26,42
Ezek 46:14
Dan 7:7; 8:7
11:31
Rev 12:4

8:12
Isa 59:14

8:13
Deut 33:2
Isa 63:18
Dan 4:13,23
12:6,8
Lk 10:22; 21:24
Heb 10:29
Rev 6:10; 11:2

8:14
Dan 7:25
12:7,11
Rev 11:2,3
12:14; 13:5

8:15
Dan 7:13
10:16,18

three of them. 25He will defy the Most High God, and wear down the saints with persecution, and try to change all laws, morals, and customs. God's people will be helpless in his hands for three and a half years.

26"But then the Ancient of Days will come and open his court of justice and take all power from this vicious king, to consume and destroy it until the end. 27Then every nation under heaven, and all their power, shall be given to the people of God; they shall rule all things forever, and all rulers shall serve and obey them."

28That was the end of the dream. When I awoke, I was greatly disturbed, and my face was pale with fright, but I told no one what I had seen.

Daniel dreams of a ram and goat

8 In the third year of the reign of King Belshazzar, I had another dream similar to the first.

2This time I was at Susa, the capital in the province of Elam, standing beside the Ulai River. 3As I was looking around, I saw a ram with two long horns standing on the river bank; and as I watched, one of these horns began to grow, so that it was longer than the other. 4The ram butted everything out of its way and no one could stand against it or help its victims. It did as it pleased and became very great.

5While I was wondering what this could mean, suddenly a buck goat appeared from the west, so swiftly that it didn't even touch the ground. This goat, which had one very large horn between its eyes, 6rushed furiously at the two-horned ram. 7And the closer he came, the angrier he was. He charged into the ram and broke off both his horns. Now the ram was helpless and the buck goat knocked him down and trampled him, for there was no one to rescue him.

8The victor became both proud and powerful, but suddenly, at the height of his power, his horn was broken, and in its place grew four good-sized horns pointing in four directions. 9One of these, growing slowly at first, soon became very strong and attacked the south and east, and warred against the land of Israel. 10He fought against the people of God and defeated some of their leaders. 11He even challenged the Commander of the army of heaven by canceling the daily sacrifices offered to him, and by defiling his Temple. 12But the army of heaven was restrained from destroying him for this transgression. As a result, truth and righteousness perished, and evil triumphed and prospered.

13Then I heard two of the holy angels talking to each other. One of them said, "How long will it be until the daily sacrifice is restored again? How long until the destruction of the Temple is avenged and God's people triumph?"

14The other replied, "Twenty-three hundred days must first go by."

15As I was trying to understand the meaning of this vision, suddenly a man was standing in front of me—or at least he looked like a man— 16and I heard a man's

7:25 *change all laws, morals, and customs,* literally, "change the times and the law." Perhaps the meaning is, "change right to wrong and wrong to right." **7:26** *the Ancient of Days will come,* implied in vs 22. **7:27** *the people of God,* literally, "the people of the saints of the Most High." **8:10** *the people of God and . . . some of their leaders,* literally, "host of heaven" and the "starry host." See 8:24. **8:12** *and evil triumphed and prospered,* or, "and great indignities were perpetrated against the Temple ceremonies, so truth and righteousness perished." The Hebrew text is obscure.

8:1 This chapter precedes chapter 5 chronologically: the dream probably occurred in 551 B.C. when Daniel was about 70 years old. It gives us more details about the Medo-Persian and Greek empires, the two kingdoms which immediately followed Babylon.

8:2 Susa (Shushan) was one of the Babylonian Empire's capitals at this time. Located in what is now Iran, it was a well-developed city. The earliest known code of law, the Code of Hammurabi, was found there. Susa rivaled Babylon itself in sophistication.

8:3 The two horns were the kings of Media and Persia (8:20). The longer horn represented the growing dominance of Persia in the Medo-Persian Empire.

8:5–7 The goat represented Greece, and its large horn, Alexander the Great (8:21). This is an amazing prediction because Greece was not considered a world power when this prophecy was given. Alexander the Great conquered the world with great

speed and military strategy, indicated by the goat's rapid movement. Breaking off both horns symbolized Alexander breaking both parts of the Medo-Persian Empire.

8:8 Alexander the Great died in his thirties at the height of his power. His kingdom was split into four parts under four generals: Ptolemy I of Egypt and Palestine; Seleucus of Babylonia and Syria; Antigonus of Asia Minor; and Antipater of Macedonia and Greece.

8:9 Israel was attacked by Antiochus IV Epiphanes in the second century B.C. A further fulfillment of this prophecy will occur in the future with the coming of the Antichrist (see 8:17, 19, 23).

8:14 The 2,300 days (literally 2,300 mornings and evenings) refers to the time from the desecration of the altar in the Temple by Antiochus IV Epiphanes to the restoration of Temple worship under Judas Maccabees in 165 B.C.

voice calling from across the river, "Gabriel, tell Daniel the meaning of his dream."

17So Gabriel started toward me. But as he approached, I was too frightened to stand, and fell down with my face to the ground. "Son of man," he said, "you must understand that the events you have seen in your vision will not take place until the end times come."

18Then I fainted, lying face downward on the ground. But he roused me with a touch, and helped me to my feet. 19"I am here," he said, "to tell you what is going to happen in the last days of the coming time of terror—for what you have seen pertains to that final event in history.

20"The two horns of the ram you saw are the kings of Media and Persia; 21the shaggy-haired goat is the nation of Greece, and its long horn represents the first great king of that country. 22When you saw the horn break off, and four smaller horns replace it, this meant that the Grecian Empire will break into four sections with four kings, none of them as great as the first.

23"Toward the end of their kingdoms, when they have become morally rotten, an angry king shall rise to power with great shrewdness and intelligence. 24His power shall be mighty, but it will be satanic strength and not his own. Prospering wherever he turns, he will destroy all who oppose him, though their armies be mighty, and he will devastate God's people.

25"He will be a master of deception, defeating many by catching them off guard as they bask in false security. Without warning he will destroy them. So great will he fancy himself to be that he will even take on the Prince of Princes in battle; but in so doing he will seal his own doom, for he shall be broken by the hand of God, though no human means could overpower him.

26"And then in your vision you heard about the twenty-three hundred days to pass before the rights of worship are restored. This number is literal, and means just that. But none of these things will happen for a long time, so don't tell anyone about them yet."

27Then I grew faint and was sick for several days. Afterward I was up and around again and performed my duties for the king, but I was greatly distressed by the dream and did not understand it.

Daniel prays for his people

9 It was now the first year of the reign of King Darius, the son of Ahasuerus. (Darius was a Mede but became king of the Chaldeans.) 2In that first year of his reign, I, Daniel, learned from the book of Jeremiah the prophet, that Jerusalem must lie desolate for seventy years. 3So I earnestly pleaded with the Lord God [to end our captivity and send us back to our own land].

Cross-references (right margin):

8:17
Gen 17:3
Ezek 1:28; 6:2
44:4
Dan 2:46; 8:19
11:35,40

8:18
Ezek 2:2
Dan 10:9,10,
16,18
Lk 9:32

8:19
Dan 8:15-17

8:24
Dan 8:11-13
12:7
Rev 13:3-9
16:6; 17:12-17

8:25
Job 34:20
Dan 2:34,45

8:27
Dan 7:28; 8:17
Hab 3:16

9:1
Dan 5:31; 11:1

9:2
2 Chron 36:21
Ezra 1:1
Jer 25:11; 29:10
Zech 7:5

8:23 *with great shrewdness and intelligence,* literally, "one who understands riddles"; an alternate rendering might read, "skilled in intrigues." **8:24** *but it will be satanic strength and not his own,* implied. Literally, "but not with his power." **8:26** *This number is literal, and means just that,* literally, "The vision of the evenings and the mornings which has been told is true." Vs 14 is the basis for the meaning expressed in the paraphrase. **9:3** *to end our captivity and send us back to our own land,* implied.

8:17 The end times, in this case, refer to the whole period from the end of the exile until the Second Coming of Christ. Many of the events that would happen under Antiochus IV Epiphanes would be repeated on a broader scale just before Christ's Second Coming. During these times, God deals with Israel in a radically different way, with divine discipline coming through Gentile nations. This period is sometimes referred to as the "times of the Gentiles."

8:23 This angry king may symbolize both Antiochus IV Epiphanes and the Antichrist at the end of human history.

8:25 This Prince of Princes is God himself. No human power could defeat the king whom Daniel saw in his vision; but God would bring him down. Antiochus IV Epiphanes died insane in Persia in 163 B.C.

9:1 The story of Belshazzar's feast (chapter five) fits chronologically between chapters eight and nine. This Darius is the person mentioned in chapter six. The Ahasuerus mentioned here is not Esther's husband. The events described in the book of Esther happened about 50 years later.

9:2, 3 Daniel pleaded with God to bring about the promised return of his people to their land. The prophet Jeremiah had written that God would not allow the captives to return to their land for 70 years (Jeremiah 25:11, 12; 29:10). Daniel had read this prophecy and knew that this 70-year period was coming to an end.

9:3-19 Daniel knew how to pray. He had read God's words and believed them. As he prayed, he fasted, confessed his sins, and pleaded that God would reveal his will. He prayed with complete surrender to God and with complete openness to what God was saying to him. When you pray, do you speak openly to God? Examine your attitude. Talk to God with openness, vulnerability, and honesty.

As I prayed, I fasted, and wore rough sackcloth, and sprinkled myself with ashes, 4and confessed my sins and those of my people.

"O Lord," I prayed, "you are a great and awesome God; you always fulfill your promises of mercy to those who love you and who keep your laws. 5But we have sinned so much; we have rebelled against you and scorned your commands. 6We have refused to listen to your servants the prophets, whom you sent again and again down through the years, with your messages to our kings and princes and to all the people.

7"O Lord, you are righteous; but as for us, we are always shamefaced with sin, just as you see us now; yes, all of us—the men of Judah, the people of Jerusalem, and all Israel, scattered near and far wherever you have driven us because of our disloyalty to you. 8O Lord, we and our kings and princes and fathers are weighted down with shame because of all our sins.

9"But the Lord our God is merciful, and pardons even those who have rebelled against him.

10"O Lord our God, we have disobeyed you; we have flouted all the laws you gave us through your servants, the prophets. 11All Israel has disobeyed; we have turned away from you and haven't listened to your voice. And so the awesome curse of God has crushed us—the curse written in the law of Moses your servant. 12And you have done exactly as you warned us you would do, for never in all history has there been a disaster like what happened at Jerusalem to us and our rulers. 13Every curse against us written in the law of Moses has come true; all the evils he predicted—all have come. But even so we still refuse to satisfy the Lord our God by turning from our sins and doing right.

14"And so the Lord deliberately crushed us with the calamity he prepared; he is fair in everything he does, but we would not obey. 15O Lord our God, you brought lasting honor to your name by removing your people from Egypt in a great display of power. Lord, do it again! Though we have sinned so much and are full of wickedness, 16yet because of all your faithful mercies, Lord, please turn away your furious anger from Jerusalem, your own city, your holy mountain. For the heathen mock at you because your city lies in ruins for our sins.

17"O our God, hear your servant's prayer! Listen as I plead! Let your face shine again with peace and joy upon your desolate sanctuary—for your own glory, Lord.

18"O my God, bend down your ear and listen to my plea. Open your eyes and see our wretchedness, how your city lies in ruins—for everyone knows that it is yours. We don't ask because we merit help, but because you are so merciful despite our grievous sins.

19"O Lord, hear; O Lord, forgive. O Lord, listen to me and act! Don't delay—for your own sake, O my God, because your people and your city bear your name."

20Even while I was praying and confessing my sin and the sins of my people, and desperately pleading with the Lord my God for Jerusalem, his holy mountain,

9:4
Deut 7:9,21
Neh 9:32
Nah 1:2-7
Jas 2:5
1 Jn 5:2,3

9:5
Isa 53:6
Lam 1:18,20
Dan 9:11

9:6
Jer 44:4,5,21

9:7
Ezra 9:6,7
Jer 2:26,27
3:25; 23:6
33:16
Dan 9:18

9:9
Neh 9:17
Dan 9:5,6

9:10
2 Kgs 17:13-15
18:12

9:12
Isa 44:26
Jer 44:2-6
Zech 1:6

9:13
Lev 26:14-45
Deut 28:15-68
Isa 9:13
Jer 2:30; 5:3
Dan 9:11

9:14
Jer 31:28; 44:27
Dan 9:7

9:15
Deut 5:15
Neh 9:10
Jer 32:20
2 Cor 1:10

9:16
Ezek 5:14
Dan 9:20
Joel 3:17
Zech 8:3
Mt 23:31,32

9:17
Num 6:24-26
Ps 80:3,7,19
Lam 5:18

9:18
Ps 80:14
Isa 37:17
Jer 7:12; 36:7
Ezek 36:22

9:20
Isa 6:5; 58:9
Dan 9:3; 10:12

9:4ff God is merciful even to rebels, if they confess their sins and return to him. Don't let past disobedience keep you from returning to God. He is waiting for you with open arms.

9:6 God had sent many prophets to speak to his people through the years, but their messages were ignored. The truth was too painful to hear. God still speaks infallibly and authoritatively through the Bible, and he also speaks through preachers, teachers, and concerned friends. Sometimes the truth hurts, and we would rather accept soothing falsehoods. If you are unwilling to listen to God's Word, ask yourself if you are trying to avoid making a painful change. Don't settle for a soothing lie which will bring harsh judgment, when you could have great blessings after a painful but brief change.

9:11–13 Daniel mentioned the blessings and curses outlined in Deuteronomy 28. God had given the people of Israel a choice: obey me and be blessed, or disobey me and face curses. The

affliction was meant to turn the people to God. When we face difficult circumstances, we should ask ourselves if God has reason to send judgment. If we think so, we must beg his forgiveness. Then we can ask him to help us through our troubles.

9:15 Daniel recalled Israel's deliverance from Egypt (see Exodus 12); then he said, "Do it again Lord!" His faith reached in two directions. When we pray, we should recall what God has done in history and in our own lives. Reviewing these past mighty acts will give us the confidence to pray for help today and tomorrow. Don't be afraid to ask God to "do it again."

9:18 Daniel begged for mercy, not for help, because he knew his people didn't deserve God's help. God sends his help, not because we deserve it, but because he wants to show great mercy when we need him. If God refuses to help us because of our sin, how can we complain? But if he sends help despite our sin, how can we withhold our praise?

21Gabriel, whom I had seen in the earlier vision, flew swiftly to me at the time of the evening sacrifice, 22and said to me, "Daniel, I am here to help you understand God's plans. 23The moment you began praying, a command was given. I am here to tell you what it was, for God loves you very much. Listen, and try to understand the meaning of the vision that you saw!

24"The Lord has commanded 490 years of further punishment upon Jerusalem and your people. Then at last they will learn to stay away from sin, and their guilt will be cleansed; then the kingdom of everlasting righteousness will begin, and the Most Holy Place (in the Temple) will be rededicated, as the prophets have declared. 25Now listen! It will be forty-nine years plus 434 years from the time the command is given to rebuild Jerusalem, until the Anointed One comes! Jerusalem's streets and walls will be rebuilt despite the perilous times.

26"After this period of 434 years, the Anointed One will be killed, his kingdom still unrealized . . . and a king will arise whose armies will destroy the city and the Temple. They will be overwhelmed as with a flood, and war and its miseries are decreed from that time to the very end. 27This king will make a seven-year treaty with the people, but after half that time, he will break his pledge and stop the Jews from all their sacrifices and their offerings; then, as a climax to all his terrible deeds, the Enemy shall utterly defile the sanctuary of God. But in God's time and plan, his judgment will be poured out upon this Evil One."

Daniel sees a heavenly messenger

10 In the third year of the reign of Cyrus, king of Persia, Daniel (also called Belteshazzar) had another vision. It concerned events certain to happen in the future: times of great tribulation—wars and sorrows, and this time he understood what the vision meant.

2When this vision came to me (Daniel said later) I had been in mourning for three full weeks. 3All that time I tasted neither wine nor meat, and of course I went without desserts. I neither washed nor shaved nor combed my hair.

4Then one day early in April, as I was standing beside the great Tigris River, 5, 6I looked up and suddenly there before me stood a person robed in linen garments, with a belt of purest gold around his waist, and glowing, lustrous skin! From his face came blinding flashes like lightning, and his eyes were pools of fire; his arms and feet shone like polished brass, and his voice was like the roaring of a vast multitude of people.

7I, Daniel, alone saw this great vision; the men with me saw nothing, but they were suddenly filled with unreasoning terror and ran to hide, 8and I was left alone. When I saw this frightening vision my strength left me, and I grew pale and weak with fright.

9Then he spoke to me, and I fell to the ground face downward in a deep faint.

9:24 *490 years*, literally, "seventy weeks" or "seventy sevens" (of years). These were not in uninterrupted sequence. See vss 25-27.

Cross references (right margin):

9:22 Dan 8:16; 10:21 / Zech 1:9,14 / Rev 4:1

9:24 Lev 25:8 / Num 14:34 / 2 Chron 29:24 / Isa 51:6,8 / 53:10 / Rom 3:21; 5:10 / 2 Cor 5:18-20

9:25 Ezra 4:24 / 6:1-15 / Neh 2:1-8; 3:1 / Isa 9:6 / Jn 1:41; 4:25

9:26 Isa 53:8 / Nah 1:8 / Mt 24:2 / Mk 9:12; 13:2 / Lk 24:26

9:27 Dan 11:31 / Mt 24:15 / Mk 13:14 / Lk 21:20

10:1 Dan 1:17,21 / 2:21; 6:28

10:2 Ezra 9:4 / Neh 1:4

10:4 Ezek 1:3 / Dan 8:2

10:5 Jer 10:9 / Ezek 9:2 / Dan 12:6,7 / Rev 1:13; 15:6

10:7 2 Kgs 6:17 / Ezek 12:18 / Acts 9:7 / Heb 12:21

10:8 Gen 32:34 / Ex 3:3 / Dan 7:28; 8:27 / Hab 3:16 / Rev 1:17

9:24, 25 The expression "490 years" is literally "seventy weeks." Each week may represent one year. Scripture often uses round numbers to make a point, not to give an exact count. For example, Jesus said we are to forgive others "seventy times seven" times. He did not mean a literal 490 times only, but that we should be abundantly forgiving. Similarly, some scholars see this figure of 490 years as a figurative time period. Others, however, interpret this time period as a literal 490 years; they say Christ's death came at the end of the 69 weeks (i.e., 483 years later). One widely accepted interpretation places the seventieth week as the seven years of the great tribulation, still in the future.

9:26, 27 The Anointed One is the Messiah, rejected by his own people. His perfect eternal kingdom would have to come later. There has been much discussion on the numbers, times, and events in these verses, and there are two basic views: (1) this was fulfilled in the past, either at the desecration of the Temple by Antiochus IV Epiphanes or at the destruction of the Temple by the

Roman general Titus Vespasian; or (2) this is still to be fulfilled in the future under the Antichrist.

10:1ff This is Daniel's final vision (536 B.C.). In it, he is given further insight into the great spiritual battle between those who protect God's people and those who want to destroy them. There is also more detailed information on the future, specifically the struggles between the Ptolemies (kings of the South) and the Seleucids (kings of the North).

10:1ff Why didn't Daniel return to Jerusalem? He may have been too old to make the long, hazardous journey (he was over 80); his government duties could have prevented him; or God may have told him to stay behind to complete the work he was called to do.

10:5, 6 The person seen by Daniel was a heavenly being. This is believed by some commentators to be an appearance of Christ (see Revelation 1:13–15), while others say it is an angel (because he required Michael's help—10:13). In either case, Daniel caught a glimpse of the battle between good and evil supernatural powers.

10:11
Ezek 2:1
Dan 8:16,17

10:12
Dan 9:20-23
10:2,3,19

10:13
Dan 10:21; 12:1
Zech 3:1
Eph 6:12
Jude 9
Rev 12:7

10:14
Dan 2:28; 8:26
12:4,9
Hos 3:5
2 Thess 3:1

10:15
Ezek 24:27
33:22
Lk 1:20

10:16
Ex 4:10
Josh 5:14
Isa 6:7
Jer 1:9
Dan 7:15
8:17,27; 10:8,9

10:17
Ex 24:10,11
Isa 6:1-5
Mt 22:43,44

10:19
Josh 1:6-9
Isa 35:4; 43:1
Dan 10:12

[10]But a hand touched me and lifted me, still trembling, to my hands and knees. [11]And I heard his voice—"O Daniel, greatly beloved of God," he said, "stand up and listen carefully to what I have to say to you, for God has sent me to you." So I stood up, still trembling with fear.

[12]Then he said, "Don't be frightened, Daniel, for your request has been heard in heaven and was answered the very first day you began to fast before the Lord and pray for understanding; that very day I was sent here to meet you. [13]But for twenty-one days the mighty Evil Spirit who overrules the kingdom of Persia blocked my way. Then Michael, one of the top officers of the heavenly army, came to help me, so that I was able to break through these spirit rulers of Persia. [14]Now I am here to tell you what will happen to your people, the Jews, at the end times—for the fulfillment of this prophecy is many years away."

[15]All this time I was looking down, unable to speak a word. [16]Then someone—he looked like a man—touched my lips and I could talk again, and I said to the messenger from heaven, "Sir, I am terrified by your appearance and have no strength. [17]How can such a person as I even talk to you? For my strength is gone and I can hardly breathe."

[18]Then the one who seemed to be a man touched me again, and I felt my strength returning. [19]"God loves you very much," he said; "don't be afraid! Calm yourself; be strong—yes, strong!"

Suddenly, as he spoke these words, I felt stronger and said to him, "Now you can go ahead and speak, sir, for you have strengthened me."

[20, 21]He replied, "Do you know why I have come? I am here to tell you what is written in the 'Book of the Future.' Then, when I leave, I will go again to fight my way back, past the prince of Persia; and after him, the prince of Greece. Only Michael, the angel who guards your people Israel, will be there to help me.

The messenger predicts the future

11:3
Dan 5:19
8:4,5,21
11:16,36

11:4
Jer 49:36
Ezek 37:9
Dan 7:2; 8:8
Zech 2:6
Lk 12:20
Rev 7:1

11 "I was the one sent to strengthen and help Darius the Mede in the first year of his reign. [2]But now I will show you what the future holds. Three more Persian kings will reign, to be succeeded by a fourth, far richer than the others. Using his wealth for political advantage, he will plan total war against Greece.

[3]"Then a mighty king will rise in Greece, a king who will rule a vast kingdom and accomplish everything he sets out to do. [4]But at the zenith of his power, his kingdom will break apart and be divided into four weaker nations, not even ruled by his sons. For his empire will be torn apart and given to others. [5]One of them, the

10:13 *the . . . Evil Spirit,* literally, "the prince of Persia." **10:20, 21** *your people Israel,* literally, "your prince."

10:10–18 Daniel was frightened by this vision, but the messenger's hand calmed his fears; Daniel lost his speech, but the messenger's touch restored it; Daniel felt weak, but the messenger's words strengthened him. God can bring us healing when we are hurt, peace when we are troubled, and strength when we are weak. Ask God to minister to you as he did to Daniel.

10:12, 13 Although God sent a messenger to Daniel, powerful obstacles detained the messenger for three weeks. Daniel faithfully continued praying and fasting, and God's messenger eventually arrived. Answers to our prayers may be hindered by unseen obstacles. Don't expect God's answers to come too easily or too quickly. Prayer may be challenged by evil forces, so pray fervently and pray earnestly. Then expect God to answer in his good timing.

10:20, 21 Historians record past events and interpret them for today. Newspapers and magazines record today's events. But only God can write the "Book of the Future" because only God knows the future. When a messenger comes from God with a word about the future, listen carefully.

11:1ff Babylon was defeated by Medo-Persia. Persia was defeated by Greece under Alexander the Great, who conquered most of the Mediterranean and Middle Eastern lands. After Alexander's death, the empire was divided into four parts. The

Ptolemies gained control of the southern section of Palestine, and the Seleucids took the northern part. Verses 1–20 show the conflict between the Ptolemies and Seleucids over control of Palestine in 300–200 B.C. Verses 21–39 describe the persecution of Israel under Antiochus IV Epiphanes. In verses 40–45 the prophecy shifts to the end times. Antiochus IV fades from view and the Antichrist of the last days becomes the center of attention from that point on.

11:1, 2 The angelic messenger was revealing Israel's future (see 10:20, 21). Only God can reveal future events so clearly. God's work not only deals with the sweeping panorama of history, but also focuses on the intricate details of people's lives. And his plans—whether for nations or individuals—are unshakable.

11:2 The fourth Persian king may be Xerxes I, also known as Ahasuerus in the book of Esther (486–465 B.C.), who launched an all-out effort against Greece.

11:3 This mighty king of Greece is Alexander the Great who conquered Medo-Persia and built a huge empire in only four years. He did indeed rule a "vast kingdom."

11:4, 5 The four weaker nations were comprised of the following regions: (1) Egypt, (2) Babylonia and Syria, (3) Asia Minor, and (4) Macedonia and Greece. The king of Egypt was Ptolemy II.

king of Egypt, will increase in power, but this king's own officials will rebel against him and take away his kingdom and make it still more powerful.

6"Several years later an alliance will be formed between the king of Syria and the king of Egypt. The daughter of the king of Egypt will be given in marriage to the king of Syria as a gesture of peace, but she will lose her influence over him and not only will her hopes be blighted, but those of her father, the king of Egypt, and of her ambassador and child. 7But when her brother takes over as king of Egypt, he will raise an army against the king of Syria, and march against him and defeat him. 8When he returns again to Egypt he will carry back their idols with him, along with priceless gold and silver dishes and for many years afterward he will leave the Syrian king alone.

9"Meanwhile the king of Syria will invade Egypt briefly, but will soon return again to his own land. 10, 11However, the sons of this Syrian king will assemble a mighty army that will overflow across Israel into Egypt, to a fortress there. Then the king of Egypt, in great anger, will rally against the vast forces of Syria and defeat them. 12Filled with pride after this great victory, he will have many thousands of his enemies killed, but his success will be short-lived.

13"A few years later the Syrian king will return with a fully-equipped army far greater than the one he lost, 14and other nations will join him in a crusade against Egypt. Insurgents among your own people, the Jews, will join them, thus fulfilling prophecy, but they will not succeed. 15Then the Syrian king and his allies will come and lay siege to a fortified city of Egypt and capture it, and the proud armies of Egypt will go down to defeat.

16"The Syrian king will march onward unopposed; none will be able to stop him. And he will also enter 'The Glorious Land' of Israel, and pillage it. 17This will be his plot for conquering all Egypt: he too will form an alliance with the Egyptian king, giving him a daughter in marriage, so that she can work for him from within. But the plan will fail.

18"After this he will turn his attention to the coastal cities and conquer many. But a general will stop him and cause him to retreat in shame. 19He will turn homeward again, but will have trouble on the way, and disappear.

20"His successor will be remembered as the king who sent a tax collector into Israel, but after a very brief reign, he will die mysteriously, neither in battle nor in riot.

21"Next to come to power will be an evil man not directly in line for royal succession. But during a crisis he will take over the kingdom by flattery and intrigue. 22Then all opposition will be swept away before him, including a leader of the priests. 23His promises will be worthless. From the first his method will be deceit; with a mere handful of followers, he will become strong. 24He will enter the richest areas of the land without warning and do something never done before: he will take the property and wealth of the rich and scatter it out among the people. With great success he will besiege and capture powerful strongholds throughout his dominions, but this will last for only a short while. 25Then he will stir up his courage and raise a great army against Egypt; and Egypt, too, will raise a mighty army, but to no avail, for plots against him will succeed.

26"Those of his own household will bring his downfall; his army will desert, and many be killed.

11:6
Dan 11:7,13,15, 40

11:7
Dan 11:19,38, 39

11:8
Isa 37:19
46:1,2
Jer 43:12,13

11:10
Isa 8:8
Jer 46:7,8
51:42
Dan 11:26,40

11:13
Dan 4:16; 12:7

11:15
Jer 6:6
Ezek 4:2; 17:17

11:16
Josh 1:5
Dan 5:19; 8:9
11:3,36,41

11:17
2 Kgs 12:17
Ezek 4:3,7
Lk 9:51; 11:23
Rom 8:31

11:18
Gen 10:5
Zeph 2:11

11:19
Ps 27:2; 37:36
Jer 46:6
Ezek 26:21

11:24
Num 13:20
Neh 9:25
Ezek 34:14

11:14 *thus fulfilling prophecy,* literally, "in order to fulfill the vision."

11:6, 7 These prophecies seem to have been fulfilled many years later in the Seleucid wars between Egypt and Syria. In 252 B.C., Ptolemy II of Egypt gave his daughter Berenice in marriage to Antiochus II of Syria to conclude a peace treaty. But Berenice was murdered in Antioch by Antiochus II's former wife, Laodice. Berenice's brother, Ptolemy III, ascended the Egyptian throne and declared war against the Seleucids to avenge his sister's murder.

11:9-11 The king of Syria is Seleucus II, and the king of Egypt is Ptolemy IV.

11:13 This Syrian king is possibly Antiochus III the Great, who was later defeated by the Romans at Magnesia (see 11:18).

11:20 This successor is Seleucus IV, successor of Antiochus III. He sent Heliodorus to rob and desecrate the Temple in Jerusalem.

11:21 Seleucus IV was succeeded by his brother, Antiochus IV Epiphanes, who ingratiated himself with the Romans and took over after his brother's death.

11:27
Jer 9:3-5
Dan 11:35,40
Hab 2:3
Acts 17:31

11:31
Ezek 24:21,24
Dan 8:11-13
9:27; 12:11
Mt 24:15
Mk 13:14

11:32
Dan 11:21,34
Zech 9:13-16
10:3-6
Rev 12:7-11

11:33
Zech 8:20-23
Mt 24:9
Jn 16:2
Heb 11:36-38
Rev 1:9; 6:9
7:14

11:34
Dan 11:21,32
Mt 7:15
Rom 16:18
Rev 2:20
13:11-14

11:35
Deut 8:16
Prov 17:3
Dan 12:10
Zech 13:9
Rev 14:15
17:17

11:36
Deut 10:17
Isa 10:25
14:13; 26:20
Dan 2:47; 5:20
7:8,11; 8:11
9:27; 11:3
Acts 4:28
Rev 10:7
13:5,6

11:40
Jer 4:13
Dan 11:27,35
12:4,9
Zech 9:14

11:41
Jer 48:47; 49:6

27"Both these kings will be plotting against each other at the conference table, attempting to deceive each other. But it will make no difference, for neither can succeed until God's appointed time has come.

28"The Syrian king will then return home with great riches, first marching through Israel and destroying it. 29Then, at the predestined time, he will once again turn his armies southward, as he had threatened, but now it will be a very different story from those first two occasions. 30, 31For Roman warships will scare him off, and he will withdraw and return home. Angered by having to retreat, the Syrian king will again pillage Jerusalem and pollute the sanctuary, putting a stop to the daily sacrifices, and worshiping idols inside the Temple. He will leave godless Jews in power when he leaves—men who have abandoned their fathers' faith. 32He will flatter those who hate the things of God, and win them over to his side. But the people who know their God shall be strong and do great things.

33"Those with spiritual understanding will have a wide ministry of teaching in those days. But they will be in constant danger, many of them dying by fire and sword, or being jailed and robbed. 34Eventually these pressures will subside, and some ungodly men will come, pretending to offer a helping hand, only to take advantage of them.

35"And some who are most gifted in the things of God will stumble in those days and fall, but this will only refine and cleanse them and make them pure until the final end of all their trials, at God's appointed time.

36"The king will do exactly as he pleases, claiming to be greater than every god there is, even blaspheming the God of gods, and prospering—until his time is up. For God's plans are unshakable. 37He will have no regard for the gods of his fathers, nor for the god beloved of women, nor any other god, for he will boast that he is greater than them all. 38Instead of these he will worship the Fortress god—a god his fathers never knew—and lavish on him costly gifts! 39Claiming his help he will have great success against the strongest fortresses. He will honor those who submit to him, appointing them to positions of authority and dividing the land to them as their reward.

40"Then at the time of the end, the king of the south will attack him again, and the northern king will react with the strength and fury of a whirlwind; his vast army and navy will rush out to bury him with their might. 41He will invade various lands on the way, including Israel, the Pleasant Land, and overthrow the governments of many nations. Moab, Edom, and most of Ammon will escape, 42but Egypt and

11:30, 31 *For Roman warships*, or, "from Cyprus." *pollute the sanctuary.* By offering swine on the altar. **11:38** *the Fortress god,* literally, "the god of Fortresses."

11:27 These two treacherous kings are probably Antiochus IV of Syria and Ptolemy VI of Egypt. Treachery and deceit are a power broker's way to position himself over another. But when two power brokers try to do this to one another, it is a mutually weakening and self-destructive process. It is also futile because God ultimately holds all power in his hands.

11:30, 31 The sanctuary was polluted when Antiochus IV Epiphanes sacrificed pigs on an altar erected in honor of Zeus. According to Jewish law, pigs were unclean and were not to be touched or eaten. To sacrifice a pig in the Temple was the worst kind of insult an enemy could level against the Jews. This happened in 168–167 B.C.

11:32 This reference may be to Menelaus, the High Priest, who was won over by Antiochus and conspired with him against the Jews who were loyal to God. Those who are "strong and do great things" could be the Maccabees and their sympathizers, but a further fulfillment may lie in the future.

11:33 Trying times remind us of our weaknesses and inability to cope. We reach out for answers, for leadership, for clear direction. God's Word begins to interest even those who, in better times, would never look at it. We who are believers should prepare ourselves to meet opportunities to share God's Word in needy

times. We must also prepare ourselves for persecution and rejection as we teach God's Word.

11:35 God's messenger describes a time of trial when even gifted believers may stumble. This could mean (1) falling into sin, (2) being fearful and losing faith, (3) mistakenly following wrong teaching, or (4) experiencing severe suffering and martyrdom. If we endure and persevere in faith, this experience will only refine us and make us purer. No matter how God has blessed you, there is still more purifying to be done. Are you facing trials? Recognize them as opportunities through which you can be refined by God.

11:36–39 These verses could refer to Antiochus IV Epiphanes, Titus Vespasian, or the Antichrist. Some of these events seem to have been fulfilled in the past, and some seem yet to be fulfilled.

11:37 The god beloved of women is Tammuz-Adonis, a Babylonian fertility god. (See Ezekiel 8:14.)

11:38 The "Fortress god" is sometimes believed to be Jupiter or Zeus. The implication is that this king will make *war* his god. More than all his predecessors, he will wage war and glorify its horrors.

11:40 The prophecy takes a turn here. Antiochus IV fades from view and the Antichrist of the last days becomes the center of attention from this point through the rest of the book of Daniel.

many other lands will be occupied. 43He will capture all the treasures of Egypt, and the Libyans and Ethiopians shall be his servants.

44"But then news from the east and north will alarm him and he will return in great anger to destroy as he goes. 45He will halt between Jerusalem and the sea, and there pitch his royal tents, but while he is there his time will suddenly run out and there will be no one to help him.

A prophecy of the last days

12 "At that time Michael, the mighty angelic prince who stands guard over your nation, will stand up [and fight for you in heaven against satanic forces], and there will be a time of anguish for the Jews greater than any previous suffering in Jewish history. And yet every one of your people whose names are written in the Book will endure it.

2"And many of those whose bodies lie dead and buried will rise up, some to everlasting life and some to shame and everlasting contempt.

3"And those who are wise—the people of God—shall shine as brightly as the sun's brilliance, and those who turn many to righteousness will glitter like stars forever.

4"But Daniel, keep this prophecy a secret; seal it up so that it will not be understood until the end times, when travel and education shall be vastly increased!"

5Then I, Daniel, looked and saw two men on each bank of a river. 6And one of them asked the man in linen robes who was standing now above the river, "How long will it be until all these terrors end?"

7He replied, with both hands lifted to heaven, taking oath by him who lives forever and ever, that they will not end until three and a half years after the power of God's people has been crushed.

8I heard what he said but I didn't understand what he meant, so I said, "Sir, how will all this finally end?"

9But he said, "Go now, Daniel, for what I have said is not to be understood until the time of the end. 10Many shall be purified by great trials and persecutions. But the wicked shall continue in their wickedness, and none of them will understand. Only those who are willing to learn will know what it means.

11"From the time the daily sacrifice is taken away and the Horrible Thing is set

Cross-references (right margin):

11:43
Ezek 30:4,5
Nah 3:9

12:1
Jer 30:7
Ezek 5:9
Dan 7:10; 9:12
10:21; 12:4
Mk 13:19

12:2
Isa 26:19
Jn 5:28,29

12:3
Isa 53:11
Jn 5:35

12:4
Isa 8:16; 11:9

12:6
Ezek 9:2
Dan 8:13,16
10:5; 12:8
Zech 1:12,13
Mt 24:3
Mk 13:4

12:7
Ezek 20:5
Dan 7:25; 8:24
Lk 21:24
Rev 10:7
11:7-15; 12:14

12:10
Isa 32:6,7
Dan 12:3
Rev 3:18
9:20,21; 16:11
22:11

12:11
Dan 9:27; 11:31
Mt 24:15
Mk 13:14
Rev 11:2; 12:6
13:5

12:1 *and fight for you in heaven against satanic forces,* implied. **12:5** *two men.* Hebrew: "two others," probably angels. **12:7** *three and a half years,* literally, "a time, times, and half a time . . . when the shattering of the power of the holy people comes to an end." **12:11** *1,290 days.* Three and a half years (vs 7) plus one month.

12:1 Great suffering is in store for Israel throughout the years ahead. This way of describing the future is also used by Jeremiah (Jeremiah 30:7) and Jesus (Matthew 24:21ff). Yet great suffering is tempered by a great promise of hope for true believers.

12:2 This is a clear reference to the resurrection of both the righteous and the wicked, although the eternal fates of each will be quite different. Up to this point in time, teaching about the resurrection was not common, although every Israelite believed that one day he or she would be included in the restoration of the new kingdom. This reference to a bodily resurrection of both the saved and the lost was a dramatic idea. (See also Job 19:25, 26; Psalm 16:10; and Isaiah 26:19 for other Old Testament references to the resurrection.)

12:3 Many people strive to be "stars" in the transient world of entertainment, only to find their stardom temporary. God tells us how we can be eternal "stars"—by "turning many to *God's* righteousness." If we share our Lord with others, we can be true stars—radiantly beautiful in God's sight!

12:4 Why was the prophecy sealed and kept secret? It was to be sealed and preserved to give people in the end times the needed hope that God will ultimately conquer all evil. Daniel did not understand the exact meaning of the times and events in his vision. We can see events as they unfold, for we are in the "end

times." The whole book will not be understood until the climax of earth's history.

12:7 "The power of God's people" seems to be crushed again and again throughout history. God's recurring purpose in this is to break the pride and self-sufficiency of his people and to bring them to accept him as their Lord.

12:10 Daniel was told that to understand what is happening, people have to be willing to learn. Trials and persecutions, when we are in the midst of them, make very little sense. But they can purify us if we are willing to learn from them. After you survive a difficult time, seek to learn from it so that it can help you in the future.

12:11 "The Horrible Thing" set up in the Temple refers to the altar of Zeus that Antiochus IV Epiphanes set up in the Temple and on which he sacrificed pigs. Some think it will have a double fulfillment and refer to the Antichrist or one of his horrible acts of evil. More likely, this and the predictions at the early part of the chapter refer specifically to Antiochus IV Epiphanes, and then the prophecy shifts to the end times.

12:11, 12 Either these are further calculations relating to the persecution of the Jews under Antiochus IV Epiphanes, or they refer to the end times. The removal of the daily sacrifices means the removal of worship of the true God and oppression of

12:12
Dan 8:14
Rev 11:2

12:13
Ps 16:5
Rev 16:5

up to be worshiped, there will be 1,290 days. 12And blessed are those who wait and remain until the 1335th day!

13"But go on now to the end of your life and your rest; for you will rise again and have your full share of those last days."

12:13 *of those last days,* literally, "at the end of the days."

---

believers. There is much speculation about these numbers. Their meanings were closed to Daniel, and they are closed to us, to be opened when they need to be understood. The point is that this time of persecution has an end, God is in control of it, and he will be victorious over evil.

12:13 The promise of resurrection is reaffirmed to Daniel. He would one day see the fulfillment of his words, but he was not to spend the rest of his life wondering what his visions might mean. Instead, he was to rest in the comfort of God's sovereignty and look forward to the time when he would share eternal life with God. God does not reveal all things to us in this life. We must be content with the partial picture until it is his good time for us to see more. He will tell us all we need to know.

12:13 Daniel stands tall in the gallery of God's remarkable servants. Born of royal heritage, yet taken into captivity when only a teenager, Daniel determined to remain faithful to God in the land of his captivity. Even at great personal cost, Daniel spent his entire lifetime advising his captors with unusual wisdom. God chose him as his servant to record some of the events of the captivity and some significant events concerning the future. As an old man, having been faithful to God throughout his years, Daniel is assured by God that he will be resurrected from the dead and receive his portion in God's eternal kingdom. Faithfulness to God has a rich reward, not necessarily in this life, but most certainly in the life to come.

HOSEA

Jeroboam II
becomes
king of
Israel
793 B.C.

Amos
becomes
a prophet
760

VITAL STATISTICS

PURPOSE:
To illustrate God's love for his sinful people

AUTHOR:
Hosea, son of Beeri. ("Hosea" means "salvation.")

TO WHOM WRITTEN:
Israel (the Northern Kingdom) and God's people everywhere

DATE WRITTEN:
Approximately 715 B.C., recording events from about 753–715 B.C.

SETTING:
Hosea began his ministry during the end of the prosperous but morally declining reign of Jeroboam II of Israel (the upper classes were doing well, but they were oppressing the poor). He prophesied until shortly after the fall of Samaria in 722 B.C.

KEY VERSE:
"Then the Lord said to me, 'Go, and get your wife again and bring her back to you and love her, even though she loves adultery. For the Lord still loves Israel though she has turned to other gods and offered them choice gifts' " (3:1).

KEY PEOPLE:
Hosea, Gomer, their children

KEY PLACES:
The Northern Kingdom (Israel), Samaria, Ephraim

SPECIAL FEATURES:
Hosea employs many images from daily life—God is depicted as husband, father, lion, leopard, she-bear, dew, rain, moth, and others; Israel is pictured as wife, sick person, grapevine, grapes, early fig, olive tree, woman in labor, oven, morning mist, chaff, and smoke, to name a few.

GROOMSMEN stand at attention as the music swells and the bride begins her long walk down the aisle, arm in arm with her father. The smiling, but nervous, husband-to-be follows every step, his eyes beaming with love. Happy tears are shed, vows stated, and families merged. A wedding is a joyous celebration of love. It is the holy mystery of two becoming one, of beginning life together, and of commitment. Marriage is ordained by God and illustrates his relationship with his people. There is perhaps no greater tragedy, therefore, than the violation of those sacred vows.

God told Hosea to find a wife, and told him ahead of time that she would be unfaithful to him. Although she would bear many children, some of these offspring would be fathered by others. In obedience to God, Hosea married Gomer. His relationship with her, her adultery, and their children became living, prophetic examples to Israel.

The book of Hosea is a love story—real, tragic, and true. Transcending the tale of young man and wife, it tells of God's love for his people and the response of his "bride." A covenant had been made and God had been faithful. His love was steadfast and his commitment unbroken. But Israel, like Gomer, was adulterous and unfaithful, spurning God's love and turning instead to false gods. After warning of judgment, God reaffirms his love and offers reconciliation. His love and mercy overflow, but justice will be served.

The book begins with God's marriage instructions to Hosea. After Hosea's marriage, children are born, each bearing a name signifying a divine message (chapter 1). Then, as predicted, Gomer leaves Hosea to pursue her lusts (chapter 2). But Hosea (whose name means "salvation") finds her, redeems her, and brings her home again, fully reconciled (chapter 3). Images of God's love, judgment, grace, and mercy are woven into their relationship. Next, God outlines his case against the people of Israel—their sins will ultimately cause their destruction (chapters 4, 6, 7, 12), and will rouse his anger, resulting in punishment (chapters 5, 8—10, 12, 13). But even in the midst of Israel's immorality, God is merciful and offers hope, expressing his infinite love for his people (chapter 11) and the fact that their repentance will bring about blessing (chapter 14).

The book of Hosea dramatically portrays our God's constant and persistent love. As you read this book, watch the prophet submit himself willingly to his Lord's direction. Grieve with him over the unfaithfulness of his wife and his people. Hear the clear warning of judgment, and reaffirm your commitment to being God's person, faithful in your love and true to your vows.

THE BLUEPRINT

A. HOSEA'S WAYWARD WIFE (1:1—3:5)

Hosea was commanded by God to marry a woman who was faithless in marriage and would cause him many heartaches. Just as Gomer lost interest in Hosea and ran after other lovers, we too can easily lose appreciation for our special relationship with God and pursue dreams and goals that do not include him. When we compromise our Christian life-styles and adopt the ways of the world, we are being faithless.

B. GOD'S WAYWARD PEOPLE (4:1—14:9)
1. Israel's sinfulness
2. Israel's punishment
3. God's love for Israel

God wanted the people in the Northern Kingdom to turn from their sin and return to worshiping him alone, but they persisted in their wickedness. Throughout the book, Israel is described as ignorant of God, with no desire to please him. Israel did not understand God at all, just as Gomer did not understand Hosea. Like a loving husband or patient father, God wants people to know him and to turn to him daily.

MEGATHEMES

THEME	EXPLANATION	IMPORTANCE
The nation's sin	Just as Hosea's wife, Gomer, was unfaithful to him, so the nation of Israel had been unfaithful to God. Israel's idolatry was like adultery. They sought "illicit" relationships with Assyria and Egypt to give them military might, and they mixed Baal worship with the worship of God.	Like Gomer, we can chase after other loves—love of power, pleasure, money, or recognition. The temptations in this world can be very seductive. Are we loyal to God, remaining completely faithful, or have other loves taken his rightful place?
God's judgment	Hosea was solemnly warning Judah against following Israel's example. Because Judah broke the covenant, turned away from God, and forgot her maker, she experienced a devastating invasion and exile. Sin has terrible consequences.	Disaster surely follows ingratitude toward God and rebellion. The Lord is our only true refuge. If we harden our hearts against him, there is no safety or security anywhere else. We cannot escape God's judgment.
God's love	Just as Hosea went after his unfaithful wife to bring her back, so the Lord pursues us with his love. His love is tender, loyal, unchanging, and undying. No matter what, God still loves us.	Have you forgotten God and become disloyal to him? Don't let prosperity diminish your love for him or let success blind you to your need for his love.
Restoration	Although God will discipline his people for sin, he encourages and restores those who have repented. True repentance opens the way to a new beginning. God forgives and restores.	There is still hope for those who turn back to God. No loyalty, achievement, or honor can be compared to loving him. Turn to the Lord while the offer is still good. No matter how far you have strayed, God is willing to bring you back.

A. HOSEA'S WAYWARD WIFE (1:1—3:5)

Hosea highlights the parallels between his relationship with Gomer and God's relationship with the nation of Israel. Although Israel made a covenant with the one true God, she sought after other false gods. In the same way, Hosea married Gomer, knowing ahead of time that she would leave him. Hosea tenderly dealt with his wife in spite of her sin. And God was merciful toward the people of Israel despite their sins. God has not changed, he is still merciful and forgiving.

Hosea's wife and children

1 These are the messages from the Lord to Hosea, son of Beeri, during the reigns of these four kings of Judah: Uzziah, Jotham, Ahaz, and Hezekiah; and one of the kings of Israel, Jereboam, son of Joash.

1:1
1 Kgs 13:1-34
2 Kgs 15:32-38
16:1; 18:1
2 Chron
10:12-16
26:1-23
Mic 1:1

2Here is the first message:

The Lord said to Hosea, "Go and marry a girl who is a prostitute, so that some of her children will be born to you from other men. This will illustrate the way my people have been untrue to me, committing open adultery against me by worshiping other gods."

1:2
Hos 3:1

3So Hosea married Gomer, daughter of Diblaim, and she conceived and bore him a son.

4, 5And the Lord said, "Name the child Jezreel, for in the Valley of Jezreel I am about to punish King Jehu's dynasty to avenge the murders he committed; in fact, I will put an end to Israel as an independent kingdom, breaking the power of the nation in the Valley of Jezreel."

1:4
Josh 17:16
Judg 6:33
2 Kgs 9:14-36
10:1-28
2 Chron 22:8,9

6Soon Gomer had another child—this one a daughter. And God said to Hosea, "Name her Lo-ruhamah (meaning 'No more mercy') for I will have no more mercy upon Israel, to forgive her again. 7But I *will* have mercy on the tribe of Judah. I will

1:7
Ps 44:3-7
Isa 30:18

1:1 Hosea was a prophet to the Northern Kingdom of Israel. He served from 753 to 715 B.C. Under the reign of Jeroboam II, the Northern Kingdom had prospered materially but had decayed spiritually. The people were greedy and had adopted the moral behavior and idolatrous religion of the surrounding Canaanites.

Hosea's role was to show how the Northern Kingdom had been unfaithful to God, their "husband" and provider, and had married themselves to Baal and the gods of Canaan. He warned that unless they repented of their sin and turned back to God they were headed for destruction. Hosea spoke of God's characteristics—his powerful love and fierce justice—and how these should affect their lives and make them return to him. Unfortunately, the people had broken their covenant with God, and they would receive the punishments God had promised (Deuteronomy 27, 28).

1:2 God told Hosea to marry Gomer, and he warned him before the marriage took place that she would be unfaithful to him. Hosea's life as a husband to an unfaithful woman would illustrate God's relationship to the unfaithful nation of Israel.

1:2 It is hard to imagine Hosea's feelings when God told him to marry a woman who would be unfaithful to him. He may not have wanted to do this. But he obeyed. God often asked extraordinary obedience from his prophets who were facing extraordinary times. He may ask you to do something difficult and extraordinary too. If he does, how will you respond? Will you obey him, trusting that he who knows everything has a special purpose for his request? Will you be satisfied with the knowledge that the pain involved in obedience may benefit those you serve, and not you personally?

1:2, 3 Did God really order his prophet to marry a prostitute? Some who find it difficult to believe God could make such a request view this story as an illustration, not an historial event. Many, however, think the story is historical and give one of these explanations: (1) According to God's law, a priest could not marry a prostitute (Leviticus 21:7), but Hosea was not a priest. (2) It is possible that Gomer was not a prostitute when Hosea married her, and that God was letting Hosea know that Gomer would later turn to adultery and prostitution. In any case, Hosea knew ahead of

time that his wife would be unfaithful and that their married life would become a living object lesson to the adulterous Northern Kingdom to whom he prophesied.

1:4, 5 Elijah had predicted that Ahab's family would be destroyed because of their evil (1 Kings 21:20–22), but Jehu went too far in carrying out God's command (2 Kings 10:9–11). Therefore, Jehu's dynasty would also be punished—in Jezreel, the very place where he carried out the massacre of Ahab's family. God's promise to put an end to Israel as an independent kingdom came true 25 years later when the Assyrians conquered the Northern Kingdom and carried the people into captivity.

1:6–8 In 1:3, we read that Gomer "bore him [Hosea] a son." In 1:6 and 1:8, we learn that Gomer gave birth to two more children, but there is no indication that Hosea was their natural father, and some translations imply that he was not. Whether or not they were his, the key to this part of the story is found in the names God chose for the children, showing his reaction to Israel's unfaithfulness. His reaction to unfaithfulness is no different today.

1:7 Israel and Judah had been a united kingdom under David and Solomon. After Solomon's death a civil dispute arose, and the land was divided into a Northern Kingdom (Israel, whose capital was Samaria) and a Southern Kingdom (Judah, whose capital was Jerusalem). Although Hosea spoke mainly to the Northern Kingdom, his concern, like God's, was for the entire nation of Israelites including those from the kingdom of Judah. Just as Hosea prophesied, God helped Judah because Judah had a few kings who honored him. Shortly after defeating Israel, the Assyrian Emperor Sennacherib invaded Judah and beseiged Jerusalem. He was driven off by an angel's intervention (Isaiah 36, 37).

1:7 God said he would personally rescue the people of Judah from their enemies with no help from their armies or weapons. Although God asks us to do our part, we should remember that he is not dependent on our help. He often chooses to work through people, but only because it is good for *them*. He can accomplish all his purposes without any help from us if he so chooses. You are very important to God, but on your own you have neither the ability to fulfill nor the power to disrupt God's plans.

personally free her from her enemies without any help from her armies or her weapons."

8After Gomer had weaned Lo-ruhamah, she again conceived and this time gave birth to a son. 9And God said, "Call him Lo-ammi (meaning 'Not mine'), for Israel is not mine and I am not her God.

10"Yet the time will come when Israel shall prosper and become a great nation; in that day her people will be too numerous to count—like sand along a seashore! Then, instead of saying to them, 'You are not my people,' I will tell them, 'You are my sons, children of the Living God.' 11Then the people of Judah and Israel will unite and have one leader; they will return from exile together; what a day that will be—the day when God will sow his people in the fertile soil of their own land again."

Punishment and restoration

2 O Jezreel, rename your brother and sister. Call your brother Ammi (which means "Now you are mine"); name your sister Ruhamah ("Pitied"), for now God will have mercy upon her!

2Plead with your mother, for she has become another man's wife—I am no longer her husband. Beg her to stop her harlotry, to quit giving herself to others. 3If she doesn't, I will strip her as naked as the day she was born, and cause her to waste away and die of thirst as in a land riddled with famine and drought. 4And I will not

1:10
Gen 22:17
Isa 63:16; 64:8
Jer 33:22

1:11
Jer 30:21
Hos 3:5

2:1
Hos 1:4,5,11

2:3
Isa 20:2,3
32:13,14
Jer 14:3
Ezek 16:7,22,29
Hos 13:15
Amos 8:11-13

1:11 *the day when God will sow his people in the fertile soil of their own land again,* literally, "the day of Jezreel ('God sows')"; see 2:23.   2:1 *Jezreel is implied in the preceding chapter and verse.*

HOSEA
served as a
prophet to Israel
(the Northern
Kingdom) from
753–715 B.C.

Climate of the times	Israel's last six kings were especially wicked; they promoted heavy taxes, oppression of the poor, idol worship, and total disregard for God. Israel was subjected to Assyria and was forced to pay tribute, which robbed its few remaining resources.
Main message	The people of Israel had sinned against God, as an adulterous woman sins against her husband. Judgment was sure to come for living in total disregard for God and fellow man. Hosea saw the nation fall to Assyria in 722 B.C.
Importance of message	When we sin we sever our relationship with God, breaking our commitment to him. While all must answer to God for their sins, those who seek God's forgiveness are spared eternal judgment.
Contemporary prophets	Jonah (793–753)
	Amos (760–750)
	Micah (742–687)
	Isaiah (740–681)

1:9 Here God uses his covenant name, *Yahweh* or *I Am*. He is literally saying, "I am no longer the *I Am* to Israel." God's warnings recorded in Deuteronomy 28:15–68 were beginning to come true: Israel was abandoning him, and in turn, he was leaving them alone and without his blessings.

1:10 The Old Testament prophetic books sometimes use the word "Israel" to refer to the united kingdom (North and South) and sometimes just to the Northern Kingdom. In talking about past events, Hosea usually thought of Israel as the Northern Kingdom with its capital in Samaria. But when Hosea spoke about future events relating to God's promises of restoration, it is difficult to understand his words as applying only to the Northern Kingdom because the exiled northerners became hopelessly interbred with their conquerors. Thus the promises of return are seen by most as either: (1) conditional—the Israelites chose not to return to God and therefore were not entitled to the blessings included in the promises of restoration, or (2) unconditional—God's promises of restoration are fulfilled in Jesus Christ and therefore the church (the new Israel) receives his blessings.

1:10, 11 Although Israel was unfaithful, God's commitment remained unchanged. This promise of a future reuniting reiterates the covenant made with Moses (Deuteronomy 18:15–18) and foreshadows the prophecies of Jeremiah (Jeremiah 29:11–14; 31:31–40) and Ezekiel (Ezekiel 11:16–21). It is a prediction of the day when all the people of God will be united under Christ. Today all believers everywhere are God's chosen people, a nation of priests (see 1 Peter 2:9).

2:1ff The themes of this chapter are Israel's punishment and restoration. As in a court case, the adulteress is brought to trial and found guilty. But after her punishment, she is joyfully and tenderly restored to God.

2:3 Hosea had supplied his wife with clothing, and God had provided Israel with plenty of rain for their crops. Whether the picture is of Hosea and Gomer or of God and Israel, it warns of the punishment that results from unfaithfulness. Just as a husband might refuse to support an unfaithful wife, God would not tolerate Israel's unfaithfulness. He would strip the land, and famine would result.

give special favors to her children as I would to my own, for they are not my children; they belong to other men.

5For their mother has committed adultery. She did a shameful thing when she said, "I'll run after other men and sell myself to them for food and drinks and clothes."

6But I will fence her in with briars and thornbushes; I'll block the road before her to make her lose her way, so that 7when she runs after her lovers she will not catch up with them. She will search for them but not find them. Then she will think, "I might as well return to my husband, for I was better off with him than I am now."

8She doesn't realize that all she has, has come from me. It was I who gave her all the gold and silver she used in worshiping Baal, her god!

9But now I will take back the wine and ripened corn I constantly supplied, and the clothes I gave her to cover her nakedness—I will no longer give her rich harvests of grain in its season, or wine at the time of the grape harvest. 10Now I will expose her nakedness in public for all her lovers to see, and no one will be able to rescue her from my hand.

11I will put an end to all her joys, her parties, holidays, and feasts. 12I will destroy her vineyards and her orchards—gifts she claims her lovers gave her—and let them grow into a jungle; wild animals will eat their fruit.

13For all the incense she burned to Baal her idol and for the times when she put on her earrings and jewels and went out looking for her lovers, and deserted me: for all these things I will punish her, says the Lord.

14But I will court her again, and bring her into the wilderness, and speak to her tenderly there. 15There I will give back her vineyards to her, and transform her Valley of Troubles into a Door of Hope. She will respond to me there, singing with joy as in days long ago in her youth, after I had freed her from captivity in Egypt.

16In that coming day, says the Lord, she will call me "My Husband" instead of "My Master." 17O Israel, I will cause you to forget your idols, and their names will not be spoken anymore.

18At that time I will make a treaty between you and the wild animals, birds, and snakes, not to fear each other any more; and I will destroy all weapons, and all wars will end.

Then you will lie down in peace and safety, unafraid; 19and I will bind you to me

2:5
Jer 2:25
3:1,2
Ezek 23:16,17,
40-45

2:6
Job 19:8

2:7
2 Chron
28:20-22
Jer 2:2; 3:1
Ezek 23:4
Hos 2:5; 5:13

2:8
Hos 2:13; 8:4
13:2

2:10
Ezek 16:37
Hos 2:3

2:11
Jer 7:34; 16:9

2:12
Jer 5:17; 8:13

2:13
Jer 7:9
Ezek 23:40-42
Hos 4:13; 11:2

2:14
Ezek 20:33-38

2:15
Josh 7:26
Isa 65:10
Jer 2:1-3
Ezek 16:8,22

2:16
Isa 54:5
Hos 2:7

2:18
Lev 26:5,6
Isa 2:4
Jer 33:16
Ezek 34:25
39:1-10
Mic 4:3

2:5-7 The Israelites were thanking false gods (specifically Baal) for their food, shelter, and clothing, instead of the true God who gave those blessings. Therefore, God would fence Israel in and "block the road" by making the rewards of her idol worship so disappointing that she would be persuaded to turn back to God. Despite Israel's unfaithfulness, God was still faithful and merciful. He would continue to seek out his people, even to the point of placing obstacles in their wayward path to turn them back to him.

2:7 Just as Gomer would return to her husband if she thought she would be better off with him, so people often return to God when they find life's struggle too difficult to handle. Returning to God out of desperation is better than rebelling against him, but it is better yet to turn to him out of gratitude for his care.

2:8 Material possessions are success symbols in most societies. Israel was a wealthy nation at this time, and Gomer had acquired gold and silver. But Gomer didn't realize that Hosea gave her what she owned, and Israel did not recognize God as the Giver of blessings. Both Gomer and Israel used their possessions unfaithfully as they ran after other lovers and other gods. How do you use your possessions? Use what God has given you to return glory to him.

2:12 The Israelites were so immersed in idolatry that they actually believed heathen gods gave them their orchards and vineyards. They had forgotten that the entire land was a gift from God (Deuteronomy 32:49). Today many people give credit to everything but God for their prosperity—luck, hard work, quick thinking, the right contacts. When you succeed, who gets the credit?

2:13 Baal was the most important of the Canaanite gods, but his name came to be used to describe all the local deities worshiped throughout the land occupied by Israel. Unfortunately, Israel did not get rid of the idols and heathen worship centers as they had been commanded. Instead, they tolerated and frequently joined Baal worshipers, often through the influence of corrupt kings. One Israelite king noted for his Baal worship was Ahab. The prophet Elijah, in a dramatic showdown with Ahab's hired prophets, proved God's power far superior to Baal's (1 Kings 18).

2:14 God would court Israel in the wilderness of captivity, far away from Canaan's tempting idols. In his great mercy, God spoke tenderly to his people who had forsaken him to worship Baal, wanting to restore his relationship with them.

2:14, 15 God was promising: (1) to bring the people to the wilderness where there were no distractions so he could clearly communicate with them, and (2) to change what had been a time of difficulty into a day of hope. God uses even the negative experiences in our lives to create opportunities for us to turn back to him. As you face problems and trials, remember that God speaks to you in the desert, not just in times of prosperity.

2:16 Not until Judah's exile would the entire nation begin to come to its senses, give up its idols, and turn back to God; and not until God rules through Jesus the Messiah will the relationship between God and his people be restored. In that day, God will no longer be like a master or owner to them; he will be like a husband. The relationship will be deep and personal, the kind of relationship we can know, though imperfectly, in marriage (Isaiah 54:4-8).

2:20
Jer 31:34
Hos 6:6; 13:4

forever with chains of righteousness and justice and love and mercy. 20I will betroth you to me in faithfulness and love, and you will really know me then as you never have before.

2:21
Isa 55:10
Jer 31:27
Zech 8:12

21, 22In that day, says the Lord, I will answer the pleading of the sky for clouds, to pour down water on the earth in answer to its cry for rain. Then the earth can answer the parched cry of the grain, the grapes, and the olive trees for moisture and for dew—and the whole grand chorus shall sing together that "God sows!" He has given all!

2:23
Hos 1:6,9

23At that time I will sow a crop of Israelites and raise them for myself! I will pity those who are "not pitied," and I will say to those who are "not my people," "Now you are my people"; and they will reply, "You are our God!"

Hosea is reconciled to his wife

3:1
2 Sam 6:19
1 Chron 16:3
Song 2:5

3 Then the Lord said to me, "Go, and get your wife again and bring her back to you and love her, even though she loves adultery. For the Lord still loves Israel though she has turned to other gods and offered them choice gifts."

2:21, 22 *"God sows,"* literally, "Jezreel." **2:23** *"not pitied,"* see 1:6, 9, 10.

SPIRITUAL UNFAITHFULNESS
Spiritual adultery and physical adultery are alike in many ways and both are dangerous. God was disappointed with his people because they had committed spiritual adultery against him, as Gomer had committed physical adultery against Hosea.

Parallels
Both spiritual and physical adultery are against God's law.

Both spiritual and physical adultery begin with disappointment and dissatisfaction—either real or imagined—with an already existing relationship.

Both spiritual and physical adultery begin with diverting affection from one object of devotion to another.

Both spiritual and physical adultery involve a process of deterioration; it is not usually an impulsive decision.

Both spiritual and physical adultery involve the creation of a fantasy about what a new object of love can do for you.

The danger
When we break God's law in full awareness of what we're doing, our hearts become hardened to the sin and our relationship with God is broken.

The feeling that God disappoints can lead you away from him. Feelings of disappointment and dissatisfaction are normal and, when endured, will pass.

The diverting of our affection is the first step in the blinding process that leads into sin.

The process is dangerous because you don't always realize it is happening until it is too late.

Such fantasy creates unrealistic expectations of what a new relationship can do and only leads to disappointment in all existing and future relationships.

2:19, 20 By running after lovers, Gomer lost her freedom, just as Israel and Judah would lose theirs by running after strange gods. Now God offered to exchange their chains of captivity for chains of love. In our obsession to be independent, free from all rules and restraints, we run the risk of becoming slaves to our own desires. God's chains, by contrast, do not enslave us, thwart us, hinder us, or stifle us. Instead, they offer us the freedom for which we were created—the freedom to choose what is right and thus to grow in relationship with God.

2:19, 20 The time will come when unfaithfulness will be impossible—God will bind us to himself in his perfect righteousness, love, and mercy. Betrothal in Hosea's time was more than a simple agreement to marry. It was a binding engagement, a deep commitment between two families for a future, permanent relationship. God was promising a fresh new beginning, not just a repair job on a tired old agreement. (See Jeremiah 31:31–34.)

2:19, 20 God's wedding gift to his people, both in Hosea's day and in our own, is his mercy. Through no merit of our own, he forgives us and makes us right with him. There is no way for us by our own efforts to reach God's high standard for moral and spiritual life, but he graciously accepts us, forgives us, and draws us into a relationship with himself. In that relationship we have personal and intimate communion with him.

2:20 Although Israel was unfaithful and was condemned for her idolatry, God—unchanging in his love—would offer forgiveness and a renewed relationship with himself, one even better than any she had previously experienced. Why? Because he loved Israel with an everlasting love. Have you been unfaithful to God? God loves you still. If you turn back to him, he will forgive you. He wants you to know him as you never have before.

3:1 Here Hosea may be talking about the entire nation—Judah and Israel. This short chapter pictures the nation's exile and return. Israel would experience a time of purification in a foreign land, but God would still love the people and would be willing to accept them back. He commanded Hosea to show the same forgiving spirit to Gomer. Although Gomer had no merit of her own and although Hosea had good reason to divorce her, he was told to buy her back and love her.

3:1 God is asking Hosea to do something almost unthinkable—to buy back his adulterous, unrepentant wife and continue to love her! When those who knew about Gomer's adultery heard Hosea say that God loved idolatrous Israel as much as he loved Gomer, they must have been amazed. *They* were acting like Gomer, and yet God still loved them! The people had heard God's words many times, but they felt the impact of those words when they saw them acted out in Hosea's troubled home life.

²So I bought her [back from her slavery] for a couple of dollars and eight bushels of barley, ³and I said to her, "You must live alone for many days; do not go out with other men nor be a prostitute, and I will wait for you."

⁴This illustrates the fact that Israel will be a long time without a king or prince, and without an altar, temple, priests, or even idols!

⁵Afterward they will return to the Lord their God, and to the Messiah, their King, and they shall come trembling, submissive to the Lord and to his blessings, in the end times.

3:2
Ruth 4:10

3:4
Judg 17:5
18:17-24

3:5
Isa 55:3,4
Jer 50:4,5
Ezek 34:24
Amos 9:11
Acts 15:16-18

B. GOD'S WAYWARD PEOPLE (4:1—14:9)

The rest of the book deals with Israel's sin and her impending judgment. Hosea points out the moral and spiritual decay of the nation. He describes the punishment awaiting them and pleads with them to return to God. Although judgment and condemnation of sin are prevalent in the book, a strand of love and restoration runs throughout. Even in the midst of judgment, God is merciful and will restore those who repent and turn to him.

1. Israel's sinfulness

God charges Israel with sins

4 Hear the word of the Lord, O people of Israel. The Lord has filed a lawsuit against you listing the following charges: There is no faithfulness, no kindness, no knowledge of God in your land. ²You swear and lie and kill and steal and commit adultery. There is violence everywhere, with one murder after another.

³That is why your land is not producing; it is filled with sadness, and all living things grow sick and die; the animals, the birds, and even the fish begin to disappear.

⁴Don't point your finger at someone else, and try to pass the blame to him! Look,

4:1
Isa 50:4
Jer 7:28
Hos 12:2
Mic 6:2

4:3
Isa 24:4; 33:9

4:4
Deut 17:12
Ezek 3:26
Amos 5:10,13

3:2 *back from her slavery,* implied. **3:5** *to the Messiah, their King,* literally, "to David, their king." Christ was "the Greater David."

3:2 Gomer apparently was on her own for a while. Needing to support herself, she must have either sold herself into slavery or become the mistress of another man. In either case, Hosea had to pay to get her back—although the required amount was pitifully small. Gomer was no longer worth much to anyone except Hosea, but he loved her just as God loved Israel. No matter how low we sink, God is willing to "buy us back"—to redeem us—and to lift us up again.

3:3 After this, Gomer is no longer mentioned by Hosea. This is explained in 3:4. Gomer's absence and isolation show how God will deal with the Northern Kingdom. It is dangerous to rebel against God. If he were ever to withdraw his love and mercy, we would be without hope.

3:4, 5 The Northern Kingdom rebelled against the house of David under Jeroboam (1 Kings 12, 13). Their rebellion was both political and religious. At that time, they reverted back to the worship of golden idols. In the time of Messiah's rule, all people will stand before him humble and submissive. Those who won't accept his blessings now will face his power and judgment later. How much better to love and follow him now than face his anger later.

4:1ff In this chapter, God brings a charge of disobedience against Israel. The religious leaders had failed to turn the people to God, and ritual prostitution had replaced right worship. The nation had declined spiritually and morally, breaking the laws God had given them. The people found it easy to condemn Hosea's wife. They were not so quick to see that *they* were faithless to God.

4:1-3 God used the courtroom image to point out the reasons for Israel's suffering. Their lawless behavior had brought the twin judgments of increased violence and ecological crisis. There is not always a direct cause-and-effect relationship between our actions and the problems we face. Nevertheless, when we are surrounded with difficulties, we should seriously ask, "Have I done anything

sinful or irresponsible that has caused my suffering?" If we discover we are at fault, even partially, we can change our ways to get some relief.

4:2 This verse may allude to the assassinations of kings during Hosea's lifetime. Shallum killed Zechariah (the king, not the prophet) and took the throne. Then Menahem killed Shallum and destroyed an entire city because it refused to accept him as king (2 Kings 15:8–16). God pointed out that even murder was being taken casually in Israel.

4:4 We often blame others if we fear punishment for wrongdoing. Hosea warned the priests not to blame anyone else; the nation's sins were largely their fault. Israel's priests pointed out the people's sins, but God would not allow them to overlook their own irresponsible actions. Instead of instructing the nation in religion and morality, they had led the way toward idolatry and immorality. Their failure to lead the people in God's ways placed most of the blame for Israel's destruction on them. Knowing that God will not allow us to blame others for our mistakes should cause us to deal with our sins head on. We are responsible for our own sinful actions. Beware of the tendency to blame others because it can keep you from feeling the need to repent.

4:4–10 Hosea leveled his charges against the religious leaders. Who were these religious leaders? When Jeroboam I rebelled against Solomon's son Rehoboam and set up a rival kingdom in the north, he also set up his own religious system (see 1 Kings 12:25–33). In violation of God's law, he made two gold calf-idols and told the people to worship them. He also appointed his own priests, who were not descendants of Aaron. At first the residents of the Northern Kingdom continued to worship God, even though they were doing it in the wrong way; but very soon they also began to worship Canaanite gods. Before long they substituted Baal for God and no longer worshiped God at all. It is not surprising that Jeroboam's false priests were unable to preserve the true worship of God.

4:5
Ezek 14:3,7
Hos 5:5

4:6
Hos 4:14
Zech 11:8,9,
15-17

4:7
Hos 2:16; 10:1
13:6
Rom 1:21-23

4:9
Isa 24:2
Jer 5:31
Mt 15:13,14

4:11
Isa 5:12; 28:7

4:12
1 Chron 10:13
Isa 19:3
Ezek 21:21

4:13
Jer 2:20; 3:6
Ezek 6:13
Hos 2:13; 11:2

4:14
Deut 23:17

4:16
Ps 23:2,3; 78:8
Isa 5:17; 7:25

4:19
Hos 12:1; 13:15
Zech 5:9-11

priest, I am pointing my finger at *you*. 5As a sentence for your crimes, you priests will stumble in broad daylight as well as in the night, and so will your false "prophets" too; and I will destroy your mother, Israel. 6My people are destroyed because they don't know me, and it is all your fault, you priests, for you yourselves refuse to know me; therefore I refuse to recognize you as my priests. Since you have forgotten my laws, I will "forget" to bless your children. 7The more my people multiplied, the more they sinned against me. They exchanged the glory of God for the disgrace of idols.

8The priests rejoice in the sins of the people; they lap it up and lick their lips for more! 9And thus it is: "Like priests, like people"—because the priests are wicked, the people are too. Therefore, I will punish both priests and people for all their wicked deeds. 10They will eat and still be hungry. Though they do a big business as prostitutes, they shall have no children, for they have deserted me and turned to other gods.

11Wine, women, and song have robbed my people of their brains. 12For they are asking a piece of wood to tell them what to do. "Divine Truth" comes to them through tea leaves! Longing after idols has made them foolish. For they have played the harlot, serving other gods, deserting me. 13They sacrifice to idols on the tops of mountains; they go up into the hills to burn incense in the pleasant shade of oaks and poplars and sumac trees.

There your daughters turn to prostitution and your brides commit adultery. 14But why should I punish them? For you men are doing the same thing, sinning with harlots and temple prostitutes. Fools! Your doom is sealed, for you refuse to understand.

15But though Israel is a prostitute, may Judah stay far from such a life. O Judah, do not join with those who insincerely worship me at Gilgal and at Bethel. Their worship is mere pretense. 16Don't be like Israel, stubborn as a heifer, resisting the Lord's attempts to lead her in green pastures. 17Stay away from her, for she is wedded to idolatry.

18The men of Israel finish up their drinking bouts, and off they go to find some whores. Their love for shame is greater than for honor.

19Therefore, a mighty wind shall sweep them away; they shall die in shame, because they sacrifice to idols.

4:12 *"Divine Truth" comes to them through tea leaves*, literally, "their staff." There is no modern parallel to this ancient practice used by sorcerers, whose predictions were based on how their staffs landed on the ground when thrown or allowed to fall. **4:18** *Their love for shame is greater than for honor.* The Hebrew text is uncertain. The translation follows the Greek version.

4:6–9 God accused the religious leaders of keeping the people from knowing him. They were supposed to be spiritual leaders, but they became leaders in wrongdoing. The people may have said to one another, "It must be OK if the priests do it." Spiritual leadership is a heavy responsibility. Whether you teach a Sunday school class, hold a church office, or lead a Bible study, don't take your leadership responsibilities lightly. Be a leader who leads to God.

4:8 The priests rejoiced in the people's sins. Every time a person brought a sin offering, the priest received a portion of it. The more the people sinned, the more the priests received. Since they couldn't eat all of the offerings themselves, they sold some and gave some to their relatives. The priests profited from the continuation of sin; it gave them power and position in the community. So instead of trying to lead the people out of sin, they encouraged it to have greater profit.

4:10 What was ritual prostitution? The chief Canaanite gods, Baal and Ashtoreth, represented the power of fertility and sexual reproduction. Not surprisingly, their worship included rituals with vile sexual practices. Male worshipers had sex with female temple prostitutes, or priestesses, and young women wishing to bear children had sex with male priests.

4:11 God created wine to make man glad (Psalm 104:15) and he tells him, "rejoice in the wife of your youth" (Proverbs 5:18). But all of God's good gifts can be misused. Celebration can turn into drunkenness and pleasure in marriage can be replaced by illicit sex. When any of God's gifts become more important than the Giver, abuses are sure to follow.

4:13, 14 By divorcing themselves from God's authoritative religion centered in Jerusalem, inhabitants of the Northern Kingdom had effectively cut themselves off from his Word and from his way of forgiveness. The drive to be free and independent from all restrictions can move us completely out of God's will.

4:15 God sent a warning to the Southern Kingdom of Judah and her priests not to become like Israel. Israel's priests who remained in the North had forgotten their spiritual heritage and sold out to Baal. They now promoted idol worship and ritual prostitution. Israel would not escape punishment, but Judah could if she refused to follow Israel's example.

4:19 The mighty wind that would sweep Israel away refers to the Assyrian invasion that destroyed the nation about 20 years later.

God's judgment against Israel

5 Listen to this, you priests and all of Israel's leaders; listen, all you men of the royal family: You are doomed! For you have deluded the people with idols at Mizpah and Tabor, ²and dug a deep pit to trap them at Acacia. But never forget—I will settle up with all of you for what you've done.

³I have seen your evil deeds: Israel, you have left me as a prostitute leaves her husband; you are utterly defiled. ⁴Your deeds won't let you come to God again, for the spirit of adultery is deep within you, and you cannot know the Lord.

⁵The very arrogance of Israel testifies against her in my court. She will stumble under her load of guilt, and Judah, too, shall fall. ⁶Then at last, they will come with their flocks and herds to sacrifice to God, but it will be too late—they will not find him. He has withdrawn from them and they are left alone.

⁷For they have betrayed the honor of the Lord, bearing children that aren't his. Suddenly they and all their wealth will disappear. ⁸Sound the alarm! Warn with trumpet blasts in Gibeah and Ramah, and on over to Beth-aven; tremble, land of Benjamin! ⁹Hear this announcement, Israel: When your day of punishment comes, you will become a heap of rubble.

¹⁰The leaders of Judah have become the lowest sort of thieves. Therefore, I will pour my anger down upon them like a waterfall, ¹¹and Ephraim will be crushed and broken by my sentence because she is determined to follow idols. ¹²I will destroy her as a moth does wool; I will sap away the strength of Judah like dry rot.

¹³When Ephraim and Judah see how sick they are, Ephraim will turn to Assyria, to the great king there, but he can neither help nor cure.

¹⁴I will tear Ephraim and Judah as a lion rips apart its prey; I will carry them off and chase all rescuers away.

¹⁵I will abandon them and return to my home until they admit their guilt and look to me for help again, for as soon as trouble comes, they will search for me and say:

6 "Come, let us return to the Lord; it is he who has torn us—he will heal us. He has wounded—he will bind us up. ²In just a couple of days, or three at the most, he will set us on our feet again, to live in his kindness! ³Oh, that we might know the Lord! Let us press on to know him, and he will respond to us as surely as the coming of dawn or the rain of early spring."

2. Israel's punishment

God wants Israel's love

⁴O Ephraim and Judah, what shall I do with you? For your love vanishes like

5:3 *the lowest sort of thieves,* literally, "as those who move a boundary marker." See Deut 19:14; 27:17. **6:2** *In just a couple of days,* literally, "In two days."

Cross references (right margin):

5:3 Amos 5:12 / Heb 4:13
5:4 Hos 4:6,14
5:5 2 Kgs 17:19,20 / Ezek 23:31-35
5:6 Ezek 8:6
5:7 Hos 2:4
5:9 Isa 28:1-4; 37:3 / Hos 9:11-17 / Amos 3:14,15
5:10 Deut 27:17 / Ps 32:6; 93:3,4 / Prov 22:28 / Ezek 7:8
5:12 Ps 39:11 / Isa 51:8
5:14 Ps 7:2 / Hos 13:7
6:1 Isa 30:26; 61:1 / Zeph 2:1-3
6:3 Isa 2:3; 5:6 / Hos 14:5 / Mic 4:2

5:1, 2 With both civil and religious leaders hopelessly corrupt, the people of Israel did not have much of a chance. They looked to their leaders for guidance, and in God's plan they should have found it. Today we can often choose our own leaders, but we still need to beware of whether they are taking us toward or away from God. God held the people responsible for what they did. Similarly, he holds us individually responsible for our actions and choices.

5:4 Persistent sin hardens a person's heart and makes it difficult to repent. Deliberately choosing to disobey God can sear the conscience; each sin makes the next one easier to commit. Don't allow sin to wear down a hard path deep within you. Steer as far away from sinful practices as possible.

5:11, 13 Ephraim is another name for Israel, the Northern Kingdom, because Ephraim was the most powerful of the ten tribes in the north. In the same way, the Southern Kingdom was called Judah after its most powerful tribe.

5:13 During the reigns of Menahem and Hoshea, Israel turned to Assyria for help (2 Kings 15:19, 20), but these attempts did not work because they were grounded in man's ability to deliver, not God's. Even the great world powers of that time could not help Israel. For God himself had determined to judge the nation. If we

neglect God's call to repentance, how can we escape? (See Hebrews 2:3.)

6:1-3 This is presumption, not genuine repentance. The people did not understand the depth of their sins. They did not turn from idols, pledge to change, or regret their sins. They thought God's wrath would last only a few days; little did they know that their nation would soon be taken into exile. Israel was interested in God only for the material benefits he provided; they did not value the eternal benefits that come from worshiping him. Before judging them, however, consider your attitude. What do you hope to gain from your religion? Do you "repent" easily, without seriously considering what changes need to take place in your life?

6:3 God had shown his faithfulness to Israel many times. They knew that if they sought to know him and his ways, he would reveal himself to them, and they were right (see 2:20 for a promise of God's faithfulness). The problem was that they were so deep in sin, they did not really want to know him. They wanted blessings, but not his discipline or guidance.

6:4 God answered his people, pointing out that their profession of loyalty, like a mist, easily evaporated and had no substance. Many find it easy and comfortable to maintain the appearance of being

6:4
Ps 78:34-37
Hos 13:3

6:5
Isa 49:2
Heb 4:12

6:6
Mt 9:13; 12:7

6:9
Jer 7:9
Hos 4:2

6:11
Jer 51:33
Joel 3:13

7:1
Jer 51:9
Ezek 24:13
Hos 7:13

7:3
Hos 7:5
Mic 7:3

7:4
Jer 9:2; 23:10

7:5
Prov 20:1
Isa 5:11,22,23
28:1

morning clouds, and disappears like dew. ⁵I sent my prophets to warn you of your doom; I have slain you with the words of my mouth, threatening you with death. Suddenly, without warning, my judgment will strike you as surely as day follows night.

⁶I don't want your sacrifices—I want your love; I don't want your offerings—I want you to know me.

⁷But like Adam, you broke my covenant; you refused my love. ⁸Gilead is a city of sinners, tracked with footprints of blood. ⁹Her citizens are gangs of robbers, lying in ambush for their victims; packs of priests murder along the road to Shechem and practice every kind of sin. ¹⁰Yes, I have seen a horrible thing in Israel—Ephraim chasing other gods, Israel utterly defiled.

¹¹O Judah, for you also there is a plentiful harvest of punishment waiting—and I wanted so much to bless you!

Israel is like a crooked bow

7 I wanted to forgive Israel, but her sins were far too great—no one can even live in Samaria without being a liar, thief, and bandit!

²Her people never seem to recognize that I am watching them. Their sinful deeds give them away on every side; I see them all. ³The king is glad about their wickedness; the princes laugh about their lies. ⁴They are all adulterers; as a baker's oven is constantly aflame—except after he kneads the dough and waits for it to rise again—so are these people constantly aflame with lust.

⁵On the king's birthday, the princes get him drunk; he makes a fool of himself and drinks with those who mock him. ⁶Their hearts blaze like a furnace with

---

OBEDIENCE VS. SACRIFICES	1 Samuel 15:22, 23	Obedience is far better than sacrifice.
God says many times that he doesn't want our gifts and sacrifices when we give them out of ritual or hypocrisy. God wants us first to love and obey him.	Psalm 40:6–8	God doesn't want burnt animals; he wants our life-long service.
	Psalm 51:16–19	God isn't interested in penance; he wants a broken and contrite heart.
	Jeremiah 7:21–23	It isn't offerings God wants; he desires our obedience and promises that he will be our God and we shall be his people.
	Hosea 6:6	God doesn't want sacrifices, he wants love; he doesn't want offerings, he wants us to know him.
	Amos 5:21–24	God hates pretense and hypocrisy; he wants to see a flood of justice.
	Micah 6:6–8	God is not satisfied with sacrifices; he wants us to be fair and just and merciful, and to walk humbly with him.
	Matthew 9:13	God doesn't want gifts; he wants us to be merciful.

---

committed, but is their loyalty deep and sincere? If you profess loyalty to God, back it up with your words and actions.

6:6 Religious rituals can help people understand God and nourish their relationship with him. That is why God instituted circumcision and the sacrificial system in the Old Testament and baptism and the Lord's Supper in the New. But a religious ritual is helpful only if it is carried out with an attitude of love and obedience to God. If one's heart is far from God, ritual becomes empty mockery. God didn't want the Israelites' rituals; he wanted their hearts. Why do you worship? What is the motive behind your "offerings" and "sacrifices"?

6:7 One of Hosea's key themes is that Israel had broken the treaty, or covenant, they had made with God at Mount Sinai (Exodus 19, 20). God wanted to make Israel a light to all the nations, and if they obeyed him and proclaimed him to the world, he would give them special blessings. If they broke the covenant, however, they would suffer severe penalties, as they should have known (see Deuteronomy 28:15–68). Sadly, like Adam in the Garden of Eden, the people broke the treaty and proved

themselves unfaithful to God. How about us? Have we also broken faith with God? What about our forgotten promises to serve him?

6:8, 9 Gilead and Shechem were once sacred places, but now they were corrupt. Shechem was a City of Refuge (Joshua 20:7) and was supposed to be a place of safety for fugitives. But the roads leading to Shechem were unsafe—bands of evil priests lay in wait to murder travelers passing through the territory.

6:11 So that Judah would not become proud as they saw the Northern Kingdom's destruction, Hosea interjected a solemn warning. God's Temple was in Judah (Jerusalem), and the people thought that what happened in Israel could never happen to them. But when they had become utterly corrupt, they too were led off into captivity (see 2 Kings 25).

7:1, 2 God sees and knows everything. Like Israel we often forget this. Thoughts like "No one will ever know," or "No one is watching," may tempt us to try to get away with sin. If you are facing difficult temptations, you will be less likely to give in if you remind yourself that God is watching. When faced with the choice to sin, remember God's words to Israel—"I see them all."

intrigue. Their plot smolders through the night, and in the morning it flames forth like raging fire.

7They kill their kings one after another, and none cries out to me for help.

8My people mingle with the heathen, picking up their evil ways; thus they become as good-for-nothing as a half-baked cake!

9Worshiping foreign gods has sapped their strength, but they don't know it. Ephraim's hair is turning gray, and he doesn't even realize how weak and old he is. **10**His pride in other gods has openly condemned him; yet he doesn't return to his God, nor even try to find him.

11Ephraim is a silly, witless dove, calling to Egypt, flying to Assyria. **12**But as she flies, I throw my net over her and bring her down like a bird from the sky; I will punish her for all her evil ways.

13Woe to my people for deserting me; let them perish, for they have sinned against me. I wanted to redeem them but their hard hearts would not accept the truth. **14**They lie there sleepless with anxiety, but won't ask my help. Instead, they worship heathen gods, asking them for crops and for prosperity.

15I have helped them, and made them strong, yet now they turn against me. **16**They look everywhere except to heaven, to the Most High God. They are like a crooked bow that always misses targets; their leaders will perish by the sword of the enemy for their insolence to me. And all Egypt will laugh at them.

Israel will reap the whirlwind

8 Sound the alarm! They are coming! Like a vulture, the enemy descends upon the people of God because they have broken my treaty and revolted against my laws.

2Now Israel pleads with me and says, "Help us, for you are our God!" **3**But it is too late! Israel has thrown away her chance with contempt, and now her enemies will chase her. **4**She has appointed kings and princes, but not with my consent. They have cut themselves off from my help by worshiping the idols that they made from their silver and gold.

5O Samaria, I reject this calf—this idol you have made. My fury burns against you. How long will it be before one honest man is found among you? **6**When will you admit this calf you worship was made by human hands! It is not God! Therefore, it must be smashed to bits.

7They have sown the wind and they will reap the whirlwind. Their cornstalks

Margin refs: 7:6 Ps 21:9 Dan 3:6 | 7:9 Isa 57:1-11 | 7:12 Job 19:6 Ezek 12:13 | 7:15 Ps 2:1 Nah 1:9 | 7:16 Hos 8:13; 9:3,6 Lk 8:13 | 8:1 Jer 48:40 Hab 1:8 | 8:5 Jer 13:27 | 8:7 Job 38:1 Nah 1:3 Zech 7:14; 9:14

7:7 Three Israelite kings were assassinated during Hosea's lifetime—Zechariah, Shallum, and Pekahiah (2 Kings 15:8–26). Their foreign relations and domestic lives were ruined because they ignored God and his Word.

7:8 Israel had intermarried with heathen people and had picked up their evil ways. When we spend a lot of time with people, we can easily pick up their attitudes and begin to imitate their actions. When you work, live, or play with unbelievers, beware of the influence they may have on you. Instead of drifting into bad habits, see if you can have a positive influence and point them to God.

7:10 Pride keeps a person from returning to God, because pride acknowledges no need of help from anyone, human or divine. To be proud of an idol means to value an object you have made rather than the One who made you. Pride intensifies all our other sins, because we cannot repent of any of them without first giving up our pride.

7:11 Israel's King Menahem had paid Assyria to support him in power (2 Kings 15:19, 20); King Hoshea turned against Assyria and went to Egypt for help (2 Kings 17:4). Israel's kings went back and forth allying themselves with different nations when they should have allied themselves with God.

7:16 A warped bow is unreliable. Its arrows miss the target. Life without God is as unreliable as a warped bow. Without God's direction, our lives are filled with lust, cheating, selfishness, and deceit. As long as our lives are warped by sin, we will never become the kind of people God created us to be.

7:16 People look everywhere except to God for happiness and fulfillment, filling their lives with possessions, activities, and relationships. In reality, only God can truly satisfy the deep longings of the soul. Look first to heaven, "to the Most High God." He will meet your needs.

8:1, 2 This descending enemy is Assyria coming to attack Israel and take her people into captivity (2 Kings 15:28, 29). The people will call to God, but it will be too late because they had stubbornly refused to give up their idols. We, like Israel, often call upon God to ease our pain without wanting him to change our lives. We, like Israel, may repent after it is too late to avoid the painful consequences of sin.

8:5 Samaria was the capital of the Northern Kingdom. Jeroboam I had set up a calf-idol there and had encouraged the people to worship it (1 Kings 12:25–33). Thus the people were worshiping the image of a created animal rather than the Creator.

8:7 Crop yield is the result of good seed planted in good soil and given the proper proportions of sunlight, moisture, and fertilizer. A single seed can produce multiple fruit in good conditions. Israel, however, had sown her spiritual seed to the wind—she had invested herself in activities without substance. Like the wind that comes and goes, her idolatry and foreign alliances offered no protection. In seeking self-preservation apart from God, she brought about her own destruction. Like a forceful whirlwind, God's

stand there barren, withered, sickly, with no grain; if it has any, foreigners will eat it.

8:8
Isa 30:14
Jer 48:38

8Israel is destroyed; she lies among the nations as a broken pot. 9She is a lonely, wandering wild ass. The only friends she has are those she hires; Assyria is one of them.

8:9
Job 39:5-8
Jer 2:24
Ezek 16:33

10But though she hires "friends" from many lands, I will send her off to exile. Then for a while at least she will be free of the burden of her wonderful king! 11Ephraim has built many altars, but they are not to worship me! They are altars of sin! 12Even if I gave her ten thousand laws, she'd say they weren't for her—that they applied to someone far away. 13Her people love the ritual of their sacrifice, but to me it is meaningless! I will call for an accounting of their sins and punish them; they shall return to Egypt.

8:10
Hos 10:10

8:13
Hos 7:2; 9:9
1 Cor 4:5

8:14
2 Sam 7:2
1 Kgs 7:1-12
2 Kgs 18:13
Neh 1:1
Jer 17:27
Dan 4:29; 8:2
Hos 2:13; 4:6

14Israel has built great palaces; Judah has constructed great defenses for her cities, but they have forgotten their Maker. Therefore, I will send down fire upon those palaces and burn those fortresses.

Wandering aimlessly without God

9 O Israel, rejoice no more as others do, for you have deserted your God and sacrificed to other gods on every threshing floor.

9:1
Isa 17:11
22:12,13

9:3
Ezek 4:13
Dan 1:8
Acts 10:14

9:4
Ex 29:40
Lev 22:4-9
23:13
Hag 2:14

9:5
Hos 2:11
Joel 1:13

9:6
Prov 24:31
Isa 5:6; 7:23
Hos 10:8

2Therefore your harvests will be small; your grapes will blight upon the vine. 3You may no longer stay here in this land of God; you will be carried off to Egypt and Assyria, and live there on scraps of food. 4There, far from home, you are not allowed to pour out wine for sacrifice to God. For no sacrifice that is offered there can please him; it is polluted, just as food of mourners is; all who eat such sacrifices are defiled. They may eat this food to feed themselves, but may not offer it to God. 5What then will you do on holy days, on days of feasting to the Lord, 6when you are carried off to Assyria as slaves? Who will inherit your possessions left behind? Egypt will! She will gather your dead; Memphis will bury them. And thorns and thistles will grow up among the ruins.

7The time of Israel's punishment has come; the day of recompense is almost here

---

judgment would come upon Israel by means of the Assyrians. When we seek security in anything besides God, we expose ourselves to great danger. Without God there is no lasting security.

8:12 It is easy to listen to a sermon and think of all the people we know who should be listening, or to read the Bible and think of those who should do what the passage teaches. The Israelites did this constantly, applying God's laws to others but not to themselves. This is just another way to deflect God's Word and avoid making needed changes. As you think of others who need to apply what you are hearing or reading, check to see if the same application could fit you. Apply the lessons to your own life first because often our own faults are the very ones we see first in others.

8:13 We have rituals too—attending church, observing a regular quiet time, celebrating Christian holidays, praying before dinner. Rituals give us security in a changing world. Because they are repeated often, they drive God's lessons deep within us. But rituals can be abused. Beware if you find yourself observing a religious ritual for any of the following reasons: (1) to gain community approval, (2) to avoid the risks of doing something different, (3) to make thought unnecessary, (4) to substitute for personal relationships, (5) to make up for bad behavior, (6) to earn God's favor. We should not reject the rituals of our worship, but we must be careful with them. Think about why you do them; focus on God; and perform every act with sincere devotion.

8:13 In Egypt, the Israelites had been slaves (Exodus 1:11). The people would not literally return to Egypt, but they would return to slavery—this time scattered throughout the Assyrian Empire.

8:14 Israel put her confidence in military strength, strong defenses, and economic stability, just as nations do today. But because of the people's inner moral decay, their apparent sources

of strength were inadequate. There is a tendency in many nations toward removing all traces of God from daily life. But if a nation forgets its Maker, its strengths may prove worthless when put to the test.

9:1ff Hosea probably spoke these words at a national festival, the Feast of Tabernacles, when it was customary to live in tents to commemorate God's care for his people in the wilderness (Leviticus 23:33–44).

9:1 A threshing floor was a flat area, often built on a hilltop, where harvesters beat the wheat and separated it from the chaff. Often men would stay overnight at the threshing floor to protect their grain, so this was a natural gathering place. Because of their elevation, threshing floors began to be used as places to sacrifice to false gods.

9:5, 6 Israel's leaders vacillated between alliances with Egypt and alliances with Assyria. Hosea was saying that both were wrong. Breaking an alliance with untrustworthy Assyria and fleeing for help to the equally untrustworthy Egypt would cause Israel's destruction. Their only hope was to return to God.

9:7 By the time Israel began to experience the consequences of her sins, she was no longer listening to God's messengers. Refusing to hear the truth from prophets who spoke out so clearly about her sins, she did not hear God's warnings about what was soon to happen to her. We all listen and read selectively—focusing on what seems to support our present life-style, ignoring what demands a radical reordering of our priorities. In doing this, we are likely to miss the warnings we need most. Listen to people who think your approach is all wrong. Read articles that present viewpoints you would be unlikely to take. Ask yourself, "Is God speaking to me through these speakers and writers? Is there something I need to change?"

and soon Israel will know it all too well. "The prophets are crazy"; "The inspired men are mad." Yes, so they mock, for the nation is weighted with sin, and shows only hatred for those who love God.

8I appointed the prophets to guard my people, but the people have blocked them at every turn and publicly declared their hatred, even in the Temple of the Lord. 9The things my people do are as depraved as what they did in Gibeah long ago. The Lord does not forget. He will surely punish them.

10O Israel, how well I remember those first delightful days when I led you through the wilderness! How refreshing was your love! How satisfying, like the early figs of summer in their first season! But then you deserted me for Baal-peor, to give yourselves to other gods, and soon you were as foul as they. 11The glory of Israel flies away like a bird, for your children will die at birth, or perish in the womb, or never even be conceived. 12And if your children grow, I will take them from you; all are doomed. Yes, it will be a sad day when I turn away and leave you alone.

13In my vision I have seen the sons of Israel doomed. The fathers are forced to lead their sons to slaughter. 14O Lord, what shall I ask for your people? I will ask for wombs that don't give birth, for breasts that cannot nourish.

15All their wickedness began at Gilgal; there I began to hate them. I will drive them from my land because of their idolatry. I will love them no more, for all their leaders are rebels. 16Ephraim is doomed. The roots of Israel are dried up; she shall bear no more fruit. And if she gives birth, I will slay even her beloved child.

17My God will destroy the people of Israel because they will not listen or obey. They will be wandering Jews, homeless among the nations.

Hosea predicts punishment

10 How prosperous Israel is—a luxuriant vine all filled with fruit! But the more wealth I give her, the more she pours it on the altars of her heathen gods; the richer the harvests I give her, the more beautiful the statues and idols she erects. 2The hearts of her people are false toward God. They are guilty and must be punished. God will break down their heathen altars and smash their idols. 3Then they will say, "We deserted the Lord and he took away our king. But what's the difference? We don't need one anyway!"

4They make promises they don't intend to keep. Therefore punishment will spring up among them like poisonous weeds in the furrows of the field. 5The people

9:7
Isa 10:3
Jer 10:15
Jer 29:26
Lam 2:14
Ezek 7:2-7
13:3,10
Amos 8:2

9:9
Isa 24:4,5; 31:6
Hos 7:2; 8:13

9:10
Num 13:21-23
25:1-9
Josh 22:17,18
Jer 24:2
Mic 7:1

9:11
Hos 4:7

9:15
Hos 5:2
Amos 4:4; 5:5

9:16
Ezek 24:21

10:1
1 Kgs 14:23
Isa 5:1-7
Ezek 15:1-5

10:2
1 Kgs 18:21
Mic 5:13
Zeph 1:5

10:3
Mic 4:9

10:4
Ezek 17:13-19

9:9 A couple had stopped to stay overnight in Gibeah when a gang of sex perverts gathered around the house and demanded that the man come out. Instead, the traveler gave them his wife. They raped and abused her all night and then left her dead on the doorstep (Judges 19:14–30). That horrible act revealed the depths to which the people had sunk. Gibeah was destroyed for its evil (Judges 20:8–48), but Hosea said that the whole nation was now as evil as that city. Just as the city didn't escape punishment, neither would the nation.

9:10 Baal-peor was the god of Peor, a city in Moab. In Numbers 23, Balaam, a freelance prophet, was hired by King Balak of Moab to curse the Israelites as they were coming through his land. The Moabites enticed the young Israelites into sexual sin and Baal worship. Before long, they became as corrupt as the gods they worshiped. People can take on the characteristics of what or whom they love. What do you worship? Are you becoming more like God, or are you becoming more like someone or something else?

9:14 Hosea prayed this prayer when he foresaw the destruction that Israel's sins would bring upon them (2 Kings 17). This vision of Israel's terrible fate moved him to pray that women would not get pregnant and that children would die as infants so they would not have to experience the tremendous suffering and pain that lay ahead.

9:15 At Gilgal, both the political and the religious failure of the nation began. Here idols and kings were substituted for God. Saul,

the united nation's first king, was crowned at Gilgal (1 Samuel 11:15), but by Hosea's time, Baal worship flourished there (4:15; 12:11).

10:1 Israel prospered under Jeroboam II, gaining military and economic strength. But the more prosperous she became, the more she lavished on her idols. It seems as if the more God gives, the more we spend. We want bigger houses, better cars, finer clothes, and more expensive education. But the finest things the world offers line the pathway to destruction. As you prosper, consider where your money is going. Is it being used for God's purposes, or are you consuming it all on yourself?

10:3 This statement shows Israel's unrepentant attitude. First they put their confidence in a king. When their king was taken away, however, they did not turn back to God. Instead, they said in effect, "So what?" and continued in their sinful ways.

10:4 God was angry with Israel for their insincere promises to him, and in response he said that punishment would come. People break their promises, but God always keeps his. Are you remaining true to your promises, both to other people and to God? If not, ask God for forgiveness and help to get back on track. Then be careful about the promises you make. Never make a promise unless you are sure you can keep it.

10:5 If the Israelites' idols were really gods, they should have been able to protect the people. How ironic that the people were fearing for their gods' safety! For more information on these

of Samaria tremble lest their calf-god idols at Beth-aven should be hurt; the priests and people, too, mourn over the departed honor of their shattered gods. 6This idol—this calf-god thing—will be carted with them when they go as slaves to Assyria, a present to the great king there. Ephraim will be laughed at for trusting in this idol; Israel will be put to shame. 7As for Samaria, her king shall disappear like a chip of wood upon an ocean wave. 8And the idol altars of Aven at Bethel where Israel sinned will crumble. Thorns and thistles will grow up to surround them. And the people will cry to the mountains and hills to fall upon them and crush them.

9O Israel, ever since that awful night in Gibeah, there has been only sin, sin, sin! You have made no progress whatever. Was it not right that the men of Gibeah were wiped out? 10I will come against you for your disobedience; I will gather the armies of the nations against you to punish you for your heaped-up sins.

11Ephraim is accustomed to treading out the grain—an easy job she loves. I have never put her under a heavy yoke before; I have spared her tender neck. But now I will harness her to the plow and harrow. Her days of ease are gone.

12Plant the good seeds of righteousness and you will reap a crop of my love; plow the hard ground of your hearts, for now is the time to seek the Lord, that he may come and shower salvation upon you.

13But you have cultivated wickedness and raised a thriving crop of sins. You have earned the full reward of trusting in a lie—believing that military might and great armies can make a nation safe!

14Therefore the terrors of war shall rise among your people, and all your forts will fall, just as at Beth-arbel, which Shalman destroyed; even mothers and children were dashed to death there. 15That will be your fate, too, you people of Israel, because of your great wickedness. In one morning the king of Israel shall be destroyed.

3. God's love for Israel
God's fatherly love

11 When Israel was a child I loved him as a son and brought him out of Egypt. 2But the more I called to him, the more he rebelled, sacrificing to Baal and burning incense to idols. 3I trained him from infancy, I taught him to walk, I held

Marginal references

10:5
1 Kgs 12:28-32
2 Chron 11:15
Hos 10:6

10:6
Hos 10:5

10:8
Hos 5:8; 9:6
10:5

10:11
Deut 28:48
Jer 28:14

10:12
Prov 11:18
Isa 32:20

10:13
Ps 33:16
Eccles 9:11

10:14
2 Kgs 17:6
18:9,10

11:1
Ex 4:22

---

calf-gods, see the notes on 3:4, 5 and 8:5.

10:9 For information on "that awful night," see the note on 9:9 or read Judges 19 and 20. Gibeah stands for cruelty and sensuality.

10:12 Hosea repeatedly uses illustrations about fields and crops. Here he speaks of a plowed field, ground that is ready to receive seeds. It is no longer stony and hard; it has been carefully prepared, and it is available. Is your life ready for God to work in it? You can plow the hard ground of your heart by acknowledging your sins and opening your heart to God's forgiveness.

10:12, 13 When we think of reaping what we sow, we usually think of negative results. Here we see that the results can be positive or negative. Just as small seeds eventually produce large crops, our small everyday actions can produce far-reaching results for good or for evil. What kind of crop are you sowing today? What might be the long-term effects of some of your actions?

10:13 The Israelites trusted in the lie that military power could keep them safe. Believers today are also capable of falling for lies. Those who want to lead others astray often follow these rules for effective lying: make it big; keep it simple; repeat it often. Believers can avoid falling for lies by asking: (1) Am I believing this because there is personal gain in it for me? (2) Am I discounting important facts? (3) Does it conflict with a direct command of Scripture? (4) Are there any biblical parallels to the situation I'm facing that would help me know what to believe?

10:14 Shalman was probably Salaman, king of Moab, who invaded Gilead around 740 B.C. Shalman destroyed the city of Beth-arbel, killing many people, including women and children. Hosea was saying that Israel's fate will be like that of Beth-arbel.

10:15 Israel put their confidence in military might rather than in God, and as a result, they would be destroyed by military power. Israel's king, who had led the people into idol worship, would be the first to fall. Divine judgment is *sometimes* swift, but it is *always* sure.

11:1ff In the final four chapters, Hosea shifts to the theme of God's intense love for Israel. God had always loved Israel as a parent loves a stubborn child, and that is why he would not release her from the consequences of her behavior. The Israelites were sinful, and they would be punished like a wayward son brought by his parents before the elders (Deuteronomy 21:18–21). All through Israel's sad history, God repeatedly offered to restore her if she would only turn to him. By stubbornly refusing his invitation, the Northern Kingdom sealed her doom. She would be destroyed, never to rise again. Even so, Israel as a nation was not finished. A remnant of faithful Israelites would return to Jerusalem, where one day the Messiah would come, offering pardon and reconciliation to all who would faithfully follow him.

11:3 God had consistently provided for his people, but they refused to see what he had done, and they showed no interest in thanking him. Ungratefulness is a common human fault. For example, when was the last time you thanked your parents for caring for you? Your pastor for the service he gives your church? Your child's teacher for the care taken with each day's activities? Your heavenly Father for his guidance? Many of the blessings we enjoy are the result of loving actions done long ago. Look for hidden acts of nurturing, and thank those who make the world better through their love. But begin by thanking God for all his blessings.

him in my arms. But he doesn't know or even care that it was I who raised him.

⁴As a man would lead his favorite ox, so I led Israel with my ropes of love. I loosened his muzzle so he could eat. I myself have stooped and fed him. ⁵But my people shall return to Egypt and Assyria because they won't return to me.

⁶War will swirl through their cities; their enemies will crash through their gates and trap them in their own fortresses. ⁷For my people are determined to desert me. And so I have sentenced them to slavery, and no one shall set them free.

⁸Oh, how can I give you up, my Ephraim? How can I let you go? How can I forsake you like Admah and Zeboiim? My heart cries out within me; how I long to help you! ⁹No, I will not punish you as much as my fierce anger tells me to. This is the last time I will destroy Ephraim. For I am God and not man; I am the Holy One living among you, and I did not come to destroy.

¹⁰For the people shall walk after the Lord. I shall roar as a lion [at their enemies] and my people shall return trembling from the west. ¹¹Like a flock of birds, they will come from Egypt—like doves flying from Assyria. And I will bring them home again; it is a promise from the Lord.

¹²Israel surrounds me with lies and deceit, but Judah still trusts in God and is faithful to the Holy One.

God invites his people to return to him

12 Israel is chasing the wind, yes, shepherding a whirlwind—a dangerous game! For she has given gifts to Egypt and Assyria to get their help, and in return she gets their worthless promises.

²But the Lord is bringing a lawsuit against Judah. Jacob will be justly punished for his ways. ³When he was born, he struggled with his brother; when he became a man, he even fought with God. ⁴Yes, he wrestled with the Angel and prevailed. He wept and pleaded for a blessing from him. He met God there at Bethel face to face. God spoke to him— ⁵the Lord, the God of heaven's armies—Jehovah is his name.

⁶Oh, come back to God. Live by the principles of love and justice, and always be expecting much from him, your God.

⁷But no, my people are like crafty merchants selling from dishonest scales—they

11:4 *As a man would lead his favorite ox,* implied.   **12:1** *a dangerous game,* implied.

11:4
Ex 16:32
Jer 31:2,3

11:6
Isa 9:14; 18:5

11:7
Jer 8:5
Hos 4:16

11:8
Gen 14:8
Deut 29:23
Hos 6:4; 7:1

11:9
Ex 32:10-14
Deut 13:17
Isa 5:24; 12:6
Jer 31:1-3

11:10
Isa 66:2,5
Jer 5:22; 25:30
Joel 3:16
Amos 1:2; 3:4

11:11
Isa 11:11; 60:8
Zech 10:10

12:1
Jer 22:22
Ezek 17:10

12:3
Gen 25:26
Rom 9:11

12:4
Gen 28:13-15
32:24-30
35:10-15

12:6
Mic 7:7

12:7
Prov 11:1
Hos 7:14
Amos 8:5
Mic 6:11

11:4 God's discipline requires times of leading and times of feeding. Sometimes the rope is taut, sometimes it is slack. It is always loving, and its object is always the well-being of the beloved. When you are called to discipline others—children, students, employees, or church members—do not be rigid. Vary your approach according to the goals you are seeking to accomplish. In each case, ask yourself: does this person need guidance, or does he need to be nurtured?

11:5 The Northern Kingdom survived only two centuries after the break with Jerusalem. Its spiritual and political leaders did not help the people learn the way to God, so as a nation they would never repent. Hosea prophesied its downfall, which happened when Shalmaneser of Assyria conquered Israel in 722 B.C. Judah also would go into captivity, but a remnant would return to their homeland.

11:8 Admah and Zeboiim were cities of the plain that perished with Sodom and Gomorrah (Genesis 14:8; Deuteronomy 29:23).

11:9 "I am God and not man." It is easy for us to define God in terms of our own expectations and behavior. In so doing, we make him just slightly larger than ourselves. In reality, he is infinitely greater than we are. We should seek to become like him rather than attempting to remake him in our image.

11:12 Unlike Israel, Judah had some fairly good kings—Asa, Jehoshaphat, Joash, Amaziah, Azariah, Jotham, and especially Hezekiah and Josiah. Under some of these kings, God's law was dusted off and taught to the people. The priests continued to serve

in God's appointed Temple in Jerusalem, and the feasts were celebrated at least some of the time. Unfortunately, none of the political or religious leaders were able to completely wipe out idol worship and pagan rites (although Hezekiah and Josiah came close), which continued to fester until they eventually erupted and infected the whole country. Still, the influence of the good kings enabled Judah to survive more than 150 years longer than Israel, and it fortified a small group—a remnant—of faithful people who would one day return and restore their land and Temple.

12:2–5 Jacob, whose name was later changed to Israel, was the common ancestor of all 12 tribes of Israel (both Northern and Southern Kingdoms). Like the nations that descended from him, Jacob practiced deceit. Unlike Israel and Judah, however, he constantly searched for God. Jacob wrestled with the Angel in order to be blessed, but his descendants thought their blessings came from their own successes. Jacob purged his house of idols (Genesis 35:2), but his descendants could not seem to banish idol worship from their midst.

12:6 The two principles Hosea called his nation to live by, love and justice, are at the very foundation of God's character. They are essential to his followers, but they are not easy to keep in balance. Some people are loving—to the point that they excuse wrongdoing. Others are just—to the extent that they forget mercy. Love without justice, because it is not aiming at a higher standard, leaves people in their sins. Justice without love, because it has no heart, drives people away from God. To specialize in one at the expense of the other is to distort our witness. Today's church, just like Hosea's nation, must live by both principles.

12:8
Ps 62:10
Zech 11:5

12:10
Isa 20:2-5
Jer 25:4

12:12
Gen 28:5; 29:20

12:13
Ex 12:50

12:14
1 Kgs 2:33,34
2 Kgs 17:7-18
Ezek 18:13
23:2-10

13:2
1 Kgs 19:18
Isa 44:17-20
Jer 10:2-5

13:3
Ps 68:2
Isa 17:13
Hos 6:4

13:4
Ex 20:3
Isa 43:11

13:5
Deut 2:7; 8:15
32:10

13:6
Hos 2:13; 4:6

13:10
2 Kgs 17:4
Hos 8:4

love to cheat. 8Ephraim boasts, "I am so rich! I have gotten it all by myself!" But riches can't make up for sin.

9I am the same Lord, the same God, who delivered you from slavery in Egypt, and I am the one who will consign you to living in tents again, as you do each year at the Tabernacle Feast. 10I sent my prophets to warn you with many a vision and many a parable and dream. 11But the sins of Gilgal flourish just the same. Row on row of altars—like furrows in a field—are used for sacrifices to your idols. And Gilead, too, is full of fools who worship idols. 12Jacob fled to Syria and earned a wife by tending sheep. 13Then the Lord led his people out of Egypt by a prophet, who guided and protected them. 14But Ephraim has bitterly provoked the Lord. The Lord will sentence him to death as payment for his sins.

God expresses his anger against Israel

13 It used to be when Israel spoke, the nations shook with fear, for he was a mighty prince; but he worshiped Baal and sealed his doom.

2And now the people disobey more and more. They melt their silver to mold into idols, formed with skill by the hands of men. "Sacrifice to these!" they say—men kissing calves! 3They shall disappear like morning mist, like dew that quickly dries away, like chaff blown by the wind, like a cloud of smoke.

4I alone am God, your Lord, and have been ever since I brought you out from Egypt. You have no God but me, for there is no other Savior. 5I took care of you in the wilderness, in that dry and thirsty land. 6But when you had eaten and were satisfied, then you became proud and forgot me. 7So I will come upon you like a lion, or a leopard lurking along the road. 8I will rip you to pieces like a bear whose cubs have been taken away, and like a lion I will devour you.

9O Israel, if I destroy you, who can save you? 10Where is your king? Why don't you call on him for help? Where are all the leaders of the land? You asked for them,

12:11 fools, or, "vanity."

CYCLES OF JUDGMENT/ SALVATION IN HOSEA

Judgment	1:2–9; 2:2–13; 4:1—5:14; 6:4—11:7; 11:12—13:16
Salvation	1:10—2:1; 2:14—3:5; 5:15—6:3; 11:8–11; 14:1–9

God promises to judge, but he also promises mercy. Here you can see the cycles of judgment and salvation in Hosea. Prophecies of judgment are consistently followed by prophecies of forgiveness.

12:7, 8 In Israel, dishonesty had become an accepted means of attaining wealth. Israelites who were financially successful could not imagine that God would consider them sinful. They thought their wealth was a sign of his blessing, and they didn't bother to consider how they had gotten it. But God said Israel's riches would not make up for her sin. Remember that God's measure of success is different from ours. He calls us to faithfulness, not to affluence. Our character is more important to him than our pocketbook.

12:8 Rich people and nations often claim that their material success is due to their own hard work, initiative, and intelligence. Because they have every possession they want, they don't feel the need for God. They believe that their riches are their own, and they feel they have the right to use them any way they please. If you find yourself feeling proud of your accomplishments, remember that all your opportunities, abilities, and resources come from God, and that you hold them in sacred trust for him.

12:9 Once a year the Israelites spent a week living in tents during the Festival of Tabernacles, which commemorated God's protection as they wandered in the wilderness for 40 years (see Deuteronomy 1:19—2:1). Now, because of their sin, God would cause them to live in tents again—this time not as part of a festival, but in actual bondage.

12:12 Hosea was using this reference to Jacob to say "Don't forget your humble beginnings. What you have is not a result of your own efforts, but is yours because God has been gracious to you."

12:13 The prophet who led Israel out of Egypt was Moses (Exodus 13:17–19).

13:1 Israel had a history of greatness, but by Hosea's time the people had rebelled against God and lost their authority. Greatness in the past is no guarantee of greatness in the future. It is good to remember what God has done for you and through you, but it is equally important to keep your relationship with him up to date. Commit yourself to God day by day and moment by moment, and you will continue to grow and thrive.

13:4–6 When Israel's possessions made her feel self-sufficient, she turned her back on God and forgot him. Self-sufficiency is as destructive today as it was in Hosea's time. Do you see your constant need of God's presence and help? Learn to rely on him both in good times and bad. If you are traveling along a smooth and easy path right now, beware of thinking you deserve your good fortune. Don't depend on your gifts; depend on the Giver.

now let them save you! ¹¹I gave you kings in my anger, and I took them away in my wrath. ¹²Ephraim's sins are harvested and stored away for punishment.

¹³New birth is offered him, but he is like a child resisting in the womb—how stubborn! how foolish! ¹⁴Shall I ransom him from hell? Shall I redeem him from Death? O Death, bring forth your terrors for his tasting! O Grave, demonstrate your plagues! For I will not relent!

¹⁵He was called the most fruitful of all his brothers, but the east wind—a wind of the Lord from the desert—will blow hard upon him and dry up his land. All his flowing springs and green oases will dry away, and he will die of thirst. ¹⁶Samaria must bear her guilt, for she rebelled against her God. Her people will be killed by the invading army, her babies dashed to death against the ground, her pregnant women ripped open with a sword.

13:11	1 Sam 8:7 1 Kgs 14:7-10
13:12	Deut 32:34,35
13:13	Mic 4:9,10
13:14	Isa 25:8 Ezek 37:12,13 1 Cor 15:55
13:15	Jer 51:36 Hos 12:1
13:16	2 Kgs 15:16

Repentance will bring restoration

14 O Israel, return to the Lord, your God, for you have been crushed by your sins. ²Bring your petition. Come to the Lord and say, "O Lord, take away our sins; be gracious to us and receive us, and we will offer you the sacrifice of praise. ³Assyria cannot save us, nor can our strength in battle; never again will we call the idols we have made 'our gods'; for in you alone, O Lord, the fatherless find mercy."

⁴Then I will cure you of idolatry and faithlessness, and my love will know no bounds, for my anger will be forever gone! ⁵I will refresh Israel like the dew from heaven; she will blossom as the lily and root deeply in the soil like cedars in Lebanon. ⁶Her branches will spread out, as beautiful as olive trees, fragrant as the forests of Lebanon. ⁷Her people will return from exile far away and rest beneath my shadow. They will be a watered garden and blossom like grapes and be as fragrant as the wines of Lebanon.

⁸O Ephraim! Stay away from idols! I am living and strong! I look after you and care for you. I am like an evergreen tree, yielding my fruit to you throughout the year. My mercies never fail.

14:2	Mic 7:18,19
14:3	Ps 68:5 Mic 5:10-14
14:4	Isa 57:18 Jer 3:22 Zeph 3:17
14:6	Ps 52:8 Jer 11:16
14:7	Ps 91:1 Isa 32:1,2
14:8	Isa 41:19

13:11 *I gave you kings in my anger, and I took them away.* Probably an allusion to the kings of Israel assassinated during her last tempestuous years: Zechariah, Shallum, Pekahiah.

13:11 God had warned Israel that kings would cause more problems than they would solve, and he reluctantly gave them Saul as their first king (1 Samuel 8:4–22). David was a good king, and Solomon had his strengths, but once the nation divided in two, the Northern Kingdom never had another good ruler. Evil kings led the nation deeper and deeper into idolatry and unwise political alliances. Assassinations became common, and cities and roads grew unsafe. Eventually the evil kings destroyed the nation, and with Hoshea, Israel's kings were cut off (2 Kings 17:1–6).

13:12 Ephraim's (Israel's) sins were recorded for later punishment. This was not a special case. All our sins are known and will be revealed at the Day of Judgment (2 Corinthians 5:10; Revelation 20:11–15).

14:1ff Verses 1–3 are Hosea's call to repent. Verses 4–8 are God's promise of restoration. God must punish Israel for her gross and repeated violations of his law, but he does so with a heavy heart. What he really wants to do is restore the nation and make it prosper.

14:1, 2 The people could return to God by asking him to take away their sins. The same is true for us: we can pray Hosea's prayer and know our sins are forgiven because Christ died for them on the cross (John 3:16).

Forgiveness begins when we see the destructiveness of sin and the futility of life without God. Then we must admit we cannot save ourselves; our only hope is in God's mercy. When we request forgiveness, we must recognize that we do not deserve it and therefore cannot demand it. Our appeal must be for God's love

and mercy, not for his justice. Although we cannot demand forgiveness, we can be confident we have received it, because God is gracious and loving and wants to restore us to himself, just as he wanted to restore Israel.

14:2 A sacrifice of praise means offering praise to God rather than going to the Temple and offering a sacrifice on the altar. This was a verbal rather than physical sacrifice. An animal sacrifice was made to atone for sin, while a sacrifice of praise was thanking God for forgiving sins. Believers can continually offer sacrifices of praise to God today (Hebrews 13:15; 1 Peter 2:5).

14:8 When our will is weak, when our reason is confused, when our conscience is burdened with a load of guilt, we must remember that God's mercies never fail. When friends and family desert us, when co-workers don't understand us, when we are tired of being good, God's mercies never fail. When we can't see the way or seem to hear God's voice, when we lack courage to go on, God's mercies never fail. When our shortcomings beset us and awareness of our sins overcomes us, God's mercies never fail.

14:9 Hosea closes with an appeal to listen, learn, and benefit from God's Word. To those receiving the Lord's message through Hosea, this meant the difference between life and death. For you, the reader of the book of Hosea, the choice is similar: either listen to the book's message and follow God's ways, or refuse to walk along the Lord's path. But a person who insists on following his own direction without God's guidance "gropes and stumbles in the dark" (Proverbs 4:18, 19). If you are lost, you can find the way by turning from your sin and following God.

14:9
Job 34:10-12
Prov 1:5,6; 4:18
Rom 9:32

9Whoever is wise, let him understand these things. Whoever is intelligent, let him listen. For the paths of the Lord are true and right, and good men walk along them. But sinners trying it will fail.

14:9 God's concern for *justice* that requires faithfulness and *mercy* that offers forgiveness can be seen in his dealings with Hosea. We can err by forgetting God's love and feeling that our sins are hopeless; but we can also err by forgetting his wrath against our sins and thinking he will continue to accept us no matter how we act. *Forgiveness* is a key word: when God forgives us, he judges the sin but shows mercy to the sinner. We should never be afraid to come to God for a clean slate and a renewed life.

JOEL

King Ahab dies in battle 853 B.C.	Elisha becomes a prophet 848	Jehu becomes king of Israel; Athaliah siezes Judah's throne 841	Joel becomes a prophet; Joash becomes king of Judah 835

VITAL STATISTICS

PURPOSE:
To warn Judah of God's impending judgment because of their sins and to urge them to turn back to God

AUTHOR:
Joel, son of Pethuel

TO WHOM WRITTEN:
The people of Judah, the Southern Kingdom, and God's people everywhere

DATE WRITTEN:
Probably during the time Joel prophesied, from about 835 to 796 B.C.

SETTING:
The people of Judah had become prosperous and complacent. Taking God for granted, they had turned to self-centeredness, idolatry, and sin. Joel warns them that this kind of life-style will inevitably bring down God's judgment.

KEY VERSES:
"That is why the Lord says, 'Turn to me now, while there is time. Give me all your hearts. Come with fasting, weeping, mourning. Let your remorse tear at your hearts and not your garments.' Return to the Lord your God, for he is gracious and merciful. He is not easily angered; he is full of kindness, and anxious not to punish you" (2:12, 13).

KEY PEOPLE:
Joel, the people of Judah

KEY PLACE:
Jerusalem

A SINGLE bomb devastates a city and the world is ushered into the nuclear age. A split atom reveals power and force such as we have never seen. At a launch site, rockets roar and a payload is thrust into space. Discoveries dreamed of for centuries are ours as we begin to explore the universe.

Volcanoes, earthquakes, tidal waves, hurricanes, and tornadoes unleash uncontrollable and unstoppable force. And we can only avoid them and then pick up the pieces.

Power, strength, might—we stand in awe at the natural and man-made display. But these forces cannot touch the power of omnipotent God. Creator of galaxies, atoms, and natural laws, the sovereign Lord rules all there is and ever will be. How silly to live without him; how foolish to run and hide from him; how ridiculous to disobey him. But we do. Since Eden, we have sought independence from his control, as though we were gods and could control our destiny. And he has allowed our rebellion. But soon *the Day of the Lord* will come.

It is about this day that the prophet Joel spoke, and it is the theme of his book. On this day God will judge all unrighteousness and disobedience—all accounts will be settled and the crooked made straight.

We know very little about Joel, only that he was a prophet and the son of Pethuel. And he may have lived in Jerusalem, for his audience was Judah, the Southern Kingdom. Whoever he was, Joel speaks forthrightly and forcefully in this short and powerful book. His message is one of foreboding and warning, but it is also filled with hope. Joel states that our Creator, the omnipotent Judge, is also merciful, and he wants to bless all those who trust him.

Joel begins by describing a terrible plague of locusts that covers the land and devours the crops. The devastation wrought by these creatures is but a foretaste of the coming judgment of God. Joel, therefore, urges the people to turn from their sin and turn back to God. Woven into this message of judgment and repentance is an affirmation of God's kindness and the blessings he promises for all who follow him. In fact, "everyone who calls upon the name of the Lord will be saved" (2:32).

As you read Joel, catch his vision of the power and might of God and of his ultimate judgment on sin. Choose to follow, obey, and worship God alone as your sovereign Lord.

THE BLUEPRINT

1. The day of the locusts (1:1—2:27)
2. The Day of the Lord (2:28—3:21)

The locust plague was only a foretaste of the judgment to come in the Day of the Lord. This is a timeless call to repentance with the promise of blessing. Just as the people faced the tragedy of their crops being destroyed, we too will face tragic judgment if we live in sin. But God's grace is available to us both now and in that coming day.

MEGATHEMES

THEME	EXPLANATION	IMPORTANCE
Punishment	Like a destroying army of locusts, God's punishment for sin is overwhelming, dreadful, and unavoidable. When it comes, there will be no food, no water, no protection, and no escape. The day for settling accounts with God for how we have lived is fast approaching.	God is the one with whom we all must reckon—not nature, the economy, or a foreign invader. We can't ignore or offend God forever. We must pay attention to his message now, or we will face his anger later.
Forgiveness	God stood ready to forgive and restore all those who would come to him and turn away from sin. God wanted to shower his people with his love and restore them to a proper relationship with him.	Forgiveness comes by turning from sin and turning toward God. It is not too late to receive God's forgiveness. God's greatest desire is for you to come to him.
Promise of the Holy Spirit	Joel predicts the time when God will pour out his Holy Spirit on all people. It will be the beginning of new and fresh worship of God by those who believe in him, but also the beginning of judgment on all who reject him.	God is in control. Justice and restoration are in his hands. The Holy Spirit confirms God's love for us just as he did for the first Christians (Acts 2). We must be faithful to God and place our lives under the guidance and power of his Holy Spirit.

1. The day of the locusts

Joel predicts a plague of locusts

1:2
Jer 30:7

1:3
Ex 10:2
Deut 6:4-9

1 This message came from the Lord to Joel, son of Pethuel:

²Listen, you aged men of Israel! Everyone, listen! In all your lifetime, yes, in all your history, have you ever heard of such a thing as I am going to tell you? ³In years to come, tell your children about it; pass the awful story down from

1:1 Joel was a prophet to the nation of Judah, also known as the Southern Kingdom. The book does not mention when he lived, but it is likely he prophesied during the reign of King Joash (835–796 B.C.). Basing their argument on verses such as 3:1, however, some have suggested that he wrote after the Jews had returned from exile. Those who suggest an earlier date point to 3:4, claiming that Tyre, Sidon, and Philistia were contemporary nations of Judah *before* their captivity (586 B.C.). But the date of Joel's book is not

nearly so important as its timeless message. Sin brings God's judgment. Yet with God's justice there is also great mercy.

1:3 God urged adults to pass their history down to their children, telling them over and over the important lessons they learned. One of the greatest gifts you can give younger people is your life's story to help them understand the successes you've had and the mistakes you've made.

generation to generation. ⁴After the cutter-locusts finish eating your crops, the
swarmer-locusts will take what's left! After them will come the hopper-locusts!
And then the stripper-locusts, too!

⁵Wake up and weep, you drunkards, for all the grapes are ruined and all your
wine is gone! ⁶A vast army of locusts covers the land. It is a terrible army too
numerous to count, with teeth as sharp as those of lions! ⁷They have ruined my
vines and stripped the bark from the fig trees, leaving trunks and branches white
and bare.

⁸Weep with sorrow, as a virgin weeps whose fiancé is dead. ⁹Gone are the
offerings of grain and wine to bring to the Temple of the Lord; the priests are
starving. Hear the crying of these ministers of God. ¹⁰The fields are bare of crops.
Sorrow and sadness are everywhere. The grain, the grapes, the olive oil are gone.

¹¹Well may you farmers stand so shocked and stricken; well may you vinedressers weep. Weep for the wheat and the barley too, for they are gone. ¹²The
grapevines are dead; the fig trees are dying; the pomegranates wither; the apples
shrivel on the trees; all joy has withered with them.

Joel calls the people to repent

¹³O priests, robe yourselves in sackcloth. O ministers of my God, lie all night
before the altar, weeping. For there are no more offerings of grain and wine for
you. ¹⁴Announce a fast; call a solemn meeting. Gather the elders and all the people
into the Temple of the Lord your God, and weep before him there.

¹⁵Alas, this terrible day of punishment is on the way. Destruction from the
Almighty is almost here! ¹⁶Our food will disappear before our eyes; all joy and
gladness will be ended in the Temple of our God. ¹⁷The seed rots in the ground; the
barns and granaries are empty; the grain has dried up in the fields. ¹⁸The cattle
groan with hunger; the herds stand perplexed for there is no pasture for them; the
sheep bleat in misery.

¹⁹Lord, help us! For the heat has withered the pastures and burned up all the
trees. ²⁰Even the wild animals cry to you for help, for there is no water for them.
The creeks are dry and the pastures are scorched.

Joel warns of the approaching judgment

2 Sound the alarm in Jerusalem! Let the blast of the warning trumpet be heard
upon my holy mountain! Let everyone tremble in fear, for the day of the Lord's
judgment approaches.

1:6 *a vast army of locusts,* literally, "a nation." **1:15** *this terrible day of punishment,* or, "the Day of the Lord."

Marginal references:

1:4
Isa 33:4
Jer 51:14
Joel 2:25

1:6
Joel 1:4

1:7
Amos 4:9

1:9
Hos 9:4
Joel 1:13; 2:14

1:11
Ezra 9:3
Amos 5:16

1:12
Song 2:3
Joel 1:7
Hab 3:17,18
Hag 2:19

1:13
1 Kgs 21:27
Jer 4:8

1:15
Isa 13:9
Ezek 7:2-13
Joel 2:1

1:16
Isa 3:7
Amos 4:6,7

1:17
Isa 17:10,11

1:19
Ps 50:15; 91:15
Mic 7:7

1:20
1 Kgs 17:7; 18:5
Ps 104:21
Joel 1:18

2:1
Joel 1:15
2:11,15,31
3:14

1:4 A locust plague can be as devastating as an invading army.
The locusts gather in swarms too great to number (1:6) and fly
several feet above the ground, seemingly darkening the sun as
they pass by (2:2). When they land, they devour almost every
piece of vegetation (1:7–12), invading everything in their path
(2:9).

1:4 Joel's detailed description has caused many to believe that
he was referring to an actual locust plague that had come or was
about to come upon the land. Another common view is that the
locusts symbolize an invading enemy army. Regardless of the
correct view, Joel's point was that God would punish the people
because of their sin. Joel calls this judgment the "Day of the Lord"
(see the note on 1:15).

1:5 The people's moral senses were dulled, making them
oblivious to sin. Joel called them to awaken from their
complacency and admit their sins before it was too late. Otherwise,
everything would be destroyed, even the grapes and wine that
caused their drunkenness. Our times of peace and prosperity can
lull us to sleep. We must never let material abundance be a
substitute for spiritual readiness.

1:14 A fast was a period of time when no food was eaten and
people approached God with humility, sorrow for sin, and urgent
prayer. In the Old Testament, people often fasted during times of

calamity in order to focus their attention on God and to
demonstrate their change of heart and true devotion (see, for
example, Judges 20:26; 1 Kings 21:27; Ezra 8:21; Jonah 3:4, 5).

1:15 This "terrible day of punishment," also called "the Day of the
Lord," is a common phrase in the Old Testament and in the book of
Joel (see 2:1, 11, 31; 3:14). It always refers to some extraordinary
happening, whether a present event (like a locust plague), an
event in the near future (like the destruction of Jerusalem or the
defeat of enemy nations), or the final period of history when God
will defeat all the forces of evil.

Even when the Day of the Lord refers to a present event, it also
pictures the *final* day of the Lord. This final event of history has two
aspects to it: (1) the last judgment on all evil and sin and (2) the
final reward for faithful believers. Righteousness and truth will
prevail, but not before much suffering (Zechariah 14:1–3). The final
day of the Lord is a time of hope, because all who survive will be
united forever with God.

1:15–19 Without God, devastation is sure. Those who have no
personal relationship with God will stand before him with no
appeal. Be sure to call upon God's love and mercy while you have
the opportunity (2:32).

2:1ff Joel was still describing the devastating effects of the locust
plague (see 2:25). The alarm showed that the crisis was at hand.

2:2
Dan 9:12
Joel 1:2
2:5,10,11,15

2:3
Gen 2:8
Isa 51:3
Amos 7:4

2:5
Isa 5:24; 30:30
Nah 2:3; 3:2

2:6
Jer 30:6

2:9
Ex 10:6
Jer 9:21
Jn 10:1

2:10
Isa 13:10
Joel 2:31; 3:15
Nah 1:5
Mt 24:29; 27:51
Acts 2:20

2:11
Ps 46:6
Isa 42:13
Joel 2:1; 3:16

2:12
Deut 4:29,30

2:13
Ex 34:6
Num 14:18
Ps 106:45
Amos 7:2-6

2:14
Hag 2:19

2:15
Joel 2:1

2:17
Ps 44:13; 79:10
Isa 37:20
Mic 7:10

²It is a day of darkness and gloom, of black clouds and thick darkness. What a mighty army! It covers the mountains like night! How great, how powerful these "people" are! The likes of them have not been seen before, and never will again throughout the generations of the world! ³Fire goes before them and follows them on every side! Ahead of them the land lies fair as Eden's Garden in all its beauty, but they destroy it to the ground; not one thing escapes. ⁴They look like tiny horses, and they run as fast. ⁵Look at them leaping along the tops of the mountain! Listen to the noise they make, like the rumbling of chariots, or the roar of fire sweeping across a field, and like a mighty army moving into battle.

⁶Fear grips the waiting people; their faces grow pale with fright. ⁷These "soldiers" charge like infantry; they scale the walls like picked and trained commandos. Straight forward they march, never breaking ranks. ⁸They never crowd each other. Each is right in place. No weapon can stop them. ⁹They swarm upon the city; they run upon the walls; they climb up into the houses, coming like thieves through the windows. ¹⁰The earth quakes before them and the heavens tremble. The sun and moon are obscured and the stars are hid.

¹¹The Lord leads them with a shout. This is his mighty army and they follow his orders. The day of the judgment of the Lord is an awesome, terrible thing. Who can endure it?

Return to the Lord your God

¹²That is why the Lord says, "Turn to me now, while there is time. Give me all your hearts. Come with fasting, weeping, mourning. ¹³Let your remorse tear at your hearts and not your garments." Return to the Lord your God, for he is gracious and merciful. He is not easily angered; he is full of kindness, and anxious not to punish you.

¹⁴Who knows? Perhaps even yet he will decide to let you alone and give you a blessing instead of his terrible curse. Perhaps he will give you so much that you can offer your grain and wine to the Lord as before!

¹⁵Sound the trumpet in Zion! Call a fast and gather all the people together for a solemn meeting. ¹⁶Bring everyone—the elders, the children, and even the babies. Call the bridegroom from his quarters and the bride from her privacy.

¹⁷The priests, the ministers of God, will stand between the people and the altar, weeping; and they will pray, "Spare your people, O our God; don't let the heathen rule them, for they belong to you. Don't let them be disgraced by the taunts of the

JOEL	Climate of the times	Wicked queen Athaliah seized power in a bloody coup, but was overthrown after a few years. Joash was crowned as king, but he was only seven years old and in great need of spiritual guidance. Joash followed God in his early years, but then turned away from him.
served as a prophet to Judah from 835–796 B.C.	Main message	A plague of locusts had come to discipline the nation. Joel called the people to turn back to God before an even greater judgment occurred.
	Importance of message	God judges all people for their sins, but is merciful to those who turn to him, and offers them eternal salvation.
	Contemporary prophets	Elisha (848–797) Jonah (793–753)

However, Joel implied that the locust plague was only the forerunner of an even greater crisis if the people didn't turn from their sins.

2:3 Eden's Garden was Adam and Eve's first home (Genesis 2:8). Known for its beauty, here it is used to describe the beauty of the land prior to its destruction.

2:12, 13 God told the people to turn to him while there was still time. Time was running out and destruction would soon be upon

them. Time is also running out for us. Because we don't know when our lives will end, we should turn to the Lord now, while we can. Don't let anything hold you back from turning to God.

2:13 Deep remorse was often shown by tearing one's clothes. But God didn't want an outward display of penitence without true inward repentance (1 Samuel 16:7; Matthew 23:1–36). Be sure your attitude toward God is correct, not just your outward actions.

heathen who say, 'Where is this God of theirs? How weak and helpless he must be!' "

¹⁸Then the Lord will pity his people and be indignant for the honor of his land! ¹⁹He will reply, "See, I am sending you much corn and wine and oil, to fully satisfy your need. No longer will I make you a laughingstock among the nations. ²⁰I will remove these armies from the north and send them far away; I will turn them back into the parched wastelands where they will die; half shall be driven into the Dead Sea and the rest into the Mediterranean, and then their rotting stench will rise upon the land. The Lord has done a mighty miracle for you."

²¹Fear not, my people; be glad now and rejoice, for he has done amazing things for you.

²²"Let the flocks and herds forget their hunger; the pastures will turn green again. The trees will bear their fruit; the fig trees and grape vines will flourish once more.

²³"Rejoice, O people of Jerusalem, rejoice in the Lord your God! For the rains he sends are tokens of forgiveness. Once more the autumn rains will come, as well as those of spring. ²⁴The threshing floors will pile high again with wheat, and the presses overflow with olive oil and wine. ²⁵And I will give you back the crops the locusts ate!—my great destroying army that I sent against you. ²⁶Once again you will have all the food you want.

"Praise the Lord, who does these miracles for you. Never again will my people experience disaster such as this. ²⁷And you will know that I am here among my people Israel, and that I alone am the Lord, your God. And my people shall never again be dealt a blow like this.

2. The Day of the Lord
God will pour out his Spirit

²⁸"After I have poured out my rains again, I will pour out my Spirit upon all of you! Your sons and daughters will prophesy; your old men will dream dreams, and your young men see visions. ²⁹And I will pour out my Spirit even on your slaves, men and women alike, ³⁰and put strange symbols in the earth and sky—blood and fire and pillars of smoke.

³¹"The sun will be turned into darkness and the moon to blood before the great and terrible Day of the Lord shall come.

³²"Everyone who calls upon the name of the Lord will be saved; even in Jerusalem some will escape, just as the Lord has promised, for he has chosen some to survive.

2:18
Deut 32:36
Isa 60:10
2:19
Ezek 34:29
39:29
2:20
Deut 11:24
Jer 1:14,15
Zech 14:8

2:23
Ps 28:6; 72:6
95:1-3
Hos 6:3
Zech 10:1
Phil 3:1
1 Thess 5:16
2:26
Ps 67:5-7
Isa 45:17
Rom 10:11
2:27
Lev 26:11,12
Isa 45:5,6,18
Ezek 39:22,28
Joel 3:17,21

2:28
Isa 32:15
Acts 2:16-18
2:29
1 Cor 12:13

2:31
Joel 2:1,10
3:15
2:32
Isa 4:2
Acts 2:21
Rom 10:13
11:26

2:18 This is a turning point in the book. Joel moves from prophesying about an outpouring of God's judgment to prophesying about an outpouring of God's forgiveness and blessing. But this would come only if the people sought to live as God wanted them to, giving up their sins. Where there is repentance, there is hope. This section of the book feeds that hope. If it were not there, Joel's prophecy could bring only despair. This promise of forgiveness should have encouraged the people to repent.

2:21 Joel contrasts the fear of God's judgment (2:1) with the joy of God's intervention (2:21). Sin will bring judgment on the Day of the Lord, and only God's forgiveness will bring rejoicing. Unless you repent, your sin will result in judgment. Let God intervene in your life, and you can rejoice in that day because you have nothing to fear.

2:22-26 God does not promise that all his followers will be wealthy. When God pardons, he restores our relationship with him, but this does not guarantee individual wealth. Instead, God promises to meet the deepest needs of those who love him—if not immediately, then certainly in eternity.

2:26, 27 If the Jews would never again experience a disaster like

this locust plague, how does one explain the captivity in Babylon, the Jews' slavery under the Greeks and Romans, and their persecution under Hitler? It is important not to take this verse out of context. It is still part of the "blessings" section of Joel's prophecy. Only if the people truly repented would they avoid a disaster like the one Joel had described. God's blessings are promised only to those who sincerely and consistently follow him. God does promise that after the final day of Judgment, his people will never again experience this kind of disaster (Zechariah 14:9-11; Revelation 21).

2:28-32 Peter quoted this passage on the day of Pentecost (Acts 2:16-21); the outpouring of the Spirit predicted by Joel occurred on Pentecost. Ezekiel also spoke of an outpouring of the Spirit (Ezekiel 39:28, 29) which, some think will come after Christ returns. God's Spirit is available now to anyone who calls upon the Lord (2:32).

2:31, 32 Judgment and mercy go hand in hand. Joel had said that if the people repented, the Lord would save them from judgment (2:12-14). In the midst of this judgment and catastrophe, therefore, some will be saved. God's intention is not to destroy but to heal. However, we must accept his salvation or we will certainly perish with the unrepentant.

The Day of the Lord is near

3 "At that time, when I restore the prosperity of Judah and Jerusalem," says the Lord, 2"I will gather the armies of the world into the 'Valley Where Jehovah Judges' and punish them there for harming my people, for scattering my inheritance among the nations and dividing up my land.

3"They divided up my people as their slaves; they traded a young lad for a prostitute, and a little girl for wine enough to get drunk. 4Tyre and Sidon, don't you try to interfere! Are you trying to take revenge on me, you cities of Philistia? Beware, for I will strike back swiftly, and return the harm to your own heads.

5"You have taken my silver and gold and all my precious treasures and carried them off to your heathen temples. 6You have sold the people of Judah and Jerusalem to the Greeks, who took them far from their own land. 7But I will bring them back again from all these places you have sold them to, and I will pay you back for all that you have done. 8I will sell your sons and daughters to the people of Judah and they will sell them to the Sabeans far away. This is a promise from the Lord."

9Announce this far and wide: Get ready for war! Conscript your best soldiers; collect all your armies. 10Melt your plowshares into swords and beat your pruning hooks into spears. Let the weak be strong. 11Gather together and come, all nations everywhere.

And now, O Lord, bring down your warriors! 12Collect the nations; bring them to the Valley of Jehoshaphat, for there I will sit to pronounce judgment on them all. 13Now let the sickle do its work; the harvest is ripe and waiting. Tread the winepress, for it is full to overflowing with the wickedness of these men.

14Multitudes, multitudes waiting in the valley for the verdict of their doom! For the Day of the Lord is near, in the Valley of Judgment.

15The sun and moon will be darkened and the stars withdraw their light. 16The Lord shouts from his Temple in Jerusalem and the earth and sky begin to shake. But to his people Israel, the Lord will be very gentle. He is their Refuge and Strength. 17"Then you shall know at last that I am the Lord your God in Zion, my holy mountain. Jerusalem shall be mine forever; the time will come when no foreign armies will pass through her any more.

18"Sweet wine will drip from the mountains, and the hills shall flow with milk. Water will fill the dry stream beds of Judah, and a fountain will burst forth from the Temple of the Lord to water Acacia Valley. 19Egypt will be destroyed, and Edom

3:2 *Valley Where Jehovah Judges,* or, "Valley of Jehoshaphat."

Cross references (left margin):

3:2
Isa 66:18
Joel 3:12,14
Zeph 3:8

3:3
Obad 11
Nah 3:10

3:5
2 Kgs 12:18
Dan 5:2,3

3:9
Isa 34:1
Jer 46:3; 51:27
Zech 14:2,3

3:10
Isa 2:4
Mic 4:3

3:12
Ps 76:8,9
Isa 3:13
Rev 19:11

3:13
Hos 6:11
Mt 13:39
Mk 4:29

3:14
Isa 34:2-8
Ezek 38:8-23
Joel 2:1; 3:2,12

3:15
Joel 12:10,31

3:16
Ps 18:2; 19:21
Hos 11:10
Amos 1:2; 3:8
Zech 12:5-9

3:17
Isa 11:9
Ezek 20:40
Zech 8:3

3:18
Ex 3:8
Isa 55:12,13
Amos 9:13

3:19
Amos 1:11
Obad 10

3:1, 2 The phrase "at that time" refers to the time when those who call upon the Lord will be saved (2:32). God will not only bless believers with everything they need: he will bless them by destroying all evil, ending the pain and suffering on earth. This prophecy had an immediate, ongoing, and final fulfillment. Its immediate interpretation could apply to King Jehoshaphat's recent battle against several enemy nations, including Moab and Ammon (2 Chronicles 20). Its ongoing fulfillment could be the partial restoration of the people to their land after the exile to Babylon. The final fulfillment will come in the great battle that precedes the Messiah's reign over the earth (Revelation 20:7–9).

3:4 Tyre and Sidon were major cities in Phoenicia to the north of Israel; Philistia was the nation southwest of Judah. Phoenicia and Philistia were small countries who rejoiced at the fall of Judah and Israel because they would benefit from the increased trade. God would judge them for their wrong attitude.

3:6 Some think this verse indicates that Joel lived after the captivity in Babylon, when the Greek culture began to flourish. But archaeological studies have shown that the Greeks were trading with Phoenicia as early as 800 B.C.

3:8 The Sabeans came from Sheba, a nation in southwest Arabia. One of Sheba's queens had visited Solomon over a century earlier (1 Kings 10:1–13).

3:14 Joel described multitudes waiting in the Valley of Judgment. Billions of people have lived on earth, and every one of them— dead, living, and yet to be born—will face judgment. Look around you. See your friends, those with whom you work and live. Have they received God's forgiveness? Have they been warned about sin's consequences? If we understand the severity of God's final judgment, we will want to take God's offer of hope to them.

3:17 The last word will be God's; his ultimate sovereignty will be revealed in the end. We cannot predict when that end will come, but we can have confidence in his control over the world's events. The world's history, as well as our own, is in God's hands. How much better to acknowledge this now rather than later.

3:18 The picture of this restored land is one of perfect beauty, similar to the Garden of Eden. The life-giving water flowing from the Temple illustrates the blessings that come from God's presence. Those who attach themselves to God will be forever fruitful. (See also Ezekiel 47:1–12; Revelation 22:1, 2.)

3:19 Egypt and Edom were two of Israel's most persistent enemies. They represent all the nations hostile to God's people. God's promise that they would be destroyed is also a promise that all evil in the world will one day be destroyed.

too, because of their violence against the Jews, for they killed innocent people in those nations.

²⁰"But Israel will prosper forever, and Jerusalem will thrive as generations pass. ²¹For I will avenge the blood of my people; I will not clear their oppressors of guilt. For my home is in Jerusalem with my people."

3:20
Ezek 37:25
Amos 9:15

3:21
Isa 4:4
Ezek 36:25,29
Mt 27:25

3:20, 21 The word *Israel* is used here to refer to all God's people—anyone who has called on the name of the Lord. There is full assurance of victory and peace for those who trust in God (2:32).

3:21 Joel began with a prophecy about the destruction of the land and ended with a prophecy about its restoration. He began by stressing the need for repentance and ended with the promise of forgiveness that repentance brings. Joel was trying to convince the people to wake up (1:5), get rid of their complacency, and realize the danger of living apart from God. His message to us is that there is still time; anyone who calls on God's name can be saved (2:12–14, 32). Those who do this will enjoy the blessings mentioned in Joel's prophecy; those who refuse to turn to God will face destruction.

AMOS

WHEN we hear, "he's a man of God," the images that most often come to our minds are some famous evangelist, a "Reverend," or the campus minister—professionals, Christian workers, those who preach and teach the Word as a vocation.

Surely Amos was a man of God—a person whose life was devoted to serving the Lord and whose life-style reflected this devotion—but he was a layman. Herding sheep and tending sycamore-fig trees in the Judean countryside, Amos was not the son of a prophet; he was not the son of a priest. As a humble herdsman, he could have stayed in Tekoa, doing his job, providing for his family, and worshiping his God. But God gave Amos a vision of the future (1:2), and told him to take his message to Israel, the Northern Kingdom (7:15). Amos obeyed, and thus proved he was a man of God.

Amos means *burden* or *burden-bearer*. He carried the heavy burden of God's message to Israel. Amos' message has had an impact upon God's people throughout the centuries, and it needs to be heard today, by individuals and nations. Although they were divided from their southern brothers and sisters in Judah, the northern Israelites were still God's people. But they were living beneath a pious veneer of religion, worshiping idols, and oppressing the poor. Amos, a fiery, fearless, and honest shepherd from the south, confronted them with their sin and warned them of the impending judgment.

The book of Amos opens with this humble herdsman watching his sheep. God then gives him a vision of what was about to happen to the nation of Israel. God condemns all the nations who have sinned against him and harmed his people. Beginning with Syria, he moves quickly through Philistia, Tyre, Edom, Ammon, and Moab. All are condemned, and we can almost hear the Israelites shouting, "Amen!" And then, even Judah, Amos' homeland, is included in God's scathing denunciation (2:4, 5). How Amos' listeners must have enjoyed hearing those words! Suddenly, however, Amos turns to the people of Israel and pronounces God's judgment on *them*. The next four chapters enumerate and describe their sins. It is no wonder that Amaziah, the priest, intervenes and tries to stop the preaching (7:10–13). Fearlessly, Amos continues to relate the visions of future judgment which God gave to him (chapters 8, 9). After all the chapters on judgment, the book concludes with a message of hope. Eventually God will restore his people and make them great again (9:8–15).

As you read Amos' book, put yourself in the place of those Israelites and listen to God's message. Have you grown complacent? Have other concerns taken God's place in your life? Do you ignore those in need or oppress the poor? Picture yourself as Amos, faithfully doing what God calls you to do. You, too, can be God's person. Listen for his clear call and do what he says, wherever it leads.

VITAL STATISTICS

PURPOSE:
To pronounce God's judgment upon Israel, the Northern Kingdom, for their complacency, idolatry, and oppression of the poor

AUTHOR:
Amos

TO WHOM WRITTEN:
Israel, the Northern Kingdom, and God's people everywhere

DATE WRITTEN:
Probably during the reigns of Jeroboam II of Israel and Uzziah of Judah (about 760–750 B.C.)

SETTING:
The wealthy people of Israel were enjoying peace and prosperity. They were quite complacent and were oppressing the poor, even selling them into slavery. Soon, however, Israel would be conquered by Assyria, and the rich would themselves be made slaves.

KEY VERSE:
"I want to see a mighty flood of justice—a torrent of doing good" (5:24).

KEY PEOPLE:
Amos, Amaziah, Jeroboam II

KEY PLACES:
Bethel, Samaria

SPECIAL FEATURES:
Amos uses striking metaphors from his shepherding and farming experience—an overloaded wagon (2:13), a roaring lion (3:8), a torn lamb (3:12), fat cows (4:1), and a basket of fruit (8:1, 2).

THE BLUEPRINT

1. Announcement of judgment (1:1—2:16)
2. Reasons for judgment (3:1—6:14)
3. Visions of judgment (7:1—9:15)

Amos speaks with brutal frankness in denouncing sin. He collided with the false religious leaders of his day and was not intimidated by priest or king. He continued to speak his message boldly. God requires truth and goodness from all people and nations today as well. Many of the conditions in Israel during Amos' time are evident in today's societies. We need Amos' courage to ignore danger and stand against sin.

MEGATHEMES

THEME	EXPLANATION	IMPORTANCE
Everyone answers to God	Amos pronounced judgment from God on all the surrounding nations. Then he included Judah and Israel. God is in supreme control of all the nations. Everyone is accountable to him.	All people will have to account for their sin. When those who reject God seem to get ahead, don't envy their prosperity or feel sorry for yourself. Remember that we all must answer to God for how we live.
Complacency	Everyone was optimistic, business was booming, people were happy (except for the poor and oppressed). With all the comfort and luxury came self-sufficiency and a false sense of security. But prosperity brought corruption and destruction.	A complacent present leads to a disastrous future. Don't congratulate yourself for the blessings and benefits you now enjoy. They are from God. If you are more satisfied with yourself than with God, remember everything is meaningless without him. A self-sufficient attitude may be your downfall.
Oppressing the poor	The wealthy and powerful people of Samaria, the capital of Israel, had become prosperous, greedy, and unfair. Illegal and immoral slavery came as the result of over-taxation and land-grabbing. There was also cruelty and indifference towards the poor. God is weary of greed and will not tolerate injustice.	God made all people; therefore, to ignore the poor is to ignore those whom God loves and whom Christ came to save. We must go beyond feeling bad for the poor and oppressed. We must act compassionately to stop injustice and to help care for those in need.
Superficial religion	Although many people had abandoned real faith in God, they still pretended to be religious. They were carrying on nominal religious performances instead of having spiritual integrity and practicing heartfelt obedience toward God.	Merely participating in ceremony or ritual falls short of true religion. God wants simple trust in him, not showy external motions. Don't settle for impressing others with external rituals when God wants heartfelt obedience and commitment.

1. Announcement of judgment
God will punish the surrounding nations

1 Amos was a herdsman living in the village of Tekoa. [All day long he sat on the hillsides watching the sheep, keeping them from straying.] ²One day, in a vision, God told him some of the things that were going to happen

1:1
2 Sam 14:2
2 Chron 11:6

1:1 *All day long he sat . . . keeping them from straying,* implied.

1:1 Amos was a shepherd and fig grower from the Southern Kingdom (Judah), but he prophesied to the Northern Kingdom (Israel). Israel was politically at the height of its power with a prosperous economy, but the nation was spiritually corrupt. Idols were worshiped throughout the land, and especially at Bethel, which was supposed to be the nation's religious center. Like Hosea, Amos was sent by God to denounce this social and religious corruption. About 30 or 40 years after Amos prophesied, Assyria destroyed the capital city, Samaria, and conquered the nation (722 B.C.). Uzziah reigned in Judah from 792–740; Jeroboam II reigned in Israel from 793–753.

1:1 Tekoa, Amos' hometown, was located in the rugged sheep country of Judah, ten miles south of Jerusalem. Long before Amos was born, a woman of Tekoa helped reconcile David and his

rebellious son, Absalom (2 Samuel 14:1–23).

1:1 All day long Amos took care of sheep—not a particularly "spiritual" job—yet he became a channel of God's message to others. Your job may not cause you to feel spiritual or successful, but it is a vital work if you are in the place God wants you to be. God can work through you to do extraordinary things, no matter how ordinary your occupation.

1:2 The prophet Zechariah and other historical records from this period mention an earthquake at this time (Zechariah 14:5).

1:2 In the Bible, God is often pictured as a shepherd and his people as sheep. As a shepherd, he leads and protects his flock. But here he is depicted as a ferocious lion ready to devour those who are evil or unfaithful. (See also Hosea 11:10.)

1:2
Isa 42:13
Jer 12:4; 14:2
Joel 3:16
Zech 14:5

1:3
Isa 8:4
Amos 1:6,9,11,
13; 2:1,4,6

1:5
Jer 50:36; 51:30
Lam 2:9
Nah 3:13

1:6
1 Sam 6:17
2 Chron 28:16
Ezek 35:5
Amos 1:9,11

1:8
Isa 14:29-31
Jer 47:1-7
Ezek 25:16
Zeph 2:4-7

1:9
2 Sam 5:11
1 Kgs 5:1
9:11-14
Isa 23:1-18
Zech 9:2-4

1:11
Gen 27:40
Num 20:14-21
Isa 34:1-17
63:1-3
Jer 49:7-22
Ezek 25:12-14

1:12
Gen 36:11
Jer 49:7,20

to his nation, Israel. This vision came to him at the time Uzziah was king of Judah, and while Jeroboam (son of Joash) was king of Israel—two years before the earthquake.

This is his report of what he saw and heard: The Lord roared—like a ferocious lion from his lair—from his Temple on Mount Zion. And suddenly the lush pastures of Mount Carmel withered and dried, and all the shepherds mourned.

³The Lord says, "The people of Damascus have sinned again and again, and I will not forget it. I will not leave her unpunished any more. For they have threshed my people in Gilead as grain is threshed with iron rods. ⁴So I will set fire to King Hazael's palace, destroying the strong fortress of Ben-hadad. ⁵I will snap the bars that locked the gates of Damascus, and kill her people as far away as the plain of Aven, and the people of Syria shall return to Kir as slaves." The Lord has spoken.

⁶The Lord says, "Gaza has sinned again and again, and I will not forget it. I will not leave her unpunished any more. For she sent my people into exile, selling them as slaves in Edom. ⁷So I will set fire to the walls of Gaza, and all her forts shall be destroyed. ⁸I will kill the people of Ashdod, and destroy Ekron and the king of Ashkelon; all Philistines left will perish." The Lord has spoken.

⁹The Lord says, "The people of Tyre have sinned again and again and I will not forget it. I will not leave them unpunished any more. For they broke their treaty with their brother, Israel; they attacked and conquered him, and led him into slavery to Edom. ¹⁰So I will set fire to the walls of Tyre, and it will burn down all his forts and palaces."

¹¹The Lord says, "Edom has sinned again and again, and I will not forget it. I will not leave him unpunished any more. For he chased his brother, Israel, with the sword; he was pitiless in unrelenting anger. ¹²So I will set fire to Teman, and it will burn down all the forts of Bozrah."

AMOS
served as a
prophet to Israel
(the Northern
Kingdom) from
760–750 B.C.

Climate of the times	Israel was enjoying economic prosperity and peace. But this had caused her to become a selfish, materialistic society. Those who were well-off ignored the needs of those less fortunate. The people were self-centered and indifferent toward God.
Main message	Amos spoke against those who exploited or ignored the needy.
Importance of message	Believing in God is more than a personal matter. God calls all believers to work against injustices in society and to aid those less fortunate.
Contemporary prophets	Jonah (793–753)
	Hosea (753–715)

1:3 Damascus was the capital of Syria. In the past, Syria had been one of Israel's formidable enemies. After the defeat of Syria by Assyria in 802 B.C., Damascus was no longer a real threat.

1:3—2:6 Amos pronounced God's judgment on nation after nation around Israel's borders—even Judah. Perhaps the people of Israel cheered when they heard the rebukes leveled against those nations. But then Amos proclaimed God's judgment on Israel. They could not excuse their own sin because they thought the sins of their neighbors were worse. God is no respecter of persons. He judges all people fairly and equally.

1:3—2:6 The accusation that these nations "have sinned again and again" echoes through these verses, as God evaluates nation after nation. Each had persistently refused to follow God's commands. Sin has a way of becoming part of our lives. Ignoring or denying the problem will not help us. We must begin the process of correction by confessing our sins to God and asking him to forgive us. Otherwise, we have no hope but to continue our pattern of sin.

1:5 The Syrians had been slaves in Kir and were now free (9:7). Decreeing that the Syrians should go back to Kir was like saying the Israelites should go back to Egypt as slaves (Exodus 1).

1:7, 8 Ashdod, Ekron, Gaza, and Ashkelon were four of the five major city-states of Philistia, an enemy who often threatened Israel. The fifth city-state, Gath, had already been destroyed. Therefore, Amos was saying that the entire nation of Philistia would be destroyed for her sins.

1:9 Tyre was one of two major cities in Phoenicia. Several treaties had been made with this city because it supplied the cedar lumber used to build David's palace and God's Temple (2 Samuel 5:11; 1 Kings 5).

1:11, 12 Edom and Israel both descended from Isaac: Edom from Isaac's son Esau, and Israel from Esau's twin brother, Jacob (Genesis 25:19–28; 27). But these two nations, like the two brothers, were always at odds. Edom rejoiced at Israel's misfortunes. As a result, God promised to destroy Edom completely, from Teman in the north to Bozrah in the south.

13The Lord says, "The people of Ammon have sinned again and again, and I will not forget it. I will not leave them unpunished any more. For in their wars in Gilead to enlarge their borders, they committed cruel crimes, ripping open pregnant women with their swords.

14"So I will set fire to the walls of Rabbah, and it will burn down their forts and palaces; there will be wild shouts of battle like a whirlwind in a mighty storm. 15And their king and his princes will go into exile together." The Lord has spoken.

2 The Lord says, "The people of Moab have sinned again and again, and I will not forget it. I will not leave them unpunished any more. For they desecrated the tombs of the kings of Edom, with no respect for the dead. 2Now in return I will send fire upon Moab, and it will destroy all the palaces in Kerioth. Moab shall go down in tumult as the warriors shout and trumpets blare. 3And I will destroy their king and slay all the leaders under him." The Lord has spoken.

4The Lord says, "The people of Judah have sinned again and again, and I will not forget it. I will not leave them unpunished any more. For they have rejected the laws of God, refusing to obey him. They have hardened their hearts and sinned as their fathers did. 5So I will destroy Judah with fire, and burn down all Jerusalem's palaces and forts."

God will punish Israel

6The Lord says, "The people of Israel have sinned again and again, and I will not forget it. I will not leave them unpunished any more. For they have perverted justice by accepting bribes, and sold into slavery the poor who can't repay their debts; they trade them for a pair of shoes. 7They trample the poor in the dust and kick aside the meek.

"And a man and his father defile the same temple-girl, corrupting my holy name. 8At their religious feasts they lounge in clothing stolen from their debtors, and in my own Temple they offer sacrifices of wine they purchased with stolen money.

9"Yet think of all I did for them! I cleared the land of the Amorites before them—the Amorites, as tall as cedar trees, and strong as oaks! But I lopped off their fruit and cut their roots. 10And I brought you out from Egypt and led you through the desert forty years, to possess the land of the Amorites. 11And I chose your sons

2:11 *to be Nazirites, see* Num 6.

1:13
Jer 49:1-6
Hos 13:16

1:14
Isa 9:5; 30:30
Dan 11:40
Zech 7:14

1:15
Jer 49:3

2:1
Isa 15:1-9
Zech 2:8,9

2:2
Isa 9:5
Jer 48:24,41,45

2:4
Lev 26:14,15
Judg 2:17-20
2 Kgs 17:19
Hos 6:11

2:5
Jer 17:27
37:8-10
Hos 8:14

2:6
Joel 3:3,6
Mic 3:2,3

2:7
Lev 18:8,15
Prov 28:21
Ezek 22:11

2:9
Josh 11:21,22

2:10
Num 14:34
Deut 2:7; 8:2-4

2:11
Num 6:1-21
1 Kgs 17:1; 22:8

1:13–15 The Ammonites descended from an incestuous relationship between Lot and his younger daughter (Genesis 19:30- 38). They were hostile to Israel, and although Israel began to worship their idols, they still attacked her (Judges 10:6–8). After Saul was anointed Israel's king, his first victory in battle was against the Ammonites (1 Samuel 11). Rabbah was Ammon's capital city. Amos' prophecy of Ammon's destruction was fulfilled through the Assyrian invasion.

2:1–3 The Moabites descended from an incestuous relationship between Lot and his older daughter (Genesis 19:30–38). Balak, King of Moab, tried to hire the seer, Balaam, to curse the Israelites so they could be defeated (Numbers 22—24). Balaam refused, but some of the Moabites succeeded in getting Israel to worship Baal (Numbers 25:1–3). The Moabites were known for their atrocities (2 Kings 3:26, 27). An archaeological artifact, the Moabite stone, reveals that Moab was always ready to profit from the downfalls of others.

2:4, 5 After Solomon's reign, the kingdom divided, and the tribes of Judah and Benjamin became the Southern Kingdom (Judah) under Solomon's son, Rehoboam. The other ten tribes became the Northern Kingdom (Israel) and followed Jeroboam, who had rebelled against Rehoboam.

God judged other nations harshly for their evil actions and atrocities. But God also promised to judge both Israel and Judah because they ignored the revealed Word of God. The other nations were ignorant, but Judah and Israel, God's people, knew what God

wanted. Still they ignored him and joined pagan nations in worshiping idols.

2:6 Amos won his audience as he proclaimed God's judgment against the evil nations surrounding Israel. He even spoke against his own nation, Judah, before focusing on God's indictment of Israel.

2:6, 7 Amos spoke to the upper class. There was no middle class in the country—only the very rich and the very poor. The rich kept religious rituals. They gave extra tithes, went to places of worship, and offered sacrifices. But they were greedy and unjust, and they took advantage of the helpless. Be sure that you do not neglect the needs of the poor while you faithfully attend church and fulfill religious rituals. God expects us to live out our faith, and this means responding to those in need.

2:6ff God condemned Israel for five specific sins: (1) selling the poor as slaves (see Deuteronomy 15:7–11; Amos 8:6), (2) exploiting the poor (see Exodus 23:6; Deuteronomy 16:19), (3) engaging in perverse sexual sins, (4) taking illegal collateral for loans (see Exodus 22:26, 27; Deuteronomy 24:6, 12, 13), and (5) worshiping false gods (see Exodus 20:3–5).

2:9–11 The prophets were constantly challenging people to remember what God had done! When we read a list like this one, we are amazed at Israel's forgetfulness. But what would the prophets say about us? God's past faithfulness should have reminded the Israelites to obey him; likewise, what he has done for us should remind us to live for him.

to be Nazirites and prophets—can you deny this, Israel?" asks the Lord. ¹²"But you caused the Nazirites to sin by urging them to drink your wine, and you silenced my prophets, telling them, 'Shut up!'

¹³"Therefore I will make you groan as a wagon groans that is loaded with sheaves. ¹⁴Your swiftest warriors will stumble in flight. The strong will all be weak, and the great ones can no longer save themselves. ¹⁵The archer's aim will fail, the swiftest runners won't be fast enough to flee, and even the best of horsemen can't outrun the danger then. ¹⁶The most courageous of your mighty men will drop their weapons and run for their lives that day." The Lord God has spoken.

2. Reasons for judgment
Sin separates the people from God

3 Listen! This is your doom! It is spoken by the Lord against both Israel and Judah—against the entire family I brought from Egypt:

²"Of all the peoples of the earth, I have chosen you alone. That is why I must punish you the more for all your sins. ³For how can we walk together with your sins between us?

⁴"Would I be roaring as a lion unless I had a reason? The fact is, I am getting ready to destroy you. Even a young lion, when it growls, shows it is ready for its food. ⁵A trap doesn't snap shut unless it is stepped on; your punishment is well deserved. ⁶The alarm has sounded—listen and fear! For I, the Lord, am sending disaster into your land.

⁷"But always, first of all, I warn you through my prophets. This I now have done."

⁸The Lion has roared—tremble in fear. The Lord God has sounded your doom—I dare not refuse to proclaim it.

⁹Call together the Assyrian and Egyptian leaders, saying, "Take your seats now on the mountains of Samaria to witness the scandalous spectacle of all Israel's crimes. ¹⁰My people have forgotten what it means to do right," says the Lord. "Their beautiful homes are full of the loot from their thefts and banditry. ¹¹Therefore," the Lord God says, "an enemy is coming! He is surrounding them and will shatter their forts and plunder those beautiful homes."

Cross-references (left margin):

2:12
Jer 11:21
Amos 7:13,16
2:13
Joel 13:13
2:14
Isa 30:16,17
Jer 9:23
Amos 9:1-3
2:15
Ps 33:16,17
Isa 31:3

3:1
Jer 8:3
33:24-26
Ezek 37:16
3:2
Ex 19:5,6
Deut 7:6
3:3
Gen 5:22; 6:9
Lev 26:23,24
3:4
Ps 104:21
Hos 11:10
3:6
Isa 14:24-27
Jer 4:5
Ezek 33:3
Hos 5:8
Zeph 1:16
3:7
Gen 18:17
Dan 9:22-27
3:8
Jer 20:9
3:10
Hab 2:8-11
Zeph 1:9
Zech 5:3,4

2:11 The Nazirites took vows to abstain from wine and to let their hair grow long. But instead of being respected for their disciplined and temperate lives, they were being urged to break their vows. If the Nazirites were corrupted, there would remain little influence for good among the Israelites.

2:16 *That day* refers to when Assyria would attack Israel, destroy Samaria, and take the people captive (722 B.C.). This military defeat came only a few decades after this pronouncement.

2:16 Television and movies are filled with images of people who seem to have no fear. Many today have sought to model their lives after these images—they want to be tough at any cost. But God is not impressed with tough actions. He says that even the toughest of men will run in fear when God's judgment comes. Can you think of people who consider themselves tough enough to make it without God? Don't be swayed by their self-assured rhetoric. Recognize that God fears no one, and one day all people will fear him.

3:2 God chose Israel to be the people through whom all other nations of the world could know God. He made this promise to Abraham, father of the Israelites (Genesis 12:1–3). Israel didn't have to do anything to be chosen; God gave them this special privilege because he wanted to, not because they deserved special treatment (Deuteronomy 9:4–6). Pride in their privileged position, however, hardened Israel to the Word of God and to the plight of others.

3:3 When you have an unresolved conflict with someone, you may feel that a wall separates you from that person. The joy of being with a close friend is the closeness God wants to have with us. If your sin has put a wall of separation between you and God, ask him to forgive you so you can again walk with him as with a close friend.

3:7 If we have been warned about our sin, we have no excuse when punishment comes. God had warned his people, so they could not rationalize or complain when God punished them for refusing to repent.

3:7 Even in anger, God is merciful: he always warned his people through prophets before punishing them. Warnings about sin and judgment apply to people today just as they did to Israel. Do not take lightly warnings in God's Word about judgment. His warnings are a way of showing mercy to you.

3:9 Amos pictured Assyria and Egypt coming to witness Israel's great sins. Even Israel's most wicked neighbors would witness God's judgment of Israel's sins.

3:10 Israel had forgotten how to do what was right. The more they sinned, the harder it was to remember what God wanted. The same is true for us. The longer we fail to deal with sin, the greater its hold on us. Finally, we forget what it means to do right. Are you on the verge of forgetting?

3:11–13 The approaching enemy was Assyria, who conquered the nation and did as Amos predicted. The people were scattered to foreign lands, and foreigners were placed in the land to keep the peace. Israel's leaders had robbed their defenseless fellow countrymen, and now they would be rendered defenseless by the Assyrians. Amos added that even if they tried to repent then, it would be too late. The destruction would be so complete that nothing of value would be left.

12The Lord says, "A shepherd tried to rescue his sheep from a lion, but it was too late; he snatched from the lion's mouth two legs and a piece of ear. So it will be when the Israelites in Samaria are finally rescued—all they will have left is half a chair and a tattered pillow.

13"Listen to this announcement, and publish it throughout all Israel," says the Lord, the Lord Almighty: 14"On the same day that I punish Israel for her sins, I will also destroy the idol altars at Bethel. The horns of the altar will be cut off and fall to the ground.

15"And I will destroy the beautiful homes of the wealthy—their winter mansions and their summer houses, too—and demolish their ivory palaces."

The people refuse to turn to God

4 Listen to me, you "fat cows" of Bashan living in Samaria—you women who encourage your husbands to rob the poor and crush the needy—you who never have enough to drink! 2The Lord God has sworn by his holiness that the time will come when he will put hooks in your noses and lead you away like the cattle you are; they will drag the last of you away with fishhooks! 3You will be hauled from your beautiful homes and tossed out through the nearest breach in the wall. The Lord has said it.

4Go ahead and sacrifice to idols at Bethel and Gilgal. Keep disobeying—your sins are mounting up. Sacrifice each morning and bring your tithes twice a week! 5Go through all your proper forms and give extra offerings. How you pride yourselves and crow about it everywhere!

6"I sent you hunger," says the Lord, "but it did no good; you still would not return to me. 7I ruined your crops by holding back the rain three months before the harvest. I sent rain on one city, but not another. While rain fell on one field, another was dry and withered. 8People from two or three cities would make their weary journey for a drink of water to a city that had rain, but there wasn't ever enough. Yet you wouldn't return to me," says the Lord.

9"I sent blight and mildew on your farms and your vineyards; the locusts ate your figs and olive trees. And still you wouldn't return to me," says the Lord. 10"I sent you plagues like those of Egypt long ago. I killed your lads in war and drove away your horses. The stench of death was terrible to smell. And yet you refused to come. 11I destroyed some of your cities, as I did Sodom and Gomorrah; those left are like half-burned firebrands snatched away from fire. And still you won't return to me," says the Lord.

12"Therefore I will bring upon you all these further evils I have spoken of. Prepare to meet your God in judgment, Israel. 13For you are dealing with the one who formed the mountains and made the winds, and knows your every thought; he turns the morning to darkness and crushes down the mountains underneath his feet: Jehovah, the Lord, the Lord Almighty, is his name."

3:12
1 Sam 17:34-37

3:13
Ezek 2:7

3:14
Amos 4:4
5:5,6; 7:10,13

3:15
Judg 3:20
1 Kgs 22:39
Jer 36:22

4:1
Deut 32:14,15

4:2
Isa 37:29
Jer 16:16
Ezek 29:4; 38:4

4:3
2 Kgs 25:4
Ezek 12:5,12

4:5
Lev 7:13
22:18-21

4:6
Lev 26:26
Deut 28:38

4:7
1 Kgs 8:35,36

4:8
1 Kgs 18:5
Isa 41:17,18
Jer 14:3,4

4:9
Deut 28:22,42
1 Kgs 8:37
Joel 2:25

4:10
Ex 9:3-6
Jer 11:22; 18:21
Isa 9:13

4:11
Gen 19:24,25
Jer 23:14

4:12
Isa 47:3
Ezek 13:5

4:13
Deut 32:13
Job 38:4-11
Dan 2:28,30
Hab 3:19

3:14 God's judgment against Israel's altars showed that he was rejecting Israel's entire religious system because it was so polluted. The altar was a place of protection (1 Kings 1:49–53). The people's sanctuary, protection, and refuge would soon be gone. They would have no place to hide when judgment came.

4:1 Israel's wealthy women were compared to the cows of Bashan—pampered, sleek, and well-fed (see Psalm 22:12). These women selfishly pushed their husbands to oppress the helpless in order to supply their lavish life-styles. Be careful not to desire material possessions so much that you are willing to oppress others and displease God to get them.

4:4 Amos sarcastically invited the people to sin in Bethel and Gilgal where they worshiped idols instead of God. At Bethel, God had renewed his covenant to Abraham with Jacob (Genesis 28:10–22). Now Bethel was the religious center of the Northern Kingdom, and Jeroboam had placed an idol there to discourage the people from traveling to Jerusalem in the Southern Kingdom for worship (1 Kings 12:26–29). Gilgal was Israel's first campground

after entering the Promised Land (Joshua 4:19). Here Joshua renewed the covenant and the rite of circumcision, and the people celebrated the Passover (Joshua 5:2–10). Saul was crowned Israel's first king in Gilgal (1 Samuel 11:15).

4:4, 5 The Israelites were tithing and thanking God for the wealth they had achieved by oppressing the poor. Wealth is not necessarily a blessing from God. It is good to thank God for prosperity, but God must also be involved in the process leading to prosperity.

4:6–13 No matter how God warned the people—through famine, drought, blight, locusts, plagues, or war—they still ignored him. Because they didn't get the message, they would have to meet him face to face in judgment. No longer would they ignore God; they would have to face the One they had rejected, the One they had refused to obey when he commanded them to care for the poor. One day each of us will meet God face to face to account for what we have done or refused to do. Have we listened to his Word that tells us how to prepare ourselves to meet him?

Amos mourns for Israel

5:1
Jer 9:10
Ezek 19:1,14
Mic 2:4

5:4
Deut 4:29
30:1-8
32:46,47

5:6
Ex 22:6
Deut 4:24

5:7
Amos 2:3; 5:12

5:8
Gen 7:11-20
Job 9:9; 12:22
37:13; 38:31-34
Amos 9:6

5:9
Amos 2:14
Mic 5:11

5:10
Jer 17:16,17
Amos 5:15
Jn 7:7; 8:45-47

5:11
Deut 28:30
Isa 65:21,23
Mic 6:15

5:12
Ps 26:9,10
Isa 1:23
Mic 3:11; 7:3

5:15
1 Kgs 20:31
Ps 34:14; 97:10
Joel 2:14
Jonah 3:9

5:16
Isa 15:2-5
Amos 8:3,10
Joel 1:8,11
Mic 1:8,2:4

5:17
Isa16:10
32:10-12

5:18
Isa 5:30
Jer 30:7
Zeph 1:14
2 Pet 3:10

5 Sadly I sing this song of grief for you, O Israel: ²"Beautiful Israel lies broken and crushed upon the ground and cannot rise. No one will help her. She is left alone to die." ³For the Lord God says, "The city that sends a thousand men to battle, a hundred will return. The city that sends a hundred, only ten will come back alive."

⁴The Lord says to the people of Israel, "Seek me—and live. ⁵Don't seek the idols of Bethel, Gilgal, or Beer-sheba; for the people of Gilgal will be carried off to exile, and those of Bethel shall surely come to grief."

⁶Seek the Lord and live, or else he will sweep like fire through Israel and consume her, and none of the idols in Bethel can put it out.

⁷O evil men, you make "justice" a bitter pill for the poor and oppressed. "Righteousness" and "fair play" are meaningless fictions to you!

⁸Seek him who created the Seven Stars and the constellation Orion, who turns darkness into morning, and day into night, who calls forth the water from the ocean and pours it out as rain upon the land. The Lord, Jehovah, is his name. ⁹With blinding speed and violence he brings destruction on the strong, breaking all defenses.

¹⁰How you hate honest judges! How you despise people who tell the truth! ¹¹You trample the poor and steal their smallest crumb by all your taxes, fines, and usury; therefore you will never live in the beautiful stone houses you are building, nor drink the wine from the lush vineyards you are planting.

¹²For many and great are your sins. I know them all so well. You are the enemies of everything good; you take bribes; you refuse justice to the poor. ¹³Therefore those who are wise will not try to interfere with the Lord in the dread day of your punishment.

¹⁴Be good, flee evil—and live! Then the Lord, the Lord Almighty, will truly be your Helper, as you have claimed he is. ¹⁵Hate evil and love the good; remodel your courts into true halls of justice. Perhaps even yet the Lord God of Hosts will have mercy on his people who remain.

¹⁶Therefore the Lord God says this: "There will be crying in all the streets and every road. Call for the farmers to weep with you, too; call for professional mourners to wail and lament. ¹⁷There will be sorrow and crying in every vineyard, for I will pass through and destroy. ¹⁸You say, 'If only the Day of the Lord were here, for then God would deliver us from all our foes.' But you have no idea what you ask. For that day will *not* be light and prosperity, but darkness and doom! How

---

5:1 Amos shocked his listeners by singing a song of grief for them as if they had already been destroyed. The Israelites believed their wealth and religious ritual made them secure, but Amos lamented their sure destruction.

5:4 There is one sure remedy for a world that is sick and dying in sin—seek God and live. Sin seeks to destroy, but hope is found in seeking God. In times of difficulty, seek God. In personal discomfort and struggle, seek God. When others are struggling, encourage them to seek God too.

5:7 The law courts should have been places of justice where the poor and oppressed could find relief. Instead, they had become places of greed and injustice.

5:8 For thousands of years, navigators have staked lives and fortunes on the reliability of the stars. The constancy of the heavens challenges us to look beyond them to their Creator.

5:10-12 A society is in trouble when those who try to do right are hated for their justice. Any society that exploits the poor and defenseless or hates the truth is bent on destroying itself.

5:12 Why does God put so much emphasis on the way we treat the poor? How we treat the rich, or those of equal station, often reflects what we hope to get from them. But since the poor can give us nothing, how we treat them reflects our true character. Do we, like Christ, give without thought of gain? We should treat the poor the same way we would like God to treat us.

5:15 If Israel swept away the corrupt system of false accusations, bribery, and corruption, and insisted that only just decisions be given, this would show their change of heart. We dare not read this passage lightly or write it off simply as encouragement to be good. Instead, it is a command to reform our own legal and social system.

5:16 Failure to honor the dead was considered horrible in Israel, so loud weeping was common at funerals. Paid mourners, usually women, cried and mourned loudly with dirges and eulogies. Amos said there would be so many funerals that there would be a shortage of professional mourners, so farmers would be called from the fields to help. (See also Jeremiah 9:17-20.)

5:18 Here "the Day of the Lord" means the imminent destruction by the Assyrian army as well as the future day of the Lord's judgment. For the faithful, that day will be glorious; but for the unfaithful it will be darkness and doom. (See Joel 1:15 for more discussion of the Day of the Lord.)

5:18-24 We, like these people, often cry for justice. But God says, "You don't know what you are asking for." Justice would bring us the punishment we deserve for our sins. We really need mercy, not justice.

terrible the darkness will be for you; not a ray of joy or hope will shine. ¹⁹In that day you will be as a man who is chased by a lion—and met by a bear, or a man in a dark room who leans against a wall—and puts his hand on a snake. ²⁰Yes, that will be a dark and hopeless day for you.

²¹"I hate your show and pretense—your hypocrisy of 'honoring' me with your religious feasts and solemn assemblies. ²²I will not accept your burnt offerings and thank offerings. I will not look at your offerings of peace. ²³Away with your hymns of praise—they are mere noise to my ears. I will not listen to your music, no matter how lovely it is.

²⁴"I want to see a mighty flood of justice—a torrent of doing good.

25, 26, 27"You sacrificed to me for forty years while you were in the desert, Israel—but always your real interest has been in your heathen gods—in Sakkuth your king, and in Kaiwan, your god of the stars, and in all the images of them you made. So I will send them into captivity with you far to the east of Damascus," says the Lord, the Lord Almighty.

God despises Israel's pride

6 Woe to those lounging in luxury at Jerusalem and Samaria, so famous and popular among the people of Israel. ²Go over to Calneh and see what happened there; then go to great Hamath and down to Gath in the Philistines' land. Once they were better and greater than you, but look at them now. ³You push away all thought of punishment awaiting you, but by your deeds you bring the Day of Judgment near.

⁴You lie on ivory beds surrounded with luxury, eating the meat of the tenderest lambs and the choicest calves. ⁵You sing idle songs to the sound of the harp, and fancy yourselves to be as great musicians as King David was.

⁶You drink wine by the bucketful and perfume yourselves with sweet ointments, caring nothing at all that your brothers need your help. ⁷Therefore you will be the first to be taken as slaves; suddenly your revelry will end.

⁸Jehovah the Almighty Lord has sworn by his own name, "I despise the pride and false glory of Israel, and hate their beautiful homes. I will turn over this city and everything in it to her enemies."

⁹If there are as few as ten of them left, and even one house, they too will perish.

5:19
Job 20:24
Amos 9:1,2

5:20
Amos 5:18

5:21
Prov 15:8; 21:27
Isa 1:11-16
Jer 14:12
Hos 5:6

5:22
Lev 6:9-23
7:11-21

5:24
Jer 22:3
Amos 5:7
Mic 6:8

6:1
Judg 18:7
Isa 32:9-11

6:2
Gen 10:10
1 Sam 17:23
2 Kgs 17:24,30
19:13
Isa 10:9

6:3
Amos 5:18; 9:10

6:4
Ezek 34:2,3

6:5
1 Chron 15:16
23:5

6:8
Lev 26:11
Zech 11:8

5:21–23 God does not hate worship, but he hates false worship by people who do it out of pretense or for show. If we are living sinful lives and use religious ritual and traditions to make ourselves look good, God will despise our worship and will not accept what we offer. He wants sincere hearts, not the songs of hypocrites. When we worship at church, are we more concerned about our image or our attitude toward God?

5:24 Here are eight common excuses for not helping the poor: (1) They don't deserve help. They got themselves into poverty; let them get themselves out. (2) God's call to help the poor applies to another time. (3) We don't have any people like this. (4) I have my own needs. (5) Any money I give will be wasted, stolen, or spent on other things. The poor will never see it. (6) I may become a victim myself. (7) I don't know where to start, and I don't have time. (8) My little bit won't make any difference.

Instead of making lame excuses, ask what can be done to help the poor. Does your church have programs that help the needy? Could you volunteer to work with a community group that fights poverty? As one individual, you may not be able to accomplish much, but join up with similarly motivated people and watch mountains begin to move.

5:25–27 Sakkuth and Kaiwan were heathen gods associated with Saturn. Israel had turned to worshiping stars and planets, preferring nature over nature's God. Heathen religion allowed them to indulge themselves in sexual immorality and to become wealthy through any means. Because they refused to worship and obey the one true God, they would cause their own destruction.

5:25–27 Israel's captivity was indeed far to the east of Damascus—the people were taken to Assyria. God's punishment was more than defeat; it was complete exile from their homeland.

6:1–5 Amos leveled his attack at those living in luxury in both Israel and Judah. Great wealth and comfortable life-styles may make people think they are secure; but God is not pleased if we isolate ourselves from others' needs. Using our wealth to help others is one way to guard against pride.

6:2 Great cities to the east, north, and west had been destroyed because of their pride. What happened to them would happen to Israel because her sin was just as great as theirs.

6:4 Ivory was an imported luxury, rare and extremely expensive. Even a small amount of ivory symbolized wealth, and something as extravagant as an ivory bed shows the gross waste of resources that should have been used to help the poor.

6:4–7 God wants us to care for others as he cares for us. His kingdom has no place for selfishness or indifference. We must learn to put the needs of others before our wants.

6:8, 11 The people had built luxurious homes to flaunt their achievements. While it is not wrong to live in comfortable homes, we must not let them become sources of pride and self-glorification. God gave our homes to us, and they are to be used for his glory. Remember that everything keeping us from God will one day be destroyed.

6:10
1 Sam 31:12
Amos 5:13; 8:3

[10]A man's uncle will be the only one left to bury him, and when he goes in to carry his body from the house, he will ask the only one still alive inside, "Are any others left?" And the answer will be, "No," and he will add, "Shhh . . . don't mention the name of the Lord—he might hear you."

6:12
Amos 5:7,11,12

[11]For the Lord commanded this: That homes both great and small should be smashed to pieces. [12]Can horses run on rocks? Can oxen plow the sea? Stupid even to ask, but no more stupid than what you do when you make a mockery of justice, and corrupt and sour all that should be good and right. [13]And just as stupid is your rejoicing in how great you are, when you are less than nothing! And priding yourselves on your own tiny power!

6:14
Num 34:7,8
2 Kgs 14:25

[14]"O Israel, I will bring against you a nation that will bitterly oppress you from your northern boundary to your southern tip, all the way from Hamath to the brook of Arabah," says the Lord, the Lord Almighty.

3. Visions of judgment
Amos sees a swarm of locusts

7:1
Ex 10:12-16
Nah 3:15-17
7:2
Ex 10:15
Num 14:17-19
Jer 14:7; 42:2
Ezek 9:8
Rev 9:4

7 This is what the Lord God showed me in a vision: He was preparing a vast swarm of locusts to destroy all the main crop that sprang up after the first mowing, which went as taxes to the king. [2]They ate everything in sight. Then I said, "O Lord God, please forgive your people! Don't send them this plague! If you turn against Israel, what hope is there? For Israel is so small!" [3]So the Lord relented, and did not fulfill the vision. "I won't do it," he told me.

Amos sees a great fire

7:4
Isa 66:15,16
Amos 2:5

[4]Then the Lord God showed me a great fire he had prepared to punish them; it had burned up the waters and was devouring the entire land.

[5]Then I said, "O Lord God, please don't do it. If you turn against them, what hope is there? For Israel is so small!"

7:6
Amos 7:3

[6]Then the Lord turned from this plan too, and said, "I won't do that either."

Amos sees a plumbline

[7]Then he showed me this: The Lord was standing beside a wall built with a

AMOS' VISIONS	Vision	Reference	Significance
	Swarm of locusts	7:1–3	God was preparing punishment which he delayed only because of Amos' intervention.
	Fire	7:4–6	God was preparing to devour the land, but Amos intervened on behalf of the people.
	Wall and plumbline	7:7–9	God would see if the people were crooked and, if they were, he would punish them.
	Basket of ripe fruit	8:1ff	The people were ripe for punishment; though once beautiful, they were now rotten.
	God standing beside the altar	9:1ff	Punishment was executed.

Amos had a series of visions concerning God's judgment on Israel. God was planning to judge Israel by sending a swarm of locusts or fire. In spite of Amos' intercession on Israel's behalf, God would still carry out his judgment because Israel persisted in her disobedience.

6:10 Amos gives us a picture of God's fearful judgment: the people will be afraid even to speak God's name, lest they attract his attention.

6:14 This northern enemy is Assyria, who would destroy Israel (2 Kings 17).

7:1ff The following series of visions conveyed God's message to the people using images that were familiar to them—insects, fire, tools.

7:1–9 Twice Amos was shown a vision of Israel's impending

punishment, and his immediate response was to pray that God would spare Israel. Prayer is a powerful privilege. Amos' prayers should remind us to pray for our nation.

7:7–9 A plumbline was a device used to ensure the straightness of a wall. A wall that is not straight will eventually collapse. God wants people to be right with him; he wants the sin that makes us crooked removed immediately. God's Word is the plumbline that helps us be aware of our sin. How do you measure up to this plumbline?

plumbline, checking it with a plumbline to see if it was straight. 8And the Lord said to me, "Amos, what do you see?"

I answered, "A plumbline."

And he replied, "I will test my people with a plumbline. I will no longer turn away from punishing. 9The idol altars and temples of Israel will be destroyed, and I will destroy the dynasty of King Jeroboam by the sword."

10But when Amaziah, the priest of Bethel, heard what Amos was saying, he rushed a message to Jeroboam, the king: "Amos is a traitor to our nation and is plotting your death. This is intolerable. It will lead to rebellion all across the land. 11He says you will be killed, and Israel will be sent far away into exile and slavery."

12Then Amaziah sent orders to Amos, "Get out of here, you prophet, you! Flee to the land of Judah and do your prophesying there! 13Don't bother us here with your visions, not here in the capital, where the king's chapel is!"

14But Amos replied, "I am not really one of the prophets. I do not come from a family of prophets. I am just a herdsman and fruit picker. 15But the Lord took me from caring for the flocks and told me, 'Go and prophesy to my people Israel.'

16"Now therefore listen to this message to you from the Lord. You say, 'Don't prophesy against Israel.' 17The Lord's reply is this: 'Because of your interference, your wife will become a prostitute in this city, and your sons and daughters will be killed and your land divided up. You yourself will die in a heathen land, and the people of Israel will certainly become slaves in exile, far from their land.'"

Amos sees a basket of fruit

8 Then the Lord God showed me, in a vision, a basket full of ripe fruit. 2"What do you see, Amos?" he asked.

I replied, "A basket full of ripe fruit."

Then the Lord said, "This fruit represents my people Israel—ripe for punishment. I will not defer their punishment again. 3The riotous sound of singing in the Temple will turn to weeping then. Dead bodies will be scattered everywhere. They will be carried out of the city in silence." The Lord has spoken.

4Listen, you merchants who rob the poor, trampling on the needy; 5you who long for the Sabbath to end and the religious holidays to be over, so you can get out and start cheating again—using your weighted scales and under-sized measures; 6you who make slaves of the poor, buying them for their debt of a piece of silver or a pair of shoes, or selling them your moldy wheat— 7the Lord, the Pride of Israel, has sworn: "I won't forget your deeds! 8The land will tremble as it awaits its doom, and everyone will mourn. It will rise up like the river Nile at floodtime, toss about, and sink again. 9At that time I will make the sun go down at noon and darken the earth in the daytime.

10"And I will turn your parties into times of mourning, and your songs of joy will be turned to cries of despair. You will wear funeral clothes and shave your heads as signs of sorrow, as if your only son had died; bitter, bitter will be that day. 11The time is surely coming," says the Lord God, "when I will send a famine on the land—not a famine of bread or water, but of hearing the words of the Lord. 12Men

7:8
Isa 28:17; 34:11

7:9
2 Kgs 15:8-10

7:10
1 Kgs 12:31
18:17
2 Kgs 14:23,24

7:12
1 Sam 9:9
2 Chron 16:10

7:13
1 Kgs 12:29,32
13:1
Amos 2:12

7:14
1 Kgs 20:35
2 Kgs 2:3-7
2 Chron 16:7

7:15
Jer 1:7
Ezek 2:3,4

7:16
Isa 31:10
Mic 2:6

7:17
Isa 13:16
Jer 14:16; 20:6
Hos 4:13,14

8:2
Isa 28:4
Jer 24:1-3

8:3
Hos 10:5,6
Amos 5:23

8:5
Ex 20:8-10
Neh 13:15-21
Hos 12:7

8:7
Deut 33:26-29
Ps 10:11; 47:4
68:34
Hos 7:2; 8:13

8:8
Isa 8:7,8
Jer 4:24-26
46:8
Hag 2:6,7

8:9
Ex 10:21-23
Amos 4:13; 5:8
Mic 3:6
Mt 24:29; 27:45

8:10
Isa 15:2,3
Ezek 7:18

8:12
Ezek 20:3,31

7:10 Prophets like Amos were often seen as traitors because they spoke out against the king and his advisors, undermining their authority and exposing their sin. The king saw the prophet as an enemy rather than as one who was really trying to help him and the nation.

7:10ff Amaziah was the chief priest in Bethel, representing Israel's official religion. He was not concerned about hearing God's message; he was only worried about his own position. Maintaining his position was more important than listening to the truth.

7:14, 15 Without any special preparation, education, or upbringing, Amos obeyed God's call to "go and prophesy to my people Israel." Obedience is the test of a faithful servant of God. Are you obeying God's Word?

8:5 These merchants kept the religious holidays, but not in spirit. Their real interest was in making money, even if that meant cheating. Do you take a day to rest and worship God at least once a week, or is making money more important to you than anything else? When you give time to God, is your heart in your worship, or is your religion only a front for unethical practices?

8:11–13 The people had no appetite for God's Word when prophets like Amos brought it. Because of their apathy, God said he would take away even the opportunity to hear his Word. We have God's Word, the Bible. But many still look everywhere for answers to life's problems *except* in Scripture. You can help them by directing them to the Bible, showing them the parts that speak to their special needs and questions. God's Word is available to us. Let us help people know it before a time comes when they cannot find it.

8:13
Isa 41:17
Hos 2:3

will wander everywhere from sea to sea, seeking the Word of the Lord, searching, running here and going there, but will not find it.

8:14
1 Kgs 12:28,29
2 Kgs 10:29
Hos 8:5

13"Beautiful girls and fine young men alike will grow faint and weary, thirsting for the Word of God. 14And those who worship the idols of Samaria, Dan, and Beersheba shall fall and never rise again."

Israel will be destroyed

9:1
2 Chron 18:18
Zeph 2:14

9 I saw the Lord standing beside the altar, saying, "Smash the tops of the pillars and shake the Temple until the pillars crumble and the roof crashes down upon the people below. Though they run, they will not escape; they all will be killed.

9:2
Job 26:6
Ps 139:7-10
Isa 14:13-16

2"Though they dig down to Sheol, I will reach down and pull them up; though they climb into the heavens, I will bring them down. 3Though they hide among the

9:3
Job 34:22
Ps 139:9-11

rocks at the top of Carmel, I will search them out and capture them. Though they hide at the bottom of the ocean, I will send the sea-serpent after them to bite and

9:4
Lev 26:33,36-39
Deut 28:63-65
Jer 24:6; 44:11

destroy them. 4Though they volunteer for exile, I will command the sword to kill them there. I will see to it that they receive evil and not good."

9:5
Ps 46:6
Isa 64:1
Rev 20:11

5The Lord Almighty touches the land and it melts, and all its people mourn. It rises like the river Nile in Egypt, and then sinks again. 6The upper stories of his home are in the heavens, the first floor on the earth. He calls for the vapor to rise

9:6
Ps 104:3,6,13

from the ocean and pours it down as rain upon the ground. Jehovah, the Lord, is his name.

9:7
2 Chron 14:9,12
Isa 20:4; 43:3

7"O people of Israel, are you any more to me than the Ethiopians are? Have not I, who brought you out of Egypt, done as much for other people, too? I brought the Philistines from Caphtor and the Syrians out of Kir.

9:8
Deut 4:31; 6:15
1 Kgs 13:34
Jer 5:10
Hos 9:11-17
Joel 2:32

8"The eyes of the Lord God are watching Israel, that sinful nation, and I will root her up and scatter her across the world. *Yet I have promised that this rooting out will not be permanent.* 9For I have commanded that Israel be sifted by the other

9:9
Lev 26:33
Deut 28:64

nations as grain is sifted in a sieve, yet not one true kernel will be lost. 10But all these sinners who say, 'God will not touch us,' will die by the sword.

Israel will be restored

9:11
Isa 9:6,7
16:5; 63:11
Ezek 21:25-27

11"Then, at that time I will rebuild the City of David, which is now lying in ruins, and return it to its former glory, 12and Israel will possess what is left of Edom, and of all the nations that belong to me." For so the Lord, who plans it all, has said.

9:1 Judgment would begin at the altar, the center of the nation's life, the place where the people expected protection and blessing. This judgment would cover all 12 tribes. Commentators disagree concerning this altar—some think it was the altar at Bethel; others think it was the altar in the Temple in Jerusalem.

9:2-4 No one can escape God's judgment. This was good news for the faithful but bad news for the unfaithful. Whether we go to the mountaintops or the bottom of the sea, God will find us and judge us for our deeds. Amos pictured the judgment of the wicked as a sea-serpent, relentlessly pursuing the condemned. For God's faithful followers, however, the judgment brings a new earth of peace and prosperity. Does God's judgment sound like good news or bad news to you?

9:7 Ethiopia, south of Egypt, was a remote and exotic land to the Israelites. Caphtor is Crete, where the Philistines originally lived. God would judge Israel no differently than he judges foreign nations. He is not just the God of Israel; he is God of the universe and he controls all nations.

9:8 Amos assured the Israelites that God's punishment "will not be permanent." God wants to redeem, not punish. But when punishment is necessary he doesn't withhold it. Like a loving father, God disciplines those he loves in order to correct them. If he disciplines you, accept it as a sign of his love.

9:8, 9 Although Assyria would destroy Israel and take her people into exile, some would be preserved. This exile had been predicted hundreds of years earlier (Deuteronomy 28:63-68). Although the nation was purified through this invasion and captivity, not one true believer would be eternally lost. Our system of justice is not always perfect, but God is. Sinners will not get away; the faithful will not be forgotten. True believers will not be lost.

9:11, 12 God's covenant with David stated that one of David's descendants would always sit on his throne (2 Samuel 7:12-16). The exile made this seem impossible. But "in that day" God will raise and restore the kingdom to its promised glory. This was a promise to both Israel and Judah, not to be fulfilled by an earthly, political ruler, but by the Messiah, who would renew the spiritual kingdom and rule forever.

James quoted this verse (Acts 15:16, 17), finding its fulfillment in Christ's resurrection and in the presence of both Jews and Gentiles in the church. When God brings in the Gentiles, he is repairing the broken down "Tabernacle." After the Gentiles are called together, God will renew and restore the fortunes of the new Israel. All the land that was once under David's rule will again be part of God's nation.

13"The time will come when there will be such abundance of crops, that the harvest time will scarcely end before the farmer starts again to sow another crop, and the terraces of grapes upon the hills of Israel will drip sweet wine! 14I will restore the fortunes of my people Israel, and they shall rebuild their ruined cities, and live in them again, and they shall plant vineyards and gardens and eat their crops and drink their wine. 15I will firmly plant them there upon the land that I have given them; they shall not be pulled up again," says the Lord your God.

9:13
Isa 55:13
Ezek 36:35
Hos 2:21-23
Joel 3:18,20
9:14
Ps 53:6
Isa 61:4
Jer 30:3
Ezek 36:33-36

9:13–15 The Jews of Amos' day had lost sight of God's care and love for them. The rich were carefree and comfortable, refusing to help others in need. They observed their religious rituals in hopes of appeasing God, but they did not truly love him. Amos announced God's warnings of destruction for their evil ways.

We must not assume that going to church and being good is enough. God expects our belief in him to penetrate all areas of our lives and conduct and extend to all people and circumstances. We should let Amos' words inspire us to live faithfully as God would have us live.

AFTER months of growth and development, the newborn bursts forth into the world. "She has your mother's eyes," "I can sure tell who her parents are," relatives and friends exclaim as they gaze into the little face and see a resemblance to her mom and dad. Mother and father rejoice in their little daughter, a miracle, a new member of the family. As loving parents, they will protect, nurture, feed, guide, and discipline her. This is their duty and joy.

God has children too—men and women whom he has chosen as his very own. God even chose a nation to be his own—the nation of Israel. Israel was to be God's country, and her people, his very own sons and daughters. Through the following centuries, there was discipline and punishment, but always love and mercy. God, the eternal Father, protected and cared for his children.

Obadiah, the shortest book in the Old Testament, is a dramatic example of God's response to anyone who would harm his children. Edom was a mountainous nation, occupying the region southeast of the Dead Sea including Petra, the spectacular city discovered by archaeologists a few decades ago. As descendants of Esau (Genesis 25:19—27:45), the Edomites were blood relatives of Israel and, like their father, they were rugged, fierce, and proud warriors with a seemingly invincible mountain home. Of all people, they should have rushed to the aid of their northern brothers. Instead, however, they gloated over Israel's problems, captured and delivered fugitives to the enemy, and even looted Israel's countryside.

Obadiah gives God's message to Edom. Because of their indifference and defiance of God, their cowardice and pride, and their treachery toward their brothers in Judah, they stand condemned and will be destroyed. The book begins with the announcement that disaster is coming to Edom (1:1–9). Despite their "impregnable" cliffs and mountains, they will not be able to escape God's judgment. Obadiah then gives the reasons for their destruction (1:10–14)—their blatant arrogance toward God and their persecution of his children. This concise prophecy ends with a description of the Day of the Lord, when judgment will fall on all who have harmed God's people (1:15–21).

Today, God's holy nation is his church—all who have trusted Christ for their salvation and have given their lives to him. These men and women are his born again and adopted children. As you read Obadiah, catch a glimpse of what it means to be God's child, under his love and protection. See how the heavenly Father responds to all who would attack those whom he loves.

VITAL STATISTICS

PURPOSE:
To show that God judges those who have harmed his people

AUTHOR:
Obadiah. Very little is known about this man whose name means "servant of the Lord" or "worshiper of Jehovah"

TO WHOM WRITTEN:
The Edomites, the Jews in Judah, and God's people everywhere

DATE WRITTEN:
Possibly during the reign of Jehoram in Judah, 853–841 B.C.

SETTING:
Historically, Edom had constantly harassed the Jews. Prior to the time this book was written, they had participated in attacks against Judah. Given the dates above, this prophecy comes after the division of Israel into the northern and southern kingdoms and before the conquering of Judah by Nebuchadnezzar in 586 B.C.

KEY VERSE:
"The Lord's vengeance will soon fall upon all Gentile nations. As you have done to Israel, so will it be done to you. Your acts will boomerang upon your heads" (1:15).

KEY PEOPLE:
The Edomites

KEY PLACES:
Edom, Jerusalem

SPECIAL FEATURES:
The book of Obadiah uses vigorous poetic language and is written in the form of a dirge of doom.

THE BLUEPRINT

1. Edom's destruction (1:1–16)
2. Israel's restoration (1:17–21)

The book of Obadiah shows the end of the ancient feud between Edom and Israel. Edom was proud of its high position, but God would bring her down. Those who are high and powerful today should not be overconfident in themselves, whether they are a nation, a corporation, a church, or a family. Just as Edom was destroyed for its pride, so will anyone who lives in defiance of God.

MEGATHEMES

THEME	EXPLANATION	IMPORTANCE
Justice	Obadiah predicted that God would destroy Edom as punishment for helping Babylon invade Judah. Because of their treachery, Edom's land would be given to Judah in the day when God rights the wrongs against his people.	God will judge and fiercely punish all who harm his people. We can be confident in God's final victory. He is our champion and we can trust him to bring about true justice.
Pride	Because of their seemingly invincible rock fortress, the Edomites were proud and self-confident. But God humbled them and their nation disappeared from the face of the earth.	All those who defy God will meet their doom as Edom did. Any nation who trusts in its power, wealth, technology, or wisdom more than in God will be brought low. All who are proud will one day be shocked to discover that no one is exempt from God's justice.

1. Edom's destruction

1 *In a vision the Lord God showed Obadiah the future of the land of Edom.* "A report has come from the Lord," he said, "that God has sent an ambassador to the nations with this message: 'Attention! You are to send your armies against Edom and destroy her!' "

²I will cut you down to size among the nations, Edom, making you small and despised.

³You are proud because you live in those high, inaccessible cliffs. "Who can ever reach us way up here!" you boast. Don't fool yourselves! ⁴Though you soar as high as eagles, and build your nest among the stars, I will bring you plummeting down, says the Lord.

1:1
Isa 34:5-15
63:1-6
Jer 49:7-22
Ps 137:7
Ezek 25:12-14
Amos 1:11,12

1:2
Num 24:15-19

1:3
Jer 49:15,16

1:4
Job 39:26-30
Isa 14:12-15

1:1 Obadiah was a prophet from Judah who told of God's judgment against the nation of Edom. Two commonly accepted dates for this prophecy are (1) between 848 and 841 B.C., when King Jehoram and Jerusalem were attacked by a Philistine/Arab coalition (2 Chronicles 21:16ff), or (2) 586 B.C., when Jerusalem was completely destroyed by the Babylonians (2 Kings 25; 2 Chronicles 36). Edom had rejoiced over the misfortunes of both Israel and Judah, and yet the Edomites and Jews descended from two brothers—Esau and Jacob (Genesis 25:19–26). But just as these two brothers were constantly at odds, Israel and Edom were rarely at peace. God pronounced judgment on Edom for their callous and malicious actions toward his people.

1:3 Edom was Judah's southern neighbor, sharing a common boundary. But neighbors are not always friends, and Edom liked nothing about Judah. Edom's capital at this time was Petra, a city considered impregnable because it was cut into a solid rock cliff and set in a canyon that could be entered only through a narrow gap. What Edom perceived as strengths would be its downfall: (1) safety in their city (1:3, 4)—God would send them plummeting from the heights; (2) pride in their self-sufficiency (1:4)—God would humble them; (3) wealth (1:5, 6)—thieves would steal all they had; (4) allies (1:7)—God would cause them to turn against

Edom; (5) wisdom (1:8, 9)—they would be confused.

1:3 The Edomites felt secure, and they were proud of their self-sufficiency. But they were fooling themselves because there is no lasting security apart from God. Is your security in objects or people? Ask yourself how much lasting security they really offer. Possessions and people can disappear in a moment, but God does not change. Only he can supply true security.

1:4 The Edomites were proud of their city carved right into the rock. Today it is considered one of the marvels of the ancient world, but only as a tourist attraction. The Bible warns that pride is the surest route to self-destruction (Proverbs 16:18). Just as Petra and Edom fell, so will proud people fall. A humble person is more secure than a proud person, because humility gives one a more accurate perspective of oneself and the world.

1:4–9 God did not pronounce these harsh judgments against Edom out of vengeance but in order to bring about justice. God is morally perfect and demands complete justice and fairness. The Edomites were simply getting what they deserved. Because they murdered, they would be murdered. Because they robbed, they would be robbed. Because they took advantage of others, they would be used. Don't talk yourself into sin, thinking that "nobody will know" or "I won't get caught." God knows all our sins, and he will be just.

1:5
Jer 49:9,10

⁵Far better it would be for you if thieves had come at night to plunder you—for they would not take everything! Or if your vineyards were robbed of all their fruit—for at least the gleanings would be left! ⁶Every nook and cranny will be searched and robbed, and every treasure found and taken.

1:7
Ps 55:12-14
Isa 19:11-14
Jer 4:30
1:8
Job 5:12-14
Isa 19:3,13,14
29:14
1:9
Jer 49:20-22
Amos 2:16
1:10
Num 20:14-22
Ps 83:5-8
109:29
Ezek 7:18
25:12-14
1:11
2 Kgs 25:8-21
2 Chron 36:19,
20
Jer 52:12-30
1:12
Ps 22:17
Mic 4:11
1:13
2 Kgs 24:13-16
2 Chron 36:18
1:15
Jer 9:25,26
25:15
Joel 1:15

⁷All your allies will turn against you and help to push you out of your land. They will promise peace while plotting your destruction. Your trusted friends will set traps for you and all your counterstrategy will fail. ⁸In that day not one wise man will be left in all of Edom! says the Lord. For I will fill the wise men of Edom with stupidity. ⁹The mightiest soldiers of Teman will be confused, and helpless to prevent the slaughter.

¹⁰And why? Because of what you did to your brother Israel. Now your sins will be exposed for all to see; ashamed and defenseless, you will be cut off forever. ¹¹For you deserted Israel in his time of need. You stood aloof, refusing to lift a finger to help him when invaders carried off his wealth and divided Jerusalem among them by lot; you were as one of his enemies.

¹²You should not have done it. You should not have gloated when they took him far away to foreign lands; you should not have rejoiced in the day of his misfortune; you should not have mocked in his time of need. ¹³You yourselves went into the land of Israel in the day of his calamity and looted him. You made yourselves rich at his expense. ¹⁴You stood at the crossroads and killed those trying to escape; you captured the survivors and returned them to their enemies in that terrible time of his distress.

¹⁵The Lord's vengeance will soon fall upon all Gentile nations. As you have done to Israel, so will it be done to you. Your acts will boomerang upon your heads. ¹⁶You drank my cup of punishment upon my holy mountain, and the nations round about will drink it, too; yes, drink and stagger back and disappear from history, no longer nations any more.

HISTORY OF THE CONFLICT BETWEEN ISRAEL AND EDOM	The nation of Israel descended from Jacob; the nation of Edom descended from Esau	Genesis 25:23
	Jacob and Esau struggled in their mother's womb	Genesis 25:19–26
	Esau sold his birthright and blessing to Jacob	Genesis 25:29–34
	Edom refused to let the Israelites pass through their land	Numbers 20:14–22
	Israel's kings had constant conflict with Edom	
	● Saul	1 Samuel 14:47, 48
	● David	2 Samuel 8:13, 14
	● Solomon	1 Kings 11:14–22
	● Jehoram	2 Kings 8:20–22; 2 Chronicles 21:8ff
	● Ahaz	2 Chronicles 28:16
	Edom encouraged Babylon to destroy Jerusalem	Psalm 137:7

1:8 Edom was noted for her wise men. There is a difference, however, between man's wisdom and God's wisdom. The Edomites may have been wise in the ways of the world, but they were foolish because they ignored and even mocked God.

1:9 Eliphaz, one of Job's three friends (Job 2:11), was from Teman, five miles east of Petra. Teman was named after Esau's grandson (Genesis 36:10–12).

1:10, 11 The Israelites descended from Jacob, and the Edomites from his brother, Esau (Genesis 25:19–26). Instead of helping Israel and Judah when they were in need, Edom let them be destroyed and even plundered what was left behind. Edom, therefore, was an enemy and would be punished. Anyone who does not help God's people is God's enemy. If you have withheld your help from someone in a time of need, this is sin. Sin includes not only what we do, but also what we refuse to do. Don't ignore or refuse to help those in need.

1:12 Edom was glad to see Judah in trouble. Their hatred made them want the nation destroyed. For this wrong, God obliterated

Edom. How often do you find yourself rejoicing at the misfortunes of others? Because God alone is the judge, we must never be happy about others' misfortunes, even if we think they deserve them (see Proverbs 24:17).

1:12–14 Of all Israel and Judah's neighbors, Edom was the only one not promised any mercy from God. This was because they looted Jerusalem and rejoiced at the misfortunes of Israel and Judah. They betrayed their blood brothers in times of crisis and aided their enemies. (See also Psalm 137:7; Jeremiah 49:7–22; Ezekiel 25:12–14; Amos 1:11, 12.)

1:15 Why will God's vengeance fall on the Gentile nations? Edom was not the only nation to rejoice at Judah's fall. All nations and individuals will be judged for the way they treat God's people. Some nations today treat God's people favorably, while others are hostile toward them. God will judge all people according to the way they treat others, especially believers (Revelation 20:12, 13). Jesus talked about this in Matthew 25:31–46.

2. Israel's restoration

17But Jerusalem will become a refuge, a way of escape. Israel will reoccupy the land. 18Israel will be a fire that sets the dry fields of Edom aflame. There will be no survivors, for the Lord has spoken.

19Then my people who live in the Negeb shall occupy the hill country of Edom; those living in Judean lowlands shall possess the Philistine plains, and repossess the fields of Ephraim and Samaria. And the people of Benjamin shall possess Gilead.

20The Israeli exiles shall return and occupy the Phoenician coastal strip as far north as Zarephath. Those exiled in Asia Minor shall return to their homeland and conquer the Negeb's outlying villages. 21For deliverers will come to Jerusalem and rule all Edom. And the Lord shall be King!

1:17
Isa 14:1,2
Joel 3:19-21
Amos 9:11-15

1:19
Num 24:15-19
Jer 31:5; 32:44
Ezek 36:6-12
47:13-20

1:20
1 Kgs 17:9

1:21
Zech 9:11-17
Lk 1:32,33
Rev 11:15; 19:6

Climate of the times	Edom was a constant thorn in Judah's side. They often participated in attacks initiated by other enemies.	**OBADIAH** served as a prophet to Judah around 853 B.C.
Main message	God will judge Edom for its evil actions towards God's people.	
Importance of message	Just as Edom was destroyed and disappeared as a nation, so God will destroy proud and wicked people.	
Contemporary prophets	Elijah (875–848)	
	Micaiah (865–853)	
	Jehu (855–840?)	

1:17-21 The Edomites were routed by Judas Maccabeus in 185 B.C. The nation no longer existed by the first century A.D. At the time of Obadiah's prophecy, Edom may have seemed more likely to survive than Judah. Yet Edom has vanished and Judah still exists. This demonstrates the absolute certainty of God's Word and of the punishment awaiting all who have mistreated God's people.

1:21 Obadiah brought God's message of judgment on Edom. God was displeased with both their inward and their outward rebellion. People today are much the same as those in Obadiah's time. We see arrogance, envy, and dishonesty, and we wonder where it will all end. Regardless of sin's effects, however, God is in control. As you struggle, don't despair or give up hope. Know that when all is said and done, the Lord will still be King, and the confidence you place in him will not be in vain.

1:21 Edom is an example to all the nations who are hostile to God. Nothing can break God's promise to protect his people from complete destruction. In the book of Obadiah we see four aspects of God's message of judgment: (1) evil will certainly be punished; (2) those faithful to God have hope for a new future; (3) God is sovereign in human history; (4) God's ultimate purpose is to establish his eternal kingdom. The Edomites had been cruel to God's people. They were arrogant and proud, and they took advantage of others' misfortunes. Any nation who mistreats those people who obey God will be punished, regardless of how invincible they appear. Similarly we, as individuals, cannot allow ourselves to feel so comfortable with our wealth or security that we fail to help God's people in need. This is sin. And because God is just, people will reap punishment if they sow sin.

JONAH

SIN runs rampant in society—daily headlines and overflowing prisons bear dramatic witness to that fact. With child abuse, pornography, serial killings, terrorism, anarchy, and ruthless dictatorships, the world seems to be filled to overflowing with violence, hatred, and corruption. Reading, hearing, and perhaps even experiencing these tragedies, we begin to understand the necessity of God's judgment. We may even find ourselves wishing for vengeance by any means upon the violent perpetrators. Surely they are beyond redemption! But suppose that in the midst of such thoughts, God told you to take the gospel to the worst of these offenders—how would you respond?

Jonah was given such a task. Assyria—a great, but evil empire—was Israel's most dreaded enemy. The Assyrians flaunted their power before God and the world through numerous acts of heartless cruelty. So when Jonah heard God tell him to go to Assyria and call the people to repentance, he ran in the opposite direction.

The book of Jonah tells the story of this prophet's flight and how God stopped him and turned him around. But it is much more than a story of a man and a great fish—Jonah's story is a profound illustration of God's mercy and grace. No one deserved God's favor less than the people of Nineveh, Assyria's capital. Jonah knew this. But he knew that God would forgive and bless them if they turned from their sin and worshiped him. He also knew the power of God's message, that even through his weak preaching, they would respond and be spared God's judgment. But Jonah hated the Assyrians, and he wanted vengeance, not mercy, and so he ran. Eventually, Jonah obeyed and preached in the streets of Nineveh and the people repented and were delivered from judgment. Then Jonah sulked and complained to God, "I knew you were a gracious God, merciful, slow to get angry, and full of kindness; I knew how easily you could cancel your plans for destroying these people" (4:2). In the end, God confronted Jonah about his self-centered values and lack of compassion, saying, "Why shouldn't I feel sorry for a great city like Nineveh with its 120,000 people in utter spiritual darkness?" (4:11).

As you read Jonah, see the full picture of God's love and compassion and realize that no one is beyond redemption. The gospel is for all who will repent and believe. Begin to pray for those who seem to be farthest from the kingdom, and look for ways to tell them about God. Learn from the story of this reluctant prophet and determine to obey God, doing whatever and going wherever he leads.

VITAL STATISTICS

PURPOSE:
To show the extent of God's grace—the message of salvation is for *all* people

AUTHOR:
Jonah, son of Amittai

TO WHOM WRITTEN:
Israel and God's people everywhere

DATE WRITTEN:
Approximately 785–760 B.C.

SETTING:
Jonah preceded Amos and ministered under Jeroboam II, Israel's most powerful king (793–753 B.C., see 2 Kings 14:23–25). Assyria was Israel's great enemy, and Israel was conquered by them in 722 B.C. Nineveh's repentance must have been short-lived.

KEY VERSE:
"Why shouldn't I feel sorry for a great city like Nineveh with its 120,000 people in utter spiritual darkness?" (4:11).

KEY PEOPLE:
Jonah, the boat's captain and crew

KEY PLACES:
Joppa, Nineveh

SPECIAL FEATURES:
This book is different from the other prophetic books because it tells the story of the prophet and does not center on his prophecies. In fact, only one verse summarizes his message to the people of Nineveh (3:4). Jonah is an historical narrative. It is also mentioned by Jesus as a picture of his death and resurrection (Matthew 12:38–42).

THE BLUEPRINT

1. Jonah forsakes his mission (1:1—2:10)
2. Jonah fulfills his mission (3:1—4:11)

Jonah was a reluctant prophet given a mission which he found distasteful. He chose to run away from God rather than obey him. Like Jonah, we may have to do things in life which we don't want to do. Sometimes, we find ourselves wanting to turn and run. But it is better to obey God than to defy him or run away. Often, in spite of our defiance, God in his mercy will give us another chance to serve him when we return to him.

MEGATHEMES

THEME	EXPLANATION	IMPORTANCE
God's sovereignty	Although the prophet Jonah tried to run away from God, God was in control. By controlling the stormy seas and a great fish, God displayed his absolute, yet loving guidance.	Rather than running from God, trust him with your past, present, and future. Saying ''no'' to God quickly leads to disaster. Saying ''yes'' brings new understanding of God and his purpose in the world.
God's message to all the world	God had given Jonah a purpose—to preach to the great Assyrian city of Nineveh. Jonah hated Nineveh, and so he responded with anger and indifference. Jonah had yet to learn that God loves all people. Through Jonah, God reminded Israel of their missionary purpose.	God wants his people to proclaim his love in words and actions to the whole world. He wants us to be his missionaries wherever we are, wherever he sends us.
Repentance	When the reluctant preacher went to Nineveh, there was a great response. The people repented and turned to God. This was a powerful rebuke to Israel who thought themselves better and yet refused to respond to God's message. God will forgive all those who turn from their sin.	God doesn't honor sham or pretense. He wants the sincere devotion of each person. It is not enough to share the privileges of Christianity; we must ask God to forgive us and to remove our sin. Refusing to repent is the same as loving our sin.
God's compassion	God's message of love and forgiveness was not for the Jews alone. God loves all the people of the world. The Assyrians didn't deserve it, but God spared them when they repented. In his mercy, God did not reject Jonah for aborting his mission. God has great love, patience, and forgiveness.	God loves each of us even when we fail him. But he also loves other people, including those not of our group, background, race, or denomination. When we accept his love, we must also learn to accept all those whom he loves. We will find it much easier to love others when we love God.

1. Jonah forsakes his mission

Jonah runs away from God

1 *The Lord sent this message to Jonah, the son of Amittai:* 2"Go to the great city of Nineveh, and give them this announcement from the Lord: 'I am going to destroy you, for your wickedness rises before me; it smells to highest heaven.' "

3But Jonah was afraid to go and ran away from the Lord. He went down to the

1:1
2 Kgs 14:25
Mt 12:39-41
Lk 11:29,30,32

1:2
2 Kgs 19:36
Jonah 3:3

1:1 Jonah is mentioned in 2 Kings 14:25. He prophesied during the reign of Jeroboam II, the king of Israel from 793–753 B.C. He may have been one of the young prophets of the school mentioned in connection with Elisha's ministry (2 Kings 2:3).

God called Jonah to preach to Nineveh, the most important city in Assyria, the rising world power of Jonah's day. Within 50 years, Nineveh would become the capital of the vast Assyrian Empire. Jonah doesn't say much about Nineveh's wickedness, but the prophet Nahum gives us more insight. He says that Nineveh was guilty of (1) evil plots against God (Nahum 1:9, 10), (2) exploitation of the helpless (Nahum 2:12), (3) cruelty in war (Nahum 2:12, 13), (4) idolatry (Nahum 3:4), and (5) prostitution and witchcraft

(Nahum 3:4). God told Jonah to go to Nineveh, about 500 miles northeast of Israel, to warn of judgment and to declare that the people could receive mercy and forgiveness if they repented.

1:3 Nineveh was a powerful and wicked city. Jonah grew up hating the Assyrians and fearing their atrocities. His hatred was so strong that he didn't want them to receive God's mercy. Jonah was actually afraid the people would repent (4:2). Jonah's attitude is representative of Israel's reluctance to share God's love and mercy with others, even though this was their God-given mission (Genesis 12:3). They, like Jonah, did not want non-Jews (Gentiles) to obtain God's favor.

1:3 Jonah was afraid. He knew God had a specific job for him,

1:3
Gen 3:8; 4:16
2 Chron 2:16
9:21
Isa 23:6
Acts 9:36

1:5
1 Kgs 18:26
Isa 44:17-20
Acts 27:18,19,
38

1:6
Ps 107:28
Jer 2:28

1:7
Judg 20:9,10
Esth 3:7
Prov 16:33

1:8
Gen 47:3

1:9
Gen 1:9,10
Ezra 1:2; 5:11
Neh 1:4; 9:6

seacoast, to the port of Joppa, where he found a ship leaving for Tarshish. He bought a ticket, went on board, and climbed down into the dark hold of the ship to hide there from the Lord.

⁴But as the ship was sailing along, suddenly the Lord flung a terrific wind over the sea, causing a great storm that threatened to send them to the bottom. ⁵Fearing for their lives, the desperate sailors shouted to their gods for help and threw the cargo overboard to lighten the ship. And all this time Jonah was sound asleep down in the hold.

⁶So the captain went down after him. "What do you mean," he roared, "sleeping at a time like this? Get up and cry to your god, and see if he will have mercy on us and save us!"

⁷Then the crew decided to draw straws to see which of them had offended the gods and caused this terrible storm; and Jonah drew the short one.

⁸"What have you done," they asked, "to bring this awful storm upon us? Who are you? What is your work? What country are you from? What is your nationality?"

⁹, ¹⁰And he said, "I am a Jew; I worship Jehovah, the God of heaven, who made the earth and sea." Then he told them he was running away from the Lord.

The men were terribly frightened when they heard this. "Oh, why did you do it?"

1:9 *I am a Jew,* literally, "a Hebrew."

JONAH
served as a
prophet to Israel
and Assyria from
793–753 B.C.

Climate of the times	Nineveh was the most important city in Assyria and would soon become the capital of the huge Assyrian Empire. But Nineveh was also a very wicked city.
Main message	Jonah, who hated the powerful and wicked Assyrians, was called by God to warn the Assyrians that they would receive judgment if they did not repent.
Importance of message	Jonah didn't want to go to Nineveh, so he tried to run from God. But God has ways of teaching us to obey and follow him. When Jonah preached, the city repented and God withheld his judgment. Even the most wicked will be saved if they truly repent of their sins and turn to God.
Contemporary prophets	Joel (853–796?)
	Amos (760–750)

---

but he didn't want to do it. When God gives us directions through his Word, sometimes we run in fear, claiming that God is asking too much. Fear made Jonah run. But running got him into worse trouble. In the end, he knew it was best to do what God had asked in the first place. But by then he had paid a costly price for running. It is far better to obey from the start.

1:4 Before settling in the Promised Land, the Israelites had been a nomadic people. They wandered from place to place, seeking good pastureland for their flocks. Although they were not a seafaring people, their location along the Mediterranean Sea and the neighboring maritime powers of Phoenicia and Philistia allowed much contact with ships and sailors. The ship Jonah sailed on was probably a large trading vessel with a deck.

1:4 Jonah's disobedience to God endangered the lives of the ship's crew. We have a great responsibility to obey God's Word because our sin and disobedience will hurt others around us.

1:4, 5 While the storm raged, Jonah was sound asleep in the ship's hold. Even as he ran from God, he apparently didn't have a guilty conscience. But the absence of guilt isn't always a barometer of whether we are doing right. Because we can deny reality, we cannot measure obedience by our feelings. Instead, we must compare our lives with God's standards for living.

1:7 The crew drew straws to find the guilty person, relying on their superstitions to give them the answer. Their system worked, but only because God intervened to let Jonah know he couldn't run from him.

1:9–12 You cannot seek God's love and run from him at the same time. Jonah soon realized that no matter where he went, he

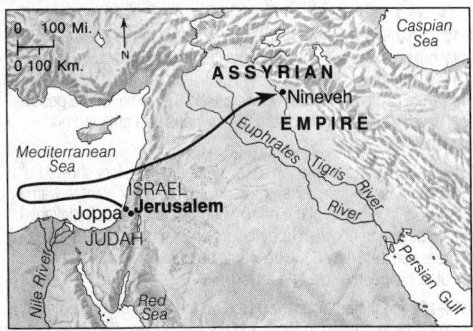

JONAH'S ROUNDABOUT JOURNEY God told Jonah to go to Nineveh, the capital of the Assyrian Empire. Many of Jonah's countrymen had experienced the atrocities of these fierce people. The last place Jonah wanted to go on a missionary trip was to Nineveh! So he went in the opposite direction. He boarded a ship in Joppa which was headed for Tarshish in Spain. But Jonah could not run from God.

couldn't get away from God. But before Jonah could return to God, he first had to stop running away from him. What has God told you to do? If you want more of God's love and power, you must be willing to carry out the responsibilities he gives you. You cannot say that you truly believe in God if you don't do what he says.

they shouted. 11"What should we do to you to stop the storm?" For it was getting worse and worse.

12"Throw me out into the sea," he said, "and it will become calm again. For I know this terrible storm has come because of me."

1:12
Jn 11:50

13They tried harder to row the boat ashore, but couldn't make it. The storm was too fierce to fight against. 14Then they shouted out a prayer to Jehovah, Jonah's God. "O Jehovah," they pleaded, "don't make us die for this man's sin, and don't hold us responsible for his death, for it is not our fault—you have sent this storm upon him for your own good reasons."

15Then they picked up Jonah and threw him overboard into the raging sea—and the storm stopped!

1:15
Ps 89:9
Mk 4:34

16The men stood there in awe before Jehovah, and sacrificed to him and vowed to serve him.

1:16
Gen 28:20
Ps 66:13,14

17Now the Lord had arranged for a great fish to swallow Jonah. And Jonah was inside the fish three days and three nights.

1:17
Jonah 1:1; 2:1

Jonah prays inside the fish

2 Then Jonah prayed to the Lord his God from inside the fish:

2:1
Ps 130:1
Jonah 1:17

2"In my great trouble I cried to the Lord and he answered me; from the depths of death I called, and Lord, you heard me! 3You threw me into the ocean depths; I sank down into the floods of waters and was covered by your wild and stormy waves. 4Then I said, 'O Lord, you have rejected me and cast me away. How shall I ever again see your holy Temple?'

2:2
Ps 18:4-6; 22:24
2:3
Ps 42:7
2:4
1 Kgs 8:38
Ps 5:7
Ps 77:1-7
Isa 38:10-14

5"I sank beneath the waves, and death was very near. The waters closed above me; the seaweed wrapped itself around my head. 6I went down to the bottoms of the mountains that rise from off the ocean floor. I was locked out of life and imprisoned in the land of death. But, O Lord my God, you have snatched me from the yawning jaws of death!

2:5
Lam 3:54
2:6
Ps 30:3; 65:6
Isa 38:17; 40:12

7"When I had lost all hope, I turned my thoughts once more to the Lord. And my earnest prayer went to you in your holy Temple. 8(Those who worship false gods have turned their backs on all the mercies waiting for them from the Lord!)

2:7
2 Chron 30:27
Ps 18:6; 142:3

9"I will never worship anyone but you! For how can I thank you enough for all

---

1:12 Jonah knew he had disobeyed and that the storm was his fault, but he didn't say anything until the crew drew straws and he got the short one (1:7). Then he was willing to give his life to save the sailors (although he had refused to do the same for the people of Nineveh). Jonah's hatred for the Assyrians had affected his perspective.

1:13 By trying to save Jonah's life, the heathen sailors showed more compassion than Jonah did, for Jonah did not want to warn the people of Nineveh of the coming judgment of God. Believers should be ashamed when unbelievers show more concern and compassion than they do. God wants us to become concerned about all his people, lost and saved.

1:14-16 Jonah had disobeyed God. In the midst of running away, however, he submitted to God, and the ship's crew began to worship God because they saw the storm quiet down. God is able to use even our mistakes to help others come to know him. It may be painful, but admitting our sins can be a powerful example to those who don't know God. How ironic that the pagan sailors did what the entire nation of Israel would not do—prayed to God and vowed to serve him.

1:17 Many have tried to explain away this miraculous event, but the Bible does not describe it as a dream or a legend. We should not explain away this miracle as if we could pick and choose which of the miracles in the Bible we want to believe and which ones we don't. This kind of attitude allows us to question any part of the Bible, causing us to lose our trust in it as God's true and reliable Word. Jonah's experience was used by Christ himself as an illustration of his death and resurrection (Matthew 12:39, 40).

2:1ff This is a prayer of thanksgiving, not a prayer for deliverance. Jonah was simply thankful that he had not been drowned. He was delivered in a most spectacular way and was overwhelmed that he had escaped certain death. Even from inside the fish, Jonah's prayer was heard by God. We can pray anywhere and at any time, and God will hear us. Your sin is never too great, your predicament never too difficult, for God.

2:1-7 Jonah said, "When I had lost all hope, I turned my thoughts once more to the Lord" (2:7). Often we act the same way. When life is going well, we tend to take God for granted, but when we lose hope, we cry out to him. This kind of relationship with God can result only in an inconsistent, up-and-down spiritual life. A consistent, daily commitment to God promotes a solid relationship with him. Look to God during both the good and bad times, and you will have a stronger spiritual life.

2:9 Jonah was obviously not in a position to bargain with God. Instead, he simply thanked God for saving his life. Our troubles should cause us to cling tightly to God, not make an attempt at bargaining our way out of the pain. We can thank him and praise him for what he has already done for us by being merciful and loving towards us.

2:9 It took a miracle of deliverance to get Jonah to do as God had commanded. As a prophet, he was obligated to obey God's Word, but he had tried to escape his responsibilities. He now pledged to keep his vows. Jonah's story began with a tragedy, but a greater tragedy would have happened if God had allowed him to keep running. When you know God wants you to do something, don't run. God may not stop you as he did Jonah.

2:9
Lev 27:1-33
Deut 23:21
Ps 50:14; 68:20

you have done? I will surely fulfill my promises. For my deliverance comes from the Lord alone."

¹⁰And the Lord ordered the fish to spit up Jonah on the beach, and it did.

2. Jonah fulfills his mission
Jonah preaches at Nineveh

3:2
Jer 1:17
Ezek 2:7; 3:17
Mt 3:8

3 Then the Lord spoke to Jonah again: "Go to that great city, Nineveh," he said, "and warn them of their doom, as I told you to before!"

3:3
Jonah 1:2; 4:11

³So Jonah obeyed, and went to Nineveh. Now Nineveh was a very large city, with many villages around it—so large that it would take three days to walk through it.

3:4
2 Kgs 20:1,6
2 Chron 20:3
Ezra 8:21
Dan 9:3
Mt 12:41
Lk 11:32

⁴, ⁵But the very first day when Jonah entered the city and began to preach, the people repented. Jonah shouted to the crowds that gathered around him, "Forty days from now Nineveh will be destroyed!" And they believed him and declared a fast; from the king on down, everyone put on sackcloth—the rough, coarse garments worn at times of mourning.

3:7
2 Chron 30:1-10

3:8
Ps 130:1,2
Isa 1:16-19
Jonah 1:6,14
Acts 3:19

⁶For when the king of Nineveh heard what Jonah was saying, he stepped down from his throne and laid aside his royal robes and put on sackcloth and sat in ashes. ⁷And the king and his nobles sent this message throughout the city: "Let no one, not even the animals, eat anything at all, nor even drink any water. ⁸Everyone must wear sackcloth and cry mightily to God, and let everyone turn from his evil ways, from his violence and robbing. ⁹Who can tell? Perhaps even yet God will decide to let us live, and will hold back his fierce anger from destroying us."

3:9
2 Sam 12:22
Joel 2:14

3:10
1 Kgs 21:27-29
Jer 18:8

¹⁰And when God saw that they had put a stop to their evil ways, he abandoned his plan to destroy them, and didn't carry it through.

God's mercy makes Jonah angry

4:2
Jer 20:7
Hos 11:8,9

4 This change of plans made Jonah very angry. ²He complained to the Lord about it: "This is exactly what I thought you'd do, Lord, when I was there in

3:4, 5 the rough, coarse garments worn at times of mourning, implied.

3:1, 2 Jonah had ignored God and rebelled against him, but God still showed him compassion. When we ignore God, he may punish us, but he will offer compassion and forgiveness if we turn from our sins and obey him.

3:1, 2 Jonah ran away from God, but he was given a second chance to participate in God's work. You may feel you are disqualified from serving him because of past mistakes. But serving God is not an earned position. None of us qualifies for God's service, but he asks us to be a part of his work. You may yet have another chance.

3:1, 2 Jonah was to preach only what God told him—a message of doom to the most powerful city in the world. This was not the most desirable assignment, but those who bring God's Word to others should not let society, social pressures, or fear of people dictate their words. They are called to preach God's message and his truth, no matter how unpopular it may be.

3:3 The Hebrew text makes no distinction between the city proper (the walls of which were only about eight miles in circumference, accomodating a population of about 175,000 persons) and the administrative district of Nineveh which was about 30 to 60 miles across.

3:4, 5 God's message is for everyone. Despite the wickedness of the Ninevite people, they were open to God's message and repented immediately. If we simply proclaim what we know of God, we may be surprised at how many people will listen.

3:10 The heathen people of Nineveh believed Jonah's message and repented. What a miraculous effect God's words had on these evil people! Their repentance stood in stark contrast to Israel's stubbornness. The people of Israel heard many messages from the prophets, but they refused to repent. The people of Nineveh only

needed to hear God's message once. Jesus said that at the Judgment Day, these Ninevites will rise up to condemn the Israelites for their failure to repent (Matthew 12:39–41). It is not the hearing of God's Word that pleases him, but an obedient response to it.

3:10 God responded in mercy by canceling his threatened punishment. God himself said that any nation on which he pronounced judgment would be saved if they repented (Jeremiah 18:7–10). God forgave Nineveh just as he had forgiven Jonah. The purpose of God's judgment is correction, not revenge. He is always ready to show compassion to anyone willing to seek him.

4:1 Why did Jonah become angry when God spared Nineveh? The Jews did not want to share God's message with Gentile nations in Jonah's day, just as in Paul's day (1 Thessalonians 2:14–16). They forgot their original purpose as a nation—to be a blessing to the rest of the world by sharing God's message with other nations (Genesis 22:18). Jonah thought God should not freely give his salvation to a wicked heathen nation. Yet this is exactly what he does for all who come to him today in faith.

4:1 Jonah was angry that God had spared Nineveh. He forgot that God forgave his own sin of disobedience and spared his life. How much better it would have been if he had rejoiced that sinners had repented (compare Luke 15:10)!

4:1, 2 Jonah reveals the reason for his reluctance to go to Nineveh (1:3). He didn't want the Ninevites forgiven; he wanted them destroyed. Jonah did not understand that the God of Israel is also the God of the whole world. Are you surprised when some unexpected person turns to God? Is it possible that your view is as narrow as Jonah's? We must not forget that, in reality, *we* do not deserve to be forgiven by God.

my own country and you first told me to come here. That's why I ran away to Tarshish. For I knew you were a gracious God, merciful, slow to get angry, and full of kindness; I knew how easily you could cancel your plans for destroying these people.

3"Please kill me, Lord; I'd rather be dead than alive [when nothing that I told them happens]."

4:3
1 Kgs 19:4
Job 6:8,9

4Then the Lord said, "Is it right to be *angry* about *this?*"

5So Jonah went out and sat sulking on the east side of the city, and he made a leafy shelter to shade him as he waited there to see if anything would happen to the city. 6And when the leaves of the shelter withered in the heat, the Lord arranged for a vine to grow up quickly and spread its broad leaves over Jonah's head to shade him. This made him comfortable and very grateful.

7But God also prepared a worm! The next morning the worm ate through the stem of the plant, so that it withered away and died.

4:7
Joel 1:12

8Then, when the sun was hot, God ordered a scorching east wind to blow on Jonah, and the sun beat down upon his head until he grew faint and wished to die. For he said, "Death is better than this!"

4:8
Isa 49:10
Ezek 19:12
Hos 13:15
Rev 7:16

9And God said to Jonah, "Is it right for you to be angry because the plant died?"
"Yes," Jonah said, "it is; it is right for me to be angry enough to die!"

10Then the Lord said, "You feel sorry for yourself when your shelter is destroyed, though you did no work to put it there, and it is, at best, short-lived. 11And why shouldn't I feel sorry for a great city like Nineveh with its 120,000 people in utter spiritual darkness, and all its cattle?"

4:11
Jonah 3:10

4:3 *when nothing that I told them happens,* implied.   **4:5** *sat sulking,* implied.   **4:11** *with its 120,000 people in utter spiritual darkness,* or "with its 120,000 children who don't know their right hands from their left."

God caused a great storm	1:4	**MIRACLES IN**
God arranged a great fish to swallow Jonah	1:17	**THE BOOK OF**
God ordered the fish to spit up Jonah	2:10	**JONAH**
God made a vine to shade Jonah	4:6	
God prepared a worm to eat the vine	4:7	
God ordered a scorching wind to blow on Jonah	4:8	

4:3 Jonah had run from the job of delivering God's message of destruction to Nineveh (1:2); now he wanted to die because the destruction wouldn't happen. How quickly Jonah had forgotten God's mercy on him when he was in the fish (2:10). He was happy when God saved him, but angry when Nineveh was saved. But Jonah was learning a valuable lesson about God's mercy and forgiveness. God's forgiveness was not only for Jonah or for Israel alone, it extends to all who repent and believe.

4:3 Jonah was more concerned about his own reputation than God's. He knew that if the people repented, none of his warnings to Nineveh would come true. This would embarrass him, although it would give glory to God. Are you more interested in getting glory for God or for yourself?

4:6–10 God ministered tenderly to Jonah just as he did to Nineveh and to Israel, and just as he does to us. He could have destroyed Jonah for his defiant anger, but instead he gently taught him a lesson. If we will obey God's Word he will gently lead us. His harsh judgment is reserved for those who persist in rebellion.

4:9 Jonah was angry at the death of the plant, but not over what could have happened to Nineveh. Most of us have cried at the death of a pet or when an object with sentimental value is broken, but have we cried over the fact that a friend does not know God? How easy it is to be more sensitive to our own interests than to the spiritual needs of people around us.

4:10, 11 Sometimes people wish that judgment and destruction would come upon sinful people whose wickedness seems to demand immediate punishment. But God is more merciful than we can imagine. He feels compassion for the sinners we want judged, and he devises plans to bring them to himself. What is your attitude toward those who are especially wicked? Do you want them destroyed? Or do you wish that they could experience God's mercy and forgiveness?

4:11 God spared the sailors when they pleaded for mercy. God saved Jonah when he prayed from the belly of the fish. God saved the people of Nineveh when they responded to Jonah's preaching. God answers the prayers of those who call upon him. God will always work his will, and he desires that all come to him, trust in him, and be saved. We can be saved if we heed God's warnings to us through his Word. If we respond in obedience, he will be gracious, and we will receive his mercy, not his judgment.

MICAH

"I HATE YOU!" she screams, and runs from the room. Words from a child, thrown as emotional darts. Perhaps she learned the phrase from mom and dad, or maybe it just burst forth from that inner well of "sinful nature." Whatever the case, hate and love have become society's by-words, almost tired clichés, tossed carelessly at objects, situations, and even people.

The casual use of such words as "love" and "hate" has emptied them of their meaning. We no longer understand statements which describe a loving God who hates sin. So we picture God as gentle and kind—a cosmic "pushover"; and our concept of what he hates is tempered by our misconceptions and wishful thinking.

The words of the prophets stand in stark contrast to such misconceptions. God's hatred is real—burning, consuming, and destroying. He hates sin, and he stands as the righteous judge, ready to mete out just punishment to all who defy his rule. God's love is also real. So real that he sent his Son, the Messiah to save and accept judgment in the sinner's stead. Love and hate are together—both unending, irresistable, and unfathomable.

In seven short chapters, Micah presents this true picture of God—the Almighty Lord who hates sin and loves the sinner. Much of the book is devoted to describing God's judgment on Israel (the Northern Kingdom), on Judah (the Southern Kingdom), and on all the earth. This judgment will come "because of the sins of Israel and Judah. . . . The idolatry and oppression centering in the capital cities, Samaria and Jerusalem!" (1:5). And the prophet lists their despicable sins, including fraud (2:2), theft (2:8), greed (2:9), debauchery (2:11), oppression (3:3), hypocrisy (3:4), heresy (3:5), injustice (3:9), extortion and lying (6:12), murder (7:2), and other offenses. God's judgment will come.

In the midst of this overwhelming prediction of destruction, Micah gives hope and consolation, because he also describes God's love. The truth is that judgment comes only after countless opportunities to repent, to turn back to true worship and obedience—"to be fair and just and merciful, and to walk humbly with your God" (6:8). But even in the midst of judgment, God promises to deliver the small minority who have continued to follow him. He states, "The Messiah will lead you out of exile and bring you through the gates of your cities of captivity, back to your own land. Your King will go before you—the Lord leads on" (2:13). The Messiah, of course, is Jesus; and we read in 5:2 that he will be born as a baby in Bethlehem, an obscure Judean village.

As you read Micah, catch a glimpse of God's anger in action as he judges and punishes sin. See God's love in action as he offers eternal life to all who repent and believe. And then determine to join the faithful remnant of God's people who live according to his will.

VITAL STATISTICS

PURPOSE:
To warn God's people that judgment is coming and to offer pardon to all who repent

AUTHOR:
Micah, a native of Moresheth, near Gath, about 20 miles southwest of Jerusalem

TO WHOM WRITTEN:
The people of Israel (the Northern Kingdom) and of Judah (the Southern Kingdom)

DATE WRITTEN:
Possibly during the reigns of Jotham, Ahaz, and Hezekiah (742–687 B.C.)

SETTING:
The political situation is described in 2 Kings 15—20 and 2 Chronicles 26—30. Micah was a contemporary of Isaiah and Hosea.

KEY VERSE:
"No, he [God] has told you what he wants, and this is all it is: *to be fair and just and merciful, and to walk humbly with your God*" (6:8).

KEY PEOPLE:
The people of Samaria and Jerusalem

KEY PLACES:
Samaria, Jerusalem, Bethlehem

SPECIAL FEATURES:
This is a beautiful example of classical Hebrew poetry. There are three parts, each beginning with "Attention" or "Listen" (1:2; 3:1; 6:1) and closing with a promise.

THE BLUEPRINT

1. The trial of the capitals (1:1—2:13)
2. The trial of the leaders (3:1—5:15)
3. The trial of the people (6:1—7:20)

Micah emphasized the need for justice and peace. Like a lawyer, he set forth God's case against Israel and Judah, their leaders, and their people. Throughout the book are prophecies about Jesus the Messiah who will gather the people into one nation. He will be their king and ruler, acting mercifully toward them. Micah makes it clear that God hates unkindness, idolatry, injustice, and empty ritual—and he still hates these today. But God is very willing to pardon the sins of any who repent.

MEGATHEMES

THEME	EXPLANATION	IMPORTANCE
Perverting faith	God will judge the false prophets, dishonest leaders, and selfish priests in Israel and Judah. While they publicly carried out religious ceremonies, they were privately seeking to gain money and influence. To mix selfish motives with an empty display of religion is to pervert faith.	Don't try to mix your own selfish desires with true faith in God. One day God will reveal how foolish it is to substitute anything for loyalty to him. Coming up with your own private blend of religion will pervert your faith.
Oppression	Micah predicted ruin for all nations and leaders who were oppressive towards others. The upper classes oppressed and exploited the poor. Yet no one was speaking against them or doing anything to stop them. God will not put up with such injustice.	We dare not ask God to help us while we ignore those who are needy and oppressed, or silently condone the actions of those who oppress them.
The Messiah— King of Peace	God promised to provide a new king to bring strength and peace to his people. Hundreds of years before Christ's birth, God promised that the eternal king would be born in Bethlehem. It was God's great plan to restore his people through the Messiah.	Christ our king leads us just as God promised. But until his final judgment, his leadership is only visible among those who welcome his authority. We can have God's peace now by giving up our sins and welcoming him as king.
Pleasing God	Micah preached that God's greatest desire was not the offering of sacrifices at the Temple. God delights in faith that produces fairness, love to others, and obedience to him.	True faith in God generates kindness, compassion, justice, and humility. We can please God by seeking these results in our work, our family, our church, and our neighborhoods.

1. The trial of the capitals

1 These are messages from the Lord to Micah, who lived in the town of Moresheth during the reigns of King Jotham, King Ahaz, and King Hezekiah, all kings of Judah. The messages were addressed to both Samaria and Judah, and came to Micah in the form of visions.

2Attention! Let all the peoples of the world listen. For the Lord in his holy Temple has made accusations against you!

3Look! He is coming! He leaves his throne in heaven and comes to earth, walking on the mountaintops. 4They melt beneath his feet, and flow into the valleys like wax in fire, like water pouring down a hill.

5And why is this happening? Because of the sins of Israel and Judah. What sins?

1:1
Jer 26:18

1:2
Deut 32:1
Ps 50:7
Jer 6:19

1:3
Isa 26:21
64:1-3

1:4
Ps 97:5
Amos 9:5

1:5
2 Chron 34:3,4

1:1 Micah and Isaiah lived at the same time, about 750–680 B.C., and undoubtedly knew each other. Micah directed his message mainly to Judah, the Southern Kingdom, but he also had some words for Israel, the Northern Kingdom. Judah enjoyed great prosperity at this time. Of the three kings mentioned, Jotham (750–735) and Hezekiah (715–686) tried to follow God (2 Kings 15:32–38; 18–20), but Ahaz was one of the most evil kings

ever to reign in Judah (see 2 Kings 16).

1:3–6 Jerusalem was the capital city of Judah (the Southern Kingdom); Samaria was the capital city of Israel (the Northern Kingdom). The destruction of Samaria was literally fulfilled during Micah's lifetime, in 722 B.C. (2 Kings 17:1–18), just as he had predicted.

1:5 There are two sins identified in Micah's message—the

The idolatry and oppression centering in the capital cities, Samaria and Jerusalem!

1:6
Jer 51:25
Lam 4:1
Ezek 13:14
1:7
Lev 26:30
Deut 9:21; 23:18
Joel 3:3
1:8
Job 30:29
Isa 13:21,22
1:9
Isa 1:5,6; 3:26
Jer 15:18
30:11-15
Mic 1:11
1:11
Mic 1:8
1:12
Isa 59:9-11
Jer 8:15; 14:19
1:13
Josh 10:3; 15:39
Amos 2:14
1:14
Josh 15:44
1:15
Josh 15:35
2 Chron 11:7
1:16
Deut 28:32,41
2 Kgs 17:6
Isa 22:12
Jer 7:29

6Therefore the entire city of Samaria will crumble into a heap of rubble, and become an open field, her streets plowed up for planting grapes! The Lord will tear down her wall and her forts, exposing their foundations, and pour their stones into the valleys below. 7All her carved images will be smashed to pieces; her ornate idol temples, built with the gifts of worshipers, will all be burned.

8I will wail and lament, howling as a jackal, mournful as an ostrich crying across the desert sands at night. I will walk naked and barefoot in sorrow and shame; 9for my people's wound is far too deep to heal. The Lord stands ready at Jerusalem's gates to punish her. 10Woe to the city of Gath. Weep, men of Bakah. In Beth-le-aphrah roll in the dust in your anguish and shame. 11There go the people of Shaphir, led away as slaves—stripped, naked and ashamed. The people of Zaanan dare not show themselves outside their walls. The foundations of Beth-ezel are swept away—the very ground on which it stood. 12The people of Maroth vainly hope for better days, but only bitterness awaits them as the Lord stands poised against Jerusalem.

13Quick! Use your swiftest chariots and flee, O people of Lachish, for you were the first of the cities of Judah to follow Israel in her sin of idol worship. Then all the cities of the south began to follow your example.

14Write off Moresheth of Gath; there is no hope of saving her. The town of Achzib has deceived the kings of Israel, for she promised help she cannot give. 15You people of Mareshah will be a prize to your enemies. They will penetrate to Adullam, the "Pride of Israel."

16Weep, weep for your little ones. For they are snatched away and you will never

1:7 *will all be burned,* literally, "they shall return to the hire of an harlot."

MICAH served as a prophet to Judah from 742–687 B.C.	Climate of the times	King Ahaz set up pagan idols in the Temple and finally nailed the Temple door shut. Four different nations harassed Judah. When Hezekiah became king, the nation began a slow road to recovery and economic strength. Hezekiah probably heeded much of Micah's advice.
	Main message	Predicted the fall of both the Northern Kingdom of Israel and the Southern Kingdom of Judah. This was God's discipline upon the people, actually showing how much he cared for them. Hezekiah's good reign helped postpone Judah's punishment.
	Importance of message	Choosing to live a life apart from God is making a commitment to sin. Sin leads to judgment and death. God alone shows us the way to eternal peace. His discipline often keeps us on the right path.
	Contemporary prophets	Hosea (753–715) Isaiah (740–681)

perversion of worship (1:7; 3:5–7, 11; 5:12, 13) and injustice toward others (2:1, 2, 8, 9; 3:2, 3, 9–11; 7:2–6). Rampant in the capital cities, these sins infiltrated and infected the entire country.

1:9 Samaria's sins were beyond healing, and God's judgment on her had already begun. Her sin was not like a gash in the skin, but more like a stab from a vital organ. Sin had caused an injury that would soon prove fatal (Samaria was, in fact, destroyed early in Micah's ministry). Tragically, Samaria's sin had influenced Jerusalem, and judgment would come to its very gates. This probably refers to Sennacherib's siege in 701 B.C. (see 2 Kings 18, 19).

1:10–16 There is a clever word play in the Hebrew of these verses. Micah bitterly denounces each town by using puns. *Shaphir* sounds like the Hebrew word for "beauty"; *Zaanan* sounds like the verb meaning "to go forth"; and *Beth-ezel* sounds like a word for "foundation." Read 1:11 aloud, substituting the meaning for each city's name, and you will realize the effect of Micah's word choice.

1:13 The people of Lachish influenced many to follow their evil example. We often do the same when we sin. Regardless of whether you consider yourself a leader, your daily actions and words are observed by others more than you suspect, and they may choose to follow your example, whether you know it or not.

1:14 Moresheth was Micah's hometown (1:1).

1:15 This verse can also be translated, "the glory of Israel will enter Adullam." The terrain surrounding Adullam had numerous caves. Micah was warning that when the enemy approached, Judah's proud princes would be forced to flee and hide in these caves.

1:16 Micah pictured the devastating sorrow of parents seeing their children taken away to be slaves in a distant land. This happened frequently in both Israel and Judah, most horribly when each nation was completely conquered—Israel in 722 B.C. and Judah in 586 B.C.

see them again. They have gone as slaves to distant lands. Shave your heads in sorrow.

God will remove injustice

2 Woe to you who lie awake at night, plotting wickedness; you rise at dawn to carry out your schemes; because you can, you do. ²You want a certain piece of land, or someone else's house (though it is all he has); you take it by fraud and threats and violence.

³But the Lord God says, I will reward your evil with evil; nothing can stop me; never again will you be proud and haughty after I am through with you. ⁴Then your enemies will taunt you and mock your dirge of despair: "We are finished, ruined. God has confiscated our land and sent us far away, and given what is ours to others." ⁵Others will set your boundaries then. "The People of the Lord" will live where they are sent.

⁶"Don't say such things," the people say. "Don't harp on things like that. It's disgraceful, that sort of talk. Such evils surely will not come our way."

⁷Is that the right reply for you to make, O House of Jacob? Do you think the Spirit of the Lord likes to talk to you so roughly? No! His threats are for your good, to get you on the path again.

⁸Yet to this very hour my people rise against me. For you steal the shirts right off the backs of those who trusted you, who walk in peace.

⁹You have driven out the widows from their homes, and stripped their children of every God-given right. ¹⁰Up! Begone! This is no more your land and home, for you have filled it with sin and it will vomit you out.

¹¹"I'll preach to you the joys of wine and drink"—that is the kind of drunken, lying prophet that you like!

¹²The time will come, O Israel, when I will gather you—all that are left—and bring you together again like sheep in a fold, like a flock in a pasture—a noisy, happy crowd. ¹³The Messiah will lead you out of exile and bring you through the gates of your cities of captivity, back to your own land. Your King will go before you—the Lord leads on.

2. The trial of the leaders

3 Listen, you leaders of Israel—you are supposed to know right from wrong, ²yet you are the very ones who hate good and love evil; you skin my people and strip them to the bone.

2:13 *The Messiah*, literally, "He who opens the breach."

Cross references

2:1 Isa 32:7 / Hos 7:6,7 / Rom 1:30
2:2 Prov 3:27
2:3 Deut 28:32-35 / Isa 2:11,12 / 28:14-18 / Jer 11:8
2:4 Isa 14:4 / Jer 6:12; 8:10 / Hab 2:6
2:5 Deut 32:8 / Josh 18:4,10
2:6 Isa 30:10 / Jer 26:8,9 / Amos 2:12
2:7 Jer 15:16 / Rom 7:13
2:8 Isa 9:21 / Jer 12:8 / Mic 3:2,3
2:9 Mt 23:14 / Mk 12:40
2:10 Lev 18:24-28 / Ps 106:38
2:11 Mic 3:5,11
2:12 Isa 11:11
3:1 Deut 16:18 / Ps 14:4

2:1, 2 Micah warned against those who use their position to take advantage of others. Less than a century earlier, King Ahab of Israel had pouted because he couldn't get Naboth's vineyard. So his wife, Jezebel, had Naboth killed in order to give the garden to Ahab (1 Kings 21:1–15). This kind of immorality had spread throughout Judah and, like a disease, was destroying the nation from the inside out.

Countless people today are victims of unethical attempts to take what little they have and give it to those who are more powerful. Some of these actions may be legally permissible, but they are not morally acceptable to God. Being legal doesn't necessarily mean being right.

2:1, 2 Micah spoke out against those who planned evil deeds at night and rose at dawn to do them. A person's thoughts reflect his character. What do you think about as you lie down to sleep? Do your desires involve greed or stepping on others to achieve your goals? Evil thoughts lead to evil deeds as surely as morning follows night.

2:6, 7 If the messages in this book seem harsh to us, we must remember that God did not want to take revenge on Israel; he only wanted to get them back on the right path. The harsh reality is that the people had rejected what was true and right, and they needed

stern discipline. Children may think discipline is harsh, but it helps keep them on the right path. If we only want God's comforting messages, we may miss what he has for us. Listen whenever God speaks to you, even when the message is hard to take.

2:11 The people liked the false prophets who told them only what they wanted to hear. Micah spoke against prophets who encouraged the people to feel comfortable in their sinful life-styles. Preachers are popular when they don't ask too much of us, when they tell us our greed or lust might even be good for us, and tell us not to worry about hell. But a true teacher of God speaks the truth, regardless of what the listeners want to hear.

2:12, 13 Micah's prophecy telescopes two great events—Judah's return from captivity in Babylon, and the great gathering of all believers when the Messiah returns. God gave his prophets visions of various future events, but not necessarily the ability to discern when these events would happen. For example, they could not see the long period of time between the Babylonian captivity and the coming of the Messiah, but they could clearly see that the Messiah was coming. The purpose of this prophecy was not to predict exactly *how* this would occur, but *that* it would. This gave the people hope and helped them turn from sin.

3:1ff Micah denounced the sins of the leaders, priests, and

3:3
Ps 14:4; 27:2

3:4
Jer 33:5

3:5
Isa 9:15
Jer 6:14

3:6
Ps 74:9
Isa 8:20-22
29:10; 59:10
Amos 8:9,10

3:7
1 Sam 28:6,15
Zech 13:4

3:8
Isa 58:1; 61:1,2
Ezek 16:2
Mt 3:7-12

3:10
Jer 22:13-17
Ezek 22:25-28
Hab 2:9-12

3:11
Jer 7:8-12
Mic 7:3

³You devour them, flog them, break their bones, and chop them up like meat for the cooking pot— ⁴and then you plead with the Lord for his help in times of trouble! Do you really expect him to listen? He will look the other way! ⁵You false prophets! You who lead his people astray! You who cry "Peace" to those who give you food, and threaten those who will not pay!

This is God's message to you: ⁶The night will close about you and cut off all your visions; darkness will cover you, with never a word from God. The sun will go down upon you, and your day will end. ⁷Then at last you will cover your faces in shame, and admit that your messages were not from God.

⁸But as for me, I am filled with power, with the Spirit of the Lord, fearlessly announcing God's punishment on Israel for her sins.

⁹Listen to me, you leaders of Israel who hate justice and love unfairness, ¹⁰and fill Jerusalem with murder and sin of every kind— ¹¹you leaders who take bribes; you priests and prophets who won't preach and prophesy until you're paid. (And yet you fawn upon the Lord and say, "All is well—the Lord is here among us. No harm can come to us.") ¹²It is because of you that Jerusalem will be plowed like a field, and become a heap of rubble; the mountaintop where the Temple stands will be overgrown with brush.

MICAH'S CHARGES OF INJUSTICE

Micah charged the people with injustice of many kinds.

Plotting wickedness	2:1
Fraud, threats, violence	2:2
Stealing, dishonesty	2:8
Driving out widows	2:9
Hating good, loving evil	3:1, 2
Hating justice, loving unfairness	3:9
Murder	3:10
Taking bribes	3:11

---

prophets—those responsible for teaching the people right from wrong. Elders, who were supposed to live among the people, had moved into Jerusalem and become an elite ruling class. The leaders, who should have known the law and taught it to the people, had set the law aside and become the worst of sinners. They took advantage of the very people they were supposed to serve. All sin is bad, but the sin that leads others astray is the worst of all.

3:1, 2 The dividing line between right and wrong often seems blurred, but spiritual leaders are supposed to help others see it. The Bible is God's guidebook to show us how to distinguish right and wrong. Leaders must understand the Bible's principles and teach them to others. Leaders cannot force people to do right, but they should point them in that direction by their teaching and example.

3:3, 4 The leaders had no compassion or respect for those they were supposed to serve. They treated the people miserably in order to satisfy their own desires and then had the gall to ask for God's help when they found themselves in trouble. We, like the leaders, should not treat God like a light switch to be turned on only as needed. Instead, we should always rely on him.

3:5–7 Micah remained true to his calling and proclaimed God's words. In contrast, the false prophets' messages were geared to the favors they received. Not all those who claim to have messages from God really do. Micah prophesied that one day the false prophets would be shamed by their actions.

3:8 Micah attributed the power of his ministry to God's Spirit. Our power comes from the same source. Jesus told his followers they

would receive power to witness about him when the Holy Spirit came to them (Acts 1:8). You can't witness effectively by relying on your own strength, because fear will keep you from speaking out for God. Only by relying on the power of the Holy Spirit can you live and witness for him.

3:11 Micah severely condemned religious leaders who ministered only if they got paid for it. Jesus came to serve, not to promote a big-business gospel. When people "minister" for personal gain, servanthood is lost. Preaching and teaching should never be motivated by the promise of personal gain. When God calls you to do something, obey him, even if there is no monetary reward.

3:11 Micah warned the ministers of his day to avoid bribes. Pastors today accept bribes when they allow those who contribute much to control the church. When fear of losing money influences a pastor to remain silent when he should speak up for what is right, his church is in danger. We should remember that Judah was finally destroyed because of the behavior of its religious leaders. A similar warning must be directed at those who have money—*never* use your resources to influence or manipulate God's ministers, because that is bribery.

3:12 Jerusalem would be destroyed just as Samaria was (1:6). This happened in 586 B.C. when Nebuchadnezzar and the Babylonian army attacked the city (2 Kings 25). Although Micah blamed the corrupt leaders, the people were not without fault. They allowed the corruption to continue without turning to God or calling for justice.

The Lord will be king

4 But in the last days Mount Zion will be the most renowned of all the mountains of the world, praised by all nations; people from all over the world will make pilgrimages there.

2"Come," they will say to one another, "let us visit the mountain of the Lord, and see the Temple of the God of Israel; he will tell us what to do, and we will do it." For in those days the whole world will be ruled by the Lord from Jerusalem! He will issue his laws and announce his decrees from there.

3He will arbitrate among the nations, and dictate to strong nations far away. They will beat their swords into plowshares and their spears into pruning-hooks; nations shall no longer fight each other, for all war will end. There will be universal peace, and all the military academies and training camps will be closed down.

4Everyone will live quietly in his own home in peace and prosperity, for there will be nothing to fear. The Lord himself has promised this. 5(Therefore we will follow the Lord our God forever and ever, even though all the nations around us worship idols!)

6In that coming day, the Lord says that he will bring back his punished people—sick and lame and dispossessed— 7and make them strong again in their own land, a mighty nation, and the Lord himself shall be their King from Mount Zion forever. 8O Jerusalem—the Watchtower of God's people—your royal might and power will come back to you again, just as before.

9But for now, now you scream in terror. Where is your king to lead you? He is dead! Where are your wise men? All are gone! Pain has gripped you like a woman in labor. 10Writhe and groan in your terrible pain, O people of Zion, for you must leave this city and live in the fields; you will be sent far away into exile in Babylon. But there I will rescue you and free you from the grip of your enemies.

11True, many nations have gathered together against you, calling for your blood, eager to destroy you. 12But they do not know my thoughts nor understand my plan, for the time will come when the Lord will gather together the enemies of his people like sheaves upon the threshing floor, 13helpless before Israel.

Rise, thresh, O daughter of Zion; I will give you horns of iron and hoofs of brass and you will trample to pieces many people, and you will give their wealth as offerings to the Lord, the Lord of all the earth.

A ruler will come from Bethlehem

5 Mobilize! The enemy lays siege to Jerusalem! With a rod they shall strike the Judge of Israel on the face.

4:1
Ps 22:27; 86:9
Dan 2:28; 10:14
Mic 3:12
Zeph 3:9,10

4:2
Deut 6:1
Ps 25:8-12
Isa 2:3; 42:1-4
Jer 31:6
Hos 6:3
Zech 8:20-23
Acts 1:8
Rom 15:19

4:3
Ps 82:8; 98:9
Isa 11:3-5

4:4
Isa 1:20; 40:5
58:14

4:5
2 Kgs 17:29,34
Jer 2:10,11

4:6
Isa 35:3-7
Zeph 3:19

4:7
Isa 9:6,7; 24:23

4:8
Ps 48:12
Dan 7:18

4:9
Jer 4:21; 8:19

4:10
2 Kgs 20:18
2 Chron 36:20
Hos 2:14
Mic 7:8-12

4:12
Ps 147:19,20
Isa 55:8

4:13
Isa 18:7
41:15,16; 60:9
Jer 51:33
Mic 5:8-15
Rom 15:25-28

5:1
Jer 5:7
Lam 3:30

4:1ff The phrase, "in the last days," describes the days when God will reign over his perfect kingdom (see 4:1–8). This will be an era of peace and blessing, when war will be forever ended. We cannot pinpoint its date, but God has promised that it *will* arrive (see also Isaiah 2:2; Jeremiah 16:14, 15; Daniel 8:19; Joel 3:1ff; Zechariah 14:9–11; Malachi 3:17, 18; Revelation 19—22).

Verses 9–13 speak of the Babylonian captivity in 586 B.C., even before Babylon became a powerful empire. Just as God promises a time of peace and prosperity, he also promises judgment and punishment for all who refuse to follow him. Both results are certain.

4:9–13 Micah predicted the end of the kings—a drastic statement to the people of Judah who thought their kingdom would last forever. He also said that Babylon would destroy the land of Judah and carry away its king, but that after a while God would help his people return to their land. This all happened just as Micah prophesied, and these events are recorded in 2 Chronicles 36:9–23 and Ezra 1, 2.

4:12 When God reveals the future, his purpose goes beyond satisfying our curiosity. He wants us to change our present behavior because of what we know about the future. Forever begins now; and a glimpse of God's plan for his followers should motivate us to serve him now.

5:1ff Jerusalem's leaders were obsessed with wealth and position, but Micah prophesied that mighty Jerusalem, with all its wealth and power, would be besieged and destroyed. Its king could not save it. In contrast, Bethlehem, a tiny town, would be the birthplace of the only king who could save his people. This deliverer, the Messiah, would be born as a baby in Bethlehem (Luke 2:4–6), and eventually would reign as the eternal king (Revelation 19—22).

5:1 This judge was probably King Zedekiah who was reigning in Jerusalem when Nebuchadnezzar conquered the city (2 Kings 25:1). Zedekiah was the last of the kings in David's line to sit on the throne in Jerusalem. Micah said that the next king in David's line would be the Messiah, who would establish a kingdom that would never end.

5:2
Jer 30:21
Zech 9:9
Mt 2:6
Jn 1:1-3; 7:42

5:3
Isa 10:20-22
Mic 4:10; 5:7,8
7:13

5:4
Ps 72:8
Isa 52:10
Mic 7:14

5:5
Isa 8:7,8
37:31-36
Jer 33:15

5:6
Gen 10:8-11
2 Kgs 19:32-35
Nah 2:11-13

5:7
Deut 32:2
Ps 72:6

5:8
Gen 49:9
Zech 9:15

5:11
Isa 2:12-17
Ezek 38:11
Amos 5:9

5:12
Deut 18:10-12

²O Bethlehem Ephrathah, you are but a small Judean village, yet you will be the birthplace of my King who is alive from everlasting ages past! ³God will abandon his people to their enemies until she who is to give birth has her son; then at last his fellow countrymen—the exile remnants of Israel—will rejoin their brethren in their own land.

⁴And he shall stand and feed his flock in the strength of the Lord, in the majesty of the name of the Lord his God, and his people shall remain there undisturbed, for he will be greatly honored all around the world. ⁵He will be our Peace. And when the Assyrian invades our land and marches across our hills, he will appoint seven shepherds to watch over us, eight princes to lead us. ⁶They will rule Assyria with drawn swords and enter the gates of the land of Nimrod. He will deliver us from the Assyrians when they invade our land.

⁷Then the nation of Israel will refresh the world like a gentle dew or the welcome showers of rain, ⁸and Israel will be as strong as a lion. The nations will be like helpless sheep before her! ⁹She will stand up to her foes; all her enemies will be wiped out.

¹⁰At that same time, says the Lord, I will destroy all the weapons you depend on, ¹¹and tear down your walls and demolish the defenses of your cities. ¹²I will put an end to all witchcraft—there will be no more fortune-tellers to consult— ¹³and destroy all your idols. Never again will you worship what you have made, ¹⁴and I will abolish the heathen shrines from among you, and destroy the cities where your idol temples stand.

¹⁵And I will pour out my vengeance upon the nations who refuse to obey me.

3. The trial of the people
God has a complaint against his people

6 Listen to what the Lord is saying to his people:
Stand up and state your case against me. Let the mountains and hills be called to witness your complaint.

6:2
Hos 4:1; 12:2

6:3
Jer 2:5,31

6:4
Ex 20:1,2
Ps 77:20

²And now, O mountains, listen to the Lord's complaint! For he has a case against his people Israel! He will prosecute them to the full. ³O my people, what have I done that makes you turn away from me? Tell me why your patience is exhausted! Answer me! ⁴For I brought you out of Egypt, and cut your chains of slavery. I gave you Moses, Aaron, and Miriam to help you.

5:2 This king is Jesus, the Messiah. Micah accurately predicted Christ's birthplace hundreds of years before he was born. The promised eternal king in David's line, who would come to live as a man, had been alive forever—"from everlasting ages past." Although eternal, he entered human history as the man, Jesus of Nazareth.

5:5 Micah's prophecy of seven shepherds and eight princes is a figurative way of saying that the Messiah will raise up many good leaders when he returns to reign. In sharp contrast are Micah's words in chapter three about Judah's corrupt leaders. Assyria symbolically refers to all nations in every age that oppose God's people. These good leaders will help Christ defeat all evil in the world.

5:5 This chapter provides one of the clearest Old Testament prophecies of Christ's coming. The key descriptive phrase is "He will be our Peace." In one of Christ's closing talks he said, "I am leaving you with a gift—peace of mind and heart! And the peace I give isn't fragile like the peace the world gives. So don't be troubled or afraid" (John 14:27). With Christ's first coming we have the opportunity for peace with God. No more fear of judgment, no more conflict and guilt. Christ's peace gives us assurance even though wars continue. With Christ's second coming all wars and weapons will be destroyed (4:3–5).

5:6 The land of Nimrod is another name for Assyria, which, in this case, is a symbol of all the evil nations in the world.

5:10 When God rules in his eternal kingdom, our strength will not be found in military might but in God's almighty power. He will destroy all the weapons that people use for security. There will be no need for armies, because God will rule in the heart of every person. Our hearts should not be ruled by fear of invasion or nuclear attack. Our confidence should be in God.

6:1ff Here Micah pictures a courtroom. God, the judge, tells his people what he requires of them and recites all the ways they have wronged both him and others. Chapters four and five are full of hope; chapters six and seven proclaim judgment and appeal to the people to repent.

6:1, 2 God called to the mountains to confirm the people's guilt. The mountains would serve as excellent witnesses, for it was in the "high places" that the people had built pagan altars and sacrificed to false gods (1 Kings 14:23; Jeremiah 17:2, 3; Ezekiel 20:27, 28).

6:3 The people would never be able to answer this question because God had done nothing wrong. In fact, he had been exceedingly patient with them, had always lovingly guided them, and had given them every opportunity to return to him. If God asked you this question, how would you reply?

5Don't you remember, O my people, how Balak, king of Moab, tried to destroy you through the curse of Balaam, son of Beor, but I made him bless you instead? That is the kindness I showed you again and again. Have you no memory at all of what happened at Acacia and Gilgal, and how I blessed you there?

6:5
Num 22:5,6

6"How can we make up to you for what we've done?" you ask. "Shall we bow before the Lord with offerings of yearling calves?"

6:6
Lev 1:3,6:9-13

Oh, no! 7For if you offered him thousands of rams and ten thousands of rivers of olive oil—would that please him? Would he be satisfied? If you sacrificed your oldest child, would that make him glad? Then would he forgive your sins? Of course not!

6:7
Lev 18:21
20:1-5
Ps 50:9
Isa 40:16

8No, he has told you what he wants, and this is all it is: *to be fair and just and merciful, and to walk humbly with your God.* 9The Lord's voice calls out to all Jerusalem—listen to the Lord if you are wise! The armies of destruction are coming; the Lord is sending them.

6:8
Lev 26:41
Deut 10:12,13
Isa 57:15

10For your sins are very great—is there to be no end of getting rich by cheating? The homes of the wicked are full of ungodly treasures and lying scales. 11Shall I say "Good!" to all your merchants with their bags of false, deceitful weights? How could God be just while saying that? 12Your rich men are wealthy through extortion and violence; your citizens are so used to lying that their tongues can't tell the truth!

6:10
Prov 10:2; 11:1
20:10,23; 21:6
Jer 5:26,27
Amos 3:10

6:11
Mic 6:10

6:12
Isa 3:10

13Therefore I will wound you! I will make your hearts miserable for all your sins. 14You will eat but never have enough; hunger pangs and emptiness will still remain. And though you try and try to save your money, it will come to nothing at the end, and what little you succeed in storing up I'll give to those who conquer you! 15You will plant crops but not harvest them; you will press out the oil from the olives, and not get enough to anoint yourself! You will trample the grapes, but get no juice to make your wine.

6:13
Lev 26:16
Isa 1:5,6
Jer 14:18
Acts 12:23

6:14
Lev 26:26
Isa 9:20; 30:6

16The only commands you keep are those of Omri; the only example you follow is that of Ahab! Therefore I will make an awesome example of you—I will destroy you. I will make you the laughingstock of the world; all who see you will snicker and sneer!

6:15
Deut 28:38-40
Isa 62:8,9

6:16
1 Kgs 16:29-33
Jer 18:15,16
Ezek 8:17,18

God promises eventual restoration

7 Woe is me! It is as hard to find an honest man as grapes and figs when harvest days are over. Not a cluster to eat, not a single early fig, however much I long

7:1
Ps 12:1
Mic 3:10

6:14 See Haggai 1:6.

6:5 The story of Balak and Balaam is found in Numbers 22—24. Acacia was the Israelites' campsite on the east of the Jordan River just before they entered the Promised Land (Joshua 2:1). There the people received many of God's instructions and promises about how to live. Gilgal, their first campsite after crossing the Jordan (Joshua 4:19), was where the people renewed their covenant with God (Joshua 5:3–9). These two places represent God's loving care for his people: his willingness both to bless them greatly and to warn them about potential troubles. In Micah's day, the people had forgotten this covenant and its blessings and had turned away from God.

6:5 God continued to be kind to his forgetful people, but their short memory and lack of thankfulness condemned them. When people refuse to see how fortunate they are and begin to take God's blessings for granted, they become self-centered. Regularly remember God's goodness and thank him. Remembering God's past blessings will help you see your present blessings.

6:6-8 Israel responded to God's request by trying to appease him with sacrifices, hoping he would then leave them alone. But sacrifices and other religious rituals aren't enough; God wants changed lives. He wants his people to be fair, just, merciful, and humble. God wants us to become *living* sacrifices (Romans 12:1, 2), not just doing religious deeds, but living rightly (Jeremiah 4:4; Hebrews 9:14). It is impossible to live such a life consistently without God's transforming love in our hearts.

6:8 People have tried all kinds of ways to please God (6:6, 7), but God has made his wishes clear: he wants his people to be fair, just, and merciful, and to walk humbly with him. In your efforts to please God, examine these areas on a regular basis. Are you fair in your dealings with people? Do you show mercy to those who wrong you? Are you learning humility? Only those who obey God because they want to please him live in a proper relationship with him.

6:16 Omri reigned over Israel and led the people into idol worship (1 Kings 16:21–26). Ahab, his son, was Israel's most wicked king (1 Kings 16:29–33). If the people were following only the commands and examples of these kings, they were in bad shape. Such pervasive evil was ripe for punishment.

7:1ff This chapter begins in gloom (7:1–6) and ends in hope (7:7–20). Micah watched as society rotted around him. Rulers demanded gifts; judges accepted bribes; corruption was universal. But God promised to lead the people out of the darkness of sin and into his light. Then the people would praise him for his faithfulness. God alone is perfectly faithful.

7:1-4 Micah could not find an honest person anywhere in the land. Even today, real honesty is difficult to find. Society rationalizes sin, and even Christians sometimes compromise Christian principles in order to do what they want. It is easy to convince ourselves that we deserve a few breaks, especially when "everyone else" is doing it. But the standards for honesty come

for it! The good men have disappeared from the earth; not one fairminded man is left. They are all murderers, turning against even their own brothers.

³They go at their evil deeds with both hands, and how skilled they are in using them! The governor and judge alike demand bribes. The rich man pays them off and tells them whom to ruin. Justice is twisted between them. ⁴Even the best of them are prickly as briars; the straightest is more crooked than a hedge of thorns. But your judgment day is coming swiftly now; your time of punishment is almost here; confusion, destruction, and terror will be yours.

⁵Don't trust anyone, not your best friend—not even your wife! ⁶For the son despises his father; the daughter defies her mother; the bride curses her mother-in-law. Yes, a man's enemies will be found in his own home.

⁷As for me, I look to the Lord for his help; I wait for God to save me; he will hear me. ⁸Do not rejoice against me, O my enemy, for though I fall, I will rise again! When I sit in darkness, the Lord himself will be my Light. ⁹I will be patient while the Lord punishes me, for I have sinned against him; then he will defend me from my enemies, and punish them for all the evil they have done to me. God will bring me out of my darkness into the light, and I will see his goodness. ¹⁰Then my enemy will see that God is for me, and be ashamed for taunting me, "Where is that God of yours?" Now with my own eyes I see them trampled down like mud in the street.

¹¹Your cities, people of God, will be rebuilt, much larger and more prosperous than before. ¹²Citizens of many lands will come and honor you—from Assyria to Egypt, and from Egypt to the Euphrates, from sea to sea and from distant hills and mountains.

¹³But first comes terrible destruction to Israel for the great wickedness of her people. ¹⁴O Lord, come and rule your people; lead your flock; make them live in peace and prosperity; let them enjoy the fertile pastures of Bashan and Gilead as they did long ago.

¹⁵"Yes," replies the Lord, "I will do mighty miracles for you, like those when I brought you out of slavery in Egypt. ¹⁶All the world will stand amazed at what I will do for you, and be embarrassed at their puny might. They will stand in silent awe, deaf to all around them." ¹⁷They will see what snakes they are, lowly as worms crawling from their holes. They will come trembling out from their fortresses to meet the Lord our God. They will fear him; they will stand in awe.

¹⁸Where is another God like you, who pardons the sins of the survivors among his people? You cannot stay angry with your people, for you love to be merciful. ¹⁹Once again you will have compassion on us. You will tread our sins beneath your feet; you will throw them into the depths of the ocean! ²⁰You will bless us as you promised Jacob long ago. You will set your love upon us, as you promised our father Abraham!

7:13 *But first comes terrible destruction to Israel,* literally, "But the land will be desolate because of its inhabitants."

---

from God, not society. We are honest because God is truth, and we are to be like him.

7:5, 6 Sin had affected the government leaders and society in general. Deceit had even ruined the family, the core of society. As a result, the only way left to purify the people was God's judgment. This would draw the nation back to him and restore them from the inside out.

7:7–9 Micah showed great faith in God as he proclaimed that (1) he would wait upon God because God hears and saves when help is needed, (2) God would bring him through when times were tough, (3) he would be patient in punishment because God would bring him out of the darkness, and (4) his enemies would be punished. We too can have a relationship with God that can allow us to have confidence like Micah's. It doesn't take unusual talent; it simply takes faith in God and a willingness to act on that faith.

7:9 Micah realized that if he was patient and obedient through punishment, God would forgive his people and show his goodness again (Lamentations 3:39–41). Punishment does not mean

rejection. The nation of Judah was being punished in order to bring her people to God, not to send them away from him. When you face trials because of your sin, do not be angry with God or be afraid that he has rejected you. Instead, turn away from your sin and turn to God.

7:18 God loves to be merciful! He does not forgive grudgingly, but is glad when we repent and offers forgiveness to all who come back to him. Today you can confess your sins and receive his loving forgiveness. Don't be too proud to accept God's mercy.

7:20 In an age when religion was making little difference in people's lives, Micah said that God expected his people to be fair, just, and merciful (6:8). He requires the same of Christians today. In a world that is unfair, we must act justly. In a world of tough breaks, we must be merciful. In a world of pride and self-sufficiency, we must walk humbly with God. Only when we live God's way will our lives begin to affect our homes, our society, and our world.

NAHUM

Manasseh
becomes
king of
Judah
697 B.C.

Ashurbanipal
becomes
king of
Assyria
669

The fall
of Thebes;
Nahum
becomes
a prophet
663

VITAL STATISTICS

PURPOSE:
To pronounce God's judgment on Assyria and to comfort Judah with this truth

AUTHOR:
Nahum

TO WHOM WRITTEN:
The people of Nineveh and Judah

DATE WRITTEN:
Sometime during Nahum's prophetic ministry (probably between 663 and 654 B.C.)

SETTING:
This particular prophecy takes place after the fall of Thebes in 661 B.C. (see 3:8–10)

KEY VERSES:
"The Lord is good. When trouble comes, he is the place to go! And he knows everyone who trusts in him! But he sweeps away his enemies with an overwhelming flood; he pursues them all night long. What are you thinking of, Nineveh, to defy the Lord? He will stop you with one blow; he won't need to strike again" (1:7–9).

KEY PLACE:
Nineveh, the capital of Assyria

THE SHRILL whistle pierces the air and all the action on the court abruptly stops. Pointing to the offending player, the referee shouts, "Foul!"

Rules, fouls, and penalties are part of any game, and are regulated and enforced vigorously by referees, umpires, judges, and other officials. Every participant knows that boundaries must be set and behavior monitored, or the game will degenerate into chaos.

There are laws in the world as well—boundaries and rules for living established by God. But men and women regularly flaunt these regulations, hiding their infractions or overpowering others, declaring that "might makes right." God calls this sin—willful disobedience, rebellion against his control, or apathy. And, at times, it seems as though the violators succeed—no whistles blow, no fouls are called, and individual despots rule. The truth is, however, that ultimately justice will be served in the world. God will settle all accounts.

Assyria was the most powerful nation on earth. Proud in their self-sufficiency and military might, the Assyrians plundered, oppressed, and slaughtered their victims. One hundred years earlier, Jonah had preached in the streets of the capital city, Nineveh; the people heard God's message and turned from their evil. But generations later, evil is again reigning, and the prophet Nahum pronounces judgment on this wicked nation. Nineveh is called a "city of blood" (3:1), a city of cruelty (3:19), and the Assyrians are judged for their arrogance (1:11), idolatry (1:14), murder, lies, treachery, and social injustice (3:1–19). Because of their sins, Nahum predicts that this proud and powerful nation will be utterly destroyed. The end came within 50 years.

In this judgment of Assyria and its capital city, Nineveh, God is judging a sinful world. And the message is clear—disobedience, rebellion, and injustice will not prevail, but will be punished severely by a righteous and holy God who rules over all the earth.

As you read Nahum, sense God's wrath as he avenges sin and brings about justice. Decide to live under his guidance and within his rules, commands, and guidelines for life.

THE BLUEPRINT

1. Nineveh's judge (1:1–15)
2. Nineveh's judgment (2:1—3:19)

Nineveh, the capital of the Assyrian Empire, is the subject of Nahum's prophecy. The news of its coming destruction was a relief for Judah, who was subject to Assyrian domination. No longer would Judah be forced to pay tribute as insurance against invasions. Judah was comforted to know that God was still in control. Nineveh is an example to all rulers and nations of the world today. God is sovereign over even those who are seemingly invincible. We can be confident that God's power and justice will one day conquer all evil.

MEGATHEMES

THEME	EXPLANATION	IMPORTANCE
God judges	God would judge the city of Nineveh for its idolatry, arrogance, and oppression. Although Assyria was the leading military power in the world, God would completely destroy this "invincible" nation. God allows no person or power to assume or scoff at his authority.	Anyone who remains arrogant and resists God's authority will face his anger. No ruler or nation will get away from rejecting him. No individual will be able to hide from his judgment. Yet those who keep trusting God will be kept safe forever.
God rules	God rules over all the earth, even over those who don't acknowledge him. God is all-powerful and no one can thwart his plans. God will overcome any who attempt to defy him. Human power is futile against God.	If you are impressed by or afraid of any weapons, armies, or powerful people, remember that God alone can truly rescue you from fear or oppression. We must place our confidence in God because he alone rules all of history, all the earth, and our lives.

1. Nineveh's judge
God's patience and power

1:1
Isa 13:1
Ezek 40:2
Zeph 2:13
Rev 1:1

1 This is the vision God gave to Nahum, who lived in Elkosh, concerning the impending doom of Nineveh:

2God is jealous over those he loves; that is why he takes vengeance on those who hurt them. He furiously destroys their enemies. 3He is slow in getting angry, but when aroused, his power is incredible, and he does not easily forgive. He shows his power in the terrors of the cyclone and the raging storms; clouds are billowing dust beneath his feet! 4At his command the oceans and rivers become dry sand; the lush pastures of Bashan and Carmel fade away; the green forests of Lebanon wilt. 5In his presence mountains quake and hills melt; the earth crumbles and its people are destroyed.

1:2
Ex 20:5
Deut 4:24; 32:35
Rom 12:19

1:5
Ps 68:8; 97:5
Isa 2:12-18

6Who can stand before an angry God? His fury is like fire; the mountains tumble down before his anger.

1:6
Mal 3:2
Rev 6:17

1:1 Nahum, like Jonah, was a prophet to Nineveh, the capital of the Assyrian Empire, and he prophesied between 663 and 654 B.C. Jonah had seen the city repent a century earlier (see the book of Jonah), but it had fallen back into wickedness. Assyria, the world power controlling the Fertile Crescent, seemed unstoppable. Her ruthless and savage warriors had already conquered Israel, the Northern Kingdom, and were causing great suffering in Judah. So Nahum proclaimed God's anger against Assyria's evil. Within a few decades, Nineveh would be toppled by Babylon.

1:2 God alone has the right to be jealous and to carry out vengeance. Jealousy and vengeance may be surprising terms to associate with God. When humans are jealous and take vengeance, they are usually acting in a spirit of selfishness. But it is appropriate for God to insist on our complete allegiance, and it is just for him to punish unrepentant evildoers. His jealousy and vengeance are unmixed with selfishness. Their purpose is to remove sin and restore peace to the world (Deuteronomy 4:24; 5:9).

1:3 God is slow to get angry, but when he is ready to punish, even the earth trembles. Often people avoid God because they see evildoers in the world and hypocrites in the church. They don't realize that because God is slow to anger, he gives his true followers time to share his love and truth with evildoers. But judgment *will* come; God will not allow sin to go unchecked forever. When people wonder why God doesn't punish evil immediately, help them remember that if he did, none of us would be here. We can all be thankful that God gives people time to turn to him.

1:6 No person on earth can safely defy God, the Almighty, the Creator of all the universe. God, who controls the sun, the galaxies, and the vast stretches beyond, also controls the rise and fall of nations. How could a small temporal kingdom like Assyria, no matter how powerful, challenge his awesome power? If only Assyria could have looked ahead to see the desolate mound of rubble that she would become—and yet God would still be alive and well! Don't defy God; he will be here forever with greater power than that of all armies and nations combined.

7The Lord is good. When trouble comes, he is the place to go! And he knows everyone who trusts in him! 8But he sweeps away his enemies with an overwhelming flood; he pursues them all night long.

1:7
Ps 25:8; 100:5
1:8
Isa 8:7,8

God will rescue Judah

9What are you thinking of, Nineveh, to defy the Lord? He will stop you with one blow; he won't need to strike again. 10He tosses his enemies into the fire like a tangled mass of thorns. They burst into flames like straw. 11Who is this king of yours who dares to plot against the Lord? 12But the Lord is not afraid of him! "Though he build his army millions strong," the Lord declares, "it will vanish.

"O my people, I have punished you enough! 13Now I will break your chains and release you from the yoke of slavery to this Assyrian king." 14And to the king he says, "I have ordered an end to your dynasty; your sons will never sit upon your throne. And I will destroy your gods and temples, and I will bury you! For how you stink with sin!"

15See, the messengers come running down the mountains with glad news: "The invaders have been wiped out and we are safe!" O Judah, proclaim a day of thanksgiving, and worship only the Lord, as you have vowed. For this enemy from Nineveh will never come again. He is cut off forever; he will never be seen again.

1:9
Job 9:4
Ps 2:1-4; 21:11
Prov 21:30
1:10
Isa 9:18; 10:17
Mal 4:1
Rev 14:10,11
1:13
Ps 107:14
Isa 9:4
Jer 2:20
1:14
Nah 3:4-6
1:15
Ps 107:15,
21,22
Isa 29:7,8
Lk 2:10,14
Rom 10:15-17

2. Nineveh's judgment

The city will fall

2 Nineveh, you are finished! You are already surrounded by enemy armies! Sound the alarm! Man the ramparts! Muster your defenses, full force, and keep a sharp watch for the enemy attack to begin! 2For the land of the people of God lies empty and broken after your attacks but the Lord will restore their honor and power again!

3Shields flash red in the sunlight! The attack begins! See their scarlet uniforms! See their glittering chariots moving forward side by side, pulled by prancing steeds! 4Your own chariots race recklessly along the streets and through the squares, darting like lightning, gleaming like torches. 5The king shouts for his officers; they stumble in their haste, rushing to the walls to set up their defenses. 6But too late! The river gates are open! The enemy has entered! The palace is in panic!

2:1
Isa 10:12
37:36,37
Zeph 2:13-15
2:2
Hos 2:14-23
11:11
2:4
Nah 3:2

1:11 Who is this king, implied in vss 11, 13, and 3:18.

Climate of the times	Manasseh, one of Judah's most wicked kings, ruled the land. He openly defied God and persecuted God's people. Assyria, the world power at that time, made Judah one of its vassal states. The people of Judah wanted to be like the Assyrians, who seemed to have all the power and possessions they wanted.	**NAHUM** served as a prophet to Judah and Assyria from 663–654 B.C.
Main message	The mighty empire of Assyria that oppressed God's people would soon tumble.	
Importance of message	Those who do evil and oppress others will one day meet a bitter end.	
Contemporary prophet	Zephaniah (640–621)	

1:6, 7 To those who refuse to believe, God's punishment is like an angry fire, consuming but not consumed. To those who love him, his mercy is security and peace, supplying all our needs without diminishing his supply. The relationship we have is up to us. Which kind of relationship will you choose?

1:11 The king who plots against the Lord could have been (1) Ashurbanipal (669–627 B.C.), king of Assyria during much of Nahum's life and the one who brought Assyria to the zenith of its power; (2) Sennacherib (705–681), who openly defied God (2 Kings 18:13–35), epitomizing rebellion against God; (3) no one

king in particular, but the entire evil monarchy. The point is that Nineveh would be destroyed for rebelling against God.

1:15 The good news for Judah, whom Assyria destroyed, was that her conquerors and tormentors would be destroyed and would never rise to torment her again. Nineveh was so completely wiped out that her ruins were not identified until 1845.

2:1 This chapter predicts the events of 612 B.C., when the combined armies of the Babylonians and the Medes sacked the impregnable Nineveh.

2:2 Assyria had plundered and crushed the Northern Kingdom

2:8
Nah 3:3

2:9
Gen 14:21,24
Ex 15:9
2 Chron 25:13
Isa 33:4

2:10
Lev 26:33
Isa 24:1; 34:10
Jer 4:23

2:13
Ps 46:9

3:1
Ezek 22:2-5
24:6-9
Zeph 3:13

3:2
Nah 2:4

3:3
Nah 2:3,6,8

3:4
Rev 17:1-6
18:2,3

3:5
Rev 18:3-7

3:6
Lam 3:15

3:7
Isa 51:19

3:8
Jer 46:25
Ezek 30:14-16

3:9
Isa 20:5,6
Jer 46:9

7The queen of Nineveh is brought out naked to the streets, and led away, a slave, with all her maidens weeping after her; listen to them mourn like doves, and beat their breasts! 8Nineveh is like a leaking water tank! Her soldiers slip away, deserting her; she cannot hold them back. "Stop, stop," she shouts, but they keep on running.

9Loot the silver! Loot the gold! There seems to be no end of treasures. Her vast, uncounted wealth is stripped away. 10Soon the city is an empty shambles; hearts melt in horror; knees quake; her people stand aghast, pale-faced and trembling.

11Where now is that great Nineveh, lion of the nations, full of fight and boldness, where even the old and feeble, as well as the young and tender, lived unafraid?

12O Nineveh, once mighty lion! You crushed your enemies to feed your children and your wives, and filled your city and your homes with captured goods and slaves.

13But now the Lord Almighty has turned against you. He destroys your weapons. Your chariots stand there, silent and unused. Your finest youth lie dead. Never again will you bring back slaves from conquered nations; never again will you rule the earth.

The people will be scattered

3 Woe to Nineveh, City of Blood, full of lies, crammed with plunder. 2Listen! Hear the crack of the whips as the chariots rush forward against her, wheels rumbling, horses' hoofs pounding, and chariots clattering as they bump wildly through the streets! 3See the flashing swords and glittering spears in the upraised arms of the cavalry! The dead are lying in the streets—bodies, heaps of bodies, everywhere. Men stumble over them, scramble to their feet, and fall again.

4All this because Nineveh sold herself to the enemies of God. The beautiful and faithless city, mistress of deadly charms, enticed the nations with her beauty, then taught them all to worship her false gods, bewitching people everywhere.

5"No wonder I stand against you," says the Lord Almighty; "and now all the earth will see your nakedness and shame. 6I will cover you with filth and show the world how really vile you are." 7All who see you will shrink back in horror: "Nineveh lies in utter ruin." Yet no one anywhere regrets your fate!

8Are you any better than Thebes, straddling the Nile, protected on all sides by the river? 9Ethiopia and the whole land of Egypt were her mighty allies, and she could call on them for infinite assistance, as well as Put and Libya. 10Yet Thebes fell and her people were led off as slaves; her babies were dashed to death against the stones

3:4 *taught them all to worship her false gods,* literally, "who betrays nations with her harlotries." **3:8** *Are you any better than Thebes . . .* Thebes was conquered by the Assyrians fifty-one years before this prophecy.

---

and deported her people in 722 B.C. (2 Kings 17:3–6; 18:9, 10). Assyria had also attacked the Southern Kingdom and forced it to pay tribute. Later Judah, the Southern Kingdom, was conquered and taken into captivity in three separate invasions by the Babylonians (605, 597, and 586 B.C.).

2:6 This reference to the opening of river gates could refer either to the enemy flowing into Nineveh like a flood of water (1:8) or to an actual flood of water. Some scholars suggest that dam gates, which have been found in archaeological excavations, were closed to dam up the river. When an enormous amount of water had been accumulated, the gates were opened, allowing the water to flood Nineveh.

2:12—3:1 The major source of the Assyrian economy was the plunder taken from other nations. The Assyrians had taken the food of innocent people to maintain their luxurious standard of living, depriving others to supply their excesses. Depriving innocent people to support the luxury of a few is a sin that angers God. As Christians we must stand firm against this evil practice.

2:13 God had given the people of Nineveh a chance to repent, which they did after hearing Jonah (see the book of Jonah). But now they had returned to their sin, and its consequences were destroying them. There is a point for people, cities, and nations

after which there is no turning back; Assyria had crossed that point. We must warn others to repent while there is still time.

3:4 Nineveh used her beauty, prestige, and power to seduce other nations. Like a prostitute, she enticed them into false friendships. Then when the other nations relaxed, thinking Assyria was a friend, Assyria destroyed and plundered them. Beautiful and impressive on the outside, Nineveh was vicious and deceitful on the inside. Beneath beautiful facades sometimes lie seduction and death. Don't let an attractive institution, company, movement, or person seduce you into lowering your standards.

3:8-10 Thebes was a city in Egypt, the previous world power, which stood in the path of Assyria's expansion in the South. The Assyrians conquered Thebes 51 years before this prophecy was given. To Judah, surrounded to the north and south by Assyria, the situation appeared hopeless. But God said that the same horrible things done in Thebes would happen in Nineveh.

3:8-10 No power on earth can protect us from God's judgment or be a suitable substitute for his power in our lives. Thebes and Assyria put their trust in alliances and military power, but history would show these inadequate. Don't insist on learning through personal experience; instead, learn the lessons history has already taught. Put your trust in God above all else.

of the streets. Soldiers drew straws to see who would get her officers as servants. All her leaders were bound in chains.

11Nineveh, too, will stagger like a drunkard and hide herself in fear. 12All your forts will fall. They will be devoured like first-ripe figs that fall into the mouths of those who shake the trees. 13Your troops will be weak and helpless as women. The gates of your land will be opened wide to the enemy and set on fire and burned. 14Get ready for the siege! Store up water! Strengthen the forts! Prepare many bricks for repairing your walls! Go into the pits to trample the clay, and pack it in the molds!

15But in the middle of your preparations, the fire will devour you; the sword will cut you down; the enemy will consume you like young locusts that eat up everything before them. There is no escape, though you multiply like grasshoppers. 16Merchants, numerous as stars, filled your city with vast wealth, but your enemies swarm like locusts and carry it away. 17Your princes and officials crowd together like grasshoppers in the hedges in the cold, but all of them will flee away and disappear, like locusts when the sun comes up and warms the earth.

18O Assyrian king, your princes lie dead in the dust; your people are scattered across the mountains; there is no shepherd now to gather them. 19There is no healing for your wound—it is far too deep to cure. All who hear your fate will clap their hands for joy, for where can one be found who has not suffered from your cruelty?

3:10
2 Kgs 8:12
Ps 137:9

3:11
Hos 13:16
Nah 3:8
Mt 2:16-18

3:11
Isa 29:9; 49:26
Jer 25:15-27
51:57

3:13
Isa 19:16
Jer 50:37; 51:30

3:14
2 Chron 32:3,
4,11
Isa 8:9,10
22:9-11; 37:25
Nah 2:1

3:15
Isa 66:15,16

3:18
Jer 50:18
Ezek 32:22,23

3:19
Job 27:23
Jer 30:13-15
Ezek 25:6
Nah 2:2

3:19 All the nations hated to be ruled by the merciless Assyrians, but they wanted to be like Assyria—powerful wealthy, prestigious—and they courted her friendship. In the same way, we don't like the idea of being ruled harshly, so we do what we can to stay on good terms with a powerful leader. And deep down, we would like to have that kind of power. The thought of being on top can be captivating. But power is seductive, so we should not scheme to get it or hold on to it. Those who lust after power will be powerfully destroyed, as was the mighty Assyrian Empire.

HABAKKUK

FROM innocent childhood queries to complex university discussions, life is filled with questions. Asking how and why and when, we probe beneath the surface to find satisfying answers. But not all questions have answers. These unanswered interrogations beget more questions and nagging, spirit-destroying doubt. Some choose to live with their doubts, ignoring them and moving on with life. Others become cynical and hardened. But there are those who reject those options and continue to ask, looking for answers.

Habakkuk was such a man. Troubled by what he observed, he asked difficult questions. These questions were not merely intellectual exercises or bitter complaints. Habakkuk saw a dying world, and it broke his heart. Why is there evil in the world? Why do the wicked seem to be winning? He boldly and confidently took his complaints directly to God. And God answered him with an avalanche of proof and prediction.

The prophet's questions and God's answers are recorded in this book. As we turn the pages, we are immediately confronted with his urgent cries, "O Lord, how long must I call for help before you will listen? I shout to you in vain; there is no answer. . . . Must I forever see this sin and sadness all around me?" (1:2, 3). In fact, most of the first chapter is devoted to his questions. As chapter two begins, Habakkuk declares that he will wait to hear God's answers to his complaints. Then God begins to speak, telling the prophet to write his answer in large letters so that all will see and understand. It may seem, God says, as though the wicked triumph, but eventually they will be judged, and righteousness will prevail. It may not come quickly, but it will happen. God's answers fill chapter two. Then Habakkuk concludes his book with a prayer of triumph. With questions answered and a new understanding of God's power and love, Habakkuk rejoices in who God is and in what he will do. "Yet I will rejoice in the Lord; I will be happy in the God of my salvation. The Lord is my Strength, and he will give me the speed of a deer and bring me safely over the mountains" (3:18, 19).

Listen to Habakkuk's profound questions which he boldly brings to God, and realize that you can also bring your doubts and inquiries to him. Listen to God's answers and rejoice that he is at work in the world and in your life.

VITAL STATISTICS

PURPOSE:
To show that God is still in control of the world despite the apparent triumph of evil

AUTHOR:
Habakkuk

TO WHOM WRITTEN:
Judah (the Southern Kingdom), and God's people everywhere

DATE WRITTEN:
Between 612 and 589 B.C.

SETTING:
Babylon was becoming the dominant world power and Judah would soon feel Babylon's destructive force

KEY VERSE:
"O Lord, now I have heard your report, and I worship you in awe for the fearful things you are going to do. In this time of our deep need, begin again to help us, as you did in years gone by. Show us your power to save us. In your wrath, remember mercy" (3:2).

KEY PEOPLE:
Habakkuk, the Chaldeans (Babylonians)

KEY PLACE:
Judah

THE BLUEPRINT

1. Habakkuk's doubt (1:1—2:20)
2. Habakkuk's prayer (3:1–19)

When Habakkuk was troubled he brought his concerns directly to God. After receiving God's answers, he responded with a prayer of faith. Habakkuk's example is one that should encourage us as we struggle to move from doubt to faith. We don't have to be afraid to ask questions of God. The problem is not with God's ways, but with our limited understanding of him.

MEGATHEMES

THEME	EXPLANATION	IMPORTANCE
Struggle and doubt	Habakkuk asked God why the people of Judah were not being punished for their sin. He couldn't understand why a just God would allow such evil to exist. God promised to use the Babylonians to punish Judah. When Habakkuk cried out for answers in his time of struggle, God answered him with words of hope.	God wants us to come to him with our struggles and doubts. But his answers may not be what we expect. God sustains us by revealing himself to us. Trusting him leads to quiet hope, not bitter resignation.
God's sovereignty	Habakkuk asked God why he would use the wicked Babylonians to punish his people. God said that he would also punish the Babylonians after they had fulfilled his purpose.	God is still in control of this world in spite of the apparent triumph of evil. God doesn't overlook sin. One day he will rule the whole earth with perfect justice.
Hope	God is the Creator; he is all-powerful. He has a plan and he will carry it out. He will punish sin. He is our strength and our place of safety. We can have confidence that he will love us and guard our relationship with him forever.	Hope means going beyond our unpleasant daily experiences to the joy of knowing God. We live by trusting in him, not in the benefits, happiness, or success we may experience in this life. Our hope comes from God.

1. Habakkuk's doubt

Habakkuk questions God

1 This is the message that came to the prophet Habakkuk in a vision from God: ²O Lord, how long must I call for help before you will listen? I shout to you in vain; there is no answer. "Help! Murder!" I cry, but no one comes to save. ³Must I forever see this sin and sadness all around me?

Wherever I look there is oppression and bribery and men who love to argue and to fight. ⁴The law is not enforced and there is no justice given in the courts, for the wicked far outnumber the righteous, and bribes and trickery prevail.

⁵The Lord replied: "Look, and be amazed! You will be astounded at what I am about to do! For I am going to do something in your own lifetime that you will have to see to believe. ⁶I am raising a new force on the world scene, the Chaldeans, a cruel and violent nation who will march across the world and conquer it. ⁷They are notorious for their cruelty. They do as they like, and no one can interfere. ⁸Their horses are swifter than leopards. They are a fierce people, more fierce than wolves at dusk. Their cavalry move proudly forward from a distant land; like eagles they come swooping down to pounce upon their prey. ⁹All opposition melts away before the terror of their presence. They collect captives like sand.

1:4
2 Kgs 24:1-5
2 Chron 36:4-8

1:5
Isa 28:21

1:6
Deut 28:49-57
2 Kgs 24:2, 10-20; 25:1-23
2 Chron 36:6-13
Isa 48:14
Jer 21:3,4
Dan 9:1

1:7
Jer 39:5-9

1:8
Deut 28:49
Isa 5:26-30
Lam 4:19

1:9
2 Kgs 24:14,15
2 Chron 36:18

1:1 Habakkuk lived in Judah during the reign of Jehoiakim (2 Kings 23:36—24:5). He prophesied between the fall of Nineveh (the capital of Assyria) in 612 B.C. and the invasion of Judah in 589 B.C. With Assyria in disarray, Babylon was becoming the dominant world power. This book records the prophet's dialogue with God concerning the questions, "Why does God often seem indifferent in the face of evil? Why do evil people seem to go unpunished?" While other prophetic books brought God's Word to men, this brought men's questions to God.

1:2–4 Habakkuk was saddened by the corruption he saw around him. In response, he poured out his heart to God. Today injustice is still rampant, but don't let your concern cause you to doubt God or rebel against him. Instead, consider the message God gave Habakkuk and recognize God's long-range plans and purposes. Realize that God is doing right, even if you do not understand why he works as he does.

1:3–5 When circumstances around us become almost unbearable, we wonder if God has forgotten us. But remember, he is in control. He has a plan and will judge evildoers in his time. If we are truly humble, we will be willing to accept God's answers and await his timing.

1:5 God told the inhabitants of Jerusalem that they would be astounded at what he was about to do. The people would see a series of unbelievable events: (1) their own independent and prosperous kingdom, Judah, would suddenly become a vassal nation; (2) Egypt, a world power for centuries, would be crushed almost overnight; (3) Nineveh, the capital of the Assyrian Empire, would be so completely ransacked that people would forget where it had been; and (4) the Chaldeans (Babylonians) would rise to power. Though these words were indeed astounding, the people saw them fulfilled during their lifetime.

1:6 The Chaldeans (Babylonians), who lived northwest of the Persian Gulf, made a rapid rise to power around 630 B.C. They began to assert themselves against the Assyrian Empire, and by 605 B.C. had conquered Assyria to become the strongest world power. But they were as wicked as the Assyrians, for they loved to collect captives (1:9), were proud of their warfare tactics (1:10), and trusted in their idols and military strength (1:11).

1:10
2 Kgs 25:6,7
2 Chron 36:6
Jer 32:24
33:4,5; 52:4-7
Ezek 26:7-11

1:12
Deut 32:4,30,31
2 Kgs 19:25
Isa 10:5-7
Jer 25:8-14

1:13
Job 15:15
Ps 5:4; 11:7
1 Pet 1:15,16

1:15
Jer 16:16
Ezek 29:4,5

1:16
Jer 7:18
44:17,18
Hab 1:11

2:2
Deut 27:8
Isa 8:1
Rev 1:19; 14:13

2:3
Dan 8:17-19
9:24-27
2 Thess 2:6-14

¹⁰"They scoff at kings and princes, and scorn their forts. They simply heap up dirt against their walls and capture them! ¹¹They sweep past like wind and are gone, but their guilt is deep, for they claim their power is from their gods."

¹²O Lord my God, my Holy One, you who are eternal—is your plan in all of this to wipe us out? Surely not! O God our Rock, you have decreed the rise of these Chaldeans to chasten and correct us for our awful sins. ¹³We are wicked, but they far more! Will you, who cannot allow sin in any form, stand idly by while they swallow us up? Should you be silent while the wicked destroy those who are better than they?

¹⁴Are we but fish, to be caught and killed? Are we but creeping things that have no leader to defend them from their foes? ¹⁵Must we be strung up on their hooks and dragged out in their nets, while they rejoice? ¹⁶Then they will worship their nets and burn incense before them! "These are the gods who make us rich," they'll say.

¹⁷Will you let them get away with this forever? Will they succeed forever in their heartless wars?

God explains his ways to Habakkuk

2 I will climb my watchtower now, and wait to see what answer God will give to my complaint.

²And the Lord said to me, "Write my answer on a billboard, large and clear, so that anyone can read it at a glance and rush to tell the others. ³But these things I plan won't happen right away. Slowly, steadily, surely, the time approaches when the vision will be fulfilled. If it seems slow, do not despair, for these things will surely

1:11 The Hebrew text of this verse is very uncertain. **2:2** *on a billboard,* literally, "on the tablets." **2:3** *if it seems slow,* or, "if he seems slow."

HABAKKUK served as a prophet to Judah from 612–589 B.C.

Climate of the times	Judah's last four kings were wicked men who rejected God and oppressed their own people. Babylon invaded Judah twice before finally destroying her in 586. It was a time of fear, oppression, persecution, lawlessness, and immorality.
Main message	Habakkuk couldn't understand why God seemed to do nothing about the wickedness in society. Then he realized that faith in God alone would supply the answers to his questions.
Importance of message	Instead of questioning the ways of God, we should realize that he is totally just, and we should have faith that he is in control and that one day evil will be utterly destroyed.
Contemporary prophets	Jeremiah (627–586)
	Daniel (605–536)
	Ezekiel (593–571)

1:13 Judah's forthcoming punishment would be at the hands of the Babylonians. Habakkuk was appalled that God would use a nation more wicked than Judah for Judah's punishment. But the Babylonians did not know they were being used by God to help Judah return to him, and Babylon's pride in its victories would be its fall. Evil is self-destructive, and it is never beyond God's control. God may use whatever unusual instrument he chooses to correct us or punish us. When we deserve punishment or correction, how can we complain about the kind of "rod" God uses on us?

1:14–16 Babylon was proud of its military might, strategies, armies, and weapons. With no regard for humanity, the armies brought home riches, booty, slaves, and tribute from the nations they plundered. Such is the essence of idolatry—asking the gods we make to help us get all we want. The essence of Christianity is asking the God *who made us* to help us give all we can in service to him.

2:1 The watchtower, often used by the prophets to show an attitude of expectation (Isaiah 21:8, 11; Jeremiah 6:17; Ezekiel 3:17), is a picture of Habakkuk's attitude of patient waiting and watching for God's response. These stone towers were built on city walls or ramparts so watchmen could see people (enemies or messengers) approaching their city while they were still at a distance. Watchtowers were also erected in vineyards to help guard the ripening grapes. Habakkuk wanted to be in the best position to receive God's message.

2:2ff This chapter records God's answers to Habakkuk's questions: (1) How long would evil prevail (1:2, 3)? (2) Why was Babylon chosen to punish Judah (1:13)? God said that the judgment, though slow to come, was certain. Though God used Babylon against Judah, he was aware of Babylon's sins and would punish her in due time.

2:3 Evil seems to have the upper hand in the world. Like Habakkuk, Christians often feel angry and discouraged as they see what goes on. Habakkuk complained vigorously to God about it. God's answer to him is the same answer he would give us, "Be patient! God will work out his plans." It isn't easy to be patient, but it helps to remember that God hates sin even more than we do. Punishment of sin will certainly come. As God told Habakkuk, "Don't despair." To trust God fully means to trust him even when we don't understand why events occur as they do.

come to pass. Just be patient! They will not be overdue a single day!

4"Note this: Wicked men trust themselves alone [as these Chaldeans do], and fail; but the righteous man trusts in me, and lives! 5What's more, these arrogant Chaldeans are betrayed by all their wine, for it is treacherous. In their greed they have collected many nations, but like death and hell, they are never satisfied. 6The time is coming when all their captives will taunt them, saying: 'You robbers! At last justice has caught up with you! Now you will get your just deserts for your oppression and extortion!'

7"Suddenly your debtors will rise up in anger and turn on you and take all you have, while you stand trembling and helpless. 8You have ruined many nations; now they will ruin you. You murderers! You have filled the countryside with lawlessness and all the cities too.

9"Woe to you for getting rich by evil means, attempting to live beyond the reach of danger. 10By the murders you commit, you have shamed your name and forfeited your lives. 11The very stones in the walls of your homes cry out against you, and the beams in the ceilings echo what they say.

12"Woe to you who build cities with money gained from murdering and robbery! 13Has not the Lord decreed that godless nations' gains will turn to ashes in their hands? They work so hard, but all in vain!

14("The time will come when all the earth is filled, as the waters fill the sea, with an awareness of the glory of the Lord.)

15"Woe to you for making your neighboring lands reel and stagger like drunkards beneath your blows, and then gloating over their nakedness and shame. 16Soon your own glory will be replaced by shame. Drink down God's judgment on yourselves. Stagger and fall! 17You cut down the forests of Lebanon—now you will be cut down! You terrified the wild animals you caught in your traps—now terror will strike you because of all your murdering and violence in cities everywhere.

18"What profit was there in worshiping all your man-made idols? What a foolish lie that they could help! What fools you were to trust what you yourselves had made. 19Woe to those who command their lifeless wooden idols to arise and save them, who call out to the speechless stone to tell them what to do. Can images speak for God? They are overlaid with gold and silver, but there is no breath at all inside!

20"But the Lord is in his holy Temple; let all the earth be silent before him."

2. Habakkuk's prayer

3 This is the prayer of triumph that Habakkuk sang before the Lord:

2O Lord, now I have heard your report, and I worship you in awe for the

2:4 *as these Chaldeans do,* implied. *the righteous trusts in me, and lives,* or, "the righteous shall live by his faith."
3:1 *This is the prayer of triumph,* literally, "according to Shigionoth"—thought by some to mean a mournful dirge.

(Cross-references, right margin:)
2:4 Prov 3:6; 16:3; Rom 1:17; Gal 3:11; Heb 10:38
2:6 Mic 2:4,5; Hab 2:9,12,15,19
2:8 Isa13:16-18; Jer 27:7,8; 50:10,34-46
2:9 Ps 10:3-11; 52:7
2:11 Josh 24:27; Lk 19:40
2:12 Mic 3:10; Hab 2:9,15,19
2:14 Ps 22:27; 86:9; Isa 6:3; Zech 14:9; Rev 11:15; 15:3,4
2:15 Hos 7:5; Hab 2:9,12,19
2:16 Isa 51:21-23; Jer 25:15,16; Rev 14:10; 18:6
2:17 Lev 26:16,17; Deut 28:25,28, 29,66-68
2:18 1 Kgs 18:26-27; Isa 42:17; Jer 2:28; 50:2
2:19 Ex 32:2-4; Isa 40:19; 46:6; Jer 10:4,5; Acts 17:29
2:20 Zeph 1:7; Zech 2:13
3:2 Hab 3:16; Heb 11:7

2:4 Another translation of this passage is "the righteous shall live by his faith." This verse has inspired countless Christians. Paul refers to it in Romans 1:17 and quotes it in Galatians 3:11. The writer of Hebrews quotes it in 10:38, just before the famous chapter on faith. And it is helpful to all Christians who must live through difficult times without seeing the outcome. Christians must trust that God is directing all things according to his purposes.

2:4–8 Babylon was proud, trusted in herself and her military might, and lived to satisfy her own lusts at the expense of her captives. But these very sins would rise up to judge her, and the captives she wronged would strip Babylon and taunt her. Justice would come slowly, but it would come.

2:9–13 Babylon's riches came from the misfortunes of others, and these riches would turn to worthless ashes in her hands. The victims and their cities would cry out against Babylon. Money is not evil, but God condemns the love of riches and all evil means of acquiring it (1 Timothy 6:10). Be careful not to hunger for wealth so much that you lose your appetite for God. Do not allow money to take the place of family, friends, or God.

2:18 Idolatry may seem like a sin that modern people need not fear. But idolatry is not just bowing down to idols; it is trusting in what one has made, and therefore, in one's own power as creator and sustainer. If we say we worship God, but we put our trust in bank accounts, homes, businesses, and organizations, then we are idolaters. Do you trust God more than you trust what your hands have made?

2:20 Idols have no life, no personhood, no power; they are empty chunks of wood or stone. Temples built to idols are equally empty; no one lives there. But the Lord *is* in his Temple. He is a real person—alive and powerful. He is truly and fully God. Idolaters command their idols to save them, but we who worship the living God come to him in silent awe, great respect, and reverence. We acknowledge that he is in control and knows what he is doing. Idols remain silent, because they cannot answer. The living God, by contrast, speaks through his prophets. Approach God reverently and wait silently to hear what he has to say.

3:3
Ex 24:15-17
Ps 48:10; 113:4
Rev 5:13,14

3:4
Ex 14:20
Ps 18:12; 104:1
1 Tim 6:16

3:5
Deut 32:24,25

3:6
Josh 10:40-42
Neh 9:22-25

3:7
1 Chron 1:5-9

3:8
Ex 14:21,22
Josh 3:12-17
2 Kgs 2:11,12

3:10
Ps 93:3; 96:11

3:11
Josh 10:12-14

3:12
Hab 3:6

3:13
Ps 18:38; 68:21

3:14
Judg 7:22
Dan 11:40

3:15
Hab 3:8

3:16
Isa 6:5

3:17
Deut 28:15-19
Jer 14:2-6
Joel 1:10,12
Hag 2:16,17
Mt 21:19,20

3:18
Ps 25:5; 27:1
Isa 12:2
Phil 4:4

3:19
Ps 18:2,3; 46:1
Phil 14:13

fearful things you are going to do. In this time of our deep need, begin again to help us, as you did in years gone by. Show us your power to save us. In your wrath, remember mercy.

³I see God moving across the deserts from Mount Sinai. His brilliant splendor fills the earth and sky; his glory fills the heavens, and the earth is full of his praise! What a wonderful God he is! ⁴From his hands flash rays of brilliant light. He rejoices in his awesome power. ⁵Pestilence marches before him; plague follows close behind. ⁶He stops; he stands still for a moment, gazing at the earth. Then he shakes the nations, scattering the everlasting mountains and leveling the hills. His power is just the same as always! ⁷I see the people of Cushan and of Midian in mortal fear.

⁸, ⁹Was it in anger, Lord, you smote the rivers and parted the sea? Were you displeased with them? No, you were sending your chariots of salvation! All saw your power! Then springs burst forth upon the earth at your command! ¹⁰The mountains watched and trembled. Onward swept the raging water. The mighty deep cried out, announcing its surrender to the Lord. ¹¹The lofty sun and moon began to fade, obscured by brilliance from your arrows and the flashing of your glittering spear.

¹²You marched across the land in awesome anger, and trampled down the nations in your wrath. ¹³You went out to save your chosen people. You crushed the head of the wicked and laid bare his bones from head to toe. ¹⁴You destroyed with their own weapons those who came out like a whirlwind, thinking Israel would be an easy prey.

¹⁵Your horsemen marched across the sea; the mighty waters piled high. ¹⁶I tremble when I hear all this; my lips quiver with fear. My legs give way beneath me and I shake in terror. I will quietly wait for the day of trouble to come upon the people who invade us.

¹⁷Even though the fig trees are all destroyed, and there is neither blossom left nor fruit, and though the olive crops all fail, and the fields lie barren; even if the flocks die in the fields and the cattle barns are empty, ¹⁸yet I will rejoice in the Lord; I will be happy in the God of my salvation. ¹⁹The Lord God is my Strength, and he will give me the speed of a deer and bring me safely over the mountains.

(A note to the choir director: When singing this ode, the choir is to be accompanied by stringed instruments.)

3:3 *from Mount Sinai,* literally, "from Teman . . . from Mount Paran." **3:4** *He rejoices in his awesome power.* Or, "He veils his power." **3:8, 9** Literally, "Was the Lord displeased against the rivers? Were you angry with them? Was your wrath against their sin that you rode upon your horses? Your chariots were salvation. Your bow was pulled from its sheath and you put arrows to the string. You ribboned the earth with rivers." **3:10** *announcing its surrender to the Lord,* literally, "and lifts high its hands."

3:1ff Habakkuk praised God for answering his questions of chapter two. Evil will not triumph forever; God is in control and he can be completely trusted to vindicate those who are faithful to him. We must quietly wait for him to act (3:16).

3:2 Habakkuk knew that God was going to discipline the people of Judah, and that it wasn't going to be a pleasant experience. But he accepted God's will, asking for help and mercy. Habakkuk did not ask to escape the discipline, but accepted the truth that Judah needed to learn a lesson. God still disciplines in love, to bring his children back to him (Hebrews 12:5, 6). Accept his discipline gladly, and ask him to help you change.

3:3–16 In these verses, Habakkuk paints the picture of God delivering his people out of Egypt in the dramatic exodus event (see Exodus 14). God's awesome power is not restricted to creating scenic wonders; he also uses it to execute righteousness and justice. It is not enough to be awed by God's power. We need discipline in order to learn how to obey and live for him.

3:17–19 Crop failure and the death of flocks would devastate Judah. But Habakkuk affirmed that even in the midst of starvation, he would still rejoice in the Lord. Habakkuk's feelings were not

controlled by the events around him but by faith in God's ability to give him strength. When nothing makes sense, and when troubles seem more than you can bear, remember that God gives strength. Take your eyes off your difficulties and look to God.

3:19 God will give his followers surefooted confidence through difficult times. They will run like deer across rough and dangerous terrain. At the proper time, God will bring about his justice and completely rid the world of evil. In the meantime, God's people need to live in the strength of his Spirit, confident in his ultimate victory over evil.

3:19 The note to the choir director was to be used when this passage was sung as a psalm in Temple worship.

3:19 Habakkuk had asked God why evil people prosper while the righteous suffer. God's answer: they don't, not in the long run. Habakkuk saw his own limitations in contrast to God's unlimited control of all the world's events. God is alive and in control of the world and its events. We cannot see all that God is doing, and we cannot see all that God will do. But we can be assured that he is God and will do what is right. Knowing this brings us confidence and hope in the midst of a confusing world.

ZEPHANIAH

VITAL STATISTICS

PURPOSE:
To shake the people of Judah out of their complacency and urge them to return to God

AUTHOR:
Zephaniah

TO WHOM WRITTEN:
Judah and all nations

DATE WRITTEN:
Probably near the end of Zephaniah's ministry (640–621 B.C.), when King Josiah's great reforms began

SETTING:
King Josiah of Judah was attempting to reverse the evil trends set by the two previous kings of Judah—Manasseh and Amon. Josiah was able to extend his influence because there wasn't a strong superpower dominating the world at that time (Assyria was declining rapidly). Zephaniah's prophecy may have been the motivating factor in Josiah's reform. Zephaniah was a contemporary of Jeremiah.

KEY VERSE:
"Beg him to save you, all who are humble—all who have tried to obey. Walk humbly and do what is right; perhaps even yet the Lord will protect you from his wrath in the day of doom" (2:3).

KEY PLACE:
Jerusalem

OVERWHELMING grief, prolonged distress, incessant abuse, continual persecution, and imminent punishment breed hopelessness and despair. "If only," we cry as we search our minds for a way out and look to the skies for rescue. With just a glimmer of hope, we would take courage and carry on, enduring until the end.

Hope is the silver shaft of sun breaking through the storm-darkened sky, words of comfort in the intensive care unit, a letter from across the sea, the first spring bird perched on a snow-covered twig, and the finish line in sight. It is a rainbow, a song, a loving touch. Hope is knowing God and resting in his love.

As God's prophet, Zephaniah was bound to speak the truth—this he did clearly, thundering certain judgment and horrible punishment for all who would defy the Lord. God's awful wrath would sweep away everything in the land and destroy it. "Mankind and all the idols that he worships—all will vanish. Even the birds of the air and the fish in the sea will perish" (1:3). No living thing in the land would escape. And that terrible day was coming soon: "Swiftly it comes—a day when strong men will weep bitterly. It is a day of the wrath of God poured out; it is a day of terrible distress and anguish, a day of ruin and desolation, of darkness, gloom, clouds, blackness" (1:14, 15). One can sense the oppression and depression his listeners must have felt. They were judged guilty and doomed.

But in the midst of this terrible pronouncement, there is hope. Chapter one of Zephaniah's prophecy is filled with terror. In chapter two, however, a whispered promise appears. "Beg him to save you, all who are humble—all who have tried to obey. Walk humbly and do what is right; perhaps even yet the Lord will protect you from his wrath in that day of doom" (2:3). And a few verses later we read of a "remnant of Judah" who will be "pastured and restored" (2:7).

Finally in chapter three, the quiet refrain grows to a crescendo as God's salvation and deliverance for those who are faithful to him is declared. "Sing, O daughter of Zion; shout, O Israel; be glad and rejoice with all your heart. . . . For the Lord will remove his hand of judgment. . . . And the Lord himself, the King of Israel, will live among you! At last your troubles will be over—you need fear no more" (3:14, 15). This is true hope, grounded in the knowledge of God's justice and his love for his people.

As you read Zephaniah, listen carefully to the words of judgment. God does not take sin lightly, and it will be punished. But be encouraged by the words of hope—our God reigns, and he will rescue his own. Decide to be part of that faithful remnant of souls who humbly worship and obey the living Lord.

Josiah dies in battle 609	First captives taken to Babylon 605	Babylon's second attack on Judah 597	Judah (the Southern Kingdom) falls 586

THE BLUEPRINT

1. The day of wrath (1:1—3:8)
2. The day of hope (3:9—20)

Zephaniah warned the people of Judah that if they refused to repent, the entire nation, including Jerusalem, would be lost. The people knew that God would eventually bless them, but Zephaniah made it clear that there would be judgment first, then blessing. This judgment would not be merely punishment for sin, but also a process of purifying the people. Though we live in a fallen world surrounded by evil, we can hope in the perfect Kingdom of God to come and we can allow any punishment that touches us now to purify us from sin.

MEGATHEMES

THEME	EXPLANATION	IMPORTANCE
Day of judgment	Destruction was coming because Judah had forsaken the Lord. The people worshiped Baal, Molech, and nature. Even the priests mixed pagan practices with faith in God. God's punishment for sin was on the way.	To escape God's judgment we must listen to him, accept his correction, trust him, and seek his guidance. If we accept him as our Lord, we can escape his condemnation.
Indifference to God	Although there had been occasional attempts at renewal, Judah had no sorrow for her sins. The people were prosperous and they no longer cared about God. God's demands for righteous living seemed irrelevant to Judah, whose security and wealth made them complacent.	Don't let material comfort be a barrier to your commitment to God. Prosperity can produce an attitude of proud self-sufficiency. The only antidote is to admit that money won't save us and that we cannot save ourselves. Only God can save us and cure our indifference to spiritual matters.
Day of cheer	The day of judgment will also be a day of cheer. God will judge all those who mistreat his people. He will purify his people, purging away all sin and evil. God will restore his people and give them hope.	When people are purged of sin, there is great relief and hope. No matter how difficult our experience now, we can look forward to the day of celebration when God will completely restore us. It will truly be our day of cheer.

1. The day of wrath
Zephaniah predicts the destruction of Judah

1:1
2 Kgs 22:1—23:28
2 Chron 34:1—35:26
1:2
2 Kgs 22:15-20
Isa 6:11
Ezek 33:27-29

1 Subject: a message from the Lord.

To: Zephaniah (son of Cushi, grandson of Gedaliah, great-grandson of Amariah, and great-great-grandson of Hezekiah). *When:* During the reign of Josiah (son of Amon) king of Judah.

²"I will sweep away everything in all your land," says the Lord. "I will destroy it to the ground. ³I will sweep away both men and animals alike. Mankind and all

---

1:1 Zephaniah prophesied in the days of Josiah, king of Judah (640–609 B.C.). Josiah sought after God, and during his reign the books of the Law were discovered in the Temple. After reading them, Josiah began a great religious revival in Judah (2 Kings 22:1—23:25). Zephaniah helped the revival by warning the people that judgment would come if they did not turn from their sins. Although this great revival brought the nation toward God, it did not fully eliminate idolatry, and it lasted only a short time. Twelve

years later Judah was conquered by Babylon and sent into exile.

1:2ff The people of Judah were clearly warned by the highest authority of all—God. They refused to listen either because they doubted God's prophet and thus did not believe the message was from God, or because they doubted God himself and thus did not believe he would do what he said. If we refuse to listen to God's Word, the Bible, we are as shortsighted as the people of Judah.

the idols that he worships—all will vanish. Even the birds of the air and the fish in the sea will perish. ⁴I will crush Judah and Jerusalem with my fist, and destroy every remnant of those who worship Baal; I will put an end to their idolatrous priests, so that even the memory of them will disappear. ⁵They go up on their roofs and bow to the sun, moon and stars. They 'follow the Lord,' but worship Molech, too! I will destroy them. ⁶And I will destroy those who formerly worshiped the Lord, but now no longer do, and those who never loved him and never wanted to."

⁷Stand in silence in the presence of the Lord. For the awesome Day of his Judgment has come; he has prepared a great slaughter of his people and has chosen their executioners. ⁸"On that Day of Judgment I will punish the leaders and princes of Judah, and all others wearing heathen clothing. ⁹Yes, I will punish those who follow heathen customs and who rob and kill to fill their masters' homes with evil gain of violence and fraud. ¹⁰A cry of alarm will begin at the farthest gate of Jerusalem, coming closer and closer until the noise of the advancing army reaches the very top of the hill where the city is built.

¹¹"Wail in sorrow, you people of Jerusalem. All your greedy businessmen, all your loan sharks—all will die.

¹²"I will search with lanterns in Jerusalem's darkest corners to find and punish those who sit contented in their sins, indifferent to God, thinking he will let them alone. ¹³They are the very ones whose property will be plundered by the enemy, whose homes will be ransacked; they will never have a chance to live in the new homes they have built. They will never drink wine from the vineyards they have planted."

¹⁴"That terrible day is near. Swiftly it comes—a day when strong men will weep bitterly. ¹⁵It is a day of the wrath of God poured out; it is a day of terrible distress and anguish, a day of ruin and desolation, of darkness, gloom, clouds, blackness, ¹⁶trumpet calls and battle cries; down go the walled cities and strongest battlements!

¹⁷"I will make you as helpless as a blind man searching for a path, because you have sinned against the Lord; therefore your blood will be poured out into the dust and your bodies will lie there rotting on the ground.

1:7 *Has chosen their executioners,* literally is: "He has prepared a sacrifice and sanctified his guests."

1:4 When the Israelites arrived in the Promised Land, they did not completely rid the land of its heathen Canaanite inhabitants who worshiped idols. Gradually the Israelites began to worship the gods of the Canaanites. Although there were many gods, Baal was the chief god; he was the symbol of strength and fertility. God was greatly displeased when his people turned from him to Baal.

1:4-6 History is littered with idols and their worship, and idol worship is prevalent even today. An idol is anything reverenced more than God. But ultimately all idols will prove worthless, and the true God will prevail. Seek God first (Matthew 6:33), and put no other gods before him (Exodus 20:3).

1:5 The people had become polytheistic, worshiping the Lord *and* all the other gods of the land. They added the "best" of pagan worship to true faith in God, and this corrupted them. One of these other gods was Molech, the national god of the Ammonites. Molech worship included child sacrifice, an abominable sin. From the time of Moses, the Israelites had been warned about worshiping this false god (Leviticus 18:21; 20:5), but they refused to take heed.

1:7 Many think these prophecies have a double fulfillment—one for the near future (soon after the prophecy was made) and another for the distant future (possibly during the end times). A day of judgment and a great slaughter occurred during the lifetime of these people when Babylon invaded the land. Some scholars understand these prophecies of judgment to refer to events entirely in the future. The prophet saw these prophecies as future events, but he could not see when or in what order these events would take place.

1:8, 9 Wearing heathen clothing showed a desire for foreign gods and foreign ways. Leaders who should have been good examples to the people were adopting foreign practices and thus showing their contempt for the Lord by ignoring his commands against adopting pagan culture.

1:12 Within 20 years, the Babylonians would enter Jerusalem, drag people out of hiding, and take them captive or kill them. Because the people did not search their own hearts, and because they were content with their sins and indifferent to God, God would use the Babylonians to judge them. No one would escape God's judgment; there would be no place to hide.

1:12, 13 Some people think of God as an indulgent heavenly grandfather, nice to have around, but not a real force in shaping modern life. They don't believe in his power or his coming judgment. But God is holy, and therefore he will actively judge and justly punish everyone who is content to live in sin, indifferent to him, or unconcerned about justice. When people are indifferent to God, they tend to think he is indifferent to them and their sin.

1:14-18 The terrible day of the Lord was near; the Babylonians would soon come and destroy Jerusalem. The day of the Lord is also near to us. God promises a final judgment, a day of worldwide destruction. The Babylonian conquest occurred just as surely and horribly as Zephaniah predicted. And God's final day of judgment is also sure—but so is his ability to save. To be spared from judgment, recognize that you have sinned, that your sin will bring judgment, that you cannot save yourself, and that God alone can save you.

1:4 2 Kgs 21:12-15; 23:4-7; 2 Chron 34:3-7
1:5 Lev 20:2-5; 2 Kgs 21:3-5; Acts 7:42
1:6 Isa 43:22; Rom 3:11
1:7 Ezek 39:17-21
1:8 Isa 10:12; 24:21-23
1:9 Neh 5:15
1:10 2 Chron 33:14; Neh 3:3; 12:39
1:11 Ezek 22:12; Hos 12:7,8
1:12 Jer 16:16; Amos 9:1-3; Obad 6
1:13 Deut 28:30; Isa 5:8,9; Amos 5:11
1:14 Ezek 7:16-18
1:15 Joel 2:2
1:16 Isa 2:12-15
1:17 Deut 28:28,29; Ps 79:3; 83:10; Jer 8:2; 9:22; Mt 15:13,14

1:18
Deut 32:21-25
Ps 49:6-9
Zeph 3:8

2:2
Ezek 33:11
Rom 2:4
2 Pet 3:9
2:3
2 Kgs 22:18,19
2 Chron 7:14,15
Ps 25:8,9
Zeph 3:12

2:4
Jer 25:19,20
47:1-7
Amos 1:6-8
2:5
Isa 14:29,31
2:7
Ps 85:1-3
Amos 9:14
Zeph 3:20
2:8
Ps 83:4-8
Zeph 2:10

18Your silver and gold will be of no use to you in that day of the Lord's wrath. You cannot ransom yourselves with it. For the whole land will be devoured by the fire of his jealousy. He will make a speedy riddance of all the people of Judah.

2 Gather together and pray, you shameless nation, 2while there still is time—before judgment begins, and your opportunity is blown away like chaff; before the fierce anger of the Lord falls and the terrible day of his wrath begins. 3Beg him to save you, all who are humble—all who have tried to obey.

Walk humbly and do what is right; perhaps even yet the Lord will protect you from his wrath in that day of doom.

Judgment will come to the surrounding nations

4Gaza, Ashkelon, Ashdod, Ekron—these Philistine cities, too, will be rooted out and left in desolation. 5And woe to you Philistines living on the coast and in the land of Canaan, for the judgment is against you, too. The Lord will destroy you until not one of you is left. 6The coastland will become a pasture, a place of shepherd camps and folds for sheep.

7There the little remnant of the tribe of Judah will be pastured. They will lie down to rest in the abandoned houses in Ashkelon. For the Lord God will visit his people in kindness and restore their prosperity again.

8"I have heard the taunts of the people of Moab and Ammon, mocking my people

1:18 *you cannot ransom yourselves with it,* implied. **2:5** *Philistines,* literally, "Cherethites [or Cretans]." With the Philistines they were part of a great wave of immigrants to the southern coast of Palestine around 1200 B.C.

ZEPHANIAH
served as a
prophet to
Judah from
640–621 B.C.

Climate of the times	Josiah was the last good king in Judah. His bold attempts to reform the nation and turn it back to God were probably influenced by Zephaniah.
Main message	A day will come when God, as Judge, will severely punish all nations. But after judgment, he will show mercy to all who have been faithful to him.
Importance of message	We will all be judged for our disobedience to God; but if we remain faithful to him, he will show us mercy.
Contemporary prophet	Jeremiah (627–586)

1:18 Money and wealth are good in their place, but they are useless before God. In this life, money can warp our perspective, giving us feelings of security and power. At the judgment, only Christ's redemptive work on our behalf matters. He alone will ransom us if we believe in him. Don't trust money, trust Christ.

2:1-3 There was still time to avert judgment. The people simply had to turn from their sins, humble themselves, and obey God. The Old Testament prophets announced news of destruction, but they also offered the only means of escape and protection—turning from sin and walking with God (Micah 6:8).

2:1-3 God's judgment against Judah came with ample warning, so the people had no excuse. God told them to (1) pray together, (2) beg to be saved, and (3) humbly do what is right. As God warned Judah, so he also warns us concerning the final day of judgment. We must (1) pray for forgiveness of sin, (2) ask God to bring us into his heavenly kingdom, and (3) humbly obey him. At the end of time, when God comes to judge, you cannot say, "But no one told me." Turn to God today for salvation.

2:4—3:8 God's judgment on the nations is universal—no one will escape. He punishes his own people for their sin; but he also punishes the surrounding nations for their wickedness, their idolatry, and their treatment of his people.

2:4 The Philistines lived west of Judah along the coast. Age-old enemies of Israel from the days of Joshua, they were known for their cruelty. God judged them for their idolatry and their constant taunting of Israel. These four cities were four of the five capitals.

The fifth (Gath) had already been destroyed.

2:7 All the prophets, even while prophesying doom and destruction, speak of a remnant—a small group of God's people who remain faithful to him and whom God will restore to the land. Although God said he would destroy Judah, he also promised to save a remnant, thus keeping his original covenant to preserve Abraham's descendants (Genesis 17:4-8). God is holy, and he cannot allow sin to continue. But he is also faithful to his promises. He "cannot stay angry" forever with Israel, or with you, if you are his child, because like a good parent he loves his children and always seeks their good.

2:8 The Moabites and Ammonites lived to the east of Judah, and they often attacked Judah. These nations, whose ancestors were born of Lot's incest with his daughters (Genesis 19:36-38), worshiped Chemosh and Molech (1 Kings 11:7). Moab's king once sacrificed his son on the city wall to stop an invasion (2 Kings 3:26, 27). God would judge them for their wickedness and for their treatment of God's people.

2:8-11 Judah had been taunted and mocked by the neighboring nations, Moab and Ammon, but God reminded them that he had "heard the taunts" (2:8), and that "they [would] receive the wages of their pride" (2:10). At times the whole world seems to mock God and ridicule those who have faith in him. In the midst of mockery or ridicule, remember that God hears and he will answer. Eventually, in God's timing, justice will be served.

and invading their land. ⁹Therefore as I live," says the Lord Almighty, God of Israel, "Moab and Ammon will be destroyed like Sodom and Gomorrah, and become a place of stinging nettles and salt pits and eternal desolation; those of my people who are left will plunder and possess them." ¹⁰They will receive the wages of their pride, for they have scoffed at the people of the Lord Almighty. ¹¹The Lord will do terrible things to them. He will starve out all those gods of foreign powers, and everyone shall worship him, each in his own land throughout the world.

¹²You Ethiopians, too, will be slain by his sword, ¹³and so will the lands of the north; he will destroy Assyria and make its great capital Nineveh a desolate wasteland like a wilderness. ¹⁴That once proud city will become a pastureland for sheep. All sorts of wild animals will have their homes in her. Hedgehogs will burrow there; the vultures and the owls will live among the ruins of her palaces, hooting from the gaping windows; the ravens will croak from her doors. All her cedar paneling will lie open to the wind and weather.

¹⁵This is the fate of that vast, prosperous city that lived in such security, that said to herself, "In all the world there is no city as great as I." But now—see how she has become a place of utter ruins, a place for animals to live! Everyone passing that way will mock, or shake his head in disbelief.

Judgment will come to Jerusalem

3 Woe to filthy, sinful Jerusalem, city of violence and crime. ²In her pride she won't listen even to the voice of God. No one can tell her anything; she refuses all correction. She does not trust the Lord, nor seek for God.

³Her leaders are like roaring lions hunting for their victims—out for everything that they can get. Her judges are like ravenous wolves at evening time, who by dawn have left no trace of their prey.

⁴Her "prophets" are liars seeking their own gain; her priests defile the Temple by their disobedience to God's laws.

⁵But the Lord is there within the city, and he does no wrong. Day by day his justice is more evident, but no one heeds—the wicked know no shame.

⁶"I have cut off many nations, laying them waste to their farthest borders; I have left their streets in silent ruin and their cities deserted without a single survivor to

2:10
Isa 16:6-10
Jer 48:28-31
Dan 5:20,21
Obad 3,4
Zeph 2:8
2:11
Joel 2:11
2:12
Isa 20:3,4; 43:3
2:13
Nah 3:7
2:14
Lev 11:13-19
Deut 14:11-18
Ps 102:6
Isa 14:23; 34:11
2:15
1 Kgs 9:7,8
Isa 10:12-14
22:2-7
Lam 2:15,16
Mt 27:39

3:1
Jer 6:6
3:2
Ps 78:22
Jer 32:33
3:3
Ps 10:8-10
Ezek 22:6-12
3:4
Hos 4:6-5
Mal 2:7-9
3:5
Jer 3:3; 6:15
3:6
Isa 10:1-33
15:1-9; 16:1-14
Zeph 2:4,5

2:9 The nations of Moab and Ammon began with Lot and his daughters after they escaped the destruction of evil Sodom and Gomorrah (Genesis 19). It is ironic that Moab and Ammon would face the same kind of destruction that God sent those evil cities. Sodom and Gomorrah symbolize total destruction—so complete that the exact location of those cities is still unknown.

2:12 Ethiopia, at the southern end of the Red Sea, controlled Egypt at this time. Zephaniah mentioned the large nation to the south and then moved to the nation of the north, Assyria. No one can escape deserved judgment. The Ethiopians were "slain by his sword" when the Assyrians invaded Egypt in 670 B.C. (See Isaiah 18 and Ezekiel 30:9 for other prophecies concerning Ethiopia.)

2:13 Assyria, though declining, was still the strongest military power of the day. She had dominated the world for three centuries, destroying anyone in her path. Nineveh, her large capital city, was considered impregnable. It was wiped out in 612 B.C. by the Babylonians, who would become the next world power.

2:15 To predict the destruction of Nineveh ten years before it happened would be equivalent to predicting the destruction of Tokyo, Moscow, or New York. Nineveh was the Middle Eastern center for culture, technology, and beauty. It had great libraries, buildings, and a vast irrigation system that created lush gardens in the city. The city wall was 60 miles long, 100 feet high, and over 30 feet wide and was fortified with 1,500 towers. Yet the entire city was destroyed so completely that its very existence was questioned until it was discovered, with great difficulty, by 19th century archaeologists. The area where it reigned in splendour had indeed become a pastureland.

3:1 After predicting the destruction of the surrounding nations, Zephaniah returned to the problem at hand—sin in Jerusalem. The city of God and God's people had become as sinful as its heathen neighbors. The people pretended worship and devotion to God, but in their hearts they had rejected him and they continued to be complacent about their sins. They no longer cared about the consequences of turning away from God.

3:2 Do you know people who refuse to listen when someone disagrees with their opinions? Those who are proud often refuse to listen to anything that contradicts their inflated self-esteem, and God's people had become so proud that they would not hear or accept God's correction. Do you find it difficult to listen to the spiritual counsel of others or God's words from the Bible? You will be more willing to listen when you consider how weak and sinful you really are.

3:3, 4 Leading God's people is a privilege and a responsibility. Through Zephaniah, God rebukes all types of leadership in Jerusalem—judges, prophets, and priests—because of their callous disobedience, irresponsibility, and sin. If you are a leader in the church, consider yourself in a privileged position, but be careful. God holds you responsible for the purity of your actions, the quality of your example, and the truth of your words.

3:5 Jerusalem's citizens, of all people, had no excuse for their sins. Jerusalem, where the Temple was located, was the religious center of the nation. But even though the people didn't follow God, he was "there within the city," present in the midst of corruption, persecution, and unbelief. No matter how spiritually desolate the world seems, God is there and he is at work. Ask yourself, "What is he doing now, and how can I be part of his work?"

remember what happened. 7I thought, 'Surely they will listen to me now—surely they will heed my warnings, so that I'll not need to strike again.' But no; however much I punish them, they continue all their evil ways from dawn to dusk and dusk to dawn. 8But the Lord says, "Be patient; the time is coming soon when I will stand up and accuse these evil nations. For it is my decision to gather together the kingdoms of the earth, and pour out my fiercest anger and wrath upon them. All the earth shall be devoured with the fire of my jealousy.

2. The day of hope

9"At that time I will change the speech of my returning people to pure Hebrew so that all can worship the Lord together. 10My scattered people who live in the Sudan, beyond the rivers of Ethiopia, will come with their offerings, asking me to be their God again. 11And then you will no longer need to be ashamed of your-selves, for you will no longer be rebels against me. I will remove all your proud and arrogant people from among you; there will be no pride or haughtiness on my holy mountain. 12Those who are left will be the poor and the humble, and they will trust in the name of the Lord. 13They will not be sinners, full of lies and deceit. They will live quietly, in peace, and lie down in safety, and no one will make them afraid."

14Sing, O daughter of Zion; shout, O Israel; be glad and rejoice with all your heart, O daughter of Jerusalem. 15For the Lord will remove his hand of judgment, and disperse the armies of your enemy. And the Lord himself, the King of Israel, will live among you! At last your troubles will be over—you need fear no more.

16On that day the announcement to Jerusalem will be, "Cheer up, don't be afraid. 17, 18For the Lord your God has arrived to live among you. He is a mighty Savior. He will give you victory. He will rejoice over you in great gladness; he will love you and not accuse you." Is that a joyous choir I hear? No, it is the Lord himself exulting over you in happy song:

"I have gathered your wounded and taken away your reproach. 19And I will deal severely with all who have oppressed you. I will save the weak and helpless ones, and bring together those who were chased away. I will give glory to my former exiles, mocked and shamed.

20"At that time, I will gather you together and bring you home again, and give you a good name, a name of distinction among all the peoples of the earth, and they will praise you when I restore your fortunes before your very eyes," says the Lord.

3:9 *I will change the speech . . . to pure Hebrew*, literally "I will change the speech of the peoples to a pure speech. . . ." See Isa 19:18.   **3:10** *in the Sudan*, implied.

Marginal references

3:8
Ezek 38:14-23
Zeph 1:18

3:9
Isa 19:18

3:10
Isa 11:11

3:11
Num 16:3
Isa 11:9
48:1,2; 54:4
Dan 9:16,20
Mt 3:9
Rom 2:17-20
9:33
1 Pet 2:6

3:12
Nah 1:7
Zeph 2:3
1 Pet 1:21

3:13
Lev 26:6
Hos 2:18

3:15
Ps 21:1-7
24:1-10
Isa 33:22

3:16
Isa 35:3,4
43:1-4
Hag 2:4,5
Heb 12:12,13

3:17
Isa 63:1
Heb 7:25

3:19
Isa 61:7
Ezek 39:26-29

3:20
Zeph 2:7

3:7 We may wonder how the Israelites could have such clear warnings and still not turn to God. The problem was not that they were ignorant, but that they had allowed sin to so harden them that they no longer cared to follow God. They refused to heed God's warnings and they refused to repent. If you disobey God now, your heart may grow hard, and you may lose your desire for God.

3:7 When God teaches, he expects us to listen and learn. If we do not learn, he must "strike again" in order to teach us. God doesn't want us to suffer, but he will continue to chasten us until we learn the lesson he has for us. Be teachable, not unreachable.

3:8 Don't try to avenge yourself. Be patient, and God's justice will come. In the last days, God will judge all people according to their deeds (Revelation 20:12). Justice will prevail; evildoers will be punished and the obedient will be blessed.

3:9 God will purify and unify language so that all his people from all nations will be able to worship him in unison. In the new earth, all believers will speak the same language; the confusion of languages at the Tower of Babel will be reversed (Genesis 11).

3:9 Throughout Scripture, prophets who mention judgment for God's people follow it with the promise of redemption. There is hope for those who obey and trust him. Today, as in Bible times, God offers redemption to those who turn to him.

3:12 God is opposed to the proud and haughty of every generation. But the poor and humble, both physically and spiritually, will be blessed because they trust in God. Self-reliance and arrogance have no place among God's people or in his kingdom.

3:14-18 We sin when we pursue happiness by cutting ourselves off from fellowship with God—the only person who can make us truly happy. Zephaniah points out that "great gladness" results when we allow God to be with us. We do that by faithfully following him and obeying his Word. Then God rejoices over us in song. If you want to be happy, draw close to the source of happiness by obeying God.

3:20 "Before your very eyes" does not mean this promise will be fulfilled during Zephaniah's generation. Rather, it means that the restoration will be an obvious work of the Lord.

3:20 The message of doom in the beginning of the book becomes a message of hope by the end. There will be a new day when God will bless his people. If the leaders in the church today were to hear a message from a prophet of God, the message would probably resemble the book of Zephaniah. Under Josiah's religious reforms, the people did return to God *outwardly*, but their hearts were far from him. Zephaniah encouraged the nation to gather together and pray for salvation. We must also ask ourselves, is our reform merely an outward show, or is it changing our hearts and lives? We need to gather together and pray, to walk humbly with God, to do what is right, and to hear the message of hope regarding the new world to come.

Daniel taken to Babylon 605 B.C.	Ezekiel taken to Babylon 597	Jerusalem falls 586		Babylon overthrown by Cyrus 539	Cyrus' decree allowing the exiles to return 538	Exiles return to Jerusalem 537	Temple construc begins 536

VITAL STATISTICS

PURPOSE:
To call the people to complete the rebuilding of the Temple

AUTHOR:
Haggai

TO WHOM WRITTEN:
The people living in Jerusalem and those who had returned from exile

DATE WRITTEN:
520 B.C.

SETTING:
The Temple in Jerusalem had been destroyed in 586 B.C. Cyrus allowed the Jews to return to their homeland and rebuild their Temple in 538 B.C. They began the work, but were unable to complete it. Through the ministry of Haggai and Zechariah, the Temple was completed (520–515 B.C.).

KEY VERSE:
"Is it then the right time for you to live in luxurious homes, when the Temple lies in ruins?" (1:4).

KEY PEOPLE:
Haggai, Zerubbabel, Joshua

KEY PLACE:
Jerusalem

SPECIAL FEATURES:
Haggai was the first of the post-exilic prophets. The other two were Zechariah and Malachi. The literary style of this book is simple and direct.

PRESSURES, demands, expectations, and tasks push in from all sides and assault our schedules. Do this! Be there! Finish that! Call them! It seems as though everyone wants something from us—family, employer, school, church, clubs. Soon there is little left to give, as we run out of energy and time. We find ourselves rushing through life, attending to the necessary, the immediate, and the urgent. Too often, the important is left in the dust. Our problem is not the volume of demands or lack of scheduling skills, but values—what is *truly* important to us.

Our values and priorities are reflected in how we use our resources—time, money, strength, and talent. Often our actions belie our words. We say God is number one, but then we relegate him to a lesser number on our "to do" lists.

Twenty-five centuries ago, a voice was heard, calling men and women to the right priorities. Haggai knew what was important and what had to be done, and he challenged God's people to respond.

In 586 B.C., the armies of Babylon had destroyed the Temple in Jerusalem—God's house, the symbol of his presence with them. In 538 B.C. King Cyrus decreed that Jews could return to their beloved city and rebuild the Temple. So they traveled to Jerusalem and began the work. But then they forgot their purpose and lost their priorities, as opposition and apathy brought the work to a standstill (Ezra 4:4, 5). Then Haggai speaks, calling them back to God's values. "Is it then the right time for you to live in luxurious homes, when the Temple lies in ruins?" (1:4). The people were more concerned with their own needs than with doing God's will and, as a result, they suffered. Then Haggai calls them to action, " 'Think it over,' says the Lord Almighty. 'Consider how you have acted, and what has happened as a result? Then go up into the mountains and bring down timber, and rebuild my Temple, and I will be pleased with it and appear there in my glory,' says the Lord" (1:7, 8). And God's message through his servant Haggai became the catalyst for finishing the work.

Although Haggai is a small book, it is filled with challenge and promise, reminding us of God's claim on our lives and our priorities. As you read Haggai, imagine him walking the streets and alleys of Jerusalem, urging the people to get back to doing God's work. And listen to Haggai speaking to you, urging you to reorder your priorities in accordance with God's will. What has God told you to do? Put aside all else, and obey him.

| Temple work halted 530 | Haggai, Zechariah become prophets; Temple work resumed 520 | Temple completed 516 | Ezra comes to Jerusalem 458 | Nehemiah comes to Jerusalem 445 |

THE BLUEPRINT

1. The call to rebuild the Temple (1:1–15)
2. Encouragement to complete the Temple (2:1–23)

When the exiles first returned from Babylon, they set about rebuilding the Temple right away. Although they began with the right attitudes, they slipped back into wrong behavior and the work came to a standstill. In the same way, we need to be on guard to keep our priorities straight. Our spiritual state is more important than our material state, but it is easy to get these confused. Remain active in your service to God and continue to put first things first.

MEGATHEMES

THEME	EXPLANATION	IMPORTANCE
Right priorities	God had given the Jews the assignment to finish the Temple in Jerusalem when they returned from captivity. After 15 years, they still had not completed it. They were more concerned about building their own homes than finishing God's work. Haggai told them to get their priorities straight.	It is easy to make other priorities more important than doing God's work. But God wants us to follow through and build up his kingdom. Don't stop and don't make excuses. Set your heart on what is right and do it. Get your priorities straight.
God's encouragement	Haggai encouraged the people as they worked. He assured them of the divine presence of the Holy Spirit, of final victory, and the hope that the Messiah would reign.	If God gives you a task, don't be afraid to get started. His resources are infinite. God will help you complete it by giving you encouragement from others along the way.

1. The call to rebuild the Temple

1:1
Ezra 2:2; 3:8
4:1-3,24
5:1,2; 6:6-14
Neh 12:1-7

1 Subject: a message from the Lord.

To: Haggai the prophet, who delivered it to Zerubbabel (son of Shealtiel), governor of Judah; and to Joshua (son of Josedech), the High Priest—for it was addressed to them.

When: In late August of the second year of the reign of King Darius I.

2"Why is everyone saying it is not the right time for rebuilding my Temple?" asks the Lord.

3, 4His reply to them is this: "Is it then the right time for you to live in luxurious

1:1ff The Jews who had returned from Babylon in 537 B.C. to rebuild the Temple in Jerusalem were not able to finish their work because they were frustrated by their enemies. There was no further work done on the Temple for over 15 years. In August, 520 B.C., Haggai delivered a message to encourage the people to rebuild the Temple! Haggai was probably born in captivity in Babylon and returned to Jerusalem with Zerubbabel in 537 B.C. (Ezra 1—2). Haggai and Zechariah, two prophets who encouraged the Temple rebuilding, are mentioned in Ezra 5:1.

1:1 Zerubbabel, governor of Judah, and Joshua, the High Priest, were key leaders in rebuilding the Temple. They had already reestablished the altar, but work had slowed. Haggai sent a letter of encouragement to these outstanding leaders.

1:2ff Haggai wanted to encourage the people to finish rebuilding the Temple. Opposition from hostile neighbors had caused them to feel discouraged, neglect the Temple, and neglect God. But Haggai's message turned them around and motivated them to pick up their tools and continue the work they had begun.

1:3–6 God asked his people, "How can you live in luxury when my house lies in ruins?" The Temple was a symbol of Judah's relationship with God, but it was still unfinished. The harder the people worked for themselves, the less they had, because they ignored their spiritual lives. The same happens to us. If we put God first, he will provide for our deepest needs. If we put him in any other place, all our efforts are futile. Caring only for your physical needs while ignoring your relationship with God will lead to ruin.

homes, when the Temple lies in ruins? 5Look at the result: 6You plant much but harvest little. You have scarcely enough to eat or drink, and not enough clothes to keep you warm. Your income disappears, as though you were putting it into pockets filled with holes!

7"Think it over," says the Lord Almighty. "Consider how you have acted, and what has happened as a result! 8Then go up into the mountains and bring down timber, and rebuild my Temple, and I will be pleased with it and appear there in my glory," says the Lord.

9"You hope for much but get so little. And when you bring it home, I blow it away—it doesn't last at all. Why? Because my Temple lies in ruins and you don't care. Your only concern is your own fine homes. 10That is why I am holding back the rains from heaven and giving you such scant crops. 11In fact, I have called for a drought upon the land, yes, and in the highlands, too; a drought to wither the grain and grapes and olives and all your other crops, a drought to starve both you and all your cattle, and ruin everything you have worked so hard to get."

12Then Zerubbabel (son of Shealtiel), the governor of Judah, and Joshua (son of Josedech), the High Priest, and the few people remaining in the land obeyed Haggai's message from the Lord their God; they began to worship him in earnest.

13Then the Lord told them (again sending the message through Haggai, his messenger), "I am with you; I will bless you." 14, 15And the Lord gave them a desire to rebuild his Temple; so they all gathered in early September of the second year of King Darius' reign, and volunteered their help.

2. Encouragement to complete the Temple

2 In early October of the same year, the Lord sent them this message through Haggai:

2Ask this question of the governor and High Priest and everyone left in the land: 3"Who among you can remember the Temple as it was before? How glorious it was! In comparison, it is nothing now, is it? 4But take courage, O Zerubbabel and Joshua and all the people; take courage and work, for 'I am with you,' says the Lord Almighty. 5'For I promised when you left Egypt that my Spirit would remain among you; so don't be afraid.'

6"For the Lord Almighty says, 'In just a little while I will begin to shake the heavens and earth—and the oceans, too, and the dry land— 7I will shake all

1:6
Lev 26:14-20
Deut 28:15-19,
22,24,30-34
Hag 1:9; 2:16
1:8
Ezra 3:7-13
1:9
Hag 1:6
1:10
Deut 28:24
1 Kgs 8:35,36
17:1
Joel 1:18-20
1:11
Lev 26:18-22
Deut 28:22-24
Jer 14:1-6
1:12
Ps 112:1
Eccles 12:13
Isa 50:10
Hag 1:1
1:13
2 Chron
20:15-17
Ps 46:7
Isa 8:9,10; 43:2
Hag 2:4,5
1:14,15
Ezra 3:1; 4:24
Neh 4:6; 11:2
Hag 1:1; 2:10

2:3
Ezra 3:12
2:5
Ex 29:45,46
2 Chron
20:15-17
Jn 14:15-17
2:6
Isa 13:10; 34:4
Ezek 38:20
Mt 24:29
Mk 13:24,25
Lk 21:25,26
Rev 6:12-17

1:6 Because the people had not given God first place in their lives, their material possessions did not satisfy. They concentrated on building and beautifying their own homes, but God's blessing was withheld because they no longer put him in first place. Moses predicted that this would be the result if the people neglected God (Deuteronomy 28:38–40).

1:9 Judah's problem was confused priorities: Like Judah, our priorities relating to work, family, and God's work are often confused. Jobs, homes, vacations, and leisure activities may rank higher on our list of importance than God. What is most important to you? Where does God rank?

1:11 Grain, grapes, and olives were Israel's major crops at this time.

1:14, 15 The people began rebuilding the Temple just 23 days after Haggai's first message. Rarely did a prophet's message produce such a quick response. How often we hear a sermon and respond, "That was an excellent point—we ought to do that," only to leave church and forget to act. These people put their words into action. When you hear a good sermon or lesson, ask what you should *do* about it, and then make plans to put it into practice.

2:1–9 This is Haggai's second message, given during the Feast of Tabernacles, October, 520 B.C. The older people could remember the incredible beauty of Solomon's Temple, destroyed 66 years earlier. Many were discouraged because the rebuilt Temple was inferior to Solomon's. But Haggai encouraged them

with God's message that the splendor of this Temple would surpass that of its predecessor. The most important part of the Temple is God's presence. Five hundred years later, Jesus would walk in the Temple courts.

2:4 "Take courage and work." Judah had already returned to worshiping God, and God had promised to bless their efforts. Now it was time for them to *work*. We must be people of prayer, Bible study, and worship; but eventually we must get out and *do* what God has in mind for us. He wants to change the world through us. God has given you a job to do in the church, at your place of employment, and at home. The time has come to take courage and work!

2:5 The Israelites had been led from captivity in Egypt to their Promised Land. They were God's chosen people, whom he guided and cared for. He never left them, despite their sins (Exodus 29:45, 46).

2:6 When God promised to shake all the nations with his judgment, he was speaking of both present judgment on evil nations and future judgment during the last days.

2:6–9 The focus shifts from the local Temple being rebuilt in Jerusalem to the worldwide reign of the Messiah on earth. The words "in just a little while" are not limited to the immediate historical context; they refer to God's control of history—he can act any time he chooses. God will act *in his time* (Hebrews 12:26, 27).

2:7–9 The Desire of All Nations (literally, "the Treasures," or "that

2:7
1 Kgs 8:11
Ps 80:1
Rom 15:9-13
Gal 3:8,9

2:8,9
Ps 84:8
Isa 9:6
Lk 2:14

2:10
Hag 1:14

2:12
Ex 29:37
Ezek 44:19

2:13
Lev 11:28,40
22:4-6
Num 19:11,12,
22

2:14
Prov 21:4,24
Isa 1:11-15
Tit 1:15

2:15
Ezra 4:24

2:16
Hag 1:9

2:18
Hag 2:10

nations, and the Desire of All Nations shall come to this Temple, and I will fill this place with my glory,' says the Lord Almighty. 8, 9'The future splendor of this Temple will be greater than the splendor of the first one! For I have plenty of silver and gold to do it! And here I will give peace,' says the Lord."

10In early December, in the second year of the reign of King Darius, this message came from the Lord through Haggai the prophet:

11Ask the priests this question about the law: 12"If one of you is carrying a holy sacrifice in his robes, and happens to brush against some bread or wine or meat, will it too become holy?"

"No," the priests replied. "Holiness does not pass to other things that way."

13Then Haggai asked, "But if someone touches a dead person, and so becomes ceremonially impure, and then brushes against something, does it become contaminated?"

And the priests answered, "Yes."

14Haggai then made his meaning clear. "You people," he said (speaking for the Lord), "were contaminating your sacrifices by living with selfish attitudes and evil hearts—and not only your sacrifices, but everything else that you did as a 'service' to me. 15And so everything you did went wrong. But all is different now, because you have begun to build the Temple. 16, 17Before, when you expected a twenty-bushel crop, there were only ten. When you came to draw fifty gallons from the olive press, there were only twenty. I rewarded all your labor with rust and mildew and hail. Yet, even so, you refused to return to me," says the Lord.

18, 19"But now note this: From today, this 24th day of the month, as the foundation of the Lord's Temple is finished, and from this day onward, I will bless you. Notice, I am giving you this promise now before you have even begun to rebuild the Temple structure, and before you have harvested your grain, and before the grapes and figs and pomegranates and olives have produced their next crops: *From this day I will bless you.*"

20Another message came to Haggai from the Lord that same day:

2:18, 19 *24th day of the month, i.e., of Kislev, which is early in December, according to our calendar.*

HAGGAI served as a prophet to Judah about 520 B.C. after the return from exile.	Climate of the times	The people of Judah had been exiled to Babylon in 586 B.C. and Jerusalem and the Temple had been destroyed. Under Cyrus, king of Persia, the Jews were allowed to return to Judah and rebuild their Temple.
	Main message	The people returned to Jerusalem to begin rebuilding the Temple, but they never finished. Haggai's message encouraged the people to finish rebuilding God's Temple.
	Importance of message	The Temple lay half-finished while the people lived in beautiful homes. Haggai warned them against putting their possessions and jobs ahead of God. We must put God first in our lives.
	Contemporary prophets	Zechariah (520–480)

---

which is choice") has two possible meanings: (1) It refers to the Messiah, Jesus, who, 500 years later, would enter the Temple and fill it with his splendor and his peace. (2) It could also refer to the riches which would flow into the Temple, given as blessings to God's people.

2:8, 9 God wanted the Temple to be rebuilt, and he had the resources to do it, but he needed willing hands. God has chosen to do his work through people. He provides the resources, but willing hands must do the work. Are your hands available for God's work in the world?

2:10–19 The example given in this message (delivered in December, 520 B.C.) makes it clear that holiness will not rub off on others, but contamination will. Now that the people were beginning to obey God, he promised to bless them. But they needed to understand that activities in the Temple would not clean up their sin; only repentance and obedience could do that. If we insist on

harboring wrong attitudes and sins or on maintaining close relationships with sinful people, we will be contaminated. Holy living will come only when we are empowered by God's Holy Spirit.

2:14 When a child eats spaghetti sauce, it isn't long before face, hands, and clothes are red. Sin and selfish attitudes produce the same result: they stain everything they touch. Even good works done for God can be tainted by sinful attitudes. The only remedy is God's cleansing.

2:18, 19 The people built the Temple foundation, and immediately God blessed them. He did not wait for the project to be completed. God often sends his blessing with our first few steps. He is eager to bless us!

2:20–23 Haggai's final message acknowledges that Haggai is merely the messenger who brings the word of the Lord. It is addressed to Zerubbabel, the governor of Judah.

21Tell Zerubbabel, the governor of Judah, "I am about to shake the heavens and **2:21** the earth, 22and to overthrow thrones and destroy the strength of the kingdoms of Hag 2:6 the nations. I will overthrow their armed might, and brothers and companions will kill each other. 23But when that happens, I will take you, O Zerubbabel my servant, and honor you like a signet ring upon my finger; for I have specially chosen you," says the Lord Almighty.

2:23 A signet ring was used to guarantee the authority and authenticity of a letter. It served as a signature when impressed in soft wax on a written document. God was reaffirming and guaranteeing his promise of a Messiah through David's line (Matthew 1:17).

2:23 God closes his message to Zerubbabel with this tremendous affirmation: "I have specially chosen you!" Such a proclamation is

ours as well—each of us has been chosen by God (Ephesians 1:4). This truth should make us see our value in God's eyes and motivate us to work for him. When you feel down, remind yourself, "God has chosen me!"

2:23 Haggai's message to the people sought to get their priorities straight, help them quit worrying, and motivate them to build the Temple. Like them, we often place a higher priority on our personal comfort than on God's work and true worship.

ZECHARIAH

THE FUTURE—that vast uncharted sea of unknown, holding joy or terror, comfort or pain, love or loneliness. Some people fear the days to come, wondering what evils lurk in their shadows; others consult seers and future-telling charlatans, trying desperately to see what will happen to them. But tomorrow's story is known only to God and to those special messengers, called prophets, to whom he has revealed a chapter or two.

A prophet's primary task was to proclaim the Word of the Lord, pointing out sin, explaining its consequences, and calling men and women to repentance and obedience. Elijah, Elisha, Isaiah, Jeremiah, Ezekiel, Hosea, and Amos stand with scores of others who faithfully delivered God's message despite rejection, ridicule, and persecution. And at times they were given prophetic visions foretelling coming events.

Nestled near the end of the Old Testament, among what are known as "minor prophets," is the book of Zechariah. As one of three post-exilic prophets, along with Haggai and Malachi, Zechariah ministered to the small remnant of Jews who had returned to Judah to rebuild the Temple and their nation. Like Haggai, he encouraged them to finish rebuilding the Temple, but his message went far beyond those physical walls and contemporary issues. With spectacular apocalyptic imagery and graphic detail, Zechariah told of the Messiah, the one whom God would send to rescue his people and to reign over all the earth. Zechariah is one of our most important prophetic books, giving detailed messianic references which were clearly fulfilled in the life of Jesus Christ. The rebuilding of the Temple, he says, was just the first act in the drama of the end and the ushering in of the messianic age. Zechariah proclaimed a stirring message of hope to these ex-captives and exiles—their King was coming!

Jesus is Messiah, the promised "great deliverer" of Israel. Unlike Zechariah's listeners, we can look back at his ministry and mission. As you study his prophecy, you will see details of Christ's life which were written 500 years before their fulfillment. Read and stand in awe of our God who keeps his promises. But there is also a future message which has not yet been fulfilled—the return of Christ at the end of the age. As you read Zechariah, therefore, think through the implications of this promised event. *Your King is coming,* and he will reign forever and ever.

God knows and controls the future. We may never see a moment ahead, but we can be secure if we trust in him. Read Zechariah and strengthen your faith in God—he alone is your hope and security.

VITAL STATISTICS

PURPOSE:
To give hope to God's people by revealing God's future deliverance through the Messiah

AUTHOR:
Zechariah

TO WHOM WRITTEN:
The Jews in Jerusalem who had returned from their captivity in Babylon and to God's people everywhere

DATE WRITTEN:
Chapters 1—8 were written about 520—518 B.C. Chapters 9—14 were written around 480 B.C.

SETTING:
The exiles had returned from Babylon to rebuild the Temple, but the work had been thwarted and stalled. Haggai and Zechariah confronted the people with their task and encouraged them to complete it.

KEY VERSES:
"Rejoice greatly, O my people! Shout with joy! For look—your King is coming! He is the Righteous One, the Victor! Yet he is lowly, riding on a donkey's colt! I will disarm all peoples of the earth, including my people in Israel, and he shall bring peace among the nations. His realm shall stretch from sea to sea, from the river to the ends of the earth" (9:9, 10).

KEY PEOPLE:
Zerubbabel, Joshua

KEY PLACE:
Jerusalem

SPECIAL FEATURES:
This book is the most apocalyptic and messianic of all the minor prophets.

THE BLUEPRINT

A. MESSAGES WHILE REBUILDING THE TEMPLE (1:1—8:23)
1. Zechariah's night visions
2. Zechariah's words of encouragement

Zechariah encouraged the people to put away the sin in their lives and to continue rebuilding the Temple. His visions described the judgment of Israel's enemies, the blessings to Jerusalem, and the need for God's people to remain pure—avoiding hypocrisy, superficiality, and sin. Zechariah's visions provided hope for the people. We also need to carefully follow the instruction to remain pure until Christ returns again.

B. MESSAGES AFTER COMPLETING THE TEMPLE (9:1—14:21)

Besides encouragement and hope, Zechariah's messages were also a warning that God's messianic Kingdom would not begin as soon as the Temple was complete. Israel's enemies would be judged and the King would come, but they would face many difficult circumstances before experiencing the blessing of the messianic Kingdom. We too may face much sorrow, disappointment, and tribulation before coming into Christ's eternal Kingdom.

MEGATHEMES

THEME	EXPLANATION	IMPORTANCE
God's jealousy	God was angry at his people for neglecting his prophets through the years, and he was concerned that they not follow the careless and false leaders who exploited them. Disobedience was the root of their problems and the cause of their misery. God was jealous for their devotion to him.	God is jealous for our devotion. To avoid Israel's ruin, don't walk in their steps. Don't reject God, follow false teachers, or lead others astray. Turn to God, faithfully obey his Word, and make sure you are leading others correctly.
Rebuild the Temple	The Jews were discouraged. they were free from exile, yet the Temple was not completed. Zechariah encouraged them to rebuild it. God would both protect his workmen and also empower them by his Holy Spirit to carry out and complete his work.	More than the rebuilding of the Temple was at stake—the people were staging the first act in God's wonderful drama of the end times. Those of us who believe in God must complete his work. To do so we must have the Holy Spirit's help. God will empower us with his Spirit.
The King is coming	The Messiah will come both to rescue people from sin and to reign as king. He will establish his kingdom, conquer all his enemies, and rule over all the earth. Everything will one day be under his loving and powerful control.	The Messiah came as a servant to die for us. He will return as a victorious king. At that time, he will usher in peace through-out the world. Submit to his leadership now to be ready for the King's triumphant return.
God's protection	There was opposition to God's plan in Zechariah's day, and he prophesied future times of trouble. But God's Word endures. God remembers the agreements he makes with his people. He cares for his people and will deliver them from all the world powers that oppress them.	Although evil is still present, God's infinite love and personal care have been demonstrated through the centuries. God keeps his promises. Although our bodies may be destroyed, we need never fear our ultimate destiny if we love and obey him.

A. MESSAGES WHILE REBUILDING THE TEMPLE (1:1—8:23)

Zechariah begins by describing eight visions that came to him at night. Then he gives a collection of messages about the crowning of Joshua, answers about feasting and fasting, and encouragment to continue rebuilding the Temple. We, too, can be inspired to continue following God in faithfulness throughout our lives.

1. Zechariah's night visions

Return to the Lord

1:1
Ezra 5:1
Neh 12:4,16

1:2
2 Kgs 23:26
2 Chron 36:16

1:3
2 Chron 15:4
Neh 9:28
Isa 31:6
Joel 2:12

1:4
2 Chron 24:19
29:6-10; 36:15
Ezra 9:7

1:5
Deut 28:45
Jer 12:16
Amos 9:10

1:8
Neh 8:15
Isa 41:19; 55:13

1 *Subject: messages from the Lord. These messages from the Lord were given to Zechariah (son of Berechiah, and grandson of Iddo the prophet) in early November of the second year of the reign of King Darius.*

²The Lord Almighty was very angry with your fathers. ³But he will turn again and favor you if only you return to him. ⁴Don't be like your fathers were! The earlier prophets pled in vain with them to turn from all their evil ways.

"Come, return to me," the Lord God said. But no, they wouldn't listen; they paid no attention at all.

⁵, ⁶Your fathers and their prophets are now long dead, but remember the lesson they learned, that *God's Word endures!* It caught up with them and punished them. Then at last they repented.

"We have gotten what we deserved from God," they said. "He has done just what he warned us he would."

Zechariah sees a man among the myrtle trees

⁷The following February, still in the second year of the reign of King Darius, another message from the Lord came to Zechariah (son of Berechiah and grandson of Iddo the prophet), in a vision in the night: ⁸I saw a Man sitting on a red horse that was standing among the myrtle trees beside a river. Behind him were other horses, red and bay and white, each with its rider.

⁹An angel stood beside me, and I asked him, "Sir, what are all those horses for?"

"I'll tell you," he replied.

1:8 *each with its rider,* implied.

ZECHARIAH served as a prophet to Judah about 520 B.C., after the return from exile.	*Climate of the times*	The exiles had returned from captivity to rebuild their Temple. But work on the Temple had stalled and the people were neglecting their service to God.
	Main message	Zechariah, like Haggai, encouraged the people to finish rebuilding the Temple. His visions gave the people hope. He told the people of a future king who would one day establish an eternal kingdom.
	Importance of message	Even in times of discouragement and despair, God is working out his plan. God protects and guides us; we must trust and follow him.
	Contemporary prophets	Haggai (about 520 B.C.)

1:1 Born in Babylon during the exile, Zechariah was a fairly young man when he returned to Jerusalem in 538 B.C. King Cyrus of Persia had defeated Babylon in 539 and decreed that captives in exile could return to their homelands. Zechariah and Haggai were among the first to leave. Zechariah, a prophet and a priest, began ministering at the same time as the prophet Haggai (520–518 B.C.). His first prophecy was delivered two months after Haggai's first prophecy.

Like Haggai, Zechariah encouraged the people to continue rebuilding the Temple, whose reconstruction had been halted for nearly 15 years. Zechariah combated the people's spiritual apathy, despair over pressures from their enemies, and discouragement about the smaller scale of the new Temple foundation. Neglect of our spiritual priorities can be just as devastating to fulfilling God's purpose today.

1:2, 3 The familiar phrase, "Like father, like son," implies that children turn out like their parents. But God warned Israel *not* to be like their fathers who disobeyed him and reaped the consequences—his judgment. We are responsible before God for our actions. We aren't trapped by our heredity or environment, and we can't use these as excuses for our sins. We can choose, and we must individually return to God and follow him.

1:5, 6 The words God had spoken through his prophets a century earlier, before the captivity, still applied to Zechariah's generation, and they are still relevant for us. God's Word endures. Because God's Word endures, we must read, study, and apply it. Learn the lessons of God's Word so you will not have to repeat the mistakes of others.

1:7–17 The horses and their colors were symbols of God's involvement in world governments. The full meaning of the colors is unknown, although the red horse is often associated with war and the white horse with final victory.

¹⁰Then the rider on the red horse—he was the Angel of the Lord—answered me, "The Lord has sent them to patrol the earth for him."

¹¹Then the other riders reported to the Angel of the Lord, "We have patrolled the whole earth, and everywhere there is prosperity and peace."

¹²Upon hearing this, the Angel of the Lord prayed this prayer: "O Lord Almighty, for seventy years your anger has raged against Jerusalem and the cities of Judah. How long will it be until you again show mercy to them?"

¹³And the Lord answered the angel who stood beside me, speaking words of comfort and assurance.

¹⁴Then the angel said, "Shout out this message from the Lord Almighty: Don't you think I care about what has happened to Judah and Jerusalem? I am as jealous as a husband for his captive wife. ¹⁵I am very angry with the heathen nations sitting around at ease, for I was only a little displeased with my people, but the nations afflicted them far beyond my intentions. ¹⁶Therefore the Lord declares: I have returned to Jerusalem filled with mercy; my Temple will be rebuilt, says the Lord Almighty, and so will all Jerusalem. ¹⁷Say it again: The Lord Almighty declares that the cities of Israel will again overflow with prosperity, and the Lord will again comfort Jerusalem and bless her and live in her."

Zechariah sees four horns and four blacksmiths

¹⁸Then I looked and saw four animal horns!

¹⁹"What are these?" I asked the angel.

He replied, "They represent the four world powers that have scattered Judah, Israel, and Jerusalem."

²⁰Then the Lord showed me four blacksmiths.

²¹"What have these men come to do?" I asked.

The angel replied, "They have come to take hold of the four horns that scattered Judah so terribly, and to pound them on the anvil and throw them away."

Zechariah sees a man with a yardstick

2 When I looked around me again, I saw a man carrying a yardstick in his hand. ²"Where are you going?" I asked.

"To measure Jerusalem," he said. "I want to see whether it is big enough for all the people!"

³Then the angel who was talking to me went over to meet another angel coming toward him.

⁴"Go tell this young man," said the other angel, "that Jerusalem will some day be so full of people that she won't have room enough for all! Many will live outside the city walls, with all their many cattle—and yet they will be safe. ⁵For the Lord himself will be a wall of fire protecting them and all Jerusalem; he will be the glory of the city.

⁶,⁷" 'Come, flee from the land of the north, from Babylon,' says the Lord to all

Cross-references (margin):

1:10
Job 2:1,2
Zech 1:19
4:4,5,13; 6:4

1:11
Zech 1:15
1 Thess 5:3

1:12
2 Chron 36:21
Ps 74:10; 69:5
Isa 64:9-12
Jer 25:11,12
Dan 9:2
Rev 6:10

1:13
Isa 40:1,2
Zech 1:17

1:14
Zech 1:17

1:16
Ezra 6:14,15
Isa 12:1
54:8-10
Zech 2:10

1:17
Isa 52:9; 54:8

1:19
1 Kgs 22:11

1:21
Zech 1:18,19
9:12-16
10:3-5; 12:2-6

2:1
Ezek 40:3,5

2:2
Jer 31:39
Rev 21:15-17

2:4
Ezek 38:11
Jer 1:6
Dan 1:17
1 Tim 4:12

2:5
Isa 60:18,19
Zech 2:10,11

2:6
Num 16:26
Deut 28:64
Jer 3:18; 31:10
Rev 18:4

1:11 The angel saw that all the nations were at peace and prosperous while Israel was still conquered and despised. But God was planning a change. He had released his people, and he would allow them to return and rebuild his Temple.

1:12 Seventy years was the time God had decreed for Israel to remain in captivity (Jeremiah 25:11; 29:10). This time was now completed, and the angel asked God to act swiftly to complete the promised return of his people to Jerusalem.

1:13 God's people had lived under his judgment for 70 years during their captivity in Babylon. But now God spoke words of comfort and assurance. God promises that when we return to him, he will heal us (Hosea 6:1). If you feel wounded and torn by the events of your life, turn to God so he can heal and comfort you.

1:14 Captive women often faced all kinds of abuse while separated from their husbands or even in their presence. A loving husband would be tormented with jealousy, anger, and longing for

his wife. The people just coming out of captivity understood Zechariah's language. It revealed God's love for his people and his desire to have them as his own.

1:15 Although the heathen nations afflicted God's people beyond his intentions, he was not powerless to stop them. God used these nations to punish his sinful people. When they went beyond his plans by trying to destroy Israel as a nation, he intervened.

1:16 The Temple foundation had been completed, and the entire Temple was finished four years later under Zerubbabel's leadership. Jerusalem's wall was completed a few years after that under Nehemiah's leadership.

1:18-21 The horns were the four world powers who oppressed Israel—Egypt, Assyria, Babylon, and Medo-Persia. The blacksmiths (1:20) were the nations used to overthrow Israel's enemies. God raised them up to judge the oppressors of his people.

ZECHARIAH'S VISIONS	Vision	Reference	Significance
	Zechariah sees scouts reporting to God that the surrounding nations who have oppressed Judah are living in careless and sinful ease.	1:7–17	Israel was asking, "Why isn't God punishing the wicked?" Wicked nations may prosper, but not forever. God will bring upon them the judgment they deserve.
	Zechariah sees four animal horns, representing the four world powers that oppressed and scattered the people of Judah and Israel. Then he sees four blacksmiths who will pound the horns.	1:18–21	God will do what he promised. After the evil nations have carried out his will in punishing his people, God will destroy those nations for their sin.
	Zechariah sees a man measuring the city of Jerusalem. The city will one day be full of people and God himself will be a wall around the city.	2:1–13	The city will be restored in God's future kingdom. God will keep his promise to protect his people.
	Zechariah sees Joshua, the High Priest, standing before God. His filthy rags are exchanged for clean clothes; Satan's accusations against him are rejected by God.	3:1–10	Joshua's position as High Priest pictures how the filthy rags of sin are replaced with the pure linen of God's righteousness. Christ has taken our rags of sin and replaced them with God's righteousness. (See Ephesians 4:24; 1 John 1:9.)
	Zechariah sees a lampstand that is continually kept burning by an unlimited reservoir of oil. This picture reminds the people that it is only through God's Spirit that they will succeed, not by their own might and resources.	4:1–14	The Spirit of God is given without measure. Human effort does not make a difference. The work of God is not accomplished in human strength.
	Zechariah sees a flying scroll which represents God's curse.	5:1–4	By God's Word and Spirit every person will be judged. The individual's sin is the focus here, not the sins of the nation. Each person is responsible for his or her deeds; no one has an excuse. God's curse is a symbol of destruction; all sin will be judged and removed.
	Zechariah sees a vision of a woman in a basket. She represents the wickedness of the nations. The angel packed the woman back into the basket and sent her back to Babylon.	5:5–11	Sins of the individual were judged in the last vision (5:1–4); now sin is being removed from society. Sin has to be eradicated in order to clean up the nation and the individual.
	Zechariah sees a vision of four horses and chariots. The horses represent God's judgment on the world—one is sent north, the direction from which most of Judah's enemies came. The other horses are patrolling the world, ready to execute judgment at God's command.	6:1–8	Judgment will come upon those who oppress God's people—it will come in God's time and at his command.

his exiles there; 'I scattered you to the winds but I will bring you back again. Escape, escape to Zion now!' says the Lord.

8"The Lord of Glory has sent me against the nations that oppressed you, for he who harms you sticks his finger in Jehovah's eye!

9" 'I will smash them with my fist and their slaves will be their rulers! *Then you will know it was the Lord Almighty who sent me.* 10Sing, Jerusalem, and rejoice! For I have come to live among you,' says the Lord. 11, 12"At that time many nations will be converted to the Lord, and they too shall be my people; I will live among them all. *Then you will know it was the Lord Almighty who sent me to you.* And Judah shall be the Lord's inheritance in the Holy Land, for God shall once more choose to bless Jerusalem.'

13"Be silent, all mankind, before the Lord, for he has come to earth from heaven, from his holy home."

Zechariah sees the High Priest

3 Then the Angel showed me (in my vision) Joshua the High Priest standing before the Angel of the Lord; and Satan was there too, at the Angel's right hand, accusing Joshua of many things.

2And the Lord said to Satan, "I reject your accusations, Satan; yes, I, the Lord, for I have decided to be merciful to Jerusalem—I rebuke you. I have decreed mercy to Joshua and his nation; they are like a burning stick pulled out of the fire."

3Joshua's clothing was filthy as he stood before the Angel of the Lord.

4Then the Angel said to the others standing there, "Remove his filthy clothing." And turning to Joshua he said, "See, I have taken away your sins, and now I am giving you these fine new clothes."

5, 6Then I said, "Please, could he also have a clean turban on his head?" So they gave him one.

Then the Angel of the Lord spoke very solemnly to Joshua and said, 7"The Lord

2:8	Deut 32:10 / Isa 60:7-14
2:9	Isa 10:32 / 11:15; 14:2 / 19:16 / Jer 27:7
2:10	Zech 9:9
2:11	Ex 19:5,6 / Deut 32:9 / Isa 52:15 / Mic 4:2
2:13	Deut 26:15 / 2 Chron 30:27 / Hab 2:20
3:1	Ezra 5:2 / Job 1:6-12 / 2:1-8 / Hag:1:1 / Zech 6:11
3:3	Ezra 9:15 / Isa 64:6 / Dan 9:18
3:4	Isa 43:25; 61:10 / Zech 3:9 / Mt 22:11-13 / Lk 15:22 / Rev 7:14
3:5	Ex 28:37-40 / Lev 8:9 / Ezek 44:18

3:2 *I reject your accusations, Satan,* literally, "The Lord rebuke you, O Satan; even the Lord, who has chosen Jerusalem, rebuke you. Is not this a brand plucked out of the fire?"

2:6, 7 Many of the captive Israelites did not return to Jerusalem because they preferred to stay with the wealth they had accumulated in Babylon. But Zechariah instructed them to leave Babylon quickly. This was an urgent request because Babylon would be destroyed and because its decadent culture would cause his people to forget their spiritual priorities. About 90 percent of the Israelites rejected these warnings and remained in Babylon.

2:8 Believers are precious to God (Psalm 116:15), they are his very own children (Psalm 103:13). Treating any believer unkindly is the same as treating God that way. As Jesus told his disciples, when we help others we are helping him; when we neglect them we are neglecting him (Matthew 25:34–46). Be careful, therefore, how you treat fellow believers—that is the way you are treating God.

2:9–12 *Me* (2:9) may refer to the Messiah who, in the end, will judge all who have oppressed God's people. God promises to live among his people, and he says that many nations will come to know him (John 1:4; Revelation 21:3).

2:11, 12 God did not forget his words to Abraham, "The entire world will be blessed because of you" (Genesis 12:3). Abraham, the father of the nation of Israel, was promised that his descendants would bless the whole world. Since the coming of Jesus, the Messiah, this promise is being fulfilled—people from all nations are coming to God through him.

3:1 Joshua was Israel's High Priest when the remnant returned to Jerusalem and began rebuilding the walls (Haggai 1:1, 12; 2:4).

3:1 Satan accused Joshua (representing the nation of Israel here). The accusations were accurate—Joshua stood in filthy rags (sins). Yet God revealed his mercy, stating that he chose to save his people anyway. Satan is always accusing people of their sins

before God (Job 1:6; Colossians 2:15). But he greatly misunderstands the breadth of God's mercy and forgiveness toward those who believe in him. Satan the Accuser will ultimately be destroyed (Revelation 12:10), while everyone who is a believer will be saved (John 3:16).

3:2 God punished Judah through the fire of great trials, but he rescued her before she was completely destroyed.

3:2–4 Zechariah's vision graphically portrays how we obtain God's mercy. We do nothing ourselves. It is at God's initiative that our filthy garments (sins) are removed, and God provides us with new, clean clothes (the righteousness of Christ—2 Corinthians 5:21 [see textual note]; Revelation 19:8). All we need to do is repent and ask God to forgive us. When Satan tries to make you feel dirty and unworthy, remember that the clean clothes of Christ's righteousness make you worthy to draw near to God.

3:5–7 There was no priesthood during the exile, so it had to be reinstated upon the return to the land. The Greek name for Joshua is Jesus, "Jehovah saves." This Joshua should not be confused with the warrior of the book of Joshua. Both the warrior Joshua and the High Priest Joshua, however, have been seen as symbols of Jesus, the Messiah.

3:7–10 In this vision, Joshua was installed as High Priest. One of the High Priest's duties was to offer a sacrifice on the Day of Atonement to make amends for all the sins of the people. The priest was the mediator between God and the nation. Thus, he represented the coming Messiah (Isaiah 11:1), who would change the entire order of God's dealing with man's sin (Hebrews 10:8–14 explains this in detail). Jesus, the Messiah, was the High Priest who offered, once for all, the sacrifice of himself to take away our sins. In his new order, every Christian is a priest offering a holy, cleansed life to God (1 Peter 2:9; Revelation 5:10).

3:7
1 Kgs 3:14
Isa 62:9

3:8
Isa 4:2; 8:18
11:1; 53:2
Jer 33:15
Ezek 12:11
24:24
Zech 6:12

3:10
1 Kgs 4:25
Mic 4:4

4:2
Ex 25:31,37
37:17-24
Zech 5:2
Rev 4:5

4:3
Zech 4:11,12,
14
Rev 11:4

4:6
2 Chron 14:11
Ezra 3:1,2
Isa 11:2-4
Hag 2:4,5
Eph 6:17

4:7
Ezra 3:11-13
6:15-17
Rev 5:9-13

4:9
Ezra 3:8-10
5:16
Zech 6:12,13

4:10
Amos 7:2,7,8
Hag 2:3
Zech 3:9

Almighty declares: 'If you will follow the paths I set for you and do all I tell you to, then I will put you in charge of my Temple, to keep it holy; and I will let you walk in and out of my presence with these angels. 8Listen to me, O Joshua the High Priest, and all you other priests, you are illustrations of the good things to come. Don't you see?—Joshua represents my servant the Branch whom I will send. 9He will be the Foundation Stone of the Temple that Joshua is standing beside, and I will engrave this inscription on it seven times: *I will remove the sins of this land in a single day.* 10And after that,' the Lord Almighty declares, 'you will all live in peace and prosperity and each of you will own a home of your own where you can invite your neighbors.' "

Zechariah sees the golden lampstand

4 Then the angel who had been talking with me woke me, as though I had been asleep.

2"What do you see now?" he asked.

I answered, "I see a gold lampstand holding seven lamps, and at the top there is a reservoir for the olive oil that feeds the lamps, flowing into them through seven tubes. 3And I see two olive trees carved upon the lampstand, one on each side of the reservoir. 4What is it, sir?" I asked. "What does this mean?"

5"Don't you really know?" the angel asked.

"No, sir," I said, "I don't."

6Then he said, "This is God's message to Zerubbabel: 'Not by might, nor by power, but by my Spirit, says the Lord Almighty—you will succeed because of my Spirit, though you are few and weak.' 7Therefore no mountain, however high, can stand before Zerubbabel! For it will flatten out before him! And Zerubbabel will finish building this Temple with mighty shouts of thanksgiving for God's mercy, declaring that all was done by grace alone."

8Another message that I received from the Lord said:

9"Zerubbabel laid the foundation of this Temple, and he will complete it. (Then you will know these messages are from God, the Lord Almighty.) 10Do not despise this small beginning, for the eyes of the Lord rejoice to see the work begin, to see the plumbline in the hand of Zerubbabel. For these seven lamps represent the eyes of the Lord that see everywhere around the world."

11Then I asked him about the two olive trees on each side of the lampstand, 12and about the two olive branches that emptied oil into gold bowls through two gold tubes.

13"Don't you know?" he asked.

"No, sir," I said.

3:9 *I will engrave this inscription on it seven times,* literally, "See the stone with seven facets I have set before Joshua, and I will engrave its inscription." **4:7** *will finish building this Temple,* literally, "He will bring forth the capstone." *all was done by grace alone,* or, "with mighty shouts, 'How beautiful it is!' " or, "The Lord bless it!"

3:8, 9 These verses were fulfilled hundreds of years later by Jesus Christ, who is also called the Foundation (1 Corinthians 3:11). God said, "I will remove the sins of this land in a single day," and this was fulfilled in Christ who "died once for the sins of all . . . that he might bring us safely home to God" (1 Peter 3:18). You cannot remove your sins by your own effort. You must allow God to remove them through Christ.

3:10 God promises that each person will have his own home during Christ's reign (see also Micah 4:4). This is a symbol of peace and prosperity.

4:6 Zerubbabel was the governor of Judah in the days of Zechariah. He was given the responsibility of rebuilding the Temple in Jerusalem (Haggai 1:1; 2:23). While the prophets Haggai and Zechariah gave the moral and spiritual encouragement to resume work on the Temple, Zerubbabel saw that the task was carried out. As the work was being completed, the prophets encouraged Zerubbabel and told him of a time when spiritual apathy and foreign oppression would forever be abolished.

4:6 Many people believe that to survive in this world a person must be tough, strong, unbending, and harsh. But God says, "You will succeed because of my Spirit, though you are few and weak." The key words are "because of my Spirit." It is *only* through his Spirit that anything of lasting value is accomplished. The returned exiles were indeed weak—harassed by their enemies, tired, discouraged, and poor. But actually they had God on their side! As you live for God, determine not to trust in your own strength or abilities. Instead, depend on God and work in the power of his Spirit!

4:9 The Temple was completed in 516 B.C.

4:10 Many of the older Jews were disheartened when they realized this new Temple would not match the size and beauty of the previous one. But bigger and more beautiful is not always better. What you do for God may seem small and insignificant at the time, but God rejoices in what is right, not necessarily in what is big. Be faithful in the small opportunities. Begin where you are and do what you can, and leave the results to God.

14Then he told me, "They represent the two anointed ones who assist the Lord of all the earth."

Zechariah sees a flying scroll

5 I looked up again and saw a scroll flying through the air.

2"What do you see?" he asked.

"A flying scroll!" I replied. "It appears to be about thirty feet long and fifteen feet wide!"

3"This scroll," he told me, "represents the words of God's curse going out over the entire land. It says that all who steal and lie have been judged and sentenced to death."

4"I am sending this curse into the home of every thief and everyone who swears falsely by my name," says the Lord Almighty. "And my curse shall remain upon his home and completely destroy it."

Zechariah sees a flying basket

5Then the angel left me for awhile, but he returned and said, "Look up! Something is traveling through the sky!"

6"What is it?" I asked.

He replied, "It is a bushel basket filled with the sin prevailing everywhere throughout the land."

7Suddenly the heavy lead cover on the basket was lifted off, and I could see a woman sitting inside the basket!

8He said, "She represents wickedness," and he pushed her back into the basket and clamped down the heavy lid again.

9Then I saw two women flying toward us, with wings like those of a stork. And they took the bushel basket and flew off with it, high in the sky.

10"Where are they taking her?" I asked the angel.

11He replied, "To Babylon where they will build a temple for the basket, to worship it!"

Zechariah sees four chariots

6 Then I looked up again and saw four chariots coming from between what looked like two mountains made of brass. 2The first chariot was pulled by red horses, the second by black ones, 3the third by white horses and the fourth by dappled-greys.

4"And what are these, sir?" I asked the angel.

5He replied, "These are the four heavenly spirits who stand before the Lord of all the earth; they are going out to do his work. 6The chariot pulled by the black horses will go north, and the one pulled by white horses will follow it there, while the dappled-greys will go south."

7The red horses were impatient to be off, to patrol back and forth across the earth, so the Lord said, "Go. Begin your patrol." So they left at once.

8Then the Lord summoned me and said, "Those who went north have executed my judgment and quieted my anger there."

5:11 *To Babylon* (the land of Shinar). Babylon had, by the time of Zechariah, become a symbol, the center of world idolatry and wickedness. **6:6** *will follow it there,* or, "will go west." **6:7** *red,* implied. **6:8** *Those who went north have executed my judgment,* implied.

4:14 The two anointed ones may be Joshua and Zerubbabel, dedicated for this special task. Also note that in Revelation 11:4, two prophets (witnesses) arise to prophesy to the nations during the time of tribulation. They will be killed but will rise again.

5:1–11 The judgment of the flying scroll was leveled against those who violated God's law, specifically by stealing and lying. The woman in the basket personified wickedness, and so this vision showed that wickedness would be not only severely punished (the vision of the flying scroll), but also banished (the vision of the woman in the basket).

5:9–11 Wickedness and sin (as represented by the woman) were taken away from Israel. One day sin will be removed from the entire earth. When Jesus Christ reigns, all sin will be eliminated and people will live in safety and security. When Christ died, he removed sin's power and penalty. When we trust him to forgive us, he removes the penalty of sin and gives us the power to overcome sin in our lives. When he returns, he will remove sin's presence from the earth.

6:8 Zechariah said the execution of judgment had quieted God's anger. God is angry with sin and with the wicked (Psalm 7:11), and his anger is expressed in judgment. Much as we like to concentrate on God's love and mercy, anger and judgment are

Cross-refs: 4:14 Dan 9:24-26; 5:1 Jer 36:1-6, Ezek 2:9,10, Rev 10:2,8-11; 5:3 Ex 20:15, Deut 27:15-26, Isa 24:6, Jer 26:6; 5:4 Lev 14:34-45, Deut 7:26, Jer 2:26, Hab 2:9-11, Mal 3:5; 5:6 Lev 19:36, Amos 8:5; 5:8 Hos 12:7, Mic 6:11; 5:9 Lev 11:13-19, Deut 14:11-18, Ps 104:17, Jer 8:7; 5:11 Isa 11:11, Dan 1:2; 6:1 Zech 6:5; 6:5 Dan 7:2; 11:4, Zech 6:1, Mt 24:31, Rev 7:1; 6:6 Jer 1:14,15, 25:9, Ezek 1:4, Dan 11:5,6, 9,40; 6:8 Zech 1:15

2. Zechariah's words of encouragement

The symbolic crowning of Joshua

⁹In another message the Lord said:

^{10, 11}"Heldai, Tobijah, and Jedaiah will bring gifts of silver and gold from the Jews exiled in Babylon. The same day they arrive, meet them at the home of Josiah (son of Zephaniah), where they will stay. Accept their gifts and make from them a crown from the silver and gold. Then put the crown on the head of Joshua (son of Josedech) the High Priest. ¹²Tell him that the Lord Almighty says, 'You represent the Man who will come, whose name is "The Branch"—he will grow up from himself—and will build the Temple of the Lord. ¹³To him belongs the royal title. He will rule both as King and as Priest, with perfect harmony between the two!'

¹⁴"Then put the crown in the Temple of the Lord, to honor those who gave it—Heldai, Tobijah, Jedaiah, and also Josiah. ¹⁵These three who have come from so far away represent many others who will some day come from distant lands to rebuild the Temple of the Lord. And when this happens you will know my messages have been from God, the Lord Almighty. But none of this will happen unless you carefully obey the commandments of the Lord your God."

The people urged to be just and merciful

7 Another message came to me from the Lord in late November of the fourth year of the reign of King Darius.

²The Jews of the city of Bethel had sent a group of men headed by Sharezer, the chief administrative officer of the king, and Regem-melech, to the Lord's Temple at Jerusalem, to seek his blessing, ³and to speak with the priests and prophets about whether they must continue their traditional custom of fasting and mourning during the month of August each year, as they had been doing so long.

⁴This was the Lord's reply:

⁵"When you return to Bethel, say to all your people and your priests, 'During those seventy years of exile when you fasted and mourned in August and October, were you really in earnest about leaving your sins behind, and coming back to me? No, not at all! ⁶And even now in your holy feasts to God, you don't think of me, but only of the food and fellowship and fun. ⁷Long years ago, when Jerusalem was prosperous and her southern suburbs out along the plain were filled with people, the prophets warned them that this attitude would surely lead to ruin, as it has.' "

^{8, 9}Then this message from the Lord came to Zechariah. "Tell them to be honest and fair—and not to take bribes—and to be merciful and kind to everyone. ¹⁰Tell them to stop oppressing widows and orphans, foreigners and poor people, and to

6:12 *he will grow up from himself,* literally, "he will grow up in his place."

Cross-references: 6:10 Ezra 7:14-16; 8:26-30; Ps 21:3; Song 3:11; Zech 3:1. 6:12 Isa 4:2,3; 11:1; Jer 23:5,6; Zech 3:8; 4:6-9. 6:13 Ps 110:4; Isa 9:6; 11:10; Dan 7:13,14; Heb 3:1; 4:14-16; 10:12,13. 6:15 Isa 56:6-8; 60:10; Zech 3:7. 7:2 Zech 8:21. 7:3 Ezra 3:10-12. 7:5 Isa 1:11,12; Zech 1:12; Mt 5:16-18; 6:2,5,16; 23:5. 7:7 Deut 34:3; Jer 17:26; 22:21; Zech 1:4. 7:8 2 Sam 9:7; Mic 6:8; Zech 8:16. 7:10 Ex 22:22; Deut 24:14-18; Prov 22:22,23; Zech 8:17.

also part of his righteous character. If you have unconfessed or habitual sin in your life, confess it and turn away from it. Confession releases God's mercy, but refusing to repent invites his judgment.

6:9–15 This vision is about the Messiah, the King-Priest. In the days of the kings and during the exile, Judah's government was to be ruled by two distinct persons—the king, ruling the nation's political life, and the High Priest, ruling its religious life. Kings and priests had often been corrupt. God was telling Zechariah that someone would come who would rule as both king and priest—an unlikely combination for that day. This King-Priest, the Messiah, would rule both over his people and in the hearts of those who believe in him.

6:15 Some of God's promises are conditional—we must obey him to receive them. The rebuilding of the Temple required careful obedience. God would protect the people as long as they obeyed. Casual or occasional obedience, the result of a half-hearted or divided commitment, would not lead to blessing. Many of God's blessings come to us as a result of diligent obedience. Inconsistent obedience can't produce consistent blessing.

7:1ff The fourth year of King Darius' reign was 518 B.C. For the previous 70 years, the people had been holding a fast in August to remember the destruction of Jerusalem. Now that Jerusalem was being rebuilt, they came to the Temple to ask if they had to continue this annual fast. God did not answer their question directly. Instead, he told them that their behavior was more important than their religious holidays. What he wanted from his people was honesty in business and compassion for the weak.

7:5–7 The Israelites had lost their sincere desire for God. Zechariah told them that they were celebrating religious rites—such as fasting or feasting on holy days—without a proper attitude of repentance or worship. They were doing these rites with no thought of God. When you go to church, pray, or fellowship with other believers, are you doing these from habit or for what you get out of it? God says that an attitude of worship without a sincere desire for him will lead to ruin.

7:8–10 God is just, and he wants his people to reflect his justice in their lives. Here God tells Zechariah what he expects of his people: (1) be honest and fair; (2) don't take bribes; (3) be merciful and kind. This sounds like an easy prescription for justice, but are you fair and just in *all* your dealings—the small as well as the large?

stop plotting evil against each other. 11Your fathers would not listen to this message. They turned stubbornly away and put their fingers in their ears to keep from hearing me. 12They hardened their hearts like flint, afraid to hear the words that God, the Lord Almighty, commanded them—the laws he had revealed to them by his Spirit through the early prophets. That is why such great wrath came down on them from God. 13I called but they refused to listen, so when they cried to me, I turned away. 14I scattered them as with a whirlwind among the far-off nations. Their land became desolate; no one even traveled through it; the Pleasant Land lay bare and blighted."

Judah will be blessed

8 Again the Lord's message came to me:
2"The Lord Almighty says, I am greatly concerned—yes, furiously angry—because of all that Jerusalem's enemies have done to her. 3Now I am going to return to my land and I, myself, will live within Jerusalem, and Jerusalem shall be called 'The Faithful City,' and 'The Holy Mountain,' and 'The Mountain of the Lord Almighty.'"

4The Lord Almighty declares that Jerusalem will have peace and prosperity so long that there will once again be aged men and women hobbling through her streets on canes, 5and the streets will be filled with boys and girls at play. 6The Lord says, "This seems unbelievable to you—a remnant, small, discouraged as you are—but it is no great thing for me. 7You can be sure that I will rescue my people from east and west, wherever they are scattered. 8I will bring them home again to live safely in Jerusalem, and they will be my people, and I will be their God, just and true and yet forgiving them their sins!"

9The Lord Almighty says, "Get on with the job and finish it! You have been listening long enough! For since you began laying the foundation of the Temple, the prophets have been telling you about the blessings that await you when it's finished. 10Before the work began there were no jobs, no wages, no security; if you left the city, there was no assurance you would ever return, for crime was rampant.

11"But it is all so different now!" says the Lord Almighty. 12"For I am sowing peace and prosperity among you. Your crops will prosper; the grapevines will be weighted down with fruit; the ground will be fertile, with plenty of rain; all these blessings will be given to the people left in the land. 13'May you be as poor as Judah,' the heathen used to say to those they cursed! But no longer! For now

8:8 forgiving them their sins, literally, "I will be their God in truth and in righteousness."

7:11
Neh 9:29
Acts 7:57

7:12
2 Chron 36:16
Jer 17:1; 26:19

7:13
Prov 1:24-28
Isa 1:15; 50:2
Jer 11:10,14

7:14
Jer 12:10; 44:6

8:4
Isa 65:20-22
Lam 2:20

8:5
Jer 30:19,20
Zech 2:4

8:6
Jer 32:17,27

8:7
Ps 107:2,3
Amos 9:14,15

8:8
Zech 10:10

8:9
Ezra 5:1; 6:14

8:10
Isa 19:2
Amos 3:6; 9:4
Hag 1:6-11
2:16-19

8:12
Gen 27:28
1 Kgs 17:1
Hag 1:10

8:13
Deut 28:37
Ps 72:17
Jer 29:18
Dan 9:11
Mic 5:7
Zech 10:6-9
14:11

7:12 Zechariah explained to the people that their ancestors brought God's great wrath on themselves by hardening their hearts. Any sin seems more natural the second time—as we become hardened, each repetition is easier. Ignoring or refusing God's warning hardens you each time you do wrong. Zechariah compared the resulting attitudes to the hardest substance the Jews knew—flint. Read God's Word and apply it to your life. Sensitivity and submission to God's Word can soften your heart and allow you to live as you should.

8:3 One day Christ will reign in his kingdom on earth. There all his people will live with him. This truth encourages us to look forward to the Messiah's reign.

8:4, 5 In troubled times, the very old and very young are the first to suffer and die. But both groups are plentiful in this vision, filling the streets with their normal everyday activities. This is a sign of the complete peace and prosperity of God's new earth.

8:6 The remnant was the small group of exiles who had returned from Babylon to rebuild Jerusalem and the Temple. Struggling to survive in the land, they became discouraged over the opposition they often faced from hostile neighbors. It was hard to believe that one day God himself would reign from this city and that their land would enjoy great peace and plenty.

8:6 What is impossible to us is "no great thing" for God. God reminded Zechariah of this truth when predicting his deliverance of Jerusalem. Our God is all-powerful; he can do anything! When confronting seemingly impossible tasks or situations, remember that "with God, everything is possible!" (Matthew 19:26).

8:8 This promise of forgiveness and unity refers to all God's people wherever they may be found, not just the Jews. (For his promise to the Jews specifically, see Exodus 6:6, 7; Deuteronomy 6:4ff; Ruth 1; Jeremiah 31:1,33.)

8:9 God had to give the Temple workers a little push to get them moving. He said, "Get on with the job and finish it! You have been listening long enough!" We need to listen to what God says, but once he has made our course of action plain, we need to "get on with the job and finish it."

8:13-15 For more than 15 years God and his prophets had been urging the people to finish building the Temple. Once more God encouraged them with visions of the future. We are tempted to slow down for many reasons: people aren't responding; we feel physically or emotionally drained; the workers are uncooperative; the work is distasteful, too difficult, or not worth the effort. God's promises about the future should encourage us now. He knows what the results of our labors will be, and thus he can give us a perspective that will help us continue in our work for him.

'Judah' is a word of blessing, not a curse. 'May you be as prosperous and happy as Judah is,' they'll say. So don't be afraid or discouraged! Get on with rebuilding the Temple! ¹⁴, ¹⁵If you do, I will certainly bless you. And don't think that I might change my mind. I did what I said I would when your fathers angered me and I promised to punish them, and I won't change this decision of mine to bless you. ¹⁶Here is your part: Tell the truth. Be fair. Live at peace with everyone. ¹⁷Don't plot harm to others; don't swear that something is true when it isn't! How I hate all that sort of thing!" says the Lord.

¹⁸Here is another message that came to me from the Lord Almighty:

¹⁹"The traditional fasts and times of mourning you have kept in July, August, October, and January are ended. They will be changed to joyous festivals if you love truth and peace! ²⁰, ²¹People from around the world will come on pilgrimages and pour into Jerusalem from many foreign cities to attend these celebrations. People will write their friends in other cities and say, 'Let's go to Jerusalem to ask the Lord to bless us, and be merciful to us. I'm going! Please come with me. Let's go now!' ²²Yes, many people, even strong nations, will come to the Lord Almighty in Jerusalem to ask for his blessing and help. ²³In those days ten men from ten different nations will clutch at the coat sleeves of one Jew and say, 'Please be my friend, for I know that God is with you.' "

B. MESSAGES AFTER COMPLETING THE TEMPLE (9:1—14:21)

After the Temple was completed, Zechariah gave several prophecies about Israel's future, which describe the first and second comings of Jesus Christ. This book contains more about the person, work, and future glory of Christ than the other minor prophets combined. Israel's King would come, but he would be rejected by his people. They would later repent and be restored to God. The King who is coming is our king. May we be found faithful and pure in his sight when we meet him face to face.

Israel's enemies will be judged

9 This is the message concerning God's curse on the lands of Hadrach and Damascus, for the Lord is closely watching all mankind, as well as Israel. ²"Doomed is Hamath, near Damascus, and Tyre, and Zidon, too, shrewd though they be. ³Though Tyre has armed herself to the hilt, and become so rich that silver is like dirt to her, and fine gold like dust in the streets, ⁴yet the Lord will dispossess her, and hurl her fortifications into the sea; and she shall be set on fire and burned to the ground.

⁵"Ashkelon will see it happen and be filled with fear; Gaza will huddle in desperation and Ekron will shake with terror, for their hopes that Tyre would stop the enemies' advance will all be dashed. Gaza will be conquered, her king killed, and Ashkelon will be completely destroyed.

⁶"Foreigners will take over the city of Ashdod, the rich city of the Philistines. ⁷I will yank her idolatry out of her mouth, and pull from her teeth her sacrifices that she eats with blood. Everyone left will worship God and be adopted into Israel as a new clan: the Philistines of Ekron will intermarry with the Jews, just as the

8:19 *July, August, October, and January,* literally, "fourth, fifth, seventh, and tenth months," of the Hebrew calendar. **9:1** *for the Lord is closely watching all mankind,* or, "for the cities of Syria belong to the Lord, as much as do the tribes of Israel."

Cross-references (margin)
8:14 Jer 4:28; 29:11-14; Mic 4:10-13
8:16 Zech 8:3
8:17 Jer 4:2; Zech 5:3,4; 7:10; Mal 3:5
8:19 Esth 8:17; Isa 12:1; Zech 7:3-5; 8:16; Lk 1:74,75
8:20 Zech 2:11; 14:16
8:22 Isa 49:6,22,23; 52:15; 60:3-12
8:23 Isa 45:14; 60:14
9:1 Gen 14:15; Amos 1:3-5; 3:12
9:2 Num 13:21; 1 Kgs 17:9; 2 Kgs 25:21; Isa 23:1-18; Ezek 28:3-5; 12:21-26
9:3 1 Kgs 10:27; Isa 23:8; Ezek 27:33
9:4 Isa 23:1-7; Ezek 27:26-36; 28:16,18; Joel 3:8
9:5 Jer 47:4-7; Zeph 2:4

8:14–17 God promised to give his people rich rewards; and he reassured the people that despite punishments, he would not change his mind. But he also said they had a job to do. God will be faithful, but we also have responsibilities: to tell the truth, be fair, and live peacefully. If you expect God to do his part, be sure to do yours.

8:20–22 There will come a time when fasting for sins will be replaced by feasting and joy. People from all nations will worship God and ask for his blessing and help. This is also promised in 2:11, 12.

8:23 In the past, Jerusalem had often borne the brunt of cruel jokes from other nations. The city was not respected; its citizens had sinned so much that God let them be "kicked around" by their enemies. But eventually, says Zechariah, Jerusalem will be a holy place—respected highly throughout the world because its people will have a change of heart toward God. People from other nations will see how God has rewarded his people for their faithfulness and will want to be included in their great blessings.

9:1–17 The last six chapters of the book are two messages delivered late in Zechariah's life which point to the Messiah and his second coming. Some of these prophecies were fulfilled before the Messiah came, perhaps by Alexander the Great; others were fulfilled during the Messiah's time on earth; and others will be fulfilled when he returns. Those who oppressed Jerusalem—Syria, Philistia, Phoenicia—would be crushed. The promised king would come—first as a servant on a donkey's colt, then as a powerful ruler and judge.

Jebusites did so long ago. 8And I will surround my Temple like a guard to keep invading armies from entering Israel. I am closely watching their movements and I will keep them away; no foreign oppressors will again overrun my people's land.

9:8
Isa 54:14
Zech 14:11

The coming of the King

9"Rejoice greatly, O my people! Shout with joy! For look—your King is coming! He is the Righteous One, the Victor! Yet he is lowly, riding on a donkey's colt! 10I will disarm all peoples of the earth, including my people in Israel, and he shall bring peace among the nations. His realm shall stretch from sea to sea, from the river to the ends of the earth.

9:9
Isa 9:6,7; 12:6
57:15
Jer 23:5,6
Zeph 3:5
Mt 11:29

11"I have delivered you from death in a waterless pit because of the covenant I made with you, sealed with blood. 12Come to the place of safety, all you prisoners, for there is yet hope! I promise right now, I will repay you two mercies for each of your woes! 13Judah, you are my bow! Ephraim, you are my arrow! Both of you will be my sword, like the sword of a mighty soldier brandished against the sons of Greece."

9:10
Ps 72:17
Isa 57:18,19
Mic 4:2-10; 5:4
Rev 11:15
9:11
Ex 24:8
Heb 9:10-26
9:12
Isa 40:2; 52:2
Joel 3:16

14The Lord shall lead his people as they fight! His arrows shall fly like lightning; the Lord God shall sound the trumpet call and go out against his enemies like a whirlwind off the desert from the south. 15He will defend his people and they will subdue their enemies, treading them beneath their feet. They will taste victory and shout with triumph. They will slaughter their foes, leaving horrible carnage everywhere. 16, 17The Lord their God will save his people in that day, as a Shepherd caring for his sheep. They shall shine in his land as glittering jewels in a crown. How wonderful and beautiful all shall be! The abundance of grain and grapes will make the young men and girls flourish; they will be radiant with health and happiness.

9:13
Dan 11:32-34
Joel 3:6-8
Mic 4:2,3
9:14
Josh 6:4,5
Isa 18:3; 27:13
9:16
Ps 27:4
Isa 40:10; 62:3
Jer 31:12,14
Ezek 34:22-26
Hag 2:23

Israel and Judah are lost sheep

10 Ask the Lord for rain in the springtime, and he will answer with lightning and showers. Every field will become a lush pasture. 2How foolish to ask the idols for anything like that! Fortune-tellers' predictions are all a bunch of silly lies; what comfort is there in promises that don't come true? Judah and Israel have been led astray and wander like lost sheep; everyone attacks them, for they have no shepherd to protect them.

10:1
Deut 11:14
Hos 6:3
10:2
Jer 23:25-27
Ezek 21:29
Mic 3:6-11
Mt 9:36

3"My anger burns against your 'shepherds'—your leaders—and I will punish them—these goats. For the Lord Almighty has arrived to help his flock of Judah.

10:3
Isa 10:12
Ezek 34:2,7,12

9:10 *from the river to the ends of the earth,* or, "to the ends of the land" of Palestine. Either interpretation is possible from the Hebrew text, but many other passages indicate Christ's universal rule.

9:8 Several centuries after Zechariah's day Antiochus IV Epiphanes would invade Israel; and in A.D. 70, Titus, a Roman general, completely destroyed the Temple. This promise, therefore, may have been conditional upon the people's obedience. The day will come, however, when God's people will never again have to worry about invading enemies (Joel 3:17).

9:9 The Triumphal Entry of Jesus riding into Jerusalem (Matthew 21:1–11) is predicted here 500 years before it happened. Just as this prophecy was fulfilled when Jesus came to earth, so the prophecies of his second coming are just as certain to come true. We are to be ready for his return, for he is coming!

9:10 When we view two distant mountains, they appear to be close together, perhaps even to touch each other. But as we approach them, we can see that they are in fact far apart, even separated by a huge valley. This is the situation with many Old Testament prophecies. Verse 9 was clearly fulfilled in Christ's first coming, but verse 10 can now be seen to refer to his second coming. At that time all nations will be subject to Christ. His reign will cover the whole earth. In Philippians 2:9, 10, we are told that every knee will bow to Christ and every tongue confess him as Lord.

9:11 Covenants in Old Testament times were sealed or confirmed with blood, much as we would sign our name to a contract. The old covenant was sealed by the blood of sacrifices, pointing to the blood Christ would shed at Calvary, his "signature" which confirmed God's new covenant with his people. Because God had made a covenant with these people, he delivered them from the "waterless pit," the cistern-like prison of exile.

9:13–17 *Ephraim* is another name for the Northern Kingdom of Israel. After Solomon's reign, the kingdom was divided into the Northern Kingdom (called Israel or Ephraim) and the Southern Kingdom (called Judah). This prophecy says that all Israel, north and south, will someday be reunited. The first part of this chapter tells how God will help his people avoid war; now God explains that he will help his people when war is inevitable. Verses 14–17 explain how the Jews will win over the Greeks, but it is also a figurative picture of the ultimate future victory over evil by God's people.

10:2 How often we create idols of money, power, fame, or success, and then expect them to give us happiness and security. But these idols can't supply what we need any more than a stone image can make it rain. How foolish it is to trust in idols. Instead, trust God's promises for your future.

10:5
2 Sam 22:8

10:6
Isa 54:8
Zech 1:16; 8:11

10:7
Isa 38:19; 54:13

10:8
Isa 5:26
7:18,19
Jer 33:22
Ezek 36:11

10:9
Deut 30:1-4
1 Kgs 8:47,48
Jer 51:50
Ezek 6:9

10:10
Isa 11:11-16
49:19-21
Mic 7:11,12

10:11
Ps 66:10-12
Isa 11:15,16
19:5-7
Zeph 2:13
Ezek 30:13

10:12
Isa 2:5
Mic 4:5

11:1
Ezek 31:3

11:3
Jer 2:15
25:34-36; 50:44

11:5
Jer 50:7
Ezek 34:2-6
Hos 12:8

11:6
Isa 9:19-21
Jer 13:14

11:7
Lev 27:32
Ps 27:4; 90:17
Ezek 37:16-23
Jn 17:21-23

I will make them strong and glorious like a proud steed in battle. 4From them will come the Cornerstone, the Peg on which all hope hangs, the Bow that wins the battle, the Ruler over all the earth. 5They will be mighty warriors for God, grinding their enemies' faces into the dust beneath their feet. The Lord is with them as they fight; their enemy is doomed.

6"I will strengthen Judah, yes, and Israel too; I will re-establish them because I love them. It will be as though I had never cast them all away, for I, the Lord their God, will hear their cries. 7They shall be like mighty warriors. They shall be happy as with wine. Their children, too, shall see the mercies of the Lord and be glad. Their hearts shall rejoice in the Lord. 8When I whistle to them, they'll come running, for I have bought them back again. From the few that are left, their population will grow again to former size. 9Though I have scattered them like seeds among the nations, still they will remember me and return again to God; with all their children, they will come home again to Israel. 10I will bring them back from Egypt and Assyria, and resettle them in Israel—in Gilead and Lebanon; there will scarcely be room for all of them! 11They shall pass safely through the sea of distress, for the waves will be held back. The Nile will become dry—the rule of Assyria and Egypt over my people will end."

12The Lord says, "I will make my people strong with power from me! They will go wherever they wish, and wherever they go, they will be under my personal care."

11 Open your doors, O Lebanon, to judgment. You will be destroyed as though by fire raging through your forests. 2Weep, O cypress trees, for all the ruined cedars; the tallest and most beautiful of them are fallen. Cry in fear, you oaks of Bashan, as you watch the thickest forests felled. 3Listen to the wailing of Israel's leaders—all these evil shepherds—for their wealth is gone. Hear the young lions roaring—the princes are weeping, for their glorious Jordan valley lies in ruins.

The two shepherds

4Then said the Lord my God to me, "Go and take a job as shepherd of a flock being fattened for the butcher. 5This will illustrate the way my people have been bought and slain by wicked leaders, who go unpunished. 'Thank God, now I am rich!' say those who have betrayed them—their own shepherds have sold them without mercy. 6And I won't spare them either," says the Lord, "for I will let them fall into the clutches of their own wicked leaders, and they will slay them. They shall turn the land into a wilderness and I will not protect it from them."

7So I took two shepherd's staffs, naming one "Grace" and the other "Union," and

10:11 *the sea of distress,* or, "the Sea of Egypt," referring to the Red Sea which the people of Israel were miraculously brought through when God delivered them out of slavery the first time. **11:1** *to judgment,* implied.

10:4 Zechariah's prophecy, 500 years before Christ's first coming, calls him a Cornerstone (see also Isaiah 28:16), a Peg (see also Isaiah 22:23, 24), and a Ruler (see also Genesis 49:10; Micah 5:2). This Messiah would be strong, stable, victorious, and trustworthy—in all, the answer to Israel's problems. Only in the Messiah will all the promises to God's people be fulfilled.

10:6 One day God will unite all his people. This verse tells about his reuniting the Jews (see also Jeremiah 31:10). This was a startling idea: the people of the Northern Kingdom of Israel were so completely absorbed into other cultures after 722 B.C. that a regathering could not be done by human means, but only by God.

10:6, 12 God promises to strengthen his people, and 10:12 reveals that this strength comes from God. When we stay close to God, his Spirit enables us to do his will, despite the obstacles. When we stray from God, we are cut off from our power source.

10:10 This pictured return from Egypt and Assyria was a symbolic way of saying that the people would be returned from all the countries where they had been dispersed. Egypt and Assyria evoked memories of slavery and separation.

10:11 The "sea of distress" refers to the Red Sea through which the Israelites were miraculously delivered from Egypt. As the Israelites returned once again from Egypt and other lands, they would once again be protected by God's miraculous power.

11:1–17 In this message, God asks Zechariah to act out the roles of two different kinds of shepherds. The first shepherd was to demonstrate how God would reject his people (the sheep) because they rejected him (the shepherd). The second shepherd was to demonstrate how God would give over his people to evil shepherds. (See Ezekiel 34.)

11:4 God told Zechariah to take a job as shepherd of a flock of sheep being fattened for butchering. The flock represented the people feeding on their own greed and evil desires until they were ripe for God's judgment.

11:7 Zechariah took two shepherd's staffs and named them *Grace* and *Union;* he broke the first one ("Grace") to show that God's gracious covenant with his people was broken and he broke the second one ("Union") to show "that the bond of unity between Judah and Israel was broken" (11:14).

I fed the flock as I had been told to do. 8And I got rid of their three evil shepherds in a single month. But I became impatient with these sheep—this nation—and they hated me too.

11:8
Hos 5:7

9So I told them, "I won't be your shepherd any longer. If you die, you die; if you are killed, I don't care. Go ahead and destroy yourselves!"

11:9
Ps 69:22-28
Jer 15:2,3

10And I took my staff called "Grace" and snapped it in two, showing that I had broken my contract to lead and protect them. 11That was the end of the agreement. Then those who bought and sold sheep, who were watching, realized that God was telling them something through what I did.

12And I said to their leaders, "If you like, give me my pay, whatever I am worth; but only if you want to."

11:12
1 Kgs 3:5
Mt 26:15
27:9,10
Jn 13:2,27-30

So they counted out thirty little silver coins as my wages.

13And the Lord told me, "Use it to buy a field from the pottery makers—this magnificent sum they value you at!"

11:13
Mt 27:3-10,12
Acts 1:18,19

So I took the thirty coins and threw them into the Temple for the pottery makers. 14Then I broke my other staff, "Union," to show that the bond of unity between Judah and Israel was broken.

11:14
Zech 11:6

15Then the Lord told me to go again and get a job as a shepherd; this time I was to act the part of a worthless, wicked shepherd.

11:15
Jer 2:26,27
Ezek 13:3
Zech 11:17

16And he said to me, "This illustrates how I will give this nation a shepherd who will not care for the dying ones, nor look after the young, nor heal the broken bones, nor feed the healthy ones, nor carry the lame that cannot walk; instead, he will eat the fat ones, even tearing off their feet. 17Woe to this worthless shepherd who doesn't care for the flock. God's sword will cut his arm and pierce through his right eye; his arm will become useless and his right eye blinded."

11:16
Jer 23:2,22
Ezek 34:2-6

11:17
Zech 10:2
11:15

God will destroy his people's enemies

12 This is the fate of Israel, as pronounced by the Lord, who stretched out the heavens and laid the foundation of the earth, and formed the spirit of man within him:

12:1
Gen 2:7
Ps 102:23,26
Isa 57:16
Jer 51:15

2"I will make Jerusalem and Judah like a cup of poison to all the nearby nations that send their armies to surround Jerusalem. 3Jerusalem will be a heavy stone burdening the world. And though all the nations of the earth unite in an attempt to move her, they will all be crushed.

12:2
Isa 51:17,22,23
Jer 49:12

12:3
Dan 2:34,35
Mt 21:44

4"In that day," says the Lord, "I will bewilder the armies drawn up against her,

11:13 *Use it to buy a field,* literally, "Throw it to the pottery-makers."

11:8 The identity of the three evil shepherds is not known, but God knew they were unfit to shepherd his people, and so he removed them. Obviously they could not be blamed for the people's sins because the people kept right on sinning without them.

11:10, 11 Breaking the staff called *Grace* showed that God was revoking his agreement to protect Israel, because the people had rejected the good shepherd.

11:12 To pay this shepherd 30 pieces of silver was an insult—this was the price paid to an owner for a slave gored by an ox (Exodus 21:32). This is also the amount Judas received for betraying Jesus (Matthew 27:3-9). The priceless Messiah was sold for the price of a slave.

11:13 "Toss it into the Temple treasury" is sometimes translated "cast it to the potter." Potters were in the lowest social class. The "magnificent sum" (a sarcastic comment) was so little that it could be thrown to the potter. It is significant that the 30 pieces of silver paid to Judas for betraying Jesus were returned to the Temple and used to buy a potter's field (Matthew 27:1-10).

11:14 Because the people rejected the Messiah, God would reject them—symbolized by Zechariah breaking the staff called *Union.* Not long after Zechariah's time, the Jews began to divide

into numerous factions—Pharisees, Sadducees, Essenes, Herodians, and Zealots. The discord among these groups was a key factor leading to the destruction of Jerusalem in A.D. 70.

11:15-17 Israel would not only reject the true shepherd; they would accept instead a foolish (worthless) shepherd. This shepherd would serve his own concerns rather than the concerns of his flock and would destroy rather than defend them (Revelation 13:7). "Woe" is his rightful condemnation. Because he trusted his arm (military might) and his eye (intellect), God would destroy both areas.

11:17 It is a great tragedy for God's people when their leaders fail to care for them adequately. God holds leaders particularly accountable for the condition of his people. The New Testament tells church leaders, "When we teachers of religion, who should know better, do wrong, our punishment will be greater than it would be for others" (James 3:1). If God puts you in a position of leadership, remember that it is also a place of great responsibility.

12:1-14 This chapter pictures the final siege against the people of Jerusalem.

12:3, 4 This speaks of a great future battle against Jerusalem. Some say it is Armaggedon, the last great battle on earth. Those who go against God's people will not prevail forever. Evil, pain, and oppression will one day be abolished once and for all.

and make fools of them, for I will watch over the people of Judah, but blind all her enemies.

5"And the clans of Judah shall say to themselves, 'The people of Jerusalem have found strength in the Lord Almighty, their God.'

6"In that day I will make the clans of Judah like a little fire that sets the forest aflame—like a burning match among the sheaves; they will burn up all the neighboring nations right and left, while Jerusalem stands unmoved. 7The Lord will give victory to the rest of Judah first, before Jerusalem, so that the people of Jerusalem and the royal line of David won't be filled with pride at their success.

8"The Lord will defend the people of Jerusalem; the weakest among them will be as mighty as King David! And the royal line will be as God, like the Angel of the Lord who goes before them! 9For my plan is to destroy all the nations that come against Jerusalem.

10"Then I will pour out the spirit of grace and prayer on all the people of Jerusalem, and they will look on him they pierced, and mourn for him as for an only son, and grieve bitterly for him as for an oldest child who died. 11The sorrow and mourning in Jerusalem at that time will be even greater than the grievous mourning for the godly King Josiah, who was killed in the valley of Megiddo.

12, 13, 14"All of Israel will weep in profound sorrow. The whole nation will be bowed down with universal grief—king, prophet, priest, and people. Each family will go into private mourning, husbands and wives apart, to face their sorrow alone.

A fountain of cleansing

13 "At that time a Fountain will be opened to the people of Israel and Jerusalem, a Fountain to cleanse them from all their sins and defilement."

2And the Lord Almighty declares, "In that day I will get rid of every vestige of idol worship throughout the land, so that even the names of the idols will be forgotten. All false prophets and fortune-tellers will be wiped out, 3and if anyone begins false prophecy again, his own father and mother will slay him! 'You must die,' they will tell him, 'for you are prophesying lies in the name of the Lord.'

4"No one will be boasting then of his prophetic gift! No one will wear prophet's clothes to try to fool the people then.

5"'No,' he will say. 'I am not a prophet; I am a farmer. The soil has been my livelihood from my earliest youth.'

6"And if someone asks, 'Then what are these scars on your chest and your back?' he will say, 'I got into a brawl at the home of a friend!'

7"Awake, O sword, against my Shepherd, the man who is my associate and equal," says the Lord Almighty. "Strike down the Shepherd and the sheep will

12:6
Isa 10:16-18
Obad 18
12:7
Isa 2:11-17
Amos 9:11
Zech 4:6; 11:11
12:8
Gen 22:15-17
Ex 14:19
Lev 26:8
Ps 82:6
Mic 7:8
Zech 9:14,15
12:10
Ps 22:16,17
Isa 32:15
Joel 2:28,29
Jn 19:34-37
Heb 12:2
Rev 1:7
12:11
Jer 6:26
Amos 8:10
Mt 24:30; 26:75
13:1
Lev 15:2
Num 19:9-22
13:2
Ex 23:13
Deut 12:3
Jer 8:10-12
13:3
Deut 13:6-11
Jer 23:25
13:4
Isa 20:2
Jer 2:26; 6:15
Mic 3:6,7
Mt 3:4; 11:8,9
13:5
Amos 7:14
13:7
Isa 9:6; 40:11
53:4,5,10
Hos 12:3-5

12:11 *King Josiah.* Implied in 2 Chron 35:24, 25. Literally, "Like the mourning of Hadad-rimmon in the valley of Megiddo." **13:6** *these scars on your chest and your back.* Evidently self-inflicted cuts, as practiced by false prophets. See 1 Kgs 18:28. *at the home of a friend,* literally, "[These are] wounds I received in the house of my friends." Some think this refers to Christ; others believe this refers to a false prophet who is lying about the reasons for his scars.

12:7 As water flows downhill, so a city's influence usually flows to its surrounding countryside. But this time, the countryside of Judah would have priority over Jerusalem so that the people of Jerusalem would not become proud. Don't think you have to witness first to the "important" people—professional athletes, movie stars, and top businessmen. Christ came to seek and save the lost, even the "down-and-out" lost. We must be careful to avoid spiritual pride or we, like Jerusalem, may be the last to know what God is doing.

12:10 The Holy Spirit was poured out at Pentecost, 50 days after Christ's resurrection (see Acts 2). Zechariah calls the Spirit "the spirit of grace and prayer." It is this Spirit who convicts us of sin, reveals to us God's righteousness and judgment, and helps us as we pray (see Romans 8:26).

12:10–14 Eventually *all* people will realize that Jesus, the man who was pierced and killed, was indeed the Messiah. There will be an awakening and a revival. The crucified Messiah will be clearly

revealed (Philippians 2:10; Revelation 5:13).

13:1ff There will be a never-ending supply of God's mercy, forgiveness, and cleansing power. This picture is similar to the never-ending stream flowing out of the Temple (Ezekiel 47:1). The fountain is used in Scripture to symbolize God's forgiveness. Isaiah 12:3 says "Oh, the joy of drinking deeply from the Fountain of Salvation"; and in John 4, Jesus tells of his "living water" that satisfies completely. Are you spiritually thirsty? Do you need to experience God's forgiveness? Drink from the fountain—ask Jesus to forgive you and give you his salvation.

13:2, 3 This chapter pictures the final days of the earth as we know it. For God's new era to begin, all evil must be abolished.

13:7 Just before his arrest, Jesus quoted from this verse, referring to himself and his disciples (Matthew 26:31, 32). He knew beforehand that his disciples would scatter when he was arrested. The Roman "sword" was the military power that put Christ to death.

scatter, but I will come back and comfort and care for the lambs. ⁸Two-thirds of all the nation of Israel will be cut off and die, but a third will be left in the land. ⁹I will bring the third that remain through the fire and make them pure, as gold and silver are refined and purified by fire. They will call upon my name and I will hear them; I will say, 'These are my people,' and they will say, 'The Lord is our God.' "

13:8
Zech 11:6-9
13:9
Zech 12:10

The Lord will rule

14 Watch, for the day of the Lord is coming soon! On that day the Lord will gather together the nations to fight Jerusalem; the city will be taken, the houses rifled, the loot divided, the women raped; half the population will be taken away as slaves, and half will be left in what remains of the city.

14:1
Isa 2:12
Mal 4:1
Rev 16:14

³Then the Lord will go out fully armed for war, to fight against those nations. ⁴That day his feet will stand upon the Mount of Olives, to the east of Jerusalem, and the Mount of Olives will split apart, making a very wide valley running from east to west, for half the mountain will move toward the north and half toward the south. ⁵You will escape through that valley, for it will reach across to the city gate. Yes, you will escape as your people did long centuries ago from the earthquake in the days of Uzziah, king of Judah, and the Lord my God shall come, and all his saints and angels with him.

14:4
Ezek 47:1-10
Zech 4:7
14:5
Isa 29:6

⁶The sun and moon and stars will no longer shine, ⁷yet there will be continuous day! Only the Lord knows how! There will be no normal day and night—at evening time it will still be light. ⁸Life-giving waters will flow out from Jerusalem, half toward the Dead Sea and half toward the Mediterranean, flowing continuously both in winter and in summer.

14:6
Isa 60:1-3
Acts 2:16,19
14:7
Amos 8:9
Rev 21:23; 22:5

⁹And the Lord shall be King over all the earth. In that day there shall be one Lord—his name alone will be worshiped. ¹⁰All the land from Geba (the northern border of Judah) to Rimmon (the southern border) will become one vast plain, but Jerusalem will be on an elevated site, covering the area all the way from the Gate of Benjamin over to the site of the old gate, then to the Corner Gate, and from the Tower of Hananel to the king's wine presses. ¹¹And Jerusalem shall be inhabited, safe at last, never again to be cursed and destroyed.

14:8
Lk 24:47
Jn 4:10,14
14:9
Deut 6:4
Zech 9:9
14:16,17
14:10
Josh 15:32
21:17
2 Kgs 14:13
2 Chron 25:23
Neh 12:39
Jer 31:8
14:11
Jer 31:40
Rev 22:3

¹²And the Lord will send a plague on all the people who fought Jerusalem. They will become like walking corpses, their flesh rotting away; their eyes will shrivel in their sockets, and their tongues will decay in their mouths.

¹³They will be seized with terror, panic-stricken from the Lord, and will fight against each other in hand-to-hand combat. ¹⁴All Judah will be fighting at Jerusalem. The wealth of all the neighboring nations will be confiscated—great quantities of gold and silver and fine clothing. ¹⁵(This same plague will strike the horses, mules, camels, donkeys, and all the other animals in the enemy camp.)

14:14
Zech 14:1

14:5 *for it will reach across to the city gate,* literally, "for the valley of my mountain shall touch Azel"—apparently a hamlet on the eastern outskirts of Jerusalem. *all his saints and angels,* literally, "his holy ones." **14:6** *The sun and moon and stars will no longer shine.* The Hebrew is uncertain. **14:14** *at Jerusalem,* or, "against Jerusalem."

13:9 A remnant is a small part of the whole. Throughout the history of Israel, whenever the whole nation seemed to turn against God, God said that a righteous remnant still trusted and followed him. These believers were refined like silver and gold through the fire of their difficult circumstances. Determine to be part of God's remnant, that small part of the whole that is obedient to him. Obey him no matter what the rest of the world does. This may mean trials and troubles at times; but as fire purifies gold and silver, you will be purified and made more like Christ.

14:1ff The eventual triumph of the Messiah over all the earth and his reign over God's people are pictured in this chapter.

14:1-21 This chapter portrays important future events, but their chronological order is not clear. They show that God has various ways of dealing with his people. He is in control and has provided the way for purification to those who call on him (13:7, 8). Now we are to *watch* (14:1) as the events unfold and God provides an escape for his people.

14:1, 2 Many times in the Bible we are encouraged to watch for the Day of the Lord which is coming soon. What if you knew exactly when this would happen? Would you live differently? He could come at any moment. Watch for him by studying the Scriptures carefully and making sure you live as he intends for you to live—in obedience and spiritual readiness.

14:4 On the Mount of Olives, Jesus talked to his disciples about the end times (Matthew 24). Near this same mount, an angel promised that he would return in the same manner as he had left (Acts 1:11; see also Ezekiel 11:23).

14:5 Only God's people will escape God's punishment (Matthew 24:16-20). In this time of confusion, God will clearly know who his people are. (See the note on Amos 1:2 concerning the earthquake in King Uzziah's day.)

14:10 Jerusalem is honored as the city of God and the focal point of all the world's worship. Jerusalem's elevation is a dramatic way of showing God's supremacy.

14:16
Lev 23:34-44
Isa 60:6-9
66:18-21
14:17
1 Kgs 17:1
Jer 14:3-6

14:20
Ex 28:36; 39:30
Lev 6:28
Ezek 46:20-24
Rev 20:6
14:21
Deut 12:7,12
Neh 8:10
Rom 14:6,7
1 Cor 10:31
1 Tim 4:3-5

16In the end, those who survive the plague will go up to Jerusalem each year to worship the King, the Lord Almighty, to celebrate a time of thanksgiving. 17And any nation anywhere in all the world that refuses to come to Jerusalem to worship the King, the Lord Almighty, will have no rain. 18But if Egypt refuses to come, God will punish her with some other plague. 19And so Egypt and the other nations will all be punished if they refuse to come.

20In that day the bells on the horses will have written on them, "These Are Holy Property"; and the trash cans in the Temple of the Lord will be as sacred as the bowls beside the altar. 21In fact, every container in Jerusalem and Judah shall be sacred to the Lord Almighty; all who come to worship may use any of them free of charge to boil their sacrifices in; there will be no more grasping traders in the Temple of the Lord Almighty!

14:16 *to celebrate a time,* literally, "the Feast of Tabernacles," or "Booths."   **14:20** *These Are Holy Property,* literally, "Holy to the Lord."

14:16 This Feast of Tabernacles (see textual note) is the only feast still appropriate in Messiah's reign. The Feast of Passover was fulfilled in Christ's death, the Feast of Atonement in acceptance of Christ's salvation, the Feast of First Fruits in his resurrection, and Pentecost with the arrival of the Holy Spirit. But the Feast of Tabernacles, a feast of thanksgiving, celebrates the harvest of human souls for the Lord. Jesus may have alluded to it in John 4:35.

14:18 Egypt will be punished with some plague other than lack of rainfall, because they have very little rainfall anyway. Since they are watered by the Nile River, a drought would not be an effective punishment.

14:20, 21 In the future, even such common objects as horses' bells and trash cans will be holy. This vision of a restored, holy Jerusalem is in stark contrast to her broken walls and unpleasant living conditions. One day God would fulfill their dreams for Jerusalem beyond what they could imagine. God still wants to do much more for us than we can imagine (Ephesians 3:20). When we walk with him, we discover this more deeply each day.

14:21 Zechariah was speaking to a people enduring hardships—they were being harassed by neighbors; they were discouraged over their small numbers and inadequate Temple; and their worship was apathetic. But God said, "Don't you think I care about what has happened?" (1:14). He promised to restore their land, their city, and their Temple. Like other prophets, Zechariah blended prophecies of the present, near future, and final days into one sweeping panorama. Through his message we learn that our hope is found in God and his Messiah, who are in complete control of the world and its nations.

MALACHI

VITAL STATISTICS

PURPOSE:
To confront the people with their sins and to restore their relationship with God

AUTHOR:
Malachi

TO WHOM WRITTEN:
The Jews in Jerusalem and God's people everywhere

DATE WRITTEN:
About 430 B.C.

SETTING:
Malachi, Haggai, and Zechariah were post-exilic prophets to Judah (the Southern Kingdom). Haggai and Zechariah rebuked the people for their failure to rebuild the Temple. Malachi confronted them with their neglect of the Temple and their false and profane worship.

KEY VERSES:
" 'Watch now,' the Lord Almighty declares, 'the day of judgment is coming, burning like a furnace. . . . But for you who fear my name, the Sun of Righteousness will rise with healing in his wings. And you will go free, leaping with joy like calves let out to pasture' " (4:1, 2).

KEY PEOPLE:
Malachi, the priests

KEY PLACES:
Jerusalem, the Temple

SPECIAL FEATURES:
Malachi's literary style displays a continual use of questions asked by God and his people (for example, see 3:7, 8).

A VASE shatters, brushed by a careless elbow; a toy breaks, pushed beyond its limit by young fingers; and fabric rips, pulled by strong and angry hands. Spills and breakages take time to clean up or repair and money to replace, but far more costly are shattered relationships. Unfaithfulness, untruths, hateful words, and forsaken vows tear and rip delicate personal bonds and inflict wounds not easily healed. Most tragic, however, are broken relationships with God.

God loves perfectly and completely. And his love is a love of action—giving, guiding, and guarding. He is altogether faithful, true to his promises to his chosen people. But consistently they spurn their loving God, breaking the covenant, following other gods, and living for themselves. So the relationship is shattered.

But the breach is not irreparable; all hope is not lost. God can heal and mend and reweave the fabric. Forgiveness is available. And that is grace.

This is the message of Malachi, God's prophet in Jerusalem. His words reminded the Jews, God's chosen nation, of their willful disobedience, beginning with the priests (1:1—2:9) and then including every person (2:10—3:15). They had dishonored God's name (1:6), offered false worship (1:7–14), led others into sin (2:7–9), broken God's laws (2:11–16), called evil "good" (2:17), kept God's tithes and offerings for themselves (3:8–12), and become arrogant and proud (3:13–15). The relationship was broken, and judgment and punishment would be theirs. In the midst of this wickedness, however, there were a faithful few—the remnant— who loved and honored God. God would shower his blessings upon these men and women (3:16–18).

This litany of unfaithfulness is terrible and surely worthy of punishment; but woven throughout this message is hope—the possibility of forgiveness. This is beautifully expressed in 4:2—"But for you who fear my name, the Sun of Righteousness will rise with healing in his wings. And you will go free, leaping with joy like calves let out to pasture."

Malachi concludes with a promise of the coming of another "prophet like Elijah" who will offer God's forgiveness to all people through repentance and faith (4:5, 6).

The book of Malachi forms a bridge between the Old Testament and the New Testament. As you read Malachi, see yourself as the recipient of this word of God to his people. Evaluate the depth of your commitment, the sincerity of your worship, and the direction of your life. Then allow God to restore your relationship with him through his love and forgiveness.

THE BLUEPRINT

1. The sinful priests (1:1—2:9)
2. The sinful people (2:10—3:15)
3. The faithful few (3:16—4:6)

Malachi rebuked the people and the priests for neglecting the worship of God and failing to live according to God's Word. If the priests were unfaithful, how could they lead the people? They had become stumbling blocks instead of spiritual leaders. If the people were divorcing their wives and marrying heathen women, how could they lead their children? Their relationship to God had become inconsequential. When our relationship with God becomes less important than it should be, we can strengthen it by setting aside our sinful habits, thinking often of our Lord, and giving God our best each day.

MEGATHEMES

THEME	EXPLANATION	IMPORTANCE
God's love	God loves his people even when they neglect or disobey him. He has great blessings to bestow on those who are faithful to him. His love never ends.	Because God loves us so much, he hates hypocrisy and careless living. This kind of living denies him the relationship he wants to have with us. What we give and how we live reflects the sincerity of our love for God.
The sin of the priests	Malachi singled out the priests for condemnation. They knew what God required, yet their sacrifices were unworthy, their service was insincere, and they were lazy, arrogant, and insensitive. They had a casual attitude toward the worship of God and observance of God's standards.	If religious leaders go wrong, how will the people be led? We are all leaders in some capacity. Don't neglect your responsibilities or be ruled by what is convenient. Neglect and insensitivity are acts of disobedience. God wants leaders who are faithful and sincere.
The sin of the people	The people had not learned the lesson of the exile nor listened to the prophets. Men were callously divorcing their faithful wives to marry younger, pagan women. This was against God's law because it disobeyed his commands about marriage and threatened the religious training of the children. But pride had hardened the hearts of the people.	God deserves our very best honor, respect, and faithfulness. But sin hardens our hearts to our true condition. Don't let pride keep you from giving God your devotion, money, marriage, and family.
The Lord's coming	God's love for his faithful people is demonstrated by the Messiah's coming. The Messiah will lead the people to the realization of all their fondest hopes. It will be a day of comfort and healing for a faithful few, and a day of judgment for those who reject him.	Christ's coming the first time refined and purified all those who believe in him. His return will expose and condemn those who are proud, insensitive, or unprepared. Yet God can heal and mend. Forgiveness is available to all who come to him for it.

1. The sinful priests

God's love for his people

1 Here is the Lord's message to Israel, given through the prophet Malachi: 2, 3"I have loved you very deeply," says the Lord.

But you retort, "Really? When was this?"

And the Lord replies, "I showed my love for you by loving your father, Jacob. I didn't need to. I even rejected his very own brother, Esau, and destroyed Esau's mountains and inheritance, to give it to the jackals of the desert. 4And if his descendants should say, 'We will rebuild the ruins,' then the Lord Almighty will say, 'Try to if you like, but I will destroy it again,' for their country is named 'The Land of Wickedness' and their people are called 'Those Whom God Does Not Forgive.' "

5O Israel, lift your eyes to see what God is doing all around the world; then you will say, "Truly, the Lord's great power goes far beyond our borders!"

God rejects the imperfect sacrifice

6"A son honors his father, a servant honors his master. I am your Father and Master, yet you don't honor me, O priests, but you despise my name."

"Who? Us?" you say. "When did we ever despise your name?"

7"When you offer polluted sacrifices on my altar."

"Polluted sacrifices? When have we ever done a thing like that?"

"Every time you say, 'Don't bother bringing anything very valuable to offer to God!' 8You tell the people, 'Lame animals are all right to offer on the altar of the Lord—yes, even the sick and the blind ones.' And you claim this isn't evil? Try it on your governor sometime—give him gifts like that—and see how pleased he is!

9" 'God have mercy on us,' you recite; 'God be gracious to us!' But when you bring that kind of gift, why should he show you any favor at all?

10"Oh, to find one priest among you who would shut the doors and refuse this kind of sacrifice. I have no pleasure in you," says the Lord Almighty, "and I will not accept your offerings.

11"But my name will be honored by the Gentiles from morning till night. All around the world they will offer sweet incense and pure offerings in honor of my

1:1 Isa 13:1 Zech 9:1
1:2 Rom 9:13
1:4 Isa 9:9
1:5 Ps 35:27 58:10,11 Mic 5:4
1:6 Ex 20:12 Deut 1:31 Prov 30:11,17 Isa 1:2 Jer 31:9
1:7 Lev 21:6,8 Deut 15:21
1:8 Lev 22:19-25 Mal 1:14
1:9 Jer 27:18 Joel 1:13,14
1:10 Isa 1:13 Jer 6:20 14:10,12
1:11 Ps 50:1; 141:2 Isa 45:6; 60:6 Jer 10:6,7

1:1 Malachi, the last Old Testament prophet, preached after Haggai, Zechariah, and Nehemiah—about 430 B.C. The Temple had been rebuilt for almost a century, and the people were losing their enthusiasm for worship. Apathy and disillusionment had set in because the exciting messianic prophecies of Isaiah, Jeremiah, and Micah had not been fulfilled. Many of the sins that brought the downfall of Jerusalem in 586 B.C. were still practiced in Judah. Malachi confronted the hypocrites with their sin by portraying a graphic dialogue between a righteous God and his hardened people.

1:2, 3 God's first message through Malachi was "I have loved you very deeply." Although this message applied specifically to Israel, it is a message of hope for all people in all times. Unfortunately, many people are cynical about God's love, using political and economic progress as a measure of success. Because the government was corrupt and the economy poor, the Israelites assumed that God didn't love them. They were wrong. God loves all people because he made them; however, his *eternal* rewards go only to those who are faithful to him.

1:2–5 The phrase, "I even rejected . . . Esau" simply means that God chose Jacob to be the one through whom the nation of Israel and the Messiah would come. It does not refer to Esau's eternal destiny. God allowed Esau to father a nation, but this nation, Edom, later became one of Israel's chief enemies. The story is found in Genesis 25:19–34; 27:30–43. Because God chose Jacob and his descendants as the nation through whom the world would be blessed, God cared for them in a special way. Ironically, they rejected God after he chose them.

1:6ff God charged the priests with failing to honor him and failing to be good spiritual examples to the people. The Temple had been rebuilt in 516 B.C., and worship was being conducted there, but the priests did not worship God properly. Ezra, the priest, had sparked a great revival, but by Malachi's time, many years after Ezra's death, the priesthood was in decline. The worship of God had lost its vitality and had become more of a business for the priests than heartfelt adoration.

1:6–8 God accused Israel of dishonoring him by offering imperfect sacrifices. Our lives should be living sacrifices to God (Romans 12:1). If we give God only our leftover time, money, and energy, we repeat the same sin as these worshipers who didn't want to bring anything valuable to God. What we give God reflects our true attitude toward him.

1:7, 8 From a practical standpoint, it made sense for the Jews to keep the best animals for themselves and to sacrifice the unwanted ones. But these sacrifices were to God, and God deserves the very best. By giving our best to him, we honor him and demonstrate our trust in his provision. To give second best to God implies that he is second rate in our lives. What are you giving to God? Do convenience and expedience govern your giving?

1:7, 8 The people sacrificed to God wrongly through (1) expedience—being as cheap as possible, (2) neglect—not caring how they offered the sacrifice, and (3) outright disobedience—sacrificing their own way and not as God had commanded. Their methods of giving showed their real attitudes toward God.

name. For my name shall be great among the nations," says the Lord Almighty. 12"But you dishonor it, saying that my altar is not important, and encouraging people to bring cheap, sick animals to offer to me on it.

13"You say, 'Oh, it's too difficult to serve the Lord and do what he asks.' And you turn up your noses at the rules he has given you to obey. Think of it! Stolen animals, lame and sick—as offerings to God! Should I accept such offerings as these?" asks the Lord. 14"Cursed is that man who promises a fine ram from his flock, and substitutes a sick one to sacrifice to God. For I am a Great King," says the Lord Almighty, "and my name is to be mightily revered among the Gentiles."

God warns his priests

2 Listen, you priests, to this warning from the Lord Almighty:
"If you don't change your ways and give glory to my name, then I will send terrible punishment upon you, and instead of giving you blessings as I would like to, I will turn on you with curses. Indeed, I have cursed you already because you haven't taken seriously the things that are most important to me.

3"Take note that I will rebuke your children and I will spread on your faces the manure of these animals you offer me, and throw you out like dung. 4Then at last you will know it was I who sent you this warning to return to the laws I gave your father Levi," says the Lord Almighty. 5"The purpose of these laws was to give him life and peace, to be a means of showing his respect and awe for me, by keeping them. 6He passed on to the people all the truth he got from me. He did not lie or cheat; he walked with me, living a good and righteous life, and turned many from their lives of sin.

1:13
Lev 6:4
22:19-23
Isa 43:22; 61:8
1:14
Ps 47:2; 68:35
Zeph 2:11
Zech 14:9
Mal 1:13

2:1
Lev 26:14-17
Deut 28:15-20

2:4
Num 3:45; 18:21

2:5
Num 25:7,8,13

2:6
Ps 37:30
Ps 119:142

MALACHI served as a prophet to Judah about 430 B.C. He was the last of the Old Testament prophets.	*Climate of the times*	The city of Jerusalem and the Temple had been rebuilt for almost a century, but the people had become complacent in their worship of God.
	Main message	The people's relationship with God was broken because of their sin and they would soon be punished. But the few who repented would receive God's blessing, illustrated in his promise to send a Messiah.
	Importance of message	Hypocrisy, neglecting God, and careless living have devastating consequences. Serving and worshiping God must be the primary focus of our lives, both now and in eternity.
	Contemporary prophets	None

1:10 As intermediaries between God and the people, priests were responsible for reflecting God's attitudes and character. By accepting imperfect sacrifices, they led the people to believe that God accepted those sacrifices as well. As Christians, we are often in the same position as these priests because we reflect God to our friends and family. What image of God's character and attitudes do they see in you? If you casually accept sin, you are like these priests in Malachi's day.

1:11 A theme that can be heard throughout the Old Testament is affirmed in this book—"My name will be honored by the Gentiles. My name shall be great among the nations." God had a chosen people, the Jews, through whom he planned to save and bless the entire world. Today God still wants to save and bless the world through his people, but now his people are all who believe in him—Jews and Gentiles. Christians are now his chosen people, and our sweet sacrifice to the Lord is our new life in Christ (see 2 Corinthians 2:14, 15). Are you available to God to be used in making his name great to the nations? This mission begins in your home and in your neighborhood.

1:13 Too many think that following God is supposed to make life easier or more comfortable. They are looking for a God of convenience. The truth is that it often takes hard work to live by

God's high standards. He may call us to lives of poverty or suffering. But if serving God is more important to us than anything else, what we must give up is of little importance compared to what we gain—eternal life with God.

2:1, 2 When God asks us to give glory to his name, he is asking us to worship him. Worshiping God means acknowledging him for who he is—the almighty Creator of the universe who alone is perfect and who reaches down to sinful mankind with perfect love.

2:1, 2 The priests didn't take seriously the things most important to God, even though he had reminded them through his Word many times. How do you find out what is most important to God? Begin by loving him with all your heart, soul, and might (Deuteronomy 6:5). This means listening to what he says in his Word and then setting your heart, mind, and will on doing what he says. When we love God, his Word is a shining light that guides our daily activities. The priests in Malachi's day had stopped loving God, and thus they did not know nor care what he wanted.

2:4 Levi founded the tribe that bears his name. The Levites became God's ministers, first in the Tabernacle, then in the Temple. They were a tribe set apart for service to God (Numbers 1:47–54).

7"Priests' lips should flow with the knowledge of God so the people will learn God's laws. The priests are the messengers of the Lord Almighty, and men should come to them for guidance. 8But not to you! For you have left God's paths. Your 'guidance' has caused many to stumble in sin. You have distorted the covenant of Levi, and made it into a grotesque parody," says the Lord Almighty. 9"Therefore I have made you contemptible in the eyes of all the people; for you have not obeyed me, but you let your favorites break the law without rebuke."

2:7
Lev 10:11
Num 27:21
Deut 17:8-11
Ezra 7:10
Neh 8:2-8
2:8
Neh 13:29
Isa 9:16
Jer 18:15
Ezek 44:10

2. The sinful people
Treachery in Jerusalem

10We are children of the same father, Abraham, all created by the same God. And yet we are faithless to each other, violating the covenant of our fathers! 11In Judah, in Israel, and in Jerusalem, there is treachery, for the men of Judah have defiled God's holy and beloved Temple by marrying heathen women who worship idols. 12May the Lord cut off from his covenant every last man, whether priest or layman, who has done this thing!

2:10
Ex 19:4-6
Josh 24:3
Isa 63:16
Jer 9:4
2:11
Lev 20:26
Ezra 9:1,2
Jer 3:7-9
Ezek 18:13
2:12
Lev 18:29
Num 15:30,31
2:13
Isa 1:11-15
Jer 11:14; 14:12
2:15
Ex 20:14
Lev 20:10
Hos 1:10
Mal 2:14

13Yet you cover the altar with your tears because the Lord doesn't pay attention to your offerings anymore, and you receive no blessing from him. 14"Why has God abandoned us?" you cry. I'll tell you why; it is because the Lord has seen your treachery in divorcing your wives who have been faithful to you through the years, the companions you promised to care for and keep. 15You were united to your wife by the Lord. In God's wise plan, when you married, the two of you became one person in his sight. And what does he want? Godly children from your union. Therefore guard your passions! Keep faith with the wife of your youth.

16For the Lord, the God of Israel, says he hates divorce and cruel men. Therefore control your passions—let there be no divorcing of your wives.

2:16
Deut 24:1
Mt 5:31; 19:6-8
2:17
Isa 5:19
43:22,24
Jer 17:15
Zeph 1:12

17You have wearied the Lord with your words.

"Wearied him?" you ask in fake surprise. "How have we wearied him?"

By saying that evil is good, that it pleases the Lord! Or by saying that God won't punish us—he doesn't care.

2:7, 8 Malachi was angry at the priests because they did not know God's Word, and this lack of knowledge caused them to lead God's people astray. Their ignorance was willful and inexcusable. Pastors and leaders of God's people *must* know God's Word— what it says, what it means, and how it applies to daily life. How much time do you spend in God's Word?

2:9 The priests had allowed influential and favored people to break the law. They were so dependent on these people for support that they could not afford to confront them when they did wrong. In your church, are certain people allowed to do wrong without criticism? There should be no double standard based on wealth or position. Let your standards be those presented in God's Word. Don't play favorites and become contemptible in God's sight (see James 2:1-4).

2:10-16 The people were being unfaithful in their homes. They were not openly saying they rejected God, but they were living as if he did not exist. Divorce was common, occurring for no reason other than a desire for change. People acted as if they could do anything without being punished. We cannot successfully separate our dealings with God from the rest of our lives. He must be Lord of all.

2:11, 12 After the Temple had been rebuilt and the walls completed, the people were excited to see past prophecies coming true. But as time passed, the prophecies about the destruction of God's enemies and a coming Messiah were not fulfilled. People became discouraged, and they grew complacent about obeying all of God's laws. This complacency gradually led to

blatant sin, such as marriage to those who worshiped idols. Ezra and Nehemiah also confronted this problem years earlier (Ezra 9, 10; Nehemiah 13:23-31).

2:14 The people were complaining about their adverse circumstances when they had only themselves to blame. People often try to avoid guilt feelings by shifting the blame. This doesn't solve the problem, however. When you face problems, look first at yourself. If you changed your attitude or behavior, would the problem be solved?

2:14, 15 Divorce in these times was practiced exclusively by men. They broke faith with their wives, divorcing them so they could marry younger women. They ignored the bonding between a husband and a wife that God instills (the two become one person) and his purpose for them (raising godly children). Not only were men breaking faith with their wives, they were ignoring the bonding relationship and spiritual purpose of being united with God.

2:15, 16 To "guard your passions" means to have the same commitment to marriage that God has to his promises with his people. We need passion in the marriage relationship to keep the commitment and intimacy satisfying, but this passion should be focused on our spouse.

2:17—3:6 God was tired of the way the people twisted his truths. He would punish those who insisted that, because God was silent, he approved of their actions. He would also punish those who casually professed a counterfeit faith. The apostle Peter warns us to guard against these same false attitudes by becoming better acquainted with Jesus Christ (2 Peter 3:15-18).

The coming of the Lord

3:1
Isa 63:9

3 "Listen: I will send my messenger before me to prepare the way. And then the one you are looking for will come suddenly to his Temple—the Messenger of God's promises, to bring you great joy. Yes, he is surely coming," says the Lord Almighty. 2"But who can live when he appears? Who can endure his coming? For he is like a blazing fire refining precious metal and he can bleach the dirtiest garments! 3Like a refiner of silver he will sit and closely watch as the dross is burned away. He will purify the Levites, the ministers of God, refining them like gold or silver, so that they will do their work for God with pure hearts. 4Then once more the Lord will enjoy the offerings brought to him by the people of Judah and Jerusalem, as he did before. 5At that time my punishments will be quick and certain; I will move swiftly against wicked men who trick the innocent, against adulterers, and liars, against all those who cheat their hired hands, or oppress widows and orphans, or defraud strangers, and do not fear me," says the Lord Almighty.

6"For I am the Lord—I do not change. That is why you are not already utterly destroyed [for my mercy endures forever].

3:2
Isa 4:4
Ezek 22:14
Zech 13:9
Mt 3:10-12

3:3
Ps 51:19
Ezek 22:18-22
Dan 12:10

3:4
2 Chron 7:1-3
Ps 51:17-19
Jer 2:2
Zech 8:3

3:5
Ex 22:22-24
Deut 5:11
18:10; 27:19
Jer 5:2; 7:9
Ezek 22:9-11

God's people rob him

3:7
Zech 1:3

7"Though you have scorned my laws from earliest time, yet you may still return to me," says the Lord Almighty. "Come and I will forgive you.

"But you say, 'We have never even gone away!'

8"Will a man rob God? Surely not! And yet you have robbed me.

" 'What do you mean? When did we ever rob you?'

"You have robbed me of the tithes and offerings due to me. 9And so the awesome curse of God is cursing you, for your whole nation has been robbing me. 10Bring all the tithes into the storehouse so that there will be food enough in my Temple; if you do, I will open up the windows of heaven for you and pour out a blessing so great you won't have room enough to take it in!

"Try it! Let me prove it to you! 11Your crops will be large, for I will guard them from insects and plagues. Your grapes won't shrivel away before they ripen," says the Lord Almighty. 12"And all nations will call you blessed, for you will be a land sparkling with happiness. These are the promises of the Lord Almighty.

13"Your attitude toward me has been proud and arrogant," says the Lord. "But you say, 'What do you mean? What have we said that we shouldn't?'

3:8
Lev 5:15,16
Neh 13:11

3:10
Ps 78:23-29
Ezek 34:26

3:11
Joel 1:4; 2:25

3:12
Deut 8:7-10
Ps 72:17
Isa 61:9; 62:4
Zech 8:23

3:1 *the one,* literally, "the Lord." **3:6** *for my mercy endures forever,* implied. **4:5** *another prophet like Elijah,* literally, "like the prophet Elijah." Compare Mt. 17:10-12 and Lk 1:17.

3:1 There are two messengers in this verse. The first is usually understood to be John the Baptist (Matthew 11:10; Luke 7:27). The second messenger is Jesus, the Messiah, for whom both Malachi and John the Baptist prepared the way.

3:3 In the process of refining metals, the raw metal is heated with fire until it melts. The impurities separate from it and rise to the surface. They are then skimmed off, leaving the pure metal. Without this heating and melting, there could be no purifying. As the impurities are skimmed off the top, the reflection of the metallurgist appears in the smooth, pure surface. As we are purified by God, his reflection in our lives will become more and more clear to those around us. God says that leaders (here the Levites) should be especially open to his purification process in their lives.

3:6-12 Malachi urged the people to stop holding back their tithes, to stop keeping from God what he deserved. The tithing system began during the time of Moses (Leviticus 27:30-34; Deuteronomy 14:22). The Levites received some of the tithe because they could not possess land of their own (Numbers 18:20, 21). During Malachi's day, the tithes were not being used to support God's workers, so the Levites went to work to earn a living. Everything we have is from God; so when we refuse to return to him a part of what he has given, we rob him. Do you selfishly want

to keep 100 percent of what you have been given, or are you willing to return the first part for advancing God's Kingdom?

3:7 God's patience seems endless! Throughout history, his people have disobeyed, even scorned, his laws; but he has always been willing to accept them back. Here, however, they have the nerve to say they never disobeyed! Many people have turned their backs on forgiveness and restoration because they have refused to admit their sin. Don't follow their example. God is ready to forgive, but he will not say evil is good.

3:8-12 The people of Malachi's day ignored God's command to give a tithe of their income to his Temple. They may have feared losing what they had worked so hard to get, but in this they misjudged God. "If you give, you will get!" he says (Luke 6:38). When we give, we must remember that the blessings God promises are not always material and may not be experienced completely here on earth, but we will certainly receive them in our future life with him.

3:13-15 These verses deal with the people's arrogant attitude toward God. When we say, "What good does it do to worship God?" we are really saying, "What good does it do for *me?*" Our focus is selfish. Our real question should be, "What good does it do for God?" We must worship God just because he is God and deserves to be worshiped.

14, 15"Listen; you have said, 'It is foolish to worship God and obey him. What good does it do to obey his laws, and to sorrow and mourn for our sins? From now on, as far as we're concerned, "Blessed are the arrogant." For those who do evil shall prosper, and those who dare God to punish them shall get off scot-free.' "

3:14,15
Ps 73:8-13
Isa 58:3
Jer 7:10
Zeph 1:12

3. The faithful few

16Then those who feared and loved the Lord spoke often of him to each other. And he had a Book of Remembrance drawn up in which he recorded the names of those who feared him and loved to think about him.

3:16
Isa 4:31
Dan 12:1

17"They shall be mine," says the Lord Almighty, "in that day when I make up my jewels. And I will spare them as a man spares an obedient and dutiful son. 18Then you will see the difference between God's treatment of good men and bad, between those who serve him and those who don't.

3:17
Neh 13:22
1 Pet 1:13-16

3:18
Ps 58:10,11
Amos 5:15

The great judgment day of the Lord

4 "Watch now," the Lord Almighty declares, "the day of judgment is coming, burning like a furnace. The proud and wicked will be burned up like straw; like a tree, they will be consumed—roots and all.

4:1
Isa 5:24
9:18,19
Mt 3:12

2"But for you who fear my name, the Sun of Righteousness will rise with healing in his wings. And you will go free, leaping with joy like calves let out to pasture. 3Then you will tread upon the wicked as ashes underfoot," says the Lord Almighty. 4"Remember to obey the laws I gave all Israel through Moses my servant on Mount Horeb.

4:2
2 Sam 23:4
Isa 30:26; 35:6
Jer 30:17,33:6

4:4
Ex 20:3
Deut 4:5,6

5"See, I will send you another prophet like Elijah before the coming of the great and dreadful judgment day of God. 6His preaching will bring fathers and children together again, to be of one mind and heart, for they will know that if they do not repent, I will come and utterly destroy their land."

4:5
Mt 11:14
Mk 9:11-13

4:6
Isa 24:6
Mt 11:21
Rev 19:15

3:16 The Book of Remembrance may or may not be an actual book. The point is that God will remember those who remain faithful to him, and who love, fear, honor, and respect him.

3:17 God's people are called jewels. A jewel is made from raw material that is exposed to time, heat, and pressure to change it into a valuable gemstone. The stone must then be cut in order for its real beauty to be seen. A craftsman takes a stone and chips away a rough edge, minimizes a fault, polishes, and puts it into just the right setting to display its beauty. Be willing to allow God to make you a jewel; ask him to chip and polish where needed; and be patient while he works. Be sure you are ready to change, because when God begins to make a jewel, he doesn't stop until it is perfect.

4:2 At the day of judgment, God's wrath toward the wicked will be like the blasting heat of a furnace (4:1). But he will be like the healing warmth of the sun to those who love and obey him. John the Baptist prophesied that with the coming of Jesus, the dawn was about to break with light for those in sin's darkness (Luke 1:76–79). In Isaiah 60:20 and Revelation 21:23, 24 we learn that no light will be needed in God's holy city because God himself will be the light.

4:2 These last verses of the Old Testament are filled with hope. Regardless of how life looks now, God controls the future and everything will be made right. We who have loved and served God look forward to a joyful celebration. This hope for the future is ours as soon as we trust God with our lives.

4:4 These laws, given to Moses on Mount Horeb (Sinai), are the foundation of the nation's civil, moral, and ceremonial life (Exodus 20; Deuteronomy 4:5, 6). We still must obey these moral laws; they apply to all generations.

4:5, 6 Elijah was one of the greatest prophets who ever lived (his story is recorded in 1 Kings 17—2 Kings 2). With Malachi's death, the voice of God's prophets would be silent for 400 years. Then a prophet would come, like Elijah, to herald Christ's coming (Matthew 17:10–13; Luke 1:17). This prophet was John the Baptist. He prepared people's hearts for Jesus by urging people to repent of their sins. This would bring unity and peace, but also judgment on those who refused to turn from their sins.

4:6 Malachi gives us practical guidelines about commitment to God. God deserves the best we have to offer (1:7–10). We must be willing to change our wrong ways of living (2:1, 2). We should make family a lifelong priority (2:13–15). We should be ready for God's refining process in our lives (3:3). We should tithe our income (3:8–12). There is no room for pride (3:13–15).

Malachi closes his messages by pointing to that great last day of judgment. For those who are committed to God, it will be a day of joy because it will usher in eternity in God's presence. Those who have ignored God will "be burned up like straw" (4:1). To help the people prepare for that day, God would send a prophet like Elijah (John the Baptist) who would prepare the way for Jesus, the Messiah. The New Testament begins with this prophet calling the people to turn from their sins and turn toward God. Such a commitment to God demands great sacrifice on our part, but we can be sure it will be worth it all in the end.

THE NEW TESTAMENT

VITAL STATISTICS

PURPOSE:
To prove that Jesus is the Messiah, the eternal King

AUTHOR:
Matthew (Levi)

TO WHOM WRITTEN:
Matthew wrote especially to the Jews

DATE WRITTEN:
Probably between A.D. 60–65

SETTING:
Matthew was a Jewish tax collector who became one of Jesus' disciples. This Gospel forms the connecting link between the Old and New Testaments because of its emphasis on the fulfillment of prophecy.

KEY VERSE:
"Don't misunderstand why I have come—it isn't to cancel the laws of Moses and the warnings of the prophets. No, I came to fulfill them" (5:17).

KEY PEOPLE:
Jesus, Mary, Joseph, John the Baptist, the disciples, the religious leaders, Caiaphas, Pilate, Mary Magdalene

KEY PLACES:
Bethlehem, Jerusalem, Capernaum, Galilee, Judea

SPECIAL FEATURES:
Matthew is filled with messianic language ("Son of David" is used throughout) and Old Testament references (53 quotes and 76 other references). This Gospel is not written as a chronological account; its purpose is to present the clear evidence that Jesus is the Messiah, the Savior.

MOTORCADES herald the approach of heads of state. Pomp and ceremony are symbols of their position and importance. Whether they are leaders by birth or election, we honor and respect them.

The Jews waited for a leader who had been promised centuries before by prophets. They believed that this leader—the Messiah ("anointed one")—would rescue them from their Roman oppressors and establish a new kingdom. As their king, he would rule the world with justice.

However, many Jews overlooked prophecies which also spoke of this king as a suffering servant who would be rejected and killed. It is no wonder, then, that few recognized Jesus as the Messiah. How could this humble teacher from Nazareth be their king? But Jesus was and is the King of all the earth!

Matthew (Levi) was one of Jesus' 12 disciples. Once he was a despised tax collector, but his life was changed by this man from Galilee. Matthew wrote this Gospel to his fellow Jews to prove that Jesus is the Messiah and to explain God's Kingdom.

Matthew begins his account by giving Jesus' genealogy. He then tells of Jesus' birth and early years, including the family's escape to Egypt from the murderous Herod and their return to Nazareth. Following his baptism by John (3:17) and his defeat of Satan in the desert, Jesus begins his public ministry by calling his first disciples and giving the "Sermon on the Mount" (chapters 5—7). Matthew shows Christ's authority by reporting his miracles of healing the sick and the demon-possessed, and even raising the dead.

Despite opposition from the Pharisees and others in the religious establishment (chapters 12—15), Jesus continued to teach concerning the Kingdom of Heaven (chapters 16—20). During this time, Jesus spoke with his disciples about his imminent death and resurrection (16:21), and revealed his true identity to Peter, James, and John (17:1–5). Near the end of his ministry, Jesus entered Jerusalem in a triumphant procession (21:1–11). But soon opposition mounted and Jesus realized that his death was near. So he taught his disciples about the future—what they could expect before his return (chapter 24) and how to live until then (chapter 25).

In Matthew's finale (chapters 26—28), he focuses on Jesus' final days on earth—the Last Supper, his prayer in Gethsemane, the betrayal by Judas, the flight of the disciples, Peter's denial, the trials before Caiaphas and Pilate, Jesus' final words on the cross, and his burial in a borrowed tomb. But the story does not end there, for the Messiah rose from the dead—conquering death and then telling his followers to continue his work by making disciples in all nations.

As you read this Gospel, listen to Matthew's clear message: Jesus is the Christ, the King of kings and Lord of lords. Celebrate his victory over evil and death, and make Jesus the Lord of your life.

THE BLUEPRINT

A. BIRTH AND PREPARATION OF JESUS, THE KING (1:1—4:11)

The people of Israel were waiting for the Messiah, their king. Matthew begins his book by showing how Jesus Christ was a descendant of David. But Matthew goes on to show that God did not send Jesus to be an earthly king, but a heavenly king. Jesus did not come to reign over people's land but to rule in people's lives. His Kingdom would be much greater than David's, because it would never end. Even at his birth, many recognized Jesus as a king. Herod, the ruler, as well as Satan, was afraid of Jesus' kingship and tried to stop him, but others worshiped him and brought royal gifts. We must be willing to recognize Jesus for who he really is and worship him as king of our lives.

B. MESSAGE AND MINISTRY OF JESUS, THE KING (4:12—25:46)
 1. Jesus begins his ministry
 2. Jesus gives the Sermon on the Mount
 3. Jesus performs many miracles
 4. Jesus teaches about the Kingdom
 5. Jesus encounters differing reactions to his ministry
 6. Jesus faces conflict with the religious leaders
 7. Jesus teaches on the Mount of Olives

Jesus gave the Sermon on the Mount, directions for living in his kingdom. He also told many parables about the difference between his Kingdom and the kingdoms of earth. Forgiveness, peace, and putting others first are some of the characteristics that make one great in the future Kingdom of God. And to be great in God's Kingdom, we must live by God's standards right now. Jesus came to show us how to live as faithful subjects in his Kingdom.

C. DEATH AND RESURRECTION OF JESUS, THE KING (26:1—28:20)

Jesus was formally presented to the nation of Israel, but rejected. How strange for the king to be accused, arrested, and crucified. But Jesus demonstrated his power even over death through his resurrection, and gained access for us into his Kingdom. With all this evidence that Jesus is God's Son, we, too, should accept him as our Lord.

MEGATHEMES

THEME	EXPLANATION	IMPORTANCE
Jesus Christ, the King	Jesus is revealed as the King of kings. His miraculous birth, his life and teaching, his miracles, and his triumph over death show his true identity.	Jesus cannot be compared with any person or power. He is the supreme ruler of time and eternity, heaven and earth, men and angels. We should give him his rightful place as king of our lives.
The Messiah	Jesus was the Messiah, the one for whom the Jews had waited to deliver them from Roman oppression. Yet tragically, they didn't recognize him when he came because his kingship was not what they expected. The true purpose of God's anointed deliverer was to die for all people to free them from sin's oppression.	Because Jesus was sent by God, we can trust him with our lives. It is worth everything we have to recognize him and give ourselves to him because he came to be our Messiah, our Savior.
Kingdom of God	Jesus came to earth to begin his Kingdom. His full Kingdom will be realized at his return and will be made up of anyone who has faithfully followed him.	The way to enter God's Kingdom is by faith—believing in Christ to save us from sin and change our lives. We must do the work of his Kingdom now to be prepared for his return.
Teachings	Jesus taught the people through sermons, illustrations, and parables. Through them, he showed the true ingredients of faith and how to guard against a fruitless and hypocritical life.	Jesus' teachings show us how to prepare for life in his Kingdom by living properly right now. His life was an example of his teachings, as our lives should be.

Resurrection	When Jesus rose from the dead, he rose in power as the true king. In his victory over death, he established his credentials as king and his power and authority over evil.	The resurrection shows Jesus' all-powerful life for us—not even death could stop his plan of offering eternal life. Those who believe in Jesus can hope for a resurrection like his. Our role is to tell his story to all the earth so that everyone may share in his victory.

KEY PLACES IN MATTHEW

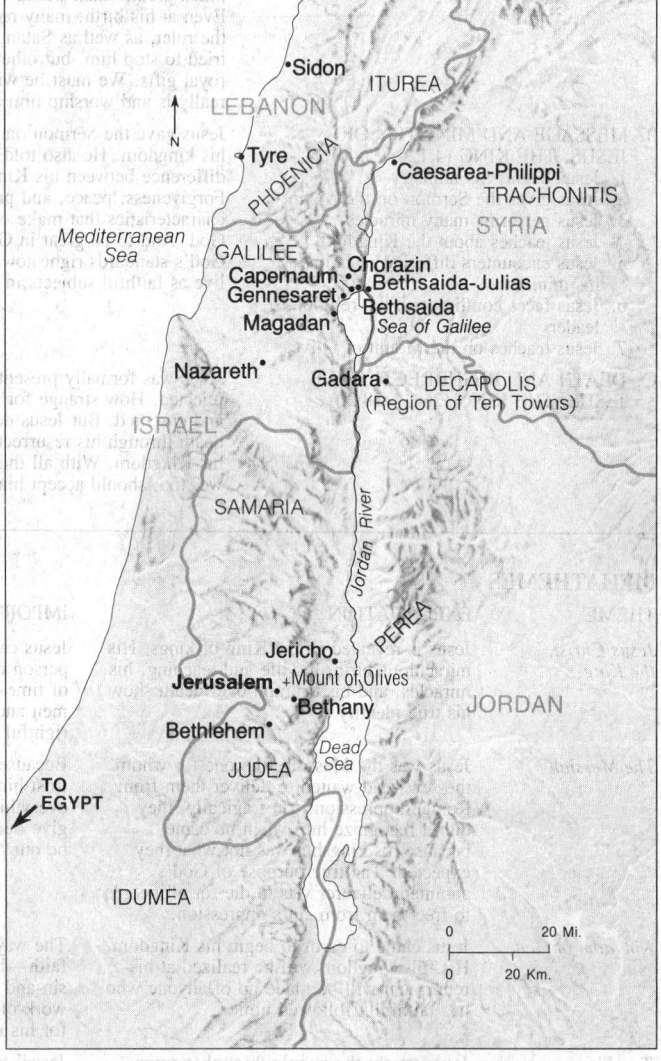

Jesus' earthly story begins in the town of Bethlehem in the Roman province of Judea (2:1). A threat to kill the infant king led Joseph to take his family to Egypt (2:14). When they returned, God led them to settle in Nazareth in Galilee (2:22, 23). At about age 30, Jesus was baptized in the Jordan River and was tempted by Satan in the Judean wilderness (3:13; 4:1). He set up his base of operations in Capernaum (4:12, 13) and from there ministered throughout Israel, telling parables, teaching about the Kingdom, and healing the sick. He traveled to the country of the Gadarenes and healed two demon-possessed men (8:28ff); fed over 5,000 people with five small loaves and two fish on the shores of Galilee near Bethsaida-Julias (14:15ff); healed the sick in Gennesaret (14:34ff); ministered to the Gentiles in Tyre and Sidon (15:21ff); visited Caesarea-Philippi where Peter declared him as the Messiah (16:13ff); and taught in Perea, across the Jordan (19:1). As he set out on his last visit to Jerusalem, he told the disciples what would happen to him there (20:17ff). He spent some time in Jericho (20:29) then stayed in Bethany at night as he went back and forth into Jerusalem during his last week (21:17ff). In Jerusalem he would be crucified, but he would rise again.

A. BIRTH AND PREPARATION OF JESUS, THE KING (1:1—4:11)

Matthew opens his Gospel with a genealogy to prove that Jesus is the descendant of both King David and Abraham, just as the Old Testament had predicted. Jesus' birth didn't go unnoticed, for both shepherds and wise kings came to worship him. The Jewish people were waiting for the Messiah to appear. Finally, he was born, but the Jews didn't recognize him because they were looking for a different kind of king.

The ancestors of Jesus
(3/Luke 3:23–38)

1:1
Gen 22:18
2 Sam 7:12-14
Ps 89:3,4
Ps 132:11
Isa 9:6; 11:1
Mt 22:42
Lk 3:23-28
Jn 7:42
Acts 2:30
Rom 1:3
Gal 3:16
Rev 22:16

1:3
Ruth 4:18
1 Chron 2:5,9

1:4
Num 1:2-15

1:5
Josh 6:25
Heb 11:31

1:6
1 Sam 16:1
2 Sam 12:24

1:7
1 Chron 3:10-14

1:10
2 Kgs 20:21

1:11
2 Kgs 25:11
Jer 27:20; 52:11
Dan 1:1

1:12
Ezra 3:2
Neh 12:1
Hag 1:1

1:16
Gen 3:15
Isa 9:6; 53:2
Mt 27:17,22
Lk 2:11
Jn 3:14; 4:25
Rom 9:5
1 Tim 3:16

1 These are the ancestors of Jesus Christ, a descendant of King David and of Abraham:

2Abraham was the father of Isaac; Isaac was the father of Jacob; Jacob was the father of Judah and his brothers.

3Judah was the father of Perez and Zerah (Tamar was their mother); Perez was the father of Hezron; Hezron was the father of Aram;

4Aram was the father of Amminadab; Amminadab was the father of Nahshon; Nahshon was the father of Salmon;

5Salmon was the father of Boaz (Rahab was his mother); Boaz was the father of Obed (Ruth was his mother); Obed was the father of Jesse;

6Jesse was the father of King David. David was the father of Solomon (his mother was the widow of Uriah);

7Solomon was the father of Rehoboam; Rehoboam was the father of Abijah; Abijah was the father of Asa;

8Asa was the father of Jehoshaphat; Jehoshaphat was the father of Joram; Joram was the father of Uzziah;

9Uzziah was the father of Jotham; Jotham was the father of Ahaz; Ahaz was the father of Hezekiah;

10Hezekiah was the father of Manasseh; Manasseh was the father of Amos; Amos was the father of Josiah;

11Josiah was the father of Jechoniah and his brothers (born at the time of the exile to Babylon).

12After the exile: Jechoniah was the father of Shealtiel; Shealtiel was the father of Zerubbabel;

13Zerubbabel was the father of Abiud; Abiud was the father of Eliakim; Eliakim was the father of Azor;

14Azor was the father of Zadok; Zadok was the father of Achim; Achim was the father of Eliud;

15Eliud was the father of Eleazar; Eleazar was the father of Matthan; Matthan was the father of Jacob;

16Jacob was the father of Joseph (who was the husband of Mary, the mother of Jesus Christ the Messiah).

1:1ff More than 400 years had passed since the last Old Testament prophecies, and faithful Jews all over the world were still awaiting the Messiah (Luke 3:15). Matthew wrote this book to Jews to present Jesus as King and Messiah, the promised descendant of King David who would reign forever (Isaiah 11:1–5). The Gospel of Matthew links the Old and New Testaments and contains many references to how Jesus fulfilled Old Testament prophecy.

1:1ff Jesus entered history when the land of Israel was controlled by Rome and considered an insignificant outpost of the vast and mighty Roman Empire. The presence of Roman soldiers in Israel gave the Jews military peace, but at the price of oppression, slavery, injustice, and immorality. Into this kind of world came the promised Messiah.

1:1 This genealogy was one of the most interesting ways Matthew could begin a book for a Jewish audience. Because a person's family line proved his or her standing as one of God's chosen people, Matthew begins by showing that Jesus was a descendant of Abraham, the father of all Jews, and a direct descendant of King

David, fulfilling Old Testament prophecies about the Messiah's line. The facts of this ancestry were carefully preserved. This is the first of many proofs recorded by Matthew to show that Jesus is the true Messiah.

1:1–17 In the first 17 verses we meet 46 people, spanning 2,000 years. All were ancestors of Jesus, but they varied considerably in personality, spirituality, and experience. Some were heroes of faith—like Abraham, Isaac, Ruth, and David. Some had shady reputations—like Rahab and Tamar. Many were very ordinary—like Hezron, Aram, Nahshon, and Achim. And others were evil—like Manasseh and Abijah. God's work in history is not limited by human failures or sins, and he works through ordinary people. Just as God used all kinds of people to bring his Son into the world, he uses all kinds today to accomplish his will.

1:16 Because Mary was a virgin when she became pregnant, Matthew lists Joseph only as the husband of Mary, not the father of Jesus. Matthew's genealogy gives Jesus' legal (or royal) lineage through Joseph. Mary's ancestral line is recorded in Luke 3:23–38. Both Mary and Joseph were direct descendants of King David.

¹⁷These are fourteen of the generations from Abraham to King David; and fourteen from King David's time to the exile; and fourteen from the exile to Christ.

1:17
2 Kgs 24:14
Jer 27:20

An angel appears to Joseph
(8)

¹⁸These are the facts concerning the birth of Jesus Christ: His mother, Mary, was engaged to be married to Joseph. But while she was still a virgin she became pregnant by the Holy Spirit. ¹⁹Then Joseph, her fiancé, being a man of stern principle, decided to break the engagement but to do it quietly, as he didn't want to publicly disgrace her.

1:18
Lk 1:27,35
Gal 4:4
Heb 10:5
1:19
Deut 24:1

²⁰As he lay awake considering this, he fell into a dream, and saw an angel standing beside him. "Joseph, son of David," the angel said, "don't hesitate to take Mary as your wife! For the child within her has been conceived by the Holy Spirit. ²¹And she will have a Son, and you shall name him Jesus (meaning 'Savior'), for he will save his people from their sins. ²²This will fulfill God's message through his prophets—

1:20
Lk 1:35
1:21
Dan 9:24
Lk 1:31; 2:11,21
Jn 1:29
Acts 5:31; 13:23
Heb 7:25
Rev 1:5

> ²³*'Listen! The virgin shall conceive a child!* She shall give birth to a Son, and he shall be called "Emmanuel" (meaning "God is with us").' "

1:23
Isa 7:14; 9:6
Jn 1:14
1 Tim 3:16

²⁴When Joseph awoke, he did as the angel commanded, and brought Mary home

1:17 *These are fourteen,* literally, "So all the generations from Abraham unto David are fourteen." **1:19** *her fiancé,* literally, "her husband." *a man of stern principle,* literally, "a just man." **1:20** *As he lay awake,* implied in remainder of verse.

1:17 Matthew breaks Israel's history into three sets of 14 generations, but there were probably more than those listed here. Genealogies often compressed history, meaning that not every generation of ancestors was specifically listed. Thus the phrase "father of" can also be translated "ancestor of."

1:18 Why is the virgin birth important to the Christian faith? Jesus Christ, God's Son, had to be free from the sinful nature passed on to all other human beings from Adam. Because he was born of a woman, he was a human being; but because he was the Son of God, he was born without any trace of human sin. He was both fully human and fully divine.

Because Jesus lived as a man, we know that he fully understands our experiences and struggles (Hebrews 4:15, 16). Because he is God, he has the power and authority to deliver us from sin (Colossians 2:15). We can tell him all our thoughts, feelings, and needs. He has been where we are now, and he has the ability to help.

1:18 There were three steps in a Jewish marriage. A couple became engaged when their two families agreed to their union. When a public announcement was made, the couple became "betrothed." Betrothal (called "engagement" in the text) was considered binding and could be broken only by death or divorce. No sexual relationship was allowed, however, until after the couple was married. Because Mary and Joseph were betrothed, Mary's apparent unfaithfulness carried a severe social stigma. According to Jewish civil law, Joseph had a right to divorce her, and the Jewish authorities could have her stoned to death (Deuteronomy 22:23, 24).

1:18-24 Joseph was faced with a difficult choice after discovering Mary was pregnant. Although he knew that taking Mary as his wife could be humiliating, he chose to obey God's command to marry her. His action revealed four admirable qualities: (1) stern principle (1:19), (2) discretion and sensitivity (1:19), (3) responsiveness to God (1:24), and (4) self-discipline (1:25).

1:19 Perhaps Joseph thought he had only two options: divorce Mary quietly or have her stoned. But God had a third option—marry her (1:20-23). In view of the circumstances, this had not occurred to Joseph. But God often shows us that there are more options available than we think. Although Joseph seemed to

be doing right by breaking the engagement, only God's guidance helped him make the best decision. When our decisions affect the lives of others, we must always seek God's wisdom.

1:20-23 The angel declared to Joseph that Mary's child was conceived by the Holy Spirit and that it would be a son. This reveals an important truth about Jesus—he is both God and man. God took on the limitations of humanity so he could live and die for the salvation of all who believe in him.

1:20 The conception and birth of Jesus Christ are supernatural events beyond human logic or reasoning. Because of this, God sent angels to help certain people understand the significance of what was happening (see Matthew 1:20; 2:13, 19; Luke 1:11, 12, 26; 2:9).

Angels are spiritual beings created by God who help carry out his work on earth. They bring God's messages to people (Luke 1:26), protect God's people (Daniel 6:22), offer encouragement (Genesis 16:7ff), give guidance (Exodus 14:19), bring punishment (2 Samuel 24:16), patrol the earth (Zechariah 1:10, 11), and fight the forces of evil (2 Kings 6:16-18; Revelation 20:1). There are both good and bad angels (Revelation 12:7), but because bad angels are allied with Satan, they have considerably less power and authority.

1:21 *Jesus* means "Savior." Jesus came to earth to save us because we can't save ourselves from sin's consequences. No matter how good we are, we can't eliminate the sinful nature present in all of us. Only Jesus can do that. Jesus didn't come to help people save themselves; he came to be their Savior from the power and penalty of sin. Thank Christ for his death on the cross for your sin, and then ask him to take control of your life. Your new life begins the moment you do that.

1:23 Jesus was to be called *Emmanuel* ("God with us"), as predicted by Isaiah the prophet (Isaiah 7:14). Jesus was God in the flesh; thus God was literally among us. Through the Holy Spirit, Christ is present today in the life of every believer. Perhaps not even Isaiah understood how far-reaching the meaning of "Emmanuel" would be.

1:24 Joseph changed his plans quickly after discovering that Mary had not been unfaithful to him (1:20). He obeyed God and proceeded with the marriage plans. Although others may have disapproved of his decision, Joseph went ahead with what he

to be his wife, 25but she remained a virgin until her Son was born; and Joseph named him "Jesus."

Visitors arrive from eastern lands
(12)

2:1
1 Kgs 4:30
Lk 2:4

2 Jesus was born in the town of Bethlehem, in Judea, during the reign of King Herod.

At about that time some astrologers from eastern lands arrived in Jerusalem, asking, 2"Where is the newborn King of the Jews? for we have seen his star in far-off eastern lands, and have come to worship him."

2:2
Jer 23:5; 30:9

GOSPEL ACCOUNTS FOUND ONLY IN MATTHEW	Passage	Subject
	1:20–24	Joseph's vision*
	2:1–12	The visit of the wise men
	2:13–15	Escape to Egypt*
	2:16–19	Slaughter of the children*
	27:3–10	The death of Judas*
	27:19	The dream of Pilate's wife
	27:52	The extra resurrections
	28:11–15	The bribery of the guards
	28:19, 20	The baptism emphasis in the Great Commission*

Matthew records nine special events that are not mentioned in any of the other Gospels. In each case, the most apparent reason for Matthew's choice has to do with his purpose in communicating the gospel to Jewish people. Five cases are fulfillments of Old Testament prophecies (marked with asterisks above). The other four would have been of particular interest to the Jews of Matthew's day.

---

knew was right. We sometimes avoid doing right because of what others might think. Like Joseph, we must choose to obey God rather than seek the approval of others.

THE FLIGHT TO EGYPT
Herod planned to kill the baby Jesus whom he perceived to be a future threat to his position. Warned of this treachery in a dream, Joseph took his family to Egypt until Herod's death which occurred a year or two later. They then planned to return to Judea, but God led them instead to Nazareth in Galilee.

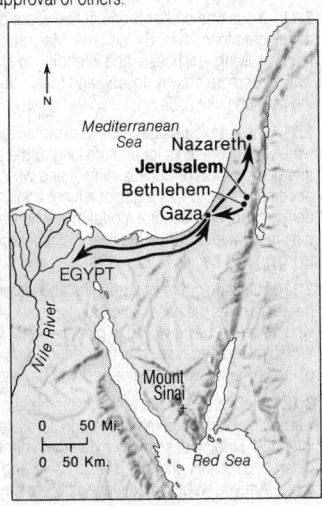

2:1 Bethlehem is a small town five miles south of Jerusalem. It sits on a high ridge over 2,000 feet above sea level. It is mentioned in more detail in the Gospel of Luke. The Luke account also explains why Joseph and Mary were in Bethlehem when Jesus was born, rather than Nazareth, their hometown.

2:1 The land of Israel was divided into four political districts and several lesser terrorities. Judea was to the south, Samaria in the middle, Galilee to the north, and Idumea to the east. Bethlehem of Judea had been prophesied as the Messiah's birthplace (Micah 5:2). Jerusalem was also in Judea and was the seat of government for Herod the Great, king over all four political districts. After Herod's death, the districts were divided among

three separate rulers (see the note on 2:19–22). Although he was a ruthless, evil man who murdered many in his own family, Herod the Great supervised the renovation of the Temple, making it much larger and more beautiful. This made him popular with many Jews. Jesus would visit Jerusalem many times because the great Jewish festivals were held there.

2:1 Not much is known about these astrologers (wise men). We don't know where they came from or how many there were. Tradition says they were men of high position from Parthia, near the site of ancient Babylon. How did they know the star represented the Messiah? (1) They could have been Jewish people who remained in Babylon after the exile and knew the Old Testament predictions of the Messiah's coming. (2) They may have been Eastern astrologers who studied ancient manuscripts from around the world. Because of the Jewish exile centuries earlier, they would have had copies of the Old Testament in their land. (3) They may have had a special message from God directing them to the Messiah. Some scholars say these astrologers were each from a different land, representing the entire world as bowing before Jesus. These men from faraway lands recognized Jesus as the Messiah when most of God's chosen people in Israel did not. Matthew pictures Jesus as King over the whole world, not just Judea.

2:1, 2 The astrologers traveled thousands of miles to see the King of the Jews. When they finally found him, they responded with joy, worship, and gifts. How different from the approach people often take today. We expect God to come looking for us, to explain himself, prove who he is, and give *us* gifts. But those who are wise still seek and worship Jesus today, not for what they can get, but for who he is.

2:2 The astrologers (magi) said they saw Jesus' star. Balaam referred to a coming "star of Jacob" (Numbers 24:17). Some say this star may have been a conjunction of Jupiter, Saturn, and Mars in 6 B.C., and others offer other explanations. But couldn't God, who created the heavens, have created a special star to announce the arrival of his Son? Whatever the nature of the star, these wise men traveled thousands of miles searching for a king, and they found him.

3King Herod was deeply disturbed by their question, and all Jerusalem was filled with rumors. 4He called a meeting of the Jewish religious leaders.
"Did the prophets tell us where the Messiah would be born?" he asked.
5"Yes, in Bethlehem," they said, "for this is what the prophet Micah wrote:

6'O little town of Bethlehem, you are not just an unimportant Judean village, for a Governor shall rise from you to rule my people Israel.'"

7Then Herod sent a private message to the astrologers, asking them to come to see him; at this meeting he found out from them the exact time when they first saw the star. Then he told them, 8"Go to Bethlehem and search for the child. And when you find him, come back and tell me so that I can go and worship him too!"

9After this interview the astrologers started out again. And look! The star appeared to them again, standing over Bethlehem. 10Their joy knew no bounds! 11Entering the house where the baby and Mary his mother were, they threw themselves down before him, worshiping. Then they opened their presents and gave him gold, frankincense and myrrh. 12But when they returned to their own land, they didn't go through Jerusalem to report to Herod, for God had warned them in a dream to go home another way.

2:4
Ps 2:1
Mal 2:7

2:5
Jn 7:42
Rev 2:27

2:6
Mic 5:2

2:11
Ps 2:12; 22:29
72:10
Isa 49:7; 60:6
Jn 5:23

2:12
Job 33:14,15
Mt 1:20; 2:19,20

The escape to Egypt
(13)

13After they were gone, an angel of the Lord appeared to Joseph in a dream. "Get up and flee to Egypt with the baby and his mother," the angel said, "and stay there until I tell you to return, for King Herod is going to try to kill the child." 14That

2:3 *and all Jerusalem was filled with rumors,* literally, "and all Jerusalem with him." 2:5 *Micah,* implied. Micah 5:2.
2:9 *standing over Bethlehem,* literally, "went before them until it came and stood over where the baby lay."

2:3 Herod the Great was quite disturbed when the astrologers asked about a newborn king of the Jews because: (1) Herod was not the rightful heir to the throne of David; therefore many Jews hated him as a usurper. If Jesus really was an heir, trouble would arise. (2) Herod was ruthless and, because of his many enemies, he was suspicious that someone would try to overthrow him. (3) Herod didn't want the Jews, a religious people, to unite around a religious figure. (4) If these astrologers were of Jewish descent and from Parthia (the region most powerful, next to Rome), they would have welcomed a Jewish king who could swing the balance of power away from Rome. The land of Israel, far from Rome, would have been easy prey for a nation trying to gain more control.

2:4 Herod's counselors on religious matters were aware of Micah 5:2 and other prophecies about the Messiah. The astrologers' news troubled Herod because he knew the Jewish people expected the Messiah to come soon (Luke 3:15). Most Jews expected the Messiah to be a great military and political deliverer, like Alexander the Great. Herod's counselors would have told Herod this. No wonder Herod took no chances and ordered all the babies in Bethlehem killed!

2:5, 6 Matthew often quoted Old Testament prophets. This prophecy from Micah was delivered seven centuries earlier. The words here are slightly different from those in Micah because Matthew paraphrased the thought of this Old Testament passage in applying it to Christ. In addition, New Testament writers often combined similar verses when citing the Scripture to get their point across.

2:6 Most religious leaders believed in a literal fulfillment of all Old Testament prophecy; therefore, they believed the Messiah would be born in Bethlehem. Ironically, when Jesus was born, these same religious leaders became his greatest enemies. When the Messiah for whom they had been waiting finally came, they didn't recognize him.

2:8 Herod did not want to worship Christ—he was lying. This was a trick to get the astrologers to return to him and reveal the whereabouts of the newborn king. Herod's plan was to kill him.

2:11 Jesus was probably one or two years old when the astrologers found him. By this time, Mary and Joseph were married, living in a house, and intending to stay in Bethlehem for a while. For more on why Joseph and Mary stayed in Bethlehem, see the note on Luke 2:39.

2:11 The astrologers gave these expensive gifts because they were worthy presents for a future king. Bible students have seen in the gifts symbols of Christ's identity and what he would accomplish. Gold was a gift for a king; frankincense, a gift for deity; myrrh, a spice for a mortal man who was going to die. These gifts may have provided the financial resources for the family's trip to Egypt and back.

2:11 The astrologers brought gifts and worshiped Jesus for who he was. This is the essence of true worship—honoring Christ for who he is and being willing to give him what is valuable to you. Worship God because he is the perfect, just, and almighty Creator of the universe, worthy of the best you have to give.

2:12 After finding Jesus and worshiping him, the astrologers were warned by God not to return through Jerusalem as they had intended. Finding Jesus may mean that your life must take a different direction, one that is responsive and obedient to God's Word. Are you willing to be led a different way?

2:13 This is the second dream or vision that Joseph received from God. His first dream revealed that Mary's child would be the Messiah (1:20, 21). His second dream told him how to protect the child's life. Although Joseph was not Jesus' natural father, he was his legal father and was responsible for his safety and well-being. Divine guidance comes only to prepared hearts. Since his first vision from God, Joseph had not become proud, but had remained receptive to God's guidance.

2:14, 15 Going to Egypt was not unusual, because there were several colonies of Jews in several major cities there. These colonies began during the time of the great captivity (see Jeremiah 43, 44). There is an interesting parallel between this flight to Egypt

2:15
Ex 4:22,23
Hos 11:1

same night he left for Egypt with Mary and the baby, [15]and stayed there until King Herod's death. This fulfilled the prophet's prediction,

"I have called my Son from Egypt."

[16]Herod was furious when he learned that the astrologers had disobeyed him. Sending soldiers to Bethlehem, he ordered them to kill every baby boy two years

2:14 *same,* implied.   **2:15** Hosea 11:1.

JOSEPH

The strength of what we believe is measured by how much we are willing to suffer for those beliefs. Joseph was a man with strong beliefs. He was prepared to do what was right despite the pain he knew it would cause. But Joseph had another trait—he not only tried to do what was right, he tried to do it in the right way.

When Mary told Joseph about her pregnancy, Joseph knew the child was not his. His respect for Mary's character and the story she told him, as well as her attitude toward the expected child, must have made it hard to think his bride had done something wrong. Still, someone else was the child's father—and it was difficult to accept that the "someone else" was God.

Joseph decided he had to break the engagement, but he was determined to do it in a way that would not cause public shame to Mary. He intended to act with justice and love.

At this point, God sent a messenger to Joseph to confirm Mary's story and open another way of obedience for Joseph—to take Mary as his wife. Joseph obeyed God, married Mary, and honored her virginity until the baby was born.

We do not know how long Joseph lived his role as Jesus' earthly father—he is last mentioned when Jesus was 12 years old. But Joseph trained his son in the trade of carpentry, made sure he had good spiritual training in Nazareth, and took the whole family on the yearly trip to Jerusalem for the Passover, which Jesus continued to observe during his adult years.

Joseph knew Jesus was someone special from the moment he heard the angel's words. His strong belief in that fact, and his openness to God's words to him, enabled him to be Jesus' chosen earthly father.

Strengths and accomplishments:
- A man of integrity
- A descendant of King David
- Jesus' legal and earthly father
- Sensitive to God's guidance and willing to do God's will no matter what the consequence

Lessons from his life:
- God honors integrity
- Social position is of little importance when God chooses to use us
- Being obedient to the guidance we have from God leads to more guidance from him
- Feelings are not accurate measures of the rightness or wrongness of an action

Vital statistics:
- Where: Nazareth, Bethlehem
- Occupation: Carpenter
- Relatives: Wife: Mary. Sons: Jesus, James, Joseph, Judas, Simon.
- Contemporaries: Herod the Great, John the Baptist, Simeon, Anna

Key verses:
"Then Joseph, her fiancé, being a man of stern principle, decided to break the engagement but to do it quietly, as he didn't want to publicly disgrace her. As he lay awake considering this, he fell into a dream, and saw an angel standing beside him. 'Joseph, son of David,' the angel said, 'don't hesitate to take Mary as your wife! For the child within her has been conceived by the Holy Spirit' " (Matthew 1:19, 20).

Joseph's story is told in Matthew 1:16—2:23; Luke 1:26—2:52.

---

and Israel's history. When Israel was an infant nation, she went to Egypt, as Jesus did as a child. God led Israel out (Hosea 11:1); God brought Jesus back. Both events show God working to save his people.

2:16 Herod, the king of the Jews, killed all the boys under two years of age in an obsessive attempt to kill Jesus, the newborn King. He stained his hands with blood, but he did not harm Jesus. Herod was king by a human appointment; Jesus was King by a divine appointment. No one can thwart God's plans—people only

hurt themselves in trying to do so.

2:16-18 Herod was afraid that this newborn king would one day take his throne. He completely misunderstood the reason for Christ's coming. Jesus didn't want Herod's throne, he wanted to be king of Herod's life. He wanted to give him eternal life, not take away his present life. Today people are often afraid that Christ wants to take things away when, in reality, he wants to give them real freedom, peace, and joy.

old and under, both in the town and on the nearby farms, for the astrologers had told him the star first appeared to them two years before. 17This brutal action of Herod's fulfilled the prophecy of Jeremiah,

18"Screams of anguish come from Ramah,
   Weeping unrestrained;
Rachel weeping for her children,
Uncomforted—
   For they are dead."

2:18
Jer 31:15

The return to Nazareth
(14)

19When Herod died, an angel of the Lord appeared in a dream to Joseph in Egypt, and told him, 20"Get up and take the baby and his mother back to Israel, for those who were trying to kill the child are dead."

21So he returned immediately to Israel with Jesus and his mother. 22But on the way he was frightened to learn that the new king was Herod's son, Archelaus. Then, in another dream, he was warned not to go to Judea, so they went to Galilee instead, 23and lived in Nazareth. This fulfilled the prediction of the prophets concerning the Messiah,
   "He shall be called a Nazarene."

2:23
Judg 13:5
Isa 11:1
Lk 2:39
Jn 1:45,46
Acts 4:10; 24:5

John the Baptist prepares the way for Jesus
(16/Mark 1:1–8; Luke 3:1–18)

3 While they were living in Nazareth, John the Baptist began preaching out in the Judean wilderness. His constant theme was, 2"Turn from your sins . . . turn to

3:1
Mal 3:1

2:18 Ramah, or, "the region of Ramah."   **3:1** While they were living in Nazareth, literally, "in those days."   **3:2** is coming soon, or, "has arrived." Literally, "is at hand."

2:17, 18 Rachel was the wife of Jacob, one of the great men of God in the Old Testament. From Jacob's 12 sons came the 12 tribes of Israel. Rachel was buried near Bethlehem (Genesis 35:19). For more about the significance of this verse see Jeremiah 31:15 from which this verse was quoted.

2:19–22 Herod the Great died in 4 B.C. of an incurable disease. Rome trusted him, but not his sons. Herod knew Rome wouldn't give his successor as much power, so he divided his kingdom into three parts, one for each son. Archelaus got Judea, Samaria, and Idumea; Herod Antipas received Galilee and Perea; Herod Philip II got Trachonitis. Archelaus, a violent man, began his reign by slaughtering 3,000 influential people. He was banished nine years later. God didn't want Joseph's family to go into the region of this evil ruler.

2:23 Nazareth sat in the hilly area of southern Galilee near the crossroads of great caravan trade routes. The people of Nazareth had constant contact with people from all over the world, so world news reached them quickly. The town itself was rather small. The Roman garrison in charge of Galilee was housed there, making Nazareth despised by many Jews. This may have been why Nathanael commented (John 1:46), "Can anything good come from there?"

2:23 The Old Testament does not specifically record this statement, "He shall be called a Nazarene." Many scholars believe, however, that Matthew was referring to Isaiah 11:1 where the Hebrew word for "branch" is similar to the word for "Nazarene." Or he may have been referring to an unrecorded prophecy. In any case, Matthew painted the picture of Jesus as the true Messiah, spoken of by God through the prophets, and he made the point that Jesus, the Christ, had very unexpected and humble beginnings, just as the Old Testament predicted (see Micah 5:2).

3:1, 2 Almost 30 years had passed since the events of chapter 2. Now John the Baptist burst onto the scene. His theme was "turn from your sins; . . . turn to God." He meant that we must do an

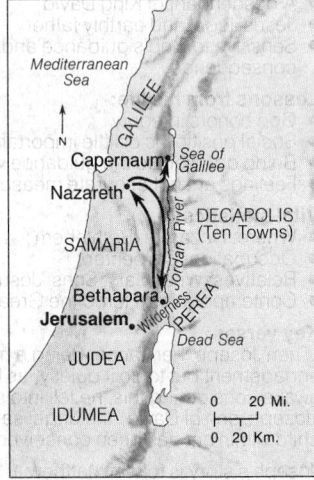

JESUS BEGINS HIS MINISTRY
From his childhood home, Nazareth, Jesus set out to begin his earthly ministry. He was baptized by John the Baptist in the Jordan River, tempted by Satan in the wilderness, and then returned to Galilee. Between the temptation and his move to Capernaum (4:12, 13), he ministered in Judea, Samaria, and Galilee (see John 1-4).

about-face—a 180-degree turn—from the kind of self-centeredness that leads to wrong actions such as lying, cheating, stealing, gossiping, revenge, abuse, and sexual immorality. Instead, we must follow God's prescribed way of living found in his Word. The first step in turning to God is to admit your sin, as John urged. Then God will receive you and help you live the way he wants you to. Remember that only God can get rid of sin. He doesn't expect us to clean up our lives before we come to him.

3:2 The Kingdom of Heaven began when God himself entered human history as a man. Today Jesus Christ reigns in the hearts of believers, but the Kingdom of Heaven will not be fully realized until

3:3
Isa 40:3
Lk 1:76

God . . . . for the Kingdom of Heaven is coming soon." ³Isaiah the prophet had told about John's ministry centuries before! He had written,

"I hear a shout from the wilderness, 'Prepare a road for the Lord—straighten out the path where he will walk.'"

3:3 *I hear,* implied. Isa 40:3.

HEROD

The Bible records history. It has proven itself an accurate and reliable record of people, events, and places. Independent historical records back up the Bible's descriptions and details of many famous lives. One of these was the father of the Herodian family, Herod the Great.

Herod is remembered as a builder of cities and lavish rebuilder of the Temple in Jerusalem. But he also destroyed people. He showed little greatness in either his personal actions or his character. He was ruthless in ruling his territory. His suspicions and jealousy led to the murder of several of his children and the death of his wife Mariamne.

Herod's title, king of the Jews, was granted by Rome but never accepted by the people. He was not part of the Davidic family line, and he was only partly Jewish. Although Israel benefited from Herod's lavish efforts to repair the Temple in Jerusalem, he won little admiration because he also rebuilt various pagan temples. Herod's costly attempt to gain the loyalty of the people failed because it was superficial. His only loyalty was to himself.

Because his royal title was not genuine, Herod was constantly worried about losing his position. His actions when hearing from the wise men about their search for the new king are consistent with all that we know about Herod. He planned to locate and kill the child before he could become a threat. The murder of innocent children that followed is a tragic lesson in what can happen when actions are motivated by selfishness. Herod's suspicions did not spare even his own family. His life was self-destructing.

Strengths and accomplishments:
- Was given the title king of the Jews by the Romans
- Held onto his power for more than 30 years
- Was an effective, though ruthless, ruler
- Sponsored a great variety of large building projects

Weaknesses and mistakes:
- Tended to treat those around him with fear, suspicion, and jealousy
- Had several of his own children and at least one wife killed
- Ordered the killing of the infants in Bethlehem
- Although claiming to have become Jewish, he was still involved in many forms of pagan religion

Lessons from his life:
- Great power brings neither peace nor security
- No one can prevent God's plans from being carried out
- Superficial loyalty does not impress people or God

Vital statistics:
- Occupation: King of Judea from 37–4 B.C.
- Relatives: Father: Antipater. Sons: Archelaus, Antipater, Antipas, Philip, and others. Wives: Doris, Mariamne, and others.
- Contemporaries: Zacharias, Elizabeth, Mary, Joseph, Mark Antony, Augustus.

Notes about Herod the Great are found in Matthew 2:1–22 and Luke 1:5.

---

all evil in the world is judged and removed. Christ came to earth first as a suffering servant; he will come again as king and judge to rule over all the earth as victor.

3:3 The prophet quoted is Isaiah (40:3), one of the greatest prophets of the Old Testament and one of the most quoted in the New. Like Isaiah, John was a prophet who urged the people to confess their sins and live for God. Both prophets taught that the message of repentance is good news to those who listen and seek the healing forgiveness of God's love, but terrible news to those who refuse to listen and cut off their only source of eternal hope.

3:3 John the Baptist *prepared* the way for Jesus. People who do not know Jesus may need to be prepared to meet him. We can prepare them by explaining their need for forgiveness, demonstrating Christ's teachings in our lives, and telling them how Christ can give their lives meaning. We can straighten out the path by correcting misconceptions that might be hindering them from approaching Christ. Someone you know may be open to a relationship with Christ. What can you do to prepare the way for this person?

4John's clothing was woven from camel's hair and he wore a leather belt; his food was locusts and wild honey. 5People from Jerusalem and from all over the Jordan Valley, and, in fact, from every section of Judea went out to the wilderness to hear him preach, 6and when they confessed their sins, he baptized them in the Jordan River.

7But when he saw many Pharisees and Sadducees coming to be baptized, he denounced them.

"You sons of snakes!" he warned. "Who said that you could escape the coming wrath of God? 8Before being baptized, prove that you have turned from sin by doing worthy deeds. 9Don't try to get by as you are, thinking, 'We are safe for we are Jews—descendants of Abraham.' That proves nothing. God can change these stones here into Jews!

10"And even now the axe of God's judgment is poised to chop down every unproductive tree. They will be chopped and burned.

11"With water I baptize those who repent of their sins; but someone else is coming, far greater than I am, so great that I am not worthy to carry his shoes! He shall baptize you with the Holy Spirit and with fire. 12He will separate the chaff

3:4
Lev 11:22
2 Kgs 1:8
Zech 13:4

3:6
Acts 19:4

3:7
Mt 12:34; 23:33
Jn 8:44
Rom 5:9
1 Thess 1:10
1 Jn 3:8,10

3:9
Jn 8:33,39
Acts 13:26
Rom 4:1

3:10
Jn 15:6
Heb 6:8

3:11
Jn 1:26,33
Acts 1:5; 2:3,4

3:12
Mal 3:2,3; 4:1

3:9 *God can change these stones here into Jews*, literally, "God is able of these stones to raise up children unto Abraham."   **3:11** *With water ... with the Holy Spirit*, or, "in water," and "in the Holy Spirit and in fire."

3:4-6 John must have had a strange image! Many people came to hear this preacher who wore odd clothes and ate unusual food. Some probably came simply out of curiosity and ended up repenting of their sins as they listened to his powerful message. People may be curious about our Christian lifestyle and values. We can use their simple curiosity as an opener to share how Christ makes a difference in our lives.

3:4 John was markedly different from other religious leaders of his day. While many were greedy, selfish, and concerned mostly with winning the praise of the people, John was concerned only with the praise of God. Having separated himself from the evil and hypocrisy of his day, he lived differently from other people to show that his message was new. John not only preached about God's law, he *lived* it.

3:5 Why did John attract so many people? He was the first true prophet in 400 years. He blasted both King Herod and the religious leaders, something that was not only daring, but fascinating to the common people. But John also had strong words for them—they too were sinners and needed to repent. His message was powerful and true. The people were expecting a prophet like Elijah (Malachi 4:5), and John seemed to be the one!

3:6 The Jordan river is about 70 miles long, its main section stretching between the Sea of Galilee and the Dead Sea. Jerusalem lies about 20 miles west of it. This river was Israel's eastern border, and many significant events in the nation's history took place there. It was by the Jordan River that the Israelites renewed their covenant with God (Joshua 1, 2). Here John the Baptist calls them to do the same thing.

3:6 When you wash dirty hands, the results are immediately visible. But repentance happens inside with a cleansing that isn't immediately seen. So John used a symbolic action that people could see: baptism. Baptism was used by the Jews to initiate converts to Judaism, so John's audience was familiar with the rite. Here, baptism was used as a sign of repentance and forgiveness. Repent means "to turn," implying a change in behavior. It is turning from sin toward God. Have you repented of sin in your life? Can others see the difference it makes in you? A changed life with new and different behavior makes your repentance real and visible.

3:7 The Jewish religious leaders were divided into several groups. Two of the most prominent were the Pharisees and the Sadducees. The Pharisees separated themselves from anything non-Jewish and carefully followed both the Old Testament laws and the oral traditions which had been handed down through the centuries. The Sadducees believed the Pentateuch alone

(Genesis—Deuteronomy) to be God's Word. They were descended mainly from priestly nobility, while the Pharisees came from all classes of people. The two groups disliked each other greatly, and, as a whole, both opposed Jesus. John the Baptist criticized the Pharisees for being legalistic and hypocritical, following the letter of the law while ignoring its true intent. He criticized the Sadducees for using religion to advance their political position.

3:8 John the Baptist called people to more than words or ritual; he told them to change their lives. God looks beyond our words and religious activities to see if our lives back up our words, and he judges our words by the actions that accompany them. Do your actions agree with your words?

3:9, 10 Just as a fruit tree is expected to bear fruit, God's people should produce a crop of good deeds. God has no use for those who call themselves Christians but do nothing about it. Like many people in John's day who were God's people in name only, we are of no value if we are Christians in name only. If others can't see our faith in the way we live, we may not be God's people at all.

3:10 God's message hasn't changed since the Old Testament—people will be judged for their unproductive lives. God calls us to be *active* in our obedience. John compared people who say they believe God but don't live for God to "unproductive trees" which will be chopped down. To be productive for God, we must obey his teachings, resist temptation, actively serve and help our fellow man, and share our faith. How productive are you for God?

3:11 John baptized people as a sign that they had asked God to forgive their sins and purposed to live as he wanted them to live. Baptism was an *outward* sign. But the real sign of the people's repentance was whether their lives changed for the better. It wasn't the water of baptism that changed their lives, but their inner heart attitude. John said that Jesus would baptize with the Holy Spirit and fire. This looks ahead to Pentecost (Acts 2), when the Holy Spirit would be sent by Jesus in the form of tongues of fire, empowering his followers to preach the gospel. It also symbolizes the work of the Holy Spirit in bringing God's judgment on those who refuse to repent. Everyone will one day be baptized—either now by God's Holy Spirit, or later by the fire of his judgment.

3:12 The grain is the part of the plant that is useful; chaff is the worthless outer shell. Because it is useless, chaff is burned; grain, however, is stored. The unrepentant people will be judged and discarded because they have no value in God's work; those who repent and believe will be saved and used by God.

from the grain, burning the chaff with never-ending fire, and storing away the grain."

→ John baptizes Jesus
(17/Mark 1:9–11; Luke 3:21, 22)

3:13
Mk 1:9-11
Lk 3:21,22
Jn 1:31-34

¹³Then Jesus went from Galilee to the Jordan River to be baptized there by John. ¹⁴John didn't want to do it.

"This isn't proper," he said. "I am the one who needs to be baptized by you."

3:16
Isa 11:2

¹⁵But Jesus said, "Please do it, for I must do all that is right." So then John baptized him.

3:17
Mt 12:18; 17:5
Mk 9:7
Isa 42:1
Lk 9:35
Jn 12:28

⅄ ¹⁶After his baptism, as soon as Jesus came up out of the water, the heavens were opened to him and he saw the Spirit of God coming down in the form of a dove. ¹⁷And a voice from heaven said, "This is my beloved Son, and I am wonderfully pleased with him."

3:15 *do all that is right,* literally, "fulfill all righteousness."

THE PHARISEES AND SADDUCEES	Name	Positive Characteristics	Negative Characteristics
The Pharisees and Sadducees were the two major religious groups in Israel at the time of Christ. The Pharisees were more religiously minded while the Sadducees were more politically minded. Although the groups disliked and distrusted each other, they became allies in their common hatred for Jesus.	PHARISEES	• Were committed to obeying all of God's Word • Were admired by the common people for their apparent piety • Believed in a bodily resurrection and eternal life • Believed in angels and demons	• Behaved as though their own religious rules were just as important as God's rules for living • Their piety was often hypocritical and their efforts often forced others to try to live up to standards they themselves could not live up to • Believed that salvation came from perfect obedience to the law and was not based on forgiveness of sins • Became so obsessed with obeying their legal interpretations in every detail that they completely ignored God's message of mercy and grace • Were more concerned with appearing to be good than obeying God
	SADDUCEES	• Believed God's Word was limited to the first five books of the Bible: Genesis to Deuteronomy • Were more practically minded than the Pharisees	• Relied on logic while placing little importance on faith • Did not believe all the Old Testament was God's Word • Did not believe in a bodily resurrection or eternal life • Did not believe in angels or demons • Were often willing to compromise their values with the Romans and others in order to maintain their status and influential positions

---

3:13, 14 John had explained that Jesus' baptism would be much greater than his, when suddenly Jesus was there to be baptized! John did not feel qualified. He wanted Jesus to baptize him. Why was it right for Jesus to be baptized? It was not for repentance for sin because he never sinned. Jesus was baptized because (1) he was personally confessing the sin of the nation, as Nehemiah, Ezra, Moses, and Daniel had done; (2) he was showing support for what John was doing; (3) he was inaugurating his public ministry; (4) he was identifying with the common people, not with the critical Pharisees who were only watching; (5) he was portraying his coming ministry of death and resurrection. God showed his approval of Jesus as the perfect man who didn't need baptism for sin but accepted baptism in obedient service to the Father.

3:15 Put yourself in John's shoes. Your work is going well, people are taking notice, everything is growing. But you know that the purpose of your work is to prepare the hearts of the people for Jesus (3:11; John 1:36). Now Jesus has arrived, and with him, the real test of your integrity. Will you be able to turn your followers over to him? John passed the test by publicly baptizing Jesus. Soon he would say, "He must become greater and greater, and I must become less and less" (John 3:30). Can we, like John, put our egos and profitable work aside in order to point others to Jesus? Are we willing to lose some of our status so that everyone will benefit?

3:16 The doctrine of the Trinity means that God is three persons and yet one in essence. In this passage, all three persons of the Trinity are present and active. God the Father spoke; God the Son was baptized; God the Holy Spirit descended on Jesus. God is one, yet in three persons at the same time. This is one of God's incomprehensible mysteries. Other Bible references that speak of the Father, Son, and Holy Spirit are Matthew 28:19; John 15:26; 1 Corinthians 12:4–13; 2 Corinthians 13:14; Ephesians 2:18; 1 Thessalonians 1:2–5; and 1 Peter 1:2.

Satan tempts Jesus in the wilderness
(18/Mark 1:12, 13; Luke 4:1–13)

4 Then Jesus was led out into the wilderness by the Holy Spirit, to be tempted there by Satan. ²For forty days and forty nights he ate nothing and became very hungry. ³Then Satan tempted him to get food by changing stones into loaves of bread.

4:1
1 Kgs 18:12
Ezek 3:14
Mk 1:12,13
Lk 4:1-13
Acts 8:39

Temptation	Real needs used as basis for temptation	Possible doubts that made the temptations real	Potential weaknesses Satan sought to exploit	Jesus' answer	**THE TEMPTATIONS**
Make bread	Physical need: Hunger	Would God provide food?	Hunger, impatience, need to "prove his Sonship"	Deuteronomy 8:3 "Depend on God" Focus: God's purpose	
Dare God to rescue you (based on misapplied Scripture, Psalm 91:11, 12)	Emotional need: Security	Would God protect?	Pride, insecurity, need to test God	Deuteronomy 6:16 "Don't test God" Focus: God's plan	
Worship me! (Satan)	Psychological need: Significance, power, achievement	Would God direct?	Desire for quick power, easy solutions, need to prove equality with God	Deuteronomy 6:13 "No compromise with evil" Focus: God's person	

As if going through a final test of preparation, Jesus was tempted by Satan in the wilderness. Three specific parts of the temptation are listed by Matthew. They are familiar because we face the same kinds of temptations. As the chart shows, temptation is often the combination of a real need and a possible doubt that create an inappropriate desire. Jesus demonstrates both the importance and effectiveness of knowing and applying Scripture to combat temptation.

4:1ff This temptation by Satan shows us that Jesus was human, and it provided the opportunity for Jesus to reaffirm God's plan for his ministry. It also gives us an example to follow when we are tempted. Jesus' temptation was important because it demonstrated his sinlessness. He would face temptation and not give in.

4:1 This time of testing showed that Jesus really was the Son of God, able to overcome Satan and his temptations. A person has not shown true obedience if he has never had an opportunity to be disobedient. In Deuteronomy 8:2, God led Israel into the wilderness to humble and test them. He wanted to find out how they would respond and whether or not they would really obey him. We too will be tested. Because we know that testing will come, we should be alert and ready for it. Otherwise, as Matthew 26:41 says, "temptation will overpower you." Remember, your convictions are only as good as they are under pressure!

4:1 Satan tempted Eve in the garden, and here he tempts Jesus in the wilderness. Satan is a fallen angel. He is *real,* not symbolic, and is constantly fighting against those who follow and obey God. Satan's temptations are real, and he is always trying to get us to do things his way or ours rather than God's way. Jesus will one day reign over all creation, but Satan tried to force his hand and get him to declare his kingship prematurely. If Jesus had given in, his mission on earth—to die for our sins and give us the opportunity to have eternal life—would have been lost. When temptations seem especially strong, or when you think they can be rationalized, consider whether Satan may be trying to block God's purposes for your life.

4:1 Jesus was tempted by Satan, but he never sinned! Although we may feel dirty after being tempted, we should remember that temptation itself is not sin. We sin when we give in and disobey God. Remembering this will help us walk away from the temptation.

4:1 Jesus wasn't tempted in the Temple or at his baptism, but in the wilderness, where he was tired, alone, and hungry, and thus most vulnerable. Satan often tempts us when we are vulnerable—when we are tired, lonely, weighing big decisions, or faced with uncertainty. But Satan also likes to tempt us through our strengths where we are susceptible to pride (see the note on Luke 4:3ff). We must be on guard at all times against his attacks.

4:1-10 Satan's temptations focused on three crucial areas: (1) physical desires, (2) possessions and power, and (3) pride (see 1 John 2:15, 16 for a similar list). But Jesus did not give in. Hebrews 4:15, 16 says that Jesus was tempted just like we are, but he never once gave in and sinned. He knows firsthand what we are experiencing, and he is willing and able to help us in our struggles. When tempted, turn to him for strength.

4:3, 4 Jesus was hungry and weak after fasting for 40 days, but he chose not to use his divine power to satisfy his natural desire for food. Food, hunger, and eating are good, but the timing was wrong. He had given up the unlimited, independent use of his divine power in order to fully experience humanity. We also may be tempted to satisfy a perfectly normal desire in a wrong way or at the wrong time. If we indulge in sex before marriage or if we steal to get food, we are trying to satisfy God-given desires in ways God disapproves. Remember, many of your desires are normal and good, but they must be satisfied in the right way and at the right time.

4:3, 4 Jesus was able to resist all of Satan's temptations because he not only knew Scripture; he obeyed it. Ephesians 6:17 says that God's Word is a weapon—like a two-edged sword—to use in spiritual combat. Knowing Bible verses is an important step in helping us resist Satan's attacks, but we must obey the Bible as well. Note that Satan, too, had memorized Scripture, but he failed to obey it. Knowing and obeying the Bible helps us follow God's desires rather than Satan's.

"It will prove you are the Son of God," he said.

4:4
Deut 8:3
Eph 6:17

⁴But Jesus told him, "No! For the Scriptures tell us that bread won't feed men's souls: obedience to every word of God is what we need."

4:6
Ps 91:11

⁵Then Satan took him to Jerusalem to the roof of the Temple. ⁶"Jump off," he said, "and prove you are the Son of God; for the Scriptures declare, 'God will send his angels to keep you from harm,' . . . they will prevent you from smashing on the rocks below."

4:7
Deut 6:16

⁷Jesus retorted, "It also says not to put the Lord your God to a foolish test!"

⁸Next Satan took him to the peak of a very high mountain and showed him the nations of the world and all their glory. ⁹"I'll give it all to you," he said, "if you will only kneel and worship me."

4:10
Deut 6:13
4:11
Heb 1:14
Jas 4:7

¹⁰"Get out of here, Satan," Jesus told him. "The Scriptures say, 'Worship only the Lord God. Obey only him.' "

¹¹Then Satan went away, and angels came and cared for Jesus.

B. MESSAGE AND MINISTRY OF JESUS, THE KING (4:12—25:46)

Matthew features Jesus' sermons. The record of his actions are woven around great passages of his teaching. This section of Matthew, then, is topical rather than chronological. Matthew records for us the Sermon on the Mount, the Parables of the Kingdom, Jesus' teachings on forgiveness, and parables about the end of the age.

1. Jesus begins his ministry
Jesus preaches in Galilee
(30/Mark 1:14, 15; Luke 4:14, 15; John 4:43–45)

4:12
Mark 1:14
Lk 3:19,20
Jn 4:1-3

¹²,¹³When Jesus heard that John had been arrested, he left Judea and returned home to Nazareth in Galilee; but soon he moved to Capernaum, beside the Lake of Galilee, close to Zebulun and Naphtali. ¹⁴This fulfilled Isaiah's prophecy:

4:15,16
Isa 9:1,2; 42:6,7
Lk 2:32

¹⁵, ¹⁶"The land of Zebulun and the land of Naphtali, beside the Lake, and the countryside beyond the Jordan River, and Upper Galilee where so many

4:12, 13 *returned home,* implied.   **4:15, 16** *broke through upon them,* Isa 9:1, 2.

4:5 The Temple was the religious center of the entire nation and the place where the Jews expected the Messiah to arrive (Malachi 3:1). Herod the Great had renovated the Temple in hope of gaining the Jews' confidence. The Temple was the tallest building in the area, and the pinnacle of the Temple was probably the corner wall that jutted out of the hillside, overlooking the valley below. From this spot, Jesus could see all of Jerusalem behind him and the country for miles in front of him.

4:5–9 God is not our magician in the sky. In response to Satan's temptations, Jesus said not to put God to a foolish test (Deuteronomy 6:16). You may want to ask God to do a special favor for you to prove his existence or his love for you. A man once asked Jesus for a special sign to be sent to help people believe. Jesus told him that people who don't believe through what is written in the Bible wouldn't believe if someone came back from the dead to warn them (Luke 16:31)! Asking God for signs amounts to manipulating him. He wants us to live by faith, not by chance. Don't tempt God or try to manipulate him.

4:6 Satan used Scripture to try to convince Jesus to sin! Sometimes friends will present attractive and convincing reasons why you should try something you know is wrong. They may even find Bible verses which *seem* to support their viewpoint. Study the Bible carefully, especially the broader contexts of specific verses, so that you understand God's principles for living and what he wants for your life. Only if you really understand what the *whole* Bible says, can you recognize errors of interpretation when people take verses out of context and twist them to say what they want them to say.

4:8, 9 Did Satan have the power to give Jesus the kingdoms of the world? Didn't God, the Creator of the world, have control over them? Satan may have been lying about his implied power, or he may have been referring to his temporary control and free rein over

the earth because of humanity's sinful nature. The temptation was to take the world as a political ruler, *now.* Satan was trying to distort Jesus' perspective by making him focus on worldly power and not on God's plans.

4:8–10 Satan offered all the world to Jesus if he would only kneel and worship him. Today Satan offers us the world by trying to entice us with materialism and power. We can resist temptations the same way Jesus did. If you find yourself craving something that the world offers, quote Deuteronomy 6:13, "Worship only the Lord God. Obey only him."

4:11 Angels, like these ministering to Jesus, have a significant role as God's messengers. They are spiritual beings who were involved in Jesus' life on earth by (1) announcing his birth to Mary, (2) reassuring Joseph, (3) naming Jesus, (4) announcing his birth to the shepherds, (5) protecting Jesus by sending his family to Egypt, (6) ministering to him in Gethsemane. For more on angels, see the note on 1:20.

4:12, 13 Jesus moved from Nazareth, his hometown, to Capernaum, about 20 miles farther north. Capernaum became Jesus' home base during his ministry in Galilee. He probably moved (1) to get away from intense opposition and also from apathy in Nazareth, (2) to have an impact on the greatest number of people (Capernaum was a busy city and Jesus' message could reach more people and spread more quickly), (3) to utilize extra resources and support for his ministry.
    Jesus' move fulfilled the prophecy of Isaiah 9:1, 2, which states that the Messiah will be a light to the land of Zebulun and Naphtali, the region of Galilee in which Capernaum was located.

4:14–16 Matthew continues to tie Jesus' ministry into the Old Testament by quoting Isaiah. This was helpful for his Jewish listeners, who were familiar with these Scriptures.

foreigners live—there the people who sat in darkness have seen a great Light; they sat in the land of death, and the Light broke through upon them."

17From then on, Jesus began to preach, "Turn from sin, and turn to God, for the Kingdom of Heaven is near."

4:17
Mt 10:7

Four fishermen follow Jesus
(33/Mark 1:16–20)

18One day as he was walking along the beach beside the Lake of Galilee, he saw two brothers—Simon, also called Peter, and Andrew—out in a boat fishing with a net, for they were commercial fishermen.

4:18
Mk 1:16-20
Lk 5:1-11

19Jesus called out, "Come along with me and I will show you how to fish for the souls of men!" 20And they left their nets at once and went with him.

4:19
Mt 16:18
Jn 1:42

21A little farther up the beach he saw two other brothers, James and John, sitting in a boat with their father Zebedee, mending their nets; and he called to them to come too. 22At once they stopped their work and, leaving their father behind, went with him.

4:20
Mk 10:28
Lk 18:28

Jesus preaches throughout Galilee
(36/Mark 1:35–39; Luke 4:42–44)

23Jesus traveled all through Galilee teaching in the Jewish synagogues, everywhere preaching the Good News about the Kingdom of Heaven. And he healed every kind of sickness and disease. 24The report of his miracles spread far beyond the borders of Galilee so that sick folk were soon coming to be healed from as far away as Syria. And whatever their illness and pain, or if they were possessed by demons, or were insane, or paralyzed—he healed them all. 25Enormous crowds followed him wherever he went—people from Galilee, and the Ten Cities, and Jerusalem, and from all over Judea, and even from across the Jordan River.

4:23
Mt 9:35
Mk 1:39
Lk4:15

4:17 is near, or, "is at hand," or, "has arrived."   **4:18** out in a boat, implied.

4:17 The "Kingdom of Heaven" means the same thing as the "Kingdom of God" in Mark and Luke. Matthew uses this phrase because the Jews, out of their intense reverence and respect, did not pronounce God's name. The Kingdom of Heaven is near, for it has arrived in our hearts. See the note on 3:2 for more on the Kingdom of Heaven.

4:17 Jesus started his ministry with the very words people had heard John the Baptist say, "Turn from sin and turn to God." The message is the same today as when Jesus and John gave it. Becoming a follower of Christ means turning away from our self-centeredness and "self" control and turning our lives over to Christ's direction and control.

4:18 This lake is also called the Sea of Galilee. About 30 fishing towns surrounded this sea during Jesus' day, and Capernaum was the largest.

4:18–20 Jesus told Peter and Andrew to leave their fishing business and "fish for people's souls." He meant that he could show them how to help others find God. Jesus was calling them from their productive trades to be productive spiritually. We all need to fish for souls. If we follow Christ's example and teachings and put them into practice, we will be able to draw those around us to Christ like a fisherman who pulls fish into his boat with nets.

4:19, 20 These men already knew Jesus. He had talked to Peter and Andrew previously (John 1:41, 42) and had been preaching in the area. When Jesus called them, they knew what kind of man he was and were willing to follow him. They were not in a hypnotic trance when they followed, but instead were thoroughly convinced that following him would change their lives forever.

4:21, 22 James and his brother, John, along with Peter and Andrew, were the first disciples Jesus called to work with him.

Jesus' call motivated these men to get up and leave their jobs—immediately. They didn't make excuses about why now wasn't a good time. They left at once and followed. Jesus calls each of us to follow him. When Jesus asks us to serve him, we must be like the disciples and do it at once.

4:23 Jesus was teaching, preaching, and healing. These were the three main aspects of his ministry. Teaching shows Jesus' concern for understanding; preaching shows his concern for commitment; and healing shows his concern for wholeness. His miracles of healing authenticated his teaching and preaching, showing that he truly was from God.

4:23 Jesus soon developed a powerful preaching ministry and often spoke in the synagogues. Most towns that had ten or more Jewish families had a synagogue. The building served as a local gathering place on the Sabbath and as a school during the week. The leader of the synagogue was not a preacher as much as an administrator. His job was to find and invite rabbis to teach and preach. It was customary to invite visiting rabbis like Jesus to speak.

4:23, 24 Jesus preached the Good News to everyone who wanted to hear it. The Good News is that the Kingdom of Heaven has come, that God is with us, and that he cares for us. He can heal us, not just of physical sickness, but of spiritual sickness as well. There's no sin or problem too great or too small for him to handle. Jesus' words were good news because they offered freedom, hope, peace of heart, and eternal life with God.

4:25 The Ten Cities were located east of the Sea of Galilee. They formed a league of Gentile cities joined for better trade and mutual defense. The word about Jesus was out, and Jews and Gentiles were coming long distances to hear him.

2. Jesus gives the Sermon on the Mount

Jesus gives the Beatitudes
(49/Luke 6:17–26)

5:1
Lk 6:20-23

5 One day as the crowds were gathering, he went up the hillside with his disciples and sat down and taught them there.

KEY LESSONS FROM THE SERMON ON THE MOUNT	Beatitude	Old Testament anticipation	Clashing worldly values	God's reward	How to develop this attitude
	Humility (5:3)	Isaiah 57:15	Pride and personal independence	Kingdom of Heaven	James 4:7–10
	Mourning (5:4)	Isaiah 61:1, 2	Happiness at any cost	Comfort (2 Corinthians 1:4)	Psalm 51 James 4:7–10
	Meekness and lowliness (5:5)	Psalm 37:5–11	Power	Wide world belongs to you	Matthew 11:27–30
	Justice and goodness (5:6)	Isaiah 11:5; 42:1–4	Pursuing personal needs	Complete satisfaction	John 16:5–11 Philippians 3:7–11
	Kindness and mercy (5:7)	Psalm 41:1	Strength without feeling	Receive mercy	Ephesians 5:1, 2
	Hearts that are pure (5:8)	Psalm 24:3, 4; 51:10	Deception is acceptable	To see God	1 John 3:1–3
	Peace (5:9)	Isaiah 57:18, 19; 60:17	Personal peace is pursued without concern for the world's chaos	Be called sons of God	Romans 12:9–21 Hebrews 12:10, 11
	Faithfulness (5:10)	Isaiah 52:13; 53:12	Weak commitments	Will inherit the Kingdom of God	2 Timothy 3:12

In his longest recorded sermon, Jesus began by describing the traits he was looking for in his followers. He called those who lived out those traits fortunate because God had something special in store for them. Each beatitude is an almost direct contradiction of society's typical way of life. In the last beatitude, Jesus even points out that a serious effort to develop these traits is bound to create opposition. The best example of each trait is found in Jesus himself. If our goal is to become like him, the beatitudes will challenge the way we live each day.

5:1ff Matthew 5—7 is called the "Sermon on the Mount" because Jesus gave it on a hillside near Capernaum. This "sermon" probably covered several days of preaching. In it, Jesus proclaimed his attitude toward the law. Position, authority, and money are not important in his Kingdom—what matters is faithful obedience from the heart. The Sermon on the Mount challenged the proud and legalistic religious leaders of the day. It called them back to the messages of the Old Testament prophets who, like Jesus, taught that heartfelt obedience is more important than legalistic observance.

Some commentators think this sermon is probably the same discourse as that recorded in Luke 6:17–49. Luke provided far less detail than Matthew, with considerable variation. Other commentators believe the two sermons are different discourses containing shared material. Those who affirm the second view indicate that the sermons were given at different times: Matthew, during Jesus' first preaching tour; Luke, after Jesus' selection of the Twelve. It is apparent that Jesus repeated some of his weightier sayings in different forms, with varied application, to meet the need of the situation.

5:1, 2 Enormous crowds were following Jesus—he was the talk of the town and everyone wanted to see him. The disciples, who were the closest associates of this popular man, were certainly tempted to feel important, proud, and possessive. Being with Jesus gave them not only prestige, but great opportunity for gaining wealth.

The crowds were gathering once again. But before speaking to them, Jesus pulled his disciples aside and warned them about the temptations they would face as his associates. Jesus' "beatitudes" (5:1–12), as well as his whole Sermon on the Mount, may have been directed to the disciples, although the crowds listened in. Don't expect fame and fortune, Jesus was saying, but mourning, hunger, and persecution. Nevertheless, Jesus assured his disciples, you will be rewarded—but perhaps not in this life. There may be times when following Jesus will bring us great popularity. If we don't live by Jesus' words in this sermon, we will find ourselves using God's message only to promote our personal interests.

3"Humble men are very fortunate!" he told them, "for the Kingdom of Heaven is given to them. 4Those who mourn are fortunate! for they shall be comforted. 5The meek and lowly are fortunate! for the whole wide world belongs to them.

6"Happy are those who long to be just and good, for they shall be completely satisfied. 7Happy are the kind and merciful, for they shall be shown mercy. 8Happy are those whose hearts are pure, for they shall see God. 9Happy are those who strive for peace—they shall be called the sons of God. 10Happy are those who are persecuted because they are good, for the Kingdom of Heaven is theirs.

11"When you are reviled and persecuted and lied about because you are my followers—wonderful! 12Be *happy* about it! Be *very glad!* for a *tremendous reward* awaits you up in heaven. And remember, the ancient prophets were persecuted too.

Jesus teaches about salt and light
(50)

13"You are the world's seasoning, to make it tolerable. If you lose your flavor, what will happen to the world? And you yourselves will be thrown out and trampled underfoot as worthless. 14You are the world's light—a city on a hill, glowing in the night for all to see. 15, 16Don't hide your light! Let it shine for all; let your good deeds glow for all to see, so that they will praise your heavenly Father.

Jesus teaches about the Law
(51)

17"Don't misunderstand why I have come—it isn't to cancel the laws of Moses

5:3
Ps 37:11; 51:17
Isa 57:15; 66:2

5:5
1 Pet 3:4

5:7
Ps 41:1

5:8
1 Jn 3:2,3

5:10
2 Tim 2:12
1 Pet 3:13,14

5:12
2 Chron 36:16
Mt 23:37
Acts 7:52

5:14
Phil 2:15

5:16
Jn 15:8

5:3-12 Here are at least four ways to understand the Beatitudes: (1) They are a code of ethics for the disciples and a standard of conduct for all believers. (2) They contrast kingdom values (what is eternal) and worldly values (what is temporary). (3) They contrast the superficial "faith" of the Pharisees with the real faith Christ wants. (4) They show how the Old Testament expectations will be fulfilled in the new kingdom. These Beatitudes cannot be taken like multiple choice—pick what you like and leave the rest. They must be taken as a whole. They describe what we should be like as Christ's followers.

5:3-12 Each beatitude tells how to be *fortunate* and *happy*. Other translations use the word *blessed*. These words don't mean laughter, pleasure, or earthly prosperity. Jesus turns the world's idea of happiness upside down. To Jesus, happiness means hope and joy, independent of outward circumstances. To find hope and joy, the deepest form of happiness, get closer to God by serving and obeying him.

5:3-12 With Jesus' announcement that the Kingdom was near (4:17), people were naturally asking, "How do I qualify to be in God's Kingdom?" Jesus said they must live differently than their leaders had been telling them. They must seek benefits and rewards far different from those the Pharisees and Sadducees were pushing. Many people seek happiness, but it easily fades. Very few seek God's joy, which never fades. Are your attitudes a carbon copy of the world's selfishness, pride, and lust for power, or do they reflect the ideal to which Jesus called you?

5:3-12 Jesus began his sermon with words that seem to contradict each other. But God's way of living usually contradicts the world's. If you want to live for God you must be ready to say and do what seems strange to the world. You must be willing to give when others take, to love when others hate, to help when others abuse. In doing this, you will one day receive everything, while the others will end up with nothing.

5:11, 12 Jesus said to be happy when we're persecuted. Persecution can be good because: (1) it takes our eyes off earthly rewards, (2) it strips away superficial believers, (3) it strengthens the faith of those who endure, and (4) it serves as an example to others who may follow us. We can be comforted to know that God's greatest prophets were persecuted in the past (Elijah, Jeremiah, Daniel). Our persecution in the present means we have

shown ourselves to be faithful. In the future God will reward the faithful by letting them enter his eternal kingdom where there is no more persecution.

5:13 If a seasoning has no flavor, it has no value. If Christians make no effort to have an effect on the world around them, they are of little value to God. If we are too much like the world, we are worthless. Christians should not blend in with everyone else. Instead, we should affect them positively, just as seasoning brings out the best flavor in food.

5:14-16 Can you hide a city that is sitting on top of a hill? Its light at night can be seen for miles. If we live for Christ, we will glow like lights, showing others what Christ is like. We hide our light by (1) being quiet when we should speak, (2) going along with the crowd, (3) denying the light, (4) letting sin dim our light, (5) not explaining our light to others, or (6) ignoring the needs of others. Be a beacon of truth—don't shut your light off from the rest of the world.

5:17 God's moral and ceremonial laws were given to help people love God with all their hearts and minds. Throughout Israel's history, however, these laws were often misquoted and misapplied. By the time of Jesus, lawyers and religious leaders had turned the law into a confusing mass of rules. When Jesus was talking about a new way to understand God's law, he was actually trying to bring people back to its *original* purpose. He did not speak against the law itself, but against the abuses and excesses to which it had been subjected.

5:17-20 If Jesus did not come to cancel the law, does that mean all the Old Testament laws still apply to us today? In the Old Testament, there were three categories of law: ceremonial, civil, and moral.

(1) The *ceremonial law* related specifically to Israel's worship (see Leviticus 1:2, 3, for example). Its primary purpose was to point forward to Jesus Christ; these laws, therefore, were no longer necessary after Jesus' death and resurrection. While we are no longer bound by ceremonial laws, the principles behind them—to worship and love a holy God—still apply. Jesus was often accused by the Pharisees of violating ceremonial law.

(2) The *civil law* applied God's law to daily living in Israel (see Deuteronomy 24:10, 11, for example). Because modern society and culture are so radically different, all of these guidelines cannot be followed specifically. But the principles behind the commands

and the warnings of the prophets. No, I came to fulfill them, and to make them all come true. [18]With all the earnestness I have I say: Every law in the Book will continue until its purpose is achieved. [19]And so if anyone breaks the least commandment, and teaches others to, he shall be the least in the Kingdom of Heaven. But those who teach God's laws *and obey them* shall be great in the Kingdom of Heaven.

5:18
Lk 16:17

5:19
Jas 2:10

[20]"But I warn you—unless your goodness is greater than that of the Pharisees and other Jewish leaders, you can't get into the Kingdom of Heaven at all!

5:20
Rom 10:3

Jesus teaches about anger
(52)

[21]"Under the laws of Moses the rule was, 'If you murder, you must die.' [22]But I have added to that rule, and tell you that if you are only *angry*, even in your own home, you are in danger of judgment! If you call your friend an idiot, you are in

5:21
Ex 20:13
Deut 5:17

5:18 *until its purpose is achieved*, literally, "until all things be accomplished." **5:20** *goodness*, literally, "righteousness." **5:21, 22** *But I have added to that rule*, literally, "But I say." *even in your own home*, literally, "with your brother."

SIX WAYS TO THINK LIKE CHRIST	Reference	Example	It's not enough to:	We must also:
	5:21, 22	Murder	Avoid killing	Avoid anger and hatred
	5:23–26	Sacrifices	Offer regular sacrifices	Have right relationships with God and others
	5:27–30	Adultery	Avoid adultery	Keep our hearts from lusting and be faithful
	5:31, 32	Divorce	Be legally married	Live out our marriage commitments
	5:33–37	Vows	Make a vow	Avoid casual and irresponsible commitments to God
	5:38–46	Revenge	Seek justice for ourselves	Show mercy and love to others

We are, more often than not, guilty of avoiding the extreme sins while regularly committing the types of sins with which Jesus was most concerned. In these six examples, our real struggle with sin is exposed. Jesus pointed out what kind of lives would be required of his followers. Are you living as Jesus taught?

---

are timeless and should guide our conduct. Jesus fulfilled these by example.

(3) The *moral law* (such as the Ten Commandments) is the direct command of God and it requires strict obedience (see Exodus 20:13, for example). It reveals the nature and will of God, and it still applies today. Jesus obeyed the moral law completely.

5:19 Some of those in the crowd were experts at telling others what to do, but they missed the central point of God's laws themselves. The religious leaders thought that teaching others was the ultimate goal in life. Jesus made it clear, however, that obedience to God was to be the highest goal. It's much easier to study God's laws and tell others to obey them than it is to really put them into practice.

5:20 The Pharisees were exacting and scrupulous in their attempts to follow the law. So how could Jesus reasonably call us to a greater righteousness than theirs? The Pharisees' weakness was that they were content to obey the law outwardly without allowing it to change their hearts (or attitudes). Jesus was saying, therefore, that the *quality* of our goodness needs to be greater than that of the Pharisees. We can look pious and still be far from the Kingdom of God. God judges our hearts as well as our deeds, for it is in the heart where our real allegiance lies. Be just as concerned about your attitudes, which people don't see, as your actions, which are seen by all.

5:20 Jesus was saying that his listeners needed a different kind of goodness altogether, not just a more intense version of the Pharisees' goodness. Our goodness must (1) come from what God

does in us, not what we can do by ourselves, (2) be God-centered, not self-centered, (3) be based on reverence for God, not approval from people, and (4) go beyond keeping the law to loving the principles behind it.

5:21, 22 When Jesus said, "But I have added to that rule," he was not doing away with the law or adding his own beliefs. Rather, he was giving a fuller understanding of why God made that law in the first place. For example, when Moses said, "Don't murder," Jesus said, "Don't even become angry enough to murder, for then you have already committed murder in your heart." The Pharisees read this law and, not having murdered, felt very righteous. Yet they were angry enough with Jesus that they would soon plot his murder, though they would not do the dirty work themselves. We miss the true intent of God's Word when we read his rules for living without trying to understand why he made them. Are there ways you keep God's rules but miss his true intent?

5:21, 22 Killing is a terrible sin, but *anger* is a great sin too because it also violates God's command to love. Anger in this case refers to a seething, brooding bitterness against someone. It is a dangerous emotion which always threatens to leap out of control, leading to violence, emotional hurt, increased mental stress, and other destructive results. There is spiritual damage as well. Anger keeps us from developing a spirit pleasing to God. Have you ever been proud that you didn't strike out and say what was really on your mind? Self-control is good, but Christ wants us to practice thought-control as well. Jesus said we will be held accountable even for our attitudes.

danger of being brought before the court. And if you curse him, you are in danger of the fires of hell.

23"So if you are standing before the altar in the Temple, offering a sacrifice to God, and suddenly remember that a friend has something against you, 24leave your sacrifice there beside the altar and go and apologize and be reconciled to him, and then come and offer your sacrifice to God. 25Come to terms quickly with your enemy before it is too late and he drags you into court and you are thrown into a debtor's cell, 26for you will stay there until you have paid the last penny.

5:25
Prov 25:8
Lk 12:58

Jesus teaches about lust
(53)

27"The laws of Moses said, 'You shall not commit adultery.' 28But I say: Anyone who even looks at a woman with lust in his eye has already committed adultery with her in his heart. 29So if your eye—even if it is your best eye!—causes you to lust, gouge it out and throw it away. Better for part of you to be destroyed than for all of you to be cast into hell. 30And if your hand—even your right hand—causes you to sin, cut it off and throw it away. Better that than find yourself in hell.

5:27
Ex 20:17
Deut 5:18

5:29
Mt 18:9
Mk 9:43-47

5:30
Mt 18:8

Jesus teaches about divorce
(54)

31"The law of Moses says, 'If anyone wants to be rid of his wife, he can divorce her merely by giving her a letter of dismissal.' 32But I say that a man who divorces his wife, except for fornication, causes her to commit adultery if she marries again. And he who marries her commits adultery.

5:31
Deut 24·

5:32
Rom 7:3
1 Cor 7:10

Jesus teaches about vows
(55)

33"Again, the law of Moses says, 'You shall not break your vows to God, but

5:21, 22 *the fires of hell,* literally, "the hell of fire."   **5:29** *your best eye,* literally, "your right eye."

5:23, 24 Broken relationships can hinder our relationship with God. If we have a problem or grievance with a friend, we should resolve the problem as soon as possible. We are hypocrites if we claim to have a right relationship with God while we have wrong relationships with others. Our relationships with others reflect our relationship with God (1 John 4:20).

5:25, 26 In Jesus' day, someone who couldn't pay a debt was thrown into prison until the debt was paid. Unless someone came to pay the debt for the prisoner, he would probably die there. It is practical advice to resolve our differences with our enemies before their anger causes more trouble (Proverbs 25:8–10). You may not get into a disagreement that takes you to court, but even small conflicts mend more easily if we try to make peace right away. In a broader sense, these verses advise us to get things right with our fellow man before we have to stand before God.

5:27, 28 The Old Testament Law said that it is wrong for a person to have sex with someone other than his or her spouse (Exodus 20:14). But Jesus said that the *desire* to have sex with someone other than your spouse is mental adultery and thus sin. Jesus emphasized that if the *act* is wrong, then so is the *intention.* To be faithful to your spouse with your body but not your mind is to break the trust so vital to a strong marriage. Jesus is not condemning natural interest in the opposite sex or even a healthy sexual desire, but he does condemn the deliberate and repeated filling of one's mind with fantasies that would be evil if acted out.

5:27, 28 Some believe that if lustful thoughts are sin, they might as well do the lustful actions too. This is harmful in several ways: (1) it causes you to excuse your sin rather than eliminate it; (2) it destroys marriages; (3) it is deliberate rebellion against God's Word; and (4) it always hurts someone else, in addition to yourself. While desire is not as dangerous as action, it is just as damaging to righteousness. Left unchecked, wrong desires will result in wrong actions and turn you away from God.

5:29, 30 When Jesus said to get rid of your hand or your eye, he was speaking figuratively. He didn't mean literally to gouge out your eye because even a blind person can lust. But if that were the only choice, it would be better to go into heaven with one eye or hand than to go to hell with two. The point is that we sometimes tolerate sins in our lives which will eventually destroy us. It is better to experience the pain of removal (getting rid of a bad habit or something we treasure, for instance) than to allow the sin to bring judgment and condemnation. Examine your life for anything that causes you to sin, and take every necessary action to remove it.

5:31, 32 Divorce is as hurtful and destructive today as in Jesus' day. God intends marriage to be a lifetime commitment (Genesis 2:24). When entering into marriage, people should never consider divorce an option for resolving problems, or a way out of a relationship that seems dead. In these verses, Jesus is also attacking those who purposefully abuse the marriage contract, using divorce to satisfy their lustful desire to marry someone else. Are your actions today helping your marriage grow stronger, or are you tearing it apart?

5:32 Jesus said that divorce is not permissible except if one's partner is unfaithful. This does not mean that divorce should automatically occur when a spouse commits adultery. Those who discover that their partner has been unfaithful should first attempt to forgive, reconcile, and restore their relationship. We are always to look for reasons to restore our relationship rather than for excuses to leave it.

5:33ff In this passage, Jesus is emphasizing the importance of telling the truth. People were breaking promises and using sacred language casually and carelessly. Keeping vows and promises is important; it builds trust and makes committed human relationships possible. If you make a vow, remember that the Bible has strong words for making it casually, for giving it knowing you won't keep it, or for swearing falsely in God's name (Exodus 20:7; Leviticus

5:34
Isa 66:1
Jas 5:12
5:35
Ps 48:2
Isa 66:1
5:37
Col 4:6

must fulfill them all.' 34But I say: Don't make any vows! And even to say, 'By heavens!' is a sacred vow to God, for the heavens are God's throne. 35And if you say 'By the earth!' it is a sacred vow, for the earth is his footstool. And don't swear 'By Jerusalem!' for Jerusalem is the capital of the great King. 36Don't even swear 'By my head!' for you can't turn one hair white or black. 37Say just a simple 'Yes, I will' or 'No, I won't.' Your word is enough. To strengthen your promise with a vow shows that something is wrong.

✪ Jesus teaches about retaliation
(56)

5:38
Lev 24:20
5:39
Rom 12:17
1 Cor 6:7
1 Pet 3:9
5:42
Deut 15:8

38"The law of Moses says, 'If a man gouges out another's eye, he must pay with his own eye. If a tooth gets knocked out, knock out the tooth of the one who did it.' 39But I say: Don't resist violence! If you are slapped on one cheek, turn the other too. 40If you are ordered to court, and your shirt is taken from you, give your coat too. 41If the military demand that you carry their gear for a mile, carry it two. 42Give to those who ask, and don't turn away from those who want to borrow.

Jesus teaches about loving enemies
(57/Luke 6:27–36)

43"There is a saying, 'Love your *friends* and hate your enemies.' 44But I say:

5:38 *pay with his own eye . . . knock out the tooth,* literally, "an eye for an eye and a tooth for a tooth."

JESUS AND THE OLD TESTAMENT LAW	Reference	Examples of Old Testament mercy in justice:
	Leviticus 19:18	"Don't seek vengeance. Don't bear a grudge; but love your neighbor as yourself, for I am Jehovah."
	Proverbs 24:28, 29	"Don't testify spitefully against an innocent neighbor. Why lie about him? Don't say, 'Now I can pay him back for all his meanness to me!'"
	Proverbs 25:21, 22	"If your enemy is hungry, give him food! If he is thirsty, give him something to drink! This will make him feel ashamed of himself, and God will reward you."
	Lamentations 3:30, 31	"Let him turn the other cheek to those who strike him, and accept their awful insults, for the Lord will not abandon him forever."

What seems to be a case of Jesus contradicting the laws of the Old Testament deserves a careful look. It is too easy to overlook how much mercy was written into the Old Testament laws. Above are several examples. What God designed as a system of justice with mercy had been distorted over the years into a license for revenge. It was this misapplication of the law that Jesus attacked.

19:12; Numbers 30:1, 2; Deuteronomy 19:16–20). Oaths are needed in certain situations only because we live in a sinful society that breeds distrust.

5:33–37 Vows were common, but Jesus told his followers not to use them—their word alone should be enough (see James 5:12). Are you known as a person of your word? Truthfulness seems so rare that we feel we must end our statements with "I promise." If we tell the truth all the time, we will have less pressure to back up our words with an oath or promise.

5:38 Jesus explained that God's purpose for this law was mercy. It was given to judges and said, in effect, "Make the punishment fit the crime"—it was not a guide for personal revenge (Exodus 21:23–25; Leviticus 24:19, 20; Deuteronomy 19:21). These laws were given to *limit* vengeance and help the court mete out punishment that was neither too strict nor too lenient. Some people, however, were using this phrase to justify their vendettas against others. People still try to excuse their acts of revenge by saying, "I was just doing to him what he did to me."

5:38–42 When we are wronged, often our first reaction is to get even. Instead Jesus said we should do *good* to those who wrong us! Our desire should not be to keep score, but to love and forgive. This is not natural—it is supernatural, and only God can give us the

strength to love like he does. Instead of planning vengeance, pray for those who hurt you.

5:39–44 To many Jews of the day, these statements were radical and offensive. Any Messiah who would turn the other cheek was not the military leader they wanted to lead a revolt against Rome. Under Roman oppression, they were used to retaliation and hatred against their enemies. But Jesus suggests a new response to injustice. Instead of demanding our rights, he asks us to give them up freely. Jesus' radical statement says that it is more important to *give* justice and mercy than to demand it.

5:43, 44 By calling us to nonretaliation, Jesus keeps us from taking the law into our own hands. By loving and praying for our enemies rather than retaliating, we can overcome evil with good.
   The Pharisees interpreted Leviticus 19:18 as teaching that they should love only those who love in return, and Psalm 139:19–22 and 140:9–11 as meaning that they should hate their enemies. But Jesus says we are to love our enemies. If you love your enemies and treat them well, you will truly show that Jesus is Lord of your life. This is possible only for those who give themselves fully to God, because only he can deliver people from natural selfishness. We must trust the Holy Spirit to help us love those for whom we may not *feel* love.

Love your *enemies!* Pray for those who *persecute* you! 45In that way you will be acting as true sons of your Father in heaven. For he gives his sunlight to both the evil and the good, and sends rain on the just and on the unjust too. 46If you love only those who love you, what good is that? Even scoundrels do that much. 47If you are friendly only to your friends, how are you different from anyone else? Even the heathen do that. 48But you are to be perfect, even as your Father in heaven is perfect.

5:48
Lev 19:1
Col 1:28
1 Pet 1:15

— *Jesus teaches about giving to the needy*
(58)

6 "Take care! Don't do your good deeds publicly, to be admired, for then you will lose the reward from your Father in heaven. 2When you give a gift to a beggar, don't shout about it as the hypocrites do—blowing trumpets in the synagogues and streets to call attention to their acts of charity! I tell you in all earnestness, they have received all the reward they will ever get. 3But when you do a kindness to someone, do it secretly—don't tell your left hand what your right hand is doing. 4And your Father who knows all secrets will reward you.

6:1
2 Cor 9:9
6:2
Mt 23:5

6:4
Mt 6:6,18

Jesus teaches about prayer
(59)

5"And now about prayer. When you pray, don't be like the hypocrites who pretend piety by praying publicly on street corners and in the synagogues where everyone can see them. Truly, that is all the reward they will ever get. 6But when you pray, go away by yourself, all alone, and shut the door behind you and pray to your Father secretly, and your Father, who knows your secrets, will reward you. 7,8"Don't recite the same prayer over and over as the heathen do, who think prayers are answered only by repeating them again and again. Remember, your Father knows exactly what you need even before you ask him!
9"Pray along these lines: 'Our Father in heaven, we honor your holy name. 10We

6:5
Lk 18:11,12
6:6
Jer 17:10
6:7
1 Kgs 18:26
6:9
Mt 23:9
Lk 11:2
Rom 8:15,16
6:10
Ps 103:20

5:48 How can we be perfect? (1) *In character.* In this life we cannot be flawless, but we can aspire to be as much like Christ as possible, seeking moral perfection and sinless behavior. (2) *In holiness.* Like the Pharisees, we are to separate ourselves from the world's sinful values. But unlike the Pharisees, we are to be devoted to God's desires rather than our own, and carry his love and mercy into the world. (3) *In maturity.* We can't achieve Christlike character and holy living all at once, but must grow toward perfection. Just as we expect different behavior from a baby, a child, a teenager, and an adult, so God expects different behavior from us depending on our stage of spiritual development. We can be perfect if our behavior is appropriate for our maturity level—perfect, yet with much room to grow. Our tendency to sin must never deter us from striving to be more like Christ. Christ calls all of his disciples to excel, to rise above mediocrity and to mature in every area, becoming like him. Those who strive to become perfect will one day be perfect even as he is perfect (1 John 3:2).

6:2 The term *hypocrite*, as used here, means a person who does good acts for appearances only—not out of compassion or other good motives. His actions may be good, but his motives are hollow. These empty acts are his only reward, while God will reward those who are sincere in their faith.

6:3 When Jesus says not to tell your right hand what your left hand is doing, he is explaining that our motives for giving must be pure. It is easy to give with mixed motives, to do something for someone if it will benefit us in return. But believers should avoid all scheming and give for the sake of giving.

6:3, 4 It's easy to do right for recognition and praise. To be sure our motives are not selfish, we should do our good deeds quietly or in secret, with no thought of reward. Jesus says we should check our motives in three areas: generosity (6:4), prayer (6:6),

and fasting (6:18). Those acts should not be self-centered, but God-centered; not done to make us look good, but to make God look good. The reward God promises is not material, and it is never given to those who seek it. Doing something only for ourselves is not a loving sacrifice. With your next good deed, ask, "Would I still do this if no one would ever know I did it?"

6:5–15 Jesus also teaches about prayer in Luke 11:1–13.

6:5, 6 Some people, especially the religious leaders, wanted to be seen as "holy," and public prayer was one way to get attention. Jesus saw through their self-righteous acts, however, and taught that the essence of prayer is not what is said (or how or where), but communication with God. There is a place for public prayer, but to pray only where others will notice you is an indication that your real audience is not God.

6:7, 8 Some people think that repeating the same words over and over—like a magic incantation—will insure that God will hear them. It's not wrong to come to God with the same requests—Jesus encourages *persistent* prayer. But he condemns the shallow repetition of words that are not offered with a sincere heart. We can never pray too much if our prayers are honest and sincere. Before you start to pray, make sure you mean what you say.

6:9 This is often called the Lord's prayer because Christ gave it to the disciples. It can be a pattern for our prayers. We should praise God, pray for his work in the world, pray for our daily needs, and pray for help in our daily struggles.

6:9 The phrase "Our Father in heaven" indicates that God is not only majestic and holy, but also personal and loving. The first line of this model prayer is a statement of praise and a commitment to honor God's holy name. We can honor God's name by being careful to use it respectfully. If we use God's name lightly, we aren't remembering God's holiness.

6:11
Prov 30:8

6:13
Lk 22:40,46
Jn 17:15

6:14
Eph 4:32
Col 3:13

ask that your kingdom will come now. May your will be done here on earth, just as it is in heaven. 11Give us our food again today, as usual, 12and forgive us our sins, just as we have forgiven those who have sinned against us. 13Don't bring us into temptation, but deliver us from the Evil One. Amen.' 14, 15Your heavenly Father will forgive you if you forgive those who sin against you; but if *you* refuse to forgive *them, he* will not forgive *you.*

Jesus teaches about fasting
(60)

6:16
Isa 58:5,6

16"And now about fasting. When you fast, declining your food for a spiritual purpose, don't do it publicly, as the hypocrites do, who try to look wan and disheveled so people will feel sorry for them. Truly, that is the only reward they will ever get. 17But when you fast, put on festive clothing, 18so that no one will suspect you are hungry, except your Father who knows every secret. And he will reward you.

Jesus teaches about money
(61)

6:19
Prov 23:4,5

6:20
Mt 19:21
Lk 12:33,34
6:23
Rom 1:21
2 Cor 3:15; 4:4

6:24
1 Jn 2:15

19"Don't store up treasures here on earth where they can erode away or may be stolen. 20Store them in heaven where they will never lose their value, and are safe from thieves. 21If your profits are in heaven your heart will be there too.

22"If your eye is pure, there will be sunshine in your soul. 23But if your eye is clouded with evil thoughts and desires, you are in deep spiritual darkness. And oh, how deep that darkness can be!

24"You cannot serve two masters: God and money. For you will hate one and love the other, or else the other way around.

6:13 the Evil One, or, "from evil." Some manuscripts add here, "For yours is the kingdom and the power and the glory forever, Amen."

6:10 The phrase "We ask that your kingdom will come now" is a reference to God's spiritual reign, not a request that the Israelite nation be freed from Rome's control. God's Kingdom was announced in the covenant with Abraham (8:11; Luke 13:28), is present in Christ's reign in believers' hearts (Luke 17:21), and will be complete when all evil is destroyed and he establishes the new heaven and earth (6:10).

6:10 When we pray "Your will be done," we are not resigning ourselves to fate, but praying that God's perfect purpose will be accomplished in this world as well as in the next.

6:11 When we pray, "Give us our food again today," we are acknowledging that God is our Sustainer and Provider, as opposed to the misconception that we provide for our needs ourselves. We are also showing that we trust God *daily* to provide what he knows we need.

6:13 Jesus is not implying that God leads us into temptation. He is simply asking for deliverance from Satan and his deceit. All Christians struggle with temptation. Sometimes it is so subtle that we don't even realize what is happening to us. God has promised that he won't allow us to be tempted beyond our endurance (1 Corinthians 10:13). Ask God to help you recognize temptation and to be strong enough to overcome it and choose God's way. For more on temptation, see the notes on 4:1.

6:14, 15 Jesus gives a startling warning about forgiveness: if we refuse to forgive others, he will also refuse to forgive us. Why? Because when we don't forgive others, we are denying our common ground as sinners in need of God's forgiveness. God's forgiveness of sin is not the direct result of our forgiving others, but it is based on our realizing what forgiveness means (see Ephesians 4:32). How forgiven would you be if God's forgiveness were based on the way you forgive others? It is easy to ask God for forgiveness, but difficult to grant it to others. Whenever we ask God to forgive us for sin, we should ask ourselves, "Have I forgiven the people who have hurt or wronged me?"

6:16 Fasting—going without food in order to spend time in prayer—is noble *and* difficult. It gives us time to pray, teaches self-discipline, reminds us that we can live with a lot less, and helps us appreciate God's gifts. Jesus was not condemning fasting, but hypocrisy—fasting in order to gain approval from people. Fasting was mandatory for the Jewish people only once a year, on the Day of Atonement (Leviticus 23:32). The Pharisees voluntarily fasted twice a week to impress the people with their "holiness." Jesus commended acts of self-sacrifice done quietly and sincerely. He wanted people to serve him for the right reasons, not from a selfish desire for praise.

6:22, 23 Spiritual vision is our capacity to see clearly what God wants to do with our lives in this world. But this spiritual insight can be easily clouded by our thoughts and desires. Self-serving desires, interests, and goals block that vision. Serving God is the best way to restore it.

6:24 Jesus says we can have only one master. We live in a materialistic society where many people serve money. They spend all their lives collecting and storing it, only to die and leave it behind. Their desire for money and what it can buy far outweighs their commitment to God and spiritual matters. Whatever you store up, you will spend all your time and energy thinking about. Don't fall into the materialistic trap, because "the love of money is the first step toward all kinds of sin" (1 Timothy 6:10). Can you honestly say that God is your Master, and not money? One test is to ask which one occupies more of your thoughts, time, and efforts.

6:24 Jesus contrasted heavenly values with earthly values when he explained that our first loyalty should be to those things that never fade, cannot be stolen or used up, and never wear out. We should not be fascinated with our possessions lest *they* possess *us.* This means we may have to do some cutting back if our possessions are becoming too important to us. Jesus is calling for a decision that allows us to live contentedly with whatever we have because we have chosen what is eternal and lasting.

Jesus teaches about worry
(62)

25"So my counsel is: Don't worry about *things*—food, drink, and clothes. For you already have life and a body—and they are far more important than what to eat and wear. 26Look at the birds! They don't worry about what to eat—they don't need to sow or reap or store up food—for your heavenly Father feeds them. And you are far more valuable to him than they are. 27Will all your worries add a single moment to your life?

28"And why worry about your clothes? Look at the field lilies! They don't worry about theirs. 29Yet King Solomon in all his glory was not clothed as beautifully as they. 30And if God cares so wonderfully for flowers that are here today and gone tomorrow, won't he more surely care for you, O men of little faith?

31,32"So don't worry at all about having enough food and clothing. Why be like the heathen? For they take pride in all these things and are deeply concerned about them. But your heavenly Father already knows perfectly well that you need them, 33and he will give them to you if you give him first place in your life and live as he wants you to.

34"So don't be anxious about tomorrow. God will take care of your tomorrow too. Live one day at a time.

Jesus teaches about criticizing others
(63/Luke 6:37–42)

7 "Don't criticize, and then you won't be criticized. 2For others will treat you as you treat them. 3And why worry about a speck in the eye of a brother when you have a board in your own? 4Should you say, 'Friend, let me help you get that speck out of your eye,' when you can't even see because of the board in your own? 5Hypocrite! First get rid of the board. Then you can see to help your brother.

6:25 Lk 12:22-31 / Phil 4:6,19 / 1 Pet 5:7

6:26 Job 38:41 / Ps 39:5,6

6:29 1 Kgs 10:4-7

6:30 Mt 8:26; 16:8

6:31 Ps 23:1

6:33 Ps 34:9; 37:25 / Mk 10:29,30

7:1 Lk 6:37,38 / Rom 2:1-3; 14:4 / 1 Cor 4:5 / Jas 4:11

7:3 Lk 6:41,42

6:34 *Live one day at a time*, literally, "Sufficient unto the day is the evil thereof."

6:25	The same God who created life in you can be trusted with the details of your life.	**SEVEN REASONS NOT TO WORRY**
6:26	Worrying about the future hampers your efforts for today.	
6:27	Worrying is more harmful than helpful.	
6:28–30	God does not ignore those who depend on him.	
6:32	Worry shows a lack of faith and understanding of God.	
6:33	There are real challenges God wants us to pursue, and worrying keeps us from them.	
6:34	Living one day at a time keeps us from being consumed with worry.	

6:25 Because of its ill effects, Jesus tells us not to worry about those needs that God promises to supply. How many ill effects are you experiencing? Worry (1) affects you physically—making you unable to sleep or eat, (2) causes the object of your worry to consume your thoughts, (3) disrupts your productivity, (4) negatively affects the way you treat others, and (5) reduces your ability to trust in God. Here is the difference between worry and genuine concern—worry immobilizes, but concern moves you to action.

6:33 To give God first place in your life means to turn to him first for help, to fill your thoughts with his desires, to take his character for your pattern, and to serve and obey him in everything. What is really important to you? People, objects, goals, and other desires all compete for priority. Any of these can quickly bump God out of first place if you don't actively choose to give him first place in *every* area of your life.

6:34 Planning for tomorrow is time well spent; worrying about tomorrow is time wasted. Sometimes it's difficult to tell the difference. Careful planning is thinking ahead about goals, steps, and schedules, and trusting in God's guidance. When done well, it can help alleviate worry. The worrier is consumed by fear and finds it difficult to trust God. The worrier lets his plans interfere with his relationship with God. Don't let worries about tomorrow affect your relationship with God today.

7:1-5 Jesus' statement "Don't criticize" is against the kind of hypercritical, judgmental attitude that tears others down in order to build oneself up. It is not a blanket statement against all criticism, but a call to be *discerning* rather than negative. Paul taught clearly that we should discern false teachers (7:15–23), exercise church discipline (1 Corinthians 5:1, 2), and trust God to be the final judge (1 Corinthians 4:3–5).

7:1, 2 Jesus tells us to examine our own lives instead of criticizing others. The traits that bother us in others are often the habits we dislike in ourselves. Our unbroken bad habits and behavior patterns are the very ones we most want to change in others. Do you find it easy to magnify others' faults while ignoring your own? If you are ready to criticize someone, check to see if you deserve the same criticism. Judge yourself first, and then lovingly forgive and help your neighbor.

6"Don't give holy things to depraved men. Don't give pearls to swine! They will trample the pearls and turn and attack you.

Jesus teaches about asking, seeking, knocking
(64)

7:7
Mt 21:22
Mk 11:24
Lk 11:9-13
Jn 14:13,14
15:7; 16:23
Jas 1:5,6
1 Jn 3:21,22;
5:14,15

7"Ask, and you will be given what you ask for. Seek, and you will find. Knock, and the door will be opened. 8For everyone who asks, receives. Anyone who seeks, finds. If only you will knock, the door will open. 9If a child asks his father for a loaf of bread, will he be given a stone instead? 10If he asks for fish, will he be given a poisonous snake? Of course not! 11And if you hardhearted, sinful men know how to give good gifts to your children, won't your Father in heaven even more certainly give good gifts to those who ask him for them?

7:12
Lk 6:31
Rom 13:8-10
Gal 5:14

12"Do for others what you want them to do for you. This is the teaching of the laws of Moses in a nutshell.

Jesus teaches about the way to heaven
(65)

7:13
Lk 13:24

13"Heaven can be entered only through the narrow gate! The highway to hell is broad, and its gate is wide enough for all the multitudes who choose its easy way.

7:14
Jn 14:6

14But the Gateway to Life is small, and the road is narrow, and only a few ever find it.

Jesus teaches about fruit in people's lives
(66/Luke 6:43–45)

7:15
Deut 13:1-4
Jer 23:16
Acts 20:29
Rom 16:17
2 Pet 2:1
1 Jn 4:1
7:16-20
Mt 12:33
Lk 6:43-49

15"Beware of false teachers who come disguised as harmless sheep, but are wolves and will tear you apart. 16You can detect them by the way they act, just as you can identify a tree by its fruit. You need never confuse grapevines with thorn bushes or figs with thistles. 17Different kinds of fruit trees can quickly be identified by examining their fruit. 18A variety that produces delicious fruit never produces an inedible kind. And a tree producing an inedible kind can't produce what is good. 19So the trees having the inedible fruit are chopped down and thrown on the fire.

7:12 *This is the teaching of the laws of Moses in a nutshell,* literally, "This is the law and the prophets." **7:13** *The highway to hell,* literally, "The way that leads to destruction."

7:6 Pigs were unclean animals according to God's law (Deuteronomy 14:8). Anyone who touched an unclean animal became "ceremonially unclean" and could not go to the Temple to worship until the uncleanness was removed. Jesus says that we should not entrust holy teachings to unholy or unclean people. It is futile to try to teach holy concepts to people who don't want to listen and will only tear apart what we say. This does not mean we should stop giving God's Word to unbelievers—we should always tell the Good News—but we should be wise and discerning in what we teach to whom so we will not be wasting our time.

7:7, 8 Jesus tells us to persist in pursuing God. People often give up after a few halfhearted efforts and conclude that God cannot be found. But knowing God takes effort, and Jesus assures us that our efforts will be rewarded. Don't give up in your efforts to seek God. Continue to ask him for more knowledge, patience, wisdom, love, and understanding. He will give them to you.

7:9, 10 The child in Jesus' example asked his father for bread and fish—good and necessary items. If the child had asked for a poisonous snake, would the wise father have granted his request? Sometimes, though we persist in our prayers, God knows we are praying for "snakes" and does not give us what we ask for. As we learn to know God better as a loving Father, we learn to ask for things that are good for us, and then he gives them.

7:11 Christ is showing us the heart of God the Father. He is not selfish, begrudging, or stingy. We don't have to beg or grovel as

we come with our requests. He is a loving Father who understands, cares, and comforts. If humans can be kind, imagine how kind God, the Creator of kindness, can be.

7:12 This is commonly known as the Golden Rule. In many religions, it is stated negatively: "Don't do to others what you don't want done to you." By stating it positively, Jesus made it more significant. It is not so hard to refrain from harming others; it is much more difficult to take the initiative in doing something good for them. The Golden Rule as Jesus formulated it is the foundation of active goodness and mercy—the kind God shows to us every day.

7:13, 14 The Gateway to eternal life (John 10:7–9) is called small. This does not mean it is difficult to become a Christian. It means there are many ways to live your life, but only *one* way to live eternally with God. Believing in Jesus is the only way to heaven, because he alone died for our sins and made us right before God. Living his way may not be easy, but it is true and right.

7:15 False prophets were common in Old Testament times. They prophesied only what the king and the people wanted to hear, claiming it was God's message. False teachers are just as common today. Jesus says to beware of those whose words sound religious but who are motivated by money, prestige, or promoting their own ideas. You can tell who they are because in their teaching they minimize Christ and glorify themselves.

20Yes, the way to identify a tree or a person is by the kind of fruit produced.

Jesus teaches about those who build houses on rock and sand
(67/Luke 6:46–49)

21"Not all who sound religious are really godly people. They may refer to me as 'Lord,' but still won't get to heaven. For the decisive question is whether they obey my Father in heaven. 22At the Judgment many will tell me, 'Lord, Lord, we told others about you and used your name to cast out demons and to do many other great miracles.' 23But I will reply, 'You have never been mine. Go away, for your deeds are evil.'

24"All who listen to my instructions and follow them are wise, like a man who builds his house on solid rock. 25Though the rain comes in torrents, and the floods rise and the storm winds beat against his house, it won't collapse, for it is built on rock.

26"But those who hear my instructions and ignore them are foolish, like a man who builds his house on sand. 27For when the rains and floods come, and storm winds beat against his house, it will fall with a mighty crash." 28The crowds were amazed at Jesus' sermons, 29for he taught as one who had great authority, and not as their Jewish leaders.

7:21
Lk 6:46
Jas 1:22
7:22
Acts 19:13-15
7:23
Mt 25:11,12,41
Lk 13:24-27
7:24
2 Tim 2:19
Jas 1:22-24
7:28
Isa 50:4
Mt 13:54
Mk 1:22; 6:2
Lk 4:32
Jn 7:46

3. Jesus performs many miracles
Jesus heals a man with leprosy
(38/Mark 1:40–45; Luke 5:12–16)

8 Large crowds followed Jesus as he came down the hillside. 2Look! A leper is approaching. He kneels before him, worshiping. "Sir," the leper pleads, "if you want to, you can heal me."

8:2
Lev 14:3
Mk 1:40-44
Lk 5:12-14

7:20 or a person, implied.   **7:22** At the Judgment, literally, "in that day."   **7:23** You have never been mine, literally, "I never knew you."   **7:29** not as their Jewish leaders, literally, "not as the scribes."

7:20 We should evaluate a teacher's words by examining his life. Just as a tree is consistent in the kind of fruit it produces, a good teacher will consistently exhibit good behavior and high moral character as he attempts to live out the truths of Scripture. This does not mean we should have witch hunts, throwing out Sunday school teachers, pastors, and others who are less than perfect. Every one of us is subject to sin, and we must show the same mercy to others that we need for ourselves. Jesus is talking about teachers who deliberately teach false doctrine. We must examine the teachers' motives, the direction they are taking, and the results they are seeking.

7:21 Some sports fans can "talk" a great game, but that tells you nothing about their athletic skills. And not everyone who talks about heaven belongs to God's Kingdom. Jesus is more concerned about our walk than our talk. He wants us to do right, not just say the right words. Your house (which represents your life, 7:25) will withstand the storms of life only if you do what is right instead of just talking about it. What you do cannot be separated from what you believe.

7:21-23 Jesus exposed those people who sounded religious but had no personal relationship with him. At the Day of Judgment, only our relationship with Christ—our acceptance of him as Savior and our obedience to him—will matter. Many people think that if they are "good" and sound religious, they will be rewarded with eternal life. In reality, faith in Christ is what will count at the Judgment.

7:22 The Judgment is the final day of reckoning when God will settle all accounts, judging sin and rewarding faith.

7:26 Like a house of cards, the fool's life crumbles. Most people do not deliberately seek a false or inferior foundation upon which to build their lives; instead, they just don't think about their life's purpose. Many people are headed for destruction, not out of stubbornness but out of thoughtlessness. Part of our responsibility

as believers is to help others stop and think about where their lives are headed and to point out the consequences of ignoring Christ's message.

7:29 The religious leaders spent much of their time citing traditions and quoting previous authorities to support their arguments and interpretations. But Jesus spoke with a new authority—his own. He didn't need to quote anyone because he was the original Word (John 1:1).

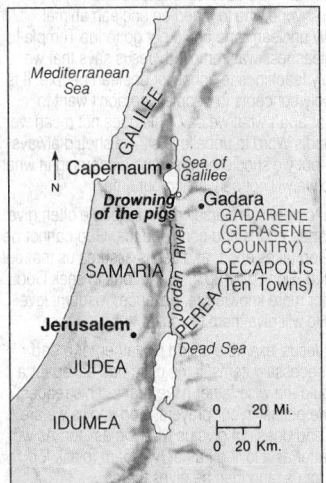

JESUS' MIRACULOUS POWER DISPLAYED Jesus finished the sermon he had given on a hillside near Galilee and returned to Capernaum. As he and his disciples crossed the Sea of Galilee, Jesus calmed a fierce storm. But the disciples were to see yet another miracle for, in the Gentile Gadarene country, Jesus commanded demons to come out of two men.

³*Jesus touches the man. "I want to," he says. "Be healed." And instantly the leprosy disappears.*

8:4
Mk 1:43,44
Lk 5:14; 17:14

⁴*Then Jesus says to him, "Don't stop to talk to anyone; go right over to the priest to be examined; and take with you the offering required by Moses' law for lepers who are healed—a public testimony of your cure."*

A Roman soldier demonstrates faith
(68/Luke 7:1–10)

8:5
Lk 7:1-10

⁵, ⁶When Jesus arrived in Capernaum, a Roman army captain came and pled with him to come to his home and heal his servant boy who was in bed paralyzed and racked with pain.

⁷"Yes," Jesus said, "I will come and heal him."

8:9
Ps 107:20

⁸, ⁹Then the officer said, "Sir, I am not worthy to have you in my home; [and it isn't necessary for you to come]. If you will only stand here and say, 'Be healed,' my servant will get well! I know, because I am under the authority of my superior officers and I have authority over my soldiers, and I say to one, 'Go,' and he goes, and to another, 'Come,' and he comes, and to my slave boy, 'Do this or that,' and he does it. And I know you have authority to tell his sickness to go—and it will go!"

8:11
Isa 2:2; 11:10
Lk 13:28,29
Acts 10:45
11:18; 14:27
Eph 3:6

8:12
Mt 13:41,42
21:43

¹⁰Jesus stood there amazed! Turning to the crowd he said, "I haven't seen faith like this in all the land of Israel! ¹¹And I tell you this, that many Gentiles [like this Roman officer], shall come from all over the world and sit down in the Kingdom of Heaven with Abraham, Isaac, and Jacob. ¹²And many an Israelite—those for whom the Kingdom was prepared—shall be cast into outer darkness, into the place of weeping and torment."

¹³Then Jesus said to the Roman officer, "Go on home. What you have believed has happened!" And the boy was healed that same hour!

Jesus heals Peter's mother-in-law and many others
(35/Mark 1:29–34; Luke 4:38–41)

¹⁴When Jesus arrived at Peter's house, Peter's mother-in-law was in bed with a

8:4 talk, literally, "See you tell no man."   **8:8, 9** and it isn't necessary for you to come, implied.   **8:11** like this Roman officer, implied.

8:3 Leprosy was a feared disease because there was no known cure. In Jesus' day, the word *leprosy* was used for a variety of similar diseases, and some forms were contagious. If a person contracted the contagious type, a priest declared him a leper and banished him from his home and city. He was sent to live in a community with other lepers until he either got better or died. Yet when the leper begged Jesus to heal him, Jesus reached out and touched him, even though his skin was covered with the dread disease.

Like leprosy, sin is an incurable disease—and we all have it. Only Christ's healing touch can miraculously take away our sins and restore us to real living. But first, just like the leper, we must realize our inability to cure ourselves and ask for Christ's saving help.

8:4 The law required a healed leper to be examined by the priest (Leviticus 14:1–15). Jesus wanted this man to give his story firsthand to the priest so he could prove that his leprosy was completely gone and could be restored to his community.

8:5, 6 The Roman army captain could have let many obstacles stand between him and Jesus—pride, doubt, money, language, distance, time, self-sufficiency, power, race. But he didn't. If he did not let these barriers block off his approach to Jesus, we don't need to either.

8:8–12 A centurion was a career military officer in the Roman army with control over 100 soldiers. Roman soldiers, of all people, were hated by the Jews for their oppression, control, and ridicule. Yet this man's faith amazed Jesus! This hated Gentile's genuine faith put to shame the stagnant piety of many of the Jewish religious leaders.

8:10–12 Jesus told the crowd that many religious Jews who should be in the Kingdom would be excluded because of their lack of faith. They were so entrenched in their religious traditions that they could not accept Christ and his new message. We must be careful not to become so set in our religious habits that we expect God to work only in specified ways.

8:11, 12 The Jews should have known that when the Messiah came, his blessings would be for Gentiles too (see Isaiah 25:6–8). But this message came as a shock because they were too wrapped up in their own affairs and destiny. In claiming God's promises, we must not apply them so personally that we forget to see what God wants to do to reach all the people he loves.

8:11, 12 Matthew emphasizes this universal theme—Jesus' message is for everyone. The Old Testament prophets knew this (see Isaiah 56:3, 6; 66:12, 19; Malachi 1:11, 14), but many New Testament Jewish leaders chose to ignore it. Each individual has to choose to accept or reject the Good News, and no one can become part of God's Kingdom on the basis of heritage or family connections.

8:14 Peter was one of Jesus' 12 disciples. His Profile is found in chapter 27.

8:14, 15 Peter's mother-in-law gives us a beautiful example to follow. Her response to Jesus' touch was to serve him immediately. Has God ever helped you through a dangerous or difficult situation? If so, you should ask, "How can I express my gratitude to him?" Because God has promised us all the rewards of his Kingdom, we should look for ways to serve him now.

high fever. 15But when Jesus touched her hand, the fever left her; and she got up and prepared a meal for them!

16That evening several demon-possessed people were brought to Jesus; and when he spoke a single word, all the demons fled; and all the sick were healed. 17This fulfilled the prophecy of Isaiah, "He took our sicknesses and bore our diseases."

8:17
1 Pet 2:24

Jesus teaches about the cost of following him
(122/Luke 9:51–62)

18When Jesus noticed how large the crowd was growing, he instructed his disciples to get ready to cross to the other side of the lake.

19Just then one of the Jewish religious teachers said to him, "Teacher, I will follow you no matter where you go!"

8:19
Lk 9:57-60

20But Jesus said, "Foxes have dens and birds have nests, but I, the Messiah, have no home of my own—no place to lay my head."

8:20
Dan 7:13,14
Mt 24:27; 26:24
Jn 1:11
Acts 7:56

21Another of his disciples said, "Sir, when my father is dead, then I will follow you."

22But Jesus told him, "Follow me *now!* Let those who are spiritually dead care for their own dead."

8:22
Mt 9:9
Mk 2:14
Lk 9:59
Jn 1:43; 21:19

Jesus calms the storm
(87/Mark 4:35–41; Luke 8:22–25)

23Then he got into a boat and started across the lake with his disciples. 24Suddenly a terrible storm came up, with waves higher than the boat. But Jesus was asleep.

8:23
Mk 4:35-41
Lk 8:22-25

25The disciples went to him and wakened him, shouting, "Lord, save us! We're sinking!"

26But Jesus answered, "O you men of little faith! Why are you so frightened?" Then he stood up and rebuked the wind and waves, and the storm subsided and all was calm. 27The disciples just sat there, awed! "Who is this," they asked themselves, "that even the winds and the sea obey him?"

8:26
Job 38:8-11
Ps 65:7; 89:9
107:29
Prov 30:4
Phil 4:6

Jesus sends demons into a herd of pigs
(88/Mark 5:1–20; Luke 8:26–39)

28When they arrived on the other side of the lake, in the country of the Gada-

8:15 *prepared a meal for them,* literally, "ministered unto them." 8:17 *bore our diseases,* Isa 53:4. 8:19 *Just then,* implied. *one of the Jewish religious teachers,* literally, "a scribe." 8:20 *Messiah,* literally, "Son of Man." 8:21 *then I will follow you,* or, "let me first go and bury my father." 8:22 *now,* implied. *spiritually dead,* implied.

8:16, 17 Matthew continues to show Jesus' kingly nature. Through a single touch, he heals (8:3, 15); when he speaks a single word, demons flee his presence (8:16). Jesus has authority over all evil powers and all earthly disease. He also has power and authority to conquer sin. Sickness and evil are consequences of living in a fallen world. But in the future, when God cleanses the earth from sin, there will be no more sickness and death. Jesus' healing miracles were a taste of what the whole world will one day experience.

8:19, 20 Following Jesus is not always an easy or comfortable road. Often it means great cost and sacrifice, with no earthly rewards or security. Jesus didn't have a place to call home. You may find that following Christ costs you popularity, friendships, leisure time, or treasured habits. But while the costs of following Christ may be high, the value of being Christ's disciple is an investment which lasts for eternity and yields incredible rewards.

8:21, 22 Jesus was always direct with those who wanted to follow him. He made sure they counted the cost and set aside any conditions they might have for following him. As God's Son, Jesus did not hesitate to demand complete loyalty. Even the burial of the dead was not to take priority over the demands of obedience. His direct challenge forces us to ask ourselves about our own priorities in following him. The decision to follow Christ should not be put off, even when an important event is at hand. Nothing should be placed above a total commitment to living for Christ.

8:23 This would have been a fishing boat, because many of Jesus' disciples were fishermen. Josephus, an ancient historian, wrote that there were usually more than 300 fishing boats on the Sea of Galilee at one time. This boat was large enough to hold Jesus and his 12 disciples and was powered by both oars and sails. During a storm, however, the sails were taken down to keep them from ripping and to make the boat easier to control.

8:24 The Sea of Galilee is an unusual body of water. It is relatively small (13 miles long, 7 miles wide) but 150 feet deep, and the shoreline is 680 feet below sea level. Sudden storms can appear with little warning over the surrounding mountains, stirring the water into violent 20-foot waves. The disciples had not foolishly set out in a storm. They had been caught without warning, and their danger was great.

8:25 Although the disciples had witnessed many miracles, they panicked in this storm. As experienced sailors, they knew its danger; what they did not know was that Christ could control the forces of nature. There is always a dimension of our lives where we feel God can't or won't work. When we truly understand who he is, however, we will understand that he controls both the storms of nature and the storms of the troubled heart. Jesus' power that calmed this storm can also calm the storms raging in our lives. He is willing to help if we only ask him. We do not need to exclude him from any area of our lives.

8:28 The country of the Gadarenes is located southeast of the

renes, two men with demons in them met him. They lived in a cemetery and were so dangerous that no one could go through that area.

²⁹They began screaming at him, "What do you want with us, O Son of God? You have no right to torment us yet."

³⁰A herd of pigs was feeding in the distance, ³¹so the demons begged, "If you cast us out, send us into that herd of pigs."

³²"All right," Jesus told them. "Begone."

And they came out of the men and entered the pigs, and the whole herd rushed over a cliff and drowned in the water below. ³³The herdsmen fled to the nearest city with the story of what had happened, ³⁴and the entire population came rushing out to see Jesus, and begged him to go away and leave them alone.

Jesus heals a paralyzed man
(39/Mark 2:1–12; Luke 5:17–26)

9 So Jesus climbed into a boat and went across the lake to Capernaum, his home town.

²Soon some men brought him a paralyzed boy on a mat. When Jesus saw their faith, he said to the sick boy, "Cheer up, son! For I have forgiven your sins!"

³"Blasphemy! This man is saying he is God!" exclaimed some of the religious leaders to themselves.

⁴Jesus knew what they were thinking and asked them, "Why are you thinking such evil thoughts? ^{5, 6}I, the Messiah, have the authority on earth to forgive sins. But talk is cheap—anybody could say that. So I'll prove it to you by healing this

8:29 *You have no right to torment us yet,* literally, "Have you come here to torment us before the time?" **9:1** *his home town,* literally, "his own city." **9:5, 6** *the Messiah,* literally, "the Son of Man."

Margin references:

8:29 Mk 1:23,24 / Lk 4:33,34 / 2 Pet 2:4
8:30 Deut 14:8
8:34 Lk 5:8
9:2 Mk 2:2-12 / Lk 5:17-26
9:3 Mt 8:10 / Eph 1:7
9:4 Mt 12:25 / Lk 6:8; 9:47; 11:17
9:5 Acts 5:31

Sea of Galilee. Luke calls it the region of the Gerasenes, near the town of Gadara, the capital of the region (see map). Gadara was a member of the Ten Towns (or Decapolis; see the note on Mark 5:20). These were ten cities that had independent governments and were largely inhabited by Gentiles, which explains the herd of pigs. The Jews did not raise pigs because they were considered unclean and thus unfit to eat.

8:28 Demons are probably fallen angels who joined Satan in his rebellion against God and are now evil spirits under Satan's control. They help Satan tempt people to sin and have great destructive powers. But whenever they were confronted by Jesus, they lost their power. Demons recognized Jesus as God's Son (8:29), but they didn't think they had to obey him. You may believe Jesus is the Son of God, but just believing is not enough (see James 2:19 for a discussion of belief and demons). Faith is more than belief. By faith, you must accept what he has done for you, receive him as the only one who can save you from sin, and live out your faith by obeying his Word.

8:28 Matthew says there were two demon-possessed men, while Mark and Luke refer only to one. Apparently Mark and Luke mention only the man who did the talking.

8:28 According to Jewish ceremonial laws, the men Jesus encountered were unclean in three ways: they were Gentiles (non-Jews), they were demon-possessed, and they lived in a graveyard. Jesus helped them anyway. We should not turn our backs on people who are "unclean" or repulsive to us. Instead, we must realize that every human individual is a unique creation of God who needs to be touched by his love.

8:29 The Bible tells us that at the end of the world, Satan and his angels will be thrown into the Lake of Fire (25:41; Revelation 20:14). When the demons said that Jesus could not torment them "yet," they showed they knew their ultimate fate.

8:32 When the demons entered the pigs, they drove the animals into the sea. The demons' action proves their destructive intent—if they could not destroy the men, they would destroy the pigs. Jesus' action, by contrast, shows the value he places on each human life.

8:34 Why did the people ask Jesus to leave? Unlike the pagan gods they worshiped, Jesus could not be contained, controlled, or appeased. They feared Jesus' supernatural power, a power they had never before witnessed. And they were upset about losing a herd of pigs more than they were glad about the deliverance of the demon-possessed men. Are you more concerned about property and programs than people? Human beings are created in God's image and have eternal value. How foolish and yet how easy to value possessions, investments, and even animals above human life.

9:1 Capernaum was a good choice for Jesus' base of operations. It was a wealthy city due to fishing and trade. Situated on the Sea of Galilee in a densely populated area, it had a Roman garrison to keep peace in the region. The city was a cultural melting pot, greatly influenced by Greek and Roman manners, dress, architecture, and politics.

9:2 The first words Jesus said to the paralyzed man were "I have forgiven your sins." Then he healed the man. We must be careful not to concentrate on God's power to heal physical sickness more than on his power to forgive spiritual sickness in the form of sin. Jesus saw that in addition to needing physical health, this man needed spiritual health. Spiritual health comes only from Jesus' healing touch.

9:2 Both the man's body and his spirit were paralyzed—he could not walk and he did not know Jesus. But the man's spiritual state was Jesus' first concern. If God does not heal us or someone we love, we need to remember that physical healing is not Christ's only concern. We will all be completely healed in Christ's coming Kingdom; but first we have to come to know Jesus.

9:3 Blasphemy is claiming to be God and applying his characteristics to yourself. The religious leaders rightly saw that Jesus was claiming to be God. What they did not understand was that he *is* God and thus has the authority to heal and forgive sins.

9:5, 6 "Talk is cheap," Jesus replied to the hostile leaders. He then backed up his words by healing the man's legs. Talk is indeed cheap. Our words lack meaning if our actions do not back them up.

man." Then, turning to the paralyzed man, he commanded, "Pick up your stretcher and go on home, for you are healed."

7And the boy jumped up and left!

8A chill of fear swept through the crowd as they saw this happen right before their eyes. How they praised God for giving such authority to a man!

9:8
Mt 15:31
Mk 2:12
Lk 7:16

─◉ *Jesus eats with sinners at Matthew's house*
(40/Mark 2:13–17; Luke 5:27–32)

9As Jesus was going on down the road, he saw a tax collector, Matthew, sitting at a tax collection booth. "Come and be my disciple," Jesus said to him, and Matthew jumped up and went along with him.

9:9
Mt 10:3
Mk 2:13-17; 3:18
Lk 5:27-32; 6:15
15:1,2
Acts 1:14

10Later, as Jesus and his disciples were eating dinner [at Matthew's house], there were many notorious swindlers there as guests!

11The Pharisees were indignant. "Why does your teacher associate with men like that?"

9:11
Mt 11:19
Mk 2:16
Lk 5:30; 15:2

12"Because people who are well don't need a doctor! It's the sick people who do!" was Jesus' reply. 13Then he added, "Now go away and learn the meaning of this verse of Scripture,

'It isn't your sacrifices and your gifts I want—I want you to be merciful.'

For I have come to urge sinners, not the self-righteous, back to God."

9:13
Prov 21:3
Hos 6:6
Mic 6:6-8
Mt 12:7; 18:11
Lk 19:9,10
1 Tim 1:15

Religious leaders ask Jesus about fasting
(41/Mark 2:18–22; Luke 5:33–39)

14One day the disciples of John the Baptist came to Jesus and asked him, "Why don't your disciples fast as we do and as the Pharisees do?"

9:14
Mk 2:18-22
Lk 5:33-39
18:12

15"Should the bridegroom's friends mourn and go without food while he is with them?" Jesus asked. "But the time is coming when I will be taken from them. Time enough then for them to refuse to eat.

9:15
Jn 3:29
Acts 13:2; 14:23

16"And who would patch an old garment with unshrunk cloth? For the patch would tear away and make the hole worse. 17And who would use old wineskins to

9:9 *Matthew.* The Matthew who wrote this book.   **9:10** *at Matthew's house,* implied.   **9:13** *to be merciful,* see Hosea 6:6.   **9:15** *I,* literally, "the Bridegroom."   **9:17** *old wineskins.* These were leather bags for storing wine.

───

9:9 Matthew was a Jew who was appointed by the Romans to be the area's tax collector. He collected taxes from the citizens as well as from merchants passing through town. Tax collectors were expected to take a commission on the taxes they collected, but most of them overcharged and vastly enriched themselves. Tax collectors were thus hated by the Jews because of their reputation for cheating and their support of Rome.

9:9 When Jesus called Matthew to be one of his disciples, Matthew jumped up and followed, leaving a lucrative career. When God calls you to follow or obey him, do you do it with as much abandon as Matthew? Sometimes the decision to follow Christ requires some difficult or painful choices. Like Matthew, we must decide to leave behind those things that would keep us from following Christ.

9:10–13 When he visited Matthew, Jesus hurt his reputation. Matthew was cheating the people, but Jesus found and changed him. We are not to be afraid to reach out to those with different lifestyles, because God's message can change anyone.

9:11, 12 The Pharisees constantly tried to trap Jesus, and they thought his association with these "low lives" was the perfect opportunity. They were more concerned with their own appearance of holiness than in helping people, with criticism than encouragement, with outward respectability than practical help. But God is concerned for all people, including the sinful and hurting ones. The Christian life is not a popularity contest! Following Jesus' example, we should share the Good News with the poor, lonely, and outcast, not just the good, talented, and popular.

9:13 The self-righteous can't be saved because the first step in

following Jesus is acknowledging our need and admitting that we don't have all the answers.

9:14 John's disciples fasted to repent of sin and prepare for the coming of the Messiah. Jesus' disciples did not need to fast to prepare for the Messiah's coming because he was with them! Jesus did not condemn fasting—he himself fasted (Matthew 4:2). He emphasized that fasting must be done for the right reasons.

9:15 The Kingdom of Heaven is like a wedding feast, and it had arrived in the person of Jesus. His disciples, therefore, were filled with joy. It would not be right to mourn or fast when the bridegroom was present.

9:17 In Bible times, wine was not kept in bottles, but in goatskins sewn around the edges to form watertight bags. New wine would expand as it fermented, stretching its wineskin. After the wine had aged, the stretched skin would burst if more new wine were poured into it. New wine, therefore, was always put into new wineskins.

9:17 Jesus did not come to "patch up" the old religious system of Judaism with its rules and traditions. If he had, his message would damage it. His purpose was to bring in something new, yet something that had been prophesied for centuries. This new message, the gospel, said that Jesus Christ, God's Son, came to earth to offer all people forgiveness of sins and restoration with God. This new message of faith and love did not fit in the old rigid legalistic system of religion. It needed a fresh start. The message will always remain "new" because it must be accepted and applied in every generation. When we follow Christ, we must be prepared for new ways to live, new ways to look at people, and new ways to serve.

store new wine? For the old skins would burst with the pressure, and the wine would be spilled and skins ruined. Only new wineskins are used to store new wine. That way both are preserved."

Jesus heals a bleeding woman and restores a girl to life
(89/Mark 5:21–43; Luke 8:40–56)

9:18
Mk 5:22-43
Lk 8:41-56

18As he was saying this, the rabbi of the local synagogue came and worshiped him. "My little daughter has just died," he said, "but you can bring her back to life again if you will only come and touch her."

19As Jesus and the disciples were going to the rabbi's home, 20a woman who had been sick for twelve years with internal bleeding came up behind him and touched a tassel of his robe, 21for she thought, "If I only touch him, I will be healed."

MATTHEW

More than any other disciple, Matthew had a clear idea of how much it would cost to follow Jesus, yet he did not hesitate a moment. When he left his tax-collecting booth, he guaranteed himself unemployment. For several of the other disciples, there was always fishing to return to, but for Matthew, there was no turning back.

Two changes happened to Matthew when he decided to follow Jesus. First, Jesus gave him a new life. He not only belonged to a new group; he belonged to the Son of God. He was not just accepting a different way of life; he was now an accepted person. For a despised tax collector, that change must have been wonderful! Second, Jesus gave Matthew a new purpose for his skills. When he followed Jesus, the only tool from his past job that he carried with him was his pen. From the beginning, God had made him a record-keeper. Jesus' call eventually allowed him to put his skills to their finest work. Matthew was a keen observer, and he must have mentally recorded what he saw going on around him. The Gospel that bears his name came as a result.

Matthew's experience points out that each of us, from the beginning, is one of God's works in progress. Much of what God has for us he gives long before we are able to consciously respond to him. He trusts us with skills and abilities ahead of schedule. He has made us each capable of being his servant. When we trust him with what he has given us, we begin a life of real adventure. Matthew couldn't have known that God would use the very skills he had sharpened as a tax collector to record the greatest story ever lived. And God has no less meaningful a purpose for each one of us. Have you recognized Jesus saying to you, "Come be my disciple"? What has been your response?

Strengths and accomplishments:
• Was one of Jesus' 12 disciples
• Responded immediately to Jesus' call
• Invited many friends to his home to meet Jesus
• Compiled the Gospel of Matthew
• Clarified for his Jewish audience Jesus' fulfillment of Old Testament prophecies

Lessons from his life:
• Jesus consistently accepted people from every level of society
• Matthew was given a new life, and his God-given skills of record-keeping and attention to detail were given new purpose
• Having been accepted by Jesus, Matthew immediately tried to bring others into contact with Jesus

Vital statistics:
• Where: Capernaum
• Occupation: Tax collector, disciple of Jesus
• Relatives: Father: Alphaeus
• Contemporaries: Jesus, Pilate, Herod, other disciples

Key verse:
"As he was walking up the beach he saw Levi [Matthew], the son of Alphaeus, sitting at his tax collection booth. 'Come with me,' Jesus told him. 'Come be my disciple.' And Levi jumped to his feet and went along" (Mark 2:14).

Matthew's story is told in the Gospels. He is also mentioned in Acts 1:13.

9:18 Mark and Luke call this man the synagogue leader and say his name was Jairus (Mark 5:22; Luke 8:41). As the ruler of the synagogue, he was responsible for administration, which included looking after the building, supervising worship, running the school on weekdays, and finding rabbis to teach on the Sabbath. For more information on synagogues, read the note on Mark 1:21.

9:19–22 In our times of desperation, we don't have to worry about the correct way to reach out to God. Like this woman, we can simply reach out in faith. He will respond.

22Jesus turned around and spoke to her. "Daughter," he said, "all is well! Your faith has healed you." And the woman was well from that moment.

23When Jesus arrived at the rabbi's home and saw the noisy crowds and heard the funeral music, 24he said, "Get them out, for the little girl isn't dead; she is only sleeping!" Then how they all scoffed and sneered at him!

25When the crowd was finally outside, Jesus went in where the little girl was lying and took her by the hand, and she jumped up and was all right again! 26The report of this wonderful miracle swept the entire countryside.

Jesus heals the blind and mute (90)

27As Jesus was leaving her home, two blind men followed along behind, shouting, "O Son of King David, have mercy on us."

28They went right into the house where he was staying, and Jesus asked them, "Do you believe I can make you see?"

"Yes, Lord," they told him, "we do."

29Then he touched their eyes and said, "Because of your faith it will happen."

30And suddenly they could see! Jesus sternly warned them not to tell anyone about it, 31but instead they spread his fame all over the town.

32Leaving that place, Jesus met a man who couldn't speak because a demon was inside him. 33So Jesus cast out the demon, and instantly the man could talk. How the crowds marveled! "Never in all our lives have we seen anything like this," they exclaimed.

34But the Pharisees said, "The reason he can cast out demons is that he is demon-possessed himself—possessed by Satan, the demon king!"

Jesus urges the disciples to pray for workers (92)

35Jesus traveled around through all the cities and villages of that area, teaching in

9:31 all over the town, literally, "in all that land."

9:22
Mt 9:29; 15:28
Mk 10:52
Lk 7:50; 17:19
18:42

9:23
2 Chron 35:25
Jer 9:17,18

9:24
Jn 11:11-13
Acts 20:10

9:27
Mt 15:22; 20:30
Mk 10:47
Lk 18:38

9:30
Ps 146:8
Lk 5:14

9:31
Mk 7:36

9:32
Lk 11:14,15

9:34
Mt 12:24
Mk 3:22
Lk 11:15
Jn 7:20

9:22 God changed a situation that had been a problem for years. Like the leper and the demon-possessed man (see the notes on 8:3 and 8:28), this bleeding woman was considered unclean. For 12 years, she too had been one of the "untouchables" and had not been able to live a normal life. But Jesus changed that and restored her. Sometimes we are tempted to give up on people or situations which have not changed for many years. God can change what seems unchangeable, giving new life and hope.

9:23-26 The local synagogue rabbi didn't come to Jesus until his daughter was dead—it was too late for anyone else to help. But Jesus simply went to the girl and raised her! In our lives, Christ can make a difference when it seems too late for anyone else to help. He can bring healing to broken marriages, release from addicting habits, and forgiveness and change to scarred lives. If your situation looks hopeless, remember that Christ can do the impossible.

9:27-30 Jesus didn't respond immediately to the blind men's pleas. He waited to see how earnest they were. Not everyone who says he wants help really wants it badly enough to do something about it. Jesus may have waited and questioned these men to make their desire and faith stronger. If, in your prayers, it seems as if God is too slow in giving his answer, maybe he is testing you as he did the blind men. Do you believe God can help you? Do you really want his help?

9:27 "O Son of King David" was a popular way of addressing Jesus as the Messiah, because it was known that the Messiah would be a descendant of King David (Isaiah 9:7). This is the first time the title is used in Matthew. Jesus' ability to heal the blind was prophesied in Isaiah 29:18; 35:5; 42:7.

9:28 These blind men were persistent. They went right into the

house where Jesus was staying. They knew Jesus could heal them and they would let nothing stop them—that's faith. If you believe Jesus is the answer to your every need, don't let anything or anyone stop you from reaching him.

9:30 Jesus told the people to keep quiet about his healings because his purpose was not to be known only as a miracle worker. He healed because he had compassion on people, but he also wanted to bring spiritual healing to a sin-sick world.

9:32 While Jesus was on earth, demonic forces seemed to have been especially active. Although we cannot be sure why or how demon possession occurs, it causes both physical and mental problems. In this case, the demon caused a physical problem—the inability to talk. For more on demons and demon possession, read the notes on 8:28 and Mark 1:23.

9:34 In chapter 9, the Pharisees accuse Jesus of four different sins: blasphemy, immorality, impiety, and demon possession. Matthew shows how Jesus was maligned by those who should have received him most gladly. Why did the Pharisees do this? (1) Their religious authority had been bypassed. (2) Their control over the people was weakening. (3) Their personal beliefs were being challenged. (4) Their insincere motives were being exposed.

9:34 While the Pharisees questioned, debated, and dissected Jesus, people were being healed right in front of them and lives were being changed. Their skepticism was not based on insufficient evidence but on jealousy of Jesus' popularity.

9:35 The Good News about the Kingdom was that the promised and long-awaited Messiah had finally come. His healing was a sign that his teaching was true.

9:35-38 Jesus needs workers who know how to deal with people's problems. We can comfort others and show them the way

the Jewish synagogues and announcing the Good News about the Kingdom. And wherever he went he healed people of every sort of illness. 36And what pity he felt for the crowds that came, because their problems were so great and they didn't know what to do or where to go for help. They were like sheep without a shepherd.

37"The harvest is so great, and the workers are so few," he told his disciples. 38"So pray to the one in charge of the harvesting, and ask him to recruit more workers for his harvest fields."

9:37
Lk 10:2
Jn 4:35

9:38
Acts 13:2
2 Thess 3:1

Jesus sends out the twelve disciples
(93/Mark 6:7–13; Luke 9:1–6)

10 Jesus called his twelve disciples to him, and gave them authority to cast out evil spirits and to heal every kind of sickness and disease.

2, 3, 4Here are the names of his twelve disciples: Simon (also called Peter), Andrew (Peter's brother), James (Zebedee's son), John (James' brother), Philip, Bartholomew, Thomas, Matthew (the tax collector), James (Alphaeus' son), Thaddaeus, Simon (a member of "The Zealots," a subversive political party), Judas Iscariot (the one who betrayed him).

10:4
Jn 13:26

10:5
2 Kgs 17:24
Jn 4:9

10:6
Isa 53:6
Jer 50:6,17
Mt 15:24
Acts 3:25,26
13:46

5Jesus sent them out with these instructions: "Don't go to the Gentiles or the Samaritans, 6but only to the people of Israel—God's lost sheep. 7Go and announce to them that the Kingdom of Heaven is near. 8Heal the sick, raise the dead, cure the lepers, and cast out demons. Give as freely as you have received!

9"Don't take any money with you; 10don't even carry a duffle bag with extra clothes and shoes, or even a walking stick; for those you help should feed and care for you. 11Whenever you enter a city or village, search for a godly man and stay in

10:7 *is near,* or, "at hand," or, "has arrived."

---

to live because we have been helped in our problems by God (2 Corinthians 1:3–7).

9:36 Ezekiel had also compared Israel to sheep without a shepherd (Ezekiel 34:5, 6). Jesus came to be the Shepherd, the one who could show people how to avoid life's pitfalls (see John 10:14).

9:37, 38 Jesus looked at the crowds following him and referred to them as a field ripe for harvest. Many people are ready to give their lives to Christ if someone will show them the way. Jesus commands us to pray that people will respond to this need for workers. Often, when we pray for something, God answers our prayers by using *us.* Be prepared for God to use you to show another person the way to him.

10:1 Jesus *called* his 12 disciples. He didn't draft them, force them, or ask them to volunteer. Being called means being chosen to serve Christ in a special way. If you truly know him, you can do nothing else. Christ calls us today. He doesn't twist our arms and make us do something we don't want to do. We can choose to join him or remain behind. Christ is also calling you to follow him. Are you responding?

10:2–4 The list of Jesus' 12 disciples doesn't give us many details—probably because there weren't many impressive details to tell. Jesus called people from all walks of life—fishermen, political activists, tax collectors. He called common men and leaders; rich and poor; educated and uneducated. Today, many people discriminate about who is fit to follow Christ, but this was not the attitude of the Master himself. God can use anyone no matter how insignificant he feels. He uses ordinary people to do his extraordinary work.

10:4 The Zealots were a radical political party working for the violent overthrow of Roman rule in Israel.

10:4 In this list, Bartholomew is probably Nathanael whom we meet in John 1:45–51. Thaddaeus is also known as Judas, son of James. The disciples are also listed in Mark 3:16–19; Luke 6:14–16; and Acts 1:14.

10:5, 6 Why didn't Jesus send the disciples to the Gentiles or the

Samaritans? A Gentile is anyone who is not a Jew. The Samaritans were a race that resulted from intermarriage between Jews and Gentiles after the Old Testament captivities (see 2 Kings 17:24). Jesus asked his disciples to go only to the Jews because he came *first* to the Jews. They were chosen by God to be the ones who would tell the rest of the world about God. And this is what eventually happened: Jewish disciples and apostles preached the Good News of the risen Christ all around the Roman Empire, and soon Gentiles were pouring into the Church. The Bible clearly teaches that God's message of salvation is for *all* people, regardless of race, sex, or national origin (Genesis 12:3; Isaiah 25:6; 56:3–7; Malachi 1:11; Acts 10:34, 35; Romans 3:29, 30; Galatians 3:28).

10:7 The Jews were waiting for the Messiah to usher in his kingdom. They hoped for a political and military kingdom that would free them from Roman rule and return the days of glory under David and Solomon. But Jesus was talking about a spiritual kingdom. The Good News today is that the kingdom is still *near.* Jesus, the Messiah, has already begun his kingdom on earth in the hearts of his followers. One day the kingdom will be fully realized. Then evil will be destroyed and all people will live in peace with one another.

10:8 Jesus gave the disciples a principle to guide their actions as they ministered to others: "Give as freely as you have received!" Because God has showered us with his blessings, we should give generously to others of our time, love, and possessions.

10:10 Matthew said that those who minister are to be cared for—the disciples were to expect food and shelter because of the spiritual service they provided. Who ministers to you? Make sure you take care of the pastors, missionaries, and teachers who serve God by serving you (see 1 Corinthians 9:10 and 1 Timothy 5:17).

10:10 Mark's account (9:8) says to take a walking stick, and Matthew and Luke (9:3) say not to. Jesus may have meant that they were not to take an *extra* set of sandals, staff, and bag. In any case, the principle was that they were to go out, ready for duty and travel, unencumbered by excess material goods.

his home until you leave for the next town. ¹²When you ask permission to stay, be friendly, ¹³and if it turns out to be a godly home, give it your blessing; if not, keep the blessing. ¹⁴Any city or home that doesn't welcome you—shake off the dust of that place from your feet as you leave. ¹⁵Truly, the wicked cities of Sodom and Gomorrah will be better off at Judgment Day than they.

10:14 Acts 13:51
10:15 Mt 11:23,24; 2 Pet 2:6; Jude 7

Jesus prepares the disciples for persecution
(94)

¹⁶"I am sending you out as sheep among wolves. Be as wary as serpents and harmless as doves. ¹⁷But beware! For you will be arrested and tried, and whipped in the synagogues. ¹⁸Yes, and you must stand trial before governors and kings for my sake. This will give you the opportunity to tell them about me, yes, to witness to the world.

¹⁹"When you are arrested, don't worry about what to say at your trial, for you will be given the right words at the right time. ²⁰For it won't be you doing the talking—it will be the Spirit of your heavenly Father speaking through you!

²¹"Brother shall betray brother to death, and fathers shall betray their own children. And children shall rise against their parents and cause their deaths. ²²Everyone shall hate you because you belong to me. But all of you who endure to the end shall be saved.

²³"When you are persecuted in one city, flee to the next! I will return before you have reached them all!

²⁴"A student is not greater than his teacher. A servant is not above his master. ²⁵The student shares his teacher's fate. The servant shares his master's! And since

10:16 Mk 13:8-13; Lk 21:12-19; 1 Cor 14:20
10:17 Acts 5:40
10:18 Acts 12:1; 24:10
10:19 Lk 12:11,12
10:20 2 Sam 23:2; Acts 4:8; 6:10
10:21 Mic 7:6
10:22 Gal 6:9
10:23 Mt 16:28; Acts 14:6
10:24 Jn 13:16; 15:20

10:23 *l*, literally, "the Son of Man."

Who may oppose us?	Natural response	Possible pressures	Needed truth	COUNTING THE COST OF FOLLOWING CHRIST
GOVERNMENT 10:18–19		THREATS 10:26	→ The truth will be revealed (10:26)	Jesus helped his disciples prepare for the rejection many of them would experience by being Christians. Being God's person will usually create reaction from others who are resisting him.
		PHYSICAL HARM 10:28	→ Our soul cannot be harmed (10:28)	
RELIGIOUS PEOPLE 10:17	FEAR AND WORRY	PUBLIC RIDICULE	→ God himself will acknowledge us if we acknowledge him (10:33)	
FAMILY 10:21		REJECTION BY LOVED ONES 10:34–37	→ God's love can sustain us (10:31)	

10:14 Why did Jesus tell his disciples to shake the dust off their feet if a city or home didn't welcome them? When leaving Gentile cities, pious Jews often shook the dust from their feet to show their separation from Gentile practices. If the disciples shook the dust of a *Jewish* town from their feet, it would show their separation from Jews who had rejected their Messiah. This gesture was to show the people that they were making a wrong choice—that the opportunity to choose Christ might not present itself again. Are you receptive to teaching from God? If you ignore the Spirit's prompting, you may not get another chance.

10:15 The cities of Sodom and Gomorrah were destroyed by fire from heaven because of their wickedness (Genesis 19:24, 25). Jesus was saying that those who reject the Good News when they hear it will be worse off than the wicked people of these destroyed cities who never heard it at all.

10:17, 18 Later the disciples experienced these hardships (Acts 5:40; 12:1), not only from without (governments, courts), but also from within (friends, family) (10:21). Living for God often brings on persecution, but with it comes the opportunity to tell the Good

News of salvation. In the midst of persecution, we can be confident because Jesus has "overcome the world" (John 16:33). And those who "endure to the end" will be saved (10:22).

10:19, 20 Jesus told the disciples that when arrested for preaching the gospel, they should not worry about what to say in their defense—God's Spirit would speak through them. This prediction was fulfilled in Acts 4:8–15 and elsewhere. Some mistakenly think this means we don't have to prepare to present the gospel because God will take care of everything. Scripture teaches, however, that we are to make carefully prepared, thoughtful statements (Colossians 4:6). Jesus is not telling us to stop preparing, but to stop worrying.

10:22 Enduring to the end is not a way to be saved but the evidence that you are really committed to Jesus. Persistence is not a means to earn salvation, but the by-product of a truly devoted life.

10:23 We have plenty of work to do and people to reach. Our work won't be finished until Christ returns. And only after he returns will the whole world discover who he is (see Matthew 24:14).

10:26
Lk 12:1-9

10:27
Lk 12:3

10:28
Isa 8:13
Jer 1:8
Heb 10:31

10:29
Lk 12:6

10:30
Lk 21:18
Acts 27:34

10:32
Lk 12:8
Rom 10:9
Rev 3:5

10:33
Lk 9:26
2 Tim 2:12

10:34
Lk 12:51-53

10:36
Mic 7:6

10:37
Lk 14:26

10:38
Mt 16:24
Mk 8:34
Lk 9:23; 14:27

10:39
Mt 16:25
Mk 8:35
Lk 9:24; 17:33
Jn 12:25

10:40
Jn 12:44; 13:20

10:41
2 Kgs 4:8

I, the master of the household, have been called 'Satan,' how much more will you! 26But don't be afraid of those who threaten you. For the time is coming when the truth will be revealed: their secret plots will become public information.

27"What I tell you now in the gloom, shout abroad when daybreak comes. What I whisper in your ears, proclaim from the housetops!

28"Don't be afraid of those who can kill only your bodies—but can't touch your souls! Fear only God who can destroy both soul and body in hell. 29Not one sparrow (What do they cost? Two for a penny?) can fall to the ground without your Father knowing it. 30And the very hairs of your head are all numbered. 31So don't worry! You are more valuable to him than many sparrows.

32"If anyone publicly acknowledges me as his friend, I will openly acknowledge him as my friend before my Father in heaven. 33But if anyone publicly denies me, I will openly deny him before my Father in heaven.

34"Don't imagine that I came to bring peace to the earth! No, rather, a sword. 35I have come to set a man against his father, and a daughter against her mother, and a daughter-in-law against her mother-in-law— 36a man's worst enemies will be right in his own home! 37If you love your father and mother more than you love me, you are not worthy of being mine; or if you love your son or daughter more than me, you are not worthy of being mine. 38If you refuse to take up your cross and follow me, you are not worthy of being mine.

39"If you cling to your life, you will lose it; but if you give it up for me, you will save it.

40"Those who welcome you are welcoming me. And when they welcome me they are welcoming God who sent me. 41If you welcome a prophet because he is a man of God, you will be given the same reward a prophet gets. And if you welcome good and godly men because of their godliness, you will be given a reward like theirs.

42"And if, as my representatives, you give even a cup of cold water to a little child, you will surely be rewarded."

10:25 The Pharisees did, in fact, call Jesus "Satan" (see 9:34). Good is sometimes labeled evil. If Jesus, who is perfect, was called evil, his followers can expect similar accusations directed at them. But those who endure (10:22) will be vindicated.

10:29-31 Jesus said that God cares for the sparrows' every need, and we are far more valuable to God than these little birds, so valuable that God sent his only Son to die for us (John 3:16). You are of great worth to God. You are never lost in his inventory. Because God places such value on us, we need never fear personal threats or difficult trials. These can't dislodge God's love and Spirit from within us.

But don't think that because you are valuable to God he will take away all your troubles (see 10:16). The real test of value is how well something holds up under the wear, tear, and abuse of everyday life. Those who stand up for Christ in spite of their troubles truly have lasting value and will receive great rewards (see 5:11, 12).

10:34 Jesus did not come to bring the kind of peace that glosses over deep differences just for the sake of superficial harmony. Conflict and disagreement will arise between those who choose to follow Christ and those who don't (see Isaiah 9:6; Matthew 5:9; John 14:27). Yet we can look forward to the day when all conflict will be resolved.

10:34-39 Christian commitment may separate friends and loved ones. In saying this, Jesus was not encouraging disobedience to parents or conflict at home. Rather, he was showing that his presence demands a decision. Since some will follow him and some won't, inevitable conflict will arise. As we "take up our cross and follow him," our different values, morals, goals, and purposes inevitably will set us apart from others. Don't neglect your family, but don't neglect your higher mission. God should be your first priority.

10:37 Christ calls us to a higher mission than to find comfort and tranquility in this life. Love of family is a law of God, but even this love can be self-serving and an excuse not to serve God or do his work.

10:38 To take up our cross and follow Jesus, we must lay down other cares and priorities—only then can we pick up our commitment to Christ. We should be totally commited to God (10:39) and willing to face anything, even suffering and death, for his sake.

10:39 This verse is a positive and negative statement of the same truth: clinging to this life may cause us to forfeit the best from Christ in this world *and* in the next. The more we love this life's rewards (leisure, power, popularity, financial security), the more we discover how empty they really are. The best way to enjoy life, therefore, is to loosen our greedy grasp on earthly rewards to be free to follow Christ (Matthew 16:25). In doing so, we will inherit eternal life and begin at once to experience the benefits of following him.

10:42 How much we love God can be measured by how well we treat others. Jesus' example of giving a cup of cold water to a thirsty child is a good model of unselfish service. A child usually can't or won't return a favor. God notices every good deed we do or don't do as if he were the one receiving it. Is there something unselfish you can do for someone else today? Although no one else may see you, it won't go unnoticed by God.

—◉ 4. Jesus teaches about the kingdom

Jesus eases John's doubt
(70/Luke 7:18–35)

11 When Jesus had finished giving these instructions to his twelve disciples, he went off preaching in the cities where they were scheduled to go.

²John the Baptist, who was now in prison, heard about all the miracles the Messiah was doing, so he sent his disciples to ask Jesus, ³"Are you really the one we are waiting for, or shall we keep on looking?"

⁴Jesus told them, "Go back to John and tell him about the miracles you've seen me do— ⁵the blind people I've healed, and the lame people now walking without help, and the cured lepers, and the deaf who hear, and the dead raised to life; and tell him about my preaching the Good News to the poor. ⁶Then give him this message, 'Blessed are those who don't doubt me.' "

⁷When John's disciples had gone, Jesus began talking about him to the crowds. "When you went out into the barren wilderness to see John, what did you expect him to be like? Grass blowing in the wind? ⁸Or were you expecting to see a man dressed as a prince in a palace? ⁹Or a prophet of God? Yes, and he is more than just a prophet. ¹⁰For John is the man mentioned in the Scriptures—a messenger to precede me, to announce my coming, and prepare people to receive me.

¹¹"Truly, of all men ever born, none shines more brightly than John the Baptist. And yet, even the lesser lights in the Kingdom of Heaven will be greater than he is! ¹²And from the time John the Baptist began preaching and baptizing until now, ardent multitudes have been crowding toward the Kingdom of Heaven, ¹³for all the laws and prophets looked forward [to the Messiah]. Then John appeared, ¹⁴and if you are willing to understand what I mean, he is Elijah, the one the prophets said would come [at the time the Kingdom begins]. ¹⁵If ever you were willing to listen, listen now!

¹⁶"What shall I say about this nation? These people are like children playing, who say to their little friends, ¹⁷'We played wedding and you weren't happy, so we played funeral but you weren't sad.' ¹⁸For John the Baptist doesn't even drink wine and often goes without food, and you say, 'He's crazy.' ¹⁹And I, the Messiah, feast and drink, and you complain that I am 'a glutton and a drinking man, and hang

11:2 Mt 14:3 / Lk 7:18-35
11:3 Num 24:17 / Deut 18:15 / Mal 3:1 / Jn 6:14
11:5 Isa 42:7; 61:1 / Lk 4:18,19 / Jn 5:36 / Jas 2:5
11:6 Mt 13:57 / 1 Pet 2:8
11:9 Lk 1:76
11:10 Isa 40:3 / Mal 3:1 / Mk 1:2
11:12 Lk 16:16
11:14 Mal 4:5 / Mt 17:11-13 / Mk 9:11-13 / Lk 1:17 / Jn 1:23
11:15 Mt 13:9,43 / Mk 4:9,23 / Lk 8:8 / Rev 2:7,11,17, 29; 3:6,13,22
11:18 Mt 3:4 / Lk 1:15
11:19 Lk 15:2

11:1 *where they were scheduled to go,* literally, "to teach and preach in their cities." Lk 10:1 remarks, "The Lord now chose seventy other disciples and sent them on ahead in pairs to all the towns and villages he planned to visit later."
11:10 *prepare people to receive me,* literally, "prepare your way before you."   **11:13** *to the Messiah,* implied.
11:14 *at the time the Kingdom begins,* implied.   **11:18** *He's crazy,* literally, "He has a demon."   **11:19** *the Messiah,* literally, "the Son of Man." *you can justify your every inconsistency,* literally, "wisdom is justified by her children."

11:1 This verse could be included with Jesus' instructions given in chapter 10. Jesus may have visited the cities where the disciples had first announced his coming.

11:2, 3 John had been put in prison by Herod. Herod had married his own sister-in-law, and John publicly rebuked Herod's flagrant sin (14:3–5). John's Profile is found in John 1. Herod's Profile is found in Mark 6.

11:4–6 As John sat in prison, he began to experience some doubts about whether Jesus really was the Messiah. If John's purpose was to prepare people for the coming Messiah (3:3), and if Jesus really was that Messiah, then why was John in prison when he could have been preaching to the crowds, preparing their hearts?

Jesus answered John's doubts by pointing to his acts of healing the blind, lame, and deaf, curing the lepers, raising the dead, and preaching the Good News about God. With so much evidence, Jesus' identity was obvious. If you sometimes doubt your salvation, the forgiveness of your sins, or God's work in your life, look at the evidence in Scripture and the changes in your life. When you doubt, don't turn away from Christ, turn *to* him.

11:11 Jesus contrasted John's spiritual life to his physical life. Of all people, no man fulfilled his God-given purpose better than John. Yet, in God's coming kingdom, all those present would have

a greater spiritual heritage than John because they would have seen and known Christ and his finished work on the cross.

11:12 There are three common views about the meaning of this verse. (1) Jesus may have been referring to a vast movement toward God, the momentum of which began with John's preaching. (2) A more literal translation of this verse reads, "The Kingdom of Heaven suffers violence, and men of violence take it by force." Most of the Jews in Jesus' day expected God's Kingdom to come through a violent overthrow of Rome. They wanted a kingdom, but not Jesus' kind. (3) A third translation reads, "The Kingdom of Heaven has been forcefully advancing, and forceful men lay hold of it." The emphasis of this alternative is that entering the Kingdom takes courage, unwavering faith, determination, and endurance because of persecution leveled at Jesus' followers.

11:14 John was not a resurrected Elijah, but he took Elijah's prophetic role—boldly confronting sin and pointing people to God (Malachi 3:1).

11:16–19 Jesus condemned the attitude of his generation. No matter what he said or did, they would take the opposite view. They were cynical and skeptical because their comfortable, secure, and self-centered lifestyles were being challenged. We too often justify our inconsistencies because listening to God may require us to change the way we live.

around with the worst sort of sinners!' But brilliant men like you can justify your every inconsistency!"

Jesus promises rest for the soul
(71)

11:20
Lk 10:12-15

11:21
Mk 8:22,23
Lk 6:17,18; 9:10,
11; 10:13-15

11:22
Ezek 26:19,20
Mt 10:15

11:23
Isa 14:13,15
Ezek 31:14

11:25
Lk 10:21-22
Eph 1: 17,18

11:27
Mt 28:18
Jn 1:18; 3:35
6:46; 10:15
17:2,26

11:29,30
Jn 13:15
Eph 4:20
Phil 2:5-8
1 Pet 2:21

20Then he began to pour out his denunciations against the cities where he had done most of his miracles, because they hadn't turned to God.

21"Woe to you, Chorazin, and woe to you, Bethsaida! For if the miracles I did in your streets had been done in wicked Tyre and Sidon their people would have repented long ago in shame and humility. 22Truly, Tyre and Sidon will be better off on the Judgment Day than you! 23And Capernaum, though highly honored, shall go down to hell! For if the marvelous miracles I did in you had been done in Sodom, it would still be here today. 24Truly, Sodom will be better off at the Judgment Day than you."

25And Jesus prayed this prayer: "O Father, Lord of heaven and earth, thank you for hiding the truth from those who think themselves so wise, and for revealing it to little children. 26Yes, Father, for it pleased you to do it this way! . . .

27"Everything has been entrusted to me by my Father. Only the Father knows the Son, and the Father is known only by the Son and by those to whom the Son reveals him. 28Come to me and I will give you rest—all of you who work so hard beneath a heavy yoke. 29, 30Wear my yoke—for it fits perfectly—and let me teach you; for I am gentle and humble, and you shall find rest for your souls; for I give you only light burdens."

The disciples pick wheat on the Sabbath
(45/Mark 2:23–28; Luke 6:1–5)

12:2
Ex 20:10
Deut 5:14
Mt 12:10
Lk 13:14; 14:3
Jn 5:10; 7:23

12:3
1 Sam 21:6

12:4
Ex 25:30
29:32,33

12 About that time, Jesus was walking one day through some grainfields with his disciples. It was on the Sabbath, the Jewish day of worship, and his disciples were hungry; so they began breaking off heads of wheat and eating the grain.

2But some Pharisees saw them do it and protested, "Your disciples are breaking the law. They are harvesting on the Sabbath."

3But Jesus said to them, "Haven't you ever read what King David did when he and his friends were hungry? 4He went into the Temple and they ate the special

11:21 *Tyre and Sidon*, cities destroyed by God for their wickedness. Also *Sodom* in vs 23.   **11:23** *highly honored*, i.e., highly honored by Christ's being there.

11:21–24 Tyre, Sidon, and Sodom were ancient cities with a longstanding reputation for wickedness (Genesis 18; 19; Ezekiel 27; 28). Each had been destroyed by God for its evil. The people of Bethsaida, Chorazin, and Capernaum saw Jesus firsthand, and yet they stubbornly refused to repent of their sins and believe in him. Jesus said that if some of the wickedest cities in the world had seen him, they would have repented. Because Bethsaida, Chorazin, and Capernaum saw Jesus and didn't believe, they would suffer greater punishment than the wicked cities who didn't see Jesus. Similarly, those nations and cities that have churches on every corner and Bibles in every home will have no excuse on Judgment Day if they do not repent and believe.

11:25 Jesus mentions two kinds of people in his prayer: the "wise"—arrogant in their own knowledge—and the "children"—humbly open to receive the truth of God's Word.

11:28–30 A yoke is a heavy wooden harness that fits onto one or more oxen. It is attached to a piece of equipment the oxen are to pull. When an ox wears a yoke, it means that the animal is going to have a long day of hard work. The "heavy yoke" Jesus mentioned here can mean (1) the burden of sin, (2) the burden of the law (the excessive demands of the religious leaders, 23:4; Acts 15:10), (3) government oppression, (4) weariness in the search for God.

Jesus frees people from all these burdens. The rest Jesus promises is peace with God, not the end of all effort.

12:1, 2 The Pharisees had established 39 general categories of actions forbidden on the Sabbath. These were based on interpretations of God's law and on Jewish custom. Harvesting was one of those forbidden actions. By picking wheat and rubbing it in their hands, the disciples were technically harvesting, according to the religious leaders. Jesus and the disciples were picking grain because they were hungry, not because they wanted to harvest the grain for a profit. Jesus and the disciples were not working on the Sabbath. The Pharisees, however, could not (and did not want to) see beyond the law's technicalities. They had no room for compassion, and they were determined to accuse Jesus of wrongdoing.

12:4 This story is recorded in 1 Samuel 21:1–6. The Bread of the Presence was replaced every week, and the old loaves were eaten by the priests. The loaves given to David were the old loaves that had just been replaced with fresh ones. Although the priests were the only ones allowed to eat the bread, God did not punish David because his need for food was more important than the legal technicalities. Jesus was saying, "If you condemn me, you must also condemn David," something the religious leaders could never do without causing a great uproar among the people. It must be emphasized that Jesus was not condoning disobedience to God's laws. Instead he was emphasizing discernment and compassion regarding enforcement of the laws.

bread permitted to the priests alone. That was breaking the law too. 5And haven't you ever read in the law of Moses how the priests on duty in the Temple may work on the Sabbath? 6And truly, one is here who is greater than the Temple! 7But if you had known the meaning of this Scripture verse, 'I want you to be merciful more than I want your offerings,' you would not have condemned those who aren't guilty! 8For I, the Messiah, am master even of the Sabbath."

12:5
Num 28:9

12:6
Mal 3:1

12:7
1 Sam 15:22
Hos 6:6
Mic 6:6-8

Jesus heals a man's hand on the Sabbath
(46/Mark 3:1–6; Luke 6:6–11)

9Then he went over to the synagogue, 10and noticed there a man with a deformed hand. The Pharisees asked Jesus, "Is it legal to work by healing on the Sabbath day?" (They were, of course, hoping he would say "Yes," so they could arrest him!) 11This was his answer: "If you had just one sheep, and it fell into a well on the Sabbath, would you work to rescue it that day? Of course you would. 12And how much more valuable is a person than a sheep! Yes, it is right to do good on the Sabbath." 13Then he said to the man, "Stretch out your arm." And as he did, his hand became normal, just like the other one!

14Then the Pharisees called a meeting to plot Jesus' arrest and death.

12:9
Mk 3:1-6
Lk 6:6-11

12:10
Lk 13:14; 14:3
Jn 9:16

12:11
Deut 22:4
Lk 14:5

12:12
Mt 10:31

Huge crowds follow Jesus
(47/Mark 3:7–12)

15But he knew what they were planning, and left the synagogue, with many following him. He healed all the sick among them, 16but he cautioned them against spreading the news about his miracles. 17This fulfilled the prophecy of Isaiah concerning him:

12:15
Mk 3:7
Heb 4:13

12:8 the Messiah, literally, "the Son of Man." **12:10** The Pharisees, implied. arrest, literally, "accuse." **12:11** Of course you would, implied.

12:5 The Ten Commandments prohibit work on the Sabbath (Exodus 20:8–11). That was the *letter* of the law. But because the *purpose* of the Sabbath is to rest and to worship God, the priests were allowed to work by performing sacrifices and conducting worship services. This "Sabbath work" was serving and worshiping God. Jesus always emphasized the intent of the law, the meaning behind the letter. The Pharisees had lost the spirit of the law and rigidly demanded that the letter (and their interpretation of it) be obeyed.

12:6 The Pharisees were so concerned about religious rituals that they missed the whole purpose of the Temple—to bring people to God. And because Jesus Christ is even greater than the Temple, how much better can he bring people to God. God is far more important than the created instruments of worship. If we become more concerned with the means and feelings of worship than with the One we worship, we will miss God even as we think we are worshiping him.

12:7 Jesus repeated to the Pharisees words the Jewish people had heard time and again throughout their history (1 Samuel 15:22, 23; Psalm 40:6–8; Isaiah 1:11–17; Jeremiah 7:21–23; Hosea 6:6). Our heart attitude toward God comes first. Only then can we properly obey and observe religious regulations and rituals.

12:8 When Jesus said he is "master of the Sabbath," he revealed to the Pharisees that he created the Sabbath. The Creator is always greater than the creation; thus Jesus had the authority to overrule their traditions and regulations.

12:9 For more information on synagogues, read the notes on Mark 1:21 and 5:22.

12:10 As they pointed to the man with the deformed hand, the Pharisees tried to trick Jesus by asking him if it was legal to *work* by healing on the Sabbath. Their Sabbath rules said that people could be helped on the Sabbath only if their lives were in danger. Jesus healed on the Sabbath several times, and none of those healings could be classed as emergencies. If Jesus had waited until another day, he would have been submitting to the Pharisees'

authority, showing that their petty rules were equal to God's law. If he healed the man, the Pharisees could claim that because he broke their rules, his power was not from God. But Jesus made it clear to all those watching how ridiculous and petty their rules were. God is a God of people, not rules. The best time to reach out to someone is when he needs help.

12:10–12 The Pharisees placed their laws above human need. They were so concerned about Jesus breaking one of their rules that they did not care about the man's deformed hand. What is your attitude toward others? If your convictions don't allow you to help certain people, your convictions may not be in tune with God's Word.

12:14 The Pharisees plotted Jesus' death because they were outraged that he had overruled their authority (Luke 6:11). Jesus exposed their evil attitudes before the entire crowd in the synagogue. He showed that they were more loyal to their religious system than to God.

12:15 Up to now, Jesus had been aggressively confronting the Pharisees and their hypocrisy. Here he decided to withdraw from the synagogue before a major confrontation developed because it was not time for him to die. Jesus had many lessons still to teach his disciples and the people.

12:16 Jesus did not want those he healed to tell others about his miracles because he didn't want the people coming to him for the wrong reasons—this would hinder his teaching ministry. But the news of his miracles spread, and many came to see for themselves (see Mark 3:7, 8).

12:17–21 Matthew quoted the Old Testament Scriptures often because he wanted to prove to his Jewish audience that Jesus was the Messiah. The Jews held the Bible as their highest authority. They believed it pointed to a coming Messiah, but they didn't believe Jesus was the one. Matthew showed that Jesus was, in fact, the Messiah prophesied by Old Testament prophets. This particular prophecy teaches that Jesus was not to be the high-profile Messiah the Jews were expecting. Instead, the

12:18-21
Isa 42:1-4

> 18"Look at my Servant.
> See my Chosen One.
> He is my Beloved, in whom my soul delights.
> I will put my Spirit upon him,
> And he will judge the nations.
> 19He does not fight nor shout;
> He does not raise his voice!
> 20He does not crush the weak,
> Or quench the smallest hope;
> He will end all conflict with his final victory,
> 21And his name shall be the hope of all the world."

Religious leaders accuse Jesus of being Satan (74/Mark 3:20–30)

12:22
Mk 3:20-30
Lk 11:14-23

12:24
Mt 9:34

12:25
Ps 139:2
Mt 9:4
Jn 2:25

12:27
Mt 9:34

12:28
Lk 1:33
17:20,21

12:30
Mk 9:40
Lk 9:50; 11:23

12:31,32
Mt 11:19
Lk 12:10
1 Jn 5:16

12:33
Mt 7:15-20
Lk 6:43-45

12:34
Mt 3:7; 23:33

22Then a demon-possessed man—he was both blind and unable to talk—was brought to Jesus, and Jesus healed him so that he could both speak and see. 23The crowd was amazed. "Maybe Jesus is the Messiah!" they exclaimed.

24But when the Pharisees heard about the miracle they said, "He can cast out demons because he is Satan, king of devils."

25Jesus knew their thoughts and replied, "A divided kingdom ends in ruin. A city or home divided against itself cannot stand. 26And if Satan is casting out Satan, he is fighting himself, and destroying his own kingdom. 27And if, as you claim, I am casting out demons by invoking the powers of Satan, then what power do your own people use when they cast them out? Let them answer your accusation! 28But if I am casting out demons by the Spirit of God, then the Kingdom of God has arrived among you. 29One cannot rob Satan's kingdom without first binding Satan. Only then can his demons be cast out! 30Anyone who isn't helping me is harming me.

31,32"Even blasphemy against me or any other sin, can be forgiven—all except one: speaking against the Holy Spirit shall never be forgiven, either in this world or in the world to come.

33"A tree is identified by its fruit. A tree from a select variety produces good fruit; poor varieties don't. 34You brood of snakes! How could evil men like you

12:23 the Messiah, literally, "the Son of David." **12:24** Satan, literally, "Beelzebub." **12:29** without first binding Satan, literally, "the strong." Only then can his demons be cast out, literally, "Then will he spoil his house." **12:31, 32** me, literally, "the Son of Man."

Messiah would come as a servant, helping and healing, not leading into battle (Isaiah 42:1–4).

12:20 The people expected the Messiah to be a king. This quotation from Isaiah's prophecy shows he is indeed a king, but illustrates what kind of king. His final victory puts the cross before a crown, brings justice without courtly pomp, and yields victory without an army. As a servant, he brings hope. He brings life by offering his own. Like the crowd, we want Christ to rule as a king and bring great and visible victories in our lives. But often his work is quiet, and it happens according to his perfect timing, not ours.

12:24 Jesus had been accused before of being Satan (9:34). The Pharisees are trying to discredit Jesus by using an emotional argument. They refused to believe he was God, so they said he was Satan. Jesus easily exposed the foolishness of their argument.

12:25 As a man, Jesus did not share supernatural ability to know everything, but he still had profound insight into human nature. His discernment stopped the religious leaders' attempts to trick him. The resurrected Christ knows all our thoughts. This can be both a comfort and a threat. It can be a comfort because he knows what we really mean when we speak to him, and he can offer help. It can be a threat because we cannot hide from him, and he knows when we're acting out of selfish motives.

12:29 At Jesus' birth, Satan's power and control were disrupted. In the wilderness, Jesus overcame Satan's temptations, and at the resurrection, he defeated Satan's ultimate weapon, death. Eventually Satan will be constrained forever (Revelation 20:10),

and evil will no longer pervade the earth. Jesus has complete power and authority over Satan and all his forces.

12:30 It is impossible to be neutral about Christ. Anyone who is not actively following him has chosen to reject him. Any person who tries to remain neutral in the cosmic struggle of good against evil is choosing to be separated from God who alone is good. To refuse to follow Christ is to choose to play for Satan's team.

12:31, 32 Blasphemy against the Holy Spirit is denying that the Holy Spirit convicts us of sin. Because a person can be saved only through the Holy Spirit's work, to refuse repentance and to refuse even to acknowledge our sin is to refuse God's forgiveness of our sins. Sometimes believers worry that they have accidently committed this unforgivable sin. But only those who have turned their backs on God and rejected all faith have any need to worry. Jesus said they can't be forgiven—not because their sin is worse than any other, but because they will never ask for forgiveness. Whoever rejects the prompting of the Holy Spirit removes himself from the only force that can lead him to repentance and restoration to God.

12:34–36 Jesus reminds us that what we say reveals what is in our hearts. What kinds of words come from your mouth? That is an indication of what your heart is really like. You can't solve a heart problem, however, just by cleaning up your speech. You must allow the Holy Spirit to fill you with new attitudes and motives; then your speech will be cleansed at its source.

speak what is good and right? For a man's heart determines his speech. 35A good man's speech reveals the rich treasures within him. An evil-hearted man is filled with venom, and his speech reveals it. 36And I tell you this, that you must give account on Judgment Day for every idle word you speak. 37Your words now reflect your fate then: either you will be justified by them or you will be condemned."

12:36
Eph 5:4

Religious leaders ask Jesus for a miracle
(75)

38One day some of the Jewish leaders, including some Pharisees, came to Jesus asking him to show them a miracle.

12:38
Mt 16:1-4
Mk 8:11,12
Lk 11:16,29-32
Jn 2:18
1 Cor 1:22

39, 40But Jesus replied, "Only an evil, faithless nation would ask for further proof; and none will be given except what happened to Jonah the prophet! For as Jonah was in the great fish for three days and three nights, so I, the Messiah, shall be in the heart of the earth three days and three nights. 41The men of Nineveh shall arise against this nation at the judgment and condemn you. For when Jonah preached to them, they repented and turned to God from all their evil ways. And now a greater than Jonah is here—and you refuse to believe him. 42The Queen of Sheba shall rise against this nation in the judgment, and condemn it; for she came from a distant land to hear the wisdom of Solomon; and now a greater than Solomon is here—and you refuse to believe him.

12:39
Jn 4:48

12:40
Jonah 1:17

12:41
Jonah 3:5
Rom 9:5

12:42
1 Kgs 10:1
2 Chron 9:1
Mt 12:6

43, 44, 45"This evil nation is like a man possessed by a demon. For if the demon leaves, it goes into the deserts for a while, seeking rest but finding none. Then it says, 'I will return to the man I came from.' So it returns and finds the man's heart clean but empty! Then the demon finds seven other spirits more evil than itself, and all enter the man and live in him. And so he is worse off than before."

12:43
Lk 11:24-26
1 Pet 5:8

12:45
2 Pet 2:20

Jesus describes his true family
(76/Mark 3:31–35; Luke 8:19–21)

46, 47As Jesus was speaking in a crowded house his mother and brothers were outside, wanting to talk with him. When someone told him they were there, 48he remarked, "Who is my mother? Who are my brothers?" 49He pointed to his disciples. "Look!" he said, "these are my mother and brothers." 50Then he added, "Anyone who obeys my Father in heaven is my brother, sister and mother!"

12:46
Mk 3:31-35; 6:3
Lk 8:19-21
Jn 7:3-5
Acts 1:14
1 Cor 9:5
Gal 1:19

12:35, the Messiah, literally, "the Son of Man." **12:41** you refuse to believe him, implied. Also in vs 42. **12:43-45** goes into the deserts, literally, "passes through waterless places." **12:46, 47** in a crowded house, implied in Mk 3:32.

12:38–40 The Pharisees were asking for another miracle, but they were not sincerely seeking to know Jesus. Jesus knew they had already seen enough miraculous proof to convince them that he was the Messiah, if they would just open their hearts. But they had already decided not to believe in him, and more miracles would not change that.

Many people have thought, "If I could just see a real miracle, then I could really believe in God." But Jesus' response to the Pharisees applies to us. We have plenty of evidence—Jesus' death, resurrection, and ascension, and centuries of his work in the lives of believers around the world. Instead of looking for additional evidence or miracles, accept what God has already given and move forward. He may use your life as evidence to reach another person.

12:39–41 Jonah was a prophet sent to the Assyrian city of Nineveh (see the book of Jonah). Because Assyria was such a cruel and warlike nation, Jonah tried to run from his assignment and ended up spending three days in the belly of a great fish. When he got out, he grudgingly went to Nineveh, preached God's message, and saw the city repent. By contrast, when Jesus came to his people, they refused to repent. Here he is clearly saying that his resurrection would prove he is the Messiah. Three days after his death he would come back to life, just as Jonah was given a new chance at life after three days in the fish.

12:41, 42 In Jonah's day, Nineveh was the capital of the Assyrian empire, and it was as powerful as it was evil (Jonah 1:2). But the entire city repented at Jonah's preaching. The Queen of Sheba traveled far to see Solomon, king of Israel, and learn about his great wisdom (1 Kings 10:1–10). These Gentiles recognized the truth about God when it was presented to them, but the religious leaders ignored the truth even though it stared them in the face.

12:43–45 Jesus was describing the attitude of the nation of Israel and the religious leaders in particular. Just cleaning up one's life without filling it with God leaves plenty of room for Satan to enter. The book of Ezra records how the people rid themselves of idolatry, but failed to replace it with God's love and obedience to him. Wanting to rid our lives of sin is the first step—then we must fill our lives with God's Word and the Holy Spirit.

12:48–50 Jesus was not denying his responsibility to his earthly family. On the contrary, he had earlier criticized the Jewish leaders for not following the Old Testament command to honor their parents. He provided for his mother's security as he hung on the cross (John 19:25, 26). His mother Mary and brother James were present in the upper room at Pentecost (Acts 1:14). Instead Jesus was pointing out that spiritual relationships are as binding as physical ones, and he was paving the way for a new community of believers (the church).

Jesus tells the parable of the four soils
(77/Mark 4:1–9; Luke 8:4–8)

13:1
Mk 4:1-20
Lk 8:4-15

13 Later that same day, Jesus left the house and went down to the shore, 2, 3where an immense crowd soon gathered. He got into a boat and taught from it while the people listened on the beach. He used many illustrations such as this one in his sermon:

"A farmer was sowing grain in his fields. 4As he scattered the seed across the ground, some fell beside a path, and the birds came and ate it. 5And some fell on rocky soil where there was little depth of earth; the plants sprang up quickly enough in the shallow soil, 6but the hot sun soon scorched them and they withered and died, for they had so little root. 7Other seeds fell among thorns, and the thorns choked out the tender blades. 8But some fell on good soil, and produced a crop that was thirty, sixty, and even a hundred times as much as he had planted. 9If you have ears, listen!"

Jesus explains the parable of the four soils
(78/Mark 4:10–25; Luke 8:9–18)

13:11
Mt 11:25; 16:17
1 Cor 2:10
Col 1:26,27
1 Jn 2:27

10His disciples came and asked him, "Why do you always use these hard-to-understand illustrations?"

11Then he explained to them that only they were permitted to understand about the Kingdom of Heaven, and others were not.

13:12
Mk 4:25
Lk 19:26

12, 13"For to him who has will more be given," he told them, "and he will have great plenty; but from him who has not, even the little he has will be taken away. That is why I use these illustrations, so people will hear and see but not understand.

13:13
Jer 5:21

13:14
Isa 6:9,10
Ezek 12:2
Jn 12:39,40
Acts 28:26,27
Rom 11:8
2 Cor 3:14

14"This fulfills the prophecy of Isaiah:

'They hear, but don't understand; they look, but don't see! 15For their hearts are fat and heavy, and their ears are dull, and they have closed their eyes in sleep, 16so they won't see and hear and understand and turn to God again, and let me heal them.'

13:17
Lk 10:23,24
Jn 8:56
Heb 11:13
1 Pet 1:10-12

But blessed are your eyes, for they see; and your ears, for they hear. 17Many a prophet and godly man has longed to see what you have seen, and hear what you have heard, but couldn't.

13:19
Ezek 11:19
2 Cor 4:3,4
Eph 4:17,18

18"Now here is the explanation of the story I told about the farmer planting grain: 19The hard path where some of the seeds fell represents the heart of a person who hears the Good News about the Kingdom and doesn't understand it; then Satan comes and snatches away the seeds from his heart. 20The shallow, rocky soil represents the heart of a man who hears the message and receives it with real joy,

13:21
Col 2:7

13:22
Jer 4:3
Ezek 33:31
Mt 19:23
Eph 2:2
1 Tim 6:9,10,17
2 Tim 4:4,10

21but he doesn't have much depth in his life, and the seeds don't root very deeply, and after a while when trouble comes, or persecution begins because of his beliefs, his enthusiasm fades, and he drops out. 22The ground covered with thistles repre-

13:10 Why do you always use these hard-to-understand illustrations? is implied.   **13:19** Satan, literally, "the evil."

13:2, 3 Jesus used many illustrations, or *parables*, when speaking to the crowds. A parable compares something familiar to something unfamiliar. It helps us understand spiritual truth by using everyday objects and relationships. Parables compel the listener to discover truth, while at the same time concealing the truth from those too lazy or too stubborn to see it. To those who are honestly searching, the truth becomes clear. We must be careful not to read too much into parables, forcing them to say what they don't mean. All parables have one meaning unless otherwise specified by Jesus.

13:8 This parable should encourage spiritual "farmers"—those who teach, preach, and lead others. The farmer sowed good seed, but not all responses brought high yield. Some seed did not sprout, and even the plants that grew had varying yields. Don't be discouraged if no one seems to be listening to you as you faithfully teach the Word. Belief cannot be forced to follow a mathematical formula (i.e., a 4:1 ratio of good yield). Rather, it is a miracle of

God's Holy Spirit as he uses your words to move others to come to him.

13:9 Human ears hear many sounds, but there is a deeper kind of listening that results in spiritual understanding. If you honestly seek God's will, you have spiritual hearing, and these parables will give you new perspectives.

13:10 When speaking in parables, Jesus was not hiding truth from sincere seekers, for those who were receptive to spiritual truth understood the illustrations. To others they were only stories without meaning. This allowed Jesus to give spiritual food to those who hungered for it while preventing his enemies from turning against him sooner than they might have otherwise.

13:12, 13 This phrase means we are responsible to use well what we have. When we reject Jesus, our hardness of heart will drive away even the little understanding we had.

13:14–16 This prophecy is found in Isaiah 6:9, 10.

sents a man who hears the message, but the cares of this life and his longing for money choke out God's Word, and he does less and less for God. 23The good ground represents the heart of a man who listens to the message and understands it and goes out and brings thirty, sixty, or even a hundred others into the Kingdom."

13:23
Gen 26:12

Jesus tells the parable of the weeds
(80)

24Here is another illustration Jesus used: "The Kingdom of Heaven is like a farmer sowing good seed in his field; 25but one night as he slept, his enemy came and sowed thistles among the wheat. 26When the crop began to grow, the thistles grew too.

13:24
Mk 4:26-29

27"The farmer's men came and told him, 'Sir, the field where you planted that choice seed is full of thistles!'

28" 'An enemy has done it,' he exclaimed.

" 'Shall we pull out the thistles?' they asked.

29" 'No,' he replied. 'You'll hurt the wheat if you do. 30Let both grow together until the harvest, and I will tell the reapers to sort out the thistles and burn them, and put the wheat in the barn.' "

13:30
Mt 3:12

Jesus tells the parable of the mustard seed
(81/Mark 4:30-34)

31, 32Here is another of his illustrations: "The Kingdom of Heaven is like a tiny mustard seed planted in a field. It is the smallest of all seeds, but becomes the largest of plants, and grows into a tree where birds can come and find shelter."

13:31,32
Gen 1:11,12
Ezek 17:22,23
31:6

Jesus tells the parable of the yeast
(82)

33He also used this example:

"The Kingdom of Heaven can be compared to a woman making bread. She takes a measure of flour and mixes in the yeast until it permeates every part of the dough."

13:33
Lev 7:13; 23:17
Mt 16:6,12
Lk 13:20,21
1 Cor 5:6-8
Gal 5:8,9

34, 35Jesus constantly used these illustrations when speaking to the crowds. In fact, because the prophets said that he would use so many, he never spoke to them without at least one illustration. For it had been prophesied, "I will talk in parables; I will explain mysteries hidden since the beginning of time."

13:34,35
Ps 78:2,3
Mk 4:34
Jn 10:6; 16:25
Rom 16:25
1 Cor 2:7

Jesus explains the parable of the weeds
(83)

36Then, leaving the crowds outside, he went into the house. His disciples asked him to explain to them the illustration of the thistles and the wheat.

37"All right," he said, "I am the farmer who sows the choice seed. 38The field is the world, and the seed represents the people of the Kingdom; the thistles are the

13:36
Mt 15:15
13:38
Mk 16:15
Lk 24:27
Jn 8:44

13:23 *even a hundred others into the Kingdom,* literally, "produces a crop many times greater than the amount planted—thirty, sixty, or even a hundred times as much." **13:35** *beginning of time,* see Psalm 78:2. **13:37** *I,* literally, "the Son of Man."

13:23 The four types of soil represent the different responses we can have to God's message. We respond differently because we are in different states of readiness. Some people are hardened, others are shallow, others are contaminated by distracting cares, and some are receptive. How has God's Word taken root in your life? What kind of soil are you?

13:24ff Jesus gives the meaning of this illustration in verses 36–43. All of the parables in this chapter teach us about God and his Kingdom. They explain what the Kingdom is really like as opposed to our expectations of it. The Kingdom of Heaven is not necessarily a geographic place, but a spiritual realm in which God rules and in which we have God's eternal life.

13:30 The young thistles and the young blades of wheat look the same and can't be distinguised until they are grown and ready for harvest. Thistles (unbelievers) and wheat (believers) must live side

by side in this world. God is allowing unbelievers to remain for a while just as a farmer allows thistles to remain in his field so the surrounding wheat isn't uprooted with them. At the harvest, however, the thistles will be uprooted and thrown away. God's harvest (Judgment) of all mankind is coming. We are to make ourselves ready by making sure our faith is sincere.

13:31, 32 The mustard seed was the smallest seed a farmer used. Jesus used this illustration to show that the Kingdom has small beginnings but will grow and produce great results.

13:33 In other Bible passages, yeast is often a symbol of evil or uncleanness. Here it is a positive symbol of growth. Although yeast looks like a minor ingredient, it permeates the whole loaf. While the beginning of the Kingdom was small and nearly invisible, it would soon grow and have a great impact on the world.

13:39
Joel 3:13
Rev 14:15
13:41
Mt 24:31
25:31-46
13:42
Mt 8:12; 13:50
22:13
13:43
Dan 12:3

people belonging to Satan. ³⁹The enemy who sowed the thistles among the wheat is the devil; the harvest is the end of the world, and the reapers are the angels.

⁴⁰"Just as in this story the thistles are separated and burned, so shall it be at the end of the world: ⁴¹I will send my angels and they will separate out of the Kingdom every temptation and all who are evil, ⁴²and throw them into the furnace and burn them. There shall be weeping and gnashing of teeth. ⁴³Then the godly shall shine as the sun in their Father's Kingdom. Let those with ears, listen!

Jesus tells the parable of the hidden treasure (84)

13:44
1 Cor 6:20
Phil 3:7

⁴⁴"The Kingdom of Heaven is like a treasure a man discovered in a field. In his excitement, he sold everything he owned to get enough money to buy the field—and get the treasure, too!

Jesus tells the parable of the pearl merchant (85)

⁴⁵"Again, the Kingdom of Heaven is like a pearl merchant on the lookout for choice pearls. ⁴⁶He discovered a real bargain—a pearl of great value—and sold everything he owned to purchase it!

Jesus tells the parable of the fishing net (86)

13:47,48
Mt 22:10

⁴⁷,⁴⁸"Again, the Kingdom of Heaven can be illustrated by a fisherman—he casts a net into the water and gathers in fish of every kind, valuable and worthless. When the net is full, he drags it up onto the beach and sits down and sorts out the edible ones into crates and throws the others away. ⁴⁹That is the way it will be at the end of the world—the angels will come and separate the wicked people from the godly,

13:50
Mt 8:12

⁵⁰casting the wicked into the fire; there shall be weeping and gnashing of teeth. ⁵¹Do you understand?"

"Yes," they said, "we do."

⁵²Then he added, "Those experts in Jewish law who are now my disciples have double treasures—from the Old Testament as well as from the New!"

13:41 *I*, literally, "the Son of Man." **13:52** *from the Old Testament as well as from the New,* literally, "brings back out of his treasure things both new and old." The paraphrase is of course highly anachronistic!

13:40–43 At the end of the world, angels will separate those who are evil from those who are good. There are true and false believers in churches today, but we should be cautious in our judgments because the final separation will be made by Christ himself. If you start judging, you may damage some of the good "plants." It's more important to judge our own response to God than to analyze others.

13:42 Matthew often uses these terms to refer to the coming judgment. The weeping indicates sorrow or remorse, and gnashing of teeth is the response to extreme anxiety or pain. Those who say they don't care what happens to them after they die don't realize what they are saying. They will be punished for living in selfishness and indifference to God.

13:43 Those who receive God's favor stand in bright contrast to those who receive his judgment. A similiar illustration is used in Daniel 12:3.

13:44–46 The Kingdom of Heaven is more valuable than anything else we can have, so a person must be willing to give up everything to obtain it. The man who discovered the treasure in the field stumbled upon it by accident, but knew its value when he found it. The merchant was earnestly searching for the choice

pearl and, when he found it, sold everything he had to purchase it.

13:49 The parable of the fishing net has the same meaning as the parable of the weeds. We are to follow God's desires and tell others about his grace and goodness, but we are not to say who is part of the Kingdom of Heaven and who is not. This sorting will be done at the last judgment by those infinitely more qualified than we.

13:52 There is a double benefit for those who understand and utilize both Old and New Testaments. The Old Testament Scriptures point the way to Jesus the Messiah. Jesus always upheld their authority and relevance. The New Testament reveals Christ himself, who is now available to anyone who accepts his spiritual kingship. Both the Old and New teach about God and give practical guidelines for living in the world. The religious leaders, however, were trapped in the Old and blind to the New. They were looking for a future kingdom *preceded* by judgment. Jesus, however, taught that the kingdom was *now* and the judgment was future. The religious leaders were looking for a physical and temporal kingdom (via military rebellion and physical rule), but were blind to the spiritual significance of the kingdom Christ brought.

5. Jesus encounters differing reactions to his ministry

The people of Nazareth refuse to believe in Jesus
(91/Mark 6:1–6)

53, 54When Jesus had finished giving these illustrations, he returned to his home town, Nazareth in Galilee, and taught there in the synagogue and astonished everyone with his wisdom and his miracles.

13:53
Mt 2:23
Mk 6:1-6
Lk 3:23; 4:16-24

55"How is this possible?" the people exclaimed. "He's just a carpenter's son, and we know Mary his mother and his brothers—James, Joseph, Simon, and Judas. 56And his sisters—they all live here. How can he be so great?" 57And they became angry with him!

13:55
Ps 69:8
Mt 12:46
Mk 15:40
Jn 6:42

Then Jesus told them, "A prophet is honored everywhere except in his own country, and among his own people!" 58And so he did only a few great miracles there, because of their unbelief.

13:57
Ps 6
Isa 53:2,3
Jn 4:44

Herod kills John the Baptist
(95/Mark 6:14–29; Luke 9:7–9)

14 When King Herod heard about Jesus, 2he said to his men, "This must be John the Baptist, come back to life again. That is why he can do these miracles." 3For Herod had arrested John and chained him in prison at the demand of his wife Herodias, his brother Philip's ex-wife, 4because John had told him it was wrong for him to marry her. 5He would have killed John but was afraid of a riot, for all the people believed John was a prophet.

14:1
Mk 6:14-29
Lk 9:7-9
3:19,20

14:4
Lev 18:16; 20:21
Eph 5:11
2 Tim 4:2

6But at a birthday party for Herod, Herodias' daughter performed a dance that greatly pleased him, 7so he vowed to give her anything she wanted. 8Consequently, at her mother's urging, the girl asked for John the Baptist's head on a tray.

14:5
Mt 21:26
Lk 20:6

9The king was grieved, but because of his oath, and because he didn't want to back down in front of his guests, he issued the necessary orders.

10So John was beheaded in the prison, 11and his head was brought on a tray and given to the girl, who took it to her mother.

12Then John's disciples came for his body and buried it, and came to tell Jesus what had happened.

13:53, 54 *Nazareth in Galilee*, implied.   **14:3** *at the demand of*, literally, "on account of."

NAZARETH REJECTS JESUS

Chronologically, this return to Nazareth occurred after Jesus was in the Gerasene country and healed the demon-possessed men (8:28–34) then re-crossed the sea to Capernaum. From there he traveled to Nazareth, where he had grown up, only to discover that the people refused to believe he could be the Christ.

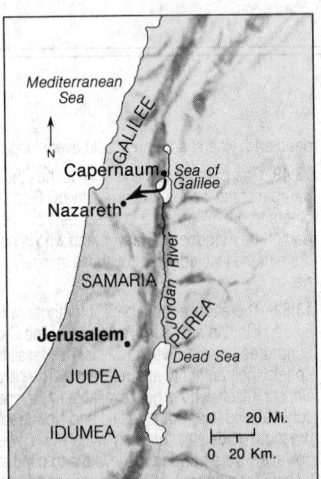

13:55 The residents of Jesus' hometown had known him since he was a young child and were acquainted with his family, yet they could not bring themselves to believe in his message. They were too close to the situation. Jesus had come to them as a prophet,

one who challenged them to respond to unpopular spiritual truth. They did not listen to the timeless message because they could not see beyond the man.

13:57 Jesus was not the first prophet to be rejected in his own country. Jeremiah experienced the rejection of his hometown and even members of his own family (Jeremiah 12:5, 6).

14:1 Herod was called a "Tetrarch," one of four rulers over the four districts of Palestine. His territory included the regions of Galilee and Perea. This is the son of Herod the Great who ordered the killing of the babies (2:16). Also known as Herod Antipas, he judged Jesus before his crucifixion (Luke 23:6–12). His Profile is found in Mark 6.

14:3 Philip, Herod's half brother, was one of the four rulers of Palestine (see 4:1 note). His territories were Iturea and Trachonitis, northeast of the Sea of Galilee (Luke 3:1). Philip's wife, Herodias, left him to live with Herod. John the Baptist condemned the two for living immorally (see Mark 6:17, 18).

14:9 Herod did not want to kill John the Baptist, but he gave the order so he wouldn't be embarrassed in front of his guests. How easy it is to give in to crowd pressure and to let ourselves be coerced into doing wrong. Don't place yourself in a position where it is too embarrassing to do what is right. Do what is right no matter how embarrassing or painful it may be.

14:13, 14 Jesus sought solitude after the news of John's death. Sometimes we may need to deal with our grief alone. Jesus, however, did not dwell on his grief; he returned to his ministry.

Jesus feeds five thousand
(96/Mark 6:30–44; Luke 9:10–17; John 6:1–15)

14:13
Mk 6:30-45
Lk 9:10-17
Jn 6:1-13

13As soon as Jesus heard the news, he went off by himself in a boat to a remote area to be alone. But the crowds saw where he was headed, and followed by land from many villages.

14:14
Mt 9:36
Mk 1:41
Heb 2:17,18
4:15; 5:1-3

14So when Jesus came out of the wilderness, a vast crowd was waiting for him and he pitied them and healed their sick.

15That evening the disciples came to him and said, "It is already past time for supper, and there is nothing to eat here in the desert; send the crowds away so they can go to the villages and buy some food."

14:16
2 Kgs 4:42-44

16But Jesus replied, "That isn't necessary—you feed them!"

17"What!" they exclaimed. "We have exactly five small loaves of bread and two fish!"

18"Bring them here," he said.

14:19
Mt 15:35-38
Lk 22:19

19Then he told the people to sit down on the grass; and he took the five loaves and two fish, looked up into the sky and asked God's blessing on the meal, then broke the loaves apart and gave them to the disciples to place before the people. 20And everyone ate until full! And when the scraps were picked up afterwards, there were twelve basketfuls left over! 21(About 5,000 men were in the crowd that day, besides all the women and children.)

Jesus walks on water
(97/Mark 6:45–52; John 6:16–21)

22Immediately after this, Jesus told his disciples to get into their boat and cross to the other side of the lake while he stayed to get the people started home.

14:23
Mk 6:46-56
Jn 6:15-21

23, 24Then afterwards he went up into the hills to pray. Night fell, and out on the lake the disciples were in trouble. For the wind had risen and they were fighting heavy seas.

14:25
Job 9:8

25About four o'clock in the morning Jesus came to them, walking on the water! 26They screamed in terror, for they thought he was a ghost.

27But Jesus immediately spoke to them, reassuring them. "Don't be afraid!" he said.

28Then Peter called to him: "Sir, if it is really you, tell me to come over to you, walking on the water."

14:19–22 Jesus multiplied five loaves and two fish to feed over 5,000 people. What he was originally given seemed insufficient, but in his hands it became more than enough. We often feel that our contribution to Jesus is meager, but he can use and multiply whatever we give him, whether it is talent, time, or treasure. It is when we give them to Jesus that our resources are multiplied.

14:21 The text states there were 5,000 men present, *plus* women and children. Therefore, the total of people Jesus fed could have been 10 to 15 thousand. The number of men is listed separately because in the Jewish culture of the day, men and women usually ate separately.

14:23, 24 Seeking solitude was an important priority for Jesus (see also 14:13). He made room in his busy schedule to be alone with the Father. Spending time with God in prayer nurtures a vital relationship and equips us to meet life's challenges and struggles. Develop the discipline of spending time alone with God—it will help you grow spiritually and become more and more like Christ.

14:28 Peter was not testing Jesus, something we are told not to do (4:7). Instead he was the only one in the boat to react in faith. His impulsive request led him to experience a rather unusual demonstration of God's power. Peter started to sink because he took his eyes off Jesus and focused on the high waves around him. Then his faith wavered when he realized what he was doing. We may not walk on water, but we do walk through tough situations. If we focus on the waves of difficult circumstances around us without looking to Christ for help, we too may despair and sink. To maintain

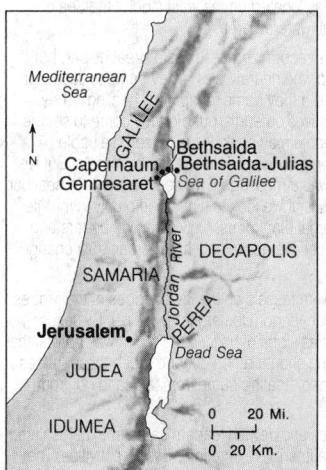

JESUS WALKS ON THE SEA
The miraculous feeding of the 5,000 occurred on the shores of the Sea of Galilee near Bethsaida-Julias. Jesus then sent his disciples across the lake. Several hours later, they encountered a storm, and Jesus came to them—walking on the water. The boat then landed at Gennesaret.

your faith in the midst of difficult situations, keep your eyes on Christ's power rather than on your inadequacies.

29"All right," the Lord said, "come along!"

So Peter went over the side of the boat and walked on the water toward Jesus. 30But when he looked around at the high waves, he was terrified and began to sink. "Save me, Lord!" he shouted.

31Instantly Jesus reached out his hand and rescued him. "O man of little faith," Jesus said. "Why did you doubt me?" 32And when they had climbed back into the boat, the wind stopped.

33The others sat there, awestruck. "You really are the Son of God!" they exclaimed.

14:32
Ps 107:29
14:33
Ps 2:7
Mt 16:16; 26:63
Mk 1:1
Lk 4:41
Jn 1:49; 6:69
11:27
Acts 8:37
Rom 1:4

Jesus heals all who touch him
(98/Mark 6:53–56)

34They landed at Gennesaret. 35The news of their arrival spread quickly throughout the city, and soon people were rushing around, telling everyone to bring in their sick to be healed. 36The sick begged him to let them touch even the tassel of his robe, and all who did were healed.

Jesus teaches about inner purity
(102/Mark 7:1–23)

15 Some Pharisees and other Jewish leaders now arrived from Jerusalem to interview Jesus.

2"Why do your disciples disobey the ancient Jewish traditions?" they demanded. "For they ignore our ritual of ceremonial handwashing before they eat." 3He replied, "And why do your traditions violate the direct commandments of God? 4For instance, God's law is 'Honor your father and mother; anyone who reviles his parents must die.' 5, 6But you say, 'Even if your parents are in need, you may give their support money to the church instead.' And so, by your man-made rule, you

15:1
Mk 7:1-23
15:2
Lk 11:37,38
Gal 1:14
15:4
Ex 20:12; 21:17
Lev 19:2; 20:9
Deut 5:16; 27:16
Prov 20:20
30:17
Eph 6:2

15:5, 6 to the church, literally, "to God."

14:30, 31 Although we start out with good intentions, sometimes our faith falters. This doesn't necessarily mean we have failed. When Peter's faith faltered, he reached out to Christ, the only one who could help. He was afraid, but he still looked to Christ. When we are apprehensive about the troubles around us and doubt Christ's presence or ability to help, we must remember that he is the only one who can really help.

14:34 Gennesaret was located on the west side of the Sea of Galilee in a fertile, well-watered area.

14:35, 36 The people recognized Jesus as a great healer, but how many understood who he truly was? They came to Jesus for physical healing, but did they come for spiritual healing? They came to prolong their lives on earth, but did they come to secure their eternal lives? People may seek Jesus to learn valuable lessons from his life or in hopes of finding relief from pain. But we have missed Jesus' whole message if we seek him only to heal our bodies but not our souls, if we look to him for help only in this life, rather than for his eternal plan for us. Only when we understand the real Jesus Christ can we appreciate how he can truly change our lives.

14:36 Jewish men wore tassels on the lower edges of their robes according to God's command (Deuteronomy 22:12). By Jesus' day, these were seen as signs of holiness (23:5). It was natural that people seeking healing should reach out and touch these, but as one sick woman learned, healing came from faith and not from Jesus' robe (9:19–22).

15:1, 2 The Pharisees and Jewish leaders came from Jerusalem, the center of Jewish authority, to scrutinize Jesus' activities. They had added hundreds of religious traditions to God's laws and considered them all equally important. Many traditions are not bad in themselves. Certain religious traditions can add richness and meaning to our lives. But we must not fall into the trap of assuming that because our traditions have been practiced for years they should be elevated to a sacred standing. God's law never changes, and it

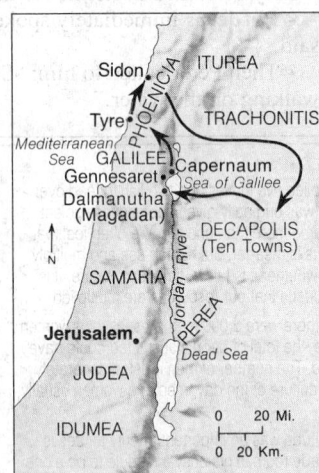

MINISTRY IN PHOENICIA
After preaching again in Capernaum, Jesus left Galilee for Phoenicia, where he preached in Tyre and Sidon. On his return, he traveled through the region of the Ten Towns, fed the 4,000 beside the sea, then crossed to Magadan.

doesn't need additions. Traditions should help us understand God's laws better, not become laws themselves.

15:5, 6 This was known as the law of *Corban*. Anyone who made a Corban vow was required to dedicate money that otherwise would have gone to support his parents to a worthy cause, usually the Temple. It had become a religiously acceptable way to neglect parents, circumventing the child's responsibility to them. Although their actions seemed worthy (tithing more money to God), they were neglecting God's command to care for needy parents.

nullify the direct command of God to honor and care for your parents. 7You hypocrites! Well did Isaiah prophesy of you, 8'These people say they honor me, but their hearts are far away. 9Their worship is worthless, for they teach their man-made laws instead of those from God.' "

15:7,8
Ezek 33:31

10Then Jesus called to the crowds and said, "Listen to what I say and try to understand: 11You aren't made unholy by eating non-kosher food! It is what you *say* and *think* that makes you unclean."

15:9
Col 2:8,18,22
1 Tim 1:6,7
Tit 1:13,14

12Then the disciples came and told him, "You offended the Pharisees by that remark."

15:11
Acts 10:15
Rom 14:14
1 Tim 4:4

13, 14Jesus replied, "Every plant not planted by my Father shall be rooted up, so ignore them. They are blind guides leading the blind, and both will fall into a ditch."

15:13
Isa 60:21; 61:3
Jn 15:2
1 Cor 3:9

15Then Peter asked Jesus to explain what he meant when he said that people are not defiled by non-kosher food.

15:14
Isa 9:16
Mal 2:8
Mt 23:16
Lk 6:39

16"Don't you understand?" Jesus asked him. 17"Don't you see that anything you eat passes through the digestive tract and out again? 18But evil words come from an evil heart, and defile the man who says them. 19For from the heart come evil thoughts, murder, adultery, fornication, theft, lying and slander. 20These are what defile; but there is no spiritual defilement from eating without first going through the ritual of ceremonial handwashing!"

15:16
Mt 16:9

15:18
Jas 3:6

15:19
Prov 6:14
Jer 17:9
Gal 5:19-21

Jesus sends a demon out of a girl
(103/Mark 7:24–30)

15:21
Mk 7:24-30

21Jesus then left that part of the country and walked the fifty miles to Tyre and Sidon.

22A woman from Canaan who was living there came to him, pleading, "Have mercy on me, O Lord, King David's Son! For my daughter has a demon within her, and it torments her constantly."

23But Jesus gave her no reply—not even a word. Then his disciples urged him to send her away. "Tell her to get going," they said, "for she is bothering us with all her begging."

15:24
Isa 53:6
Mt 10:5,6
Acts 3:25,26
13:46

24Then he said to the woman, "I was sent to help the Jews—the lost sheep of Israel—not the Gentiles."

15:9 *those from God,* see Isa 29:13. **15:11** *It is what you say and think that makes you unclean,* implied. Literally, "what comes out of a man defiles a man." **15:21** *walked the fifty miles,* implied. Literally, "withdrew into the parts of Tyre and Sidon."

15:8, 9 The prophet Isaiah also criticized the hypocrites in his day (Isaiah 29:13). Jesus applied his words to these religious leaders. When we claim to honor God while our hearts are far from him, our worship means nothing. It is not enough to act religious. Our actions and our attitudes must be sincere. If they are not, Isaiah's words will also describe us.

15:9 The Pharisees knew a lot about God, but they didn't know God. It is not enough to study about religion or even to study the Bible. We must respond to God himself.

15:13, 14 Jesus told his disciples to ignore the Pharisees because they were blind to God's truth. Anyone who listened to their teaching would risk spiritual blindness as well. Not all religious leaders are good Christian leaders. Make sure those you listen to and learn from are those with good spiritual eyesight.

15:15 Later on, Peter would be faced with the issue of nonkosher food (Acts 10:9–17). Then he would learn that nothing should be a barrier to proclaiming the gospel to the Gentiles (non-Jews).

15:16–20 We work hard to keep our outward appearance attractive, but what is in our hearts is even more important. The way we are deep down (where others can't see) matters much to God. What are you like inside? When people become Christians, God changes them and actually makes them different on the inside. He will continue to help change them if they only ask.

15:22 This woman is called a Syrophoenician in Mark's Gospel (7:26), indicating she was from the territory northwest of Galilee where the cities of Tyre and Sidon were located. Matthew calls her a Canaanite, naming her ancient ancestors, who were enemies of Israel. Matthew's Jewish audience would immediately understand the significance of Jesus helping this woman.

15:23 The disciples asked Jesus to get rid of the woman because she was bothering them with her begging. They showed no compassion for her or sensitivity to her needs. It is possible to become so occupied with spiritual matters that we miss real spiritual needs right around us, whether out of prejudice or simply the inconvenience they cause. Instead of being bothered, be aware of the opportunities that surround you. Be open to the beauty of God's message for all people.

15:24 Jesus' words do not contradict the truth that God's message is for all people (Deuteronomy 32:21; Psalm 22:27; Isaiah 56:3; Matthew 28:19; Romans 15:9–12). After all, Jesus himself was in Gentile territory on a mission to Gentile people. He ministered to Gentiles on many occasions during his ministry. Jesus was simply telling the woman that Jews have the first opportunity to accept him as the Messiah because God wanted them to present the message of salvation to the rest of the world (see Genesis 12:3). This woman was not being rejected. Jesus may have wanted to test her faith, or he may have wanted to use the situation as another opportunity to teach a lesson about faith's being available to all people.

25But she came and worshiped him and pled again, "Sir, help me!"

26"It doesn't seem right to take bread from the children and throw it to the dogs," he said.

27"Yes, it is!" she replied, "for even the puppies beneath the table are permitted to eat the crumbs that fall."

28"Woman," Jesus told her, "your faith is large, and your request is granted." And her daughter was healed right then.

15:26
Mt 7:6
Eph 2:12

The crowd marvels at Jesus' healings
(104/Mark 7:31–37)

29Jesus now returned to the Sea of Galilee, and climbed a hill and sat there. 30And a vast crowd brought him their lame, blind, maimed, and those who couldn't speak, and many others, and laid them before Jesus, and he healed them all. 31What a spectacle it was! Those who hadn't been able to say a word before were talking excitedly, and those with missing arms and legs had new ones; the crippled were walking and jumping around, and those who had been blind were gazing about them! The crowds just marveled, and praised the God of Israel.

15:29
Mk 7:31
15:30
Isa 35:5,6
Mt 4:23; 11:5
Lk 7:22

Jesus feeds four thousand
(105/Mark 8:1–9)

32Then Jesus called his disciples to him and said, "I pity these people—they've been here with me for three days now, and have nothing left to eat; I don't want to send them away hungry or they will faint along the road."

33The disciples replied, "And where would we get enough here in the desert for all this mob to eat?"

34Jesus asked them, "How much food do you have?" And they replied, "Seven loaves of bread and a few small fish!"

35Then Jesus told all of the people to sit down on the ground, 36and he took the seven loaves and the fish, and gave thanks to God for them, and divided them into pieces, and gave them to the disciples who presented them to the crowd. 37, 38And everyone ate until full—4,000 men besides the women and children! And afterwards, when the scraps were picked up, there were seven basketfuls left over!

39Then Jesus sent the people home and got into the boat and crossed to Magadan.

15:32
Ps 103:13
111:4-5
Mk 1:41; 8:1,10
Heb 2:17; 4:15
5:1-3
15:33
Num 11:21,22
2 Kgs 4:43
15:36
1 Sam 9:13
Mt 14:19
Lk 22:19
15:37
Ps 104:28
145:15
15:39
Mk 8:10

Religious leaders ask for a sign in the sky
(106/Mark 8:10–12)

16 One day the Pharisees and Sadducees came to test Jesus' claim of being the Messiah by asking him to show them some great demonstrations in the skies.

16:1
Mt 12:38
Mk 8:11-21
Lk 11:16

15:26–28 *Dog* was a term the Jews commonly applied to any Gentiles, because the Jews considered these pagan people no more likely than dogs to receive God's blessing. Jesus was not degrading the woman by using this term, but reflecting the Jews' attitude so as to show its contrast with his own. The woman did not argue. Using Jesus' choice of words, she agreed to be considered a dog as long as she could receive God's blessing for her daughter. Ironically, many Jews would lose God's blessing and salvation because they rejected Jesus, and many Gentiles would find salvation because they recognized Jesus.

15:29–31 A vast crowd was brought to Jesus to be healed, and he healed them all. Jesus is still able to heal broken lives, and we can be the ones who bring others to him. Do you know some who need the healing touch of Jesus? You can bring them to Jesus through prayer or by explaining the reason for your faith. Then let Christ do the healing.

15:32ff This feeding of 4,000 is a separate event from the feeding of the 5,000 (14:13–21), confirmed by Mark 8:19, 20. This was the beginning of Jesus' expanded ministry to the Gentiles.

15:33 Jesus had already fed more than 5,000 people with five

loaves and two fish. Now, in a similar situation, the disciples were again perplexed. How easily we throw up our hands in despair when faced with tough situations. Like the disciples, we often forget that if God has cared for us in the past, he will do the same now. If you are facing a difficult situation, remember when God cared for you and trust him to work faithfully again.

15:39 Magadan was located on the west shore of the Sea of Galilee. Also known as Magdala or Dalmanutha (Mark 8:10), this town was Mary Magdalene's home.

16:1 The Pharisees and Sadducees were Jewish religious leaders of two different parties, and their views were diametrically opposed on many issues. The Pharisees carefully followed their religious rules and traditions, believing that this was the way to God. They also believed in the authority of all Scripture and in the resurrection of the dead. The Sadducees accepted only the books of Moses as Scripture and did not believe in life after death. In Jesus, however, these two groups had a common enemy, and they joined forces to try to kill him. For more information on the Pharisees and Sadducees, see the charts in Matthew 3 and Mark 2.

16:1 The Pharisees and Sadducees demanded a sign *in the sky.*

16:2
Isa 7:14
Lk 12:54-56

16:4
Mt 12:39

2, 3He replied, "You are good at reading the weather signs of the skies—red sky tonight means fair weather tomorrow; red sky in the morning means foul weather all day—but you can't read the obvious signs of the times! 4This evil, unbelieving nation is asking for some strange sign in the heavens, but no further proof will be given except the miracle that happened to Jonah." Then Jesus walked out on them.

Jesus warns against wrong teaching
(107/Mark 8:13–21)

5Arriving across the lake, the disciples discovered they had forgotten to bring any food.

16:6
Mt 7:15
Lk 12:1
Rom 16:17,18
Phil 3:2
Col 2:8
2 Pet 3:17

16:9
Mt 14:19; 15:36

16:11
Lk 12:1

6"Watch out!" Jesus warned them; "beware of the yeast of the Pharisees and Sadducees."

7They thought he was saying this because they had forgotten to bring bread.

8Jesus knew what they were thinking and told them, "O men of little faith! Why are you so worried about having no food? 9Won't you ever understand? Don't you remember at all the 5,000 I fed with five loaves, and the basketfuls left over? 10Don't you remember the 4,000 I fed, and all that was left? 11How could you even think I was talking about food? But again I say, 'Beware of the yeast of the Pharisees and Sadducees.'"

12Then at last they understood that by "yeast" he meant the *wrong teaching* of the Pharisees and Sadducees.

Peter says Jesus is the Messiah
(109/Mark 8:27–30; Luke 9:18–20)

16:13
Mk 8:27-30
Lk 9:18-21

13When Jesus came to Caesarea Philippi, he asked his disciples, "Who are the people saying I am?"

16:13 /, literally, "the Son of Man."

They might try to explain away Jesus' other miracles as sleight of hand, coincidence, or use of evil power, but they believed only God could do a sign in the sky. This, they were sure, would be a feat beyond Jesus' power. Although Jesus could have easily impressed them, he refused. He knew that even a miracle in the sky would not convince them he was the Messiah because they had already decided not to believe in him.

16:4 In using the illustration of Jonah, who was inside a great fish for three days, Jesus was predicting his death and resurrection (see also 12:38–42).

16:4 Many people, like these Jewish leaders, want a miracle so they can believe. But Jesus knew that miracles would never convince them. Jesus had been healing, raising people from the dead, and feeding thousands, and still people wanted him to prove himself. Do you doubt Christ because you haven't *seen* a miracle? Do you expect God to prove himself to you personally before you believe? Jesus says, "Blessed are those who haven't seen me and believe anyway" (John 20:29). We have all the miracles recorded in the Old and New Testaments, 2,000 years of church history, and the witness of thousands. With all this evidence, those who don't believe are proud or stubborn. If you simply step forward in faith and believe, then you will begin to notice miracles happening in your own life!

16:12 Yeast is put into bread to make it rise, and it takes only a little to affect a whole batch of dough. Jesus used yeast as an example of how a small amount of evil can affect a large group of people. The wrong teachings of the Pharisees and Sadducees were leading many people astray. Beware of the tendency to say, "How can this little wrong possibly affect anyone?"

16:13 Caesarea Philippi was located several miles north of the Sea of Galilee, in the territory ruled by the tetrarch Philip. The influence of Greek and Roman culture was everywhere, and pagan temples and idols abounded. When Philip became tetrarch, he rebuilt and renamed the city after the emperor (Caesar) and himself. The city was originally called Caesarea, the same name as

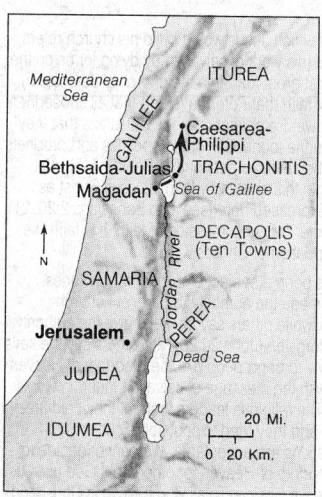

JOURNEY TO CAESAREA-PHILIPPI
Jesus left Magadan, crossed the lake, and landed in Bethsaida-Julias. There he healed a man who had been born blind. From there, he and his disciples went to Caesarea-Philippi, where Peter confessed Jesus as indeed the Messiah and Son of God.

the capital city of his brother Herod's territory.

16:13–17 The disciples answered Jesus' question with the common view people held—that Jesus was one of the great prophets come back to life. This belief may have stemmed from Deuteronomy 18:18, where God said he would raise up a prophet from among the people. (John the Baptist's Profile is in John; Elijah's Profile is in 1 Kings and Jeremiah's Profile is in Jeremiah.) Peter, however, confesses Jesus as divine and as the promised and long-awaited Messiah. If Jesus asked you this question, how would you answer? Is he your Lord and Messiah?

14"Well," they replied, "some say John the Baptist; some, Elijah; some, Jeremiah or one of the other prophets."

15Then he asked them, "Who do *you* think I am?"

16Simon Peter answered, "The Christ, the Messiah, the Son of the living God."

17"God has blessed you, Simon, son of Jonah," Jesus said, "for my Father in heaven has personally revealed this to you—this is not from any human source. 18You are Peter, a stone; and upon this rock I will build my church; and all the powers of hell shall not prevail against it. 19And I will give you the keys of the Kingdom of Heaven; whatever doors you lock on earth shall be locked in heaven; and whatever doors you open on earth shall be open in heaven!"

20Then he warned the disciples against telling others that he was the Messiah.

Jesus predicts his death the first time
(110/Mark 8:31—9:1; Luke 9:21–27)

21From then on Jesus began to speak plainly to his disciples about going to Jerusalem, and what would happen to him there—that he would suffer at the hands of the Jewish leaders, that he would be killed, and that three days later he would be raised to life again.

22But Peter took him aside to remonstrate with him. "Heaven forbid, sir," he said. "This is not going to happen to you!"

23Jesus turned on Peter and said, "Get away from me, you Satan! You are a dangerous trap to me. You are thinking merely from a human point of view, and not from God's."

24Then Jesus said to the disciples, "If anyone wants to be a follower of mine, let him deny himself and take up his cross and follow me. 25For anyone who keeps his life for himself shall lose it; and anyone who loses his life for me shall find it again.

16:21 *the Jewish leaders,* literally, "of the elders, and chief priests, and scribes."

16:14
Mal 4:5

16:16
Mt 1:16; 14:33
Jn 6:69; 11:27
20:31

16:17
Gal 1:16

16:18
Jn 1:42
1 Cor 3:11
Eph 2:20-22
4:15-16
1 Pet 2:4,5

16:19
Jn 20:23

16:21
Mk 8:31 9:1
Lk 9:22-27

16:23
Rom 8:7

16:24
1 Thess 3:3
2 Tim 3:12

16:18 The rock upon which Jesus would build his church refers either to Jesus himself (his work of salvation for us on the cross), to Peter (the first great leader in the church at Jerusalem), or to the confession of faith that Peter gave and that all subsequent true believers would give. Peter later reminds Christians that they are the church built on the foundation of the apostles and prophets with Jesus Christ as the chief Cornerstone (1 Peter 2:4–6). All believers are joined into this church by faith in Jesus Christ as Savior, just as Peter expressed here (see also Ephesians 2:20, 21). Jesus was praising Peter for his confession of faith. It is faith like Peter's that is the foundation of Christ's Kingdom.

16:19 This verse has been a subject of debate for centuries. Some say the "keys" mean the authority to carry out church discipline (18:15–18), while others say the keys give the authority to announce sins as forgiven (John 20:23). Still others say the keys may be the opportunity to bring people to the Kingdom of Heaven by presenting them with the message of salvation found in God's Word (Acts 15:7–9). The religious leaders thought they held the keys to the kingdom, and they tried to shut some out.

All three interpretations are acceptable. We cannot decide to open or close the Kingdom of Heaven for others, but God uses us to help others find the way inside. To all who believe in Christ and obey his words, the Kingdom doors are swung wide open.

16:20 Jesus warned the disciples not to publicize Peter's confession, because they did not yet fully understand what kind of Messiah he had come to be—not a military commander but a suffering servant. They needed to come to a full understanding of Jesus and their mission as disciples before they could proclaim it to others in a way that would not precipitate rebellion. They would have a difficult time understanding what he came to do until his earthly mission was complete.

16:21 "From then on" marks a turning point. In 4:17 it signals Jesus' announcement of the Kingdom of Heaven. Here it points to his new emphasis on his death and resurrection. Still, the disciples

didn't grasp Jesus' true purpose because of their preconceived notions about what the Messiah should be. This is the first of three times Jesus predicted his death (see 17:22, 23; 20:18 for others).

16:21–28 The death of Jesus and the suffering of his followers correspond to Daniel's prophecies: the Messiah would be cut off (Daniel 9:26); there would be a period of trouble (9:27); and the king would come in glory (7:13, 14). The disciples would endure the same suffering as their King and, like him, would be rewarded in the end.

16:22 Peter, Jesus' friend and devoted follower who had just eloquently proclaimed his true identity, sought to protect him from the suffering he prophesied. Great temptations can come from those who love us and seek to protect us. Be cautious of advice from a friend who says, "Surely God doesn't want you to face this." Often our most difficult temptations come from those who are only trying to protect us from discomfort.

16:23 The same message Jesus heard in his wilderness temptations (that he did not have to die—4:6) he now heard from Peter. Peter had just recognized Jesus as Messiah; now, however, he forsook God's perspective and evaluated the situation from a human one. Satan is always trying to get us to leave God out of the picture. Jesus rebuked Peter for this kind of attitude.

16:24 When Jesus used this picture of his followers' taking up their crosses to follow him, the disciples knew what he meant. Crucifixion was a common Roman method of execution, and condemned criminals had to carry their crosses through the streets to the execution site. Following Jesus, therefore, meant a true commitment, the risk of death, and no turning back (see 10:39).

16:25 If we protect ourselves from pain, we make our own prisons because we begin to die spiritually and emotionally. Our lives turn inward, and we lose our intended purpose. When we give our lives in service to Christ, however, we discover the real purpose of living.

16:26
Ps 49:7-9

16:27
Mt 25:31
2 Cor 5:10
Jude 14,15
Rev 22:12

26What profit is there if you gain the whole world—and lose eternal life? What can be compared with the value of eternal life? 27For I, the Son of Mankind, shall come with my angels in the glory of my Father and judge each person according to his deeds. 28And some of you standing right here now will certainly live to see me coming in my Kingdom."

Jesus is transfigured on the mountain
(111/Mark 9:2–13; Luke 9:28–36)

17:1
Mk 9:2-8
Lk 9:28-36

17 Six days later Jesus took Peter, James, and his brother John to the top of a high and lonely hill, 2and as they watched, his appearance changed so that his face shone like the sun and his clothing became dazzling white.

3Suddenly Moses and Elijah appeared and were talking with him. 4Peter blurted out, "Sir, it's wonderful that we can be here! If you want me to, I'll make three shelters, one for you and one for Moses and one for Elijah."

17:5
Deut 18:15
Isa 42:1
Mk 1:11
Lk 3:22
Acts 3:22
Heb 12:25
2 Pet 1:17,18

5But even as he said it, a bright cloud came over them, and a voice from the cloud said, "This is my beloved Son, and I am wonderfully pleased with him. Obey him."

6At this the disciples fell face downward to the ground, terribly frightened. 7Jesus came over and touched them. "Get up," he said, "don't be afraid."

8And when they looked, only Jesus was with them.

17:9
Mk 9:9-13

9As they were going down the mountain, Jesus commanded them not to tell anyone what they had seen until after he had risen from the dead.

17:10
Mal 4:5

10His disciples asked, "Why do the Jewish leaders insist Elijah must return before the Messiah comes?"

17:11
Lk 1:17

11Jesus replied, "They are right. Elijah must come and set everything in order.

17:12
Mt 14:3

12And, in fact, he has already come, but he wasn't recognized, and was badly mistreated by many. And I, the Messiah, shall also suffer at their hands."

13Then the disciples realized he was speaking of John the Baptist.

17:4 *three shelters,* literally, "three tabernacles" or "tents." What was in Peter's mind is not explained. **17:5** *Obey him,* literally, "hear him." **17:10** *Elijah must return before the Messiah comes,* implied. Literally, "that Elijah must come first." **17:12** *the Messiah,* literally, "the Son of Man."

16:26 When we don't know Christ, we make choices as though this life is all we have. In reality, this life is just the introduction to eternity. How we live this brief span, however, determines our eternal state. What we accumulate on earth has no value in purchasing eternal life. Even the highest social or civic honors cannot earn for us eternal life. Begin, therefore, to evaluate all that happens from an eternal perspective.

16:27 Jesus Christ has been given the authority to judge all the earth (Philippians 2:9–11). Although his judgment is already working in our lives, there is a future, final judgment when Christ returns (25:31–46) and everyone's life is reviewed and evaluated. This will not be confined to nonbelievers; Christians too will face a judgment. Their eternal destiny is secure, but Jesus will look at how they handled gifts, opportunities, and responsibilities in order to determine their heavenly rewards. At the time of judgment, God will deliver the righteous and condemn the wicked. We should not judge others' salvation; that is God's work.

16:28 Since all the disciples died *before* Christ's return, many believe Jesus' words here were fulfilled at the transfiguration when Peter, James, and John saw his glory (17:1–3). Others say they refer to Pentecost (Acts 2) and the beginning of Christ's church. In either case, certain disciples were eyewitnesses to the power and glory of Christ's Kingdom.

17:1ff The transfiguration foreshadowed the glory of the King (16:27, 28). This was a special revelation of Jesus' divinity to three of the disciples, and it was God's divine affirmation of everything Jesus had done and was about to do.

17:3–5 Moses and Elijah were two of the greatest prophets in the Old Testament. Moses represents the law. He wrote the Pentateuch, and he predicted the coming of a great Prophet (Deuteronomy 18:15–19). Elijah represents the prophets who foretold the coming of the Messiah (Malachi 4:5, 6). Their presence with Jesus confirms his messianic mission—to fulfill God's law and the words of God's prophets. Just as God's voice in the cloud over Mount Sinai gave authority to his law (Exodus 19:9), God's voice at the transfiguration gave authority to Jesus' words.

17:4 Peter wanted to build a place for these three great men to stay. But he had the wrong idea. He wanted to act, but this was a time for worship and adoration. He wanted to capture the moment, but he was supposed to learn and move on. He saw Christ as equal to the others, but Christ is infinitely greater and not to be compared with anyone.

17:5 Jesus is more than just a great leader, more than just a good example, a good influence, or a prophet. He is, in fact, the Son of God. When you understand this profound truth, the only adequate response is worship. When you have a correct understanding of Christ, you will obey him.

17:9 Jesus told Peter, James, and John not to tell what they had seen until after his resurrection, because Jesus knew that they didn't fully understand what they had seen and heard and could not explain what they didn't understand. Their questions (17:10ff) revealed their misunderstandings. They knew that he was the Messiah, but they had much more to learn about the significance of his death and resurrection.

17:11, 12 Jesus was referring to John the Baptist, not to the Old Testament prophet Elijah. John the Baptist took Elijah's prophetic role—boldly confronting sin and pointing people to God. Malachi had earlier prophesied that a prophet like Elijah would come (Malachi 4:5).

Jesus heals the demon-possessed boy
(112/Mark 9:14–29; Luke 9:37–43)

14When they arrived at the bottom of the hill, a huge crowd was waiting for them. A man came and knelt before Jesus and said, 15"Sir, have mercy on my son, for he is mentally deranged, and in great trouble, for he often falls into the fire or into the water; 16so I brought him to your disciples, but they couldn't cure him."

17Jesus replied, "Oh, you stubborn, faithless people! How long shall I bear with you? Bring him here to me." 18Then Jesus rebuked the demon in the boy and it left him, and from that moment the boy was well.

19Afterwards the disciples asked Jesus privately, "Why couldn't we cast that demon out?"

20"Because of your little faith," Jesus told them. "For if you had faith even as small as a tiny mustard seed you could say to this mountain, 'Move!' and it would go far away. Nothing would be impossible. 21But this kind of demon won't leave unless you have prayed and gone without food."

17:14
Mk 9:14-29
Lk 9:37-43

17:20
Mt 21:21
Mk 11:22,23
Lk 17:6
Jn 11:40
1 Cor 13:2

Jesus predicts his death the second time
(113/Mark 9:30–32; Luke 9:44, 45)

22,23One day while they were still in Galilee, Jesus told them, "I am going to be betrayed into the power of those who will kill me, and on the third day afterwards I will be brought back to life again." And the disciples' hearts were filled with sorrow and dread.

17:22
Mt 16:21
20:17-19
Mk 9:30-32
10:33,34
Lk 9:22,43-45

Peter finds the coin in the fish's mouth
(114)

24On their arrival in Capernaum, the Temple tax collectors came to Peter and asked him, "Doesn't your master pay taxes?"

25"Of course he does," Peter replied.

Then he went into the house to talk to Jesus about it, but before he had a chance

17:24
Mk 12:14-17

17:21 This verse is omitted in many of the ancient manuscripts.

17:17 This is an indirect message to the nine disciples who were left at the bottom of the hill (17:20). Jesus' purpose was not to criticize the disciples, but to encourage them to greater faith.

17:17-20 The disciples were unable to cast out this demon, so they asked Jesus why. He pointed to their little faith which was small even in comparison with a mustard seed. The mustard seed produced a great plant, but their faith produced little. Perhaps they had tried to cast out the demon with their own ability rather than God's. There is great power in even a little faith when God is with us. If we feel weak or powerless as Christians, we should examine our faith, making sure we are trusting not in our own abilities to produce results, but in God's.

17:20 Jesus wasn't condemning the disciples for substandard faith; he was trying to show how important faith would be in their future ministry. If you are facing a problem that seems as big and immovable as a mountain, turn your eyes from the mountain and look to Christ for more faith. Only then will your work for him become useful and vibrant.

17:21 Jesus was teaching that some work for God is more difficult than others and requires a greater than usual dependence on God. This verse does not mean that prayer and fasting alone would have accomplished the miracle. Prayer and fasting indicate faith and humility before God, without which there can be no hope of success.

17:22, 23 Once again Jesus predicted his death; but more important, he told of his resurrection. Unfortunately, the disciples heard only the first part of Jesus' words and became discouraged. They couldn't understand why Jesus wanted to go back to Jerusalem where he would walk right into trouble.

The disciples didn't fully comprehend the purpose of Jesus'

death and resurrection until Pentecost (Acts 2). We shouldn't get upset at ourselves for being slow to understand everything about Jesus. After all, the disciples were with him, saw his miracles, heard his words, and still had difficulty understanding. Despite their questions and doubts, however, they still believed. We can do no less.

17:22, 23 The disciples didn't understand why Jesus kept talking about his death, because they expected him to set up a political kingdom—his death would dash their hopes. They didn't know that Jesus' death and resurrection would make his kingdom possible.

17:24 All Jewish males had to pay a Temple tax to support Temple upkeep (Exodus 30:11–16). Tax collectors set up booths to collect these taxes. Only Matthew records this incident—perhaps because he had been a tax collector himself.

17:24–27 As usual, Peter answered a question without really knowing the answer, putting Jesus and the disciples in an awkward position. Jesus used this situation, however, to emphasize his kingly role. Just as kings pay no taxes and collect none from their family, Jesus, the King, owed no taxes. But Jesus supplied the tax payment for both himself and Peter rather than offend those who didn't understand his kingship. Although Peter was given the tax money, he had to go and get it. Ultimately all that we have comes to us from God's supply, but he may want us to be active in the process.

17:24–27 As God's people, we are foreigners on earth because our loyalty is always to our real King—Jesus. Still we have to cooperate with the authorities and be responsible citizens. An ambassador to another country keeps the local laws in order to represent well the one who sent him. We are Christ's ambassadors. Are you being a good foreign ambassador for him to this world?

to speak, Jesus asked him, "What do you think, Peter? Do kings levy assessments against their own people, or against conquered foreigners?"

26, 27"Against the foreigners," Peter replied.

"Well, then," Jesus said, "the citizens are free! However, we don't want to offend them, so go down to the shore and throw in a line, and open the mouth of the first fish you catch. You will find a coin to cover the taxes for both of us; take it and pay them."

17:27
Mt 18:6-9
1 Cor 8:13; 10:32

The disciples argue about who would be the greatest
(115/Mark 9:33–37; Luke 9:46–48)

18:3
Mt 19:14
Mk 10:14
Lk 18:16,17
1 Cor 14:20
1 Pet 2:2
18:4
Mt 20:27
1 Pet 5:5,6
18:5
Mt 10:42
18:6
Lk 17:1-3
1 Cor 8:12,13

18 About that time the disciples came to Jesus to ask which of them would be greatest in the Kingdom of Heaven!

2Jesus called a small child over to him and set the little fellow down among them, 3and said, "Unless you turn to God from your sins and become as little children, you will never get into the Kingdom of Heaven. 4Therefore anyone who humbles himself as this little child, is the greatest in the Kingdom of Heaven. 5And any of you who welcomes a little child like this because you are mine, is welcoming me and caring for me. 6But if any of you causes one of these little ones who trusts in me to lose his faith, it would be better for you to have a rock tied to your neck and be thrown into the sea.

Jesus warns against temptation
(117/Mark 9:43–50)

18:8
Mt 5:29,30

7"Woe upon the world for all its evils. Temptation to do wrong is inevitable, but woe to the man who does the tempting. 8So if your hand or foot causes you to sin, cut it off and throw it away. Better to enter heaven crippled than to be in hell with both of your hands and feet. 9And if your eye causes you to sin, gouge it out and throw it away. Better to enter heaven with one eye than to be in hell with two.

Jesus warns against looking down on others
(118)

18:10
Ps 34:7
Lk 1:19
Acts 12:15
Heb 1:14
18:12
Lk 15:3-7

10"Beware that you don't look down upon a single one of these little children. For I tell you that in heaven their angels have constant access to my Father. 11And I, the Messiah, came to save the lost.

12"If a man has a hundred sheep, and one wanders away and is lost, what will he do? Won't he leave the ninety-nine others and go out into the hills to search for the

18:6 *to lose his faith,* literally, "cause to stumble."   **18:7** *for all its evils,* literally, "because of occasions of stumbling." **18:10** *have constant access,* or, "do always behold . . ."   **18:11** *the Messiah,* literally, "the Son of Man." This verse is left out of many manuscripts, some ancient.

18:1 From Mark's Gospel we learn that Jesus precipitated this conversation by asking the disciples what they had been discussing among themselves earlier (Mark 9:33, 34).

18:1–4 Jesus used a child to help his self-centered disciples get the point. We are not to be *childish* (like the disciples, arguing over petty issues), but rather *childlike,* with humble and sincere hearts. Are you being childlike or childish?

18:2 The disciples had become so preoccupied with the organization of Jesus' earthly kingdom, they had lost sight of its divine purpose. Instead of seeking a place of service, they sought positions of advantage. How easy it is to lose our eternal perspective and compete for promotions in the church. How hard it is to identify with the "little children"—weak and dependent people with no status or influence.

18:6 Children are trusting by nature. They trust adults, and through that trust their capacity to trust God grows. Parents and adults who influence young children are held accountable by God for how they affect these little ones' ability to trust. Jesus warned that anyone who turns little children away from faith will receive severe punishment.

18:7ff Jesus warned the disciples about three ways to cause "little ones" to lose faith: tempting them (18:7–9), neglecting or demeaning them (18:10–14), and teaching false doctrine to them (18:15–26). As leaders, we are to help young or new believers avoid anything or anyone that could cause them to stumble in their faith and lead them to sin. We must never take lightly the spiritual education and protection of children and children in the faith.

18:8, 9 We must remove stumbling blocks that cause us to sin. This does not mean to cut off a part of the body; it means that any person, program, or teaching in the church that threatens the spiritual growth of the body must be removed. Jesus says it would be better to go to heaven with one hand than to hell with both. Sin, however, affects more than our hands; it affects our minds and hearts.

18:10 Our concern for children must parallel God's treatment of them. Certain angels are assigned to watch over children, and they have direct access to God. These words ring out sharply in cultures where children are taken lightly, ignored, or aborted. If their angels have constant access to God, the least we can do is to allow children to approach us easily in spite of our far-too-busy schedules.

lost one? 13And if he finds it, he will rejoice over it more than over the ninety-nine others safe at home! 14Just so, it is not my Father's will that even one of these little ones should perish.

Jesus teaches about how to treat a believer who sins (119)

15"If a brother sins against you, go to him privately and confront him with his fault. If he listens and confesses it, you have won back a brother. 16But if not, then take one or two others with you and go back to him again, proving everything you say by these witnesses. 17If he still refuses to listen, then take your case to the church, and if the church's verdict favors you, but he won't accept it, then the church should excommunicate him. 18And I tell you this—whatever you bind on earth is bound in heaven, and whatever you free on earth will be freed in heaven.

19"I also tell you this—if two of you agree down here on earth concerning anything you ask for, my Father in heaven will do it for you. 20For where two or three gather together because they are mine, I will be right there among them."

18:15
Lk 17:3
Gal 6:1
2 Thess 3:15
Jas 5:19,20

18:16
Deut 19:15

18:17
Rom 16:17
1 Cor 6:1-8
1 Tim 5:20

18:18
Mt 16:19
Jn 20:23

Jesus tells the parable of the unforgiving debtor (120)

21Then Peter came to him and asked, "Sir, how often should I forgive a brother who sins against me? Seven times?"

22"No!" Jesus replied, "seventy times seven!

23"The Kingdom of Heaven can be compared to a king who decided to bring his accounts up to date. 24In the process, one of his debtors was brought in who owed

18:21
Lk 17:4

18:22
Col 3:13
18:23
Mt 25:19

18:17 *should excommunicate him,* literally, "let him be to you as the Gentile and the publican."   **18:24** $10,000,000, literally, "10,000 talents." Approximately £3,000,000.

Jesus forgave	Reference	**JESUS AND**
the paralyzed man lowered on a stretcher through the roof.	Matthew 9:2–8	**FORGIVENESS**
the woman caught in adultery.	John 8:3–11	
the woman who anointed his feet with oil.	Luke 7:47–50	
Peter, for denying he knew Jesus.	John 18:15–18, 25–27; 21:15–19	
the thief on the cross.	Luke 23:39–43	
the people who crucified him.	Luke 23:34	

Jesus not only taught frequently about forgiveness, he also demonstrated his own willingness to forgive. Here are several examples that should be an encouragement to recognize his willingness to forgive us also.

18:14 Just as a shepherd is concerned enough for one lost sheep to go search the hills for it, so God is concerned about every human being he creates ("He is not willing that any should perish," 2 Peter 3:9). We come in contact with children who need Christ at home, at school, in church, and in our neighborhood. Steer them toward him by your example, your words, and your acts of kindness.

18:15-17 These are Jesus' guidelines for dealing with those who sin against us. They were meant for (1) Christians, not unbelievers, (2) sins against *you* and not others, and (3) conflict resolution that is done in the context of the church, not the community at large. Jesus' words are not a license for a frontal attack on every person who hurts or slights us. They are not a license to start a destructive gossip campaign or church trial. They are designed to reconcile those who disagree so that all Christians can live in harmony.

When someone wrongs us, we often do the opposite of what Jesus recommends. We turn away in hatred or resentment, seek revenge, or gossip. By contrast, we should go to that person *first*, as difficult as that may be. Then we should forgive him as often as he needs it (18:20–22). This will give you a much better chance of restoring the relationship.

18:18 This *binding* and *loosing* refers to the decisions of the church in conflicts. There is no court of appeals among believers beyond the church. Ideally, its decisions should be God-guided and based on discernment from his Word. There is great responsibility on believers, therefore, to bring their problems to the church *and* on the church to utilize God's guidance in seeking to resolve conflicts. Handling problems God's way will have an impact now and for eternity.

18:19, 20 Jesus looks ahead to a new day when he will be present with them not in body, but through his Holy Spirit. In the body of believers (the Church), the sincere agreement of two people is more powerful than the superficial agreement of thousands, because Christ's Holy Spirit is with them. Two or more believers, *filled with the Holy Spirit*, will pray according to God's will, not their own, and thus their requests will be granted.

18:22 The rabbis taught that Jews should forgive those who offend them three times. Peter, in trying to be especially generous, asked Jesus if seven (the "perfect" number) was enough times to forgive someone. But Jesus answered, "Seventy times seven," meaning that we shouldn't even keep track of how many times we forgive someone. We should always forgive those who are truly repentant, no matter how many times they ask.

18:25
Ex 21:2
Lev 25:39
2 Kings 4:1
Neh 5:5

him $10,000,000! 25He couldn't pay, so the king ordered him sold for the debt, also his wife and children and everything he had.

26"But the man fell down before the king, his face in the dust, and said, 'Oh, sir, be patient with me and I will pay it all.'

27"Then the king was filled with pity for him and released him and forgave his debt.

28"But when the man left the king, he went to a man who owed him $2,000 and grabbed him by the throat and demanded instant payment.

29"The man fell down before him and begged him to give him a little time. 'Be patient and I will pay it,' he pled.

30"But his creditor wouldn't wait. He had the man arrested and jailed until the debt would be paid in full.

31"Then the man's friends went to the king and told him what had happened.
32And the king called before him the man he had forgiven and said, 'You evil-hearted wretch! Here I forgave you all that tremendous debt, just because you asked me to— 33shouldn't you have mercy on others, just as I had mercy on you?'

18:33
Mt 7:2
Eph 4:32; 5:2
Col 3:13

18:34
Mark 11:25
Jas 2:13

34"Then the angry king sent the man to the torture chamber until he had paid every last penny due. 35So shall my heavenly Father do to you if you refuse to truly forgive your brothers."

6. Jesus faces conflict with the religious leaders
Jesus teaches about marriage and divorce
(173/Mark 10:1–12)

19:3
Mk 10:2-12

19 After Jesus had finished this address, he left Galilee and circled back to Judea from across the Jordan River. 2Vast crowds followed him, and he healed their sick. 3Some Pharisees came to interview him, and tried to trap him into saying something that would ruin him.

"Do you permit divorce?" they asked.

19:4
Gen 1:27; 5:2

19:5
Gen 2:24
Mal 2:15
1 Cor 6:16
Eph 5:31

4"Don't you read the Scriptures?" he replied. "In them it is written that at the beginning God created man and woman, 5, 6and that a man should leave his father and mother, and be forever united to his wife. The two shall become one—no longer two, but one! And no man may divorce what God has joined together."

18:28 *$2,000,* approximately £700.

18:30 In Bible times, serious consequences awaited those who could not repay their debts. A person lending money could seize the borrower who couldn't pay him back and force him or his family to work until the debt was paid. The debtor could also be thrown into prison, or his family could be sold into slavery to help pay off the debt. It was hoped the debtor, while in prison, would sell off his landholdings or that relatives would pay the debt. If not, the debtor could remain in prison for life.

18:35 Because God has forgiven all our sins, we should not withhold forgiveness from others. Realizing how completely Christ has forgiven us should produce a free and generous attitude of forgiveness toward others. When we don't forgive others, we are setting ourselves outside and above Christ's law of love.

19:3–12 John was put in prison and killed for his public opinions on marriage and divorce, and the Pharisees hoped to trap Jesus too. They were trying to trick Jesus by having him choose sides in a theological controversy. Two main groups had two opposing views of divorce. One group supported divorce for almost any reason. The other believed divorce could be allowed only for marital unfaithfulness. This conflict hinged on how each group interpreted Deuteronomy 24:1–4. But in his answer, Jesus focused on marriage rather than divorce. He pointed out that Scripture intended marriage to be permanent, and he gave four reasons for the importance of marriage (19:1–6).

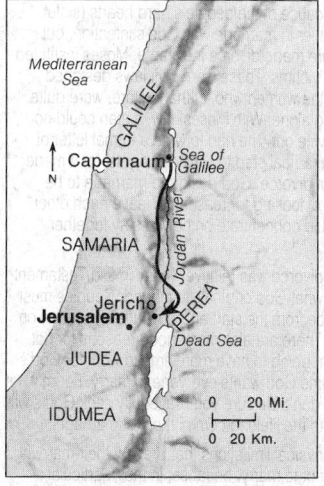

JESUS TRAVELS TOWARD JERUSALEM Jesus left Galilee for the last time—heading toward his death in Jerusalem. He again crossed the Jordan, spending some time in Perea before going on to Jericho.

7"Then, why," they asked, "did Moses say a man may divorce his wife by merely writing her a letter of dismissal?"

8Jesus replied, "Moses did that in recognition of your hard and evil hearts, but it was not what God had originally intended. 9And I tell you this, that anyone who divorces his wife, except for fornication, and marries another, commits adultery."

10Jesus' disciples then said to him, "If that is how it is, it is better not to marry!"

11"Not everyone can accept this statement," Jesus said. "Only those whom God helps. 12Some are born without the ability to marry, and some are disabled by men, and some refuse to marry for the sake of the Kingdom of Heaven. Let anyone who can, accept my statement."

Jesus blesses little children
(174/Mark 10:13–16; Luke 18:15–17)

13Little children were brought for Jesus to lay his hands on them and pray. But the disciples scolded those who brought them. "Don't bother him," they said.

14But Jesus said, "Let the little children come to me, and don't prevent them. For of such is the Kingdom of Heaven." 15And he put his hands on their heads and blessed them before he left.

Jesus speaks to the rich young man
(175/Mark 10:17–31; Luke 18:18–30)

16Someone came to Jesus with this question: "Good master, what must I do to have eternal life?"

17"When you call me good you are calling me God," Jesus replied, "for God alone is truly good. But to answer your question, you can get to heaven if you keep the commandments."

18"Which ones?" the man asked.

And Jesus replied, "Don't kill, don't commit adultery, don't steal, don't lie, 19honor your father and mother, and love your neighbor as yourself!"

20"I've always obeyed every one of them," the youth replied. "What else must I do?"

21Jesus told him, "If you want to be perfect, go and sell everything you have and

19:7
Deut 24:1
Mt 5:31,32

19:9
Lk 16:18
1 Cor 7:10,11

19:11
1 Cor 7:7-9,17
19:12
1 Cor 7:32,34

19:13
Mk 10:13-16
Lk 18:15-17
19:14
Mt 18:3

19:16
Mk 10:17-31
Lk 10:25
18:18-30
19:18
Ex 20:12-17
Deut 5:16-21
19:19
Lev 19:18
Mt 15:4; 22:39
Mk 12:31
19:21
Lk 12:33
Acts 2:45
4:34,35
1 Tim 6:18

19:9 "And the man who marries a divorced woman commits adultery." This sentence is added in some ancient manuscripts.   **19:12** Some are born without the ability to marry, literally, "born eunuchs," or, "born emasculated."
19:17 for God alone is truly good, implied from Lk 18:19.

19:7, 8 This law is found in Deuteronomy 24:1–4. In Moses' day, as well as in Jesus' day, the practice of marriage fell far short of God's intention. The same is true today. Jesus said that Moses gave this law only because of the people's hard hearts (sinful nature). Staying together in marriage was God's intention, but because human nature made divorce inevitable, Moses instituted some laws to help its victims. These were civil laws designed especially to protect the women who, in that culture, were quite vulnerable when living alone. With Moses' law, a man could no longer just throw his wife out—he had to write a formal letter of dismissal. This was a radical step toward civil rights, for it made men think twice about divorce. God designed marriage to be indissoluble. Instead of looking for reasons to leave each other, married couples should concentrate on how to stay together (19:3–9).

19:10–12 Although divorce was relatively easy in Old Testament times (19:7), it is not what God originally intended. Couples must decide against divorce from the start and build their marriage on mutual commitment. There are also many good reasons for not marrying, one of them being to have more time to work for God's Kingdom. Don't assume God wants everyone to marry. For many it may be better if they don't. Be sure you prayerfully seek God's will before you plunge into the lifelong commitment of marriage.

19:12 Some have physical limitations that prevent their marrying, while others choose not to marry, because, in their particular situation, they can serve God better as single people. Jesus was

not teaching us to avoid marriage because it is inconvenient or takes away our freedom. This is selfishness. A good reason to remain single is to use the time and freedom to serve God. Paul elaborates on this in 1 Corinthians 7.

19:13–15 The disciples must have forgotten what Jesus had said about children (18:4–6). Jesus wanted little children to come because he loves them and because they have the kind of attitude needed to approach God. He didn't mean that heaven is only for children, but that people need childlike attitudes of trust in God. The receptiveness of little children was a great contrast to the stubbornness of the religious leaders who let their religious education and sophistication stand in the way of the simple faith needed to believe in Jesus.

19:16 This man was seeking assurance that he could have eternal life. Jesus pointed out that he could not save himself through good deeds that are not based on love for God. This man needed a whole new starting point. He needed to discover God's love and plan for him.

19:17 In response to the young man's question about how to have eternal life, Jesus told him to keep God's Ten Commandments. Jesus then listed six of them, all referring to relationships with others. When the young man replied that he had kept them, Jesus told him he must do something more—sell everything and give the money to the poor. This request showed the man's weakness. In reality, his wealth was his god, his "graven image," and he would not give it up.

give the money to the poor, and you will have treasure in heaven; and come, follow me." 22But when the young man heard this, he went away sadly, for he was very rich.

19:23
Job 31:24-28
Mt 13:22
1 Cor 1:26
1 Tim 6:9

23Then Jesus said to his disciples, "It is almost impossible for a rich man to get into the Kingdom of Heaven. 24I say it again—it is easier for a camel to go through the eye of a needle than for a rich man to enter the Kingdom of God!"

25This remark confounded the disciples. "Then who in the world can be saved?" they asked.

19:26
Gen 18:14
Job 42:2
Jer 32:17
Zech 8:6
19:27
Mt 4:20
Lk 5:11

26Jesus looked at them intently and said, "Humanly speaking, no one. But with God, everything is possible."

27Then Peter said to him, "We left everything to follow you. What will we get out of it?"

28And Jesus replied, "When I, the Messiah, shall sit upon my glorious throne in the Kingdom, you my disciples shall certainly sit on twelve thrones judging the twelve tribes of Israel. 29And anyone who gives up his home, brothers, sisters, father, mother, wife, children, or property, to follow me, shall receive a hundred times as much in return, and shall have eternal life. 30But many who are first now will be last then; and some who are last now will be first then."

19:28
Lk 22:28-30
1 Cor 6:2,3
Rev 2:26
19:30
Mt 20:16

Jesus tells the parable of the workers paid equally (176)

20:1
Song 1:6; 8:11,12
20:2

20 Here is another illustration of the Kingdom of Heaven. "The owner of an estate went out early one morning to hire workers for his harvest field. 2He agreed to pay them $20 a day and sent them out to work.

3"A couple of hours later he was passing a hiring hall and saw some men standing around waiting for jobs, 4so he sent them also into his fields, telling them he would pay them whatever was right at the end of the day. 5At noon and again around three o'clock in the afternoon he did the same thing.

6"At five o'clock that evening he was in town again and saw some more men standing around and asked them, 'Why haven't you been working today?'

7" 'Because no one hired us,' they replied.

" 'Then go on out and join the others in my fields,' he told them.

20:8
Lev 19:13

8"That evening he told the paymaster to call the men in and pay them, beginning

19:28 *the Messiah,* literally, "the Son of Man." *in the Kingdom,* literally, "in the regeneration." **19:29** *wife,* omitted here in many manuscripts but included in Lk 18:29. **20:2** *$20 a day,* literally, "a denarius," the payment for a day's labor; equivalent to $20 in modern times, or £7.

19:21 Should all believers sell everything they own? No, because we must be responsible for caring for our own needs and the needs of our families so as not to be a burden on others. We should, however, be willing to give up anything if God asks us to do so. This kind of attitude allows nothing to come between us and God and keeps us from using our God-given wealth selfishly.

19:22 We cannot love God with all our hearts and keep our money to ourselves. Loving him totally means using our money in ways that please him.

19:24 Because it is impossible for a camel to go through the eye of a needle, it appears impossible for a rich person to get into heaven. Jesus explained, however, that with God "everything is possible." Even rich men can enter the Kingdom if God brings them in. Faith in him, not in self or riches, is what counts. On what are you counting for salvation?

19:25, 26 The disciples were confused because they thought that if anyone could be saved it would be the rich—who were thought in Jewish culture to be especially blessed by God.

19:27 In the Bible, God gives rewards to his people according to his justice. In the Old Testament, obedience often brought reward in this life (Deuteronomy 28), but obedience and reward are not always linked. If they were, good people would always be rich, and suffering would always be a sign of sin. As believers, our true reward is God's presence and power through the Holy Spirit. And

later we will be rewarded in eternity for our faith and service. If material rewards in this life came to us for every faithful deed, we would be tempted to boast in our achievements and soil our motives.

19:29 Jesus assured the disciples that anyone who gives up something valuable for his sake will be repaid many times over in this life, although not necessarily in the same form. For example, a person may be rejected by his family for accepting Christ, but he will gain the larger family of believers.

19:30 Jesus turned the world's values upside down. Consider the most powerful or well-known people in our world—how many got where they are by being mild-tempered, self-effacing, and gentle? Not many! But in the life to come, the last will be first—if they got in last place by choosing to follow Jesus. Don't forfeit eternal rewards for temporary benefits. Be willing to make sacrifices now for greater rewards later. Be willing to accept man's disapproval for God's approval.

20:1ff Jesus further clarified the membership rules of the Kingdom of Heaven—entrance is by God's grace alone. In this parable, God is the estate owner and the believers are those who work for him. This parable was for those who felt superior because of heritage or favored position, to those who felt superior because they had spent so much time with Christ, and to new believers as reassurance of God's grace.

with the last men first. ⁹When the men hired at five o'clock were paid, each received $20. ¹⁰So when the men hired earlier came to get theirs, they assumed they would receive much more. But they, too, were paid $20.

¹¹, ¹²"They protested, 'Those fellows worked only one hour, and yet you've paid them just as much as those of us who worked all day in the scorching heat.'

20:12
Mt 4:8
Lk 1:11

¹³" 'Friend,' he answered one of them, 'I did you no wrong! Didn't you agree to work all day for $20? ¹⁴Take it and go. It is my desire to pay all the same; ¹⁵is it against the law to give away my money if I want to? Should you be angry because I am kind?' ¹⁶And so it is that the last shall be first, and the first, last."

20:15
Rom 9:21
20:16
Mt 19:30

Jesus predicts his death the third time
(177/Mark 10:32–34; Luke 18:31–34)

¹⁷As Jesus was on the way to Jerusalem, he took the twelve disciples aside, ¹⁸and talked to them about what would happen to him when they arrived.

20:17
Mk 10:32-34
Lk 18:31-33

"I will be betrayed to the chief priests and other Jewish leaders, and they will condemn me to die. ¹⁹And they will hand me over to the Roman government, and I will be mocked and crucified, and the third day I will rise to life again."

20:19
Mt 16:21; 27:2
Jn 18:28
Acts 2:23; 3:13

Jesus teaches about serving others
(178/Mark 10:35–45)

²⁰Then the mother of James and John, the sons of Zebedee, brought them to Jesus and respectfully asked a favor.

20:20
Mt 28:56; 4:21
Mk 10:35-45
15:40

²¹"What is your request?" he asked. She replied, "In your Kingdom, will you let my two sons sit on two thrones next to yours?"

20:21
Mt 19:28
Jas 4:3

²²But Jesus told her, "You don't know what you are asking!" Then he turned to James and John and asked them, "Are you able to drink from the terrible cup I am about to drink from?"

20:22
Mt 26:39
Mk 14:36
Jn 18:11

"Yes," they replied, "we are able!"

²³"You shall indeed drink from it," he told them. "But I have no right to say who will sit on the thrones next to mine. Those places are reserved for the persons my Father selects."

20:23
Acts 12:2
Rom 8:17
Rev 1:9

²⁴The other ten disciples were indignant when they heard what James and John had asked for.

20:24
Lk 22:24

²⁵But Jesus called them together and said, "Among the heathen, kings are tyrants and each minor official lords it over those beneath him. ²⁶But among you it is quite

20:26
Mt 23:11
Mk 9:35
1 Pet 5:3

20:18 I, literally, "the Son of Man."   **20:21** sit on two thrones, implied. Also in vs 23.

20:15 This parable is not about rewards but about salvation. It is a strong teaching about grace, God's generosity. We shouldn't begrudge those who turn to God in the last moments of life, because, in reality, no one deserves eternal life.

Many people we don't expect to see in the kingdom may be there. The thief who repented as he was dying (Luke 23:40–43) will be there as well as the person who has believed and served God for many years. Do you resent God's gracious acceptance of the despised, the outcast, and the sinners who have turned to him for forgiveness? Are you ever jealous of what God has given to another person? Instead, focus on God's gracious benefits to you, and be thankful for what you have.

20:17-19 Jesus predicted his death and resurrection for the third time (see 16:21 and 17:23 for the first two times). But the disciples didn't understand what he meant. They continued to argue greedily over their positions in Christ's Kingdom (20:20–28).

20:20 The mother of James and John asked Jesus to give her sons special positions in his Kingdom. Parents naturally want to see their children promoted and honored, but this desire can cause them to lose sight of God's specific will for their children. God may have different work for them—not as glamorous, but just as important. Thus parents' desires for their children's advancement must be held in check as they pray that God's

will be done in their children's lives.

20:20 According to 27:56, the mother of James and John was at the cross when Jesus was crucified. Some have suggested she was the sister of Mary, the mother of Jesus. A close family relationship could have prompted her to make this request for her sons.

20:22 James, John, and their mother failed to grasp Jesus' previous teachings on rewards (19:16–30) and eternal life (20:1–16). They failed to understand the suffering they would face before living in the glory of God's Kingdom. The terrible cup was the suffering and crucifixion Christ faced. Both James and John would also face great suffering. James would be put to death for his faith, and John would be exiled.

20:23 Jesus was showing that he was under the authority of the Father, who alone makes the decisions about leadership in heaven. Such rewards are not granted as favors. They are for those who have maintained their commitment to Jesus in spite of severe trials.

20:24 The other disciples were upset because James and John were trying to grab the top positions. All the disciples wanted to be the greatest (18:1), but Jesus taught them that the greatest person in God's Kingdom is the servant of all.

20:27
Mt 18:4

20:28
Phil 2:7
1 Pet 1:19

different. Anyone wanting to be a leader among you must be your servant. 27And if you want to be right at the top, you must serve like a slave. 28Your attitude must be like my own, for I, the Messiah, did not come to be served, but to serve, and to give my life as a ransom for many."

Jesus heals a blind beggar
(179/Mark 10:46–52; Luke 18:35–43)

20:29
Mk 10:46-52
Lk 18:35-43

29As Jesus and the disciples left the city of Jericho, a vast crowd surged along behind.

30Two blind men were sitting beside the road and when they heard that Jesus was coming that way, they began shouting, "Sir, King David's Son, have mercy on us!"

31The crowd told them to be quiet, but they only yelled the louder.

32, 33When Jesus came to the place where they were he stopped in the road and called, "What do you want me to do for you?"

"Sir," they said, "we want to see!"

34Jesus was moved with pity for them and touched their eyes. And instantly they could see, and followed him.

Jesus rides into Jerusalem on a donkey
(183/Mark 11:1–11; Luke 19:28–44; John 12:12–19)

21:1
Zech 14:4
Mk 11:1-10
Lk 19:28-40
Jn 12:12-19

21 As Jesus and the disciples approached Jerusalem, and were near the town of Bethphage on the Mount of Olives, Jesus sent two of them into the village ahead.

21:3
Ps 24:1

2"Just as you enter," he said, "you will see a donkey tied there, with its colt beside it. Untie them and bring them here. 3If anyone asks you what you are doing, just say, 'The Master needs them,' and there will be no trouble."

21:5
Zech 9:9

4This was done to fulfill the ancient prophecy, 5"Tell Jerusalem her King is coming to her, riding humbly on a donkey's colt!"

6The two disciples did as Jesus said, 7and brought the animals to him and threw

20:28 Your attitude, implied. the Messiah, literally, "the Son of Man."   **21:7** threw their garments over the colt, implied.

20:27 Jesus described leadership from a new perspective. Instead of using people, we are to serve them. Jesus' purpose in life was to serve others and to give his life away. A real leader has a servant's heart. He appreciates others' worth and realizes he's not above any job. If you see something that needs to be done, don't wait to be asked. Take the initiative and do it like a faithful servant.

20:28 A ransom was the price paid to release a slave from bondage. Jesus often told his disciples that he must die, but here he told them why he had to die—to redeem all people from the bondage of sin and death. The disciples thought that as long as Jesus was alive, he could save them. But Jesus revealed that only his death would save them and the world.

20:29–34 Matthew records that there were two blind men, while Mark and Luke mention only one. This is probably the same event, but Mark and Luke singled out the more vocal of the two men.

20:30 The blind men called Jesus "King David's Son" because the Jews knew that the Messiah would be a descendant of King David (see Isaiah 9:6, 7; 11:1; Jeremiah 23:5, 6). This poor blind beggar could *see* that Jesus was the long-awaited Messiah, while the religious leaders who witnessed Jesus' miracles were blind to his identity, refusing to open their eyes to the truth. Seeing with your eyes doesn't guarantee seeing with your heart.

20:32, 33 Although Jesus was concerned about the coming events in Jerusalem, he demonstrated what he had just told the disciples about service (20:28) by stopping to care for the blind men.

21:2–4 Matthew mentions a donkey and a colt, while the other Gospels mention only the colt. This was the same event, but

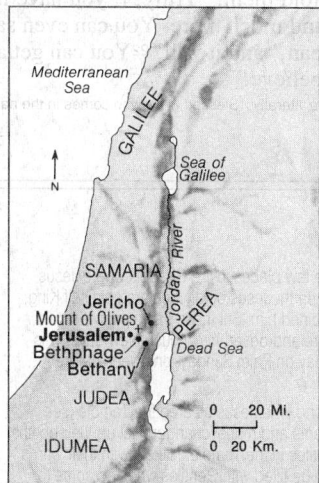

Mediterranean Sea

GALILEE

N

Sea of Galilee

SAMARIA

Jericho
Mount of Olives
Jerusalem
Bethphage
Bethany

Jordan River

PEREA

Dead Sea

JUDEA

0   20 Mi.

0   20 Km.

IDUMEA

PREPARATION FOR THE TRIUMPHAL ENTRY
On their way from Jericho, Jesus and the disciples neared the village of Bethphage, on the slope of the Mount of Olives just outside Jerusalem. Two disciples went into the village, as Jesus told them, to bring back a donkey and its colt. Jesus rode into Jerusalem on the donkey, an unmistakable sign of his kingship.

Matthew focuses on the prophecy in Zechariah 9:9, where a donkey and a colt are mentioned. He shows how Jesus' actions fulfilled the words of the prophet, thus proving that Jesus was indeed the Messiah. Jesus' entering Jerusalem on a donkey's colt affirmed his messianic royalty as well as his humility.

their garments over the colt for him to ride on. ⁸And some in the crowd threw down their coats along the road ahead of him, and others cut branches from the trees and spread them out before him.

⁹Then the crowds surged on ahead and pressed along behind, shouting, "God bless King David's Son!" . . . "God's Man is here!" . . . Bless him, Lord!" . . . "Praise God in highest heaven!"

21:9
Ps 118:26
Mt 22:42
Mk 12:35-37
Rom 1:3

¹⁰The entire city of Jerusalem was stirred as he entered. "Who is this?" they asked.

21:11
Mt 2:23
Lk 7:16
Jn 6:14; 7:40
9:17

¹¹And the crowds replied, "It's Jesus, the prophet from Nazareth up in Galilee."

Jesus clears the Temple again
(184/Mark 11:12–19; Luke 19:45–48)

¹²Jesus went into the Temple, drove out the merchants, and knocked over the moneychangers' tables and the stalls of those selling doves.

21:12
Deut 14:24-26
Mk 11:15-19
Lk 19:45-48
Jn 2:13-16

¹³"The Scriptures say my Temple is a place of prayer," he declared, "but you have turned it into a den of thieves."

21:13
Isa 56:7
Jer 7:11

¹⁴And now the blind and crippled came to him and he healed them there in the Temple. ¹⁵But when the chief priests and other Jewish leaders saw these wonderful miracles, and heard even the little children in the Temple shouting, "God bless the Son of David," they were disturbed and indignant and asked him, "Do you hear what these children are saying?"

21:14
Isa 35:5,6

21:15
Ps 8:2

¹⁶"Yes," Jesus replied. "Didn't you ever read the Scriptures? For they say, 'Even little babies shall praise him!' "

¹⁷Then he returned to Bethany, where he stayed overnight.

21:17
Mk 11:11
Jn 11:18

Jesus says the disciples can pray for anything
(188/Mark 11:20–25)

¹⁸In the morning, as he was returning to Jerusalem, he was hungry, ¹⁹and noticed a fig tree beside the road. He went over to see if there were any figs, but there were only leaves. Then he said to it, "Never bear fruit again!" And soon the fig tree withered up.

21:18
Mk 11:12-14

²⁰The disciples were utterly amazed and asked, "How did the fig tree wither so quickly?"

21:21
Mt 17:20
Lk 17:6
1 Cor 13:2
Jas 1:6

²¹Then Jesus told them, "Truly, if you have faith, and don't doubt, you can do things like this and much more. You can even say to this Mount of Olives, 'Move over into the ocean,' and it will. ²²You can get anything—*anything* you ask for in prayer—if you believe."

21:22
Mt 7:7
Mt 11:24
Lk 11:9
Jas 5:16
1 Jn 3:22; 5:14

21:9 *God's Man is here,* literally, "Blessed is he who comes in the name of the Lord."   **21:19** *soon,* or "immediately."

21:8 This is one of the few places in the Gospels where Jesus' glory is recognized on earth. Jesus boldly declared himself King, and the crowd gladly joined him. But these same people would bow to political pressure and desert him in just a few days. This event is celebrated today on Palm Sunday, one week before Easter.

21:12 This is the second time Jesus cleared the Temple (see John 2:13–25). Merchants and moneychangers set up their booths in the Court of the Gentiles in the Temple, filling it with their wares instead of allowing it to be filled with Gentiles who had come to worship God. The merchants sold sacrificial animals at high prices, taking advantage of those who had come long distances. The moneychangers exchanged all secular currency for Temple currency—the only kind of money the merchants would accept. They often deceived foreigners who didn't know the exchange rate. Not only were the merchants and moneychangers dishonest; they also took advantage of those who had come to worship God. Their commercialism in God's house frustrated people's attempts

at worship. This, of course, greatly angered Jesus. Any practice that interferes with worshiping God should be stopped.

21:19 Why did Jesus curse the fig tree? This was not a thoughtless, angry act, but an acted-out parable. Jesus was showing his anger at religion without substance. Just as the fig tree looked good from a distance but was fruitless at close examination, so the Temple looked impressive at first glance, but its sacrifices and other activities were hollow because they were not done to worship God sincerely. If you only appear to have faith without putting it to work in your life, you are like the fig tree that withered and died because it bore no fruit. Genuine faith means bearing fruit for God's Kingdom.

21:22 This is not a guarantee that we can get anything we want simply by asking Jesus. God does not grant requests that would hurt us or others, or that violate his own nature or will. Jesus' statement is not a blank check—our prayers must focus on the work of God's Kingdom. If we *truly* believe, our prayers will be in line with God's will, and God will be happy to grant them.

→ *Religious leaders challenge Jesus' authority*
(189/Mark 11:26–33; Luke 20:1–8)

21:23
Mk 11:26-33
Lk 20:1-8
Acts 4:7; 7:27

23When he had returned to the Temple and was teaching, the chief priests and other Jewish leaders came up to him and demanded to know by whose authority he had thrown out the merchants the day before.

21:24
Job 5:13

24"I'll tell you if you answer one question first," Jesus replied. 25"Was John the Baptist sent from God, or not?"

They talked it over among themselves. "If we say, 'From God,' " they said,

21:26
Mt 14:5
Mk 6:20

"then he will ask why we didn't believe what John said. 26And if we deny that God sent him, we'll be mobbed, for the crowd all think he was a prophet." 27So they finally replied, "We don't know!"

And Jesus said, "Then I won't answer your question either.

Jesus tells the parable of the two sons
(190)

28"But what do you think about this? A man with two sons told the older boy, 'Son, go out and work on the farm today.' 29'I won't,' he answered, but later he changed his mind and went. 30Then the father told the youngest, 'You go!' and he said, 'Yes, sir, I will.' But he didn't. 31Which of the two was obeying his father?"

They replied, "The first, of course."

Then Jesus explained his meaning: "Surely evil men and prostitutes will get into

21:32
Mt 3:2
Lk 3:3,12
7:29,30

the Kingdom before you do. 32For John the Baptist told you to repent and turn to God, and you wouldn't, while very evil men and prostitutes did. And even when you saw this happening, you refused to repent, and so you couldn't believe.

Jesus tells the parable of the wicked farmers
(191/Mark 12:1–12; Luke 20:9–19)

21:33
Mk 12:1-12
Lk 20:9-19

33"Now listen to this story: A certain landowner planted a vineyard with a hedge around it, and built a platform for the watchman, then leased the vineyard to some farmers on a sharecrop basis, and went away to live in another country.

21:35
2 Chron 36:15, 16
Mt 23:34
Acts 7:52

34"At the time of the grape harvest he sent his agents to the farmers to collect his share. 35But the farmers attacked his men, beat one, killed one and stoned another.

21:37
Gal 4:4

36"Then he sent a larger group of his men to collect for him, but the results were the same. 37Finally the owner sent his son, thinking they would surely respect him.

21:38
Jn 11:53

38"But when these farmers saw the son coming they said among themselves, 'Here comes the heir to this estate; come on, let's kill him and get it for ourselves!'

21:41
Lk 21:24

39So they dragged him out of the vineyard and killed him.

40"When the owner returns, what do you think he will do to those farmers?"

21:42
Ps 118:22,23
Isa 28:16
Acts 4:11
Eph 2:20
1 Pet 2:6,7

41The Jewish leaders replied, "He will put the wicked men to a horrible death, and lease the vineyard to others who will pay him promptly."

42Then Jesus asked them, "Didn't you ever read in the Scriptures: 'The stone

21:23 *by whose authority he had thrown out the merchants the day before,* literally, "By what authority do you do these things?"   **21:42** *the honored cornerstone,* literally, "the head of the corner."

→ **21:24, 25** The Pharisees demanded to know where Jesus got his authority. If Jesus said his authority came from God, they would accuse him of blasphemy. If he said he acted on his own authority, the crowds would be convinced that the Pharisees had the greater authority. But Jesus answered them with a seemingly unrelated question that exposed their real motives. They didn't really want an answer to their question; they only wanted to trap him. Jesus showed that the Pharisees used the truth only if it supported their own views and causes.

21:30 The son who said he would obey and then didn't represented the nation of Israel in Jesus' day. They said they wanted to do God's will, but they constantly disobeyed. It is dangerous to pretend to obey God when our hearts are far from him, because God knows the intentions of our hearts. Our actions must match our words.

21:33 The main characters in this parable are (1) the landowner—God, (2) the vineyard—Israel, (3) the farmers—the Jewish religious leaders, (4) the landowner's men—the prophets and priests who remained faithful to God and preached to Israel, (5) the son—Jesus (21:38), and (6) the others—Gentiles. Jesus was exposing the religious leaders' murderous plot (21:45).

21:37 In trying to reach us with his love, God finally sent his own Son. His perfect life, his words of truth, and his sacrifice of love are meant to cause us to listen and to follow Christ as Lord. When we ignore this gracious act on God's part, we are rejecting God.

21:42 Jesus refers to himself as the stone rejected by the builders. Though rejected by many of his people, he would become the Cornerstone of his new building, the church (see Acts 4:11).

rejected by the builders has been made the honored cornerstone; how remarkable! what an amazing thing the Lord has done'?

43"What I mean is that the Kingdom of God shall be taken away from you, and given to a nation that will give God his share of the crop. 44All who stumble on this rock of truth shall be broken, but those it falls on will be scattered as dust."

21:44
Isa 8:14,15
Dan 2:44,45

45When the chief priests and other Jewish leaders realized that Jesus was talking about them—that they were the farmers in his story— 46they wanted to get rid of him, but were afraid to try because of the crowds, for they accepted Jesus as a prophet.

21:46
Jn 7:40-44

Jesus tells the parable of the wedding feast
(192)

22 Jesus told several other stories to show what the Kingdom of Heaven is like. "For instance," he said, "it can be illustrated by the story of a king who prepared a great wedding dinner for his son. 3Many guests were invited, and when the banquet was ready he sent messengers to notify everyone that it was time to come. But all refused! 4So he sent other servants to tell them, 'Everything is ready and the roast is in the oven. Hurry!'

22:1
Lk 14:15-24

5"But the guests he had invited merely laughed and went on about their business, one to his farm, another to his store; 6others beat up his messengers and treated them shamefully, even killing some of them.

7"Then the angry king sent out his army and destroyed the murderers and burned their city. 8And he said to his servants, 'The wedding feast is ready, and the guests I invited aren't worthy of the honor. 9Now go out to the street corners and invite everyone you see.'

22:7
Dan 9:26
22:8
Acts 13:46

10"So the servants did, and brought in all they could find, good and bad alike; and the banquet hall was filled with guests. 11But when the king came in to meet the guests he noticed a man who wasn't wearing the wedding robe [provided for him].

22:12
Rom 3:19

12" 'Friend,' he asked, 'how does it happen that you are here without a wedding robe?' And the man had no reply.

22:13
Mt 8:12; 25:30

13"Then the king said to his aides, 'Bind him hand and foot and throw him out into the outer darkness where there is weeping and gnashing of teeth.' 14For many are called, but few are chosen."

22:14
Mt 24:22
2 Pet 1:10
Rev 17:14

Religious leaders question Jesus about paying taxes
(193/Mark 12:13–17; Luke 20:20–26)

15Then the Pharisees met together to try to think of some way to trap Jesus into

21:43 *that will give God his share of the crop,* literally, "bringing forth the fruits." **21:44** *on this rock of truth,* literally, "on this stone." **22:11** *provided for him,* implied.

21:44 Jesus is quoting from several Old Testament texts: Isaiah 8:14, 15; Isaiah 28:16; Daniel 2:34, 44, 45. He uses this metaphor to show that one stone can affect people different ways, depending on how they relate to it. Ideally many will build on it; many, however, will trip over it. And at the Last Judgment it will crush God's enemies. Christ, the "building block," will in the end become the "crushing stone." He is offering mercy and forgiveness *now* and promising judgment later. We should not wait to make our choice.

22:1-14 In this culture, two invitations were expected when banquets were given. The first asked the guests to attend; the second announced that all was ready. Here the king, God, invited his guests three times—and each time they rejected his invitations. God wants us to join him at his banquet, which will last for eternity. That's why he sends us invitations again and again. Have you accepted his invitation?

22:11, 12 It was customary for wedding guests to be given a garment to wear to the banquet. It was unthinkable to refuse to wear the garment. This would insult the host, who could only

assume the guest did not want to take part in the wedding celebration. Jesus is speaking here of the garment of righteousness needed to enter God's banquet in the Kingdom. This robe is a picture of the total acceptance in God's eyes given to every believer by Christ. Christ has provided this garment for everyone, but each person must choose to put it on in order to enter the king's banquet (eternal life). For more on the imagery of garments of righteousness and salvation, see Psalm 132:16; Isaiah 61:10; Zechariah 3:3–5; Revelation 3:4, 5; 19:7, 8.

22:15-17 The Pharisees were a religious group who opposed the Roman occupation of Palestine. The Herodians were a Jewish political party who supported Herod Antipas and the policies instituted by Rome. Normally, these two groups were bitter enemies, but here they united against Jesus. Together, men from these two groups asked Jesus a question about paying Roman taxes, thinking they had a foolproof plan to corner him. If Jesus agreed that it was right to pay taxes to Caesar, the Pharisees would say he was opposed to God, the only King they recognized. If Jesus said the taxes should not be paid, the Herodians would hand him over to Herod for rebellion. The Pharisees were not motivated by love for God's laws, and the Herodians were not

saying something for which they could arrest him. 16They decided to send some of their men along with the Herodians to ask him this question: "Sir, we know you are very honest and teach the truth regardless of the consequences, without fear or favor. 17Now tell us, is it right to pay taxes to the Roman government or not?"

18But Jesus saw what they were after. "You hypocrites!" he exclaimed. "Who are you trying to fool with your trick questions? 19Here, show me a coin." And they handed him a penny.

20"Whose picture is stamped on it?" he asked them. "And whose name is this beneath the picture?"

21"Caesar's," they replied.

"Well, then," he said, "give it to Caesar if it is his, and give God everything that belongs to God."

22His reply surprised and baffled them and they went away.

Religious leaders question Jesus about the resurrection
(194/Mark 12:18–27; Luke 20:27–40)

23But that same day some of the Sadducees, who say there is no resurrection after death, came to him and asked, 24"Sir, Moses said that if a man died without children, his brother should marry the widow and their children would get all the dead man's property. 25Well, we had among us a family of seven brothers. The first of these men married and then died, without children, so his widow became the second brother's wife. 26This brother also died without children, and the wife was passed to the next brother, and so on until she had been the wife of each of them. 27And then she also died. 28So whose wife will she be in the resurrection? For she was the wife of all seven of them!"

29But Jesus said, "Your error is caused by your ignorance of the Scriptures and of God's power! 30For in the resurrection there is no marriage; everyone is as the angels in heaven. 31But now, as to whether there is a resurrection of the dead—don't you ever read the Scriptures? Don't you realize that God was speaking directly to you when he said, 32'I *am* the God of Abraham, Isaac, and Jacob'? So God is not the God of the dead, but of the *living*."

22:16 The Herodians were a Jewish political party.   **22:32** *of the living*, i.e., if Abraham, Isaac, and Jacob, long dead, were not alive in the presence of God, then God would have said, "I *was* the God of Abraham, etc."

Cross-references column:

22:17
Mt 17:24

22:21
Rom 13:7

22:22
Job 5:12,13

22:23
Mk 12:18-27
Lk 10:27-40
Acts 23:8
1 Cor 15:12

22:24
Gen 38:8
Deut 25:5

22:29
Jn 20:9

22:32
Ex 3:6,15
Acts 7:32

---

motivated by love for Roman justice. Jesus' answer exposed their evil motives and embarrassed them.

22:17 The Jews were required to pay taxes to support the Roman government. The Jews hated this taxation because the money went directly into Caesar's treasury, where some of it went to support the pagan temples and decadent lifestyle of the Roman aristocracy. Caesar's image on the coins was a constant reminder of Israel's subjection to Rome.

22:21 Jesus avoided this trap by showing that we have a dual citizenship (1 Peter 2:17). Our citizenship in the state requires that we pay money for the services and benefits we receive. Our citizenship in the Kingdom of Heaven requires that we pledge to God the obedience and commitment of our souls.

22:23ff After the Pharisees and Herodians failed to trap Jesus, the Sadducees smugly stepped in to try. They did not believe in the resurrection because the Pentateuch (Genesis—Deuteronomy) has no direct teaching on it. The Pharisees had never been able to come up with a convincing argument from the Pentateuch for the resurrection, and the Sadducees thought they had trapped Jesus for sure. But he was about to show them otherwise (see 22:31, 32 for Jesus' answer).

22:24 For information on Moses, see his Profile in Exodus 16.

22:24 The law said that when a woman's husband died without having a son, the man's unmarried brother had a responsibility to marry and care for the widow (Deuteronomy 25:5, 6). This protected women who were left alone, because in that culture they usually had no other means to live.

22:29 The Sadducees asked Jesus what marriage would be like in eternity. Jesus said it was more important to understand God's power than know what it will be like. In every generation and culture, views about heaven or eternal life tend to be based upon images and experiences of present life. Jesus said these faulty views are caused by ignorance of God's Word. We must not make up our own ideas about eternity by trying to put it and God into human terms. We should concentrate more on our relationship with God than about what heaven will look like. Eventually we will find out, and it will be far beyond our greatest expectations.

22:31, 32 Since the Sadducees accepted only the Pentateuch as Scripture, Jesus answered them from the book of Exodus (3:6). God would not have said, "I *am* the God of your fathers" if God thought of Abraham, Isaac, and Jacob as being dead. From God's perspective, they were alive. Jesus' use of the present tense pointed to the resurrection and the eternal life that all believers enjoy in him.

Religious leaders question Jesus about the greatest commandment
(195/Mark 12:28–34)

33The crowds were profoundly impressed by his answers— 34, 35but not the Pharisees! When they heard that he had routed the Sadducees with his reply, they thought up a fresh question of their own to ask him. One of them, a lawyer, spoke up: 36"Sir, which is the most important command in the laws of Moses?"

37Jesus replied, " 'Love the Lord your God with all your heart, soul, and mind.' 38, 39This is the first and greatest commandment. The second most important is similar: 'Love your neighbor as much as you love yourself.' 40All the other commandments and all the demands of the prophets stem from these two laws and are fulfilled if you obey them. Keep only these and you will find that you are obeying all the others."

22:33
Mt 7:28
22:34
Mk 12:28-31
22:35
Lk 10:25
22:37
Deut 6:5
10:12,13; 30:6
22:38
Lev 19:18
Mt 7:12
Rom 13:9

Religious leaders cannot answer Jesus' question
(196/Mark 12:35–37; Luke 20:41–44)

41Then, surrounded by the Pharisees, he asked them a question: 42"What about the Messiah? Whose son is he?" "The son of David," they replied.

43"Then why does David, speaking under the inspiration of the Holy Spirit, call him 'Lord'?" Jesus asked. "For David said,

44'God said to my Lord, Sit at my right hand until I put your enemies beneath your feet.'

45Since David called him 'Lord,' how can he be merely his son?"

46They had no answer. And after that no one dared ask him any more questions.

22:41
Mk 12:35-37
Lk 20:41-44
22:43
2 Sam 23:2
Acts 2:30
2 Pet 1:20,21
22:44
Ps 110:1
Mt 26:64
Acts 2:34
Heb 1:13; 10:12
22:46
Lk 14:6; 20:40

Jesus warns against the religious leaders
(197/Mark 12:38–40; Luke 20:45–47)

23 Then Jesus said to the crowds, and to his disciples, 2"You would think these Jewish leaders and these Pharisees were Moses, the way they keep making up so many laws! 3And of course you should obey their every whim! It may be all right to do what they say, but above anything else, *don't follow their example*. For they don't do what they tell you to do. 4They load you with impossible demands that they themselves don't even try to keep.

5"Everything they do is done for show. They act holy by wearing on their arms

23:2
Ezra 7:6,25
Neh 8:1-4
Lk 11:46
Acts 15:10
Rom 2:17-23
Gal 6:13
23:5
Num 15:37-40
Mt 6:1,2

23:2 *the way they keep making up so many laws,* literally, "sit on Moses' seat." **23:5** *act holy,* implied. *Scripture verses inside,* literally, "enlarge their phylacteries."

22:33-35 We might think the Pharisees would have been glad to see the Sadducees silenced. The question with which the Sadducees had always trapped them was finally answered by Jesus. But the Pharisees were too proud to be impressed. Jesus' answer gave them a theological victory over the Sadducees, but they were more interested in trapping and stopping Jesus than in learning truth.

22:36-40 The Pharisees, who had classified over 600 laws, often tried to distinguish the more important from the less important. So they asked Jesus to identify the most important law. Jesus quoted from Deuteronomy 6:5 and Leviticus 19:18. By fulfilling these two commands, a person keeps all the others. They summarize the Ten Commandments and the other Old Testament moral laws.

22:37-40 Jesus says that if we truly love God and our neighbor, we will naturally keep the commandments. This is looking at God's law positively. Rather than worrying about all we should *not* do, we should concentrate on all we *can* do to show our love for God and others.

22:41-45 The Pharisees, Herodians, and Sadducees had asked their questions. Now Jesus turned the tables and asked them a penetrating question—what they thought about the Messiah's identity. The Pharisees knew the Messiah would be a descendant of David, but they did not understand he would be God himself. Jesus quoted from Psalm 110:1 to show that the Messiah would be

greater than David. (Hebrews 1:13 uses the same text as proof of Christ's deity.) The most important question we will ever answer is what we believe about Christ. Other spiritual questions are irrelevant until we believe that Jesus is who he said he is.

23:2, 3 The Pharisees' traditions and their interpretations and applications of the law had become as important to them as the law itself. Their laws were not all bad—some were beneficial. The problem came when the religious leaders (1) took man-made rules as seriously as God's laws, (2) told the people to obey these rules but did not do so themselves, (3) obeyed the rules not to honor God but to make themselves look good. Usually Jesus did not condemn what they taught, but what they *were*—hypocrites.

23:5 These little prayer boxes, called *phylacteries,* contained Bible verses. The Pharisees wore them because Exodus 13:9, 16 commands people to keep God's Word close to their hearts, and they took this literally. But these little prayer boxes had become more important for the status they gave than for the truth they contained.

23:5-7 Jesus again exposed the hypocritical attitudes of the religious leaders. They knew the Scriptures but did not live by them. They didn't care about *being* holy—just *looking* holy in order to receive the people's admiration and praise. Today, like the Pharisees, many people who know the Bible do not let it change their lives. They say they follow Jesus but don't live by his

little prayer boxes with Scripture verses inside, and by lengthening the memorial fringes of their robes. 6And how they love to sit at the head table at banquets, and in the reserved pews in the synagogue! 7How they enjoy the deference paid them on the streets, and to be called 'Rabbi' and 'Master'! 8Don't ever let anyone call you that. For only God is your Rabbi and all of you are on the same level, as brothers. 9And don't address anyone here on earth as 'Father,' for only God in heaven should be addressed like that. 10And don't be called 'Master,' for only one is your master, even the Messiah.

11"The more lowly your service to others, the greater you are. To be the greatest, be a servant. 12But those who think themselves great shall be disappointed and humbled; and those who humble themselves shall be exalted.

Jesus condemns the religious leaders
(198)

13, 14"Woe to you, Pharisees, and you other religious leaders. Hypocrites! For you won't let others enter the Kingdom of Heaven, and won't go in yourselves. And you pretend to be holy, with all your long, public prayers in the streets, while you are evicting widows from their homes. Hypocrites! 15Yes, woe upon you hypocrites. For you go to all lengths to make one convert, and then turn him into twice the son of hell you are yourselves. 16Blind guides! Woe upon you! For your rule is that to swear 'By God's Temple' means nothing—you can break that oath, but to swear 'By the gold in the Temple' is binding! 17Blind fools! Which is greater, the gold, or the Temple that sanctifies the gold? 18And you say that to take an oath 'By the altar' can be broken, but to swear 'By the gifts on the altar' is binding! 19Blind! For which is greater, the gift on the altar, or the altar itself that sanctifies the gift? 20When you swear 'By the altar' you are swearing by it and everything on it, 21and when you swear 'By the Temple' you are swearing by it, and by God who

23:9
Mal 1:6

23:11
Mt 20:26
Mk 9:35
10:43-45
Lk 9:48

23:12
Job 22:29
Prov 15:33
29:23
Dan 4:37
Lk 14:11; 18:14
Jas 4:6
1 Pet 5:5,6

23:13
Lk 11:39-52

23:16
Isa 56:10
Mt 5:33-35
15:14

23:19
Ex 29:37; 30:29

23:21
1 Kgs 8:12,13
2 Chron 6:1
Ps 26:8; 132:14

THE SEVEN WOES		
	23:14	Not letting others enter the Kingdom of Heaven and not entering yourselves
	23:15	Converting people away from God to be like yourselves
	23:16–22	Blindly leading God's people to follow man-made traditions instead of God's Word
	23:23, 24	Involving yourself in insignificant details and ignoring what is really important: justice, mercy, and faith
	23:25, 26	Keeping up appearances while your private world is corrupt
	23:27, 28	Acting spiritual to cover sin
	23:29–36	Pretending to have learned from past history, but your present behavior shows you have learned nothing

Jesus mentioned seven ways to guarantee God's anger, often called the "seven woes." These seven statements about the religious leaders must have been spoken with a mixed tone of judgment and sorrow. They were strong and unforgettable. They are still applicable any time we become so involved in perfecting the practice of religion that we forget that God is also concerned with mercy, real love, and forgiveness.

---

standards of love. People who live this way are hypocrites. We must make sure our actions match our beliefs.

23:5–7 People desire positions of leadership not only in business but also in the church. This becomes dangerous if love for the position grows stronger than loyalty to God. This is what happened to the Pharisees. Jesus is not against all leadership—we need Christian leaders—but against leadership that serves itself rather than others.

23:11, 12 Jesus challenged society's norms. To him, greatness comes from serving—giving of yourself to help God and others. Service keeps us aware of others' needs, and it stops us from focusing only on ourselves. Jesus came as a servant. What kind of greatness do you seek?

23:13, 14 Being a religious leader in Jerusalem was very different from being a pastor in a secular society today. The nation's history,

culture, and daily life centered around its relationship with God. The religious leaders were the most well-known, powerful, and respected of all leaders. Jesus gave his stinging accusations because their hunger for more power, money, and status had made them lose sight of God, and their blindness was spreading to the whole nation.

23:15 The Pharisees' converts were attracted to pharisaism, not to God. By getting caught up in the details of their additional laws and regulations, they missed God to whom the laws pointed. A religion of works puts pressure on people to surpass others in what they know and do. Thus, a hypocritical teacher was likely to have students who were even more hypocritical. We must make sure we are not creating Pharisees by emphasizing outward obedience at the expense of inner renewal.

lives in it. 22And when you swear 'By heavens' you are swearing by the Throne of
God and by God himself.
23"Yes, woe upon you, Pharisees, and you other religious leaders—hypocrites!
For you tithe down to the last mint leaf in your garden, but ignore the important
things—justice and mercy and faith. Yes, you should tithe, but you shouldn't leave
the more important things undone. 24Blind guides! You strain out a gnat and
swallow a camel.
25"Woe to you, Pharisees, and you religious leaders—hypocrites! You are so
careful to polish the outside of the cup, but the inside is foul with extortion and
greed. 26Blind Pharisees! First cleanse the inside of the cup, and then the whole cup
will be clean.
27"Woe to you, Pharisees, and you religious leaders! You are like beautiful
mausoleums—full of dead men's bones, and of foulness and corruption. 28You try
to look like saintly men, but underneath those pious robes of yours are hearts
besmirched with every sort of hypocrisy and sin.
29, 30"Yes, woe to you, Pharisees, and you religious leaders—hypocrites! For
you build monuments to the prophets killed by your fathers and lay flowers on the
graves of the godly men they destroyed, and say, 'We certainly would never have
acted as our fathers did.'
31"In saying that, you are accusing yourselves of being the sons of wicked men.
32And you are following in their steps, filling up the full measure of their evil.
33Snakes! Sons of vipers! How shall you escape the judgment of hell?
34"I will send you prophets, and wise men, and inspired writers, and you will kill
some by crucifixion, and rip open the backs of others with whips in your synagogues, and hound them from city to city, 35so that you will become guilty of all the
blood of murdered godly men from righteous Abel to Zechariah (son of Barachiah),
slain by you in the Temple between the altar and the sanctuary. 36Yes, all the
accumulated judgment of the centuries shall break upon the heads of this very
generation.

23:22 Ps 11:4; Acts 7:48,49
23:23 1 Sam 15:22; Hos 6:6; Mic 6:8; Mt 9:13; 12:7
23:25 Mk 7:4; Tit 1:15
23:27 Lk 11:44; Acts 23:3
23:31 Acts 7:51
23:32 Gen 15:16; 1 Thess 2:16
23:33 Mt 3:7; 12:34; Lk 3:7
23:34 Acts 5:40; 7:58; 22:19; 2 Cor 11:23-25
23:35 Gen 4:8; 1 Jn 3:12; Rev 18:24

Jesus grieves over Jerusalem again
(199)

37"O Jerusalem, Jerusalem, the city that kills the prophets, and stones all those
God sends to her! How often I have wanted to gather your children together as a hen
gathers her chicks beneath her wings, but you wouldn't let me. 38And now your

23:37 Deut 32:11
23:38 Ezek 10:4,18,19

23:23, 24 It's possible to obey the details of the law but still be disobedient in our general behavior. For example, we could be very precise and faithful about giving 10 percent of our money to God, but refuse to give one minute of our time in helping others. Tithing is important, but paying tithe does not exempt us from fulfilling God's other directives.

23:24 The Pharisees strained their water so they wouldn't accidentally swallow a gnat—an unclean insect according to the law. They were so meticulous about the details of ceremonial cleanliness that they lost their perspective on true purity. Ceremonially clean on the outside, they had corrupt hearts.

23:25–28 Jesus condemned the Pharisees and religious leaders for appearing saintly and holy outwardly but inwardly remaining full of corruption and greed. Living our Christianity merely as a show for others is like washing a cup on the outside only. When we are clean on the inside, our cleanliness on the outside won't be a sham.

23:34–36 These prophets, wise men, and writers who would be sent could refer to the disciples, Stephen, Paul, and other leaders in the early church who were hounded, flogged, and sometimes crucified, as Jesus predicted. The people of Jesus' generation said they would not act as their fathers did in killing the prophets whom God sent to them (23:30), but they were about to kill the Messiah himself and his faithful followers. Thus all the judgment from across the centuries would fall on their heads.

23:35 Jesus was giving a brief summary of Old Testament martyrdom. Abel was the first martyr (Genesis 4); Zechariah was the last (because the Hebrew Bible ended with 2 Chronicles). Zechariah was a classic example of a man of God being killed by those who claimed to be God's people (see 2 Chronicles 24:21).

23:37 Jesus wanted to gather his people together as a hen protects her chicks under her wings, but they wouldn't let him. Jesus also wants to protect us if we will come to him. Many times we hurt and don't know where to turn. We reject Christ's help because we don't think he can give us what we need. But who knows our needs better than our Creator? Those who turn to Jesus will find that he helps and comforts as no one else can.

23:37 Jerusalem was the capital city of God's chosen people; the ancestral home of David, Israel's greatest king; and the location of the Temple, the earthly dwelling place of God. It was intended to be the center of worship of the true God and a model of justice to all people, but Jerusalem had become blind to God and insensitive to human need. Here we see the depth of Jesus' feelings for lost people and for his beloved city, which would soon be destroyed.

23:39
Ps 118:26
Mt 21:9

house is left to you, desolate. 39For I tell you this, you will never see me again until you are ready to welcome the one sent to you from God."

7. Jesus teaches on the Mount of Olives

Jesus tells about the future
(201/Mark 13:1–20; Luke 21:5–24)

24:2
Jer 7:14; 26:18
Mic 3:12
Lk 19:44

24 As Jesus was leaving the Temple grounds, his disciples came along and wanted to take him on a tour of the various Temple buildings.

2But he told them, "All these buildings will be knocked down, with not one stone left on top of another!"

24:3
1 Thess 5:1

3"When will this happen?" the disciples asked him later, as he sat on the slopes of the Mount of Olives. "What events will signal your return, and the end of the world?"

24:4
1 Jn 4:1

24:5
Jer 14:14; 23:21
Jn 5:43

4Jesus told them, "Don't let anyone fool you. 5For many will come claiming to be the Messiah, and will lead many astray. 6When you hear of wars beginning, this does not signal my return; these must come, but the end is not yet. 7The nations and kingdoms of the earth will rise against each other and there will be famines and earthquakes in many places. 8But all this will be only the beginning of the horrors to come.

24:9
Acts 7:59; 12:1

24:10
2 Tim 4:10,16

24:11
Acts 20:29
1 Tim 4:1
2 Pet 2:1

9"Then you will be tortured and killed and hated all over the world because you are mine, 10and many of you shall fall back into sin and betray and hate each other. 11And many false prophets will appear and lead many astray. 12Sin will be rampant everywhere and will cool the love of many. 13But those enduring to the end shall be saved.

24:12
2 Tim 3:1-5

24:13
Mt 10:22
Rev 2:7

24:14
Mk 13:14-23
Lk 21:20-24

14"And the Good News about the Kingdom will be preached throughout the whole world, so that all nations will hear it, and then, finally, the end will come.

23:39 *from God,* literally, "in the name of the Lord." **24:3** *world,* literally, "age."

24:1 Although no one knows exactly how this Temple looked, it must have been beautiful. Herod had helped the Jews remodel and beautify it, no doubt to stay on friendly terms with his subjects. Next to the inner Temple, where the sacred objects were kept and the sacrifices offered, there was a large area called the Court of the Gentiles (this was where the moneychangers and merchants had their booths). Outside these courts were long porches. Solomon's Porch was 1,562 feet long; the Royal Portico was decorated with 160 columns stretching along its 921-foot length. While gazing at this glorious and massive structure, the disciples found Jesus' words about its destruction difficult to believe. But the Temple was indeed destroyed only 40 years later when the Romans sacked Jerusalem in A.D. 70.

24:3ff Jesus was sitting on the Mount of Olives, the very place where the prophet Zechariah predicted the Messiah would stand when he came to establish his Kingdom (Zechariah 14:4). It was a fitting place for the disciples to ask Jesus when he would come into power and what they could expect then. Jesus' reply emphasized the events that would take place before the end of the age. He pointed out that they should be less concerned with knowing the exact date and more concerned with being prepared—living God's way consistently so that no matter when Jesus came, he would claim them as his own.

24:9–13 You may not be facing intense persecution now, but Christians in other parts of the world are. As you hear about Christians suffering for their faith, remember that they are your brothers and sisters in Christ. Pray for them. Ask God what you can do to help them in their troubles. When one part suffers, the *whole* body suffers. But when all the parts join together to ease the suffering, the whole body benefits.

24:11 The Old Testament frequently mentions false prophets (see 2 Kings 3:13; Isaiah 44:25; Jeremiah 23:16; Ezekiel 13:2, 3; Micah 3:5; Zechariah 13:2). They were people who claimed to receive messages from God, but who preached a "health and wealth" message. They told the people only what they wanted to hear, even when the nation was not following God as it should. There were false prophets in Jesus' day, and we have them today. They are the popular leaders who spout a false gospel, telling people what they want to hear—such as "God wants you to be rich," "Do whatever your desires tell you," or "There is no such thing as sin or hell." Jesus said false teachers would come, and he warned his disciples, as he warns us, not to listen to their dangerous words.

24:12 With false teaching and loose morals comes a particularly destructive disease—the loss of true love for God and others. Sin cools your love for God and others by turning your focus on yourself. You cannot truly love if you think only of yourself.

24:13 Jesus predicted that his followers could expect to be severely persecuted by those who hated him, but that in the midst of terrible persecutions, they could have hope, knowing that salvation was theirs. Times of trial serve to sift true Christians from false or fair-weather Christians. When you are pressured to give up and turn your back on Christ, don't give in. Remember the benefits of endurance, and continue to live for Christ.

24:14 Jesus said that before he returns, the Good News about the Kingdom (the message of salvation) would be preached throughout the world. This was the disciples' mission—and is ours today. Jesus talked about the end times and final judgment to show his followers the urgency of spreading the Good News of salvation to everyone.

15"So, when you see the horrible thing (told about by Daniel the prophet) standing in a holy place (Note to the reader: You know what is meant!), 16then those in Judea must flee into the Judean hills. 17Those on their porches must not even go inside to pack before they flee. 18Those in the fields should not return to their homes for their clothes.

24:15
Dan 9:27; 11:31
12:11

19"And woe to pregnant women and to those with babies in those days. 20And pray that your flight will not be in winter, or on the Sabbath. 21For there will be persecution such as the world has never before seen in all its history, and will never see again.

24:21
Dan 12:1
Joel 2:2
Rev 3:10; 7:14

22"In fact, unless those days are shortened, all mankind will perish. But they will be shortened for the sake of God's chosen people.

24:22
Isa 65:8,9

Jesus tells about his return
(202/Mark 13:21–31; Luke 21:25–33)

23"Then if anyone tells you, 'The Messiah has arrived at such and such a place, or has appeared here or there,' don't believe it. 24For false Christs shall arise, and false prophets, and will do wonderful miracles, so that if it were possible, even God's chosen ones would be deceived. 25See, I have warned you.

24:24
2 Thess 2:9
1 Jn 4:1-3
Rev 13:13,14

26"So if someone tells you the Messiah has returned and is out in the desert, don't bother to go and look. Or, that he is hiding at a certain place, don't believe it! 27For as the lightning flashes across the sky from east to west, so shall my coming be, when I, the Messiah, return. 28And wherever the carcass is, there the vultures will gather.

24:28
Job 39:30
Lk 17:37
Rev 19:17,18

29"Immediately after the persecution of those days the sun will be darkened, and the moon will not give light, and the stars will seem to fall from the heavens, and the powers overshadowing the earth will be convulsed.

24:29
Isa 13:10
Ezek 32:7,8
Joel 2:31; 3:15
Mk 13:24-37
Lk 21:25-36
Acts 2:20
Rev 6:12

30"And then at last the signal of my coming will appear in the heavens and there will be deep mourning all around the earth. And the nations of the world will see me arrive in the clouds of heaven, with power and great glory. 31And I shall send forth my angels with the sound of a mighty trumpet blast, and they shall gather my chosen ones from the farthest ends of the earth and heaven.

24:30
Dan 7:13
Zech 12:10-14
Rev 1:7

24:31
1 Cor 15:52
1 Thess 4:16
Rev 11:15

32"Now learn a lesson from the fig tree. When her branch is tender and the leaves begin to sprout, you know that summer is almost here. 33Just so, when you see all these things beginning to happen, you can know that my return is near, even at the doors. 34Then at last this age will come to its close.

24:33
Mt 16:28
Jas 5:9

24:15 *the horrible thing,* literally, "the abomination of desolation." *Daniel,* see Dan 9:27, 11:31, 12:11. *Note to the reader: You know what is meant,* literally, "Let the reader take note." **24:17** *porches,* literally, "roof tops," which, being flat, were used as porches at that time. See Acts 10:9. **24:20** *on the Sabbath.* The city gates were closed on the Sabbath. **24:22** *chosen people,* literally, "the elect." **24:24** *chosen ones,* literally, "the elect." **24:27** *the Messiah,* literally, "the Son of Man." **24:29** *the stars will seem to fall,* literally, "the stars shall fall from heaven." *the earth will be convulsed,* literally, "the powers of the heavens shall be shaken." See Eph 6:12. **24:30** *of my coming,* literally, "of the coming of the Son of Man." **24:31** *from the farthest ends of the earth and heaven,* literally, "from the four winds, from one end of heaven to the other." **24:33** *my return is near,* literally, "He is nigh." **24:34** *this age will come to its close* is literally, "this generation shall pass away."

24:15, 16 What was this "horrible thing" (or "the abomination of desolation," see textual note) mentioned by both Daniel and Jesus? Rather than one specific object, event, or person, it could be seen as any deliberate attempt to mock and destroy God's presence. Daniel's prediction came true in 168 B.C. when Antiochus Epiphanes sacrificed a pig to Zeus on the sacred Temple altar (Daniel 9:27; 11:30, 31). Jesus' words were remembered in A.D. 70, when Titus placed an idol on the site of the burned Temple after destroying Jerusalem. In the end times the Antichrist will set up a statue to himself and order everyone to worship it (2 Thessalonians 2:4; Revelation 13:14, 15). These are all "horrible things" which seek to desecrate that which is holy.

24:21, 22 Jesus, talking about the end times, telescoped near future and far future events, as did the Old Testament prophets. Many of these persecutions have already occurred; more are yet to come. But God is in control of even the length of persecutions. He will not forget his people. This is all we need to know about the future to motivate us to live rightly now.

24:23, 24 Jesus' warnings about false teachers still hold true. Upon close examination it becomes clear that many nice-sounding messages don't agree with God's message in the Bible. Only a solid foundation in God's Word can equip us to perceive the errors and distortions in false teaching.

24:24–28 In the midst of persecution even strong believers will find it difficult to be loyal. To keep from being deceived by false messiahs, we must understand that Jesus' return will be unmistakable (Mark 13:26). When he returns, there will be no doubt that it is he. If you have to be told that the Messiah has come, then he hasn't (24:27). Christ's coming will be obvious to everyone.

24:30 There will be "deep mourning" because unbelievers will suddenly realize they have chosen the wrong side. Everything they have scoffed about will be happening, and it will be too late for them.

35"Heaven and earth will disappear, but my words remain forever.

Jesus tells about remaining watchful
(203/Mark 13:32–37; Luke 21:34–38)

24:36
Acts 1:7
1 Thess 5:2
2 Pet 3:10

36But no one knows the date and hour when the end will be—not even the angels. No, nor even God's Son. Only the Father knows.

24:37
Gen 6:3; 7:1
Lk 17:26
1 Pet 3:20

37, 38"The world will be at ease—banquets and parties and weddings—just as it was in Noah's time before the sudden coming of the flood; 39people wouldn't believe what was going to happen until the flood actually arrived and took them all away. So shall my coming be.

24:40
Lk 17:34-36

40"Two men will be working together in the fields, and one will be taken, the other left. 41Two women will be going about their household tasks; one will be taken, the other left.

24:42
Lk 12:29; 21:36
1 Thess 5:6
Rev 3:3,16:15

42"So be prepared, for you don't know what day your Lord is coming.

43"Just as a man can prevent trouble from thieves by keeping watch for them, 44so you can avoid trouble by always being ready for my unannounced return.

24:45
Lk 12:40-47
1 Cor 4:2
Heb 3:5

45"Are you a wise and faithful servant of the Lord? Have I given you the task of managing my household, to feed my children day by day? 46Blessings on you if I return and find you faithfully doing your work. 47I will put such faithful ones in charge of everything I own!

48"But if you are evil and say to yourself, 'My Lord won't be coming for a while,' 49and begin oppressing your fellow servants, partying and getting drunk,

24:51
Mt 25:30

50your Lord will arrive unannounced and unexpected, 51and severely whip you and send you off to the judgment of the hypocrites; there will be weeping and gnashing of teeth.

Jesus tells the parable of the ten bridesmaids
(204)

25:1
Isa 61:10
Mt 9:15
Jn 3:29
Rev 19:7
21:2,9

25 "The Kingdom of Heaven can be illustrated by the story of ten bridesmaids who took their lamps and went to meet the bridegroom. 2, 3, 4But only five of them were wise enough to fill their lamps with oil, while the other five were foolish and forgot.

24:36 No, nor even God's Son, literally, "neither the Son." Many ancient manuscripts omit this phrase. **24:37** The world will be at ease, implied. **24:39** wouldn't believe, literally, "knew not." **25:1** bridesmaids, literally, "virgins."

24:36 It is good that we don't know exactly when Christ will return. If we knew the precise date, we might be tempted to be lazy in our work for Christ, or worse yet, to keep sinning and then turn to God right at the end. Heaven is not our only goal; we have work to do here. And we must keep on doing it until death or until we see the unmistakable return of our Savior.

24:40–42 Christ's Second Coming will be swift and sudden. There will be no opportunity for afterthought, last-minute repentance, or bargaining. The choice we have already made will determine our eternal destiny.

24:44 Jesus' purpose in telling about his return is not to stimulate predictions and calculations about the date, but to warn us to be prepared. Will you be found "faithfully doing his work"? The only safety is to obey him today (24:46).

24:45–47 Jesus asks us to spend the waiting time in taking care of his people and his work here on earth, both within the church and outside it. This is the best way to prepare for Christ's return.

24:50 Knowing that Christ's return will be sudden should motivate us always to be prepared. We are not to live irresponsibly—(1) sitting and waiting, doing nothing; (2) seeking self-serving pleasure; (3) using his tarrying as an excuse not to do God's work of building his Kingdom; (4) developing a false security based on precise calculations of events; or (5) letting our curiosity about the end times divert us from doing God's work.

24:51 "Weeping and gnashing of teeth" is a phrase used to describe despair. God's coming judgment is as certain as Jesus' return to earth.

25:1ff Jesus gave the following parables to further clarify what it means to be ready for his return and how to live until he comes. In the story of the bridesmaids (25:1–13), we are taught that every person is responsible for his or her own spiritual condition. The story of the talents (25:14–30) shows the necessity of using well what God has entrusted to us. The parable of the sheep and goats (25:31–46) stresses the importance of serving others in need. No parable by itself completely describes our preparation. Instead, each paints one part of the whole picture.

25:1ff This parable is about a wedding. In Jewish culture, a couple was engaged for a long time before the actual marriage, and the engagement promise was just as binding as the marriage vows. On the wedding day the bridegroom went to the bride's house for the ceremony; then the bride and groom, along with a great parade, returned to the groom's house where a feast took place, often lasting a full week.

These bridesmaids were waiting for the parade, and they hoped to take part in the wedding banquet. But when the groom didn't come when they expected, five of them let their lamps run out of oil. By the time they had purchased extra oil, it was too late to join the feast.

When Jesus returns to take his people to heaven, we must be ready. Spiritual preparation cannot be bought or borrowed at the last minute. Our relationship with God must be our own.

5, 6"So, when the bridegroom was delayed, they lay down to rest until midnight, when they were roused by the shout, 'The bridegroom is coming! Come out and welcome him!'

25:5
1 Thess 4:16
5:6
2 Pet 3:4-9

7, 8"All the girls jumped up and trimmed their lamps. Then the five who hadn't any oil begged the others to share with them, for their lamps were going out.

25:7
Lk 12:35-40

9"But the others replied, 'We haven't enough. Go instead to the shops and buy some for yourselves.'

10"But while they were gone, the bridegroom came, and those who were ready went in with him to the marriage feast, and the door was locked.

25:10
Lk 13:24,25

11"Later, when the other five returned, they stood outside, calling, 'Sir, open the door for us!'

12"But he called back, 'Go away! It is too late!'

13"So stay awake and be prepared, for you do not know the date or moment of my return.

25:13
Mt 24:42
Mk 13:33
Rev 16:15

Jesus tells the parable of the loaned money (205)

14"Again, the Kingdom of Heaven can be illustrated by the story of a man going into another country, who called together his servants and loaned them money to invest for him while he was gone.

15"He gave $5,000 to one, $2,000 to another, and $1,000 to the last—dividing it in proportion to their abilities—and then left on his trip. 16The man who received the $5,000 began immediately to buy and sell with it and soon earned another $5,000. 17The man with $2,000 went right to work, too, and earned another $2,000.

25:15
Rom 12:6
Eph 4:11
1 Pet 4:10

18"But the man who received the $1,000 dug a hole in the ground and hid the money for safekeeping.

19"After a long time their master returned from his trip and called them to him to account for his money. 20The man to whom he had entrusted the $5,000 brought him $10,000.

21"His master praised him for good work. 'You have been faithful in handling this small amount,' he told him, 'so now I will give you many more responsibilities. Begin the joyous tasks I have assigned to you.'

25:21
Mt 24:46,47
Lk 12:42-44
22:28-30
2 Tim 2:12

22"Next came the man who had received the $2,000, with the report, 'Sir, you gave me $2,000 to use, and I have doubled it.'

23" 'Good work,' his master said. 'You are a good and faithful servant. You have been faithful over this small amount, so now I will give you much more.'

24, 25"Then the man with the $1,000 came and said, 'Sir, I knew you were a hard man, and I was afraid you would rob me of what I earned, so I hid your money in the earth and here it is!'

26"But his master replied, 'Wicked man! Lazy slave! Since you knew I would demand your profit, 27you should at least have put my money into the bank so I could have some interest. 28Take the money from this man and give it to the man with the $10,000. 29For the man who uses well what he is given shall be given

25:29
Lk 8:18
Jn 15:2
1 Cor 15:10

25:12 *It is too late,* literally, "I know you not." **25:13** *of my return,* implied. **25:24, 25** *I was afraid you would rob me of what I earned,* literally, "reaping where you didn't sow, and gathering where you didn't scatter, and I was afraid. . . ."

25:15 The master divided the money up among his servants according to their abilities—no one received more or less money than he could handle. If he failed in his master's assignment, his excuse could not be that he was overwhelmed. Failure could come only from laziness or hatred for the master. Money, as used here, represents any kind of resource we are given. God gives us time, abilities, gifts, and other resources according to our abilities, and he expects us to invest them wisely until he returns. We are responsible to use well what God has given us. The issue is not how much we have, but what we do with what we have.

25:21 Jesus is coming back—we know this is true. Does this mean we must drop our jobs in order to serve God? No, it means

we are diligently to use our time, talents, and treasures in order to serve God completely in whatever we do. For a few people, this means changing professions. For most of us, it means doing our daily work out of love for God.

25:24–30 This last man was thinking only of himself—playing it safe and protecting himself from his hard taskmaster. He was judged for his self-centeredness. We must not make excuses to avoid what God calls us to do. If God truly is our Master, we must obey willingly. Our time, abilities, and money aren't ours in the first place—we are caretakers, not owners. When we ignore, squander, or abuse what we are given, we are rebellious and deserve to be punished.

25:30
Mt 8:12
Lk 13:28

more, and he shall have abundance. But from the man who is unfaithful, even what little responsibility he has shall be taken from him. 30And throw the useless servant out into outer darkness: there shall be weeping and gnashing of teeth.'

Jesus tells about the final judgment (206)

25:31
Zech 14:5
Acts 1:11; 3:20
1 Thess 4:16
2 Thess 1:7

31"But when I, the Messiah, shall come in my glory, and all the angels with me, then I shall sit upon my throne of glory. 32And all the nations shall be gathered before me. And I will separate the people as a shepherd separates the sheep from the goats, 33and place the sheep at my right hand, and the goats at my left.

25:32
Ezek 20:34-38
34:17
Rev 20:12

34"Then I, the King, shall say to those at my right, 'Come, blessed of my Father, into the Kingdom prepared for you from the founding of the world. 35For I was hungry and you fed me; I was thirsty and you gave me water; I was a stranger and you invited me into your homes; 36naked and you clothed me; sick and in prison, and you visited me.'

25:34
Lk 12:32
1 Cor 2:9; 6:9
Heb 11:16
Rev 21:7

25:35
Isa 58:7
2 Tim 1:16
Heb 13:2,3
Jas 2:15

37"Then these righteous ones will reply, 'Sir, when did we ever see you hungry and feed you? Or thirsty and give you anything to drink? 38Or a stranger, and help you? Or naked, and clothe you? 39When did we ever see you sick or in prison, and visit you?'

25:40
Prov 14:31
19:17
Heb 6:10

40"And I, the King, will tell them, 'When you did it to these my brothers you were doing it to me!' 41Then I will turn to those on my left and say, 'Away with you, you cursed ones, into the eternal fire prepared for the devil and his demons. 42For I was hungry and you wouldn't feed me; thirsty, and you wouldn't give me anything to drink; 43a stranger, and you refused me hospitality; naked, and you wouldn't clothe me; sick, and in prison, and you didn't visit me.'

25:41
Mt 13:41
2 Pet 2:4
Jude 6

25:45
Prov 17:5
Zech 2:8
Acts 9:5

44"Then they will reply, 'Lord, when did we ever see you hungry or thirsty or a stranger or naked or sick or in prison, and not help you?'

45"And I will answer, 'When you refused to help the least of these my brothers, you were refusing help to me.'

25:46
Dan 12:2
Jn 3:15,36; 5:29
Acts 13:46,48
Rom 2:7,8; 6:23
Gal 6:8
1 Jn 5:11

46"And they shall go away into eternal punishment; but the righteous into everlasting life."

25:31 *the Messiah,* literally, "the Son of Man."   **25:32** *separate the people,* literally, "separate the nations."

25:29, 30 This parable describes the consequences of two attitudes to Christ's return. The worker who diligently and usefully prepares for it by investing his time and talent to serve God will be rewarded. The worker who has no heart for the work of the Kingdom will be punished. God rewards faithfulness. Those who bear no fruit for God's Kingdom cannot expect to be treated the same as the faithful.

25:31–46 God will separate his obedient followers from pretenders and unbelievers. The real evidence of our belief is the way we act. To treat all persons we encounter as if they are Jesus is no easy task. What we do for others demonstrates what we really think about Jesus' words to us—feed the hungry, give the homeless a place to stay, visit the sick. How well do your actions separate you from pretenders and unbelievers?

25:32 Jesus used sheep and goats to show the division between believers and unbelievers. Sheep and goats often grazed together but were separated when it came time to shear the sheep. Ezekiel 34:17–24 also refers to the separation of sheep and goats.

25:34–40 This parable describes acts of mercy we all can do every day. These acts are not dependent on wealth, ability, or intelligence; they are simple acts freely given and freely received. We have no excuse to neglect those who have deep needs, and we cannot hand over this responsibility to the church or government. Jesus demands personal involvement in caring for others' needs (Isaiah 58:7).

25:40 There has been much discussion about the identity of the

"brothers." Some have said it refers to the Jews; others say it refers to all Christians; still others say it refers to suffering people everywhere. Such a debate is much like the lawyer's earlier question to Jesus, "Who is my neighbor?" (Luke 10:29). The point of this parable is not the *who*, but the *what*—the act of serving where service is needed. The focus of this parable is that we should love every person and serve anyone we can. Such love for others is glorifying to God, because it reflects our love for him.

25:46 Eternal punishment takes place in hell, the place of punishment after death for all those who refuse to repent (5:29). In the Bible, three words have been translated "hell."

(1) *Sheol* is used in the Old Testament to mean the grave, the place of the dead, generally thought to be under the earth. (See Job 24:19; Psalm 16:10; Isaiah 38:10.)

(2) *Hades* is the Greek word for the underworld, the realm of the dead. It is the word used in the New Testament for Sheol.

(3) *Gehenna* was named after the valley of Hinnom near Jerusalem where children were sacrificed by fire to the pagan gods (see 2 Kings 23:10; 2 Chronicles 28:3). This is the place of eternal fire (Mark 9:43) prepared for the devil, his angels, and all those who do not believe in God (25:46; Revelation 20:9, 10). This is the final and eternal state of the wicked after the resurrection and the Last Judgment.

When Jesus warns against unbelief, he is trying to save us from agonizing punishment.

C. DEATH AND RESURRECTION OF JESUS, THE KING (26:1—28:20)

After facing much opposition for his teaching, Jesus is betrayed by Judas, denied by the disciples, crucified, and dies. Three days later he rises from the dead and appears to the disciples, confirming that he is indeed king over life and death. The long-awaited King has brought in his Kingdom, but it is different than expected, for he reigns in our hearts until the day he comes again to establish a new and perfect world.

Religious leaders plot to kill Jesus
(207/Mark 14:1, 2; Luke 22:1, 2)

26 When Jesus had finished this talk with his disciples, he told them, 2" As you know, the Passover celebration begins in two days, and I shall be betrayed and crucified."

26:1
Mk 14:1,2
Lk 22:1,2

3At that very moment the chief priests and other Jewish officials were meeting at the residence of Caiaphas the High Priest, 4to discuss ways of capturing Jesus quietly, and killing him. 5"But not during the Passover celebration," they agreed, "for there would be a riot."

26:3
Ps 2:2
Jn 11:47,48
Acts 4:25,26

A woman anoints Jesus with expensive perfume
(182/Mark 14:3–9; John 12:1–11)

6Jesus now proceeded to Bethany, to the home of Simon the leper. 7While he was eating, a woman came in with a bottle of very expensive perfume, and poured it over his head.

26:6
Mk 14:3-9
Jn 12:1-8

26:7
Mt 21:17
Jn 11:1

8, 9The disciples were indignant. "What a waste of good money," they said. "Why, she could have sold it for a fortune and given it to the poor."

10Jesus knew what they were thinking, and said, "Why are you criticizing her? For she has done a good thing to me. 11You will always have the poor among you, but you won't always have me. 12She has poured this perfume on me to prepare my body for burial. 13And she will always be remembered for this deed. The story of what she has done will be told throughout the whole world, wherever the Good News is preached."

26:11
Deut 15:11
Jn 17:11

Judas agrees to betray Jesus
(208/Mark 14:10, 11; Luke 22:3–6)

14Then Judas Iscariot, one of the twelve apostles, went to the chief priests, 15and
26:2 *I,* literally, "the Son of Man."

26:3 Caiaphas was the ruling High Priest during Jesus' ministry. He was the son-in-law of Annas, the previous High Priest. The Roman government had taken over the process of appointing all political and religious leaders. Caiaphas served for 18 years, longer than most High Priests, suggesting that he was good at cooperating with the Romans. He was the first to recommend Jesus' death in order to "save" the nation (John 11:49, 50).

26:4 This was a deliberate plot to kill Jesus. Without this plot, there would have been no groundswell of popular opinion against him. In fact, because of Jesus' popularity, the religious leaders were afraid to arrest him during the Passover. They did not want their actions to incite a riot.

26:6–13 Matthew and Mark placed this event just before the Last Supper, while John placed it a week earlier, just before the Triumphal Entry. We must remember that the main purpose of the Gospel writers was to give an accurate record of Jesus' message, not to present an exact chronological account of his life. Matthew and Mark may have chosen to place this event here to contrast the complete devotion of Mary with the betrayal of Judas, the next event in both Gospels.

26:7 This woman was Mary, the sister of Martha and Lazarus, who lived in Bethany (John 12:1–3).

26:8 The disciples were all indignant, but John's Gospel singles out Judas Iscariot as especially so (John 12:4).

26:11 Jesus refers to Deuteronomy 15:11 which says, "There will always be some among you who are poor." This is not a

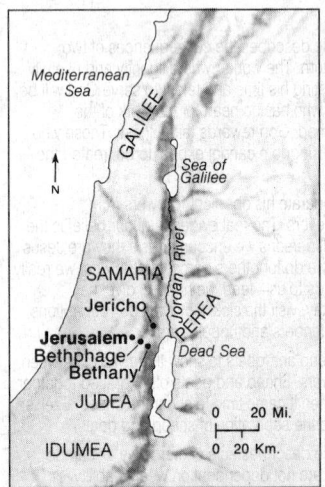

justification of ignoring the needs of the poor. Scripture continually calls us to care for the needy. Rather, Jesus said this to highlight the special sacrifice Mary made for him.

26:14, 15 Why would Judas want to betray Jesus? Judas, like the

VISIT IN BETHANY
Chronologically, the events of Matt. 26:6–13 precede the events of 21:1ff. In 20:29, Jesus left Jericho, heading toward Jerusalem. Then he arrived in Bethany, where a woman anointed him. From there he went toward Bethphage where he sent two of his disciples to get the donkey on which he would ride into Jerusalem.

asked, "How much will you pay me to get Jesus into your hands?" And they gave him thirty silver coins. ¹⁶From that time on, Judas watched for an opportunity to betray Jesus to them.

Disciples prepare for the Passover
(209/Mark 14:12–16; Luke 22:7–13)

26:17
Ex 12:6
Lev 23:5,6

¹⁷On the first day of the Passover ceremonies, when bread made with yeast was purged from every Jewish home, the disciples came to Jesus and asked, "Where shall we plan to eat the Passover?"

MARY LAZARUS' SISTER

Hospitality is an art. Making sure a guest is welcomed, warmed, and well-fed requires creativity, organization, and teamwork. Their ability to accomplish these makes Mary and her sister Martha one of the best hospitality teams in the Bible. Their frequent guest was Jesus Christ.

For Mary, hospitality meant giving more attention to the guest himself than to the needs he might have. She would rather talk than cook. She was more interested in her guest's words than in the cleanliness of her home or the timeliness of her meals. She let her older sister Martha take care of those details. Mary's approach to events shows her to be mainly a "responder." She did little preparation—her role was participation. Unlike her sister, who had to learn to stop and listen, Mary needed to learn that action is often appropriate and necessary.

We first meet Mary during a visit Jesus paid to her home. She simply sat at his feet and listened. When Martha became irritated at her sister's lack of help, Jesus stated that Mary's choice to enjoy his company was the most appropriate response at the time. Our last glimpse of Mary shows her to have become a woman of thoughtful and worshipful action. Again she was at Jesus' feet, washing them with perfume and wiping them with her hair. She seemed to understand, better even than the disciples, why Jesus was going to die. Jesus said her act of worship would be told everywhere, along with the Good News, as an example of costly service.

What kind of hospitality does Jesus receive in your life? Are you so busy planning and running your life that you neglect precious time with him? Or do you respond to him by listening to his Word, then finding ways to worship him with your life? That is that kind of hospitality he longs for from each of us.

Strengths and accomplishments:
- Perhaps the only person who understood and accepted Jesus' coming death, taking time to anoint his body while he was still living
- Learned when to listen and when to act

Lessons from her life:
- The busy-ness of serving God can become a barrier to knowing him personally
- Small acts of obedience and service have widespread effects

Vital statistics:
- Where: Bethany
- Relatives: Sister: Martha. Brother: Lazarus.

Key verses:
"She has poured this perfume on me to prepare my body for burial. And she will always be remembered for this deed. The story of what she has done will be told throughout the whole world, wherever the Good News is preached" (Matthew 26:12, 13).

Mary's story is told in Matthew 26:6–13; Mark 14:3-9; Luke 10:38-42; John 11:17-45; 12:1–11.

other disciples, expected Jesus to start a political rebellion and overthrow Rome. As treasurer, Judas certainly assumed (as did the other disciples—see Mark 10:35–37) that he would be given an important position in Jesus' new government. But when Jesus praised Mary for pouring out the perfume, worth a year's salary, Judas may have realized that Jesus' Kingdom was not physical or political, but spiritual. Judas' greedy desire for money and status could not be realized if he followed Jesus, so he betrayed him in exchange for money and favor from the religious leaders.

26:15 Matthew alone records the exact amount of money Judas accepted to betray Jesus—30 pieces of silver. The religious leaders had planned to wait until after the Passover to take Jesus, but with Judas' unexpected offer, they accelerated their plans.

26:17 The Passover was one night and one meal, but the Feast of Unleavened Bread, which was celebrated with it, continued for a week. The people removed all yeast from their homes in commemoration of their ancestors' exodus from Egypt, when they did not have time to let the bread dough rise. Thousands of people poured into Jerusalem from all over the Roman Empire. For more information on how the Passover was celebrated, see the notes on Mark 14:1 and in Exodus 12.

18He replied, "Go into the city and see Mr. So-and-So, and tell him, 'Our Master says, my time has come, and I will eat the Passover meal with my disciples at your house.'" 19So the disciples did as he told them, and prepared the supper there.

Jesus and the disciples have the Last Supper
(211/Mark 14:17–25; Luke 22:14–30; John 13:21–30)

20, 21That evening as he sat eating with the Twelve, he said, "One of you will betray me."

22Sorrow chilled their hearts, and each one asked, "Am I the one?"

23He replied, "It is the one I served first. 24For I must die just as was prophesied, but woe to the man by whom I am betrayed. Far better for that one if he had never been born."

25Judas, too, had asked him, "Rabbi, am I the one?" And Jesus had told him, "Yes."

26As they were eating, Jesus took a small loaf of bread and blessed it and broke it apart and gave it to the disciples and said, "Take it and eat it, for this is my body."

27And he took a cup of wine and gave thanks for it and gave it to them and said, "Each one drink from it, 28for this is my blood, sealing the New Covenant. It is poured out to forgive the sins of multitudes. 29Mark my words—I will not drink this wine again until the day I drink it new with you in my Father's Kingdom."

Jesus again predicts Peter's denial
(222/Mark 14:26–31)

30And when they had sung a hymn, they went out to the Mount of Olives.
31Then Jesus said to them, "Tonight you will all desert me. For it is written in the

26:23 It is the one I served first, literally, "he that dipped his hand with me in the dish." **26:24** For I must die, literally, "the Son of Man goes." **26:31** in the Scriptures, see Zech 13:7.

26:23
Ps 41:9

26:24
Gen 3:15
Isa 53:8
Dan 9:26
Lk 24:25-27,46
1 Pet 1:10,11

26:26
Mk 14:22-26
Lk 22:19,20,39
1 Cor 10:16
11:23

26:28
Ex 24:8
Lev 17:11
Jer 31:31
Rom 5:15
Heb 9:22

26:29
Acts 10:41

26:31
Zech 13:7

26:26 Each name we use for this sacrament brings out a different dimension to it. It is the *Lord's Supper* because it commemorates the Passover meal Jesus ate with his disciples; it is the *Eucharist* (thanksgiving) because in it we thank God for Christ's work for us; it is *communion* because through it we commune with God and with other believers. As we eat the bread and drink the wine, we should be sober as we recall Jesus' death and his promise to come again, grateful for God's wonderful gift to us, and joyful as we meet with Christ and the body of believers.

26:28 How does Jesus' blood seal the New Covenant? People under the Old Covenant (those who lived before Jesus) could approach God only through a priest and an animal sacrifice. Now all people can come directly to God through faith because Jesus' death has made us acceptable in God's eyes (Romans 3:21–24).

The Old Covenant was a picture of the New (Jeremiah 31:31), pointing forward to the day when Jesus himself would be the final and ultimate sacrifice for sin. Rather than a lamb without blemish on the altar, the perfect Lamb of God was slain on the cross, a sinless sacrifice so that all our sins could be forgiven once and for all. All those who believe in him receive that forgiveness.

26:29 Again Jesus assured his disciples of victory over death and of their future with him. The next few hours would bring apparent defeat, but soon they would experience the power of the Holy Spirit and witness the wild spread of the gospel message. And one day, they would all be together again in God's new Kingdom.

26:30 It is possible that the hymn the disciples sang was from Psalms 115—118, the traditional psalms sung as part of the Passover meal.

26:35 All the disciples declared that they would die before deserting Jesus. A few hours later, however, they all scattered. Talk is cheap. It is easy to say we are devoted to Christ, but our claims are meaningful only when they are tested in the crucible of

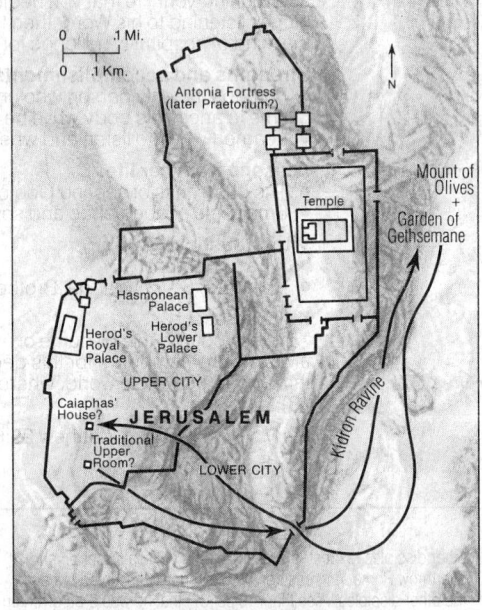

THE PASSOVER MEAL AND GETHSEMANE Jesus, who would soon be the final Passover Lamb, ate the traditional Passover meal with his disciples in the upper room of a house in Jerusalem. During the meal they partook of the wine and bread which would be the element of future communion celebrations and then went out to the Garden of Gethsemane on the Mount of Olives.

Scriptures that God will smite the Shepherd, and the sheep of the flock will be scattered. 32But after I have been brought back to life again I will go to Galilee, and meet you there."

33Peter declared, "If everyone else deserts you, I won't."

26:34
Mt 26:75
Mk 14:30
Lk 22:34
Jn 13:38

34Jesus told him, "The truth is that this very night, before the cock crows at dawn, you will deny me three times!"

35"I would die first!" Peter insisted. And all the other disciples said the same thing.

Jesus agonizes in the garden
(223/Mark 14:32–42; Luke 22:39–46)

26:36
Mk 14:32-42
Lk 22:39-46
Jn 18:1

36Then Jesus brought them to a garden grove, Gethsemane, and told them to sit down and wait while he went on ahead to pray. 37He took Peter with him and Zebedee's two sons James and John, and began to be filled with anguish and despair.

26:38
Jn 12:27

38Then he told them, "My soul is crushed with horror and sadness to the point of death . . . stay here . . . stay awake with me."

26:39
Mt 20:22
Jn 5:30; 6:38
Heb 5:7

39He went forward a little, and fell face downward on the ground, and prayed, "My Father! If it is possible, let this cup be taken away from me. But I want your will, not mine."

26:41
Eph 6:18
1 Pet 5:8

40Then he returned to the three disciples and found them asleep. "Peter," he called, "couldn't you even stay awake with me one hour? 41Keep alert and pray. Otherwise temptation will overpower you. For the spirit indeed is willing, but how weak the body is!"

42Again he left them and prayed, "My Father! If this cup cannot go away until I drink it all, your will be done."

43He returned to them again and found them sleeping, for their eyes were heavy, 44so he went back to prayer the third time, saying the same things again.

26:45
Jn 12:23-27
13:1,31

45Then he came to the disciples and said, "Sleep on now and take your rest . . . but no! The time has come! I am betrayed into the hands of evil men! 46Up! Let's be going! Look! Here comes the man who is betraying me!"

Jesus is betrayed and arrested
(224/Mark 14:43–52; Luke 22:47–53; John 18:1–11)

26:47
Mk 14:43-52
Lk 22:47-53
Jn 18:1-12

47At that very moment while he was still speaking, Judas, one of the Twelve, arrived with a great crowd armed with swords and clubs, sent by the Jewish leaders. 48Judas had told them to arrest the man he greeted, for that would be the

26:45 *l*, literally, "the Son of Man."

---

persecution. How strong is your faith? Is it strong enough to stand under intense trial? For the second time that evening, Jesus predicted that his disciples would desert him (see Luke 22:31–38; John 13:31–38 for the first prediction).

26:37, 38 Jesus was in great anguish over his coming physical pain, separation from the Father, and death for the sins of the world. The divine course was set; but he, in his human nature, still struggled (Hebrews 5:7–9). Because of the anguish he faced, he can relate to our suffering. His strength to obey came from his relationship with God the Father, who is also the source of our strength (John 17:11, 15, 16, 21, 26).

26:39 Jesus was not rebelling against his Father's will when he asked that the cup be taken away. In fact, he reaffirmed his desire to do God's will by saying, "I want your will, not mine!" His prayer reveals to us his terrible suffering. His agony was worse than death as he paid personally for *all* sin by being separated from God. The "cup" was this suffering and separation. The sinless Son of God took our sins upon himself to save us from suffering and separation.

26:39 This was a difficult night for Jesus because he knew what lay ahead, and he struggled with it. But he also knew the reason for his terrible death. We cannot see the future and often don't know the purpose of our struggles. What does it take for you to be able to say, "I want your will, not mine"? It takes trust in God's plans, prayer, and obedience each step of the way.

26:40 Jesus used Peter's drowsiness to warn him about the kinds of temptation he would soon face. The way to overcome temptation is to be alert to it and pray. Being alert involves being aware of the possibilities of temptation, sensitive to the subtleties, and spiritually equipped to fight it. Because temptation strikes where we are most vulnerable, we can't resist it alone. Prayer is essential, because it strengthens us to defeat Satan's power.

26:48 Judas had told the Temple guards to arrest the man he greeted. This was not an arrest by Roman soldiers under Roman law, but an arrest by the religious leaders. Judas pointed Jesus out not because he was hard to recognize, but because Judas had agreed to be the formal accuser in case a trial was called. Judas was able to lead them to one of Jesus' retreats where no crowds would interfere with the arrest.

one they were after. 49So now Judas came straight to Jesus and said, "Hello, Master!" and embraced him in friendly fashion.

50Jesus said, "My friend, go ahead and do what you have come for." Then the others grabbed him.

51One of the men with Jesus pulled out a sword and slashed off the ear of the High Priest's servant.

52"Put away your sword," Jesus told him. "Those using swords will get killed. 53Don't you realize that I could ask my Father for thousands of angels to protect us, and he would send them instantly? 54But if I did, how would the Scriptures be fulfilled that describe what is happening now?" 55Then Jesus spoke to the crowd. "Am I some dangerous criminal," he asked, "that you had to arm yourselves with swords and clubs before you could arrest me? I was with you teaching daily in the Temple and you didn't stop me then. 56But this is all happening to fulfill the words of the prophets as recorded in the Scriptures."

At that point, all the disciples deserted him and fled.

Caiaphas questions Jesus
(226/Mark 14:53–65)

57Then the mob led him to the home of Caiaphas the High Priest, where all the Jewish leaders were gathering. 58Meanwhile, Peter was following far to the rear, and came to the courtyard of the High Priest's house and went in and sat with the soldiers, and waited to see what was going to be done to Jesus.

59The chief priests and, in fact, the entire Jewish Supreme Court assembled there and looked for witnesses who would lie about Jesus, in order to build a case against him that would result in a death sentence. 60, 61But even though they found many who agreed to be false witnesses, these always contradicted each other.

Finally two men were found who declared, "This man said, 'I am able to destroy the Temple of God and rebuild it in three days.' "

62Then the High Priest stood up and said to Jesus, "Well, what about it? Did you say that, or didn't you?" 63But Jesus remained silent.

Then the High Priest said to him, "I demand in the name of the living God that you tell us whether you claim to be the Messiah, the Son of God."

64"Yes," Jesus said, "I am. And in the future you will see me, the Messiah, sitting at the right hand of God and returning on the clouds of heaven."

65, 66Then the High Priest tore at his own clothing, shouting, "Blasphemy! What need have we for other witnesses? You have all heard him say it! What is your verdict?"

They shouted, "Death!—Death!—Death!"

26:49 *embraced,* literally, "kissed," the greeting still used among men in Eastern lands.   **26:64** *the Messiah,* literally, "the Son of Man."

26:50 Ps 41:9 55:12,13
26:52 Gen 9:6 Rev 13:10
26:53 2 Kgs 6:16,17 Ps 91:11 Dan 7:10
26:55 Mk 12:35; 14:49 Lk 4:20; 19:47 20:1; 21:37 Jn 7:14,28; 8:20 18:20
26:56 Isa 53:7 Lam 4:20 Dan 9:26 Jn 18:15
26:57 Mk 14:53-65
26:58 Lk 22:54,55
26:60 Deut 19:15 1 Kgs 21:10 Ps 27:12
26:61 Mt 27:40 Jn 2:19 Acts 6:14
26:62 Mt 27:12
26:63 Lev 5:1
26:64 Ps 110:1 Dan 7:13 Acts 7:55 1 Thess 4:16 Rev 1:7
26:65 Lev 24:16 2 Kgs 18:37 Jn 19:7 Acts 3:15; 7:52

		BETRAYED!
Cain betrayed Abel and killed him.	Genesis 4:1–15	
Delilah betrayed Samson to the Philistines.	Judges 16:18–21	
Absalom betrayed David, his father.	2 Samuel 15:10–16	
Jehu betrayed Joram and killed him.	2 Kings 9:14–27	
Servants betrayed Joash and killed him.	2 Kings 12:20, 21	
Judas betrayed Jesus.	Matthew 26:46–56	

Scripture records a number of occasions in which a person or group was betrayed. The tragedies caused by these violations of trust are a strong lesson about the importance of keeping our commitments.

26:51-53 The man who cut off the servant's ear was Peter (John 18:10). Peter was trying to prevent what he saw as *defeat.* He didn't realize that Jesus had to die in order to have *victory.* But Jesus demonstrated perfect commitment to his Father's will. His Kingdom would not be advanced with swords, but with faith and obedience.

26:55 Although the religious leaders could have arrested Jesus at any time, they came at night because they were afraid of the crowds who followed him each day (see 26:5).

26:56 A few hours earlier, this band of men had said they would rather die than desert their Lord (see the note on 26:35).

26:57 Earlier in the evening, Jesus had been questioned by Annas (the former High Priest and father-in-law of Caiaphas). Annas then sent Jesus to Caiaphas' home to be questioned (John 18:12–24). Because of their haste to complete the trial and see Jesus die before the Sabbath, less than 24 hours away, the religious leaders met in Caiaphas' home at night instead of waiting for daylight and meeting in the Temple.

26:67
Isa 50:6; 53:3
Mic 5:1

67Then they spat in his face and struck him and some slapped him, 68saying, "Prophesy to us, you Messiah! Who struck you that time?"

Peter denies knowing Jesus
(227/Mark 14:66–72; Luke 22:54–65; John 18:25–27)

26:69
Mk 14:66-72
Lk 22:55-62
Jn 18:25-27

69Meanwhile, as Peter was sitting in the courtyard a girl came over and said to him, "You were with Jesus, for both of you are from Galilee."

70But Peter denied it loudly. "I don't even know what you are talking about," he angrily declared.

71Later, out by the gate, another girl noticed him and said to those standing around, "This man was with Jesus—from Nazareth."

72Again Peter denied it, this time with an oath. "I don't even know the man," he said.

73But after a while the men who had been standing there came over to him and said, "We know you are one of his disciples, for we can tell by your Galilean accent."

74Peter began to curse and swear. "I don't even know the man," he said.

26:75
Mt 26:34

And immediately the cock crowed. 75Then Peter remembered what Jesus had said, "Before the cock crows, you will deny me three times." And he went away, crying bitterly.

26:69 *from Galilee*, literally, "with Jesus the Galilean." **26:73** *Galilean*, implied.

JESUS' TRIAL After Judas singled Jesus out for arrest, the mob took Jesus first to Caiaphas, the High Priest. This trial, a mockery of justice, ended at daybreak with their decision to kill him—but the Jews needed Rome's permission for the death sentence. Jesus was taken to Pilate (who was probably in the Antonia Fortress), then to Herod (Luke 23:5–12), and back to Pilate who sentenced him to die.

26:59 The Jewish Supreme Court, also called the Sanhedrin, was the most powerful religious and political body of the Jewish people. Although the Romans controlled Israel's government, they gave the people power to handle religious disputes and some civil disputes, so the Sanhedrin made many of the local decisions affecting daily life. But a death sentence had to be approved by the Romans.

26:60, 61 The Jewish Supreme Court tried to find witnesses who would distort some of Jesus' teachings. Finally they found two witnesses who distorted Jesus' words about the Temple (see John 2:19). They claimed that Jesus had said he could destroy the Temple—a blasphemous boast. Actually, Jesus had said, "You destroy this temple and I will raise it up." Jesus, of course, was talking about his body, not the building. Ironically, the religious leaders were about to destroy Jesus' body just as he had said, and three days later he would rise from the dead.

26:64 Jesus declared his royalty in no uncertain terms. Although he literally said he was the Son of Man, everyone present knew he was claiming to be the Messiah. He knew this declaration would be his undoing, but he did not panic. He was calm, courageous, and determined.

26:65, 66 The High Priest accused Jesus of blasphemy—calling himself God. To the Jews, this was a great crime, punishable by death. The religious leaders refused even to consider that Jesus' words might be true. They had decided against Jesus, and in so doing they sealed their own fate as well as his. Like the Jewish Court members, you must decide whether Jesus' words are blasphemy or truth. The implication of your decision is eternal.

26:69ff There were three stages to Peter's denial. First he acted confused and tried to divert attention from himself by changing the subject. Second, he vehemently denied Jesus. Third, he denied Jesus with an oath. Believers who deny Christ often begin doing so subtly by pretending not to know him. When opportunities to discuss religious issues come up, they walk away or pretend they don't know the answers. With only a little more pressure, they can be induced to flatly deny their relationship with Christ. If you find yourself subtly avoiding occasions to talk about Christ, watch out. You may be on the road to denying him.

26:72–74 That Peter denied Christ with an oath and with cursing and swearing does not mean he used foul language. This was the kind of swearing one does in a court of law. Peter was swearing that he did not know Jesus and was invoking a curse on himself if his words were untrue. In effect he was saying, "May God strike me dead if I am lying."

The council of religious leaders condemns Jesus
(228/Mark 15:1; Luke 22:66–71)

27 When it was morning, the chief priests and Jewish leaders met again to discuss how to induce the Roman government to sentence Jesus to death. ²Then they sent him in chains to Pilate, the Roman governor.

27:1
Ps 2:2
27:2
Mt 20:19

Judas kills himself
(229)

³About that time Judas, who betrayed him, when he saw that Jesus had been condemned to die, changed his mind and deeply regretted what he had done, and brought back the money to the chief priests and other Jewish leaders. ⁴"I have sinned," he declared, "for I have betrayed an innocent man."

"That's your problem," they retorted.

⁵Then he threw the money onto the floor of the Temple and went out and hanged himself. ⁶The chief priests picked the money up. "We can't put it in the collection," they said, "since it's against our laws to accept money paid for murder."

⁷They talked it over and finally decided to buy a certain field where the clay was used by potters, and to make it into a cemetery for foreigners who died in Jerusalem. ⁸That is why the cemetery is still called "The Field of Blood."

⁹This fulfilled the prophecy of Jeremiah which says,

"They took the thirty pieces of silver—the price at which he was valued by the people of Israel— ¹⁰and purchased a field from the potters as the Lord directed me."

27:3
Job 20:5
Mt 26:14
2 Cor 7:10

27:5
Acts 1:18

27:9,10
Jer 18:1-4; 19:2,
11; 32:6-9
Zech 11:12,13

Jesus stands trial before Pilate
(230/Mark 15:2–5; Luke 23:1–5; John 18:28–38)

¹¹Now Jesus was standing before Pilate, the Roman governor. "Are you the Jews' Messiah?" the governor asked him.

"Yes," Jesus replied.

¹²But when the chief priests and other Jewish leaders made their many accusations against him, Jesus remained silent.

27:11
1 Tim 6:13

27:12
Isa 53:7
Mt 26:63
Jn 19:9
1 Pet 2:22

27:1 *to sentence Jesus to death,* literally, "took counsel against Jesus to put him to death." **27:3** *regretted what he had done,* literally, "repented himself." **27:11** *the Jews' Messiah,* literally, " 'King' of the Jews."

27:1 The religious leaders had to induce the Roman government to sentence Jesus to death because they did not have the authority to do it themselves. The Romans had taken away the religious leaders' authority to inflict capital punishment. Politically, it looked better for the religious leaders anyway if someone else was responsible for killing Jesus. They wanted the death to appear Roman so the crowds couldn't blame them. They had arrested Jesus on theological grounds—blasphemy; but since this charge would be thrown out of a Roman court, they had to come up with a political reason for Jesus' death. Their strategy was to show Jesus as a rebel who claimed to be God and thus higher than Caesar.

27:2 Pilate was the Roman governor for the regions of Samaria and Judea from A.D. 26–36. Jerusalem was located in Judea. Pilate took special pleasure in demonstrating his authority over the Jews by doing such things as impounding money from the Temple treasuries to build an aqueduct. He was not popular, but the religious leaders had no other way to get rid of Jesus than to go to Pilate. Ironically, when Jesus, a Jew, came before him for trial, Pilate found him innocent. He could not find a single fault in Jesus, nor could he contrive one.

27:3, 4 Jesus' formal accuser (see 26:48 note) wanted to drop his charges, but the religious leaders refused to halt the trial. When he first betrayed Jesus, perhaps Judas was trying to force his hand to get him to lead a revolt against Rome. This did not work, of course. Whatever his reason, Judas changed his mind, but it was too late. Many of the plans we set into motion cannot be reversed. It is best to think of the potential consequences before we launch into an action we may later regret.

27:4 The priests' job was to teach people about God and act as intercessors for them, helping with the sacrifices to cover their sins. Judas returned to the priests, exclaiming that he had sinned. But rather than helping him find forgiveness, the priests said, "That's your problem." Not only had they rejected the Messiah, they had rejected their role as priests.

27:5 In this passage, Judas hanged himself. Acts 1:18, however, says he fell and burst open. The best explanation is that the limb from which he was hanging broke and the resulting fall split open his body.

27:6 These chief priests felt no guilt in giving Judas money to betray an innocent man, but when Judas returned the money, the priests couldn't accept it because it was wrong to accept money given for a murder! Their hatred for Jesus had indeed caused them to lose all sense of justice.

27:9 This prophecy is found specifically in Zechariah 11:12, 13, but may also have been taken from Jeremiah 17:2, 3; 18:1–4; 19:1–11; or 32:6–15.

27:12 Before Pilate, the religious leaders accused Jesus of different crimes from the ones for which they had arrested him. They arrested him for blasphemy (claiming to be God), but that charge would mean nothing to the Romans. So the religious leaders had to accuse Jesus of crimes that would have concerned the Roman government, such as encouraging the people not to pay taxes, claiming to be a king, and causing riots. These accusations were not true, but they were determined to kill Jesus; and they broke several commandments in order to do so.

13"Don't you hear what they are saying?" Pilate demanded.

14But Jesus said nothing, much to the governor's surprise.

Pilate hands Jesus over to be crucified
(232/Mark 15:6–15; Luke 23:13–25; John 18:39—19:16)

15Now the governor's custom was to release one Jewish prisoner each year during the Passover celebration—anyone they wanted. 16This year there was a particularly notorious criminal in jail named Barabbas, 17and as the crowds gathered before Pilate's house that morning he asked them, "Which shall I release to you—Barabbas, or Jesus your Messiah?" 18For he knew very well that the Jewish leaders had arrested Jesus out of envy because of his popularity with the people.

19Just then, as he was presiding over the court, Pilate's wife sent him this

27:18
Acts 7:9
27:19
Job 33:14,15

27:17 *Jesus your Messiah,* literally, "Jesus who is called Christ."

PETER

Jesus' first words to Simon Peter were, "Come, follow me" (Mark 1:17). His last words to him were, "*You* follow me" (John 21:22). Every step of the way between those two challenges, Peter never failed to follow—even though he often stumbled.

When Jesus entered Peter's life, this plain fisherman became a new person with new goals and new priorities. He did not become a perfect person, however, and he never stopped being Simon Peter. We may wonder what Jesus saw in Simon that made him greet this potential disciple with a new name, Peter—"the Rock." Impulsive Peter certainly didn't act like a rock much of the time. But when Jesus chose his followers, he wasn't looking for models, he was looking for men. He chose people who could be changed by his love, and then he sent them out to communicate that his acceptance was available to anyone—even to those who often fail.

We may wonder what Jesus sees in us when he calls us to follow him. But we know Jesus accepted Peter, and, in spite of his failures, Peter went on to do great things for God. Are you willing to keep following Jesus, even when you fail?

Strengths and accomplishments:
- Became the recognized leader among Jesus' disciples—one of the inner group of three
- Was the first great voice of the gospel during and after Pentecost
- Probably knew Mark and gave him information for the Gospel of Mark
- Wrote 1 and 2 Peter

Weaknesses and mistakes:
- Often spoke without thinking; was brash and impulsive
- During Jesus' trial, denied three times that he even knew Jesus
- Later, found it hard to treat Gentile Christians as equals

Lessons from his life:
- Enthusiasm has to be backed up by faith and understanding or it fails
- God's faithfulness can compensate for our greatest unfaithfulness
- It is better to be a follower who fails than one who fails to follow

Vital statistics:
- Occupation: Fisherman, disciple
- Relatives: Father: Jonah. Brother: Andrew.
- Contemporaries: Jesus, Pilate, Herod

Key verse:
"You are Peter, a stone; and upon this rock I will build my church; and all the powers of hell shall not prevail against it" (Matthew 16:18).

Peter's story is told in the Gospels and the book of Acts. He is mentioned in Galatians 1:18; 2:7–14; and he wrote the books of 1 and 2 Peter.

27:14 Jesus' silence fulfilled the words of the prophet (Isaiah 53:7). Pilate was amazed that Jesus didn't try to defend himself. He recognized the obvious plot against Jesus and wanted to let him go, but Pilate was already under pressure from Rome to keep peace in his territory. The last thing he needed was a rebellion over this quiet and seemingly insignificant man.

27:15 Barabbas had taken part in a rebellion against the Roman government (Mark 15:7). Although an enemy to Rome, he may have been a hero to the Jews. Ironically, Barabbas was guilty of

the crime for which Jesus was accused. *Barabbas* means "son of the father," which was actually Jesus' position with God.

27:19 For a leader who was supposed to administer justice, Pilate proved to be concerned more about political expediency than about doing what was right. He had several opportunities to make the right decision. His conscience told him Jesus was innocent; Roman law said an innocent man should not be put to death; and his wife had a troubled dream. Pilate had no good excuse to condemn Jesus, but he was afraid of the mob.

message: "Leave that good man alone; for I had a terrible nightmare concerning him last night."

20Meanwhile the chief priests and Jewish officials persuaded the crowds to ask for Barabbas' release, and for Jesus' death. 21So when the governor asked again, "Which of these two shall I release to you?" the crowd shouted back their reply: "Barabbas!"

22"Then what shall I do with Jesus, your Messiah?" Pilate asked.
And they shouted, "Crucify him!"

23"Why?" Pilate demanded. "What has he done wrong?" But they kept shouting, "Crucify! Crucify!"

24When Pilate saw that he wasn't getting anywhere, and that a riot was developing, he sent for a bowl of water and washed his hands before the crowd, saying, "I am innocent of the blood of this good man. The responsibility is yours!"

25And the mob yelled back, "His blood be on us and on our children!"

26Then Pilate released Barabbas to them. And after he had whipped Jesus, he gave him to the Roman soldiers to take away and crucify.

27:20 Acts 3:14

27:22 Mt 1:16

27:24 Deut 21:5-9 Ps 26:6

27:25 Deut 19:10 Acts 5:28

27:26 Isa 53:5

Roman soldiers mock Jesus
(233/Mark 15:16–20)

27But first they took him into the armory and called out the entire contingent. 28They stripped him and put a scarlet robe on him, 29and made a crown from long thorns and put it on his head, and placed a stick in his right hand as a scepter and knelt before him in mockery. "Hail, King of the Jews," they yelled. 30And they spat on him and grabbed the stick and beat him on the head with it.

31After the mockery, they took off the robe and put his own garment on him again, and took him out to crucify him.

27:28 Lk 23:11

27:29 Ps 69:19

27:30 Job 30:10 Isa 50:6

27:31 Isa 53:8

Jesus is led away to be crucified
(234/Mark 15:21–24; Luke 23:26–31; John 19:17)

32As they were on the way to the execution grounds they came across a man from Cyrene, in Africa—Simon was his name—and forced him to carry Jesus' cross. 33Then they went out to an area known as Golgotha, that is, "Skull Hill," 34where the soldiers gave him drugged wine to drink; but when he had tasted it, he refused.

27:32 Mk 15:21-32 Lk 23:26,32-43 Jn 19:17-24

27:34 Ps 69:21

Jesus is placed on the cross
(235/Mark 15:25–32; Luke 23:32–43; John 19:18–27)

35After the crucifixion, the soldiers threw dice to divide up his clothes among themselves. 36Then they sat around and watched him as he hung there. 37And they put a sign above his head, "This is Jesus, the King of the Jews."

38Two robbers were also crucified there that morning, one on either side of him. 39And the people passing by hurled abuse, shaking their heads at him and saying,

27:35 Ps 22:18

27:38 Isa 53:12

27:39 Ps 22:7,8

27:21 when the governor asked again, implied.

27:21 Crowds are fickle. If they loved Jesus on Sunday because they thought he was going to inaugurate his Kingdom, they could easily hate him on Friday when his power appeared broken. In the face of the mass uprising against Jesus, his friends were afraid to speak up.

27:21 Faced with a clear choice, the people chose Barabbas, a revolutionary and murderer, over the Son of God. Faced with the same choice today, people are still choosing "Barabbas." They would rather have the tangible force of human power than the salvation offered by the Son of God.

27:24 At first Pilate hesitated to give the religious leaders permission to crucify Jesus. He thought they were simply jealous of a teacher who was more popular with the people than they were. But when the Jews threatened to report Pilate to Caesar (John 19:12), he became afraid. Historical records indicate that the Jews had already threatened to lodge a formal complaint against Pilate

for his stubborn flouting of their traditions—and such a complaint would most likely have led to his recall by Rome. His job was in jeopardy. The Roman government could not afford to put large numbers of troops in all the regions under their control, so one of Pilate's main duties was to do whatever was necessary to maintain peace.

27:24 In making no decision, Pilate made the decision to let the crowds crucify Jesus. Although he washed his hands, the guilt remained. Washing your hands of a tough situation doesn't cancel your guilt. It merely gives you a false sense of peace. Don't make excuses—take responsibility for the decisions you make.

27:29 People still make fun of Christians for their faith. But believers can take courage that Jesus himself was mocked as greatly as anyone. Taunting may hurt our feelings, but we should never let it change our faith (see 5:11, 12).

27:40
Mt 26:61
Jn 2:19

40"So! You can destroy the Temple and build it again in three days, can you? Well, then, come on down from the cross if you are the Son of God!"

41, 42, 43And the chief priests and Jewish leaders also mocked him. "He saved others," they scoffed, "but he can't save himself! So you are the King of Israel, are you? Come down from the cross and we'll believe you! He trusted God—let God show his approval by delivering him! Didn't he say, 'I am God's Son'?"

44And the robbers also threw the same in his teeth.

Jesus dies on the cross
(236/Mark 15:33–41; Luke 23:44–49; John 19:28–37)

27:45
Isa 50:3
Amos 8:9
Mk 15:33-41
Lk 23:44-49
27:46
Ps 22:1

45That afternoon, the whole earth was covered with darkness for three hours, from noon until three o'clock.

46About three o'clock, Jesus shouted, "Eli, Eli, lama sabachthani?" which means, "My God, my God, why have you forsaken me?"

27:48
Ps 69:21
Jn 19:29,30

47Some of the bystanders misunderstood and thought he was calling for Elijah. 48One of them ran and filled a sponge with sour wine and put it on a stick and held it up to him to drink. 49But the rest said, "Leave him alone. Let's see whether Elijah will come and save him."

27:51
Ex 26:31-33
Heb 10:19,20

50Then Jesus shouted out again, dismissed his spirit, and died.

27:52
Ps 69:20

51And look! The curtain secluding the Holiest Place in the Temple was split apart from top to bottom; and the earth shook, and rocks broke, 52and tombs opened, and

27:45 *earth,* or "land."   27:51 *secluding the Holiest Place,* implied.

THE WAY OF THE CROSS   The Roman soldiers took Jesus to the armory (a part of the Praetorium) and mocked him, dressing him with a scarlet robe and a crown of thorns. They then led him to the crucifixion site outside the city. He was so weakened by his beatings that he could not carry his cross, and a man from Cyrene was forced to carry it to Golgotha.

27:34 The wine was offered to Jesus to help deaden his pain. But Jesus refused—he would suffer fully conscious and with a clear mind.

27:35 The soldiers customarily took the clothing of those they crucified. These soldiers threw dice and divided Jesus' clothing among themselves, fulfilling the prophecy in Psalm 22:18.

27:44 Later one of these robbers repented. Jesus promised he would join him in Paradise (Luke 23:39–43).

27:45 We do not know how this darkness occurred, but it is clear that God caused it. Nature testified to the gravity of Jesus' death, while Jesus' friends and enemies alike fell silent in the encircling gloom. The darkness on that Friday afternoon was both physical and spiritual.

27:46 Jesus was not questioning God; he was quoting the first line of Psalm 22—a deep expression of the anguish he felt when he took on the sins of the world and thus was separated from his Father. *This* was what Jesus dreaded as he prayed to God in the garden to take the cup from him (26:39). The physical agony was horrible, but even worse was the period of spiritual separation from God. Jesus suffered this double death so that we would never have to experience eternal separation from God.

27:47 The bystanders misinterpreted Jesus' words and thought he was calling for Elijah. Because Elijah ascended into heaven without dying (2 Kings 2:11), they thought he would return again to rescue them from great trouble (Malachi 4:5). At their annual Passover feast, each family set an extra place for Elijah in expectation of his return.

27:51 The Temple had three main parts—the courts, the Holy Place (where only the priests could enter), and the Holy of Holies (where only the High Priest could enter, and then only once a year, to atone for the sins of the nation—Leviticus 16:1–35). The curtain separating the Holy Place from the Holy of Holies was split in two at Christ's death, symbolizing that the barrier between God and people was removed. Now all people are free to approach God because of Christ's sacrifice for our sins (see Hebrews 9:1–14; 10:19–22).

27:52, 53 Christ's death was accompanied by at least four miraculous events: darkness, the splitting of the curtain in the Temple, an earthquake, and dead people rising from their tombs. Jesus' death, therefore, could not have gone unnoticed. Everyone knew something significant had happened.

many godly men and women who had died came back to life again. 53After Jesus' resurrection, they left the cemetery and went into Jerusalem, and appeared to many people there.

54The soldiers at the crucifixion and their sergeant were terribly frightened by the earthquake and all that happened. They exclaimed, "Surely this was God's Son."

27:54
Ex 20:18-20

55And many women who had come down from Galilee with Jesus to care for him were watching from a distance. 56Among them were Mary Magdalene and Mary the mother of James and Joseph, and the mother of James and John (the sons of Zebedee).

27:56
Lk 8:2

Jesus is laid in the tomb
(237/Mark 15:42–47; Luke 23:50–56; John 19:38–42)

57When evening came, a rich man from Arimathea named Joseph, one of Jesus' followers, 58went to Pilate and asked for Jesus' body. And Pilate issued an order to release it to him. 59Joseph took the body and wrapped it in a clean linen cloth, 60and placed it in his own new rock-hewn tomb, and rolled a great stone across the entrance as he left. 61Both Mary Magdalene and the other Mary were sitting nearby watching.

27:57
Mk 15:42-47
Lk 23:50-56
Jn 19:38-42

27:60
Isa 53:9

Guards are posted at the tomb
(238)

62The next day—at the close of the first day of the Passover ceremonies—the chief priests and Pharisees went to Pilate, 63and told him, "Sir, that liar once said, 'After three days I will come back to life again.' 64So we request an order from you sealing the tomb until the third day, to prevent his disciples from coming and stealing his body and then telling everyone he came back to life! If that happens we'll be worse off than we were at first."

65"Use your own Temple police," Pilate told them. "They can guard it safely enough."

66So they sealed the stone and posted guards to protect it from intrusion.

27:62
Ps 2:1-6

27:63
Mt 16:21; 17:23
20:19
Mk 8:31; 10:34
Lk 9:22; 18:33
Jn 2:19
2 Cor 6:8

27:66
Dan 6:17

27:54 God's Son, or, "a godly man."   **27:62** at the close of the first day of the Passover ceremonies, implied; literally, "on the morrow, which is after the Preparation."

"Father, forgive these people, for they don't know what they are doing."	Luke 23:34	**THE SEVEN LAST WORDS OF JESUS ON THE CROSS**
"Today you will be with me in Paradise. This is a solemn promise."	Luke 23:43	
Speaking to John and Mary, "He is your son. . . . She is your mother!"	John 19:26, 27	
"My God, my God, why have you forsaken me?"	Matthew 27:46; Mark 15:34	
"I'm thirsty."	John 19:28	
"It is finished."	John 19:30	
"Father, I commit my spirit to you."	Luke 23:46	

The statements that Jesus made from the cross have been treasured by all who have followed him as Lord. They demonstrate both his manhood and his divinity. They also capture the last moments of all that Jesus went through to gain our forgiveness.

27:57, 58 Joseph of Arimathea was a secret follower of Jesus. He was a religious leader, an honored member of the Supreme Court. In the past, Joseph had been afraid to speak against the religious leaders who opposed Jesus; now he was bold, courageously asking to take Jesus' body from the cross and bury it. The disciples who publicly followed Jesus had fled, but this Jewish leader, who followed Jesus in secret, came forward and did what was right.

27:60 The tomb where Jesus was laid was probably a man-made cave cut out of one of the many limestone hills in the area. These caves were often large enough to walk into.

27:64 The religious leaders took Jesus' resurrection claims more

seriously than the disciples did. The disciples didn't remember Jesus' teaching about his resurrection (20:17–19); but the religious leaders did. Because of his claims, they were almost as afraid of Jesus after his death as when he was alive. They tried to take every precaution that his body would remain in the tomb.

27:66 The Pharisees were so afraid of Jesus' predictions about his resurrection that they made sure the tomb was thoroughly sealed and guarded. Because the tomb was hewn out of rock in the side of a hill, there was only one entrance. The tomb was sealed by stringing a cord across the stone that was rolled over the entrance. The cord was sealed at each end with clay. But the religious leaders took a further precaution, asking that guards be

Jesus rises from the dead
(239/Mark 16:1–8; Luke 24:1–12; John 20:1–9)

28:1
Mt 27:56
Mk 16:1-11
Lk 24:1-11
Jn 20:1,2,11-18

28:3
Dan 7:9; 10:5,6
Rev 1:16

28:5
Rev 1:17,18

28:6
Mt 12:40; 16:21
17:23; 20:19

28:7
Mt 26:32
Mk 16:7

28:10
Jn 20:17
Rom 8:29
Heb 2:11

28 Early on Sunday morning, as the new day was dawning, Mary Magdalene and the other Mary went out to the tomb.

²Suddenly there was a great earthquake; for an angel of the Lord came down from heaven and rolled aside the stone and sat on it. ³His face shone like lightning and his clothing was a brilliant white. ⁴The guards shook with fear when they saw him, and fell into a dead faint.

⁵Then the angel spoke to the women. "Don't be frightened!" he said. "I know you are looking for Jesus, who was crucified, ⁶but he isn't here! For he has come back to life again, just as he said he would. Come in and see where his body was lying. . . . ⁷And now, go quickly and tell his disciples that he has risen from the dead, and that he is going to Galilee to meet them there. That is my message to them."

Jesus appears to the women
(241)

⁸The women ran from the tomb, badly frightened, but also filled with joy, and rushed to find the disciples to give them the angel's message. ⁹And as they were running, suddenly Jesus was there in front of them!

"Good morning!" he said. And they fell to the ground before him, holding his feet and worshiping him.

¹⁰Then Jesus said to them, "Don't be frightened! Go tell my brothers to leave at once for Galilee, to meet me there."

28:9 *Good morning,* literally, "All hail!"

**HOW JESUS'
TRIAL WAS
ILLEGAL**

1. Even before the trial began, it had been determined that Jesus must die (John 11:50; Mark 14:1). There was no "innocent before being proven guilty" approach.
2. False witnesses were sought to testify against Jesus (Matthew 26:59). Usually the religious leaders went through an elaborate system of screening witnesses to insure justice.
3. No defense for Jesus was sought or allowed (Luke 22:67–71).
4. The trial was conducted by night (Luke 22:53–55), which was illegal according to the religious leaders' own laws.
5. The High Priest put Jesus under oath, but then incriminated him for what he said (Matthew 26:63–66).
6. Cases involving such serious charges were to be tried only in the Sanhedrin's regular meeting place, not in the High Priest's palace (Luke 22:54).

The religious leaders were not interested in giving Jesus a fair trial. In their minds, Jesus had to die. This blind obsession led them to pervert the justice they were appointed to protect. Here are many examples of the actions taken by the religious leaders that were illegal according to their own laws.

---

placed at the tomb's entrance. With such precautions, the only way the tomb could be empty would be for Jesus to rise from the dead. The Pharisees failed to understand that no rock, seal, guard, or army could prevent the Son of God from rising again.

28:1 The other Mary was not Jesus' mother. She could have been the wife of Cleopas (John 19:25). Or, if she was the mother of James and John, she may have been Jesus' aunt.

28:5, 6 Jesus' resurrection is the key to the Christian faith. Why? (1) "Just as he said," Jesus rose from the dead. We can be confident, therefore, that he will accomplish all he has promised. (2) Jesus' bodily resurrection shows that the living Christ is ruler of God's eternal kingdom, not a fale prophet or imposter. (3) We can be certain of our resurrection because he was resurrected. Death is not the end—there is future life. (4) The power that brought Jesus back to life is available to us to bring our spiritually dead selves back to life. (5) The resurrection is the basis for the church's witness to the world.

28:5–7 The angel who announced the Good News of the

resurrection to the women gave them four messages: (1) *Don't be frightened.* The reality of the resurrection brings joy, not fear. When you are afraid, remember the empty tomb. (2) *He isn't here.* Jesus is not dead and is not to be looked for among the dead. He is alive, with his people. (3) *Come in and see.* The women could check the evidence themselves. The tomb was empty then, and is empty today. The resurrection is a historical fact. (4) *Go quickly and tell.* They were to spread the joy of the resurrection. We too are to spread the Good News about Jesus' resurrection.

28:10 By "brothers," Jesus meant his disciples. This showed that he had forgiven them, even after they had denied and deserted him. Their relationship would now be even stronger than before.

28:10 Jesus told the women to pass a message on to the disciples—that he would meet them in Galilee, as he had previously told them (Mark 14:28). But the disciples, afraid of the religious leaders, stayed hidden behind locked doors in Jerusalem (John 20:19). So Jesus met them first there (Luke 24:36) and then later in Galilee (John 21).

Religious leaders bribe the guards
(242)

11As the women were on the way into the city, some of the Temple police who had been guarding the tomb went to the chief priests and told them what had happened. 12, 13A meeting of all the Jewish leaders was called, and it was decided to bribe the police to say they had all been asleep when Jesus' disciples came during the night and stole his body.

14"If the governor hears about it," the Council promised, "we'll stand up for you and everything will be all right."

15So the police accepted the bribe and said what they were told to. Their story spread widely among the Jews, and is still believed by them to this very day.

Jesus gives the Great Commission
(248/Mark 16:15–18)

16Then the eleven disciples left for Galilee, going to the mountain where Jesus had said they would find him. 17There they met him and worshiped him—but some of them weren't sure it really was Jesus!

28:18
Mt 26:64
Eph 1:19-22
1 Pet 3:22

18He told his disciples, "I have been given all authority in heaven and earth.
19Therefore go and make disciples in all the nations, baptizing them into the name of the Father and of the Son and of the Holy Spirit, 20and then teach these new disciples to obey all the commands I have given you; and be sure of this—that I am with you always, even to the end of the world."

28:19
Lk 24:47
Acts 2:38,41,42

28:20
Mt 1:23; 18:20
Jn 14:17-20
Heb 13:5

28:19 *in all the nations*, literally, "of all nations."   **28:20** *world*, or, "age."

28:11–15 Jesus' resurrection was already causing a great stir in Jerusalem. A group of women was moving quickly through the streets, looking for the disciples to tell them the amazing news that Jesus was alive. At the same time, a group of religious leaders was plotting how to cover up the resurrection.

Today there is still a great stir over the resurrection, and there are still only two choices—to believe that Jesus rose from the dead, or to be closed to the truth, denying it, ignoring it, or rationalizing it away.

28:18 God gave Jesus authority over heaven and earth. On the basis of that authority, Jesus told his disciples to make more disciples as they preached, baptized, and taught. With this same authority, Jesus still commands us to tell others the Good News and make them disciples for the Kingdom.

28:18–20 When someone is dying or leaving us, his last words are very important. Jesus left the disciples with these last words of instruction: they were under his authority; they were to make more disciples; they were to baptize and teach them to obey him; he would be with them always. Whereas in previous missions Jesus had sent his disciples only to the Jews (10:5, 6), their mission from now on would be worldwide. Jesus is Lord of the earth, and he died for the sins of all people.

We are to go—whether it is next door or to another country—and make disciples. It is not an option, but a command to all who call Jesus "Lord." We are not all evangelists, but we have all received gifts that we can use in helping to fulfill the Great Commission. As we obey we have comfort in the knowledge that Jesus is always with us.

28:19 Jesus' words affirm the reality of the Trinity. Some people accuse theologians of making up the concept of the Trinity and reading it into Scripture. As we see here, the concept comes directly from Jesus himself. He did not say baptize them into the *names*, but into the *name* of the Father, Son, and Holy Spirit. The word *Trinity* does not occur in Scripture, but it well describes the three-in-one nature of the Father, Son, and Holy Spirit.

28:19 The disciples were to baptize people because baptism unites a believer with Jesus Christ in his death to sin and resurrection to new life. Baptism shows submission to Christ and a willingness to live God's way.

28:20 How is Jesus present with us? Jesus was with the disciples physically until he ascended into heaven, and then spiritually through the Holy Spirit (Acts 1:4). The Holy Spirit would be Jesus' presence that would never leave them (John 14:26). Jesus continues to be with us today through his Spirit.

28:20 The Old Testament prophecies and genealogies in the book of Matthew present Jesus' credentials for being King of the world—not a military or political leader as the disciples had originally hoped, but a spiritual King who can overcome all evil and reign in the heart of every person. If we refuse to serve the King faithfully, we are disloyal subjects, fit only to be banished from the Kingdom. We must make Jesus King of our lives and worship him as our Savior, King, and Lord.

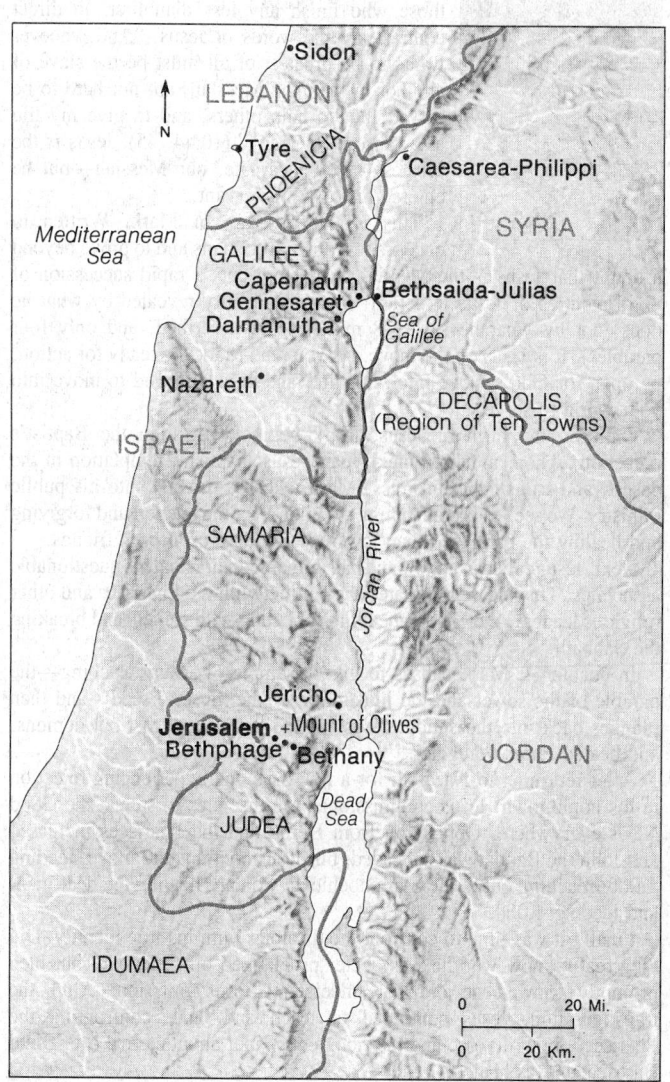

Of the four Gospels, Mark's narrative is the most chronological—that is, most of the stories are positioned in the order they actually occurred. Though the shortest of the four, the Gospel of Mark contains the most events; it is action-packed. Most of this action centers in Galilee, where Jesus began his ministry. Capernaum served as his base of operation (1:21; 2:1; 9:33), from which he would go out to cities like Bethsaida-Julias—where he healed a blind man (8:22ff); Gennesaret—where he performed many healings (6:53ff); Tyre and Sidon (to the far north)—where he cured many, cast out demons, and met the Syrophoenician woman (3:8; 7:24ff); and Caesarea-Philippi—where Peter declared him to be the Messiah (8:27ff). After his ministry in Galilee and the surrounding regions, Jesus headed south for Jerusalem (10:1). Before going there, Jesus told his disciples three times that he would be crucified there and then come back to life (8:31; 9:31; 10:33, 34).

MARK

VITAL STATISTICS

PURPOSE:
To present the person, work, and teachings of Jesus

AUTHOR:
John Mark. He was not one of the twelve disciples but he accompanied Paul on his first missionary journey (Acts 13:13).

TO WHOM WRITTEN:
The Christians in Rome, where he wrote the Gospel

DATE WRITTEN:
Between A.D. 55 and 65

SETTING:
The Roman Empire under Tiberius Caesar. The Empire, with its common language and excellent transportation and communication systems, was ripe to hear Jesus' message, which spread quickly from nation to nation.

KEY VERSE:
"For even I, the Messiah, am not here to be served, but to help others, and to give my life as a ransom for many" (10:45).

KEY PEOPLE:
Jesus, the twelve disciples, Pilate, the Jewish religious leaders

KEY PLACES:
Capernaum, Nazareth, Caesarea Philippi, Jericho, Bethany, Mount of Olives, Jerusalem, Golgotha

SPECIAL FEATURES:
Mark was the first Gospel written. The other Gospels quote all but 31 verses of Mark. Mark records more miracles than does any other Gospel.

EVERYONE wants to be a winner. Losers are those who finish any less than first. In direct contrast are the words of Jesus, "And whoever wants to be greatest of all must be the slave of all. For even I, the Messiah, am not here to be served, but to help others, and to give my life as a ransom for many" (10:44, 45). Jesus *is* the greatest—God incarnate, our Messiah—but he entered history as a servant.

This is the message of Mark. Written to encourage Roman Christians and to prove beyond a doubt that Jesus is the Messiah, Mark presents a rapid succession of vivid pictures of Jesus in action—his true identity revealed by what he does, not by what he says (18 miracles are described, and only four parables). It is Jesus on the move. As you read Mark, be ready for action, be open for God's move into your life, and be challenged to move into your world to serve.

Omitting the birth of Jesus, Mark begins with John the Baptist's preaching. Then, moving quickly past Jesus' baptism, temptation in the desert, and call of the disciples, Mark takes us directly into his public ministry. We see Jesus confronting a demon, healing a leper, and forgiving and healing the paralyzed man lowered into his presence by friends.

Next, Jesus called Matthew and had dinner with him and his questionable associates. This incident initiated the conflict with the Pharisees and other religious leaders who condemned him for eating with sinners and breaking the Sabbath.

In chapter 4, Mark pauses to give a sample of Jesus' teaching—the parable of the sower and the illustration of the mustard seed—and then plunges back into the action. Jesus calmed the waves, cast out demons, and healed Jairus' daughter.

After returning to Nazareth for a few days and experiencing rejection in his home town, Jesus commissioned the disciples to spread the Good News everywhere. Opposition from Herod and the Pharisees increased and John the Baptist was beheaded, but Jesus continued to move, feeding 5,000, reaching out to the Syrophoenician woman, healing the deaf man, and feeding 4,000.

Finally it was time to confront the disciples with his true identity. Did they really know who he was? Peter proclaimed him Messiah, but then promptly showed he did not understand Jesus' mission. After the transfiguration, Jesus continued to teach and heal, confronting the Pharisees about divorce and the rich young ruler about eternal life. Blind Bartimaeus was healed.

Events rapidly move toward a climax. The Last Supper, the betrayal, the crucifixion, and the resurrection are dramatically portrayed, along with more examples of Jesus' teachings. Mark shows us Jesus—moving, serving, sacrificing, and saving!

Tiberius Caesar becomes Emperor 14	John's ministry begins 26	Jesus begins his ministry 26/27	Jesus chooses Twelve disciples 28	Jesus feeds 5,000 29	Jesus is crucified, rises again, and ascends 30

THE BLUEPRINT

A. BIRTH AND PREPARATION OF JESUS, THE SERVANT (1:1–13)

Jesus did not arrive unannounced or unexpected. The Old Testament prophets had clearly predicted the coming of a great One, sent by God himself, who would offer salvation and eternal peace to Israel and the entire world. Then came John the Baptist, who announced that the long-awaited Messiah had finally come, and would soon be among the people. In God's work in the world today, Jesus does not come unannounced, or unexpected. Yet many still reject him. We have the witness of the Bible to show the way, but some choose to ignore it as they ignored John the Baptist in his day.

B. MESSAGE AND MINISTRY OF JESUS, THE SERVANT (1:14—13:37)
1. Jesus' ministry in Galilee
2. Jesus' ministry beyond Galilee
3. Jesus' ministry in Jerusalem

Jesus had all the power of almighty God—he raised the dead, gave sight to the blind, restored deformed bodies, and quieted stormy seas. But with all this power, Jesus came to mankind as a servant. We can use his life as a pattern for how to live today. As Jesus served God and others, so should we.

C. DEATH AND RESURRECTION OF JESUS, THE SERVANT (14:1—16:20)

Jesus came as a servant, so many did not recognize or acknowledge him as the Messiah. We, too, must be careful we don't reject God or his will because it doesn't quite fit our image of how God should be.

MEGATHEMES

THEME	EXPLANATION	IMPORTANCE
Jesus Christ	Jesus Christ alone is the Son of God. In Mark, Jesus demonstrates his divinity by overcoming disease, demons, and death. Although he had the power to be king of the earth, Jesus chose to obey the Father and die for us.	When Jesus rose from the dead, he proved that he was God, that he could forgive sin, and that he has the power to change our lives. By trusting in him for forgiveness, we can begin a new life with him as our guide.
Servant	As the "Messiah," Jesus fulfilled the prophecies of the Old Testament by coming to earth. He did not come as a conquering king; he came as a servant. He helped mankind by telling them about God and healing them. Even more, by giving his life as a sacrifice for sin, he did the ultimate act of service.	Because of Jesus' example, we should be willing to serve God and others. Real greatness in Christ's kingdom is shown by service and sacrifice. Ambition, love of power or position, should not be our motive; instead, we should do God's work because we love him.
Miracles	Mark records more of Jesus' miracles than sermons. Jesus is clearly a man of power and action, not just words. Jesus did miracles to convince the people who he was and to teach the disciples his true identity as God.	The more convinced we become that Jesus is God, the more we will see his power and his love. His mighty works show us he is able to save anyone regardless of their past. His miracles of forgiveness bring healing, wholeness, and changed lives to those who trust him.
Spreading the Gospel	Jesus directed his public ministry to the Jews first. When the Jewish leaders opposed him, Jesus also went to the non-Jewish world, healing and preaching. Roman soldiers, Syrians, and other Gentiles heard the Good News. Many believed and followed him. Jesus' final message to his disciples challenged them to go into all the world and preach the gospel of salvation.	Jesus crossed national, racial, and economic barriers to spread his Good News. Jesus' message of faith and forgiveness is for the whole world not just our church, neighborhood, or nation. We must reach out beyond our own people and needs to fulfill the worldwide vision of Jesus Christ that people everywhere might hear this great message and be saved from sin and death.

A. BIRTH AND PREPARATION OF JESUS, THE SERVANT (1:1–13)

Mark, the shortest of the four Gospels, opens with Jesus' baptism and temptation. Moving right into action, Mark quickly prepares us for Christ's ministry. The Gospel of Mark is concise, straightforward, and chronological.

John the Baptist prepares the way for Jesus
(16/Matthew 3:1–12; Luke 3:1–18)

1 Here begins the wonderful story of Jesus the Messiah, the Son of God. ²In the book written by the prophet Isaiah, God announced that he would send his Son to earth, and that a special messenger would arrive first to prepare the world for his coming.

³"This messenger will live out in the barren wilderness," Isaiah said, "and will proclaim that everyone must straighten out his life to be ready for the Lord's arrival."

⁴This messenger was John the Baptist. He lived in the wilderness and taught that all should be baptized as a public announcement of their decision to turn their backs on sin, so that God could forgive them. ⁵People from Jerusalem and from all over Judea traveled out into the Judean wastelands to see and hear John, and when they confessed their sins he baptized them in the Jordan River. ⁶His clothes were woven

1:1
Ps 2:7
Mt 3:1-6,11
Lk 1:35
3:1-6,16
Jn 1:34
Rom 8:3
1 Jn 4:15

1:2,3
Isa 40:3
Mal 3:1
Jn 1:23

1:4
Acts 19:4

1:6
Lev 11:22

1:2 *his Son*, implied.   **1:4** *so that God could forgive them*, literally, "preaching a baptism of repentance for the forgiveness of sins."

1:1 When you experience the excitement of a big event, you naturally want to tell someone. Telling the story can bring back that original thrill as you relive the experience. Reading Mark's first words, you can sense his excitement. Picture yourself in the crowd as Jesus heals and teaches. Imagine yourself as one of the disciples. Respond to his words of love and encouragement. And remember that Jesus came for every man and woman, for us who live today as well as those who lived two thousand years ago.

1:1 Mark was not one of the twelve disciples of Jesus, but he probably knew Jesus personally. He wrote his Gospel in the form of a fast-paced story, like a popular novel. The book portrays Jesus as a man who backed up his words with action that constantly proved who he is—the Son of God. Because he wrote the Gospel for Christians in Rome where many gods were worshiped, Mark wanted them to know that Jesus is *the one true* Son of God.

1:2 Why did Jesus come at this time in history? The entire civilized world was relatively peaceful under Roman rule, travel was easy, and there was a common language. The news about Jesus' life, death, and resurrection could spread quickly throughout the vast Roman Empire.

In Israel, common men and women were ready for Jesus too. There had been no God-sent prophets for 400 years, since the days of Malachi (who wrote the last book of the Old Testament). There was growing anticipation that a great prophet, or the Messiah mentioned in the Old Testament Scriptures, would soon come (see Luke 3:15).

1:2, 3 Isaiah was one of the greatest prophets of the Old Testament. The second half of the book of Isaiah is devoted to the promise of salvation. Isaiah wrote about the coming of the Messiah, Jesus Christ, and the man who would announce his coming, John the Baptist. John's call for people to "straighten out" their lives meant that they should give up their selfish way of living, renounce sins, seek God's forgiveness, and establish a relationship with almighty God by believing and obeying his words as found in the Bible (Isaiah 1:18–20; 57:15).

1:2, 3 Mark 1:2, 3 is a composite quotation, taken first from Malachi 3:1 and then from Isaiah 40:3. Isaiah is cited first because it was customary for biblical writers to credit the more prominent prophet. The earliest manuscripts read "Isaiah"; later manuscripts read "the prophets."

1:2, 3 Hundreds of years earlier, the prophet Isaiah had predicted that John the Baptist and Jesus would come. How did he know? God promised Isaiah that a Deliverer would come to Israel, and

that a voice crying in the wilderness would prepare the way for him. Isaiah's words comforted many people as they looked forward to the Messiah, and knowing that God keeps his promises should comfort us too.

1:4 Why does the Gospel of Mark begin with the story of John the Baptist, while not mentioning the story of Jesus' birth? Important Roman officials of this day were always preceded by an announcer or herald. When the herald arrived in town, the people knew that someone of prominence would soon arrive. Since Mark's audience was primarily Roman Christians, he began his book with John the Baptist, the one whose mission it was to announce the coming of Jesus, the most important man who ever lived. Roman Christians wouldn't have been as interested in Jesus' birth as they would be in this herald.

1:4 John chose to live in the wilderness: (1) to get away from distractions so he could hear God's instructions; (2) to capture the undivided attention of the people; (3) to symbolize a sharp break with the hypocrisy of the religious leaders who preferred their luxurious homes and positions of authority over doing God's work; (4) to fulfill Old Testament prophecies which said that John would be a voice "crying in the wilderness" (Isaiah 40:3).

1:4 In John's ministry, baptism was a visible sign that a person had decided to change his or her life, giving up a sinful and selfish way of living and turning to God. John took a known custom and gave it new meaning. The Jews often baptized non-Jews who had converted to Judaism. But to baptize a Jew as a sign of repentance was a radical departure from Jewish custom. The early church took baptism a step further, associating it with Jesus' death and resurrection (see, for example, 1 Peter 3:21).

1:5 The purpose of John's preaching was to prepare people to accept Jesus as God's Son. When John challenged the people to confess sin individually, he signaled the start of a new approach to having a relationship with God.

Is change needed in your life before you can hear and understand Jesus' message? People have to admit that they need forgiveness before they can accept forgiveness; thus true repentance must come before a person can have true faith in Jesus Christ. To prepare to receive Christ, we must repent, denouncing the world's dead-end attractions, sinful temptations, and harmful attitudes.

1:6 John's clothes were not the latest style of his day. He dressed much like the prophet Elijah (2 Kings 1:8) in order to distinguish himself from the religious leaders whose long flowing robes reflected their great pride in their position. John's striking

1:7
Jn 1:15

from camel's hair and he wore a leather belt; locusts and wild honey were his food. 7Here is a sample of his preaching:

1:8
Joel 2:28
Acts 2:4; 10:45
11:15,16

"Someone is coming soon who is far greater than I am, so much greater that I am not even worthy to be his slave. 8I baptize you with water but he will baptize you with God's Holy Spirit!"

John baptizes Jesus
(17/Matthew 3:13–17; Luke 3:21, 22)

1:9
Mt 3:13-17
Lk 3:21,22
Jn 1:32-34

9Then one day Jesus came from Nazareth in Galilee, and was baptized by John there in the Jordan River. 10The moment Jesus came up out of the water, he saw the heavens open and the Holy Spirit in the form of a dove descending on him, 11and a voice from heaven said, "You are my beloved Son; you are my Delight."

Satan tempts Jesus in the wilderness
(18/Matthew 4:1–11; Luke 4:1–13)

1:12
Mt 4:1-11
Lk 4:1-13
1 Tim 3:16

12, 13Immediately the Holy Spirit urged Jesus into the desert. There, for forty days, alone except for desert animals, he was subjected to Satan's temptations to sin. And afterwards the angels came and cared for him.

1:7 *I am not even worthy to be his slave,* literally, "Whose shoes I am not worthy to unloose." **1:8** *with water,* or "in water." The Greek word is not clear on this controversial point. *with God's Holy Spirit,* or "in God's Holy Spirit"; the Greek is not clear. **1:12, 13** *afterwards,* implied in parallel passages.

---

appearance reflected his striking message.

1:7, 8 Although John was regarded as the first genuine prophet in 400 years, Jesus the Messiah would be infinitely greater than he. John was pointing out how insignificant he was compared to the One who was coming. He was not even worthy of doing the most menial tasks for him, like untying his shoes. What John began, Jesus finished. What John prepared, Jesus fulfilled.

1:8 John said Jesus would baptize with the Holy Spirit; Jesus would send the Holy Spirit to live within each believer. John's baptism with water prepared a person to receive Christ's message. It demonstrated humility and willingness to turn from sin. This was the *beginning* of the spiritual process.

When Jesus baptizes with the Holy Spirit, however, the entire person will be transformed by the Holy Spirit's power. This baptism is the result of the completed work of Jesus.

1:9 If John's baptism was only for the repentance of sin, why was Jesus baptized? While even the greatest prophets (Isaiah, Jeremiah, Ezekiel) had to confess their sinfulness and need for repentance, Jesus didn't need to admit sin—he was sinless. Although it was unnecessary, Jesus was baptized for the following reasons: (1) to acknowledge his commitment to his mission to bring the message of salvation to all people; (2) to demonstrate that he truly was God's Son and that God approved and endorsed his mission; (3) to officially begin his public ministry (John 1:31–34); (4) to identify with our humanness and sin; (5) to give us an example to follow. John's baptism was different than Christian baptism in the church.

1:9 Jesus grew up in Nazareth, where he had lived since he was a young boy (Matthew 2:22, 23). Nazareth was a small town in Galilee, located about halfway between the Sea of Galilee and the Mediterranean Sea. The city was despised and avoided by many Jews because it was an outpost for Roman troops in the region. Devout Jews hated the Romans for making them pay taxes and for showing little respect for God.

1:10, 11 The Holy Spirit descended dovelike upon Jesus and the voice from heaven proclaimed the Father's approval of Jesus as his divine Son. Here we see all three members of the Trinity together—the Father, Son, and Holy Spirit.

1:12, 13 Jesus left the crowds and went into the desert, where he was tempted by Satan. Temptation is bad for us only when we give in. Times of inner testing should not be hated and resented, because through them our character can be strengthened and

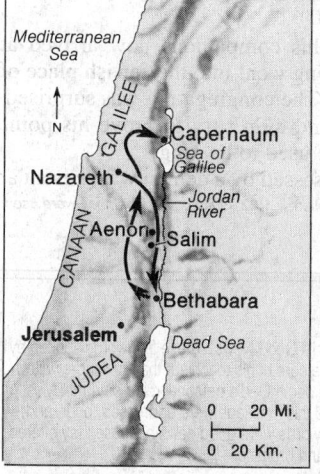

JESUS BEGINS HIS MINISTRY
When Jesus came from his home in Nazareth to begin his ministry, he first took two steps in preparation— baptism by John in the Jordan River, and temptation by Satan in the rough wilderness of Judea. After the temptations, Jesus returned to Galilee and later set up his home base in Capernaum.

God can teach us valuable lessons. When you face Satan and must deal with his temptations and the turmoil he brings, remember Jesus. He used God's Word against Satan and won. You can do the same.

1:12, 13 Satan is an angel who rebelled against God. He is real, not symbolic, and is constantly working against God and those who obey him. He tempted Eve in the garden and persuaded her to sin; he tempted Jesus in the wilderness and did not persuade him to fall. To be tempted is not a sin. Tempting others or giving in to temptation is sin. For a more detailed account of Jesus' temptation read Matthew 4:1–11.

1:12, 13 To identify fully with human beings, Jesus had to endure Satan's temptations. Because Jesus faced temptations and overcame them, he can assist us in two important ways: (1) as an example of how to face temptation without sinning, and (2) as our helper who knows just what we need, since he went through the same experience. (See Hebrews 4:15, 16 for more on Jesus and temptation.)

B. MESSAGE AND MINISTRY OF JESUS, THE SERVANT (1:14—13:37)

Mark tells us dramatic, action-packed stories. He gives us the most vivid account of Christ's activities. He features facts and actions, rather than teachings. Seeing Jesus live his life is the perfect example of how we should live our lives today.

1. Jesus' ministry in Galilee

Jesus preaches in Galilee
(30/Matthew 4:12–17; Luke 4:14, 15; John 4:43–45)

¹⁴Later on, after John was arrested by King Herod, Jesus went to Galilee to preach God's Good News.

¹⁵"At last the time has come!" he announced. "God's Kingdom is near! Turn from your sins and act on this glorious news!"

1:14
Mt 4:12,17,23
Lk 4:14,15

1:15
Dan 2:44; 9:24,25
Gal 4:4

Four fishermen follow Jesus
(33/Matthew 4:18–22)

¹⁶One day as Jesus was walking along the shores of the Sea of Galilee, he saw Simon and his brother Andrew fishing with nets, for they were commercial fishermen.

¹⁷Jesus called out to them, "Come, follow me! And I will make you fishermen for the souls of men!" ¹⁸At once they left their nets and went along with him.

¹⁹A little farther up the beach, he saw Zebedee's sons, James and John, in a boat mending their nets. ²⁰He called them too, and immediately they left their father Zebedee in the boat with the hired men and went with him.

1:16
Mt 4:18-22
Lk 5:1-11
Jn 1:35-42

1:18
Mt 19:27

Jesus teaches with great authority
(34/Luke 4:31–37)

²¹Jesus and his companions now arrived at the town of Capernaum and on Saturday morning went into the Jewish place of worship—the synagogue—where he preached. ²²The congregation was surprised at his sermon because he spoke as an authority, and didn't try to prove his points by quoting others—quite unlike what they were used to hearing!

²³A man possessed by a demon was present and began shouting, ²⁴"Why are you

1:21
Lk 4:31-41

1:22
Mt 7:28

1:24
Mt 8:29
Jn 6:69
Acts 3:14
Jas 2:19

1:14 *King Herod,* implied.   **1:22** *Quite unlike what they were used to hearing,* literally, "not as the scribes."

1:14, 15 What is God's Good News? These first words spoken by Jesus in Mark give the core of his teaching: that the long-awaited Messiah has come to begin God's personal reign on earth. Most of the people who heard this message were oppressed, poor, and without hope. Jesus' words were good news because they offered freedom, blessings, and promise.

1:16 Fishing was a major industry around the Sea of Galilee. Fishing with nets was the most common method. Capernaum, which became Jesus' new home (Matthew 4:12, 13), was the largest of more than 30 fishing villages around the sea at that time.

1:16–20 We often assume that Jesus' disciples were great men of faith from the first time they met Jesus. But they had to grow in their faith just as all believers do (Mark 14:48–50, 66–72; John 14:1–9; 20:26–29). This is apparently not the only time Jesus called Peter, James, and John to follow him (see Luke 5:1–11 and John 1:35–42 for two other times). It took time for Jesus' call and his message to get through, but the important thing is this: though the disciples had much growing to do, they *followed.*

1:21 Because the Temple in Jerusalem was too far for many Jews to travel to for regular worship, many towns had synagogues which served both as places of worship and as schools. Beginning in the days of Ezra, about 450 B.C., a group of ten Jewish families could start up a synagogue. There, during the week, Jewish boys were taught the Old Testament law and Jewish religion. Girls could not attend. Each Saturday, the Sabbath, the Jewish men would gather to listen to a rabbi teach from God's Word. Because there was no permanent rabbi or teacher, it was customary for the synagogue

leader to ask visiting teachers to speak. This is why Jesus often spoke in the towns he visited.

1:21 Jesus had recently moved to Capernaum from Nazareth (Matthew 4:12, 13). Capernaum was a thriving city with great wealth as well as great sin and decadence. Because it was the headquarters for many Roman troops, pagan influences from all over the Roman Empire were everywhere. This was an ideal place for Jesus to challenge both Jews and non-Jews with the Good News of God's kingdom.

1:22 The Jewish teachers often quoted from well-known rabbis to give their words more authority. But Jesus didn't need to do that. Since he was God, he knew exactly what the Scriptures said and meant. He was the ultimate authority.

1:23 What are demons? Demons are evil spirits who are ruled by Satan. They work to tempt people to sin. They were not created by Satan, because God is the Creator of all; rather they are fallen angels who joined Satan in his rebellion. In their degenerate state they can cause a person to become mute, deaf, blind, or insane. But in every case where they confronted Jesus, they lost their power. Thus God limits what they can do; they can do nothing without his permission. During Jesus' life on earth demons were allowed to be very active to show once and for all Christ's power and authority over them.

1:23ff Many psychologists dismiss accounts of demon possession as a primitive way to describe mental illness. Clearly, however, a demon controlled the man described here. Mark emphasizes Jesus' conflict with evil powers to show his superiority

bothering us, Jesus of Nazareth—have you come to destroy us demons? I know who you are—the holy Son of God!"

1:26
Mk 9:20

25Jesus curtly commanded the demon to say no more and to come out of the man. 26At that the evil spirit screamed and convulsed the man violently and left him. 27Amazement gripped the audience and they began discussing what had happened.

"What sort of new religion is this?" they asked excitedly. "Why, even evil spirits obey his orders!"

28The news of what he had done spread quickly through that entire area of Galilee.

Jesus heals Peter's mother-in-law and many others
(35/Matthew 8:14–17; Luke 4:38–41)

1:29
Mt 8:14-17
Lk 4:18-31

29, 30Then, leaving the synagogue, he and his disciples went over to Simon and Andrew's home, where they found Simon's mother-in-law sick in bed with a high fever. They told Jesus about her right away. 31He went to her bedside, and as he took her by the hand and helped her to sit up, the fever suddenly left, and she got up and prepared dinner for them!

1:32
Mt 8:16,17
Lk 4:40,41
1:34
Mk 3:12
Acts 16:16,17

32, 33By sunset the courtyard was filled with the sick and demon-possessed, brought to him for healing; and a huge crowd of people from all over the city of Capernaum gathered outside the door to watch. 34So Jesus healed great numbers of sick folk that evening and ordered many demons to come out of their victims. (But he refused to allow the demons to speak, because they knew who he was.)

Jesus preaches throughout Galilee
(36/Matthew 4:23–25; Luke 4:42–44)

1:35
Lk 4:42-44
Heb 5:7

35The next morning he was up long before daybreak and went out alone into the wilderness to pray.

36, 37Later, Simon and the others went out to find him, and told him, "Everyone is asking for you."

1:38
Isa 61:1

38But he replied, "We must go on to other towns as well, and give my message to them too, for that is why I came."

1:39
Mt 4:23

39So he traveled throughout the province of Galilee, preaching in the synagogues and releasing many from the power of demons.

---

over them, and so he records many stories about Jesus casting out demons. Jesus didn't have to conduct an elaborate exorcism ritual. His word was enough to send out the demons.

1:23, 24 The demon knew at once that Jesus was the Son of God. Mark, by including this event in his Gospel, was establishing Jesus' credentials, showing that even the underworld recognized Jesus as the Messiah.

1:29-31 Each Gospel writer had a slightly different perspective as he wrote; thus the comparable stories in the gospels often highlight different details. In Matthew, Jesus touched the woman's hand. In Mark, he helped her sit up. In Luke, he spoke to the fever and it left her. The accounts do not conflict. Each writer chose to emphasize different details of the story in order to highlight a certain characteristic of Jesus.

1:32, 33 The people came to Jesus in the evening as the sun was setting. This was the Sabbath (verse 21), their day of rest, lasting from sunset Friday to sunset Saturday. The Jewish leaders had proclaimed that it was against the law to be healed on the Sabbath (Matthew 12:10; Luke 13:14). The people didn't want to break this law or the Jewish law that prohibited traveling on the Sabbath, so they waited until sunset. After the sun went down, the crowds were free to find Jesus so he could heal them.

1:34 Why didn't Jesus want the demons to reveal who he was? (1) By commanding the demons to remain silent, he proved his

authority and power over them. (2) Jesus wanted the people to believe he was the Messiah because of what he said and did, not because of the demons' words. (3) He wanted to reveal his identity as the Messiah according to his timetable, not according to Satan's timetable. Satan wanted the people to follow Jesus based on his popularity, not because he was the Son of God.

1:35 Jesus took time to pray. Finding time to pray is not easy, but prayer is the vital link between us and God. Like Jesus, we must find time away from others to talk with God, even if we have to get up before daybreak to do it!

1:36, 37 "The others" probably refers to the disciples Jesus had already called—Andrew, James, John, and perhaps Philip and Nathanael.

1:39 The Romans divided the land of Israel into three separate regions: Galilee, Samaria, and Judea. Galilee was the northernmost region, an area about 60 miles long and 30 miles wide. Jesus spent much of his ministry in this area, an ideal place for him to teach because there were over 250 towns concentrated in this small area. Jesus didn't have far to walk to spread his great message.

Jesus heals a man with leprosy
(38/Matthew 8:1–4; Luke 5:12–16)

40Once a leper came and knelt in front of him and begged to be healed. "If you want to, you can make me well again," he pled.

41And Jesus, moved with pity, touched him and said, "I want to! Be healed!" 42Immediately the leprosy was gone—the man was healed!

43, 44Jesus then told him sternly, "Go and be examined immediately by the Jewish priest. Don't stop to speak to anyone along the way. Take along the offering prescribed by Moses for a leper who is healed, so that everyone will have proof that you are well again."

45But as the man went on his way he began to shout the good news that he was healed; as a result, such throngs soon surrounded Jesus that he couldn't publicly enter a city anywhere, but had to stay out in the barren wastelands. And people from everywhere came to him there.

1:40
Jer 32:17
Mt 8:2-4
Lk 5:12-16
1:41
Heb 2:17; 4:15

1:44
Lev 14:1-32
1:45
Mk 3:7; 6:31-34

Jesus heals a paralyzed man
(39/Matthew 9:1–8; Luke 5:17–26)

2 Several days later he returned to Capernaum, and the news of his arrival spread quickly through the city. 2Soon the house where he was staying was so packed with visitors that there wasn't room for a single person more, not even outside the door. And he preached the Word to them. 3Four men arrived carrying a paralyzed man on a stretcher. 4They couldn't get to Jesus through the crowd, so they dug through the clay roof above his head and lowered the sick man on his stretcher, right down in front of Jesus.

5When Jesus saw how strongly they believed that he would help, Jesus said to the sick man, "Son, your sins are forgiven!"

6But some of the Jewish religious leaders said to themselves as they sat there, 7"What? This is blasphemy! Does he think he is God? For only God can forgive sins."

8Jesus could read their minds and said to them at once, "Why does this bother you? 9, 10, 11I, the Messiah, have the authority on earth to forgive sins. But talk is cheap—anybody could say that. So I'll prove it to you by healing this man." Then, turning to the paralyzed man, he commanded, "Pick up your stretcher and go on home, for you are healed!"

2:1
Mt 9:1-8
Lk 5:17-26
2:2
Eph 2:17
Heb 2:3

2:5
Ps 103:3

2:7
Ps 130:4
Isa 43:25
Rom 8:33
2:8
Heb 4:13

2:4 *right down in front of Jesus,* implied.   **2:6** *religious leaders,* literally, "scribes."   **2:9-11** *Messiah,* literally, "Son of Man."

1:40, 41 Jewish leaders declared lepers unclean. This meant they were unfit to participate in any religious or social activity. Because their law said that contact with any unclean person made them unclean too, some even threw rocks at lepers to keep them at a safe distance. But Jesus touched this leper.

The real value of a person is inside, not outside. Although a person's body may be diseased or deformed, the person inside is no less valuable to God. No person is too disgusting for his touch. In a sense, we are all lepers, because we have all been deformed by the ugliness of sin. But God, by sending his Son Jesus, has touched us, giving us the opportunity to be healed. When you feel repulsed by someone, stop and remember how God feels about that person—and about you.

1:43, 44 The Old Testament laws about lepers are found in Leviticus 13, 14. When a leper was cured, he or she had to go to a priest to be examined. Then the leper was to give an offering of thanks at the Temple. Jesus adhered to these laws by sending the man to the priest, demonstrating his complete regard for God's law. Sending a healed leper to a priest was also a way to verify Jesus' great miracle to the community.

2:3 The paralyzed man's need moved his friends to action, and they brought him to Jesus. When you recognize someone's need, do you act? Many people have physical and spiritual needs you can meet, either by yourself or with others who are also concerned.

Human need moved these four men; let it also move you to compassionate action.

2:4 Houses in Bible times were built of stone. They had flat roofs made of mud mixed with straw. Outside stairways led to the roofs. These friends, therefore, could have carried the lame man up the outside stairs to the roof. They then could easily have taken apart the mud and straw mixture to make a hole through which to lower their friend to Jesus.

2:7 Instead of saying to the paralyzed man, "You are healed," Jesus said, "Your sins are forgiven." To the Jewish leaders this was blasphemy, claiming to do something only God could do. According to Jewish law, this sin deserved death (Leviticus 24:15, 16). The religious leaders understood correctly that Jesus was claiming to be the Messiah, but their judgment of him was wrong. Jesus was not blaspheming, because his claim was true. Jesus is God, and he proved his claim by healing the paralyzed man (verses 9–11).

2:9–11 This is the first time in Mark that Jesus calls himself the "Son of Man" (see textual note). The title *Son of Man* emphasizes that Jesus is fully human, while *Son of God* (see, for example, John 20:31) emphasizes that he is fully God. As God's Son, Jesus has the authority to forgive sin. As a man, he can identify with our deepest needs and sufferings and help us overcome sin.

2:12
Mt 9:33

12The man jumped up, took the stretcher, and pushed his way through the stunned onlookers! Then how they praised God. "We've never seen anything like this before!" they all exclaimed.

Jesus eats with sinners at Matthew's house
(40/Matthew 9:9–13; Luke 5:27–32)

2:13
Mt 9:9-13
Lk 5:27-32

13Then Jesus went out to the seashore again, and preached to the crowds that gathered around him. 14As he was walking up the beach he saw Levi, the son of Alphaeus, sitting at his tax collection booth. "Come with me," Jesus told him. "Come be my disciple."

And Levi jumped to his feet and went along.

15That night Levi invited his fellow tax collectors and many other notorious sinners to be his dinner guests so that they could meet Jesus and his disciples. (There were many men of this type among the crowds that followed him.) 16But when some of the Jewish religious leaders saw him eating with these men of ill repute, they said to his disciples, "How can he stand it, to eat with such scum?"

2:16
Isa 65:5

2:17
Mt 18:11
Lk 19:9,10
1 Tim 1:15

17When Jesus heard what they were saying, he told them, "Sick people need the doctor, not healthy ones! I haven't come to tell good people to repent, but the bad ones."

Religious leaders ask Jesus about fasting
(41/Matthew 9:14–17; Luke 5:33–39)

2:18
Mt 9:14-17
Lk 5:33-39

18John's disciples and the Jewish leaders sometimes fasted, that is, went without food as part of their religion. One day some people came to Jesus and asked why his disciples didn't do this too.

2:19
Isa 54:5
Jn 3:29
Rev 19:7

19Jesus replied, "Do friends of the bridegroom refuse to eat at the wedding feast? Should they be sad while he is with them? 20But some day he will be taken away from them, and then they will mourn. 21[Besides, going without food is part of the old way of doing things.] It is like patching an old garment with unshrunk cloth! What happens? The patch pulls away and leaves the hole worse than before. 22You know better than to put new wine into old wineskins. They would burst. The wine

2:22
Gal 3:1-3

2:16 *religious leaders*, literally, "the scribes of the Pharisees." **2:21** *way of doing things*, implied.

2:14 Levi is another name for the disciple Matthew, who wrote the Gospel of Matthew. See Matthew's Profile in Matthew 9 for more information.

2:14 Capernaum was a key military center for Roman troops as well as a thriving business community. Several major highways intersected in Capernaum, with merchants passing through from as far away as Egypt to the south and Mesopotamia to the north.

Matthew was a Jew who was appointed by the Romans to be the area's tax collector. He collected taxes from the citizens as well as from the merchants passing through town. Tax collectors were expected to take a commission on the taxes they collected, but most of them overcharged and vastly enriched themselves. Tax collectors were hated by the Jews because of their reputation for cheating and their support of Rome. The Jews also hated to think that some of the money collected went to support pagan religions and temples.

2:14, 15 The day that Levi met Jesus, he held a meeting at his house to introduce others to him. He didn't waste any time starting to witness! Some people feel that new believers should wait for time, maturity, or training before they start telling others about Jesus. But like Levi, new believers can tell others about their faith right away with whatever knowledge, skill, or experience they already have.

2:16, 17 "Such scum," the self-righteous Pharisees said, describing the people with whom Jesus ate. But Jesus associated with sinners because he loved them and because he knew they needed to hear what he had to say. He spent time with whoever needed or wanted to hear his message—poor, rich, evil, good. We, too, must befriend those who need Christ, even if they do not

seem to be ideal companions. Are there people you have been neglecting because of their reputation? They may be the ones who most need to see and hear the message of Christ's love from you.

2:18ff John had two purposes: to cause people to repent of their sin, and to prepare them for Christ's coming. This was a time of sober reflection, and so it included fasting, an outward sign of humility and regret for sin. Fasting empties the body of food; repentance empties our lives of sin. Jesus' disciples did not need to fast to prepare for his coming, because he was with them. Jesus did not condemn fasting however. He himself fasted for 40 days (Matthew 4:2). Nevertheless, he emphasized fasting with the right motives. The Pharisees fasted twice a week to show how holy they were. Jesus explained that if people fast only to impress others, they have missed the purpose of fasting.

2:19 Jesus compared himself to a bridegroom because in the Old Testament, the term *bride* is often used for Israel and *bridegroom* for the God who loves her (Jeremiah 2:2; Ezekiel 16:8–14).

2:21, 22 A wineskin was a goatskin sewed together at the edges to form a watertight bag. New wine, expanding as it aged, stretched the wineskin. New wine, therefore, could not be put into a wineskin that had already been stretched. The old rigid skin would burst.

The Pharisees had become rigid like old wineskins. They could not accept faith in Jesus which cannot be contained or limited by man-made ideas or rules. Your heart, like a wineskin, can become rigid and prevent you from accepting the new life that Christ offers. Keep your heart open and pliable to accept the life-changing truths of Jesus' message.

would be spilled out and the wineskins ruined. New wine needs fresh wineskins."

➤ The disciples pick wheat on the Sabbath
(45/Matthew 12:1–8; Luke 6:1–5)

23Another time, on a Sabbath day as Jesus and his disciples were walking through the fields, the disciples were breaking off heads of wheat and eating the grain.

24Some of the Jewish religious leaders said to Jesus, "They shouldn't be doing that! It's against our laws to work by harvesting grain on the Sabbath."

2:23 *eating the grain,* implied.

2:23
Deut 23:25
Mt 12:1-8
Lk 6:1-5

Name and Selected References	Description	Agreement with Jesus	Disagreement with Jesus	PROMINENT JEWISH RELIGIOUS AND POLITICAL GROUPS
PHARISEES Matthew 5:20 Matthew 23:1–36 Luke 6:2 Luke 7:36–47	Strict religious group of Jews, who advocated minute obedience to the Jewish law and traditions. Very influential in the synagogues.	Respect for the Law, belief in the resurrection of the dead, committed to obeying God's will.	Rejected Jesus' claim to be Messiah because he did not follow all their traditions and associated with notoriously wicked people.	
SADDUCEES Matthew 3:7 Matthew 16:11, 12 Mark 12:18	Wealthy, upper class Jewish priestly party. Rejected the authority of the Bible beyond the five books of Moses. Profited from business in the Temple. They, along with the Pharisees, were the two major parties of the Jewish Supreme Court.	Showed great respect for the five books of Moses, as well as the sanctity of the Temple.	Denied the resurrection of the dead. Thought the Temple could also be used as a place to transact business.	
SCRIBES Matthew 7:29 Mark 2:6 Mark 2:16	Professional interpreters of the Law—who especially emphasized the traditions. Many scribes were Pharisees.	Respect for the Law. Committed to obeying God.	Denied Jesus' authority to reinterpret the Law. Rejected Jesus as Messiah because he did not obey all of their traditions.	
HERODIANS Matthew 22:16 Mark 3:6 Mark 12:13	A Jewish political party of King Herod's supporters.	Unknown. In the Gospels they tried to trap Jesus with questions and plotted to kill him.	Afraid of Jesus causing political instability. They saw Jesus as a threat to their political future, at a time when they were trying to regain from Rome some of their lost political power.	
ZEALOTS Matthews 10:4 Luke 6:15 Acts 1:14	A fiercely dedicated group of Jewish patriots determined to end Roman rule in Israel.	Concerned about the future of Israel. Believed in the Messiah but did not recognize Jesus as the One sent by God.	Believed that the Messiah must be a political leader who would deliver Israel from Roman occupation.	
ESSENES none	Jewish monastic group practicing ritual and ceremonial purity as well as personal holiness.	Emphasized justice, honesty, commitment.	Fulfilling detailed ceremonial rituals was an essential aspect of righteousness.	

2:23 Jesus and his disciples were not stealing when they were picking grain in the field. Leviticus 19:9, 10 and Deuteronomy 23:25 say that Jewish farmers were to leave the corners and edges of their fields unharvested so that the grain could be picked by travelers and by the poor. Just as walking on a sidewalk is not trespassing on private property, eating grain at the edge of a field was not stealing.

2:24 God's law said that crops should not be harvested on the Sabbath (Exodus 34:21). This law prevented farmers from becoming greedy and ignoring God on the Sabbath. It also protected laborers from being overworked. The Pharisees

interpreted the action of Jesus and his disciples—picking off the heads of grain and rubbing them in their hands—as harvesting; and so they judged Jesus a lawbreaker. But Jesus and the disciples clearly were not picking the wheat for personal gain; they were simply looking for something to eat. The Pharisees focused so intently on the specific rule that they missed its true intent.

2:24 The Jewish religious leaders were so caught up in their man-made laws that they lost sight of what was good and right. Jesus implied in Mark 3:4 that the Sabbath is a day to do good. God provided the Sabbath as a day of rest and worship, but he didn't mean that concern for rest should keep us from lifting a

2:25
Ex 25:30
29:32,33
Lev 24:9
1 Sam 21:1-6
2:27
Ex 23:12
Deut 5:14
Jn 7:21-24

25, 26But Jesus replied, "Didn't you ever hear about the time King David and his companions were hungry, and he went into the house of God—Abiathar was High Priest then—and they ate the special bread only priests were allowed to eat? That was against the law too. 27But the Sabbath was made to benefit man, and not man to benefit the Sabbath. 28And I, the Messiah, have authority even to decide what men can do on Sabbath days!"

Jesus heals a man's hand on the Sabbath
(46/Matthew 12:9–14; Luke 6:6–11)

3:1
Mt 12:9-16
Lk 6:6-11,17-19

3 While in Capernaum Jesus went over to the synagogue again, and noticed a man there with a deformed hand. 2Since it was the Sabbath, Jesus' enemies watched him closely. Would he heal the man's hand? If he did, they planned to arrest him! 3Jesus asked the man to come and stand in front of the congregation. 4Then turning to his enemies he asked, "Is it all right to do kind deeds on Sabbath days? Or is this a day for doing harm? Is it a day to save lives or to destroy them?" But they wouldn't answer him. 5Looking around at them angrily, for he was deeply disturbed by their indifference to human need, he said to the man, "Reach out your hand." He did, and instantly his hand was healed!

3:6
Mt 22:16

6At once the Pharisees went away and met with the Herodians to discuss plans for killing Jesus.

Large crowds follow Jesus
(47/Matthew 12:15–21)

3:7
Mt 12:15-21
Lk 6:17-19

7, 8Meanwhile, Jesus and his disciples withdrew to the beach, followed by a huge crowd from all over Galilee, Judea, Jerusalem, Idumea, from beyond the Jordan River, and even from as far away as Tyre and Sidon. For the news about his miracles had spread far and wide and vast numbers came to see him for themselves. 9He instructed his disciples to bring around a boat and to have it standing ready to rescue him in case he was crowded off the beach. 10For there had been many healings that day and as a result great numbers of sick people were crowding around him, trying to touch him.

2:25, 26 *special bread,* literally "shewbread." **2:28** *the Messiah,* literally, "the Son of Man."

finger to help others. Don't allow your Sabbath to become a time of selfish indulgence.

2:27, 28 Jesus used the example of King David to point out how ridiculous the Pharisees' accusations were. Jesus said that God created the Sabbath for our benefit, not his own. God derives no benefit from having us rest on the Sabbath, but we are restored both physically and spiritually when we take time to rest and focus on God. For the Pharisees, Sabbath laws had become more important than the reason for the Sabbath. Both David and Jesus understood that the true intent of God's law is to promote love for God and for others. Don't blindly keep a law without looking carefully at the reasons for the law. The spirit of the law is usually more important than the letter.

3:2 Already the Jewish leaders had turned against Jesus. They were jealous of his popularity, his miracles, and his speaking authority. They valued their status in the community and their opportunity for personal gain so much that they lost sight of their goal as religious leaders—to point people toward God. Of all people, they should have recognized the Messiah, but they refused to acknowledge him because they were not willing to give up their treasured position and power. When Jesus exposed their true attitudes, he became their enemy instead of their Messiah, and they began looking for ways to turn the people against him to stop his growing popularity.

3:4 Jesus did a good deed, but the Pharisees accused him of breaking their law that said medical attention could be given to no one on the Sabbath except in matters of life and death. Ironically, the Pharisees were accusing Jesus of breaking the Sabbath by

healing someone, while at the same time they were plotting murder.

3:5 Jesus was angry about the Pharisees' uncaring attitudes. Anger itself is not wrong. It depends on what makes us angry and what we do with our anger. Too often we express our anger in selfish and harmful ways. By contrast, Jesus expressed his anger by correcting a problem—healing the man's hand. Use your anger to find constructive solutions rather than to add to the problem by tearing people down.

3:6 The Pharisees were a Jewish religious group who zealously followed Old Testament law as well as their own religious traditions. They were highly respected in the community, but they hated Jesus because he challenged their proud attitudes and dishonorable motives.

The Herodians were a Jewish political party that hoped to restore Herod the Great's line to the throne. Jesus was a threat to them as well because he challenged their political ambitions. The Pharisees and Herodians, normally enemies, joined forces against Jesus because he exposed them for what they were and undermined their power and reputations.

3:7, 8 While Jesus was drawing fire from the religious leaders, he was gaining great popularity among the people. Some were curious, some sought healing, some wanted evidence to use against him, and others wanted to know if he truly was the Messiah. Most of them only dimly guessed the real scope of what was happening among them. Today crowds still follow Jesus, and they come for the same variety of reasons. What is your primary reason for following Jesus?

11And whenever those possessed by demons caught sight of him they would fall
down before him shrieking, "You are the Son of God!" 12But he strictly warned
them not to make him known.

3:11
Mk 1:24,25,34
Lk 4:41
Acts 16:16,17

Jesus selects the twelve disciples
(48/Luke 6:12–16)

13Afterwards he went up into the hills and summoned certain ones he chose,
inviting them to come and join him there; and they did. 14, 15Then he selected twelve
of them to be his regular companions and to go out to preach and to cast out
demons. 16–19These are the names of the twelve he chose: Simon (he renamed him
"Peter"), James and John (the sons of Zebedee, but Jesus called them "Sons of
Thunder"), Andrew, Philip, Bartholomew, Matthew, Thomas, James (the son of
Alphaeus), Thaddaeus, Simon (a member of a political party advocating violent
overthrow of the Roman government), Judas Iscariot (who later betrayed him).

3:13
Mt 10:2-4
Lk 6:12-16
3:14
Lk 9:1
3:16
Jn 1:42

Religious leaders accuse Jesus of being Satan
(74/Matthew 12:22–37)

20When he returned to the house where he was staying, the crowds began to
gather again, and soon it was so full of visitors that he couldn't even find time to
eat. 21When his friends heard what was happening they came to try to take him
home with them.

"He's out of his mind," they said.

22But the Jewish teachers of religion who had arrived from Jerusalem said, "His
trouble is that he's possessed by Satan, king of demons. That's why demons obey
him."

23Jesus summoned these men and asked them (using proverbs they all understood), "How can Satan cast out Satan? 24A kingdom divided against itself will
collapse. 25A home filled with strife and division destroys itself. 26And if Satan is
fighting against himself, how can he accomplish anything? He would never survive. 27[Satan must be bound before his demons are cast out], just as a strong man
must be tied up before his house can be ransacked and his property robbed.

28"I solemnly declare that any sin of man can be forgiven, even blasphemy

3:20
Mk 6:31

3:22
Mt 9:34; 10:25
12:22-32
Lk 11:14-23
Jn 8:48,52
10:20

3:26
Mt 4:10

3:27
Isa 49:24,25

3:27 cast out, implied.

3:11 The demons knew that Jesus was God's Son, but they
refused to turn from their evil purpose. Knowing about Jesus, or
even believing that he is God's Son, does not guarantee salvation.
You must also want to follow and obey him (James 2:17).

3:12 Jesus warned the demons not to make him known as
Messiah because they would be reinforcing a popular
misconception. The huge crowds were looking for a political and
military leader who would free them from Rome's control, and they
thought the Messiah predicted by the Old Testament prophets
would be this kind of man. Jesus wanted to teach the people about
the kind of Messiah he really was—far different from their
expectations. His kingdom is spiritual. It begins, not with the
overthrow of governments, but with the overthrow of sin in people's
hearts.

3:14 Jesus was surrounded by followers, from whom he chose
twelve to be his regular companions. He did not choose these
twelve because of their faith, because their faith faltered. He didn't
choose them because of their talent and ability, because no one
stood out with unusual ability. The disciples represented a wide
range of backgrounds and life experiences, but apparently they
had no more leadership potential than those who were not chosen.
The one characteristic they all shared was their willingness to obey
and follow Jesus. After Jesus' ascension, they were filled with the
Holy Spirit and carried out special roles in the growth of the early
church. We should not disqualify ourselves from service to Christ
because we do not have the right credentials. Being a good
disciple is simply a matter of following Jesus with a willing heart.

3:14–16 Why did Jesus choose twelve men? The number twelve
corresponds to the twelve tribes of Israel (Matthew 19:28), showing
the continuity between the old religious system and the new,
based on Jesus' message. Many people followed Jesus, but these
twelve received the most intense training. We see the impact of
these men throughout the rest of the New Testament.

3:21 With the crowds pressing in on him, Jesus didn't even take
time to eat. Because of this, his friends and family came from
Nazareth to take him home (verses 31, 32), thinking he had gone
"over the edge" as a religious fanatic. They were concerned for
him, but they missed the point of his ministry. Even those who were
closest to Jesus were slow to understand his true identity.

3:22–26 The Pharisees could not deny Jesus' miracles and
supernatural power. They refused to believe that his power was
from God, however, because then they would have had to accept
him as the Messiah. Their pride would not let them do that. So in an
attempt to destroy his popularity among the people, they accused
him of having power from Satan. We can see from Jesus' reply in
verses 23–26 that the argument of the Jewish leaders didn't make
sense.

3:27 Although God permits Satan to work in our world, God is still
in control. Jesus, because he is God, has power over Satan; he is
able to cast out demons and end their terrible work in people's
lives. One day Satan will be bound forever, never again to do his
evil work in the world (Revelation 20:10).

3:28, 29 Christians sometimes wonder if they have committed this
sin of blaspheming the Holy Spirit. This is not a sin about which

3:29
Lk 12:10
1 Jn 5:16

against me; 29but blasphemy against the Holy Spirit can never be forgiven. It is an eternal sin."

30He told them this because they were saying he did his miracles by Satan's power [instead of acknowledging it was by the Holy Spirit's power].

Jesus describes his true family
(76/Matthew 12:46–50; Luke 8:19–21)

3:31
Mt 12:46-50; 13:55
Mk 6:3
Lk 8:19-21
Jn 7:3-5

31, 32Now his mother and brothers arrived at the crowded house where he was teaching, and they sent word for him to come out and talk with them. "Your mother and brothers are outside and want to see you," he was told.

3:34
Rom 8:29
Heb 2:11

33He replied, "Who is my mother? Who are my brothers?" 34Looking at those around him he said, "These are my mother and brothers! 35Anyone who does God's will is my brother, and my sister, and my mother."

Jesus tells the parable of the four soils
(77/Matthew 13:1–9; Luke 8:4–8)

4:1
Mt 13:1-23
Lk 8:4-15

4 Once again an immense crowd gathered around him on the beach as he was teaching, so he got into a boat and sat down and talked from there. 2His usual method of teaching was to tell the people stories. One of them went like this:

3"Listen! A farmer decided to sow some grain. As he scattered it across his field, 4some of it fell on a path, and the birds came and picked it off the hard ground and ate it. 5, 6Some fell on thin soil with underlying rock. It grew up quickly enough, but soon wilted beneath the hot sun and died because the roots had no nourishment in the shallow soil. 7Other seeds fell among thorns that shot up and crowded the young plants so that they produced no grain. 8But some of the seeds fell into good soil and yielded thirty times as much as he had planted—some of it even sixty or a hundred times as much! 9If you have ears, listen!"

4:9
Mk 4:23

Jesus explains the parable of the four soils
(78/Matthew 13:10–23; Luke 8:9–18)

4:11,12
Isa 6:9; 44:18
Jer 5:21
Jn 12:39,40
Acts 28:26,27
Rom 11:8
1 Cor 2:10

10Afterwards, when he was alone with the twelve and with his other disciples, they asked him, "What does your story mean?"

11, 12He replied, "You are permitted to know some truths about the kingdom of God that are hidden to those outside the kingdom:

3:30 *instead of acknowledging it was by the Holy Spirit's power,* implied.

Christians need worry; it is a heart-attitude of unbelief and unrepentance. Deliberate, ongoing rejection of the work of the Holy Spirit is blasphemy because it is rejecting God himself. The religious leaders accused Jesus of blasphemy, but ironically they were the guilty ones when they looked him in the face and called him Satan.

3:31-35 Jesus' mother was Mary (Luke 1:30, 31) and his brothers were probably the other children Mary and Joseph had after Jesus. Many Christians, however, believe the ancient tradition that Jesus was Mary's only child. If this is true, the "brothers" were possibly cousins (cousins were often called brothers in those days). Jesus' family did not yet fully understand his ministry, as can be seen in verse 21. Jesus explained that our spiritual family forms relationships that are ultimately more important and longer lasting than those formed in our physical families.

3:33-35 God's family is open and doesn't exclude anyone. Although Jesus cared for his mother and brothers, he also cared for all those who loved him. Jesus did not show partiality; he allowed everyone the privilege of obeying God and becoming part of his family. He shows us how to relate to other believers in a new way. In our increasingly computerized, impersonal world, warm relationships among members of God's family take on major importance. The church can give loving, personalized care that many people find nowhere else.

4:2 Jesus taught the people by telling stories, often called *parables.* A parable uses familiar scenes to explain deeper spiritual truth. This method of teaching compels the listener to think. It conceals the truth from those who are too stubborn to hear what is taught. Most parables have one main point, so we must be careful not to go beyond what Jesus intended to teach.

4:3 Seed was planted, or sowed, by hand. As the farmer walked across the field, he threw handfuls of seed onto the ground from a large bag slung across his shoulders. The plants did not grow in neat rows as with today's machine planting. No matter how skillful he may have been, no farmer could keep all his seed from falling on the path or among rocks and thorns or from being carried off by the wind. He threw the seed liberally, however, and enough fell on good ground to ensure the harvest.

4:9 We hear with our ears, but there is a deeper kind of listening with the mind and heart that is necessary in order to gain spiritual understanding from Jesus' words. Some people in the crowd were looking for evidence to use against Jesus; others truly wanted to learn and grow. Jesus' words were for the honest seekers.

4:11, 12 Some people do not understand God's truth because they are not ready for it. God reveals truth to people who will act on it, who will make it evident in their lives. When you talk with people about God, be aware that they will not understand if they are not yet ready.

THE TWELVE

Name	Occupation	Outstanding Characteristics	Major Events in His Life
SIMON PETER (son of John)	Fisherman	Impulsive; later—bold in preaching Jesus	One of three in core group of disciples; recognized Jesus as the Messiah; denied Christ and repented; preached Pentecost sermon; a leader of the Jerusalem church; baptized Gentiles; wrote 1 and 2 Peter.
JAMES, son of Zebedee. He and his brother John were called the "Sons of Thunder"	Fisherman	Ambitious, short-tempered, judgmental, deeply committed to Jesus	Also in core group; he and his brother John asked Jesus for places of honor in his kingdom; wanted to command fire to fall on a Samaritan village; first disciple to be martyred.
JOHN (son of Zebedee), James' brother, and "the disciple Jesus loved"	Fisherman	Ambitious, judgmental, later—very loving	Third disciple in core group; asked Jesus for a place of honor in his kingdom; wanted to call down fire on a Samaritan village; a leader of the Jerusalem church; wrote the Gospel of John and 1, 2, 3 John and Revelation.
ANDREW (Peter's brother)	Fisherman	Eager to bring others to Jesus	Accepted John the Baptist's testimony about Jesus; told Peter about Jesus; he and Philip told Jesus that Greeks wanted to see him.
PHILIP	Fisherman	Questioning attitude	Told Nathanael about Jesus; wondered how Jesus could feed the 5,000; asked Jesus to show his followers God the Father; he and Andrew told Jesus that Greeks wanted to see him.
BARTHOLOMEW (Nathanael)	Unknown	Honesty and straight-forwardness	Initially rejected Jesus because he was from Nazareth but acknowledged Jesus as the "Son of God" and "King of Israel" when they met.
MATTHEW (Levi)	Tax collector	Despised outcast because of his dishonest career	Abandoned his corrupt (and financially profitable) way of life to follow Jesus; invited Jesus to a party with his notorious friends; wrote the Gospel of Matthew.
THOMAS (the Twin)	Unknown	Courage and doubt	Suggested the disciples go with Jesus to Bethany—even if it meant death; asked Jesus about where he was going; refused to believe Jesus was risen until he would see Jesus alive and touch his wounds.
JAMES (son of Alphaeus)	Unknown	Unknown	Became one of Jesus' disciples.
THADDAEUS (Judas, son of James)	Unknown	Unknown	Asked Jesus why he would reveal himself to his followers and not to the world.
SIMON THE ZEALOT	Unknown	Fierce patriotism	Became a disciple of Jesus.
JUDAS ISCARIOT	Unknown	Treacherous and greedy	Became one of Jesus' disciples; betrayed Jesus; killed himself.

Jesus' faithful disciples were ordinary men who became extraordinary because of Jesus Christ. Despite their confusion and misunderstanding during his lifetime, they became powerful witnesses to his resurrection. Their lives were transformed by God's power. The story of Jesus' disciples does not end with the Gospels. It continues in the book of Acts and many of the epistles.

DISCIPLES

What Jesus Said about Him	*A Key Lesson from His Life*	*Selected References*
Named him Peter, "a rock"; called him "Satan" when he urged Jesus to reject the Cross; said he would become a fisherman of men's souls; he received revelation from God; he would deny Jesus; he would later be crucified for his faith.	Christians falter at times; but when they return to Jesus, he forgives them and strengthens their faith.	Matthew 4:18–20 Mark 8:29–33 Luke 22:31–34 John 21:15–19 Acts 2:14–41, 10:1–11:18
Called James and John "Sons of Thunder"; said they would fish for the souls of men; they would drink the cup Jesus drank; they did not understand their own hearts.	Christians must be willing to die for Jesus.	Mark 3:17 Mark 10:35–40 Luke 9:52–56 Acts 12:1, 2
Called James and John "Sons of Thunder"; said he would fish for the souls of men; would drink the cup Jesus drank; did not understand his own heart; would take care of Jesus' mother after his death.	The transforming power of the love of Christ is available to all.	Mark 1:19 Mark 10:35–40 Luke 9:52–56 John 19:26, 27 John 21:20–24
Said he would become a fisherman of men's souls.	Christians are to tell other people about Jesus.	Matthew 4:18–20 John 1:35–42; 6:8, 9 John 12:20–22
Asked if Philip realized that to know and see him was to know and see the Father.	God uses our questions to teach us.	Matthew 10:3 John 1:43–46; 6:2–7 John 12:20–22; 14:8–11
Called him "an honest man" and "a true son of Israel."	Jesus respects honesty in people—even if they challenge him because of it.	Mark 3:18 John 1:45–51 John 21:1–13
Called him to be a disciple.	Christianity is not for people who think they're already good; it is for people who know they've failed and want help.	Matthew 9:9–13 Mark 2:15–17 Luke 5:27–32
Said Thomas believed because he actually saw Jesus after the resurrection.	Even when Christians experience serious doubts, Jesus reaches out to them to restore their faith.	Matthew 10:3 John 14:5; 20:24–29 John 21:1–13
Unknown	Unknown	Matthew 10:3 Mark 3:18 Luke 6:15
Unknown	Christians follow Jesus because they believe in him; they do not always understand the details of God's plan.	Matthew 10:3 Mark 3:18 John 14:22
Unknown	If we are willing to give up our plans for the future, we can participate in Jesus' plans.	Matthew 10:4 Mark 3:18 Luke 6:15
Called him "a devil"; said he would betray Jesus.	It is not enough to be familiar with Jesus' teachings. Jesus' true followers love and obey him.	Matthew 26:20–25 Luke 22:47, 48 John 12:4–8

'Though they see and hear, they will not understand or turn to God, or be forgiven for their sins.'

13But if you can't understand *this* simple illustration, what will you do about all the others I am going to tell?

14"The farmer I talked about is anyone who brings God's message to others, trying to plant good seed within their lives. 15The hard pathway, where some of the seed fell, represents the hard hearts of some of those who hear God's message; Satan comes at once to try to make them forget it. 16The rocky soil represents the hearts of those who hear the message with joy, 17but, like young plants in such soil, their roots don't go very deep, and though at first they get along fine, as soon as persecution begins, they wilt.

18"The thorny ground represents the hearts of people who listen to the Good News and receive it, 19but all too quickly the attractions of this world and the delights of wealth, and the search for success and lure of nice things come in and crowd out God's message from their hearts, so that no crop is produced.

20"But the good soil represents the hearts of those who truly accept God's message and produce a plentiful harvest for God—thirty, sixty, or even a hundred times as much as was planted in their hearts. 21Then he asked them, "When someone lights a lamp, does he put a box over it to shut out the light? Of course not! The light couldn't be seen or used. A lamp is placed on a stand to shine and be useful.

22"All that is now hidden will someday come to light. 23If you have ears, listen! 24And be sure to put into practice what you hear. The more you do this, the more you will understand what I tell you. 25To him who has shall be given; from him who has not shall be taken away even what he has.

Jesus tells the parable of the growing seed
(79)

26"Here is another story illustrating what the Kingdom of God is like:
"A farmer sowed his field, 27and went away, and as the days went by, the seeds grew and grew without his help. 28For the soil made the seeds grow. First a leaf-blade pushed through, and later the wheat-heads formed and finally the grain ripened, 29and then the farmer came at once with his sickle and harvested it."

Jesus tells the parable of the mustard seed
(81/Matthew 13:31, 32)

30Jesus asked, "How can I describe the Kingdom of God? What story shall I use to illustrate it? 31, 32It is like a tiny mustard seed! Though this is one of the smallest of seeds, yet it grows to become one of the largest of plants, with long branches where birds can build their nests and be sheltered."

4:14
Eph 3:8
Jas 1:18
1 Pet 1:23-25
4:15
2 Cor 4:4
1 Pet 5:8

4:19
Prov 23:4,5
Lk 18:24
1 Tim 6:9,10,17
1 Jn 2:15,16
4:20
Jn 15:5
4:21
Mt 5:15
Lk 8:16-18
11:33
4:22
Mt 10:26
Lk 12:2
4:23
Mt 11:15; 13:43
4:25
Mt 13:12; 25:29
Lk 6:38; 19:26
2 Cor 9:6

4:26,27
1 Cor 3:6,7
4:28,29
Mt 9:37,38
Jn 4:35
1 Cor 15:36-38
Rev 14:15

4:30
Mt 13:31,32
Lk 13:18,19
4:31,32
Ezek 17:22,23

4:14–20 The four soils represent four different ways people respond to God's Word. Usually we think that Jesus was talking about four different kinds of people. But he may also have been talking about (1) different times or phases in a person's life, or (2) how we willingly receive God's message in some areas of our life and resist it in others. For example, you may be open to God about your future, but closed concerning how you spend your money. You may respond like good soil to God's demand for worship, but like rocky soil to his demand to give to those in need. We must strive to be like good soil in every area of our life at all times.

4:21 If a lamp doesn't help people see, it is useless. Does your life show other people how to find God and how to live for him? If not, ask what "boxes" have shut out your light. Complacency, resentment, stubbornness of heart, or disobedience could be "boxes" that keep God's light from shining through you to others.

4:21–24 The light of Jesus' truth is revealed to us, not hidden. But we may not be able to see or to use all of that truth right now. Only as we put God's teachings into practice will we understand and

see more of the truth. The truth is clear, but our ability to understand is imperfect. As we obey, we will sharpen our vision and increase our understanding (James 1:22–25).

4:25 This phrase simply means we are responsible to use well what we have. It doesn't matter how much we have but what we do with it.

4:26–29 This parable about the Kingdom of God, recorded only by Mark, reveals that spiritual growth is a continual, gradual process that is finally consummated in a harvest of spiritual maturity. We can understand the process of spiritual growth by comparing it to the slow but certain growth of a plant.

4:30–32 Jesus used this parable to explain that although Christianity had very small beginnings, it would grow into a worldwide community of believers. When you feel alone in your stand for Christ, realize that God is building a worldwide kingdom. He has faithful followers in every part of the world, and your faith, no matter how small, can join with that of others to accomplish great things.

4:33
Mt 13:34,35
4:34
Jn 10:6; 16:25

33He used many such illustrations to teach the people as much as they were ready to understand. 34In fact, he taught only by illustrations in his public teaching, but afterwards, when he was alone with his disciples, he would explain his meaning to them.

Jesus calms the storm
(87/Matthew 8:23–27; Luke 8:22–25)

4:35
Mt 8:23-27
Lk 8:22-25

35As evening fell, Jesus said to his disciples, "Let's cross to the other side of the lake." 36So they took him just as he was and started out, leaving the crowds behind (though other boats followed). 37But soon a terrible storm arose. High waves began to break into the boat until it was nearly full of water and about to sink. 38Jesus was asleep at the back of the boat with his head on a cushion. Frantically they wakened him, shouting, "Teacher, don't you even care that we are all about to drown?"

4:39
Job 38:11
Ps 65:7; 89:9; 93:4

39Then he rebuked the wind and said to the sea, "Quiet down!" And the wind fell, and there was a great calm!

40And he asked them, "Why were you so fearful? Don't you even yet have confidence in me?"

4:41
Ps 33:8,9

41And they were filled with awe and said among themselves, "Who is this man, that even the winds and seas obey him?"

Jesus sends the demons into a herd of pigs
(88/Matthew 8:28–34; Luke 8:26–39)

5:1
Mt 8:28-34
Lk 8:26-39

5 When they arrived at the other side of the lake a demon-possessed man ran out from a graveyard, just as Jesus was climbing from the boat. 3, 4This man lived among the gravestones, and had such strength that whenever he was put into handcuffs and shackles—as he often was—he snapped the handcuffs from his wrists and smashed the shackles and walked away. No one was strong enough to control him. 5All day long and through the night he would wander among the tombs and in the wild hills, screaming and cutting himself with sharp pieces of stone.

4:33 *as much as they were ready to understand,* literally, "as they were able to hear."

4:33, 34 Jesus adapted his methods to his audience's ability and desire to understand. He didn't speak in parables to confuse people, but to challenge sincere seekers to discover the true meaning of his words. Much of Jesus' teaching was against hypocrisy and impure motives, characteristics of the religious leaders. Had Jesus spoken against the leaders directly, his public ministry would have been hampered. Those who truly listened to Jesus knew what he was talking about.

4:37, 38 The Sea of Galilee is 680 feet below sea level, and it is surrounded by hills. Winds blowing across the land intensify close to the sea, causing violent and unexpected storms. The disciples were seasoned fishermen who had spent their lives fishing on this huge lake, but in this storm they panicked.

4:38–40 The disciples panicked because the storm threatened to destroy them all, and Jesus seemed unaware and unconcerned. Theirs was a physical storm, but storms come in other forms too. Think about the storms in your life—the situations that cause you great anxiety. Whatever your difficulty, you have two options. You can worry and assume that Jesus no longer cares, or you can resist fear, putting your trust in him. When you feel like panicking, confess your need for God and then trust him to care for you.

4:41 The disciples lived with Jesus, but they underestimated him. They did not see that his power applied to their own situation. We've had 20 centuries of Jesus with us, and yet we, like the disciples, underestimate his power to handle crises in our lives. The disciples did not yet know enough about Jesus. We cannot claim the same excuse.

5:1 Although we cannot be sure why demon possession occurs, we know that it uses the body in a destructive way to distort and destroy man's relationship with God and likeness to him. Even

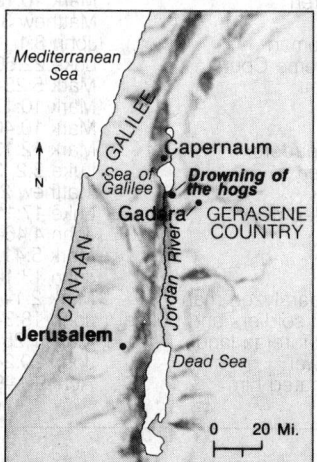

HEALING A DEMON-POSSESSED MAN
From Capernaum, Jesus and his disciples crossed the Sea of Galilee. A storm blew up unexpectedly, but Jesus calmed it. Landing in the country of the Gadarenes, Jesus sent demons out of a man and into a herd of swine that plunged over the steep bank into the sea.

today, demons are dangerous, powerful, and destructive. While it is important to recognize their evil activity so we can stay away from them, we must avoid any curiosity about or involvement with demonic forces or the occult (Deuteronomy 18:10–12). If we resist the devil and his influences, he will flee from us (James 4:7).

6When Jesus was still far out on the water, the man had seen him and had run to meet him, and fell down before him.

7,8Then Jesus spoke to the demon within the man and said, "Come out, you evil spirit."

5:7,8
Lk 8:28
Acts 16:17
Heb 7:1

It gave a terrible scream, shrieking, "What are you going to do to me, Jesus, Son of the Most High God? For God's sake, don't torture me!"

9"What is your name?" Jesus asked, and the demon replied, "Legion, for there are many of us here within this man."

10Then the demons begged him again and again not to send them to some distant land.

11Now as it happened there was a huge herd of hogs rooting around on the hill above the lake. 12"Send us into those hogs," the demons begged.

5:11
Deut 14:8
Isa 65:4

13And Jesus gave them permission. Then the evil spirits came out of the man and entered the hogs, and the entire herd plunged down the steep hillside into the lake and drowned.

5:13
Job 1:12; 2:6; 12:16
Mt 28:18
Lk 4:36
Col 2:10
Heb 2:8

14The herdsmen fled to the nearby towns and countryside, spreading the news as they ran. Everyone rushed out to see for themselves. 15And a large crowd soon gathered where Jesus was; but as they saw the man sitting there, fully clothed and

5:15
1 Jn 3:8

Jesus Talked with . . .	Reference	**THE TOUCH OF JESUS**
A despised tax collector	Matthew 9:9	What kind of people did Jesus associate with? Whom did he consider important enough to touch? Here we see many of the people Jesus came to know. Some reached out to him; he reached out to them all. Regardless of how great or unknown, rich or poor, young or old, sinner or saint— Jesus cares equally for all. No person is beyond the loving touch of Jesus.
An insane hermit	Mark 5:1–15	
The Roman governor	Mark 15:1–15	
A young boy	Mark 9:17–27	
A prominent religious leader	John 3:1–21	
A homemaker	Luke 10:38–42	
A lawyer	Matthew 22:34, 35	
A criminal	Luke 23:40–43	
A synagogue ruler	Mark 5:22	
A fisherman	Matthew 4:18–20	
A king	Luke 23:7–11	
A poor widow	Luke 7:11–17; 21:1–4	
A Roman army captain	Luke 7:1–10	
A group of children	Mark 10:13–16	
A prophet	Matthew 3	
An adulterous woman	John 8:1–11	
The Jewish Supreme Court	Luke 22:66–71	
A sick old woman	Mark 5:25–34	
A rich man	Mark 10:17–23	
A blind beggar	Mark 10:46	
Jewish political leaders	Mark 12:13	
A group of women	Luke 8:2, 3	
The High Priest	Matthew 26:62–68	
An outcast with leprosy	Luke 17:11–19	
A city official	John 4:46–53	
A young girl	Mark 5:41, 42	
A traitor	John 13:1–3	
A helpless and paralyzed man	Mark 2:1–12	
An angry mob of soldiers and police	John 18:3–9	
A woman from a foreign land	Mark 7:25–30	
A doubting follower	John 20:24–29	
An enemy who hated him	Acts 9:1–9	

5:9 The demon said its name was "Legion." A legion was the largest unit of the Roman army, consisting of 3,000 to 6,000 soldiers. Obviously this man was possessed by not one but many demons.

5:10 Mark often highlights the supernatural struggle between Jesus and Satan. The demons' goal was to control the humans they inhabited; Jesus' goal was to give people freedom from sin and Satan's control. The demons knew they had no power over Jesus, so when they saw him, they begged not to be sent to a distant land (called the Bottomless Pit in Luke 8:31). Jesus granted

their request (verse 13) but ended their destructive work in people. He could have sent them to hell, but he did not because the time for judgment had not yet come. In the end, of course, all demons will be sent into eternal fire (Matthew 25:41).

5:11 According to Old Testament law (Leviticus 11:7), pigs were "unclean" animals. This meant they could not be eaten or even touched by a Jew. This incident took place southeast of the Sea of Galilee in the Gerasene country, a Gentile region, which explains how a herd of pigs could be involved.

perfectly sane, they were frightened. ¹⁶Those who saw what happened were telling everyone about it, ¹⁷and the crowd began pleading with Jesus to go away and leave them alone! ¹⁸So he got back into the boat. The man who had been possessed by the demons begged Jesus to let him go along. ¹⁹But Jesus said no.

"Go home to your friends," he told him, "and tell them what wonderful things God has done for you; and how merciful he has been."

²⁰So the man started off to visit the Ten Towns of that region and began to tell everyone about the great things Jesus had done for him; and they were awestruck by his story.

Jesus heals a bleeding woman and restores a girl to life
(89/Matthew 9:18–26; Luke 8:40–56)

²¹When Jesus had gone across by boat to the other side of the lake, a vast crowd gathered around him on the shore.

²²The leader of the local synagogue, whose name was Jairus, came and fell down before him, ²³pleading with him to heal his little daughter.

"She is at the point of death," he said in desperation. "Please come and place your hands on her and make her live."

²⁴Jesus went with him, and the crowd thronged behind. ²⁵In the crowd was a woman who had been sick for twelve years with a hemorrhage. ²⁶She had suffered much from many doctors through the years and had become poor from paying them, and was no better but, in fact, was worse. ²⁷She had heard all about the wonderful miracles Jesus did, and that is why she came up behind him through the crowd and touched his clothes.

²⁸For she thought to herself, "If I can just touch his clothing, I will be healed." ²⁹And sure enough, as soon as she had touched him, the bleeding stopped and she knew she was well!

³⁰Jesus realized at once that healing power had gone out from him, so he turned around in the crowd and asked, "Who touched my clothes?"

³¹His disciples said to him, "All this crowd pressing around you, and you ask who touched you?"

³²But he kept on looking around to see who it was who had done it. ³³Then the

5:20 *to visit the Ten Towns*, or, "to visit Decapolis."

5:17
Job 21:14; 22:17
Lk 5:8

5:18
Ps 116:12

5:20
Isa 63:7; 116:16
1 Tim 1:13,14

5:21
Mt 9:1,18-26
Lk 8:40-56

5:23
Mk 6:5; 7:32; 8:23;
16:18
Lk 4:40; 13:13
Acts 6:6; 9:17; 28:8

5:27
Mk 3:10
Acts 19:11,12

5:30
Lk 6:19

5:17 After such a wonderful miracle of saving a man's life, why did the people want Jesus to leave? The people asked Jesus to leave because they were afraid of his supernatural power, a power that seemed uncontrollable. They may have also feared that Jesus would continue to eliminate their source of livelihood by destroying their pigs. They would rather give up Jesus than their source of income and security.

5:19 Jesus told this man to tell his friends about the miraculous healing. Most of the time, Jesus urged those he healed to keep quiet. Why the change? Here are possible answers: (1) The demon-possessed man had been alone and unable to speak. Telling others what Jesus did for him would prove that he was healed. (2) This was mainly a Gentile and pagan area, so Jesus was not expecting great crowds to follow him. (3) By sending the man away with this good news, Jesus was expanding his ministry to the Gentiles.

5:19, 20 This man had been demon possessed but now was a living example of Jesus' power. He wanted to go with Jesus, but Jesus told him to go home and share his story there. If you have experienced Jesus' power, you too are a living example. Are you, like this man, enthusiastic about sharing the good news with those around you? Just as we would tell others about a doctor who cured a physical disease, we should tell about Christ who cures our sin.

5:20 The region of the Ten Towns, called the Decapolis in Greek, was located southeast of the Sea of Galilee. Ten cities, each with its own independent government, formed an alliance for protection and to increase trade. These cities had been settled several

centuries earlier by Greek traders and immigrants. Although Jews also lived in the area, they were not in the majority. Many people from these ten towns followed Jesus (Matthew 4:25).

5:22 Jesus recrossed the Sea of Galilee, probably landing at Capernaum. Jairus was the elected ruler of the local synagogue. He was responsible for supervising worship, running the weekly school, and caring for the building. Many synagogue rulers had close ties to the Pharisees. It is likely, therefore, that some synagogue rulers had been pressured not to support Jesus. For Jairus to bow before Jesus was a significant and perhaps daring act of respect and worship.

5:25-34 This woman had an incurable condition causing her to bleed constantly. This may have been a menstrual or uterine disorder which would have made her ritually unclean (Leviticus 15:25–27) and excluded her from most social contact with other Jews. She desperately wanted Jesus to heal her, but she knew her bleeding would cause Jesus to be "unclean" under Jewish law if she touched him. Still, she reached out by faith and was healed. Sometimes we feel our problems will keep us from God. But he is always ready to help, and we should never allow our fear to keep us from approaching him.

5:32-34 Jesus was not angry with this woman for touching him. Jesus knew she had touched him, but he stopped and asked who did it in order to teach her something about faith. Although she was healed when she touched him, Jesus said her faith caused the cure. Genuine faith involves action. Faith that isn't put into action is no faith at all.

frightened woman, trembling at the realization of what had happened to her, came and fell at his feet and told him what she had done. 34And he said to her, "Daughter, your faith has made you well; go in peace, healed of your disease."

35While he was still talking to her, messengers arrived from Jairus' home with the news that it was too late—his daughter was dead and there was no point in Jesus' coming now. 36But Jesus ignored their comments and said to Jairus, "Don't be afraid. Just trust me."

37Then Jesus halted the crowd and wouldn't let anyone go on with him to Jairus' home except Peter and James and John. 38When they arrived, Jesus saw that all was in great confusion, with unrestrained weeping and wailing. 39He went inside and spoke to the people.

"Why all this weeping and commotion?" he asked. "The child isn't dead; she is only asleep!"

40They laughed at him in bitter derision, but he told them all to leave, and taking the little girl's father and mother and his three disciples, he went into the room where she was lying.

41, 42Taking her by the hand he said to her, "Get up, little girl!" (She was twelve years old.) And she jumped up and walked around! Her parents just couldn't get over it. 43Jesus instructed them very earnestly not to tell what had happened, and told them to give her something to eat.

The people of Nazareth refuse to believe
(91/Matthew 13:53–58)

6 Soon afterwards he left that section of the country and returned with his disciples to Nazareth, his home town. 2, 3The next Sabbath he went to the synagogue to teach, and the people were astonished at his wisdom and his miracles because he was just a local man like themselves.

Marginal references (right column):

5:34
Mk 10:52
Lk 7:50; 17:19
18:42
Acts 14:9

5:36
Jn 11:25,40

5:39
Jn 11:11

5:40
Acts 9:40

5:41,42
Ps 33:9
Lk 7:14

5:43
Mt 12:16; 17:9
Mk 3:12; 5:19
Lk 5:14

6:1
Mt 13:53-58

6:2,3
Ps 69:8
Mt 11:6

5:36 Jairus' crisis made him feel confused, afraid, and without hope. Jesus' words to Jairus in the midst of crisis speak to us as well: "Don't be afraid. Just trust me." The next time you feel as Jairus did, remember to see your problem from Jesus' point of view. He is the source of all hope and promise.

5:38 Loud mourning and crying was customary at a person's death. Lack of it was the ultimate disgrace and disrespect. Some people, usually women, made mourning a profession, and were paid by the dead person's family to weep over the body. On the day of death, the body was carried through the streets, followed by the mourners and others who felt obligated to join the procession.

5:39, 40 The mourners began to mock Jesus when he said, "She isn't dead; she is only asleep." The girl was dead, but Jesus used the image of sleep to indicate that her condition was temporary and she would be restored. Whether Jesus was talking about her physical or spiritual life doesn't matter. In either case, her life would continue.

Jesus tolerated the crowd's abuse in order to teach an important lesson about maintaining hope and trust in him. Today most of the world laughs at God's claims, which seem ridiculous to them. When you are belittled for expressing faith in Jesus and hope for eternal life, remember that unbelievers don't see from God's perspective.

5:41, 42 Jesus not only demonstrated great power; he also showed tremendous compassion. Jesus' power over nature, demons, and death was motivated by compassion—for a demonic man who lived among tombs, for a diseased woman, and for the family of a dead girl. The rabbis of the day considered such people unclean. Polite society avoided them. But Jesus reached out and helped anyone in need.

5:43 Jesus told the girl's parents not to spread the news of the miracle. He wanted the facts to speak for themselves, and the time was not yet right for a major confrontation with the religious

leaders. Jesus still had much to accomplish, and he didn't want people following him just to see his miracles.

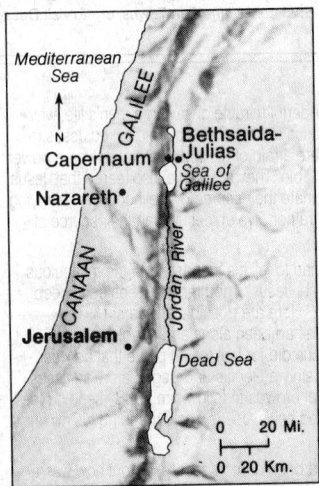

Mediterranean Sea — GALILEE — Capernaum — Bethsaida-Julias — Sea of Galilee — Nazareth — CANAAN — Jordan River — Jerusalem — Dead Sea — 0   20 Mi. — 0   20 Km. — N

PREACHING IN GALILEE
After returning to his home town, Nazareth, from Capernaum Jesus preached in the villages of Galilee and sent his disciples out to preach as well. After meeting back in Capernaum, they left by boat to rest in a "quieter spot" only to be met by the crowds who followed the boat along the shore.

6:2, 3 Jesus was teaching effectively and wisely, but the people of his hometown saw him as only a carpenter. "He's no better than us—he's just a common laborer," they said. They were offended that others could be impressed by him and follow him. They rejected his authority because he was one of their peers. They thought they knew him, but their preconceived notions made it impossible for them to accept his message. Don't let prejudice blind you to truth. Try to see Jesus for who he really is.

"He's no better than we are," they said. "He's just a carpenter, Mary's boy, and a brother of James and Joseph, Judas and Simon. And his sisters live right here among us." And they were offended!

6:4
Jn 4:44

⁴Then Jesus told them, "A prophet is honored everywhere except in his home town and among his relatives and by his own family." ⁵And because of their unbelief he couldn't do any mighty miracles among them except to place his hands on a few sick people and heal them. ⁶And he could hardly accept the fact that they wouldn't believe in him.

Then he went out among the villages, teaching.

Jesus sends out the twelve disciples
(93/Matthew 10:1–15; Luke 9:1–6)

6:7
Mt 10:1,9-14; 11:1
Lk 9:1-6
10:1-11

⁷And he called his twelve disciples together and sent them out two by two, with power to cast out demons. ⁸, ⁹He told them to take nothing with them except their walking sticks—no food, no knapsack, no money, not even an extra pair of shoes or a change of clothes.

¹⁰"Stay at one home in each village—don't shift around from house to house while you are there," he said. ¹¹"And whenever a village won't accept you or listen

6:11
Acts 13:51; 18:6
Heb 10:31

to you, shake off the dust from your feet as you leave; it is a sign that you have abandoned it to its fate."

6:13
Jas 5:14

¹²So the disciples went out, telling everyone they met to turn from sin. ¹³And they cast out many demons, and healed many sick people, anointing them with olive oil.

Herod kills John the Baptist
(95/Matthew 14:1–12; Luke 9:7–9)

6:14
Mt 14:1-12
Lk 9:7-9
6:15
Mt 16:14

¹⁴King Herod soon heard about Jesus, for his miracles were talked about everywhere. The king thought Jesus was John the Baptist come back to life again. So the people were saying, "No wonder he can do such miracles." ¹⁵Others thought Jesus was Elijah the ancient prophet, now returned to life again; still others claimed he was a new prophet like the great ones of the past.

¹⁶"No," Herod said, "it is John, the man I beheaded. He has come back from the dead."

6:17
Lev 18:15, 16
20:21
Lk 3:19
2 Tim 4:2
Heb 13:4

¹⁷, ¹⁸For Herod had sent soldiers to arrest and imprison John because he kept saying it was wrong for the king to marry Herodias, his brother Philip's wife.

6:4 Jesus said that a prophet (in other words, a worker for God) is never honored in his hometown. But that doesn't make his work any less important. A person doesn't need to be respected or honored to be useful to God. If friends, neighbors, or family don't respect your Christian work, don't let their rejection keep you from serving God.

6:5 Jesus could have done greater miracles in Nazareth, but he chose not to because of the people's pride and unbelief. The miracles he did had little effect on the people because they did not want to accept his message or believe he was from God. Therefore, Jesus looked elsewhere, seeking those who would respond to his miracles and message.

6:7 The disciples were sent out in pairs. Individually they could have reached more areas of the country, but this was not Christ's plan. One advantage in going out by twos was that they could strengthen and encourage each other, especially when they faced rejection. Our strength comes from God, but he meets many of our needs through our teamwork with others.

6:11 Pious Jews shook the dust from their feet after passing through Gentile cities or territory to show their separation from Gentile influences and practices. When the disciples shook the dust from their feet after leaving a *Jewish* town, it was a vivid sign that the people had rejected Jesus and his message. Jesus made it clear that the people were responsible for how they responded to the gospel. The disciples were not to blame if the message was

rejected, as long as they had faithfully and carefully presented it. We are not responsible when others reject Christ's message of salvation, but we do have the responsibility to share it faithfully with others.

6:15 Herod, along with many others, wondered who Jesus really was. Unable to accept Jesus' claim to be God's Son, many people made up their own explanations for his power and authority. Herod thought Jesus was John the Baptist come back to life, while those who were familiar with the Old Testament thought he was Elijah (Malachi 4:5). Still others believed he was a teaching prophet in the tradition of Moses, Isaiah, or Jeremiah. Today people still have to make up their minds about Jesus. Some think that if they can name what he is—prophet, teacher, good man—they can weaken the power of his claim on their lives. But what they *think* does not change who Jesus *is*.

6:17-19 Palestine was divided into four territories, each ruled by a "tetrarch." Herod Antipas, called King Herod in the Gospels, was ruler over Galilee; his brother Philip ruled over Trachonitus and Idumea. Philip's wife was Herodias, but she left him to marry Herod Antipas. When John confronted the two for committing adultery, Herodias formulated a plot to kill him. Instead of trying to get rid of her sin, she tried to get rid of the one who brought it to public attention. This is exactly what the religious leaders were trying to do to Jesus.

19Herodias wanted John killed in revenge, but without Herod's approval she was powerless. 20And Herod respected John, knowing that he was a good and holy man, and so he kept him under his protection. Herod was disturbed whenever he talked with John, but even so he liked to listen to him.

21Herodias' chance finally came. It was Herod's birthday and he gave a stag party for his palace aides, army officers, and the leading citizens of Galilee. 22, 23Then Herodias' daughter came in and danced before them and greatly pleased them all.

6:21
Gen 40:20
6:22
Esth 5:3,6; 7:2

"Ask me for anything you like," the king vowed, "even half of my kingdom, and I will give it to you!"

24She went out and consulted her mother, who told her, "Ask for John the Baptist's head!"

25So she hurried back to the king and told him, "I want the head of John the Baptist—right now—on a tray!"

26Then the king was sorry, but he was embarrassed to break his oath in front of his guests. 27So he sent one of his bodyguards to the prison to cut off John's head and bring it to him. The soldier killed John in the prison, 28and brought back his head on a tray, and gave it to the girl and she took it to her mother.

6:27
Rev 6:9

29When John's disciples heard what had happened, they came for his body and buried it in a tomb.

6:29
Acts 8:2

Jesus feeds five thousand
(96/Matthew 14:13–21; Luke 9:10–17; John 6:1–15)

30The apostles now returned to Jesus from their tour and told him all they had done and what they had said to the people they visited.

6:30
Mt 14:13-22
Lk 9:10-17
Jn 6:1-15

31Then Jesus suggested, "Let's get away from the crowds for a while and rest." For so many people were coming and going that they scarcely had time to eat. 32So they left by boat for a quieter spot. 33But many people saw them leaving and ran on ahead along the shore and met them as they landed. 34So the usual vast crowd was there as he stepped from the boat; and he had pity on them because they were like sheep without a shepherd, and he taught them many things they needed to know.

6:31
Mk 3:20

6:34
Ps 145:8,9
Isa 61:1
Mt 9:36
Heb 5:1-3

35,36Late in the afternoon his disciples came to him and said, "Tell the people to go away to the nearby villages and farms and buy themselves some food, for there is nothing to eat here in this desolate spot, and it is getting late."

37But Jesus said, *"You* feed them."

6:37
Num 11:13,22
2 Kgs 4:43
Mt 15:33
Mk 8:4

6:37 *It would take a fortune,* literally, "200 denarii," a year's wages.

Herod as a leader	Jesus as a leader	**REAL LEADERSHIP**
Selfish	Compassionate	Mark gives us
Murder	Healer	some of the best
Immoral	Just and good	insights into
Political opportunist	Servant	Jesus' character.
King over small territory	King over all creation	

6:20 Herod arrested John the Baptist under pressure from his wife and advisors. Though he respected John's integrity, in the end he had him killed because of pressure from his peers and family. What you do under pressure often shows what you are really like.

6:22, 23 As a tetrarch under Roman authority, Herod had no kingdom to give. His offer of half his kingdom was his way to say he would give Herodias' daughter almost anything she wanted. When Herodias asked for John's head, Herod would have been greatly embarrassed in front of his guests if he had denied her request. Words are powerful. Because they can lead to great sin, we should use them with great care.

6:30 Mark uses the word *apostles* only once. *Apostle* means "one sent" as messenger or missionary. The word became an official

title for Jesus' twelve disciples after his death and resurrection (Acts 2:14; Ephesians 2:20).

6:31 When the disciples had returned from their mission, Jesus took them away to rest. Doing God's work is very important, but Jesus recognized that to do God's work effectively requires periodic rest and renewal. Jesus and his disciples, however, did not always find it easy to get the rest they needed!

6:34 This crowd was as pitiful as a flock of sheep without a shepherd. Sheep are easily scattered; without a shepherd they are in grave danger. Jesus knew he was the Shepherd who could teach them what they needed to know and keep them from straying from God. See Psalm 23; Isaiah 61:1; and Ezekiel 34:5–10 for descriptions of the Good Shepherd.

"With what?" they asked. "It would take a fortune to buy food for all this crowd!"

38"How much food do we have?" he asked. "Go and find out."

They came back to report that there were five loaves of bread and two fish. 39, 40 Then Jesus told the crowd to sit down, and soon colorful groups of fifty or a hundred each were sitting on the green grass.

Most people dislike having their sins pointed out, especially in public. The shame of being exposed is often worse than the guilt brought on by the wrongdoing. Herod Antipas was a man experiencing both guilt and shame.

Herod's ruthless ambition was public knowledge, as was his illegal marriage to his brother's wife, Herodias. One man made Herod's sin a public issue. That man was John the Baptist. John had been preaching in the desert, and thousands flocked to hear him. Apparently John used Herod's life-style as a negative example. Herodias was particularly anxious to have John silenced. As a solution, Herod imprisoned John.

Herod liked John. John was probably one of the few people he met who spoke only the truth. But the truth about his sin was a bitter pill to swallow, and Herod wavered at the point of conflict: he couldn't afford to have John constantly reminding the people of their leader's sinfulness, but he was afraid to have John killed. He put off the choice. Eventually Herodias forced his hand, and John was executed. Of course, this only served to increase Herod's guilt.

Upon hearing about Jesus, Herod immediately identified him with John. He couldn't decide what to do about Jesus. He didn't want to repeat the mistake he had made with John, so he tried to threaten Jesus just before his final journey to Jerusalem. When the two met briefly during Jesus' trial, Jesus would not speak to Herod. Herod had proved himself a poor listener to John, and Jesus had nothing to add to John's words. Herod responded with spite and mocking. Having rejected the messenger, he found it easy to reject the Messiah. For each person, God chooses the best possible ways to reveal himself. He uses his Word, circumstances, our minds, or other people to get our attention. He is persuasive and persistent, but never forces himself on us. To miss or resist God's message, as did Herod, is tragedy. How aware are you of God's attempts to enter your life? Have you welcomed him?

Strengths and accomplishments:
- Built the city of Tiberias and other architectural projects
- Ruled the region of Galilee for the Romans

Weaknesses and mistakes:
- Consumed with his quest for power
- Put off decisions or made wrong ones under pressure
- Divorced his wife to marry the wife of his half-brother, Philip
- Imprisoned John the Baptist and later ordered his execution
- Had a minor part in the execution of Jesus

Lessons from his life:
- A life motivated by ambition is usually characterized by self-destruction
- Opportunities to do good usually come to us in the form of choices to be made

Vital statistics:
- Where: Jerusalem
- Occupation: Roman tetrarch of the region of Galilee and Perea
- Relatives: Father: Herod the Great. Mother: Malthace. First wife: daughter of Aretas IV. Second wife: Herodias.
- Contemporaries: John the Baptist, Jesus, Pilate

Key verse:
"And Herod respected John, knowing that he was a good and holy man, and so he kept him under his protection. Herod was disturbed whenever he talked to John, but even so he liked to listen to him" (Mark 6:20).

Herod Antipas' story is told in the Gospels. He is also mentioned in Acts 4:27; 13:1.

6:37 In this chapter different people have examined Jesus' life and ministry: his neighbors and family, Herod the king, and the disciples. Yet none of these appreciate him for who he is. The disciples are still pondering, still unclear, still unbelieving. They do not realize that Jesus can provide for them. They are so preoccupied with the impossibility of the task that they cannot see the possible. Do you let what seems impossible about Christianity keep you from believing?

6:37-42 Jesus asked the disciples to provide food for over 5,000 people. They responded, "With what?" How do you react when you are given an impossible task? A situation that seems impossible with human means is simply an opportunity for God. The disciples did everything they could—they gathered the available food and organized the people into groups. Then, in answer to prayer, God did the impossible.

⁴¹He took the five loaves and two fish and looking up to heaven, gave thanks for the food. Breaking the loaves into pieces, he gave some of the bread and fish to each disciple to place before the people. ⁴²And the crowd ate until they could hold no more!

⁴³, ⁴⁴There were about 5,000 men there for that meal, and afterwards twelve basketfuls of scraps were picked up off the grass!

6:41
1 Sam 9:13
Mt 26:26
1 Tim 4:4,5

Jesus walks on water
(97/Matthew 14:22–33; John 6:16–21)

⁴⁵Immediately after this Jesus instructed his disciples to get back into the boat and strike out across the lake to Bethsaida, where he would join them later. He himself would stay and tell the crowds good-bye and get them started home.

⁴⁶Afterwards he went up into the hills to pray. ⁴⁷During the night, as the disciples in their boat were out in the middle of the lake, and he was alone on land, ⁴⁸he saw that they were in serious trouble, rowing hard and struggling against the wind and waves.

6:47
Mt 14:23-36
Jn 6:16-21

About three o'clock in the morning he walked out to them on the water. He started past them, ⁴⁹but when they saw something walking along beside them they screamed in terror, thinking it was a ghost, ⁵⁰for they all saw him.

But he spoke to them at once. "It's all right," he said. "It is I! Don't be afraid." ⁵¹Then he climbed into the boat and the wind stopped!

They just sat there, unable to take it in! ⁵²For they still didn't realize who he was, even after the miracle the evening before! For they didn't want to believe!

6:52
Mk 16:14

Jesus heals all who touch him
(98/Matthew 14:34–36)

⁵³When they arrived at Gennesaret on the other side of the lake they moored the boat, ⁵⁴and climbed out.

6:53
Mt 14:34-36
Jn 6:24,25

The people standing around there recognized him at once, ⁵⁵and ran throughout the whole area to spread the news of his arrival, and began carrying sick folks to him on mats and stretchers. ⁵⁶Wherever he went—in villages and cities, and out on

6:56
Mk 5:28
Acts 5:15

6:52 *For they didn't want to believe,* literally, "For their hearts were hardened."

JESUS WALKS ON THE WATER
After feeding the people who had followed to hear him at Bethsaida-Julias, Jesus sent the people home, sent his disciples by boat toward Bethsaida, and went to pray. The disciples encountered a storm and Jesus walked to them on the water. They landed at Gennesaret.

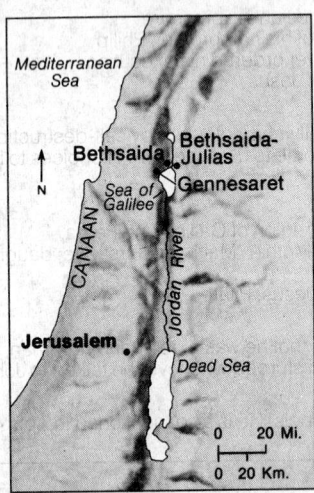

6:50 The disciples were afraid, but Jesus' presence calmed their fears. We all experience fear. Do we try to deal with it ourselves, or do we let Jesus deal with it? In times of fear and uncertainty, it is calming to know that Christ is always with us. To recognize his presence is the antidote for fear.

6:52 The disciples didn't want to believe, perhaps because (1) they couldn't accept the fact that this human named Jesus was really the Son of God; (2) they dared not believe that the Messiah would choose them as his followers—it was too good to be true; (3) they still did not understand the real purpose for Jesus' coming to earth. Their disbelief took the form of misunderstanding.

Even after watching Jesus miraculously feed 5,000 people, they still could not take the final step of faith to believe he was God's Son. If they had, they would not have been amazed that he could walk on water. They did not transfer the truth they already knew about him to their own lives. We read that Jesus walked on the water, and yet we often marvel that he is able to work in our life. We must not only believe these miracles really occurred; we must also transfer the truth to our own life situations.

6:53 Gennesaret was a small fertile plain located on the west side of the Sea of Galilee. Capernaum, Jesus' home, sat at the northern edge of this plain.

6:56 Jewish men wore ankle-length robes called tunics. Over the tunic they wore a waist-length vest called a tallith. Four tassels were sewed to the four lower corners of the fringe of the tallith. The people probably expected Jesus' healing power to be released when they touched these tassels on the fringe of his tallith (Matthew 9:20, 21). They may not have realized that it was faith in Jesus, not magical power, that healed them.

6:49 The disciples were surprised to see Jesus walking beside them on the water. But they should have realized he would help them when they were in trouble. Though they had lost sight of him, he had not lost sight of them. His concern for them overcame their lack of faith. The next time you are in "deep water," remember that Christ knows your struggle and cares for you.

the farms—they laid the sick in the market plazas and streets, and begged him to let them at least touch the fringes of his clothes; and as many as touched him were healed.

Jesus teaches about inner purity
(102/Matthew 15:1–20)

7:1
Mt 15:1-20

7:2
Lk 11:38

7:3
Gal 1:14
Col 2:8

7 One day some Jewish religious leaders arrived from Jerusalem to investigate him, 2and noticed that some of his disciples failed to follow the usual Jewish rituals before eating. 3(For the Jews, especially the Pharisees, will never eat until they have sprinkled their arms to the elbows, as required by their ancient traditions. 4So when they come home from the market they must always sprinkle themselves in this way before touching any food. This is but one of many examples of laws and regulations they have clung to for centuries, and still follow, such as their ceremony of cleansing for pots, pans and dishes.)

5So the religious leaders asked him, "Why don't your disciples follow our age-old customs? For they eat without first performing the washing ceremony."

7:6,7
Isa 29:13
Tit 1:16

6, 7Jesus replied, "You bunch of hypocrites! Isaiah the prophet described you very well when he said, 'These people speak very prettily about the Lord but they have no love for him at all. Their worship is a farce, for they claim that God commands the people to obey their petty rules.' How right Isaiah was! 8For you ignore God's specific orders and substitute your own traditions. 9You are simply rejecting God's laws and trampling them under your feet for the sake of tradition.

7:9
Isa 24:4,5

7:10
Ex 20:12; 21:17
Lev 20:19
Deut 5:16
Prov 20:20
1 Tim 5:8

10For instance, Moses gave you this law from God: 'Honor your father and mother.' And he said that anyone who speaks against his father or mother must die. 11But you say it is perfectly all right for a man to disregard his needy parents, telling them, 'Sorry, I can't help you! For I have given to God what I could have given to you.' 12, 13And so you break the law of God in order to protect your man-made tradition. And this is only one example. There are many, many others."

7:11
Lev 1:2

7:3 *sprinkled their arms to the elbows,* literally, "to wash with the fist."

GOSPEL ACCOUNTS FOUND ONLY IN MARK	Section	Topic	Significance
	4:26–29	Story of the growing seeds	We must share the good news of Jesus with other people, but only God makes it grow in their lives.
	7:31–37	Jesus heals a deaf man with a speech impediment	Jesus cares about our physical as well as spiritual needs.
	8:22–26	Jesus heals the blind man of Bethsaida	Jesus is considerate because he makes sure this man's sight is fully restored.

7:1ff The religious leaders sent some investigators from their headquarters in Jerusalem to check up on Jesus. They didn't like what they found, however, because Jesus scolded them for keeping the law in order to look holy instead of to honor God. The prophet Isaiah accused the religious leaders of his day for doing the same (Isaiah 29:13). Jesus used Isaiah's words to accuse these men.

7:3, 4 Mark explained these Jewish rituals because he was writing to a non-Jewish audience. Before each meal, devout Jews performed a short ceremony, washing their hands and arms in a specific way. To them, this was a symbol of being cleansed from any contact they might have had with anything considered unclean. Jesus said the Pharisees were wrong in thinking they were acceptable to God because they were clean on the outside.

7:6, 7 Hypocrisy is pretending to be something you are not. Jesus called the Pharisees hypocrites because they worshiped God not because they loved him, but because it was profitable, it made them look holy, and it increased their status in the community. We become hypocrites when we (1) pay more attention to reputation than to character, (2) carefully follow certain religious practices while allowing our hearts to remain distant from God, and (3)

emphasize our virtues but others' sins.

7:8, 9 The Pharisees added hundreds of their own petty rules and regulations to God's holy laws, and then tried to force people to follow them. These men claimed to know God's will in every detail of life. Religious leaders today still try to add rules and regulations to God's Word, causing much confusion among believers. It is idolatry to claim your interpretation of God's Word is as important as God's Word itself. It is especially dangerous to set up non-biblical standards for *others* to follow. Instead, look to Christ for guidance about your own behavior, and let him lead others in the details of their lives.

7:10, 11 The Pharisees used God as an excuse to avoid helping their families, especially their parents. They thought it was more important to put money in the Temple treasury than to help their needy parents, although God's law specifically says to honor fathers and mothers (Exodus 20:12) and to care for those in need (Leviticus 25:35–43). We should give money and time to God, but we must never use God as an excuse to neglect our responsibilities. Helping those in need is one of the most important ways to honor God.

14Then Jesus called to the crowd to come and hear. "All of you listen," he said, "and try to understand. 15, 16Your souls aren't harmed by what you eat, but by what you think and say!"

7:15
Acts 10:14,15
1 Cor 8:8
1 Tim 4:4

17Then he went into a house to get away from the crowds, and his disciples asked him what he meant by the statement he had just made.

7:17
Mk 2:1,2; 3:20
9:28

18"Don't you understand either?" he asked. "Can't you see that what you eat won't harm your soul? 19For food doesn't come in contact with your heart, but only passes through the digestive system." (By saying this he showed that every kind of food is kosher.)

7:19
Lk 11:41
Acts 10:15; 11:9

20And then he added, "It is the thoughtlife that pollutes. 21For from within, out of men's hearts, come evil thoughts of lust, theft, murder, adultery, 22wanting what belongs to others, wickedness, deceit, lewdness, envy, slander, pride, and all other folly. 23All these vile things come from within; they are what pollute you and make you unfit for God."

7:20
Rom 14:1-12
Col 2:16

7:21
Gal 5:19
Tit 1:15

2. Jesus' ministry beyond Galilee
Jesus sends a demon out of a girl
(103/Matthew 15:21–28)

24Then he left Galilee and went to the region of Tyre and Sidon, and tried to keep it a secret that he was there, but couldn't. For as usual the news of his arrival spread fast.

7:24
Mt 15:21-28

25Right away a woman came to him whose little girl was possessed by a demon. She had heard about Jesus and now she came and fell at his feet, 26and pled with him to release her child from the demon's control. (But she was Syrophoenician—a "despised Gentile!")

27Jesus told her, "First I should help my own family—the Jews. It isn't right to take the children's food and throw it to the dogs."

7:27
Mt 10:5,6
Acts 13:46
Rom 9:4
Eph 2:11,12

7:15, 16 Verse 16 is omitted in many of the ancient manuscripts. "If any man has ears to hear, let him hear." *Your souls aren't harmed by what you eat, but by what you think and say,* literally, "what proceeds out of the man defiles the man." **7:27** *First I should help my own family—the Jews,* literally, "Let the children eat first."

7:18 Do we worry more about what is in our diets than what is in our hearts and minds? As they interpreted the dietary laws (Leviticus 11), the Jews believed they could be clean before God because of what they *did not* eat. But Jesus pointed out that sin actually begins in the attitudes and intentions of the inner person. He did not downgrade the law, but he paved the way for the change made clear in Acts 10:9–29 when God removed the cultural restrictions regarding food. We are not pure because of outward acts—we become pure on the inside as Christ renews our minds and makes us over in his image.

7:20-23 An evil action begins with a single thought. Our thoughts can pollute us, leading us into sin. Allowing our thoughts to dwell on lust, envy, hate, or revenge will lead to evil actions. Don't be made unfit for God. Instead, "think about things that are pure and lovely, and dwell on the fine good things in others. Think about all you can praise God for and be glad about" (Philippians 4:8).

7:24 Jesus traveled about 50 miles to Tyre and then went to Sidon. These were two port cities on the Mediterranean Sea north of Israel. Both cities had flourishing trade and were very wealthy.
In David's day, Tyre was on friendly terms with Israel (2 Samuel 5:11), but soon afterward the city became known for its wickedness. Its king, Ethbaal, even claimed to be God (Ezekiel 28:1ff). Tyre rejoiced when Jerusalem was destroyed in 586 B.C. because without Israel's competition, Tyre's trade and profits would increase. It was into this evil and materialistic culture that Jesus brought his message. It is interesting that he stressed the importance of inner purity just before visiting Tyre.

7:26 This woman is called a Syrophoenician in Mark and a Canaanite in Matthew. Mark's designation refers to her political background. His Roman audience would easily identify her by the part of the Empire that was her home. Matthew's description was designed for his Jewish audience, who remembered the

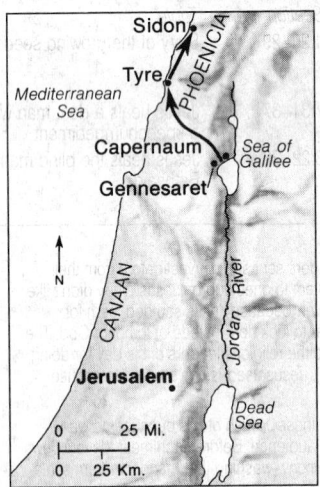

MINISTRY IN PHOENICIA
Jesus' ministry was to all people—first to Jews but also to Gentiles. Jesus took his disciples from Galilee to Tyre and Sidon, large cities in Phoenicia, where he healed a Gentile woman's daughter.

Canaanites as bitter enemies when Israel was settling the Promised Land.

7:27 *Dog* was a term the Jews commonly applied to any Gentiles, because the Jews considered these pagan people no more likely than dogs to receive God's blessing. Jesus, however, was not degrading the woman by using this term, but simply explaining to her God's plan to present his message first to Jews. The woman did not try to argue. Using Jesus' choice of words, she pointed out

28She replied, "That's true, sir, but even the puppies under the table are given some scraps from the children's plates."

7:29
Mt 9:29

29"Good!" he said, "You have answered well—so well that I have healed your little girl. Go on home, for the demon has left her!"

7:30
Josh 21:45

30And when she arrived home, her little girl was lying quietly in bed, and the demon was gone.

The crowd marvels at Jesus' healings
(104/Matthew 15:29–31)

7:31
Mt 15:29-31

31From Tyre he went to Sidon, then back to the Sea of Galilee by way of the Ten Towns. 32A deaf man with a speech impediment was brought to him, and everyone begged Jesus to lay his hands on the man and heal him.

7:33
Mk 8:23
Jn 9:6

33Jesus led him away from the crowd and put his fingers into the man's ears, then spat and touched the man's tongue with the spittle. 34Then, looking up to heaven, he sighed and commanded, "Open!" 35Instantly the man could hear perfectly and speak plainly!

7:34
Isa 35:5,6
Mt 11:5
Mk 6:41
Jn 11:41; 17:1

7:36
Mk 5:43

36Jesus told the crowd not to spread the news, but the more he forbade them, the more they made it known, 37for they were overcome with utter amazement. Again and again they said, "Everything he does is wonderful; he even corrects deafness and stammering!"

Jesus feeds four thousand
(105/Matthew 15:32–39)

8:2
Ps 111:4,5
145:9
Mk 1:41
Heb 2:17; 4:15
5:1-3

8 One day about this time as another great crowd gathered, the people ran out of food again. Jesus called his disciples to discuss the situation.

"I pity these people," he said, "for they have been here three days, and have nothing left to eat. 3And if I send them home without feeding them, they will faint along the road! For some of them have come a long distance."

8:4
Num 11:21,22
2 Kgs 4:42,43

4"Are we supposed to find food for them here in the desert?" his disciples scoffed.

8:5
Mk 6:38

5"How many loaves of bread do you have?" he asked.

"Seven," they replied. 6So he told the crowd to sit down on the ground. Then he took the seven loaves, thanked God for them, broke them into pieces and passed them to his disciples; and the disciples placed them before the people. 7A few small

8:6
1 Tim 4:4,5

8:7
Mt 14:19

---

that she was willing to be considered a dog as long as she could receive God's blessing for her daughter. Ironically, many Jews would lose God's blessing and salvation because they rejected Jesus. Many Gentiles, whom the Jews considered "dogs," would find salvation because they recognized Jesus.

7:29 This miracle shows that Jesus' power over demons is so great that he doesn't need to be present physically in order to free someone. His power spans any distance.

7:36 Jesus asked the people not to spread the news of this healing because he didn't want to be seen simply as a miracle worker. He didn't want the people to miss his real message.

8:1 This is a different miracle from the feeding of the 5,000 described in chapter 6. At that time, those fed were mostly Jews. This time Jesus was ministering to a Gentile crowd in the Gentile region of the Ten Towns, or Decapolis. Jesus' work and message were beginning to have an impact on large numbers of Gentiles.

8:1–3 Do you ever feel God is so busy with important concerns that he can't possibly be aware of your needs? Just as Jesus was concerned about those people's need for food, he is concerned about our daily needs. At another time Jesus said, "Don't worry at all about having enough food and clothing. Your heavenly Father already knows perfectly well that you need them" (Matthew 6:31, 32). Do you have concerns that you think would not interest God? There is no concern too large for him to handle and no need too small to escape his interest.

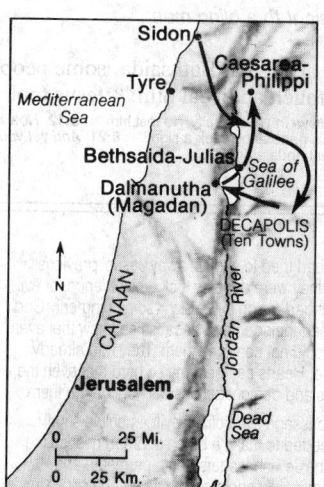

CONTINUED MINISTRY
After taking a roundabout way back to Galilee through the Ten Towns. Jesus returned to Dalmanutha where Jewish leaders questioned his authority. From there he went to Bethsaida-Julias and on to Caesarea-Philippi. Here he talked with his disciples about his authority and coming events.

fish were found, too, so Jesus also blessed these and told the disciples to serve them.

8,9And the whole crowd ate until they were full, and afterwards he sent them home. There were about 4,000 people in the crowd that day and when the scraps were picked up after the meal, there were seven very large basketfuls left over!

Religious leaders ask for a sign in the sky
(106/Matthew 16:1–4)

10Immediately after this he got into a boat with his disciples and came to the region of Dalmanutha.

8:10
Mt 15:39—16:12

11When the local Jewish leaders learned of his arrival they came to argue with him.

"Do a miracle for us," they said. "Make something happen in the sky. Then we will believe in you."

8:11
Mt 12:38
16:1-10
Lk 11:16
Jn 6:30
1 Cor 1:22

12He sighed deeply when he heard this and he said, "Certainly not. How many more miracles do you people need?"

Jesus warns against wrong teaching
(107/Matthew 16:5–12)

13So he got back into the boat and left them, and crossed to the other side of the lake. 14But the disciples had forgotten to stock up on food before they left, and had only one loaf of bread in the boat.

15As they were crossing, Jesus said to them very solemnly, "Beware of the yeast of King Herod and of the Pharisees."

8:15
Lk 12:1

16"What does he mean?" the disciples asked each other. They finally decided that he must be talking about their forgetting to bring bread.

17Jesus realized what they were discussing and said, "No, that isn't it at all! Can't you understand? Are your hearts too hard to take it in? 18'Your eyes are to see with—why don't you look? Why don't you open your ears and listen?' Don't you remember anything at all?

8:17
Mk 6:52
8:18
Ezek 12:2

19"What about the 5,000 men I fed with five loaves of bread? How many basketfuls of scraps did you pick up afterwards?"

"Twelve," they said.

8:19
Mt 14:20
Mk 6:43,44
Lk 9:17
Jn 6:13

20"And when I fed the 4,000 with seven loaves, how much was left?"

"Seven basketfuls," they said.

8:20
Mt 15:37
Mk 8:8,9

21"And yet you think I'm worried that we have no bread?"

Jesus restores sight to a blind man
(108)

22When they arrived at Bethsaida, some people brought a blind man to him and begged him to touch and heal him. 23Jesus took the blind man by the hand and led

8:23
Mk 7:33
Jn 9:6

8:11 Then we will believe in you, literally, "to test him." **8:12** How many more miracles do you people need? literally, "Why does this generation seek a sign?" **8:21** And yet you think I'm worried that we have no bread? literally, "Do you not yet understand?"

8:11 The Pharisees had tried to explain away Jesus' previous miracles by claiming they were done by luck, coincidence, or evil power. So they demanded a sign in the sky—something only God could do. Jesus refused their demand because he knew that even this kind of miracle would not convince them. They had already decided not to believe. Hearts can become so hard that even the most convincing facts and demonstrations will not change them.

8:15ff Yeast in this passage symbolizes evil. As only a small amount of yeast is needed to make a batch of bread rise, so the hardheartedness of the Jewish leaders could permeate and contaminate the entire society and make it rise up against Jesus.

8:15 Mark mentions the "yeast of King Herod and the Pharisees," while Matthew talks about the "yeast of the Sadducees and Pharisees." Mark's audience, mostly non-Jews, would have known

about King Herod, but not necessarily about the Jewish religious sect of the Sadducees. Thus Mark quoted the part of Jesus' statement that his readers would understand. When Mark refers to King Herod he is talking about the Herodians, a group of Jews who supported King Herod. Many Herodians were also Sadducees.

8:17, 18 How could the disciples experience so many of Jesus' miracles and yet be so slow to comprehend his true identity? They had already seen Jesus feed over 5,000 people with five loaves and two fish (6:35–44), yet now they doubted whether he could feed another large group. Sometimes we are also slow to catch on. Although Christ has brought us through trials and temptations in the past, we are slow to believe he will do it in the future. Is your heart too closed to take in all that God can do for you? Don't be like the disciples. Remember what Christ has done, and have faith that he will do it again.

him out of the village, and spat upon his eyes, and laid his hands over them. "Can you see anything now?" Jesus asked him.

²⁴The man looked around. "Yes!" he said, "I see men! But I can't see them very clearly; they look like tree trunks walking around!"

²⁵Then Jesus placed his hands over the man's eyes again and as the man stared intently, his sight was completely restored, and he saw everything clearly, drinking in the sights around him.

8:26
Mt 8:4

²⁶Jesus sent him home to his family. "Don't even go back to the village first," he said.

Peter says Jesus is the Messiah
(109/Matthew 16:13–20; Luke 9:18–20)

8:27
Mt 16:13-20
Lk 9:18-21

²⁷Jesus and his disciples now left Galilee and went out to the villages of Caesarea Philippi. As they were walking along he asked them, "Who do the people think I am? What are they saying about me?"

8:28
Mt 14:2

²⁸"Some of them think you are John the Baptist," the disciples replied, "and others say you are Elijah or some other ancient prophet come back to life again."

8:29
Jn 6:69; 11:27

²⁹Then he asked, "Who do you think I am?" Peter replied, "You are the Messiah." ³⁰But Jesus warned them not to tell anyone!

Jesus predicts his death the first time
(110/Matthew 16:21–28; Luke 9:21–27)

8:31
Mt 16:21-28; 17:22, 23
Lk 9:22-27

³¹Then he began to tell them about the terrible things he would suffer, and that he would be rejected by the elders and the Chief Priests and the other Jewish leaders—and be killed, and that he would rise again three days afterwards. ³²He talked about it quite frankly with them, so Peter took him aside and chided him. "You shouldn't say things like that," he told Jesus.

8:33
Rom 8:7

³³Jesus turned and looked at his disciples and then said to Peter very sternly, "Satan, get behind me! You are looking at this only from a human point of view and not from God's."

8:31 *he would suffer*, literally, "the Son of Man would suffer."   **8:32** *chided him*, "began to rebuke him."

8:25 Why did Jesus touch the man a second time before he could see? This miracle was not too difficult for Jesus, but he chose to do it in stages, possibly to show the disciples that some healing would be gradual rather than instantaneous or to demonstrate that spiritual truth is not always perceived clearly at first. Before Jesus left, however, the man was healed completely.

8:27 Caesarea Philippi was an especially pagan city, known for its worship of Greek gods and its temples devoted to the ancient god Baal. Herod Philip, mentioned in Mark 6:18, changed the city's name from Caesarea to Caesarea Philippi so that it would not be confused with the coastal city of Caesarea (Acts 8:40), the capital of the territory ruled by his brother, Herod Antipas. This pagan city, where many gods were recognized, was a fitting place for Jesus to ask the disciples to recognize his identity as the Son of God.

8:28 For the story of John the Baptist, see Mark 1:1–11 and 6:14–29. For Elijah's story, see 1 Kings 17—20 and 2 Kings 1, 2.

8:29 Jesus asked the disciples who others thought he was; then he focused on them: "Who do *you* think I am?" It is not enough to know what others say about Jesus: you must know, understand, and accept for yourself that he is the Messiah. You must move from curiosity to commitment, from admiration to adoration.

8:30 Why did Jesus warn his own disciples not to tell anyone the truth about him? Jesus knew they needed more instruction about the work he would accomplish through his death and resurrection. Without more teaching, the disciples would have only half the

picture. When they confessed Jesus as the Christ, they still didn't know all that it meant.

8:31 From this point on, Jesus spoke plainly and directly to his disciples about his death and resurrection. He began to prepare them for what was going to happen to him by telling them three times that he would soon die (8:31; 9:31; 10:33, 34).

8:32, 33 In this moment, Peter was not considering God's purposes, but only his natural human desires and feelings. He wanted Christ to be King, but not the suffering servant prophesied in Isaiah 53. He was ready to receive the glory of following the Messiah, but not the persecution. The Christian life is not a paved road to wealth and ease. It often involves hard work, persecution, privation, and deep suffering. Peter saw only part of the picture. Don't repeat his mistake—instead, focus on the good that God can bring out of apparent evil, and the resurrection that follows crucifixion.

8:33 Peter was often the spokesman for all the disciples. In singling him out, Jesus may have been addressing all of them indirectly. Unknowingly, the disciples were trying to prevent Jesus from going to the cross, his real mission on earth. Satan tempted Jesus to do the same thing (Matthew 4). Whereas Satan's motives were evil, the disciples were motivated by love and admiration for Jesus. Nevertheless, the disciples' job was not to guide and protect Jesus, but to follow him. Only after Jesus' death and resurrection would they fully understand why he had to die.

34Then he called his disciples and the crowds to come over and listen. "If any of you wants to be my follower," he told them, "you must put aside your own pleasures and shoulder your cross, and follow me closely. 35If you insist on saving your life, you will lose it. Only those who throw away their lives for my sake and for the sake of the Good News will ever know what it means to really live.

36"And how does a man benefit if he gains the whole world and loses his soul in the process? 37For is anything worth more than his soul? 38And anyone who is ashamed of me and my message in these days of unbelief and sin, I, the Messiah, will be ashamed of him when I return in the glory of my Father, with the holy angels."

9 Jesus went on to say to his disciples, "Some of you who are standing here right now will live to see the Kingdom of God arrive in great power!"

Jesus is transfigured on the mountain
(111/Matthew 17:1–13; Luke 9:28–36)

2Six days later Jesus took Peter, James and John to the top of a mountain. No one else was there.

Suddenly his face began to shine with glory, 3and his clothing became dazzling white, far more glorious than any earthly process could ever make it! 4Then Elijah and Moses appeared and began talking with Jesus!

5"Teacher, this is wonderful!" Peter exclaimed. "We will make three shelters here, one for each of you. . . ."

6He said this just to be talking, for he didn't know what else to say and they were all terribly frightened.

7But while he was still speaking these words, a cloud covered them, blotting out the sun, and a voice from the cloud said, *"This* is my beloved Son. Listen to *him."*

8:38 *the Messiah,* literally, "the Son of Man."

8:34 Mt 10:38 Lk 14:27

8:35 Lk 17:33 Jn 12:25 Rev 12:11

8:38 Mt 10:33 Lk 12:9 Rom 1:16 2 Thess 1:7 2 Tim 1:8; 2:12 Heb 11:16

9:1 Mt 16:28; 24:30 Lk 9:27; 22:18

9:2 Mt 17:1-13 Lk 9:28-36

9:3 Dan 7:9 Mt 28:3

9:7 Ex 40:34 2 Pet 1:17,18 Heb 1:2; 2:3; 12:25

8:34 The Romans, Mark's original audience, knew what shouldering a cross meant. Death on a cross was a form of execution used by Rome for dangerous criminals. A prisoner carried his own cross to the place of execution, signifying submission to Rome's power.

Jesus used carrying a cross to illustrate the ultimate submission required to follow him. He is not against pleasure, nor is he saying that we should seek pain needlessly. He is talking about the heroic effort needed to follow him moment by moment, to do his will even when the work is difficult and the future looks bleak.

8:35 To throw away our lives for the sake of the Good News doesn't mean our lives are useless. Rather, it means that nothing—not even life itself—can compare to what we can gain with Christ. Jesus wants us to *choose* to follow him rather than to lead a life of sin and self-satisfaction. He wants us to stop trying to control our own lives and to let him be in charge. This makes good sense because, as the Creator, only he knows what real life is about. He asks for submission, not self-hatred; he asks us to throw away the self-centeredness that says we know better than God how to run our lives.

8:36, 37 Many people spend their lives seeking pleasure. Jesus said, however, that the world of pleasure centered on possessions, position, or power is ultimately worthless. Whatever we have on earth is only temporary; it cannot be exchanged for our souls. If you work hard at getting what you want, you might eventually have a "pleasurable" life, but in the end you will find it hollow and empty. Are you willing to make the pursuit of God more important than the selfish pursuit of pleasure? Follow Jesus, and you will know what it means to really live in this life and to have life eternal as well.

8:38 Jesus constantly turns the world's perspective upside down with talk of saving and losing, throwing away and finding. Here he faces us with a choice. Those so embarrassed by Jesus now that they reject him in this life will see him clearly at the time of judgment, but it will be too late. Those who see him clearly now and accept him will escape the shame of being rejected at his final judgment.

9:1 What did Jesus mean when he said that some of the disciples would see the Kingdom arrive? There are several possibilities. He could have been foretelling his transfiguration, his resurrection and ascension, the coming of the Holy Spirit at Pentecost, or his second coming. The transfiguration is a strong possibility because it follows immediately in the text. In the transfiguration (9:2–8), Peter, James, and John saw Jesus' true identity and power as the Son of God (2 Peter 1:16).

9:2 We don't know why Jesus singled out Peter, James, and John for this special revelation. Perhaps they were the ones most ready to understand and accept this great truth revealed about Jesus. These three disciples were the inner circle of the group of twelve. They were among the first to hear Jesus' call (1:16–19). They headed the Gospel lists of disciples (3:16). And they were present at certain healings where others were excluded (Luke 8:51).

9:2 Jesus took the disciples to either Mount Hermon or Mount Tabor. A mountain was often associated with closeness to God and readiness to receive his words. God had appeared to both Moses (Exodus 24:12–18) and Elijah (1 Kings 19:8–18) on mountains.

9:3ff The transfiguration revealed Christ's true nature as God's Son. God's voice singled Jesus out from Moses and Elijah as the long-awaited Messiah with full divine authority. Moses represented the law, and Elijah, the prophets. With their appearance, Jesus was shown as the fulfillment of both the Old Testament law and the prophetic promises.

Jesus was not a reincarnation of Elijah or Moses. He was not merely one of the prophets. As God's only Son, he far surpasses their authority and power. Many voices try to tell us how to live and how to know God personally. Some of these are helpful; many are not. We must first listen to Jesus, and then evaluate all other authorities in light of his revelation.

⁸Then suddenly they looked around and Moses and Elijah were gone, and only Jesus was with them.

⁹As they descended the mountainside he told them never to mention what they had seen until after he had risen from the dead. ¹⁰So they kept it to themselves, but often talked about it, and wondered what he meant by "rising from the dead."

¹¹Now they began asking him about something the Jewish religious leaders often spoke of, that Elijah must return [before the Messiah could come]. ¹²,¹³Jesus agreed that Elijah must come first and prepare the way—and that he had, in fact, already come! And that he had been terribly mistreated, just as the prophets had predicted. Then Jesus asked them what the prophets could have been talking about when they predicted that the Messiah would suffer and be treated with utter contempt.

Jesus heals a demon-possessed boy
(112/Matthew 17:14–21; Luke 9:37–43)

¹⁴At the bottom of the mountain they found a great crowd surrounding the other nine disciples, as some Jewish leaders argued with them. ¹⁵The crowd watched Jesus in awe as he came toward them, and then ran to greet him. ¹⁶"What's all the argument about?" he asked.

¹⁷One of the men in the crowd spoke up and said, "Teacher, I brought my son for you to heal—he can't talk because he is possessed by a demon. ¹⁸And whenever the demon is in control of him it dashes him to the ground and makes him foam at the mouth and grind his teeth and become rigid. So I begged your disciples to cast out the demon, but they couldn't do it."

¹⁹Jesus said [to his disciples], "Oh, what tiny faith you have; how much longer must I be with you until you believe? How much longer must I be patient with you? Bring the boy to me."

9:9 *after he had risen,* literally, "after the Son of Man had risen." **9:11** *before the Messiah could come,* implied. **9:12, 13** *the Messiah,* literally, "the Son of Man." **9:18** *and become rigid,* or, "is growing weaker day by day." **9:19** *to his disciples,* implied. *Oh, what tiny faith you have,* literally, "O unbelieving generation."

9:11
Mal 4:5
Mt 11:14

9:12,13
Gen 3:15
Ps 22:6,7
Isa 50:6; 53:2,3
Dan 9:26
Mt 11:13,14
Lk 1:17; 23:11
Jn 3:14

9:14
Mt 17:14-21
Lk 9:37-43

9:19
Jn 4:48

KEY WORDS IN MARK'S GOSPEL	Word	Selected References	Significance
	Follow	1:17; 8:34; 10:21	Christians must be willing to sacrifice everything for Jesus.
	Listen	4:3; 7:14; 9:7	In order to understand Jesus, we must be open to what he says.
	Understand	4:24; 4:33; 7:18	The more we obey Jesus, the more we will understand his message.
	Immediately (Instantly)	1:20; 1:42; 7:35	Mark uses this word to emphasize Jesus' authority and to keep the story fast-paced.
	Kingdom of God	1:15; 4:30–32; 9:47	Jesus' coming signals a new reign of God on earth.

9:9, 10 Jesus instructed Peter, James, and John not to speak about what they had seen because they would not fully understand what they saw until Jesus had risen from the dead. Then they would realize that only through death could he rise again, showing his power over death and his authority to be King of all. The disciples could not be powerful witnesses for God until they had grasped this truth completely.

It was natural for the disciples to be confused about Jesus' death and resurrection because they could not see into the future. We, on the other hand, have God's entire revealed Word, the Bible, to give us the full meaning of Jesus' death and resurrection. We have no excuse for our unbelief.

9:11–13 When Jesus said Elijah had indeed come, he was speaking of John the Baptist (Matthew 17:11–13).

9:12, 13 It was difficult for the disciples to understand that their Messiah would have to suffer. The Jews who studied the Old Testament prophecies expected the Messiah to be a great king like David, who would overthrow the enemy, Rome. Their vision was limited to their own time and experience.

They could not grasp that the values of God's eternal kingdom were different from the values of the world. They wanted relief from their present problems, but deliverance from sin is far more important than deliverance from physical suffering or political oppression. Our appreciation for Jesus must go beyond what he can do for us here and now.

9:18 Why couldn't the disciples cast out the demon? In Mark 6:12 we read that they cast out demons while on their mission to the villages. Perhaps they had special authority only for that trip; or perhaps their faith had lapsed. Mark tells this story to show that the battle with Satan is a difficult, ongoing struggle. Victory over sin and temptation comes through faith in Jesus Christ, not through our own effort.

20So they brought the boy, but when he saw Jesus the demon convulsed the child horribly, and he fell to the ground writhing and foaming at the mouth.

21"How long has he been this way?" Jesus asked the father.

And he replied, "Since he was very small, 22and the demon often makes him fall into the fire or into water to kill him. Oh, have mercy on us and do something if you can."

23"If I can?" Jesus asked. *"Anything* is possible if you have faith."

24The father instantly replied, "I *do* have faith; oh, help me to have *more!"*

25When Jesus saw the crowd was growing he rebuked the demon.

"O demon of deafness and dumbness," he said, "I command you to come out of this child and enter him no more!"

26Then the demon screamed terribly and convulsed the boy again and left him; and the boy lay there limp and motionless, to all appearance dead. A murmur ran through the crowd—"He is dead." 27But Jesus took him by the hand and helped him to his feet and he stood up and was all right! 28Afterwards, when Jesus was alone in the house with his disciples, they asked him, "Why couldn't we cast that demon out?"

29Jesus replied, "Cases like this require prayer."

Jesus predicts his death the second time
(113/Matthew 17:22, 23; Luke 9:44, 45)

30, 31Leaving that region they traveled through Galilee where he tried to avoid all publicity in order to spend more time with his disciples, teaching them. He would say to them, "I, the Messiah, am going to be betrayed and killed and three days later I will return to life again."

32But they didn't understand and were afraid to ask him what he meant.

The disciples argue about who would be the greatest
(115/Matthew 18:1–6; Luke 9:46–48)

33And so they arrived at Capernaum. When they were settled in the house where they were to stay he asked them, "What were you discussing out on the road?"

34But they were ashamed to answer, for they had been arguing about which of them was the greatest!

35He sat down and called them around him and said, "Anyone wanting to be the greatest must be the least—the servant of all!"

9:29 *Cases like this require prayer.* "And fasting" is added in some manuscripts, but not the most ancient.

Marginal references:
9:20 Mk 1:26
9:23 Mk 11:22-24 / Lk 17:6 / Jn 11:40 / Acts 14:9
9:24 Eph 2:8
9:25 Acts 10:38
9:30 Mt 17:22,23 / Lk 9:43-45
9:31 Mt 16:21 / Mk 8:31 / Lk 9:22
9:33 Mt 18:1-11 / Lk 9:46-50
9:34 Prov 13:10 / Lk 22:24,26
9:35 Mt 20:26,27; 23:11

9:23 These words of Jesus do not mean we can automatically obtain anything we want if we just think positively. Jesus meant that anything is *possible* with faith because nothing is too difficult for God. This is not a teaching on how to pray as much as a statement about God's power to overcome obstacles in his work. We cannot have everything we pray for; but with faith, we can have everything we need to serve him.

9:24 Faith is not something tangible to be taken like medicine. It is an attitude of trusting and believing (Hebrews 11:1, 6). But even our ability to believe is a gift from God (Ephesians 2:8, 9). No matter how much faith we have, we never reach the point of being self-sufficient. Faith is not stored away like money in the bank. Growing in faith is a constant process of daily renewing our trust in Jesus.

9:29 Jesus was telling the disciples that they would face difficult situations that could be resolved only through prayer. Prayer is the key that unlocks faith in our lives. Effective prayer needs both an attitude—complete dependence—and an action—asking. Prayer demonstrates our reliance on God as we humbly invite God to fill us with faith and power. There is no substitute for prayer, especially in circumstances that seem unconquerable.

9:30, 31 At times Jesus limited his public ministry in order to train his disciples in depth. He knew the importance of equipping them to carry on when he returned to heaven. It takes time to learn.

Deep spiritual growth isn't instant, regardless of the quality of experience or teaching. If even the disciples needed to lay aside their work periodically in order to learn from the Master, how much more do we need to alternate working and learning.

9:30, 31 Leaving Caesarea Philippi, Jesus began his last tour through the region of Galilee.

9:32 Why were the disciples afraid to ask Jesus about his prediction of his death? Perhaps it was because the last time they reacted to Jesus' words they were scolded (8:32, 33). In their minds, Jesus seemed morbidly preoccupied with death. Actually it was the disciples who were wrongly preoccupied—constantly thinking about the kingdom they hoped Jesus would bring and their positions in it. They were worried about what would happen to them if Jesus died, and consequently they preferred not to talk about his predictions.

9:34 The disciples had been caught up in their constant struggle for personal success, and they were embarrassed to answer Jesus' question. It is always painful to compare our motives with Christ's. It is not wrong for believers to be industrious or ambitious, but inappropriate ambition is sin. Pride or insecurity can cause us to value position and prestige more than service. In God's kingdom, such motives are destructive. Our ambition should be for Christ's kingdom, not for our own advancement.

9:37
Mt 10:40
Mk 10:16
Jn 13:20

36Then he placed a little child among them; and taking the child in his arms he said to them, 37"Anyone who welcomes a little child like this in my name is welcoming me, and anyone who welcomes me is welcoming my Father who sent me!"

The disciples forbid another to use Jesus' name
(116/Luke 9:49, 50)

9:38
Num 11:26-29

38One of his disciples, John, told him one day, "Teacher, we saw a man using your name to cast out demons; but we told him not to, for he isn't one of our group."

9:39
1 Cor 12:3

9:40
Mt 12:30

9:41
Mt 10:42

9:42
Lk 17:1-3

39"Don't forbid him!" Jesus said. "For no one doing miracles in my name will quickly turn against me. 40Anyone who isn't against us is for us. 41If anyone so much as gives you a cup of water because you are Christ's—I say this solemnly—he won't lose his reward. 42But if someone causes one of these little ones who believe in me to lose faith—it would be better for that man if a huge millstone were tied around his neck and he were thrown into the sea.

Jesus warns against temptation
(117/Matthew 18:7-9)

9:43
Deut 13:6-10
Mt 5:29,30

9:48
Isa 66:24
2 Thess 1:9

9:49
Lev 2:13
Ezek 43:24

9:50
Mt 5:13
Lk 14:34

43, 44"If your hand does wrong, cut it off. Better live forever with one hand than be thrown into the unquenchable fires of hell with two! 45, 46If your foot carries you toward evil, cut it off! Better be lame and live forever than have two feet that carry you to hell.

47"And if your eye is sinful, gouge it out. Better enter the Kingdom of God half blind than have two eyes and see the fires of hell, 48where the worm never dies, and the fire never goes out— 49where all are salted with fire.

50"Good salt is worthless if it loses its saltiness; it can't season anything. So don't lose your flavor! Live in peace with each other."

9:39 *will quickly turn against me,* literally, "will be able to speak evil of me." **9:43, 44** Vss 44, 46 (which are identical with vs 48) are omitted in some of the ancient manuscripts. **9:49** *where all are salted with fire,* literally, "For everyone shall be salted with fire."

9:36, 42 Luke 9:48 states, "Your care for others is the measure of greatness." In Jesus' eyes, whoever welcomes a child welcomes Jesus; giving a cup of cold water to one in need is the same as giving an offering to God. By contrast, harming others or even failing to care for them is a sin. It is possible for thoughtless, selfish people to gain a measure of greatness in the world's eyes, but enduring greatness is measured only by God's standards. What do you use as your measure of greatness—personal achievement or unselfish service?

9:36, 37 Jesus taught the disciples to welcome the children. This was a new approach in a society where children were usually treated as second-class citizens. It is important not only to treat children well, but also to teach them about Jesus. Sunday School should never be regarded as less important than adult Bible study.

9:38 More concerned about their own group's position than in helping free those troubled by demons, the disciples were jealous of a man who healed in Jesus' name. We do the same today when we refuse to participate in worthy causes because (1) they are not affiliated with our denomination, (2) they do not involve the kind of people with whom we feel most comfortable, (3) they don't do things the way we are used to, (4) our efforts won't receive enough recognition. Correct theology is important, but it should never be an excuse to avoid helping those in need.

9:40 Jesus was not saying that being indifferent or neutral toward him is as good as being committed. As he explained in Matthew 12:30, "Anyone who isn't helping me is harming me." Jesus taught that many different people follow him and do work in his name, and they should all get along. Those who share a common faith in Christ should be able to cooperate. People don't have to be just like us to be following Jesus with us.

9:42 This caution against harming little ones in the faith applies both to what we do individually as teachers and examples and to what we allow in our Christian fellowship. Our thoughts and actions must be motivated by love (1 Corinthians 13) and we must be careful about judging others (Matthew 7:1-5; Romans 14:1—15:4). However, we also have a responsibility to confront flagrant sin within the church (1 Corinthians 5:12, 13).

9:43ff Jesus used startling language to stress the importance of cutting sin out of our lives. Painful discipline is required of his true followers. Giving up a relationship, job, or habit that is against God's will may seem just as painful as cutting off a hand. Our high goal, however, is worth any sacrifice; Christ is worth any possible loss. Nothing should stand in the way of faith. We must be ruthless in removing sins from our lives now in order to avoid being stuck with them for eternity. Make your choices from an eternal perspective.

9:48, 49 With these strange words, Jesus pictured the serious and eternal consequences of sin. To the Jews, worms and fire represented both internal and external pain.

9:50 Jesus used salt to illustrate three qualities which should be found in the lives of his people: (1) *We should remember God's faithfulness,* just as salt was used with a sacrifice to recall God's covenant with his people (Leviticus 2:13). (2) *We should be effective in Christian living,* just as salt is effective in giving flavor to food (see Matthew 5:13). When we lose this desire to "salt" the earth with the love and message of God, we become useless to him. (3) *We should live morally* so that we can counteract the decay in society, just as salt preserves food from decay.

Jesus teaches about marriage and divorce
(173/Matthew 19:1–12)

10 Then he left Capernaum and went southward to the Judean borders and into the area east of the Jordan River. And as always there were the crowds; and as usual he taught them.

²Some Pharisees came and asked him, "Do you permit divorce?" Of course they were trying to trap him.

10:2
Mt 19:3-12

³"What did Moses say about divorce?" Jesus asked them.

⁴"He said it was all right," they replied. "He said that all a man has to do is write his wife a letter of dismissal."

10:4
Deut 24:1-3
Mt 5:31

⁵"And why did he say that?" Jesus asked. "I'll tell you why—it was a concession to your hardhearted wickedness. 6, 7But it certainly isn't God's way. For from the very first he made man and woman to be joined together permanently in marriage; therefore a man is to leave his father and mother, ⁸and he and his wife are united so that they are no longer two, but one. ⁹And no man may separate what God has joined together."

10:6
Gen 1:27; 2:24

10:8
1 Cor 6:16
Eph 5:31

¹⁰Later, when he was alone with his disciples in the house, they brought up the subject again.

¹¹He told them, "When a man divorces his wife to marry someone else, he commits adultery against her. ¹²And if a wife divorces her husband and remarries, she, too, commits adultery."

10:11
Mt 5:32
Lk 16:18
Rom 7:2,3

Jesus blesses little children
(174/Matthew 19:13–15; Luke 18:15–17)

¹³Once when some mothers were bringing their children to Jesus to bless them, the disciples shooed them away, telling them not to bother him.

10:13
Mt 19:13-15
Lk 18:15-17

¹⁴But when Jesus saw what was happening he was very much displeased with his

10:1 *Then he left Capernaum,* literally, "And rising up, he went from there." Mentioned here so quietly, this was his final farewell to Galilee. He never returned until after his death and resurrection.   **10:13** *mothers,* implied.

FINAL TRIP TO JUDEA

Jesus quietly left Capernaum, heading toward the borders of Judea before crossing the Jordan River. He preached there before going to Jericho. This trip from Galilee was his last; he would not return before his death.

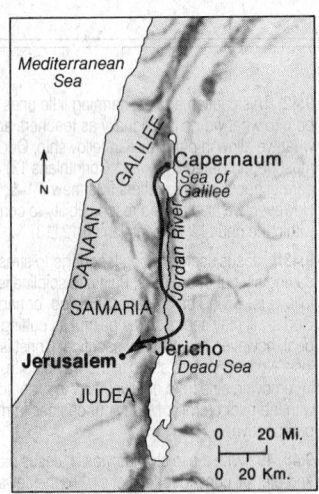

God's intended purpose for marriage and to expose the Pharisees' selfish motives. They were not thinking about what God intended for marriage, but had settled for marriages of convenience. In addition, they were quoting Moses unfairly and out of context. Jesus showed these legal experts how superficial their knowledge really was.

10:5–9 God allowed divorce as a concession to people's sinfulness. Divorce was not approved, but it was instituted to protect the injured party in the midst of a bad situation. Unfortunately, the Pharisees used Deuteronomy 24:1 as an excuse for divorce. Jesus explained that this was not God's intent; instead, God wants married people to consider their marriage permanent. Don't enter marriage with the option of getting out, but be committed to permanence. You'll stand a much better chance of making your marriage work. Don't be hard-hearted like these Pharisees, but be hardheaded in your determination, with God's help, to stay together.

10:6, 7 Women were often treated as property. Marriage and divorce were regarded as transactions similar to buying and selling land. But Jesus condemned this practice, clarifying God's original intention—that marriage bring oneness (Genesis 2:24). Jesus held up God's ideal for marriage and told his followers to live by it.

10:13–16 Jesus was often criticized for spending too much time with the wrong people—children, sinners (Matthew 9:11), tax collectors (Luke 15:1, 2; 19:7). Some, including the disciples, thought Jesus should be spending more time with important leaders and the devout, because this was the way to improve his position and avoid criticism. But Jesus didn't need to improve his position. He was God, and he wanted to speak to those who needed him most.

10:14 Adults are not as trusting as little children. All children need in order to feel secure is a loving look and gentle touch from

10:2 The Pharisees were trying to trap Jesus with their question. If Jesus said he supported divorce, he would be upholding the Pharisees' procedures; and they doubted that he would do that. If he spoke against divorce, however, the crowds would dislike his position. More important, he might incur the wrath of King Herod, who had already killed John the Baptist for speaking out against divorce and adultery (6:17–28). This is what the Pharisees wanted.

The Pharisees saw divorce as a legal issue rather than a spiritual one. Jesus used this test as an opportunity to review

10:15
Mt 18:3
1 Cor 14:20
1 Pet 2:2

disciples and said to them, "Let the children come to me, for the Kingdom of God belongs to such as they. Don't send them away! 15I tell you as seriously as I know how that anyone who refuses to come to God as a little child will never be allowed into his Kingdom."

10:16
Isa 40:11

16Then he took the children into his arms and placed his hands on their heads and he blessed them.

Jesus speaks to the rich young man
(175/Matthew 19:16–30; Luke 18:18–30)

10:17
Mt 19:16-30
Lk 18:18-30

17As he was starting out on a trip, a man came running to him and knelt down and asked, "Good Teacher, what must I do to get to heaven?"

10:19
Ex 20:12-17
Deut 5:16-20
Rom 13:9

18"Why do you call me good?" Jesus asked. "Only God is truly good! 19But as for your question—you know the commandments: don't kill, don't commit adultery, don't steal, don't lie, don't cheat, respect your father and mother."

10:20
Jas 2:10

20"Teacher," the man replied, "I've never once broken a single one of those laws."

10:21
Mt 6:19,20
Lk 12:33
Acts 2:44,45
1 Tim 6:17-19

21Jesus felt genuine love for this man as he looked at him. "You lack only one thing," he told him; "go and sell all you have and give the money to the poor—and you shall have treasure in heaven—and come, follow me."

22Then the man's face fell, and he went sadly away, for he was very rich.

23Jesus watched him go, then turned around and said to his disciples, "It's almost impossible for the rich to get into the Kingdom of God!"

10:24
Ps 52:7

24This amazed them. So Jesus said it again: "Dear children, how hard it is for those who trust in riches to enter the Kingdom of God. 25It is easier for a camel to go through the eye of a needle than for a rich man to enter the Kingdom of God." 26The disciples were incredulous! "Then who in the world can be saved, if not a rich man?" they asked.

10:27
Jer 32:17
Heb 7:25

27Jesus looked at them intently, then said, "Without God, it is utterly impossible. But with God everything is possible."

10:20 *never once*, literally, "from my youth." **10:24** *for those who trust in riches.* Some of the ancient manuscripts do not contain the words, "for those who trust in riches."

---

someone who cares. Complete intellectual understanding is not one of their requirements. They believe us if they trust us. Jesus said that all must believe in him with this kind of childlike faith. We should not have to understand all the mysteries of the universe; it should be enough to know that God loves us and provides forgiveness for our sin. This doesn't mean we should be childish or immature, but we should trust God with a child's simplicity and purity.

10:17–23 This young man wanted to be sure he would get eternal life, so he asked what he could *do*. He said he'd never once broken any of the laws Jesus mentioned (verse 19), and perhaps he had kept the Pharisees' loophole-filled version of them. But Jesus lovingly broke through his pride with a challenge that brought out his true motives: "Sell all you have and give to the poor." Here was the barrier that could keep this young man out of the Kingdom: his love of money. Money represented his pride of accomplishment and self-effort. Ironically, his attitude made him unable to keep the first commandment, to let nothing be more important than God (Exodus 20:3). He could not meet the one requirement Jesus gave—to turn his whole heart and life over to God. The man came to Jesus wondering what he could do; he left seeing what he was unable to do. What barriers are keeping you from turning your life over to Christ?

10:18 When Jesus asked this question, he was saying, "Do you really know to whom you are talking?" Because only God is truly good, the man was calling Jesus God. This was true, of course, but he may not have realized it.

10:21 What does your money mean to you? Although Jesus wanted this man to sell everything and give his money to the poor,

this does not mean that all believers should sell all their possessions. Most of his followers did not sell everything, although they used their possessions to bless others. Instead, this story shows us that we must not let anything keep us from following Jesus. We must remove all barriers to serving him fully. If Jesus asked you to, could you give up your house? your car? your way of eating? Could you move to a crowded apartment in a poor neighborhood, ride the city buses, and never know where your next meal was coming from, if that was how Jesus wanted you to serve him? Your reaction may show your attitude toward money—whether it is your servant or your master.

10:21 Jesus showed genuine love for this man, even though he knew he might not follow him. Genuine love is able to give tough advice; it doesn't hedge around the truth. Christ loved us enough to die for us, but he still gives tough advice. If his love were superficial, he would give us only approval; but because his love is complete, he gives us life-changing challenges.

10:23 Jesus said it was very difficult for the rich to get into the kingdom of God because the rich have most of their basic physical needs met and can become self-reliant. When they feel empty, they can buy something new to dull the pain that was meant to drive them toward God. Their abundance becomes their deficiency. The person who has everything on earth can still lack what is most important—eternal life.

10:26 The disciples were incredulous. Was not wealth a blessing from God, a reward for being good? This misconception is still common today. Although many believers enjoy material prosperity, many others live in hardship. Wealth is not a sign of faith or of partiality on God's part.

28Then Peter began to mention all that he and the other disciples had left behind. "We've given up everything to follow you," he said.

10:28
Mk 1:18

29And Jesus replied, "Let me assure you that no one has ever given up anything—home, brothers, sisters, mother, father, children, or property—for love of me and to tell others the Good News, 30who won't be given back, a hundred times over, homes, brothers, sisters, mothers, children, and land—with persecutions!

10:30
Acts 14:22
1 Thess 3:3
2 Tim 3:12

"All these will be his here on earth, and in the world to come he shall have eternal life. 31But many people who seem to be important now will be the least important then; and many who are considered least here shall be greatest there."

10:31
Mt 20:16
Lk 13:30

Jesus predicts his death the third time
(177/Matthew 20:17–19; Luke 18:31–34)

32Now they were on the way to Jerusalem, and Jesus was walking along ahead; and as the disciples were following they were filled with terror and dread.

10:32
Mt 20:17-19
Lk 18:31-34

Taking them aside, Jesus once more began describing all that was going to happen to him when they arrived at Jerusalem.

33"When we get there," he told them, "I, the Messiah, will be arrested and taken before the chief priests and the Jewish leaders, who will sentence me to die and hand me over to the Romans to be killed. 34They will mock me and spit on me and flog me with their whips and kill me; but after three days I will come back to life again."

10:33
Mt 16:21; 26:67
27:30
Mk 8:31; 9:31;
14:65
Lk 9:22
1 Cor 15:3,4

Jesus teaches about serving others
(178/Matthew 20:20–28)

35Then James and John, the sons of Zebedee, came over and spoke to him in a low voice. "Master," they said, "we want you to do us a favor."

10:35
Mt 20:20-28

36"What is it?" he asked.

37"We want to sit on the thrones next to yours in your kingdom," they said, "one at your right and the other at your left!"

38But Jesus answered, "You don't know what you are asking! Are you able to

10:38
Lk 12:50

10:33 *the Messiah,* literally, "the Son of Man."   10:35 *spoke to him in a low voice,* literally, "came up to him."

10:29, 30 Jesus assured the disciples that anyone who gives up something valuable for his sake will be repaid a hundred times over in this life, although not necessarily in the same form. For example, someone may be rejected by his family for accepting Christ, but he will gain the larger family of believers. Along with these rewards, however, we receive persecution because the world hates God. Jesus emphasized persecution to make sure we do not selfishly follow him only for rewards.

10:31 Jesus explained that in the world to come, the values of this world will be reversed. Those who seek status and importance here will have none in heaven. Those who are humble here will be great in heaven. The corrupt condition of our society encourages this confusion in values. We are bombarded by messages that tell us how to be important and feel good, and Jesus' teaching on service to others seems alien. But those who serve others are most qualified to be great in heaven.

10:32 The disciples were afraid of what they thought awaited them in Jerusalem because Jesus had just spoken to them about facing persecution.

10:33 Jesus' death and resurrection should have come as no surprise to the disciples. Here he clearly explained to them what would happen to him. Unfortunately, they didn't really hear what he was saying. Jesus said he was the Messiah, but they thought the Messiah would be a conquering king. He spoke to them of

resurrection, but they wondered how a person could come back to life after being dead. Because Jesus often spoke in parables, the disciples may have thought his words on death and resurrection were another parable they didn't understand. The Gospels include Jesus' predictions of his death and resurrection to show that they were God's plan from the beginning, not an accident.

10:35 Mark records that John and James went to Jesus with their request; in Matthew, their mother also made the request. There is no contradiction in the accounts—mother and sons were in agreement in making the request for honored places in Christ's Kingdom.

10:37 The disciples, like most Jews of that day, had the wrong idea of the Messiah's kingdom as predicted by the Old Testament prophets. They thought Jesus would establish an earthly kingdom that would free Israel from Rome's oppression, and James and John wanted honored places in it. But Jesus' kingdom is not of this world; it is not centered in palaces and thrones, but in the hearts and lives of his followers. The disciples did not understand this until after Jesus' resurrection.

10:38 James and John said they were willing to face any trial for Christ. Both did suffer: James died as a martyr (Acts 12:2), and John was forced to live in exile (Revelation 1:9). It is easy to say we'll suffer anything for Christ, and yet most of us complain every day when even little irritations come. If we say we are willing to suffer on a large scale for Christ, we must also be willing to suffer in little ways.

drink from the bitter cup of sorrow I must drink from? Or to be baptized with the baptism of suffering I must be baptized with?"

10:39
Acts 12:2
Rev 1:9

39"Oh, yes," they said, "we are!"

10:40
Jas 4:3

And Jesus said, "You shall indeed drink from my cup and be baptized with my baptism, 40but I do not have the right to place you on thrones next to mine. Those appointments have already been made."

10:42
Lk 22:25,26

10:43
Mk 9:35
Lk 9:48

41When the other disciples discovered what James and John had asked, they were very indignant. 42So Jesus called them to him and said, "As you know, the kings and great men of the earth lord it over the people; 43but among you it is different. Whoever wants to be great among you must be your servant. 44And whoever wants to be greatest of all must be the slave of all. 45For even I, the Messiah, am not here to be served, but to help others, and to give my life as a ransom for many."

10:45
Jn 13:14
Phil 2:7
1 Tim 2:5,6
Tit 2:14

Jesus heals a blind beggar
(179/Matthew 20:29–34; Luke 18:35–43)

10:46
Mt 20:29-34
Lk 18:35-43

46And so they reached Jericho. Later, as they left town, a great crowd was following. Now it happened that a blind beggar named Bartimaeus (the son of Timaeus) was sitting beside the road as Jesus was going by.

10:47
Isa 11:1
Jer 23:5,6
Rom 1:3
Rev 22:16

47When Bartimaeus heard that Jesus from Nazareth was near, he began to shout out, "Jesus, Son of David, have mercy on me!"

48"Shut up!" some of the people yelled at him.

But he only shouted the louder, again and again, "O Son of David, have mercy on me!"

49When Jesus heard him he stopped there in the road and said, "Tell him to come here."

So they called the blind man. "You lucky fellow," they said, "come on, he's calling you!" 50Bartimaeus yanked off his old coat and flung it aside, jumped up and came to Jesus.

51"What do you want me to do for you?" Jesus asked.

"O Teacher," the blind man said, "I want to see!"

10:52
Isa 35.5
Mt 9:22

52And Jesus said to him, "All right, it's done. Your faith has healed you." And instantly the blind man could see, and followed Jesus down the road!

10:45 *the Messiah*, literally, "the Son of Man." **10:49** *You lucky fellow*, literally, "be of good cheer." **10:52** *All right, it's done*, literally. "Go your way."

10:38 Jesus didn't ridicule James and John for asking, but he denied their request. We can feel free to ask God for anything, but we may be denied. God wants to give us what is best for us, not merely what we want. Some requests are denied for our own good.

10:42–44 James and John wanted the highest positions in Jesus' kingdom. But Jesus told them that true greatness comes in serving others. Peter, one of the disciples who heard this message, expands this thought in 1 Peter 5:1–4. Most businesses, organizations, and institutions in our world measure greatness by high personal achievement. In Christ's kingdom, however, service is the way to get ahead. The desire to be on top won't be a help but a hindrance.

10:45 A ransom was the price paid to release a slave. Jesus paid a ransom for us, since we could not pay it ourselves. His death released all of us from our slavery to sin. That is why Christ died. The disciples thought Jesus' life and power would save them from Rome; Jesus said his *death* would save them from sin, an even greater slavery than Rome's. More about the ransom Jesus paid for us is found in 1 Peter 1:18, 19.

10:46 Jericho was a popular resort city rebuilt by Herod the Great in the Judean desert, not far from the Jordan River crossing. Jesus was on his way to Jerusalem (verse 32) and, after crossing over from Perea, would naturally enter Jericho.

10:46 Beggars were a common sight in most towns. Since most occupations of that day required physical labor, anyone with a crippling disease or handicap was at a severe disadvantage and was usually forced to beg, even though God's laws commanded care for such needy people (Leviticus 25:35–38). Blindness was considered a curse from God for sin; but Jesus refuted this idea when he reached out to heal those who were blind. Jesus' ability to heal the blind was prophesied in Isaiah 29:18; 35:5; 42:7.

10:47 "Son of David" was a popular way of addressing Jesus as the Messiah, because it was known that the Messiah would be a descendant of King David (Isaiah 9:7). The fact that Bartimaeus called Jesus the Son of David shows that he recognized Jesus as the Messiah. His faith in Jesus as the Messiah brought about his healing.

◄ 3. Jesus' ministry in Jerusalem

Jesus rides into Jerusalem on a donkey
(183/Matthew 21:1–11; Luke 19:28–44; John 12:12–19)

11 As they neared Bethphage and Bethany on the outskirts of Jerusalem and came to the Mount of Olives, Jesus sent two of his disciples on ahead. ²"Go into that village over there," he told them, "and just as you enter you will see a colt tied up that has never been ridden. Untie him and bring him here. ³And if anyone asks you what you are doing, just say, 'Our Master needs him and will return him soon.' "

4, 5Off went the two men and found the colt standing in the street, tied outside a house. As they were untying it, some who were standing there demanded, "What are you doing, untying that colt?"

⁶So they said what Jesus had told them to, and then the men agreed.

⁷So the colt was brought to Jesus and the disciples threw their cloaks across its back for him to ride on. ⁸Then many in the crowd spread out their coats along the road before him, while others threw down leafy branches from the fields.

⁹He was in the center of the procession with crowds ahead and behind, and all of them shouting, "Hail to the King!" "Praise God for him who comes in the name of the Lord!" . . . ¹⁰"Praise God for the return of our father David's kingdom. . . ." "Hail to the King of the universe!"

¹¹And so he entered Jerusalem and went into the Temple. He looked around carefully at everything and then left—for now it was late in the afternoon—and went out to Bethany with the twelve disciples.

Jesus clears the Temple again
(184/Matthew 21:12–17; Luke 19:45–48)

¹²The next morning as they left Bethany, he felt hungry. ¹³A little way off he noticed a fig tree in full leaf, so he went over to see if he could find any figs on it. But no, there were only leaves, for it was too early in the season for fruit.

11:1
Mt 21:1-9
Lk 19:29-40
Jn 12:12-19
Acts 1:12

11:7
Zech 9:9

11:9
Ps 118:25,26

11:11
Mt 21:10,17

11:12-14
Mt 21:18,19

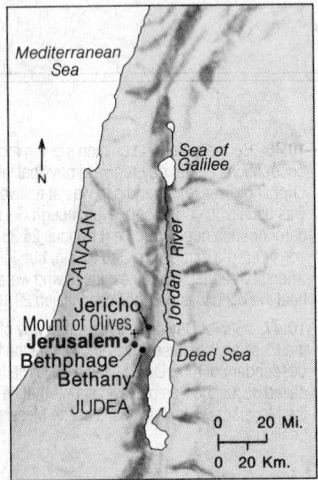

JESUS NEARS JERUSALEM
Leaving Jericho, Jesus headed toward acclaim, then crucifixion, in Jerusalem. During his last week, he stayed outside the city in Bethany, a village on the Mount of Olives, entering Jerusalem to teach, eat the Passover, and finally be crucified.

Mediterranean Sea
Sea of Galilee
N
CANAAN
Jordan River
Jericho
Mount of Olives
Jerusalem
Bethphage
Bethany
JUDEA
Dead Sea
0   20 Mi.
0   20 Km.

Jesus did come, not as a king, but on a donkey's colt that had never been ridden. Kings often rode to war on horses or in wheeled vehicles, but Zechariah 9:9 had predicted that the Messiah would come in peace riding on a lowly donkey. Jesus knew that those who heard him teach at the Temple would return to their homes throughout the world and announce the coming of the Messiah.

11:9, 10 The people exclaimed "Hail to the king!" They were fulfilling the prophecy in Zechariah 9:9. (See also Psalm 24:7–10; 118:26.) They spoke of the return of David's kingdom because of God's words to David in 2 Samuel 7:12–14. The crowd correctly saw Jesus as the fulfillment of these prophecies, but they did not understand where Jesus' kingship would lead him. This same crowd cried out, "Crucify him!" when Jesus stood on trial only a few days later.

11:11–24 There are two parts to this unusual incident: the cursing of the fig tree and the cleansing of the Temple. The cursing of the fig tree was an acted-out parable related to the cleansing of the Temple. The Temple was supposed to be a place of worship, but true worship had disappeared. The fig tree showed promise of fruit, but it produced none. Jesus was showing his anger at religious life without substance. If you "go through the motions" of faith without putting it to work in your life, you are like the fig tree that withered and died. Genuine faith has great potential; ask God to help you bear fruit for his kingdom.

◄ **11:1, 2** This was Sunday of the week Jesus would be crucified, and the great Passover festival was about to begin. Jews came to Jerusalem from all over the Roman world during this week-long celebration to remember the great exodus from Egypt (see Exodus 13). Many in the crowds had heard of or seen Jesus and were hoping he would come to the Temple (John 11:55–57).

¹⁴Then Jesus said to the tree, "You shall never bear fruit again!" And the disciples heard him say it.

11:15
Mt 21:12-17
Lk 19:45-48
Jn 2:13-17

¹⁵When they arrived back to Jerusalem he went to the Temple and began to drive out the merchants and their customers, and knocked over the tables of the money-changers and the stalls of those selling doves, ¹⁶and stopped everyone from bringing in loads of merchandise.

11:17
Isa 56:7
Jer 7:11

¹⁷He told them, "It is written in the Scriptures, 'My Temple is to be a place of prayer for all nations,' but you have turned it into a den of robbers."

KEY CHARACTER-ISTICS OF CHRIST IN THE GOSPELS	Characteristic	References
	Jesus is the Son of God	Matthew 16:15, 16; Mark 1:1 Luke 22:70, 71; John 8:24
	Jesus is God who became human	John 1:1, 2, 14; 20:28
	Jesus is the Christ, the Messiah	Matthew 26:63, 64; Mark 14:61, 62 Luke 9:20; John 4:25, 26
	Jesus came to help sinners	Luke 5:32; Matthew 9:13
	Jesus has power to forgive sins	Mark 2:9–12; Luke 24:47
	Jesus has authority over death	Mark 5:22–24, 35–42 John 11:1–44; Luke 24:5, 6 Matthew 28:5, 6
	Jesus has power to give eternal life	John 10:28; 17:2
	Jesus healed the sick	Matthew 8:5–13; Mark 1:32–34 Luke 5:12–15; John 9:1–7
	Jesus taught with authority	Mark 1:21, 22; Matthew 7:29
	Jesus was compassionate	Mark 1:41; Mark 8:3; Matthew 9:36
	Jesus experienced sorrow	Matthew 26:38; John 11:35
	Jesus never disobeyed God	Matthew 3:15; John 8:46

11:13–25 Fig trees, an inexpensive and popular source of food in Israel, require three years from the time they are planted until they can bear fruit. Each tree yields a great amount of fruit, which is harvested twice a year in late spring and in early autumn. This incident occurred early in the spring fig season when the leaves were beginning to bud. The figs normally grow as the leaves fill out, but this tree, though full of leaves, had no figs; thus, it would not have given fruit that year. The tree looked promising, but offered no fruit. Jesus' harsh words meant that the nation of Israel was like the fig tree. It was supposed to be fruitful, but was spiritually barren.

11:14, 15 Jesus became angry, but he did not sin in his anger. There is a place for righteous indignation. Christians should be upset about sin and injustice and should take a stand against them. Unfortunately, believers are often passive about these important issues and get angry instead over personal insults and petty irritations.

11:15–17 Moneychangers and merchants did big business during Passover. Those who came from foreign countries had to have their money changed into Jewish currency because this was the only money accepted for the Temple tax and for the purchase of animals for the sacrifices. Often the inflated exchange rate enriched the moneychangers, and the exorbitant prices of animals made the merchants wealthy. Their stalls were set up in the Court of the Gentiles in the Temple, frustrating the intentions of non-Jews who had come to worship God (Isaiah 56:6, 7).

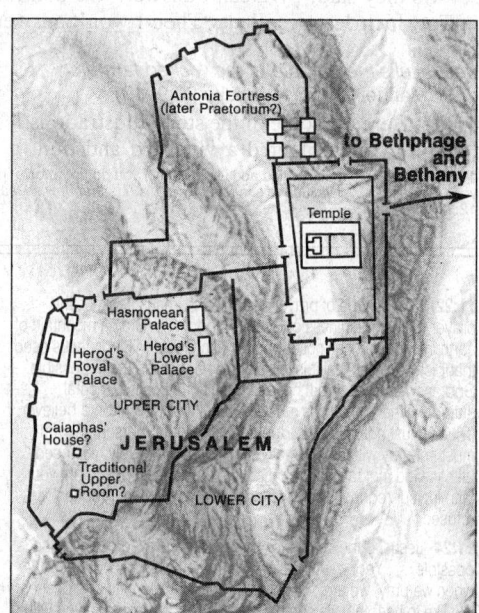

CLEANSING THE TEMPLE On Monday morning of his last week, Jesus left Bethany, entered Jerusalem, and cleansed the Temple of moneychangers and merchants.

18When the chief priests and other Jewish leaders heard what he had done they began planning how best to get rid of him. Their problem was their fear of riots because the people were so enthusiastic about Jesus' teaching.

19That evening as usual they left the city.

11:18
Mt 21:46
Mk 12:12
Lk 4:32; 20:19
Jn 7:1

Jesus says the disciples can pray for anything
(188/Matthew 21:18–22)

20Next morning, as the disciples passed the fig tree he had cursed, they saw that it was withered from the roots! 21Then Peter remembered what Jesus had said to the tree on the previous day, and exclaimed, "Look, Teacher! The fig tree you cursed has withered!"

11:20
Mt 21:20-22

22, 23In reply Jesus said to the disciples, "If you only have faith in God—this is the absolute truth—you can say to this Mount of Olives, 'Rise up and fall into the Mediterranean,' and your command will be obeyed. All that's required is that you really believe and have no doubt! 24Listen to me! You can pray for *anything,* and *if you believe, you have it;* it's yours! 25But when you are praying, first forgive anyone you are holding a grudge against, so that your Father in heaven will forgive you your sins too."

11:22
Mt 17:20
Lk 17:6
11:24
Mt 7:7
Lk 11:9
Jn 14:12-14; 15:7;
16:24
Jas 1:5-8
11:25
Mt 6:14,15
Eph 4:32

Religious leaders challenge Jesus' authority
(189/Matthew 21:23–27; Luke 20:1–8)

26, 27, 28By this time they had arrived in Jerusalem again, and as he was walking through the Temple area, the chief priests and other Jewish leaders came up to him demanding, "What's going on here? Who gave you the authority to drive out the merchants?"

11:26
Mt 21:23-27
Lk 20:1-8

29Jesus replied, "I'll tell you if you answer one question! 30What about John the Baptist? Was he sent by God, or not? Answer me!"

31They talked it over among themselves. "If we reply that God sent him, then he will say, 'All right, why didn't you accept him?' 32But if we say God didn't send him, then the people will start a riot." (For the people all believed strongly that John was a prophet.)

11:32
Mt 14:5
Mk 6:20

33So they said, "We can't answer. We don't know."
To which Jesus replied, "Then I won't answer your question either!"

11:33
Job 5:12,13

Jesus tells the parable of the wicked farmers
(191/Matthew 21:33–46; Luke 20:9–19)

12 Here are some of the story-illustrations Jesus gave to the people at that time: "A man planted a vineyard and built a wall around it and dug a pit for

12:1
Isa 5:1,2

11:26 Many ancient authorities add vs 26, "but if you do not forgive, neither will your Father who is in heaven forgive your trespasses." All include this in Mt 6:15. **11:27** *other Jewish leaders,* literally, "scribes and elders." Also in 12:12.

11:22, 23 The type of prayer about which Jesus spoke is the prayer for the fruitfulness of God's Kingdom. To pray a mountain of earth into the sea has nothing to do with God's will, but Jesus used that picture to say that it is possible for God to do the impossible. God answers prayer, but not as a result of a positive mental attitude. Other conditions must be met: (1) you must be a believer; (2) you must not hold a grudge against another person; (3) you must not pray with selfish motives. To pray effectively, you need faith in God, not faith in the object of your request. If you put your faith in your request, you will have nothing when your request is refused.

11:24 Jesus, our example for prayer, once prayed, "Everything is possible. . . . Yet I want your will, not mine" (Mark 14:36). Often when we pray, we are motivated by our own interests and desires. We like to hear that we can have anything. But Jesus prayed with God's interests in mind. When we pray, we are to express our desires, but want his will above ours. Check yourself to see if your prayers are focusing on your interests or on God's.

11:26–30 The Pharisees asked Jesus who gave him the authority

to chase away the merchants and moneychangers. Their request, however, was a trap. If Jesus said his authority was from God, they would accuse him of blasphemy; if he said his authority was his own, they would overrule him and dismiss him as a fanatic. To expose their real motives, Jesus countered their question with a question about John the Baptist. The Pharisees' silence proved they were not interested in the truth. They simply wanted to get rid of Jesus because he was undermining their authority.

12:1 The story-illustrations Jesus used are also called parables. A parable uses something familiar to help us understand something new. This method of teaching compels the listener to discover truth for himself. The message gets through only to those who are willing to listen and learn.

12:1ff In this parable, the landowner is God; the vineyard is the nation Israel; the farmers are the Jewish religious leaders; the landowner's men are the prophets and priests who remained faithful to God; the son is Jesus; the others are the Gentiles. By telling this story, Jesus let the religious leaders know he knew exactly what they were thinking, and he exposed their plot to kill

pressing out the grape juice, and built a watchman's tower. Then he leased the farm to tenant farmers and moved to another country. 2At grape-picking time he sent one of his men to collect his share of the crop. 3But the farmers beat up the man and sent him back empty-handed.

4"The owner then sent another of his men, who received the same treatment, only worse, for his head was seriously injured. 5The next man he sent was killed; and later, others were either beaten or killed, until 6there was only one left—his only son. He finally sent him, thinking they would surely give him their full respect.

7"But when the farmers saw him coming they said, 'He will own the farm when his father dies. Come on, let's kill him—and then the farm will be ours!' 8So they caught him and murdered him and threw his body out of the vineyard.

9"What do you suppose the owner will do when he hears what happened? He will come and kill them all, and lease the vineyard to others. 10Don't you remember reading this verse in the Scriptures? 'The Rock the builders threw away became the cornerstone, the most honored stone in the building! 11This is the Lord's doing and it is an amazing thing to see.'"

12The Jewish leaders wanted to arrest him then and there for using this illustration, for they knew he was pointing at them—they were the wicked farmers in his story. But they were afraid to touch him for fear of a mob. So they left him and went away.

Religious leaders question Jesus about paying taxes
(193/Matthew 22:15–22; Luke 20:20–26)

13But they sent other religious and political leaders to talk with him and try to trap him into saying something he could be arrested for.

14"Teacher," these spies said, "we know you tell the truth no matter what! You aren't influenced by the opinions and desires of men, but sincerely teach the ways of God. Now tell us, is it right to pay taxes to Rome, or not?"

15Jesus saw their trick and said, "Show me a coin and I'll tell you."

16When they handed it to him he asked, "Whose picture and title is this on the coin?" They replied, "The emperor's."

17"All right," he said, "if it is his, give it to him. But everything that belongs to God must be given to God!" And they scratched their heads in bafflement at his reply.

12:5
2 Chron 24:21
36:15,16
Neh 9:26
Mt 23:34-37
Acts 7:52
1 Thess 2:15

12:6
Rom 8:3
Gal 4:4

12:7
Acts 4:27

12:8
Acts 2:23

12:9
Acts 28:23-29

12:10,11
Ps 118:22,23
Rom 9:33
Eph 2:20
1 Pet 2:5-7

12:12
Mt 11:18
Jn 7:26,30,44

12:13
Mt 22:15-40,46
Lk 20:20-40

---

him. He pointed out that their sins would not go unpunished.

12:1 Israel, pictured as a vineyard, was the place God had cultivated to bring salvation to the world. The nation's leaders not only frustrated the purpose of the vineyard, but they also killed those trying to take care of it. They were so jealous that they forgot the welfare of the very people they were supposed to be leading.

12:10 Jesus referred to himself as the Rock thrown away by the builders. Although he would be rejected by the Jews, he would become the cornerstone of a new "building," the church (Acts 4:11, 12). The cornerstone was used as a base to make sure the other stones of the building were straight and level. Likewise, Jesus' life and teaching would be the church's foundation, or base.

12:13 These religious and political leaders were the Pharisees and Herodians. The Pharisees were primarily a religious group; the Herodians, a Jewish political group.

The Pharisees did not like Jesus because he exposed their hypocrisy. The Herodians also saw Jesus as a threat. Supporters of the dynasty of Herod the Great, they had lost political control when, as a result of reported unrest, Rome deposed Herod's son and replaced him with a Roman governor. The Herodians feared

that Jesus would cause still more instability in Judea, and that Rome might react by never allowing the Roman leaders to step down and be replaced by a descendant of Herod.

12:14 Anyone avoiding taxes faced harsh penalties. The Jews hated to pay taxes to Rome because the money supported their oppressors and symbolized their subjection. Much of this tax also went to support the pagan temples and luxurious life-styles of Rome's upper class. The Pharisees and Herodians hoped to trap Jesus with this tax question. Either a yes or no could lead him into trouble. A yes would mean he supported Rome, which would turn the people against him. A no would bring accusations of treason and rebellion against Rome.

12:17 The Pharisees and Herodians thought they had the perfect question to trap Jesus. But Jesus answered wisely, once again exposing their self-interest and wrong motives. Jesus said that the coin bearing the emperor's image should be given to the emperor. But whatever bears God's image—our lives—belongs to God. Are you giving God all that is rightfully his? Make sure your life is given to God—you bear his image.

Religious leaders question Jesus about the resurrection
(194/Matthew 22:23–32; Luke 20:27–40)

¹⁸Then the Sadducees stepped forward—a group of men who say there is no resurrection. Here was their question:

¹⁹"Teacher, Moses gave us a law that when a man dies without children, the man's brother should marry his widow and have children in his brother's name. ²⁰, ²²Well, there were seven brothers and the oldest married and died, and left no children. So the second brother married the widow, but soon he died too, and left no children. Then the next brother married her, and died without children, and so on until all were dead, and still there were no children; and last of all, the woman died too.

²³"What we want to know is this: In the resurrection, whose wife will she be, for she had been the wife of each of them?"

²⁴Jesus replied, "Your trouble is that you don't know the Scriptures, and don't know the power of God. ²⁵For when these seven brothers and the woman rise from the dead, they won't be married—they will be like the angels.

²⁶"But now as to whether there will be a resurrection—have you never read in the book of Exodus about Moses and the burning bush? God said to Moses, 'I *am* the God of Abraham, and I *am* the God of Isaac, and I *am* the God of Jacob.' ²⁷"God was telling Moses that these men, though dead for hundreds of years, were still very much alive, for he would not have said, 'I *am* the God' of those who don't exist! You have made a serious error."

Religious leaders question Jesus about the greatest commandment
(195/Matthew 22:33–40)

²⁸One of the teachers of religion who was standing there listening to the discussion realized that Jesus had answered well. So he asked, "Of all the commandments, which is the most important?"

²⁹Jesus replied, "The one that says, 'Hear, O Israel! The Lord our God is the one and only God. ³⁰And you must love him with all your heart and soul and mind and strength.'

12:23 *what we want to know is this,* implied.   **12:27** *though dead for hundreds of years,* implied.

12:18 Mt 22:23-33 Lk 20:27-38 Acts 23:8 1 Cor 15:12	
12:19 Gen 38:8 Deut 25:5	
12:24 Dan 12:2 Rom 4:17 1 Tim 1:7 2 Pet 1:19	
12:25 1 Cor 15:42, 49,52 1 Jn 3:2	
12:26 Ex 3:6 Lk 20:37	
12:27 Mt 22:32 Lk 20:38	
12:29 Deut 6:4,5	
12:30 Lk 10:27	

12:18 After the Pharisees and Herodians failed to trap Jesus with their tax question, the Sadducees stepped in with a question they were sure would stump Jesus. This was a question they had successfully used against the Pharisees, who could not come up with an answer. The Sadducees did not believe in life after death because the Pentateuch (Genesis—Deuteronomy) had no direct teaching about it, and those writings of Moses were the only Scriptures they followed. But Jesus was about to point out that Moses' books support the idea of eternal life (verse 26).

12:20–22 According to Old Testament law, when a woman's husband died without a son, the man's brother had to marry the woman in order to ensure children to care for the widow and allow the family line to continue. The first son of this marriage was considered the child of the dead man (Deuteronomy 25:5, 6).

12:24 Jesus said that not only were the Sadducees ignorant of Scripture, but they didn't understand God's power. Heaven is far beyond our ability to understand or imagine (Isaiah 64:4; 1 Corinthians 2:9). We must be careful not to create questions about heaven that cannot be answered from our human perspective. We need not be afraid of heaven because of the unknowns. Instead of wondering what God's coming Kingdom will be like, we should concentrate on our relationship with Jesus right now, because when we are in the new Kingdom we will be with him. How we live *now* will make a difference then.

12:25 Jesus' statement does not mean that a person will not recognize his or her partner in the coming Kingdom. It simply means that God's new order will not be an extension of this

life—the same physical and natural rules won't apply. In our fallen world, relationships are limited by time, death, and human institutions, but in God's new and restored world they will not be.

12:26 Jesus answered their real question—"Will there be a resurrection?" Because the Sadducees believed only in the Pentateuch, Jesus quoted from Exodus 3:6 to prove that there is life after death. The Pharisees had overlooked this verse in their debates with the Sadducees over this issue. God spoke of Abraham, Isaac, and Jacob years after their death as if they *still lived.* God's covenant with all people exists beyond death.

12:28 By Jesus' time, the Jews had accumulated hundreds of laws—613, by one count. Some religious leaders tried to distinguish between major and minor laws, and some taught that all laws were equally binding and that it was dangerous to make any distinctions. This teacher's question could have provoked controversy among these groups, but Jesus' answer summarized all of God's laws.

12:29–31 God's laws are not burdensome in number or detail. They can be reduced to two simple rules for life: love God, and love others. These commands are from the Old Testament (Leviticus 19:18; Deuteronomy 6:5). When you love God completely and care for others as you care for yourself, then you have fulfilled the intent of the Ten Commandments and the other Old Testament laws. According to Jesus, these two rules summarize all God's laws. Let them rule your thoughts, decisions, and actions. When you are uncertain about what to do, ask yourself which course of action best demonstrates love for God and love for others.

12:31
Lev 19:18
Rom 13:9

12:32
Deut 4:35,39
Isa 45:5,6,14
1 Cor 8:4-6

12:33
1 Sam 15:22
Hos 6:6
Mic 6:6-8

12:35
Mt 22:41-46
Lk 20:41-44

12:36
2 Sam 23:2
Ps 110:1

12:37
Rom 1:3; 9:5
Rev 22:16

31"The second is: 'You must love others as much as yourself.' No other commandments are greater than these."

32The teacher of religion replied, "Sir, you have spoken a true word in saying that there is only one God and no other. 33And I know it is far more important to love him with all my heart and understanding and strength, and to love others as myself, than to offer all kinds of sacrifices on the altar of the Temple."

34Realizing this man's understanding, Jesus said to him, "You are not far from the Kingdom of God." And after that, no one dared ask him any more questions.

Religious leaders cannot answer Jesus' question
(196/Matthew 22:41–46; Luke 20:41–44)

35Later, as Jesus was teaching the people in the Temple area, he asked them this question:

"Why do your religious teachers claim that the Messiah must be a descendant of King David? 36For David himself said—and the Holy Spirit was speaking through him when he said it—'God said to my Lord, sit at my right hand until I make your enemies your footstool.' 37Since David called him his Lord, how can he be his son?"

(This sort of reasoning delighted the crowd and they listened to him with great interest.)

WHAT JESUS SAID ABOUT LOVE

In Mark 12:28 a teacher of religion asked Jesus which of all the commandments was the most important to follow. Jesus mentioned two commandments, one from Deuteronomy 6:5, the other from Leviticus 19:18. Both had to do with love. Why is love so important? Jesus said that all of the commandments were given for two simple reasons—to help us love God and love others as we should.

What else did Jesus say about love?	Reference
God loves us.	John 3:16
We are to love God.	Matthew 22:37
Because God loves us, he cares for us.	Matthew 6:25–34
God wants everyone to know how much he loves them.	John 17:23
God loves even those who hate him; we are to do the same.	Matthew 5:43–47; Luke 6:35
God seeks out even those most alienated from him.	Luke 15
God must be your first love.	Matthew 6:24; 10:37
You love God when you obey him.	John 14:21; 15:10
God loves Jesus his Son.	John 5:20; 10:17
Jesus loves God.	John 14:31
Those who refuse Jesus don't have God's love.	John 5:41–44
Jesus loves us just as God loves Jesus.	John 15:9
Jesus proved his love for us by dying on the cross so that we could live eternally with him.	John 3:14, 15; 15:13, 14
The love between God and Jesus is the perfect example of how we are to love others.	John 17:21–26
We are to love one another (John 13:34, 35) and demonstrate that love.	Matthew 5:40–42; 10:42
We are *not* to love the praise of men (John 12:43), selfish recognition (Matthew 23:6), earthly belongings (Luke 16:19–31), or anything more than God.	Luke 16:13
Jesus' love extends to each individual.	John 10:11–15; Mark 10:21
Jesus wants us to love him through the good and difficult times.	Matthew 26:31–35
Jesus wants our love to be genuine.	John 21:15–17

12:33, 34 All the commands in the Old Testament lead to Christ. This man had caught the intent of God's law as it is so often stressed in the Old Testament—that heartfelt love is better than outward compliance, or that "obedience is better than sacrifice" (1 Samuel 15:22). His next step was faith in Jesus himself, and this was the most difficult step to take.

12:35, 36 Jesus quoted Psalm 110:1 to show that the Messiah would be different from an ordinary man. The religious leaders did not understand that the Messiah would be far more than a human descendant of David; he would be God himself in human form.

Jesus warns against the religious leaders
(197/Matthew 23:1–12; Luke 20:45–47)

38Here are some of the other things he taught them at this time:

"Beware of the teachers of religion! For they love to wear the robes of the rich and scholarly, and to have everyone bow to them as they walk through the markets. 39They love to sit in the best seats in the synagogues, and at the places of honor at banquets— 40but they shamelessly cheat widows out of their homes and then, to cover up the kind of men they really are, they pretend to be pious by praying long prayers in public. Because of this, their punishment will be the greater."

12:38
Mt 23:1-10,14
Lk 20:45-47

12:39
Lk 11:43

A poor widow gives all she has
(200/Luke 21:1–4)

41Then he went over to the collection boxes in the Temple and sat and watched as the crowds dropped in their money. Some who were rich put in large amounts. 42Then a poor widow came and dropped in two pennies.

43, 44He called his disciples to him and remarked, "That poor widow has given more than all those rich men put together! For they gave a little of their extra fat, while she gave up her last penny."

12:41
2 Kgs 12:9
Lk 21:1-4
Jn 8:20

12:43
Lk 8:43,44
2 Cor 8:12

Jesus tells about the future
(201/Matthew 24:1–22; Luke 21:5–24)

13 As he was leaving the Temple that day, one of his disciples said, "Teacher, what beautiful buildings these are! Look at the decorated stonework on the walls."

13:1
Mt 24:1-51
Lk 21:5-36

2Jesus replied, "Yes, look! For not one stone will be left upon another, except as ruins."

13:2
Lk 19:43,44

3, 4And as he sat on the slopes of the Mount of Olives across the valley from Jerusalem, Peter, James, John, and Andrew got alone with him and asked him, "Just when is all this going to happen to the Temple? Will there be some warning ahead of time?

5So Jesus launched into an extended reply. "Don't let anyone mislead you," he

12:43, 44 *a little of their extra fat,* literally, "out of their surplus."

12:38–40 Jesus again exposed the Pharisees' impure motives. These religious leaders received no pay, so they depended upon the hospitality extended by devout Jews. Some of them used this custom to exploit people, cheating the poor out of everything they had and taking advantage of the rich. They acted spiritual to gain status, recognition, and respect.

12:38–40 Jesus warned against the teachers of religion who loved to appear holy and receive honor when, in reality, they were phonies. True followers of Christ are not distinguished by showy acts. Reading the Bible, praying in public, or following church rituals can be phony if the motive for doing them is to be noticed or honored. Let your actions be consistent with your beliefs. You must live for Christ, even when no one is looking.

12:40 The punishment of the religious leaders would be greater because, as teachers and leaders, they carried great responsibility in shaping the faith of those they taught. But they saddled people with petty rules while forgetting the God they were supposed to worship, and their greed and impure motives led many people astray.

12:41 There were several boxes in the Temple where money was placed. Some were for collection of the Temple tax from Jewish males; the others were for free-will offerings. These collection boxes were probably in the Court of Women.

12:41–44 In the Lord's eyes, this poor widow gave more than all the others put together, although her gift was by far the smallest. The value of a gift is not determined by its amount, but by the spirit in which it is given. A gift given grudgingly or for recognition loses its value. When you give, take heart—small gifts are more pleasing

to God than large gifts when they are given out of gratitude.

13:1, 2 About fifteen years before Jesus was born (20 B.C.) Herod the Great began to remodel and rebuild the Temple, which had stood for nearly five hundred years, since the days of Ezra (Ezra 6:14, 15). Herod made the Temple one of the most beautiful buildings in Jerusalem, not to honor God, but to appease the Jews whom he ruled. The magnificent building project was not completely finished until A.D. 64. Jesus' prophecy that not one stone would be left upon another was fulfilled in A.D. 70, when the Romans completely destroyed the Temple and the entire city of Jerusalem.

13:3ff The disciples wanted to know when the Temple would be destroyed. Jesus gave them a prophetic picture of that time, including events leading up to it. He also talked about other future events which would signal his return. Jesus predicted both near and distant events without trying to put them in chronological order. The disciples lived to see the destruction of Jerusalem in A.D. 70. This event would assure them that everything else Jesus predicted would also happen.

Jesus warned them about the future so that they could learn how to live in the present. Many predictions Jesus made in this passage have not yet been fulfilled. He did not make them so that we would guess when they might happen, but to help us remain spiritually alert and prepared at all times, waiting for his return.

13:3, 4 The Mount of Olives rises above Jerusalem to the east of the city. From its slopes a person can look down into the city and see the Temple. Zechariah 14:1–4 predicts that the Messiah will stand on this very mountain when he returns to set up his eternal kingdom.

said, 6"for many will come declaring themselves to be your Messiah, and will lead many astray. 7And wars will break out near and far, but this is not the signal of the end-time.

8"For nations and kingdoms will proclaim war against each other, and there will be earthquakes in many lands, and famines. These herald only the early stages of the anguish ahead. 9But when these things begin to happen, watch out! For you will be in great danger. You will be dragged before the courts, and beaten in the synagogues, and accused before governors and kings of being my followers. This is your opportunity to tell them the Good News. 10And the Good News must first be made known in every nation before the end-time finally comes. 11But when you are arrested and stand trial, don't worry about what to say in your defense. Just say what God tells you to. Then you will not be speaking, but the Holy Spirit will.

12"Brothers will betray each other to death, fathers will betray their own children, and children will betray their parents to be killed. 13And everyone will hate you because you are mine. But all who endure to the end without renouncing me shall be saved.

14"When you see the horrible thing standing in the Temple—reader, pay attention!—flee, if you can, to the Judean hills. 15, 16Hurry! If you are on your rooftop porch, don't even go back into the house. If you are out in the fields, don't even return for your money or clothes.

17"Woe to pregnant women in those days, and to mothers nursing their children. 18And pray that your flight will not be in winter. 19For those will be days of such horror as have never been since the beginning of God's creation, nor will ever be

13:9
Mt 10:17-22
13:10
Rom 10:18
13:11
Lk 12:11,12; 21:14, 15
Acts 2:4; 4:8,31
13:12
Mic 7:6
13:13
Jn 15:18-21
2 Tim 4:7,8
Heb 3:6,14
Rev 2:10
13:14
Dan 9:27
11:31; 12:11
Mt 24:15
13:17
Lk 23:29
13:19
Jer 30:7
Dan 12:1
Joel 2:2
Rev 3:10

13:10 *before the end-time finally comes,* implied.   **13:14** *standing in the Temple,* literally, "standing where he ought not."

JESUS' PROPHECIES IN THE OLIVET DISCOURSE

Type of Prophecy	Old Testament References	Other New Testament References
The Last Days	Daniel 9:26 27	John 15:21
Mark 13:1–23	Daniel 11:31	Revelation 11:2
Matthew 24:1–28	Joel 2:2	1 Timothy 4:1, 2
Luke 21:5–24		
The Second Coming of Christ	Isaiah 13:6–10	Revelation 6:12
Mark 13:24–27	Ezekiel 32:7	Mark 14:62
Luke 21:25–28	Daniel 7:13, 14	1 Thessalonians 4:16
Matthew 24:29–31		

In Mark 13, often called the Olivet Discourse, Jesus talked a lot about two things: the end times and his Second Coming. Jesus was not trying to encourage his disciples to speculate about exactly when he would return by sharing these prophecies with them. Instead, he urges all his followers to be watchful and prepared for his coming. If we serve Jesus faithfully now, we will be ready when he returns.

13:5–7 What are the signs of the end times? There have been people in every generation since Christ's resurrection claiming to know exactly when Jesus would return. No one has been right yet, however, because Christ will return on God's timetable, not man's. Jesus predicted that many believers would be misled before his return by false teachers claiming to have revelations from God. In Scripture, the one clear sign of Christ's return is that all mankind will see him coming in the clouds (13:26). In other words, you do not have to wonder whether a certain person is the Messiah or whether these are the "end times." When Jesus returns, *you will know* beyond a doubt. Beware of groups that claim special knowledge of the last days because no one knows when this time will be.

13:9, 10 As the early church began to grow, most of the disciples experienced the kind of persecution Jesus was talking about. Since the time of Christ, Christians have been persecuted in their own lands and on foreign mission fields. Though you may be safe from persecution now, your vision of God's Kingdom must not be limited by what happens only to you. Many Christians in other parts of the world face hardships and persecution. Persecutions are an opportunity for Christians to witness for Christ.

13:11 Jesus is not saying that studying the Bible and gaining knowledge are useless or wrong. Before and after his resurrection Jesus himself taught his disciples what to say and how to say it. But Jesus is telling us what attitude we can have when we must take a stand for the gospel. We don't have to be fearful or defensive about our faith because the Holy Spirit will be present to give us the right words to say.

13:13 To believe in Jesus "to the end" will take perseverance because our faith will be challenged and opposed. These trials will sift true Christians from fair-weather believers. Enduring to the end does not earn salvation for us, but marks us as those already saved. The assurance of our salvation will keep us going in the midst of persecution.

13:14 The "horrible thing" Jesus mentioned is the desecra- tion of the Temple by those who insult God's holiness. In A.D. 38, the emperor Caligula planned to put his own statue in the Temple, but he died before his plans were carried out. In A.D. 70, the emperor Titus placed an idol on the site of the burned-out Temple after the destruction of Jerusalem.

again. 20And unless the Lord shortens that time of calamity, not a soul in all the earth will survive. But for the sake of his chosen ones he will limit those days.

Jesus tells about his return
(202/Matthew 24:23–35; Luke 21:25–33)

21"And then if anyone tells you, 'This is the Messiah,' or, 'That one is,' don't pay any attention. 22For there will be many false Messiahs and false prophets who will do wonderful miracles that would deceive, if possible, even God's own children. 23Take care! I have warned you!

24"After the tribulation ends, then the sun will grow dim and the moon will not shine, 25and the stars will fall—the heavens will convulse.

26"Then all mankind will see me, the Messiah, coming in the clouds with great power and glory. 27And I will send out the angels to gather together my chosen ones from all over the world—from the farthest bounds of earth and heaven.

28"Now, here is a lesson from a fig tree. When its buds become tender and its leaves begin to sprout, you know that spring has come. 29And when you see these things happening that I've described, you can be sure that my return is very near, that I am right at the door.

30"Yes, these are the events that will signal the end of the age. 31Heaven and earth shall disappear, but my words stand sure forever.

Jesus tells about remaining watchful
(203/Matthew 24:36–51; Luke 21:34–38)

32"However, no one, not even the angels in heaven, nor I myself, knows the day or hour when these things will happen; only the Father knows. 33And since you don't know when it will happen, stay alert. Be on the watch [for my return].

34"My coming can be compared with that of a man who went on a trip to another country. He laid out his employees' work for them to do while he was gone, and told the gatekeeper to watch for his return.

35, 36, 37"Keep a sharp lookout! For you do not know when I will come, at evening, at midnight, early dawn or late daybreak. Don't let me find you sleeping. *Watch for my return!* This is my message to you and to everyone else."

13:21 Lk 17:23
13:22 Mt 7:15; 24:24 2 Thess 2:9
13:23 2 Pet 3:17
13:24 Isa 13:10 Ezek 32:7,8 Joel 2:31; 3:15 Rev 6:12
13:26 Dan 7:13 Mt 16:27 Acts 1:11 Rev 1:7
13:27 Deut 30:3,4
13:31 Ps 102:25-27
13:32 Acts 1:7
13:33 Rom 13:11 Eph 6:17,18 Col 4:2 1 Thess 5:6
13:34 Mt 25:14 Lk 19:9
13:35-37 Lk 12:39,40

13:22 *God's own children,* literally, the "elect of God." **13:26** *the Messiah,* literally, "the Son of Man." **13:30** *of the age,* literally, "of this generation." **13:32** *I myself,* literally, "the Son." **13:33** *for my return,* implied. **13:34** *My coming,* literally, "You do not know when the master of the house will come." **13:35-37** *I,* implied.

13:22, 23 Is it possible for Christians to be deceived? Yes. So convincing will be the arguments and proofs from deceivers in the end times that it will be difficult *not* to fall away from Christ. If we are prepared, Jesus says, we can remain faithful, but if we are not prepared we will not endure. To penetrate the disguises of false teachers we can ask: (1) Have their predictions come true, or do they have to revise them to fit what's already happened? (2) Does any teaching utilize a small section of the Bible to the neglect of the whole? (3) Does the teaching go against what is said in the Bible about God? (4) Are the practices meant to glorify the teacher or Christ? (5) Do the teachings promote hostility toward other Christians?

13:31 In Jesus' day the world seemed very concrete and dependable, giving the impression of permanence. Nowadays many people fear its destruction by nuclear power. Jesus tells us, however, that while we can be sure the earth will pass away, the truth of his words will never be changed or abolished. God and his Word provide the only stability in our unstable world. How shortsighted to spend so much of our time learning about this temporary world and accumulating its possessions, while neglecting the Bible and its eternal truths.

13:32 When Jesus said that even he did not know the time of the end, he was affirming his humanity. Of course God the Father knows the time, and Jesus and the Father are one, but when Jesus became a man, he voluntarily gave up the unlimited use of his divine attributes. The emphasis of this verse is not on Jesus' lack of knowledge, but rather on the fact that no one knows. It is God the Father's secret to be revealed when he wills. No one can predict by Scripture or science the exact day of Jesus' return. Jesus is teaching that preparation, not calculation, is needed.

13:33, 34 Months of planning go into a wedding, the birth of a baby, a career change, a speaking engagement, the purchase of a home. Do we place the same importance on preparing for Christ's return? His return is the most important event in our lives. Its results will last for eternity. You dare not postpone preparing for it because you do not know when it will occur. The only way to prepare is to study God's Word and then determine to live by its instructions each day. Only then will you be ready.

13:35 This entire passage (verses 3–37) tells us how to live while we wait for Christ's return: (1) We are not to be misled by confusing claims or idle interpretations of what will happen (verses 5, 6). (2) We should not be afraid to tell anyone about Christ, despite what they might say or do to us (verses 9–11). (3) We must endure by faith and not be surprised by persecutions (verse 13). (4) We must be morally alert and obedient to the commands for living found in God's Word. This chapter was not given to promote discussions on events in prophecy, but to stimulate talk about right living for God in a world where God is largely ignored.

C. DEATH AND RESURRECTION OF JESUS, THE SERVANT (14:1—16:20)

Mark tells us about Jesus' ultimate deed of servanthood—dying for us on the cross. Jesus died for our sin so we wouldn't have to. Now we can have eternal fellowship with God instead of eternal suffering and death. When first written in Rome, this Gospel was encouraging to Roman Christians during times of persecution. Christ's victory through suffering can encourage us during difficult times too.

Religious leaders plot to kill Jesus
(207/Matthew 26:1-5; Luke 22:1, 2)

14:1
Mt 26:1-5
Lk 22:1,2
Jn 11:55-57

14 The Passover observance began two days later—an annual Jewish holiday when no bread made with yeast was eaten. The chief priests and other Jewish leaders were still looking for an opportunity to arrest Jesus secretly and put him to death.

²"But we can't do it during the Passover," they said, "or there will be a riot."

A woman anoints Jesus with expensive perfume
(182/Matthew 26:6-13; John 12:1-11)

14:3
Mt 26:6-13
Lk 7:37-39
Jn 12:1-8

³Meanwhile Jesus was in Bethany, at the home of Simon the leper; during supper a woman came in with a beautiful flask of expensive perfume. Then, breaking the seal, she poured it over his head.

⁴, ⁵Some of those at the table were indignant among themselves about this "waste," as they called it.

"Why, she could have sold that perfume for a fortune and given the money to the poor!" they snarled.

14:7
Deut 15:11

⁶But Jesus said, "Let her alone; why berate her for doing a good thing? ⁷You always have the poor among you, and they badly need your help, and you can aid them whenever you want to; but I won't be here much longer.

14:8
Mk 16:1
Lk 24:1
Jn 19:40

⁸"She has done what she could, and has anointed my body ahead of time for burial. ⁹And I tell you this in solemn truth, that wherever the Good News is preached throughout the world, this woman's deed will be remembered and praised."

Judas agrees to betray Jesus
(208/Matthew 26:14-16; Luke 22:3-6)

14:11
Zech 11:12
1 Tim 6:10
Jude 11

¹⁰Then Judas Iscariot, one of his disciples, went to the chief priests to arrange to betray Jesus to them.

¹¹When the chief priests heard why he had come, they were excited and happy

---

14:1 For the festival of the Passover, all Jewish males over 12 years of age were required to go to Jerusalem. The Passover commemorated the night the Israelites were freed from Egypt (Exodus 12) when God "passed over" homes marked by the blood of a lamb while killing firstborn sons in unmarked homes. The Day of Passover was followed by a seven-day festival called the Feast of Unleavened Bread. This, too, recalled the Israelites' quick escape from Egypt when they didn't have time to let their bread rise, so they baked it without yeast. This Jewish holiday found people gathering for a special meal that included lamb, wine, bitter meats, and unleavened bread. Eventually the whole week came to be called Passover because it immediately followed the special Passover holiday.

14:3 Bethany is located on the eastern slope of the Mount of Olives (Jerusalem is on the western side). This town was the home of Jesus' friends Lazarus, Mary, and Martha, who were also present at this dinner (John 11:1). The woman who anointed Jesus' feet was Mary, Lazarus' and Martha's sister (John 12:1-3).

14:3-9 Matthew and Mark placed this event just before the Last Supper, while John placed it a week earlier, just before the Triumphal Entry. It must be remembered that the main purpose of the Gospel writers was not to present an exact chronological account of Christ's life, but to give an accurate record of his message. Matthew and Mark may have chosen to place this event

here to contrast the complete devotion of Mary with the betrayal of Judas, the next event in both Gospels.

14:4, 5 Where Mark says "some of those at the table," John specifically mentions Judas (John 12:4). Judas' indignation over Mary's act of worship was not out of concern for the poor but out of greed. Since he was the treasurer of Jesus' ministry and had embezzled funds (John 12:6), he no doubt wanted the perfume sold so that the proceeds could be put into his care.

14:6 Jesus was not saying that we should neglect the poor, nor was he justifying indifference to them. He was praising Mary for her unselfish act of worship. The essence of worshiping Christ is to regard him with utmost love, respect, and devotion and to be willing to sacrifice to him what is most precious.

14:10 Why would Judas want to betray Jesus? Judas, like the other disciples, expected Jesus to start a political rebellion and overthrow Rome. As treasurer, Judas certainly assumed (as did the other disciples—see 10:35-37) that he would be given an important position in Jesus' new government. But when Jesus praised Mary for pouring out the perfume, thought to be worth half a year's salary, Judas finally realized that Jesus' kingdom was not physical or political, but spiritual. Judas' greedy desire for money and status could not be realized if he followed Jesus, so he betrayed him in exchange for money and favor from the religious leaders.

and promised him a reward. So he began looking for the right time and place to betray Jesus.

Disciples prepare for the Passover
(209/Matthew 26:17–19; Luke 22:7–13)

¹²On the first day of the Passover, the day the lambs were sacrificed, his disciples asked him where he wanted to go to eat the traditional Passover supper. ¹³He sent two of them into Jerusalem to make the arrangements.

"As you are walking along," he told them, "you will see a man coming toward you carrying a pot of water. Follow him. ¹⁴At the house he enters, tell the man in charge, 'Our Master sent us to see the room you have ready for us, where we will eat the Passover supper this evening!' ¹⁵He will take you upstairs to a large room all set up. Prepare our supper there."

14:12
Deut 16:5
Mt 26:17-19
Lk 22:7-13
1 Cor 5:7,8

14:14
Ex 12:8
Lev 23:5

Day	Event	References	MAJOR EVENTS OF PASSION WEEK
Sunday	Triumphal entry into Jerusalem	Matthew 21:1–11 Mark 11:1–10 Luke 19:29–40 John 12:12–19	Sunday through Wednesday Jesus spent each night in Bethany, just
Monday	Jesus cleanses the Temple	Matthew 21:12, 13 Mark 11:15–17 Luke 19:45, 46	two miles east of Jerusalem on the opposite slope of
Tuesday	Jesus' authority challenged in the Temple	Matthew 21:23–27 Mark 11:26–33 Luke 20:1–8	the Mount of Olives. He
	Jesus teaches in stories and confronts the Jewish leaders	Matthew 21:28–23:36 Mark 12:1–40 Luke 20:9–47	probably stayed at the home of Mary, Martha, and
	Greeks ask to see Jesus	John 12:20–26	Lazarus. Jesus
	The Olivet Discourse	Matthew 24 Mark 13 Luke 21:5–38	spent Thursday night praying in the Garden of Gethsemane.
	Judas agrees to betray Jesus	Matthew 26:14–16 Mark 14:10, 11 Luke 22:3–6	Friday and Saturday nights Jesus' body lay in
Wednesday	The Bible does not say what Jesus did on this day. He probably remained in Bethany with his disciples		the Garden Tomb.
Thursday	The Last Supper	Matthew 26:26–29 Mark 14:22–25 Luke 22:14–20	
	Jesus speaks to the disciples in the Upper Room	John 13—17	
	Jesus struggles in Gethsemane	Matthew 26:36–46 Mark 14:32–42 Luke 22:39–46 John 18:1	
	Jesus is betrayed and arrested	Matthew 26:47–56 Mark 14:43–52 Luke 22:47–53 John 18:2–12	
Friday	Jesus is tried by Jewish and Roman authorities and denied by Peter	Matthew 26:57—27:2, 11–31 Mark 14:53—15:20 Luke 22:54—23:25 John 18:13—19:16	
	Jesus is crucified	Matthew 27:31–56 Mark 15:20–41 Luke 23:26–49 John 19:17–30	
Sunday	The resurrection	Matthew 28:1–10 Mark 16:1–11 Luke 24:1–12 John 20:1–18	

16So the two disciples went on ahead into the city and found everything as Jesus had said, and prepared the Passover.

Jesus and the disciples have the Last Supper
(211/Matthew 26:20–29; Luke 22:14–30; John 13:21–30)

14:17
Mt 26:20-30
Lk 22:14-23
Jn 13:21-30

17In the evening Jesus arrived with the other disciples, 18and as they were sitting around the table eating, Jesus said, "I solemnly declare that one of you will betray me, one of you who is here eating with me."

19A great sadness swept over them, and one by one they asked him, "Am I the one?"

14:21
Ps 22:1-21
Isa 53:3-8

20He replied, "It is one of you twelve eating with me now. 21I must die, as the prophets declared long ago; but, oh, the misery ahead for the man by whom I am betrayed. Oh, that he had never been born!"

14:22
1 Cor 10:16
11:23-26

22As they were eating, Jesus took bread and asked God's blessing on it and broke it in pieces and gave it to them and said, "Eat it—this is my body."

23Then he took a cup of wine and gave thanks to God for it and gave it to them; and they all drank from it. 24And he said to them, "This is my blood, poured out for

14:24
Heb 9:13-15

many, sealing the new agreement between God and man. 25I solemnly declare that I shall never again taste wine until the day I drink a different kind in the Kingdom of God."

Jesus again predicts Peter's denial
(222/Matthew 26:30–35)

26Then they sang a hymn and went out to the Mount of Olives.

14:21 *I,* literally, "the Son of Man." **14:24** *sealing,* literally, "This is my blood of the covenant." Some ancient manuscripts read "new covenant." **14:25** *drink a different kind,* literally, "drink it new."

UPPER ROOM AND GETHSEMANE Jesus and the disciples ate the traditional Passover meal in an upper room in the city and then went to the Mount of Olives into a garden called Gethsemane. In the cool of the evening, Jesus prayed for strength to face the trial and suffering ahead.

14:13 The two men Jesus sent were Peter and John (Luke 22:8).

14:14, 15 Many homes had large upstairs rooms, sometimes with stairways both inside and outside the house. The preparations for the Passover would have included setting the table and buying and preparing the Passover lamb, unleavened bread, sauces, and other ceremonial food and drink.

14:19 Judas, the very man who would betray Jesus, was at the table with the others. He had already determined to betray Jesus, but in cold-blooded hypocrisy he shared the fellowship of this meal. It is easy to become enraged or shocked by what Judas did, yet when we profess commitment to Christ and then deny him with our lives we also betray him. We deny Christ's truth because he taught us how to live and we live otherwise. We deny Christ's love by not obeying him. And we deny Christ's deity by rejecting his authority. Do your words and actions match? If not, consider a change of mind and heart that will protect you from making a terrible mistake.

14:22–25 Mark records the origin of the Lord's Supper, also called Communion or Eucharist, which is still celebrated in worship services today. Jesus and his disciples ate a meal, sang Psalms, read Scripture, and prayed. Then Jesus took two traditional parts of the Passover meal, the passing of bread and the drinking of wine, and gave them new meaning as his body and blood. He used the bread and wine to explain the significance of what he was about to do on the cross. For more on the significance of the Last Supper, see 1 Corinthians 11:23–29.

14:24 Jesus' death for us on the cross seals a new agreement between God and mankind. The old agreement involved forgiveness of sins through the blood of an animal sacrifice (Exodus 24:6–8). But, instead of a spotless lamb on the altar, Jesus came as the Lamb of God to sacrifice himself to forgive sin once and for all. Jesus was the final sacrifice for sins, and his blood sealed the new agreement between God and us (also called the "new covenant" or "new testament"). Now all of us can come to God through Jesus, in full confidence that he will hear us and save us from our sins.

14:26 The hymn they sang was most likely taken from Psalms 115—118, which were sung to conclude the Passover meal.

27"All of you will desert me," Jesus told them, "for God has declared through the prophets, 'I will kill the Shepherd, and the sheep will scatter.' 28But after I am raised to life again, I will go to Galilee and meet you there."

29Peter said to him, "I will never desert you no matter what the others do!"

30"Peter," Jesus said, "before the cock crows a second time tomorrow morning you will deny me three times."

31"No!" Peter exploded. "Not even if I have to die with you! I'll *never* deny you!" And all the others vowed the same.

— ### Jesus agonizes in the garden
(223/Matthew 26:36–46; Luke 22:39–46)

32And now they came to an olive grove called the Garden of Gethsemane, and he instructed his disciples, "Sit here, while I go and pray."

33He took Peter, James and John with him and began to be filled with horror and deepest distress. 34And he said to them, "My soul is crushed by sorrow to the point of death; stay here and watch with me."

35He went on a little further and fell to the ground and prayed that if it were possible the awful hour awaiting him might never come.

36"Father, Father," he said, "everything is possible for you. Take away this cup from me. Yet I want your will, not mine."

37Then he returned to the three disciples and found them asleep.

"Simon!" he said. "Asleep? Couldn't you watch with me even one hour? 38Watch with me and pray lest the Tempter overpower you. For though the spirit is willing enough, the body is weak."

39And he went away again and prayed, repeating his pleadings. 40Again he returned to them and found them sleeping, for they were very tired. And they didn't know what to say.

41The third time when he returned to them he said, "Sleep on; get your rest! But no! The time for sleep has ended! Look! I am betrayed into the hands of wicked men. 42Come! Get up! We must go! Look! My betrayer is here!"

Jesus is betrayed and arrested
(224/Matthew 26:47–56; Luke 22:47–53; John 18:1–11)

43And immediately, while he was still speaking, Judas (one of his disciples) arrived with a mob equipped with swords and clubs, sent out by the chief priests and other Jewish leaders.

44Judas had told them, "You will know which one to arrest when I go over and greet him. Then you can take him easily." 45So as soon as they arrived he walked up to Jesus. "Master!" he exclaimed, and embraced him with a great show

14:35 *the awful hour . . . might never come*, literally, "that the hour might pass away from him."   14:41 *I*, literally, "the Son of Man."   14:44 *greet*, literally, "kiss," the usual oriental greeting, even to this day.

Reference column (right margin):

14:27
Zech 13:7
Mt 26:31-35
Lk 22:31-34
Jn 13:36-38

14:28
Mk 16:7

14:32
Mt 26:36-46
Lk 22:39-46
Jn 18:1

14:33
Mt 17:1
Mk 9:2
Lk 9:28

14:35
Jn 12:27
Heb 5:7

14:36
Mt 20:22
Jn 5:30; 6:38; 18:11
Rom 8:15
Gal 4:6

14:38
Rom 7:23
Gal 5:17

14:43
Mt 26:47-56
Lk 22:47-53
Jn 18:2-11

14:45
Jn 20:16

14:27 It's easy to think that Satan temporarily gained the upper hand in this drama about Jesus' death. But we see later that God is in control even in the death of his Son. Satan gained no victory—everything occurred exactly as God had planned.

14:27 This is the second time in the same evening that Jesus predicted the disciples' denial and desertion, which probably explains why they reacted so strongly (verse 31). For Jesus' earlier prediction of their denial see Luke 22:31–38 and John 13:31–38.

— **14:35, 36** Was Jesus trying to get out of his task? Jesus expressed his true feelings, but he did not deny or rebel against God's will. He reaffirmed his desire to do what God wanted. His prayer highlights the terrible suffering he had to endure—an agony worse than dying, because he had to take on the sins of the whole world. This "cup" was the alienation Jesus knew would occur when he was separated from God, his Father, at the cross (Hebrews 5:7–9). The sinless Son of God took on our sins and was separated in that moment from God in order that we could be saved.

14:36-38 While praying, Jesus was aware of what doing the Father's will would cost him. He understood the suffering he was about to encounter, and he did not want to have to endure the horrible experience. But Christ prayed, "I want your will, not mine." What does your commitment to God cost you? Anything worth having costs something. Be willing to pay the price to have something worthwhile in the end.

14:41 In times of great stress we are vulnerable to temptation, even if we have a willing spirit. Jesus gave us an example of what to do to resist: (1) pray to God (verse 35); (2) seek support of friends and loved ones (verses 33, 37, 40, 41); (3) focus on the purpose God has given us (verse 36).

14:43-45 Judas was given a contingent of Jewish Temple police as well as some Roman soldiers (John 18:3) in order to seize Jesus and bring him before the religious court for trial. The religious leaders had issued the warrant for Jesus' arrest, and Judas was acting as Jesus' official accuser.

JUDAS ISCARIOT

It is easy to overlook the fact that Jesus chose Judas to be his disciple. We may also forget that while Judas betrayed Jesus, *all* the disciples abandoned him. With the other disciples, Judas shared a persistent misunderstanding of Jesus' mission. They all expected Jesus to make the right political moves. When he kept talking about dying, they all felt varying degrees of anger, fear, and disappointment. They didn't understand why they had been chosen if Jesus' mission was doomed to fail.

We do not know the exact motivation behind Judas' betrayal. What is clear is that Judas allowed his desires to place him in a position where Satan could manipulate him. He got paid to set Jesus up for the religious leaders. He identified Jesus for the guards in the dimly lit garden of Gethsemane. It is possible that he was trying to force Jesus' hand—would he or would he not rebel against Rome and set up a new political government?

Whatever his plan, though, at some point Judas realized he didn't like the way things were turning out. He tried to undo the evil he had done by returning the money to the priests, but it was too late. The wheels of God's sovereign plan had been set into motion. How sad that Judas ended his life in despair without ever experiencing the gift of reconciliation God could give even to him through Jesus Christ.

Human feelings toward Judas have always been mixed. Some have fervently hated him for his betrayal. Others have pitied him for not realizing what he was doing. A few have tried to make him a hero for his part in ending Jesus' earthly mission. Some have questioned God's fairness in allowing one man to bear such guilt. While there are many feelings about Judas, there are some facts to consider as well. He, by his own choice, betrayed God's Son into the hands of Roman soldiers (Luke 22:48). He was a thief (John 12:6). Jesus knew that Judas' life of evil would not change (John 6:70). Judas' betrayal of Jesus was part of God's sovereign plan (Psalm 41:9; Zechariah 11:12, 13; Matthew 20:18; 26:20–25; Acts 1:16, 20).

In betraying Jesus, Judas made the greatest mistake in history. But just the fact that Jesus knew Judas would betray him doesn't mean that Judas was a puppet of God's will. Judas made the choice. God knew what that choice would be and confirmed it. Judas didn't lose his relationship with Jesus; rather, he had never found Jesus. He is called the "son of hell" (John 17:12) because he was never saved.

Judas does a favor if he makes us think a second time about our commitment to God and the presence of his Spirit within us. Are we true disciples and followers, or uncommitted pretenders? We can choose despair and death, or we can choose repentance, forgiveness, hope, and eternal life. Judas' betrayal sent Jesus to the cross to guarantee that second choice, our only chance. Will we accept his free gift, or like Judas, betray him?

Strengths and accomplishments:
- He was chosen as one of the twelve disciples; the only non-Galilean
- He kept the money bag for the expenses of the group
- He was able to recognize the evil in his betrayal of Jesus

Weaknesses and mistakes:
- He was greedy (John 12:6)
- He betrayed Jesus
- He committed suicide instead of seeking forgiveness

Lessons from his life:
- Evil plans and motives leave us open to being used by Satan for even greater evil
- The consequences of evil are so devastating that even small lies and little wrongdoings have serious results
- God's plan and his purposes are worked out even in the worst possible events

Vital statistics:
- Where: probably from the town of Kerioth
- Occupation: disciple of Jesus
- Relatives: Father: Simon
- Contemporaries: Jesus, Pilate, Herod, the other 11 disciples

Key verses:
"Then Satan entered into Judas Iscariot, who was one of the twelve disciples, and he went over to the chief priests and captains of the Temple guards to discuss the best way to betray Jesus to them" (Luke 22:3, 4).

Judas' story is told in the Gospels. He is also mentioned in Acts 1:18, 19.

of friendliness. [46]Then the mob arrested Jesus and held him fast. [47]But someone pulled a sword and slashed at the High Priest's servant, cutting off his ear.

14:47
Jn 18:10

[48]Jesus asked them, "Am I some dangerous robber, that you come like this, armed to the teeth to capture me? [49]Why didn't you arrest me in the Temple? I was there teaching every day. But these things are happening to fulfill the prophecies about me."

14:49
Ps 22:6-18
Isa 53:7-9
Dan 9:26
Lk 24:44

[50]Meanwhile, all his disciples had fled. [51], [52]There was, however, a young man following along behind, clothed only in a linen nightshirt. When the mob tried to grab him, he escaped, though his clothes were torn off in the process, so that he ran away completely naked.

14:50
Ps 88:8
Jn 16:32

Caiaphas questions Jesus
(226/Matthew 26:57–68)

[53]Jesus was led to the High Priest's home where all of the chief priests and other Jewish leaders soon gathered. [54]Peter followed far behind and then slipped inside the gates of the High Priest's residence and crouched beside a fire among the servants.

14:53
Mt 26:57-68
Lk 22:54,63-71
Jn 18:12-14,19-24

14:54
Mt 26:3
Jn 18:18

[55]Inside, the chief priests and the whole Jewish Supreme Court were trying to find something against Jesus that would be sufficient to condemn him to death. But their efforts were in vain. [56]Many false witnesses volunteered, but they contradicted each other.

14:55
Dan 6:4
1 Pet 3:16

14:56
Ps 35:11
Prov 6:16-19
19:5

[57]Finally some men stood up to lie about him and said, [58]"We heard him say, 'I will destroy this Temple made with human hands and in three days I will build another, made without human hands!' " [59]But even then they didn't get their stories straight!

14:58
Mk 15:29,30
Jn 2:19

14:51, 52 in a linen nightshirt, literally, "wearing only a linen cloth."

14:47 According to John 18:10, the person who pulled the sword was Peter. Luke 22:51 records that Jesus immediately healed the man's ear and prevented any further bloodshed.

14:50 Just hours earlier, these disciples had vowed never to desert Jesus (verse 31).

14:51, 52 Tradition says that this young man might have been John Mark, the writer of this Gospel. The incident is not mentioned in any of the other accounts.

14:53ff This trial by the Jewish Supreme Court had two phases. A small group met at night (John 18:12–24), and then the full council met at daybreak (Luke 22:66–71). They tried Jesus for religious offenses such as calling himself the Son of God, which, according to law, was blasphemy. The trial was obviously fixed, because these religious leaders had already decided to kill Jesus (Luke 22:2).

14:55 The Romans controlled Israel, but the Jews were given some power to handle religious and minor civil disputes. This Jewish ruling body, called the Supreme Court (or Sanhedrin), was made up of 71 of Israel's religious leaders. It was assumed that these men, as religious leaders, would be fair and just. Instead they showed great injustice in the trial of Jesus, even to the point of making up lies to use against him (verse 57).

14:58 This claim about which the false witnesses finally agreed twisted Jesus' actual words. He did not say, "I will destroy this Temple;" he said, "Destroy this sanctuary and in three days I will raise it up!" (John 2:19). Jesus was not talking about Herod's Temple, but about his own death and resurrection.

14:61–64 To the first question, Jesus made no reply because the evidence itself was confusing and erroneous. Not answering was wiser than trying to clarify the fabricated accusations. But if Jesus had refused to answer the second question, it could have been taken as a denial of his mission. Instead, his answer predicted a powerful role-reversal. Sitting at the right hand of God meant he would come to judge *them* and they would be answering *his* questions (Psalm 110:1; Revelation 20:11–13).

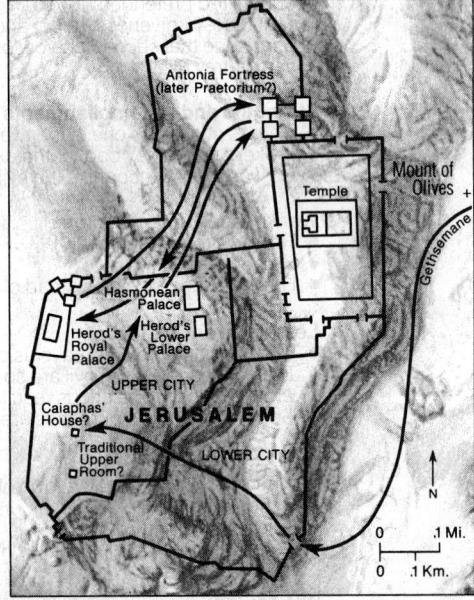

JESUS' TRIAL From Gethsemane, Jesus' trial began at the home of Caiaphas, the High Priest. He was then taken to Pilate, the Roman governor. Luke records that Pilate sent him to Herod, who was in Jerusalem—presumably in one of his two palaces (Luke 23:5–12). Herod sent him back to Pilate, who sentenced him to be crucified.

60Then the High Priest stood up before the Court and asked Jesus, "Do you refuse to answer this charge? What do you have to say for yourself?"

61To this Jesus made no reply.

Then the High Priest asked him. "Are you the Messiah, the Son of God?"

62Jesus said, "I am, and you will see me sitting at the right hand of God, and returning to earth in the clouds of heaven."

63, 64Then the High Priest tore at his clothes and said, "What more do we need? Why wait for witnesses? You have heard his blasphemy. What is your verdict?" And the vote for the death sentence was unanimous.

65Then some of them began to spit at him, and they blindfolded him and began to hammer his face with their fists.

"Who hit you that time, you prophet?" they jeered. And even the bailiffs were using their fists on him as they led him away.

Peter denies knowing Jesus
(227/Matthew 26:69–75; Luke 22:54–65; John 18:25–27)

66, 67Meanwhile Peter was below in the courtyard. One of the maids who worked for the High Priest noticed Peter warming himself at the fire.

She looked at him closely and then announced, *"You* were with Jesus, the Nazarene."

68Peter denied it. "I don't know what you're talking about!" he said, and walked over to the edge of the courtyard.

Just then, a rooster crowed.

69The maid saw him standing there and began telling the others, "There he is! There's that disciple of Jesus!"

70Peter denied it again.

A little later others standing around the fire began saying to Peter, "You are, too, one of them, for you are from Galilee!"

71He began to curse and swear. "I don't even know this fellow you are talking about," he said.

72And immediately the rooster crowed the second time. Suddenly Jesus' words flashed through Peter's mind: "Before the cock crows twice, you will deny me three times." And he began to cry.

The council of religious leaders condemns Jesus
(228/Matthew 27:1, 2; Luke 22:66–71)

15 Early in the morning the chief priests, elders and teachers of religion—the entire Supreme Court—met to discuss their next steps. Their decision was to send Jesus under armed guard to Pilate, the Roman governor.

14:62 *me,* literally, "the Son of Man." **14:68** *a rooster crowed.* This statement is found in only some of the manuscripts. **15:1** *the Roman governor,* implied.

Cross references (left margin):
14:61
Isa 53:7
1 Pet 2:23
14:62
Ps 110:1
Dan 7:13
Mt 16:27; 24:30
Mk 8:38; 13:26
Acts 1:11
1 Thess 4:16
2 Thess 1:7
Rev 1:7; 22:20
14:63
Lev 24:15,16
Jn 19:7
Acts 6:11
14:65
Isa 50:6; 53:5
14:66
Mt 26:69-75
Lk 22:55-62
Jn 18:15-18; 25-27
14:70
Acts 2:7
14:71
Prov 29:25
1 Cor 10:12
14:72
2 Cor 7:10
15:1
Jn 18:28-40
Acts 4:27

14:63, 64 Of all people, the High Priest and other religious leaders should have recognized the Messiah because they knew the Scriptures thoroughly. Their job was to point people to God, but they were more concerned about their own reputations and holding onto what authority they had. They valued their human security more than their eternal security.

14:66, 67 Caiaphas' house, where Jesus was tried (verse 53), was part of a huge palace with several courtyards. John was apparently acquainted with the High Priest and some of his servants, and he was let into the courtyard along with Peter (John 18:15, 16).

14:71 Peter's curse was more than just a common swear word. He was making the strongest denial he could think of by denying with an oath that he did not know Jesus. He said, in effect, "May God strike me dead if I'm lying."

14:71 It is easy to get angry at the Jewish Supreme Court for their injustice in condemning Jesus, but Peter and the rest of the disciples contributed to Jesus' pain by deserting him (verse 50).

While most of us are not like the Jewish leaders, we are all like the disciples, for all of us have been guilty of denying Christ as Lord in vital areas of our life. We may pride ourselves that we have not committed certain sins, but we are all guilty of sin. Don't excuse yourself by pointing the finger at others whose sins seem worse than yours.

15:1 Why did the Jews send Jesus to Pilate, the Roman governor? The Romans had taken away the Jews' right to inflict capital punishment, so in order for Jesus to be condemned to death, he had to be sentenced by a Roman leader. More important, the Jewish leaders wanted Jesus executed on a cross, a method of death they believed brought a curse from God (see Deuteronomy 21:23). They hoped to persuade the people that Jesus was cursed, not blessed by God.

Jesus stands trial before Pilate
(230/Matthew 27:11–14; Luke 23:1–5; John 18:28–38)

2Pilate asked him, "Are you the King of the Jews?"
"Yes," Jesus replied, "it is as you say."

15:2
1 Tim 6:13

3, 4Then the chief priests accused him of many crimes, and Pilate asked him, "Why don't you say something? What about all these charges against you?" 5But Jesus said no more, much to Pilate's amazement.

15:5
Isa 53:7
Jn 19:9
1 Pet 2:23

Pilate hands Jesus over to be crucified
(232/Matthew 27:15–26; Luke 23:13–25; John 18:39—19:16)

6Now, it was Pilate's custom to release one Jewish prisoner each year at Passover time—any prisoner the people requested. 7One of the prisoners at that time was Barabbas, convicted along with others for murder during an insurrection.

8Now a mob began to crowd in toward Pilate, asking him to release a prisoner as usual.

9"How about giving you the 'King of Jews'?" Pilate asked. "Is he the one you want released?" 10(For he realized by now that this was a frameup, backed by the chief priests because they envied Jesus' popularity.)

15:9
Ps 2:6
Jer 23:5,6
Mic 5:2
Lk 1:31-33
Acts 3:13,14

11But at this point the chief priests whipped up the mob to demand the release of Barabbas instead of Jesus.

12"But if I release Barabbas," Pilate asked them, "what shall I do with this man you call your king?"

13They shouted back, "Crucify him!"

The Problem	We have all done things that are wrong, and we have failed to obey God's law. Because of this, we have been separated from God our Creator. Separation from God is death; but, by ourselves, we can do nothing to become united with God.	**WHY DID JESUS HAVE TO DIE?**
Why Jesus Could Help	Jesus was not only a man; he was God's unique Son. Because Jesus never disobeyed God and never sinned, only he can bridge the gap between the sinless God and sinful mankind.	
The Solution	Jesus freely offered his life for us, dying on the cross in our place, taking all our wrongdoing upon himself, and saving us from the consequences of sin—including God's judgment and death.	
The Results	Jesus took our past, present, and future sins upon himself so that we could have new life. Because all our wrongdoing is forgiven, we are reconciled to God. Furthermore, Jesus' resurrection from the dead is the proof that his substitutionary sacrifice on the cross was acceptable to God, and his resurrection has become the source of new life for whoever believes that Jesus is the Son of God. All who believe in him may have this new life and live it in union with him.	

15:3, 4 The Jews had to fabricate new accusations against Jesus when they brought him before Pilate. The charge of blasphemy would mean nothing to the Roman governor, so they accused Jesus of three other crimes: (1) encouraging the people not to pay their taxes to Rome, (2) claiming he was a king—"the King of the Jews," and (3) causing riots all over the countryside. Tax evasion, treason, and terrorism—all of these would be cause for Pilate's concern.

15:5 Why didn't Jesus answer Pilate's questions? It would have been futile to answer, and the time had come to give his life to save the world. He had no reason to try to prolong the trial or save himself. His was the ultimate example of self-assurance and peace, which no ordinary criminal could imitate. Nothing would stop him from completing the work he had come to earth to do (Isaiah 53:7).

15:7 Barabbas was arrested for his part in a rebellion against the Roman government, and although he'd committed a murder, he may have been a hero among the Jews. The fiercely independent Jews hated to be ruled by pagan Romans. They hated paying taxes to support the despised government and its gods. Most of

the Roman authorities, who had to settle Jewish disputes, hated the Jews in return. This period in history, therefore, was ripe for rebellion.

15:8 This mob was most likely a group of Jews loyal to the Jewish leaders. But where were the disciples and the crowds who days earlier had shouted, "Hail to the king" (11:9)? Jesus' sympathizers were afraid of the Jewish leaders, so they went into hiding. Another possibility is that the mob included many people who were in the Palm Sunday parade, but who turned against Jesus when they saw he was not going to be an earthly conqueror.

15:10 The Jews hated Pilate, but they went to him for the favor of condemning Jesus to crucifixion. Pilate could obviously see this was a frame-up. Why else would these people, who hated him and the Roman empire he represented, ask him to convict of treason and give the death penalty to one of their fellow Jews?

15:13 Crucifixion was the Roman penalty for rebellion. Only slaves or those who were not Roman citizens could be crucified. If Jesus died by crucifixion, he would die the death of a rebel and slave, not of the king he claimed to be. This is just what the Jewish religious leaders wanted as they whipped the mob into a frenzy. In

¹⁴"But why?" Pilate demanded. "What has he done wrong?" They only roared the louder, "Crucify him!"

15:15
Prov 29:25

¹⁵Then Pilate, afraid of a riot and anxious to please the people, released Barabbas

---

PILATE

In Jesus' day, any death sentence had to be approved by the top Roman official of the area. Pontius Pilate was in charge of the area where Jerusalem was located. When the Jewish leaders had Jesus in their power and wanted to kill him, their final obstacle was obtaining Pilate's permission. So it was that early one morning Pilate found a crowd at his door demanding a man's death.

Pilate's relationship with the Jews had always been stormy. His Roman toughness and fairness had been weakened by cynicism, compromises, and mistakes. On several occasions his actions had deeply offended the religious leaders. The resulting riots and chaos must have made Pilate wonder what he had gotten himself into. He was trying to control people who treated their Roman conquerors without respect. Jesus' trial was another episode in Pilate's ongoing problems.

For Pilate, there was never a doubt about Jesus' innocence. Three separate times he declared Jesus not guilty. He couldn't understand what made these people want to kill Jesus, but his fear of the pressure the Jews would place on him controlled his decision to allow Jesus' crucifixion. Because of their threat to inform the emperor that Pilate hadn't eliminated a rebel against Rome, Pilate went against what he knew was right. In desperation, he chose the opposite.

We share a common humanity with Pilate. At times we know the right and choose the wrong. He had his moment in history and now we have ours. What have we done with our opportunities and responsibilities? What judgment have we passed on Jesus?

Strengths and accomplishments:
- Roman governor of Judea

Weaknesses and mistakes:
- He failed in his attempt to rule a people who were defeated militarily but never dominated by Rome
- His constant political struggles made him a cynical and uncaring compromiser, susceptible to pressure
- Although he realized Jesus was innocent, he bowed to the public demand for his execution

Lessons from his life:
- Great evil can happen when truth is at the mercy of political pressures
- Resisting the truth leaves a person without purpose or direction

Vital statistics:
- Where: Judea
- Occupation: Roman governor (or procurator) of Judea
- Relatives: Wife, unnamed
- Contemporaries: Jesus, Caiaphas, Herod

Key verses:
"What is truth?" Pilate exclaimed. Then he went out again to the people and told them, "He is not guilty of any crime. But you have a custom of asking me to release someone from prison each year at Passover. So if you want me to, I'll release the 'King of the Jews' " (John 18:38, 39).

Pilate's story is told in the Gospels. He is also mentioned in Acts 3:13; 4:27; 13:28; 1 Timothy 6:13.

---

addition, crucifixion would make it look as if the Romans were responsible for killing Jesus, and thus the religious leaders could not be blamed by the crowds.

15:15 The region of Judea where Pilate ruled as governor was little more than a dusty outpost of the Roman empire. Because it was so far from Rome, Pilate was given just a small army. His primary job was to keep peace. We know from historical records that Pilate had already been warned about other uprisings in his region. Although he may have seen no guilt in Jesus and no reason to condemn him to death, he wavered when the Jews in the crowd threatened to report him to Caesar (John 19:12). Such a report, accompanied by a riot, could cost him his position and hopes for advancement.

15:15 Although Jesus was innocent according to Roman law,

Pilate caved in under political pressure. He abandoned what he knew was right. He tried to second-guess the Jewish leaders and give a decision that would please everyone while keeping himself safe. When we lay aside God's clear statements of right and wrong and make decisions based on our audience, we fall into compromise and lawlessness. God promises to honor those who do right, not those who make everyone happy.

15:15 Who was guilty of Jesus' death? In reality, everyone was at fault. The disciples deserted him in fear. Peter denied that he even knew Jesus. Judas betrayed him. The crowds who had followed him stood by and did nothing. Pilate tried to blame the crowds. The religious leaders actively promoted Jesus' death. The Roman soldiers tortured him. If you had been there, watching these trials, what would your response have been?

to them. And he ordered Jesus flogged with a leaded whip, and handed him over to be crucified.

Roman soldiers mock Jesus
(233/Matthew 27:27–31)

16, 17Then the Roman soldiers took him into the barracks of the palace, called out the entire palace guard, dressed him in a purple robe, and made a crown of long, sharp thorns and put it on his head. 18Then they saluted, yelling, "Yea! King of the Jews!" 19And they beat him on the head with a cane, and spat on him and went down on their knees to "worship" him.

20When they finally tired of their sport, they took off the purple robe and put his own clothes on him again, and led him away to be crucified.

15:16
Mt 27:27-31
Jn 19:1-3,16

Jesus is led away to be crucified
(234/Matthew 27:32–34; Luke 23:26–31; John 19:17)

21Simon of Cyrene, who was coming in from the country just then, was pressed into service to carry Jesus' cross. (Simon is the father of Alexander and Rufus.)

22And they brought Jesus to a place called Golgotha. (Golgotha means skull.) 23Wine drugged with bitter herbs was offered to him there, but he refused it. 24And then they crucified him—and threw dice for his clothes.

15:21
Rom 16:13
15:23
Ps 69:21
15:24
Ps 22:18

Jesus is placed on the cross
(235/Matthew 27:35–44; Luke 23:32–43; John 19:18–27)

25It was about nine o'clock in the morning when the crucifixion took place. 26A signboard was fastened to the cross above his head, announcing his crime. It read, "The King of the Jews."

27Two robbers were also crucified that morning, their crosses on either side of his. 28And so the Scripture was fulfilled that said, "He was counted among evil men."

15:25
Jn 19:14
15:26
Ps 2:6
Jer 23:5
Lk 1:31-33
15:28
Lk 22:37

15:28 This verse is omitted in some of the ancient manuscripts. The quotation is from Isa 53:12.

15:21 Colonies of Jews existed outside Judea; Simon came from Cyrene in Africa, making a pilgrimage to Jerusalem for the Passover. His sons, Alexander and Rufus, are mentioned here because they evidently became well-known in the early church (Romans 16:13).

15:24 The dice the soldiers threw were used to decide, by chance, who would receive Jesus' clothing. The Roman soldiers had the right to take for themselves the clothing of those crucified. This act fulfilled the prophecy of Psalm 22:18.

15:25 Crucifixion was a feared and shameful form of capital punishment. The victim was forced to carry his cross along the longest possible route to the crucifixion site as a warning to the people. There were several shapes for crosses, as well as different methods of crucifixion. Jesus was nailed to the cross; condemned men were sometimes tied to their crosses with ropes. In either case, death came by suffocation because the weight of the body made breathing more and more difficult as the person lost strength.

15:26 A sign stating the condemned man's crime was often placed on a cross as a warning to the people. Because Jesus was never found guilty, the only accusation placed on his sign was the "crime" of being King of the Jews.

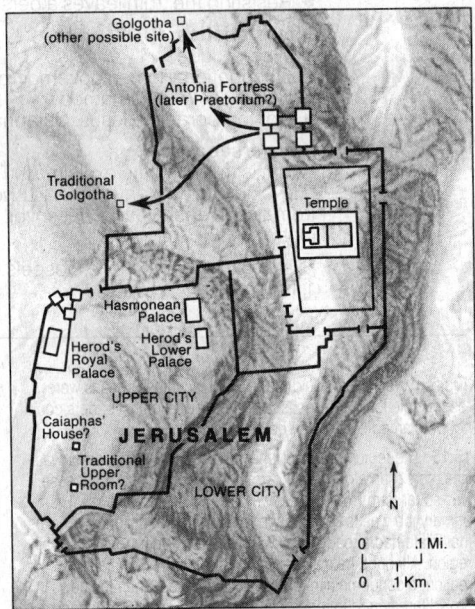

JESUS' ROUTE TO GOLGOTHA After being sentenced by Pilate, Jesus was taken from the Praetorium to a place outside the city, Golgotha, for crucifixion.

15:29,30
Ps 22:7
Mk 14:58
Jn 2:19
Acts 6:14

29, 30The people jeered at him as they walked by, and wagged their heads in mockery.

"Ha! Look at you now!" they yelled at him. "Sure, you can destroy the Temple and rebuild it in three days! If you're so wonderful, save yourself and come down from the cross."

31The chief priests and religious leaders were also standing around joking about Jesus.

"He's quite clever at 'saving' others," they said, "but he can't save himself!"

15:32
Heb 12:2,3

32"Hey there, Messiah!" they yelled at him. "You 'King of Israel'! Come on down from the cross and we'll believe you!"

And even the two robbers dying with him, cursed him.

Jesus dies on the cross
(236/Matthew 27:45–56; Luke 23:44–49; John 19:28–37)

15:33
Mt 27:45-56
Lk 23:44-49
Jn 19:28-30

33About noon, darkness fell across the entire land, lasting until three o'clock that afternoon.

15:34
Ps 22:1

34Then Jesus called out with a loud voice, "Eli, Eli, lama sabachthani?" ("My God, my God, why have you deserted me?")

15:36
Ps 69:21

35Some of the people standing there thought he was calling for the prophet Elijah. 36So one man ran and got a sponge and filled it with sour wine and held it up to him on a stick.

"Let's see if Elijah will come and take him down!" he said.

37Then Jesus uttered another loud cry, and dismissed his spirit.

15:38
Ex 26:31-33
Eph 2:14
Heb 6:19
10:19,20

38And the curtain in the Temple was split apart from top to bottom.

39When the Roman officer standing beside his cross saw how he dismissed his spirit, he exclaimed, "Truly, this was the Son of God!"

15:40
Ps 38:11
Lk 8:2

40Some women were there watching from a distance—Mary Magdalene, Mary (the mother of James the Younger and of Joses), Salome, and others. 41They and many other Galilean women who were his followers had ministered to him when he was up in Galilee, and had come with him to Jerusalem.

15:33 *the entire land,* or, "over the entire world."   **15:34** *Eli, Eli, lama sabachthani.* He spoke here in Aramaic. The onlookers, who spoke Greek and Latin, misunderstood his first two words ("Eloi, Eloi") and thought he was calling for the prophet Elijah.

15:31 Jesus could have saved himself, but he endured this suffering because of his love for us. He could have chosen not to take the pain and humiliation; he could have killed those who mocked him—but he suffered through it all because he loved even his enemies. We had a significant part in the drama that afternoon because our sin was on the cross, too. Jesus died on that cross for us, and the penalty for our sin was paid by his death. The only adequate response we can make is to confess our sin and freely accept the fact that Jesus paid for it so we wouldn't have to. Don't insult God with indifference toward the greatest act of genuine love in history.

15:32 When James and John asked Jesus for the places of honor next to him in his Kingdom, he told them they didn't know what they were asking (10:35-39). Now that Jesus was preparing to inaugurate his Kingdom through his death, the places on his right and on his left were taken by dying men—criminals. This illustrates that Jesus' death is for *all* people. As Jesus explained to his two power-hungry disciples, a person who wants to be close to Jesus must be prepared to suffer and die as he himself was doing. The way to the Kingdom is the way of the cross. If we want the glory of the Kingdom, we must be willing to be united with the crucified Christ.

15:32 Luke records that one of these robbers repented before his death and Jesus promised him that he would be with him in Paradise (Luke 23:39-43).

15:34 Jesus did not ask this question in surprise or despair. He

was quoting the first line of Psalm 22. The whole Psalm is a prophecy expressing the deep agony of the Messiah's death for the world's sin. Jesus knew this temporary separation from God would come the moment he took upon himself the sins of the world. This separation was what Jesus dreaded as he prayed in Gethsemane. The physical agony was horrible, but the spiritual separation from God was the ultimate pain.

15:37 This loud cry of Jesus was probably his last words, "It is finished" (John 19:30).

15:38 A heavy veil hung in front of the Temple room called the Holy of Holies, a place reserved by God for himself. Symbolically, the veil separated the holy God from sinful mankind. The room was entered only once a year, on the Day of Atonement, by the High Priest as he made a sacrifice to gain forgiveness for the sins of all the people. When Jesus died, the veil was split in two, showing that his death for our sins had opened up the way for us to approach our Holy God. Read Hebrews 9 for a more complete explanation of this.

Jesus is laid in the tomb
(237/Matthew 27:57–61; Luke 23:50–56; John 19:38–42)

42, 43This all happened the day before the Sabbath. Late that afternoon Joseph from Arimathea, an honored member of the Jewish Supreme Court (who personally was eagerly expecting the arrival of God's Kingdom), gathered his courage and went to Pilate and asked for Jesus' body.

44Pilate couldn't believe that Jesus was already dead so he called for the Roman officer in charge and asked him. 45The officer confirmed the fact, and Pilate told Joseph he could have the body.

46Joseph bought a long sheet of linen cloth and, taking Jesus' body down from the cross, wound it in the cloth and laid it in a rock-hewn tomb, and rolled a stone in front of the entrance.

47(Mary Magdalene and Mary the mother of Joses were watching as Jesus was laid away.)

15:42,43
Deut 21:22,23
Mt 27:57-61
Lk 2:25
23:50-56
Jn 19:38-42

15:46
Isa 53:9
Acts 13:29

Jesus rises from the dead
(239/Matthew 28:1–7; Luke 24:1–12; John 20:1–9)

16 The next evening, when the Sabbath ended, Mary Magdalene and Salome and Mary the mother of James went out and purchased embalming spices. Early the following morning, just at sunrise, they carried them out to the tomb. 3On the way they were discussing how they could ever roll aside the huge stone from the entrance.

4But when they arrived they looked up and saw that the stone—a *very* heavy one—was already moved away and the entrance was open! 5So they entered the tomb—and there on the right sat a young man clothed in white. The women were startled, 6but the angel said, "Don't be so surprised. Aren't you looking for Jesus,

16:3
Mt 27:60
Mk 15:46

16:5
John 20:11,12
Acts 1:10; 10:30
16:6
Acts 2:23-32
Rom 1:3,4
1 Cor 15:4,12-20
Rev 1:18

15:42, 43 The Sabbath began at sundown on Friday and ended at sundown on Saturday. Jesus died just a few hours before sundown on Friday. It was against Jewish law to do physical work or to travel on the Sabbath. It was also against Jewish law to let a dead body remain exposed overnight (Deuteronomy 21:23). Joseph came to bury Jesus' body before the Sabbath began. If Jesus had died on the Sabbath when Joseph was unavailable, his body would have been taken down by the Romans. Had the Romans taken Jesus' body, no Jews could have confirmed his death, and they could have disputed his resurrection.

15:42, 43 After Jesus died on the cross, Joseph of Arimathea asked for his body and then sealed it in a new tomb. Although an honored member of the Jewish Supreme Court, Joseph was a secret disciple of Jesus. Not all the religious leaders hated Jesus. Joseph risked his reputation as a religious leader to give a proper burial to the One he followed. It is frightening to risk one's reputation even for what is right. If your Christian witness endangers your reputation, consider Joseph. Today he is well known in the Christian church. How many of the other members of the Jewish Supreme Court can you name?

15:44 Pilate was surprised that Jesus had died so quickly, so he asked a soldier to double-check to make absolutely certain the report was true. Today, in an effort to deny the resurrection, there are those who say that Jesus didn't really die. His death, however, was confirmed by the soldier, Pilate, Joseph, the religious leaders, and the women who witnessed his burial. Jesus suffered true physical death on the cross.

15:46 This tomb was probably a man-made cave hewn from a hill and large enough to walk into. Joseph wrapped Jesus' body, placed it in the tomb, and rolled a heavy stone across the entrance. The religious leaders also watched where Jesus was buried, stationed guards by the tomb, and sealed the stone to make sure no one would try to steal Jesus' body and claim he had risen from the dead (Matthew 27:62–66).

15:47 These women could do very little—they couldn't speak before the Sanhedrin in Jesus' defense, they couldn't appeal to

Pilate, they couldn't stand against the crowds, they couldn't overpower the Roman guards. But they did what they could. They stayed at the cross when the disciples had fled; they followed Jesus' body to its tomb; and they prepared spices for his body. Because they used the opportunities they had, they were the first to witness the resurrection. God blessed their devotion and diligence. As believers, we should take advantage of the opportunities we have and do what we *can* for Christ, instead of worrying about what we *cannot* do.

16:1, 2 The women purchased the spices on Saturday evening after the Sabbath had ended so they could go to the tomb early the next morning. The women did not want to use the spices for embalming Jesus' body, but for anointing it as a sign of love, devotion, and respect. Bringing spices to the tomb was like bringing flowers to a grave today.

16:4 The angels did not roll away the stone so Jesus could get out, but so others could get in and see for themselves that Jesus had indeed risen from the dead, just as he said.

16:5 Mark says that one angel met the women at the tomb, while Luke records that there were two angels. These accounts are not contradictory. Each Gospel writer chose to highlight different details as he explained the same story, just as eyewitnesses to a news story each may highlight a different aspect of that event. Mark probably emphasized only the angel who spoke. The unique emphasis of each Gospel shows that they were written independently and that all four accounts are true and reliable.

16:6 The resurrection is vitally important for many reasons: (1) Jesus kept his promise to rise from the dead, so we can believe he will keep all his other promises. (2) The resurrection ensures that the ruler of God's eternal kingdom will be the living Christ, not just an idea, hope, or dream. (3) Christ rose from the dead, giving us the assurance that we also will be resurrected. (4) The power of God that brought Christ's body back from the dead is available to us to bring our morally and spiritually dead selves back to life so we can change and grow (1 Corinthians 15:12–19). (5) The resurrection provides the substance of the church's witness to the

the Nazarene who was crucified? He isn't here! He has come back to life! Look, that's where his body was lying. 7Now go and give this message to his disciples including Peter:

16:7
Mt 26:32
Mk 14:28
Jn 21:1

" 'Jesus is going ahead of you to Galilee. You will see him there, just as he told you before he died!' "

8The women fled from the tomb, trembling and bewildered, too frightened to talk.

Jesus appears to Mary Magdalene
(240/John 20:10–18)

16:9
Mt 28:9,10
Lk 24:11
Jn 20:11-18

9It was early on Sunday morning when Jesus came back to life, and the first person who saw him was Mary Magdalene—the woman from whom he had cast out seven demons. 10, 11She found the disciples wet-eyed with grief and exclaimed that she had seen Jesus, and he was alive! But they didn't believe her!

Jesus appears to two believers traveling on the road
(243/Luke 24:13–35)

16:12
Lk 24:13-33
1 Cor 15:35-45

12Later that day he appeared to two who were walking from Jerusalem into the country, but they didn't recognize him at first because he had changed his appear-

16:9 Vss 9-20 are not found in the most ancient manuscripts, but may be considered an appendix giving additional facts.   **16:12** *Later that day,* literally, "after these things."

EVIDENCE THAT JESUS ACTUALLY DIED AND AROSE	Proposed Explanations for Empty Tomb	Evidence Against These Explanations	References
This evidence demonstrates Jesus' uniqueness in history and proves that he is God's Son. No one else was able to predict his own resurrection and then accomplish it.	Jesus was only unconscious and later revived.	A Roman soldier told Pilate Jesus was dead.	Mark 15:44, 45
		The Roman soldiers did not break Jesus' legs, because he had already died, and one of them pierced Jesus' side with a spear.	John 19:32–34
		Joseph of Arimathea and Nicodemus wrapped Jesus' body and placed it in the tomb.	John 19:38–40
	The women made a mistake and went to the wrong tomb.	Mary Magdalene and Mary the mother of Joses saw Jesus placed in the tomb.	Matthew 27:59–61 Mark 15:47 Luke 23:55
		On Sunday morning Peter and John also went to the same tomb.	John 20:3–9
	Unknown thieves stole Jesus' body.	The tomb was sealed and guarded by the Temple police and probably Roman soldiers, too.	Matthew 27:65, 66
	The disciples stole Jesus' body.	The disciples were ready to die for their faith. Stealing Jesus' body would have been admitting their faith was meaningless.	Acts 12:2
		The tomb was guarded and sealed.	Matthew 27:66
	The religious leaders stole Jesus' body to secure it.	If the religious leaders had taken Jesus' body, they would have produced it to stop the rumors of his resurrection.	none

world. We do not merely tell lessons from the life of a good teacher; we proclaim the reality of the resurrection of Jesus Christ.

16:7 The angel made special mention of Peter to show that, in spite of Peter's denials, Jesus had not denied him. Jesus still had great responsibilities for Peter to fill in the church that was not yet born.

16:7 The angel told the disciples to meet Jesus in Galilee as Jesus had told them before (Mark 14:28). This is where he called

most of them to be "fishers of men" (Matthew 4:19), and it would be where this mission would be restated (John 21). But the disciples, filled with fear, remained behind locked doors in Jerusalem (John 20:19). Jesus met them first in Jerusalem (Luke 24:36) and later in Galilee (John 21). Then he returned to Jerusalem where he ascended into heaven from the Mount of Olives (Acts 1:12).

ance. 13When they finally realized who he was, they rushed back to Jerusalem to tell the others, but no one believed them.

16:13
Lk 24:33-35

Jesus appears to the disciples including Thomas
(245/John 20:24–31)

14Still later he appeared to the eleven disciples as they were eating together. He rebuked them for their unbelief—their stubborn refusal to believe those who had seen him alive from the dead.

16:14
Lk 24:36
Jn 20:19-23
1 Cor 15:5

Jesus gives the Great Commission
(248/Matthew 28:16–20)

15And then he told them, "You are to go into all the world and preach the Good News to everyone, everywhere. 16Those who believe and are baptized will be saved. But those who refuse to believe will be condemned.

17"And those who believe shall use my authority to cast out demons, and they shall speak new languages. 18They will be able even to handle snakes with safety, and if they drink anything poisonous, it won't hurt them; and they will be able to place their hands on the sick and heal them."

16:15
Col 1:23

16:16
Acts 2:38; 16:31
Rom 10:9
1 Pet 3:21

16:17
Acts 2:4; 19:6

16:18
Acts 28:5

Jesus ascends into heaven
(250/Luke 24:50–53)

19When the Lord Jesus had finished talking with them, he was taken up into heaven and sat down at God's right hand.

20And the disciples went everywhere preaching, and the Lord was with them and confirmed what they said by the miracles that followed their messages.

16:19
Lk 24:50,51
Rom 8:34
Heb 1:3
Rev 3:21

16:17 *speak new languages*, literally, "they will speak in new tongues." Some ancient manuscripts omit "new."

16:13 When the two men finally realized who Jesus was, they rushed back to Jerusalem. It's not enough to read about Christ as a personality or to study his teachings. By believing that he is God, you trust him to save you and accept him as Lord of your life. This is the difference between knowing Jesus and knowing about him. Only when you know him will you be motivated to share with others what he has done for you.

16:15 Jesus told his disciples to "go into all the world" telling everyone he paid the penalty for sin and that those who believe in him can be forgiven and live eternally with God. Christian disciples today are living in all parts of the world, telling this good news to people who haven't heard it. The driving power that carries missionaries around the world and sets Christ's church in motion is the faith that comes from the resurrection. Do you ever feel you don't have the skill or determination to be a witness for Christ? You must personally realize that Jesus rose from the dead and lives for you today. As you grow in your relationship with him, he will provide you with both the opportunities and the inner strength to tell his message.

16:16 It is not the water of baptism that saves, but God's grace accepted through faith in Christ. Baptism is an outward sign of inward faith. Because of Jesus' response to the thief on the cross who died with him, we know it is possible to be saved without

being baptized (Luke 23:43). Baptism alone without faith does not automatically bring a person to heaven. Those who refuse to believe will be condemned, regardless of whether or not they have been baptized.

16:18 There are times when God intervenes miraculously to protect his followers. Occasionally he gives them special powers. Paul handled snakes safely (Acts 28:5), and the disciples healed the sick (Matthew 10:1; Acts 3:7, 8). This does not mean, however, that we should test God by putting ourselves in dangerous situations.

16:19 When Jesus ascended into heaven, his physical presence left the disciples (Acts 1:9). Jesus' sitting at God's right hand signifies the completion of his work, his authority as God, and his coronation as King.

16:20 Mark's Gospel emphasizes Christ's power as well as his servanthood. Jesus' life and teaching turn the world upside down. The world's view of power is to control others in order to get your way. But Jesus, with all authority and power in heaven and earth, chose to serve others. He held children in his arms, healed the sick, washed the disciples' feet, and died for the sins of the world. Following Jesus means receiving this same power to serve. We are called, as believers, to be servants of Christ. As Christ served, we are to serve.

Mediterranean Sea

LEBANON

ITUREA

Sidon

Tyre

PHOENICIA

TRACHONITIS
SYRIA

GALILEE

Chorazin
Capernaum

Bethsaida-Julias
Bethsaida

Sea of Galilee

Nazareth
Nain

Gadara

DECAPOLIS
(Region of Ten Towns)

ISRAEL

SAMARIA

Jordan River

Arimathea

PEREA

Jericho

Emmaus
Jerusalem
Bethphage
Bethlehem

Mount of Olives
Bethany

JORDAN

Dead Sea

JUDEA

IDUMEA

0   20 Mi.

0   20 Km.

Luke begins his account in the Temple in Jerusalem, giving us the background for the birth of John the Baptist, then moves on to the city of Nazareth and the story of Mary, chosen to be Jesus' mother (1:26ff). As a result of Caesar's call for a census, Mary and Joseph had to travel to Bethlehem, where Jesus was born in fulfillment of prophecy (2:1ff). Jesus grew up in Nazareth and began his earthly ministry by being baptized by John (3:21, 22) and tempted by Satan (4:1ff). Much of his ministry focused in Galilee—he set up his "home" in Capernaum (4:31ff) and from there he taught throughout the region (8:1ff). Later he visited the Gerasene country where he healed a demon-possessed man from Gadara (8:36ff). He fed more than 5,000 people with one lunch on the shores of the Sea of Galilee near Bethsaida-Julias (9:10ff). Jesus always traveled to Jerusalem for the major festivals, and enjoyed visiting friends in nearby Bethany (10:38ff). He healed ten lepers on the border between Galilee and Samaria (17:11), and helped a dishonest tax collector in Jericho turn his life around (19:1ff). The little villages of Bethphage and Bethany on the Mount of Olives were Jesus' resting places during his last days on earth. He was crucified outside Jerusalem's walls, but he would rise again. Two men on the road leading to Emmaus were among the first to see the resurrected Christ (24:13ff).

LUKE

VITAL STATISTICS

PURPOSE:
To present an accurate account of the life of Christ and to present Christ as the perfect man and Savior

AUTHOR:
Luke—a doctor (Colossians 4:14), a Greek and Gentile Christian. He is the only known Gentile author in the New Testament. He was a close friend and companion of Paul. He also wrote Acts, and the two books go together.

TO WHOM WRITTEN:
Theophilus ("lover of God"), Gentiles, and people everywhere

DATE WRITTEN:
About A.D. 60

SETTING:
Luke wrote from Caesarea or from Rome.

KEY VERSES:
"Jesus told him, 'This shows that salvation has come to this home today. This man was one of the lost sons of Abraham, and I, the Messiah, have come to search for and to save such souls as his' " (19:9, 10).

KEY PEOPLE:
Jesus, Elizabeth, Zacharias, John the Baptist, Mary, the disciples, Herod the Great, Pilate, Mary Magdalene

KEY PLACES:
Bethlehem, Galilee, Judea, Jerusalem

SPECIAL FEATURES:
This is the most comprehensive Gospel. The general vocabulary and diction show that the author was educated. He makes frequent references to illnesses and diagnoses. Luke stresses Jesus' relationships with people; emphasizes prayer, miracles, angels; records inspired hymns of praise; and gives a prominent place to women. Most of 9:51—18:35 is not found in any other Gospel.

EVERY birth is a miracle, and every child is a gift from God. But nearly 20 centuries ago, there was a truly miraculous birth; the Son of God was born a man. With divine Father and human mother, Jesus entered history—God in the flesh.

Luke affirms Christ's divinity, but the real emphasis of his book is to show his humanity—Jesus, the Son of God, is also the Son of Man. As a doctor, Luke was a man of science, and as a Greek, he was a man of detail. It is not surprising, then, that he begins by outlining his extensive research and explaining that he is reporting the facts (1:1–4). In addition, Luke was a close friend and traveling companion of Paul, so he could interview the other disciples, had access to other historical accounts, and was an eyewitness to the birth and growth of the early church. His Gospel and book of Acts are reliable, historical documents.

Luke's story begins with angels appearing to Zacharias and then Mary, telling them of the birth of their sons. From Zacharias and Elizabeth would come John the Baptist who would prepare the way for Christ. And Mary would conceive by the Holy Spirit and bear Jesus, the Son of God. Soon after John's birth, Caesar Augustus declared a census, and so Mary and Joseph traveled to Bethlehem, the city of David, their ancient ancestor. There the child was born. Angels announced the joyous event to shepherds who rushed to the manger. When they left, they were praising God and spreading the news. Eight days later, Jesus was circumcised and then dedicated to God in the Temple where Simeon and Anna confirmed his identity as the Savior, their Messiah.

Luke gives us a glimpse of Jesus at age 12—discussing theology with the teachers of the Law at the Temple (2:41–52). The next event occurs 18 years later, when we read of John the Baptist preaching in the wilderness. Jesus came to John to be baptized before beginning his public ministry (3:1–38). At this point, Luke traces Jesus' geneology on his stepfather Joseph's side, through David and Abraham back to Adam, underscoring his identity as the Son of Man.

After the temptation in the Judean wastelands (4:1–13), Jesus returned to Galilee and began to preach, teach, and heal (4:14—21:38). During this time, he solidified his group of 12 disciples, calling Peter, James, John (5:1–10), and Matthew (5:27–29). Later Jesus commissioned the disciples and sent them out to proclaim the Kingdom of God. When they returned, he revealed to them his mission, his true identity, and what it means to be his disciple (9:18–62). His mission—to be the Savior of the world—would take him to Jerusalem (9:51–53), where he would be rejected, tried, and crucified.

While carrying his cross to Golgotha, some women in Jerusalem wept for him; but Jesus told them to weep for themselves and their children (23:28). But Luke's Gospel does not end in sadness. It concludes with the thrilling account of Jesus' resurrection from the dead, his appearances to the disciples, and his promise to send the Holy Spirit (24:1–53). Read Luke's beautifully written and accurate account of the life of Jesus, Son of Man and Son of God. Then praise God for sending the Savior for all men—our risen and triumphant Lord.

THE BLUEPRINT

A. BIRTH AND PREPARATION OF JESUS, THE SAVIOR (1:1—4:13)

From an infant who could do nothing on his own, Jesus grew to become completely able to fulfill his mission on earth. He became fully human, developing in all ways like us. Yet he remained fully God. He took no short-cuts and was not isolated from the pressures and temptations of life. There are no short-cuts for us either, as we prepare for a life of service to God.

B. MESSAGE AND MINISTRY OF JESUS, THE SAVIOR (4:14—21:38)
1. Jesus' ministry in Galilee
2. Jesus' ministry on the way to Jerusalem
3. Jesus' ministry in Jerusalem

Jesus taught great crowds of people, especially through parables, which are stories with great truths. But only those with ears to hear will understand. We should pray that God's Spirit would help us understand the implications of these truths for our lives so we can become more and more like Jesus.

C. DEATH AND RESURRECTION OF JESUS, THE SAVIOR (22:1—24:53)

The Savior of the world was arrested and executed. But death could not destroy him, and Jesus came to life again and ascended to heaven. In Luke's careful, historical account, we receive the facts about Jesus' resurrection. We must not only believe that these facts are true, but must also trust Christ as our Savior. It is shortsighted to neglect the facts, but how sad to accept the facts and neglect the forgiveness that Jesus offers to each of us.

MEGATHEMES

THEME	EXPLANATION	IMPORTANCE
Jesus Christ, the Savior	Luke describes how God's Son entered human history. Jesus lived as the perfect example of a man. After a perfect ministry, he provided a perfect sacrifice for our sin so we could be saved.	Jesus is our perfect leader and Savior. He offers forgiveness to all who will accept him as Lord of their lives and believe that what he says is true.
History	Luke was a medical doctor and historian. He put great emphasis on dates and details, connecting Jesus to events and people in history.	Luke gives details so we can believe in the reliability of the history of Jesus' life. Even more important, we can believe with certainty that Jesus is God.
People	Jesus was deeply interested in people and relationships. He showed warm concern for his followers and friends—men, women, and children.	Jesus' love for people is good news for everyone. His message is for all people in every nation. Each one of us has an opportunity to respond to him in faith.
Compassion	As a perfect human, Jesus showed tender sympathy to the poor, the despised, the hurt, and the sinful. No one was rejected or ignored by him.	Jesus is more than an idea or teacher—he cares for you. Only this kind of deep love can satisfy your need.
Holy Spirit	The Holy Spirit was present at Jesus' birth, baptism, ministry, and resurrection. As a perfect example for us, Jesus lived in dependence on the Holy Spirit.	The Holy Spirit was sent by God as confirmation of Jesus' authority. The Holy Spirit is given to enable people to live for Christ. By faith we can have the Holy Spirit's presence and power to witness and to serve.

A. BIRTH AND PREPARATION OF JESUS, THE SAVIOR (1:1—4:13)

Luke gives us the most detailed account of Jesus' birth. In describing Jesus' birth, childhood, and human development, Luke lifts up the humanity of Jesus. Our Savior was the ideal man. Fully prepared, the ideal man was now ready to live the perfect life.

Luke's purpose in writing
(1)

1 Dear friend who loves God:

1, 2Several biographies of Christ have already been written using as their source material the reports circulating among us from the early disciples and other eyewitnesses. 3However, it occurred to me that it would be well to recheck all these accounts from first to last and after thorough investigation to pass this summary on to you, 4to reassure you of the truth of all you were taught.

1:1,2
Jn 15:27
Acts 1:21,22
1 Tim 3:16
Heb 2:3
2 Pet 1:16
1 Jn 1:1-4
1:3
Acts 1:1; 11:4

An angel promises the birth of John to Zacharias
(4)

5My story begins with a Jewish priest, Zacharias, who lived when Herod was king of Judea. Zacharias was a member of the Abijah division of the Temple service corps. (His wife Elizabeth was, like himself, a member of the priest tribe of the Jews, a descendant of Aaron.) 6Zacharias and Elizabeth were godly folk, careful to obey all of God's laws in spirit as well as in letter. 7But they had no children, for Elizabeth was barren; and now they were both very old.

8, 9One day as Zacharias was going about his work in the Temple—for his division was on duty that week—the honor fell to him by lot to enter the inner sanctuary and burn incense before the Lord. 10Meanwhile, a great crowd stood outside in the Temple court, praying as they always did during that part of the service when the incense was being burned.

1:5
1 Chron 24:10,19
Neh 12:4
Mt 2:1
1:6
2 Kgs 20:3
Phil 3:6
1:7
1 Sam 1:5
1:8
2 Chron 8:14
1:9
Ex 30:7,8

1:1 *Dear friend who loves God.* From vs 3. Literally, "most excellent Theophilus." The name means "one who loves God." **1:3** *to pass this summary on to you,* literally, "an account of the things accomplished among us." **1:8, 9** *by lot.* Probably by throwing dice or something similar—"drawing straws" would be a modern equivalent.

1:1 "Friend who loves God," a translation of the name Theophilus, for whom the book was written and/or dedicated. The book of Acts, also written by Luke, begins this same way.

1:1 *Christ,* one of Jesus' titles, is the Greek form of the Hebrew word *Messiah,* meaning "God's anointed one." This book is the biography of Jesus, also known as the Christ. For his Greek audience, who admired and valued perfection, Luke depicts Jesus as the perfect man. He portrays Jesus as entirely human and yet entirely divine. Luke is the only New Testament writer known to be a Gentile (someone who is not a Jew).

1:1-4 There was a lot of interest in Jesus, and many people had written personal accounts of experiences with him. Luke set out to put these accounts into an historical, thorough, and complete form using all available resources. Because it was important to him to know what was true, he relied heavily on eyewitness accounts. Christianity doesn't say, "Close your eyes and believe," but rather "Check it out for yourself." The Bible encourages you to thoroughly investigate its claims (John 1:46; 21:24; Acts 17:11, 12), because your conclusions about Jesus are a life-and-death matter.

1:3 As a medical doctor, Luke knew the importance of a thorough checkup. He used his skills in observation and analysis to do a thorough investigation of the stories about Jesus. His diagnosis? The gospel of Jesus Christ is true! You can read Luke's account of Jesus' life with confidence that it was written by a clear thinker and a thoughtful researcher. Because the gospel is founded on historical truth, our spiritual growth must involve careful, disciplined, thorough investigation of God's Word. If this kind of study is not part of your life, find a pastor, teacher, or book to help you get started and to guide you in this important part of Christian growth.

1:5 A Jewish priest was a minister who worked at the Temple

managing its upkeep, teaching the people God's Word, and directing the worship services. At this time there were about twenty thousand priests throughout the country—far too many to minister in the Temple at one time. Therefore the priests were divided into 24 separate groups of about 1,000 each, according to King David's directions (1 Chronicles 24:3–19).

Zacharias was a member of the Abijah division, on duty this particular week. Each morning a priest was to enter the inner sanctuary of the Temple and burn incense. Lots were cast (a procedure like throwing dice) to decide who would enter the sacred room, and one day the lot fell to Zacharias. But it was not by chance that Zacharias was on duty and that he was chosen to enter the inner sanctuary—a once-in-a-lifetime opportunity—that day. God was guiding the events of history to prepare the way for Jesus to come to earth.

1:5 This was Herod the Great, confirmed by the Roman Senate as king of the Jews. Only half Jewish himself and eager to please his Roman superiors, he expanded and beautified the Jerusalem Temple—but placed a Roman eagle over the entrance. When he helped the Jews, it was for political purposes and not because he cared about their God. Herod the Great later ordered a massacre of infants in a futile attempt to kill the infant Jesus whom some were calling the new "King of the Jews" (Matthew 2:16–18).

1:6 Zacharias and Elizabeth not only went through the motions of following God's laws; they backed up their outward compliance with inward obedience. To obey in spirit means to understand God's intention and to obey that rather than to distort his purposes by obeying the letter of his law only.

1:10 Incense was burned in the Temple twice daily. When the people saw the smoke from the burning incense, they prayed. The smoke drifting heavenward symbolized their prayers ascending to God's throne.

11, 12Zacharias was in the sanctuary when suddenly an angel appeared, standing to the right of the altar of incense! Zacharias was startled and terrified. 13But the angel said, "Don't be afraid, Zacharias! For I have come to tell you that God has heard your prayer, and your wife Elizabeth will bear you a son! And you are to name him John. 14You will both have great joy and gladness at his birth, and many will rejoice with you. 15For he will be one of the Lord's great men. He must never touch wine or hard liquor—and he will be filled with the Holy Spirit, even from before his birth! 16And he will persuade many a Jew to turn to the Lord his

ZACHARIAS

Zacharias was told before anyone else that God was setting in motion his own visit to earth. Zacharias and his wife, Elizabeth, were known for their personal holiness. They were well suited to doing a special work for God. But they shared the pain of not having children—long seen by Jews as proof of not having God's blessing. Zacharias and Elizabeth were old, and they had stopped even asking for children.

This trip to the Temple in Jerusalem for Zacharias' turn at duty had included an unexpected blessing. Zacharias was chosen to be the priest who would enter the Holy of Holies to offer incense to God for the people. Suddenly, much to his surprise and terror, he found himself face to face with an angel. The angel's message was too good to be true! But Zacharias did not respond to the news of the coming Savior as much as he expressed doubts about his own ability to father the child the angel promised him. His age spoke more loudly than God's promise. As a result, God prevented Zacharias from speaking until the promise became reality.

The record of the prayer in Luke 1 is our last glimpse of Zacharias. Like so many of God's most faithful servants, he passed quietly from the scene once his part was done. He becomes our hero for times when we doubt God yet are willing to obey. We gain hope from Zacharias that God can do great things through anyone who is available to him.

Strengths and accomplishments:
• Known as a righteous man
• Was a priest for God
• One of the few people to be directly addressed by an angel
• Fathered John the Baptist

Weaknesses and mistakes:
• Momentarily doubted the angel's promise of a son because of his old age

Lessons from his life:
• Physical limitations do not limit God
• God accomplishes his will, sometimes in unexpected ways

Vital statistics:
• Occupation: Priest
• Relatives: Wife: Elizabeth. Son: John the Baptist.

Key verses:
"Zacharias and Elizabeth were godly folk, careful to obey all of God's laws in spirit as well as in letter. But they had no children, for Elizabeth was barren; and now they were both very old" (Luke 1:6, 7).

Zacharias' story is told in Luke 1.

1:11, 12 Angels are spirit beings who live in God's presence and do his will. Only two are mentioned by name in Scripture—Michael and Gabriel—but there are many who act as God's messengers. Here Gabriel (1:19) delivered a special message to Zacharias. This was not a dream or a vision. The angel appeared in visible form and spoke audible words to the priest.

1:13 Zacharias, while offering incense on the altar, was also praying, perhaps for a son or for the coming of the Messiah. In either case, his prayer was answered. He would soon have a son who would prepare the way for the Messiah. God answers prayer in his own way and in his own time. He worked in an "impossible" situation—Zacharias' wife was barren—to bring about the fulfillment of all the prophecies concerning the Messiah. If we want to have our prayers answered, we must be open to what God can do in impossible situations. And we must wait for him to work in his way, in his time.

1:13 John means "the Lord is gracious," and Jesus means "Savior." Both names were prescribed by God, not chosen by human parents. Throughout the Gospels, God acts graciously and gives salvation to his people.

1:15 John was set apart for special service to God. He may have been forbidden to drink as part of the Nazirite vow, an ancient vow of consecration to God (see Numbers 6:1–4). Samson (Judges 13) was under the Nazirite vow and Samuel may have been also (1 Samuel 1:11).

1:15 This is Luke's first mention of the Holy Spirit, the third person of the Trinity. Here, as in the Old Testament when people are said to be filled with the Spirit, he came for a specific purpose, to accomplish a particular task. Since Pentecost (Acts 2:2–4), the Holy Spirit comes to indwell people permanently.

God. 17He will be a man of rugged spirit and power like Elijah, the prophet of old; and he will precede the coming of the Messiah, preparing the people for his arrival. He will soften adult hearts to become like little children's, and will change disobedient minds to the wisdom of faith."

18Zacharias said to the angel, "But this is impossible! I'm an old man now, and my wife is also well along in years."

19Then the angel said, "I am Gabriel! I stand in the very presence of God. It was he who sent me to you with this good news! 20And now, because you haven't believed me, you are to be stricken silent, unable to speak until the child is born. For my words will certainly come true at the proper time."

21Meanwhile the crowds outside were waiting for Zacharias to appear and wondered why he was taking so long. 22When he finally came out, he couldn't speak to them, and they realized from his gestures that he must have seen a vision in the Temple. 23He stayed on at the Temple for the remaining days of his Temple duties and then returned home. 24Soon afterwards Elizabeth his wife became pregnant and went into seclusion for five months.

25"How kind the Lord is," she exclaimed, "to take away my disgrace of having no children!"

1:17 rugged, implied. *and will change disobedient minds to the wisdom of faith,* literally, "to turn the hearts of the fathers to the children, and the disobedient to the wisdom of the just."

1:17
Isa 40:3
Mal 4:5
Mt 11:14
Mk 9:12
Rom 9:5

1:18
Gen 17:17

1:19
Dan 8:16
9:21-23
Heb 1:14

1:20
Ezek 3:26; 24:27

1:25
Gen 30:23

Person/Group	Methods	Reference	GOD'S UNUSUAL METHODS
Jacob, Zacharias, Mary, Shepherds	Angels	Genesis 32:22–32; Luke 1:13, 30; 2:10	One of the best ways to under-stand God's willingness to communicate to people is to note the various methods, some of them quite unexpected, that he has used to give his message. Following is a sample of his methods and the people he contacted.
Jacob, Isaiah, Joseph, Pharaoh, a baker, a butler, the wise men	Dreams	Genesis 28:10–22; 37:5–10; 40:5; 41:7, 8; Isaiah 1:1; Matthew 1:20; 2:12, 13	
Belshazzar	Handwriting on the wall	Daniel 5:5–9	
Balaam	Talking donkey	Numbers 22:21–35	
People of Israel	Pillar of cloud and fire	Exodus 13:21, 22	
Jonah	Being swallowed by a fish	Jonah 2	
Abraham, Moses, Jesus at his baptism, Paul, others	Verbally	Genesis 12:1–4; Exodus 7:8; Matthew 3:13–17; Acts 18:9	
Moses	Fire	Exodus 3:2	
Us	God's Son	Hebrews 1:1, 2	

1:17 John's role was to be almost identical to that of an Old Testament prophet—to encourage people to turn away from sin and back to God. He is often compared to the great prophet Elijah, known for standing up to evil rulers (Malachi 4:5; Matthew 11:14; 17:10–13). See Elijah's profile in 1 Kings 18.

1:17 In preparing people for the Messiah's arrival, John would do "heart transplants." He would take stony adult hearts and exchange them for hearts that were soft and childlike—pliable, trusting, and open to change. (See Ezekiel 11:19, 20 and 36:25–29 for more on "heart transplants.") While adults should not be *childish,* their faith must have these *childlike* qualities. Are you as open to God as you should be? Or do you need a change of heart?

1:18 When told he would have a son, Zacharias doubted the angel's word. From his human perspective, his doubts were understandable—but with God, anything is possible. Although Zacharias and Elizabeth were past the age of childbearing, God gave them a child. It is easy to doubt or misunderstand what God wants to do in our lives. Even God's people sometimes make the mistake of trusting their reason or experience rather than God. When tempted to think that one of God's promises is impossible, we should try to look at the situation from God's perspective. He is not bound by our human limitations.

1:20 Zacharias thought it incredible that he and his wife, at their old age, could conceive a child. But what God promises, he delivers. And he delivers *on time!* You can have complete confidence that God will keep his promises. It may not be the next day, but it will be at his proper time. If you are waiting for God to answer some request or fill some need, remain patient. No matter how impossible God's promises may seem, what he has said in his Word will come true at the right time.

1:21 The people were waiting outside for Zacharias to come out and pronounce the customary blessing upon them as found in Numbers 6:22–27.

1:25 Zacharias and Elizabeth were both faithful people, and yet they were suffering. Some Jews at that time did not believe in a bodily resurrection, so their hope of immortality was in their children. In addition, children cared for their parents in their old age, and they added to the family's wealth and social status. Children were considered a blessing, and childlessness was seen as a curse. Zacharias and Elizabeth had been childless for many years, and now they were too old to expect any change in their situation. They felt humiliated and hopeless. But God was waiting for the right time to bless them and take away their disgrace.

An angel promises the birth of Jesus to Mary
(5)

1:26
Mt 2:23

1:27
Isa 7:14

1:31
Mt 1:21,25

1:32
2 Sam 7:11
Ps 132:11
Isa 9:6,7; 16:5
Jer 23:5
Phil 2:10
1 Tim 6:15

1:33
Dan 2:44;
7:14,18,27
Heb 1:8

1:35
Mt 14:33; 26:63
Mk 1:1
Jn 1:34; 20:31
Rom 1:4

26The following month God sent the angel Gabriel to Nazareth, a village in Galilee, 27to a virgin, Mary, engaged to be married to a man named Joseph, a descendant of King David.

28Gabriel appeared to her and said, "Congratulations, favored lady! The Lord is with you!"

29Confused and disturbed, Mary tried to think what the angel could mean. 30"Don't be frightened, Mary," the angel told her, "for God has decided to wonderfully bless you! 31Very soon now, you will become pregnant and have a baby boy, and you are to name him 'Jesus.' 32He shall be very great and shall be called the Son of God. And the Lord God shall give him the throne of his ancestor David. 33And he shall reign over Israel forever; his Kingdom shall never end!"

34Mary asked the angel, "But how can I have a baby? I am a virgin."

35The angel replied, "The Holy Spirit shall come upon you, and the power of God shall overshadow you; so the baby born to you will be utterly holy—the Son of God. 36Furthermore, six months ago your Aunt Elizabeth—'the barren one,'

1:28 *The Lord is with you.* Some ancient versions add, "Blessed are you among women," as in vs 42 which appears in all manuscripts. **1:36** *Aunt,* literally, "relative."

DOUBTERS IN THE BIBLE

Doubter	Doubtful Moment	Reference
Abraham	When God told him he would be a father in old age	Genesis 17:17
Sarah	When she heard she would be a mother in old age	Genesis 18:12
Moses	When God told him to return to Egypt to lead the people	Exodus 3:10–15
Israelites	Whenever they faced difficulties in the wilderness	Exodus 16:1–3
Gideon	When told he would be a judge and lead the people	Judges 6:14–23
Zacharias	When told he would be a father in old age	Luke 1:18
Thomas	When told Jesus had risen from the dead	John 20:24–25

Many of the people God used to accomplish great things started out as real doubters. With all of them, God showed great patience. Honest doubt was not a bad starting point as long as they didn't stay there. How great a part does doubt have in your willingness to trust God?

1:26 Gabriel appeared not only to Zacharias and to Mary but also to the prophet Daniel more than 500 years earlier (Daniel 8:15; 9:21). Each time he appeared, he brought important messages from God.

1:26 Nazareth, Joseph's and Mary's hometown, was remote from Jerusalem, the center of Jewish life and worship. Located on a major trade route, it was frequently visited by Gentile merchants and Roman soldiers. For these reasons its reputation was tarnished among the Jews (John 1:46). Jesus was born in Bethlehem but grew up in Nazareth. Nevertheless, the people of Nazareth would reject him as the Messiah (4:22–30).

1:28 Mary was young, poor, female—all characteristics that, to the people of her day, would make her seem unusable by God for any major task. But God chose Mary for one of the most important acts of obedience he has ever demanded of anyone. You may feel that your situation in life makes you an unlikely candidate for God's service. Don't limit God's choices. He can use you if you trust him.

1:30, 31 God's blessing does not automatically bring instant success, fame, or favor. His blessing on Mary, the honor of being the mother of the Messiah, would lead to much pain: her peers would ridicule her; her fiancé would come close to leaving her; her son would be rejected and murdered. But through her son would come the world's only hope, and this is why Mary has been praised by countless generations as "blessed among women." Her submission led to our salvation. If your blessings lead to sorrows, think of Mary and wait patiently for God to finish working out his plan.

1:31–33 *Jesus,* a Greek form of the Hebrew word *Joshua,* was a common name meaning "Savior." Just as Joshua led Israel into the Promised Land (see Joshua 1:2), so Jesus would lead his people into eternal life. The symbolism of his name was not lost on the people of his day, who took names seriously and saw them as a source of power. In Jesus' name people were healed, demons were banished, and sins were forgiven.

1:32, 33 Centuries earlier, God had promised King David that his kingdom would last forever (2 Samuel 7:16). This promise was fulfilled in the coming of Jesus, a direct descendant of David, whose reign will continue throughout eternity.

1:34 The birth of Jesus to a virgin is a miracle that many people find hard to believe. These three facts can aid our faith: (1) Luke was a medical doctor, and he knew perfectly well how babies are made. It would have been just as hard for him to believe in a virgin birth as it is for us, and yet he reports it as fact. (2) Luke was a painstaking researcher who based his Gospel on eyewitness accounts. Tradition holds that he talked with Mary about the events in the first two chapters. This is her story, not a fictional invention. (3) Christians and Jews, who worship God as the creator of the universe, should believe he has the power to create a child in a virgin's womb.

1:35 Jesus was born without the sin that entered the world through Adam. He was born holy, just as Adam was created sinless. In contrast to Adam, who disobeyed God, Jesus obeyed God and is thus able to be our substitute for sin's consequences and make us acceptable to God (Romans 5:14–19).

they called her—became pregnant in her old age! 37For every promise from God shall surely come true."

1:37
Gen 18:14
Jer 32:17
Rom 4:21

38Mary said, "I am the Lord's servant, and I am willing to do whatever he wants. May everything you said come true." And then the angel disappeared.

Mary visits Elizabeth
(6)

39, 40A few days later Mary hurried to the highlands of Judea to the town where Zacharias lived, to visit Elizabeth.

1:39
Josh 20:7; 21:9,
11

41At the sound of Mary's greeting, Elizabeth's child leaped within her and she was filled with the Holy Spirit.

1:42
Judg 5:24
1:43
Lk 2:11
1:46
1 Sam 2:1-10
Ps 34:2,3
1:47
1 Tim 1:1; 2:3
Tit 1:3; 2:10; 3:4
1:48
1 Sam 1:11

42She gave a glad cry and exclaimed to Mary, "You are favored by God above all other women, and your child is destined for God's mightiest praise. 43What an honor this is, that the mother of my Lord should visit me! 44When you came in and greeted me, the instant I heard your voice, my baby moved in me for joy! 45You believed that God would do what he said; that is why he has given you this wonderful blessing."

46Mary responded, "Oh, how I praise the Lord. 47How I rejoice in God my Savior! 48For he took notice of his lowly servant girl, and now generation after

---

Person	Reference	
Abraham	Genesis 15:1	**TO FEAR**
Moses	Numbers 21:34	**OR**
	Deuteronomy 3:2	**NOT TO FEAR**
Joshua	Joshua 8:1	
Jeremiah	Lamentations 3:57	
Daniel	Daniel 10:12, 19	
Zacharias	Luke 1:13	
Mary	Luke 1:30	
Shepherds	Luke 2:10	
Peter	Luke 5:10	
Paul	Acts 27:24	
John	Revelation 1:17, 18	

People in the Bible who were confronted by God or his angels all had one consistent response—fear. To each of them, God's response was always the same—don't be afraid. As soon as they sensed that God accepted them and wanted to communicate with them, then fear subsided. He had given them freedom to be his friends. Has he given you the same freedom?

1:38 A young unmarried girl who became pregnant risked disaster. Unless the father of the child agreed to marry her, she would probably remain unmarried for life. If her own father rejected her, she could be forced into begging or prostitution in order to earn her living. And Mary, with her story about being made pregnant by the Holy Spirit, risked being considered crazy as well. Still she said, despite the possible costs, "I am willing." When Mary said that, she didn't know about the tremendous blessing she would receive. She only knew God was asking her to serve him, and she willingly obeyed. Don't wait to see the bottom line before offering your life to God. Offer yourself willingly, even when the results of doing so look disastrous.

1:38 The announcement of a child's birth was met with various responses throughout Scripture. Sarah, Abraham's wife, laughed (Genesis 18:9–15). Manoah, Samson's father, panicked (Judges 13:22). Zacharias doubted (Luke 1:18). By contrast, Mary submitted. She believed the angel's words and agreed to bear the child, even under humanly impossible circumstances. God is able to do the impossible. Our response to his demands should not be laughter, fear, or doubt, but willing acceptance.

1:41–43 Apparently the Holy Spirit told Elizabeth that Mary's child was the Messiah, for Elizabeth called her young niece "the mother

of my Lord" as she greeted her. As she rushed off to visit her aunt, Mary must have been wondering if the events of the last few days were real. Elizabeth's greeting would have strengthened her faith. Mary's pregnancy may have seemed impossible, but her wise old aunt believed and rejoiced in it.

1:42, 43 Even though she herself was pregnant with a long-awaited son, Elizabeth could have envied Mary, whose son would be even greater than her own. Instead she was filled with joy that the mother of her Lord would visit her. Have you ever envied people whom God has apparently singled out for special blessing? A cure for jealousy is to rejoice with them, realizing that God uses his people in ways best suited to his purpose.

1:46–55 This song is often called the *Magnificat*, the first word in the Latin translation of this passage. It has often been used as the basis for choral music and hymns. Like Hannah, the mother of Samuel (1 Samuel 2:1–10), Mary glorified God in song for what he was going to do for the world through her. Notice that in both songs, God is pictured as a champion of the poor, the oppressed, and the despised.

1:48 When Mary said, "Generation after generation forever shall call me blest of God," was she being proud? No, she was recognizing and accepting the gift God had given her. If Mary had

1:50
Gen 17:7
Ex 20:6
Ps 103:17

1:51
Ps 33:10; 98:1
118:15

1:52
1 Sam 2:6

1:53
Ps 34:10; 107:9

1:54
Ps 98:3
Jer 31:3,20

1:55
Gen 17:9

generation forever shall call me blest of God. 49For he, the mighty Holy One, has done great things to me. 50His mercy goes on from generation to generation, to all who reverence him.

51"How powerful is his mighty arm! How he scatters the proud and haughty ones! 52He has torn princes from their thrones and exalted the lowly. 53He has satisfied the hungry hearts and sent the rich away with empty hands. 54And how he has helped his servant Israel! He has not forgotten his promise to be merciful. 55For he promised our fathers—Abraham and his children—to be merciful to them forever."

56Mary stayed with Elizabeth about three months and then went back to her own home.

ELIZABETH

In societies like Israel in which a woman's value was largely measured by her ability to bear children, aging without children often led to personal hardship and public shame. For Elizabeth, childless aging was a painful and lonely time during which she remained faithful to God.

Both Elizabeth and Zacharias came from priestly families. Elizabeth had to give up her husband for two weeks each year so he could be at the Temple in Jerusalem for his priestly duties. Life had probably settled into a well-worn routine when Zacharias returned excited, but speechless from one of these trips. His news was a wonderful surprise. What had been a faded dream would become an exciting reality! Soon she became pregnant and she knew God had given her a gift she had not dared to hope for in a long time.

News traveled fast among the family. Seventy miles to the north, in Nazareth, Elizabeth's niece, Mary, also unexpectedly became pregnant. Within days after the angel's message that she would bear the Messiah, Mary went to visit Elizabeth. They were instantly bound by the unique gifts God had given them. Elizabeth knew that Mary's son would be even greater than her own, for John would be the messenger for Mary's son.

When the baby was born, Elizabeth insisted on his God-given name: John. Zacharias' written agreement freed his tongue, and everyone in town wondered what would become of this obviously special child.

Elizabeth whispered her praise as she cared for God's gift. Knowing about Mary must have made her marvel at God's timing. Things had worked out even better than she could have planned. In our own lives, we need to remember that God is in control of every situation. When did you last pause to recognize God's timing in the events of your life?

Strengths and accomplishments:
- Known as a deeply spiritual woman
- Showed no doubts about God's ability to fulfill his promise
- Mother of John the Baptist
- The first woman besides Mary to hear of the coming Savior

Lessons from her life:
- God does not forget those who have been faithful to him
- God's timetable and methods do not have to conform to what we expect

Vital statistics:
- Occupation: Homemaker
- Relatives: Husband: Zacharias. Son: John the Baptist. Niece: Mary.
- Contemporaries: Joseph, Herod the Great

Key verses:
"What an honor this is, that the mother of my Lord should visit me! When you came in and greeted me, the instant I heard your voice, my baby moved in me for joy! You believed that God would do what he said; that is why he has given you this wonderful blessing" (Luke 1:43–45).

Elizabeth's story is told in Luke 1:5–80.

---

denied her incredible position, she would have been throwing God's blessing back at him. Pride is refusing to accept God's gifts; humility is accepting them and using them to praise and serve him. Don't deny your gifts. Thank God for them and use them to his glory.

1:54, 55 God kept his promise to Abraham to be merciful to his people forever (Genesis 22:16–18). Christ's birth fulfilled the promise, and Mary understood this. She was not surprised when

her special son eventually announced that he was the Messiah. She had known his mission from before his birth. Some of God's promises to Israel are found in 2 Samuel 22:50, 51; Psalms 89:2–4; 103:17, 18; Micah 7:18–20.

1:56 Because travel was not easy, long visits were customary. Mary must have been a great help to Elizabeth, who was experiencing the difficulties of a first pregnancy in her old age.

John the Baptist is born
(7)

⁵⁷By now Elizabeth's waiting was over, for the time had come for the baby to be born—and it was a boy. ⁵⁸The word spread quickly to her neighbors and relatives of how kind the Lord had been to her, and everyone rejoiced.

⁵⁹When the baby was eight days old, all the relatives and friends came for the circumcision ceremony. They all assumed the baby's name would be Zacharias, after his father.

⁶⁰But Elizabeth said, "No! He must be named John!"

⁶¹"What?" they exclaimed. "There is no one in all your family by that name."

⁶²So they asked the baby's father, talking to him by gestures.

⁶³He motioned for a piece of paper and to everyone's surprise wrote, "His name is *John!*" ⁶⁴Instantly Zacharias could speak again, and he began praising God.

⁶⁵Wonder fell upon the whole neighborhood, and the news of what had happened spread through the Judean hills. ⁶⁶And everyone who heard about it thought long thoughts and asked, "I wonder what this child will turn out to be? For the hand of the Lord is surely upon him in some special way."

⁶⁷Then his father Zacharias was filled with the Holy Spirit and gave this prophecy:

⁶⁸"Praise the Lord, the God of Israel, for he has come to visit his people and has redeemed them. ⁶⁹He is sending us a Mighty Savior from the royal line of his servant David, ⁷⁰just as he promised through his holy prophets long ago— ⁷¹someone to save us from our enemies, from all who hate us.

⁷², ⁷³"He has been merciful to our ancestors, yes, to Abraham himself, by remembering his sacred promise to him, ⁷⁴and by granting us the privilege of serving God fearlessly, freed from our enemies, ⁷⁵and by making us holy and acceptable, ready to stand in his presence forever.

⁷⁶"And you, my little son, shall be called the prophet of the glorious God, for you will prepare the way for the Messiah. ⁷⁷You will tell his people how to find salvation through forgiveness of their sins. ⁷⁸All this will be because the mercy of our God is very tender, and heaven's dawn is about to break upon us, ⁷⁹to give light to those who sit in darkness and death's shadow, and to guide us to the path of peace."

⁸⁰The little boy greatly loved God and when he grew up he lived out in the lonely wilderness until he began his public ministry to Israel.

1:62 *talking to him by gestures.* Zacharias was apparently stone deaf as well as speechless, and had not heard what his wife had said.   **1:80** *greatly loved God,* "became strong in spirit."

1:59
Gen 17:12
Lev 12:3
Lk 2:21
Phil 13:5

1:66
Lk 2:19
Acts 11:21

1:67
Joel 2:28

1:68
Lk 2:38
Acts 1:6
Heb 9:12

1:69
1 Sam 2:1,10
Ps 18:2; 132:17
Ezek 29:21

1:70
Jer 23:5; 30:10
Dan 9:24
Acts 3:21
Rom 1:2-4

1:71
Ps 106:10

1:72,73
Lev 26:42
Ps 105:8; 106:45
Mic 7:20
Heb 6:13

1:75
Jer 32:39
Eph 4:24

1:76
Isa 40:3
Mal 3:1

1:77
Jer 31:34
Mk 1:4

1:78
Eph 5:14
2 Pet 1:19

1:79
Isa 9:2

1:80
Lk 2:40

1:59 The circumcision ceremony was an important event in the family of a Jewish baby boy. God commanded it when he was beginning to form his holy nation (Genesis 17:4–14) and reaffirmed it through Moses (Leviticus 12:3). Still practiced today in Jewish homes, it is a day of joy when friends and family members celebrate the baby's becoming part of God's covenant with Israel.

1:59 Family lines and family names were important to the Jews. The people naturally assumed the child would receive, if not Zacharias' name, at least a family name. Thus they were surprised that both Elizabeth and Zacharias wanted to name him John.

1:62 Zacharias' relatives talked to him by gestures because he was apparently stone deaf as well as speechless and had not heard what his wife had said.

1:67–79 Zacharias praised God with his first words after months of silence. In a song that is often called the *Benedictus* after its first words in the Latin translation of this passage, he prophesied the coming of a Savior who would redeem his people, and he predicted that his son John would prepare the Messiah's way. All the Old Testament prophecies were coming true—no wonder Zacharias praised God! The Messiah would come in his lifetime, and his son had been chosen to pave the way.

1:71 The Jews were eagerly awaiting the Messiah, but they thought he would come to save them from the powerful Roman Empire. They were ready for a military Savior, but not for a peaceful Messiah who would conquer sin.

1:72, 73 This was God's promise to Abraham to bless all nations through him (see Genesis 12:3). It would be fulfilled through the Messiah, Abraham's descendant.

1:76, 80 Zacharias had just recalled hundreds of years of God's sovereign work in history, beginning with Abraham and ending in eternity. Then, in tender contrast, he personalized the story—"You, my little son," have a part to play in God's plan. His son had been chosen for a key role in the drama of the ages. Although he has unlimited power, God has chosen to work through frail humans who begin as helpless babies.

1:80 Why did John live out in the wilderness? Prophets used the isolation of the wilderness to enhance their spiritual growth and to focus their message on God. By being in the wilderness, John showed his separation from the economic and political powers so that he could aim his message against them. It also showed his separation from the hypocritical religious leaders of his day. His message was different from theirs, and his life proved it.

Jesus is born in Bethlehem
(9)

2:1
Mt 1:18-25

2 About this time Caesar Augustus, the Roman Emperor, decreed that a census should be taken throughout the nation. ²(This census was taken when Quirinius was governor of Syria.)

2:4
1 Sam 16:1
Mic 5:2
Mt 1:16
Lk 1:27
Jn 7:42

³Everyone was required to return to his ancestral home for this registration. ⁴And because Joseph was a member of the royal line, he had to go to Bethlehem in Judea, King David's ancient home—journeying there from the Galilean village of Nazareth. ⁵He took with him Mary, his fiancée, who was obviously pregnant by this time.

2:7
Mt 1:25
Gal 4:4

⁶And while they were there, the time came for her baby to be born; ⁷and she gave birth to her first child, a son. She wrapped him in a blanket and laid him in a manger, because there was no room for them in the village inn.

Shepherds visit Jesus
(10)

⁸That night some shepherds were in the fields outside the village, guarding their

2:7 *in a blanket,* literally, "swaddling clothes."

THE JOURNEY TO BETHLEHEM Caesar's decree for a census of the entire Roman Empire made it necessary for Joseph and Mary to leave their hometown, Nazareth, and journey the 70 miles to the Judean village of Bethlehem.

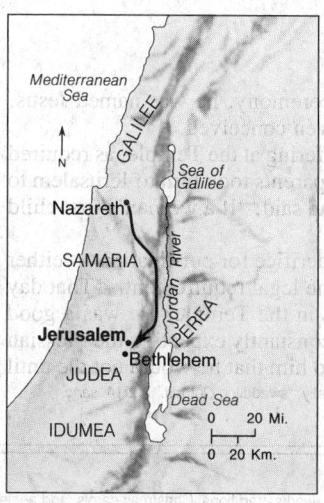

2:4 God controls all history. By the decree of Caesar Augustus, Jesus was born in the very town prophesied for his birth (Micah 5:2), even though his parents did not live there.

2:4 Joseph and Mary were both descendants of King David. The Old Testament is filled with prophecies that the Messiah would be born in David's royal line (see, for example, Isaiah 11:1; Jeremiah 33:15; Ezekiel 37:24; Hosea 3:5).

2:7 This mention of the manger is the basis for the traditional belief that Jesus was born in a stable. Stables were often caves with feeding troughs (mangers) carved into the rock walls. Despite popular Christmas card pictures, the surroundings were dark and dirty. This was not the atmosphere the Jews expected as the birthplace of the Messiah King. They thought their promised Messiah would be born in royal surroundings. We should not limit God by our expectations. He is at work wherever he is needed in our sin-darkened and dirty world.

2:7 Literally, she "wrapped him in swaddling clothes"—that is, strips of cloth. Swaddling clothes kept a baby warm and gave it a sense of security. They were believed to protect its internal organs. The custom of swaddling infants is still practiced in many Eastern countries.

2:7 Although our first impression of Jesus is as a baby in a manger, it must not be our last. The Christ child in the manger makes a beautiful Christmas scene, but we cannot leave him there. This tiny, helpless baby lived an amazing life, died for us, ascended to heaven, and will come back to this earth as King of kings. He will rule the world and judge all people according to their decisions about him. Do you still picture Jesus as a baby in a manger—or is he your Lord? Make sure you don't underestimate Jesus. Let him grow up in your life.

2:8 God continued to reveal his Son, but not to those we might expect. Luke records that Jesus' birth was announced to shepherds in the fields. These may have been the shepherds who supplied the lambs for the Temple sacrifices, performed for the forgiveness of sin. Angels now invited these shepherds to greet the Lamb of God (John 1:36), who would take away the sins of the whole world forever.

2:1 Luke is the only Gospel writer who relates the events he records to world history. His account was addressed to a predominantly Greek audience who would have been interested in and familiar with the political situation. Palestine was under the rule of the Roman Empire; Caesar Augustus, the first Roman emperor, was in charge. The Roman rulers, considered gods, stood in stark contrast to the tiny baby in a manger who was truly God in the flesh.

2:1 A Roman census was taken to aid military conscription or tax collection. The Jews didn't have to serve in the Roman army, but they could not avoid paying taxes. Augustus' decree went out in God's perfect timing and according to his perfect plan to bring his Son into the world.

2:3–6 The government forced Joseph to make a 70-mile trip just to pay his taxes. His fiancée, who had to go with him, was going to have their baby any moment. But when they arrived in Bethlehem, they couldn't even find a place to stay. When we do God's will, we are not guaranteed a comfortable life; we are promised only that even our discomfort has meaning in God's plan.

2:8–11 What a birth announcement! The shepherds were terrified, but their fear turned to joy as the angels announced the Messiah's birth. First they ran to see the baby; then they spread the word. Jesus is *your* Messiah, *your* Savior. Do you look forward to meeting him in prayer and in his Word each day? Is your relationship so special that you can't help sharing your joy with your friends?

flocks of sheep. 9Suddenly an angel appeared among them, and the landscape shone bright with the glory of the Lord. They were badly frightened, 10but the angel reassured them.

"Don't be afraid!" he said. "I bring you the most joyful news ever announced, and it is for everyone! 11The Savior—yes, the Messiah, the Lord—has been born tonight in Bethlehem! 12How will you recognize him? You will find a baby wrapped in a blanket, lying in a manger!"

13Suddenly, the angel was joined by a vast host of others—the armies of heaven—praising God:

14"Glory to God in the highest heaven," they sang, "and peace on earth for all those pleasing him."

15When this great army of angels had returned again to heaven, the shepherds said to each other, "Come on! Let's go to Bethlehem! Let's see this wonderful thing that has happened, which the Lord has told us about."

16They ran to the village and found their way to Mary and Joseph. And there was the baby, lying in the manger. 17The shepherds told everyone what had happened and what the angel had said to them about this child. 18All who heard the shepherds' story expressed astonishment, 19but Mary quietly treasured these things in her heart and often thought about them.

20Then the shepherds went back again to their fields and flocks, praising God for the visit of the angels, and because they had seen the child, just as the angel had told them.

Mary and Joseph bring Jesus to the Temple (11)

21Eight days later, at the baby's circumcision ceremony, he was named Jesus, the name given him by the angel before he was even conceived.

22When the time came for Mary's purification offering at the Temple, as required by the laws of Moses after the birth of a child, his parents took him to Jerusalem to present him to the Lord; 23for in these laws God had said, "If a woman's first child is a boy, he shall be dedicated to the Lord."

24At that time Jesus' parents also offered their sacrifice for purification—"either a pair of turtledoves or two young pigeons" was the legal requirement. 25That day a man named Simeon, a Jerusalem resident, was in the Temple. He was a good man, very devout, filled with the Holy Spirit and constantly expecting the Messiah to come soon. 26For the Holy Spirit had revealed to him that he would not die until

2:11 in Bethlehem, literally, "in the city of David." **2:12** a blanket, literally, "swaddling clothes." **2:14** sang, literally, "said." **2:25** the Messiah, literally, "the Consolation of Israel."

2:9 Lk 1:11; 24:4 Acts 5:19; 12:7
2:10 Mt 28:19 Acts 13:47 Col 1:23
2:11 Isa 9:6 Mt 1:16,21 16:16,20 Jn 4:42; 11:21 20:31 Acts 2:36; 10:36 Phil 2:11
2:13 Gen 28:12 Ps 103:20 Rev 5:11
2:14 Isa 57:19 Eph 2:14,18 Col 1:20 2 Thess 2:16
2:21 Gen 17:12 Lev 12:3 Mt 1:21
2:22 Lev 12:2-6
2:23 Ex 13:2,12
2:24 Lev 12:8
2:25 Isa 40:1 Mk 15:43
2:26 Ps 89:48 Jn 8:51 Heb 11:5

2:9, 10 The greatest event in history had just happened! The Messiah was born! For ages the Jews had waited for this, and when it finally happened, the announcement came to humble shepherds. The good news about Jesus is that he comes to all, including the plain and the ordinary. He comes to anyone with a heart humble enough to accept him. Whoever you are, whatever you do, you can have Jesus in your life. Don't think you need extraordinary qualifications—he accepts you as you are.

2:11-14 Some of the Jews were waiting for the Messiah to deliver them from Roman rule; others hoped he would deliver them from physical ailments. But Jesus, while healing their illnesses and establishing a spiritual kingdom, delivered them from sin. He outstripped all their expectations. People often set their own agenda for Jesus, and thus expect too little from him. His work is more far-reaching than anyone could imagine. He has paid the price for sin and opened the way to God. He offers us more than superficial political or physical changes—he offers us new hearts which will be ours for eternity.

2:14 The story of Jesus' birth resounds with music that has inspired composers for two thousand years. The angels' song is an all-time favorite. Often called the Gloria after its first word in the Latin translation of this verse, it is the basis of modern choral

works, traditional Christmas carols, and ancient liturgical chants.

2:21-23 Jewish families went through several ceremonies soon after a baby's birth: (1) Circumcision. Every boy was circumcised and named on the eighth day after birth (Leviticus 12:3; Luke 1:59, 60). Circumcision symbolized the Jews' separation from Gentiles and their unique relationship with God (see the note on 1:59). (2) Redemption of the firstborn. A firstborn son was presented to God one month after birth (Exodus 13:2, 11–16; Numbers 18:15, 16). The ceremony included buying back—"redeeming"—the child from God through an offering. Thus the parents acknowledged that the child belonged to God, who alone has the power to give life. (3) Purification of the mother. For 40 days after the birth of a son and 80 days after the birth of a daughter, the mother was ceremonially unclean and could not enter the Temple. At the end of her time of separation, the parents were to bring a lamb for a burnt offering and a dove for a sin offering. The priest would sacrifice these animals and would declare her clean. If a lamb was too expensive, the parents could bring a second dove instead. This is what Mary and Joseph did.

Jesus was God's Son, and his family carried out these ceremonies according to God's law. He was not born above the law; instead, he fulfilled it perfectly.

2:27
Rev 1:10

2:30
Isa 52:10
Acts 4:12

2:32
Isa 9:2
42:6,7; 49:6
Acts 13:47
26:23

he had seen him—God's anointed King. 27The Holy Spirit had impelled him to go to the Temple that day; and so, when Mary and Joseph arrived to present the baby Jesus to the Lord in obedience to the law, 28Simeon was there and took the child in his arms, praising God.

29, 30, 31"Lord," he said, "now I can die content! For I have seen him as you promised me I would. I have seen the Savior you have given to the world. 32He is the Light that will shine upon the nations, and he will be the glory of your people Israel!"

Motherhood is a painful privilege. Young Mary of Nazareth had the unique privilege of being mother to the very Son of God. Yet the pains and pleasures of her motherhood are understood by mothers everywhere. Mary was the only human present at Jesus' birth who also witnessed his death. She saw him arrive as her baby son, and she watched him die as her Savior.

Until Gabriel's unexpected visit, Mary's life was going about as well as she could hope. She had recently become engaged to a local carpenter, Joseph, and was anticipating married life. But Mary's life was about to change forever.

Angels don't usually make appointments before visiting. As if she were being congratulated as the grand winner of a contest she had never entered, Mary found the angel's greeting puzzling and his presence frightening. What she heard next was the news almost every woman in Israel hoped to hear—that her child would be the Messiah, God's promised Savior. Mary did not doubt the message, but rather asked how pregnancy would be possible. Gabriel told her the baby would be God's Son. Her answer was one that God has been waiting in vain to hear from so many other people: "I am the Lord's servant, and I am willing to do whatever he wants" (Luke 1:38). Later, her song of joy to Elizabeth shows us how well she knew God, for her thoughts were filled with his words from the Old Testament.

Within days after his birth, Jesus was taken to the Temple to be dedicated to God. There Joseph and Mary were met by two prophets, Simeon and Anna, who recognized the child as the Messiah and praised God. Simeon added some words to Mary that must have come to her mind many times in the years that followed: "A sword shall pierce your soul" (Luke 2:34). A big part of her painful privilege of motherhood would be to see her son rejected and crucified by the people he came to save.

We can imagine that even if she had known all she would suffer as Jesus' mother, Mary would have given the same response. Are you as available to be used by God as Mary was?

Strengths and accomplishments:
- The mother of Jesus, the Messiah
- The one human who was with Jesus from birth to death
- Willing to be available to God
- Knew and applied God's Word

Lessons from her life:
- God's best servants are often plain people available to him
- God's plans involve extraordinary events in ordinary people
- A person's character is revealed by his or her response to the unexpected

Vital statistics:
- Where: Nazareth, Bethlehem
- Occupation: Homemaker
- Relatives: Husband: Joseph. Uncle and Aunt: Zacharias and Elizabeth. Sons: Jesus, James, Joseph, Judas, and Simon, plus daughters.

Key verse:
"I am the Lord's servant, and I am willing to do whatever he wants. May everything you said come true" (Luke 1:38).

Mary's story is told throughout the Gospels. She is also mentioned in Acts 1:14.

2:28-32 When Mary and Joseph brought Jesus to the Temple to be dedicated to God, they met an old man who told them what their child would become. Simeon's song is often called the *Nunc Dimittis*, which comes from the first words of the Latin translation of this passage. Simeon could die in peace now, because he had seen the Messiah.

2:32 The Jews were well acquainted with the Old Testament

prophecies that spoke of the Messiah's blessings to their nation. They did not always give equal attention to the prophecies saying he would bring salvation to the entire world, not just the Jews (see, for example, Isaiah 49:6). Many thought he had come to save only his own people. Luke made sure his Greek audience understood that Jesus came to save *all* who believe.

33Joseph and Mary just stood there, marveling at what was being said about Jesus.

34, 35Simeon blessed them but then said to Mary, "A sword shall pierce your soul, for this child shall be rejected by many in Israel, and this to their undoing. But he will be the greatest joy of many others. And the deepest thoughts of many hearts shall be revealed."

2:34,35
Isa 8:14
Hos 14:9
Acts 24:5,14
28:22
1 Cor 1:23
1 Pet 2:7,8,12

2:35
Ps 42:10
1 Cor 11:19

36, 37Anna, a prophetess, was also there in the Temple that day. She was the daughter of Phanuel, of the Jewish tribe of Asher, and was very old, for she had been a widow for eighty-four years following seven years of marriage. She never left the Temple but stayed there night and day, worshiping God by praying and often fasting.

2:37
Acts 21:9; 26:7
1 Tim 5:5,9

38She came along just as Simeon was talking with Mary and Joseph, and she also began thanking God and telling everyone in Jerusalem who had been awaiting the coming of the Savior that the Messiah had finally arrived.

2:38
Lam 3:25,26
Mk 15:43
Lk 24:21

39When Jesus' parents had fulfilled all the requirements of the Law of God they returned home to Nazareth in Galilee. 40There the child became a strong, robust lad, and was known for wisdom beyond his years; and God poured out his blessings on him.

2:39
Mt 2:23

Jesus speaks with the religious teachers (15)

41, 42When Jesus was twelve years old he accompanied his parents to Jerusalem for the annual Passover Festival, which they attended each year. 43After the celebration was over they started home to Nazareth, but Jesus stayed behind in Jerusalem. His parents didn't miss him the first day, 44for they assumed he was with friends among the other travelers. But when he didn't show up that evening, they started to look for him among their relatives and friends; 45and when they couldn't find him, they went back to Jerusalem to search for him there.

2:41
Deut 16:1-6

46, 47Three days later they finally discovered him. He was in the Temple, sitting

2:46
Isa 11:1-4

2:38 *awaiting the coming of the Savior,* literally, "looking for the redemption of Jerusalem."

2:33 Joseph and Mary marveled for three reasons: Simeon said Jesus was a gift from God; he recognized him as the Messiah; and he said Jesus would be a light to the entire world. This was at least the second time that Mary was greeted with a prophecy about her son; the first time was when Elizabeth had welcomed her as the mother of her Lord (1:42-45).

2:34, 35 Simeon prophesied that with Jesus, there would be no neutral ground: people would either joyfully accept him or totally reject him. As Jesus' mother, Mary would be grieved by the widespread rejection he would face. This is the first note of sorrow in Luke's Gospel.

2:36 Although Simeon and Anna were very old, they still hoped to see the Messiah. Led by the Holy Spirit, they were among the first to bear witness to Jesus. In the Jewish culture, elders were respected, and Simeon's and Anna's prophecies carried extra weight because they were not young. Our society, however, values youthfulness over wisdom, and potential contributions by the elderly are often ignored. As Christians, we should reverse those values wherever we can. Encourage older people to share their wisdom and experience. Listen carefully when they speak. Offer them your friendship and help them find ways to continue to serve God.

2:36, 37 Anna was called a prophetess, indicating she was unusually close to God. Prophets and prophetesses did not necessarily predict the future. Their main role was to speak for God, proclaiming his truth.

2:39 Did Mary and Joseph return immediately to Nazareth, or did they remain in Bethlehem for a time (as implied in Matthew 2)? Apparently there is a gap of several years between verses 38 and 40—ample time for them to take a house in Bethelehem, flee to Egypt to escape Herod's wrath, and return to Nazareth

when it was safe to do so.

2:40 Jesus demonstrated wisdom beyond his years, which is not surprising since he stayed in close contact with his heavenly Father. James 1:5 says God "is always ready to give a bountiful supply of wisdom to all who ask him." Like Jesus, we can grow in wisdom by walking with God.

2:41, 42 According to God's law, every male was required to go to Jerusalem three times a year for the great festivals (Deuteronomy 16:16). In the spring, the Passover was celebrated, followed immediately by the week-long Feast of Unleavened Bread. Passover commemorated the night of the Jews' escape from Egypt when the angel of the Lord killed the Egyptian firstborn but passed over Israelite homes (see Exodus 12:21-36). Passover was the most important of the three annual festivals.

2:43-45 At age 12, Jesus was considered almost an adult, and so he didn't spend a lot of time with his parents during the festival. Those who attended these festivals often traveled in caravans for protection from robbers along the Palestine roads. It was customary for the women and children to travel at the front of the caravan, with the men bringing up the rear. A 12-year-old boy could have been in either group, and Mary and Joseph assumed Jesus was with the others. But when the caravan left Jerusalem, Jesus stayed behind, absorbed in his discussion with the religious leaders.

2:46, 47 The Temple school, a kind of seminary, was famous throughout Judea. The apostle Paul studied there under Gamaliel, one of its foremost teachers (Acts 22:3). At the time of the Passover, the greatest rabbis of the land would assemble to teach and to discuss great truths among themselves. The coming Messiah would no doubt have been a popular discussion topic, for "everyone was expecting the Messiah to come soon" (3:15). Jesus

2:47
Mt 7:28
Mk 1:22
Jn 7:15

2:48
Mt 12:26
Lk 4:22

2:49
Jn 2:16; 4:34
6:38; 8:29

2:50
Lk 9:45; 18:34

2:51
Dan 7:28

2:52
1 Sam 2:26

among the teachers of Law, discussing deep questions with them and amazing everyone with his understanding and answers.

48His parents didn't know what to think. "Son!" his mother said to him. "Why have you done this to us? Your father and I have been frantic, searching for you everywhere."

49"But why did you need to search?" he asked. "Didn't you realize that I would be here at the Temple, in my Father's House?" 50But they didn't understand what he meant.

51Then he returned to Nazareth with them and was obedient to them; and his mother stored away all these things in her heart. 52So Jesus grew both tall and wise, and was loved by God and man.

➤ **John the Baptist prepares the way for Jesus**
(16/Matthew 3:1–12; Mark 1:1–8)

3:1
Mt 3:1-12
Mk 1:1-8

3:2
Jn 11:49; 18:13

3:3
Mal 4:6
Mt 3:1
Lk 1:77
Acts 13:24; 19:4

3 In the fifteenth year of the reign of Emperor Tiberius Caesar, a message came from God to John (the son of Zacharias), as he was living out in the deserts. (Pilate was governor over Judea at that time; Herod, over Galilee; his brother Philip, over Iturea and Trachonitis; Lysanias, over Abilene; and Annas and Caiaphas were High Priests.) 3Then John went from place to place on both sides of the Jordan River, preaching that people should be baptized to show that they had turned to God and away from their sins, in order to be forgiven.

3:3 *preaching that people should be baptized to show that they had turned to God and away from their sins, in order to be forgiven*, or, "preaching the baptism of repentance for remission of sins."

---

would have been eager to listen and to ask probing questions. It was not his youth, but the depth of his thought, that astounded these teachers.

2:48 Mary had to let go of her child and let him become a man, God's Son, the Messiah. Fearful that she hadn't been careful enough with this God-given child, she searched frantically for him. But she was looking for a boy, not the young man who was in the Temple astounding the religious leaders with his questions. It is hard to let go of people or projects we have nurtured. It is both sweet and painful to see our children as adults, our students as teachers, our subordinates as managers, our inspirations as institutions. But when the time comes to step back and let go, we must do so in spite of the hurt. Then our proteges can exercise their wings, take flight, and soar to the heights God intended for them.

2:49 This is the first hint that Jesus realized he was God's Son. But even though he knew his real Father, he did not reject his earthly parents. He went back to Nazareth with them and lived under their authority for another 18 years. God's people do not despise human relationships or family responsibilities. If the Son of God obeyed his human parents, how much more should we honor our family members!

2:50 Jesus' parents didn't understand what he meant about his Father's House. They didn't realize he was making a distinction between his earthly father and his heavenly Father. Although they knew he was God's Son, they didn't understand what his mission would involve. Besides, they had to raise him, along with his brothers and sisters (Matthew 13:55, 56), as a normal child. They knew he was unique, but they did not know what was going on in his mind.

2:52 The Bible does not record any events of the next 18 years of Jesus' life, but he was learning and maturing. As the oldest in a large family, he assisted Joseph in his carpentry work. Joseph probably died during this time, leaving Jesus to provide for the family. The normal routines of his daily life gave him a solid understanding of the Judean people.

2:52 The second chapter of Luke shows us that although Jesus was unique, he had a normal childhood and youth. In terms of development, he was like us. He grew physically and mentally; he related to other people and he was loved by God. A full human life

is not unbalanced. It was important to Jesus—and it should be important to all believers—to develop harmoniously in each of these key areas: physical, mental, social, and spiritual.

➤ **3:1** Tiberius, the Roman emperor, ruled from A.D. 14–37. Pilate was the Roman governor responsible for the province of Judea; Herod Antipas and Philip were halfbrothers and sons of the cruel Herod the Great, who had been dead more than 20 years. Antipas, Philip, Pilate, and Lysanias apparently had equal powers in governing their separate territories. All were subject to Rome and responsible for keeping peace in their respective lands.

3:1 This is John the Baptist, whose birth story is told in chapter 1.

3:1 Pilate, Herod, and Caiaphas were the most powerful leaders in Palestine, but they were upstaged by a desert prophet from rural Judea. God chose to speak through the loner John the Baptist, who has gone down in history as greater than any of the rulers of his day. How often we judge people by our culture's standards—power, wealth, beauty—and miss the truly great people through whom God works! Greatness is not measured by what you have, but by what you do for God. Like John, give yourself entirely to him so his power can work through you.

3:1, 2 Under Jewish law there was only one High Priest. God appointed him from Aaron's line, and he held his position for life. By this time, however, the religious system had been corrupted, and the Roman government was appointing its own religious leaders to maintain greater control over the Jews. The Roman authorities had apparently deposed the Jewish-appointed Annas and replaced him with his son-in-law, Caiaphas. Nevertheless, Annas retained his title (see Acts 4:6) and probably also much of the power it carried. Because the Jews believed the High Priest's position to be for life, they would have continued to call Annas their High Priest.

3:3 Repentance has two sides—turning away from sins, and turning toward God. To be forgiven, we must do both. We can't just say we believe and then live any way we want to (see 3:7, 8), and neither can we simply live a morally correct life without reference to God, because that alone cannot bring forgiveness from sin. Determine to rid your life of any sins God points out, and put your trust in him alone to save you from sins' consequences.

4In the words of Isaiah the prophet, John was "a voice shouting from the barren wilderness, 'Prepare a road for the Lord to travel on! Widen the pathway before him! 5Level the mountains! Fill up the valleys! Straighten the curves! Smooth out the ruts! 6And then all mankind shall see the Savior sent from God.'"

7Here is a sample of John's preaching to the crowds that came for baptism: "You brood of snakes! You are trying to escape hell without truly turning to God! That is why you want to be baptized! 8First go and prove by the way you live that you really have repented. And don't think you are safe because you are descendants of Abraham. That isn't enough. God can produce children of Abraham from these desert stones! 9The axe of his judgment is poised over you, ready to sever your roots and cut you down. Yes, every tree that does not produce good fruit will be chopped down and thrown into the fire."

10The crowd replied, "What do you want us to do?"

11"If you have two coats," he replied, "give one to the poor. If you have extra food, give it away to those who are hungry."

12Even tax collectors—notorious for their corruption—came to be baptized and asked, "How shall we prove to you that we have abandoned our sins?"

13"By your honesty," he replied. "Make sure you collect no more taxes than the Roman government requires you to."

14"And us," asked some soldiers, "what about us?"

John replied, "Don't extort money by threats and violence; don't accuse anyone of what you know he didn't do; and be content with your pay!"

15Everyone was expecting the Messiah to come soon, and eager to know whether

3:4 Isa 40:3 / MT 3:3 / Mk 1:3 / Jn 1:23
3:5 Isa 40:4
3:6 Ps 98:2 / Isa 40:5; 52:10 / Jn 1:14
3:7 Mt 3:7 / Jn 8:44
3:8 Acts 26:20
3:9 Mt 3:10; 7:19 / Jn 15:2,6
3:11 Jas 2:15 / 1 Jn 3:17
3:12 Mt 21:32
3:13 Mic 6:8 / Lk 19:8
3:14 Ex 23:1 / Lev 19:11
3:15 Jn 1:19,20

3:13 *Roman,* implied.

3:4, 5 In John's day, before a king took a trip, messengers would tell the ones he was planning to visit to prepare the roads for him. Similarly John told his listeners to make their lives ready so the Lord could come to them. What have you done to prepare the way for Jesus to come to you?

3:6 This book was written to a non-Jewish audience. Luke quotes from Isaiah to show that salvation is for all people, not just the Jews (Isaiah 40:3–5; 52:10). John the Baptist called all mankind to prepare to meet Jesus. That includes you, no matter what your standing is with religious organizations and authorities. Don't let feelings of being an outsider cause you to hold back. No one who wants to follow Jesus is an outsider in God's Kingdom.

3:7 What motivates your faith—fear of the future, or a desire to be a better person in a better world? Some people wanted to be baptized by John so they could escape eternal punishment, but they didn't turn to God for salvation. John had harsh words for such people. He knew that God values reformation above ritual. Is your faith rooted in a desire for a new, changed life, or is it only a vaccination or an insurance policy against possible disaster?

3:8 Many of John's hearers were shocked when he said that being Abraham's descendants was not enough for God. The religious leaders relied more on their family line than on their faith for their standing with God. For them, religion was inherited. But a relationship with God is not handed down from parents to children. Everyone has to find it on his or her own. Don't rely on someone else for your salvation. Put your own faith in Jesus, and then exercise your faith by acting on it every day.

3:8, 9 Faith and works are inseparable. Faith without works is a lifeless faith. Jesus' harshest words were to the respectable religious leaders who lacked true faith. Repentance must be tied to action, or it isn't real. Is the fruit of your faith ripening as your faith grows, or is it rotting as you fail to act upon what God shows you?

3:12 Tax collectors were notorious for their dishonesty. Romans gathered funds for their government by farming out the collection

privilege to whoever promised to get the most money from a given area. This tax collector earned his own living by adding a sizable sum—whatever he could get away with—to the total and keeping this money for himself. Unless the people revolted and risked Roman fury, they had to pay whatever was demanded. Obviously they hated the tax collectors, who were dishonest, greedy, and ready to betray their own countrymen for cold cash. Yet, said John, God would accept even these men if they repented and truly changed their ways.

3:11–14 John's message demanded at least two specific responses: (1) share what you have with those who need it, and (2) whatever your job, do it well. John had no time to address comforting messages to those who lived careless or selfish lives—he was calling the people to right living. What changes can you make in sharing what you have and doing your work honestly and well?

3:12 John's message took root in unexpected places—among the poor, the criminals, even the hated occupation army. They were people painfully aware of their needs. Too often we confuse respectability with right living. They are not the same. Respectability can even hinder right living if it keeps us from seeing our need for God. If you had to choose between them, would you protect your character even if it ruined your reputation?

3:14 These soldiers were the Roman troops who were sent to keep peace in this distant province. They oppressed the poor and used their power to take advantage of all the people. John called them to repent and change their ways by demonstrating their faith in front of others.

3:15 There had not been a prophet in Israel for more than 400 years. It was widely believed that when the Messiah came, prophecy would reappear (Joel 2:28, 29; Malachi 3:1; 4:5). When John burst upon the scene, the people were excited—he was obviously a great prophet, and they were sure that the eagerly awaited age of the Messiah had come. John spoke like the

or not John was he. This was the question of the hour, and was being discussed everywhere.

16John answered the question by saying, "I baptize only with water; but someone is coming soon who has far higher authority than mine; in fact, I am not even worthy of being his slave. He will baptize you with fire—with the Holy Spirit. 17He will separate chaff from grain, and burn up the chaff with eternal fire and store away the grain." 18He used many such warnings as he announced the Good News to the people.

3:16
Mt 3:11
Mk 1:7,8
Jn 1:26,33
1 Cor 12:13

3:17
Mic 4:12
Mt 13:20

Herod puts John in prison
(26)

19, 20(But after John had publicly criticized Herod, governor of Galilee, for marrying Herodias, his brother's wife, and for many other wrongs he had done, Herod put John in prison, thus adding this sin to all his many others.)

3:19,20
Mt 14:3
Mk 6:17
Jn 3:24

John baptizes Jesus
(17/Matthew 3:13–17; Mark 1:9–11)

21Then one day, after the crowds had been baptized, Jesus himself was baptized; and as he was praying, the heavens opened, 22and the Holy Spirit in the form of a dove settled upon him, and a voice from heaven said, "You are my much loved Son, yes, my delight."

3:21
Mt 3:13-17
Mk 1:9-11
Jn 1:32

3:16 *of being his slave,* literally, "of loosing the sandal strap of his shoe."

---

prophets of old: turn from your sin to avoid punishment, turn to God to reap blessing. It is a message for all times and places, but John spoke it with particular urgency—he was preparing the people for the coming Messiah.

3:16 John's baptism with water symbolized the washing away of sins. It coordinated with his message of repentance and reformation. Jesus' baptism by fire includes the power needed to do God's will. It began on the day of Pentecost (Acts 2) when the Holy Spirit in the form of tongues of fire came upon the believers, empowering them to proclaim Jesus' resurrection in many languages. The baptism by fire also symbolizes the work of the Holy Spirit in bringing God's judgment on those who refuse to repent.

3:17 John warns of impending judgment by comparing those who refuse to live for God to chaff, the useless outer husk of the grain. By contrast, he compares those who repent and reform their lives to the nourishing grain itself. Those who refuse to be used by God will be discarded because they have no value in furthering God's work. Those who repent and believe, however, hold great value in God's eyes because they are beginning a new life of productive service for him.

3:19, 20 These two verses are in parentheses to show the reader that Luke is flashing forward to continue his explanation about John the Baptist. See the Harmony of the Gospels for the chronological order of events.

3:19, 20 This was Herod Antipas (see Mark 6 for his Profile). Herodias was Herod's niece and also his brother's wife. She treacherously plotted John the Baptist's death (Matthew 14:1–12). The Herods were an incestuous, murderous, deceitful family. Rebuking a tyrannical Roman official who could imprison and execute him was extremely dangerous, yet that is what John did. Herod seemingly had the last word, but the story is not finished yet. At the Last Judgment, Herod, not John, will be the one in danger.

3:21 Luke emphasizes Jesus' human side. He came to humble parents, unannounced except to shepherds and foreigners. This baptism was the first public declaration of his ministry. Instead of going to Jerusalem and identifying with the established religious leaders, Jesus went to a river and identified himself with those who were repenting of sin. When Jesus, at age 12, visited the Temple, he understood his mission (2:49). Eighteen years later, at his baptism, he began carrying it out. And as he prayed, God spoke to him and confirmed his decision to act. God was breaking into human history through Jesus Christ.

3:21, 22 If baptism was a sign of repentance from sin, why did Jesus ask to be baptized? Jesus' mission on earth was to identify with our humanness and sin, thus he was portraying his upcoming death and resurrection for our salvation. He was also giving us an example to follow by endorsing the act of baptism. Jesus' baptism was the beginning of his public ministry and because he had come to take away people's sin, he was perhaps confessing the sins of the nation through his baptism. The Holy Spirit coming in the form of a dove showed that God approved of what Jesus was doing. Jesus was the perfect man who didn't need baptism for sin, but was baptized anyway to demonstrate that he would take away our sin.

3:21, 22 This is one of several places in Scripture where all members of the Trinity are mentioned—Father, Son, and Holy Spirit. In the traditional words of the church, the one God exists in three persons but one substance, co-eternal and co-equal. No amount of explanation can adequately portray the power and intricacy of this unique relationship. There are no perfect analogies in nature because there is no other relationship like the Trinity.

The ancestors of Jesus
(3/Matthew 1:1–17)

23-38 Jesus was about thirty years old when he began his public ministry.

Jesus was known as the son of Joseph. Joseph's father was Heli; Heli's father was Matthat; Matthat's father was Levi; Levi's father was Melchi; Melchi's father was Jannai; Jannai's father was Joseph; Joseph's father was Mattathias; Mattathias' father was Amos; Amos' father was Nahum; Nahum's father was Esli; Esli's father was Naggai; Naggai's father was Maath; Maath's father was Mattathias; Mattathias' father was Semein; Semein's father was Josech; Josech's father was Joda; Joda's father was Joanan; Joanan's father was Rhesa; Rhesa's father was Zerubbabel; Zerubbabel's father was Shealtiel; Shealtiel's father was Neri; Neri's father was Melchi; Melchi's father was Addi; Addi's father was Cosam; Cosam's father was Elmadam; Elmadam's father was Er; Er's father was Joshua; Joshua's father was Eliezer; Eliezer's father was Jorim; Jorim's father was Matthat; Matthat's father was Levi; Levi's father was Simeon; Simeon's father was Judah; Judah's father was Joseph; Joseph's father was Jonam; Jonam's father was Eliakim; Eliakim's father was Melea; Melea's father was Menna; Menna's father was Mattatha; Mattatha's father was Nathan; Nathan's father was David; David's father was Jesse; Jesse's father was Obed; Obed's father was Boaz; Boaz' father was Salmon; Salmon's father was Nahshon; Nahshon's father was Amminadab; Amminadab's father was Admin; Admin's father was Arni; Arni's father was Hezron; Hezron's father was Perez; Perez' father was Judah; Judah's father was Jacob; Jacob's father was Isaac; Isaac's father was Abraham; Abraham's father was Terah; Terah's father was Nahor; Nahor's father was Serug; Serug's father was Reu; Reu's father was Peleg; Peleg's father was Eber; Eber's father was Shelah; Shelah's father was Cainan; Cainan's father was Arphaxad; Arphaxad's father was Shem; Shem's father was Noah; Noah's father was Lamech; Lamech's father was Methuselah; Methuselah's father was Enoch; Enoch's father was Jared; Jared's father was Mahalaleel; Mahalaleel's father was Cainan; Cainan's father was Enos; Enos' father was Seth; Seth's father was Adam; Adam's father was God.

3:23
Num 4:3,35,
39,47
Mt 1:1-17; 13:55
Jn 6:42

3:31
2 Sam 5:14
1 Chron 3:5
Zech 12:12

3:32
Ruth 4:18
1 Chron 2:10

3:34
Gen 11:24,26

3:36
Gen 11:10,12

3:38
Gen 1:26,27
2:7; 5:1,2
Isa 64:8

Satan tempts Jesus in the wilderness
(18/Matthew 4:1–11; Mark 1:12, 13)

4 Then Jesus, full of the Holy Spirit, left the Jordan River, being urged by the Spirit out into the barren wastelands of Judea, where Satan tempted him for forty days. He ate nothing all that time, and was very hungry.

4:1
Isa 11:2; 61:1
Mt 4:1-11
Jn 1:33; 3:34

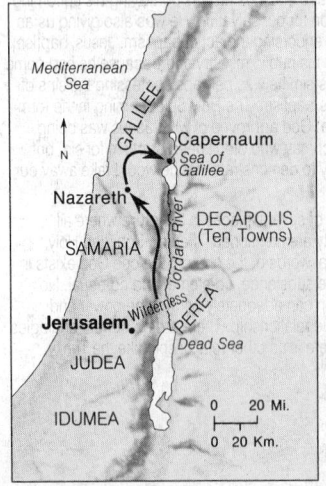

**JESUS'
TEMPTATION
AND RETURN
TO GALILEE**
Jesus was tempted by Satan in the rough wilderness of Judea before returning to his boyhood home, Nazareth. John's Gospel tells of his journeys in Galilee, Samaria, and Judea (see John 1–4) before he moved to Capernaum to set up his base of operations (see Matthew 4:12, 13).

3:23 Imagine the Savior of the world driving nails in a small-town carpenter's shop until he was 30 years old! It seems incredible that Jesus would have been content to remain in Nazareth all that time, but he patiently trusted the Father's timing for his life and ministry. Thirty was the prescribed age for priests to begin their ministry (Numbers 4:3). Joseph was 30 years old when he began serving the king of Egypt (Genesis 41:46), and David was 30 years old when he began to reign over Judah (2 Samuel 5:4). Age 30, then, was a good time to begin an important task in the Jewish culture. Like Jesus, we need to work within God's timing, resisting the temptation to jump ahead before receiving the Spirit's direction. Are you waiting and wondering what your next step should be? Don't jump ahead—trust God's timing.

3:23-38 Here Jesus' genealogy is traced back through Mary. The genealogy recorded in Matthew 1:1–17 traces his line through Joseph, his legal but not actual father. Matthew's genealogy goes back to Abraham and shows that Jesus was related to all Jews. Luke's goes back to Adam, showing he is related to all human beings. This is consistent with Luke's picture of Jesus as the Savior of the whole world.

3:23 Heli was actually Joseph's father-in-law. Thus this is actually Mary's genealogy, which Luke may have received personally from

4:2
Ex 34:28
1 Kgs 19:8
Heb 2:18; 4:15

4:4
Deut 8:3
Eph 6:17

4:6
Jn 12:31; 14:30
1 Jn 5:19
Rev 13:2,7

4:8
Deut 6:13; 10:20

4:9
Mt 4:5
1 Pet 5:8

4:11
Ps 91:11

4:12
Deut 6:16

4:13
Jn 14:30

3Satan said, "If you are God's Son, tell this stone to become a loaf of bread."

4But Jesus replied, "It is written in the Scriptures, 'Other things in life are much more important than bread!' "

5Then Satan took him up and revealed to him all the kingdoms of the world in a moment of time; 6, 7and the devil told him, "I will give you all these splendid kingdoms and their glory—for they are mine to give to anyone I wish—if you will only get down on your knees and worship me."

8Jesus replied, "We must worship God, and him alone. So it is written in the Scriptures."

9, 10, 11Then Satan took him to Jerusalem to a high roof of the Temple and said, "If you are the Son of God, jump off! For the Scriptures say that God will send his angels to guard you and to keep you from crashing to the pavement below!"

12Jesus replied, "The Scriptures also say, 'Do not put the Lord your God to a foolish test.' "

13When the devil had ended all the temptations, he left Jesus for a while and went away.

4:4 *Other things in life are much more important than bread,* literally, "Man shall not live by bread alone," cf Deut 8:3.

---

her. It is fitting that Luke would show Mary's genealogy because of the prominence he gives women in his Gospel.

4:1 Sometimes we feel that if the Holy Spirit leads us, it will always be "beside the still waters." But that is not necessarily true. He led Jesus into the desert for a long and difficult time of testing, and he may also lead us into difficult situations. When facing trials, first make sure you haven't brought them on yourself through sin or unwise choices. If you find no sin to confess or unwise behavior to change, then ask God to strengthen you for your test. Finally, be careful to faithfully follow where the Holy Spirit leads.

4:1 Temptation often comes after a high point in our spiritual lives or ministries (see 1 Kings 18, 19 for Elijah's story of great victory followed by despair). Remember that Satan chooses the times for his attacks. We need to be on our guard in times of victory just as much as in times of discouragement. See note on Matthew 4:1ff for how Satan tempts us when we're vulnerable.

4:1, 2 Satan tempted Eve in the garden, and he also tempted Jesus in the wilderness. Satan is a real being, not a symbol or an idea. He constantly fights against God and those who follow and obey God. Jesus was a prime target for his temptations. Satan succeeded with Eve, and he hoped to succeed with Jesus too.

4:1–13 Knowing and obeying God's Word is an effective weapon against temptation, the only *offensive* weapon provided in the Christian's "armor" (Ephesians 6:17). Jesus used Scripture to counter Satan's attacks, and you can too. But to use it effectively you must have faith in God's promises, because Satan also knows Scripture and is adept at twisting it to suit his purpose. Obeying the Scriptures is more important than simply having a verse to quote, so read them daily and apply them to your life. Then your "sword" will always be sharp.

4:3 Why was it necessary for Jesus to be tempted? First, temptation is part of the human experience. For Jesus to be fully human, for him to understand us completely, he had to face temptation (see Hebrews 4:15). Second, Jesus had to undo Adam's work. Adam, though created perfect, gave in to temptation and passed on sin to the whole human race. Jesus, by contrast, resisted Satan. His victory offers salvation to all of Adam's descendants (see Romans 5:12–19).

4:3 Satan frequently raises questions about what God has said. He knows that once we begin to question God, it's far easier to get us to do what he wants. Times of questioning can help us sort out our beliefs and strengthen our faith, but they can also be

dangerous. If you are dealing with doubt in your life, realize that you are especially vulnerable to temptation. Even as you search for answers, protect yourself by meditating on the unshakable truths of God's Word.

4:3 Sometimes what we are tempted to do isn't wrong in itself. Turning stones into bread wasn't necessarily bad. The sin was not in the act but in the reason for it. Satan was trying to get Jesus to take a shortcut, to solve his immediate problem at the expense of his long-range goals. Satan often works that way—persuading us to do things, even good things, for the wrong reason. The fact that something is not wrong in itself does not mean it is good for you at a given time. First ask, "Is the Holy Spirit leading me to do this? Or is Satan nudging me to do this in order to get me off the track?"

4:3ff Often we are tempted not through our weaknesses, but through our strengths. Satan tempted Jesus where he was strong. Jesus had power over stones, the kingdoms of the world, and even angels, and Satan wanted him to use that power without regard to his mission. When we give in to Satan and wrongly use our strengths, we become proud and self-reliant. Trusting in our own powers, we feel little need of God. To avoid this trap, we must realize that all our strengths are God's gifts to us, and we must dedicate them to his service. Satan also tempts us when we are vulnerable. For how he does this see note on Matthew 4:1ff.

4:6, 7 Satan arrogantly hoped to succeed in his rebellion against God by diverting Jesus from his mission and winning his worship. "This world is mine, not God's," he was saying, "and if you hope to do anything worthwhile here, you'd better recognize that fact." Jesus didn't argue with Satan about who owns the world, but he refused to validate Satan's claim by bowing to him. Jesus knew he would redeem the world through giving up his life on the cross, not through making an alliance with a corrupt angel.

4:9–11 Here Satan didn't misquote Scripture, but he misinterpreted it. The intention of Psalm 91 is to show God's protection of his people, not to incite them to use God's power for sensational or foolish displays.

4:13 Christ's defeat of Satan was decisive but not final. Throughout his ministry, Jesus would confront Satan in many forms. Too often we see temptation as once and for all. In reality, we need to be constantly on guard against the devil's ongoing attacks. Where are you most susceptible to temptation right now? How are you preparing to withstand it?

B. MESSAGE AND MINISTRY OF JESUS, THE SAVIOR (4:14—21:38)

Luke accurately records the actions and teachings of Christ, helping us understand the way of salvation. There is much unique material in Luke, especially the parables of Jesus. Jesus came to teach us how to live and how to find salvation. How carefully, then, we should study the words and life of our Savior.

1. Jesus' ministry in Galilee

Jesus preaches in Galilee
(30/Matthew 4:12–17; Mark 1:14, 15; John 4:43–45)

14Then Jesus returned to Galilee, full of the Holy Spirit's power. Soon he became well known throughout all that region 15for his sermons in the synagogues; everyone praised him.

4:14
Mt 4:12-17
Mk 1:14,15
Jn 4:43-45

Jesus is rejected at Nazareth
(32)

16When he came to the village of Nazareth, his boyhood home, he went as usual to the synagogue on Saturday, and stood up to read the Scriptures. 17The book of Isaiah the prophet was handed to him, and he opened it to the place where it says: 18, 19"The Spirit of the Lord is upon me; he has appointed me to preach Good News to the poor; he has sent me to heal the brokenhearted and to announce that captives shall be released and the blind shall see, that the downtrodden shall be freed from their oppressors, and that God is ready to give blessings to all who come to him."

4:16
Mt 2:23
13:54-58
Mk 6:1-6
Acts 13:14

4:18
Isa 61:1-2
Dan 9:24

4:19
Lev 25:8-10
2 Cor 6:2

20He closed the book and handed it back to the attendant and sat down, while everyone in the synagogue gazed at him intently. 21Then he added, "These Scriptures came true today!"

22All who were there spoke well of him and were amazed by the beautiful words that fell from his lips. "How can this be?" they asked. "Isn't this Joseph's son?"

23Then he said, "Probably you will quote me that proverb, 'Physician, heal yourself'—meaning, 'Why don't you do miracles here in your home town like those you did in Capernaum?' 24But I solemnly declare to you that no prophet is accepted in his own home town! 25, 26For example, remember how Elijah the prophet used a miracle to help the widow of Zarephath—a foreigner from the land of Sidon. There were many Jewish widows needing help in those days of famine, for there had been no rain for three and one-half years, and hunger stalked the land; yet Elijah was not sent to them. 27Or think of the prophet Elisha, who healed Naaman, a Syrian, rather than the many Jewish lepers needing help."

28These remarks stung them to fury; 29and jumping up, they mobbed him and took him to the edge of the hill on which the city was built, to push him over the cliff. 30But he walked away through the crowd and left them.

4:22
Ps 45:2
Lk 2:47
Jn 1:16; 6:42

4:23
Mt 4:13; 11:23
Mk 1:21-28
2:1-12
Jn 4:46-54

4:24
Mt 13:57
Mk 6:4
Jn 4:44

4:25,26
1 Kgs 17:9; 18:1
Jas 5:17

4:27
2 Kgs 5:14

4:29
Num 15:35
Acts 7:58
Heb 13:12

4:30
Jn 8:59; 10:39

4:18, 19 *to give blessings to all who come to him,* literally, "to proclaim the acceptable year of the Lord."

4:16 Synagogues were very important in Jewish religious life. During the exile when the Jews no longer had their Temple, synagogues were established as places of worship during the Sabbath and as schools for young boys during the week. They continued after the Temple was rebuilt. A synagogue could be set up in any town where there were at least ten Jewish families. It was run by one leader and an assistant. At the synagogue, the leader often invited a visiting rabbi to read from the Scriptures and to teach.

4:16 Jesus went to the synagogue "as usual." Even though he was the perfect Son of God, and his local synagogue left much to be desired, he attended services every week. His example makes most excuses for not attending church sound weak and self-serving. Make regular worship a part of your life.

4:18, 19 Jesus quoted this verse from Isaiah 61:1, 2 stopping in the middle of verse 2 just before "and the day of his wrath to their enemies." He did this because the time of God's blessings is fulfilled in Jesus' first coming, but the time of God's wrath awaits

his second coming. His hearers were expecting just the opposite of the Messiah: they thought he would crush their enemies first, and then usher in God's blessings.

4:22 To know Christ is to know the truth, and knowledge of the truth is what this world needs. People today are confused and lost. If we want people to turn to God, we will have to let them see the truth that is within us. Is your life so full of Jesus' love that others know it by your words and actions?

4:24 Even Jesus himself was not accepted as a prophet in his hometown. We have a similar attitude—an expert is anyone who carries a briefcase and comes from more than 200 miles from home. Don't be surprised when your Christian life and faith are not easily understood or accepted by those who know you well.

4:28 These remarks stung the people of Nazareth to fury because Jesus was saying that Gentiles were more interested in God's Good News than the Jews were. Jesus accused them of being as unbelieving as the citizens of the Northern Kingdom of Israel in the days of Elijah and Elisha, a time notorious for its great wickedness.

Jesus teaches with great authority
(34/Mark 1:21–28)

4:31
Mt 4:13-16
8:14-17
Mk 1:21-34

31Then he returned to Capernaum, a city in Galilee, and preached there in the synagogue every Saturday. 32Here, too, the people were amazed at the things he said. For he spoke as one who knew the truth, instead of merely quoting the opinions of others as his authority.

4:32
Mt 7:28,29
Tit 2:15

4:34
Isa 49:7
Dan 9:24
Lk 1:35

33Once as he was teaching in the synagogue, a man possessed by a demon began shouting at Jesus, 34"Go away! We want nothing to do with you, Jesus from Nazareth. You have come to destroy us. I know who you are—the Holy Son of God."

4:35
Lk 4:39,41

35Jesus cut him short. "Be silent!" he told the demon. "Come out!" The demon threw the man to the floor as the crowd watched, and then left him without hurting him further.

4:37
Mic 5:4

36Amazed, the people asked, "What is in this man's words that even demons obey him?" 37The story of what he had done spread like wildfire throughout the whole region.

Jesus heals Peter's mother-in-law and many others
(35/Matthew 8:14-17; Mark 1:29-34)

4:38
Mt 8:14-17
Mk 1:29-34

38After leaving the synagogue that day, he went to Simon's home where he found Simon's mother-in-law very sick with a high fever. "Please heal her," everyone begged.

4:39
Ps 103:3

39Standing at her bedside he spoke to the fever, rebuking it, and immediately her temperature returned to normal and she got up and prepared a meal for them!

4:40
Mt 8:16,17
Mk 1:32-34

4:41
Mk 3:11

40As the sun went down that evening, all the villagers who had any sick people in their homes, no matter what their diseases were, brought them to Jesus; and the touch of his hands healed every one! 41Some were possessed by demons; and the demons came out at his command, shouting, "You are the Son of God." But because they knew he was the Christ, he stopped them and told them to be silent.

4:39 *prepared a meal for them,* literally, "ministered unto them."

4:31 Jesus had recently moved to Capernaum from Nazareth (Matthew 4:12, 13). Capernaum was a thriving city with great wealth as well as great sin and decadence. Because it was the headquarters for many Roman troops, pagan influences from all over the Roman Empire were everywhere.

4:31 If the religious leaders were so opposed to Jesus, why did they let him preach in the synagogues? Jesus was taking advantage of their custom of allowing visitors to teach. Itinerant preachers were always welcome to speak to those gathered each Sabbath in the synagogues. The apostle Paul also profited from this custom (see Acts 13:5; 14:1).

4:33 A man possessed by a demon was in the synagogue where Jesus was teaching. He made his way into the place of worship and verbally abused Jesus himself. It is naive to think we are sheltered from evil in the church. Satan is happy to invade our presence wherever and whenever he can. But Jesus' authority is much greater than his, and where Jesus is present, demons cannot stay for long.

4:34, 35 The people were amazed at Jesus' authority to cast out demons—evil spirits ruled by Satan and sent to tempt people to sin. Like their leader, they are probably fallen angels who have joined him in rebellion against God. Demons can cause a person to become mute, deaf, blind, or insane. Jesus faced many demons during his time on earth, and he always exerted authority over them. Not only did the demon leave this man; Luke records that the man was not even hurt.

4:36 Evil permeates our world, and it is no wonder that people are often fearful. But Jesus' power is far greater than that of Satan. The first step toward conquering fear of evil is to recognize Jesus' authority. He has overcome all evil, including Satan himself.

4:39 Jesus healed Peter's mother-in-law so completely that not only did the fever leave, but her strength was restored and immediately she got up and served them dinner. What a beautiful attitude of service she showed. God gives us health so that we may serve others.

4:40 The villagers came to Jesus "as the sun went down" because this was the Sabbath (4:31), their day of rest. Sabbath lasted from sunset on Friday to sunset on Saturday. The people didn't want to break the law that prohibited travel on the Sabbath, so they waited until the Sabbath hours were over before coming to Jesus. Then, as Luke the physician notes, they came "no matter what their diseases," and Jesus healed every one.

4:41 Why didn't Jesus want the demons to reveal who he was? (1) He commanded the demons to remain silent to show his authority over them. (2) He wanted his listeners to believe he was the Messiah because of his words, not because of the demons' words. (3) He was going to reveal his identity according to God's timetable, and he would not be pushed by Satan's evil plans. The demons called Jesus "Son of God," or "Christ." But Jesus was going to show himself to be the suffering servant before he became the great king. To reveal his identity as King too soon would stir up the crowds with the wrong expectations of what he came to do.

Jesus preaches throughout Galilee
(36/Matthew 4:23–25; Mark 1:35–39)

42Early the next morning he went out into the desert. The crowds searched everywhere for him and when they finally found him they begged him not to leave them, but to stay at Capernaum. 43But he replied, "I must preach the Good News of the Kingdom of God in other places too, for that is why I was sent." 44So he continued to travel around preaching in synagogues throughout Judea.

4:42
Mt 4:23
Mk 1:35-39
4:43
Mk 1:14,15
Acts 10:38
Rom 15:8

Jesus provides a miraculous catch of fish
(37)

5 One day as he was preaching on the shore of Lake Gennesaret, great crowds pressed in on him to listen to the Word of God. 2He noticed two empty boats standing at the water's edge while the fishermen washed their nets. 3Stepping into one of the boats, Jesus asked Simon, its owner, to push out a little into the water, so that he could sit in the boat and speak to the crowds from there.

5:1
Mt 4:18-22
Mk 1:16-20

4When he had finished speaking, he said to Simon, "Now go out where it is deeper and let down your nets and you will catch a lot of fish!"

5:4
Jn 21:6

5"Sir," Simon replied, "we worked hard all last night and didn't catch a thing. But if you say so, we'll try again."

5:5
Jn 21:3

6And this time their nets were so full that they began to tear! 7A shout for help brought their partners in the other boat and soon both boats were filled with fish and on the verge of sinking.

5:8
2 Sam 6:9
Job 42:5,6
Dan 8:17

8When Simon Peter realized what had happened, he fell to his knees before Jesus and said, "Oh, sir, please leave us—I'm too much of a sinner for you to have around." 9For he was awestruck by the size of their catch, as were the others with him, 10and his partners too—James and John, the sons of Zebedee. Jesus replied, "Don't be afraid! From now on you'll be fishing for the souls of men!"

5:10
Ezek 47:9,10

5:11
Mt 19:27
Lk 18:28
Phil 3:7,8

11And as soon as they landed, they left everything and went with him.

Jesus heals a man with leprosy
(38/Matthew 8:1–4; Mark 1:40–45)

12One day in a certain village he was visiting, there was a man with an advanced

---

4:42 Jesus had to get up very early just to get some time alone. If Jesus needed solitude for prayer and refreshment, how much more is this true for us? Don't become so busy that life turns into a flurry of activity leaving no room for quiet fellowship alone with God. No matter how much you have to do, you always have time for prayer.

4:43 Why is the Kingdom of God good news? Since the time of the Babylonian captivity, the Jews had been awaiting the coming of the promised Messiah. The Kingdom of God was good news for them, because it meant the end of their waiting. It is good news for us, because it means freedom from slavery to sin and selfishness. The Kingdom of God is here and now, because the Holy Spirit lives in the hearts of believers. Yet it is also in the future, because Jesus will return to reign over a perfect kingdom where sin and evil no longer exist.

4:44 Matthew and Mark record that Jesus continued to travel throughout Galilee rather than Judea. In writing to a Gentile audience, Luke may have used the word "Judea" because it often referred to the entire region of Palestine (see Acts 10:37; 26:20). Luke may also have been referring to Jesus' earlier Judean ministry recorded in John 2:13—4:3.

5:1 Lake Gennesaret was also known as the Sea of Galilee or the Sea of Tiberius.

5:2 Fishermen on the Sea of Galilee used nets, often bell shaped with lead weights around the edges. A net was thrown flat on the water, and the lead weights caused it to sink and cover the fish. The fisherman then pulled on a cord, drawing the net around the fish. Nets had to be kept in good condition, so they were washed to remove weeds and then mended.

5:8 Peter was awestruck at this miracle, and his first response was to feel his own insignificance in comparison to this man's greatness. Peter knew Jesus had healed the sick and cast out demons, but he was amazed that Jesus cared about his day-to-day routine and understood his needs. God is interested not only in saving us, but also in helping us in our daily lives.

5:11 There are two preconditions for following God. We must recognize our sinful human nature—we can't save ourselves; only God can save us. And we must recognize the futility of human effort—these men had fished all night without success.

5:11 This is the disciples' second call. After the first call (Matthew 4:18–22; Mark 1:16–20), Peter, Andrew, James, and John went back to fishing. They continued to watch Jesus, however, as he established his authority in the synagogue, healed the sick, and cast out demons. Now he also established his authority in their lives—he met them on their level and helped them in their work. From this point on, they left their nets and remained with Jesus. For us, to follow Jesus is more than just acknowledging him as Savior. It means leaving our past behind and devoting our future to him.

5:12 Leprosy was a feared disease because it was highly contagious and incurable. It destroyed nerve endings, causing lepers to unknowingly damage their fingers, toes, and noses. Those with advanced cases usually had lost much body tissue. While leprosy is relatively rare today, the impact it had on ancient society is similar to that of other diseases today, such as AIDS (Acquired Immune Deficiency Syndrome). Because AIDS has no known cure at present, the fear of AIDS has caused people to treat those inflicted with the disease with disgust, as outcasts, and even with outright violence. The stigma and fear of AIDS is similar to the stigma that these lepers faced.

case of leprosy. When he saw Jesus he fell to the ground before him, face downward in the dust, begging to be healed.

"Sir," he said, "if you only will, you can clear me of every trace of my disease." 13Jesus reached out and touched the man and said, "Of course I will. Be healed." And the leprosy left him instantly! 14Then Jesus instructed him to go at once without telling anyone what had happened and be examined by the Jewish priest. "Offer the sacrifice Moses' law requires for lepers who are healed," he said. "This will prove to everyone that you are well." 15Now the report of his power spread even faster and vast crowds came to hear him preach and to be healed of their diseases. 16But he often withdrew to the wilderness for prayer.

Jesus heals a paralyzed man
(39/Matthew 9:1–8; Mark 2:1–12)

17One day while he was teaching, some Jewish religious leaders and teachers of the Law were sitting nearby. (It seemed that these men showed up from every village in all Galilee and Judea, as well as from Jerusalem.) And the Lord's healing power was upon him.

18, 19Then—look! Some men came carrying a paralyzed man on a sleeping mat. They tried to push through the crowd to Jesus but couldn't reach him. So they went up on the roof above him, took off some tiles and lowered the sick man down into the crowd, still on his sleeping mat, right in front of Jesus.

20Seeing their faith, Jesus said to the man, "My friend, your sins are forgiven!" 21"Who does this fellow think he is?" the Pharisees and teachers of the Law exclaimed among themselves. "This is blasphemy! Who but God can forgive sins?"

22Jesus knew what they were thinking, and he replied, "Why is it blasphemy? 23, 24I, the Messiah, have the authority on earth to forgive sins. But talk is cheap— anybody could say that. So I'll prove it to you by healing this man." Then, turning to the paralyzed man, he commanded, "Pick up your stretcher and go on home, for you are healed!"

25And immediately, as everyone watched, the man jumped to his feet, picked up his mat and went home praising God! 26Everyone present was gripped with awe and fear. And they praised God, remarking over and over again, "We have seen strange things today."

Jesus eats with sinners at Matthew's house
(40/Matthew 9:9–13; Mark 2:13–17)

27Later on as Jesus left the town he saw a tax collector—with the usual reputation

5:17 *Jewish religious leaders,* literally, "Pharisees."   5:23, 24 *the Messiah,* literally, "the Son of Man."

5:13 Lepers were considered untouchable because people feared contracting their disease. Yet Jesus reached out and touched the leper to heal him. We may consider certain people untouchable or repulsive. We must not be afraid to reach out and touch them with God's love. Who do you know that needs God's touch of love in his or her life?

5:16 People were clamoring to hear Jesus preach and have their diseases healed, but Jesus made sure he often withdrew to quiet, solitary places to pray. Many things clamor for our attention, and we often run ourselves ragged attending to them. Like Jesus, however, we should take time to withdraw to a quiet place to pray. Strength comes from God, and we can get it only by spending time with him.

5:17 The religious leaders spent much time defining and discussing the huge body of religious tradition that had been accumulating for more than 400 years since the Jews' return from exile. They were so concerned with these man-made traditions, in fact, that they often lost sight of Scripture. Now these leaders felt threatened because Jesus challenged the sincerity of their laws and the people were flocking to him.

5:18, 19 In Bible times, houses were built of stone and had flat roofs made of mud mixed with straw. Outside stairways led to the roof. These men carried their friend up the stairs to the roof where they took apart as much of the mud and straw mixture as was necessary to lower him through to Jesus.

5:18–20 It wasn't the sick man's faith that impressed Jesus, but the faith of his friends. Jesus responded to their faith and healed the man. For better or worse, our faith affects others. We cannot make another person a Christian, but we can do much through our words, actions, and love to give him or her a chance to respond. Look for opportunities to bring your friends to the living Christ.

5:21 When Jesus told the paralyzed man his sins were forgiven, the Jewish leaders accused him of blasphemy—claiming to be God or to do what only God can do. In Jewish law, blasphemy was punishable by death (Leviticus 24:16). In labeling Jesus' claim to forgive sins blasphemous, the religious leaders did not understand that he *is* God, and he has God's power to heal both the body and the soul. Forgiveness of sins was a sign that the messianic age had come (Isaiah 40:2; Joel 2:32; Micah 7:18, 19; Zechariah 13:1).

for cheating—sitting at a tax collection booth. The man's name was Levi. Jesus said to him, "Come and be one of my disciples!" 28So Levi left everything, sprang up and went with him.

29Soon Levi held a reception in his home with Jesus as the guest of honor. Many of Levi's fellow tax collectors and other guests were there.

5:29
Lk 15:1

30But the Pharisees and teachers of the Law complained bitterly to Jesus' disciples about his eating with such notorious sinners.

31Jesus answered them, "It is the sick who need a doctor, not those in good health. 32My purpose is to invite sinners to turn from their sins, not to spend my time with those who think themselves already good enough."

5:32
1 Tim 1:15

Religious leaders ask Jesus about fasting
(41/Matthew 9:14–17; Mark 2:18–22)

33Their next complaint was that Jesus' disciples were feasting instead of fasting. "John the Baptist's disciples are constantly going without food, and praying," they declared, "and so do the disciples of the Pharisees. Why are yours wining and dining?"

5:33
Mt 9:14-17
Mk 2:18-22

34Jesus asked, "Do happy men fast? Do wedding guests go hungry while celebrating with the groom? 35But the time will come when the bridegroom will be killed; then they won't want to eat."

5:34
Mt 22:2
Lk 14:16-23
2 Cor 11:2
Rev 19:7; 21:2

36Then Jesus used this illustration: "No one tears off a piece of a new garment to make a patch for an old one. Not only will the new garment be ruined, but the old garment will look worse with a new patch on it! 37And no one puts new wine into old wineskins, for the new wine bursts the old skins, ruining the skins and spilling the wine. 38New wine must be put into new wineskins. 39But no one after drinking the old wine seems to want the fresh and the new. 'The old ways are best,' they say."

5:35
Zech 13:7
Mt 6:16,17
Jn 7:33; 16:6,
20,22
Acts 13:2,3
1 Cor 7:5

The disciples pick wheat on the Sabbath
(45/Matthew 12:1–8; Mark 2:23–28)

6 One Sabbath as Jesus and his disciples were walking through some grainfields, they were breaking off the heads of wheat, rubbing off the husks in their hands and eating the grains.

6:1
Mt 12:1-8
Mk 2:23-28

2But some Pharisees said, "That's illegal! Your disciples are harvesting grain, and it's against the Jewish law to work on the Sabbath."

6:2
Ex 20:10
Mark 7:2

5:35 killed, literally, "taken away from them."

5:28 For more about Levi, who became Matthew the disciple and author of the Gospel of Matthew, see his Profile in Matthew 9.

5:28, 29 Levi responded as Jesus would want all his followers to do—he followed his Lord immediately, and he called his friends together to meet him too. Levi left a lucrative, though probably dishonest, tax-collecting business to follow Jesus. Then he held a reception for his fellow tax collectors and other "notorious sinners" so they could meet Jesus too. Levi, who left behind a material fortune in order to gain a spiritual fortune, was proud to be associated with Jesus.

5:30–32 The Pharisees wrapped their sin in respectability. They made themselves appear good by publicly doing good deeds and pointing at the sins of others. Jesus chose to spend time, not with these self-righteous religious leaders, but with people who sensed their own sin and knew they were not good enough for God. In order to come to God, you must repent; and in order to repent, you must recognize your sin.

5:35 Jesus knew his death was coming. After that time, fasting would be in order. Although he was fully human, Jesus knew he was God and knew why he had come—to die for the sins of the world.

5:36–39 Wineskins were goatskins sewed together at the edges to form a watertight bag. New wine expands as it ages, so it had to

be put in new, pliable wineskins. A used skin, more rigid, would burst and spill the wine. Like old wineskins, the Pharisees were too rigid to accept Jesus, who could not be contained in their traditions or rules. Jesus' way could not simply be superimposed on the old ways. Christianity required new approaches, new traditions, new structures. We, too, must be careful that our hearts do not become so rigid that they prevent us from accepting the new way of thinking that Christ brings. We need to keep our hearts pliable so we can accept Jesus' life-changing message.

6:1, 2 The Pharisees had written in the Mishnah, their handbook of rabbinic law, 39 categories of activities that were forbidden on the Sabbath—and harvesting was one of them. They even went so far as to describe different methods of harvesting, one of which was rubbing the heads of grain between the hands, as the disciples were doing here. Since God's law said farmers were to leave the edges of their fields unplowed so travelers and the poor could eat from this bounty (Deuteronomy 23:25), the disciples were not stealing grain. Neither were they breaking the Sabbath by doing their daily work on it. They were not breaking any divine law, only a human law against harvesting on the Sabbath.

6:2 The Pharisees thought their religious system had all the answers. They could not accept Jesus, because he did not fit into their system. We could miss Christ for the same reason. Beware of thinking you or your church has all the answers. No religious

6:3
1 Sam 21:6

6:4
Ex 29:23,33
Lev 24:9

3Jesus replied, "Don't you read the Scriptures? Haven't you ever read what King David did when he and his men were hungry? 4He went into the Temple and took the shewbread, the special bread that was placed before the Lord, and ate it—illegal as this was—and shared it with others." 5And Jesus added, "I am master even of the Sabbath."

Jesus heals a man's hand on the Sabbath
(46/Matthew 12:9–14; Mark 3:1–6)

6:6
Mt 12:9-14
Mk 3:1-6
Lk 13:14; 14:3
Jn 9:16

6On another Sabbath he was in the synagogue teaching, and a man was present whose right hand was deformed. 7The teachers of the Law and the Pharisees watched closely to see whether he would heal the man that day, since it was the Sabbath. For they were eager to find some charge to bring against him.

6:8
1 Sam 16:7
Mt 9:4
Lk 5:22
Jn 2:24,25
6:64; 21:17
Acts 1:24
Rev 2:23

8How well he knew their thoughts! But he said to the man with the deformed hand, "Come and stand here where everyone can see." So he did.

9Then Jesus said to the Pharisees and teachers of the Law, "I have a question for you. Is it right to do good on the Sabbath day, or to do harm? To save life, or to destroy it?"

6:9
Jn 7:23

10He looked around at them one by one and then said to the man, "Reach out your hand." And as he did, it became completely normal again. 11At this, the enemies of Jesus were wild with rage, and began to plot his murder.

→ Jesus selects the twelve disciples
(48/Mark 3:13–19)

6:12
Mt 10:2-4; 14:23
Mk 3:13-19

6:13
Mt 10:1

6:14
Jn 1:42

6:16
Acts 1:13

12One day soon afterwards he went out into the mountains to pray, and prayed all night. 13At daybreak he called together his followers and chose twelve of them to be the inner circle of his disciples. (They were appointed as his "apostles," or "missionaries.") 14, 15, 16Here are their names: Simon (he also called him Peter), Andrew (Simon's brother), James, John, Philip, Bartholomew, Matthew, Thomas, James (the son of Alphaeus), Simon (a member of the Zealots, a subversive political party), Judas (son of James), Judas Iscariot (who later betrayed him).

6:5 *l, literally, "the Son of Man."*

---

system is big enough to contain Christ or perfectly describe his activity in the world.

6:3–5 Each week 12 consecrated loaves of bread, representing the 12 tribes of Israel, were placed on a table in the Temple. This bread was called shewbread, or the bread of the presence. After its week in the Temple, it was to be eaten only by priests. Jesus, accused of Sabbath-breaking, appealed to a story about David (1 Samuel 21:1–6). Once when fleeing from King Saul, he and his men ate this consecrated bread. Their need was more important than ceremonial regulations. Jesus was appealing to the same principle: human need was more important than petty laws about Sabbath observance. By comparing himself and his disciples with David and his companions, he was saying, "If you condemn me, you must also condemn King David."

6:6, 7 The religious leaders had invented a law that said no healing could be done on the Sabbath. They determined that healing was practicing medicine and thus part of a doctor's profession. And a person could not practice his or her profession on the Sabbath. It was more important for the religious leaders to protect their laws than to free a person from painful suffering.

6:9 When Jesus said he is master of the Sabbath he revealed to the Pharisees that he had the authority to overrule their traditions and regulations because he had created the Sabbath. The creator is always greater than the creation.

6:11 Jesus' enemies were wild with rage. Not only had he read their minds; he also flouted their laws and exposed the hatred in their hearts. It is ironic that their hatred combined with their zeal for the law drove them to plot murder—clearly against the law.

6:12 The Gospel writers note that before every important event in Jesus' life, he took time to go off by himself and pray. This time he was preparing to choose his inner circle, the twelve disciples. Make sure that all important decisions in your life are grounded in prayer and meditation.

6:13–16 Jesus selected ordinary men to be his disciples, and they were a real mixture of backgrounds and personalities. They were "ordinary" people with a high calling. Today, God calls "ordinary" people together to build his church, teach salvation's message, and serve others out of love. Alone we may feel unqualified to serve Christ effectively, but together we make up a group strong enough to serve God in any way. Ask for patience to accept the differences in people in your church, and build on the variety of strengths represented in your group.

6:14 Jesus had many *disciples*, (learners), but he chose only 12 *apostles* (messengers). The apostles were his inner circle to whom he gave special training, and he sent them out with his own authority. These were the men who started the Christian church. In the Gospels these 12 men are usually called the disciples, but in the book of Acts they are called apostles.

6:14–16 There are several differences between the names in this list and those listed in Mark 3:13–19. Jesus gave several of his disciples new names. For example, Simon is called Peter, Levi is called Matthew. Bartholomew is thought to be the same person as Nathanael (John 1:45), and Judas, son of James, is thought to be Thaddaeus.

Jesus gives the beatitudes
(49/Matthew 5:1–12)

17, 18When they came down the slopes of the mountain, they stood with Jesus on a large, level area, surrounded by many of his followers who, in turn, were surrounded by the crowds. For people from all over Judea and from Jerusalem and from as far north as the seacoasts of Tyre and Sidon had come to hear him or to be healed. And he cast out many demons. 19Everyone was trying to touch him, for when they did healing power went out from him and they were cured.

20Then he turned to his disciples and said, "What happiness there is for you who are poor, for the Kingdom of God is yours! 21What happiness there is for you who are now hungry, for you are going to be satisfied! What happiness there is for you who weep, for the time will come when you shall laugh with joy! 22What happiness it is when others hate you and exclude you and insult you and smear your name because you are mine! 23When that happens, rejoice! Yes, leap for joy! For you will have a great reward awaiting you in heaven. And you will be in good company—the ancient prophets were treated that way too!

24"But, oh, the sorrows that await the rich. For they have their only happiness down here. 25They are fat and prosperous now, but a time of awful hunger is before them. Their careless laughter now means sorrow then. 26And what sadness is ahead for those praised by the crowds—for *false* prophets have *always* been praised.

Jesus teaches about loving enemies
(57/Matthew 5:43–48)

27"Listen, all of you. Love your *enemies*. Do *good* to those who *hate* you. 28Pray for the happiness of those who *curse* you; implore God's blessing on those who *hurt* you.

29"If someone slaps you on one cheek, let him slap the other too! If someone demands your coat, give him your shirt besides. 30Give what you have to anyone who asks you for it; and when things are taken away from you, don't worry about getting them back. 31Treat others as you want them to treat you.

32"Do you think you deserve credit for merely loving those who love you? Even the godless do that! 33And if you do good only to those who do you good—is that so wonderful? Even sinners do that much! 34And if you lend money only to those who can repay you, what good is that? Even the most wicked will lend to their own kind for full return!

6:22 *because you are mine,* literally, "on account of the Son of Man."

6:17
Mt 4:25

6:19
Mt 14:36
Mk 5:30

6:20
Mt 5,6,7; 8:1
11:5
Jas 2:5

6:21
Isa 55:1; 61:3
1 Cor 4:11
Rev 7:14-17

6:22
Jn 9:22; 16:2
1 Pet 2:19
3:14; 4:14

6:23
Acts 5:41; 7:51
Col 1:24

6:24
Amos 6:1
Jas 5:1

6:25
Isa 65:13
Prov 14:13

6:27
Ex 23:4
Prov 25:21
Rom 12:20

6:28
Lk 23:34
Acts 7:60

6:29
1 Cor 6:7

6:30
Deut 15:7
Prov 3:27

6:31
Phil 4:8

6:17, 18 This may be Luke's account of the sermon Matthew records in Matthew 5—7, or it may be that Jesus gave a similar sermon on several different occasions. It is believed by many that this was not one sermon, but a composite based on Jesus' customary teachings.

6:19 Once Jesus' healing power became known, crowds gathered just to touch him. For many, he had become a symbol of good fortune, a lucky charm, or a country magician. Instead of desiring God's pardon and love, they only wanted physical healing or a chance to see spectacular events. Some people still see God as a cosmic magician, and prayer only as a way to ease their pain or get him to do his tricks. But God is not a magician—he is the Master. Prayer is not a way for us to control him; it is a way for us to put ourselves under his control.

6:20–26 These "happiness" verses are called the *Beatitudes,* from the Latin word meaning "blessing." They describe what it means to be Christ's follower. They are a standard of conduct. They contrast Kingdom values with worldly values, showing what Christ's followers can expect from the world and what God will give them. They contrast fake piety with true humility. And finally, they show how the Old Testament expectations will be fulfilled in God's Kingdom.

6:21 Some believe that the hunger of which Jesus spoke is a

hunger for righteousness (Matthew 5:6). Others say this is physical hunger, which is in line with Old Testament Scriptures that speak of God's concern for the poor. In a nation where riches were seen as a sign of God's favor, Jesus startled his hearers by pronouncing blessings on the hungry. In doing so, however, he was in line with an ancient tradition. See, for example, 1 Samuel 2:5; Psalm 146:7; Isaiah 58:6, 7; and his own mother's prayer in Luke 1:53.

6:24 If you are trying to find fulfillment through riches, wealth is the only reward you will ever get—and it does not last.

6:26 There were many false prophets in Old Testament times. They were praised by kings and crowds because their predictions—prosperity and victory in war—were popular rather than true. But popularity is fickle. Sadness lies ahead for those who chase after the crowd's praise rather than God's approval.

6:27 The Jews despised the Romans because they oppressed God's people, but Jesus told them to love these enemies. Such words turned many away from Christ. But Jesus wasn't talking about having affection for enemies; he was talking about an act of the will. You can't "fall into" this kind of love—it takes conscious effort. Loving our enemies means acting in their best interests. We can pray for them, and we can think of ways to help them. Jesus loved the whole world, even though the world was in rebellion against God. He asks us to follow his example by loving our enemies.

6:35
Lev 25:35
Ps 37:26
Acts 14:17
1 Jn 3:1

6:36
Eph 5:1,2

35"Love your *enemies!* Do good to *them!* Lend to *them!* And don't be concerned about the fact that they won't repay. Then your reward from heaven will be very great, and you will truly be acting as sons of God: for he is kind to the *unthankful* and to those who are *very wicked*.

36"Try to show as much compassion as your Father does.

Jesus teaches about criticizing others
(63/Matthew 7:1–6)

6:37
Jas 4:11

6:38
Ps 79:12
Prov 19:17
Mk 4:24
Jas 2:13

6:39
Mt 15:14

6:40
Mt 10:24
Jn 13:16; 15:20

6:42
Prov 18:17

37"Never criticize or condemn—or it will all come back on you. Go easy on others; then they will do the same for you. 38For if you give, you will get! Your gift will return to you in full and overflowing measure, pressed down, shaken together to make room for more, and running over. Whatever measure you use to give—large or small—will be used to measure what is given back to you."

39Here are some of the story-illustrations Jesus used in his sermons: "What good is it for one blind man to lead another? He will fall into a ditch and pull the other down with him. 40How can a student know more than his teacher? But if he works hard, he may learn as much.

41"And why quibble about the speck in someone else's eye—his little fault— when a board is in your own? 42How can you think of saying to him, 'Brother, let me help you get rid of that speck in your eye,' when you can't see past the board in yours? Hypocrite! First get rid of the board, and then perhaps you can see well enough to deal with his speck!

Jesus teaches about fruit in people's lives
(66/Matthew 7:15–20)

6:43
1 Tim 3:1-9
6:44
Mt 12:33
6:45
Rom 8:5-8

43"A tree from good stock doesn't produce scrub fruit nor do trees from poor stock produce choice fruit. 44A tree is identified by the kind of fruit it produces. Figs never grow on thorns, or grapes on bramble bushes. 45A good man produces good deeds from a good heart. And an evil man produces evil deeds from his hidden wickedness. Whatever is in the heart overflows into speech.

Jesus teaches about those who build houses on rock and sand
(67/Matthew 7:21–29)

6:46
Mal 1:6
Mt 25:11
Rom 2:13
6:48
1 Cor 3:11

46"So why do you call me 'Lord' when you won't obey me? 47, 48But all those who come and listen and obey me are like a man who builds a house on a strong foundation laid upon the underlying rock. When the floodwaters rise and break against the house, it stands firm, for it is strongly built.

6:37 *Go easy on others; then they will do the same for you,* literally, "release, and you shall be released." **6:41** *his little fault,* implied.

6:35 Love means action. One way to put love to work is to take the initiative in meeting specific needs. This is easy to do with people who love us, people whom we trust; but love means doing this even to those who dislike us or plan to hurt us. The money we give to others should be considered a gift, not a point of leverage or an IOU. Give it as though you are giving it to God.

6:38 If we are critical rather than compassionate, we will also receive criticism. If we treat others generously, graciously, and compassionately, however, these qualities will come back to us in full measure. We are to love others, not judge them.

6:39, 40 Make sure you're following the right teachers and leaders, because you will go no farther than they do. Look for leaders who will show you more about faith and whose guidance you can trust.

6:41 Jesus doesn't mean we should ignore wrongdoing, but we are not to be so worried about others' sins that we overlook our own. We often rationalize our sins by pointing out the same mistakes in others. What kinds of specks in others' eyes are the easiest for you to criticize? Remember your own logs when you feel like criticizing, and you may find you have less to say.

6:42 We should not be so afraid of the label *hypocrite* that we stand still in our Christian life, hiding our faith and making no attempts to grow. A person who tries to do the right thing but often fails is not a hypocrite. Neither is a person whose actions are different from his feelings—it is often necessary and good to set aside our feelings and do what needs doing. It is not hypocrisy to be weak in faith. What then is a hypocrite? A hypocrite is a person who puts on religious behavior in order to gain attention, approval, acceptance, or admiration from others.

6:45 Jesus reminds us that our speech and actions reveal our real, underlying beliefs. The good impressions we try to make cannot last if our hearts are deceptive. What is in your heart will come out in your speech and behavior.

6:46–49 Obeying God is compared to building a house on a strong, solid foundation that stands firm when storms come. When life is calm, our foundations don't seem to matter. But when crises come, our foundations are tested. Be sure your life is built on the solid foundation of Jesus Christ.

49"But those who listen and don't obey are like a man who builds a house without a foundation. When the floods sweep down against that house, it crumbles into a heap of ruins."

6:49
Job 8:13
Prov 1:29-31
2 Pet 2:20,21

A Roman soldier demonstrates faith
(68/Matthew 8:5–13)

7 When Jesus had finished his sermon he went back into the city of Capernaum. 2Just at that time the highly prized slave of a Roman army captain was sick and near death. 3When the captain heard about Jesus, he sent some respected Jewish elders to ask him to come and heal his slave. 4So they began pleading earnestly with Jesus to come with them and help the man. They told him what a wonderful person the captain was.

"If anyone deserves your help, it is he," they said, 5"for he loves the Jews and even paid personally to build us a synagogue!"

6, 7, 8Jesus went with them; but just before arriving at the house, the captain sent some friends to say, "Sir, don't inconvenience yourself by coming to my home, for I am not worthy of any such honor or even to come and meet you. Just speak a word from where you are, and my servant boy will be healed! I know, because I am under the authority of my superior officers, and I have authority over my men. I only need to say 'Go!' and they go; or 'Come!' and they come; and to my slave, 'Do this or that,' and he does it. So just say, 'Be healed!' and my servant will be well again!"

9Jesus was amazed. Turning to the crowd he said, "Never among all the Jews in Israel have I met a man with faith like this."

10And when the captain's friends returned to his house, they found the slave completely healed.

7:1
Mt 8:5-13

7:6-8
Ps 33:9
Lk 4:36
Jn 11:43

7:9
Rom 3:1,2; 9:4

Jesus raises a widow's son from the dead
(69)

11Not long afterwards Jesus went with his disciples to the village of Nain, with
7:2 *Roman*, implied.

6:49 Why would people build their houses on sand? Perhaps they want to avoid the hard work of preparing a stone foundation, or maybe they are short of time. Possibly the waterfront scenery is more attractive, or beach houses have higher social status than cliff houses. Perhaps they are joining their friends who have already settled in sandy areas. Maybe they haven't heard about the violent storms coming, or they have discounted the reports, or for some reason they think disaster can't happen to them. Whatever their reason, sand-builders have these features in common: they are shortsighted, and they will be sorry. When you find yourself listening but not obeying, what are your reasons?

7:2 This army captain was a *centurion*, in charge of 100 men in the Roman army. He came to Jesus not as a last resort or magic charm, but because he believed Jesus was sent from God. Apparently he recognized that the Jews had God's message for mankind—he had paid to build a synagogue. Thus it was natural for him to turn to Jesus in his need.

7:3 Why did the centurion send Jewish elders to Jesus instead of going himself? Well aware of the Jewish hatred for Roman soldiers, he may not have wanted to interrupt a Jewish gathering. As an army captain, he daily delegated jobs and sent groups on missions, so this was how he chose to get his message to Jesus.

7:3 Matthew 8:5 says the Roman army captain visited Jesus himself, while Luke 7:3 says he sent Jewish elders to present his request to Jesus. In dealing with the messengers, Jesus was dealing with the centurion. For his Jewish audience, Matthew emphasized the man's faith. For his Gentile audience, Luke highlighted the good relationship between the Jewish elders and the Roman army captain.

7:9 The Roman army captain didn't come to Jesus, and he didn't

expect Jesus to come to him. Just as he did not need to be present to have his orders carried out, so Jesus didn't need to be present to heal. The captain's faith was especially amazing because he was a Gentile who had not been brought up to know a loving God.

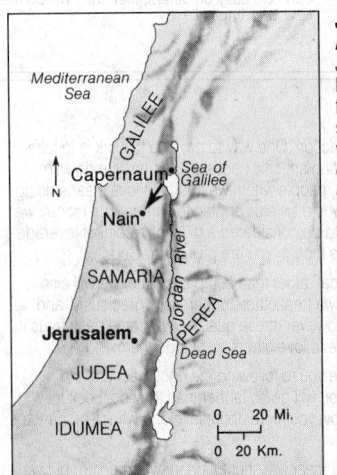

JESUS RAISES A DEAD BOY
Jesus traveled to Nain, and met a funeral procession leaving the village. A widow's only son had died, leaving her virtually helpless, but Jesus brought the boy back to life. This miracle, recorded only in Luke, reveals Jesus' compassion for people's needs.

7:11–17 This story illustrates salvation. The whole world was dead in sin (Ephesians 2:1), just as the widow's son was dead. Being

the usual great crowd at his heels. 12A funeral procession was coming out as he approached the village gate. The boy who had died was the only son of his widowed mother, and many mourners from the village were with her.

13When the Lord saw her, his heart overflowed with sympathy. "Don't cry!" he said. 14Then he walked over to the coffin and touched it, and the bearers stopped. "Laddie," he said, "come back to life again."

15Then the boy sat up and began to talk to those around him! And Jesus gave him back to his mother.

16A great fear swept the crowd, and they exclaimed with praises to God, "A mighty prophet has risen among us," and, "We have seen the hand of God at work today."

17The report of what he did that day raced from end to end of Judea and even out across the borders.

Jesus eases John's doubt
(70/Matthew 11:1–19)

18The disciples of John the Baptist soon heard of all that Jesus was doing. When they told John about it, 19he sent two of his disciples to Jesus to ask him, "Are you really the Messiah? Or shall we keep on looking for him?"

20, 21, 22The two disciples found Jesus while he was curing many sick people of their various diseases—healing the lame and the blind and casting out evil spirits. When they asked him John's question, this was his reply: "Go back to John and tell him all you have seen and heard here today: how those who were blind can see. The lame are walking without a limp. The lepers are completely healed. The deaf can hear again. The dead come back to life. And the poor are hearing the Good News. 23And tell him, 'Blessed is the one who does not lose his faith in me.' "

24After they left, Jesus talked to the crowd about John. "Who is this man you went out into the Judean wilderness to see?" he asked. "Did you find him weak as grass, moved by every breath of wind? 25Did you find him dressed in expensive clothes? No! Men who live in luxury are found in palaces, not out in the wilderness. 26But did you find a prophet? Yes! And more than a prophet. 27He is the one to whom the Scriptures refer when they say, 'Look! I am sending my messenger ahead of you, to prepare the way before you.' 28In all humanity there is no one

7:19 *the Messiah,* literally, "the one who is coming."   **7:23** *Blessed is the one who does not lose his faith in me,* literally, "Blessed is he who keeps from stumbling over me."

Cross-references (left margin):

7:13 Lam 3:32 / Jn 11:33,35 / Heb 4:15

7:14 Lk 8:54 / Jn 11:43 / Acts 9:40 / Rom 4:17

7:16 Lk 1:65,68 / 24:19 / Jn 4:19; 6:14 / 9:17

7:17 Mt 9:26

7:18 Mt 11:2-30

7:19 Ezek 21:27 / Dan 9:24-26 / Mic 5:2 / Zech 9:9 / Mal 3:1-3

7:22 Isa 29:18; 35:5 / 42:6; 61:1 / Lk 4:18 / Jas 2:5

7:25 Mt 3:4 / Mk 1:6

7:27 Isa 40:3 / Mal 3:1; 4:5

---

dead, we could do nothing to help ourselves—we couldn't even ask for help. But God's "heart overflowed with sympathy," and he sent Jesus to raise us to life with him (Ephesians 2:4–7). The dead boy did not earn his second chance at life, and we cannot earn our new life in Christ. But we can accept it, praise God for it, and use it to do his will.

7:11–15 The widow's situation was serious. She had lost her husband, and now her only son was dead—her last means of support. The crowd of mourners would go home, and she would be left penniless and friendless. She was probably past the age of childbearing and would not marry again. Unless a relative came to her aid, her future was bleak. She would be an easy prey for swindlers, and she would likely be reduced to begging for food. In fact, as Luke repeatedly emphasizes, she was just the kind of person Jesus came to help—and help her he did. Jesus has the power to bring hope out of any tragedy.

7:12 Honoring the dead was important in Jewish tradition. A funeral procession—the relatives of the dead person following the body which was wrapped and carried on a kind of stretcher—made its way through town, and bystanders were expected to join it. In addition, hired mourners cried aloud and drew attention to the procession. The family's mourning continued for 30 days.

7:16 The people thought of Jesus as a prophet because, like the Old Testament prophets, he boldly proclaimed God's message

and sometimes raised the dead. Both Elijah and Elisha raised children from the dead (1 Kings 17:17–24; 2 Kings 4:18–37). The people were correct in thinking Jesus was a prophet, but he is much more than that—he is God himself.

7:18–23 John was confused because the reports he received about Jesus were unexpected and incomplete. His doubts were natural, and Jesus didn't rebuke him for them. Instead, he responded in a way John would understand by explaining that he had in fact accomplished those things that the Messiah was supposed to accomplish. God also can handle our doubts, and he welcomes our questions.

7:20–22 The proofs listed here for Jesus' being the Messiah are significant. They consist of observable deeds, not theories—actions that Jesus' contemporaries saw and reported for us to read today. The prophets had said that the Messiah would do these very acts (see Isaiah 35:5, 6; 61:1). These physical proofs helped John—and will help all of us—to recognize who Jesus is.

7:28 Of all people, no one fulfilled his God-given purpose better than John. Yet in God's Kingdom, all who come after John have a greater spiritual heritage than his, because they have clearer knowledge of the purpose of Jesus' death and resurrection. John was the last of the Old Testament prophets, the last to prepare the people for the coming Messianic age. Jesus was not contrasting the man John with individual Christians; he was contrasting life before Christ with life in the fullness of his Kingdom.

greater than John. And yet the least citizen of the Kingdom of God is greater than he."

29And all who heard John preach—even the most wicked of them—agreed that God's requirements were right, and they were baptized by him. 30All, that is, except the Pharisees and teachers of Moses' Law. They rejected God's plan for them and refused John's baptism.

31"What can I say about such men?" Jesus asked. "With what shall I compare them? 32They are like a group of children who complain to their friends, 'You don't like it if we play "wedding" and you don't like it if we play "funeral" '! 33For John the Baptist used to go without food and never took a drop of liquor all his life, and you said, 'He must be crazy!' 34But I eat my food and drink my wine, and you say, 'What a glutton Jesus is! And he drinks! And has the lowest sort of friends!' 35But I am sure you can always justify your inconsistencies."

A sinful woman anoints Jesus' feet
(72)

36One of the Pharisees asked Jesus to come to his home for lunch and Jesus accepted the invitation. As they sat down to eat, 37a woman of the streets—a prostitute—heard he was there and brought an exquisite flask filled with expensive perfume. 38Going in, she knelt behind him at his feet, weeping, with her tears falling down upon his feet; and she wiped them off with her hair and kissed them and poured the perfume on them.

39When Jesus' host, a Pharisee, saw what was happening and who the woman was, he said to himself, "This proves that Jesus is no prophet, for if God had really sent him, he would know what kind of woman this one is!"

40Then Jesus spoke up and answered his thoughts. "Simon," he said to the Pharisee, "I have something to say to you."

"All right, Teacher," Simon replied, "go ahead."

41Then Jesus told him this story: "A man loaned money to two people—$5,000 to one and $500 to the other. 42But neither of them could pay him back, so he kindly forgave them both, letting them keep the money! Which do you suppose loved him most after that?"

43"I suppose the one who had owed him the most," Simon answered.

"Correct," Jesus agreed.

44Then he turned to the woman and said to Simon, "Look! See this woman kneeling here! When I entered your home, you didn't bother to offer me water to

7:29 Mt 3:5 / Lk 3:12 / Acts 18:25; 19:3
7:30 Acts 20:27
7:33 Mt 3:4 / Mk 1:6 / Lk 1:15
7:35 1 Cor 1:23,24
7:36 Mt 26:6 / Mk 14:3 / Jn 11:2
7:37 Lk 8:2
7:38 Zech 12:10
7:39 Lk 15:2 / Jn 7:52
7:41 Mt 18:28
7:42 Isa 1:18; 43:25 44:22
7:44 Gen 18:4 / 1 Tim 5:10

7:29 even the most wicked of them, literally, "even the tax collectors," i.e., the publicans. **7:32** You don't like it if we play "wedding" and you don't like it if we play "funeral." Literally, "We played the flute for you and you didn't dance; we sang a dirge and you didn't weep." **7:33** He must be crazy, literally, "He has a demon." **7:34** has the lowest sort of friends, literally, "is a friend of tax gatherers and sinners." **7:35** But I am sure you can always justify your inconsistencies, literally, "But wisdom is justified of all her children."

7:29, 30 The wicked people heard John's message and repented. In contrast, the religious leaders rejected his words. Wanting to live their own way, they refused to listen to other ideas. Rather than trying to force your plans on God, try to discover his plan for you.

7:31–35 Jesus had some strong words for many of the religious leaders of his day, who thought they alone had God's answers to life. But Jesus, who is God, lived by: (1) spending time with sinners, (2) speaking and living the truth, (3) judging others' hearts, not their actions, and (4) being righteous. The religious leaders, however, lived by (1) avoiding the "unclean" people, (2) being hypocrites, (3) judging others' actions, not hearts, and (4) being "self-righteous."

7:35 The Pharisees were good at rationalizing their inconsistencies. This helped them keep up a good appearance, but it also kept them from changing where change was needed. If we excuse our wrong actions or inconsistent attitudes, we will strengthen them. If we face up to our inconsistencies, then we will grow in wisdom. Jesus was saying that if the Pharisees were really wise, the people would be able to see it by their consistent behavior.

7:36 A similar but separate incident occurred later in Jesus' ministry (see Matthew 26:6–13; Mark 14:3–9; John 12:1–11).

7:38 Although the woman was not an invited guest, she entered the house anyway and knelt behind Jesus at his feet. In Jesus' day, it was customary to recline while eating. Dinner guests lay on couches with their heads near the table, propping themselves up on one elbow and stretching their feet out behind them. The woman could easily anoint Jesus' feet without going up to the table.

7:44 Again the Pharisees are contrasted with sinners—and again the sinners come out ahead. Simon had committed a social error in neglecting to wash Jesus' feet (a courtesy that was extended to guests, because sandaled feet got very dirty), anoint his head with oil, and offer him the kiss of greeting. Did he perhaps feel he was too good to treat Jesus as an equal? The sinful woman, by contrast, lavished tears, expensive perfume, and kisses on her Savior. In this story it is the generous prostitute, not the stingy religious leader, whose sins are forgiven. Sinners who seek forgiveness will be accepted into God's Kingdom, while those who think they're too good to sin will not be accepted.

7:45
1 Cor 16:20
2 Cor 13:12

7:46
2 Sam 12:20
Ps 23:5

wash the dust from my feet, but she has washed them with her tears and wiped them with her hair. ⁴⁵You refused me the customary kiss of greeting, but she has kissed my feet again and again from the time I first came in. ⁴⁶You neglected the usual courtesy of olive oil to anoint my head, but she has covered my feet with rare perfume. ⁴⁷Therefore her sins—and they are many—are forgiven, for she loved me much; but one who is forgiven little, shows little love."

⁴⁸And he said to her, "Your sins are forgiven."

7:49
Isa 53:3
Mt 9:3
Mk 2:7
Jn 1:10

⁴⁹Then the men at the table said to themselves, "Who does this man think he is, going around forgiving sins?"

⁵⁰And Jesus said to the woman, "Your faith has saved you; go in peace."

➤ Women accompany Jesus and the disciples
(73)

8:1
Mt 4:23

8 Not long afterwards he began a tour of the cities and villages of Galilee to announce the coming of the Kingdom of God, and took his twelve disciples

8:2
Mt 27:55,56
Mk 16:9
Lk 23:49
8:3
Mt 14:1

with him. ²Some women went along, from whom he had cast out demons or whom he had healed; among them were Mary Magdalene (Jesus had cast out seven demons from her), ³Joanna, Chuza's wife (Chuza was King Herod's business manager and was in charge of his palace and domestic affairs), Susanna, and many others who were contributing from their private means to the support of Jesus and his disciples.

Jesus tells the parable of the four soils
(77/Matthew 13:1–9; Mark 4:1–9)

8:4
Mt 13:1-53
Mk 4:1-34

⁴One day he gave this illustration to a large crowd that was gathering to hear him—while many others were still on the way, coming from other towns.

8:1 *and villages of Galilee,* implied.

JESUS AND WOMEN		
Jesus raises a widow's son from the dead	Luke 7:11–17
A sinful woman anoints Jesus' feet	Luke 7:36–50
The adulterous woman	John 8:1–11
The group of women travel with Jesus	Luke 8:1–3
Jesus visits Mary and Martha	Luke 10:38–42
Jesus heals a handicapped woman	Luke 13:10–17
Jesus heals the daughter of a Gentile woman	Mark 7:24–30
Weeping women follow Jesus on his way to the cross	Luke 23:27–31
Jesus' mother and other women gather at the cross	John 19:25–27
Jesus appears to Mary Magdalene	Mark 16:9–11
Jesus appears to other women after his resurrection	Matthew 28:8–10

As a non-Jew recording the words and works of Jesus' life, Luke demonstrates a special sensitivity to other "outsiders" with whom Jesus came into contact. For instance, Luke records five events involving women that are not mentioned in the other Gospels. In first-century Jewish culture, women were usually treated as second-class citizens and had few of the rights men had. But Jesus crossed those barriers, and Luke showed the special care Jesus had for women. Jesus treated all people with equal respect. Above are his encounters with women.

7:47 Overflowing love is the natural response to forgiveness. But only those who realize the depth of their sin can appreciate the complete forgiveness God offers them. Jesus has rescued all of his followers, whether they were once extremely wicked or whether they were conventionally good, from eternal death. Are you aware of the wideness of his mercy? Are you grateful for his forgiveness?

7:49, 50 The Pharisees believed that only God could forgive sins, so they wondered why this man Jesus was saying the woman's sins were forgiven. They did not grasp the fact that Jesus is indeed God.

8:2, 3 Jesus raised women from degradation and servitude to fellowship and service. In Jewish culture, women were not supposed to learn from rabbis. By allowing these women to travel

with him, Jesus was showing that all people are equal under God. These women supported Jesus' ministry with their own money. They owed a great debt to him, for he had cast demons out of some and healed others.

8:4 Jesus' illustrations are often called *parables.* A parable takes a familiar object or situation and gives it a spiritual application. By linking the known with the hidden, it can help us understand spiritual truths. A parable compels listeners to discover the truth for themselves, and it conceals the truth from those too lazy or prejudiced to look for it. In reading Jesus' parables, we must be careful not to read too much into them. Most have only one point and one meaning.

5"A farmer went out to his field to sow grain. As he scattered the seed on the ground, some of it fell on a footpath and was trampled on; and the birds came and ate it as it lay exposed. 6Other seed fell on shallow soil with rock beneath. This seed began to grow, but soon withered and died for lack of moisture. 7Other seed landed in thistle patches, and the young grain stalks were soon choked out. 8Still other fell on fertile soil; this seed grew and produced a crop one hundred times as large as he had planted." (As he was giving this illustration he said, "If anyone has listening ears, use them now!")

Jesus explains the parable of the four soils
(78/Matthew 13:10–23; Mark 4:10–25)

9His apostles asked him what the story meant.

10He replied, "God has granted you to know the meaning of these parables, for they tell a great deal about the Kingdom of God. But these crowds hear the words and do not understand, just as the ancient prophets predicted.

11"This is its meaning: The seed is God's message to men. 12The hard path where some seed fell represents the hard hearts of those who hear the words of God, but then the devil comes and steals the words away and prevents people from believing and being saved. 13The stony ground represents those who enjoy listening to sermons, but somehow the message never really gets through to them and doesn't take root and grow. They know the message is true, and sort of believe for awhile; but when the hot winds of persecution blow, they lose interest. 14The seed among the thorns represents those who listen and believe God's words but whose faith afterwards is choked out by worry and riches and the responsibilities and pleasures of life. And so they are never able to help anyone else to believe the Good News.

15"But the good soil represents honest, good-hearted people. They listen to God's words and cling to them and steadily spread them to others who also soon believe."

16[Another time he asked,] "Who ever heard of someone lighting a lamp and then covering it up to keep it from shining? No, lamps are mounted in the open where they can be seen. 17This illustrates the fact that someday everything [in men's hearts] shall be brought to light and made plain to all. 18So be careful how you listen; for whoever has, to him shall be given more; and whoever does not have, even what he thinks he has shall be taken away from him."

8:16 *Another time he asked,* implied. See Mt 5:16.　　**8:17** *in men's hearts,* implied.

8:10
Isa 6:9

8:11
Acts 20:27,32
1 Pet 1:23

8:12
2 Cor 2:11; 4:3
2 Thess 2:10
Jas 1:23,24
1 Pet 5:8

8:14
Mt 19:23
1 Tim 6:9,10
2 Tim 4:10

8:15
Ps 32:2,5
Eph 2:4
2 Pet 1:5-10

8:16
Mt 5:15
Lk 11:33
Phil 2:15,16

8:17
Mt 10:26
Lk 12:2

8:18
Mt 25:29
Lk 19:26
Jn 15:2

8:5 Why would a farmer allow precious seed to land in the road, in a thorn patch, or among rocks? This is not a picture of an irresponsible farmer scattering seeds at random. The farmer is using the acceptable method of hand-seeding a large field—casting it by handfuls as he walks through the field. His goal is to get as much seed as possible to take root in good soil, but there is inevitable waste as some falls or is blown into less productive places. The fact that some of the seed produced no crop was not the fault of the faithful farmer or of the seed—the results depended on the condition of the soil on which the seed fell. It is our responsibility to spread the seed (God's message), but we should not give up when some of our efforts fail. Remember, not every seed falls on good soil.

8:10 Why didn't the crowds understand Jesus' words? Perhaps they were looking for a physical, military leader and could not fit his words into their preconceived idea. Perhaps they were afraid of pressure from religious leaders, so they did not want to look too deep into Jesus' words. God told Isaiah that people would hear his words and see great miracles and still not understand their meaning (Isaiah 6:9), and the same thing happened to Jesus. The parable of the soil was an accurate picture of the people's reaction to his parables.

8:11–15 Hard-rock people, like the religious leaders, refused to believe God's message. Stony-ground people, like the crowds who followed Jesus, trusted God but never got around to doing anything about it. Thistle-patch people, overcome by materialism, left no room in their lives for God. Good-soil people, by contrast to all the other groups, followed no matter what the cost. Which type of soil are you?

8:16–18 In God's eyes, people's hearts—their thoughts and motives—are as visible as a lamp mounted in the open. No matter how hard we try to cover up bad attitudes, deeds, or words, we cannot deceive God. Instead of hiding our faults, we should ask God to change our lives so we no longer have to be ashamed. If you are trying to hide anything from God it won't work. Only when you confess your hidden sins and seek God's forgiveness will you have the help you need to do right.

8:18 This is a principle of growth in physical, mental, and spiritual life. For example, a muscle, when exercised, grows stronger; but an unused muscle grows weak and flabby. If you are not growing, you are weakening; it is impossible to stand still for long. What are you doing with what God has given you?

Jesus describes his true family
(76/Matthew 12:46–50; Mark 3:31–35)

8:19
Mt 12:46-50
13:55
Mk 3:31-35
Jn 7:5
Acts 1:14

19Once when his mother and brothers came to see him, they couldn't get into the house where he was teaching, because of the crowds. 20When Jesus heard they were standing outside and wanted to see him, 21he remarked, "My mother and my brothers are all those who hear the message of God and obey it."

Jesus calms the storm
(87/Matthew 8:23–27; Mark 4:35–41)

8:22
Job 28:11; 38:11
Ps 29:10; 65:7
89:9
Mt 8:18,23-27
Mk 4:35-41

22One day about that time, as he and his disciples were out in a boat, he suggested that they cross to the other side of the lake. 23On the way across he lay down for a nap, and while he was sleeping the wind began to rise. A fierce storm developed that threatened to swamp them, and they were in real danger.

24They rushed over and woke him up. "Master, Master, we are sinking!" they screamed.

So he spoke to the storm: "Quiet down," he said, and the wind and waves subsided and all was calm! 25Then he asked them, "Where is your faith?"

8:25
Ps 33:8,9
Mk 6:51

And they were filled with awe and fear of him and said to one another, "Who is this man, that even the winds and waves obey him?"

Jesus sends demons into a herd of pigs
(88/Matthew 8:28–34; Mark 5:1–20)

8:26
Mt 8:28-34
Mk 5:1-20

26So they arrived at the other side, in the Gerasene country across the lake from Galilee. 27As he was climbing out of the boat a man from the city of Gadara came to meet him, a man who had been demon-possessed for a long time. Homeless and naked, he lived in a cemetery among the tombs. 28As soon as he saw Jesus he

8:28
Acts 16:16,17
Phil 2:10,11

shrieked and fell to the ground before him, screaming, "What do you want with me, Jesus, Son of God Most High? Please, I beg you, oh, don't torment me!"

29For Jesus was already commanding the demon to leave him. This demon had often taken control of the man so that even when shackled with chains he simply broke them and rushed out into the desert, completely under the demon's power,

---

8:21 Jesus' true relatives are those who hear *and* obey his words. Hearing without obeying is not enough. As Jesus loved his mother (see John 19:25-27), so he loves us. He offers us an intimate family relationship with him.

8:23 The Sea of Galilee is still the scene of fierce storms, sometimes with waves as high as 20 feet. Jesus' disciples were not frightened without cause. Even though several of them were expert fishermen and knew how to handle a boat, their peril was real.

8:25 When caught in the storms of life, it is easy to think that God has lost control and that we're at the mercy of the winds of fate. In reality, God is sovereign. He controls the history of the world and our personal destinies. Just as Jesus calmed the waves, he can calm whatever storms you may face.

8:26 The Gerasene country was a Gentile region southeast of the Sea of Galilee, home of the Decapolis, or the Ten Towns. These were Greek cities that belonged to no country but were self-governing. Although Jews would not have raised pigs, which the Jewish religion labeled unclean, the Gentiles had no objections to them.

8:27, 28 These demons recognized Jesus immediately. They knew who he was and what his great power could do to them. Demons, Satan's messengers, are powerful and destructive. Still active today, they attempt to distort and destroy man's relationship with God. Demons and demon possession are real. It is vital that believers recognize the power of Satan and his demons, but we shouldn't let curiosity lead us to get involved with demonic forces (Deuteronomy 18:10–12). If we resist the devil, he will leave us alone (James 4:7).

8:29–31 The demons begged Jesus to spare them from the

HEALING A DEMON-POSSESSED MAN
As he traveled through Galilee, Jesus gave many parables and met many people as recorded in Matthew and Mark. Later, from Capernaum, Jesus and the disciples set out in a boat, only to encounter a fierce storm. Jesus calmed the storm and, when they landed, exorcised a "legion" of demons.

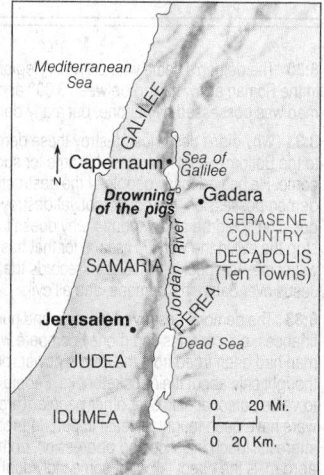

Bottomless Pit. The Bottomless Pit (literally, "the abyss") is also mentioned in Revelation 9:1 and 20:1–3 as the place of confinement for Satan and his messengers. They, of course, knew about this place of confinement; they begged not to be sent there.

30"What is your name?" Jesus asked the demon. "Legion," they replied—for the man was filled with thousands of them! 31They kept begging Jesus not to order them into the Bottomless Pit.

8:31
Rev 9:1; 20:3

32A herd of pigs was feeding on the mountainside nearby, and the demons pled with him to let them enter into the pigs. And Jesus said they could. 33So they left the man and went into the pigs, and immediately the whole herd rushed down the mountainside and fell over a cliff into the lake below, where they drowned. 34The herdsmen rushed away to the nearby city, spreading the news as they ran.

8:32
Lev 11:7
Deut 14:8
Job 1:12; 12:16
Rev 20:7

35Soon a crowd came out to see for themselves what had happened and saw the man who had been demon-possessed sitting quietly at Jesus' feet, clothed and sane! And the whole crowd was badly frightened. 36Then those who had seen it happen told how the demon-possessed man had been healed. 37And everyone begged Jesus to go away and leave them alone (for a deep wave of fear had swept over them). So he returned to the boat and left, crossing back to the other side of the lake. 38The man who had been demon-possessed begged to go too, but Jesus said no.

8:35
1 Jn 3:8
Rom 16:20

8:37
1 Sam 16:4
Job 21:14
Mk 1:24
Lk 4:34; 5:8
Acts 16:39

39"Go back to your family," he told him, "and tell them what a wonderful thing God has done for you."

8:38
Lk 18:43

So he went all through the city telling everyone about Jesus' mighty miracle.

Jesus heals a bleeding woman and restores a girl to life
(89/Matthew 9:18–26; Mark 5:21–43)

40On the other side of the lake the crowds received him with open arms, for they had been waiting for him.

8:40
Mt 9:1,18-26
Mk 5:21-43

41And now a man named Jairus, a leader of a Jewish synagogue, came and fell down at Jesus' feet and begged him to come home with him, 42for his only child was dying, a little girl twelve years old. Jesus went with him, pushing through the crowds.

43, 44As they went a woman who wanted to be healed came up behind and touched him, for she had been slowly bleeding for twelve years, and could find no cure (though she had spent everything she had on doctors). But the instant she touched the edge of his robe, the bleeding stopped.

8:43
Lev 15:25

8:44
Acts 5:15; 19:12

45"Who touched me?" Jesus asked.

8:43, 44 *though she had spent everything she had on doctors.* This clause is not included in some of the ancient manuscripts.

8:30 The demon's name was Legion. A legion was the largest unit in the Roman army, having between 3,000 and 6,000 soldiers. The man was possessed by not one, but many demons.

8:33 Why didn't Jesus just destroy these demons—or send them to the Bottomless Pit? Because his time for such work had not yet come. He healed many people of the destructive work of demon-possession, but he did not yet destroy demons. The same question could be asked today—why doesn't Jesus destroy or stop the evil in the world? His time for that has not yet come. But it will come. The book of Revelation records the future victory of Jesus over Satan, his demons, and all evil.

8:33 The demons destroyed the pigs and hurt the herdsmen's finances, but can pigs and money compare with a human life? A man had been freed from the devil's power, but the villagers thought only about their pocketbooks. People have always tended to value personal gain over other people. Throughout history most wars have been fought, at least in part, to protect economic interests. Much injustice and oppression, both at home and abroad, is the direct fallout of some individual's or company's urge to get rich. People are continually being sacrificed to money. Don't think more highly of "pigs" than of people. Think carefully about how your decisions will affect other human beings, and be willing to choose a simpler lifestyle if it would keep other people from being harmed.

8:38, 39 Often Jesus asked those he healed to be quiet about the healing, but he urged this man to return to his family and tell them what God had done for him. Why? (1) He knew the man would be

an effective witness to those who knew his previous condition and could attest to the miraculous healing. (2) He wanted to expand his ministry by introducing his message into this Gentile area. (3) He knew that the Gentiles, since they were not expecting a Messiah, would not divert his ministry by trying to crown him king. When God touches your life, don't be afraid to share the wonderful events with your family and friends.

8:41 The synagogue was the local center of worship. The synagogue leader was responsible for administration, building maintenance, and worship supervision. It would have been quite unusual for a respected synagogue leader to fall at the feet of an itinerant preacher and beg him to heal his daughter. Jesus honored this man's humble trust (8:50, 54–56).

8:41-48 Many people surrounded Jesus as he made his way through the crowds. It was virtually impossible to get through the mass of people, but one woman fought her way desperately through the crowd in order to touch Jesus. As soon as she did so, she was healed. What a difference between the crowds that contact Jesus and the few that reach out and touch him! Many people are faintly familiar with him, but nothing in their lives is changed or bettered because of this vague acquaintance. It is only the touch of faith that releases God's healing power. Are you only slightly acquainted with God, or are you reaching out to him in faith, knowing that touching him will bring healing to your soul and spirit?

8:45 It wasn't that Jesus didn't know who had touched him, but he wanted the woman to step forward and identify herself. He wanted

Everyone denied it, and Peter said, "Master, so many are crowding against you. . . ."

8:46
Lk 5:17; 6:19

46But Jesus told him, "No, it was someone who deliberately touched me, for I felt healing power go out from me."

47When the woman realized that Jesus knew, she began to tremble and fell to her knees before him and told why she had touched him and that now she was well. 48"Daughter," he said to her, "your faith has healed you. Go in peace."

49While he was still speaking to her, a messenger arrived from the Jairus' home with the news that the little girl was dead. "She's gone," he told her father; "there's no use troubling the Teacher now."

8:50
2 Chron 20:20
Mk 9:23

50But when Jesus heard what had happened, he said to the father, "Don't be afraid! Just trust me, and she'll be all right."

8:52
Jn 11:11,13

51When they arrived at the house Jesus wouldn't let anyone into the room except Peter, James, John, and the little girl's father and mother. 52The home was filled with mourning people, but he said, "Stop the weeping! She isn't dead; she is only asleep!" 53This brought scoffing and laughter, for they all knew she was dead.

8:54
Lk 7:14
Jn 11:43

8:55
Deut 32:39
Ps 33:9

54Then he took her by the hand and called, "Get up, little girl!" 55And at that moment her life returned and she jumped up! "Give her something to eat!" he said.

8:56
Mt 8:4; 9:30

56Her parents were overcome with happiness, but Jesus insisted that they not tell anyone the details of what had happened.

Jesus sends out the twelve disciples
(93/Matthew 10:1–15; Mark 6:7–13)

9:1
Mt 9:36-11:1
Mk 3:13; 6:7-13

9 One day Jesus called together his twelve apostles and gave them authority over all demons—power to cast them out—and to heal all diseases. 2Then he sent them away to tell everyone about the coming of the Kingdom of God and to heal the sick.

9:2
Lk 10:1,9
Tit 2:12,14

9:3
Ps 37:3
Lk 10:4; 22:35
2 Tim 2:4

3"Don't even take along a walking stick," he instructed them, "nor a beggar's bag, nor food, nor money. Not even an extra coat. 4Be a guest in only one home at each village.

9:5
Acts 13:51

5"If the people of a town won't listen to you when you enter it, turn around and

---

to teach her that his robe did not contain magical properties, but that her faith in him had healed her. He may also have wanted to teach the crowds a lesson. According to Jewish law, a man who touched a menstruating woman became ceremonially defiled (Leviticus 15:19–28). This was true whether her bleeding was normal or, as in this woman's case, the result of illness. To protect themselves from such defilement, Jewish men carefully avoided touching, speaking to, or even looking at women. By contrast, Jesus proclaimed to hundreds of people that this "unclean" woman had touched him—and then he healed her. In Jesus' mind, women were not potential sources of defilement. They were human beings who deserved recognition and respect.

8:56 Why did Jesus tell the parents not to talk about their daughter's healing? He knew the facts would speak for themselves. Besides, he was concerned for his ministry. He did not want to be known as just the miracle-worker; he wanted people to listen to his words that would heal their broken spiritual lives.

9:2 Why did Jesus announce his Kingdom by both preaching and healing? If he had limited himself to preaching, people might have seen his Kingdom as spiritual only. On the other hand, if he had healed without preaching, people might have not realized the spiritual importance of his mission. Most of his listeners expected a Messiah who would bring wealth and power to their nation; they preferred material blessings to spiritual discernment. The truth about Jesus is that he is both God and man, both spiritual and physical; and the salvation he offers is both for the soul and the body. Any group or teaching that emphasizes soul at the expense

of body or body at the expense of soul is in danger of distorting Jesus' Good News.

9:3 Why were the disciples instructed to depend on others while they went from town to town announcing the Good News? Their purpose was to blanket Judea with Jesus' message, and by traveling light they could move quickly. Their dependence on others had other good effects as well: (1) it clearly showed that the Messiah had not come to offer wealth to his followers; (2) it forced the disciples to rely on God's power and not on their own provision; (3) it involved the villagers and made them more eager to hear the message. This was an excellent approach for their short-term mission; it was not intended, however, to be a permanent way of life for them.

9:4 Why were the disciples to stay in only one home in each village? They were not to offend their hosts by moving to a home that was more comfortable or socially prominent. This did not burden their host because their stay in each community was short.

9:5 Shaking the dust of unaccepting towns from their feet had deep cultural implications. Pious Jews would shake the dust from their feet after passing through Gentile cities to show their separation from Gentile practices. If the disciples shook the dust of a *Jewish* town from their feet, it would show their separation from Jews who rejected their Messiah. This action also showed that the disciples were not responsible for how the people responded to their message. Neither are we responsible. If we have carefully and truthfully presented Christ and our message is rejected, we are not to blame. Like the disciples, we must move on.

leave, demonstrating God's anger against it by shaking its dust from your feet as you go."

⁶So they began their circuit of the villages, preaching the Good News and healing the sick.

9:6
Lk 8:1

Herod kills John the Baptist
(95/Matthew 14:1–12; Mark 6:14–29)

⁷When reports of Jesus' miracles reached Herod, the governor, he was worried and puzzled, for some were saying, "This is John the Baptist come back to life again"; ⁸and others, "It is Elijah or some other ancient prophet risen from the dead." These rumors were circulating all over the land.

9:7
Mt 14:1-12
Mk 6:14-29
9:8
Mt 16:14

⁹"I beheaded John," Herod said, "so who is this man about whom I hear such strange stories?" And he tried to see him.

9:9
Lk 23:8

Jesus feeds five thousand
(96/Matthew 14:13–21; Mark 6:30–44; John 6:1–15)

¹⁰After the apostles returned to Jesus and reported what they had done, he slipped quietly away with them toward the city of Bethsaida. ¹¹But the crowds found out where he was going, and followed. And he welcomed them, teaching them again about the Kingdom of God and curing those who were ill.

9:10
Mt 14:13-23
Mk 6:30-46
Jn 6:1-15

¹²Late in the afternoon all twelve of the disciples came and urged him to send the people away to the nearby villages and farms, to find food and lodging for the night. "For there is nothing to eat here in this deserted spot," they said.

¹³But Jesus replied, *"You* feed them!"

"Why, we have only five loaves of bread and two fish among the lot of us," they protested; "or are you expecting us to go and buy enough for this whole mob?" ¹⁴For there were about 5,000 men there!

9:13
Num 11:22
2 Kgs 4:42,43
Ps 78:19,20

"Just tell them to sit down on the ground in groups of about fifty each," Jesus replied. ¹⁵So they did.

¹⁶Jesus took the five loaves and two fish and looked up into the sky and gave thanks; then he broke off pieces for his disciples to set before the crowd. ¹⁷And everyone ate and ate; still, twelve basketfuls of scraps were picked up afterwards!

9:17
Ps 145:15,16
Prov 10:22

9:5 *demonstrating God's anger against it,* literally, "as a testimony against them."   **9:7** *Herod, the governor,* literally, "Herod the Tetrarch."

9:1–6 How did Jesus lead his disciples? He empowered them (9:1), gave them specific instructions so they knew what to do (9:3, 4), told them how to deal with tough times (9:5), and held them accountable (9:10). As you lead others, study the Master Leader's pattern. Which of these elements do you need to incorporate into your leadership?

9:7 For more information on Herod, also known as Herod Antipas, see his Profile in Mark 6.

9:7 It was so difficult for the people to accept Jesus for who he was that they tried to come up with other solutions—most of which sound quite unbelievable to our ears. Many thought he must be someone come back to life, perhaps John the Baptist or another prophet. Some suggested he was Elijah, the great prophet who did not die but was taken to heaven in a chariot of fire (2 Kings 2:1–11). Very few found the correct answer, as Peter did (9:20). It may not be easier today to accept Jesus as the fully human yet fully divine Son of God, and people are still trying to find alternate explanations—a great prophet, a radical political leader, a self-deceived rabble-rouser. None of these explanations can account for Jesus' miracles or, especially, his glorious resurrection—so these too have to be explained away. In the end, the attempts to explain Jesus away are far more difficult to believe than the truth.

9:9 For the story of how Herod had John beheaded, see Mark 6:14–29.

9:11 Jesus had tried to slip quietly away from the crowds, but they found out where he was going and followed him. Instead of showing impatience at this interruption, Jesus welcomed the people and ministered to their needs. How do you see people who interrupt your schedule—as nuisances, or as the reason for your life and ministry?

9:11 The Kingdom of God was a focal point of Jesus' teaching. He explained that it was not just a future Kingdom; it was among them, embodied in him, the Messiah. Even though the Kingdom will not be complete until Jesus comes again in glory, we do not have to wait to taste it. The Kingdom of God begins in the hearts of those who believe in Jesus. It is as present with us today as it was with the Judeans two thousand years ago.

9:13, 14 When the disciples expressed concern about where the crowd of thousands would eat, Jesus offered a solution—"*You* feed them!" They protested, focusing their attention on what they didn't have (food and money). Do you think God would ask you to do something that you and he together couldn't handle?

9:16, 17 Why did Jesus bother to feed these people? He could just as easily have sent them on their way. But Jesus does not ignore needs. He is concerned with every aspect of our lives—the physical as well as the spiritual. As we work to bring wholeness to people's lives, we must never ignore the fact that all of us have both physical and spiritual needs. It is impossible to minister effectively to one type of need without considering the other.

Peter says Jesus is the Messiah
(109/Matthew 16:13–20; Mark 8:27–30)

9:18
Mt 16:13-20
Mk 8:27-30

9:19
Mt 14:2

9:20
Jn 6:69
Rom 10:9
1 Jn 4:14,15

¹⁸One day as he was alone, praying, with his disciples nearby, he came over and asked them, "Who are the people saying I am?"

¹⁹"John the Baptist," they told him, "or perhaps Elijah or one of the other ancient prophets risen from the dead."

²⁰Then he asked them, "Who do you think I am?"

Peter replied, "The Messiah—the Christ of God!"

Jesus predicts his death the first time
(110/Matthew 16:21–28; Mark 8:31—9:1)

9:22
Mt 16:21-28
17:22; 20:17
Mk 8:31—9:1,31
Lk 18:31
24:6,7

9:23
Mt 10:38
Lk 14:27

9:24
Mt 10:39

9:26
Mt 10:33
2 Tim 2:12

²¹He gave them strict orders not to speak of this to anyone. ²²"For I, the Messiah, must suffer much," he said, "and be rejected by the Jewish leaders—the elders, chief priests, and teachers of the Law—and be killed; and three days later I will come back to life again!"

²³Then he said to all, "Anyone who wants to follow me must put aside his own desires and conveniences and carry his cross with him every day and *keep close to me!* ²⁴Whoever loses his life for my sake will save it, but whoever insists on keeping his life will lose it; ²⁵and what profit is there in gaining the whole world when it means forfeiting one's self?

²⁶"When I, the Messiah, come in my glory and in the glory of the Father and the holy angels, I will be ashamed then of all who are ashamed of me and of my words now. ²⁷But this is the simple truth—some of you who are standing here right now will not die until you have seen the Kingdom of God."

Jesus is transfigured on the mountain
(111/Matthew 17:1–13; Mark 9:2–13)

9:29
Ex 34:29,35

²⁸Eight days later he took Peter, James, and John with him into the hills to pray. ²⁹And as he was praying, his face began to shine, and his clothes became dazzling

9:22 *the Messiah,* literally, "the Son of Man." Also in vs 26.   **9:29** *his face began to shine,* literally, "the appearance of his face changed."

9:18-20 The Christian faith goes beyond knowing what others believe. It requires us to hold beliefs for ourselves. When Jesus asks, "Who do you think I am?" he wants us to take a stand. Who do *you* say Jesus is?

9:21 Jesus told his disciples not to tell anyone he was the Messiah because, at this point, they didn't fully understand the significance of that statement—nor would anyone else. Everyone still expected the Messiah to come as a conquering king. But Jesus, as the Messiah, still had to suffer, be rejected by the leaders, be killed, and rise from the dead. When the disciples saw all this happen to Jesus, they would understand what the Messiah came to do. Only then would they be equipped to share the Good News around the world.

9:22 This is the turning point in Jesus' instruction of his disciples. He now began teaching clearly and specifically about what was going to happen to him and what they could expect, so they would not need to be surprised when it happened. He explained that he would not *now* be the conquering Messiah because he first had to suffer, die, and rise again. But one day he would return in great glory to set up his eternal Kingdom.

9:23-27 People are willing to pay a high price for something they value. Is it any surprise that Jesus should demand this much commitment from those who would follow him? There are at least three conditions that must be met by people who want to follow Jesus. They must be willing to deny self, to carry their crosses, and to give up their lives. Anything less is superficial lip service.

9:23 "Keep close to me" is literally translated "follow me!" The Christian follows his Lord by imitating his life and obeying his commands. To carry our cross means to deny our selfish desires to do things our own way. Living in this way is costly now, but well worth the pain and effort in the long run.

9:24, 25 If this life is most important to you, you will do everything you can to protect it. You will not want to do anything that might endanger your safety, your health, or your comfort. By contrast, if following Jesus is most important to you, you may find yourself in some very unsafe, unhealthy, and uncomfortable places. You will risk death, but you will not fear it because you know Jesus will raise you to eternal life. The person who is concerned only with this life has no such assurance. His earthly life may be longer, but it will most likely be marred by feelings of boredom and worthlessness.

9:26 Luke's Greek audience would have found it difficult to understand a God who could die, just as Jesus' Jewish audience would have been perplexed by a Messiah who would let himself be captured. Both would be ashamed of him if they did not look past his death to his glorious resurrection and second coming. Then they would see him, not as a loser, but as the Lord of the universe who, through his death, accomplished salvation for all people.

9:27 When Jesus said some would not die without seeing the Kingdom, he was referring to (1) Peter, James, and John, who would witness the Transfiguration eight days later, or in a broader sense, (2) all who would take part in the spread of the church after Pentecost. Jesus' listeners were not going to have to wait for another, future Messiah—the Kingdom was among them, and it would soon (after the resurrection, at Pentecost) come in power (though the work of the Holy Spirit).

9:29 Jesus took Peter, James, and John to the top of a mountain to show them who he really was—not just a great prophet, but God's own Son. Moses, representing the law, and Elijah, representing the prophets, appeared with Jesus, and God's voice singled out Jesus as the long-awaited Messiah with divine authority. Jesus would fulfill both the law and the prophets.

white and blazed with light. 30Then two men appeared and began talking with
him—Moses and Elijah! 31They were splendid in appearance, glorious to see; and
they were speaking of his death at Jerusalem, to be carried out in accordance with
God's plan.

9:30
2 Kgs 2:11
Rom 3:21

9:31
Rom 3:21
Col 3:4

32Peter and the others had been very drowsy and had fallen asleep. Now they
woke up and saw Jesus covered with brightness and glory, and the two men
standing with him. 33As Moses and Elijah were starting to leave, Peter, all
confused and not even knowing what he was saying, blurted out, "Master, this is
wonderful! We'll put up three shelters—one for you and one for Moses and one for
Elijah!"

2 Pet 1:15
1 Jn 3:2

9:32
Dan 8:18; 10:9

34But even as he was saying this, a bright cloud formed above them; and terror
gripped them as it covered them. 35And a voice from the cloud said, "This is my
Son, my Chosen One; listen to him."

9:35
Ex 23:21
Deut 18:15,18
Mt 3:17

36Then, as the voice died away, Jesus was there alone with his disciples. They
didn't tell anyone what they had seen until long afterwards.

Acts 3:22
Heb 2:3
2 Pet 1:16,17

Jesus heals a demon-possessed boy
(112/Matthew 17:14–21; Mark 9:14–29)

37The next day as they descended from the hill, a huge crowd met him, 38and a
man in the crowd called out to him, "Teacher, this boy here is my only son, 39and
a demon keeps seizing him, making him scream; and it throws him into convul-
sions so that he foams at the mouth; it is always hitting him and hardly ever leaves
him alone. 40I begged your disciples to cast the demon out, but they couldn't."

9:37
Mt 17:14-21
Mk 9:14-29

9:38
Lk 7:12

41"O you stubborn faithless people," Jesus said [to his disciples], "how long
should I put up with you? Bring him here."

42As the boy was coming the demon knocked him to the ground and threw him
into a violent convulsion. But Jesus ordered the demon to come out, and healed the
boy and handed him over to his father.

43Awe gripped the people as they saw this display of the power of God.
Meanwhile, as they were exclaiming over all the wonderful things he was doing,
Jesus said to his disciples,

9:43
Mt 17:22,23
Mk 9:30-32
2 Pet 1:16

Jesus predicts his death the second time
(113/Matthew 17:22, 23; Mark 9:30–32)

44"Listen to me and remember what I say. I, the Messiah, am going to be
betrayed." 45But the disciples didn't know what he meant, for their minds had been
sealed and they were afraid to ask him.

9:44
Mt 17:22,23

9:45
Lk 2:50; 18:34

9:41 to his disciples, implied.   9:44 the Messiah, literally, "the Son of Man."

9:33 Peter may have been thinking of the Feast of Tabernacles,
where booths were set up to commemorate the Exodus, God's
deliverance from slavery in Egypt. Peter wanted to keep Moses
and Elijah there, and to stay there with them. But Peter was to
discover that this was not what God wanted. Peter's wish to build
shelters for Jesus, Moses, and Elijah may also show he wished to
build a church on three cornerstones: the law, the prophets, and
Jesus. But Peter grew in his understanding, and eventually he
would write of Jesus as the "carefully chosen, precious
Cornerstone" of the church (1 Peter 2:6).

9:33 Peter, James, and John experienced a wonderful moment on
the mountain, and they didn't want to leave. Sometimes we too
have such an exciting experience we want to stay where we
are—away from the reality and problems of our daily lives.
Knowing that struggles await us in the valley encourages us to
retreat from reality. Yet staying on top of a mountain does not allow
us to minister to others. Instead of becoming spiritual giants, we
would soon become giants of self-centeredness. We need times of
retreat and renewal, but only so we can return to minister to the
world. Our faith must make sense off the mountain as well as on it.

9:35 As God's Son, Jesus has God's power and authority; thus

his words should be our final authority. If a person's teaching is
true, it will go along with Jesus' teachings. Test everything you
hear against Jesus' words, and you will not be led astray.

9:35 God clearly identified Jesus as his Son, his Chosen One,
and said that Peter and the others were to listen to him, not to their
own ideas and desires. The power to follow Jesus comes from an
assurance of who he is.

9:37-43 As the disciples came down the mountain with Jesus,
they passed from a special experience of God's presence to a
frightening experience of evil. The beauty they had just seen made
the ugliness seem even uglier. As our spiritual vision improves and
allows us to see and understand God better, we will also be able to
see and understand evil better. We would be overcome by its
horror if we did not have Jesus at our sides to take us through it in
safety.

9:40 Why couldn't the disciples cast out the demon? In Mark 6:13
we read that they cast out demons while on their mission to the
villages. Perhaps they had special authority only for that trip; or
perhaps their faith had lapsed. The battle with Satan is a difficult,
ongoing struggle. Victory over sin and temptation comes through
faith in Jesus Christ, not through our own effort.

The disciples argue about who would be the greatest
(115/Matthew 18:1–6; Mark 9:33–37)

9:47
Mt 9:4
Jn 2:24,25

9:48
Mt 10:40
23:11,12
Lk 18:17; 22:26

46Now came an argument among them as to which of them would be greatest [in the coming Kingdom]! 47But Jesus knew their thoughts, so he stood a little child beside him 48and said to them, "Anyone who takes care of a little child like this is caring for me! And whoever cares for me is caring for God who sent me. Your care for others is the measure of your greatness."

The disciples forbid another from using Jesus' name
(116/Mark 9:38–42)

9:49
Num 11:28

9:50
Mt 12:30
Lk 11:23
1 Cor 12:3

49His disciple John came to him and said, "Master, we saw someone using your name to cast out demons. And we told him not to. After all, he isn't in our group."

50But Jesus said, "You shouldn't have done that! For anyone who is not against you is for you."

2. Jesus' ministry on the way to Jerusalem
Jesus teaches about the cost of following him
(122/Matthew 8:18–22)

9:51
Mt 19:1,2
8:18-22
Mk 10:1; 16:19
Lk 13:22; 17:11
18:31
19:28; 24:51
Acts 1:2

9:54
2 Kgs 1:10,12

9:55
Rom 10:2

51As the time drew near for his return to heaven, he moved steadily onward toward Jerusalem with an iron will.

52One day he sent messengers ahead to reserve rooms for them in a Samaritan village. 53But they were turned away! The people of the village refused to have anything to do with them because they were headed for Jerusalem.

54When word came back of what had happened, James and John said to Jesus, "Master, shall we order fire down from heaven to burn them up?" 55But Jesus turned and rebuked them, 56and they went on to another village.

57As they were walking along someone said to Jesus, "I will always follow you no matter where you go."

58But Jesus replied, "Remember, I don't even own a place to lay my head. Foxes have dens to live in, and birds have nests, but I, the Messiah, have no earthly home at all."

59Another time, when he invited a man to come with him and to be his disciple, the man agreed—but wanted to wait until his father's death.

9:60
Mt 4:23

60Jesus replied, "Let those without eternal life concern themselves with things

9:46 *the coming Kingdom,* implied.   **9:55** Later manuscripts add to vss 55, 56, "And Jesus said, You don't realize what your hearts are like. For the Son of Man has not come to destroy men's lives, but to save them."   **9:58** *the Messiah,* literally, "the Son of Man."   **9:59** *but wanted to wait until his father's death,* literally, "But he said, 'Lord, suffer me first to go and bury my father,'" perhaps meaning that the man could, when his father died, collect the inheritance and have some security.   **9:60** *Let those without eternal life concern themselves with things like that,* or, "Let those who are spiritually dead care for their own dead."

9:45, 46 The disciples didn't understand Jesus' words about his death. They still thought of Jesus as only an earthly king, and they were concerned about their places in the kingdom he would set up. So they ignored his words about his death and began arguing about who would be greatest.

9:48 How much care do you show to others? This is a vital question that can accurately measure your greatness in God's eyes. How have you expressed your care for others lately, especially the helpless, the needy, the poor—those who can't return your care and concern? Your honest answer to that question will give you a good idea of your real greatness.

9:49, 50 The disciples were jealous. Nine of them together were unable to cast out a single demon (9:40), but when they saw a man who was not one of their group casting out demons, they told him to stop. Our pride is hurt when someone else succeeds where we have failed, but Jesus says there is no room for such jealousy in the spiritual warfare of his Kingdom. Share Jesus' open-arms attitude to Christian workers outside your group.

9:51 Although Jesus knew he would face persecution and death in Jerusalem, he moved steadily toward the city. That kind of determination should characterize our lives too. When God gives

us a course of action, we must move steadily toward our destination, no matter what potential hazards await us there.

9:53 After Assyria invaded Israel, the Northern Kingdom, and resettled it with its own people (2 Kings 17:24–41), the mixed race that developed became known as the Samaritans. "Purebred" Jews hated these "half-breeds," and the Samaritans in turn hated the Jews. So many tensions arose between the two peoples that Jewish travelers between Galilee and Southern Judea often walked around rather than through Samaritan territory, even though this lengthened their trip considerably. Jesus held no such prejudices, and he sent messengers ahead to get rooms in a Samaritan village. But the village refused to welcome these Jewish travelers.

9:54 When the disciples were rejected by the Samaritan village, they didn't want to stop at shaking the dust from their feet (9:5). They wanted to retaliate by calling down fire from heaven, as God had done to the wicked cities of Sodom and Gomorrah (Genesis 19). When others reject or scorn us, we too may feel like retaliating. We must remember that judgment belongs to God, and we must not expect him to use his power to carry out our personal vendettas.

like that. Your duty is to come and preach the coming of the Kingdom of God to all the world."

61Another said, "Yes, Lord, I will come, but first let me ask permission of those at home."

62But Jesus told him, "Anyone who lets himself be distracted from the work I plan for him is not fit for the Kingdom of God."

9:61
1 Kgs 19:20

9:62
Phil 3:13
Heb 6:4

Jesus sends out seventy messengers
(130)

10 The Lord now chose seventy other disciples and sent them on ahead in pairs to all the towns and villages he planned to visit later.

2These were his instructions to them: "Plead with the Lord of the harvest to send out more laborers to help you, for the harvest is so plentiful and the workers so few. 3Go now, and remember that I am sending you out as lambs among wolves. 4Don't take any money with you, or a beggar's bag, or even an extra pair of shoes. And don't waste time along the way.

5"Whenever you enter a home, give it your blessing. 6If it is worthy of the blessing, the blessing will stand; if not, the blessing will return to you.

7"When you enter a village, don't shift around from home to home, but stay in one place, eating and drinking without question whatever is set before you. And don't hesitate to accept hospitality, for the workman is worthy of his wages!

8, 9"If a town welcomes you, follow these two rules:

(1) Eat whatever is set before you.

(2) Heal the sick; and as you heal them, say, 'The Kingdom of God is very near you now.'

10"But if a town refuses you, go out into its streets and say, 11'We wipe the dust of your town from our feet as a public announcement of your doom. Never forget how close you were to the Kingdom of God!' 12Even wicked Sodom will be better

10:1
Mt 10:1
Mk 6:7

10:2
Jer 3:15
Mt 9:37,38
Jn 4:35
1 Cor 12:28
2 Thess 3:1

10:3
Mt 10:16

10:4
2 Kgs 4:29
Mt 10:9
Mk 6:8
Lk 9:3

10:5
Mt 10:12

10:7
Mt 10:10,11
1 Cor 9:4; 10:27
Eph 5:15
1 Tim 5:18

10:9
Isa 2:2
Mt 3:2; 10:7
Lk 9:2

10:12
Mt 10:15

9:61 *ask permission of those at home,* literally, "bid them farewell at home." **10:4** *And don't waste time along the way,* literally, "Salute no one in the way."

9:62 What does Jesus want from us? Total dedication, not halfhearted commitment. We can't pick and choose among Jesus' ideas and follow him selectively; we have to accept the cross along with the crown, judgment as well as mercy. We must count the cost and be willing to abandon everything else that has given us security. With our focus on Jesus, we should allow nothing to distract us from the manner of living he calls good and true.

10:1 Far more than 12 people have been following Jesus. Now he designates a group of 70 to prepare a number of towns he will visit later. These disciples were not unique in their qualifications. They were not better educated, of higher status, or superior in their teaching abilities. What equipped them for this mission was their awareness of Jesus' power and their vision to reach all the people. It is important to dedicate your skills to God's Kingdom, but it is even more important to have a personal experience of his power and a clear vision of what he wants to do in the world.

10:2 Jesus was sending out 35 teams of two to reach the multitudes. They were not to try to do the job without help; rather, they were to ask God for more workers. In doing the work of evangelism, you may want to begin working immediately to reach unsaved people by yourself. This story suggests a different approach: begin by mobilizing people to pray. And before praying for the unsaved people, pray that other concerned people will join you in reaching out to them.

10:2 In Christian service, there is no unemployment. God has work enough for everyone. Don't just sit back and watch the others work—look for ways to get in on the harvest.

10:3, 4 Jesus said he was sending his disciples out "as lambs among wolves." They would have to be careful, for they would surely meet with opposition. We too are sent into the world as

lambs among wolves. So "watch out" and remember that we are not to face our enemies with aggression but with love and gentleness. Our mission may be dangerous so our commitment must be sincere.

10:7 Jesus' direction to stay in one home avoided certain problems. Shifting from home to home could offend the families who first took them in. The families might begin to compete for the disciples' presence, and some might think they weren't good enough to hear their message. If the disciples appeared not to appreciate the hospitality offered them, the village might not accept Jesus when he followed them there. In addition, by staying in one place the disciples did not have to worry continually about getting good accommodations. They could settle down and do the task they came to do.

10:7 Jesus told his disciples to accept hospitality graciously, because their work entitled them to it. Ministers of the gospel deserve to be supported, and it is our responsibility to make sure they have what they need. There are several ways to support the efforts of those who serve God in his church. First, see that they have an adequate salary. Second, see that they are supported emotionally, inviting them over for a meal or expressing your appreciation for something they have done. Third, lift their spirits with occasional surprises that will encourage them. If ministers know we are giving to them cheerfully and generously, they will not feel guilty about accepting our gifts.

10:8, 9 Jesus gave two rules for the disciples as they traveled. They were to eat what was put before them—meaning they were to accept hospitality without being picky, and they were to heal the sick. Because of the healings people would be willing to listen to them proclaim the Good News.

10:13
Ezek 3:6
Mt 11:21
Jn 3:5

10:15
Gen 11:4
Deut 1:28
Isa 14:13
Jer 51:53
Ezek 26:20

10:16
Mt 10:40
Jn 5:23; 13:20
1 Thess 4:8

off than such a city on the Judgment Day. ¹³What horrors await you, you cities of Chorazin and Bethsaida! For if the miracles I did for you had been done in the cities of Tyre and Sidon, their people would have sat in deep repentance long ago, clothed in sackcloth and throwing ashes on their heads to show their remorse. ¹⁴Yes, Tyre and Sidon will receive less punishment on the Judgment Day than you. ¹⁵And you people of Capernaum, what shall I say about you? Will you be exalted to heaven? No, you shall be brought down to hell."

¹⁶Then he said to the disciples, "Those who welcome you are welcoming me. And those who reject you are rejecting me. And those who reject me are rejecting God who sent me."

JAMES

Jesus singled out three of his 12 disciples for special training. James, his brother John, and Peter made up this inner circle. Each eventually played a key role in the early church. Peter became a great speaker, John became the main writer, and James was the first of the 12 disciples to die for the faith.

The way in which the names of James and John are mentioned together indicates that James was the older brother. Zebedee, their father, owned a fishing business where they worked along with Peter and Andrew. When Peter, Andrew, and John left Galilee to see John the Baptist, James stayed back with the boats and fishing nets. Later, when Jesus called them, he was as eager as his partners to follow.

James enjoyed being in the inner circle of Jesus' disciples, but he misunderstood Jesus' purpose. He and his brother even tried to secure their role in Jesus' Kingdom by asking Jesus to promise them each a special position. Like all the disciples, James had a limited view of what Jesus was doing on earth, picturing only an earthly kingdom that would overthrow Rome and restore Israel's former glory. But above all, James wanted to be with Jesus. He had found the right leader, even though he was still on the wrong timetable. It took Jesus' death and resurrection to correct James' view.

James was the first of many to die for the gospel. He was willing to die because he knew Jesus had conquered death, which was now only the doorway to eternal life. Our expectations about life will be limited if this life is all we can see. Jesus promised eternal life to those willing to trust him. If we believe this promise, he will give us the courage to stand for him even during dangerous times.

Strengths and accomplishments:
- One of the 12 disciples
- One of a special inner circle of three with Peter and John
- First of the 12 disciples to be killed for his faith

Weaknesses and mistakes:
- There are two outbursts from James that indicate struggles with temper (Luke 9:54) and selfishness (Mark 10:37). Both times, he and his brother, John, spoke as one

Lessons from his life:
- Many of Jesus' followers do not consider the loss of life too heavy a price to pay

Vital statistics:
- Where: Galilee
- Occupation: Fisherman, disciple
- Relatives: Father: Zebedee. Mother: Salome. Brother: John.
- Contemporaries: Jesus, Pilate, Herod Agrippa

Key verses:
"Then James and John, the sons of Zebedee, came over and spoke to him in a low voice. 'Master,' they said, 'we want you to do us a favor.' 'What is it?' he asked. 'We want to sit on the thrones next to yours in your kingdom,' they said, 'one at your right and the other at your left' " (Mark 10:35–37).

James' story is told in the Gospels. He is also mentioned in Acts 1:14 and 12:2.

10:12 Sodom was an evil city that God destroyed for its great sinfulness (Genesis 19). The city's name is often used to symbolize wickedness. Sodom will suffer at Judgment Day, but these cities who saw the Messiah and rejected him will suffer even more.

10:13 Tyre and Sidon were cities destroyed by God as punishment for their wickedness (see Ezekiel 26—28).

10:15 Capernaum was Jesus' base for his Galilean ministry. The city was at an important crossroads used by traders and the Roman army, and a message proclaimed in Capernaum was likely to go far. But many people of Capernaum did not understand Jesus' miracles or believe his teaching, and the city was included among those who would be judged for rejecting Jesus.

The seventy messengers return
(131)

17When the seventy disciples returned, they joyfully reported to him, "Even the demons obey us when we use your name."

18"Yes," he told them, "I saw Satan falling from heaven as a flash of lightning! 19And I have given you authority over all the power of the Enemy, and to walk among serpents and scorpions and to crush them. Nothing shall injure you! 20However, the important thing is not that demons obey you, but that your names are registered as citizens of heaven."

21Then he was filled with the joy of the Holy Spirit and said, "I praise you, O Father, Lord of heaven and earth, for hiding these things from the intellectuals and worldly wise and for revealing them to those who are as trusting as little children. Yes, thank you, Father, for that is the way you wanted it. 22I am the Agent of my Father in everything; and no one really knows the Son except the Father, and no one really knows the Father except the Son and those to whom the Son chooses to reveal him."

23Then, turning to the twelve disciples, he said quietly, "How privileged you are to see what you have seen. 24Many a prophet and king of old has longed for these days, to see and hear what you have seen and heard!"

Jesus tells the parable of the good Samaritan
(132)

25One day an expert on Moses' laws came to test Jesus' orthodoxy by asking him this question: "Teacher, what does a man need to do to live forever in heaven?"
26Jesus replied, "What does Moses' law say about it?"

27"It says," he replied, "that you must love the Lord your God with all your heart, and with all your soul, and with all your strength, and with all your mind. And you must love your neighbor just as much as you love yourself."

10:21 little children, literally, "babies."

Cross references:

10:18 Jn 12:31; 1 Jn 3:8; Rev 9:1; 12:8,9

10:19 Acts 28:5

10:20 Ex 32:32; Ps 69:28; Isa 4:3; Phil 4:3; Rev 20:12

10:21 Mt 11:25; 1 Cor 1:19; 2 Cor 2:6

10:22 Mt 28:18; Jn 1:18; 3:35; 5:27; 17:2; Eph 1:21; 2:9

10:23 Mt 13:16

10:24 1 Pet 1:10

10:25 Mt 22:34-40; Mk 12:28-31

10:27 Deut 6:5; Lev 19:18

10:17-20 The disciples had seen tremendous results as they ministered in Jesus' name and with his authority. They were elated by the victories they had witnessed, and Jesus shared their enthusiasm. He brought them down to earth, however, by reminding them of their most important victory—that their names were registered among the citizens of heaven. This honor was more important than any of their accomplishments. As we see God's wonders at work in us and through us, we should not lose sight of the greatest wonder of all—our heavenly citizenship.

10:18 Jesus may have been looking ahead to his victory over Satan at the cross. John 12:31, 32 indicates that Satan would be judged and cast out at the time of Jesus' death. On the other hand, Jesus may have been warning his disciples against pride. Perhaps he was referring to Isaiah 14:12-17, which begins, "How you are fallen from heaven, O Lucifer, son of the morning! . . . For you said to yourself, I will ascend to heaven and rule the angels." Many interpreters identify Lucifer with Satan and say that his pride led to all the evil we see on earth today. To his disciples, who were thrilled with their power over evil spirits, Jesus gave this kind of warning: "Yours is the kind of pride that led to Satan's downfall. Be careful!"

10:21 Jesus Christ was conceived by the Holy Spirit (Matthew 1:20), baptized by the Holy Spirit (Matthew 3:16), anointed by the Holy Spirit (Luke 4:18), guided by the Holy Spirit (Matthew 4:1; Luke 4:1), and empowered by the Holy Spirit (Luke 4:14). He lived in union with the Holy Spirit, dependent upon him. Here we see him filled with the joy of the Holy Spirit. Jesus' relationship with the Holy Spirit is a model for our Christian life. We need to be filled with the Holy Spirit and live by his power and joy.

10:21 Jesus thanked God that spiritual truth was for everyone, not just the elite. Many of life's rewards seem to go to the intelligent, the rich, the good-looking, or the powerful, but the Kingdom of God is equally available to all, regardless of position or abilities. We come to Jesus not through strength or brains, but through childlike trust. Jesus is not against those engaged in scholarly pursuits; he is against spiritual pride (being wise in your own eyes). Join Jesus in thanking God that we all have equal access to him. Trust in God, not in your personal qualifications or your citizenship in the Kingdom.

10:22 Christ's mission was to reveal God the Father to people. His Word brought difficult ideas down to earth. He explained God's love through parables, teachings, and most of all his life. By examining Jesus' actions, principles, and attitudes we can understand God more clearly.

10:23, 24 The disciples had a fantastic opportunity—they were eyewitnesses to Christ, the Son of God. But for many months they took Jesus for granted, not really listening to him or obeying him. We also have a privileged position—two thousand years of church history, the Bible in hundreds of languages and translations, many excellent pastors and speakers. Yet how often we take them for granted, forgetting our tremendous blessings. Remember, with privilege comes responsibility. Because we are privileged to know so much about Christ, we must be careful to follow him.

10:24 Old Testament men such as King David and the prophet Isaiah made many God-inspired predictions that Jesus fulfilled. As Peter later wrote, they wondered what their words could possibly mean (1 Peter 1:10-13), and Jesus said that they "longed for these days"—earnestly desired to see God's Kingdom in its fullness.

10:27 This expert in Moses' law was quoting Leviticus 19:18 and Deuteronomy 6:5. Jesus talked more about these laws elsewhere (see Matthew 19:16-22 and Mark 10:17-22).

10:28
Lev 18:5
Neh 9:29
Ezek 20:11
Rom 10:5

28"Right!" Jesus told him. *"Do* this and *you* shall live!"

10:29
Lk 16:15

29The man wanted to justify (his lack of love for some kinds of people), so he asked, "Which neighbors?"

30Jesus replied with an illustration: "A Jew going on a trip from Jerusalem to Jericho was attacked by bandits. They stripped him of his clothes and money and beat him up and left him lying half dead beside the road.

10:31
Ps 38:11

31"By chance a Jewish priest came along; and when he saw the man lying there, he crossed to the other side of the road and passed him by. 32A Jewish Temple-assistant walked over and looked at him lying there, but then went on.

10:33
Jn 4:9

33"But a despised Samaritan came along, and when he saw him, he felt deep pity. 34Kneeling beside him the Samaritan soothed his wounds with medicine and bandaged them. Then he put the man on his donkey and walked along beside him till they came to an inn, where he nursed him through the night. 35The next day he handed the innkeeper two twenty-dollar bills and told him to take care of the man. 'If his bill runs higher than that,' he said, 'I'll pay the difference the next time I am here.'

10:35
Philem 18

36"Now which of these three would you say was a neighbor to the bandits' victim?"

37The man replied, "The one who showed him some pity."

Then Jesus said, "Yes, now go and do the same."

Jesus visits Mary and Martha (133)

10:38
Jn 11:1,5,19,30,
39; 12:2

38As Jesus and the disciples continued on their way to Jerusalem they came to a village where a woman named Martha welcomed them into her home. 39Her sister Mary sat on the floor, listening to Jesus as he talked.

10:29 *wanted to justify (his lack of love for some kinds of people)*, literally, "wanting to justify himself." **10:32** *Jewish Temple-assistant*, literally, "Levite." **10:33** *a despised Samaritan*, literally, "a Samaritan." All Samaritans were despised by Jews and the feeling was mutual, due to historic reasons. **10:34** *nursed him through the night*, literally, "took care of him." **10:35** *two twenty-dollar bills*, literally, "two denarii," each the equivalent of a modern day's wage. **10:38** *on their way to Jerusalem*, implied.

A COLLECTION OF ATTITUDES

To the lawyer, the wounded man was a subject to discuss.

To the thieves, the wounded man was someone to use and exploit.

To the religious men, the wounded man was a problem to be avoided.

To the innkeeper, the wounded man was a customer to serve for a fee.

To the Samaritan, the wounded man was a human being worth being cared for and loved.

To Jesus, all of them and all of us were worth dying for.

The needs of others bring out various attitudes in us. Jesus used the story of the good but despised Samaritan to make clear what attitude was acceptable to him. If we are honest, we often will find ourselves in the place of the lawyer, needing to learn again who our neighbor is. Note these different attitudes toward the wounded man.

10:27-37 The legal experts treated the wounded man as a topic for discussion; the thieves, as an object to exploit; the priest, as a problem to avoid; and the temple assistant, as an object of curiosity. Only the Samaritan treated him as a person to love.

10:27-37 From the parable we learn three principles about loving our neighbor: (1) lack of love is often easy to justify; (2) our neighbor is anyone of any race or creed or social background who is in need; and (3) love means acting to meet the need. Wherever you live, there are needy people close by. There is no good rationale for refusing to help.

10:33 There was deep hatred between Jews and Samaritans. The Jews saw themselves as pure descendants of Abraham, while the Samaritans were a mixed race produced when Jews from the Northern Kingdom intermarried with other peoples after Israel's

exile. To this expert in Jewish law, the person least likely to act correctly would be the Samaritan. The expert's attitude betrayed his lack of love, which he had earlier said the law commanded.

10:33-37 This parable pictures the love Jesus has for us. Like the traveler, we have been wounded and left to die, and we can do nothing to save ourselves. But Jesus came along and took us to a place of healing. Our salvation is his doing, not our own.

10:38-42 Mary and Martha both loved Jesus. On this occasion they were both serving him. But Martha implied that Mary's style of serving was inferior to hers. She didn't realize that in her desire to serve, she was actually neglecting him. Are you so busy doing things *for* Jesus that you're not spending any time *with* him? Don't let your service become self-serving. It is important to know *whom* you are serving.

⁴⁰But Martha was the jittery type, and was worrying over the big dinner she was preparing.

She came to Jesus and said, "Sir, doesn't it seem unfair to you that my sister just sits here while I do all the work? Tell her to come and help me."

⁴¹But the Lord said to her, "Martha, dear friend, you are so upset over all these details! ⁴²There is really only one thing worth being concerned about. Mary has discovered it—and I won't take it away from her!"

10:41
Mt 6:25

10:42
Ps 27:4
Phil 3:13,14

Jesus teaches his disciples about prayer
(134)

11 Once when Jesus had been out praying, one of his disciples came to him as he finished and said, "Lord, teach us a prayer to recite just as John taught one to his disciples."

²And this is the prayer he taught them: "Father, may your name be honored for its holiness; send your Kingdom soon. ³Give us our food day by day. ⁴And forgive our sins—for we have forgiven those who sinned against us. And don't allow us to be tempted."

⁵, ⁶Then, teaching them more about prayer, he used this illustration: "Suppose you went to a friend's house at midnight, wanting to borrow three loaves of bread. You would shout up to him, 'A friend of mine has just arrived for a visit and I've nothing to give him to eat.' ⁷He would call down from his bedroom, 'Please don't ask me to get up. The door is locked for the night and we are all in bed. I just can't help you this time.'

⁸"But I'll tell you this—though he won't do it as a friend, if you keep knocking

11:1
2 Cor 3:5

11:2
Isa 11:9; 63:16
Dan 7:14

11:4
Eph 4:32
1 Cor 10:13
Jas 1:13
Rev 3:10

11:8
Lk 18:1

10:41 *Martha, dear friend,* literally, "Martha, Martha." **11:1** *to recite,* implied. **11:5, 6** *Then, teaching them more about prayer.* Some ancient manuscripts add at this point additional portions of the Lord's Prayer as recorded in Mt 6:9-13.

JESUS VISITS MARY AND MARTHA
Jesus, after teaching throughout Galilee, returned to Jerusalem for the Tabernacle Ceremonies (John 7:2). He spoke in Jerusalem and then visited his friends Mary and Martha in the tiny village of Bethany on the slope of the Mount of Olives.

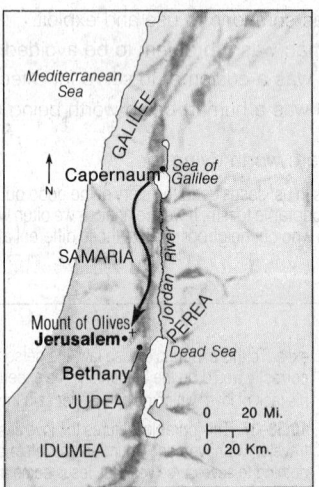

10:42 Jesus did not blame Martha for being concerned about household chores. He was only asking her to set priorities. It is possible for service to Christ to degenerate into mere busy-work that is no longer full of devotion to God.

11:1–4 Notice the order in this prayer. First Jesus praises God; then he makes his requests. Praising God first puts us in the right frame of mind to tell him about our needs. Too often our prayers are more like shopping lists than conversations.

11:2–13 These verses focus on three aspects of prayer: its content (11:2–4), our persistence (11:5–10), and God's faithfulness (11:11–13).

11:3 God's provision is daily, not once for all. We cannot store it up and then cut off communication with God, and we dare not be self-satisfied. If you are running low on strength, ask yourself—how long have I been away from the Source?

11:4 When Jesus taught his disciples to pray, he made forgiveness the cornerstone of their relationship with God. God has forgiven our sins; we must now forgive those who have wronged us. To remain unforgiving shows we have not understood that we ourselves, along wih all other human beings, deeply need to be forgiven. Think of some people who have wronged you. Have you truly forgiven them, or do you still carry a grudge against them? How will God deal with you if he treats you as you treat others?

11:8 Persistence in prayer overcomes our insensitiveness, not God's. It does more to change our hearts and minds than his. It helps us understand and express the intensity of our need. It is helpful to pray as if the answer depended on our prayer, but then to trust that the answer depends on God. Persistence in prayer helps us recognize God's work when we see it.

11:13 Good fathers, even though they make mistakes, treat their children well. How much better our perfect heavenly Father treats his children! The most important gift he ever gives us is the Holy Spirit (Acts 2:1–4), which he promised to give to all believers after his death, resurrection, and return to heaven (John 15:26).

long enough he will get up and give you everything you want—just because of your

11:9
Mt 7:7; 21:22
Mk 11:24
Jn 15:7
Jas 1:6
1 Jn 3:22; 5:14

11:11
Mt 7:9

11:13
Isa 44:3
Jas 1:15

persistence. 9And so it is with prayer—keep on asking and you will keep on getting; keep on looking and you will keep on finding; knock and the door will be opened. 10Everyone who asks, receives; all who seek, find; and the door is opened to everyone who knocks.

11"You men who are fathers—if your boy asks for bread, do you give him a stone? If he asks for fish, do you give him a snake? 12If he asks for an egg, do you give him a scorpion? [Of course not!]

13"And if even sinful persons like yourselves give children what they need, don't

11:12 *Of course not,* implied.

MARTHA

Many older brothers and sisters have an irritating tendency to take charge, a habit developed while growing up. We can easily see this pattern in Martha, the older sister of Mary and Lazarus. She was used to being in control.

The fact that Martha, Mary, and Lazarus are remembered for their hospitality takes on added significance when we note that hospitality was a social requirement in Jewish culture at the time. It was considered shameful to turn anyone away from your door. Apparently this family did very well at this practice.

Martha worried about details. She wished to please, to serve, to do the right thing— but she often succeeded in making everyone around her uncomfortable. Perhaps as the oldest, she felt the fear of shame if her home did not measure up to expectations. She tried to do everything she could to make sure that wouldn't happen. As a result, she found it hard to relax and enjoy her guests. She found it even harder to accept Mary's lack of cooperation in all the preparations. Her feelings were so intense that she finally asked Jesus to settle the matter. He gently corrected her attitude and showed her that while her priorities were good, they were not the best. The attention she gave to her guests should be more important than what she tried to do for them.

Later, following her brother Lazarus' death, Martha could hardly help but be herself on two brief occasions. When she heard Jesus was finally coming, though too late, she rushed out to meet him. She expressed her inward conflict of disappointment and hope. Jesus pointed out that her hope was too limited—he was not only Lord beyond death, he was Lord over death—the resurrection and the life! Moments later, Martha again spoke without thinking, pointing out that four-day old corpses are well on their way to decomposition. Her awareness of details sometimes kept her from seeing the whole picture! Jesus was consistently patient with her.

In our last picture of Martha, she is once again serving a meal to Jesus and his disciples. She has not stopped serving. But the Bible records her silence this time. She has begun to learn what her younger sister already knew, that worship begins with silence and listening.

Strengths and accomplishments:
• Known as a hospitable homeowner
• A friend of Jesus, she believed in him with growing faith
• Had a strong desire to do everything exactly right

Weaknesses and mistakes:
• Expected others to agree with her priorities
• Was overly concerned with details
• Tended to feel sorry for herself when her efforts were not recognized
• Limited Jesus' power to this life

Lessons from her life:
• Getting caught up in details can make us forget the main reasons for our actions
• There is a proper time to listen to Jesus and a proper time to work for him

Vital statistics:
• Where: Bethany
• Relatives: Sister: Mary. Brother: Lazarus.

Key verse:
"But Martha was the jittery type, and was worrying over the big dinner she was preparing. She came to Jesus and said, 'Sir, doesn't it seem unfair to you that my sister just sits here while I do all the work? Tell her to come and help me' " (Luke 10:40).

Martha's story is told in Luke 10:38–42 and John 11:17–45.

you realize that your heavenly Father will do at least as much, and give the Holy Spirit to those who ask for him?"

Jesus answers hostile accusations
(135)

14Once, when Jesus cast out a demon from a man who couldn't speak, his voice returned to him. The crowd was excited and enthusiastic, 15but some said, "No wonder he can cast them out. He gets his power from Satan, the king of demons!" 16Others asked for something to happen in the sky to prove his claim of being the Messiah.

17He knew the thoughts of each of them, so he said, "Any kingdom filled with civil war is doomed; so is a home filled with argument and strife. 18Therefore, if what you say is true, that Satan is fighting against himself by empowering me to cast out his demons, how can his kingdom survive? 19And if I am empowered by Satan, what about your own followers? For they cast out demons! Do you think this proves they are possessed by Satan? Ask *them* if you are right! 20But if I am casting out demons because of power from God, it proves that the Kingdom of God has arrived.

21"For when Satan, strong and fully armed, guards his palace, it is safe— 22until someone stronger and better-armed attacks and overcomes him and strips him of his weapons and carries off his belongings.

23"Anyone who is not for me is against me; if he isn't helping me, he is hurting my cause.

24"When a demon is cast out of a man, it goes to the deserts, searching there for rest; but finding none, it returns to the person it left, 25and finds that its former home is all swept and clean. 26Then it goes and gets seven other demons more evil than itself, and they all enter the man. And so the poor fellow is seven times worse off than he was before."

27As he was speaking, a woman in the crowd called out, "God bless your

11:14
Mt 9:32
12:22-32,38-45
Mk 3:22-30

11:15
Mt 9:34

11:16
Mt 16:1

11:17
Jn 2:25
Rev 2:23

11:19
Mk 9:38
Lk 9:49

11:20
Ex 8:19
Jn 3:2
Acts 2:22; 10:38

11:21
Eph 2:2; 6:12
1 Pet 5:8

11:22
Isa 53:12
Col 2:15
Heb 7:25

11:26
Jn 5:14
Heb 6:4; 10:26
2 Pet 2:20

11:27
Lk 1:28,48

11:15 *from Satan,* literally, "from Beelzebub." **11:16** *Others asked for something to happen in the sky to prove his claim of being the Messiah,* implied. Literally, "Others, tempting, sought of him a sign from heaven." **11:21** *Satan,* literally, "the Strong." **11:25** *is all swept and clean.* But empty, since the person is neutral about Christ. **11:26** *seven times,* implied.

11:14-23 A similar but separate event is reported in Matthew 12:22-45 and Mark 3:20-30. These are different because the event described by Luke happened in Judea while the other two accounts took place in Galilee. According to Luke, Jesus spoke to the crowds; in Matthew and Mark he accused the Pharisees.

11:19 There are two common interpretations to these verses: (1) Some of the Pharisees' followers actually performed exorcisms to cast out demons. If this was so, the Pharisees' accusations were becoming more desperate. To accuse Jesus of being empowered by Satan because he was casting out demons was to say their own people were doing Satan's work as well. Jesus turned the leaders' accusation into words against them. (2) Another possibility, as indicated by other translations, is that the Pharisees' followers were *not* casting out demons; and if they had tried, they did not succeed. Jesus first dismisses their claim as absurd (why would the devil cast out his own demons?—11:18). Then he engages in a little irony—"What about your own followers?" (Another translation reads, "by whom do your followers drive them out?") Finally he concludes that his work of casting out demons proves that the Kingdom of God has arrived.

Satan, who had controlled the kingdom of this world for thousands of years, was now being controlled and defeated by Jesus and the Kingdom of Heaven. Jesus' Kingdom began to take power at his birth, grew as he resisted the wilderness temptations, established itself through his teachings and healings, blossomed in victory at his resurrection and at Pentecost, and will become permanent and universal at his Second Coming. Though these two interpretations differ, they arrive at the same conclusion—the Kingdom of God has arrived with the coming of Jesus Christ.

11:21 The word "Satan" here is literally "the strong man." Jesus may have taken his words from Isaiah 49:24-26. Regardless of how great Satan's power is, Jesus is stronger and will bind Satan and dispose of him for eternity (see Revelation 20:2, 10).

11:23 Jesus says, "Anyone who is not for me is against me," while earlier he stated, "Anyone who is not against *you*, is for *you.*" People who are neutral toward Christians are actually helping them more than hurting them because they are not setting up barriers. But while people can be neutral toward Christians, they cannot be neutral in their relationship with Jesus. You can't be neutral in the battle between Jesus and Satan. You can't be aloof or noncommittal, because there are only two sides. Since God has already won the battle, why be on the losing side? If you aren't actively for Christ, you are against him.

11:24-26 Jesus is illustrating an unfortunate human tendency—our desire to reform often does not last long. In Judea's history, almost as soon as a good king pulled down idols, a bad king set them up again. It is not enough to be emptied of evil; we must then be filled with the power of the Holy Spirit to accomplish God's new purpose in our lives (see also Matthew 12:43-45; Galatians 5:22).

11:27, 28 Jesus was speaking to people who put extremely high value on family ties. Their genealogies were important guarantees that they were part of God's chosen people. A man's value came from his ancestors, and a woman's value came from the sons she bore. Jesus' response to the woman meant that a person's individual decisions are more important than his or her place on the family tree. Consistent with Luke's emphasis on Jesus' ministry to women, Jesus' response also showed that a woman is important

mother—the womb from which you came, and the breasts that gave you suck!"

11:28
Mt 7:21
Lk 8:21
Jas 1:25

28He replied, "Yes, but even more blessed are all who hear the Word of God and put it into practice."

Jesus warns against unbelief
(136)

11:29
Mt 12:38-40

29, 30As the crowd pressed in upon him, he preached them this sermon: "These are evil times, with evil people. They keep asking for some strange happening in the skies [to prove I am the Messiah], but the only proof I will give them is a miracle like that of Jonah, whose experiences proved to the people of Nineveh that God had sent him. My similar experience will prove that God has sent me to these people.

11:30
Jonah 1:17; 2:10

11:31
1 Kgs 10:1
Isa 9:6
Rom 9:5
Phil 2:10
Tit 2:13

31"And at the Judgment Day the Queen of Sheba shall arise and point her finger at this generation, condemning it, for she went on a long, hard journey to listen to the wisdom of Solomon; but one far greater than Solomon is here [and few pay any attention].

11:32
Jn 3:5

32"The men of Nineveh, too, shall arise and condemn this nation, for they repented at the preaching of Jonah; and someone far greater than Jonah is here [but this nation won't listen].

Jesus teaches about the light within
(137)

11:33
Mt 5:15
Mk 4:21
Lk 8:16

33"No one lights a lamp and hides it! Instead, he puts it on a lampstand to give light to all who enter the room. 34Your eyes light up your inward being. A pure eye lets sunshine into your soul. A lustful eye shuts out the light and plunges you into darkness. 35So watch out that the sunshine isn't blotted out. 36If you are filled with light within, with no dark corners, then your face will be radiant too, as though a floodlight is beamed upon you."

11:34
Mt 6:22

Jesus criticizes the religious leaders
(138)

11:38
Mk 7:3

37, 38As he was speaking, one of the Pharisees asked him home for a meal. When Jesus arrived, he sat down to eat without first performing the ceremonial washing required by Jewish custom. This greatly surprised his host.

11:39
Mt 23:25
2 Tim 3:5
Tit 1:15

39Then Jesus said to him, "You Pharisees wash the outside, but inside you are still dirty—full of greed and wickedness! 40Fools! Didn't God make the inside as well as the outside? 41Purity is best demonstrated by generosity.

11:41
Isa 58:7

11:31 the Queen of Sheba, literally, "Queen of the South." See 1 Kgs 10.   **11:32** but this nation won't listen, implied.

---

for more than her reproductive ability.

11:29, 30 When Jesus used Jonah's experience to illustrate his approaching death and resurrection, he was also affirming the historical fact of Jonah's life and the validity of his story in the book of Jonah. God asked Jonah to preach repentance from sin to the Gentiles (non-Jews). Jesus was affirming his message. Salvation is not only for Jews, but all people.

11:29-32 The cruel, warlike men of Assyria repented when Jonah preached to them—and Jonah did not really care about them. The heathen Queen of Sheba praised the God of Israel when she heard Solomon's wisdom, and Solomon was full of faults. By contrast, Jesus, the perfect Son of God, came to people that he loved dearly—and they rejected him. Thus God's chosen people made themselves more liable to judgment than either a notoriously wicked nation or a powerful pagan queen. Compare Luke 10:10-15 where Jesus says the evil cities of Sodom, Gomorrah, Tyre, and Sidon will be judged less harshly than the cities of Judea and Galilee who rejected Jesus' message.

11:31, 32 The people of Nineveh and the Queen of Sheba had turned to God with far less evidence than Jesus was giving his

listeners—and far less than we have today. We have eyewitness reports of the risen Jesus, the continuing power of the Holy Spirit unleashed at Pentecost, easy access to the Bible, and knowledge of 2,000 years of Christ acting through his church in history. Do you take full advantage of your opportunities to know God?

11:33-36 The light is Christ; the eye represents spiritual understanding and insight. Lust—the unnatural or greedy desire for anything, not just sex—makes the eye less sensitive and blots out the light of Christ's presence. If you have a hard time seeing God at work, check your vision. Are any sinful desires blinding you to Christ?

11:37-39 This washing was not done for health reasons, but as a symbol of moral purity. Not only had the Pharisees made the practice a public show; they had also commanded everyone to follow a practice originally intended only for the priests.

11:41 The Pharisees loved to think of themselves as pure, but their stinginess toward God and the poor proved they were not as pure as they thought. How do you use the resources God has entrusted to you? Are you generous in meeting the needs around you? Your generosity reveals much about the purity of your heart.

42"But woe to you Pharisees! For though you are careful to tithe even the smallest part of your income, you completely forget about justice and the love of God. You should tithe, yes, but you should not leave these other things undone.

43"Woe to you Pharisees! For how you love the seats of honor in the synagogues and the respectful greetings from everyone as you walk through the markets! 44Yes, awesome judgment is awaiting you. For you are like hidden graves in a field. Men go by you with no knowledge of the corruption they are passing."

45"Sir," said an expert in religious law who was standing there, "you have insulted my profession, too, in what you just said."

46"Yes," said Jesus, "the same horrors await you! For you crush men beneath impossible religious demands—demands that you yourselves would never think of trying to keep. 47Woe to you! For you are exactly like your ancestors who killed the prophets long ago. 48Murderers! You agree with your fathers that what they did was right—you would have done the same yourselves.

49"This is what God says about you: 'I will send prophets and apostles to you, and you will kill some of them and chase away the others.'

50"And you of this generation will be held responsible for the murder of God's servants from the founding of the world— 51from the murder of Abel to the murder of Zechariah who perished between the altar and the sanctuary. Yes, it will surely be charged against you.

52"Woe to you experts in religion! For you hide the truth from the people. You won't accept it for yourselves, and you prevent others from having a chance to believe it."

53, 54The Pharisees and legal experts were furious; and from that time on they plied him fiercely with a host of questions, trying to trap him into saying something for which they could have him arrested.

11:42
Mt 23:23
1 Sam 15:22
Hos 6:6

11:43
Mt 23:6,7
Mk 12:38,39

11:46
Mt 23:4

11:47
Mt 23:29-36
Acts 7:51,52

11:48
Acts 8:1; 22:20

11:49
Prov 8:12,22-31
Mt 11:19; 23:34
Lk 7:35
1 Cor 1:24,30
Col 2:3

11:50
1 Thess 2:15

11:51
Gen 4:8
2 Chron 24:20,21

11:52
Mt 23:13

11:53
Mk 12:13

Jesus speaks against hypocrisy
(139)

12 Meanwhile the crowds grew until thousands upon thousands were milling about and crushing each other. He turned now to his disciples and warned

12:1
Mt 16:6,11,12

11:42 It is easy to rationalize not helping others because we have already given to the church, but a person who follows Jesus should share with needy neighbors. While tithing is important to the life of the church, our compassion must not stop there. Where we can help, we should help.

11:44 The Old Testament laws said a person who touched a grave was unclean (Numbers 19:16). Jesus accused the Pharisees of making other men unclean by their spiritual rottenness. Like graves hidden in a field, they corrupted everyone that came in contact with them.

11:46 These "impossible religious demands" were the details the Pharisees had added to God's law. To the commandment, "Remember to observe the Sabbath as a holy day" (Exodus 20:8), for example, they had added instructions regarding how far a person could walk on the Sabbath, which kinds of knots could be tied, and how much weight could be carried. Healing a person was considered unlawful work on the Sabbath, although rescuing a trapped animal was permitted (14:5). No wonder Jesus condemned their additions to the law.

11:49 God's prophets had been persecuted and murdered throughout history. But this generation was rejecting more than a human prophet—they were rejecting God himself. This quotation is not from the Old Testament. Jesus was prophesying a message from God.

11:50, 51 Abel's death is recorded in Genesis 4:8. For more about him, see his Profile in Genesis 5. The prophet Zechariah's death is recorded in 2 Chronicles 24:20–22 (the last book in the Hebrew canon). Why were all these sins charged against this particular generation? Because they were rejecting Christ in the

flesh, the one to whom all their history and prophecy was pointing.

11:52 How did the experts in religion hide the truth? Through their erroneous interpretations of Scripture and their added man-made rules, they made God's truth hard to understand and practice. On top of that, they were bad examples, arguing their way out of demands they placed on others. Caught up in a religion of their own making, they could no longer lead the people to God. They had closed the door of God's love to the people and thrown away the key.

11:52 Jesus criticized the Pharisees harshly because they (1) washed their hands but not their hearts, (2) remembered to tithe but forgot justice, (3) loved people's praise, (4) made impossible religious demands, and (5) would not accept the truth about Jesus and prevented others from believing it as well. They went wrong by focusing on outward appearances and ignoring the inner condition of their hearts. We do the same when our service is motivated by a desire to be seen rather than from a pure heart and love for others. Others may be fooled, but God isn't. Don't be a Christian on the outside only. Bring your inner life under God's control, and your outer life will naturally reflect him.

11:53, 54 The Pharisees hoped to arrest Jesus for blasphemy, heresy, and law breaking. They were stung to fury by Jesus' words about them, but they couldn't arrest him for that. They had to find a legal way to get rid of Jesus.

12:1, 2 As Jesus watched the huge crowds approach to hear him, he warned his disciples against hypocrisy—trying to appear good when one's heart is far from God. The Pharisees could not keep their attitudes hidden forever. Their selfishness would grow like yeast, and soon they would expose themselves for what they really

them, "More than anything else, beware of these Pharisees and the way they pretend to be good when they aren't. But such hypocrisy cannot be hidden forever. ²It will become as evident as yeast in dough. ³Whatever they have said in the dark shall be heard in the light, and what you have whispered in the inner rooms shall be broadcast from the housetops for all to hear!

⁴"Dear friends, don't be afraid of these who want to murder you. They can only kill the body; they have no power over your souls. ⁵But I'll tell you whom to fear—fear God who has the power to kill and then cast into hell.

⁶"What is the price of five sparrows? A couple of pennies? Not much more than that. Yet God does not forget a single one of them. ⁷And he knows the number of hairs on your head! Never fear, you are far more valuable to him than a whole flock of sparrows.

⁸"And I assure you of this: I, the Messiah, will publicly honor you in the presence of God's angels if you publicly acknowledge me here on earth as your Friend. ⁹But I will deny before the angels those who deny me here among men. ¹⁰(Yet those who speak against me may be forgiven—while those who speak against the Holy Spirit shall never be forgiven.)

¹¹"And when you are brought to trial before these Jewish rulers and authorities in the synagogues, don't be concerned about what to say in your defense, ¹²for the Holy Spirit will give you the right words even as you are standing there."

Jesus tells the parable of the rich fool (140)

¹³Then someone called from the crowd, "Sir, please tell my brother to divide my father's estate with me."

¹⁴But Jesus replied, "Man, who made me a judge over you to decide such things as that? ¹⁵Beware! Don't always be wishing for what you don't have. For real life and real living are not related to how rich we are."

12:3 they, literally, "you."   **12:8** the Messiah, literally, "the Son of Man."   **12:10** me, literally, "the Son of Man."

12:2
Mt 10:26-33
Mk 4:22
Lk 8:17

12:5
Heb 10:31
Rev 1:17,18

12:8
Rom 10:9-11
Rev 3:5

12:9
Mk 8:38
Lk 9:26
2 Tim 2:12

12:10
Mt 12:31,32
Mk 3:28,29
1 Jn 5:16

12:11
Ex 4:12
Mt 10:19,20
Mk 13:11
Lk 21:14,15
1 Pet 5:7

12:14
Acts 7:27

12:15
1 Tim 6:6-10
Heb 13:5

---

were—power-hungry impostors, not devoted religious leaders. Is your heart close to or far from God?

12:4, 5 Fear of opposition or ridicule can weaken our witness for Christ. Often we cling to peace and comfort, even at the cost of our walk with God. Jesus reminds us here that we should fear eternal, not merely temporal, consequences. Don't allow fear of a person or some group to keep you from standing up for Christ.

12:7 Our true value is God's estimate of our worth, not our peers'. Other people evaluate and categorize us according to how we perform, what we achieve, and how we look. But God's love gives us the real basis for our worth—we belong to him.

12:8, 9 We deny Jesus when we: (1) hope no one will think we are Christians; (2) decide *not* to speak up for what is right, (3) are silent about our relationship with God; (4) blend into society; (5) accept our culture's non-Christian values. By contrast, we acknowledge him when we: (1) live moral, upright, Christ-honoring lives; (2) look for opportunities to share our faith with others; (3) help others in need, (4) take a stand for justice; (5) love others; (6) acknowledge our loyalty to him; (7) use our life and resources to carry out his desires rather than our own.

12:10 Jesus says that the sin against the Holy Spirit is unforgivable. This has worried many sincere Christians, but it does not need to. The sin against the Holy Spirit involves deliberate and ongoing rejection of his work and thus of God himself. A person who has committed this sin has shut himself off from God so thoroughly that he is unaware of any sin at all. A person who fears having committed it shows, by his very concern, that he has not sinned in this way.

12:11, 12 The disciples knew they could never dominate a religious dispute with the well-educated Jewish leaders.

Nevertheless, they would not be left unprepared. Jesus promised that the Holy Spirit would supply the needed words. The disciples' testimony might not make them look impressive, but it would still point out God's work in the world through Jesus' life. We need to pray for opportunities to speak for God, and then trust him to help us with our words. This promise of courage, however, does not compensate for lack of preparation. Remember that these disciples had three years of teaching and practical application. We too must study God's Word. Then God will bring his truths to mind when we most need them, helping us to present them in the most effective way.

12:13ff Problems like this were often brought to rabbis for them to settle. Jesus' response, though not directly to the topic, is not a change of subject. Rather, Jesus is pointing to a higher issue—a correct attitude toward the accumulation of wealth. Life is more than material goods; far more important is our relationship with God. Jesus put his finger on this questioner's heart. When we bring problems to God in prayer he often does the same—showing us how we need to change and grow in our attitude toward the problem. This is often a different, but more effective answer than we are looking for.

12:15 Jesus says that the good life has nothing to do with being wealthy. This is the exact opposite of what society usually says. Advertisers spend millions of dollars to entice us to think that if we buy more and more of their products, we will be happier, more in tune, more comfortable. How do you respond to the constant pressure to buy? Learn to tune out expensive enticements and concentrate on the truly good life—living in a relationship with God and doing his work.

16Then he gave an illustration: "A rich man had a fertile farm that produced fine crops. 17In fact, his barns were full to overflowing—he couldn't get everything in. He thought about his problem, 18and finally exclaimed, 'I know—I'll tear down my barns and build bigger ones! Then I'll have room enough. 19And I'll sit back and say to myself, "Friend, you have enough stored away for years to come. Now take it easy! Wine, women, and song for you!" '

20"But God said to him, 'Fool! Tonight you die. Then who will get it all?'

21"Yes, every man is a fool who gets rich on earth but not in heaven."

Jesus warns about worry
(141)

22Then turning to his disciples he said, "Don't worry about whether you have enough food to eat or clothes to wear. 23For life consists of far more than food and clothes. 24Look at the ravens—they don't plant or harvest or have barns to store away their food, and yet they get along all right—for God feeds them. And you are far more valuable to him than any birds!

25"And besides, what's the use of worrying? What good does it do? Will it add a single day to your life? Of course not! 26And if worry can't even do such little things as that, what's the use of worrying over bigger things?

27"Look at the lilies! They don't toil and spin, and yet Solomon in all his glory was not robed as well as they are. 28And if God provides clothing for the flowers that are here today and gone tomorrow, don't you suppose that he will provide clothing for you, you doubters? 29And don't worry about food—what to eat and drink; don't worry at all that God will provide it for you. 30All mankind scratches for its daily bread, but your heavenly Father knows your needs. 31He will always give you all you need from day to day if you will make the Kingdom of God your primary concern.

32"So don't be afraid, little flock. For it gives your Father great happiness to give you the Kingdom. 33Sell what you have and give to those in need. This will fatten your purses in heaven! And the purses of heaven have no rips or holes in them. Your treasures there will never disappear; no thief can steal them; no moth can destroy them. 34Wherever your treasure is, there your heart and thoughts will also be.

Jesus warns about preparing for his coming
(142)

35"Be prepared—all dressed and ready— 36for your Lord's return from the

12:19 *Wine, women, and song for you,* literally, "Eat, drink, and be merry."

Cross references:
12:19 Prov 27:1; 1 Cor 15:32; Jas 5:1-5
12:20 Job 27:8; Ps 39:5,6
12:21 Hab 2:9; 1 Tim 6:18,19; Jas 2:5
12:22 Mt 6:25-33; Phil 4:6
12:24 Job 38:41; Ps 147:9
12:25 Ps 39:5
12:27 1 Kgs 10:1-10
12:30 Mt 6:8; Phil 4:19
12:32 Dan 7:27; Eph 1:5
12:33 Mt 6:19-21; 19:21; Acts 2:45; 4:34

12:16-21 The man in Jesus' story died before he could begin to use what was stored in his big barns. Planning for retirement—preparing for life *before* death—is wise, but neglecting life *after* death is disastrous. If you accumulate wealth only to enrich yourself, with no concern for helping others, you will enter eternity empty-handed.

12:18, 19 Why do you save money? To retire? To buy more expensive cars or toys? For security? Jesus challenges us to think beyond earthbound goals and to use what we have been given to help others.

12:22-34 Jesus commands us not to worry. But how can we avoid it? Only our faith can free us from the anxiety that is caused by greed and covetousness. It is good to work and plan responsibly; it is bad to dwell on all the ways our planning could go wrong. Worry is pointless because it can't fill any of our needs; worry is foolish because the Creator of the universe loves us and knows what we need.

12:31 Making the Kingdom of God your primary concern means making Jesus the Lord and King of your life. He must control every area—your work, your play, your plans, your relationships. Is the Kingdom only one of your many concerns, or is it central to all you

do? Are you holding back any areas of your life from God's control? As your Lord and Creator, he is interested in helping provide what you need as well as guiding how you use what he provides.

12:33 Money used as an end in itself quickly traps us and cuts us off from both God and the needy. The key to using money wisely is to see how much we can use for God's purposes, not how much we can accumulate for ourselves. Does God's love touch your wallet? Does your money free you to help others? If so, you are storing up lasting treasures in heaven.

12:34 You cannot separate what you do from what you believe. What you treasure reveals your true priorities. If your priorities were judged by where you put your time, your money, and your energy, what would the verdict be? How should you change the way you use your resources so it more accurately reflects kingdom values?

12:35 In his teaching, Jesus repeatedly said he would leave this world but would return at some future time (see Matthew 24, 25; John 14:1-3). He also says a kingdom is being prepared for his followers. Many Greeks envisioned this as a heavenly, noncorporeal kingdom. Jews—like Isaiah and John the writer of Revelation—saw it as a restored earthly kingdom.

wedding feast. Then you will be ready to open the door and let him in the moment he arrives and knocks. 37There will be great joy for those who are ready and waiting for his return. He himself will seat them and put on a waiter's uniform and serve them as they sit and eat! 38He may come at nine o'clock at night—or even at midnight. But whenever he comes there will be joy for his servants who are ready!

39"Everyone would be ready for him if they knew the exact hour of his return—just as they would be ready for a thief if they knew when he was coming. 40So be ready all the time. For I, the Messiah, will come when least expected."

41Peter asked, "Lord, are you talking just to us or to everyone?"

42, 43, 44And the Lord replied, "I'm talking to any faithful, sensible man whose master gives him the responsibility of feeding the other servants. If his master returns and finds that he has done a good job, there will be a reward—his master will put him in charge of all he owns.

45"But if the man begins to think, 'My Lord won't be back for a long time,' and begins to whip the men and women he is supposed to protect, and to spend his time at drinking parties and in drunkenness— 46well, his master will return without notice and remove him from his position of trust and assign him to the place of the unfaithful. 47He will be severely punished, for though he knew his duty he refused to do it.

48"But anyone who is not aware that he is doing wrong will be punished only lightly. Much is required from those to whom much is given, for their responsibility is greater.

Jesus warns about coming division
(143)

49"I have come to bring fire to the earth, and, oh, that my task were completed! 50There is a terrible baptism ahead of me, and how I am pent up until it is accomplished!

51"Do you think I have come to give peace to the earth? *No!* Rather, strife and division! 52From now on families will be split apart, three in favor of me, and two against—or perhaps the other way around. 53A father will decide one way about me; his son, the other; mother and daughter will disagree; and the decision of an honored mother-in-law will be spurned by her daughter-in-law."

12:40 *the Messiah,* literally, "the Son of Man." 12:53 *the decision of an honored mother-in-law,* implied by ancient custom.

Margin references:

12:37
Jn 13:4

12:39
1 Thess 5:2
Rev 16:15
12:40
Mk 13:32,33

12:42
Mt 24:45-51
1 Cor 4:2
1 Pet 5:4

12:46
1 Thess 5:3
12:47
Num 15:31
Deut 25:1-3
12:48
Lev 5:17
Jn 9:41; 15:22
1 Tim 1:13
Jas 4:17

12:50
Mk 10:38

12:51
Mt 10:34-36
Mic 7:6
Jn 7:43; 9:16
10:19

12:40 Christ's return at an unexpected time is not a trap, a trick by which God hopes to catch us off guard. In fact, God is delaying his return so more will have a better chance to follow Christ (see 2 Peter 3:9). During this time before his return, we have the *opportunity* to live out our beliefs and to reflect Jesus' love as we relate to others.

People who are ready for their Lord's return are (1) not hypocritical, but sincere (12:1); (2) not fearful, but ready to witness (12:4–9); (3) not anxious, but trusting (12:25, 26); (4) not greedy, but generous (12:34); (5) not lazy, but diligent (12:44). Is your life growing more like Christ's so that when he comes, you will be ready to greet him joyfully?

12:42–44 Jesus talks about a reward for those who have been faithful to the Master. While we sometimes experience immediate and material rewards for our obedience to God, this is not always the case. If material rewards came to us for every faithful deed, we would be tempted to boast about our achievements and do good only for what we get. Jesus said that if we look for rewards now, we will lose them later (see Mark 8:36). Our heavenly rewards will be the most accurate reflection of what we have done on earth—and they will be far greater than we could imagine.

12:48 Jesus has told us how to live until he comes. We must watch for him and work diligently to obey his commands. Such attitudes are especially necessary for leaders. Watchful and faithful leaders will be given increased opportunities and responsibilities. The more resources, talent, and understanding we have, the more responsible we are to use them effectively. We must not hesitate, refuse, or serve grudgingly.

12:50 The "terrible baptism" to which Jesus referred is his coming crucifixion. He was talking about both the incredible physical pain and the spiritual pain of experiencing complete separation from God in order to die for the sins of the world.

12:51–53 In these strange and unsettling words, Jesus revealed that his coming often results in conflict. He demands a response, and close groups can be torn apart when some choose to follow him and others refuse to do so. There is no middle ground with Jesus. Loyalties must be declared and commitments made, sometimes the severing of other relationships. Life is easiest when a family unitedly believes in Christ, of course; but this often does not happen. Are you willing to risk your family's approval in order to gain eternal life?

Jesus warns about the future crisis
(144)

54Then he turned to the crowd and said, "When you see clouds beginning to form in the west, you say, 'Here comes a shower.' And you are right. **12:54** Mt 16:2,3

55"When the south wind blows you say, 'Today will be a scorcher.' And it is. **12:55** Job 37:17 56Hypocrites! You interpret the sky well enough, but you refuse to notice the warnings all around you about the crisis ahead. 57Why do you refuse to see for yourselves what is right? **12:56** Lk 21:30,31

58"If you meet your accuser on the way to court, try to settle the matter before it reaches the judge, lest he sentence you to jail; 59for if that happens you won't be free again until the last penny is paid in full." **12:58** Prov 25:8-10 Mt 5:25,26

Jesus calls the people to repent
(145)

13 About this time he was informed that Pilate had butchered some Jews from Galilee as they were sacrificing at the Temple in Jerusalem.

2"Do you think they were worse sinners than other men from Galilee?" he asked. "Is that why they suffered? 3Not at all! And don't you realize that you also will perish unless you leave your evil ways and turn to God? **13:2** Jn 9:2 **13:3** Ezek 18:30

4"And what about the eighteen men who died when the Tower of Siloam fell on them? Were they the worst sinners in Jerusalem? 5Not at all! And you, too, will perish unless you repent." **13:4** Isa 8:6 Jn 9:7,11

6Then he used this illustration: "A man planted a fig tree in his garden and came again and again to see if he could find any fruit on it, but he was always disappointed. 7Finally he told his gardener to cut it down. 'I've waited three years and there hasn't been a single fig!' he said. 'Why bother with it any longer? It's taking up space we can use for something else.' **13:6** Isa 5:2 Mt 21:18,19 Mk 11:12-14,20, 21 Rom 2:4,5

8" 'Give it one more chance,' the gardener answered. 'Leave it another year, and I'll give it special attention and plenty of fertilizer. 9If we get figs next year, fine; if not, I'll cut it down.' " **13:7** Mt 3:10 Lk 3:9 **13:8** 2 Pet 3:9

Jesus heals the handicapped woman
(146)

10One Sabbath as he was teaching in a synagogue, 11he saw a seriously handicapped woman who had been bent double for eighteen years and was unable to straighten herself. **13:10** Mt 4:23

12Calling her over to him Jesus said, "Woman, you are healed of your sickness!"

12:54–57 For most of recorded history, the world's major occupation was farming. The farmer depended directly on the weather for his livelihood. He needed just the right amounts of sun and rain—not too much, not too little—to make his living, and he grew skilled in interpreting natural signs. Jesus was preaching an earth-shaking event that would be even more important than the year's crops—the coming of God's Kingdom. The Kingdom, like a rainstorm or a sunny day, was giving signs that it would soon arrive. But Jesus' hearers, even though they were skilled at interpreting weather signs, were intentionally ignoring the signs of the times. Their values were misplaced.

13:1–5 Pilate may have killed the Galileans because he thought they were rebelling against Rome; those killed by the Tower of Siloam may have been working for the Romans on an aqueduct there. The Pharisees, who were opposed to using force to deal with Rome, would have said the Galileans deserved to die for rebelling. The Zealots, a group of anti-Roman terrorists, would have said the aqueduct workers deserved to die for cooperating. Jesus said that neither the Galileans nor the workers should be blamed for their calamity. Instead, everyone should look to his or her own day of judgment.

13:5 Being killed or staying alive is not a measure of righteousness. Everyone will die; that's part of being human. But not everyone needs to stay dead. Jesus promises that those who believe in him "will not perish but will have eternal life" (John 3:16).

13:6–9 In the Old Testament, a fruitful tree was often used as a symbol of godly living (see, for example, Psalm 1:3 and Jeremiah 17:7, 8). Jesus pointed out what would happen to the other kind of tree—the kind that took time and space and still produced nothing for the patient gardener. This was one way he warned his listeners that God would not tolerate their lack of productivity forever. Luke 3:9 records John the Baptist's version of the same message. Have you been enjoying God's special treatment without giving anything in return? If so, respond to the gardener's patient care and start preparing to bear fruit by living for God.

13:10–17 Why was healing considered work? The religious leaders saw healing as part of a doctor's profession, and practicing one's profession on the Sabbath was prohibited. The synagogue leader could not see beyond the law to Jesus' compassion in healing this handicapped woman. Jesus shamed him and the other leaders by pointing out their hypocrisy. They would untie their cattle and care for them, but they refused to rejoice when a human being was freed from Satan's bondage.

13:13
Mk 5:23

¹³He touched her, and instantly she could stand straight. How she praised and thanked God!

13:14
Ex 20:8,9
Mt 12:9-12
Mk 3:2
Lk 6:7; 14:3
Rom 10:1-4

¹⁴But the local Jewish leader in charge of the synagogue was very angry about it because Jesus had healed her on the Sabbath day. "There are six days of the week to work," he shouted to the crowd. "Those are the days to come for healing, not on the Sabbath!"

13:15
Lk 14:5

¹⁵But the Lord replied, "You hypocrite! You work on the Sabbath! Don't you untie your cattle from their stalls on the Sabbath and lead them out for water? ¹⁶And

13:16
Lk 19:9

is it wrong for me, just because it is the Sabbath day, to free this Jewish woman from the bondage in which Satan has held her for eighteen years?"

13:17
Lk 18:43

¹⁷This shamed his enemies. And all the people rejoiced at the wonderful things he did.

Jesus teaches about the Kingdom of God
(147)

13:18
Gen 1:11,12
Ps 104:12
Ezek 17:22,23
Dan 4:12,21
Mt 13:31,32
Mk 4:30-32

¹⁸Now he began teaching them again about the Kingdom of God: "What is the Kingdom like?" he asked. "How can I illustrate it? ¹⁹It is like a tiny mustard seed planted in a garden; soon it grows into a tall bush and the birds live among its branches.

13:20
Mt 13:33

²⁰, ²¹"It is like yeast kneaded into dough, which works unseen until it has risen high and light."

Jesus teaches about entering the Kingdom
(153)

13:22
Mt 9:35
Mk 6:6

²²He went from city to city and village to village, teaching as he went, always pressing onward toward Jerusalem.

13:24
Mt 7:13,14

²³Someone asked him, "Will only a few be saved?"
And he replied, ²⁴, ²⁵"The door to heaven is narrow. Work hard to get in, for the

---

**SEVEN
SABBATH
MIRACLES**

Jesus sends a demon out of a man	Mark 1:21-28
Jesus heals Peter's mother-in-law	Mark 1:29-31
Jesus heals a lame man by Bethesda Pool	John 5:1-18
Jesus heals a man with a withered hand	Mark 3:1-6
Jesus restores a handicapped woman	Luke 13:10-17
Jesus heals a man with dropsy	Luke 14:1-6
Jesus heals a man born blind	John 9:1-16

Over the centuries, the Jewish religious leaders had added rule after rule to God's law. For example, God's law said the Sabbath is a day of rest (Exodus 20:10, 11). But the religious leaders added to that law, creating one that said, "you cannot heal on the Sabbath" because that is "work." Seven times Jesus healed people on the Sabbath. In doing this, he was challenging these religious leaders to look beneath their rules to their true purpose—to honor God by helping those in need. Would God have been pleased if Jesus had ignored these people?

13:15, 16 The Pharisees hid behind their own set of laws to avoid love's obligations. We too can use the letter of the law to rationalize away our obligation to care for others (for example, tithing regularly then refusing to give help to a needy neighbor). But peoples' needs are more important than laws. Take time to lovingly help others, even if doing so might make you look less spiritual.

13:16 In our fallen world, disease is common. Its causes are many and often multiple—inadequate nutrition, contact with a source of infection, lowered defenses, and even direct attack by Satan. Whatever the immediate cause of our illness, we can trace its original source to Satan, the author of all the evil in our world. The Good News is that Jesus is more powerful than any devil or any disease. He often offers physical healing in this life, and when he returns he will put an end to all disease, injuries, and handicaps.

13:18-21 The general expectation among Jesus' hearers was that the Messiah would come as a great king and leader, freeing

the nation from Rome and restoring Israel's former glory. But Jesus said his Kingdom was beginning small and quietly. Like the tiny mustard seed that grows into an enormous bush or the spoonful of yeast that makes the bread dough double, the Kingdom of God would eventually push outward until the whole world was changed.

13:22 This is the second time Luke has reminded us that Jesus was going intentionally to Jerusalem (the other time is in 9:51). Knowing he was on his way to his death, he continued preaching to large crowds and healing. The prospect of death did not turn Jesus from his mission.

13:24, 25 Finding salvation requires more concentration and effort than most people are willing to put forth. Obviously we cannot save ourselves—there is no way we can work ourselves into God's favor. The work Jesus is recommending is diligently desiring to know God, earnestly striving to establish a relationship with him whatever the cost. We dare not put off doing this work, because the door will not stay open forever.

truth is that many will try to enter but when the head of the house has locked the door, it will be too late. Then if you stand outside knocking, and pleading, 'Lord, open the door for us,' he will reply, 'I do not know you.'

26" 'But we ate with you, and you taught in our streets,' you will say.

27"And he will reply, 'I tell you, I don't know you. You can't come in here, guilty as you are. Go away.'

28"And there will be great weeping and gnashing of teeth as you stand outside and see Abraham, Isaac, Jacob, and all the prophets within the Kingdom of God— 29for people will come from all over the world to take their places there. 30And note this: some who are despised now will be greatly honored then; and some who are highly thought of now will be least important then."

13:26
Tit 1:16
13:27
Ps 6:18
Mt 25:41
13:28
Mt 8:10-12
13:41,42
13:29
Gen 28:14
Isa 49:6-12
60:3
Rev 5:9; 7:9
13:30
Mt 19:30; 20:16
Mk 10:31

Jesus grieves over Jerusalem
(154)

31A few minutes later some Pharisees said to him, "Get out of here if you want to live, for King Herod is after you!"

32Jesus replied, "Go tell that fox that I will keep on casting out demons and doing miracles of healing today and tomorrow; and the third day I will reach my destination. 33Yes, today, tomorrow, and the next day! For it wouldn't do for a prophet of God to be killed except in Jerusalem!

34"O Jerusalem, Jerusalem! The city that murders the prophets. The city that stones those sent to help her. How often I have wanted to gather your children together even as a hen protects her brood under her wings, but you wouldn't let me. 35And now—now your house is left desolate. And you will never again see me until you say, 'Welcome to him who comes in the name of the Lord.' "

13:32
Lk 24:26
Heb 2:10; 5:5,9
7:28
13:33
Mt 16:21
Jn 11:7-10
13:34
Mt 23:37-39
Lk 19:41-44
13:35
Ps 69:25
118:26
Ezek 10:4,18,19
Lk 19:38; 21:24

Jesus heals a man with dropsy
(155)

14 One Sabbath as he was in the home of a member of the Jewish Council, the Pharisees were watching him like hawks to see if he would heal a man who was present who was suffering from dropsy.

3Jesus said to the Pharisees and legal experts standing around, "Well, is it within the Law to heal a man on the Sabbath day, or not?"

4And when they refused to answer, Jesus took the sick man by the hand and healed him and sent him away.

14:1
Mt 12:9-13
Mk 3:1-5
Lk 6:6-11
13:10-16

13:26 27 Jesus is dramatically illustrating the point that the Kingdom of God will be populated with many of the people we least expect.

13:27 The people were eager to know who would be saved. Jesus explained that although many people know something about God, only a few have accepted his forgiveness. Just listening to his words and admiring his miracles is not enough—it is vital to turn from sin and trust in God to save us.

13:29 God's Kingdom will include people from every part of the world. Israel's rejection of Jesus as Messiah would not stop God's plan. True Israel includes all people who believe in God. This is an important fact for Luke to stress as he directs his Gospel to a Gentile audience (see also Romans 4:16-25; Galatians 3:6-9).

13:30 There will be many surprises in God's Kingdom. Some who are despised now will be greatly honored then; some influential people here will be left outside the gates. Many "great" people on this earth (in God's eyes) are virtually ignored by the rest of the world. What matters to God is not one's earthly popularity, status, wealth, heritage, or power, but one's commitment to Christ. How do your values match what the Bible tells us to value? Make sure you put God in first place so you will join the people from all over the world who will take their places in the Kingdom of Heaven.

13:31, 33 Jesus saw the Pharisees as Herod's messengers who would report him. They urged him to leave, because they wanted to stop him from going to Jerusalem. But Jesus' life, work, and death were not to be determined by Herod or the Pharisees. His life was planned and directed by God himself, and his mission would unfold in God's time according to God's plan.

13:33, 34 Why was Jesus aiming for Jerusalem? Jerusalem, the city of God, symbolized the entire nation. It was Israel's largest city and the nation's spiritual and political capital, and Jews from around the world visited it frequently. But Jerusalem had a history of rejecting the prophets sent by God (2 Chronicles 24:19; 1 Kings 19:10; Jeremiah 2:30), and it would reject the Messiah just as it had rejected his forerunners.

14:1-6 Earlier Jesus had been invited to a Pharisee's home for discussion (7:36). This time it was specifically to trap him into saying or doing something for which he could be arrested. It may be surprising to see him on their turf after he had denounced them so many times, but Jesus was unafraid to face the Pharisees even though he knew their motive was to trick him into breaking their laws.

14:2 Luke, the doctor, uses the medical term for this man's disease—he was suffering from *dropsy*. This disease results in an abnormal accumulation of fluid in body tissues and cavities.

5Then he turned to them: "Which of you doesn't work on the Sabbath?" he asked. "If your cow falls into a pit, don't you proceed at once to get it out?"

6Again they had no answer.

Jesus teaches about seeking honor
(156)

7When he noticed that all who came to the dinner were trying to sit near the head of the table, he gave them this advice: 8"If you are invited to a wedding feast, don't always head for the best seat. For if someone more respected than you shows up, 9the host will bring him over to where you are sitting and say, 'Let this man sit here instead.' And you, embarrassed, will have to take whatever seat is left at the foot of the table!

10"Do this instead—start at the foot; and when your host sees you he will come and say, 'Friend, we have a better place than this for you!' Thus you will be honored in front of all the other guests. 11For everyone who tries to honor himself shall be humbled; and he who humbles himself shall be honored." 12Then he turned to his host. "When you put on a dinner," he said, "don't invite friends, brothers, relatives, and rich neighbors! For they will return the invitation. 13Instead, invite the poor, the crippled, the lame, and the blind. 14Then at the resurrection of the godly, God will reward you for inviting those who can't repay you."

Jesus tells the parable of the great feast
(157)

15Hearing this, a man sitting at the table with Jesus exclaimed, "What a privilege it would be to get into the Kingdom of God!"

16Jesus replied with this illustration: "A man prepared a great feast and sent out many invitations. 17When all was ready, he sent his servant around to notify the guests that it was time for them to arrive. 18But they all began making excuses. One said he had just bought a field and wanted to inspect it, and asked to be excused. 19Another said he had just bought five pair of oxen and wanted to try them out. 20Another had just been married and for that reason couldn't come.

21"The servant returned and reported to his master what they had said. His master was angry and told him to go quickly into the streets and alleys of the city and to invite the beggars, crippled, lame, and blind. 22But even then, there was still room.

14:10
Prov 15:33
18:12; 25:6,7

14:11
Ps 18:27
Prov 29:23
Mt 23:12
Lk 18:14
Jas 4:6
1 Pet 5:5

14:13
Job 31:17

14:14
Jn 5:28,29
Acts 24:15

14:15
Mt 22:1-10

14:16
Rev 19:9

14:20
Deut 24:15
1 Cor 7:33

14:21
Acts 13:46

14:7–14 Jesus taught two lessons here. First he spoke to the guests, telling them not to seek places of honor. Service is more important in God's Kingdom than status. Second he told the host not to be exclusive about whom he invites. God opens his Kingdom to everyone—especially to those who can never repay his invitation.

14:7–11 Jesus advised people not to rush for the best seats at a feast. People today are just as eager to raise their social status, whether by being with the right people, dressing for success, or driving the right car. Wanting a nice car or hoping to be successful in your work is not wrong in itself—it is wrong only when you want these things just to impress others. Whom do you try to impress? Rather than aiming for prestige, look for a place where you can serve. If God wants you to serve on a wider scale, he will invite you to take a higher place.

14:11 How can we humble ourselves? Some people try to give the appearance of humility in order to manipulate others. But truly humble people compare themselves only with Christ, realize their own sinfulness, and understand their limitations in ability, moral performance, and knowledge. Humility is not self-degradation; it is realistic affirmation. Truly humble people do not get that way by trying to be humble; they are humble because of their relationship with God.

14:15–24 The man with Jesus saw the glory of the Kingdom of God, but failed to see how to get in. Jesus' story shows how we often resist God's invitation to his banquet because it's

inconvenient. Whether the excuse is business, marriage, wealth, or anything else, we can resist or delay responding to God's invitation. Are you making excuses to avoid responding to God's call? Jesus says not to make excuses. The time will come when God will stop inviting us, and it will be too late to get into the banquet.

14:16ff It was customary to send two invitations to a party—the first to announce it, the second to tell the guests that all was ready. The guests in Jesus' story insulted the host by making excuses when he issued the second invitation. In Israel's history, God's first invitation came from the prophets; the second came from his Son. The religious leaders accepted the first invitation. They believed the prophets, but they insulted God by refusing to believe his Son. Thus, as the master in the story sent his servant into the streets to invite the needy to his banquet, so God sent his Son to the whole world of needy people to tell them God's Kingdom had arrived and was ready for them.

14:16ff In this chapter we read Jesus' words against status-seeking and in favor of hard work and even suffering. Let's not lose sight of the purpose of all our humility and self-sacrifice—a joyous banquet with our Lord! God never asks us to suffer for the sake of suffering. He never asks us to give up something good unless he plans to replace it with something even better. He is not calling us to join him in a labor camp but in a feast—the wedding feast of the Lamb (Revelation 19:6–9), when God and his beloved church will be joined forever.

23" 'Well, then,' said his master, 'go out into the country lanes and out behind the hedges and urge anyone you find to come, so that the house will be full. 24For none of those I invited first will get even the smallest taste of what I had prepared for them.' "

14:24
Mt 8:12; 21:43
Heb 3:18,19

Jesus teaches about the cost of being a disciple
(158)

25Great crowds were following him. He turned around and addressed them as follows: 26"Anyone who wants to be my follower must love me far more than he does his own father, mother, wife, children, brothers, or sisters—yes, more than his own life—otherwise he cannot be my disciple. 27And no one can be my disciple who does not carry his own cross and follow me.

14:26
Mt 10:37,38
Rev 12:11
14:27
Mt 16:24
Mk 8:34
Lk 9:23

28"But don't begin until you count the cost. For who would begin construction of a building without first getting estimates and then checking to see if he has enough money to pay the bills? 29Otherwise he might complete only the foundation before running out of funds. And then how everyone would laugh!

30" 'See that fellow there?' they would mock. 'He started that building and ran out of money before it was finished!'

31"Or what king would ever dream of going to war without first sitting down with his counselors and discussing whether his army of 10,000 is strong enough to defeat the 20,000 men who are marching against him?

14:33
Mt 19:27,28
Lk 18:29,30
Phil 3:7
Heb 11:26

32"If the decision is negative, then while the enemy troops are still far away, he will send a truce team to discuss terms of peace. 33So no one can become my disciple unless he first sits down and counts his blessings—and then renounces them all for me.

14:34
Mt 5:13
Mk 9:50

34"What good is salt that has lost its saltiness? 35Flavorless salt is fit for nothing—not even for fertilizer. It is worthless and must be thrown out. Listen well, if you would understand my meaning."

14:35
Mt 11:15
13:9,43
Mk 4:9,23
Lk 8:8
Rev 2:11

Jesus tells the parable of the lost sheep
(159)

15 Dishonest tax collectors and other notorious sinners often came to listen to Jesus' sermons; 2but this caused complaints from the Jewish religious leaders and the experts on Jewish law because he was associating with such despicable people—even eating with them!

15:1
Mt 9:10,11
Lk 5:29,30
19:7
Acts 11:3
Gal 2:12
1 Tim 1:15,16

3, 4So Jesus used this illustration: "If you had a hundred sheep and one of them

14:26 *must love me far more than . . .* literally, "If anyone comes to me and does not hate his father and mother. . . ."
14:28 *But don't begin until you count the cost,* implied in vs 33.

14:27 Jesus' audience was well aware of what it meant to carry one's own cross. When the Romans led a criminal to his execution site, he was forced to carry the cross on which he was to be hanged. This showed his submission to Rome and warned observers that they'd better submit too. Jesus gave this teaching to get the crowds to think through their enthusiasm for him. He encouraged the superficial either to go deeper or to turn back. Following Christ means total submission to him—perhaps even to death.

14:33 When a builder doesn't count the cost or figures it inaccurately, his building may be left half completed. Will your Christian life be only half built and then abandoned because you did not count the cost of commitment to Jesus? What are those costs? A Christian may face loss of social status or wealth. He may have to give up control over his money, his time, or his career. He may be hated, separated from his family, and even put to death. Following Christ does not mean a trouble-free life. We must carefully count the cost of becoming Christ's disciples so that we know what we are getting into and are not later tempted to turn back.

14:34 Salt can lose its flavor. When it gets wet and then dries, nothing is left but a tasteless residue. Many Christians blend into

the world and avoid the cost of standing for Christ, but Jesus says if Christians lose their distinctive saltiness, they become worthless. Just as salt flavors and preserves food, we are to preserve the good in the world, help keep it from spoiling, and bring new flavor to life. This requires planning, willing sacrifice, and unswerving commitment to Christ's Kingdom. Being "salty" is not easy, but if a Christian fails in this function, he fails to represent Christ in the world. How salty are you?

15:2 Why were the Pharisees bothered that Jesus associated with these people? The religious leaders were always careful to stay "clean" according to Old Testament law. In fact, they went well beyond the law in their avoidance of certain people and situations and in their ritual washings. By contrast, Jesus took the concept of "cleanness" lightly. He risked defilement by touching lepers and by neglecting to wash in the Pharisees' prescribed manner, and he showed complete disregard for the sanctions against associating with certain classes of sinners. He came to offer salvation to sinners, to show that God loves them. Jesus didn't worry about these accusations. Instead he continued going to those who needed him, regardless of their sinfulness and the effect they might have on his reputation.

15:3–6 It seems foolish for the shepherd to leave the 99 sheep to

15:4
Ezek 34:11,12
Jn 10:11

15:6
1 Pet 2:25

15:7
Lk 5:32

strayed away and was lost in the wilderness, wouldn't you leave the ninety-nine others to go and search for the lost one until you found it? ⁵And then you would joyfully carry it home on your shoulders. ⁶When you arrived you would call together your friends and neighbors to rejoice with you because your lost sheep was found.

⁷"Well, in the same way heaven will be happier over one lost sinner who returns to God than over ninety-nine others who haven't strayed away!

Jesus tells the parable of the lost coin
(160)

15:10
Ezek 18:23

⁸"Or take another illustration: A woman has ten valuable silver coins and loses one. Won't she light a lamp and look in every corner of the house and sweep every nook and cranny until she finds it? ⁹And then won't she call in her friends and neighbors to rejoice with her? ¹⁰In the same way there is joy in the presence of the angels of God when one sinner repents."

Jesus tells the parable of the lost son
(161)

15:12
Deut 21:17

¹¹To further illustrate the point, he told them this story: "A man had two sons. ¹²When the younger told his father, 'I want my share of your estate now, instead of waiting until you die!' his father agreed to divide his wealth between his sons.

¹³"A few days later this younger son packed all his belongings and took a trip to a distant land, and there wasted all his money on parties and prostitutes. ¹⁴About the time his money was gone a great famine swept over the land, and he began to starve. ¹⁵He persuaded a local farmer to hire him to feed his pigs. ¹⁶The boy became so hungry that even the pods he was feeding the swine looked good to him. And no one gave him anything.

15:18
Lam 3:40
Lk 18:13,14

¹⁷"When he finally came to his senses, he said to himself, 'At home even the hired men have food enough and to spare, and here I am, dying of hunger! ¹⁸I will go home to my father and say, "Father, I have sinned against both heaven and you, ¹⁹and am no longer worthy of being called your son. Please take me on as a hired man."'

15:20
Gen 45:14; 46:29

²⁰"So he returned home to his father. And while he was still a long distance away, his father saw him coming, and was filled with loving pity and ran and embraced him and kissed him.

---

go search for just one. But God's love for each individual is so great that he seeks each one out and rejoices when he or she is "found." Jesus associated with sinners because he was going to the lost sheep—sinners who were considered beyond hope—to bring them the Good News of God's Kingdom.

15:8-10 Palestinian women received ten silver coins as a wedding gift. These coins held sentimental value like that of a wedding ring, and to lose one was extremely distressing. Just as a woman would rejoice at finding her lost coin or ring, so the angels would rejoice over a repentant sinner. Each individual is precious to God. He grieves over every loss and rejoices whenever one of his children is found and brought into his Kingdom.

15:10 We can perhaps understand a God who would forgive sinners who crawl to him for mercy, but a God who searches for sinners and then forgives them must have extraordinary love! This is the kind of love that prompted Jesus to come to earth to search for lost people and save them. This is the kind of extraordinary love God has for you. If you feel far from God, don't despair. He is seaching for you.

15:12 The younger son's share of the estate was one third (Deuteronomy 21:17). In most cases he would have received this at his father's death, although fathers sometimes chose to divide up their inheritance early and retire from managing their estates. What is unusual here is that the younger one initiated the division of the estate. This showed disregard for his father's

authority as head of the family.

15:15 According to Moses' law, pigs were unclean animals (Leviticus 11:2–8; Deuteronomy 14:8). This meant that they could not be eaten or used for sacrifices. And to protect themselves from defilement, Jews would not even touch them. For a Jew to stoop to feeding pigs was a great humiliation, and for this young man to eat food the pigs had touched was to be degraded beyond belief. The younger son had truly sunk to the depths.

15:17 Some people need to hit bottom in order to come to their senses. The son's attitude was based on a desire to be free to live as he pleased. That is not so different from the desires of most people in our world today. It may take great sorrow and tragedy to cause them to look up to the only One who can help them. Are you trying to live life your way, selfishly pushing aside anything that gets in your way? Don't take leave of your senses—stop and look before you hit bottom, and save yourself and your family much grief.

15:20 In the two preceding stories, the seeker actively looked for the coin and the sheep, who could not return by themselves. In this story, the father watched and waited. He was dealing with a human being with a will of his own, but he was ready should his son return. God's love is constant and waiting. He will search for us and give us opportunities to respond, but he does not force us to come to him. Like the father, he waits patiently for us to come to our senses.

21"His son said to him, 'Father, I have sinned against heaven and you, and am not worthy of being called your son—'

22"But his father said to the slaves, 'Quick! Bring the finest robe in the house and put it on him. And a jeweled ring for his finger; and shoes! 23And kill the calf we have in the fattening pen. We must celebrate with a feast, 24for this son of mine was dead and has returned to life. He was lost and is found.' So the party began.

15:22
Isa 61:10
Zech 3:4
Rev 6:11
15:24
Rom 11:15
Eph 2:1-5
Col 2:13

25"Meanwhile, the older son was in the fields working; when he returned home, he heard dance music coming from the house, 26and he asked one of the servants what was going on.

27" 'Your brother is back,' he was told, 'and your father has killed the calf we were fattening and has prepared a great feast to celebrate his coming home again unharmed.'

28"The older brother was angry and wouldn't go in. His father came out and begged him, 29but he replied, 'All these years I've worked hard for you and never once refused to do a single thing you told me to; and in all that time you never gave me even one young goat for a feast with my friends. 30Yet when this son of yours comes back after spending your money on prostitutes, you celebrate by killing the finest calf we have on the place.'

15:29
Mt 20:11-15
15:30
Prov 29:3

31" 'Look, dear son,' his father said to him, 'you and I are very close, and everything I have is yours. 32But it is right to celebrate. For he is your brother; and he was dead and has come back to life! He was lost and is found!' "

15:32
Lk 15:7

Jesus tells the parable of the shrewd accountant (162)

16 Jesus now told this story to his disciples: "A rich man hired an accountant to handle his affairs, but soon a rumor went around that the accountant was thoroughly dishonest.

2"So his employer called him in and said, 'What's this I hear about your stealing from me? Get your report in order, for you are to be dismissed.'

16:2
Rom 14:12

3"The accountant thought to himself, 'Now what? I'm through here, and I haven't the strength to go out and dig ditches, and I'm too proud to beg. 4I know just the thing! And then I'll have plenty of friends to take care of me when I leave!'

5, 6"So he invited each one who owed money to his employer to come and discuss the situation. He asked the first one, 'How much do you owe him?' 'My debt is 850 gallons of olive oil,' the man replied. 'Yes, here is the contract you signed,' the accountant told him. 'Tear it up and write another one for half that much!'

7" 'And how much do you owe him?' he asked the next man. 'A thousand bushels of wheat,' was the reply. 'Here,' the accountant said, 'take your note and replace it with one for only 800 bushels!'

15:24 The coin was lost through no fault of its own (15:8); the sheep was lost because it foolishly wandered away (15:3, 4); and the son left out of selfishness (15:12). God's great love reaches out and finds sinners no matter why they became lost.

15:25-31 It would be just as difficult to accept the younger brother today as it was in Jesus' day. People who repent after being notorious for their sinful lives are often held in suspicion; churches are sometimes even unwilling to admit them to membership. Instead, we should rejoice like the angels in heaven when an unbeliever repents and turns to God. Like the father, accept repentant sinners wholeheartedly and give them the support and encouragement they need to grow in Christ.

15:30 In the story of the prodigal son, there is a contrast between the father's response and the older brother's reaction. The father was forgiving and overjoyed. The brother was unforgiving and bitter. The father forgave because he was joyful, and the son refused to forgive because he was bitter. The difference between

bitterness and joy is our capacity to forgive. If you are refusing to forgive people, you are missing a wonderful opportunity of experiencing joy and sharing it with them.

15:32 When Jesus told this story, the older brother represented the Pharisees, who were angry and resentful that sinners were being welcomed into God's Kingdom. After all, they thought, we have sacrificed and done so much for God. How easy it is to resent God's gracious forgiveness of others whom we consider far worse sinners than we. But when our self-righteousness gets in the way of rejoicing at God's mercy, we are no better than the Pharisees.

16:1-8 People have offered many explanations for this difficult story. Here are some of them: (1) Don't waste the resources you have because they belong to God, not you. (2) Money can be used for good or evil; use yours for good. (3) Money has a lot of power, so use it carefully and thoughtfully. (4) We must use our material goods in a way that will help us in the next life (see Luke 12:33, 34).

16:8
Jn 12:36
Eph 5:8,9
1 Thess 5:5

16:10
Mt 25:21
Lk 19:17

16:13
Mt 6:24

16:14
Mt 23:13,14
1 Tim 3:2

16:15
1 Sam 16:7
2 Chron 16:30
Ps 7:9
Prov 15:11; 21:2
Jer 17:10
Mt 23:28
Heb 4:13

16:16
Mt 11:12,13

16:17
Isa 40:8
Mt 5:17,18
Lk 21:33
1 Pet 1:25

16:18
Mt 5:32; 19:9
Mk 10:11,12
1 Cor 7:10,11

16:20
Acts 3:2

8"The rich man had to admire the rascal for being so shrewd. And it is true that the citizens of this world are more clever [in dishonesty!] than the godly are. 9But shall I tell *you* to act that way, to buy friendship through cheating? Will this ensure your entry into an everlasting home in heaven? 10*No!* For unless you are honest in small matters, you won't be in large ones. If you cheat even a little, you won't be honest with greater responsibilities. 11And if you are untrustworthy about worldly wealth, who will trust you with the true riches of heaven? 12And if you are not faithful with other people's money, why should you be entrusted with money of your own?

13"For neither you nor anyone else can serve two masters. You will hate one and show loyalty to the other, or else the other way around—you will be enthusiastic about one and despise the other. You cannot serve both God and money."

14The Pharisees, who dearly loved their money, naturally scoffed at all this.

15Then he said to them, "You wear a noble, pious expression in public, but God knows your evil hearts. Your pretense brings you honor from the people, but it is an abomination in the sight of God. 16Until John the Baptist began to preach, the laws of Moses and the messages of the prophets were your guides. But John introduced the Good News that the Kingdom of God would come soon. And now eager multitudes are pressing in. 17But that doesn't mean that the Law has lost its force in even the smallest point. It is as strong and unshakable as heaven and earth.

18"So anyone who divorces his wife and marries someone else commits adultery, and anyone who marries a divorced woman commits adultery."

Jesus tells about the rich man and the beggar (163)

19"There was a certain rich man," Jesus said, "who was splendidly clothed and lived each day in mirth and luxury. 20One day Lazarus, a diseased beggar, was laid

16:8 *The rich man had to admire the rascal for being so shrewd,* or, "Do you think the rich man commended the scoundrel for being so shrewd?" *in dishonesty,* implied. *godly,* literally, "sons of the light." **16:9** *Will this ensure your entry into an everlasting home in heaven?* Literally, and probably ironically, "Make to yourselves friends by means of the mammon of unrighteousness; that when it shall fail you, they may receive you into the eternal tabernacles." Some commentators would interpret this to mean: "Use your money for good, so that it will be waiting to befriend you when you get to heaven." But this would imply the end justifies the means, an unbiblical idea.

16:10, 11 Our integrity often meets its match in money matters. God calls us to be honest even in small details we could rationalize away. Heaven's riches are far more valuable than earthly wealth—but if we are untrustworthy with our earthly wealth (no matter how much or little we have), we are unfit to handle the vast riches of God's Kingdom. Don't let your integrity slip in small matters, and it will not fail you in crucial decisions either.

16:13 Money has the power to take God's place in your life. It can become your master. How can you tell if you are a slave to money? (1) Do you worry about it frequently? (2) Do you give up doing what you should do or would like to do in order to make more money? (3) Do you spend a great deal of your time caring for your possessions? (4) Is it hard for you to give money away? (5) Are you in debt?

Money is a hard master and a deceptive one. Money promises power and control, but it often cannot deliver. Great fortunes can be made—and lost—overnight, and no amount of money can provide health, happiness, or eternal life. How much better to let God be your master. His servants have peace of mind and security both now and forever.

16:14 The Pharisees loved money and took exception with Jesus' teaching. We too may be fond of our money. Do we also scoff at Jesus' warnings against serving money? Do we try to explain them away? Do we apply them to someone else—the Pharisees, for example? Unless we take Jesus' statements seriously, we may be acting like Pharisees ourselves.

16:15 The Pharisees acted pious to get praise from others, but God knew what was in their hearts. Is your spirituality genuine, or is it merely aimed at impressing others? Remember, that which is only a show for the general public is disgusting to God.

16:16, 17 John the Baptist was the dividing line between the Old and New Testaments (John 1:15–18). With Jesus came the realization of all the prophets' hopes. Jesus emphasized that his Kingdom fulfilled the law (the Old Testament); it did not cancel it. His was not a new system but the culmination of the old. The same God who worked through Moses was working through him.

16:18 Most religious leaders of Jesus' day permitted a man to divorce his wife for nearly any reason. Jesus' words about divorce went beyond Moses' (Deuteronomy 24:1–4). Stricter than any of the then-current schools of thought, they shocked his hearers (see Matthew 19:10) just as they shake today's readers. Jesus says in unmistakable terms that marriage is a lifetime commitment. To leave your spouse for another person may be legal, but it is adultery in God's eyes. As you think about marriage, remember that God intends it to be a permanent commitment.

16:19–31 The Pharisees considered wealth a proof of righteousness. Jesus startled them with this story in which a diseased beggar is rewarded and a rich man is punished. The rich man did not go to hell because of his wealth but because he was selfish with it. He did not feed Lazarus, take him in, or care for his health. He was hard-hearted in spite of his great blessings. The amount of money we have is not so important as the way we use it. Rich people can be generous or stingy—and so can poor people. What is your attitude toward your possessions? Do you hoard them selfishly for yourself, or do you use them to bless others?

16:20 This Lazarus should not be confused with the Lazarus whom Jesus raised from the dead in John 11.

at his door. 21As he lay there longing for scraps from the rich man's table, the dogs would come and lick his open sores. 22Finally the beggar died and was carried by the angels to be with Abraham in the place of the righteous dead. The rich man also died and was buried, 23and his soul went into hell. There, in torment, he saw Lazarus in the far distance with Abraham.

16:22
Ps 103:20,21
Mt 8:11
Jn 1:18
Heb 1:14
Jas 2:5

24" 'Father Abraham,' he shouted, 'have some pity! Send Lazarus over here if only to dip the tip of his finger in water and cool my tongue, for I am in anguish in these flames.'

16:24
Mk 9:44
Lk 3:8

25"But Abraham said to him, 'Son, remember that during your lifetime you had everything you wanted, and Lazarus had nothing. So now he is here being comforted and you are in anguish. 26And besides, there is a great chasm separating us, and anyone wanting to come to you from here is stopped at its edge; and no one over there can cross to us.'

16:25
Job 21:7-14
Lk 6:24,25

16:26
2 Thess 1:9

27"Then the rich man said, 'O Father Abraham, then please send him to my father's home— 28for I have five brothers—to warn them about this place of torment lest they come here when they die.'

16:28
Acts 2:40; 10:42
18:5

29"But Abraham said, 'The Scriptures have warned them again and again. Your brothers can read them any time they want to.'

16:29
Jn 5:39,45-47
Acts 15:21
2 Tim 3:15

30"The rich man replied, 'No, Father Abraham, they won't bother to read them. But if someone is sent to them from the dead, then they will turn from their sins.'

31"But Abraham said, 'If they won't listen to Moses and the prophets, they won't listen even though someone rises from the dead.' "

16:31
Jn 12:9,10

Jesus teaches about forgiveness and faith (164)

17 "There will always be temptations to sin," Jesus said one day to his disciples, "but woe to the man who does the tempting. 2, 3If he were thrown into the sea with a huge rock tied to his neck, he would be far better off than facing the punishment in store for those who harm these little children's souls. I am warning you!

17:1
Mt 18:6,7
Mk 9:42
1 Cor 8:12

17:3
Lev 19:17
Mt 18:15,21,22
Jas 5:19

"Rebuke your brother if he sins, and forgive him if he is sorry. 4Even if he wrongs you seven times a day and each time turns again and asks forgiveness, forgive him."

5One day the apostles said to the Lord, "We need more faith; tell us how to get it."

6"If your faith were only the size of a mustard seed," Jesus answered, "it would be large enough to uproot that mulberry tree over there and send it hurtling into the

17:6
Mt 17:20; 21:21
Mk 9:23
11:22,23

16:22 *to be with Abraham in the place of the righteous dead*, literally, "into Abraham's bosom." **16:23** *into hell*, literally, "into Hades." **16:31** *even though someone rises from the dead*. Even Christ's resurrection failed to convince the Pharisees, to whom he gave this illustration.

16:29–31 The rich man thought his five brothers would surely believe a messenger who was raised from the dead. But Jesus said that if they did not believe Moses and the prophets, who spoke constantly of the duty to care for the poor, not even a resurrection would convince them. Notice the irony in Jesus' statement; on his way to Jerusalem to die, he was fully aware that even when he had returned from the dead most of the religious leaders would not accept him. They were set in their ways, and neither Scripture nor God's Son himself could shake them loose.

17:1–3 Jesus may have been directing this warning at the religious leaders who taught their converts their own hypocritical ways (see Matthew 23:15). They were perpetuating an evil system. A person who teaches others has a solemn responsibility (James 3:1). Like physicians, a teacher should keep this ancient oath in mind: "First, do no harm."

17:3, 4 To rebuke does not mean to point out every sin we see; it means to bring sin to a person's attention with the purpose of restoring him or her to God and to fellow humans. When you feel you must rebuke another Christian for a sin, check your attitudes before opening your mouth. Do you love the person? Are you

willing to forgive? Unless rebuke is tied to forgiveness, it will not help the sinning person.

17:6 The disciples' question (17:5) was genuine; they wanted the faith necessary to do what Jesus had been telling them to do. But Jesus didn't directly answer their question because faith is not something we "get." The amount of faith is not as important as its object and its genuineness. What is faith? It is total dependence on God and a willingness to do his will. It is not something we use to put on a show for others. It is complete and humble obedience to God's will, readiness to do whatever he calls us to do. The amount of faith isn't as important as the right kind of faith—faith in our all-powerful God.

17:6 A mustard seed is small, but it is alive and growing. Like this tiny seed, a small amount of genuine faith in God will take root and grow. Almost invisible at first, it will begin to spread, first underground and then visibly. Although each change will be gradual and imperceptible, soon this faith will have produced major results that will uproot and destroy competing loyalties. We don't need more faith; a tiny seed of faith is enough, if it is alive and growing.

sea! Your command would bring immediate results! 7, 8, 9When a servant comes in from plowing or taking care of sheep, he doesn't just sit down and eat, but first prepares his master's meal and serves him his supper before he eats his own. And he is not even thanked, for he is merely doing what he is supposed to do. 10Just so, if you merely obey me, you should not consider yourselves worthy of praise. For you have simply done your duty!"

17:10
1 Cor 9:16-18

Jesus heals ten lepers
(169)

17:11
Lk 9:51; 13:22
17:12
Lev 13:45,46
17:14
Lev 14:3
Mt 8:4
Mk 1:43,44
Lk 5:14
17:16
2 Kgs 17:24
Jn 8:48
17:19
Mt 9:22
Lk 18:42

11As they continued onward toward Jerusalem, they reached the border between Galilee and Samaria, 12and as they entered a village there, ten lepers stood at a distance, 13crying out, "Jesus, sir, have mercy on us!"

14He looked at them and said, "Go to the Jewish priest and show him that you are healed!" And as they were going, their leprosy disappeared.

15One of them came back to Jesus, shouting, "Glory to God, I'm healed!" 16He fell flat on the ground in front of Jesus, face downward in the dust, thanking him for what he had done. This man was a despised Samaritan.

17Jesus asked, "Didn't I heal ten men? Where are the nine? 18Does only this foreigner return to give glory to God?"

19And Jesus said to the man, "Stand up and go; your faith has made you well."

Jesus teaches about the coming of the Kingdom of God
(170)

17:20
Mt 12:28
Lk 11:20; 19:11
Jn 3:3; 18:36
Acts 1:6
17:22
Mt 9:15

20One day the Pharisees asked Jesus, "When will the Kingdom of God begin?" Jesus replied, "The Kingdom of God isn't ushered in with visible signs. 21You won't be able to say, 'It has begun here in this place or there in that part of the country.' For the Kingdom of God is within you."

22Later he talked again about this with his disciples. "The time is coming when

17:16 *despised,* implied. Samaritans were despised by Jews as being only "half-breed" Hebrews.   **17:21** *within you,* or "among you."   **17:22** *long for me,* or, "long for the Son of Man."

17:7–10 If we have obeyed God, we have only done our duty. This means that God never owes us anything, no matter how good we are. It also means we win no awards for avoiding sin—this too is our duty. Do you sometimes feel you deserve extra credit for serving God? Obedience is our duty, not just an act of charity.

17:11–14 These lepers were required to try to stay apart from other people and to announce their presence if they had to come near. Sometimes leprosy went into remission; if a leper thought his leprosy had gone away, he was supposed to present himself to a priest who could declare him clean (Leviticus 14). Jesus sent the ten lepers to the priest *before* they were healed—and they went! They responded in faith, and Jesus healed them on the way. Is your trust in God so strong that you act on what he says even before it happens?

17:16 Jesus healed all ten lepers, but only one returned to thank him. It is possible to receive God's great gifts with an ungrateful spirit—nine of the lepers did so. Only the thankful leper, however, learned that his faith had played a role in his healing; and only grateful Christians grow in understanding of God's grace. God does not demand that we thank him, but he is pleased when we do so, and he uses our spirit of thankfulness to teach us more about his Kingdom.

17:16 Not only was this man a leper, he was also a Samaritan—a race despised by the Jews as idolatrous half-breeds (see the note on 10:33). Once again Luke is pointing out that God's grace is for everybody.

17:20, 21 The Kingdom of God is not like an earthly kingdom with geographical boundaries. Instead, it consists of the work of God's Spirit in people's lives and relationships. Still today we must resist looking to institutions or programs for evidence of the progress of God's Kingdom. Instead, we should look for what God is doing in people's hearts.

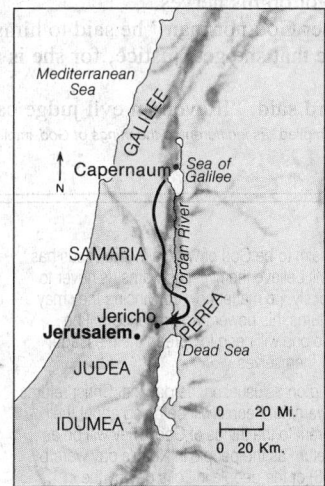

LAST TRIP FROM GALILEE
Jesus left Galilee for the last time—he would not return before his death. He passed through Samaria, met and healed ten lepers, and continued to Jerusalem. He spent some time east of the Jordan (Mark 10:1), before going to Jericho (19:1).

17:21 Some versions say "the Kingdom of God is *among* you"; the word can be translated either way. If Jesus meant a kingdom *within,* he was emphasizing that it would begin with spiritual change in his followers. If he meant a kingdom *among* them, he was saying that he, the King, was in their midst. Perhaps he chose a word with both meanings because both possibilities were true.

you will long for me to be with you even for a single day, but I won't be here," he said. 23"Reports will reach you that I have returned and that I am in this place or that; don't believe it or go out to look for me. 24For when I return, you will know it beyond all doubt. It will be as evident as the lightning that flashes across the skies. 25But first I must suffer terribly and be rejected by this whole nation.

26"[When I return] the world will be [as indifferent to the things of God] as the people were in Noah's day. 27They ate and drank and married—everything just as usual right up to the day when Noah went into the ark and the flood came and destroyed them all.

28"And the world will be as it was in the days of Lot: people went about their daily business—eating and drinking, buying and selling, farming and building— 29until the morning Lot left Sodom. Then fire and brimstone rained down from heaven and destroyed them all. 30Yes, it will be 'business as usual' right up to the hour of my return.

31"Those away from home that day must not return to pack; those in the fields must not return to town— 32remember what happened to Lot's wife! 33Whoever clings to his life shall lose it, and whoever loses his life shall save it. 34That night two men will be asleep in the same room, and one will be taken away, the other left. 35, 36Two women will be working together at household tasks; one will be taken, the other left; and so it will be with men working side by side in the fields."

37"Lord, where will they be taken?" the disciples asked.

Jesus replied, "Where the body is, the vultures gather!"

Jesus tells the parable of the persistent widow (171)

18 One day Jesus told his disciples a story to illustrate their need for constant prayer and to show them that they must keep praying until the answer comes.

2"There was a city judge," he said, "a very godless man who had great contempt for everyone. 3A widow of that city came to him frequently to appeal for justice against a man who had harmed her. 4, 5The judge ignored her for a while, but eventually she got on his nerves.

" 'I fear neither God nor man,' he said to himself, 'but this woman bothers me. I'm going to see that she gets justice, for she is wearing me out with her constant coming!' "

6Then the Lord said, "If even an evil judge can be worn down like that, 7don't

17:26 *When I return,* implied. *as indifferent to the things of God,* implied.   **17:30** *the hour of my return,* or, "the hour I am revealed."

Cross references (right margin):

17:23 — Mt 24:23,26,27 / Mk 13:21 / Lk 21:8
17:24 — 1 Tim 6:15
17:25 — Mt 16:21 / Mk 8:31 / Lk 9:22
17:26 — Gen 6:12,13 / Mt 24:37-39
17:29 — Gen 19:24-26
17:30 — 2 Thess 1:7
17:31 — Mt 24:17,18 / Mk 13:15,16
17:33 — Mt 10:39; 16:25 / Mk 8:35 / Lk 9:24 / Jn 12:25
17:35 — Mt 24:40,41 / 1 Thess 4:17
17:37 — Job 39:30 / Mt 24:28
18:1 — Rom 12:12 / Eph 6:18 / Col 4:2 / 1 Thess 5:17
18:4,5 — Lk 11:8
18:7 — Mt 24:22 / Rom 8:33 / Rev 6:10

17:23, 24 Many will claim to be God or will claim that Jesus has returned—and many will believe them. Jesus warns us never to take such reports seriously, no matter how convincing they may sound. When Jesus returns, his power and presence will be evident to everyone. No one will need to spread the message, because all will see for themselves.

17:23 Life will be going on as usual on the day that Christ returns. There will be no prior warning. People will be going about their everyday tasks, indifferent to the things of God. They will be as surprised by Christ's return as the people in Noah's day were by the flood (Genesis 6—8) or the people in Lot's day by the destruction of Sodom (Genesis 19). We don't know the day or the hour of Christ's return, but we do know he is coming. It may be today, or tomorrow, or centuries in the future. Whenever it is, we must be ready. Live as if Jesus were coming today, and then you will be ready for his return.

17:26—36 Jesus warned against false security. We are to abandon the values and attachments of this world in order to be ready for Christ's return. His return will happen suddenly, and when he comes, there will be no second chances. Some will be taken to be with him; the rest will be left behind.

17:37 To answer the disciples' question, Jesus quoted a familiar proverb. One vulture circling overhead does not mean much; but a gathering of vultures means a dead body is nearby. Likewise, one "sign of the end" may not be significant; but when the signs come hard and fast, the Second Coming is near.

18:1 To repeat our prayers until the answer comes does not mean endless repetition or painfully long prayer sessions. Constant prayer means keeping our requests constantly before God as we live for him day by day, always believing he will answer. When we thus live by faith, we are not to give up. God may delay answering, but his delays always have good reasons, and we must not confuse them with neglect. As we persist in prayer we grow in character, faith, and hope.

18:3 Widows and orphans were among the most vulnerable of all God's people, and both Old Testament prophets and New Testament apostles insisted that they be properly cared for. See, for example, Exodus 22:22–24; Isaiah 1:17; 1 Timothy 5:3; James 1:27.

18:6, 7 If evil judges respond to constant pressure, how much more will a great and loving God respond to us. If we have felt his love, we can believe he will hear our cries.

you think that God will surely give justice to his people who plead with him day and night? 8Yes! He will answer them quickly! But the question is: When I, the Messiah, return, how many will I find who have faith [and are praying]?"

18:8
1 Tim 4:1

Jesus tells the parable of two men who prayed
(172)

9Then he told this story to some who boasted of their virtue and scorned everyone else:

18:9
Rom 14:10

10"Two men went to the Temple to pray. One was a proud, self-righteous Pharisee, and the other a cheating tax collector. 11The proud Pharisee 'prayed' this prayer: 'Thank God, I am not a sinner like everyone else, especially like that tax collector over there! For I never cheat, I don't commit adultery, 12I go without food twice a week, and I give to God a tenth of everything I earn.'

18:11
Isa 58:2
Mt 6:5
Rev 3:17
18:13
Ps 40:12

13"But the corrupt tax collector stood at a distance and dared not even lift his eyes to heaven as he prayed, but beat upon his chest in sorrow, exclaiming, 'God, be merciful to me, a sinner.' 14I tell you, this sinner, not the Pharisee, returned home forgiven! For the proud shall be humbled, but the humble shall be honored."

18:14
Job 22:29
Mt 23:12
Lk 14:11
Jas 4:6
1 Pet 5:5,6

Jesus blesses little children
(174/Matthew 19:13–15; Mark 10:13–16)

15One day some mothers brought their babies to him to touch and bless. But the disciples told them to go away.

18:15
Mt 19:13-15
Mk 10:13-16

16, 17Then Jesus called the children over to him and said to the disciples, "Let the little children come to me! Never send them away! For the Kingdom of God belongs to men who have hearts as trusting as these little children's. And anyone who doesn't have their kind of faith will never get within the Kingdom's gates."

18:17
Mt 18:3
1 Cor 14:20
1 Pet 2:2

Jesus speaks to the rich young man
(175/Matthew 19:16–30; Mark 10:17–31)

18Once a Jewish religious leader asked him this question: "Good sir, what shall I do to get to heaven?"

18:18
Mt 19:16-22
Mk 10:17-22

19"Do you realize what you are saying when you call me 'good'?" Jesus asked him. "Only God is truly good, and no one else.

20"But as to your question, you know what the ten commandments say—don't commit adultery, don't murder, don't steal, don't lie, honor your parents, and so on." 21The man replied, "I've obeyed every one of these laws since I was a small child."

18:20
Ex 20:12-16
Deut 5:16-20

22"There is still one thing you lack," Jesus said. "Sell all you have and give the

18:22
Mt 6:19-21
1 Tim 6:18,19

18:8 *the Messiah,* literally, *"the Son of Man." and are praying,* implied.

18:10 The people who lived near Jerusalem often went to the Temple to pray. The Temple was the center of their worship (Isaiah 56:7).

18:11–14 The Pharisee did not go to the Temple to pray to God but to announce to all within earshot how good he was. The tax collector went recognizing his sin and begging for mercy. Self-righteousness is dangerous. It leads to pride, causes a person to despise others, and prevents him or her from learning anything from God. The tax collector's prayer should be our prayer because we all need God's mercy every day. Don't let pride disqualify you.

18:15–17 It was customary for a mother to bring her children to a rabbi for a blessing, and that is why these mothers gathered about Jesus. The disciples, however, thought the children were unworthy of the Master's time—less important than whatever else he was doing. But Jesus welcomed them because little children have the kind of faith and trust needed to enter God's Kingdom. It is important to introduce our children to Jesus and that we ourselves approach him with childlike attitudes of acceptance and trust.

18:18ff This religious leader sought reassurance, some way of knowing for sure he had eternal life. He wanted Jesus to measure and grade his qualifications, or to give him some task he could do

to assure his own immortality. So Jesus gave him a task—the one thing the religious leader felt he could not do. "Then how can *anyone* be saved?" the bystanders asked. "No one can, by his own achievements," Jesus' answer implied. "But God can do what men can't." Salvation cannot be earned—it is God's gift (see Ephesians 2:8–10).

18:19 Jesus' question to the religious leader who came and called him "Good sir," was, in essence, "Do you know who I am?" Undoubtedly the religious leader did not catch the implications of Jesus' statement—that he was right in calling him good, because Jesus truly is God.

18:22, 23 This man's wealth smoothed his life and gave him power and prestige. When Jesus told him to sell everything he owned, he was touching the man's very security. The man did not understand that he would be even more secure if he followed Jesus than he was with all his wealth. Jesus does not ask all believers to sell everything they have, although this may be his will for some. He does ask us all, however, to get rid of anything that has become more important to us than God. What is the ultimate source of your security?

money to the poor—it will become treasure for you in heaven—and come, follow me."

23But when the man heard this he went sadly away, for he was very rich.

24Jesus watched him go and then said to his disciples, "How hard it is for the rich to enter the Kingdom of God! 25It is easier for a camel to go through the eye of a needle than for a rich man to enter the Kingdom of God."

26Those who heard him say this exclaimed, "If it is that hard, how can *anyone* be saved?"

27He replied, "God can do what men can't!"

28And Peter said, "We have left our homes and followed you."

29"Yes," Jesus replied, "and everyone who has done as you have, leaving home, wife, brothers, parents, or children for the sake of the Kingdom of God, 30will be repaid many times over now, as well as receiving eternal life in the world to come."

Jesus predicts his death the third time
(177/Matthew 20:17–19; Mark 10:32–34)

31Gathering the Twelve around him he told them, "As you know, we are going to Jerusalem. And when we get there, all the predictions of the ancient prophets concerning me will come true. 32I will be handed over to the Gentiles to be mocked and treated shamefully and spat upon, 33and lashed and killed. And the third day I will rise again."

34But they didn't understand a thing he said. He seemed to be talking in riddles.

Jesus heals a blind beggar
(179/Matthew 20:29–34; Mark 10:46–52)

35As they approached Jericho, a blind man was sitting beside the road, begging from travelers. 36When he heard the noise of a crowd going past, he asked what was happening. 37He was told that Jesus from Nazareth was going by, 38so he began shouting, "Jesus, Son of David, have mercy on me!"

39The crowds ahead of Jesus tried to hush the man, but he only yelled the louder, "Son of David, have mercy on me!"

40When Jesus arrived at the spot, he stopped. "Bring the blind man over here," he said. 41Then Jesus asked the man, "What do you want?"

"Lord," he pleaded, "I want to see!"

42And Jesus said, "All right, begin seeing! Your faith has healed you."

43And instantly the man could see, and followed Jesus, praising God. And all who saw it happen praised God too.

18:23
Ezek 33:31
18:24
Mt 19:23-30
Mk 10:23-31
1 Tim 6:9
Jas 2:5

18:27
Jer 32:17
18:28
Lk 5:11
18:30
Job 42:10

18:31
Ps 22
Isa 53
Lk 9:22,44-45
17:25
18:32
Mt 16:21; 17:22
27:2

18:35
Mt 20:29-34
Mk 10:46-52
18:38
Heb 2:17

18:42
Mt 9:22
Lk 7:50; 17:19
18:43
Isa 35:5
Mt 9:8
Lk 19:37
Acts 4:21

18:24-27 Because money represents power, authority, and success, often it is difficult for wealthy people to realize their need and their powerlessness to save themselves. Unless God reaches down into their lives, they will not come to him. Jesus surprised some of his hearers by offering salvation to the poor; he may surprise some people today by offering it to the rich. It is difficult for a rich person to realize his need and come to Jesus, but "God can do what men can't!"

18:26-30 Peter and the other disciples had paid a high price—leaving their homes and jobs—to follow Jesus. But Jesus reminded Peter that following him has its benefits as well as its sacrifices. Any believer who has had to give up something to follow Christ will be paid back in this life as well as in the next. For example, if you must give up a secure job, you will find that God offers a secure relationship with himself now and forever. If you must give up your family's approval, you will gain the love of the family of God. The disciples had begun to pay the price of following Jesus, and Jesus said they would be rewarded. Don't dwell on what you have given up; think about what you have gained and give thanks for it. You can never outgive God.

18:31-34 Some predictions about what would happen to Jesus are found in Psalm 41:9 (betrayal); Psalm 22:16–18 and Isaiah

53:4–7 (crucifixion); Psalm 16:10 (resurrection). The disciples didn't understand what Jesus said, apparently because they focused on what he said about his death and ignored what he said about his resurrection. Even though Jesus spoke plainly, they would not grasp the significance of his words until they saw the risen Christ face to face.

18:35 Beggars often waited along the roads near cities, because that was where they would be able to contact the most people. Usually handicapped in some way, they were unable to earn a living. Medical help was not available for their problems, and the people tended to ignore their obligation to care for the needy (Leviticus 25:35–38). Thus beggars had little hope of escaping their degrading way of life. But this blind beggar took hope in the Messiah. He shamelessly cried out for Jesus' attention, and Jesus said his faith made him see. No matter how desperate your situation may seem, if you call out to Jesus in faith, he will help you.

18:38 The blind man called Jesus "Son of David." This means he understood Jesus to be the long-awaited Messiah. This poor blind beggar could *see* that Jesus was the Messiah, while the religious leaders who saw his miracles were blinded to his identity and refused to recognize him as the Messiah.

Jesus brings salvation to Zacchaeus' home
(180)

19 As Jesus was passing through Jericho, a man named Zacchaeus, one of the most influential Jews in the Roman tax-collecting business (and, of course, a very rich man), 3tried to get a look at Jesus, but he was too short to see over the crowds. 4So he ran ahead and climbed into a sycamore tree beside the road, to watch from there.

5When Jesus came by he looked up at Zacchaeus and called him by name! "Zacchaeus!" he said. "Quick! Come down! For I am going to be a guest in your home today!"

6Zacchaeus hurriedly climbed down and took Jesus to his house in great excitement and joy.

7But the crowds were displeased. "He has gone to be the guest of a notorious sinner," they grumbled.

8Meanwhile, Zacchaeus stood before the Lord and said, "Sir, from now on I will give half my wealth to the poor, and if I find I have overcharged anyone on his taxes, I will penalize myself by giving him back four times as much!"

9, 10Jesus told him, "This shows that salvation has come to this home today. This man was one of the lost sons of Abraham, and I, the Messiah, have come to search for and to save such souls as his."

19:9, 10 *This shows,* implied. *the Messiah,* literally, "the Son of Man."

19:1
Josh 6:26
1 Kgs 16:34
Lk 18:35

19:4
1 Kings 10:27
2 Chron 1:15

19:7
Mt 9:11; 11:19
Lk 5:30; 15:2

19:8
Ex 22:1
Num 5:7
2 Sam 12:6
Lk 3:12,13

19:9
Mt 9:13; 15:24
18:11
Lk 5:32
Rom 4:11,12,
16,17
Gal 3:7
1 Tim 1:15

19:1–10 To finance their great world empire, the Romans levied heavy taxes against all nations under their control. The Jews opposed these taxes because they supported a secular government and its pagan gods, but they were still forced to pay. Tax collectors were among the most unpopular people in Israel. Jews by birth who chose to work for Rome were considered traitors. Besides, it was common knowledge that tax collectors made themselves rich by gouging their fellow Jews. No wonder the crowds were displeased when Jesus went home with the tax collector Zacchaeus. But despite the fact that Zacchaeus was both dishonest and a turncoat, Jesus loved him, and in response, the little tax collector was converted. In every society certain groups of people are considered "untouchable" because of their politics, their immoral behavior, or their lifestyle. We should not give in to social pressure to avoid these people. Jesus loves them, and they need to hear his Good News.

19:8 Judging from the crowd's reaction to him, Zacchaeus was, no doubt, a very crooked tax collector. But after he met Jesus, he realized that his life needed straightening out. By giving to the poor and making restitution—with generous interest—to those he had cheated, Zacchaeus demonstrated inward change by outward action. It is not enough to follow Jesus in your head or heart alone. You must show your changed life by changed behavior. Has your faith resulted in action? What changes do you need to make?

19:9, 10 When Jesus said Zacchaeus was one of the lost sons of Abraham, he meant he was one of God's chosen people who was not following his ways. A person is not saved by a good heritage or condemned by a bad one; faith is more important than genealogy. Jesus still loves to bring the lost into his Kingdom, no matter what their background or previous way of life. Through faith, they are forgiven and made new.

Jesus tells the parable of the king's ten servants
(181)

¹¹And because Jesus was nearing Jerusalem, he told a story to correct the impression that the Kingdom of God would begin right away.

¹²"A nobleman living in a certain province was called away to the distant capital of the empire to be crowned king of his province. ¹³Before he left he called together ten assistants and gave them each $2,000 to invest while he was gone. ¹⁴But some of his people hated him and sent him their declaration of independence, stating that they had rebelled and would not acknowledge him as their king.

¹⁵"Upon his return he called in the men to whom he had given the money, to find out what they had done with it, and what their profits were.

¹⁶"The first man reported a tremendous gain—ten times as much as the original amount!

¹⁷" 'Fine!' the king exclaimed. 'You are a good man. You have been faithful with the little I entrusted to you, and as your reward, you shall be governor of ten cities.'

¹⁸"The next man also reported a splendid gain—five times the original amount.

¹⁹" 'All right!' his master said. 'You can be governor over five cities.'

²⁰"But the third man brought back only the money he had started with. 'I've kept it safe,' he said, ²¹'because I was afraid [you would demand my profits], for you are a hard man to deal with, taking what isn't yours and even confiscating the crops that others plant.' ²²'You vile and wicked slave,' the king roared. 'Hard, am I? That's exactly how I'll be toward you! If you knew so much about me and how tough I am, ²³then why didn't you deposit the money in the bank so that I could at least get some interest on it?'

²⁴"Then turning to the others standing by he ordered, 'Take the money away from him and give it to the man who earned the most.'

²⁵" 'But, sir,' they said, 'he has enough already!'

²⁶" 'Yes,' the king replied, 'but it is always true that those who have, get more, and those who have little, soon lose even that. ²⁷And now about these enemies of mine who revolted—bring them in and execute them before me.' "

3. Jesus' ministry in Jerusalem

Jesus rides into Jerusalem on a donkey
(183/Matthew 21:1–11; Mark 11:1–11; John 12:12–19)

²⁸After telling this story, Jesus went on toward Jerusalem, walking along ahead of his disciples. ²⁹As they came to the towns of Bethphage and Bethany, on the Mount of Olives, he sent two disciples ahead, ³⁰with instructions to go to the next village, and as they entered they were to look for a donkey tied beside the road. It would be a colt, not yet broken for riding.

19:11 Acts 1:6
19:12 Mt 25:14-30 Mk 13:34
19:13 1 Pet 4:10,11
19:14 Jn 1:11
19:17 Lk 16:10
19:22 Job 15:6 Mt 12:37 Tit 3:11
19:26 Mt 13:12 Mk 4:25 Lk 8:18
19:27 Lk 19:14
19:28 Mk 10:32 19:29 Mt 21:1-9 Mk 11:1-10 Jn 12:12-18

19:11 The people still hoped for a political leader who would set up an earthly kingdom and get rid of Roman domination. Jesus' parable showed that his Kingdom would not take this form right away. First he would go away for a while, and his followers would need to be faithful and productive during his absence. Upon his return, he would inaugurate the powerful Kingdom they were expecting.

19:11ff This story showed Jesus' followers what they were to do during the time between Jesus' departure and his Second Coming. Because we live in that time, it applies directly to us. We have been given excellent resources to build and enlarge God's Kingdom. Jesus expects us to use these talents so that they multiply and the Kingdom expands. He asks each of us, "What are you doing with what I have given you?" While awaiting the coming of the Kingdom of God in glory, we must do his work.

19:20-27 Why was the king so hard on this man who had not increased the money? He punished the man because (1) he didn't share his master's interest in the kingdom; (2) he didn't trust his master's intentions; and (3) his only loyalty was to himself. Like the king in this story, God has given you gifts to use for the benefit of his Kingdom. Do you want the Kingdom to grow? Do you trust God to govern it fairly? Are you as concerned for others' welfare as for your own? If you can answer yes to these questions, you are faithfully using what he has entrusted to you.

19:26, 27 The background of this story is civil war. Some of the king's subjects refuse to acknowledge him. As he tries to consolidate his kingdom in absentia, he discovers among his own servants one who seems more influenced by the rebels than by the loyal subjects. Like the kingdom in the story, our world is in a state of civil war. Some people are loyal to God, their King in heaven; while others refuse to acknowledge his Lordship. Even among God's servants, people can be found who act more like enemies than loyal subjects. One day the Lord will return to put an end to the civil war by destroying his enemies and recreating the earth. On which side will you be?

"Untie him," Jesus said, "and bring him here. 31And if anyone asks you what you are doing, just say, 'The Lord needs him.'"

32They found the colt as Jesus said, 33and sure enough, as they were untying it, the owners demanded an explanation.

"What are you doing?" they asked. "Why are you untying our colt?"

34And the disciples simply replied, "The Lord needs him!" 35So they brought the colt to Jesus and threw some of their clothing across its back for Jesus to sit on.

36, 37Then the crowds spread out their robes along the road ahead of him, and as they reached the place where the road started down from the Mount of Olives, the whole procession began to shout and sing as they walked along, praising God for all the wonderful miracles Jesus had done.

38"God has given us a King!" they exulted. "Long live the King! Let all heaven rejoice! Glory to God in the highest heavens!"

39But some of the Pharisees among the crowd said, "Sir, rebuke your followers for saying things like that!"

40He replied, "If they keep quiet, the stones along the road will burst into cheers!"

41But as they came closer to Jerusalem and he saw the city ahead, he began to cry. 42"Eternal peace was within your reach and you turned it down," he wept, "and now it is too late. 43Your enemies will pile up earth against your walls and encircle you and close in on you, 44and crush you to the ground, and your children within you; your enemies will not leave one stone upon another—for you have rejected the opportunity God offered you."

Jesus clears the Temple again
(184/Matthew 21:12–17; Mark 11:12–19)

45Then he entered the Temple and began to drive out the merchants from their

Cross-references (margin):

19:36
2 Kgs 9:13

19:38
Ps 118:26
Mt 2:2; 25:34
Lk 2:14; 13:35
1 Tim 1:17

19:40
Hab 2:11

19:41
Lk 13:34
Jn 11:35

19:43
Eccles 9:14
Isa 29:3
Jer 6:6
Ezek 4:1-3
Lk 21:6,20

19:44
1 Kgs 9:6-9
Dan 9:26
Mic 3:12
Mt 24:2
Mk 13:2
Lk 21:6

LAST WEEK IN JERUSALEM

As they neared Jerusalem from Jericho (19:1), Jesus and the disciples came to the villages of Bethany and Bethphage, nestled on the eastern slope of the Mount of Olives, only a few miles outside Jerusalem. Jesus stayed in Bethany during the nights of that last week, entering Jerusalem during the day.

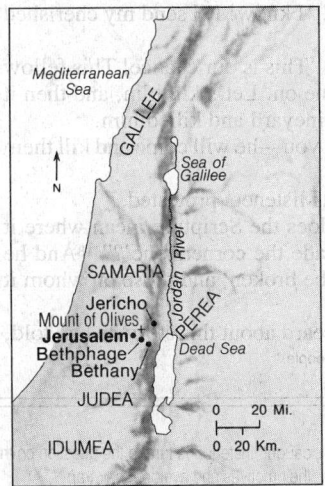

Righteous One, the Victor! Yet he is lowly, riding on a donkey's colt!" To announce that he was indeed the Messiah, Jesus chose a *time* when all Israel would be gathered at Jerusalem, a *place* where huge crowds could see him, and a *way* of proclaiming his mission that was unmistakable. The people went wild. Now they were sure their liberation was at hand.

19:38 The people who were praising God for giving them a king had the wrong idea about Jesus. They were sure he would be a national leader who would restore their nation to its former glory, and thus they were deaf to the words of their prophets and blind to Jesus' real mission. When it became apparent that Jesus was not going to fulfill their hopes, many people turned against him.

19:39 The Pharisees thought the crowd's words were sacrilegious and blasphemous. They didn't want someone upsetting their power and authority, and they didn't want a revolt that would bring the Roman army down on them. So they asked Jesus to keep his people quiet. But Jesus said that if the people were quiet, even the stones would shout with joy. Why? Not because Jesus was setting up a powerful political kingdom, but because he was establishing God's eternal Kingdom, a cause for the greatest celebration of all.

19:41–44 The Jews had rejected their king (19:47). The leaders had gone too far. They had refused God's offer of salvation in Jesus Christ, and soon they would suffer. God continues to offer salvation to the people he loves, both Jews and Gentiles. Eternal peace is within your reach—accept it before it is too late.

19:42, 44 About 40 years after Jesus said these words, they came true. In A.D. 66, the Jews revolted against Roman control. Three years later Titus, son of the emperor Vespasian, was sent to crush the rebellion. Roman soldiers attacked Jerusalem and broke through the northern wall but still couldn't take the city. Finally they laid siege to it, and in A.D. 70 they were able to enter the severely weakened city and burn it. Six hundred thousand Jews were killed during Titus' onslaught.

19:30–35 By this time Jesus was extremely well known. Everyone coming to Jerusalem for the Passover feast had heard of him, and for a time the popular mood was in his favor. "The Lord needs him" was all the disciples needed to say, and the colt's owners gladly turned their animal over to the disciples.

19:36, 37 This is the event Christians celebrate on Palm Sunday. The people lined the highway, praising God, waving palm branches, and throwing their cloaks in front of the colt as it passed before them. "Long live the King" was the meaning of their joyful shouts, because they knew Jesus was intentionally fulfilling the prophecy in Zechariah 9:9: "Your King is coming! He is the

stalls, 46saying to them, "The Scriptures declare, 'My Temple is a place of prayer; but you have turned it into a den of thieves.' "

47After that he taught daily in the Temple, but the chief priests and other religious leaders and the business community were trying to find some way to get rid of him. 48But they could think of nothing, for he was a hero to the people—they hung on every word he said.

19:46
Isa 56:7
Jer 7:11

19:47
Mt 26:55
Lk 21:37; 22:53
Jn 18:20

Religious leaders challenge Jesus' authority
(189/Matthew 21:23–27; Mark 11:26–33)

20 On one of those days when he was teaching and preaching the Good News in the Temple, he was confronted by the chief priests and other religious leaders and councilmen. 2They demanded to know by what authority he had driven out the merchants from the Temple.

3"I'll ask you a question before I answer," he replied. 4"Was John sent by God, or was he merely acting under his own authority?"

5They talked it over among themselves. "If we say his message was from heaven, then we are trapped because he will ask, 'Then why didn't you believe him?' 6But if we say John was not sent from God, the people will mob us, for they are convinced that he was a prophet." 7Finally they replied, "We don't know!"

8And Jesus responded, "Then I won't answer your question either."

20:1
Mt 21:23-27
Mk 11:26-33
Acts 4:1; 6:12

20:2
Jn 2:18
Acts 4:7,10

20:6
Mt 14:5
Lk 7:29

20:7
Rom 1:18,21

20:8
Job 5:12,13

Jesus tells the parable of the wicked farmers
(191/Matthew 21:33–46; Mark 12:1–12)

9Now he turned to the people again and told them this story: "A man planted a vineyard and rented it out to some farmers, and went away to a distant land to live for several years. 10When harvest time came, he sent one of his men to the farm to collect his share of the crops. But the tenants beat him up and sent him back empty-handed. 11Then he sent another, but the same thing happened; he was beaten up and insulted and sent away without collecting. 12A third man was sent and the same thing happened. He, too, was wounded and chased away.

13" 'What shall I do?' the owner asked himself. 'I know! I'll send my cherished son. Surely they will show respect for him.'

14"But when the tenants saw his son, they said, 'This is our chance! This fellow will inherit all the land when his father dies. Come on. Let's kill him, and then it will be ours.' 15So they dragged him out of the vineyard and killed him.

"What do you think the owner will do? 16I'll tell you—he will come and kill them and rent the vineyard to others."

"But they would never do a thing like that," his listeners protested.

17Jesus looked at them and said, "Then what does the Scripture mean where it says, 'The Stone rejected by the builders was made the cornerstone'?" 18And he added, "Whoever stumbles over that Stone shall be broken; and those on whom it falls will be crushed to dust."

19When the chief priests and religious leaders heard about this story he had told,

20:9
Isa 5:1-7
Mt 21:33-46
Mk 12:1-12

20:10
2 Kgs 17:13,14
2 Chron 36:15,
16
Acts 7:52

20:13
Jn 3:16
Rom 8:3
Gal 4:4

20:14
Heb 1:2

20:15
Acts 3:15
1 Thess 2:15

20:17
Ps 118:22
Acts 4:11
Eph 2:20
1 Pet 2:7,8

20:18
Isa 8:14,15
Dan 2:34,35

19:47 *the business community*, literally, "the leading men among the people."

19:47 Why would the business community—which included the leading political, commercial, and judicial men among the people—want to get rid of Jesus? Obviously he had damaged business in the Temple by driving the merchants out. In addition, he preached against injustice, and his teachings often favored the poor over the rich. Further, his great popularity was in danger of attracting Rome's attention, and the leaders of Israel wanted as little as possible to do with Rome.

20:1-8 This group of leaders wanted to get rid of Jesus, so they tried to trap him with their question. If Jesus answered that his authority came from God—if he stated openly that he was the Messiah and the Son of God—they would accuse him of blasphemy and bring him to trial. Jesus did not let himself be

caught. Instead, he turned the question on them. Thus he exposed their motives and avoided their trap.

20:9-19 The characters in this story are easily identified. Even the religious leaders understood it. The landowner is God; the vineyard is Israel; the tenant farmers are the religious leaders; the landowner's men are the prophets and priests God sent to Israel to denounce their sins; the son is the Messiah, Jesus; and the others are the Gentiles. Jesus' parable indirectly answered the religious leaders' question about his authority; it also showed them that he knew their plan to kill him.

20:18 There is no difference between those who ignore Christ because they don't understand him, and those who refuse to believe in him. All who stumble over Jesus, the Cornerstone, will be judged in the end.

they wanted him arrested immediately, for they realized that he was talking about them. They were the wicked tenants in his illustration. But they were afraid that if they themselves arrested him there would be a riot. So they tried to get him to say something that could be reported to the Roman governor as reason for arrest by him.

Religious leaders question Jesus about paying taxes
(193/Matthew 22:15–22; Mark 12:13–17)

20:20
Mt 22:15-22
Mk 12:13-17

20Watching their opportunity, they sent secret agents pretending to be honest men. 21They said to Jesus, "Sir, we know what an honest teacher you are. You always tell the truth and don't budge an inch in the face of what others think, but teach the ways of God. 22Now tell us—is it right to pay taxes to the Roman government or not?"

23He saw through their trickery and said, 24"Show me a coin. Whose portrait is this on it? And whose name?"

They replied, "Caesar's—the Roman emperor's."

20:25
Lk 23:2
Rom 13:7

25He said, "Then give the emperor all that is his—and give to God all that is his!"

26Thus their attempt to outwit him before the people failed; and marveling at his answer, they were silent.

Religious leaders question Jesus about the resurrection
(194/Matthew 22:23–32; Mark 12:18–27)

20:27
Mt 22:15-33
Mk 12:18-27
Acts 23:8

27Then some Sadducees—men who believed that death is the end of existence, that there is no resurrection— 28came to Jesus with this:

20:28
Gen 38:8
Deut 25:5

"The laws of Moses state that if a man dies without children, the man's brother shall marry the widow and their children will legally belong to the dead man, to carry on his name. 29We know of a family of seven brothers. The oldest married and then died without any children. 30His brother married the widow and he, too, died. Still no children. 31And so it went, one after the other, until each of the seven had married her and died, leaving no children. 32Finally the woman died also. 33Now here is our question: Whose wife will she be in the resurrection? For all of them were married to her!"

20:36
Rom 8:23
1 Cor 15:42,49, 52
1 Jn 3:1,2

34, 35Jesus replied, "Marriage is for people here on earth, but when those who are counted worthy of being raised from the dead get to heaven, they do not marry. 36And they never die again; in these respects they are like angels, and are sons of God, for they are raised up in new life from the dead.

20:20–26 Jesus turned his enemies' attempt to trap him into a powerful lesson: God's followers have legitimate obligations to both God and the government. But what is important is to keep our priorities straight. When the two authorities conflict, our duty to God always comes before our duty to the government.

20:21 These secret agents, pretending to be honest men, flattered Jesus before asking him their trick question, hoping to catch him off guard. But Jesus knew what they were trying and stayed out of their trap. Beware of flattery. With God's help, you can detect it and stay out of its grasp.

20:22 This was indeed a loaded question. The Jews were enraged at having to pay taxes to Rome, thus supporting the pagan government and its gods. They hated the system that allowed tax collectors to charge exorbitant rates and keep the extra for themselves. If Jesus said they should pay taxes, they would call him a traitor to their nation and their religion. But if he said they should not, they could report him to Rome as a rebel. Jesus' questioners thought they had him this time, but he outwitted them again.

20:27–38 The Sadducees, a group of conservative religious

leaders, honored only the Pentateuch—Genesis through Deuteronomy—as Scripture and did not believe in a resurrection of the dead because they could find no mention of it in these books. They decided to try their hand at tricking Jesus, so they brought him a question that had always stumped the Pharisees. After addressing their question about marriage, Jesus answered their *real* question about resurrection. Basing his answer on the writings of Moses—an authority they respected—he upheld belief in resurrection.

20:28 The Sadducees' riddle could have been based on an actual case. See Deuteronomy 25:5, 6 for Moses' law providing for widows.

20:34, 35 Jesus' statement does not mean people will not recognize their partners in heaven. It simply means we must not think of heaven as an extension of life as we now know it. Our relationships in this life are limited by time, death, and sin. We don't know everything about our resurrection life, but Jesus affirms that relationships will be different from what we are used to here and now.

37, 38"But as to your real question—whether or not there is a resurrection—why, even the writings of Moses himself prove this. For when he describes how God appeared to him in the burning bush, he speaks of God as 'the God of Abraham, the God of Isaac, and the God of Jacob.' To say that the Lord *is* some person's God means that person is *alive*, not dead! So from God's point of view, all men are living."

39"Well said, sir!" remarked some of the experts in the Jewish law who were standing there. 40And that ended their questions, for they dared ask no more!

20:37
Ex 3:6
Jn 11:25
Acts 7:32
Rom 4:17
2 Cor 5:15
Heb 11:10,35

20:40
Mt 22:41-46
Mk 12:34-37

Religious leaders cannot answer Jesus' question
(196/Matthew 22:41–46; Mark 12:35–37)

41Then he presented *them* with a question. "Why is it," he asked, "that Christ, the Messiah, is said to be a descendant of King David? 42, 43For David himself wrote in the book of Psalms: 'God said to my Lord, the Messiah, "Sit at my right hand until I place your enemies beneath your feet." ' 44How can the Messiah be both David's son and David's God at the same time?"

20:42
Ps 110:1
Acts 2:34
1 Cor 15:25

Jesus warns against the religious leaders
(197/Matthew 23:1–12; Mark 12:38–40)

45Then, with the crowds listening, he turned to his disciples and said, 46"Beware of these experts in religion, for they love to parade in dignified robes and to be bowed to by the people as they walk along the street. And how they love the seats of honor in the synagogues and at religious festivals! 47But even while they are praying long prayers with great outward piety, they are planning schemes to cheat widows out of their property. Therefore God's heaviest sentence awaits these men."

20:45
Mt 23:1-7,13-14
Mk 12:38-40
Lk 11:43

20:47
Lk 12:47
Jas 4:17

A poor widow gives all she has
(200/Mark 12:41–44)

21 As he stood in the Temple, he was watching the rich tossing their gifts into the collection box. 2Then a poor widow came by and dropped in two small copper coins.

21:1
Prov 3:9,10
11:24,25
Mk 12:41-44

20:37, 38 *the Lord* is *some person's God.* Otherwise the statement would be, "He *had been* that person's God."

20:37, 38 The Sadducees came to Jesus with a trick question. Not believing in the resurrection, they wanted Jesus to say something they could refute. Even so, Jesus did not ignore or belittle their question. He answered it, then went beyond it to the real issue. When people ask you tough religious questions—"How can a loving God allow people to starve?" "If God knows what I'm going to do, do I have any free choice?"—follow Jesus' example. First answer the question to the best of your ability; then look for the real issue—hurt over a personal tragedy, for example, or difficulty in making a decision. Often the spoken question is only a test—not of your ability to answer hard questions, but of your willingness to listen and care.

20:41-44 The Pharisees and Sadducees had asked their questions. Now Jesus turned the tables and asked them a question that went right to the heart of the matter—what they thought about the identity of the Messiah. The Pharisees knew that the Messiah would be a descendant of David, but they did not understand that the Scriptures also said he would be more than a human descendant—he was God himself. Jesus quoted from Psalm 110:1 to show that David recognized that Jesus would be both man *and* God. The Pharisees expected only a human ruler to restore Israel's greatness as in the days of David and Solomon.

The central issue of life is what we believe about Jesus. Other spiritual questions are irrelevant without deciding first to believe that Jesus is who he said he is. The Pharisees and Sadducees could not do this and remained divided and confused over his identity.

20:45, 46 The religious experts loved the benefits associated with their position, and they sometimes cheated the poor in order to get even more benefits. Every job has its rewards, but they should never become more important than doing the job faithfully. God will punish people who use their position of responsibility to cheat others. Whatever trust you have been given, use it to help others and not just yourself.

20:47 How strange to think that the religious leaders would receive the worst punishment. But behind their appearance of holiness and respectability, they were arrogant, crafty, selfish, and uncaring. Jesus exposed their evil hearts. He showed that despite their pious words, they neglected God's laws and did as they pleased. Religious works do not cancel sin. Jesus said God's heaviest sentence awaited these leaders because they should have been living examples of mercy and justice.

21:1, 2 Jesus was in the area of the Temple called the Court of the Women, and the treasury was located there or in an adjoining walkway. In this area were seven boxes in which men could deposit their Temple tax and six boxes for freewill offerings like the one this woman gave. Not only was she poor; as a widow she had few resources for making money. Her small gift was a sacrifice, but she gave it willingly.

21:1, 2 This widow gave all she had, in stark contrast to the way most of us handle our money. When we consider giving a certain percentage of our income a great accomplishment, we resemble "the rest of them" who gave only a little of what they didn't need. Here, Jesus is admiring sacrificial giving. As believers, we should increase our giving—whether of money, time, or talents—to a point

3"Really," he remarked, "this poor widow has given more than all the rest of them combined. 4For they have given a little of what they didn't need, but she, poor as she is, has given everything she has."

Jesus tells about the future
(201/Matthew 24:1–22; Mark 13:1–20)

5Some of his disciples began talking about the beautiful stonework of the Temple and the memorial decorations on the walls.

6But Jesus said, "The time is coming when all these things you are admiring will be knocked down, and not one stone will be left on top of another; all will become one vast heap of rubble."

7"Master!" they exclaimed. "When? And will there be any warning ahead of time?"

8He replied, "Don't let anyone mislead you. For many will come announcing themselves as the Messiah, and saying, 'The time has come.' But don't believe them! 9And when you hear of wars and insurrections beginning, don't panic. True, wars must come, but the end won't follow immediately— 10for nation shall rise against nation and kingdom against kingdom, 11and there will be great earthquakes, and famines in many lands, and epidemics, and terrifying things happening in the heavens.

12"But before all this occurs, there will be a time of special persecution, and you will be dragged into synagogues and prisons and before kings and governors for my name's sake. 13But as a result, the Messiah will be widely known and honored.

21:5
Mk 24:1-22
Mk 13:1-23
21:6
1 Kgs 9:8
Mic 3:12
Lk 19:44

21:8
Lk 17:23

21:12
Mt 10:17,18
Acts 4:3; 5:18
12:4; 16:24
25:23
Rev 2:10
21:13
Phil 1:12,13

21:8 *will come announcing themselves as the Messiah,* literally, "will come in my name." **21:13** *the Messiah will be widely known and honored,* literally, "It shall turn out unto you for a testimony."

---

beyond that which is convenient or safe.

21:5 The Temple the disciples were admiring was not Solomon's Temple—that was destroyed by the Babylonians in the seventh century B.C. This Temple was built by Ezra after the return from exile in the sixth century B.C., desecrated by the Seleucids in the second century B.C., reconsecrated by the Maccabees soon afterward, and enormously expanded by Herod the Great over a 46-year period. It was a beautiful, imposing structure with a significant history, but Jesus said it would be completely destroyed. This happened in A.D. 70 when a Roman army burned Jerusalem.

21:7ff Jesus did not leave his disciples unprepared for the difficult years ahead. He warned them against false messiahs, natural disasters, and persecutions; but he assured them he would be with them to protect them and make his Kingdom known through them. In the end, he promised, he would return in power and glory to save them. Jesus' warnings and promises to his disciples still apply to us as we look forward to his return.

21:8 Jesus was sitting on the Mount of Olives, the very place where the prophet Zechariah predicted the Messiah would stand when he came to establish his Kingdom (Zechariah 14:4). It was a fitting place for the disciples to ask Jesus when he would come into power and what they could expect then. Jesus' reply emphasized the events that would take place before the end of the age. He pointed out that they should be less concerned with knowing the exact date and more concerned with being prepared – living God's way consistently so that no matter when Jesus came, he would claim them as his own.

21:12, 13 These persecutions soon began. Luke recorded many of them in the book of Acts. Paul wrote from prison that he anticipated suffering because it helped him know Christ better and do Christ's work for the church (Philippians 3:10; Colossians 1:24). The early church thrived despite intense persecution. In fact, late in the second century the church father Tertullian wrote, "The blood of Christians is seed."

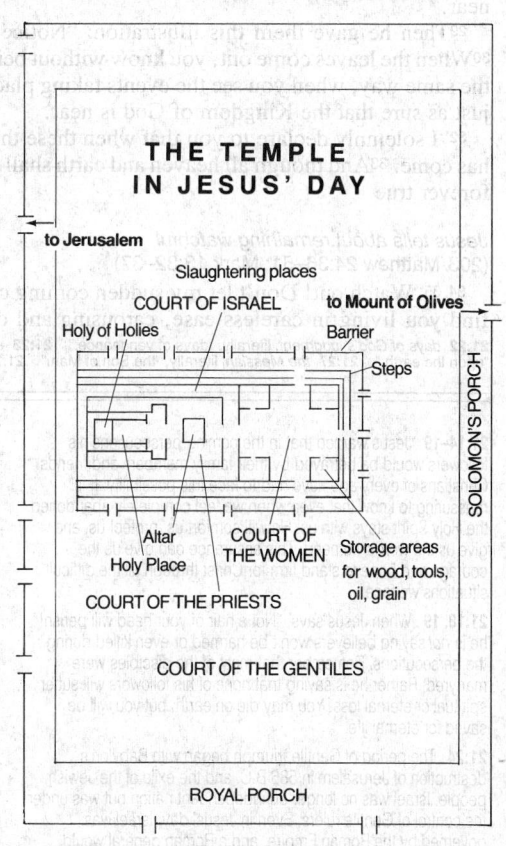

THE TEMPLE IN JESUS' DAY

to Jerusalem

Slaughtering places

COURT OF ISRAEL   to Mount of Olives

Holy of Holies   Barrier

                          Steps

                                    SOLOMON'S PORCH

Altar   COURT OF
Holy Place THE WOMEN   Storage areas
                           for wood, tools,
COURT OF THE PRIESTS   oil, grain

COURT OF THE GENTILES

ROYAL PORCH

14Therefore, don't be concerned about how to answer the charges against you, 15for I will give you the right words and such logic that none of your opponents will be able to reply! 16Even those closest to you—your parents, brothers, relatives, and friends will betray you and have you arrested; and some of you will be killed. 17And everyone will hate you because you are mine and are called by my name. 18But not a hair of your head will perish! 19For if you stand firm, you will win your souls.

20"But when you see Jerusalem surrounded by armies, then you will know that the time of its destruction has arrived. 21Then let the people of Judea flee to the hills. Let those in Jerusalem try to escape, and those outside the city must not attempt to return. 22For those will be days of God's judgment, and the words of the ancient Scriptures written by the prophets will be abundantly fulfilled. 23Woe to expectant mothers in those days, and those with tiny babies. For there will be great distress upon this nation and wrath upon this people. 24They will be brutally killed by enemy weapons, or sent away as exiles and captives to all the nations of the world; and Jerusalem shall be conquered and trampled down by the Gentiles until the period of Gentile triumph ends in God's good time.

Jesus tells about his return
(202/Matthew 24:23–35; Mark 13:21–31)

25"Then there will be strange events in the skies—warnings, evil omens and portents in the sun, moon and stars; and down here on earth the nations will be in turmoil, perplexed by the roaring seas and strange tides. 26The courage of many people will falter because of the fearful fate they see coming upon the earth, for the stability of the very heavens will be broken up. 27Then the peoples of the earth shall see me, the Messiah, coming in a cloud with power and great glory. 28So when all these things begin to happen, stand straight and look up! For your salvation is near."

29Then he gave them this illustration: "Notice the fig tree, or any other tree. 30When the leaves come out, you know without being told that summer is near. 31In the same way, when you see the events taking place that I've described you can be just as sure that the Kingdom of God is near.

32"I solemnly declare to you that when these things happen, the end of this age has come. 33And though all heaven and earth shall pass away, yet my words remain forever true.

Jesus tells about remaining watchful
(203/Matthew 24:36–51; Mark 13:32–37)

34, 35"Watch out! Don't let my sudden coming catch you unawares; don't let me find you living in careless ease, carousing and drinking, and occupied with the

21:22 *days of God's judgment,* literally, "days of vengeance."   21:23 *upon this nation,* literally, "upon the land," or "upon the earth."   21:27 *the Messiah,* literally, "the Son of Man."   21:32 *this age,* "this generation."

Cross references:
21:14 Mt 10:19,20 / Lk 12:11,12 / Acts 6:10
21:16 Mic 7:6 / Mt 10:21,22 / Acts 7:60; 12:2
21:17 2 Tim 3:12
21:19 Rom 2:7 / 1 Pet 1:6-9
21:22 Isa 61:2 / Dan 9:26,27 / Hos 9:7 / Rom 11:25 / Rev 11:2
21:24 Dan 8:13 / Rom 11:25 / Rev 11:2
21:25 Mt 24:29-31 / Mk 13:24-27 / 2 Pet 3:10,12
21:27 Dan 7:13 / Acts 1:11 / Rev 1:7; 14:14
21:29 Mt 24:32-35 / Mk 13:28-31
21:31 Mk 1:15
21:33 Isa 40:6-8 / Mt 5:18 / Lk 6:17 / 1 Pet 1:23-25
21:34 Rom 13:12,13 / 1 Thess 5:2

21:14-19 Jesus warned that in the coming persecutions his followers would be betrayed by their family members and friends. Christians of every age have had to face this possibility. It is reassuring to know that even when we feel completely abandoned, the Holy Spirit stays with us. He will comfort us, protect us, and give us the words we need. This assurance can give us the courage and hope to stand firm for Christ through all the difficult situations we face.

21:18, 19 When Jesus says, "Not a hair of your head will perish!" he is *not* saying believers won't be harmed or even killed during the persecutions. Remember that most of the disciples were martyred. Rather he is saying that none of his followers will suffer spiritual or eternal loss. You may die on earth, but you will be saved for eternal life.

21:24 The period of Gentile triumph began with Babylon's destruction of Jerusalem in 586 B.C. and the exile of the Jewish people. Israel was no longer an independent nation but was under the control of Gentile rulers. Even in Jesus' day, Israel was governed by the Roman Empire, and a Roman general would

destroy the city in A.D. 70. In this verse Jesus was saying that this Gentile domination would continue until God decided to end it. The Gentile triumph refers not just to the repeated destructions of Jerusalem, but also to the continued and mounting persecution of God's people until the end.

21:28 The picture of the coming persecutions and natural disasters is gloomy, but ultimately they are cause not for worry but for great joy. When believers see these events happening, they will know that the return of their Messiah is near, and they can look forward to his reign of justice and peace. Rather than being terrified by what is happening in our world, we should confidently await Christ's return.

21:34, 35 Jesus told the disciples to keep a constant watch for his return. Although nearly two thousand years have passed since he spoke these words, their truth remains: he is coming again, and we need to watch and be ready. This means working faithfully at the tasks God has given us. Our attitude toward all we do should be colored with our joyful expectation of Christ's return.

21:36
Mt 25:13
Mk 13:33
Eph 6:13,18
1 Thess 5:17
1 Jn 2:28

problems of this life, like all the rest of the world. ³⁶Keep a constant watch. And pray that if possible you may arrive in my presence without having to experience these horrors."

21:37,38
Lk 22:39
Jn 8:1,2

³⁷,³⁸Every day Jesus went to the Temple to teach, and the crowds began gathering early in the morning to hear him. And each evening he returned to spend the night on the Mount of Olives.

➤ C. DEATH AND RESURRECTION OF JESUS, THE SAVIOR (22:1—24:53)

The perfect man was a high ideal in Greek culture. Written with Greeks in mind, Luke shows how Jesus was the perfect man given as the perfect sacrifice for the sin of all mankind. Christ is the ideal man—the perfect model for us to follow. We must stand in awe of his character, living up to man's highest ideals as well as God's demand for an atonement for sin. He is, at once, our model and our Savior.

Religious leaders plot to kill Jesus
(207/Matthew 26:1–5; Mark 14:1, 2)

22:1
Mt 26:1-5,14-16
Mk 14:1,2,10
22:2
Ps 2:2
Acts 4:27

22 And now the Passover celebration was drawing near—the Jewish festival when only bread made without yeast was used. ²The chief priests and other religious leaders were actively plotting Jesus' murder, trying to find a way to kill him without starting a riot—a possibility they greatly feared.

Judas agrees to betray Jesus
(208/Matthew 26:14–16; Mark 14:10, 11)

22:3
Jn 13:2,27

³Then Satan entered into Judas Iscariot, who was one of the twelve disciples, ⁴and he went over to the chief priests and captains of the Temple guards to discuss the best way to betray Jesus to them. ⁵They were, of course, delighted to know that he was ready to help them and promised him a reward. ⁶So he began to look for an opportunity for them to arrest Jesus quietly when the crowds weren't around.

22:5
Zech 11:12
1 Tim 6:10

Disciples prepare for the Passover
(209/Matthew 26:17–19; Mark 14:12–16)

22:7
Ex 12:3,4,17
Deut 16:1
Mt 26:17-19
Mk 14:12-16

⁷Now the day of the Passover celebration arrived, when the Passover lamb was killed and eaten with the unleavened bread. ⁸Jesus sent Peter and John ahead to find a place to prepare their Passover meal.

22:8
Acts 3:1; 4:13
Gal 2:9

⁹"Where do you want us to go?" they asked.

22:10
1 Sam 10:3

¹⁰And he replied, "As soon as you enter Jerusalem, you will see a man walking along carrying a pitcher of water. Follow him into the house he enters, ¹¹and say to the man who lives there, 'Our Teacher says for you to show us the guest room where he can eat the Passover meal with his disciples.' ¹²He will take you upstairs to a large room all ready for us. That is the place. Go ahead and prepare the meal there."

21:36 *without having to experience these horrors,* or, "Pray for strength to pass safely through these coming horrors."
22:10 *Jerusalem,* literally, "the city."

21:36 Only days after telling the disciples to pray that they might escape persecution, Jesus himself asked God, if possible, to spare him the agonies of the cross (Luke 22:41, 42). It is abnormal to *want* to suffer, but Jesus' followers are willing to suffer if by doing so they can help build God's Kingdom. We have two wonderful promises to help us as we suffer: God will always be with us (Matthew 28:20), and he will one day rescue us and give us eternal life (Revelation 21:1–4).

22:1 All Jewish males over the age of 12 were required to go to Jerusalem for the Passover festival, followed by a seven-day festival called the Feast of Unleavened Bread. For these feasts Jews from all over the Roman Empire converged on Jerusalem to celebrate one of the most important events in their history. To learn more about the Passover and the Feast of Unleavened Bread, see the note on Mark 14:1.

22:3 Satan's part in the betrayal of Jesus does not remove any of the responsibility from Judas. Disillusioned because Jesus was talking about dying rather than about setting up his Kingdom,

Judas may have been trying to force his hand and make him use his power to prove he was the Messiah. Or perhaps Judas, not understanding Jesus' mission, no longer believed he was God's chosen one. (For more information on Judas, see his profile in Mark 14.) Whatever Judas thought, Satan assumed that Jesus' death would end his mission and thwart God's plan. Like Judas, he did not know Jesus' death was the most important part of God's plan all along.

22:7, 8 The Passover meal included lamb because when the Jews were getting ready to leave Egypt, God told them to kill a lamb and paint its blood on the doorposts of their homes and prepare the meat for food. Peter and John had to buy and prepare the lamb as well as the unleavened bread, sauces, wine, and other cermonial food.

22:10 Ordinarily women, not men, went to the well and brought home the water. This man, then, would have stood out in the crowd.

13They went off to the city and found everything just as Jesus had said, and prepared the Passover supper.

Jesus and the disciples have the Last Supper
(211/Matthew 26:20–29; Mark 14:17–25; John 13:21–30)

14Then Jesus and the others arrived, and at the proper time all sat down together at the table; 15and he said, "I have looked forward to this hour with deep longing, anxious to eat this Passover meal with you before my suffering begins. 16For I tell you now that I won't eat it again until what it represents has occurred in the Kingdom of God."

17Then he took a glass of wine, and when he had given thanks for it, he said, "Take this and share it among yourselves. 18For I will not drink wine again until the Kingdom of God has come."

19Then he took a loaf of bread; and when he had thanked God for it, he broke it apart and gave it to them, saying, "This is my body, given for you. Eat it in remembrance of me."

20After supper he gave them another glass of wine, saying, "This wine is the token of God's new agreement to save you—an agreement sealed with the blood I shall pour out to purchase back your souls. 21But here at this table, sitting among us as a friend, is the man who will betray me. 22I must die. It is part of God's plan. But, oh, the horror awaiting that man who betrays me."

23Then the disciples wondered among themselves which of them would ever do such a thing.

24And they began to argue among themselves as to who would have the highest rank [in the coming Kingdom].

25Jesus told them, "In this world the kings and great men order their slaves around, and the slaves have no choice but to like it! 26But among you, the one who serves you best will be your leader. 27Out in the world the master sits at the table

22:14
Mt 26:20,26-29
Mk 14:17,22-25

22:16
Lk 14:15
Rev 19:9

22:19
1 Cor 10:16
11:23-26

22:20
Jer 31:31
Heb 9:15-18

22:21
Ps 41:9
Mt 26:20-25
Mk 14:17-21
Jn 13:21-30

22:22
Acts 2:23; 4:28

22:24
Mk 9:34
Lk 9:46

22:25
Mt 20:25-28
Mk 10:42-45

22:26
Mt 23:11
Mk 9:35
Lk 9:48
1 Pet 5:5

22:27
Jn 13:14
Phil 2:7

22:20 *This wine is the token . . . to purchase back your souls,* literally, "This cup of the new covenant in my blood, poured out for you." 22:22 *I,* literally, "the Son of Man." 22:24 *in the coming Kingdom,* implied. 22:25 *the slaves have no choice but to like it,* literally, "they the kings and great men are called 'benefactors.' "

22:16 The Passover commemorated Israel's escape from Egypt when the blood of a lamb, painted on their doorposts, saved them from the angel of death who was killing the firstborn in all the homes in Egypt. This event foreshadowed Jesus' work on the cross. As the spotless Lamb of God, his blood would be spilled in order to save his people from the death brought by sin and judgment.

22:17 Luke mentions two glasses of wine (22:17, 20), while Matthew and Mark mention only one. Actually, in the traditional Passover meal, the wine is served four times. Christ spoke the words about his body and his blood when he offered the fourth and last cup.

22:17-20 Christians differ in their interpretation of the meaning of the commemoration of the Lord's Supper. There are three main views: (1) the bread and wine actually become Christ's body and blood; (2) the bread and wine remain unchanged, yet Christ is spiritually present by faith in and through them; (3) the bread and wine, which remain unchanged, are lasting memorials of Christ's sacrifice. No matter which view you favor, all Christians agree that the Lord's Supper commemorates Christ's death on the cross for our sins and points to the coming of his Kingdom in glory. When we partake of it, we show our acceptance of his work and our faith is strengthened.

22:20 In Old Testament times, God agreed to forgive people's sins if they brought animals for the priests to sacrifice. When this sacrificial system was inaugurated, the agreement between God and man was sealed with the blood of animals (Exodus 24:8). But animal blood did not in itself remove sin, and animal sacrifices had to be repeated day by day and year by year. Jesus instituted a

new agreement—sometimes called the new covenant—between man and God. Under this new agreement, Jesus would die in the place of sinners. Unlike the blood of animals, his blood would truly remove the sins of all who put their faith in him. And his sacrifice would never have to be repeated; it would be good for all eternity. The prophets looked forward to this new agreement, which would fulfill the old sacrificial agreement (Jeremiah 31:31-34), and John the Baptist called Jesus the "Lamb of God who takes away the world's sin" (John 1:29).

22:21 From the accounts of Mark and John we know that this friend is Judas Iscariot. Although the other disciples were confused by Jesus' words, Judas knew what he meant.

22:24 The most important event in human history was about to take place, and the disciples were still arguing about their prestige in the Kingdom! Looking back, we say, "This was no time to worry about status." But the disciples, wrapped up in their own concerns, did not perceive what Jesus had been trying to tell them about his approaching death and resurrection. What are your major concerns today? Twenty years from now, as you look back, will these worries look petty and inappropriate? Get your eyes off yourself and look for signs of the Kingdom of God, which is about to break into human history for the second time.

22:24-26 The world's system of leadership is very different from the Kingdom's. Worldly leaders are often selfish and arrogant as they claw their way to the top. But among Christians, the leader is to be the one who *serves* best. There are different styles of leadership—some lead through public speaking, some through administering, some through relationships—but all leaders need a servant's heart. Ask the people you lead how you can serve them better.

and is served by his servants. But not here! For I am your servant. 28Nevertheless, because you have stood true to me in these terrible days, 29and because my Father has granted me a Kingdom, I, here and now, grant you the right 30to eat and drink at my table in that Kingdom; and you will sit on thrones judging the twelve tribes of Israel.

Jesus predicts Peter's denial
(212/John 13:31–38)

31"Simon, Simon, Satan has asked to have you, to sift you like wheat, 32but I have pleaded in prayer for you that your faith should not completely fail. So when you have repented and turned to me again, strengthen and build up the faith of your brothers."

33Simon said, "Lord, I am ready to go to jail with you, and even to die with you."

34But Jesus said, "Peter, let me tell you something. Between now and tomorrow morning when the rooster crows, you will deny me three times, declaring that you don't even know me."

35Then Jesus asked them, "When I sent you out to preach the Good News and you were without money, duffle bag, or extra clothing, how did you get along?"

"Fine," they replied.

36"But now," he said, "take a duffle bag if you have one, and your money. And if you don't have a sword, better sell your clothes and buy one! 37For the time has come for this prophecy about me to come true: 'He will be condemned as a criminal!' Yes, everything written about me by the prophets will come true."

38"Master," they replied, "we have two swords among us."

"Enough!" he said.

Jesus agonizes in the garden
(223/Matthew 26:36–46; Mark 14:32–42)

39Then, accompanied by the disciples, he left the upstairs room and went as usual to the Mount of Olives. 40There he told them, "Pray God that you will not be overcome by temptation."

41,42He walked away, perhaps a stone's throw, and knelt down and prayed this prayer: "Father, if you are willing, please take away this cup of horror from me. But I want your will, not mine." 43Then an angel from heaven appeared and strengthened him, 44for he was in such agony of spirit that he broke into a sweat of blood, with great drops falling to the ground as he prayed more and more earnestly.

22:28 *because you have stood true to me in these terrible days,* literally, "you have continued with me in my temptation." **22:32** *not completely fail,* literally, "fail not." **22:40** *that you will not be overcome by temptation,* literally, "that you enter not into temptation."

Marginal references:

22:30
Mt 8:11; 19:28
Lk 14:15
1 Cor 6:2
2 Tim 2:12
Rev 3:21; 19:9

22:31
Amos 9:9
Mt 26:31-35
Mk 14:27-31
1 Pet 5:8

22:32
Ps 51:13
Jn 17:9,11,15
21:15
2 Cor 1:3,4

22:33
Jn 13:37,38

22:35
Mt 10:9,10
Lk 9:3

22:37
Isa 53:12
Mk 15:28

22:39
Mt 26:30,36-46
Mk 14:26,32-42
Jn 18:1

22:40
Mt 6:13

22:41
Mk 10:38
Jn 5:30; 6:38
18:11

22:31, 32 Satan wanted to crush Peter like a grain of wheat. He hoped to find only chaff and blow it away. But Jesus assured Peter that his faith, although it would falter, would not be destroyed. It would be renewed, and he would become a powerful leader.

22:33, 34 Jesus predicts that Judas will betray him and says that horror is awaiting the traitor (22:22). He then predicts that Peter will deny him but then repent and lead his brethren. Betraying and denying—one is just about as bad as the other. But the two men have entirely different fates because one believed and repented.

22:35-38 Now Jesus reverses his earlier advice regarding how to travel (9:3). The disciples were to bring a bag, money, and a sword. They would be facing hatred and persecution and would need to be prepared. When Jesus said "Enough," he may have meant that two swords were enough or that they had talked enough. In either case, their need for a sword vividly communicated the trials they were soon to face.

22:39 The Mount of Olives was located just to the east of Jerusalem. Jesus went up the southwestern slope to an olive grove called Gethsemane, which means "oil press."

22:40 Jesus asked the disciples to pray that they would not be overcome by temptation because he knew he would soon be

leaving them. He also knew they would need extra strength to face the temptations ahead—temptations to run away, or to deny their relationship with him. Also, they were about to see him die—would they still think he was the Messiah? Their strongest temptation would be to think they had been deceived.

22:41, 42 Was Jesus trying to get out of his mission? It is never wrong to express our true feelings to God. Jesus exposed his dread of the coming trials, but he also reaffirmed his commitment to do what God wanted. The cup he spoke of means the terrible agony he knew he would endure—not only the horror of the crucifixion but, even worse, the total separation from God he would have to experience in order to die for the world's sins.

22:43, 44 Only Luke tells us of Jesus' sweating drops of blood. Jesus was in extreme agony, but he did not give up or give in. He went ahead with the mission for which he had come. "If you want to keep from becoming fainthearted and weary," says the writer of Hebrews, "think about his patience as sinful men did such terrible things to him. After all, you have never yet struggled against sin and temptation until you sweat great drops of blood" (Hebrews 12:3, 4).

45At last he stood up again and returned to the disciples—only to find them asleep, exhausted from grief.

46"Asleep!" he said. "Get up! Pray God that you will not fall when you are tempted."

Jesus is betrayed and arrested
(224/Matthew 26:47–56; Mark 14:43–52; John 18:1–11)

47But even as he said this, a mob approached, led by Judas, one of his twelve disciples. Judas walked over to Jesus and kissed him on the cheek in friendly greeting.

22:47
Mt 26:47-56
Mk 14:43-50
Jn 18:1-11

48But Jesus said, "Judas, how can you do this—betray the Messiah with a kiss?"

49When the other disciples saw what was about to happen, they exclaimed, "Master, shall we fight? We brought along the swords!" 50And one of them slashed at the High Priest's servant, and cut off his right ear.

51But Jesus said, "Don't resist any more." And he touched the place where the man's ear had been and restored it. 52Then Jesus addressed the chief priests and captains of the Temple guards and the religious leaders who headed the mob. "Am I a robber," he asked, "that you have come armed with swords and clubs to get me? 53Why didn't you arrest me in the Temple? I was there every day. But this is your moment—the time when Satan's power reigns supreme."

22:53
Gen 3:15
Lk 19:47
Jn 7:30

Peter denies knowing Jesus
(227/Matthew 26:69–75; Mark 14:66–72; John 18:25–27)

54So they seized him and led him to the High Priest's residence, and Peter followed at a distance. 55The soldiers lit a fire in the courtyard and sat around it for warmth, and Peter joined them there.

22:54
Mt 26:57,58
Mk 14:53,54
Jn 18:25-27

22:47 walked over . . . and kissed him on the cheek in friendly greeting, literally, "approached Jesus to kiss him."

Event	Probable reasons	References	**JESUS' TRIAL**
Trial before Annas (powerful ex-High Priest)	Although no longer the High Priest, may have still wielded much power	John 18:13–23	Jesus' trial was actually a series of hearings, carefully controlled to accomplish the death of Jesus. The verdict was predecided, but certain "legal" procedures were necessary. A lot of effort went into condemning and crucifying an innocent man. Jesus went through an unfair trial in our place so that we would not have to face a fair trial and receive just punishment for our sins.
Trial before Caiaphas (the ruling High Priest)	To gather evidence for the full Supreme Court hearing to follow	Matthew 26:57–68 Mark 14:53–65 Luke 22:54, 63–65 John 18:24	
Trial before the Supreme Court	Formal religious trial and condemnation to death	Matthew 27:1 Mark 15:1 Luke 22:66–71	
Trial before Pilate (highest Roman authority)	All death sentences needed Roman approval	Matthew 27:2, 11–14 Mark 15:1–5 Luke 23:1–6 John 18:28–38	
Trial before Herod (ruler of Galilee)	A courtesy and guilt-sharing act by Pilate because Jesus was from Galilee, Herod's district	Luke 23:7–12	
Trial before Pilate	Pilate's last effort to avoid condemning an obviously innocent man	Matthew 27:15–26 Mark 15:6–15 Luke 23:13–25 John 18:39—19:16	

22:47 A kiss was and still is the traditional greeting among men in certain parts of the world. In this case, it was also the agreed upon signal to point out Jesus (Matthew 26:48).

22:50 We learn from the Gospel of John that the man who drew his sword was Peter (John 18:10).

22:53 The religious leaders had not arrested Jesus in the Temple for fear of a riot. Instead, they came secretly at night, under the influence of the prince of darkness, Satan himself. Although it looked as if Satan was getting the upper hand, everything was proceeding according to God's plan. It was now time for Jesus to die.

⁵⁶A servant girl noticed him in the firelight and began staring at him. Finally she spoke: "This man was with Jesus!"

⁵⁷Peter denied it. "Woman," he said, "I don't even know the man!"

⁵⁸After a while someone else looked at him and said, "You must be one of them!" "No sir, I am not!" Peter replied.

⁵⁹About an hour later someone else flatly stated, "I know this fellow is one of Jesus' disciples, for both are from Galilee."

22:61
Jn 13:38

⁶⁰But Peter said, "Man, I don't know what you are talking about." And as he said the words, a rooster crowed.

22:62
2 Cor 7:10

⁶¹At that moment Jesus turned and looked at Peter. Then Peter remembered what he had said—"Before the rooster crows tomorrow morning, you will deny me three times." ⁶²And Peter walked out of the courtyard, crying bitterly.

22:63
Isa 52:14
Mt 26:67,68
Mk 14:65
Jn 18:22

⁶³, ⁶⁴Now the guards in charge of Jesus began mocking him. They blindfolded him and hit him with their fists and asked, "Who hit you that time, prophet?" ⁶⁵And they threw all sorts of other insults at him.

The council of religious leaders condemns Jesus
(228/Matthew 27:1, 2; Mark 15:1)

22:66
Mt 26:63-66
27:1
Mk 14:61-64
15:1

⁶⁶Early the next morning at daybreak the Jewish Supreme Court assembled, including the chief priests and all the top religious authorities of the nation. Jesus was led before this Council, ⁶⁷, ⁶⁸and instructed to state whether or not he claimed to be the Messiah.

But he replied, "If I tell you, you won't believe me or let me present my case.

22:69
Dan 7:13,14
Acts 3:21
Heb 1:3; 8:1

⁶⁹But the time is soon coming when I, the Messiah, shall be enthroned beside Almighty God."

⁷⁰They all shouted, "Then you claim you are the Son of God?"

22:69 *the Messiah,* literally, "the Son of Man."

JESUS' TRIAL Taken from Gethsemane, Jesus first appeared before the Jewish Supreme Court which had convened at daybreak at Caiaphas' house. From there he went first to Pilate, the Roman governor, then to Herod, tetrarch of Galilee, who was visiting in Jerusalem, and back to Pilate who, in desperation, sentenced Jesus to die.

22:54 Jesus was immediately taken to the High Priest's residence, even though this was the middle of the night. The Jewish leaders were in a hurry—they wanted to complete the execution before the Sabbath and get on with the Passover celebration. This residence was a palace with outer walls enclosing a courtyard where servants and soldiers warmed themselves around a fire.

22:55 Peter's experiences in the next few hours would change his life. For more information on Peter, see his Profile in Matthew 27.

22:62 Peter wept bitterly, not only because he realized he had denied his Lord, the Messiah, but also because he had turned away from a very dear friend, a person who had loved and taught him for three years. Peter had said he would *never* deny Christ, despite Jesus' prediction (22:33, 34), but when frightened he went against all he had boldly promised. Unable to stand up for his Lord for even 12 hours, he had failed as a disciple and as a friend. We need to be aware of our own breaking points and not become overconfident or self-sufficient. If we fail, we must remember that Christ can use those who recognize their failure. From this humiliating experience Peter learned much that would help him in the leadership responsibilities he would soon assume.

22:70 Jesus didn't actually say he was God; he simply answered yes to the High Priest's quesion, by saying "I Am." But Jesus identified himself with God by using a familiar title for him found in the Old Testament: "I Am" (Exodus 3:14). The High Priest recognized Jesus' claim and accused him of blasphemy. Although claiming to be God is blasphemy, blasphemy includes attacks on God as well as claiming to have his attributes. For any other man this claim would have been blasphemy, but in this case it was true. Blasphemy, the sin of claiming to be God, was punishable by death. The Jewish leaders had the evidence they wanted.

And he replied, "Yes, I am."

71"What need do we have for other witnesses?" they shouted. "For we ourselves have heard him say it."

Jesus stands trial before Pilate
(230/Matthew 27:11–14; Mark 15:2–5; John 18:28–38)

23 Then the entire Council took Jesus over to Pilate, the governor. 2They began at once accusing him: "This fellow has been leading our people to ruin by telling them not to pay their taxes to the Roman government and by claiming he is our Messiah—a King."

3So Pilate asked him, "Are you their Messiah—their King?""Yes," Jesus replied, "it is as you say."

4Then Pilate turned to the chief priests and to the mob and said, "So? That isn't a crime!"

5Then they became desperate. "But he is causing riots against the government everywhere he goes, all over Judea, from Galilee to Jerusalem!"

23:1
Mt 27:2,11-14
Mk 15:1-5
Jn 18:28,33-38
23:2
Mt 17:24-27
22:21
Mk 12:17
Jn 19:12
Acts 17:7; 24:5
23:3
1 Tim 6:13
23:4
Jn 19:4
1 Pet 2:22

Jesus stands trial before Herod
(231)

6"Is he then a Galilean?" Pilate asked.

7When they told him yes, Pilate said to take him to King Herod, for Galilee was under Herod's jurisdiction; and Herod happened to be in Jerusalem at the time. 8Herod was delighted at the opportunity to see Jesus, for he had heard a lot about him and had been hoping to see him perform a miracle.

9He asked Jesus question after question, but there was no reply. 10Meanwhile, the chief priests and the other religious leaders stood there shouting their accusations.

11Now Herod and his soldiers began mocking and ridiculing Jesus; and putting a kingly robe on him, they sent him back to Pilate. 12That day Herod and Pilate—enemies before—became fast friends.

23:7
Lk 3:1
23:8
Mt 14:1
Mk 6:14
Lk 9:9
23:9
Jn 19:9

23:12
Acts 4:27

Pilate hands Jesus over to be crucified
(232/Matthew 27:15–26; Mark 15:6–15; John 18:39—19:16)

13Then Pilate called together the chief priests and other Jewish leaders, along with the people, 14and announced his verdict:

23:1 *the governor,* implied.   **23:3** *Are you their Messiah—their King?* Literally, "Are you the King of the Jews?"
23:14 *of leading a revolt against the Roman government,* literally, "as one who perverts the people."

23:1 Pilate was the Roman governor of Judea, where Jerusalem was located. He seemed to take special pleasure in harassing the Jews. For example, he took money from the Temple treasuries and used it to build an aqueduct, and he insulted the Jewish religion by bringing imperial images into the city. As Pilate well knew, however, such acts could backfire. If the people lodged a formal complaint against his administration, Rome might remove him from his post. Pilate was already beginning to feel insecure in his position when the Jewish leaders brought Jesus to trial. Would he continue to badger the Jews and risk his political future, or would he give in to their demands and condemn a man who, he was quite sure, was innocent? That was the quesion facing Pilate that springtime Friday morning nearly two thousand years ago. For more about Pilate, see his profile in Mark 15.

23:7 Herod, also called Herod Antipas, was in Jerusalem that weekend for the Passover celebration. (This was the Herod who killed John the Baptist.) Pilate hoped to pass Jesus off on Herod, because he knew Jesus had lived and worked in Galilee. But Herod was not much help. He was curious about Jesus and enjoyed making fun of him, but when he sent Jesus back to Pilate it

was with the verdict of innocent. For more about Herod Antipas, see his Profile in Mark 6.

23:12 Herod was the part-Jewish ruler of Galilee and Perea. Pilate was the Roman governor of Judea and Samaria. These four provinces, together with several others, had been united under King Herod the Great, but when he died in 4 B.C. the kingdom was divided among four of his sons, none of whom was called king but tetrarch (meaning "one fourth"). Archelaus, the son who had received Judea and Samaria, was removed from office within ten years, and his provinces were then ruled by a succession of Roman governors of whom Pilate was the fifth.

Herod Antipas had two advantages over Pilate: he came from a hereditary, part-Jewish monarchy, and he had held his position much longer. But Pilate had two advantages over Herod: he was a Roman citizen and an envoy of the emperor, and his position was created to replace that of Herod's ineffective half brother. It is not surprising that the two men were uneasy around each other. Jesus' trial, however, brought them together. Because Pilate recognized Herod's authority over Galilee, Herod stopped feeling threatened by the Roman politician. And because neither man knew what to do in this predicament, their common problem united them.

"You brought this man to me, accusing him of leading a revolt against the Roman government. I have examined him thoroughly on this point and find him innocent. 15Herod came to the same conclusion and sent him back to us—nothing this man has done calls for the death penalty. 16I will therefore have him scourged with leaded thongs, and release him."

17, 18But now a mighty roar rose from the crowd as with one voice they shouted. "Kill him, and release Barabbas to us!" 19(Barabbas was in prison for starting an insurrection in Jerusalem against the government, and for murder.) 20Pilate argued with them, for he wanted to release Jesus. 21But they shouted, "Crucify him! Crucify him!"

22Once more, for the third time, he demanded, "Why? What crime has he committed? I have found no reason to sentence him to death. I will therefore scourge him and let him go." 23But they shouted louder and louder for Jesus' death, and their voices prevailed.

24So Pilate sentenced Jesus to die as they demanded. 25And he released Barabbas, the man in prison for insurrection and murder, at their request. But he delivered Jesus over to them to do with as they would.

Jesus is led away to be crucified
(234/Matthew 27:32–34; Mark 15:21–24; John 19:17)

26As the crowd led Jesus away to his death, Simon of Cyrene, who was just coming into Jerusalem from the country, was forced to follow, carrying Jesus' cross. 27Great crowds trailed along behind, and many grief-stricken women.

23:17 Some ancient authorities add vs 17, "For it was necessary for him to release unto them at the feast one prisoner."

Side references (left margin):
23:15 Lk 9:9
23:16 Jn 19:1 / Acts 16:37
23:17 Mt 27:15-26 / Mk 15:6-15 / Jn 18:39,40
23:18 Acts 3:14
23:23 Ex 23:2,3
23:24 Jn 19:16
23:25 Prov 17:15
23:26 Mt 27:32 / Mk 15:21 / Jn 19:17

23:13–25 Pilate wanted to release Jesus, but the crowd loudly demanded his death, so Pilate sentenced Jesus to die. No doubt Pilate did not want to risk losing his position, which may already have been shaky, by allowing a riot to occur in his province. As a career politician, he knew the importance of compromise, and he saw Jesus more as a political threat than as a human being with rights and dignity.

When the stakes are high, it is hard to stand up for what is right, and it is easy to see our opponents as problems to be solved rather than as people to be respected. Had Pilate been a man of real courage, he would have released Jesus no matter what the consequences. But the crowd roared, and Pilate buckled. When you have a difficult decision to make, don't discount the effects of peer pressure. Realize beforehand that the right decision could have unpleasant consequences: social rejection, career derailment, public ridicule. Then think of Pilate and resolve to stand up for what is right no matter what other people pressure you to do.

23:15 Jesus was tried six times, by both Jewish and Roman authorities, but never was he convicted of a crime deserving death. Even when he was turned over to the Jews for execution, he had been convicted of no felony. Still today, no one is able to find fault in Jesus. But, just like Pilate, Herod, and the religious leaders, many still refuse to acknowledge him as Lord.

23:17–19 Barabbas had been part of a rebellion against the Roman government (Mark 15:7). As a political insurgent, he was no doubt a hero among some of the Jews. How ironic that Barabbas, who was released, was guilty of the very crime Jesus was accused of (23:14).

23:17–19 Who was Barabbas? Jewish men had names that identified them with their fathers. Simon Peter, for example, is called Simon Bar-jona (Matthew 16:17; also translated "Simon, son

of Jonah"). Barabbas is never identified by his given name, and this name is not much help either—*bar-abbas* means "son of papa." He could have been anybody's son—and that's just the point. Barabbas, son of an unnamed papa, committed a crime. Because Jesus died in his place, this man was set free. We too are sinners and criminals against God's holy law. Like Barabbas, we deserve to die. But Jesus has died in our place, for our sins, and we have been set free. We don't have to be important to accept our freedom in Christ. In fact, thanks to Jesus, God adopts us all as his own sons and daughters and gives us the right to call him Abba—"papa" (see Galatians 4:4–6).

23:22 Scourging in itself could have left Jesus dead. The usual procedure was to bare the upper half of the victim's body and tie his hands to a pillar before whipping him with a three-pronged whip. The number of lashes was determined by the severity of the crime; up to 40 were permitted under Jewish law. After being scourged, Jesus also endured other agonies as recorded in Matthew and Mark. He was slapped, struck with fists, and mocked. A crown of thorns was placed on his head, and he was beaten with a stick and stripped before being hung on the cross.

23:23, 24 Pilate did not want to give Jesus the death sentence. He thought the Jewish leaders were simply jealous and wanted to get rid of a rival. When they threatened to report Pilate to Caesar (John 19:12), however, Pilate became frightened. Historic records indicate that Pilate had already been warned by Roman authorities about tensions in this region. The last thing he needed was a riot in Jerusalem at Passover time, when the city was crowded with Jews from all over the Empire. So he turned Jesus over to the mob to do with as they pleased.

28But Jesus turned and said to them, "Daughters of Jerusalem, don't weep for me, but for yourselves and for your children. 29For the days are coming when the women who have no children will be counted fortunate indeed. 30Mankind will beg the mountains to fall on them and crush them, and the hills to bury them. 31For if such things as this are done to me, the Living Tree, what will they do to you?"

23:29
Lk 21:23

23:30
Isa 2:19
Hos 10:8
Rev 6:16

➤ Jesus is placed on the cross
(235/Matthew 27:35–44; Mark 15:25–32; John 19:18–27)

32, 33Two others, criminals, were led out to be executed with him at a place called "The Skull." There all three were crucified—Jesus on the center cross, and the two criminals on either side.

23:32
Isa 53:12
Mt 27:33-44
Mk 15:22-32
Jn 19:18-24
Heb 13:12

34"Father, forgive these people," Jesus said, "for they don't know what they are doing."

And the soldiers gambled for his clothing, throwing dice for each piece. 35The crowd watched. And the Jewish leaders laughed and scoffed. "He was so good at helping others," they said, "let's see him save himself if he is really God's Chosen One, the Messiah."

23:34
Mt 5:44
Acts 3:17; 7:60
1 Cor 2:8

23:35
Ps 22:16-18

36The soldiers mocked him, too, by offering him a drink—of sour wine. 37And they called to him, "If you are the King of the Jews, save yourself!"

23:36
Mt 27:48

38A signboard was nailed to the cross above him with these words: "This is the King of the Jews."

23:31 *For if such things as this are done to me, the Living Tree, what will they do to you?* Literally, "For if they do this when the tree is green, what will happen when it is dry?"

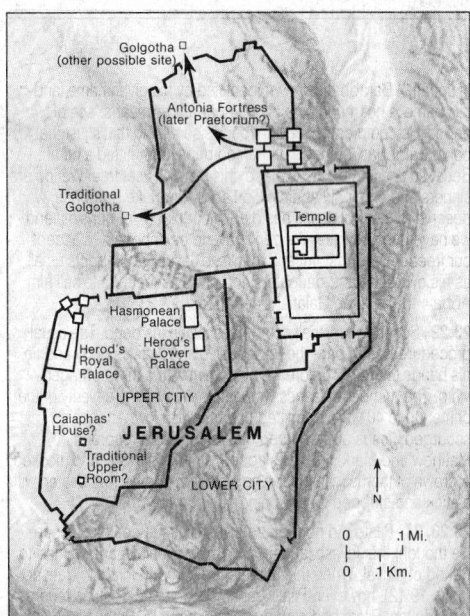

Golgotha □
(other possible site)

Antonia Fortress
(later Praetorium?)

Traditional
Golgotha □

Temple

Hasmonean
Palace □

Herod's
Royal
Palace

Herod's
Lower
Palace

UPPER CITY

Caiaphas'
House? □   **JERUSALEM**

Traditional
Upper
□Room?   LOWER CITY

N

0   .1 Mi.

0   .1 Km.

JESUS LED AWAY TO DIE As Jesus was led away through the streets of Jerusalem, he could no longer carry his cross, and Simon of Cyrene was given the burden. Jesus was crucified, along with common criminals, on a hill outside Jerusalem.

23:28–31 Luke alone mentions the tears of the Jewish women while Jesus was being led through the streets to his execution. He told them not to weep for him but for themselves. He knew that in only about 40 years, Jerusalem and the Temple would be destroyed by the Romans.

➤ **23:32, 33** The Skull, also called Golgotha, was probably a hill outside Jerusalem along a main road. The Romans made executions public displays as examples to the people.

23:32, 33 When James and John asked Jesus for the places of honor next to him in his Kingdom, he told them they didn't know what they were asking (Mark 10:35–39). Now that Jesus was preparing to inaugurate his Kingdom through his death, the places on his right and on his left were taken by dying men—criminals. This illustrates that Jesus' death is for *all* people. As Jesus explained to his two power-hungry disciples, a person who wants to be close to Jesus must be prepared to suffer and die as he himself was doing. The way to the Kingdom is the way of the cross.

23:34 Jesus asked God to forgive the people who were putting him to death—Jewish leaders, Roman politicians and soldiers, bystanders—and God answered that prayer by opening up the way of salvation even to Jesus' murderers. The Roman officer and soldiers who witnessed the crucifixion said, "Surely this was God's Son" (Matthew 27:54). Soon many priests were converted to the Christian faith (Acts 6:7). Since we are all sinners, we all played a part in putting Jesus to death. The Good News is that God is gracious. He will forgive us and give us new life through his Son.

23:34 Roman soldiers customarily divided up the clothing of executed criminals among themselves. When they threw dice for Jesus' clothes, they fulfilled the prophecy in Psalm 22:18.

23:38 This sign was meant to be ironic. A king, stripped and executed in public view, had obviously lost his Kingdom forever. But Jesus, who turns the world's wisdom upside down, was just coming into his Kingdom. His death and resurrection would strike the deathblow to Satan's rule and would establish his eternal authority over the earth. Few people reading that sign that bleak afternoon understood its real meaning, but the sign was absolutely true. All was not lost. Jesus was King of the Jews—and the Gentiles, and the whole universe.

39One of the criminals hanging beside him scoffed, "So you're the Messiah, are you? Prove it by saving yourself—and us, too, while you're at it!"

40, 41But the other criminal protested. "Don't you even fear God when you are dying? We deserve to die for our evil deeds, but this man hasn't done one thing wrong." 42Then he said, "Jesus, remember me when you come into your Kingdom."

43And Jesus replied, "Today you will be with me in Paradise. This is a solemn promise."

Jesus dies on the cross
(236/Matthew 27:45–56; Mark 15:33–41; John 19:28–37)

44By now it was noon, and darkness fell across the whole land for three hours, until three o'clock. 45The light from the sun was gone—and suddenly the thick veil hanging in the Temple split apart.

46Then Jesus shouted, "Father, I commit my spirit to you," and with those words he died.

47When the captain of the Roman military unit handling the executions saw what had happened, he was stricken with awe before God and said, "Surely this man was innocent."

48And when the crowd that came to see the crucifixion saw that Jesus was dead they went home in deep sorrow. 49Meanwhile, Jesus' friends, including the women who had followed him down from Galilee, stood in the distance watching.

Jesus is laid in the tomb
(237/Matthew 27:57–61; Mark 15:42–47; John 19:38–42)

50, 51, 52Then a man named Joseph, a member of the Jewish Supreme Court, from the city of Arimathea in Judea, went to Pilate and asked for the body of Jesus. He was a godly man who had been expecting the Messiah's coming and had not agreed with the decision and actions of the other Jewish leaders. 53So he took down Jesus' body and wrapped it in a long linen cloth and laid it in a new, unused tomb hewn into the rock [at the side of a hill]. 54This was done late on Friday afternoon, the day of preparation for the Sabbath.

55As the body was taken away, the women from Galilee followed and saw it

23:44 *the whole land,* or "the whole world." 23:45 *and suddenly,* implied. 23:46 *he died,* literally, "yielded up the spirit." 23:47 *innocent,* literally, "righteous." 23:53 *at the side of a hill,* implied.

Margin references: 23:42 Heb 8:1 | 23:43 2 Cor 12:3,4; Rev 2:7 | 23:44 Mt 27:45-51; Mk 15:33-38; Jn 19:14,28-30 | 23:45 Ex 26:33; Heb 9:8; 10:19 | 23:46 Ps 31:5 | 23:47 Mt 27:54-56; Mk 15:39-41; Jn 19:25 | 23:50 Mt 27:57-61; Mk 15:42-47; Lk 2:25,38; Jn 19:38-42 | 23:53 Isa 53:9 | 23:55 Lk 8:2

23:39-43 As this man was about to die, he turned to Christ for forgiveness, and Christ accepted him. This shows that our works don't save us—our faith in Christ does. It is never too late to turn to God. Even in his misery, Jesus had mercy on this criminal who decided to believe in him. Our lives are much more useful and fulfilling if we turn to God early, but even those who repent at the very last moment will be with God in his Kingdom.

23:42, 43 The dying criminal had more faith than the rest of Jesus' followers put together. Although the disciples continued to love Jesus, their hopes for the Kingdom were shattered. Most of them had gone into hiding. As one of his followers sadly said two days later, "We had thought he was the glorious Messiah and that he had come to rescue Israel" (24:21). By contrast, the criminal looked at the man dying next to him and said, "Remember me when you come into your Kingdom." By all appearances, the Kingdom was finished. How awe-inspiring is the faith of this man who alone saw beyond the present shame to the coming glory!

23:44 Darkness covered the entire land for about three hours in the middle of the day. All nature seemed to mourn over the stark tragedy of the death of God's Son.

23:45 This significant event symbolized Christ's work on the cross. The Temple had three parts: the courts for all the people; the Holy Place, where only priests could enter; and the Holy of Holies, where the High Priest alone could enter once a year to atone for the sins of the people. It was in the Holy of Holies that the

Ark of the Covenant, and God's presence with it, rested. The curtain that split was the one that closed off the Holy of Holies from view. At Christ's death, the barrier between God and man was torn apart. Now all people are able to approach God directly through Christ (Hebrews 9:1–14; 10:19–22).

23:50–52 Joseph of Arimathea was a wealthy and honored member of the Jewish Supreme Court. He was also a secret disciple of Jesus (John 19:38). The disciples who had publicly followed Jesus fled, but Joseph boldly took a stand that could cost him dearly. He cared enough about Jesus to ask for his body so he could give it a proper burial.

23:53 This tomb was likely a man-made cave cut out of one of the many limestone hills in the area around Jerusalem. Such a tomb was large enough to walk into. After burial, a large stone would have been rolled across the entrance (John 20:1).

23:55 The Galilean women followed Joseph to the tomb, and so they knew exactly where to find Jesus' body when they returned after the Sabbath with their spices and ointments. These women could not do great things for Jesus—they were not permitted to stand up before the Jewish Supreme Court or the Roman governor and testify on his behalf—but they did what they could. They stayed at the cross when most of the disciples had fled, and they got ready to embalm their Lord's body. Because of their devotion, they were the first to know about the resurrection.

carried into the tomb. 56Then they went home and prepared spices and ointments to embalm him; but by the time they were finished it was the Sabbath, so they rested all that day as required by the Jewish law.

23:56
Ex 20:10; 35:2
Lev 23:3
Deut 5:14

Jesus rises from the dead
(239/Matthew 28:1–7; Mark 16:1–8; John 20:1–9)

24 But very early on Sunday morning they took the ointments to the tomb— 2and found that the huge stone covering the entrance had been rolled aside. 3So they went in—but the Lord Jesus' body was gone.

4They stood there puzzled, trying to think what could have happened to it. Suddenly two men appeared before them, clothed in shining robes so bright their eyes were dazzled. 5The women were terrified and bowed low before them. Then the men asked, "Why are you looking in a tomb for someone who is alive? 6, 7He isn't here! He has come back to life again! Don't you remember what he told you back in Galilee—that the Messiah must be betrayed into the power of evil men and be crucified and that he would rise again the third day?"

8Then they remembered, 9and rushed back to Jerusalem to tell his eleven disciples—and everyone else—what had happened. 10(The women who went to the tomb were Mary Magdalene and Joanna and Mary the mother of James, and several others.) 11But the story sounded like a fairy tale to the men—they didn't believe it.

12However, Peter ran to the tomb to look. Stooping, he peered in and saw the empty linen wrappings; and then he went back home again, wondering what had happened.

24:1
Mt 28:1-8
Mk 16:1-11
Jn 20:1,2,10-13

24:4
Acts 1:10

24:5
Rev 1:17,18

24:6
Mt 16:21
Mk 8:31
Lk 9:22

24:8
Jn 2:22

24:10
Mt 27:56
Lk 8:3

24:11
Mk 16:11

24:12
Lk 24:34
Jn 20:2-10

Jesus appears to two believers traveling on the road
(243/Mark 16:12, 13)

13That same day, Sunday, two of Jesus' followers were walking to the village of

24:6, 7 the Messiah, literally, "the Son of Man."   **24:9** rushed back to Jerusalem, literally, "returned from the tomb."

24:1 The women brought ointments to the tomb as we would bring flowers—as a sign of love and respect. Ordinarily a body was embalmed at burial and not a day and a half later, but Jesus died only a few hours before sundown Friday, when the Sabbath began. By the time Joseph had received Pilate's permission to take the body and had put it in his tomb, there was no longer time for embalming. The women went home and kept Sabbath as the law required, from sundown Friday to sundown Saturday, before gathering up their spices and returning to the tomb.

24:1–9 The two angels asked the women why they were looking in a tomb for someone who was alive. Often we run into people who are looking for God among the dead. They study the Bible as a mere historical document and go to church as if to a memorial service. But Jesus is not among the dead—he lives! He reigns in the hearts of Christians, and he is the head of his church. Do you look for Jesus among the living? Do you expect him to be active in the world and in the church? Look for signs of his power—they are all around you.

24:4 We learn from the other Gospel accounts that these men were angels. When angels appeared to men, they looked like men.

24:6, 7 The angels reminded the women that Jesus had accurately predicted all that had happened to him (9:22, 44; 18:31–33).

24:6, 7 The resurrection of Jesus from the dead is the central fact of Christian history. On it, the church is built; without it, there would be no Christian church today. Jesus' resurrection is unique. Other religions have strong ethical systems, concepts about Paradise, and various holy scriptures. Only Christianity has a God who became man, literally died for his people, and was raised again in power and glory to rule his church forever.

Why is the resurrection so important? (1) Because Christ was raised from the dead, we know that the Kingdom of Heaven has broken into earth's history. Our world is now headed for redemption, not disaster. God's mighty power is at work destroying sin, creating new lives, and preparing us for Jesus' Second Coming. (2) Because of the resurrection, we know that death has been conquered, and we too will be raised from the dead to live forever with Christ. (3) The resurrection gives authority to the church's witness in the world. Look at the early evangelistic sermons in the book of Acts: the apostles' most important message was the proclamation that Jesus Christ had been raised from the dead! (4) The resurrection gives meaning to the church's regular feast, the Lord's Supper. Like the disciples on the Emmaus Road, we break bread with our risen Lord, who comes in power to save us. (5) The resurrection helps us find meaning even in the midst of great tragedy. No matter what happens to us as we walk with the Lord, the resurrection gives us hope for the future. (6) The resurrection assures us that Christ is alive and ruling his Kingdom. He is not legend; he is alive and real. (7) God's power that brought Jesus back from the dead is available to us so that we can live for him in an evil world.

Christians can look very different from one another; they can hold widely varying beliefs about politics, lifestyle, and even theology. But one central belief unites and inspires all true Christians—Jesus Christ rose from the dead! (For more on the importance of the resurrection, see 1 Corinthians 15:12–58.)

24:11, 12 People who hear about the resurrection for the first time may need time before they can comprehend this amazing story. Like the disciples, they may pass through four stages of belief. (1) At first, they may think it is a fairy tale, impossible to believe. (2) Like Peter, they may check out the facts but still be puzzled about what happened. (3) Only when they encounter Jesus personally are they able to accept the fact of the resurrection. (4) Then, as they commit themselves to him and devote their lives to serving Jesus, they begin fully to understand the reality of his presence with them.

24:12 From John 20:3, 4, we learn that John also ran to the tomb with Peter.

24:15
Mt 18:20
24:16
Jn 20:14; 21:4

24:18
Jn 19:25

24:19
Acts 2:22

24:20
Lk 23:13
Acts 13:27
24:21
Lk 1:68
Acts 1:6

24:25
2 Cor 4:14,15

24:26
Mt 26:24
Lk 24:7,44
Jn 12:23,24
13:31,32
Acts 17:3
Heb 2:10; 5:5

Emmaus, seven miles out of Jerusalem. ¹⁴As they walked along they were talking of Jesus' death, ¹⁵when suddenly Jesus himself came along and joined them and began walking beside them. ¹⁶But they didn't recognize him, for God kept them from it.

¹⁷"You seem to be in a deep discussion about something," he said. "What are you so concerned about?" They stopped short, sadness written across their faces. ¹⁸And one of them, Cleopas, replied, "You must be the only person in Jerusalem who hasn't heard about the terrible things that happened there last week."

¹⁹"What things?" Jesus asked.

"The things that happened to Jesus, the Man from Nazareth," they said. "He was a Prophet who did incredible miracles and was a mighty Teacher, highly regarded by both God and man. ²⁰But the chief priests and our religious leaders arrested him and handed him over to the Roman government to be condemned to death, and they crucified him. ²¹We had thought he was the glorious Messiah and that he had come to rescue Israel.

"And now, besides all this—which happened three days ago— ²², ²³some women from our group of his followers were at his tomb early this morning and came back with an amazing report that his body was missing, and that they had seen some angels there who told them Jesus was alive! ²⁴Some of our men ran out to see, and sure enough, Jesus' body was gone, just as the women had said."

²⁵Then Jesus said to them, "You are such foolish, foolish people! You find it so hard to believe all that the prophets wrote in the Scriptures! ²⁶Wasn't it clearly

24:18 *there last week*, literally, "in these days."

ON THE ROAD TO EMMAUS
After Jesus' death, two of his followers were walking from Jerusalem back towards Emmaus when a stranger joined them. After dinner in Emmaus, Jesus revealed himself to these men, then disappeared. They immediately returned to Jerusalem to tell the disciples the good news that Jesus was alive!

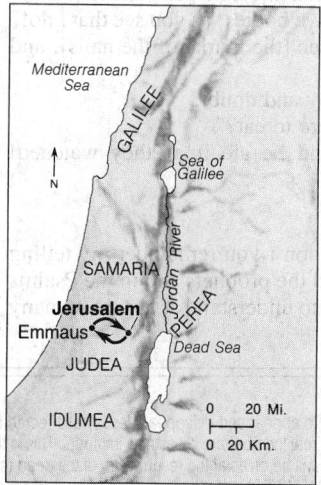

Mediterranean Sea

GALILEE

N

Sea of Galilee

Jordan River

SAMARIA

Jerusalem
Emmaus

PEREA

Dead Sea

JUDEA

IDUMEA

0   20 Mi.
0   20 Km.

24:18 The disciples from Emmaus were counting on Jesus to rescue Israel. Most Jews believed that the Old Testament prophecies pointed to a military and political Messiah; they didn't realize that the Messiah had come to rescue people's souls. When Jesus died, therefore, they lost all hope. They didn't understand that Jesus' death offered the greatest hope available.

24:24 These men knew the tomb was empty, but still they didn't understand that Jesus had risen, and they were filled with sadness. Despite the evidence and the witness of the women, and the biblical prophecies of this very event, they didn't believe. Today the resurrection still catches people by surprise. In spite of 2,000 years of evidence and witness, many people still refuse to believe. What more will it take? For these disciples it took the living, breathing Jesus in their midst. For many people today, it takes the presence of living, breathing Christians.

24:25 Why did Jesus call these men foolish? Even though they well knew the biblical prophecies, they failed to understand that Christ's suffering was his path to glory. They could not understand why God did not intervene to save Jesus from the cross. They were so caught up in the world's admiration of political power and military might that they were unprepared for the reversal of values in God's Kingdom—that the last will be first, and that life grows out of death. The world has not changed its values: the concept of a suffering servant is no more popular today than it was 2,000 years ago. But we have not only the witness of the Old Testament prophets; we have also the witness of the New Testament apostles and the history of the Christian church all pointing to Jesus' victory over death. Will we step outside the values of our culture and put our faith in Jesus? Or will we foolishly continue to be baffled by his Good News?

24:25–27 After the two disciples told Jesus they were puzzled, he answered them by going to Scripture and applying it to his ministry. When we are puzzled by questions or problems, we too can go to Scripture and find authoritative help. If we, like these two disciples, do not understand what the Bible means, we can turn to other believers who know the Bible and have the wisdom to apply it to our situation.

24:13ff The two disciples returning to Emmaus missed the significance of history's greatest event because they were too focused on their disappointments and problems—so much so that they didn't recognize that it was Jesus walking beside them. To compound the problem, they were walking in the wrong direction—away from the fellowship of believers in Jerusalem. We are likely to miss Jesus and withdraw from the strength found in other believers when we become preoccupied with our dashed hopes and frustrated plans. Only when we are looking for Jesus in our midst will we experience the power and help he can bring.

24:18 The news about Jesus' crucifixion had spread throughout Jerusalem. Because this was Passover week Jewish pilgrims visiting the city from all over the Roman empire now knew about his death. This was not a small, insignificant event, affecting only the disciples—the whole nation was interested.

predicted by the prophets that the Messiah would have to suffer all these things before entering his time of glory?"

27Then Jesus quoted them passage after passage from the writings of the prophets, beginning with the book of Genesis and going right on through the Scriptures, explaining what the passages meant and what they said about himself.

28By this time they were nearing Emmaus and the end of their journey. Jesus would have gone on, 29but they begged him to stay the night with them, as it was getting late. So he went home with them. 30As they sat down to eat, he asked God's blessing on the food and then took a small loaf of bread and broke it and was passing it over to them, 31when suddenly—it was as though their eyes were opened—they recognized him! And at that moment he disappeared!

32They began telling each other how their hearts had felt strangely warm as he talked with them and explained the Scriptures during the walk down the road.

33, 34Within the hour they were on their way back to Jerusalem, where the eleven disciples and the other followers of Jesus greeted them with these words, "The Lord has really risen! He appeared to Peter!"

35Then the two from Emmaus told their story of how Jesus had appeared to them as they were walking along the road and how they had recognized him as he was breaking the bread.

Jesus appears to the disciples behind locked doors
(244/John 20:19–23)

36And just as they were telling about it, Jesus himself was suddenly standing there among them, and greeted them. 37But the whole group was terribly frightened, thinking they were seeing a ghost!

38"Why are you frightened?" he asked. "Why do you doubt that it is really I? 39Look at my hands! Look at my feet! You can see that it is I, myself! Touch me and make sure that I am not a ghost! For ghosts don't have bodies, as you see that I do!" 40As he spoke, he held out his hands for them to see [the marks of the nails], and showed them [the wounds in] his feet.

41Still they stood there undecided, filled with joy and doubt.

Then he asked them, "Do you have anything here to eat?"

42They gave him a piece of broiled fish, 43and he ate it as they watched!

Jesus appears to the disciples in Jerusalem
(249)

44Then he said, "When I was with you before, don't you remember my telling you that everything written about me by Moses and the prophets and in the Psalms must all come true?" 45Then he opened their minds to understand at last these many

24:40 the marks of the nails and the wounds in, implied.

24:27
Gen 3:15
14:18-20; 26:4
49:10
Ex 3:6; 12:3-11
16:15; 17:6
Num 21:8,9
24:17
Deut 18:15,18
2 Sam 7:12-14
Job 19:25
Ps 2:2,6-9,12
8:4-6; 16:8-11
22:1-22; 31:5
34:20; 41:9
45:6,7; 68:18
69:4,9,21
89:3,4
97:7; 110:1,2,4
118:22,26
132:11
Prov 8:22-31
Isa 4:2; 6:15
7:14; 8:14,15,
18; 9:1,2,6,7
11:1-10
22:22-24; 25:8,9
32:1-4; 35:5
6; 40:3-11
42:1-9;
49:1-10
50:5-7; 52:10,13
53:1-12
61:1,2
Jer 23:5,6; 30:9
33:15
Ezek 34:23,24
37:24,25
Dan 2:34,35,44,
45; 7:13
9:25,26
Hos 11:1
Mic 5:2
Zech 3:8,9;
6:12,13; 9:9
11:12,13; 12:10
13:1,7
Mal 3:1; 4:2,5
24:34
1 Cor 15:5
24:36
Mk 16:14
Jn 20:19,20
24:44
Lk 24:27

24:27 From the promised seed in Genesis, through the suffering servant in Isaiah and the pierced one in Zechariah, to the promised one in Malachi, Jesus reintroduced these disciples to the Old Testament. Christ is the thread woven through all the Scriptures, the central theme that binds them together. We can see that God loves us in his careful preparation and the detail of all his efforts to make salvation available to us. Following are several key passages Jesus probably mentioned on this walk to Emmaus: Genesis 3, 12; Psalms 22, 69, 110; Isaiah 53; Jeremiah 31; Zechariah 9, 13; Malachi 3. See cross references for additional verses.

24:33, 34 Paul also mentions that Jesus appeared to Peter alone (1 Corinthians 15:5). This event is not described in the Gospels. Jesus showed individual concern for Peter because Peter felt completely unworthy after denying his Lord. But Peter repented, and Jesus met and forgave him. Soon God would use Peter in building Christ's church (see the first half of the book of Acts).

24:36 Jesus' body wasn't just a vision or a ghost—the disciples touched him, and he ate food. On the other hand, his body wasn't just a restored human body like Lazarus' (John 11)—he was able

to appear and disappear. Jesus' resurrected body was even more real than before: it was now immortal. This is the kind of body we will be given at the resurrection of the dead (see 1 Corinthians 15:42–50).

24:44 We can assume that many days elapsed between verses 43 and 44, because Jesus and his followers traveled to Galilee and back before he returned to heaven (Matthew 28:16; John 21). In his second book, Acts, Luke makes it clear that Jesus spent 40 days with his disciples between his resurrection and ascension.

24:44, 46 "Moses and the prophets and the Psalms" is a way to describe the entire Old Testament Scripture. In other words, the entire Old Testament points to the Messiah. For example, his sufferings were prophesied in Psalm 22 and Isaiah 53; his resurrection was predicted in Psalm 16:9–11 and Isaiah 53:10, 11.

24:45 Jesus opened these people's minds to understand the Scriptures. The Holy Spirit does this in our lives today when we study the Bible. Have you ever wondered how to understand a difficult Bible passage? Besides reading surrounding passages, asking other people, and consulting reference works, pray that the

24:47
Acts 2:38; 5:31
10:43; 13:38
26:18

24:48
Jn 15:27

24:49
Isa 44:3
Joel 2:28
Acts 2:1-4

Scriptures! 46And he said, "Yes, it was written long ago that the Messiah must suffer and die and rise again from the dead on the third day; 47and that this message of salvation should be taken from Jerusalem to all the nations: *There is forgiveness of sins for all who turn to me.* 48You have seen these prophecies come true.

49"And now I will send the Holy Spirit upon you, just as my Father promised. Don't begin telling others yet—stay here in the city until the Holy Spirit comes and fills you with power from heaven."

Jesus ascends into heaven
(250/Mark 16:19, 20)

24:51
Mk 16:19,20
Eph 1:20; 4:8

24:53
Acts 2:46; 5:42

50Then Jesus led them out along the road to Bethany, and lifting his hands to heaven, he blessed them, 51and then began rising into the sky, and went on to heaven. 52And they worshiped him, and returned to Jerusalem filled with mighty joy, 53and were continually in the Temple, praising God.

24:49 *the Holy Spirit,* implied. Literally, "the promise of my Father." *Don't begin telling others,* literally, "but wait here in the city until. . . ." The paraphrase relates this to vs 47. **24:50** *along the road to Bethany,* implied. Bethany was a mile or so away, across the valley on the Mount of Olives.

Holy Spirit will open your mind to understand, giving you the needed insight to put God's Word into action in your life.

24:47 Luke wrote to the Greek-speaking world. He wanted them to know that Christ's message of God's love and forgiveness should go to all the world. We must never ignore the worldwide scope of Christ's gospel. God wants all the world to hear the Good News of salvation.

24:50-53 As the disciples stood and watched, Jesus began rising into the air, and soon he disappeared into heaven. Seeing Jesus leave must have been frightening, but they knew he would keep his promise to be with them in the Spirit. This same Jesus who lived with the disciples, who died and rose from the dead, and who loves us, promises to be with us always. We can get to know him better through studying the Scriptures, praying, and allowing the Holy Spirit to make us more like him.

24:51 Jesus' physical presence left the disciples when he returned to heaven (Acts 1:9), but the Holy Spirit soon came to comfort them and empower them to spread the Good News of salvation (Acts 2:1–4). Today Jesus' work of salvation is completed; and he is sitting at God's right hand, where he has authority over heaven and earth.

24:53 Luke's Gospel portrays Jesus as the perfect example of a life lived according to God's plan—as a child with the religious leaders in the Temple, as a young man living without sin, as an adult serving God and others, and in his death suffering without complaint. This emphasis was well suited to his Greek audience, who placed high value on examples and self-improvement, and who often discussed the meaning of perfection. The Greeks, however, had a hard time understanding the spiritual importance of the physical world. To them, the spiritual was always more important than the physical. To help them understand the God-man who united the spiritual and the physical, Luke emphasized that Jesus was not a phantom but a real human being, who healed and fed people because he was concerned with their physical health as well as the state of their souls.

As believers living according to God's plan, we too should obey our Lord in every detail as we seek to restore people's bodies and souls to the health and salvation God has in store for them. If we want to know how to live a perfect life, we can look to Jesus as our example.

JOHN

VITAL STATISTICS

PURPOSE:
To prove conclusively that Jesus is the Son of God and that all who believe in him will have eternal life

AUTHOR:
John, the apostle, son of Zebedee, brother of James, called a "Son of Thunder"

TO WHOM WRITTEN:
New Christians and searching non-Christians

DATE WRITTEN:
Probably A.D. 85–90

SETTING:
Written after the destruction of Jerusalem in A.D. 70 and before John's exile to the island of Patmos

KEY VERSES:
"Jesus' disciples saw him do many other miracles besides the ones told about in this book, but these are recorded so that you will believe that he is the Messiah, the Son of God, and that believing in him you will have life" (20:30, 31).

KEY PEOPLE:
Jesus, John the Baptist, the disciples, Mary, Martha, Lazarus, Jesus' mother, Pilate, Mary Magdalene

KEY PLACES:
Judean countryside, Samaria, Galilee, Bethany, Jerusalem

SPECIAL FEATURES:
Of the eight miracles recorded, six are unique (among the Gospels) to John, as is the "Upper Room Discourse" (chapters 14—17). Over 90% of John is unique to his Gospel—John does not contain a genealogy or any record of Jesus' birth, childhood, temptation, transfiguration, appointment of the disciples, and no parables, ascension, or Great Commission.

HE SPOKE and galaxies whirled into place, stars burned the heavens, and planets began orbiting their suns—words of awesome, unlimited, unleashed power. He spoke again and the waters and lands were filled with plants and creatures, running, swimming, growing, and multiplying—words of animating, breathing, pulsing life. Again he spoke and man and woman were formed, thinking, speaking, and loving—words of personal and creative glory. Eternal, infinite, unlimited—he was, is, and always will be the Maker and Lord of all that exists.

And then he came in the flesh to a speck in the universe called planet earth. The mighty Creator became a part of the creation, limited by time and space and susceptible to age, sickness, and death. But love propelled him, and so he came to rescue and save those who were lost and to give them the gift of eternity. He is *the Word;* he is Jesus, the Christ.

It is this truth that the apostle John brings to us in this book. John's Gospel is not a life of Christ; it is a powerful argument for the incarnation, a conclusive demonstration that Jesus was, and is, the very heaven-sent Son of God and the only source of eternal life.

John discloses Christ's identity with his very first words, "Before anything else existed, there was Christ [the Word], with God. He has always been alive and is himself God" (1:1, 2); and the rest of the book continues the theme. John, the eyewitness, chooses eight of Christ's miracles (or signs, as he calls them), to reveal Christ's divine/human nature and his life-giving mission. These signs are (1) turning water to wine (2:1–11), (2) healing the nobleman's son (4:46–54), (3) healing the cripple at Bethesda (5:1–9), (4) feeding the 5,000 with just a few loaves and fish (6:1–14), (5) walking on the water (6:15–21), (6) restoring sight to the blind man (9:1–41), (7) raising Lazarus from the dead (11:1–44), and, after the resurrection, (8) giving the disciples an overwhelming catch of fish (21:1–14).

In every chapter Jesus' deity is revealed. And John underscores Jesus' true identity through the titles he is given—Word, only begotten, Lamb of God, Son of God, true Bread, Life, Resurrection, Vine. And the formula is "I am." When Jesus uses this phrase, he affirms his preexistence and eternal deity. Jesus says, *I am* the Bread of Life (6:35); *I am* the Light of the world (8:12; 9:5); *I am* the Gate (10:7); *I am* the Good Shepherd (10:11, 14); *I am* the resurrection and the life (11:25); *I am* the Way, the Truth, and the Life (14:6); and *I am* the true Vine (15:1).

The greatest sign, of course, is the resurrection, and John provides a stirring eyewitness account of finding the empty tomb. Then he records various post-resurrection appearances by Jesus.

John, the devoted follower of Christ, has given us a personal and powerful look at Jesus Christ, the eternal Son of God. As you read his story commit yourself to believe and follow him.

THE BLUEPRINT

A. THE BIRTH AND PRESENTATION OF JESUS, THE SON OF GOD (1:1—2:12)

John makes it clear that Jesus is not just a man; he is the eternal Son of God. He is the light of the world because he offers this gift of eternal life to all mankind. How blind and foolish to call Jesus nothing more than an unusually good man or moral teacher. Yet we sometimes act as if this were true when we casually toss around his words and go about living our own way. If Jesus is the eternal Son of God, we should pay attention to his divine identity and life-giving message.

B. MESSAGE AND MINISTRY OF JESUS, THE SON OF GOD (2:13—12:50)
1. Jesus encounters belief and unbelief from the people
2. Jesus encounters conflict with the religious leaders
3. Jesus encounters crucial events in Jerusalem

Jesus meets with individuals, preaches to great crowds, trains his disciples, and debates with the religious leaders. The message, that he is the Son of God, receives a mixed reaction. Some worship him, some are puzzled, some shrink back, and some move to silence him. We see the same varied reactions today. Times have changed, but people's hearts remain hard. May we see ourselves in these encounters Jesus had with people, and may our response be to worship and follow him.

C. DEATH AND RESURRECTION OF JESUS, THE SON OF GOD (13:1—21:25)
1. Jesus teaches his disciples
2. Jesus completes his mission

Jesus carefully instructed the disciples how to continue to believe even after his death, yet they could not take it in. After he died and the first reports came back that Jesus was alive, the disciples could not believe it. Thomas is especially remembered as one who refused to believe even when he heard the eyewitness accounts from other disciples. May we not be like Thomas, demanding a physical face-to-face encounter, but may we accept the eyewitness of the disciples that John has recorded in this Gospel.

MEGATHEMES

THEME	EXPLANATION	IMPORTANCE
Jesus Christ, Son of God	John shows us that Jesus is unique as God's special Son, yet he is fully God. Because he is fully God, Jesus is able to reveal God to us clearly and accurately.	Because Jesus is God's Son, we can perfectly trust what he says. By trusting him, we can gain an open mind to understand God's message and fulfill his purpose in our lives.
Eternal life	Because Jesus is God, he lives forever. Before the world began, he lived with God, and he will reign forever with him. In John we see Jesus revealed in power and magnificence even before his resurrection.	Jesus offers eternal life to us. We are invited to begin living in a personal, eternal relationship with him that begins now. Although we must grow old and die, by trusting him we can have a new life that lasts forever.
Believe	John records eight specific signs or miracles that show the nature of Jesus' power and love. We see his power over everything created, and we see his love of all people. These signs encourage us to believe in him.	Believing is active, living, and continuous trust in Jesus as God. When we believe in his life, his words, his death, and his resurrection, we are cleansed from sin and receive power to follow him. But we must respond to him by believing.
Holy Spirit	Jesus taught his disciples that the Holy Spirit would come after he ascended from earth. The Holy Spirit would then indwell, guide, counsel, and comfort those who follow Jesus. Through the Holy Spirit, Christ's presence and power are multiplied in all who believe.	Through God's Holy Spirit we are drawn to him in faith. We must know the Holy Spirit to understand all Jesus taught. We can experience Jesus' love and guidance as we allow the Holy Spirit to do his work in us.

| Resurrection | On the third day after he died, Jesus rose from the dead. This was verified by his disciples and many eyewitnesses. This reality changed the disciples from frightened deserters to dynamic leaders in the new church. This fact is the foundation of the Christian faith. | We can be changed as the disciples were, and have confidence that our bodies will one day be raised to live with Christ forever. The same power that raised Christ to life can give you the ability to follow Christ each day. |

KEY PLACES IN JOHN

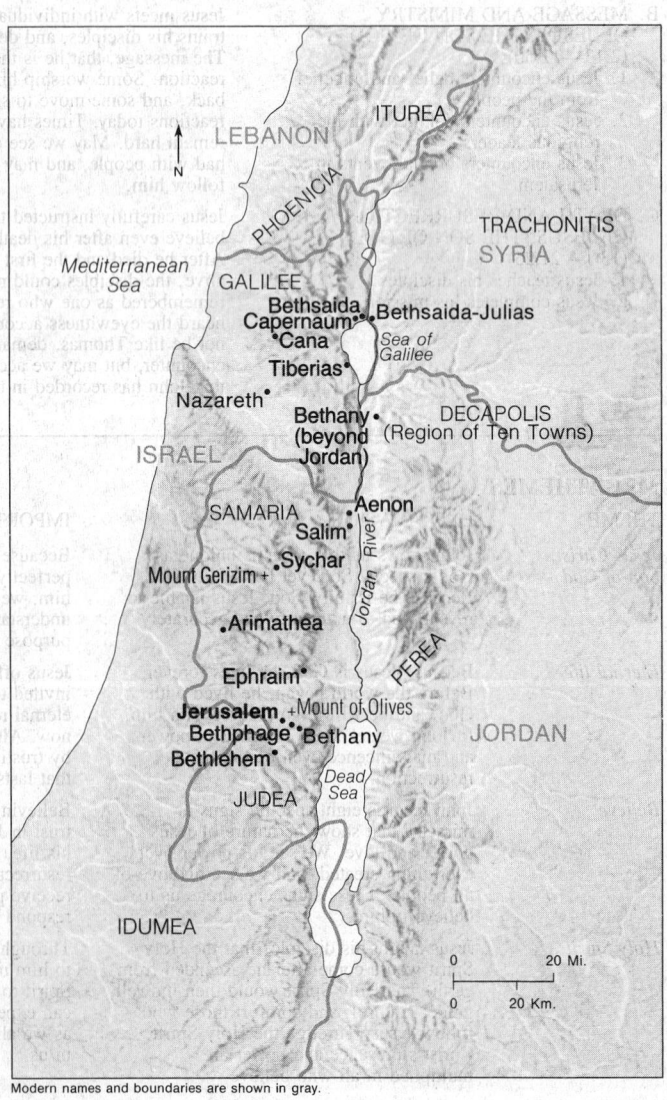

John's story begins as John the Baptist ministers near Bethany beyond the Jordan (1:28ff). Jesus also begins his ministry, talking to some of the men who would later become his 12 disciples. Jesus' ministry in Galilee began with a visit to a wedding in Cana (2:1ff). Then he went to Capernaum, which became his new home (2:12). He journeyed to Jerusalem for the special feasts (2:13) and there met with Nicodemus, a religious leader (3:1ff). When he left Judea, he traveled through Samaria and ministered to the Samaritans (4:1ff). Jesus did miracles in Galilee (4:46ff) and in Judea and Jerusalem (5:1ff). We follow him as he fed 5,000 near Bethsaida-Julias beside the Sea of Galilee (6:1ff), walked on the water to his frightened disciples (6:16ff), preached through Galilee (7:1), returned to Jerusalem (7:2ff), preached beyond the Jordan in Perea (10:40), raised Lazarus from the dead in Bethany (11:1ff), and finally entered Jerusalem for the last time to celebrate the Passover with his disciples and give them key teachings about what was to come and how they should act. His last hours before his crucifixion were spent in the city (13:1ff), in the Garden of Gethsemane (18:1ff), and finally in various buildings in Jerusalem during his trial (18:12ff). He would be crucified, but he would rise again as he had promised.

Map labels: ITUREA · LEBANON · PHOENICIA · TRACHONITIS · SYRIA · Mediterranean Sea · GALILEE · Bethsaida · Bethsaida-Julias · Capernaum · Cana · Sea of Galilee · Tiberias · Nazareth · Bethany (beyond Jordan) · DECAPOLIS (Region of Ten Towns) · ISRAEL · SAMARIA · Aenon · Salim · Sychar · Mount Gerizim · Jordan River · Arimathea · PEREA · Ephraim · Jerusalem · Mount of Olives · Bethphage · Bethany · JORDAN · Bethlehem · Dead Sea · JUDEA · IDUMEA

0   20 Mi.
0   20 Km.

Modern names and boundaries are shown in gray.

A. BIRTH AND PREPARATION OF JESUS, THE SON OF GOD (1:1—2:12)

John provides unique material about Jesus' birth. He did not come into being when he was born, because he is eternal.

God became a human being
(2)

1:1
Gen 1:1
Phil 2:6
1 Jn 5:21
1:3
1 Cor 8:6
Col 1:16,17
Heb 1:2
1:4
Jn 3:15,16,36
6:35,48; 8:12
11:25; 14:6
1 Jn 5:12,20
1:5
Jn 3:19; 9:5
1:7
Jn 5:33
1:9
1 Jn 2:8
1:12
Rom 8:15,16,29
1 Jn 3:1,23

1 Before anything else existed, there was Christ, with God. He has always been alive and is himself God. ³He created everything there is—nothing exists that he didn't make. ⁴Eternal life is in him, and this life gives light to all mankind. ⁵His life is the light that shines through the darkness—and the darkness can never extinguish it.

⁶,⁷God sent John the Baptist as a witness to the fact that Jesus Christ is the true Light. ⁸John himself was not the Light; he was only a witness to identify it.

⁹Later on, the one who is the true Light arrived to shine on everyone coming into the world.

¹⁰But although he made the world, the world didn't recognize him when he came. ¹¹,¹²Even in his own land and among his own people, the Jews, he was not accepted. Only a few would welcome and receive him. But to all who received him, he gave the right to become children of God. All they needed to do was to trust him to save them. ¹³All those who believe this are reborn!—not a physical rebirth resulting from human passion or plan—but from the will of God.

1:1, 2 *Before anything else existed,* literally, "In the beginning." *Christ,* literally, "the Word," meaning Christ, the wisdom and power of God and the first cause of all things; God's personal expression of himself to men.   **1:11, 12** *to trust him to save them,* literally, "to believe on his name."   **1:13** *not a physical rebirth,* literally, "not of blood."

1:1 What Jesus taught and what he did are tied inseparably to who he is. John shows Jesus as fully human and fully God. Although Jesus took upon himself full humanity and lived as a man, he never ceased to be the eternal God who has always existed, who is Creator of the universe, the binding force that holds creation together, and the source of eternal life. This is the truth about Jesus, and the foundation of all truth. If we cannot or do not believe this basic truth, we will not have enough faith to trust our eternal destiny to him. That is why John wrote this Gospel—to build faith and confidence in Jesus Christ so that we may believe he truly was and is God in the flesh (20:30, 31).

1:1 John wrote to believers everywhere, both Jews and non-Jews (Gentiles). As one of Jesus' 12 disciples, John was an eyewitness, so his story is accurate. His book is not a biography (like Luke), but a thematic presentation of Jesus' life. Many in John's original audience had a Greek background. Greek culture encouraged worship of many mythological gods, whose supernatural characteristics were as important to Greeks as genealogies were to Jews. John shows that Jesus is not only different from, but superior to these gods of mythology.

1:3 When God created, he made something from nothing. Because we are created beings, we have no basis for pride. Remember that you exist only because God made you, and you have special gifts only because God gave them to you. With God you are something special; apart from God you are nothing, because you are not fulfilling the purpose for which you were made.

1:3–5 Do you ever feel your life is so complex that God would never understand? Remember, God created the entire universe, and nothing is too complex for him to understand. He created you, he is alive today, and his love is bigger than any problem you may face.

1:4 Why is eternal life in Christ a light to all mankind? Because death brings eternal darkness, and only Christ's eternal life planted in us will keep us alive in his new Kingdom for eternity. Christ is eternally alive because he is God. He came to earth to offer

mankind the hope and light of his eternal life. It can't be bought, only received as a gift. But Jesus gives it only to those who want it—those who want to live the way God's citizens will live in his future, eternal Kingdom.

1:4 Jesus Christ was the creator of life, and his life brings light to mankind. In his light, we see ourselves as we really are (sinners in need of a Savior). When we follow Jesus, the Light, we can avoid walking blind and falling into sin. He lights the path ahead of us so we can see how to live. He removes the darkness of sin from our lives. Have you allowed the light of Christ to shine into your life? Let Christ bring light to your life, and you'll never need to stumble in darkness.

1:8 In this book, the name *John* refers to John the Baptist. For more information on John the Baptist, see his Profile in John 1.

1:8 We, like John the Baptist, are not the source of God's light; we merely reflect that light. Jesus Christ is the true Light; he helps us see our way to God and shows us how to walk along that way. But Christ has chosen to reflect his light from his followers to an unbelieving world, perhaps because unbelievers are not able to bear the full blazing glory of his light firsthand. The word *witness* indicates our role as reflectors of Christ's light. We are never to present ourselves as the light to others, but are always to point them to Christ, the Light.

1:10–12 Although Christ created the world, the people he created didn't recognize him (1:10). Even the people chosen by God to prepare the rest of the world for the Messiah rejected him (1:11, 12), although the entire Old Testament pointed to his coming.

1:13 All who welcome Jesus Christ as Lord of their lives are reborn spiritually, receiving new life from God. Through faith in Christ, this new birth changes us from the inside out—rearranging our attitudes, desires, and motives. Being born makes you physically alive and places you in your parents' family. Being reborn makes you spiritually alive and puts you in God's family. Have you asked Christ to make you a new person? This fresh start in life is available to all who believe in Christ.

14And Christ became a human being and lived here on earth among us and was full of loving forgiveness and truth. And some of us have seen his glory—the glory of the only Son of the heavenly Father!

15John pointed him out to the people, telling the crowds, "This is the one I was talking about when I said, 'Someone is coming who is greater by far than I am—for he existed long before I did!' " 16We have all benefited from the rich blessings he brought to us—blessing upon blessing heaped upon us! 17For Moses gave us only the Law with its rigid demands and merciless justice, while Jesus Christ brought us loving forgiveness as well. 18No one has ever actually seen God, but, of course, his only Son has, for he is the companion of the Father and has told us all about him.

1:14
Ex 40:34,35
Rom 1:3; 8:3
Gal 4:4
Phil 2:6-8
Col 2:9
1 Tim 3:16
Heb 2:14
1 Jn 1:1; 4:2,3

1:17
Ex 20:1

1:18
Ex 33:20
2 Cor 4:4,6
Col 1:15

John the Baptist declares his mission
(19)

19The Jewish leaders sent priests and assistant priests from Jerusalem to ask John whether he claimed to be the Messiah.

20He denied it flatly. "I am not the Christ," he said.

21"Well then, who are you?" they asked. "Are you Elijah?"

"No," he replied.

"Are you the Prophet?" "No."

1:20
Lk 3:15
Jn 3:28

1:21
Deut 18:15
Mal 4:5
Mt 11:14

22"Then who are you? Tell us, so we can give an answer to those who sent us. What do you have to say for yourself?"

23He replied, "I am a voice from the barren wilderness, shouting as Isaiah prophesied, 'Get ready for the coming of the Lord!' "

1:23
Isa 40:3

24,25Then those who were sent by the Pharisees asked him, "If you aren't the Messiah or Elijah or the Prophet, what right do you have to baptize?"

26John told them, "I merely baptize with water, but right here in the crowd is

1:26
Mal 3:1
Mt 3:11
Mk 1:8
Lk 3:16

1:14 Christ, literally, "the Word." loving forgiveness, literally, "grace." seen his glory, see Mt 17:2. the only Son of the heavenly Father, literally, "his unique Son." 1:19 the Jewish leaders, literally, "the Jews." 1:21 See Deut 18:15, 18. 1:26, 31 with, or "in." So also with or in the Holy Spirit in vs 33.

1:14 By becoming human, Christ became (1) the perfect teacher—in Jesus' life we see how God thinks and therefore how we should think (Philippians 2:5–11); (2) the perfect example—he is a model of what we are to become, and he shows us how to live and gives the power to live that way (1 Peter 2:21–23); (3) the perfect sacrifice—Jesus came as a sacrifice for all sins, and his death satisfied God's requirements for the obliteration of sin (Colossians 1:15–23).

1:14 When Christ was born, God became a man. He was not part man and part God; he was completely human and completely divine (Colossians 2:9). Before Christ came, people could know God partially. After Christ came, people could know God fully because he became visible and tangible in Christ. Christ is the perfect expression of God in human form. The two most common errors are to minimize Jesus' humanity or to minimize his divinity. Jesus is both God and man.

1:17 Love and justice are both aspects of God's nature that he uses in dealing with us. Moses emphasized God's Law and justice, while Jesus Christ came to highlight God's mercy, love, and forgiveness. Moses could only be the vehicle of the Law, while Christ came to fulfill it. The nature and will of God were revealed in the Law; now the nature and will of God are revealed in Jesus Christ. Rather than coming from cold stone tablets, God's revelation now comes from the life of a person.

1:18 God communicated through various people in the Old Testament, usually prophets who were told to give specific messages. But no one ever saw God. In Christ, God revealed his nature and essence in a way that could be seen and touched. In Christ, God became a man who lived on earth.

1:19 These Jewish leaders were Pharisees (1:24). They were part of the Sanhedrin—a court of religious leaders in charge of the nation's spiritual welfare. Both John the Baptist and Jesus often denounced these Pharisees. Many of them outwardly obeyed

God's laws to look pious, while inwardly their hearts were filled with pride and greed. The Pharisees believed that their own oral traditions were just as important as God's inspired Word. For more information on the Pharisees, see the charts in Matthew 3 and Mark 2.

These leaders came to see John the Baptist for several reasons: (1) Their duty as guardians of the faith caused them to want to investigate any new preaching (Deuteronomy 13:1–5; 18:20–22). (2) They were checking when out to see if he had the credentials of a prophet. (3) John had quite a following, and it was growing. They were probably jealous and wanted to see why this man was so popular.

1:21–23 In the Pharisees' minds, there were four options regarding John the Baptist's identity: he was (1) the Prophet who would speak God's words (Deuteronomy 18:15), (2) Elijah (Malachi 4:5), (3) the Messiah, or (4) a false prophet. John denied being the first three personages, and instead referred to himself, in the words of the Old Testament prophet Isaiah, as the voice shouting in the wilderness. The leaders kept pressing him to say who he was, because people were expecting the Messiah to come (Luke 3:15). But John emphasized only why he had come—to prepare the way for the Messiah. The Pharisees missed the point. They wanted to know who John was, but John wanted them to know who Jesus was.

1:26 John was baptizing Jews. The Essenes (a strict, monastic sect of Judaism) practised baptism for purification, but normally only non-Jews (Gentiles) were baptized when they converted to Judaism. When the Pharisees asked by what authority he was baptizing, they were asking, "Why are you treating God's chosen people like Gentiles?" John said, "I merely baptize with water"—he was merely helping the people perform a symbolic act of repentance. But soon one would come who would truly forgive sins, a role only the Son of God—the Messiah—could fill.

1:27
Mk 1:7

someone you have never met, ²⁷who will soon begin his ministry among you, and I am not even fit to be his slave."

1:28
Jn 3:26; 10:40

²⁸This incident took place at Bethany, a village on the other side of the Jordan River where John was baptizing.

JOHN THE BAPTIST

There's no getting around it—John the Baptist was unique. He wore odd clothes and ate strange food and preached an unusual message to the Judeans who went into the wastelands to see him.

But John did not aim at uniqueness for its own sake. Instead, he aimed at obedience. He knew he had a specific role to play in the world—announcing the coming of the Savior—and he put all his energies into this task. Luke tells us that John was in the desert when God's word of direction came to him. John was ready and waiting. The angel who had announced John's birth to Zacharias had made it clear this child was to be a Nazirite—one set apart for God's service. John remained faithful to that description.

This wild-looking man had no power or position in the Jewish political system, but he spoke with almost irresistible authority. People were moved by his words because he spoke the truth, challenging them to turn from their sins and baptizing them as a symbol of their repentance. They responded by the hundreds. But even as people crowded to him, he pointed beyond himself, never forgetting that his main role was to announce the coming of the Savior.

The words of truth that moved many to repentance goaded others to resistance and resentment. John even challenged King Herod to admit his sin. Herodias, the woman whom Herod had married illegally, decided to get rid of this desert preacher. Although she was able to have him killed, she was not able to stop his message. The One John had announced was already on the move. John had accomplished his mission.

God has given each of us a purpose for living, and we can trust him to guide us. John did not have the complete Bible as we know it today. Yet he focused his life on the truth he knew from the available Old Testament Scriptures. Likewise we can discover in God's Word the truths he wants us to know. And as these truths work in us, others will be drawn to him. God can use you unlike anyone else. Let him know your willingness to follow him today.

Strength and accomplishments:
- The God-appointed messenger to announce the arrival of Jesus
- A preacher whose theme was repentance
- A fearless confronter
- Known for his remarkable life-style
- Uncompromising

Weaknesses and mistakes:
- Momentary doubt about Jesus' identity

Lessons from his life:
- God does not guarantee an easy or safe life to those who serve him
- Doing what God desires is the greatest possible life-investment
- Standing for the truth is more important than life itself

Vital statistics:
- Where: Judea
- Occupation: Prophet
- Relatives: Father: Zacharias. Mother: Elizabeth. Distant cousin: Jesus.
- Contemporaries: Herod, Herodias

Key Verse:
"Truly, of all men ever born, none shines more brightly than John the Baptist. And yet, even the lesser lights in the Kingdom of Heaven will be greater than he is!" (Matthew 11:11).

John's story is told in all four Gospels. His coming was predicted in Isaiah 40:3 and Malachi 4:5ff; and he is mentioned in Acts 1:5, 22; 10:37; 11:16; 13:24, 25; 18:25; 19:3, 4.

1:27 John the Baptist said he was not even fit to be Christ's slave. But in Luke 7:28, Jesus said that in all humanity, there is no person greater than John. If such a great human being felt inadequate to be Christ's slave, how much more should we lay aside our pride to serve Christ! When we truly understand who Christ is, our pride and self-importance melt away.

John the Baptist proclaims Jesus as the Messiah
(20)

29The next day John saw Jesus coming toward him and said, "Look! There is the Lamb of God who takes away the world's sin! 30He is the one I was talking about when I said, 'Soon a man far greater than I am is coming, who existed long before me!' 31I didn't know he was the one, but I am here baptizing with water in order to point him out to the nation of Israel."

32Then John told about seeing the Holy Spirit in the form of a dove descending from heaven and resting upon Jesus.

33"I didn't know he was the one," John said again, "but at the time God sent me to baptize he told me, 'When you see the Holy Spirit descending and resting upon someone—he is the one you are looking for. He is the one who baptizes with the Holy Spirit.' 34I saw it happen to this man, and I therefore testify that he is the Son of God."

The first disciples follow Jesus
(21)

35The following day as John was standing with two of his disciples, 36Jesus walked by. John looked at him intently and then declared, "See! There is the Lamb of God!"

37Then John's two disciples turned and followed Jesus.
38Jesus looked around and saw them following. "What do you want?" he asked them.

"Sir," they replied, "where do you live?"

39"Come and see," he said. So they went with him to the place where he was staying and were with him from about four o'clock that afternoon until the evening. 40(One of these men was Andrew, Simon Peter's brother.)

41Andrew then went to find his brother Peter and told him, "We have found the Messiah!" 42And he brought Peter to meet Jesus.

1:29 Isa 53:7 1 Cor 5:7 1 Pet 1:19
1:30 Jn 1:15,27
1:32 Mt 3:16 Mk 1:10 Lk 3:22
1:33 Lk 3:16 Acts 1:5
1:34 Jn 1:49; 10:36 11:27; 20:30,31
1:40 Mt 4:18-22 Mk 1:16 Lk 5:2-11
1:41 Job 23:3 Dan 9:25 Jn 4:25
1:42 Mt 16:18 1 Cor 15:5 1 Pet 2:5 Rev 21:14

1:29 Every morning and evening, a lamb was sacrificed in the Temple for the sins of the people (Exodus 29:38–42). Isaiah 53:7 prophesied that the Messiah, God's Servant, would be led to slaughter like a lamb. To pay the penalty for sin, a life had to be given—and God chose to provide the sacrifice himself. The sins of the world were removed when Jesus died as the perfect sacrifice. This is the way our sins are forgiven (1 Corinthians 5:7). The "world's sin" means everyone's sin, the sin of each individual. Jesus paid the price of *your* sin by his death. You can receive forgiveness by confessing your sin to him and asking for his forgiveness.

1:30 Although John the Baptist was a well-known preacher and attracted large crowds, he was content for Jesus to take the higher place. This is true humility, the basis for greatness in preaching, teaching, or any other work we do for Christ. When you are content to do what God wants you to do and let Jesus Christ be honored for it, God will do great things through you.

1:31 At Jesus' baptism, John the Baptist declared him the Messiah. At this time God gave John a sign to show him that Jesus was truly sent from God (1:33). John and Jesus were second cousins, so John knew who he was. But it wasn't until his baptism that he understood Jesus to be the Messiah. Jesus' baptism is described in Matthew 3:13–17; Mark 1:9–11; and Luke 3:21, 22.

1:33 John the Baptist's baptism by water was preparatory, because it was for repentance and symbolized the washing away of sins. But Jesus would baptize with the Holy Spirit, meaning that he would send the Holy Spirit upon all believers, empowering them to live and teach the message of salvation. This began after Jesus had risen from the dead and ascended into heaven (see John 20:22; Acts 2).

1:34 John the Baptist's job was to point people to Jesus, the Messiah for whom they were looking. Today people are looking for someone to give them security in an insecure world. Our job is to point them to Christ and to show that he is the One they seek.

1:35ff These new disciples used several names for Jesus: Lamb of God (1:36), Sir (literally, Rabbi or Teacher) (1:38), Messiah (1:41, 45), Son of God (1:49), King of Israel (1:49). As they got to know Jesus, their appreciation for him grew. The more time we spend getting to know Christ, the more we understand and appreciate who he is. We may be drawn to him for his teaching, but we will come to know him as the Son of God. Although these disciples made this verbal shift in a few days, they would not fully understand until three years later (Acts 2). What they so easily professed had to be worked out in experience. We may find that words of faith come easily, but deep appreciation for Christ comes with living by faith.

1:37 One of the two disciples was Andrew (1:40). The other is either John, the writer of this book, or Philip, who is often mentioned. Why did these disciples leave John the Baptist? Because that's what John wanted them to do—he pointed the way to Jesus, whom he had prepared them to follow. These were Jesus' first disciples, along with Peter (1:42) and Nathanael (1:45).

1:38 When the two disciples began to follow Jesus, he asked them, "What do you want?" Following Christ is not enough; we must follow him for the right reasons. To follow Christ for our own purposes is asking Christ to follow us—to align with us to build our cause, not his. We must examine our motives for following him—are they for his glory or ours?

1:40 Andrew accepted John the Baptist's testimony about Jesus and immediately went to tell his brother, Simon Peter, about him. There was no question in his mind that Jesus was the Messiah. Not only did he tell Peter, but throughout the Gospels we find Andrew eager to introduce people to Jesus (see John 6:8, 9; 12:22).

1:42 Jesus saw not only who Peter was, but who he would

1:43
Jn 6:5,6
12:20-22
1:45
Gen 3:15; 26:4
49:10
Num 21:8,9
Deut 18:15,18
Ps 2; 16:8-11,22
110; 132:11
Isa 6:5; 7:14; 9:6
11:1-10; 32:1-5
42:1-9; 49:1-13
50:6,53
Jer 23:5,6
33:15
Ezek 34:23
37:25
Dan 7:13; 9:25
Mic 5:2
Zech 3:8,9;
6:12; 9:9; 13:1,7
1:49
Jn 1:34
1:51
Gen 28:12

2:1
Jn 1:29,35,43
2:4
Eccles 3:1
Mt 12:46-49
Jn 7:6; 8:20
19:26

Jesus looked intently at Peter for a moment and then said, "You are Simon, John's son—but you shall be called Peter, the rock!"

43The next day Jesus decided to go to Galilee. He found Philip and told him, "Come with me." 44(Philip was from Bethsaida, Andrew and Peter's home town.)

45Philip now went off to look for Nathanael and told him, "We have found the Messiah!—the very person Moses and the prophets told about! His name is Jesus, the son of Joseph from Nazareth!"

46"Nazareth!" exclaimed Nathanael. "Can anything good come from there?"

"Just come and see for yourself," Philip declared.

47As they approached, Jesus said, "Here comes an honest man—a true son of Israel."

48"How do you know what I am like?" Nathanael demanded.

And Jesus replied, "I could see you under the fig tree before Philip found you."

49Nathanael replied, "Sir, you are the Son of God—the King of Israel!"

50Jesus asked him, "Do you believe all this just because I told you I had seen you under the fig tree? You will see greater proofs than this. 51You will even see heaven open and the angels of God coming back and forth to me, the Messiah."

Jesus turns water into wine
(22)

2 Two days later Jesus' mother was a guest at a wedding in the village of Cana in Galilee, 2and Jesus and his disciples were invited too. 3The wine supply ran out during the festivities, and Jesus' mother came to him with the problem.

4"I can't help you now," he said. "It isn't yet my time for miracles."

5But his mother told the servants, "Do whatever he tells you to."

1:51 *the Messiah,* literally, "the Son of Man." **2:4** *"I can't help you now," he said,* literally, "Woman, what have I to do with you?"

---

become. Peter is not presented as "rock-solid" throughout the Gospels, but he became a solid "rock" in the days of the early church, as recorded in the book of Acts. By giving Peter a new name, Jesus introduced a change in character.

1:46 Nazareth was despised by the Jews because a Roman army garrison was located there. Nathanael's harsh comment reflected the common view. Nathanael's hometown was Cana, about four miles from Nazareth.

1:46 When Nathanael heard that Jesus was from Nazareth, he was surprised and questioned Philip. Philip responded by saying, "Come and see for yourself!" Fortunately, Nathanael went to meet Jesus and became a disciple. If he had acted on his prejudice without investigating further, he would have missed the Messiah!

2:1, 2 Weddings in Jesus' day were week-long festivals. Banquets were prepared for many guests, and the week was spent celebrating the new life of the married couple. Often the whole town was invited, and people came—it was considered an insult to refuse an invitation to a wedding. To accommodate many people, careful planning was needed. To run out of wine was an embarrassment and broke the strong unwritten laws of hospitality. Jesus was about to respond to a need.

2:1, 2 Jesus was on a mission to save the world, the greatest mission in the history of mankind. Yet he took time to attend a wedding and take part in its festivities. We may be tempted to think we should not take time out from our "important" work for social occasions. But maybe these social occasions are part of our mission. Jesus valued these wedding festivities because they involved people, and Jesus came to be with people. Our mission can often be accomplished in joyous times of celebration with others. Bring balance to your life by bringing Jesus into times of pleasure as well as times of work.

2:4 "It isn't yet my time for miracles" can also be translated, "My time has not yet come." Mary was probably not asking Jesus to do a miracle but to help with this major dilemma and find some wine. Tradition says that Joseph, Mary's husband, was dead, so she

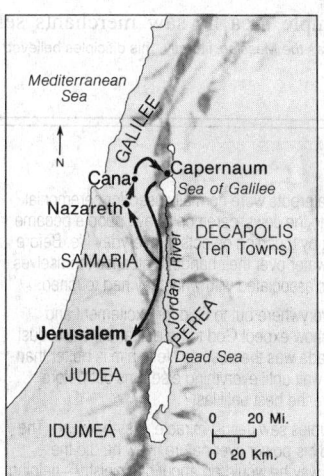

JESUS' FIRST TRAVELS
After his baptism by John in the Jordan River and temptation by Satan in the wilderness (see the map in Mark 1), Jesus returned to Galilee. He visited Nazareth, Cana, and Capernaum, and then returned to Jerusalem for the Passover.

probably was used to asking for her son's help in difficult problems. Jesus' answer to Mary is difficult to understand, but maybe that is the point. Although Mary did not understand what Jesus was going to do, she trusted him to do the right thing. Those who believe in Jesus but run into situations they cannot understand must continue to trust that he will work in the best way.

2:5 Mary submitted to Jesus' way of doing things. She recognized that Jesus was more than her human son—he was the Son of God. When we bring our problems to Christ, we may think we know how he should take care of them. But he may have a completely different plan. Like Mary, we should submit and allow him to deal with the problem as he sees best.

⁶Six stone waterpots were standing there; they were used for Jewish ceremonial purposes and held perhaps twenty to thirty gallons each. ⁷, ⁸Then Jesus told the servants to fill them to the brim with water. When this was done he said, "Dip some out and take it to the master of ceremonies."

⁹When the master of ceremonies tasted the water that was now wine, not knowing where it had come from (though, of course, the servants did), he called the bridegroom over.

¹⁰"This is wonderful stuff!" he said. "You're different from most. Usually a host uses the best wine first, and afterwards, when everyone is full and doesn't care, then he brings out the less expensive brands. But you have kept the best for the last!"

¹¹This miracle at Cana in Galilee was Jesus' first public demonstration of his heaven-sent power. And his disciples believed that he really was the Messiah.

¹²After the wedding he left for Capernaum for a few days with his mother, brothers, and disciples.

2:6
Mk 7:3,4
Jn 3:25

2:9
Jn 4:46

2:11
Jn 2:23; 3:2
4:54; 6:14; 11:47
12:37

2:12
Mt 12:46-50

B. MESSAGE AND MINISTRY OF JESUS, THE SON OF GOD (2:13—12:50)

John stresses the deity of Christ. He gives us seven miracles that serve as signs that Jesus is the Messiah. In this section he records Jesus describing himself as the bread of life, the water of life, the light of the world, the door, and the good shepherd. John provides teachings of Jesus found nowhere else. This is the most theological of the four Gospels.

1. Jesus encounters belief and unbelief from the people

Jesus clears the Temple
(23)

¹³Then it was time for the annual Jewish Passover celebration, and Jesus went to Jerusalem.

¹⁴In the Temple area he saw merchants selling cattle, sheep, and doves for

2:13
Ex 12:14
Num 28:16
Deut 16:1

2:11 *that he really was the Messiah,* literally, "his disciples believed him."

2:6 The six stone waterpots were normally used for ceremonial washing. According to the Jews' ceremonial law, people became symbolically unclean by touching objects of everyday life. Before eating, they poured water over their hands to cleanse themselves of any bad influences associated with what they had touched.

2:10 People look everywhere but to God for excitement and meaning. They somehow expect God to be dull and lifeless. Just as the wine Jesus made was the best, so life in him is better than life on our own. Why wait until everything else runs out before trying God? Why save the best until last?

2:11 When the disciples saw Jesus' miracle, they believed. The miracle itself showed his power over nature. How he did the miracle revealed the way he would go about his ministry—helping others, speaking with authority, and being in personal touch with people.

2:11 Miracles are not merely superhuman happenings, but happenings that demonstrate God's power. Almost every miracle Jesus did was a renewal of fallen creation—restoring sight, making the lame to walk, even restoring life to the dead. Believe in him, not because he is a superman, but because he is God continuing his creation, even in those of us who are poor, or weak, or crippled, or orphaned, or blind, or lame, or with some other desperate need to be re-created.

2:12 Capernaum became Jesus' home base during his ministry in Galilee. Located on a major trade route, it was an important city in the region with a Roman garrison and a customs station. At

Capernaum, Matthew was called to be a disciple (Matthew 9:9), and it was also the home of several other disciples (Matthew 4:13), and a high-ranking government official (4:46). It had at least one major synagogue. Although Jesus made this city his base of operations in Galilee, he condemned it for the people's unbelief (Matthew 11:23; Luke 10:15).

2:13 The Passover celebration took place yearly at the Temple in Jerusalem. Every Jewish male was expected to make a pilgrimage to Jerusalem during this time (Deuteronomy 16:16). This was a week-long festival—the Passover was one day, and the Feast of Unleavened Bread lasted the rest of the week. The entire week commemorated the freeing of the Jews from slavery in Egypt (Exodus 12:1–13).

2:13 Jerusalem was both the religious and political seat of Palestine, and the place where the Messiah was expected to arrive. The Temple was located there, and many Jewish families from all over the world traveled to Jerusalem during the key feasts. The Temple was built on an imposing site, a hill overlooking the city. Solomon built the first Temple on this same site almost 1,000 years earlier (949 B.C.), but his Temple was destroyed by the Babylonians (2 Kings 25). The Temple was rebuilt in 515 B.C., and Herod the Great enlarged and remodeled it.

2:14 John records this first cleansing of the Temple. A second cleansing occurred at the end of Jesus' ministry, about three years later, and is recorded in Matthew 21:12–17; Mark 11:12–19; Luke 19:45–48.

2:16
Lk 2:49
Jn 14:2
2:17
Ps 69:9
2:18
Mt 12:38
2:19
Mt 26:61; 27:40
Mk 14:58
Acts 6:14
2:20
Ezra 5:16
2:21
Jn 10:38
14:2,10; 17:21
1 Cor 3:16; 6:19
2 Cor 6:16
Eph 2:21,22
Col 2:9
1 Pet 2:4-7
2:22
Ps 2:7; 16:10
Lk 24:8,25,26
Jn 12:16; 14:26
2:24
1 Sam 16:7
1 Chron 28:9
Mt 9:4
Mk 2:8

sacrifices, and moneychangers behind their counters. 15Jesus made a whip from some ropes and chased them all out, and drove out the sheep and oxen, scattering the moneychangers' coins over the floor and turning over their tables! 16Then, going over to the men selling doves, he told them, "Get these things out of here. Don't turn my Father's House into a market!"

17Then his disciples remembered this prophecy from the Scriptures: "Concern for God's House will be my undoing."

18"What right have you to order them out?" the Jewish leaders demanded. "If you have this authority from God, show us a miracle to prove it."

19"All right," Jesus replied, "this is the miracle I will do for you: Destroy this sanctuary and in three days I will raise it up!"

20"What!" they exclaimed. "It took forty-six years to build this Temple, and you can do it in three days?" 21But by "this sanctuary" he meant his body. 22After he came back to life again, the disciples remembered his saying this and realized that what he had quoted from the Scriptures really did refer to him, and had all come true!

23Because of the miracles he did in Jerusalem at the Passover celebration, many people were convinced that he was indeed the Messiah. 24, 25But Jesus didn't trust them, for he knew mankind to the core. No one needed to tell him how changeable human nature is!

2:18 the Jewish leaders, literally, "the Jews."

2:14 The Temple tax had to be paid in local currency, so foreigners had to have their money changed by moneychangers, who were often dishonest and charged high exchange rates. The people were also required to make a sacrifice for sin. Because of the long journey, many could not bring their own animals. Some who did bring animals had them rejected for being imperfect. Thus animal merchants did a flourishing business in the Temple courtyard. The price of sacrificial animals was much higher in the Temple area than elsewhere. Jesus was angry at the dishonest, greedy practices of the moneychangers and merchants. They should not have been working in the Temple itself. Their presence made a mockery of the Temple, the place of worship to God.

2:14 The Temple area was always crowded during Passover with thousands of people. The religious leaders crowded it even further by allowing moneychangers and merchants to set up booths in the Court of the Gentiles. They rationalized this practice as a convenience for the worshipers and as a way to make money for Temple upkeep. But the religious leaders did not seem to care that the Court of the Gentiles was so full of merchants that foreigners found it difficult to worship. And worship was the main purpose for visiting the Temple. No wonder Jesus was angry!

2:14-16 God's Temple was being misused by people who turned it into a marketplace. They forgot, or didn't care, that God's house is a place of worship, not a marketplace for making a profit. Our attitude toward the church is wrong if we see it as a place for personal contacts or business advantage. Make sure you attend a church meeting to worship God.

2:15, 16 Jesus was obviously angry at the merchants who exploited those who had come to God's house to worship. There is a difference between uncontrolled rage and righteous indignation—yet both are called anger. We must be very careful how we use the powerful emotion of anger. It is right to be angry about injustice and sin; it is wrong to be angry over trivial personal offenses.

2:15, 16 Jesus made a whip and chased out the moneychangers; does that permit us to use violence against wrongdoers? Certain authority is granted to some, but not to all. For example, the authority to use weapons and restrain people is granted to police officers, but not to the general public. The authority to imprison people is granted to judges, but not to individual citizens. Jesus had God's authority, something we cannot have. While we want to live Christlike lives, we should never try to claim his authority where it has not been given to us.

2:17 This quotation from Psalm 69:9 is also translated, "Zeal for God's house will consume me" (ASV). Jesus took the evil acts in the Temple as an insult against God and thus did not deal with them halfheartedly. He was consumed with righteous anger against sin and disrespect for God.

2:19, 20 This was the Temple Zerubbabel had built over 500 years earlier, but Herod the Great had begun remodeling it—making it much larger and far more beautiful. It had been 46 years since this remodeling had started (20 B.C.), and it still wasn't completely finished; therefore, Jesus' words that it could be torn down and rebuilt in three days were startling.

2:21 Jesus was giving his credentials, his right to take direct action against the Temple merchants. This statement refers to his body, not the literal Temple. Christ's resurrection (rebuilding in three days) would prove his authority to drive out the merchants (1:18), heal, cast out demons, and forgive sins.

2:23-25 Jesus, the Son of God, knows all about human nature. He was well aware of the truth of Jeremiah 17:9, which states, "The heart is the most deceitful thing there is, and desperately wicked. No one can really know how bad it is!" Some of the same people calling Jesus "Messiah" would later yell "Crucify him!" It's easy to believe when it is exciting and everyone else believes the same way. But true faith remains firm when it isn't popular to believe.

Nicodemus visits Jesus at night
(24)

3 After dark one night a Jewish religious leader named Nicodemus, a member of the sect of the Pharisees, came for an interview with Jesus. "Sir," he said, "we all know that God has sent you to teach us. Your miracles are proof enough of this."

3Jesus replied, "With all the earnestness I possess I tell you this: Unless you are born again, you can never get into the Kingdom of God."

4"Born again!" exclaimed Nicodemus. "What do you mean? How can an old man go back into his mother's womb and be born again?"

5Jesus replied, "What I am telling you so earnestly is this: Unless one is born of water and the Spirit, he cannot enter the Kingdom of God. 6Men can only reproduce human life, but the Holy Spirit gives new life from heaven; 7so don't be surprised at my statement that you must be born again! 8Just as you can hear the wind but can't tell where it comes from or where it will go next, so it is with the Spirit. We do not know on whom he will next bestow this life from heaven."

9"What do you mean?" Nicodemus asked.

10, 11Jesus replied, "You, a respected Jewish teacher, and yet you don't under-

3:1
Jn 7:50; 19:39
3:2
Jn 9:33
Acts 2:22; 10:38
3:3
Jn 1:13
1 Pet 1:23
3:5
Acts 2:38
Tit 3:4,5
1 Pet 3:21
3:6
Ezek 36:26,27
Jn 1:13
Rom 8:15,16
1 Cor 15:50
Gal 4:6
3:8
Eccles 11:5
Ezek 37:5,9,10,14

THE VISIT IN SAMARIA
Jesus went to Jerusalem for the Passover, cleansed the Temple, and talked with Nicodemus, a religious leader, about eternal life. He then left Jerusalem and traveled in Judea. On his way to Galilee, he visited Sychar and other villages in Samaria. Unlike most Jews of the day, he did not try to avoid the region of Samaria.

world (3:16), not just the Jews, and that Nicodemus wouldn't be a part of it unless he was personally born again (3:5). This was a revolutionary concept; the Kingdom is personal, not national or ethnic, and its entrance requirements are repentance and spiritual rebirth. Jesus later taught that God's Kingdom has *already begun* in the hearts of believers through the presence of the Holy Spirit. It will be fully realized when Jesus will return again to judge the world and abolish evil forever (see Luke 8:1; 9:11, note; 11:20; Revelation 21, 22).

3:5, 6 "By water and the Spirit" could be referring to (1) the contrast between physical birth (water) and spiritual birth (Spirit), or (2) being regenerated by the Spirit and demonstrating that rebirth by baptism. The water may also represent the cleansing action of God's Holy Spirit (Titus 3:5). Jesus is explaining the importance of a spiritual rebirth, saying we don't enter the Kingdom by living a better life, but by being spiritually reborn.

3:6 Jesus says that the Holy Spirit gives new life from heaven. Who is the Holy Spirit? God is three persons in one—the Father, the Son, and the Holy Spirit. God became a man in Jesus so that Jesus could die for our sins. He rose from the dead to offer salvation to all people through spiritual renewal and rebirth. When Jesus ascended into heaven, his physical presence left the earth, but he promised to send the Holy Spirit so his spiritual presence would still be among mankind (see Luke 24:49). Whereas in Old Testament days the Holy Spirit empowered specific individuals only for specific purposes, now all believers have the power of the Holy Spirit available to them. The Holy Spirit first became available to all believers at Pentecost (Acts 2). For more on the Holy Spirit, read 14:16–28; Romans 8:9; 1 Corinthians 12:13; and 2 Corinthians 1:22.

3:8 Jesus explained that we cannot control the work of the Holy Spirit. He works in ways we cannot predict or understand. Just as you did not control your physical birth, so you cannot control your spiritual birth. It is a gift from God, given by the Holy Spirit (Romans 8:16; 1 Corinthians 2:10–12; 1 Thessalonians 1:5, 6).

3:8 Are there people you disregard, thinking they could never be brought to God—such as a world leader for whom you have not prayed or a successful person to whom you have never witnessed? Don't ever assume that a certain person will never respond to the gospel. God, through his Holy Spirit, can reach anyone, and you should pray diligently for whomever he brings to your mind. Be a witness and example to everyone with whom you have contact. God may touch those you think most unlikely—and he may use you to do it.

3:1 Nicodemus was a teacher and a member of the Pharisees, a group of religious leaders whom Jesus and John the Baptist often criticized for being hypocrites (see the note on Matthew 3:7 for more on the Pharisees). Most Pharisees were intensely jealous of Jesus because he undermined their authority and challenged their views. But Nicodemus was searching, and he believed Jesus had some answers. A learned teacher, he came to be taught. No matter how intelligent and well educated you are, you must come to Jesus with an open mind and heart so he can teach you the truth about God.

3:1ff Nicodemus came to Jesus personally, although he could have sent one of his assistants. He wanted to examine Jesus for himself to separate fact from rumor. Perhaps he was afraid of what his peers, the Pharisees, would say about his visit, so he came after dark. Later, when he understood that Jesus was truly the Messiah, he spoke up boldly in his defense (7:50). Like Nicodemus, we must examine Jesus for ourselves—others cannot do it for us. Then, if we believe he is who he says, we will want to speak up for him.

3:3 What did Nicodemus know about the Kingdom? From the Bible he knew it would be ruled by God, it would be restored on earth, and it would incorporate God's people. Jesus revealed to this devout Pharisee that the Kingdom would come to the whole

3:10, 11 This Jewish teacher of the Bible knew the Old Testament thoroughly, but he didn't understand what it said about the Messiah. Knowledge is not salvation. You should know the Bible;

3:13
Jn 6:38,42
16:28
Rom 10:6
Eph 4:9,10
3:14
Num 21:8,9
3:15
1 Jn 5:11,12
3:16
Rom 5:8; 8:32

stand these things? I am telling you what I know and have seen—and yet you won't believe me. 12But if you don't even believe me when I tell you about such things as these that happen here among men, how can you possibly believe if I tell you what is going on in heaven? 13For only I, the Messiah, have come to earth and will return to heaven again. 14And as Moses in the wilderness lifted up the bronze image of a serpent on a pole, even so I must be lifted up upon a pole, 15so that anyone who believes in me will have eternal life. 16For God loved the world so much that he gave his only Son so that anyone who believes in him shall not perish but have

3:13 *the Messiah,* literally, "the Son of Man."   3:16 *his only Son,* or, "the unique Son of God." So also in vs 18.

NICODEMUS

God specializes in finding and changing people we consider out of reach. In Nicodemus' case, it took awhile for him to come out of the dark, but God was patient with this "undercover" believer.

Afraid of being discovered, Nicodemus made an appointment to see Jesus at night. Daylight conversations between Pharisees and Jesus tended to be antagonistic, but Nicodemus really wanted to learn. He probably got a lot more than he expected—a challenge to a new life! We know very little about Nicodemus, but we know that he left that evening's encounter a changed man. He came away with a whole new understanding of both God and himself.

Nicodemus next appears as part of the Supreme Court. As it discussed ways to eliminate Jesus, Nicodemus raised the question of justice. Although his objection was overruled, he had spoken up. He had begun to change.

Our last picture of Nicodemus shows him joining Joseph of Arimathea in asking for Jesus' body to bury. Realizing what he was risking, Nicodemus was making a bold move. He was continuing to grow.

God looks for steady growth, not instant perfection. How well does your present degree of spiritual growth match up with how long you have known Jesus?

Strengths and accomplishments:
• One of the few religious leaders who believed in Jesus
• A member of the powerful Supreme Court
• A Pharisee who was attracted by Jesus' character and miracles
• Joined with Joseph of Arimathea in burying Jesus

Weaknesses and mistakes:
• Limited by his fear of being publicly exposed as Jesus' follower

Lessons from his life:
• Unless we are born again, we can never get into the Kingdom of God
• God is able to change those we might consider unreachable
• God is patient, but persistent
• If we are available, God can use us

Vital statistics:
• Where: Jerusalem
• Occupation: Religious leader
• Contemporaries: Jesus, Annas, Caiaphas, Pilate, Joseph of Arimathea

Key verse:
" 'Born again!' exclaimed Nicodemus. 'What do you mean? How can an old man go back into his mother's womb and be born again?' " (John 3:4).

Nicodemus' story is told in John 3:1–21; 7:50–52; and 19:39, 40.

---

but even more important, you should understand the God it reveals and the salvation he offers.

3:14, 15 When the Israelites were wandering in the wilderness, God sent a plague of snakes to punish the people for their rebellious attitudes. Those doomed to die from snakebites could be cured by obeying God's command to look up at the elevated bronze serpent and believing that God would heal them if they did (see Numbers 21:8, 9). Looking to Jesus for our salvation happens the same way. You will be saved from sin's deadly "bite" by looking to Jesus and believing he will save you.

3:16 Many people are repulsed by thinking about living forever because their lives are miserable. But eternal life is not the extension of man's miserable, mortal life; eternal life is God's life (Ephesians 4:18) embodied in Christ (14:6) given to all believers now as a guarantee that they will live forever. In this life there is no

death, sickness, enemies, evil, and sin. When we don't know Christ, we make choices as though this life were all we have. In reality, this life is just the introduction to eternity. Begin, therefore, to evaluate all that happens from an eternal perspective.

3:16 The entire gospel comes to a focus in this verse. True love is not static or self-centered; it reaches out and draws others in. God sets the pattern of true love here, the basis for all love relationships—if you love someone dearly, you are willing to pay dearly for that person's responsive love. God paid dearly with the life of his Son, the highest price he could pay. Jesus accepted our punishment, paid the price for our sins, and then offered us the new life he bought for us. When we share the gospel with others, our love must be like his—willingly giving up our own comfort and security so that others might join us in receiving God's love.

eternal life. 17God did not send his Son into the world to condemn it, but to save it.

18"There is no eternal doom awaiting those who trust him to save them. But those who don't trust him have already been tried and condemned for not believing in the only Son of God. 19Their sentence is based on this fact: that the Light from heaven came into the world, but they loved the darkness more than the Light, for their deeds were evil. 20They hated the heavenly Light because they wanted to sin in the darkness. They stayed away from that Light for fear their sins would be exposed and they would be punished. 21But those doing right come gladly to the Light to let everyone see that they are doing what God wants them to."

3:17
Jn 12:47
3:18
Jn 5:24
Rom 8:1
3:19
Jn 1:4,5; 7:7
8:12; 12:46
3:20
Eph 5:11-13
3:21
1 Jn 1:7

— *John the Baptist tells more about Jesus* (25)

22Afterwards Jesus and his disciples left Jerusalem and stayed for a while in Judea and baptized there.

3:22
Jn 4:2

23, 24At this time John the Baptist was not yet in prison. He was baptizing at Aenon, near Salim, because there was plenty of water there. 25One day someone began an argument with John's disciples, telling them that Jesus' baptism was best. 26So they came to John and said, "Master, the man you met on the other side of the Jordan River—the one you said was the Messiah—he is baptizing too, and everybody is going over there instead of coming here to us."

3:24
Mt 4:12
3:26
Jn 1:6,7,34

27John replied, "God in heaven appoints each man's work. 28My work is to prepare the way for that man so that everyone will go to him. You yourselves know how plainly I told you that I am not the Messiah. I am here to prepare the way for him—that is all. 29The crowds will naturally go to the main attraction—the bride will go where the bridegroom is! A bridegroom's friends rejoice with him. I am the Bridegroom's friend, and I am filled with joy at his success. 30He must become greater and greater, and I must become less and less.

3:27
1 Cor 4:7
Heb 5:4
3:28
Mal 3:1
Jn 1:20,23
3:29
Isa 62:5
2 Cor 11:2
Rev 21:9

31"He has come from heaven and is greater than anyone else. I am of the earth, and my understanding is limited to the things of earth. 32He tells what he has seen and heard, but how few believe what he tells them! 33, 34Those who believe him discover that God is a fountain of truth. For this one—sent by God—speaks God's words, for God's Spirit is upon him without measure or limit. 35The Father loves this man because he is his Son, and God has given him everything there is.

3:32
Jn 3:11
3:33
1 Jn 5:10
3:34
Lk 4:18,19
Jn 6:63
3:35
Jn 5:20; 17:2,24

3:25 *best,* literally, "about purification."   **3:29** *The crowds will naturally go to the main attraction,* implied.

3:18 As people try to save themselves from their fears, they may trust in themselves, their good works, or their money and possessions. But only God can save us from the one thing we really need to fear—eternal condemnation. We trust in God by recognizing the insufficiency of our own efforts to find salvation and by asking him to do his work in us. When Jesus talks about "those who don't trust him," he is referring to those who reject or ignore him completely, not those who have momentary doubts.

3:19–21 Many people don't want their lives exposed to God's light because they are afraid of what it will reveal. They don't want to be changed. Don't be surprised when these same people are threatened by your desire to obey God and do what is right, because they are afraid that the light in you may expose some of the darkness in their lives. Don't be discouraged, however. Keep praying that they will come to see how much better it is to live in light than in darkness.

— **3:25** Some people look for points of disagreement to sow seeds of discord, discontent, and doubt. John the Baptist ended this theological argument by focusing on his devotion to Christ. It is divisive to try to force others to believe our way. Instead, let's witness about our own personal devotion to Christ and what he has done for us. How can anyone argue with us about that?

3:26 John the Baptist's disciples were disturbed because people were following Jesus instead of John. It is easy to grow jealous of the popularity of another person's ministry. But we must remember that our true mission is to win people to follow Christ, not us.

3:27 Why did John the Baptist continue to baptize after Jesus came onto the scene? Why didn't he become a disciple too? John said, "God in heaven appoints each man's work." John had to continue the work God called him to do—being Jesus' disciple would not have allowed him to do that. John's main purpose was to point people to Christ. Even with Jesus beginning his own ministry, John could still point people to him.

3:27 John believed God had appointed him. If God appoints us to a task, it becomes a high and holy privilege. We should accept it with great enthusiasm.

3:30 John said that Christ must become greater while he became less. Pastors and other Christian leaders can be tempted to focus more on the success of their ministries than on Christ. Beware of those who put more emphasis on their own achievements than on God's Kingdom.

3:33–35 Our whole spiritual life comes to a focus in one question, "Who is Jesus Christ?" If you accept Jesus as only a prophet or teacher, you have rejected his prophetic teaching, for he claimed to be God's Son, even God himself. The heartbeat of John's Gospel is the dynamic truth that Jesus Christ is God's Son, the Messiah, the Savior, who was from the beginning and will continue to live forever. The dynamic truth is that this same Jesus has invited us to accept him and live with him forever. When we understand who Jesus is, we are compelled to accept him personally.

3:36 Jesus says that those who believe in him *have* eternal life

3:36
Hab 2:4
Jn 3:16
Rom 1:17

36 And all who trust him—God's Son—to save them have eternal life; those who don't believe and obey him shall never see heaven, but the wrath of God remains upon them."

Jesus talks to a woman at the well (27)

4 When the Lord knew that the Pharisees had heard about the greater crowds coming to him than to John to be baptized and to become his disciples— (though Jesus himself didn't baptize them, but his disciples did)— 3he left Judea and returned to the province of Galilee.

4:4
Lk 9:52

4He had to go through Samaria on the way, 5, 6and around noon as he approached the village of Sychar, he came to Jacob's Well, located on the parcel of ground Jacob gave to his son Joseph. Jesus was tired from the long walk in the hot sun and sat wearily beside the well.

4:5,6
Gen 33:19
48:22
Josh 24:32

4:7
Gen 24:11

7Soon a Samaritan woman came to draw water, and Jesus asked her for a drink. 8He was alone at the time as his disciples had gone into the village to buy some food. 9The woman was surprised that a Jew would ask a "despised Samaritan" for anything—usually they wouldn't even speak to them!—and she remarked about this to Jesus.

4:9
2 Kgs 17:24
Ezra 4
Mt 10:5
Jn 8:48
Acts 10:48

4:10
Isa 12:3; 44:3
Jer 2:13
Jn 7:37-39
1 Cor 12:13
Rev 21:6; 22:17

10He replied, "If you only knew what a wonderful gift God has for you, and who I am, you would ask me for some *living* water!"

11"But you don't have a rope or a bucket," she said, "and this is a very deep well! Where would you get this living water? 12And besides, are you greater than our ancestor Jacob? How can you offer better water than this which he and his sons and cattle enjoyed?"

4:14
Jn 6:35
7:37,38

13Jesus replied that people soon became thirsty again after drinking this water. 14"But the water I give them," he said, "becomes a perpetual spring within them, watering them forever with eternal life."

(not *will* have eternal life). Thus, eternal life begins at the moment of spiritual rebirth. To receive eternal life is to possess God's life, which by nature is eternal. The reception of this life now guarantees an eternal life with God.

3:36 John the writer has been demonstrating that Jesus is the true Son of God. He sets before us the greatest choice of life. We are responsible to decide today whom we will obey (Joshua 24:15), and God wants us to choose life (Deuteronomy 30:15–20). To decide to put off the choice is to choose not to follow Christ. Indecision is a fatal decision.

4:1–3 Already opposition was rising against Jesus, especially from the Pharisees. They resented Jesus' popularity as well as his message, which challenged much of their teachings. Because Jesus was still in the beginning of his ministry, it wasn't yet time to confront these leaders openly; so he left Jerusalem and traveled north toward the region of Galilee.

4:4 When the Northern Kingdom with its capital at Samaria fell to the Assyrians, many Jews were deported to Assyria, and foreigners were brought in to settle the land and help keep the peace (2 Kings 17:24). The intermarriage between foreigners and the Jews who were left in the land resulted in a mixed race, impure in the opinion of Jews who lived in Judah, the Southern Kingdom. Thus the pure Jews hated this mixed race called Samaritans because they felt they had betrayed their people and nation. The Jews did everything they could to avoid traveling through Samaria. But Jesus had no reason to live by such cultural restrictions, and so he traveled directly through Samaria.

4:5–7 Jacob's well was part of the property originally owned by Jacob. The well itself was probably more than 200 feet deep. It was not a spring-fed well, but a well into which water seeped from rain and dew, collecting at the bottom. Wells were almost always

located outside the city along the main road. Twice each day, morning and evening, women came to draw water. This woman came at noon, however, probably to avoid meeting people because of her reputation. Here Jesus gave this woman an extraordinary message about fresh and pure water that would quench her spiritual thirst forever.

4:7–9 This woman (1) was a Samaritan, a member of the hated mixed race, (2) had a bad reputation, and (3) was in a public place. No respectable Jewish man would talk to a woman under such circumstances. But Jesus did. The gospel is for every person, no matter what his or her race, social position, or past sins. We must be prepared to share this gospel at any time in any place. Jesus crossed all barriers to share the Good News, and we who follow him must do no less.

4:10 What did Jesus mean by "living water?" In the Old Testament, many verses speak of thirsting after God as one thirsts for water (Psalm 42:1; Isaiah 55:1; Jeremiah 2:13; Zechariah 13:1). God is called the Fountain of life (Psalm 36:9; Jeremiah 17:13). In saying he would bring living water that could forever quench one's thirst for God, Jesus was claiming to be the Messiah. Only the Messiah could give this free gift that satisfies the desire of the soul.

4:13–15 Many functions of one's spiritual life parallel the functions of the physical life. As our bodies hunger and thirst, so do our souls. But our souls need *spiritual* food and water. The woman confused the two kinds of water, perhaps because no one had ever talked with her about her spiritual hunger and thirst before. We would not think of depriving our bodies of food and water when they hunger or thirst. Why then should we deprive our souls? The living Word, Jesus Christ, and the written Word, the Bible, can satisfy our hungry and thirsty souls.

15"Please, sir," the woman said, "give me some of that water! Then I'll never be thirsty again and won't have to make this long trip out here every day."

16"Go and get your husband," Jesus told her.

17, 18"But I'm not married," the woman replied.

"All too true!" Jesus said. "For you have had five husbands, and you aren't even married to the man you're living with now."

19"Sir," the woman said, "you must be a prophet. 20But say, tell me, why is it that you Jews insist that Jerusalem is the only place of worship, while we Samaritans claim it is here [at Mount Gerizim], where our ancestors worshiped?"

21-24Jesus replied, "The time is coming, ma'am, when we will no longer be concerned about whether to worship the Father here or in Jerusalem. For it's not *where* we worship that counts, but *how* we worship—is our worship spiritual and real? Do we have the Holy Spirit's help? For God is Spirit, and we must have his help to worship as we should. The Father wants this kind of worship from us. But you Samaritans know so little about him, worshiping blindly, while we Jews know all about him, for salvation comes to the world through the Jews."

25The woman said, "Well, at least I know that the Messiah will come—the one they call Christ—and when he does, he will explain everything to us."

26Then Jesus told her, "I am the Messiah!"

Jesus tells about the spiritual harvest (28)

27Just then his disciples arrived. They were surprised to find him talking to a woman, but none of them asked him why, or what they had been discussing.

28, 29Then the woman left her waterpot beside the well and went back to the village and told everyone, "Come and meet a man who told me everything I ever did! Can this be the Messiah?" 30So the people came streaming from the village to see him.

31Meanwhile, the disciples were urging Jesus to eat. 32"No," he said, "I have some food you don't know about."

33"Who brought it to him?" the disciples asked each other.

34Then Jesus explained: "My nourishment comes from doing the will of God who sent me, and from finishing his work. 35Do you think the work of harvesting will not begin until the summer ends four months from now? Look around you!

4:20 *at Mount Gerizim,* implied.

Cross-references (right margin)

4:15 Jn 6:34

4:19 Lk 7:16

4:20 Gen 12:6,7 33:18 Judg 9:7 Deut 12:5 2 Chron 7:12

4:21 Mal 1:11 1 Tim 2:8

4:22 2 Kings 17:28-41 Isa 2:3 Acts 17:24-29 Rom 3:1,2 9:4,5

4:23,24 2 Cor 3:17,18 Phil 3:3

4:25 Deut 18:15

4:26 Mk 14:61,62 Jn 8:24; 9:35-37

4:29 Jn 7:26,31

4:34 Job 23:12 Jn 5:30,36 6:38; 17:4 19:28,30

4:35 Mt 9:37,38 Lk 10:2

4:15 The woman mistakenly believed that if she received the water Jesus offered, she would not have to return to the well each day. She was interested in Jesus' message because she thought it could make her life easier. But if that were always the case, people would accept Christ's message only to make life easier, healthier, or wealthier. Instead, Christ's message is supposed to change us on the inside. He doesn't take away challenges, but helps us deal with them from a proper perspective.

4:15 The woman did not immediately understand what Jesus was talking about. It takes time to accept something that changes the very foundations of your life. Jesus allowed the woman time to ask questions and put pieces together for herself. Sharing the gospel does not always have immediate results. When you ask people to let Jesus change their lives, give them time to weigh the matter.

4:16–19 When this woman found that Jesus knew all about her private life, she quickly changed the subject. Often people are uncomfortable talking about their sins or problems and try to change the subject. In our witness we should gently turn the conversation back to what the person will decide to do about Christ.

4:20–24 The woman brought up a popular theological issue—the correct place to worship. But Jesus turned the conversation back to her personal needs. Her question, "Where do I worship?" was a smokescreen to cover up her deepest need. Jesus brought her back to "How do I worship, and whose help will I need?"

4:21–24 How does the Holy Spirit help us worship? The Holy Spirit prays for us (Romans 8:26), teaches us the words of Christ (John 14:26), and helps us feel loved (Romans 5:5).

4:24 When Jesus said, "Salvation comes to the world through the Jews," he was saying that only through Jesus, a Jew, would the whole world find salvation. God promised that through the Jewish race all nations and people would be blessed (Genesis 12:3). The Old Testament prophets called the Jews to be a light to the other nations of the world, to bring them to a knowledge of God; and they predicted the coming of a Jewish Messiah to save the nation and the world. The woman at the well knew of these passages, because she was expecting the Messiah to come. But she didn't realize she was talking to the one of whom the Old Testament passages spoke!

4:34 The nourishment about which Jesus was speaking did not include just Bible study, prayer, or attending church. We also are nourished by doing God's will and helping to bring his work of salvation to completion. We are nourished not only by what we take in, but also by what we give out for God.

4:35 Sometimes Christians excuse themselves from witnessing by saying their family or friends aren't ready to believe. Jesus, however, makes it clear that around us a continual harvest waits to be reaped. Don't let Jesus find you making excuses. Look around. You will find people ready to hear God's Word.

4:36
Dan 12:3
1 Cor 3:8,9
9:17-19
4:37
Job 31:8
Mic 6:15

Vast fields of human souls are ripening all around us, and are ready now for reaping. 36The reapers will be paid good wages and will be gathering eternal souls into the granaries of heaven! What joys await the sower and the reaper, both together! 37For it is true that one sows and someone else reaps. 38I sent you to reap where you didn't sow; others did the work, and you received the harvest."

Many Samaritans believe in Jesus
(29)

4:42
Isa 49:6
Mt 1:21
Lk 2:29-31
Jn 1:29; 17:8
Acts 5:31; 13:23
Eph 2:13
Phil 3:20
1 Tim 1:15
1 Jn 4:14

39Many from the Samaritan village believed he was the Messiah because of the woman's report: "He told me everything I ever did!" 40, 41When they came out to see him at the well, they begged him to stay at their village; and he did, for two days, long enough for many of them to believe in him after hearing him. 42Then they said to the woman, "Now we believe because we have heard him ourselves, not just because of what you told us. He is indeed the Savior of the world."

➡ Jesus preaches in Galilee
(30/Matthew 4:12–17; Mark 1:14, 15; Luke 4:14, 15)

4:43,44
Mt 13:57
Mk 6:4
Lk 4:24
4:45
Deut 16:16

43, 44At the end of the two days' stay he went on into Galilee. Jesus used to say, "A prophet is honored everywhere except in his own country!" 45But the Galileans welcomed him with open arms; for they had been in Jerusalem at the Passover celebration and had seen some of his miracles.

Jesus heals a government official's son
(31)

4:46
Jn 2:1,11,23

46, 47In the course of his journey through Galilee he arrived at the town of Cana, where he had turned the water into wine. While he was there, a man in the city of Capernaum, a government official, whose son was very sick, heard that Jesus had come from Judea and was traveling in Galilee. This man went over to Cana, found Jesus, and begged him to come to Capernaum with him and heal his son, who was now at death's door.

4:48
1 Cor 1:22
Heb 2:4

48Jesus asked, "Won't any of you believe in me unless I do more and more miracles?"

49The official pled, "Sir, please come now before my child dies."

50Then Jesus told him, "Go back home. Your son is healed!" And the man

4:45 *some of his miracles,* see John 2:23.

4:36–38 The wages Jesus offers are the joy of working for him and seeing the harvest of believers. Usually a sower sees nothing but the seed, while the reaper sees the great reward of the harvest. But in Jesus' work, both will be rewarded by seeing new believers come into Christ's Kingdom. The phrase "others did the work" (4:38) could refer to the Old Testament prophets and/or John the Baptist.

4:39 The Samaritan woman immediately shared her experience with others. Despite her reputation, many took her invitation and came out to meet Jesus. Perhaps there are sins in our past of which we're ashamed. But Christ changes us. As people see these changes, they become curious. Use these opportunities to introduce them to Christ.

4:46, 47 This government official was probably an officer in Herod's service. He walked 20 miles to see Jesus and addressed him as "Sir," putting himself under Jesus even though he had legal authority over Jesus.

4:48 This miracle was a sign to all the people, not merely a favor to this official. John's Gospel, written to all mankind, shows another group of Gentiles affected by Jesus' ministry. An official in the government had faith that Jesus could do what he claimed. He believed; *then* he saw.

4:50 This government official not only believed Jesus could heal; he also obeyed Jesus by returning home, thus demonstrating his faith. It isn't enough for us to say we believe Jesus can take care of our problems. We need to act as if he can. When you pray about a

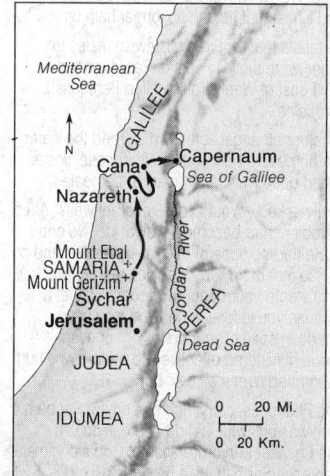

JESUS RETURNS TO GALILEE
Jesus stayed in Sychar for two days, then went on to Galilee. He visited Nazareth and various towns in Galilee before arriving at Cana. From there he spoke the word of healing, and a government official's son in Capernaum was healed. The Gospel of Matthew tells us Jesus then settled in Capernaum (Matthew 4:12, 13).

need or problem, live as though you believe Jesus can do what he says.

believed Jesus and started home. ⁵¹While he was on his way, some of his servants met him with the news that all was well—his son had recovered. ⁵²He asked them when the lad had begun to feel better, and they replied, "Yesterday afternoon at about one o'clock his fever suddenly disappeared!" ⁵³Then the father realized it was the same moment that Jesus had told him, "Your son is healed." And the officer and his entire household believed that Jesus was the Messiah.

⁵⁴This was Jesus' second miracle in Galilee after coming from Judea.

4:53
Acts 11:14
16:34

4:54
Jn 2:11

Jesus heals a lame man by the pool
(42)

5 Afterwards Jesus returned to Jerusalem for one of the Jewish religious holidays. ²Inside the city, near the Sheep Gate, was Bethesda Pool, with five covered platforms or porches surrounding it. ³Crowds of sick folks—lame, blind, or with paralyzed limbs—lay on the platforms (waiting for a certain movement of the water, ⁴for an angel of the Lord came from time to time and disturbed the water, and the first person to step down into it afterwards was healed).

5:1
Lev 23:1,2
Deut 16:1
Jn 2:13

5:2
Neh 3:1; 12:39

⁵One of the men lying there had been sick for thirty-eight years. ⁶When Jesus saw him and knew how long he had been ill, he asked him, "Would you like to get well?"

5:6
Ps 72:13
113:5,6
Heb 4:13

⁷"I can't," the sick man said, "for I have no one to help me into the pool at the movement of the water. While I am trying to get there, someone else always gets in ahead of me."

⁸Jesus told him, "Stand up, roll up your sleeping mat and go on home!" ⁹Instantly, the man was healed! He rolled up the mat and began walking!

But it was on the Sabbath when this miracle was done. ¹⁰So the Jewish leaders objected. They said to the man who was cured, "You can't work on the Sabbath! It's illegal to carry that sleeping mat!"

¹¹"The man who healed me told me to," was his reply.

¹²"Who said such a thing as that?" they demanded.

5:8
Mt 9:6
Mk 2:11
Lk 5:24

5:10
Ex 20:10
Neh 13:19
Jer 17:21
Mt 12:2
Mk 2:24; 3:4
Lk 6:2; 13:14

5:3b, 4 Many of the ancient manuscripts omit the material within the parentheses.

4:51 This shows that Jesus' miracles were not mere illusions. Although the official's son was 20 miles away, he was healed when Jesus spoke the word. Distance was no problem because Christ has mastery over space. We can never put so much space between ourselves and Christ that he can no longer help us.

5:1 There were three feasts that required all Jewish males to come to Jerusalem. They were the (1) Feast of Passover and Unleavened Bread, (2) Feast of Weeks (also called Pentecost), and (3) Feast of Tabernacles.

5:3, 4 It is unclear whether an angel actually disturbed the water, or if this was just what the people believed. In either case, Jesus healed this man who had been waiting for years to be healed.

5:6 Jesus appropriately asked, "Would you like to get well?" After 38 years, this man's problem had become a way of life. No one had ever helped him. He had no hope of ever being healed and no desire to help himself. No matter how trapped you feel in your infirmities, God can minister to your deepest needs. Don't let a problem or hardship cause you to lose hope. God may have special work for you to do in spite of your condition, or even because of it. Many have ministered effectively to people who hurt, because they have triumphed over their own hurts.

5:10 According to the Pharisees, carrying a mat on the Sabbath was work and therefore was unlawful. It did not break an Old Testament law, but the Pharisees' interpretation of God's command to "remember to observe the Sabbath as a holy day" (Exodus 20:8). This was just one of hundreds of rules they had added to the Old Testament law.

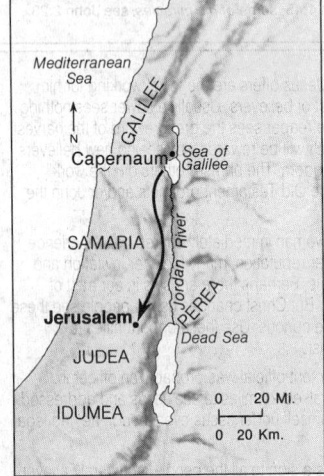

JESUS TEACHES IN JERUSALEM
Between chapters four and five of John, Jesus ministered throughout Galilee, especially in Capernaum. He had been calling certain men to follow him, but it wasn't until after this trip to Jerusalem (5:1) that he chose his 12 disciples from among them.

5:10 A man who hadn't walked for 38 years was healed, but the Pharisees were more concerned about their petty rules than the life and health of a human being. It is easy to get so caught up in our man-made structures and rules that we forget the people involved. Are your guidelines for living God-made or man-made? Are they helping people, or have they become needless stumbling blocks?

5:14
Jn 8:11

¹³The man didn't know, and Jesus had disappeared into the crowd. ¹⁴But afterwards Jesus found him in the Temple and told him, "Now you are well; don't sin as you did before, or something even worse may happen to you."

¹⁵Then the man went to find the Jewish leaders and told them it was Jesus who had healed him.

Jesus claims to be God's Son
(43)

5:17
Jn 9:4; 14:10
5:18
Isa 9:6
Jn 1:1,18
10:30,33; 20:28
Phil 2:6
Tit 2:13
2 Pet 1:1
1 Jn 5:21

5:19
Jn 8:28; 12:49
14:10

¹⁶So they began harassing Jesus as a Sabbath breaker.

¹⁷But Jesus replied, "My Father constantly does good, and I'm following his example."

¹⁸Then the Jewish leaders were all the more eager to kill him because in addition to disobeying their Sabbath laws, he had spoken of God as his Father, thereby making himself equal with God.

¹⁹Jesus replied, "The Son can do nothing by himself. He does only what he sees the Father doing, and in the same way. ²⁰For the Father loves the Son, and tells him everything he is doing; and the Son will do far more awesome miracles than this

5:14 *"don't sin as you did before,"* implied. Literally, "sin no more." **5:17** *"My Father constantly does good,"* implied. Literally, "My Father works even until now, and I work."

THE CLAIMS OF CHRIST	Jesus claimed to be:	Matthew	Mark	Luke	John
Those who read the life of Christ are faced with one unavoidable question—was Jesus God? Part of any reasonable conclusion has to include the fact that he did claim to be God. We have no other choice but to agree or disagree with his claim. Eternal life is at stake in the choice.	the fulfillment of Old Testament prophecies	5:17; 14:33; 16:16, 17; 26:31, 53–56; 27:43	14:21, 61, 62	4:16–21; 7:18–23; 18:31; 22:37; 24:44	2:22; 5:45–47; 6:45; 7:40; 10:34–36; 13:18; 15:25; 20:9
	the Son of Man	8:20; 12:8; 16:27; 19:28; 20:18, 19; 24:27, 44; 25:31; 26:2, 45, 64 (see textual notes)	8:31, 38; 9:9; 10:45; 14:41 (see textual notes)	6:22; 7:33, 34; 12:8; 17:22; 18:8, 31; 19:10; 21:36 (see textual notes)	1:51; 3:13, 14; 6:27, 53; 12:23, 34 (see textual notes)
	the Son of God	11:27; 14:33; 16:16, 17; 27:43	3:11, 12; 14:61, 62	8:28; 10:22	1:18; 3:35, 36; 5:18–26; 6:40; 10:36; 11:4; 17:1; 19:7
	the Messiah/ the Christ	23:9, 10; 26:63, 64	8:29, 30	4:41; 23:1, 2; 24:25–27	4:25, 26; 10:24, 25; 11:27
	Teacher/Master	26:18			13:13, 14
	One with authority to forgive		2:1–12	7:48, 49	
	Lord		5:19		13:13, 14; 20:28
	Savior			19:10	3:17; 10:9

5:14 This man had been lame, or paralyzed, but now he could walk. This was a great miracle. But he needed an even greater miracle—to have his sins forgiven. The man was delighted to be physically healed, but he had to turn from his sins and seek God's forgiveness to be spiritually healed. God's forgiveness is the greatest gift you will ever receive.

5:16, 17 The Jewish leaders saw a mighty miracle of healing and a broken rule. They threw the miracle aside as they focused their attention on the broken rule, for the rule was more important to them than the miracle. God is prepared to do great things in our lives, but we can shut out his miracles by limiting our views about how God works.

5:17 This is also translated, "My Father is always at his work." In other words, Jesus was saying, "What if God stopped all *his* work

on the Sabbath?" Nature would fall into chaos, and sin would overrun the world. Jesus was explaining that when the opportunity to do good (or God's work) presents itself, it should not be ignored, even on the Sabbath.

5:17ff Jesus was identifying himself with God, his Father. The Pharisees also called God their Father, but they realized Jesus was claiming a unique relationship with him. Because of Jesus' claim, the Pharisees had two choices: to believe him, or to accuse him of blasphemy. They chose the second.

5:19–23 Because of his unity with God, Jesus lived as God wanted him to live. Because of our identification with Jesus, we must live as he wants us to live. The questions "What would Jesus do?" and "What would Jesus have me do?" may help us make the right choices.

man's healing. 21He will even raise from the dead anyone he wants to, just as the
Father does. 22And the Father leaves all judgment of sin to his Son, 23so that
everyone will honor the Son, just as they honor the Father. But if you refuse to
honor God's Son, whom he sent to you, then you are certainly not honoring the
Father.

24"I say emphatically that anyone who listens to my message and believes in God
who sent me has eternal life, and will never be damned for his sins, but has already
passed out of death into life.

25"And I solemnly declare that the time is coming, in fact, it is here, when the
dead shall hear my voice—the voice of the Son of God—and those who listen shall
live. 26The Father has life in himself, and has granted his Son to have life in
himself, 27and to judge the sins of all mankind because he is the Son of Man.
28Don't be so surprised! Indeed the time is coming when all the dead in their graves
shall hear the voice of God's Son, 29and shall rise again—those who have done
good, to eternal life; and those who have continued in evil, to judgment.

30"But I pass no judgment without consulting the Father. I judge as I am told.
And my judgment is absolutely fair and just, for it is according to the will of God
who sent me and is not merely my own.

Jesus supports his claim
(44)

31"When I make claims about myself they aren't believed, 32, 33but someone
else, yes, John the Baptist, is making these claims for me too. You have gone out
to listen to his preaching, and I can assure you that all he says about me is true!
34But the truest witness I have is not from a man, though I have reminded you about
John's witness so that you will believe in me and be saved. 35John shone brightly
for a while, and you benefited and rejoiced, 36but I have a greater witness than
John. I refer to the miracles I do; these have been assigned me by the Father, and
they prove that the Father has sent me. 37And the Father himself has also testified
about me, though not appearing to you personally, or speaking to you directly.
38But you are not listening to him, for you refuse to believe me—the one sent to you
with God's message.

39"You search the Scriptures, for you believe they give you eternal life. And the
Scriptures point to me! 40Yet you won't come to me so that I can give you this life
eternal!

41, 42"Your approval or disapproval means nothing to me, for as I know so well,
you don't have God's love within you. 43I know, because I have come to you
representing my Father and you refuse to welcome me, though you readily enough

5:32, 33 *John the Baptist,* implied. However, most commentators believe the reference is to the witness of his Father.
See vs 37.

5:21
Jn 11:25
5:22
Jn 5:27
5:23
1 Jn 2:23
5:24
20:30,31
1 Jn 3:14; 5:13
5:25
Jn 4:21; 6:63,68
5:26
Jn 1:4; 6:57
1 Jn 5:11,12
5:27
Dan 7:13,14
Jn 9:39
Acts 10:42; 17:31
5:29
Dan 12:2
Mt 25:31-46
Acts 24:15
1 Cor 15:52
5:30
Jn 5:19; 6:38
5:31
Jn 8:14
5:32
Jn 1:6,7,15
5:36
Jn 10:25,37,38
14:11; 15:24
1 Jn 5:9
5:37
Deut 4:12
Jn 1:18; 8:18
5:38
Jn 8:37
1 Jn 2:14
5:39
Isa 34:16
Lk 16:29; 24:25
Jn 5:46,47; 7:52
Acts 13:27
17:11
Rom 2:17
5:41
Jn 7:18

5:24 Eternal life—living forever with God—begins when you
accept Jesus Christ as Savior. At that moment, new life begins in
you (2 Corinthians 5:17). You still face physical death, but when
Christ returns again, your body will be resurrected to live forever.

5:25 In saying that the dead would hear his voice, Jesus was
talking about the spiritually dead who hear, understand, and
accept him. Those who accept God's Word will have eternal life.

5:26 God is the source and Creator of life, for there is no life apart
from God, here or hereafter. The life in us is a gift from him (see
Deuteronomy 30:20; Psalm 36:9). Because Jesus is eternally
existent with God, the Creator, he too is "the Life" (John 14:6)
through whom we may live eternally (see 1 John 5:11).

5:27 The Old Testament mentioned three signs of the coming
Messiah. In this chapter, John shows that Jesus has fulfilled all
three signs. All power and dominion are given to him as the Son of
Man (cf. 5:27 with Daniel 7:1–14). The lame and sick are healed
(cf. 5:20, 26 with Isaiah 35:6; Jeremiah 31:8, 9). The dead are
raised to life (cf. 5:21, 28 with Deuteronomy 32:39; 1 Samuel
2:6; 2 Kings 4:32-36).

5:29 Those who have rebelled against Christ will be resurrected
too, but to hear God's judgment against them and to be sentenced
to eternity apart from him.

5:31ff Jesus claimed to be equal with God (5:18), to give eternal
life (5:24), to be the source of life (5:26), and to judge sin (5:27).
These statements make it clear that Jesus claimed to be divine.

5:39 The religious leaders knew what the Bible said, but failed to
apply its words to their lives. They knew the teachings of the
Scriptures, but failed to see the Messiah to whom the Scriptures
pointed. They knew the rules but missed the Savior. Entrenched in
their own religious system, they refused to let the Son of God
change their lives.

5:41 Whose approval do you seek? The religious leaders enjoyed
great prestige in Israel, but their stamp of approval meant nothing
to Jesus. He was concerned about God's approval. This is a good
principle for us. If even the highest officials in the world approve of
our actions and God does not, we should be concerned. But if
God approves, even though others don't, we should be content.

5:45
Jn 9:28
Rom 2:17
5:46
Gen 3:15; 12:3
18:18; 22:18
49:10
Deut 18:15,18
Lk 24:27,44
Acts 26:22,23
5:47
Lk 16:31

receive those who aren't sent from him, but represent only themselves! ⁴⁴No wonder you can't believe! For you gladly honor each other, but you don't care about the honor that comes from the only God!

⁴⁵"Yet it is not I who will accuse you of this to the Father—Moses will! Moses, on whose laws you set your hopes of heaven. ⁴⁶For you have refused to believe Moses. He wrote about me, but you refuse to believe him, so you refuse to believe in me. ⁴⁷And since you don't believe what he wrote, no wonder you don't believe me either."

Jesus feeds five thousand
(96/Matthew 14:13–21; Mark 6:30–44; Luke 9:10–17)

6:2
Mt 14:14
Mk 6:35
Lk 9:12

6 After this, Jesus crossed over the Sea of Galilee, also known as the Sea of Tiberias. ²⁻⁵And a huge crowd, many of them pilgrims on their way to Jerusalem for the annual Passover celebration, were following him wherever he went, to watch him heal the sick. So when Jesus went up into the hills and sat down with his disciples around him, he soon saw a great multitude of people climbing the hill, looking for him.

Turning to Philip he asked, "Philip, where can we buy bread to feed all these people?" ⁶(He was testing Philip, for he already knew what he was going to do.)

6:6
Num 11:21,22
6:7
Mk 6:37

⁷Philip replied, "It would take a fortune to begin to do it!"

6:9
2 Kgs 4:43,44

⁸, ⁹Then Andrew, Simon Peter's brother, spoke up. "There's a youngster here with five barley loaves and a couple of fish! But what good is that with all this mob?"

6:10
Mt 14:21
Mk 6:43,44
Lk 9:14
6:11
1 Tim 4:4,5

¹⁰"Tell everyone to sit down," Jesus ordered. And all of them—the approximate count of the men only was 5,000—sat down on the grassy slopes. ¹¹Then Jesus took the loaves and gave thanks to God and passed them out to the people. Afterwards he did the same with the fish. And everyone ate until full!

¹²"Now gather the scraps," Jesus told his disciples, "so that nothing is wasted." ¹³And twelve baskets were filled with the leftovers!

6:2-5 *annual Passover celebration,* literally, "Now the Passover, the feast of the Jews, was at hand." **6:7** *take a fortune,* literally, 200 denarii, a denarius being a full day's wage.

5:45 The Pharisees prided themselves on being the true followers of their ancestor Moses. They followed every one of his laws to the letter and even added some of their own. Jesus' warning that Moses would accuse them would have indeed stung them to fury. Moses wrote about Jesus (Genesis 3:15; Numbers 21:9; 24:17; Deuteronomy 18:15), yet the religious leaders refused to believe Jesus when he came.

6:5 If anyone knew where to get food, it would have been Philip, because he was from nearby Bethsaida, a town about nine miles away (1:44). Jesus was testing him to strengthen his faith. By asking for a human solution (knowing that there was none), Jesus highlighted the miraculous act he was about to perform.

6:5–7 Jesus asked Philip where they could buy a great amount of bread. Philip started assessing the probable cost. Jesus wanted to teach him that financial resources are not the most important ones. We can limit what God does in our lives by assuming what is and is not possible. Is there some impossible task you feel God wants you to do? Don't let your estimate of what can't be done keep you from taking on the task. God can do the miraculous; trust him to provide the resources.

6:8, 9 The disciples are contrasted with the youngster who brought what he had. They certainly had more resources than he did, but they knew they didn't have enough, so they didn't give anything at all. The youngster gave what little he had, and it made all the difference. If we offer nothing to God, he will have nothing to use. But he can take what little we have and make it great.

6:8, 9 In performing his miracles, Jesus usually preferred to work through people. Here he used what a young child offered to accomplish one of the greatest miracles recorded in the Gospels. Age is no barrier to being used for Christ's service. Never feel that

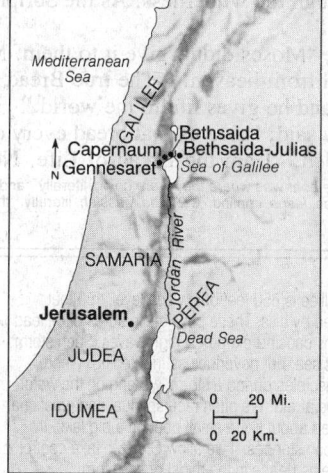

JESUS WALKS ON THE WATER
Jesus fed the 5,000 on a hillside near the Sea of Galilee at Bethsaida-Julias. The disciples set out across the sea toward Bethsaida or Capernaum. But they encountered a storm—and Jesus came walking to them on the water! The boat landed at Gennesaret (Mark 6:53). From there they went, by sea or by land, back to Capernaum.

you are too young or old to be of service to him.

6:13 There is a lesson in the leftovers. God gives in abundance. He takes whatever we can offer him in time, ability, or resources and multiplies its effectiveness beyond our wildest expectations. If you take the first step in making yourself available to him, he will show you how greatly you can be used to advance the work of his Kingdom.

14When the people realized what a great miracle had happened, they exclaimed, "Surely, he is the Prophet we have been expecting!"

15Jesus saw that they were ready to take him by force and make him their king, so he went higher into the mountains alone.

Jesus walks on water
(97/Matthew 14:22–33; Mark 6:45–52)

16That evening his disciples went down to the shore to wait for him. 17But as darkness fell and Jesus still hadn't come back, they got into the boat and headed out across the lake toward Capernaum. 18, 19But soon a gale swept down upon them as they rowed, and the sea grew very rough. They were three or four miles out when suddenly they saw Jesus walking toward the boat! They were terrified, 20but he called out to them and told them not to be afraid. 21Then they were willing to let him in, and immediately the boat was where they were going!

Jesus is the true bread from heaven
(99)

22, 23The next morning, back across the lake, crowds began gathering on the shore [waiting to see Jesus]. For they knew that he and his disciples had come over together and that the disciples had gone off in their boat, leaving him behind. Several small boats from Tiberias were nearby, 24so when the people saw that Jesus wasn't there, nor his disciples, they got into the boats and went across to Capernaum to look for him.

25When they arrived and found him, they said, "Sir, how did you get here?" 26Jesus replied, "The truth of the matter is that you want to be with me because I fed you, not because you believe in me. 27But you shouldn't be so concerned about perishable things like food. No, spend your energy seeking the eternal life that I, the Messiah, can give you. For God the Father has sent me for this very purpose."

28They replied, "What should we do to satisfy God?"

29Jesus told them, "This is the will of God, that you believe in the one he has sent."

30, 31They replied, "You must show us more miracles if you want us to believe you are the Messiah. Give us free bread every day, like our fathers had while they journeyed through the wilderness! As the Scriptures say, 'Moses gave them bread from heaven.' "

32Jesus said, "Moses didn't give it to them. My Father did. And now he offers you true Bread from heaven. 33The true Bread is a Person—the one sent by God from heaven, and he gives life to the world."

34"Sir," they said, "give us that bread every day of our lives!"

35Jesus replied, "I am the Bread of Life. No one coming to me will ever be

6:14
Gen 49:10
Deut 18:15,18
Isa 7:14; 9:6
Mt 11:3
Jn 1:21; 7:40-42

6:16
Mt 14:23-27
Mk 6:47-51

6:27
Isa 55:2
Mt 3:17; 17:5
Mk 1:11; 9:7
Lk 3:22
Jn 1:33; 5:37
8:18
Acts 2:22
Rom 6:23
2 Pet 1:17,18

6:29
1 Thess 1:3
1 Jn 3:23

6:31
Ex 16:4,15
Num 11:7
Neh 9:15
Ps 78:24; 105:40
Mt 12:38
Mk 8:11
1 Cor 10:3

6:33
Jn 6:41,50

6:35
Jn 4:14; 6:48
7:37,38

6:21 *immediately the boat was where they were going,* literally, "and straightway the boat was at the land." **6:22, 23** *waiting to see Jesus,* implied. **6:27** *the Messiah,* literally, "the Son of Man." So also in vss 53, 62. **6:32** *My Father did,* implied.

6:18 The Sea of Galilee is 650 feet below sea level, 150 feet deep, and surrounded by hills. These physical features often lead to sudden windstorms causing extremely high waves. Such storms are part of life on this sea, but nevertheless frightening. When Jesus came to the disciples during a storm, walking on the water, he told them not to be afraid. We often face spiritual and emotional storms and feel tossed about like a small boat on a big lake. In spite of terrifying circumstances, if we allow Christ to take control in our lives, he can give us peace in the midst of any storm.

6:18, 19 The disciples, terrified, thought they were seeing a ghost (Matthew 14:26). But if they had believed all they had already seen Jesus do, they could have accepted this miracle. They were frightened—they didn't expect him to come, and they weren't prepared for his help. Faith is a mindset that *expects* God to act. When we live with this expectation, we can overcome our fears.

6:26 Jesus criticized the people who followed him only for the physical and temporal benefits, not because they were spiritually

hungry. We should follow Christ because we need the truth. Many people use religion to gain prestige, comfort, or votes. But those are self-centered motives. True believers follow Jesus simply because they know his way is the way to live.

6:28, 29 Jesus answered a question that still puzzles many sincere seekers for God: what should we do to satisfy God? The religions of the world are mankind's attempts to answer this question. But Jesus' reply is brief and simple: we must believe in the One whom God has sent. Satisfying God does not come from what we *do*, but from whom we *believe*. The first step is accepting that Jesus is who he claims to be. All spiritual development follows on this affirmation. Declare in prayer to Jesus, "You are the Christ, the Son of the living God," and embark on a life of belief that is satisfying to your Creator.

6:35 People eat bread to satisfy physical hunger and to sustain physical life. We can satisfy spiritual hunger and sustain spiritual life only by a right relationship with Jesus Christ. No wonder he

6:37
Jn 10:28,29
17:2,24

6:38
Jn 4:34; 5:30

6:39
Jn 5:24; 10:28
17:12; 18:9
Col 3:3

6:40
Jn 1:14,18; 3:16

6:41
Jn 6:33,51,58

6:42
Jn 7:27

6:44
Jer 31:3
Hos 11:4
Jn 6:65; 12:32

6:45
Isa 54:13
Jer 31:34
Mic 4:2
1 Thess 4:9
Heb 8:10,11

6:46
Mt 11:27
Lk 10:22
Jn 1:18; 5:37
7:29
2 Cor 4:6

6:47
Jn 3:16

6:48
Jn 6:58
Heb 10:5,10

6:51
Jn 10:10,11

hungry again. Those believing in me will never thirst. 36But the trouble is, as I have told you before, you haven't believed even though you have seen me. 37But some will come to me—those the Father has given me—and I will never, never reject them. 38For I have come here from heaven to do the will of God who sent me, not to have my own way. 39And this is the will of God, that I should not lose even one of all those he has given me, but that I should raise them to eternal life at the Last Day. 40For it is my Father's will that everyone who sees his Son and believes on him should have eternal life—that I should raise him at the Last Day."

The Jews disagree that Jesus is from heaven (100)

41Then the Jews began to murmur against him because he claimed to be the Bread from heaven.

42"What?" they exclaimed. "Why, he is merely Jesus the son of Joseph, whose father and mother we know. What is this he is saying, that he came down from heaven?"

43But Jesus replied, "Don't murmur among yourselves about my saying that. 44For no one can come to me unless the Father who sent me draws him to me, and at the Last Day I will cause all such to rise again from the dead. 45As it is written in the Scriptures, 'They shall all be taught of God.' Those the Father speaks to, who learn the truth from him, will be attracted to me. 46(Not that anyone actually sees the Father, for only I have seen him.)

47"How earnestly I tell you this—anyone who believes in me already has eternal life! 48–51Yes, I am the Bread of Life! When your fathers in the wilderness ate bread from the skies, they all died. But the Bread from heaven gives eternal life to everyone who eats it. I am that Living Bread that came down out of heaven. Anyone eating this Bread shall live forever; this Bread is my flesh given to redeem humanity."

52Then the Jews began arguing with each other about what he meant. "How can this man give us his flesh to eat?" they asked.

53So Jesus said it again, "With all the earnestness I possess I tell you this: Unless

---

called himself the Bread of Life. But bread must be eaten to give life, and Christ must be invited into our daily walk to give spiritual life.

6:38 Jesus did not work independently of God the Father, but in union with him. This gives us even more assurance of our security in him. Jesus' purpose was to do the will of God, not to satisfy his human desires. When we follow Jesus, we should have the same purpose.

6:39 Jesus said he would not lose even one person that the Father had given him. Thus anyone who makes a sincere commitment to believe in Jesus Christ as Savior is secure in God's promise of eternal life. Christ will not let his people be overcome by Satan and lose their salvation (see also 17:12; Philippians 1:6).

6:40 Those who put their faith in Jesus will be resurrected from physical death to eternal life with God when Christ comes again (see 1 Corinthians 15:52; 1 Thessalonians 4:16).

6:41 When John says, "Jews," he is referring to the Jewish leaders who were hostile to Jesus, not to Jews in general. John himself was a Jew.

6:41 The religious leaders murmured because they could not accept Jesus' claim of divinity. They saw him only as a carpenter from Nazareth. They refused to believe he was God's divine Son, and they could not tolerate his message. Many people reject Christ because they say they cannot believe he is the Son of God. In reality, the claims he makes on their lives are what they can't accept. So to protect themselves from the message, they deny the Messenger.

6:44 God, not people, plays the most active role in salvation.

When someone chooses to believe in Jesus Christ as Savior, he does so only in response to the urging of God's Holy Spirit. God does the urging; then we decide whether or not to believe. Thus no one can believe in Jesus without God's help.

6:45 Jesus is referring to an Old Testament view of the messianic Kingdom where all people will be taught directly by God (Isaiah 54:13; Jeremiah 31:31–34; Hebrews 8:8–11). He is stressing the importance of not merely hearing, but learning. We are taught by God through the Bible, our experiences, the thoughts the Holy Spirit brings, and other Christians.

6:47 *Believes* as used here means "continues to believe." We do not believe merely once; we keep on believing or trusting him.

6:47 The religious leaders frequently asked Jesus to prove to them why he was better than the prophets they already had. Jesus here refers to the bread from heaven (manna—see Numbers 11:7-9) that Moses gave their ancestors. This bread was physical and temporal. The people ate it, and it sustained them for a day; but they had to get more bread every day, and this bread could not keep them from dying. Jesus, who is much greater than Moses, offers himself as the spiritual Bread from heaven that satisfies completely and leads to eternal life.

6:51 How can Jesus give us his flesh as bread to eat? To eat Living Bread means to unite ourselves with Christ. We are united with Christ in two ways: (1) by believing in his death and resurrection and (2) by devoting ourselves to living as he requires, depending on his teaching for guidance, and trusting in the Holy Spirit for power.

you eat the flesh of the Messiah and drink his blood, you cannot have eternal life within you. ⁵⁴But anyone who does eat my flesh and drink my blood has eternal life, and I will raise him at the Last Day. ⁵⁵For my flesh is the true food, and my blood is the true drink. ⁵⁶Everyone who eats my flesh and drinks my blood is in me, and I in him. ⁵⁷I live by the power of the living Father who sent me, and in the same way those who partake of me shall live because of me! ⁵⁸I am the true Bread from heaven; and anyone who eats this Bread shall live forever, and not die as your fathers did—though they ate bread from heaven." ⁵⁹(He preached this sermon in the synagogue in Capernaum.)

6:54
Jn 6:39
6:56
Jn 15:4; 14:20
17:21-23
Rom 8:9,10
6:57
Jn 5:26; 14:19
15:5
2 Pet 1:3,4
6:58
Jn 6:31
6:59
Mt 4:23

Many disciples desert Jesus
(101)

⁶⁰Even his disciples said, "This is very hard to understand. Who can tell what he means?"

⁶¹Jesus knew within himself that his disciples were complaining and said to them, "Does *this* offend you? ⁶²Then what will you think if you see me, the Messiah, return to heaven again? ⁶³Only the Holy Spirit gives eternal life. Those born only once, with physical birth, will never receive this gift. But now I have told you how to get this true spiritual life. ⁶⁴But some of you don't believe me." (For Jesus knew from the beginning who didn't believe and knew the one who would betray him.)

⁶⁵And he remarked, "That is what I meant when I said that no one can come to me unless the Father attracts him to me."

⁶⁶At this point many of his disciples turned away and deserted him.

⁶⁷Then Jesus turned to the Twelve and asked, "Are you going too?"

⁶⁸Simon Peter replied, "Master, to whom shall we go? You alone have the words that give eternal life, ⁶⁹and we believe them and know you are the holy Son of God."

⁷⁰Then Jesus said, "I chose the twelve of you, and one is a devil." ⁷¹He was speaking of Judas, son of Simon Iscariot, one of the Twelve, who would betray him.

6:62
Mk 16:19
Jn 3:13
Acts 1:9
Eph 4:8
6:63
Jn 3:34
Rom 8:2
1 Cor 15:45
2 Cor 3:6
Heb 4:12
6:64
Mt 10:4
Jn 13:11
6:65
Jn 6:37,44
6:66
Lk 9:62
Heb 10:38
1 Jn 2:19
Jn 3:34,5:25,26
6:63
6:69
Lk 4:34
Acts 3:14
1 Jn 2:20
6:70
Mt 10:2-4
Jn 13:2,27

6:62 *the Messiah,* literally, "the Son of Man." **6:63** *"Only the Holy Spirit gives eternal life,"* literally, "It is the Spirit who quickens." *physical birth,* see 1:13. Literally, "the flesh profits nothing."

6:56 This was a shocking message—to eat flesh and drink blood seemed cannibalistic. These religious leaders could not tolerate Jesus' statement because the law forbade drinking blood (Leviticus 17:10, 11). Jesus was not talking about literal blood, of course. He was saying that his life had to become their own, but they could not accept this concept. The apostle Paul later used the body and blood imagery in talking about communion (see 1 Corinthians 11:23-26).

6:63, 65 The Holy Spirit gives spiritual life (3:6); without the work of the Holy Spirit we cannot even see our need for it (14:17). All spiritual renewal begins and ends with God as he reveals truth to us and then lives within us as we respond to that truth.

6:66 Why did Jesus' words cause many of his followers to desert him? (1) They may have realized that he wasn't going to be the conquering Messiah-king they expected. (2) He refused to give in to their self-centered requests. (3) He emphasized faith, not works. (4) His teachings were difficult to understand, and some of his words were very offensive. As we grow in our faith, we may be tempted to turn away because Jesus' lessons are hard. Will your response be to give up, ignore certain teachings, or reject Christ? Instead, ask God to show you what the teachings mean and how they apply to your life. Then have the courage to act upon God's truth.

6:67 There is no middle ground with Jesus. When he asked the disciples if they would also leave, he was showing that they could either accept or reject him. Jesus was not trying to repel people with his teachings. He was simply telling the truth. The more the people heard Jesus' real message, the more they divided into two camps—the honest seekers who wanted to understand more, and those who rejected Jesus because they didn't like what they heard.

6:67, 68 After many of Jesus' followers had deserted him, he asked the 12 disciples if they were also going to leave. Peter responded, "Where else can we go?" In his straightforward way, Peter answered for all of us—there is no other way. Jesus alone gives life. People look everywhere for eternal life and miss Christ, the only source. Stay with him, especially when you are confused or feel alone.

6:70 In response to Jesus' message, some people left; others stayed and truly believed; and some, like Judas, stayed but tried to use Jesus for personal gain. Many today turn away from Christ. Others pretend to follow, going to church for status, votes, or business contacts. But there are only two real responses to Jesus—you either accept or reject him. How have you responded to Christ?

6:71 For more information on Judas, see his Profile in Mark 14.

2. Jesus encounters conflict with the religious leaders

Jesus' brothers ridicule him
(121)

7 After this, Jesus went to Galilee, going from village to village, for he wanted to stay out of Judea where the Jewish leaders were plotting his death. 2But soon it was time for the Tabernacle Ceremonies, one of the annual Jewish holidays, 3and Jesus' brothers urged him to go to Judea for the celebration.

"Go where more people can see your miracles!" they scoffed. 4"You can't be famous when you hide like this! If you're so great, prove it to the world!" 5For even his brothers didn't believe in him.

6Jesus replied, "It is not the right time for me to go now. But you can go anytime and it will make no difference, 7for the world can't hate you; but it does hate me, because I accuse it of sin and evil. 8You go on, and I'll come later when it is the right time." 9So he remained in Galilee.

Jesus teaches openly at the Temple
(123)

10But after his brothers had left for the celebration, then he went too, though secretly, staying out of the public eye. 11The Jewish leaders tried to find him at the celebration and kept asking if anyone had seen him. 12There was a lot of discussion about him among the crowds. Some said, "He's a wonderful man," while others said, "No, he's duping the public." 13But no one had the courage to speak out for him in public for fear of reprisals from the Jewish leaders.

14Then, midway through the festival, Jesus went up to the Temple and preached openly. 15The Jewish leaders were surprised when they heard him. "How can he know so much when he's never been to our schools?" they asked.

16So Jesus told them, "I'm not teaching you my own thoughts, but those of God who sent me. 17If any of you really determines to do God's will, then you will certainly know whether my teaching is from God or is merely my own. 18Anyone presenting his own ideas is looking for praise for himself, but anyone seeking to honor the one who sent him is a good and true person. 19None of *you* obeys the laws of Moses! So why pick on *me* for breaking them? Why kill *me* for this?"

7:8 *I'll come later,* literally, "I go up yet unto this feast." The word "yet" is included in the text of many ancient manuscripts.

Cross-references (margin)

7:1
Jn 5:18; 7:19
8:37
7:2
Lev. 23:23,24
Deut 16:16
Zech 14:16
7:3
Mt 12:46
Mk 3:31,32
Acts 1:14
7:6
Jn 2:4
7:7
Jn 3:19
15:18,19
7:11
Jn 11:56
7:12
Mt 21:45,46
Lk 7:16
Jn 7:40-43
9:16; 10:19
7:13
Jn 9:22,23
7:15
Acts 4:13; 22:3
2 Tim 3:15
7:16
Jn 8:28; 12:49
14:10
7:17
Hos 6:1-3
7:18
Jn 5:41; 8:50,54
7:19
Jn 1:17; 7:1

7:2 The Tabernacle Ceremonies, also called the Feast of Tabernacles, are described in Leviticus 23:33ff. This event occurred in October, about six months after the Passover celebration mentioned in 6:2-5. The Feast commemorated the days when the Israelites wandered in the wilderness and lived in tents (Leviticus 23:43).

7:3-5 Jesus' brothers had a difficult time believing in him. Some of these brothers would eventually become leaders in the church, but here they are still wondering if Jesus will prove once and for all his messianic claims. After Jesus died and rose again, they finally believed. We today have every reason to believe, because we have the full record of Jesus' miracles, death, and resurrection. We also have the evidence of what the gospel has done in people's lives for hundreds of years. Don't miss this opportunity to believe in God's Son.

7:7 Because the world hated Jesus, we who follow him can expect that many people will hate us as well. If things are going too well, ask if you are following him as you should. We can be grateful if life goes well, but not at the cost of following Jesus halfheartedly or not at all.

7:10 Jesus came with the greatest gift ever offered, so why did he often remain in secret? The religious leaders hated him and would refuse his gift of salvation no matter what he said or did. The more he taught and worked publicly, the more these leaders would cause trouble for Jesus and his followers. So it was necessary for Jesus to teach and work as quietly as possible. Many people today have the privilege of teaching, preaching, and worshiping publicly

with little persecution. These believers should thankfully take advantage of their freedom.

7:13 The religious leaders had a great deal of power over the common people. It is apparent that they couldn't do much to Jesus at this time, but they threatened anyone who might publicly support him. Excommunication from the synagogue was one of the reprisals for believing in Jesus (9:22, 23). To a Jew, this was one of the worst possible social stigmas.

7:13 Everyone was talking about Jesus! But when it came time to speak up for him in public, no one said a word. All were afraid. Fear can stifle our witness. Although many people talk about Christ in church, when it comes to making a public statement about their faith, they are often embarrassed. Jesus says that he will acknowledge us before God if we acknowledge him before others (Matthew 10:32). Be courageous! Speak up for Christ!

7:16-18 Have you ever listened to religious speakers and wondered if they were telling the truth? Test them—(1) ask if their words agree with or contradict the Bible; and (2) ask if their words point to Christ or to themselves.

7:19 The Pharisees spent their lives trying to appear holy by keeping the meticulous rules they had added to God's laws. Jesus' accusation that they didn't keep Moses' laws stung them deeply. In spite of their pompous pride in themselves and their rules, they did not even fulfill a legalistic religion, for they were living far below what the law of Moses required. Jesus' followers should do *more* than the moral law requires, going beyond and beneath the mere dos and don'ts of the law to the spirit of the law.

20The crowd replied, "You're out of your mind! Who's trying to kill you?" 21, 22, 23Jesus replied, "I worked on the Sabbath by healing a man, and you were surprised. But you work on the Sabbath, too, whenever you obey Moses' law of circumcision (actually, however, this tradition of circumcision is older than the Mosaic law); for if the correct time for circumcising your children falls on the Sabbath, you go ahead and do it, as you should. So why should I be condemned for making a man completely well on the Sabbath? 24Think this through and you will see that I am right."

25Some of the people who lived there in Jerusalem said among themselves, "Isn't this the man they are trying to kill? 26But here he is preaching in public, and they say nothing to him. Can it be that our leaders have learned, after all, that he really is the Messiah? 27But how could he be? For we know where this man was born; when Christ comes, he will just appear and no one will know where he comes from."

28So Jesus, in a sermon in the Temple, called out, "Yes, you know me and where I was born and raised, but I am the representative of one you don't know, and he is Truth. 29I know him because I was with him, and he sent me to you."

30Then the Jewish leaders sought to arrest him; but no hand was laid on him, for God's time had not yet come.

31Many among the crowds at the Temple believed on him. "After all," they said, "what miracles do you expect the Messiah to do that this man hasn't done?"

Religious leaders attempt to arrest Jesus (124)

32When the Pharisees heard that the crowds were in this mood, they and the chief priests sent officers to arrest Jesus. 33But Jesus told them, "[Not yet!] I am to be here a little longer. Then I shall return to the one who sent me. 34You will search for me but not find me. And you won't be able to come where I am!"

35The Jewish leaders were puzzled by this statement. "Where is he planning to go?" they asked. "Maybe he is thinking of leaving the country and going as a missionary among the Jews in other lands, or maybe even to the Gentiles! 36What does he mean about our looking for him and not being able to find him, and, 'You won't be able to come where I am'?"

37On the last day, the climax of the holidays, Jesus shouted to the crowds, "If anyone is thirsty, let him come to me and drink. 38For the Scriptures declare that rivers of living water shall flow from the inmost being of anyone who believes in me." 39(He was speaking of the Holy Spirit, who would be given to everyone believing in him; but the Spirit had not yet been given, because Jesus had not yet returned to his glory in heaven.)

7:33 Not yet, implied.

7:20
Jn 8:48-52
10:20

7:21,22
Gen 17:9,10
Lev 12:3
Jn 5:8
Acts 7:8

7:23
Jn 5:10

7:24
Isa 11:3
Jn 8:15

7:27
Jn 7:41,42
9:29

7:28
Jn 1:18; 5:43
8:14,26,55

7:29
Mt 11:27
Jn 3:17; 8:55
10:15; 17:25

7:33
Jn 14:19
16:5,10,16-18

7:34
Jn 8:21; 13:33

7:37
Isa 55:1
Jn 4:10,14
6:35
Rev 22:17

7:38
Isa 12:3; 44:3
58:11
Ezek 47:1-10
Joel 3:18

7:39
Jn 14:17,18; 16:7
20:22
Rom 8:9
1 Cor 15:45
2 Cor 3:17

7:20 Most of the people were probably not aware of the plot to kill Jesus (5:18). There was a small group looking for the right opportunity to kill him, but most were still trying to decide what they believed about him.

7:21–23 According to Moses' law, circumcision was to be performed eight days after a baby's birth (Genesis 17:9, 10; Leviticus 12:3). It was done to all Jewish males to demonstrate their identity as part of God's covenant people. If the eighth day after birth was a Sabbath, the circumcision was still performed (even though it was considered work). While the religious leaders allowed certain exceptions to Sabbath laws, they allowed none to Jesus, who was simply showing mercy to those who needed healing.

7:26 This chapter shows the many reactions people had toward Jesus. They called him wonderful (7:12, 16), a deceiver (7:12), a madman (7:20), the Messiah (7:26), a prophet (7:40), and a man who should be arrested (7:44). We must make up our own minds about who Jesus is, knowing that whatever we decide will have eternal consequences.

7:27 There was a popular tradition that the Messiah would simply appear. But those who believed this tradition were ignoring the Scriptures, which clearly predicted the Messiah's birthplace (Micah 5:2).

7:37 Jesus' words "come to me and drink" allude to the theme of many Bible passages that talk about the Messiah's life-giving blessings (Isaiah 12:2, 3; 44:3, 4; 58:11). In promising to give the Holy Spirit to all who believed, Jesus was claiming to be the Messiah, for that was something only the Messiah could do.

7:38 Jesus used the term living water in 4:10 to indicate eternal life. Here he uses the term to refer to the Holy Spirit. The two go together: having eternal life includes the Holy Spirit's presence. Wherever the Holy Spirit is accepted, he brings eternal life. Jesus teaches more about the Holy Spirit in chapters 14—16. The Holy Spirit empowered Jesus' followers at Pentecost (Acts 2) and has since been available to all who believe in Jesus as Savior.

7:40
Deut 18:15
Jn 1:21; 6:14

7:41,42
1 Sam 16:1
2 Sam 7:12
Ps 132:11
Mic 5:2
Mt 1:1; 2:5-10
Lk 2:4
Jn 7:52

7:43
Jn 9:16; 10:19

7:46
Lk 4:22

7:48
1 Cor 1:20

7:50
Jn 3:1,2; 19:39

7:51
Ex 23:1
Deut 17:2-8
19:15-19
Prov 18:13

7:52
Isa 9:1,2
Mt 4:14-16
Jn 1:46

8:5
Ex 20:14
Lev 18:20; 20:10
Deut 5:18; 22:22
Job 31:9-11
Mt 5:27,28

40When the crowds heard him say this, some of them declared, "This man surely is the prophet who will come just before the Messiah." 41, 42Others said, "He *is* the Messiah." Still others, "But he *can't* be! Will the Messiah come from *Galilee?* For the Scriptures clearly state that the Messiah will be born of the royal line of David, in *Bethlehem,* the village where David was born." 43So the crowd was divided about him. 44And some wanted him arrested, but no one touched him.

45The Temple police who had been sent to arrest him returned to the chief priests and Pharisees. "Why didn't you bring him in?" they demanded.

46"He says such wonderful things!" they mumbled. "We've never heard anything like it."

47"So you also have been led astray?" the Pharisees mocked. 48"Is there a single one of us Jewish rulers or Pharisees who believes he is the Messiah? 49These stupid crowds do, yes; but what do they know about it? A curse upon them anyway!"

50Then Nicodemus spoke up. (Remember him? He was the Jewish leader who came secretly to interview Jesus.) 51"Is it legal to convict a man before he is even tried?" he asked.

52They replied, "Are you a wretched Galilean too? Search the Scriptures and see for yourself—no prophets will come from Galilee!"

53Then the meeting broke up and everybody went home.

Jesus forgives an adulterous woman (125)

8 Jesus returned to the Mount of Olives, 2but early the next morning he was back again at the Temple. A crowd soon gathered, and he sat down and talked to them. 3As he was speaking, the Jewish leaders and Pharisees brought a woman caught in adultery and placed her out in front of the staring crowd.

4"Teacher," they said to Jesus, "this woman was caught in the very act of adultery. 5Moses' law says to kill her. What about it?"

6They were trying to trap him into saying something they could use against him,

7:49 *A curse upon them anyway,* literally, "This multitude is accursed." **7:53** Most ancient manuscripts omit John 7:53–8:11.

7:40–43 The crowd was asking questions about Jesus. As a result, some believed, others were hostile, and others disqualified Jesus as the Messiah because he was from Nazareth, not Bethlehem (Micah 5:2). But he *was* born in Bethlehem (Luke 2:1–7), although he grew up in Nazareth. If they had looked more carefully, they would not have jumped to the wrong conclusions. When you search for God's truth, make sure you look carefully and thoughtfully at the Bible with an open heart and mind. Don't jump to conclusions before knowing more of what the Bible says.

7:44, 45 Although the Romans ruled Palestine, they gave the Jewish religious leaders authority over minor civil and religious affairs. The religious leaders controlled their own Temple police and gave them power to arrest anyone causing a disturbance or breaking any of their ceremonial laws. Because these leaders had developed hundreds of trivial laws, it was almost impossible for anyone, even the leaders themselves, not to break, neglect, or ignore at least a few of them. But these police couldn't find one reason to arrest Jesus. And as they listened to him to try to find evidence, they couldn't help hearing the wonderful words he said.

7:46–50 The Jewish leaders saw themselves as an elite group who alone had the truth, and they resisted the truth about Christ because it wasn't *theirs* to begin with. It is easy to think we have the truth about everything and those who disagree with us do not have any at all. But God's truth is available to everyone. Don't repeat the Pharisees' self-centered and cultish attitude.

7:50 This verse offers additional insight into Nicodemus, the Pharisee who visited Jesus at night (chapter 3). Apparently Nicodemus had become a secret believer. Since most of the

Pharisees hated Jesus and wanted to kill him, Nicodemus risked his reputation and high position in speaking up for Jesus. This statement was bold, and the Pharisees immediately became suspicious. After Jesus' death, Nicodemus brought spices for Jesus' body (19:39). That is the last time he is mentioned in Scripture, but tradition says he was baptized by Peter and John and was later forced to step down from his position as a member of the Supreme Court.

7:51 Nicodemus confronted the Pharisees with their failure to keep their own laws. The Pharisees saw themselves losing ground—the Temple police came back impressed by Jesus (7:46), and one of their own, Nicodemus, was defending him. With their hypocritical motives being exposed and their prestige slowly eroding, they began to move to protect themselves. Pride would interfere with their ability to reason, and soon they would become obsessed with getting rid of Jesus just to save face. What was good and right no longer mattered; they began to break their own laws by plotting to murder Jesus.

8:6 Because the woman was caught in the act of adultery, the Jewish leaders had already disregarded the law by bringing her without the man. The law required that both parties be stoned (Leviticus 20:10; Deuteronomy 22:22). The leaders were using the woman as a trap so they could trick Jesus. If Jesus said the woman should not be stoned, they would arrest him for violating Moses' law. If he urged them to execute her, they would report him to the Romans, who did not permit the Jews to carry out their own executions.

but Jesus stooped down and wrote in the dust with his finger. 7They kept demanding an answer, so he stood up again and said, "All right, hurl the stones at her until she dies. But only he who never sinned may throw the first!"

8:7
Deut 17:7

8Then he stooped down again and wrote some more in the dust. 9And the Jewish leaders slipped away one by one, beginning with the eldest, until only Jesus was left in front of the crowd with the woman.

10Then Jesus stood up again and said to her, "Where are your accusers? Didn't even one of them condemn you?"

11"No, sir," she said.

And Jesus said, "Neither do I. Go and sin no more."

8:11
Jn 5:14

Jesus is the light of the world
(126)

12Later, in one of his talks, Jesus said to the people, "I am the Light of the world. So if you follow me, you won't be stumbling through the darkness, for living light will flood your path."

8:12
Isa 9:1,2
Jn 1:4,5,9; 3:19
9:5; 12:35,36,46
2 Cor 4:6

13The Pharisees replied, "You are boasting—and lying!"

8:14
Jn 7:28; 18:37
Rev 1:5

14Jesus told them, "These claims are true even though I make them concerning myself. For I know where I came from and where I am going, but you don't know this about me. 15You pass judgment on me without knowing the facts. I am not judging you now; 16but if I were, it would be an absolutely correct judgment in every respect, for I have with me the Father who sent me. 17Your laws say that if two men agree on something that has happened, their witness is accepted as fact. 18Well, I am one witness, and my Father who sent me is the other."

8:16
Jn 5:30
14:10,11; 16:32
8:17
Deut 17:6; 19:15
2 Cor 13:1
Heb 10:28
8:18
Jn 5:37

19"Where is your father?" they asked.

Jesus answered, "You don't know who I am, so you don't know who my Father is. If you knew me, then you would know him too."

8:19
Jn 14:7,9

20Jesus made these statements while in the section of the Temple known as the Treasury. But he was not arrested, for his time had not yet run out.

8:20
Mk 12:41
Lk 21:1
Jn 7:30

Jesus warns of coming judgment
(127)

21Later he said to them again, "I am going away; and you will search for me, and die in your sins. And you cannot come where I am going."

8:21
Jn 7:34; 13:33

8:7 This is a significant statement about judging others. By mentioning the throwing of stones, Jesus could not be accused of being against the law. But by saying that only a sinless person could throw the first stone, he highlighted the importance of compassion and forgiveness. When others are caught in sin, are you quick to pass judgment? To do so is to act as though you have never sinned. It is God's role to judge, not ours. Our role is to show forgiveness and compassion.

8:9 When Jesus said that only those who had not sinned should throw the first stone, the leaders slipped away, the eldest to the youngest. Evidently the older men were more aware of their sins than the younger. Age and experience temper youthful idealism and self-righteousness. But whatever your age, take an honest look at your life; recognize your sinful nature; and spend more time looking for ways to help others rather than hurt them.

8:11 Jesus didn't condemn the woman accused of adultery, but neither did he ignore or condone her sin. He told her to go and sin no more. Jesus stands ready to forgive any sin in your life, but confession and repentance mean a change of heart. With God's help we can accept Christ's forgiveness and stop our wrongdoing.

8:12 What does it mean to follow Christ? As a soldier follows his captain, so we should follow Christ as our commander. As a slave follows his master, so we should follow Christ as our Lord. As we follow the advice of a trusted counselor, so we should follow Jesus' commands to us in Scripture. As we follow the laws of a nation, so we follow Christ's laws because we are citizens of heaven.

8:12 Jesus called himself the Light of the world. For what he meant by this, see the note on 1:4.

8:12 Jesus was speaking in the part of the Temple known as the Treasury (8:20), where candles burned to symbolize the pillar of fire that led the people of Israel through the wilderness (Exodus 13:21, 22). In this context, Jesus called himself the Light of the world. The pillar of fire represented God's presence, protection, and guidance. Jesus brings God's presence, protection, and guidance. Is he the light of *your* world?

8:13, 14 The Pharisees thought Jesus was either insane or a liar. Jesus provided them with a third alternative: he was telling the truth. Because the Pharisees refused to consider the third alternative, they would never recognize him as Messiah and Lord. If you are seeking to know who Jesus is, do not close any door before looking through it honestly. Only with an open mind will you know the truth that he is Messiah and Lord.

8:18 The Jews argued that Jesus' claim was legally invalid because he had no other witnesses. Jesus responded that his confirming witness was God himself. He and God made two witnesses, the number required by the law (Deuteronomy 19:15).

8:20 The Temple Treasury was located in the Court of Women. In this area, 13 collection boxes were set up to receive money offerings. Seven of the boxes were for the Temple tax; the other six were for freewill offerings. On another occasion, a widow placed her money in one of these boxes and Jesus taught a profound lesson from her action (Luke 21:1, 2).

8:22
Jn 7:35,36

8:23
Jn 3:31; 15:19
17:16
1 Jn 4:5

8:24
Ex 3:14,15
Jn 4:26; 8:28,58
13:19

8:26
Jn 3:32-34
12:49; 15:15

8:28
Jn 3:11,14,15
5:19,8:24; 12:32
Rom 1:4

8:29
Jn 4:34; 6:38
14:10; 16:32

8:31
Jn 15:7

8:32
Rom 8:2
2 Cor 3:17
Gal 5:1,13
1 Pet 2:16

8:33
Lev 25:42
Mt 3:9

8:34
Rom 6:16
2 Pet 2:19

8:35
Gen 21:10
Gal 4:30

8:39
Mt 3:9
Rom 3:28; 9:7
Gal 3:7,29

8:41
Deut 32:6
Isa 63:16; 64:8
Mal 1:6

8:42
Jn 1:14; 3:16
5:43; 16:27
Gal 4:4

8:44
Gen 3:1,4
1 Jn 2:4; 3:8

22The Jews asked, "Is he planning suicide? What does he mean, 'You cannot come where I am going'?"

23Then he said to them, "You are from below; I am from above. You are of this world; I am not. 24That is why I said that you will die in your sins; for unless you believe that I am the Messiah, the Son of God, you will die in your sins."

25"Tell us who you are," they demanded.

He replied, "I am the one I have always claimed to be. 26I could condemn you for much and teach you much, but I won't, for I say only what I am told to by the one who sent me; and he is Truth." 27But they still didn't understand that he was talking to them about God.

28So Jesus said, "When you have killed the Messiah, then you will realize that I am he and that I have not been telling you my own ideas, but have spoken what the Father taught me. 29And he who sent me is with me—he has not deserted me—for I always do those things that are pleasing to him."

Jesus speaks about God's true children (128)

30, 31Then many of the Jewish leaders who heard him say these things began believing him to be the Messiah.

Jesus said to them, "You are truly my disciples if you live as I tell you to, 32and you will know the truth, and the truth will set you free."

33"But we are descendants of Abraham," they said, "and have never been slaves to any man on earth! What do you mean, 'set free'?"

34Jesus replied, "You are slaves of sin, every one of you. 35And slaves don't have rights, but the Son has every right there is! 36So if the Son sets you free, you will indeed be free— 37(Yes, I realize that you are descendants of Abraham!) And yet some of you are trying to kill me because my message does not find a home within your hearts. 38I am telling you what I saw when I was with my Father. But you are following the advice of *your* father."

39"Our father is Abraham," they declared.

"No!" Jesus replied, "for if he were, you would follow his good example. 40But instead you are trying to kill me—and all because I told you the truth I heard from God. Abraham wouldn't do a thing like that! 41No, you are obeying your *real* father when you act that way."

They replied, "We were not born out of wedlock—our true Father is God himself."

42Jesus told them, "If that were so, then you would love me, for I have come to you from God. I am not here on my own, but he sent me. 43Why can't you understand what I am saying? It is because you are prevented from doing so! 44For you are the children of your father the devil and you love to do the evil things he

8:27 *God,* literally, "the Father."   **8:28** *When you have killed the Messiah,* literally, "When you have lifted up the Son of Man."

8:24 People will die in their sins if they reject Christ, because they are rejecting the only way to be rescued from sin. Sadly, many are so taken up with the values of this world that they are blind to the priceless gift Christ offers.

8:32 Jesus himself is the truth that sets us free. He is the source of truth, the perfect standard of what is right. He frees us from the consequences of sin, from self-deception, and from deception by Satan. He shows us clearly the way to eternal life with God. Thus Jesus does not give us freedom to do what we want, but freedom to follow God. As we seek to live for God, Jesus' perfect truth frees us to be all that God meant us to be.

8:34, 35 Sin has a way of enslaving us, controlling us, dominating us, and dictating our actions. Jesus can free you from this slavery that keeps you from becoming the person God created you to be. If sin is restraining, mastering, or enslaving you, Jesus can break its power over your life.

8:41 Jesus made a distinction between hereditary sons and *true*

sons. The religious leaders were hereditary sons of Abraham (founder of the Jewish nation) and therefore claimed to be sons of God. But their actions showed them to be true sons of Satan, for they lived under Satan's guidance. True sons of Abraham (faithful followers of God) would not act as they did. Your church membership and family connections will not make you true sons of God. Your true father is the one you obey.

8:43 The religious leaders were prevented from believing because they refused to believe. Satan used their own stubbornness, pride, and prejudices to prevent them from believing in Jesus.

8:44, 45 The attitudes and actions of these leaders clearly identified them as followers of Satan. They may not have been conscious of this, but their hatred of truth, their lies, and their murderous intentions indicated how much control Satan had over them. They were tools in carrying out his plans. Satan still uses people to squelch God's work in the world.

does. He was a murderer from the beginning and a hater of truth—there is not an iota of truth in him. When he lies, it is perfectly normal; for he is the father of liars. ⁴⁵And so when I tell the truth, you just naturally don't believe it!

⁴⁶"Which of you can truthfully accuse me of one single sin? [No one!] And since I am telling you the truth, why don't you believe me? ⁴⁷Anyone whose Father is God listens gladly to the words of God. Since you don't, it proves you aren't his children."

Jesus states he is eternal
(129)

⁴⁸"You Samaritan! Foreigner! Devil!" the Jewish leaders snarled. "Didn't we say all along you were possessed by a demon?"

⁴⁹"No," Jesus said, "I have no demon in me. For I honor my Father—and you dishonor me. ⁵⁰And though I have no wish to make myself great, God wants this for me and judges [those who reject me]. ⁵¹With all the earnestness I have I tell you this—no one who obeys me shall ever die!"

⁵²The leaders of the Jews said, "Now we know you are possessed by a demon. Even Abraham and the mightiest prophets died, and yet you say that obeying you will keep a man from dying! ⁵³So you are greater than our father Abraham, who died? And greater than the prophets, who died? Who do you think you are?" ⁵⁴Then Jesus told them this: "If I am merely boasting about myself, it doesn't count. But it is my Father—and you claim him as your God—who is saying these glorious things about me. ⁵⁵But you do not even know him. I do. If I said otherwise, I would be as great a liar as you! But it is true—I know him and fully obey him. ⁵⁶Your father Abraham rejoiced to see my day. He knew I was coming and was glad."

⁵⁷*The Jewish leaders:* "You aren't even fifty years old—sure, you've seen Abraham!"

⁵⁸*Jesus:* "The absolute truth is that I was in existence before Abraham was ever born!"

⁵⁹At that point the Jewish leaders picked up stones to kill him. But Jesus was hidden from them, and walked past them and left the Temple.

Jesus heals the man who was born blind
(148)

9 As he was walking along, he saw a man blind from birth. ²"Master," his disciples asked him, "why was this man born blind? Was it a result of his own sins or those of his parents?"

8:46 *No one,* implied. **8:50** *those who reject me,* implied. Literally, "There is one who seeks and judges."

Cross references (right margin):

8:45 Jn 18:37
8:47 1 Jn 4:6
8:49 Jn 7:20
8:50 Jn 5:41,42
8:51 Jn 5:24 11:25,26
8:53 Jn 4:12
8:54 Jn 16:14; 17:1 Acts 3:13
8:55 Jn 7:29; 15:10
8:56 Gen 22:17,18 Lk 10:24 Gal 3:8,9,16 Heb 11:10,13
8:58 Ex 3:14 Isa 9:6; 43:13 Mic 5:2 Jn 8:24,28 13:19 Col 1:17 Heb 13:8 Rev 1:8
9:1 Ex 20:5 Lk 13:2 Jn 9:34

8:46 No one could accuse Jesus of a single sin. People who hated him and wanted him dead scrutinized his life but could find nothing wrong. Jesus proved he was God in the flesh by his sinless life. He is the only perfect example to follow.

8:46 In a number of places Jesus intentionally challenged his listeners to test him. He welcomed those who wanted to question his claims and character as long as they were willing to follow through on what they discovered. His challenge clarifies the two ways people most frequently miss encountering him: (1) they never accept his challenge to test him, or (2) they do test him but are not willing to believe what they discover. Have you made either of those mistakes?

8:51 Obedience is a continuous process, so we must frequently ask God's forgiveness when we sin. When Jesus says those who obey won't die, he is talking about spiritual death, not physical death. Those who follow him are promised eternal life.

8:56 God told Abraham, father of the Jewish nation, that through him all nations would be blessed (Genesis 12:1–3). Jesus, a descendant of Abraham, blessed all people through his death, resurrection, and offer of salvation.

8:58 This is one of the most powerful statements uttered by Jesus. When he says he existed before Abraham was born, he undeniably proclaims his divinity. Other translations say, "Before Abraham was, *I Am.*" Not only did Jesus say he existed before Abraham; he also applied God's holy name (*I Am*—Exodus 3:14) to himself. This claim demands a response. It cannot be ignored. The Jewish leaders tried to stone him for blasphemy because he claimed equality with God. But Jesus is God. Have you truly recognized that fact?

8:59 In accordance with the law in Leviticus 24:16, the religious leaders were ready to stone Jesus for claiming to be God. They well understood what Jesus was claiming, and since they didn't believe him, they charged him with blasphemy. How ironic that they were really the blasphemers, cursing and attacking the very God they claimed to serve!

9:1ff In chapter 9, we see four different reactions to Jesus. The neighbors revealed surprise and skepticism; the Pharisees showed disbelief and prejudice; the parents believed but kept quiet for fear of excommunication; and the healed man showed consistent, growing belief.

9:2, 3 A common belief in Jewish culture was that calamity or suffering was the result of some great sin. But Christ used this

9:3
Jn 11:4

9:4
Jn 4:34
5:19,36; 11:9
12:35; 17:4

9:5
Isa 9:2; 42:6
49:6
Lk 2:32
Jn 1:5,9; 3:19
8:12; 12:46

9:6
Mk 7:33; 8:23

9:7
2 Kgs 5:14
Neh 3:15
Isa 35:5

9:8
Acts 3:2,10

3"Neither," Jesus answered. "But to demonstrate the power of God. 4All of us must quickly carry out the tasks assigned us by the one who sent me, for there is little time left before the night falls and all work comes to an end. 5But while I am still here in the world, I give it my light."

6Then he spat on the ground and made mud from the spittle and smoothed the mud over the blind man's eyes, 7and told him, "Go and wash in the Pool of Siloam" (the word "Siloam" means "Sent"). So the man went where he was sent and washed and came back seeing!

8His neighbors and others who knew him as a blind beggar asked each other, "Is this the same fellow—that beggar?"

9Some said yes, and some said no. "It can't be the same man," they thought, "but he surely looks like him!"

And the beggar said, "I *am* the same man!"

10Then they asked him how in the world he could see. What had happened?

11And he told them, "A man they call Jesus made mud and smoothed it over my eyes and told me to go to the Pool of Siloam and wash off the mud. I did, and I can see!"

12"Where is he now?" they asked.

"I don't know," he replied.

Religious leaders question the blind man (149)

9:14
Jn 5:9

13Then they took the man to the Pharisees. 14Now as it happened, this all occurred on a Sabbath. 15Then the Pharisees asked him all about it. So he told them how Jesus had smoothed the mud over his eyes, and when it was washed away, he could see!

9:16
Jn 3:2; 7:12,43

16Some of them said, "Then this fellow Jesus is not from God, because he is working on the Sabbath."

Others said, "But how could an ordinary sinner do such miracles?" So there was a deep division of opinion among them.

9:17
Deut 18:15
Mt 21:11
Jn 4:19; 6:14

17Then the Pharisees turned on the man who had been blind and demanded, "This man who opened your eyes—who do you say he is?"

"I think he must be a prophet sent from God," the man replied.

18The Jewish leaders wouldn't believe he had been blind, until they called in his parents 19and asked them, "Is this your son? Was he born blind? If so, how can he see?"

20His parents replied, "We know this is our son and that he was born blind, 21but we don't know what happened to make him see, or who did it. He is old enough to speak for himself. Ask him."

9:22
Jn 7:13; 12:42
16:2; 19:38
Acts 5:13

9:24
Josh 7:19

22, 23They said this in fear of the Jewish leaders who had announced that anyone saying Jesus was the Messiah would be excommunicated.

24So for the second time they called in the man who had been blind and told him, "Give the glory to God, not to Jesus, for we know Jesus is an evil person."

---

man's suffering to teach about faith and to glorify God. We live in a fallen world where good behavior is not always rewarded and bad behavior not always punished. Therefore, innocent people sometimes suffer. If God took suffering away whenever we asked, we would follow him for comfort and convenience, not out of love and devotion. Regardless of the reasons for our suffering, Jesus has the power to help us deal with it. When you suffer from a disease, tragedy, or handicap, try not to ask, "Why did this happen to me?" or "What did I do wrong?" Instead, ask God to give you strength through the trial and offer you a deeper perspective on what is happening.

9:7 The Pool of Siloam was made by King Hezekiah. His workers built an underground tunnel from a spring outside the city walls which carried water into the city. Thus the people could always get

water without fear of being attacked. This was especially important in times of siege (see 2 Kings 20:20; 2 Chronicles 32:30).

9:13–17 While the Pharisees questioned and debated about Jesus, people were being healed and lives were being changed. Their skepticism was based not on insufficient evidence, but on jealousy of Jesus' popularity.

9:14–16 The Jewish Sabbath, Saturday, was the weekly holy day of rest. The Pharisees had made a long list of specific dos and don'ts regarding the Sabbath. Kneading the clay and healing the man were considered work and therefore were forbidden. By making the clay, Jesus may have wanted to make his point about the Sabbath—that it is right to care for others' needs even on a day of rest.

25"I don't know whether he is good or bad," the man replied, "but I know this: *I was blind, and now I see!"*

26"But what did he do?" they asked. "How did he heal you?"

27"Look!" the man exclaimed. "I told you once; didn't you listen? Why do you want to hear it again? Do you want to become his disciples too?"

28Then they cursed him and said, "You are his disciple, but we are disciples of Moses. 29We know God has spoken to Moses, but as for this fellow, we don't know anything about him."

30"Why, that's very strange!" the man replied. "He can heal blind men, and yet you don't know anything about him! 31Well, God doesn't listen to evil men, but he has open ears to those who worship him and do his will. 32Since the world began there has never been anyone who could open the eyes of someone born blind. 33If this man were not from God, he couldn't do it."

34"You illegitimate bastard, you!" they shouted. "Are you trying to teach *us?"* And they threw him out.

Jesus teaches about spiritual blindness (150)

35When Jesus heard what had happened, he found the man and said, "Do you believe in the Messiah?"

36The man answered, "Who is he, sir, for I want to."

37"You have seen him," Jesus said, "and he is speaking to you!"

38"Yes, Lord," the man said, "I believe!" And he worshiped Jesus.

39Then Jesus told him, "I have come into the world to give sight to those who are spiritually blind and to show those who think they see that they are blind."

40The Pharisees who were standing there asked, "Are you saying we are blind?"

41"If you were blind, you wouldn't be guilty," Jesus replied. "But your guilt remains because you claim to know what you are doing.

Jesus is the Good Shepherd (151)

10 "Anyone refusing to walk through the gate into a sheepfold, who sneaks over the wall, must surely be a thief! 2For a shepherd comes through the gate. 3The gatekeeper opens the gate for him, and the sheep hear his voice and come to him; and he calls his own sheep by name and leads them out. 4He walks ahead of them; and they follow him, for they recognize his voice. 5They won't follow a stranger but will run from him, for they don't recognize his voice."

6Those who heard Jesus use this illustration didn't understand what he meant, 7so he explained it to them.

"I am the Gate for the sheep," he said. 8"All others who came before me were thieves and robbers. But the true sheep did not listen to them. 9Yes, I am the Gate. Those who come in by way of the Gate will be saved and will go in and out and find

9:34 You illegitimate bastard, literally, "You were altogether born in sin."   **9:35** the Messiah, literally, "the Son of Man."

9:28 Jn 5:45; Rom 2:17
9:29 Jn 1:10; 8:14
9:31 Job 27:8,9; Ps 34:15; 66:18; 145:19; Prov 15:29; Isa 1:15; Jer 11:11; 14:12; Mic 3:4; Zech 7:13
9:33 Jn 3:2
9:34 Jn 12:42
9:35 Mt 16:16; Mk 1:1
9:37 Jn 4:26
9:39 Lk 4:18,19
9:40 Rom 2:19
9:41 Prov 26:12; Jn 15:22
10:1 Isa 56:10
10:2 Acts 20:28
10:5 Prov 19:27; Gal 1:8; Eph 4:14
10:6 Jn 16:25; 2 Pet 2:22
10:7 Jn 14:6
10:8 Jer 23:1; 50:6; Ezek 34:2

9:25 By now the man who had been blind had heard the same questions over and over. He did not know how he was healed, but he knew that his life had been miraculously changed, and he was not afraid to tell the truth. You don't need to know all the answers in order to share Christ with others. It is important to tell them what Christ has done for you and how he has changed your life. Then trust that God will use your words to help others believe in him too.

9:28, 34 The man's new faith was severely tested by some of the authorities. He was cursed and evicted from the Temple. You also may expect persecution when you follow Jesus. You may lose friends; you may even lose your life. But no one can ever take away the eternal life you have been given by Jesus.

9:30-33 The longer this man experienced his new life through Christ, the more confident he became in the One who healed him.

He gained not only physical sight but also spiritual sight as he recognized Jesus as Master, then prophet, then Lord. When you turn to Christ, you begin to see him differently. The longer you walk with him, the better you understand who he is. Peter tells us to "grow in spiritual strength and become better acquainted with our Lord and Savior Jesus Christ" (2 Peter 3:18). If you want to know more about Jesus, keep walking with him.

10:1 At night, sheep were often gathered into a sheepfold to protect them from thieves, weather, or wild animals. The sheepfolds were caves, sheds, or open areas surrounded by walls made of stones or branches. The shepherd often slept in the fold to protect the sheep. Just as a shepherd cares for his sheep, Jesus, the Good Shepherd, cares for his flock (those who follow him). The prophet Ezekiel, in predicting the coming of the Messiah, called him a Shepherd (Ezekiel 34:23).

10:10
Jn 5:40
Acts 20:29
2 Pet 2:1

10:11
Isa 40:11
Ezek 34:11-16,
23; 37:24
Heb 13:20,21
1 Pet 2:25; 5:4
1 Jn 3:16
Rev 7:17

10:14
Phil 3:10
2 Tim 2:19

10:16
Isa 56:6,7
Ezek 37:21,22
Jn 11:52
17:20-24
Eph 2:14; 3:6

10:17
Isa 53:6,7
2 Cor 5:15
Heb 2:9
1 Jn 3:16

10:18
Jn 11:25; 19:11
Heb 5:8; 7:16

green pastures. ¹⁰The thief's purpose is to steal, kill and destroy. My purpose is to give life in all its fullness.

¹¹"I am the Good Shepherd. The Good Shepherd lays down his life for the sheep. ¹²A hired man will run when he sees a wolf coming and will leave the sheep, for they aren't his and he isn't their shepherd. And so the wolf leaps on them and scatters the flock. ¹³The hired man runs because he is hired and has no real concern for the sheep.

¹⁴"I am the Good Shepherd and know my own sheep, and they know me, ¹⁵just as my Father knows me and I know the Father; and I lay down my life for the sheep. ¹⁶I have other sheep, too, in another fold. I must bring them also, and they will heed my voice; and there will be one flock with one Shepherd.

¹⁷"The Father loves me because I lay down my life that I may have it back again. ¹⁸No one can kill me without my consent—I lay down my life voluntarily. For I have the right and power to lay it down when I want to and also the right and power to take it again. For the Father has given me this right."

¹⁹When he said these things, the Jewish leaders were again divided in their opinions about him. ²⁰Some of them said, "He has a demon or else is crazy. Why listen to a man like that?"

²¹Others said, "This doesn't sound to us like a man possessed by a demon! Can a demon open the eyes of blind men?"

THE NAMES OF JESUS	Reference	Name	Significance
In different settings, Jesus gave himself names that pointed to special roles he was ready to fulfill for people. Some of these refer back to the Old Testament promises of the Messiah. Others were ways to help people understand him.	6:27 (see textual note)	Son of Man	Jesus' favorite reference to himself. It emphasized his humanity—but the way he used it, it was a claim to divinity.
	6:35	Bread of life	Refers to his life-giving role—that he is the only source of eternal life.
	8:12	Light of the world	Light is a symbol of spiritual truth. Jesus is the universal answer for man's need of spiritual truth.
	10:7	Gate for the sheep	Jesus is the only way into God's Kingdom.
	10:11	Good Shepherd	Jesus appropriated the prophetic images of the Messiah pictured in the Old Testament. This is a claim to divinity, focusing on his love and guidance.
	11:25	The one who raises the dead	Not only is Jesus the source of life, he is the power over death.
	14:6	The Way, the Truth, and the Life	Jesus is the method, the message, and the meaning for all people. With this title he summarized his purpose in coming to earth.
	15:1	The Vine	This title has an important second part, "and you are the branches." As in so many of his other names, Jesus reminds us that just as branches gain life from the vine and cannot live apart from it, so we are completely dependent on Christ for spiritual life.

10:11, 12 A hired man tends the sheep for money, while the shepherd does it for love. The shepherd is committed to his sheep. Jesus is not merely doing a job; he is committed to love us and even lay down his life for us. False teachers and false prophets do not have this commitment.

10:16 The "other sheep" refers to people who are not Jews. Jesus came to save Gentiles as well as Jews. This is an insight into his worldwide mission—to die for the sins of the whole world.

10:17, 18 Jesus is talking about his death and resurrection which, as part of God's plan for the salvation of the world, were under God's full control.

10:19, 20 If Jesus had been merely a man, he would have been a madman because of his claims to be God. But his miracles proved his words true—he really was God. The Jewish leaders could not see beyond their own prejudices, and they tried to put Jesus in a human "box." But Jesus was not limited by their limited vision.

**Religious leaders surround Jesus at the Temple
(152)**

22, 23It was winter, and Jesus was in Jerusalem at the time of the Dedication Celebration. He was at the Temple, walking through the section known as Solomon's Hall. 24The Jewish leaders surrounded him and asked, "How long are you going to keep us in suspense? If you are the Messiah, tell us plainly."

25"I have already told you, and you don't believe me," Jesus replied. "The proof is in the miracles I do in the name of my Father. 26But you don't believe me because you are not part of my flock. 27My sheep recognize my voice, and I know them, and they follow me. 28I give them eternal life and they shall never perish. No one shall snatch them away from me, 29for my Father has given them to me, and he is more powerful than anyone else, so no one can kidnap them from me. 30I and the Father are one."

31Then again the Jewish leaders picked up stones to kill him.

32Jesus said, "At God's direction I have done many a miracle to help the people. For which one are you killing me?"

33They replied, "Not for any good work, but for blasphemy; you, a mere man, have declared yourself to be God."

34, 35, 36"In your own Law it says that men are gods!" he replied. "So if the Scripture, which cannot be untrue, speaks of those as gods to whom the message of God came, do you call it blasphemy when the one sanctified and sent into the world by the Father says, 'I am the Son of God'? 37Don't believe me unless I do miracles of God. 38But if I do, believe them even if you don't believe me. Then you will become convinced that the Father is in me, and I in the Father."

39Once again they started to arrest him. But he walked away and left them, 40and went beyond the Jordan River to stay near the place where John was first baptizing. 41And many followed him.

"John didn't do miracles," they remarked to one another, "but all his predictions

10:25 *I have already told you,* see 5:19; 8:36, 56, 58, etc.

10:23
Acts 3:11; 5:12
10:24
Lk 22:67
10:25
Jn 5:36
10:38; 14:10,11
10:26
Jn 8:47
1 Jn 4:6
10:28
Jn 6:37,39
17:2,3
1 Jn 5:11,12
10:29
Jn 14:28
17:2,6
10:30
Isa 9:6
Jn 1:1; 10:38
14:8-11
17:21-24
10:33
Lev 24:15,16
Jn 1:1,18
Jn 5:18; 20:28
Rom 9:5
Phil 2:6
Tit 2:13
Heb 1:8,9
2 Pet 1:1
1 Jn 5:20
10:34
Ps 82:1,6
10:37
Jn 15:24

MINISTRY BEYOND THE JORDAN
Jesus had been in Jerusalem for the Tabernacle Ceremonies (7:2); then he preached in various towns, probably in Judea, before returning to Jerusalem for the Dedication Celebration. He again angered the religious leaders who tried to arrest him, but he left the city and went beyond the Jordan to preach.

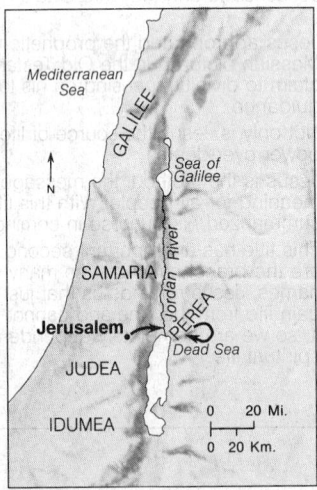

Mediterranean Sea
GALILEE
Sea of Galilee
N
Jordan River
SAMARIA
PEREA
Jerusalem
JUDEA
Dead Sea
IDUMEA
0   20 Mi.
0   20 Km.

10:23 Solomon's Hall, also called Solomon's Colonnade, was a roofed porch, supported by large stone columns, just inside the courtyard walls.

10:24 These leaders were waiting for the signs and answers *they* thought would convince them of Jesus' identity. Thus they couldn't hear the truth Jesus was giving them. Jesus tried to correct their mistaken ideas, but they clung to the wrong idea of what kind of Messiah God would send. Such blindness still keeps people away from Jesus. They want him on their own terms; they do not want him if it means changing their whole lives.

10:28, 29 Just as a shepherd protects his sheep, Jesus protects his people from eternal harm. While believers can expect to suffer on earth, their souls cannot be harmed by Satan. Their eternal life with God cannot be taken away. There are many reasons to be afraid here on earth, because this is Satan's domain. But if you choose to follow Jesus, he will give you everlasting safety.

10:30, 31 This is one of the clearest statements of Jesus' divinity—he and the Father are one. They are not the same person, but they are one in essence and nature. Thus Jesus is not merely a good teacher—he is God. His claim to be God is unmistakable. The religious leaders wanted to kill him for it, because their laws said that anyone claiming to be God should die. Nothing could persuade them that Jesus' claim was true.

10:22, 23 The Dedication Celebration commemorated the cleansing of the Temple under Judas Maccabeus in 164 B.C. after Antiochus Epiphanes defiled it by sacrificing a pig on the altar of burnt offering. It was celebrated toward the end of December. This is also the present-day Feast of Lights, Hanukkah.

10:31 The Jewish leaders attempted to carry out the direction found in Leviticus 24:15, 16 regarding those who blaspheme (claim to be God). They were going to stone Jesus.

10:34–36 This is a clear statement of the truth of the Bible. If we accept Christ as Lord, we also accept his confirmation of the Bible as God's Word.

10:42
Jn 7:31
8:30,31; 11:45

11:1
Mt 21:17
Lk 10:38

11:2
Mt 26:7
Mk 14:3
Lk 7:37,38
Jn 12:3

11:4
Jn 9:3

11:8
Jn 8:59; 10:31

11:9
Ps 97:11
119:105,130
Prov 4:18; 13:9
Lk 13:33
Jn 9:4

11:10
Job 12:24,25
Jn 12:35
1 Jn 2:11

11:11
Dan 12:2
Acts 7:60
1 Cor 15:51

11:16
Mt 10:3
Jn 14:5
20:24-28; 21:2

concerning this man have come true." ⁴²And many came to the decision that he was the Messiah.

3. Jesus encounters crucial events in Jerusalem
Lazarus becomes ill and dies
(165)

11 Do you remember Mary, who poured the costly perfume on Jesus' feet and wiped them with her hair? Well, her brother Lazarus, who lived in Bethany with Mary and her sister Martha, was sick. ³So the two sisters sent a message to Jesus telling him, "Sir, your good friend is very, very sick."

⁴But when Jesus heard about it he said, "The purpose of his illness is not death, but for the glory of God. I, the Son of God, will receive glory from this situation."

⁵Although Jesus was very fond of Martha, Mary, and Lazarus, ⁶he stayed where he was for the next two days and made no move to go to them. ⁷Finally, after the two days, he said to his disciples, "Let's go to Judea."

⁸But his disciples objected. "Master," they said, "only a few days ago the Jewish leaders in Judea were trying to kill you. Are you going there again?"

⁹Jesus replied, "There are twelve hours of daylight every day, and during every hour of it a man can walk safely and not stumble. ¹⁰Only at night is there danger of a wrong step, because of the dark." ¹¹Then he said, "Our friend Lazarus has gone to sleep, but now I will go and waken him!"

¹², ¹³The disciples, thinking Jesus meant Lazarus was having a good night's rest, said, "That means he is getting better!" But Jesus meant Lazarus had died.

¹⁴Then he told them plainly, "Lazarus is dead. ¹⁵And for your sake, I am glad I wasn't there, for this will give you another opportunity to believe in me. Come, let's go to him."

¹⁶Thomas, nicknamed "The Twin," said to his fellow disciples, "Let's go too—and die with him."

10:42 *many came to the decision that he was the Messiah,* literally, "Many believed on him there." **11:1** *wiped them with her hair,* see John 12:3.

JESUS RAISES LAZARUS
Jesus had been preaching in the villages beyond the Jordan, probably in Perea, when he received the news of Lazarus' sickness. Jesus did not leave immediately, but waited two days before returning to Judea. He knew Lazarus would be dead when he arrived in Bethany, but he was going to do a great miracle.

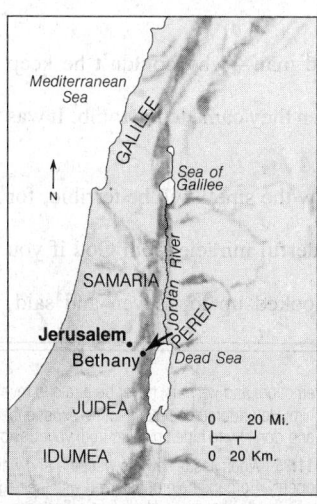

11:1, 2 The village of Bethany was located about two miles east of Jerusalem on the road to Jericho.

11:3 As their brother grew very sick, Mary and Martha turned to Jesus for help. They believed in his ability to help because they had seen his miracles. We too know of his miracles, both from

Scripture and through changed lives. When we need extraordinary help, Jesus offers extraordinary resources. We should not hesitate to ask him for help.

11:4 Any difficult situation a believer faces can ultimately bring glory to God because God can bring good out of any bad situation. When trouble comes, do you whine, complain, and blame God, or do you see your problems as opportunities to honor him?

11:5-7 Jesus loved this family and often stayed with them. He knew their pain but did not respond immediately. His delay had a specific purpose. God's timing, especially his delays, may make us think he is not answering or is not answering the way we want. But he will meet all our needs according to his perfect schedule and purpose. Patiently await his timing.

11:9, 10 *Daylight* means the knowledge of God's will; *night* means absence of this knowledge. When we move ahead in darkness, we are likely to stumble.

11:14, 15 If Jesus had been with Lazarus during the final moments of his sickness, he might have healed him rather than let him die. But Lazarus died so Jesus' power over death could be shown to his disciples and others. Sometimes we must experience hurt to reveal God's power over that hurt.

11:16 The disciples knew the dangers of going with Jesus to Jerusalem, and they tried to talk him out of it. When their objections failed, they were willing to go and even die with him. They may not have understood the reason Jesus would die, but they were loyal. There are unknown dangers in doing God's work. It is wise to consider the high cost of being Jesus' disciple.

Jesus comforts Mary and Martha
(166)

17When they arrived at Bethany, they were told that Lazarus had already been in his tomb for four days. 18Bethany was only a couple of miles down the road from Jerusalem, 19and many of the Jewish leaders had come to pay their respects and to console Martha and Mary on their loss. 20When Martha got word that Jesus was coming, she went to meet him. But Mary stayed at home.

21Martha said to Jesus, "Sir, if you had been here, my brother wouldn't have died. 22And even now it's not too late, for I know that God will bring my brother back to life again, if you will only ask him to."

23Jesus told her, "Your brother will come back to life again."

24"Yes," Martha said, "when everyone else does, on Resurrection Day."

25Jesus told her, "I am the one who raises the dead and gives them life again. Anyone who believes in me, even though he dies like anyone else, shall live again. 26He is given eternal life for believing in me and shall never perish. Do you believe this, Martha?"

27"Yes, Master," she told him. "I believe you are the Messiah, the Son of God, the one we have so long awaited."

28Then she left him and returned to Mary and, calling her aside from the mourners, told her, "He is here and wants to see you." 29So Mary went to him at once.

30Now Jesus had stayed outside the village, at the place where Martha met him. 31When the Jewish leaders who were at the house trying to console Mary saw her leave so hastily, they assumed she was going to Lazarus' tomb to weep; so they followed her.

32When Mary arrived where Jesus was, she fell down at his feet, saying, "Sir, if you had been here, my brother would still be alive."

33When Jesus saw her weeping and the Jewish leaders wailing with her, he was moved with indignation and deeply troubled. 34"Where is he buried?" he asked them.

They told him, "Come and see." 35Tears came to Jesus' eyes.

36"They were close friends," the Jewish leaders said. "See how much he loved him."

Jesus raises Lazarus from the dead
(167)

37,38But some said, "This fellow healed a blind man—why couldn't he keep Lazarus from dying?"

And again Jesus was moved with deep anger. Then they came to the tomb. It was a cave with a heavy stone rolled across its door.

39"Roll the stone aside," Jesus told them.

But Martha, the dead man's sister, said, "By now the smell will be terrible, for he has been dead four days."

40"But didn't I tell you that you will see a wonderful miracle from God if you believe?" Jesus asked her.

41So they rolled the stone aside. Then Jesus looked up to heaven and said,

Cross references (right margin):

11:17 Jn 11:39
11:20 Lk 10:38-42
11:22 Jn 9:31
11:23 Dan 12:2; Phil 3:21; 1 Thess 4:14
11:24 Jn 5:28,29; Acts 24:15
11:25 Jn 1:4; 3:36; 5:21; 6:39,40; 14:6; Col 1:18; 3:4; 1 Jn 1:1,2; 5:10,11; Rev 1:17,18
11:26 Jn 6:47-51; 8:51
11:27 Mt 16:16; Jn 4:42; 6:14,68,69
11:35 Isa 53:3; Lk 19:41; Rom 12:15; Heb 4:15
11:37 Jn 9:6,7
11:39 Jn 11:17
11:41 Mt 11:25; 27:60; Lk 24:2

11:25 Jesus has power over life and death as well as power to forgive sins. This is because he is the Creator of life (see John 14:6). He who *is* Life can surely restore life.

11:27 Martha is best known for being too busy to sit down and talk with Jesus (Luke 10:38–42). But here we see her as a woman of deep faith.

11:33–38 John stresses that we have a God who cares. This contrasts with the Greek concept of God that was popular in his day—a God with no emotions and no messy involvement with humans. Here we see many of Jesus' emotions—compassion, indignation, sorrow, even frustration. He often expressed deep

emotion, and we must never be afraid to reveal our true feelings to him. He understands them, for he experienced them. Be honest, and don't try to hide anything from your Savior. He cares.

11:35 When Jesus saw the weeping and wailing, he too wept openly. Perhaps he empathized with their sorrow, or perhaps he was troubled at their unbelief. In either case, Jesus showed that he cares enough for us to weep with us.

11:37, 38 Tombs at this time were usually caves carved in the limestone rock of a hillside. A tomb was often large enough for people to walk inside. Several bodies were usually placed in one tomb. After burial, a large stone was rolled across the entrance to the tomb.

11:42
Jn 12:30

11:43
Deut 32:39
1 Sam 2:6
Lk 7:14; 8:54
Acts 3:15; 9:40

"Father, thank you for hearing me. ⁴²(You always hear me, of course, but I said it because of all these people standing here, so that they will believe you sent me.)" ⁴³Then he shouted, "Lazarus, come out!"

⁴⁴And Lazarus came—bound up in the gravecloth, his face muffled in a head swath. Jesus told them, "Unwrap him and let him go!"

Religious leaders plot to kill Jesus
(168)

⁴⁵And so at last many of the Jewish leaders who were with Mary and saw it

---

Caiaphas was the leader of the religious group called the Sadducees. Educated and wealthy, they controlled the political power of the nation. As the elite group, they were on fairly good terms with Rome. They hated Jesus because he endangered their secure lifestyles and taught a message they could not accept. A kingdom in which leaders *served* had no appeal to them.

Caiaphas' usual policy was to remove any threats to his power by whatever means necessary. For Caiaphas, whether Jesus should die was not in question; the only point to be settled was *when* his death should take place. Not only did Jesus have to be captured and tried; the Jewish Supreme Court also needed Roman approval before they could carry out the death sentence. Caiaphas' plans were unexpectedly helped by Judas' offer to betray Christ.

Caiaphas did not realize, however, that his actions were actually part of a wonderful plan God was carrying out. Caiaphas' willingness to sacrifice another man to preserve his own security was a clear act of selfishness. By contrast, God's willingness to die for us was the clearest example of loving self-sacrifice. Caiaphas thought he had won the battle as Jesus hung on the cross, but he did not count on the resurrection!

Caiaphas' mind was closed. He couldn't accept the resurrection even when the evidence was overwhelming, and he attempted to silence those whose lives had been forever changed by the risen Christ (Matthew 28:12, 13). Caiaphas represents those people who will not believe because they think it will cost them too much to accept Jesus as Lord. They choose the fleeting power, prestige, and pleasures of this life instead of the eternal forgiveness, direction, and life that God offers to those who receive his Son. What is your choice?

Strengths and accomplishments:
• High Priest for 18 years

Weaknesses and mistakes:
• One of those most directly responsible for Jesus' death
• Used his office as a means to power and personal security
• Planned Jesus' capture, carried out his illegal trial, forced Pilate to approve of the crucifixion, attempted to prevent the resurrection, and later tried to cover up the fact of the resurrection
• Kept up religious appearances while compromising with Rome
• Involved in the later persecution of Christians

Lessons from his life:
• God uses even the twisted motives and actions of his enemies to bring about his will
• When we cover selfish motives with spiritual objectives and words, God still sees our intentions

Vital statistics:
• Where: Jerusalem
• Occupation: High Priest
• Relatives: Father-in-law: Annas
• Contemporaries: Jesus, Pilate, Herod Antipas

Key verses:
"And one of them, Caiaphas, who was High Priest that year, said, 'You stupid idiots— let this one man die for the people—why should the whole nation perish?' " (John 11:49, 50).

11:44 Jesus raised others from the dead, including Jairus' daughter (Matthew 9:18-26; Mark 5:41; Luke 8:40-56) and a widow's son (Luke 7:11–17).

11:45–53 Even when confronted point-blank with the power of Jesus' deity, some refused to believe. These eyewitnesses even rejected him and plotted his murder. They were so hardened that they were ready to reject God's Son rather than admit they were wrong. Beware of pride. If we allow it to grow, it can lead us into enormous sin.

happen, finally believed on him. 46But some went away to the Pharisees and reported it to them.

47Then the chief priests and Pharisees convened a council to discuss the situation.

"What are we going to do?" they asked each other. "For this man certainly does miracles. 48If we let him alone the whole nation will follow him—and then the Roman army will come and kill us and take over the Jewish government."

49And one of them, Caiaphas, who was High Priest that year, said, "You stupid idiots— 50let this one man die for the people—why should the whole nation perish?"

51This prophecy that Jesus should die for the entire nation came from Caiaphas in his position as High Priest—he didn't think of it by himself, but was inspired to say it. 52It was a prediction that Jesus' death would not be for Israel only, but for all the children of God scattered around the world. 53So from that time on the Jewish leaders began plotting Jesus' death.

54Jesus now stopped his public ministry and left Jerusalem; he went to the edge of the desert, to the village of Ephraim, and stayed there with his disciples.

55The Passover, a Jewish holy day, was near, and many country people arrived in Jerusalem several days early so that they could go through the cleansing ceremony before the Passover began. 56They wanted to see Jesus, and as they gossiped in the Temple, they asked each other, "What do you think? Will he come for the Passover?" 57Meanwhile the chief priests and Pharisees had publicly announced that anyone seeing Jesus must report him immediately so that they could arrest him.

11:47
Ps 2:2
Jn 12:19
Acts 4:16

11:48
Dan 9:26,27

11:49
Mt 26:3
Lk 3:1,2
Acts 4:6

11:50
Jn 18:14

11:51
Ex 28:30
Num 27:21
Ezra 2:62,63

11:52
Isa 49:6
Jn 10:16
Acts 13:47
Gal 3:28
Eph 2:14-19; 3:6
1 Pet 5:9
1 Jn 2:2

11:53
Mt 26:3,4

11:55
Ex 19:10
2 Chron 30:17-19
Mt 26:1,2
Mk 14:1
Lk 22:1
Jn 18:28

— *A woman anoints Jesus with expensive perfume*
(182/Matthew 26:6–13; Mark 14:3–9)

12 Six days before the Passover ceremonies began, Jesus arrived in Bethany where Lazarus was—the man he had brought back to life. 2A banquet was

12:1
Jn 11:43

What was expected	What Jesus did	Reference	**GREAT EXPECTATIONS**
A man looked for healing	Jesus also forgave his sins	Mark 2:1–12	Wherever he went, Jesus exceeded people's expectations.
The disciples were expecting an ordinary day of fishing	They found the Savior	Luke 5:1–11	
A widow was resigned to bury her dead son	Jesus restored her son to life	Luke 7:11–17	
The religious leaders wanted a miracle	Jesus offered them the Creator of miracles	Matthew 12:38–45	
A woman who wanted to be healed touched Jesus	Jesus helped her see it was her faith that made her well	Mark 5:25–34	
The disciples thought the crowd should be sent home because there was no food	Jesus used a small meal to feed thousands, and there were leftovers!	John 6:1–15	
The crowds looked for a political leader to set up a new kingdom to overthrow Rome's control	Jesus offered them an eternal, spiritual Kingdom to overthrow sin's control	A theme throughout the Gospels	
The disciples wanted to eat the Passover meal with Jesus, their Master	Jesus washed their feet, showing he was also their servant	John 13:1–20	
The religious leaders wanted Jesus killed and got their wish	But Jesus rose from the dead!	John 11:53; 19:30; 20:1–29	

11:48 The Jewish leaders knew if they didn't stop Jesus, the Romans would discipline them. Rome gave partial freedom to the Jews as long as they were quiet and obedient. Jesus' miracles often caused a disturbance. The leaders feared that Rome's displeasure would cause them to lose their jobs or be punished.

12:3
Lk 10:38-41
Jn 11:1,2
12:4
Jn 6:70,71
12:6
Prov 28:20,22
Jn 13:29
1 Cor 5:10,11
6:10
Eph 5:5
1 Tim 6:9,10
12:7
Mt 26:10-13
Mk 14:8,9
Jn 19:40
12:8
Deut 15:11
Mk 14:7
12:10
Lk 16:31
12:12
Mt 21:4-9
Mk 11:7-10
Lk 19:35-38
12:13
Ps 118:26
1 Tim 1:17
12:15
Zech 9:9
12:16
Jn 2:22; 7:39

prepared in Jesus' honor. Martha served, and Lazarus sat at the table with him. ³Then Mary took a jar of costly perfume made from essence of nard, and anointed Jesus' feet with it and wiped them with her hair. And the house was filled with fragrance.

⁴But Judas Iscariot, one of his disciples—the one who would betray him—said, ⁵"That perfume was worth a fortune. It should have been sold and the money given to the poor." ⁶Not that he cared for the poor, but he was in charge of the disciples' funds and often dipped into them for his own use!

⁷Jesus replied, "Let her alone. She did it in preparation for my burial. ⁸You can always help the poor, but I won't be with you very long."

⁹When the ordinary people of Jerusalem heard of his arrival, they flocked to see him and also to see Lazarus—the man who had come back to life again. ¹⁰Then the chief priests decided to kill Lazarus too, ¹¹for it was because of him that many of the Jewish leaders had deserted and believed in Jesus as their Messiah.

Jesus rides into Jerusalem on a donkey
(183/Matthew 21:1–11; Mark 11:1–11; Luke 19:28–44)

¹²The next day, the news that Jesus was on the way to Jerusalem swept through the city, and a huge crowd of Passover visitors ¹³took palm branches and went down the road to meet him, shouting, "The Savior! God bless the King of Israel! Hail to God's Ambassador!"

¹⁴Jesus rode along on a young donkey, fulfilling the prophecy that said: ¹⁵"Don't be afraid of your King, people of Israel, for he will come to you meekly, sitting on a donkey's colt!"

¹⁶(His disciples didn't realize at the time that this was a fulfillment of prophecy;

TIME WITH THE DISCIPLES
Lazarus' return to life became the last straw for the religious leaders who were bent on killing Jesus. So Jesus stopped his public ministry and took his disciples away from Jerusalem to Ephraim. From there they returned to Galilee for a while (see the map in Luke 17:11).

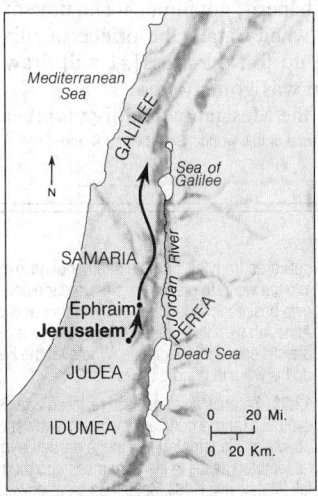

Mediterranean Sea
GALILEE
Sea of Galilee
N
SAMARIA
Jordan River
Ephraim
Jerusalem
PEREA
Dead Sea
JUDEA
IDUMEA
0   20 Mi.
0   20 Km.

was a unique act for a specific occasion—an anointing for Jesus' burial and a public declaration of faith in him as Messiah. Jesus' words should have taught Judas a valuable lesson about the worth of money. Unfortunately, he did not take heed; soon he would sell his Master's life for 30 pieces of silver.

12:10, 11 The chief priests' blindness and hardness of heart caused them to sink ever deeper into sin. They rejected the Messiah, planned to kill him, and now plotted to murder Lazarus also. One sin leads to another. From the Jewish leaders' point of view, they could accuse Jesus of blasphemy because he claimed equality with God. But Lazarus had done nothing of the kind. They wanted him dead simply because he was a living example of Jesus' power. This is a warning to us. Sin leads to more sin, a downward spiral that can be stopped only by repentance and asking for forgiveness.

12:13 We celebrate this day of Jesus' triumphal entry as Palm Sunday. Jesus entered his last week on earth riding into Jerusalem on a donkey under a canopy of palm branches, with crowds hailing him as their king. To announce that he was indeed the Messiah, Jesus chose a time when all Israel would be gathered at Jerusalem, a place where huge crowds could see him, and a way of proclaiming his mission that was unmistakable.

12:13 The people who were praising God for giving them a king had the wrong idea about Jesus. They were sure he would be a national leader who would restore their nation to its former glory, and thus they were deaf to the words of their prophets and blind to Jesus' real mission. When it became apparent that Jesus was not going to fulfill their hopes, many people turned against him.

12:16 After Jesus' resurrection, the disciples understood many of the prophecies which they had missed along the way. Jesus' words and actions took on new meaning and made more sense. In retrospect, they saw how Jesus had led them into a deeper and better understanding of his truth. Stop now and think about the events in your life leading up to where you are now. How has God led you to this point? As you grow older, you will look back and see God's involvement more clearly than you do now. Let this truth encourage you to live a life of faith today.

12:3 Nard was a fragrant ointment imported from the mountains of India. Thus it was very expensive. The amount Mary used was worth a year's wages. Nard was used to anoint kings; Mary may have been anointing Jesus as her kingly Messiah.

12:4–6 Judas often dipped into the disciples' funds for his own use. Jesus, of course, knew this, but apparently never did or said anything about it. Similarly, when we choose the way of sin, God may not immediately do anything to stop us, but this does not mean he approves our actions. What we deserve is coming.

12:5, 6 Judas used a pious phrase to hide his true motives. But Jesus knew what was in his heart. Jesus' knowledge of us should make us want to keep our actions consistent with our words.

12:7, 8 This act and Jesus' response to it do not teach us to ignore the poor so we can do extravagant things for Christ. This

but after Jesus returned to his glory in heaven, then they noticed how many prophecies of Scripture had come true before their eyes.)

17And those in the crowd who had seen Jesus call Lazarus back to life were telling all about it. 18That was the main reason why so many went out to meet him—because they had heard about this mighty miracle.

19Then the Pharisees said to each other, "We've lost. Look—the whole world has gone after him!"

Jesus explains why he must die
(185)

20Some Greeks who had come to Jerusalem to attend the Passover 21paid a visit to Philip, who was from Bethsaida, and said, "Sir, we want to meet Jesus." 22Philip told Andrew about it, and they went together to ask Jesus.

23, 24Jesus replied that the time had come for him to return to his glory in heaven, and that "I must fall and die like a kernel of wheat that falls into the furrows of the earth. Unless I die I will be alone—a single seed. But my death will produce many new wheat kernels—a plentiful harvest of new lives. 25If you love your life down here—you will lose it. If you despise your life down here—you will exchange it for eternal glory.

26"If these Greeks want to be my disciples, tell them to come and follow me, for my servants must be where I am. And if they follow me, the Father will honor them. 27Now my soul is deeply troubled. Shall I pray, 'Father, save me from what lies ahead'? But that is the very reason why I came! 28Father, bring glory and honor to your name."

Then a voice spoke from heaven saying, "I have already done this, and I will do it again." 29When the crowd heard the voice, some of them thought it was thunder, while others declared an angel had spoken to him.

30Then Jesus told them, "The voice was for your benefit, not mine. 31The time of judgment for the world has come—and the time when Satan, the prince of this world, shall be cast out. 32And when I am lifted up [on the cross], I will draw everyone to me." 33He said this to indicate how he was going to die.

34"Die?" asked the crowd. "We understood that the Messiah would live forever

12:17	Jn 11:42
12:18	Jn 12:11
12:21	Jn 1:43,44
12:23,24	Jn 13:32; 17:1 / Rom 6:4,5 / 1 Cor 15:36-45
12:25	Mt 20:39 / Lk 9:24; 17:33
12:27	Lk 12:50; 22:53
12:28	Mt 3:17; 17:5 / Mk 1:11; 9:7 / Lk 3:22; 9:35 / 2 Pet 1:17,18
12:31	Jn 14:30; 16:11 / Eph 6:12 / Heb 2:14
12:32	Jn 3:14; 6:44 / Heb 2:9
12:34	2 Sam 7:13 / Ps 89:35,36 / 110:4 / Isa 9:7 / Ezek 37:24,25 / Dan 7:14 / Mic 4:7

12:26 *If these Greeks,* literally, "If any man." **12:31** *Satan,* literally, "prince of this world." See 2 Cor 4:4 and Eph 2:2 and 6:12. **12:32** *on the cross,* implied.

12:18 The people came to Jesus because they had heard of his great miracle in raising Lazarus from the dead. Their adoration was short-lived and their commitment shallow, for in a few days they would do nothing to stop his crucifixion. Devotion based only on curiosity or popularity fades quickly.

12:20, 21 These Greeks were converts to the Jewish faith. They probably went to Philip because, though he was a Jew, he had a Greek name.

12:23–25 This is a beautiful picture of the necessary sacrifice of Jesus. Unless a grain of wheat is buried, it will not become a blade of wheat producing many more grains. Jesus died to show his power over death. His resurrection proves he has eternal life. Because of his authority as God, he can give this same eternal life to all who believe in him.

12:25 We must be so committed to living for Christ that we "hate" our lives by comparison. This does not mean that we long to die, but that we are willing to die if doing so will glorify Christ.

12:26 Many believed that Jesus came for the Jews only. But no matter who the sincere seekers are, Jesus welcomes them. His message is for everyone. Don't allow social or racial differences to become barriers to the gospel. Take the Word to all people.

12:27 Jesus knew his crucifixion lay ahead, and he dreaded it. He knew he would have to take the sins of the world on himself, and he knew this would separate him from his Father. He wanted to be delivered from this horrible death, but he knew that God sent him into the world to die for our sins, in our place. Jesus said no to his own desires in order to obey his Father and bring glory to him. Although we will never have to face such a difficult situation, we are still called to obedience. Whatever the Father asks, we should do his will and bring glory to his name.

12:31 Satan is an angel who rebelled against God. He is real, not symbolic, and is constantly working against God and those who obey him. He tempted Eve in the garden and persuaded her to sin; he tempted Jesus in the wilderness and did not persuade him to fall (Matthew 4:1–11). Satan has great power, but people can be delivered from his reign of spiritual darkness because of Christ's victory on the cross. Satan is powerful, but Jesus is much more powerful. Jesus' resurrection shattered Satan's power over death (Colossians 1:13, 14).

12:34 The crowd could not believe the Messiah would die. They were waving palm branches for a victorious Messiah who they thought would set up a political, earthly kingdom that would never end. From their reading of certain scriptural passages, they thought the Messiah would never die (Psalms 89:35, 36; 110:4; Isaiah 9:7). Other passages, however, showed that he would (Isaiah 53:5–9). Jesus' words did not fit their concept of the Messiah. First he had to suffer and die—then he would one day set up his eternal Kingdom. For what kind of Messiah, or Savior, are you looking? Beware of trying to force Jesus into your own mold—he won't fit.

12:35
Jer 13:16
Jn 8:12; 9:5
12:46

12:36
Lk 16:8
Jn 8:12; 12:46
Eph 5:8
1 Thess 5:5
1 Jn 2:9,10

and never die. Why are you saying he will die? What Messiah are you talking about?"

35Jesus replied, "My light will shine out for you just a little while longer. Walk in it while you can, and go where you want to go before the darkness falls, for then it will be too late for you to find your way. 36Make use of the Light while there is still time; then you will become light bearers." After saying these things, Jesus went away and was hidden from them.

Most of the people do not believe in Jesus
(186)

12:38
Isa 53:1
Rom 10:16
12:40
Isa 6:9,10
Mt 13:14
12:41
Isa 6:1

12:42
Jn 7:13,48
9:22,23; 12:11
12:43
Jn 5:44

37But despite all the miracles he had done, most of the people would not believe he was the Messiah. 38This is exactly what Isaiah the prophet had predicted: "Lord, who will believe us? Who will accept God's mighty miracles as proof?" 39But they couldn't believe, for as Isaiah also said: 40"God has blinded their eyes and hardened their hearts so that they can neither see nor understand nor turn to me to heal them." 41Isaiah was referring to Jesus when he made this prediction, for he had seen a vision of the Messiah's glory.

42However, even many of the Jewish leaders believed him to be the Messiah but wouldn't admit it to anyone because of their fear that the Pharisees would excommunicate them from the synagogue; 43for they loved the praise of men more than the praise of God.

Jesus summarizes his message
(187)

12:45
Jn 14:9
12:46
Jn 1:4,5,9
3:19; 8:12
9:5,39
12:47
Jn 3:17; 5:45
8:15,16
12:48
Deut 18:18,19

44Jesus shouted to the crowds, "If you trust me, you are really trusting God. 45For when you see me, you are seeing the one who sent me. 46I have come as a Light to shine in this dark world, so that all who put their trust in me will no longer wander in the darkness. 47If anyone hears me and doesn't obey me, I am not his judge—for I have come to save the world and not to judge it. 48But all who reject me and my message will be judged at the Day of Judgment by the truths I have spoken. 49For these are not my own ideas, but I have told you what the Father said to tell you. 50And I know his instructions lead to eternal life; so whatever he tells me to say, I say!"

12:36 *you will become light bearers,* literally, "sons of light."   **12:38** *Who will accept God's mighty miracles as proof?* Literally, "To whom has the arm of the Lord been revealed?" (Isa 53:1).   **12:40** *God,* literally, "He." The Greek here is a very free rendering, or paraphrase, of Isa 6:10.

12:35, 36 Jesus said he would be with them in person for only a short time, and they should take advantage of his presence while they had it. If they did this, their lives would shine with his light in places of darkness (that is, where Jesus' message had not yet been heard), revealing the truth and pointing people to God. As Christians, we are to be Christ's "light bearers," letting his light shine through our lives. How brightly is your light shining?

12:37, 38 Jesus had performed many miracles, but most people still didn't believe in him. Likewise, many today won't believe despite all God does. Don't be discouraged if your witness for Christ doesn't turn as many to him as you'd like. Your job is to continue as a faithful witness. You are not responsible for the decisions of others, but simply to reach out to others.

12:40 People in Jesus' time, like those in Isaiah's time, would not believe despite the evidence (12:37). As a result, Jesus says, God "hardened their hearts." Does that mean God intentionally prevented these people from believing in him? No, he simply confirmed that they had chosen a lifetime of resisting God and had become so set in their ways that they wouldn't even try to understand Jesus' message. For such people, it is virtually impossible to come to God—their hearts have been permanently hardened. Other instances of hardened hearts because of constant stubbornness are recorded in Exodus 9:12, Romans 1:24–28, and 2 Thessalonians 2:8–12.

12:42, 43 Along with those who refused to believe, many believed but refused to admit it. This is just as bad, and Jesus had strong words for such people (see Matthew 10:32, 33). People who do this are afraid of rejection or ridicule from others. Many Jewish leaders wouldn't admit faith in Jesus because they feared excommunication from the Temple (which was their livelihood) and loss of their prestigious place in the community. But the praise of others is fickle and shortlived. We should be concerned much more about God's eternal acceptance than the temporary approval of other people.

12:45 We often wonder what God is like. How can we know the Creator when he doesn't make himself visible? Jesus said plainly that those who know what he is like know what God is like, because he *is* God. If you want to know what God is like, study the person and words of Jesus Christ.

12:48 The purpose of Jesus' first mission on earth was not to judge people, but to show them the way to find salvation and eternal life. When he comes again, one of his main purposes will be to judge people for how they lived on earth. On the Day of Judgment, those who lived Jesus' way will be raised to eternal life (1 Corinthians 15:51–57; 1 Thessalonians 4:15–18; Revelation 21:1–8), and those who rejected Jesus and lived any way they pleased will face eternal punishment (Revelation 20:11–15). Decide now which side you'll be on, for the consequences of your decision last forever.

C. DEATH AND RESURRECTION OF JESUS, THE SON OF GOD (13:1—21:25)

John begins his Gospel with eternity and ends with Jesus coming to earth again. He features Jesus teaching his disciples privately just before his arrest and death. We see, clearly, the deep love Jesus has for the believer, and the peace that comes from faith. Knowing the love Jesus has for believers, we too should believe and allow Jesus to forgive our sins. Only then will we experience peace in a world filled with turmoil.

1. Jesus teaches his disciples

Jesus washes the disciples' feet
(210)

13 Jesus knew on the evening of Passover Day that it would be his last night on earth before returning to his Father. During supper the devil had already suggested to Judas Iscariot, Simon's son, that this was the night to carry out his plan to betray Jesus. Jesus knew that the Father had given him everything and that he had come from God and would return to God. And how he loved his disciples! ⁴So he got up from the supper table, took off his robe, wrapped a towel around his loins, ⁵poured water into a basin, and began to wash the disciples' feet and to wipe them with the towel he had around him.

⁶When he came to Simon Peter, Peter said to him, "Master, you shouldn't be washing our feet like this!"

⁷Jesus replied, "You don't understand now why I am doing it; some day you will."

⁸"No," Peter protested, "you shall never wash my feet!"

"But if I don't, you can't be my partner," Jesus replied.

⁹Simon Peter exclaimed, "Then wash my hands and head as well—not just my feet!"

¹⁰Jesus replied, "One who has bathed all over needs only to have his feet washed to be entirely clean. Now you are clean—but that isn't true of everyone here." ¹¹For Jesus knew who would betray him. That is what he meant when he said, "Not all of you are clean."

¹²After washing their feet he put on his robe again and sat down and asked, "Do you understand what I was doing? ¹³You call me 'Master' and 'Lord,' and you do well to say it, for it is true. ¹⁴And since I, the Lord and Teacher, have washed your feet, you ought to wash each other's feet. ¹⁵I have given you an example to follow: do as I have done to you. ¹⁶How true it is that a servant is not greater than his master. Nor is the messenger more important than the one who sends him. ¹⁷You know these things—now do them! That is the path of blessing.

¹⁸"I am not saying these things to all of you; I know so well each one of you I chose. The Scripture declares, 'One who eats supper with me will betray me,' and this will soon come true. ¹⁹I tell you this now so that when it happens, you will believe on me.

13:1
Jn 3:35; 16:28
17:2
1 Cor 15:27
13:2
Lk 22:3
Jn 6:70,71
13:4
Lk 12:37; 22:27
13:5
Lk 7:44
13:8
Ps 51:2,7
Isa 52:14,15
Ezek 36:25
Jn 3:5
Acts 2:38
1 Cor 6:11
Eph 5:26
Tit 3:5
Heb 9:13,14
10:22
13:10
Ex 29:4
30:18-21; 40:12
Jn 15:3
13:11
Jn 6:64; 13:2
13:12
Jn 13:4
13:13
1 Cor 8:6; 12:3
13:14
Lk 22:27
Rom 12:10
1 Pet 5:5
13:15
Phil 2:5-7
1 Pet 5:3-5
1 Jn 2:6
13:17
Jas 1:25
13:18
Ps 41:9
2 Tim 2:19

13:1ff Chapters 13—17 tell us what Jesus said to his disciples the night before his death. These words were all spoken in one evening when, with only the disciples as his audience, he gave final instructions to comfort and prepare them for his death and resurrection, events that would change their lives forever.

13:1-3 For more information on Judas Iscariot, see his Profile in Mark 14.

13:1-17 Jesus was the model servant, and he showed this attitude to his disciples. Washing guests' feet was a job for a household servant when guests arrived. But Jesus wrapped a towel around him, as the lowliest slave would do, and washed his disciples' feet. If even he, God in the flesh, is willing to serve, we his followers must also be servants, willing to serve in any way in order to glorify God. Are you willing to follow Christ's example of serving? Whom can you serve today?

13:3 There is a deep truth in the simple phrase, "And how he loved his disciples!" Jesus knew he would be betrayed by one of them and denied by another, and that all of them would desert him

for a time. Still he loved them. God knows us completely, as Jesus knew his disciples. He knows the sins we have committed and the ones we will yet commit. Still, he loves us. How do you respond to that kind of love?

13:6, 7 Imagine being Peter and watching Jesus wash the others' feet, moving closer to you. Seeing his Master behave like a slave must have confused him. But Jesus graphically explained that to be his disciple, Peter had to follow his example. To be a leader, he must be a servant. This is not a comfortable passage for many people with leadership responsibilities who find it hard to serve those under them. How do you treat those who work under you (whether children, employees, or volunteers)?

13:12 Jesus did not wash his disciples' feet just to get them to be nice to each other. His far greater goal was to extend his mission on earth after he was gone. They were to move into the world serving God, serving each other, and serving all people to whom they took the message of salvation.

13:20
Mt 10:40
Lk 10:16

20"Truly, anyone welcoming my messenger is welcoming me. And to welcome me is to welcome the Father who sent me."

Jesus and the disciples have the Last Supper
(211/Matthew 26:20–29; Mark 14:17–25; Luke 22:14–30)

13:21
Mt 26:20-25
Mk 14:18-21
Lk 22:21-23

13:23
Jn 19:26

13:25
Jn 21:20

21Now Jesus was in great anguish of spirit and exclaimed, "Yes, it is true—one of you will betray me." 22The disciples looked at each other, wondering whom he could mean. 23Since I was sitting next to Jesus at the table, being his closest friend, 24Simon Peter motioned to me to ask him who it was who would do this terrible deed.

25So I turned and asked him, "Lord, who is it?"

13:23 *Since I*, literally, "There was one at the table." All commentators believe him to be John, the writer of this book. *was sitting next*, literally, "reclining on Jesus' bosom." The custom of the period was to recline around the table, leaning on the left elbow. John, next to Jesus, was at his side.   **13:25** *So I turned*, literally, "leaning back against Jesus' chest," to whisper his inquiry.

JOHN

Being loved is the most powerful motivation in the world! Our ability to love is often shaped by our experience of love. We usually love others as we have been loved.

Some of the greatest statements about God's loving nature were written by a man who experienced God's love in a unique way. John, Jesus' disciple, expressed his relationship to the Son of God by calling himself "the disciple Jesus loved" (John 21:20). Although Jesus' love is clearly communicated in all the Gospels, in John's Gospel it is a central theme. Because his own experience of Jesus' love was so strong and personal, John was sensitive to those words and actions of Jesus that illustrated how the One, who *is* love, loved others.

Jesus knew John fully and loved him fully. He gave John and his brother James the nickname "Sons of Thunder," perhaps from an occasion when the brothers asked Jesus for permission to "order fire down from heaven" (Luke 9:54) on a village that had refused to welcome Jesus and the disciples. In this Gospel and his letters, we see the great God of love, while the thunder of God's justice bursts from the pages of Revelation.

Jesus confronts each of us as he confronted John. We cannot know the depth of his love unless we are willing to face the fact that he knows us completely. Otherwise we are fooled into believing he must love the people we pretend to be, not the sinners we actually are. John and all the disciples convince us that God is able and willing to accept us as we are. Realizing his love is a great motivator for change. His love is not given in exchange for our efforts; his love frees us to really live. Have you accepted that love?

Strengths and accomplishments:
• Before following Jesus, one of John the Baptist's disciples
• One of the 12 disciples and, with Peter and James, one of the inner three, closest to Jesus
• Wrote five New Testament books: the Gospel of John; 1, 2, and 3 John; and Revelation

Weaknesses and mistakes:
• Along with James, shared a tendency to outbursts of selfishness and anger
• Asked for a special position in Jesus' kingdom

Lessons from his life:
• Those who realize how much they are loved are able to love much
• When God changes a life, he does not take away personality characteristics, but puts them to effective use in his service

Vital statistics:
• Occupation: Fisherman, disciple
• Relatives: Father: Zebedee. Mother: Salome. Brother: James.
• Contemporaries: Jesus, Pilate, Herod

Key verses:
"Dear brothers, I am not writing out a new rule for you to obey, for it is an old one you have always had, right from the start. You have heard it all before. Yet it is always new, and works for you just as it did for Christ; and as we obey this commandment, *to love one another*, the darkness in our lives disappears and the new light of life in Christ shines in" (1 John 2:7, 8).

John's story is told throughout the Gospels, Acts, and Revelation.

26He told me, "It is the one I honor by giving the bread dipped in the sauce." And when he had dipped it, he gave it to Judas, son of Simon Iscariot.

27As soon as Judas had eaten it, Satan entered into him. Then Jesus told him, "Hurry—do it now."

28None of the others at the table knew what Jesus meant. 29Some thought that since Judas was their treasurer, Jesus was telling him to go and pay for the food or to give some money to the poor. 30Judas left at once, going out into the night.

Jesus predicts Peter's denial
(212/Luke 22:31–38)

31As soon as Judas left the room, Jesus said, "My time has come; the glory of God will soon surround me—and God shall receive great praise because of all that happens to me. 32And God shall give me his own glory, and this so very soon. 33Dear, dear children, how brief are these moments before I must go away and leave you! Then, though you search for me, you cannot come to me—just as I told the Jewish leaders.

34"And so I am giving a new commandment to you now—love each other just as much as I love you. 35Your strong love for each other will prove to the world that you are my disciples."

36Simon Peter said, "Master, where are you going?"

And Jesus replied, "You can't go with me now; but you will follow me later."

37"But why can't I come now?" he asked, "for I am ready to die for you."

38Jesus answered, "Die for me? No—three times before the cock crows tomorrow morning, you will deny that you even know me!

Jesus is the way to the Father
(213)

14 "Let not your heart be troubled. You are trusting God, now trust in me. 2, 3There are many homes up there where my Father lives, and I am going to prepare them for your coming. When everything is ready, then I will come and get

13:26
Jn 6:71
13:27
Lk 22:3
13:29
Jn 12:6
13:30
Lk 22:53
13:31,32
Lk 24:26
Jn 12:23; 17:1,5
1 Cor 15:42
Heb 5:5
13:33
Jn 7:33,34
13:34
Lev 19:18
Eph 5:2
1 Thess 4:9
Heb 13:1
Jas 2:8
1 Pet 1:22
1 Jn 2:8; 3:11
4:20,21
13:35
Acts 2:44-46
13:36
Jn 14:2; 21:18
2 Pet 1:13,14
14:2
Ps 90:1
Jn 2:16,19-21
14:6

13:26 The honored guest at a meal was singled out in this way.

13:27 Satan's part in the betrayal of Jesus does not remove any of the responsibility from Judas. Disillusioned because Jesus was talking about dying rather than setting up his Kingdom, Judas may have been trying to force his hand and make him use his power to prove he was the Messiah. Or perhaps Judas, not understanding Jesus' mission, no longer believed he was God's chosen one. Whatever Judas thought, Satan assumed that Jesus' death would end his mission and thwart God's plan. Like Judas, he did not know Jesus' death was the most important part of God's plan all along.

13:27-38 John describes these few moments in clear detail. We can see that Jesus knew exactly what was going to happen. He knew about Judas and about Peter, but he did not change the situation, nor did he stop loving them. In the same way, Jesus knows exactly what you will do to hurt him at certain times in your life. Yet he still loves you unconditionally and will forgive you whenever you ask for it. Judas couldn't understand this, and his life ended tragically. Peter understood, and despite his shortcomings, his life ended triumphantly because he never let go of his faith.

13:34, 35 Jesus says that our Christlike love will prove we are his disciples. Do people see petty bickering, jealousy, and division in your church? Or do they know you are Jesus' followers by your love for one another?

13:34 To love others was not a new commandment (see Leviticus 19:18), but to love others as much as Christ loved others was revolutionary. Now we are to love others based on Jesus' sacrificial love for us. Such love will not only bring unbelievers to Christ; it will also keep believers strong and united in a world hostile to God.

Jesus was a living example of God's love, as we are to be living examples of Jesus' love.

13:35 Love is not simply warm feelings; it is instead an attitude that reveals itself in action. How can we love others as Christ loves us? By helping when it's not convenient, by giving when it hurts, by devoting energy to others' welfare rather than our own, by absorbing hurts from others without complaining or fighting back. This kind of loving is hard to do. That is why people will notice when you do it and will know you are empowered by a supernatural source. The Bible has another beautiful description of love in 1 Corinthians 13.

13:37, 38 Peter proudly told Jesus that he was ready to die for him. But Jesus corrected him. He knew Peter would deny him that very night to protect himself (18:25–27). In our enthusiasm, it is easy to make promises, but God knows the extent of our commitment. Paul tells us to be honest in our estimates of ourselves (Romans 12:3). Instead of bragging, show your commitment step by step as you grow in your knowledge of God's Word and in your faith.

14:1-3 Jesus' words show that the unseen way to eternal life is not an unsure way. Heaven is as certain as your trust in Jesus. He has already prepared the way to eternal life—that is sure. The only unsettled issue is your willingness to believe.

14:2, 3 There are few verses in Scripture that describe eternal life, but they are rich with promises. Here Jesus says, "I *am going* to prepare," and "*When* everything is ready, then *I will come and get you.*" We can look forward to eternal life because Jesus has promised it to all who believe in him. Although the details of eternity are unknown, we need not fear, because Jesus is preparing for us and will spend eternity with us.

14:3
Jn 10:38
14:10,11,18,20
16:16,19-22
17:21-24

14:6
Jn 1:4,14,16
8:32; 10:9,10
11:25
Rom 5:2
Eph 2:18
Heb 10:20
1 Jn 5:20

14:7
Jn 6:46; 8:19
1 Jn 2:13

14:9
Jn 1:14,18
12:45
2 Cor 4:4
Col 1:15
Heb 1:3

14:10
Jn 5:19; 10:38
17:11,21-24

14:12
Acts 5:15
19:11,12

14:16
Jn 14:26; 15:26

14:17
Rom 8:15,16
1 Jn 3:24

14:18
Rom 8:9-11
2 Cor 3:17,18

you, so that you can always be with me where I am. If this weren't so, I would tell you plainly. ⁴And you know where I am going and how to get there."

⁵"No, we don't," Thomas said. "We haven't any idea where you are going, so how can we know the way?"

⁶Jesus told him, "I am the Way—yes, and the Truth and the Life. No one can get to the Father except by means of me. ⁷If you had known who I am, then you would have known who my Father is. From now on you know him—and have seen him!"

⁸Philip said, "Sir, show us the Father and we will be satisfied."

⁹Jesus replied, "Don't you even yet know who I am, Philip, even after all this time I have been with you? Anyone who has seen me has seen the Father! So why are you asking to see him? ¹⁰Don't you believe that I am in the Father and the Father is in me? The words I say are not my own but are from my Father who lives in me. And he does his work through me. ¹¹Just believe it—that I am in the Father and the Father is in me. Or else believe it because of the mighty miracles you have seen me do.

¹²,¹³"In solemn truth I tell you, anyone believing in me shall do the same miracles I have done, and even greater ones, because I am going to be with the Father. You can ask him for *anything,* using my name, and I will do it, for this will bring praise to the Father because of what I, the Son, will do for you. ¹⁴Yes, ask *anything,* using my name, and I will do it!

Jesus promises the Holy Spirit
(214)

¹⁵,¹⁶"If you love me, obey me; and I will ask the Father and he will give you another Comforter, and he will never leave you. ¹⁷He is the Holy Spirit, the Spirit who leads into all truth. The world at large cannot receive him, for it isn't looking for him and doesn't recognize him. But you do, for he lives with you now and some day shall be in you. ¹⁸No, I will not abandon you or leave you as orphans in the storm—I will come to you. ¹⁹In just a little while I will be gone from the world, but

---

14:4-6 This is one of the most basic and important passages in Scripture. It asks, "How can I find God?" and answers, "Only through Jesus." Jesus is the Way because he is both God and man. By uniting our lives with his, we are united with God. Trust Jesus to take you to the Father, and all the benefits of being God's child will be yours.

14:6 Jesus says he is the *only* way to God the Father. Some people may argue that this is too narrow. In reality, it is wide enough for the whole world, if the world chooses to accept it. Instead of worrying about how limited it sounds to have only one way, we should be saying, "Thank you God, for providing a sure way to get to you!"

14:6 Jesus says he is "the Way, the Truth, and the Life." As the Way, he is our path to the Father. As the Truth, he is the reality of all God's promises. As the Life, he joins his divine life to ours, both now and eternally.

14:9 Jesus is the visible, tangible image of the invisible God. He is the complete revelation of what God is like. Jesus explained to Philip, who wanted to *see* the Father, that to know Jesus is to know God. The search for God, for truth and reality, ends in Christ. (See also Colossians 1:15; Hebrews 1:1-4.)

14:12, 13 Jesus is not saying that his disciples will do more amazing miracles—after all, raising the dead is about as amazing as you can get. Rather, the disciples, working in the power of the Holy Spirit, would carry the Good News of God's Kingdom out of Palestine and into the whole world.

14:14 When Jesus says we can ask for anything, we must remember that our asking must be in his name—meaning according to God's character and will. God will not grant requests contrary to his nature or his will, and we cannot use his name as a magic formula to fulfill our selfish desires. If we are sincerely

following God and seeking his will for us, then our requests will be in line with what he wants, and he will grant them.

14:15, 16 The disciples must have been perplexed, wondering how Jesus could leave them and still be with them. The Comforter—the Spirit of God himself—would come after Jesus was gone to care for and guide the disciples. This happened at Pentecost (Acts 2), shortly after Jesus ascended to heaven. The Holy Spirit is the very presence of God within us and all believers, helping us live as God wants.

14:16 The word for *Comforter* combines the ideas of comfort and counsel. The Holy Spirit is a powerful person on our side, working for and with us.

14:17 The following chapters teach these truths about the Holy Spirit: he will never leave us (14:16); he leads us into all truth (14:17); the world at large cannot recognize him (14:17); he lives with us and in us (14:17); he teaches us (14:26); he reminds us of Jesus' words (14:26; 15:26); he is the source of all truth (15:26); he convinces us of sin, the availability of God's goodness, and the certainty of God's judgment (16:8); he gives insight into future events (16:13); he shows Christ's glory (16:14). The Holy Spirit has been active among people from the beginning of time, but after Pentecost (Acts 2), he came to live in all believers.

14:19-21 Sometimes people wish they knew the future so they could prepare for it. God has chosen not to give us this knowledge—he alone knows what will happen. But he tells us all we need to know to *prepare* for the future: when we live by his standards, he will not leave us; he will come to us; he will be within us; and he will reveal himself to us. God knows what will happen, and, because he will be with us through it, we need not fear. We don't have to know the future to have faith in God; we have to have faith in God to be secure about our future.

I will still be present with you. For I will live again—and you will too. 20When I come back to life again, you will know that I am in my Father, and you in me, and I in you. 21The one who obeys me is the one who loves me; and because he loves me, my Father will love him; and I will too, and I will reveal myself to him."

22Judas (not Judas Iscariot, but his other disciple with that name) said to him, "Sir, why are you going to reveal yourself only to us disciples and not to the world at large?"

23Jesus replied, "Because I will only reveal myself to those who love me and obey me. The Father will love them too, and we will come to them and live with them. 24Anyone who doesn't obey me doesn't love me. And remember, I am not making up this answer to your question! It is the answer given by the Father who sent me.

25"I am telling you these things now while I am still with you. 26But when the Father sends the Comforter instead of me—and by the Comforter I mean the Holy Spirit—he will teach you much, as well as remind you of everything I myself have told you.

27"I am leaving you with a gift—peace of mind and heart! And the peace I give isn't fragile like the peace the world gives. So don't be troubled or afraid. 28Remember what I told you—I am going away, but I will come back to you again. If you really love me, you will be very happy for me, for now I can go to the Father, who is greater than I am. 29I have told you these things before they happen so that when they do, you will believe [in me].

30"I don't have much more time to talk to you, for the evil prince of this world approaches. He has no power over me, 31but I will freely do what the Father requires of me so that the world will know that I love the Father. Come, let's be going.

Jesus teaches about the Vine and the branches
(215)

15 "I am the true Vine, and my Father is the Gardener. 2He lops off every branch that doesn't produce. And he prunes those branches that bear fruit

14:26 *the Comforter,* or, "helper." *instead of me,* literally, "in my name."   **14:27** *So don't be troubled or afraid,* implied.   **14:29** *in me,* implied.

Cross-references

14:20
Jn 10:38,15:4,5
16:16,23
17:21-24

14:21
Prov 8:17
Jn 15:10; 16:27
1 Jn 2:5
2 Jn 6

14:22
Lk 6:14-16
Acts 10:40

14:23
Ps 91:1
Jn 15:10
Eph 3:17
1 Jn 4:16; 5:3
Rev 3:20; 21:3

14:24
Jn 7:16; 14:10

14:26
Lk 24:49
Jn 1:33; 15:26
16:7; 20:22
1 Jn 2:20,27

14:27
Jn 16:33; 20:19
Phil 4:7
Col 3:15

14:28
1 Cor 11:3

14:29
Jn 13:19

14:30
Jn 12:31
Heb 4:15

14:31
Jn 10:18; 12:49

15:1
Ps 80:8
Isa 5:1-7

14:21 Jesus said that his followers show their love by obeying God. Love is more than lovely words; it is commitment and conduct. If you love Christ, then prove it by obeying what he says in his Word.

14:22, 23 Because the disciples were still expecting the Messiah to establish an earthly kingdom and to overthrow Rome, they found it hard to understand why Jesus did not tell the world at large that he was the Messiah. Ever since Pentecost, the Good News of the Kingdom has been proclaimed in the whole world. Not everyone is receptive to it, however. Jesus saves the deepest revelations of himself for those who love and obey him.

14:26 Jesus promised the disciples that the Holy Spirit would help them remember what he had been teaching them. This promise underscores the validity of the New Testament. The disciples were eyewitnesses of Jesus' life and teachings, and the Holy Spirit helped them remember without taking away their individual perspective. We can be confident that the Gospels are accurate records of what Jesus taught and did (see 1 Corinthians 2:10–14).

14:27 The result of the Holy Spirit's work in our lives is deep and lasting peace. Unlike worldly peace, which is usually defined as the absence of conflict, this peace is confident assurance in any circumstance; with this kind of peace, we have no need to fear the present or the future. If your life is full of stress, allow God to fill you with his true peace (see Philippians 4:6, 7 for more on experiencing God's peace).

14:27–29 Sin, fear, uncertainty, doubt, and numerous other forces are at war within us. The peace of God moves into our hearts and lives to restrain these hostile forces and offer comfort in place of conflict. Jesus said he will give us that peace if we are willing to accept it from him.

14:28 As God the Son, Jesus willingly submits to God the Father. On earth, Jesus also submitted to many of the physical limitations of being human.

14:30, 31 Although Satan was unable to overpower Jesus (Matthew 4), he still had the arrogance to try. Satan's power exists only because God allows him to act. But because Jesus is sinless, Satan has no power or claim over him. The more you obey Jesus and align yourself with God's purposes, the less power Satan will have over you.

14:31 "Come, let's be going" suggests that chapters 15—17 were probably spoken en route to the Garden of Gethsemane. Another view is that Jesus was asking the disciples to get ready to leave the Upper Room, but they did not actually do so until 18:1.

15:1ff Christ is the Vine, and God is the Gardener who cares for the branches to make them fruitful. The branches are all who claim to be followers of Christ. The fruitful branches are true believers who by their living union with Christ produce much fruit. But those who become unproductive will be separated from the Vine—such are the people who have turned back from Christ after making a superficial commitment. The unproductive followers are as good as dead and will be cut off and cast aside.

15:1 The grapevine is a prolific plant; a single vine bears many grapes. In the Old Testament, grapes were a symbol of Israel's fruitfulness in doing God's work on the earth (Psalm 80:8; Isaiah

15:3
Jn 17:17

15:4
Jn 6:56; 14:20
1 Jn 4:12,13

for even larger crops. 3He has already tended you by pruning you back for greater strength and usefulness by means of the commands I gave you. 4Take care to live in me, and let me live in you. For a branch can't produce fruit when severed from the vine. Nor can you be fruitful apart from me.

15:5
Hos 14:8

15:6
Mt 3:10; 7:19
Heb 6:4-6

15:8
Mt 5:15,16

15:9
Jn 3:35
17:23-26

15:10
Jn 8:29
14:15,16,31

15:11
Jn 16:24; 17:13
1 Jn 1:4

15:12
1 Thess 4:9
1 Pet 4:8
1 Jn 3:11

15:13
Jn 10:11
Rom 5:6-8
Eph 5:2

5"Yes, I am the Vine; you are the branches. Whoever lives in me and I in him shall produce a large crop of fruit. For apart from me you can't do a thing. 6If anyone separates from me, he is thrown away like a useless branch, withers, and is gathered into a pile with all the others and burned. 7But if you stay in me and obey my commands, you may ask any request you like, and it will be granted! 8My true disciples produce bountiful harvests. This brings great glory to my Father.

9"I have loved you even as the Father has loved me. Live within my love. 10When you obey me you are living in my love, just as I obey my Father and live in his love. 11I have told you this so that you will be filled with my joy. Yes, your cup of joy will overflow! 12I demand that you love each other as much as I love you. 13And here is how to measure it—the greatest love is shown when a person lays down his life for his friends; 14and you are my friends if you obey me. 15I no longer call you slaves, for a master doesn't confide in his slaves; now you are my friends, proved by the fact that I have told you everything the Father told me.

16"You didn't choose me! I chose you! I appointed you to go and produce lovely fruit always, so that no matter what you ask for from the Father, using my name, he will give it to you.

Jesus warns about the world's hatred (216)

15:18
Jn 7:7
1 Jn 3:1,13

15:19
Mt 10:22; 24:9
Jn 17:14
1 Jn 4:5,6

17I demand that you love each other, 18for you get enough hate from the world! But then, it hated me before it hated you. 19The world would love you if you belonged to it; but you don't—for I chose you to come out of the world, and so it hates you. 20Do you remember what I told you? 'A slave isn't greater than his master!' So since they persecuted me, naturally they will persecute you. And if

---

5:1–7; Ezekiel 19:10–14). In the Passover meal, the fruit of the vine was a symbol of God's goodness to his people.

15:2, 3 Jesus makes a distinction between two kinds of pruning: (1) separating (15:2), and (2) cutting back branches (15:3). Fruitful branches are cut back to promote growth. In other words, God must sometimes discipline us to strengthen our character and faith. But branches that don't bear fruit are cut off at the trunk—they are not only worthless, they often infect the rest of the tree. Those who won't bear fruit for God or who try to block the efforts of God's followers will be cut off from the divine flow of life.

15:5 Fruit is not limited to soul-winning. In this chapter, prayer, joy, and love are mentioned as fruit (15:7, 11, 12). Galatians 5:22, 23 and 2 Peter 1:5-8 describe additional fruit. These are qualities of the Christian character.

15:5, 6 Living in Christ means: (1) believing he is God's Son (1 John 4:15), (2) receiving him as Savior and Lord (John 1:12), (3) doing what God says (1 John 3:24), (4) continuing in faith (1 John 2:24), and (5) relating to the community of believers, Christ's body.

15:5–8 Many people try to do good, be honest, and do what is right. But Jesus says the only way to live a truly good life is to stay close to him, like a branch attached to the vine. Apart from him our efforts are unfruitful. Are you receiving the nourishment and life offered by Christ, the Vine? If not, you are missing a special gift he has for you.

15:8 A rich harvest honors the harvester, for he has gathered the fruits. The harvest also honors the sower and the caretaker, for without them there would be nothing to harvest. Most of all, the harvest honors God, the Lord of the harvest, for daily he sent the sunshine and rain to make the crops grow. Even when the sower and caretaker slept, he nurtured each tiny plant and prepared it to blossom. What a moment of glory for the Lord of the harvest when the harvest is brought into the barns, safe and ready for use! He

made it all happen! This farming analogy shows how God is glorified when Jesus' disciples bring people into a right relationship with him. We who harvest people for his Kingdom may be honored, but the Lord is glorified!

15:11 When things are going well, we feel elated. When hardships come, we sink into depression. But true joy transcends these waves of circumstance. Joy comes from a consistent relationship with Jesus Christ. When our lives are intertwined with his, he will help us walk through adversity without sinking into lows and manage prosperity without moving into deceptive highs. The joy of living with Jesus Christ daily keeps us levelheaded no matter how high or low our circumstances.

15:12, 13 We are to love one another as Jesus loved us, and he loved us enough to give his life for us. We may not have to die for someone, but there are other ways we can demonstrate our sacrificial love for others: listening, helping, encouraging, giving. Think of someone in particular who needs this kind of love today. Give all the love you can, and then try to give a little more.

15:15 Because Jesus Christ is Lord and Master, he should call us slaves, but instead he calls us friends. Because he is Lord and Master, our obedience should be unqualified and blind, but Jesus asks us to obey him because we love him (14:23, 24).

15:16 Jesus made the first choice—to love and to die for us, to invite us to live with him forever. We make the next choice—to accept or reject his offer. Without *his* choice, we would have no choice to make.

15:17, 18 Christians will get plenty of hatred from the world; from each other we need love and support. Do you allow small problems to get in the way of loving other believers? Jesus commands that you love them, and he will give you the strength to do it.

they had listened to me, they would listen to you! ²¹The people of the world will persecute you because you belong to me, for they don't know God who sent me.

²²"They would not be guilty if I had not come and spoken to them. But now they have no excuse for their sin. ²³Anyone hating me is also hating my Father. ²⁴If I hadn't done such mighty miracles among them they would not be counted guilty. But as it is, they saw these miracles and yet they hated both of us—me and my Father. ²⁵This has fulfilled what the prophets said concerning the Messiah, 'They hated me without reason.'

²⁶"But I will send you the Comforter—the Holy Spirit, the source of all truth. He will come to you from the Father and will tell you all about me. ²⁷And you also must tell everyone about me, because you have been with me from the beginning.

16 "I have told you these things so that you won't be staggered [by all that lies ahead]. ²For you will be excommunicated from the synagogues, and indeed the time is coming when those who kill you will think they are doing God a service. ³This is because they have never known the Father or me. ⁴Yes, I'm telling you these things now so that when they happen you will remember I warned you. I didn't tell you earlier because I was going to be with you for a while longer.

— *Jesus teaches about the Holy Spirit*
(217)

⁵"But now I am going away to the one who sent me; and none of you seems interested in the purpose of my going; none wonders why. ⁶Instead you are only filled with sorrow. ⁷But the fact of the matter is that it is best for you that I go away, for if I don't, the Comforter won't come. If I do, he will—for I will send him to you.

⁸"And when he has come he will convince the world of its sin, and of the availability of God's goodness, and of deliverance from judgment. ⁹The world's sin is unbelief in me; ¹⁰there is righteousness available because I go to the Father and you shall see me no more; ¹¹there is deliverance from judgment because the prince of this world has already been judged.

¹²"Oh, there is so much more I want to tell you, but you can't understand it now. ¹³When the Holy Spirit, who is truth, comes, he shall guide you into all truth, for

15:21	Jn 17:25; 1 Pet 4:14
15:22	Jn 9:41
15:24	Jn 5:36-38; 10:37,38
15:25	Ps 35:19; 69:4
15:26	Jn 14:15-17,26; Acts 2:33
15:27	Jn 19:35; 21:24; 1 Jn 1:1,2
16:2	Acts 8:1; 9:1; 26:9; Rev 6:9
16:3	Acts 3:17
16:4	Jn 13:19; 14:29
16:5	Jn 7:33; 13:36
16:7	Jn 14:26
16:8	1 Pet 1:2
16:9	Rom 1:18-23; 3:9,10; 14:23
16:10	Acts 3:14; 7:52
16:11	Lk 10:18; Jn 12:31; Heb 2:14
16:13	Jn 14:26

16:1 *by all that lies ahead,* implied. 16:5 *none wonders why,* literally, "none of you is asking me whither I am going." 16:8 *of deliverance from judgment,* literally, "he will convict the world of sin and righteousness and judgment."

15:25–27 Once again Jesus offers hope. The Holy Spirit gives strength to endure the hatred and evil in our world and the hostility many have toward Christ. This is especially comforting for those facing persecution.

15:26 Jesus uses two names for the Holy Spirit—*Comforter* and *the source of all truth.* The word *Comforter* conveys the helping, encouraging, and strengthening work of the Spirit. *Source of all truth* points to the teaching, illuminating, and reminding work of the Spirit. If we tend to emphasize one dimension over the other, we should remember that he both comforts and teaches us, so both dimensions are important.

16:1–16 In his last moments with his disciples, Jesus (1) warned them about further persecution, (2) told them where he was going, when he was leaving, and why, and (3) assured them they would not be left alone, but that the Spirit would come. He knew what lay ahead, and he did not want their faith shaken or destroyed. God wants you to know you are not alone in the world. You have the Holy Spirit to comfort you, teach you truth, and help you.

16:2 A vivid fulfillment of this prediction happened when Stephen was expelled from the synagogue and was stoned to death (Acts 7:57–60). Saul (who later became Paul), under the direction of the High Priest, went through the land hunting down and persecuting Christians (Acts 9:1).

16:5 Although the disciples had asked Jesus about his death (13:36; 14:5), they had never wondered about its meaning. They were mostly concerned about themselves. If Jesus went, what would become of them?

16:7 Unless Jesus did what he came to do, there would be no gospel. If he did not die, he could not remove our sins; if he did not die, he could not rise again and defeat death. If he did not go back to the Father, the Holy Spirit would not come. Christ's presence on earth was limited to one place at a time. His leaving meant he could be present to the whole world through the Holy Spirit.

16:9 According to Jesus, unbelief in him is *sin.*

16:8–11 Three important tasks of the Holy Spirit are (1) convincing the world of its sin, (2) showing the availability of God's righteousness to anyone who believes, and (3) demonstrating Christ's judgment over Satan.

16:10, 11 Christ's death on the cross made a personal relationship with God available to us. When we confess our sin, God declares us righteous and delivers us from judgment for our sins.

16:13 Jesus said the Holy Spirit would tell the disciples about the future—the nature of their mission, the opposition they would face, and the final outcome of their efforts. They didn't fully understand these promises until the Holy Spirit came after Jesus' death and

16:14
Phil 1:19

16:15
Mt 11:27
Jn 17:10
Col 2:9,10

16:16
Jn 14:3,19-25

he will not be presenting his own ideas, but will be passing on to you what he has heard. He will tell you about the future. 14He shall praise me and bring me great honor by showing you my glory. 15All the Father's glory is mine; this is what I mean when I say that he will show you my glory.

16"In just a little while I will be gone, and you will see me no more; but just a little while after that, and you will see me again!" *Cover of Christ.*

Jesus teaches about using his name in prayer
(218)

17, 18"Whatever is he saying?" some of his disciples asked. "What is this about 'going to the Father'? We don't know what he means."

16:20
Mk 16:10
Lk 23:27
Jn 20:19,20

16:21
Isa 26:16-19
Acts 13:33
Col 1:18

16:22
Jn 20:19,20

16:23
Jn 14:20
15:16; 16:26

16:24
Jn 15:11

16:25
Jn 10:6; 16:29

16:27
Jn 8:42; 14:21
17:8

16:28
Jn 1:14
6:32,46
8:42; 13:1,3
17:11,13

16:32
Zech 13:7
Mt 26:31
Jn 8:29

16:33
Jn 14:27
Acts 14:22
Rom 5:1; 8:37
1 Cor 15:27
2 Cor 2:14
Eph 2:14
Col 1:20
Rev 3:19

19Jesus realized they wanted to ask him so he said, "Are you asking yourselves what I mean? 20The world will greatly rejoice over what is going to happen to me, and you will weep. But your weeping shall suddenly be turned to wonderful joy [when you see me again]. 21It will be the same joy as that of a woman in labor when her child is born—her anguish gives place to rapturous joy and the pain is forgotten. 22You have sorrow now, but I will see you again and then you will rejoice; and no one can rob you of that joy. 23At that time you won't need to ask me for anything, for you can go directly to the Father and ask him, and he will give you what you ask for because you use my name. 24You haven't tried this before, [but begin now]. Ask, using my name, and you will receive, and your cup of joy will overflow.

25"I have spoken of these matters very guardedly, but the time will come when this will not be necessary and I will tell you plainly all about the Father. 26Then you will present your petitions over my signature! And I won't need to ask the Father to grant you these requests, 27for the Father himself loves you dearly because you love me and believe that I came from the Father. 28Yes, I came from the Father into the world and will leave the world and return to the Father."

29"At last you are speaking plainly," his disciples said, "and not in riddles. 30Now we understand that you know everything and don't need anyone to tell you anything. From this we believe that you came from God."

31"Do you finally believe this?" Jesus asked. 32"But the time is coming—in fact, it is here—when you will be scattered, each one returning to his own home, leaving me alone. Yet I will not be alone, for the Father is with me. 33I have told you all this so that you will have peace of heart and mind. Here on earth you will have many trials and sorrows; but cheer up, for I have overcome the world."

16:20 *when you see me again,* implied.   **16:24** *but begin now,* implied.   **16:26** *petitions over my signature,* literally, "you shall ask *in my name."* The above paraphrase is the modern equivalent of this idea, otherwise obscure. **16:30** *don't need anyone to tell you anything,* literally, "and need not that anyone should ask you," i.e., discuss what is true.

---

resurrection. Then the Holy Spirit revealed truths to the disciples that they wrote down in the books that came to form the New Testament.

16:13 The truth into which the Holy Spirit guides us is the truth about Christ.

16:16 Jesus was referring to his death. But three days later he would rise again and show himself to the disciples.

16:20 What a contrast between the disciples and the world! The world rejoiced as they wept, but they would see him again (in three days) and rejoice. The world's values are often the opposite of God's values. This can cause Christians to feel like misfits. But even if life is difficult now, one day we will rejoice. Keep your eye on the future and on God's promises!

16:23–27 Jesus is talking about a new relationship between the believer and God. Previously, people approached God through priests. After Jesus' resurrection, any believer could approach God directly. A new day has dawned and now all believers are priests,

talking with God personally and directly (see Hebrews 10:19–23). We approach God, not because of our own merit, but because Jesus, our great High Priest, has made us acceptable to God.

16:30 Jesus knew everything, and this caused the disciples to believe. But their belief was only a first step toward the great faith they would experience when the Holy Spirit came to dwell in them.

16:32 The disciples scattered after Jesus was arrested (see Mark 14:50).

16:33 Jesus sums up all he has told them this night, tying together themes from 14:27–29; 16:1–4; and 16:9–11. With these words he is telling his disciples to take courage. In spite of the inevitable struggles they will face, they are not alone. Besides, the ultimate victory has already been won!

Jesus prays for himself
(219)

17 When Jesus had finished saying all these things he looked up to heaven and said, "Father, the time has come. Reveal the glory of your Son so that he can give the glory back to you. ²For you have given him authority over every man and woman in all the earth. He gives eternal life to each one you have given him. ³And this is the way to have eternal life—by knowing you, the only true God, and Jesus Christ, the one you sent to earth! ⁴I brought glory to you here on earth by doing everything you told me to. ⁵And now, Father, reveal my glory as I stand in your presence, the glory we shared before the world began.

17:1
Jn 7:39
13:31,32
17:2
Jn 3:35; 6:37
10:28
17:3
Phil 3:8,10
1 Jn 5:20
17:5
Jn 1:1,2; 17:24
Phil 2:6

Jesus prays for his disciples
(220)

⁶"I have told these men all about you. They were in the world, but then you gave them to me. Actually, they were always yours, and you gave them to me; and they have obeyed you. ⁷Now they know that everything I have is a gift from you, ⁸for I have passed on to them the commands you gave me; and they accepted them and know of a certainty that I came down to earth from you, and they believe you sent me.

⁹"My plea is not for the world but for those you have given me because they belong to you. ¹⁰And all of them, since they are mine, belong to you; and you have given them back to me with everything else of yours, and so *they are my glory!* ¹¹Now I am leaving the world, and leaving them behind, and coming to you. Holy Father, keep them in your own care—all those you have given me—so that they will be united just as we are, with none missing. ¹²During my time here I have kept safe within your family all of these you gave me. I guarded them so that not one perished, except the son of hell, as the Scriptures foretold.

¹³"And now I am coming to you. I have told them many things while I was with them so that they would be filled with my joy. ¹⁴I have given them your commands. And the world hates them because they don't fit in with it, just as I don't. ¹⁵I'm not asking you to take them out of the world, but to keep them safe from Satan's power. ¹⁶They are not part of this world any more than I am. ¹⁷Make them pure and holy through teaching them your words of truth. ¹⁸As you sent me into the world, I am

17:6
Jn 17:26
17:8
Jn 15:15; 16:50
17:9
1 Jn 5:19
17:10
Rom 8:29,30
Eph 3:21
17:11
Jn 10:30; 17:21
Rom 12:4,5
Gal 3:28
17:12
Jn 6:39; 10:28
Acts 1:20
Heb 2:13
1 Jn 2:19
17:13
Jn 7:33; 15:11
17:14
Jn 15:19
1 Jn 3:13
17:15
1 Jn 5:18
17:17
Jn 15:3
17:18
Jn 20:21

17:12 *I have kept safe . . . all of these you gave me,* literally, "kept in your name those whom you have given me."

17:1ff This entire chapter is Jesus' prayer. From it, we learn that the world is a tremendous battleground where the forces under Satan's power and those under God's authority are at war. Satan and his forces are motivated by bitter hatred for Christ and his forces.

Jesus prayed for his disciples, including those of us who follow him today. He prayed that God would keep his chosen believers safe from Satan's power, making them pure and holy, uniting them through his truth.

17:3 How do we get eternal life? Jesus tells us clearly here—by knowing God the Father himself through his Son, Jesus Christ. Eternal life requires entering into a personal relationship with God in Jesus Christ. When we admit our sin and turn away from it, Christ's love lives in us by the Holy Spirit.

17:5 Before Jesus came to earth, he was one with God. Now that his mission on earth was almost finished, he was asking his Father to restore him to his original place with God. Jesus' resurrection and ascension—and Stephen's dying exclamation (Acts 7:56)—attest that Jesus did return to his exalted position at the right hand of God.

17:10 Jesus said that his disciples are his glory. What a fantastic truth, that Jesus glories in us and that our lives can bring him joy. Are you living in a way that brings him joy? Does he glory in you?

17:11 Jesus is asking that the disciples be united as the Father, Son, and Holy Spirit are united—the strongest of all unions.

17:12 Judas was the "son of hell," who perished because he betrayed Jesus (see Psalm 41:9).

17:13 Joy is a common theme in Christ's teachings—he wants us to be joyful (see 15:11, 16:24, 33). The key to joy is living in close contact with him, the source of all joy.

17:14 The world hates Christians because Christians' values differ from the world's, thus showing the world's immorality. They don't cooperate with the world by joining in their sin; thus they are living accusations against the world's way of life. The world follows Satan's agenda, and Satan is the avowed enemy of Jesus and his people.

17:17 A person becomes pure and holy through believing and obeying the Word of God (Hebrews 4:12), and accepting the forgiveness of our sins through Christ's sacrificial death (Hebrews 7:26, 27). The process of becoming holy and pure involves God's workmanship with respect to our past, present, and future. Through Christ we have been saved from sin; through the Holy Spirit we are growing in our Christian life; according to God's plan, we will be made perfect when Christ returns (Hebrews 9:24–28).

17:18 Jesus didn't ask God to take believers *out* of the world but instead to use them *in* the world. Because Jesus sends us into the world, we should not try to escape from the world or avoid all relationships with non-Christians. We are called to be salt and light (Matthew 5:13–16), and we are to do the work God sent us to do.

17:19
1 Cor 1:30
Heb 2:11

sending them into the world, 19and I consecrate myself to meet their need for growth in truth and holiness.

Jesus prays for future believers
(221)

17:20
Acts 2:40,41
4:29,31; 10:44
17:21
Jn 10:30,38
14:11; 17:11
Eph 4:3-6
17:22
2 Cor 4:6
Eph 3:16,21
17:23
Jn 10:38
16:27; 17:11
17:24
Jn 1:14; 12:26

17:26
Jn 15:9

20"I am not praying for these alone but also for the future believers who will come to me because of the testimony of these. 21My prayer for all of them is that they will be of one heart and mind, just as you and I are, Father—that just as you are in me and I am in you, so they will be in us, and the world will believe you sent me.

22"I have given them the glory you gave me—the glorious unity of being one, as we are— 23I in them and you in me, all being perfected into one—so that the world will know you sent me and will understand that you love them as much as you love me. 24Father, I want them with me—these you've given me—so that they can see my glory. You gave me the glory because you loved me before the world began!

25"O righteous Father, the world doesn't know you, but I do; and these disciples know you sent me. 26And I have revealed you to them, and will keep on revealing you so that the mighty love you have for me may be in them, and I in them."

2. Jesus completes his mission
Jesus is betrayed and arrested
(224/Matthew 26:47-56; Mark 14:43-52; Luke 22:47-53)

18:1
2 Sam 15:23
2 Kgs 23:4,6,12
2 Chron 15:16
29:16; 30:14

18 After saying these things Jesus crossed the Kidron ravine with his disciples and entered a grove of olive trees. 2Judas, the betrayer, knew this place, for Jesus had gone there many times with his disciples.

3The chief priests and Pharisees had given Judas a squad of soldiers and police to

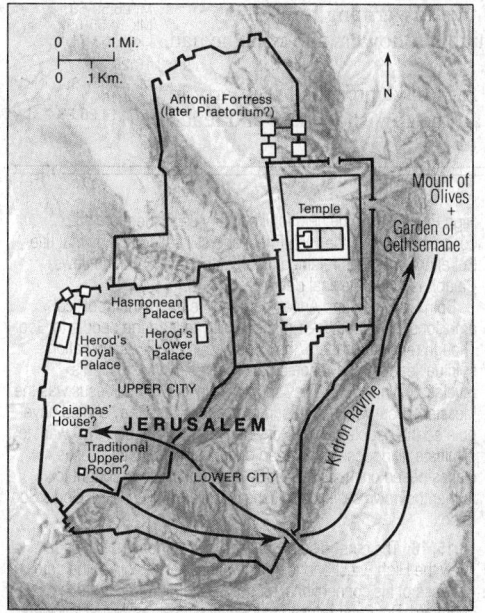

17:20 Jesus prayed for all who would follow him, so he was praying for you and others you know. He prayed for unity (17:11), protection from Satan (17:15), and purity (17:17). Knowing that Jesus prayed for us should give us confidence as we work for his Kingdom.

17:21-23 Jesus' great desire for his disciples was that they become one. He wanted them unified as a powerful witness to the reality of God's love. Are you helping to unify the body of Christ, the church? You can pray for other Christians, avoid gossip, build others up, work together in humility, give your time and money, lift up Christ, and refuse to get sidetracked arguing over matters that divide us.

17:21-23 Jesus prayed for unity among the believers based on the believers' oneness with him and the Father. Christians can know unity among themselves if they are living in union with God. For example, each branch living in union with the Vine is united with all the other branches doing the same.

18:3 The police would have been the Temple police; they were Jews given authority by the religious leaders to make arrests for minor infractions. The soldiers may have been a small contingent of Roman soldiers who did not participate in the arrest but accompanied the police to make sure matters didn't get out of control.

BETRAYAL IN THE GARDEN After eating the Passover meal in the Upper Room, Jesus and his disciples went to Gethsemane, where Judas led the Temple police to arrest Jesus. Jesus was then taken to Caiaphas' house for his first of many trials.

accompany him. Now with blazing torches, lanterns, and weapons they arrived at the olive grove.

4, 5Jesus fully realized all that was going to happen to him. Stepping forward to meet them he asked, "Whom are you looking for?"

"Jesus of Nazareth," they replied.

"I am he," Jesus said. 6And as he said it, they all fell backwards to the ground! 7Once more he asked them, "Whom are you searching for?"

And again they replied, "Jesus of Nazareth."

8"I told you I am he," Jesus said; "and since I am the one you are after, let these others go." 9He did this to carry out the prophecy he had just made, "I have not lost a single one of those you gave me. . . ."

10Then Simon Peter drew a sword and slashed off the right ear of Malchus, the High Priest's servant.

11But Jesus said to Peter, "Put your sword away. Shall I not drink from the cup the Father has given me?"

Annas questions Jesus (225)

12So the Jewish police, with the soldiers and their lieutenant, arrested Jesus and tied him. 13First they took him to Annas, the father-in-law of Caiaphas, the High Priest that year. 14Caiaphas was the one who told the other Jewish leaders, "Better that one should die for all."

15Simon Peter followed along behind, as did another of the disciples who was acquainted with the High Priest. So that other disciple was permitted into the courtyard along with Jesus, 16while Peter stood outside the gate. Then the other disciple spoke to the girl watching at the gate, and she let Peter in. 17The girl asked Peter, "Aren't you one of Jesus' disciples?"

"No," he said, "I am not!"

18The police and the household servants were standing around a fire they had made, for it was cold. And Peter stood there with them, warming himself.

19Inside, the High Priest began asking Jesus about his followers and what he had been teaching them.

20Jesus replied, "What I teach is widely known, for I have preached regularly in the synagogue and Temple; I have been heard by all the Jewish leaders and teach

18:9
Jn 17:12

18:10
Mt 26:51
Mk 14:47
Lk 22:49,50

18:11
Mt 20:22
26:39,42

18:12
Mt 26:57

18:13
Lk 3:1,2
Acts 4:6

18:14
Jn 11:50

18:15
Mt 26:58
Lk 22:54

18:16
Mt 26:69

18:18
Mk 14:54

18:19
Mt 26:59-68
Mk 14:55-65
Lk 22:63-71

18:20
Mt 26:55
Lk 4:15
Jn 7:14,26,28

18:4, 5 John does not record Judas' kiss of greeting (Matthew 26:49; Mark 14:45; Luke 22:47, 48); but his kiss marked a turning point for the disciples because with Jesus' arrest each one's life would be radically different. For the first time, Judas openly betrayed Jesus before the other disciples. For the first time, Jesus' loyal disciples ran away from him (Matthew 26:56). The band of disciples would undergo severe testing before they were transformed from uncertain followers to dynamic leaders.

18:6 The men may have been startled by Jesus' statement or by the words "I am," a declaration of his divinity (Exodus 3:14). Or perhaps they were overcome by his obvious power and authority.

18:10, 11 Trying to protect Jesus, Peter pulled a sword and wounded one of the Temple police. But Jesus told him to put away his sword and allow God's plan to unfold. At times it is tempting to take matters into our own hands, to force the issue. Instead we must trust God to work out his plan. Think of it—if Peter had had his way, Jesus would not have gone to the cross, and God's plan of redemption would have been halted.

18:11 The cup means the suffering, isolation, and death that Jesus would have to endure in order to atone for the sins of the world.

18:13 Both Annas and Caiaphas are called High Priests. Annas was Israel's High Priest from A.D. 6 to 15 when he was deposed by Roman rulers. Caiaphas, Annas' son-in-law, was appointed High Priest from A.D. 18 to 36/37. According to Jewish law, the office of

High Priest was to be held for life. Many Jews therefore still considered Annas the High Priest and still called him by that title. But although Annas retained much authority among the Jews, Caiaphas made the final decisions.

Both Caiaphas and Annas cared more about their political ambitions than about their responsibility to lead the people to God. Though religious leaders, they had become evil. As the nation's spiritual leaders, they should have been sensitive to God's revelation in his Word. They should have known that Jesus was the Messiah about whom the Scriptures spoke, and they should have pointed the people to him. But when men pursue evil, they want to eliminate all opposition. Instead of honestly evaluating Jesus' claims based on their knowledge of Scripture, they sought to further their own selfish ambitions and were willing to kill God's Son to do it.

18:15, 16 The other disciple is John, the author of this Gospel. He knew the High Priest and identified himself to the girl at the gate. Because of his connections, he got himself and Peter into the courtyard. But Peter refused to identify himself as Jesus' follower. Peter's experiences in the next few hours would change his life. For more information about Peter, see this Profile in Matthew 27.

18:19ff During the night, Jesus had two pretrial hearings before he was taken before the entire Jewish Supreme Court (see 18:24 for mention of the second). The religious leaders knew they had no grounds on which to charge him, so they tried to build evidence against him by using false witnesses.

nothing in private that I have not said in public. 21Why are you asking me this question? Ask those who heard me. You have some of them here. They know what I said."

22One of the soldiers standing there struck Jesus with his fist. "Is that the way to answer the High Priest?" he demanded.

23"If I lied, prove it," Jesus replied. "Should you hit a man for telling the truth?" 24Then Annas sent Jesus, bound, to Caiaphas the High Priest.

Peter denies knowing Jesus
(227/Matthew 26:69–75; Mark 14:66–72; Luke 22:54–65)

25Meanwhile, as Simon Peter was standing by the fire, he was asked again, "Aren't you one of his disciples?"

18:22
Isa 50:6
Mic 5:1
Jn 19:3

18:23
Mt 5:39
Acts 23:2
Heb 12:3
1 Pet 2:21-23

18:25
Mt 26:73-75

THE SIX STAGES OF JESUS' TRIAL			
Although Jesus' trial lasted less than 18 hours, he was taken to six different hearings.	BEFORE JEWISH AUTHORITIES	Preliminary Hearing before Annas (John 18:12–24)	Because the office of High Priest was for life, Annas was still the "official" High Priest in the eyes of the Jews, even though the Romans had appointed another. Thus Annas still carried much weight among the Jewish Supreme Court.
		Hearing before Caiaphas (Matthew 26:57–68)	Like the hearing before Annas, this hearing was conducted at night in secrecy. It was full of illegalities that made a mockery of justice (see the chart in Matthew 28).
		Trial before the Supreme Court (Matthew 27:1, 2)	Just after daybreak, 70 members of the Jewish Supreme Court met to rubber-stamp their approval of the previous hearings to make them appear legal. The purpose of this trial was not to determine justice, but to justify their own preconceptions of Jesus' guilt.
	BEFORE ROMAN AUTHORITIES	First Hearing before Pilate (Luke 23:1–5)	The religious leaders had condemned Jesus to death on religious grounds, but only the Roman government could grant the death penalty. Thus, they took Jesus to Pilate, the Roman governor, and accused him of treason and rebellion, crimes for which the Roman government gave the death penalty. Pilate saw at once that Jesus was innocent, but he was afraid about the uproar being caused by the religious leaders.
		Hearing before Herod (Luke 23:6–12)	Since Jesus' home was in the region of Galilee, Pilate sent Jesus to Herod Agrippa, the ruler of Galilee, who was in Jerusalem for the Passover celebration. Herod was eager to see Jesus do a miracle, but when Jesus remained silent, Herod wanted nothing to do with him and sent him back to Pilate.
		Last Hearing before Pilate (Luke 23:13–25)	Pilate didn't like the religious leaders. He wasn't interested in condemning Jesus because he knew Jesus was innocent. However, he knew that another uprising in his district might cost him his job. First he tried to compromise with the religious leaders by having Jesus beaten, an illegal action in itself. But finally he gave in and handed Jesus over to be executed. His self-interest was stronger than his sense of justice.

18:22-27 We can easily get angry at the Jewish Supreme Court for their injustice in condemning Jesus, but Peter and the rest of the disciples also contributed to Jesus' pain by deserting and denying him (Matthew 26:56). While most of us are not like the religious leaders, we are all like the disciples, for all of us have been guilty of denying Christ as Lord in vital areas of our lives. Don't excuse yourself by pointing at others whose sins seem worse than yours. Instead, come to Jesus for forgiveness and healing.

18:25 The other three Gospels say that Peter's three denials happened near the same fire outside Caiaphas' palace. John places the first denial outside Annas' home, the other two outside Caiaphas' home. This was no doubt the same courtyard. The High Priest's residence was large, and Annas and Caiaphas probably lived near each other.

"Of course not," he replied.

26But one of the household slaves of the High Priest—a relative of the man whose ear Peter had cut off—asked, "Didn't I see you out there in the olive grove with Jesus?"

27Again Peter denied it. And immediately a rooster crowed.

18:27
Jn 13:38

Jesus stands trial before Pilate
(230/Matthew 27:11–14; Mark 15:2–5; Luke 23:1–5)

28Jesus' trial before Caiaphas ended in the early hours of the morning. Next he was taken to the palace of the Roman governor. His accusers wouldn't go in themselves for that would "defile" them, they said, and they wouldn't be allowed to eat the Passover lamb. 29So Pilate, the governor, went out to them and asked, "What is your charge against this man? What are you accusing him of doing?"

18:28
Mt 27:2
Mk 15:1
Lk 23:1
Jn 11:55
Acts 11:3

30"We wouldn't have arrested him if he weren't a criminal!" they retorted.

31"Then take him away and judge him yourselves by your own laws," Pilate told them.

"But we want him crucified," they demanded, "and your approval is required." 32This fulfilled Jesus' prediction concerning the method of his execution.

18:32
Mt 20:19
Jn 12:32,33

33Then Pilate went back into the palace and called for Jesus to be brought to him. "Are you the King of the Jews?" he asked him.

18:33
Lk 23:3
Jn 19:12

34" 'King' as *you* use the word or as the *Jews* use it?" Jesus asked.

18:36
Isa 9:6
Dan 2:44; 7:14
Mt 26:53
Lk 17:20,21
Jn 6:15

35"Am I a Jew?" Pilate retorted. "Your own people and their chief priests brought you here. Why? What have you done?"

36Then Jesus answered, "I am not an earthly king. If I were, my followers would

18:31 *your approval is required,* literally, "It is not lawful for us to put any man to death."

18:27 This fulfilled Jesus' words to Peter after he promised he would never deny him (13:38).

18:28 This Roman governor, Pilate, was in charge of Judea (the region where Jerusalem was located) from A.D. 26 to 36. Pilate was unpopular with the Jews because he had raided the Temple treasuries for money to build an aqueduct. He did not like the Jews, but when Jesus, the King of the Jews, stood before him, Pilate found him innocent.

18:28 By Jewish law, entering the house of a Gentile would cause a Jewish person to be ceremonially defiled. As a result, he could not take part in worship at the Temple or feasts. Afraid of being defiled, these men stayed outside the home where they had taken Jesus for trial. They kept the pretenses of religion while harboring murder and treachery in their hearts.

18:30 Pilate knew what was going on; he knew that the religious leaders hated Jesus, and he did not want to act as their executioner. They could not sentence him to death themselves—permission had to come from a Roman leader. But Pilate refused to sentence Jesus without sufficient evidence. Jesus' life became a pawn in a political power struggle.

18:31ff Pilate made four attempts to deal with Jesus: (1) he tried to put the responsibility on someone else (18:31); (2) he tried to find a way of escape so he could release Jesus (18:39); (3) he tried to compromise with the people—beating Jesus rather than handing him over to die (19:1–3); and (4) he tried a direct appeal to the sympathy of the accusers (19:15). Everyone has a responsibility to decide what he or she will do with Jesus. Pilate tried to let everyone else decide—and in the end, he lost.

18:32 This prediction is recorded in Matthew 20:19. Crucifixion was a common method of execution for criminals who were not Roman citizens.

18:34 If Pilate was asking as the Roman governor, he would be inquiring whether Jesus was setting up a rebel government. But the Jews were using the word "King" to mean their religious ruler, the Messiah. Israel was a captive nation, under the authority of the Roman Empire. A king might have threatened Rome; a Messiah could have been a purely religious leader.

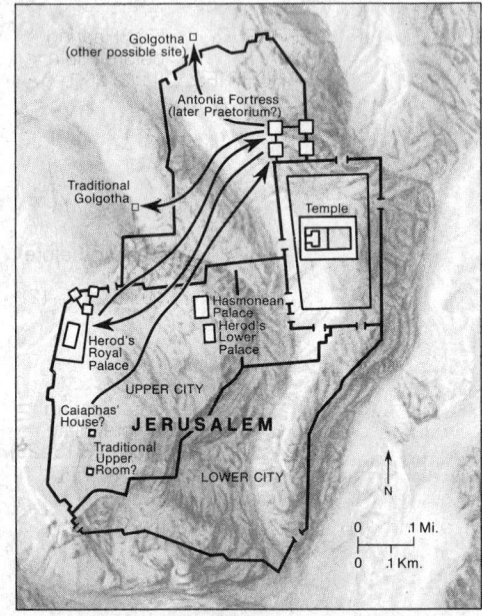

JESUS' TRIAL AND CRUCIFIXION Jesus was taken from trial before the Jewish Supreme Court to trial before the Roman procurator, Pilate, in the Antonia Fortress. Pilate sent him to Herod (Luke 23:5–12), but Herod just returned Jesus to Pilate. Responding to threats from the mob, Pilate finally turned Jesus over to be crucified.

have fought when I was arrested by the Jewish leaders. But my Kingdom is not of the world."

18:37
Jn 8:47
1 Pet 1:23
1 Jn 3:19; 4:6
Rev 1:5

37Pilate replied, "But you are a king then?"

"Yes," Jesus said. "I was born for that purpose. And I came to bring truth to the world. All who love the truth are my followers."

18:38
Jn 19:4,6

38"What is truth?" Pilate exclaimed.Then he went out again to the people and told them, "He is not guilty of any crime.

Pilate hands Jesus over to be crucified
(232/Matthew 27:15–26; Mark 15:6–15; Luke 23:13–25)

18:39
Mt 27:15-18,
20-23
Mk 15:6-15
Lk 23:17-19

39But you have a custom of asking me to release someone from prison each year at Passover. So if you want me to, I'll release the 'King of the Jews.' "

40But they screamed back. "No! Not this man, but Barabbas!" Barabbas was a robber.

19:1
Isa 50:6
Mt 27:26-30
Mk 15:15-19
Lk 18:32,33

19 Then Pilate laid open Jesus' back with a leaded whip, 2and the soldiers made a crown of thorns and placed it on his head and robed him in royal purple. 3"Hail, 'King of the Jews!' " they mocked, and struck him with their fists.

19:3
Jn 18:22

4Pilate went outside again and said to the Jews, "I am going to bring him out to you now, but understand clearly that I find him *not guilty."*

19:4
Jn 18:38
2 Cor 5:21

5Then Jesus came out wearing the crown of thorns and the purple robe. And Pilate said, "Behold the man!"

19:6
Acts 3:13

6At sight of him the chief priests and Jewish officials began yelling, "Crucify! Crucify!"

"You crucify him," Pilate said. "I find him *not guilty."*

19:7
Lev 24:15,16
Mt 26:63-66

7They replied, "By our laws he ought to die because he called himself the Son of God."

19:9
Isa 53:7
Mt 27:12,14
Acts 8:32

8When Pilate heard this, he was more frightened than ever. 9He took Jesus back into the palace again and asked him, "Where are you from?" but Jesus gave no answer.

19:11
Acts 2:23; 3:13
Rom 13:1

10"You won't talk to me?" Pilate demanded. "Don't you realize that I have the power to release you or to crucify you?"

11Then Jesus said, "You would have no power at all over me unless it were given

19:11 *those,* literally, "he."

18:36, 37 Pilate asked Jesus a straightforward question and Jesus answered clearly. He is a King, but one whose Kingdom is not of this world. There seems to have been no question in Pilate's mind that Jesus spoke the truth and was innocent of any crime. It also seems apparent that while recognizing the truth, Pilate chose to reject it. It is a tragedy when we fail to recognize the truth. It is a greater tragedy when we recognize the truth but fail to heed it.

18:38 Pilate probably thought all truth was relative. To many government officials, truth was whatever the majority of people agreed with or whatever helped their own personal power and political advancement.

18:40 Barabbas was a rebel against Rome and, although he had committed murder, was probably a hero among the Jews. The Jews hated being governed by Rome and paying taxes to the despised government. Barabbas, who had led a rebellion and failed, was released instead of Jesus, the only one who could truly help Israel. For more on Barabbas, see the note on Luke 23:17–19.

19:1ff To grasp the full picture of Jesus' crucifixion, read John's perspective along with the other three accounts in Matthew 27, Mark 15, and Luke 23. Each writer adds meaningful details, but each has the same message—Jesus died on the cross, in fulfillment of Old Testament prophecy. And Jesus died so that we could be saved from our sins and given eternal life.

19:1–3 Scourging could have killed Jesus. The usual procedure was to bare the upper half of the victim's body and tie his hands to a pillar before whipping him with a three-pronged whip. The number of lashes was determined by the severity of the crime; up

to 40 were permitted under Jewish law (Deuteronomy 25:3).

19:2–5 The soldiers went beyond their orders to whip Jesus—they also mocked and beat him. They mocked his claim to royalty by placing a crown on his head and a royal robe on his shoulders.

19:7 The truth finally came out—the religious leaders had not brought Jesus to Pilate because he was causing rebellion against Rome, but because they thought he had broken their religious laws. Blasphemy was one of the most serious crimes in Jewish law and was given the death penalty. Accusing Jesus of blasphemy would give credibility to their case in the eyes of Jews; accusing Jesus of treason would give credibility to their case in the eyes of the Romans. They didn't care which accusation Pilate listened to, as long as he would cooperate with them in killing Jesus.

19:10 Throughout the trial we see that Jesus was in control, not Pilate or the religious leaders. Pilate vacillated; the Jewish leaders reacted out of hatred and anger; but Jesus remained composed. He knew the truth, he knew God's plan, he knew the reason for his trial. Despite the pressure and persecution, Jesus remained unmoved. It was really Pilate and the religious leaders who were on trial, not Jesus. When you are questioned or ridiculed because of your faith, remember that while you may be on trial before your accusers, they are on trial before God.

19:11 When Jesus said their sin was greater, he was not excusing Pilate for reacting to the political pressure placed on him. Pilate also was responsible for his decision about Jesus. The religious leaders were more guilty because they premeditated his murder.

to you from above. So those who brought me to you have the greater sin."

¹²Then Pilate tried to release him, but the Jewish leaders told him, "If you release this man, you are no friend of Caesar's. Anyone who declares himself a king is a rebel against Caesar."

19:12
Lk 23:2
Acts 17:7

¹³At these words Pilate brought Jesus out to them again and sat down at the judgment bench on the stone-paved platform. ¹⁴It was now about noon of the day before Passover.

19:13
Mt 27:19

And Pilate said to the Jews, "Here is your king!"

¹⁵"Away with him," they yelled. "Away with him—crucify him!"

"What? Crucify your king?" Pilate asked.

"We have no king but Caesar," the chief priests shouted back.

¹⁶Then Pilate gave Jesus to them to be crucified.

19:16
Mt 27:26,31
Mk 15:15
Lk 23:24

Jesus is led away to be crucified
(234/Matthew 27:32–34; Mark 15:21–24; Luke 23:26–31)

¹⁷So they had him at last, and he was taken out of the city, carrying his cross to the place known as "The Skull," in Hebrew, "Golgotha."

19:17
Num 15:36
Heb 13:12

Jesus is placed on the cross
(235/Matthew 27:35–44; Mark 15:25–32; Luke 23:32–43)

¹⁸There they crucified him and two others with him, one on either side, with Jesus between them. ¹⁹And Pilate posted a sign over him reading, "Jesus of Nazareth, the King of the Jews." ²⁰The place where Jesus was crucified was near the city; and the signboard was written in Hebrew, Latin, and Greek, so that many people read it.

19:18
Gal 3:13
19:19
Isa 53:12
Mt 27:37
Mk 15:26
Lk 23:38

²¹Then the chief priests said to Pilate, "Change it from 'The King of the Jews' to 'He said, I am King of the Jews.' "

²²Pilate replied, "What I have written, I have written. It stays exactly as it is."

²³, ²⁴When the soldiers had crucified Jesus, they put his garments into four piles, one for each of them. But they said, "Let's not tear up his robe," for it was seamless. "Let's throw dice to see who gets it." This fulfilled the Scripture that says,

19:23,24
Ps 22:18

19:13 *on the stone-paved platform,* literally, "the judgment seat in a place that is called The Pavement, but in Hebrew, Gabbatha."

19:12, 13 These words pressured Pilate into allowing Jesus to be crucified. As Roman governor of the area, Pilate was expected to keep peace. Because Rome could not afford to keep large numbers of troops in the outlying regions, they maintained control by crushing rebellions immediately with brute force. Pilate was afraid that reports to Caesar of insurrection in his region would cost him his job, and perhaps even his life. When we face a tough decision, we can take the easy way out, or we can stand for what is right, regardless of the cost. If we know to do right and don't do it, it is sin (James 4:17).

19:13 This stone-paved platform was part of the Tower of Antonia bordering the northwest corner of the Temple complex.

19:15 The Jewish leaders were so desperate to get rid of Jesus that despite their intense hatred for Rome, they shouted, "We have no king but Caesar." How ironic that they feigned allegiance to Rome while rejecting their own Messiah! The priests had truly lost their reasons for being—instead of turning people to God, they claimed allegiance to Rome in order to kill their Messiah.

19:17 This place called "The Skull" or Golgotha was probably a hill outside Jerusalem along a main road. Many executions took place here so the Romans could use them as an example to the people.

19:18 Crucifixion was a Roman form of punishment. The victim sentenced to this type of execution was forced to carry his cross along a main road to the execution site, as a warning to the people. Crosses and methods of crucifixion varied. Jesus was nailed to his cross; others were sometimes tied with ropes. Death came by suffocation, because the weight of the body made breathing difficult as the victim lost strength. Crucifixion was a hideously slow and painful death.

19:19 This sign was meant to be ironic. A king, stripped naked and executed in public view, had obviously lost his kingdom forever. But Jesus, who turns the world's wisdom upside down, was just coming into his Kingdom. His death and resurrection would strike the deathblow to Satan's rule and would establish his eternal authority over the earth. Few people reading the sign that bleak afternoon understood its real meaning, but the sign was absolutely true. All was not lost. Jesus was King of the Jews—and the Gentiles, and the whole universe.

19:20 The signboard was written in three languages: Hebrew for the native Jews; Latin for the Romans in the area; and Greek for foreigners and Jews visiting from other lands.

19:23, 24 Roman soldiers in charge of crucifixions customarily took for themselves the clothes of the condemned men. They

19:25
Mt 27:55,56
Lk 8:2,3; 24:18

"They divided my clothes among them, and cast lots for my robe." 25So that is what they did.

Standing near the cross were Jesus' mother, Mary, his aunt, the wife of Cleopas, and Mary Magdalene. 26When Jesus saw his mother standing there beside me, his close friend, he said to her, "He is your son."

19:26
Jn 2:4; 13:23
21:24

27And to me he said, "She is your mother!" And from then on I took her into my home.

Jesus dies on the cross
(236/Matthew 27:45–56; Mark 15:33–41; Luke 23:44–49)

19:28
Ps 2:1-3
22:1-21; 69:21
Isa 53
Mt 27:48-50
Mk 15:36,37
Lk 23:36

28Jesus knew that everything was now finished, and to fulfill the Scriptures said, "I'm thirsty." 29A jar of sour wine was sitting there, so a sponge was soaked in it and put on a hyssop branch and held up to his lips.

19:30
Lk 23:46
Heb 10:1-14

30When Jesus had tasted it, he said, "It is finished," and bowed his head and dismissed his spirit.

19:31
Num 28:17
Deut 21:22,23

31The Jewish leaders didn't want the victims hanging there the next day, which was the Sabbath (and a very special Sabbath at that, for it was the Passover), so they asked Pilate to order the legs of the men broken to hasten death; then their bodies could be taken down. 32So the soldiers came and broke the legs of the two men crucified with Jesus; 33but when they came to him, they saw that he was dead already, so they didn't break his. 34However, one of the soldiers pierced his side with a spear, and blood and water flowed out. 35I saw all this myself and have given an accurate report so that you also can believe. 36, 37The soldiers did this in fulfillment of the Scripture that says, "Not one of his bones shall be broken," and, "They shall look on him whom they pierced."

19:35
Jn 20:30,31
21:24
1 Jn 1:1

19:36,37
Ex 12:46
Num 9:12
Ps 34:20
Zech 12:10
Rev 1:7

19:26 *standing there beside me, his close friend,* literally, "standing by the disciple whom he loved." **19:27** *And to me,* literally, "to the disciple." **19:30** *had tasted,* literally, "had received." **19:35** *so that you also can believe,* literally, "And he who has seen has borne witness, and his witness is true; and he knows what he says is true, that you also may believe."

---

divided Jesus' clothing, but cast lots to determine who would get his robe, the most valuable piece of clothing. This fulfilled the prophecy in Psalm 22:18.

19:25–27 Even while dying on the cross, Jesus was concerned about his family. He instructed John to care for Mary, his mother. Our families are precious gifts from God, and we should value and care for them under all circumstances. What can you do today to show your love to your family?

19:27 Jesus asked his close friend John, the writer of this Gospel, to care for his mother, Mary, whose husband, Joseph, was probably dead by this time. Why didn't Jesus assign this task to his brothers? As the eldest son, Jesus entrusted his mother to a person who was there with him at the cross—and that was John.

19:29 This jar of sour wine was a cheap wine that the Roman soldiers drank while waiting for those crucified to die.

19:30 Until this time, a complicated system of sacrifices atoned for sins. Sin separates people from God, and only through the sacrifice of an animal, a substitute, could people be forgiven of sin and become clean before God. But people sin continually, so frequent sacrifices were required. Jesus, however, became the final and ultimate sacrifice for sin. The word *finished* is the same as "paid in full." Jesus came to *finish* God's work of salvation (John 4:34; 17:4), to pay the full penalty for our sins. With his death, the complex sacrificial system ended because Jesus took all sin upon himself. Now we can freely approach God because of what Jesus did for us. Those who believe in Jesus' death and resurrection can live eternally with God and escape the death which comes from sin.

19:31 It was against God's law to have the body of a dead person exposed overnight (Deuteronomy 21:23), and it was also against the law to work after sundown on Friday, when the Sabbath began. This is why the religious leaders urgently wanted to get Jesus' body off the cross and buried by sundown.

19:31–35 These Romans were experienced soldiers. They knew from many previous crucifixions whether a man was dead or alive. There was no question that Jesus was dead when they checked him, so they decided not to break his legs as they had done to the other victims. Piercing his side and seeing the separation of blood and water was further proof of his death. Some people say Jesus didn't really die, that he only passed out—and that's how he "came back to life." But we have proof from an impartial party, the Roman soldiers, that Jesus died on the cross (see Mark 15:44, 45).

19:32 The Roman soldiers broke victims' legs to hurry the death process. When a person hung on a cross, death came by suffocation, but the victim could push against the cross with his legs to hold up his body and keep breathing. With broken legs, he would suffocate immediately.

19:34, 35 The graphic details of Jesus' death are especially important in John's record because he was an eyewitness.

19:36, 37 Jesus died when the lambs for the Passover meal were being slain. Not a bone was to be broken in these sacrificial lambs (Exodus 12:46; Numbers 9:12). Jesus, the Lamb of God, was the perfect sacrifice for the sins of the world (1 Corinthians 5:7).

Jesus is laid in the tomb
(237/Matthew 27:57–61; Mark 15:42–47; Luke 23:50–56)

³⁸Afterwards Joseph of Arimathea, who had been a secret disciple of Jesus for fear of the Jewish leaders, boldly asked Pilate for permission to take Jesus' body down; and Pilate told him to go ahead. So he came and took it away. ³⁹Nicodemus, the man who had come to Jesus at night, came too, bringing a hundred pounds of embalming ointment made from myrrh and aloes. ⁴⁰Together they wrapped Jesus' body in a long linen cloth saturated with the spices, as is the Jewish custom of burial. ⁴¹The place of crucifixion was near a grove of trees, where there was a new tomb, never used before. ⁴²And so, because of the need for haste before the Sabbath, and because the tomb was close at hand, they laid him there.

19:39
2 Chron 16:13, 14
Mt 26:12
Mk 14:8
Jn 3:1,2; 7:50
12:7

19:40
Lk 23:56
Jn 11:44

19:41
Mt 27:60
Lk 23:52

Jesus rises from the dead
(239/Matthew 28:1–7; Mark 16:1–8; Luke 24:1–12)

20 Early Sunday morning, while it was still dark, Mary Magdalene came to the tomb and found that the stone was rolled aside from the entrance.

²She ran and found Simon Peter and me and said, "They have taken the Lord's body out of the tomb, and I don't know where they have put him!"

^{3,4}We ran to the tomb to see; I outran Peter and got there first, ⁵and stooped and looked in and saw the linen cloth lying there, but I didn't go in. ⁶Then Simon Peter arrived and went on inside. He also noticed the cloth lying there, ⁷while the swath that had covered Jesus' head was rolled up in a bundle and was lying at the side. ⁸Then I went in too, and saw, and believed [that he had risen]— ⁹for until then we hadn't realized that the Scriptures said he would come to life again!

20:2
Jn 13:23

20:3
Lk 24:12

20:5
Jn 19:40

20:6
Lk 24:12

20:7
Jn 11:44; 19:40

20:9
Ps 2:7; 16:8-11

19:39 *at night,* see chapter 3.   **19:41** *a grove of trees,* literally, "a garden."   **20:1** *Early Sunday,* literally, "on the first day of the week."   **20:2** *and me,* literally, "the other disciple whom Jesus loved."   **20:3, 4** *We,* literally, "Peter and the other disciple." *I,* literally, "the other disciple also, who came first."   **20:8** *that he had risen,* implied.

19:38–42 Joseph of Arimathea and Nicodemus were secret followers of Jesus. They were afraid to make this known because of their positions in the Jewish community. Joseph was a leader and honored member of the Supreme Court. Nicodemus, also a member of the Court, had come to Jesus by night (3:1) and later tried to defend him before the other religious leaders (7:50–52). Yet they risked their reputations to bury Jesus. Are you a secret believer? Do you hide from your friends and fellow workers? This is an appropriate time to step out of hiding and let others know of your faith.

19:38, 39 Four people were changed in the process of Jesus' death. The criminal, dying on the cross beside Jesus, asked Jesus to include him in his Kingdom (Luke 23:40–42). The Roman captain proclaimed that surely Jesus was the Son of God (Mark 15:39). Joseph and Nicodemus, members of the Jewish Supreme Court and secret followers of Jesus (7:50–52), came out of hiding. These men were changed more by Christ's death than they had been affected by his life. They realized who he was, and that realization brought out their belief, proclamation, and action. When confronted with Jesus and his death, we should be changed—to believe, proclaim, and act.

19:42 This tomb was probably a cave carved out of the stone hillside. It was large enough for a man to walk into, so Joseph and Nicodemus carried Jesus' body into it. A large stone was rolled in front of the entrance.

19:42 As they buried Jesus, Nicodemus and Joseph had to hurry to avoid working on the Sabbath, which began Friday evening at sundown.

20:1 Other women came to the tomb along with Mary Magdalene. The other Gospel accounts give their names. For more information on Mary Magdalene, see her Profile in John 20.

20:1 The stone was not rolled away from the entrance to the tomb so Jesus could get out. He could have easily left without moving the stone. It was rolled away so others could get *in* and see that Jesus was gone.

20:1ff People who hear about the resurrection for the first time may need time before they can comprehend this amazing story. Like Mary and the disciples, they may pass through four stages of belief. (1) At first, they may think it is a fabrication, impossible to believe (20:2). (2) Like Peter, they may check out the facts but still be puzzled about what happened (20:6). (3) Only when they encounter Jesus personally are they able to accept the fact of the resurrection (20:16). (4) Then, as they commit themselves to him and devote their lives to serving Jesus, they begin to understand fully the reality of his presence with them (20:28).

20:7 The cloths that had been wrapped around Jesus' body had been neatly folded. They would not have been arranged that way if there had been a grave robbery.

20:9 As further proof that the disciples did not fabricate this story, we find that Peter and John were surprised that Jesus was not in the tomb. When John saw the grave cloths neatly folded, he believed Jesus had risen. It wasn't until after they had seen the empty tomb that they remembered what the Scriptures and Jesus had said—he would die, but he would also rise again!

20:9 Jesus' resurrection is the key to the Christian faith. Why? (1) "Just as he said," Jesus rose from the dead. We can be confident, therefore, that he will accomplish all he has promised. (2) Jesus' bodily resurrection shows us that the living Christ, not a false prophet or imposter, is ruler of God's eternal kingdom. (3) We can be certain of our own resurrection because he was resurrected. Death is not the end—there is future life. (4) The divine power that brought Jesus back to life is now available to us to bring our spiritually dead selves back to life. (5) The resurrection is the basis for the church's witness to the world.

Jesus appears to Mary Magdalene
(240/Mark 16:9–11)

¹⁰We went on home, ¹¹and by that time Mary had returned to the tomb and was standing outside crying. And as she wept, she stooped and looked in ¹²and saw two white-robed angels sitting at the head and foot of the place where the body of Jesus had been lying.

20:12
Mt 28:2
Mk 16:5
Lk 24:4

¹³"Why are you crying?" the angels asked her.

"Because they have taken away my Lord," she replied, "and I don't know where they have put him."

¹⁴She glanced over her shoulder and saw someone standing behind her. It was Jesus, but she didn't recognize him!

20:14
Mt 28:9
Mk 16:9
Jn 21:4

¹⁵"Why are you crying?" he asked her. "Whom are you looking for?"

She thought he was the gardener. "Sir," she said, "if you have taken him away, tell me where you have put him, and I will go and get him."

¹⁶"Mary!" Jesus said. She turned toward him.

"Master!" she exclaimed.

20:10 *We,* literally, "the disciples."

MARY MAGDALENE

The absence of women among the 12 disciples has bothered a few people. But it is clear that there were many women among Jesus' followers. It is also clear that Jesus did not treat women as his culture did; he treated them with dignity, as people with worth.

Mary of Magdala was an early follower of Jesus and certainly deserves to be called a disciple. An energetic, impulsive, caring woman, she not only traveled with Jesus, but also contributed to the needs of the group. She was present at the crucifixion and was on her way to embalm Jesus' body on Sunday morning when she discovered the empty tomb. Mary was the first to see Jesus after his resurrection.

Mary Magdalene is a heartwarming example of thankful living. Her life was miraculously freed by Jesus—he cast seven demons out of her. In every glimpse we have of her, she was acting out her appreciation for the freedom Christ had given her. That freedom allowed her to stand under Christ's cross when all the disciples except John were hiding in fear. She stayed close to her Lord. After his death, her intention was to give his body every respect. Like all Jesus' followers, she never expected his bodily resurrection—but she was overjoyed to discover it.

Mary did not have a complicated faith—it was direct and genuine. She was more eager to believe and obey than to understand everything. Jesus honored her childlike faith by granting her to see his first resurrection appearance and by entrusting her with the first message of his resurrection.

Strengths and accomplishments:
- Contributed to the needs of Jesus and his disciples
- One of the few faithful followers present at Jesus' death on the cross
- First to see the risen Christ

Weaknesses and mistakes:
- Jesus had to cast seven demons out of her

Lessons from her life:
- Those who are obedient grow in understanding
- Women are vital to Jesus' ministry
- Jesus relates to women as he created them—as equal reflectors of God's image

Vital statistics:
- Where: Magdala
- Occupation: We are not told, but she seems to have been wealthy
- Contemporaries: Jesus, the 12 disciples, Mary, Martha, Lazarus, Jesus' mother Mary

Key verse:
"It was early on Sunday morning when Jesus came back to life, and the first person who saw him was Mary Magdalene—the woman from whom he had cast out seven demons" (Mark 16:9).

Mary Magdalene's story is told in Luke 8 and Mark 15, 16. She is also mentioned in Matthew 27, 28 and John 19, 20.

20:14 Mary didn't recognize Jesus at first. Her grief had blinded her; she couldn't see him because she didn't expect to see him. Then he spoke her name, and immediately she recognized him.

Imagine the love that flooded her heart when she heard her Savior saying her name. Jesus is near you, and he is calling your name. Can you, like Mary, answer him by saying, "Master!"?

17"Don't touch me," he cautioned, "for I haven't yet ascended to the Father. But go find my brothers and tell them that I ascend to my Father and your Father, my God and your God."

20:17
Mt 28:10
Jn 16:28
Rom 8:29
Col 1:18
Heb 2:11
1 Pet 1:3

18Mary Magdalene found the disciples and told them, "I have seen the Lord!" Then she gave them his message.

Jesus appears to the disciples behind locked doors
(244/Luke 24:36–43)

19That evening the disciples were meeting behind locked doors, in fear of the Jewish leaders, when suddenly Jesus was standing there among them! After greeting them, 20he showed them his hands and side. And how wonderful was their joy as they saw their Lord!

20:19
Mk 16:14
Lk 24:36-43
1 Cor 15:5,42-45

21He spoke to them again and said, "As the Father has sent me, even so I am sending you." 22Then he breathed on them and told them, "Receive the Holy Spirit. 23If you forgive anyone's sins, they are forgiven. If you refuse to forgive them, they are unforgiven."

20:21
Mt 28:18-20
Jn 17:18

20:22
Jn 7:37-39
14:16-18,26

Jesus appears to the disciples including Thomas
(245/Mark 16:14)

24One of the disciples, Thomas, "The Twin," was not there at the time with the others. 25When they kept telling him, "We have seen the Lord," he replied, "I won't believe it unless I see the nail wounds in his hands—and put my fingers into them—and place my hand into his side."

20:24
Jn 11:16

26Eight days later the disciples were together again, and this time Thomas was with them. The doors were locked; but suddenly, as before, Jesus was standing among them and greeting them.

27Then he said to Thomas, "Put your finger into my hands. Put your hand into my side. Don't be faithless any longer. Believe!"

28"My Lord and my God!" Thomas said.

20:28
Jn 1:1,18
10:30; 14:9
Phil 2:6
Col 2:9
Tit 2:13
2 Pet 1:1
1 Jn 5:20

20:17 "Don't touch me" can also be translated, "Don't hold onto me" or "Don't cling to me." Mary did not want to lose Jesus again. She had not yet understood the resurrection. But Jesus did not want to be detained by the tomb. Both he and Mary had important work to do.

20:18 Mary did not meet the risen Christ until she had discovered the empty tomb. She responded with joy and obedience in telling the disciples. We cannot truly meet Christ until we discover that he is indeed alive, that his tomb is empty. Are we filled with joy and do we share this good news with others?

20:21 Jesus again identified himself with his Father. He told the disciples by whose authority he did his work. Now he passed the job to his disciples of spreading the Good News of salvation around the world. Whatever God has asked you to do, remember: (1) your authority comes from God, and (2) Jesus has demonstrated by words and actions how to accomplish the job he has given you. As the Father sent Jesus, Jesus sends his followers.

20:22 This is a special filling of the Holy Spirit for the disciples, a foretaste of what all believers would experience from the time of Pentecost (Acts 2) and forever after.

20:22 There is life in the breath of God. Man was created but did not come alive until God breathed into him the breath of life (Genesis 2:7). His first breath made man different from all other forms of creation. Now, through the breath of Jesus, God imparted eternal, spiritual life. With this inbreathing came the power to do God's will on earth.

20:23 Jesus is telling the disciples their mission—to preach the Good News about Jesus so people's sins might be forgiven. The disciples in and of themselves did not have the power to forgive

sins, for no human can do that (Acts 10:43). Jesus gave them the privilege of telling new believers that their sins *have been* forgiven because they have accepted Jesus' message. All believers have this same privilege. Conversely, those who publicly reject Jesus cannot be forgiven, and believers can announce this to them. People cannot receive the message of forgiveness until they receive the one who forgives, Jesus.

20:24–29 Have you wished you could actually see Jesus, touch him, hear his words? Are there times you want to sit down with him and get his advice? Thomas wanted Jesus' physical presence. But God's plan is wiser. He has not kept himself contained in one physical body; he wants to be present with all of us at all times. Even now he is with you in the form of the Holy Spirit. You can talk to him, and you can find his words to you in the pages of the Bible. He can be as real to you as he was to Thomas.

20:25 Jesus wasn't hard on Thomas for his doubts. Despite his skepticism, Thomas was still loyal to the believers and to Jesus himself. Some need to doubt before they believe. If doubt leads to questions and questions lead to answers and the answers are accepted, then doubt has done good work. It is when doubt becomes stubbornness and stubbornness becomes a lifestyle that doubt harms faith. When you doubt, don't stop there, but let your doubt deepen your faith as you continue to search for the answer.

20:27 Jesus' resurrected body was a unique kind of physical body. It was not the same kind of flesh and blood Lazarus had when he came back to life. Jesus' body was no longer subject to the same laws of nature as before his death—he could appear in a locked room. Yet he was not a ghost or apparition; he could be touched and could eat. Jesus' resurrection was *literal* and *physical*—he was not a disembodied spirit.

20:29
2 Cor 5:7
1 Pet 1:8
20:30,31
Jn 3:15,16
5:24; 19:35
21:25

21:1
Jn 21:14

²⁹Then Jesus told him, "You believe because you have seen me. But blessed are those who haven't seen me and believe anyway."

³⁰,³¹Jesus' disciples saw him do many other miracles besides the ones told about in this book, but these are recorded so that you will believe that he is the Messiah, the Son of God, and that believing in him you will have life.

Jesus appears to the disciples while they are fishing
(246)

21 Later Jesus appeared again to the disciples beside the Lake of Galilee. This is how it happened:

THOMAS

Thomas, so often remembered as "Doubting Thomas," deserves to be respected for his faith. He was a doubter, but his doubts had a purpose—he wanted to know the truth. Thomas did not idolize his doubts; he gladly believed when given reasons to do so. He expressed his doubts fully and had them answered completely. Doubting was only his way of responding, not his way of life.

Although our glimpses of Thomas are brief, his character comes through with consistency. He struggled to be faithful to what he knew, despite what he felt. At one point, when it was plain to everyone that Jesus' life was in danger, only Thomas put into words what most were feeling, "Let's go too—and die with him" (John 11:16). He didn't hesitate to follow Jesus.

We don't know why Thomas was absent the first time Jesus appeared to the disciples after the resurrection, but he was reluctant to believe their witness to Christ's resurrection. Not even ten friends could change his mind!

We can doubt without having to live a doubting way of life. Doubt encourages rethinking. Its purpose is much more to sharpen the mind than to change it. Doubt can be used to pose the question, get an answer, and push for a decision. But doubt was never meant to be a permanent condition. Doubt is one foot lifted, poised to step forward or back. There is no motion until the foot comes down.

When you experience doubt, take encouragement from Thomas. He didn't stay in his doubt, but allowed Jesus to bring him to belief. Take encouragement also from the fact that countless other followers of Christ have struggled with doubts. The answers God gave them may be of great help. Don't settle into doubts, but move on from them to decision and belief. Find another believer with whom you can share your doubts. Silent doubts rarely find answers.

Strengths and accomplishments:
* One of Jesus' 12 disciples
* Had a great capacity for intensity, both in doubt and belief
* Was a loyal and honest man

Weaknesses and mistakes:
* Along with the others, abandoned Jesus at his arrest
* Refused to believe the others' claims to have seen Christ and demanded proof
* Struggled with a pessimistic outlook

Lessons from his life:
* Jesus does not reject doubts that are honest and directed toward belief
* Better to doubt out loud than to disbelieve in silence

Vital statistics:
* Where: Galilee, Judea, Samaria
* Occupation: Disciple of Jesus
* Contemporaries: Jesus, other disciples, Herod, Pilate

Key verses:
"Then he [Jesus] said to Thomas, 'Put your finger into my hands. Put your hand into my side. Don't be faithless any longer. Believe!' 'My Lord and my God!' Thomas said" (John 20:27, 28).

Thomas' story is told in the Gospels. He is also mentioned in Acts 1:13.

20:29 Some people think they would believe in Jesus if they could see a definite sign or miracle. But Jesus says we are blessed if we can believe without seeing. We have all the proof we need in the words of the Bible and the testimony of believers.

20:30, 31 To understand the life and mission of Jesus more fully, all we need to do is study the Gospels. John tells us that in his Gospel are only a few of the many events in Jesus' life on earth. But what is written is everything we need to know to believe that Jesus is the Christ, the Son of God, through whom we receive eternal life.

21:1ff This chapter tells how Jesus commissioned Peter. Perhaps Peter needed special encouragement after his denial.

²A group of us were there—Simon Peter, Thomas, "The Twin," Nathanael from Cana in Galilee, my brother James and I and two other disciples.

³Simon Peter said, "I'm going fishing."

"We'll come too," we all said. We did, but caught nothing all night. ⁴At dawn we saw a man standing on the beach but couldn't see who he was.

⁵He called, "Any fish, boys?""No," we replied.

⁶Then he said, "Throw out your net on the right-hand side of the boat, and you'll get plenty of them!" So we did, and couldn't draw in the net because of the weight of the fish, there were so many!

⁷Then I said to Peter, "It is the Lord!" At that, Simon Peter put on his tunic (for he was stripped to the waist) and jumped into the water [and swam ashore]. ⁸The rest of us stayed in the boat and pulled the loaded net to the beach, about 300 feet away. ⁹When we got there, we saw that a fire was kindled and fish were frying over it, and there was bread.

¹⁰"Bring some of the fish you've just caught," Jesus said. ¹¹So Simon Peter went out and dragged the net ashore. By his count there were 153 large fish; and yet the net hadn't torn.

¹²"Now come and have some breakfast!" Jesus said; and none of us dared ask him if he really was the Lord, for we were quite sure of it. ¹³Then Jesus went around serving us the bread and fish.

¹⁴This was the third time Jesus had appeared to us since his return from the dead.

Jesus talks with Peter
(247)

¹⁵After breakfast Jesus said to Simon Peter, "Simon, son of John, do you love me more than these others?""Yes," Peter replied, "You know I am your friend."

"Then feed my lambs," Jesus told him.

¹⁶Jesus repeated the question: "Simon, son of John, do you *really* love me?"

"Yes, Lord," Peter said, "you know I am your friend."

21:2 *my brother James and I,* literally, "the sons of Zebedee." **21:5** *boys,* literally, "children." **21:7** *Then I,* literally, "that disciple therefore whom Jesus loved." *and swam ashore,* implied. **21:15** *more than these others,* literally, "more than these." See Mk 14:29.

21:2 Mt 4:21,22 / Jn 1:45-51

21:6 Lk 5:4-7

21:7 Jn 13:21; 21:20

21:9 Jn 6:9,11

21:12 Acts 10:41

21:14 Jn 20:19,26

21:15 Mt 26:33 / Acts 20:28 / Eph 4:11

21:16 Heb 13:20,21 / 1 Pet 2:25,5:2

		JESUS' APPEARANCES AFTER HIS RESURRECTION
Mary Magdalene	Mark 16:9–11; John 20:10–18	
The other women at the tomb	Matthew 28:8–10	
Peter in Jerusalem	Luke 24:34; 1 Corinthians 15:5	
The two travelers on the road	Mark 16:9–11; John 20:10–18	
Ten disciples behind closed doors	Mark 16:14; Luke 24:36–43; John 20:19–25	
All the disciples, with Thomas (excluding Judas Iscariot)	John 20:26–31; 1 Corinthians 15:5	
Seven disciples while fishing	John 21:1–14	
Eleven disciples on the mountain	Matthew 28:16–20	
A crowd of 500	1 Corinthians 15:6	
His brother James	1 Corinthians 15:7	
Those who watched him ascend into heaven	Luke 24:44–49; Acts 1:3–8	

The truth of Christianity rests heavily on the resurrection. If Jesus rose from the grave, who saw him? How trustworthy were the witnesses? Those who claimed to have seen the risen Jesus went on to turn the world upside down. Most of them also died for being followers of Christ. People rarely die for half-hearted belief. These are the people who saw Jesus risen from the grave.

21:7 John recognized Jesus, undoubtedly because Jesus had performed a similar miracle earlier (Luke 5:1–11).

21:15-17 In this beach scene, Jesus led Peter through an experience which would remove the cloud of his denial. Peter had denied Jesus three times. Three times Jesus asked Peter if he loved him. When Peter answered yes, Jesus told him to feed his sheep. It is one thing to say you love Jesus, but the real test is

willingness to serve him. Peter had repented, and now Jesus asked him to commit his life.

21:15-19 Peter's life changed when he finally realized who Jesus was. His occupation changed from fisherman to evangelist; his identity changed from impetuous to "rock"; and his relationship to Jesus changed—now he was forgiven and fully understood the significance of Jesus' words about his death and resurrection.

"Then take care of my sheep," Jesus said.

21:17
1 Chron 28:9
29:17
2 Chron 6:30
Jer 17:10
Jn 2:24,25
13:38
Rom 8:27
1 Thess 2:4

17Once more he asked him, "Simon, son of John, are you even my friend?" Peter was grieved at the way Jesus asked the question this third time. "Lord, you know my heart; you know I am," he said.

Jesus said, "Then feed my little sheep. 18When you were young, you were able to do as you liked and go wherever you wanted to; but when you are old, you will stretch out your hands and others will direct you and take you where you don't want to go." 19Jesus said this to let him know what kind of death he would die to glorify God. Then Jesus told him, "Follow me."

21:19
2 Pet 1:13,14

21:20
Jn 13:23-25

20Peter turned around and saw the disciple Jesus loved following, the one who had leaned around at supper that time to ask Jesus, "Master, which of us will betray you?" 21Peter asked Jesus, "What about him, Lord? What sort of death will he die?"

21:22
Deut 29:29
1 Cor 4:5; 11:26
Rev 2:25; 3:11
22:7,20

22Jesus replied, "If I want him to live until I return, what is that to you? *You* follow me."

21:24
Jn 1:14; 15:27
19:35
1 Jn 1:1-3
3 Jn 12

23So the rumor spread among the brotherhood that that disciple wouldn't die! But that isn't what Jesus said at all! He only said, "If I want him to live until I come, what is that to you?"

24*I am that disciple!* I saw these events and have recorded them here. And we all know that my account of these things is accurate.

21:25
Jn 20:30,31

25And I suppose that if all the other events in Jesus' life were written, the whole world could hardly contain the books!

21:17 *you know my heart,* literally, "all things."   **21:21** *What sort of death will he die?* implied. Literally, "and this man, what?"   **21:22** *live,* literally, "tarry." So also in vs 23.

21:17 Jesus asked Peter three times if he loved him. The first time Jesus said, "Do you love (Greek, *agape:* signifying volitional, self-sacrificial love) me more than these others?" The second time, Jesus focused on Peter alone and still used the Greek word *agape.* The third time, Jesus used the Greek word *phileo,* (signifying affection, affinity, or brotherly love) and asked, "Are you even my friend?" Each time Peter responded with the Greek word *phileo.* Jesus doesn't settle for quick, superficial answers. He has a way of getting to the heart of the matter. Peter had to face his true feelings and motives when confronted by Christ. How would you respond if Jesus asked you, "Do you love me?" Do you really love Jesus? Are you his friend?

21:18, 19 This was a prediction of Peter's death by crucifixion. Tradition indicates that Peter was crucified for his faith—upside down, because he did not feel worthy of dying as his Lord did. Despite what his future held, Jesus told Peter to follow him. We may be uncertain and fearful about our future. But we are assured that God is in control, and we can confidently follow Christ.

21:21, 22 Peter asked Jesus how John would die. Jesus replied that Peter should not concern himself with that. We tend to compare our lives to others, whether to rationalize our own level of devotion to Christ or to question God's justice. When evidence is presented in the courtroom, those who hear it must make a choice. Jesus responds to us as he did to Peter: "What is that to you? *You* follow me!"

21:23 Tradition says that John, after spending several years as an exile on the island of Patmos, returned to Ephesus, where he died as an old man near the end of the first century.

21:25 John's stated purpose for writing his Gospel was to show that Jesus was the Son of God. He clearly and systematically presented the evidence for Jesus' claims. When evidence is presented in the courtroom, those who hear it must make a choice—is Jesus the Son of God, or isn't he? You are the jury. The evidence has been clearly presented. You must decide. Read John's Gospel and believe!

250 EVENTS IN THE LIFE OF CHRIST/ A HARMONY OF THE GOSPELS

All four books in the Bible that tell the story of Jesus Christ—Matthew, Mark, Luke, and John—stand alone, emphasizing a unique aspect of Jesus' life. But when these are blended into one complete account, or harmonized, we gain new insights about the life of Christ.

This harmony combines the four Gospels into a single chronological account of Christ's life on earth. It includes every chapter and verse of each Gospel, leaving nothing out.

The harmony is divided into 250 events. The title of each event is identical to the title found in the corresponding Gospel. Parallel passages found in more than one Gospel have identical titles, helping you to identify them quickly.

Each of the 250 events in the harmony is numbered. The number of the event corresponds to the number next to the title in the Bible text. When reading one of the Gospel accounts you will notice, at times, that some numbers are missing or out of sequence. The easiest way to locate these events is to refer to the harmony.

In addition, if you are looking for a particular event in the life of Christ, the harmony can help you locate it more rapidly than paging through all four Gospels. Each of the 250 events has a distinctive title keyed to the main emphasis of the passage to help you locate and remember the events.

This harmony will help you better visualize the travels of Jesus, study the four Gospels comparatively, and appreciate the unity of their message.

I. BIRTH AND PREPARATION OF JESUS CHRIST

	Matthew	Mark	Luke	John
1 Luke's purpose in writing			1:1–4	
2 God became a human being				1:1–18
3 The ancestors of Jesus	1:1–17		3:23–38	
4 An angel promises the birth of John to Zacharias			1:5–25	
5 An angel promises the birth of Jesus to Mary			1:26–38	
6 Mary visits Elizabeth			1:39–56	
7 John the Baptist is born			1:57–80	
8 An angel appears to Joseph	1:18–25			
9 Jesus is born in Bethlehem			2:1–7	
10 Shepherds visit Jesus			2:8–20	
11 Mary and Joseph bring Jesus to the Temple			2:21–40	
12 Visitors arrive from eastern lands	2:1–12			
13 The escape to Egypt	2:13–18			
14 The return to Nazareth	2:19–23			
15 Jesus speaks with the religious teachers			2:41–52	
16 John the Baptist prepares the way for Jesus	3:1–12	1:1–8	3:1–18	
17 John baptizes Jesus	3:13–17	1:9–11	3:21, 22	
18 Satan tempts Jesus in the wilderness	4:1–11	1:12, 13	4:1–13	
19 John the Baptist declares his mission				1:19–28

	Matthew	Mark	Luke	John
20 John the Baptist proclaims Jesus as the Messiah				1:29–34
21 The first disciples follow Jesus				1:35–51
22 Jesus turns water into wine				2:1–12

II. MESSAGE AND MINISTRY OF JESUS CHRIST

	Matthew	Mark	Luke	John
23 Jesus clears the Temple				2:13–25
24 Nicodemus visits Jesus at night				3:1–21
25 John the Baptist tells more about Jesus				3:22–36
26 Herod puts John in prison			3:19, 20	
27 Jesus talks to a woman at the well				4:1–26
28 Jesus tells about the spiritual harvest				4:27–38
29 Many Samaritans believe in Jesus				4:39–42
30 Jesus preaches in Galilee	4:12–17	1:14, 15	4:14, 15	4:43–45
31 Jesus heals a government official's son				4:46–54
32 Jesus is rejected at Nazareth			4:16–30	
33 Four fishermen follow Jesus	4:18–22	1:16–20		
34 Jesus teaches with great authority		1:21–28	4:31–37	
35 Jesus heals Peter's mother-in-law and many others	8:14–17	1:29–34	4:38–41	
36 Jesus preaches throughout Galilee	4:23–25	1:35–39	4:42–44	
37 Jesus provides a miraculous catch of fish			5:1–11	
38 Jesus heals a man with leprosy	8:1–4	1:40–45	5:12–16	
39 Jesus heals a paralyzed man	9:1–8	2:1–12	5:17–26	
40 Jesus eats with sinners at Matthew's house	9:9–13	2:13–17	5:27–32	
41 Religious leaders ask Jesus about fasting	9:14–17	2:18–22	5:33–39	
42 Jesus heals a lame man by the pool				5:1–15
43 Jesus claims to be God's Son				5:16–30
44 Jesus supports his claim				5:31–47
45 The disciples pick wheat on the Sabbath	12:1–8	2:23–28	6:1–5	
46 Jesus heals a man's hand on the Sabbath	12:9–14	3:1–6	6:6–11	
47 Large crowds follow Jesus	12:15–21	3:7–12		
48 Jesus selects the twelve disciples		3:13–19	6:12–16	
49 Jesus gives the beatitudes	5:1–12		6:17–26	
50 Jesus teaches about salt and light	5:13–16			
51 Jesus teaches about the law	5:17–20			
52 Jesus teaches about anger	5:21–26			
53 Jesus teaches about lust	5:27–30			
54 Jesus teaches about divorce	5:31, 32			
55 Jesus teaches about vows	5:33–37			
56 Jesus teaches about retaliation	5:38–42			
57 Jesus teaches about loving enemies	5:43–48		6:27–36	
58 Jesus teaches about giving to the needy	6:1–4			
59 Jesus teaches about prayer	6:5–15			
60 Jesus teaches about fasting	6:16–18			
61 Jesus teaches about money	6:19–24			
62 Jesus teaches about worry	6:25–34			
63 Jesus teaches about criticizing others	7:1–6		6:37–42	
64 Jesus teaches about asking, seeking, knocking	7:7–12			
65 Jesus teaches about the way to heaven	7:13, 14			
66 Jesus teaches about fruit in people's lives	7:15–20		6:43–45	
67 Jesus teaches about those who build houses on rock and sand	7:21–29		6:46–49	
68 A Roman soldier demonstrates faith	8:5–13		7:1–10	
69 Jesus raises a widow's son from the dead			7:11–17	
70 Jesus eases John's doubt	11:1–19		7:18–35	
71 Jesus promises rest for the soul	11:20–30			
72 A sinful woman anoints Jesus' feet			7:36–50	
73 Women accompany Jesus and the disciples			8:1–3	
74 Religious leaders accuse Jesus of being Satan	12:22–37	3:20–30		

	Matthew	Mark	Luke	John
75 Religious leaders ask Jesus for a miracle	12:38–45			
76 Jesus describes his true family	12:46–50	3:31–35	8:19–21	
77 Jesus tells the parable of the four soils	13:1–9	4:1–9	8:4–8	
78 Jesus explains the parable of the four soils	13:10–23	4:10–25	8:9–18	
79 Jesus tells the parable of the growing seed		4:26–29		
80 Jesus tells the parable of the weeds	13:24–30			
81 Jesus tells the parable of the mustard seed	13:31, 32	4:30–34		
82 Jesus tells the parable of the yeast	13:33–35			
83 Jesus explains the parable of the weeds	13:36–43			
84 Jesus tells the parable of hidden treasure	13:44			
85 Jesus tells the parable of the pearl merchant	13:45, 46			
86 Jesus tells the parable of the fishing net	13:47–52			
87 Jesus calms the storm	8:23–27	4:35–41	8:22–25	
88 Jesus sends the demons into a herd of pigs	8:28–34	5:1–20	8:26–39	
89 Jesus heals a bleeding woman and restores a girl to life	9:18–26	5:21–43	8:40–56	
90 Jesus heals the blind and mute	9:27–34			
91 The people of Nazareth refuse to believe	13:53–58	6:1–6		
92 Jesus urges the disciples to pray for workers	9:35–38			
93 Jesus sends out the twelve disciples	10:1–15	6:7–13	9:1–6	
94 Jesus prepares the disciples for persecution	10:16–42			
95 Herod kills John the Baptist	14:1–12	6:14–29	9:7–9	
96 Jesus feeds five thousand	14:13–21	6:30–44	9:10–17	6:1–15
97 Jesus walks on water	14:22–33	6:45–52		6:16–21
98 Jesus heals all who touch him	14:34–36	6:53–56		
99 Jesus is the true bread from heaven				6:22–40
100 The Jews disagree that Jesus is from heaven				6:41–59
101 Many disciples desert Jesus				6:60–71
102 Jesus teaches about inner purity	15:1–20	7:1–23		
103 Jesus sends a demon out of a girl	15:21–28	7:24–30		
104 The crowd marvels at Jesus' healings	15:29–31	7:31–37		
105 Jesus feeds four thousand	15:32–39	8:1–9		
106 Religious leaders ask for a sign in the sky	16:1–4	8:10–12		
107 Jesus warns against wrong teaching	16:5–12	8:13–21		
108 Jesus restores sight to a blind man		8:22–26		
109 Peter says Jesus is the Messiah	16:13–20	8:27–30	9:18–20	
110 Jesus predicts his death the first time	16:21–28	8:31–9:1	9:21–27	
111 Jesus is transfigured on the mountain	17:1–13	9:2–13	9:28–36	
112 Jesus heals a demon-possessed boy	17:14–21	9:14–29	9:37–43	
113 Jesus predicts his death the second time	17:22, 23	9:30–32	9:44, 45	
114 Peter finds the coin in the fish's mouth	17:24–27			
115 The disciples argue about who would be the greatest	18:1–6	9:33–37	9:46–48	
116 The disciples forbid another to use Jesus' name		9:38–42	9:49, 50	
117 Jesus warns against temptation	18:7–9	9:43–50		
118 Jesus warns against looking down on others	18:10–14			
119 Jesus teaches how to treat a believer who sins	18:15–20			
120 Jesus tells the parable of the unforgiving debtor	18:21–35			
121 Jesus' brothers ridicule him				7:1–9
122 Jesus teaches about the cost of following him	8:18–22		9:51–62	
123 Jesus teaches openly at the Temple				7:10–31
124 Religious leaders attempt to arrest Jesus				7:32–53
125 Jesus forgives an adulterous woman				8:1–11
126 Jesus is the light of the world				8:12–20
127 Jesus warns of coming judgment				8:21–29
128 Jesus speaks about God's true children				8:30–47
129 Jesus states he is eternal				8:48–59
130 Jesus sends out seventy messengers			10:1–16	
131 The seventy messengers return			10:17–24	
132 Jesus tells the parable of the good Samaritan			10:25–37	
133 Jesus visits Mary and Martha			10:38–42	
134 Jesus teaches his disciples about prayer			11:1–13	
135 Jesus answers hostile accusations			11:14–28	
136 Jesus warns against unbelief			11:29–32	

	Matthew	Mark	Luke	John
137 Jesus teaches about the light within			11:33–36	
138 Jesus criticizes the religious leaders			11:37–54	
139 Jesus speaks against hypocrisy			12:1–12	
140 Jesus tells the parable of the rich fool			12:13–21	
141 Jesus warns about worry			12:22–34	
142 Jesus warns about preparing for his coming			12:35–48	
143 Jesus warns about coming division			12:49–53	
144 Jesus warns about the future crisis			12:54–59	
145 Jesus calls the people to repent			13:1–9	
146 Jesus heals the handicapped woman			13:10–17	
147 Jesus teaches about the Kingdom of God			13:18–21	
148 Jesus heals the man who was born blind				9:1–12
149 Religious leaders question the blind man				9:13–34
150 Jesus teaches about spiritual blindness				9:35–41
151 Jesus is the Good Shepherd				10:1–21
152 Religious leaders surround Jesus at the Temple				10:22–42
153 Jesus teaches about entering the Kingdom			13:22–30	
154 Jesus grieves over Jerusalem			13:31–35	
155 Jesus heals a man with dropsy			14:1–6	
156 Jesus teaches about seeking honor			14:7–14	
157 Jesus tells the parable of the great feast			14:15–24	
158 Jesus teaches about the cost of being a disciple			14:25–35	
159 Jesus tells the parable of the lost sheep			15:1–7	
160 Jesus tells the parable of the lost coin			15:8–10	
161 Jesus tells the parable of the lost son			15:11–32	
162 Jesus tells the parable of the shrewd accountant			16:1–18	
163 Jesus tells about the rich man and the beggar			16:19–31	
164 Jesus tells about forgiveness and faith			17:1–10	
165 Lazarus becomes ill and dies				11:1–16
166 Jesus comforts Mary and Martha				11:17–36
167 Jesus raises Lazarus from the dead				11:37–44
168 Religious leaders plot to kill Jesus				11:45–57
169 Jesus heals ten lepers			17:11–19	
170 Jesus teaches about the coming of the Kingdom of God			17:20–37	
171 Jesus tells the parable of the persistent widow			18:1–8	
172 Jesus tells the parable of two men who prayed			18:9–14	
173 Jesus teaches about marriage and divorce	19:1–12	10:1–12		
174 Jesus blesses little children	19:13–15	10:13–16	18:15–17	
175 Jesus speaks to the rich young man	19:16–30	10:17–31	18:18–30	
176 Jesus tells the parable of the workers paid equally	20:1–16			
177 Jesus predicts his death the third time	20:17–19	10:32–34	18:31–34	
178 Jesus teaches about serving others	20:20–28	10:35–45		
179 Jesus heals a blind beggar	20:29–34	10:46–52	18:35–43	
180 Jesus brings salvation to Zacchaeus' home			19:1–10	
181 Jesus tells the parable of the king's ten servants			19:11–27	
182 A woman anoints Jesus with perfume	26:6–13	14:3–9		12:1–11
183 Jesus rides into Jerusalem on a donkey	21:1–11	11:1–11	19:28–44	12:12–19
184 Jesus clears the Temple again	21:12–17	11:12–19	19:45–48	
185 Jesus explains why he must die				12:20–36
186 Most of the people do not believe in Jesus				12:37–43
187 Jesus summarizes his message				12:44–50
188 Jesus says the disciples can pray for anything	21:18–22	11:20–25		
189 Religious leaders challenge Jesus' authority	21:23–27	11:26–33	20:1–8	
190 Jesus tells the parable of the two sons	21:28–32			
191 Jesus tells the parable of the wicked farmers	21:33–46	12:1–12	20:9–19	
192 Jesus tells the parable of the wedding feast	22:1–14			
193 Religious leaders question Jesus about paying taxes	22:15–22	12:13–17	20:20–26	
194 Religious leaders question Jesus about the resurrection	22:23–32	12:18–27	20:27–40	
195 Religious leaders question Jesus about the greatest commandment	22:33–40	12:28–34		
196 Religious leaders cannot answer Jesus' question	22:41–46	12:35–37	20:41–44	

	Matthew	Mark	Luke	John
197 Jesus warns against the religious leaders	23:1–12	12:38–40	20:45–47	
198 Jesus condemns the religious leaders	23:13–36			
199 Jesus grieves over Jerusalem again	23:37–39			
200 A poor widow gives all she has		12:41–44	21:1–4	
201 Jesus tells about the future	24:1–22	13:1–20	21:5–24	
202 Jesus tells about his return	24:23–35	13:21–31	21:25–33	
203 Jesus tells about remaining watchful	24:36–51	13:32–37	21:34–38	
204 Jesus tells the parable of the ten bridesmaids	25:1–13			
205 Jesus tells the parable of the loaned money	25:14–30			
206 Jesus tells about the final judgment	25:31–46			

III. DEATH AND RESURRECTION OF JESUS CHRIST

	Matthew	Mark	Luke	John
207 Religious leaders plot to kill Jesus	26:1–5	14:1, 2	22:1, 2	
208 Judas agrees to betray Jesus	26:14–16	14:10, 11	22:3–6	
209 Disciples prepare for the Passover	26:17–19	14:12–16	22:7–13	
210 Jesus washes the disciples' feet				13:1–20
211 Jesus and the disciples have the Last Supper	26:20–29	14:17–25	22:14–30	13:21–30
212 Jesus predicts Peter's denial			22:31–38	13:31–38
213 Jesus is the way to the Father				14:1–14
214 Jesus promises the Holy Spirit				14:15–31
215 Jesus teaches about the Vine and the branches				15:1–16
216 Jesus warns about the world's hatred				15:17—16:4
217 Jesus teaches about the Holy Spirit				16:5–16
218 Jesus teaches about using his name in prayer				16:17–33
219 Jesus prays for himself				17:1–5
220 Jesus prays for his disciples				17:6–19
221 Jesus prays for future believers				17:20–26
222 Jesus again predicts Peter's denial	26:30–35	14:26–31		
223 Jesus agonizes in the garden	26:36–46	14:32–42	22:39–46	
224 Jesus is betrayed and arrested	26:47–56	14:43–52	22:47–53	18:1–11
225 Annas questions Jesus				18:12–24
226 Caiaphas questions Jesus	26:57–68	14:53–65		
227 Peter denies knowing Jesus	26:69–75	14:66–72	22:54–65	18:25–27
228 The council of religious leaders condemns Jesus	27:1, 2	15:1	22:66–71	
229 Judas kills himself	27:3–10			
230 Jesus stands trial before Pilate	27:11–14	15:2–5	23:1–5	18:28–38
231 Jesus stands trial before Herod			23:6–12	
232 Pilate hands Jesus over to be crucified	27:15–26	15:6–15	23:13–25	18:39— 19:16
233 Roman soldiers mock Jesus	27:27–31	15:16–20		
234 Jesus is led away to be crucified	27:32–34	15:21–24	23:26–31	19:17
235 Jesus is placed on the cross	27:35–44	15:25–32	23:32–43	19:18–27
236 Jesus dies on the cross	27:45–56	15:33–41	23:44–49	19:28–37
237 Jesus is laid in the tomb	27:57–61	15:42–47	23:50–56	19:38–42
238 Guards are posted at the tomb	27:62–66			
239 Jesus rises from the dead	28:1–7	16:1–8	24:1–12	20:1–9
240 Jesus appears to Mary Magdalene		16:9–11		20:10–18
241 Jesus appears to the women	28:8–10			
242 Religious leaders bribe the guards	28:11–15			
243 Jesus appears to two believers traveling on the road		16:12, 13	24:13–35	
244 Jesus appears to the disciples behind locked doors			24:36–43	20:19–23
245 Jesus appears to the disciples including Thomas		16:14		20:24–31
246 Jesus appears to the disciples while fishing				21:1–14
247 Jesus talks with Peter				21:15–25

**THE PARABLES
OF JESUS**

I. Teaching Parables

    A. About the Kingdom of God
1. The Soils (Matthew 13:3–8; Mark 4:4–8; Luke 8:5–8)
2. The Thistles (Matthew 13:24–30)
3. The Mustard Seed (Matthew 13:31, 32; Mark 4:30–32; Luke 13:18, 19)
4. The Yeast (Matthew 13:33; Luke 13:20, 21)
5. The Treasure (Matthew 13:44)
6. The Pearl (Matthew 13:45, 46)
7. The Fishing Net (Matthew 13:47–50)
8. The Growing Wheat (Mark 4:26–29)

    B. About Service and Obedience
1. The Workers in the Harvest (Matthew 20:1–16)
2. The Loaned Money (Matthew 25:14–30)
3. The Nobleman's Servants (Luke 19:11–27)
4. The Servant's Role (Luke 17:7–10)

    C. About Prayer
1. The Friend at Midnight (Luke 11:5–8)
2. The Unjust Judge (Luke 18:1–8)

    D. About Neighbors
1. The Good Samaritan (Luke 10:30–37)

    E. About Humility
1. The Wedding Feast (Luke 14:7–11)
2. The Proud Pharisee and the Corrupt Taxpayer (Luke 18:9–14)

    F. About Wealth
1. The Wealthy Fool (Luke 12:16–21)
2. The Great Feast (Luke 14:16–24)
3. The Dishonest Accountant (Luke 16:1–9)

II. Gospel Parables

    A. About God's Love
1. The Lost Sheep (Matthew 18:12–14; Luke 15:3–7)
2. The Lost Coin (Luke 15:8–10)
3. The Lost Son (Luke 15:11–32)

    B. About Thankfulness
1. The Forgiven Loans (Luke 7:41–43)

III. Parables of Judgment and the Future

    A. About Christ's Return
1. The Ten Virgins (Matthew 25:1–13)
2. The Wise and Faithful Servants (Matthew 24:45–51; Luke 12:42–48)
3. The Traveling Boss (Mark 13:34–37)

    B. About God's Values
1. The Two Sons (Matthew 21:28–32)
2. The Wicked Farmers (Matthew 21:33, 34; Mark 12:1–9; Luke 20:9–16)
3. The Unproductive Fig Tree (Luke 13:6–9)
4. The Marriage Feast (Matthew 22:1–14)
5. The Unforgiving Servant (Matthew 18:23–35)

	Matthew	Mark	Luke	John	JESUS' MIRACLES
Five thousand people are fed	14:15–21	6:35–44	9:12–17	6:5–14	John and the other gospel writers were able to record only a fraction of the people who were touched and healed by Jesus. But enough of Jesus' words and works have been saved so that we also might be able to know him and be his disciples in this day. There follows a listing of the miracles that are included in the Gospels. They were supernatural events that pointed people to God, and they were acts of love by one who is love.
Stilling the storm	8:23–27	4:35–41	8:22–25		
Demons sent into the pigs	8:28–34	5:1–20	8:26–39		
Jairus' daughter raised	9:18–26	5:22–24, 35–43	8:41, 42, 49–56		
Diseased woman healed	9:20–22	5:25–34	8:43–48		
Jesus heals a paralyzed man	9:1–8	2:1–12	5:17–26		
A leper is healed at Gennesaret	8:1–4	1:40–45	5:12–15		
Peter's mother-in-law healed	8:14–17	1:29–31	4:38, 39		
A withered hand is restored	12:9–13	3:1–5	6:6–11		
A demon-possessed boy is cured	17:14–21	9:14–29	9:37–42		
Jesus walks on the sea	14:22–33	6:45–52		6:17–21	
Blind Bartimaeus receives sight	20:29–34	10:46–52	18:35–43		
A girl is freed from a demon	15:21–28	7:24–30			
Four thousand are fed	15:32–38	8:1–9			
Cursing the fig tree	21:18–22	11:12–14, 20–24			
A centurion's servant is healed	8:5–13		7:1–10		
A demon is sent out of a man		1:23–27	4:33–36		
A dumb demoniac is healed	12:22		11:14		
Two blind men find sight	9:27–31				
Jesus heals the mute man	9:32, 33				
A coin in a fish's mouth	17:24–27				
A deaf and dumb man is healed		7:31–37			
A blind man sees at Bethsaida		8:22–26			
The first miraculous catch of fish			5:1–11		
A widow's son is raised			7:11–16		
A handicapped woman is healed			13:10–17		
Jesus cures a sick man			14:1–6		
Ten lepers are cured			17:11–19		
Jesus restores a man's ear			22:49–51		
Jesus turns water into wine				2:1–11	
A nobleman's son is healed at Cana				4:46–54	
A lame man is cured				5:1–16	
Jesus heals a man born blind				9:1–7	
Lazarus is raised from the dead				11:1–45	
The second miraculous catch of fish				21:1–14	

	Matthew	Mark	Luke	John	COMPARISON OF THE FOUR GOSPELS
Jesus is . . .	The promised King	The Servant of God	The Son of Man	The Son of God	All four Gospels present the life and teachings of Jesus. Each book, however, focuses on a unique facet of Jesus and his character. To understand more about the specific characteristics of Jesus, read any one of the four Gospels.
The original readers were . . .	Jews	Gentiles, Romans	Greeks	Christians throughout the world	
Significant themes . . .	Jesus is the Messiah because he fulfilled Old Testament prophecy	Jesus backed up his words with action	Jesus was God but also fully human	Belief in Jesus is required for salvation	
Character of the writer . . .	Teacher	Storyteller	Historian	Theologian	
Greatest emphasis is on . . .	Jesus' sermons and words	Jesus' miracles and actions	Jesus' humanity	The principles of Jesus' teaching	

MESSIANIC PROPHECIES AND FULFILLMENTS
For the Gospel writers, one of the main reasons for believing in Jesus was the way his life fulfilled the Old Testament prophecies about the Messiah. Following is a list of some of the main prophecies.

		Old Testament Prophecies	New Testament Fulfillment
1.	Messiah was to be born in Bethlehem	Micah 5:2	Matthew 2:1–6 Luke 2:1–20
2.	Messiah was to be born of a virgin	Isaiah 7:14	Matthew 1:18–25 Luke 1:26–38
3.	Messiah was to be a prophet like Moses	Deuteronomy 18:15, 18, 19	John 7:40
4.	Messiah was to enter Jerusalem in triumph	Zechariah 9:9	Matthew 21:1–9 John 12:12–16
5.	Messiah was to be rejected by his own people	Isaiah 53:1, 3 Psalm 118:22	Matthew 26:3, 4 John 12:37–43 Acts 4:1–12
6.	Messiah was to be betrayed by one of his followers	Psalm 41:9	Matthew 26:14–16, 47–50 Luke 22:19–23
7.	Messiah was to be tried and condemned	Isaiah 53:8	Luke 23:1–25 Matthew 27:1, 2
8.	Messiah was to be silent before his accusers	Isaiah 53:7	Matthew 27:12–14 Mark 15:3–4, Luke 23:8–10
9.	Messiah was to be struck and spat upon by his enemies	Isaiah 50:6	Matthew 26:67 Matthew 27:30 Mark 14:65
10.	Messiah was to be mocked and taunted	Psalm 22:7, 8	Matthew 27:39–44 Luke 23:11, 35
11.	Messiah was to die by crucifixion	Psalm 22:14, 16, 17	Matthew 27:31 Mark 15:20, 25
12.	Messiah was to suffer with criminals and pray for his enemies	Isaiah 53:12	Matthew 27:38 Mark 15:27, 28 Luke 23:32–34
13.	Messiah was to be given vinegar and gall	Psalm 69:21	Matthew 27:34 John 19:28–30
14.	Others were to cast lots for Messiah's garments	Psalm 22:18	Matthew 27:35 John 19:23, 24
15.	Messiah's bones were not to be broken	Exodus 12:46	John 19:31–36
16.	Messiah was to die as a sacrifice for sin	Isaiah 53:5, 6, 8, 10, 11, 12	John 1:29; 11:49–52 Acts 10:43; 13:38, 39
17.	Messiah was to be raised from the dead	Psalm 16:10	Acts 2:22–32 Matthew 28:1–10
18.	Messiah is now at God's right hand	Psalm 110:1	Mark 16:19 Luke 24:50, 51

ACTS

VITAL STATISTICS

PURPOSE:
To give an accurate account of the birth and growth of the Christian church

AUTHOR:
Luke

TO WHOM WRITTEN:
Theophilus

DATE WRITTEN:
Between A.D. 63 and 70

SETTING:
Acts is the connecting link between Christ's life and the life of the church, between the Gospels and the Epistles

KEY VERSE:
"But when the Holy Spirit has come upon you, you will receive power to testify about me with great effect, to the people in Jerusalem, throughout Judea, in Samaria, and to the ends of the earth . . . " (1:8).

KEY PEOPLE:
Peter, John, James, Stephen, Philip, Paul, Barnabas, Cornelius, James (Jesus' brother), Timothy, Lydia, Silas, Titus, Apollos, Agabus, Ananias, Felix, Festus, Agrippa, Luke

KEY PLACES:
Jerusalem, Samaria, Lydda, Joppa, Antioch, Cyprus, Antioch in Pisidia, Iconium, Lystra, Derbe, Philippi, Thessalonica, Beroea, Athens, Corinth, Ephesus, Caesarea, Malta, Rome

SPECIAL FEATURES:
Acts is a sequel to the Gospel of Luke. Because it ends so abruptly, Luke may have planned to write a third book, continuing the story.

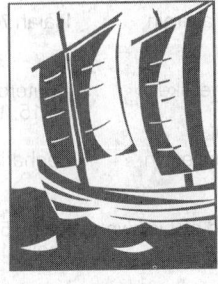

WITH a flick of the fingers, friction occurs and a spark leaps from match to tinder. A small flame burns the edges and grows, fueled by wood and air. Heat builds, and soon the kindling is licked by orange-red tongues. Higher and wider it spreads, consuming the wood. The flame has become a fire.

Nearly 2,000 years ago, a match was struck in Palestine. At first, just a few in that corner of the world were touched and warmed; but the fire spread beyond Jerusalem and Judea out to the world and to all people. Acts provides an eyewitness account of the flame and fire—the birth and spread of the church. Beginning in Jerusalem with a small group of disciples, the message traveled across the Roman empire. Empowered by the Holy Spirit, this courageous band preached, taught, healed, and demonstrated love in synagogues, schools, homes, markets, and courtrooms; on streets, hills, ships, and desert roads—wherever God sent them, lives and history were changed.

Written by Luke as a sequel to his Gospel, Acts is an accurate historical record of the early church. But Acts is also a theological book, with lessons and living examples of the work of the Holy Spirit, church relationships and organization, the implications of grace, and the law of love. And Acts is an apologetic work, building a strong case for the validity of Christ's claims and promises.

The book of Acts begins with the outpouring of the promised Holy Spirit and the commencement of the proclamation of the gospel of Jesus Christ. This Spirit-inspired evangelism begins in Jerusalem and eventually speads to Rome, covering most of the Roman empire. The gospel first goes to the Jews; but they, as a nation, continually reject it. A remnant of Jews, of course, gladly received the Good News. But the continual rejection of the gospel by the vast majority of the Jews led to the ever-increasing proclamation of the gospel to the Gentiles. Now this was according to Jesus' plan: the gospel was to go from Jerusalem, to Judea, to Samaria, and to the ends of the earth (1:8). This, in fact, is the pattern that the Acts narrative follows. The glorious proclamation begins in Jerusalem (chapters 1—7), goes to Judea and Samaria (chapter 8 and following), and to the countries beyond Judea (11:19; 13:4 and on to the end of Acts). The second half of Acts is focused primarily on Paul's missionary journeys to many countries north of the Mediterranean Sea. He, with his companions, takes the gospel first to the Jews and then to the Gentiles. Some of the Jews believe, and many of the Gentiles receive the Good News with joy. New churches are started, and new believers begin to grow in the Christian life.

As you read Acts, put yourself in the place of the disciples—feel with them as they are filled with the Holy Spirit, and thrill with them as they see thousands respond to the gospel message. Sense their commitment as they give every ounce of talent and treasure to Christ. And as you read, watch the Spirit-led boldness of these first-century believers, who through suffering and in the face of death take every opportunity to tell of their crucified and risen Lord. Then decide to be a 20th-century version of those men and women of God.

Paul's third missionary journey 53-57	Nero becomes emperor 54	Paul imprisoned in Caesarea 57-59	Paul's voyage to Rome 59	Paul released from prison 62	Paul martyred 67?	Rome destroys Jerusalem 70

THE BLUEPRINT

A. PETER'S MINISTRY (1:1—12:25)
1. Establishment of the church
2. Expansion of the church

After the resurrection of Jesus Christ, Peter preached boldly and performed many miracles. This demonstrates vividly the source and effects of Christian power. Because of the Holy Spirit, God's people were empowered so they could accomplish their tasks. The Holy Spirit is still available to empower believers today. We should turn to the Holy Spirit to give us the strength, courage, and insight to accomplish our work for God.

B. PAUL'S MINISTRY (13:1—28:31)
1. First missionary journey
2. Meeting of the church council
3. Second missionary journey
4. Third missionary journey
5. Paul on trial

Paul's missionary adventures show us the progress of Christianity. The gospel could not be confined to one corner of the world. This was a faith that offered hope to all mankind. We too should venture forth and share in this heroic task to witness for Christ in all the world.

MEGATHEMES

THEME	EXPLANATION	IMPORTANCE
Church beginnings	Acts is the history of how Christianity was founded and organized and solved its problems. The community of believers began by faith in the risen Christ and in the power of the Holy Spirit, who enabled them to witness, to love, and to serve.	New churches are continually being founded. By faith in Jesus Christ and in the power of the Holy Spirit, the church can be a vibrant agent for change. As we face new problems, Acts gives important remedies for solving them.
Holy Spirit	The church did not start or grow by its own power or enthusiasm. The disciples were empowered by God's Holy Spirit. He was the promised Comforter and Guide sent when Jesus went to heaven.	The Holy Spirit's work demonstrated that Christianity was supernatural. Thus the church became more Holy Spirit-conscious than problem-conscious. By faith, any believer can claim the Holy Spirit's power to do Christ's work.
Church growth	Acts presents the history of a dynamic, growing community of believers from Jerusalem to Syria, Africa, Asia, and Europe. In the first century it spread from believing Jews to non-Jews in 39 cities and 30 countries, islands, or provinces.	When the Holy Spirit works, there is movement, excitement, and growth. He gives us the motivation, energy, and ability to get the gospel to the whole world. How are you fitting into God's plan for expanding Christianity? What is your place in this movement?
Witnessing	Peter, John, Philip, Paul, Barnabas, and thousands more witnessed to their new faith in Christ. By personal testimony, preaching, or defense before authorities, they told the story with boldness and courage to groups of all sizes.	We are God's people, chosen to be part of his plan to reach the world. In love and by faith, we can have the Holy Spirit's help as we witness or preach. Witnessing is also beneficial to us because it strengthens our faith as we confront those who challenge it.
Opposition	Through imprisonment, beatings, plots, and riots, Christians were persecuted by both Jews and Gentiles. But the opposition became a catalyst for the spread of Christianity. This showed that Christianity was not the work of man, but of God.	God can work through any opposition. When severe treatment from hostile unbelievers comes, realize that it has come because you have been a faithful witness and look for the opportunity to present the Good News about Christ. Seize the opportunities that opposition brings.

KEY PLACES IN ACTS

Modern names and boundaries are shown in gray.

The apostle Paul, whose missionary journeys fill much of this book, traveled tremendous distances as he tirelessly spread the gospel across much of the Roman empire. His combined trips, by land and ship, equal more than 13,000 airline miles, to say nothing of the circuitous land routes he walked and climbed.

1 **Judea**   Jesus ascended to heaven from the Mount of Olives outside Jerusalem, and his followers returned to the city to await the infilling of the Holy Spirit, which occurred at Pentecost. Peter gave a powerful sermon that was heard by Jews from across the empire. The Jerusalem church grew, but Stephen was martyred for his faith by Jewish leaders who did not believe in Jesus (1:1—7:59).

2 **Samaria**   After Stephen's death, persecution of Christians intensified, but it caused the believers to leave Jerusalem and spread the gospel to other cities in the empire. Philip took the gospel into Samaria, and even to a man from Ethiopia (8:1–40).

3 **Syria**   Paul began his story as a persecutor of Christians, only to be met by Jesus himself on the road to Damascus. He became a believer, but his new faith caused opposition, so he returned to Tarsus, his home, for safety. Barnabas sought out Paul in Tarsus and brought him to the church in Antioch in Syria, where they worked together. Meanwhile, Peter had received a vision that led him to Caesarea, where he presented the gospel to a Gentile family, who became believers (9:1—12:25).

4 **Cyprus and Galatia**   Paul and Barnabas were dedicated by the church in Antioch in Syria for God's work of spreading the gospel to other cities. They set off on their first missionary journey through Cyprus and Galatia (13:1—14:28).

5 **Jerusalem**   Controversy between Jewish Christians and Gentile Christians over the matter of keeping the law led to a special council, with delegates from the churches in Antioch and Jerusalem meeting in Jerusalem. Together, they resolved the conflict and the news was taken back to Antioch (15:1–35).

6 **Macedonia**   Barnabas traveled to Cyprus while Paul took a second missionary journey. He revisited the churches in Galatia and headed toward Ephesus, but the Holy Spirit said no. He then turned north toward Bithynia and Pontus, but again was told not to go. He then received the "Macedonian call," and followed the Spirit's direction into the cities of Macedonia (15:36—17:14).

7 **Achaia**   Paul traveled from Macedonia to Athens and Corinth in Achaia, then traveled by ship to Ephesus before returning to Caesarea, Jerusalem, and finally back to Antioch (17:15—18:22).

8 **Ephesus**   Paul's third missionary journey took him back through Cilicia and Galatia, this time straight to Ephesus in Asia. He visited other cities in Asia before going back to Macedonia and Achaia. He returned to Jerusalem by ship, despite his knowledge that arrest awaited him there (18:23—23:30).

9 **Caesarea**   Paul was arrested in Jerusalem and taken to Antipatris, then on to Caesarea under Roman guard. Paul always took advantage of any opportunity to share the gospel, and he did so before many Gentile leaders. But because Paul appealed to Caesar, he began the long journey to Rome (23:31—26:32).

10 **Rome**   After storms, layovers in Crete, and shipwreck on the island of Malta, Paul arrived in Sicily, and finally in Italy, where he traveled by land, under guard, to his long-awaited destination, Rome, the capital of the empire.

A. PETER'S MINISTRY (1:1—12:25)

The book of Acts begins where the Gospels leave off, reporting on the actions of the apostles and the work of the Holy Spirit. Beginning in Jerusalem, the church is established and grows rapidly, then faces intense persecution, which drives the believers out into the surrounding areas. Through this dispersion, Samaritans and Gentiles hear the Good News and believe.

1. Establishment of the church

Jesus ascends to heaven

1:1
Lk 1:3
1:2
Mt 28:19,20
Lk 24:49-51
Jn 20:22,23
1:3
Mk 16:12,14
Lk 24:33-36
Jn 20:19,26
21:1,14
1:4
Jn 14:16,17,26
Lk 24:49
Acts 2:33
1:5
Acts 2:4; 11:16

1 Dear friend who loves God:

In my first letter I told you about Jesus' life and teachings and how he returned to heaven after giving his chosen apostles further instructions from the Holy Spirit. ³During the forty days after his crucifixion he appeared to the apostles from time to time, actually alive, and proved to them in many ways that it was really he himself they were seeing. And on these occasions he talked to them about the Kingdom of God.

⁴In one of these meetings he told them not to leave Jerusalem until the Holy Spirit came upon them in fulfillment of the Father's promise, a matter he had previously discussed with them.

⁵"John baptized you with water," he reminded them, "but you shall be baptized with the Holy Spirit in just a few days."

➤ 1:5 *with water,* or, "in water." *with the Holy Spirit,* or "in the Holy Spirit."

1:1 The book of Acts continues the story Luke began in his Gospel, covering the 30 years after Jesus' ascension. In that short time the church was established and the gospel of salvation was taken throughout the world, even to the capital of the Roman Empire. Those preaching the gospel, though ordinary people with human frailties and limitations, were empowered by the Holy Spirit to turn the world "upside down" (17:6). Throughout the book of Acts we learn about the nature of the church and how we today are also to go about turning our world upside down.

1:1 Luke's first writing was the Gospel of Luke; it was also addressed to Theophilus, whose name means "dear friend who loves God." (See note on Luke 1:1.)

1:1–3 Luke says that the disciples were eyewitnesses to all that had happened to Jesus Christ. It is important to know this so we can have confidence in their testimony. Twenty centuries later we can still be confident that our faith is based on fact, not mere enthusiasm.

1:3 Verses 1–8 are the bridge between the events recorded in the Gospels and the life of the early church. Jesus spent 40 days teaching his disciples, and they were changed drastically. Before, they had argued with each other, deserted their Lord, even lied about knowing Jesus. Now, in a series of meetings with the living, resurrected Christ, the disciples had many questions answered. They became convinced about the resurrection, learned about the Kingdom of God, and learned about their power source—the Holy Spirit. By reading the Bible, we can sit with the resurrected Christ in his school of discipleship. By believing in him, we can receive his power by the Holy Spirit to be new people. By joining with other Christians in his church, we can take part in doing his work.

1:3 Jesus explained that with his coming, the Kingdom of God was inaugurated. When he ascended into heaven, God's Kingdom would remain in the hearts of all believers through the presence of the Holy Spirit. But the Kingdom of God will not be fully realized until Jesus Christ comes again to judge all people and remove all evil from the world. Before that time, believers are to work to spread God's Kingdom across the world. The book of Acts records how this was begun. We must continue the work the early church started.

1:3 Today there are still people who doubt Jesus' resurrection. But Jesus appeared to the apostles on many occasions after his resurrection, proving he was alive. Look at the change the resurrection made in the disciples' lives. At Jesus' death, they

scattered. They were disillusioned and feared for their lives. After seeing the resurrected Christ, they were fearless and risked everything to spread the Good News about him around the world. They faced imprisonment, beatings, rejection, and martyrdom yet never compromised their mission. These men would not have risked their lives for something they knew was a fraud. They knew Jesus was raised from the dead, and the early church was fired with their enthusiasm to tell others.

1:4 The *Trinity* is a description of the unique relationship of God the Father, the Son, and the Holy Spirit. If Jesus had stayed on earth, his physical presence would have limited the spread of the gospel, for physically he could be in only one place at a time. After his ascension, he would be spiritually present everywhere through the Holy Spirit. The Holy Spirit was sent so God would be with and within his followers after Jesus returned to heaven. His Spirit would comfort them, guide them to know his truth, remind them of Jesus' words, give them the right words to say, and fill them with power (John 14—16).

1:4 Jesus instructed his disciples to witness to people of all nations about him. But they were told to wait first for the Holy Spirit. God has important work for you to do for him, but you must do it by the power of the Holy Spirit. We often like to get on with the job, even if it means running ahead of God. But waiting is sometimes part of God's plan. Are you waiting and listening for God's complete instructions, or are you running ahead of his plans? We need God's timing and power to be truly effective.

1:5 At Pentecost (Acts 2:4) the Holy Spirit was made available to all who believe in Jesus. We receive the Holy Spirit (are baptized by him) when we receive Jesus Christ. The baptism of the Holy Spirit must be understood in the light of his total work in Christians.

(1) The Spirit marks the beginning of the Christian experience. We cannot belong to Christ without his Spirit (Romans 8:9); we cannot be united to Christ without his Spirit (1 Corinthians 6:17); we cannot be adopted as his children without his Spirit (Romans 8:14–17; Galatians 4:6, 7); we cannot be in the body of Christ except by baptism in the Spirit (1 Corinthians 12:13).(2) The Spirit is the power of our new lives. He begins a lifelong process of change as we become more like Christ (1 John 3:2; Philippians 1:6). When we receive Christ by faith, we begin an immediate personal relationship with God. The Holy Spirit works in us to help us become like Christ.(3) The Spirit unites the Christian community in Christ (Ephesians 2:22). The Holy Spirit can be experienced by all and works through all (1 Corinthians 12:11; Ephesians 4:4).

6And another time when he appeared to them, they asked him, "Lord, are you going to free Israel [from Rome] now and restore us as an independent nation?"

7"The Father sets those dates," he replied, "and they are not for you to know. 8But when the Holy Spirit has come upon you, you will receive power to testify about me with great effect, to the people in Jerusalem, throughout Judea, in Samaria, and to the ends of the earth, about my death and resurrection."

9It was not long afterwards that he rose into the sky and disappeared into a cloud, leaving them staring after him. 10As they were straining their eyes for another glimpse, suddenly two white-robed men were standing there among them, 11and said, "Men of Galilee, why are you standing here staring at the sky? Jesus has gone away to heaven, and some day, just as he went, he will return!"

Matthias is chosen to replace Judas

12They were at the Mount of Olives when this happened, so now they walked the half mile back to Jerusalem 13and held a prayer meeting in an upstairs room of the house where they were staying.

14Here is the list of those who were present at the meeting: Peter, John, James, Andrew, Philip, Thomas, Bartholomew, Matthew, James (son of Alphaeus), Simon (also called "The Zealot"), Judas (son of James), And the brothers of Jesus. Several women, including Jesus' mother, were also there.

15This prayer meeting went on for several days. During this time, on a day when about 120 people were present, Peter stood up and addressed them as follows:

16"Brothers, it was necessary for the Scriptures to come true concerning Judas,

1:6 *from Rome,* implied.

1:6
Dan 7:27
Amos 9:11
1 Cor 15:7

1:7
Mt 24:36
1 Thess 5:1,2

1:8
Mt 28:19
Lk 24:48,49
Jn 15:27
Acts 2:4; 8:1
Rom 10:18

1:11
Zech 14:4
Rev 1:7

1:12
Lk 24:50

1:13
Lk 22:12
Acts 12:12; 20:8

1:14
Mt 10:2-4
Mk 3:16-19
Lk 6:14-16

1:16
Ps 41:9
Jn 18:3

1:6 During the years of Jesus' ministry on earth, the disciples continually wondered about his kingdom. When would it come? What would be their role? In the traditional view, the Messiah would be an earthly conqueror who would free Israel from Rome. But the kingdom Jesus spoke about was first a *spiritual* kingdom established in the hearts and lives of believers. God's presence and power dwell in believers in the person of the Holy Spirit.

1:6, 7 Like other Jews, the disciples chafed under their Roman rulers. They wanted Jesus to free Israel from Roman power and then become their king. Jesus replied that God the Father sets the timetable for all events—worldwide, national, and personal. If you want changes that God isn't making immediately, don't become impatient. It is not God, but you who should adjust your timetable.

1:8 This verse describes a series of ever-widening circles. The gospel was to spread, geographically, from Jerusalem, into Judea and Samaria, and finally to the whole world. It would begin with the devout Jews in Jerusalem and Samaria, spread to the mixed race in Samaria, and finally be offered to the Gentiles in the uttermost parts of the earth. God's gospel has not reached its final destination if someone in your family, your workplace, your school, or your community hasn't heard about Jesus Christ. Make sure that you are contributing in some way to the ever-widening circle of God's loving message.

1:8 Power from the Holy Spirit is not limited to strength beyond the ordinary—it involves courage, boldness, confidence, insight, ability, and authority. The disciples would need all these to fulfill their mission. If you believe in Jesus Christ, you can experience the power of the Holy Spirit in your life.

1:8 Jesus promised the apostles that they would receive power to witness after they received the Holy Spirit. Notice the progression: (1) they received the Holy Spirit, (2) he gave them power, and (3) they witnessed with extraordinary results. We often try to reverse the order and witness by our own power and authority. Witnessing is not showing what we can do for God, but showing and telling what God has done for us.

1:9 It was important for the disciples to see Jesus ascend. Then they knew without a doubt that he was God and that his home is in heaven.

1:9-11 After 40 days with his disciples, Jesus ascended into heaven. Two angels proclaimed to the disciples that one day Jesus would return in the same way he went—bodily and visibly. History is not haphazard; it is moving toward a specific point—the return of Jesus to judge and rule over the earth. We should be ready for his sudden return (1 Thessalonians 5:2), not by standing around "gazing into the sky," but by working hard to share the gospel so others will be able to share in God's great blessings.

1:12, 13 After Christ ascended into heaven, the apostles immediately returned to Jerusalem and had a prayer meeting. Jesus had said they would be baptized with the Holy Spirit in a few days, so they waited and prayed. When you face a difficult task, an important decision, or a baffling dilemma, your first step should be to pray for the Holy Spirit's power and guidance. Don't rush into the work and hope it happens the way it should.

1:14 Jesus' brothers are now with the disciples. During Jesus' lifetime they did not believe he was the Messiah, but his resurrection must have convinced them. Jesus' special appearance to James, one of his brothers, may have been an especially significant event in their conversion (see 1 Corinthians 15:7).

1:15-26 This was the first church business meeting. The small group of 11 had already grown to more than 120. The main order of business was to appoint a new disciple, or apostle, as the 12 were now called. While the apostles waited, they were doing what they could—praying, seeking God's guidance, and getting organized. Waiting for God to work does not mean sitting around doing nothing. We must do what we can, while we can, as long as we don't run ahead of God.

1:16 How could someone who had been with Jesus daily betray him? Judas received the same calling and teaching as everyone else. But he chose to reject Christ's warning as well as his offers of mercy. He hardened his heart and joined in the plot with Jesus' enemies to betray him. He remained unrepentant to the end, and he finally committed suicide. Although Jesus predicted this would happen, it was Judas' choice. Those privileged to be *close* to the truth are not necessarily *committed* to the truth. See Judas' Profile in Mark 14 for more information on his life.

who betrayed Jesus by guiding the mob to him, for this was predicted long ago by the Holy Spirit, speaking through King David. 17Judas was one of us, chosen to be an apostle just as we were. 18He bought a field with the money he received for his treachery and falling headlong there, he burst open, spilling out his bowels. 19The news of his death spread rapidly among all the people of Jerusalem, and they named the place 'The Field of Blood.' 20King David's prediction of this appears in the Book of Psalms, where he says, 'Let his home become desolate with no one living in it.' And again, 'Let his work be given to someone else to do.'

21, 22"So now we must choose someone else to take Judas' place and to join us as witnesses of Jesus' resurrection. Let us select someone who has been with us constantly from our first association with the Lord—from the time he was baptized by John until the day he was taken from us into heaven."

23The assembly nominated two men: Joseph Justus (also called Barsabbas) and Matthias. 24, 25Then they all prayed for the right man to be chosen. "O Lord," they said, "you know every heart; show us which of these men you have chosen as an apostle to replace Judas the traitor, who has gone on to his proper place."

26Then they drew straws, and in this manner Matthias was chosen and became an apostle with the other eleven.

The Holy Spirit comes at Pentecost

2 Seven weeks had gone by since Jesus' death and resurrection, and the Day of Pentecost had now arrived. As the believers met together that day, 2suddenly there was a sound like the roaring of a mighty windstorm in the skies above them and it filled the house where they were meeting. 3Then, what looked like flames or tongues of fire appeared and settled on their heads. 4And everyone present was filled with the Holy Spirit and began speaking in languages they didn't know, for the Holy Spirit gave them this ability.

5Many godly Jews were in Jerusalem that day for the religious celebrations, having arrived from many nations. 6And when they heard the roaring in the sky

1:26 they drew straws, literally, "cast lots," or "threw dice." **2:4** in languages they didn't know, literally, "in other tongues."

Marginal references:
1:17 Jn 6:70,71; Acts 1:24,25; 20:24; 21:19
1:18 Mt 26:14,15; 27:3-10
1:20 Ps 69:25; 109:8
1:21,22 Mk 1:1-4; Acts 1:2; 2:32
1:24 1 Sam 16:7; Acts 6:6; 15:8
1:25 Acts 1:17; Rom 1:5
1:26 Lev 16:8; Josh 14:1,2; 1 Sam 14:41; Prov 16:33
2:1 Lev 23:15,16; Deut 16:9,10; Acts 1:14,15; 20:16
2:2 Acts 4:31
2:4 Mk 16:7; Acts 4:8,31; 10:46; 13:9,19:6; 1 Cor 12:10; 13:1; Eph 5:18

1:18 Matthew says Judas hanged himself (Matthew 27:5); Acts says he fell. The traditional explanation is that when Judas hanged himself, the rope or branch broke, Judas fell, and his body burst open.

1:21, 22 The disciples became *apostles*. *Disciple* means follower or learner, and *apostle* means messenger or missionary. These men now had the special assignment of spreading the Good News of Jesus' death and resurrection.

1:21, 22 There were many who consistently followed Jesus throughout his ministry on earth. The 12 apostles were his inner circle, but others shared their level of love and commitment.

1:21, 22 The apostles had to choose a replacement for Judas Iscariot. They outlined specific criteria for making the choice. When the "finalists" had been chosen, the apostles prayed, asking God to guide the selection process. This gives us a good example of how to proceed when we are making important decisions. Set up criteria consistent with the Bible, examine the alternatives, and pray for wisdom and guidance to reach a wise decision.

2:1 Held 50 days after Passover, Pentecost was also called the Feast of Weeks and Feast of Harvests. It was one of three major feasts of the year (Leviticus 23:16), a festival of thanksgiving for the harvested crops. Jesus was crucified at Passover, and he ascended 40 days later. The Holy Spirit came 50 days after the crucifixion, 10 days after the ascension. Jews of many nations gathered in Jerusalem for this festival. Thus Peter's speech was given to an international audience. It resulted in a worldwide harvest of new believers—the first converts to Christianity.

2:3 This was a fulfillment of John the Baptist's words (Luke 3:16)

about the Holy Spirit's baptizing with fire. Verses 3 and 4 are also a fulfillment of Joel 2:28, 29 about the outpouring of the Holy Spirit.

Why tongues of fire? Tongues symbolize speech and the communication of the gospel. Fire symbolizes God's purifying presence, burning away the undesirable elements of our lives and setting our hearts aflame to ignite the lives of others. On Mount Sinai, God confirmed the validity of the Old Testament law with fire from heaven (Exodus 19:16–18). At Pentecost, God confirmed the validity of the Holy Spirit's ministry by sending fire. At Mount Sinai, fire came down on one place; at Pentecost, fire came down on many believers, symbolizing that God's presence is now available to all who believe in him.

2:3, 4 God made his presence known to this group of believers in a spectacular way—roaring wind, fire, and his Holy Spirit. Would you like God to reveal himself to you in such recognizable ways? He may, but be wary of forcing your expectations on God. In 1 Kings 19:11, 12, Elijah also needed a message from God. There was a mighty wind, then an earthquake, and finally a fire. But God's message came in a gentle whisper. God may use dramatic methods to work in your life—or he may speak in gentle whispers. Wait patiently and always listen.

2:4 These people literally spoke in other languages—a miraculous attention-getter for the crowds gathered in town for the feast. All the nationalities represented recognized their own languages being spoken. But more than miraculous speaking drew people's attention; they saw the presence and power of the Holy Spirit. The apostles continued to minister in the power of the Holy Spirit wherever they went.

above the house, crowds came running to see what it was all about, and were stunned to hear their own languages being spoken by the disciples.

7"How can this be?" they exclaimed. "For these men are all from Galilee, 8and yet we hear them speaking all the native languages of the lands where we were born! 9Here we are—Parthians, Medes, Elamites, men from Mesopotamia, Judea,

2:7
Mt 26:73
Acts 1:11

2:9
Acts 6:9; 19:10
1 Pet 1:1

Beginning with a brief summary of Jesus' last days on earth with his disciples, his ascension, and the replacement for Judas Iscariot, Luke moves quickly to his subject—the spread of the gospel and the growth of the church. Pentecost, celebrated by the filling of the Holy Spirit (2:1–13) and Peter's powerful sermon (2:14–42), was the beginning. Then the Jerusalem church grew daily through the bold witness of Peter and John and the love of the believers (2:43—4:37). The infant church was not without problems, however, with external opposition (resulting in imprisonment, beatings, and death) and internal deceit and complaining. Greek-speaking Jewish believers were appointed to help with the administration of the church to free the apostles to preach. Stephen and Philip were among the first deacons, and Stephen became the church's first martyr (5:1—8:3).

Instead of stopping Christianity, opposition and persecution served as catalysts for its spread, for the believers took the message with them wherever they fled (8:4). Soon there were converts throughout Samaria and even in Ethiopia (8:5–40).

At this point, Luke introduces us to a bright young Jew, zealous for the law and intent on ridding Judaism of the Jesus heresy. But on the way to Damascus to capture believers, Saul was converted, confronted in person by the risen Christ (9:1–9). Through the ministry of Ananias and the sponsorship of Barnabas, Saul (Paul) was welcomed into the fellowship and then sent to Tarsus for safety (9:10–30).

Meanwhile, the church continued to thrive throughout Judea, Galilee, and Samaria. Luke recounts Peter's preaching and how he healed Aeneas in Lydda and Dorcas in Joppa (9:31–43). While in Joppa, Peter learned through a vision that he could take the gospel to the "unclean" Gentiles. Peter understood and he faithfully shared the truth with Cornelius, whose entire household became believers (chapter 10). This was startling news to the Jerusalem church; but when Peter told his story, they praised God for his plan for all people to hear the Good News (11:1–18). This pushed the church into even wider circles as the message was preached to Greeks in Antioch, where Barnabas went to encourage the believers and find Paul (11:20–26).

To please the Jewish leaders, Herod joined in the persecution of the Jerusalem church, killing James (John's brother) and imprisoning Peter. But God freed Peter, and he walked from prison to a prayer meeting on his behalf at John Mark's house (chapter 12).

Here Luke shifts the focus to Paul's ministry. Commissioned by the Antioch church for a missionary tour (13:1–3), Paul and Barnabas took the gospel to Cyprus and south Galatia with great success (13:4—14:28). But the Jewish-Gentile controversy still smoldered, and with so many Gentiles responding to Christ, it threatened to divide the church. So a council met in Jerusalem to rule on the relationship of Gentile Christians to the Old Testament laws. After hearing both sides, James (Jesus' brother and the leader of the Jerusalem church) resolved the issue and sent messengers to the churches with the decision (15:1–31).

After the council, Paul and Silas preached in Antioch. Then they left for Syria and Cilicia as Barnabas and Mark sailed for Cyprus (15:36–41). On this second missionary journey, Paul and Silas traveled throughout Macedonia and Achaia, establishing churches in Philippi, Thessalonica, Beroea, Corinth, and Ephesus before returning to Antioch (16:1—18:21). Luke also tells of the ministry of Apollos (18:24–28).

On Paul's third missionary trip he traveled through Galatia, Phrygia, Macedonia, and Achaia, encouraging and teaching the believers (19:1—21:9). During this time, he felt compelled to go to Jerusalem; and although he was warned by Agabus and others of impending imprisonment (21:10–12), he continued his journey in that direction.

While in Jerusalem, Paul was accosted in the Temple by an angry mob and taken into protective custody by the Roman commander (21:17—22:30). Now we see Paul as a prisoner and on trial before the Jewish Council (23:1–9), Governor Felix (23:22—24:27), and Festus and Agrippa (25:1—26:32). In each case, Paul gave a strong and clear witness for his Lord.

Because he appealed to Caesar, however, they sent him to Rome for the final hearing of his case. But on the way the ship was destroyed in a storm, and the sailors and prisoners had to swim ashore. Even in this circumstance Paul shared his faith (27:1—28:11). Eventually the journey continued, and Paul arrived in Rome where he was held under house arrest while awaiting trial (28:12–31).

Luke ends Acts abruptly, with the encouraging word that Paul had freedom in his captivity to tell visitors and guards with boldness "about the Kingdom of God and about the Lord Jesus Christ; and no one tried to stop him" (28:31).

A JOURNEY THROUGH THE BOOK OF ACTS

2:10
Ex 12:48
Mt 23:15; 27:32
Acts 13:13; 16:6

Cappadocia, Pontus, Asia minor, ¹⁰Phrygia, Pamphylia, Egypt, the Cyrene language areas of Libya, visitors from Rome—both Jews and Jewish converts—¹¹Cretans, and Arabians. And we all hear these men telling in our own languages about the mighty miracles of God!"

2:13
1 Cor 2:14; 14:23
Eph 5:18

¹²They stood there amazed and perplexed. "What can this mean?" they asked each other.

¹³But others in the crowd were mocking. "They're drunk, that's all!" they said.

Peter preaches to the crowd

2:16
Joel 2:28-32

2:17
Isa 44:3
Ezek 11:10
36:27
Zech 12:10
Acts 10:45

2:18
1 Cor 12:10

2:20
Mt 24:29

2:21
Ps 55:16;
88:9 116:2,4,13,
17; 145:18
Acts 9:14,21 22:16
Rom 10:13

2:22
Jn 17:4
Acts 10:38
Heb 2:4

2:23
Acts 3:17,18
1 Pet 1:11,20
Rev 13:8

2:24
Acts 3:15;
10:40; 17:31

2:25-27
Ps 16:8-11
Acts 13:30-35

¹⁴Then Peter stepped forward with the eleven apostles, and shouted to the crowd, "Listen, all of you, visitors and residents of Jerusalem alike! ¹⁵Some of you are saying these men are drunk! It isn't true! It's much too early for that! People don't get drunk by 9 A.M.! ¹⁶No! What you see this morning was predicted centuries ago by the prophet Joel— ¹⁷'In the last days,' God said, 'I will pour out my Holy Spirit upon all mankind, and your sons and daughters shall prophesy, and your young men shall see visions, and your old men dream dreams. ¹⁸Yes, the Holy Spirit shall come upon all my servants, men and women alike, and they shall prophesy. ¹⁹And I will cause strange demonstrations in the heavens and on the earth—blood and fire and clouds of smoke; ²⁰the sun shall turn black and the moon blood-red before that awesome Day of the Lord arrives. ²¹But anyone who asks for mercy from the Lord shall have it and shall be saved.'

²²"O men of Israel, listen! God publicly endorsed Jesus of Nazareth by doing tremendous miracles through him, as you well know. ²³But God, following his prearranged plan, let you use the Roman government to nail him to the cross and murder him. ²⁴Then God released him from the horrors of death and brought him back to life again, for death could not keep this man within its grip.

²⁵"King David quoted Jesus as saying:

'I know the Lord is always with me. He is helping me. God's mighty power supports me.

²⁶'No wonder my heart is filled with joy and my tongue shouts his praises! For I know all will be well with me in death—

2:23 *the Roman government,* literally, "men without the Law." See Rom 2:12.

2:7, 8 Christianity is not limited to any race or group of people. Christ offers salvation to all people without regard to nationality. Visitors in Jerusalem were surprised to hear the apostles speaking in their native languages, but they need not have been. God works all kinds of miracles to spread the gospel, using many languages as he calls all people to become his followers. No matter what your race, color, nationality, or language, God speaks to you. Are you listening?

2:9–11 Why are all these places mentioned? This is a list of many lands from which Jews came to the festivals in Jerusalem. These Jews were not living in Palestine, because through captivities and persecutions they had been widely dispersed throughout the world. The Jews who responded to Peter's message returned to their homelands with God's Good News of salvation. Thus God prepared the way for the spread of the gospel. As you read Acts, you will see how the way was often prepared for Paul and others through people who became believers at Pentecost. The church at Rome, for example, was begun by such Jewish believers—not by Peter, Paul, or any of the other apostles.

2:14ff Peter tells the people why they should listen to the believers: because the Old Testament prophecies had been entirely fulfilled in Jesus (2:14–21), because Jesus is the Messiah (2:25–36), and because the risen Christ could change their lives (2:37–40).

2:14 Peter had been an unstable leader during Jesus' ministry, letting his bravado be his downfall, even denying that he knew Jesus (John 18:15–18, 25–27). But Christ forgave and restored him after his denial. This is a new Peter, humble but bold. His

confidence comes from the Holy Spirit, who makes him a powerful and dynamic speaker. Have you ever felt as if you've made such bad mistakes that God could never forgive and use you? No matter what sins you have committed, God promises to forgive them and make you useful for his kingdom. Allow him to forgive you and use you effectively to serve him.

2:16–21 Not everything mentioned in Joel 2:28, 29 was happening that particular morning. The "last days" include all the days between Christ's first and second comings, another way of saying "from now on." "The Day of the Lord" denotes the whole Christian age. Even Moses yearned for the Lord to pour his Spirit on everyone (Numbers 11:29). At Pentecost the Holy Spirit was released throughout the entire world—to men, women, sons, daughters, Jews, Gentiles. Now *everyone* can receive the Spirit. This was a revolutionary thought for first-century Jews.

2:24 Peter began with a public proclamation of the resurrection, at a time when it could be verified by many witnesses. This was a powerful statement because many of the people listening to Peter's words were in Jerusalem 50 days earlier at Passover and may have seen or heard about the crucifixion of this "great teacher." Jesus' resurrection was the ultimate sign that what he said about himself was true. Without the resurrection, we would have no reason to believe in Jesus.

2:25–32 *Hell* (2:27) is literally *Hades,* and the audience understood this as the grave, not the place of final punishment. The emphasis here is that Jesus' body was *not* left to decay, but was resurrected and glorified.

27'You will not leave my soul in hell or let the body of your Holy Son decay.
28'You will give me back my life, and give me wonderful joy in your presence.'

29"Dear brothers, think! David wasn't referring to himself when he spoke these words I have quoted, for he died and was buried, and his tomb is still here among us. 30But he was a prophet, and knew God had promised with an unbreakable oath that one of David's own descendants would [be the Messiah and] sit on David's throne. 31David was looking far into the future and predicting the Messiah's resurrection, and saying that the Messiah's soul would not be left in hell and his body would not decay. 32He was speaking of Jesus, and we all are witnesses that Jesus rose from the dead.

33"And now he sits on the throne of highest honor in heaven, next to God. And just as promised, the Father gave him the authority to send the Holy Spirit—with the results you are seeing and hearing today.

34"[No, David was not speaking of himself in these words of his I have quoted], for he never ascended into the skies. Moreover, he further stated, "God spoke to my Lord, the Messiah, and said to him, Sit here in honor beside me 35until I bring your enemies into complete subjection.'

36"Therefore I clearly state to everyone in Israel that God has made this Jesus you crucified to be the Lord, the Messiah!"

37These words of Peter's moved them deeply, and they said to him and to the other apostles, "Brothers, what should we do?"

38And Peter replied, "Each one of you must turn from sin, return to God, and be baptized in the name of Jesus Christ for the forgiveness of your sins; then you also shall receive this gift, the Holy Spirit. 39For Christ promised him to each one of you who has been called by the Lord our God, and to your children and even to those in distant lands!"

40Then Peter preached a long sermon, telling about Jesus and strongly urging all his listeners to save themselves from the evils of their nation. 41And those who believed Peter were baptized—about 3,000 in all!

The believers become the first church

42They joined with the other believers in regular attendance at the apostles' teaching sessions and at the Communion services and prayer meetings. 43A deep sense of awe was on them all, and the apostles did many miracles.

44And all the believers met together constantly and shared everything with each other, 45selling their possessions and dividing with those in need. 46They wor-

2:29
1 Kings 2:10
Neh 3:16
Acts 13:35,36
2:30
2 Sam 7:12-14
Ps 89:3,4
Lk 1:32
2 Tim 2:8
2:31
Acts 13:35,36
2:33
Lk 24:49
Jn 14:26
Acts 1:4,8
Eph 4:8
Phil 2:9
Heb 10:12
2:34
Ps 110:1
2:35
1 Cor 15:25
2:36
Lk 2:11
Acts 5:31
2:37
Zech 12:10
Acts 16:30
2:38
Mk 16:16
Lk 24:47
Acts 3:19;
5:31 8:12; 22:16
2:39
Isa 44:3
Joel 2:32
Rom 9:8
Eph 2:13,17
2:40
Phil 2:15
2:42
Acts 20:7
2:44
Acts 4:32-37
2:45
Isa 58:7

2:30 be the Messiah and, implied in vs 31.   **2:34** No, David was not speaking of himself in these words of his I have quoted, implied in vs 31.   **2:42** at the Communion services, literally, "the breaking of bread," i.e., "The Lord's Supper."

2:37 After Peter's powerful, Spirit-filled message, the people were deeply moved and asked, "What should we do?" This is the basic question we must ask. It is not enough to be sorry for our sins—we must let God forgive them, and then we must live like forgiven people. Has God spoken to you through his Word or through the words of another believer? Like Peter's audience, ask him what you should do, and then obey.

2:38, 39 If you want to receive salvation, you must turn from sin, changing the direction of your life from selfishness and rebellion against God's laws. At the same time, you must turn to Christ, depending on him for forgiveness, mercy, guidance, and purpose. We cannot save ourselves—only God can save us. Baptism shows identification with Christ and with the community of believers.

2:40–43 About 3,000 people became new believers when Peter preached the Good News about Christ. These new Christians were "joined with the other believers," taught by the apostles, and included in the prayer meetings and fellowship. New believers in Christ need to be in a group where they can learn God's Word, pray, and mature in the faith. If you have just begun a relationship

with Christ, seek out other believers for fellowship, prayer, and teaching. This is the way to grow.

2:42 These communion services were celebrated in remembrance of Jesus and were patterned after the last supper that Jesus had with his disciples before his death (Matthew 26:26–29).

2:44 Recognizing the other believers as brothers and sisters in the family of God, the Christians in Jerusalem shared all they had so that all could benefit from God's blessings. It is tempting—especially if we have material wealth—to cut ourselves off from one another, each taking care of his own, each providing for and enjoying his own little piece of the world. But as part of God's spiritual family, we have a responsibility to help one another in every way possible. God's family works best when its members work together.

2:46 A common misconception about the first Christians (who were Jews) was that they rejected the Jewish religion. But these believers saw Jesus' message and resurrection as the fulfillment of everything they knew and believed from the Old Testament. The

shiped together regularly at the Temple each day, met in small groups in homes for Communion, and shared their meals with great joy and thankfulness, 47praising God. The whole city was favorable to them, and each day God added to them all who were being saved.

Peter heals a crippled beggar

3 Peter and John went to the Temple one afternoon to take part in the three o'clock daily prayer meeting. 2As they approached the Temple, they saw a man lame from birth carried along the street and laid beside the Temple gate—the one called The Beautiful Gate—as was his custom every day. 3As Peter and John were passing by, he asked them for some money.

4They looked at him intently, and then Peter said, "Look here!"

5The lame man looked at them eagerly, expecting a gift.

6But Peter said, "We don't have any money for you! But I'll give you something else! I command you in the name of Jesus Christ of Nazareth, *walk!*"

7, 8Then Peter took the lame man by the hand and pulled him to his feet. And as he did, the man's feet and ankle-bones were healed and strengthened so that he came up with a leap, stood there a moment and began walking! Then, walking, leaping, and praising God, he went into the Temple with them.

9When the people inside saw him walking and heard him praising God, 10and realized he was the lame beggar they had seen so often at The Beautiful Gate, they were inexpressibly surprised! 11They all rushed out to Solomon's Hall, where he was holding tightly to Peter and John! Everyone stood there awed by the wonderful thing that had happened.

Peter preaches in the Temple

12Peter saw his opportunity and addressed the crowd. "Men of Israel," he said, "what is so surprising about this? And why look at us as though we by our own power and godliness had made this man walk? 13For it is the God of Abraham, Isaac, Jacob and of all our ancestors who has brought glory to his servant Jesus by doing this. I refer to the Jesus whom you rejected before Pilate, despite Pilate's determination to release him. 14You didn't want him freed—this holy, righteous

---

Jewish believers at first did not separate from the rest of the Jewish community. They still went to the Temple and synagogues for worship and instruction in God's Word. But their belief in Jesus created great friction with Jews who didn't believe Jesus was the Messiah. Thus believing Jews were forced to meet in private homes for communion, prayer, and teaching about Jesus. By the end of the first century, many of these Jewish believers were excommunicated from their synagogues altogether.

2:46, 47 A healthy Christian community attracts people to Christ. The Jerusalem church's zeal for worship and brotherly love was contagious. A healthy, loving church will grow. What are you doing to make your church the kind of place that will attract others to Christ?

3:1 The Jews observed three times of prayer—morning (9:00 a.m.), afternoon (3:00 p.m.), and evening (sunset). At these times devout Jews and God-fearing Gentiles often went to the Temple to pray.

3:2 The Beautiful Gate was an entrance to the Temple, not to the city. It was one of the favored entrances, and many people passed through it on their way to worship. The lame man was begging where he would be seen by the most people.

3:6 The lame beggar asked for money, but Peter gave him something much better—the use of his legs. We often ask God to solve a small problem, but he wants to give us a new life and help for *all* our problems. When we ask God for help, he may say, "I've got something even better for you." Ask God for what you want, but don't be surprised when he gives you what you really *need*.

3:6 "In the name of Jesus" means "by the authority of Jesus." The

apostles were doing this healing through the Holy Spirit's power, not their own.

3:7-10 In his excitement the formerly lame man began to jump and run around. He also praised God! And then others too were awed by God's power. Don't forget to thank people who help you, but also remember to praise God for his blessings.

3:12 Peter had an audience, and he capitalized on the opportunity to share Jesus Christ. He clearly presented his message by telling (1) who Jesus is, (2) how they had rejected him, (3) why their rejection was fatal, and (4) what they needed to do to change the situation. He told them that they still had a choice: God still offered them the opportunity to believe and receive Jesus as their Messiah and as their Lord. Displays of God's mercy and grace such as the healing of this lame man often create teachable moments. Pray to have courage like Peter to see these opportunities and speak up for Christ.

3:13 The word *servant* is the same word used in Isaiah 52:13. By choosing this word, Peter indicated that the servant in Isaiah's prophecy is Jesus Christ. Jesus came to serve God and people by dying on the cross for our sin and by giving us an example of perfect service (Mark 10:44, 45).

3:13 Pilate had decided to release Jesus, but the people had clamored to have Barabbas released instead (see Luke 23:13-25). When Peter said "You," he meant it literally. Jesus' trial and death had occurred right there in Jerusalem only weeks earlier. It wasn't an event of the distant past—most of these people had heard about it, and some had probably taken part in condemning him.

one. Instead you demanded the release of a murderer. ¹⁵And you killed the Author of Life; but God brought him back to life again. And John and I are witnesses of this fact, for after you killed him we saw him alive!

¹⁶"Jesus' name has healed this man —and you know how lame he was before. Faith in Jesus' name—faith given us from God—has caused this perfect healing.

¹⁷"Dear brothers, I realize that what you did to Jesus was done in ignorance; and the same can be said of your leaders. ¹⁸But God was fulfilling the prophecies that the Messiah must suffer all these things. ¹⁹Now change your mind and attitude to God and turn to him so he can cleanse away your sins and send you wonderful times of refreshment from the presence of the Lord ²⁰and send Jesus your Messiah back to you again. ²¹, ²²For he must remain in heaven until the final recovery of all things from sin, as prophesied from ancient times. Moses, for instance, said long ago, 'The Lord God will raise up a Prophet among you, who will resemble me! Listen carefully to everything he tells you. ²³Anyone who will not listen to him shall be utterly destroyed.'

²⁴"Samuel and every prophet since have all spoken about what is going on today. ²⁵You are the children of those prophets; and you are included in God's promise to your ancestors to bless the entire world through the Jewish race—that is the promise God gave to Abraham. ²⁶And as soon as God had brought his servant to life again, he sent him first of all to you men of Israel, to bless you by turning you back from your sins."

Peter and John face the Sanhedrin

4 While they were talking to the people, the chief priests, the captain of the Temple police, and some of the Sadducees came over to them, ²very disturbed

3:15 *Acts 2:24; 5:31,32 Heb 2:10; 5:9*
3:17 *Lk 23:34 Acts 13:27 1 Cor 2:8 1 Tim 1:13*
3:18 *Ps 22: 41:9 69:4,21; Isa 50:6; 53:4-11 Zech 12:10; 13:7 1 Pet 1:10*
3:19 *Acts 2:38; 26:20*
3:21 *Rom 8:21*
3:22 *Deut 18:15,18 Jn 1:20,21 7:40,41,52*
3:23 *Deut 18:19*
3:25 *Gen 12:3; 22:18 Rom 9:4-8*
3:26 *Acts 13:46*
4:1 *Lk 22:4*

3:21, 22 *who will resemble me,* literally, "like unto me." **3:23** *be utterly destroyed,* literally, "destroyed from among the people." **4:1** *the Sadducees,* who were members of a Jewish religious sect that denied the resurrection of the dead.

3:15 The religious leaders thought they had put an end to Jesus when they crucified him. But their confidence was shaken when Peter told them that Jesus was alive again and that this time they could not harm him. Peter's message emphasized that (1) the religious leaders killed Jesus, (2) God brought him back to life, and (3) the apostles were witnesses to this fact. After pointing out the sin and injustice of these leaders, Peter showed the significance of the resurrection, God's triumph and power over death.

3:16 Jesus, not the apostles, received the glory for the healing. In those days a man's name represented his character; it stood for his authority and power. By using Jesus' name, Peter showed who gave him the authority and power to heal. The apostles did not emphasize what they could do, but what God could do through them. Jesus' name is not to be used as magic—it must be used by faith. When we pray in Jesus' name, we must remember that it is Jesus himself, not merely the sound of his name, that gives our prayers their power.

3:18 These prophecies are found in Psalm 22 and Isaiah 50:6 and 53:5. Peter was explaining the kind of Messiah God sent to earth. The Jews expected a great governor, not a suffering servant.

3:19 John the Baptist prepared the way for Jesus by preaching repentance. The apostles' call to salvation also included repentance—acknowledging personal sin and turning away from it. Many people want the benefits of being identified with Christ without turning from sin and acknowledging their own disobedience. The first step to being forgiven is to confess your sin and turn from it (see 2:38).

3:19 When we repent, God promises not only to wipe away our sin, but to bring spiritual refreshment. Repentance may at first seem painful because it is hard to give up certain sins. But God will give you a better way. As Hosea promised, "Let us press on to know him, and he will respond to us as surely as the coming of dawn or the rain of early spring" (Hosea 6:3). Do you feel a need to be refreshed?

3:21 The "recovery of all things from sin" points to the Second Coming, the last judgment, and the removal of sin from the universe.

3:21, 22 Most Jews thought that Joshua was this Prophet predicted by Moses (Deuteronomy 18:15). Peter was saying that he was Jesus Christ. Peter wanted to show them that their long-awaited Messiah had come! He and all the apostles were calling the Jewish nation to realize what they had done to their Messiah, to repent, and to believe. From this point on in Acts, we see many Jews rejecting the gospel. So the message went also to the Gentiles, many of whom had hearts open to receive Jesus.

3:24 The prophet Samuel lived during the transition between the judges and the kings of Israel, and he was seen as the first in a succession of prophets. He anointed David king, founding David's royal line, from which the Messiah eventually came. All the prophets point forward to a future Messiah. For more on Samuel, see his Profile in 1 Samuel 8.

3:25 God promised Abraham that he would bless the world through his descendants, the Jewish race (Genesis 12:3), from which the Messiah would come. God intended the Jewish nation to be a separate and holy nation that would teach the world about God, introduce the Messiah, and then carry on his work in the world. After the days of Solomon, the nation gave up its mission to tell the world about God, and now, in apostolic times, it also rejected its Messiah.

4:1 The chief priests were prominent priests, often close relatives of the high priests, as well as priests of special ability or influence. The Temple police were guards set around the Temple to insure order. The Sadducees were members of a Jewish religious sect who did not believe in the resurrection of the dead. Most of those who engineered and carried out Jesus' arrest and crucifixion were from these three groups.

4:2 Peter and John spoke to the people during the afternoon prayer time. The Sadducees moved in quickly to investigate.

4:3
Acts 5:18
4:4
Acts 4:21

that Peter and John were claiming that Jesus had risen from the dead. 3They arrested them and since it was already evening, jailed them overnight. 4But many of the people who heard their message believed it, so that the number of believers now reached a new high of about 5,000 men!

4:6
Mt 26:3
Lk 3:1,2
Jn 11:49; 18:13
4:7
Mt 21:23

5The next day it happened that the Council of all the Jewish leaders was in session in Jerusalem— 6Annas the High Priest was there, and Caiaphas, John, Alexander, and others of the High Priest's relatives. 7So the two disciples were brought in before them.

"By what power, or by whose authority have you done this?" the Council demanded.

4:8
Lk 12:1

4:10
Acts 2:22,24; 3:6

4:11
Ps 118:22
Isa 28:16
Mt 21:42
Rom 9:33
4:12
Mt 1:21
Acts 10:43
Rom 3:24
1 Tim 2:5

8Then Peter, filled with the Holy Spirit, said to them, "Honorable leaders and elders of our nation, 9if you mean the good deed done to the cripple, and how he was healed, 10let me clearly state to you and to all the people of Israel that it was done in the name and power of Jesus from Nazareth, the Messiah, the man you crucified—but God raised back to life again. It is by his authority that this man stands here healed! 11For Jesus the Messiah is (the one referred to in the Scriptures when they speak of) a 'stone discarded by the builders which became the capstone of the arch.' 12There is salvation in no one else! Under all heaven there is no other name for men to call upon to save them."

4:13
Mt 11:25
1 Cor 1:27

4:16
Jn 11:47
Acts 3:7-10
4:17
Jn 15:20,21

13When the Council saw the boldness of Peter and John, and could see that they were obviously uneducated non-professionals, they were amazed and realized what being with Jesus had done for them! 14And the Council could hardly discredit the healing when the man they had healed was standing right there beside them! 15So they sent them out of the Council chamber and conferred among themselves.

16"What shall we do with these men?" they asked each other. "We can't deny that they have done a tremendous miracle, and everybody in Jerusalem knows about it. 17But perhaps we can stop them from spreading their propaganda. We'll

4:11 *became the capstone of the arch,* implied. Literally, "became the head of the corner."

Because they did not believe in the resurrection, they were disturbed with what the apostles were saying. Peter and John were refuting one of their fundamental beliefs and thus threatening their authority as religious teachers. Even under Roman rule, the Sadducees had almost unlimited power over the Temple grounds. Thus they were able to arrest Peter and John for no other reason than teaching something that contradicted their beliefs.

4:3 Not often will our witnessing send us to prison as it did Peter and John. Still, we run risks in trying to win others to Christ. We might be willing to face a night in prison if it would bring 2,000 people to Christ, but shouldn't we also be willing to suffer for even one? What do you risk in witnessing—vulnerability, rejection, persecution? Whatever the risks, realize that nothing done for God is ever wasted.

4:5 This Council of Jewish leaders was the Sanhedrin or Jewish Supreme Court—the same Council that had condemned Jesus to death. It had 70 members plus the current High Priest, who presided. The Sadducees held a majority in this ruling group. These were the wealthy, intellectual, and powerful men of Jerusalem. Jesus' followers stood before this Council just as he had.

4:6 Annas had been deposed as High Priest by the Romans, who then appointed Caiaphas, Annas' son-in-law, in his place. But since the Jews considered the office of High Priest a lifetime position, they still called Annas by that title and gave him respect and authority within the Council. Annas and Caiaphas had played significant roles in Jesus' trial (John 18:24, 28). It did not please Annas or Caiaphas that the man they thought they had sacrificed for the good of the nation (John 11:50, 51) had followers who were just as persistent and promised to be just as troublesome as he was.

4:7 The Council asked Peter and John by whose power they had

healed the man (3:6) and by what authority they preached (3:12–26). The actions and words of Peter and John threatened these religious leaders who, for the most part, were more interested in their reputations and positions than in God. Through the help of the Holy Spirit (Mark 13:11), Peter spoke boldly before the Council, actually putting the Council on trial by showing them that the one they had crucified had risen again. Instead of being defensive, the apostles were going on the offensive, boldly speaking out for God and presenting the gospel to these leaders.

4:11 A capstone is the center stone of an arch, and it holds the arch in place. The cornerstone unites two walls at the corner of a building and holds the building together. Peter said the Jews rejected Jesus, but now he has become the cornerstone of the church (or the capstone of the arch—Psalm 118:22; Mark 12:10; 1 Peter 2:7). Without him there would be no church, because it could not stand.

4:12 Many people react negatively to the fact that there is no other name than that of Jesus to call upon for salvation. Yet this is not something the Church decided; it is the specific teaching of Jesus himself (John 14:6). Christians are to be open-minded on many issues, but not on how we are saved from sin. No other religious teacher could die for the sins of the whole human race; no other religious teacher came to earth as God's only Son; no other religious teacher rose from the dead. Our focus should be on Jesus, whom God offered as a way to have an eternal relationship with himself.

4:13 The Council knew Peter and John were uneducated, and they were amazed at what being with Jesus had done for them. A changed life convinces people of Jesus' power. One of your greatest testimonies is the difference others see in your life and attitudes since you have believed in Jesus.

tell them that if they do it again we'll really throw the book at them." 18So they
called them back in, and told them never again to speak about Jesus.

19But Peter and John replied, "You decide whether God wants us to obey you
instead of him! 20We cannot stop telling about the wonderful things we saw Jesus
do and heard him say."

21The Council then threatened them further, and finally let them go because they
didn't know how to punish them without starting a riot. For everyone was praising
God for this wonderful miracle— 22the healing of a man who had been lame for
forty years.

The believers pray for boldness

23As soon as they were freed, Peter and John found the other disciples and told
them what the Council had said.

24Then all the believers united in this prayer:

"O Lord, Creator of heaven and earth and of the sea and everything in them—
25, 26you spoke long ago by the Holy Spirit through our ancestor King David, your
servant, saying, 'Why do the heathen rage against the Lord, and the foolish nations
plan their little plots against Almighty God? The kings of the earth unite to fight
against him, and against the anointed Son of God!'

27"That is what is happening here in this city today! For Herod the king, and
Pontius Pilate the governor, and all the Romans—as well as the people of Israel—are united against Jesus, your anointed Son, your holy servant. 28They won't
stop at anything that you in your wise power will let them do. 29And now, O Lord,
hear their threats, and grant to your servants great boldness in their preaching,
30and send your healing power, and may miracles and wonders be done by the
name of your holy servant Jesus."

31After this prayer, the building where they were meeting shook and they were
all filled with the Holy Spirit and boldly preached God's message.

The believers share their possessions

32All the believers were of one heart and mind, and no one felt that what he
owned was his own; everyone was sharing. 33And the apostles preached powerful
sermons about the resurrection of the Lord Jesus, and there was warm fellowship
among all the believers, 34, 35and no poverty—for all who owned land or houses

4:33 *there was warm fellowship among all the believers,* literally, "great grace was upon them all."

Cross references (right margin):

4:18 Act 5:28

4:19 Acts 5:29

4:20 Acts 1:8; 1 Cor 9:16; 1 Jn 1:1

4:21 Mt 21:26; Lk 20:6; 22:2; Acts 3:7,8

4:24 Ex 20:11; Ps 103:1; 107:1; 146:6

4:25,26 Ps 2:1,2

4:27 Isa 61:1; Lk 23:12; Acts 3:13

4:28 Acts 2:23

4:29 Eph 6:19; 2 Thess 3:1

4:30 Acts 3:6,16; 5:12

4:31 Acts 2:2,4; 16:26; Phil 1:14

4:32 Acts 2:44; Phil 2:2

4:33 Lk 24:48

4:20 We are sometimes afraid to share our faith in God because people might feel uncomfortable and disapprove. But Peter and John's zeal for the Lord was so strong that they could not keep quiet, even when threatened. If your courage to witness for God has weakened, pray that your boldness may increase. Remember Jesus' promise, "If anyone publicly acknowledges me as his friend, I will openly acknowledge him as my friend before my Father in heaven" (Matthew 10:32).

4:24–30 Notice how the believers prayed. First they praised God; then they told God their specific problem and asked for his help. They did not ask God to remove the problem, but to help them deal with it. This is a model for us to follow when we pray. We may ask God to remove our problems, and he may choose to do so, but we must recognize that often he will leave the problem in place and give us the grace to deal with it.

4:27 This was Herod Antipas, appointed by the Romans to rule over the territory of Galilee. For more information on Herod, see his Profile in Mark 6. Pontius Pilate was the Roman governor over Judea. He bent to pressure from the crowd and sentenced Jesus to death. For more information on Pilate, see his Profile in Mark 15.

4:29–31 Boldness is not reckless impulsiveness. Boldness requires courage to press through our fears and do what we know is right. How can we be more bold? Like the disciples, we need to pray with others for that courage. To gain boldness, you can (1) pray for the power of the Holy Spirit to give you courage, (2) look

for opportunities in your family and neighborhood to talk about Christ, (3) realize that rejection, social discomfort, and embarrassment are not persecution, and (4) start where you are by being bolder in small ways.

4:32 Differences of opinion are inevitable among human personalities and can actually be helpful if handled well. But spiritual unity is essential—loyalty, commitment, and love for God and his Word. Without spiritual unity, the church could not survive. Paul wrote the letter of 1 Corinthians to urge the church in Corinth toward greater unity.

4:32 None of these Christians felt what they had was their own, and so they were able to give and share, eliminating poverty among them. They would not let a brother or sister suffer when others had plenty. How do you feel about your possessions? We should adopt the attitude, "Everything we have comes from God, and we are only sharing what is already his."

4:32–35 The early church was able to share possessions and property as a result of the unity brought by the Holy Spirit working in and through the believers' lives. This is different from communism because (1) it was voluntary sharing; (2) it didn't involve *all* private property, but only as much as was needed; (3) it was not a membership requirement in order to be a part of the church. The spiritual unity and generosity of these early believers attracted others to them. This organizational structure is not a biblical command, but it offers vital principles for us to follow.

4:36
Acts 9:27
11:19-30
12:25; 13:1-4
15:39
4:37
Prov 11:24,25

sold them and brought the money to the apostles to give to others in need. 36For instance, there was Joseph (the one the apostles nicknamed "Barnabas, the encourager"! He was of the tribe of Levi, from the island of Cyprus). 37He was one of those who sold a field he owned and brought the money to the apostles for distribution to those in need.

The judgment of Ananias and Sapphira

5:2
Acts 4:37
1 Tim 6:10
5:3
Num 30:1,2
Deut 23:21
Eccles 5:4
Isa 29:15

5:5
Ezek 11:13

5 But there was a man named Ananias (with his wife Sapphira) who sold some property, 2and brought only part of the money, claiming it was the full price. (His wife had agreed to this deception.)

3But Peter said, "Ananias, Satan has filled your heart. When you claimed this was the full price, you were lying to the Holy Spirit. 4The property was yours to sell or not, as you wished. And after selling it, it was yours to decide how much to give. How could you do a thing like this? You weren't lying to us, but to God."

5As soon as Ananias heard these words, he fell to the floor, dead! Everyone was terrified, 6and the younger men covered him with a sheet and took him out and buried him.

7About three hours later his wife came in, not knowing what had happened. 8Peter asked her, "Did you people sell your land for such and such a price?"

"Yes," she replied, "we did."

5:9
Deut 6:16
Mt 4:7
Lk 4:12
1 Cor 10:9

9And Peter said, "How could you and your husband even think of doing a thing like this—conspiring together to test the Spirit of God's ability to know what is going on? Just outside that door are the young men who buried your husband, and they will carry you out too."

10Instantly she fell to the floor, dead, and the young men came in and, seeing that she was dead, carried her out and buried her beside her husband. 11Terror gripped the entire church and all others who heard what had happened.

The apostles heal many people

5:12
Mk 16:15-20
Jn 10:23
Acts 3:10
Heb 2:4
5:13
Jn 9:22,23
12:42
Acts 2:47

12Meanwhile, the apostles were meeting regularly at the Temple in the area known as Solomon's Hall, and they did many remarkable miracles among the people. 13The other believers didn't dare join them, though, but all had the highest regard for them. 14And more and more believers were added to the Lord, crowds both of men and women. 15Sick people were brought out into the streets on beds and mats so that at least Peter's shadow would fall across some of them as he went

5:9 to test the Spirit of God's ability to know what is going on, literally, "to try the Spirit of the Lord."

4:36 Barnabas (which means "son of encouragement" or "son of consolation") was a respected leader of the church. He traveled with Paul on his first missionary journey (13:1–4). For more information on Barnabas, see his Profile in chapter 13.

5:1ff In Acts 5:1—8:3 we see both internal and external problems facing the church. Inside, there was dishonesty (5:1–11) and adminstrative headaches (6:1–7); outside, the church was being pressured by persecution. While church leaders were careful and sensitive in dealing with the internal problems, there was not much they could do to prevent the external pressures. Through it all, the leaders kept their focus on what was most important—spreading the gospel about Jesus Christ.

5:3 Although Satan was defeated by Christ at the cross, he was still actively trying to make the believers stumble—as he does today (Ephesians 6:12; 1 Peter 5:8). Satan's overthrow is inevitable, but it will not occur until the last days, when Christ returns to judge the world (Revelation 20:10).

5:5 The sin Ananias and Sapphira committed was not stinginess or holding back part of the money—they could choose whether or not to sell the land and how much to give. Their sin was lying to God and God's people—saying they gave the whole amount but holding back some for themselves, trying to make themselves appear more generous than they really were. This act was judged harshly because dishonesty and covetousness are destructive in a

church, preventing the Holy Spirit from working effectively. All lying is bad, but when we lie to try to deceive God and his people about our relationship with him, we destroy our testimony for Christ.

5:11 God's judgment on Ananias and Sapphira produced shock and fear among the believers, making them realize how seriously God regards sin in the church.

5:12, 13 Solomon's Hall was part of the Temple complex built by King Herod the Great in an attempt to strengthen his relationship with the Jews. Jesus taught and performed miracles in the Temple many times. When the apostles went to the Temple, they were near the same religious leaders who had conspired to kill Jesus.

5:13 Believers did not dare join the apostles or work beside them because they were afraid to face the same kind of persecution the apostles had just faced (4:17).

5:14 What makes Christianity attractive? It is easy to be drawn to churches because of programs, good speakers, size, beautiful facilities, or fellowship. Believers were attracted to the early church by God's power and miracles, the generosity, sincerity, honesty, and unity of the members, and the character of the leaders. Have our standards slipped? God wants to add to his church, not just to programs or congregations.

5:15 These people were not healed by Peter's shadow, but by God's power working through Peter.

by! 16And crowds came in from the Jerusalem suburbs, bringing their sick folk and those possessed by demons; and every one of them was healed.

The apostles meet furious opposition

17The High Priest and his relatives and friends among the Sadducees reacted with violent jealousy 18and arrested the apostles, and put them in the public jail.

19But an angel of the Lord came at night, opened the gates of the jail and brought them out. Then he told them, 20"Go over to the Temple and preach about this Life!"

21They arrived at the Temple about daybreak, and immediately began preaching! Later that morning the High Priest and his courtiers arrived at the Temple, and, convening the Jewish Council and the entire Senate, they sent for the apostles to be brought for trial. 22But when the police arrived at the jail, the men weren't there, so they returned to the Council and reported, 23"The jail doors were locked, and the guards were standing outside, but when we opened the gates, no one was there!"

24When the police captain and the chief priests heard this, they were frantic, wondering what would happen next and where all this would end! 25Then someone arrived with the news that the men they had jailed were out in the Temple, preaching to the people!

26, 27The police captain went with his officers and arrested them (without violence, for they were afraid the people would kill them if they roughed up the disciples) and brought them in before the Council.

28"Didn't we tell you never again to preach about this Jesus?" the High Priest demanded. "And instead you have filled all Jerusalem with your teaching and intend to bring the blame for this man's death on us!"

29But Peter and the apostles replied, "We must obey God rather than men. 30The God of our ancestors brought Jesus back to life again after you had killed him by hanging him on a cross. 31Then, with mighty power, God exalted him to be a Prince and Savior, so that the people of Israel would have an opportunity for repentance, and for their sins to be forgiven. 32And we are witnesses of these things, and so is the Holy Spirit, who is given by God to all who obey him."

33At this, the Council was furious, and decided to kill them. 34But one of their

5:21 *Later that morning,* implied. | 5:24 *the police captain,* literally, "the captain of the Temple."

Cross references (right margin):

5:17 Acts 4:1,2
5:18 Lk 21:12
5:19 Ps 34:7; Acts 12:7; 16:26; Heb 1:14
5:20 Jn 6:63,68; 17:3; 1 Jn 5:11
5:21 Acts 4:5,6
5:26 Mt 14:5; 21:26
5:28 Mt 23:35; 27:25; Acts 2:23; 3:15; 4:18; 7:52
5:29 Acts 4:19
5:30 Acts 10:39-41; 1 Pet 2:24
5:31 Isa 9:6; Mt 1:21; Acts 2:33; Phil 2:9; Heb 2:10; 12:2; Rev 1:5
5:32 Lk 24:28; Jn 15:26; Rom 8:16; Heb 2:4
5:33 Acts 2:37; 7:54

5:16 What did these miraculous healings do for the early church? (1) They attracted believers. (2) They confirmed the truth of the apostles' teaching. (3) They demonstrated that the power of the Messiah who had been crucified and risen was now with his followers.

5:17 The religious leaders were jealous—Peter and the apostles were already commanding more respect than they had ever received. The difference, however, was that the religious leaders demanded respect and reverence for themselves; the apostles' goal was to bring respect and reverence to God. The apostles were respected not because they demanded it, but because they deserved it.

5:17, 18 The apostles had power to do miracles, great boldness in preaching, and God's presence in their lives; yet they were not free from hatred and persecution. They were arrested and put in jail, beaten with rods and whips, and slandered by community leaders. Faith in God does not make troubles disappear; it makes troubles appear less fearsome because it puts them in the right perspective. You cannot expect everyone to react favorably when you share something as dynamic as your faith in Christ. Some will be jealous of you, frightened, or threatened. Expect some negative reactions. But remember that you must be more concerned about God's reactions than peoples'.

5:21 The Jewish Council and Senate are not two different groups—this phrase simply means they convened the entire group, the 70 men of the Jewish Council (also called the Supreme Court or Sanhedrin). This was going to be no small trial. The religious leaders would do anything to stop these apostles from challenging their authority, threatening their secure position, and exposing their hypocritical motives to the people.

5:21 Suppose someone threatened to kill you if you didn't stop talking about God. You might be tempted to keep quiet. But the apostles, after being threatened by powerful leaders, arrested, beaten, jailed, and finally released, went back to preaching. This was nothing less than God's power working through this group of men (4:13). When we are convinced of the power of Christ's resurrection and have experienced the presence of his Holy Spirit, we can have the confidence to speak out for Christ.

5:21 The Temple at daybreak was a busy place. Many people stopped at the Temple to pray and worship at sunrise, and the apostles were already there, ready to tell them the Good News.

5:29 The apostles knew their priorities. While we should try to keep peace with everyone (Romans 12:18), conflict with the world and its authorities is sometimes inevitable for a Christian (John 15:18). There will be situations where you cannot obey both God and man. Then you must obey God and trust his Word. Let Jesus' words encourage you: "What happiness it is when others hate you and exclude you and insult you and smear your name because you are mine! When that happens, rejoice! Yes, leap for joy! For you will have a great reward awaiting you in heaven" (Luke 6:22, 23).

5:34 The Pharisees were the other major party in the Jewish Council with the Sadducees (5:17). They were the strict keepers of the law—not only God's law, but hundreds of other rules they had added to God's law. They were careful about outward purity, but many had hearts full of impure motives. Jesus confronted the

members, a Pharisee named Gamaliel (an expert on religious law and very popular with the people), stood up and requested that the apostles be sent outside the Council chamber while he talked.

35Then he addressed his colleagues as follows:

"Men of Israel, take care what you are planning to do to these men! 36Some time ago there was that fellow Theudas, who pretended to be someone great. About 400 others joined him, but he was killed, and his followers were harmlessly dispersed.

37"After him, at the time of the taxation, there was Judas of Galilee. He drew away some people as disciples, but he also died, and his followers scattered.

38"And so my advice is, leave these men alone. If what they teach and do is merely on their own, it will soon be overthrown. 39But if it is of God, you will not be able to stop them, lest you find yourselves fighting even against God."

40The Council accepted his advice, called in the apostles, had them beaten, and then told them never again to speak in the name of Jesus, and finally let them go. 41They left the Council chamber rejoicing that God had counted them worthy to suffer dishonor for his name. 42And every day, in the Temple and in their home Bible classes, they continued to teach and preach that Jesus is the Messiah.

➤ *The church appoints seven deacons*

6 But with the believers multiplying rapidly, there were rumblings of discontent. Those who spoke only Greek complained that their widows were being discriminated against, that they were not being given as much food, in the daily distribution, as the widows who spoke Hebrew. 2So the Twelve called a meeting of all the believers.

Cross references (left margin)
5:36 Acts 8:9
5:37 Lk 2:1
5:38 Ps 127:1
5:39 Prov 21:30; Isa 46:9,10; Mt 16:18; Acts 9:5; 1 Cor 1:25
5:40 Mt 10:17; Mk 13:9
5:41 Mt 5:11,12; Jn 15:20,21; Rom 5:3; Phil 1:29; Heb 10:34; 1 Pet 4:13,14,16
6:1 Ex 18:17; Acts 2:47; 4:35; 1 Tim 5:3

Pharisees often during his ministry on earth.

5:34 Gamaliel was an unexpected ally for the apostles, although he probably did not support their teachings. He was a distinguished member of the Jewish Council and a teacher. While he may have saved their lives, his real intentions were to keep the Council from being divided over them and to avoid arousing the Romans. Sometimes one time will tell if they are merely the work the people and killing them would probably start a riot. But Gamaliel's advice to the Council gave the apostles some breathing room to continue their work. The Council waited and hoped that this would all fade away harmlessly. They couldn't have been more wrong. Ironically, Paul, who would become one of the greatest apostles, was tutored by Gamaliel (22:3).

5:39 Gamaliel presented some sound advice about reacting to religious movements. Unless they endorse obviously dangerous doctrine or practices, it is often wiser to be tolerant rather than repressive. Sometimes only time will tell if they are merely the work of men or if God is trying to say something through them. Next time a group promotes differing religious ideas, consider Gamaliel's advice, "lest you find yourselves fighting even against God."

5:40 Peter and John were warned repeatedly not to preach, but they continued in spite of the threats. We, too, should live as Christ has asked, sharing our faith no matter what the cost. We may not be beaten or thrown in jail, but we may be ridiculed, ostracized, or slandered. To what extent are you willing to suffer for the sake of sharing the gospel with others?

5:41 Have you ever thought of persecution as a blessing? This beating suffered by Peter and John was the first time any of the apostles had been physically abused for their faith. These men knew how Jesus had suffered, and they praised God that he allowed them to be persecuted like their Lord. If you are mocked or persecuted for your faith, it isn't because you're doing something wrong, but that God has counted you "worthy to suffer dishonor for his name."

5:42 Home Bible studies are not new. The apostles had to teach in homes because the synagogues and the Temple were not open to their teaching. Home Bible studies met the needs of believers

and also introduced new people to the Christian faith. During later times of persecution, this became the primary method of passing on Bible knowledge. Christians throughout the world still use home Bible study both as a strategy under persecution and as a way to build up believers.

➤ **6:1ff** Another internal problem developed in the early church. The native Jewish Christians spoke Aramaic, a semitic language. The Greek-speaking Christians were probably Jews from other lands who were converted at Pentecost. The Greek-speaking Christians complained that their widows were being unfairly treated. This favoritism may not have been intentional, but was caused by a language barrier. To correct the problem, the apostles put seven respected Greek-speaking men in charge of the food distribution program. This put an end to the problem and allowed the apostles to keep their focus on their ministry of teaching and preaching the Good News about Jesus.

6:1 When we read the descriptions of the early church—the miracles, the sharing and generosity—we may wish we could have been a part of this "perfect" church. But in reality, they had problems just as we do today. No church has ever been or will ever be perfect until Christ and his church are united at his Second Coming. All churches have problems. If your church's shortcomings distress you, ask yourself: "Would a perfect church let me be a member?" Then do what you can to make your church better. A church does not have to be perfect to be faithful.

6:2 The Twelve are the 11 original disciples and Matthias, who was chosen to replace Judas Iscariot (1:26).

6:2–4 As the early church increased in size, their needs also increased. One need was to organize the distribution of food to the needy. The apostles needed to focus on preaching, so they chose others to administer the food program. Each person has a necessary part to play in the life of the church (see 1 Corinthians 12:27, 28). If you are in a position of leadership and find yourself bogged down, determine *your* God-given abilities and priorities and then find others to help. If you are not in leadership, you have gifts that can be used by God in various areas of the church's ministry. Offer these gifts in service to him.

"We should spend our time preaching, not administering a feeding program," they said. ³"Now look around among yourselves, dear brothers, and select seven men, wise and full of the Holy Spirit, who are well thought of by everyone; and we will put them in charge of this business. ⁴Then we can spend our time in prayer, preaching, and teaching."

⁵This sounded reasonable to the whole assembly, and they elected the following: Stephen (a man unusually full of faith and the Holy Spirit), Philip, Prochorus, Nicanor, Timon, Parmenas, Nicolaus of Antioch (a Gentile convert to the Jewish faith, who had become a Christian). ⁶These seven were presented to the apostles, who prayed for them and laid their hands on them in blessing.

⁷God's message was preached in ever-widening circles, and the number of disciples increased vastly in Jerusalem; and many of the Jewish priests were converted too.

Stephen is arrested

⁸Stephen, the man so full of faith and the Holy Spirit's power, did spectacular miracles among the people.

⁹But one day some of the men from the Jewish cult of "The Freedmen" started an argument with him, and they were soon joined by Jews from Cyrene, Alexandria in Egypt, and the Turkish provinces of Cilicia, and Asia minor. ¹⁰But none of them was able to stand against Stephen's wisdom and spirit.

¹¹So they brought in some men to lie about him, claiming they had heard Stephen curse Moses, and even God.

¹²This accusation roused the crowds to fury against Stephen, and the Jewish leaders arrested him and brought him before the Council. ¹³The lying witnesses testified again that Stephen was constantly speaking against the Temple and against the laws of Moses.

¹⁴They declared, "We have heard him say that this fellow Jesus of Nazareth will destroy the Temple, and throw out all of Moses' laws." ¹⁵At this point everyone in the Council chamber saw Stephen's face become as radiant as an angel's!

6:3 Acts 2:4
Eph 5:18
1 Tim 3:7,8
6:4 Acts 1:14; 2:42
6:5 Acts 8:5; 21:8
6:6 Num 8:10
Acts 1:24; 13:3
1 Tim 4:14
2 Tim 1:6
6:7 Jn 12:42
Acts 12:24; 19:20
21:20
Col 1:6
6:8 Jn 14:12
6:9 Mt 27:32
Acts 2:10;
18:24 21:39; 24:18
6:10 Ex 4:12
Lk 21:15
6:11 Mt 26:59
6:12 Lk 20:1
Acts 4:1
6:13 Mt 26:59
Acts 7:58; 21:28
6:14 Jn 2:19-21
Heb 9; 10
6:15 Mt 28:3

6:8 *full of faith and the Holy Spirit's power*, literally, "full of grace and truth." See vs 5.   **6:12** *the Jewish leaders*, literally, "the elders and the scribes."

6:3 This administrative task was not taken lightly. Notice the requirements for the men who were to handle the feeding program: (1) wise, (2) full of the Holy Spirit, and (3) well thought of by everyone. Jobs that require responsibility and dealing with people need leaders with these qualities. We must look for those who are wise, spiritually mature, and with good reputations to lead our churches today.

6:4 The apostles' priorities were correct. The ministry of the Word should never be neglected because of administrative burdens. Pastors should never try, or be expected, to do everything. The work of the church should be spread out among its members.

6:6 Spiritual leadership is serious business and must not be taken lightly by the church or the leaders. In the early church, the chosen men were commissioned (set apart by prayer and laying on of hands) by the apostles. Laying hands on someone, an ancient Jewish practice, was a way to set a person apart for special service (see Numbers 27:23; Deuteronomy 34:9).

6:7 Jesus had told the apostles that they were to witness first in Jerusalem (1:8). In a short time, their message had infiltrated the entire city and all levels of society. Even some priests were being converted, going against the directives of the Jewish Council and endangering their position.

6:7 The gospel spread in "ever-widening circles" like ripples on a pond where, from a single center, each wave touches the next,

spreading wider and farther. The gospel still spreads this way today. You don't have to change the world single-handedly—it is enough just to be part of the wave, touching those around you, who in turn will touch others until all have felt the movement. Don't ever feel that your part is insignificant or unimportant.

6:8-10 The most important prerequisite for any kind of Christian service is to be filled with the Holy Spirit. By the Spirit's power, Stephen was a good administrator, miracle worker (6:8), and evangelist (6:10). By the Spirit's power, you can exercise the gifts God has given you.

6:9 The Freedmen were a group of Jewish slaves who had been freed by Rome and had formed their own synagogue in Jerusalem.

6:11 The Sadducees were the dominant party in the Jewish Council. They accepted and studied only the writings of Moses (Genesis through Deuteronomy). In their view, to curse Moses was a crime. But from Stephen's speech (chapter 7), we learn that this accusation was false. Stephen based his review of Israel's history on Moses' writings.

6:14 When Stephen was brought before the Council of religious leaders, the Freedmen used the same false accusation that the religious leaders had used against Jesus (Matthew 26:61). They falsely accused Stephen of wanting to do away with Moses' laws because they knew that the Sadducees, who controlled the Council, believed *only* in Moses' laws.

Stephen addresses the Sanhedrin

7:2
Gen 15:7
7:3
Gen 12:1
7:4
Gen 11:31; 12:4
Heb 11:8

7 Then the High Priest asked him, "Are these accusations true?" 2This was Stephen's lengthy reply: "The glorious God appeared to our ancestor Abraham in Iraq before he moved to Syria, 3and told him to leave his native land, to say good-bye to his relatives and to start out for a country that God would direct him to. 4So he left the land of the Chaldeans and lived in Haran, in Syria, until his

7:2 *Iraq,* literally, "Mesopotamia." *Syria,* literally, "Haran," a city in the area we now know as Syria.

STEPHEN

Around the world, the gospel has most often taken root in places prepared by the blood of martyrs. Before a person can *give* his life for the gospel, however, he must first *live* his life for the gospel. One way God trains his servants is to place them in insignificant positions. Their desire to serve Christ is translated into the reality of serving others. Stephen was an effective administrator and messenger before becoming a martyr.

Stephen was named among the managers of food distribution in the early church. Long before violent persecution broke out against Christians, there was already social ostracism. Jews who accepted Jesus as Messiah were usually cut off from their families. As a result, the believers depended on each other for support. The sharing of homes, food, and resources was both a practical and necessary mark of the early church. Eventually, the number of believers made it necessary to organize the sharing. People were being overlooked. There were complaints. Those chosen to help manage were chosen for their integrity and sensitivity to God.

Stephen, besides being a good administrator, was also a powerful speaker. When confronted in the Temple by various antagonistic groups, Stephen's logic in responding was convincing. This is clear from the defense he made before the Court. He presented a summary of the Jews' own history and made powerful applications that stung his listeners. During his defense Stephen must have known he was speaking his own death sentence. Members of the Court could not stand to have their evil motives exposed. They stoned him to death while he prayed for their forgiveness. His final words show how much like Jesus he had become in a short time. His death had a lasting impact on young Saul (Paul) of Tarsus, who would move from being a violent persecutor of Christians to being one of the greatest champions of the gospel the church has known.

Stephen's life is a continual challenge to all Christians. Because he was the first to die for the faith, his sacrifice raises questions: How many risks do we take in being Jesus' followers? Would we be willing to die for him? Are we really willing to live for him?

Strengths and accomplishments:
● One of seven leaders chosen to supervise food distribution to the needy in the early church
● Known for his spiritual qualities of faith, wisdom, grace, and power, and for the Spirit's presence in his life
● Outstanding leader, teacher, and debater
● First to give his life for the gospel

Lessons from his life:
● Striving for excellence in small assignments prepares one for greater responsibilities
● Real understanding of God always leads to practical and compassionate actions toward people

Vital statistics:
● Church responsibilities: Deacon—distributing food to the needy
● Contemporaries: Paul, Caiaphas, Gamaliel, the apostles

Key verses:
"And as the murderous stones came hurtling at him, Stephen prayed, 'Lord Jesus, receive my spirit.' And he fell to his knees, shouting, 'Lord, don't charge them with this sin!' and with that, he died" (Acts 7:59, 60).

Stephen's story is told in Acts 6:3—8:2. He is also mentioned in Acts 11:19; 22:20.

7:1 This High Priest was Caiaphas, the same High Priest who had earlier questioned and condemned Jesus (John 18:24).

7:2ff Stephen launched into a long speech about Israel's relationship with God. From Old Testament history he showed that the Jews had constantly rejected God's message and his prophets, and that this Council had rejected the Messiah, God's Son. He made three main points: (1) Israel's history is the history of God's acts in the world; (2) men worshiped God long before there was a temple, for God does not live in a temple; (3) Jesus' death

was just one more example of Israel's rebellion and rejection of God.

7:2ff Stephen wasn't really defending himself. Instead he took the offensive, seizing the opportunity to summarize his teaching about Jesus. Stephen was accusing these religious leaders of failing to obey God's laws—the laws they prided themselves in following so meticulously. This was the same accusation Jesus leveled against them. When we witness for Jesus, we don't need to be on the defensive, but instead simply share our faith.

father died. Then God brought him here to the land of Israel, 5but gave him no property of his own, not one little tract of land.

"However, God promised that eventually the whole country would belong to him and his descendants—though as yet he had no children! 6But God also told him that these descendants of his would leave the land and live in a foreign country and there become slaves for 400 years. 7'But I will punish the nation that enslaves them,' God told him, 'and afterwards my people will return to this land of Israel and worship me here.'

8"God also gave Abraham the ceremony of circumcision at that time, as evidence of the covenant between God and the people of Abraham. And so Isaac, Abraham's son, was circumcised when he was eight days old. Isaac became the father of Jacob, and Jacob was the father of the twelve patriarchs of the Jewish nation. 9These men were very jealous of Joseph and sold him to be a slave in Egypt. But God was with him, 10and delivered him out of all of his anguish, and gave him favor before Pharaoh, king of Egypt. God also gave Joseph unusual wisdom, so that Pharaoh appointed him governor over all Egypt, as well as putting him in charge of all the affairs of the palace.

11"But a famine developed in Egypt and Canaan and there was great misery for our ancestors. When their food was gone, 12Jacob heard that there was still grain in Egypt, so he sent his sons to buy some. 13The second time they went, Joseph revealed his identity to his brothers, and they were introduced to Pharaoh. 14Then Joseph sent for his father Jacob and all his brothers' families to come to Egypt, seventy-five persons in all. 15So Jacob came to Egypt, where he died, and all his sons. 16All of them were taken to Shechem and buried in the tomb Abraham bought from the sons of Hamor, Shechem's father.

17, 18"As the time drew near when God would fulfill his promise to Abraham to free his descendants from slavery, the Jewish people greatly multiplied in Egypt; but then a king was crowned who had no respect for Joseph's memory. 19This king plotted against our race, forcing parents to abandon their children in the fields.

20"About that time Moses was born—a child of divine beauty. His parents hid him at home for three months, 21and when at last they could no longer keep him hidden, and had to abandon him, Pharaoh's daughter found him and adopted him as her own son, 22and taught him all the wisdom of the Egyptians, and he became a mighty prince and orator.

23"One day as he was nearing his fortieth birthday, it came into his mind to visit his brothers, the people of Israel. 24During this visit he saw an Egyptian mistreating a man of Israel. So Moses killed the Egyptian. 25Moses supposed his brothers would realize that God had sent him to help them, but they didn't.

26"The next day he visited them again and saw two men of Israel fighting. He tried to be a peacemaker. 'Gentlemen,' he said, 'you are brothers and shouldn't be fighting like this! It is wrong!'

27"But the man in the wrong told Moses to mind his own business. 'Who made

7:12 *his sons*, literally, "our fathers."

7:5
Gen 12:7
13:15,16
17:7,8; 26:3

7:6
Gen 15:13
Ex 12:40
Gal 3:17
1 Pet 2:11

7:7
Ex 3:12

7:8
Gen 17:9,10
21:1,2; 25:26
35:23-26
1 Chron 1:34
Mt 1:2

7:9
Gen 37:4,11,28
39:2
Ps 105:17

7:10
Gen 42:6
Ps 37:23; 105:21

7:11
Gen 41:54

7:12
Gen 42:2

7:13
Gen 45:1-4

7:14
Gen 45:9; 46:27
Deut 10:22

7:15
Gen 49:33
Ex 1:6

7:16
Gen 23:16

7:17,18
Gen 15:13
Ex 1:7,8

7:19
Ex 1:10,15,16

7:20
Ex 2:1,2
Heb 11:23

7:22
1 Kgs 4:30

7:23
Ex 2:11

7:24
Ex 2:12

7:27,28
Ex 2:14

Stephen's death was not in vain. Below are some of the events that were by-products (either directly or indirectly) of the persecution that began with Stephen's martyrdom.
1. Philip's evangelistic tour (Acts 8:4–40)
2. Paul's conversion (Acts 9:1–30)
3. Peter's missionary tour (Acts 9:32—11:18)
4. The church in Antioch in Syria founded (Acts 11:1ff)

THE EFFECTS OF STEPHEN'S DEATH

7:8 Circumcision was a sign of the promise made between God, Abraham, and the entire nation of Israel (Genesis 17:9–13). Stephen's speech was a summary of Israel's history, thus a summary of how this covenant fared over time. Stephen pointed out that God always kept his side of the promise, but Israel failed again and again to uphold its end. Although the Jews in Stephen's day still adhered to the ceremony of circumcision, they neglected to obey. The people's hearts were far from God, and so they had gone back on their side of the promise.

you a ruler and judge over us?' he asked. 28'Are you going to kill me as you killed that Egyptian yesterday?'

29"At this, Moses fled the country, and lived in the land of Midian, where his two sons were born.

30"Forty years later, in the desert near Mount Sinai, an Angel appeared to him in a flame of fire in a bush. 31Moses saw it and wondered what it was, and as he ran to see, the voice of the Lord called out to him, 32'I am the God of your ancestors—of Abraham, Isaac and Jacob.' Moses shook with terror and dared not look.

33"And the Lord said to him, 'Take off your shoes, for you are standing on holy ground. 34I have seen the anguish of my people in Egypt and have heard their cries. I have come down to deliver them. Come, I will send you to Egypt.' 35And so God sent back the same man his people had previously rejected by demanding, 'Who made *you* a ruler and judge over us?' Moses was sent to be their ruler and savior. 36And by means of many remarkable miracles he led them out of Egypt and through the Red Sea, and back and forth through the wilderness for forty years.

37"Moses himself told the people of Israel, 'God will raise up a Prophet much like me from among your brothers.' 38How true this proved to be, for in the wilderness, Moses was the go-between—the mediator between the people of Israel and the Angel who gave them the Law of God—the Living Word—on Mount Sinai.

39"But our fathers rejected Moses and wanted to return to Egypt. 40They told Aaron, 'Make idols for us, so that we will have gods to lead us back; for we don't know what has become of this Moses, who brought us out of Egypt.' 41So they made a calf-idol and sacrificed to it, and rejoiced in this thing they had made.

42"Then God turned away from them and gave them up, and let them serve the sun, moon and stars as their gods! In the book of Amos' prophecies the Lord God asks, 'Was it to me you were sacrificing during those forty years in the desert, Israel? 43No, your real interest was in your heathen gods—Sakkuth, and the star god Kaiway, and in all the images you made. So I will send you into captivity far away beyond Babylon.'

44"Our ancestors carried along with them a portable Temple, or Tabernacle, through the wilderness. In it they kept the stone tablets with the Ten Commandments written on them. This building was constructed in exact accordance with the plan shown to Moses by the Angel. 45Years later, when Joshua led the battles against the Gentile nations, this Tabernacle was taken with them into their new territory, and used until the time of King David.

46"God blessed David greatly, and David asked for the privilege of building a permanent Temple for the God of Jacob. 47But it was Solomon who actually built it. 48, 49However, God doesn't live in temples made by human hands. 'The heaven is my throne,' says the Lord through his prophets, 'and earth is my footstool. What kind of home could you build?' asks the Lord. 'Would I stay in it? 50Didn't I make both heaven and earth?'

51"You stiff-necked heathen! Must you forever resist the Holy Spirit? But your fathers did, and so do you! 52Name one prophet your ancestors didn't persecute! They even killed the ones who predicted the coming of the Righteous One—the

7:37 *much like me,* literally, "like unto me."

Cross-references (left margin)

7:29 Ex 2:15
7:30 Ex 3:2 / Deut 33:16
7:32 Ex 3:6
7:33 Josh 5:15
7:34 Ex 3:7,10
7:35 Ex 14:19 / Num 20:16
7:36 Ex 7:3; 12:40,41
7:37 Deut 18:15 / Mt 17:5 / Acts 3:22
7:38 Ex 19:2,3,17 / Deut 32:47 / Rom 3:2
7:39 Num 14:3
7:40 Ex 32:1,23
7:42 Deut 17:2,3 / Josh 24:20 / 2 Kgs 17:16 / Amos 5:25-27
7:44 Ex 25:8,40 / Heb 8:5
7:45 Josh 3:13,14 / 18:1; 22:19 / 2 Sam 7:6 / 1 Chron 17:5 21:29 / 2 Chron 1:3
7:46 2 Sam 7:1-14 / 1 Kgs 8:17 / Ps 132:1-5
7:47 2 Sam 7:12,13 / 1 Kgs 8:20
7:48 2 Chron 2:6 / Isa 57:15 / Eph 2:22 / 1 Pet 2:5
7:49,50 Isa 66:1-2
7:51 Ex 32:9 / Isa 48:4 / Ezek 44:9
7:52 2 Chron 36:16 / Mt 23:30-34

7:37 The Jews originally thought this "Prophet" was Joshua. But Moses was prophesying of the coming Messiah (Deuteronomy 18:15). Peter also quotes this verse in referring to the Messiah (Acts 3:22).

7:38 From Galatians 3:19 and Hebrews 2:2, it appears that God gave the law to Moses through angels. Exodus 31:18 says God wrote the Ten Commandments himself ("written with the finger of God"). Apparently God used angelic messengers to deliver his law to Moses.

7:44-50 Stephen had been accused of speaking against the Temple (6:13). Although he recognized the importance of the

Temple, he knew that it was not more important than God. God is not limited; he doesn't live only in a sanctuary, but wherever hearts of faith are open to receive him. Solomon knew this when he prayed at the dedication of the Temple (2 Chronicles 6:18; Isaiah 66:1, 2.)

7:52 Many prophets indeed were persecuted: Jeremiah (Jeremiah 38:1-6); Isaiah (tradition says he was killed by King Manasseh; see 2 Kings 21:16); Amos (Amos 7:10-13); Zechariah (2 Chronicles 24:20-22); Elijah (1 Kings 19:2). Jesus also told a parable about how the Jews had constantly rejected God's messages and persecuted his messengers (Luke 20:9-15).

Messiah whom you betrayed and murdered. ⁵³Yes, and you deliberately destroyed God's Laws, though you received them from the hands of angels."

7:53
Ex 20:1
Gal 3:19

Stephen is martyred by stoning

⁵⁴The Jewish leaders were stung to fury by Stephen's accusation, and ground their teeth in rage. ⁵⁵But Stephen, full of the Holy Spirit, gazed steadily upward into heaven and saw the glory of God and Jesus standing at God's right hand. ⁵⁶And he told them, "Look, I see the heavens opened and Jesus the Messiah standing beside God, at his right hand!"

7:55
Mt 26:64
Heb 1:3,13

7:56
Mt 3:16
Heb 9:24

⁵⁷Then they mobbed him, putting their hands over their ears, and drowning out his voice with their shouts, ⁵⁸and dragged him out of the city to stone him. The official witnesses—the executioners—took off their coats and laid them at the feet of a young man named Paul.

7:58
Lev 24:14-16
Deut 17:7

⁵⁹And as the murderous stones came hurtling at him, Stephen prayed, "Lord Jesus, receive my spirit." ⁶⁰And he fell to his knees, shouting, "Lord, don't charge them with this sin!" and with that, he died.

7:59
Ps 31:5
Lk 23:46

7:60
Mt 5:44
Lk 6:28; 23:34

2. Expansion of the church

Widespread persecution scatters the believers

8 Paul was in complete agreement with the killing of Stephen. And a great wave of persecution of the believers began that day, sweeping over the church in Jerusalem, and everyone except the apostles fled into Judea and Samaria. ²(But some godly Jews came and with great sorrow buried Stephen.) ³Paul was like a wild man, going everywhere to devastate the believers, even entering private homes and dragging out men and women alike and jailing them.

8:1
Acts 7:58

8:3
Acts 9:1; 22:4
26:10
1 Cor 15:9
Gal 1:13

⁴But the believers who had fled Jerusalem went everywhere preaching the Good News about Jesus! ⁵Philip, for instance, went to the city of Samaria and told the people there about Christ. ⁶Crowds listened intently to what he had to say because of the miracles he did. ⁷Many evil spirits were cast out, screaming as they left their victims, and many who were paralyzed or lame were healed, ⁸so there was much joy in that city!

8:4
Acts 11:19

8:5
Acts 6:5

8:7
Mt 10:1

7:53 *God's Laws, though you received them from the hands of angels,* literally, "the Law as it was ordained by angels." **7:56** *the Messiah,* literally, "the Son of Man." **7:58** *Paul,* also known as Saul. **8:2** *godly Jews,* literally, "devout men." It is not clear whether these were Christians who braved the persecution, or whether they were godly and sympathetic Jews. **8:4** *the believers,* literally, "the church."

7:55 Stephen saw the glory of God and Jesus the Messiah standing at God's right hand. Stephen's words are similar to Jesus' words spoken before the Council (Matthew 26:64; Mark 14:62; Luke 22:69). Stephen's vision supported Jesus' claim and angered the Jewish leaders who had condemned Jesus to death for blasphemy. They would not tolerate Stephen's words, so they mobbed him and killed him. People may not kill us for witnessing about Christ, but they will let us know they don't want to hear the truth and will often try to silence us. Keep honoring God in your conduct and words; though many will turn against you and your message, some will turn to Christ.

7:58 When Luke introduces Paul, Paul is hating and persecuting Jesus' followers. This is a great contrast to the Paul about whom Luke will write for most of the rest of the book of Acts—a devoted follower of Christ and a gifted gospel preacher. Paul was uniquely qualified to talk to the Jews about Jesus because he had once opposed him, and he understood how the opposition felt about him. In other translations, the name here is "Saul," which was his Hebrew name; Paul, his Greek name, was used after his conversion.

7:59 The penalty for blasphemy, speaking irreverently about God, was death by stoning (Leviticus 24:14). The religious leaders, in a rage and without trial or verdict, had Stephen stoned. They did not understand that Stephen's words were truth, because they were

not seeking the truth. They only wanted support for their own views. Stephen did not have widespread public support as Jesus had, so the leaders felt secure in stoning him.

7:60 As Stephen died, he repeated what Jesus had said as he died on the cross (Luke 23:34). The early believers were glad to suffer as Jesus had suffered, because that meant they were counted worthy (5:41). Stephen was ready to suffer like Jesus, even to the point of asking forgiveness for his murderers. Such a forgiving response comes only from the Holy Spirit. The Spirit can also help us respond as Stephen did and love our enemies (Luke 6:27). How would you respond if someone hurt you because of what you believe?

8:1-4 Persecution forced the Christians out of Jerusalem and into Judea and Samaria—thus fulfilling the next part of Jesus' command (see 1:8). The persecution helped spread the gospel. All the believers suffered, but God would bring great results from their suffering.

8:4 Persecution forced the believers out of their homes in Jerusalem, and with them went the gospel. Often we have to become uncomfortable before we'll move. Discomfort may be unwanted, but it is not undesirable, for out of our hurting, God works his purposes. The next time you are tempted to complain about uncomfortable or painful circumstances, stop and ask if God may be preparing you for a special task.

— *Philip and Simon the sorcerer*

8:9
Acts 5:36; 13:6

9, 10, 11A man named Simon had formerly been a sorcerer there for many years; he was a very influential, proud man because of the amazing things he could do—in fact, the Samaritan people often spoke of him as the Messiah. 12But now they believed Philip's message that Jesus was the Messiah, and his words concerning

8:12
Acts 1:3; 2:38

8:9-11 *the Messiah,* literally, "this man is that Power of God which is called great."

MISSIONARIES OF THE NEW TESTAMENT AND THEIR JOURNEYS	Name	Journey Purpose	Scripture Reference in Acts
	Philip	One of the first to preach the gospel outside Jerusalem	8:4–40
	Peter and John	Visited new Samaritan believers to encourage them	8:14–25
	Paul (journey to Damascus)	Set out to capture Christians but was captured by Christ	9:1–25
	Peter	Led by God to one of the first Gentile families to become Christian—Cornelius' family	9:32—10:48
	Barnabas	Went to Antioch as an encourager; traveled on to Troas to bring Paul back to Jerusalem from Antioch	11:25–30
	Barnabas, Paul, John Mark	Left Antioch for Cyprus, Pamphylia, and Galatia on the first missionary journey	13:1—14:28
	Barnabas and John Mark	After a break with Paul, they left Antioch for Cyprus	15:36–41
	Paul, Silas, Timothy, Luke	Left Antioch to revisit churches in Galatia, then traveled on to Asia, Macedonia, and Achaia on a second missionary journey	15:36—18:22
	Apollos	Left Alexandria for Ephesus; learned the complete gospel story from Priscilla and Aquila; preached in Athens and Corinth	18:24–28
	Paul, Timothy, Erastus	Third major missionary journey revisiting churches in Galatia, Asia, Macedonia, and Achaia	18:23; 19:1—21:14

PHILIP'S MINISTRY
To escape persecution in Jerusalem, Philip fled to Samaria, where he continued preaching the gospel. While he was there, an angel commanded him to meet an Ethiopian official on the road between Jerusalem and Gaza. The official became a believer before continuing to Ethiopia. Philip then went from Azotus to Caesarea.

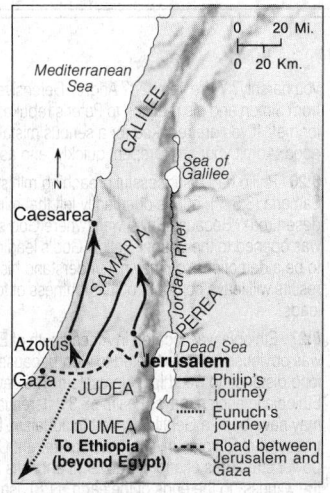

north, Samaria in the middle, and Judea in the south. The city of Samaria (in the region of Samaria) had been the capital of the Northern Kingdom of Israel in the days of the divided kingdom, before it was conquered by Assyria in 722 B.C. The Assyrian king took many captives, leaving only the poorest people in the land and resettling it with foreigners. These foreigners intermarried with the Jews who were left, and the mixed race became known as Samaritans. The Samaritans were considered half-breeds by the "pure" Jews in the Southern Kingdom of Judah, and there was intense hatred between the two groups. But Jesus himself went into Samaria (John 4), and he commanded his followers to spread the gospel even there (1:8).

8:7 Jesus encountered and cast out many demons during his ministry on earth. Demons, or evil spirits, are ruled by Satan. They are probably fallen angels who joined Satan in his rebellion against God, and they can cause a person to be mute, deaf, blind, or insane. They also tempt people to sin. Demons are real and active, but Jesus has authority over them, and he gave this authority to his followers. Although he permits Satan to work in our world, God is in complete control. His power can cast demons out and end their destructive work in people's lives. Eventually Satan and his demons will be bound forever, ending their evil work in the world (Revelation 20:10).

8:5 This is not the apostle Philip (see John 1:43, 44), but a Greek-speaking Jew, "wise and full of the Holy Spirit," who was one of the seven deacons chosen to help with the food distribution program in the church (6:5).

8:5 Israel was divided into three main regions—Galilee in the

— **8:9–11** In the days of the early church, sorcerers and magicians were numerous and influential. They worked wonders, performed healings and exorcisms, and practiced astrology. Simon the sorcerer had done so many wonders that some even thought he was the Messiah, but his powers did not come from God (see 8:18–24).

the Kingdom of God; and many men and women were baptized. 13Then Simon himself believed and was baptized and began following Philip wherever he went, and was amazed by the miracles he did.

8:13
Acts 19:11

14When the apostles back in Jerusalem heard that the people of Samaria had accepted God's message, they sent down Peter and John. 15As soon as they arrived, they began praying for these new Christians to receive the Holy Spirit, 16for as yet he had not come upon any of them. For they had only been baptized in the name of the Lord Jesus. 17Then Peter and John laid their hands upon these believers, and they received the Holy Spirit.

8:14
Acts 8:1
8:15
Acts 2:38
19:2
8:16
Acts 10:48
8:17
Acts 2:4

18When Simon saw this—that the Holy Spirit was given when the apostles placed their hands upon people's heads—he offered money to buy this power.

8:20
Mic 3:11,12
Mt 10:8
Acts 2:38

19"Let me have this power too," he exclaimed, "so that when I lay my hands on people, they will receive the Holy Spirit!"

8:21
Jer 17:9
Eph 5:5

20But Peter replied, "Your money perish with you for thinking God's gift can be bought! 21You can have no part in this, for your heart is not right before God. 22Turn from this great wickedness and pray. Perhaps God will yet forgive your evil thoughts— 23for I can see that there is jealousy and sin in your heart."

8:22
Isa 55:7
Dan 4:27
8:23
Heb 12:15

24"Pray for me," Simon exclaimed, "that these terrible things won't happen to me."

8:24
Gen 20:7
Ex 8:8
Num 21:7
Job 42:8
Jas 5:16

25After testifying and preaching in Samaria, Peter and John returned to Jerusalem, stopping at several Samaritan villages along the way to preach the Good News to them too.

Philip and the Ethiopian official

26But as for Philip, an angel of the Lord said to him, "Go over to the road that runs from Jerusalem through the Gaza Desert, arriving around noon." 27So he did, and who should be coming down the road but the Treasurer of Ethiopia, a eunuch of great authority under Candace the queen. He had gone to Jerusalem to worship, 28and was now returning in his chariot, reading aloud from the book of the prophet Isaiah.

8:26
Ps 91:11
Heb 1:14
8:27
1 Kgs 8:41,42
Ps 68:29
Isa 43:6; 53:7
56:3
Zeph 3:10

29The Holy Spirit said to Philip, "Go over and walk along beside the chariot."

8:23 *jealousy*, literally, "the gall of bitterness."

8:14 Peter and John were sent to Samaria to find out whether or not the Samaritans were truly becoming believers. The Jewish Christians, even the apostles, were still unsure whether Gentiles (non-Jews) and half-Jews could receive the Holy Spirit. It wasn't until Peter's experience with Cornelius (chapter 10) that the apostles became fully convinced that the Holy Spirit was for all people. It was John who had asked Jesus if they should call fire down from heaven to burn up a Samaritan village which refused to welcome them (Luke 9:49–55). Now he and Peter went to the Samaritans to pray with them.

8:15–17 This was a crucial moment in the spread of the gospel and the growth of the church, and the apostles, Peter and John, had to go to Samaria to help keep this new group of believers from becoming segregated from other believers. When Peter and John saw the Holy Spirit working in these people, they were assured that the Holy Spirit worked through all believers—Gentiles and mixed races as well as the "pure" Jews.

8:17–20 "Everything has a price" seems to be true in our world of bribes, wealth, and materialism. Simon thought he could buy the Holy Spirit's power, but Peter harshly rebuked him. The only way to receive God's power is to do as Peter told Simon—turn from sin, ask God for forgiveness, and be filled with his Spirit. No amount of money can buy salvation, forgiveness of sin, or God's power. These are only gained by repentance and belief in Christ as Savior.

8:24 Do you remember the last time a parent or friend rebuked

you harshly? Were you hurt? Angry? Defensive? Learn a lesson from Simon and his reaction to Peter's rebuke. He exclaimed, "Pray for me!" If you are rebuked for a serious mistake, it is for your good. Admit your error, repent quickly, and ask for prayer.

8:26 Philip had a successful preaching ministry to great crowds in Samaria (8:5–7), but he obediently left that ministry to go to a desert road. Because Philip went where God sent him, Ethiopia was opened to the gospel. Follow God's leading, even if it appears to be a demotion. You may not understand his plans at first, but the results will leave no doubt of the rightness of following wherever he leads.

8:27 Ethiopia was located in Africa south of Egypt. The eunuch was obviously very dedicated to God because he came such a long distance to worship in Jerusalem. The Jews had contact with Ethiopia in ancient days (Psalm 68:31; Jeremiah 38:7), so this man may have been a Gentile convert to Judaism. Because he was the treasurer of Ethiopia, his conversion brought Christianity into the power structures of another government. This is the beginning of the witness "to the ends of the earth" (1:8). Isaiah had prophesied that Gentiles and eunuchs would be blessed (Isaiah 56:3–5).

8:29–35 Philip found the Ethiopian man reading the Scriptures, and he took advantage of this opportunity to explain the gospel by asking if the man understood what he was reading. Philip (1) followed the Spirit's leading, (2) began the discussion from where the man was—immersed in the prophecies of Isaiah, and (3)

30Philip ran over and heard what he was reading and asked, "Do you understand it?"

8:31
2 Cor 3:14

31"Of course not!" the man replied. "How can I when there is no one to instruct me?" And he begged Philip to come up into the chariot and sit with him.

8:32,33
Isa 53:7,8
Phil 2:7,8

32The passage of Scripture he had been reading from was this:

"He was led as a sheep to the slaughter, and as a lamb is silent before the shearers, so he opened not his mouth; 33in his humiliation, justice was denied him; and who can express the wickedness of the people of his generation? For his life is taken from the earth."

34The eunuch asked Philip, "Was Isaiah talking about himself or someone else?"

8:35
Lk 24:27
Acts 18:28

35So Philip began with this same Scripture and then used many others to tell him about Jesus.

36As they rode along, they came to a small body of water, and the eunuch said, "Look! Water! Why can't I be baptized?"

8:37
Mt 16:16; 28:19
Mk 16:16
Jn 6:69; 11:27
Rom 10:10

37"You can," Philip answered, "if you believe with all your heart."

And the eunuch replied, "I believe that Jesus Christ is the Son of God."

8:39
1 Kgs 18:12
2 Kgs 2:16
Ezek 3:12

38He stopped the chariot, and they went down into the water and Philip baptized him. 39And when they came up out of the water, the Spirit of the Lord caught away Philip, and the eunuch never saw him again, but went on his way rejoicing. 40Meanwhile, Philip found himself at Azotus! He preached the Good News there and in every city along the way, as he traveled to Caesarea.

Paul is converted on the way to Damascus

9:1
Acts 8:3
Gal 1:13
1 Tim 1:13

9 But Paul, threatening with every breath and eager to destroy every Christian, went to the High Priest in Jerusalem. 2He requested a letter addressed to synagogues in Damascus, requiring their cooperation in the persecution of any believers he found there, both men and women, so that he could bring them in chains to Jerusalem.

9:2
Acts 22:5; 26:10

8:33 *who can express the wickedness of the people of his generation,* implied. Literally, "Who can declare his generation?" Alternatively, "Who will be able to speak of his posterity? For . . ." **8:37** Many ancient manuscripts omit vs 37 wholly or in part.

---

explained how Jesus Christ fulfilled Isaiah's prophecies. When we share the gospel, we should start where the other person's concerns are focused. Then we can bring the gospel to bear on those concerns.

8:30, 31 The eunuch begged Philip to explain a passage of Scripture which he did not understand. When we do not understand the Bible, we should ask others to help us. We must never let our pride get in the way of understanding God's Word.

8:35 Some think the Old Testament is not relevant today, but Philip led this man to faith in Jesus Christ by using Old Testament Scripture. Jesus Christ is found in the pages of both the Old and New Testaments. God's entire Word is applicable to all people in all ages. We must not neglect to use the Old Testament, because it too is God's Word.

8:39, 40 Why was Philip suddenly transported to a different city? This miraculous sign showed the urgency of bringing the Gentiles to belief in Christ.

9:2 Why would the Jews in Jerusalem want to persecute Christians as far away as Damascus? There are several possibilities: (1) to seize the Christians who had fled, (2) to contain and prevent the spread of Christianity to other major cities, (3) to keep the Christians from provoking any problems with Rome, (4) to advance Paul's career and build his reputation as a true Pharisee zealous for the law, (5) to unify the factions of Judaism by giving them a common enemy.

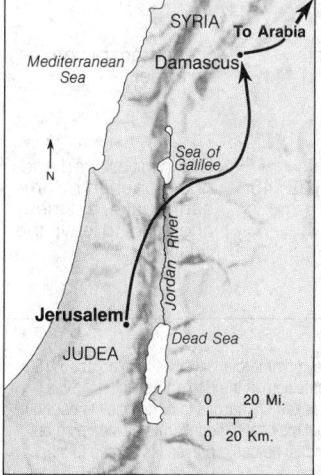

PAUL TRAVELS TO DAMASCUS Many Christians fled Jerusalem when persecution began after Stephen's death, seeking refuge in other cities and countries. Paul tracked them down, even traveling 150 miles to Damascus in Syria to bring Christians back in chains to Jerusalem. But as he neared the ancient city, he discovered that God had other plans for him (9:15).

³As he was nearing Damascus on this mission, suddenly a brilliant light from heaven spotted down upon him! ⁴He fell to the ground and heard a voice saying to him, "Paul! Paul! Why are you persecuting me?"

9:3
Acts 22:6,7
26:12,13
1 Cor 15:8

GREAT ESCAPES IN THE BIBLE

Who escaped	Reference	What happened	What the escape accomplished	Application
Jacob	Genesis 31:1–55	Left his father-in-law, Laban, after almost 20 years of service	Allowed Jacob to return home for Isaac's death and for reconciliation with Esau, his brother	A time away from home often puts the really important things into perspective
Moses	Exodus 2:11–15	Fled Egypt after killing an Egyptian in defense of a fellow Israelite	Saved his own life and began another part of God's training	God even fits our mistakes into his plan
Israelites	Exodus 12:28–42	Escaped Egypt after 430 years, most of that time in slavery	God confirmed his choice of Abraham's descendants	God will not forget his promises
Spies	Joshua 2:1–24	Escaped searchers in Jericho by hiding in Rahab's house	Prepared the destruction of Jericho, preserved Rahab who would become one of David's ancestors—as well as an ancestor of Jesus	God's plan weaves lives together in a pattern beyond our understanding
Ehud	Judges 3:15–30	Assassinated the Moabite King Eglon, but escaped undetected	Broke the control of Moab over Israel and began 80 years of peace	Punishments by God are often swift and deadly
Samson	Judges 16:1–3	Escaped a locked city by ripping the gates from their hinges	Merely postponed Samson's self-destruction because of his lack of self-control	Without dependence on God and his guidance, even great ability is wasted
Elijah	1 Kings 19:1–18	Fled into the desert out of fear of Queen Jezebel	Preserved Elijah's life, but also displayed his human weakness	Even at moments of real success, our personal weaknesses are our greatest challenges
Paul	Acts 9:25	Lowered over the wall in a basket to get out of Damascus	Saved this new Christian for great service to God	God has a purpose for every life, which becomes a real adventure for those willing to cooperate
Peter	Acts 12:1–11	Freed from prison by an angel	Saved Peter for God's further plans for his life	God can use extraordinary means to carry out his plan—often when we least expect it
Paul and Silas	Acts 16:22–40	Chains loosened and doors opened by an earthquake, but they chose not to leave the prison	Pointed out the powerlessness of men before God	When our dependence and attention are focused on God rather than our problems, he is able to offer help in unexpected ways

---

9:3 Damascus, a key commercial city, was located about 150 miles northeast of Jerusalem in the Roman province of Syria. Several trade routes linked Damascus to other cities throughout the Roman world. Paul may have thought that by stamping out Christianity in Damascus, he could prevent its spread to other areas.

9:2, 3 As Paul traveled to Damascus, pursuing Christians, he was confronted by the risen Christ and brought face to face with the truth of the gospel. Sometimes God breaks into a life in a spectacular manner, and sometimes conversion is a quiet experience. Beware of people who insist you must have a particular type of conversion experience. The right way to come to faith in Jesus is whatever way God brings *you*.

9:3 Paul refers to this experience as the start of his new life in Christ (1 Corinthians 9:1; 15:8; Galatians 1:15, 16). At the center of this wonderful experience was Jesus Christ—Paul did not see a vision, he saw the risen Christ himself (9:17). Paul recognized

9:5
Acts 5:39

9:7
Dan 10:7
Acts 22:9; 26:14

9:10
Acts 10:3;
11:5; 12:9; 22:12

9:11
Acts 21:39

5"Who is speaking, sir?" Paul asked.

And the voice replied, "I am Jesus, the one you are persecuting! 6Now get up and go into the city and await my further instructions."

7The men with Paul stood speechless with surprise, for they heard the sound of someone's voice but saw no one! 8, 9As Paul picked himself up off the ground, he found that he was blind. He had to be led into Damascus and was there three days, blind, going without food and water all that time.

10Now there was in Damascus a believer named Ananias. The Lord spoke to him in a vision, calling, "Ananias!"

"Yes, Lord!" he replied.

11And the Lord said, "Go over to Straight Street and find the house of a man named Judas and ask there for Paul of Tarsus. He is praying to me right now, for

---

PHILIP

Jesus' last words to his followers were a command to take the gospel everywhere, but they seemed reluctant to leave Jerusalem. It took intense persecution to scatter the believers from Jerusalem and into Judea and Samaria, where Jesus had instructed them to go. Philip, one of the deacons in charge of food distribution, left Jerusalem and, like most Jewish Christians, spread the gospel wherever he went; but unlike most of them, he did not limit his audience to other Jews. He went directly to Samaria, the last place many Jews would go, due to age-old prejudice.

The Samaritans responded in large numbers. When word got back to Jerusalem, Peter and John were sent to evaluate Philip's ministry. They quickly became involved themselves, seeing firsthand God's acceptance of those who previously were considered unacceptable.

In the middle of all this success and excitement, God directed Philip out to the desert for an appointment with an Ethiopian eunuch, another foreigner, who had been in Jerusalem. Philip went immediately. His effectiveness in sharing the gospel with this man placed a Christian in a significant position in a distant country, and may well have had an effect on an entire nation.

Philip ended up in Caesarea, where events allowed him to be Paul's host many years later. Paul, who as the leading persecutor of the Christians had been instrumental in pushing Philip and others out of Jerusalem, had himself become an effective believer. The conversion of the Gentiles begun by Philip was continued across the entire Roman empire by Paul.

Whether or not you are a follower of Christ, Philip's life presents a challenge. To those still outside the gospel, he is a reminder that the gospel is for you also. To those who have accepted Christ, he is a reminder that we are not free to disqualify anyone from hearing about Jesus. How much like Philip would your neighbors say you are?

Strengths and accomplishments:
• One of the seven organizers of food distribution in the early church
• Became an evangelist, one of the first traveling missionaries
• One of the first to obey Jesus' command to take the gospel to all people
• A careful student of the Bible who could explain its meaning clearly

Lessons from his life:
• God finds great and various uses for those willing to obey wholeheartedly
• The gospel is universal Good News
• The whole Bible, not just the New Testament, helps us understand more about Jesus
• Both mass response (the Samaritans) and individual response (the man from Ethiopia) to the gospel are valuable

Vital statistics:
• Occupation: Deacon, evangelist
• Relatives: Four daughters
• Contemporaries: Paul, Stephen, the apostles

Key verse:
"So Philip began with this same Scripture and then used many others to tell him about Jesus" (Acts 8:35).

Philip's story is told in Acts 6:1–7; 8:5–40; 21:8–10.

Jesus as Lord, realized his own sin, surrendered his life to Jesus, and resolved to obey. True conversion comes from a personal encounter with Jesus Christ and leads to a new life in relationship with him.

9:5 Paul thought he was persecuting heretics, but he was persecuting Jesus himself. Anyone who persecutes believers today is also guilty of persecuting Jesus (see Matthew 25:45), because believers are the body of Christ on earth.

12I have shown him a vision of a man named Ananias coming in and laying his hands on him so that he can see again!"

13"But Lord," exclaimed Ananias, "I have heard about the terrible things this man has done to the believers in Jerusalem! 14And we hear that he has arrest warrants with him from the chief priests, authorizing him to arrest every believer in Damascus!"

15But the Lord said, "Go and do what I say. For Paul is my chosen instrument to take my message to the nations and before kings, as well as to the people of Israel. 16And I will show him how much he must suffer for me."

17So Ananias went over and found Paul and laid his hands on him and said, "Brother Paul, the Lord Jesus, who appeared to you on the road, has sent me so that you may be filled with the Holy Spirit and get your sight back."

18Instantly (it was as though scales fell from his eyes) Paul could see, and was immediately baptized.

19Then he ate and was strengthened.

Paul preaches boldly

He stayed with the believers in Damascus for a few days 20and went at once to the synagogue to tell everyone there the Good News about Jesus—that he is indeed the Son of God!

21All who heard him were amazed. "Isn't this the same man who persecuted Jesus' followers so bitterly in Jerusalem?" they asked. "And we understand that he came here to arrest them all and take them in chains to the chief priests."

22Paul became more and more fervent in his preaching, and the Damascus Jews couldn't withstand his proofs that Jesus was indeed the Christ.

23After a while the Jewish leaders determined to kill him. 24But Paul was told about their plans, that they were watching the gates of the city day and night prepared to murder him. 25So during the night some of his converts let him down in a basket through an opening in the city wall!

26Upon arrival in Jerusalem he tried to meet with the believers, but they were all afraid of him. They thought he was faking! 27Then Barnabas brought him to the apostles and told them how Paul had seen the Lord on the way to Damascus, what the Lord had said to him, and all about his powerful preaching in the name of Jesus. 28Then they accepted him, and after that he was constantly with the believers 29and preached boldly in the name of the Lord. But then some Greek-speaking Jews with whom he had argued plotted to murder him. 30However, when the other believers

Cross-references (margin):

9:13 Acts 26:10

9:14 1 Cor 1:2

9:15 Acts 13:2; 22:21; 26:1-18; Rom 1:1,5; 11:13; Gal 1:15,16; Eph 3:7; 1 Tim 2:7; 2 Tim 1:11

9:16 Acts 20:23; 21:11; 2 Cor 11:23-27

9:17 Acts 2:4; 13:52; 22:12,13

9:19 Acts 26:20

9:21 Acts 8:3; Gal 1:13

9:22 Acts 18:28

9:23 Gal 1:17,18

9:24 Acts 20:3; 23:12; 25:3; 2 Cor 11:32

9:25 Josh 2:15; 1 Sam 19:12

9:26 Acts 22:17,18

9:27 Acts 4:36; 11:24; 13:2

9:13 "Not him, Lord, that's impossible. He could never become a Christian!" This was the essence of Ananias' response when God told him of Paul's conversion. After all, Paul had pursued believers to their death. Despite these understandable feelings, Ananias obeyed God and ministered to Paul. We must not limit God. He can do anything. We must obey, following God's leading even to difficult people and places.

9:15, 16 Christianity involves not only great blessings but often great suffering too. Paul would suffer for his faith (see 2 Corinthians 11:23-27). God calls us to commitment, not to comfort. He promises to be with us through suffering and hardship, not to spare us from them.

9:17 Ananias found Paul, as he had been instructed, and greeted him as "Brother Paul." Ananias feared this meeting; after all, Paul had come to Damascus to persecute the believers and take them in chains to Jerusalem (9:2). Yet in obedience to the Holy Spirit he greeted Paul lovingly. It is not always easy to show love to others, especially if we are afraid of them or doubt their motives. Nevertheless, we must follow Jesus' command (John 13:34) and Ananias' example, showing loving acceptance to other believers.

9:20 Immediately after receiving his sight, Paul went to the synagogue to tell the Jews about Jesus Christ. Some Christians counsel new believers to wait until they are thoroughly grounded in their faith before attempting to share the gospel. Paul took time alone to learn about Jesus before beginning his worldwide ministry, but he did not wait to witness. Although we should not rush into a ministry unprepared, we do not need to wait before telling others what has happened to us.

9:23 According to Galatians 1:17, 18, Paul left Damascus and traveled to Arabia, the desert region just southeast of Damascus, where he lived for three years. It is unclear whether his three-year stay occurred between verses 22 and 23, or between verses 25 and 26. Some commentators say that "a while" could mean a long period of time. They suggest that when Paul returned to Damascus, the governor under Aretas ordered his arrest (2 Corinthians 11:32), probably trying to keep peace with influential Jews.

The other possibility is that Paul's night escape occurred during his first stay in Damascus, just after his conversion when the Pharisees were especially upset over his defection from their ranks. He would have fled to Arabia to let the Jewish religious leaders cool down as well as to spend time alone with God. Regardless of which theory is correct, there was a period of at least three years between Paul's conversion (9:3–6) and his trip to Jerusalem (9:26).

PAUL

No person, apart from Jesus himself, shaped the history of Christianity like the apostle Paul. Even before he was a believer, his actions were significant. His frenzied persecution of Christians following Stephen's death got the church started in obeying Christ's final command to take the gospel worldwide. Paul's personal encounter with Jesus changed his life. He never lost his fierce intensity, but from then on it was channeled for the gospel.

Paul was very religious. His training under Gamaliel was the finest available. His intentions and efforts were sincere. He was a good Pharisee, knew the Bible, and sincerely believed that this Christian movement was dangerous to Judaism. Thus Paul hated the Christian faith and persecuted Christians without mercy.

Paul got permission to travel to Damascus to capture Christians and bring them back to Jerusalem. But God stopped him in his hurried tracks on the Damascus road. Paul personally met Jesus Christ, and his life was never the same.

Until Paul's conversion, little had been done about carrying the gospel to non-Jews. Philip had preached in Samaria and to an Ethiopian man; Cornelius, a Gentile, was converted under Peter; and in Antioch in Syria, some Greeks had joined the believers. When Barnabas was sent from Jerusalem to check on this situation, he went to Tarsus to find Paul and bring him to Antioch, and together they worked among the believers there. They were then sent on a missionary journey, the first of three Paul would take, that would carry the gospel across the Roman Empire.

The thorny issue of whether Gentile believers had to obey Jewish laws before they could become Christians caused many problems in the early church. Paul worked hard to convince the Jews that Gentiles were acceptable to God, but he spent even more time convincing the Gentiles that they were acceptable to God. The lives Paul touched were changed and challenged by meeting Christ through him.

God did not waste any part of Paul—his background, his training, his citizenship, his mind, or even his weaknesses. Are you willing to let God do the same for you? You will never know all he can do with you until you allow him to have all that you are!

Strengths and accomplishments:
- Transformed by God from a persecutor of Christians to a preacher for Christ
- Preached for Christ throughout the Roman Empire on three missionary journeys
- Wrote letters to various churches, which became part of the New Testament
- Was never afraid to face an issue head-on and deal with it
- Was sensitive to God's leading and, despite his strong personality, always did as God directed
- Is often called the apostle to the Gentiles

Weaknesses and mistakes:
- Witnessed and approved of Stephen's stoning
- Set out to destroy Christianity by persecuting Christians

Lessons from his life:
- The Good News is that forgiveness and eternal life are a gift of God's grace received by faith in Christ and available to all people
- Obedience results from a relationship with God, but obedience will never create or earn that relationship
- Real freedom doesn't come until we no longer have to prove our freedom
- God does not waste our time—he will use our past and present so we may serve him with our future

Vital statistics:
- Where: Born in Tarsus, but became a world traveler for Christ
- Occupations: Trained as a Pharisee, learned the tentmaking trade, served as a missionary
- Contemporaries: Gamaliel, Stephen, the apostles, Luke, Barnabas, Timothy

Key verses:
"For to me, living means opportunities for Christ, and dying—well, that's better yet! But if living will give me more opportunities to win people to Christ, then I really don't know which is better, to live or die" (Philippians 1:21, 22).

Paul's story is told in Acts 7:58—28:31 and throughout his New Testament letters.

9:27 It is difficult to change your reputation, and Paul had a terrible reputation with the Christians. But Barnabas, one of the Jewish converts mentioned in 4:36, became the bridge between Paul and the apostles. New Christians especially need sponsors, people who will come alongside, encourage, teach, and introduce them to other believers. Find ways that you can become a Barnabas to new believers.

9:27 Galatians 1:18, 19 tells us that Paul was in Jerusalem only 15 days and that he met only with Peter and James.

heard about his danger, they took him to Caesarea and then sent him to his home in Tarsus.

31Meanwhile, the church had peace throughout Judea, Galilee and Samaria, and grew in strength and numbers. The believers learned how to walk in the fear of the Lord and in the comfort of the Holy Spirit.

9:31
Acts 5:11; 8:1

➤ Peter heals Aeneas and Dorcas

32Peter traveled from place to place to visit them, and in his travels came to the believers in the town of Lydda. 33There he met a man named Aeneas, paralyzed and bedridden for eight years.

9:32
Acts 8:14

34Peter said to him, "Aeneas! Jesus Christ has healed you! Get up and make your bed." And he was healed instantly. 35Then the whole population of Lydda and Sharon turned to the Lord when they saw Aeneas walking around.

9:34
Mt 9:6
Jn 5:8
Acts 3:6; 4:10

36In the city of Joppa there was a woman named Dorcas ("Gazelle"), a believer who was always doing kind things for others, especially for the poor. 37About this time she became ill and died. Her friends prepared her for burial and laid her in an upstairs room. 38But when they learned that Peter was nearby at Lydda, they sent two men to beg him to return with them to Joppa. 39This he did; as soon as he arrived, they took him upstairs where Dorcas lay. The room was filled with weeping widows who were showing one another the coats and other garments Dorcas had made for them. 40But Peter asked them all to leave the room; then he knelt and prayed. Turning to the body he said, "Get up, Dorcas," and she opened her eyes! And when she saw Peter, she sat up! 41He gave her his hand and helped her up and called in the believers and widows, presenting her to them.

9:35
Acts 11:21

9:36
Prov 31:31
1 Tim 2:9,10
5:10
Tit 3:8
Jas 1:27

9:40
1 Kgs 17:19-23
2 Kgs 4:32-36
Mt 9:25
Mk 5:41,42
Jn 11:43

9:32 *to visit them,* implied.   **9:40** *Dorcas,* literally, "Tabitha," her name in Hebrew.

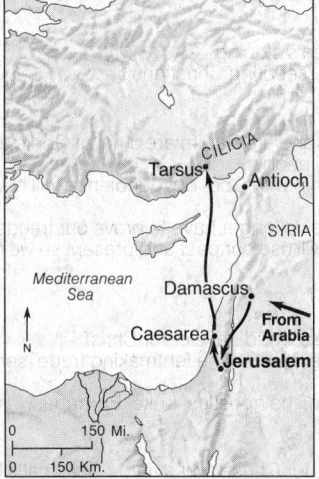

PAUL'S RETURN TO TARSUS
At least three years elapsed between Acts 9:22 and 9:26. After time alone in Arabia (see Galatians 1:16–18), Paul returned to Damascus and then to Jerusalem. The apostles were reluctant to believe that this former persecutor could be one of them. He escaped this time to Caesarea where he caught a ship and returned to Tarsus, his hometown.

9:36–42 Dorcas made an enormous impact on her community by "always doing kind things for others, especially for the poor." When she died, the room was filled with mourners, people she had helped. And when she was brought back to life, the news raced through the town. God uses great preachers like Peter and Paul, but he also uses those who have gifts of kindness like Dorcas. Rather than wishing you had other gifts, make good use of the gifts God has given you.

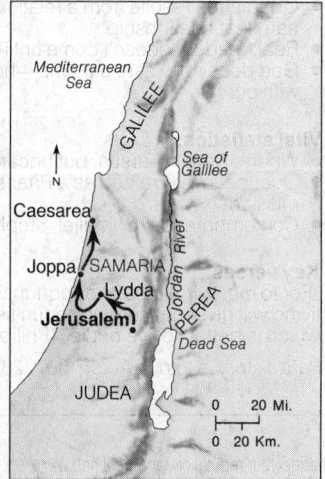

PETER'S MINISTRY
Peter traveled to the ancient crossroads town of Lydda, where he healed crippled Aeneas. The believers in Joppa, an old port city, sent for him after a wonderful woman died, and Peter brought her back to life. While in Joppa, Peter had a vision that led him to open the gospel to Cornelius, a Gentile, in Caesarea.

9:31 Paul's visit to Tarsus helped quiet conflicts with the Jews and allowed Paul time to prove his commitment. After Paul, the most zealous persecutor, was converted, the church enjoyed a brief time of relative peace.

9:36 The important harbor city of Joppa sits 125 feet above sea level overlooking the Mediterranean Sea. Joppa was the town into which the cedars of Lebanon were floated to be shipped to Jerusalem and used in the Temple construction (2 Chronicles 2:16; Ezra 3:7). The prophet Jonah left the port of Joppa on his ill-fated trip (Jonah 1:3).

9:42
Jn 11:45; 12:11

42The news raced through the town, and many believed in the Lord. 43And Peter stayed a long time in Joppa, living with Simon, the tanner.

Peter and Cornelius

10:1
Acts 8:40; 27:1
10:2
Gen 18:19
Josh 24:15
10:3
Ps 34:7
Acts 11:13
Heb 1:14
10:4
2 Chron 7:15
Ps 65:1,2
141:2
Prov 15:29
Heb 6:10; 13:16
Jas 5:16
1 Pet 3:2
Rev 5:8; 8:4
10:6
Acts 9:43; 11:14
10:9
Ps 55:17
Acts 11:5
10:11
Ezek 1:1-3
Mt 3:16
Acts 7:56
Rev 19:11
10:14
Lev 11:4-7
20:25
Deut 14:3-5
Ezek 4:14
10:15
Mt 15:11
Rom 14:14,17, 20
1 Cor 10:25
1 Tim 4:4
Tit 1:15
10:19
Acts 8:29; 11:12
10:20
Mt 28:19
Mk 16:15
Acts 15:7

10 In Caesarea there lived a Roman army officer, Cornelius, a captain of an Italian regiment. 2He was a godly man, deeply reverent, as was his entire household. He gave generously to charity and was a man of prayer. 3While wide awake one afternoon he had a vision—it was about three o'clock—and in this vision he saw an angel of God coming toward him.

"Cornelius!" the angel said.

4Cornelius stared at him in terror. "What do you want, sir?" he asked the angel.

And the angel replied, "Your prayers and charities have not gone unnoticed by God! 5, 6Now send some men to Joppa to find a man named Simon Peter, who is staying with Simon, the tanner, down by the shore, and ask him to come and visit you."

7As soon as the angel was gone, Cornelius called two of his household servants and a godly soldier, one of his personal bodyguard, 8and told them what had happened and sent them off to Joppa.

9, 10The next day, as they were nearing the city, Peter went up on the flat roof of his house to pray. It was noon and he was hungry, but while lunch was being prepared, he fell into a trance. 11He saw the sky open, and a great canvas sheet, suspended by its four corners, settle to the ground. 12In the sheet were all sorts of animals, snakes and birds [forbidden to the Jews for food].

13Then a voice said to him, "Go kill and eat any of them you wish."

14"Never, Lord," Peter declared, "I have never in all my life eaten such creatures, for they are forbidden by our Jewish laws."

15The voice spoke again, "Don't contradict God! If he says something is kosher, then it is."

16The same vision was repeated three times. Then the sheet was pulled up again to heaven.

17Peter was very perplexed. What could the vision mean? What was he supposed to do?

Just then the men sent by Cornelius had found the house and were standing outside at the gate, 18inquiring whether this was the place where Simon Peter lived!

19Meanwhile, as Peter was puzzling over the vision, the Holy Spirit said to him, "Three men have come to see you. 20Go down and meet them and go with them. All is well, I have sent them."

10:11 *a great canvas sheet,* implied.

9:43 In Joppa, Peter stayed at the home of Simon, a tanner. Tanners made animal hides into leather. It is significant that Peter was at Simon's house, because tanning involved contact with dead animals, and Jewish law considered it an unclean job. Peter was already beginning to break down his prejudice against people and customs that did not adhere to Jewish religious tradition.

10:1 This Caesarea, sometimes called Palestinian Caesarea, was located on the coast of the Mediterranean Sea, 32 miles north of Joppa. The largest and most important port city on the Mediterranean in Palestine, it served as the capital of the Roman province of Judea. This was the first city to have Gentile Christians and a non-Jewish church.

10:1 This Roman officer was a *centurion,* a commander of 100 soldiers. Although stationed in Caesarea, Cornelius would probably soon return to Rome. Thus his conversion was a major stepping stone for spreading the gospel to the capital city.

10:2 "What about the heathen who have never heard about

Christ?" This is a common question asked about God's justice. Cornelius wasn't a Christian, but he was seeking God, and he was a reverent and generous man. Therefore God sent Peter to tell Cornelius about Jesus. Cornelius is an example that God "rewards those who sincerely look for him" (Hebrews 11:6). Those who sincerely seek God will find him! God made Cornelius' knowledge complete.

10:12 According to Jewish law, certain foods were forbidden (see Leviticus 11). The food laws made it hard for Jews to eat with Gentiles without risking defilement. In fact, the Gentiles themselves were often seen as "unclean." Peter's vision meant that he was not to look upon the Gentiles as inferior people whom God would not redeem. Before having the vision, Peter would have thought a Gentile Roman officer could not accept Christ. Afterward, he understood that he should go with the messengers into a Gentile home and tell Cornelius the Good News of salvation in Jesus Christ.

21So Peter went down. "I'm the man you're looking for," he said. "Now what is it you want?"

22Then they told him about Cornelius the Roman officer, a good and godly man, well thought of by the Jews, and how an angel had instructed him to send for Peter to come and tell him what God wanted him to do.

23So Peter invited them in and lodged them overnight.

The next day he went with them, accompanied by some other believers from Joppa.

24They arrived in Caesarea the following day, and Cornelius was waiting for him, and had called together his relatives and close friends to meet Peter. 25As Peter entered his home, Cornelius fell to the floor before him in worship.

26But Peter said, "Stand up! I'm not a god!"

27So he got up and they talked together for a while and then went in where the others were assembled.

28Peter told them, "You know it is against the Jewish laws for me to come into a Gentile home like this. But God has shown me in a vision that I should never think of anyone as inferior. 29So I came as soon as I was sent for. Now tell me what you want."

30Cornelius replied, "Four days ago I was praying as usual at this time of the afternoon, when suddenly a man was standing before me clothed in a radiant robe! 31He told me, 'Cornelius, your prayers are heard and your charities have been noticed by God! 32Now send some men to Joppa and summon Simon Peter, who is staying in the home of Simon, a tanner, down by the shore.' 33So I sent for you at once, and you have done well to come so soon. Now here we are, waiting before the Lord, anxious to hear what he has told you to tell us!"

Peter preaches in Cornelius' house

34Then Peter replied, "I see very clearly that the Jews are not God's only favorites! 35In every nation he has those who worship him and do good deeds and are acceptable to him. 36, 37I'm sure you have heard about the Good News for the people of Israel—that there is peace with God through Jesus, the Messiah, who is Lord of all creation. This message has spread all through Judea, beginning with John the Baptist in Galilee. 38And you no doubt know that Jesus of Nazareth was anointed by God with the Holy Spirit and with power, and he went around doing good and healing all who were possessed by demons, for God was with him.

39"And we apostles are witnesses of all he did throughout Israel and in Jerusalem, where he was murdered on a cross. 40, 41But God brought him back to life again three days later and showed him to certain witnesses God had selected beforehand—not to the general public, but to us who ate and drank with him after he rose from the dead. 42And he sent us to preach the Good News everywhere and to testify that Jesus is ordained of God to be the Judge of all—living and dead. 43And all the prophets have written about him, saying that everyone who believes in him will have their sins forgiven through his name."

44Even as Peter was saying these things, the Holy Spirit fell upon all those listening! 45The Jews who came with Peter were amazed that the gift of the Holy

10:22
Acts 10:2

10:23
Acts 10:45; 11:12

10:24
Acts 8:40; 10:1

10:26
Lk 4:8
Acts 14:14
Col 2:18
Rev 19:10; 22:9

10:28
Jn 4:9
Acts 11:3; 15:9
Gal 2:12

10:30
Acts 10:3-6

10:31
Prov 14:31
Dan 10:12
Mt 6:4; 10:42
Heb 6:10

10:34
Rom 2:11
Col 3:11,25

10:35
Rom 3:9-24
Eph 2:13; 3:6

10:36
Rom 5:1
Eph 2:17

10:38
Lk 4:18,19

10:39
Lk 24:40

10:40,41
Jn 21:13

10:42
Mt 28:19
2 Cor 5:10

10:43
Isa 53:11
Jer 31:34

10:44
Acts 11:15; 15:8

10:34, 35 Perhaps the greatest barrier to the spread of the gospel in the first century was the Jewish-Gentile conflict. Most of the early believers were Jewish, and to them it was scandalous even to think of associating with Gentiles. But God told Peter to take the gospel to a Roman, and Peter obeyed despite his background and personal feelings. (Later he struggled with this again—see Galatians 2:12.) But God was making it clear that the Good News of Christ is for everyone! We should not allow any barrier—language, culture, prejudice, geography, economic class, or education—to keep us from spreading the gospel.

10:35 In every nation there are hearts bent toward God, ready to receive the gospel—but someone must take it to them. Seeking God is not enough—people must find him. How then shall seekers find God without someone to point the way? Is God asking you to show someone the way to him? (See Romans 10:14, 15.)

10:43 Two examples of prophets writing about Jesus and his forgiveness of sin are Isaiah 52:13—53:1 and Ezekiel 36:25, 26.

10:45 Cornelius and Peter were two very different people. Cornelius was wealthy, a Gentile, a military man. Peter was a Jewish fisherman turned preacher. But God's plan included both of them. In Cornelius' house that day, a new chapter in Christian history was written as a Jewish Christian leader and a Gentile Christian convert each discovered something significant about God at work in the other person. Cornelius needed Peter and his gospel to know he could be saved. Peter needed Cornelius and his salvation experience to know Gentiles were included in God's

10:46
Acts 2:4,19:6
10:47
Acts 8:36; 11:17
10:48
Acts 2:38
8:16; 19:5

Spirit would be given to Gentiles too! 46, 47But there could be no doubt about it, for they heard them speaking in tongues and praising God.

Peter asked, "Can anyone object to my baptizing them, now that they have received the Holy Spirit just as we did?" 48So he did, baptizing them in the name of Jesus, the Messiah. Afterwards Cornelius begged him to stay with them for several days.

10:46, 47 *But there could be no doubt about it,* implied.

The early days of Christianity were exciting as God's Spirit moved and people's lives were changed. Converts were pouring in from surprising backgrounds. Even the dreaded Saul (Paul) became a Christian, and non-Jews were responding to the Good News about Jesus. Among the first of these was the Roman centurion, Cornelius.

Because of frequent outbreaks of violence, Roman soldiers had to be stationed to keep peace throughout Israel. But most Romans, hated as conquerors, did not get along well in the nation. As an army officer, Cornelius was in a difficult position. He represented Rome, but his home was in Caesarea. During his years in Israel, he had himself been conquered by the God of Israel. He had a reputation as a godly man who put his faith into action, and he was respected by the Jews.

Four significant aspects of Cornelius' character are noted in Acts. He actively sought after God, he revered God, he was generous in meeting other people's needs, and he prayed. God told him to send for Peter, because Peter would give him more knowledge about the God he was already seeking to please.

When Peter entered Cornelius' home, he broke a whole list of Jewish rules. Peter confessed he wasn't comfortable, but here was an eager audience and he couldn't hold back his message. He had no sooner started sharing the gospel when God gave overwhelming approval by filling that Roman family with his Holy Spirit. Peter saw he had no choice but to baptize them and welcome them as equals in the growing Christian church. Another step had been taken in carrying the gospel to the whole world.

Cornelius is a welcome example of God's willingness to use extraordinary means to reach those who desire to know him. He does not play favorites, and he does not hide from those who want to find him. God sent his Son because he loves the whole world—and that includes Peter, Cornelius, and you.

Strengths and accomplishments:
- A godly and generous Roman
- Although an officer in the occupying army, he seems to have been well-respected by the Jews
- He responded to God and encouraged his family to do the same
- His conversion helped the young church realize that the Good News was for all people, both Jews and Gentiles

Lessons from his life:
- God reaches those who want to know him
- The gospel is open to all people
- There are those eager to believe everywhere
- When we are willing to seek the truth and be obedient to the light God gives us, God will reward us richly

Vital statistics:
- Where: Caesarea
- Occupation: Roman centurion
- Contemporaries: Peter, Philip, the apostles

Key verse:
"He was a godly man, deeply reverent, as was his entire household. He gave generously to charity and was a man of prayer" (Acts 10:2).

Cornelius' story is told in Acts 10:1—11:18.

---

plan. You and another believer may also need each other to understand how God works!

10:48 Cornelius wanted Peter to stay with him for several days. He was a new believer and realized his need for teaching and fellowship. Are you as eager to learn more about Jesus? Recognize your need to be with more mature Christians, and strive to learn from them.

Peter defends his preaching to Gentiles

11 Soon the news reached the apostles and other brothers in Judea that Gentiles also were being converted! 2But when Peter arrived back in Jerusalem, the Jewish believers argued with him.

3"You fellowshiped with Gentiles and even ate with them," they accused. 4Then Peter told them the whole story. 5"One day in Joppa," he said, "while I was praying, I saw a vision—a huge sheet, let down by its four corners from the sky. 6Inside the sheet were all sorts of animals, reptiles and birds [which we are not to eat]. 7And I heard a voice say, 'Kill and eat whatever you wish.'

8" 'Never, Lord,' I replied. 'For I have never yet eaten anything forbidden by our Jewish laws!'

9"But the voice came again, 'Don't say it isn't right when God declares it is!'

10"This happened *three times* before the sheet and all it contained disappeared into heaven. 11Just then three men who had come to take me with them to Caesarea arrived at the house where I was staying! 12The Holy Spirit told me to go with them and not to worry about their being Gentiles! These six brothers here accompanied me, and we soon arrived at the home of the man who had sent the messengers. 13He told us how an angel had appeared to him and told him to send messengers to Joppa to find Simon Peter! 14'He will tell you how you and all your household can be saved!' the angel had told him.

15"Well, I began telling them the Good News, but just as I was getting started with my sermon, the Holy Spirit fell on them, just as he fell on us at the beginning! 16Then I thought of the Lord's words when he said, 'Yes, John baptized with water, but you shall be baptized with the Holy Spirit.' 17And since it was *God* who gave these Gentiles the same gift he gave us when we believed on the Lord Jesus Christ, who was I to argue?"

18When the others heard this, all their objections were answered and they began praising God! "Yes," they said, "God has given to the Gentiles, too, the privilege of turning to him and receiving eternal life!"

The Gentile church in Antioch

19Meanwhile, the believers who fled from Jerusalem during the persecution after Stephen's death traveled as far as Phoenicia, Cyprus, and Antioch, scattering the Good News, but only to Jews. 20However, some of the believers who went to Antioch from Cyprus and Cyrene also gave their message about the Lord Jesus to some Greeks. 21And the Lord honored this effort so that large numbers of these Gentiles became believers.

11:6 *which we are not to eat*, implied.   **11:16** *baptized with*, or, "baptized in."

11:3
Mt 9:11
Acts 10:28
Gal 2:12

11:5
Acts 10:9,10

11:8
Ezek 4:14

11:12
Jn 16:13
Acts 10:23; 15:7

11:13
Acts 10:30

11:14
Acts 10:2; 16:15
18:8
1 Cor 1:16

11:15
Acts 2:4

11:16
Isa 44:3
Joel 2:28
Mt 3:11
Jn 1:26,33

11:17
Acts 10:47
15:8,9

11:18
Rom 10:12; 15:9

11:19
Acts 8:1; 13:1
14:25-27; 15:3

11:20
Acts 6:1

11:21
Lk 1:66

11:1 A Gentile was anyone who was not a Jew. Most Jewish believers thought God offered salvation only to the Jews because God had given his law to them (Exodus 19, 20). One group in Jerusalem believed that Gentiles could be saved, but only if they followed all the Jewish laws and traditions—in essence, if they became Jews. Both groups were mistaken. God chose the Jews and taught them his laws so they could bring the message of salvation to *all* people (see Genesis 12:3; Psalm 22:27; Isaiah 42:4; 49:6; 56:3; 60:1-3; Jeremiah 16:19-21; Zechariah 2:11; Malachi 1:11; Romans 15:9-12).

11:2-18 When Peter brought the news of Cornelius' conversion back to Jerusalem, the believers were shocked that he had eaten with Gentiles. After they heard the whole story, however, they began praising God (11:18). Their reactions teach us how to handle disagreements with other believers. Before judging the behavior of fellow believers, it is important to hear them out. The Holy Spirit may have something important to teach us through them.

11:8 God had promised throughout Scripture that he would reach the Gentiles. This began with his general promise to Abraham (Genesis 12:3; 18:18) and became very specific in Malachi's

statement that God's name "will be honored by the Gentiles from morning till night" (Malachi 1:11). But this was an extremely difficult truth for Jews, even Jewish believers, to accept. The Jewish believers understood how certain prophecies were fulfilled in Christ, but they overlooked other Old Testament teachings. Too often we are inclined to accept only the parts of God's Word that appeal to us, ignoring the teachings we don't like. We must accept all of God's Word as absolute truth.

11:12ff Peter's defense for eating with Gentiles was a simple restatement of what happened. He brought six witnesses with him to back him up, and then he quoted Jesus' promise about the coming of the Holy Spirit (11:16). These Gentiles' lives had been changed, and that was all the evidence Peter and the other believers needed. Changed lives are an equally powerful evidence today.

11:18 The intellectual questions ended and the theological discussion stopped with the report that God had given the Holy Spirit to the Gentiles. This was a turning point for the early church. They had to accept those whom God had chosen, even if they were Gentiles. But joy over the conversion of Gentiles was not unanimous. Throughout the first century this continued to be a struggle for some Jewish Christians.

11:22
Acts 9:27
13:43; 14:22,23

11:23
Deut 10:20
1 Cor 15:58
Col 2:6

11:24
Acts 2:4,47
5:14

11:25
Acts 9:30

11:27
Acts 2:17; 13:1
1 Cor 16:1
2 Cor 9:1

11:28
Acts 21:10

11:29
Rom 15:25,26

11:30
1 Pet 5:1

22When the church at Jerusalem heard what had happened, they sent Barnabas to Antioch to help the new converts. 23When he arrived and saw the wonderful things God was doing, he was filled with excitement and joy, and encouraged the believers to stay close to the Lord, whatever the cost. 24Barnabas was a kindly person, full of the Holy Spirit and strong in faith. As a result large numbers of people were added to the Lord.

25Then Barnabas went on to Tarsus to hunt for Paul. 26When he found him, he brought him back to Antioch; and both of them stayed there for a full year, teaching the many new converts. (It was there at Antioch that the believers were first called "Christians.")

27During this time some prophets came down from Jerusalem to Antioch, 28and one of them, named Agabus, stood up in one of the meetings to predict by the Spirit that a great famine was coming upon the land of Israel. (This was fulfilled during the reign of Claudius.) 29So the believers decided to send relief to the Christians in Judea, each giving as much as he could. 30This they did, consigning their gifts to Barnabas and Paul to take to the elders of the church in Jerusalem.

11:28 *the land of Israel,* literally, "upon the earth."

BARNABAS AND PAUL IN ANTIOCH

Persecution spread the believers into Phoenicia, Cyprus, and Antioch, and the gospel went with them. Most spoke only to Jews, but in Antioch, some Gentile Greeks were converted. The church sent Barnabas to investigate, and he was pleased with what he found. Barnabas went to Tarsus to bring Paul back to Antioch.

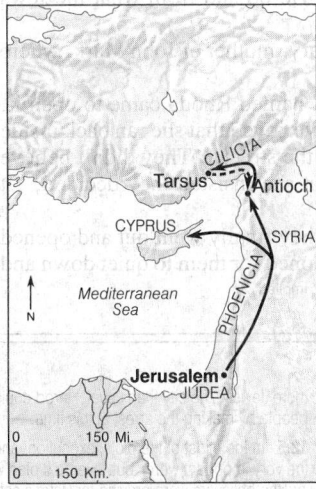

commercial center—the gateway to the eastern world. Antioch was a key city both to Rome and to the early church.

11:22-26 Barnabas gives us a wonderful example of how to help new Christians. He demonstrated strong faith; he ministered joyfully with kindness and encouragement; and he taught them further lessons about God. Remember Barnabas when you see new believers, and think of ways to help them grow in their faith.

11:25 Paul had been sent to his home in Tarsus to protect him from danger (9:30). He stayed there for several years before Barnabas brought him to help the church at Antioch.

11:26 The young church at Antioch was a curious mixture of Jews (who spoke Greek or Aramaic) and Gentiles. It is significant that this is the first place where the believers were called Christians, because all they had in common was Christ—not race, culture, or even language. Christ can cross all boundaries and unify all people.

11:26 Barnabas and Paul stayed at Antioch for a full year, teaching the new believers. They could have left for new cities, but they saw the importance of follow-through and training. Have you helped someone believe in God? Spend time teaching and encouraging that person. Are you a new believer? Remember, you are just beginning your Christian life. Your faith needs to grow and mature through consistent Bible study and learning.

11:27 Prophets were found not only in the Old Testament, but also in the early church. Their role was to present God's will to the people and to instruct them in God's Word. Sometimes they, like Agabus, also had the gift of predicting the future.

11:28, 29 There were serious food shortages during the reign of the Roman emperor Claudius (A.D. 41–54) because of a drought that extended across much of the Roman empire for many years. It is significant that the church in Antioch assisted the church in Jerusalem. The daughter church had grown enough to be able to help the established church.

11:19-21 When the church accepted Peter's testimony that the gospel was also for Gentiles, Christianity exploded into Gentile areas and large numbers became believers. The seeds of this missionary work had been sown after Stephen's death when many believing Jews were persecuted and scattered, settling in faraway cities and spreading the gospel.

11:20, 21 It was in Antioch that Christianity was launched on its worldwide mission and where the believers aggressively preached to the Gentiles. Philip had preached in Samaria, but the Samaritans were already partly Jewish (8:5); Peter preached to Cornelius, but he already worshiped God (10:46, 47). Believers who scattered after the outbreak of persecution in Jerusalem spread the gospel to other Jews in the lands they fled to (11:19). But now the believers began actively sharing the Good News with Gentiles.

11:22 With the exception of Jerusalem, Antioch played a more important role in the early church than any other city. After Rome and Alexandria, Antioch was the largest city in the Roman world. In Antioch, the first Gentile church was founded, and the believers were first called Christians. Paul used the city as his home base during his missionary journeys. Antioch was the center of worship for several pagan cults, promoting much sexual immorality and other forms of evil common to pagan religions. It was also a vital

11:29 The people of Antioch were motivated to give generously because they cared about the needs of others. This is "cheerful giving," which the Bible commends (2 Corinthians 9:7). Reluctant giving reflects a lack of concern for people. Focus your concern on the needy, and you will be motivated to give.

11:30 Elders were appointed to manage the affairs of the congregation. At this point, not much is known about their responsibilities, but it appears that their main role was to respond to the believers' needs.

An angel rescues Peter from prison

12 About that time King Herod moved against some of the believers, ²and killed the apostle James (John's brother). ³When Herod saw how much this pleased the Jewish leaders, he arrested Peter during the Passover celebration ⁴and imprisoned him, placing him under the guard of sixteen soldiers. Herod's intention was to deliver Peter to the Jews for execution after the Passover. ⁵But earnest prayer was going up to God from the church for his safety all the time he was in prison.

⁶The night before he was to be executed, he was asleep, double-chained between two soldiers with others standing guard before the prison gate, ⁷when suddenly there was a light in the cell and an angel of the Lord stood beside Peter! The angel slapped him on the side to awaken him and said, "Quick! Get up!" And the chains fell off his wrists! ⁸Then the angel told him, "Get dressed and put on your shoes." And he did. "Now put on your coat and follow me!" the angel ordered.

⁹So Peter left the cell, following the angel. But all the time he thought it was a dream or vision, and didn't believe it was really happening. ¹⁰They passed the first and second cell blocks and came to the iron gate to the street, and this opened to them of its own accord! So they passed through and walked along together for a block, and then the angel left him.

¹¹Peter finally realized what had happened! "It's really true!" he said to himself. "The Lord has sent his angel and saved me from Herod and from what the Jews were hoping to do to me!"

¹²After a little thought he went to the home of Mary, mother of John Mark, where many were gathered for a prayer meeting.

¹³He knocked at the door in the gate, and a girl named Rhoda came to open it. ¹⁴When she recognized Peter's voice, she was so overjoyed that she ran back inside to tell everyone that Peter was standing outside in the street. ¹⁵They didn't believe her. "You're out of your mind," they said. When she insisted they decided, "It must be his angel. [They must have killed him.]"

¹⁶Meanwhile Peter continued knocking. When they finally went out and opened the door, their surprise knew no bounds. ¹⁷He motioned for them to quiet down and

12:2 *and killed the apostle,* implied.   **12:15** *They must have killed him,* implied.

12:1 Mt 10:17

12:2 Mt 4:21; 20:20-23; Mk 10:39

12:3 Ex 12:14,15

12:4 Jn 21:18

12:5 2 Cor 1:11; Eph 6:18

12:7 Acts 5:19; 21:33; Heb 1:14

12:9 Ps 126:1; Acts 10:3

12:10 Acts 5:19; 16:26

12:11 Job 5:19; Ps 33:18,19; 34:7; 97:10; Dan 3:28; 6:22; 2 Pet 2:9

12:12 Acts 12:25; 13:5 15:37; Col 4:10; 1 Pet 5:13

12:15 Mt 18:10

12:17 Acts 15:35; 21:18

12:1 This King Herod was Herod Agrippa I, the son of Aristobulus and grandson of Herod the Great. His sister was Herodias, who was responsible for the death of John the Baptist (see Mark 6:17–28). He was partly Jewish. The Romans had appointed him to rule over most of Palestine, including the territories of Galilee, Perea, Judea, and Samaria. He moved against the Christians in order to please the Jewish leaders who opposed them, hoping that would solidify his position. Agrippa I died suddenly in A.D. 44 (see 12:20–23). His death is also recorded by the historian Josephus.

12:2 James and John were two of the original 12 disciples who followed Jesus. James and John had asked Jesus for special recognition in his kingdom (Mark 10:35–37). Jesus said that recognition in his kingdom often means suffering for him (drink from the same cup—Mark 10:38, 39). James and John did indeed suffer—Herod executed James, and John was later exiled (see Revelation 1:9).

12:2–12 Why did God allow James to die and yet miraculously save Peter? Life is full of difficult questions like this. Why is one child physically handicapped and another child athletically gifted? Why do people die before realizing their potential? These are questions we cannot possibly answer in this life because we do not see all that God sees. He has chosen to allow evil in this world for a time, but we can trust his leading because he has promised to destroy all evil one day. In the meantime, we know he will help us use our suffering in a way that strengthens us and glorifies him. For more on this question, see the notes on Job 1:1ff; 2:10; 3:23–26.

12:3 Peter was arrested during the Passover because there were more Jews in the city than usual. Herod could impress the most people by making the arrest at this time.

12:5 In the midst of the plots, execution, and arrest, Luke injects the very important word "but." Herod's plan was to execute Peter, *but* the believers were praying for Peter's safety. The earnest prayer of the church significantly affected the outcome of these events. We know from the testimony of the Bible that prayer changes attitudes and events. So pray often and pray with confidence.

12:7 God sent an angel to rescue Peter. Angels are God's messengers. They are divinely created beings with supernatural powers, and they sometimes take on human appearance in order to talk to people. Angels should not be worshiped because they, too, serve God.

12:12 John Mark wrote the Gospel of Mark. His mother's house was large enough to accommodate a meeting of many believers. An upstairs room in this house may have been the location of Jesus' last supper with his disciples.

12:13–15 The prayers of the little group of believers were answered, even as they prayed. But when the answer arrived at the door, they didn't believe it. We should be people of faith who believe that God answers the prayers of those who seek his will. When you pray, believe you'll get an answer—and when the answer comes, don't be surprised!

12:17 This James was Jesus' brother, who became a leader in the Jerusalem church (Galatians 1:19). The James who was killed (12:2) was John's brother and one of the original 12 disciples.

told them what had happened and how the Lord had brought him out of jail. "Tell James and the others what happened," he said—and left for safer quarters.

18At dawn, the jail was in great commotion. What had happened to Peter?

12:19
Acts 8:40; 16:27

19When Herod sent for him and found that he wasn't there, he had the sixteen guards arrested, court-martialed and sentenced to death. Afterwards he left to live in Caesarea for a while.

The judgment of Herod

20While he was in Caesarea, a delegation from Tyre and Sidon arrived to see him. He was highly displeased with the people of those two cities, but the delegates

---

HEROD AGRIPPA I

For good or evil, families have lasting and powerful influence on their children. Traits and qualities are passed on to the next generation, and often the mistakes and sins of the parents are repeated by the children. Four generations of the Herod family are mentioned in the Bible. Each leader left his evil mark: Herod the Great murdered Bethlehem's children; Herod Antipas was involved in Jesus' trial and had John the Baptist executed; Herod Agrippa I murdered the apostle James; and Herod Agrippa II was one of Paul's judges.

Herod Agrippa I related fairly well to his Jewish subjects. Because he had a Jewish grandmother of royal blood (Mariamne), he was grudgingly accepted by the people. Although as a youth he had been temporarily imprisoned by the emperor Tiberias, he was now trusted by Rome and got along well with the emperors Caligula and Claudius.

An unexpected opportunity for Herod to gain new favor with the Jews was created by the Christian movement. Gentiles began to be accepted into the church in large numbers. Many Jews had been tolerating this new movement as a sect within Judaism, but its rapid growth alarmed them. Persecution of Christians was revived, and even the apostles were not spared. James was killed, and Peter was thrown into prison.

But soon, Herod made a fatal error. During a visit to Caesarea, the people called him a god and he accepted their praise. Herod was immediately struck with a painful disease, and he died within a week.

Like his grandfather, uncle, and son after him, Herod Agrippa I came close to the truth but missed it. Because religion was important only as an aspect of politics, he had no reverence and no qualms about taking praise that only God should receive. His mistake is a common one. Whenever we are proud of our own abilities and accomplishments, not recognizing them as gifts from God, we repeat Herod's sin.

Strengths and accomplishments:
- Capable administrator and negotiator
- Managed to maintain good relations with the Jews in his region and with Rome

Weaknesses and mistakes:
- Arranged the murder of the apostle James
- Imprisoned Peter with plans to execute him
- Allowed the people to praise him as a god

Lessons from his life:
- Those who set themselves against God are doomed to ultimate failure
- There is great danger in accepting praise that only God deserves
- Family traits can influence children toward great good or great evil

Vital statistics:
- Where: Jerusalem
- Occupation: Roman-appointed King of the Jews
- Relatives: Grandfather: Herod the Great. Father: Aristobulus. Uncle: Herod Antipas. Sister: Herodias. Wife: Cypros. Son: Herod Agrippa II. Daughters: Bernice, Mariamne, Drusilla.
- Contemporaries: Emperors Tiberias, Caligula, and Claudius. James, Peter, the apostles.

Key verse:
"Instantly, an angel of the Lord struck Herod with a sickness so that he was filled with maggots and died—because he accepted the people's worship instead of giving the glory to God" (Acts 12:23).

Herod Agrippa I's story is told in Acts 12:1–23.

12:19 Under Roman law, if guards allowed their prisoner to escape, they were subject to the same punishment the prisoner was to receive. Thus these 16 guards were sentenced to death.

12:20 The Jews considered Jerusalem their capital, but the Romans made Caesarea their headquarters in Palestine. This is where Herod Agrippa lived.

made friends with Blastus, the royal secretary, and asked for peace, for their cities were economically dependent upon trade with Herod's country. 21An appointment with Herod was granted, and when the day arrived he put on his royal robes, sat on his throne and made a speech to them. 22At its conclusion the people gave him a great ovation, shouting, "It is the voice of a god and not of a man!"

23Instantly, an angel of the Lord struck Herod with a sickness so that he was filled with maggots and died—because he accepted the people's worship instead of giving the glory to God.

24God's Good News was spreading rapidly and there were many new believers.

25Barnabas and Paul now visited Jerusalem and, as soon as they had finished their business, returned to Antioch, taking John Mark with them.

12:23
Deut 28:58,59
1 Sam 25:37,38
2 Sam 24:16
2 Kgs 19:35
Isa 42:8; 48:11
Dan 4:30-37
Rev 15:3,4
12:24
Isa 55:11
Acts 6:7; 19:20
12:25
Acts 11:29,30
15:37

➤ B. PAUL'S MINISTRY (13:1—28:31)
The book focuses now on the ministry to the Gentiles and the spread of the church around the world, and Paul replaces Peter as the central figure in the book. Paul completes three missionary journeys and ends up being imprisoned in Jerusalem and transported to Rome. The book of Acts ends abruptly, showing that the history of the church is not yet complete. We are to be a part of the sequel.

1. First missionary journey
Barnabas and Paul are sent out to preach

13 Among the prophets and teachers of the church at Antioch were Barnabas and Symeon (also called "The Black Man"), Lucius (from Cyrene), Manaen (the foster-brother of King Herod), and Paul. 2One day as these men were worshiping and fasting the Holy Spirit said, "Dedicate Barnabas and Paul for a special job I have for them." 3So after more fasting and prayer, the men laid their hands on them—and sent them on their way.

13:1
Acts 11:22
Rom 16:21
13:2
Eph 3:7-9
13:3
Acts 6:6

Paul curses a sorcerer in Cyprus

4Directed by the Holy Spirit they went to Seleucia and then sailed for Cyprus.

12:25 *returned to Antioch,* implied.

12:23 Herod died a horrible death with intense pain; he was literally eaten alive, from the inside out, by maggots or worms. Pride is a serious sin, and in this case, God chose to punish it immediately. God does not immediately judge all sin, but he will judge it (Hebrews 9:27). Accept Christ's offer of forgiveness today. No one can afford to wait.

12:25 John Mark was Barnabas' nephew. His mother, Mary, often opened her home to the apostles, so John Mark would have been exposed to most of the great men and teachings of the early church. John Mark later joined Paul and Barnabas on their first missionary journey, but for unknown reasons, left them in the middle of the trip. John Mark was criticized for abandoning the mission, but he wrote the Gospel of Mark and was later acclaimed by Paul as a vital help in the growth of the early church.

➤ **13:1** What variety there is in the church! The common thread among these five men was their deep faith in Christ. We must never exclude anyone whom Christ has called to follow him.

13:2, 3 The church dedicated Barnabas and Paul to the work God had for them. *Dedicating* means setting apart for a special purpose. We too should dedicate our pastors, missionaries, and Christian workers for their tasks. We can also dedicate ourselves with our time, money, and talents for God's work. Ask God what he wants you to dedicate to him.

13:2, 3 This was the beginning of Paul's first missionary journey. The church was involved in sending Paul and Barnabas, but it was God's plan. Why did Paul and Barnabas go where they did? (1) The Holy Spirit led them. (2) They followed the communication routes of the Roman empire—this made travel easier. (3) They visited key population and cultural centers to reach as many

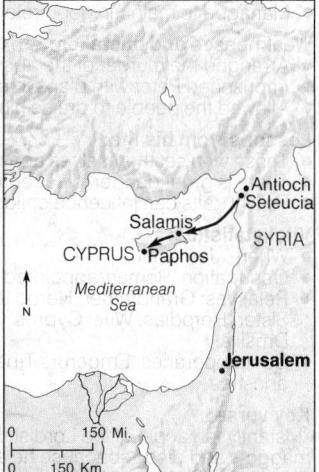

people as possible. (4) They went to cities with synagogues, speaking first to the Jews in hopes that they would see Jesus as the Messiah and help spread the Good News to everyone.

13:4 Located in the Mediterranean Sea, the island of Cyprus, with a large Jewish population, was Barnabas' home. Their first stop was into familiar territory.

MINISTRY IN CYPRUS
The leaders of the church in Antioch chose Paul and Barnabas to take the gospel westward. Along with John Mark, they boarded ship at Seleucia and set out across the Mediterranean for Cyprus. They preached in Salamis, the largest city, and went across the island to Paphos.

13:5
Acts 9:20; 12:25
1 Pet 5:13

13:6
Ex 7:11
Mt 7:15
Acts 8:9
2 Tim 3:8

⁵There, in the town of Salamis, they went to the Jewish synagogue and preached. (John Mark went with them as their assistant.)

⁶, ⁷Afterwards they preached from town to town across the entire island until finally they reached Paphos where they met a Jewish sorcerer, a fake prophet named Bar-Jesus. He had attached himself to the governor, Sergius Paulus, a man of considerable insight and understanding. The governor invited Barnabas and Paul

---

JOHN MARK

Mistakes are effective teachers. Their consequences have a way of making lessons painfully clear. But those who learn from their mistakes are likely to develop wisdom. John Mark was a good learner who just needed some time and encouragement.

Mark was eager to do the right thing, but he had trouble staying with a task. In his Gospel, Mark mentions a young man (probably referring to himself) who fled in such fear during Jesus' arrest that he left his clothes behind. This tendency to run was to reappear later when Paul and Barnabas took him as their assistant on their first missionary journey. At their second stop, Mark left them and returned to Jerusalem. It was a decision Paul did not easily accept. In preparing for their second journey two years later, Barnabas again suggested Mark as a traveling companion, but Paul flatly refused. As a result, the team was divided. Barnabas took Mark with him, and Paul chose Silas. Barnabas was patient with Mark, and the young man repaid his investment. Paul and Mark were later reunited, and the older apostle became a close friend of the young disciple.

Mark was a valuable companion to three early Christian leaders—Barnabas, Paul, and Peter. The material in Mark's Gospel seems to have come mostly from Peter. Mark's role as a serving assistant allowed him to be an observer. He heard Peter's accounts of the years with Jesus over and over, and he was one of the first to put Jesus' life in writing.

Barnabas played a key role in Mark's life. He stood beside the young man despite his failure, giving him patient encouragement. Mark challenges us to learn from our mistakes and appreciate the patience of others. Is there a Barnabas in your life you need to thank for his or her encouragement to you?

Strengths and accomplishments:
• Wrote the Gospel of Mark
• He and his mother provided their home as one of the main meeting places for the Christians in Jerusalem
• Persisted beyond his youthful mistakes
• Was an assistant and traveling companion to three of the greatest early missionaries

Weaknesses and mistakes:
• Probably the nameless young man described in the Gospel of Mark who fled in panic when Jesus was arrested
• Left Paul and Barnabas for unknown reasons during the first missionary journey

Lessons from his life:
• Personal maturity usually comes from a combination of time and mistakes
• Mistakes are not usually as important as what can be learned from them
• Effective living is not measured as much by what we accomplish as by what we overcome in order to accomplish it
• Encouragement can change a person's life

Vital statistics:
• Where: Jerusalem
• Occupation: Missionary-in-training, Gospel writer, traveling companion
• Relatives: Mother: Mary. Uncle: Barnabas.
• Contemporaries: Paul, Peter, Timothy, Luke, Silas

Key verse:
"Only Luke is with me. Bring Mark with you when you come, for I need him" (Paul writing in 2 Timothy 4:11).

John Mark's story is told in Acts 12:25—13:13 and 15:36-39. He is also mentioned in Colossians 4:10, 11; 2 Timothy 4:11; Philemon 1:24; 1 Peter 5:13.

13:6, 7 Governors often kept private wizards. Bar-Jesus realized   that if Sergius Paulus believed in Jesus, he'd soon be out of a job.

to visit him, for he wanted to hear their message from God. 8But the sorcerer, Elymas (his name in Greek), interfered and urged the governor to pay no attention to what Paul and Barnabas said, trying to keep him from trusting the Lord.

9Then Paul, filled with the Holy Spirit, glared angrily at the sorcerer and said, 10"You son of the devil, full of every sort of trickery and villainy, enemy of all that is good, will you never end your opposition to the Lord? 11And now God has laid his hand of punishment upon you, and you will be stricken awhile with blindness."

Instantly mist and darkness fell upon him, and he began wandering around begging for someone to take his hand and lead him. 12When the governor saw what happened he believed and was astonished at the power of God's message.

13:9
Acts 2:4; 4:8
13:10
Mt 13:38
Jn 8:44
2 Pet 2:15
1 Jn 3:8
13:11
2 Kgs 6:18

Paul preaches to the Jews in Antioch in Pisidia

13Now Paul and those with him left Paphos by ship for Turkey, landing at the port town of Perga. There John deserted them and returned to Jerusalem. 14But Barnabas and Paul went on to Antioch, a city in the province of Pisidia.

On the Sabbath they went into the synagogue for the services. 15After the usual readings from the Books of Moses and from the Prophets, those in charge of the service sent them this message: "Brothers, if you have any word of instruction for us come and give it!"

16So Paul stood, waved a greeting to them and began. "Men of Israel," he said,

13:13
Acts 14:24,25
15:38
13:14
Acts 14:19,21
24
13:15
Lk 14:16
Acts 15:21
2 Cor 3:14
13:16
Acts 10:2,13:26

13:13 *Turkey,* literally, "Pamphylia." *deserted them,* literally, "departed from them." See 15:38.   **13:16** *waved a greeting to them,* literally, "beckoning with the hand." *Let me begin my remarks with a bit of history,* implied.

13:13 No reason is given why John Mark left Paul and Barnabas. Some suggestions are: (1) he was homesick, (2) he resented the change in leadership from Barnabas (his uncle) to Paul, (3) he became ill (this may have affected all of them—see Galatians 4:13), (4) he was unable to withstand the rigors and dangers of the missionary journey, (5) he may have planned to go only that far but had not communicated this to Paul and Barnabas. Paul accused John Mark of lacking courage and commitment, calling him a deserter (see 15:38). It is clear from Paul's later letters, however, that Paul grew to respect Mark (Colossians 4:10) and needed him in his work (2 Timothy 4:11).

13:14 This is Antioch of Pisidia, different from Antioch of Syria where there was already a flourishing church (11:26). Antioch of Pisidia was a hub of good roads and trade and had a large Jewish population.

13:14 What happened in a synagogue service? First the *Shema* was recited (see Numbers 15:37–41; Deuteronomy 6:4–9; 11:13–21). Certain prayers were given; then there was a reading from the Law (the books of Genesis through Deuteronomy), a reading from the Prophets intending to illustrate the Law, and a sermon. The synagogue leader decided who was to lead the service and give the sermon. A different person was chosen to lead each week. Since it was customary for the synagogue leader to invite visiting rabbis to speak, Paul and Barnabas usually had an open door when they first went to a synagogue. But as soon as they spoke about Jesus as Messiah, the door slammed. They were usually not invited back by the religious leaders, and sometimes they were thrown out of town!

13:14 When they went to a new town to witness for Christ, Paul and Barnabas went first to the synagogue. The Jews who went to the synagogue believed in God and diligently studied the Scriptures. Tragically, however, many could not accept Jesus as the promised Messiah because they had the wrong idea of what kind of Messiah he would be. He was not a military king who would overthrow Rome's control, but a servant king who would overthrow

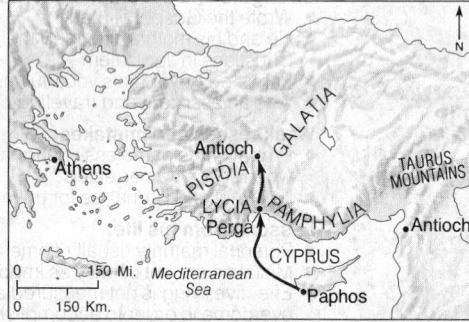

MINISTRY IN PAMPHYLIA AND GALATIA Paul, Barnabas, and John Mark left Paphos and landed at Perga in the humid region of Pamphylia, a narrow strip of land between the sea and the Taurus Mountains. John Mark deserted them in Perga, but Paul and Barnabas traveled up the steep road into the higher elevation of Pisidia in Galatia. When the Jews rejected his message, Paul preached to Gentiles, and the Jews drove Paul and Barnabas out of the Pisidian city of Antioch.

sin in people's hearts. (Only later, when he returns, will he overthrow the nations of the world.) Paul and Barnabas did not separate themselves from the synagogues but tried to show clearly that the Scriptures the Jews studied pointed to Jesus.

13:16ff Paul's message to the Jews in the synagogue in Antioch began with an emphasis on God's covenant with Israel. He began with a point of agreement, for all Jews were proud to be God's chosen people. Then Paul went on to explain how the gospel fulfilled this covenant, and some Jews found this message hard to take.

"and all others here who reverence God, [let me begin my remarks with a bit of history].

13:17
Deut 7:6-8
Acts 7:36
13:19,20
Deut 7:1
Judg 2:16
13:21
1 Sam 8:5; 10:1

17"The God of this nation Israel chose our ancestors and honored them in Egypt by gloriously leading them out of their slavery. 18And he nursed them through forty years of wandering around in the wilderness. 19, 20Then he destroyed seven nations in Canaan, and gave Israel their land as an inheritance. Judges ruled for about 450 years, and were followed by Samuel the prophet.

21"Then the people begged for a king, and God gave them Saul (son of Kish), a

BARNABAS

Every group needs an "encourager," because everyone needs encouragement at one time or another. However, the value of encouragement is often missed because it tends to be private rather than public. In fact, people most need encouragement when they feel most alone. A man named Joseph was such an encourager that he earned the nickname "son of encouragement," or Barnabas, from the Jerusalem Christians.

Barnabas was drawn to people he could encourage, and he was a great help to those around him. It is delightful that wherever Barnabas encouraged Christians, non-Christians flocked to become believers!

Barnabas' actions were crucial to the early church. In a way, we can thank him for most of the New Testament. God used his relationship with Paul at one point and with Mark at another to keep these two men going when either might have failed. Barnabas did wonders with encouragement!

When Paul arrived in Jerusalem for the first time following his conversion, the local Christians were understandably reluctant to welcome him. They thought his story was a trick to capture more Christians. Only Barnabas proved willing to risk his life to meet with Paul and then convince the others that their former enemy was now a vibrant believer in Jesus. We can only wonder what might have happened to Paul without Barnabas.

It was Barnabas who encouraged Mark to go with him and Paul to Antioch. Mark joined them on their first missionary journey, but decided during the trip to return home. Later, Barnabas wanted to invite Mark to join them for another journey, but Paul would not agree. As a result, the partners went separate ways, Barnabas with Mark and Paul with Silas. This actually doubled the missionary effort. Barnabas' patient encouragement was confirmed by Mark's eventual effective ministry. Paul and Mark were later reunited in missionary efforts.

As Barnabas' life shows, we are rarely in a situation where there isn't someone we can encourage. Our tendency, however, is to criticize instead. It may be important at times to point out someone's shortcomings, but before we have the right to do this, we must build that person's trust through encouragement. Are you prepared to encourage those with whom you come in contact today?

Strengths and accomplishments:
- One of the first to sell possessions to help the Christians in Jerusalem
- First to travel with Paul as a missionary team
- Was an encourager, as his nickname shows, and thus one of the most quietly influential people in the early days of Christianity
- Called an apostle, although not one of the original Twelve

Weaknesses and mistakes:
- With Peter, temporarily stayed aloof from Gentile believers until Paul corrected him

Lessons from his life:
- Encouragement is one of the most effective ways to help
- Sooner or later, true obedience to God will involve risk
- There is always someone who needs encouragement

Vital statistics:
- Where: Cyprus, Jerusalem, Antioch
- Occupation: Missionary, teacher
- Relatives: Sister: Mary. Nephew: John Mark.
- Contemporaries: Peter, Silas, Paul, Herod Agrippa I

Key verses:
"When he arrived and saw the wonderful things God was doing, he was filled with excitement and joy, and encouraged the believers to stay close to the Lord, whatever the cost. Barnabas was a kindly person, full of the Holy Spirit and strong in faith. As a result large numbers of people were added to the Lord" (Acts 11:23, 24).

Barnabas' story is told in Acts 9:27—15:39. He is also mentioned in 1 Corinthians 9:6; Galatians 2:1, 9, 13; Colossians 4:10.

man of the tribe of Benjamin, who reigned for forty years. 22But God removed him
and replaced him with David as king, a man about whom God said, 'David (son of
Jesse) is a man after my own heart, for he will obey me.' 23And it is one of King
David's descendants, Jesus, who is God's promised Savior of Israel!

24"But before he came, John the Baptist preached the need for everyone in Israel
to turn from sin to God. 25As John was finishing his work he asked, 'Do you think
I am the Messiah? No! But he is coming soon—and in comparison with him, I am
utterly worthless.'

26"Brothers—you sons of Abraham, and also all of you Gentiles here who
reverence God—this salvation is for all of us! 27The Jews in Jerusalem and their
leaders fulfilled prophecy by killing Jesus; for they didn't recognize him, or realize
that he is the one the prophets had written about, though they heard the prophets'
words read every Sabbath. 28They found no just cause to execute him, but asked
Pilate to have him killed anyway. 29When they had fulfilled all the prophecies
concerning his death, he was taken from the cross and placed in a tomb.

30"But God brought him back to life again! 31And he was seen many times during
the next few days by the men who had accompanied him to Jerusalem from
Galilee—these men have constantly testified to this in public witness.

32, 33"And now Barnabas and I are here to bring you this Good News—that God's
promise to our ancestors has come true in our own time, in that God brought Jesus
back to life again. This is what the second Psalm is talking about when it says
concerning Jesus, 'Today I have honored you as my Son.'

34"For God had promised to bring him back to life again, no more to die. This is
stated in the Scripture that says, 'I will do for you the wonderful thing I promised
David.' 35In another Psalm he explained more fully, saying, 'God will not let his
Holy One decay.' 36This was not a reference to David, for after David had served
his generation according to the will of God, he died and was buried, and his body
decayed. 37[No, it was a reference to another]—someone God brought back to life,
whose body was not touched at all by the ravages of death.

38"Brothers! Listen! In this man Jesus, there is forgiveness for your sins! 39Ev-
eryone who trusts in him is freed from all guilt and declared righteous—something
the Jewish law could never do. 40Oh, be careful! Don't let the prophets' words
apply to you. For they said, 41'Look and perish, you despisers [of the truth], for I
am doing something in your day—something that you won't believe when you hear
it announced.' "

42As the people left the synagogue that day, they asked Paul to return and speak
to them again the next week. 43And many Jews and godly Gentiles who worshiped
at the synagogue followed Paul and Barnabas down the street as the two men urged
them to accept the mercies God was offering.

Paul turns to the Gentiles

44The following week almost the entire city turned out to hear them preach the
Word of God.

45But when the Jewish leaders saw the crowds, they were jealous, and cursed and
argued against whatever Paul said.

46Then Paul and Barnabas spoke out boldly and declared, "It was necessary that

13:22 1 Sam 16:1,13

13:23 Isa 11:1 Lk 1:32; 2:11

13:24 Mk 1:1-14

13:25 Mt 3:11 Mk 1:7 Lk 3:16 Jn 1:26,27

13:27 Acts 3:17 1 Cor 2:8

13:28 Acts 3:14 **13:29** Lk 23:52,53

13:30 Mt 28:6 Acts 2:24

13:31 Lk 24:48 Acts 1:11 1 Cor 15:5

13:32 Rom 1:2-4 Gal 3:16

13:33 Ps 2:7 Heb 1:5; 5:5

13:34 Isa 55:3

13:35 Ps 16:10

13:36 1 Kgs 2:10

13:37 Acts 2:24 1 Cor 15:42

13:38 Jer 31:34 Col 1:13,14

13:39 Isa 53:11 Rom 3:28; 10:4 Gal 2:16

13:41 Hab 1:5

13:45 Acts 14:2; 18:6 1 Thess 2:15,16 Jude 10

13:46 Deut 32:21 Rom 1:16; 10:19

13:33 *Today I have honored you as my Son,* literally, "This day have I begotten you." **13:37** *No, it was a reference to another,* implied. *was not touched at all by the ravages of death,* literally, "saw no corruption." **13:41** *of the truth,* implied. **13:45** *the Jewish leaders,* literally, "the Jews." *cursed,* or "blasphemed."

13:38, 39 This is the Good News of the gospel—that forgiveness of sins and freedom from guilt are available to all people through faith in Christ—including *you.* Have you received this forgiveness? Are you refreshed by it each day?

13:42-45 The Jewish leaders brought theological arguments against Paul and Barnabas, but the Bible tells us that the real reason for their denunciation was jealousy (5:17). When we see others succeeding where we haven't or receiving the affirmation we crave, it is hard to rejoice with them. Jealousy is our natural

reaction. But how tragic when our own jealous feelings make us try to stop God's work. If a work is God's work, rejoice in it—no matter who is doing it.

13:46 Why was it necessary for the gospel to go first to the Jews? God planned that through the Jewish nation *all* the world would come to know God (Genesis 12:3). Paul, a Jew himself, loved his people (Romans 9:1–3) and wanted to give them every opportunity to join him in proclaiming God's salvation. Unfortunately, many Jews did not recognize Jesus as Messiah, and they did not

this Good News from God should be given first to you Jews. But since you have rejected it, and shown yourselves unworthy of eternal life—well, we will offer it to Gentiles. 47For this is as the Lord commanded when he said, 'I have made you a light to the Gentiles, to lead them from the farthest corners of the earth to my salvation.' "

48When the Gentiles heard this, they were very glad and rejoiced in Paul's message; and as many as wanted eternal life, believed. 49So God's message spread all through that region.

50Then the Jewish leaders stirred up both the godly women and the civic leaders of the city and incited a mob against Paul and Barnabas, and ran them out of town. 51But they shook off the dust of their feet against the town and went on to the city of Iconium. 52And their converts were filled with joy and with the Holy Spirit.

Paul and Barnabas preach boldly at Iconium

14 At Iconium, Paul and Barnabas went together to the synagogue and preached with such power that many—both Jews and Gentiles—believed.
2But the Jews who spurned God's message stirred up distrust among the Gentiles against Paul and Barnabas, saying all sorts of evil things about them. 3Nevertheless, they stayed there a long time, preaching boldly, and the Lord proved their message was from him by giving them power to do great miracles. 4But the people of the city were divided in their opinion about them. Some agreed with the Jewish leaders, and some backed the apostles.

5, 6When Paul and Barnabas learned of a plot to incite a mob of Gentiles, Jews, and Jewish leaders to attack and stone them, they fled for their lives, going to the cities of Lycaonia, Lystra, Derbe, and the surrounding area, 7and preaching the Good News there.

Paul heals a cripple in Lystra

8While they were at Lystra, they came upon a man with crippled feet who had been that way from birth, so he had never walked. 9He was listening as Paul

13:48 *wanted,* or, "were disposed to," or, "ordained to."   **13:52** *their converts,* literally, "the disciples."

13:47
Isa 42:6; 49:6
Lk 2:32

13:48
Rom 8:29,30
Eph 1:4,5,11
1 Pet 1:2

13:51
Mt 10:14
Lk 9:5
Acts 18:6
2 Tim 3:11

13:52
1 Pet 1:8

14:2
2 Tim 3:11

14:3
Mk 16:20
Rom 15:19
Heb 2:4

14:4
Acts 27:4,5
19:9; 28:24

14:5
Acts 14:19; 16:1
1 Thess 2:14-16

14:8
Acts 3:2

---

understand that in Jesus God was offering salvation to anyone, Jew or Gentile, who comes to him in faith.

13:47 God had planned for Israel to be this light (Isaiah 49:6). Through Israel came Jesus, the light of the nations (Luke 2:32). This light would spread out and enlighten the Gentiles.

13:50 Instead of hearing the truth, the Jewish leaders ran Paul and Barnabas out of town. When confronted by a disturbing truth, people often turn away and refuse to listen. When God's Spirit points out needed changes in our lives, we must listen to him, or else we risk pushing the truth so far away that it no longer affects us.

13:51 Jesus had told his disciples to shake from their feet the dust of any village that would not accept or listen to them (Mark 6:11). The disciples were not to blame if the message was rejected as long as they had faithfully presented it. When we share Christ carefully and sensitively, God does not hold us responsible for the other person's decision.

14:3, 4 We may wish we could perform a miraculous act that would convince everyone once and for all that Jesus is the Lord, but we see here that even if we could, it wouldn't convince everyone. God gave these men power to do great miracles as proof, but people were still divided. Don't spend your time and energy wishing for miracles. Sow your seeds of Good News on the best ground you can find in the best way you can, and leave the convincing to the Holy Spirit.

14:5, 6 Iconium, Lystra, and Derbe were three cities Paul visited in the region of Galatia. Paul wrote a letter to these churches—the letter to the Galatians—because many Jewish Christians were

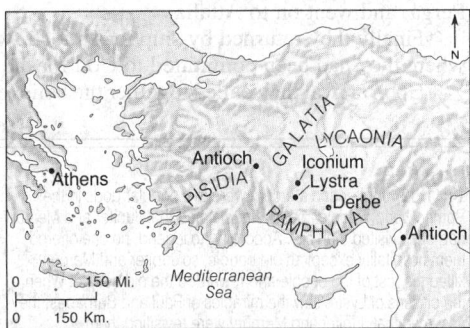

CONTINUED MINISTRY IN GALATIA Paul and Barnabas, thrown out of Antioch in Pisidia, descended the mountains, going east into Lycaonia. They went first to Iconium, a commercial center on the road between Asia and Syria. After preaching there, they had to flee to Lystra, 25 miles south. Paul was stoned in Lystra, but he and Barnabas traveled the 50 miles to Derbe, a frontier town. The pair then boldly retraced their steps.

claiming that non-Jewish Christians couldn't be saved unless they followed Jewish laws and customs. Paul's letter refuted this and brought the believers back to a right understanding of faith in Jesus (see Galatians 3:3, 5). Paul wrote his letter soon after leaving the region (see the note on 14:28).

preached, and Paul noticed him and realized he had faith to be healed. ¹⁰So Paul called to him, "Stand up!" and the man leaped to his feet and started walking! ¹¹When the listening crowd saw what Paul had done, they shouted (in their local dialect, of course), "These men are gods in human bodies!" ¹²They decided that Barnabas was the Greek god Jupiter, and that Paul, because he was the chief speaker, was Mercury! ¹³The local priest of the Temple of Jupiter, located on the outskirts of the city, brought them cartloads of flowers and prepared to sacrifice oxen to them at the city gates before the crowds.

¹⁴But when Barnabas and Paul saw what was happening they ripped at their clothing in dismay and ran out among the people, shouting, ¹⁵"Men! What are you doing? We are merely human beings like yourselves! We have come to bring you the Good News that you are invited to turn from the worship of these foolish things and to pray instead to the living God who made heaven and earth and sea and everything in them. ¹⁶In bygone days he permitted the nations to go their own ways, ¹⁷but he never left himself without a witness; there were always his reminders—the kind things he did such as sending you rain and good crops and giving you food and gladness."

¹⁸But even so, Paul and Barnabas could scarcely restrain the people from sacrificing to them!

¹⁹Yet only a few days later, some Jews arrived from Antioch and Iconium and turned the crowds into a murderous mob that stoned Paul and dragged him out of the city, apparently dead. ²⁰But as the believers stood around him, he got up and went back into the city!

Paul and Barnabas appoint elders on the return trip home

The next day he left with Barnabas for Derbe. ²¹After preaching the Good News there and making many disciples, they returned again to Lystra, Iconium and Antioch, ²²where they helped the believers to grow in love for God and each other. They encouraged them to continue in the faith in spite of all the persecution, reminding them that they must enter into the Kingdom of God through many tribulations. ²³Paul and Barnabas also appointed elders in every church and prayed for them with fasting, turning them over to the care of the Lord in whom they trusted.

²⁴Then they traveled back through Pisidia to Pamphylia, ²⁵preached again in Perga, and went on to Attalia.

²⁶Finally they returned by ship to Antioch, where their journey had begun, and where they had been committed to God for the work now completed.

²⁷Upon arrival they called together the believers and reported on their trip, telling

14:10
Isa 35:6
Acts 3:8

14:11
Acts 28:6

14:13
Dan 2:46

14:15
Ex 20:11
Deut 32:21
Jer 14:22
Mt 16:16
1 Thess 1:9
Rev 14:7; 19:10

14:16
Ps 81:12

14:17
Deut 11:14
Ps 65:10-12
147:8
Acts 17:27
Rom 1:19,20

14:19
Acts 13:45
2 Cor 1:8; 11:25
2 Tim 3:11

14:20
Acts 14:6

14:22
Mt 10:38 16:24
Jn 15:18
Rom 8:17
2 Tim 2:11; 3:12

14:23
Tit 1:5

14:24
Acts 13:13,14

14:26
Acts 11:26
13:1-3

14:27
1 Cor 16:9
Col 4:3
Rev 3:8

14:11, 12 Jupiter and Mercury were two popular gods in the Roman world. People from Lystra claimed that Jupiter and Mercury had once visited their city. According to legend, no one offered them hospitality except an old couple, so Jupiter and Mercury killed the rest of the people and rewarded the old couple. When the citizens of Lystra saw the miracles of Paul and Barnabas, they assumed that Jupiter and Mercury were revisiting them. Remembering what had happened to their citizens before, they immediately hailed Paul and Barnabas.

14:15-18 Responding to the people of Lystra, Paul and Barnabas reminded them that God never leaves himself "without a witness." Rain and crops, for example, are evidence of his goodness. Later Paul wrote that this evidence in nature leaves people without an excuse for unbelief (Romans 1:20). When in doubt about God, look around and you will see abundant evidence that he is at work in our world.

14:18-20 Paul and Barnabas were persistent in their preaching of the Good News. They considered the cost to themselves to be nothing in comparison with obedience to Christ. They had just narrowly escaped being stoned at Iconium (14:1-7). However, Jews from Antioch and Iconium tracked Paul down and stoned him.

They thought he was dead. But Paul got up and went back into the city to preach the Good News—that's true commitment! Being a disciple of Christ calls for costly commitment. As Christians, we no longer belong to ourselves, but to our Lord, for whom we are called to suffer.

14:21, 22 Paul and Barnabas returned to visit the believers in all the cities where they had recently been threatened and physically attacked. They knew the dangers they faced, yet they believed they had a responsibility to encourage the new believers. No matter how inconvenient or uncomfortable the task may seem, we must never fail to support new believers who need our help and encouragement. It was not convenient or comfortable for Jesus to go to the cross for us!

14:23 Part of the reason Paul and Barnabas took their lives in their hands to return to these cities was to organize the churches' leadership. They were not just following up on a loosely knit group; they were helping the believers get organized with Spirit-led leaders who could help them grow. Churches grow under Spirit-led leaders, both laypersons and pastors. Pray for your church leaders and support them; and if God urges you, humbly accept the responsibility of a leadership role in your church.

how God had opened the door of faith to the Gentiles too. 28And they stayed there
with the believers at Antioch for a long while.

2. Meeting of the church council
The leaders meet in Jerusalem

15:1
Gen 17:9-11
Lev 12:3
Gal 5:2
Phil 3:2,3

15:2
Gal 2:1-10

15:3
Acts 14:27

15 While Paul and Barnabas were at Antioch, some men from Judea arrived
and began to teach the believers that unless they adhered to the ancient
Jewish custom of circumcision, they could not be saved. 2Paul and Barnabas
argued and discussed this with them at length, and finally the believers sent them
to Jerusalem, accompanied by some local men, to talk to the apostles and elders
there about this question. 3After the entire congregation had escorted them out of
the city the delegates went on to Jerusalem, stopping along the way in the cities of

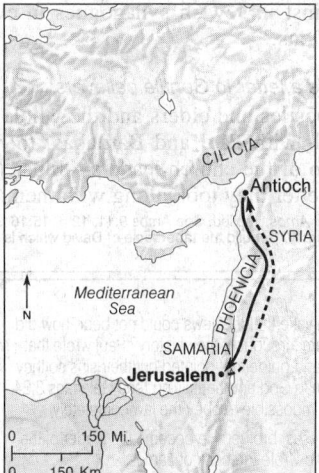

THE END OF THE FIRST JOURNEY From Antioch in Pisidia, Paul and Barnabas went down the mountains back to
Pamphylia on the coast. Stopping first in Perga, where they
had landed, they went west to Attalia, the main port that sent
goods from Asia to Syria and Egypt. There they found a ship
bound for Seleucia, the port of Antioch in Syria. This ended
their first missionary journey.

14:28 Paul probably wrote his letter to the Galatians while he was
staying in Antioch (A.D. 48 or 49) after completing his first
missionary journey. There are several theories as to what part of
Galatia Paul was addressing, but most agree that Iconium, Lystra,
and Derbe were part of that region. Galatians was probably written
before the Jerusalem Council (Acts 15), because in the letter the
question of whether Gentile believers should be required to follow
Jewish law was not yet resolved. The Council met to solve that
problem.

15:1ff The delegates to the council at Jerusalem came from the
churches in Jerusalem and Antioch. The conversion of Gentiles
was raising an urgent question for the early church—do the
Gentiles have to adhere to the laws of Moses and other Jewish
traditions to be saved? One group of Jewish Christians insisted
that following the law, including circumcision, was necessary for
salvation. The Gentiles did not think they needed to become
Jewish first in order to become Christians. So Paul and Barnabas
discussed this problem with the leaders of the church. The council
upheld the convictions expressed by Paul and Barnabas that
following the Jewish laws, including circumcision, was not
essential for salvation and that Jewish and Gentile Christians could
eat together without the Jews' becoming defiled.

15:1 The real problem for the Jewish Christians was not over
whether Gentiles could be saved, but whether Gentiles had to
adhere to the laws of Moses. The test of following these laws was

circumcision. The Jewish Christians were worried because soon
there would be more Gentile than Jewish Christians, and the Jews
were afraid of weakening moral standards among believers if they
did not follow Jewish laws. Paul, Barnabas, and the other church
leaders believed that the Old Testament law was very important,
but it was not a prerequisite to salvation. The law cannot save; only
faith in Jesus Christ is what one needs to be saved.

15:2, 3 It is helpful to see how the churches in Antioch and
Jerusalem resolved their conflict: (1) they sent a delegation to help
seek a solution; (2) they met with the church leaders to give their
reports and set another date to continue the discussion; (3) Paul
and Barnabas gave their report; (4) James summarized the reports
and made the decision; (5) everyone abided by the decision; (6)
the council sent a letter with delegates back to Antioch to report
the decision.

This is a wise way to handle conflicts within the church.
Problems must be confronted, and all sides of the argument must
be given a fair hearing. The discussion should be held before
leaders who are spiritually mature and trusted to make wise
decisions. Everyone should then abide by the decisions.

**THE
JERUSALEM
COUNCIL**
A dispute arose
when some Jude-
ans taught that
Gentile believers
had to be circum-
cised to be
saved. Paul and
Barnabas went to
Jerusalem to dis-
cuss this situation
with the leaders
there. After the
Jerusalem council
made its decision,
Paul and Barna-
bas returned to
Antioch with the
news.

Phoenicia and Samaria to visit the believers, telling them—much to everyone's joy—that the Gentiles, too, were being converted.

4Arriving in Jerusalem, they met with the church leaders—all the apostles and elders were present—and Paul and Barnabas reported on what God had been doing through their ministry. 5But then some of the men who had been Pharisees before their conversion stood to their feet and declared that all Gentile converts must be circumcised and required to follow all the Jewish customs and ceremonies.

6So the apostles and church elders set a further meeting to decide this question.

7At the meeting, after long discussion, Peter stood and addressed them as follows: "Brothers, you all know that God chose me from among you long ago to preach the Good News to the Gentiles, so that they also could believe. 8God, who knows men's hearts, confirmed the fact that he accepts Gentiles by giving them the Holy Spirit, just as he gave him to us. 9He made no distinction between them and us, for he cleansed their lives through faith, just as he did ours. 10And now are you going to correct God by burdening the Gentiles with a yoke that neither we nor our fathers were able to bear? 11Don't you believe that all are saved the same way, by the free gift of the Lord Jesus?"

12There was no further discussion, and everyone now listened as Barnabas and Paul told about the miracles God had done through them among the Gentiles.

13When they had finished, James took the floor. "Brothers," he said, "listen to me. 14Peter has told you about the time God first visited the Gentiles to take from them a people to bring honor to his name. 15And this fact of Gentile conversion agrees with what the prophets predicted. For instance, listen to this passage from the prophet Amos:

16'Afterwards' [says the Lord], 'I will return and renew the broken contract with David, 17so that Gentiles, too, will find the Lord—all those marked with my name.'

18That is what the Lord says, who reveals his plans made from the beginning.

19"And so my judgment is that we should not insist that the Gentiles who turn to God must obey our Jewish laws, 20except that we should write to them to refrain from eating meat sacrificed to idols, from all fornication, and also from eating unbled meat of strangled animals. 21For these things have been preached against in Jewish synagogues in every city on every Sabbath for many generations."

The council sends a letter to Gentile believers

22Then the apostles and elders and the whole congregation voted to send delegates to Antioch with Paul and Barnabas, to report on this decision. The men chosen were two of the church leaders—Judas (also called Barsabbas) and Silas. 23This is the letter they took along with them:

15:15 *from the prophet Amos,* implied. See Amos 9:11, 12. **15:16** *says the Lord,* implied. *renew the broken contract with David,* literally, "rebuild the tabernacle of David which is fallen."

15:5
1 Cor 7:18
Gal 5:2-11

15:7
Acts 10:19-29

15:8
1 Chron 28:9
Jer 17:10
Acts 10:44,47
Heb 4:13

15:9
Acts 10:43
Rom 10:11,12

15:10
Mt 23:4
Gal 5:1

15:11
Rom 3:23,24
5:15
2 Cor 13:14
Eph 1:7,8; 2:8

15:12
Acts 14:27; 15:4

15:13
Acts 12:17

15:15
Isa 11:10
54:1-5

15:16
Amos 9:11,12

15:18
Isa 45:21

15:19
Acts 21:15

15:20
Gen 9:4
Ex 20:3,4
Lev 3:17
Deut 12:16
Ezek 20:30
Dan 1:8
1 Cor 8:7; 10:7
1 Thess 4:3,4

15:21
Acts 13:15

15:22
Acts 1:23
15:27; 16:19
17:4
1 Pet 5:12

15:10 If the law was a yoke that the Jews could not bear, how did having the law help them throughout their history? Paul wrote that the law was a teacher and guide that pointed out their sins so they could repent and return to God and right living (see Galatians 3:24, 25). It was, and still is, impossible to obey the law completely.

15:13 This James is Jesus' brother. He became the leader of the church in Jerusalem and wrote the book of James.

15:20 Gentile believers did not have to abide by the Jewish law of circumcision, but they were asked by the council to stay away from idolatry, sexual immorality (a common part of idol worship), and eating meat of unbled animals (reflecting the biblical teaching that the life is in the blood—Leviticus 17:14). If Gentile Christians would abstain from these three practices, they would please God and get along better with fellow Jewish Christians. Of course, there were

other actions inappropriate for believers, but the Jews were especially concerned about these three. This compromise helped the church grow unhindered by the cultural differences of Jews and Gentiles. When we share our message across cultural and economic boundaries, we must be sure that the requirements for faith we set up are God's, not people's.

15:22 Apostleship was not a church office, but a position and function based on specific gifts. Elders were appointed to lead and manage the church. In this meeting, apostles submitted to the decision of an elder—James, Jesus' brother.

15:22 Silas would later accompany Paul on his second missionary journey in place of Barnabas, who visited different cities.

15:23–29 This letter answered their questions and brought great joy to the Gentile Christians in Antioch (15:31). Beautifully written, it

◄   *"From:* The apostles, elders and brothers at Jerusalem.

"To: The Gentile brothers in Antioch, Syria and Cilicia. Greetings!

15:24
Gal 1:7; 2:4; 5:12
Tit 1:10

24"We understand that some believers from here have upset you and questioned your salvation, but they had no such instructions from us. 25So it seemed wise to us, having unanimously agreed on our decision, to send to you these two official representatives, along with our beloved Barnabas and Paul. 26These men—Judas and Silas, who have risked their lives for the sake of our Lord Jesus Christ—will confirm orally what we have decided concerning your question.

15:26
Acts 13:50
14:19
1 Cor 15:30
2 Cor 11:23,26

27, 28, 29"For it seemed good to the Holy Spirit and to us to lay no greater burden of Jewish laws on you than to abstain from eating food offered to idols and from unbled meat of strangled animals, and, of course, from fornication. If you do this, it is enough. Farewell."

15:29
Lev 17:14
Acts 21:25
Rev 2:14

30The four messengers went at once to Antioch, where they called a general meeting of the Christians and gave them the letter. 31And there was great joy throughout the church that day as they read it.

15:32
Acts 13:1

32Then Judas and Silas, both being gifted speakers, preached long sermons to the

15:24 *questioned your salvation,* literally, "subverted your souls."   **15:27-29** *and from unbled meat of strangled animals,* literally, "and from blood."   **15:32** *gifted speakers,* or, "prophets."

THE FIRST CHURCH CONFERENCE	Group	Position	Reasons
	Judaizers (some Jewish Christians)	Gentiles must become Jewish first to be eligible for salvation	1. These were devout, practicing Jews who found it difficult to set aside a tradition of gaining merit with God by keeping the law 2. They thought grace was too easy for the Gentiles 3. They were afraid of seeming too non-Jewish in their new faith—which could lead to death 4. The demands on the Gentiles were a way of maintaining control and authority in the movement
	Gentile Christians	Faith in Christ as Savior is the only requirement for salvation	1. To submit to Jewish demands would be to doubt what God had already done for them by faith alone 2. They resisted exchanging a system of Jewish rituals for their pagan rituals—neither of which had power to save 3. They sought to obey Christ by baptism (rather than by circumcision) as a sign of their new faith
	Peter and James	Faith is the only requirement, but there must be evidence of change by rejecting parts of the old lifestyle	1. Tried to distinguish between what was still true from God's Word and what was just human tradition 2. Had Christ's command to preach to all the world 3. Wanted to preserve unity 4. Saw that Christianity could never survive as just a sect within Judaism

As long as most of the first Christians were Jewish, there was little difficulty in welcoming new believers. However, Gentiles (non-Jews) began to accept Jesus' offer of salvation. The evidence from their lives and the presence of God's Spirit in them showed that God was accepting them. Some of the early Christians believed that non-Jewish Christians needed to meet certain conditions before they could be worthy to accept Christ. The issue could have destroyed the church, so a conference was called in Jerusalem and the issue was formally settled there, although it continued to be a problem for many years following. Above is an outline of the three points of view at the conference.

appeals to the Holy Spirit's guidance and explains what is to be done as though the readers already know it. It is helpful when believers learn to be careful not only in what they say, but also in how they say it. We may be correct in our content, but we can lose our audience by our tone of voice or attitude.

15:31 The debate over circumcision could have split the church, but Paul, Barnabas, and the Jews in Antioch made the right decision—they sought counsel from the apostles and God's Word. Our differences should be settled the same way, by seeking wise counsel and abiding by the decisions. Don't let disagreements divide you from other believers. Third-party assistance is a sound method for resolving problems and preserving unity.

believers, strengthening their faith. ³³They stayed several days, and then Judas and
Silas returned to Jerusalem taking greetings and appreciation to those who had sent
them. ³⁴, ³⁵Paul and Barnabas stayed on at Antioch to assist several others who
were preaching and teaching there.

15:33
Mt 4:24
Acts 6:9; 11:20
15:41
Gal 1:21

3. Second missionary journey
Paul and Barnabas separate

³⁶Several days later Paul suggested to Barnabas that they return again to Turkey,
and visit each city where they had preached before, to see how the new converts
were getting along. ³⁷Barnabas agreed, and wanted to take along John Mark. ³⁸But
Paul didn't like that idea at all, since John had deserted them in Pamphylia. ³⁹Their
disagreement over this was so sharp that they separated. Barnabas took Mark with
him and sailed for Cyprus, ⁴⁰, ⁴¹while Paul chose Silas and, with the blessing of the
believers, left for Syria and Cilicia, to encourage the churches there.

15:36
Acts 13:4,13,
14,51
14:5,6,24-28

15:37
Col 4:10
2 Tim 4:11

15:38
Acts 13:13

Timothy joins Paul and Silas at Lystra

16 Paul and Silas went first to Derbe and then on to Lystra where they met
Timothy, a believer whose mother was a Christian Jewess but his father a
Greek. ²Timothy was well thought of by the brothers in Lystra and Iconium, ³so
Paul asked him to join them on their journey. In deference to the Jews of the area,
he circumcised Timothy before they left, for everyone knew that his father was a
Greek [and hadn't permitted this before]. ⁴Then they went from city to city, making

16:1
Acts 14:5,6
Phil 2:19-22
2 Tim 1:2,5; 3:15

16:3
1 Cor 9:20
Gal 2:3; 5:2

15:33 *stayed several days,* literally, "spent some time." **15:36** *return again to Turkey, and visit each city where they had preached before,* implied. Literally, "return now and visit every city wherein we proclaimed the word of the Lord." **16:3** *and hadn't permitted this before,* implied.

15:37–39 Paul and Barnabas disagreed sharply over Mark. Paul didn't want to take him along because he had left them earlier (13:13). This disagreement caused the two great preachers to lead two teams, opening up two missionary endeavors instead of one. God works even through conflict and disagreements. Later, Mark became vital to Paul's ministry (Colossians 4:10). Christians do not always agree, but problems can be solved by agreeing to disagree and letting God work his will.

15:40 Paul's second missionary journey, this time with Silas as his partner, began approximately three years after his first one ended. The two visited many of the cities covered on Paul's first journey, plus others. This journey laid the groundwork for the church in Greece.

15:40 Silas was involved in the Jerusalem council and was one of the two men chosen to represent the Jerusalem church by taking the letter and decision back to Antioch (15:22). Paul, from the Antioch church, chose Silas, from the Jerusalem church, and they traveled together to many cities to spread the Good News. This teamwork revealed the church's unity after the Jerusalem council's decision.

16:1 Timothy is the first second-generation Christian mentioned in the New Testament. His mother, Eunice, and grandmother, Lois (2 Timothy 1:5), had become believers and had faithfully influenced him for the Lord. Although Timothy's father apparently was not a Christian, the faithfulness of his mother and grandmother prevailed. Never underestimate the far-reaching consequences of raising one small child to love the Lord.

16:2, 3 Timothy and his mother, Eunice, were from Lystra. Eunice had probably heard Paul's preaching when he was there during his first missionary journey (Acts 14:5, 6). Timothy was the son of a Jewish mother and Greek father—to the Jews, a half-breed like a Samaritan. So Paul asked Timothy to be circumcised to erase some of the stigma he may have had with Jewish believers. Timothy was not required to be circumcised (the Jerusalem council had decided that—chapter 15), but he voluntarily did this to overcome any barriers to his witness for Christ. Sometimes we need to go beyond the minimum requirements in order to help our audience receive our testimony.

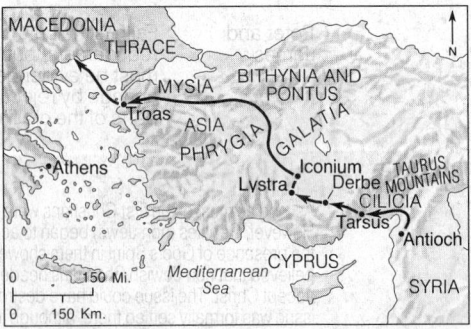

THE SECOND JOURNEY BEGINS Paul and Silas set out on a second missionary journey to visit the cities Paul had preached in earlier. This time they set out by land rather than sea, traveling the Roman road through Cilicia and the Cilician Gates—a gorge through the Taurus Mountains—then northwest toward Derbe, Lystra, and Iconium. The Spirit told them not to go into Asia, so they turned northward toward Bithynia. Again the Spirit said no, so they turned west through Mysia to the harbor city of Troas.

16:5
Acts 9:31

known the decision concerning the Gentiles, as decided by the apostles and elders in Jerusalem. 5So the church grew daily in faith and numbers.

Paul has a vision directing them to Macedonia

16:7
Rom 8:9
Gal 2:20
Phil 1:19

16:8
2 Cor 2:12
2 Tim 4:13

16:9
Num 12:6
Acts 10:3,30
Rom 15:26
18:5; 20:3

6Next they traveled through Phrygia and Galatia, because the Holy Spirit had told them not to go into the Turkish province of Asia minor at that time. 7Then going along the borders of Mysia they headed north for the province of Bithynia, but again the Spirit of Jesus said no. 8So instead they went on through Mysia province to the city of Troas.

9That night Paul had a vision. In his dream he saw a man over in Macedonia, Greece, pleading with him, "Come over here and help us." 10Well, that settled it. We would go to Macedonia, for we could only conclude that God was sending us to preach the Good News there.

Lydia is converted in Philippi

16:11
2 Cor 2:12

16:12
Acts 20:6
1 Thess 2:2

11We went aboard a boat at Troas, and sailed straight across to Samothrace, and the next day on to Neapolis, 12and finally reached Philippi, a Roman colony just inside the Macedonian border, and stayed there several days.

13On the Sabbath, we went a little way outside the city to a river bank where we understood some people met for prayer; and we taught the Scriptures to some women who came.

16:9 *That night,* literally, "in the night."   **16:12** *Roman,* implied.

16:6 We don't know how the Holy Spirit told Paul that he and his men were not to go into Asia. It may have been through a prophet, a vision, an inner conviction, or some other circumstance. To know God's will does not mean we must hear his voice. He leads in different ways. When seeking God's will (1) make sure your plan is in harmony with God's Word; (2) ask mature Christians for their advice; (3) check your own motives—are you seeking to do what you want or what you think God wants?—and (4) pray for God to open and close the doors of circumstances.

16:7–9 The Spirit of Jesus is another name for the Holy Spirit (16:6). The Holy Spirit closed the door twice for Paul, so he must have wondered which geographical direction he should take in spreading the gospel. Then, in a vision (16:9), Paul was given definite direction, and he and his companions obediently traveled into Greece. The Holy Spirit guides us to the right places, but he also guides us away from the wrong places. As we seek God's will, it is important to know what God wants us to do and where he wants us to go, but it is equally important to know what God does not want us to do and where he does not want us to go.

16:10 The use of the pronoun *we* indicates that Luke, the author of the Gospel of Luke and of this book, joined Paul, Silas, and Timothy on their journey. He was an eyewitness to most of the remaining incidents in this book.

16:12 Philippi was the key city in the region of Macedonia (northern Greece today). Paul founded a church during this visit (A.D. 50–51). Later Paul wrote a letter to the church, the book of Philippians, probably from a prison in Rome (A.D. 61). The letter was personal and tender, showing Paul's deep love and friendship for the believers there. In his letter to them he thanked them for a gift they had sent, alerted them to a coming visit by Timothy and Epaphroditus, urged the church to clear up any disunity, and encouraged the believers not to give in to persecution.

16:13 Inscribed on the arches outside the city of Philippi was a prohibition against bringing an unrecognized religion into the city; therefore, this prayer meeting was held outside the city, beside the river.

16:13, 14 After following the Holy Spirit's leading into Macedonia, Paul made his first evangelistic contact with a small group of

women. Paul never allowed sexual or cultural boundaries to keep him from preaching the gospel. He preached to these women; and Lydia, an influential merchant, believed. This threw open the door for ministry in that region. In the early church God often worked in and through women.

16:13ff Luke highlights the stories of three individuals who became believers through Paul's ministry in Philippi: Lydia, the influential businesswoman (16:14), the demon-possessed slave girl (16:18), and the jailer (16:29). The gospel was affecting all strata of society, just as it does today.

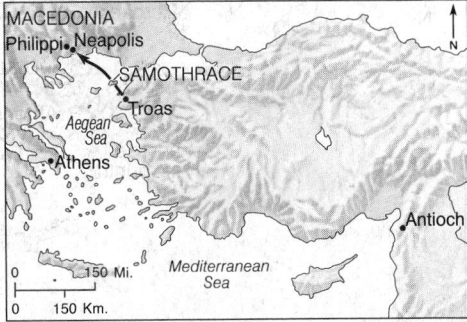

PAUL TRAVELS TO MACEDONIA At Troas, Paul received the Macedonian call (16:9), and he, Silas, Timothy, and Luke boarded a ship. They sailed to the island of Samothrace, then on to Neapolis, the port for the city of Philippi. Philippi sat on the Egnatian Way, a main transportation artery connecting the eastern provinces with Italy.

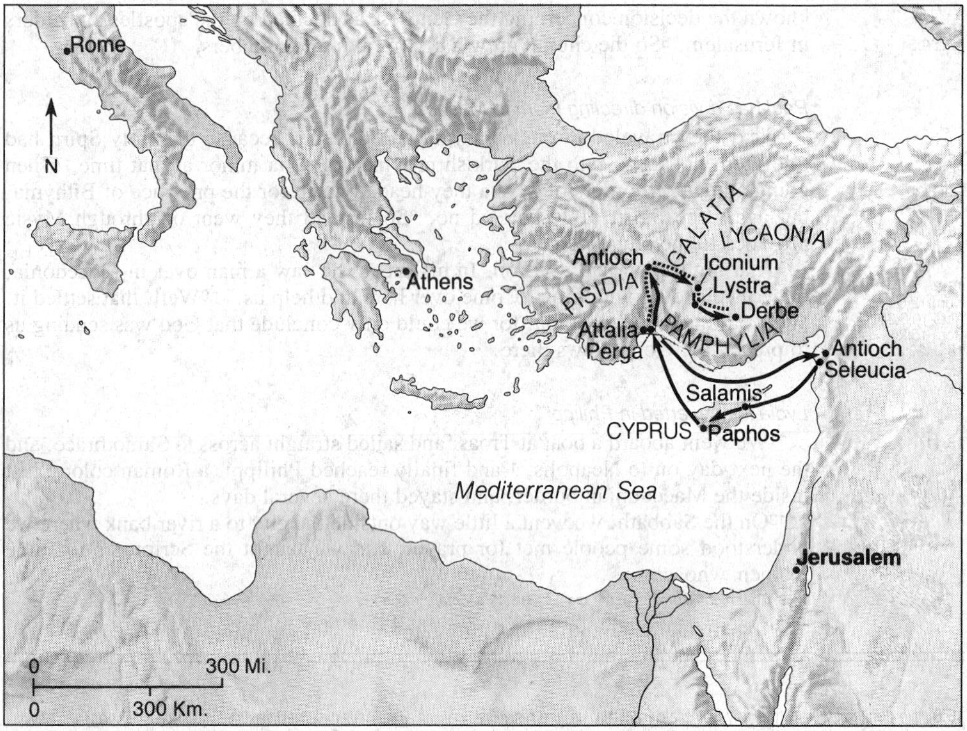

PAUL'S FIRST MISSIONARY JOURNEY

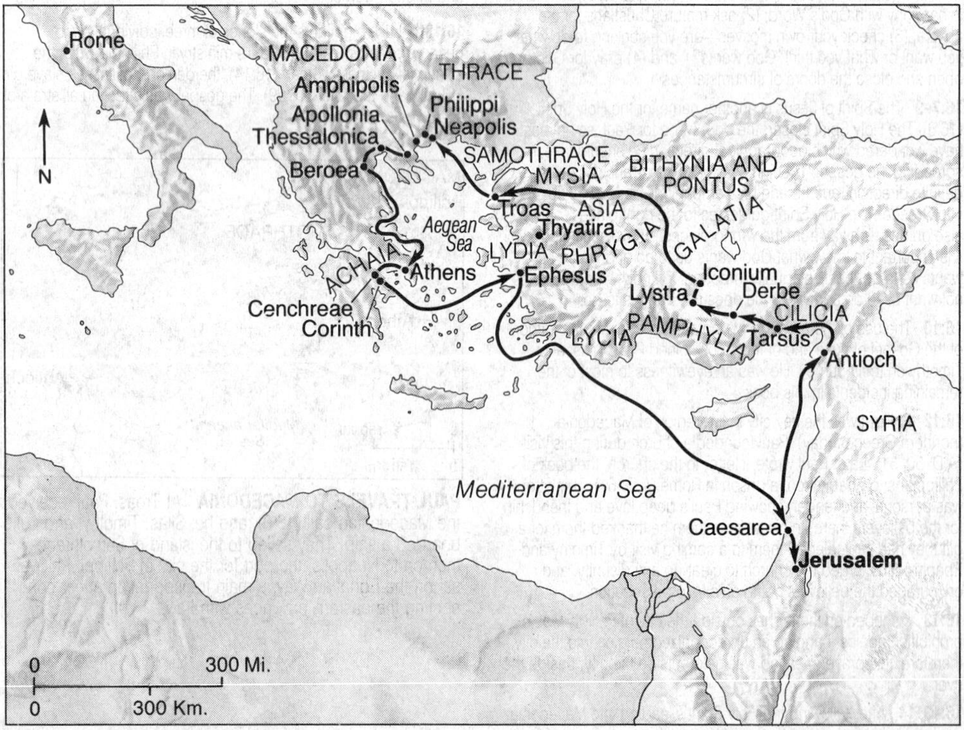

PAUL'S SECOND MISSIONARY JOURNEY

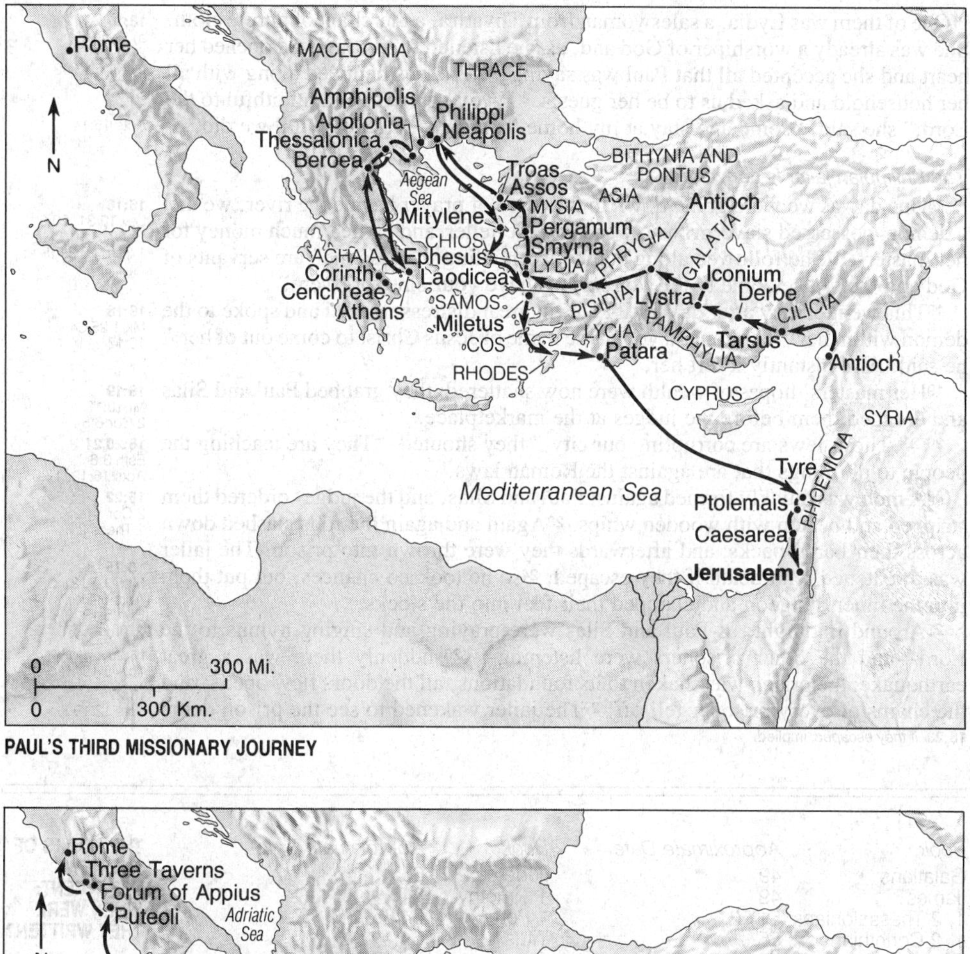

PAUL'S THIRD MISSIONARY JOURNEY

PAUL'S VOYAGE TO ROME

14One of them was Lydia, a saleswoman from Thyatira, a merchant of purple cloth. She was already a worshiper of God and, as she listened to us, the Lord opened her heart and she accepted all that Paul was saying. 15She was baptized along with all her household and asked us to be her guests. "If you agree that I am faithful to the Lord," she said, "come and stay at my home." And she urged us until we did.

16:14
a) Rev 1:11
2:18-29
b) Acts 13:43
18:7

16:15
Acts 16:14

The Philippian jailer is converted

16One day as we were going down to the place of prayer beside the river, we met a demon-possessed slave girl who was a fortune-teller, and earned much money for her masters. 17She followed along behind us shouting, "These men are servants of God and they have come to tell you how to have your sins forgiven."

16:16
Lev 19:31; 20:6
Deut 18:10,11
1 Sam 28:3,7,8

18This went on day after day until Paul, in great distress, turned and spoke to the demon within her. "I command you in the name of Jesus Christ to come out of her," he said. And instantly it left her.

16:18
Mk 1:25,34
16:17

19Her masters' hopes of wealth were now shattered; they grabbed Paul and Silas and dragged them before the judges at the marketplace.

16:19
Mt 10:18
2 Cor 6:5

20, 21"These Jews are corrupting our city," they shouted. "They are teaching the people to do things that are against the Roman laws."

16:20,21
Esth 3:8
Acts 16:12; 17:6

22A mob was quickly formed against Paul and Silas, and the judges ordered them stripped and beaten with wooden whips. 23Again and again the rods slashed down across their bared backs; and afterwards they were thrown into prison. The jailer was threatened with death if they escaped, 24so he took no chances, but put them into the inner dungeon and clamped their feet into the stocks.

16:22
2 Cor 11:23
1 Thess 2:2

16:25
Mt 5:10-12
Acts 5:41
Eph 5:19
2 Tim 1:8

25Around midnight, as Paul and Silas were praying and singing hymns to the Lord—and the other prisoners were listening— 26suddenly there was a great earthquake; the prison was shaken to its foundations, all the doors flew open—and the chains of every prisoner fell off! 27The jailer wakened to see the prison doors

16:26
Acts 5:19; 12:7,10

16:27
Acts 12:19

16:23 *if they escaped,* implied.

Book	Approximate Date	Book	Approximate Date	
Galatians	49	Jude	65	**THE BOOKS OF**
James	49	1 Timothy	64	**THE NEW**
1, 2 Thessalonians	51/52	1 Peter	64/65	**TESTAMENT:**
1, 2 Corinthians	55	Titus	64	**WHEN WERE**
Romans	57	Acts	66/68	**THEY WRITTEN?**
Mark	58/60	2 Peter	66/68	
Ephesians	60	2 Timothy	66/67	
Colossians	60	Hebrews	68/70	
Philemon	60	John	85	
Philippians	61	1, 2, 3 John	85/90	
Matthew	61/64	Revelation	95	
Luke	61/64			

16:14 Lydia was a merchant of purple cloth, so she was probably wealthy. Purple cloth was valuable and expensive. It was usually worn as a sign of nobility or royalty.

16:16 Fortune-telling was a common practice in Greek and Roman culture. There were many superstitious methods by which people thought they could foretell future events, from interpreting omens in nature to communicating with the spirits of the dead. This young slave girl had an evil spirit, and she made her master rich by interpreting signs and telling people their fortunes. The master was exploiting her unfortunate condition for personal gain.

16:17 What the slave girl said was true although the source of her knowledge was a demon. Why did a demon announce the truth about Paul, and why did this annoy him? If Paul accepted the demon's words, he would appear to be linking the gospel and demon-related activities. This would damage his message about

Christ. Truth and evil do not mix.

16:22-25 Paul and Silas were stripped, beaten, whipped, and placed in stocks in the inner dungeon. Despite this dismal situation, they praised God, praying and singing as the other prisoners listened. No matter what our circumstances, we should praise God. Others may come to Christ because of our example.

16:24 Stocks were made of two boards joined with iron clamps, leaving holes just big enough for the ankles. The prisoner's legs were placed across the lower board and then the upper board was closed over them. Sometimes both wrists and ankles were placed in stocks. Paul, who had committed no crime and was a peaceful man, was put in stocks designed for holding the most dangerous prisoners in absolute security.

16:27 The jailer drew his sword to kill himself because Roman officials had threatened his life if anyone escaped (16:23).

wide open, and assuming the prisoners had escaped, he drew his sword to kill himself.

28But Paul yelled to him, "Don't do it! We are all here!"

29Trembling with fear, the jailer called for lights and ran to the dungeon and fell down before Paul and Silas. 30He brought them out and begged them, "Sirs, what must I do to be saved?"

31They replied, "Believe on the Lord Jesus and you will be saved, and your entire household."

32Then they told him and all his household the Good News from the Lord. 33That

16:30
Acts 2:37

16:31
Jn 3:16,36
Acts 11:14
Rom 10:9

SILAS

The lives of the first Christian missionaries can be described with many words, but "boring" is not one of them. There were days of great excitement as men and women who had never heard of Jesus responded to the gospel. There were dangerous journeys over land and sea. Health risks and hunger were part of the daily routine. And there was open and hostile resistance to Christianity in many cities. Silas was one of the first missionaries, and he found out that serving Jesus Christ was certainly not boring!

The majority of early Christians were Jews who realized Jesus was the fulfillment of God's Old Testament promises to his people; however, the universal application of those promises had been overlooked. Thus, many felt that becoming Jewish was a prerequisite to becoming a Christian. The idea that God could accept a Gentile pagan was too incredible. But Gentiles began to accept Christ as Savior, and the transformation of their lives and the presence of God's Spirit confirmed their conversions. Some Jews were still reluctant, though, and insisted these new Christians take on various Jewish customs. The issue came to a boiling point at the Jerusalem meeting, but was peacefully resolved. Silas was one of the representatives from Jerusalem sent with Paul and Barnabas back to Antioch with an official letter of welcome and acceptance to the Gentile Christians. Having fulfilled this mission, Silas returned to Jerusalem. Within a short time, however, he was back in Antioch at Paul's request to join him on his second missionary journey.

Paul, Silas, and Timothy began a far-ranging ministry that included some exciting adventures. Paul and Silas spent a night singing in a Philippian prison after being severely beaten. Later, they narrowly missed another beating in Thessalonica, prevented by an evening escape. In Beroea there was more trouble, but Silas and Timothy stayed to teach the young believers while Paul traveled on to Athens. The team was finally reunited in Corinth. In each place they visited, they left behind a small group of Christians.

Silas leaves the story as suddenly as he entered it. Peter mentions him as the co-author of 1 Peter, but we do not know when he joined Peter. He was an effective believer before leaving Jerusalem, and he doubtless continued to minister after his work with Paul was completed. He took advantage of opportunities to serve God and was not discouraged by the setbacks and opposition he met along the way. Silas, though not the most famous of the early missionaries, was certainly a hero worth imitating.

Strengths and accomplishments:
- A leader in the Jerusalem church
- Represented the church in carrying the "acceptance letter" prepared by the Jerusalem council to the Gentile believers in Antioch
- Was closely associated with Paul from the second missionary journey on
- When imprisoned with Paul in Philippi, sang songs of praise to God
- Worked as a writing secretary for both Paul and Peter, using "Silvanus" as his pen name

Lessons from his life:
- Partnership is a significant part of effective ministry
- God never guarantees that his servants will not suffer
- Obedience to God will often mean giving up what makes us feel secure

Vital statistics:
- Where: Roman citizen living in Jerusalem
- Occupation: One of the first career missionaries
- Contemporaries: Paul, Timothy, Peter, Mark, Barnabas

Key verse:
"These men—Judas and Silas, who have risked their lives for the sake of our Lord Jesus Christ—will confirm orally what we have decided concerning your question" (Acts 15:26).

Silas' story is told in Acts 15:22—19:10. He is also mentioned in 2 Corinthians 1:19; 1 Thessalonians 1:1; 2 Thessalonians 1:1; 1 Peter 5:12.

same hour he washed their stripes and he and all his family were baptized. 34Then
he brought them up into his house and set a meal before them. How he and his
household rejoiced because all were now believers! 35The next morning the judges
sent police officers over to tell the jailer, "Let those men go!" 36So the jailer told
Paul they were free to leave.

37But Paul replied, "Oh, no they don't! They have publicly beaten us without
trial and jailed us—and we are Roman citizens! So now they want us to leave
secretly? Never! Let them come themselves and release us!"

38The police officers reported to the judges, who feared for their lives when they
heard Paul and Silas were Roman citizens. 39So they came to the jail and begged
them to go, and brought them out and pled with them to leave the city. 40Paul and
Silas then returned to the home of Lydia where they met with the believers and
preached to them once more before leaving town.

Paul preaches in Thessalonica

17 Now they traveled through the cities of Amphipolis and Apollonia and came
to Thessalonica, where there was a Jewish synagogue. 2As was Paul's
custom, he went there to preach, and for three Sabbaths in a row he opened the
Scriptures to the people, 3explaining the prophecies about the sufferings of the
Messiah and his coming back to life, and proving that Jesus is the Messiah. 4Some
who listened were persuaded and became converts—including a large number of
godly Greek men, and also many important women of the city.

5But the Jewish leaders were jealous and incited some worthless fellows from the
streets to form a mob and start a riot. They attacked the home of Jason, planning to
take Paul and Silas to the City Council for punishment.

6Not finding them there, they dragged out Jason and some of the other believers,

16:34
1 Sam 2:1,2
1 Chron 16:10
Ps 119:111
Rom 5:2
1 Pet 1:8

16:37
Mt 10:16
Acts 22:25-29

16:38
Acts 22:29

16:40
Acts 16:14,15

17:1
Phil 4:16
1 Thess 1:1
2 Thess 1:1

17:2
Acts 9:20
13:5,14; 14:1
17:10,17; 19:8

17:3
Lk 24:26
Acts 3:18; 9:22
18:5

17:5
Rom 16:21

17:6
Acts 16:20,21

17:4 *also many important women of the city.* Some manuscripts read, "many of the wives of the leading men."

16:37 Paul refused to take his freedom and run, in order to teach
the rulers in Philippi a lesson and to protect the other believers
from the treatment he and Silas had received. The word would
spread that Paul and Silas had been found innocent and freed by
the leaders, and that believers should not be persecuted—
especially if they were Roman citizens.

16:38 Roman citizenship carried with it certain privileges. These
Philippian authorities were frightened because it was illegal to whip
a Roman citizen. In addition, every citizen had the right to a fair
trial—which Paul and Silas had not been given.

17:1 Thessalonica was one of the wealthiest and most influential
cities in Macedonia. This is the first city Paul visited where his
teachings attracted a large group of socially prominent citizens.
The church he planted grew quickly, but in A.D. 50–51, Paul was
forced out of the city by a mob (17:5, 6, 10). Paul later sent Timothy
back to Thessalonica to see how the Christians were doing. Soon
afterward, Paul wrote 1 and 2 Thessalonians, two letters to the
Thessalonian believers, encouraging them to remain faithful and to
refuse to listen to false teachers who tried to refute their beliefs.

17:1, 2 A synagogue, a group of Jews who gathered for teaching
and prayer, could be established wherever there were ten Jewish
males. Paul's regular practice was to preach in synagogues as
long as the Jews allowed it. Often those who weren't Jews came to
these services and heard Paul's preaching. For what a synagogue
service was like, see the note on 13:14.

17:2, 3 When Paul spoke in the synagogues, he wisely began by
talking about Old Testament writings and explaining how the
Messiah fulfilled them, moving from the known to the unknown.
This is a good strategy for us. When we witness for Christ, we
should begin where people are, affirming the truth they do know,
and then present Christ, the One who is Truth.

17:5 The Jewish leaders didn't refute the theology of Paul and
Silas, but they were jealous of the popularity of these itinerant

**MINISTRY IN
MACEDONIA**
Luke stayed in
Philippi while
Paul, Silas, and
Timothy continued
on the Egnatian
Way to Amphipo-
lis, Apollonia, and
Thessalonica. But
trouble arose in
Thessalonica, and
they fled to Be-
roea. When their
enemies from
Thessalonica pur-
sued them, Paul
set out by sea to
Athens, leaving
Silas and Timothy
to encourage the
believers.

preachers. Their motives for causing the uproar were rooted in
personal jealousy, not doctrinal purity.

17:6 What a reputation these early Christians had; they truly
"turned the world upside down!" The power of the gospel
revolutionized lives, crossed all social barriers, threw open prison
doors, caused people to care deeply for one another, and stirred
them to worship God. Our world needs to be turned upside down,
to be transformed. The gospel is not in the business of merely
improving programs and conduct, but of dynamically transforming
lives.

and took them before the Council instead. "Paul and Silas have turned the rest of the world upside down, and now they are here disturbing our city," they shouted,

17:7
Lk 23:2

7"and Jason has let them into his home. They are all guilty of treason, for they claim another king, Jesus, instead of Caesar."

8, 9The people of the city, as well as the judges, were concerned at these reports and let them go only after they had posted bail.

Those at Beroea search the Scriptures

10That night the Christians hurried Paul and Silas to Beroea, and, as usual, they

17:10 *as usual*, implied.

LUKE

One of the essential qualities of a good doctor is compassion. People need to know that their doctor cares. Even if he or she doesn't know what is wrong or isn't sure what to do, real concern is always a doctor's good medicine. Doctor Luke was a person of compassion.

Although we know few facts of his life, Luke has left us a strong impression of himself by what he wrote. In his Gospel, he emphasizes Jesus Christ's compassion. He vividly recorded both the power demonstrated by Christ's life and the care with which he treated people. Luke highlighted the relationships Jesus had with women. His writing in Acts is full of sharp verbal pictures of real people caught up in the greatest events of history.

Luke was also a doctor. He had a traveling medical practice as Paul's companion. Since the gospel was often welcomed with whips and stones, the doctor was seldom without patients. It is even possible that Paul's "thorn in the flesh" was some kind of physical ailment that needed Luke's regular attention. Paul deeply appreciated Luke's skills and faithfulness.

God also made special use of Luke as the historian of the early church. Repeatedly, the details of Luke's descriptions have been proven accurate. The first words in his Gospel indicate his interest in the truth.

Luke's compassion reflected his Lord's. His skill as a doctor helped Paul. His passion for the facts as he recorded the life of Christ, the spread of the early church, and the lives of Christianity's missionaries gives us dependable sources for the basis of our faith. He accomplished all this while staying out of the spotlight. Perhaps his greatest example is the challenge to greatness even when we are not the center of attention.

Strengths and accomplishments:
- A humble, faithful, and useful companion of Paul
- A well-educated and trained physician
- A careful and exact historian
- Writer of both the Gospel of Luke and the Acts of the Apostles

Lessons from his life:
- The words we leave behind will be a lasting picture of who we are
- Even the most successful person needs the personal care of others
- Excellence is shown by how we work when no one is noticing

Vital statistics:
- Where: Probably met Paul in Troas
- Occupation: Doctor, historian, traveling companion
- Contemporaries: Paul, Timothy, Silas, Peter

Key verses:
"Dear friend who loves God: Several biographies of Christ have already been written using as their source material the reports circulating among us from the early disciples and other eyewitnesses. However, it occurred to me that it would be well to recheck all these accounts from first to last and after thorough investigation to pass this summary on to you, to reassure you of the truth of all you were taught" (Luke 1:1–4).

Luke includes himself in the *we* sections of Acts 16—28. He is also mentioned in Luke 1:3; Acts 1:1; Colossians 4:14; 2 Timothy 4:11; Philemon 24.

17:7 The Jewish leaders had difficulty manufacturing an accusation that would be heard by the city government. The Romans did not care about theological disagreements between the Jews and these preachers. Treason, however, was a serious offense in the Roman Empire. Although Paul and Silas were not advocating rebellion against Roman law, their loyalty to another king sounded suspicious.

17:8, 9 "Posting bail" was not the process we think of—putting up cash for freedom. Instead Jason had to promise that the trouble would cease or his own property and possibly his life would be taken.

went to the synagogue to preach. ¹¹But the people of Beroea were more open minded than those in Thessalonica, and gladly listened to the message. They searched the Scriptures day by day to check up on Paul and Silas' statements to see if they were really so. ¹²As a result, many of them believed, including several prominent Greek women and many men also.

17:11
Isa 34:16
Lk 16:29
Jn 5:39
Acts 26:22,23

¹³But when the Jews in Thessalonica learned that Paul was preaching in Beroea, they went over and stirred up trouble. ¹⁴The believers acted at once, sending Paul on to the coast, while Silas and Timothy remained behind. ¹⁵Those accompanying Paul went on with him to Athens, and then returned to Beroea with a message for Silas and Timothy to hurry and join him.

17:13
1 Thess 2:15
17:14
Mt 10:23
17:15
Acts 18:5
1 Thess 3:1

In Athens Paul tells about the unknown God

¹⁶While Paul was waiting for them in Athens, he was deeply troubled by all the idols he saw everywhere throughout the city. ¹⁷He went to the synagogue for discussions with the Jews and the devout Gentiles, and spoke daily in the public square to all who happened to be there.

17:16
Acts 18:1

¹⁸He also had an encounter with some of the Epicurean and Stoic philosophers. Their reaction, when he told them about Jesus and his resurrection, was, "He's a dreamer," or, "He's pushing some foreign religion."

17:18
1 Cor 1:20-24
4:10

¹⁹But they invited him to the forum at Mars Hill. "Come and tell us more about this new religion," they said, ²⁰"for you are saying some rather startling things and we want to hear more." ²¹(I should explain that all the Athenians as well as the foreigners in Athens seemed to spend all their time discussing the latest new ideas!)

²²So Paul, standing before them at the Mars Hill forum, addressed them as follows:

"Men of Athens, I notice that you are very religious, ²³for as I was out walking I saw your many altars, and one of them had this inscription on it—'To the Unknown God.' You have been worshiping him without knowing who he is, and now I wish to tell you about him.

17:23
Jn 4:22
2 Thess 2:4
17:24
1 Kgs 8:27
Isa 42:5
Acts 7:48,49

²⁴"He made the world and everything in it, and since he is Lord of heaven and earth, he doesn't live in man-made temples; ²⁵and human hands can't minister to his needs—for he has no needs! He himself gives life and breath to everything, and

17:25
Ps 50:10-12
Dan 4:35
Rom 11:36

17:11 How do you evaluate sermons and teachings? The people in Beroea opened the Scriptures for themselves and searched for truths to verify or disprove the message they heard. Always compare what you hear with what the Bible says. A preacher or teacher who gives God's true message will never contradict or explain away anything in God's Word.

17:15 Athens, with its magnificent buildings and many gods, was a center for Greek culture, philosophy, and education. Philosophers and educated men were always ready to hear something new, so they invited Paul to speak to them at Mars Hill.

17:18 The Epicureans and Stoics were the dominant philosophers in Greek culture. The Epicureans believed that seeking happiness or pleasure was the primary goal of life. By contrast, the Stoics placed thinking above feeling and tried to live in harmony with nature and reason, suppressing their desire for pleasure. Thus they were very disciplined.

17:19 At one time the supreme court met on Mars Hill. As Paul stood on Mars Hill and spoke about the one true God, his audience could look down on the city and see the many idols representing gods Paul claimed were worthless.

17:22 Paul was well prepared to speak to this group. He came from Tarsus, an educational center, and had the training and knowledge to present his beliefs clearly and persuasively. Paul was a rabbi, taught by the finest scholar of his day, Gamaliel, and he had spent much of his life thinking and reasoning through the Scriptures.

It is not enough to teach or preach with conviction. Like Paul, we must be prepared. The more we know about the Bible, what it means, and how to apply it to our lives, the more convincing our words will be. This does not mean we should avoid presenting the gospel until we feel adequately prepared. We should work with what we know, but always want to know more in order to reach more people and answer their questions and arguments more effectively.

17:22ff Paul's address is a good example of how to communicate the gospel. Paul did not begin by reciting Jewish history, as he usually did, for this would have been meaningless to his Greek audience. He began by building a case for the one true God, using examples they understood. Then he established common ground by emphasizing what they agreed about God (17:22, 23). Finally he moved his message to the person of Christ, centering on the resurrection (17:30, 31). When you witness to others, you can use Paul's approach: use examples, establish common ground, and then move people toward a decision about Jesus Christ.

17:23 The Athenians built an idol to the unknown god for fear of missing blessings or receiving punishment. Paul's opening statement to the men of Athens was about their unknown god. Paul was not endorsing this god, but using the inscription as a point of entry for his witness to the one true God.

17:23 Paul explained the one true God to these educated men of Athens; although they were, in general, very religious, they did not know him. Today we have a "Christian" society, but to most people, God is still unknown. We need to proclaim who he is and make it clear what he did for all mankind through his Son Jesus Christ. We cannot assume that even religious people around us truly know Jesus or understand the importance of faith in him.

17:26
Job 12:23; 14:5

17:27
Jer 23:23,24
Acts 14:17
Rom 1:20

17:28
Job 12:10
Dan 5:23
Col 1:17-19
Heb 1:3

17:29
Isa 40:18-25
Rom 1:23

17:30
Acts 14:16,17
Rom 3:25

17:31
Ps 96:13
Acts 2:24; 10:42
Rom 2:16; 4:25
1 Cor 15

satisfies every need there is. 26He created all the people of the world from one man, Adam, and scattered the nations across the face of the earth. He decided beforehand which should rise and fall, and when. He determined their boundaries.

27"His purpose in all of this is that they should seek after God, and perhaps feel their way toward him and find him—though he is not far from any one of us. 28For in him we live and move and are! As one of your own poets says it, 'We are the sons of God.' 29If this is true, we shouldn't think of God as an idol made by men from gold or silver or chipped from stone. 30God tolerated man's past ignorance about these things, but now he commands everyone to put away idols and worship only him. 31For he has set a day for justly judging the world by the man he has appointed, and has pointed him out by bringing him back to life again."

32When they heard Paul speak of the resurrection of a person who had been dead, some laughed, but others said, "We want to hear more about this later." 33That ended Paul's discussion with them, 34but a few joined him and became believers. Among them was Dionysius, a member of the City Council, and a woman named Damaris, and others.

The governor releases Paul at Corinth

18:2
Rom 16:3
1 Cor 16:19

18:3
Acts 20:34
1 Cor 4:12; 9:15
2 Cor 11:7

18:5
Acts 17:3
18:28

18:6
Ezek 3:18,19
Mt 10:14
27:24,25
Acts 13:46
20:26; 28:26-28

18:8
1 Cor 1:2,14

18:10
Isa 41:10
Jer 1:18
2 Tim 2:19

18 Then Paul left Athens and went to Corinth. 2, 3There he became acquainted with a Jew named Aquila, born in Pontus, who had recently arrived from Italy with his wife, Priscilla. They had been expelled from Italy as a result of Claudius Caesar's order to deport all Jews from Rome. Paul lived and worked with them, for they were tentmakers just as he was.

4Each Sabbath found Paul at the synagogue, trying to convince the Jews and Greeks alike. 5And after the arrival of Silas and Timothy from Macedonia, Paul spent his full time preaching and testifying to the Jews that Jesus is the Messiah. 6But when the Jews opposed him and blasphemed, hurling abuse at Jesus, Paul shook off the dust from his robe and said, "Your blood be upon your own heads—I am innocent—from now on I will preach to the Gentiles."

7After that he stayed with Titus Justus, a Gentile who worshiped God and lived next door to the synagogue. 8However, Crispus, the leader of the synagogue, and all his household believed in the Lord and were baptized—as were many others in Corinth.

9One night the Lord spoke to Paul in a vision and told him, "Don't be afraid! Speak out! Don't quit! 10For I am with you and no one can harm you. Many people

17:26 *Adam,* implied.

17:30, 31 Paul did not leave his message unfinished. He confronted his listeners with Jesus' resurrection and its meaning to all people—either blessing or punishment. The Greeks had no concept of judgment. Most of them preferred worshiping many gods over just one, and the concept of resurrection was unbelievable and offensive to them. Paul did not hold back the truth, however, no matter what they might think of it. He changed his approach to fit his audience, but he never changed his basic message.

17:32–34 Paul's speech received a mixed reaction: some laughed, some kept searching for more information, and a few believed. Don't hesitate to tell others about Christ because you fear that some will not believe you. And don't expect a unanimously positive response to your witnessing. Even if only a few believe, it's worth the effort.

18:1 Corinth was the political and commercial center of Greece, surpassing Athens in importance. It had a reputation for great wickedness and immorality. A temple to Aphrodite—goddess of love and war—had been built on the large hill behind the city. In this popular religion, people worshiped the goddess by giving money to the temple and taking part in sexual acts with male and female temple prostitutes. Paul found Corinth a challenge and a great ministry opportunity. Later, he wrote a series of letters to the Corinthians dealing in part with the problems of immorality. The Bible books of 1 and 2 Corinthians are two of those letters.

18:2, 3 Each Jewish boy learned a trade and tried to earn his living with it. Paul and Aquila had been trained in tentmaking, cutting and sewing the woven cloth of goat's hair into tents. Many tents were used to house soldiers, and so these tents may have been sold to the Roman army. As a tentmaker, Paul was able to go wherever God led him, carrying his livelihood with him. The word "tentmaker" in Greek was also used to describe a leather worker.

18:6 Paul told the Jews he had done all he could for them. Since they rejected Jesus as their Messiah, he would go to the Gentiles who would be more receptive.

18:10, 11 Others who became Christians in Corinth were Phoebe (Romans 16:1), Tertius (Romans 16:22), Erastus (Romans 16:23), Quartus (Romans 16:23), Chloe (1 Corinthians 1:11), Gaius (1 Corinthians 1:14), Stephanas and his household (1 Corinthians 16:15), Fortunatus (1 Corinthians 16:17), and Achaicus (1 Corinthians 16:17).

here in this city belong to me." ¹¹So Paul stayed there the next year and a half, teaching the truths of God.

¹²But when Gallio became governor of Achaia, the Jews rose in concerted action against Paul and brought him before the governor for judgment. ¹³They accused Paul of "persuading men to worship God in ways that are contrary to Roman law." ¹⁴But just as Paul started to make his defense, Gallio turned to his accusers and said, "Listen, you Jews, if this were a case involving some crime, I would be obliged to listen to you, ¹⁵but since it is merely a bunch of questions of semantics and personalities and your silly Jewish laws, you take care of it. I'm not interested and I'm not touching it." ¹⁶And he drove them out of the courtroom.

¹⁷Then the mob grabbed Sosthenes, the new leader of the synagogue, and beat him outside the courtroom. But Gallio couldn't have cared less.

18:12
Rom 15:26
1 Thess 1:7; 2:16

18:15
Acts 23:29
25:19

18:17
Acts 18:8
1 Cor 1:1

18:17 *Then the mob,* implied.

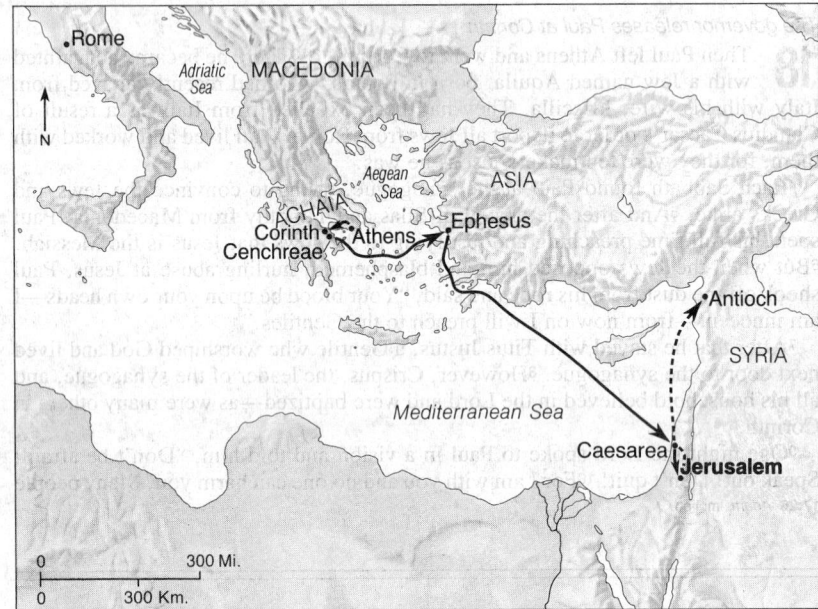

MINISTRY IN CORINTH AND EPHESUS
Paul left Athens and traveled on to Corinth, located on a narrow neck of land offering direct passage between the Aegean and Adriatic seas. When he left from the port of Corinth at Cenchreae, he visited Ephesus. He then traveled to Caesarea, from which he went on to Jerusalem to report on his trip before returning to Antioch.

18:11 During the year and a half that Paul stayed in wicked Corinth, he established a church there and wrote two letters to the believers in Thessalonica (the books of 1 and 2 Thessalonians). Although he had been in Thessalonica for only a short time (17:1–15), he commended the believers there for their loving deeds, strong faith, and steadfast hope. While encouraging them to stay away from immorality, he dealt with the themes of salvation, suffering, and the Second Coming of Jesus Christ. He told them to continue to work hard while they awaited Christ's return.

18:12 Gallio was governor of Achaia and the brother of Seneca the philosopher. He came to power in A.D. 51–52.

18:13 Paul was unjustly charged with treason. He was not encouraging obedience to a human king other than Caesar (see 17:7), nor was he speaking against the Roman empire. Instead he was speaking about the eternal Kingdom of Jesus Christ.

18:14–16 This was an important judicial decision for the spread of the gospel in the Roman empire. Judaism was a recognized

religion under Roman law. As long as Christians were seen as part of Judaism, the court refused to hear cases brought against them. If they had claimed to be a new religion, they could easily have been outlawed by the government.

18:17 Crispus had been the leader of the synagogue, but he and his family were converted and joined the Christians (18:8). Sosthenes was chosen to take his place. The mob could have been Greeks venting their feelings against the Jews for causing turmoil. Or they may have been Jews who beat Sosthenes for losing the case and leaving the synagogue worse off than before. A Sosthenes is mentioned in 1 Corinthians 1:1, and many believe this was the same man who, in time, became a convert and companion of Paul.

18:18 This was probably a temporary Nazirite vow that ended with shaving his head and offering the hair as a sacrifice (Numbers 6:18).

↘ *The return to Jerusalem and Antioch*

18:18
Num 6:2,18
Acts 18:2,26
21:24
Rom 16:1
1 Cor 9:20

18:19
Eph 1:1
Rev 1:11; 2:1

18Paul stayed in the city several days after that and then said good-bye to the Christians and sailed for the coast of Syria, taking Priscilla and Aquila with him. At Cenchreae, Paul had his head shaved according to Jewish custom, for he had taken a vow. 19Arriving at the port of Ephesus, he left us aboard ship while he went over to the synagogue for a discussion with the Jews. 20They asked him to stay for a few days, but he felt that he had no time to lose.

Some couples know how to make the most of life. They complement each other, utilize each other's strengths, and form an effective team. Their united efforts affect those around them. Aquila and Priscilla were such a couple. They are never mentioned apart from one another in the Bible. In marriage and ministry, they were always together.

Priscilla and Aquila met Paul in Corinth while Paul was on his second missionary journey. They had just been expelled from Rome by Emperor Claudius' decree against the Jews. The emperor expelled the Jews from Rome for rioting (apparently over questions about the Messiah). Their home was as movable as the tents they made to support themselves. They opened their home to Paul, and he joined them in tentmaking. He shared with them his wealth of spiritual wisdom.

Priscilla and Aquila made the most of their spiritual education. They listened carefully to sermons and evaluated what they heard. When they heard Apollos speak, they were impressed by his ability as an orator, but realized that the content of his message was not complete. Instead of open confrontation, the couple quietly took Apollos home and shared with him what he needed to know. Until then, Apollos had only known John the Baptist's message about Christ. Priscilla and Aquila told him about Jesus' life, death, and resurrection, and the reality of God's indwelling Spirit. Apollos continued to preach powerfully—but now with the full story.

As for Priscilla and Aquila, they went on using their home as a warm place for training and worship. Back in Rome years later, they hosted one of the house churches that developed. The early Christians did not meet in church buildings, but in the homes of its members. This informal atmosphere provided opportunity for intimate fellowship.

In an age when the focus is mostly on what happens *between* husband and wife, Aquila and Priscilla are an example of what can happen *through* husband and wife. Their effectiveness together speaks about their relationship with each other. Their hospitality opened the doorway of salvation to many. The Christian home is still one of the best tools for spreading the gospel. Do guests find Christ in your home?

Strengths and accomplishments:
• Outstanding husband/wife team who ministered in the early church
• Supported themselves by tentmaking while serving Christ
• Close friends of Paul
• Explained to Apollos the full message of Christ

Lessons from their lives:
• Couples can have an effective ministry together
• The home is a valuable tool for evangelism
• Every believer needs to be well educated in the faith, whatever his or her role in the church

Vital statistics:
• Where: Originally from Rome, moved to Corinth, then Ephesus
• Occupation: Tentmakers
• Contemporaries: Emperor Claudius, Paul, Timothy, Apollos

Key verses:
"Tell Priscilla and Aquila 'hello.' They have been my fellow workers in the affairs of Christ Jesus. In fact, they risked their lives for me; and I am not the only one who is thankful to them: so are all the Gentile churches" (Romans 16:3, 4).

Their story is told in Acts 18. They are also mentioned in Romans 16:3–5; 1 Corinthians 16:19; 2 Timothy 4:19.

AQUILA, PRISCILLA

21"I must by all means be at Jerusalem for the holiday," he said. But he promised to return to Ephesus later if God permitted; and so he set sail again.

18:21
Acts 19:1
Jas 4:15

22The next stop was at the port of Caesarea from where he visited the church [at Jerusalem] and then sailed on to Antioch.

18:22
Acts 8:40; 11:19

⟶ 4. Third missionary journey
Apollos is instructed at Ephesus

23After spending some time there, he left for Turkey again, going through Galatia and Phrygia visiting all the believers, encouraging them and helping them grow in the Lord.

18:23
Isa 35:3
Acts 16:6
Gal 1:2; 4:14

24As it happened, a Jew named Apollos, a wonderful Bible teacher and preacher, had just arrived in Ephesus from Alexandria in Egypt. 25, 26While he was in Egypt, someone had told him about John the Baptist and what John had said about Jesus, but that is all he knew. He had never heard the rest of the story! So he was preaching boldly and enthusiastically in the synagogue, "The Messiah is coming! Get ready to receive him!" Priscilla and Aquila were there and heard him—and it was a powerful sermon. Afterwards they met with him and explained what had happened to Jesus since the time of John, and all that it meant!

18:24
Acts 19:1
1 Cor 1:12
4:1,6; 16:12
Tit 3:13

18:25
Acts 18:2,18
19:3

18:27
1 Cor 3:6

27Apollos had been thinking about going to Greece, and the believers encouraged him in this. They wrote to their fellow-believers there, telling them to welcome him. And upon his arrival in Greece, he was greatly used of God to strengthen the church, 28for he powerfully refuted all the Jewish arguments in public debate, showing by the Scriptures that Jesus is indeed the Messiah.

18:28
Ps 22
Isa 7:14
9:6; 53
Jer 23:5,6
Dan 9:25,26
Mic 5:2
Mal 3:1
Lk 24:27

Christians in Ephesus receive the Holy Spirit

19 While Apollos was in Corinth, Paul traveled through Turkey and arrived in Ephesus, where he found several disciples. 2"Did you receive the Holy Spirit when you believed?" he asked them.

"No," they replied, "we don't know what you mean. What is the Holy Spirit?"
3"Then what beliefs did you acknowledge at your baptism?" he asked.

And they replied, "What John the Baptist taught."

4Then Paul pointed out to them that John's baptism was to demonstrate a desire to turn from sin to God and that those receiving his baptism must then go on to believe in Jesus, the one John said would come later.

5As soon as they heard this, they were baptized in the name of the Lord Jesus.
6Then, when Paul laid his hands upon their heads, the Holy Spirit came on them,

19:1
Acts 28:21

19:2
Jn 7:39
Acts 8:15,16

19:3
Lk 7:29
Acts 18:25,26

19:4
Acts 1:5; 11:16

19:5
Acts 8:12,16
10:48
Gal 3:27

19:6
Acts 2:4; 10:46

18:21 *holiday,* literally, "feast." This entire sentence is omitted in many of the ancient manuscripts.   **18:22** *at Jerusalem,* implied.   **18:26** *explained what had happened to Jesus since the time of John, and all that it meant!* Literally, "explained to him the way of God more accurately."   **19:5** *baptized in,* or, "baptized into."

18:21 This holiday was either Passover or Pentecost.

⟶ **18:22** This verse marks the end of Paul's second missionary journey and the beginning of the third, which lasted from A.D. 53–57. Leaving the church at Antioch (his home base), Paul headed toward Ephesus, but along the way he revisited the churches in Galatia and Phrygia. The heart of this trip was a lengthy stay (2 to 3 years) in Ephesus. Before returning to Jerusalem, he also visited believers in Macedonia and Greece.

18:25, 26 Apollos had heard only what John the Baptist had said about Jesus (see Luke 3:1–18), so his message was not the complete story. John focused on repentance from sin, the first step to faith in Christ. Apollos did not know about Jesus' life, crucifixion, and resurrection, nor did he know about the coming of the Holy Spirit. Priscilla and Aquila explained this to him.

18:27, 28 Apollos was from Alexandria in Egypt, the second largest city in the Roman Empire, home of a great university. He was a scholar, orator, and debater, and after his knowledge about Christ was made more complete, God greatly used these gifts to strengthen and encourage the church. Reason is a powerful tool in the right hands and the right situation. Apollos used it to convince many in Greece of the truth of the gospel. You don't have to turn off your mind when you turn to Christ. If you have an ability in logic or debate, use it to bring others to God.

18:27, 28 Not all the work of the minister or missionary is drudgery, setback, or suffering. Chapter 18 is triumphant, showing victories in key cities and the addition of exciting new leaders such as Priscilla, Aquila, and Apollos, to the church. Rejoice in the victories Christ brings, and don't let the hazards create a negative mindset.

and they spoke in other languages and prophesied. 7The men involved were about twelve in number.

Paul ministers powerfully in Ephesus

19:8
Acts 1:3; 28:23,31

8Then Paul went to the synagogue and preached boldly each Sabbath day for three months, telling what he believed and why, and persuading many to believe in Jesus. 9But some rejected his message and publicly spoke against Christ, so he left, refusing to preach to them again. Pulling out the believers, he began a separate meeting at the lecture hall of Tyrannus and preached there daily. 10This went on for the next two years, so that everyone in the Turkish province of Asia minor—both Jews and Greeks—heard the Lord's message.

19:10
Acts 16:6;
19:20,22
20:31

19:11
Mk 16:20

11And God gave Paul the power to do unusual miracles, 12so that even when his handkerchiefs or parts of his clothing were placed upon sick people, they were healed, and any demons within them came out.

19:12
2 Kgs 4:29
Jn 14:12
Acts 5:15

13A team of itinerant Jews who were traveling from town to town casting out demons planned to experiment by using the name of the Lord Jesus. The incantation they decided on was this: "I adjure you by Jesus, whom Paul preaches, to come

19:13
Mt 12:26-28
Mk 9:38,39
Lk 9:49,50
11:19

19:8 *each Sabbath day,* implied. *telling what he believed and why,* literally, "concerning the Kingdom of God."

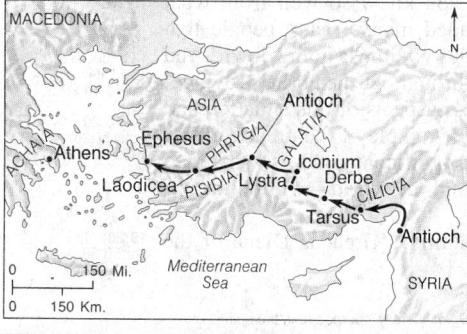

PAUL TAKES A THIRD JOURNEY What prompted Paul's third journey may have been the spread of his opponents' message in the churches Paul had planted. So he hurried north, then west, returning to many of the cities he had previously visited. This time, however, he stayed on a more direct westward route toward Ephesus.

19:1 Ephesus was the capital and leading business center of the Roman province of Asia (part of present-day Turkey). A hub of sea and land transportation, it ranked with Antioch in Syria and Alexandria in Egypt as one of the great cities on the Mediterranean Sea. Paul stayed in Ephesus for a little over two years. There he wrote his first letter to the Corinthians to counter several problems they were facing. Later, while imprisoned in Rome, Paul wrote a letter to the Ephesian church (the book of Ephesians).

19:2–4 John's baptism was a sign of repentance from sin only, not a sign of new life in Christ. Like Apollos (18:24–26), these Ephesian believers needed further instruction on the message and ministry of Jesus Christ. By faith they believed in Jesus as the Messiah, but they did not understand the significance of Jesus' death and resurrection or the work of the Holy Spirit. Therefore they had not experienced the presence and power of the Holy Spirit.

In the book of Acts, believers received the Holy Spirit in a variety of ways. Usually the Holy Spirit filled a person as soon as he or she professed faith in Christ. In this case, however, God allowed it to happen later. God was confirming to these believers,

who did not initially know about the Holy Spirit, that they too were a part of the church. The Holy Spirit's filling endorsed them as believers.

Pentecost was the formal outpouring of the Holy Spirit to the church. The other outpourings in the book of Acts were God's way of uniting new believers to the church. The mark of the true church is not merely right doctrine, but evidence of the Holy Spirit's working.

19:4 Paul was quick to point out that salvation requires repentance *and* faith. People need to be confronted with their sin and their need to repent, but this is only half the story. They must also accept the Good News of forgiveness and new life through Jesus.

19:6 When Paul laid his hands on these disciples, they received the Holy Spirit just as the disciples did at Pentecost. This also happened when the Holy Spirit came upon Gentiles, or non-Jews (10:46, 47).

19:9 Lecture halls were used in the morning for teaching philosophy, but were empty during the hot part of the day (about 11 a.m. to 4 p.m.). Since many people did not work during those hours, they came to hear Paul's preaching.

19:13 Many Ephesians engaged in exorcism and occult practices for profit, even sending demons from people (see 19:18, 19). The sons of Sceva were impressed by Paul's work, whose power to cast out demons came from God's Holy Spirit, not from witchcraft, and was obviously more powerful than theirs. They discovered, however, that one cannot control or duplicate God's power. These men were calling upon the name without knowing the person. The power to change people is in the person of Jesus Christ. It cannot be tapped by reciting his name like a magic charm. He works his power only through those he chooses.

out!" [14]Seven sons of Sceva, a Jewish priest, were doing this. [15]But when they tried it on a man possessed by a demon, the demon replied, "I know Jesus and I know Paul, but who are you?" [16]And he leaped on two of them and beat them up, so that they fled out of his house naked and badly injured.

[17]The story of what happened spread quickly all through Ephesus, to Jews and Greeks alike; and a solemn fear descended on the city, and the name of the Lord Jesus was greatly honored. [18, 19]Many of the believers who had been practicing black magic confessed their deeds and brought their incantation books and charms and burned them at a public bonfire. (Someone estimated the value of the books at $10,000.) [20]This indicates how deeply the whole area was stirred by God's message.

The tradesmen cause a riot

[21]Afterwards, Paul felt impelled by the Holy Spirit to go across to Greece before returning to Jerusalem. "And after that," he said, "I must go on to Rome!" [22]He sent his two assistants, Timothy and Erastus, on ahead to Greece while he stayed awhile longer in Asia minor.

[23]But about that time, a big blowup developed in Ephesus concerning the Christians. [24]It began with Demetrius, a silversmith who employed many craftsmen to manufacture silver shrines of the Greek goddess Diana. [25]He called a meeting of his men, together with others employed in related trades, and addressed them as follows:

"Gentlemen, this business is our income. [26]As you know so well from what you've seen and heard, this man Paul has persuaded many, many people that handmade gods aren't gods at all. As a result, our sales volume is going down! And this trend is evident not only here in Ephesus, but throughout the entire province! [27]Of course, I am not only talking about the business aspects of this situation and our loss of income, but also of the possibility that the temple of the great goddess Diana will lose its influence, and that Diana—this magnificent goddess worshiped not only throughout this part of Turkey but all around the world—will be forgotten!"

[28]At this their anger boiled and they began shouting, "Great is Diana of the Ephesians!"

19:15
Mt 8:29
Mk 1:24
Lk 4:34
Acts 16:16-18
Jas 2:19

19:17
Lk 7:16

19:18
Isa 30:22
Jer 3:13

19:20
Acts 6:7; 12:24
19:10

19:21
Acts 20:1,22
23:11
Rom 15:24-26
1 Cor 16:5

19:22
Acts 16:9
Rom 16:23
2 Tim 4:20

19:23
2 Cor 1:8

19:24
Acts 16:16,19

19:25
1 Tim 6:10

19:26
1 Chron 16:26
Ps 115:4
Isa 44:10-20
46:7
Jer 16:20
Acts 17:29
1 Cor 8:4

19:28
Jer 50:38
Hab 2:18-20

19:19 *$10,000,* approximately £3,500.   **19:21** *felt impelled by the Holy Spirit,* literally, "purposed in the spirit."

19:18, 19 Ephesus was considered a center for black magic and other occult practices. The people sought spells to give them wealth, happiness, and success in marriage. Superstition and sorcery were commonplace. God clearly forbids such practices (Deuteronomy 18:9–13). You cannot be a believer and hold onto the occult, black magic, or sorcery. Once you begin to dabble in these areas, it is extremely easy to become obsessed by them because Satan is very powerful. But God's power is even greater (1 John 4:4; Revelation 20:10). If you are mixed up in the occult, learn a lesson from the Ephesians and get rid of anything that lures you into such practices.

19:21 Why did Paul say he had to go to Rome? Wherever he went, he could see Rome's influence. Paul wanted to take the message of Christ to the world's center of influence and power.

19:22 Paul mentions Timothy in more detail in the books of 1 and 2 Timothy. Erastus was a committed follower of God who was not only Paul's helpful assistant, but also the city treasurer of Corinth (see Romans 16:23).

19:26 When Paul preached in Ephesus, Demetrius and his fellow shrinemakers did not quarrel with his doctrine. Their anger boiled because his preaching threatened their profits. They made statues

of the goddess Diana and her temple, and if people started believing in God and discarding their idols, their livelihood would suffer.

Jesus does not promise us escape from persecution, but a way through it. He also promises not to send us through it alone. He said, "I am with you always, even to the end of the world" (Matthew 28:20).

19:27 Demetrius' strategy for stirring up a riot was to appeal to the people's love of money and then hide their greed behind the mask of patriotism and religious loyalty. The rioters couldn't see the selfish motives for their rioting—instead they saw themselves as heroes for the sake of their land and beliefs.

19:29 Paul often sought others to help him in his work. On this occasion, his traveling companions were Aristarchus (who would accompany him on other journeys; see 20:3, 4 and 27:1, 2), and Gaius (probably not the same Gaius mentioned in Romans 16:23 or 1 Corinthians 1:14).

19:31 These men were not military officers, but government officials responsible for the religious and political order of the region. Paul's message had reached all levels of society, crossing all social barriers and giving Paul friends in high places.

19:29
Acts 20:4; 27:2
Rom 16:23
1 Cor 1:14
Col 4:10
Philem 24

19:32
Acts 21:34

29A crowd began to gather and soon the city was filled with confusion. Everyone rushed to the amphitheater, dragging along Gaius and Aristarchus, Paul's traveling companions, for trial. 30Paul wanted to go in, but the disciples wouldn't let him. 31Some of the Roman officers of the province, friends of Paul, also sent a message to him, begging him not to risk his life by entering.

32Inside, the people were all shouting, some one thing and some another—everything was in confusion. In fact, most of them didn't even know why they were there.

APOLLOS

Some people have an amazing natural talent for public speaking. A few even have a great message to go along with it. When Apollos arrived in Ephesus shortly after Paul's departure, he made an immediate impact. He spoke boldly in public, interpreting and applying the Old Testament Scriptures effectively. He debated opponents of Christianity forcefully and effectively. It didn't take long for him to be noticed by Priscilla and Aquila.

The couple quickly realized that Apollos did not have the whole story. His preaching was based on the Old Testament and John the Baptist's message. He was probably urging people to repent and prepare for the coming Messiah. Priscilla and Aquila took him home with them and brought him up to date on all that had happened. As they told him of the life of Jesus, his death and resurrection, and the coming of the Holy Spirit, Apollos must have seen Scripture after Scripture become clear. He was filled with new energy and boldness now that he had the complete gospel.

Apollos next decided to travel to Achaia. His friends in Ephesus were able to send along a glowing letter of introduction. He quickly became the verbal champion of the Christians in Corinth, debating the opponents of the gospel in public. As often happens, Apollos' abilities eventually created a problem. Some of the Corinthians began to follow Apollos rather than his message. Paul had to confront the Corinthians about their divisiveness. They had been forming little groups named after their favorite preacher. Apollos left Corinth and hesitated to return. Paul wrote warmly of Apollos as a fellow minister who had "watered" the seeds of the gospel that Paul had planted in Corinth. Paul last mentions Apollos briefly to Titus. He was still a traveling representative of the gospel who deserved Titus' help.

Although his natural abilities could have made him proud, Apollos proved himself willing to learn. God used Priscilla and Aquila, fresh from months of learning from Paul, to give Apollos the complete gospel. Because Apollos did not hesitate to be a student, he became an even better teacher. How much does your willingness to learn affect God's efforts to help you become all he wants you to be?

Strengths and accomplishments:
• A gifted and persuasive preacher and apologist in the early church
• Willing to be taught
• One of the possible candidates for the unknown author of Hebrews

Lessons from his life:
• Effective communication of the gospel includes an accurate message delivered with God's power
• A clear verbal defense of the gospel can be a real encouragement to believers, while convincing non-believers of its truth

Vital statistics:
• Where: From Alexandria in Egypt
• Occupation: Traveling preacher, apologist
• Contemporaries: Priscilla, Aquila, Paul

Key verses:
"While he was in Egypt, someone had told him about John the Baptist and what John had said about Jesus, but that is all he knew. He had never heard the rest of the story! So he was preaching boldly and enthusiastically in the synagogue, 'The Messiah is coming! Get ready to receive him!' Priscilla and Aquila were there and heard him—and it was a powerful sermon. Afterwards they met with him and explained what had happened to Jesus since the time of John, and all that it meant!" (Acts 18:25, 26).

Apollos' story is told in Acts 18:24–28; 19:1. He is also mentioned in 1 Corinthians 1:12; 3:4–6, 22; 4:1, 6; 16:12; Titus 3:13.

³³Alexander was spotted among the crowd by some of the Jews and dragged forward. He motioned for silence and tried to speak. ³⁴But when the crowd realized he was a Jew, they started shouting again and kept it up for two hours: "Great is Diana of the Ephesians! Great is Diana of the Ephesians!"

³⁵At last the mayor was able to quiet them down enough to speak. "Men of Ephesus," he said, "everyone knows that Ephesus is the center of the religion of the great Diana, whose image fell down to us from heaven. ³⁶Since this is an indisputable fact, you shouldn't be disturbed no matter what is said, and should do nothing rash. ³⁷Yet you have brought these men here who have stolen nothing from her temple and have not defamed her. ³⁸If Demetrius and the craftsmen have a case against them, the courts are currently in session and the judges can take the case at once. Let them go through legal channels. ³⁹And if there are complaints about other matters, they can be settled at the regular City Council meetings; ⁴⁰for we are in danger of being called to account by the Roman government for today's riot, since there is no cause for it. And if Rome demands an explanation, I won't know what to say."

⁴¹Then he dismissed them, and they dispersed.

Paul raises Eutychus from the dead at Troas

20 When it was all over, Paul sent for the disciples, preached a farewell message to them, said good-bye and left for Macedonia, ²preaching to the believers along the way, in all the cities he passed through. ³He was in Greece three months and was preparing to sail for Syria when he discovered a plot by the Jews against his life, so he decided to go north to Macedonia first.

⁴Several men were traveling with him, going as far as Turkey; they were Sopater of Beroea, the son of Pyrrhus; Aristarchus and Secundus, from Thessalonica; Gaius, from Derbe; and Timothy; and Tychicus and Trophimus, who were returning to their homes in Turkey, ⁵and had gone on ahead and were waiting for us at Troas. ⁶As soon as the Passover ceremonies ended, we boarded ship at Philippi in

19:35 *is the center,* literally, "is the temple-keeper."   **20:4** *Turkey,* literally, "Asia."

19:33
1 Tim 1:20
2 Tim 4:14

20:3
Acts 9:24; 20:19
23:12,13
2 Cor 11:26

20:4
Acts 16:1
19:22,29; 21:29
Eph 6:21
2 Tim 4:12,20
Tit 3:12

20:6
Ex 23:15
2 Cor 2:12

19:33, 34 The mob had become anti-Jewish as well as anti-Christian. This Alexander may have been pulled forward by the Jews as a spokesman to explain that the Jews had no part in the Christian community, and thus had no part in the economic problem of the silversmiths.

19:40 The city of Ephesus was under the domination of the Roman empire. The main responsibility of the local city leaders was simply to maintain peace and order. If they failed to control the people, Rome would remove them from office. An additional threat was that the entire town might be put under martial law, taking away many civic freedoms.

19:41 The riot in Ephesus showed Paul that it was time to move on, but it also showed that the law still provided some protection for Christians as they confronted the worship of the goddess Diana, the largest idolatrous religion in Asia.

20:1–3 While in Greece, Paul spent much of his time in Corinth. From there he wrote the letter to the Romans. Although he had not yet been to Rome, believers had already started a church there (2:10; 18:2), and Paul wrote that he planned to visit the Roman believers. The letter to the Romans is a theological essay on the meaning of salvation and faith, an explanation of the relation between Jews and Gentiles in Christ, and a list of practical guidelines for the church.

20:4 These men traveling with Paul represented churches he had started in Asia. Each man was carrying an offering from his home church to the believers in Jerusalem. Paul's strategy of having each man deliver the gift gave the gift a personal touch and promoted the unity of believers. It was also an effective way to

THROUGH MACEDONIA AND ACHAIA
A riot in Ephesus sent Paul to Troas, then through Macedonia to the region of Achaia. In Achaia he went to Corinth to deal with problems there. Paul had planned to sail from there straight to Antioch in Syria, but a plot against his life was discovered. So he retraced his steps through Macedonia.

teach the church about giving, for the men were able to report to their churches what they had seen. Paul discussed this gift in one of his letters to the Corinthian church (see 2 Corinthians 8:1–21).

20:6 Jewish believers celebrated the Passover according to Moses' instructions (see Exodus 12:43–51) even if they couldn't go to Jerusalem.

northern Greece and five days later arrived in Troas, Turkey, where we stayed a week.

7On Sunday, we gathered for a communion service, with Paul preaching. And since he was leaving the next day, he talked until midnight! 8The upstairs room where we met was lighted with many flickering lamps; 9and as Paul spoke on and on, a young man named Eutychus, sitting on the window sill, went fast asleep and fell three stories to his death below. 10, 11, 12Paul went down and took him into his arms. "Don't worry," he said, "he's all right!" And he was! What a wave of awesome joy swept through the crowd! They all went back upstairs and ate the Lord's Supper together; then Paul preached another long sermon—so it was dawn when he finally left them!

Paul's farewell to the elders of Ephesus

13Paul was going by land to Assos, and we went on ahead by ship. 14He joined us there and we sailed together to Mitylene; 15the next day we passed Chios; the next, we touched at Samos; and a day later we arrived at Miletus.

16Paul had decided against stopping at Ephesus this time, as he was hurrying to get to Jerusalem, if possible, for the celebration of Pentecost.

17But when we landed at Miletus, he sent a message to the elders of the church at Ephesus asking them to come down to the boat to meet him.

18When they arrived he told them, "You men know that from the day I set foot in Turkey until now 19I have done the Lord's work humbly—yes, and with tears—and have faced grave danger from the plots of the Jews against my life. 20Yet I never shrank from telling you the truth, either publicly or in your homes. 21I have had one message for Jews and Gentiles alike—the necessity of turning from sin to God through faith in our Lord Jesus Christ.

22"And now I am going to Jerusalem, drawn there irresistibly by the Holy Spirit, not knowing what awaits me, 23except that the Holy Spirit has told me in city after city that jail and suffering lie ahead. 24But life is worth nothing unless I use it for

20:7 Acts 2:42; 1 Cor 10:16,17; 11:20-34; 16:2; Rev 1:10

20:10 1 Kgs 17:21; 2 Kgs 4:34; Mt 9:23-25; Mk 5:39-42

20:15 Acts 21:4,12; 24:17; 2 Tim 4:20

20:18 Acts 18:19; 19:1,10

20:21 Lk 24:47; Acts 2:38; 11:18; 26:20

20:22 Acts 19:21

20:23 Acts 9:16; 21:4,11,33

20:24 Acts 21:13; 2 Tim 4:7

20:7 On Sunday, or, "on Saturday night." Literally, "the first day of the week," by Jewish reckoning, from sundown to sundown. **20:22** by the Holy Spirit, or, "by an inner compulsion."

20:7 A fellowship meal—much like a potluck supper—was eaten just before the Lord's Supper was celebrated with the breaking of bread and drinking of the cup (20:10–12).

20:16 Paul had missed attending the Passover feast in Jerusalem, so he was especially interested in arriving on time for Pentecost, which was 50 days after Passover. He was carrying with him gifts for the Jerusalem believers from churches in Asia and Greece (see Romans 15:25, 26; 1 Corinthians 16:1ff; 2 Corinthians 8, 9). The Jerusalem church was experiencing difficult times. Paul may have been anxious to deliver this gift to the believers at Pentecost because it was a day of celebration and thanksgiving to God for his provision.

20:18–21 The way of the believer is not an easy road; being a Christian does not solve all problems. Paul sowed humbly and "with tears," but he never quit, never gave up. The message of salvation was so important that he never missed an opportunity to share it. The Christian life will have its rough times, its tears, and its joys, but we should always be ready to tell others what good things God has done for us. His blessings far outweigh life's difficulties.

20:23 The Holy Spirit showed Paul that he would be imprisoned and would suffer. Even knowing this, Paul did not shrink from fulfilling his mission. His strong character was a good example to the Ephesian elders, some of whom would also suffer for Christ.

20:24 We often feel that life is a failure unless we're getting a lot out of it: recognition, fun, money, success. But Paul thought life was worth *nothing* unless he used it for God's work. What he put *into* life was far more important than what he got out. Which is more important to you—what you get out of life, or what you put into it?

PAUL TRAVELS FROM TROAS TO MILETUS
From Troas, Paul traveled overland to Assos, then boarded a ship to Mitylene and Samos on its way to Miletus. He summoned the elders of the Ephesian church to say farewell to them, for he knew he would probably not see them again.

20:24 Single-mindedness is a quality needed by anyone who wishes to do God's work. Paul was a single-minded person, and the single most important goal of his life was to tell others about Christ (Philippians 3:13). It is no wonder that Paul was the greatest missionary who ever lived. God is looking for more men and women who focus on that one great task God has given them.

doing the work assigned me by the Lord Jesus—the work of telling others the Good News about God's mighty kindness and love.

25"And now I know that none of you among whom I went about teaching the Kingdom will ever see me again. 26Let me say plainly that no man's blood can be laid at my door, 27for I didn't shrink from declaring all God's message to you.

28"And now beware! Be sure that you feed and shepherd God's flock—his church, purchased with his blood—for the Holy Spirit is holding you responsible as overseers. 29I know full well that after I leave you, false teachers, like vicious wolves, will appear among you, not sparing the flock. 30Some of you yourselves will distort the truth in order to draw a following. 31Watch out! Remember the three years I was with you—my constant watchcare over you night and day and my many tears for you.

32"And now I entrust you to God and his care and to his wonderful words which are able to build your faith and give you all the inheritance of those who are set apart for himself.

33"I have never been hungry for money or fine clothing— 34you know that these hands of mine worked to pay my own way and even to supply the needs of those who were with me. 35And I was a constant example to you in helping the poor; for I remembered the words of the Lord Jesus, 'It is more blessed to give than to receive.'"

36When he had finished speaking, he knelt and prayed with them, 37and they wept aloud as they embraced him in farewell, 38sorrowing most of all because he said that he would never see them again. Then they accompanied him down to the ship.

Paul continues to Jerusalem

21 After parting from the Ephesian elders, we sailed straight to Cos. The next day we reached Rhodes and then went to Patara. 2There we boarded a ship sailing for the Syrian province of Phoenicia. 3We sighted the island of Cyprus, passed it on our left and landed at the harbor of Tyre, in Syria, where the ship unloaded. 4We went ashore, found the local believers and stayed with them a week. These disciples warned Paul—the Holy Spirit prophesying through them—not to go on to Jerusalem. 5At the end of the week when we returned to the ship, the entire congregation including wives and children walked down to the beach with us where we prayed and said our farewells. 6Then we went aboard and they returned home.

7The next stop after leaving Tyre was Ptolemais where we greeted the believers, but stayed only one day. 8Then we went on to Caesarea and stayed at the home of Philip the Evangelist, one of the first seven deacons. 9He had four unmarried daughters who had the gift of prophecy.

21:9 *unmarried,* literally, "virgins."

Cross-references

20:26
Acts 18:6
20:28
Jn 21:15-17
1 Pet 1:19; 5:2
Rev 5:9
20:29
Ezek 22:27
Mt 7:15
Jn 10:10,12
20:31
Acts 19:10
20:32
Jn 17:17
Acts 9:31; 26:18
Eph 1:18
Col 3:24
1 Pet 1:4; 2:2
20:33
1 Sam 12:3
1 Cor 9:12
2 Cor 7:2
11:8,9; 12:17
20:34
1 Cor 4:12
1 Thess 2:9
2 Thess 3:8
20:35
2 Cor 8:9
1 Thess 4:11
5:14
Heb 13:1,3

21:4
Acts 20:23; 21:11
21:5
Acts 20:36
21:8
Acts 6:3,5
8:26,40
Eph 4:11
21:9
Joel 2:28
Acts 2:17

20:28 The Ephesian elders were told to feed the believers under their care by teaching them God's Word, and to shepherd them by being examples of God's love. All leaders of the church carry these two major responsibilities—to nourish others with God's truth and to exemplify God's truth at work in their lives. God's truth must be talked out and lived out.

20:31, 36-38 Paul's relationship with these believers is a beautiful example of Christian fellowship. He had cared for them and loved them, and even cried over their needs. They responded with love and care for him and sorrow over his leaving. They had prayed together and comforted one another. Like Paul, you can build strong relationships with other Christians by sharing, caring, sorrowing, rejoicing, and praying with them. You will gather others around you only by giving yourself away to them.

20:33 Paul was satisfied with whatever he had, wherever he was, as long as he could do God's work. Examine your attitudes toward wealth and comfort. If you focus more on what you don't have than on what you do have, it's time to reexamine your priorities and put God's work back in first place.

20:34 Paul worked to show he was free of covetousness, not to grow rich. He supported himself and others working with him (he also mentions this in some of his letters; see Philippians 4:11–13; 1 Thessalonians 2:9).

20:35 These words of Jesus are not recorded in the Gospels. Obviously, not all of Jesus' words were written down (John 21:25); this saying may have been passed on orally through the apostles.

21:4 Did Paul disobey the Holy Spirit by going to Jerusalem? Probably not. More likely, the Holy Spirit warned these believers about the suffering Paul would face in Jerusalem. They drew the conclusion that he should not go because of that danger. This is supported by 21:10–12 where the local believers, after hearing that Paul would be turned over to the Romans, beg him to turn back.

21:8 This is the Philip mentioned in Acts 6:5 and 8:26–40.

21:9 Obviously the gift of prophecy was given to both men and women. Women actively participated in God's work (2:17;

21:10
Acts 11:28

21:11
Acts 20:23; 21:3
Eph 6:20

[10]During our stay of several days, a man named Agabus, who also had the gift of prophecy, arrived from Judea [11]and visited us. He took Paul's belt, bound his own feet and hands with it and said, "The Holy Spirit declares, 'So shall the owner of this belt be bound by the Jews in Jerusalem and turned over to the Romans.' " [12]Hearing this, all of us—the local believers and his traveling companions—begged Paul not to go on to Jerusalem.

21:13
Acts 20:24
2 Cor 4:10
Col 1:24

21:14
Mt 26:42

[13]But he said, "Why all this weeping? You are breaking my heart! For I am ready not only to be jailed at Jerusalem, but also to die for the sake of the Lord Jesus." [14]When it was clear that he wouldn't be dissuaded, we gave up and said, "The will of the Lord be done."

[15]So shortly afterwards, we packed our things and left for Jerusalem. [16]Some disciples from Caesarea accompanied us, and on arrival we were guests at the home of Mnason, originally from Cyprus, one of the early believers; [17]and all the believers at Jerusalem welcomed us cordially.

5. Paul on trial

Paul arrives at Jerusalem

21:19
Rom 15:18

21:20
Acts 15:1,5
Gal 3:10,11

[18]The second day Paul took us with him to meet with James and the elders of the Jerusalem church. [19]After greetings were exchanged, Paul recounted the many things God had accomplished among the Gentiles through his work.

[20]They praised God but then said, "You know, dear brother, how many

PAUL RETURNS TO JERUSALEM
The ship sailed from Miletus to Cos, Rhodes, and Patara. Paul and his companions then boarded a cargo ship bound for Phoenicia. They passed Cyprus and landed at Tyre, then Ptolemais, and finally Caesarea, where Paul disembarked and returned by land to Jerusalem.

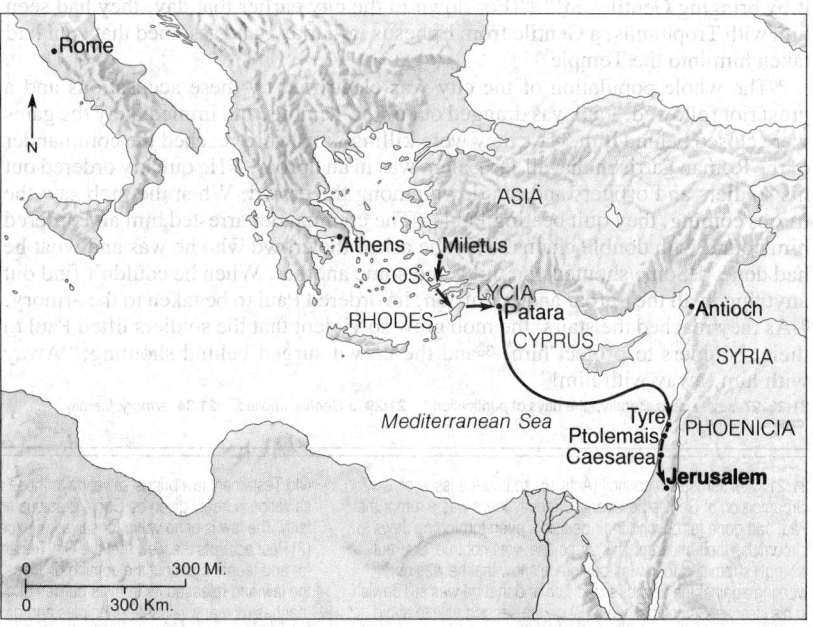

Philippians 4:3). Other women who prophesied include Miriam (Exodus 15:20), Deborah (Judges 4:4), Huldah (2 Kings 22:14), Noadiah (Nehemiah 6:14), Isaiah's wife (Isaiah 8:3), and Anna (Luke 2:36–38).

21:10 This is the Agabus who, 15 years earlier, had predicted the famine in Jerusalem (11:27–29).

21:13, 14 Paul knew he would be imprisoned in Jerusalem. His friends pleaded with him to not go there, but he knew he had to because God wanted him to. No one wants to face hardship or

suffering, but a faithful disciple wants above all else to please God. Our desire to please God should overshadow our desire to avoid hardship and suffering. When we really want to do God's will, we must accept all that comes with it—even the pain. Then we can say with Paul, "The will of the Lord be done."

21:18 James, Jesus' brother, was the leader of the Jerusalem church (15:13–21; Galatians 1:19; 2:9). He was called an apostle even though he wasn't one of the original 12 who followed Jesus.

thousands of Jews have also believed, and they are all very insistent that Jewish believers must continue to follow the Jewish traditions and customs. 21Our Jewish Christians here at Jerusalem have been told that you are against the laws of Moses, against our Jewish customs, and that you forbid the circumcision of their children. 22Now what can be done? For they will certainly hear that you have come.

21:21
Acts 16:3
Gal 2:3

23"We suggest this: We have four men here who are preparing to shave their heads and take some vows. 24Go with them to the Temple and have your head shaved too—and pay for theirs to be shaved.

21:23
Acts 18:18
21:24
Num 6:2,13-21
1 Cor 9:20

"Then everyone will know that you approve of this custom for the Hebrew Christians and that you yourself obey the Jewish laws and are in line with our thinking in these matters.

25"As for the Gentile Christians, we aren't asking them to follow these Jewish customs at all—except for the ones we wrote to them about: not to eat food offered to idols, not to eat unbled meat from strangled animals, and not to commit fornication."

21:25
Acts 15:19-29

26, 27So Paul agreed to their request and the next day went with the men to the Temple for the ceremony, thus publicizing his vow to offer a sacrifice seven days later with the others.

21:27
Acts 24:18
26:21
Rom 8:35
2 Cor 4:9
2 Tim 3:12

Paul is arrested at the Temple

The seven days were almost ended when some Jews from Turkey saw him in the Temple and roused a mob against him. They grabbed him, 28yelling, "Men of Israel! Help! Help! This is the man who preaches against our people and tells everybody to disobey the Jewish laws. He even talks against the Temple and defiles it by bringing Gentiles in!" 29(For down in the city earlier that day, they had seen him with Trophimus, a Gentile from Ephesus in Turkey, and assumed that Paul had taken him into the Temple.)

21:28
Mt 5:11
Lk 6:22; 11:49
21:12; 23:2
Jn 15:10
Acts 6:13
16:20,21; 17:6
24:5,6
1 Cor 4:12

30The whole population of the city was electrified by these accusations and a great riot followed. Paul was dragged out of the Temple, and immediately the gates were closed behind him. 31As they were killing him, word reached the commander of the Roman garrison that all Jerusalem was in an uproar. 32He quickly ordered out his soldiers and officers and ran down among the crowd. When the mob saw the troops coming, they quit beating Paul. 33The commander arrested him and ordered him bound with double chains. Then he asked the crowd who he was and what he had done. 34Some shouted one thing and some another. When he couldn't find out anything in all the uproar and confusion, he ordered Paul to be taken to the armory. 35As they reached the stairs, the mob grew so violent that the soldiers lifted Paul to their shoulders to protect him, 36and the crowd surged behind shouting, "Away with him, away with him!"

21:29
Acts 20:4
2 Tim 4:20
21:32
Acts 23:27
21:33
Acts 20:23; 28:20
Eph 6:20
21:36
Lk 23:18
Jn 19:15
Acts 22:22

21:26, 27 seven days, literally, "the days of purification."   **21:29** a Gentile, implied.   **21:34** armory, literally, "castle," or "fort."

21:21 The Jerusalem council (Acts 15) settled the issue of circumcision of Gentile believers. Evidently there was a rumor that Paul had gone far beyond their decision, even forbidding Jews to circumcise their children. This, of course, was not true. So Paul willingly submitted to Jewish custom to show that he was not working against the council's decision and that he was still Jewish in his lifestyle. Sometimes we must go the second mile to avoid offending others, especially when offending them would hinder the gospel.

21:23, 24 Paul submitted himself to this Jewish custom to keep peace in the Jerusalem church. Although Paul was a man of strong conviction, he was willing to compromise on nonessential points, becoming all things to all men that he might win some (1 Corinthians 9:19-23). Often a church is split over disagreements about minor issues or traditions. Like Paul, we should remain firm on Christian essentials but flexible on nonessentials. Of course, no one should violate his true convictions, but sometimes we need to exercise the gift of mutual submission for the sake of the gospel.

21:23, 24 There are two ways to think of the Jewish law. Paul rejects one and accepts the other. (1) Paul rejects the idea that

Old Testament law brings salvation to those who keep it. Our salvation is freely given by God's gracious act. We receive it by faith. The law is of no value for salvation except to show us our sin. (2) Paul accepts the view that the Old Testament laws prepared us for and taught us about the coming of Jesus Christ. Christ fulfilled the law and released us from its burden of guilt. But the law still teaches us many valuable principles and gives us guidelines for living. Paul was not observing the law for salvation. He was simply keeping the law as custom to avoid offending those he wished to reach with the gospel (see Romans 3:21-31; 7:4-6; 13:9, 10). For more on the law, see Galatians 3:23-29; 4:21-31.

21:28, 29 These men knew how effective Paul's work had been in Asia. Their strategy was to discredit Paul so his work would be weakened. Be alert when you hear accusations against God's workers. Someone may be trying to discredit them or to hinder their work. Keep an open mind and pray for the workers. They will be strengthened by your support.

21:31 Since Jerusalem was under Roman control, an uproar in the city would be investigated by Roman authorities. The ruler at this time was Claudius Lysias (23:26).

Paul speaks to the crowd

37, 38 As Paul was about to be taken inside, he said to the commander, "May I have a word with you?"

"Do you know Greek?" the commander asked, surprised. "Aren't you that Egyptian who led a rebellion a few years ago and took 4,000 members of the Assassins with him into the desert?"

39 "No," Paul replied, "I am a Jew from Tarsus in Cilicia which is no small town. I request permission to talk to these people."

40 The commander agreed, so Paul stood on the stairs and motioned to the people to be quiet; soon a deep silence enveloped the crowd, and he addressed them in Hebrew as follows:

22 "Brothers and fathers, listen to me as I offer my defense." 2(When they heard him speaking in Hebrew, the silence was even greater.) 3"I am a Jew," he said, "born in Tarsus, a city in Cilicia, but educated here in Jerusalem under Gamaliel, at whose feet I learned to follow our Jewish laws and customs very carefully. I became very anxious to honor God in everything I did, just as you have tried to do today. 4And I persecuted the Christians, hounding them to death, binding and delivering both men and women to prison. 5The High Priest or any member of the Council can testify that this is so. For I asked them for letters to the Jewish leaders in Damascus, with instructions to let me bring any Christians I found to Jerusalem in chains to be punished.

6"As I was on the road, nearing Damascus, suddenly about noon a very bright light from heaven shone around me. 7And I fell to the ground and heard a voice saying to me, 'Saul, Saul, why are you persecuting me?'

8" 'Who is it speaking to me, sir?' I asked. And he replied, 'I am Jesus of Nazareth, the one you are persecuting.' 9The men with me saw the light but didn't understand what was said.

10"And I said, 'What shall I do, Lord?'

"And the Lord told me, 'Get up and go into Damascus, and there you will be told what awaits you in the years ahead.'

11"I was blinded by the intense light, and had to be led into Damascus by my companions. 12There a man named Ananias, as godly a man as you could find for obeying the law, and well thought of by all the Jews of Damascus, 13came to me, and standing beside me said, 'Brother Saul, receive your sight!' And that very hour I could see him!

14"Then he told me, 'The God of our fathers has chosen you to know his will and to see the Messiah and hear him speak. 15You are to take his message everywhere, telling what you have seen and heard. 16And now, why delay? Go and be baptized, and be cleansed from your sins, calling on the name of the Lord.'

17, 18"One day after my return to Jerusalem, while I was praying in the Temple, I fell into a trance and saw a vision of God saying to me, 'Hurry! Leave Jerusalem, for the people here won't believe you when you give them my message.'

19" 'But Lord,' I argued, 'they certainly know that I imprisoned and beat those in

21:37, 38 *a few years ago,* literally, "before these days." 22:14 *Messiah,* literally, "Righteous One."

21:39
Acts 9:11
2 Cor 11:22
Gal 3:5
1 Pet 3:15; 4:16
21:40
Acts 26:14

22:3
Acts 5:34-40
26:5
Rom 10:2
2 Cor 11:22
Gal 1:14
Phil 3:5
22:4
Acts 8:3
1 Tim 1:13
22:5
Acts 9:2,3

22:6
Acts 9:3-8
26:12,13

22:8
Acts 26:15
22:9
Dan 10:7
Acts 9:7; 26:13

22:11
Acts 9:8
22:12,13
Acts 9:10,17,18
22:14
Acts 3:13; 26:16
1 Cor 9:1; 15:8
Gal 1:12
22:15
Acts 26:16
22:16
Ps 116:13
Acts 2:38
Rom 10:13
1 Cor 6:11
Heb 10:22
22:19
Acts 8:3; 22:4
26:11

21:37, 38 By speaking in Greek, Paul showed that he was a cultured man and not just a common rebel starting riots in the streets. The language grabbed the commander's attention and gave Paul protection and the opportunity to give his defense.

21:37, 38 The historian Josephus tells of an Egyptian who led a revolt of 4,000 people in Jerusalem in A.D. 54 and then disappeared. The commander assumed that Paul was this rebel.

22:1, 2 Paul was speaking in Hebrew, the language of the Old Testament. He spoke this language not only to communicate in the language of his listeners, but also to show that he was a devout Jew, had respect for the Jewish laws and customs, and was learned in Hebrew. Paul spoke Greek to the Roman officials and Hebrew to the Jews. If you want to minister to people with maximum effectiveness, you must be able to use their language.

22:3 Gamaliel was the most honored rabbi of the first century. He was well known and respected as an expert on religious law (5:34) and as a voice for moderation. Paul was showing his credentials as a well-educated man trained under the most respected Jewish rabbi.

22:3 When Paul said "just as you have tried to do today," he acknowledged their sincere motives in trying to kill him and recognized that he would have done the same to Christian leaders a few years earlier. Paul always tried to establish a common point of contact with his audience before launching into a full-scale defense of Christianity. When you witness for Christ, first identify yourself with your audience. They are much more likely to listen to you if they feel a common bond with you.

every synagogue who believed on you. 20And when your witness Stephen was
killed, I was standing there agreeing—keeping the coats they laid aside as they
stoned him.'

21"But God said to me, 'Leave Jerusalem, for I will send you far away to the
Gentiles!' "

22The crowd listened until Paul came to that word, then with one voice they
shouted, "Away with such a fellow! Kill him! He isn't fit to live!" 23They yelled
and threw their coats in the air and tossed up handfuls of dust.

22:20
Acts 7:58-8:1

22:21
Acts 13:2; 18:6
26:17
Rom 15:15,16
1 Tim 2:7

22:22
Acts 21:36
25:24

Paul reveals his Roman citizenship

24So the commander brought him inside and ordered him lashed with whips to
make him confess his crime. He wanted to find out why the crowd had become so
furious!

25As they tied Paul down to lash him, Paul said to an officer standing there, "Is
it legal for you to whip a Roman citizen who hasn't even been tried?"

26The officer went to the commander and asked, "What are you doing? This man
is a Roman citizen!"

27So the commander went over and asked Paul, "Tell me, are you a Roman
citizen?"

"Yes, I certainly am."

28"I am too," the commander muttered, "and it cost me plenty!"

"But I am a citizen by birth!"

29The soldiers standing ready to lash him, quickly disappeared when they heard
Paul was a Roman citizen, and the commander was frightened because he had
ordered him bound and whipped.

22:25
Acts 16:37

22:29
Acts 16:38

Paul appears before the Sanhedrin

30The next day the commander freed him from his chains and ordered the chief
priests into session with the Jewish Council. He had Paul brought in before them to
try to find out what the trouble was all about.

23 Gazing intently at the Council, Paul began:
"Brothers, I have always lived before God in all good conscience!"

2Instantly Ananias the High Priest commanded those close to Paul to slap him on
the mouth.

3Paul said to him, "God shall slap you, you whitewashed pigpen. What kind of
judge are you to break the law yourself by ordering me struck like that?"

4Those standing near Paul said to him, "Is that the way to talk to God's High
Priest?"

5"I didn't realize he was the High Priest, brothers," Paul replied, "for the
Scriptures say, 'Never speak evil of any of your rulers.' "

6Then Paul thought of something! Part of the Council were Sadducees, and part

23:1
1 Cor 4:4
2 Cor 1:12; 4:2
Heb 13:18

23:2
Jn 18:22
Acts 24:1

23:3
Lev 19:15
Ezek 13:10-15
Jn 7:51

23:5
Ex 22:28

23:3 *you whitewashed pigpen,* literally, "you whitewashed wall."

22:21, 22 These people listened intently to Paul, waiting to trap
and accuse him. The word *Gentile* brought out all their anger and
pride. They were supposed to be a light to the Gentiles, telling
them about the one true God. But they had renounced that mission
by becoming separatist and exclusive. God's plan, however, was
not thwarted; the Gentiles would hear the Good News through
Jewish Christians such as Paul and Peter.

22:25 Paul's question stopped the officers because, by law, a
Roman citizen could not be whipped until he had been proven
guilty of a crime. Paul was born a Roman citizen, whereas the
commander had bought his citizenship. Buying citizenship was a
common practice and a good source of money for the Roman
government, but bought citizenship was considered inferior to
citizenship by birth.

22:30 God used Paul's persecution as an opportunity for him to
witness. Now even his enemies were creating a platform for him to

address the entire Jewish Council. If we are sensitive to the Holy
Spirit's leading, we will notice increased opportunities to share our
faith, even in the heat of opposition.

23:2, 3 Josephus, a respected first-century historian, described
Ananias as profane, greedy, and hot tempered. Paul's outburst
came as a result of the illegal command Ananias had given. He
had violated Jewish law by assuming that Paul was guilty without a
trial and ordering his punishment (see Deuteronomy 19:15). Paul
didn't recognize Ananias as the High Priest, probably because
Ananias' command broke the law he was pledged to represent.
We are pledged to represent Christ. When those around us say, "I
didn't know you were a Christian," we have failed to represent him
as we should. As Christians, we are not merely Christ's followers;
we are Christ's representatives to others, as the High Priest was
the law's representative to the people.

23:6 The Sadducees and Pharisees were both religious leaders,

were Pharisees! So he shouted, "Brothers, I am a Pharisee, as were all my ancestors! And I am being tried here today because I believe in the resurrection of the dead!"

7This divided the Council right down the middle—the Pharisees against the Sadducees— 8for the Sadducees say there is no resurrection or angels or even eternal spirit within us, but the Pharisees believe in all of these.

9So a great clamor arose. Some of the Jewish leaders jumped up to argue that Paul was all right. "We see nothing wrong with him," they shouted. "Perhaps a spirit or angel spoke to him [there on the Damascus road]."

10The shouting grew louder and louder, and the men were tugging at Paul from both sides, pulling him this way and that. Finally the commander, fearing they would tear him apart, ordered his soldiers to take him away from them by force and bring him back to the armory.

11That night the Lord stood beside Paul and said, "Don't worry, Paul; just as you have told the people about me here in Jerusalem, so you must also in Rome."

The plan to kill Paul

12, 13The next morning some forty or more of the Jews got together and bound themselves by a curse neither to eat nor drink until they had killed Paul! 14Then they went to the chief priests and elders and told them what they had done. 15"Ask the

23:8 Mt 22:23
Mk 12:18
Lk 20:27
Acts 24:5

23:9 Prov 16:7
Jn 12:29
Acts 5:39; 22:7

23:11 Ps 46:1
Isa 41:10; 43:2
Acts 18:9
22:1-21
27:23

23:12 Acts 9:23

23:15 Ps 37:32

23:8 or even eternal spirit within us, literally, "nor spirit." **23:9** Jewish leaders, literally, "scribes." there on the Damascus road, implied.

UNSUNG HEROES IN ACTS
When we think of the success of the early church, we often think of the work of the apostles. But the church could have died if it hadn't been for the "unsung" heroes, the men and women who through some small but committed act moved the church forward.

Hero	Reference	Heroic action
Lame beggar	3:9–12	After his healing, he praised God. With the crowds gathering to see what happened, Peter used the opportunity to tell many about Jesus.
Five deacons	6:2–5	Everyone knows Stephen and many people know Philip, but there were five other men chosen to be deacons. They not only laid the foundation for service in the church, but their hard work gave the apostles the time they needed to preach the gospel.
Ananias	9:10–19	He had the responsibility of being the first to demonstrate Christ's love to Paul after his conversion.
Cornelius	10:34, 35	His example showed Peter that the gospel was for *all* people, Jews and Gentiles.
Rhoda	12:13–15	Her persistence brought Peter inside Mary's home where he would be safe.
James	15:13–21	He took command of the Jerusalem council and had the courage and discernment to make a decision that would affect literally millions of Christians over generations.
Lydia	16:13–15	Opened her home to Paul from which he led many to Christ and founded a church in Philippi.
Jason	17:5–7	Risked his life for the gospel by allowing Paul to stay in his home. He stood up for what was true and right, even though he faced persecution for it.
Paul's nephew	23:16–24	Saved Paul's life by telling officials of a plot to murder Paul.
Julius	27:43	Spared Paul's life when the other soldiers wanted to kill him.

---

but with strikingly different beliefs. While the Pharisees believed in a bodily resurrection, the Sadducees did not because they adhered only to the Old Testament books of Genesis through Deuteronomy, which contain no explicit teaching on resurrection. Paul's words moved the debate away from himself and toward their raging controversy about the resurrection. The Jewish Council was split.

23:6 Paul's sudden insight is an example of the power Jesus promised to believers (Mark 13:9–11). God will help us when we

are under fire for our faith. Like Paul, we should always be ready to present our testimony. The Holy Spirit will give us power to speak boldly.

23:14, 15 When the Pharisee-Sadducee controversy died down, the religious leaders refocused their attention on Paul. To these leaders, politics and position had become more important than God. They were ready to plan another murder, as they had done with Jesus. But as always, God was in control.

commander to bring Paul back to the Council again," they requested. "Pretend you want to ask a few more questions. We will kill him on the way."

16But Paul's nephew got wind of their plan and came to the armory and told Paul.

17Paul called one of the officers and said, "Take this boy to the commander. He has something important to tell him."

18So the officer did, explaining, "Paul, the prisoner, called me over and asked me to bring this young man to you to tell you something."

19The commander took the boy by the hand, and leading him aside asked, "What is it you want to tell me, lad?"

20"Tomorrow," he told him, "the Jews are going to ask you to bring Paul before the Council again, pretending they want to get some more information. 21But don't do it! There are more than forty men hiding along the road ready to jump him and kill him. They have bound themselves under a curse to neither eat nor drink till he is dead. They are out there now, expecting you to agree to their request."

22"Don't let a soul know you told me this," the commander warned the boy as he left.

Paul is sent to Caesarea

23, 24Then the commander called two of his officers and ordered, "Get 200 soldiers ready to leave for Caesarea at nine o'clock tonight! Take 200 spearmen and 70 mounted cavalry. Give Paul a horse to ride and get him safely to Governor Felix."

25Then he wrote this letter to the governor:

26"*From:* Claudius Lysias

"*To:* His Excellency, Governor Felix.

"Greetings!

27"This man was seized by the Jews and they were killing him when I sent the soldiers to rescue him, for I learned that he was a Roman citizen. 28Then I took him to their Council to try to find out what he had done. 29I soon discovered it was something about their Jewish beliefs, certainly nothing worthy of imprisonment or death. 30But when I was informed of a plot to kill him, I decided to send him on to you and will tell his accusers to bring their charges before you."

31So that night, as ordered, the soldiers took Paul to Antipatris. 32They returned

23:16
Job 5:12,13

23:21
Ps 10:9
37:12,13,32

23:27
Acts 21:33
22:25-29
23:28
Acts 22:30
23:29
Acts 18:15
25:19; 26:31
28:18
23:30
Acts 24:8,19
25:16

IMPRISONMENT IN CAESAREA
Paul brought news of his third journey to the elders of the Jerusalem church, who rejoiced at his ministry. But Paul's presence soon stirred up the Jews, who persuaded the Romans to arrest him. A plot to kill Paul was uncovered, so Paul was taken by night to Antipatris, then transferred to the provincial prison in Caesarea.

[Map: Mediterranean Sea, Sea of Galilee, Jordan River, Caesarea, Antipatris, Jerusalem, Dead Sea; 0 20 Mi., 0 20 Km.]

23:16-22 It is easy to overlook children, assuming that they aren't old enough to do much for the Lord. But a young boy played an important part in protecting Paul's life. God can use anyone, of any age, who is willing to yield to him. Jesus made it clear that children are important (Matthew 18:2-6). Do you give children the importance God gives them?

23:23, 24 The Roman commander ordered Paul sent to Caesarea. Jerusalem was the seat of Jewish government, but Caesarea was the Roman headquarters for the area. God works in amazing and amusing ways. God chose to use the Roman army to deliver Paul from his enemies. God's ways are not our ways—ours are limited, his are not. Don't limit God by asking him to respond your way. When God intervenes, anything can happen, much more and much better than you can anticipate.

23:26 Felix was the Roman procurator or governor of Judea from A.D. 52 to 59. This was the same position Pontius Pilate had held. While the Jews were given much freedom to govern themselves, the governor ran the army, kept the peace, and gathered the taxes.

23:26 How did Luke know what was written in the letter from Claudius Felix? In his concern for historical accuracy, Luke used many documents to make sure his writings were correct (see Luke 1:1-4). This letter was probably read aloud in court when Paul came before Felix to answer the Jews' accusations. Also, a copy may have been given to Paul as a courtesy, because he was a Roman citizen.

to the armory the next morning, leaving him with the cavalry to take him on to Caesarea.

23:33
Acts 8:40
23:34
Acts 21:39
23:35
Acts 24:1,19
25:16

33When they arrived in Caesarea, they presented Paul and the letter to the governor. 34He read it and then asked Paul where he was from.

"Cilicia," Paul answered.

35"I will hear your case fully when your accusers arrive," the governor told him, and ordered him kept in the prison at King Herod's palace.

Paul appears before Felix

24:1
Acts 21:26,27
23:2,24-30

24 Five days later Ananias the High Priest arrived with some of the Jewish leaders and the lawyer Tertullus, to make their accusations against Paul. 2When Tertullus was called forward, he laid charges against Paul in the following address to the governor:

"Your Excellency, you have given quietness and peace to us Jews and have greatly reduced the discrimination against us. 3And for this we are very, very grateful to you. 4But lest I bore you, kindly give me your attention for only a moment as I briefly outline our case against this man. 5For we have found him to be a troublemaker, a man who is constantly inciting the Jews throughout the entire world to riots and rebellions against the Roman government. He is a ringleader of the sect known as the Nazarenes. 6Moreover, he was trying to defile the Temple when we arrested him.

24:5
Mt 5:11
Lk 23:2
Jn 15:20
Acts 16:20,21
17:6; 24:14
1 Thess 2:14-16
2 Tim 3:2
1 Pet 2:12,19
24:6
Jn 18:31
Acts 21:28
24:7
Acts 21:33
24:8
Acts 23:30

"We would have given him what he justly deserves, 7but Lysias, the commander of the garrison, came and took him violently away from us, 8demanding that he be tried by Roman law. You can find out the truth of our accusations by examining him yourself."

9Then all the other Jews chimed in, declaring that everything Tertullus said was true.

24:11
Acts 21:26,27

10Now it was Paul's turn. The governor motioned for him to rise and speak.

24:12
Acts 15:8
24:13
Acts 15:7
24:14
Lk 24:27
Acts 9:2; 26:22
2 Tim 1:3

Paul began: "I know, sir, that you have been a judge of Jewish affairs for many years, and this gives me confidence as I make my defense. 11You can quickly discover that it was no more than twelve days ago that I arrived in Jerusalem to worship at the Temple, 12and you will discover that I have never incited a riot in any synagogue or on the streets of any city; 13and these men certainly cannot prove the things they accuse me of doing.

24:15
Dan 12:2
Mt 22:31,32
Jn 5:28,29
Acts 23:6
26:6-8
1 Thess 4:14
Rev 20:12
24:16
Acts 23:1

14"But one thing I do confess, that I believe in the way of salvation, which they refer to as a sect; I follow that system of serving the God of our ancestors; I firmly believe in the Jewish law and everything written in the books of prophecy; 15and I believe, just as these men do, that there will be a resurrection of both the righteous and ungodly. 16Because of this I try with all my strength to always maintain a clear conscience before God and man.

24:17
Acts 11:29
Rom 15:25-28
1 Cor 16:3
2 Cor 8:4
24:18
Acts 21:26,27

17"After several years away, I returned to Jerusalem with money to aid the Jews, and to offer a sacrifice to God. 18My accusers saw me in the Temple as I was presenting my thank offering. I had shaved my head as their laws required, and there was no crowd around me, and no rioting! But some Jews from Turkey were there 19(who ought to be here if they have anything against me)— 20but look! Ask

24:1 *Jewish leaders,* literally, "elders." *lawyer,* literally, "orator."   24:18 *as I was presenting my thank offering,* implied.

24:1 The accusers arrived—Ananias, the High Priest; Tertullus, the lawyer; and several Jewish leaders. They traveled 60 miles to Caesarea, the Roman center of government, to give their false accusations against Paul. Their murder plot had failed (23:12–15), but they persisted in trying to kill him. This attempted murder was both premeditated and persistent.

24:2ff Tertullus was a special orator called to present the religious leaders' case before the Roman governor. He made three accusations against Paul: (1) he was a renegade, inciting the Jews around the world; (2) he was the ringleader of an unrecognized religious sect, which was against Roman law; and (3) he had profaned the Temple. The religious leaders hoped that these accusations would persuade Felix to execute Paul to keep the peace in Palestine.

24:10ff Tertullus and the religious leaders seemed to have a strong argument against Paul, but Paul refuted their accusation point by point. Paul was also able to present the gospel message through his defense. Paul's accusers were unable to present specific evidence to support their general accusations. For example, Paul was accused of starting trouble among the Jews in Turkey, but the Jews in Turkey were not present to confirm this.

these men right here what wrongdoing their Council found in me, 21except that I
said one thing I shouldn't when I shouted out, 'I am here before the Council to
defend myself for believing that the dead will rise again!' "

24:21
Acts 23:6

22Felix, who knew Christians didn't go around starting riots, told the Jews to
wait for the arrival of Lysias, the garrison commander, and then he would decide
the case. 23He ordered Paul to prison but instructed the guards to treat him gently
and not to forbid any of his friends from visiting him or bringing him gifts to make
his stay more comfortable.

24:23
Acts 27:3; 28:16

24A few days later Felix came with Drusilla, his legal wife, a Jewess. Sending for
Paul, they listened as he told them about faith in Christ Jesus. 25And as he reasoned
with them about righteousness and self-control and the judgment to come, Felix
was terrified.

24:25
Acts 10:42
Gal 5:23
Tit 2:12
2 Pet 1:6

"Go away for now," he replied, "and when I have a more convenient time, I'll
call for you again."

26He also hoped that Paul would bribe him, so he sent for him from time to time
and talked with him. 27Two years went by in this way; then Felix was succeeded by
Porcius Festus. And because Felix wanted to gain favor with the Jews, he left Paul
in chains.

24:26
Acts 24:17
24:27
Acts 25:9,
24-27; 26:24

Paul appears before Festus

25 Three days after Festus arrived in Caesarea to take over his new responsibilities, he left for Jerusalem, 2where the chief priests and other Jewish leaders
got hold of him and gave him their story about Paul. 3They begged him to bring
Paul to Jerusalem at once. (Their plan was to waylay and kill him.) 4But Festus
replied that since Paul was at Caesarea and he himself was returning there soon,
5those with authority in this affair should return with him for the trial.

25:2
Acts 23:12-21
24:1

6Eight or ten days later he returned to Caesarea and the following day opened
Paul's trial.

7On Paul's arrival in court the Jews from Jerusalem gathered around, hurling
many serious accusations which they couldn't prove. 8Paul denied the charges: "I
am not guilty," he said. "I have not opposed the Jewish laws or desecrated the
Temple or rebelled against the Roman government."

25:7
Esth 3:8
Acts 24:13,27
25:8
Acts 6:13
24:12; 28:17
Rom 13:1-7

9Then Festus, anxious to please the Jews, asked him, "Are you willing to go to
Jerusalem and stand trial before me?"

10, 11But Paul replied, "No! I demand my privilege of a hearing before the
Emperor himself. You know very well I am not guilty. If I have done something
worthy of death, I don't refuse to die! But if I am innocent, neither you nor anyone
else has a right to turn me over to these men to kill me. *I appeal to Caesar.*"

25:10
Acts 25:21
26:32
25:11
Acts 23:11
27:24; 28:19

24:21 *except that I said one thing I shouldn't,* literally, "except it be for this one voice." **24:22** *who knew Christians
didn't go around starting riots,* literally, "having more accurate knowledge." **24:24** *his legal wife,* literally, "his own
wife."

24:22 Felix had been governor for six years and would have
known about the Christians, a topic of conversation among the
Roman leaders. The Christians' peaceful lifestyles had shown the
Romans that "Christians didn't go around starting riots."

24:25 Paul's talk with Felix became so personal that Felix felt
convicted. Felix, like Herod Antipas (Mark 6:17, 18), had taken
another man's wife. Paul's words were interesting until they
focused on "righteousness and self-control and the judgment to
come." Many people will be glad to discuss the gospel with you as
long as it doesn't touch their lives too personally. When it does,
some will resist or run away. But this is what the gospel is all
about—God's power to change lives. The gospel is not effective
until it moves from principles and doctrine into a life-changing
dynamic. When someone resists or runs from your witness, you
have made the gospel personal.

24:27 Felix lost his job as governor and was called back to Rome.
Porcius Festus took over as governor in late 59 or early 60. He was
more just than Felix, who had kept Paul in prison for two years in

order to keep the Jews happy. When Festus came into office, he
immediately ordered Paul's trial to resume.

24:27 The Jews were in the majority, and the political leaders
wanted to defer to them because their job was to keep the peace.
Paul seemed to incite problems among the Jews everywhere he
went. By keeping him in prison, Felix left office on good terms with
the Jews.

25:10, 11 Every Roman citizen had the right to appeal to Caesar.
This didn't mean that Caesar himself would hear the case, but that
his case would be tried by the highest courts in the empire. Festus
saw Paul's appeal as a way to send him out of the country and
thus calm the Jews. Paul wanted to go to Rome to preach the
gospel (Romans 1:10), and he knew his appeal would give him the
opportunity. To go there as a prisoner was better than not to go at
all.

25:11 Paul knew he was blameless of the charges against him
and could appeal to Caesar's judgment. He knew his rights as a
Roman citizen and as an innocent person. Paul had met his

12Festus conferred with his advisors and then replied, "Very well! You have appealed to Caesar, and to Caesar you shall go!"

13A few days later King Agrippa arrived with Bernice for a visit with Festus. 14During their stay of several days Festus discussed Paul's case with the king. "There is a prisoner here," he told him, "whose case was left for me by Felix. 15When I was in Jerusalem, the chief priests and other Jewish leaders gave me their side of the story and asked me to have him killed. 16Of course I quickly pointed out to them that Roman law does not convict a man before he is tried. He is given an opportunity to defend himself face to face with his accusers.

17"When they came here for the trial, I called the case the very next day and ordered Paul brought in. 18But the accusations made against him weren't at all what I supposed they would be. 19It was something about their religion, and about someone called Jesus who died, but Paul insists is alive! 20I was perplexed as to how to decide a case of this kind and asked him whether he would be willing to stand trial on these charges in Jerusalem. 21But Paul appealed to Caesar! So I ordered him back to jail until I could arrange to get him to the Emperor."

22"I'd like to hear the man myself," Agrippa said.

And Festus replied, "You shall—tomorrow!"

Paul witnesses to Agrippa

23So the next day, after the king and Bernice had arrived at the courtroom with great pomp, accompanied by military officers and prominent men of the city, Festus ordered Paul brought in.

24Then Festus addressed the audience: "King Agrippa and all present," he said, "this is the man whose death is demanded both by the local Jews and by those in Jerusalem! 25But in my opinion he has done nothing worthy of death. However, he appealed his case to Caesar, and I have no alternative but to send him. 26But what shall I write the Emperor? For there is no real charge against him! So I have brought him before you all, and especially you, King Agrippa, to examine him and then tell me what to write. 27For it doesn't seem reasonable to send a prisoner to the Emperor without any charges against him!"

26 Then Agrippa said to Paul, "Go ahead. Tell us your story."

So Paul, with many gestures, presented his defense:

2"I am fortunate, King Agrippa," he began, "to be able to present my answer before you, 3for I know you are an expert on Jewish laws and customs. Now please listen patiently!

4"As the Jews are well aware, I was given a thorough Jewish training from my earliest childhood in Tarsus and later at Jerusalem, and I lived accordingly. 5If they would admit it, they know that I have always been the strictest of Pharisees when it comes to obedience to Jewish laws and customs. 6But the real reason behind their accusations is something else—it is because I am looking forward to the fulfillment of God's promise made to our ancestors. 7The twelve tribes of Israel strive night and day to attain this same hope I have! Yet, O King, for me it is a crime, they say!

25:13 *arrived with Bernice.* She was his sister.   **26:1** *with many gestures,* literally, "stretched forth his hand."
26:4 *my earliest childhood in Tarsus,* literally, "my own nation."

25:14
Acts 24:27

25:15
Acts 25:2

25:16
Acts 23:30

25:19
Acts 18:15
23:29
1 Cor 15:2-8

25:22
Acts 9:15

25:24
Acts 22:22

25:25
Acts 23:22

26:4
Phil 3:5

26:6
Gen 3:15
22:18; 26:4
Deut 18:15
Isa 7:14; 9:6,7
Jer 23:5,6
33:14
Ezek 34:23
37:24
Dan 9:24
Mal 3:1; 4:2
Acts 13:32,33

26:7
Phil 3:11

---

responsibilities as a Roman, and so he had the opportunity to claim Rome's protection. The good reputation and clear conscience that result from our walk with God can help us remain not only guilt-free before God, but blame-free before the world as well.

25:13 This was Herod Agrippa II, son of Herod Agrippa I, and a descendant of Herod the Great. He had power over the Temple, controlled the Temple treasury, and could appoint and remove the High Priest. Bernice was the sister of Herod Agrippa II. She married her uncle Herod Chalcis, became a mistress to her brother Agrippa II, and then became mistress to the emperor Titus. Here Agrippa and Bernice were making an official visit to Festus.

Agrippa, of Jewish descent, could help clarify this "Jewish situation" to the Roman governor. Agrippa and Festus were anxious to cooperate in governing their neighboring territories.

25:19 Even though Festus knew little about Christianity, he understood that the resurrection was central to Christian belief.

25:23 Paul was in prison, but that didn't stop him from making the most of his situation. Military officers and prominent city leaders met in the palace room with Agrippa to hear this case. Paul saw this new audience as yet another opportunity to present the gospel. Rather than complain about your present situation, seek for ways to use every opportunity to serve God and share him with others. Our problems may be opportunities in disguise.

8But is it a crime to believe in the resurrection of the dead? Does it seem incredible to you that God can bring men back to life again?

26:8
Dan 12:2

9"I used to believe that I ought to do many horrible things to the followers of Jesus of Nazareth. 10I imprisoned many of the saints in Jerusalem, as authorized by the High Priests; and when they were condemned to death, I cast my vote against them. 11I used torture to try to make Christians everywhere curse Christ. I was so violently opposed to them that I even hounded them in distant cities in foreign lands.

26:9
Jn 15:21; 16:2
1 Tim 1:13

26:10
Acts 8:3; 22:5

26:11
Acts 9:1; 22:19

12"I was on such a mission to Damascus, armed with the authority and commission of the chief priests, 13when one day about noon, sir, a light from heaven brighter than the sun shone down on me and my companions. 14We all fell down, and I heard a voice speaking to me in Hebrew, 'Saul, Saul, why are you persecuting me? You are only hurting yourself.'

26:15
Acts 9:5; 22:8

26:16
Acts 22:15
Gal 1:12
Col 1:25
1 Tim 1:12

15" 'Who are you, sir?' I asked.

"And the Lord replied, 'I am Jesus, the one you are persecuting. 16Now stand up! For I have appeared to you to appoint you as my servant and my witness. You are to tell the world about this experience and about the many other occasions when I shall appear to you. 17And I will protect you from both your own people and the Gentiles. Yes, I am going to send you to the Gentiles 18to open their eyes to their true condition so that they may repent and live in the light of God instead of in Satan's darkness, so that they may receive forgiveness for their sins and God's inheritance along with all people everywhere whose sins are cleansed away, who are set apart by faith in me.'

26:17
Acts 13:46-48
22:21
Rom 11:13
15:16
Gal 1:15,16
2:7-9
1 Tim 2:7
2 Tim 1:11

26:18
Isa 35:5; 42:6,7
Lk 1:77,79
Eph 1:11; 5:8
Col 1:13
1 Pet 2:9

19"And so, O King Agrippa, I was not disobedient to that vision from heaven! 20I preached first to those in Damascus, then in Jerusalem and through Judea, and also to the Gentiles that all must forsake their sins and turn to God—and prove their repentance by doing good deeds. 21The Jews arrested me in the Temple for preaching this, and tried to kill me, 22but God protected me so that I am still alive today to tell these facts to everyone, both great and small. I teach nothing except what the prophets and Moses said— 23that the Messiah would suffer, and be the First to rise from the dead, to bring light to Jews and Gentiles alike."

26:20
Mt 3:8
Acts 9:20,26
13:46

26:21
Acts 21:30

26:22
Jn 5:46
Rom 3:21,22

26:23
Ps 2:7
6:8-11,22
Isa 53:1-12
Lk 24:26,27,46,
47
Rom 1:3,4
1 Cor 15:20
Col 1:18
Rev 1:5

24Suddenly Festus shouted, "Paul, you are insane. Your long studying has broken your mind!"

25But Paul replied, "I am not insane, Most Excellent Festus. I speak words of sober truth. 26And King Agrippa knows about these things. I speak frankly for I am sure these events are all familiar to him, for they were not done in a corner! 27King Agrippa, do you believe the prophets? But I know you do—"

26:24
1 Cor 1:23

26:26
Acts 26:3

28Agrippa interrupted him. "With trivial proofs like these, you expect me to become a Christian?"

29And Paul replied, "Would to God that whether my arguments are trivial or

26:9 the followers of Jesus of Nazareth, literally, "the name." 26:14 You are only hurting yourself, literally, "It is hard for you to kick against the oxgoad." 26:28 With trivial proofs like these, literally, "with little persuasion ."

26:18 Paul took every opportunity to remind his audience that the Gentiles have an equal share in God's inheritance. This inheritance is the promise and blessing of the covenant God made with Abraham (see Ephesians 2:19; 1 Peter 1:3, 4).

26:24 Paul was risking his life for an argument that was offensive to the Jews and unbelievable to the Gentiles. Jesus received the same response to his message (Mark 3:21; John 10:20). To a worldly, materialistic mind, it seems crazy to risk so much to gain what seems so little. But as you follow Christ, you discover that temporary possessions look small next to even the smallest eternal reward.

26:26 Paul was appealing to the facts—people were still alive who had heard Jesus and seen his miracles; the empty tomb could still be seen; and the Christian message was turning the world upside down (17:6). The history of Jesus' life and the early church are facts that are still open for us to examine. We still have

eyewitness accounts of Jesus' life in the Bible as well as historical and archaeological records of the early church to study. Examine the events and facts as verified by many witnesses. Reconfirm your faith with the truth of these accounts.

26:28 Agrippa answered Paul's presentation with a sarcastic remark. Paul didn't react to the brush-off, but made a personal appeal to which he hoped all his listeners would respond. Paul's response is a good example for us as we tell others about God's plan of salvation. A sincere personal appeal or personal testimony can show the depth of our concern and break through hardened hearts.

26:28, 29 Paul's heart is revealed here in his words: he was more concerned for the salvation of these strangers than for the removal of his own bonds. Ask God to help you share Paul's burning desire to see others come to him—a desire so strong that it overshadows your problems.

strong, both you and everyone here in this audience might become the same as I am, except for these chains."

26:31
Acts 23:9; 25:25

30Then the king, the governor, Bernice, and all the others stood and left. 31As they talked it over afterwards they agreed, "This man hasn't done anything worthy of death or imprisonment."

26:32
Acts 25:11

32And Agrippa said to Festus, "He could be set free if he hadn't appealed to Caesar!"

➤ Paul sails for Rome

27:1
Acts 25:12,25

27:2
Acts 19:29; 20:4
Col 4:10

27:3
Mt 11:21
Acts 24:23
27:43; 28:16

27 Arrangements were finally made to start us on our way to Rome by ship; so Paul and several other prisoners were placed in the custody of an officer named Julius, a member of the imperial guard. 2We left on a boat which was scheduled to make several stops along the Turkish coast. I should add that Aristarchus, a Greek from Thessalonica, was with us.

3The next day when we docked at Sidon, Julius was very kind to Paul and let him go ashore to visit with friends and receive their hospitality. 4Putting to sea from there, we encountered headwinds that made it difficult to keep the ship on course,

27:2 *a boat*, literally, "a ship of Adramyttium." *the Turkish coast*, literally, "the coast of Asia."

HEROD AGRIPPA II

Like great-grandfather, like grandfather, like father, like son—this tells the story of Herod Agrippa II. He inherited the effects of generations of powerful men with flawed personalities. Each son followed his father in weaknesses, mistakes, and missed opportunities. Each generation had a confrontation with God, but each failed to realize the importance of the decision. Herod Agrippa's great-uncle, Herod Antipas, actually met Jesus during his trial, but failed to see Jesus for who he was. Agrippa II heard the gospel from Paul, but considered the message mild entertainment. He found it humorous that Paul actually tried to convince him to become a Christian.

Like so many before and after, Agrippa II stopped within hearing distance of the Kingdom of God. He left himself without excuse. He heard the gospel but decided it wasn't worth responding to personally. Unfortunately, his mistake isn't uncommon. Many who read his story also will not believe. Their problem, like his, is not really that the gospel isn't convincing or that they don't need to know God personally; it is that they choose not to respond.

What has been your response to the gospel? Has it turned your life around and given you the hope of eternal life, or has it been a message to resist or reject? Perhaps it has just been entertainment. It may seem like too great a price to give God control of your life, but it is an even greater price by far to live eternally apart from him because you chose not to be his child.

Strengths and accomplishments:
- Last of the Herod dynasty that ruled parts of Palestine from 40 B.C. to A.D. 100
- Continued his father's success in mediating between Rome and Palestine
- Continued the family tradition of building and improving cities

Weaknesses and mistakes:
- Was not convinced by the gospel and consciously rejected it
- Carried on an incestuous relationship with his sister Bernice

Lessons from his life:
- Families pass on both positive and negative influences to children
- There are no guarantees of multiple opportunities to respond to God

Vital statistics:
- Occupation: Ruler of northern and eastern Palestine
- Relatives: Great-grandfather: Herod the Great. Father: Herod Agrippa I. Great-uncle: Herod Antipas. Sisters: Bernice, Drusilla.
- Contemporaries: Paul, Felix, Festus, Peter, Luke

Key verse:
"Agrippa interrupted him [Paul]. 'With trivial proofs like these, you expect me to become a Christian?' " (Acts 26:28).

Herod Agrippa II's story is told in Acts 25:13—26:32.

➤ **27:2** Use of the pronoun *we* indicates that Luke accompanied Paul on this journey. Aristarchus is the man who was dragged into the amphitheater at the beginning of the riot in Ephesus (19:29; 20:4; Philemon 24).

so we sailed north of Cyprus between the island and the mainland, 5and passed along the coast of the provinces of Cilicia and Pamphylia, landing at Myra, in the province of Lycia. 6There our officer found an Egyptian ship from Alexandria, bound for Italy, and put us aboard.

7, 8We had several days of rough sailing, and finally neared Cnidus; but the winds had become too strong, so we ran across to Crete, passing the port of Salome. Beating into the wind with great difficulty and moving slowly along the southern coast, we arrived at Fair Havens, near the city of Lasea. 9There we stayed for several days. The weather was becoming dangerous for long voyages by then, because it was late in the year, and Paul spoke to the ship's officers about it.

10"Sirs," he said, "I believe there is trouble ahead if we go on—perhaps shipwreck, loss of cargo, injuries, and death." 11But the officers in charge of the prisoners listened more to the ship's captain and the owner than to Paul. 12And since Fair Havens was an exposed harbor—a poor place to spend the winter—most of the crew advised trying to go further up the coast to Phoenix, in order to winter there; Phoenix was a good harbor with only a northwest and southwest exposure.

The storm at sea

13Just then a light wind began blowing from the south, and it looked like a perfect day for the trip; so they pulled up anchor and sailed along close to shore.

14, 15But shortly afterwards, the weather changed abruptly and a heavy wind of typhoon strength (a "northeaster," they called it) caught the ship and blew it out to sea. They tried at first to face back to shore but couldn't, so they gave up and let the ship run before the gale.

16We finally sailed behind a small island named Clauda, where with great

27:6 Acts 28:11

27:10 Amos 3:7

27:7, 8 *Cnidus,* a port on the southeast coast of Turkey. **27:9** *because it was late in the year,* literally, "because the Fast was now already gone by." It came about the time of the autumn equinox. **27:12** *exposed,* implied.

Reference	What happened	
21:30	When Paul arrived in Jerusalem, a riot broke out. Seeing the riot, Roman soldiers put Paul into protective custody. Paul asked for a chance to defend himself to the people. His speech was interrupted by the crowd when he spoke about the Gentiles.	**PAUL'S JOURNEY TO ROME** One of Paul's most important journeys was to Rome, but he didn't get there the way he expected. It turned out to be more of a legal journey than a missionary journey because through a series of legal trials and transactions, Paul was delivered to Rome where his presentation of the gospel would penetrate even into the walls of the emperor's palace. Sometimes when our plans don't work out as we want them to, they work out even better than we expected.
22:24	A Roman commander ordered a beating to get a confession from Paul. Paul claimed Roman citizenship and escaped the whip.	
22:30	Paul was brought before the Jewish Council. Because of his Roman citizenship, he was rescued from the religious leaders who wanted to kill him.	
23:10	The Roman commander put Paul back under protective custody.	
23:12	Due to a plot to kill Paul, the commander transferred him to Caesarea, which was under Governor Felix's control.	
23:35	Paul was in prison until the Jews arrived to accuse him. Paul defended himself before Felix.	
24:26	Paul was in prison for two years, speaking occasionally to Felix and Drusilla.	
24:27	Felix replaced by Festus.	
25:1	New accusations against Paul—Jews wanted him back in Jerusalem for a trial. Paul claimed his right to a hearing before Caesar.	
25:12	Festus promised to send him to Rome.	
25:13	Festus discussed Paul's case with Agrippa II.	
26:1	Agrippa and Festus heard Paul speak. Paul again told his story.	
26:24–28	Agrippa interrupted with sarcastic rejection of the gospel.	
26:30	Group consensus was that Paul was guilty of nothing and could be released if he had not appealed to Rome.	
27:1, 2	Paul left for Rome, by courtesy of the Roman Empire.	

27:9 Ships in ancient times had no compasses and navigated by the stars. Overcast weather made sailing almost impossible and very dangerous. Sailing was doubtful in September and impossible by November. This event occurred in October (A.D. 59).

difficulty we hoisted aboard the lifeboat that was being towed behind us, 17and then banded the ship with ropes to strengthen the hull. The sailors were afraid of being driven across to the quicksands of the African coast, so they lowered the topsails and were thus driven before the wind.

18The next day as the seas grew higher, the crew began throwing the cargo overboard. 19The following day they threw out the tackle and anything else they could lay their hands on. 20The terrible storm raged unabated many days, until at last all hope was gone.

21No one had eaten for a long time, but finally Paul called the crew together and said, "Men, you should have listened to me in the first place and not left Fair Havens—you would have avoided all this injury and loss! 22But cheer up! Not one of us will lose our lives, even though the ship will go down.

23"For last night an angel of the God to whom I belong and whom I serve stood beside me, 24and said, 'Don't be afraid, Paul—for you will surely stand trial before Caesar! What's more, God has granted your request and will save the lives of all those sailing with you.' 25So take courage! For I believe God! It will be just as he said! 26But we will be shipwrecked on an island."

The shipwreck

27About midnight on the fourteenth night of the storm, as we were being driven to and fro on the Adriatic Sea, the sailors suspected land was near. 28They sounded, and found 120 feet of water below them. A little later they sounded again, and found only ninety feet. 29At this rate they knew they would soon be driven ashore;

27:18
Jonah 1:5

27:21
Acts 27:10

27:23
Acts 18:9; 23:11
27:44
2 Tim 4:17

27:24
Isa 41:10,14
43:1,2
Acts 19:21
23:11; 25:11

27:25
2 Chron 20:20
Lk 1:45
Rom 4:20
Heb 6:17

27:26
Acts 28:1

27:17 *were afraid of being driven across to the quicksands of the African coast,* literally, "fearing lest they should be cast upon the Syrtis." **27:20** *The terrible storm raged unabated many days,* literally, "Neither sun nor stars shone upon us."

THE TRIP TOWARD ROME
Paul began his 2,000-mile trip to Rome at Caesarea. To avoid the open seas, the ship went north, following the coastline. At Myra, Paul was put on a vessel bound for Italy. It arrived with difficulty at Cnidus, then went to Crete, landing at the port of Fair Havens. The next stop was Phoenix, but the ship was blown south around the island of Clauda, then drifted for two weeks until it was shipwrecked on the island of Malta.

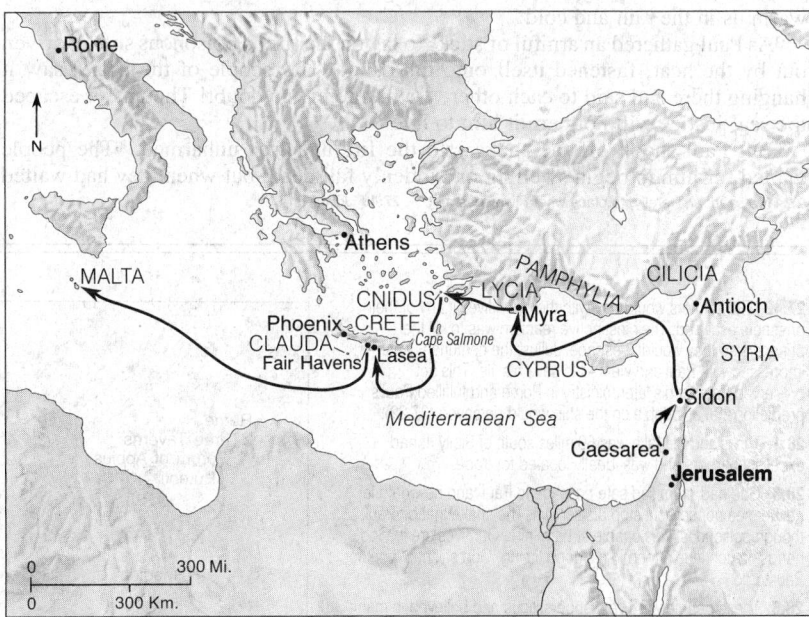

27:21 Why would Paul talk to the crew this way? Paul was not taunting them with an "I told you so," but was reminding them that, with God's guidance, he had predicted this very problem. In the future, they listened to him (27:30–32) and their lives were spared because of it.

27:28 Soundings were made by throwing a weighted, marked line into the water. When the lead hit the bottom, sailors could tell the depth of the water from the marks on the rope.

and fearing rocks along the coast, they threw out four anchors from the stern and prayed for daylight.

30Some of the sailors planned to abandon the ship, and lowered the emergency boat as though they were going to put out anchors from the prow. 31But Paul said to the soldiers and commanding officer, "You will all die unless everyone stays aboard." 32So the soldiers cut the ropes and let the boat fall off.

33As the darkness gave way to the early morning light, Paul begged everyone to eat. "You haven't touched food for two weeks," he said. 34"Please eat something now for your own good! For not a hair of your heads shall perish!"

35Then he took some hardtack and gave thanks to God before them all, and broke off a piece and ate it. 36Suddenly everyone felt better and began eating, 37all two hundred seventy-six of us—for that is the number we had aboard. 38After eating, the crew lightened the ship further by throwing all the wheat overboard.

39When it was day, they didn't recognize the coastline, but noticed a bay with a beach and wondered whether they could get between the rocks and be driven up onto the beach. 40They finally decided to try. Cutting off the anchors and leaving them in the sea, they lowered the rudders, raised the foresail and headed ashore. 41But the ship hit a sandbar and ran aground. The bow of the ship stuck fast, while the stern was exposed to the violence of the waves and began to break apart.

42The soldiers advised their commanding officer to let them kill the prisoners lest any of them swim ashore and escape. 43But Julius wanted to spare Paul, so he told them no. Then he ordered all who could swim to jump overboard and make for land, 44and the rest to try for it on planks and debris from the broken ship. So everyone escaped safely ashore!

Paul is bitten by a snake on Malta

28 We soon learned that we were on the island of Malta. The people of the island were very kind to us, building a bonfire on the beach to welcome and warm us in the rain and cold.

3As Paul gathered an armful of sticks to lay on the fire, a poisonous snake, driven out by the heat, fastened itself onto his hand! 4The people of the island saw it hanging there and said to each other, "A murderer, no doubt! Though he escaped the sea, justice will not permit him to live!"

5But Paul shook off the snake into the fire and was unharmed. 6The people waited for him to begin swelling or suddenly fall dead; but when they had waited

27:41 *a sandbar*, literally, "a place where two seas met."   27:43 *Julius*, implied.

27:34
Mt 10:30
Lk 12:7; 21:18
27:35
Mt 14:19
Jn 6:11
1 Tim 4:4,5
27:38
Jonah 1:5
Acts 27:18

27:41
2 Cor 11:25

27:44
Ps 107:30

28:1
Acts 27:26
28:4
Lk 13:2,4
28:5
Mk 16:18
Lk 10:19
28:6
Acts 14:11

27:42 The soldiers would pay with their own lives if any of their prisoners escaped. Their instinctive reaction was to kill the prisoners so they wouldn't escape. Julius, the centurion, was impressed with Paul and wanted to save his life. This act preserved Paul for his later ministry in Rome and fulfilled Paul's prediction that all people on the ship would be saved (27:22).

28:1 The island of Malta was 60 miles south of Sicily. It had excellent harbors and was ideally located for trade.

28:3 God had promised safe passage to Paul, and he would let neither sea nor serpent stop his servant. The snake that bit Paul, though poisonous, was unable to harm him. Our lives are in God's hands, to continue or end in his good timing. God still had work for Paul to do.

28:6 These people were very superstitious and believed in many gods. When they saw that Paul was unhurt by the poisonous snake, they thought he was a god. A similar situation is reported in 14:11–18.

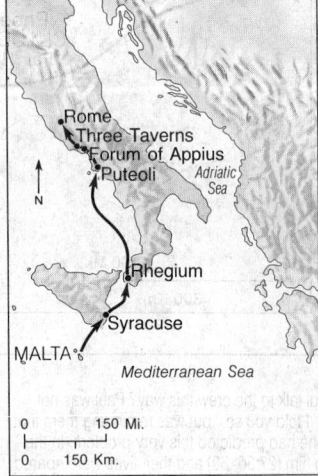

```
          Rome
          Three Taverns
          Forum of Appius
          Puteoli        Adriatic
  ↑                        Sea
  N

                    Rhegium

                  Syracuse
  MALTA
              Mediterranean Sea

  0        150 Mi.
  |————————|
  0        150 Km.
```

PAUL ARRIVES IN ROME
The shipwreck had occurred on the island of Malta where the ship's company spent three months. Finally another ship gave them passage for the 100 miles to Syracuse, capital of Sicily, then on to Rhegium, finally dropping anchor at Puteoli. Paul was taken along the Appian Way to the Forum, and to the Three Taverns before arriving in Rome.

a long time and no harm came to him, they changed their minds and decided he was a god.

7Near the shore where we landed was an estate belonging to Publius, the governor of the island. He welcomed us courteously and fed us for three days. 8As it happened, Publius' father was ill with fever and dysentery. Paul went in and prayed for him, and laying his hands on him, healed him! 9Then all the other sick people in the island came and were cured. 10As a result we were showered with gifts, and when the time came to sail, people put on board all sorts of things we would need for the trip.

28:8
Mk 5:23
Acts 19:11
1 Cor 12:9,28
Jas 5:14

11It was three months after the shipwreck before we set sail again, and this time it was in *The Twin Brothers* of Alexandria, a ship that had wintered at the island. 12Our first stop was Syracuse, where we stayed three days. 13From there we circled around to Rhegium; a day later a south wind began blowing, so the following day we arrived at Puteoli, 14where we found some believers! They begged us to stay with them seven days. Then we went on to Rome.

28:11
Acts 27:6

Paul lives under guard in Rome

15The brothers in Rome had heard we were coming and came to meet us at the Forum on the Appian Way. Others joined us at The Three Taverns. When Paul saw them, he thanked God and took courage.

16When we arrived in Rome, Paul was permitted to live wherever he wanted to, though guarded by a soldier.

28:16
Acts 24:33; 27:3

17Three days after his arrival, he called together the local Jewish leaders and spoke to them as follows:

28:17
Acts 24:12; 25:8

"Brothers, I was arrested by the Jews in Jerusalem and handed over to the Roman government for prosecution, even though I had harmed no one nor violated the customs of our ancestors. 18The Romans gave me a trial and wanted to release me, for they found no cause for the death sentence demanded by the Jewish leaders. 19But when the Jews protested the decision, I felt it necessary, with no malice against them, to appeal to Caesar. 20I asked you to come here today so we could get acquainted and I could tell you that it is because I believe the Messiah has come that I am bound with this chain."

28:18
Acts 23:29

28:19
Acts 25:11; 26:32
28:20
Acts 26:6

21They replied, "We have heard nothing against you! We have had no letters from Judea or reports from those arriving from Jerusalem. 22But we want to hear what you believe, for the only thing we know about these Christians is that they are denounced everywhere!"

28:22
Acts 24:14
1 Pet 2:12; 3:16
4:16

23So a time was set and on that day large numbers came to his house. He told them about the Kingdom of God and taught them about Jesus from the Scriptures—from the five books of Moses and the books of prophecy. He began lecturing in the morning and went on into the evening!

28:23
Lk 24:27
Acts 1:3; 23:11
28:31

28:10 *gifts,* literally, "honors." **28:20** *the Messiah,* literally, "the hope of Israel." But perhaps he is referring here, as in his other defenses, to his belief in the resurrection of the dead. **28:21** *from Jerusalem,* implied.

28:15 Where did the Roman believers come from? The gospel message had spread to Rome by various methods. Many Jews who lived in Rome visited Jerusalem for religious festivals. Some were probably present at Pentecost (chapter 2), believed in Jesus, and brought the message back to Rome. Also, Paul had written his letter to the Romans before he visited there.

28:15 The Forum was a town about 43 miles south of Rome; The Three Taverns was located about 35 miles south of Rome. A *tavern* was a place that provided food and lodging for travelers. The Christians openly went to meet Paul and encourage him.

28:17 The Edict of Claudius expelling Jews from Rome (18:2) must have been temporary because Jewish leaders were back in Rome.

28:17-20 Paul wanted to preach the gospel in Rome, and he eventually got there—in chains, through shipwreck, and after many trials. Although he may have wished for an easier passage, he

knew that God had blessed him greatly in allowing him to meet the believers in Rome and preach the message to both Jews and Gentiles in that great city. God "worked all things for good" (Romans 8:28) for Paul, and you can trust him to do the same for you. God may not make you comfortable or secure, but he will provide the opportunity to do his work.

28:22 Christians were denounced everywhere by the Romans because they were seen as a threat to the Roman establishment. They believed in one God, whereas the Romans had many gods, including Caesar. The Christians were committed to an authority higher than Caesar.

28:23 Paul used the Old Testament to teach the Jews that Jesus was the Messiah, the fulfillment of God's promises. The book of Romans, written ten years earlier, reveals the ongoing dialogue Paul had with the Jews in Rome.

24Some believed, and some didn't. 25But after they had argued back and forth among themselves, they left with this final word from Paul ringing in their ears: "The Holy Spirit was right when he said through Isaiah the prophet,

26" 'Say to the Jews, "You will hear and see but not understand, 27for your hearts are too fat and your ears don't listen and you have closed your eyes against understanding, for you don't want to see and hear and understand and turn to me to heal you." ' 28, 29So I want you to realize that this salvation from God is available to the Gentiles too, and they will accept it."

30Paul lived for the next two years in his rented house and welcomed all who visited him, 31telling them with all boldness about the Kingdom of God and about the Lord Jesus Christ; and no one tried to stop him.

28:24
Acts 14:4

28:25-27
Isa 6:9-10
Jn 12:39,40

28:28
Ps 98:3
Lk 2:30-32
Acts 9:15;
13:26,46

28:31
Acts 20:25;
28:23

28:28, 29. Some of the ancient manuscripts add, "And when he had said these words, the Jews departed, having much dissenting among themselves."   **28:30** *in his rented house*, or, "at his own expense."

28:27 Paul was quoting from Isaiah 6:9, 10.

28:30 While Paul was under house arrest, he did more than speak to the Jews. He wrote letters, commonly called his Prison Epistles, to the Ephesians, Colossians, and Philippians, as well as personal letters, such as the one to Philemon. Timothy often visited him (Philippians 1:1; Colossians 1:1; Philemon 1), as did Tychicus (Ephesians 6:21), Epaphroditus (Philippians 4:18), and Mark (John Mark, Colossians 4:10). Paul witnessed to the Roman guard (Philippians 1:13) and was involved with the Roman believers.

28:30 Tradition says that Paul was released after two years of house arrest in Rome and set off on a fourth missionary journey. Some reasons for this tradition are as follows: (1) Luke does not give us an account of his trial before Caesar, and Luke was a detailed chronicler; (2) the prosecution had two years to bring the case to trial, and time may have run out; (3) in his letter to the Philippians, written during his imprisonment in Rome, Paul implied that he would soon be released and would go further traveling; (4) Paul mentions several places where he intended to take the gospel, but he never visited those places in his first three journeys; and (5) early Christian literature talks plainly about other travels by Paul.

It may be that during Paul's time of freedom, he continued his travels extensively, even going to Spain (see Romans 15:24, 28) and back to the churches in Greece. The books of 1 Timothy and

Titus were written during this time. Later, Paul was imprisoned again, probably in Rome, where he wrote his last epistle (2 Timothy).

28:31 Why does the book of Acts end here? The book is not about the life of Paul, but about the spread of the gospel, and that has been clearly presented. God apparently thought it was not necessary for someone to write an additional book describing the continuing history of the early church. Now that the gospel had been preached and established at the center of trade and government, it would spread across the world.

28:31 The book of Acts deals with the history of the Christian church and its expansion in ever-widening circles touching Jerusalem, Antioch, Ephesus, and Rome—the most influential cities in the western world. Acts also shows the mighty miracles and testimonies of the heroes and martyrs of the early church—Peter, Stephen, James, Paul. All the ministry was prompted and held together by the Holy Spirit working in the lives of ordinary people—merchants, travelers, slaves, jailers, church leaders, males, females, Gentiles, Jews, rich, poor. Many unsung heroes of the faith continued the acts of the Holy Spirit through succeeding generations, changing the world with a changeless message—that Jesus Christ is Savior and Lord for all who call upon him. We today can be the unsung heroes in the continuing story of the spread of the gospel. It is that same message that we Christians are to take to our world, so it too may hear and believe.

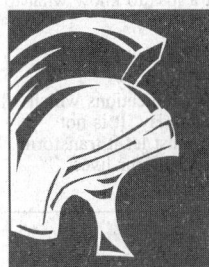

KNOWLEDGEABLE and experienced, the District Attorney makes his case. Calling key witnesses to the stand, he presents the evidence. He discredits the testimonies of witnesses for the defense by skillfully cross-examining them. Then he concludes with an airtight summary and stirring challenge for the jury. The announced verdict is no surprise. "Guilty" states the foreman; and justice is served.

The apostle Paul was intelligent, articulate, and committed to his calling. Like a skilled lawyer, he presents the case for the gospel clearly and forthrightly in his letter to the church at Rome.

Paul had heard of the church at Rome, but he had never been there, nor had any of the other apostles. Evidently the church was begun by Jews who had come to faith during Pentecost (Acts 2). They spread the faith on their return to Rome and the church grew.

Although many barriers separated them, Paul felt a bond with these Romans. They were his brothers and sisters in Christ, and he longed to see them face to face. He had never met most of the Christians in Rome, yet he loved them. He sent this letter to introduce himself and to make a clear declaration of the faith.

After a brief introduction, Paul presents the facts of the gospel (1:3) and declares his allegiance to it (1:16, 17). He continues by building an airtight case for the lostness of mankind and the necessity for God's intervention (1:18—3:20).

Then Paul presents the Good News—salvation is available to all, regardless of their identity, sin, or heritage. We are saved by *grace* (unearned, undeserved favor from God) through *faith* (complete trust) in Christ and his finished work. Through him we can stand before God justified, "not guilty" (3:21—5:21). With this foundation Paul moves directly into a discussion of the freedom that comes from being saved—freedom from the power of sin (6:1–23), freedom from the domination of the law (7:1–25), freedom to become like Christ and discover God's limitless love (8:1–39).

Speaking directly to his Jewish brothers and sisters, Paul shares his concern for them and explains how they fit into God's plan (9:1—11:12). God has made the way for Jews and Gentiles to be united in the body of Christ—both groups can praise God for his wisdom and love (11:13–36).

Paul explains what it means to live in complete submission to Christ—using spiritual gifts to serve others (12:3–8), genuinely loving others (12:9–21), and being good citizens (13:1–14). Freedom must be guided by love as we build each other up in the faith, being sensitive and helpful to those who are weak (14:1—15:4). Paul stresses unity, especially between Gentiles and Jews (15:5–13). He concludes by reviewing his reasons for writing, outlining his personal plans (15:22–33), greeting his friends, and giving a few final thoughts and greetings from his traveling companions (16:1–27).

As you read Romans, reexamine your commitment to Christ and reconfirm your relationships with other believers in Christ's body.

VITAL STATISTICS

PURPOSE:
To introduce Paul to the Romans and to give a sample of his message before he arrives in Rome

AUTHOR:
Paul

TO WHOM WRITTEN:
The Christians in Rome and believers everywhere

DATE WRITTEN:
About A.D. 57, from Corinth, as Paul was preparing for his visit to Jerusalem

SETTING:
Apparently Paul had finished his work in the east, and he planned to visit Rome on his way to Spain after first bringing a collection to Jerusalem for the poor Christians there (15:22–28). The Roman church was mostly Jewish but also contained a great number of Gentiles.

KEY VERSE:
"So now, since we have been made right in God's sight by faith in his promises, we can have real peace with him because of what Jesus Christ our Lord has done for us" (5:1).

KEY PEOPLE:
Paul, Phoebe

KEY PLACE:
Rome

SPECIAL FEATURES:
Paul writes Romans as an organized and carefully presented statement of his faith—it does not have the form of a typical letter. He does, however, spend considerable time greeting people in Rome at the end of the letter.

THE BLUEPRINT

A. WHAT TO BELIEVE (1:1—11:36)
1. Sinfulness of mankind
2. Forgiveness of sin through Christ
3. Freedom from sin's grasp
4. Israel's past, present, and future

Paul clearly sets forth the foundations of the Christian faith. All men are sinful; Christ died to forgive sin; we are made right with God through faith; this begins a new life with a new relationship with God. Like a sports team that constantly reviews the basics, we will be greatly helped in our faith by keeping close to these foundations. If we study Romans carefully, we will never be at a loss to know what to believe.

B. HOW TO BEHAVE (12:1—16:27)
1. Personal responsibility
2. Personal notes

Paul gives clear, practical guidelines for the believers in Rome. The Christian life is not abstract theology unconnected with life, but has practical implications which will affect how we choose to behave each day. It is not enough merely to know the gospel, we must let it transform our lives and let God impact every aspect of our lives.

MEGATHEMES

THEME	EXPLANATION	IMPORTANCE
Sin	Sin means refusing to do God's will and failing to do all that God wants. Since Adam's rebellion against God, our nature is to disobey him. Our sin cuts us off from God. Sin causes us to want to live our own way rather than God's way. Because God is morally perfect, just, and fair, he is right to condemn sin.	Each person has sinned, either by rebelling against God or by ignoring his will. No matter what our background or how hard we try to live good and moral lives, we cannot earn salvation or remove our sin. Only Christ can save us.
Salvation	Our sin points out our need to be forgiven and cleansed. Although we don't deserve it, God, in his kindness, reached out to love and forgive us. He provides the way for us to be saved. Christ's death paid the penalty for our sin.	It is good news that God saves us from our sin. But we must believe in Jesus Christ and that he forgave our sin in order to enter into a wonderful new relationship with God.
Growth	By God's power, believers are sanctified—made holy. This means we are set apart from sin, enabled to obey and to become more like Christ. When we are growing in our relationship with Christ, the Holy Spirit frees us from the demands of the law and from fear of judgment.	Because we are free from sin's control, the law's demands, and fear of God's punishment, we can grow in our relationship with Christ. By trusting in the Holy Spirit and allowing him to help us, we can overcome sin and temptation.
Sovereignty	God oversees and cares about his people—past, present, and future. God's ways of dealing with people are always fair. Because God is in charge of all creation, he can save whomever he wills.	Because of God's mercy, both Jews and Gentiles can be saved. We all must respond to his mercy and accept his gracious offer of forgiveness. Because he is sovereign, let him reign in your heart.
Service	When our purpose is to give credit to God for his love, power, and perfection in all we do, we can serve him properly. Serving him unifies all believers and enables them to show love and sensitivity to others.	Each one of us can't be fully Christlike by ourselves—it takes the entire body of Christ to fully express Christ. By actively and vigorously building up other believers, Christians can be a symphony of service to God.

A. WHAT TO BELIEVE (1:1—11:36)

Paul begins his message to the Romans by vividly portraying the sinfulness of all mankind, explaining how forgiveness is available through faith in Christ, and showing what believers experience in life through their new faith. In this section, we learn of the centrality of faith to becoming a Christian and to living the Christian life. Apart from faith, we have no hope in life.

1. Sinfulness of mankind

1 Dear friends in Rome: ¹This letter is from Paul, Jesus Christ's slave, chosen to be a missionary, and sent out to preach God's Good News. ²This Good News was promised long ago by God's prophets in the Old Testament. ³It is the Good News about his Son, Jesus Christ our Lord, who came as a human baby, born into King David's royal family line; ⁴and by being raised from the dead he was proved to be the mighty Son of God, with the holy nature of God himself.

1:2
Rom 3:21
Tit 1:2
1:3
Mt 1:1-17
1:4
Rom 8:11

THE GOSPEL GOES TO ROME
When Paul wrote his letter to the church in Rome, he had not yet been there, but he had taken the gospel "all the way from Jerusalem clear over into Illyricum" (15:19). He planned to visit and preach in Rome one day, and hoped to continue to take the gospel farther west—even to Spain.

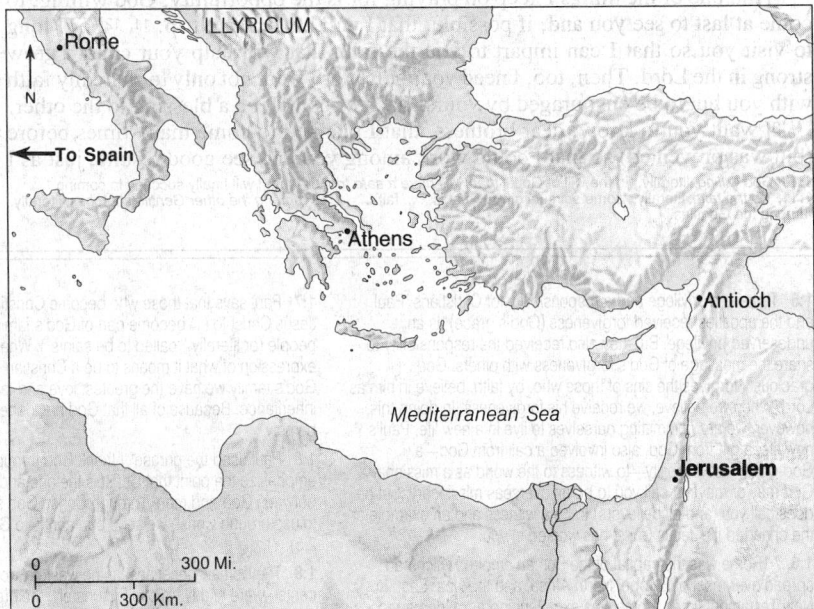

1:1 Paul wrote this letter to the church in Rome. None of the church leaders (James, Peter, Paul) had yet been to Rome; the Roman church was established by believers who had been at Jerusalem for Pentecost (Acts 2:10) and travelers who had heard the message in other places and brought it back to Rome (for example, Priscilla and Aquila, Acts 18:2; Romans 16:3–5). Paul wrote the letter to the Romans during his ministry in Corinth (at the end of his third missionary journey just before returning to Jerusalem; Acts 20:3; Romans 15:25; 16:1) to encourage the believers and to express his desire to visit them someday (within three years he would). The Roman church had no New Testament, since the Gospels were probably not yet being circulated in their final written form. Thus, this letter may well have been the first piece of Christian literature the Roman believers had seen. Written to both Jewish and Gentile Christians, the letter to the Romans is a systematic presentation of the Christian faith.

1:1 When Paul, a devout Jew who had at first persecuted the Christians, became a believer, God used him to spread the gospel throughout the world. Although he was a prisoner at the time, Paul did eventually preach in Rome (Acts 28), perhaps even to Caesar himself. Paul's Profile is found in Acts 9.

1:1 Paul humbly calls himself a slave to Jesus Christ. For a

Roman citizen—which Paul was—to choose to be a slave was unthinkable, but Paul chose to be completely dependent on and obedient to his beloved master. What is your attitude toward Christ, your master? Our obedience to him enables us to be useful and usable servants to do work that really matters.

1:2 Some of the prophecies predicting the Good News of Jesus Christ are Genesis 12:3; Psalms 16:10; 40:6–10; 118:22; Isaiah 11:1ff; Zechariah 9:9–11; 12:1–10; Malachi 4:1–6.

1:3–5 Here Paul summarizes the Good News about Jesus Christ who (1) came as a human, (2) was part of the Jewish royal line, (3) died and was raised from the dead, and (4) opened the door for God's kindness to be poured out on us. The book of Romans is an expansion of these themes. As we read it we discover what Paul meant by Good News.

1:3 Paul believed that Jesus is the Son of God, the promised Messiah, and the resurrected Lord. Paul called Jesus a descendant of King David to emphasize that Jesus truly fulfilled the Old Testament Scriptures predicting that the Messiah would come from David's line. With this statement of faith, Paul declared his agreement with the teaching of all Scripture and of the apostles.

⁵And now, through Christ, all the kindness of God has been poured out upon us undeserving sinners; and now he is sending us out around the world to tell all people everywhere the great things God has done for them, so that they, too, will believe and obey him.

⁶,⁷And you, dear friends in Rome, are among those he dearly loves; you, too, are invited by Jesus Christ to be God's very own—yes, his holy people. May all God's mercies and peace be yours from God our Father and from Jesus Christ our Lord.

Paul declares the power of the gospel

⁸Let me say first of all that wherever I go I hear you being talked about! For your faith in God is becoming known around the world. How I thank God through Jesus Christ for this good report, and for each one of you. ⁹God knows how often I pray for you. Day and night I bring you and your needs in prayer to the one I serve with all my might, telling others the Good News about his Son.

¹⁰And one of the things I keep on praying for is the opportunity, God willing, to come at last to see you and, if possible, that I will have a safe trip. ¹¹, ¹²For I long to visit you so that I can impart to you the faith that will help your church grow strong in the Lord. Then, too, I need your help, for I want not only to share my faith with you but to be encouraged by yours: Each of us will be a blessing to the other.

¹³I want you to know, dear brothers, that I planned to come many times before (but was prevented) so that I could work among you and see good results, just as I

1:5
Acts 9:15
Rom 16:26
Gal 1:16
Eph 3:8,9

1:6
1 Cor 1:3
2 Cor 1:2
Gal 1:3
Eph 1:1,2

1:8
Rom 16:19
Phil 1:3
1 Thess 1:8

1:9
Eph 1:16
Phil 1:3
1 Thess 1:2
2 Tim 1:3
Philem 4-7

1:10
Rom 15:32
Jas 4:15

1:11
Rom 15:29

1:13
Rom 15:22,23

1:10 *God willing,* literally, "in the will of God." *that I will have a safe trip,* or, "that I will finally succeed in coming."
1:11, 12 *the faith,* literally, "some spiritual gift . . . that is, . . . faith."   **1:13** *among the other Gentile churches,* literally, "among the Gentiles."

1:5 There is a privilege and a responsibility for Christians. Paul and the apostles received forgiveness (God's grace) as an undeserved privilege. But they also received the responsibility to share the message of God's forgiveness with others. God graciously forgives the sins of those who, by faith, believe in him as Lord. When we believe, we receive his forgiveness. In doing this, however, we are committing ourselves to live in a new life. Paul's new life, a gift from God, also involved a call from God—a God-given responsibility—to witness to the world as a missionary. God may or may not call you to be an overseas missionary, but he does call you (and all believers) to be a witness and an example of the changed life Jesus Christ has worked in you.

1:6, 7 Rome was the capital of the Roman empire, which had spread over most of Europe, North Africa, and the Near East. In New Testament times, Rome was experiencing a "golden age." The city was wealthy, literary, and artistic. It was a cultural center, but in terms of moral standards it was decadent in many respects. The Romans worshiped many pagan gods. Even some of the emperors were worshiped as deities. In stark contrast to the Romans, the followers of Christ believed in only one God and lived morally.

1:6, 7 Christianity was at odds with many elements in the Roman culture. (1) The Romans trusted in their strong military power to protect them against all enemies. Christians needed to be reminded that God was the only permanent source of their security and salvation. (2) Many Romans were naively pragmatic—that is, any means to accomplish the intended task was good. And for Romans, nothing worked better than physical might. Christians needed to learn the value of moral restraints in their new faith—restraints that often seemed foolish in the macho Roman society.

1:6–9 Paul showed his warm attitude toward the Roman church by expressing God's love for them and his own thanks and prayers for them. To have an effect on people's lives, you need to love them and believe in them. Paul's passion to teach these people and have fellowship with them began with his love for them. Thank God for your Christian brothers and sisters, and let them know how deeply you care for them (see, for example, Paul's commands to Philemon in Philemon 1:7).

1:7 Paul says that those who become Christians are invited by Jesus Christ to (1) become part of God's family, and (2) be holy people (or literally, "called to be saints"). What a wonderful expression of what it means to be a Christian. In being reborn into God's family we have the greatest love and the greatest inheritance. Because of all that God has done for us, we strive to be holy.

1:8 Paul used the phrase "I thank God through Jesus Christ" to emphasize the point that Christ is the one and only mediator between God and man. Through Christ, God sends his blessings to us; through Christ, we send our thanks to God (see 1 Timothy 2:5).

1:8 The Roman Christians, at the western world's political power center, were highly visible. Fortunately, their reputation was excellent: their strong faith was making itself known around the world. When people talk about your congregation or your denomination, what do they say? Are their comments accurate? Would you rather they noticed other features? What is the best way to get the public to recognize your faith?

1:9, 10 When you pray continually about a concern, don't be surprised at how God answers. Paul prayed to visit Rome so he could teach the Christians there. When he finally arrived in Rome, it was as a prisoner (see Acts 28:16). Paul prayed for a safe trip, and he did arrive safely—after getting arrested, slapped in the face, shipwrecked, and, among other things, bitten by a poisonous snake. God's ways of answering our prayers are often far from what we expect. When you pray, expect God to answer—although sometimes in ways you do not expect.

1:11, 12 Paul prayed for the chance to visit these Christians so that he could encourage them and be encouraged by them. As God's missionary, he could help them understand the meaning of the Good News about Jesus. As God's holy people, they could offer him fellowship and comfort. When Christians gather, everyone should give *and* receive.

1:13 By the end of his third missionary journey, Paul had traveled through Syria, Galatia, Asia, Macedonia, and Achaia. The churches in these areas were called Gentile churches because their members were mostly Gentiles.

1:14
Ps 40:9
1 Cor 9:16
1:15
Rom 15:20

1:16
Acts 3:26
1 Cor 1:18
2 Tim 1:8-12
1:17
Hab 2:4
Jn 3:36
Rom 3:21
Gal 3:11
Phil 3:9
Heb 10:38

have among the other Gentile churches. ¹⁴For I owe a great debt to you and to everyone else, both to civilized people and uncivilized alike; yes, to the educated and uneducated alike. ¹⁵So, to the fullest extent of my ability, I am ready to come also to you in Rome to preach God's Good News.

¹⁶For I am not ashamed of this Good News about Christ. It is God's powerful method of bringing all who believe it to heaven. This message was preached first to the Jews alone, but now everyone is invited to come to God in this same way. ¹⁷This Good News tells us that God makes us ready for heaven—makes us right in God's sight—when we put our faith and trust in Christ to save us. This is accomplished from start to finish by faith. As the Scripture says it, "The man who finds life will find it through trusting God."

1:17 *This is accomplished from start to finish by faith,* literally, " this righteousness of God is *revealed* from faith to faith." *"The man who finds life will find it through trusting God"* (Hab 2:4).

FAITH

Faith is a word with many meanings. It can mean faithfulness (Matthew 24:45). It can mean absolute trust, as shown by some of the people who came to Jesus for healing (Luke 7:2–10). It can mean confident hope (Hebrews 11:1). Or, as James points out, it can even mean a barren belief that does not result in good works (James 2:14–26). What does Paul mean when, in Romans, he speaks of saving faith?

We must be very careful to understand faith as Paul uses the word, because he ties faith so closely to salvation. It is *not* something we must do in order to earn salvation—if that were true, then faith would be just one more work, and Paul clearly states that human works can never save us (Galatians 2:16). Instead, faith is a gift God gives us *because* he is saving us (Ephesians 2:8). It is God's grace, not our faith, that saves us. In his mercy, however, when he saves us he gives us faith—a relationship with his Son that helps us become like him. Through the faith he gives us, he carries us from death into life (John 5:24).

Even in Old Testament times grace, not works, was the basis of salvation. As Hebrews points out, "it is not possible for the blood of bulls and goats really to take away sins" (10:4). God intended for his people to look beyond the animal sacrifices to him, but all too often they, instead, put their confidence in fulfilling the requirements of the law—that is, performing the required sacrifices. When Jesus triumphed over death, he cancelled the charges against us and opened the way to the Father (Colossians 2:12–15). Because he is merciful, he offers us faith. How tragic if we turn faith into a work and try to develop it on our own! We can never come to God through our own faith, any more than his Old Testament people could come through their own sacrifices. Instead, we must accept his gracious offer with thanksgiving and allow him to plant the seed of faith within us.

1:14 What was Paul's debt? After his experience with Christ on the Damascus Road (Acts 9), his whole life was consumed with spreading the Good News of salvation. His debt was to Christ for being his Savior, and it was payable to the entire world. He paid his debt by proclaiming Christ's salvation to *all* people—both Jews and Gentiles, across all cultural, social, racial, and economic lines. We owe Christ this same debt because he took on the punishment we deserve for our sin. How will we begin to pay this "debt" back to him?

1:16 Jews and Christians alike stood against the idolatrous Roman religions, and Roman officials often confused the two groups. This was especially easy to do since the Christian church in Rome was originally composed of Jewish converts who attended the feast of Pentecost (see Acts 2:10ff). By the time Paul wrote Romans, however, many Gentiles had joined the church. The Jews and the Gentiles needed to know the relationship between Judaism and Christianity.

1:16, 17 Paul was not ashamed, because his message was *Good News.* It was powerful, it was for everyone, and it was part of God's revealed plan. When you are tempted to be ashamed, remember what the Good News is all about. If you focus on God and on what God is doing in the world rather than on your own inadequacy, your embarrassment will soon disappear.

1:16 Why did the message go to the Jews first? They had been God's special people for more than a thousand years, ever since God chose Abraham and promised great blessings to his descendants (Genesis 12:1–3). God did not choose them because they deserved to be chosen (Deuteronomy 7:7, 8; 9:4–6), but because he wanted to bless them, teach them, and prepare them to welcome his Messiah into the world. He chose them, not to play favorites, but to tell the world about his plan of salvation.

For centuries the Jews had been learning about God by obeying his laws, keeping his feasts, and living according to his moral principles. Often they forgot God's blessings; often they had to be disciplined; but still they had a precious heritage of belief in and obedience to the one true God. Of all the people on earth, the Jews should have been the most ready to welcome the Messiah and to understand his mission and message—and some of them were (see Luke 2:25, 36–38). Of course, the disciples and the great apostle Paul were faithful Jews who recognized in Jesus God's most precious gift to the human race.

1:17 Paul was quoting Habakkuk 2:4. When Habakkuk spoke of life, he may have meant this present life only, but Paul extends this to include eternal life. As we trust God, we are saved: we find life both now and forever.

God's anger at sin

18But God shows his anger from heaven against all sinful, evil men who push away the truth from them. 19For the truth about God is known to them instinctively; God has put this knowledge in their hearts. 20Since earliest times men have seen the earth and sky and all God made, and have known of his existence and great eternal power. So they will have no excuse [when they stand before God at Judgment Day].

21Yes, they knew about him all right, but they wouldn't admit it or worship him or even thank him for all his daily care. And after awhile they began to think up silly ideas of what God was like and what he wanted them to do. The result was that their foolish minds became dark and confused. 22Claiming themselves to be wise without God, they became utter fools instead. 23And then, instead of worshiping the glorious, ever-living God, they took wood and stone and made idols for themselves, carving them to look like mere birds and animals and snakes and puny men.

24So God let them go ahead into every sort of sex sin, and do whatever they wanted to—yes, vile and sinful things with each other's bodies. 25Instead of

1:18
Rom 5:9
Eph 5:6
Col 3:6
1:19
Jn 1:9
Acts 14:17
1:20
Ps 19:1
Acts 17:24
1:21
2 Kgs 17:15
Ps 106:13
Eph 4:17,18
1:22
Jer 10:14
1 Cor 1:20
1:23
Ps 106:20
Isa 40:18
Jer 2:11
1:24
Lev 18:22

1:19 *is known to them instinctively,* literally, "is manifest in them."   **1:20** *when they stand before God at Judgment Day,* implied. Or, "They have no excuse for saying there is no God."   **1:23** *puny,* literally, "mortal."

1:18ff Romans 1:18—3:20 develops Paul's argument that no one can claim to be good in God's sight—not the masses, not the Romans, not even the Jews. All people everywhere deserve God's condemnation.

1:18 Why is God angry at sinful people? Because even though God is holy and free of all evil, and even though he created people to love him and give glory to him, Adam and Eve rebelled and went their own way. Now all people are sinful. No one, except for Jesus, has ever been able to live perfectly. The holy God, who is the source of all life and hope, cannot live with sin, which brings death. He wants to remove the sin and restore the sinner—if the sinner does not push away the truth. But his anger erupts against those who insist and persist in living a sinful life.

1:18–20 In these verses, Paul answers a common objection: How could a loving God send anyone to hell, especially someone who has never heard the Good News of Jesus? In fact, says Paul, God has revealed himself plainly to *all* people. Everyone knows what God requires, but no one lives up to it. Put another way, our moral standards are always better than our behavior. If people suppress God's truth in order to live their own way, they have no excuse. They know the truth, and they will have to endure the consequences of ignoring it.

1:18–20 Does anyone have an excuse for not believing in God? The Bible answers an emphatic *no.* God has revealed his existence in his creation. Every person, therefore, either accepts or rejects God. Don't be fooled. When the day comes for God to judge your response to him, there will be no excuses. Begin today to give him what he deserves—your devotion and worship.

1:18–20 Some say, "Why do we need missionaries if people can know about God through nature (the things that have been made)?" (1) Although people know that God exists, they suppress that truth by their wickedness and thus deny him. (2) Although people may believe in God, they refuse to respond to him properly. (3) People who reject God need to be convinced of the consequences of their actions. (4) Most importantly, people need to hear about Jesus. Missionaries are needed to bring the Good News about Jesus. (5) Jesus commanded us to make disciples throughout the world (Matthew 28:19, 20). Missionaries are needed in order to help the church to be obedient to the great commission of our Lord.

Knowing that God exists is not enough. People must learn that God is loving. They must understand what he did to show that love to us. They must accept his forgiveness and live their lives in his service (see 10:14, 15).

1:20 What kind of God does nature reveal? Nature shows us a

God of might, power, orderliness, and intricate detail; a God of love and beauty; a God who controls all things. But too often people try to create gods they can control rather than submit to the God who controls all things.

1:20 God reveals himself through nature, even though nature's testimony has been distorted by the Fall. Adam's sin resulted in a divine curse upon the whole natural order (Genesis 3:17–19); thorns and thistles were an immediate result, and natural disasters have been common from Adam's day to ours. If we want to know something *about* God, we can observe nature. But if we are to fully *understand* God and relate to him properly, we need more than nature—we also need his revelation in Scripture and in his Son. In Romans 8:19–21, Paul says that nature itself is eagerly awaiting its own redemption from the effects of sin (see Revelation 22:3).

1:21–24 How could intelligent people turn to idolatry? Idolatry begins when people reject what they know about God. Instead of looking to him as the Creator and sustainer of life, they see themselves as the center of the universe. They soon invent "gods" that are convenient projections of their own selfish plans and decrees. These gods may be wooden figures, but they may also be goals such as money, power, or comfort. They may even be misrepresentations of God himself—making God in our image, instead of the reverse. The common denominator is this—idolators worship the things God made rather than God himself. What are your priorities? Where are your dreams, your plans, your hopes? Do you worship God or idols of your own making?

1:21–32 Paul clearly portrays the inevitable downward spiral into sin. First people reject God; next they make up their own ideas of what a god should be and do; then they fall into sin—sexual sin, greed, hatred, envy, murder, fighting, lying, bitterness, gossip. Finally they grow to hate God and encourage others to do so. God does not cause this steady progression toward evil. Rather, when people reject him, he allows them to live as they choose. Once caught in the downward spiral, no one can pull himself out. Sinners must trust Christ alone to put them on the path of escape.

1:24–32 These people chose to reject God, and God allowed them to do it. God does not usually stop us from making choices against his will. He lets us declare our supposed independence from him, even though he knows that in time we will become slaves to our own rebellious choices—we will lose our freedom not to sin. Does life without God look like freedom to you? Look more closely. There is no worse slavery than slavery to sin.

1:25 People tend to believe lies that reinforce their own selfish, personal beliefs. Today more than ever we need to be careful about the input we allow to form our beliefs. With TV, music,

believing what they knew was the truth about God, they deliberately chose to believe lies. So they prayed to the things God made, but wouldn't obey the blessed God who made these things.

1:26
1 Thess 4:5
Jude 1

26That is why God let go of them and let them do all these evil things, so that even their women turned against God's natural plan for them and indulged in sex sin

1:27
Lev 18:22; 20:13
1 Cor 6:9,10

with each other. 27And the men, instead of having a normal sex relationship with women, burned with lust for each other, men doing shameful things with other men and, as a result, getting paid within their own souls with the penalty they so richly deserved.

1:28
Eph 5:4

28So it was that when they gave God up and would not even acknowledge him, God gave them up to doing everything their evil minds could think of. 29Their lives became full of every kind of wickedness and sin, of greed and hate, envy, murder, fighting, lying, bitterness, and gossip.

1:30
2 Tim 3:2

30They were backbiters, haters of God, insolent, proud braggarts, always thinking of new ways of sinning and continually being disobedient to their parents.

1:31
2 Tim 3:3

31They tried to misunderstand, broke their promises, and were heartless—without

1:32
Rom 6:21,23

pity. 32They were fully aware of God's death penalty for these crimes, yet they went right ahead and did them anyway, and encouraged others to do them, too.

God's judgment of sin

2:1
2 Sam 12:5-9
Mt 7:1

2:2
2 Thess 1:6

2:3
Prov 11:21

2 "Well," you may be saying, "what terrible people you have been talking about!" But wait a minute! You are just as bad. When you say they are wicked and should be punished, you are talking about yourselves, for you do these very same things. 2And we know that God, in justice, will punish anyone who does such things as these. 3Do you think that God will judge and condemn others for doing

1:31 *tried to misunderstand,* or "were confused fools."

---

movies, and the rest of the media often presenting something less than wholesome values, we find ourselves constantly bombarded by philosophies and assumptions that are in direct opposition to the Bible. Be careful about what you allow to form your opinions. The Bible is the only standard of truth. Look at all other opinions in light of its teachings.

1:26, 27 God's *natural* plan is God's ideal for his creation. Unfortunately, what comes *naturally* to human nature is sin. Sin often means not only denying God, but also denying the way we are made. When our society says that any sex act is acceptable so long as nobody gets hurt, it is fooling itself. In the long run (and often in the short run), sin hurts people—individuals, families, whole societies. How sad that people who worship the things God made instead of the Creator so often distort and destroy the very things they claim to value! But it is impossible to understand God's natural plan without knowing the Creator himself.

1:27 Homosexuality is strictly forbidden in Scripture (Leviticus 18:22). Homosexuality is considered an acceptable practice by many in our world today—even by some churches. Many homosexuals believe that their desires are normal and that they have a right to express them. But God does not obligate nor encourage us to fulfill all of our desires (even normal ones). Those desires that violate his laws are wrong and are to be avoided.

If you have this desire, you can and must resist acting upon it. Consciously avoid places or activities you know will kindle temptations of this kind. Don't underestimate the power of Satan to tempt you nor the potential for serious harm if you yield to these temptations. Remember, God can and will forgive sexual sins just as he forgives other sins. Surrender yourself to the grace and mercy of God, asking him to show you the way out of sin and into the light of his freedom and his love. Prayer, Bible study, and strong Christian fellowship in a Bible-believing church can help you to gain strength to resist these powerful temptations. If you are already deeply involved in this sin, you may need to seek help from a trustworthy, professional, pastoral counselor.

1:32 How were these people aware of God's death penalty?

Human beings, created in God's image, have a basic moral nature and a conscience. This truth is understood beyond religious circles. Psychologists, for example, say that the rare person who seems to have no conscience has a serious personality disorder, one that is extremely difficult to treat. Most people instinctively know when they do wrong—but they may not care. Some people will even trade an early death for the freedom to indulge their desires now. "I know it's wrong, but I really want it," they say; or, "I know it's dangerous, but it's worth the risk." For such people, part of the "fun" is going against God's law, the community's moral standards, common sense, or their own sense of right and wrong. But deep down inside they know that sin deserves the punishment of death (Romans 6:23).

2:1ff When Paul's letter was read in the Roman church, no doubt many heads nodded as he condemned idol worshipers, homosexual practices, and violent people. But what surprise his listeners must have felt when he turned on them and said, "You are just as bad!" Paul was emphatically making a point that is central to understanding the Good News—*nobody* is good enough to save himself. All of us in the entire human family, if we want to avoid punishment and live eternally with Christ, must depend totally on God's grace. This is true whether we have been murderers and child molesters or whether we have been honest, hardworking, solid citizens. Paul is not discussing whether some sins are worse than others. He is simply saying that *any* sin is enough to cause us to depend on Jesus Christ for salvation and eternal life. There is no way apart from Christ to be saved from sin, and we have all sinned repeatedly.

2:1 Whenever we find ourselves feeling justifiably angry about some sin we have observed in our community, we should be careful. We need to speak out against sin, but we must do so in a spirit of humility. Often the sins we see most clearly in others are the ones that have taken root in us. If we look closely at ourselves, we may find that we are committing the same sin in more socially acceptable forms. For example, one who gossips may be very critical of others who gossip about him.

them and overlook you when you do them, too? 4Don't you realize how patient he is being with you? Or don't you care? Can't you see that he has been waiting all this time without punishing you, to give you time to turn from your sin? His kindness is meant to lead you to repentance.

5But no, you won't listen; and so you are saving up terrible punishment for yourselves because of your stubbornness in refusing to turn from your sin; for there is going to come a day of wrath when God will be the just Judge of all the world. 6He will give each one whatever his deeds deserve. 7He will give eternal life to those who patiently do the will of God, seeking for the unseen glory and honor and eternal life that he offers. 8But he will terribly punish those who fight against the truth of God and walk in evil ways—God's anger will be poured out upon them. 9There will be sorrow and suffering for Jews and Gentiles alike who keep on sinning. 10But there will be glory and honor and peace from God for all who obey him, whether they are Jews or Gentiles. 11For God treats everyone the same.

12-15He will punish sin wherever it is found. He will punish the heathen when they sin, even though they never had God's written laws, for down in their hearts they know right from wrong. God's laws are written within them; their own conscience accuses them, or sometimes excuses them. And God will punish the Jews for sinning because they have his written laws but don't obey them. They know what is right but don't do it. After all, salvation is not given to those who know what to do, unless they do it. 16The day will surely come when at God's command Jesus Christ will judge the secret lives of everyone, their inmost thoughts and motives; this is all part of God's great plan which I proclaim.

God's law is broken

17You Jews think all is well between yourselves and God because he gave his laws to you; you brag that you are his special friends. 18Yes, you know what he wants; you know right from wrong and favor the right because you have been taught his laws from earliest youth. 19You are so sure of the way to God that you

2:7 *who patiently do the will of God,* literally, "who patiently do good." *seeking for the unseen glory and honor and eternal life that he offers,* implied. **2:10** *all who obey him,* literally, "all who do good." **2:17** *gave his laws to you,* or, "you rely upon the law for your salvation."

2:4
Ex 34:5,6
Rom 9:22,23
11:22
Eph 1:7
2 Pet 3:9

2:5
Ps 110:5
Jas 5:3

2:6
Mt 16:27

2:7
Mt 25:46
Lk 8:15
2 Cor 4:17
Heb 10:36
Jude 21
Rev 2:7

2:8
Isa 3:11
2 Thess 2:12

2:11
Job 34:19

2:12-15
Mt 7:21-26
Jn 13:17
Acts 10:35
Jas 1:22

2:16
Jn 5:22
Acts 10:42
Rom 16:25,26
Rev 20:12

2:17
Mic 3:11

2:18
Deut 4:8

Romans 3:23	Everyone has sinned.	**SALVATION'S**
Romans 6:23	The penalty for our sin is death.	**FREEWAY**
Romans 5:8	Jesus Christ died for sin.	
Romans 10:8–10	To be forgiven for our sin, we must believe and confess that Jesus is Lord. Salvation comes through Jesus Christ.	

2:4 It is easy to mistake God's patience for approval of the wrong way we are living. Self-evaluation is difficult, and it is even more difficult to expose our lives to God and let him tell us where we need to change. But as Christians we must pray constantly that God will point out our sins, so that he can heal them. Unfortunately, we are more likely to be amazed at God's patience with others than humbled at his patience with us.

2:5-11 Although we usually are not punished immediately for each sin, God's eventual judgment is certain. We don't know exactly when it will happen, but we know that no one will escape that final encounter with the Creator. For more on judgment, see John 12:48 and Revelation 20:11-15.

2:7 Paul says that those who *do* God's will find eternal life. He is not contradicting his previous statement that salvation comes by faith alone (1:16, 17). We are not saved by good works, but when we commit our lives fully to God, we want to please him and do his will. As such, our good works are a grateful *response* to what God has done, not a prerequisite to earning his grace.

2:12-15 People are condemned not for what they don't know, but for what they do with what they know. Those who know God's

written Word and his law will be judged by them. Those who have never seen a Bible still know right from wrong, and they will be judged because they did not keep even those standards which they did know.

2:12-15 If you traveled around the world, you would find evidence in every society and culture of God's moral law. For example, all cultures prohibit murder, and yet in all societies that law has been broken. We belong to a stubborn race. We know what's right, but we insist on doing what's wrong. It is not enough to know what's right; we must also do it. Admit to yourself and to God that you fit the human pattern and frequently fail to live up to your own standards (much less to God's standards). That's the first step to forgiveness and healing.

2:17ff Paul continues to build his argument that all stand guilty before God. After describing the fate of the unbelieving, pagan Gentiles, he moves to that of the religiously privileged. Despite their knowledge of God's will, they are guilty because they too have refused to live by their beliefs. Those who have grown up in Christian families are the religiously privileged of today. Paul's condemnation applies to them if they do not live up to what they know.

could point it out to a blind man. You think of yourselves as beacon lights, directing men who are lost in darkness to God. ²⁰You think that you can guide the simple and teach even children the affairs of God, for you really know his laws, which are full of all knowledge and truth.

²¹Yes, you teach others—then why don't you teach yourselves? You tell others not to steal—do *you* steal? ²²You say it is wrong to commit adultery—do *you* do it? You say, "Don't pray to idols," and then make money your god instead.

²³You are so proud of knowing God's laws, *but you dishonor him by breaking them*. ²⁴No wonder the Scriptures say that the world speaks evil of God because of you.

²⁵Being a Jew is worth something if you obey God's laws; but if you don't, then you are no better off than the heathen. ²⁶And if the heathen obey God's laws, won't God give them all the rights and honors he planned to give the Jews? ²⁷In fact, those heathen will be much better off than you Jews who know so much about God and have his promises but don't obey his laws.

²⁸For you are not real Jews just because you were born of Jewish parents or because you have gone through the Jewish initiation ceremony of circumcision. ²⁹No, a real Jew is anyone whose heart is right with God. For God is not looking for those who cut their bodies in actual body circumcision, but he is looking for those with changed hearts and minds. Whoever has that kind of change in his life will get his praise from God, even if not from you.

God remains faithful

3 Then what's the use of being a Jew? Are there any special benefits for them from God? Is there any value in the Jewish circumcision ceremony? ²Yes, being a Jew has many advantages.

First of all, God trusted them with his laws [so that they could know and do his will]. ³True, some of them were unfaithful, but just because they broke their promises to God, does that mean God will break his promises? ⁴Of course not!

2:22 *make money your god instead,* literally, "do you rob temples?" **2:27** *will be much better off,* literally, "will condemn you." **3:2** *so that they could know and do his will,* implied.

2:20
2 Tim 3:5
2:21
Mt 23:3
2:22
Mal 3:8
2:23
Jn 5:45
Rom 9:4
2:24
2 Sam 12:14
Isa 52:5
Ezek 36:20
2:25
Gal 5:3
2:26
Acts 10:34
2:28
Mt 3:9
Jn 8:39
Gal 6:15
Rev 2:9
2:29
Jn 1:47
Rom 7:6
2 Cor 3:6
Phil 3:3
Col 2:11
1 Pet 3:4

3:2
Deut 4:8
Ps 147:19
Acts 7:38
3:3
Num 23:18,19
3:4
Ps 51:4; 62:9

2:21-27 These verses are a scathing criticism of hypocrisy. It is much easier to tell others how to behave than to behave properly ourselves. It is easier to say the right words than to allow them to take root in our lives. Knowing God's will, however, is not the same as doing it. Do you ever tell others to do something you are unable to do yourself? Make sure your actions match your words.

2:21, 22 Paul explained to the Jews that they needed to judge *themselves,* not others, by their law. They knew the law so well that they had learned how to excuse their own actions while criticizing others. But the law is more than the "letter"—it is a guideline for living according to God's will, and it is also a reminder that we cannot live righteously without a relationship with God. As Jesus pointed out, even withholding what rightfully belongs to someone else is stealing (Mark 7:9-13), and looking on another person with lustful, adulterous intent is adultery (Matthew 5:27, 28). Before we accuse others, we must look at ourselves and see if that sin, in any form, exists within us.

2:24 If you claim to be one of God's people, your life should reflect what God is like. When you disobey God, you dishonor his name, and people may even speak evil of God because of you. What do people think about God from watching your life?

2:28, 29 To be a Jew meant you were in God's family, an heir to all his promises. Yet Paul made it clear that membership in God's family is based on internal, not external, qualities. All whose hearts are right with God are real Jews—that is, part of God's family (see also Galatians 3:7). Attending church or being baptized, confirmed, or accepted for membership are not enough, just as circumcision was not enough for the Jews.

3:1ff In this chapter Paul continues to build his case that all men stand guilty before God. Paul has dismantled the common excuses

of people who refuse to admit they are sinners: (1) "There is no God" or "I follow my conscience"—1:18-32; (2) "I'm not as bad as other people"—2:1-16; (3) "I'm a church member" or "I'm a religious person"—2:17-29. No one will be exempted from God's judgment on sin. Every person must accept that he or she is sinful and condemned by God. Only then can God's wonderful gift of salvation be understood and received.

3:1ff What a depressing picture Paul is painting! All of us—pagan Gentiles, humanitarians, or religious people—are condemned by our own actions. The law, which God gave to show the way to live, holds up our evil deeds to public view. Is there any hope for us? Yes, says Paul. The law condemns us, it is true, but the law is not the basis of our hope. God himself is. He, in his righteousness and wonderful love, offers us eternal life. We receive our salvation not through law but through faith in Jesus Christ.

3:2 The Jewish nation had many advantages. (1) They were entrusted with God's laws (Exodus 19, 20; Deuteronomy 4:8); (2) They were the race through whom the Messiah would come to earth (Isaiah 11:1-10). (3) They were the beneficiaries of covenants with God himself (Genesis 17:1-16; Exodus 19:3-6). But these privileges did not make them better than anyone else (see 3:9). In fact, because of them the Jews were even more responsible to live up to God's requirements.

3:4 This promise that God's words will always prove true, no matter what anyone says or does, is both a comfort and a challenge. It is a comfort to have something solid and unchanging on which to build our lives. It is a challenge to make the changes that God's words require. If you have been struggling with habits, attitudes, or ideas that do not agree with God's words, a fresh recognition of his unchanging truth will help you toward change.

Though everyone else in the world is a liar, God is not. Do you remember what the book of Psalms says about this? That God's words will always prove true and right, no matter who questions them.

5"But," some say, "our breaking faith with God is good, our sins serve a good purpose, for people will notice how good God is when they see how bad we are. Is it fair, then, for him to punish us when our sins are helping him?" (That is the way some people talk.) 6God forbid! Then what kind of God would he be, to overlook sin? How could he ever condemn anyone? 7For he could not judge and condemn me as a sinner if my dishonesty brought him glory by pointing up his honesty in contrast to my lies. 8If you follow through with that idea you come to this: the worse we are, the better God likes it! But the damnation of those who say such things is just. Yet some claim that this is what I preach!

3:5 Rom 5:8; 7:7 Gal 3:15

3:6 Job 34:17

3:7 Rom 9:19,20

3:8 Rom 5:20

All people are sinners

9Well, then, are we Jews *better* than others? No, not at all, for we have already shown that all men alike are sinners, whether Jews or Gentiles. 10As the Scriptures say,

"No one is good—no one in all the world is innocent."

11No one has ever really followed God's paths, or even truly wanted to.

12Every one has turned away; all have gone wrong. No one anywhere has kept on doing what is right; not one.

13Their talk is foul and filthy like the stench from an open grave. Their tongues are loaded with lies. Everything they say has in it the sting and poison of deadly snakes.

14Their mouths are full of cursing and bitterness.

15They are quick to kill, hating anyone who disagrees with them.

16Wherever they go they leave misery and trouble behind them, 17and they have never known what it is to feel secure or enjoy God's blessing.

18They care nothing about God nor what he thinks of them.

19So the judgment of God lies very heavily upon the Jews, for they are responsi-

3:9 Rom 1:18-32 2:1-29 Gal 3:21,22

3:10 Ps 14:1-3 53:1-4

3:13 Ps 5:9; 140:3

3:14 Ps 10:7

3:15 Prov 1:16 Isa 59:7

3:18 Ps 36:1

3:19 Rom 2:2,12

3:13 *Their talk is foul and filthy like the stench from an open grave,* literally, "Their throat is an open grave." Perhaps the meaning is "Their speech injures others." **3:15** *hating anyone who disagrees with them,* implied.

ELECTION Romans 9:10–13	God's choice of an individual or group for a specific purpose or destiny.	**CRUCIAL CONCEPTS IN ROMANS**
JUSTIFICATION Romans 4:25; 5:18	God's act of declaring us "not guilty" for our sins.	
PROPITIATION/EXPIATION Romans 3:25	The removal of God's punishment for sin through the perfect sacrifice of Jesus Christ.	
REDEMPTION Romans 3:24; 8:23	Jesus Christ has paid the price so we can go free. The price of sin is death; Jesus paid the price.	
SANCTIFICATION Romans 5:2; 15:16	Becoming more and more like Jesus Christ through the work of the Holy Spirit.	
GLORIFICATION Romans 8:18, 19	The ultimate state of the believer after death when he or she becomes like Christ (1 John 4:4).	

3:5 Some of us think we don't have to worry about sin because (1) it's God's job to forgive; (2) God is so loving, he won't judge us; (3) sin isn't so bad—it teaches us valuable lessons, or (4) we need to stay in touch with the culture around us. It is far too easy to take God's grace for granted. But God cannot overlook sin. Sinners, no matter how many excuses they make, will have to answer to God for their sin.

3:10–12 Paul is referring to Psalm 14:1-3. "No one is good" means "no one is innocent." Every person is valuable in God's eyes because God created us in his image and he loves us, but no one is righteous (that is, no one can earn right standing with God). Though valuable, we have fallen into sin. But God, through Jesus his Son, has redeemed us and offers to forgive us if we return to him in faith.

3:10–18 Paul uses these Old Testament references to show that humanity in general, in its present sinful condition, is unacceptable before God. Have you ever thought to yourself, "Well, I'm not too bad. I'm a pretty good person"? Look at these verses and see if any of them apply to you. Have you ever lied? Have you ever hurt someone's feelings by your words or tone of voice? Are you bitter toward anyone? Do you become angry with those who strongly disagree with you? In thought, word, and deed you, like everyone else in the world, stand guilty before God. We must remember who we are in his sight—alienated sinners. Don't deny that you are a sinner. Instead, allow that knowledge to point you toward Christ.

3:19 The last time someone accused you of wrongdoing, what was your reaction? Denial, argument, and defensiveness? The Bible tells us the world stands hushed and guilty before Almighty

ble to keep God's laws instead of doing all these evil things; not one of them has any excuse; in fact, all the world stands hushed and guilty before Almighty God.

3:20
Ps 143:2
Acts 13:39
Rom 4:15; 7:7
Gal 2:16; 3:11

20Now do you see it? No one can ever be made right in God's sight by doing what the law commands. For the more we know of God's laws, the clearer it becomes that we aren't obeying them; his laws serve only to make us see that we are sinners.

➤ 2. Forgiveness of sin through Christ
Christ took our punishment

3:21
Rom 1:2,17
9:30

3:22
Rom 4:16; 10:4,12
Gal 2:16
Col 3:11
Heb 11:4
1 Pet 1:10
2 Pet 1:1

3:23
Rom 3:9
Gal 3:21,22

3:24
Eph 1:7; 2:8
Heb 9:12
1 Pet 1:18,19

3:25
Lev 16:15
Acts 17:30
Heb 9:13,14
1 Pet 1:19
1 Jn 2:2; 4:10

3:27
Rom 2:17; 4:2
1 Cor 1:29
Eph 2:9

3:28
Acts 13:39

3:29
Rom 9:24
10:12; 15:9
Gal 3:28

21, 22But now God has shown us a different way to heaven—not by "being good enough" and trying to keep his laws, but by a new way (though not new, really, for the Scriptures told about it long ago). Now God says he will accept and acquit us—declare us "not guilty"—if we trust Jesus Christ to take away our sins. And we all can be saved in this same way, by coming to Christ, no matter who we are or what we have been like. 23Yes, all have sinned; all fall short of God's glorious ideal; 24yet now God declares us "not guilty" of offending him if we trust in Jesus Christ, who in his kindness freely takes away our sins.

25For God sent Christ Jesus to take the punishment for our sins and to end all God's anger against us. He used Christ's blood and our faith as the means of saving us from his wrath. In this way he was being entirely fair, even though he did not punish those who sinned in former times. For he was looking forward to the time when Christ would come and take away those sins. 26And now in these days also he can receive sinners in this same way, because Jesus took away their sins.

But isn't this unfair for God to let criminals go free, and say that they are innocent? No, for he does it on the basis of their trust in Jesus who took away their sins.

27Then what can we boast about doing, to earn our salvation? Nothing at all. Why? Because our acquittal is not based on our good deeds; it is based on what Christ has done and our faith in him. 28So it is that we are saved by faith in Christ and not by the good things we do.

29And does God save only the Jews in this way? No, the Gentiles, too, may come to him in this same manner. 30God treats us all the same; all, whether Jews or

3:21, 22 *God has shown us a different way to heaven,* literally, "A righteousness of God has been manifested."
3:25 *saving us from his wrath,* literally, "to be a propitiation." **3:28** *saved,* literally, "justified."

God. No excuses or arguments are left. Have you reached the point with God where you are ready to hang up your defenses and await his decision? If you haven't, stop now and admit your sin to him. If you have, the next five verses are truly good news for you!

➤ **3:20, 21** In these verses we see two purposes of God's law. First, it shows us where we go wrong. Because of the law, we know we are helpless sinners, and we are driven to Jesus Christ for mercy. Second, the moral code revealed in the law can serve to guide our actions by holding up God's moral standards. We do not earn salvation by keeping the law (no one except Christ ever kept or could keep the law perfectly), but we do please God when our lives conform to his revealed will for us.

3:21–29 After all this bad news about our sinfulness and God's condemnation, Paul now gives the wonderful news. There is a way to be declared not guilty—by trusting Jesus Christ to take away our sins. Trusting means putting our confidence in him to forgive our sins, to make us right with God, and to empower us to live the way he wants us to live. This is God's solution, and it is available to all of us regardless of our background or past behavior.

3:23 Some sins seem bigger than others because their obvious consequences are much more serious. Murder, for example, seems to us to be worse than hatred, and adultery seems worse than lust. But this does not mean we can get away with some sins and not with others. All sin makes us sinners, and all sin cuts us off from our holy God. All sin, therefore, leads to death (because it disqualifies us from living with God), regardless of how great or small it seems. Don't minimize "little" sins or overrate "big" sins. They all separate us from God, but they all can be forgiven.

3:24 When a judge in a court of law declares the defendant not guilty, all the charges are removed from his record. Legally, it is as if the person had never been accused. When God forgives our sins, our record is wiped clean. From his perspective, it is as though we had never sinned.

3:25 What happened to people who lived before Christ came and died for sin? If God condemned them, is he being unfair? If he saved them, was Christ's sacrifice unnecessary? Paul shows that God forgave all human sin at the cross of Jesus. Old Testament believers looked forward by faith to Christ's coming and were saved, even though they did not know Jesus' name or the details of his earthly life. New Testament believers look back in faith to their crucified Savior. Unlike the Old Testament believers, you know about the God who loved the world so much that he gave his own Son (John 3:16). Have you put your trust in him?

3:27, 28 Most religions prescribe specific duties that must be performed to make a person acceptable to God. Christianity is unique in teaching that the good things we do will not put us right with God. No amount of human achievement or progress in personal development will close the gap between God's moral perfection and our imperfect daily performance. Good deeds are fine, but they will not earn us eternal life. We are saved only by trusting in what God has done for us (see Ephesians 2:8–10).

3:28 Why does God save us by faith alone? (1) Faith eliminates human pride. (2) Faith exalts God, not people. (3) Faith makes salvation available to all. (4) Faith admits that we can't keep the law or measure up to God's standards—we need help. (5) Faith is based on a relationship with God, not on performance for God.

Gentiles, are acquitted if they have faith. ³¹Well then, if we are saved by faith, does this mean that we no longer need obey God's laws? Just the opposite! In fact, only when we trust Jesus can we truly obey him.

3:31
Mt 5:17
Lk 20:16

— *Abraham was justified by faith*

4 Abraham was, humanly speaking, the founder of our Jewish nation. What were his experiences concerning this question of being saved by faith? Was it because of his good deeds that God accepted him? If so, then he would have something to boast about. But from God's point of view Abraham had no basis at all for pride. ³For the Scriptures tell us Abraham *believed God,* and that is why God canceled his sins and declared him "not guilty."

4:2
1 Cor 1:31
4:3
Gen 15:6
Gal 3:6
Jas 2:23

⁴, ⁵But didn't he earn his right to heaven by all the good things he did? No, for being saved is a gift; if a person could earn it by being good, then it wouldn't be free—but it is! It is *given* to those who do *not* work for it. For God declares sinners to be good in his sight if they have faith in Christ to save them from God's wrath.

4:4,5
Josh 24:2
Acts 13:38,39
Rom 11:6
Gal 2:16

⁶King David spoke of this, describing the happiness of an undeserving sinner who is declared "not guilty" by God. ⁷"Blessed, and to be envied," he said, "are those whose sins are forgiven and put out of sight. ⁸Yes, what joy there is for anyone whose sins are no longer counted against him by the Lord."

4:6
1 Cor 1:30
2 Cor 5:19
4:7
Ps 32:1,2

⁹Now then, the question: Is this blessing given only to those who have faith in Christ but also keep the Jewish laws, or is the blessing also given to those who do not keep the Jewish rules, but only trust in Christ? Well, what about Abraham? We say that he received these blessings through his faith. Was it by faith alone? Or because he also kept the Jewish rules?

4:8
Ps 32:1,2
2 Cor 5:19
4:9
Gen 15:6
Rom 3:30

¹⁰For the answer to that question, answer this one: *When* did God give this blessing to Abraham? It was *before he became a Jew*—before he went through the Jewish initiation ceremony of circumcision.

4:10
Gen 15:6
17:10,11
4:11
Gen 17:1-11
Lk 19:9
Jn 8:39
Rom 4:16

¹¹It wasn't until later on, *after* God had promised to bless him *because of his faith,* that he was circumcised. The circumcision ceremony was a sign that Abra-

4:5 *if they have faith in Christ to save them from God's wrath,* literally, "faith is reckoned for righteousness."
4:6 *"not guilty,"* literally "righteous." **4:8** *by the Lord,* see Psalm 32:1, 2.

3:31 This verse can also be translated: "Do we then overthrow the law by this faith? By no means! On the contrary, we uphold the law." There were some misunderstandings between Jewish and Gentile Christians at Rome. Worried Jewish Christians were asking Paul, "Does faith wipe out everything Judaism stands for? Does it cancel our Scriptures, put an end to our customs, declare that God is no longer working through us?" (This is essentially the question used to open chapter 3.) "Absolutely not!" says Paul. When we understand the way of salvation through faith, we understand the Jewish religion better. We know why Abraham was chosen, why the Mosiac law was given, why God worked patiently with Israel for centuries. Faith does not wipe out the Old Testament. Rather, it makes God's dealings with the Jewish people understandable. In chapter 4, Paul will expand on this theme (see also 5:20, 21; 8:3, 4; 13:9, 10; Galatians 3:24–29; and 1 Timothy 1:8 for more on this concept).

4:1 The Jews were proud to be called children of Abraham. Paul used Abraham as a good example of someone who was saved by faith. By emphasizing faith, Paul was not saying God's laws are unimportant (4:13), but that it is impossible to be saved simply by obeying them. For more about Abraham, see his Profile in Genesis 17.

4:5 Some people, when they learn that we are saved through faith, start to worry. "Do I have enough faith?" they wonder, "Is my faith strong enough to save me?" These people miss the point. It is Jesus Christ who saves us, not *our* feelings or actions, and he is strong enough to save us no matter how weak our faith is. Jesus

offers us salvation as a gift, because he loves us, not because we have earned it through our powerful faith. What, then, is the role of faith? Faith is believing and trusting in Jesus Christ, reaching out to accept his wonderful gift of salvation. Faith is effective whether it is great or small, timid or bold—because God loves us.

4:6 What can we do with guilt? King David was guilty of terrible sins—adultery, murder, lies—and yet he experienced the joy of forgiveness. We too can have this joy when we (1) quit denying our guilt and recognize we have sinned, (2) admit our guilt to God and ask his forgiveness, and (3) let go of our guilt and believe God has forgiven us. This can be difficult when a sin has taken root and grown over many years, when it is very serious, or when it involves others; but we must remember that Jesus is willing and able to forgive all possible sins. In view of the tremendous price he paid on the cross, it is arrogant to think any of our sins are too great for him to cover.

4:10 Circumcision was an outward sign for the Jews that they were a people special to God. Circumcision of all Jewish boys set the Jewish people apart from the nations who worshiped other gods; thus it was a very important ceremony. God gave the blessing and the command for this ceremony to Abraham (Genesis 17:9–14).

4:10–12 Rituals did not earn any blessings for Abraham; he was blessed long before the circumcision ceremony was introduced. Genesis 12:1–4 tells of God's call to Abraham when he was 75 years old; the circumcision ceremony was introduced when he was

ham already had faith and that God had already accepted him and declared him just and good in his sight—before the ceremony took place. So Abraham is the spiritual father of those who believe and are saved without obeying Jewish laws. We see, then, that those who do not keep these rules are justified by God through faith. 12And Abraham is also the spiritual father of those Jews who have been circumcised. They can see from his example that it is not this ceremony that saves them, for Abraham found favor with God by faith alone, *before he was circumcised.*

4:13
Gen 12:3; 17:4-6
22:17,18
Rom 9:8
Gal 3:16,29

4:14
Gal 3:18

4:15
Rom 3:20; 7:7
1 Cor 15:55,56
Gal 3:10

13It is clear, then, that God's promise to give the whole earth to Abraham and his descendants was not because Abraham obeyed God's laws but because he trusted God to keep his promise. 14So if you still claim that God's blessings go to those who are "good enough," then you are saying that God's promises to those who have faith are meaningless, and faith is foolish. 15But the fact of the matter is this: when we try to gain God's blessing and salvation by keeping his laws we always end up under his anger, for we always fail to keep them. The only way we can keep from breaking laws is not to have any to break!

4:16
Rom 9:8
Col 3:11

4:17
Gen 17:5
Isa 51:2
Jn 5:21
1 Cor 1:28-30

16So God's blessings are given to us by faith, as a free gift; we are certain to get them whether or not we follow Jewish customs if we have faith like Abraham's, for Abraham is the father of us all when it comes to these matters of faith. 17That is what the Scriptures mean when they say that God made Abraham the father of many nations. God will accept all people in every nation who trust God as Abraham did. And this promise is from God himself, who makes the dead live again and speaks of future events with as much certainty as though they were already past.

4:18
Gen 15:5

4:19
Gen 17:17; 18:11
Heb 11:11,12

4:22
Rom 4:3

18So, when God told Abraham that he would give him a son who would have many descendants and become a great nation, Abraham believed God even though such a promise just couldn't come to pass! 19And because his faith was strong, he didn't worry about the fact that he was too old to be a father, at the age of one hundred, and that Sarah his wife, at ninety, was also much too old to have a baby.

4:23
Acts 13:30
Rom 15:4
1 Cor 10:11
2 Tim 3:16

20But Abraham never doubted. He believed God, for his faith and trust grew ever stronger, and he praised God for this blessing even before it happened. 21He was completely sure that God was well able to do anything he promised. 22And because of Abraham's faith God forgave his sins and declared him "not guilty."

4:25
Isa 53:5
Rom 8:32-34
1 Cor 15:12-20
2 Cor 5:15
Heb 9:28
1 Pet 1:21; 3:18

23Now this wonderful statement—that he was accepted and approved through his faith—wasn't just for Abraham's benefit. 24It was for us, too, assuring us that God will accept us in the same way he accepted Abraham—when we believe the promises of God who brought back Jesus our Lord from the dead. 25He died for our sins and rose again to make us right with God, filling us with God's goodness.

4:19 *at ninety,* see Gen 17:17.   **4:25** *rose again to make us right with God,* literally "raised for our justification."

---

99 (Genesis 17:1–14). Ceremonies and rituals serve as reminders of our faith. They are not important in themselves, and we should not think that they give us any special merit before God. They are outward symbols that demonstrate an inner change of heart and attitude. The focus of our faith should be on Christ and his saving actions, not on our own actions.

4:16 Paul explains that Abraham was blessed through his faith alone, before he ever heard about the rituals that would become so important to the Jewish people. We too are saved by faith plus nothing. It is not by loving God and doing good that we are saved; neither is it by faith plus love or faith plus good works. We are saved only through faith in Christ, trusting him to forgive all our sins.

4:17 The promise (or covenant) God gave Abraham said that Abraham would be the father of many nations (Genesis 17:2–4) and that the entire world would be blessed through him (Genesis 12:3). This promise was fulfilled in Jesus Christ. Jesus was from Abraham's line, and truly the whole world was blessed through him. Paul points out that the promise to Abraham to be the father of

many nations extended beyond Israel to all nations of the world.

4:20–22 Abraham never doubted that God would fulfill his promise. His life was marked by mistakes, sins, and failures as well as by wisdom and goodness, but he consistently trusted God. His life is an example of faith in action. If he had looked only at his own resources for subduing Canaan and founding a nation, he would have given up in despair. But he looked to God, obeyed him, and waited for God to fulfill his word to him.

4:25 When we believe, an exchange takes place. We give Christ our sins, and he gives us his goodness and forgiveness (see 2 Corinthians 5:21). There is nothing we can do to earn this. Only through Christ can we receive God's goodness. What an incredible bargain for us, but many still choose to pass it up to continue "enjoying" their sin.

Faith brings joy

5 So now, since we have been made right in God's sight by faith in his promises, we can have real peace with him because of what Jesus Christ our Lord has done for us. ²For because of our faith, he has brought us into this place of highest privilege where we now stand, and we confidently and joyfully look forward to actually becoming all that God has had in mind for us to be.

³We can rejoice, too, when we run into problems and trials for we know that they are good for us—they help us learn to be patient. ⁴And patience develops strength of character in us and helps us trust God more each time we use it until finally our hope and faith are strong and steady. ⁵Then, when that happens, we are able to hold our heads high no matter what happens and know that all is well, for we know how dearly God loves us, and we feel this warm love everywhere within us because God has given us the Holy Spirit to fill our hearts with his love.

⁶When we were utterly helpless with no way of escape, Christ came at just the right time and died for us sinners who had no use for him. ⁷Even if we were good, we really wouldn't expect anyone to die for us, though, of course, that might be barely possible. ⁸But God showed his great love for us by sending Christ to die for us while we were still sinners. ⁹And since by his blood he did all this for us as sinners, how much more will he do for us now that he has declared us not guilty? Now he will save us from all of God's wrath to come. ¹⁰And since, when we were

5:1
Eph 2:14
Col 1:20

5:2
Eph 2:18; 3:12
Heb 3:6; 10:19

5:3
Mt 5:11
Phil 2:17

5:5
2 Cor 1:22
Gal 4:6
Eph 1:13
Phil 1:20

5:6
Gal 2:20; 4:4
Eph 5:2

5:8
Jn 3:16; 15:13
1 Pet 3:18

5:9
Rom 1:18
1 Thess 1:10
1 Jn 1:7

5:10
Rom 8:34
2 Cor 5:18
Eph 2:3

What we have as Adam's children	What we have as God's children	**WHAT WE HAVE**
Ruin 5:9	Rescue 5:8	**AS CHILDREN**
Sin 5:12, 15, 21	Righteousness 5:18	
Death 5:12, 16, 21	Eternal life 5:17, 21	
Separation from God 5:18	Relationship with God 5:11, 19	
Disobedience 5:12, 19	Obedience 5:19	
Judgment 5:18	Deliverance 5:10, 11	
Law 5:20	Grace 5:20	

5:1-5 These verses introduce a section that contains some difficult concepts. To understand the next four chapters, it helps to keep in mind the two-sided reality of the Christian life. On the one hand, we are complete in Christ (our acceptance with him is secure); on the other hand, we are growing in Christ (we are becoming more and more like him). At the same time we have the status of kings and the duties of slaves. We feel both the presence of Christ and the pressure of sin. We enjoy the peace that comes from being made right with God, but we still face daily problems that help us grow. If we remember these two sides of the Christian life, we will not grow discouraged as we face temptations and problems. Instead, we will learn to depend on the power available to us from Christ, who lives in us in the person of the Holy Spirit.

5:1 We now have peace *with* God, which differs from peaceful feelings such as assurance, security, and confidence. Peace with God means that we have been reconciled with him. There is no more hostility between us, no sin blocking our relationship with him. Peace with God is possible only because Jesus paid the price for our sins with his death on the cross.

5:2 Paul states that, as believers, we now stand in a place of highest privilege. Not only has God declared us not guilty; he has drawn us close to him. Instead of enemies, we have become his friends—in fact, his own children (John 15:15; Galatians 4:5).

5:2-5 As Paul states clearly in 1 Corinthians 13:13, faith, hope, and love are at the heart of the Christian life. Our relationship with God begins with *faith*, which helps us realize that we are delivered from our past by Christ's death. *Hope* grows as we learn all that God has in mind for us; it gives us the promise of the future. And God's *love* fills our lives and gives us the ability to reach out to others.

5:3, 4 Paul tells us that in the future we will *become,* but until then

we must *overcome.* This means we will experience difficulties that help us grow. Problems we run into will develop our patience—which in turn will strengthen our character, deepen our trust in God, and give us greater confidence about the future. You probably find your patience tested in some way every day. Thank God for these opportunities to grow, and deal with them in his strength (see also James 1:2–4; 1 Peter 1:6, 7).

5:5 All three members of the Trinity are involved in salvation. The Father loved us so much that he sent his Son to bridge the gap between us (John 3:16). The Father and the Son send the Holy Spirit to fill our lives with love and to enable us to live by his power (Acts 1:8).

5:6 We were helpless because we could do nothing on our own to save ourselves. Someone had to come and rescue us. Not only did Christ come at a good time in history; he came at exactly the right time—according to God's own schedule. God controls all history, and he controlled the timing, methods, and results of Jesus' death.

5:8 *While we were still sinners*—these are amazing words. God sent Jesus Christ to die for us, not because we were good enough, but because he loved us so much. Whenever you feel uncertain about God's love for you, remember that he loved you even before you turned to him.

5:9, 10 The love that caused Christ to die is the same love that sends the Holy Spirit to live in us and bless us every day. The power that raised Christ from the dead is the same power that saved you and is available to you in your daily life. Be assured that, having begun a life with Christ, you have a reserve of power and love to call on each day for help to meet every challenge or trial. Just as you can pray for forgiveness, you can pray for God's power and love as you need it.

his enemies, we were brought back to God by the death of his Son, what blessings he must have for us now that we are his friends, and he is living within us! ¹¹Now we rejoice in our wonderful new relationship with God—all because of what our Lord Jesus Christ has done in dying for our sins—making us friends of God.

➤ Adam and Christ contrasted

¹²When Adam sinned, sin entered the entire human race. His sin spread death throughout all the world, so everything began to grow old and die, for all sinned. ¹³[We know that it was Adam's sin that caused this] because although, of course, people were sinning from the time of Adam until Moses, God did not in those days judge them guilty of death for breaking his laws—because he had not yet given his laws to them, nor told them what he wanted them to do. ¹⁴So when their bodies died it was not for their own sins since they themselves had never disobeyed God's special law against eating the forbidden fruit, as Adam had.

What a contrast between Adam and Christ who was yet to come! ¹⁵And what a difference between man's sin and God's forgiveness!

For this one man, Adam, brought death to many through his *sin*. But this one man, Jesus Christ, brought forgiveness to many through God's *mercy*. ¹⁶Adam's *one* sin brought the penalty of death to many, while Christ freely takes away *many* sins and gives glorious life instead. ¹⁷The sin of this one man, Adam, caused *death to be king over all*, but all who will take God's gift of forgiveness and acquittal are *kings of life* because of this one man, Jesus Christ. ¹⁸Yes, Adam's *sin* brought *punishment* to all, but Christ's *righteousness* makes men *right with God*, so that they can live. ¹⁹Adam caused many to be sinners because he *disobeyed* God, and Christ caused many to be made acceptable to God because he *obeyed*.

²⁰The Ten Commandments were given so that all could see the extent of their failure to obey God's laws. But the more we see our sinfulness, the more we see God's abounding grace forgiving us. ²¹Before, sin ruled over all men and brought them to death, but now God's kindness rules instead, giving us right standing with God and resulting in eternal life through Jesus Christ our Lord.

5:12 *grow old and die*, literally, "Sin entered into the world and death through sin."   **5:13** *We know that it was Adam's sin that caused this*, implied.   **5:14** *so when their bodies died it was not for their own sins*, implied.   **5:17** *are kings of life*, literally, "reign in life."

Cross-references (left margin):

5:12
Gen 2:17
Ezek 18:4
Rom 6:23
1 Cor 15:21,22,56

5:13
1 Jn 3:4

5:14
Hos 6:7
1 Cor 15:45

5:15
Isa 53:11

5:17
Gen 2:17
3:6,19
1 Cor 15:21

5:18
Rom 4:25
Heb 2:9

5:19
Rom 11:32
Phil 2:8

5:20
Lk 7:47
Jn 15:22
Rom 3:20; 4:15
7:8
Gal 3:19
1 Tim 1:14

5:21
Jn 1:17
Rom 6:23

5:11 How does Christ's death make us friends with God? God is holy, and he will not be associated with sin. All people are sinful, and all sin deserves punishment. Instead of punishing us with the death we deserve, however, Christ took our sins upon himself and paid the price for them with his own death. Now the way to friendship with God has been opened. Through faith in *his* work, we become his friends rather than enemies and outcasts.

5:12 How can we be declared guilty for something Adam did thousands of years ago? Many feel it isn't right for God to judge us because of Adam's sin, yet each of us confirms our solidarity with Adam by our sins. We are made of the same stuff, prone to rebel, and we are judged for the sins *we* commit. Because we are sinners, it isn't fairness we need—it's mercy.

5:13, 14 Paul has abundantly shown that keeping the law does not bring salvation. Now he adds that breaking the Mosiac law is not what brings death. Death is the result of Adam's sin and of the sins we all commit, even if they don't resemble Adam's. For thousands of years, he reminds his readers, the law had not yet been explicitly given, and yet people died. The law was added, he explains in 5:20, to help people see their sinfulness, to show them the seriousness of their offenses, and to drive them to God for mercy and pardon. This was true in Moses' day, and it is still true today. Sin is a profound rupture between who we are and who we were created to be. The law points out our sin and places the responsibility for it squarely on our shoulders, but the law offers no remedy for it. When we're convicted of sin, we must turn to Jesus Christ for healing.

5:15–19 We are all born into Adam's physical family—the family line that leads to certain death. All of us reap the results of Adam's sin. We have inherited his guilt, the tendency to sin, and God's punishment. Because of Jesus, however, we can trade judgment for forgiveness. We can trade our sin for Jesus' goodness. Jesus offers us the opportunity to be born into his spiritual family—the family line that begins with forgiveness and leads to eternal life. If we do nothing, we have death through Adam; but if we come to God by faith, we have life through Christ. Which family line do you now belong to?

5:20 As a sinner, separated from God, you see his law from below, as a ladder to be climbed to get to God. Perhaps you have repeatedly tried to climb it, only to fall to the ground every time you have advanced one or two rungs. Or perhaps the sheer height of the ladder is so overwhelming that you have never even started up. In either case, what relief you should feel to see Jesus offering with open arms to lift you above the ladder of the law, to take you directly to God! Once Jesus lifts you into God's presence, you are free to obey—out of love, not necessity; through God's power, not your own. You know that if you stumble, you will not fall back to the ground. Instead, you will be caught and held in Jesus' loving arms.

3. Freedom from sin's grasp

Sin's power is broken

6 Well then, shall we keep on sinning so that God can keep on showing us more and more kindness and forgiveness?

2,3Of course not! Should we keep on sinning when we don't have to? For sin's power over us was broken when we became Christians and were baptized to become a part of Jesus Christ; through his death the power of your sinful nature was shattered. 4Your old sin-loving nature was buried with him by baptism when he died, and when God the Father, with glorious power, brought him back to life again, you were given his wonderful new life to enjoy.

5For you have become a part of him, and so you died with him, so to speak, when he died; and now you share his new life, and shall rise as he did. 6Your old evil desires were nailed to the cross with him; that part of you that loves to sin was crushed and fatally wounded, so that your sin-loving body is no longer under sin's control, no longer needs to be a slave to sin; 7for when you are deadened to sin you are freed from all its allure and its power over you. 8And since your old sin-loving nature "died" with Christ, we know that you will share his new life. 9Christ rose from the dead and will never die again. Death no longer has any power over him. 10He died once for all to end sin's power, but now he lives forever in unbroken fellowship with God. 11So look upon your old sin nature as dead and unresponsive

6:5 *when he died*, literally, "united with him in the likeness of his death."

— MASTER A OR B —

6:1 Rom 3:5,8; 6:15

6:2 Col 2:20; 3:3

6:3 Gal 3:27

6:4 Eph 4:22 Col 2:12; 3:10

6:5 Jn 14:19,20

6:6 Rom 7:24 Gal 2:20 Col 2:11,12

6:7 1 Pet 4:1

6:8 Jn 14:19

6:9 Acts 2:24

6:11 Rom 7:4 Col 2:20; 3:3

He has given us . . .				**WHAT HAS GOD DONE ABOUT SIN?**
New life	6:2, 3	Sin's power is broken.	We can be certain that sin's power is broken.	
	6:4	Sin-loving nature is buried.		
	6:6	You are no longer under sin's control.		
New nature	6:5	Now you share his new life.	We can see ourselves as unresponsive to the old power and alive to the new.	
	6:11	Look upon your old sin nature as dead and unresponsive, and instead be alive to God.		
New freedom	6:12	Do not let sin control you.	We can commit ourselves to obey Christ in perfect freedom.	
	6:13	Give yourselves completely to God.		
	6:14	You are free.		
	6:16	You can choose your own master.		

6:1—8:39 This section deals with *sanctification*—the change God makes in our lives when we become Christians. Chapter 6 explains that believers are free from sin's control. Chapter 7 discusses the continuing struggle believers have with sin. Chapter 8 describes how we can have victory over sin.

6:1 If God loves to forgive, why not give him more to forgive? If forgiveness is guaranteed, do we have the freedom to sin as much as we like? Paul's forceful answer is *no!* Such an attitude—deciding ahead of time to take advantage of God—would only make our sin worse. God's forgiveness does not make sin less serious. To the contrary, his Son's death for sin shows us how dreadfully serious sin is. We must never take lightly the price Jesus paid for our sin. Make it a regular habit to confess your sins to God and to ask his forgiveness.

6:1-4 In the church in Paul's day, immersion was the usual form of baptism—that is, new Christians were completely "buried" in water. They understood this form of baptism to symbolize the death and burial of the old way of life, followed by resurrection to life with Christ. If we think of our old, sinful life as dead and buried, we have a powerful motive to resist sin. Not wanting the ugly old life to come back to power again, we can consciously choose to treat it as if it were dead. Then we can continue to enjoy our wonderful new life with Jesus (see Galatians 3:27 and Colossians

3:1-4 for more on this concept).

6:5ff We can enjoy our new life in Christ because we have joined him in his death and resurrection. Our evil desires, our bondage to sin, and our love of sin died with him. Now, joining him in his resurrection life, we have unbroken fellowship with God and freedom from sin. For more on the difference between our new life in Christ and our old sinful nature read Ephesians 4:23, 24 and Colossians 3:3-15.

6:6 The penalty of sin and its power over our lives died with Christ on the cross. Paul has already stated that through faith in Christ we stand acquitted, "not guilty" before God. Here Paul emphasizes that we need no longer live under sin's power. God does not take us out of the world or make us robots—we will still feel like sinning, and sometimes we will sin. The difference is that before we were saved, we were slaves to our sinful nature, but now we can choose to live for Christ (see Galatians 2:20).

6:9-11 These verses offer wonderful assurances for your life as a believer in Jesus Christ. Because of him you need never fear death. This frees you to do his will, to be in unbroken fellowship with your Lord. This will affect all your activities—your work and your worship, your play and your Bible study, your quiet times and your times of caring for others. When you know you are free from death's power, you will experience a new vigor in life as a result.

to sin, and instead be alive to God, alert to him, through Jesus Christ our Lord.

6:12
Eph 4:22

12Do not let sin control your puny body any longer; do not give in to its sinful desires. 13Do not let any part of your bodies become tools of wickedness, to be used for sinning; but give yourselves completely to God—every part of you—for you are back from death and you want to be tools in the hands of God, to be used for his good purposes. 14Sin need never again be your master, for now you are no longer tied to the law where sin enslaves you, but you are free under God's favor and mercy.

6:13
Rom 12:1
2 Cor 5:14
Col 3:5

6:14
Rom 7:4,6
8:2,12
Gal 5:18
Tit 2:14

Slaves to righteousness

6:16
Jn 8:34
1 Cor 6:9,15
2 Pet 2:19

15Does this mean that now we can go ahead and sin and not worry about it? (For our salvation does not depend on keeping the law, but on receiving God's grace!) Of course not!

6:17
2 Tim 1:13

16Don't you realize that you can choose your own master? You can choose sin (with death) or else obedience (with acquittal). The one to whom you offer yourself—he will take you and be your master and you will be his slave. 17Thank God that though you once chose to be slaves of sin, now you have obeyed with all your heart the teaching to which God has committed you. 18And now you are free from your old master, sin; and you have become slaves to your new master, righteousness.

6:18
1 Cor 7:22
Gal 5:1
1 Pet 2:16

6:19
Mt 6:24

6:21
Jer 12:13
Rom 1:32; 8:6
Gal 6:8

19I speak this way, using the illustration of slaves and masters, because it is easy to understand: just as you used to be slaves to all kinds of sin, so now you must let yourselves be slaves to all that is right and holy.

6:22
Jn 8:32
Rom 8:2
1 Cor 7:22
1 Pet 1:9; 2:16

20In those days when you were slaves of sin you didn't bother much with goodness. 21And what was the result? Evidently not good, since you are ashamed now even to think about those things you used to do, for all of them end in eternal doom. 22But now you are free from the power of sin and are slaves of God, and his benefits to you include holiness and everlasting life. 23For the wages of sin is death, but the free gift of God is eternal life through Jesus Christ our Lord.

6:23
Mt 25:46
Jn 3:16; 4:10
17:2
Rom 5:21
Gal 6:8

No longer bound to the law

7:2
Mt 19:5,6
1 Cor 7:39

7 Don't you understand yet, dear Jewish brothers in Christ, that when a person dies the law no longer holds him in its power?

2Let me illustrate: when a woman marries, the law binds her to her husband as long as he is alive. But if he dies, she is no longer bound to him; the laws of

6:14 *Sin need never again be your master,* literally, "Sin will never again be your master."   **7:1** *dear Jewish brothers,* implied. Literally, "men who know the law."

6:14, 15 If we're no longer tied to the law, are we now free to sin? Paul says, "Of course not." When we were tied to the law, sin was our master—the law does not justify us or help us overcome sin. But now that we are bound to Christ, he is our master, and he gives us power to do good rather than evil.

6:16–18 In certain skilled crafts, an apprentice trains under a "master," who trains, shapes, and molds his apprentice in the finer points of his craft. As spiritual people, we choose a master and pattern ourselves after him. Without Jesus, we would have no choice—we would have to apprentice ourselves to sin, and the results would be guilt, suffering, and separation from God. Thanks to Jesus, however, we can now choose God as our master. Following him, we can enjoy new life and learn the ways of the kingdom. Are you continuing with your first master, sin? Or have you apprenticed yourself to God?

6:17 To obey with all your heart means to give yourself fully to God, to love him "with all your heart, soul, and mind" (Matthew 22:37). And yet so often our efforts to know and obey God's commands can best be described as "half-hearted." How do you rate your heart's obedience? God is more than willing to give you the power to obey him with all your heart.

6:17 The "teaching" committed to them is the Good News that Jesus died for their sins and was raised to give them new life.

6:19–22 It is impossible to be neutral. Every person has a master—either God or sin. A Christian is not someone who cannot sin or who never sins, but someone who is no longer a slave to sin. He belongs to God, not to sin.

6:23 Each of the two masters pays with his own kind of currency. The currency of sin is death. Christ's currency is eternal life—new life with God that begins on earth and continues forever with God.

7:1ff There is a progression in chapter 7 that parallels the progression in the first three chapters. Paul shows that the law is powerless to save the pagan (7:7–14), the lawkeeper (7:15–22), and even the man with a new nature (7:23–25). The pagan is condemned by it; the lawkeeper can't live up to it; and the man with the new nature finds himself sabotaged by the remaining old nature. Thus this chapter summarizes everything that has gone before—and once again, Paul declares that salvation cannot be found by obeying the law. No matter who we are, only Jesus Christ can set us free.

marriage no longer apply to her. ³Then she can marry someone else if she wants to. That would be wrong while he was alive, but it is perfectly all right after he dies.

⁴Your "husband," your master, used to be the Jewish law; but you "died," as it were, with Christ on the cross; and since you are "dead," you are no longer "married to the law," and it has no more control over you. Then you came back to life again when Christ did, and are a new person. And now you are "married," so to speak, to the one who rose from the dead, so that you can produce good fruit, that is, good deeds for God. ⁵When your old nature was still active, sinful desires were at work within you, making you want to do whatever God said not to, and producing sinful deeds, the rotting fruit of death. ⁶But now you need no longer worry about the Jewish laws and customs because you "died" while in their captivity, and now you can really serve God; not in the old way, mechanically obeying a set of rules, but in the new way, [with all of your hearts and minds].

God's law reveals sin

⁷Well then, am I suggesting that these laws of God are evil? Of course not! No, the law is not sinful but it was the law that showed me my sin. I would never have known the sin in my heart—the evil desires that are hidden there—if the law had not said, "You must not have evil desires in your heart." ⁸But sin used this law against evil desires by reminding me that such desires are wrong and arousing all kinds of forbidden desires within me! Only if there were no laws to break would there be no sinning.

⁹That is why I felt fine so long as I did not understand what the law really demanded. But when I learned the truth, I realized that I had broken the law and was a sinner, doomed to die. ¹⁰So as far as I was concerned, the good law which

7:3
Mt 5:32
Mk 10:12
Lk 16:18
1 Cor 6:9
Heb 13:4

7:4
Rom 6:2
Gal 5:18
1 Pet 2:24

7:5
Rom 6:21; 8:8
Gal 5:19-21

7:6
2 Cor 3:6
Gal 5:22
Phil 3:3

7:7
Ex 20:17
Rom 3:20
4:15; 5:20

7:8
Rom 3:20; 4:15
1 Cor 15:56

7:10
Ezek 20:13
Rom 10:15
2 Cor 3:7
Gal 3:12

7:6 *But now you need no longer worry about the Jewish laws and customs,* literally, "But now we are delivered from the law." *with all of your hearts and minds,* implied.

7:3–6 Paul uses marriage to illustrate our relationship to the law. When a spouse dies, the law of marriage no longer applies. Because we have died with Christ, the law can no longer condemn us. The law gave us no power to live a righteous life, but the Spirit enables us to produce good fruit for God. As new people living new lives in the power of the Spirit, we are bound to Christ and will serve him with our hearts and minds.

7:4 What does it mean to be a "new person"? When you acknowledge Christ as your Lord, your life changes forever. An unbeliever's mindset is centered on his own personal gratification. His source of power is his own self-determination. By contrast, the center of a Christian's life is God. He supplies the power for the Christian's daily living. Many believers find that their whole way of looking at the world changes when they come to Christ.

7:6 Some people try to earn their way to God by keeping a set of rules. All they earn for their efforts, of course, is frustration and discouragement. What a relief when these people discover that, because of Christ's sacrifice, the way to God is already open, and they can become his children simply by putting their faith in him. Strangely enough, once they feel secure in God's love, their behavior improves. No longer trying to reach God by keeping rules, they nevertheless become more and more like Jesus as they live with him day by day. But perhaps it isn't so strange after all. When the Holy Spirit turns our eyes away from our own performance and toward Jesus' love, our lives can't help but reflect him.

7:6 A lot of Christians think the law means only "a set of rules for ethical behavior." But in Paul's day, *the law* often meant "the whole Jewish economy." Few of Paul's Jewish readers thought they would obtain eternal life because they kept the Sabbath, didn't murder, didn't bear false witness, etc. They thought they had already made it because they were part of the Jewish system—the men were circumcised, they all participated in the feasts, they kept away from ceremonial defilement, and men and women both

thought they were saved by the law; i.e., by their participation in Jewish religious and cultural life.

During Luther's day a parallel situation had developed: people thought they were saved by the sacramental system of the Catholic church. If they were baptized, took communion, and confessed to a priest, they thought they would be saved. But Luther, like Paul, knew in his heart that this was not enough. The church was not taking away sin any more than the Jewish sacrificial system was: only God could do this, and he would do it only in response to faith.

7:6 Keeping a set of rules is often not extremely difficult. How many times this week—this year—have you seriously considered bowing to an idol, murdering someone, or stealing something?

But, keeping the rules doesn't save us. Even if we could keep our actions pure (which we don't), we would still know we're doomed in God's eyes because our hearts aren't right. Like Paul, we can find no relief in the synagogue or church until we look to Jesus Christ himself for our salvation—which he gives us freely, whether we come from a Jewish, Muslim, or Christian background. But if we do come to Jesus, we are flooded with relief and gratitude. Will we keep the rules any better? We should want to try, especially if we need to improve our morals. But we may still have problems with some sins even when we're saved. But keeping the law is not the purpose of Christ—Christ is the purpose for the law. When we realize that *he* saves us and not the law, we can focus less on what we should and shouldn't be doing and more on how we can best serve him in love and service.

7:9–11 If people feel fine without the law, why did God give it? Because sin is real, and it is dangerous. Imagine a sunny day at the beach. You have just plunged into the surf, and you've never felt better. Suddenly you notice a sign on the pier: "No swimming: sharks in water." Your day is ruined. Is it the sign's fault? Are you angry with the people who put it up? The law is like the sign. It is essential, and we are grateful for it—but it doesn't get rid of the sharks.

was supposed to show me the way of life resulted instead in my being given the death penalty. 11Sin fooled me by taking the good laws of God and using them to make me guilty of death. 12But still, you see, the law itself was wholly right and good.

13But how can that be? Didn't the law cause my doom? How then can it be good? No, it was sin, devilish stuff that it is, that used what was good to bring about my condemnation. So you can see how cunning and deadly and damnable it is. For it uses God's good laws for its own evil purposes.

The struggle within

14The law is good, then, and the trouble is not there but with *me*, because I am sold into slavery with Sin as my owner.

15I don't understand myself at all, for I really want to do what is right, but I can't. I do what I don't want to—what I hate. 16I know perfectly well that what I am doing is wrong, and my bad conscience proves that I agree with these laws I am breaking. 17But I can't help myself, because I'm no longer doing it. It is sin inside me that is stronger than I am that makes me do these evil things.

18I know I am rotten through and through so far as my old sinful nature is concerned. No matter which way I turn I can't make myself do right. I want to but I can't. 19When I want to do good, I don't; and when I try not to do wrong, I do it anyway. 20Now if I am doing what I don't want to, it is plain where the trouble is: sin still has me in its evil grasp.

21It seems to be a fact of life that when I want to do what is right, I inevitably do what is wrong. 22I love to do God's will so far as my new nature is concerned; 23, 24, 25but there is something else deep within me, in my lower nature, that is at war with my mind and wins the fight and makes me a slave to the sin that is still within me. In my mind I want to be God's willing servant but instead I find myself still enslaved to sin.

So you see how it is: my new life tells me to do right, but the old nature that is still inside me loves to sin. Oh, what a terrible predicament I'm in! Who will free

7:11 Gen 3:13

7:12 Ps 19:8 1 Tim 1:8

7:14 Rom 3:9; 6:6

7:15 1 Kgs 21:20-25 Gal 5:17

7:16 1 Tim 1:8

7:18 Gen 8:21 Jn 3:6 Rom 8:3

7:21 Rom 8:2

7:22 Ps 1:2

7:23-25 Rom 8:2 1 Cor 15:57 Gal 5:17 Col 2:11 Jas 4:1 1 Pet 2:11

7:11 Sin has always fooled people by misusing the law. When Eve encountered the serpent in the Garden of Eden (Genesis 3), the serpent fooled her by taking her focus off the freedom God had given her and putting it on the one restriction he had made. Ever since then, we have all been rebels. Sin looks good to us precisely because God has said it is bad. Instead of paying attention to his warnings, we use them as a "to do" list. When we feel rebellious, we need to back off and look at the law from a wider perspective—in the light of God's grace and mercy. If we focus on his great love for us, we will understand why he asks us to restrict our behavior. He only restricts us from things that ultimately will harm us.

7:15 Paul gives three lessons he learned in trying to deal with his old sinful desires. (1) Knowledge is not the answer (7:9). Paul felt fine as long as he did not understand what the law demanded. When he learned the truth, he knew he was doomed. (2) Self-determination doesn't succeed (7:15). Paul found himself sinning in ways that weren't even attractive to him. (3) Even a profound Christian experience does not instantly stamp out all sin from the believer's life (7:22-25). Becoming like Christ is a lifelong process; Paul likens Christian growth to a strenuous race or fight (1 Corinthians 9:24-27; 2 Timothy 4:7). Thus, as Paul has been emphasizing since the beginning of his letter to the Romans, *no one* in the world is innocent; no one deserves to be saved—not the pagan who doesn't know God's laws, not the Christian or Jew who knows them and tries to keep them. All of us must depend totally on the work of Christ for our salvation. We cannot earn it by our good behavior.

7:15 This is more than the cry of one desperate man—it describes the experience of any Christian struggling against sin. We must never underestimate the power of sin. Satan is a crafty tempter, and we have a great ability to make excuses. Instead of trying to overcome sin with human willpower, we must take hold of the tremendous power of Christ that is available to us. This is God's provision for victory over sin; he sends the Holy Spirit to live in us and give us power. And when we fall, he lovingly reaches out to us and helps us up.

7:17 "The devil made me do it." It sounds like a lame excuse, but it may be true. Without Christ's help, sin is stronger than we are, and sometimes we are unable to defend ourselves against its attacks. That is why we should never stand up to sin all alone. Jesus Christ, who has conquered sin once and for all, promises to fight by our side. If we look to him for help, we will not have to give in to sin.

7:23-25 The sin deep within us is sometimes called the "flesh" or the "law of our members." This is our vulnerability to sin; it refers to everything within us that is more loyal to the world and self than to God.

7:23-25 The inward confusion about sin we sometimes feel was as real for Paul as it is for us. From Paul we learn what to do about it. Whenever he felt lost, he would return to the beginning of his spiritual life, remembering that he had already been freed by Jesus Christ. When you feel confused, follow his example: thank God he has given you freedom through Jesus Christ. Let the reality of Christ's power lift you up to real victory over sin.

me from my slavery to this deadly lower nature? Thank God! It has been done by Jesus Christ our Lord. He has set me free.

The Holy Spirit frees us from sin

8 So there is now no condemnation awaiting those who belong to Christ Jesus. ²For the power of the life-giving Spirit—and this power is mine through Christ Jesus—has freed me from the vicious circle of sin and death. ³We aren't saved from sin's grasp by knowing the commandments of God, because we can't and don't keep them, but God put into effect a different plan to save us. He sent his own Son in a human body like ours—except that ours are sinful—and destroyed sin's control over us by giving himself as a sacrifice for our sins. ⁴So now we can obey God's laws if we follow after the Holy Spirit and no longer obey the old evil nature within us.

⁵Those who let themselves be controlled by their lower natures live only to please themselves, but those who follow after the Holy Spirit find themselves doing those things that please God. ⁶Following after the Holy Spirit leads to life and peace, but following after the old nature leads to death, ⁷because the old sinful nature within us is against God. It never did obey God's laws and it never will. ⁸That's why those who are still under the control of their old sinful selves, bent on following their old evil desires, can never please God.

⁹But you are not like that. You are controlled by your new nature if you have the Spirit of God living in you. (And remember that if anyone doesn't have the Spirit of Christ living in him, he is not a Christian at all.) ¹⁰Yet, even though Christ lives within you, your body will die because of sin; but your spirit will live, for Christ has pardoned it. ¹¹And if the Spirit of God, who raised up Jesus from the dead, lives in you, he will make your dying bodies live again after you die, by means of this same Holy Spirit living within you.

¹²So, dear brothers, you have no obligations whatever to your old sinful nature to do what it begs you to do. ¹³For if you keep on following it you are lost and will perish, but if through the power of the Holy Spirit you crush it and its evil deeds, you shall live. ¹⁴For all who are led by the Spirit of God are sons of God.

8:1
Rom 8:30,34

8:2
Rom 8:11
2 Cor 3:6
Gal 2:19; 5:1

8:3
Acts 13:39
2 Cor 5:21
Phil 2:7
Heb 2:14; 4:15

8:4
Gal 5:16,25

8:5
Gal 5:19-22

8:6
Gal 6:8

8:9
Jn 14:17,18,23
15:5; 17:23,26
Gal 4:6
Phil 1:19
1 Pet 1:11

8:10
Jn 14:20;
15:5; 17:23,26
2 Cor 13:5
Col 1:26,27

8:11
Rom 6:4,5
1 Cor 6:14; 15:45

8:13
Gal 6:8
Col 3:5

8:14
Jn 1:12
Gal 3:26
Rev 21:7

7:25 *It has been done,* or, "It will be done," literally, "I thank God through Jesus Christ our Lord." **8:10** *for Christ has pardoned it,* or possibly, "but the Holy Spirit who lives in you will give you life, for he has already given you righteousness." Literally, "but the Spirit is life because of righteousness."

8:1 "Not guilty; let him go free"—what would those words mean to you if you were on death row? The fact is, of course, that the whole human race *is* on death row, justly condemned for repeatedly breaking God's holy law. Without Jesus we would have no hope at all. But thank God! He has declared us not guilty and has offered us freedom from sin and power to do his will.

8:2 This life-giving Spirit is the Holy Spirit. He was present at the creation of the world (Genesis 1:2), and he is the power behind the rebirth of every Christian. He gives us the power we need to live the Christian life. For more about the Holy Spirit read the notes on John 3:6; Acts 1:4; 1:5.

8:3 Jesus gave himself as a *sacrifice* for our sins. In Old Testament times, animal sacrifices were continually offered at the Temple. The sacrifices showed the Israelites the seriousness of sin: blood had to be shed before sins could be pardoned (see Leviticus 17:11). But animal blood could not really remove sins (Hebrews 10:4). The sacrifices could only point to Jesus' sacrifice, which paid the penalty for all sins.

8:5, 6 Paul divides people into two categories—those who let themselves be controlled by their lower natures, and those who follow after the Holy Spirit. All of us would be in the first category if Jesus hadn't offered us a way out. Once we have said yes to Jesus, we will want to continue following him, because his way brings life and peace. Daily we must consciously choose to center our lives on God. Use the Bible to discover God's guidelines, and then follow them. Ask yourself in every perplexing situation, "What would Jesus want me to do?" When the Holy Spirit points out what

is right, do it eagerly. For more on our lower natures versus our new life in Christ, see 6:6–8; Ephesians 4:23, 24; Colossians 3:3–15.

8:9 Have you ever worried about whether or not you really are a Christian? A Christian is anyone who has the Spirit of God living in him. If you have sincerely trusted Christ for your salvation and acknowledged him as Lord, then the Holy Spirit has come into your life, and you are a Christian. You won't know the Holy Spirit has come if you are waiting for a certain feeling; you will know he has come because Jesus promised he would. When the Holy Spirit is working within you, you will believe that Jesus Christ is God's Son and that eternal life comes through him (1 John 5:5–8); you will begin to act as Christ directs (Romans 8:5; Galatians 5:22, 23); you will find help in your daily problems and in your praying (Romans 8:26, 27); you will be empowered to serve God and do his will (Acts 1:8; Romans 12:6ff); and you will become part of God's plan to build up his church (Ephesians 4:12, 13).

8:14–17 Paul uses adoption to illustrate the believer's new relationship with God. In Roman culture, the adopted person lost all rights in his old family and gained all the rights of a legitimate child in his new family. He became a full heir to his new father's estate. Likewise, when a person becomes a Christian, he gains all the privileges and responsibilities of a child in God's family. One of these outstanding privileges is being led by the Spirit (see Galatians 4:5, 6).

8:14–17 We are no longer cringing and fearful slaves; instead, we are the Master's children. What a privilege! Because we are God's

8:15
Gal 4:5,6

8:16
2 Cor 1:22
Eph 1:13

8:17
Gal 3:29; 4:7
Tit 3:7

15And so we should not be like cringing, fearful slaves, but we should behave like God's very own children, adopted into the bosom of his family, and calling to him, "Father, Father." 16For his Holy Spirit speaks to us deep in our hearts, and tells us that we really are God's children. 17And since we are his children, we will share his treasures—for all God gives to his Son Jesus is now ours too. But if we are to share his glory, we must also share his suffering.

The future glory

8:18
2 Cor 4:17
Col 3:4
1 Pet 1:6,7

8:19
2 Pet 3:13
1 Jn 3:2

8:20
Gen 3:17-19

8:21
Acts 3:21
2 Pet 3:13
Rev 21:1

8:22
Jer 12:4,11

8:23
Lk 20:36
2 Cor 1:22; 5:3-6
Phil 3:21

8:24
2 Cor 5:7
1 Thess 5:8
Heb 11:1

8:25
1 Thess 1:3

8:26
Zech 12:10
Mt 20:22
Jn 14:16

8:27
1 Thess 2:4
1 Jn 5:14

18Yet what we suffer now is nothing compared to the glory he will give us later. 19For all creation is waiting patiently and hopefully for that future day when God will resurrect his children. 20, 21For on that day thorns and thistles, sin, death, and decay—the things that overcame the world against its will at God's command—will all disappear, and the world around us will share in the glorious freedom from sin which God's children enjoy.

22For we know that even the things of nature, like animals and plants, suffer in sickness and death as they await this great event. 23And even we Christians, although we have the Holy Spirit within us as a foretaste of future glory, also groan to be released from pain and suffering. We, too, wait anxiously for that day when God will give us our full rights as his children, including the new bodies he has promised us—bodies that will never be sick again and will never die.

24We are saved by trusting. And trusting means looking forward to getting something we don't yet have—for a man who already has something doesn't need to hope and trust that he will get it. 25But if we must keep trusting God for something that hasn't happened yet, it teaches us to wait patiently and confidently.

26And in the same way—by our faith—the Holy Spirit helps us with our daily problems and in our praying. For we don't even know what we should pray for, nor how to pray as we should; but the Holy Spirit prays for us with such feeling that it cannot be expressed in words. 27And the Father who knows all hearts knows, of course, what the Spirit is saying as he pleads for us in harmony with God's own

8:19 *waiting . . . for that future day,* literally, "waiting for the revelation of the sons of God." **8:20, 21** *thorns and thistles, sin, death, and decay,* implied. **8:22** *suffer in sickness and death as they await this great event,* literally, "the whole creation has been groaning in travail together until now." **8:26** *by our faith,* implied. Literally, "in like manner."

---

children, we share in great treasures. God has already given us his best gifts: his Son, forgiveness, and eternal life; and he encourages us to ask him for whatever we need.

8:17 There is a price for being identified with Jesus. Along with the great treasures, Paul mentions the suffering that Christians must face. What kinds of suffering are we to endure? For first-century believers, there were economic and social consequences, and many faced persecution and death. We too must pay a price for following Jesus. In many parts of today's world, Christians face pressures just as severe as those faced by Christ's first followers. Even in countries where Christianity is tolerated or encouraged, Christians must not become complacent. To live as Jesus did—serving others, giving up one's own rights, resisting pressures to conform to the world—always exacts a price. Nothing we suffer, however, can compare to the great price Jesus paid to save us.

8:19-22 All creation, not just humans, suffered when sin came into the world. By saying we live in a "fallen" world, we mean that sin has caused all creation to fall from the perfect state in which God created it.

8:19-22 Christians see the world as it is—physically decaying and spiritually infected with sin. But Christians do not need to be pessimistic, for they have hope. They look forward to the new heaven and new earth God has promised, and they wait for God's new order that will free the world of sin, sickness, and evil. In the meantime, they go with Christ into the world, where they heal people's bodies and souls and fight the evil effects of sin.

8:23 We will be resurrected with bodies, but they will be glorified bodies like the body Christ now has in heaven (see 1 Corinthians 15:25-53).

8:24, 25 It is natural for children to trust their parents, even though parents sometimes fail to keep their promises. Our heavenly Father, however, never makes promises he won't keep. Nevertheless, his plan may take more time than we expect. Rather than acting like impatient children as we wait for it to unfold, we should place our confidence in God's trustworthiness.

8:24, 25 In Romans, Paul presents the idea that salvation is both present and future. It is present because the moment we believe in Jesus Christ as Savior we *are* saved (3:21-26; 5:1-11; 6:1-11; 6:22, 23); our new life (eternal life) begins. But at the same time, we have not fully received all the benefits and blessings of salvation that will be ours when Christ's new kingdom is completely established. While we can be confident of our salvation, we still look ahead with hope and trust toward that which lies beyond this life, that which we cannot see but yet know is more wonderful than we can comprehend.

8:26, 27 Believers are not left to their own resources to cope with problems. Even when you don't have words to pray, the Holy Spirit prays with and for you, and God answers. With God helping you pray, you don't need to be afraid to come before him. Ask the Holy Spirit to plead for you "in harmony with God's own will." Then, when you bring your requests to God, trust that he will always do what is best.

will. 28And we know that all that happens to us is working for our good if we love God and are fitting into his plans.

29For from the very beginning God decided that those who came to him—and all along he knew who would—should become like his Son, so that his Son would be the First, with many brothers. 30And having chosen us, he called us to come to him; and when we came, he declared us "not guilty," filled us with Christ's goodness, gave us right standing with himself, and promised us his glory.

Nothing can separate us from God's love

31What can we ever say to such wonderful things as these? If God is on our side, who can ever be against us? 32Since he did not spare even his own Son for us but gave him up for us all, won't he also surely give us everything else?

33Who dares accuse us whom God has chosen for his own? Will God? No! He is the one who has forgiven us and given us right standing with himself.

34Who then will condemn us? Will Christ? *No!* For he is the one who died for us and came back to life again for us and is sitting at the place of highest honor next to God, pleading for us there in heaven.

35Who then can ever keep Christ's love from us? When we have trouble or calamity, when we are hunted down or destroyed, is it because he doesn't love us anymore? And if we are hungry, or penniless, or in danger, or threatened with death, has God deserted us?

36No, for the Scriptures tell us that for his sake we must be ready to face death at every moment of the day—we are like sheep awaiting slaughter; 37but despite all this, overwhelming victory is ours through Christ who loved us enough to die for us. 38For I am convinced that nothing can ever separate us from his love. Death can't, and life can't. The angels won't, and all the powers of hell itself cannot keep God's love away. Our fears for today, our worries about tomorrow, 39or where we are—high above the sky, or in the deepest ocean—nothing will ever be able to separate us from the love of God demonstrated by our Lord Jesus Christ when he died for us.

8:28
2 Cor 4:17
Eph 1:11
2 Tim 1:9
8:29
a) Eph 1:5
2 Tim 2:19
1 Pet 1:2
b) Heb 1:6

8:31
Ps 118:6
8:32
Jn 3:16
Rom 4:25; 5:8
8:33
Isa 50:8,9
8:34
Heb 7:25
1 Jn 2:1

8:35
2 Cor 4:7-12

8:36
Ps 44:22
8:37
Jn 16:33
1 Cor 15:57
1 Jn 5:4
8:38
Jn 10:28
Col 3:3
8:39
Rom 5:3-8

8:28 God works out all things—not just isolated incidents—for our good. This does not mean that all that happens to us is good. Evil is prevalent in our fallen world, but God is able to turn it around for our long-range good. Note that God is not working to make us happy, but to fulfill his purpose. Note also that this promise is not for everybody. It can be claimed only by those who love God and are fitting into God's plans. Such people have a new perspective, a new mindset on life. They trust in God, not life's treasures; they look to their security in heaven, not on earth; they learn to accept pain and persecution on earth, not resent it, because it brings them closer to God.

8:29 God's ultimate goal for us is to make us like Christ (1 John 3:2). As we become more and more like him, we discover our true selves, the persons we were created to be.

8:29, 30 Some say these verses mean that before the beginning of the world, God chose certain people to receive his gift of salvation. They point to verses like Ephesians 1:11, which says "we were chosen from the beginning to be his." Others say that God *knew* who would and would not be saved, but he did not specially *choose* some and condemn others. They point to verses like 2 Peter 3:9, which says God "is not willing that *any* should perish." What is clear is that God's *purpose* for man was not an afterthought; it was settled before the foundation of the world. Mankind is to serve and glorify God. God has always known who would and would not be saved. This sovereignty of God should be a reason for rejoicing and confidence, not of puzzlement or doubt.

8:31–34 Do you ever think that, because you aren't good enough

for God, he will not save you? Do you ever feel as if salvation is for everyone else but you? Then these verses are especially for you. If God gave his Son for you, he isn't going to hold back the gift of salvation! If Christ gave his life for you, he isn't going to turn around and condemn you! The book of Romans is more than a theological explanation of God's redeeming grace—it is a letter of comfort and confidence addressed to you.

8:34 Paul says that Jesus is pleading with God for us in heaven. For more on the concept of Christ as our advocate, see note in Hebrews 4:14.

8:35, 36 These words were written to a church that would soon undergo terrible persecution. In just a few years, Paul's hypothetical situations would turn into painful realities. This passage reaffirms God's profound love for his people. No matter what happens to us or where we are, we can never be lost to his love. When suffering comes, it should not drive us away from God, but help us to identify with him further and allow his love to reach us and heal us.

8:35–39 These verses contain one of the most comforting promises in all Scripture. Believers have always had to face hardships in many forms: persecution, illness, imprisonment, even death. These could cause them to fear that they have been abandoned by Christ. But Paul exclaims that it is *impossible* to be separated from Christ. His death for us is proof of his unconquerable love. Nothing can stop his constant presence with us. God tells us how great his love is so that we will feel totally secure in him. If we believe these overwhelming assurances, we will not be afraid.

4. Israel's past, present, and future

God's sovereignty

9 Oh, Israel, my people! Oh, my Jewish brothers! How I long for you to come to Christ. My heart is heavy within me and I grieve bitterly day and night because of you. Christ knows and the Holy Spirit knows that it is no mere pretense when I say that I would be willing to be forever damned if that would save you. 4God has given you so much, but still you will not listen to him. He took you as his own special, chosen people and led you along with a bright cloud of glory and told you how very much he wanted to bless you. He gave you his rules for daily life so you would know what he wanted you to do. He let you worship him, and gave you mighty promises. 5Great men of God were your fathers, and Christ himself was one of you, a Jew so far as his human nature is concerned, he who now rules over all things. Praise God forever!

6Well then, has God failed to fulfill his promises to the Jews? No! [For these promises are only to those who are truly Jews.] And not everyone born into a Jewish family is truly a Jew! 7Just the fact that they come from Abraham doesn't make them truly Abraham's children. For the Scriptures say that the promises apply only to Abraham's son Isaac and Isaac's descendants, though Abraham had other children too. 8This means that not all of Abraham's children are children of God, but only those who believe the promise of salvation which he made to Abraham.

9For God had promised, "Next year I will give you and Sarah a son." 10-13And years later, when this son, Isaac, was grown up and married, and Rebecca his wife was about to bear him twin children, God told her that Esau, the child born first, would be a servant to Jacob, his twin brother. In the words of the Scripture, "I chose to bless Jacob, but not Esau." And God said this before the children were even born, before they had done anything either good or bad. This proves that God was doing what he had decided from the beginning; it was not because of what the children did but because of what God wanted and chose.

14Was God being unfair? Of course not. 15For God had said to Moses, "If I want to be kind to someone, I will. And I will take pity on anyone I want to." 16And so God's blessings are not given just because someone decides to have them or works hard to get them. They are given because God takes pity on those he wants to.

17Pharaoh, king of Egypt, was an example of this fact. For God told him he had given him the kingdom of Egypt for the very purpose of displaying the awesome power of God against him: so that all the world would hear about God's glorious name. 18So you see, God is kind to some just because he wants to be, and he makes some refuse to listen.

19Well then, why does God blame them for not listening? Haven't they done what he made them do?

20No, don't say that. Who are you to criticize God? Should the thing made say to the one who made it, "Why have you made me like this?" 21When a man makes a jar out of clay, doesn't he have a right to use the same lump of clay to make one jar

9:6 *For these promises are only to those who are truly Jews,* implied.   **9:17** *that all the world would hear about God's glorious name,* literally, "that my name might be published abroad in all the earth."

9:1–3 Paul expressed concern for his people Israel by saying he would willingly take their punishment if that could save them. While the only one who can save us is Christ, Paul showed a rare depth of love. Like Jesus, he was willing to sacrifice for others. How concerned are you for those who don't know Christ? Are you willing to sacrifice your time, money, energy, comfort, and safety to see them come to faith in Jesus?

9:6 God's promises were made to Abraham. Covenant people, the true children of Abraham, are not just his biological descendants. They are all those who trust in God and in what Jesus Christ has done for them. (See also 2:29; Galatians 3:7.)

9:14 Was it right for God to choose Jacob, the younger, to be over Esau? Keep in mind the kind of God we worship: he is

sovereign; he works for our good in everything; he is trustworthy; he will save all who believe in him. When we understand these qualities of God, we know his choices are good even if we don't understand all his reasons. Besides, if we wanted what was right, we would deserve death for our sins; it is not "fair" for God to punish Christ in our place. But would you think of asking God to take back his offer of salvation because you don't deserve it?

9:21 Paul is not saying that some of us are worth more than others, but simply that the Creator has control over the created object. The created object, therefore, has no right to demand anything from its Creator—its very existence depends on him. Keeping this perspective removes any temptation to have pride in personal achievement.

beautiful, to be used for holding flowers, and another to throw garbage into? 22Does not God have a perfect right to show his fury and power against those who are fit only for destruction, those he has been patient with for all this time? 23, 24And he has a right to take others such as ourselves, who have been made for pouring the riches of his glory into, whether we are Jews or Gentiles, and to be kind to us so that everyone can see how very great his glory is.

9:22
Prov 16:4
Rom 2:4
1 Thess 5:9

9:23
Acts 9:15
Rom 8:29

25Remember what the prophecy of Hosea says? There God says that he will find other children for himself (who are not from his Jewish family) and will love them, though no one had ever loved them before. 26And the heathen, of whom it once was said, "You are not my people," shall be called "sons of the Living God."

9:24
Rom 3:29

9:25
Hos 2:23

9:26
Hos 1:10
1 Pet 2:10

27Isaiah the prophet cried out concerning the Jews that though there would be millions of them, only a small number would ever be saved. 28"For the Lord will execute his sentence upon the earth, quickly ending his dealings, justly cutting them short."

9:27
Isa 10:22
Rom 11:5

9:28
Isa 28:22

29And Isaiah says in another place that except for God's mercy all the Jews would be destroyed—all of them—just as everyone in the cities of Sodom and Gomorrah perished.

9:29
Isa 1:9; 13:19
Lam 3:22

Israel's unbelief of the gospel

30Well then, what shall we say about these things? Just this, that God has given the Gentiles the opportunity to be acquitted by faith, even though they had not been really seeking God. 31But the Jews, who tried so hard to get right with God by keeping his laws, never succeeded. 32Why not? Because they were trying to be saved by keeping the law and being good instead of by depending on faith. They have stumbled over the great stumbling stone. 33God warned them of this in the Scriptures when he said, "I have put a Rock in the path of the Jews, and many will stumble over him (Jesus). Those who believe in him will never be disappointed."

9:30
Gal 2:16
Heb 11:7

9:31
Isa 51:1
Gal 5:4

9:32
Isa 8:14,15

9:33
Ps 118:22
Isa 28:16

10 Dear brothers, the longing of my heart and my prayer is that the Jewish people might be saved. 2I know what enthusiasm they have for the honor of God, but it is misdirected zeal. 3For they don't understand that Christ has died to

10:3
Rom 1:17
Phil 3:9

9:27 *millions*, literally, "as the sand of the sea," i.e., numberless. **9:29** *perished,* see Isa 1:9. **9:33** *never be disappointed,* see Isa 28:16.

9:25, 26 Seven hundred years before Jesus' birth, Hosea told of God's intention to bring Gentiles into his family after the Jews rejected his plan. Verse 25 is a quotation from Hosea 2:23 and verse 26 is from Hosea 1:10.

9:27-29 Isaiah prophesied that only a small number—a remnant—of God's original people, the Jews, would be saved. Paul saw this happening in every city where he preached. Even though he went to the Jews first, relatively few ever accepted the message. Verses 27 and 28 are based on Isaiah 10:22, 23; and 9:29 is from Isaiah 1:9.

9:31-33 Sometimes we are like these people, trying "hard to get right with God by keeping his laws." We may think church attendance, church work, giving offerings, and being nice will be enough. After all, we've played by the rules, haven't we? But Paul's words sting—this approach never succeeds. Paul explains that God's plan is not for those who try to earn his favor by being good; it is for those who realize they can never be good enough and so must depend on Christ. Only by putting our faith in what Jesus Christ has done will we be saved. If we do that, we will "never be disappointed."

9:32 The Jews had a worthy goal—to honor God. But they tried to achieve it the wrong way—by rigid and painstaking obedience to the law. Thus some of them became more dedicated to the law than to God. They thought that if they kept the law, God would have to accept them as his people. But God cannot be controlled. The Jews did not see that their Scriptures, the Old Testament, taught salvation by faith, and not by human effort (see Genesis 15:6).

9:32 The stumbling stone was Jesus. The Jews did not believe in

him because he didn't meet their expectations for the Messiah. Some people still stumble over Christ because salvation by faith doesn't make sense to them. They would rather try to work their way to God, or else they expect him simply to overlook their shortcomings. Others stumble over Christ because his values are the opposite of the world's. He asks for humility, not success; and many are unwilling to humble themselves before him. Some simply refuse to acknowledge any authority over them, and thus they stumble over the Lordship of Christ.

10:1 What will happen to the Jewish people who believe in God but not in Christ? Since they believe in the same God, won't they be saved? If that were true, Paul would not have worked so hard and sacrificed so much to teach them about Christ. Since Jesus is the most complete revelation of God, and we cannot fully know God apart from Christ; and since God appointed Jesus to bring God and man together, we cannot come to God by another path. The Jews, like everyone else, can find salvation only through Jesus Christ (John 14:6; Acts 4:12). Like Paul, we should wish that all Jews might be saved. We should pray for them and lovingly share the Good News with them.

10:3, 4 Why did God give the law when he knew people couldn't keep it? According to Paul, one reason the law was given was to show men how guilty they are (Galatians 3:19). The law was a shadow of Christ—that is, the sacrificial system educated the people so that when the true sacrifice came, they would be able to understand his work. The system of ceremonial laws was to last until the coming of Christ. The law points to Christ, the reason for all those animal sacrifices.

10:3-5 Rather than living by faith in God, the Jews established

10:4
Gal 3:24

10:5
Lev 18:4,5
Ezek 20:11,
13,21
Rom 7:10

10:6
Deut 30:11-14

10:7
1 Cor 15:3,4

10:8
Deut 30:14

10:9
Mt 10:32
Lk 12:8
Acts 2:24; 16:31
Rom 4:24

10:11
Isa 28:16

10:12
Acts 15:9
Eph 2:4-7

10:13
Joel 2:32
Acts 2:21

10:14
Acts 8:28-31
Tit 1:3

10:15
Isa 52:7
Rom 1:15; 15:20

10:16
Isa 53:1
Jn 12:38
Heb 4:2

10:17
Gal 3:2,5
Col 3:16

10:18
Ps 19:4
Mt 24:14

10:19
Deut 32:21

10:20
Isa 65:1,2

10:21
1 Sam 12:22
Jer 31:37

make them right with God. Instead they are trying to make themselves good enough to gain God's favor by keeping the Jewish laws and customs, but that is not God's way of salvation. ⁴They don't understand that Christ gives to those who trust in him everything they are trying to get by keeping his laws. He ends all of that.

⁵For Moses wrote that if a person could be perfectly good and hold out against temptation all his life and never sin once, only then could he be pardoned and saved. ⁶But the salvation that comes through faith says, "You don't need to search the heavens to find Christ and bring him down to help you," and, ⁷"You don't need to go among the dead to bring Christ back to life again."

⁸For salvation that comes from trusting Christ—which is what we preach—is already within easy reach of each of us; in fact, it is as near as our own hearts and mouths. ⁹For if you tell others with your own mouth that Jesus Christ is your Lord, and believe in your own heart that God has raised him from the dead, you will be saved. ¹⁰For it is by believing in his heart that a man becomes right with God; and with his mouth he tells others of his faith, confirming his salvation.

¹¹For the Scriptures tell us that no one who believes in Christ will ever be disappointed. ¹²Jew and Gentile are the same in this respect: they all have the same Lord who generously gives his riches to all those who ask him for them. ¹³Anyone who calls upon the name of the Lord will be saved.

¹⁴But how shall they ask him to save them unless they believe in him? And how can they believe in him if they have never heard about him? And how can they hear about him unless someone tells them? ¹⁵And how will anyone go and tell them unless someone sends him? That is what the Scriptures are talking about when they say, "How beautiful are the feet of those who preach the Gospel of peace with God and bring glad tidings of good things." In other words, how welcome are those who come preaching God's Good News!

¹⁶But not everyone who hears the Good News has welcomed it, for Isaiah the prophet said, "Lord, who has believed me when I told them?" ¹⁷Yet faith comes from listening to this Good News—the Good News about Christ.

¹⁸But what about the Jews? Have they heard God's Word? Yes, for it has gone wherever they are; the Good News has been told to the ends of the earth. ¹⁹And did they understand [that God would give his salvation to others if they refused to take it]? Yes, for even back in the time of Moses, God had said that he would make his people jealous and try to wake them up by giving his salvation to the foolish heathen nations. ²⁰And later on Isaiah said boldly that God would be found by people who weren't even looking for him. ²¹In the meantime, he keeps on reaching out his hands to the Jews, but they keep arguing and refusing to come.

10:10 *confirming his salvation,* literally, "confession is made unto salvation." **10:15** *good things,* see Isa 52:7. **10:16** *When I told them?,* see Isa 53:1. **10:19** *that God would give his salvation to others if they refused to take it,* implied. **10:20** *looking for him,* see Isa 65:1. **10:21** *arguing,* literally, "disobedient, obstinate."

---

customs and traditions (in addition to God's law) to try to make themselves acceptable in God's sight. But human effort, no matter how sincere, can never substitute for the goodness God offers us by faith. The only way to *earn* salvation is to be perfect—and that is impossible. We can only hold out our empty hands and receive it as a gift.

10:6–8 People have always looked for God through dramatic experiences. Hoping for a life-changing encounter, some travel across the world to meet a spiritual leader. But God's salvation is right in front of us. He will come to us wherever we are. All we need to do is to respond and accept his gift of salvation.

10:8–12 Have you ever been asked, "How do I become a Christian?" These verses give you the beautiful answer—salvation is as close as your own heart and mouth. People think it must be a complicated process, but it is not. If they believe in their hearts and say with their mouths that Christ is the risen Lord, they will be saved.

10:11 This verse must be read in context. Paul is not saying Christians will be free of all disappointments. There will be times

when people will let us down and when circumstances will take a turn for the worse. Paul is saying that God's offer of salvation will never disappoint us. Jesus Christ will never let us down: *everyone* who believes in him will be saved.

10:14, 15 God's great message of salvation must be taken to others, so they can have the chance to respond to the Good News. How will your loved ones and neighbors hear it unless someone tells them? Is God calling you to take a part in making his message known in your community? Think of one person who needs to hear the Good News, and think of something you can do to help him or her hear it. Then do that act as soon as possible.

10:20 Many Jews who were looking for the Messiah missed him. Many Gentiles who didn't even know about a Messiah found him. Today some of the most spiritually blind people are religious, and those who have never set foot in a church are sometimes the most responsive. Since appearances are deceiving and we can't see into people's hearts, beware of judging beforehand who will respond to the gospel and who will not.

God's mercy on Israel

11 I ask then, has God rejected and deserted his people the Jews? Oh no, not at all. Remember that I myself am a Jew, a descendant of Abraham and a member of Benjamin's family.

2,3No, God has not discarded his own people whom he chose from the very beginning. Do you remember what the Scriptures say about this? Elijah the prophet was complaining to God about the Jews, telling God how they had killed the prophets and torn down God's altars; Elijah claimed that he was the only one left in all the land who still loved God, and now they were trying to kill him too.

4And do you remember how God replied? God said, "No, you are not the only one left. I have seven thousand others besides you who still love me and have not bowed down to idols!"

5It is the same today. Not all the Jews have turned away from God; there are a few being saved as a result of God's kindness in choosing them. 6And if it is by God's kindness, then it is not by their being good enough. For in that case the free gift would no longer be free—it isn't free when it is earned.

7So this is the situation: Most of the Jews have not found the favor of God they are looking for. A few have—the ones God has picked out—but the eyes of the others have been blinded. 8This is what our Scriptures refer to when they say that God has put them to sleep, shutting their eyes and ears so that they do not understand what we are talking about when we tell them of Christ. And so it is to this very day.

9King David spoke of this same thing when he said, "Let their good food and other blessings trap them into thinking all is well between themselves and God. Let these good things boomerang on them and fall back upon their heads to justly crush them. 10Let their eyes be dim," he said, "so that they cannot see, and let them walk bent-backed forever with a heavy load."

11Does this mean that God has rejected his Jewish people forever? Of course not! His purpose was to make his salvation available to the Gentiles, and then the Jews would be jealous and begin to want God's salvation for themselves. 12Now if the whole world became rich as a result of God's offer of salvation, when the Jews stumbled over it and turned it down, think how much greater a blessing the world will share in later on when the Jews, too, come to Christ.

13As you know, God has appointed me as a special messenger to you Gentiles. I lay great stress on this and remind the Jews about it as often as I can, 14so that if

11:1
1 Sam 12:22
Jer 31:36,37
2 Cor 11:22
Phil 3:5

11:2
1 Kgs 19:10

11:4
1 Kgs 19:18

11:5
2 Kgs 19:4
Rom 9:27

11:6
Rom 4:4,5

11:7
Mk 6:52
2 Cor 3:14,15

11:8
Deut 29:4
Isa 6:9-13
29:10
Mt 13:14
Jn 12:40
Acts 28:26,27

11:9
Ps 69:22

11:10
Ps 69:23

11:11
Ezek 18:23
33:11
Acts 18:6

11:12
Jer 30:3-9,11
Zech 2:11

11:13
Acts 9:15

11:14
Rom 9:3
1 Cor 9:20
2 Tim 1:9

11:1ff In this chapter Paul points out that not *all* Jews have rejected God's message of salvation. Paul himself, after all, was a Jew, and so were Jesus' disciples and nearly all of the early Christian missionaries.

11:2, 3 God chose the Jews to be the people through whom the rest of the world could find salvation. But this did not mean the entire Jewish nation would be saved; only those who were faithful to God were considered true Jews. People are saved through faith in Christ, not because they are part of a nation, religion, or family. On what are you depending for salvation?

11:6 This great truth can be hard to grasp. Do you think it's easier for God to love you when you're good? Do you secretly suspect God chose you because you deserved to be chosen? Do you think some people's behavior is so bad that God couldn't possibly save them? If you ever think this way, you don't entirely understand the Good News that salvation is a free gift. It cannot be earned, in whole or in part; it can only be accepted with thankfulness and praise.

11:8–10 These verses describe the punishment for hardened hearts predicted by the prophet Isaiah (Isaiah 6:9–13). If people refuse to hear God's Good News, they eventually will be unable to understand it. Paul saw this happening in the synagogues he visited. (Verse 8 is based on Deuteronomy 29:4 and Isaiah 29:10.

Verses 9 and 10 are from Psalm 69:22, 23.)

11:11ff Paul had a vision for a church in which all Jews and Gentiles were united in their love of God and obedience to Christ. While respecting God's law, this ideal church would look to Christ alone for salvation and eternal life. One's ethnic background and social status would be irrelevant (see Galatians 3:28)—what mattered would be one's faith in Christ.

But Paul's vision has not yet come true. In his day many Jewish people rejected the Good News. They looked to their heritage for salvation, and they did not have the "heart religion" that was so important to the Old Testament prophets and to Paul.

Soon after Paul's day, once Gentiles were in control of most Christian churches, another obstacle to Jewish/Christian unity arose. Rather than loving those Jews who wanted to come into the church and yearning for their salvation, as Paul did, many Gentile Christians began rejecting them and even persecuting them. Unfortunately, this has often been continued through the centuries.

True Christians—those who follow Jesus from the heart—should not do such things, of course. But both Christians and Jews have done so much damage to the cause of the God they claim to serve that Paul's vision often seems impossible to fulfill.

Yet the truth remains—God chose the Jews, just as he chose the Christians, and he is still working to unite Jew and Gentile in a new Israel, a new Jerusalem, ruled by his Son.

possible I can make them want what you Gentiles have and in that way save some of them. 15And how wonderful it will be when they become Christians! When God turned away from them it meant that he turned to the rest of the world to offer his salvation; and now it is even more wonderful when the Jews come to Christ. It will be like dead people coming back to life. 16And since Abraham and the prophets are God's people, their children will be too. For if the roots of the tree are holy, the branches will be too.

17But some of these branches from Abraham's tree, some of the Jews, have been broken off. And you Gentiles who were branches from, we might say, a wild olive tree, were grafted in. So now you, too, receive the blessing God has promised Abraham and his children, sharing in God's rich nourishment of his own special olive tree.

18But you must be careful not to brag about being put in to replace the branches that were broken off. Remember that you are important only because you are now a part of God's tree; you are just a branch, not a root.

19"Well," you may be saying, "those branches were broken off to make room for me so I must be pretty good."

20Watch out! Remember that those branches, the Jews, were broken off because they didn't believe God, and you are there only because you do. Do not be proud; be humble and grateful—and careful. 21For if God did not spare the branches he put there in the first place, he won't spare you either.

22Notice how God is both kind and severe. He is very hard on those who disobey, but very good to you if you continue to love and trust him. But if you don't, you too will be cut off. 23On the other hand, if the Jews leave their unbelief behind them and come back to God, God will graft them back into the tree again. He has the power to do it.

24For if God was willing to take you who were so far away from him—being part of a wild olive tree—and graft you into his own good tree—a very unusual thing to do—don't you see that he will be far more ready to put the Jews back again, who were there in the first place?

God's mercy on all

25I want you to know about this truth from God, dear brothers, so that you will not feel proud and start bragging. Yes, it is true that some of the Jews have set themselves against the Gospel now, but this will last only until all of you Gentiles have come to Christ—those of you who will. 26And then all Israel will be saved.

Do you remember what the prophets said about this? "There shall come out of Zion a Deliverer, and he shall turn the Jews from all ungodliness. 27At that time I will take away their sins, just as I promised."

28Now many of the Jews are enemies of the Gospel. They hate it. But this has been a benefit to you, for it has resulted in God's giving his gifts to you Gentiles.

11:15 Lk 15:24,32 Rom 5:11

11:17 Jer 11:16 Eph 2:11-16

11:18 Jn 4:22 1 Cor 10:12

11:20 Rom 12:16 Phil 2:12

11:22 Jn 15:2 Heb 3:6

11:23 2 Cor 3:14-16

11:25 Lk 21:24 Rom 11:12; 16:25 Eph 3:3-6

11:26 Ps 14:7 Isa 59:20 Jer 3:18

11:27 Jer 31:31 Heb 8:8; 10:16

11:15 In the early days following Pentecost, the Christian church was predominantly Jewish, and Gentiles were the exception. But because of the missionary efforts of Peter, Philip, Paul, and others, Gentiles became believers and soon became the majority in the church. However, this does not mean there is no longer any place in the church for Jews. When a Jew comes to Christ, there is great rejoicing, as if a dead person had come back to life.

11:17-21 Paul, speaking to Gentile Christians, is warning them not to feel superior because God rejected some Jews. The Jewish religion, he says, is like the root of a tree, and the Jewish people are the tree's natural branches. Gentile believers have been grafted into the tree, and now Jews and Gentiles share its nourishment. Both Jews and Gentiles depend on Christ for life; neither can rest on heritage, culture, or theological beliefs for salvation.

11:26 Some say the phrase "And then all Israel will be saved" means that the majority of Jews in the final generation before Christ's return will turn to Christ for salvation. Others say that Paul is using the term "Israel" in the sense of the "spiritual" nation of Israel made up of everyone—Jew and Gentile—who has received salvation through faith in Christ. Thus "all Israel" (or all believers) will receive God's promised gift of salvation. God chose the nation of Israel, and he has never rejected it. He also chose the church, through Jesus Christ, and he will never reject it either. This does not mean, of course, that all Jews or all church members will be saved. It is possible to belong to a nation or to an organization without ever responding in faith to Jesus.

11:28-32 In this passage Paul shows how the Jews and the Gentiles benefit each other. Whenever God shows mercy on one group, the other shares the blessing. In God's original plan, the Jews would freely share their blessings with the Gentiles (see Genesis 12:3). When the Jews neglected to do this, God blessed the Gentiles anyway through the Jewish Messiah. Now it is the Gentiles' turn to bless the Jews. God's plans will not be thwarted: he will "have mercy upon all alike." For a beautiful picture of Jews and Gentiles being blessed together, see Isaiah 60.

Yet the Jews are still beloved of God because of his promises to Abraham, Isaac, and Jacob. 29For God's gifts and his call can never be withdrawn; he will never go back on his promises. 30Once you were rebels against God, but when the Jews refused his gifts God was merciful to you instead. 31And now the Jews are the rebels, but some day they, too, will share in God's mercy upon you. 32For God has given them all up to sin so that he could have mercy upon all alike.

33Oh, what a wonderful God we have! How great are his wisdom and knowledge and riches! How impossible it is for us to understand his decisions and his methods! 34For who among us can know the mind of the Lord? Who knows enough to be his counselor and guide? 35And who could ever offer to the Lord enough to induce him to act? 36For everything comes from God alone. Everything lives by his power, and everything is for his glory. To him be glory evermore.

11:29
Num 23:18-24
Heb 7:21
11:32
Rom 3:9
Gal 3:22
11:33
Job 11:7; 15:8
Eph 3:8,10
11:34
Isa 40:13
1 Cor 2:16
11:35
Job 35:7; 41:11
Col 1:16
11:36
1 Cor 8:6

B. HOW TO BEHAVE (12:1—16:27)

Moving from theological to practical, Paul gives guidelines for living as a redeemed people in a fallen world. We are to give ourselves to Christ as living sacrifices, obey the government, love our neighbors, and take special care of those who are weak in the faith. He closes with personal remarks. Throughout this section, we learn how to live our faith each day.

1. Personal responsibility
A living sacrifice to God

12 And so, dear brothers, I plead with you to give your bodies to God. Let them be a living sacrifice, holy—the kind he can accept. When you think of what he has done for you, is this too much to ask? 2Don't copy the behavior and customs of this world, but be a new and different person with a fresh newness in all you do and think. Then you will learn from your own experience how his ways will really satisfy you.

3As God's messenger I give each of you God's warning: Be honest in your estimate of yourselves, measuring your value by how much faith God has given you. 4, 5Just as there are many parts to our bodies, so it is with Christ's body. We are all parts of it, and it takes every one of us to make it complete, for we each have different work to do. So we belong to each other, and each needs all the others.

6God has given each of us the ability to do certain things well. So if God has

12:1
Rom 6:12,13
12:2
Gal 1:4
Eph 4:23
Col 3:10
12:3
1 Cor 12:7
Phil 2:3-5
Eph 4:7
12:4,5
1 Cor 10:17
12:12-14
Eph 4:4,12,25
12:6
1 Pet 4:10,11

11:32 *has given them all up to sin,* literally, "shut up all unto disobedience."

12:1 When sacrificing an animal according to God's law, a priest killed the animal, cut it in pieces, and placed it on the altar. Sacrifice was important, but even in the Old Testament God made it clear that obedience from the heart was much more important (see 1 Samuel 15:22; Psalm 40:6; Amos 5:21–24). God wants us to offer ourselves, not animals, as *living* sacrifices—daily laying aside our own desires to follow him. We do this out of gratitude that our sins have been forgiven.

12:1, 2 God has good, pleasing, and perfect plans for his children. He wants us to be new people with freshness of thought, alive to glorify him. Since he wants only what is best for us, and since he gave his Son to make our new lives possible, we should joyfully offer ourselves as living sacrifices for him.

12:2 "The behavior and customs of this world" are usually selfish and often corrupting, and many Christians wisely decide that much worldly behavior is off-limits for them. Our refusal to conform to the world, however, must go even deeper than the level of behavior and customs—it must be firmly founded in our minds. This verse is also translated "Do not be conformed to this world, but be transformed by the renewal of your mind." It is possible to avoid most worldly customs and still be proud, covetous, selfish, stubborn, and arrogant. Only when our minds are renewed by the new attitude Christ gives us are we truly transformed. If our character is like Christ's, we can be sure our behavior will honor God.

12:3 We hear a lot about the importance of healthy self-esteem.

Paul warns us, however, not to go too far in self-love—another translation says that no one should "think of himself more highly than he ought to think." Some of us think too little of ourselves; some think too much. The key to an honest and accurate evaluation is knowing the basis of our self-worth—our new identity in Christ. Apart from him, we aren't worth very much by eternal standards; in him, our worth as a creation of God is infinite. Evaluating yourself by the worldly standards of success and achievement can cause you to think too much about your worth in the eyes of others and miss your true value in God's eyes.

12:4, 5 Paul uses the concept of the human body to teach how Christians should live and work together. Just as the parts of the body function under the direction of the brain, so Christians are to work under the command and authority of Jesus Christ (see 1 Corinthians 12:12–31; Ephesians 4:1–16).

12:4–8 God gives us gifts so we can build up his church. To use them effectively, we must (1) realize that all gifts and abilities come from God; (2) understand that not everyone has the same gifts; (3) know who we are and what we do best; (4) dedicate our gifts to God's service and not to our personal success; (5) be willing to spend our gifts generously, not holding back anything from God's service.

12:6 *Prophecy* in Scripture is not always predicting the future. Often it means preaching God's messages (1 Corinthians 14:1).

12:6–8 Look at this list of gifts and imagine the kinds of people who would have each gift. Prophets are often bold and articulate.

12:7
1 Cor 12:8,28

12:8
Acts 15:32
20:27,28
1 Cor 14:3,4
1 Pet 5:2

12:9
Amos 5:15
1 Tim 1:5

12:10
Jn 13:34
Phil 2:3,4
1 Thess 4:9
2 Pet 1:7

12:11
Acts 18:25
20:19
Rev 3:15

12:12
Rom 5:2,3
Heb 3:6; 10:32

12:13
Heb 6:10
13:1-3

12:14
1 Pet 3:9

12:15
Job 30:25
Heb 13:3

12:16
2 Cor 13:11
Phil 2:2; 4:2

12:17
Prov 20:22

given you the ability to prophesy, then prophesy whenever you can—as often as your faith is strong enough to receive a message from God. ⁷If your gift is that of serving others, serve them well. If you are a teacher, do a good job of teaching. ⁸If you are a preacher, see to it that your sermons are strong and helpful. If God has given you money, be generous in helping others with it. If God has given you administrative ability and put you in charge of the work of others, take the responsibility seriously. Those who offer comfort to the sorrowing should do so with Christian cheer.

⁹Don't just pretend that you love others: really love them. Hate what is wrong. Stand on the side of the good. ¹⁰Love each other with brotherly affection and take delight in honoring each other. ¹¹Never be lazy in your work but serve the Lord enthusiastically.

¹²Be glad for all God is planning for you. Be patient in trouble, and prayerful always. ¹³When God's children are in need, you be the one to help them out. And get into the habit of inviting guests home for dinner or, if they need lodging, for the night.

¹⁴If someone mistreats you because you are a Christian, don't curse him; pray that God will bless him. ¹⁵When others are happy, be happy with them. If they are sad, share their sorrow. ¹⁶Work happily together. Don't try to act big. Don't try to get into the good graces of important people, but enjoy the company of ordinary folks. And don't think you know it all!

¹⁷Never pay back evil for evil. Do things in such a way that everyone can see you are honest clear through. ¹⁸Don't quarrel with anyone. Be at peace with everyone, just as much as possible.

¹⁹Dear friends, never avenge yourselves. Leave that to God, for he has said that

---

Servers are faithful and loyal. Teachers are clear thinkers. Preachers know how to motivate others. Givers are generous and trusting. Administrators are good organizers and managers. Comforters are caring people who are happy to give their time to others. It would be difficult for one person to embody all these gifts. An assertive prophet would not usually make a good counselor, and a generous giver might fail as an administrator. When you identify your own gifts (and you don't have to stop with this list—it is far from complete), ask how you can use them to God's glory. At the same time, realize that your gifts can't do the work of the church all alone. Be thankful for people whose gifts are completely different from yours. Let your strengths balance their weaknesses, and be grateful that their abilities make up for your deficiencies. Together you can build the church.

12:9 Most of us have learned how to pretend to love others—how to speak kindly, avoid hurting their feelings, and appear to take an interest in them. We may even be skilled in pretending to ourselves—we feel moved with compassion when we hear of others' needs, or we become indignant when we learn of injustice. But God calls us to real love that goes far beyond surface behaviors and emotions. Real love requires work. It means doing something for the people we love so that they will be better people. It demands our time, our money, and our personal involvement. No individual has the resources to love a whole community, but a church—the body of Christ in your town—can do this. Look for people who need your active love, and look for ways you and your fellow believers can get together and love your community in the name of Christ.

12:10 We can honor others two ways. The world's way has an ulterior motive. In the world, we honor our bosses so they will reward us, our employees so they will work harder, the wealthy so they will contribute to our cause, the powerful so they will use their power for us and not against us. God's way of honoring others is different. As Christians, we honor people because they have been created in God's image, because they are our brothers and sisters in Christ, because we are grateful for the ways they are building up the body of Christ.

12:13 Christian hospitality is different from the world's way of entertaining. Entertaining focuses on the host family—their home must be spotless; their food must be well prepared and abundant; they must appear relaxed and good natured. Hospitality, by contrast, focuses on the guests. Their needs—whether for a place to stay, nourishing food, a listening ear, acceptance—are of first importance. Hospitality can happen in a messy home. It can happen around a dinner table where the main dish is canned soup. It can even happen while the host and the guest are doing chores together. Don't be afraid to offer hospitality just because you are too tired, too busy, or too poor to entertain.

12:17-21 These verses summarize the real core of Christian living. If we love someone the way Christ loves us, we will be willing to forgive. If we have experienced God's grace, we will want to pass it on to others. And remember, grace is *undeserved* favor. By giving an enemy a drink, we're not excusing his misdeeds. We're recognizing them, forgiving them, and loving the individual in spite of them—just as Christ did in our case.

12:19-21 In this day of constant lawsuits and incessant demands for legal rights, Paul's command sounds almost impossible. When someone hurts you deeply, instead of giving him what he deserves, Paul says to befriend him. Why does Paul tell us to forgive our enemies? (1) Forgiveness may break a cycle of retaliation and lead to mutual reconciliation. (2) It may make the enemy feel ashamed and change his ways. (3) By contrast, returning evil for evil hurts you just as much as it hurts your enemy. Even if your enemy never repents, forgiving him will free you of a heavy load of bitterness.

12:19-21 Forgiveness involves both attitudes and action. If you find it hard to *feel* forgiving of someone who has hurt you, try *acting* forgiving. If appropriate, tell this person you would like to heal your relationship. Give him a helping hand. Send him a gift. Smile at him. Many times you will discover that right actions lead to right feelings.

he will repay those who deserve it. [Don't take the law into your own hands.] ²⁰Instead, feed your enemy if he is hungry. If he is thirsty give him something to drink and you will be "heaping coals of fire on his head." In other words, he will feel ashamed of himself for what he has done to you. ²¹Don't let evil get the upper hand but conquer evil by doing good.

12:20
Prov 25:21
Mt 5:44
12:21
1 Pet 2:21

⟶ Obedience to the government

13 Obey the government, for God is the one who has put it there. There is no government anywhere that God has not placed in power. ²So those who refuse to obey the laws of the land are refusing to obey God, and punishment will follow. ³For the policeman does not frighten people who are doing right; but those doing evil will always fear him. So if you don't want to be afraid, keep the laws and you will get along well. ⁴The policeman is sent by God to help you. But if you are doing something wrong, of course you should be afraid, for he will have you punished. He is sent by God for that very purpose. ⁵Obey the laws, then, for two reasons: first, to keep from being punished, and second, just because you know you should.

13:1
Dan 2:21; 4:32
Jn 19:11
Tit 3:1
13:3
1 Pet 2:14

13:5
Eccles 8:2
1 Pet 2:13

⁶Pay your taxes too, for these same two reasons. For government workers need to be paid so that they can keep on doing God's work, serving you. ⁷Pay everyone whatever he ought to have: pay your taxes and import duties gladly, obey those over you, and give honor and respect to all those to whom it is due.

13:7
Mt 17:24,25
22:21
Lk 20:25

Love fulfills God's requirements

⁸Pay all your debts except the debt of love for others—never finish paying that! For if you love them, you will be obeying all of God's laws, fulfilling all his requirements. ⁹If you love your neighbor as much as you love yourself you will not want to harm or cheat him, or kill him or steal from him. And you won't sin with his wife or want what is his, or do anything else the Ten Commandments say is wrong. All ten are wrapped up in this one, to love your neighbor as you love yourself. ¹⁰Love does no wrong to anyone. That's why it fully satisfies all of God's requirements. It is the only law you need.

13:8
Mt 7:12; 22:39
Jn 13:34
Jas 2:8
13:9
Ex 20:13-17
Lev 19:18
13:10
Mt 22:39
Jn 13:34,35
Gal 5:13,14

12:19 Don't take the law into your own hands, implied.

13:1ff Christians understand Romans 13 in different ways. All Christians agree that we are to live at peace with the state as long as the state allows us to live by our religious convictions. For hundreds of years, however, there have been at least three interpretations of how we are to do this. (1) Some Christians believe that the state is so corrupt that Christians should have as little to do with it as possible. Although they should be good citizens as long as they can do so without compromising their beliefs, they should not work for the government, vote, or serve in the military. (2) Others believe God has given the state authority in certain areas and the church authority in others. Christians can be loyal to both and can work for either. They should not, however, confuse the two. In this view, church and state are concerned with two totally different spheres—the spiritual and the physical—and thus complement each other but do not work together. (3) Still others believe that Christians have a responsibility to make the state better. They can do this politically, by electing Christian or other high-principled leaders. They can also do this morally, by serving as an influence for good in society. In this view, church and state ideally work together for the good of all.

None of these views advocate rebelling against or refusing to obey the government's laws or regulations unless they clearly require you to violate the moral standards revealed by God. Wherever we find ourselves, we must be responsible citizens, as well as responsible Christians.

13:1 Are there times when we should not obey the government? We can never allow government to force us to disobey God. Jesus and his apostles never disobeyed the government for personal reasons; when they disobeyed, it was in order to follow their higher loyalty to God. Their disobedience was not cheap: they were threatened, beaten, thrown into jail, tortured, and executed for their convictions. Like them, if we are compelled to disobey, we must be ready to accept the consequences.

13:3 When the police are unjust, good people are afraid. In this verse, Paul is talking about police who are doing their duty. When the police are just, people who are doing right have nothing to fear.

13:8 Why is love for others called a debt? We are permanently in debt to Christ for the lavish love he has poured out on us. The only way we can even begin to repay this debt is by loving others in turn. Since Christ's love will always be infinitely greater than ours, we will always have the obligation to love our neighbors.

13:9 Somehow many of us have gotten the idea that self-love is wrong. But if this were the case, it would be pointless to love our neighbors as ourselves. But Paul explains what he means by self-love. Even if you have low self-esteem, you probably don't willingly let yourself go hungry. You clothe yourself reasonably well. You make sure there's a roof over your head if you can. You try not to let yourself be cheated or injured. And you get angry if someone tries to ruin your marriage. This is the kind of love we need to have for our neighbors. Do we see that others are fed, clothed, and housed as well as they can be? Are we concerned about issues of social justice? Are our morals above reproach? Loving others as ourselves means to be actively working to see that their needs are met. Interestingly, people who focus on others rather than on themselves rarely suffer from low self-esteem.

13:11
1 Cor 7:29
1 Thess 5:6
Jas 5:8
1 Pet 4:7
Rev 1:3

13:12,13
Eph 5:11; 6:13
Phil 4:8
Col 3:5-10
1 Thess 5:8
Jas 3:14

¹¹Another reason for right living is this: you know how late it is; time is running out. Wake up, for the coming of the Lord is nearer now than when we first believed. ¹², ¹³The night is far gone, the day of his return will soon be here. So quit the evil deeds of darkness and put on the armor of right living, as we who live in the daylight should! Be decent and true in everything you do so that all can approve your behavior. Don't spend your time in wild parties and getting drunk or in adultery and lust, or fighting, or jealousy. ¹⁴But ask the Lord Jesus Christ to help you live as you should, and don't make plans to enjoy evil.

— *Weak and strong believers*

14:1
1 Cor 9:22
14:2
1 Cor 10:25

14:3
Col 2:16

14 Give a warm welcome to any brother who wants to join you, even though his faith is weak. Don't criticize him for having different ideas from yours about what is right and wrong. ²For instance, don't argue with him about whether or not to eat meat that has been offered to idols. You may believe there is no harm in this, but the faith of others is weaker; they think it is wrong, and will go without any meat at all and eat vegetables rather than eat that kind of meat. ³Those who think it is all right to eat such meat must not look down on those who won't. And if you are one of those who won't, don't find fault with those who do. For God has

13:12, 13 *his return,* literally, "our salvation." **14:1** *Don't criticize him . . . about what is right and wrong,* literally, "Receive him that is weak in faith, not for decisions of scruples." Perhaps the meaning is, "Receive those whose consciences hurt them when they do things others have no doubts about." Accepting them might cause discord in the church, but Paul says to welcome them anyway.

13:10 Christians must obey the law of love, which supersedes both religious and civil laws. How easy it is to excuse our indifference to others merely because we have no legal obligation to help them, even to justify harming them if our actions are technically legal! But Jesus does not leave loopholes in the law of love. Whenever love demands it, we are to go beyond human legal requirements and imitate the God of love. See James 2:8, 9; 4:11 and 1 Peter 2:16, 17 for more about this law of love.

13:12, 13 Some people are surprised that Paul lists jealousy and lust with the gross and obvious sins of drunkenness, adultery, and fighting. Like Jesus in his Sermon on the Mount (Matthew 5—7), Paul considers attitudes as important as actions. Just as hatred leads to murder, so jealousy leads to fighting and lust to adultery. When Christ returns, he wants to find his people clean on the inside as well as on the outside.

14:1 This verse assumes there will be differences of opinion in the church. These differences should not be feared or avoided, but accepted and handled with love. Don't expect everyone, even in the best church, to agree on every subject. Through sharing ideas we can come to a fuller understanding of what the Bible teaches. Accept, listen to, and respect others. Differences of opinion need not cause division. They can be a source of learning and richness in our relationships.

14:1ff What is weak faith? It is not faith mixed with works. In all his letters, Paul is violently opposed to any attempt to gain salvation through works of the law. Rather, Paul is speaking about immature faith, faith that has not yet developed the muscle it needs to stand against external pressures. For example, if a person who once worshiped idols became a Christian, he might understand perfectly well that Christ saved him through faith and that idols have no real power. Still, because of his past associations, he might be badly shaken if he knowingly ate meat that had been used in idol worship as part of a heathen ritual. If a person who once worshiped God on the required Jewish holy days became a Christian, he might well know that Christ saved him through faith, not through his keeping of the law. Still, when the feast days came, he might feel empty and unfaithful if he didn't dedicate them to God.

Paul responds to both weak brothers in love. Both are acting according to their consciences, but their honest scruples do not

need to be made into rules for the church. Certainly some issues are central to the faith and worth fighting for—but many are based on individual differences and should not be legislated. Someone has said that a general principle in these matters is this: "In essentials, unity; in nonessentials, liberty; in everything, love."

14:1 Who is weak in faith and who is strong? We are all weak in some areas and strong in others. Our faith is strong in an area if we can survive contact with sin without falling into it. It is weak if we must avoid certain activities or places in order to protect our spiritual life. It is important to take a self-inventory in order to find out where we are weak and where we are strong. Whenever we feel called to go into the world in whatever capacity, we should ask. "Can I do that without sinning? Can I influence others for good, rather than being influenced by them for evil?" Our answer will show whether our faith is weak or strong in that area, at that time.

In areas of strength, we should not fear that we will be defiled by the world. Rather, from our position of strength we should lead the world. In areas of weakness, however, we need to play it safe. If we have a strong faith but shelter it, we are not doing Christ's work in the world. If we have a weak faith but expose it, we are being extremely foolish. Strength and weakness are not permanent conditions. Strength may diminish if it is not put to the test, and areas of weakness may develop by God's power into areas of strength.

14:2 How would Christians end up eating meat that had been offered to idols? The ancient system of sacrifice was at the center of the religious, social, and domestic life of the Roman world. After a sacrifice was presented to a god in a heathen temple, only part of it was burned. The remainder was often sent to the market to be sold. Thus a Christian might easily—even unknowingly—buy such meat in the marketplace or eat it at the home of a friend. Should a Christian question the source of his meat? Some thought there was nothing wrong with eating meat that had been offered to idols, since idols were not real gods. Others carefully checked the source of their meat, or else gave up meat altogether, in order to avoid a guilty conscience. The problem was especially acute for Christians who had once been idol worshipers. For them, such a strong reminder of their pagan days might weaken their newfound faith. Paul also deals with this problem in 1 Corinthians 8.

accepted them to be his children. 4They are God's servants, not yours. They are responsible to him, not to you. Let him tell them whether they are right or wrong. And God is able to make them do as they should.

5Some think that Christians should observe the Jewish holidays as special days to worship God, but others say it is wrong and foolish to go to all that trouble, for every day alike belongs to God. On questions of this kind everyone must decide for himself. 6If you have special days for worshiping the Lord, you are trying to honor him; you are doing a good thing. So is the person who eats meat that has been offered to idols; he is thankful to the Lord for it; he is doing right. And the person who won't touch such meat, he, too, is anxious to please the Lord, and is thankful. 7We are not our own bosses to live or die as we ourselves might choose. 8Living or dying we follow the Lord. Either way we are his. 9Christ died and rose again for this very purpose, so that he can be our Lord both while we live and when we die.

10You have no right to criticize your brother or look down on him. Remember, each of us will stand personally before the Judgment Seat of God. 11For it is written, "As I live," says the Lord, "every knee shall bow to me and every tongue confess to God." 12Yes, each of us will give an account of himself to God.

13So don't criticize each other any more. Try instead to live in such a way that you will never make your brother stumble by letting him see you doing something he thinks is wrong.

14As for myself, I am perfectly sure on the authority of the Lord Jesus that there is nothing really wrong with eating meat that has been offered to idols. But if someone believes it is wrong, then he shouldn't do it because for him it is wrong. 15And if your brother is bothered by what you eat, you are not acting in love if you go ahead and eat it. Don't let your eating ruin someone for whom Christ died. 16Don't do anything that will cause criticism against yourself even though you know that what you do is right.

17For, after all, the important thing for us as Christians is not what we eat or drink but stirring up goodness and peace and joy from the Holy Spirit. 18If you let Christ be Lord in these affairs, God will be glad; and so will others. 19In this way aim for harmony in the church and try to build each other up.

20Don't undo the work of God for a chunk of meat. Remember, there is nothing wrong with the meat, but it is wrong to eat it if it makes another stumble. 21The right thing to do is to quit eating meat or drinking wine or doing anything else that offends your brother or makes him sin. 22You may know that there is nothing wrong with what you do, even from God's point of view, but keep it to yourself; don't flaunt your faith in front of others who might be hurt by it. In this situation, happy is the man who does not sin by doing what he knows is right. 23But anyone

14:5
Rom 14:23
Gal 4:10

14:6
1 Cor 10:31
1 Tim 4:3

14:7
1 Cor 6:19
2 Cor 5:15
Gal 2:20

14:8
Phil 1:20
1 Thess 5:10

14:9
Phil 2:11
Rev 1:18

14:10
Mt 25:31,32
Rom 2:16
2 Cor 5:10

14:11
Isa 45:23

14:12
Mt 12:36

14:13
Mt 7:1
1 Cor 8:9

14:14
1 Cor 8:7

14:15
1 Cor 8:11

14:16
1 Cor 10:29,30
Tit 2:5

14:17
Rom 15:13
Gal 5:22

14:19
Ps 34:14

14:20
Acts 10:15
1 Cor 8:9

14:21
1 Cor 8:13

14:22
1 Jn 3:21

14:4 Each person is accountable to Christ, not to others. While the church must be uncompromising in its stand against activities expressly forbidden by Scripture (adultery, homosexuality, murder, theft), it should not create additional rules and regulations and give them equal standing with God's law. Many times Christians base their moral judgments on opinion, personal dislikes, or cultural bias rather than on the Word of God. When they do this, they show that their own faith is weak. They do not think God is powerful enough to guide his children.

14:10-15 Both "strong" and "weak" Christians can cause their brothers to stumble. The strong but insensitive Christian may flaunt his freedom and intentionally offend others' consciences. The scrupulous but weak Christian may fence in others with petty rules and regulations until they can't take it any longer. Paul wants his readers to be both strong in the faith and sensitive to others' needs. Since we are all strong in some areas and weak in others, we need constantly to monitor the effect of our behavior on others.

14:13ff Some Christians use an invisible weaker brother to support their own opinions, prejudices, or standards. "You must live by these standards," they say, "or you will be offending the weaker brother." In truth, you will often be offending no one but the

speaker. While Paul urges us to be sensitive to those whose faith may be harmed by our actions, we should not sacrifice our liberty in Christ just to satisfy the selfish motives of those who are trying to force their opinion on us. Neither fear them nor criticize them, but follow Christ as closely as you are able.

14:14 At the Jerusalem council (Acts 15), the Jewish church in Jerusalem asked the Gentile church in Antioch not to eat meat offered to idols. Paul was at the Jerusalem council, and he accepted this request not because he felt this practice was wrong in itself, but because this practice would deeply offend many Jewish believers. Paul did not think the issue was worth dividing the church; his desire was to promote unity.

14:22 Sin is not just a private matter. Everything we do affects others, and we have to think of them constantly. God created us to be interdependent, not independent.

14:23 We try to steer clear of actions forbidden by Scripture, of course; but sometimes Scripture is silent. Then we should follow our conscience. When God shows us something is wrong for us, we should avoid it. But we should not look down on other Christians who exercise their freedom in those areas.

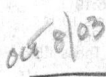

who believes that something he wants to do is wrong shouldn't do it. He sins if he does, for he thinks it is wrong, and so for him it *is* wrong. Anything that is done apart from what he feels is right is sin.

Live to please others

15 Even if we believe that it makes no difference to the Lord whether we do these things, still we cannot just go ahead and do them to please ourselves; for we must bear the "burden" of being considerate of the doubts and fears of others—of those who feel these things are wrong. Let's please the other fellow, not ourselves, and do what is for his good and thus build him up in the Lord. 3Christ didn't please himself. As the Psalmist said, "He came for the very purpose of suffering under the insults of those who were against the Lord." 4These things that were written in the Scriptures so long ago are to teach us patience and to encourage us, so that we will look forward expectantly to the time when God will conquer sin and death.

5May God who gives patience, steadiness, and encouragement help you to live in complete harmony with each other—each with the attitude of Christ toward the other. 6And then all of us can praise the Lord together with one voice, giving glory to God, the Father of our Lord Jesus Christ.

Fellowship among believers

7So, warmly welcome each other into the church, just as Christ has warmly welcomed you; then God will be glorified. 8Remember that Jesus Christ came to show that God is true to his promises and to help the Jews. 9And remember that he came also that the Gentiles might be saved and give glory to God for his mercies to them. That is what the Psalmist meant when he wrote: "I will praise you among the Gentiles, and sing to your name."

10And in another place, "Be glad, O you Gentiles, along with his people the Jews."

11And yet again, "Praise the Lord, O you Gentiles, let everyone praise him."

12And the prophet Isaiah said, "There shall be an Heir in the house of Jesse, and he will be King over the Gentiles; they will pin their hopes on him alone."

13So I pray for you Gentiles that God who gives you hope will keep you happy and full of peace as you believe in him. I pray that God will help you overflow with hope in him through the Holy Spirit's power within you.

2. Personal notes
Paul explains his reason for writing

14I know that you are wise and good, my brothers, and that you know these things so well that you are able to teach others all about them. 15, 16But even so I have been bold enough to emphasize some of these points, knowing that all you need is this reminder from me; for I am, by God's grace, a special messenger from Jesus Christ to you Gentiles, bringing you the Gospel and offering you up as a fragrant sacrifice to God; for you have been made pure and pleasing to him by the Holy Spirit. 17So it is right for me to be a little proud of all Christ Jesus has done through me. 18I dare not judge how effectively he has used others, but I know this:

15:1,2
Rom 14:1
1 Cor 9:19,22
10:23,24
Gal 6:2
Phil 2:4,5

15:3
Ps 69:9

15:4
Rom 4:23
2 Tim 3:16

15:5
1 Cor 1:10
2 Cor 1:3,4

15:6
Rev 1:6

15:7
Rom 5:2

15:8
Mt 15:24
Jn 1:11
Acts 3:25,26
Rom 3:3,4
2 Cor 1:20

15:9
Ps 18:49
Jn 10:16
Rom 9:23

15:10
Deut 32:43

15:11
Ps 117:1

15:12
Isa 11:10
Rev 5:5; 22:16

15:14
2 Pet 1:12
1 Jn 2:21

15:15,16
Acts 9:15
Gal 1:15; 2:7-9
1 Tim 2:7

15:17
Phil 3:3

15:18
Rom 1:5

15:4 The knowledge of the Scriptures affects our attitude toward the present and the future. The more we know about what God has done in years past, the greater the confidence we have about what he will do in the days ahead. We should read our Bibles diligently to increase our trust that God's will is the best choice for us.

15:5, 6 To accept Jesus' lordship in all areas of life means to share his values and his perspective. Just as we take Jesus' view on the authority of Scripture, the nature of heaven, and the resurrection, we are to have his attitude of love toward other

Christians as well. As we grow in faith and come to know Jesus better, we become more capable of maintaining this attitude throughout each day. Christ's attitude is explained in more detail in Philippians 2.

15:17 Paul was not proud of what he had done, but of what God had done through him. Being proud of God's work is not a sin—it is worship. If you are not sure whether your pride is selfish or holy, ask yourself this question: Are you just as proud of what God is doing through other people as of what he is doing through you?

he has used me to win the Gentiles to God. ¹⁹I have won them by my message and
by the good way I have lived before them, and by the miracles done through me as
signs from God—all by the Holy Spirit's power. In this way I have preached the
full Gospel of Christ all the way from Jerusalem clear over into Illyricum.

²⁰But all the while my ambition has been to go still farther, preaching where the
name of Christ has never yet been heard, rather than where a church has already
been started by someone else. ²¹I have been following the plan spoken of in the
Scriptures where Isaiah says that those who have never heard the name of Christ
before will see and understand. ²²In fact that is the very reason I have been so long
in coming to visit you.

Paul explains his travel plans

²³But now at last I am through with my work here, and I am ready to come after
all these long years of waiting. ²⁴For I am planning to take a trip to Spain, and when
I do, I will stop off there in Rome; and after we have had a good time together for
a little while, you can send me on my way again.

²⁵But before I come, I must go down to Jerusalem to take a gift to the Jewish
Christians there. ²⁶For you see, the Christians in Macedonia and Achaia have taken
up an offering for those in Jerusalem who are going through such hard times.
²⁷They were very glad to do this, for they feel that they owe a real debt to the
Jerusalem Christians. Why? Because the news about Christ came to these Gentiles
from the church in Jerusalem. And since they received this wonderful spiritual gift
of the Gospel from there, they feel that the least they can do in return is to give some
material aid. ²⁸As soon as I have delivered this money and completed this good
deed of theirs, I will come to see you on my way to Spain. ²⁹And I am sure that
when I come the Lord will give me a great blessing for you.

³⁰Will you be my prayer partners? For the Lord Jesus Christ's sake, and because
of your love for me—given to you by the Holy Spirit—pray much with me for my
work. ³¹Pray that I will be protected in Jerusalem from those who are not Christians. Pray also that the Christians there will be willing to accept the money I am
bringing them. ³²Then I will be able to come to you with a happy heart by the will
of God, and we can refresh each other.

³³And now may our God, who gives peace, be with you all. Amen.

Paul greets his friends

16 Phoebe, a dear Christian woman from the town of Cenchreae, will be
coming to see you soon. She has worked hard in the church there. Receive
her as your sister in the Lord, giving her a warm Christian welcome. Help her in
every way you can, for she has helped many in their needs, including me.

15:19 *I have preached the full Gospel,* or, "I have fully accomplished my gospel ministry."   **15:27** *the least they can
do in return is to give some material aid,* literally, "For if the Gentiles have come to share in their spiritual blessings,
they ought also to be of service to them in material blessings."

15:19 Acts 19:11 / 1 Cor 2:4 / 1 Thess 1:5

15:20 Rom 1:15 / 1 Cor 3:10 / 2 Cor 10:13,15

15:21 Isa 52:14,15

15:22 Rom 1:13 / 1 Thess 2:18

15:23 Acts 19:21 / Rom 1:10

15:24 Acts 15:3 / Rom 1:12

15:25 Acts 19:21; 24:17

15:26 1 Cor 16:1,5 / 2 Cor 8:1; 9:2

15:27 1 Cor 9:11

15:29 Acts 19:21 / Rom 1:10,11

15:30 2 Cor 1:11 / Col 1:8; 4:12

15:31 2 Cor 8:4 / 2 Thess 3:2

15:32 2 Cor 7:13 / 2 Tim 1:16 / Philem 7

15:33 Rom 16:20 / Heb 13:20

16:1 Acts 18:18

16:2 Phil 2:29 / 3 Jn 5,6

15:19 Illyricum was a Roman territory on the Adriatic Sea between
present-day Italy and Greece. It covers much the same territory as
present-day Yugoslavia. See map in Romans 1 for its location.

15:22 Paul wanted to visit the church at Rome, but he had
delayed his visit because he had heard many good reports about
the believers there and he knew they were doing well on their own.
It was more important for him to preach in areas that had not yet
heard the Good News.

15:23, 24 Paul was referring to his work in Corinth, the city from
which he most likely wrote this letter. Most of Paul's three-month
stay in Achaia (see Acts 20:3) was probably spent in Corinth. He
believed he had done what God wanted him to do there—he was
now looking forward to taking the gospel to new lands west of
Rome. When Paul eventually went to Rome, however, it was as a
prisoner under house arrest (see Acts 28). Tradition holds that Paul

was released for a time, and that he used this opportunity to go to
Spain to preach the Good News. This journey is not mentioned in
the book of Acts.

15:31 Because of several prophecies he had received en route,
Paul knew trouble awaited him in Jerusalem. See Acts 21:4, 10–14
for the story.

15:33 This phrase sounds like the end of the book, and it does
signal the end of Paul's teaching. He concludes his letter, then,
with personal greetings and remarks.

16:1 Phoebe was known as a servant (the Greek word used here
is often translated "deacon") and a helper. She apparently was
wealthy and helped support Paul's ministry financially. She was
highly regarded in the church, and she may have delivered this
letter from Corinth to Rome. This provides evidence that women

³Tell Priscilla and Aquila "hello." They have been my fellow workers in the affairs of Christ Jesus. ⁴In fact, they risked their lives for me; and I am not the only one who is thankful to them: so are all the Gentile churches.

16:5
1 Cor 16:15,19
Col 4:15
Philem 1,2

⁵Please give my greetings to all those who meet to worship in their home. Greet my good friend Epaenetus. He was the very first person to become a Christian in Asia. ⁶Remember me to Mary, too, who has worked so hard to help us. ⁷Then there

16:7
Rom 16:11,21
2 Cor 11:23
Col 4:10
Philem 23

are Andronicus and Junias, my relatives who were in prison with me. They are respected by the apostles, and became Christians before I did. Please give them my greetings. ⁸Say "hello" to Ampliatus, whom I love as one of God's own children, ⁹and Urbanus, our fellow worker, and beloved Stachys.

16:10
1 Cor 1:11

16:11
Rom 16:7,21

¹⁰Then there is Apelles, a good man whom the Lord approves; greet him for me. And give my best regards to those working at the house of Aristobulus. ¹¹Remember me to Herodion my relative. Remember me to the Christian slaves over at Narcissus House. ¹²Say "hello" to Tryphaena and Tryphosa, the Lord's workers,

16:13
Mk 15:21
Eph 1:4
2 Jn 1

and to dear Persis, who has worked so hard for the Lord. ¹³Greet Rufus for me, whom the Lord picked out to be his very own; and also his dear mother who has been such a mother to me. ¹⁴And please give my greetings to Asyncritus, Phlegon, Hermes, Patrobas, Hermas, and the other brothers who are with them. ¹⁵Give my love to Philologus, Julia, Nereus and his sister, and to Olympas, and all the

16:16
1 Thess 5:26
1 Pet 5:14

Christians who are with them. ¹⁶Shake hands warmly with each other. All the churches here send you their greetings.

☛ Paul gives final instructions

16:17
Acts 15:1-29
1 Cor 5:9
2 Thess 3:6
1 Tim 6:3
2 Tim 3:5,6
Tit 3:10
2 Jn 10

¹⁷And now there is one more thing to say before I end this letter. Stay away from those who cause divisions and are upsetting people's faith, teaching things about Christ that are contrary to what you have been taught. ¹⁸Such teachers are not working for our Lord Jesus, but only want gain for themselves. They are good speakers, and simple-minded people are often fooled by them. ¹⁹But everyone

16:18
Phil 3:19
Col 2:4
2 Pet 2:3

knows that you stand loyal and true. This makes me very happy. I want you always to remain very clear about what is right, and to stay innocent of any wrong. ²⁰The God of peace will soon crush Satan under your feet. The blessings from our Lord

16:19
Mt 10:16

Jesus Christ be upon you.

16:20
Gen 3:15

²¹Timothy my fellow-worker, and Lucius and Jason and Sosipater, my relatives, send you their good wishes. ²²I, Tertius, the one who is writing this letter for Paul,

16:21
Acts 13:1; 16:1
17:5
1 Tim 1:2

send my greetings too, as a Christian brother. ²³Gaius says to say "hello" to you for him. I am his guest, and the church meets here in his home. Erastus, the city treasurer, sends you his greetings and so does Quartus, a Christian brother. ²⁴Goodbye. May the grace of our Lord Jesus Christ be with you all.

---

had important roles in the early church. Cenchreae, the town where Phoebe lived, was the eastern port of Corinth, six miles from the city center.

16:3 Priscilla and Aquila were a married couple who became Paul's close friends. They, along with all other Jews, had been expelled from Rome by the emperor (Acts 18:2, 3), and they had moved to Corinth. There they met Paul and invited him to live with them. They were Christians before they met Paul, and probably told him much about the Roman church. Like Paul, Priscilla and Aquila were missionaries. They helped believers in Ephesus (Acts 18:18–28), in Rome when they were allowed to return, and again at Ephesus (2 Timothy 4:19).

16:5ff Paul's personal greetings went to Romans and Greeks, Jews and Gentiles, men and women, prisoners and prominent citizens. The church's base was broad: it crossed cultural, social, and economic lines. From this list we learn that the Christian community was mobile. Though Paul had not yet been to Rome, he had met these people in other places on his journeys.

16:7 Some translations say that Andronicus and Junias were "of note among the apostles"—very likely they had distinguished themselves as missionaries. Scholars are not sure whether the second name should be Junias (masculine) or Junia (feminine). If Junia is correct, some suggest she was Andronicus' wife.

➤ 16:17-20 When we read books or listen to sermons, we should check the content of what is written or said and not be fooled by smooth style. Christians who study God's Word do not need to be fooled, even if superficial listeners are easily taken in. For an example of believers who carefully checked God's Word, see Acts 17:10–12.

16:21 Timothy was a key person in the growth of the early church, traveling with Paul on his second missionary journey (Acts 16:1–3). Later Paul wrote two letters to him as he worked to strengthen the churches in Ephesus—1 and 2 Timothy. See his Profile in the book of 1 Timothy.

25, 26, 27 I commit you to God, who is able to make you strong and steady in the Lord, just as the Gospel says, and just as I have told you. This is God's plan of salvation for you Gentiles, kept secret from the beginning of time. But now as the prophets foretold and as God commands, this message is being preached everywhere, so that people all around the world will have faith in Christ and obey him. To God, who alone is wise, be the glory forever through Jesus Christ our Lord. Amen.

Sincerely, Paul

16:25
1 Cor 2:1,7; 4:1
Eph 3:3-5
1 Col 1:27; 2:2
2 Tim 1:10
1 Pet 1:20
16:26
Rom 1:2,5
16:27
Rom 11:36

16:25-27 Paul exclaims that it is wonderful to be alive when God's secret—his way of saving the Gentiles—is becoming known throughout the world! All the Old Testament prophecies were coming true, and God was using Paul as his instrument to tell this Good News.

16:25-27 As Jerusalem was the center of Jewish life, Rome was the world's political, religious, social, and economic center. There the major governmental decisions were made, and from there the gospel spread to the ends of the earth. The church in Rome was a cosmopolitan mixture of Jews, Gentiles, slaves, free people, men, women, Roman citizens, and world travelers; therefore, it had potential for both great influence and great conflict.

Paul had not yet been to Rome to meet all the Christians there, and, of course, he has not yet met us. We too live in a cosmopolitan setting with the entire world open to us. We also have the potential for both widespread influence and wrenching conflict. We should listen carefully to Paul's teaching about unity, service, and love.

ON A BED of grass, a chameleon's skin turns green. On the earth, it becomes brown. The animal changes to match the environment. Many creatures blend into nature with God-given camouflage suits to aid their survival. It's natural to fit in and adapt to the environment. But followers of Christ are *new creations,* born from above and changed from within, with values and life-styles which confront the world and clash with accepted morals. True believers don't blend in very well.

The Christians in Corinth were struggling with their environment. Surrounded by corruption and every conceivable sin, they felt the pressure to adapt to their environment. They knew they were free in Christ, but what did this freedom mean? How should they view idols or sexuality? What should they do about marriage, women in the church, and the gifts of the Spirit? These were more than theoretical questions—the church was being undermined by immorality and spiritual immaturity. Their faith was being tried in the crucible of immoral Corinth, and some of them were failing the test.

Paul heard of their struggles and wrote this letter to address their problems, heal their divisions, and answer their questions. Paul confronted them with their sin and their need for corrective action and clear commitment to Christ.

After a brief introduction (1:1-9), Paul immediately turns to the question of unity (1:10—4:21). He emphasizes the clear and simple gospel message around which all believers should rally; he explains the role of church leaders; and he urges them to grow up in their faith.

Paul then deals with the immorality of certain church members and lawsuits among Christians (5:1—6:8). He tells them to exercise church discipline and to settle their internal matters themselves. Because so many of the problems in the Corinthian church involved sex, Paul denounces sexual sin in the strongest possible terms (6:9-20).

Next Paul answers some questions which the Corinthians had. Because prostitution and immorality were pervasive, marriages in Corinth were in shambles, and Christians weren't sure how to react. Paul gives pointed and practical answers (7:1-40). Concerning the question of meat sacrificed to idols, Paul suggests that we show complete commitment to Christ and sensitivity to other believers, especially weaker brothers and sisters (8:1—11:2).

Paul goes on to talk about worship, and he carefully explains the role of women, the Lord's supper, and spiritual gifts (11:3—14:39). Sandwiched in the middle of this section is his magnificent description of the greatest gift—love (chapter 13). Then Paul concludes with a discussion of the resurrection (15:1-58), some final thoughts, greetings, and a benediction (16:1-24).

In this letter Paul confronts the Corinthians about their sins and shortcomings. And 1 Corinthians calls all Christians to be careful not to blend in with the world, accepting its values and life-styles. We must live Christ-centered, blameless, loving lives that make a difference for God. As you read 1 Corinthians, examine your values in light of complete commitment to Christ.

VITAL STATISTICS

PURPOSE:
To identify problems in the Corinthian church, to offer solutions, and to teach the believers how to live for Christ in a corrupt society

AUTHOR:
Paul

TO WHOM WRITTEN:
The church in Corinth

DATE WRITTEN:
About A.D. 55 near the end of Paul's three-year ministry in Ephesus during his third missionary journey

SETTING:
Corinth was a major cosmopolitan city, a seaport and major trade center—the most important city in Achaia. It was also filled with idolatry and immorality. The church was largely made up of Gentiles. Paul had established this church on his second missionary journey.

KEY VERSE:
"But, dear brothers, I beg you in the name of the Lord Jesus Christ to stop arguing among yourselves. Let there be real harmony so there won't be splits in the church. I plead with you to be of one mind, united in thought and purpose" (1:10).

KEY PEOPLE:
Paul, Timothy, members of Chloe's household

KEY PLACES:
Worship meetings in Corinth

SPECIAL FEATURES:
This is a strong, straightforward letter.

THE BLUEPRINT

A. PAUL ADDRESSES CHURCH PROBLEMS (1:1—6:20)
1. Divisions in the church
2. Disorders in the church

Without Paul's presence, the Corinthian church had fallen into divisiveness and disorder. This resulted in many problems which Paul addressed squarely. We must be concerned for unity and order in our local churches, but we should not mistake inactivity for order and cordiality for unity. We too must squarely address problems in our churches.

B. PAUL ANSWERS CHURCH QUESTIONS (7:1—16:24)
1. Instruction on Christian marriage
2. Instruction on Christian freedom
3. Instruction on public worship
4. Instruction on the resurrection

The Corinthians had sent Paul a list of questions, and he answered them in a way to correct abuses in the church and to show how important it is that they live what they believe. Paul gives us a Christian approach to problem-solving. He analyzed the problem thoroughly to uncover the underlying issue, and then highlighted the biblical values that should guide our actions.

MEGATHEMES

THEME	EXPLANATION	IMPORTANCE
Loyalties	The Corinthians were rallying around various church leaders and teachers—Peter, Paul, and Apollos. These loyalties led to intellectual pride and created a spirit of division in the church.	Our loyalty to human leaders or human wisdom must never divide Christians into camps. We must care for our fellow believers, not strive with them. Your allegiance must be to Christ. Let him lead you.
Immorality	Paul received a report of uncorrected sexual sin in the church at Corinth. The people had grown indifferent to immorality. Others had misconceptions about marriage. We are to live morally because our bodies are to be ready to serve God.	Christians must never compromise with sinful ideas and practices. We should not blend in with people around us. You must live up to God's standard of morality and not condone immoral behavior.
Freedom	Paul taught freedom of choice on practices not expressly forbidden in Scripture. Some believers felt certain actions—like buying meat from animals used in pagan rituals—were corrupt by association. Others felt free from the law to do such actions without sin.	We are free in Christ, yet we must not abuse our Christian freedom by being inconsiderate and insensitive to others. We must never encourage others to do wrong by anything we do. Let love guide your behavior.
Worship	Paul addressed disorder in worship. People were taking the Lord's Supper without first confessing sin. There was misuse of spiritual gifts and confusion over women's role in the church.	Worship must be carried out properly and in an orderly manner. Everything we do to worship God should be done in a manner worthy of his high honor. Make sure that worship is harmonious, useful, and builds up all believers.
Resurrection	Some people denied that Christ rose from the dead. Others felt that people would not physically be resurrected. Christ's resurrection assures us that we will have new, living bodies after we die. The hope of the resurrection forms the secret of Christian confidence.	Since we will be raised again to life after we die, our life is not in vain. We must stay faithful to God in our morality and our service. We are to live today knowing we will spend eternity with Christ.

A. PAUL ADDRESSES CHURCH PROBLEMS (1:1—6:20)

Through various sources, Paul had received reports of problems in the Corinthian church, including jealousy, divisiveness, sexual immorality, and failure to discipline members. Churches today must also address the problems they face. We can learn a great deal by observing how Paul handled these delicate situations.

1:1
Acts 18:17
Rom 1:1

1:2
Rom 8:28
Rom 10:12,13
2 Tim 2:22

1 *From:* Paul, chosen by God to be Jesus Christ's missionary, and from brother Sosthenes.

²*To:* The Christians in Corinth, invited by God to be his people and made acceptable to him by Christ Jesus. *And to:* All Christians everywhere—whoever calls upon the name of Jesus Christ, our Lord and theirs.

1:2 *made acceptable to him by Christ Jesus,* or "chosen by Christ Jesus," literally, "sanctified in Christ Jesus."

CORINTH AND EPHESUS
Paul wrote this letter to Corinth during his three-year visit in Ephesus during his third missionary journey. The two cities sat across from each other on the Aegean Sea—both were busy and important ports. Titus may have carried this letter from Ephesus to Corinth (2 Corinthians 12:18).

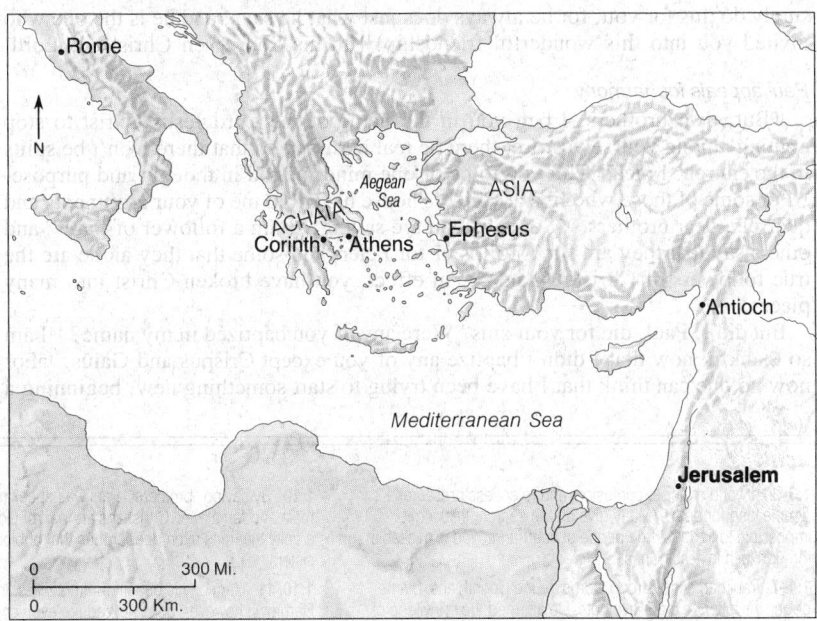

1:1 Paul, visiting Ephesus, was in the middle of his third missionary journey (Acts 19:1—20:1) when he wrote this letter to the church in Corinth. Corinth and Ephesus faced each other across the Aegean Sea. Paul knew the Corinthian church well because he had spent 18 months in Corinth during his second missionary journey (Acts 18:1–18). While in Ephesus, he heard about problems in Corinth (1:11). About the same time, a delegation from the Corinthian church visited Paul to ask his advice about their divisions (16:17). Paul wrote this letter to help correct those problems as well as to answer questions church members had asked in a previous letter (7:1).

1:1 Paul was specially selected by God to preach about Jesus Christ. Each Christian has a job to do. One may seem more spectacular than another, but all are necessary to carry out God's greater plans for the world (12:12–27). Be useful to God by using your gifts in his service. As you discover what he wants, be ready to serve.

1:1 Sosthenes may have been Paul's secretary who wrote this letter as Paul dictated it. He was probably the Jewish synagogue leader in Corinth (Acts 18:17) who was beaten during an attack on Paul. If so, he later became a believer. Sosthenes was well known to the members of the Corinthian church; therefore, Paul included his familiar name in the opening of his letter.

1:2 Corinth was a giant cultural melting pot with great diversion of wealth, religions, intellect, and moral standards. It had a reputation

for being fiercely independent and as decadent as any city in the world. The Romans destroyed Corinth in 146 B.C. after a rebellion, but in 46 B.C. the Roman emperor Julius Caesar rebuilt it because of its strategic seaport. By Paul's day (A.D. 50), the Romans had made Corinth the capital of Achaia (present-day Greece). It was a large city, offering Rome great profits through trade as well as the military protection of its ports. But the city's prosperity made it ripe for all sorts of corruption. Idolatry flourished, and there were more than a dozen pagan temples employing at least a thousand prostitutes. Prostitutes in other cities were called "Corinthian girls."

1:2 By including a salutation to "all Christians everywhere," Paul made it clear that this was not a private letter. Although it dealt with specific issues facing the church at Corinth, all believers could learn from it. The Corinthian church must have included a great cross-section of believers—wealthy merchants, common laborers, former temple prostitutes, middle-class families. Because there was such a wide diversity of people and backgrounds, Paul took great pains to stress unity in his letter.

1:2 A personal invitation makes a person feel wanted and welcome. Through his Word, God has personally invited us to become citizens of his eternal Kingdom. But Jesus Christ, God's Son, is the only one who can bring us into this glorious Kingdom, because he removes our sins. Accepting God's invitation means accepting his Son, Jesus Christ, and trusting in the work he did on the cross to forgive our sins.

³May God our Father and the Lord Jesus Christ give you all of his blessings, and great peace of heart and mind.

1:3
Rom 1:7

1. Divisions in the church

Paul thanks God

⁴I can never stop thanking God for all the wonderful gifts he has given you, now that you are Christ's: ⁵he has enriched your whole life. He has helped you speak out for him and has given you a full understanding of the truth; ⁶what I told you Christ could do for you has happened! ⁷Now you have every grace and blessing; every spiritual gift and power for doing his will are yours during this time of waiting for the return of our Lord Jesus Christ. ⁸And he guarantees right up to the end that you will be counted free from all sin and guilt on that day when he returns. ⁹God will surely do this for you, for he always does just what he says, and he is the one who invited you into this wonderful friendship with his Son, even Christ our Lord.

1:4,5
Rom 15:14
2 Cor 8:7; 9:11
1:7
Rom 8:19,23
Phil 3:20
2 Pet 3:12
1:8
Phil 1:6
1 Thess 5:23
2 Thess 3:3
1:9
1 Jn 1:3

Paul appeals for harmony

¹⁰But, dear brothers, I beg you in the name of the Lord Jesus Christ to stop arguing among yourselves. Let there be real harmony so that there won't be splits in the church. I plead with you to be of one mind, united in thought and purpose. ¹¹For some of those who live at Chloe's house have told me of your arguments and quarrels, dear brothers. ¹²Some of you are saying, "I am a follower of Paul"; and others say that they are for Apollos or for Peter; and some that they alone are the true followers of Christ. ¹³And so, in effect, you have broken Christ into many pieces.

But did I, Paul, die for your sins? Were any of you baptized in my name? ¹⁴I am so thankful now that I didn't baptize any of you except Crispus and Gaius. ¹⁵For now no one can think that I have been trying to start something new, beginning a

1:10
Rom 12:16
1 Cor 11:18
Phil 1:27
1:12
Jn 1:42
Acts 18:24
1 Cor 3:4
1:13
Acts 2:38
Eph 4:5

1:14
Acts 18:8
Rom 16:23

1:3 In a world of noise, confusion, and relentless pressures, people long for peace. Many give up the search, thinking it impossible to find, but true peace of heart and mind is available through faith in Jesus Christ.

1:4–7 Paul had some strong words for the Corinthians, but he began his letter on a positive note. He affirmed their privilege of being in God's family and of having the power of the Holy Spirit in their lives. When we must correct others, we should begin by affirming what God has already accomplished in them.

1:7 The Corinthian church members had all the spiritual gifts they needed to live the Christian life, to witness for Christ, and to stand against the paganism and immorality of Corinth. But instead of using what God had given them, they were arguing over which gifts were more important. Paul addresses this issue in depth in chapters 12—14.

1:7–9 The Corinthian believers were guaranteed that they would be counted free from sin when Christ returned (see Ephesians 1:7–10). This was not because of their great gifts (1:4) or performance, but because of what Jesus Christ accomplished through his death and resurrection (see Colossians 2:15). A guarantee is a promise. God says he will count *all* who obey his Word free from sin when Jesus Christ returns (1 Thessalonians 3:13; Hebrews 9:28); and God does what he says (1 Thessalonians 5:24). If you have faith in Christ, you *are* and *will be* saved.

1:10 Paul founded the church in Corinth on his second missionary journey. After he left, 18 months later, the church began to slip toward the immoral lifestyle prevalent in the city. Paul wrote this letter to recommend that immediate corrective action be taken to clear up their confusion about right and wrong and to remove the immorality among them. Corinthians had a reputation for jumping from fad to fad; Paul wanted to keep Christianity from degenerating into another fad.

1:10 By saying "brothers," Paul was speaking to all believers, male and female. All Christians are part of God's family and share a unity that runs even deeper than that of blood brothers and sisters.

1:10, 11 Harmony is beautiful—in families, in friendships, at work. Harmony, however, does not require everyone to believe just like everyone else. There is a difference between having opposing viewpoints and being divisive. A group of people will not completely agree on every issue, but they can work together harmoniously if they agree on what truly matters—Jesus Christ as Lord of all. In your church, talk and behave in a way that will reduce arguments and increase harmony. Petty differences should never divide Christians.

1:12ff In this large and diverse Corinthian church, the believers favored different preachers. Because there was as yet no written New Testament, the believers depended heavily on preaching and teaching for spiritual insight into the meaning of the Old Testament. Some followed Paul, who had founded their church; some who had heard Peter in Jerusalem followed him; while others listened only to Apollos, an eloquent and popular preacher who had had a dynamic ministry in Corinth (Acts 18:24; 19:1). Although these three preachers were united in their message, their personalities attracted different people. Now the church was in danger of dividing. By mentioning Jesus Christ ten times in the first ten verses, Paul makes it clear what all preachers and teachers should emphasize. The message is more important than the messenger.

1:12, 13 The Corinthians' arguing had "broken Christ into many pieces," a graphic picture of what happens when the church (the body of Christ) is divided. With the many opportunities for worship available today, we could get caught up in the same game of "my preacher is better than yours!" But this would divide Christ once more. Make sure your teachers are helping you learn more about Christ, and not merely trying to bring recognition and glory to themselves.

1:16
1 Cor 16:15

1:17
Acts 26:17
2 Cor 10:10
11:16

"Church of Paul." 16Oh, yes, and I baptized the family of Stephanas. I don't remember ever baptizing anyone else. 17For Christ didn't send me to baptize, but to preach the Gospel; and even my preaching sounds poor, for I do not fill my sermons with profound words and high sounding ideas, for fear of diluting the mighty power there is in the simple message of the cross of Christ.

Christ brings us life from God

1:18
Acts 17:18
Rom 1:16
1 Cor 2:14
2 Cor 2:15,16

1:19
Isa 29:14

18I know very well how foolish it sounds to those who are lost, when they hear that Jesus died to save them. But we who are saved recognize this message as the very power of God. 19For God says, "I will destroy all human plans of salvation no matter how wise they seem to be, and ignore the best ideas of men, even the most brilliant of them."

1:20
Job 12:17
Isa 44:25
1 Cor 2:6

1:21
Lk 10:21

1:22
Mt 12:38
Lk 11:16

20So what about these wise men, these scholars, these brilliant debaters of this world's great affairs? God has made them all look foolish, and shown their wisdom to be useless nonsense. 21For God in his wisdom saw to it that the world would never find God through human brilliance, and then he stepped in and saved all those who believed his message, which the world calls foolish and silly. 22It seems foolish to the Jews because they want a sign from heaven as proof that what is preached is true; and it is foolish to the Gentiles because they believe only what agrees with their philosophy and seems wise to them. 23So when we preach about Christ dying to save them, the Jews are offended and the Gentiles say it's all nonsense. 24But God has opened the eyes of those called to salvation, both Jews and Gentiles, to see that Christ is the mighty power of God to save them; Christ himself is the center of God's wise plan for their salvation. 25This so-called "foolish" plan of God is far wiser than the wisest plan of the wisest man, and God in his weakness—Christ dying on the cross—is far stronger than any man.

1:23
Isa 8:14,15
Mt 11:6

1:24
Rom 1:4

1:25
2 Cor 4:7; 13:4

1:26
Mt 11:25
Jn 7:48
1 Cor 2:8

1:27
Ps 8:2

1:28
Job 34:19
Rom 4:17
1 Cor 2:6

26Notice among yourselves, dear brothers, that few of you who follow Christ have big names or power or wealth. 27Instead, God has deliberately chosen to use ideas the world considers foolish and of little worth in order to shame those people considered by the world as wise and great. 28He has chosen a plan despised by the world, counted as nothing at all, and used it to bring down to nothing those the

1:18 *are lost,* or "are being lost." *are saved,* or "are being saved."

1:17 When Paul said Christ didn't send him to baptize, he wasn't putting down baptism. Baptism was commanded by Jesus himself (Matthew 28:19) and practiced by the early church (Acts 2:41). Paul was emphasizing that he couldn't do everything; he needed others to use their gifts to help him. Paul's gift was preaching, and that's what he did.

This is a model for us. Christian ministry should be a team effort; no preacher or teacher is a complete link between God and people, and no individual should think he can do everything the apostles did. We must be content with the job God has given us.

1:17 Some speakers are big on words but small on content. Paul wanted to make sure he was big on content and practical help for his listeners. He wanted them to be impressed with his *message*, not just his style (see 2:1–5). You don't need to be a great speaker with a large vocabulary to share the gospel effectively. The persuasive power is in the story, not the storyteller. Paul was not speaking against those who carefully prepare what they say (see 2:6), but against those who try to impress others only with their knowledge or speaking ability.

1:18-25 The message of Christ's death for sins sounds foolish to those who don't believe. Death seems to be the end of the road, the ultimate weakness. But Jesus did not stay dead. His resurrection shows his power even over death, and he will save us from eternal death and give us everlasting life if we trust him as Savior and Lord. This sounds so simple that many people won't accept it. They try other ways to obtain eternal life (being good, being wise, etc.). But their attempts will not work. The "foolish" people who simply accept Christ's offer are actually the wisest of all, because they alone will live eternally with God.

1:19 In this verse Paul summarizes Isaiah 29:14 to emphasize a point Jesus often made during his ministry on earth: God's way is not like the world's way, but God offers eternal life while the world cannot.

1:22 Many Jews thought the Good News of Jesus Christ was foolish because they had been taught the Messiah would be a conquering king, not a suffering servant. Jesus had not restored David's throne as they expected. Besides, he was executed as a common criminal, and how could a common criminal be a savior? Greeks, too, considered the gospel foolish: they did not believe in a bodily resurrection; they did not see in Jesus the powerful characteristics of their mythological gods; and they thought no reputable person would be crucified. Death was defeat, not victory.

The Good News of Jesus Christ still sounds foolish to many. Our society worships power, influence, and wealth. Jesus came as a humble, poor servant, and he offers his Kingdom to those with faith, not works. This looks backward to the world, but it is the way God has chosen to save it.

1:28-31 Paul continues to emphasize that the way to receive salvation is so ordinary and simple that *any* person who wants to can understand it. Skill does not get you into God's Kingdom—simple faith does. God planned it this way so no one could boast that his achievements helped him secure eternal life. Salvation is totally from God through Jesus' death, which allowed us to become perfect in God's eyes. There is *nothing* we can do to become acceptable to God; we need only accept what Jesus has already done for us. He has done the work; we acknowledge that work; we acknowledge his position as God.

world considers great, 29so that no one anywhere can ever brag in the presence of God.

30For it is from God alone that you have your life through Christ Jesus. He showed us God's plan of salvation; he was the one who made us acceptable to God; he made us pure and holy and gave himself to purchase our salvation. 31As it says in the Scriptures, "If anyone is going to boast, let him boast only of what the Lord has done."

The Spirit gives wisdom

2 Dear brothers, even when I first came to you I didn't use lofty words and brilliant ideas to tell you God's message. 2For I decided that I would speak only of Jesus Christ and his death on the cross. 3I came to you in weakness—timid and trembling. 4And my preaching was very plain, not with a lot of oratory and human wisdom, but the Holy Spirit's power was in my words, proving to those who heard them that the message was from God. 5I did this because I wanted your faith to stand firmly upon God, not on man's great ideas.

6Yet when I am among mature Christians I do speak with words of great wisdom, but not the kind that comes from here on earth, and not the kind that appeals to the great men of this world, who are doomed to fall. 7Our words are wise because they are from God, telling of God's wise plan to bring us into the glories of heaven. This plan was hidden in former times, though it was made for our benefit before the world began. 8But the great men of the world have not understood it; if they had, they never would have crucified the Lord of Glory.

9That is what is meant by the Scriptures which say that no mere man has ever seen, heard or even imagined what wonderful things God has ready for those who

1:29 Eph 2:8-10

1:30 Rom 3:24; 8:1,2
2 Cor 5:21
Eph 1:7

1:31 Jer 9:23,24
2 Cor 10:17

2:1 1 Cor 1:17

2:2 Gal 6:14
Phil 3:8

2:3 2 Cor 10:1
Gal 4:13

2:4 1 Cor 4:20

2:5 2 Cor 4:7; 6:7

2:6 Eph 4:13
Heb 5:14

2:7 Rom 8:29; 16:25
Eph 3:3-5

2:8 Acts 13:27

2:9 Isa 64:4; 65:17

1:30 he made us pure and holy, or, "he brought us near to God." to purchase our salvation, or, "to free us from slavery to sin."

		HIGHLIGHTS OF 1 CORINTHIANS
The Meaning of the Cross 1:18—2:16	Be considerate of one another because of what Christ has done for us. There is no place for pride or a know-it-all attitude. We are to have the mind of Christ.	
The Story of the Last Supper 11:23–29	The Last Supper is a time of reflection on Christ's final words to his disciples before he died on the cross; we must celebrate this in an orderly and correct manner.	
The Poem of Love 13:1–13	Love is to guide all we do. We have different gifts, abilities, likes, dislikes—but we are called, without exception, to love.	
The Christian's Destiny 15:42–58	We are promised by Christ who died for us that, as he came back to life after death, so our perishable bodies will be exchanged for heavenly bodies. Then we will live and reign with Christ.	

2:1 Paul is referring to his first visit to Corinth (A.D. 51), when he founded the church during his second missionary journey (Acts 18:1ff).

2:1–5 A brilliant scholar, Paul could have overwhelmed his listeners with intellectual arguments and persuasive oratory. Instead he shared the simple message of Jesus Christ by allowing the Holy Spirit to guide his words. In sharing the gospel with others, we should follow Paul's example and keep our message simple and basic. The Holy Spirit will give power to our words and use them to bring glory to Jesus.

2:4 Paul's confidence was not in his keen intellect or speaking ability, but in his knowledge that the Holy Spirit was helping and guiding him. Paul is not writing off the importance of study and preparation for preaching—he had a thorough education in the Scriptures. Effective preaching must combine studious preparation with the work of the Holy Spirit.

2:7 God's "wise plan" was his offer of salvation to all people. Originally unknown to mankind, this plan became crystal clear

when Jesus rose from the dead. His resurrection proved that he had power over sin and death and could now offer us this power as well (see 1 Peter 1:10, 11 and the note on Romans 16:25–27 for more about God's plan). God's plan, however, is still hidden to unbelievers because they either refuse to accept it, choose to ignore it, or simply haven't heard about it.

2:8 Jesus was misunderstood and rejected by those whom the world considered wise and great. He was put to death by the leaders in Palestine—the High Priest, King Herod, Pilate, and the Pharisees and Sadducees. Jesus' rejection by these leaders was predicted in Isaiah 53:3 and Zechariah 12:10, 11.

2:9 We cannot imagine all that God has in store for us both in this life and for eternity. He will create a new heaven and a new earth (Isaiah 65:17; Revelation 21:1), and we will live with him forever. Until then, his Holy Spirit comforts and guides us. Knowing the future that awaits us should give us hope and courage to press on in this life, to endure hardship, and to avoid giving in to temptation. This world is not all there is.

2:10
Mt 11:25; 16:17
Jn 14:26;
15:26; 16:13-15
1 Jn 2:27

2:11
Prov 20:27
Jer 17:9
Rom 11:33

2:12
Rom 8:15
1 Cor 1:27

2:13
Mt 16:23
Rom 8:5
2 Pet 1:20,21

2:14
Jn 14:17
Jude 19

2:15
Prov 28:5

2:16
Ps 25:14
Jn 15:15
Rom 11:34

love the Lord. 10But we know about these things because God has sent his Spirit to tell us, and his Spirit searches out and shows us all of God's deepest secrets. 11No one can really know what anyone else is thinking, or what he is really like, except that person himself. And no one can know God's thoughts except God's own Spirit. 12And God has actually given us his Spirit (not the world's spirit) to tell us about the wonderful free gifts of grace and blessing that God has given us. 13In telling you about these gifts we have even used the very words given to us by the Holy Spirit, not words that we as men might choose. So we use the Holy Spirit's words to explain the Holy Spirit's facts. 14But the man who isn't a Christian can't understand and can't accept these thoughts from God, which the Holy Spirit teaches us. They sound foolish to him, because only those who have the Holy Spirit within them can understand what the Holy Spirit means. Others just can't take it in. 15But the spiritual man has insight into everything, and that bothers and baffles the man of the world, who can't understand him at all. 16How could he? For certainly he has never been one to know the Lord's thoughts, or to discuss them with him, or to move the hands of God by prayer. But, strange as it seems, we Christians actually do have within us a portion of the very thoughts and mind of Christ.

Paul condemns division in the church

3:1
Gal 6:1
Eph 4:14

3:2
Heb 5:12-13
1 Pet 2:2,3

3:3
Rom 13:12-13
1 Cor 1:10; 11:18

3:4
1 Cor 1:12

3:5
Rom 12:3,6
2 Cor 6:4

3:6
Isa 55:10
Acts 18:4; 19:1

3 Dear brothers, I have been talking to you as though you were still just babies in the Christian life, who are not following the Lord, but your own desires; I cannot talk to you as I would to healthy Christians, who are filled with the Spirit. 2I have had to feed you with milk and not with solid food, because you couldn't digest anything stronger. And even now you still have to be fed on milk. 3For you are still only baby Christians, controlled by your own desires, not God's. When you are jealous of one another and divide up into quarreling groups, doesn't that prove you are still babies, wanting your own way? In fact, you are acting like people who don't belong to the Lord at all. 4There you are, quarreling about whether I am greater than Apollos, and dividing the church. Doesn't this show how little you have grown in the Lord?

5Who am I, and who is Apollos, that we should be the cause of a quarrel? Why, we're just God's servants, each of us with certain special abilities, and with our help you believed. 6My work was to plant the seed in your hearts, and Apollos' work was to water it, but it was God, not we, who made the garden grow in your

2:13 to explain the Holy Spirit's facts, or, "interpreting spiritual truth in spiritual language." **2:16** to move the hands of God by prayer, or, "who can advise him?" **3:4** Doesn't this show how little you have grown in the Lord? Literally, "Are you not mere men?"

2:10 These secrets are Jesus' resurrection and God's plan of salvation, revealed only to those who believe that what God says is true. Those who believe in the resurrection and put their faith in Christ will know all they need to know to be saved. This knowledge, however, can't be grasped by even the wisest people unless they accept God's message. All who reject God's message are foolish, no matter how wise the world thinks they are.

2:13 Paul's words are authoritative because their source is the Holy Spirit. In one sense, every believer has the ability to interpret Scripture because of the illuminating work of the Holy Spirit. In a unique sense, however, Paul was writing directly under the inspiration of the Holy Spirit. His words are the very words of God.

2:14, 15 Just as a tone-deaf person cannot appreciate fine music, the person who rejects God cannot understand God's beautiful message. The lines of communication are broken, and he cannot hear what God is saying to him.

2:14 Non-Christians cannot comprehend God, and they cannot grasp the concept that God's Spirit lives in believers. Don't expect most people to approve of or understand your decision to follow Christ. It all seems silly to them.

2:15, 16 No one can comprehend God by human effort (Romans 11:34), but by his Spirit many of his thoughts are revealed to us.

Believers are spiritual people having insight into some of God's plans, thoughts, and actions. By his Holy Spirit we can begin to know his thoughts, discuss them with him, and expect his answers to our prayers. Are you spending enough time with Christ to have his very mind in you? An intimate relationship with Christ comes only from consistent time spent in his presence and in his Word. Read Philippians 2:5ff for more on the mind of Christ.

3:1-3 Paul called the Corinthians babies in the Christian life because they were not yet spiritually healthy and mature. The proof was that they quarreled like children. Baby Christians are controlled by their own desires; mature believers by God's desires. How much influence do your own desires have on your life? Our goal is to let God's desires be our own.

3:6 Paul's work was to plant the seed of God's Word in people's hearts. He was a missionary pioneer, one who brought the message of salvation. Apollos' role was to water—to help the believers grow stronger in the faith Paul had helped them discover. Paul founded the church in Corinth, and Apollos built on that foundation. Tragically, the believers in Corinth had split into factions, pledging loyalty to different teachers (see 1:11-13). Paul wanted them to see that the preachers were merely their guides to point them to God.

hearts. 7The person who does the planting or watering isn't very important, but God is important because he is the one who makes things grow. 8Apollos and I are working as a team, with the same aim, though each of us will be rewarded for his own hard work. 9We are only God's co-workers. You are *God's* garden, not ours; you are *God's* building, not ours.

10God, in his kindness, has taught me how to be an expert builder. I have laid the foundation and Apollos has built on it. But he who builds on the foundation must be very careful. 11And no one can ever lay any other real foundation than that one we already have—Jesus Christ. 12But there are various kinds of materials that can be used to build on that foundation. Some use gold and silver and jewels; and some build with sticks, and hay, or even straw! 13There is going to come a time of testing at Christ's Judgment Day to see what kind of material each builder has used. Everyone's work will be put through the fire so that all can see whether or not it keeps its value, and what was really accomplished. 14Then every workman who has built on the foundation with the right materials, and whose work still stands, will get his pay. 15But if the house he has built burns up, he will have a great loss. He himself will be saved, but like a man escaping through a wall of flames.

16Don't you realize that all of you together are the house of God, and that the Spirit of God lives among you in his house? 17If anyone defiles and spoils God's home, God will destroy him. For God's home is holy and clean, and you are that home.

18Stop fooling yourselves. If you count yourself above average in intelligence, as judged by this world's standards, you had better put this all aside and be a fool rather than let it hold you back from the true wisdom from above. 19For the wisdom of this world is foolishness to God. As it says in the book of Job, God uses man's own brilliance to trap him; he stumbles over his own "wisdom" and falls. 20And again, in the book of Psalms, we are told that the Lord knows full well how the human mind reasons, and how foolish and futile it is.

21So don't be proud of following the wise men of this world. For God has already given you everything you need. 22He has given you Paul and Apollos and Peter as your helpers. He has given you the whole world to use, and life and even death are

3:21 *So don't be proud of following the wise men of this world,* literally, "Let no one glory in men."

3:8
Ps 62:12
Rom 2:6
Rev 2:23; 22:12

3:9
Isa 61:3
Jn 15:1-5
Eph 2:20
Col 2:7
1 Pet 2:5

3:10
Rom 15:20
1 Pet 4:11

3:11
Isa 28:16
Mt 16:18
1 Pet 2:4

3:13
2 Tim 1:12,18
4:8

3:14
1 Cor 9:25
Gal 6:4

3:15
Jude 23

3:16
2 Cor 6:16
Eph 2:21

3:17
Heb 3:1

3:18
Isa 5:21
1 Cor 8:2
Gal 6:3

3:19
Job 5:13
1 Cor 1:20

3:20
Ps 94:11

3:21
Rom 8:28,32

3:22
Rom 8:38

3:7-9 God's work in the world involves many different individuals with a variety of gifts and abilities. There are no superstars in this task, only team members performing their own special roles. We become useful members of God's team by setting aside the desire to receive glory for what we do. The praise that comes from people is comparatively worthless; invaluable approval comes from God.

3:10, 11 The foundation of the church—of all believers—is Jesus Christ, and this is the foundation Paul laid when he began the church at Corinth. Whoever builds on the foundation—teachers, preachers, parents, and others—must build with high quality materials (3:12ff) that match God's standards, including right doctrine as taught in the Bible and right living as taught by Christ.

3:10 Those who build the church have a great responsibility. Paul was not criticizing Apollos, but challenging future church leaders to realize the heavy responsibility of preaching and teaching.

3:10-17 The foundation of the church is Jesus Christ, and ideally each church member will be mature, spiritually sensitive, and doctrinally sound. The Corinthian church was filled with "wood, hay, and straw," members who were immature, insensitive to each other, and eagerly accepting wrong doctrine (3:1-4). No wonder they had so many problems. Local churches must be built on Christ, and their members should be those who know him well and are deeply committed to him.

3:11 A building is only as solid as its foundation. The foundation of our lives is Jesus Christ; he is our base, our reason for being. Everything we are and do must fit into the pattern provided by Jesus Christ. Are you building your life on the only real and lasting foundation, or are you building on another foundation such as

wealth, security, or success? What is your reason for living?

3:13 Two ways to destroy a building are to tamper with the foundation or to build with inferior materials. You cannot build a true church on any person or principle except Jesus Christ. Christ will evaluate each minister's contribution to the life of the church. The day of judgment will reveal the sincerity of each person's work. God will determine whether or not he or she has been faithful to Jesus' instructions.

3:16 Paul not only said that our bodies are the home of the Holy Spirit (6:19), but that the local church or Christian community is the house of God. Just as the Temple was not to be defiled, the church is not to be spoiled and ruined by divisions, controversy, or other sins as its members come together to worship God.

3:18, 19 Paul is not telling the Corinthian believers to neglect the pursuit of knowledge, but if one has to choose between earthly knowledge and heavenly wisdom, choose heavenly wisdom even though you may look foolish to the world. Worldly wisdom, if it holds you back from God, is no wisdom at all. The Corinthians were using so-called worldly wisdom to evaluate their leaders and teachers. Their pride made them value the presentation of the message more than its content.

3:22 Paul said that both life and death are our servants. How can this be? While nonbelievers are victims of life, swept along by its current and wondering if there is meaning to it, believers use life well because they understand its true purpose. Nonbelievers can only fear death. For believers, however, death holds no terrors, because Christ has conquered them all. Through him, they will live eternally in God's presence.

3:23
1 Cor 11:3
your servants. He has given you all of the present and all of the future. All are yours, 23and you belong to Christ, and Christ is God's.

Paul counsels his beloved children

4:1
Rom 16:25-27
1 Cor 2:1,7
Eph 3:3-5
4 So Apollos and I should be looked upon as Christ's servants who distribute God's blessings by explaining God's secrets. 2Now the most important thing about a servant is that he does just what his master tells him to. 3What about me? Have I been a good servant? Well, I don't worry over what you think about this, or

4:2
Ps 143:1,2
Lk 12:42-45
Acts 23:1
Rom 2:12,13
2 Cor 1:12
what anyone else thinks. I don't even trust my own judgment on this point. 4My conscience is clear, but even that isn't final proof. It is the Lord himself who must examine me and decide.

4:5
Mt 7:1
Rom 2:16,29
2 Cor 5:10
Rev 20:12
5So be careful not to jump to conclusions before the Lord returns as to whether someone is a good servant or not. When the Lord comes, he will turn on the light so that everyone can see exactly what each one of us is really like, deep down in our hearts. Then everyone will know why we have been doing the Lord's work. At that time God will give to each one whatever praise is coming to him.

4:6
1 Cor 1:12,31
4:18
6I have used Apollos and myself as examples to illustrate what I have been saying: that you must not have favorites. You must not be proud of one of God's teachers more than another. 7What are you so puffed up about? What do you have

4:7
Jn 3:27
Rom 12:3,6
1 Pet 4:10
that God hasn't given you? And if all you have is from God, why act as though you are so great, and as though you have accomplished something on your own?

4:8
Rev 3:17
8You seem to think you already have all the spiritual food you need. You are full and spiritually contented, rich kings on your thrones, leaving us far behind! I wish

4:9
Ps 44:22
Rom 8:36
2 Cor 4:11
you really were already on your thrones, for when that time comes you can be sure that we will be there, too, reigning with you. 9Sometimes I think God has put us apostles at the very end of the line, like prisoners soon to be killed, put on display at the end of a victor's parade, to be stared at by men and angels alike.

4:10
1 Cor 1:18,19
2 Cor 11:19,20
13:9
10Religion has made us foolish, you say, but of course you are all such wise and sensible Christians! We are weak, but not you! You are well thought of, while we

4:11
Acts 23:2
Rom 8:35
2 Cor 11:23-27
are laughed at. 11To this very hour we have gone hungry and thirsty, without even enough clothes to keep us warm. We have been kicked around without homes of

4:12
Mt 5:44
Acts 18:2,3
1 Tim 4:9,10
1 Pet 3:9
our own. 12We have worked wearily with our hands to earn our living. We have blessed those who cursed us. We have been patient with those who injured us.

4:14
1 Cor 6:5; 15:34
2 Cor 6:13
12:14
13We have replied quietly when evil things have been said about us. Yet right up to the present moment we are like dirt under foot, like garbage.

4:15
Rom 15:20
Gal 4:19
14I am not writing about these things to make you ashamed, but to warn and counsel you as beloved children. 15For although you may have ten thousand others to teach you about Christ, remember that you have only me as your father. For I

4:1, 2 Paul urged the Corinthians to think of him, Peter, and Apollos not as leaders of parties, but as servants of Christ. A servant does what his master tells him to do. We must do what God tells us to do in the Bible and through his Holy Spirit. Daily God confronts us with needs and opportunities that challenge us to do what we know is right.

4:5 It is tempting to judge a fellow Christian, evaluating whether or not he or she is a good follower of Christ. But only God knows a person's heart, and he is the only one with the right to judge. Paul's warning to the Corinthians should also warn us. We are to help those who are sinning (see 5:12, 13), but we must not judge who is a better servant for Christ. When you judge someone, you automatically consider yourself better, and this is pride.

4:6-13 The Corinthians had split into various cliques, each following its own superstar preacher (Paul, Apollos, Peter, etc.). Each clique really believed it was the only one who had the whole truth, and thus felt spiritually proud. But Paul told the groups not to boast about being tied to a particular preacher because even the

superstars were simply humble servants who had each suffered many things for the same message of salvation in Jesus Christ. No preacher of God has more authority than another.

4:6, 7 How easy it is for us to become attached to a spiritual leader. When someone has helped us, it's natural to feel loyalty. But Paul warns against having such pride in our favorite leaders that we cause divisions in the church. Any true spiritual leader is a representative of Christ and has nothing to offer that God hasn't given him. Don't let your loyalty cause fighting, slander, or broken relationships. Make sure your deepest loyalties are to Christ and not to his human agents. Those who spend more time debating church leadership than declaring Christ's message don't have Christ as their top priority.

4:15 In an attempt to unify the church, Paul appealed to his relationship with them. By "father," he meant he was the church's founder. Because he started the church, he could be trusted to have its best interests at heart. Paul's tough words were motivated by love—like the love a good father has for his children.

was the one who brought you to Christ when I preached the Gospel to you. 16So I beg you to follow my example, and do as I do.

17That is the very reason why I am sending Timothy—to help you do this. For he is one of those I won to Christ, a beloved and trustworthy child in the Lord. He will remind you of what I teach in all the churches wherever I go.

18I know that some of you will have become proud, thinking that I am afraid to come to deal with you. 19But I will come, and soon, if the Lord will let me, and then I'll find out whether these proud men are just big talkers or whether they really have God's power. 20The Kingdom of God is not just talking; it is living by God's power. 21Which do you choose? Shall I come with punishment and scolding, or shall I come with quiet love and gentleness?

4:16
1 Cor 11:1
Phil 3:17

4:17
Acts 16:1; 19:22
1 Tim 1:2

4:19
Acts 19:21
1 Cor 11:34; 16:5
2 Cor 1:15

4:20
1 Thess 1:5

4:21
2 Cor 1:23; 2:1

2. Disorders in the church
Paul condemns immorality in the church

5 Everyone is talking about the terrible thing that has happened there among you, something so evil that even the heathen don't do it: you have a man in your church who is living in sin with his father's wife. 2And are you still so conceited, so "spiritual"? Why aren't you mourning in sorrow and shame, and seeing to it that this man is removed from your membership?

3, 4Although I am not there with you, I have been thinking a lot about this, and in the name of the Lord Jesus Christ I have already decided what to do, just as though I were there. You are to call a meeting of the church—and the power of the Lord Jesus will be with you as you meet, and I will be there in spirit— 5and cast out this

5:1 *his father's wife,* possibly his stepmother.

5:1
Lev 18:7,8
Deut 27:20
2 Cor 7:12
Eph 5:3

5:3,4
Mt 18:15-18
Jn 20:23
2 Cor 2:5-10
13:3,4

5:5
Acts 26:18
1 Tim 1:20

Situations	Steps (Matthew 18:15–17)	**CHURCH DISCIPLINE**
Unintentional error and/or private sin	1. Go to the brother or sister, reprove him or her in private.	The church, at times, must exercise discipline toward members who have sinned. But church discipline must be handled carefully, straightforwardly, and in love.
Public sin and/or those done with prior knowledge and flagrantly	2. If he/she does not listen, go with one or two witnesses.	
	3. If he/she refuses to listen, take the matter before the church.	

After these steps have been carried out, the next steps are:
1. Remove the one in error from the fellowship (1 Corinthians 5:2–13).
2. The church gives united disapproval, but forgiveness and comfort is in order if he/she chooses to repent (2 Corinthians 2:5–7).
3. Do not associate with the disobedient person; and if you must, speak to him/her as one who needs a warning (2 Thessalonians 3:14, 15.)
4. After two warnings, reject the person from the fellowship (Titus 3:10).

4:16 Paul told the Corinthians to follow his example. He was able to make this statement because he walked close to God, spent time in God's Word and in prayer, and was aware of God's presence in his life at all times. God was his example; therefore, his life could be an example to other Christians. Paul wasn't expecting others to copy everything he did, because people are all different. But they should copy those aspects of his life that modeled Christ's way of living.

4:17 Timothy had traveled with Paul on his second missionary journey (see Acts 16:1–3) and was a key person in the growth of the early church. Timothy may have delivered this letter to Corinth, but more likely he arrived there shortly after the letter (see 16:10). His role was to see that Paul's advice was received, read, and implemented. He was then to return to Paul and report on the church's progress.

4:18–20 Some people talk a lot about faith, but that's all it is—talk. They may know all the right words to say, but their lives are not examples of Christian living. Paul says the Kingdom of God is to be *lived,* not just discussed. There is a big difference between

knowing the right words and living them out. Don't be content to have the right answers about Christ. Let your life put flesh on your words.

4:19 It is not known whether Paul ever returned to Corinth, but it is likely. In 2 Corinthians 2:1, he says he decided not to make *another* painful visit, implying that he had had a previous painful confrontation with the Corinthian believers.

5:1ff The church must discipline flagrant sin among its members—such actions, left unchecked, can polarize and paralyze a church. The correction, however, is never to be vengeful. Instead, it is intended to bring about a cure. The Corinthian church had a specific sin in their midst, but they had refused to deal with it. In this case, a man was having an affair with his mother (or stepmother), and the church members were trying to ignore the situation. Paul was telling the church that they had a responsibility to maintain standards of morality found in God's Word. God tells us not to judge others, but he also tells us not to tolerate flagrant sin that opposes his holiness and has a dangerous influence on the lives of other believers (5:6).

man from the fellowship of the church and into Satan's hands, to punish him, in the hope that his soul will be saved when our Lord Jesus Christ returns.

6What a terrible thing it is that you are boasting about your purity, and yet you let this sort of thing go on. Don't you realize that if even one person is allowed to go on sinning, soon all will be affected? 7Remove this evil cancer—this wicked person—from among you, so that you can stay pure. Christ, God's Lamb, has been slain for us. 8So let us feast upon him and grow strong in the Christian life, leaving entirely behind us the cancerous old life with all its hatreds and wickedness. Let us feast instead upon the pure bread of honor and sincerity and truth.

9When I wrote to you before I said not to mix with evil people. 10But when I said that I wasn't talking about unbelievers who live in sexual sin, or are greedy cheats and thieves and idol worshipers. For you can't live in this world without being with people like that. 11What I meant was that you are not to keep company with anyone who claims to be a brother Christian but indulges in sexual sins, or is greedy, or is a swindler, or worships idols, or is a drunkard, or abusive. Don't even eat lunch with such a person.

12It isn't our job to judge outsiders. But it certainly is our job to judge and deal strongly with those who are members of the church, and who are sinning in these ways. 13God alone is the Judge of those on the outside. But you yourselves must deal with this man and put him out of your church.

Believers should not sue each other

6 How is it that when you have something against another Christian, you "go to law" and ask a heathen court to decide the matter instead of taking it to other Christians to decide which of you is right? 2Don't you know that some day we Christians are going to judge and govern the world? So why can't you decide even these little things among yourselves? 3Don't you realize that we Christians will judge and reward the very angels in heaven? So you should be able to decide your problems down here on earth easily enough. 4Why then go to outside judges who are not even Christians? 5I am trying to make you ashamed. Isn't there anyone in

6:4 *Why then go to outside judges who are not even Christians?* Or, "Even the least capable people in the church should be able to decide these things for you." Both interpretations are possible.

Margin references:
5:6 Mt 13:33; 16:6,11; Gal 5:9
5:7 Ex 12:21; Isa 53:7; Jn 1:29; 19:14; 1 Pet 1:19; Rev 5:6
5:8 Ex 12:15-19; Deut 16:3
5:9 2 Cor 6:14
5:10 Jn 17:15
5:11 Mt 18:17; Rom 16:17; 2 Thess 3:6; 2 Jn 1:10
5:12 1 Tim 3:7
5:13 Eccles 12:14; Heb 13:4
6:1 Mt 18:15-17
6:2 Dan 7:18,22; Lk 22:30; Rev 2:26; 20:4
6:3 2 Pet 2:4; Jude 6
6:5 1 Cor 4:14; 15:34

5:5 Why was it necessary to cast this man out of the church? To cast this man into Satan's hands meant to exclude him from the fellowship of believers. Without the spiritual support of Christians, he would be left alone with his sin and Satan, and perhaps this emptiness would drive him to repentance. Putting someone out of the church should be a last resort in disciplinary action. It should not be done out of vengeance, but out of love, just as parents punish children to correct them. The church's role is to help the offender, not to hurt him, motivating him to repent of his sins and to return to the fellowship of the church.

5:6 Paul was talking to those who wanted to ignore this church problem, not realizing that allowing blatant sin to exist in the church body affects all its members. Paul was not expecting anyone to be sinless—all believers struggle with sin on a daily basis. Instead, he was speaking against those who deliberately sinned, felt no guilt, and would not repent. This kind of sin cannot be tolerated in the church because it affects others. We have a responsibility to other believers. Blatant sins, left uncorrected, confuse and divide the congregation. While believers should encourage, pray for, and build up one another, they must also be intolerant of sin when it jeopardizes the spiritual health of the church.

5:9 Paul was referring to an earlier letter to the Corinthian church, often called the lost letter because it has not been preserved.

5:10, 11 Paul makes it clear that we should not dissociate ourselves from unbelievers—otherwise, we could not carry out Christ's command to tell them about salvation (Matthew 28:18–20). But we are to distance ourselves from the person who claims to be a Christian, yet indulges in sins explicitly forbidden in Scripture and then rationalizes his actions. By sinning, a person harms others for whom Christ died and dims the image of God in himself. A church that includes greedy people and sexual sinners is hardly fit to be the light of the world. It is distorting the picture of Christ it presents to the world. Instead of joining Christ's Kingdom with its constant fight to replace darkness with light, it is adding to the darkness.

5:12 The Bible consistently tells us not to criticize others by gossiping or making rash judgments. At the same time, however, we are to judge and deal with sin that can hurt others. Paul's instructions are not to be used to handle trivial matters or to take revenge; nor are they to be applied to individual problems between believers. These verses are instructions for dealing with open sin in the church, with a person who claims to be a Christian and yet who sins without remorse. The church's responsibility is to confront and discipline such a person in love. Also see the notes on 4:5 and 5:1ff.

6:1-6 In chapter 5 Paul discussed what to do with blatant sinners in the congregation. In chapter 6 he discusses how the congregation should handle smaller problems between believers. Society has set up a legal system where disagreements can be solved in courts. But Paul says that disagreeing Christians should not have to go to a secular court to resolve their differences. As Christians we have the Holy Spirit and the mind of Christ, so why should we turn to those who lack God's wisdom? With all that we have been given as believers, and the power that we will have in the future to judge the world and the angels, we should be able to deal with the disputes between ourselves.

all the church who is wise enough to decide these arguments? 6But, instead, one Christian sues another and accuses his Christian brother in front of unbelievers. 7To have such lawsuits at all is a real defeat for you as Christians. Why not just accept mistreatment and leave it at that? It would be far more honoring to the Lord to let yourselves be cheated. 8But, instead, you yourselves are the ones who do wrong, cheating others, even your own brothers.

Use your body to give God glory

9, 10Don't you know that those doing such things have no share in the Kingdom of God? Don't fool yourselves. Those who live immoral lives, who are idol worshipers, adulterers or homosexuals—will have no share in his Kingdom. Neither will thieves or greedy people, drunkards, slanderers, or robbers. 11There was a time when some of you were just like that but now your sins are washed away, and you are set apart for God, and he has accepted you because of what the Lord Jesus Christ and the Spirit of our God have done for you.

12I can do anything I want to if Christ has not said no, but some of these things aren't good for me. Even if I am allowed to do them, I'll refuse to if I think they might get such a grip on me that I can't easily stop when I want to. 13For instance, take the matter of eating. God has given us an appetite for food and stomachs to digest it. But that doesn't mean we should eat more than we need. Don't think of eating as important, because some day God will do away with both stomachs and food.

But sexual sin is never right: our bodies were not made for that, but for the Lord, and the Lord wants to fill our bodies with himself. 14And God is going to raise our bodies from the dead by his power just as he raised up the Lord Jesus Christ. 15Don't you realize that your bodies are actually parts and members of Christ? So

6:7
Prov 20:22
Mt 5:39
Rom 12:17
1 Thess 5:15
6:8
1 Thess 4:6

6:9,10
Isa 3:11
Acts 20:32
Gal 5:21
Eph 5:5

6:11
Acts 22:16
Rom 8:30
1 Cor 1:2,30
Heb 10:22

6:12
1 Cor 10:23

6:13
Mt 5:17
Col 2:22
1 Thess 4:3

6:14
Acts 2:24
Rom 6:5
1 Cor 15:23
Eph 1:19,20

6:6 Why does Paul say it isn't good to sue another Christian? (1) If the judge and jury are not Christians, they are unlikely to be sensitive to Christian values. (2) The basis for going to court is often revenge; this should never be a Christian's motive. (3) Lawsuits make the church look bad, causing unbelievers to focus on its problems rather than its purpose.

6:9–11 Paul is describing characteristics of unbelievers. He doesn't mean that adulterers, homosexuals, thieves, or greedy people are automatically and irrevocably excluded from heaven. Christians come from all backgrounds, including these. They may still struggle with evil desires, but they should not continue in these practices. In 6:11, Paul clearly states that even those who sin in these ways can have their lives changed by Christ. However, those who say they are Christians but persist in these practices with no remorse should reevaluate their lives to see if they truly believe in Christ.

6:9–11 In a permissive society it is easy for Christians to overlook or accept immoral behavior (sexual sins, greed, drunkenness, gossip, etc.) because it is so widespread. Although it surrounds us, we cannot take part in it or condone it in any way. Staying away from generally accepted sin is difficult, but it is no harder for us than it was for the Corinthians. God expects his followers in any age to have high standards.

6:12 "I can do anything if Christ has not said no" is literally translated, "All things are lawful for me." Apparently the church was quoting and misapplying this line frequently. Some Christians in Corinth were excusing many of their sins by saying that (1) Christ had taken away all sin, and so they had complete freedom to live as they pleased, or (2) what they were doing was not strictly forbidden by Scripture. Paul answered both these excuses. (1) While Christ has taken away our sin, this does not give us freedom to go on doing what we know is wrong. Scripture specifically forbids many sins (see 6:9, 10). (2) Some actions are not sinful in themselves, but they are not appropriate because they can control our lives and lead us away from God. (3) Anything we do that hurts rather than helps others is not right.

6:12, 13 Many of the world's religions think the soul is important and the body is not, and Christianity has sometimes been influenced by them. In truth, however, Christianity is a very physical religion. We worship a God who created a physical world and pronounced it good. He promises us a new earth where real people continue to live physical lives—not a pink cloud where disembodied souls listen to harp music. At the heart of Christianity is the story of God himself taking on flesh and blood and coming to live with us, offering both physical healing and spiritual restoration.

We humans, like Adam, are a combination of dust and spirit. Just as our spiritual lives affect our bodies, so our physical lives affect our souls. We cannot commit sin with our bodies without damaging our souls, because our bodies and souls are inseparably joined. In the new earth we will have resurrection bodies that are not corrupted by sin. Then we will enjoy the fullness of our salvation.

6:12, 13 Freedom is a mark of the Christian faith—freedom from sin and guilt, and freedom to use and enjoy anything that comes from God. But Christians should not abuse this freedom and hurt themselves or others. Drinking too much leads to alcoholism, gluttony leads to obesity. Be careful that what God has allowed you to enjoy doesn't grow into a bad habit that controls you. For more about Christian freedom and everyday behavior, read chapter 8.

6:13 Sexual sin is a temptation we cannot escape. In movies and on television, sex outside marriage is treated as a normal, even desirable, part of life, while marriage is often shown as confining and joyless. We can even be looked down upon by others if suspected of being pure. But God does not forbid sexual sin just to be difficult. He knows its power to destroy us physically and spiritually. No one should underestimate the power of sexual sin. It has devastated countless lives and destroyed families, communities, and even nations. God wants to protect us from damaging ourselves and others, and so he offers to fill us—our loneliness, our desires—with himself.

6:16
Gen 2:24
Mt 19:5,6
6:17
Jn 17:21
Rom 8:16
2 Cor 3:17
Eph 5:30
6:18
Rom 1:24
1 Thess 4:3,4
6:19
Rom 14:7,8
2 Cor 6:16
6:20
1 Pet 1:18,19

should I take part of Christ and join him to a prostitute? Never! 16And don't you know that if a man joins himself to a prostitute she becomes a part of him and he becomes a part of her? For God tells us in the Scripture that in his sight the two become one person. 17But if you give yourself to the Lord, you and Christ are joined together as one person.

18That is why I say to run from sex sin. No other sin affects the body as this one does. When you sin this sin it is against your own body. 19Haven't you yet learned that your body is the home of the Holy Spirit God gave you, and that he lives within you? Your own body does not belong to you. 20For God has bought you with a great price. So use every part of your body to give glory back to God, because he owns it.

B. PAUL ANSWERS CHURCH QUESTIONS (7:1—16:24)

After discussing disorders in the church, Paul moves to the list of questions which the Corinthians had sent him, including subjects of marriage, singleness, eating meat offered to idols, clothing in worship, orderliness in the Lord's Supper, spiritual gifts, and the resurrection. Questions which plague churches today are remarkably similar to these, so we can receive specific guidance in these areas.

1. Instruction on Christian marriage
Questions about marriage

7:1
1 Cor 7:8,26
7:2
Prov 5:19

7 Now about those questions you asked in your last letter: my answer is that if you do not marry, it is good. 2But usually it is best to be married, each man having his own wife, and each woman having her own husband, because otherwise you might fall back into sin.

7:3
Ex 21:10
1 Pet 3:7

3The man should give his wife all that is her right as a married woman, and the wife should do the same for her husband: 4for a girl who marries no longer has full right to her own body, for her husband then has his rights to it, too; and in the same way the husband no longer has full right to his own body, for it belongs also to his

7:5
1 Thess 3:5

wife. 5So do not refuse these rights to each other. The only exception to this rule would be the agreement of both husband and wife to refrain from the rights of

---

6:15–17 This teaching about sexual sin and prostitutes was especially important for the Corinthian church because the temple of the goddess Aphrodite was in Corinth. It employed more than a thousand prostitutes, and sex was part of the worship ritual. Paul clearly states that Christians are to have no part in sexual sin, even if it is acceptable and popular in our culture.

6:18 As Christians we are free to be all we can be for God; we are not free *from* God. God created sex to be a beautiful and essential ingredient of marriage, but sexual sin—sex outside the marriage relationship—*always* hurts someone. It hurts God because it shows we prefer following our own desires instead of the leading of the Holy Spirit. It hurts others because it violates the commitment so necessary to a relationship. It often brings disease to our bodies, and it deeply affects our personalities, which respond in anguish when we harm ourselves physically and spiritually.

6:19, 20 What did Paul mean when he said that God owns our bodies? Many people say they have the right to do whatever they want with their own bodies. Although they think this is freedom, they are really enslaved to their own desires. When we become Christians, the Holy Spirit fills our lives and lives in us. Therefore, we no longer own our bodies. If you live in a building owned by someone else, you don't violate the building rules. Since your body belongs to God, you must not violate his standards for living.

7:1 The Corinthians had written to Paul asking him several questions relating to the Christian life and problems in the church. Paul gives his answers to these questions in the remainder of this book.

7:1ff Christians in Corinth were surrounded by sexual temptation. The city had a reputation even among pagans for sexual immorality and religious prostitution. It was to this kind of society that Paul delivered these instructions on sex and marriage. The

Corinthians needed special, specific instructions because of their culture's immoral standards. Paul was especially careful with this teaching to the Corinthians because their culture was so contrary to God's plan. For more on Paul's teaching on marriage, see Ephesians 5.

7:3–5 Sexual temptations are difficult to withstand because they appeal to the normal and natural desires God has given us. Marriage is meant, in part, to satisfy these natural sexual desires and to strengthen the partners against temptation. Married couples have the responsibility to care for each other. Therefore, husbands and wives should not withhold themselves from one another, but should fulfill each other's needs and desires. (See also the note on 10:13.)

7:3–11 The Corinthian church was in turmoil because of the immorality of the culture around them. Some Greeks, in rejecting immorality, rejected sex and marriage altogether. The Corinthian Christians wondered if this was what they were to do also, so they asked Paul several questions: "Because sex is perverted, shouldn't we also abstain in marriage?" "If my spouse is unsaved, should I seek a divorce?" "Should unmarried people and widows not marry?" Paul answered many of these questions by saying, "For now, stay put. Be content in the situation in which God has placed you. Don't seek to be married or single. Live God's way one day at a time, and he will show you what to do." He then proceeded to answer the specific questions by clarifying people's responsibilities in each of these situations.

7:4 Spiritually, our bodies belong to God when we become Christians, because Jesus Christ bought us by paying the price to release us from sin (see 6:19, 20). Physically, our bodies belong to our spouses, because God designed marriage so that through the union of husband and wife, the two become one (Genesis 2:24).

marriage for a limited time, so that they can give themselves more completely to prayer. Afterwards, they should come together again so that Satan won't be able to tempt them because of their lack of self-control.

⁶I'm not saying you *must* marry; but you certainly *may* if you wish. ⁷I wish everyone could get along without marrying, just as I do. But we are not all the same. God gives some the gift of a husband or wife, and others he gives the gift of being able to stay happily unmarried. ⁸So I say to those who aren't married, and to widows—better to stay unmarried if you can, just as I am. ⁹But if you can't control yourselves, go ahead and marry. It is better to marry than to burn with lust.

¹⁰Now, for those who are married I have a command, not just a suggestion. And it is not a command from me, for this is what the Lord himself has said: A wife must not leave her husband. ¹¹But if she is separated from him, let her remain single or else go back to him. And the husband must not divorce his wife.

¹²Here I want to add some suggestions of my own. These are not direct commands from the Lord, but they seem right to me: If a Christian has a wife who is not a Christian, but she wants to stay with him anyway, he must not leave her or divorce her. ¹³And if a Christian woman has a husband who isn't a Christian, and he wants her to stay with him, she must not leave him. ¹⁴For perhaps the husband who isn't a Christian may become a Christian with the help of his Christian wife. And the wife who isn't a Christian may become a Christian with the help of her Christian husband. Otherwise, if the family separates, the children might never come to know the Lord; whereas a united family may, in God's plan, result in the children's salvation.

¹⁵But if the husband or wife who isn't a Christian is eager to leave, it is permitted. In such cases the Christian husband or wife should not insist that the other stay, for God wants his children to live in peace and harmony. ¹⁶For, after all, there is no assurance to you wives that your husbands will be converted if they stay; and the same may be said to you husbands concerning your wives.

Believers should be content where they are

¹⁷But be sure in deciding these matters that you are living as God intended, marrying or not marrying in accordance with God's direction and help, and

7:6
2 Cor 8:8; 11:17

7:7
Mt 19:12
1 Cor 9:5; 12:11

7:9
1 Tim 5:14

7:10
Mal 2:14,16
Mt 5:32; 19:5,6
Mk 10:10-12
Lk 16:18

7:12
2 Cor 11:17

7:14
Ezra 9:2
Mal 2:15

7:16
1 Pet 3:1

7:17
1 Cor 4:17
11:16; 14:33

7:6, 7 Both marriage and singleness are gifts from God. One is not better than the other, and both are valuable to accomplishing God's purposes. It is important, therefore, to accept one's present situation. When Paul said he wished more could get along without marrying, he was expressing his desire that more people would devote themselves *completely* to the ministry without the added concerns of spouse and family, as he had done. He was not criticizing marriage—after all, it is God's created way of providing companionship and populating the earth.

7:9 Sexual pressure is not the best motive for getting married, but it is better to marry the right person than to burn with lust. Many new believers in Corinth thought that all sex was wrong, and so engaged couples were deciding not to get married. In this passage, Paul is telling couples who wanted to marry that they should not deny their normal sexual drives by avoiding marriage. This does not mean, however, that people who have trouble controlling their thoughts should marry the first person who comes along. It is better to deal with the pressure of desire than to deal with an unhappy marriage.

7:11 Because of their desire to serve Christ, some people in the Corinthian church thought they ought to divorce their pagan spouses and marry Christians. But Paul affirmed the marriage commitment. God's ideal is for marriages to stay together—even when one spouse is not a believer. The Christian spouse should try to win the other to Christ. It would be easy to rationalize leaving; however, Paul makes a strong case for staying with the unbelieving spouse and being a positive influence on the marriage. Paul, like

Jesus, believed marriage is permanent (see Mark 10:1–9).

7:12 Paul's *command* about the permanence of marriage comes from the Old Testament and from Jesus. His *suggestion* is based on God's command and he applies it to the situation the Corinthians were facing. Paul ranks the command above the suggestion because one is an eternal principle, whereas the other is a specific application. Nevertheless, for people in similar situations, Paul's suggestion is the best advice they will get. Paul was a man of God, an apostle; and he had the mind of Christ.

7:15, 16 This verse is misused by some as a loophole to get out of marriage. But Paul's statements were given to encourage the Christian spouse to try to get along with the unbeliever and make the marriage work. If, however, the unbelieving spouse insists on leaving, Paul says to let him or her go. The only alternative would be for the Christian to deny his faith to preserve his marriage, and this would be the one thing worse than dissolving the marriage. It cannot be stressed enough that Paul's purpose in writing this was to urge the married couples to seek unity, not separation (see 7:17; 1 Peter 3:1, 2).

7:17 Apparently the Corinthians were ready to make wholesale changes without thinking through the ramifications. Paul was writing to say that people should be Christians where they are. You can do God's work and demonstrate your faith *anywhere*. You don't have to be married to a Christian to live for Christ. Don't assume that you are in the wrong place, stuck with the wrong person. You may be just where God wants you (see 7:20).

accepting whatever situation God has put you into. This is my rule for all the churches.

18For instance, a man who already has gone through the Jewish ceremony of circumcision before he became a Christian shouldn't worry about it; and if he hasn't been circumcised, he shouldn't do it now. 19For it doesn't make any difference at all whether a Christian has gone through this ceremony or not. But it makes a lot of difference whether he is pleasing God and keeping God's commandments. That is the important thing.

20Usually a person should keep on with the work he was doing when God called him. 21Are you a slave? Don't let that worry you—but of course, if you get a chance to be free, take it. 22If the Lord calls you, and you are a slave, remember that Christ has set you free from the awful power of sin; and if he has called you and you are free, remember that you are now a slave of Christ. 23You have been bought and paid for by Christ, so you belong to him—be free now from all these earthly prides and fears. 24So, dear brothers, whatever situation a person is in when he becomes a Christian, let him stay there, for now the Lord is there to help him.

Questions about singleness

25Now I will try to answer your other question. What about girls who are not yet married? Should they be permitted to do so? In answer to this question, I have no special command for them from the Lord. But the Lord in his kindness has given me wisdom that can be trusted, and I will be glad to tell you what I think.

26Here is the problem: We Christians are facing great dangers to our lives at present. In times like these I think it is best for a person to remain unmarried. 27Of course, if you already are married, don't separate because of this. But if you aren't, don't rush into it at this time. 28But if you men decide to go ahead anyway and get married now, it is all right; and if a girl gets married in times like these, it is no sin. However, marriage will bring extra problems that I wish you didn't have to face right now.

29The important thing to remember is that our remaining time is very short, [and so are our opportunities for doing the Lord's work]. For that reason those who have

Sidebar references (left margin):

7:18
Acts 15:4-19
Gal 5:2

7:19
Rom 2:25
Gal 5:6; 6:15
Col 3:11
1 Jn 2:3; 3:24

7:21
Gal 3:28

7:22
Gal 5:13
Eph 6:6
1 Pet 2:16

7:23
Lev 25:42
1 Cor 6:20
1 Pet 1:18

7:25
2 Cor 4:1

7:26
Lk 21:23

7:29
Rom 13:11
1 Cor 7:31
1 Pet 4:7

7:23 be free now from all these earthly prides and fears, literally, "Become not bondservants of men." **7:29** and so are our opportunities for doing the Lord's work, implied. those who have wives should stay as free as possible for the Lord, literally, "[that] those who have wives may be as though they didn't."

7:18, 19 The ceremony of circumcision was an important part of the Jews' relationship with God. In fact, before Christ came, circumcision was commanded by God for all who claimed to follow him (Genesis 17:9–14). But after Christ's death, circumcision was no longer necessary (Acts 15; Romans 2:28, 29; 4:9–11; Galatians 5:2–4; Colossians 2:11). More important than ceremonies, says Paul, is pleasing God and obeying him.

7:20 Often we are so concerned about what we *could* be doing for God somewhere else that we miss great opportunities right where we are. Paul says that when someone becomes a Christian, he should usually continue with the work he has previously been doing—provided it isn't immoral or unethical. Every job can become Christian work when you realize that the purpose of your life is to honor, serve, and speak out for Christ. Because God has placed you where you are, look carefully for opportunities to serve him there.

7:23 Slavery was common throughout the Roman empire. Some Christians in the Corinthian church were slaves. Paul said that although they were slaves to men, they were free from the power of sin in their lives. People today are slaves to sin until they commit their lives to Christ, who alone can conquer sin's power. Sin, pride, and fear no longer have claim over us, just as a slaveowner no longer has power over slaves he has sold. The Bible says we become Christ's slaves when we become Christians, but this actually means we gain our freedom, because sin no longer controls us.

7:26 Paul saw the impending persecution that the Roman government would soon bring upon Christians. He gave this practical advice because being unmarried would mean less suffering and more freedom to throw one's life into the cause of Christ (7:29), even to the point of fearlessly dying for him. Paul's advice reveals his singleminded devotion to spreading the Good News.

7:28 Many people naively think that marriage will solve all their problems. Here are some problems marriage won't solve: (1) loneliness, (2) sexual temptation, (3) satisfaction of one's deepest emotional needs, (4) elimination of life's difficulties. Marriage alone does not hold two people together, but commitment does—commitment to Christ and to each other despite conflicts and problems. As wonderful as it is, marriage does not solve problems. Whether married or single, we must be content with our situation and focus on Christ, not humans, to solve our problems.

7:29 Paul urges all believers to make the most of their time before Christ's return. Every person in every generation should have this sense of urgency about telling the Good News to others. Life is short no matter how long we live.

7:29–31 Paul urged the believers to "stay as free as possible for the Lord." This means that we should not regard marriage, home, or financial security as the ultimate goal of life. As far as possible, we should live unhindered by the cares of this world, not getting involved with mortgages, budgets, investments, or bills that will keep us from doing God's work. A married man, as Paul points out (7:33), has to think about his earthly responsibilities—but he should be careful to keep them modest and manageable.

wives should stay as free as possible for the Lord; 30happiness or sadness or wealth should not keep anyone from doing God's work. 31Those in frequent contact with the exciting things the world offers should make good use of their opportunities without stopping to enjoy them; for the world in its present form will soon be gone.

7:31
Ps 39:6
Jas 4:14
1 Jn 2:17

32In all you do, I want you to be free from worry. An unmarried man can spend his time doing the Lord's work and thinking how to please him. 33But a married man can't do that so well; he has to think about his earthly responsibilities and how to please his wife. 34His interests are divided. It is the same with a girl who marries. She faces the same problem. A girl who is not married is anxious to please the Lord in all she is and does. But a married woman must consider other things such as housekeeping and the likes and dislikes of her husband.

7:34
Lk 10:40
1 Tim 5:5

35I am saying this to help you, not to try to keep you from marrying. I want you to do whatever will help you serve the Lord best, with as few other things as possible to distract your attention from him.

36But if anyone feels he ought to marry because he has trouble controlling his passions, it is all right, it is not a sin; let him marry. 37But if a man has the willpower not to marry and decides that he doesn't need to and won't, he has made a wise decision. 38So the person who marries does well, and the person who doesn't marry does even better.

7:38
Heb 13:4

39The wife is part of her husband as long as he lives; if her husband dies, then she may marry again, but only if she marries a Christian. 40But in my opinion she will be happier if she doesn't marry again; and I think I am giving you counsel from God's Spirit when I say this.

7:39
Rom 7:2
2 Cor 6:14

7:40
1 Cor 7:6,25

2. Instruction on Christian freedom
Questions about food offered to idols

8 Next is your question about eating food that has been sacrificed to idols. On this question everyone feels that only his answer is the right one! But although being a "know-it-all" makes us feel important, what is really needed to build the church is love. 2If anyone thinks he knows all the answers, he is just showing his ignorance. 3But the person who truly loves God is the one who is open to God's knowledge.

8:1
Acts 15:20
Rom 14:19
8:2
1 Cor 3:18
13:8,9
8:3
Gal 4:9
2 Tim 2:19

4So now, what about it? Should we eat meat that has been sacrificed to idols? Well, we all know that an idol is not really a god, and that there is only one God, and no other. 5According to some people, there are a great many gods, both in heaven and on earth. 6But we know that there is only one God, the Father, who created all things and made us to be his own; and one Lord Jesus Christ, who made everything and gives us life.

8:4
Deut 4:39
Isa 44:8
Acts 15:20
8:5
Jn 10:34
8:6
Jn 1:3
Acts 17:28
Eph 4:6
Col 1:16

7However, some Christians don't realize this. All their lives they have been used to thinking of idols as alive, and have believed that food offered to the idols is really being offered to actual gods. So when they eat such food it bothers them and hurts

8:7
Rom 14:14,22
1 Cor 8:4

7:34 *in all she is and does*, literally, "pure in body and in spirit."   8:6 *who created all things*, literally, "of whom are all things."

7:32-34 Some single people feel tremendous pressure to be married. They think their lives can be complete only with a spouse. But Paul underlines one advantage of being single—the potential of a greater focus on Christ and his work. If you are unmarried, use your special opportunity to serve Christ wholeheartedly.

7:38 When Paul said the unmarried person does better, he was talking about the potential time available for service to God because the single person has fewer responsibilities related to raising a family. Singleness, however, does not insure service to God—that is up to the commitment of the individual.

8:1 Meat bought in the marketplace was likely to have been symbolically offered to an idol in one of the many pagan temples. Animals were brought to a temple, killed before an idol as part of a pagan religious ceremony, then taken to butchers who sold the meat in a temple restaurant or in the marketplace. Believers

wondered if by eating such meat they were somehow participating in the worship of pagan idols.

8:1-3 Love is more important than knowledge. Knowledge makes us look good and feel important, but one can easily develop a prideful, know-it-all attitude. Many people with strong opinions are unwilling to listen and learn from God and others. Paul says that God's knowledge, the kind needed to build the church, can be obtained only by loving him.

8:4-9 Paul addressed these words to believers who weren't bothered by eating meat that had been sacrificed to idols. Although idols were not real, and the pagan ritual of sacrificing to them was meaningless, eating such meat offended Christians with more sensitive consciences. Paul said, therefore, that if a weaker or less mature believer misunderstood their actions, they should, out of consideration, avoid eating meat offered to idols.

8:8
Rom 14:17
8:9
Rom 14:1,13,21
1 Cor 8:10
10:28
Gal 5:13
8:10
Acts 15:20
8:11
Rom 14:15,20
1 Cor 8:4
8:12
Mt 18:6
Rom 14:20
8:13
Rom 14:21
1 Cor 10:32
2 Cor 6:3; 11:29

their tender consciences. 8Just remember that God doesn't care whether we eat it or not. We are no worse off if we don't eat it, and no better off if we do. 9But be careful not to use your freedom to eat it, lest you cause some Christian brother to sin whose conscience is weaker than yours.

10You see, this is what may happen: Someone who thinks it is wrong to eat this food will see you eating at a temple restaurant, for you know there is no harm in it. Then he will become bold enough to do it too, although all the time he still feels it is wrong. 11So because you "know it is all right to do it," you will be responsible for causing great spiritual damage to a brother with a tender conscience for whom Christ died. 12And it is a sin against Christ to sin against your brother by encouraging him to do something he thinks is wrong. 13So if eating meat offered to idols is going to make my brother sin, I'll not eat any of it as long as I live, because I don't want to do this to him.

The rights of apostles

9:1
Acts 9:3; 18:9
1 Cor 3:6;
4:15; 15:8
1 Tim 2:7
2 Tim 1:11
9:2
2 Cor 3:2

9 I am an apostle, God's messenger, responsible to no mere man. I am one who has actually seen Jesus our Lord with my own eyes. And your changed lives are the result of my hard work for him. 2If in the opinion of others, I am not an apostle, I certainly am to you, for you have been won to Christ through me. 3This is my answer to those who question my rights.

4Or don't I have any rights at all? Can't I claim the same privilege the other

8:9 *conscience*, implied. Literally, "faith."

STRONGER, WEAKER BROTHERS

Advice to:

Stronger brother	Don't be proud of your maturity; don't flaunt your freedom. Act in love so you do not cause a weaker brother to stumble.
Weaker brother	Although you may not feel the same freedom in some areas as in others, take your time, pray to God, but do not force others to adhere to your stipulations. You would hinder other believers by making up rules and standards for how everyone ought to behave. Make sure your convictions are based on God's Word, not your opinions.
Pastors and leaders	Teach correctly from God's Word, helping Christians understand what is right and wrong in God's eyes, and helping them see that they can have varied opinions on other issues and still be unified. Don't allow potential problems to get out of hand, causing splits and divisions.

Paul advises those who are more mature in the faith about how they must care about their brothers and sisters in Christ who have more tender consciences; those "weaker" brothers and sisters are advised concerning their growth; and pastors and leaders are instructed on how to deal with the conflicts that easily could arise between these groups.

8:10-13 Christian freedom does not mean "anything goes." It means that our salvation is not determined by legalism, good works, or rules, but by the free gift of God (Ephesians 2:8, 9). Christian freedom, then, is inseparably tied to Christian responsibility. New believers are often very sensitive to what is right or wrong, what they should or shouldn't do. Some actions may be perfectly all right for us to do, but may harm a Christian brother or sister who is still young in the faith and learning what the Christian life is all about. We must be careful not to offend a sensitive or younger Christian or, by our example, to cause him or her to sin. When we love others, our freedom to do certain things won't be as important to us as strengthening the faith of a brother or sister in Christ.

9:1 Some Corinthians were questioning Paul's authority as an apostle. Paul gives his credentials as an apostle—he actually saw and talked with the resurrected Christ, who called him to be an apostle (see Acts 9:3-18). Such credentials make the advice he gives in this letter more persuasive. In 2 Corinthians 10—13, Paul defends his apostleship in greater detail.

9:1 Paul's hard work had visible results at Corinth—changed lives were the evidence that God was using him. Does your faith have an impact on others? You can be a life-changer, helping others grow spiritually, if you dedicate yourself to be used by God and let him make you effective.

9:4ff Paul uses himself as an illustration of giving up personal rights. Paul had the right to hospitality, to be married, to bring guests, to be paid for his work; but he willingly gave up these rights to win people to Christ. When your focus is on living for Christ, your rights become comparatively unimportant.

9:4-10 Jesus said that workers are worthy of their pay (Luke 10:7). Paul echoes this thought and urges the church to be sure to pay their Christian workers. We have the responsibility to care for our pastors, teachers, and other spiritual leaders. It is our duty to see that those who serve us in the ministry are fairly and adequately compensated.

apostles have of being a guest in your homes? 5If I had a wife, and if she were a believer, couldn't I bring her along on these trips just as the other disciples do, and as the Lord's brothers do, and as Peter does? 6And must Barnabas and I alone keep working for our living, while you supply these others? 7What soldier in the army has to pay his own expenses? And have you ever heard of a farmer who harvests his crop and doesn't have the right to eat some of it? What shepherd takes care of a flock of sheep and goats and isn't allowed to drink some of the milk? 8And I'm not merely quoting the opinions of men as to what is right. I'm telling you what God's law says. 9For in the law God gave to Moses he said that you must not put a muzzle on an ox to keep it from eating when it is treading out the wheat. Do you suppose God was thinking only about oxen when he said this? 10Wasn't he also thinking about us? Of course he was. He said this to show us that Christian workers should be paid by those they help. Those who do the plowing and threshing should expect some share of the harvest.

11We have planted good spiritual seed in your souls. Is it too much to ask, in return, for mere food and clothing? 12You give them to others who preach to you, and you should. But shouldn't we have an even greater right to them? Yet we have *never* used this right, but supply our own needs without your help. We have never demanded payment of any kind for fear that, if we did, you might be less interested in our message to you from Christ.

13Don't you realize that God told those working in his temple to take for their own needs some of the food brought there as gifts to him? And those who work at the altar of God get a share of the food that is brought by those offering it to the Lord. 14In the same way the Lord has given orders that those who preach the Gospel should be supported by those who accept it.

15Yet I have never asked you for one penny. And I am not writing this to hint that I would like to start now. In fact, I would rather die of hunger than lose the satisfaction I get from preaching to you without charge. 16For just preaching the Gospel isn't any special credit to me—I couldn't keep from preaching it if I wanted to. I would be utterly miserable. Woe unto me if I don't.

17If I were volunteering my services of my own free will, then the Lord would give me a special reward; but that is not the situation, for God has picked me out and given me this sacred trust and I have no choice. 18Under this circumstance, what is my pay? It is the special joy I get from preaching the Good News without expense to anyone, never demanding my rights.

19And this has a real advantage: I am not bound to obey anyone just because he pays my salary; yet I have freely and happily become a servant of any and all so that I can win them to Christ. 20When I am with the Jews I seem as one of them so that they will listen to the Gospel and I can win them to Christ. When I am with Gentiles who follow Jewish customs and ceremonies I don't argue, even though I don't agree, because I want to help them. 21When with the heathen I agree with them as much as I can, except of course that I must always do what is right as a Christian. And so, by agreeing, I can win their confidence and help them too.

22When I am with those whose consciences bother them easily, I don't act as though I know it all and don't say they are foolish; the result is that they are willing

9:5 Mt 8:14; 12:46 Mk 6:2,3 Lk 6:15
9:6 2 Thess 3:8
9:7 Deut 20:6 Prov 27:18 1 Cor 3:6 2 Cor 10:4 2 Tim 4:7 1 Pet 5:2
9:9 Deut 25:4 1 Tim 5:18
9:10 Rom 4:23 2 Tim 2:6
9:11 Rom 15:27
9:12 2 Cor 6:3; 11:7,12
9:13 Lev 6:16 Num 5:9,10
9:14 Mt 10:10 Lk 10:7 Gal 6:6 1 Tim 5:17
9:15 Acts 18:3; 20:33 2 Cor 11:8-10
9:16 Acts 9:15 Rom 1:14
9:17 Gal 2:7 Eph 3:1-8 Phil 1:16,17 Col 1:25
9:18 2 Cor 11:7 12:13
9:19 Gal 5:13
9:20 Acts 16:3 21:20-27 Rom 11:14
9:21 Rom 2:8-11 Gal 3:2
9:22 Rom 14:1; 15:1 1 Cor 10:33 2 Cor 11:29

9:5 *If I had a wife, and if,* implied. Literally, "Have we no right to lead about a wife that is a believer?"   **9:21** *I can win their confidence,* implied.

9:13 As part of their pay, priests in the Temple received a portion of the offerings as their food (see Numbers 18:8-24).

9:16 Preaching the gospel was Paul's gift and calling, and he said he couldn't stop preaching if he wanted to. He was driven by the desire to do what God wanted, using his gifts for God's glory. What special gifts has God given you? Are you motivated, like Paul, to glorify God with your gifts?

9:19-27 In 9:19-22 Paul says that he has freedom to do anything; in 9:24-27 he emphasizes a life of strict discipline. The Christian life involves both freedom and discipline. The goal of Paul's life was to glorify God and bring people to Christ. Thus he stayed free

of any philosophical position or material entanglement that could sidetrack him, while he strictly disciplined himself to carry out his goal and not get sidetracked by life's enticements. For Paul, both freedom and discipline were important tools to be used in God's service.

9:22, 23 Paul gives several important principles for ministry: (1) find common ground with those you contact; (2) avoid a know-it-all attitude; (3) make others feel accepted; (4) be sensitive to their needs and concerns; and (5) look for opportunities to tell them about Christ. These principles are just as valid for us as they were for Paul.

to let me help them. Yes, whatever a person is like, I try to find common ground with him so that he will let me tell him about Christ and let Christ save him. ²³I do this to get the Gospel to them and also for the blessing I myself receive when I see them come to Christ.

²⁴In a race, everyone runs but only one person gets first prize. So run your race to win. ²⁵To win the contest you must deny yourselves many things that would keep you from doing your best. An athlete goes to all this trouble just to win a blue ribbon or a silver cup, but we do it for a heavenly reward that never disappears. ²⁶So I run straight to the goal with purpose in every step. I fight to win. I'm not just shadow-boxing or playing around. ²⁷Like an athlete I punish my body, treating it roughly, training it to do what it should, not what it wants to. Otherwise I fear that after enlisting others for the race, I myself might be declared unfit and ordered to stand aside.

Avoiding idol worship

10 For we must never forget, dear brothers, what happened to our people in the wilderness long ago. God guided them by sending a cloud that moved along ahead of them; and he brought them all safely through the waters of the Red Sea. ²This might be called their "baptism"—baptized both in sea and cloud!—as

9:25 *a silver cup,* literally, "a wreath that quickly fades," given to the winners of the original Olympic races of Paul's time.

9:24
Heb 12:1
9:25
1 Tim 6:12
2 Tim 2:5
Jas 1:12
1 Pet 5:4
Rev 2:10; 3:11
9:26
2 Tim 4:7,8
Heb 12:1
9:27
2 Cor 13:5

10:1
Ex 13:21,22
14:15-22
10:2
Rom 6:2,3

WHY WE DON'T GIVE UP	Reference	The Purpose	The Plan	The Prize
Perseverance, persistence, the prize!! The Christian life was never promised as an easy way to live; instead, Paul constantly reminds us that we must have a purpose and a plan because times will be difficult and Satan will attack. But we never persevere without the promise of a prize—a promise God will keep.	1 Corinthians 9:24–27	• Run your race to win • Run straight to the goal	• Deny yourself whatever is potentially harmful • Discipline your body, training it	• A heavenly reward that never disappears
	Galatians 6:7–10	• Don't get tired of doing right • Don't get discouraged and give up • Be kind to everyone	• Plant the good things of the Spirit	• Reap everlasting life
	Ephesians 6:10–20	• Put on all of God's armor • Pray all the time	• Use all the pieces of God's armor provided for you	• Standing safe against all the strategies and tricks of Satan
	Philippians 3:12–14	• Keep working for the day when you will be all God wants you to be	• Forget the past, look forward to what lies ahead	• The heavenly prize to which God calls us
	2 Timothy 2:3–13	• Teach these great truths to people who will pass them on • Hold on to your faith, even when you feel too weak to have any left	• Take your suffering as a soldier, and don't get tied up in worldly affairs • Follow the Lord's rules, as an athlete must do in order to win • Work hard, like a farmer who tends his fields for the harvest	• We will live with Christ; we will sit and rule with him • He always remains faithful to us and always carries out his promises

9:24–27 Winning a race requires purpose and discipline. Paul used this illustration to explain that the Christian life takes hard work, self-denial, and grueling preparation. As Christians, we are running toward our heavenly reward. The essential disciplines of prayer, Bible study, and worship equip us to run with vigor and stamina. Don't merely observe from the grandstand; don't just turn out to jog a couple of laps each morning. Train diligently, because the Christian life truly is important.

9:25 At times we must give up doing something we want in order to do what God wants. Each individual's goal determines the discipline and denial he must accept. Without a goal, discipline is nothing but self-punishment. With the goal of pleasing God, our

denial seems like nothing compared to the eternal reward that is ours.

9:27 When Paul said he might be declared unfit and ordered to stand aside, he did not mean he could lose his salvation, but rather that he could lose his privilege to tell others about Christ. It is easy to tell others how to live and then not to take our own advice. We must be careful to practice what we preach.

10:1ff In chapter 9 Paul uses himself as an example of a mature Christian who disciplines himself to better serve God. In chapter 10, he uses Israel as an example of spiritual immaturity shown by their overconfidence and lack of self-discipline.

followers of Moses—their commitment to hm as their leader. ³, ⁴And by a miracle God sent them food to eat and water to drink there in the desert; they drank the water that Christ gave them. He was there with them as a mighty Rock of spiritual refreshment. ⁵Yet after all this most of them did not obey God, and he destroyed them in the wilderness.

⁶From this lesson we are warned that we must not desire evil things as they did, ⁷nor worship idols as they did. (The Scriptures tell us, "The people sat down to eat and drink and then got up to dance" in worship of the golden calf.)

⁸Another lesson for us is what happened when some of them sinned with other men's wives, and 23,000 fell dead in one day. ⁹And don't try the Lord's patience—they did, and died from snake bites. ¹⁰And don't murmur against God and his dealings with you, as some of them did, for that is why God sent his Angel to destroy them.

¹¹All these things happened to them as examples—as object lessons to us—to warn us against doing the same things; they were written down so that we could read about them and learn from them in these last days as the world nears its end.

¹²So be careful. If you are thinking, "Oh, I would never behave like that"—let this be a warning to you. For you too may fall into sin. ¹³But remember this—the wrong desires that come into your life aren't anything new and different. Many others have faced exactly the same problems before you. And no temptation is irresistible. You can trust God to keep the temptation from becoming so strong that you can't stand up against it, for he has promised this and will do what he says. He will show you how to escape temptation's power so that you can bear up patiently against it.

¹⁴So, dear friends, carefully avoid idol-worship of every kind.

10:3, 4 *and by a miracle,* implied. Literally, "all ate the same supernatural food and drink." *they drank the water that Christ gave them,* literally, "For they drank of a spiritual Rock that followed them, and the Rock was Christ."

10:3,4
Ex 16:4,13-15
17:5,6
Num 20:11
Ps 78:15
Jn 4:10
6:32-58; 7:37
Rev 22:17
10:5
Num 14:29,37
26:65
Heb 3:17
Jude 5
10:6
Num 11:4,5,34
Ps 106:14
10:7
Ex 32:4-19
10:8
Num 25:1-9
10:9
Ex 17:2,7
Num 21:6
10:10
Num 16:3,32,41
Rom 13:11; 15:4
Heb 10:25
10:11
Rom 4:23
10:12
Rom 11:20
2 Pet 3:17
10:13
2 Pet 2:9
10:14
1 Jn 5:21

If I choose one course of action:	. . . does it help my witness for Christ? (9:19–22)
	. . . am I motivated by a desire to help others to know Christ? (9:23; 10:33)
	. . . does it help me do my best? (9:25)
	. . . is it against a specific command in Scripture and thus cause me to sin? (10:12)
	. . . is it best and helpful? (10:23, 33)
	. . . am I thinking only of myself, or do I truly care about the other person? (10:24)
	. . . am I acting lovingly or selfishly? (10:28–31)
	. . . does it glorify God? (10:31)
	. . . will it encourage someone else to sin? (10:32)

MAKING CHOICES IN SENSITIVE ISSUES

All of us make hundreds of choices every day. Most choices have no right or wrong attached to them—like what you wear or what you eat. But we always face decisions that carry a little more weight. We don't want to do wrong, and we don't want to cause others to do wrong, so how can we make such decisions?

10:10, 11 Today's pressures make it easy to ignore or forget the lessons of the past. But Paul cautions us to remember the lessons the Israelites learned about God so we can avoid repeating their errors. The key to remembering is to study the Bible regularly so that these lessons become continual reminders of how God wants us to live. We need not repeat their mistakes!

10:11 Did Paul think the world was going to end soon? Neither Paul nor even Jesus himself knew when the end of the world would come—God alone knows (Mark 13:32). For all practical purposes, however, we have been living in the last days since Christ's ascension. We are to be ready for Christ's return at any moment. Anyone close to Christ feels, with Paul, the urgency of spreading the gospel.

10:13 In a culture filled with moral depravity and pressures, Paul gave strong encouragement to the Corinthians about temptation.

He said: (1) wrong desires and temptations happen to everyone, so don't feel you've been singled out; (2) others have resisted temptation, and so can you; (3) any temptation can be resisted, because God will help you resist it. God helps you resist temptation by helping you (1) recognize those people and situations that give you trouble, (2) run from anything you know is wrong, (3) choose to do only what is right, (4) pray for God's help, and (5) seek friends who love God and can offer help in times of temptation. Running from a tempting situation is the first step to victory (see 2 Timothy 2:22).

10:14 Idol worship was a serious problem in Corinth. There were several pagan temples in the city, and they were very popular. The statues of wood or stone were not bad in themselves, but people gave them credit for what only God could do, such as provide good weather, crops, and children. Idolatry is still a serious

10:16
Mt 26:26-29
Acts 2:42
1 Cor 11:25-27

10:17
Rom 12:4,5
1 Cor 12:12,13

10:18
Deut 12:17
Lev 7:15

10:19
1 Cor 8:4

10:20
Deut 32:16,17
Ps 106:36,37
Gal 4:8
Rev 9:20

10:21
Deut 32:38
Isa 65:11
2 Cor 6:15

10:22
Deut 32:21
Ezek 22:14

10:23
Rom 14:19
1 Cor 6:12

10:24
Rom 15:1,2

10:25
Acts 10:15
1 Cor 8:7
1 Tim 4:4

10:26
Ps 24:1; 105:12

10:27
Lk 10:8,9

10:28
Rom 14:16
1 Cor 8:7,10

10:31
Mt 5:15,16
Jn 15:8
Rom 14:6
Phil 1:11

10:32
Acts 24:16
1 Cor 8:13

15You are intelligent people. Look now and see for yourselves whether what I am about to say is true. 16When we ask the Lord's blessing upon our drinking from the cup of wine at the Lord's Table, this means, doesn't it, that all who drink it are sharing together the blessing of Christ's blood? And when we break off pieces of the bread from the loaf to eat there together, this shows that we are sharing together in the benefits of his body. 17No matter how many of us there are, we all eat from the same loaf, showing that we are all parts of the one body of Christ. 18And the Jewish people, all who eat the sacrifices, are united by that act.

19What am I trying to say? Am I saying that the idols to whom the heathen bring sacrifices are really alive and are real gods, and that these sacrifices are of some value? No, not at all. 20What I am saying is that those who offer food to these idols are united together in sacrificing to demons, certainly not to God. And I don't want any of you to be partners with demons when you eat the same food, along with the heathen, that has been offered to these idols. 21You cannot drink from the cup at the Lord's Table and at Satan's table, too. You cannot eat bread both at the Lord's Table and at Satan's table.

22What? Are you tempting the Lord to be angry with you? Are you stronger than he is?

23You are certainly free to eat food offered to idols if you want to; it's not against God's laws to eat such meat, but that doesn't mean that you should go ahead and do it. It may be perfectly legal, but it may not be best and helpful. 24Don't think only of yourself. Try to think of the other fellow, too, and what is best for him.

25Here's what you should do. Take any meat you want that is sold at the market. Don't ask whether or not it was offered to idols, lest the answer hurt your conscience. 26For the earth and every good thing in it belongs to the Lord and is yours to enjoy.

27If someone who isn't a Christian asks you out to dinner, go ahead; accept the invitation if you want to. Eat whatever is on the table and don't ask any questions about it. Then you won't know whether or not it has been used as a sacrifice to idols, and you won't risk having a bad conscience over eating it. 28But if someone warns you that this meat has been offered to idols, then don't eat it for the sake of the man who told you, and of his conscience. 29In this case *his* feeling about it is the important thing, not yours.

But why, you may ask, must I be guided and limited by what someone else thinks? 30If I can thank God for the food and enjoy it, why let someone spoil everything just because he thinks I am wrong? 31Well, I'll tell you why. It is because you must do everything for the glory of God, even your eating and drinking. 32So don't be a stumbling block to anyone, whether they are Jews or

---

problem today. We don't put our trust in statues of wood and stone, but in paper money and plastic cards. Thanking anything for what God alone provides is idolatry. When we understand contemporary parallels to idolatry, Paul's words to "avoid idol-worship of every kind" become much more meaningful.

10:16-21 The idea of unity with God through eating a sacrifice was strong in Judaism and Christianity as well as paganism. In Old Testament days, when a Jew offered a sacrifice, he ate a part of that sacrifice as a way of restoring his unity with God, against whom he had sinned (Deuteronomy 12:17, 18). Similarly, Christians participate in Christ's once-for-all sacrifice when they eat the bread and drink the wine symbolizing his body and blood. Recent converts from paganism could not help being affected if they knowingly ate meat offered to idols.

10:21 As followers of Christ we must give him our total allegiance. We cannot, as Paul explains, eat "both at the Lord's table and at Satan's." Eating at the Lord's table means communing with Christ and identifying with his death. Eating at Satan's table means identifying with Satan by participating in actions that worship or

promote heathen (or evil) activities. Are you trying to lead two lives, following the desires of both Christ and the crowd? The Bible says you can't do both at the same time.

10:22-24 Sometimes it's hard to know when to defer to the weaker brother. Paul gives a simple rule of thumb to help in making the decision—we should be sensitive and gracious. While we have freedom in Christ, we shouldn't exercise our freedom at the cost of hurting a Christian brother or sister. For more on the proper attitude toward the weaker brother, see the notes in 8:10–13 and Romans 14.

10:25 When we become too worried about our every action, we become legalistic and cannot enjoy life. God has given us all things richly to enjoy (10:26). If you know something is a problem, then deal with it, but don't go looking for problems. When we focus on the law, we worry only about protecting ourselves. When we focus on love, our concern is to help others.

10:31 God must so permeate our lives that all we do is for his glory. Keep this as a guiding principle by asking, "Is this glorifying God?" or "How can I glorify God through this?"

Gentiles or Christians. 33That is the plan I follow, too. I try to please everyone in everything I do, not doing what I like or what is best for me, but what is best for them, so that they may be saved.

10:33
Rom 11:14
15:1-2
1 Cor 9:22
13:1-8

3. Instruction on public worship

Questions about covering the head in worship

11 And you should follow my example, just as I follow Christ's.
2I am so glad, dear brothers, that you have been remembering and doing everything I taught you. 3But there is one matter I want to remind you about: that a wife is responsible to her husband, her husband is responsible to Christ, and Christ is responsible to God. 4That is why, if a man refuses to remove his hat while praying or preaching, he dishonors Christ. 5And that is why a woman who publicly prays or prophesies without a covering on her head dishonors her husband [for her covering is a sign of her subjection to him]. 6Yes, if she refuses to wear a head covering, then she should cut off all her hair. And if it is shameful for a woman to have her head shaved, then she should wear a covering. 7But a man should not wear anything on his head [when worshiping, for his hat is a sign of subjection to men].

God's glory is man made in his image, and man's glory is the woman. 8The first man didn't come from woman, but the first woman came out of man. 9And Adam, the first man, was not made for Eve's benefit, but Eve was made for Adam. 10So a woman should wear a covering on her head as a sign that she is under man's authority, a fact for all the angels to notice and rejoice in.

11But remember that in God's plan men and women need each other. 12For

11:1
1 Cor 4:16

11:3
Gen 3:16
1 Cor 3:23; 7:17
Gal 4:4
Eph 5:23
Phil 2:7

11:5
Lk 2:36
Acts 21:9

11:6
Num 5:18

11:7
Gen 1:26
Jas 3:9

11:8
Gen 2:21
1 Tim 2:13

11:9
Gen 2:18

11:12
Rom 11:36

11:5 *for her covering is a sign of her subjection to him,* implied in vss 7, 10. **11:7** *when worshiping, for his hat is a sign of subjection to men,* implied. **11:8** *the first woman came out of man,* Gen 2:21, 22. **11:10** *as a sign that she is under man's authority,* literally, "For this cause ought the woman to have power on her head." *a fact for all the angels to notice and rejoice in,* literally, "because of the angels."

10:33 Paul's criterion was not what he liked best, but what was best for those around him. There are several hurtful attitudes toward others: (1) being insensitive and doing what we want, no matter who is hurt by it; (2) being oversensitive and doing nothing, for fear someone may be displeased; (3) being a "yes person" by going along with everything, trying to gain approval from people rather than from God. In this age of "me first" and "looking out for number one," Paul's startling statement is a good standard. When we make the good of others one of our primary goals, we develop a servant heart.

11:1ff In this section Paul's main concern is irreverence in worship. We need to read it in the context of the situation in Corinth. The matter of wearing hats or head coverings, although seemingly insignificant, had become a big problem because two cultural backgrounds were colliding. Jewish women always covered their heads in worship. For a woman to uncover her head in public was a sign of loose morals. On the other hand, Greek women were used to worshiping without head coverings.

In this letter Paul has already spoken about divisions in the church and scruples. Both are involved in this issue. Paul's solution comes from his desire for unity among church members and appropriateness in the worship service. He accepts God's sovereignty in creating the rules for relationships.

11:1 Why did Paul say, "You should follow my example"? Paul wasn't being proud—he did not think of himself as sinless. At this time, however, the Corinthian believers did not know much about the life and ministry of Christ. Paul could not tell them to imitate Jesus, because the Gospels had not yet been written, so they did not know what Jesus was like. The best way to point these new Christians to Christ was to point them to a Christian whom they trusted (see also Galatians 4:12; Philippians 3:17; 1 Thessalonians 1:6; 2:14; 2 Thessalonians 3:7, 9). Paul had been in Corinth almost two years and had built up a relationship of trust with many of these people.

11:2–16 This section focuses on attitudes toward worship, not on

marriage or the role of women in the church. While Paul's specific instructions may be cultural (women wearing hats in worship), the principles behind his specific instructions are timeless, including respect for spouse, reverence and appropriateness in worship, and focusing all of life on God. If anything you do can easily offend members and divide the church, then change your ways to promote church unity. Thus Paul told the women who were not wearing head coverings to wear them; not because it was a Scriptural command, but because it kept the congregation from dividing over a petty issue that served only to take people's minds off Christ.

11:3, 4 Submission is a key element in the smooth functioning of any business, government, or family. God ordained submission in certain relationships to prevent chaos. It is essential to understand that submission is not surrender, withdrawal, or apathy. And it does not mean inferiority, because God created all people in his image and all have equal value. Submission is mutual commitment and cooperation.

Thus God calls for submission among *equals.* He did not make the man superior; he made a way for the man and woman to work together. Jesus Christ, although equal with God the Father, submitted to him to carrry out the plan for salvation. Likewise, although equal to man under God, the wife should submit to her husband for the sake of their marriage and family. Submission between equals is submission by choice, not force. We serve God in these relationships by willing submission to others in our church, to our spouses, and to our government leaders.

11:9–11 By referring to Adam and Eve, the first man and woman, Paul was saying that God created lines of authority in order for his created world to function smoothly. Although there must be lines of authority, even in marriage, there should *not* be lines of superiority. God created men and women with unique and complementary characteristics. One sex is not better than the other. We must not let the issue of authority and submission become a wedge to destroy oneness in marriage. Instead, we should use our unique gifts to strengthen our marriages and glorify God.

although the first woman came out of man, all men have been born from women ever since, and both men and women come from God their Creator.

11:13
Lk 12:57
13What do you yourselves really think about this? Is it right for a woman to pray in public without covering her head? 14, 15Doesn't even instinct itself teach us that women's heads should be covered? For women are proud of their long hair, while a man with long hair tends to be ashamed. 16But if anyone wants to argue about

11:16
1 Tim 6:4
this, all I can say is that we never teach anything else than this—that a woman should wear a covering when prophesying or praying publicly in the church, and all the churches feel the same way about it.

~ Order at the Lord's Supper

17Next on my list of items to write you about is something else I cannot agree with. For it sounds as if more harm than good is done when you meet together for

11:18,19
1 Cor 1:10
2 Pet 2:1
1 Tim 4:1
1 Jn 2:19
your communion services. 18Everyone keeps telling me about the arguing that goes on in these meetings, and the divisions developing among you, and I can just about believe it. 19But I suppose you feel this is necessary so that you who are always right will become known and recognized!

11:21
Jude 12
20When you come together to eat, it isn't the Lord's Supper you are eating, 21but your own. For I am told that everyone hastily gobbles all the food he can without waiting to share with the others, so that one doesn't get enough and goes hungry

11:22
Lev 19:30
1 Cor 10:32
Jas 2:6
while another has too much to drink and gets drunk. 22What? Is this really true? Can't you do your eating and drinking at home, to avoid disgracing the church and shaming those who are poor and can bring no food? What am I supposed to say about these things? Do you want me to praise you? Well, I certainly do not!

11:23
Mt 26:26-28
Mk 14:22-24
Lk 22:17-20
1 Cor 10:16
Gal 1:12
23For this is what the Lord himself has said about his Table, and I have passed it on to you before: That on the night when Judas betrayed him, the Lord Jesus took bread, 24and when he had given thanks to God for it, he broke it and gave it to his disciples and said, "Take this and eat it. This is my body, which is given for you.

11:25
Lk 22:20
1 Cor 10:16
2 Cor 3:6
Do this to remember me." 25In the same way, he took the cup of wine after supper, saying, "This cup is the new agreement between God and you that has been

11:24 *given.* Some ancient manuscripts read, "broken."

11:14, 15 In talking about head coverings and length of hair, Paul is saying that believers should look and behave in ways that are honorable within their own culture. In many cultures long hair on men is considered appropriate and masculine. In Corinth, it was thought to be a sign of sexual perversion. And women with short hair were labeled prostitutes. Paul was saying that in the Corinthian culture, women should keep their long hair. If short hair on women was a sign of prostitution, then a Christian woman with short hair would find it even more difficult to be a believable witness for Jesus Christ. The issue is similar with head coverings, considered a sign of rebellion in Jewish culture. Paul isn't saying we should adopt all the practices of our culture, but that we should avoid appearances and behavior that detract from our goal of being believable witnesses for Jesus Christ and demonstrating our Christian faith.

11:17-34 The Lord's Supper is a visible representation of the gospel, the death of Christ for our sins. It focuses on the remembrance of Christ's death and the glorious hope of his return. It is an act of fellowship among believers. And it strengthens our faith through fellowship with Christ and with other believers.

11:21 When the Lord's Supper was celebrated in the early church, it included a feast or fellowship meal followed by communion. In Corinth the fellowship meal had become a time of gluttony and excessive drinking rather than a time of preparation for communion. Although the feast was similar to a potluck, there was little sharing and caring. This certainly did not demonstrate the unity and love that should characterize the church, nor was it a preparation for communion. Paul condemned these actions and reminded the church of the real purpose of the Lord's Supper.

11:24, 25 What does the Lord's Supper mean? The early church

remembered that Jesus taught about the Lord's Supper on the night of the Passover (Luke 22:13-20). Just as Passover celebrated deliverance from slavery in Egypt, so the Lord's Supper celebrates deliverance from sin by Christ's death.

Christians have several options about what Christ meant when he said, "This is my body." Some believe that the wine and bread actually become Christ's physical blood and body. Others believe that the bread and wine remain unchanged, but Christ is spiritually present with the bread and wine. Still others believe that the bread and wine symbolize Christ's body and blood. Christians agree, however, that the important point to remember is that God is a part of the communion experience, blessing us as we remember Christ's death until he comes again.

11:25 What is this new agreement (covenant)? With the old agreement, people could approach God only through the priests and the sacrificial system. Jesus' death on the cross brought in the new agreement between God and us. Now all people can personally approach God and communicate with him. The old agreement was first made on Mount Sinai between God and the Israelites (Exodus 19, 20) and was designed to point to the day when Jesus Christ would come. The new agreement completes, rather than replaces, the old agreement, fulfilling everything the old agreement looked forward to. Eating the bread and drinking the cup shows we are regularly recommitting ourselves to this new agreement. See Jeremiah 31:31-34 for a prediction of it.

11:25 Jesus said, "Do this to remember me." How do we remember Christ in the Lord's Supper? By thinking about what he did and why he did it. If the Lord's Supper becomes just a ritual or pious habit, it no longer remembers Christ.

established and set in motion by my blood. Do this in remembrance of me whenever you drink it." 26For every time you eat this bread and drink this cup you are re-telling the message of the Lord's death, that he has died for you. Do this until he comes again.

11:26
Acts 1:11
Rev 1:7

27So if anyone eats this bread and drinks from this cup of the Lord in an unworthy manner, he is guilty of sin against the body and the blood of the Lord. 28That is why a man should examine himself carefully before eating the bread and drinking from the cup. 29For if he eats the bread and drinks from the cup unworthily, not thinking about the body of Christ and what it means, he is eating and drinking God's judgment upon himself; for he is trifling with the death of Christ. 30That is why many of you are weak and sick, and some have even died.

11:27
Heb 10:29
11:28
Mt 26:20-22
2 Cor 13:5
Gal 6:4

31But if you carefully examine yourselves before eating you will not need to be judged and punished. 32Yet, when we are judged and punished by the Lord, it is so that we will not be condemned with the rest of the world. 33So, dear brothers, when you gather for the Lord's Supper—the communion service—wait for each other; 34if anyone is really hungry he should eat at home so that he won't bring punishment upon himself when you meet together.

I'll talk to you about the other matters after I arrive.

11:31
1 Jn 1:9
Rev 3:19
11:32
2 Sam 7:14
Job 5:17
Ps 94:12
Amos 3:2
Heb 12:5-7
11:34
1 Cor 4:19

Paul teaches about spiritual gifts

12 And now, brothers, I want to write about the special abilities the Holy Spirit gives to each of you, for I don't want any misunderstanding about them. 2You will remember that before you became Christians you went around from one idol to another, not one of which could speak a single word. 3But now you are meeting people who claim to speak messages from the Spirit of God. How can you know whether they are really inspired by God or whether they are fakes? Here is the test: no one speaking by the power of the Spirit of God can curse Jesus, and no one can say, "Jesus is Lord," and really mean it, unless the Holy Spirit is helping him.

12:1
1 Cor 14:1
12:2
Isa 46:7
Hab 1:18,19
1 Thess 1:9
1 Pet 4:3
12:3
Jn 13:13
Rom 10:9
1 Jn 4:2

4Now God gives us many kinds of special abilities, but it is the same Holy Spirit who is the source of them all. 5There are different kinds of service to God, but it is the same Lord we are serving. 6There are many ways in which God works in our lives, but it is the same God who does the work in and through all of us who are his. 7The Holy Spirit displays God's power through each of us as a means of helping the entire church.

12:4
Rom 12:6
Eph 4:4
Heb 2:4
12:6
Eph 1:23
12:7
Rom 12:6
1 Cor 14:26
Eph 4:12

8To one person the Spirit gives the ability to give wise advice; someone else may be especially good at studying and teaching, and this is his gift from the same Spirit. 9He gives special faith to another, and to someone else the power to heal the

12:8
1 Cor 2:6,11
12:9
Mt 17:19,20

11:27 Paul gives specific instructions on how the Lord's Supper should be observed. (1) We should take the Lord's Supper with a repentant attitude because we are remembering that Christ died for our sins (11:26). (2) We should take it after self-examination (11:28). We are to be prepared and ready, doing it only through our belief in and love for Christ. (3) We should take it in recognition of Jesus' act of love in taking away the punishment we deserve for our sins (11:29). (4) We should take it with mutual consideration (11:33), waiting until everyone is present and eating in an orderly and unified manner.

11:27 When Paul said no one should take the Lord's Supper in an unworthy manner, he was speaking to the church members who were rushing into it without thinking of its meaning. *No one* is worthy to take the Lord's Supper. We are all sinners saved by grace. This is why we should prepare ourselves for communion through healthy introspection, confession of sin, and resolution of differences with others, removing the barriers to our relationship with Christ and with other believers. Don't let awareness of your sin keep you away from communion, but drive you to it.

11:30 This may have been a special supernatural judgment on the Corinthian church. It highlights the seriousness of the communion service. The Lord's Supper is not to be taken lightly;

this new agreement cost Jesus his life. It is not a meaningless ritual, but a sacrament given by Christ to help strengthen our faith.

12:1ff The special abilities given to each person by the Holy Spirit are called *spiritual gifts*. They enable us to minister to the needs of the body of believers. This chapter is not an exhaustive list of spiritual gifts (see Romans 12; Ephesians 4; 1 Peter 4:10, 11 for more examples). There are many gifts, people have different gifts, and one gift is not superior to another. They all come from the Holy Spirit, and their purpose is to build up Christ's body, the church.

12:1ff Instead of building and unifying the Corinthian church, spiritual gifts were splitting it. They had become symbols of spiritual power, causing rivalries and setting up hierarchies of supposedly spiritual and unspiritual people. This was a terrible misuse of spiritual gifts, because their purpose is always to help the church function more effectively, not to divide it.

12:3 Anyone can claim to speak for God, and the world is full of false teachers. Paul gives us a test to help us discern whether or not a messenger is really from God: does he or she confess Christ as Lord? Don't naively accept the words of all who claim to speak for God; test their credentials by finding what they teach about Christ.

12:9 All Christians have faith. Some, however, have the spiritual

12:10
Acts 2:4
Rom 12:6
1 Cor 14:26-32
Gal 3:5
1 Jn 4:1

12:11
Rom 12:6-8
Eph 4:7
Heb 2:4

sick. ¹⁰He gives power for doing miracles to some, and to others power to prophesy and preach. He gives someone else the power to know whether evil spirits are speaking through those who claim to be giving God's messages—or whether it is really the Spirit of God who is speaking. Still another person is able to speak in languages he never learned; and others, who do not know the language either, are given power to understand what he is saying. ¹¹It is the same and only Holy Spirit who gives all these gifts and powers, deciding which each one of us should have.

Believers are the body of Christ

12:12
Rom 12:4
1 Cor 10:17
12:27

12:13
Jn 6:63; 7:37-39
Rom 6:5
Gal 3:27,28
Eph 2:13-16,18
Col 3:11

¹²Our bodies have many parts, but the many parts make up only one body when they are all put together. So it is with the "body" of Christ. ¹³Each of us is a part of the one body of Christ. Some of us are Jews, some are Gentiles, some are slaves and some are free. But the Holy Spirit has fitted us all together into one body. We have been baptized into Christ's body by the one Spirit, and have all been given that same Holy Spirit.

¹⁴Yes, the body has many parts, not just one part. ¹⁵If the foot says, "I am not a part of the body because I am not a hand," that does not make it any less a part of the body. ¹⁶And what would you think if you heard an ear say, "I am not part of the body because I am only an ear, and not an eye"? Would that make it any less a part of the body? ¹⁷Suppose the whole body were an eye—then how would you hear? Or if your whole body were just one big ear, how could you smell anything?

12:18
Rom 12:6
1 Cor 12:28

¹⁸But that isn't the way God has made us. He has made many parts for our bodies and has put each part just where he wants it. ¹⁹What a strange thing a body would be if it had only one part! ²⁰So he has made many parts, but still there is only one body.

²¹The eye can never say to the hand, "I don't need you." The head can't say to the feet, "I don't need you."

²²And some of the parts that seem weakest and least important are really the most necessary. ²³Yes, we are especially glad to have some parts that seem rather odd! And we carefully protect from the eyes of others those parts that should not be seen, ²⁴while of course the parts that may be seen do not require this special care. So God has put the body together in such a way that extra honor and care are given to those parts that might otherwise seem less important. ²⁵This makes for happiness among the parts, so that the parts have the same care for each other that they do for themselves. ²⁶If one part suffers, all parts suffer with it, and if one part is honored, all the parts are glad.

12:27
Rom 12:4,5
1 Cor 12:12
Eph 1:22,23
4:12; 5:23,30
Col 1:24

12:28
Num 11:16,17
Acts 13:1
Rom 12:6-8
Eph 2:20; 3:5
4:11
1 Tim 5:17
Heb 13:17

²⁷Now here is what I am trying to say: All of you together are the one body of Christ and each one of you is a separate and necessary part of it. ²⁸Here is a list of some of the parts he has placed in his Church, which is his body:

---

gift of faith which is an unusual measure of trust in the Holy Spirit's power.

12:12 Paul compares the body of Christ to a human body. Each part has a specific function that is necessary to the body as a whole. The parts are different for a purpose, and in their differences they must work together. Christians must avoid two common errors: (1) being too proud of their abilities, or (2) thinking they have nothing to give to the body of believers. Instead of comparing ourselves to one another, we must use our different gifts, together, to spread the Good News of salvation.

12:13 The church is composed of many types of people from a variety of backgrounds with a multitude of gifts and abilities. It is easy for these differences to divide people, as was the case in Corinth. But despite the differences, all believers have one thing in common—faith in Christ. On this essential truth the church finds unity. All believers are baptized by one Holy Spirit into one body of believers, the church. We don't lose our individual identities, but we have an overriding oneness in Christ. When a person becomes a Christian, the Holy Spirit takes up residence and he or she is born into God's family. As members of God's family, we may have

different interests and gifts, but we have a common goal.

12:14-17 Using the analogy of the body, Paul emphasizes the importance of each church member (see the note on 12:12). If a seemingly insignificant part is taken away, the whole body becomes less effective (12:22). Thinking that your gift is more important than someone else's is spiritual pride. We should not look down on those who seem unimportant, and we should not be jealous of others who have impressive gifts. Instead, we must use the gifts we have been given and encourage others to use theirs. If we don't, the body of believers will be less effective.

12:25, 26 What is your response when a fellow Christian is honored? When someone is suffering? We are called to rejoice with those who rejoice and weep with those who weep (Romans 12:15). Too often, unfortunately, we are jealous of those who rejoice and separate ourselves from those who weep. Believers are in the world together—there is no such thing as individualistic Christianity. We can't concern ourselves only with our own relationship with God; we need to get involved in the lives of others.

Apostles,
Prophets—those who preach God's Word,
Teachers,
Those who do miracles,
Those who have the gift of healing,
Those who can help others,
Those who can get others to work together,
Those who speak in languages they have never learned.

29Is everyone an apostle? Of course not. Is everyone a preacher? No. Are all
teachers? Does everyone have the power to do miracles? 30Can everyone heal the
sick? Of course not. Does God give all of us the ability to speak in languages we've
never learned? Can just anyone understand and translate what those are saying who
have that gift of foreign speech? 31No, but try your best to have the more important
of these gifts.

First, however, let me tell you about something else that is better than any of
them!

The characteristics of love

13 If I had the gift of being able to speak in other languages without learning
them, and could speak in every language there is in all of heaven and earth,
but didn't love others, I would only be making noise. 2If I had the gift of prophecy
and knew all about what is going to happen in the future, knew everything about
everything, but didn't love others, what good would it do? Even if I had the gift of
faith so that I could speak to a mountain and make it move, I would still be worth
nothing at all without love. 3If I gave everything I have to poor people, and if I were
burned alive for preaching the Gospel but didn't love others, it would be of no value
whatever.

4Love is very patient and kind, never jealous or envious, never boastful or
proud, 5never haughty or selfish or rude. Love does not demand its own way. It is
not irritable or touchy. It does not hold grudges and will hardly even notice when
others do it wrong. 6It is never glad about injustice, but rejoices whenever truth
wins out. 7If you love someone you will be loyal to him no matter what the cost.
You will always believe in him, always expect the best of him, and always stand
your ground in defending him.

8All the special gifts and powers from God will someday come to an end, but
love goes on forever. Someday prophecy, and speaking in unknown languages,
and special knowledge—these gifts will disappear. 9Now we know so little, even
with our special gifts, and the preaching of those most gifted is still so poor. 10But
when we have been made perfect and complete, then the need for these inadequate
special gifts will come to an end, and they will disappear.

11It's like this: when I was a child I spoke and thought and reasoned as a child
does. But when I became a man my thoughts grew far beyond those of my
childhood, and now I have put away the childish things. 12In the same way, we can

12:31
1 Cor 14:1-39

13:1
1 Tim 1:5

13:2
Mk 17:20
Lk 17:6
1 Cor 12:8-10

13:3
Mt 6:1,2

13:4
1 Cor 4:6
1 Pet 4:8

13:5
1 Cor 10:24
Phil 2:4; 4:8

13:6
Ps 10:3
Prov 10:12
Rom 1:32
2 Thess 2:12
2 Jn 4

13:7
Gal 6:2

13:8
1 Cor 13:1,2

13:9
1 Cor 8:2

13:10
Isa 60:19
Jer 31:34

13:12
2 Cor 3:18; 5:7
Phil 3:12
1 Jn 3:2

12:30 Paul discusses the subject of speaking in tongues in more
detail in chapter 14.

12:31 The more important gifts are those that are more beneficial
to the body of Christ. Paul has already made it clear that one gift is
not superior to another, but he urges the believers to discover how
they can serve Christ's body best with the gifts God has given
them. Your spiritual gifts are not for your own self-advancement.
They were given for serving God and enhancing the spiritual
growth of the body.

13:1ff In chapter 12 Paul gives evidence of the Corinthians' lack
of love, chapter 13 explains what real love is, and chapter 14
shows how love works. Love is more important than all the spiritual
gifts exercised in the church body. Great faith and miracle-working
power produce very little without love. Love makes our actions and

gifts useful. Although people have different gifts, love is available
to everyone.

13:4-7 Our society confuses love and lust. Unlike lust, God's kind
of love is directed outward toward others, not inward toward
ourselves. It is utterly unselfish.

13:4-7 This love is not natural. It is possible only if God
supernaturally helps us set aside our own desires and instincts, so
we can give love while expecting nothing in return. Thus the closer
we come to Christ, the more love we will show to others.

13:10 God gives us spiritual gifts for life on earth in order to build
up, serve, and strengthen fellow Christians. The spiritual gifts are
for the church. In eternity, we will be made perfect and complete
and will be in the very presence of God. We will no longer need the
spiritual gifts, so they will come to an end.

see and understand only a little about God now, as if we were peering at his reflection in a poor mirror; but someday we are going to see him in his completeness, face to face. Now all that I know is hazy and blurred, but then I will see everything clearly, just as clearly as God sees into my heart right now.

13:13
Mt 22:37-39
Gal 5:6

13There are three things that remain—faith, hope, and love—and the greatest of these is love.

Paul teaches about the gifts of prophecy and tongues

14:1
Lev 19:18
Num 11:25
Mt 22:37-40
Mk 12:29-31
Rom 12:6
13:8-10
1 Cor 12:1
Gal 5:14
Eph 5:2
Col 3:14
1 Tim 1:5
Jas 2:8

14 Let love be your greatest aim; nevertheless, ask also for the special abilities the Holy Spirit gives, and especially the gift of prophecy, being able to preach the messages of God.

2But if your gift is that of being able to "speak in tongues," that is, to speak in languages you haven't learned, you will be talking to God but not to others, since they won't be able to understand you. You will be speaking by the power of the Spirit but it will all be a secret. 3But one who prophesies, preaching the messages of God, is helping others grow in the Lord, encouraging and comforting them. 4So a person "speaking in tongues" helps himself grow spiritually, but one who prophesies, preaching messages from God, helps the entire church grow in holiness and happiness.

14:2
Mk 16:17
Acts 2:4
10:46,47; 19:6

14:3
Rom 14:19

14:4
1 Cor 12:10,30
14:18,19,26-28

5I wish you all had the gift of "speaking in tongues" but, even more, I wish you were all able to prophesy, preaching God's messages, for that is a greater and more useful power than to speak in unknown languages—unless, of course, you can tell everyone afterwards what you were saying, so that they can get some good out of it too.

14:6
Rom 6:17
1 Cor 12:8; 13:2
Eph 1:16,17

6Dear friends, even if I myself should come to you talking in some language you don't understand, how would that help you? But if I speak plainly what God has revealed to me, and tell you the things I know, and what is going to happen, and the great truths of God's Word—that is what you need; that is what will help you. 7Even musical instruments—the flute, for instance, or the harp—are examples of the need for speaking in plain, simple English rather than in unknown languages. For no one will recognize the tune the flute is playing unless each note is sounded clearly. 8And if the army bugler doesn't play the right notes, how will the soldiers know that they are being called to battle? 9In the same way, if you talk to a person in some language he doesn't understand, how will he know what you mean? You might as well be talking to an empty room.

14:8
Num 10:9
Jer 4:19
Ezek 33:2-6
Joel 2:1

10I suppose that there are hundreds of different languages in the world, and all are excellent for those who understand them, 11but to me they mean nothing. A person talking to me in one of these languages will be a stranger to me and I will be a stranger to him. 12Since you are so anxious to have special gifts from the Holy

14:12
Rom 14:19

14:7 *simple English.* The local language, whatever it is.

13:12 Paul offers a glimpse into the future to give us hope that one day we will be complete when we see God face to face. This truth should strengthen our faith—we don't have all the answers now, but then we will. Someday we will see Christ in person and be able to see with God's perspective.

13:13 In the morally corrupt society of Corinth, love had become a mixed-up term with little meaning. Today people are still confused about love. Love is the greatest of all human qualities. It involves unselfish service to others; therefore, it gives evidence that you care. Faith is the foundation and content of God's message, hope is the attitude and focus, love is the action. When faith and hope are in line, you are free to truly love because you understand how God loved. Love is an attribute of God himself (1 John 4:8).

14:1 Prophecy may involve predicting future events, but its main purpose is to communicate God's Word to people, providing insight, warning, correction, and encouragement.

14:2 The gift of speaking in tongues was a concern of the Corinthian church because it had caused disorder in worship. Speaking in tongues is a legitimate gift of the Holy Spirit, but the Corinthian believers were using it as a sign of spiritual superiority rather than as a means to spiritual unity. Do you want God's special gifts to build up the church or to use for yourself? Spiritual gifts are beneficial only when they are properly used to help everyone in the church. We do not exercise them to make *ourselves* feel good.

14:2ff Paul makes several points about speaking in tongues: (1) it is a spiritual gift from God (14:2); (2) it is a desirable gift even though it isn't a requirement of faith (12:28–31); (3) it is less important than prophecy and teaching (14:4). Although Paul himself spoke in tongues, he stresses prophecy (preaching) because it benefits the whole church, while speaking in tongues primarily benefits the speaker. Public worship must be understandable and beneficial to the whole church.

Spirit, ask him for the very best, for those that will be of real help to the whole church.

➤ 13If someone is given the gift of speaking in unknown tongues, he should pray also for the gift of knowing what he has said, so that he can tell people afterwards, plainly. 14For if I pray in a language I don't understand, my spirit is praying but I don't know what I am saying.

14:13
1 Cor 12:10

15Well, then, what shall I do? I will do both. I will pray in unknown tongues and also in ordinary language that everyone understands. I will sing in unknown tongues and also in ordinary language, so that I can understand the praise I am giving; 16for if you praise and thank God with the spirit alone, speaking in another language, how can those who don't understand you be praising God along with you? How can they join you in giving thanks when they don't know what you are saying? 17You will be giving thanks very nicely, no doubt, but the other people present won't be helped.

14:15
Ps 47:6,7
Eph 5:19
Col 3:16

14:16
1 Chron 16:36
Neh 5:13; 8:6
Ps 106:48

14:17
Rom 14:19

18I thank God that I "speak in tongues" privately more than any of the rest of you. 19But in public worship I would much rather speak five words that people can understand and be helped by, than ten thousand words while "speaking in tongues" in an unknown language.

20Dear brothers, don't be childish in your understanding of these things. Be innocent babies when it comes to planning evil, but be men of intelligence in understanding matters of this kind. 21We are told in the ancient Scriptures that God would send men from other lands to speak in foreign languages to his people, but even then they would not listen. 22So you see that being able to "speak in tongues" is not a sign to God's children concerning his power, but is a sign to the unsaved. However, prophecy (preaching the deep truths of God) is what the Christians need, and unbelievers aren't yet ready for it. 23Even so, if an unsaved person, or someone who doesn't have these gifts, comes to church and hears you all talking in other languages, he is likely to think you are crazy. 24But if you prophesy, preaching God's Word, [even though such preaching is mostly for believers] and an unsaved person or a new Christian comes in who does not understand about these things, all these sermons will convince him of the fact that he is a sinner, and his conscience will be pricked by everything he hears. 25As he listens, his secret thoughts will be laid bare and he will fall down on his knees and worship God, declaring that God is really there among you.

14:20
Mt 11:25
Rom 16:19
Eph 4:14
Heb 5:12

14:21
Isa 28:11
Jn 10:34

14:22
1 Cor 14:1

14:23
Acts 2:12,13

14:24
1 Cor 14:1

14:25
Isa 45:14
Zech 8:23
Heb 4:12,13

Worship in an orderly way

26Well, my brothers, let's add up what I am saying. When you meet together some will sing, another will teach, or tell some special information God has given him, or speak in an unknown language, or tell what someone else is saying who is speaking in the unknown language, but everything that is done must be useful to all, and build them up in the Lord. 27No more than two or three should speak in an unknown language, and they must speak one at a time, and someone must be ready to interpret what they are saying. 28But if no one is present who can interpret, they must not speak out loud. They must talk silently to themselves and to God in the unknown language but not publicly.

14:26
Rom 14:19
1 Cor 12:8-10
14:2-6
Eph 4:12-13
5:19

14:27
1 Cor 12:10
14:2,5,13
1 Thess 5:20,21

29, 30Two or three may prophesy, one at a time, if they have the gift, while all the others listen. But if, while someone is prophesying, someone else receives a message or idea from the Lord, the one who is speaking should stop. 31In this way

14:31
Rom 12:6

14:18 *privately,* implied. See vss 19, 28.   **14:24** *even though such preaching is mostly for believers,* implied.

14:22, 23 The way the Corinthians were speaking in tongues was helping no one because believers did not understand what was being said and unbelievers thought the people speaking in tongues were crazy. Speaking in tongues was supposed to be a *sign* to unbelievers (as it was in Acts 2). After speaking in tongues, believers were supposed to explain what was said and give the credit to God. The unsaved people would then be convinced of a spiritual reality and motivated to search the Christian faith further.

While this is one way to reach unbelievers, Paul says that clear preaching is usually better (14:5).

14:26ff Everything done in worship services must be beneficial to the worshipers. This principle touches every aspect—singing, preaching, and the exercise of spiritual gifts. Those contributing to the service (singers, speakers, readers) must have love as their chief motivation, giving useful words or help that will strengthen the faith of other believers.

all who have the gift of prophecy can speak, one after the other, and everyone will
learn and be encouraged and helped. 32Remember that a person who has a message
from God has the power to stop himself or wait his turn. 33God is not one who likes
things to be disorderly and upset. He likes harmony, and he finds it in all the other
churches.

34Women should be silent during the church meetings. They are not to take part
in the discussion, for they are subordinate to men as the Scriptures also declare. 35If
they have any questions to ask, let them ask their husbands at home, for it is
improper for women to express their opinions in church meetings.

36You disagree? And do you think that the knowledge of God's will begins and
ends with you Corinthians? Well, you are mistaken! 37You who claim to have the
gift of prophecy or any other special ability from the Holy Spirit should be the first
to realize that what I am saying is a commandment from the Lord himself. 38But if
anyone still disagrees—well, we will leave him in his ignorance.

39So, my fellow believers, long to be prophets so that you can preach God's
message plainly; and never say it is wrong to "speak in tongues"; 40however, be
sure that everything is done properly in a good and orderly way.

4. Instruction on the resurrection
The resurrection of Christ

15 Now let me remind you, brothers, of what the Gospel really is, for it has not
changed—it is the same Good News I preached to you before. You welcomed it then and still do now, for your faith is squarely built upon this wonderful
message; 2and it is this Good News that saves you if you still firmly believe it,
unless of course you never really believed it in the first place.

3I passed on to you right from the first what had been told to me, that Christ died
for our sins just as the Scriptures said he would, 4and that he was buried, and that
three days afterwards he arose from the grave just as the prophets foretold. 5He was
seen by Peter and later by the rest of "the Twelve." 6After that he was seen by more
than five hundred Christian brothers at one time, most of whom are still alive,
though some have died by now. 7Then James saw him and later all the apostles.
8Last of all I saw him too, long after the others, as though I had been born almost

Marginal references (left column):
- 14:32 — 1 Jn 4:1
- 14:33 — 1 Cor 4:17; 7:17
- 14:34 — Gen 3:16 / 1 Cor 11:3,16 / Eph 5:22 / Col 3:18 / 1 Tim 2:11 / Tit 2:5 / 1 Pet 3:1
- 14:36 — Isa 2:3
- 14:37 — Lk 10:16 / 1 Cor 2:15 / 2 Cor 10:7 / 1 Jn 4:6
- 14:39 — 1 Cor 12:31 / 1 Thess 5:20
- 15:3 — Isa 53:5 / Lk 24:25-27 / 1 Pet 2:24
- 15:4 — Lk 24:25-27
- 15:5 — Mk 16:14 / Lk 24:34,35 / Jn 20:19
- 15:6 — Lk 24:13-31,36 / Jn 20:19,26,30 / 21:1
- 15:8 — Acts 9:3-12

14:32 *has the power to stop himself or wait his turn,* literally, "The spirits of the prophets are subject to the prophets." **14:34** *they are subordinate to men,* literally, "They are not authorized to speak." They are permitted to pray and prophesy (1 Cor 11:5), apparently in public meetings, but not to teach men (1 Tim 2:12). **14:38** *we will leave him in his ignorance,* or, "If he disagrees, ignore his opinion." **15:5** *the Twelve,* the name given to Jesus' twelve disciples, and still used after Judas was gone from among them.

14:33 In worship, everything must be done in harmony and with order. Even when the gifts of the Holy Spirit are being exercised, there is no excuse for disorder. When there is chaos, the church is not allowing God to work among the believers as he would like.

14:33 What did Paul mean when he said he found harmony "in all the other churches"? Some other translations end the sentence after the word, "harmony," reading, "God likes harmony." The following phrase, "As in all the [other] churches . . ." then relates to the next verse.

14:34, 35 Does this mean that women should not speak in church services today? It is clear from 11:5 that women can pray and prophesy in the church, apparently in public meetings. It is also clear in chapters 12—14 that women have spiritual gifts, and they are encouraged to exercise them in the body of Christ. Women have much to contribute and can participate in worship services.

In the Corinthian culture, women were not allowed to confront men in public. Apparently some of the women who had become Christians thought their Christian freedom gave them the right to speak up in public worship and question the men. This was causing division in the church. In addition, women of that day did not receive formal religious education as did the men. Women may have been raising questions in the worship service which could have more easily been answered at home without disrupting the church service. To promote unity, Paul was asking the women not to flaunt their Christian freedom during the worship service. The purpose of Paul's words here was to promote unity, not to teach about women's role in the church.

14:40 Worship is vital to the life of an individual and to the whole church. Our church services should be conducted in a good and orderly way so that we can worship, be taught, and be prepared to serve God. Those who are responsible for planning worship should make sure it has order and direction.

15:2 All churches have people who do not yet believe. Some are moving in the direction of belief, and others are simply pretending. Imposters, however, are not to be removed (see Matthew 13:29), for that is the Lord's work alone. The Good News saves us *if* we believe it.

15:5–8 There will always be people who say Jesus didn't rise from the dead. Paul assures us that many people saw Jesus after his resurrection, including more than 500 Christian believers. The resurrection is a historical fact. Don't be discouraged by doubters who deny the resurrection.

15:7 This is probably James, Jesus' brother, who at first did not believe Jesus was the Messiah (John 7:5). But after seeing the resurrected Christ, he became a believer and ultimately a leader of the church in Jerusalem (Acts 15:3). He also wrote the New Testament book of James.

15:8, 9 Paul's most important credential to be an apostle was that he was an eyewitness of the risen Christ (see Acts 9:3–6).

too late for this. ⁹For I am the least worthy of all the apostles, and I shouldn't even be called an apostle at all after the way I treated the church of God.

¹⁰But whatever I am now it is all because God poured out such kindness and grace upon me—and not without results: for I have worked harder than all the other apostles, yet actually I wasn't doing it, but God working in me, to bless me. ¹¹It makes no difference who worked the hardest, I or they; the important thing is that we preached the Gospel to you, and you believed it.

The resurrection of the dead

¹²But tell me this! Since you believe what we preach, that *Christ* rose from the dead, why are some of you saying that dead people will never come back to life again? ¹³For if there is no resurrection of the dead, then Christ must still be dead. ¹⁴And if he is still dead, then all our preaching is useless and your trust in God is empty, worthless, hopeless; ¹⁵and we apostles are all liars because we have said that God raised Christ from the grave, and of course that isn't true if the dead do not come back to life again. ¹⁶If they don't, then Christ is still dead, ¹⁷and you are very foolish to keep on trusting God to save you, and you are still under condemnation for your sins; ¹⁸in that case all Christians who have died are lost! ¹⁹And if being a Christian is of value to us only now in this life, we are the most miserable of creatures.

²⁰But the fact is that Christ did actually rise from the dead, and has become the first of millions who will come back to life again some day.

²¹Death came into the world because of what one man (Adam) did, and it is because of what this other man (Christ) has done that now there is the resurrection from the dead. ²²Everyone dies because all of us are related to Adam, being members of his sinful race, and wherever there is sin, death results. But all who are related to Christ will rise again. ²³Each, however, in his own turn: Christ rose first; then when Christ comes back, all his people will become alive again.

²⁴After that the end will come when he will turn the Kingdom over to God the Father, having put down all enemies of every kind. ²⁵For Christ will be King until

15:20 *the first of millions,* literally, "the first-fruits of them that are asleep."

15:9
Acts 8:3
2 Cor 12:11
Eph 3:8

15:10
2 Cor 11:23
Gal 2:8
Eph 2:7
1 Tim 4:10

15:12
Acts 17:32
2 Tim 2:18

15:13
1 Thess 4:14

15:17
Rom 4:25

15:18
1 Thess 4:16
Rev 14:13

15:19
2 Tim 3:12

15:20
Col 1:18
1 Pet 1:3
Rev 1:5

15:21
Rom 5:12

15:22
Rom 5:14-18

15:23
1 Thess 4:15-17

15:24
Dan 7:14
2 Cor 4:14

15:25
Ps 110:1
Heb 1:13

15:9 As a zealous Pharisee, Paul had been an enemy of the Christian church—even to the point of capturing and persecuting believers (see Acts 9:1–3). This is why he said he was unworthy to be called an apostle (a chosen messenger) of Christ. Though the most influential of the apostles, Paul was deeply humble. He knew he had worked hard and accomplished much, but only because God had poured out kindness and grace upon him. True humility is not convincing yourself that you are worthless, but recognizing God's work in you. It is having God's perspective on who you are and acknowledging his grace in developing your abilities.

15:10 Paul speaks of working harder than the other apostles. This is not a prideful statement because he knew that his power came from God (15:9) and that it didn't matter who worked hardest (15:11). Because of his prominent position as a Pharisee, Paul's conversion made him the object of even greater persecution than the other apostles, thus he had to work harder to preach the same message.

15:12ff Most Greeks did not believe that people's bodies would be resurrected after death. They saw the afterlife as something that happened only to the soul. According to Greek philosophers, the soul was the real person, imprisoned in a physical body, and at death the soul was released. There was no immortality for the body, but the soul entered an eternal state. In Scripture, by contrast, the body and soul will be united after resurrection. The church at Corinth was in the heart of Greek culture. Thus many believers had a difficult time believing in a bodily resurrection. Paul wrote this part of his letter to solve this confusion about the resurrection.

15:13, 14 The resurrection of Christ is the center of the Christian faith. Because Christ rose from the dead, we know that what he said is true—he is God. Because he rose, his death for our sins was validated and we can be forgiven. Because he rose, he lives and makes intercession for us. Because he rose and defeated death, we know we will also rise.

15:19 Why did Paul say people would be miserable if there were only earthly value to Christianity? In Paul's day, Christianity often brought a person persecution, ostracism from family, and, in many cases, poverty. There were few tangible benefits for being a Christian in that society. It was certainly not a step up the social or career ladder. Even more important, however, is the fact that if Christ had not been resurrected from death, Christians could not be forgiven for their sins and would have no hope of eternal life.

15:21 Death came into the world as a result of Adam and Eve's sin. In Romans 5:12–21, Paul explains why Adam's sin brought sin to all people, how death and sin spread to all humans because of this first sin, and the parallel between Adam's death and Christ's death.

15:23 Those related to Christ are Christians, who by faith become Christ's brothers and sisters and share in his resurrection. Because Christ *did* rise from the dead, we now have the certainty that we who are believers will be resurrected as well.

15:24–28 This is not a chronological sequence of events, and no specific time for these events is given. Paul's point is that the resurrected Christ will conquer all evil, including death.

15:25–28 Although God the Father and God the Son are equal, each has special roles (15:28). Christ is not inferior to the Father, but his role is to defeat all evil on earth. First he defeated sin and death on the cross, and in the final days he will defeat Satan and

15:26
1 Cor 15:54,55
2 Tim 1:10
Heb 2:14
Rev 1:18; 20:14
21:4

15:27
Ps 8:6
Mt 28:18
Eph 1:22
Heb 2:8
1 Pet 3:22

15:28
Jn 14:28
1 Cor 3:23; 11:3
Eph 1:10
Phil 3:21

15:30
Rom 8:36
2 Cor 11:26

15:31
2 Cor 4:10

15:32
Isa 22:13
Lk 12:19-21
1 Cor 16:8
2 Cor 1:8

15:34
Eph 5:14
1 Cor 6:5
1 Thess 4:5

15:35
Ezek 37:3

15:36
Jn 12:23,24

15:38
Gen 1:11
Ps 104:14

15:42
Dan 12:3
Mt 13:43
1 Cor 15:50

15:43
Phil 3:21
Col 3:4

he has defeated all his enemies, 26including the last enemy—death. This too must be defeated and ended. 27For the rule and authority over all things has been given to Christ by his Father; except, of course, Christ does not rule over the Father himself, who gave him this power to rule. 28When Christ has finally won the battle against all his enemies, then he, the Son of God, will put himself also under his Father's orders, so that God who has given him the victory over everything else will be utterly supreme.

29If the dead will not come back to life again, then what point is there in people being baptized for those who are gone? Why do it unless you believe that the dead will some day rise again?

30And why should we ourselves be continually risking our lives, facing death hour by hour? 31For it is a fact that I face death daily; that is as true as my pride in your growth in the Lord. 32And what value was there in fighting wild beasts—those men of Ephesus—if it was only for what I gain in this life down here? If we will never live again after we die, then we might as well go and have ourselves a good time: let us eat, drink, and be merry. What's the difference? For tomorrow we die, and that ends everything!

33Don't be fooled by those who say such things. If you listen to them you will start acting like them. 34Get some sense and quit your sinning. For to your shame I say it, some of you are not even Christians at all and have never really known God.

☛ The resurrection body

35But someone may ask, "How will the dead be brought back to life again? What kind of bodies will they have?" 36What a foolish question! You will find the answer in your own garden! When you put a seed into the ground it doesn't grow into a plant unless it "dies" first. 37And when the green shoot comes up out of the seed, it is very different from the seed you first planted. For all you put into the ground is a dry little seed of wheat, or whatever it is you are planting, 38then God gives it a beautiful new body—just the kind he wants it to have; a different kind of plant grows from each kind of seed. 39And just as there are different kinds of seeds and plants, so also there are different kinds of flesh. Humans, animals, fish, and birds are all different.

40The angels in heaven have bodies far different from ours, and the beauty and the glory of their bodies is different from the beauty and the glory of ours. 41The sun has one kind of glory while the moon and stars have another kind. And the stars differ from each other in their beauty and brightness.

42In the same way, our earthly bodies which die and decay are different from the bodies we shall have when we come back to life again, for they will never die. 43The bodies we have now embarrass us for they become sick and die; but they will be full of glory when we come back to life again. Yes, they are weak, dying bodies now, but when we live again they will be full of strength. 44They are just human bodies at death, but when they come back to life they will be superhuman bodies.

15:34 *have never really known God*, or, "There are some who know nothing of God." **15:40** *The angels*, literally, "There are celestial bodies." But perhaps this may refer to the sun, moon, planets, and stars.

---

all evil. World events may seem out of control and justice may seem scarce, but God is in control, allowing evil to remain for a time until he sends Jesus to earth again. Then Jesus will present to God a perfect new world.

15:29 Some believers were baptized on behalf of others who had died unbaptized. Nothing more is known about this practice, but it obviously affirms a belief in resurrection. Paul was not necessarily approving of baptism for the dead, but was using it as an illustration to reinforce his argument that the resurrection is a reality.

15:30–34 If death ended it all, enjoying the moment would be all that matters. But Christians know that there is life *beyond* the grave and that our life on earth is only a preparation for that life.

15:35ff Paul launches into a discussion about what our resurrected bodies will be like. If you could select your own body, what kind would you choose—strong, athletic, beautiful? Paul explains that we will be recognized in our resurrected bodies, yet they will be better than we can imagine, for they will be made to live forever. We will still have our own personalities and individualities, but these will be perfected through Christ's work. Scripture does not say what our resurrected bodies will be able to do, but we know they will be perfect, without sickness or disease.

15:44 *Supernatural* means "more than natural." Thus our spiritual bodies will be above and not limited to the laws of nature. This does not necessarily mean we'll be superpeople, but our bodies will be different and more capable than our present earthly bodies.

For just as there are natural, human bodies, there are also supernatural, spiritual bodies. 45The Scriptures tell us that the first man, Adam, was given a natural, human body but Christ is more than that, for he was life-giving Spirit.

46First, then, we have these human bodies and later on God gives us spiritual, heavenly bodies. 47Adam was made from the dust of the earth, but Christ came from heaven above. 48Every human being has a body just like Adam's, made of dust, but all who become Christ's will have the same kind of body as his—a body from heaven. 49Just as each of us now has a body like Adam's, so we shall some day have a body like Christ's.

50I tell you this, my brothers: an earthly body made of flesh and blood cannot get into God's Kingdom. These perishable bodies of ours are not the right kind to live forever.

51But I am telling you this strange and wonderful secret: we shall not all die, but we shall all be given new bodies! 52It will all happen in a moment, in the twinkling of an eye, when the last trumpet is blown. For there will be a trumpet blast from the sky and all the Christians who have died will suddenly become alive, with new bodies that will never, never die; and then we who are still alive shall suddenly have new bodies too. 53For our earthly bodies, the ones we have now that can die, must be transformed into heavenly bodies that cannot perish but will live forever.

54When this happens, then at last this Scripture will come true—"Death is swallowed up in victory." 55, 56O death, where then your victory? Where then your sting? For sin—the sting that causes death—will all be gone; and the law, which reveals our sins, will no longer be our judge. 57How we thank God for all of this! It is he who makes us victorious through Jesus Christ our Lord!

58So, my dear brothers, since future victory is sure, be strong and steady, always

15:45 *human body*, literally, "was made a living soul." *but Christ*, literally, "the last Adam." *is more*, implied.
15:52 *from the sky*, implied.

15:45
Gen 2:7
Jn 5:21
Rom 8:2
2 Cor 3:17
Col 3:4
1 Pet 3:18

15:47
Gen 3:19
Jn 3:13,31

15:48
Phil 3:20,21

15:49
Gen 5:3
Rom 8:29
Phil 3:21
1 Jn 3:2

15:50
Mt 16:17
Jn 3:3,5

15:51
2 Cor 5:2-4
Phil 3:21
1 Thess 4:15,16

15:52
Mt 24:31

15:53
2 Cor 5:4

15:54
Isa 25:8

15:55
Hos 13:14
Rom 4:15

15:57
Rom 7:23-25
1 Jn 5:4

Physical Bodies	Resurrection Bodies	
Die and decay	Never die	**PHYSICAL AND RESURRECTION BODIES**
Embarrassing	Full of glory	
Weak and sick	Full of strength	
Human	Superhuman	
Natural	Spiritual	
From the dust	From heaven	

We all have bodies—each looks different, each has different abilities and weaknesses. But as physical, earthly bodies, they are all alike. All believers are promised life after death and bodies like Christ's (15:49), resurrection bodies.

15:45 When Christ rose from the dead, he became "life-giving Spirit." This means he entered into a new form of existence (see note on 2 Corinthians 3:17). Christ's new glorified human body now suits his new glorified life—just as Adam's human body was suitable to his natural life. When we will be resurrected, God will give us a glorified body suited to our new eternal life.

15:50-53 We all face limitations. Those who have physical, mental, or emotional handicaps are especially aware of this. Some may be blind, but they can see a new way to live. Some may be deaf, but they can hear God's Good News. Some may be lame, but they can walk in God's love. In addition, they have the encouragement that those handicaps are only temporary. Paul tells us we shall all be given new bodies when Jesus returns, and these bodies will be without handicaps, never to die or become sick. This can give us hope in our suffering.

15:52 A trumpet blast will usher in the new heaven and earth. The Jews would understand the significance of this because trumpets were always blown to signal the start of great feasts and other extraordinary events (Numbers 10:10).

15:54-56 Satan seemed to be victorious in the Garden of Eden (Genesis 3) and when Jesus died on the cross (Mark 15:22-24). But God turned Satan's apparent victory into defeat when Jesus Christ rose from the dead (Colossians 2:15; Hebrews 2:14, 15). Thus death is no longer a source of dread or fear. Christ overcame it, and one day we will also. Death has been defeated, and we have hope beyond the grave.

15:58 Paul said that because of the resurrection, nothing we do is wasted. Sometimes we hesitate to do good because we don't see any results. But if we can maintain a heavenly perspective, we understand that we don't often see the good that results from our efforts. If we truly believe that Christ has won the ultimate victory, it must affect the way we live right now. Don't let discouragement over an apparent lack of results keep you from working. Do the good that you have opportunity to do, knowing your work will have eternal results.

abounding in the Lord's work, for you know that nothing you do for the Lord is ever wasted as it would be if there were no resurrection.

Directions for the offering

16:1
Acts 11:29
24:17
Rom 15:26
2 Cor 8:4; 9:1
Gal 2:10

16:2
Lk 24:1
Acts 20:7
Rev 1:10

16:3
2 Cor 8:19-21

16 Now here are the directions about the money you are collecting to send to the Christians in Jerusalem (and, by the way, these are the same directions I gave to the churches in Galatia). 2On every Lord's Day each of you should put aside something from what you have earned during the week, and use it for this offering. The amount depends on how much the Lord has helped you earn. Don't wait until I get there and then try to collect it all at once. 3When I come I will send your loving gift with a letter to Jerusalem, to be taken there by trustworthy messengers you yourselves will choose. 4And if it seems wise for me to go along too, then we can travel together.

Paul's final instructions

16:5
Acts 19:21
1 Cor 4:19
2 Cor 1:15,16

16:6
Acts 15:3; 17:5
21:5

16:7
Acts 18:21

16:8
Acts 2:1

16:9
Acts 14:27
19:8-10
2 Cor 2:12

16:10
Acts 16:1
Rom 16:21

16:11
1 Tim 4:12,13

16:12
Acts 18:24
1 Cor 1:12
Tit 3:13

16:13
Mt 24:42
Phil 1:27; 4:1
1 Thess 3:7,8
2 Thess 2:15

16:14
1 Cor 14:1

16:15
1 Cor 14:16

16:16
1 Thess 5:12,13

5I am coming to visit you after I have been to Macedonia first, but I will be staying there only for a little while. 6It could be that I will stay longer with you, perhaps all winter, and then you can send me on to my next destination. 7This time I don't want to make just a passing visit and then go right on; I want to come and stay awhile, if the Lord will let me. 8I will be staying here at Ephesus until the holiday of Pentecost, 9for there is a wide open door for me to preach and teach here. So much is happening, but there are many enemies.

10If Timothy comes make him feel at home, for he is doing the Lord's work just as I am. 11Don't let anyone despise or ignore him [because he is young], but send him back to me happy with his time among you; I am looking forward to seeing him soon, along with the others who are returning.

12I begged Apollos to visit you along with the others, but he thought that it was not at all God's will for him to go now; he will be seeing you later on when he has the opportunity.

13Keep your eyes open for spiritual danger; stand true to the Lord; act like men; be strong; 14and whatever you do, do it with kindness and love.

15Do you remember Stephanas and his family? They were the first to become Christians in Greece and they are spending their lives helping and serving Christians everywhere. 16Please follow their instructions and do everything you can to help them as well as all others like them who work hard at your side with such real devotion. 17I am so glad that Stephanas, Fortunatus, and Achaicus have arrived here for a visit. They have been making up for the help you aren't here to give me. 18They have cheered me greatly and have been a wonderful encouragement to me, as I am sure they were to you, too. I hope you properly appreciate the work of such men as these.

16:1 *Christians in Jerusalem,* implied.   **16:11** *because he is young,* implied in 1 Tim 4:12.

16:1ff Paul had just said that no good work is ever wasted (15:58). Now he mentions some practical works that have value for all Christians.

16:1–4 The Christians in Jerusalem were suffering from poverty and famine, and so Paul was collecting money for them. Although the Jerusalem church was where Christianity began, it was experiencing hard times (see Romans 15:25–31; 2 Corinthians 8:4; 9:1ff). Paul suggested that believers set aside a certain amount each week and give it to the church until he arrived to take it on to Jerusalem. Paul had planned to go straight to Corinth from Ephesus, but he changed his mind (2 Corinthians 1, 2). When he finally arrived, he took the gift and delivered it to the Jerusalem church (Acts 21:18; 24:17).

16:10, 11 Paul was sending Timothy ahead to Corinth. Paul respected Timothy and had worked closely with him (Philippians 2:20–22; 1 Timothy 1:2). Although Timothy was young, Paul

encouraged the Corinthian church to welcome him because he was doing the Lord's work. God's work is not limited by age. Paul wrote two personal letters to Timothy that have been preserved in the Bible (1 and 2 Timothy). See also the note on 4:17.

16:12 Apollos, who had preached in Corinth, was doing evangelistic work in Greece (see Acts 18:24–28; 1 Corinthians 3:3, 4). Apollos didn't go to Corinth right away, partly because he knew of the factions there and didn't want to cause any more divisions. Paul probably had the authority to send Apollos to Corinth, but he did not force him to go, because Apollos didn't feel it was God's will for him.

16:13, 14 As the Corinthians awaited Paul's next visit, they were directed to (1) be alert to spiritual dangers, (2) stand true to the Lord, (3) behave maturely, (4) be strong, and (5) do all things with kindness and love. Today, as we wait the return of Christ, we should follow the same instructions.

¹⁹The churches here in Asia send you their loving greetings. Aquila and Priscilla send you their love and so do all the others who meet in their home for their church service. ²⁰All the friends here have asked me to say "hello" to you for them. And give each other a loving handshake when you meet.

²¹I will write these final words of this letter with my own hand: ²²if anyone does not love the Lord, that person is cursed. Lord Jesus, come! ²³May the love and favor of the Lord Jesus Christ rest upon you. ²⁴My love to all of you, for we all belong to Christ Jesus.

Sincerely, Paul

16:19
Rom 16:5
Philem 2
Rev 1:4,11

16:21
Rom 16:22
Gal 6:11
Col 4:18
2 Thess 3:17
Philem 19

16:22
Gal 1:8,9
Heb 10:26

16:19 Aquila and Priscilla were tentmakers (or leather workers) whom Paul met in Corinth (Acts 18:1–3). They followed Paul to Ephesus and lived there with him, helping to teach others about Jesus (Romans 16:3–5). Many in the Corinthian church would have known this Christian couple. They are also mentioned in Acts 18:18, 26; Romans 16:3; 2 Timothy 4:19.

16:21 Paul had a helper, or secretary, who wrote this letter while he dictated. Paul wrote the final words, however, in his own handwriting. This is similar to adding a handwritten postscript (P.S.) to a typewritten letter. It also served to verify that this was a genuine letter from the apostle, not a forgery.

16:22 The Lord Jesus Christ is coming back to earth again. To Paul, this was a glad hope, the best he could look forward to. He was not afraid of seeing Christ—he could hardly wait! Do you share Paul's eager anticipation? Those who love Christ are looking forward to that wonderful time of his return (Titus 2:13).

16:24 The church at Corinth was a church in trouble. Paul lovingly and forcefully confronted their problems and pointed them back to Christ. He dealt with divisions and conflicts, selfishness, inconsiderate use of freedom, disorder in worship, misuse of spiritual gifts, and wrong attitudes about the resurrection.

In every church, there are enough problems to split it. We should not ignore or gloss over problems in our church or in our lives. Instead, like Paul, we should deal with problems head on as they arise. The lesson for us in 1 Corinthians is that unity and love in a church are far more important than leaders and labels.

SLITHERING through the centuries, the serpent whispers his silver-lined promises, beguiling, deceiving, and tempting—urging men and women to reject God and to follow him. Satan's emmissaries have been many—false prophets contradicting God's ancient spokesmen, "pious" leaders hurling blasphemous accusations, and heretical teachers infiltrating churches. And the deception continues. Our world is filled with cults, "isms," and ideologies, all claiming to be the way to God.

Paul constantly struggled with those who would mislead God's people, and poured his life into spreading the Good News to the uttermost parts of the world. During three missionary trips and other travels, he proclaimed Christ, made converts, and established churches. But often young believers were easy prey for false teachers. False teachers were a constant threat to the gospel and the early church. So Paul had to spend much time warning and correcting them.

The church at Corinth was weak. Surrounded by idolatry and immorality, they struggled with their Christian faith and life-style. Through personal visits and letters, Paul tried to instruct them in the faith, resolve their conflicts, and solve some of their problems. First Corinthians was sent to deal with specific moral issues in the church and to answer questions about sex, marriage, and tender consciences. That letter confronted the issues directly and was well received by most. But there were false teachers who denied Paul's authority and slandered him. Paul then wrote 2 Corinthians to defend his position and to denounce those who were twisting the truth.

Second Corinthians was a difficult letter for Paul to write because he had to list his credentials as an apostle. Paul was reluctant to do so because he was a humble servant of Christ, but he knew it was necessary. Paul also knew that most of the believers in Corinth had taken his previous words to heart and were beginning to mature in their faith. He affirmed their commitment to Christ.

Second Corinthians begins with Paul reminding his readers of (1) their relationship to him—Paul had always been honest and straightforward with them (1:12–14), (2) his itinerary—he was planning to visit them again (1:15—2:3), and (3) his previous letter (2:4–11). Paul then moves directly to the subject of false teachers (2:17), and he reviews his ministry among them to demonstrate the validity of his message, and to urge them not to turn away from the truth (3:1—7:16).

Paul next turns to the issue of collecting money for the poor Christians in Jerusalem. He tells them how others have given, and he urges them to show their love in a tangible way as well (8:1—9:15). Paul then gives a strong defense for his authority as a genuine apostle while pointing out the deception of the false apostles (10:1—13:14).

As you read this intensely personal letter, listen to Paul's words of love and exhortation, and be committed to the truth of God's Word, prepared to reject all false teaching.

VITAL STATISTICS

PURPOSE:
To affirm his own ministry, defend his authority as an apostle, and refute the false teachers in Corinth

AUTHOR:
Paul

TO WHOM WRITTEN:
The church in Corinth, and Christians everywhere

DATE WRITTEN:
About A.D. 55–57, from Macedonia

SETTING:
Paul had already written three letters to the Corinthians (two are now lost). In 1 Corinthians (the second of these letters), he used strong words to correct and teach. Most of the church had responded in the right spirit; there were, however, those who were denying Paul's authority and questioning his motives.

KEY VERSE:
"We are Christ's ambassadors. God is using us to speak to you: we beg you, as though Christ himself were here pleading with you, receive the love he offers you—be reconciled to God" (5:20).

KEY PEOPLE:
Paul, Timothy, Titus, false teachers

KEY PLACES:
Corinth, Jerusalem

SPECIAL FEATURES:
This is an intensely personal and autobiographical letter.

THE BLUEPRINT

1. Paul explains his actions (1:1—2:13)
2. Paul defends his ministry (2:14—7:16)
3. Paul defends the collection (8:1—9:15)
4. Paul defends his authority (10:1—13:14)

In responding to the attacks on his character and authority, Paul explains the nature of Christian ministry and, as an example, openly shares about his ministry. This is an important letter for all who wish to be involved in any kind of Christian ministry, because it has much to teach us about how we should handle our ministries today. Like Paul, those involved in ministry should be blameless, sincere, confident, caring, open, and willing to suffer for the sake of Christ.

MEGATHEMES

THEME	EXPLANATION	IMPORTANCE
Trials	Paul experienced great suffering, persecution, and opposition in his ministry. He even struggled with a personal weakness—a "thorn in the flesh." Through it all, Paul affirmed God's faithfulness.	God is faithful. His strength is sufficient for any trial. When trials come, they keep us from pride and teach us dependence on God. He comforts us so we can comfort others.
Church discipline	Paul defends his role in church discipline. Neither immorality nor false teaching could be ignored. The church was to be neither lax nor too severe in administering discipline. The church was to restore the corrected person when he or she repented.	The goal of all discipline in the church should be correction, not vengeance. For churches to be effective, they must confront and solve problems, not ignore them. In everything, we must act in love.
Hope	To encourage the Corinthians as they faced trials, Paul reminded them that they would receive new bodies in heaven. This would be a great victory in contrast to their present suffering.	To know we will receive new bodies offers us hope. No matter what adversity we face, we can keep going. Our faithful service will result in triumph.
Giving	Paul organized a collection of funds for the poor in the Jerusalem church. Many of the Asian churches gave money. Paul explains and defends his beliefs about giving, and he urges the Corinthians to follow through on their previous commitment.	Like the Corinthians, we should follow through on our financial commitments. Our giving must be generous, sacrificial, according to a plan, and based on need. Our generosity not only helps those in need, but enables them to thank God.
Sound doctrine	False teachers were challenging Paul's ministry and authority as an apostle. Paul asserts his authority in order to preserve correct Christian doctrine. His sincerity, his love for Christ, and his concern for the people were his defense.	We should share Paul's concern for correct teaching in our churches. But in so doing, we must share his motivation—love for Christ and people—and be sincere.

1. Paul explains his actions

1 Dear friends, This letter is from me, Paul, appointed by God to be Jesus Christ's messenger; and from our dear brother Timothy. We are writing to all of you Christians there in Corinth and throughout Greece. ²May God our Father and the Lord Jesus Christ mightily bless each one of you, and give you peace.

We pass on God's comfort to others

3, 4What a wonderful God we have—he is the Father of our Lord Jesus Christ, the source of every mercy, and the one who so wonderfully comforts and strengthens us in our hardships and trials. And why does he do this? So that when others are troubled, needing our sympathy and encouragement, we can pass on to them this same help and comfort God has given us. ⁵You can be sure that the more we undergo sufferings for Christ, the more he will shower us with his comfort and encouragement. 6, 7We are in deep trouble for bringing you God's comfort and salvation. But in our trouble God has comforted us—and this, too, to help you: to show you from our personal experience how God will tenderly comfort you when you undergo these same sufferings. He will give you the strength to endure.

⁸I think you ought to know, dear brothers, about the hard time we went through

1:1 *throughout Greece,* or, "throughout Achaia."

DIFFERENCES BETWEEN 1 AND 2 CORINTHIANS
The two letters to the Corinthian church found in the Bible are very different, with different tones and focuses.

1 Corinthians	*2 Corinthians*
Practical	Personal
Focuses on the character of the Corinthian church	Focuses on Paul as he bares his soul and tells of his love for the Corinthian church
Deals with questions on marriage, freedom, spiritual gifts, and order in the church	Deals with the problem of false teachers, whereby Paul defends his authority and the truth of his message
Paul instructs in matters concerning the church's well-being	Paul gives his testimony because he knows they trust him and that acceptance of his advice is vital to the church's well-being
Contains advice to help the church against the pagan influences in the wicked city of Corinth	Contains testimony to help the church against the havoc caused by false teachers

---

1:1 Paul visited Corinth on his second missionary journey and founded a church (Acts 18:1ff). He later wrote several letters to the church there, two of which are included in the Bible. Paul's first letter to the Corinthians is lost (1 Corinthians 5:9–11), his second letter to them is our book of 1 Corinthians, his third letter is lost as well (2:6–9; 7:12), and his fourth letter is our book of 2 Corinthians. Second Corinthians was written about a year after 1 Corinthians.

Paul wrote 1 Corinthians to deal with divisions in the church, but when his advice was not taken and their problems weren't solved, he visited Corinth a second time (called "another painful visit" in 2:1). He then planned a third visit, but delayed it and wrote 2 Corinthians instead. After writing 2 Corinthians, he visited Corinth once more (Acts 20:2).

1:1 Paul had great respect for Timothy (see Philippians 2:20; 1 Timothy 1:2; 6:11), one of his traveling companions (Acts 16:1–3). Timothy had accompanied Paul to Corinth on his second missionary journey, and Paul had recently sent him there to minister (1 Corinthians 4:17; 16:10). Timothy's report to Paul about the crisis in the Corinthian church prompted Paul to make an unplanned visit to the church to deal with the problem in person (see 2:1). For more information on Timothy, see his Profile in 1 Timothy.

1:2 The Romans had made Corinth the capital of Achaia (the southern half of present-day Greece). The city was a flourishing trade center because of its seaport, and with the thousands of sailors who disembarked there each year, it had become a center

of prostitution. Corinth had a reputation as one of the most immoral cities in the ancient world. Many heathen temples had sprung up with all forms of sexual immorality and idol worship. In fact, the Greek word for practicing sexual immorality was "to Corinthianize." A Christian church in the city would face great temptations. For more information on Corinth, see the note in 1 Corinthians 1:2.

1:3, 4 Many think that when God comforts us, our hardships should go away. But if that were always so, people would turn to God only to be relieved of pain and not out of love for him. We must understand that *comfort* can also mean receiving strength, encouragement, and hope to deal with our hardships. The more we suffer, the more comfort God gives us (1:5). If you are feeling overwhelmed, allow God to comfort you as he can. Remember that every trial you endure will later become an opportunity to minister to other people suffering similar hardships.

1:8 Paul does not say what happened to him during this "hard time" in Asia, although his accounts of all three missionary journeys record many difficult trials he faced (Acts 13:2—14:28; Acts 15:40—21:17).

1:8–10 We often depend on our own skills and abilities when life seems easy, but when we feel powerless to help ourselves, we turn to God. Dependence is not defeat, but constant contact. It is realizing that our source of truth and power is God and then keeping in touch with him. With this attitude, problems drive us to God rather than away from him. Learn how to depend on God daily.

in Asia. We were really crushed and overwhelmed, and feared we would never live through it. 9We felt we were doomed to die and saw how powerless we were to help ourselves; but that was good, for then we put everything into the hands of God, who alone could save us, for he can even raise the dead. 10And he did help us, and saved us from a terrible death; yes, and we expect him to do it again and again. 11But you must help us too, by praying for us. For much thanks and praise will go to God from you who see his wonderful answers to your prayers for our safety!

1:9
Jer 17:5,7

1:10
2 Pet 2:9

1:11
Rom 15:30
2 Cor 4:15
Phil 1:19
Philem 22

Paul's change of plans

12We are so glad that we can say with utter honesty that in all our dealings we have been pure and sincere, quietly depending upon the Lord for his help, and not on our own skills. And that is even more true, if possible, about the way we have acted toward you. 13, 14My letters have been straightforward and sincere; nothing is written between the lines! And even though you don't know me very well (I hope someday you will), I want you to try to accept me and be proud of me, as you already are to some extent; just as I shall be of you on that day when our Lord Jesus comes back again.

1:12
Acts 23:1
1 Cor 2:4
2 Cor 2:17; 4:15

1:14
2 Cor 5:12
Phil 4:1
1 Thess 2:19

1:15
Rom 1:11,12
1 Cor 4:19

15, 16It was because I was so sure of your understanding and trust that I planned to stop and see you on my way to Macedonia, as well as afterwards when I returned, so that I could be a double blessing to you and so that you could send me on my way to Judea.

1:16
1 Cor 16:5

1:17
2 Cor 10:2

17Then why, you may be asking, did I change my plan? Hadn't I really made up my mind yet? Or am I like a man of the world who says "yes" when he really means "no"? 18Never! As surely as God is true, I am not that sort of person. My "yes" means "yes."

1:19
Ex 3:14
Mt 16:16; 26:63
Lk 1:35
Acts 9:20; 18:5
Heb 13:8

19Timothy and Silvanus and I have been telling you about Jesus Christ the Son of God. He isn't one to say "yes" when he means "no." He always does exactly what he says. 20He carries out and fulfills all of God's promises, no matter how many of them there are; and we have told everyone how faithful he is, giving glory to his name. 21It is this God who has made you and me into faithful Christians and commissioned us apostles to preach the Good News. 22He has put his brand upon us—his mark of ownership—and given us his Holy Spirit in our hearts as guarantee

1:20
Rom 15:8,9
Rev 3:14

1:21
1 Jn 2:20,27

1:22
2 Cor 5:5
Eph 1:13,14
4:30
2 Tim 2:19
Rev 2:17

1:11 Pray for pastors, teachers, missionaries, and others who are on the "front lines" of spreading the gospel. Anyone making a real difference for God will be challenged by Satan.

1:12–14 Paul knew the importance of honesty in writing and speaking, especially in a situation where constructive criticism was necessary. God wants us to be real and transparent in all our relationships. If we aren't, we will give in to rumors, gossip, and second-guessing.

1:13, 14 Paul had ministered in Corinth for a year and a half (Acts 18:11), and he had visited a second time. Why then did he say they didn't know him very well? Many new believers had been added to the church, and in his letters Paul often focused on those who were wavering in their faith and who did not see Paul as a God-ordained apostle. These people did not know him or understand what he was saying about Jesus Christ.

1:15–17 Paul had recently made a brief, unscheduled visit to Corinth which was very painful for him and the church (see 2:1). After that visit, he told the church when he would come again. But Paul changed his original travel plans. Instead of sailing from Ephesus to Corinth before going to Macedonia, he traveled from Ephesus directly to Macedonia, where he wrote a letter that caused him much anguish (7:8, 9). He had made his original plans thinking the church would have solved its problems. When the time came for Paul's scheduled trip to Corinth, however, the crisis had not been fully resolved (although progress was being made in some areas; 7:11–16). So he wrote a letter instead (2:3, 4; 7:8), because another visit would only have made matters worse. Thus

Paul stayed away from Corinth because he was concerned over the church's unity, not because he was fickle.

1:17 Paul's change of plans caused some of his accusers to say he couldn't be trusted, hoping to undermine his authority. Paul explained that not indecision but concern for their feelings forced him to change his plans. The reason for his trip—to bring joy (1:24)—could not be accomplished with the present crisis. He didn't want to visit them only to rebuke them severely (1:23). Just as the Corinthians could trust God to keep his promises, they could trust Paul as God's representative to keep his. He would still visit them, but at a better time.

1:19, 20 Jesus faithfully obeyed God and never sinned (1 Peter 3:18); faithfully died for us (Hebrews 2:9); and now faithfully intercedes for us (Romans 8:34; Hebrews 4:14, 15). Because Jesus Christ is faithful, Paul was faithful in his ministry.

1:21, 22 Paul mentions two gifts God gives when we become believers: a "mark of ownership" to show who our master is, and the Holy Spirit as a guarantee that we belong to him (Ephesians 1:13, 14). With the privilege of belonging to God comes the responsibility of identifying ourselves as faithful representatives and servants of our master. Don't be ashamed to let others know you are his.

1:22 Paul calls the Holy Spirit the "first installment" for two reasons: he guarantees that salvation is ours, and yet we will receive so much more, both now and when Christ returns. The great comfort and power the Holy Spirit gives in this life is a foretaste of the benefits and blessings of our eternal life in God's presence.

that we belong to him, and as the first installment of all that he is going to give us.

1:23
1 Cor 4:21

23I call upon this God to witness against me if I am not telling the absolute truth: the reason I haven't come to visit you yet is that I don't want to sadden you with a severe rebuke. 24When I come, although I can't do much to help your faith, for it is strong already, I want to be able to do something about your joy: I want to make you happy, not sad.

1:24
Rom 11:20
1 Cor 15:1,2

2:1
1 Cor 4:21
2 Cor 12:20
2:2
2 Cor 7:8

2 "No," I said to myself, "I won't do it. I'll not make them unhappy with another painful visit." 2For if I make you sad, who is going to make me happy? You are the ones to do it, and how can you if I cause you pain? 3That is why I wrote as I did in my last letter, so that you will get things straightened out before I come. Then, when I do come, I will not be made sad by the very ones who ought to give me greatest joy. I felt sure that your happiness was so bound up in mine that you would not be happy either, unless I came with joy.

2:4
2 Cor 2:9; 7:8,9

4Oh, how I hated to write that letter! It almost broke my heart and I tell you honestly that I cried over it. I didn't want to hurt you, but I had to show you how very much I loved you and cared about what was happening to you.

Reinstate the repentant sinner

2:5,6
1 Cor 5:1-5
2 Cor 7:11

5, 6Remember that the man I wrote about, who caused all the trouble, has not caused sorrow to me as much as to all the rest of you—though I certainly have my share in it too. I don't want to be harder on him than I should. He has been punished enough by your united disapproval. 7Now it is time to forgive him and comfort him. Otherwise he may become so bitter and discouraged that he won't be able to recover. 8Please show him now that you still do love him very much.

2:7
Gal 6:1
Eph 4:32

2:10
1 Cor 5:4

9I wrote to you as I did so that I could find out how far you would go in obeying me. 10When you forgive anyone, I do too. And whatever I have forgiven (to the extent that this affected me too) has been by Christ's authority, and for your good. 11A further reason for forgiveness is to keep from being outsmarted by Satan; for we know what he is trying to do.

2:11
2 Cor 4:4; 11:3
1 Pet 5:8

2:12
Acts 14:27
2 Cor 4:3; 10:14

12Well, when I got as far as the city of Troas, the Lord gave me tremendous opportunities to preach the Gospel. 13But Titus, my dear brother, wasn't there to

2:13
2 Cor 7:5,6

2:3 *so that you will get things straightened out before I come,* implied.

1:23 The Corinthian church had written to Paul with questions about their faith (see 1 Corinthians 7:1). In response, Paul wrote 1 Corinthians. But they did not follow Paul's instructions. Paul had planned to visit them again, but instead wrote a sorrowful letter (7:8, 9) to give them another chance to change their ways. He didn't want to visit and repeat the same advice for the same problems. He wrote that emotional letter to encourage them to follow the advice he had already given in previous letters and visits.

2:1 Paul's phrase "another painful visit" indicates he had already made one difficult trip to Corinth (see notes on 1:1; 1:15–17) since founding the church. He went there to deal with those in the church who were attacking and undermining his authority as an apostle of Jesus Christ, thus confusing other believers.

2:3 Paul's "last letter" was not the book of 1 Corinthians, but a letter written between 1 and 2 Corinthians, just after his unplanned, painful visit (2:1). Paul refers to this letter again in 7:8.

2:4 Paul did not enjoy reprimanding his friends and fellow believers, but he cared enough for the Corinthians to confront them about their wrongdoing. Proverbs 27:6 says that "wounds from a friend are better than kisses from an enemy." Sometimes our friends make choices that we know are wrong. If we ignore their behavior and let them continue, we aren't showing love to them. Love means honestly sharing our concerns with those we love. When we don't move to help, we show that we are more concerned about what will happen to us than what will happen to them.

2:5–11 It was time to forgive the man who had been punished by the church and had subsequently repented. He now needed

friendship and comfort. This may have been the man who required the disciplinary action described in 1 Corinthians 5 or the chief opponent of Paul who had caused Paul the anguish described in 2:1–11. The sorrowful letter taken by Titus had finally brought about the repentance of the Corinthians (7:8–14), and their discipline of the man had led to his repentance. Church discipline should always allow for restoration. Two mistakes can be made in church discipline—being too lenient with sin and not correcting mistakes, or being too harsh and not forgiving.

2:11 We use church discipline in order to keep the church pure and to help wayward people to repent. But Satan tries to harm the church by tempting it to use discipline in an unforgiving way. This causes those exercising discipline to become proud of their purity and it causes the one being disciplined to become bitter and perhaps to leave the church entirely. We must remember that our purpose in discipline is to *restore* a person to the fellowship, not to destroy him or her. We must be cautious that personal anger is not vented under the guise of church discipline.

2:13 Titus was a Greek convert whom Paul greatly loved and trusted (the book of Titus is a letter Paul wrote to him). Titus was one of the men responsible for collecting the money for the poverty-stricken Jerusalem church (8:6). Paul had also sent Titus with the sorrowful letter. On his way to Macedonia, Paul was supposed to meet Titus in Troas. When he didn't find him there, he was worried for Titus' safety, and left Troas to search for him in Macedonia. There Paul found him (7:6), and the good news he received (7:8–16) led to this epistle. Paul would send Titus back to Corinth with this letter (8:16, 17).

meet me and I couldn't rest, wondering where he was and what had happened to him. So I said good-bye and went right on to Macedonia to try to find him.

2. Paul defends his ministry
The fragrance of Christ

14But thanks be to God! For through what Christ has done, he has triumphed over us so that now wherever we go he uses us to tell others about the Lord and to spread the Gospel like a sweet perfume. 15As far as God is concerned there is a sweet, wholesome fragrance in our lives. It is the fragrance of Christ within us, an aroma to both the saved and the unsaved all around us. 16To those who are not being saved, we seem a fearful smell of death and doom, while to those who know Christ we are a life-giving perfume. But who is adequate for such a task as this? 17Only those who, like ourselves, are men of integrity, sent by God, speaking with Christ's power, with God's eye upon us. We are not like those hucksters—and

2:14
Col 2:15

2:15
Eph 5:2

2:16
Lk 2:34
Jn 9:39
2 Cor 3:5

2:17
2 Cor 4:2

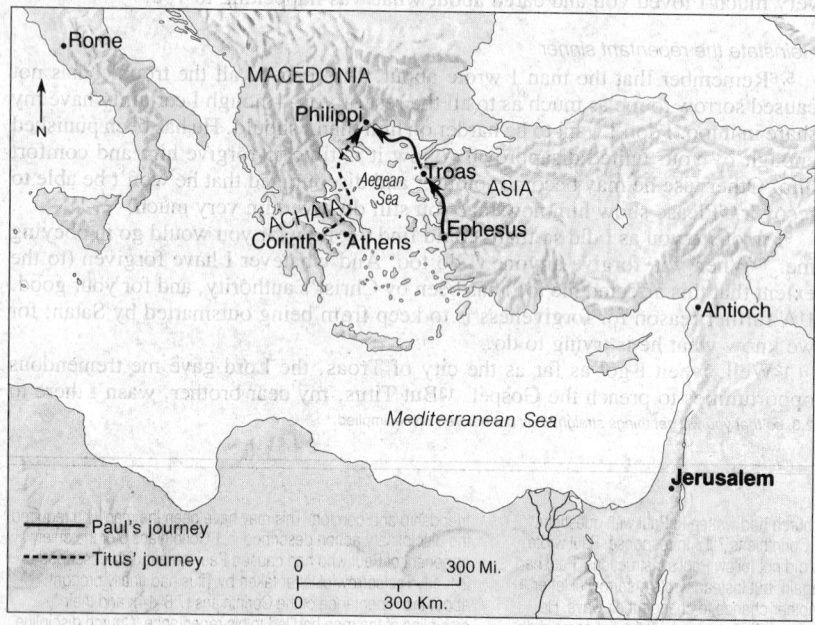

.Rome

MACEDONIA

Philippi.

Aegean
Sea

Troas

ASIA

ACHAIA

Corinth.   Athens

Ephesus

.Antioch

Mediterranean Sea

Jerusalem

——— Paul's journey
------- Titus' journey

0   300 Mi.

0   300 Km.

N

PAUL SEARCHES FOR TITUS
Paul had searched for Titus, hoping to meet him in Troas and receive news about the Corinthian church. When he did not find Titus in Troas, he went on to Macedonia (2:13), most likely to Philippi, where he found Titus.

2:14ff In the middle of discussing his unscheduled trip to Macedonia, Paul breaks off into a discussion about his ministry, his relationship with the Corinthian believers, and the way God has used him to help others wherever he went (2:14—7:4). In 7:5, Paul resumes the story of his trip to Macedonia.

2:14-16 Believers are to be like a sweet perfume whose fragrance others can't help noticing. Just as we cannot control a person's opinion about a perfume's fragrance, we cannot control a person's reaction to our Christian message and actions. But if we remain true to Christ, his Spirit working in us will attract others.

2:16 In a Roman victory procession, the Roman general would display his treasures and captives amidst a cloud of incense. To the victors, the smell was sweet; to the captives in the parade, it was the stench of death. When Christians preach the gospel, it is good news to some and repulsive to others. Believers recognize the life-giving fragrance of this news. To nonbelievers, however, it smells foul, like death—their own.

2:16, 17 When we face the task of representing Christ, we never feel adequate. Perhaps we shouldn't, for to do so would be the

basis for pride. Our adequacy is always from God (1 Corinthians 15:10; 2 Corinthians 3:5). He has already commissioned and sent us (see Matthew 28:18-20). He has given us the Holy Spirit to speak with Christ's power. He keeps his eye upon us, protecting us as we work for him. Thus, if we realize that God makes us adequate and useful for him, there is no such thing as an inadequate believer. Serving him, therefore, requires that we focus on what he can do through us, not on what we can't do by ourselves.

2:17 A huckster is a salesman who has no concern for the customers or the quality of the product—he just wants to make as much money as possible. Some preachers in Paul's day were hucksters, preaching without understanding God's message or caring about what happened to their listeners. They weren't concerned about furthering God's Kingdom—they just wanted money. Today there are still religious hucksters who care only about money, not about truth. Those who truly speak for God should have integrity and avoid preaching for profit or self-gain (1 Timothy 6:5-10).

there are many of them—whose idea in getting out the Gospel is to make a good living out of it.

God's great new covenant

3:1
Acts 18:27
2 Cor 5:12; 10:12

3 Are we beginning to be like those false teachers of yours who must tell you all about themselves and bring long letters of recommendation with them? I think you hardly need someone's letter to tell you about us, do you? And we don't need a recommendation from you, either! ²The only letter I need is you yourselves! By looking at the good change in your hearts, everyone can see that we have done a good work among you. ³They can see that you are a letter from Christ, written by us. It is not a letter written with pen and ink, but by the Spirit of the living God; not one carved on stone, but in human hearts.

3:2
1 Cor 9:2

3:3
Ex 24:12
Ps 40:8
Prov 3:3
Jer 31:33
Ezek 36:26
1 Cor 3:5

⁴We dare to say these good things about ourselves only because of our great trust in God through Christ, that he will help us to be true to what we say, ⁵and not because we think we can do anything of lasting value by ourselves. Our only power and success comes from God. ⁶He is the one who has helped us tell others about his new agreement to save them. We do not tell them that they must obey every law of God or die; but we tell them there is life for them from the Holy Spirit. The old way, trying to be saved by keeping the Ten Commandments, ends in death; in the new way, the Holy Spirit gives them life.

3:5
Jn 15:5
1 Cor 15:10

3:6
Jer 31:31
Lk 22:20
Jn 6:63
Rom 2:27; 7:6
8:2
Gal 3:10
Heb 8:6

⁷Yet that old system of law that led to death began with such glory that people could not bear to look at Moses' face. For as he gave them God's law to obey, his face shone out with the very glory of God—though the brightness was already fading away. ⁸Shall we not expect far greater glory in these days when the Holy Spirit is giving life? ⁹If the plan that leads to doom was glorious, much more glorious is the plan that makes men right with God. ¹⁰In fact, that first glory as it shone from Moses' face is worth nothing at all in comparison with the overwhelming glory of the new agreement. ¹¹So if the old system that faded into nothing was full of heavenly glory, the glory of God's new plan for our salvation is certainly far greater, for it is eternal.

3:7
Ex 34:29-35
Deut 9:10

3:8
Gal 3:5

3:9
Rom 1:17; 3:21

3:10,11
Jn 17:10,22
Heb 2:10

¹²Since we know that this new glory will never go away, we can preach with great boldness, ¹³and not as Moses did, who put a veil over his face so that the Israelis could not see the glory fade away.

3:12
Eph 6:19
1 Thess 2:2

3:13
Ex 34:33
Rom 10:4
Gal 3:23

¹⁴Not only Moses' face was veiled, but his people's minds and understanding were veiled and blinded too. Even now when the Scripture is read it seems as

3:14
Isa 6:10
Jn 12:40
Acts 13:15
Rom 11:7
2 Cor 4:4

3:1–3 Some false teachers had started carrying forged letters of recommendation to increase their authority. In no uncertain terms, Paul states that he needs no such letters. The lives of the believers whom he and his companions had converted were enough of a recommendation. Paul used letters of introduction, however, many times. For example, he wrote them for Phoebe (Romans 16:1, 2) and Timothy (1 Corinthians 16:10, 11). These letters helped Paul's trusted companions and friends find a welcome in various churches.

3:3 Paul uses powerful imagery from famous Old Testament passages predicting the promised day of new beginnings (see Jeremiah 31:33; Ezekiel 11:19; 36:26). This process of conversion isn't one for which any human minister can take credit; it is the work of God's Spirit. We do not become believers by following some manual or using some technique. Our conversion is a result of God's branding his Spirit on our hearts, guaranteeing his presence in us.

3:4, 5 Paul is not boasting; he gives God the credit for all his accomplishments. While the false teachers boasted of their own power and prestige, Paul expressed his humility before God. No one can claim to be adequate without God's help. No one is competent to carry out the responsibilities to which God has called him or her. Without the Holy Spirit's enabling, natural talent can carry us only so far. As Christ's witnesses, we need the character and special strength that only God gives.

3:6 The last sentence of this verse is literally translated "the letter kills, but the Spirit gives life." No one but Jesus has ever fulfilled the written law perfectly, and thus the whole world is condemned to death. The law makes people realize their sin, but it cannot give life. Eternal life comes from the Holy Spirit, who gives new life to all who believe in Christ. The moral law is still helpful to point out sin and show us how to live a life pleasing to God, but forgiveness comes only through the grace and mercy of Christ (see Romans 7:10—8:2).

3:7–11 Jesus Christ is far superior to the Old Testament ceremonial order (see Hebrews 8, 10 for a more complete discussion). That is saying a lot, because God himself gave the law amidst dazzling splendor. The law served its purpose until it could be translated into each person's heart by the Holy Spirit.

3:14–18 When Moses came down Mount Sinai with the Ten Commandments, his face glowed from being in God's presence (Exodus 34:29–35). He put on a veil to keep the people from being terrified by the brightness of his face. Paul adds that his veil kept them from seeing the glory fade away. Moses and his veil illustrate the fading of the old system and the veiling of the people's minds and hearts. The Jews' heritage was like a veil of pride that kept them from understanding the references to Christ in the Scriptures. When anyone becomes a Christian, Christ must remove his or her veil of pride (3:16). Don't let pride in your past keep you from eternity.

though Jewish hearts and minds are covered by a thick veil, because they cannot see and understand the real meaning of the Scriptures. For this veil of misunderstanding can be removed only by believing in Christ. 15Yes, even today when they read Moses' writings their hearts are blind and they think that obeying the Ten Commandments is the way to be saved.

16But whenever anyone turns to the Lord from his sins, then the veil is taken away. 17The Lord is the Spirit who gives them life, and where he is there is freedom [from trying to be saved by keeping the laws of God]. 18But we Christians have no veil over our faces; we can be mirrors that brightly reflect the glory of the Lord. And as the Spirit of the Lord works within us, we become more and more like him.

3:16
Isa 25:7
Rom 11:23
1 Cor 2:10

3:17
Rom 8:9
1 Cor 15:45
Gal 4:6
Phil 1:19

3:18
Rom 8:29
2 Cor 4:4,6
Col 3:10

Satan blinds, but God gives light

4 It is God himself, in his mercy, who has given us this wonderful work [of telling his Good News to others], and so we never give up. 2We do not try to trick people into believing—we are not interested in fooling anyone. We never try to get anyone to believe that the Bible teaches what it doesn't. All such shameful methods we forego. We stand in the presence of God as we speak and so we tell the truth, as all who know us will agree.

3If the Good News we preach is hidden to anyone, it is hidden from the one who is on the road to eternal death. 4Satan, who is the god of this evil world, has made him blind, unable to see the glorious light of the Gospel that is shining upon him, or to understand the amazing message we preach about the glory of Christ, who is God. 5We don't go around preaching about ourselves, but about Christ Jesus as Lord. All we say of ourselves is that we are your slaves because of what Jesus has done for us. 6For God, who said, "Let there be light in the darkness," has made us understand that it is the brightness of his glory that is seen in the face of Jesus Christ.

7But this precious treasure—this light and power that now shine within us—is held in a perishable container, that is, in our weak bodies. Everyone can see that the glorious power within must be from God and is not our own.

8We are pressed on every side by troubles, but not crushed and broken. We are perplexed because we don't know why things happen as they do, but we don't give up and quit. 9We are hunted down, but God never abandons us. We get knocked

4:2
2 Cor 2:17
1 Thess 2:3,5

4:3
Isa 6:9
1 Cor 1:18
2 Cor 3:14

4:4
Isa 6:10
Jn 1:18
12:31,40,45
2 Cor 3:14
Eph 6:12
Col 1:15
Heb 1:3

4:5
1 Cor 9:19

4:6
Gen 1:3
Ps 36:9
Jn 8:12; 12:46
Eph 5:8,14
1 Pet 2:9
2 Pet 1:19

4:7
2 Cor 5:1
2 Tim 2:20

4:8
2 Cor 7:5

4:9
Rom 8:35,36

3:17 *from trying to be saved by keeping the laws of God,* implied.   **4:1** *of telling his Good News to others,* implied.
4:4 *who is God,* literally, "who is the image of God."   **4:7** *this light and power that now shine within us,* implied.

3:17 When the Lord Jesus rose from the dead, he became life-giving Spirit (1 Corinthians 15:45). This does not mean that Jesus is now without a body or that he became the Holy Spirit; it means that he entered into a new form of existence when he was glorified. As such, he can live in heaven and in the hearts of the believers at the same time. Admittedly, this is a mystery; but those who know that Christ lives within them appreciate the reality of his presence.

3:17, 18 The glory that the Spirit imparts to the believer is greater both in quality and longevity than that which Moses experienced. The glory gradually transforms the believer into Christlikeness. Becoming Christlike is a progressive experience (see Romans 8:29; Galatians 4:19; Philippians 3:21; 1 John 3:2). The more closely we relate to him, the more we will be like him.

4:2 Preachers, teachers, and anyone who talks about Jesus Christ must remember that they stand in God's presence—he hears every word. When you tell people about Christ, be careful not to distort the message to please the audience. Proclaim the truth of God's Word.

4:3, 4 The Good News is open and revealed to everyone, except to those who refuse to believe. Satan's work is to deceive, and those who don't believe have been blinded by him (see 11:14, 15). The allure of money, power, and pleasure makes God's offer seem irrelevant. But those who refuse Christ, preferring their worldly lives, have made Satan their god.

4:5 The focus of Paul's preaching was Christ, not himself. When you witness, tell people about what Christ has done, and not about your abilities and accomplishments. People must be introduced to Christ, not to you. And if you hear someone preaching himself or his own ideas rather than Christ, beware—he is a false teacher.

4:5 Paul willingly served the Corinthian church despite the disappointments the people brought him. Any service requires a sacrifice of time and personal desires. Being Christ's follower means serving others, even when they do not measure up to our expectations.

4:7 The supremely valuable message of salvation in Jesus Christ has been entrusted by God to frail and fallible human beings. Paul's focus, however, is not on the perishable container but on its priceless contents—God's power dwelling in us. Though we are weak, God uses us to spread his Good News and gives us power to do his work. Knowing that the power is his, not ours, keeps us from pride and motivates us to keep daily contact with God, our power source. Our responsibility is to let people see God through us.

4:8–12 Paul reminds us that though we may be at the end of our rope, we are never at the end of hope. Our perishable bodies are subject to sin and suffering, but God never abandons us. Because Christ won victory over death, we have eternal life. All our risks, humiliations, and trials are opportunities to demonstrate Christ's power and presence in us.

4:10
Rom 8:17
1 Cor 15:31
Gal 6:17
Phil 3:10
Col 1:24
2 Tim 2:11
1 Pet 4:13

4:13
Ps 116:10

4:14
Acts 2:24
1 Thess 2:19

4:15
2 Cor 1:6,11

4:16
Eph 3:16
Col 3:10

4:17
Rom 8:18
1 Pet 1:6,7

4:18
Rom 8:24
2 Cor 5:7

5:1
1 Cor 15:47
2 Cor 4:7
Phil 3:21
Heb 11:10
2 Pet 1:13

5:2
Rom 8:23
1 Cor 15:53

5:3
Rom 3:18

5:4
1 Cor 15:53,54

5:5
Rom 8:23
2 Cor 1:22
Eph 1:14

down, but we get up again and keep going. ¹⁰These bodies of ours are constantly facing death just as Jesus did; so it is clear to all that it is only the living Christ within [who keeps us safe].

¹¹Yes, we live under constant danger to our lives because we serve the Lord, but this gives us constant opportunities to show forth the power of Jesus Christ within our dying bodies. ¹²Because of our preaching we face death, but it has resulted in eternal life for you.

¹³We boldly say what we believe [trusting God to care for us], just as the Psalm writer did when he said, "I believe and therefore I speak." ¹⁴We know that the same God who brought the Lord Jesus back from death will also bring us back to life again with Jesus, and present us to him along with you. ¹⁵These sufferings of ours are for your benefit. And the more of you who are won to Christ, the more there are to thank him for his great kindness, and the more the Lord is glorified.

¹⁶That is why we never give up. Though our bodies are dying, our inner strength in the Lord is growing every day. ¹⁷These troubles and sufferings of ours are, after all, quite small and won't last very long. Yet this short time of distress will result in God's richest blessing upon us forever and ever! ¹⁸So we do not look at what we can see right now, the troubles all around us, but we look forward to the joys in heaven which we have not yet seen. The troubles will soon be over, but the joys to come will last forever.

Earthly bodies are weak

5 For we know that when this tent we live in now is taken down—when we die and leave these bodies—we will have wonderful new bodies in heaven, homes that will be ours forevermore, made for us by God himself, and not by human hands. ²How weary we grow of our present bodies. That is why we look forward eagerly to the day when we shall have heavenly bodies which we shall put on like new clothes. ³For we shall not be merely spirits without bodies. ⁴These earthly bodies make us groan and sigh, but we wouldn't like to think of dying and having no bodies at all. We want to slip into our new bodies so that these dying bodies will, as it were, be swallowed up by everlasting life. ⁵This is what God has prepared for us and, as a guarantee, he has given us his Holy Spirit.

⁶Now we look forward with confidence to our heavenly bodies, realizing that every moment we spend in these earthly bodies is time spent away from our eternal

4:10 who keeps us safe, implied.   **4:13** trusting God to care for us, implied.

4:15-18 Paul faced sufferings, trials, and distress as he preached the Good News, but he knew that they would one day be over and he would obtain God's great blessings. As we face great troubles, it's easy to focus on the pain rather than on our ultimate goal. Just as athletes concentrate on the finish line and ignore their discomfort, we too must focus on the reward for our faith and the joy that lasts forever. No matter what happens to us in this life, we have the assurance of eternal life where all suffering will end.

4:16 It is easy to quit. We all have faced problems in our relationships or work that caused us to want to lay down the tools and walk away. Rather than giving up, however, Paul concentrated on developing his inner strength. Don't let fatigue, pain, or criticism force you off the job. Renew your commitment to serving Christ. Don't forsake your eternal reward because of the intensity of today's pain. Your very weakness allows the resurrection power of Christ to strengthen you moment by moment.

4:18 Our troubles should not diminish our faith or disillusion us. Instead, we should realize that there is a purpose in our suffering. Problems and human limitations have several benefits: (1) they help us remember Christ's suffering for us; (2) they help keep us from pride; (3) they help us look beyond this brief life; (4) they prove our faith to others; and (5) they give God the opportunity to demonstrate his great power. Don't resent your troubles—see them as opportunities!

5:1-10 Greeks did not believe in a bodily resurrection. Most saw

the afterlife as something that happened only to the soul—the real person, imprisoned in a physical body. At death the soul was released. There was no immortality for the body, but the soul entered an eternal state. But the Bible teaches that the body and soul are ultimately inseparable. The church at Corinth was in the heart of Greek culture, and many believers had difficulty with the concept of bodily resurrection.

Paul describes our resurrected bodies in more detail in 1 Corinthians 15:46-58. We will still have our own personalities and individualities in our resurrected bodies, but they will be made better than we can imagine through Christ's work. Scripture is unclear about what our resurrected bodies will be like, but we know they will be perfect, without sickness or disease (see Philippians 3:21).

5:1-5 The Holy Spirit within us is our guarantee that God has reserved for us brand-new everlasting bodies that he will give us at the resurrection (1:22). We have eternity in us now! Such hope should give us great courage and patience to endure anything we might experience.

5:6-8 Death is frightening for many people because it is mysterious and unknown. Paul was not afraid to die because he was confident of spending eternity with Christ. Of course, facing the unknown is cause for anxiety and leaving loved ones hurts deeply, but if we believe in Jesus Christ, we can share Paul's hope and confidence of eternal life with Christ.

home in heaven with Jesus. 7We know these things are true by believing, not by
seeing. 8And we are not afraid, but are quite content to die, for then we will be at
home with the Lord. 9So our aim is to please him always in everything we do,
whether we are here in this body or away from this body and with him in heaven.
10For we must all stand before Christ to be judged and have our lives laid bare—before him. Each of us will receive whatever he deserves for the good or bad things
he has done in his earthly body.

Be reconciled to God

11It is because of this solemn fear of the Lord, which is ever present in our minds,
that we work so hard to win others. God knows our hearts, that they are pure in this
matter, and I hope that, deep within, you really know it too.

12Are we trying to pat ourselves on the back again? No, I am giving you some
good ammunition! You can use this on those preachers of yours who brag about
how well they look and preach, but don't have true and honest hearts. You can
boast about us that we, at least, are well intentioned and honest.

13, 14Are we insane [to say such things about ourselves]? If so, it is to bring glory
to God. And if we are in our right minds, it is for your benefit. Whatever we do, it
is certainly not for our own profit, but because Christ's love controls us now. Since
we believe that Christ died for all of us, we should also believe that we have died
to the old life we used to live. 15He died for all so that all who live—having
received eternal life from him—might live no longer for themselves, to please
themselves, but to spend their lives pleasing Christ who died and rose again for
them. 16So stop evaluating Christians by what the world thinks about them or by
what they seem to be like on the outside. Once I mistakenly thought of Christ that
way, merely as a human being like myself. How differently I feel now! 17When
someone becomes a Christian he becomes a brand new person inside. He is not the
same any more. A new life has begun!

18All these new things are from God who brought us back to himself through
what Christ Jesus did. And God has given us the privilege of urging everyone to
come into his favor and be reconciled to him. 19For God was in Christ, restoring the
world to himself, no longer counting men's sins against them but blotting them out.
This is the wonderful message he has given us to tell others. 20We are Christ's
ambassadors. God is using us to speak to you: we beg you, as though Christ himself
were here pleading with you, receive the love he offers you—be reconciled to God.
21For God took the sinless Christ and poured into him our sins. Then, in exchange,
he poured God's goodness into us!

5:7
1 Cor 13:12

5:8
Phil 1:23

5:10
Mt 16:27
Acts 10:42
1 Cor 3:13-15
Rev 22:12

5:12
2 Cor 1:14; 3:1

5:14
Rom 5:15
Gal 2:20

5:15
Rom 14:7-9
1 Pet 4:2

5:16
Mt 12:50

5:17
Isa 65:17
Gal 6:15
Eph 4:24
Rev 21:5

5:18
Rom 5:10
Col 1:20-22

5:19
Isa 43:25
Rom 3:24; 4:28

5:20
Rom 5:10

5:21
Isa 53:6,9
Jer 23:6
Dan 9:24
Rom 1:17
Gal 3:13
Heb 4:15; 7:26
1 Pet 2:22

5:13, 14 to say such things about ourselves, implied.   **5:21** he poured God's goodness into us, literally, "Him who
knew no sin, he made sin on our behalf, that we might become the righteousness of God in him."

5:8 Death is not the last word. For those who believe in Christ,
death is only a prelude to eternal life with God. Our lives will
continue, both in body and in spirit. Let this confident hope inspire
you to faithful service.

5:9, 10 While eternal life is a free gift given on the basis of God's
grace (Ephesians 2:8, 9), our lives will still be judged by Christ.
This judgment is for rewards for how we have lived. Faith does not
free us from obedience. We must never use God's grace as an
excuse for laziness. All Christians must give account for how they
have lived (see Matthew 16:27; Romans 14:10–12; 1 Corinthians
3:10–15).

5:12 The false preachers or hucksters (see 2:17) were concerned
only about getting ahead in this world. They were preaching the
gospel for money, while Paul and his companions were preaching
out of concern for eternity. You can tell who false preachers are by
noticing what really motivates them. If they are more concerned
about themselves than Christ, they are false. Avoid them and their
message.

5:16, 17 Christians are brand new people on the *inside*. The Holy
Spirit gives them new life, and they are not the same any more. We

are not reformed, rehabilitated, or reeducated—we are new
creations, living in vital union with Christ (Colossians 2:6, 7). We
are not merely turning over a new leaf; we are beginning a new life
under a new Master.

5:18–21 God brings us back to himself (reconciles us) by blotting
out our sins (see also Ephesians 2:13–18) and making us
righteous. We are no longer strangers, foreigners, or enemies to
God when we trust in Christ. Because we have been reconciled to
God, he now gives us the privilege of encouraging others to do the
same.

5:20 An ambassador is an official representative from one country
to another. As believers, we are Christ's ambassadors, sent with
his message of reconciliation to the world. An ambassador of
reconciliation has an important responsibility. We dare not take this
responsibility lightly. How well are you fulfilling your commission as
Christ's ambassador?

5:21 When we trust in Christ, we make a trade—our sin for his
goodness. Our sin was poured into Christ at his crucifixion. His
righteousness is poured into us at our conversion. This is what
Christians mean by Christ's atonement for sin. In the world,

6:1
1 Cor 3:9
2 Cor 5:20
Heb 12:15

6:2
Isa 49:8

6 As God's partners we beg you not to toss aside this marvelous message of God's great kindness. 2For God says, "Your cry came to me at a favorable time, when the doors of welcome were wide open. I helped you on a day when salvation was being offered." Right now God is ready to welcome you. Today he is ready to save you.

Paul patiently endures hardship

6:3
1 Cor 8:9; 9:12

6:4
2 Cor 4:8
11:23-28

6:5
Acts 16:23
1 Cor 4:11

6:6
2 Cor 11:6

6:7
1 Cor 2:4
2 Cor 2:17; 4:2
10:4

6:8
Mt 27:63
Rom 3:8
1 Cor 4:10,13
2 Cor 4:2

6:9
Ps 118:18
Rom 8:36
1 Cor 4:9
2 Cor 1:8; 4:11

6:10
Acts 3:6
Rom 8:32
1 Cor 3:21
2 Cor 8:9

6:11
2 Cor 7:3

6:12
2 Cor 12:15

3We try to live in such a way that no one will ever be offended or kept back from finding the Lord by the way we act, so that no one can find fault with us and blame it on the Lord. 4In fact, in everything we do we try to show that we are true ministers of God.

We patiently endure suffering and hardship and trouble of every kind. 5We have been beaten, put in jail, faced angry mobs, worked to exhaustion, stayed awake through sleepless nights of watching, and gone without food. 6We have proved ourselves to be what we claim by our wholesome lives and by our understanding of the Gospel and by our patience. We have been kind and truly loving and filled with the Holy Spirit. 7We have been truthful, with God's power helping us in all we do. All of the godly man's arsenal—weapons of defense, and weapons of attack—have been ours.

8We stand true to the Lord whether others honor us or despise us, whether they criticize us or commend us. We are honest, but they call us liars.

9The world ignores us, but we are known to God; we live close to death, but here we are, still very much alive. We have been injured but kept from death. 10Our hearts ache, but at the same time we have the joy of the Lord. We are poor, but we give rich spiritual gifts to others. We own nothing, and yet we enjoy everything.

11Oh, my dear Corinthian friends! I have told you all my feelings; I love you with all my heart. 12Any coldness still between us is not because of any lack of love on my part, but because your love is too small and does not reach out to me and draw me in. 13I am talking to you now as if you truly were my very own children. Open your hearts to us! Return our love!

Be separate from unbelievers

14Don't be teamed with those who do not love the Lord, for what do the people of God have in common with the people of sin? How can light live with darkness? 15And what harmony can there be between Christ and the devil? How can a

---

bartering works only when two people exchange goods of relatively equal value. But God offers to trade righteousness for sin—something of immeasurable worth for something worthless. How grateful we should be for his goodness to us.

6:1 How could the Corinthian believers toss aside God's message? Perhaps they were doubting Paul and his words, confused by the false teachers who taught a different message. "To toss aside this message" can also be translated "to receive the grace of God in vain." The people heard God's message, but did not let it affect what they said and did. How often does God's message reach you in vain?

6:2 God is now offering salvation to all people. Sometimes we put off a decision for Christ, thinking there will be a better time—but we could easily miss our opportunity altogether. There is no time like the present to receive God's forgiveness. Don't let anything hold you back from God.

6:3, 4 In everything he did, Paul always considered what his actions communicated about Jesus Christ. If you are a believer, you are a minister for God. In the course of each day, non-Christians observe you. Consider whether your actions will keep anyone from God. Don't let your careless or undisciplined actions be another's excuse for rejecting God.

6:7 See Ephesians 6:10-18 for more about the weapons of faith.

6:8–10 What a difference knowing Jesus can make! He turns

everything around, caring for us in spite of what the world thinks. Christians don't have to give in to public opinion and pressure. Paul stood true to God whether people praised him or condemned him. He remained active, joyous, and content in the most difficult conditions. Don't let circumstances or people's expectations control you. Be firm as you stand true to God, and refuse to compromise on his standards for living.

6:12, 13 It is easy to react against those whom God has placed over us in leadership rather than to accept their exhortations as a sign of their love for us. We need an open heart rather than a hardened heart toward God's messengers.

6:14–17 Paul urged believers not to form binding relationships with nonbelievers, because this might weaken their Christian commitment, integrity, or standards. Earlier, Paul had explained that this did not mean isolating themselves from nonbelievers (see 1 Corinthians 5:9, 10). Paul even told Christians to stay with their nonbelieving spouses (1 Corinthians 7:12, 13). Paul wanted believers to be active in their witness for Christ to nonbelievers, but they should not lock themselves into personal or business relationships which could cause them to compromise their faith. Just as those in business should avoid conflicts of interest, believers should avoid situations that would force them to divide their loyalties.

Christian be a partner with one who doesn't believe? 16And what union can there be between God's temple and idols? For you are God's temple, the home of the living God, and God has said of you, "I will live in them and walk among them, and I will be their God and they shall be my people." 17That is why the Lord has said, "Leave them; separate yourselves from them; don't touch their filthy things, and I will welcome you, 18and be a Father to you, and you will be my sons and daughters."

7 Having such great promises as these, dear friends, let us turn away from everything wrong, whether of body or spirit, and purify ourselves, living in the wholesome fear of God, giving ourselves to him alone.

The church's repentance gives Paul joy

2Please open your hearts to us again, for not one of you has suffered any wrong from us. Not one of you was led astray. We have cheated no one nor taken advantage of anyone. 3I'm not saying this to scold or blame you, for, as I have said before, you are in my heart forever and I live and die with you. 4I have the highest confidence in you, and my pride in you is great. You have greatly encouraged me; you have made me so happy in spite of all my suffering.

5When we arrived in Macedonia there was no rest for us; outside, trouble was on every hand and all around us; within us, our hearts were full of dread and fear. 6Then God who cheers those who are discouraged refreshed us by the arrival of Titus. 7Not only was his presence a joy, but also the news that he brought of the wonderful time he had with you. When he told me how much you were looking forward to my visit, and how sorry you were about what had happened, and about your loyalty and warm love for me, well, I overflowed with joy!

8I am no longer sorry that I sent that letter to you, though I was very sorry for a time, realizing how painful it would be to you. But it hurt you only for a little while. 9Now I am glad I sent it, not because it hurt you, but because the pain turned you to God. It was a good kind of sorrow you felt, the kind of sorrow God wants his people to have, so that I need not come to you with harshness. 10For God sometimes uses sorrow in our lives to help us turn away from sin and seek eternal life. We should never regret his sending it. But the sorrow of the man who is not a Christian is not the sorrow of true repentance and does not prevent eternal death.

6:16
Ex 25:8; 29:45
Jer 31:33
Ezek 36:28

6:17
Isa 52:11

6:18
Jer 31:1,9
Hos 1:10

7:1
1 Pet 1:22
1 Jn 3:3

7:2
2 Cor 6:12

7:3
2 Cor 6:11

7:4
1 Cor 1:4
2 Cor 7:14; 8:24
10:8
Phil 2:17

7:5
2 Cor 2:13; 4:8

7:6
2 Cor 2:13; 7:13
2 Thess 2:16

7:8
2 Cor 2:2-4

7:10
2 Sam 12:13
Jer 31:18-20
Mt 26:75
27:4,5

Method	Reference	PRINCIPLES
Be firm	7:9; 10:2	OF
Affirm all you see that is good	7:4	CONFRON-
Be accurate and honest	7:14; 8:21	TATION IN
Know the facts	11:22–27	2 CORINTHIANS
Follow up after the confrontation	7:13; 12:14	
Be gentle after being firm	7:15; 13:11–13	
Speak words that reflect Christ's message, not your own ideas	10:3; 10:12, 13; 12:19	
Use discipline only when all else fails	13:2	

Sometimes rebuke is necessary, but it must be used with caution. The purpose of any rebuke, confrontation, or discipline is to help people, not hurt them.

6:17 Separation from the world involves more than keeping our distance from sinners; it means staying close to God (see 7:1, 2). It involves more than avoiding entertainment that leads to sin; it extends as well into how we spend our time and money. In this fallen world, there is no way to separate ourselves totally from all effects of sin. Nevertheless, we are to resist the sin around us, not give up and give in.

7:1 Purifying ourselves is a twofold action: turning *away* from sin, and turning *toward* God.

7:5 Here Paul resumes the story he left off in 2:13, where he says he went to Macedonia to look for Titus.

7:8ff "That letter" refers to the third letter (now lost) that Paul wrote the Corinthians. Apparently it had caused the people to begin to change. For an explanation of the chronology of Paul's letters to Corinth, see the note on 1:1.

7:10 True repentance means being sorry for our sins and changing our behavior. Many people are sorry only for the effects of their sins or for being caught. Compare Peter's remorse and repentance with Judas' bitterness and suicide. Both denied Christ. One repented and was restored to faith and service; the other took his own life.

7:11
Jer 50:4,5
Zech 12:10
2 Cor 2:6

11Just see how much good this grief from the Lord did for you! You no longer shrugged your shoulders, but became earnest and sincere, and very anxious to get rid of the sin that I wrote you about. You became frightened about what had happened, and longed for me to come and help. You went right to work on the problem and cleared it up [punishing the man who sinned]. You have done everything you could to make it right.

7:12
1 Cor 5:1-5

12I wrote as I did so the Lord could show how much you really do care for us. That was my purpose even more than to help the man who sinned, or his father to whom he did the wrong.

7:13
Rom 15:32
2 Cor 2:13; 7:6

13In addition to the encouragement you gave us by your love, we were made happier still by Titus' joy when you gave him such a fine welcome and set his mind at ease. 14I told him how it would be—told him before he left me of my pride in you—and you didn't disappoint me. I have always told you the truth and now my

7:15
2 Cor 2:9
Phil 2:12

boasting to Titus has also proved true! 15He loves you more than ever when he remembers the way you listened to him so willingly and received him so anxiously

7:16
2 Cor 2:3
2 Thess 3:4
Philem 21

and with such deep concern. 16How happy this makes me, now that I am sure all is well between us again. Once again I can have perfect confidence in you.

3. Paul defends the collection
Generous giving glorifies the Lord

8:1
Acts 16:9

8 Now I want to tell you what God in his grace has done for the churches in Macedonia.

8:4
Acts 24:17
Rom 15:25
1 Cor 16:1,3

2Though they have been going through much trouble and hard times, they have mixed their wonderful joy with their deep poverty, and the result has been an overflow of giving to others. 3They gave not only what they could afford, but far more; and I can testify that they did it because they wanted to, and not because of

8:5
Mt 25:40
Heb 13:16

nagging on my part. 4They begged us to take the money so they could share in the joy of helping the Christians in Jerusalem. 5Best of all, they went beyond our

7:11 *punishing the man who sinned,* implied. So also in vs 12.

NEEDS FOR A FUNDRAISING PROJECT		
Information	8:4
Definite purpose	8:4
Readiness and willingness	9:7
Dedication	8:5
Leadership	8:7
Enthusiasm	8:7, 8, 11
Persistence	8:2ff
Honesty and integrity	8:21
Accountability	9:3
Someone to keep it moving	8:18–22

The topic of fundraising is not one to be avoided or one that should embarrass us, but all fundraising efforts should be planned and conducted responsibly.

7:11 It is difficult to hear that we have sinned, and even more difficult to get rid of sin. Paul praised the Corinthians for clearing up an especially troublesome situation (see note on 2:5–11). Do you tend to be defensive when confronted? Don't let pride keep you from admitting your sins. Accept confrontation as a tool for growth, and do all you can to correct problems that are pointed out to you.

8:1ff Paul, writing from Macedonia, hoped that news of the generosity of these churches would encourage the Corinthian believers and motivate them to solve their problems and unite in fellowship.

8:2 While making his third missionary journey, Paul was collecting money for the impoverished believers in Jerusalem. The churches in Macedonia—Philippi, Thessalonica, and Beroea—gave money even though they were poor, and they gave more than Paul

expected. This was sacrificial giving—they were poor themselves, but they wanted to help. The point of giving is not so much the amount we give, but why and how we give. God does not want gifts given grudgingly. Instead, he wants us to give as these churches did—out of dedication to him, love for fellow believers, the joy of helping those in need, and because it was right to do so. How well does your giving measure up to the standards set by the Macedonian churches?

8:3–6 Through believers' concern and eagerness to help others, the Kingdom of God spreads. Here we see several churches joining to help others beyond their own circle of friends and their own city. Explore ways you might link up with a ministry outside your city, either through your church or through a Christian organization. By joining with other believers to do God's work, you increase Christian unity and help the Kingdom to grow.

highest hopes, for their first action was to dedicate themselves to the Lord and to us, for whatever directions God might give to them through us. 6They were so enthusiastic about it that we have urged Titus, who encouraged your giving in the first place, to visit you and encourage you to complete your share in this ministry of giving. 7You people there are leaders in so many ways—you have so much faith, so many good preachers, so much learning, so much enthusiasm, so much love for us. Now I want you to be leaders also in the spirit of cheerful giving.

8I am not giving you an order; I am not saying you must do it, but others are eager for it. This is one way to prove that your love is real, that it goes beyond mere words.

9You know how full of love and kindness our Lord Jesus was: though he was so very rich, yet to help you he became so very poor, so that by being poor he could make you rich.

10I want to suggest that you finish what you started to do a year ago, for you were not only the first to propose this idea, but the first to begin doing something about it. 11Having started the ball rolling so enthusiastically, you should carry this project through to completion just as gladly, giving whatever you can out of whatever you have. Let your enthusiastic idea at the start be equalled by your realistic action now. 12If you are really eager to give, then it isn't important how much you have to give. God wants you to give what you have, not what you haven't.

13Of course, I don't mean that those who receive your gifts should have an easy time of it at your expense, 14but you should divide with them. Right now you have plenty and can help them; then at some other time they can share with you when you need it. In this way each will have as much as he needs. 15Do you remember what the Scriptures say about this? "He that gathered much had nothing left over, and he that gathered little had enough." So you also should share with those in need.

16I am thankful to God that he has given Titus the same real concern for you that I have. 17He is glad to follow my suggestion that he visit you again—but I think he would have come anyway, for he is very eager to see you! 18I am sending another well-known brother with him, who is highly praised as a preacher of the Good News in all the churches. 19In fact, this man was elected by the churches to travel with me to take the gift to Jerusalem. This will glorify the Lord and show our

8:6
2 Cor 12:18

8:7
Prov 22:9; 28:27
Mt 19:21
Mk 10:21
Lk 18:22
1 Cor 1:5; 12:13
2 Cor 9:8

8:9
Mt 8:20
Lk 9:58
Phil 2:6,7

8:10
Prov 19:17
Mt 10:42
1 Tim 6:18
Heb 13:16

8:12
Mk 12:43
2 Cor 9:7

8:14
Acts 4:34,35

8:15
Ex 16:18

8:16
2 Cor 2:13,14
8:17
2 Cor 12:18
8:18
2 Cor 12:18
8:19
Acts 14:23
1 Cor 16:3

8:7, 8 Giving is a natural response of love. Paul did not order the Corinthians to give, but he encouraged them to prove that their love was real. When you love someone, you want to give him your time and attention and to provide for his needs. If you refuse to help, your love may not be as genuine as you say.

8:9 Jesus became poor by giving up his rights as God and becoming human. Incarnation means God voluntarily becoming man—the wholly human person, Jesus of Nazareth. As a man, Jesus was subject to place, time, and all other human attributes. He did not give up his eternal power to become human, but he did set aside his glory and his rights. In response to the Father's will, he limited his power and knowledge. What made Jesus' humanity unique was his freedom from sin. In his full humanity, we can see everything about God's character which can be conveyed in human terms. The incarnation is explained further in these Bible passages: John 1:1–14; Romans 1:2–5; Philippians 2:6–11; 1 Timothy 3:16; Hebrews 2:14; 1 John 1:1–3.

8:10–15 The Corinthian church had money, and Paul challenged them to share with the Jerusalem Christians just as the Macedonian churches had done. Four principles of giving emerge here: (1) your willingness to give cheerfully is more important than the amount you give; (2) you should strive to fulfill your financial commitments; (3) if you give to others in need, they will in turn help you when you are in need. (4) Nevertheless, you should give as a response to Christ, not for anything you can get out of it. How you give reflects your devotion to Christ. These principles apply regardless of your financial condition.

8:11 How do you decide how much to give? Paul gave the Corinthian church several principles to follow: (1) each person should follow through on previous promises (8:10; 9:3); (2) each person should give as much as he is able (8:12; 9:6); (3) each person must make up his own mind how much to give (9:7); and (4) each person should give in proportion to what God has given (9:10). God gives to us so we can give to others.

8:12 The attitude with which we give is more important than the amount we give. We don't have to be embarrassed if we can give only a small gift. God is concerned about *how* we give from the resources we have (see Mark 12:41–44). According to this standard, the giving of the Macedonian churches was difficult to match.

8:12 Paul says, "God wants you to give what you have, not what you haven't." Sacrificial giving must be responsible. Paul wants believers to give generously, but not to the point where those who depend on the givers must go without having their basic needs met. Give until it hurts, but don't give so that it hurts those people who depend on you (i.e., your family and/or relatives needing your financial support).

8:18–21 Paul chose more than one person to carry the gift so there would be no suspicion over the way the money was handled. The people whom Paul sent were well recommended. The church did not need to worry that these were false teachers or that they would misuse the money.

eagerness to help each other. 20By traveling together we will guard against any suspicion, for we are anxious that no one should find fault with the way we are handling this large gift. 21God knows we are honest, but I want everyone else to know it too. That is why we have made this arrangement.

22And I am sending you still another brother, whom we know from experience to be an earnest Christian. He is especially interested, as he looks forward to this trip, because I have told him all about your eagerness to help.

23If anyone asks who Titus is, say that he is my partner, my helper in helping you, and you can also say that the other two brothers represent the assemblies here and are splendid examples of those who belong to the Lord.

24Please show your love for me to these men and do for them all that I have publicly boasted you would.

- *God prizes cheerful givers*

9 I realize that I really don't even need to mention this to you, about helping God's people. 2For I know how eager you are to do it, and I have boasted to the friends in Macedonia that you were ready to send an offering a year ago. In fact, it was this enthusiasm of yours that stirred up many of them to begin helping. 3But I am sending these men just to be sure that you really are ready, as I told them you would be, with your money all collected; I don't want it to turn out that this time I was wrong in my boasting about you. 4I would be very much ashamed—and so would you—if some of these Macedonian people come with me, only to find that you still aren't ready after all I have told them!

5So I have asked these other brothers to arrive ahead of me to see that the gift you promised is on hand and waiting. I want it to be a real gift and not look as if it were being given under pressure.

6But remember this—if you give little, you will get little. A farmer who plants just a few seeds will get only a small crop, but if he plants much, he will reap much. 7Every one must make up his own mind as to how much he should give. Don't force anyone to give more than he really wants to, for cheerful givers are the ones God prizes. 8God is able to make it up to you by giving you everything you need and more, so that there will not only be enough for your own needs, but plenty left over to give joyfully to others. 9It is as the Scriptures say: "The godly man gives generously to the poor. His good deeds will be an honor to him forever."

10For God, who gives seed to the farmer to plant, and later on, good crops to harvest and eat, will give you more and more seed to plant and will make it grow so that you can give away more and more fruit from your harvest.

11Yes, God will give you much so that you can give away much, and when we take your gifts to those who need them they will break out into thanksgiving and praise to God for your help. 12So, two good things happen as a result of your gifts—those in need are helped, and they overflow with thanks to God. 13Those you help will be glad not only because of your generous gifts to themselves and to others, but they will praise God for this proof that your deeds are as good as your

8:21
Prov 3:4
Rom 12:17
Phil 4:8
1 Pet 2:12

8:23
Phil 2:25

8:24
2 Cor 7:4

9:1
Rom 15:26
1 Cor 16:1
Gal 2:10
1 Thess 4:9

9:2
2 Cor 8:6,17

9:3
1 Cor 16:2

9:5
Gen 33:11

9:6
Prov 11:24
19:17
Lk 6:38
Gal 6:7,9

9:7
Ex 35:5
Deut 15:7-10
Rom 12:8
2 Cor 8:12

9:8
Prov 28:27
Phil 4:19

9:9
Ps 112:9

9:10
Hos 10:12
Mt 6:1

9:11
2 Cor 1:11; 4:16

9:12
2 Cor 8:14

9:13
Mt 5:16
Heb 13:16

9:1 The example of giving here was at the heart of Jewish piety—for they showed their godliness by sharing with the poor. Christians today have forgotten this central idea of true godly living, largely because it is not tax-deductible! Of course, giving to organizations is still important, but we are urged to fulfill this biblical mandate by helping the poor, whether or not it is tax-deductible.

9:3, 4 Paul was reminding the Corinthians to fulfill the commitment they had already made (see also 8:10–12). He was holding them accountable to keep their promise.

9:6–8 People may hesitate to give generously to God if they worry about having enough money left over to meet their own needs. Paul assured the Corinthians that God is able to meet their needs. The person who gives only a little will receive only a little in return. Don't let a lack of faith keep you from giving freely and generously.

9:10 God gives us resources to use and invest for him. Paul used the illustration of seeds to explain that the resources God gives us are not to be hidden, foolishly devoured, or thrown away, but cultivated in order to produce more crops. When we invest what God has given us in his work, he will provide us with even more to give.

9:12 Paul emphasizes the spiritual rewards for those who give generously to God's work. We should not expect to become wealthy through giving; the rewards about which Paul speaks are treasures in heaven (see Matthew 6:19–21 for Jesus' teaching on this).

9:13, 14 Paul notes that those who receive your gifts will be glad and will pray for you. This is the unexpected result of giving—as you bless others, you yourself are blessed. Giving is a wonderful experience that only the generous fully enter into.

doctrine. 14And they will pray for you with deep fervor and feeling because of the wonderful grace of God shown through you.

15Thank God for his Son—his Gift too wonderful for words.

9:15
Jas 1:17

4. Paul defends his authority
Paul's authority is discredited

10 I plead with you—yes, I, Paul—and I plead gently, as Christ himself would do. Yet some of you are saying, "Paul's letters are bold enough when he is far away, but when he gets here he will be afraid to raise his voice!"

10:1
1 Cor 2:3
2 Cor 10:10

2I hope I won't need to show you when I come how harsh and rough I can be. I don't want to carry out my present plans against some of you who seem to think my deeds and words are merely those of an ordinary man. 3It is true that I am an ordinary, weak human being, but I don't use human plans and methods to win my battles. 4I use God's mighty weapons, not those made by men, to knock down the devil's strongholds. 5These weapons can break down every proud argument against God and every wall that can be built to keep men from finding him. With these weapons I can capture rebels and bring them back to God, and change them into men whose hearts' desire is obedience to Christ. 6I will use these weapons against every rebel who remains after I have first used them on you yourselves, and you surrender to Christ.

10:2
1 Cor 4:18,21
2 Cor 1:17; 13:2

10:4
Jer 1:10
1 Cor 9:7
Eph 6:13-17
1 Thess 5:8
10:5
Isa 2:11
1 Cor 1:19; 3:19
10:6
2 Cor 2:9; 7:15
13:2

7The trouble with you is that you look at me and I seem weak and powerless, but you don't look beneath the surface. Yet if anyone can claim the power and authority of Christ, I certainly can. 8I may seem to be boasting more than I should about my authority over you—authority to help you, not to hurt you—but I shall make good every claim. 9I say this so that you will not think I am just blustering when I scold you in my letters.

10:7
Jn 7:24
1 Cor 9:1; 14:37
2 Cor 11:23
1 Jn 4:6

10"Don't bother about his letters," some say. "He sounds big, but it's all noise. When he gets here you will see that there is nothing great about him, and you have never heard a worse preacher!" 11This time my personal presence is going to be just as rough on you as my letters are!

10:10
1 Cor 1:17; 2:3
2 Cor 11:6
Gal 4:13

12Oh, don't worry, I wouldn't dare say that I am as wonderful as these other men who tell you how good they are! Their trouble is that they are only comparing themselves with each other, and measuring themselves against their own little ideas. What stupidity!

10:12
2 Cor 3:1; 5:12

13But we will not boast of authority we do not have. Our goal is to measure up to God's plan for us, and this plan includes our working there with you. 14We are not going too far when we claim authority over you, for we were the first to come to you with the Good News concerning Christ. 15It is not as though we were trying to claim credit for the work someone else has done among you. Instead, we hope that your faith will grow and that, still within the limits set for us, our work among you will be greatly enlarged.

10:13
Rom 12:3
10:14
1 Cor 9:1
10:15
Rom 15:20
2 Thess 1:3

16After that, we will be able to preach the Good News to other cities that are far beyond you, where no one else is working; then there will be no question about

10:16
Acts 19:21

10:1 From 7:8–16 we know that the majority of Corinthian believers sided with Paul. However, a minority continued to slander him, saying that he was bold in his letters but had no authority in person. Chapters 10–13 are Paul's response to this charge.

10:3–6 The Christian must choose whose methods to use, God's or man's. Paul assures us that God's mighty weapons—prayer, faith, hope, love, God's Word, the Holy Spirit—are powerful and effective (see Ephesians 6:13–18)! When dealing with the pride that keeps people from a relationship with Christ, we may be tempted to use our own methods. But nothing can break down these barriers like God's weapons.

10:7–9 Paul reminded the Corinthians of his authority because of the opposition he was receiving from various people in their church. False teachers were encouraging them to ignore Paul, and

he wanted to protect the Corinthians from heresy.

10:10 Apparently Paul was not a powerful preacher (although he was an excellent debater). But he responded obediently to God's call, and he introduced Christianity to the Roman Empire. (Moses also had problems with speaking. Apparently preaching ability is not the first prerequisite of a powerful leader!)

10:12, 13 Paul criticized the false teachers who tried to prove their goodness by comparing themselves with others rather than with God. When we compare ourselves with others, we may feel proud because we think we're better. But when we measure ourselves against God's standards, it becomes obvious that we're not nearly good enough. Don't worry about how other people live. Instead, continually ask how your life measures up to what God wants you to be and how your life compares to that of Jesus Christ.

10:17
Jer 9:24
1 Cor 1:31

10:18
Prov 27:2

being in someone else's field. 17As the Scriptures say, "If anyone is going to boast, let him boast about what the Lord has done and not about himself." 18When someone boasts about himself and how well he has done, it doesn't count for much. But when the Lord commends him, that's different!

Paul and the false apostles

11:1
2 Cor 5:13

11:2
Hos 2:19
1 Cor 4:15

11 I hope you will be patient with me as I keep on talking like a fool. Do bear with me and let me say what is on my heart. 2I am anxious for you with the deep concern of God himself—anxious that your love should be for Christ alone, just as a pure maiden saves her love for one man only, for the one who will be her

---

PAUL'S	1:1; 1:21; 4:1	Commissioned by God
CREDENTIALS	1:18; 4:2	Spoke truthfully
One of Paul's	1:12	Acted with purity, sincerity, and dependence on God alone in his
biggest problems		dealings with them
with the church in	1:13, 14	Was straightforward and sincere in his letters
Corinth was his	1:22	Had God's Holy Spirit
concern that they	2:4; 6:11; 11:11	Loved the Corinthian believers
viewed him as no	2:17	Spoke with integrity and Christ's power
more than a	3:2, 3	Worked among them and changed their lives
blustering	3:4; 12:6	Lived as an example to the believers
preacher; thus,	4:1, 16	Never gave up
they were not	4:2	Taught the Bible with integrity
taking seriously	4:5	Had Christ as the center of his message
his advice in his	4:8–12; 6:4, 5, 9,	Endured persecution as he taught the Good News
letters and on his	10	
visits. Paul	5:11	Worked to win others and to please God
addressed this	5:12	Was well-intentioned and honest
attitude in the	5:18–20	Was Christ's ambassador, called to tell the Good News
letter of 2	6:3, 4	Tried to live a blameless life so others would not be kept from
Corinthians,		God because of his actions
pointing out his	6:6	Led a wholesome life, understood the gospel, and displayed
credentials as an		patience with the Corinthians
apostle of Christ	6:7	Was truthful and filled with God's power
and why they	6:8	Stood true to God first and always
should take his	7:2; 11:7–9	Never cheated, wronged, or took advantage of anyone
advice.	8:20, 21	Handled their money offering to be sent to Jerusalem in a
		responsible, blameless manner
	10:1–6	Used God's weapons, not his own, for God's work
	10:7, 8	Had the power and authority of Christ
	10:12, 13	Wanted to measure up to God's plan, not glorify himself
	10:14, 15	Had authority because he taught them the Good News
	11:23–33	Endured pain and danger as he fulfilled his calling
	12:2–4	Was blessed with an astounding vision
	12:7–10	Was constantly humbled by a "thorn in the flesh" that God
		refused to take away
	12:12	Did miracles among them
	12:19	Was always motivated to build up others spiritually
	13:4	Was filled with God's power
	13:5, 6	Stood the test
	13:9	Was always concerned that his spiritual children become mature
		believers

10:17, 18 When we do something well, we want to tell others and be recognized. But recognition is dangerous—it can lead to inflated pride. How much better to seek the praise of God rather than men. Interestingly, these two are usually opposites. To earn God's praise means giving up the praise of others. How should you live differently to receive God's commendation?

husband. ³But I am frightened, fearing that in some way you will be led away from your pure and simple devotion to our Lord, just as Eve was deceived by Satan in the Garden of Eden. ⁴You seem so gullible: you believe whatever anyone tells you even if he is preaching about another Jesus than the one we preach, or a different spirit than the Holy Spirit you received, or shows you a different way to be saved. You swallow it all.

⁵Yet I don't feel that these marvelous "messengers from God," as they call themselves, are any better than I am. ⁶If I am a poor speaker, at least I know what I am talking about, as I think you realize by now, for we have proved it again and again.

⁷Did I do wrong and cheapen myself and make you look down on me because I preached God's Good News to you without charging you anything? ⁸, ⁹Instead I "robbed" other churches by taking what they sent me, and using it up while I was with you, so that I could serve you without cost. And when that was gone and I was getting hungry I still didn't ask you for anything, for the Christians from Macedonia brought me another gift. I have never yet asked you for one cent, and I never will. ¹⁰I promise this with every ounce of truth I possess—that I will tell everyone in Greece about it! ¹¹Why? Because I don't love you? God knows I do. ¹²But I will do it to cut out the ground from under the feet of those who boast that they are doing God's work in just the same way we are.

¹³God never sent those men at all; they are "phonies" who have fooled you into thinking they are Christ's apostles. ¹⁴Yet I am not surprised! Satan can change himself into an angel of light, ¹⁵so it is no wonder his servants can do it too, and seem like godly ministers. In the end they will get every bit of punishment their wicked deeds deserve.

11:8, 9 *And when that was gone,* implied.

11:3
Gen 3:4
Jn 8:44
1 Thess 3:5
1 Tim 1:3; 4:1
2 Pet 3:17
Jude 4
Rev 12:9
11:4
Rom 8:15
Gal 1:6-8
11:5
2 Cor 12:11
Gal 2:6
11:6
2 Cor 10:10
Eph 3:4
11:7
Acts 18:3
2 Cor 12:13
11:9
2 Cor 12:14
11:11
2 Cor 7:3; 12:15
11:12
1 Cor 9:12
11:13
Gal 1:7
Rev 2:2
11:14
Rev 12:9
11:15
Rom 2:6; 3:8
Phil 3:19

11:3 The Corinthians' pure and simple devotion to Christ was being threatened by false teaching. Paul did not want the believers to lose their single-minded love for Christ. Keeping Christ first in our lives can be very difficult when we have so many distractions threatening to sidetrack our faith. As Eve lost her focus by listening to the serpent, we too can lose our focus by letting our lives become overcrowded and confused. Is there anything that threatens your ability to keep Christ first in your life? How can you minimize the distractions that threaten your devotion to Christ?

11:3, 4 The Corinthian believers fell for smooth talk and messages that sounded good and seemed to make sense. Today there are many false teachings that seem to make sense. Don't believe anyone simply because he sounds like an authority or says things you like to hear. Search the Bible and check people's words against God's Word. The Bible should be your authoritative guide to all teaching.

11:4 The false teachers distorted the truth about Christ and ended up preaching a different Christ, a different Spirit, and a different way of salvation. Because the Bible is God's infallible Word, those who teach anything different from what it says are both mistaken and misleading.

11:6 Paul, a brilliant thinker, may not have been a spellbinding speaker. Although his ministry was effective (see Acts 17), he was not trained in the Greek schools of oratory and speech making, as many of the false teachers probably were. Paul believed in a simple presentation of the gospel (see 1 Corinthians 1:17), and some people thought this showed simplemindedness. Thus his speaking performance was often used against him by false teachers. In all our teaching and preaching, we must make sure that the content is far more important than the presentation. Unless speaking methods help to make the message clear, they are useless. A simple, clear presentation that helps listeners understand, however, is of great value.

11:7 The Corinthians may have thought that preachers could be judged by how much money they demanded. A good speaker would charge a large sum, a fair speaker would be a little cheaper, and a poor speaker would speak for free. The false teachers may have argued that because Paul asked no fee for his preaching, he must be an amateur, with little authority. Believers today must be careful not to assume that every speaker who is well known and receives a large sum of money has something good to say.

11:7–12 Paul could have asked the Corinthian church for financial support. Jesus himself taught that those who minister for God should be supported by the people to whom they minister (Matthew 10:10). But Paul thought that asking for support in Corinth could be misunderstood. There were many false teachers who hoped to make a good profit from preaching (2:17), and Paul might look like one of them. Paul separated himself completely from these false teachers.

11:14 In one popular version of the story of Eve's temptation, Satan masqueraded as an angel. Paul may have been thinking of this story. In either case, nothing is farther from the truth than Satan, the prince of darkness (Ephesians 6:12; Colossians 1:13), pretending to represent the light. By the same token, when the false teachers claimed to represent Christ, they were lying shamelessly.

11:14, 15 Satan and his servants can deceive us by appearing attractive, good, and moral. Many unsuspecting people follow smooth-talking, Bible-quoting leaders into cults which alienate them from their families and practice immorality and deceit. Don't be fooled by external appearances. Our impressions alone are not an accurate indicator of who is or isn't a true follower of Christ; so it helps to ask these questions: (1) Do their teachings confirm Scripture (Acts 17:11)? (2) Do the teachers affirm and proclaim that Jesus Christ is God who came into the world as a man to save people from their sins (1 John 4:1–3)? (3) Is their lifestyle consistent with biblical morality (Matthew 12:33–37)?

Paul's many trials

16Again I plead, don't think that I have lost my wits to talk like this; but even if you do, listen to me anyway—a witless man, a fool—while I also boast a little as they do. 17Such bragging isn't something the Lord commanded me to do, for I am acting like a brainless fool. 18Yet those other men keep telling you how wonderful they are, so here I go: 19, 20(You think you are so wise—yet you listen gladly to those fools; you don't mind at all when they make you their slaves and take everything you have, and take advantage of you, and put on airs, and slap you in the face. 21I'm ashamed to say that I'm not strong and daring like that!

But whatever they can boast about—I'm talking like a fool again—I can boast about it, too.)

22They brag that they are Hebrews, do they? Well, so am I. And they say that they are Israelites, God's chosen people? So am I. And they are descendants of Abraham? Well, I am too.

23They say they serve Christ? But I have served him far more! (Have I gone mad to boast like this?) I have worked harder, been put in jail oftener, been whipped times without number, and faced death again and again and again. 24Five different times the Jews gave me their terrible thirty-nine lashes. 25Three times I was beaten with rods. Once I was stoned. Three times I was shipwrecked. Once I was in the open sea all night and the whole next day. 26I have traveled many weary miles and have been often in great danger from flooded rivers, and from robbers, and from my own people, the Jews, as well as from the hands of the Gentiles. I have faced grave dangers from mobs in the cities and from death in the deserts and in the stormy seas and from men who claim to be brothers in Christ but are not. 27I have lived with weariness and pain and sleepless nights. Often I have been hungry and thirsty and have gone without food; often I have shivered with cold, without enough clothing to keep me warm.

28Then, besides all this, I have the constant worry of how the churches are getting along: 29Who makes a mistake and I do not feel his sadness? Who falls without my longing to help him? Who is spiritually hurt without my fury rising against the one who hurt him?

30But if I must brag, I would rather brag about the things that show how weak I am. 31God, the Father of our Lord Jesus Christ, who is to be praised forever and ever, knows I tell the truth. 32For instance, in Damascus the governor under King Aretas kept guards at the city gates to catch me; 33but I was let down by rope and basket from a hole in the city wall, and so I got away! [What popularity!]

Paul's vision and his thorn

12 This boasting is all so foolish, but let me go on. Let me tell about the visions I've had, and revelations from the Lord.

11:33 *What popularity!* Implied.

Side references (left margin):

11:17
2 Cor 7:4

11:18
Phil 3:3

11:20
Gal 2:4; 4:9

11:21
2 Cor 10:10

11:22
Acts 22:3
Rom 11:1
Phil 3:5

11:23
Rom 8:36
1 Cor 15:10
16:23
2 Cor 6:4,5

11:24
Deut 25:3

11:25
Acts 14:19
16:22; 27:41

11:26
Acts 9:23
13:50; 14:5
17:5; 19:23
21:31; 23:10
Gal 2:4

11:27
1 Cor 4:11
2 Cor 6:5
1 Thess 2:9

11:28
Acts 20:18
Rom 1:14

11:29
1 Cor 9:22

11:31
Rom 9:5

11:32
Acts 9:24

11:33
Acts 9:25

12:1
Gal 1:12

11:22, 23 Paul presented his credentials to counteract charges the false teachers were making against him. He felt awkward speaking like this, but if the believers turned against him, they might begin to turn against the gospel he was preaching. Paul also gave a list of his credentials in his letter to the Philippians (see Philippians 3:4–8).

11:23-29 Paul was angry that the false teachers had impressed and deceived the Corinthians (11:13–15). Therefore, he had to reestablish his credibility and authority by listing the trials he had endured in his service for Christ. Some of these trials are recorded in the book of Acts (Acts 14:19; 16:22–24). Because Paul wrote this letter during his third missionary journey (Acts 18:23—21:17), he would experience yet further trials and humiliations for the cause of Christ (see Acts 21:30–33; 22:24–30). These trials showed he was sacrificing his life for the gospel, something the false teachers would never do. The trials and hurts you have experienced for Christ's sake have built your character, demonstrated your faith, and prepared you to work for the Lord.

11:25 The seaways were not as safe as they are today. Paul had been shipwrecked three times, and he would face another accident on his voyage to Rome (see Acts 27). By this time, Paul had probably made at least eight or nine voyages.

11:28, 29 Though an apostle with God's authority to preach the gospel, Paul showed enormous personal concern for individuals in the churches he served. If God has placed you in a position of leadership and authority, treat people with Paul's kind of empathy and concern.

11:32 King Aretas, king of the Nabateans (Edomites) from A.D. 9 to 40, appointed a governor to oversee the Nabatean segment of the population in Damascus. Somehow the Jews in Damascus were able to enlist this governor to help them try to capture Paul (see Acts 9:22–25). Paul recounted this incident to show what he had endured for Christ. The false teachers couldn't make such a claim.

2, 3Fourteen years ago I was taken up to heaven for a visit. Don't ask me whether my body was there or just my spirit, for I don't know; only God can answer that. But anyway, there I was in paradise, 4and heard things so astounding that they are beyond a man's power to describe or put in words (and anyway I am not allowed to tell them to others). 5That experience is something worth bragging about, but I am not going to do it. I am going to boast only about how weak I am and how great God is to use such weakness for his glory. 6I have plenty to boast about and would be no fool in doing it, but I don't want anyone to think more highly of me than he should from what he can actually see in my life and my message.

7I will say this: because these experiences I had were so tremendous, God was afraid I might be puffed up by them; so I was given a physical condition which has been a thorn in my flesh, a messenger from Satan to hurt and bother me, and prick my pride. 8Three different times I begged God to make me well again.

9Each time he said, "No. But I am with you; that is all you need. My power shows up best in weak people." Now I am glad to boast about how weak I am; I am glad to be a living demonstration of Christ's power, instead of showing off my own power and abilities. 10Since I know it is all for Christ's good, I am quite happy about "the thorn," and about insults and hardships, persecutions and difficulties; for when I am weak, then I am strong—the less I have, the more I depend on him.

Paul's concern for the Corinthians

11You have made me act like a fool—boasting like this—for you people ought to be writing about me and not making me write about myself. There isn't a single thing these other marvelous fellows have that I don't have too, even though I am really worth nothing at all. 12When I was there I certainly gave you every proof that I was truly an apostle, sent to you by God himself: for I patiently did many wonders and signs and mighty works among you. 13The only thing I didn't do for you, that I do everywhere else in all other churches, was to become a burden to you—I didn't ask me to give me food to eat and a place to stay. Please forgive me for this wrong!

14Now I am coming to you again, the third time; and it is still not going to cost you anything, for I don't want your money. I want *you!* And anyway, you are my children, and little children don't pay for their father's and mother's food—it's the other way around; parents supply food for their children. 15I am glad to give you myself and all I have for your spiritual good, even though it seems that the more I love you, the less you love me.

16Some of you are saying, "It's true that his visits didn't seem to cost us

12:2, 3 *I*, literally, "A man in Christ." *heaven*, literally, "the third heaven."

12:2
Deut 10:14
Acts 22:17
Rom 16:7
2 Cor 5:17
Gal 1:22

12:4
Lk 23:43
Rev 2:7

12:5
1 Cor 2:3
2 Cor 11:30

12:6
2 Cor 10:8

12:7
Job 2:7
Lk 13:16
Gal 4:13

12:8
Mt 26:44

12:9
Eccles 7:18
Isa 40:29; 42:10
1 Cor 10:13
Eph 3:16
Phil 4:13
Heb 2:18
1 Pet 4:14
2 Pet 2:9

12:11
1 Cor 15:9,10
2 Cor 11:15,16
Gal 2:6

12:12
Rom 15:18,19
1 Cor 9:1,2

12:13
1 Cor 1:7; 9:12, 18
2 Cor 11:7

12:14
1 Cor 4:14
9:19; 10:33
2 Cor 13:1

12:15
2 Cor 1:6; 6:12
11:11
1 Thess 2:8
Phil 2:17

12:16
2 Cor 11:9

12:2, 3 This incident cannot be positively matched with a recorded event in Paul's career. Paul tells about this incident to show that he had been uniquely touched by God.

12:7, 8 We don't know what Paul's "thorn in the flesh" was, because he doesn't tell us. Some have suggested that it was malaria, epilepsy, or a disease of the eyes (see Galatians 4:13–15). Whatever it was, it was a chronic and debilitating physical problem, which at times kept him from working. This thorn was a hindrance to his ministry, and he prayed for its removal; but God refused. It kept Paul humble, reminded him of his need for constant contact with God, and benefited those around him as they saw God at work in his life.

12:9 Although God did not remove Paul's physical affliction, he promised to demonstrate his power in Paul. The fact that God's power shows up in weak people should give us courage. If we recognize our limitations, we will not congratulate ourselves. Instead, we will turn to God to seek pathways for effectiveness. We must rely on God for our effectiveness rather than on simple energy, effort, or talent. Our weakness not only helps develop Christian character; it also deepens our worship, for in admitting our weakness, we affirm God's strength.

12:10 When we are strong in abilities or resources, we are tempted to do God's work on our own, and that leads to pride. When we are weak, when we allow God to fill us with *his* power, then we are stronger than we could ever be on our own. We must depend on God—only work done in his power makes us effective for him and has lasting value.

12:11–15 Paul is not merely revealing his feelings but defending his authority as an apostle of Jesus Christ. He was hurt that the church in Corinth was doubting and questioning him, but he was defending himself for the cause of the gospel, not to satisfy his ego. When you are "put on trial," do you think only about saving your reputation or are you more concerned about what people will think about Christ?

12:13 When Paul says, "Please forgive me for this wrong," he is using irony. He actually did more for the Corinthians than for any other church, and still they misunderstood him.

12:14 Paul had founded the church in Corinth on his first visit there (Acts 18:1). He subsequently made a second, "painful" visit (2:1). Thus, this would be his third visit (see also 13:1).

anything, but he is a sneaky fellow, that Paul, and he fooled us. As sure as anything he must have made money from us some way."

17But how? Did any of the men I sent to you take advantage of you? 18When I urged Titus to visit you, and sent our other brother with him, did they make any profit? No, of course not. For we have the same Holy Spirit, and walk in each other's steps, doing things the same way.

19I suppose you think I am saying all this to get back into your good graces. That isn't it at all. I tell you, with God listening as I say it, that I have said this to help *you*, dear friends—to build you up spiritually and not to help myself. 20For I am afraid that when I come to visit you I won't like what I find, and then you won't like the way I will have to act. I am afraid that I will find you quarreling, and envying each other, and being angry with each other, and acting big, and saying wicked things about each other and whispering behind each other's backs, filled with conceit and disunity. 21Yes, I am afraid that when I come God will humble me before you and I will be sad and mourn because many of you who have sinned became sinners and don't even care about the wicked, impure things you have done: your lust and immorality, and the taking of other men's wives.

Paul's final advice

13 This is the third time I am coming to visit you. The Scriptures tell us that if two or three have seen a wrong, it must be punished. [Well, this is my third warning, as I come now for this visit.] 2I have already warned those who had been sinning when I was there last; now I warn them again, and all others, just as I did then, that this time I come ready to punish severely and I will not spare them.

3I will give you all the proof you want that Christ speaks through me. Christ is not weak in his dealings with you, but is a mighty power within you. 4His weak, human body died on the cross, but now he lives by the mighty power of God. We, too, are weak in our bodies, as he was, but now we live and are strong, as he is, and have all of God's power to use in dealing with you.

5Check up on yourselves. Are you really Christians? Do you pass the test? Do you feel Christ's presence and power more and more within you? Or are you just pretending to be Christians when actually you aren't at all? 6I hope you can agree that I have stood that test and truly belong to the Lord.

7I pray that you will live good lives, not because that will be a feather in our caps, proving that what we teach is right; no, for we want you to do right even if we ourselves are despised. 8Our responsibility is to encourage the right at all times, not to hope for evil. 9We are glad to be weak and despised if you are really strong. Our greatest wish and prayer is that you will become mature Christians.

10I am writing this to you now in the hope that I won't need to scold and punish when I come; for I want to use the Lord's authority which he has given me, not to punish you but to make you strong.

13:1 *Well, this is my third warning, as I come now for this visit,* implied. **13:7** *a feather in our caps,* literally, "not that we may appear approved." **13:8** *not to hope for evil,* literally, "For we can do nothing against the truth, but for the truth."

12:17 2 Cor 7:2; 9:5
12:18 2 Cor 8:6,18
12:19 Rom 9:1; 1 Cor 10:33; 2 Cor 5:12; 11:31
12:20 1 Cor 4:21
12:21 1 Cor 5:1; 2 Cor 2:1,4; Gal 5:19; Phil 3:18
13:1 Num 35:30; Deut 19:15; Acts 18:1; 2 Cor 2:1; 12:14
13:2 2 Cor 1:23; 10:2; 12:21
13:3 Mt 10:20; 1 Cor 7:40; 9:2
13:4 2 Cor 10:3,4; Rom 1:4; 6:4; Phil 2:7,8; 1 Pet 3:18
13:5 Jn 14:20; 17:23, 26; Rom 8:10; 1 Cor 9:27; 11:28; Gal 4:19; Col 1:27
13:7 2 Cor 6:9
13:9 1 Cor 4:10; Eph 4:12-16; 1 Thess 3:10
13:10 Tit 1:13

12:20, 21 After reading this catalog of sins, it is hard to believe that these are the people Paul said were enriched with "every spiritual gift and power for doing his will" (1 Corinthians 1:7). Paul feared that the practices of wicked Corinth had invaded the congregation, and he wrote sternly in hope that they would straighten up their lives before he arrived. We must live differently than unbelievers, not letting secular society dictate how we are to treat others. Don't let culture invade your practices at church.

13:2 How would Paul punish unrepentant sinners? (1) He could confront and publicly denounce their behavior. (2) He could exercise church discipline by calling them before the church leaders. (3) He could excommunicate them from the church.

13:5 Just as we get physical check-ups, Paul urges us to give ourselves spiritual check-ups. We should look for a growing awareness of Christ's presence and power in our lives. Only then will we know if we are true Christians or imposters. If we're not taking active steps to grow closer to God, we are growing farther away from him.

13:8, 9 Just as parents want their children to grow into mature adults, so Paul wanted the Corinthians to grow into mature believers. As we share the Good News, our goal should be not merely to see others profess faith or begin attending church, but to see them become mature in their faith. Don't set your sights too short.

¹¹I close my letter with these last words: Be happy. Grow in Christ. Pay attention to what I have said. Live in harmony and peace. And may the God of love and peace be with you.

¹²Greet each other warmly in the Lord. ¹³All the Christians here send you their best regards. ¹⁴May the grace of our Lord Jesus Christ be with you all. May God's love and the Holy Spirit's friendship be yours.

Paul

13:11 Rom 12:16
15:33
1 Cor 1:10
1 Pet 3:8

13:13 Rom 5:5; 16:20
Phil 2:1

13:11 Paul's closing words—what he wants the Corinthians to remember about the needs for their church—are still fitting for the church today. When these qualities are not present, there are problems to be dealt with in the church. These traits do not come to a church by glossing over problems, conflicts, and difficulties. They are not produced by neglect, denial, withdrawal, or bitterness. They are the by-products of the extremely hard work of solving problems. Just as Paul and the Corinthians had to hammer out difficulties to bring peace, so we must receive and obey the principles of God's Word and not just hear them.

13:14 Paul's farewell blessing invokes all three members of the Godhead—Father, Son, and Holy Spirit. Although the doctrine of the Trinity is not explicitly taught in Scripture, verses such as this one show that it was believed.

13:14 Paul was dealing with an ongoing problem in the Corinthian church. He could have refused to communicate until they cleared up their problems, but he loved them and reached out to them again with the love of Christ. Love, however, means that sometimes we must confront those we care about. Authority and personal concern are both needed in dealing with people who are ruining their lives with sin. But there are several wrong approaches in confronting others, and these can further break relationships rather than heal them. We can be legalistic and blast people with the laws they should be obeying. We can turn away from them because we don't want to face the situation. We can isolate them by gossiping about their problem and turning others against them as well. Or, like Paul, we can seek to build relationships by taking a better approach—sharing, communicating, and caring. This is a difficult approach that can drain us emotionally; but it is best for the other person, and it is the only Christlike way to deal with others' sin.

GALATIANS

A FAMILY, executing their carefully planned escape at midnight, dashing for the border . . . a man standing outside prison walls, gulping fresh air, awash in the new sun . . . a young woman with every trace of the ravaging drug gone from her system . . . they are FREE! With fresh anticipation, they can begin life anew.

Whether fleeing oppression, stepping out of prison, or breaking a strangling habit, freedom means life. There is nothing so exhilarating as knowing that the past is forgotten and that new options await. People yearn to be free.

The book of Galatians is the charter of Christian freedom. In this profound letter, Paul proclaims the reality of our liberty in Christ—freedom from the Law and the power of sin, to serve our living Lord.

Most of the first converts and early leaders in the church were Jewish Christians who proclaimed Jesus as their Messiah. As Jewish Christians, they struggled with a dual identity: their Jewishness constrained them to be strict followers of the law; their newfound faith in Christ invited them to celebrate a holy liberty. They wondered how Gentiles (non-Jews) could be part of the Kingdom of Heaven.

This controversy wracked the early church. Judaizers—an extremist Jewish faction within the church—taught that Gentile Christians had to submit to Jewish laws and traditions *in addition to* believing in Christ. As a missionary to the Gentiles, Paul had to confront this issue many times.

Galatians was written, therefore, to refute the Judaizers and to call believers back to the pure gospel. The Good News is for all people—Jews and Gentiles alike. Salvation is by God's grace through faith in Christ Jesus *and nothing else*. Faith in Christ means true freedom.

After a brief introduction (1:1–5), Paul addresses those who were accepting the Judaizers' twisted gospel (1:6–9). He summarizes the controversy including his personal confrontation with Peter and other church leaders (1:10—2:16). He then demonstrates that salvation is by faith alone by alluding to his conversion (2:17–21), appealing to his readers' own experience of the Good News (3:1–5), and showing how the Old Testament teaches grace (3:6–20). Next, he explains the purpose of God's laws and the relationship between law, God's promises, and Christ (3:21—4:31).

Having laid the foundation, Paul builds his case for Christian liberty. We are saved by faith, not by works (5:1–12); our freedom means we are free to love and serve one another, not to do wrong (5:13–26); and Christians should bear one another's burdens and be kind to one another (6:1–10). In 6:11–18, Paul shares his final thoughts by taking the pen into his own hand.

As you read Galatians, try to understand this first-century conflict between law and grace, faith and works, but also be aware of modern parallels. Like Paul, defend the truth of the gospel and reject all those who would add to or twist this truth. You are *free* in Christ—step into the light and celebrate!

VITAL STATISTICS

PURPOSE:
To refute the Judaizers (who taught that Gentile believers must obey the Jewish law in order to be saved), and to call Christians to faith and freedom in Christ

AUTHOR:
Paul

TO WHOM WRITTEN:
The churches in southern Galatia founded on Paul's first missionary journey (including Iconium, Lystra, Derbe)

DATE WRITTEN:
About A.D. 49, from Antioch, prior to the Jerusalem council (A.D. 50)

SETTING:
The most pressing controversy of the early church was the relationship of new believers, especially Gentiles, to the Jewish laws. This was especially a problem for the converts and young churches Paul founded on his first missionary journey. Paul writes to correct this problem. Later, at the council in Jerusalem, the conflict was officially resolved by the church leaders.

KEY VERSE:
"So Christ has made us free" (5:1).

KEY PEOPLE:
Paul, Peter, Barnabas, Titus, Abraham, false teachers

KEY PLACES:
Galatia, Jerusalem

SPECIAL FEATURES:
This letter is not addressed to any specific body of believers and was probably circulated to several churches.

THE BLUEPRINT

1. Authenticity of the gospel (1:1—2:21)
2. Superiority of the gospel (3:1—4:31)
3. Freedom of the gospel (5:1—6:18)

In response to attacks from false teachers, Paul wrote to defend his apostleship and to defend the authority of the gospel. The Galatians were beginning to turn from faith to legalism. The struggle between the gospel and legalism is still a crisis. Many today would have us return to trying to earn God's favor through following rituals or obeying a set of rules. As Christians, we are not boxed in, but set free. To preserve our freedom, we must stay close to Christ and resist any who promote subtle ways of trying to earn our salvation.

MEGATHEMES

THEME	EXPLANATION	IMPORTANCE
Law	A group of Jewish teachers insisted that non-Jewish believers must obey Jewish law and traditional rules. They believed a person was saved by following the law of Moses (with emphasis on circumcision, the sign of the covenant), in addition to faith in Christ. Paul opposed them by showing that the law can't save anyone.	We can't be saved by keeping the Old Testament law, even the Ten Commandments. The law served as a guide to point out our need to be forgiven. Christ fulfilled the obligations of the law for us. We must turn to him to be saved. He alone can make us right with God.
Faith	We are saved from God's judgment and penalty for sin by God's gracious gift to us. We receive salvation by faith—trusting in him—not in anything else. Becoming a Christian is in no way based on our initiative, wise choice, or good character. We can only be right with God by believing in him.	Your acceptance with God comes by believing in Christ alone. You must never add to or twist this truth. We are saved by faith, not by the good that we do. Have you placed your whole trust and confidence in Christ? He alone can forgive you and bring you into relationship with God.
Freedom	Galatians is our charter of Christian freedom. We are not under the jurisdiction of Jewish laws and traditions, nor under the authority of Jerusalem. Faith in Christ brings true freedom from sin and from the futile attempt to be right with God by keeping the law.	We are free in Christ, and yet freedom is a privilege. We are not free to disobey Christ or be immoral, but we are free to serve the risen Christ. Let us use our freedom to love and to serve, not to do wrong.
Holy Spirit	We become Christians through the work of the Holy Spirit. He brings new life; even our faith to believe is a gift from him. The Holy Spirit instructs, guides, leads, and gives us power. He ends our bondage to evil desires, and he creates in us love, joy, peace, and many other wonderful changes.	When the Holy Spirit leads us, he produces his fruit in us. Just as we are saved by faith, not works, we also grow by faith. By believing, we can have the Holy Spirit within us, helping us live our lives. Obey Christ by following the Holy Spirit's leading.

1. Authenticity of the gospel

1 *From:* Paul the missionary and all the other Christians here.
To: The churches of Galatia. I was not called to be a missionary by any group or agency. My call is from Jesus Christ himself, and from God the Father who

---

1:1 Paul and Barnabas had just completed their first missionary journey (Acts 13:2–14:28), during which they visited Iconium, Lystra, and Derbe, cities in the Roman province of Galatia (present-day Turkey). Upon returning to Antioch, Paul was accused by some Jewish Christians of diluting Christianity to make it more appealing to Gentiles. These Jewish Christians disagreed

1:4
Jn 15:19; 17:14
Rom 4:25
1:5
Rom 11:36

raised him from the dead. ³May peace and blessing be yours from God the Father and from the Lord Jesus Christ. ⁴He died for our sins just as God our Father planned, and rescued us from this evil world in which we live. ⁵All glory to God through all the ages of eternity. Amen.

There is no other gospel

1:6
2 Cor 11:4

⁶I am amazed that you are turning away so soon from God who, in his love and mercy, invited you to share the eternal life he gives through Christ; you are already following a different "way to heaven," which really doesn't go to heaven at all.

CITIES IN GALATIA
Paul visited several cities in Galatia on each of his three missionary journeys. On his first journey he went through Antioch in Pisidia, Iconium, Lystra, and Derbe, then retraced his steps; on his second journey he went by land from Antioch in Syria through the four cities in Galatia; on his third journey he also went through those cities on the main route to Ephesus.

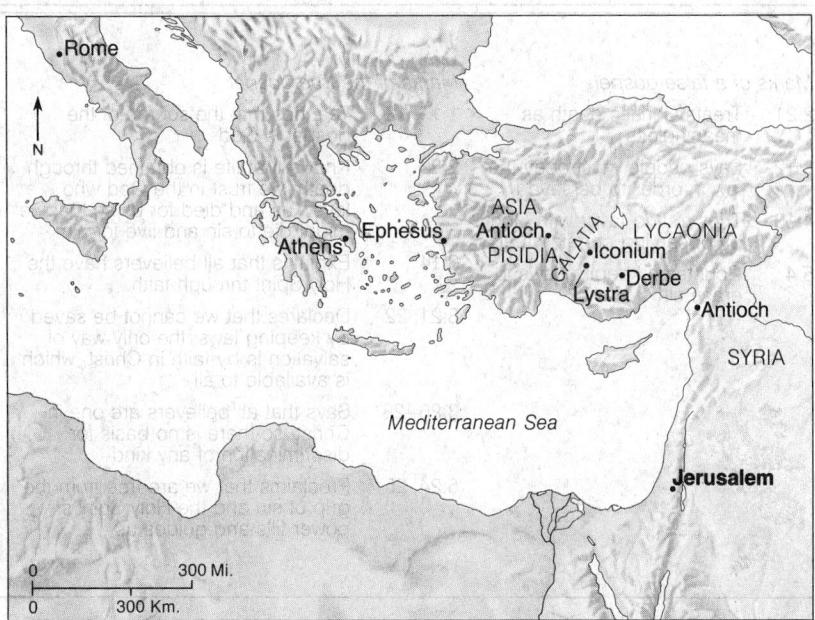

---

with Paul's statements that Gentiles did not have to follow many of the religious laws which the Jews had obeyed for centuries. Some of Paul's accusers had even followed him to those Galatian cities and told the Gentile converts that they had to be circumcised and follow all the Jewish laws and customs in order to be saved. In short, according to these men, Gentiles had to become Jews in order to become Christians.

In response to this threat, Paul wrote this letter to the Galatian churches. In it, he explains that following the Old Testament laws or the Jewish laws will not bring salvation. A person is saved by grace through faith. The Jewish law is not a condition for salvation. Paul wrote this letter about A.D. 49, shortly before the meeting of the Jerusalem council, which also dealt with the law versus grace controversy (Acts 15).

1:1 For more information about Paul's life, see his Profile in Acts 9. Paul had been a Christian for about 15 years at this time.

1:2 In Paul's time *Galatia* was the Roman province located in the center section of present-day Turkey. Much of the region rests on a large and fertile plateau and large numbers of people had moved to the region because of its favorable geography. One of Paul's goals during his missionary journeys was to visit regions with large population centers in order to reach as many people as possible.

1:2 Paul was called by Jesus Christ himself. He presented his apostolic credentials at the very outset of this letter, because some people in Galatia were questioning his authority.

1:3-5 God's plan all along was to save us by Jesus' death. We have been rescued from the power of this evil world—a world ruled by Satan, full of cruelty, tragedy, temptation, and deception. Being rescued from this evil world doesn't mean we are taken out of it, but that we are no longer enslaved to it. We have been saved to live righteous lives for God, and we have been promised eternity with him.

1:6 The different "way to heaven" was preached by people who wanted Gentile believers to follow Jewish laws in order to obtain salvation. Those proclaiming this different way believed that faith in Christ was not enough; a Christian must also follow the Jewish laws and customs, especially the rite of circumcision, in order to be saved. This message undermined the truth of the Good News that salvation is a gift, not a reward. Jesus Christ has made this gift available to all people, not just to those who are Jewish in orientation. Beware of people who say that more is needed for salvation than faith in Christ. When people set up additional requirements for salvation, they deny the power of Christ's redemptive work on the cross (see 3:1-5).

7For there is no other way than the one we showed you; you are being fooled by those who twist and change the truth concerning Christ.

8Let God's curses fall on anyone, including myself, who preaches any other way to be saved than the one we told you about; yes, if an angel comes from heaven and preaches any other message, let him be forever cursed. 9I will say it again: if anyone preaches any other Gospel than the one you welcomed, let God's curse fall upon him.

10You can see that I am not trying to please you by sweet talk and flattery; no, I am trying to please God. If I were still trying to please men I could not be Christ's servant.

1:7
Acts 15:1
Gal 5:10

1:8
2 Cor 11:14

1:9
Deut 4:2; 12:32
Prov 30:6
Rev 22:18

1:10
1 Thess 2:4

Marks of a false gospel		Marks of the true gospel		THE MARKS OF THE TRUE GOSPEL AND OF FALSE GOSPELS
2:21	Treats Christ's death as meaningless	1:11, 12	Teaches that the source of the gospel is God	
3:12	Says people must obey the law in order to be saved	2:20	Knows that life is obtained through death; we trust in the God who loved us and died for us so that we might die to sin and live for him	
4:10	Tries to find favor with God by observing certain rituals	3:14	Explains that all believers have the Holy Spirit through faith	
5:4	Counts on keeping laws to erase sin	3:21, 22	Declares that we cannot be saved by keeping laws; the only way of salvation is by faith in Christ, which is available to all	
		3:26–28	Says that all believers are one in Christ, so there is no basis for discrimination of any kind	
		5:24, 25	Proclaims that we are free from the grip of sin and the Holy Spirit's power fills and guides us	

1:7 No other person, method, or ritual can give eternal life. There is only one way to spend eternity with God—through believing in Jesus Christ as Savior and Lord. Some people think all religions are equally valid paths to God. But that is not what God says. He has provided just one way—Jesus Christ (John 14:6).

1:7 Those who fooled the Galatian believers were zealous Jewish Christians who believed that the Old Testament practices such as circumcision and dietary restrictions were required of all believers in Christ. Because these teachers wanted to turn the Gentile Christians into Jews, they were called *Judaizers.* Some time after the letter to the Galatians was sent, Paul met with the apostles in Jerusalem to discuss this matter further (see Acts 15).

1:7 The Galatian Christians were mainly Greek, unfamiliar with Jewish laws and customs. The Judaizers were an extreme faction of Jewish Christians. Both groups believed in Christ, but their lifestyles differed considerably. We do not know why the Judaizers traveled to teach their mistaken notions to the new Gentile converts. They may have been motivated by (1) a sincere wish to integrate Judaism with the new Christian faith, (2) a sincere love for their Jewish heritage, or (3) a jealous desire to destroy Paul's authority. Whether or not these Judaizers were sincere, their teaching threatened these new churches and had to be countered. Paul was not rejecting everything Jewish. He himself was a Jew who worshiped in the Temple and attended the religious festivals.

But he was concerned that *nothing* get in the way of the simple truth of his message—that salvation, to Jews and Gentiles alike, is by faith in Jesus Christ alone.

1:7 Twisted truth is sometimes more difficult to spot than outright lies. The Judaizers were twisting the truth about Christ. They claimed to follow him, but they denied that Jesus' work on the cross was sufficient for salvation. There will always be people who twist the Good News. Either they do not understand what the Bible teaches, or they are uncomfortable with the truth as it stands. How can we tell when people are twisting the truth? Before accepting the teachings of any group, find out what the group teaches about Jesus Christ. If their teaching does not match the truth in God's Word, then it is twisted.

1:8, 9 What these Judaizers were doing was so bad that Paul used strong words to denounce their actions. He said that even if an angel from heaven comes preaching another message, let that angel be cursed forever. If an angel came preaching another message, he would not be from heaven, no matter how he looked. In 2 Corinthians 11:14,15, Paul warns that Satan and his angels can turn themselves into angels of light. Here he invokes a curse on an angel who spreads a false gospel—a fitting response to an emissary of hell. Paul extended that curse to himself. His message must never change, for the truth of the gospel never changes. Paul uses strong language because he is dealing with a life-and-death issue.

☞ *Paul received the gospel from God*

1:11
1 Cor 15:1-3

1:12
1 Cor 2:10
Gal 1:15,16
Eph 3:3

1:13
Acts 8:3; 9:21
22:3-5; 26:4-11

1:14
Acts 26:3

1:15
Acts 9:15; 15:10
Eph 2:3

1:16
Rom 1:17; 8:3,
10
Gal 2:9,20
Col 1:27

1:17
1 Jn 3:8

1:18
Acts 9:26

1:19
Mt 13:55
Acts 12:17; 15:13
21:18
1 Cor 15:7
Gal 2:9,12

1:23
Acts 9:20

¹¹Dear friends, I solemnly swear that the way to heaven which I preach is not based on some mere human whim or dream. ¹²For my message comes from no less a person than Jesus Christ himself, who told me what to say. No one else has taught me.

¹³You know what I was like when I followed the Jewish religion—how I went after the Christians mercilessly, hunting them down and doing my best to get rid of them all. ¹⁴I was one of the most religious Jews of my own age in the whole country, and tried as hard as I possibly could to follow all the old, traditional rules of my religion.

¹⁵But then something happened! For even before I was born God had chosen me to be his, and called me—what kindness and grace— ¹⁶to reveal his Son within me so that I could go to the Gentiles and show them the Good News about Jesus.

When all this happened to me I didn't go at once and talk it over with anyone else; ¹⁷I didn't go up to Jerusalem to consult with those who were apostles before I was. No, I went away into the deserts of Arabia, and then came back to the city of Damascus. ¹⁸It was not until three years later that I finally went to Jerusalem for a visit with Peter, and stayed there with him for fifteen days. ¹⁹And the only other apostle I met at that time was James, our Lord's brother. ²⁰(Listen to what I am saying, for I am telling you this in the very presence of God. This is exactly what happened—I am not lying to you.) ²¹Then after this visit I went to Syria and Cilicia. ²²And still the Christians in Judea didn't even know what I looked like. ²³All they knew was what people were saying, that "our former enemy is now preaching the very faith he tried to wreck." ²⁴And they gave glory to God because of me.

1:10 Paul had to speak harshly to the Christians in Galatia because they were in serious danger. He did not apologize for his straightforward words; he knew he could not serve Christ faithfully if he allowed the Galatian Christians to remain on the wrong track. Whom are you trying to please—other people or God? Pray for the courage to put God's approval first.

1:11ff Why should the Galatians listen to Paul instead of the Judaizers? Paul answers this implicit question by furnishing his credentials: his message was directly from Christ (1:12); he had been an exemplary Jew (1:13, 14); he had a special conversion experience (1:15, 16; see also Acts 9:1–9); he was confirmed in his ministry by the other apostles (1:18, 19; 2:1–9). Paul also presented his credentials to the Corinthian and Philippian churches (2 Corinthians 11, 12; Philippians 3:4–9).

1:12 Paul did not choose to become an apostle, Christ appointed him to that task. Mere human wisdom was not the ultimate source or authority for Paul's preaching. The Good News which Paul preached rests upon the authority of Jesus Christ himself. Since Jesus appointed the apostles to be his official messengers, let us obey Christ by submitting to the apostolic teaching in the New Testament.

1:13, 14 Paul had been one of the most religious Jews of his day, scrupulously keeping the law and relentlessly persecuting Christians (see Acts 9:1, 2). Before his conversion he had been even more zealous for the law than the Judaizers were. He was sincere in his zeal—but wrong. When he met Jesus Christ, his life changed. Now he directed all his energies toward building up the Christian church.

1:15, 16 Because God was guiding his ministry, Paul wasn't doing anything God hadn't already planned and given him power to do. The great prophets Isaiah and Jeremiah knew that God had called them, even before they were born, to do special work for him (see Isaiah 49:1; Jeremiah 1:5). God knows you intimately as well, and he chose you to be his even before you were born (see Psalm 139). He wants you to draw close to him, and fulfill the job he has given you to do.

1:16 The word *Jew* refers not only to nationality but also to religion. To be fully Jewish, a person must have descended from Abraham. In addition, a faithful Jew adheres to the Jewish laws. *Gentiles* are non-Jews, whether in nationality or religion. In Paul's day, Jews thought of all Gentiles as pagans. Jews avoided Gentiles because they believed that contact with Gentiles brought spiritual corruption. Although Gentiles by nationality could become Jews in religion by undergoing circumcision and by following Jewish laws and customs, they were never fully accepted.

Many Jews had difficulty understanding that God's message is for Jews and Gentiles alike. Some Jews thought Gentiles had to become Jews before they could become Christians. But God planned to bless both Jews and Gentiles. He had revealed this plan through Old Testament prophets (see, for example, Genesis 12:3; Isaiah 42:6; 66:19), he fulfilled it through Jesus Christ, and he was proclaiming it to the Gentiles through Paul.

1:15–24 Paul tells of his conversion to show that his message came directly from God. God commissioned him to preach the Good News to the Gentiles (1:15, 16). After his call, Paul did not consult with the apostles until he had spent three years in the desert. Then he spoke with Peter and James, but he had no other contact with Jewish Christians for several more years. During those years, he was preaching to the Gentiles the message God gave him. His Good News did not come from man; it came from God.

1:18 Most believe that Paul is talking about his first visit to Jerusalem, as recorded in Acts 9:26–30.

1:24 Paul's changed life caused many comments from people who saw or heard of him. His new life astonished them, and they glorified God because only he could have turned this zealous persecutor of Christians into a Christian himself. We may not have had as dramatic a change as Paul had, but even so our new lives should glorify our Savior. When people look at us, do they recognize that God has made changes in us? If not, perhaps we are not living our new lives as we should.

The apostles accepted Paul

2 Then fourteen years later I went back to Jerusalem again, this time with Barnabas; and Titus came along too. ²I went there with definite orders from God to confer with the brothers there about the message I was preaching to the Gentiles. I talked privately to the leaders of the church so that they would all understand just what I had been teaching and, I hoped, agree that it was right. ³And they did agree; they did not even demand that Titus, my companion, should be circumcised, though he was a Gentile.

⁴Even that question wouldn't have come up except for some so-called "Christians" there—false ones, really—who came to spy on us and see what freedom we enjoyed in Christ Jesus, as to whether we obeyed the Jewish laws or not. They tried to get us all tied up in their rules, like slaves in chains. ⁵But we did not listen to them for a single moment, for we did not want to confuse you into thinking that salvation can be earned by being circumcised and by obeying Jewish laws.

⁶And the great leaders of the church who were there had nothing to add to what

2:1
Acts 15:2-29
2:2
Gal 1:6
2:3
Acts 16:3
2:4
Gal 1:7; 4:3,9
5:1
2:5
Gal 1:6; 2:14
2:6
Acts 10:34
Rom 2:11
2 Cor 12:11
Gal 6:3

What the Judaizers said about Paul	Paul's defense	JUDAIZERS VS. PAUL
They said he was perverting the truth.	He received his message from Christ himself (1:11, 12).	
They said he was a traitor to the Jewish faith.	Paul was one of the most dedicated Jews of his time. Yet, in the midst of one of his most zealous acts, God transformed him through a revelation of the Good News about Jesus (1:13–16; Acts 9:1–30).	
They said he compromised and watered down his message for the Gentiles.	The other apostles declared that the message Paul preached was the true gospel (2:1–10).	
They said he was disregarding the law of Moses.	Far from downgrading the law, Paul puts the law in its proper place. He says it shows people where they have sinned and it points them to Christ (3:19–29).	

As the debate raged between the Gentile Christians and the Judaizers, Paul found it necessary to write to the churches in Galatia. The Judaizers were trying to undermine Paul's authority and taught a false gospel. In reply, Paul defended his authority as an apostle and the truth of his message. The debate over Jewish laws and Gentile Christians was officially resolved at the Jerusalem council (Acts 15) yet, it continued to be a point of contention after that time.

2:1 Paul was converted around A.D. 35. The 14 years he mentions are probably calculated from the time of his conversion. Therefore, this trip to Jerusalem was not his first. He made his first trip to Jerusalem around A.D. 38 (see Acts 9:26–30); and other trips to Jerusalem in approximately A.D. 44 (Acts 11:30; Galatians 2:1–10); A.D. 49/50 (Acts 15); A.D. 52 (Acts 18:22); A.D. 57 (Acts 21:15ff). Paul probably visited Jerusalem on several other occasions as well.

2:1 Barnabas and Titus were two of Paul's close friends. Barnabas and Paul visited Galatia together on their first missionary journey. Paul wrote a personal letter to Titus, a faithful believer and church leader serving on the island of Crete (see the book of Titus). For more information on Barnabas, see his Profile in Acts 13. For more information on Titus, see the letter Paul wrote to him in the New Testament.

2:1 After his conversion Paul spent many years preparing for the ministry to which God had called him. This preparation period included time alone with God (1:16, 17) as well as time conferring with other Christians. Often new Christians, in their zeal, want to begin a full-time ministry without investing the necessary time studying the Bible and learning from qualified teachers. We need not wait to share Christ with our friends, but we may need more preparation before embarking on a special ministry, whether volunteer or full-time. While we wait for God's timing, we should continue to study, learn, and grow.

2:2 The essence of Paul's message to both Jews and Gentiles

was that God's salvation is offered to all people regardless of race, sex, nationality, wealth, social standing, education, or anything else. Forgiveness comes through trusting in Christ (see Romans 10:8–13).

2:2, 3 This issue threatened to divide the church. Even though God had specifically sent Paul to the Gentiles (Acts 9:15,16), Paul was willing to discuss his gospel message with the leaders of the Jerusalem church (Acts 15). This meeting prevented a major split in the church, and it formally acknowledged the apostles' approval of Paul's preaching. Sometimes we avoid conferring with others because we fear that problems or arguments may develop. Instead, we should openly discuss our plans and actions with others. This helps everyone understand the situation better, it reduces gossip, and builds unity in the church.

2:3–5 When Paul took Titus, a Greek Christian, to Jerusalem, the Judaizers said he should be circumcised. Paul adamantly refused to give in to their demands. The apostles agreed that circumcision was an unnecessary rite for Gentile converts. Several years later, Paul personally circumcised Timothy, another Greek Christian (Acts 16:3). Unlike Titus, Timothy was half Jewish. Paul did not deny Jews the right to be circumcised; he was simply saying that Gentiles should not be asked to become Jews before becoming Christians.

2:6 It's easy to rate people on the basis of their official status and to be intimidated by the "great leaders of the church." As Paul points out, however, all believers are brothers and sisters in Christ.

2:7
Acts 13:46
1 Thess 2:4

2:8
Acts 9:15; 13:2
22:21; 26:17
1 Cor 15:10

2:9
Rom 1:5

2:10
Acts 11:30
24:17

I was preaching. (By the way, their being great leaders made no difference to me, for all are the same to God.) 7, 8, 9In fact, when Peter, James, and John, who were known as the pillars of the church, saw how greatly God had used me in winning the Gentiles, just as Peter had been blessed so greatly in his preaching to the Jews—for the same God gave us each our special gifts—they shook hands with Barnabas and me and encouraged us to keep right on with our preaching to the Gentiles while they continued their work with the Jews. 10The only thing they did suggest was that we must always remember to help the poor, and I, too, was eager for that.

Paul publicly opposed Peter

2:12
Acts 10:28
11:2,3

11But when Peter came to Antioch I had to oppose him publicly, speaking strongly against what he was doing for it was very wrong. 12For when he first arrived he ate with the Gentile Christians [who don't bother with circumcision and the many other Jewish laws]. But afterwards when some Jewish friends of James came, he wouldn't eat with the Gentiles anymore because he was afraid of what these Jewish legalists, who insisted that circumcision was necessary for salvation, would say; 13and then all the other Jewish Christians and even Barnabas became hypocrites too, following Peter's example, though they certainly knew better.

2:14
Acts 11:3

14When I saw what was happening and that they weren't being honest about what they really believed, and weren't following the truth of the Gospel, I said to Peter in front of all the others, "Though you are a Jew by birth, you have long since discarded the Jewish laws; so why, all of a sudden, are you trying to make these Gentiles obey them? 15You and I are Jews by birth, not mere Gentile sinners, 16and yet we Jewish Christians know very well that we cannot become right with God by obeying our Jewish laws, but only by faith in Jesus Christ to take away our sins. And so we, too, have trusted Jesus Christ, that we might be accepted by God because of faith—and not because we have obeyed the Jewish laws. For no one will ever be saved by obeying them."

2:15
Acts 15:10
Eph 2:3
Phil 3:4

2:16
Acts 13:39
Rom 1:17; 3:20
8:3
Heb 7:18

2:12 *who* don't bother with circumcision and the many other Jewish laws, implied.

We should show respect for our spiritual leaders, but our ultimate allegiance must be to Christ. We are to serve him with our whole being. He doesn't rate us according to our status; he looks at the attitude of our hearts (1 Samuel 16:7).

2:10 Here the apostles were referring to the poor of Jerusalem. While many Gentile converts were financially comfortable, the Jerusalem church was suffering from a severe famine in Palestine (see Acts 11:28–30). Much of Paul's time was spent gathering funds for the Jewish Christians (Acts 24:17; Romans 15:25–29; 1 Corinthians 16:1–4; 2 Corinthians 8). The need for believers to care for the poor is a constant theme of Scripture, but often we do nothing about it. We get caught up in meeting our own needs and desires, or we just don't see enough poor people to remember their needs. Both in your own city and across the oceans, there are people who need help. What can you do to show them tangible evidence of God's love?

2:11 Antioch in Syria (distinguished from Antioch in Pisidia) was a major trade center in the ancient world. Heavily populated by Greeks, it eventually became a strong Christian center. In Antioch the believers were first called Christians (Acts 11:26). Antioch in Syria became the headquarters for the Gentile church and Paul's base of operations.

2:11ff The Judaizers accused Paul of watering down the gospel to make it easier for Gentiles to accept, while Paul accused the Judaizers of nullifying the truth of the gospel by adding conditions to it. The basis of salvation was the issue—is salvation through Christ alone, or does it come through Christ *and* adherence to the law? The argument came to a head when Peter, Paul, the Judaizers, and some Gentile Christians all gathered together in Antioch to share a meal. Peter probably thought that by staying aloof from the Gentiles, he was promoting harmony—he did not

want to offend the friends of James. But Paul charged that Peter's action violated the gospel. By joining the Judaizers, Peter implicitly supported their claim that Christ was not sufficient for salvation. Compromise is an important element in getting along with others, but we should never compromise the truth of God's Word. If we feel we have to change our Christian beliefs to match those of our companions, we are on dangerous ground.

2:11 Although Peter was a "pillar of the church" (2:7), he was acting like a hypocrite. Paul knew he had to confront Peter before his actions damaged the church. Therefore, Paul publicly confronted Peter. Note, however, that Paul did not go to the other "pillars," nor did he write letters to the churches telling them not to follow Peter's example. Instead, he confronted Peter face to face. Sometimes sincere Christians, even Christian leaders, make mistakes; it may take other sincere Christians to get them back on track. If you are convinced that someone is doing harm to himself or the church, a direct approach is usually the best one to take. There is no place for backstabbing in the body of Christ.

2:15,16 If the Jewish laws cannot save us, why should we still obey the Ten Commandments and other Old Testament laws? Paul was not saying the law was bad, for in another letter he wrote, "the law itself was wholly right and good" (Romans 7:12). Instead, he was saying that the law can never make us acceptable to God. The law still has an important role to play in the life of a Christian. The law: (1) guards us from sin by giving us standards for behavior; (2) convicts us of sin, leaving us the opportunity to get in tune with God by asking his forgiveness; (3) drives us to trust in the sufficiency of Christ because we can never keep the commandments perfectly. The law cannot possibly save us, but after we have become Christians, the law can be a valuable guide for living a life pleasing to God.

17But what if we trust Christ to save us and then find that we are wrong, and that
we cannot be saved without being circumcised and obeying all the other Jewish
laws? Wouldn't we need to say that faith in Christ had ruined us? God forbid that
anyone should dare to think such things about our Lord. 18Rather, we are sinners if
we start rebuilding the old systems I have been destroying, of trying to be saved by
keeping Jewish laws, 19for it was through reading the Scripture that I came to
realize that I could never find God's favor by trying—and failing—to obey the
laws. I came to realize that acceptance with God comes by believing in Christ.

20I have been crucified with Christ: and I myself no longer live, but Christ lives
in me. And the real life I now have within this body is a result of my trusting in the
Son of God, who loved me and gave himself for me. 21I am not one of those who
treats Christ's death as meaningless. For if we could be saved by keeping Jewish
laws, then there was no need for Christ to die.

— 2. Superiority of the gospel
The law and faith

3 Oh, foolish Galatians! What magician has hypnotized you and cast an evil spell
upon you? For you used to see the meaning of Jesus Christ's death as clearly as
though I had waved a placard before you with a picture on it of Christ dying on the
cross. 2Let me ask you this one question: Did you receive the Holy Spirit by trying
to keep the Jewish laws? Of course not, for the Holy Spirit came upon you only
after you heard about Christ and trusted him to save you. 3Then have you gone
completely crazy? For if trying to obey the Jewish laws never gave you spiritual life
in the first place, why do you think that trying to obey them now will make you
stronger Christians? 4You have suffered so much for the Gospel. Now are you
going to just throw it all overboard? I can hardly believe it!

5I ask you again, does God give you the power of the Holy Spirit and work

2:19 acceptance with God comes by believing in Christ, literally, "For I through the law died unto the law, that I might
live unto God."

2:17
1 Jn 3:8

2:19
Rom 6:2,14; 7:4
8:2
Heb 9:14

2:20
Rom 6:6
2 Cor 5:15
2:21
Heb 7:11

3:1
1 Cor 1:23
Gal 5:7

3:2
Acts 2:38
Rom 10:17
3:3
Gal 4:9
Heb 7:16

3:4
2 Jn 8
3:5
Phil 1:19

2:17-19 Through studying the Old Testament Scripture, Paul
realized he could not be saved by obeying God's laws. The
prophets knew that God's plan of salvation did not rest upon
keeping the law. Because we have all been infected by sin, we
cannot keep God's laws perfectly. Fortunately, God has provided a
way of salvation that depends on Jesus Christ, not on our own
efforts. We ignore God's system and try to earn our salvation whenever we think God accepts us because we do good things or because we are better than other people. In truth, only by trusting
Christ to take away our sin will we be acceptable to God.

2:20 In what senses have I been crucified with Christ? *Legally,*
God looks at me as if I had died with Christ. Because my sins died
with him, I am no longer condemned (Colossians 2:13–15).
Relationally, I have become one with Christ, and his experiences
are mine. My Christian life began when, in unity with him, I died to
my old life (see Romans 6:5–11). *In my daily life,* I have had
repeatedly to crucify sinful desires that have tried to keep me from
following Christ. This too is a kind of dying with him (Luke
9:23–25).

And yet the focus of Christianity is not dying, but living.
Because I have been crucified with Christ, I have also been raised
with him (Romans 6:5). *Legally,* I have been reconciled with God
(2 Corinthians 5:19) and am free to grow into Christ's likeness
(Romans 8:29). And *in my daily life,* as I continue to fight sin,
Christ's resurrection power is abundantly available to me
(Ephesians 1:19, 20). Christ lives in me—this is my reason for living
and my hope for the future (Colossians 1:27).

2:21 Believers today are still in danger of treating Christ's death
as meaningless. How? (1) By replacing Jewish legalism with their
own brand of Christian legalism, giving people extra laws to obey
before accepting them into fellowship; (2) by believing they can
earn acceptability with God by what they do rather than by trusting

completely in Christ's work on the cross; (3) by focusing only on
God's power to change us (sanctification) rather than giving equal
time to God's power to save us (justification). If we could be saved
by being good, then Christ did not need to die. But the cross is the
only way to salvation.

— 3:1 The Galatian believers had become fascinated by the false
teachers' arguments, almost as though they had fallen under a
magician's spell. Magic was common in Paul's day (Acts 8:9–11;
13:6, 7). Magicians used both illusions and Satan's power to
perform miracles. People were drawn into the magician's
mysterious rites, not recognizing their dangerous source.

3:2, 3 The believers in Galatia, many of whom may have been in
Jerusalem at Pentecost and received the Holy Spirit there, knew
they didn't receive God's Spirit by obeying the Jewish law. Paul
stresses that just as we were saved by faith in Christ, so also we
grow by faith in Christ. The Galatians took a step backward when
they decided to insist on keeping the Jewish laws. We must realize
that we grow spiritually because of God's work in our lives, not by
following special rules.

3:4 The Galatians were about to throw away their faith in Christ by
attempting to find Christian perfection through keeping the law
(see 1:6). Paul shouts that they need to *remember* what Christ has
done for them, how they have suffered for their faith, and what
salvation is all about! When you feel confused about your faith,
seeing different options and not knowing what is right, *remember*
your old life, *remember* how Christ has changed you, and
remember his forgiveness. Then stay true to him.

3:5 This is a rhetorical question. The Galatians knew they
received the Holy Spirit when they believed, not when they obeyed
the law. People still feel insecure in their faith because faith alone
seems too easy; people still try to become close to God by

miracles among you as a result of your trying to obey the Jewish laws? No, of course not. It is when you believe in Christ and fully trust him.

3:6
Gen 15:6
Rom 4:3

6Abraham had the same experience—God declared him fit for heaven only because he believed God's promises. 7You can see from this that the real children of Abraham are all the men of faith who truly trust in God.

3:7
Jn 8:39

3:8
Gen 12:3

8, 9What's more, the Scriptures looked forward to this time when God would save the Gentiles also, through their faith. God told Abraham about this long ago when he said, "I will bless those in every nation who trust in me as you do." And so it is: all who trust in Christ share the same blessing Abraham received.

3:10
Deut 27:26
Jer 11:3

10Yes, and those who depend on the Jewish laws to save them are under God's curse, for the Scriptures point out very clearly, "Cursed is everyone who at any time breaks a single one of these laws that are written in God's Book of the Law."

3:11
Hab 2:4

11Consequently, it is clear that no one can ever win God's favor by trying to keep the Jewish laws, because God has said that the only way we can be right in his sight is by faith. As the prophet Habakkuk says it, "The man who finds life will find it through trusting God." 12How different from this way of faith is the way of law which says that a man is saved by obeying every law of God, without one slip. 13But Christ has bought us out from under the doom of that impossible system by taking the curse for our wrongdoing upon himself. For it is written in the Scripture,

3:12
Lev 18:5
Rom 4:4; 11:6

3:13
Deut 21:23

3:13 *as Jesus was hung upon a wooden cross,* implied.

WHAT IS THE LAW? Part of the Jewish law included those laws found in the Old Testament. When Paul says that non-Jews (Gentiles) are no longer bound by these laws, he is not saying that the Old Testament laws do not apply to us today. He is saying certain types of laws may not apply to us. In the Old Testament there were three categories of laws:	Ceremonial law	This kind of law relates specifically to Israel's worship (see for example, Leviticus 1:1–13). Its primary purpose was to point forward to Jesus Christ. Therefore, these laws were no longer necessary after Jesus' death and resurrection. While we are no longer bound by ceremonial laws, the principles behind them—to worship and love a holy God—still apply. The Jewish Christians often accused the Gentile Christians of violating the ceremonial law.
	Civil law	This type of law dictated Israel's daily living (see Deuteronomy 24:10, 11, for example). Because modern society and culture are so radically different, some of these guidelines cannot be followed specifically. But the principles behind the commands should guide our conduct. At times, Paul asked Gentile Christians to follow some of these laws, not because they had to, but to promote unity.
	Moral law	This sort of law is the direct command of God—for example, the Ten Commandments (Exodus 20:1–17). It requires strict obedience. It reveals the nature and will of God and it still applies to us today. We are to obey this moral law, not to obtain salvation, but to live in ways pleasing to God.

---

following rules. By asking these questions, Paul hoped to get the Galatians to focus again on Christ as the center of their faith.

3:5 The Holy Spirit gives Christians great power to live their lives for God. Some Christians want more than this. They think that if the Holy Spirit is working in their lives, they will live in a state of perpetual excitement. The tedium of everyday living seems to say that something is wrong spiritually. These Christians may have missed the point. Often the Holy Spirit's greatest work in us is teaching us to persist, to keep on doing what is right even when it no longer seems new and interesting. The Galatians quickly turned from Paul's Good News to the teachings of the newest teachers in town; they needed the Holy Spirit's gift of persistence. If we get bored with the Christian life, we may not need the Spirit to stir us up—we may need him to settle us down and get us to see the challenge of the ordinary.

3:6–9 The main argument of the Judaizers was that Gentiles had to become Jews in order to become Christians. Paul exposed the flaw in this argument by showing that real children of Abraham are those who have faith, not those who keep the law. Abraham himself was saved by his faith (Genesis 15:6). All believers of all time and

from every nation share Abraham's blessing. This is a comforting promise, a great heritage, and a solid foundation for living.

3:10 Paul quotes Deuteronomy 27:26 to prove that, contrary to what the Judaizers claimed, the law cannot justify and save—it can only condemn. Breaking even one commandment brings a person under condemnation. Because everyone has broken the commandments, everyone is condemned, and the law can do nothing to reverse the condemnation (Romans 3:20–24). But Christ took the curse of the law upon himself when he hung on the cross (3:13). He did this so we wouldn't have to bear our own punishment and so we could be saved through him. The only condition is that we accept Christ's work on the cross (Colossians 1:20–23).

3:11 Trying to be righteous in our own power doesn't work. Good intentions such as "I'll do better next time" or "I'll never do that again" usually end in failure. Paul pointed to Habakkuk's declaration (Habakkuk 2:4) that by trusting God—believing in his provision for our sins and living each day in the power of his Spirit—we can break this cycle of failure.

"Anyone who is hanged on a tree is cursed" [as Jesus was hung upon a wooden cross].

[14]Now God can bless the Gentiles, too, with this same blessing he promised to Abraham; and all of us as Christians can have the promised Holy Spirit through this faith.

The law and the promise

[15]Dear brothers, even in everyday life a promise made by one man to another, if it is written down and signed, cannot be changed. He cannot decide afterward to do something else instead.

[16]Now, God gave some promises to Abraham and his Child. And notice that it doesn't say the promises were to his *children,* as it would if all his sons—all the Jews—were being spoken of, but to his *Child*—and that, of course, means Christ.

[17]Here's what I am trying to say: God's promise to save through faith—and God wrote this promise down and signed it—could not be canceled or changed four hundred and thirty years later when God gave the Ten Commandments. [18]If *obeying those laws* could save us, then it is obvious that this would be a different way of gaining God's favor than Abraham's way, for he simply accepted God's promise.

[19]Well then, why were the laws given? They were added after the promise was given, to show men how guilty they are of breaking God's laws. But this system of law was to last only until the coming of Christ, the Child to whom God's promise was made. (And there is this further difference. God gave his laws to angels to give to Moses, who then gave them to the people; [20]but when God gave his promise to Abraham, he did it by himself alone, without angels or Moses as go-betweens.)

[21, 22]Well then, are God's laws and God's promises against each other? Of course not! If we could be saved by his laws, then God would not have had to give us a different way to get out of the grip of sin—for the Scriptures insist we are all its prisoners. The only way out is through faith in Jesus Christ; the way of escape is open to all who believe him.

[23]Until Christ came we were guarded by the law, kept in protective custody, so to speak, until we could believe in the coming Savior.

[24]Let me put it another way. The Jewish laws were our teacher and guide until Christ came to give us right standing with God through our faith. [25]But now that Christ has come, we don't need those laws any longer to guard us and lead us to him.

Sons of God through faith

[26]For now we are all children of God through faith in Jesus Christ, [27]and we who

3:14
Isa 44:3
Joel 2:28
Acts 2:33
Eph 1:13

3:15
Heb 9:17

3:16
Gen 22:17,18

3:17
Ex 12:40
Rom 4:13,14
3:18
Rom 4:14
Heb 6:14

3:19
Ex 20:19
Deut 5:5; 33:2
Jn 15:22
Acts 7:53
1 Tim 1:9
Heb 2:2
3:20
1 Tim 2:5

3:22
Rom 11:32

3:24
Mt 5:17

3:17 God kept his promise to Abraham (Genesis 17:7, 8)—he has not revoked it, though thousands of years have passed. He saved Abraham through his faith, and he has blessed the world through Abraham by sending the Messiah as one of his descendants. Circumstances may change, but God remains constant and does not break his promises. He has promised to forgive our sins through Jesus Christ, and we can be sure he will do so.

3:18, 19 The law has two functions. On the positive side, it reveals the nature and will of God and shows people how to live. On the negative side, it points out people's sins and shows them that it is impossible to please God by obeying all his laws completely. God's promise to Abraham dealt with his faith; the law focuses on actions. The covenant with Abraham shows that faith is the only way to be saved; the law then shows how to live out our salvation. Faith does not annul the law, but the more we know God, the more we see how sinful we are. Then we are driven to depend on our faith in Christ alone for our salvation.

3:20 This is yet another reason Paul gives for the superiority of Abraham's covenant (faith) over Moses' laws (works) for salvation. The Judaizers had it backwards: the laws flowed *from* faith; they

were not a prerequisite for it. Similarly, right living is not the condition for faith, but the result of it. When we understand the transforming power of faith we will want to live in a way that demonstrates this transformation.

3:21, 22 The iron grip of sin is a reality for all people. We are trapped in sin, beaten down by past mistakes, and choked by desires for things we know are wrong. God knows we are sin's prisoners, and he has provided a way of escape: faith in Jesus Christ. All are caught in sin's grasp, and only those who place their faith in Christ ever get out of it. Look to him—he is reaching out to set you free.

3:25 The law shows the *need* for salvation; God's grace *gives* us that salvation. The Old Testament still applies today. In it, God reveals his nature, his will for man, his moral laws, and guidelines for living.

3:27 In Roman society, a youth coming of age laid aside the robe of childhood and put on a new toga. This represented his move into adult citizenship with full rights and responsibilities. Paul is saying, "You have laid aside the old clothes of the law, and now you are putting on Christ's new robe of righteousness" (see

3:28
Jn 10:16; 17:21
1 Cor 12:13
Col 3:10,11

3:29
Gen 21:10
Rom 8:17; 9:7
Gal 3:16; 4:28
Heb 11:18

have been baptized into union with Christ are enveloped by him. 28We are no longer Jews or Greeks or slaves or free men or even merely men or women, but we are all the same—we are Christians; we are one in Christ Jesus. 29And now that we are Christ's we are the true descendants of Abraham, and all of God's promises to him belong to us.

4 But remember this, that if a father dies and leaves great wealth for his little son, that child is not much better off than a slave until he grows up, even though he

THREE DISTORTIONS OF CHRISTIANITY: Almost from the beginning there were forces at work within Christianity which could have destroyed or sidetracked the movement. Of these, three created many problems then and have continued to reappear in other forms even today. The three aberrations are contrasted to true Christianity:	Group	Their definition of a Christian	Their genuine concern	The danger	Application question
	Judaized Christianity	Christians are Jews who have recognized Jesus as the promised Savior. Therefore any Gentile desiring to become a Christian must first become a Jew.	Having a high regard for God's word and his choice of Jews as his people, they did not want to see God's commands overlooked or broken.	Tends to add human traditions and standards to God's law. Also subtracts from the Scriptures God's clear concern for all nations.	Do you appreciate God's choice of a unique people through which he offered forgiveness and eternal life to all peoples?
	Legalized Christianity	Christians are those who live by a long list of "don'ts." God's favor is earned by good behavior.	Recognized that real change brought about by God should lead to changes in behavior.	Tends to make God's love something to earn rather than to accept freely. Would reduce Christianity to a set of impossible rules and transform the Good News into bad news.	As important as change in action is, can you see that God may be desiring different changes in you than in others?
	Law-less Christianity	Christians live above the law. They need no guidelines. God's word is not as important as our personal sense of God's guidance.	Recognized that forgiveness from God cannot be based on our ability to live up to his perfect standards. It must be received by faith as a gift made possible by Christ's death on the cross.	Forgets that Christians are still human and fail consistently when trying to live only by what they "feel" God wants.	Do you recognize the ongoing need for God's expressed commands as you live out your gratitude for his great salvation?
	True Christianity	Christians are those who believe inwardly and outwardly that Jesus' death has allowed God to offer them forgiveness and eternal life as a gift. They have accepted that gift by faith and are seeking to live a life of obedient gratitude for what God has done for them.	Christianity is both private and public; heart-belief and mouth-confession. Our relationship to God and the power he provides result in obedience. Having received the gift of forgiveness and eternal life, we are now daily challenged to live that life with his help.	Avoids the above dangers.	How would those closest to you describe your Christianity? Do they think you live so that God will accept you or do they know that you live because God has accepted you in Christ?

2 Corinthians 5:21; Ephesians 4:23, 24).

3:28 Jewish males greeted each new day by praying, "Lord, I thank you that I am not a Gentile, a slave, or a woman." This prayer should no longer be said, because faith in Christ transcends these differences and makes all believers one in Christ.

3:28 It's our natural inclination to feel uncomfortable around those who are different from us and to gravitate toward those who resemble us. But when we allow our differences to separate us

from our fellow believers, we are disregarding clear biblical teaching. Make a point of seeking out and appreciating people who are not just like you and your friends. You may find that you and they have a lot in common.

3:29 The original covenant with Abraham was intended for the whole world, not just for his descendants (see Genesis 12:3). All believers partake of this covenant and are blessed as children of Abraham.

actually owns everything his father had. ²He has to do what his guardians and managers tell him to, until he reaches whatever age his father set.

³And that is the way it was with us before Christ came. We were slaves to Jewish laws and rituals for we thought they could save us. ⁴But when the right time came, the time God decided on, he sent his Son, born of a woman, born as a Jew, ⁵to buy freedom for us who were slaves to the law so that he could adopt us as his very own sons. ⁶And because we are his sons God has sent the Spirit of his Son into our hearts, so now we can rightly speak of God as our dear Father. ⁷Now we are no longer slaves, but God's own sons. And since we are his sons, everything he has belongs to us, for that is the way God planned.

Paul's concern for the Galatians

⁸Before you Gentiles knew God you were slaves to so-called gods that did not even exist. ⁹And now that you have found God (or I should say, now that God has found you) how can it be that you want to go back again and become slaves once more to another poor, weak, useless religion of trying to get to heaven by obeying God's laws? ¹⁰You are trying to find favor with God by what you do or don't do on certain days or months or seasons or years. ¹¹I fear for you. I am afraid that all my hard work for you was worth nothing.

¹²Dear brothers, please feel as I do about these things, for I am as free from these chains as you used to be. You did not despise me then when I first preached to you, ¹³even though I was sick when I first brought you the Good News of Christ. ¹⁴But even though my sickness was revolting to you, you didn't reject me and turn me away. No, you took me in and cared for me as though I were an angel from God, or even Jesus Christ himself.

¹⁵Where is that happy spirit that we felt together then? For in those days I know you would gladly have taken out your own eyes and given them to replace mine if that would have helped me.

¹⁶And now have I become your enemy because I tell you the truth?

¹⁷Those false teachers who are so anxious to win your favor are not doing it for your good. What they are trying to do is to shut you off from me so that you will pay more attention to them. ¹⁸It is a fine thing when people are nice to you with good

4:3
Col 2:8
Heb 9:10

4:4
Mk 1:15
Jn 1:14
Eph 1:10
Heb 2:14

4:5
Mt 20:28
Rom 8:14,15
Eph 1:5

4:7
Rom 8:16,17

4:8
2 Chron 13:9
Rom 1:25
1 Cor 8:4
Eph 2:12
1 Thess 1:9

4:9
Col 2:20

4:10
Rom 14:5
Col 2:16

4:12
Gal 6:14

4:13
1 Cor 2:3
Gal 1:6

4:14
Mt 10:40
1 Thess 2:13

4:16
Amos 5:10

4:17
Rom 10:2

4:3-7 Paul uses the illustration of slavery to show that before Christ came and died for sins, people were in bondage to the law. Thinking they could be saved by it, they became enslaved to trying—and failing—to keep it. But the Good News is that we who were once slaves are now God's very own children with an intimate relationship with him. Because of Christ, there is no reason to be afraid of God. We can come boldly into his presence, knowing he will welcome us as members of his family.

4:4 "At just the right time" God sent Jesus to earth to die for our sins. For centuries the Jews were wondering when their Messiah would come—but God's timing was perfect. We may sometimes wonder if God will ever respond to our prayers. But we must never stop trusting him or give up hope. At the right time he will respond. Are you waiting for his timing? Trust his judgment for your best interests.

4:4, 5 Jesus was born of a woman—he was human. He was born as a Jew—he was subject to God's law and fulfilled it perfectly. Thus Jesus was the perfect sacrifice because, although he was fully human, he never sinned. His death bought freedom for us who were enslaved to sin so we could be adopted into God's family.

4:5-7 Under Roman law, an adopted child was guaranteed all legal rights to his father's property. He was not a second-class son; he was equal to any other sons, biological or adopted, in his father's family. As adopted children of God, we share with Jesus all rights to God's resources. As God's heirs, we can claim what he has provided for us—our full identity as his children (see Romans 8:15-17).

4:14 The world is often callous to people's pain and misery. Paul

commended the Galatians for not rejecting him, even though his condition was revolting (he doesn't explain what was wrong with him). Such caring was what Jesus meant when he called us to serve the homeless, hungry, sick, and imprisoned as if they were Jesus himself (Matthew 25:40). Do you avoid those in pain or facing difficulty—or are you willing to care for them as if they were Jesus Christ himself?

4:15 Paul sensed that the Galatians had lost the joy of their salvation because of legalism. How does legalism take away "that happy spirit"? (1) It makes people feel guilty rather than loved; (2) it produces self-hatred rather than humility; (3) it stresses performance over relationship; (4) it points out how far short we fall rather than how far we've come because of what Christ did for us. If you feel guilty and inadequate, check your focus. Are you putting your faith in Christ or in rule-keeping?

4:16 Paul did not gain great popularity when he rebuked the Galatians for turning away from their first faith in Christ. Human nature hasn't changed much—we still get angry when we're scolded. But don't write off someone who challenges you. There may be truth in what he says. Receive his words with humility; carefully think them over. If you discover you need to change an attitude or action, take steps to do it.

4:17 These false teachers claimed to be religious authorities, experts in Judaism and Christianity. Appealing to the believers' desire to do what is right, they drew quite a following. Paul said, however, that they were wrong and that their motives were selfish. False teachers are often respectable and persuasive. That is why all teachings need to be checked with the Bible.

motives and sincere hearts, especially if they aren't doing it just when I am with you! 19Oh, my children, how you are hurting me! I am once again suffering for you the pains of a mother waiting for her child to be born—longing for the time when you will finally be filled with Christ. 20How I wish I could be there with you right now and not have to reason with you like this, for at this distance I frankly don't know what to do.

Abraham's two children

21Listen to me, you friends who think you have to obey the Jewish laws to be saved: Why don't you find out what those laws really mean? 22For it is written that Abraham had two sons, one from his slavewife and one from his freeborn wife. 23There was nothing unusual about the birth of the slave-wife's baby. But the baby of the freeborn wife was born only after God had especially promised he would come.

24, 25Now this true story is an illustration of God's two ways of helping people. One way was by giving them his laws to obey. He did this on Mount Sinai, when he gave the Ten Commandments to Moses. Mount Sinai, by the way, is called "Mount Hagar" by the Arabs—and in my illustration Abraham's slave-wife Hagar represents Jerusalem, the mother-city of the Jews, the center of that system of trying to please God by trying to obey the Commandments; and the Jews, who try to follow that system, are her slave children. 26But our mother-city is the heavenly Jerusalem, and she is not a slave to Jewish laws.

27That is what Isaiah meant when he prophesied, "Now you can rejoice, O childless woman; you can shout with joy though you never before had a child. For I am going to give you many children—more children than the slave-wife has."

28You and I, dear brothers, are the children that God promised, just as Isaac was. 29And so we who are born of the Holy Spirit are persecuted now by those who want us to keep the Jewish laws, just as Isaac the child of promise was persecuted by Ishmael the slave-wife's son. 30But the Scriptures say that God told Abraham to send away the slave-wife and her son, for the slave-wife's son could not inherit Abraham's home and lands along with the free woman's son. 31Dear brothers, we are not slave children, obligated to the Jewish laws, but children of the free woman, acceptable to God because of our faith.

3. Freedom of the gospel

Living in the freedom of Christ

5 So Christ has made us free. Now make sure that you stay free and don't get all tied up again in the chains of slavery to Jewish laws and ceremonies. 2Listen to me, for this is serious: *if you are counting on circumcision and keeping the Jewish laws to make you right with God, then Christ cannot save you.* 3I'll say it again. Anyone trying to find favor with God by being circumcised must always obey every other Jewish law or perish. 4Christ is useless to you if you are counting on

4:19
1 Cor 4:15
Eph 3:17; 4:13

4:22
Gen 16:15; 21:2

4:23
Gen 18:10
Rom 9:7,8

4:24
Deut 32:2-4

4:26
Heb 12:22
Rev 3:12; 21:2

4:27
Isa 54:1

4:28
Rom 4:16
Gal 3:29

4:29
Gen 21:9

4:30
Gen 21:10
Jn 8:35
Gal 3:8

5:1
Jn 8:32
Acts 15:10
Gal 2:4

5:2
Acts 15:1

5:3
Gal 3:10

4:19 Paul led many people to Christ and helped them mature spiritually. Perhaps one reason for his success as a spiritual father was the deep concern he felt for his spiritual children; he compared his pain over their faithlessness to the pain of childbirth. We should have the same intense care for those to whom we are spiritual parents. When you lead people to Christ, remember to stay by to help them grow.

4:21ff People are saved because of their faith in Christ, not because of what they do. Paul contrasts those who are enslaved to the law (represented by Hagar, the slave woman) with those who are free from the law (represented by Sarah, the free woman). Hagar's abuse of Sarah (Genesis 16:4) was like the persecution Gentile Christians were getting from the Judaizers, who insisted on keeping the law in order to be saved. Eventually Sarah triumphed because her son was promised by God, just as those who worship Christ in faith will also triumph.

5:1 Christ died to set us free from sin and from a long list of laws and regulations. Christ came to set us free—not free to do whatever we want, for that would lead back into slavery to our selfish desires. Rather, thanks to Christ, we are now free and able to do what was impossible before—to live unselfishly. Those who appeal to their freedom so they can have their own way or indulge their desires are falling back into sin. Do you use your freedom for yourself or for others?

5:2 "Christ cannot save you" is literally "Christ will be of no advantage to you." Trying to be saved by keeping the law and being saved by grace are two entirely different approaches. Christ's provision for our salvation will not help us if we are trying to save ourselves. We cannot make it any easier for God to save us. All we can do is accept his grace through faith.

clearing your debt to God by keeping those laws; you are lost from God's grace.

5But we by the help of the Holy Spirit are counting on Christ's death to clear away our sins and make us right with God. 6And we to whom Christ has given eternal life don't need to worry about whether we have been circumcised or not, or whether we are obeying the Jewish ceremonies or not; for all we need is faith working through love.

7You were getting along so well. Who has interfered with you to hold you back from following the truth? 8It certainly isn't God who has done it, for he is the one who has called you to freedom in Christ. 9But it takes only one wrong person among you to infect all the others.

10I am trusting the Lord to bring you back to believing as I do about these things. God will deal with that person, whoever he is, who has been troubling and confusing you.

11Some people even say that I myself am preaching that circumcision and Jewish laws are necessary to the plan of salvation. Well, if I preached that, I would be persecuted no more—for that message doesn't offend anyone. The fact that I am still being persecuted proves that I am still preaching salvation through faith in the cross of Christ alone.

12I only wish these teachers who want you to cut yourselves by being circumcised would cut themselves off from you and leave you alone!

13For, dear brothers, you have been given freedom: not freedom to do wrong, but freedom to love and serve each other. 14For the whole Law can be summed up in

5:5 Rom 8:23
5:6 Col 3:11 1 Thess 1:3 Jas 2:18
5:7 1 Cor 9:24
5:8 Rom 8:28
5:9 1 Cor 5:6
5:10 Gal 1:7
5:11 1 Cor 1:23 15:30
5:12 Acts 15:1 1 Cor 5:13
5:13 1 Pet 2:16
5:14 Lev 19:18 Jn 13:34 Rom 13:8

5:12 would cut themselves off from you and leave you alone, or "would that those disturbing you would go and castrate themselves."

Vices
(Neglecting God and others)

Impure thoughts (Galatians 5:19)
Lust (Galatians 5:19)
Hatred (Galatians 5:20)
Fighting (Galatians 5:20)
Jealousy (Galatians 5:20)
Anger (Galatians 5:20)
Trying to be first (Galatians 5:20)
Complaining (Galatians 5:20)
Criticizing (Galatians 5:20)
Thinking you're always right (Galatians 5:20)
Envy (Galatians 5:21)
Murder (Galatians 5:21; Revelation 22:12–16)
Idolatry (Galatians 5:20; Ephesians 5:5)
Spiritism (Galatians 5:20)
Drunkenness (Galatians 5:21)
Wild parties (Galatians 5:21)
Cheating (1 Corinthians 6:8)
Adultery (1 Corinthians 6:9, 10)
Homosexuality (1 Corinthians 6:9, 10)
Greed (1 Corinthians 6:9, 10; Ephesians 5:5)
Stealing (1 Corinthians 6:9, 10)
Lying (Revelation 22:12–16)

Virtues
(The by-products of living for God)

Love (Galatians 5:22)
Joy (Galatians 5:22)
Peace (Galatians 5:22)
Patience (Galatians 5:22)
Kindness (Galatians 5:22)
Goodness (Galatians 5:22)
Faithfulness (Galatians 5:22)
Gentleness (Galatians 5:23)
Self-control (Galatians 5:23)

VICES AND VIRTUES
The Bible mentions many specific actions and attitudes that are either right or wrong. Look at the list included here. Are there too many characteristics from the wrong column that are influencing you?

5:6 We are saved by faith, not works, but love for others and for God is the response of those whom God has forgiven. God's forgiveness is complete, and Jesus said that those who are forgiven much love much (Luke 7:47). Since faith expresses itself through love, you can check up on your love to monitor your faith.

5:11 Persecution proved that Paul was preaching the gospel. If he taught what the false teachers taught, no one would be offended; but because he taught the truth, he was persecuted by both Jews and Judaizers. Have friends or loved ones rejected you because you have taken a stand for Christ? Paul's experience reminds us that this is to be expected. Jesus said not to be surprised if the world hates you, because it hated him (John 15:18,

19). Just as Paul continued faithfully proclaiming the message about Christ, you should continue doing the work God has given you to do—in spite of the obstacles others may put in your way.

5:13 Paul distinguished between freedom to sin and freedom to serve. Freedom to sin is no freedom at all, because it enslaves you to Satan, others, or your own evil desires. People who are slaves to sin are not free to live a righteous life. Christians, by contrast, should not be slaves to sin because they are free to do right and glorify God through their actions.

5:14, 15 When we are not motivated by love, we become critical of others. We stop looking for good in them and see only their faults. Soon the unity of believers is broken. Have you talked

this one command: "Love others as you love yourself." ¹⁵But if instead of showing love among yourselves you are always critical and catty, watch out! Beware of ruining each other.

Living by the Holy Spirit's power

5:16
Rom 6:12; 8:4-6

5:17
Rom 7:15,23

5:18
Rom 6:14; 8:14

5:19
Rom 13:12,13
1 Cor 3:3
Jas 3:14

5:21
1 Cor 6:9
Eph 5:5
Rev 22:15

5:22
Jas 3:17

¹⁶I advise you to obey only the Holy Spirit's instructions. He will tell you where to go and what to do, and then you won't always be doing the wrong things your evil nature wants you to. ¹⁷For we naturally love to do evil things that are just the opposite from the things that the Holy Spirit tells us to do; and the good things we want to do when the Spirit has his way with us are just the opposite of our natural desires. These two forces within us are constantly fighting each other to win control over us, and our wishes are never free from their pressures. ¹⁸When you are guided by the Holy Spirit you need no longer force yourself to obey Jewish laws.

¹⁹But when you follow your own wrong inclinations your lives will produce these evil results: impure thoughts, eagerness for lustful pleasure, ²⁰idolatry, spiritism (that is, encouraging the activity of demons), hatred and fighting, jealousy and anger, constant effort to get the best for yourself, complaints and criticisms, the feeling that everyone else is wrong except those in your own little group—and there will be wrong doctrine, ²¹envy, murder, drunkenness, wild parties, and all that sort of thing. Let me tell you again as I have before, that anyone living that sort of life will not inherit the Kingdom of God.

²²But when the Holy Spirit controls our lives he will produce this kind of fruit in us: love, joy, peace, patience, kindness, goodness, faithfulness, ²³gentleness and self-control; and here there is no conflict with Jewish laws.

| **OUR WRONG DESIRES VS. THE FRUIT OF THE SPIRIT** The will of the Holy Spirit is in constant opposition to our sinful desires. The two are on opposite sides of the spiritual battle. | *Our wrong desires are:* Evil Destructive Easy to ignite Difficult to stifle Self-centered Oppressive and possessive Decadent Sinful Deadly | *The fruit of the Spirit is:* Good Productive Difficult to ignite Easy to stifle Self-giving Liberating and nurturing Uplifting Holy Abundant life |

---

behind someone's back? Have you focused on others' shortcomings instead of their strengths? Remind yourself of Jesus' command to love others as we love ourselves (Matthew 22:39). When you begin to feel critical of someone, make a list of that person's positive qualities. And don't say anything behind his back that you wouldn't say to his face.

5:16–18 If your desires would lead to the qualities listed in 5:22, then you know the Holy Spirit is leading you. At the same time, you must beware of confusing your feelings with the Spirit's leading. Thus, being led by the Holy Spirit involves the desire to hear, and the readiness to obey, and the sensitivity to discern between your feelings and his promptings.

5:17 Paul describes the two forces at work within us—the Holy Spirit and our evil inclinations. Paul is not saying that these forces are equal. The Holy Spirit is infinitely stronger, but *we* are weak. Left to our sin, we will make wrong choices. Our only way to freedom from our natural evil desires is through the empowering of the Holy Spirit (see Romans 8:9; Ephesians 4:23, 24; Colossians 3:3–8).

5:19–21 We all have natural evil desires, and we can't ignore them. In order for us to follow the Holy Spirit's guidance, we must deal with them decisively (nail them to Christ's cross—5:24). These desires include obvious sins such as sexual immorality and

witchcraft. They also include less obvious sins such as ambition, anger, and envy. Ignoring our sins or refusing to deal with them prevents us from inheriting the Kingdom of God.

5:22 We are all controlled by some outside force. If we are controlled by the law, we are condemned by our inability to keep it. If we are controlled by sin, we are destroyed by our own evil actions. If we are controlled by the Holy Spirit, we produce the kind of fruit listed here. We do not need to fear the Spirit's control. He does not possess us against our wills or treat us as robots.

5:22 The Spirit produces character traits, not specific actions. We can't go out and *do* these things, and we can't obtain them by trying to get them. If we want the fruit of the Spirit to develop in our lives, we must recognize that all of these characteristics are found in Christ. Thus the way to grow them is to join our lives to his (see John 15:4, 5). We must know him, love him, remember him, imitate him. The result will be that we will fulfill the intended purpose of the law—loving God and man. Which of these qualities most needs further development in your life?

5:23 Because the God who sent the law also sent the Spirit, the by-products of the Spirit-filled life are in perfect harmony with the intent of God's law. A person who is rich in the fruit of the Spirit fulfills the law far better than a person who observes the rituals but has little love in his heart.

24Those who belong to Christ have nailed their natural evil desires to his cross and crucified them there.

5:24
Rom 6:6

25If we are living now by the Holy Spirit's power, let us follow the Holy Spirit's leading in every part of our lives. 26Then we won't need to look for honors and popularity, which lead to jealousy and hard feelings.

5:25
Gal 5:16
5:26
Phil 2:3

We will reap what we sow

6 Dear brothers, if a Christian is overcome by some sin, you who are godly should gently and humbly help him back onto the right path, remembering that next time it might be one of you who is in the wrong. 2Share each other's troubles and problems, and so obey our Lord's command. 3If anyone thinks he is too great to stoop to this, he is fooling himself. He is really a nobody.

6:1
1 Cor 2:15; 7:5
Jas 5:19,20
1 Jn 5:16
6:2
Rom 15:1

4Let everyone be sure that he is doing his very best, for then he will have the personal satisfaction of work well done, and won't need to compare himself with someone else. 5Each of us must bear some faults and burdens of his own. For none of us is perfect!

6:3
Rom 12:3
1 Cor 3:18
2 Cor 3:5; 12:11
6:6
Rom 15:27
1 Cor 9:11,14

6Those who are taught the Word of God should help their teachers by paying them.

6:7
1 Cor 6:9
2 Cor 9:6

7Don't be misled; remember that you can't ignore God and get away with it: a man will always reap just the kind of crop he sows! 8If he sows to please his own wrong desires, he will be planting seeds of evil and he will surely reap a harvest of spiritual decay and death; but if he plants the good things of the Spirit, he will reap the everlasting life which the Holy Spirit gives him. 9And let us not get tired of doing what is right, for after a while we will reap a harvest of blessing if we don't get discouraged and give up. 10That's why whenever we can we should always be kind to everyone, and especially to our Christian brothers.

6:8
Job 4:8
Rom 8:9-14
Jas 3:18
6:9
Mt 24:13
2 Thess 3:13
6:10
Jn 9:4
Eph 2:19
1 Tim 6:18
Heb 3:6

Paul's final warning

11I will write these closing words in my own handwriting. See how large I have to make the letters! 12Those teachers of yours who are trying to convince you to be

6:11
1 Cor 16:21

5:24 In order to accept Christ as Savior, we need to turn from our sins and willingly nail our natural evil desires to the cross. This doesn't mean, however, that we will never see traces of those desires again. As Christians we still have the capacity to sin, but we have been set free from sin's power over us and no longer have to give in to it. We must daily commit our sinful tendencies to God's control, daily nail them to Christ's cross, and moment by moment draw on the Spirit's power to overcome them (see 2:20; 6:14).

5:25 God is interested in every part of our lives, not just the spiritual part. As we live by the Holy Spirit's power, we need to submit every aspect of our lives to God—emotional, physical, social, intellectual, vocational. Paul says, "You're saved, so live like it!" The Holy Spirit is the source of your new life, so walk with him. Don't let anything or anyone else determine your values and standards in any area of your life.

5:26 We all need a certain amount of approval from others. But those who go out of their way to secure honors or to win popularity with a lot of people show they are not following the Holy Spirit's leading. Those who look to God for approval won't need to seek it from others.

6:1–3 No one should ever think he or she is totally independent and doesn't need help from others, and no one should feel excused from the task of helping. The body of Christ—the universal church—functions only when the members work together for the common good. Is there someone near you who needs help in a task of daily living? Is there a Christian brother or sister who needs correction or encouragement? Humbly and gently reach out to that person (John 13:34, 35). Any who feel they are too busy to help others take their work far too seriously.

6:4 When you do your very best, you feel good about the results

and there is no need to compare yourself with others. People make comparisons for many reasons. Some point out others' flaws in order to feel better about themselves. Others simply want reassurance that they are doing well. When you are tempted to compare, look at Jesus Christ. His example will inspire you to do your very best, and his loving acceptance will comfort you when you fall short of your goals.

6:6 Paul insisted that we fulfill our responsibility to take care of the material needs of those who teach us (1 Corinthians 9:7–12). It is easy to receive the benefit of good Bible teaching and take our spiritual leaders for granted, ignoring their financial and physical needs. We should care for them, not grudgingly or reluctantly, but with a generous spirit, showing honor and appreciation for their service (1 Timothy 5:17, 18).

6:7, 8 It would certainly be a surprise if you planted corn in the ground and pumpkins came up. But it probably would not be a surprise if you gossiped about your friends and soon found you had no friends. It's a law of life—both physical and spiritual—that you reap what you sow. Every action has results. If you plant to please your own desires, you'll reap a crop of sorrow and evil; if you plant to please God, you'll reap joy and everlasting life. What kind of seeds are you sowing in the soil of your life?

6:9, 10 It is discouraging to continue to do right and receive no word of thanks or see no tangible results. But Paul challenges the Galatians and us to keep on doing what is right and to trust God for the results. In due time, we will reap a harvest of blessing.

6:11 Up to this point, Paul had dictated the letter to a scribe. Now he took the pen into his own hands to write his final, personal greetings. He did this in other letters as well, to add emphasis to his words and validate that the letter was genuine.

circumcised are doing it for just one reason: so that they can be popular and avoid the persecution they would get if they admitted that the cross of Christ alone can save. ¹³And even those teachers who submit to circumcision don't try to keep the other Jewish laws; but they want you to be circumcised in order that they can boast that you are their disciples.

¹⁴As for me, God forbid that I should boast about anything except the cross of our Lord Jesus Christ. Because of that cross my interest in all the attractive things of the world was killed long ago, and the world's interest in me is also long dead. ¹⁵It doesn't make any difference now whether we have been circumcised or not; what counts is whether we really have been changed into new and different people. ¹⁶May God's mercy and peace be upon all of you who live by this principle and upon those everywhere who are really God's own.

¹⁷From now on please don't argue with me about these things, for I carry on my body the scars of the whippings and wounds from Jesus' enemies that mark me as his slave.

¹⁸Dear brothers, may the grace of our Lord Jesus Christ be with you all.

Sincerely, Paul

6:13
Rom 2:25

6:14
Rom 6:2,3,6
1 Cor 2:2
Gal 2:20
Col 2:20

6:15
2 Cor 5:17
Gal 5:6

6:16
Gal 3:7
Phil 3:3

6:17
2 Cor 1:5; 4:10
Col 1:24

6:18
Rom 16:20
2 Tim 4:22

6:13 Some of the Judaizers emphasized circumcision as proof of holiness—but ignored the other Jewish laws. People often choose a certain principle or prohibition and make it the measuring rod of faith. Some may abhor drunkenness but ignore gluttony. Others despise promiscuity but tolerate prejudice. The Bible in its entirety is our rule of faith and practice. We cannot pick and choose the mandates we will follow.

6:14 The world is full of enticements. We are daily confronted with both subtle cultural pressures and overt propaganda. The only way to escape these destructive influences is to ask God to help us die to them, just as Paul did. How much do the interests of this world matter to you? (See 2:20 and 5:24 for more on this concept.)

6:15 It is easy to get caught up in the externals. Beware of those who emphasize things we should or shouldn't do, with no concern for the inward condition of the heart. Living a "good" life without an inward change leads to a spiritual walk that is shallow and empty.

What matters to God is that we be completely changed from the inside out (2 Corinthians 5:17).

6:18 The Epistle of Paul to the Galatians boldly declares the freedom of the Christian. Doubtless these early Christians in Galatia wanted to grow in the Christian life, but they were being misled by those who said this could be done only by keeping certain Jewish laws.

How strange it would be for a prisoner who had been set free to walk back into his cell and refuse to leave! How strange for an animal, released from a trap, to go back inside it! How sad for a believer to be set free from the bondage of sin, only to return to rigid conformity to a set of rules and regulations! If you believe in Jesus Christ, you have been set free. Instead of going back into some form of slavery, whether legalism or sin, use your freedom to live for Christ and serve him as he desires.

VITAL STATISTICS

PURPOSE:
To strengthen the believers in Ephesus in their Christian faith by explaining the nature and purpose of the church, the body of Christ

AUTHOR:
Paul

TO WHOM WRITTEN:
The church at Ephesus, and all believers everywhere

DATE WRITTEN:
About A.D. 60, from Rome during Paul's imprisonment there

SETTING:
The letter was not written to confront any heresy or problem in the churches. It was sent with Tychicus to strengthen and encourage the churches in the area. Paul spent over three years with the Ephesian church. As a result, Paul was very close to this church. Paul met with the elders of the Ephesian church for the last time at Miletus (Acts 20:17–38)—a meeting that was filled with great sadness because Paul was leaving them for the last time. Because there are no specific references to people or problems in the Ephesian church and because the words "at Ephesus" (1:1) are not present in the earliest manuscripts, Paul may have intended this to be a circular letter—read to all the churches in the area.

KEY VERSE:
"We are all parts of one body, we have the same Spirit, and we have all been called to the same glorious future" (4:4).

KEY PEOPLE:
Paul, Tychicus

SPECIAL FEATURES:
Several pictures of the church are presented: body, temple, mystery, new man, bride, and soldier. This epistle became a circular letter distributed to many of the early churches.

OUR churches come in all styles and shapes—the secret meetings in homes; the wide-open gatherings in amphitheaters; the worship services packing thousands into the sanctuary while the overflow crowd watches on closed circuit television; the handful who kneel in an urban storefront. Buildings will vary, but the church is not confined to four walls. The church of Jesus Christ is *people*, his people, of every race and nation who love Christ and are committed to serving him.

The "church age" began at Pentecost (Acts 2). Born in Jerusalem, the church spread rapidly through the ministry of the apostles and the early believers. Fanned by persecution, the gospel flame then spread to other cities and nations. On three courageous journeys, Paul and his associates established local assemblies in scores of Gentile cities.

One of the most prominent of those churches was at Ephesus. It was established in A.D. 53 on Paul's homeward journey to Jerusalem. But he returned a year later, on his third missionary trip, and stayed there for three years, preaching and teaching with great effectiveness (Acts 19:1–20). At another time, he met with the Ephesian elders, and he sent Timothy to serve as their leader (1 Timothy 1:3). Just a few years later, Paul was sent as a prisoner to Rome. There he was visited by messengers from various churches. Among these was Tychicus of Ephesus. Paul wrote this letter to the church and sent it with Tychicus. Not written to counteract heresy or to confront any specific problem, Ephesians is a letter of encouragement. In it Paul describes the nature and appearance of the church, and he challenges believers to function as the living body of Christ on earth.

After a warm greeting (1:1, 2), Paul affirms the nature of the church—the glorious fact that believers in Christ have been showered with God's kindness (1:3–8), chosen for greatness (1:9–12), marked by the Holy Spirit (1:13, 14), filled with his power (1:15–23), freed from sin's curse and bondage (2:1–10), and brought near to God (2:11–19). As part of God's "house," we stand with the prophets, apostles, Jews, Gentiles, and Christ himself (2:20—3:11). Then, as though overcome with emotion by remembering all that God has done, Paul challenges them to live close to Christ—breaking into spontaneous praise (3:12–21).

Paul then turns his attention to the implications of being in the body of Christ, the church. Believers should have unity in their commitment to Christ and their use of spiritual gifts (4:1–16). They should have the highest moral standards (4:17—6:9)— for the individual, this means rejecting heathen practices (4:17—5:20), and for the family, this means mutual submission and love (5:21—6:9).

Paul then reminds them that the church is in a constant battle with the forces of darkness, and that they should use every spiritual weapon at their disposal (6:10–17). He concludes by asking for their prayers, commissioning Tychicus, and giving a benediction (6:18–24).

As you read this masterful description of the church, thank God for the diversity and unity in his family, pray for your brothers and sisters across the world, and draw close to those in the local church.

THE BLUEPRINT

1. Unity in Christ (1:1—3:21)
2. Unity in the church (4:1—6:24)

In this letter, Paul explains the wonderful things that we have received through Christ and refers to the church as a body, a temple, a bride, and a soldier. These all illustrate unity of purpose and show how each individual member is a part which must work together with all the other parts. In our own lives, we should work to eradicate all backbiting, gossip, criticism, jealousy, anger, and bitterness, because these are barriers to unity in the church.

MEGATHEMES

THEME	EXPLANATION	IMPORTANCE
God's purpose	According to God's eternal, loving plan, he directs, carries out, and sustains our salvation.	When we respond to Christ's love by trusting in him, his purpose becomes our mission. Have you committed yourself to fulfilling God's purpose?
Christ the center	Christ is exalted as the central meaning of the universe and the focus of history. He is the head of the body, the church.	Because Christ is central to everything, his power must be central in us. Begin by placing all your priorities in his control.
Living Church	The nature of the church is presented. The church, under Christ's control, is a living body, a family, a dwelling. God gives believers special abilities by his Holy Spirit to build the church.	We are part of Christ's body, and we must live in vital union with him. Our conduct must be consistent with this living relationship. Use your God-given abilities to equip believers for service. Fulfill your role in the living church.
New family	Because God through Christ paid our penalty for sin and forgave us, we have been reconciled—brought near to him. We are a new society, a new family. United with Christ means we are to treat one another as family members.	We are one family in Christ; so there should be no barriers, no divisions, no basis for discrimination. We all belong to him, so we should live in harmony with one another.
Christian conduct	Paul encourages all Christians to wise, dynamic Christian living, for with privileges goes family responsibility. As a new community, we are to have Christ's new standards.	God provides his Holy Spirit to enable us to live his way. To utilize his power, we must lay aside our evil desires and draw upon the power of his new life. Submit your will to Christ, and seek to love others.

1. Unity in Christ

1 Dear Christian friends at Ephesus, ever loyal to the Lord: This is Paul writing to you, chosen by God to be Jesus Christ's messenger. ²May his blessings and peace be yours, sent to you from God our Father and Jesus Christ our Lord.

1:2
Rom 1:7
Tit 1:4

God's overflowing kindness

³How we praise God, the Father of our Lord Jesus Christ, who has blessed us with every blessing in heaven because we belong to Christ.

⁴Long ago, even before he made the world, God chose us to be his very own, through what Christ would do for us; he decided then to make us holy in his eyes, without a single fault—we who stand before him covered with his love. ⁵His

1:3
Eph 1:20; 2:6
1:4
2 Thess 2:13
1 Pet 1:2,20
1:5
Rom 8:15,29

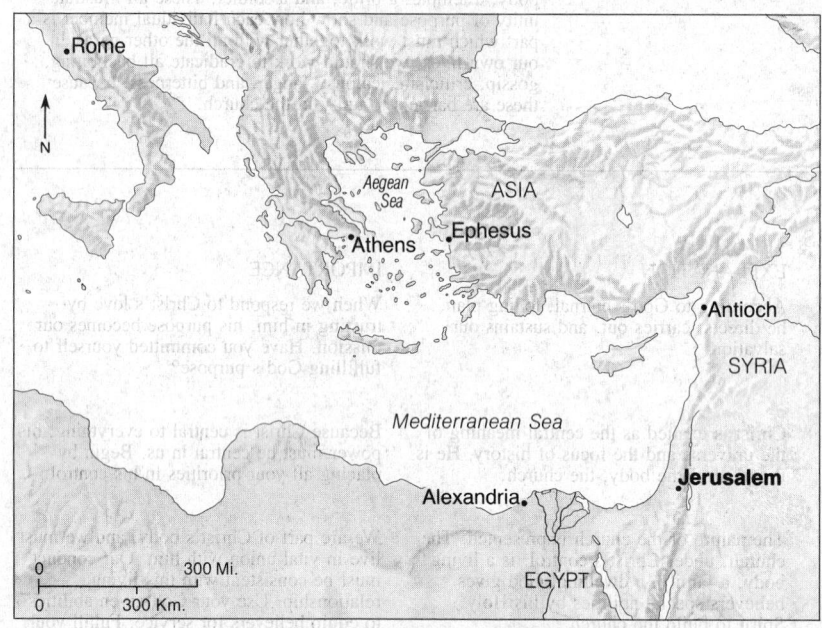

LOCATION OF EPHESUS
Ephesus was a strategic city, ranking in importance with Alexandria in Egypt and Antioch in Syria as a port. It lay on the most western edge of Asia Minor (modern-day Turkey), the most important port on the Aegean Sea on the main route from Rome to the east.

1:1 From inside the walls of a Roman prison, Paul wrote this letter to the church at Ephesus, in order to give them in-depth teaching about how to nurture and maintain the unity of the church. He wanted to circulate this important information in written form because he was in prison and could not visit the churches himself. Paul mentions no particular problems or local situations, and he offers no personal greetings. This was probably a circular letter—one sent to Ephesus and to neighboring local churches.

1:1 Paul had been a Christian for nearly 30 years. He had taken three missionary trips and established churches all around the Mediterranean Sea. When he wrote Ephesians, he was under house arrest in Rome (See Acts 28:16ff). Though a prisoner, he was free to have visitors and write letters. For more information on Paul, see his Profile in Acts 9.

1:1 Ephesus was one of the five major cities in the Roman Empire, along with Rome, Corinth, Antioch, and Alexandria. Paul first visited Ephesus on his second missionary journey (Acts 18:19-21) and, during his third missionary journey, stayed there almost three years (Acts 19). He later met again with the elders of the Ephesian church at Miletus (Acts 20:16-38). Ephesus was a commercial, political, and religious center for all of Asia Minor. The temple to the goddess Artemis (Diana) was located there.

1:1 "Ever loyal to the Lord"—what an excellent reputation! Such a label would be an honor for any believer. What would it take for others to characterize you this way? Hold fast to your faith one day

at a time; faithfully obey God even in the details of life; and like the Ephesians you will be known as loyal to the Lord.

1:3 What is heaven? Heaven is where God is. "Every blessing in heaven" means all the good things God gives us— salvation, the gifts of the Spirit, power to do God's will, the hope of eternity with Christ. Because we live in an intimate relationship with Christ, we can enjoy these blessings now. Other references to heaven in this letter include 1:20; 2:6; 3:10. They show Christ in his victorious, exalted role as ruler of all.

1:4 Paul said, "God chose us," to emphasize that salvation depends totally on God. We are not saved because we deserve it, but because God is gracious and freely gives it. We did not influence God's decision to save us; he did it according to his plan. Thus there is no way to take credit for your salvation, or to find room for pride. The mystery of salvation originated in the timeless mind of God long before we existed. It is hard to understand how God could accept us, but because of Christ we are holy and blameless in his eyes. God chose you, and when you belong to him through Jesus Christ, he looks at you as if you had never sinned.

1:5 God has adopted us as his own children. Through Jesus' sacrifice, he has brought us into his family and made us heirs along with Jesus (Romans 8:17). In Roman law, adopted children had the same rights and privileges as natural children. Paul uses this term to show how strong our relationship to God is. For more

1:6
Rom 3:24
Col 1:13

1:7
1 Cor 6:20
Col 1:14
Heb 9:12
Rev 5:9

1:9
Col 1:26,27; 2:2

1:10
Mk 1:15
Gal 4:4
Col 1:20

1:11
Rom 9:11
Eph 3:11

unchanging plan has always been to adopt us into his own family by sending Jesus Christ to die for us. And he did this because he wanted to!

6Now all praise to God for his wonderful kindness to us and his favor that he has poured out upon us, because we belong to his dearly loved Son. 7So overflowing is his kindness toward us that he took away all our sins through the blood of his Son, by whom we are saved; 8and he has showered down upon us the richness of his grace—for how well he understands us and knows what is best for us at all times.

9God has told us his secret reason for sending Christ, a plan he decided on in mercy long ago; 10and this was his purpose: that when the time is ripe he will gather us all together from wherever we are—in heaven or on earth—to be with him in Christ, forever. 11Moreover, because of what Christ has done we have become gifts to God that he delights in, for as part of God's sovereign plan we were chosen from

OUR TRUE IDENTITY IN CHRIST		
Romans 3:24	We are declared "not guilty" of sin.
Romans 8:1	No condemnation awaits us.
Romans 8:2	We are free from the vicious circle of sin and death.
1 Corinthians 1:2	We are acceptable to God through Jesus Christ.
1 Corinthians 1:30	We are pure and holy.
1 Corinthians 15:22	We will rise again.
2 Corinthians 3:17	We are free from trying to be saved by being good enough.
2 Corinthians 5:17	We are brand new people inside.
2 Corinthians 5:21	We are full of God's goodness.
Galatians 3:28	We are one in Christ with all other believers.
Ephesians 1:3	We are blessed with every spiritual blessing in heaven.
Ephesians 1:4	We are holy, faultless, and covered with God's love.
Ephesians 1:5, 6	We belong to Christ.
Ephesians 1:7	Our sins are taken away and we are forgiven.
Ephesians 1:10, 11	We will live with Christ forever; we are gifts to God.
Ephesians 1:13	We are marked as belonging to God by the Holy Spirit.
Ephesians 2:6	We have been lifted from the grave to sit with Christ in glory.
Ephesians 2:10	We have been given new lives.
Ephesians 2:13	We have been brought near to God.
Ephesians 3:6	We will receive great blessings.
Ephesians 3:12	We can come fearlessly into God's presence.
Ephesians 5:29, 30	We are part of Christ's body, the church.
Colossians 2:10	We have everything because we have Christ; we are filled with God.
Colossians 2:11	We are set free from our evil desires.
2 Timothy 2:10	We will have eternal glory.

on the meaning of adoption, see Galatians 4:5–7.

1:7 To speak of Jesus' blood was an important first-century way of speaking of Christ's death. His death points to two wonderful truths—redemption and forgiveness. *Redemption* was the price paid to gain freedom for a slave (Leviticus 25:47–54). Through his death, Jesus paid the price to release us from our slavery to sin. *Forgiveness* was granted in Old Testament times on the basis of the shedding of animals' blood (Leviticus 17:11, the death of the animal). Now we are forgiven on the basis of the shedding of Jesus' blood, because he died and was the perfect and final sacrifice. (See also Romans 5:9; Ephesians 2:13; Colossians 1:20; Hebrews 9:22; 1 Peter 1:19.)

1:8 Grace is God's voluntary and loving favor given to those he saves. We can't earn it, nor do we deserve it. No religious or moral effort can gain it, for it comes only from God's mercy and love. Without grace, no person can be saved.

1:9, 10 God was not intentionally keeping a secret, but his plan for the world could not be fully understood until Christ rose from the dead. His secret purpose for sending Christ was to unite Jews

and Gentiles in one body with Christ as the head. Many people still do not understand God's plan, but "when the time is ripe" he will gather us to be with him forever and then everyone will understand. On that day, all people will bow to Jesus as Lord, either because they love him or because they fear his power (see Philippians 2:10, 11).

1:11 What delight youngsters display when given a special gift. Joy radiates from their eyes, spreading across their faces in big, happy smiles. As adults, we rarely experience such pure delight. Yet we ourselves are gifts that inspire an infinitely higher and greater delight in the heart of God. He accepts us with joy because of what Christ did for us. When you feel that your life isn't worth much to anyone, remember that you are a special gift in God's eyes, a precious present that brings him great joy.

1:11 God has offered salvation to the world just as he planned to do long ago. God is sovereign; he is in charge. When your life seems chaotic, rest in this truth: Jesus is Lord, and God is in control. His purpose to save you cannot be thwarted, no matter what evil Satan may bring.

the beginning to be his, and all things happen just as he decided long ago. 12God's **1:12**
purpose in this was that we should praise God and give glory to him for doing these Eph 1:6,14
mighty things for us, who were the first to trust in Christ. Jas 1:18

13And because of what Christ did, all you others too, who heard the Good News **1:13**
about how to be saved, and trusted Christ, were marked as belonging to Christ by 2 Cor 1:22
the Holy Spirit, who long ago had been promised to all of us Christians. 14His Eph 4:30
presence within us is God's guarantee that he really will give us all that he Col 1:5
promised; and the Spirit's seal upon us means that God has already purchased us **1:14**
and that he guarantees to bring us to himself. This is just one more reason for us to Rom 8:23
praise our glorious God. 2 Cor 1:22; 5:5

Paul's prayer for the Ephesian believers

15That is why, ever since I heard of your strong faith in the Lord Jesus and of the
love you have for Christians everywhere, 16, 17I have never stopped thanking God **1:16**
for you. I pray for you constantly, asking God, the glorious Father of our Lord Col 1:9
Jesus Christ, to give you wisdom to see clearly and really understand who Christ is **1:17**
and all that he has done for you. 18I pray that your hearts will be flooded with light 1 Cor 2:9-12
so that you can see something of the future he has called you to share. I want you **1:18**
to realize that God has been made rich because we who are Christ's have been given Acts 26:18
to him! 19I pray that you will begin to understand how incredibly great his power is Eph 1:11; 4:4
to help those who believe him. It is that same mighty power 20that raised Christ **1:19**
from the dead and seated him in the place of honor at God's right hand in heaven, Eph 3:7,16; 6:10
21far, far above any other king or ruler or dictator or leader. Yes, his honor is far Phil 3:21
more glorious than that of anyone else either in this world or in the world to come. **1:20**
22And God has put all things under his feet and made him the supreme Head of the Acts 2:24
Church— 23which is his body, filled with himself, the Author and Giver of **1:21**
everything everywhere. Phil 2:9

1:22
Col 2:19

1:23
Eph 3:19; 4:10
3:11

The spiritually dead are made alive

2 Once you were under God's curse, doomed forever for your sins. 2You went **2:1**
along with the crowd and were just like all the others, full of sin, obeying Eph 2:5
Satan, the mighty prince of the power of the air, who is at work right now in the **2:2**
hearts of those who are against the Lord. 3All of us used to be just as they are, our Eph 5:6,8; 6:10
lives expressing the evil within us, doing every wicked thing that our passions or **2:3**
Gal 5:16
Tit 3:3

1:14 The Holy Spirit is God's guarantee to us that he will do what
he has promised. He is like a down payment, a deposit, a
validating signature on the contract. The presence of the Holy
Spirit in our lives is our assurance of eternal life with all its
blessings. His power at work in us now is transforming our lives,
and is a taste of the total change we will experience in eternity (see
2 Corinthians 1:22).

1:16, 17 Paul's prayer for the Ephesians was that they might really
understand who Christ is. Christ is our goal and our model, and the
more we know of him, the more we will be like him. Study Jesus'
life in the Bible to see what he was like on earth 2,000 years ago,
and get to know him in prayer now. Personal knowledge of Christ is
life-changing!

1:19, 20 The world fears the power of the atom, yet we belong to
the God of the universe who not only created that atomic power
but also raised Jesus Christ from the dead. We don't need to feel
inadequate. God's incomparable power is for us who believe.

1:20–22 Having been raised from the dead, Christ is now the
supreme head of the church, the ultimate authority over the world.
Christ is the Messiah, God's anointed One, the One Israel longed
for, the One who would set their broken world right. As Christians
we can be confident that God has won the final victory and is in
control of everything. We need not fear any dictator, nation, death,
or Satan himself. The contract has been signed and sealed; we are
waiting just a short while for delivery. Paul says, in Romans
8:37–39, that nothing can separate us from God and his love.

1:22, 23 When reading Ephesians, it is important to remember
that it was written not to an individual but to the church. Christ is
the head and we are the body of his church (Paul uses this
metaphor in Romans 12:4, 5; 1 Corinthians 12:12- 27; and
Colossians 3:15 as well as throughout the book of Ephesians). The
image of the body shows the church's unity. Each member is
involved with all the others as they go about doing Christ's work on
earth.

2:2 "Mighty prince of the power of the air" was understood by
Paul's readers to mean Satan and the evil spiritual forces they
thought inhabited the region between earth and sky. Satan is thus
pictured as ruling the evil spiritual world—the demons and those
who are against Christ. "Satan" means "the Adversary." He is also
called the devil (4:27) and the king of demons (Mark 3:22). In his
resurrection, Christ was victorious over Satan and his power.
Therefore Jesus Christ is the permanent ruler of the whole world;
Satan is only the temporary ruler of the part of the world that
chooses to follow him.

2:3 The fact that all people, without exception, commit sin proves
that they share in the sinful nature. Does this mean there are no
good people who are not Christians? Of course not— many people
do good to others. On a relative scale, many are moral, kind, keep
the laws, and so on. Comparing these people to criminals, we
would say they are very good indeed. But on God's absolute scale,
no one is good. Only through uniting our lives to Christ's perfect life
can we become good in God's sight.

our evil thoughts might lead us into. We started out bad, being born with evil natures, and were under God's anger just like everyone else.

2:4
Jn 3:16
Rom 10:12
Eph 1:7

4But God is so rich in mercy; he loved us so much 5that even though we were spiritually dead and doomed by our sins, he gave us back our lives again when he raised Christ from the dead—only by his undeserved favor have we ever been saved— 6and lifted us up from the grave into glory along with Christ, where we sit with him in the heavenly realms—all because of what Christ Jesus did. 7And now God can always point to us as examples of how very, very rich his kindness is, as shown in all he has done for us through Jesus Christ.

2:5
Rom 5:6; 6:4
2:6
Eph 1:3,20
Col 2:12
2:7
Tit 3:4

8Because of his kindness you have been saved through trusting Christ. And even trusting is not of yourselves; it too is a gift from God. 9Salvation is not a reward for the good we have done, so none of us can take any credit for it. 10It is God himself who has made us what we are and given us new lives from Christ Jesus; and long ages ago he planned that we should spend these lives in helping others.

2:8
Jn 4:10
Rom 4:16
2:9
Rom 3:20
2 Tim 1:9
Tit 3:5

Christ is the way to peace

2:11
Rom 2:28
Col 2:11
2:12
Rom 9:4,8
Gal 4:8

11Never forget that once you were heathen, and that you were called godless and "unclean" by the Jews. (But their hearts, too, were still unclean, even though they were going through the ceremonies and rituals of the godly, for they circumcised themselves as a sign of godliness.) 12Remember that in those days you were living

2:5 *gave us back our lives again,* literally, "he made us alive." 2:8 *And even trusting is not of yourselves,* or, "Salvation is not of yourselves."

OUR LIVES BEFORE AND AFTER CHRIST	Before	After
	Under God's curse	Loved by God
	Doomed because of our sins	Shown God's mercy and given salvation
	Went along with the crowd	Stand for Christ and truth
	God's enemies	God's children
	Enslaved to Satan	Free in Christ to love, serve, and sit with him
	Followed our evil thoughts and passions	Taken from the grave to glory
	Under God's anger	Given undeserved favor
	Spiritually dead	Given new spiritual life

2:4, 5 In the previous verses Paul is talking about our old sinful nature (2:1–3). Here Paul emphasizes that we do not need to live any longer under sin's power. The penalty of sin and its power over our lives was destroyed by Christ on the cross. Paul has already stated that through faith in Christ we stand acquitted, "not guilty" before God (Romans 3:21, 22). God does not take us out of the world or make us robots—we will still feel like sinning, and sometimes we will sin. The difference is that before we became Christians we were slaves to our sinful nature, but now we can choose to live for Christ (see also Galatians 2:20).

2:6 Because of Christ's resurrection, we know that our bodies will also be raised from the dead (1 Corinthians 15:2–23) and that we have been given the power to live the Christian life now (Ephesians 1:19). These ideas are combined in Paul's image of sitting with Christ in glory. Our eternal life in Christ is certain, because we are united in his powerful victory.

2:8, 9 When someone gives you a gift, do you say, "That's very nice—now how much do I owe you?" No, the appropriate response to a gift is "Thank you." Yet how often Christians, even after they have been given the gift of salvation, feel obligated to try to work their way to God. Because our salvation and even our faith are gifts, we should respond with gratitude, praise, and joyfulness.

2:8–10 We become Christians through God's unmerited gift to us (called "grace" in Ephesians 1:8), not as the result of any effort, ability, intelligent choice, or act of service to others on our part. However, out of gratitude for this free gift, we will seek to help and

serve others with kindness, charity, and goodness, and not merely please ourselves. While no action or "work" we do can help us obtain salvation, God's intention is that our salvation will result in works of service. We are not saved merely for our own benefit but for his—to glorify him and build up the church (Ephesians 4:12).

2:11 Pious Jews considered all non-Jews ceremonially unclean. They thought of themselves as pure and clean because of their national heritage and religious ceremonies. Paul points out that Jews and Gentiles alike are unclean before God and need to be cleansed by Christ. In order to realize how great a gift salvation is, we need to remember our natural, unclean condition.

2:11, 12 Before Christ's coming, Gentiles and Jews kept apart from each other. Jews considered Gentiles beyond God's saving power and therefore without hope. Gentiles resented Jewish claims. Christ revealed the total sinfulness of both Jews and Gentiles, and then he offered his salvation equally to both. Only Christ breaks down the walls of prejudice, reconciles all believers to God, and unifies us in one body.

2:11–13 Jews and Gentiles alike could be guilty of spiritual pride—Jews for thinking their ceremonies elevated them above everyone else, Gentiles for forgetting the hopelessness of their condition apart from Christ. Spiritual pride blinds us to our own faults and magnifies the faults of others. Be careful not to become proud of your salvation. Instead, humbly thank God for what he has done, and encourage others who might be struggling in their faith.

utterly apart from Christ; you were enemies of God's children and he had promised you no help. You were lost, without God, without hope.

¹³But now you belong to Christ Jesus, and though you once were far away from God, now you have been brought very near to him because of what Jesus Christ has done for you with his blood.

¹⁴For Christ himself is our way of peace. He has made peace between us Jews and you Gentiles by making us all one family, breaking down the wall of contempt that used to separate us. ¹⁵By his death he ended the angry resentment between us, caused by the Jewish laws which favored the Jews and excluded the Gentiles, for he died to annul that whole system of Jewish laws. Then he took the two groups that had been opposed to each other and made them parts of himself; thus he fused us together to become one new person, and at last there was peace. ¹⁶As parts of the same body, our anger against each other has disappeared, for both of us have been reconciled to God. And so the feud ended at last at the cross. ¹⁷And he has brought this Good News of peace to you Gentiles who were very far away from him, and to us Jews who were near. ¹⁸Now all of us, whether Jews or Gentiles, may come to God the Father with the Holy Spirit's help because of what Christ has done for us.

¹⁹Now you are no longer strangers to God and foreigners to heaven, but you are members of God's very own family, citizens of God's country, and you belong in God's household with every other Christian.

²⁰What a foundation you stand on now: the apostles and the prophets; and the cornerstone of the building is Jesus Christ himself! ²¹We who believe are carefully joined together with Christ as parts of a beautiful, constantly growing temple for God. ²²And you also are joined with him and with each other by the Spirit, and are part of this dwelling place of God.

Paul's special mission to Gentiles

3 I Paul, the servant of Christ, am here in jail because of you—for preaching that you Gentiles are a part of God's house. ², ³No doubt you already know that God has given me this special work of showing God's favor to you Gentiles, as I briefly mentioned before in one of my letters. God himself showed me this secret plan of his, that the Gentiles, too, are included in his kindness. ⁴I say this to explain to you how I know about these things. ⁵In olden times God did not share this plan

2:13
Acts 2:39
Col 1:20
2:14
Mic 5:5
1 Cor 12:13
2:15
2 Cor 5:17
Gal 3:28
Col 1:22; 2:14
2:16
Eph 4:4
Col 1:20
2:17
Isa 57:19
Zech 9:10
Acts 10:36
2:18
Jn 14:6,17-20
Eph 3:12; 4:4
2:19
Eph 2:12
2:20
Ps 118:22
Isa 28:16
Mt 16:18; 21:42
1 Cor 3:11
Rev 21:14
2:21
1 Cor 3:16
Eph 4:15,16
2:22
Jn 17:23
1 Pet 2:5

3:1
2 Tim 2:10
3:2
Rom 16:25
3:3
Eph 1:9; 3:4-9
Col 1:25-27
3:5
Eph 1:17

2:14 *by making us all one family,* literally, "by making us one." *breaking down the wall of contempt,* implied.

2:14ff Christ has broken down the walls people build between themselves. Since these walls have been removed, we can come to real unity with people who are not like us. This is true reconciliation. Because of Christ's death, we are all one family (2:14); our anger against each other has disappeared (2:16); we can all approach God through the Holy Spirit (2:18); we are no longer strangers to God (2:19); and we are all part of a beautiful temple with Christ as our cornerstone (2:20, 21).

2:14 There are many barriers that can divide us from other Christians: age, appearance, intelligence, political persuasion, economic status, race, theological perspective. One of the best ways to stifle Christ's love is to cater only to those for whom we have natural affinity. Fortunately, Christ has knocked down the barriers and unified all believers in one family. His cross should be the focus of our unity. The Holy Spirit helps us look beyond the barriers to the unity we are called to enjoy.

2:17, 18 The Jews were "near" to God because they already knew of him through the Scriptures and worshiped him in their religious ceremonies. The Gentiles were "far away" because they knew little or nothing about God. Because neither group could be saved by good works or sincerity, both Jews and Gentiles needed to hear about the salvation available through Jesus Christ. Both Jews and Gentiles are now free to come to God through Christ.

2:19–21 A church building is sometimes called God's house. In reality, God's house is not a building, but a group of people. He lives in us and shows himself to a watching world through us.

People can see that God is love and that Jesus is Lord as we live in harmony with each other and with what God says in his Word.

2:20 What does it mean to stand on the foundation of the apostles and the prophets? It means that the church is not built on modern ideas, but rather on the spiritual heritage given to us in the Old and New Testaments.

3:1 Paul was under house arrest in Rome for preaching about Christ. The religious leaders, who felt threatened by Christ's teachings and didn't believe he was the Messiah, pressured the Romans to arrest Paul and bring him to trial for treason and for causing rebellion among the Jews. Paul had appealed that his case be heard by the emperor, and he was awaiting trial (see Acts 28:16–31). Even though he was under arrest, Paul maintained his firm belief that God was in control of all that happened to him. Do you let circumstances convince you that God has lost control of this world? Like Paul, remember that no matter what happens, God is directing the world's affairs.

3:2, 3 "In one of my letters" is literally, "as I wrote before in brief." This could refer to a previous letter which was not preserved by the church, or it could refer to an earlier part of this letter (especially 1:9ff; 2:11ff).

3:5, 6 God's plan was hidden from previous generations, not because God wanted to keep something from his people, but because he would reveal it to everyone in his perfect timing. God planned to have Jews and Gentiles comprise one body, the church. It was known in the Old Testament that the Gentiles would

with his people, but now he has revealed it by the Holy Spirit to his apostles and prophets.

3:6
Gal 3:14
Eph 2:14-16

6And this is the secret: that the Gentiles will have their full share with the Jews in all the riches inherited by God's sons; both are invited to belong to his Church, and all of God's promises of mighty blessings through Christ apply to them both when they accept the Good News about Christ and what he has done for them. 7God

3:7
Rom 15:18
Col 1:23

has given me the wonderful privilege of telling everyone about this plan of his; and he has given me his power and special ability to do it well.

3:8
1 Cor 15:9
Col 2:2,3,9,10
3:9
1 Cor 2:7

8Just think! Though I did nothing to deserve it, and though I am the most useless Christian there is, yet I was the one chosen for this special joy of telling the Gentiles the Glad News of the endless treasures available to them in Christ; 9and to explain to everyone that God is the Savior of the Gentiles too, just as he who made all things had secretly planned from the very beginning.

3:10
Rom 11:33
1 Cor 2:7
Eph 1:21; 6:12
1 Pet 3:22

10And his reason? To show to all the rulers in heaven how perfectly wise he is when all of his family—Jews and Gentiles alike—are seen to be joined together in his Church, 11in just the way he had always planned it through Jesus Christ our Lord.

3:11
Eph 1:11

3:12
Eph 2:18
Heb 4:16

12Now we can come fearlessly right into God's presence, assured of his glad welcome when we come with Christ and trust in him.

13So please don't lose heart at what they are doing to me here. It is for you I am suffering and you should feel honored and encouraged.

The magnitude of God's love

3:14
Phil 2:9,10

3:16
Phil 4:13,19
Col 1:11

3:17
Jn 14:23
Col 1:27; 2:7

3:18
Jn 1:16
Col 2:9,10

14, 15When I think of the wisdom and scope of his plan I fall down on my knees and pray to the Father of all the great family of God—some of them already in heaven and some down here on earth— 16that out of his glorious, unlimited resources he will give you the mighty inner strengthening of his Holy Spirit. 17And I pray that Christ will be more and more at home in your hearts, living within you as you trust in him. May your roots go down deep into the soil of God's marvelous love; 18, 19and may you be able to feel and understand, as all God's children should, how long, how wide, how deep, and how high his love really is; and to experience

---

receive salvation (Isaiah 49:6; 56:3), but it was never revealed in the Old Testament that all Gentile and Jewish believers would become equal in the body of Christ. Yet this equality was accomplished when Jesus broke down the "wall of contempt" and created the "one new person" (2:14,15).

3:7 God gave the apostle Paul the ability to share effectively the gospel of Christ. You may not be an apostle or even an evangelist, but God will also give you opportunities to tell others about Christ—and with the opportunity he will provide the ability, courage, and power. Whenever an opportunity presents itself, make yourself available to God. As you focus on the other person and his or her needs, God will communicate your caring attitude, and your words will be natural, loving, and compelling.

3:8 When Paul describes himself as a useless Christian, he is saying that without God's help, he would never be able to do God's work. Yet God chose him to share the gospel with the Gentiles and gave him the power to do this. If we feel useless, we may be right—except that we have forgotten what a difference God makes. How does God want to use you? Do your part and faithfully perform the special role you play in God's plan.

3:10 The rulers in heaven are either angels (see 1 Peter 1:12), or perhaps hostile forces opposed to God (2:2; 6:12).

3:12 It is an awesome privilege to be admitted into God's presence. Most of us would be apprehensive in the presence of a powerful ruler, but thanks to Christ, we can enter directly into God's presence through prayer. We know we'll be welcomed with open arms because we are God's children through our unity with Christ. Don't be afraid of God. Talk with him about everything. He is waiting to hear from you.

3:13 Why should Paul's suffering make the Ephesians feel honored? If Paul had not preached the gospel, he would not be in jail—but then the Ephesians would not have heard the Good News and been converted either. As a mother endures the pain of childbirth in order to bring new life into the world, Paul endured the pain of persecution in order to bring new believers to Christ. Obeying Christ is never easy. He calls us to take up our crosses and follow him (Matthew 16:24)—that is, to be willing to endure pain so that God's message of salvation can reach the entire world. We should feel honored that others have suffered and sacrificed for us so that we might be blessed.

3:14, 15 The great family of God includes all who have believed in him in the past, all who believe in the present, and all who will believe in the future. We are all a family because we have the same Father. He is the source of all creation, the rightful owner of everything. God promises his love and power to his family, the church (3:16–21); if we want to receive his blessings, it is important that we stay in living contact with other believers in the body of Christ. Those who isolate themselves from God's family and try to go it alone are cutting themselves off from God's power.

3:17–19 God's love is total, says Paul. It reaches every corner of our experience. It is *long*—it continues the length of our lives. It is *deep*—it reaches to the depths of discouragement, despair, and even death. It is *wide*—it covers the breadth of our own experience, and it reaches out to the whole world. It is *high*—it rises to the heights of our celebration and elation. When you feel shut out or isolated, remember that you can never be lost to God's love. For another hymn to God's immeasurable and inexhaustible love, see Paul's words in Romans 8:38, 39.

this love for yourselves, though it is so great that you will never see the end of it or fully know or understand it. And so at last you will be filled up with God himself.

²⁰Now glory be to God who by his mighty power at work within us is able to do far more than we would ever dare to ask or even dream of—infinitely beyond our highest prayers, desires, thoughts, or hopes. ²¹May he be given glory forever and ever through endless ages because of his master plan of salvation for the Church through Jesus Christ.

3:19
Eph 1:23
Col 2:10
3:20
Eph 1:19,20
3:21
1 Tim 1:17

2. Unity in the church
We are one body in Christ

4 I beg you—I, a prisoner here in jail for serving the Lord—to live and act in a way worthy of those who have been chosen for such wonderful blessings as these. ²Be humble and gentle. Be patient with each other, making allowance for each other's faults because of your love. ³Try always to be led along together by the Holy Spirit, and so be at peace with one another.

⁴We are all parts of one body, we have the same Spirit, and we have all been called to the same glorious future. ⁵For us there is only one Lord, one faith, one baptism, ⁶and we all have the same God and Father who is over us all and in us all, and living through every part of us. ⁷However, Christ has given each of us special abilities—whatever he wants us to have out of his rich storehouse of gifts.

⁸The Psalmist tells about this, for he says that when Christ returned triumphantly

4:2
Col 3:12,13
4:3
Col 3:14
4:4
Rom 12:5
1 Cor 12:12,13
4:5
1 Cor 8:6
4:6
Rom 11:36
4:7
Rom 12:3
1 Cor 12:7
4:8
Ps 68:18

Believers are one in:	Our unity is experienced in:	**THE ONENESS OF ALL BELIEVERS**
Body	The fellowship of believers—the church	
Spirit	The Holy Spirit who activates the fellowship	
Hope	That glorious future to which we are all called	
Lord	Christ, to whom we all belong	
Faith	Our singular commitment to Christ	
Baptism	Baptism—the sign of entry into the church	
God	God, who is our Father and keeps us for eternity	

Too often believers are separated because of minor differences in doctrine. But Paul here shows those areas where Christians must agree to attain true unity. When believers have this unity of Spirit, petty differences should never be allowed to dissolve that unity.

3:21 This *doxology*—hymn of praise to God—ends Part One of Ephesians, in which Paul describes the timeless role of the church. In Part Two (chapters 4—6), he will explain how church members should live in order to bring about the unity God wants. As in most of his books, Paul first lays a doctrinal foundation, then makes practical applications of the truths he has presented.

4:1–6 "We are all parts of one body," says Paul, and we have been given many gifts and abilities. Unity does not just happen; we have to work at it. Often differences among people can lead to division, but this should not be true in the church. Instead of concentrating on what divides us, we should remember what unites us: *one* body, *one* Spirit, *one* future, *one* Lord, *one* faith, *one* baptism, *one* God! Have you learned to appreciate people who are different from you? Can you see how their differing gifts and viewpoints can help the church as it does God's work? Learn to enjoy the way we members of Christ's body complement one another (see 1 Corinthians 12:12, 13 for more on this thought).

4:1, 2 God has chosen us to be Christ's representatives on earth. In light of this truth, Paul challenges us to live worthy of the name "Christian," meaning *Christ's one.* This includes being humble, gentle, patient, understanding, and peaceful. People are watching your life. Can they see Christ in you? How well are you doing as his representative?

4:2 No one is ever going to be perfect here on earth, so we must accept and love other Christians in spite of their faults. When we

see faults in fellow believers, we should be patient and gentle. Is there someone whose actions or personality really annoys you? Rather than dwelling on that person's weaknesses, or looking for faults, pray for that person. Then do even more—spend time together and see if you can learn to like him or her.

4:3 Unity is one of the Holy Spirit's important roles. He leads, but we have to be willing to be led. We do that by focusing on God, not on ourselves. For more about who the Holy Spirit is and what he does, see the notes on John 3:6; Acts 1:5; and Ephesians 1:14.

4:4–7 All believers in Christ belong to one body; all are united under one Head, who is Christ himself (see 1 Corinthians 12:12-26). Each believer has God-given abilities that can strengthen the whole body. Your special ability may be seemingly small or large, but it is yours to use in God's service. Ask God to use your unique gifts to contribute to the strength and health of the body of believers.

4:6 God is *over us all*—this shows his overruling care (transcendence). He is *in us all*—this shows his active presence in the world and in the lives of believers (immanence). Any view of God that violates either his transcendence or his immanence is not a true picture of him.

4:8 In Psalm 68:18, God is pictured as a conqueror marching to the gates and taking tribute from the fallen foes. Paul uses that picture to teach that Christ, in his crucifixion and resurrection, was victorious over Satan. When he ascended to heaven, he gave gifts

4:9
Jn 3:13
Acts 2:27
1 Pet 3:18

4:10
Eph 1:23
1 Tim 3:16
Heb 4:14; 8:1
1 Pet 3:22

4:11
1 Cor 12:28

4:12
1 Cor 14:26

4:13
Eph 1:17
Col 2:2

4:14
Mt 11:7
1 Cor 14:20
Eph 6:11

4:15,16
Col 2:19

4:17
Jn 1:4,5
Acts 17:30; 26:18
Eph 2:2

to heaven after his resurrection and victory over Satan, he gave generous gifts to men. 9Notice that it says he returned to heaven. This means that he had first come down from the heights of heaven, far down to the lowest parts of the earth. 10The same one who came down is the one who went back up, that he might fill all things everywhere with himself, from the very lowest to the very highest.

11Some of us have been given special ability as apostles; to others he has given the gift of being able to preach well; some have special ability in winning people to Christ, helping them to trust him as their Savior; still others have a gift for caring for God's people as a shepherd does his sheep, leading and teaching them in the ways of God.

12Why is it that he gives us these special abilities to do certain things best? It is that God's people will be equipped to do better work for him, building up the Church, the body of Christ, to a position of strength and maturity; 13until finally we all believe alike about our salvation and about our Savior, God's Son, and all become full-grown in the Lord—yes, to the point of being filled full with Christ.

14Then we will no longer be like children, forever changing our minds about what we believe because someone has told us something different, or has cleverly lied to us and made the lie sound like the truth. 15, 16Instead, we will lovingly follow the truth at all times—speaking truly, dealing truly, living truly—and so become more and more in every way like Christ who is the Head of his body, the Church. Under his direction the whole body is fitted together perfectly, and each part in its own special way helps the other parts, so that the whole body is healthy and growing and full of love.

Living as a new person

17, 18Let me say this, then, speaking for the Lord: Live no longer as the unsaved do, for they are blinded and confused. Their closed hearts are full of darkness; they are far away from the life of God because they have shut their minds against him,

4:10 *from the very lowest to the very highest,* literally, "that he might fill all things." **4:15, 16** *speaking truly, dealing truly, living truly,* Amplified New Testament.

---

to the church, some of which he discusses in verses 11–13.

4:9 The "lowest parts of the earth" may be (1) the earth itself, (2) the grave, or (3) Hades (which many believe is the resting place of souls between death and resurrection). Whichever way you understand it, Christ is Lord of the whole universe, past, present, and future. Nothing or no one is hidden from him. The Lord of all came to earth and went down into death to rescue all people. No one is beyond his reach.

4:11 Our oneness in Christ does not destroy our individuality. The Holy Spirit has given each Christian special gifts for building up the church. Now that we have these gifts, it is crucial to use them. Are you spiritually mature, exercising the gifts God has given you? If you know what your gifts are, look for opportunities to serve. If you don't know, ask God to show you, perhaps through Christian friends. Then, as you begin to recognize your special area of service, use your gifts to strengthen and encourage the church.

4:12 God has given his church an enormous responsibility— to make disciples in every nation (Matthew 28:18–20). This involves preaching, teaching, healing, nurturing, giving, administering, building, and many other tasks. If we had to fulfill this command as individuals, we might as well give up without trying—it would be impossible. But God calls us as members of his body. Some of us can do one task; some can do another. Together we can obey him more fully than any of us could do alone. It is a human tendency to overestimate what we can do by ourselves and to underestimate what we can do as a group. The truth is just the opposite. Alone, we are quite ineffective. Together, as the body of Christ, we can do far more than we would ever dream possible.

4:14–16 Christ is the Truth (John 14:6), and the Holy Spirit who guides the church is the Spirit of truth (John 16:13). Satan, by contrast, is the father of liars (John 8:44). As followers of Christ, we

must be committed to the truth. This means both that our words will be honest and that our actions will reflect Christ's integrity. "Living truly" is not always easy, convenient, or pleasant; but it is necessary if the church is going to do Christ's work in the world.

4:15, 16 Some Christians fear that any mistake will destroy their witness for the Lord. They see their own weaknesses, and they know that many non-Christians seem to have stronger character than they do. How can they be new and different persons, holy and good? The Good News is that Jesus forms us into a body—into a group of individuals who are united in their purpose and in their love for one another and for Christ. If an individual stumbles, the rest of the group is there to pick him up and help him walk with his Lord again. If an individual sins, he can find restoration through the church (Galatians 6:1) even as the rest of the body continues to witness to God's truth. As part of Christ's body, you will reflect part of Christ's character and do part of his work. As you grow to be more and more like him, you will be able to give more and more thanks for your brothers and sisters in Christ, without whom you could not adequately represent the Lord.

4:17–24 People should be able to see a difference between Christians and non-Christians because of the way Christians live. Paul tells the Ephesians to leave behind the old life of sin now that they are followers of Christ. The Christian life is a process. Although we have a new nature, we don't automatically have all good thoughts and attitudes when we become new people in Christ. But if we keep listening to God, we will be changing all the time. As you look over the last year, do you see a process of change for the better in your thoughts, attitudes, and actions? Although change may be slow, it comes about if you trust God to change you. For more about our new nature as believers see Romans 6:6; 8:9; Galatians 5:16–26; Colossians 3:3–8.

and they cannot understand his ways. ¹⁹They don't care anymore about right and wrong and have given themselves over to impure ways. They stop at nothing, being driven by their evil minds and reckless lusts.

²⁰But that isn't the way Christ taught you! ²¹If you have really heard his voice and learned from him the truths concerning himself, ²²then throw off your old evil nature—the old you that was a partner in your evil ways—rotten through and through, full of lust and sham.

²³Now your attitudes and thoughts must all be constantly changing for the better. ²⁴Yes, you must be a new and different person, holy and good. Clothe yourself with this new nature.

²⁵Stop lying to each other; tell the truth, for we are parts of each other and when we lie to each other we are hurting ourselves. ²⁶If you are angry, don't sin by nursing your grudge. Don't let the sun go down with you still angry—get over it quickly; ²⁷for when you are angry you give a mighty foothold to the devil.

²⁸If anyone is stealing he must stop it and begin using those hands of his for honest work so he can give to others in need. ²⁹Don't use bad language. Say only what is good and helpful to those you are talking to, and what will give them a blessing.

³⁰Don't cause the Holy Spirit sorrow by the way you live. Remember, he is the one who marks you to be present on that day when salvation from sin will be complete.

³¹Stop being mean, bad-tempered and angry. Quarreling, harsh words, and dislike of others should have no place in your lives. ³²Instead, be kind to each other, tenderhearted, forgiving one another, just as God has forgiven you because you belong to Christ.

Living as a child of the light

5 Follow God's example in everything you do just as a much loved child imitates his father. ²Be full of love for others, following the example of Christ who loved you and gave himself to God as a sacrifice to take away your sins. And God was pleased, for Christ's love for you was like sweet perfume to him.

³Let there be no sex sin, impurity or greed among you. Let no one be able to accuse you of any such things. ⁴Dirty stories, foul talk and coarse jokes—these are not for you. Instead, remind each other of God's goodness and be thankful.

4:30 he is the one who marks you to be present, literally, "in whom you were sealed unto the day of redemption."

Cross-references (right margin):

4:19
Rom 1:24
Col 3:5

4:22
Rom 6:6
Col 3:8
Jas 1:21

4:23
Rom 12:2

4:24
2 Cor 5:17
Col 3:10

4:25
Zech 8:16
Rom 12:5
Col 3:9

4:27
Rom 12:19
Jas 4:7

4:28
1 Thess 4:11

4:29
Mt 12:34
Rom 14:19
Col 4:6

4:30
Isa 63:10
Eph 1:13
1 Thess 5:19

4:31
Col 3:8
1 Pet 2:1

4:32
Col 3:12,13

5:1
Mt 5:45

5:2
Gen 8:21
Jn 13:34
2 Cor 2:15

5:3
Col 3:5

5:4
Rom 1:28

4:25 Lying to each other disrupts unity by creating conflicts and destroying trust. It tears down relationships and leads to open war in a church.

4:26, 27 The Bible doesn't tell us we shouldn't feel angry, but it points out that it is important to handle our anger properly. If ventilated thoughtlessly, anger can hurt others and destroy relationships. If bottled up inside, it can cause us to become bitter and destroy us from within. Paul tells us to deal with our anger immediately in a way that builds relationships rather than destroying them. If we nurse our anger, we will give Satan a foothold from which he can divide us. Are you angry with someone right now? What can you do to resolve your differences? Don't let the day end before you begin to work on the conflict and mend your relationship.

4:28–32 We can cause the Holy Spirit sorrow by the way we live.

Paul warns us against bad language, meanness, improper use of anger, quarrels, harsh words, and bad attitudes toward others. Instead of acting that way, we should be forgiving, just as God has forgiven us. Are you grieving or pleasing God with your attitudes and actions? Act in love toward your brothers and sisters in Christ, just as God acted in love by sending his Son to die for your sins.

4:30 God's Spirit within us is a sign that we belong to him. For more information on this thought, see the note on 1:14.

4:32 This is Christ's law of forgiveness as taught in the Gospels (Matthew 6:14, 15; 18:35; Mark 11:25). We also see it in the Lord's prayer—"Forgive us our debts, as we forgive our debtors." God does not forgive us because we forgive others, but out of his great mercy. As we come to understand his mercy, however, we will want to be like him. Having received forgiveness, we will pass it on to others. Those who are unwilling to forgive have not become one with Christ, who was willing to forgive even those who crucified him (Luke 23:34).

5:5
1 Cor 6:9
Gal 5:21

5:8
Isa 9:2
Jn 8:12
Eph 2:2
1 Jn 2:9

5:11
Lev 19:17
1 Cor 5:9

5:13
Jn 3:20
Heb 4:13

5:14
Isa 26:19; 51:17
52:1; 60:1
Jn 5:25
Rom 6:4,5; 13:11

5:15
Col 4:5

5:17
1 Thess 4:3

5:18
Prov 20:1; 23:31
Jn 7:37-39
1 Cor 12:13

5:19
1 Cor 14:26
Col 3:16
Jas 5:13

⁵You can be sure of this: The Kingdom of Christ and of God will never belong to anyone who is impure or greedy, for a greedy person is really an idol worshiper—he loves and worships the good things of this life more than God. ⁶Don't be fooled by those who try to excuse these sins, for the terrible wrath of God is upon all those who do them. ⁷Don't even associate with such people. ⁸For though once your heart was full of darkness, now it is full of light from the Lord, and your behavior should show it! ⁹Because of this light within you, you should do only what is good and right and true.

¹⁰Learn as you go along what pleases the Lord. ¹¹Take no part in the worthless pleasures of evil and darkness, but instead, rebuke and expose them. ¹²It would be shameful even to mention here those pleasures of darkness which the ungodly do. ¹³But when you expose them, the light shines in upon their sin and shows it up, and when they see how wrong they really are, some of them may even become children of light! ¹⁴That is why God says in the Scriptures, "Awake, O sleeper, and rise up from the dead; and Christ shall give you light."

¹⁵,¹⁶So be careful how you act; these are difficult days. Don't be fools; be wise: make the most of every opportunity you have for doing good. ¹⁷Don't act thoughtlessly, but try to find out and do whatever the Lord wants you to. ¹⁸Don't drink too much wine, for many evils lie along that path; be filled instead with the Holy Spirit, and controlled by him.

¹⁹Talk with each other much about the Lord, quoting psalms and hymns and singing sacred songs, making music in your hearts to the Lord. ²⁰Always give thanks for everything to our God and Father in the name of our Lord Jesus Christ.

5:10 *Learn as you go along what pleases the Lord,* or "Your lives should be an example."

5:1, 2 Just as children imitate their parents, we should imitate Christ. His great love for us led him to sacrifice himself so that we might live. Our love for others should be of the same kind—a love that goes beyond affection to self-sacrificing service.

5:4 Foul language or talk about shameful things is so common that we begin to take it for granted. Paul cautions, however, that vulgar speech should have no place in the Christian's conversation because it does not reflect God's gracious presence in us. How can we praise God and remind others of his goodness when we are speaking coarsely (see Colossians 3:15)?

5:7 Paul is not saying that believers should keep away from all unbelievers. Jesus taught his followers to befriend sinners and lead them to him (Luke 5:30-32). Instead, Paul is speaking against condoning or adopting the lifestyles of people who excuse, love, and recommend bad behavior—whether they are in the church or outside of it. Such people can quickly pollute the church, and endanger its unity and purpose. We must befriend unbelievers if we are to lead them to Christ, but we must be wary of those who are viciously evil, immoral, or opposed to all that Christianity stands for. Such people are more likely to influence us for evil than we are likely to influence them for good.

5:8 Your actions should reflect your faith. We should live moral lives so that we can reflect God's goodness to others. Jesus stressed this in the Sermon on the Mount (Matthew 5:15, 16).

5:10-14 It is important to avoid evil pleasures, but we must go even further. Paul instructs us to rebuke and expose them, for often our silence is interpreted as approval. God needs people who will take a stand for what is right. Wherever you are, lovingly speak out for what is true and right.

5:14 This is not a direct quote from Scripture but was probably taken from a hymn well-known to the Ephesians. The hymn seems to have been based on Isaiah 26:19; 51:17; 52:1; 60:1; and Malachi 4:2. Paul was appealing to the Ephesians to wake up and realize the dangerous condition into which some of them had been slipping.

5:15, 16 By saying, "these are difficult days," Paul communicates his sense of urgency because of evil's pervasiveness. We need the same sense of urgency because our days are also difficult. We must keep our standards high, act wisely, and do good whenever we can.

5:17 It is not enough to *know* what God wants us to do; we must also *do* it. We must follow our beliefs with actions.

5:18 Paul contrasted being filled with wine, which can produce harmful effects, to being filled with the Spirit, which produces positive effects. What matters is not how much of the Holy Spirit we have, but how much of us the Holy Spirit has. We need to submit daily to his leading and draw on his power. Some effects of being filled with the Holy Spirit are mentioned in 5:19-21.

5:19 In the meetings of the early church, the Christians enjoyed speaking to one another. The content of their speech was drawn from the Old Testament Scriptures (particularly the Psalms). They not only spoke the Psalms, they sung them; and they composed other hymns and songs. Throughout the ages Christians have enjoyed singing hymns full of Scripture and praise.

5:20 When you feel down, you may find it difficult to give thanks. Take heart—God works all things out for good if we love him and are fitting into his plans (Romans 8:28). Thank God, not for your problems, but for the strength he is building in you through the difficult experiences of your life. You can be sure that God's perfect love will see you through.

Wives and husbands

²¹Honor Christ by submitting to each other. ²²You wives must submit to your husbands' leadership in the same way you submit to the Lord. ²³For a husband is in charge of his wife in the same way Christ is in charge of his body the Church. (He gave his very life to take care of it and be its Savior!) ²⁴So you wives must willingly obey your husbands in everything, just as the Church obeys Christ.

²⁵And you husbands, show the same kind of love to your wives as Christ showed to the Church when he died for her, ²⁶to make her holy and clean, washed by baptism and God's Word; ²⁷so that he could give her to himself as a glorious Church without a single spot or wrinkle or any other blemish, being holy and without a single fault. ²⁸That is how husbands should treat their wives, loving them as parts of themselves. For since a man and his wife are now one, a man is really doing himself a favor and loving himself when he loves his wife! ²⁹, ³⁰No one hates his own body but lovingly cares for it, just as Christ cares for his body the Church, of which we are parts.

³¹(That the husband and wife are one body is proved by the Scripture which says, "A man must leave his father and mother when he marries, so that he can be perfectly joined to his wife, and the two shall be one.") ³²I know this is hard to understand, but it is an illustration of the way we are parts of the body of Christ.

³³So again I say, a man must love his wife as a part of himself; and the wife must see to it that she deeply respects her husband—obeying, praising and honoring him.

5:26 *washed by baptism*, literally, "having cleansed it by washing of water with the word."

5:21
1 Pet 5:5
5:22
Gen 3:16
5:23
1 Cor 11:3
5:24
Eph 5:2
5:26
Jn 15:3; 17:17
Tit 3:5
Heb 10:22
5:27
Eph 1:4
Col 1:22
Rev 21:2
5:28
1 Pet 3:7
5:29
1 Cor 12:27
5:30
1 Cor 6:15
5:31
Gen 2:24
5:33
1 Pet 3:1,2,5

5:21, 22 *Submission* is an often misused word. It does not mean becoming a doormat. Christ—at whose name "every knee shall bow in heaven and on earth and under the earth" (Philippians 2:10)—submitted his will to the Father, and we honor Christ by following his example. When we submit to God, we become more willing to obey his command to submit to others; that is, to subordinate our rights to theirs. In a marriage relationship both husband and wife are called to submit. For the wife this means willingly following her husband's leadership in Christ. For the husband it means putting aside his own interests in order to care for his wife. Submission is rarely a problem in homes where both spouses are in a strong relationship with Christ and where each is concerned for the happiness of the other.

5:22–26 Why did Paul tell wives to submit and husbands to love? Perhaps Christian women, newly freed in Christ, found submission difficult; and Christian men, used to the Roman custom of giving unlimited power to the head of the family, were not used to treating their wives with respect and love. Of course both husbands and wives should submit to each other (5:21), just as both should love each other.

5:22–24 In Paul's day, the lot of women, children, and slaves was to submit to the head of the family—slaves until they were freed, male children until they grew up, and women and girls their whole lives. Paul emphasized the equality of all believers in Christ (Galatians 3:28), but he did not suggest overthrowing Roman society to achieve it. Instead, he counseled all believers to submit to one another by choice—wives to husbands and also husbands to wives; slaves to masters and also masters to slaves; children to parents and also parents to children. This kind of mutual submission preserves order and harmony in the family while it increases love and respect among family members.

5:22–24 Although some people have distorted Paul's teaching on submission by giving unlimited authority to husbands, we cannot get around it—Paul told wives to submit to their husbands. The fact that a teaching is not popular is no reason to discard it. According to the Bible, the man is the spiritual head of the family and his wife goes along with his leadership. But real spiritual leadership is service. Just as Christ served the disciples, even to the point of washing their feet, so the husband is to serve his wife. A wise and

Christ-honoring husband will not take advantage of his role, and a wise and Christ-honoring wife will not try to undermine her husband's leadership. Either approach causes disunity and friction in marriage.

5:25ff Some Christians have thought Paul was negative about marriage because of the counsel he gave in 1 Corinthians 7:32–38. These verses in Ephesians, however, show a high view of marriage. Here marriage is not a practical necessity or a cure for lust, but a picture of the relationship between Christ and his church! Why the apparent difference? Paul's counsel in 1 Corinthians was designed for a state of emergency during a time of persecution and crisis. Paul's counsel to the Ephesians was more a theology of marriage. Marriage, for Paul, is a holy union, a living symbol, a precious relationship that needs tender, self-sacrificing care.

5:25–30 Paul devotes twice as many words to telling husbands to love their wives as to telling wives to submit to their husbands. How should a man love his wife? (1) He should be willing to sacrifice everything for her. (2) He should make her well-being of primary importance. (3) He should care for her as he cares for his body. No wife needs to fear submitting to a man who treats her in this way.

5:26 Jesus Christ purifies the church through the work of the Holy Spirit, who draws people to Christ. In this case, Paul is using the water of baptism to mean the washing away of sin. The believer is making a commitment to be part of this purification process. Then the Spirit, who inspired the Bible, works through his people in order to build up Christ's church. Just as Christ draws his church to him and then builds her up, so a loving husband will care for his wife in ways that make her strong.

5:31–33 The union of husband and wife merges two persons in such a way that little can affect one without also affecting the other. Oneness in marriage does not mean losing your personality in the personality of the other. Instead, it means caring for your spouse as you care for yourself, learning to anticipate the other person's needs, helping the other person become all he or she can be. The creation story tells of God's plan that husband and wife should be one (Genesis 2:24), and Jesus also referred to this plan (Matthew 19:4–6).

Children and parents

6:1
Prov 23:22
Col 3:20

6:2
Ex 20:12
Mt 15:4

6:4
Col 3:21

6 Children, obey your parents; this is the right thing to do because God has placed them in authority over you. 2Honor your father and mother. This is the first of God's Ten Commandments that ends with a promise. 3And this is the promise: that if you honor your father and mother, yours will be a long life, full of blessing.

4And now a word to you parents. Don't keep on scolding and nagging your children, making them angry and resentful. Rather, bring them up with the loving discipline the Lord himself approves, with suggestions and godly advice.

Slaves and masters

6:5
Col 3:22

6:6
Col 3:22,23

6:8
Rom 2:6
2 Cor 5:10
Col 3:24

6:9
Job 31:13,14
Col 4:1

5Slaves, obey your masters; be eager to give them your very best. Serve them as you would Christ. 6, 7Don't work hard only when your master is watching and then shirk when he isn't looking; work hard and with gladness all the time, as though working for Christ, doing the will of God with all your hearts. 8Remember, the Lord will pay you for each good thing you do, whether you are slave or free.

9And you slave owners must treat your slaves right, just as I have told them to treat you. Don't keep threatening them; remember, you yourselves are slaves to Christ; you have the same Master they do, and he has no favorites.

Wearing the whole armor of God

6:11
Rom 13:12
1 Thess 5:8

6:12
Eph 3:10

10Last of all I want to remind you that your strength must come from the Lord's mighty power within you. 11Put on all of God's armor so that you will be able to stand safe against all strategies and tricks of Satan. 12For we are not fighting against people made of flesh and blood, but against persons without bodies—the evil rulers

---

6:1–4 If our faith in Christ is real, it will usually prove itself at home, in our relationships with those who know us best. Children and parents have a responsibility to each other. Children should honor their parents even if the parents are demanding and unfair. Parents should care gently for their children, even if the children are disobedient and unpleasant. Ideally, of course, Christian parents and Christian children will relate to each other with thoughtfulness and love. This will happen if both parents and children put the others' interests above their own—that is, if they submit to one another.

6:1, 2 There is a difference between obeying and honoring. To obey means to do as one is told; to honor means to show respect and love. Children are to obey until they are no longer under their parents' care, but the responsibility to honor parents continues for a lifetime.

6:3 Some societies honor their elders. They respect their wisdom, they defer to their authority, and they pay attention to their comfort and happiness. This is how Christians should act. Where elders are respected, long life is a blessing, not a burden to them.

6:4 The purpose of parental discipline is to help children grow, not to hurt or discourage them (see also Colossians 3:21). Parenting is not easy—it takes lots of patience to raise children in a loving, Christ-honoring manner. But frustration and anger should not be causes for discipline. Instead, parents should act in love, treating their children as Jesus treats the people he loves. This is vital to children's development and to their concept of the Lord.

6:5 Slaves played a significant part in Roman culture. It is estimated that there were several million slaves in the Roman Empire at this time. Since many slave owners and slaves became Christians, the early church had to deal straightforwardly with the question of master/slave relations. Paul's statement neither condemns nor condones the institution of slavery. Instead, it tells masters and slaves how to live together in Christian households. In Paul's day, women, children, and slaves had few rights. In the church, however, they had freedoms that society denied them. Paul gave firm directions to those responsible for these groups: husbands, parents, and masters.

6:6, 7 Paul's instructions encourage responsibility and integrity on the job. Christian employees should do their jobs as if Jesus Christ were their supervisor, and Christian employers should treat their employees fairly and with respect. Are you trusted in any job to do your best, whether or not the boss is around? Do you work hard and with enthusiasm? Do you treat your employees as people, not machines? Remember that no matter whom you work for, and no matter who works for you, the One you ultimately want to please is your Father in heaven.

6:9 Although Christians may be at different levels in earthly society, we are all equal before God. He does not play favorites; no one is more important than anyone else. Paul's letter to Philemon stresses the same point: Philemon, the master, and Onesimus, his slave, were brothers before God.

6:10–17 In the Christian life we battle against powerful evil forces, headed by Satan, a vicious fighter (see 1 Peter 5:8). To withstand his attacks, we must depend on God's strength and use every piece of his armor. Paul is not only giving this counsel to the church, the body of Christ, but to all individuals within the church. The whole body needs to be armed. As you do battle against "the evil rulers of the unseen world," fight in the strength of the church, whose power comes from the Holy Spirit.

6:12 These evil rulers, satanic beings, and evil princes of darkness are not people, but fallen angels over whom Satan has control. They are not mere fantasies—they are very real. We face a powerful army whose goal is to defeat Christ's church. When we believe in Christ and join his church, these beings become our enemies, and they try every device to turn us away from Christ and back to sin. Although we are assured of victory, we must engage in the struggle until Christ comes, because Satan is constantly battling against all who are on the Lord's side. We need supernatural power to defeat Satan, and God has provided that in his Holy Spirit within us and his armor surrounding us. If you feel discouraged, remember Jesus' words to Peter: "Upon this rock I will build my church; and all the powers of hell shall not prevail against it" (Matthew 16:18).

of the unseen world, those mighty satanic beings and great evil princes of darkness who rule this world; and against huge numbers of wicked spirits in the spirit world. ¹³So use every piece of God's armor to resist the enemy whenever he attacks, and when it is all over, you will still be standing up.

¹⁴But to do this, you will need the strong belt of truth and the breastplate of God's approval. ¹⁵Wear shoes that are able to speed you on as you preach the Good News of peace with God. ¹⁶In every battle you will need faith as your shield to stop the fiery arrows aimed at you by Satan. ¹⁷And you will need the helmet of salvation and the sword of the Spirit—which is the Word of God.

¹⁸Pray all the time. Ask God for anything in line with the Holy Spirit's wishes. Plead with him, reminding him of your needs, and keep praying earnestly for all Christians everywhere. ¹⁹Pray for me, too, and ask God to give me the right words as I boldly tell others about the Lord, and as I explain to them that his salvation is for the Gentiles too. ²⁰I am in chains now for preaching this message from God. But pray that I will keep on speaking out boldly for him even here in prison, as I should.

6:13
Jas 4:7
6:14
Isa 11:5; 59:17
1 Thess 5:8
6:15
Isa 52:7
6:16
1 Jn 5:4
6:17
Isa 59:17
Jn 6:63
1 Thess 5:8
Heb 4:12
6:18
Rom 8:26
Phil 4:6
Col 4:2
6:19
Col 4:3,4

Piece of Armor	Use	Application	GOD'S ARMOR FOR US
Strong Belt	Truth	Satan fights with lies, and sometimes his lies *sound* like truth; but only believers have God's truth which can defeat Satan's lies.	We are engaged in a spiritual battle—all believers find themselves subject to Satan's attacks because they are no longer on Satan's side. Thus, Paul tells us to use *every piece* of God's armor to resist Satan's attacks and to stand true to God in the midst of them.
Breastplate	God's approval	Satan often attacks our hearts—the seat of our emotions, self-worth, and trust. God's approval is the breastplate that protects our hearts. He approves of us because he loves us and sent his Son to die for us.	
Shoes	Readiness to spread the Good News	Satan wants us to think that telling others the Good News is a worthless and hopeless task—the size of the task is too big and the negative responses are too much to handle. But the "shoes" God gives us are the motivation to continue to proclaim the true peace which is available in God—news everyone needs to hear.	
Shield	Faith	What *we* see are Satan's attacks in the form of insults, setbacks, and temptations. But the shield of faith protects us from Satan's flaming arrows. With God's perspective, we can see beyond our circumstances and know that ultimate victory is ours.	
Helmet	Salvation	Satan wants to make us doubt God, Jesus, and our salvation. The helmet protects our minds from doubting God's saving work for us.	
Sword	The Spirit, the Word of God	The sword is the only weapon of *offense* in this list of armor. There are times when we need to take the offensive against Satan. When we are tempted, we need to trust in the truth of God's Word.	

6:18 How can anyone pray all the time? One way to pray constantly is to make quick, brief prayers your habitual response to every situation you meet throughout the day. Another way is to order your life around God's desires and teachings so that your very life becomes a prayer. You don't have to isolate yourself from other people and from daily work in order to pray constantly. You can make prayer your life and your life a prayer while living in a world that needs God's powerful influence.

6:20 Undiscouraged and undefeated, Paul wrote powerful letters of encouragement from prison. Paul did not ask the Ephesians to pray that his chains would be removed, but that he would continue to speak boldly for Christ in spite of them. God can use us in any circumstances to do his will. Even as we pray for a change in our circumstances, we should also pray that God will accomplish his plan through us right where we are. Knowing God's eternal purpose for our lives helps us through the difficult times.

Paul's final greetings

6:21
Acts 20:4
2 Tim 4:12
Tit 3:12

6:22
Col 4:7,8

6:23
2 Thess 3:16

21Tychicus, who is a much loved brother and faithful helper in the Lord's work, will tell you all about how I am getting along. 22I am sending him to you for just this purpose, to let you know how we are and be encouraged by his report.

23May God give peace to you, my Christian brothers, and love, with faith from God the Father and the Lord Jesus Christ. 24May God's grace and blessing be upon all who sincerely love our Lord Jesus Christ.

Sincerely, Paul

6:21 Tychicus is also mentioned in Acts 20:4, Colossians 4:7, 2 Timothy 4:12, and Titus 3:12.

6:24 This letter was written to the church at Ephesus, but it was also meant for circulation among other churches. In this epistle, Paul presents the supremacy of Christ, gives information on both the nature of the church and on how church members should live, and stresses the unity of all believers—male, female, parent, child, master, slave—regardless of sex, nationality, or social rank. The home and the church are difficult places to live the Christian life, because our real self comes through to those who know us well. Close relationships between imperfect people can lead to trouble—or to increased faith and deepened dependence on God. We can build unity in our churches through willing submission to Christ's leadership and humble service to one another.

PHILIPPIANS

VITAL STATISTICS

PURPOSE:
To thank the Philippians for the gift they had sent him and to strengthen these believers by showing them that true joy comes from Jesus Christ alone

AUTHOR:
Paul

TO WHOM WRITTEN:
All the Christians at Philippi and all believers everywhere

DATE WRITTEN:
About A.D. 61, from Rome during Paul's imprisonment there

SETTING:
Paul and his companions founded the church at Philippi on his second missionary journey (Acts 16:11–40). This was the first church established on the European continent. The Philippian church had sent a gift with Epaphroditus (one of their members) to be delivered to Paul (4:18). Paul was in a Roman prison at the time. He writes this letter to thank them for their gift and to encourage them in their faith.

KEY VERSE:
"Always be full of joy in the Lord; I say it again, rejoice!" (4:4)

KEY PEOPLE:
Paul, Timothy, Epaphroditus, Euodias and Syntyche

KEY PLACE:
Philippi

THE word *happiness* evokes visions of unwrapping gifts on Christmas morning, strolling hand in hand with the one you love, being surprised on your birthday, responding with unbridled laughter to a comedian, or vacationing in an exotic locale. Everyone wants to be happy; we make chasing this elusive ideal a lifelong pursuit: spending money, collecting things, and searching for new experiences. But if happiness depends upon our circumstances, what happens when the toys rust, loved ones die, health deteriorates, money is stolen, and the party's over? Often happiness flees and despair sets in.

In contrast to *happiness* stands *joy*. Running deeper and stronger, joy is the quiet, confident assurance of God's love and work in our lives, that he will be there no matter what! Happiness depends on happenings, but joy depends on Christ.

Philippians is Paul's joy letter. The church in that Macedonian city had been a great encouragement to Paul. The Philippian believers had enjoyed a very special relationship with Paul, so he wrote them a personal expression of his love and affection. They had brought him great joy (4:1). Philippians is also a joyful book because it emphasizes the real joy of the Christian life. The concept of *rejoicing* or *joy* appears 16 times, and the pages radiate this positive message, culminating in the exhortation to "Always be full of joy in the Lord; I say it again, rejoice!" (4:4).

In a life dedicated to serving Christ, Paul had faced excruciating poverty, abundant wealth, and everything in-between. He even wrote this joyful letter from prison. Whatever the circumstances, Paul had learned to be content (4:11, 12), finding real joy as he focused all of his attention and energy on knowing Christ (3:8) and obeying him (3:12, 13).

Paul's desire to know Christ above all else is wonderfully expressed in the following words: "Everything else is worthless when compared with the priceless gain of knowing Christ Jesus my Lord. I have put aside all else, counting it worth less than nothing, in order that I can have Christ, and become one with him. . . . Now I have given up everything else—I have found it to be the only way to really know Christ and to experience the mighty power that brought him back to life again, and to find out what it means to suffer and to die with him" (3:8–10). May we share Paul's aspiration and seek to know Jesus Christ more and more. This is the secret of a joyful Christian life.

THE BLUEPRINT

1. Joy in suffering (1:1–30)
2. Joy in serving (2:1–30)
3. Joy in believing (3:1–21)
4. Joy in giving (4:1–23)

Although Paul was writing from prison, joy is a dominant theme in this letter. The secret of his joy is grounded in his relationship with Christ. People today desperately want to be happy but are tossed and turned by daily successes, failures, and inconveniences. Christians are to be joyful in every circumstance, even when things are going badly, even when we feel like complaining, even when no one else is joyful. Christ still reigns and we still know him, so we can rejoice at all times.

MEGATHEMES

THEME	EXPLANATION	IMPORTANCE
Humility	Christ showed true humility when he laid aside his rights and privileges as God to become human. He poured out his life to pay the penalty we deserve. Laying aside self-interest is essential to all our relationships.	We are to take Christ's attitude in serving others. We must renounce personal recognition and merit. When we give up our self-interest, we can serve with joy, love, and kindness.
Self-sacrifice	Christ suffered and died so we might have eternal life. With courage and faithfulness, Paul sacrificed himself for the ministry. He preached the gospel even while he was in prison.	Christ gives us power to lay aside our personal needs and concerns. To utilize his power, we must imitate those leaders who show self-denying concern for others. We dare not be self-centered.
Unity	In every church, in every generation, there are divisive influences (issues, loyalties, and conflicts). In the midst of hardships, it is easy to turn on one another. Paul encouraged the Philippians to agree with one another, stop complaining, and work together.	As believers, we should contend against a common enemy, not against one another. When we are unified in love, Christ's strength is most abundant. Keep before you the ideals of teamwork, consideration of others, and unselfishness.
Christian living	Paul shows us how to live successful Christian lives. We can become mature by being so identified with Christ that his attitude of humility and sacrifice rules us. Christ is both our source of power and our guide.	Developing our character begins with God's work in us. But growth also requires discipline, obedience, and relentless concentration on our part.
Joy	Believers can have profound contentment, serenity, and peace no matter what happens. This joy comes from knowing Christ personally and from depending on his strength rather than our own.	We can have joy, even in hardship. Joy does not come from outward circumstances but from inward strength. As Christians, we must not rely on what we have or what we experience to give us joy, but on Christ within us.

1. Joy in suffering

1 *From:* Paul and Timothy, slaves of Jesus Christ.
To: The pastors and deacons and all the Christians in the city of Philippi.
²May God bless you all. Yes, I pray that God our Father and the Lord Jesus
Christ will give each of you his fullest blessings, and his peace in your hearts and
your lives.

1:1
Acts 16:1,12
2 Cor 1:1
Col 1:1
Philem 1
1:2
Rom 1:7

Paul's prayer for the Philippian believers

³All my prayers for you are full of praise to God! ⁴When I pray for you, my heart
is full of joy, ⁵because of all your wonderful help in making known the Good News
about Christ from the time you first heard it until now. ⁶And I am sure that God who

1:3
Col 1:3
1:6
1 Cor 1:8

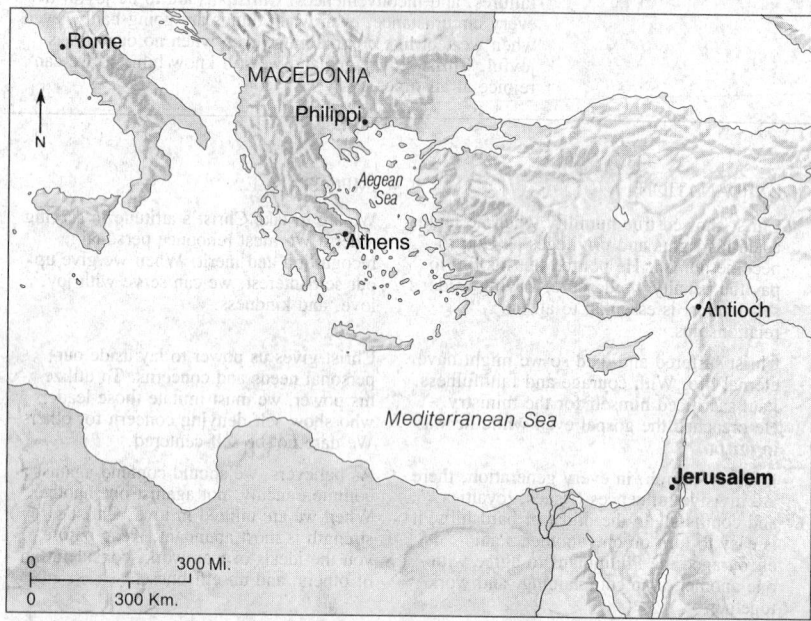

LOCATION OF PHILIPPI
Philippi sat on the Egnatian Way, the main transportation route in Macedonia, an extension of the Appian Way, which joined the eastern empire with Italy.

1:1 This is a personal letter to the Philippians, not intended for general circulation as was the letter to the Ephesians. Paul wanted to thank the believers for helping him when he had a need. He also wanted to tell them why he could be full of joy despite his imprisonment and coming trial. This is an uplifting letter in which Paul devotes only a small space to correcting the Philippians and warning them about potential problems.

1:1 On Paul's first missionary journey, he visited towns close to his headquarters in Antioch of Syria. On his second and third journeys, his travels extended even farther. Because of the great distance between the congregations which Paul had founded, he could no longer personally oversee them all. Thus he was compelled to write letters to teach and encourage the believers. Fortunately, Paul had a staff of volunteers (including Timothy, Mark, and Epaphras) who personally delivered these letters and often remained with the congregations for a while to teach and encourage them.

1:1 For more information on Paul, see his Profile in Acts 9. Timothy's Profile is found in 1 Timothy.

1:1 Pastors and deacons led the early Christian churches. "Pastors" were the "overseers" or "elders"; their qualifications and duties are explained in detail in 1 Timothy 3:1–7; Titus 1:5–9. The qualifications and duties of deacons are spelled out in 1 Timothy 3:8–13.

1:1 The Roman colony of Philippi was located in northern Greece (called Macedonia in Paul's day). This thriving commercial center sat at the crossroads between Europe and Asia. In about A.D. 50, Paul, Silas, Timothy, and Luke crossed the Aegean Sea from Asia Minor and landed at Philippi (Acts 16:11–40). The church in Philippi consisted mostly of Gentile (non-Jewish) believers. Since they were not familar with the Old Testament, Paul did not specifically quote any Old Testament passages in this letter.

1:4 This is the first of many times Paul used the word *joy* in his letter. Here he says that the Philippians were a source of joy when he prayed. By helping Paul, they were helping Christ's cause. The Philippians were willing to be used by God for whatever task he had in store for them. When others think about you, are you a source of joy for them?

1:4, 5 The Philippians first heard the Good News about ten years earlier when Paul and his companions visited Philippi (during Paul's second missionary journey) and founded the church there.

1:6 The God who begins his good work in us continues it through our lives and will finish it when we meet him face to face. God's work *for* us began when Christ died on the cross to forgive our sins. His work *in* us begins when the Holy Spirit comes into our hearts, enabling us to be more like Christ every day. Paul is describing the process of Christian growth and maturity that begins when we accept Jesus and continues until Christ returns.

began the good work within you will keep right on helping you grow in his grace until his task within you is finally finished on that day when Jesus Christ returns.

7How natural it is that I should feel as I do about you, for you have a very special place in my heart. We have shared together the blessings of God, both when I was in prison and when I was out, defending the truth and telling others about Christ. 8Only God knows how deep is my love and longing for you—with the tenderness of Jesus Christ. 9My prayer for you is that you will overflow more and more with love for others, and at the same time keep on growing in spiritual knowledge and insight, 10for I want you always to see clearly the difference between right and wrong, and to be inwardly clean, no one being able to criticize you from now until our Lord returns. 11May you always be doing those good, kind things which show that you are a child of God, for this will bring much praise and glory to the Lord.

Honor Christ by life or death

12And I want you to know this, dear brothers: Everything that has happened to me here has been a great boost in getting out the Good News concerning Christ. 13For everyone around here, including all the soldiers over at the barracks, knows that I am in chains simply because I am a Christian. 14And because of my imprisonment many of the Christians here seem to have lost their fear of chains! Somehow my patience has encouraged them and they have become more and more bold in telling others about Christ.

15Some, of course, are preaching the Good News because they are jealous of the way God has used me. They want reputations as fearless preachers! But others have purer motives, 16, 17preaching because they love me, for they know that the Lord has brought me here to use me to defend the Truth. And some preach to make me jealous, thinking that their success will add to my sorrows here in jail! 18But whatever their motive for doing it, the fact remains that the Good News about Christ is being preached and I am glad.

19I am going to keep on being glad, for I know that as you pray for me, and as the

Side references:
1:7 2 Cor 7:3 Eph 3:1; 6:20 Col 4:3 2 Tim 1:8
1:8 Rom 1:9
1:9 Col 1:9 1 Thess 3:12 Philem 6
1:10 Rom 12:2 1 Cor 1:8
1:11 Jn 15:4
1:12 Lk 21:12,13
1:13 Acts 28:30,31
1:14 Phil 1:20
1:15 Phil 2:3
1:17 1 Cor 9:17
1:19 Acts 16:7 Rom 8:9 2 Cor 1:11

1:6 Do you sometimes feel as if you'll never make progress in your spiritual life? When God starts a project, he finishes it! As with the Philippians, God will work in your life and help you grow in grace until he has completed his work in your life. When you are discouraged, remember that God won't give up on you. He promises to finish the work he has begun. Let him do it!

1:7 Paul is probably referring to his imprisonment in Philippi, recorded in Acts 16:22–36. In verses 13 and 14, Paul speaks of his Roman imprisonment. Wherever Paul was, even in prison, he faithfully preached the Good News.

1:7, 8 Have you ever longed to see a friend with whom you share fond memories? Paul had such a longing to see the Christians at Philippi. His love and affection for them was based not merely on past experiences, but upon the unity that comes when believers draw upon Christ's love. All Christians are part of God's family and thus share equally in the transforming power of his love. Do you feel a deep love for fellow Christians, friends and strangers alike? Let Christ's love for you motivate you to love other Christians, and feel free to express that love.

1:10 Paul calls for discernment—the ability to differentiate between right and wrong, good and bad, vital and trivial. This is to help us avoid the criticism of unbelievers and to keep us from compromising our Christian morals and values (Hebrews 5:14).

1:12–14 Being imprisoned would cause many people to become bitter or to give up, but Paul saw it as one more opportunity to spread the Good News of Christ. Paul realized that his current circumstances weren't as important as what he did with them. Turning a bad situation into a good one, he reached out to the Roman soldiers and encouraged those Christians who were afraid of persecution. We may not be in prison, but we still have plenty of

opportunities to be discouraged—times of indecision, financial burdens, family conflict, church conflict, or the loss of our jobs. How we act in such situations reflects what we believe. Like Paul, look for opportunities to demonstrate your faith even in bad situations. Whether or not the situation improves, your faith will grow stronger.

1:13 How did Paul end up in a Roman prison? While he was visiting Jerusalem, some Jews had him arrested for preaching the gospel, but he appealed to Caesar to hear his case (Acts 21:15—25:12). He was then escorted by soldiers to Rome, where he was placed under house arrest while awaiting trial—not a trial for breaking civil law, but for proclaiming the Good News of Christ. At that time, the Roman authorities did not consider "proclaiming the Good News" to be a serious charge. A few years later, however, Rome took a different view of Christianity and made every effort to stamp it out of existence. Paul's house arrest allowed him some degree of freedom. He could have visitors, continue to preach, and write letters such as this one. A brief record of Paul's time in Rome is found in Acts 28:11–31.

1:15–18 Paul had an amazingly selfless attitude. He knew that some were preaching to build their own reputations, but he was glad the gospel was being preached, regardless of the motives of these preachers. Many Christians serve for the wrong reasons. God doesn't excuse their motives, but, like Paul, we should be glad if God uses their message, regardless of their motives.

1:19–21 This was not Paul's final imprisonment in Rome. Awaiting trial, he knew he could either be released or executed. As it turned out, he was released from this imprisonment but arrested again two or three years later.

Holy Spirit helps me, this is all going to turn out for my good. 20For I live in eager expectation and hope that I will never do anything that will cause me to be ashamed of myself but that I will always be ready to speak out boldly for Christ while I am going through all these trials here, just as I have in the past; and that I will always be an honor to Christ, whether I live or whether I must die. 21For to me, living means opportunities for Christ, and dying—well, that's better yet! 22But if living will give me more opportunities to win people to Christ, then I really don't know which is better, to live or die! 23Sometimes I want to live and at other times I don't, for I long to go and be with Christ. How much happier for *me* than being here! 24But the fact is that I can be of more help to *you* by staying!

25Yes, I am still needed down here and so I feel certain I will be staying on earth a little longer, to help you grow and become happy in your faith; 26my staying will make you glad and give you reason to glorify Christ Jesus for keeping me safe, when I return to visit you again.

27But whatever happens to me, remember always to live as Christians should, so that, whether I ever see you again or not, I will keep on hearing good reports that you are standing side by side with one strong purpose—to tell the Good News 28fearlessly, no matter what your enemies may do. They will see this as a sign of their downfall, but for you it will be a clear sign from God that he is with you, and that he has given you eternal life with him. 29For to you has been given the privilege not only of trusting him but also of suffering for him. 30We are in this fight together. You have seen me suffer for him in the past; and I am still in the midst of a great and terrible struggle now, as you know so well.

1:20
Rom 5:5; 14:8
1 Cor 6:20
Eph 6:19

1:21
Gal 2:20
Col 1:27

1:22
Rom 1:13

1:23
2 Cor 5:8
2 Tim 4:6

1:25
Phil 2:24

1:27
Acts 4:32
Phil 4:1,2

1:28
Mt 10:28
Rom 8:17
2 Tim 2:11
Heb 13:6

1:29
Mt 5:11,12
Acts 5:41

1:30
Acts 16:19
Col 2:1
1 Thess 2:2

2. Joy in serving

Be humble like Christ

2 Is there any such thing as Christians cheering each other up? Do you love me enough to want to help me? Does it mean anything to you that we are brothers in the Lord, sharing the same Spirit? Are your hearts tender and sympathetic at all? 2Then make me truly happy by loving each other and agreeing wholeheartedly with each other, working together with one heart and mind and purpose.

3Don't be selfish; don't live to make a good impression on others. Be humble, thinking of others as better than yourself. 4Don't just think about your own affairs, but be interested in others, too, and in what they are doing.

2:1
2 Cor 13:14
Col 3:12

2:2
1 Pet 3:8

2:3
Rom 12:10,16
1 Pet 5:5

2:4
Rom 15:1,2
1 Cor 10:24

1:20, 21 To those who don't believe in God, life on earth is all there is, and so it is natural for them to strive for the things that this world values—money, popularity, power, and prestige. For Paul, however, life meant developing eternal values and telling others about Christ, who alone can help us see life from an eternal perspective. Paul's whole purpose in life was to speak out boldly for Christ and to become more like him. Thus Paul could confidently say that dying would be even better than living, because in death he would be spared from the troubles of the world and see Christ face to face (1 John 3:2, 3). If you're not ready to die, then you're not ready to live. Once you know your eternal purpose, then you're free to serve—devoting your life to what really counts without fear of dying.

1:29 Suffering, in and of itself, is not a privilege. But when we suffer because we faithfully represent Christ, we know that our message and example are having an effect and that God considers us worthy to represent him (see Acts 5:41). Suffering has these additional benefits: (1) it takes our eyes off of earthly comforts; (2) it weeds out superficial believers; (3) it strengthens the faith of those who endure; (4) it serves as an example to others who may follow us. Suffering for our faith doesn't mean we have done something wrong. In fact, the opposite is often true—it verifies that we have been faithful.

1:30 Throughout his life Paul suffered for spreading the Good News. Like the Philippians, we struggle against the forces of evil that would discredit the saving message of Christ. All true believers are in this fight together, uniting against the same enemy for the same cause.

2:1–5 Many people—even Christians—live only to make a good impression on others or to please themselves. This is self-centered living; if people are concerned only for themselves, seeds of discord are sown. Paul therefore stresses spiritual unity, asking the Philippians to love one another and to work together with one heart and purpose. When we work together, caring for the problems of others as if they were our own, we are demonstrating Christ's example of putting others first. This brings unity. Don't be concerned about making a good impression or pleasing yourself to the point where you strain your relationship to others in God's family. Let the Spirit of God work through you to attract fellow believers to himself.

2:3 Being humble means having a true perspective on ourselves (see Romans 12:3). It does not mean that we should put ourselves down. We see that we are sinners, saved only by God's grace; but we *are* saved and therefore have great worth in God's Kingdom. We should place ourselves in his hands to be used as he wants in order to spread his Word and share his love with others.

2:3, 4 Immediately after Paul calls for unity among the believers (2:2), he urges the Philippians to avoid selfishness. The cure for selfishness is servanthood, which is being like Christ (2:5). Selfish ambitions destroy church unity by pitting one Christian against another.

2:6
Isa 9:6
Jn 1:1,2
2:7
Jn 1:14
Gal 4:4
2:8
Heb 5:8; 12:2
2:9
Eph 1:20,21
Heb 1:4
2:10
Rom 14:11

⁵Your attitude should be the kind that was shown us by Jesus Christ, ⁶who, though he was God, did not demand and cling to his rights as God, ⁷but laid aside his mighty power and glory, taking the disguise of a slave and becoming like men. ⁸And he humbled himself even further, going so far as actually to die a criminal's death on a cross.

⁹Yet it was because of this that God raised him up to the heights of heaven and gave him a name which is above every other name, ¹⁰that at the name of Jesus every knee shall bow in heaven and on earth and under the earth, ¹¹and every tongue shall confess that Jesus Christ is Lord, to the glory of God the Father.

Shine like lights in a dark world

2:12
Phil 1:5
2:13
Rom 8:28
1 Cor 12:6
Heb 13:20,21

¹²Dearest friends, when I was there with you, you were always so careful to follow my instructions. And now that I am away you must be even more careful to do the good things that result from being saved, obeying God with deep reverence, shrinking back from all that might displease him. ¹³For God is at work within you, helping you want to obey him, and then helping you do what he wants.

2:7 *becoming like men*, literally, "was made in the likeness of men."　**2:8** *to die a criminal's death on a cross,* literally, "became obedient to death, even the death of the cross."

2:4 Philippi was a cosmopolitan city. The composition of the church reflected this with its people from a variety of backgrounds and walks of life. Acts 16 gives us some indication of the diverse makeup of this church. For example, Lydia was a Jewish convert from Asia, a wealthy merchant (Acts 16:14), the slave girl in Acts 16:16, 17 was probably a native Greek and the jailer serving this colony of the empire was probably Roman (Acts 16:25–36). With so many different backgrounds among the members, unity must have been difficult to achieve. Although there is no evidence of widespread division in the church, its unity had to be safeguarded (3:2; 4:2). Paul encourages us to guard against any selfishness, prejudice, or jealousy that might lead to dissension. Showing genuine interest in others is one way to strive actively for unity among believers.

2:5–11 These verses were probably from a hymn which was sung in the early Christian church. The passage holds many parallels to the prophecy of the suffering servant in Isaiah 53. As a hymn, it was not meant to be a complete statement about the nature and work of Christ, however, are inferred from this passage: (1) he has always existed with God; (2) he is equal to God because he *is* God (John 1:1ff; Colossians 1:15–19); (3) though he is God, he became a man in order to fulfill God's plan of salvation for all people; (4) he did not just pretend to have a man's body; he actually became a man to identify with man's sins; (5) he voluntarily laid aside his divine rights, privileges, and position, out of love for his Father; (6) he died on the cross for our sins, so that we wouldn't have to face eternal death; (7) God glorified him because of his obedience; (8) God raised him to his original position at the Father's right hand where he will reign forever as our Lord and Judge.

Jesus Christ was humble, willing to give up his rights in order to obey God and serve people. Like Christ, we must serve out of love for God and for others, not out of guilt or fear.

2:5–11 Often people excuse selfishness, pride, or evil by claiming their "rights." They think, "I can cheat on this test; after all, I deserve to pass this class," or "I can spend all this money on myself—I worked for it," or "I can get an abortion; I have a right to control my own body." But as believers, we should have a different attitude, an attitude that enables us to give up our rights for the good of others—in order to serve others. If we say we follow Christ, we must also say we want to live as he lived. We should develop his attitude of humble service, even when we are not likely to get

recognition for our efforts. Are you selfishly clinging to your rights, or are you willing to serve?

2:5–7 The *incarnation* was the act of the preexistent Son of God voluntarily assuming a human body and human nature. Without ceasing to be God, he became a human being, the man called Jesus. He did not give up his deity to become human, but he set aside the right to his glory and power. In submission to the Father's will, he limited his power and knowledge. Jesus of Nazareth was subject to place, time, and many other human limitations. What made his humanity unique was his freedom from sin. In his full humanity, Jesus showed us everything about God's character that can be conveyed in human terms. The incarnation is explained further in these passages: John 1:1–14; Romans 1:2–5; 2 Corinthians 8:9; 1 Timothy 3:16; Hebrews 2:14; and 1 John 1:1–3.

2:8 Crucifixion was the form of capital punishment Romans used for notorious criminals. It was excruciatingly painful, humiliating, and could last for several days. Prisoners were nailed or tied to a cross and left to die. Death usually came by suffocation when the weight of the weakened body made breathing more and more difficult. Jesus died as one who was cursed (Galatians 3:13). How amazing that the perfect man should die this most shameful death so that we would not have to face eternal punishment!

2:9–11 At the last judgment, even those who are condemned will recognize Jesus' authority and right to rule.

2:12 The Philippian Christians needed to be especially careful to obey Christ, now that Paul wasn't there to continually remind them about what was right. We too must be careful about how we live, especially when we are on our own. In the absence of cherished Christian leaders, we must focus our attention and devotion even more on Christ so that we won't be sidetracked.

2:13 God has not left us alone in our struggles to do his will. He wants to come alongside us and within us to help. He helps us want to obey him and then gives us the power to do it. The secret to changing our lives is to submit to his control and let him work in us.

2:13 To be like Christ, we must condition ourselves to think like Christ. To change our desires to be more like Christ's, we need the power of the indwelling Spirit (1:19), the influence of faithful Christians, obedience to God's Word (not just exposure to it), and sacrificial service. Often it is in *doing* God's will that we gain the *desire* for it (see 4:8, 9).

¹⁴In everything you do, stay away from complaining and arguing, ¹⁵so that no one can speak a word of blame against you. You are to live clean, innocent lives as children of God in a dark world full of people who are crooked and stubborn. Shine out among them like beacon lights, ¹⁶holding out to them the Word of Life.

Then when Christ returns how glad I will be that my work among you was so worthwhile. ¹⁷And if my lifeblood is, so to speak, to be poured out over your faith which I am offering up to God as a sacrifice—that is, if I am to die for you—even then I will be glad, and will share my joy with each of you. ¹⁸For you should be happy about this, too, and rejoice with me for having this privilege of dying for you.

2:14 Rom 14:1 / 1 Cor 10:10
2:15 Mt 5:45 / Jn 12:36 / Eph 5:1
2:16 Jn 6:63,68 / 1 Thess 2:19,20
2:17 Rom 15:16 / Col 1:24

Those who will soon come to you

¹⁹If the Lord is willing, I will send Timothy to see you soon. Then when he comes back he can cheer me up by telling me all about you and how you are getting along. ²⁰There is no one like Timothy for having a real interest in you; ²¹everyone else seems to be worrying about his own plans and not those of Jesus Christ. ²²But you know Timothy. He has been just like a son to me in helping me preach the Good News. ²³I hope to send him to you just as soon as I find out what is going to happen to me here. ²⁴And I am trusting the Lord that soon I myself may come to see you.

²⁵Meanwhile, I thought I ought to send Epaphroditus back to you. You sent him to help me in my need; well, he and I have been real brothers, working and battling side by side. ²⁶Now I am sending him home again, for he has been homesick for all of you and upset because you heard that he was ill. ²⁷And he surely was; in fact, he almost died. But God had mercy on him, and on me too, not allowing me to have this sorrow on top of everything else.

²⁸So I am all the more anxious to get him back to you again, for I know how thankful you will be to see him, and that will make me happy and lighten all my cares. ²⁹Welcome him in the Lord with great joy, and show your appreciation, ³⁰for he risked his life for the work of Christ and was at the point of death while trying to do for me the things you couldn't do because you were far away.

2:20 1 Cor 16:10
2:21 1 Cor 10:24 / 13:5
2:22 1 Cor 4:17 / 1 Tim 1:2
2:24 Phil 1:25
2:25 Phil 4:18
2:29 Rom 16:2 / 1 Cor 16:18 / 1 Thess 5:12 / 1 Tim 5:17
2:30 1 Cor 16:17

3. Joy in believing
All is worthless compared to knowing Christ

3 Whatever happens, dear friends, be glad in the Lord. I never get tired of telling you this and it is good for you to hear it again and again. ²Watch out for those wicked men—dangerous dogs, I call them—who say you

3:1 Phil 4:4
3:2 Gal 5:2

2:14-16 Why are complaining and arguing so harmful? If all that people know about a church is that its members constantly argue, complain, and gossip, they get a false impression of the gospel. Belief in Christ should unite those who trust him. If our church is always complaining and arguing, it lacks the unifying power of Jesus Christ. Stop arguing with other Christians or complaining about conditions within the church and let the world see Christ.

2:14-16 Our lives should be characterized by purity, patience, and peacefulness, so that we will shine out "like beacon lights." A transformed life is an effective witness to the power of God's Word. Is your light shining brightly, or is it clouded by complaints and arguing? Be a clean, radiant light shining out for God.

2:17 Even if he had to die, Paul was content, knowing he had helped the Philippians live for Christ. When you're totally committed to serving Christ, sacrifice is more rewarding than painful.

2:19 Timothy was with Paul in Rome at the time Paul wrote this letter. He was also with Paul on his second missionary journey when the church at Philippi was founded. For more information on Timothy, see his Profile in 1 Timothy.

2:23 Paul was in prison (either awaiting his trial or its verdict), for preaching the message of Jesus Christ. He was telling the

Philippians that when he learned of the court's decision, he would send Timothy to them with the news, but that he was ready to accept whatever came (1:21-26).

2:25 Epaphroditus delivered money from the Philippians to Paul; then he returned with this thank-you letter to Philippi. Epaphroditus may have been an elder in Philippi (2:25-30; 4:18) who, while staying with Paul, became ill (2:27, 30). After his recovery, he returned home. He is mentioned only in Philippians.

3:2, 3 These wicked men to whom Paul refers are Judaizers—Jewish Christians who wrongly believed it was essential for Gentiles to follow all the Old Testament Jewish laws, especially the rite of circumcision, in order to receive salvation. Many Judaizers were motivated by spiritual pride. Because they had invested so much time and effort in keeping their laws, they couldn't accept the fact that all their efforts wouldn't bring them a step closer to salvation.

Paul criticized the Judaizers because they looked at Christianity backwards—thinking that what they *did* made them believers rather than the free gift of grace given by Christ. What believers do is a *result* of faith, not a *prerequisite* to faith. This had been confirmed by the early church leaders at the Jerusalem council 11 years earlier (Acts 15). No person should try to add anything to

3:3
Deut 30:6
Jn 4:21-24
Rom 2:29; 7:6
Col 2:11

3:5
Acts 22:3; 23:6
Rom 11:1
2 Cor 11:22

3:6
Acts 8:3; 22:4
Rom 10:5
Gal 1:13

3:7
Mt 13:44
Lk 14:33

3:8
Isa 53:11
Jn 17:3
Eph 4:13
2 Pet 3:18

3:9
Isa 64:6
Rom 1:17;
9:30; 10:3
Gal 2:16
2 Pet 1:1

3:10
Jn 17:3
Rom 8:17,29
Eph 1:19,20
1 Pet 4:13

3:11
Acts 26:8
1 Cor 15:23

must be circumcised to be saved. 3For it isn't the *cutting of our bodies* that makes us children of God; it is *worshiping him with our spirits*. That is the only true "circumcision." We Christians glory in what Christ Jesus has done for us and realize that we are helpless to save ourselves.

4Yet if anyone ever had reason to hope that he could save himself, it would be I. If others could be saved by what they are, certainly I could! 5For I went through the Jewish initiation ceremony when I was eight days old, having been born into a pure-blooded Jewish home that was a branch of the old original Benjamin family. So I was a real Jew if there ever was one! What's more, I was a member of the Pharisees who demand the strictest obedience to every Jewish law and custom. 6And sincere? Yes, so much so that I greatly persecuted the Church; and I tried to obey every Jewish rule and regulation right down to the very last point.

7But all these things that I once thought very worthwhile—now I've thrown them all away so that I can put my trust and hope in Christ alone. 8Yes, everything else is worthless when compared with the priceless gain of knowing Christ Jesus my Lord. I have put aside all else, counting it worth less than nothing, in order that I can have Christ, 9and become one with him, no longer counting on being saved by being good enough or by obeying God's laws, but by trusting Christ to save me; for God's way of making us right with himself depends on faith—counting on Christ alone. 10Now I have given up everything else—I have found it to be the only way to really know Christ and to experience the mighty power that brought him back to life again, and to find out what it means to suffer and to die with him. 11So, whatever it takes, I will be one who lives in the fresh newness of life of those who are alive from the dead.

Forget the past and reach to the goal

12I don't mean to say I am perfect. I haven't learned all I should even yet, but I

Christ's offer of salvation by grace through faith.

3:2, 3 It is easy to place more emphasis on religious effort than on internal faith; but God values the attitude of our hearts above all else. Don't judge people's spirituality by their fulfillment of rituals or level of human activity. And don't think you will satisfy God by feverishly doing his work. God notices all you do for him and will reward you for it, but only if you first accept his free gift of salvation.

3:4-6 At first glance, it seems that Paul is boasting about his achievements. But he is actually doing the opposite, showing that human achievements, no matter how impressive, cannot earn a person salvation and eternal life with God. Paul had impressive credentials: upbringing, nationality, family background, inheritance, orthodoxy, activity, and morality (see 2 Corinthians 11; Galatians 1:13, 24, for more of his credentials). But when he was converted to faith in Christ (Acts 9), it wasn't based upon his credentials, but upon the grace of Christ. Paul did not depend on his credentials to please God, because even the most impressive credentials fall short of God's holy standards. Are you depending on Christian parents, church affiliation, or just being good to make you right with God? Credentials, accomplishments, or reputation cannot earn salvation. Like Paul, you must realize that salvation comes only through faith in Christ.

3:5 Paul belonged to the tribe of Benjamin, a heritage greatly esteemed among the Jews. From this tribe came Israel's first king, Saul (1 Samuel 10:20-24). When the kingdom was divided after Solomon's death, only the tribes of Benjamin and Judah remained loyal to David's line (1 Kings 12:20, 21). In addition, Benjamin and Judah were the only two tribes to return to Israel after the exile (Ezra 4:1). Paul was also a Pharisee, a very devout Jewish sect, which scrupulously kept its own numerous rules in addition to the laws of Moses. Jewish listeners would have been impressed by both of these facts on Paul's resumé.

3:6 Why did Paul, a devout Jewish leader, persecute the church?

In harmony with the leaders of the religious establishment, Paul thought Christianity was heretical and blasphemous. Because Jesus did not meet his expectations of what the Messiah would be like, Paul assumed Jesus' claims were false—and therefore wicked. In addition, he saw Christianity as a political menace because it threatened to disrupt the fragile harmony between the Jews and the Roman establishment.

3:8 After Paul considered everything he had accomplished in his life, he said that it was all worthless when compared with knowing Christ. This is a profound statement about values: a person's relationship with Christ is more important than anything else. To know Christ should be our ultimate goal. Consider your values. Do you place anything above your relationship with Christ? If your priorities are wrong, how can you reorder them?

3:10 Paul gave up everything—family, friendship, and political freedom—in order to know Christ and his resurrection power. We too have access to this knowledge and this power, but we may have to make sacrifices to enjoy it fully. What are you willing to give up in order to know Christ—a few minutes each day for prayer and Bible study? Your friend's approval? Some of your plans or pleasures? Whatever it is, knowing Christ is more than worth the sacrifice.

3:11 The last part of verse 11 literally reads, "if somehow I may attain to the resurrection of the dead." Just as Christ was exalted after his resurrection, so we will one day share Christ's glory (Revelation 22:1-7). Paul knew that he might die soon, but he had faith that he would be raised to life again.

3:12-14 Paul said his goal was to know Christ, to be like Christ, and to be all Christ has in mind for him. This goal absorbed all his energy. This is an example for us. We should not let anything take our eyes off our goal—Christ. With the singlemindedness of an athlete in training, we must lay aside everything harmful and forsake even the good things that may distract us from being effective Christians.

keep working toward that day when I will finally be all that Christ saved me for and wants me to be.

13No, dear brothers, I am still not all I should be but I am bringing all my energies to bear on this one thing: Forgetting the past and looking forward to what lies ahead, 14I strain to reach the end of the race and receive the prize for which God is calling us up to heaven because of what Christ Jesus did for us.

15I hope all of you who are mature Christians will see eye-to-eye with me on these things, and if you disagree on some point, I believe that God will make it plain to you— 16if you fully obey the truth you have.

17Dear brothers, pattern your lives after mine and notice who else lives up to my example. 18For I have told you often before, and I say it again now with tears in my eyes, there are many who walk along the Christian road who are really enemies of the cross of Christ. 19Their future is eternal loss, for their god is their appetite: they are proud of what they should be ashamed of; and all they think about is this life here on earth. 20But our homeland is in heaven, where our Savior the Lord Jesus Christ is; and we are looking forward to his return from there. 21When he comes back he will take these dying bodies of ours and change them into glorious bodies like his own, using the same mighty power that he will use to conquer all else everywhere.

3:13
Lk 9:62
1 Cor 9:24
Heb 6:1

3:14
2 Tim 4:7,8
Heb 12:1

3:15
1 Cor 2:6; 14:20
Gal 5:10
Phil 1:9,10

3:16
Gal 6:16

3:17
1 Cor 4:16
1 Pet 5:3

3:18
Gal 6:14

3:20
Eph 2:16,19
Col 3:1,3

3:21
Mt 17:2; 28:18
1 Cor 15:43-53
Col 3:4
Heb 7:25
1 Jn 3:2

		THREE STAGES OF PERFECTION
1. *Perfect Relationship*	We are perfect because of our eternal union with the infinitely perfect Christ. When we become his children, we are declared "not guilty," thus righteous, because of what Christ, God's beloved Son, has done for us. This perfection is absolute and unchangeable, and it is this perfect relationship that guarantees that we will one day be "completely perfect" (below). See Colossians 2:8–10; Hebrews 10:8–14.	
2. *Perfect Progress*	We can grow and mature spiritually as we continue to trust Christ, learn more about him, draw closer to him, and obey him. Our progress is changeable (in contrast to our relationship, above) because it depends on our daily walk— at times in life we mature more than at other times. But we are growing toward perfection if we "work toward it" (3:12). These good works do not perfect us; rather, as God perfects us, we do good works for him. See Philippians 3:1–15.	
3. *Completely Perfect*	When Christ returns to take us into his eternal Kingdom, we will be glorified and made completely perfect. See Philippians 3:20, 21.	

All phases of perfection are grounded in faith in Christ and what he has done, not what we can do for him. We cannot perfect ourselves; only God can work in and through us until his task is "finally finished on that day when Jesus Christ returns" (1:6).

3:13, 14 Paul had reason to feel guilty—he held the coats of those who stoned Stephen, the first Christian martyr (Acts 7:57, 58). We have all done things for which we are ashamed, and we all live in the tension of what we have been and what we want to be. Because our hope is in Christ, however, we can let go of past guilt and look forward to what he will help us become. Don't dwell on your past. Instead, grow in the knowledge of God by concentrating on your relationship with him *now*. Know you are forgiven, and then move on to a life of faith and obedience. Look forward to a fuller and more meaningful life because of your hope in Christ.

3:17 Paul challenged the Philippians to pursue Christlikeness by telling them to follow his example. This did not mean, of course, that they should copy everything he did; he had just stated that he was not perfect (3:12). But as he focused his life on being like Christ, so should we. It is likely that none of the Gospels had yet been written, so Paul could not tell them to read the Bible to see what Christ was like. Therefore he urged them to imitate him. That Paul could tell people to follow his example is a testimony to his

character. Can you do the same? What kind of follower would a new Christian become if he or she imitated you?

3:17–21 Paul criticized not only the Judaizers (see the note on 3:2, 3), but also the self-indulgent Christians. These are people who claim to be Christians but don't live up to Christ's model of servanthood and sacrifice. They satisfy their own desires before even thinking about the needs of others. Freedom in Christ does not mean freedom to be selfish. It means the opportunity to serve and to become the best person you can be.

3:20 Citizens of Philippi had the same rights and privileges as the citizens of Rome because Philippi was a Roman colony. Likewise we Christians will one day experience all the special privileges of our heavenly citizenship because we belong to Christ.

3:21 The bodies we receive when we are raised from the dead will be like Christ's resurrected body. For a more detailed discussion of our new bodies, see 1 Corinthians 15:35ff and 2 Corinthians 5:1–10.

4. Joy in giving

Think about pure and lovely things

4:2
Phil 2:2

4 Dear brother Christians, I love you and long to see you, for you are my joy and my reward for my work. My beloved friends, stay true to the Lord.

4:3
Rev 3:5; 20:12
21:27

2And now I want to plead with those two dear women, Euodias and Syntyche. Please, please, with the Lord's help, quarrel no more—be friends again. 3And I ask you, my true teammate, to help these women, for they worked side by side with me in telling the Good News to others; and they worked with Clement, too, and the rest of my fellow workers whose names are written in the Book of Life.

4:4
Phil 3:1

4:5
Heb 10:25,37
1 Pet 4:7

4:6
Mt 6:25
1 Pet 5:7

4Always be full of joy in the Lord; I say it again, rejoice! 5Let everyone see that you are unselfish and considerate in all you do. Remember that the Lord is coming soon. 6Don't worry about anything; instead, pray about everything; tell God your needs and don't forget to thank him for his answers. 7If you do this you will

TRAINING FOR THE CHRISTIAN LIFE	Reference	Metaphors	Training	Our Goal as Believers
As a great amount of training is needed for athletic activities, so we must train diligently for the Christian life. Such training takes time, dedication, energy, continued practice, and vision. We must all commit ourselves to the Christian life, but we must first know the rules as prescribed in God's Word (2 Timothy 2:5).	1 Corinthians 9:24–27	Race	Deny yourself many things in order to do your best.	We train ourselves to run the race of life. So we keep our eyes on Christ—the goal—and don't get sidetracked or slowed down. When we do this, we will win a reward in Christ's Kingdom.
	Philippians 3:13, 14	Race	Put all your energies toward winning the race.	Living the Christian life demands all of our energy. We can forget the past and strain for the goal because we know Christ promises eternity with him at the race's end.
	2 Timothy 4:7, 8	Fight	Fighting long and hard without giving up.	The Christian life is a fight against evil forces from without and temptation from within. If we stay true to God through it all, he promises an end, a rest, and a crown.
	1 Timothy 4:7–10	Exercise	Spiritual exercise will help you grow in faith and character.	As we must repeat exercises to tone our bodies, so we must steadily repeat spiritual exercises to be spiritually fit. When we do this, we will be better Christians, living in accordance with God's will. Such a life will attract others to Christ and pay dividends in this present life and the next.

4:2, 3 Paul did not warn the Philippian church of doctrinal errors, but they did have some relational problems. These two women had been workers for Christ in the church. Their broken relationship was no small matter, because many had become believers through their efforts. It is possible to believe in Christ, work hard for his Kingdom, and yet have broken relationships with others who are committed to the same cause. But there is no excuse for remaining unreconciled. Do you need to be reconciled to someone today?

4:3 Those whose names are written in the Book of Life are all who are marked out for salvation through their faith in Christ (see Luke 10:17–20; Revelation 20:11–15, for more on this concept).

4:4 It seems strange that a man in prison would be telling a church to be joyful. But Paul's attitude serves to teach us an important lesson—our inner attitudes do not have to reflect our outward circumstances. Paul was full of joy because he knew that no matter what happened to him, Jesus Christ was with him. Several times in this letter, Paul urges the Philippians to be joyful,

probably because they needed to hear this. It's easy to get discouraged about unpleasant circumstances or to take unimportant events too seriously. If you haven't been joyful lately, you may not be looking at life from the right perspective.

4:4, 5 Ultimate joy comes from Christ dwelling within us. At Christ's Second Coming we will fully realize this ultimate joy, because he who dwells within us will fulfill his final purposes for us.

4:6, 7 Imagine never having to worry about anything! It seems like an impossibility—we all have worries on the job, in our homes, at school. But Paul's advice is to turn your worries into prayers. Do you want to worry less? Then pray more! Whenever you start to worry, stop and pray.

4:7 God's peace is different from the world's peace (see John 14:27). It is not found in positive thinking, in absence of conflict, or in good feelings. Real peace comes from knowing that because God is in control, our citizenship in Christ's Kingdom is sure, our destiny is set, and our victory over sin is certain.

experience God's peace, which is far more wonderful than the human mind can understand. His peace will keep your thoughts and your hearts quiet and at rest as you trust in Christ Jesus.

8And now, brothers, as I close this letter let me say this one more thing: Fix your thoughts on what is true and good and right. Think about things that are pure and lovely, and dwell on the fine, good things in others. Think about all you can praise God for and be glad about. 9Keep putting into practice all you learned from me and saw me doing, and the God of peace will be with you.

4:8
1 Thess 5:22

4:9
Rom 15:33

Paul is grateful for their gift

10How grateful I am and how I praise the Lord that you are helping me again. I know you have always been anxious to send what you could, but for a while you didn't have the chance. 11Not that I was ever in need, for I have learned how to get along happily whether I have much or little. 12I know how to live on almost nothing or with everything. I have learned the secret of contentment in every situation, whether it be a full stomach or hunger, plenty or want; 13for I can do everything God asks me to with the help of Christ who gives me the strength and power. 14But even so, you have done right in helping me in my present difficulty.

4:10
2 Cor 11:9

4:11
1 Tim 6:6

4:12
1 Cor 4:11
2 Cor 11:9

4:13
Jn 15:5
2 Cor 12:9

4:14
Phil 1:7
Heb 10:33,34

15As you well know, when I first brought the Gospel to you and then went on my way, leaving Macedonia, only you Philippians became my partners in giving and receiving. No other church did this. 16Even when I was over in Thessalonica you sent help twice. 17But though I appreciate your gifts, what makes me happiest is the well-earned reward you will have because of your kindness.

4:15
Rom 15:26
2 Cor 11:8,9
Phil 1:5

4:17
Tit 3:14

18At the moment I have all I need—more than I need! I am generously supplied with the gifts you sent me when Epaphroditus came. They are a sweet-smelling sacrifice that pleases God well. 19And it is he who will supply all your needs from his riches in glory, because of what Christ Jesus has done for us. 20Now unto God our Father be glory forever and ever. Amen.

Sincerely, Paul

4:18
2 Cor 9:12
Phil 2:25
Heb 13:16

4:19
Ps 23:1
Prov 8:21
2 Cor 9:8

4:8 What we put into our minds determines what comes out in our words and actions. Paul tells us to fill our minds with thoughts that are "true and good and right." Do you have problems with impure thoughts and daydreams? Examine what you are putting into your mind through television, books, movies, and magazines. Replace harmful input with wholesome material. Above all, read God's Word and pray. Ask him to help you focus your mind on what is good and pure. It takes practice, but it can be done.

4:10 In 1 Corinthians 9:11-18, Paul said he didn't accept gifts from the Corinthian church because he didn't want to be accused of preaching only to get money. But Paul maintained that it was a church's responsibility to support God's ministers (1 Corinthians 9:14). Here he accepted the Philippians' gift because they gave it willingly and he was in need.

4:10-14 Are you content in any situation you face? Paul knew how to be content whether he had much or little. The secret was Christ's power in his life. Do you have great needs, or are you discontented because you don't have what you want? Learn to rely on God's promises and Christ's power to help you be content. If you always want more, ask God to remove that desire and teach you contentment in every situation. He will supply all your needs, but in a way that he knows is best for you (see note on 4:19 for more on God supplying our needs).

4:12, 13 Paul was content because he could see life from God's point of view. He focused on what he was supposed to *do*, not what he felt he should *have*. He had his priorities straight and was grateful for everything God had given him. Often the desire for more or better possessions is really a longing to fill an empty place in one's life. To what are you drawn when you feel empty inside? How can you find true contentment? The answer lies in your perspective, your priorities, and your source of power.

4:17 When we give to those in need, there is not only benefit to the receiver, but we are benefited as well. It was not the Philippians' gift, but their spirit of love and devotion that Paul appreciated most.

4:18 Paul was not referring to a sin offering but to a thank offering (Leviticus 7:12-15 contains the instructions for thank offerings). Although the Greek and Roman Christians were not Jews and had not offered sacrifices according to the Old Testament laws, they were well acquainted with the custom of offering sacrifices.

4:19 We can trust that God will always meet our needs, but we must remember that he may not supply them all in this life. Christians suffer and die (tradition says Paul himself was beheaded), and God does not always intervene to spare them. In the new earth, however, when sin has been permanently destroyed, our wants and needs will be abundantly supplied for eternity.

Paul's final greetings

4:22
2 Cor 13:13
4:23
2 Tim 4:22

21Say "hello" for me to all the Christians there; the brothers with me send their greetings too. 22And all the other Christians here want to be remembered to you, especially those who work in Caesar's palace. 23The blessings of our Lord Jesus Christ be upon your spirits.

4:22 There were many Christians in Rome; some were even in Caesar's palace. Perhaps Paul, while awaiting trial, was making converts of the Roman civil service! Paul sent greetings from these Roman Christians to the believers at Philippi. The gospel had spread to all strata of society, linking people who had no other bond but Christ. The Roman Christians and the Philippian Christians were brothers and sisters because of their unity in Christ. Believers today are also linked to others across cultural, economic, and social barriers. We are family—all believers truly are our brothers and sisters in Christ.

4:23 In many ways the Philippian church was a model congregation. It was made up of many different kinds of people who were learning to work together in unity. But Paul recognized that problems could arise, so in his thank-you letter, he prepared the Philippians for difficulties that could crop up within a body of believers. Though a prisoner in Rome, Paul had learned the true secret of joy and peace—imitating Christ and serving others. By focusing our minds on Christ we will learn unity, humility, joy, and peace. We will also be motivated to live for him. We can live confidently for him because we have "the blessings of our Lord Jesus Christ" (4:23) upon us.

VITAL STATISTICS

PURPOSE:
To combat errors in the church and to show that believers have everything they need in Christ

AUTHOR:
Paul

TO WHOM WRITTEN:
The church at Colosse, a city in Asia Minor, and all believers everywhere

DATE WRITTEN:
About A.D. 60, during Paul's imprisonment in Rome

SETTING:
Paul had never visited Colosse—evidently the church had been founded by Epaphras and other converts from Paul's missionary travels. The church, however, had been infiltrated by religious relativism with some believers attempting to combine elements of paganism and secular philosophy with Christian doctrine. Paul confronts these false teachings and affirms the sufficiency of Christ.

KEY VERSES:
"For in Christ there is all of God in human body; so you have everything when you have Christ, and you are filled with God through your union with Christ. He is the highest Ruler, with authority over every other power" (2:9, 10).

KEY PEOPLE:
Paul, Timothy, Tychicus, Onesimus, Aristarchus, Mark, Epaphras

KEY PLACES:
Colosse, Laodicea (4:15, 16)

SPECIAL FEATURES:
Christ is presented as having absolute supremacy and sole sufficiency. Colossians has similarities to Ephesians, probably because it was written at about the same time, but it has a different emphasis.

REMOVE the head coach, and the team flounders; break the fuel line, and the car won't run; unplugged the electrical appliance has no power; without the head, the body dies. Whether for leadership, power, or life, connections are vital!

Colossians is a book of connections. Writing from prison in Rome, Paul combatted false teachings which had infiltrated the Colossian church. The problem was "syncretism," combining ideas from other philosophies and religions (such as paganism, strains of Judaism, and Greek thought) with Christian truth. The resulting heresy later became known as "gnosticism," emphasizing special knowledge (*gnosis* in Greek) and denying Christ as God and Savior. To combat this devious error, Paul stressed Christ's deity and his sacrificial death on the cross for sin. Only by being connected with Christ through faith can anyone have eternal life and only through a continuing connection with him can anyone have power for living. Christ is God incarnate and the *only* way to peace with God the Father. Paul also emphasized believers' connections with each other as Christ's body on earth.

Paul's introduction to the Colossians includes a greeting, a note of thanksgiving, and a prayer for spiritual wisdom and strength for these brothers and sisters in Christ (1:1–12). He then moves into a doctrinal discussion of the person and work of Christ (1:13–23), stating that Christ is the "exact likeness of the unseen God" (1:15), the "Creator" (1:16), the "Head of the body . . . his Church" (1:18), and the "Leader of all those who arise from the dead" (1:18). His death on the cross makes it possible for us to stand in the presence of God (1:22).

Paul then explains how the world's teachings are totally empty when compared with God's plan, and he challenges the Colossians to reject shallow answers and to live in union with Christ (1:23—2:23).

Against this theological backdrop, Paul turns to practical considerations—what the divinity, death, and resurrection of Jesus should mean to all believers (3:1—4:6). Because our eternal destiny is sure, heaven should fill our thoughts (3:1–4), sexual impurity and other worldly lusts should not be named among us (3:5–8), and truth, love, and peace should mark our lives (3:9–15). Our love for Christ should also translate into love for others—friends, fellow believers, spouses, children, and parents (3:16—4:1). Furthermore, we should constantly communicate with God through prayer (4:2–4), and we should take every opportunity to tell others the Good News (4:5, 6). In Christ we have everything we need for salvation and for living the Christian life.

Paul had probably never visited Colosse, so he concludes this epistle with personal comments about their common Christian associations, providing a living lesson of the connectedness of the body of Christ.

Read Colossians as a book for an embattled church in the first century, but read it also for its timeless truths. Gain a fresh appreciation for Christ as the *fullness* of God and the *only* source for living the Christian life.

THE BLUEPRINT

1. What Christ has done (1:1—2:23)
2. What Christians should do (3:1—4:18)

In this letter Paul clearly teaches that Christ has paid for sin, that Christ has reconciled us to God, and that Christ gives us the pattern and the power to grow spiritually. Since Christ is the exact likeness of God, when we learn what he is like, we see what we need to become. Since Christ is Lord over all creation, we should crown him Lord over our lives. Since Christ is the Head of the body, his church, we should nurture our vital connection to him.

MEGATHEMES

THEME	EXPLANATION	IMPORTANCE
Christ is God	Jesus Christ is God in the flesh, Lord of all creation, and Lord of the new creation. He is the express reflection of the invisible God. He is eternal, preexistent, omnipotent, equal with the Father. He is supreme and complete.	Because Christ is supreme, our lives must be Christ centered. To recognize him as God means to regard our relationship with him most vital and to make his interests our top priority.
Christ is head of the Church	Because Christ is God, he is the head of the church, his true believers. Christ is the founder, the leader, and the highest authority on earth. He requires first place in all our thoughts and activities.	To acknowledge him as our head, we must welcome his leadership in all we do or think. No person, group, or church can regard any loyalty as more critical than that of loyalty to Christ.
Union with Christ	Because our sin has been forgiven and we have been reconciled to God, we have a union with Christ that can never be broken. In our faith connection with him, we identify with his death, burial, and resurrection.	We should live in constant contact and communication with God. When we do, we all will be unified with Christ and with one another.
Man-made religion	False teachers were promoting a heresy that stressed man-made rules (legalism). They also sought spiritual growth by asceticism and mysticism. This search created pride in their self-centered efforts.	We must not cling to our own ideas and try to blend them into Christianity. Nor should we let our hunger for a more fulfilling Christian experience cause us to trust in a teacher, a group, or a system of thought more than in Christ himself. Christ is our hope and our true source of wisdom.

1. What Christ has done

1 *From:* Paul, chosen by God to be Jesus Christ's messenger, and from Brother Timothy. **1:1**
Eph 1:1

²*To:* The faithful Christian brothers—God's people—in the city of Colosse. May God our Father shower you with blessings and fill you with his great peace. **1:2**
Rom 1:7

Paul's prayer for the Colossian believers

³Whenever we pray for you we always begin by giving thanks to God the Father of our Lord Jesus Christ, ⁴for we have heard how much you trust the Lord, and how much you love his people. ⁵And you are looking forward to the joys of heaven, and have been ever since the Gospel first was preached to you. ⁶The same Good News **1:4**
Eph 1:15
1:5
Eph 1:13
1 Pet 1:4

The Heresy	Reference	Paul's Answer
Spirit is good; matter is evil.	1:15–20	God created heaven and earth for his glory.
One must follow ceremonies, rituals, and restrictions in order to be saved or perfected.	2:11, 16–23; 3:11	These were only shadows that ended when Christ came. He is all you need to be saved.
One must deny the body and live in strict asceticism.	2:20–23	This is no help in conquering evil thoughts and desires, instead it leads to pride.
Angels must be worshiped.	2:18	Angels are not to be worshiped; Christ alone is worthy of worship.
Christ could not be both human and divine.	1:15–20; 2:2, 3	Christ is God in the flesh; he is the eternal One, Head of the body, first in everything, supreme.
One must obtain "secret knowledge" in order to be saved or perfected—and this was not available to everyone.	2:2, 18	God's secret is Christ, and he has been revealed to all.
One must adhere to human wisdom, tradition, and philosophies.	2:4, 8–10; 3:15–17	By themselves, these can be misleading and shallow because they have human origin; instead, we should remember what Christ taught and follow his words as our ultimate authority.
It is even better to combine aspects of several religions.	2:10	You have everything when you have Christ; he is all-sufficient.
There is nothing wrong with immorality.	3:1–11	Get rid of sin and evil because you have been chosen by God and must live a new life as a representative of the Lord Jesus.

THE COLOSSIAN HERESY
Paul answered the various tenets of the Colossian heresy that threatened the church. This heresy was a "mixed bag," containing elements from several different heresies, some of which contradicted each other (as the chart shows).

1:1 Colossians, along with Philippians, Ephesians, and Philemon, is called a *prison epistle* because Paul wrote it from prison in Rome. This prison was actually a house where Paul was kept under close guard at all times (probably chained to a soldier) but given certain freedoms not offered to most prisoners: he was allowed to write letters and to see any visitors he wanted to see.

1:1 Paul and Timothy worked together on other New Testament letters: 2 Corinthians, Philippians, 1 and 2 Thessalonians, and Philemon. Paul also wrote two letters to Timothy (1 and 2 Timothy). For more information on these men, two of the greatest missionaries of the early church, see Paul's Profile in Acts 9 and Timothy's Profile in 1 Timothy.

1:1 The city of Colosse was 100 miles east of Ephesus on the Lycus River. It was not as influential as the nearby city of Laodicea, but as a trading center it was a crossroads for ideas and religions. Colosse had a large Jewish population—many Jews fled there when they were forced out of Jerusalem under the persecutions of Antiochus III and IV, almost 200 years before Christ. The church in Colosse was founded by Epaphras (1:7), one of Paul's converts.

Paul had not yet visited this church. His purpose in writing was to refute a heretical teaching about Christ, which had been causing confusion among the Christians there.

1:2, 3 Letters in Paul's day frequently began with the writer's name, followed by a blessing. Paul usually added Christian elements to his greetings, reminding his readers of his call by God to spread the gospel, emphasizing that the authority for his words came from God, and giving thanks for God's blessings.

1:4, 5 Throughout this letter Paul combats a heresy related to *gnosticism* (see note on 2:4). Gnostics believed it took special knowledge to be accepted by God; for them, even if they claimed to be Christians, Christ alone was not the way of salvation (1:20). In his introductory comments, therefore, Paul commends the Colossians for their faith, hope, and love—three main emphases of Christianity (1 Corinthians 13:13). He deliberately omits any mention of knowledge because of the heresy. It is not *what* one knows that makes him a Christian, but *whom* he knows. Knowing Christ is knowing God.

1:6 Wherever Paul went, he preached the gospel—to Gentile

that came to you is going out all over the world and changing lives everywhere, just as it changed yours that very first day you heard it and understood about God's great kindness to sinners.

7Epaphras, our much-loved fellow worker, was the one who brought you this Good News. He is Jesus Christ's faithful slave, here to help us in your place. 8And he is the one who has told us about the great love for others which the Holy Spirit has given you.

9So ever since we first heard about you we have kept on praying and asking God to help you understand what he wants you to do; asking him to make you wise about spiritual things; 10and asking that the way you live will always please the Lord and

1:7
Col 4:12,13
Philem 23

1:9
Rom 12:2
Eph 1:15-17

1:10
Jn 15:16
Eph 4:1
1 Thess 2:12
4:1

LOCATION OF COLOSSE

Paul had no doubt been through Laodicea on his third missionary journey, as it lay on the main route to Ephesus, but he had never been to Colosse. Though a large city with a significant population, Colosse was smaller and less important than the nearby cities of Laodicea and Hieropolis.

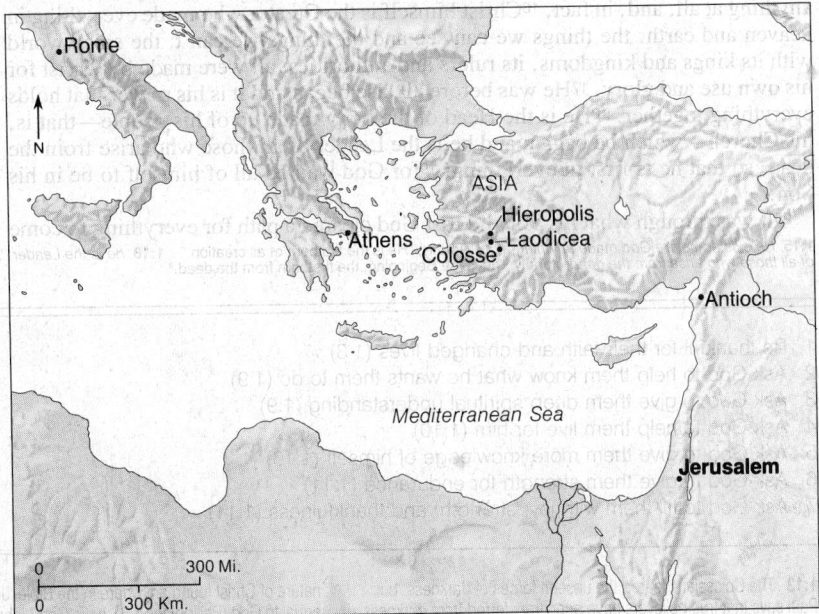

audiences, to hostile Jewish leaders, and even to his Roman guards. Whenever people believed in the message he spoke, they were changed. God's Word is not just for our information, it is for our transformation! Becoming a Christian means beginning a whole new relationship with God, not just turning over a new leaf or determining to do right. New believers have a changed purpose, direction, attitude, and behavior. They no longer seek to serve themselves, but to serve God. Can you point to any areas where hearing God's Word has changed your life, or where it should do so?

1:7 Epaphras probably founded the church at Colosse while Paul was living in Ephesus (Acts 19:10). He may have been converted in Ephesus, then returned to Colosse, his hometown. For some reason, Epaphras visited Rome and, while there, told Paul about the problem with the Colossian heresy. This prompted Paul to write this letter. Epaphras is also mentioned in Philemon 1:23 (the Colossian church met in Philemon's house).

1:8 Because of their love for one another, Christians can have an impact that goes far beyond their neighborhoods and communities. Christian love for others comes from the Holy Spirit (see Galatians 5:22). The Bible speaks of it as an action and attitude, not just an emotion. It is a by-product of our new life in Christ (see Romans 5:5; 1 Corinthians 13). Christians have no excuse for not loving others, because Christian love is not a feeling but a decision to *act* in the best interests of others.

1:9-14 Paul was exposing a heresy in the Colossian church that was a forerunner of *gnosticism* (see the note on 2:4 for more information). Gnostics valued the accumulation of knowledge, but Paul pointed out that knowledge in itself is empty. To be worth anything, it must lead to a changed life and right living. His prayer for the Colossians (1:9-14) has two dimensions—that they might *understand* what God wants, and that they might also have the power *to do* God's will. Knowledge is not merely to be accumulated; it should give us direction for living. Paul wanted the Colossians to *use* their knowledge. Knowledge of God is not a secret that only a few can discover; it is open to everyone. God wants us not only to learn more about him, but also to live for him and do his will.

1:9-14 Sometimes we wonder how to pray for missionaries and other leaders we have never met. Paul had never met the Colossians, but he faithfully prayed for them. His prayers teach us how to pray for others, whether we know them or not. We can request that they (1) understand God's will, (2) gain spiritual wisdom, (3) live lives pleasing and honoring to God, (4) do kind things for others, (5) know God better and better, (6) be filled with God's strength, (7) endure in faith, (8) stay full of Christ's joy, and (9) always be thankful. All believers have these same basic needs. When you don't know how to pray for someone, remember Paul's prayer pattern for the Colossians.

honor him, so that you will always be doing good, kind things for others, while all the time you are learning to know God better and better.

¹¹We are praying, too, that you will be filled with his mighty, glorious strength so that you can keep going no matter what happens—always full of the joy of the Lord, ¹²and always thankful to the Father who has made us fit to share all the wonderful things that belong to those who live in the Kingdom of light. ¹³For he has rescued us out of the darkness and gloom of Satan's kingdom and brought us into the Kingdom of his dear Son, ¹⁴who bought our freedom with his blood and forgave us all our sins.

1:11
Acts 5:41
Eph 3:16,20
1:12
Acts 26:18
Eph 1:11; 5:20
1:13
Acts 26:18
Heb 2:14,15
1:14
Eph 1:7

Person and work of Christ

¹⁵Christ is the exact likeness of the unseen God. He existed before God made anything at all, and, in fact, ¹⁶Christ himself is the Creator who made everything in heaven and earth, the things we can see and the things we can't; the spirit world with its kings and kingdoms, its rulers and authorities; all were made by Christ for his own use and glory. ¹⁷He was before all else began and it is his power that holds everything together. ¹⁸He is the Head of the body made up of his people—that is, his Church—which he began; and he is the Leader of all those who arise from the dead, so that he is first in everything; ¹⁹for God wanted all of himself to be in his Son.

²⁰It was through what his Son did that God cleared a path for everything to come

1:15
Jn 1:1,18; 14:9
2 Cor 4:4
Rev 3:14
1:16
Jn 1:3
Heb 1:2
1:17
Jn 1:1,2; 8:58
1:18
Eph 1:22,23
1:19
Jn 1:16
Col 2:9

1:15 *He existed before God made anything at all,* literally, "He is the firstborn of all creation." **1:18** *he is the Leader of all those who arise from the dead,* literally, "he is the Beginning, the firstborn from the dead."

---

1. Be thankful for their faith and changed lives (1:3)
2. Ask God to help them know what he wants them to do (1:9)
3. Ask God to give them deep spiritual understanding (1:9)
4. Ask God to help them live for him (1:10)
5. Ask God to give them more knowledge of himself (1:10)
6. Ask God to give them strength for endurance (1:11)
7. Ask God to fill them with joy, strength, and thankfulness (1:11)

HOW TO PRAY FOR OTHER CHRISTIANS
How many people in your life could be touched if you prayed in this way?

1:13 The Colossians feared the unseen forces of darkness, but Paul says that true believers have been transferred from darkness to light, from slavery to freedom, from guilt to forgiveness, and from the power of Satan to the power of God. We have been rescued from a rebel kingdom to serve the rightful King.

1:14 In verses 12–14, Paul lists five benefits God secured for us when Christ died on the cross: (1) he made us fit to be part of his Kingdom (see also 2 Corinthians 5:21); (2) he rescued us from Satan's domination and made us his children (see also 2:15); (3) he brought us into his eternal Kingdom (see also Ephesians 1:5, 6); (4) he bought our freedom from sin and judgment (see also Hebrews 9:12); and (5) he forgave all our sins (see also Ephesians 1:7).

1:15–23 The Colossian church had several misconceptions about Christ, which Paul directly refutes: (1) They believed that matter is evil, so they said God would not have come to earth as a true human being in bodily form. Paul states that Christ is the exact likeness of God, is himself God, and yet died on the cross as a human being. (2) They believed God did not create the world because he would not have created evil. Paul says that Jesus Christ, who was also God in the flesh, is the Creator of both heaven and earth. (3) They said Christ was not the unique Son of God, but rather one of many intermediaries between God and people. Paul explains that Christ existed before anything else and is the firstborn of those resurrected. (4) They refused to see Christ as the source of salvation, insisting that people could find God through special and secret knowledge. Paul affirms that a person can be saved through Christ alone.

1:15, 16 This is one of the strongest statements about the divine

nature of Christ found anywhere in the Bible. Jesus is not only equal to God (Philippians 2:6), he is God (John 10:30, 38; 12:45; 14:1–11). He not only reflects God, but he reveals God to us (John 1:18; 14:9). He came from heaven, not from the dust of the ground (1 Corinthians 15:47), and is Lord of all (Romans 9:5; 10:11–13; Revelation 1:5; 17:14). He is completely holy (Hebrews 7:26–28; 1 Peter 1:19; 2:22; 1 John 3:5), and he has authority to judge the world (Romans 2:16; 2 Corinthians 5:10; 2 Timothy 4:1). Therefore, he is supreme over all creation, including the spirit world. We, like the Colossian believers, must believe in the deity of Jesus Christ (that Jesus is God), or our Christian faith is hollow, misdirected, and meaningless. This is a central truth of Christianity.

1:16 Because the false teachers believed the physical world was evil, they thought God himself could not have created it. If Christ were God, they reasoned, he would be in charge only of the spiritual world. But Paul explains that both the spiritual and physical worlds were created by and are under the authority of Christ himself. He has no equal and no rival. For more on the connection between our spiritual and physical selves, see the note on 1 Corinthians 6:12, 13.

1:18 The resurrection proves Christ's lordship over the material world. All who trust in Christ will also defeat death and rise again to live eternally with him (1 Corinthians 15:20; 1 Thessalonians 4:14). See the note on Luke 24:6, 7 for more about the significance of Christ's resurrection.

1:19 Christ is fully divine (see the note on Philippians 2:5–7). Christ has always been God and will always be God.

1:20 Christ's death provided a way for all people to come to God. It cleared away the sin that keeps us from having a right

to him—all things in heaven and on earth—for Christ's death on the cross has made

1:21
Rom 5:10
2 Cor 5:18,19
Eph 2:3,12

peace with God for all by his blood. 21This includes you who were once so far away from God. You were his enemies and hated him and were separated from him by your evil thoughts and actions, yet now he has brought you back as his friends.

1:22
Rom 7:4
Eph 1:4; 5:27

22He has done this through the death on the cross of his own human body, and now as a result Christ has brought you into the very presence of God, and you are standing there before him with nothing left against you—nothing left that he could

1:23
Eph 3:17
Col 1:5,6

even chide you for; 23the only condition is that you fully believe the Truth, standing in it steadfast and firm, strong in the Lord, convinced of the Good News that Jesus died for you, and never shifting from trusting him to save you. This is the wonderful news that came to each of you and is now spreading all over the world. And I, Paul, have the joy of telling it to others.

Paul's mission and concern

1:24
Phil 2:17; 3:10
2 Tim 1:8

24But part of my work is to suffer for you; and I am glad, for I am helping to finish up the remainder of Christ's sufferings for his body, the Church.

1:25
Eph 3:2

25God has sent me to help his Church and to tell his secret plan to you Gentiles.

1:26
Eph 3:3

26, 27He has kept this secret for centuries and generations past, but now at last it has pleased him to tell it to those who love him and live for him, and the riches and

1:27
Rom 8:10; 9:23,24
Eph 3:8,9,16

glory of his plan are for you Gentiles too. And this is the secret: *that Christ in your hearts is your only hope of glory*.

1:28
Eph 4:13

28So everywhere we go we talk about Christ to all who will listen, warning them and teaching them as well as we know how. We want to be able to present each one

1:29
Eph 1:19
Col 4:12

to God, perfect because of what Christ has done for each of them. 29This is my work, and I can do it only because Christ's mighty energy is at work within me.

2:1
Col 4:12,13

2 I wish you could know how much I have struggled in prayer for you and for the church at Laodicea, and for my many other friends who have never known me

2:2
Mt 11:25-27
Eph 1:18,19
Phil 3:8
Col 2:19

personally. 2This is what I have asked of God for you: that you will be encouraged and knit together by strong ties of love, and that you will have the rich experience of knowing Christ with real certainty and clear understanding. *For God's secret*

---

relationship with our Creator. This does not mean that everyone has been saved, but that the way has been cleared for anyone who will trust Christ to be saved. God gives salvation to all those who by faith accept Christ's death for themselves.

1:21, 22 *No one* is good enough to save himself. If we want to live eternally with Christ, we must depend totally on God's grace. This is true whether we have been murderers or honest, hardworking citizens. We have all sinned repeatedly, and *any* sin is enough to cause us to depend on Jesus Christ for salvation and eternal life. Apart from Christ, there is no way to be saved from sin.

1:22, 23 The way to be declared not guilty for our sins is to trust Jesus Christ to take them away. Trusting means putting our confidence in him to forgive our sins, to make us right with God, and to empower us to live the way he wants us to live. When a judge in a court of law declares the defendant "not guilty," he has been acquitted of all the charges. Legally, it is as if the person had never been accused. When God forgives our sins, our record is wiped clean. From his perspective, it is as though we had never sinned. This is God's solution, and it is available to all of us regardless of our background or past behavior.

1:24 When Paul says he is finishing up the remainder of Christ's suffering, he does not mean Christ's suffering was inadequate to save us, nor does he mean that there is a predetermined amount of suffering that must be paid by all believers. Paul is simply saying that suffering is unavoidable in bringing the Good News of Christ to the world. It is called Christ's suffering because of our relationship to Christ. When we suffer, Christ feels it with us. But this suffering can be endured joyfully because it changes lives and brings people into God's Kingdom (see 1 Peter 4:1, 2, 12–19). For more about how Paul could be glad despite his suffering, see the note on Philippians 1:29.

1:26, 27 The false teachers in the Colossian church believed spiritual perfection was a secret and hidden plan that only a few privileged people would discover. Their secret plan was meant to be exclusive. Paul calls God's plan a secret, not in the sense that only a few would understand, but because it was hidden until Christ came. Who could have imagined that God's secret plan was to have his Son, Jesus Christ, live in the hearts of all who believe in him.

1:28 The word *perfect* means mature or complete, not flawless. Paul wanted to see each believer mature spiritually. To mature, we must grow daily in our faith.

1:28, 29 Christ's message is for everyone; so everywhere Paul and Timothy went they brought the Good News to all who would listen. An effective presentation of the gospel includes warning and teaching. The warning is that without Christ, people are doomed to eternal separation from God. The teaching is that salvation is available through faith in Christ. As Christ works in you, tell others about him, warning and teaching them in love. Do you know someone who needs to hear this message?

2:1 Laodicea was located a few miles northwest of Colosse. Like the church at Colosse, the Laodicean church was probably founded by one of Paul's converts while Paul was staying in Ephesus (Acts 19:10). The city was wealthy, a center of trade and commerce, but later the apostle John would criticize the believers for their lukewarm commitment to Christ (Revelation 3:14–22). The fact that Paul wanted this letter to be passed on to the Laodicean church (4:16) indicates that false teaching had spread there as well. Paul was counting on ties of love to bring the churches together to stand against this heresy and to encourage each other to remain true to God's plan of salvation in Christ.

plan, now at last made known, is Christ himself. ³In him lie hidden all the mighty, untapped treasures of wisdom and knowledge.

⁴I am saying this because I am afraid that someone may fool you with smooth talk. ⁵For though I am far away from you my heart is with you, happy because you are getting along so well, happy because of your strong faith in Christ.

New life in Christ

⁶And now just as you trusted Christ to save you, trust him, too, for each day's problems; live in vital union with him. ⁷Let your roots grow down into him and draw up nourishment from him. See that you go on growing in the Lord, and become strong and vigorous in the truth you were taught. Let your lives overflow with joy and thanksgiving for all he has done.

⁸Don't let others spoil your faith and joy with their philosophies, their wrong and shallow answers built on men's thoughts and ideas, instead of on what Christ has said. ⁹For in Christ there is all of God in a human body; ¹⁰*so you have everything when you have Christ,* and you are filled with God through your union with Christ. He is the highest Ruler, with authority over every other power.

¹¹When you came to Christ he set you free from your evil desires, not by a bodily operation of circumcision but by a spiritual operation, the baptism of your souls.

2:3
Isa 11:2
Rom 11:33
Eph 3:8

2:5
1 Cor 5:7

2:6
Jn 1:12
Col 1:10

2:7
Eph 2:20; 3:17

2:8
Jer 29:8
Mt 15:2,3
Col 2:20,23
Heb 13:9

2:9
Isa 7:14; 9:6
Jn 1:14
Col 1:19

2:10
Eph 1:21; 3:19
1 Pet 3:22

	Religion by Self-effort	Salvation by Faith	**SALVATION BY FAITH**
Goal	Please God by our own good works	Trust in Christ and then live to please God	
Means	Practice diligent service, discipline, and obedience, in hope of reward	Confess, submit, and commit yourself to Christ's control	
Power	Good, honest effort through self-determination	The Holy Spirit in us helps us do good work for Christ's Kingdom	
Control	Self-motivation; self-control	Christ in me; I in Christ	
Results	Chronic decision-making, apathy, depression, failure, constant desire for approval	Joy, thankfulness, love, guidance, service, forgiveness	

Salvation by faith in Christ sounds too easy for many people. They would rather think that they have done something to save themselves. Their religion becomes one of self-effort that leads either to disappointment or pride, but finally to eternal death. Christ's simple way is the only way, and it alone leads to eternal life.

2:4ff The problem Paul was combatting in the Colossian church was similar to *gnosticism* (from the Greek word for "knowledge"). This *heresy* (a teaching contrary to biblical doctrine) attacked Christianity in several basic ways: (1) It insisted that important hidden knowledge was secret from most believers; Paul, however, said that in Christ we see all we need to see of God's provision for us. (2) It taught that the body was evil; Paul countered that God himself dwelt in a body—that is, he was embodied in Jesus Christ. (3) It said that Christ seemed to be human, but was not. Paul insisted that in Jesus we see one who is fully human and fully God.

Gnosticism became fashionable in the second century. Even in Paul's day, these ideas sounded attractive to many and could easily seduce a church that didn't know Christian doctrine well. Aspects of this early heresy still pose significant problems for many in the church today. The antidote for heretical ideas is a thorough acquaintance with God's Word through personal study and sound Bible teaching.

2:6, 7 Accepting Christ as Lord of your life is the beginning of life with Christ. But you must continue to follow his leadership. Every day he desires to guide you and help you with your daily problems. You can live for Christ by (1) committing your life and submitting your will to him (Romans 12:1, 2); (2) seeking to learn from him, his life, and his teachings (3:16); and (3) recognizing the Holy Spirit's power in you (Acts 1:8; Galatians 5:22).

2:7 Paul used the illustration of our being rooted in or connected to Christ. As plants draw nourishment from the soil through their roots, so we draw our life-giving strength from Christ. The more we

draw our life from him, the less we will be fooled by those who falsely claim to have life's answers (2:8).

2:8 Paul writes against any philosophy of life based only on human ideas and experiences. Paul himself was a gifted philosopher, so he is not condemning philosophy. He was condemning teaching that credits humanity, not Christ, with being the answer to life's problems and thus becomes a false religion. The way to resist heresy is not to quit using your mind and retreat, but to focus on Christ's words as the foundation for your faith.

2:9 Again Paul asserts Christ's deity. The totality of God is embodied in Christ. See the note on 1:15, 16.

2:10 When we know Jesus Christ, we don't need to investigate other religions, cults, or unbiblical philosophies as the Colossians were doing. Christ alone holds the answers to the true meaning of life, because Christ *is* life. He is the unique source for the Christian life; therefore, no Christian needs anything he has not provided.

2:11, 12 Jewish males were circumcised as a sign of the Jews' covenant with God (Genesis 17:9–14; Deuteronomy 10:16). With the death of Christ, circumcision was no longer necessary. Now our commitment to God is written on our souls, not our bodies. In baptism we let God operate on our souls to put off the old nature and to make room for the new nature.

2:12 In the church in Paul's day, immersion was the usual form of baptism—that is, new Christians were completely "buried" in water. They understood this form of baptism to symbolize the

2:12
Rom 6:4,5
Eph 2:6

¹²For in baptism you see how your old, evil nature died with him and was buried with him; and then you came up out of death with him into a new life because you trusted the Word of the mighty God who raised Christ from the dead.

2:13
Eph 2:1,5
2:14
Eph 2:15
1 Pet 2:24
2:15
Isa 53:12
Jn 12:31
2 Cor 2:14
Eph 4:8

¹³You were dead in sins, and your sinful desires were not yet cut away. Then he gave you a share in the very life of Christ, for he forgave all your sins, ¹⁴and blotted out the charges proved against you, the list of his commandments which you had not obeyed. He took this list of sins and destroyed it by nailing it to Christ's cross. ¹⁵In this way God took away Satan's power to accuse you of sin, and God openly displayed to the whole world Christ's triumph at the cross where your sins were all taken away.

Freedom from legalism

2:16
1 Chron 23:31
Rom 14:3,5
Gal 4:10
2:17
Heb 8:5; 10:1

¹⁶So don't let anyone criticize you for what you eat or drink, or for not celebrating Jewish holidays and feasts or new moon ceremonies or Sabbaths. ¹⁷For these were only temporary rules that ended when Christ came. They were only shadows of the real thing—of Christ himself. ¹⁸Don't let anyone declare you lost when you refuse to worship angels, as they say you must. They have seen a vision, they say,

---

TRUST: YESTERDAY, TODAY, AND TOMORROW!
Living the lordship of Christ means realizing that each day brings new opportunities to trust Christ and experience his powerful work in us. Have you trusted this day to Christ?

1. Trusting Christ = living in vital union with Christ day by day (Colossians 2:2–7)

2. Accepting Christ as Head or Lord = he is in control (Colossians 1:15–18; 2:19; 3:10, 17)

3. Experiencing the power of the Holy Spirit = God's mighty energy at work in us (Colossians 1:11, 28, 29)

4. Inward and outward results =
   - assurance of forgiveness (Colossians 2:15)
   - freedom from evil desires (Colossians 2:11)
   - happiness (joy) (Colossians 2:7)
   - personal growth (Colossians 1:28)
   - opportunities to tell others the gospel (Colossians 1:4, 28)
   - thankfulness to God (Colossians 2:7)

5. Direction = God becoming involved in our decisions (Colossians 3:1, 16)

---

death and burial of the old way of life, followed by resurrection to life with Christ. If we think of our old, sinful life as dead and buried, we have a powerful motive to resist sin. Not wanting the ugly old life to come back to power again, we can consciously choose to treat it as if it were dead. Then we continue to enjoy our wonderful new life with Jesus (see Galatians 3:27 and Colossians 3:1–4 for more on this concept).

2:12-15 Before we believed in Christ, our nature was evil. The Christian, however, has a new nature. God has crucified the old rebellious nature (Romans 6:6) and replaced it with a new loving nature (Colossians 3:9, 10). The penalty of sin died with Christ on the cross. God has declared us not guilty, and we need no longer live under sin's power. God does not take us out of the world or make us robots—we will still feel like sinning, and sometimes we will sin. The difference is that before we were saved, we were slaves to our sinful nature, but now we can choose to live for Christ (see Galatians 2:20).

2:15 We can enjoy our new life in Christ because we have joined him in his death and resurrection. Our evil desires, our bondage to sin, and our love of sin died with him. Now, joining him in his resurrection life, we may have unbroken fellowship with God and freedom from sin. Our debt for sin has been paid in full; our sins are swept away and forgotten by God; and we can be clean and new. For more on the difference between our new life in Christ and our old sinful nature, read Ephesians 4:23, 24 and Colossians 3:3–15.

2:16, 17 Paul told the Colossian Christians not to let others criticize their diet or their religious ceremonies. Instead of outward observance, they should focus on Christ alone. In our worship, traditions and ceremonies can help bring us close to God, but we should never criticize fellow Christians whose traditions and ceremonies differ from ours. The Bible does not define how we should worship, only *whom*.

2:17 The purpose of the Old Testament laws, holidays, and feasts was simply to point toward Christ. Paul calls them shadows of the real thing—Christ himself. Once Christ came, he dispelled the shadows.

2:18 The false teachers claimed that God was remote and could be approached only through various levels of angels. They taught that people had to worship angels in order eventually to reach God. This is unscriptural; the Bible teaches that angels are inferior to God, and it forbids worshiping them (Exodus 20:3, 4; Revelation 22:8, 9).

2:18 The false teachers were proud of their humility! This false humility brought attention and praise to themselves rather than to God. True humility is viewing ourselves as we really are from God's perspective and acting accordingly. People today practice false humility when they talk themselves down so that others will think they are spiritual. False humility is self-centered; true humility is God centered.

2:18 The expression "clever imagination" has also been translated "fleshly minds," which is another way of saying that these men had a man-made religion. Paul pointed out that the false teachers were trying to deny the body by saying it was evil, but their desire for attention from others showed they were actually obsessed by it. Their philosophy that the flesh was evil came from the flesh itself—they made it up (2:8).

and know you should. These proud men (though they claim to be so humble) have a very clever imagination. ¹⁹But they are not connected to Christ, the Head to which all of us who are his body are joined; for we are joined together by his strong sinews and we grow only as we get our nourishment and strength from God.

²⁰Since you died, as it were, with Christ and this has set you free from following the world's ideas of how to be saved—by doing good and obeying various rules—why do you keep right on following them anyway, still bound by such rules as ²¹not eating, tasting, or even touching certain foods? ²²Such rules are mere human teachings, for food was made to be eaten and used up. ²³These rules may seem good, for rules of this kind require strong devotion and are humiliating and hard on the body, but they have no effect when it comes to conquering a person's evil thoughts and desires. They only make him proud.

2. What Christians should do

Principles of Christian living

3 Since you became alive again, so to speak, when Christ arose from the dead, now set your sights on the rich treasures and joys of heaven where he sits

2:20 *obeying various rules,* literally, "by the rudiments of the world."

2:19 Eph 1:22,23 4:15,16

2:20 Rom 6:2 Gal 2:20; 4:9

2:22 Mt 15:9 1 Cor 6:13

2:23 1 Tim 4:3

3:1 Mt 6:33 Eph 2:6

The Bible uses many illustrations to teach what happens when we choose to let Jesus be Lord of our lives. Following are some of the most vivid pictures:

FROM DEATH TO LIFE

1. Because Christ died for us, we have been crucified with him.

   Romans 6:2–13; 7:4–6
   2 Corinthians 5:14
   Galatians 2:20; 5:24; 6:14
   Colossians 2:20; 3:3–5
   1 Peter 2:24

2. Our old, rebellious nature died with Christ.

   Romans 6:6; 7:4–6
   Colossians 3:9, 10

3. Christ's resurrection guarantees our new life now and eternal life with him later.

   Romans 6:4, 11
   Colossians 2:12, 13; 3:1, 3

This process is acted out in baptism (Colossians 2:12), based on our faith in Christ: (1) The old evil nature dies (crucified); (2) We are ready to receive a new life (buried); (3) Christ gives us new life (resurrected).

2:19 The fundamental problem with the false teachers is that they were not connected to Christ. If they had been joined to him, they could not have taught false doctrine or lived evil lives. Anyone who teaches about God without being connected to him by faith is going to speak falsely about him.

2:20; 3:1 How do we die with Christ, and how are we raised with him? When a person becomes a Christian, he is given new life through the power of the Holy Spirit. See the notes on 2:12 and 2:12–15 for further information.

2:20–23 People should be able to see a difference between the way Christians and non-Christians live. Still, we should not expect instant maturity of new Christians. The Christian life is a process. Although we have a new nature, we don't automatically have all good thoughts and attitudes when we become new people in Christ. But if we keep listening to God, we will be changing all the time. As you look over the last year, what changes for the better have you seen in your thoughts and attitudes? Change may be slow, but your life will change significantly if you trust God to change you.

2:20–24 We cannot reach up to God by following rules and rituals or by practicing religion. Paul isn't saying all rules are bad (see the note on Galatians 2:16). But no keeping of laws or rules will earn salvation. The Good News is that God reaches down to man, and we respond. Man-made religions focus on human effort; Christianity focuses on Christ's work. Paul agrees that believers must put aside sinful desires, but that is the by-product of our new

life in Christ, not the cause of it. Our salvation does not depend on our own discipline and rule keeping, but on the power of Christ's death and resurrection.

2:22, 23 We can guard against man-made religions by asking these questions of any religious group: (1) Does it stress man-made rules and taboos rather than God's grace? (2) Does it foster a critical spirit about others, or does it exercise discipline discreetly and lovingly? (3) Does it stress formulas, secret knowledge, or special visions more than the Word of God? (4) Does it elevate self-righteousness, honoring those who keep the rules, rather than elevating Christ? (5) Does it neglect Christ's universal church, claiming to be an elite group? (6) Does it teach humiliation of the body as a means to spiritual growth rather than focusing on the growth of the whole person? (7) Does it disregard the family rather than holding it in high regard as the Bible does?

2:23 To the Colossians, the discipline demanded by the false teachers seemed good, and legalism still attracts many people today. Following a long list of religious rules requires strong self-discipline and can make a person appear moral, but religious rules cannot change a person's heart. Only the Holy Spirit can do that.

3:1ff In chapter 2, Paul exposed the wrong reasons for self-denial. In chapter 3, he explains true Christian behavior—putting on the new nature by accepting Christ and letting the old nature die. We change our behavior by letting Christ live within us, so that he can shape us into what we *should* be rather than merely what we might want to be in ourselves.

3:2
Phil 3:19,20

3:3
Gal 2:20

3:4
1 Cor 15:43
1 Jn 3:2

3:5
Mk 7:21-23
Rom 8:13
Gal 5:19
Eph 5:3,5

3:7
Eph 2:2

3:8
Eph 4:22,29
Jas 1:21

3:9
Eph 4:22,25

3:10
Rom 8:29; 12:2
Eph 2:10; 4:24

3:11
Rom 10:12
1 Cor 12:13
Gal 3:28

3:12
Gal 5:22
Eph 4:2,24
1 Pet 1:2

3:13
Eph 4:32

beside God in the place of honor and power. 2Let heaven fill your thoughts; don't spend your time worrying about things down here. 3You should have as little desire for this world as a dead person does. Your real life is in heaven with Christ and God. 4And when Christ who is our real life comes back again, you will shine with him and share in all his glories.

5Away then with sinful, earthly things; deaden the evil desires lurking within you; have nothing to do with sexual sin, impurity, lust and shameful desires; don't worship the good things of life, for that is idolatry. 6God's terrible anger is upon those who do such things. 7You used to do them when your life was still part of this world; 8but now is the time to cast off and throw away all these rotten garments of anger, hatred, cursing, and dirty language.

9Don't tell lies to each other; it was your old life with all its wickedness that did that sort of thing; now it is dead and gone. 10You are living a brand new kind of life that is continually learning more and more of what is right, and trying constantly to be more and more like Christ who created this new life within you. 11In this new life one's nationality or race or education or social position is unimportant; such things mean nothing. Whether a person has Christ is what matters, and he is equally available to all.

12Since you have been chosen by God who has given you this new kind of life, and because of his deep love and concern for you, you should practice tenderhearted mercy and kindness to others. Don't worry about making a good impression on them but be ready to suffer quietly and patiently. 13Be gentle and ready to forgive;

SINS VS. SIGNS OF LOVE	Sins of Sexual Attitude and Behavior	Sins of Speech	Signs of love
	Evil desires	Anger expressed	Tender-hearted mercy
	Sexual sin	Cursing	Kindness
	Impurity	Dirty language	Humility
	Lust	Lying	Patience
	Shameful desires		Gentleness
			Forgiveness

In Colossians 3:5 Paul tells us to consider ourselves dead to list 1. In 3:8 he tells us to cast off list 2. In 3:12 we're told to practice list 3. List 1 deals with sins of sexual attitudes and behavior—they are particularly destructive because of what they do to destroy any group or church. List 2 deals with sins of speech—these are the relationship-breakers. List 3 contains the relationship-builders, which we are to express as members of Christ's body.

3:2, 3 The Christian's real home is where Christ lives (John 14:2, 3). This gives us a different perspective on our lives here on earth. To let heaven fill your thoughts means to look at life from God's perspective. This is the antidote to materialism; we gain the proper perspective on material goods when we take God's view of them. The more we see the life around us as God sees it, the more we live in harmony with him. We must not become too attached to what is only temporary.

3:4 Christ gives us power to help us live now, and he gives us hope for the future—he will return again. In the rest of this chapter Paul explains how Christians should live *now* in order to be prepared for Christ's return.

3:5 We should consider ourselves dead and unresponsive to evil desires: sexual sin, impurity, lustful desires, and materialism. This is never easy, so we must make a conscious, daily decision to live according to God's values and to rely on the Holy Spirit's power.

3:8 Paul's words to "cast off and throw away" the rotten garments of sin can also be translated, "lay aside the old self and put on the new." Paul was appealing to the commitment the believers had made in their baptism (see the note on 2:12) and urging them to remain true to their confession of faith. They were to "cast off" the old life and "put on" the new life given by Christ and guided by the Holy Spirit. If you have made such a commitment, are you remaining true to it?

3:10 The Christian is in a continuing education program. The more we know of Christ and his work, the more we are being changed to be like him. Because this process is lifelong, we must never cease learning and obeying. There is no justification for drifting along, but there is an incentive to find the rich treasures of growing in him. It takes practice, review, patience, and concentration to keep in line with his will. For more on this idea, see the note on 2:12–15.

3:11 Barriers of nationality, race, education, social standing, wealth, and power should not apply in the Christian church. Christ breaks down all barriers and accepts all people who come to him. Nothing should keep us from telling others about Christ or accepting into our fellowship any and all believers (Ephesians 2:14, 15). Christians should be in the business of building bridges, not walls.

3:12–17 Paul offers a strategy to help us live for God day by day: (1) imitate Christ's merciful, forgiving spirit (3:12, 13); (2) let love guide your life (3:14); (3) let the peace of Christ rule in your heart (3:15); (4) always be thankful (3:15); (5) keep God's Word in you at all times (3:16); (6) do everything as though you were Jesus Christ's representative (3:17).

3:13 The key to forgiving others is remembering how much God has forgiven you. Realizing God's infinite love and forgiveness can help you love and forgive others.

never hold grudges. Remember, the Lord forgave you, so you must forgive others. **3:14**
¹⁴Most of all, let love guide your life, for then the whole church will stay together   Rom 13:8
in perfect harmony. ¹⁵Let the peace of heart which comes from Christ be always   **3:15**
present in your hearts and lives, for this is your responsibility and privilege as   Jn 14:27
members of his body. And always be thankful.   Eph 2:14-16
Phil 4:7

¹⁶Remember what Christ taught and let his words enrich your lives and make you   **3:16**
wise; teach them to each other and sing them out in psalms and hymns and spiritual   Jer 15:16
songs, singing to the Lord with thankful hearts. ¹⁷And whatever you do or say, let   Rom 10:17
it be as a representative of the Lord Jesus, and come with him into the presence of   Eph 5:19
2 Tim 3:15-17
God the Father to give him your thanks.   **3:17**
Eph 5:20
1 Thess 5:18

⟿ *Principles for relationships*

¹⁸You wives, submit yourselves to your husbands, for that is what the Lord has   **3:18**
planned for you. ¹⁹And you husbands must be loving and kind to your wives and   Eph 5:22
not bitter against them, nor harsh.   **3:19**
Eph 5:25

²⁰You children must always obey your fathers and mothers, for that pleases the   **3:20**
Lord. ²¹Fathers, don't scold your children so much that they become discouraged   Eph 6:1
and quit trying.   **3:21**
Eph 6:4

²²You slaves must always obey your earthly masters, not only trying to please   **3:22**
them when they are watching you but all the time; obey them willingly because of   Eph 6:5,6
your love for the Lord and because you want to please him. ²³Work hard and   **3:23**
cheerfully at all you do, just as though you were working for the Lord and not   Eph 6:7
merely for your masters, ²⁴remembering that it is the Lord Christ who is going to   **3:24**
pay you, giving you your full portion of all he owns. He is the one you are really   Eph 6:8
working for. ²⁵And if you don't do your best for him, he will pay you in a way that   **3:25**
Acts 10:34

		RULES OF
Wives, submit to your husbands (3:18).	*Husbands,* be loving and kind toward your wives (3:19).	**SUBMISSION**
Children, obey your parents (3:20).	*Parents,* don't scold your children so much that they become discouraged and quit trying (3:21).	
Slaves, obey your masters (3:22).	*Masters,* be just and fair toward your slaves (4:1).	
(*Employees,* work hard for your employers.)	(*Employers,* be just and fair with your employees.)	

The New Testament includes many instructions concerning relationships. Most people read these instructions for the other person and ignore the ones that apply to themselves. But you can't control another person's behavior, only your own. Start by following your own instructions and not insisting on the obedience of others first.

3:14, 15 Christians should live in perfect harmony. This does not mean there cannot be differences in opinion, but loving Christians will work together despite their differences. Such love is not a feeling, but a decision to meet others' needs (see 1 Corinthians 13). It leads to peace between individuals and among the members of the body of believers. Do problems in your relationship with other Christians cause open conflicts or mutual silence? Consider what you can do to heal those relationships with selfless acts of love.

3:15 Another translation of this verse is, "Let the peace of Christ rule in your hearts." The word *rule* comes from athletics: Paul tells us to let Christ's peace be "umpire" in our hearts. Our hearts are the center of conflict because there our feelings and desires clash—our fears and hopes, our distrust and trust, our jealousy and love. How can we deal with these constant conflicts and live as God wants? Paul explains that we must decide between conflicting elements on the basis of peace—which choice will promote peace in our souls and in our churches?

3:16 Although the early Christians had access to the Old Testament and freely used it, they did not yet have the New Testament or any other Christian books to study. Their stories and

teachings about Christ were memorized and passed on from person to person. Sometimes they were set to music, and so music became an important part of Christian worship and education.

3:17 As a Christian, you represent Christ at all times—wherever you go, whatever you say. What impression do people have of Christ when they see or talk with you?

3:18—4:1 Paul describes three relationships: (1) husbands and wives, (2) parents and children, and (3) masters and slaves. In each case there is mutual responsibility to submit and love, to obey and encourage, to work hard and be fair. Examine your family and work relationships. Do you relate to others as God intended? See Ephesians 5:21—6:9 for similar instructions.

3:22—4:1 Here Paul does not condemn or condone slavery, but explains that Christ transcends all divisions between people. Slaves are told to work hard as though their master were Christ himself (3:22-25); but masters should be just and fair (4:1). Perhaps Paul was thinking specifically of Onesimus and Philemon— the slave and master whose conflict lay behind the letter to Philemon (see the book of Philemon). Philemon was a slave owner in the Colossian church, and Onesimus had been his slave (4:9).

you won't like—for he has no special favorites who can get away with shirking.

4 You slave owners must be just and fair to all your slaves. Always remember that you, too, have a Master in heaven who is closely watching you.

2Don't be weary in prayer; keep at it; watch for God's answers and remember to be thankful when they come. 3Don't forget to pray for us too, that God will give us many chances to preach the Good News of Christ for which I am here in jail. 4Pray that I will be bold enough to tell it freely and fully, and make it plain, as, of course, I should.

5Make the most of your chances to tell others the Good News. Be wise in all your contacts with them. 6Let your conversation be gracious as well as sensible, for then you will have the right answer for everyone.

Paul's final greetings

7Tychicus, our much loved brother, will tell you how I am getting along. He is a hard worker and serves the Lord with me. 8I have sent him on this special trip just to see how you are, and to comfort and encourage you. 9I am also sending Onesimus, a faithful and much loved brother, one of your own people. He and Tychicus will give you all the latest news.

10Aristarchus, who is with me here as a prisoner, sends you his love, and so does Mark, a relative of Barnabas. And as I said before, give Mark a hearty welcome if he comes your way. 11Jesus Justus also sends his love. These are the only Jewish Christians working with me here, and what a comfort they have been!

12Epaphras, from your city, a servant of Christ Jesus, sends you his love. He is always earnestly praying for you, asking God to make you strong and perfect and to help you know his will in everything you do. 13I can assure you that he has worked hard for you with his prayers, and also for the Christians in Laodicea and Hierapolis.

14Dear doctor Luke sends his love, and so does Demas.

15Please give my greeting to the Christian friends at Laodicea, and to Nymphas, and to those who meet in his home. 16By the way, after you have read this letter will

4:10 *a hearty welcome*, literally, "receive him."

4:1
Lev 19:13
Eph 6:9
4:2
Lk 18:1
Acts 1:14
Eph 6:18
1 Thess 5:17
4:4
Eph 6:20
4:5
Eph 5:15,16
4:6
Eccles 10:12
Eph 4:29
1 Pet 3:15
4:7
Acts 20:4
Eph 6:21,22
4:9
Philem 10
4:10
Acts 12:12; 15:37
19:29; 20:4
27:2
2 Tim 4:11
4:11
Acts 11:2
4:12
Col 1:7,28
4:13
Col 2:1
4:14
2 Tim 4:10,11
Philem 24
4:15
Rom 16:5
1 Cor 16:19
Philem 2
4:16
1 Thess 5:27

4:2 Have you ever grown tired of praying for something or someone? Paul says, "Keep at it." Persistence demonstrates our faith that God answers our prayers. Faith shouldn't die if the answers don't come immediately, for the delay may be God's way of working his will in your life. When you feel weary in your prayers, know that God is present, always listening, always acting—maybe not in ways you had hoped, but in ways he knows are best.

4:6 When we tell others about Christ, it is important always to be gracious in what we say. No matter how much sense the message makes, we lose our effectiveness if we are not courteous. Just as we like to be respected, we must respect others if we want them to listen to what we have to say.

4:7 Tychicus was one of Paul's personal respresentatives and probably the bearer of the letters to the Colossians and Ephesians (see also Ephesians 6:21, 22). He accompanied Paul to Jerusalem with the collection for the church (Acts 20:4).

4:10 Mark left with Paul and Barnabas on their first missionary journey (Acts 12:25), but then left in the middle of the trip for unknown reasons (Acts 15:37–39). Barnabas and Mark were relatives, and when Paul refused to take Mark on another journey, Barnabas and Mark journeyed together to preach the Good News (Acts 15:39–41). Mark also worked with Peter (Acts 12:12, 13; 1 Peter 5:13). Later, Mark and Paul were reconciled (Philemon 1:24). Mark wrote the Gospel of Mark.

4:12 Epaphras founded the Colossian church (see the note on 1:7), and his report to Paul in Rome caused Paul to write this letter. Epaphras was a hero of the Colossian church, one of the believers who helped keep the church together in spite of growing troubles. His earnest prayers for the believers show his deep love and concern for them.

4:13 Laodicea was located 11 miles northwest of Colosse; Hierapolis was about five miles north of Laodicea. See the note on 2:1 for more about Laodicea.

4:14 Luke spent much time with Paul, not only accompanying him on most of his third missionary journey, but sitting with him in the prison at Rome. Luke wrote the Gospel of Luke and the book of Acts. Demas was faithful to Paul for a while, but then left him (2 Timothy 4:10).

4:15 The early Christians often met in homes. Church buildings were not common until the third century.

4:16 Some suggest that the letter to Laodicea may be the book of Ephesians. More likely there was a special letter to the Laodiceans, of which we have no record today. Paul wrote several letters that have been lost (see, for example, 2 Corinthians 2:3 and note).

you pass it on to the church at Laodicea? And read the letter I wrote to them. [17]And say to Archippus, "Be sure that you do all the Lord has told you to."

4:17
2 Tim 4:5
Philem 2

[18]Here is my own greeting in my own handwriting: Remember me here in jail. May God's blessings surround you.

4:18
Heb 13:3

Sincerely, Paul

4:17 Paul's letter to Philemon is also addressed to Archippus (Philemon 1:2). Paul called him "a soldier of the cross." He may have been a Roman soldier who had become a member of the Colossian church, or he may have been Philemon's son.

4:18 Paul usually dictated his letters to a scribe, but often ended with a short note in his own handwriting (see also 1 Corinthians 16:21; Galatians 6:11). This prevented false teachers from writing letters in the name of Paul, a problem Paul had previously faced (2 Thessalonians 3:17). It also gave the letters a personal touch.

4:18 To understand the letter to the Colossians, we need to know that the church was facing pressure from a cult-like heresy that promised deeper spiritual life through secret knowledge (an early form of gnosticism). The false teachers destroyed faith in Christ by undermining Christ's humanity and divinity, and attempted to divide the physical and spiritual.

Paul makes it clear in Colossians that Christ alone is the source of our spiritual life, the Head of the Body. He is Lord of both the physical and spiritual worlds. The path to deeper spiritual life is not through religious duties, special knowledge, or secrets; it is only through a clear connection with the Lord Jesus Christ. We must never let anything come between us and our Savior.

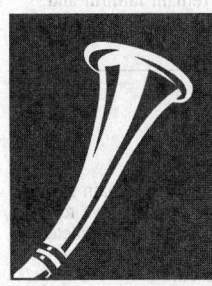

SLOWLY they walk, scattering the leaves and trampling the grass under measured and heavy steps. The minister's words still echoing in their minds, they hear workmen moving toward the terrible place, preparing to cover the casket of their loved one. Death, the enemy, has torn the bonded relationships of family and friends, leaving only memories and tears.

But like a golden shaft of sun piercing the winter sky, a singular truth shatters the oppressive gloom—death is not the end! Christ is the victor over death and there is hope of the resurrection through him.

Many first-century Christians were persecuted—whether at the hands of zealous Jews (like Paul before his conversion), angry Greeks, or ruthless Roman authorities. Persecution included stonings, beatings, crucifixions, torture, and death. To be a follower of Christ meant to be willing to give up everything in order to follow him.

Paul faced persecution when he established the church in Thessalonica during his second missionary journey (in about A.D. 51). He wrote this letter a short time later to encourage the young believers there. He wanted to assure them of his love, to praise them for their faithfulness in the midst of persecution, and to remind them of their hope—the sure return of their Lord and Savior, Jesus Christ.

Paul begins this letter with a note of affirmation, thanking God for the strong faith and good reputation of the Thessalonians (1:1–10). Then Paul reviews their relationship—how he and his companions brought the gospel to them (2:1–12), how they accepted the message (2:13–16), and how he longed to be with them again (2:17–20). Because of his concern, he sent Timothy to encourage them in their faith (3:1–13).

Paul then presents the central thrust of his message—exhortation and comfort. He challenges the Thessalonians to please God in their daily living by avoiding all sexual sin (4:1–8), to love one another (4:9, 10), and to live as good citizens in a sinful world (4:11, 12).

Paul comforts the Thessalonians by reminding them of the hope of the resurrection (4:13–18). Then he warns them to be prepared at all times, for Jesus Christ could return at any moment. When Christ returns, those Christians who are alive and those who have died will be raised to new life (5:1–11).

Paul then gives the Thessalonians a handful of reminders on how to prepare themselves for the Second Coming—warn the lazy (5:14), comfort the frightened (5:14), care for the weak (5:14), "be patient with everyone" (5:14), do good to everyone (5:15), "always be joyful" (5:16), pray continually (5:17), "be thankful" (5:18), test everything that is taught (5:20, 21), and stay away from evil (5:22). Paul concludes his letter with two benedictions and a request for prayer.

As you read this letter, listen carefully to Paul's practical advice for Christian living. When you feel overwhelmed by sorrow, remember that there is hope in Christ's return, the resurrection, and the promise of eternal life!

VITAL STATISTICS

PURPOSE:
To strengthen the Thessalonian Christians in their faith and give them the assurance of Christ's return

AUTHOR:
Paul

TO WHOM WRITTEN:
The church at Thessalonica and all believers everywhere

DATE WRITTEN:
About A.D. 51 from Corinth; one of Paul's earliest letters

SETTING:
The church at Thessalonica was very young, having been established only two or three years before this letter was written. The Thessalonian Christians needed to mature in their faith. In addition, there was a misunderstanding concerning Christ's Second Coming—some thought he would return immediately, others wondered whether those who had already died would experience a bodily resurrection at his Second Coming.

KEY VERSE:
"For since we believe that Jesus died and then came back to life again, we can also believe that when Jesus returns, God will bring back with him all the Christians who have died" (4:14).

KEY PEOPLE:
Paul, Timothy, Silas

KEY PLACE:
Thessalonica

SPECIAL FEATURES:
Paul received from Timothy a favorable report about the Thessalonians. However, he wrote this letter to correct their misconceptions about the resurrection and the Second Coming of Christ.

THE BLUEPRINT

1. Faithfulness to the Lord (1:1—3:13)
2. Watchfulness for the Lord (4:1—5:28)

Paul and his companions were faithful to bring the gospel to the Thessalonians in the midst of persecution. The Thessalonians had only recently become Christians and yet remained faithful to the Lord, despite the fact that the apostles were not with them. Others have been faithful in bringing God's Word to us. We must remain faithful and live with the expectation that Christ will return at any time.

MEGATHEMES

THEME	EXPLANATION	IMPORTANCE
Persecution	Paul and the new Christians at Thessalonica experienced persecution because of their faith in Christ. We can expect trials and troubles as well. We need to stand firm in our faith in the midst of trials, being strengthened by the Holy Spirit.	The Holy Spirit helps us to remain strong in faith, able to show genuine love to others and maintain our moral character even when we are being persecuted, slandered, or oppressed.
Paul's ministry	Paul expressed his concern for this church even while he was being slandered. Paul's commitment to share the gospel in spite of difficult circumstances is a model we should follow.	Paul not only delivered his message, but gave of himself. In our ministries, we must become like Paul—faithful and bold, yet sensitive and self-sacrificing.
Hope	One day all believers, both those who are alive and those who have died, will be united with Christ. To those Christians who die before Christ's return, there is hope—the hope of the resurrection of the body.	If we believe in Christ, we will live with him forever. All those who belong to Jesus Christ—from throughout history—will be present with him at his Second Coming.
Being prepared	No one knows the time of Christ's return. We are to live moral and holy lives, ever watchful for his coming. Believers must not neglect daily responsibilities, but always work and live as unto the Lord.	The gospel is not only what we believe, but also how we must live. The Holy Spirit leads us in faithfulness, so we can avoid lust and fraud. Live as though you expect Christ's return at any time. Don't be caught unprepared.

1. Faithfulness to the Lord

1 *From:* Paul, Silas and Timothy.
To: The Church at Thessalonica—to you who belong to God the Father and the Lord Jesus Christ: May blessing and peace of heart be your rich gifts from God our Father, and from Jesus Christ our Lord.

1:1   Jn 14:23
Rom 1:7
2 Cor 1:19
2 Thess 1:1
1 Pet 5:12

1:1 Paul and his companions probably arrived in Thessalonica in the early summer of A.D. 50. They planted the first Christian church in that city, but had to leave in a hurry because their lives were threatened (Acts 17:1–10). At the first opportunity, probably when he stopped at Corinth, Paul sent Timothy back to Thessalonica to see how the new believers were doing. Timothy returned to Paul with good news: the Christians in Thessalonica were remaining firm in the faith and were unified. But the Thessalonians did have some questions about their new faith. Paul had not had time to answer all their questions during his brief visit and other questions had arisen in the meantime. So Paul wrote to answer their questions and commend them on their faithfulness to the Good News.

1:1 For more information on Paul, see his Profile in Acts 9. Timothy's Profile is in 1 Timothy. Silas accompanied Paul on his second missionary journey (Acts 15:36—17:15). He helped Paul establish the church in Thessalonica (Acts 17:1–9). He is called Silvanus in 2 Corinthians 1:19 and in 1 Peter 5:12. His Profile is found in Acts 16.

1:1 Thessalonica was the capital and largest city of the Roman province of Macedonia. The most important Roman highway (the Egnatian Way)—extending from Rome all the way to the Orient—went through Thessalonica. This highway, along with the city's thriving seaport, made Thessalonica one of the wealthiest and most flourishing trade centers in the Roman Empire. Recognized as a free city, Thessalonica was allowed self-rule and was exempted from most of the restrictions placed by Rome on other cities in the empire. However, with its international flavor came many pagan religions and cultural influences that challenged the faith of the young Christians there.

Paul commends the faith of the Thessalonian believers

1:2
Rom 1:9
2 Thess 1:3

1:3
Heb 6:10
Jas 2:17

1:4
Col 3:12
2 Thess 2:13
2 Pet 1:10

1:5
1 Cor 2:4
2 Cor 6:6
1 Thess 2:10
2 Thess 3:7

1:6
Acts 17:1-6
1 Cor 4:16

1:8
Rom 1:8; 10:18
2 Thess 3:1

²We always thank God for you and pray for you constantly. ³We never forget your loving deeds as we talk to our God and Father about you, and your strong faith and steady looking forward to the return of our Lord Jesus Christ.

⁴We know that God has chosen you, dear brothers, much beloved of God. ⁵For when we brought you the Good News, it was not just meaningless chatter to you; no, you listened with great interest. What we told you produced a powerful effect upon you, for the Holy Spirit gave you great and full assurance that what we said was true. And you know how our very lives were further proof to you of the truth of our message. ⁶So you became our followers and the Lord's; for you received our message with joy from the Holy Spirit in spite of the trials and sorrows it brought you.

⁷Then you yourselves became an example to all the other Christians in Greece. ⁸And now the Word of the Lord has spread out from you to others everywhere, far beyond your boundaries, for wherever we go we find people telling us about your

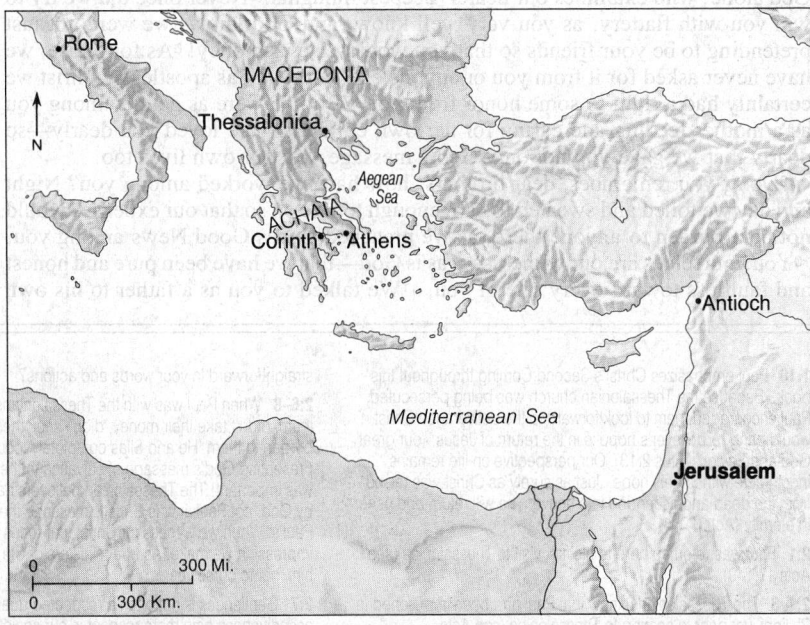

LOCATION OF THESSALONICA
Paul visited Thessalonica on his second and third missionary journeys. It was a seaport and trade center located on the Egnatian Way, a busy international highway. Paul probably wrote his two letters to the Thessalonians from Corinth.

1:3 The Thessalonian believers stood firm when they were persecuted (1:6; 3:1–4, 7, 8). Paul commends these young Christians for their loving deeds, strong faith, and deep commitment to Christ. These characteristics are the marks of an effective Christian.

1:5 The power of the Holy Spirit changes people when they believe the Good News. When we tell others about Christ, we must depend on the Holy Spirit to open their eyes and convince them that they need salvation. His power changes them—not our cleverness or persuasion. Without the work of the Holy Spirit, our words are meaningless. The Holy Spirit not only convicts people of sin but also assures them of the truth of the gospel. (For more information on the Holy Spirit, see John 14:23–26; 15:26, 27; and the notes on John 3:6 and Acts 1:4.)

1:5 The Good News produced a powerful effect upon the Thessalonians. Whenever the Word of God is heard and obeyed, lives are changed! Christianity is more than a collection of interesting facts; it is the power of God for salvation to every one who believes. What has God's power done in your life since you first put your faith in Christ?

1:5 Paul says, "our very lives were further proof." The Thessalonians could see that what Paul, Silas, and Timothy were preaching was true, because they lived it. Does your life confirm or contradict what you say you believe?

1:6 The Thessalonians received the message of salvation with great joy. Even though their new faith led to persecution from both Jews and Gentiles (3:2–4; Acts 17:5), they stood firm in their faith. Many Thessalonians were apparently concerned about the condition of those believers who had already died. What would happen to them when Christ returned? Paul answered these questions by explaining to the Thessalonian Christians what happens when believers die (see 4:13ff).

1:7–10 All of us should respond to the Good News as the Thessalonian believers did: *turn* from sin, *serve* the living and true God, and *look forward* to Jesus' return. We should turn from sin because Christ is coming to judge the earth; we should be fervent in our service because we have little time to further the work of Christ's Kingdom before he returns. We should be prepared for Jesus to return at any time because we don't know when he will come.

remarkable faith in God. We don't need to tell *them* about it, 9for *they* keep telling *us* about the wonderful welcome you gave us, and how you turned away from your idols to God so that now the living and true God only is your Master. 10And they speak of how you are looking forward to the return of God's Son from heaven—Jesus, whom God brought back to life—and he is our only Savior from God's terrible anger against sin.

1:9
1 Cor 12:2

1:10
Rom 2:7; 5:9
Phil 3:20
1 Thess 5:9
Heb 9:28
Rev 1:7

Paul reviews his relationship with the Thessalonians

2 You yourselves know, dear brothers, how worthwhile that visit was. 2You know how badly we had been treated at Philippi just before we came to you, and how much we suffered there. Yet God gave us the courage to boldly repeat the same message to you, even though we were surrounded by enemies. 3So you can see that we were not preaching with any false motives or evil purposes in mind; we were perfectly straightforward and sincere.

4For we speak as messengers from God, trusted by him to tell the truth; we change his message not one bit to suit the taste of those who hear it; for we serve God alone, who examines our hearts' deepest thoughts. 5Never once did we try to win you with flattery, as you very well know, and God knows we were not just pretending to be your friends so that you would give us money! 6As for praise, we have never asked for it from you or anyone else, although as apostles of Christ we certainly had a right to some honor from you. 7But we were as gentle among you as a mother feeding and caring for her own children. 8We loved you dearly—so dearly that we gave you not only God's message, but our own lives too.

9Don't you remember, dear brothers, how hard we worked among you? Night and day we toiled and sweated to earn enough to live on so that our expenses would not be a burden to anyone there, as we preached God's Good News among you. 10You yourselves are our witnesses—as is God—that we have been pure and honest and faultless toward every one of you. 11We talked to you as a father to his own

2:1
1 Thess 1:9

2:2
Acts 16:22; 17:2
Phil 1:30

2:3
2 Cor 4:2
2 Pet 1:16

2:4
Prov 17:3
1 Cor 7:25
Gal 1:10
1 Tim 1:11

2:5
Acts 20:33

2:7
2 Tim 2:24

2:8
Rom 1:11; 15:29
2 Cor 12:15

2:9
Acts 18:3
2 Cor 11:9
2 Thess 3:8

2:10
1 Thess 1:5

2:11
1 Cor 4:14

1:10 Paul emphasizes Christ's Second Coming throughout this book. Because the Thessalonian church was being persecuted, Paul encouraged them to look forward to the deliverance Christ would bring. A believer's hope is in the return of Jesus, "our great God and Savior" (Titus 2:13). Our perspective on life remains incomplete without this hope. Just as surely as Christ was raised from the dead and ascended into heaven, he will return and usher in eternity (Acts 1:11).

2:1 Paul was referring here to his first visit to Thessalonica (see Acts 17:1–9).

2:1–3 The Thessalonians knew that Paul had been imprisoned in Philippi just prior to coming to Thessalonica (see Acts 16:11—17:1). Fear of imprisonment did not keep Paul from preaching the Good News. If God wants us to do something, he will give us the strength and courage to do it in spite of the obstacles that may come our way.

2:3 This pointed statement may be a response to accusations from the Jewish leaders who had stirred up the crowds (Acts 17:5). Paul demonstrates the sincerity of his motives by showing that he and Silas suffered for sharing the gospel in Philippi. Paul did not seek money, fame, or popularity by sharing the Good News. We must always examine our motives for sharing the Good News.

2:4–8 In trying to persuade people, we often alter our position just enough to make our message more palatable. Paul never changed his *message* to make it more acceptable, but he did tailor his *presentation* to each audience. Although our presentation must be altered to be appropriate to the situation, the truth of the gospel must never be compromised.

2:5 We often feel disgusted when we hear someone "butter up" another person. Flattery is a false cover-up for a person's real intentions, and Christian leaders should not practice it. Christians who proclaim God's truth have a special responsibility to be honest. Can people be sure that you will always be honest and

straightforward in your words and actions?

2:6–8 When Paul was with the Thessalonians, he didn't flatter them, didn't take their money, didn't seek their praise, and wasn't a burden to them. He and Silas completely focused their efforts on presenting God's message of salvation to the Thessalonians. This was important! The Thessalonian believers had their lives changed by God, not Paul; it was Christ's message they believed, not Paul's. When we witness for Christ, our focus should not be on the impression we make. As true ministers of Christ, we should point to him, not to ourselves.

2:7 Gentleness is not often a respected quality. Power and assertiveness gain more respect in our society, even though none of us likes to be bullied. Gentleness is love in action—being considerate, meeting the needs of others, allowing time for the other person to talk, and being willing to learn. It is an essential trait for both men and women. We all need to maintain a gentle attitude in our relationships with others.

2:9 Although Paul had the right to receive financial support from the people he taught, he worked as a tentmaker (Acts 18:3) to support himself and not be a burden to the new Thessalonian believers.

2:11 No loving father would neglect the safety of his children, allowing them to walk into circumstances that might prove fatal or permanently damaging. In the same way, we must take new believers under our wings until they are mature enough to stand firm in their faith. When new Christians are strong enough to influence others for the gospel, rather than be influenced by others to practices contrary to the gospel, they are ready to be out from under our wings.

2:11, 12 By his words and example, Paul encouraged the Thessalonians to live in ways that would bring joy to God. Is there anything about your daily life that would embarrass God? What do people think of God when they examine your life? What does God

2:12
Eph 4:1
Col 1:10
1 Pet 1:15

2:13
Mt 10:40
Heb 4:2,12

2:14
Acts 17:5
1 Thess 1:6
Heb 10:33

2:15
Mt 5:12
Lk 24:20
Acts 7:52

2:16
Lk 11:52
Acts 9:23; 13:50
14:19; 17:5

2:17
1 Cor 5:3
1 Thess 3:10

2:18
Rom 1:13; 15:22

2:19
1 Cor 15:23
Phil 2:16
1 Thess 3:13
Rev 1:7; 22:12

2:20
2 Cor 1:14

3:1
Acts 17:15

3:2
Rom 16:21

3:4
1 Thess 2:14

children—don't you remember?—pleading with you, encouraging you and even demanding 12that your daily lives should not embarrass God, but bring joy to him who invited you into his Kingdom to share his glory.

13And we will never stop thanking God for this: that when we preached to you, you didn't think of the words we spoke as being just our own, but you accepted what we said as the very Word of God—which, of course, it was—and it changed your lives when you believed it.

14And then, dear brothers, you suffered what the churches in Judea did, persecution from your own countrymen, just as they suffered from their own people the Jews. 15After they had killed their own prophets, they even executed the Lord Jesus; and now they have brutally persecuted us and driven us out. They are against both God and man, 16trying to keep us from preaching to the Gentiles for fear some might be saved; and so their sins continue to grow. But the anger of God has caught up with them at last.

17Dear brothers, after we left you and had been away from you but a very little while (though our hearts never left you), we tried hard to come back to see you once more. 18We wanted very much to come and I, Paul, tried again and again, but Satan stopped us. 19For what is it we live for, that gives us hope and joy and is our proud reward and crown? It is you! Yes, you will bring us much joy as we stand together before our Lord Jesus Christ when he comes back again. 20For you are our trophy and joy.

Paul is encouraged by Timothy's good report about the Thessalonians

3 Finally, when I could stand it no longer, I decided to stay alone in Athens 2, 3and send Timothy, our brother and fellow worker, God's minister, to visit you to strengthen your faith and encourage you, and to keep you from becoming fainthearted in all the troubles you were going through. (But of course you know that such troubles are a part of God's plan for us Christians. 4Even while we were

---

think about how you live from day to day?

2:13 In the New Testament the phrase "Word of God" usually refers to the preaching of the gospel, the Old Testament Scriptures, and Jesus Christ himself. Today we often apply it only to the Scriptures. We must remember that Jesus Christ himself is the "Word" (John 1:1), the subject of our preaching and teaching.

2:14 When Paul refers to the Jews, he is talking about certain Jews who opposed his preaching of the gospel. He does not mean all Jews. Many of Paul's converts were Jewish. Paul himself was a Jew (2 Corinthians 11:22).

2:14 Just as the Jewish Christians in Jerusalem were persecuted by their own people, so the Gentile Christians in Thessalonica were persecuted by their fellow Gentiles. It is discouraging to face persecution, especially when it comes from your own people. But when we take a stand for Christ, we may face opposition, disapproval, ridicule, and persecution from our neighbors, friends, and even family members.

2:15, 16 Why were so many Jews opposed to Christianity? First, although the Jewish religion was declared "legal" by the Roman government, it still had a tenuous relationship with the government. At this time, Christianity was viewed as a sect of Judaism. The Jews were afraid that reprisals leveled against the Christians might be stretched to include them. Second, the Jewish leaders thought Jesus was a false prophet and they didn't want his teachings to spread. Third, they feared that if many Jews were drawn away, their own political position might be weakened. Fourth, they were proud of their special status as "God's chosen people" and they resented the fact that Gentiles were full members within the church.

2:18 Paul was not using the word "Satan" here symbolically—he knew that Satan was real. Satan is called "the god of this evil

world" (2 Corinthians 4:4) and "the mighty prince of the power of the air" (Ephesians 2:2). We don't know exactly what hindered Paul from returning to Thessalonica—opposition, illness, travel complications, or a direct attack by Satan—but Satan worked in some way to keep him from Thessalonica. Many of the difficulties which prevent us from accomplishing God's work can be attributed to Satan (see Ephesians 6:12).

2:20 The ultimate reward for Paul's ministry was not money, prestige, or fame, but new believers whose lives had been changed by God through the preaching of the gospel. This should be the motivation of all Christians who seek to further the Kingdom of God.

3:1-4 Because Paul could not return to Thessalonica (2:18), he sent Timothy as his representative. According to Acts 17:10, Paul left Thessalonica and went to Beroea. When trouble broke out in Beroea, some Christians took Paul to Athens while Silas and Timothy stayed behind (Acts 17:13-15). Later Paul sent Timothy to encourage the Thessalonian Christians to be strong in their faith in the face of persecution.

3:1-3 Some think that troubles are always caused by sin or a lack of faith. Here Paul states that troubles may be a part of God's plan for believers. Going through trials can build character (James 1:2-4), patience (Romans 5:3-5), and sensitivity toward others who also face trouble (2 Corinthians 1:3-7). Problems are unavoidable for godly people in an ungodly world. Your troubles may be a sign of effective Christian living.

3:4 Some people turn to God hoping to escape suffering on earth. Rather than promising escape from suffering, God gives us power to grow through our sufferings. The Christian life is marked by obedience to Christ despite temptation and hardship.

still with you we warned you ahead of time that suffering would soon come—and it did.)

5As I was saying, when I could bear the suspense no longer I sent Timothy to find out whether your faith was still strong. I was afraid that perhaps Satan had gotten the best of you and that all our work had been useless. 6And now Timothy has just returned and brings the welcome news that your faith and love are as strong as ever, and that you remember our visit with joy and want to see us just as much as we want to see you. 7So we are greatly comforted, dear brothers, in all of our own crushing troubles and suffering here, now that we know you are standing true to the Lord. 8We can bear anything as long as we know that you remain strong in him.

9How can we thank God enough for you and for the joy and delight you have given us in our praying for you? 10For night and day we pray on and on for you, asking God to let us see you again, to fill up any little cracks there may yet be in your faith.

11May God our Father himself and our Lord Jesus send us back to you again. 12And may the Lord make your love to grow and overflow to each other and to everyone else, just as our love does toward you. 13This will result in your hearts being made strong, sinless and holy by God our Father, so that you may stand before him guiltless on that day when our Lord Jesus Christ returns with all those who belong to him.

2. Watchfulness for the Lord

Live to please God

4 Let me add this, dear brothers: You already know how to please God in your daily living, for you know the commands we gave you from the Lord Jesus himself. Now we beg you—yes, we demand of you in the name of the Lord Jesus—that you live more and more closely to that ideal. 3, 4For God wants you to be holy and pure, and to keep clear of all sexual sin so that each of you will marry in holiness and honor— 5not in lustful passion as the heathen do, in their ignorance of God and his ways.

6And this also is God's will: that you never cheat in this matter by taking another man's wife, because the Lord will punish you terribly for this, as we have solemnly told you before. 7For God has not called us to be dirty-minded and full of lust, but to be holy and clean. 8If anyone refuses to live by these rules he is not disobeying the rules of men but of God who gives his *Holy* Spirit to you.

3:13 with all those who belong to him, literally, "with all his saints. Amen."

Cross-references

3:5
Mt 4:3
1 Cor 7:5
2 Cor 11:3
3:6
Phil 1:8
3:8
Phil 4:1
3:10
2 Cor 13:9
1 Thess 1:2,3
2 Tim 1:3
3:11
2 Thess 3:5
3:12
Phil 1:9
3:13
Zech 14:5
1 Cor 1:8
1 Thess 2:19
4:17
Jude 14
Rev 22:12
4:1
Eph 4:1
Col 1:10
4:3,4
1 Cor 6:18; 7:2
Heb 13:4
1 Pet 3:7
4:6
1 Cor 6:8
Heb 13:4
4:7
Lev 11:44
1 Pet 1:15
4:8
Rom 5:5
1 Jn 3:24

3:5 Satan is the most powerful of the evil spirits. His power can affect both the spiritual world (Ephesians 2:1–3; 6:10–12) and the physical world (2 Corinthians 12:7–10). Satan even tempted Jesus (Matthew 4:1–11). But Jesus defeated Satan when he died on the cross for the sins of the world and rose again to bring new life. At the proper time God will overthrow Satan forever (Revelation 20:7–10).

3:8 In the midst of persecution or pressure, believers should encourage each other. Compliments, expressions of thanks, and support for those who are wavering in the faith help to build up fellow believers.

3:9 It is great joy for a Christian to see another person come to faith in Christ and mature in that faith. Paul experienced this joy countless times. He thanked God for those who had come to know Christ and prayed for their continued growth in faith. If there are new Christians who have brought you joy, thank God for them and support them as they continue to grow in the faith.

3:11 We have no record that Paul returned to Thessalonica; but when he was traveling through Asia on his third journey, he was joined by Aristarchus and Secundus, who were from Thessalonica (Acts 20:4, 5).

3:12 If we are full of God's love, it will overflow to others. It's not enough merely to be courteous to others; we must actively and

persistently show love to others. Our love should be continually growing. If your capacity to love has remained unchanged for some time, ask God to fill you again with his never-ending supply of love. Then look for opportunities to express his love.

3:11–13 This refers to the Second Coming of Christ, when he will establish his eternal Kingdom. At that time he will gather all believers, those who have died and those who are alive, into one united family under his rule. All believers from all times, including these Thessalonians, will be with Christ in his Kingdom.

4:1–8 Sexual standards were very low in the Roman Empire, and in many societies today they are not any higher. The temptations to engage in sexual intercourse outside the marriage relationship have always been powerful. Giving in to these temptations can have disastrous results. Sexual sins always hurt someone: families, businesses, and even churches. It has not only physical consequences, but spiritual ones as well. For more on why sexual sin is so harmful, see the note on 1 Corinthians 6:18.

4:1–8 Sexual desires and activities must be placed under Christ's control. God created sex for procreation, pleasure, and as an expression of love between a husband and wife. Sexual experience must be limited to the marriage relationship to avoid hurting ourselves, our relationship to God, and our relationship to others.

4:9
Jer 31:34
Jn 6:45; 13:34
1 Jn 2:20,27
4:10
1 Thess 3:12
4:11
Eph 4:28
2 Thess 3:11,12

9But concerning the pure brotherly love that there should be among God's people, I don't need to say very much, I'm sure! For God himself is teaching you to love one another. 10Indeed, your love is already strong toward all the Christian brothers throughout your whole nation. Even so, dear friends, we beg you to love them more and more. 11This should be your ambition: to live a quiet life, minding your own business and doing your own work, just as we told you before. 12As a result, people who are not Christians will trust and respect you, and you will not need to depend on others for enough money to pay your bills.

Remember the hope of the resurrection

4:13
Lev 19:28
Deut 14:1,2
Eph 2:12
4:14
1 Cor 15:18,52
4:15
1 Cor 15:52
4:16
Joel 2:11
Mt 24:30
Acts 1:11
1 Cor 15:52
2 Thess 1:7
4:17
Dan 7:13
Acts 1:9
Rev 11:12
21:3,4

13And now, dear brothers, I want you to know what happens to a Christian when he dies so that when it happens, you will not be full of sorrow, as those are who have no hope. 14For since we believe that Jesus died and then came back to life again, we can also believe that when Jesus returns, God will bring back with him all the Christians who have died.

15I can tell you this directly from the Lord: that we who are still living when the Lord returns will not rise to meet him ahead of those who are in their graves. 16For the Lord himself will come down from heaven with a mighty shout and with the soul-stirring cry of the archangel and the great trumpet-call of God. And the believers who are dead will be the first to rise to meet the Lord. 17Then we who are still alive and remain on the earth will be caught up with them in the clouds to meet the Lord in the air and remain with him forever. 18So comfort and encourage each other with this news.

Be prepared: no one knows when the Lord will return

5:1
Mt 24:3
5:2
2 Pet 3:10
5:3
Isa 26:17

5 When is all this going to happen? I really don't need to say anything about that, dear brothers, 2for you know perfectly well that no one knows. That day of the Lord will come unexpectedly like a thief in the night. 3When people are saying, "All is well, everything is quiet and peaceful"—then, all of a sudden, disaster will

---

THE EVENTS OF CHRIST'S RETURN

1. Christ will return visibly with a mighty shout.
2. There will be an unmistakable cry from an angel.
3. There will be a trumpet fanfare such as has never been heard.
4. Believers in Christ who are dead will rise from their graves.
5. Believers who are alive will be lifted into the clouds and meet Christ.

While Christians have often disagreed about what events will lead up to the return of Christ, there has been less disagreement about what will happen once Christ does return.

4:11 This is part of what it means to live as a Christian—to be responsible in all areas of your life. You can hardly be effective when you share your faith with others if people don't respect you. Whatever you do, do it faithfully and be a positive force in society.

4:13ff The Thessalonians wondered why many of their fellow believers had died and what would happen to them when Christ returned. Paul wanted the Thessalonians to understand that death is not the end of the story. When Christ returns, all believers—dead and alive—will be reunited, never to suffer or die again.

4:15 What does Paul mean when he says, "I can tell you this directly from the Lord"? This was either something God revealed directly to Paul, or it was a teaching of Jesus which had been passed along orally by the apostles and other Christians.

4:15-18 Exactly when the dead will be raised, in relation to the other events at the Second Coming, is not as important as the purpose for which Paul wrote these words—to challenge believers to comfort and encourage one another when loved ones died. This passage can be a great comfort when any believer dies. The same love that should unite believers in this life (4:9) will unite believers when Christ returns and reigns for eternity.

4:15-18 Because Jesus Christ came back to life, so will all believers. All Christians, including those living when he returns, will

live with Jesus forever. Therefore, we need not despair when loved ones die or world events take a tragic turn. For God will turn our tragedies to triumphs, our poverty to riches, our pain to glory, and our defeat to victory. All believers throughout history will stand reunited in God's very presence, safe and secure. As Paul comforted the Thessalonians with the promise of the resurrection, so we should comfort and reassure one another with this great hope.

5:1-3 Efforts to determine the date of Christ's return are foolish. Don't be misled by anyone who claims to know. We are told here that no one knows and that even believers will be surprised. The Lord will return suddenly and unexpectedly, warns Paul, so be ready! Because no one knows when Jesus will come back to earth, we should be ready at all times. Suppose he were to return today. How would he find you living? Are you ready to meet him? Live each day prepared to welcome him.

5:2 The day of the Lord is a future time when God intervenes directly and dramatically in world affairs. Predicted and discussed often in the Old Testament (Isaiah 13:6-12; Joel 2:28-32; Zephaniah 1:14-18), the day of the Lord will include both punishment and blessing. Christ will judge sin and set up his eternal Kingdom.

fall upon them as suddenly as a woman's birth pains begin when her child is born. And these people will not be able to get away anywhere—there will be no place to hide.

4But, dear brothers, you are not in the dark about these things, and you won't be surprised as by a thief when that day of the Lord comes. 5For you are all children of the light and of the day, and do not belong to darkness and night. 6So be on your guard, not asleep like the others. Watch for his return and stay sober. 7Night is the time for sleep and the time when people get drunk. 8But let us who live in the light keep sober, protected by the armor of faith and love, and wearing as our helmet the happy hope of salvation.

9For God has not chosen to pour out his anger upon us, but to save us through our Lord Jesus Christ; 10he died for us so that we can live with him forever, whether we are dead or alive at the time of his return. 11So encourage each other to build each other up, just as you are already doing.

Paul's final instructions

12Dear brothers, honor the officers of your church who work hard among you and

		5:4
		Lk 21:34
		1 Jn 2:8
		5:5
		Jn 12:36
		Acts 26:18
		Eph 5:8
		5:7
		Acts 2:15
		5:8
		Isa 59:17
		Rom 8:24
		Eph 6:14,17
		1 Pet 1:13
		5:9
		Rom 5:9
		2 Tim 2:19
		5:10
		Rom 14:9

Reference	Example	Suggested application
5:11	Build each other up.	Point out to someone a quality you appreciate in him or her.
5:12	Give honor to leaders.	Look for ways to cooperate.
5:13	Think highly of leaders.	Withhold your next critical comment about those in positions of responsibility.
5:13	Give wholehearted love.	Say "thank you" to your leaders for their efforts.
5:13	Avoid quarreling.	Search for ways to get along with others.
5:14	Warn the lazy.	Challenge someone to join you in a project.
5:14	Comfort the frightened.	Encourage those who are frightened by reminding them of God's promises.
5:14	Tenderly care for the weak.	Support those who are weak by loving them and praying for them.
5:14	Practice patience.	Think of a situation that tries your patience and plan ahead of time how you can stay calm.
5:15	Resist revenge.	Instead of planning to get even with those who mistreat you, do good to them.
5:16	Be joyful.	Remember that even in the midst of turmoil, God is in control.
5:17	Pray continuously.	God is always with you—talk to him.
5:18	Be thankful.	Make a list of all the gifts God has given you, giving thanks to God for each one.
5:19	Do not smother the Holy Spirit.	Cooperate with the Spirit the next time he prompts you to participate in a Christian meeting.
5:20	Do not scoff at those who prophesy.	Receive God's word from those who speak for him.
5:22	Keep away from evil.	Avoid situations where you will be drawn into temptation.
5:23	Count on God's constant help.	Realize that the Christian life is to be lived not in our own strength, but through God's power.

CHECKLIST FOR ENCOURAGERS
The command to "encourage others" is found throughout the Bible. In 5:11–23, Paul gives many specific examples of how we can encourage others.

5:8 For more about the Christian's armor, see Ephesians 6:13–17.

5:9–11 As you near the end of a foot race, your legs ache, your throat burns, and your whole body cries out for you to stop. This is when supporters are most valuable. Their encouragement helps you push through the pain to the finish. In the same way, Christians are to encourage one another. A word of encouragement offered at the right moment can be the difference between finishing well and

collapsing along the way. Look around you. Be sensitive to others need for encouragement and offer supportive words or actions.

5:12, 13 Think of your pastor and other church leaders. How can you honor them? Express your appreciation, tell them how you have been helped by their leadership and teaching, and thank them for their ministry in your life. If you say nothing, how will they know where you stand? Remember, they need and deserve your

warn you against all that is wrong. 13Think highly of them and give them your wholehearted love because they are straining to help you. And remember, no quarreling among yourselves.

14Dear brothers, warn those who are lazy; comfort those who are frightened; take tender care of those who are weak; and be patient with everyone. 15See that no one pays back evil for evil, but always try to do good to each other and to everyone else. 16Always be joyful. 17Always keep on praying. 18No matter what happens, always be thankful, for this is God's will for you who belong to Christ Jesus.

19Do not smother the Holy Spirit. 20Do not scoff at those who prophesy, 21but test everything that is said to be sure it is true, and if it is, then accept it. 22Keep away from every kind of evil. 23May the God of peace himself make you entirely pure and devoted to God; and may your spirit and soul and body be kept strong and blameless until that day when our Lord Jesus Christ comes back again. 24God, who called you to become his child, will do all this for you, just as he promised. 25Dear brothers, pray for us. 26Shake hands for me with all the brothers there. 27I command you in the name of the Lord to read this letter to all the Christians. 28And may rich blessings from our Lord Jesus Christ be with you, every one.

Sincerely, Paul

5:14 Don't lie down with the lazy; warn them. Don't yell at the frightened; comfort them. At times it's difficult to distinguish between laziness and fear. Two people may be doing nothing— one because he is lazy and the other out of fear of doing something wrong. The key to ministry is sensitivity: sensing the condition of each person and offering the appropriate remedy for each situation. You can't effectively help until you know the problem. You can't apply the medicine until you know where the wound is.

5:16-18 Our joy, prayers, and thankfulness to God should not fluctuate with our circumstances or feelings. Obeying these three commands—be joyful, keep praying, and be thankful—often goes against our natural inclinations. When we make a conscious decision to do what God says, however, we will begin to see people in a new perspective. When we do God's will, we will find it easier to be joyful and thankful.

5:17 We cannot spend all our time on our knees, but it is possible to have a prayerful attitude all the time. This attitude is built upon acknowledging our dependence on God, realizing his presence within us, and determining to obey him fully. We then find it natural to pray frequent, spontaneous, short prayers. A prayerful attitude is not a substitute for regular times of prayer, but should be an outgrowth of those times.

5:18 Paul was not teaching that we should thank God *for* everything that happens to us, but *in* everything. Evil does not come from God, so we should not thank him for evil. But when evil strikes, we can still be thankful for who God is and for the good he can bring through the distress.

5:19 By warning us not to "smother the Holy Spirit," Paul means we should not ignore or toss aside the gifts the Holy Spirit gives. Here he mentions prophecy; in 1 Corinthians 14:39, he mentions tongues. Sometimes spiritual gifts are controversial and cause

division in a church. Rather than trying to solve the problems, some Christians prefer to smother the gifts. This impoverishes the church. We should not stifle the Holy Spirit's work in anyone's life but encourage the full expression of these gifts in the body of Christ.

5:20, 21 We shouldn't make fun of those who don't agree with what we believe, but we should always check their words against the Bible. We are on dangerous ground if we scoff at a person who speaks the truth. Instead we should carefully check out what people say, accepting what is true and rejecting what is false.

5:22-24 A Christian can no more avoid all evil than a boat can avoid all water. He can, however, make sure his "boat" has no leaks. Evil should never be allowed into a Christian's heart.

5:23 The spirit, soul, and body are integral parts of a person. This expression is Paul's way of saying that God must be involved in *every* aspect of our lives. It is wrong to think we can separate our spiritual lives from everything else, obeying God only in some ethereal sense or living for him only one day each week. Christ must control *all* of us, not just a "religious" part.

5:27 For every Christian to hear this letter, it had to be read in a public meeting, for there were not enough copies to circulate. Paul wanted to make sure everyone had the opportunity to hear his message because he was answering important questions and offering needed encouragement.

5:28 The Thessalonian church was young, and they needed help and encouragement. Both the persecution they faced and the temptations of their pagan culture were potential problems for these new Christians. Therefore, Paul wrote to strengthen their faith and bolster their resistance to persecution and temptation. We too have a responsibility to help new believers, to make sure they continue in their faith and don't become sidetracked by wrong beliefs or practices. First Thessalonians can better equip us to help our brothers and sisters in Christ.

VITAL STATISTICS

PURPOSE:
To clear up the confusion about
the Second Coming of Christ

AUTHOR:
Paul

TO WHOM WRITTEN:
The church at Thessalonica and
all believers everywhere

DATE WRITTEN:
About A.D. 51 or 52, a few
months after 1 Thessalonians,
from Corinth

SETTING:
Many in the church were
confused about the timing of
Christ's return. Because of
mounting persecution, they
thought the day of the Lord
must be imminent, and they
interpreted Paul's first letter to
say that the Second Coming
would be at any moment. In
light of this misunderstanding,
many persisted in being lazy
and disorderly with the excuse
of waiting for Christ's return.

KEY VERSE:
"May the Lord bring you into an
even deeper understanding of
the love of God and of the
patience that comes from Christ"
(3:5).

KEY PEOPLE:
Paul, Silas, Timothy

KEY PLACES:
Thessalonica

SPECIAL FEATURES:
This is a follow-up letter to
1 Thessalonians. In this epistle,
Paul indicates various events
that must precede the Second
Coming of Christ.

EVEN when clearly stated or written, words can
be misinterpreted and misunderstood, especially
when filtered through the sieve of prejudices and
preconceptions.

Paul faced this problem with the Thessalonians.
He had written to help them grow in the faith,
comforting and encouraging them by affirming
the reality of Christ's return. Just a few months
later, however, word came from Thessalonica
that some had misunderstood his teaching about
the Second Coming. His announcement that
Christ could come at any moment had caused some to stop working and
just wait, rationalizing their laziness by pointing to Paul's teaching.
Adding fuel to this fire was the continued persecution of the church.
Many felt that indeed this must be the "day of the Lord."

Responding quickly, Paul sent his second epistle to this young church.
In it he gave further instruction concerning the Second Coming and the
day of the Lord (2:1, 2). Second Thessalonians, therefore, continues the
subject of 1 Thessalonians and is a call to continued courage and consistent
conduct.

The letter begins with Paul's trademark—a personal greeting and a
statement of thanksgiving for their faith (1:1–3). He mentions their
patience in spite of their crushing troubles and hardships (1:4) and uses
this to broach the subject of Christ's return. At that time, Christ will
vindicate the righteous who endure and he will punish the wicked
(1:5–12).

Paul then directly answers the misunderstanding concerning the timing
of the events of the end times. He tells them not to listen to rumors and
reports that the day of the Lord has already begun (2:1, 2) because a
number of events must occur before he returns (2:3–12). Meanwhile,
they should stand firm for Christ's truth (2:13–15), receive God's comfort
and hope (2:16, 17), pray for strength and that the Lord's message will
spread (3:1–5), and warn those who are lazy (3:6–15). Paul ends with
personal greetings and a benediction (3:16–18).

Almost 2,000 years later, we stand much closer to the time of Christ's
return; but we also would be wrong to see his imminent appearance as
an excuse for idle waiting and heavenward gazing. Being prepared for
his coming means spreading the gospel, reaching out to those in need,
and building the church, his body. As you read 2 Thessalonians, then,
see clearly the reality of his return and your responsibility to live for him
until that day.

THE BLUEPRINT

1. The bright hope of Christ's return
   (1:1—2:17)
2. Living in the light of Christ's return
   (3:1–18)

Paul wrote to encourage those who were facing persecution and to correct a misunderstanding about the timing of Christ's return. The teaching about the Lord's return promoted idleness in this young church. The imminent coming of Christ should never make us lazy; we should be even more busy—living purely, using our time well, and working for his Kingdom. We must work not only during easy times when it is convenient, but also during difficult times. Christians must patiently wait, watch, and work for Christ's return.

MEGATHEMES

THEME	EXPLANATION	IMPORTANCE
Persecution	Paul encouraged the church to have patience in spite of troubles and hardships. God will bring victory to his faithful followers and judge those who persecute them.	God promises to reward our faith with his power, helping us bear persecution. Suffering for our faith will strengthen us to serve Christ.
Christ's return	Since Paul had said that the Lord would come at any moment, some of the Thessalonian believers had stopped work in order to wait for Christ.	Christ will return and bring total victory to all who trust in him. If we are ready, we need not be concerned about *when* he will return. We should stand firm, keep working, and wait for Christ.
Great rebellion	Before Christ's return, there will be a great rebellion against God led by the man of rebellion (the Antichrist). God will remove all the restraints on evil before he brings judgment on the rebels. The Antichrist will attempt to deceive many.	We should not be afraid when we see evil increase. God is in control, no matter how evil the world becomes. God guards us from Satanic attack. We can have victory over evil by remaining faithful to him.
Persistence	Because church members had quit working and become disorderly and disobedient, Paul chastised them for their laziness. He called them to show courage and true Christian conduct.	We must never get so tired of doing right that we quit. We can be persistent by making the most of our time and talent. Our endurance will be rewarded.

1. The bright hope of Christ's return

1 *From:* Paul, Silas and Timothy.

To: The church of Thessalonica—kept safe in God our Father and in the Lord Jesus Christ.

1:1
2 Cor 1:19
1 Thess 1:1

²May God the Father and the Lord Jesus Christ give you rich blessings and peace-filled hearts and minds.

1:2
Rom 1:7

Paul encourages those experiencing persecution

³Dear brothers, giving thanks to God for you is not only the right thing to do, but it is our duty to God, because of the really wonderful way your faith has grown, and because of your growing love for each other. ⁴We are happy to tell other churches

1:3
Job 17:9
Ps 84:7
1 Thess 1:2

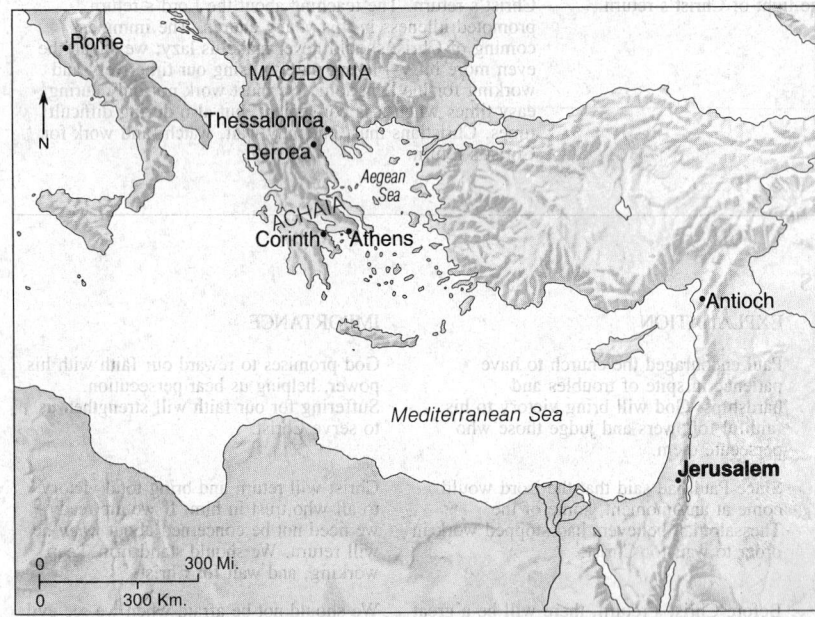

LOCATION OF THESSALONICA
After Paul visited Thessalonica on his second missionary journey, he went on to Beroea, Athens, and Corinth (Acts 17, 18). From Corinth, Paul wrote his two letters to the Thessalonian church.

1:1 Paul wrote this letter from Corinth less than a year after he wrote 1 Thessalonians. He and his companions, Timothy and Silas, had visited Thessalonica on Paul's second missionary journey (Acts 17:1–10). They started the first church there, but Paul had to leave suddenly because of persecution. This prompted him to write his first letter (1 Thessalonians), which contains words of comfort and encouragement. Paul then heard how the Thessalonians had responded to this letter. The good news was that they continued to grow in their faith, but the bad news was that false teachings about Christ's return were spreading, leading many to quit their jobs and wait for the end of the world. So Paul wrote to them again. While the purpose of Paul's first letter was to comfort the Thessalonians with the assurance of Christ's Second Coming, his second letter was to correct false teaching about the Second Coming.

1:1 Paul, Silas, and Timothy were together in Corinth (Acts 18:5). Paul wrote this letter on behalf of all three of them. He often included Timothy as a co-sender of his letters (see Philippians 1:1; Colossians 1:1; 1 Thessalonians 1:1). For more information about Paul, see his Profile in Acts 9. Timothy's Profile is found in 1 Timothy, and Silas' is in Acts 16.

1:1 Thessalonica was the capital and largest city of the Roman province of Macedonia. The most important Roman highway—extending from Rome to the Orient—went through Thessalonica. This highway, along with the city's thriving seaport, made

Thessalonica one of the wealthiest and most flourishing trade centers in the Roman Empire. Recognized as a free city, Thessalonica was allowed self-rule and was exempted from most of the restrictions placed by Rome on other cities. Because of this open climate, however, the city had many pagan religions and cultural influences that challenged the Christians' faith.

1:3 Regardless of his letters' contents, Paul's style was affirming. He began most of his letters by stating what he most appreciated about his readers and the joy he felt because of their faith in God.

1:4–6 Paul was persecuted during his first visit to Thessalonica (Acts 17:5–9). No doubt those who responded to his message and became Christians continued to be persecuted by both Jews and Gentiles. In Paul's first letter to the Thessalonians, he said that Christ's return would bring deliverance from persecution and judgment on the persecutors. But this caused the people to expect Christ's return right away to rescue and vindicate them. Thus Paul points out that while waiting for God's Kingdom, believers can learn from their suffering.

1:4, 5 The keys to surviving suffering are patience and faith. When we are faced with crushing troubles and hardships we can have faith that God is using them for our good and for his glory—these troubles will better prepare us for his Kingdom. Knowing that God is fair and just gives us confidence that he has not forgotten us in our troubles, and that, in his timing, he will relieve us of our suffering and will judge those who persecute us.

1:5
2 Tim 2:12

1:6
Ex 23:22
Rev 6:10

1:7
Mk 8:38
1 Thess 4:16
Rev 14:13

1:8
Ps 79:6
Rom 2:8
Heb 10:27

1:9
Deut 33:2
Isa 2:19
1 Thess 5:3
2 Thess 2:8

1:10
Jn 17:10
Eph 3:21

1:11
Eph 4:1
1 Thess 1:3

1:12
Phil 2:9

2:1
Mt 24:31
1 Thess 2:19
4:15-17

2:2
2 Thess 2:15
3:17

2:3
1 Tim 4:1

2:4
Isa 14:13
Mt 24:15
1 Cor 8:5,6

about your patience and complete faith in God, in spite of all the crushing troubles and hardships you are going through.

⁵This is only one example of the fair, just way God does things, for he is using your sufferings to make you ready for his Kingdom, ⁶while at the same time he is preparing judgment and punishment for those who are hurting you.

⁷And so I would say to you who are suffering, God will give you rest along with us when the Lord Jesus appears suddenly from heaven in flaming fire with his mighty angels, ⁸bringing judgment on those who do not wish to know God, and who refuse to accept his plan to save them through our Lord Jesus Christ. ⁹They will be punished in everlasting hell, forever separated from the Lord, never to see the glory of his power, ¹⁰when he comes to receive praise and admiration because of all he has done for his people, his saints. And you will be among those praising him, because you have believed what we told you about him.

¹¹And so we keep on praying for you that our God will make you the kind of children he wants to have—will make you as good as you wish you could be!—rewarding your faith with his power. ¹²Then everyone will be praising the name of the Lord Jesus Christ because of the results they see in you; and your greatest glory will be that you belong to him. The tender mercy of our God and of the Lord Jesus Christ has made all this possible for you.

Paul predicts the coming of the Antichrist

2 And now, what about the coming again of our Lord Jesus Christ, and our being gathered together to meet him? Please don't be upset and excited, dear brothers, by the rumor that this day of the Lord has already begun. If you hear of people having visions and special messages from God about this, or letters that are supposed to have come from me, don't believe them. ³Don't be carried away and deceived regardless of what they say.

For that day will not come until two things happen: first, there will be a time of great rebellion against God, and then the man of rebellion will come—the son of hell. ⁴He will defy every god there is, and tear down every other object of adoration

---

1:5 As we live for Christ, we will experience troubles and hardships. Some say troubles are a result of sin or lack of faith. But Paul teaches that they may be a part of God's plan for believers. Our problems help us look upward and forward, not inward (Mark 13:35, 36); they help build strong character (Romans 5:3, 4); and they help us be sensitive to others who also must struggle (2 Corinthians 1:3–5). In addition, problems are unavoidable because we are trying to be godly people in an ungodly world. Your troubles may well be a sign of effective Christian living.

1:5, 6 There are two dimensions of the comfort mentioned by Paul. We can be comforted in knowing that our sufferings strengthen us, making us ready for Christ's Kingdom. We can also take comfort in the fact that one day everyone will stand before God; then, wrongs will be righted, judgment will be pronounced, and evil will be terminated.

1:7–9 Paul describes hell as eternal separation from God. In hell, people no longer have any hope for salvation. Those doomed to hell don't want to know God and they refuse to accept his salvation. They will be allowed to stay away from him—forever.

1:11 When we truly love God, we are repeatedly disappointed in our performance. We want to be good, and yet we are unable to do so. God's purpose for all believers is to make them the kind of children he wants to have. This would mean becoming as good as we wish we could be. As our faith in God increases, God increases the power available in us to do good. If you want God's power in your life, believe in *his* ability to do good rather than in yours. Then when Christ comes again, he will make you better than you ever thought you could be.

2:1ff Paul launches into a discussion about the end of the world and Christ's Second Coming. He says that great suffering and trouble lie ahead, but evil will not prevail, because Christ will return

to judge all people. Although Paul presents a few signs of the end times, his emphasis, like Jesus' (Mark 13), is not on specific or current events but on each person's need to prepare for Christ's return by living rightly day by day. If we are ready, we won't have to be concerned about what will happen. God is in control of all events. (See 1 Thessalonians 4, 5 for Paul's earlier teaching on this subject.)

2:1, 2 In the Bible, the *day of the Lord* is used in two ways: the end times (which began with Christ and in which we are now living), and the final judgment day (which is yet to come). Paul emphasizes that the judgment day has not yet come.

2:3ff When Paul first wrote to the Thessalonians, they were in danger of losing hope in the Second Coming. Now they have shifted to the opposite extreme—some of them thought Jesus would be coming any minute. Paul tried to restore the balance by describing certain events that would happen before Christ's return.

2:3 Throughout history there have been antichrists— individuals who epitomized evil (see 1 John 2:18; 4:3; 2 John 7). Antichrists have occured in every generation and will continue to occur until a "man of rebellion" arises. Just before the Second Coming, a completely evil individual will arise. He will be Satan's tool with Satan's power—perhaps even Satan himself (2:9). This "son of hell" will be *the* Antichrist.

It is dangerous, however, to label certain individuals *antichrists* and try to predict Christ's coming based on those assumptions. Paul mentions the Antichrist, not necessarily to help us recognize him, but to urge us to ready ourselves for anything that might threaten our faith. If our faith is strong, we don't need to be afraid of what lies ahead. God is in control, and he will be victorious over the Antichrist. Our task is to ready ourselves for Christ and to spread his Good News so even more people will be prepared also.

and worship. He will go in and sit as God in the temple of God, claiming that he himself is God. 5Don't you remember that I told you this when I was with you? 6And you know what is keeping him from being here already; for he can come only when his time is ready.

7As for the work this man of rebellion and hell will do when he comes, it is already going on, but he himself will not come until the one who is holding him back steps out of the way. 8Then this wicked one will appear, whom the Lord Jesus will burn up with the breath of his mouth and destroy by his presence when he returns. 9This man of sin will come as Satan's tool, full of satanic power, and will trick everyone with strange demonstrations, and will do great miracles. 10He will completely fool those who are on their way to hell because they have said "no" to the Truth; they have refused to believe it and love it, and let it save them, 11so God will allow them to believe lies with all their hearts, 12and all of them will be justly judged for believing falsehood, refusing the Truth, and enjoying their sins.

Believers should stand firm

13But we must forever give thanks to God for you, our brothers loved by the Lord, because God chose from the very first to give you salvation, cleansing you by the work of the Holy Spirit and by your trusting in the Truth. 14Through us he told you the Good News. Through us he called you to share in the glory of our Lord Jesus Christ.

15With all these things in mind, dear brothers, stand firm and keep a strong grip on the truth that we taught you in our letters and during the time we were with you.

16May our Lord Jesus Christ himself and God our Father, who has loved us and given us everlasting comfort and hope which we don't deserve, 17comfort your hearts with all comfort, and help you in every good thing you say and do.

2. Living in the light of Christ's return
Paul requests prayer

3 Finally, dear brothers, as I come to the end of this letter I ask you to pray for us. Pray first that the Lord's message will spread rapidly and triumph wherever it goes, winning converts everywhere as it did when it came to you. 2Pray too that

2:13 *God chose from the very first to give you salvation*, or, "because God chose you to be among the first to believe."

2:7 Gen 6:3 / 1 Jn 4:3
2:8 Job 4:9 / Isa 11:4 / Mt 25:31 / Heb 10:27 / Rev 19:15
2:9 Mt 24:24 / Eph 2:2 / Rev 13:13
2:10 2 Cor 4:3
2:11 1 Kgs 22:22,23 / Mt 24:5 / Rom 1:24,28
2:12 Rom 1:32; 2:8
2:13 Eph 1:4 / 1 Pet 1:2
2:14 Jn 17:22 / Rom 8:29,30 / 1 Thess 2:12
2:15 1 Cor 11:2; 16:13
2:16 Jn 3:16
2:17 1 Thess 3:2; 5:11
3:1 1 Thess 1:8; 5:25
3:2 Rom 15:30,31

2:7 "The work . . . is already going on" can also be translated "the mystery of lawlessness is already at work." Paul uses the word *mystery* for something no one can discover, but which God will reveal. The mystery of lawlessness, then, is the hidden, subtle, underlying force from which all sin springs. Civilization has a veneer of decency through law enforcement, education, science, and reason. Although we are horrified by criminal acts, we have yet to see the real horror of complete lawlessness. This will happen when the restraining forces are removed. Why will God allow this to happen? To show men and nations their own sinfulness, and to show them by bitter experience the true alternative to the Lordship of Christ. Men totally without God can act no better than vicious animals. Lawlessness, to a certain extent, is already going on, but the Lawless One has not yet arrived.

2:7 Who holds back the man of rebellion? Three possibilities have been suggested: (1) government and law, which help to curb evil, (2) the ministry and activity of the church and the effects of the gospel, or (3) the Holy Spirit. The Bible is not clear on who this "restrainer" is, only that he will not restrain forever. But we should not fear this—God is far stronger than the man of rebellion, and he will save his people.

2:9 Miracles from God can help strengthen our faith and lead people to Christ, but miracles are not necessarily from God. Christ's miracles were significant not just because of their power, but also because of their purpose—to help, to heal, to point us to God. The man of rebellion will have power to do mighty miracles, but his power will be from Satan. He will use this power to destroy

and to lead people away from God and toward himself. If anyone draws attention only to himself, his work is not from God.

2:10–12 God gives people freedom to turn their backs on him and believe Satan's lies. But if they say no to the Truth, they will experience the consequences of their sin.

2:13 Paul consistently taught that salvation begins and ends with God. We can do nothing to be saved on our own merit—we must accept God's gift of salvation (see the note on Ephesians 1:4). There is no other way to receive forgiveness from sin.

2:14 God worked through Paul and his companions to tell the Good News and to call new believers to share in Christ's glory. It seems strange that God works through us—fallible, unfaithful, untrustworthy human creatures. But he has given us the fantastic privilege of accomplishing his great mission— telling the world how to find salvation.

2:15 Paul knew that the Thessalonians would face pressure from persecutions, false teachers, worldliness, and apathy to waver from the truth and to leave the faith; so he urged them to keep a "grip on the truth" and to stand firm. We are also confronted with temptations to turn away from God. We should hold on to the truth found in Christ's teachings because our lives depend on it. Never forget the reality of his life and love!

3:2, 3 Beneath the surface of the routine of daily life, a fierce struggle among invisible spiritual powers is being waged. Like the wind, the evil powers' force can be devastating. Our main defense is prayer that God will protect us from evil and that he will make us

3:3
Jn 17:15
1 Cor 1:9
2 Pet 2:9

3:4
1 Thess 4:9,10

3:5
1 Jn 4:16

we will be saved out of the clutches of evil men, for not everyone loves the Lord. ³But the Lord is faithful; he will make you strong and guard you from satanic attacks of every kind. ⁴And we trust the Lord that you are putting into practice the things we taught you, and that you always will. ⁵May the Lord bring you into an ever deeper understanding of the love of God and of the patience that comes from Christ.

Paul admonishes the church against laziness

3:6
Rom 16:17
1 Cor 5:4; 11:2
1 Thess 5:14

3:8
Acts 18:3
1 Thess 2:9

3:9
Mt 10:10
1 Cor 9:4
1 Tim 5:17
1 Pet 5:3

3:10
1 Thess 4:11

3:11
1 Tim 5:13

3:12
Rom 12:11
1 Thess 4:1,11

3:15
Gal 6:1
1 Thess 5:14

⁶Now here is a command, dear brothers, given in the name of our Lord Jesus Christ by his authority: Stay away from any Christian who spends his days in laziness and does not follow the ideal of hard work we set up for you. ⁷For you well know that you ought to follow our example: you never saw us loafing; ⁸we never accepted food from anyone without buying it; we worked hard day and night for the money we needed to live on, in order that we would not be a burden to any of you. ⁹It wasn't that we didn't have the right to ask you to feed us, but we wanted to show you, firsthand, how you should work for your living. ¹⁰Even while we were still there with you we gave you this rule: "He who does not work shall not eat."

¹¹Yet we hear that some of you are living in laziness, refusing to work, and wasting your time in gossiping. ¹²In the name of the Lord Jesus Christ we appeal to such people—we command them—to quiet down, get to work, and earn their own living. ¹³And to the rest of you I say, dear brothers, never be tired of doing right.

¹⁴If anyone refuses to obey what we say in this letter, notice who he is and stay away from him, that he may be ashamed of himself. ¹⁵Don't think of him as an enemy, but speak to him as you would to a brother who needs to be warned.

Paul's final greetings

3:16
Rom 15:33

3:17
1 Cor 16:21
Gal 6:11
Col 4:18
Philem 19

¹⁶May the Lord of peace himself give you his peace no matter what happens. The Lord be with you all.

¹⁷Now here is my greeting which I am writing with my own hand, as I do at the end of all my letters, for proof that it really is from me. This is in my own handwriting. ¹⁸May the blessing of our Lord Jesus Christ be upon you all.

Sincerely, Paul

---

strong. (See also comments on Ephesians 6:10–19 concerning our armor for spiritual warfare.) The following guidelines can help you prepare for and survive satanic attacks: (1) take the threat of spiritual attack seriously; (2) pray for strength and help from God; (3) study the Bible to recognize Satan's style and tactics, (4) memorize Scripture so it will be a source of help no matter where you are; (5) associate with those who speak the truth; and (6) practice what you are taught by spiritual leaders.

3:6–15 Some people in the Thessalonian church were falsely teaching that since Christ's Second Coming could happen any day, people should set aside their responsibilities, quit work, do no future planning, and just wait for Christ. But their lack of activity only led them into sin: They became a burden to the church, which was supporting them; they wasted time that could have been used for helping others; and they gossiped (3:11). They may have thought they were being more spiritual by not working, but Paul told them to be responsible and get back to work. Being ready for Christ means obeying him in every area of life. Because we know Christ is coming, we must do everything we can to live in a way that will please him when he arrives.

3:6–10 There's a difference between leisure and laziness. Relaxation and recreation provide a necessary and much needed

balance; but when it is time to work, Christians should be responsible. We should make the most of our talent and time, doing all we can to provide for ourselves and our dependents.

3:11, 12 Gossip is tantalizing. It is exciting to hear, and it makes us feel like insiders. But instead of building up, gossip tears down. If you often find your nose in other people's business, you may be underemployed. Look for a task to do for Christ or for your family and get to work.

3:14, 15 Paul counsels the church to stop financially supporting and to stop associating with those who persist in their laziness. Hunger and loneliness could be very effective means in making the idle become productive. Paul was not advising coldness or cruelty, but the kind of tough love one would show a brother.

3:18 The book of 2 Thessalonians is especially meaningful for those who are being persecuted or are under pressure for their faith. In chapter 1 we are told what suffering can do for us. In chapter 2 we are assured of final victory. In chapter 3 we are encouraged to continue living responsibly in spite of difficult circumstances. Christ's return is more than a doctrine; it is a promise. It is not just for the future; it has a vital impact on how we live now.

we will be saved out of the clutches of evil men, for not everyone loves the Lord.
But the Lord is faithful; he will make you strong and guard you from satanic attacks of every kind. And we trust the Lord that you are putting into practice the things we taught you, and that you always will. May the Lord bring you into an ever deeper understanding of the love of God and of the patience that comes from Christ.

VITAL STATISTICS

PURPOSE:
To give encouragement and instruction to Timothy, a young leader

AUTHOR:
Paul

TO WHOM WRITTEN:
Timothy, young church leaders, and all believers everywhere

DATE WRITTEN:
About A.D. 64, from Rome or Macedonia (possibly Philippi), probably just prior to Paul's final imprisonment in Rome

SETTING:
Timothy was one of Paul's closest companions. Paul had sent Timothy to the church at Ephesus to counter the false teaching which had arisen there (1 Timothy 1:3, 4). Timothy probably served for a time as a leader in the church at Ephesus. Paul hoped to visit Timothy (3:14, 15; 4:13), but in the meantime, he wrote this letter to give Timothy practical advice for the ministry.

KEY VERSE:
"Don't let anyone think little of you because you are young. Be their ideal; let them follow the way you teach and live; be a pattern for them in your love, your faith, and your clean thoughts" (4:12).

KEY PEOPLE:
Paul, Timothy

KEY PLACE:
Ephesus

SPECIAL FEATURES:
First Timothy is a personal letter and a handbook of church administration and discipline.

WITHOUT trying, we model our values. Parents in particular demonstrate to their children what they consider important. "Like father, like son" is not just a well-worn cliché; it is a truth often repeated in our homes. And experience proves that children often follow the life-styles of their parents, repeating their successes and mistakes.

Timothy is a prime example of one who was influenced by godly relatives. His mother, Eunice, and grandmother, Lois, were Jewish believers who helped shape his spiritual life (2 Timothy 1:5; 3:15). Timothy is the first "second generation" Christian mentioned in the New Testament.

Timothy became Paul's protegé and was probably a leader of the church at Ephesus for a time. As a young minister, Timothy faced all sorts of pressures, conflicts, and challenges from the church and his surrounding culture. To counsel and encourage Timothy, Paul sent this very personal letter.

Paul wrote 1 Timothy in about A.D. 64, probably just prior to his final Roman imprisonment. Because he had appealed to Caesar, Paul was sent as a prisoner to Rome (see Acts 25—28). Most scholars believe that Paul was released in about A.D. 62 (possibly because the "statute of limitations" had expired), and that during the next few years he was able to travel. During this time, he wrote the letters of 1 Timothy and Titus. Soon, however, the Emperor Nero began his campaign to eliminate Christianity. It is believed that during this time, Paul was imprisoned again and eventually executed. During this second Roman imprisonment, Paul wrote 2 Timothy. Titus and the two letters to Timothy comprise what are called the "pastoral epistles."

Paul's first letter to Timothy affirms their relationship (1:2). He warns Timothy about false teachers (1:3–11), and urges him to cling tightly to his faith in Christ (1:12–20). Next Paul considers public worship, emphasizing the importance of prayer (2:1–7) and order in church meetings (2:8–15). This leads to a discussion of the qualifications of church leaders—pastors (elders) and deacons. Here Paul lists specific criteria for each office (3:1–16).

Paul speaks again about false teachers, telling Timothy how to recognize them and respond to them (4:1–16). Next, he gives practical advice on pastoral care to the young and old (5:1, 2), widows (5:3–16), elders (5:17–25), and slaves (6:1, 2). Paul concludes by exhorting Timothy to guard his motives (6:3–10), to stand firm in his faith (6:11, 12), to live above reproach (6:13–16), and to minister faithfully (6:17–21).

First Timothy holds many lessons. If you are a church leader, take note of Paul's relationship with this young disciple—his careful counsel and guidance. Measure yourself against the qualifications Paul gives for elders and deacons. If you are young in the faith, follow the example of godly Christian leaders, like Timothy, who imitated Paul's life. If you are a parent, remind yourself of the profound effect a Christian home can have on family members—a faithful mother and grandmother led Timothy to Christ and his ministry helped change the world.

THE BLUEPRINT

1. Instructions on right belief (1:1–20)
2. Instructions for the church (2:1—3:16)
3. Instructions for leaders (4:1—6:21)

Paul advised Timothy on such practical topics as qualifications for church leaders, public worship, confronting false teaching, and how to treat various groups of people within the church. Right belief and right behavior are critical for anyone who desires to lead or serve effectively in the church. We should all believe rightly, participate in church actively, and minister to one another lovingly.

MEGATHEMES

THEME	EXPLANATION	IMPORTANCE
Sound doctrine	Paul instructed Timothy to preserve the Christian faith by teaching sound doctrine and modeling right living. Timothy had to oppose false teachers who were leading church members away from belief in salvation by faith in Jesus Christ alone.	We must know the truth in order to defend it. We must cling to the belief that Christ came to save us. We should stay away from those who twist the words of the Bible for their own purposes.
Public worship	Prayer in public worship must be done with a proper attitude toward God and fellow believers.	Christian character must be evident in every aspect of worship. We must rid ourselves of any anger, resentment, or offensive attire that might disrupt worship or damage church unity.
Church leadership	Paul gives specific instructions concerning the qualifications for church leaders so that the church might honor God and run smoothly.	Church leaders must be wholly committed to Christ. If you are a new or young Christian, don't be anxious to become a leader in the church. Seek to develop your Christian character first. Be sure to seek God, not your own ambition.
Personal discipline	It takes discipline to be a leader in the church. Timothy, like all church leaders, had to guard his motives, minister faithfully, and live above reproach. Any pastor must keep morally and spiritually fit.	To stay in good spiritual shape, you must discipline yourself to study God's Word and to live a godly life. Put your spiritual abilities to work!
Caring church	The church has a responsibility to care for the needs of all its members, especially the sick, the poor, and the widowed.	Caring for the family of believers demonstrates our Christ-like attitude and exhibits genuine love to nonbelievers.

1. Instructions on right belief

1 *From:* Paul, a missionary of Jesus Christ, sent out by the direct command of
God our Savior and by Jesus Christ our Lord—our only hope.
²*To:* Timothy.

Timothy, you are like a son to me in the things of the Lord. May God our Father
and Jesus Christ our Lord show you his kindness and mercy and give you great
peace of heart and mind.

1:1
Gal 1:1,2
Col 1:27
Tit 1:3; 3:4

1:2
Acts 16:1
1 Cor 4:17
2 Tim 1:2
Tit 1:4

Paul warns about false teachers

³,⁴As I said when I left for Macedonia, please stay there in Ephesus and try to
stop the men who are teaching such wrong doctrine. Put an end to their myths and
fables, and their idea of being saved by finding favor with an endless chain of
angels leading up to God—wild ideas that stir up questions and arguments instead
of helping people accept God's plan of faith. ⁵What I am eager for is that all the
Christians there will be filled with love that comes from pure hearts, and that their
minds will be clean and their faith strong.

⁶But these teachers have missed this whole idea and spend their time arguing and
talking foolishness. ⁷They want to become famous as teachers of the laws of Moses
when they haven't the slightest idea what those laws really show us. ⁸Those laws
are good when used as God intended. ⁹But they were not made for us, whom God
has saved; they are for sinners who hate God, have rebellious hearts, curse and
swear, attack their fathers and mothers, and murder. ¹⁰, ¹¹Yes, these laws are made

1:3,4
Acts 19:1,10
20:1-3
Gal 1:6,7
1 Tim 4:7; 6:3,4
Tit 3:9

1:5
Rom 13:8
Gal 5:14
2 Tim 1:5; 2:22
1 Pet 3:16

1:6
Tit 1:10

1:8
Rom 7:12,16

1:9
Gal 3:19
Rev 21:8

1:1 This letter was written to Timothy in A.D. 64 or 65, after Paul's
first imprisonment in Rome (Acts 28:16–31). Paul was apparently
released from prison for several years, during which time he
revisited many churches in Asia and Macedonia. When Paul and
Timothy returned to Ephesus, they found widespread false
teaching in the church. Paul had warned the Ephesian elders to be
on guard against the false teachers who would inevitably come
after he had left (Acts 20:29, 30). Paul sent Timothy to lead the
Ephesian church while he moved on to Macedonia. Paul may have
written this letter from somewhere within Macedonia. Paul wrote to
Timothy to help him deal with the difficult situation in the Ephesian
church. Paul was then arrested again and later executed.

1:1 For more information on Paul, see his Profile in Acts 9.

1:1 Paul called himself a missionary or, literally, an *apostle*, "one
who is sent." Paul was sent by Jesus Christ to give the message of
salvation to the Gentiles (Acts 9:1–20).

1:1 In adventure stories, the hero often rescues defenseless
victims at the last possible moment. Within this fictional world, the
bold adventurer is the only hope for the victims. Within the reality of
the spiritual realm, our only hope is Jesus Christ. Only he can save
us. Where have you placed your hope?

1:3, 4 Paul first visited Ephesus on his second missionary journey
(Acts 18:19–21). Later, on his third missionary journey, he stayed
there for almost three years (Acts 19, 20). Ephesus, along with
Rome, Corinth, Antioch, and Alexandria, was one of the major
cities in the Roman Empire. It was a center for the commerce,
politics, and religions of Asia Minor, and the place where the
temple dedicated to the goddess Artemis (Diana) was located.

1:3, 4 The church at Ephesus was probably plagued by the same
heresy that threatened the church at Colosse, the false doctrine
that to be acceptable to God one had to find favor with angels. To
aid in their salvation, some Ephesians constructed lists and
biographies of angels. The false teachers mentioned here were
motivated by their own interests rather than Christ's. They
embroiled the church in endless and irrelevant disputes (1:6, 7).
Today we have many opportunities to enter into such worthless
and irrelevant discussions. Such disputes crowd out the
life-changing message of Christ. Stay away from religious
speculation and theological haggling. It may seem harmless at
first, but it has a way of sidetracking us from the central message

of the gospel—the person and work of Jesus Christ.

1:3–11 The world is filled with people demanding allegiance,
many of whom would have us turn from Christ to follow them. Often
their influence is subtle. How can you recognize false teaching
before it does irreparable damage? (1) It stirs up questions and
arguments instead of helping people come to Jesus (1:4). (2) It is
often promoted by teachers whose motivation is to make a name
for themselves (1:7). (3) It will be contrary to the true teaching of
the Scriptures (1:6, 7; 4:1–3). Instead of listening to false teachers,
we should learn what the Bible teaches and remain steadfast in our
faith in Christ alone.

1:5 The false teachers were motivated by curiosity, power, and
prestige. By contrast, genuine Christian teachers are motivated by
love, truth, and faith. It may be exciting to explore esoteric
doctrines in order to impress people with our great "knowledge,"
but position based on falsehood is ultimately empty, a cheap and
temporary thrill. Leaders who truly follow Christ will find lasting,
eternal reward as they see his truth spread throughout the world
and his love transform people everywhere.

1:6 Theological hairsplitting—arguing about tiny details of
Scripture—can take us into interesting, but irrelevant bypaths and
cause us to miss the intent of God's message. The false teachers
at Ephesus constructed vast speculative systems and then argued
about the minor details of their wholly imaginary ideas. We should
allow nothing to distract us from the Good News of Jesus Christ,
the main point of Scripture. We need to know what the Scriptures
say, apply them to our lives daily, and teach them to others. When
we do this we will be able to evaluate all teachings in light of the
central truth about Jesus. Don't spend so much time on the minute
details of Scripture that you miss the main point of what God is
trying to teach you.

1:7–11 The "whole idea" the false teachers missed (1:6) was the
purpose of God's law. The law was not meant to give believers a
list of commands for every occasion, but to show nonbelievers
their sin and bring them to God. For more of what Paul says about
our relationship to law, see Romans 5:20, 21; 13:9, 10; Galatians
3:24–29.

1:10, 11 There are those who attempt to legitimize homosexuality
as an acceptable alternative lifestyle. Even some Christians say
people have a right to choose how they want to live. But the Bible

to identify as sinners all who are immoral and impure: homosexuals, kidnappers, liars, and all others who do things that contradict the glorious Good News of our blessed God, whose messenger I am.

1:11
2 Cor 4:4

God's mercy on Paul

1:12
2 Cor 3:5,6
Phil 4:13
Col 1:25

12How thankful I am to Christ Jesus our Lord for choosing me as one of his messengers, and giving me the strength to be faithful to him, 13even though I used to scoff at the name of Christ. I hunted down his people, harming them in every way I could. But God had mercy on me because I didn't know what I was doing, for I didn't know Christ at that time. 14Oh, how kind our Lord was, for he showed me how to trust him and become full of the love of Christ Jesus.

1:13
Lk 23:34
Acts 8:3; 26:9
1 Cor 15:9

1:14
Lk 7:47
Rom 5:20
2 Tim 1:13

15How true it is, and how I long that everyone should know it, that Christ Jesus came into the world to save sinners—and I was the greatest of them all. 16But God had mercy on me so that Christ Jesus could use me as an example to show everyone how patient he is with even the worst sinners, so that others will realize that they, too, can have everlasting life. 17Glory and honor to God forever and ever. He is the King of the ages, the unseen one who never dies; he alone is God, and full of wisdom. Amen.

1:15
Lk 19:10
Rom 5:8

1:16
Eph 2:7

1:17
1 Tim 6:15,16

→ Cling tightly to the faith

1:18
2 Cor 10:4

18Now, Timothy, my son, here is my command to you: Fight well in the Lord's battles, just as the Lord told us through his prophets that you would. 19Cling tightly to your faith in Christ and always keep your conscience clear, doing what you know is right. For some people have disobeyed their consciences and have deliberately done what they knew was wrong. It isn't surprising that soon they lost their faith in Christ after defying God like that. 20Hymenaeus and Alexander are two examples of this. I had to give them over to Satan to punish them until they could learn not to bring shame to the name of Christ.

1:19
1 Tim 6:12

1:20
1 Cor 5:5
2 Tim 2:17; 4:14

---

specifically calls homosexual behavior sin (see Leviticus 18:22; Romans 1:18–32; 1 Corinthians 6:9–11). We must be careful, however, to condemn only the practice, not the people. People who commit homosexual acts are not to be feared, ridiculed, or hated. They can be forgiven and their lives can be transformed. The church should be a haven of forgiveness and healing for homosexuals without compromising its stance against homosexual behavior. For more on this subject see the note on Romans 1:27.

1:12-17 People can feel so guilt-ridden by their past that they think God could never forgive and accept them. But consider Paul's past. He had hunted down and murdered God's own people before coming to faith in Christ (Acts 9:1–9). God forgave Paul and he can forgive you.

1:14 When we become Christians, we often feel that our love for Jesus and others is inadequate. But we can be confident that Christ will give us the faith and love we need. Even with our weak faith, we must demonstrate genuine love toward others. Christ will increase both our faith and love as our relationship with him deepens.

1:15 In this verse, often memorized and quoted, Paul summarizes the Good News: Jesus saves sinners, and no sinner is beyond his saving power. Do you believe that? Jesus didn't come just to show us how to live, or to challenge us to be better people. He came to offer us salvation that leads to eternal life. Have you accepted his offer?

→ 1:18 Paul highly valued the gift of prophecy (1 Corinthians 14:1) through which important messages of warning and encouragement came to the church. Just as pastors are set apart for ministry in today's church, Timothy was set apart for ministry when elders laid

their hands on him (see 4:14). Apparently at this ceremony, several believers prophesied about Timothy's gifts and strengths. These words from the Lord must have encouraged him throughout his ministry.

1:19 How can you keep your conscience clear? Treasure your faith in Christ more than anything else and do what you know is right. Each time you deliberately ignore your conscience, you are hardening your heart. Soon your capacity to tell right from wrong will disappear. But when you walk with God, he is able to speak to you through your conscience, letting you know the difference between right and wrong. Be sure to act on those inner tugs to do what is right—then your conscience will remain clear.

1:20 Hymenaeus' error is explained in 2 Timothy 2:17, 18. He weakened people's faith by teaching that the resurrection had already occurred. Paul says in 1 Timothy 1:20, that he gave him "over to Satan," which meant that Paul had removed him from the fellowship of the church. He did this so that Hymenaeus would see his error and repent. The ultimate purpose of this discipline was not punishment, but correction. The church today is too often lax in disciplining Christians who deliberately sin. Deliberate disobedience should be handled quickly and sternly to prevent the entire congregation from being infected. But it must be done in a way that strives to bring the offender back to Christ and into the loving embrace of the church. The definition of discipline includes these words: strengthening, purifying, training, correcting, perfecting. Therefore, condemnation, suspicion, withholding forgiveness, or permanent exile are not to be a part of church discipline.

2. Instructions for the church

Instructions about worship

2 Here are my directions: Pray much for others; plead for God's mercy upon them; give thanks for all he is going to do for them.

²Pray in this way for kings and all others who are in authority over us, or are in places of high responsibility, so that we can live in peace and quietness, spending our time in godly living and thinking much about the Lord. ³This is good and pleases God our Savior, ⁴for he longs for all to be saved and to understand this truth: ⁵*That God is on one side and all the people on the other side, and Christ Jesus, himself man, is between them to bring them together,* ⁶*by giving his life for all mankind.*

This is the message which at the proper time God gave to the world. ⁷And I have been chosen—this is the absolute truth—as God's minister and missionary to teach this truth to the Gentiles, and to show them God's plan of salvation through faith.

⁸So I want men everywhere to pray with holy hands lifted up to God, free from sin and anger and resentment. ⁹, ¹⁰And the women should be the same way, quiet and sensible in manner and clothing. Christian women should be noticed for being kind and good, not for the way they fix their hair or because of their jewels or fancy clothes. ¹¹Women should listen and learn quietly and humbly.

—¹²I never let women teach men or lord it over them. Let them be silent in your

2:1 Eph 6:18
2:2 Rom 13:1
2:3 1 Tim 1:1
2:4 1 Tim 4:10; 2 Tim 2:25
2:5 Rom 8:35
2:6 Gal 4:4
2:7 Acts 9:15; 1 Cor 9:1; 2 Tim 1:1
2:8 Ps 24:4; 63:4
2:9 1 Pet 3:3
2:11 1 Cor 14:34
2:12 Tit 2:5

2:2 *in godly living and thinking much about the Lord,* literally, "in gravity."

2:1-6 Although God is all-powerful and all-knowing, he has chosen to let us help him change the world through our prayers. How this works is a mystery to us because of our limited understanding, but it is a reality. Paul urges us to pray for each other and for our leaders in government. Our earnest prayers will have powerful results (James 5:16).

2:2 Paul's command to pray for rulers was remarkable considering that Nero was emperor at this time (A.D. 54–68). Nero was a notoriously cruel emperor. He needed a scapegoat for the great fire that destroyed much of Rome in A.D. 64, so to take the focus off himself he blamed the Roman Christians. Persecution erupted throughout the Roman Empire. Not only were Christians denied certain privileges in society, some were even publicly butchered, burned, or fed to animals. Social ostracism was widespread. When Paul wrote this letter, persecution was a growing threat to believers.

2:4 Both Peter and Paul said that God longs for all to be saved (see 2 Peter 3:9). This does not mean that all *will* be saved, because the Bible makes it clear that many reject him (Matthew 25:31–46; John 12:44–50; Hebrews 10:26–29). These verses indicate that the gospel has a universal scope; it is not limited to people of one race, one sex, or one national background. God loves the whole world and sent his Son to save it, and he is hurt by all who turn away from him.

2:2-6 We human beings are separated from God by sin, and only one person in the universe can stand between us and bring us together again—Jesus, who is both God and man. Jesus' sacrifice brought new life to all mankind. Have you let him bring you to the Father?

2:8 Besides being displeasing to God, it is difficult to pray when we have sinned or when we feel angry and resentful. That is why Jesus told us to interrupt worship, if necessary, to make peace with others (Matthew 5:23, 24). Our goal is to have a right relationship with God and also with others.

2:9-15 To understand these verses, we must understand the situation in which Paul and Timothy worked. In first-century Jewish culture, women were not allowed to study. When Paul said women should learn quietly and humbly, he was offering them new opportunities. Paul did not want the Ephesian women to teach because they didn't yet have enough knowledge or experience. The Ephesian church had a particular problem with false teachers.

Evidently the women were especially susceptible to their teaching (2 Timothy 3:1–9), because they did not yet have enough biblical knowledge to see through the false claims. In addition, some of the women were apparently flaunting their new-found Christian freedom by wearing inappropriate clothing (2:9, 10). Paul was telling Timothy not to put anyone (in this case, women) into positions of leadership who were not yet mature in the faith (see 5:22). The same principle applies to churches today (see note on 3:6).

2:9, 10 Some Christian women were apparently trying to gain respect by looking beautiful rather than becoming Christlike in their characters. Some may have thought they could win unbelieving husbands through their appearance (see Peter's counsel to such women in 1 Peter 3:1–6). It is not unscriptural for a woman to want to be attractive; the holy city itself is described as "a glorious sight, as a bride at her wedding" (Revelation 21:2). Beauty, however, begins inside a person. A gentle, modest, loving character gives a light to the face that cannot be duplicated by the best cosmetics and jewelry in the world. A carefully groomed and well-decorated exterior looks artificial and cold unless inner beauty is present.

2:12 Some interpret this passage to mean that women should never teach in the assembled church. However, other commentators say that Paul's words "I never let" can be more literally translated "I am not allowing." Paul did not believe women should never teach men. Paul's commended coworker, Priscilla, taught Apollos, the great preacher (Acts 18:24–26). In addition, Paul frequently mentions other women who held positions of responsibility in the church. Phoebe was a deaconess (see Romans 16:1 in other translations). Mary, Tryphaena, and Tryphosa were the Lord's workers (Romans 16:6, 12), as were Euodias and Syntyche (Philippians 4:2). Thus, here in 1 Timothy 2:12, Paul would have been prohibiting the Ephesian women from teaching, not all women (see note on 2:9–15).

As to women being silent in church meetings, the word *silence* here is often translated "be in quietness," expressing an attitude of being composed and not unruly. A different Greek word is used to mean "complete silence." In addition, Paul himself acknowledges that women publicly prayed and prophesied (1 Corinthians 11:5). Apparently, however, the women in the Ephesian church were abusing their newly acquired Christian freedom. Because these women were new converts and uneducated, they did not yet have the necessary experience or knowledge to teach those who already had extensive biblical education.

TIMOTHY

Painful lessons are usually doorways to new opportunities. Even the apostle Paul had much to learn. Shortly after his disappointing experience with John Mark, Paul recruited Timothy to be his assistant. Paul's intense personality may have been too much for John Mark to handle. It could easily have been the same for Timothy. But Paul seems to have learned a lesson in patience from his old friend Barnabas. As a result, Timothy became a "son" to Paul.

Timothy probably became a Christian after Paul's first missionary visit to Lystra (Acts 16:1–5). Timothy's mother and grandmother had already taught him a great deal from the Old Testament Scriptures. By the time Paul visted Lystra a second time, Timothy had become a respected disciple of Jesus in his hometown. He did not hesitate to join Paul and Silas on their journey. His willingness to be circumcised as an adult is clearly a mark of his commitment (Timothy's mixed Greek/Jewish background could have created problems on their missionary journeys, since many of their audiences would be made up of Jews who were concerned with the strict keeping of this tradition). The circumcision helped to avoid that potential problem.

Beyond the tensions of his mixed racial background, Timothy seemed to struggle with a naturally timid character. Unfortunately, many who share Timothy's character are quickly written off as too great a risk to deserve much responsibility. By God's grace, Paul saw great potential in Timothy. Paul demonstrated his confidence in Timothy by entrusting him with important responsibilities. Paul sent Timothy as his personal representative to Corinth during a particularly tense time (1 Corinthians 4:14–17). Although Timothy was apparently ineffective in that difficult mission, Paul did not give up on him. He continued to travel with Paul.

Our last pictures of Timothy come from the most personal letters in the New Testament: 1 and 2 Timothy. In them, the aging apostle Paul is near the end of his life, but his burning desire to continue his mission has not dimmed. Paul is writing to one of his closest friends: they have traveled, suffered, cried, and laughed together. Paul left Timothy in Ephesus to oversee the young church there (1 Timothy 1:3, 4). He writes to encourage Timothy and give him needed direction. These letters have provided comfort and help to countless other "Timothys" through the years. When you face a challenge which is beyond your abilities, read 1 and 2 Timothy, and remember that others have shared your experience.

Strengths and accomplishments:
- Became a believer after Paul's first missionary journey and joined him for his other two journeys
- Was a respected Christian in his hometown
- Was Paul's special representative on several occasions
- Received two personal letters from Paul
- Probably knew Paul better than any other person, becoming like a son to him

Weaknesses and mistakes:
- Struggled with a timid and reserved nature
- He allowed others to look down upon his youthfulness
- He was apparently unable to correct some of the problems in the church at Corinth when Paul sent him there

Lessons from his life:
- Youthfulness should not be an excuse for ineffectiveness
- Our inadequacies and inabilities should not keep us from being available to God

Vital statistics:
- Where: Lystra
- Occupation: Missionary-in-training
- Relatives: Mother: Eunice. Grandmother: Lois. Greek father.
- Contemporaries: Paul, Silas, Luke, Mark, Peter, Barnabas

Key verses:
"There is no one like Timothy for having a real interest in you; everyone else seems to be worrying about his own plans and not those of Jesus Christ. But you know Timothy. He has been just like a son to me in helping me preach the Good News" (Philippians 2:20–22).

Timothy's story is told in Acts, starting in chapter 16. He is also mentioned in Romans 16:21; 1 Corinthians 4:17; 16:10, 11; 2 Corinthians 1:1, 19; Philippians 1:1; 2:19–23; Colossians 1:1, 2; 1 Thessalonians 1:1–10; 2:3, 4; 3:2–6; 1 and 2 Timothy; Philemon 1:1; Hebrews 13:23.

church meetings. ¹³Why? Because God made Adam first, and afterwards he made Eve. ¹⁴And it was not Adam who was fooled by Satan, but Eve, and sin was the result. ¹⁵So God sent pain and suffering to women when their children are born, but he will save their souls if they trust in him, living quiet, good, and loving lives.

2:13
Gen 2:7,22
2:14,15
Gen 3:6,13,16

Standards for church leaders

3 It is a true saying that if a man wants to be a pastor he has a good ambition. ²For a pastor must be a good man whose life cannot be spoken against. He must have only one wife, and he must be hard working and thoughtful, orderly, and full of good deeds. He must enjoy having guests in his home, and must be a good Bible teacher. ³He must not be a drinker or quarrelsome, but he must be gentle and kind, and not be one who loves money. ⁴He must have a well-behaved family, with children who obey quickly and quietly. ⁵For if a man can't make his own little family behave, how can he help the whole church?

3:1
Acts 20:28
3:2
Tit 1:6,8
3:3
Tit 1:7
3:4
1 Tim 3:12

⁶The pastor must not be a new Christian, because he might be proud of being chosen so soon, and pride comes before a fall. (Satan's downfall is an example.) ⁷Also, he must be well spoken of by people outside the church—those who aren't Christians—so that Satan can't trap him with many accusations, and leave him without freedom to lead his flock.

3:7
2 Cor 8:21
2 Tim 2:26

⁸The deacons must be the same sort of good, steady men as the pastors. They must not be heavy drinkers and must not be greedy for money. ⁹They must be earnest, wholehearted followers of Christ who is the hidden Source of their faith. ¹⁰Before they are asked to be deacons they should be given other jobs in the church as a test of their character and ability, and if they do well, then they may be chosen as deacons.

3:8
Phil 1:1
3:9
1 Tim 1:19

¹¹Their wives must be thoughtful, not heavy drinkers, not gossipers, but faithful

3:1 *pastor,* more literally, "church leader," or "presiding elder."

2:13, 14 In previous letters Paul had talked about male/female roles in marriage (Ephesians 5:21–33; Colossians 3:18, 19). Here he talks about male/female roles within the church. Some scholars see these verses about Adam and Eve as an illustration of what was happening in the Ephesian church. Just as Eve had been deceived in the Garden of Eden, so the women in the church were being deceived by false teachers. And just as Adam was the first human created by God, so the men in the church in Ephesus should be the first to speak and teach, because they had had more experience in learning the things of God. This view, then, stresses that Paul's teaching here is not universal, but applies to churches with similar problems. Other scholars, however, contend that the roles Paul points out are God's design for his created order. He established these roles to maintain harmony in both the family and the church.

2:14 Paul was not excusing Adam for his part in the Fall (Genesis 3:6, 7, 17–19). On the contrary, in his letter to the Romans Paul placed the primary blame for mankind's sinful nature on Adam (Romans 5:12–21).

2:15 This verse is literally translated, "But women will be saved through childbirth." There are several interpretations: (1) Man sinned and was condemned to hard labor. Woman sinned and was condemned to pain in childbearing. Both men and women, however, can be saved through trusting Christ and obeying him. (2) Women who fulfill their God-given roles are demonstrating true commitment and obedience to Christ. One of the most important roles for a wife and mother is to care for her family. (3) The childbirth mentioned here refers to the birth of Jesus Christ. Women (and men) are saved spiritually because of the most important birth, that of Christ himself. (4) From the lessons learned through the trials of childbirth, women can develop qualities that teach them about love, trust, submission, and service.

3:1–13 It is good to want to be a spiritual leader, but the standards are high. Paul enumerates some of the qualifications

here. Do you hold a position of spiritual leadership, or would you like to be a leader some day? Check yourself against Paul's standard of excellence. Those with great responsibility must meet high expectations.

3:2 When Paul says elders (see textual note) should have only one wife, he is prohibiting both polygamy and promiscuity. This does not prohibit an unmarried man from becoming an elder or a widowed elder from remarrying.

3:4, 5 Christian workers and volunteers sometimes make the mistake of thinking their work is so important that they are justified in ignoring their families. Spiritual leadership, however, must begin at home. If a man is not willing to care for, discipline, and teach his children, he is not qualified to lead the church.

3:6 New believers should become secure and strong in the faith before taking a leadership role in the church. Too often, when the church is desperate for workers, they place new believers into positions of responsibility for which they are unqualified. New faith needs to pass the test of time in order to mature. New believers should have a place of service, but not be put into leadership positions until they are firmly grounded in the Christian way of life.

3:8–10 *Deacon* means "one who serves." This position was begun by the apostles in the Jerusalem church (Acts 6:1–6) to care for the physical needs of the congregation, especially the needs of the Greek-speaking widows. Deacons were leaders in the church and their qualifications resemble those of elders. In some churches today, the office of deacon has become a catch-all position in which new and young Christians are often asked to serve. That is not the New Testament pattern. Paul says men are to be tested with lesser responsibilities before being made deacons.

3:11 Some have translated *wives* as "women helpers" or "deaconesses." It is unclear whether this verse refers to wives of deacons or female leaders of the church (such as Phoebe, the deacon mentioned in Romans 16:1). In either case, Paul expects

3:12
1 Tim 3:2,4
3:13
Mt 25:21

3:15
Mt 16:16-18
Eph 2:21

3:16
Isa 7:14
Mt 4:11
Jn 1:14
Rom 1:3,4
Acts 1:9
1 Jn 4:2,3; 5:6

4:1
Jn 16:13
2 Thess 2:3
2 Pet 2:1
1 Jn 4:6

4:2
Eph 4:19

4:3
Prov 18:22
Col 2:16
Heb 13:4

4:4
1 Cor 10:26
Tit 1:15

4:6
2 Tim 3:14

4:7
1 Tim 1:4

4:8
Col 2:23

in everything they do. ¹²Deacons should have only one wife and they should have happy, obedient families. ¹³Those who do well as deacons will be well rewarded both by respect from others and also by developing their own confidence and bold trust in the Lord.

¹⁴I am writing these things to you now, even though I hope to be with you soon, ¹⁵so that if I don't come for awhile you will know what kind of men you should choose as officers for the church of the living God, which contains and holds high the truth of God.

¹⁶It is quite true that the way to live a godly life is not an easy matter. But the answer lies in Christ, who came to earth as a man, was proved spotless and pure in his Spirit, was served by angels, was preached among the nations, was accepted by men everywhere and was received up again to his glory in heaven.

3. Instructions for elders
Paul's warning about false teachers

4 But the Holy Spirit tells us clearly that in the last times some in the church will turn away from Christ and become eager followers of teachers with devil-inspired ideas. ²These teachers will tell lies with straight faces and do it so often that their consciences won't even bother them.

³They will say it is wrong to be married and wrong to eat meat, even though God gave these things to well-taught Christians to enjoy and be thankful for. ⁴For everything God made is good, and we may eat it gladly if we are thankful for it, ⁵and if we ask God to bless it, for it is made good by the Word of God and prayer.

⁶If you explain this to the others you will be doing your duty as a worthy pastor who is fed by faith and by the true teaching you have followed.

⁷Don't waste time arguing over foolish ideas and silly myths and legends. Spend your time and energy in the exercise of keeping spiritually fit. ⁸Bodily exercise is all right, but spiritual exercise is much more important and is a tonic for all you do. So exercise yourself spiritually and practice being a better Christian, because that will help you not only now in this life, but in the next life too. ⁹, ¹⁰This is the truth and everyone should accept it. We work hard and suffer much in order that people

---

the behavior of prominent women in the church to be just as responsible as that of prominent men.

3:14, 15 To be a church leader is a heavy responsibility because the church belongs to the living God. Church leaders are not to be elected because they are popular, nor should they be allowed to push their way to the top. Instead they should be chosen by the church because of their respect for truth, both in doctrine and in their personal lives.

3:15, 16 The lists of qualifications for church office show that living a godly life requires effort and self-discipline. All believers, even if they never plan to be church leaders, should strive to follow these guidelines because they are consistent with what God says is true and right. The strength to do so comes from Christ.

4:1 The "last times" began with Christ's resurrection and will continue until his return, when he will set up his Kingdom and judge all mankind.

4:1, 2 False teachers were and still are a threat to the church. Jesus and the apostles repeatedly warned against them (see, for example, Mark 13:21-23; Acts 20:28-31; 2 Thessalonians 2:1-12; 2 Peter 3:3-7). The danger Timothy faced in Ephesus seems to have come from certain people in the church who followed some Greek philosophers who held that the body is evil and that only the soul matters. They refused to believe that the God of creation was good, because his very contact with the physical world would soil him. Though these Greek-influenced church members honored Jesus, they could not believe he was truly human. Their teachings, if left unchecked, would greatly distort Christian truth.

It is not enough that a teacher appears to know what he is

talking about, is disciplined and moral, and says he is speaking for God. If his words contradict biblical teaching, his teaching is false. Paul was warning Timothy not only of this specific problem, but of any teaching that causes us to dilute or reject parts of our faith. Such false teaching can be very direct or extremely subtle.

4:1-5 Why did Paul say the false teachers were devil-inspired (4:1)? Satan deceives people by offering a clever imitation of the real thing. The false teachers were giving stringent rules and this made them look righteous. Their strict disciplines for the body, however, could not remove sin (see Colossians 2:20-23). We must look beyond a teacher's methods and disciplines to his teaching about Jesus Christ. His attitude toward Christ shows the source of his message.

4:4, 5 In opposition to the false teachers, Paul affirms that everything God made is good (see Genesis 1). We should ask his blessing on his created gifts that give us pleasure and we should thank him for them. This doesn't mean we should abuse what God has made (for example gluttony abuses God's gift of good food, lust abuses God's gift of love, and murder abuses God's gift of life). We should not abuse what God has made, but enjoy these gifts by using them to serve and honor God. Have you thanked God for the good things he has made? Are you using them in a way that is pleasing to you *and* to God?

4:7-10 Are you in shape physically and spiritually? In our society, much emphasis is placed on physical fitness, but Paul declared that spiritual health is even more important than physical health. We must develop our faith through using the abilities God has given us in the service of the church (see 4:14-16).

will believe it, for our hope is in the living God who died for all, and particularly for those who have accepted his salvation. ¹¹Teach these things and make sure everyone learns them well. ¹²Don't let anyone think little of you because you are young. Be their ideal; let them follow the way you teach and live; be a pattern for them in your love, your faith, and your clean thoughts. ¹³Until I get there, read and explain the Scriptures to the church; preach God's Word.

¹⁴Be sure to use the abilities God has given you through his prophets when the elders of the church laid their hands upon your head. ¹⁵Put these abilities to work; throw yourself into your tasks so that everyone may notice your improvement and progress. ¹⁶Keep a close watch on all you do and think. Stay true to what is right and God will bless you and use you to help others.

Caring for different groups in the church

5 Never speak sharply to an older man, but plead with him respectfully just as though he were your own father. Talk to the younger men as you would to much loved brothers. ²Treat the older women as mothers, and the girls as your sisters, thinking only pure thoughts about them.

³The church should take loving care of women whose husbands have died, if they don't have anyone else to help them. ⁴But if they have children or grandchildren, these are the ones who should take the responsibility, for kindness should begin at home, supporting needy parents. This is something that pleases God very much.

⁵The church should care for widows who are poor and alone in the world, if they are looking to God for his help and spending much time in prayer; ⁶but not if they are spending their time running around gossiping, seeking only pleasure and thus ruining their souls. ⁷This should be your church rule so that the Christians will know and do what is right.

⁸But anyone who won't care for his own relatives when they need help, especially those living in his own family, has no right to say he is a Christian. Such a person is worse than the heathen.

4:10
1 Tim 2:4; 3:15

4:11
1 Tim 5:7

4:12
1 Cor 16:11
Tit 2:7

4:13
1 Tim 3:14

4:14
Acts 6:6
1 Tim 1:8
2 Tim 1:6

5:1
Lev 19:32
Tit 2:2,6

5:4
Mt 15:4
Eph 6:2
1 Tim 2:3

5:5
Lk 2:37
1 Pet 3:5

5:6
Jas 5:5

4:12, 13 Timothy was a young leader. It would be easy for older Christians to look down on him because of his youth. He had to earn the respect of his elders by setting an example in his teaching and living, of love, faith, and purity. Regardless of your age, God can use you. Whether you are young or old, don't think of your age as a handicap. Live so others can see Christ in you.

4:14, 15 As a young leader in a church with a lot of problems, Timothy may have felt intimidated. The elders and prophets encouraged him and charged him to use his spiritual abilities responsibly. Highly skilled and talented athletes will lose their abilities if their muscles aren't toned by constant use, so we will lose our spiritual gifts if we don't put them to work. Our talents are enhanced by exercise, but failing to use them causes them to waste away from lack of practice and nourishment. What gifts and abilities has God given you? Use them regularly in serving God and others (see Romans 12:1–8; 2 Timothy 1:6–8).

5:2 Men in the ministry can avoid improper attitudes toward women by treating them as sisters, not as possessions or objects. If men see women as fellow members in God's family, they will protect them and help them grow spiritually.

5:3 Because there were no pensions, no social security, no life insurance, and few honorable jobs for women, widows were usually unable to support themselves. If a widow had no children or other family members to support her, she was doomed to poverty. From the beginning the church took care of its widows, who in turn gave valuable service to the church.

5:3ff Paul wanted Christian families to be as self-supporting as possible. He insisted that children and grandchildren take care of the widows in their families (5:4); he suggested that younger

widows remarry and start new families (5:14); and he ordered the church not to support lazy members who refused to work (2 Thessalonians 3:10). Nevertheless, when necessary, the believers pooled their resources (Acts 2:44–47); they gave generously to help disaster-ridden churches (1 Corinthians 16:1- 4); and they took care of a large number of widows (Acts 6:1–6). The church has always had limited resources, and it has always had to balance financial responsibility with generosity. It only makes sense for members to work as hard as they can and to be as independent as possible so they can adequately care for themselves and for less fortunate members. When church members are both responsible and generous, everyone's needs can be met.

5:4 The responsibility for caring for the helpless naturally falls first on their families, the people whose lives are closely linked with theirs. But families cannot always provide all the necessary care. The church should support those who have no families, and it should also help the others—whether elderly, young, handicapped, ill, or poverty stricken—with their emotional and spiritual needs. Often families who are caring for their own helpless members have heavy burdens. They may need extra money, a listening ear, a helping hand, or a word of encouragement. Interestingly, those who are helped often turn around and help others so that the church turns into a circle of caring.

5:8 Almost everyone has relatives, family of some kind. Family relationships are so important in God's eyes, Paul says, that one who neglects his family responsibilities should not call himself a Christian. Are you doing your part to meet the needs of those included in your family circle?

9A widow who wants to become one of the special church workers should be at least sixty years old and have been married only once. 10She must be well thought of by everyone because of the good she has done. Has she brought up her children well? Has she been kind to strangers as well as to other Christians? Has she helped those who are sick and hurt? Is she always ready to show kindness?

11The younger widows should not become members of this special group because after awhile they are likely to disregard their vow to Christ and marry again. 12And so they will stand condemned because they broke their first promise. 13Besides, they are likely to be lazy and spend their time gossiping around from house to house, getting into other people's business. 14So I think it is better for these younger widows to marry again and have children, and take care of their own homes; then no one will be able to say anything against them. 15For I am afraid that some of them have already turned away from the church and been led astray by Satan.

16Let me remind you again that a widow's relatives must take care of her, and not leave this to the church to do. Then the church can spend its money for the care of widows who are all alone and have nowhere else to turn.

17Pastors who do their work well should be paid well and should be highly appreciated, especially those who work hard at both preaching and teaching. 18For the Scriptures say, "Never tie up the mouth of an ox when it is treading out the grain—let him eat as he goes along!" And in another place, "Those who work deserve their pay!"

19Don't listen to complaints against the pastor unless there are two or three witnesses to accuse him. 20If he has really sinned, then he should be rebuked in front of the whole church so that no one else will follow his example.

21I solemnly command you in the presence of God and the Lord Jesus Christ and of the holy angels to do this whether the pastor is a special friend of yours or not. All must be treated exactly the same. 22Never be in a hurry about choosing a pastor; you may overlook his sins and it will look as if you approve of them. Be sure that you yourself stay away from all sin. 23(By the way, this doesn't mean you should completely give up drinking wine. You ought to take a little sometimes as medicine for your stomach because you are sick so often.)

24Remember that some men, even pastors, lead sinful lives and everyone knows it. In such situations you can do something about it. But in other cases only the judgment day will reveal the terrible truth. 25In the same way, everyone knows how much good some pastors do, but sometimes their good deeds aren't known until long afterward.

5:9 *one of the special church workers,* literally, "enrolled as a widow."

Cross references (left margin):

5:10
Gen 18:3,4
Acts 9:36

5:12
Heb 6:4-6

5:13
2 Thess 3:11
Tit 1:11

5:14
1 Cor 7:9
1 Tim 3:15
Tit 2:5

5:15
1 Tim 1:20

5:16
Ruth 2:18

5:17
Rom 12:8
Gal 6:6
1 Thess 5:12

5:18
Deut 25:4
Lk 10:7

5:19
Mt 18:16

5:20
Deut 13:11
2 Cor 7:11
Eph 5:11

5:21
1 Tim 6:13

5:22
1 Tim 4:14

5:23
1 Tim 3:8

5:24
Rev 14:13

5:9–16 Apparently older widows took a vow by which they committed themselves to work for the church in exchange for financial support. Three out of four women today eventually are widowed, and most of the older women in our churches have lost their husbands. Does your church provide an avenue of service for these women? Could you help match their gifts and abilities with your church's needs?

5:17, 18 Faithful, diligent church leaders should be supported and appreciated. Too often they are targets for criticism because the congregation has unrealistic expectations. How do you treat your church leaders? Do you enjoy finding fault, or do you show your appreciation? Do they receive enough financial support to allow them to live without worry and provide for the needs of their families? Jesus and Paul emphasized the importance of supporting ministers who lead and teach us (see Galatians 6:6 and the notes on Luke 10:7 and 1 Corinthians 9:4–10).

5:17, 18 Preaching and teaching are closely related. Preaching is proclaiming the Word of God and confronting listeners with the truth of Scripture. Teaching is explaining the truth in Scripture, helping learners understand difficult passages, and helping them apply God's Word to daily life.

5:19, 20 Church leaders are not exempt from sin, faults, and mistakes. But they are often criticized for the wrong reasons—minor imperfections, failure to meet someone's expectations, personality clashes. Thus Paul said that complaints should not even be heard unless two or three witnesses will confirm them. Sometimes church leaders should be confronted about their behavior, and sometimes they should be rebuked. But all rebuking must be done fairly, lovingly, and for the purpose of restoration.

5:22 It is a serious responsibility to choose church leaders. They must have strong faith and live upright lives, having the qualities described in 1 Timothy 3:1–7 and Titus 1:5–9. Not everyone who wants to be a church leader is eligible. Be certain of an applicant's qualifications before asking him to lead you spiritually.

6 Christian slaves should work hard for their owners and respect them; never let it be said that Christ's people are poor workers. Don't let the name of God or his teaching be laughed at because of this.

6:1
Tit 2:9

²If their owner is a Christian, that is no excuse for slowing down; rather they should work all the harder because a brother in the faith is being helped by their efforts.

6:2
1 Tim 4:11

Teach these truths, Timothy, and encourage all to obey them.

Avoid worthless arguments and the longing to be rich

³Some may deny these things, but they are the sound, wholesome teachings of the Lord Jesus Christ and are the foundation for a godly life. ⁴Anyone who says anything different is both proud and stupid. He is quibbling over the meaning of Christ's words and stirring up arguments ending in jealousy and anger, which only lead to name-calling, accusations, and evil suspicions. ⁵These arguers—their minds warped by sin—don't know how to tell the truth; to them the Good News is just a means of making money. Keep away from them.

6:3
1 Tim 1:3,10
Tit 1:1

6:4
1 Cor 8:2
1 Tim 1:4
2 Tim 2:14

6:5
Rom 16:17
2 Tim 3:8
Tit 1:11

⁶Do you want to be truly rich? You already are if you are happy and good. ⁷After all, we didn't bring any money with us when we came into the world, and we can't carry away a single penny when we die. ⁸So we should be well satisfied without money if we have enough food and clothing. ⁹But people who long to be rich soon begin to do all kinds of wrong things to get money, things that hurt them and make them evil-minded and finally send them to hell itself. ¹⁰For the love of money is the first step toward all kinds of sin. Some people have even turned away from God because of their love for it, and as a result have pierced themselves with many sorrows.

6:6
Ps 37:16
Phil 4:11
1 Tim 4:8

6:7
Job 1:21

6:8
Prov 30:8
Heb 13:5

6:9
Mt 13:22

Paul's final instructions

¹¹Oh, Timothy, you are God's man. Run from all these evil things and work instead at what is right and good, learning to trust him and love others, and to be patient and gentle. ¹²Fight on for God. Hold tightly to the eternal life which God has given you, and which you have confessed with such a ringing confession before many witnesses.

6:11
2 Tim 2:22

6:12
1 Tim 1:19
2 Tim 2:2-4; 4:7

6:13
Jn 18:37

¹³I command you before God who gives life to all, and before Christ Jesus who gave a fearless testimony before Pontius Pilate, ¹⁴that you fulfill all he has told you to do, so that no one can find fault with you from now until our Lord Jesus Christ returns. ¹⁵For in due season Christ will be revealed from heaven by the blessed and only Almighty God, the King of kings and Lord of lords, ¹⁶who alone can never die, who lives in light so terrible that no human being can approach him. No mere man has ever seen him, nor ever will. Unto him be honor and everlasting power and dominion forever and ever. Amen.

6:14
1 Thess 3:13

6:15
1 Tim 1:17
Rev 17:14; 19:16

6:16
Ex 33:20
2 Chron 5:14
Ps 104:2
Jn 1:18; 5:26
1 Tim 1:17

¹⁷Tell those who are rich not to be proud and not to trust in their money, which

6:17
Lk 12:20

6:1, 2 In Paul's culture there was a great social and legal gulf separating masters and slaves. But as Christians, masters and slaves became spiritual equals, brothers or sisters in the faith (Galatians 3:28). Paul did not speak to the evils in the institution of slavery, but he gave guidelines for Christian slaves and Christian masters. His counsel for the master/slave relationship can be applied to the employer/employee relationship today. Employees should work hard, showing respect for their employers. In turn, employers should be fair (Ephesians 6:5–9; Colossians 3:22–25). Our work should reflect our faithfulness and love for Christ.

6:3–5 Division within the church often begins with quibblings over minute points of theology. This leads to all sorts of problems. A person's understanding of the finer points of theology should not become the basis for lording it over others or making money. Instead, theology should always unify the church. Stay away from those who just want to argue.

6:6–10 Despite almost overwhelming evidence to the contrary, most people still believe that money brings happiness. Rich people

craving greater riches can be caught in an endless cycle which only ends in ruin and destruction. How can you keep away from the love of money? Paul gives us some principles: (1) realize that one day riches will all be gone (6:7, 17); (2) be content with what you have (6:8); (3) monitor what you are willing to do to get more money (6:9, 10); (4) love people more than money (6:11); (5) love God's work more than money (6:11); (6) freely share what you have with others (6:18). (See Proverbs 30:7–9.)

6:13 Jesus' trial before Pilate is recorded in the Gospels: Matthew 27:11–26; Mark 15:1–15; Luke 23:1–25; John 18:28—19:16.

6:17–19 Ephesus was a wealthy city and the Ephesian church probably had many wealthy members. Paul advised Timothy to deal with that potential problem by teaching that the possession of riches carries great responsibility. Those who have money must be generous, not arrogant because they have a lot to give. They must be careful not to put their trust in money instead of in the living God for their security. Even if we don't have material wealth, we can be rich in good works toward others. No matter how poor

will soon be gone, but their pride and trust should be in the living God who always richly gives us all we need for our enjoyment. 18Tell them to use their money to do good. They should be rich in good works and should give happily to those in need, always being ready to share with others whatever God has given them. 19By doing this they will be storing up real treasure for themselves in heaven—it is the only safe investment for eternity! And they will be living a fruitful Christian life down here as well.

20Oh, Timothy, don't fail to do these things that God entrusted to you. Keep out of foolish arguments with those who boast of their "knowledge" and thus prove their lack of it. 21Some of these people have missed the most important thing in life—they don't know God. May God's mercy be upon you.

Sincerely, Paul

6:19
Mt 6:20
1 Tim 6:12

6:20
2 Tim 2:16

6:21
1 Tim 1:19
2 Tim 2:18

---

we are, we have something to share with someone.

6:21 The book of 1 Timothy provides guiding principles for local churches, including rules for public worship and qualifications for elders (pastors), deacons, and special church workers (widows). Paul tells the church leaders to correct unsound doctrine and to deal lovingly and fairly with all people in the church. The church is not organized for the sake of organization, but so Christ can be honored and glorified in its midst. While studying these guidelines, don't lose sight of the most important things in the life of the church—knowing God, working together in loving harmony, and taking God's Good News to the world.

VITAL STATISTICS

PURPOSE:
To give final instructions and encouragement to Timothy, an elder of the church at Ephesus

AUTHOR:
Paul

TO WHOM WRITTEN:
Timothy

DATE WRITTEN:
About A.D. 66 or 67 from prison in Rome. After a year or two of freedom, Paul was arrested again and executed under Emperor Nero.

SETTING:
Paul is virtually alone in prison; only Luke is with him. He writes this letter to pass the torch to the new generation of church leaders. He also asks for visits from his friends, for his books, and especially the parchments—possibly parts of the Old Testament, the Gospels, and other biblical manuscripts.

KEY VERSE:
"Work hard so God can say to you, 'Well done.' Be a good workman, one who does not need to be ashamed when God examines your work. Know what his Word says and means" (2:15).

KEY PEOPLE:
Paul, Timothy, Luke, Mark, and others

KEY PLACES:
Rome, Ephesus

SPECIAL FEATURES:
Because this is Paul's last letter, it reveals his heart and his priorities—sound doctrine, steadfast faith, confident endurance, and enduring love.

"FAMOUS last words" is more than a cliché. When notable men and women of influence are about to die, many wait to hear their final words of insight and wisdom; and those words are repeated worldwide. This is also true with a dying loved one. Gathered at his or her side, the family strains to hear every whispered syllable of blessing, encouragement, and advice, knowing that this will be the final message.

One of the most knowledgeable, influential, and beloved men of history was the apostle Paul. And we have his famous last words.

Paul was facing death. He was not dying of a disease in a sterile hospital with loved ones gathered near. He was very much alive, but his condition was terminal. Convicted as a follower of Jesus of Nazareth, he lay in a cold Roman prison, cut off from the world, with just a visitor or two and his writing materials. Paul knew that soon he would be executed (4:6), and so he wrote his final thoughts to his "son" Timothy, passing to him the torch of leadership, reminding him of what was truly important, and encouraging him in the faith. Imagine how Timothy must have read and reread every word—this was the last message from his beloved mentor, Christ's great missionary apostle, Paul. Because of the situation and the recipient, this is the most intimate and moving of all Paul's letters, and his last.

Paul's introduction is tender, and the love he has for Timothy seeps from every phrase (1:1–5). He then reminds Timothy of the qualities necessary for a faithful minister of Jesus Christ (1:6—2:13). Timothy should remember his call and use his gifts with boldness (1:6–12), hold tightly to the truth (1:13–18), prepare others to follow him in the ministry (2:1, 2), be disciplined and ready to suffer hardship like a soldier, an athlete, and a farmer (2:3–7), and keep his eyes and mind focused on Christ (2:8–13). Paul challenges Timothy to hold to sound doctrine, reject error and foolish discussions, know the Word (2:14–19), and keep his life pure (2:20–26).

Next, Paul warns Timothy of the opposition he and other believers would face in the last days from self-centered people who use the church for their own gain and who teach new and false doctrines (3:1–9). He tells Timothy to be prepared for them by remembering his example (3:10, 11), understanding the real source of the opposition (3:12, 13), and finding strength and power in the Word of God (3:14–17). Then Paul gives Timothy a stirring charge—to preach the Word (4:1–4) and to fulfill his ministry until the end (4:5–8).

Paul concludes with personal requests and items of information. In these final words, he reveals his loneliness and his strong love for his brothers and sisters in Christ (4:9–22).

There has never been another person like Paul, the missionary apostle. He was a man of deep faith, undying love, constant hope, tenacious conviction, and profound insight. And he was inspired by the Holy Spirit to give us God's message. As you read 2 Timothy, know that you are reading the last words of this great man of God—last words to Timothy and to all who would claim to follow Christ.

THE BLUEPRINT

1. Foundations of Christian service (1:1—2:26)
2. Difficult times for Christian service (3:1—4:22)

Paul gives helpful advice to Timothy to remain solidly grounded in Christian service and endure suffering during the difficult days to come. It is easy for us to serve Christ for the wrong reasons: because it is exciting, rewarding, or personally enriching. Without a proper foundation, however, we will find it easy to quit during difficult times. All believers need a strong foundation for their service, because Christian service does not get easier as we grow older, and it will become no easier as we near the last days.

MEGATHEMES

THEME	EXPLANATION	IMPORTANCE
Boldness	In the face of opposition and persecution, Timothy was to carry out his ministry unashamed and unafraid. Paul urged him to utilize the gifts of preaching and teaching that the Holy Spirit had given him.	The Holy Spirit helps us to be wise and strong. God honors our confident testimony even when we suffer. To get over our fear of what people might say or do, we must take our eyes off of people and look only to God.
Faithfulness	Christ was faithful to all of us in dying for our sin. Paul was a faithful minister even when he was in prison. Paul urged Timothy not only to maintain sound doctrine, but also loyalty, diligence, and endurance.	We can count on opposition, suffering, and hardship as we serve Christ. But this shows that our faithfulness is having an effect on others. As we trust Christ, he counts us worthy to suffer and will give us the strength we need to be steadfast.
Preaching and Teaching	Paul and Timothy were active in preaching and teaching the Good News about Jesus Christ. Paul encouraged Timothy not only to carry the torch of truth but also to train others, passing on to them sound doctrine and enthusiasm for Christ's mission.	We must prepare people to transmit God's Word to others so that they might pass it on. Does your church carefully train others to teach?
Error	In the final days before Christ returns, there will be false teachers, spiritual dropouts, and heresy. The remedy for error is to have a solid program for teaching Christians.	Because of the deception and false teaching, we must be disciplined and ready to reject error by knowing God's Word. Know the Word of God as your sure defense against error and confusion.

1. Foundations of Christian service

1 *From:* Paul, Jesus Christ's missionary, sent out by God to tell men and women everywhere about the eternal life he has promised them through faith in Jesus Christ.

1:1
Jn 5:24
Tit 1:1,2
1 Jn 5:10,11,20

²*To:* Timothy, my dear son. May God the Father and Christ Jesus our Lord shower you with his kindness, mercy and peace.

1:2
1 Tim 1:2
Tit 1:4

Paul encourages Timothy to be faithful

³How I thank God for you, Timothy. I pray for you every day, and many times during the long nights I beg my God to bless you richly. He is my fathers' God, and mine, and my only purpose in life is to please him.

1:3
Acts 23:1; 24:14
Rom 1:9

⁴How I long to see you again. How happy I would be, for I remember your tears as we left each other.

1:4
Acts 20:37
2 Tim 4:9

⁵I know how much you trust the Lord, just as your mother Eunice and your grandmother Lois do; and I feel sure you are still trusting him as much as ever.

1:5
Acts 16:1

⁶This being so, I want to remind you to stir into flame the strength and boldness that is in you, that entered into you when I laid my hands upon your head and blessed you. ⁷For the Holy Spirit, God's gift, does not want you to be afraid of people, but to be wise and strong, and to love them and enjoy being with them.

1:6
Acts 8:18
1 Tim 4:14
1:7
Rom 8:15

⁸If you will stir up this inner power, you will never be afraid to tell others about our Lord, or to let them know that I am your friend even though I am here in jail for Christ's sake. You will be ready to suffer with me for the Lord, for he will give you strength in suffering.

1:8
Rom 1:16
Eph 3:1
2 Tim 2:3
1:9
Rom 8:28-30
11:29
Eph 1:4; 2:9
1 Thess 4:7
Tit 3:5
1:10
1 Cor 15:54

⁹It is he who saved us and chose us for his holy work, not because we deserved it but because that was his plan long before the world began—to show his love and kindness to us through Christ. ¹⁰And now he has made all of this plain to us by the

1:6 *stir into flame the strength and boldness,* implied. Literally, "stir up the gift of God."

1:1 This is a somber letter. Paul was imprisoned for the last time, and he knew he would soon die. Unlike his first imprisonment in Rome, when he was in a house (Acts 28:16, 23, 30) and continued to preach and teach, this time he was probably confined to a cold dungeon, awaiting his death (4:6–8). Emperor Nero had begun a major persecution in A.D. 64 as part of his plan to pass the blame for the great fire of Rome from himself to the Christians. This persecution spread across the empire and included social ostracism, public torture, and murder. As Paul waited to die, he wrote a letter to his dear friend Timothy. These are the last words we have from Paul, written in approximately A.D. 66–67.

1:1 For more information on the great missionary, Paul, see his Profile in Acts 9.

1:2 Paul's second letter to Timothy was written about two to four years after his first letter. Timothy had been Paul's traveling companion on the second and third missionary journeys, and Paul had left him in Ephesus to help the church there. For more information on Timothy, see his Profile in 1 Timothy.

1:3 Paul consistently prayed for Timothy, his friend, his fellow traveler, and a strong leader in the Christian church. Although the two men were separated from each other, their prayers provided a source of mutual encouragement. We too should pray consistently for others, especially for those with whom we do God's work.

1:4 We don't know when Paul and Timothy last parted, but it was probably when Paul was arrested and taken to Rome for his second imprisonment. The tears they shed at parting reveal the depth of their relationship.

1:5 Timothy's mother and grandmother, Lois and Eunice, were early Christian converts, possibly through Paul's ministry in their home city, Lystra (Acts 16:1). They communicated their strong Christian faith to Timothy, even though his father was probably not a believer. Don't hide your light at home: our families are fertile fields for planting gospel seeds. Let your parents, children, spouse, brothers, and sisters know of your faith in Jesus, and be

sure they see Christ's love, helpfulness, and joy in you.

1:6 At the time of his ordination, Timothy received special gifts of the Spirit to enable him to serve the church (see 1 Timothy 4:14). In telling Timothy to stir those gifts into flame, Paul was encouraging him to persevere. Timothy did not need new revelations or new gifts; he needed the courage and self-discipline to hang onto the truth and use the gifts he had already received (see 1:13, 14). If he would step out boldly in faith and proclaim the gospel once again, the Holy Spirit would go with him and give him power.

1:6, 7 Timothy was experiencing great opposition to his message and to himself as a leader. His youth, his association with Paul, and his leadership had come under fire. Paul urged him to be bold. When we allow people to intimidate us, we neutralize our effectiveness for God. The power of the Holy Spirit can help us overcome our fear of what some might say or do to us so we can continue to do God's work.

1:7 Paul mentions three characteristics of the effective Christian leader: wisdom, strength, and love. These are available to us because the Holy Spirit lives in us. See Galatians 5:22, 23 for a list of characteristics resulting from the Holy Spirit's control.

1:8 In this time of mounting persecution, Timothy may have been afraid to continue preaching Christ. His fears were based on fact. As Paul warned him, suffering would come: Timothy, like Paul, would be jailed for preaching the gospel (Hebrews 13:23). But Paul promised Timothy that God would give him strength and that he would be ready when it was his turn to suffer. Even when persecution is not a threat, it can be difficult to share our faith in Christ. Fortunately we, like Paul and Timothy, can call on the Holy Spirit's power to give us courage.

1:9, 10 This is a brief synopsis of the gospel. God loves us, chose us, and sent Christ to die for us. We can have eternal life through faith in him because he broke the power of death by his resurrection. We do not deserve to be saved, but God offers us salvation anyway. All we have to do is believe and accept his offer.

coming of our Savior Jesus Christ, who broke the power of death and showed us the way of everlasting life through trusting him. [11]And God has chosen me to be his missionary, to preach to the Gentiles and teach them.

[12]That is why I am suffering here in jail and I am certainly not ashamed of it, for I know the one in whom I trust, and I am sure that he is able to safely guard all that I have given him until the day of his return.

[13]Hold tightly to the pattern of truth I taught you, especially concerning the faith and love Christ Jesus offers you. [14]Guard well the splendid, God-given ability you received as a gift from the Holy Spirit who lives within you.

[15]As you know, all the Christians who came here from Asia have deserted me; even Phygellus and Hermogenes are gone. [16]May the Lord bless Onesiphorus and all his family, because he visited me and encouraged me often. His visits revived me like a breath of fresh air, and he was never ashamed of my being in jail. [17]In fact, when he came to Rome he searched everywhere trying to find me, and finally did. [18]May the Lord give him a special blessing at the day of Christ's return. And you know better than I can tell you how much he helped me at Ephesus.

Good soldiers are not afraid to suffer

2 Oh, Timothy, my son, be strong with the strength Christ Jesus gives you. [2]For you must teach others those things you and many others have heard me speak about. Teach these great truths to trustworthy men who will, in turn, pass them on to others.

[3]Take your share of suffering as a good soldier of Jesus Christ, just as I do, [4]and as Christ's soldier do not let yourself become tied up in worldly affairs, for then you cannot satisfy the one who has enlisted you in his army. [5]Follow the Lord's rules for doing his work, just as an athlete either follows the rules or is disqualified and wins no prize. [6]Work hard, like a farmer who gets paid well if he raises a large crop. [7]Think over these three illustrations, and may the Lord help you to understand how they apply to you.

[8]Don't ever forget the wonderful fact that Jesus Christ was a Man, born into King David's family; and that he was God, as shown by the fact that he rose again from

1:13 *and love Christ Jesus offers you,* literally, "and love that is in Christ Jesus."

Marginal cross-references (left column):

1:11
1 Tim 2:7

1:12
1 Tim 6:20
1 Pet 4:19

1:13
Rom 6:17
1 Tim 1:14
2 Tim 3:14
Heb 10:23

1:14
Rom 8:9,11,16
Gal 4:6

1:15
2 Tim 4:10

1:16
2 Tim 4:19
Philem 7

1:18
Heb 6:10

2:1
Eph 3:16; 6:10
Col 1:11

2:2
1 Cor 15:3-7
2 Tim 2:13

2:3
1 Cor 9:7

2:4
2 Pet 2:20

2:5
1 Cor 9:25

2:6
1 Cor 9:7,10

2:8
Acts 2:24
13:33, 34
Rom 1:3,4

1:12 Paul was in prison, but that did not stop his ministry. He carried it on through others like Timothy. Paul had lost all his material possessions, but he would never lose his faith. He trusted God to use him regardless of his circumstances. If your situation looks bleak, give your concerns to Christ. He will guard your faith and find a way to use you even in the midst of suffering.

1:12 The phrase "safely guard all that I have given him" has three main interpretations: (1) Paul knew God would guard the souls of those converted through his preaching; (2) he trusted God to guard his own soul until the Second Coming; or (3) he was confident that, though he was in prison and facing death, God would carry out the gospel ministry through others such as Timothy. Paul may have expressed his confidence to encourage Timothy, who was discouraged by the problems in Ephesus and fearful of persecution. Even in prison, Paul knew God was still in control.

1:13, 14 Timothy was in a time of transition. He had been Paul's bright young helper; soon he would be on his own as leader of a difficult, but critically important, church. Although his responsibilities were changing, Timothy was not without help. He had everything he needed to face the future, if he would hold tightly onto it. When you are facing difficult transitions, it is good to follow Paul's advice to Timothy and look back at your experience. Who is the foundation of your faith? What gifts has the Holy Spirit given you? How can you build on the foundation that has already been laid, using the gifts you have already been given?

2:2 If the church consistently followed this advice, it would

expand geometrically as well-taught believers would teach others and commission them, in turn, to teach still others. Disciples need to be equipped to pass their faith on; our work is not done until new believers are telling others the Good News they have learned (see Ephesians 4:12, 13).

2:3-7 As Timothy preached and taught, he would face suffering, but he should be willing to take it. Christian leaders are not the only ones to suffer. Soldiers, athletes, and farmers all must discipline themselves and be willing to sacrifice to achieve the results they want. Like soldiers, we have to give up worldly security and endure rigorous discipline. Like athletes, we must train hard and follow the rules. Like farmers, we must work extremely hard. We keep going in spite of suffering because of the thought of victory, the vision of winning, and the hope of harvest. All our suffering is made worthwhile by our goal of glorifying God, winning people to Christ, and one day living eternally with him.

2:8 False teachers were a problem in Ephesus (see Acts 20:29, 30; 1 Timothy 1:3-11). At the heart of false teaching is an incorrect view of Christ. In Timothy's day it was popular to assert that he is divine but not human—God but not man. Nowadays we often hear that he is human but not divine—man but not God. Either view destroys the Good News that Jesus Christ has taken our sins on himself and has reconciled God and man. In this verse, Paul firmly states that Jesus is fully God and fully man. This is the only biblical view. For more on this important concept see the note on Philippians 2:5-7.

the dead. 9It is because I have preached these great truths that I am in trouble here and have been put in jail like a criminal. But the Word of God is not chained, even though I am. 10I am more than willing to suffer if that will bring salvation and eternal glory in Christ Jesus to those God has chosen.

11I am comforted by this truth, that when we suffer and die for Christ it only means that we will begin living with him in heaven. 12And if we think that our present service for him is hard, just remember that some day we are going to sit with him and rule with him. But if we give up when we suffer, and turn against Christ, then he must turn against us. 13Even when we are too weak to have any faith left, he remains faithful to us and will help us, for he cannot disown us who are part of himself, and he will always carry out his promises to us.

Good workers are not ashamed of their work

14Remind your people of these great facts, and command them in the name of the Lord not to argue over unimportant things. Such arguments are confusing and useless, and even harmful. 15Work hard so God can say to you, "Well done." Be a good workman, one who does not need to be ashamed when God examines your work. Know what his Word says and means. 16Steer clear of foolish discussions which lead people into the sin of anger with each other. 17Things will be said that will burn and hurt for a long time to come. Hymenaeus and Philetus, in their love of argument, are men like that. 18They have left the path of truth, preaching the lie that the resurrection of the dead has already occurred; and they have weakened the faith of some who believe them.

19But God's truth stands firm like a great rock, and nothing can shake it. It is a foundation stone with these words written on it: "The Lord knows those who are

2:9 Phil 1:7

2:10 Col 1:24

2:11 Rom 6:5,8 1 Thess 5:10

2:12 Mt 10:33 Rom 8:17 1 Pet 4:13

2:13 Num 23:19 1 Cor 1:9

2:14 1 Tim 1:4; 6:4 Tit 3:9

2:17 1 Tim 1:20

2:18 1 Cor 15:12-20

2:19 Num 16:5 Nah 1:7 Jn 10:14

2:9 The truth about Jesus was no more popular in Paul's day than in ours, but that won't stop it from reaching receptive hearts. When Paul said Jesus was God, he angered the Jews who had condemned Jesus for blasphemy, but many Jews became Christians (1 Corinthians 1:24). He angered the Romans who worshiped the emperor as God, but even some in Caesar's palace turned to Jesus (Philippians 4:22). When Paul said Jesus was man, he angered the Greeks who thought divinity was soiled if it had any contact with humanity; still many Greeks accepted the faith (Acts 11:20, 21). The truth that Jesus is one person with two united natures has never been easy to accept, but it *is* being accepted by people every day. Are you one of those who has accepted this life-changing message?

2:10 We are free to choose between life and death, and yet God has chosen us. This is a mystery our finite minds cannot easily grasp. But even if we do not completely understand it, we can still choose Jesus and be grateful that he has chosen us.

2:11-13 God is faithful to his children, and although we may suffer great hardships here, he promises that someday we will live eternally with him. What will this involve? It means believers will live in Christ's Kingdom, and that we will share in the administration of that Kingdom. This was Paul's comfort as he went through suffering and death, and it can be ours, too. Are you facing hardships? Don't turn away from God—he promises you a wonderful future with him. For more information about living eternally with God, see Matthew 16:24-27; 19:28, 29; Luke 22:28-30; Romans 5:17; 6:8; 8:10, 11, 17; 1 Corinthians 15:42-58; Colossians 3:3, 4; 1 Thessalonians 4:13-18; Revelation 3:21; 21:1—22:21.

2:12, 13 Jesus will stay by our side even when we have endured so much that we seem to have no faith left. We may be faithless at times, but Jesus remains faithful to his promise to be with us always, "even to the end of the world" (see Matthew 28:20; Romans 8:38, 39).

2:15 Life on earth is not a script which we meaninglessly act out. It is a time of deciding whether we will live for God or not and then *living out* what we have decided. Because God will examine what kinds of workers we have been for him, we should build our lives on his Word and build his Word into our lives, because it alone tells us how to live for him and serve him. Believers who ignore the Bible will certainly be ashamed at the judgment. Consistent and diligent study of God's Word is vital, or else we will be lulled into neglecting God and our true purpose for living.

2:16 In important areas, we must carefully work through our disagreements. But when we bicker long hours over words and theories that are not central to the Christian faith and life, we only provoke anger and hurt feelings. Even if such "foolish discussions" lead to resolution, they gain little ground for the Kingdom. Learning and discussing are not bad in themselves unless they keep believers constantly focusing on false doctrine or unhelpful trivialities. This, in turn, keeps us from our work and service to God.

2:17 Hymenaeus is also mentioned in 1 Timothy 1:20. Paul had "handed him over to Satan" because of his false teaching.

2:18 The false teachers were denying the resurrection of the body. They believed that when a person became a Christian he was spiritually reborn, and that was the only resurrection there would ever be. To them, resurrection was symbolic and spiritual, not physical. Paul clearly taught, however, that believers will be resurrected after they die, and their bodies as well as their souls will live eternally with Christ (1 Corinthians 15:35ff; 2 Corinthians 5:1-10; 1 Thessalonians 4:15-18). We cannot shape the doctrines of Scripture to match our opinions. If we do, we are putting ourselves above God. We must instead shape our opinions into beliefs that match God's Word.

2:19 False teachers are still spouting lies. Some distort the truth; some dilute it; and some simply delete it by saying it no longer applies. But no matter how many follow the liars, God's truth never changes, is never shaken, and will never fade. When we know and believe God's truth, he will never forsake us.

really his," and "A person who calls himself a Christian should not be doing things that are wrong."

2:20
Rom 9:21

²⁰In a wealthy home there are dishes made of gold and silver as well as some made from wood and clay. The expensive dishes are used for guests, and the cheap ones are used in the kitchen or to put garbage in. ²¹If you stay away from sin you will be like one of these dishes made of purest gold—the very best in the house—so that Christ himself can use you for his highest purposes.

2:21
2 Tim 3:17

2:22
1 Tim 6:11

²²Run from anything that gives you the evil thoughts that young men have, but stay close to anything that makes you want to do right. Have faith and love, and enjoy the companionship of those who love the Lord and have pure hearts.

2:23
1 Tim 6:4
Tit 3:9

²³Again I say, don't get involved in foolish arguments which only upset people and make them angry. ²⁴God's people must not be quarrelsome; they must be gentle, patient teachers of those who are wrong. ²⁵Be humble when you are trying to teach those who are mixed up concerning the truth. For if you talk meekly and courteously to them they are more likely, with God's help, to turn away from their wrong ideas and believe what is true. ²⁶Then they will come to their senses and escape from Satan's trap of slavery to sin which he uses to catch them whenever he likes, and then they can begin doing the will of God.

2:24
1 Tim 3:2,3
Tit 1:7-9

2:25
1 Tim 2:4
Tit 3:2
1 Pet 3:15

2:26
Eph 4:27; 6:11
1 Tim 3:7

2. Difficult times for Christian service
The last days characterized by sinfulness

3:1
1 Tim 4:1
Jude 18

3 You may as well know this too, Timothy, that in the last days it is going to be very difficult to be a Christian. ²For people will love only themselves and their money; they will be proud and boastful, sneering at God, disobedient to their parents, ungrateful to them, and thoroughly bad. ³They will be hardheaded and never give in to others; they will be constant liars and troublemakers and will think nothing of immorality. They will be rough and cruel, and sneer at those who try to be good. ⁴They will betray their friends; they will be hotheaded, puffed up with pride, and prefer good times to worshiping God. ⁵They will go to church, yes, but they won't really believe anything they hear. Don't be taken in by people like that.

3:2
Lk 16:14
Rom 1:30
1 Tim 1:9

3:3
Rom 1:31

3:5
1 Tim 5:8

3:6
Jude 4

⁶They are the kind who craftily sneak into other people's homes and make friendships with silly, sin-burdened women and teach them their new doctrines. ⁷Women of that kind are forever following new teachers, but they never understand the truth. ⁸And these teachers fight truth just as Jannes and Jambres fought against

3:8
Ex 7:11

2:22 Running away is sometimes considered cowardly. But wise people realize that removing oneself physically from temptation is often prudent. Timothy, a young man, was warned to run from anything that produced evil thoughts (1 Timothy 6:11). Perhaps you experience a recurring temptation that is difficult to resist. Remove yourself physically from the situation. Knowing when to run is as important in spiritual battle as knowing when and how to fight.

2:23-26 As a teacher, Timothy helped those who were confused about the truth. Paul's advice to him, and to all who teach God's truth, is to be humble, patiently and courteously explaining the truth. Good teaching never promotes quarrels or foolish arguments. Whether you are teaching Sunday school, leading a Bible study, or preaching in church, remember to listen to people's questions and treat them respectfully. If you do this, they will be willing to hear what you have to say.

3:1 Paul's reference to the *last days* reveals his sense of urgency. The last days began after Jesus' resurrection, when the Holy Spirit came upon the believers at Pentecost, and will continue until his Second Coming.

3:1ff In many parts of the world today it does not seem especially difficult to be a Christian. No one is jailed for reading the Bible or executed for preaching Christ. But when we read Paul's descriptive list of behavior in the last days, we recognize it as a description of our society—even, unfortunately, of many Christians. There is a comfortableness about superficial Christianity that

should cause us to be uncomfortable. Check your life against this list. Don't give in to society's pressures. Stand up against its evil ways by living as God would have his people live.

3:5 "They will go to church" is a paraphrase of "Having a form of godliness." The appearance of godliness includes going to church, knowing Christian doctrine, and following a community's Christian traditions. Such practices can make a person look good, but if the inner attitudes of belief, love, and worship are lacking, the outer appearance doesn't mean a thing. Paul warns us not to be taken in by people who only look like Christians. They can be hard to distinguish from true Christians at first glance, but their lives give them away. The characteristics described in 3:2-4 are unmistakable.

3:6, 7 Because of their cultural background, women in the Ephesian church had had no formal religious training. They enjoyed their new freedom to study Christian truths, but their eagerness to learn made them a target for false teachers. Paul warned Timothy to watch out for men who would take advantage of these women. New believers need to grow in their knowledge of the Word, because ignorance can make them vulnerable to deception.

3:8, 9 Jannes and Jambres, according to tradition, were two of the magicians who counterfeited Moses' miracles before Pharaoh (Exodus 7:11, 12). Moses exposed and defeated them (Exodus 8:18, 19), just as God would overthrow the false teachers plaguing the Ephesian church.

Moses. They have dirty minds, warped and twisted, and have turned against the Christian faith.

9But they won't get away with all this forever. Some day their deceit will be well known to everyone, as was the sin of Jannes and Jambres.

3:9
Ex 8:18; 9:11

Paul's charge to Timothy

10But you know from watching me that I am not that kind of person. You know what I believe and the way I live and what I want. You know my faith in Christ and how I have suffered. You know my love for you, and my patience. 11You know how many troubles I have had as a result of my preaching the Good News. You know about all that was done to me while I was visiting in Antioch, Iconium and Lystra, but the Lord delivered me. 12Yes, and those who decide to please Christ Jesus by living godly lives will suffer at the hands of those who hate him. 13In fact, evil men and false teachers will become worse and worse, deceiving many, they themselves having been deceived by Satan.

14But you must keep on believing the things you have been taught. You know they are true for you know that you can trust those of us who have taught you. 15You know how, when you were a small child, you were taught the holy Scriptures; and it is these that make you wise to accept God's salvation by trusting in Christ Jesus. 16The whole Bible was given to us by inspiration from God and is useful to teach us what is true and to make us realize what is wrong in our lives; it straightens us out and helps us do what is right. 17It is God's way of making us well prepared at every point, fully equipped to do good to everyone.

3:10
1 Tim 6:11

3:11
Acts 13:14,45, 50; 14:19
2 Cor 1:5
11:23-27
12:10

3:12
Jn 15:20
Acts 14:22
1 Thess 3:3

3:14
2 Tim 1:13; 2:2

3:15
Jn 5:47; 20:30, 31
Rom 10:17

3:16
Rom 15:4
2 Pet 1:20,21

3:17
1 Tim 6:11
2 Tim 2:21

4 And so I solemnly urge you before God and before Christ Jesus—who will some day judge the living and the dead when he appears to set up his Kingdom— 2to preach the Word of God urgently at all times, whenever you get the chance, in season and out, when it is convenient and when it is not. Correct and

4:1
Acts 10:42

4:2
1 Tim 5:10
Tit 1:13

3:16 The whole Bible, literally, "Every Scripture."

3:9 Sin has consequences, and no one will get away with it forever. Live each day as if your actions will one day be known to all. Now is the time to change anything you would want to hide then.

3:11 In Lystra, Timothy's hometown, Paul was stoned and left for dead (Acts 14:19); and this was only one incident among many. In 2 Corinthians 11:23–33 he summarizes his lifetime of suffering for the sake of the gospel. Paul mentions his suffering here to contrast his experience with that of the false teachers.

3:14 Besieged by false teachers and the inevitable pressures of a growing ministry, Timothy could easily have abandoned his faith or modified his doctrine. Once again Paul counsels him to look to his past, to hold to the basic teachings about Jesus that are eternally true. Like Timothy, we are surrounded by false teachings, and most of us are very busy. But we must not allow our society to distort or crowd out God's eternal truth. Spend time every day thinking about the foundations of your Christian faith, the great truths on which you build your life.

3:15 Timothy was one of the first second-generation Christians: he became a Christian not because an evangelist preached a powerful sermon, but because his mother and grandmother taught him the holy Scriptures when he was a small child. The evangelist's work is important, but the parent's work is just as important. At home and in church, we should realize that teaching small children is both an opportunity and a responsibility. Jesus wanted little children to come to him (Matthew 19:13–15). Like Lois and Eunice, do your part in leading them to Christ.

3:16 The Bible is not a collection of stories, fables, myths, or merely human ideas about God. It is not just a human book. Through the Holy Spirit God revealed his person and plan to godly men, who wrote down God's message for his people (2 Peter 1:20, 21). This process is known as inspiration. The writers wrote from their own personal, historical, and cultural contexts. But even

though they used their own minds, talents, language, and style, they wrote what God wanted them to write. Scripture is completely trustworthy because God was in control of its writing, and its words are entirely authoritative for our faith and lives.

3:16 The whole Bible is God's inspired Word. Because it is inspired and trustworthy, we should read it and apply it to our lives. The Bible is our standard for testing everything else that claims to be true. It is our safeguard against false teaching and our source of guidance for how we should live. It is our only source of knowledge about how we can be saved. God wants to show you what is true and equip you to live for him. How much time do you spend in God's Word? Read it regularly to discover God's truth and become confident in your life and faith. Develop a plan for reading the whole Bible, not just the same familiar passages.

3:17 In our zeal for the truth of Scripture, we must never forget its purpose—to equip us to do good to others. We do not study God's Word simply to increase our own knowledge or to prepare us to win arguments. We do not even study it primarily to learn how to save our own souls (most people are saved before they begin intensively studying the Bible). We study Scripture so that we will know how to do Christ's work in the world. Our knowledge of God's Word is not useful unless we use it to do good to others.

4:1, 2 It was important for Timothy to preach the gospel so that the Christian faith could spread throughout the world. We believe in Christ today because people like Timothy were faithful to their mission. It is still vitally important for the church to preach the gospel. Half the people who have ever lived are alive today, and most of them do not know Jesus. He is coming soon, and he wants to find a faithful church waiting for him. It may be inconvenient to take a stand for Christ or to tell others about his love, but preaching the Word of God is the most important responsibility the church has been given. Be prepared, courageous, and sensitive to God-given opportunities to tell the Good News.

4:3
2 Tim 3:1

4:4
2 Thess 2:11
1 Tim 1:4

4:5
Col 4:17
2 Tim 1:8

4:6
Phil 1:23

4:7
1 Cor 9:24-27
Phil 3:12-14
1 Tim 6:12

4:8
1 Cor 9:25
Phil 3:11
Col 1:5
2 Tim 1:12
Rev 2:10

rebuke your people when they need it, encourage them to do right, and all the time be feeding them patiently with God's Word.

³For there is going to come a time when people won't listen to the truth, but will go around looking for teachers who will tell them just what they want to hear. ⁴They won't listen to what the Bible says but will blithely follow their own misguided ideas.

⁵Stand steady, and don't be afraid of suffering for the Lord. Bring others to Christ. Leave nothing undone that you ought to do.

⁶I say this because I won't be around to help you very much longer. My time has almost run out. Very soon now I will be on my way to heaven. ⁷I have fought long and hard for my Lord, and through it all I have kept true to him. And now the time has come for me to stop fighting and rest. ⁸In heaven a crown is waiting for me which the Lord, the righteous Judge, will give me on that great day of his return. And not just to me, but to all those whose lives show that they are eagerly looking forward to his coming back again.

Paul's final words

4:9
2 Tim 1:4

4:10
Col 4:14
Philem 24

4:11
Col 4:10,14

4:12
Acts 20:4
Eph 6:21

4:16
Acts 7:60
1 Cor 13:5

4:17
Ps 22:21
Acts 9:15
2 Tim 3:11
Tit 1:3

4:18
Ps 121:7
Rom 11:36

⁹Please come as soon as you can, ¹⁰for Demas has left me. He loved the good things of this life and went to Thessalonica. Crescens has gone to Galatia, Titus to Dalmatia. ¹¹Only Luke is with me. Bring Mark with you when you come, for I need him. ¹²(Tychicus is gone too, as I sent him to Ephesus.) ¹³When you come, be sure to bring the coat I left at Troas with Brother Carpus, and also the books, but especially the parchments.

¹⁴Alexander the coppersmith has done me much harm. The Lord will punish him, ¹⁵but be careful of him, for he fought against everything we said.

¹⁶The first time I was brought before the judge no one was here to help me. Everyone had run away. I hope that they will not be blamed for it. ¹⁷But the Lord stood with me and gave me the opportunity to boldly preach a whole sermon for all the world to hear. And he saved me from being thrown to the lions. ¹⁸Yes, and the Lord will always deliver me from all evil and will bring me into his heavenly Kingdom. To God be the glory forever and ever. Amen.

4:17 *he saved me from being thrown to the lions,* literally, "I was delivered out of the mouth of the lion."

4:3, 4 It is difficult to accept correction, to be told we have to change. But no matter how much the truth hurts, we must be willing to listen to it so we can more fully obey God.

4:5-8 As he neared the end of his life, Paul could confidently say he had been faithful to his call. Thus he faced death calmly; he knew he would be rewarded at Christ's Second Coming. Is your life preparing you for death? Do you share Paul's confident expectation of meeting Christ? The Good News is that the heavenly reward is not just for giants of the faith, like Paul, but for all who "are eagerly looking forward" to Jesus' Second Coming. Paul gave these words to encourage Timothy, and us, that no matter how difficult the fight seems—keep fighting. We will discover when we are with Jesus Christ that it was all worth it.

4:8 In Roman athletic games, a laurel wreath was given to the winners. A symbol of triumph and honor, it was the most coveted prize in ancient Rome. This is probably what Paul was thinking of when he spoke of the crown. See 2 Corinthians 5:10 and the note on Matthew 19:27 for more on the rewards awaiting us for our faith and deeds.

4:10 Demas had been one of Paul's coworkers (Colossians 4:14; Philemon 1:24), but he deserted Paul because he "loved the good things of this life," or more literally, "loved this present world." There are two ways to love the world. God loves the world as he created it and as it could be if it were rescued from evil. That is why he sacrificed his Son to save it (John 3:16). Others, like Demas, love the world as it is, sin and all. Do you love the world as

it could be if justice were done, the hungry were fed, and people loved one another? Or do you love what the world has to offer—wealth, power, pleasure—even if gaining it means hurting people and neglecting the work God has given you to do?

4:11, 12 Mentioning Demas reminded Paul of other, more faithful coworkers. Only Luke was with him, and Paul was feeling lonely. Tychicus, one of his most trusted companions (Acts 20:4; Ephesians 6:21; Colossians 4:7; Titus 3:12), had already left for Ephesus. He missed his young helpers Timothy and Mark. Mark, also called John and John Mark, had left Paul on his first missionary journey, and this had greatly angered Paul (Acts 13:13; 15:36-41). But Mark later proved himself a worthy helper, and Paul recognized him as a good friend and trusted Christian leader (Colossians 4:10; Philemon 1:24).

4:13 Paul's arrest was probably so sudden that he was not allowed to return home to gather his personal belongings. As a prisoner in a damp and chilly dungeon, Paul asked Timothy to bring him a coat. Paul wanted his parchments. These may have included parts of the Old Testament, the Gospels, copies of his own letters, or other important documents.

4:17 With his mentor in prison and his church in turmoil, Timothy was not feeling at all brave. Paul may have been subtly telling him, "The Lord has called you to preach, and he will give you the courage to do so." God always gives us the strength to do what he has commanded. This strength may not be evident, however, until we step out in faith and actually begin doing the task.

¹⁹Please say "hello" for me to Priscilla and Aquila and those living at the home of Onesiphorus. ²⁰Erastus stayed at Corinth, and I left Trophimus sick at Miletus. ²¹Do try to be here before winter. Eubulus sends you greetings, and so do Pudens, Linus, Claudia, and all the others. ²²May the Lord Jesus Christ be with your spirit.

4:19
Acts 18:2
2 Tim 1:16
4:20
Acts 19:22; 20:4
4:22
Gal 6:18

Farewell, Paul

4:19, 20 Priscilla and Aquila were fellow Christian leaders with whom Paul had lived and worked (Acts 18:2, 3). Onesiphorus visited and encouraged Paul in jail (2 Timothy 1:16–18). Erastus was one of Paul's trusted companions (Acts 19:22), as was Trophimus (Acts 20:4; 21:29).

4:22 As Paul reached the end of his life, he could look back and know he had been faithful to God's call. Now it was time to pass the torch to the next generation, preparing leaders to take his

place so that many would continue to hear the life-changing message of Jesus Christ. Timothy was Paul's living legacy, a product of Paul's faithful teaching, discipleship, and example. Because of Paul's work with many believers, including Timothy, the world is full of believers today who are also carrying on the work. What legacy will you leave behind? Whom are you training to carry on your work? It is our responsibility to keep the Word of God alive for the next generation.

TITUS

GREAT speakers and teachers gather a following, and soon a church is flourishing. Lives are being changed and led into the kingdom. But when this catalyst leaves or dies, with him or her goes the drive and the heart of the organization.

People flocked to hear Paul's teaching. Articulate, motivated, and filled with the Holy Spirit, he faithfully proclaimed the Good News throughout the Roman Empire—lives were changed and churches planted. But Paul knew that the church must be built on Christ, not on any other person.

He knew that eventually he would not be there to build, encourage, discipline, and teach, so he trained young pastors to assume leadership in the church after he was gone. Paul urged them to center their lives and preaching on the Word of God (2 Timothy 3:16, 17) and to train others to carry on the ministry (2 Timothy 2:2).

Titus was a Greek believer, probably converted to Christ through Paul's ministry. Taught and nurtured by Paul, he stood before the leaders of the church in Jerusalem as a living example of what Christ was doing among the Gentiles (Galatians 2:1-3). He was one of Paul's trusted traveling companions and closest friends. Later he became Paul's special ambassador (2 Corinthians 7:5-16) and eventually the overseer of the churches on Crete (Titus 1:5). Slowly and carefully, Paul developed Titus into a mature Christian leader. The letter to Titus is another step in this discipleship process. As with Timothy, Paul tells Titus how to organize and lead the churches.

Paul begins with a longer than usual greeting and introduction, outlining the leadership progression—Paul's ministry (1:1-3), Titus' responsibilities (1:4, 5), and those leaders whom Titus would appoint and train (1:5). Paul then lists pastoral qualifications (1:6-9), and contrasts them with the false leaders and teachers (1:10-16).

Next, Paul emphasizes the importance of good works in the life of the Christian, telling Titus how to relate to the various age groups in the church (2:2-6). He urges Titus to be a good example of a mature believer (2:7, 8) and to teach with courage and conviction (2:9-15). He then discusses the general responsibilities of Christians in society—Titus should remind the people of these (3:1-8), and he should avoid divisive arguments (3:9-11). Paul concludes with a few matters of itinerary and personal greetings (3:12-15).

As you read this pastoral epistle, you will gain insight into the organization and life of the early church and principles for structuring contemporary churches. But you should also see how to be a responsible Christian leader. Read the Epistle to Titus and determine, like Paul, to train men and women to lead and teach others.

VITAL STATISTICS

PURPOSE:
To advise Titus in his responsibility of supervising the churches on the island of Crete

AUTHOR:
Paul

TO WHOM WRITTEN:
Titus, a Greek convert, who had become Paul's special representative to the island of Crete

DATE WRITTEN:
About A.D. 64, around the same time 1 Timothy was written; probably from Macedonia when Paul traveled in between his Roman imprisonments

SETTING:
Paul sent Titus to organize and oversee the churches on Crete. This letter tells him how to do this job.

KEY VERSE:
"I left you there on the island of Crete so that you could do whatever was needed to help strengthen each of its churches, and I asked you to appoint pastors [elders] in every city who would follow the instructions I gave you" (1:5).

KEY PEOPLE:
Paul, Titus

KEY PLACES:
Crete, Nicopolis

SPECIAL FEATURES:
Titus is very similar to 1 Timothy with its instructions to pastors (elders).

THE BLUEPRINT

1. Leadership in the church (1:1–16)
2. Right living in the church (2:1–15)
3. Right living in society (3:1–15)

Paul calls for church order and right living in an island known for laziness, gluttony, lying, and evil. The Christians are to be disciplined as individuals and orderly as a church. We need to obey this message in our day when discipline is not respected or rewarded by our society. Although others may not regard our efforts, we must live upright lives, obey the government, and control our speech. We should live together peacefully in the church and be living examples of our faith in society.

MEGATHEMES

THEME	EXPLANATION	IMPORTANCE
A *Good Life*	The good news of salvation is that we can't be saved by living a good life; we are saved only by faith in Jesus Christ. But the gospel transforms people's lives, so that they eventually perform good works. Our service won't save us, but we are saved to serve.	A good life is a witness to the gospel's power. As Christians, we must have commitment and discipline to serve. Are you putting your faith in action by serving others?
Character	Titus' responsibility at Crete was to appoint pastors (elders) on Crete to maintain proper organization and discipline, so Paul listed the qualities needed for the eldership. Their conduct in their homes revealed their fitness for service in the church.	It's not enough to be educated or have a following to be Christ's kind of leader. You must have self-control, spiritual and moral fitness, and Christian character. Who you are is just as important as what you can do.
Church Relationships	Church teaching was to relate to various groups. Older Christians were to teach and to be examples to younger men and women. Every age and group has a lesson to learn and a role to play.	Right living and right relationship go along with right doctrine. Treat relationships with other believers as an outgrowth of your faith.
Citizenship	Christians must be good citizens in society, not just in church. Believers must obey the government and work honestly.	How you fulfill your civic duties is a witness to the watching world. Your community life should reflect Christ's love as much as your church life does.

1. Leadership in the church

1 *From:* Paul, the slave of God and the messenger of Jesus Christ. I have been sent to bring faith to those God has chosen and to teach them to know God's truth—the kind of truth that changes lives—so that they can have eternal life, which God promised them before the world began—and he cannot lie. ³And now in his own good time he has revealed this Good News and permits me to tell it to everyone. By command of God our Savior I have been trusted to do this work for him.

⁴*To:* Titus, who is truly my son in the affairs of the Lord.

1:1 1 Tim 2:4; 6:3 2 Tim 1:9; 2:25

1:2 1 Tim 1:9 Tit 3:7

1:3 Acts 9:15 1 Tim 1:1,11 2 Tim 4:17 Tit 2:10

1:1 Paul wrote this letter between his first and second imprisonments in Rome (before he wrote 2 Timothy) to guide Titus in working with the churches on the island of Crete. Paul had visited Crete with Titus, and he left him there to minister (1:5). Crete was a center for training Roman soldiers. Thus, there was a large pagan influence on this small island. Therefore, the church in Crete needed strong Christian leadership.

1:1 In one short phrase, Paul gives us insight into his reason for living. He calls himself a slave (or servant) of God—that is, he was committed to obeying God. This obedience led him to spend his life telling others about Christ. How would you describe your purpose in life? To what are you devoted? For more information on Paul, see his Profile in Acts 9.

1:1, 2 The foundation of our faith is trust in God's character. Because he *is* truth, he is the *source* of all truth and cannot lie. The eternal life he has promised will be ours because he keeps his promises. Build your faith on the foundation of a trustworthy God who will not lie.

1:3 God is called "our Savior" (1:3), as is Jesus (1:4). Jesus did the work of salvation by dying for our sins and therefore is our Savior. God planned the work of salvation and forgives our sins; thus, he is our Savior as well. Both the Father and the Son are involved in saving us.

1:4 Titus, a Greek, was one of Paul's most trusted and dependable coworkers. Paul sent Titus to Corinth on several

May God the Father and Christ Jesus our Savior give you his blessings and his peace.

Qualifications for church leaders

1:5
Acts 14:23

⁵I left you there on the island of Crete so that you could do whatever was needed to help strengthen each of its churches, and I asked you to appoint pastors in every city who would follow the instructions I gave you.

1:6
1 Tim 3:2-4

⁶The men you choose must be well thought of for their good lives; they must have only one wife and their children must love the Lord and not have a reputation for being wild or disobedient to their parents.

1:7
1 Cor 4:1,2
1 Tim 3:2,3

⁷These pastors must be men of blameless lives because they are God's ministers. They must not be proud or impatient; they must not be drunkards or fighters or greedy for money.

1:8
1 Tim 3:2,3

⁸They must enjoy having guests in their homes and must love all that is good. They must be sensible men, and fair. They must be clean minded and level headed.

1:9
2 Thess 2:15

⁹Their belief in the truth which they have been taught must be strong and steadfast, so that they will be able to teach it to others and show those who disagree with them where they are wrong.

1:5 *pastors,* more literally, "elders." Also in vs 7.

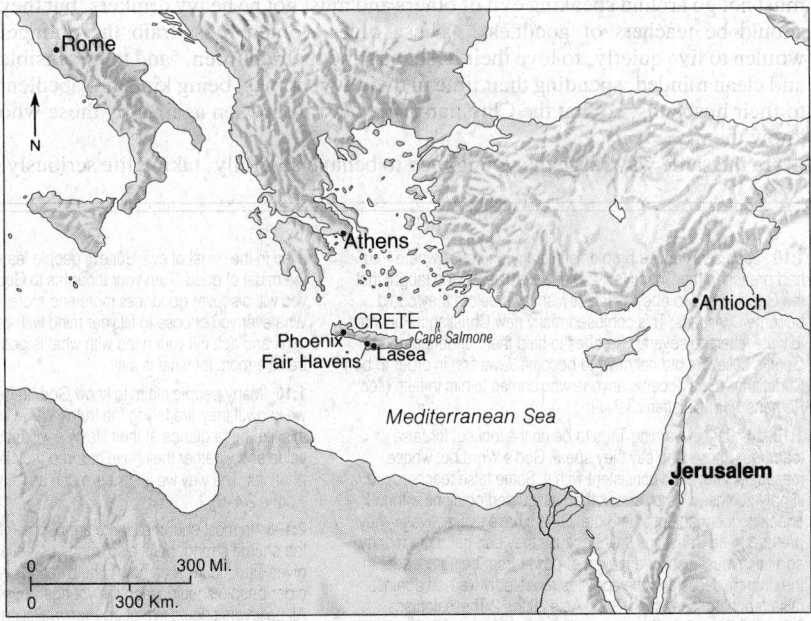

TITUS GOES TO CRETE
Tradition says that after Paul was released from prison in Rome, he and Titus traveled together for a while. They stopped in Crete, and when it was time for Paul to go, he left Titus behind to help the churches there.

special missions to help the church in its troubles (2 Corinthians 7, 8). Paul and Titus also traveled together to Jerusalem (Galatians 2:3) and Crete (1:5). Paul left Titus there to lead the new churches springing up on the island. Titus is last mentioned by Paul in 2 Timothy 4:10, his last recorded letter. Titus had leadership ability, so Paul gave him leadership responsibility, urging him to use his abilities well.

1:5 Crete, a small island in the Mediterranean Sea, had a large population of Jews. The churches there were probably founded by Cretan Jews who had been in Jerusalem at Pentecost (Acts 2:11) more than 30 years before Paul wrote this letter.

1:5 It was important for each church to have spiritual leaders, and Paul had appointed elders in various churches (Acts 14:23). These

men led the churches by helping believers mature spiritually and equipping them to live for Jesus Christ despite the opposition.

1:5-9 The Greek word for "pastors" here is "elders" (see textual note). Paul briefly describes some qualifications an elder should have. He gave Timothy a similar set of instructions for the church in Ephesus (see 1 Timothy 3:1–7; 5:22). Notice that most of the qualifications involve the elder's character, not his knowledge or skill. A person's lifestyle and relationships provide a window into his or her character. Consider these qualifications as you evaluate a person for a position of leadership. While it is important to have an elder or pastor who can effectively preach God's Word, it is even more important to have one who can live out God's Word and be an example for others to follow.

Warning against false teachers

[10]For there are many who refuse to obey; this is especially true among those who say that all Christians must obey the Jewish laws. But this is foolish talk; it blinds people to the truth, [11]and it must be stopped. Already whole families have been turned away from the grace of God. Such teachers are only after your money. [12]One of their own men, a prophet from Crete, has said about them, "These men of Crete are all liars; they are like lazy animals, living only to satisfy their stomachs." [13]And this is true. So speak to the Christians there as sternly as necessary to make them strong in the faith, [14]and to stop them from listening to Jewish folk tales and the demands of men who have turned their backs on the truth.

[15]A person who is pure of heart sees goodness and purity in everything; but a person whose own heart is evil and untrusting finds evil in everything, for his dirty mind and rebellious heart color all he sees and hears. [16]Such persons claim they know God, but from seeing the way they act, one knows they don't. They are rotten and disobedient, worthless so far as doing anything good is concerned.

1:10
Acts 15:1
2 Cor 11:13
1 Tim 1:6

1:11
1 Tim 5:13; 6:5

1:13
2 Cor 13:10
1 Tim 5:20

1:14
Col 2:22
1 Tim 1:4
2 Tim 4:4

1:15
Lk 11:39
Rom 14:14

1:16
Ezek 33:31
1 Tim 5:8
2 Tim 3:8
1 Jn 2:4

2. Right living in the church

2 But as for you, speak up for the right living that goes along with true Christianity. [2]Teach the older men to be serious and unruffled; they must be sensible, knowing and believing the truth and doing everything with love and patience.

[3]Teach the older women to be quiet and respectful in everything they do. They must not go around speaking evil of others and must not be heavy drinkers, but they should be teachers of goodness. [4]These older women must train the younger women to live quietly, to love their husbands and their children, [5]and to be sensible and clean minded, spending their time in their own homes, being kind and obedient to their husbands, so that the Christian faith can't be spoken against by those who know them.

[6]In the same way, urge the young men to behave carefully, taking life seriously.

2:1
1 Tim 6:3
Tit 1:9

2:3
1 Pet 3:3,4

2:5
Eph 5:22
Col 3:18
1 Tim 5:14

1:10 *Judaizers* caused problems in many churches where Paul had preached the Good News. These were Jews who taught that the Gentiles had to obey all the Jewish laws before they could become Christians. This confused many new Christians. Paul had to write letters to several churches to help them understand that Gentile believers did not have to become Jews first in order to be Christians—God accepts anyone who comes to him in faith (see Romans 1:17; Galatians 3:2–7).

1:10–14 Paul is warning Titus to be on the lookout for false teachers—those who say they speak God's Word but whose message is not at all consistent with it. Some false teachers are simply confused—they speak their misguided opinions without checking them against the Bible. Others have evil motives—they pretend to be Christians only because they can get more money, additional business, or a feeling of power from being a leader in the church. Jesus and the apostles repeatedly warned against false teachers (see Mark 13:22; Acts 20:29; 2 Thessalonians 2:3–12; 2 Peter 3:3–7), because their teachings attack the foundations of truth and integrity upon which the Christian faith is built. You can recognize false teachers because they will (1) focus more attention on themselves than on Christ; (2) ask you to do something that will compromise or dilute your faith; (3) de-emphasize the divine nature of Christ or the inspiration of the Bible; or (4) urge the church to make decisions based more on human judgment than on prayer and biblical guidelines.

1:12 Paul is quoting a line from a poem by Epimenides, a poet and philosopher who had lived in Crete 600 years earlier. "To play the Cretan" had become a phrase meaning to be a cheat and a liar. Paul used a familiar phrase to make a point.

1:15 Some people see good all around them, while others see nothing but evil. What is the difference? Our souls become filters through which we perceive goodness or evil. The pure of heart (those who have Christ in control of their lives) learn to see good

even in the midst of evil. But evil people learn to see evil even in the midst of good. Turn your thoughts to God and his Word, and you will discover goodness more and more, even in this evil world. Whatever you choose to fill your mind with will affect the way you think and act. Fill your mind with what is good, and then there will be little room for what is evil.

1:16 Many people claim to know God, to be born again. How can we know if they are telling the truth? We will not know for certain in this life, but a glance at their lifestyle will quickly tell us what they value and whether they have ordered their lives around Kingdom priorities. The way we live says much about what we believe (see 1 John 2:4–6).

2:1–8 In most churches there are people of all ages. This makes the church strong, but it also brings potential for problems. So Paul gives Titus counsel on how to help various types of people. The older people should teach the younger, by words *and* by example. All believers should live good lives, resisting the pagan influences of their culture as well as false teaching.

2:3–5 Women who were new Christians were to learn how to have harmony in the home by watching older women who had been Christians for some time. We have the same need today. Younger wives and mothers should learn to live in a Christian manner—loving their husbands and caring for their children—through observing exemplary women of God. If you are of an age or position where people look up to you, can you be confident that your example is motivating younger believers to live in a way that honors God?

2:6 This advice given to young men was very important. In ancient Greek society, the role of the husband/father was not viewed as a nurturing role, but merely a functional one. Many young men today have been raised in families where the father neglected his responsibilities to his wife and children. The few husbands and fathers who are good examples of Christian living in

2:7
1 Tim 4:12
1 Pet 5:3

2:8
1 Pet 2:12

2:9
Eph 6:5

2:10
Tit 1:3

2:11
Jn 1:9
1 Tim 2:4
2 Tim 1:10

2:13
John 1:1; 20:28
Rom 9:5
2 Pet 1:1
1 Jn 5:20

2:14
Deut 7:6; 14:2
Eph 2:10
1 Pet 2:9
1 Jn 1:7

2:15
1 Tim 4:12

7And here you yourself must be an example to them of good deeds of every kind. Let everything you do reflect your love of the truth and the fact that you are in dead earnest about it. 8Your conversation should be so sensible and logical that anyone who wants to argue will be ashamed of himself because there won't be anything to criticize in anything you say!

9Urge slaves to obey their masters and to try their best to satisfy them. They must not talk back, 10nor steal, but must show themselves to be entirely trustworthy. In this way they will make people want to believe in our Savior and God.

11For the free gift of eternal salvation is now being offered to everyone; 12and along with this gift comes the realization that God wants us to turn from godless living and sinful pleasures and to live good, God-fearing lives day after day, 13looking forward to that wonderful time we've been expecting, when his glory shall be seen—the glory of our great God and Savior Jesus Christ. 14He died under God's judgment against our sins, so that he could rescue us from constant falling into sin and make us his very own people, with cleansed hearts and real enthusiasm for doing kind things for others. 15You must teach these things and encourage your people to do them, correcting them when necessary as one who has every right to do so. Don't let anyone think that what you say is not important.

3. Right living in society
Obey the government

3:1
Rom 13:1

3:2
Eph 4:31
2 Tim 2:25

3:3
1 Cor 6:9-11

3:4
Rom 2:4
Tit 2:10,11

3:5
Rom 3:20; 8:16
Gal 2:16; 4:6
Eph 2:9

3:6
Joel 2:28
Rom 5:5

3:7
Rom 8:17

3:8
Tit 3:14

3 Remind your people to obey the government and its officers, and always to be obedient and ready for any honest work. 2They must not speak evil of anyone, nor quarrel, but be gentle and truly courteous to all.

3Once we, too, were foolish and disobedient; we were misled by others and became slaves to many evil pleasures and wicked desires. Our lives were full of resentment and envy. We hated others and they hated us.

4But when the time came for the kindness and love of God our Savior to appear, 5then he saved us—not because we were good enough to be saved, but because of his kindness and pity—by washing away our sins and giving us the new joy of the indwelling Holy Spirit 6whom he poured out upon us with wonderful fullness—and all because of what Jesus Christ our Savior did 7so that he could declare us good in God's eyes—all because of his great kindness; and now we can share in the wealth of the eternal life he gives us, and we are eagerly looking forward to receiving it. 8These things I have told you are all true. Insist on them so that Christians will be careful to do good deeds all the time, for this is not only right, but it brings results.

their families are extremely important role models for young men who need to *see* how it is done more than to be *told* how to do it.

2:6-8 Paul urged Titus to be a good example to those around him so that others might see his good deeds and imitate him. His life would give his words greater impact. If you want someone to act a certain way, be sure that you live that way yourself. Then you will earn the right to be heard.

2:8 Paul counseled Titus to be sensible and logical (reasonable) in his conversation, to avoid criticism. Such conversation comes from careful Bible study and listening before speaking. If we are impulsive, unreasonable, and confusing, we are likely to start arguments rather than to convince people of the truth.

2:9, 10 Slavery was common in Paul's day. Paul did not condemn slavery in any of his letters, but he advised slaves and masters to be loving and responsible in their conduct (see also Ephesians 6:5-9). The standards set by Paul apply to any employee/employer relationship. Employees should always do their best work and be trustworthy, not just when the employer is watching. Businesses in the United States lose millions of dollars a year to employee theft and time-wasting. If all Christian employees followed Paul's advice, what a transformation it would make!

2:11-14 The power to live the Christian life comes from Jesus Christ. Because Christ died and rescued us from sin, we are free

from sin's control. He gives us the power and understanding to live according to God's will, to look forward to his return, and to do good.

2:15 Paul told Titus to teach the Scriptures as well as to live them. We must also teach, encourage, and correct others when necessary. Although good teaching occurs in classrooms and small groups, much of the teaching Paul refers to must be done in the "classroom" of personal and family relationships.

3:1, 2 As Christians, our first allegiance is to Jesus as Lord, but we also must obey our government and its leaders. Christians are not above the law, but keeping the civil law is only the beginning of our Christian responsibility. In a democracy, it is also important to be involved and to serve. (See the notes on Acts 5:29 and Romans 13:1ff.)

3:3-8 Paul summarizes what Christ does for us when he saves us. We move from a life full of sin to one led by God's Holy Spirit. *All* our sins, not merely some, are washed away. We gain eternal life with *all* its treasures. We have the *fullness* of the Holy Spirit, and he continually renews our hearts. None of this occurs because we earned or deserved it; it is all a gift of God's grace.

3:4-6 All persons of the Trinity participate in the work of salvation. Based upon the redemptive work of his Son, the Father sends the Holy Spirit to wash away our sins and continually renew us.

Avoid useless arguments

⁹Don't get involved in arguing over unanswerable questions and controversial theological ideas; keep out of arguments and quarrels about obedience to Jewish laws, for this kind of thing isn't worthwhile; it only does harm. ¹⁰If anyone is causing divisions among you, he should be given a first and second warning. After that have nothing more to do with him, ¹¹for such a person has a wrong sense of values. He is sinning, and he knows it.

3:9
1 Tim 1:4
2 Tim 2:14,16,
23

3:10
Mt 18:15-17
Rom 16:2

Paul's final instructions

¹²I am planning to send either Artemas or Tychicus to you. As soon as one of them arrives, please try to meet me at Nicopolis as quickly as you can, for I have decided to stay there for the winter. ¹³Do everything you can to help Zenas the lawyer and Apollos with their trip; see that they are given everything they need. ¹⁴For our people must learn to help all who need their assistance, that their lives will be fruitful.

¹⁵Everybody here sends greetings. Please say "hello" to all of the Christian friends there. May God's blessings be with you all.

Sincerely, Paul

3:12
Acts 20:4
2 Tim 4:12,21
Col 4:9

3:13
Acts 18:24

3:14
Rom 12:13
Phil 1:11
Tit 3:8
2 Pet 1:8

3:15
Col 4:18

3:9-11 Paul warns Titus, as he warned Timothy, not to get involved in arguments over unanswerable questions (2 Timothy 2:14). This does not mean we should refuse to study, discuss, and examine different interpretations of difficult Bible passages. Paul is warning against petty quarrels, not honest discussion that leads to wisdom. When foolish arguments develop, it is best to turn the discussion back to a track that is going somewhere or politely excuse yourself from the discussion.

3:9-11 A person must be warned when he or she is causing division that threatens the unity of the church. This warning should not be a heavy-handed action, but should correct the individual's divisive nature and restore him or her to fellowship. A person who refuses to be corrected has already chosen to be outside the fellowship. As Paul says, "He is sinning and he knows it." (See also Matthew 18:15-18 and 2 Thessalonians 3:14, 15 for help in handling such problems in the church.)

3:12 The city of Nicopolis was on the western coast of Greece. Artemas or Tychicus would take over Titus' work on the island of

Crete, so Titus could meet Paul in Nicopolis. Tychicus was one of Paul's trusted companions (Acts 20:4; Ephesians 6:21; Colossians 4:7). Titus would have to leave quickly because sea travel was dangerous in the winter months.

3:13 Apollos was a famous Christian preacher. A native of Alexandria in North Africa, he became a Christian in Ephesus and was trained by Aquila and Priscilla (Acts 18:24-28; 1 Corinthians 1:12).

3:15 The letters of Paul to Titus and Timothy mark the end of Paul's writing and the end of his life and ministry. These letters are rich treasures for us today because they give vital information for church leadership. They provide a strong model for elders, pastors, and other Christian leaders as they develop younger leaders to carry on the work, following Paul's example of preparing Timothy and Titus to carry on his ministry. For practical guidelines on church leadership and problem solving, carefully study the principles found in these letters.

PHILEMON

AT THE FOREMAN'S signal, the giant ball is released, and with dynamite force and a reverberating crash, it meets the wall, snapping bricks like twigs and scattering pieces of mortar. Repeatedly, the powerful pendulum works, and soon the barrier has been reduced to rubble. Then it is carted away so that construction can begin.

Life has many walls and fences which divide, separate, and compartmentalize. Not made of wood or stone, they are personal obstructions, blocking people from each other and from God. But Christ came as the great wall remover, tearing down the sin partition which separates us from God and blasting the barriers which keep us from each other (see Ephesians 2:14–16).

Roman, Greek, and Jewish cultures had many societal barriers—people were assigned to certain social classes and were expected to remain in their place—men and women, enslaved and free, rich and poor, Jews and Gentiles, Greeks and barbarians, pious and heathen. In Christ the walls came down, and Paul could declare, "In this new life one's nationality or race or education or social position is unimportant; such things mean nothing. Whether a person has Christ is what matters, and he is equally available to all" (Colossians 3:11).

This life-changing truth forms the backdrop for the letter to Philemon. The epistle to Philemon is Paul's personal plea on behalf of a slave. Onesimus "belonged" to Paul's friend Philemon, who was probably a member of the Colossian church. But Onesimus, had run away and may have even stolen from his master. He ran to Rome where he met Paul, and there he responded to the Good News and came to faith in Christ (1:10). So Paul writes to Philemon and reintroduces Onesimus to him, explaining that he is sending him back, not just as a slave but also as a brother in Christ (1:11, 12, 15, 16). Tactfully he asks Philemon to forgive Onesimus and to accept his servant back (1:10, 13–16, 20). The social barriers of the past and the new ones erected by Onesimus' desertion and theft should no longer divide them—they are one in Christ.

This small book is a masterpiece of grace and tact and is a profound demonstration of the power of Christ and of true Christian fellowship in action. What separates you from fellow believers—race, status, wealth, education, personality? As with Philemon, God calls you to unity: break down those walls and embrace all brothers and sisters in Christ.

VITAL STATISTICS

PURPOSE:
To convince Philemon to forgive his runaway slave, Onesimus, and to accept him as a brother in the faith

AUTHOR:
Paul

TO WHOM WRITTEN:
Philemon, who was probably a wealthy member of the Colossian church

DATE WRITTEN:
About A.D. 60, during Paul's first imprisonment in Rome, at about the same time Ephesians and Colossians were written

SETTING:
Slavery was very common in the Roman Empire, and evidently some Christians had slaves. Paul does not condemn the institution in his writings, but he makes a radical statement by calling this slave Philemon's brother in Christ.

KEY VERSES:
"Perhaps you could think of it this way: that he ran away from you for a little while so that now he can be yours forever, no longer only a slave, but something much better—a beloved brother, especially to me . . ." (1:15, 16).

KEY PEOPLE:
Paul, Philemon, Onesimus

KEY PLACES:
Colosse, Rome

THE BLUEPRINT

1. Paul's appreciation of Philemon (1:1–7)
2. Paul's appeal for Onesimus (1:8–25)

Paul pleads for Onesimus, a repentant runaway slave. Paul's intercession for him illustrates what Christ has done for us. As Paul interceded for a slave, so Christ intercedes for us, slaves to sin. As Onesimus was reconciled to Philemon, so we are reconciled to God through Christ. As Paul offered to pay the debts of a slave, so Christ paid our debt of sin. Like Onesimus, we must return to God our Master and serve him with glad hearts and transformed lives.

MEGATHEMES

THEME	EXPLANATION	IMPORTANCE
Forgiveness	Philemon was Paul's friend and Onesimus' owner. Paul asked him not to punish Onesimus, but to forgive and restore him as a new Christian brother.	Christian relationships must be full of forgiveness and acceptance. Can you forgive those who have wronged you?
Barriers	Slavery was widespread in the Roman Empire, but no one is beyond God's love. Slavery was a barrier between people, but Christian love and fellowship are to overcome such barriers.	In Christ we are one family. No walls of race, economic status, or political differences should separate believers. Let Christ work through you to remove barriers between Christian brothers and sisters.
Respect	Paul was a friend of both Philemon and Onesimus. He had the authority as an apostle to tell Philemon what to do. Yet Paul chose to appeal to his friend in Christian love rather than to order him.	Tactful persuasion accomplishes a great deal more than commands, when dealing with people. Remember to exhibit courtesy and respect in dealing with people.

1. Paul's appreciation of Philemon

1 *From:* Paul, in jail for preaching the Good News about Jesus Christ, and from Brother Timothy.

To: Philemon, our much loved fellow worker, and to the church that meets in your home, and to Apphia our sister, and to Archippus who like myself is a soldier of the cross.

3May God our Father and the Lord Jesus Christ give you his blessings and his peace.

4I always thank God when I am praying for you, dear Philemon, **5**because I keep hearing of your love and trust in the Lord Jesus and in his people. **6**And I pray that as you share your faith with others it will grip their lives too, as they see the wealth of good things in you that come from Christ Jesus. **7**I myself have gained much joy and comfort from your love, my brother, because your kindness has so often refreshed the hearts of God's people.

1:1 Eph 4:1 / 2 Tim 1:8 / Philem 9,23,24
1:2 Rom 16:5 / 1 Cor 16:29 / Phil 2:25 / Col 4:17
1:4 Rom 1:8,9 / 2 Thess 1:3
1:6 Phil 1:9
1:7 2 Cor 7:13 / 2 Tim 1:16

2. Paul's appeal for Onesimus

8, 9 Now I want to ask a favor of you. I could demand it of you in the name of Christ because it is the right thing for you to do, but I love you and prefer just to ask you—I, Paul, an old man now, here in jail for the sake of Jesus Christ. **10**My plea

1:8 1 Thess 2:6

1:1, 2 Paul wrote this letter from Rome in about A.D. 60, when he was under house arrest (see Acts 28:30, 31). Onesimus was a domestic slave who belonged to Philemon, a wealthy man and a member of the church in Colosse. Onesimus had run away from Philemon and made his way to Rome where he met Paul, who apparently led him to Christ (1:10). Paul convinced Onesimus that running from his problems wouldn't solve them and he persuaded Onesimus to return to his master. Paul wrote this letter to Philemon to ask him to be reconciled to his runaway slave who was now also a Christian brother.

1:1, 2 For more information on Paul's life and ministry, see his Profile in Acts 9. Timothy's name is included with Paul's in 2 Corinthians, 1 Thessalonians, 2 Thessalonians, Philippians, Colossians, and Philemon—the last three of these letters are from a group known as the "prison epistles," (the fourth letter in this group is Ephesians). Timothy was one of Paul's trusted companions; Paul wrote two letters to him— 1 and 2 Timothy.

1:1, 2 Philemon was a Greek landowner living in Colosse. He was converted under Paul's ministry, and the Colossian church met in his home. Onesimus was one of Philemon's slaves.

1:1, 2 Archippus may have been Philemon's son or possibly an elder of the Colossian church. In either case, Paul included him as

a recipient of the letter, possibly so Archippus could read the letter with Philemon and encourage him to follow Paul's advice.

1:1, 2 The early churches often met in people's homes. Because of sporadic persecutions and the great expense involved, church buildings were not constructed at this time.

1:7 Paul reflected on Philemon's kindness, love, and comfort. He had opened his heart and his home to the church. We should do likewise, opening ourselves and our homes to others, offering Christian fellowship to refresh people's spirits.

1:8, 9 Since Paul was an elder and an apostle, he could have used his authority with Philemon, commanding him to deal kindly with his runaway slave. But Paul based his request not on his own authority, but on Philemon's Christian commitment. Paul wanted Philemon's heartfelt, not grudging obedience. When you know something is right and you have the power to demand it, do you appeal to your authority or the other person's commitment? Here Paul provides a good example of how to deal with a possible conflict between Christian friends.

1:10 A master had the legal right to kill a runaway slave. Onesimus feared for his life. So Paul wrote this letter to Philemon to help him understand his new relationship with Onesimus. Onesimus was now a Christian brother, not a mere possession.

is that you show kindness to my child Onesimus, whom I won to the Lord while here in my chains. ¹¹Onesimus (whose name means "Useful") hasn't been of much use to you in the past, but now he is going to be of real use to both of us. ¹²I am sending him back to you, and with him comes my own heart.

1:13
Phil 1:7; 2:30

¹³I really wanted to keep him here with me while I am in these chains for preaching the Good News, and you would have been helping me through him, ¹⁴but I didn't want to do it without your consent. I didn't want you to be kind because you had to but because you wanted to. ¹⁵Perhaps you could think of it this way: that he ran away from you for a little while so that now he can be yours forever, ¹⁶no longer only a slave, but something much better—a beloved brother, especially to me. Now he will mean much more to you too, because he is not only a servant but also your brother in Christ.

1:14
2 Cor 9:7

1:15
Gen 45:5,8
Rom 8:28

1:16
Mt 23:8
1 Cor 7:22
Col 3:22

1:17
2 Cor 8:23

1:19
2 Thess 3:17

1:21
2 Cor 7:16

1:22
Phil 1:24-26
2:24

1:23
Col 1:7; 4:12

1:24
Acts 12:12
19:29; 27:2
Col 4:10,14
Philem 1

1:25
Gal 6:18
2 Tim 4:22

¹⁷If I am really your friend, give him the same welcome you would give to me if I were the one who was coming. ¹⁸If he has harmed you in any way or stolen anything from you, charge me for it. ¹⁹I will pay it back (I, Paul, personally guarantee this by writing it here with my own hand) but I won't mention how much you owe me! The fact is, you even owe me your very soul! ²⁰Yes, dear brother, give me joy with this loving act and my weary heart will praise the Lord.

²¹I've written you this letter because I am positive that you will do what I ask and even more!

²²Please keep a guest room ready for me, for I am hoping that God will answer your prayers and let me come to you soon.

²³Epaphras my fellow prisoner, who is also here for preaching Christ Jesus, sends you his greetings. ²⁴So do Mark, Aristarchus, Demas and Luke, my fellow workers.

²⁵The blessings of our Lord Jesus Christ be upon your spirit.

Paul

1:10ff Paul asked Philemon to forgive his runaway slave who had become a Christian, and not only to forgive, but to accept him as a brother. As Christians, we should forgive as we have been forgiven (Matthew 6:5–15; Ephesians 4:31, 32). True forgiveness means we treat the one we've forgiven as we would want to be treated. Is there someone you say you have forgiven, but who still needs your kindness?

1:13–16 What a difference Onesimus' status as a Christian made in his relationship to Philemon. He was no longer merely a servant, he was also a brother. Now both Onesimus and Philemon were members of God's family—equals in Christ. A Christian's status as a member of God's family transcends all other distinctions among believers. Do you look down on any fellow Christians? Remember, they are your brothers and sisters, your equals before Christ (Galatians 3:28). How you treat your brothers and sisters in Christ's family reflects your true Christian commitment.

1:15, 16 Slavery was widespread throughout the Roman Empire. In these early days, Christians did not have the political power to change the slavery system. Paul didn't condemn or condone slavery but worked to transform relationships. The gospel begins to change social structures by changing the *people* within those structures. (See 1 Corinthians 7:20–24; Ephesians 6:5–9; Colossians 3:22—4:1.)

1:17–19 Paul genuinely loved Onesimus. Paul showed his love by personally guaranteeing payment for any stolen goods or injuries for which Onesimus might be responsible. Paul's investment in the life of this new believer certainly encouraged and strengthened Onesimus' faith. Are there young believers who need you to demonstrate such self-sacrifice towards them? Be grateful when you can invest in the lives of others.

1:19 When Paul said, "you even owe me your very soul," he was reminding Philemon that it was he who had led him to Christ. Because Paul was Philemon's spiritual father, he hoped Philemon would feel a debt of gratitude that he would repay by accepting Onesimus with a spirit of forgiveness.

1:22 Paul was released from prison soon after writing this letter, but the Bible doesn't say whether he returned to Colosse.

1:23 Epaphras was well known to the Colossians, since he had founded the church there (Colossians 1:7). He was a hero to this church, helping to hold it together in spite of growing persecution and struggles with false doctrine. Epaphras' earnest prayers for the Colossian Christians revealed his deep love for them (Colossians 4:12, 13). He was probably in prison with Paul for preaching the gospel.

1:24 Mark, Aristarchus, Demas, and Luke are also mentioned in Colossians 4:10, 14. Mark had accompanied Paul and Barnabas on their first missionary journey (Acts 12:25ff). John Mark also wrote the Gospel of Mark. Luke had accompanied Paul on his third missionary journey and was the writer of the Gospel of Luke and the book of Acts. Demas was faithful to Paul for a while but then deserted him (see 2 Timothy 4:9, 10).

1:25 Paul urged Philemon to be reconciled to his slave, receiving him as a brother and fellow member of God's family. *Reconciliation* means reestablishing relationship. Christ has reconciled us to God and to others. Many barriers arise between people—race, social status, sex, personality differences—but Christ can break down these barriers. Jesus Christ changed Onesimus' relationship to Philemon from slave to brother. Only in Christ can our most hopeless relationships be transformed into something wonderful.

HEBREWS

VITAL STATISTICS

PURPOSE:
To present the sufficiency and superiority of Christ

AUTHOR:
Paul, Luke, Barnabas, Apollos, Silas, Philip, Priscilla, and others have been suggested because the name of the author is not given in the biblical text itself. Whoever it was speaks of Timothy as "Brother" (13:23).

TO WHOM WRITTEN:
Hebrew Christians who may have been considering a return to Judaism, perhaps because of immaturity, due to their lack of understanding of biblical truths. They seem to be "second-generation" Christians (2:3).

DATE WRITTEN:
Probably before the destruction of the Temple in Jerusalem in A.D. 70, since the religious sacrifices and ceremonies are referred to in the book, but no mention is made of the Temple's destruction

SETTING:
These Jewish Christians were probably undergoing fierce persecution, socially and physically, both from Jews and from Romans. Christ had not returned to establish his Kingdom, and the people needed to be reassured that Christianity was true and that Jesus was indeed the Messiah.

KEY VERSE:
"God's Son shines out with God's glory, and all that God's Son is and does marks him as God. He regulates the universe by the mighty power of his command. He is the one who died to cleanse us and clear our record of all sin, and then sat down in highest honor beside the great God of heaven" (1:3).

KEY PEOPLE:
Old Testament men and women of faith (chapter 11)

SPECIAL FEATURES:
Although Hebrews is called a "letter" (13:22), it has the form and the content of a sermon.

CONSCIENTIOUS consumers shop for value. Wise parents desire only the best for their children, nourishing their growing bodies, minds, and spirits. Individuals with integrity seek the best investment of time, talents, and treasures. In every area, to settle for less would be wasteful, foolish, and irresponsible. Yet that is a natural pull, to move toward what is convenient, comfortable, and less than ideal.

Judaism was not second-rate or easy. Divinely designed, it was the best religion, expressing true worship and devotion to God. The commandments, the rituals, and the prophets described God's promises and revealed the way to forgiveness and salvation. Then Christ came, fulfilling the Law and the Prophets, conquering sin, and freely providing eternal life.

This message was difficult for Jews to accept. Although they had sought the Messiah for centuries, they were entrenched in thinking and worshiping in traditional forms. Following Jesus seemed to repudiate their marvelous heritage and profound Scriptures. With caution and questions they listened to the gospel, but many rejected it and sought to eliminate this "heresy." Those who did accept Jesus as the Messiah, often found themselves slipping back into the old and familiar.

Hebrews is a masterful document written to demonstrate the exclusiveness and superiority of the new covenant. The overarching message of Hebrews is that Christianity is superior to Judaism because Christ is supreme and is completely sufficient for salvation.

Hebrews begins by emphasizing that the old (Judaism) and the new (Christianity) are both religions "revealed" by God (1:1–3). In the doctrinal section which follows (1:4—10:23), the writer shows how Jesus is greater than angels (1:4—2:18) and Moses (3:1–19), provides a better rest (4:1–13), and is superior to the Old Testament priesthood (4:14—7:28). Christianity surpasses Judaism because it has a better covenant (8:1–13), a better sanctuary (9:1–10), and a more sufficient sacrifice for sins (9:1—10:18).

Having established the superiority of Christianity, the writer moves on to the practical implications of following Christ. The readers are exhorted to hold on to their new faith, encourage each other, and look forward to Christ's return (10:19–25). They are warned about the consequences of rejecting Christ's sacrifice for them (10:26–31) and reminded of the rewards for faithfulness (10:32–39). Then the author explains what it is to live by faith, giving illustrations of the faithful men and women in the history of Israel (11:1–40). We are exhorted to pattern our lives after Christ, allowing God to discipline us (12:1–17). This section ends by comparing the old covenant with the new (12:18–29). The writer concludes with moral exhortations (13:1–17), a request for prayer (13:18, 19), and a benediction followed by greetings (13:20–25).

Jesus Christ is the perfect revelation of God, the final and complete sacrifice for sin, and the *only* way to eternal life. Read Hebrews and begin to see history and life from God's perspective. Then give yourself unreservedly and completely to Christ. Don't settle for anything less.

THE BLUEPRINT

A. THE SUPERIORITY OF CHRIST
   (1:1—10:18)
   1. Christ is greater than the angels
   2. Christ is greater than Moses
   3. Christ is greater than the Old
      Testament priesthood
   4. The new covenant is greater than the
      old

The superiority of Christ over everyone and everything is clearly demonstrated by the author. Christianity supersedes all other religions and can never be surpassed. Where can one find anything better than Christ? Living in Christ is having the best there is in life. All competing religions are deceptions or cheap imitations.

B. THE SUPERIORITY OF FAITH
   (10:19—13:25)

Jews who had become Christians in the first century were tempted to fall back into Judaism because of uncertainty, the security of customs, and persecution. Today believers are also tempted to fall back into legalism, fulfilling minimum religious requirements, rather than pressing on in genuine faith. We must strive to live by faith each day.

MEGATHEMES

THEME	EXPLANATION	IMPORTANCE
Christ Is Superior	Hebrews reveals Jesus' true identity as God. He is the ultimate authority. He is greater than any religion or any angel. He is superior to any Jewish leader (such as Abraham, Moses, or Joshua) and superior to any priest. He is the complete revelation of God.	Jesus alone can forgive your sin. He has secured your forgiveness and salvation by his death on the cross. You can find peace with God and real meaning for life by believing in Christ.
High Priest	In the Old Testament, the High Priest represented the Jews before God. Jesus Christ links us with God. There is no other superior way to reach God. Because Jesus Christ lived a sinless life, he is the perfect substitute to die for our sin. He is our perfect representative with God.	Jesus guarantees our access to God the Father. He intercedes for us so we can boldly come to the Father with our needs. When we are weak we can come confidently to God for forgiveness and help.
Sacrifice	Christ's sacrifice was the ultimate fulfillment of all that the Old Testament sacrifices represented—God's forgiveness for sin. Because Christ is the perfect sacrifice for our sin, our sins are completely forgiven—past, present, and future.	Christ removed sin which barred us from God's presence and fellowship. But we must accept his sacrifice for us. By believing in him we are no longer guilty, but cleansed and made whole. His sacrifice makes the way for us to have eternal life.
Maturity	Though we are saved from sin when we believe in Christ, we are given the task to go on and grow in our faith. Through our relationship with Christ we can live blameless lives, be set aside for his special use, and develop maturity.	The process of maturing in our faith takes time. Daily commitment and service produce maturity. When we are mature in our faith, we are not easily swayed or shaken.
Faith	Faith is confident trust in God. God's salvation is in his son Jesus, who is the only one who can save us from sin.	If you trust in Jesus Christ for your complete salvation, he will transform you completely. A life of obedience and complete truth is pleasing to God.
Endurance	Faith enables Christians to face trials. Genuine faith includes the commitment to stay true to God when we are under fire. Endurance builds character and leads to victory.	You can have victory in your trials if you don't give up or turn your back on Christ. Stay true to Christ and pray for endurance.

A. THE SUPERIORITY OF CHRIST (1:1—10:18)

The relationship of Christianity to Judaism was a critical issue in the early church. The author clears up confusion by carefully explaining how Christ is superior to angels, Moses, and High Priests. The new covenant is shown to be far superior to the old. This can be of great encouragement to us and help us avoid drifting away from our faith in Christ.

1. Christ is greater than the angels

Jesus Christ is God's Son

1 Long ago God spoke in many different ways to our fathers through the prophets [in visions, dreams, and even face to face], telling them little by little about his plans.

1:1
Num 12:6-8

2But now in these days he has spoken to us through his Son to whom he has given everything, and through whom he made the world and everything there is.

1:2
Ps 2:8
Jn 1:1,3,18; 8:25

3God's Son shines out with God's glory, and all that God's Son is and does marks him as God. He regulates the universe by the mighty power of his command. He is the one who died to cleanse us and clear our record of all sin, and then sat down in highest honor beside the great God of heaven.

1:3
Ps 110:1
Jn 14:9
2 Cor 4:4
Col 1:15

God's Son compared to the angels

4Thus he became far greater than the angels, as proved by the fact that his name "Son of God," which was passed on to him from his Father, is far greater than the names and titles of the angels. **5, 6**For God never said to any angel, "You are my Son, and today I have given you the honor that goes with that name." But God said it about Jesus. Another time he said, "I am his Father and he is my Son." And still

1:4
Eph 1:21
Phil 2:9

1:5
a) Ps 2:7
Rev 1:5
b) 2 Sam 7:14

1:1 *in visions, dreams, and even face to face,* implied. **1:5, 6** *today I have given you the honor that goes with that name,* literally, "this day I have begotten you."

Hebrews passage	Old Testament passage	How Christ is higher than the angels	CHRIST AND THE ANGELS
1:5, 6	Psalm 2:7	Christ is called Son of God, a title never given to an angel.	
1:7, 14	Psalm 104:4	Angels are important, but servants.	
1:8, 9	Psalm 45:6	Christ's Kingdom is forever.	
1:10	Psalm 102:25	Christ is the Creator of the world.	
1:13	Psalm 110:1	Christ is given unique honor by God.	

The writer of Hebrews quotes from the Old Testament repeatedly in demonstrating Christ's greatness in comparison to the angels. His audience of first-century Jewish Christians had developed an unbalanced belief in angels and their role. Christ's lordship is affirmed without disrespect to God's valued angelic messengers.

1:1 The book of Hebrews describes in detail how Jesus Christ fulfills the promises and prophecies of the Old Testament. The Jews believed in the Old Testament Scriptures, but most rejected Jesus as the long-awaited Messiah. The recipients of this letter seem to have been Jewish Christians. They were well-versed in Scripture, and they had professed faith in Christ. Whether through doubt, persecution, or false teaching, however, they may have been in danger of giving up their Christian faith and returning to Judaism.

The authorship of this book is uncertain. Several names have been suggested including Luke, Barnabas, Apollos, Priscilla, and Paul. Most scholars do not believe Paul was the author, because the writing style of Hebrews is quite different from that of Paul's epistles. In addition, Paul identified himself in his other letters and appealed to his authority as an apostle, whereas this writer never gives his or her name and appeals to eyewitnesses of Jesus' ministry for authority. Nevertheless, the author of Hebrews evidently knew Paul well. Hebrews was probably written by one of Paul's close associates who often heard him preach.

1:1, 2 God used many approaches to send his messages to people in Old Testament times. He spoke to Isaiah in visions (Isaiah 6), to Jacob in a dream (Genesis 28:10–22), and to Abraham and Moses personally (Genesis 18; Exodus 31:18).

Jewish people familiar with these stories would not have found it hard to believe that God was still revealing his will, but it was astonishing for them to think that God had revealed *himself* by speaking through his Son, Jesus Christ. Jesus is the fulfillment and culmination of God's many revelations through the centuries.

1:2, 3 Not only is Jesus God's spokesman; he is God himself—the very God who spoke in Old Testament times. He is eternal; he worked with the Father in creating the world (John 1:3; Colossians 1:16). He is the full revelation of God. You can have no clearer view of God than by looking at him. Jesus Christ is the complete embodiment of God.

1:3 The book of Hebrews links God's saving power with his creative power. In other words, the power that brought the universe into being and that keeps it operating is the very power that removes our sins. How wrong it is, then, to think that God can't forgive us. No sin is too big for the Ruler of the universe to handle. He can and will forgive us when we come to him through his Son.

1:5, 6 Jesus is God's firstborn (unique) Son. In Jewish families the firstborn son held the place of highest privilege and responsibility. The Jewish Christians reading this message would understand that as God's firstborn, Jesus was superior to any created being.

another time—when his firstborn Son came to earth—God said, "Let all the angels of God worship him."

1:6
Ps 89:27; 97:7

7God speaks of his angels as messengers swift as the wind and as servants made of flaming fire; 8but of his Son he says, "Your Kingdom, O God, will last forever and ever; its commands are always just and right. 9You love right and hate wrong; so God, even your God, has poured out more gladness upon you than on anyone else."

1:7
Ps 104:4
1:8,9
Ps 45:6,7

10God also called him "Lord" when he said, "Lord, in the beginning you made the earth, and the heavens are the work of your hands. 11They will disappear into nothingness, but you will remain forever. They will become worn out like old clothes, 12and some day you will fold them up and replace them. But you yourself will never change, and your years will never end."

1:10-12
Ps 102:25-27

13And did God ever say to an angel, as he does to his Son, "Sit here beside me in honor until I crush all your enemies beneath your feet"?

1:13
Ps 110:1
Mt 22:44

14No, for the angels are only spirit-messengers sent out to help and care for those who are to receive his salvation.

1:14
Ps 34:7; 91:11
Rom 8:17
Heb 2:3

Warning against drifting away

2 So we must listen very carefully to the truths we have heard, or we may drift away from them. 2For since the messages from angels have always proved true and people have always been punished for disobeying them, 3what makes us think that we can escape if we are indifferent to this great salvation announced by the Lord Jesus himself, and passed on to us by those who heard him speak?

2:2
Deut 5:5; 33:2
Acts 7:38,53
Gal 3:19
2:3
Heb 1:1,2; 10:29
2:4
Mk 6:14

4God always has shown us that these messages are true by signs and wonders and

---

LESSONS FROM CHRIST'S HUMANITY

Christ is the perfect human leader	and he wants to lead you
	model	and he is worth imitating
	sacrifice	and he died for you
	conqueror	and he conquered death to give you eternal life
	High Priest	and he is merciful, loving, and understanding

God, in Christ, became a living, breathing human being. Hebrews points out many reasons why this is so important.

1:11, 12 Because the readers of Hebrews experienced the rejection of their fellow Jews, they often felt isolated. Many were tempted to exchange the changeless Christ for their familiar old faith. The writer of Hebrews warns them not to do this: Christ is the *only* security in a changing world. Whatever may happen in this world, Christ remains forever changeless. A Christian, then, is absolutely secure, because he stands on the firmest foundation in the universe—Jesus Christ.

1:12 What does it mean that Christ is changeless? It means that his character will never change. He is persistent in his love for us, committed to fairness and justice, and absolutely set on being merciful to us who are so undeserving. Rejoice today that Christ is changeless—he will always help you when you need it and offer forgiveness when you fall.

1:13 False teachers in many of the early churches taught that God could be approached only through angels. Instead of worshiping God directly, followers of these heretics bowed to angels. Hebrews clearly denounces such teaching as false. Some thought of Jesus as the highest angel of God. But Jesus is not a superior angel; and, in any case, angels are not to be worshiped (see Colossians 2:18; Revelation 19:1–10). Jesus is God, he alone deserves our worship.

1:14 Angels, God's messengers, were created by God and are under his authority (Colossians 1:16). They have several functions: serving believers (1:14), protecting the helpless (Matthew 18:10,

11), proclaiming God's messages (Revelation 14:6–12), and executing God's judgment (Acts 12:1–23; Revelation 20:1–3).

2:1–3 Listening is hard work. It involves our minds, bodies, and senses. Listening to Christ means not merely hearing, but also responding in obedience (see James 1:22–25). We must persevere in our obedience to Christ.

2:3 Eyewitnesses to Jesus' ministry had handed down his teachings to the readers of this book. These readers were second-generation believers who had not seen Christ in the flesh. They are like us; we have not seen Jesus personally, but we base our belief in Jesus on eyewitness accounts recorded in the Bible.

2:3 A central theme of Hebrews is that Christ is infinitely greater than all other proposed means to God. Your previous faith was good, the author said to his Jewish readers, but Christ is incomparably better. Just as Christ is greater than angels, so his message is more important than theirs. Don't turn your back on Christ in an attempt to escape your troubles.

2:4 In the book of Acts, miracles and gifts of the Spirit authenticated the gospel wherever it was preached (see Acts 9:31–42; 14:1–20). Paul, who discusses spiritual gifts in Romans 12, 1 Corinthians 12—14, and Ephesians 4, says that the purpose of spiritual gifts is to build up the church, making it strong and mature. When we see the gifts of the Spirit in an individual or congregation, we know God is truly present. As we receive his gifts, we should recognize him and thank him for them.

various miracles and by giving certain special abilities from the Holy Spirit to those who believe; yes, God has assigned such gifts to each of us.

Christ came as a human being

5And the future world we are talking about will not be controlled by angels. 6No, for in the book of Psalms David says to God, "What is mere man that you are so concerned about him? And who is this Son of Man you honor so highly? 7For though you made him lower than the angels for a little while, now you have crowned him with glory and honor. 8And you have put him in complete charge of everything there is. Nothing is left out."

We have not yet seen all of this take place, 9but we do see Jesus—who for awhile was a little lower than the angels—crowned now by God with glory and honor because he suffered death for us. Yes, because of God's great kindness, Jesus tasted death for everyone in all the world.

10And it was right and proper that God, who made everything for his own glory, should allow Jesus to suffer, for in doing this he was bringing vast multitudes of God's people to heaven; for his suffering made Jesus a perfect Leader, one fit to bring them into their salvation.

11We who have been made holy by Jesus, now have the same Father he has. That is why Jesus is not ashamed to call us his brothers. 12For he says in the book of Psalms, "I will talk to my brothers about God my Father, and together we will sing his praises." 13At another time he said, "I will put my trust in God along with my brothers." And at still another time, "See, here am I and the children God gave me."

14Since we, God's children, are human beings—made of flesh and blood—he became flesh and blood too by being born in human form; for only as a human being could he die and in dying break the power of the devil who had the power of death. 15Only in that way could he deliver those who through fear of death have been living all their lives as slaves to constant dread.

16We all know he did not come as an angel but as a human being—yes, a Jew. 17And it was necessary for Jesus to be like us, his brothers, so that he could be our merciful and faithful High Priest before God, a Priest who would be both merciful to us and faithful to God in dealing with the sins of the people. 18For since he

Cross references:

2:5 Heb 6:5
2:6 Ps 8:4-6
2:8 1 Cor 15:27
2:9 Acts 2:33 Phil 2:6-9
2:10 Lk 13:32; 24:46 Acts 3:15 Rom 11:36 Heb 5:9
2:11 Mt 28:10 Jn 20:17 Rom 8:29 Heb 10:10; 13:12
2:12 Ps 22:22
2:13 Isa 8:17,18 Jn 17:6,9 11,12
2:14 Jn 1:14 Rom 8:3 1 Cor 15:54,55 2 Tim 1:10 1 Jn 3:8
2:17 Phil 2:7 Heb 3:1; 4:15 5:1 1 Jn 2:2
2:18 Heb 4:15; 5:2

2:9 God has put Jesus in charge of everything and Jesus has revealed himself to us. We do not yet see Jesus reigning on earth, but we can picture him in his heavenly glory. When confused by tomorrow and anxious about the future, strive to keep a clear view of Jesus Christ—who he is, what he has done, and what he is doing for us right now. This will give stability to your decisions day by day.

2:9, 10 God's kindness led Christ to his death—what a startling juxtaposition of ideas! Yet kindness can and often does involve sacrifice and pain. Jesus did not come into the world to gain status or political power, but to suffer and die so that we could truly live. If this is difficult to understand, perhaps it is time to evaluate our own motives. Are we more interested in power or submission, domination or service, getting or giving? If kindness, not selfishness, motivates us, we too may have to suffer.

2:10 Jesus' suffering made him a perfect Leader (see 5:8, 9), and our suffering can make us better servants of God. People who have known pain are able to reach out with sensitivity to their hurting brothers and sisters. When you suffer, ask how your experience can help you serve Christ better.

2:11-13 The Psalms often look forward to Christ and his work in the world. Here a portion of Psalm 22, a messianic psalm, is quoted. Because God has adopted all believers as his children, Jesus calls them his brothers.

2:14 Jesus had to be human so he could die, so he could

overcome the same temptations we face, and so he could mediate between God and human beings. He identified with us so that we could identify with God.

2:14 By dying, Jesus became our sacrifice and delivered us from death. By rising from the dead, he defeated death, the enemy (see Romans 6:5-11; 1 Corinthians 15).

2:14, 15 Christ's death and resurrection free us from the fear of death because death has been defeated. Do some of your loved ones need the freedom from the fear of death which only Christ can give? All who live in dread of death should have the opportunity to know the truth of Christ's victory. How can you share this understanding with those close to you?

2:16, 17 In the Old Testament, the High Priest was the mediator between God and his people. His job was to regularly offer animal sacrifices according to the law and to intercede before God for the people's sins. Jesus Christ is now our High Priest. He has *once and for all* paid the penalty for all our sins by his own sacrificial death, and he continually intercedes on our behalf before God. We are released from sin's domination over us when we commit ourselves fully to Christ, trusting completely in what he has done for us (see note on 4:14 for more about Jesus as the High Priest).

2:18 Knowing that Christ suffered and was tempted helps us go through our own suffering. We know he understands our struggles, and we trust him to help us survive suffering and overcome temptation. When you face trials, go to Jesus. He understands your needs and is able to help (see 4:14-16).

himself has now been through suffering and temptation, he knows what it is like when we suffer and are tempted, and he is wonderfully able to help us.

2. Christ is greater than Moses

Jesus compared to Moses

3:1
Jn 17:3
Heb 2:17; 4:14

3 Therefore, dear brothers whom God has set apart for himself—you who are chosen for heaven—I want you to think now about this Jesus who is God's Messenger and the High Priest of our faith.

3:2
Num 12:7,8

²For Jesus was faithful to God who appointed him High Priest, just as Moses also faithfully served in God's house. ³But Jesus has far more glory than Moses, just as a man who builds a fine house gets more praise than his house does. ⁴And many people can build houses, but only God made everything.

3:3
2 Cor 3:7-11

3:5
Ex 14:31
Deut 18:15,18

⁵Well, Moses did a fine job working in God's house, but he was only a servant; and his work was mostly to illustrate and suggest those things that would happen later on. ⁶But Christ, God's faithful Son, is in complete charge of God's house. And we Christians are God's house—he lives in us!—if we keep up our courage firm to the end, and our joy and our trust in the Lord.

3:6
a) Eph 2:19-22
1 Tim 3:15
1 Pet 2:5
b) Mt 10:22
Rom 11:22

Now is the time to listen to God

3:7
2 Sam 23:2
Ps 95:7,8
Acts 1:16

⁷, ⁸And since Christ is so much superior, the Holy Spirit warns us to listen to him, to be careful to hear his voice today and not let our hearts become set against him, as the people of Israel did. They steeled themselves against his love and complained against him in the desert while he was testing them. ⁹But God was patient with them forty years, though they tried his patience sorely; he kept right on doing his mighty miracles for them to see. ¹⁰"But," God says, "I was very angry with them, for their hearts were always looking somewhere else instead of up to me, and they never found the paths I wanted them to follow."

3:9
Ps 95:9
Acts 7:36

3:10
Ps 95:10

3:11
Ps 95:11

¹¹Then God, full of this anger against them, bound himself with an oath that he would never let them come to his place of rest.

¹²Beware then of your own hearts, dear brothers, lest you find that they, too, are

---

3:1 This verse was especially meaningful to Jewish Christians. For Jews, the highest human authority was the High Priest. For Christians, the highest human authorities were God's messengers, his apostles. Jesus, God's Messenger and High Priest, is the ultimate authority in the church.

3:1–6 The author uses different pictures to explain Jesus' relationship to believers: he is (1) the Messenger of God, to whom we should listen; (2) our High Priest, by whom we come to God the Father; (3) our Creator, whom we should praise; and (4) the ruler of God's house, whom we should obey. The Bible is filled with pictures of Jesus Christ, and each one shows a different facet of his character.

3:2, 3 To the Jewish people, Moses was a great hero; he brought their ancestors, the Israelites, from Egyptian bondage to the Promised Land. He also wrote the first five books of the Old Testament and was the prophet through whom God gave the moral and the ceremonial law. But Jesus is superior to Moses, because Moses was merely a human servant of God, while Jesus is God himself (1:3). As Moses led the people of Israel out of Egypt, delivering them from bondage, so Christ leads us out of the slavery to sin. Why settle for Moses, the book of Hebrews asks its readers, when you can have Jesus Christ, who appointed Moses?

3:5 Moses was faithful to God's calling, which was not only to deliver Israel, but also to prepare the way for the Messiah. This is also true of all the Old Testament saints. Thus, knowing the Old Testament is the best foundation for understanding the New Testament. Reading the Old Testament, we see (1) how God used people to accomplish his purposes, (2) how he used events and personalities to illustrate important truths, (3) how, through prophets, he announced the Messiah, and (4) how, through worship, he prepared people to understand the Messiah's work. Include the Old Testament in your regular Bible reading, and the

New Testament will grow clearer and more meaningful to you.

3:6 Since Christ dwells within us as believers, we courageously remain firm to the end. We are not saved by persevering, but perseverance reveals our faithfulness. Without this enduring faithfulness, we could easily be blown away by the winds of persecution.

3:7–15 Many times the Bible warns us not to harden our hearts. "Hardening our hearts" is an expression that means we have set ourselves against God to the point that we are no longer able to turn to him to be saved. Such hardheartedness begins when we refuse to obey God's revealed will. The Israelites became hardhearted when they disobeyed God's command to conquer the Promised Land (see Numbers 13, 14; see also Numbers 20 and Psalm 95). Let us be careful to obey God's Word and not allow our hearts to become hardened.

3:11 *God's rest* has several meanings in Scripture: (1) the seventh day of creation and the weekly Sabbath commemorating it (Genesis 2:2; Hebrews 4:4–9), (2) the Promised Land of Canaan (Deuteronomy 12:8–12; Psalm 95), (3) peace with God now because of our relationship with him through faith (Hebrews 4:1, 3, 8–11), and (4) our future eternal life with Christ (Hebrews 4:8–11). All of these meanings were probably familiar to the Jewish Christian readers of Hebrews.

3:12–14 Our hearts lead us away from the living God when we stubbornly refuse to believe him. If we persist in our unbelief, he will eventually leave us alone. But God can give us new hearts, new desires, and a new spirit (Ezekiel 36:22–27). One antidote to a wayward heart is steadfast fellowship with other believers, talking daily about our mutual faith and encouraging one another with love and concern.

evil and unbelieving and are leading you away from the living God. ¹³Speak to each other about these things every day while there is still time, so that none of you will become hardened against God, being blinded by the glamor of sin. ¹⁴For if we are faithful to the end, trusting God just as we did when we first became Christians, we will share in all that belongs to Christ.

3:13
Eph 4:22

3:14
Heb 3:6

¹⁵But *now* is the time. Never forget the warning, "*Today* if you hear God's voice speaking to you, do not harden your hearts against him, as the people of Israel did when they rebelled against him in the desert."

3:15
Ps 95:7

¹⁶And who were those people I speak of, who heard God's voice speaking to them but then rebelled against him? They were the ones who came out of Egypt with Moses their leader. ¹⁷And who was it who made God angry for all those forty years? These same people who sinned and as a result died in the wilderness. ¹⁸And to whom was God speaking when he swore with an oath that they could never go into the land he had promised his people? He was speaking to all those who disobeyed him. ¹⁹And why couldn't they go in? Because they didn't trust him.

3:16
Deut 1:34,35

3:17
1 Cor 10:5

A rest for God's people

4 Although God's promise still stands—his promise that all may enter his place of rest—we ought to tremble with fear because some of you may be on the verge of failing to get there after all. ²For this wonderful news—the message that God wants to save us—has been given to us just as it was to those who lived in the time of Moses. But it didn't do them any good because they didn't believe it. They didn't mix it with faith. ³For only we who believe God can enter into his place of rest. He has said, "I have sworn in my anger that those who don't believe me will never get in," even though he has been ready and waiting for them since the world began.

4:2
1 Thess 2:13

4:3
Ps 95:11

⁴We know he is ready and waiting because it is written that God rested on the seventh day of creation, having finished all that he had planned to make.

4:4
Gen 2:2
Ex 31:17

⁵Even so they didn't get in, for God finally said, "They shall never enter my rest." ⁶Yet the promise remains and some get in—but not those who had the first chance, for they disobeyed God and failed to enter.

4:6
Num 14:26-30
Heb 3:18

⁷But he has set another time for coming in, and that time is now. He announced this through King David long years after man's first failure to enter, saying in the words already quoted, "Today when you hear him calling, do not harden your hearts against him."

4:7
Ps 95:7

⁸This new place of rest he is talking about does not mean the land of Israel that Joshua led them into. If that were what God meant, he would not have spoken long

4:8
Josh 22:4

3:13 *glamor*, literally, "deceitfulness."

3:15-19 The Israelites failed to enter the Promised Land because they lacked trust in God. They did not believe God would help them conquer the land (see Numbers 14, 15); and lacking trust, they failed. So God sent them into the wilderness to wander for 40 years, an unhappy alternative to the wonderful gift he had planned for them. Lack of trust in God always prevents us from receiving his best.

4:1-3 Some of the Jewish Christians who received this letter of Hebrews may have been on the verge of turning back from their promised rest in Christ, just as the people in Moses' day turned back from the Promised Land. In both cases, the difficulties of the present moment overshadowed the reality of God's promise, and people stopped believing that God was able to fulfill his promises. When we place our trust in our own efforts instead of in Christ, we too are in danger of turning back. Our own efforts are never adequate; only Christ can see us through.

4:2 The Israelites of Moses' day illustrate a problem facing many who fill our churches today. They know a great deal about Christ, but they do not know him personally. They don't mix their knowledge with faith. Let the Good News about Christ affect your life. Believe in him and respond in obedience to him.

4:4 God rested on the seventh day to celebrate the completion of creation. The world was perfect, and he was well satisfied with it. This rest is a foretaste of our eternal joy when creation is redeemed, when every mark of sin has been destroyed and the world is perfect once again. Our rest in Christ begins when we trust him to do his good and perfect work in us and through us.

4:7 God gave Israel the opportunity to enter Canaan, but they failed because they didn't trust him (Numbers 14, 15). Now God offers "another time" to enter his ultimate place of rest—he gives us the opportunity to come to Christ. *Now* is the time to believe in Christ and enter the place of rest, which is peace with God. Tomorrow may be too late.

4:8-11 God wants us to enter his rest. For the Israelites of Moses' time, this rest was the Promised Land. For Christians, it is peace with God now and eternal life in a new earth later. We do not need to wait for the next life to enjoy God's rest and peace; we may have it daily now! Our daily rest in the Lord will not terminate with death, but will mature into an eternal rest in the home Christ is preparing for us (John 14:1-4).

afterwards about "today" being the time to get in. 9So there is a full complete rest *still waiting* for the people of God. 10Christ has already entered there. He is resting from his work, just as God did after the creation. 11Let us do our best to go into that place of rest, too, being careful not to disobey God as the children of Israel did, thus failing to get in.

12For whatever God says to us is full of living power: it is sharper than the sharpest dagger, cutting swift and deep into our innermost thoughts and desires with all their parts, exposing us for what we really are. 13He knows about everyone, everywhere. Everything about us is bare and wide open to the all-seeing eyes of our living God; nothing can be hidden from him to whom we must explain all that we have done.

➤ 3. Christ is greater than the Old Testament priesthood
Jesus Christ is our High Priest

14But Jesus the Son of God is our great High Priest who has gone to heaven itself to help us; therefore let us never stop trusting him. 15This High Priest of ours understands our weaknesses, since he had the same temptations we do, though he never once gave way to them and sinned. 16So let us come boldly to the very throne of God and stay there to receive his mercy and to find grace to help us in our times of need.

5 The Jewish high priest is merely a man like anyone else, but he is chosen to speak for all other men in their dealings with God. He presents their gifts to God and offers to him the blood of animals that are sacrificed to cover the sins of the people and his own sins too. And because he is a man he can deal gently with other men, though they are foolish and ignorant, for he, too, is surrounded with the same temptations and understands their problems very well.

THE CHOICES OF MATURITY	Mature choices	Versus	Immature choices
One way to evaluate spiritual maturity is by looking at the choices we make. The writer of Hebrews notes many of the ways those choices change with personal growth.	Teaching others	rather than . . .	just being taught.
	Developing depth of understanding	rather than . . .	struggling with the basics.
	Self-evaluation	rather than . . .	self-criticism.
	Seeking unity	rather than . . .	disunity.
	Desiring spiritual challenges	rather than . . .	desiring entertainment.
	Careful study and observation	rather than . . .	opinions and half-hearted efforts.
	Active faith	rather than . . .	cautious apathy and doubt.
	Confidence	rather than . . .	fear.
	Feelings and experiences evaluated in the light of God's Word	rather than . . .	experiences evaluated according to feelings.

4:12 The Word of God is not merely words from God, a vehicle for communicating ideas; it is living, life-changing, and dynamic as it works in us. With the incisiveness of a surgeon's knife, it reveals who we are and what we are not. It discerns what is within us, both good and evil. We must not only listen to the Word; we must let it shape our lives.

4:13 Since nothing can be hidden from God, he sees all we do and knows all we think. Even when we are unaware of his presence, even when we try to hide from him, he knows. We can have no secrets from him. Remarkably, though he knows us intimately, he still loves us.

4:14 To the Jews, the High Priest was the highest religious authority in the land. He alone entered the Holy of Holies once a year to make atonement for the sins of the whole nation (Leviticus 16). Like the High Priest, Jesus mediates between God and us. As man's representative, he intercedes for us before God. As God's

representative, he assures us of God's forgiveness. Jesus has more authority than the Jewish High Priests because he is truly God and truly man. Unlike the High Priest who could go before God only once a year, Christ is always at God's right hand, interceding for us.

4:15 Jesus is like us because he experienced every kind of temptation we experience today. But he is different because, although he was tempted, he never sinned. Jesus is the only human being who has ever lived without committing sin. Now in heaven, he completely understands our weaknesses and temptations and offers forgiveness.

4:16 Prayer is our approach to God. Some Christians do it meekly with heads hung, afraid to ask God to meet their needs. Others pray flippantly with little thought. Come with reverence, for he is your King, but come with bold assurance, for he is your Friend and Counselor.

⁴Another thing to remember is that no one can be a high priest just because he wants to be. He has to be called by God for this work in the same way God chose Aaron.

⁵That is why Christ did not elect himself to the honor of being High Priest; no, he was chosen by God. God said to him, "My Son, today I have honored you." ⁶And another time God said to him, "You have been chosen to be a priest forever, with the same rank as Melchizedek."

⁷Yet while Christ was here on earth he pleaded with God, praying with tears and agony of soul to the only one who would save him from [premature] death. And God heard his prayers because of his strong desire to obey God at all times.

⁸And even though Jesus was God's Son, he had to learn from experience what it was like to obey, when obeying meant suffering. ⁹It was after he had proved himself perfect in this experience that Jesus became the Giver of eternal salvation to all those who obey him. ¹⁰For remember that God has chosen him to be a High Priest with the same rank as Melchizedek.

Go beyond elementary principles

¹¹There is much more I would like to say along these lines, but you don't seem to listen, so it's hard to make you understand.

¹²,¹³You have been Christians a long time now, and you ought to be teaching others, but instead you have dropped back to the place where you need someone to teach you all over again the very first principles in God's Word. You are like babies who can drink only milk, not old enough for solid food. And when a person is still living on milk it shows he isn't very far along in the Christian life, and doesn't know much about the difference between right and wrong. He is still a baby-Christian! ¹⁴You will never be able to eat solid spiritual food and understand the deeper things of God's Word until you become better Christians and learn right from wrong by practicing doing right.

6 Let us stop going over the same old ground again and again, always teaching those first lessons about Christ. Let us go on instead to other things and become

5:5 *I have honored you*, literally, "begotten you." **5:7** *premature*, implied.

Marginal references:
5:2 Heb 2:18; 7:28
5:3 Heb 7:27; 9:7
5:4 Ex 28:1; Num 16:40
5:5 Ps 2:7; Acts 13:33; Heb 1:5
5:6 Ps 110:4
5:7 Ps 22:1-4; Mt 26:39,53
5:8 Phil 2:8; Heb 1:2
5:10 Heb 2:17; 6:20
5:12 1 Cor 3:1,2
5:13 1 Cor 14:20; Eph 4:13,14
5:14 1 Cor 2:6,14
6:1 Phil 3:13-16; Heb 5:12,16

5:4-6 This chapter stresses both Christ's divine appointment and his humanity. (The writer uses two Old Testament verses to show Christ's divine appointment—Psalms 2:7 and 110:4.) In the days when this book was written, the Romans chose the High Priest in Jerusalem. In the Old Testament, however, God chose Aaron, and only his descendants could be High Priests. Christ, like Aaron, was chosen by God.

5:6 Melchizedek was a priest of Salem (now called Jerusalem). His Profile is found in Genesis 15. Melchizedek's position is explained in Hebrews 7.

5:7 Jesus found no pleasure in suffering and dying, but he chose to endure pain and humiliation in order to obey his Father. At times we will choose to undergo trials, not because we want to suffer, but because we want to obey God. Let Jesus' obedience sustain you and encourage you in times of trial. You can face anything when you know Jesus Christ is with you.

5:7 Have you ever felt that God didn't hear your prayers? Be sure you are praying with an obedient spirit, willing to do what God wants. God responds to his obedient children.

5:8 Jesus' life was not a script that he passively followed. It was a life he chose freely (John 10:17, 18). He chose to obey, even though obedience led to suffering and death. Because he obeyed perfectly even under trial, he can help us obey, no matter how difficult obedience seems to be.

5:9 Christ was always morally perfect. Through obedience he proved his perfection to us, not to God or to himself. In the Bible, *perfection* often means completeness or maturity. By sharing our

experience of suffering, Christ shared our human experience completely. He is now able to offer eternal salvation to those who obey him.

5:12, 13 These Jewish Christians were immature. They were reluctant to move beyond age-old traditions, established doctrines, and discussion of the basics. They wouldn't be able to understand what the writer was teaching about the high-priestly role of Christ unless they moved out of their comfortable position, cut some of their Jewish ties, and stopped trying to blend in with their culture. Commitment to Christ moves people out of the comfort zone.

5:12-14 In order to grow from a "baby" Christian to a "grown-up" Christian, each of us must learn discernment. By practice we must train our consciences, our senses, our minds, and our bodies to distinguish right from wrong. Can you recognize temptation before it controls you? Can you tell correct use of Scripture from mistaken or shallow uses?

5:14 Our capacity to feast on the deeper things of God is determined by our spiritual growth. Too often we want God's banquet before we are spiritually capable of digesting it. As you grow in the Lord, you will find that you will feast even more bountifully at his table.

6:1, 2 Certain basics are essential for all believers. Those principles that all Christians must know include repentance, baptism, faith, etc. We need to move on to a more complete theology, to a more profound understanding of the faith. And this is what the author intends to do (6:3). Christians should be teaching new Christians the basics, and then, acting on what they know, they should be learning even more from God's Word.

6:2
Acts 6:6; 8:17
17:31; 19:4
24:25
Rom 2:16

6:3
1 Cor 4:19

mature in our understanding, as strong Christians ought to be. Surely we don't need to speak further about the foolishness of trying to be saved by being good, or about the necessity of faith in God; ²you don't need further instruction about baptism and spiritual gifts and the resurrection of the dead and eternal judgment.

³The Lord willing, we will go on now to other things.

☛ **6:2** *spiritual gifts,* literally, "the laying on of hands."

ABRAHAM IN THE NEW TESTAMENT	Abraham was an ancestor of Jesus Christ	Matthew 1:1, 2, 17; Luke 3:23–38	Jesus Christ was human; he was born into the line of Abraham, whom God had chosen to be the father of a great nation through which the whole world would be blessed. We are blessed because of what Jesus Christ, Abraham's descendant, did for us.
	Abraham was the father of the Jewish nation	Matthew 3:9; Luke 3:8; Acts 13:26; Romans 4:1; 11:1; 2 Corinthians 11:22; Hebrews 6:14	God wanted to set apart a nation for himself, a nation that would tell the world about him. He began with a man of faith who, though old and childless, believed God's promise of innumerable descendants. We can trust God to do the impossible when we have faith.
	Abraham was honored by God	Hebrews 7:4	God honors those who trust him. Although the world may disdain us if we trust in God, God promises to honor us.
	Abraham, because of his faith, now sits in the Kingdom with Christ	Matthew 8:11; Luke 13:28; 16:23–31	Abraham followed God and now he is enjoying his reward—eternity with God. We will one day meet Abraham, because we have been promised eternity as well.
	God *is* Abraham's God, thus Abraham is alive with God	Matthew 22:32; Mark 12:26; Luke 20:37; Acts 7:32	As Abraham lives forever, we will live forever because we, like Abraham, have chosen the life of faith.
	Abraham received great promises from God	Luke 1:55, 72, 73; Acts 3:25; 7:17, 18; Galatians 3:6, 14–16; Hebrews 6:13–15	Many of the promises God made to Abraham seemed impossible to be realized, but Abraham trusted God. The promises to believers in God's Word also seem too incredible to believe, but we can trust God to keep all his promises.
	Abraham followed God	Acts 7:2–8; Hebrews 11:8, 17–19	Abraham followed God's leading from his homeland to an unknown territory, which became the Jews' Promised Land. When we follow God, even before he makes all his plans clear to us, we will never be disappointed.
	God blessed Abraham because of his faith	Romans 4; Galatians 3:6–9, 14–29; Hebrews 11:8, 17–19; James 2:21–24	Abraham showed faith in times of disappointment, trial, and testing. Because of his faith, God counted him righteous, his "friend." God accepts us because of our faith.
	Abraham is the father of all those who come to God by faith	Romans 9:6–8; Galatians 3:7–9, 14–29	The Jews are Abraham's children, and Christ was his descendant. We are Christ's brothers and sisters; thus all believers are Abraham's children and God's children. Abraham was righteous because of his faith; we are made righteous by faith in Christ. The promises made to Abraham apply to us because of Christ.

6:3 These Christians needed to go on to understand Christ as the perfect High Priest and fulfillment of all the Old Testament prophecies. Rather than arguing about the respective merits of Judaism and Christianity, they needed to depend on Christ and live effectively for him.

4There is no use trying to bring you back to the Lord again if you have once understood the Good News and tasted for yourself the good things of heaven and shared in the Holy Spirit, 5and know how good the Word of God is, and felt the mighty powers of the world to come, 6and then have turned against God. You cannot bring yourself to repent again if you have nailed the Son of God to the cross again by rejecting him, holding him up to mocking and to public shame.

7When a farmer's land has had many showers upon it and good crops come up, that land has experienced God's blessing upon it. 8But if it keeps on having crops of thistles and thorns, the land is considered no good and is ready for condemnation and burning off.

9Dear friends, even though I am talking like this I really don't believe that what I am saying applies to you. I am confident you are producing the good fruit that comes along with your salvation. 10For God is not unfair. How can he forget your hard work for him, or forget the way you used to show your love for him—and still do—by helping his children? 11And we are anxious that you keep right on loving others as long as life lasts, so that you will get your full reward.

12Then, knowing what lies ahead for you, you won't become bored with being a Christian, nor become spiritually dull and indifferent, but you will be anxious to follow the example of those who receive all that God has promised them because of their strong faith and patience.

God's certain promise gives hope

13For instance, there was God's promise to Abraham: God took an oath in his own name, since there was no one greater to swear by, 14that he would bless Abraham again and again, and give him a son and make him the father of a great nation of people. 15Then Abraham waited patiently until finally God gave him a son, Isaac, just as he had promised.

16When a man takes an oath, he is calling upon someone greater than himself to force him to do what he has promised, or to punish him if he later refuses to do it; the oath ends all argument about it. 17God also bound himself with an oath, so that those he promised to help would be perfectly sure and never need to wonder whether he might change his plans.

18He has given us both his promise and his oath, two things we can completely count on, for it is impossible for God to tell a lie. Now all those who flee to him to save them can take new courage when they hear such assurances from God; now they can know without doubt that he will give them the salvation he has promised them.

19This certain hope of being saved is a strong and trustworthy anchor for our

Cross references

6:4
Mt 7:22
Jn 4:10; 6:32
Eph 2:8
Heb 10:26,32
2 Pet 2:20
1 Jn 5:16

6:5
Heb 2:5
1 Pet 2:3

6:6
Heb 10:26,29

6:10
Mt 10:42; 25:40
Jn 13:20
1 Thess 1:3

6:11
Col 2:2
Heb 3:6; 10:22

6:12
Heb 1:14; 10:36
13:7

6:13
Gen 22:16
Gal 3:16

6:14
Gen 22:16,17

6:15
Gen 21:5

6:16
Ex 22:11
Gal 3:15

6:17
Ps 110:4
Rom 11:29
Heb 11:9

6:18
Tit 1:2
Heb 3:6; 12:1

6:19
Lev 16:15,16
Ps 130:7
Heb 9:7

6:4–6 In the first century, a pagan who investigated Christianity and then went back to paganism made a clean break with the church. But for Jewish Christians who decided to return to Judaism, the break was less obvious. Their lifestyle remained relatively unchanged. But by deliberately turning away from Christ, they were cutting themselves off from God's forgiveness. Those who persevere in believing are true saints; those who continue to reject Christ are unbelievers, no matter how well they behave.

6:6 Some think this verse refers to believers who turn from their salvation. Others think this refers to unbelievers who come close to salvation, then turn away. Either way, those who reject Christ will not be saved. Christ died once for all. He will not be crucified again. Apart from his cross, there is no other possible way of salvation. But the author does not really believe that his readers are in danger of missing salvation (see 6:9).

6:7, 8 Land that produces good fruit receives loving care, but land that produces thistles and thorns has to be burned off so the farmer can start over. An unproductive Christian life falls under God's condemnation. We are not saved by works or conduct, but what we do is the *evidence* of our faith. Being productive for Christ is serious business.

6:12 Hope keeps the Christian from feeling dull or becoming bored. Like an athlete, train hard and run well, remembering the reward that lies ahead (Philippians 3:14).

6:15 Abraham waited patiently—it was 25 years from the time God promised him a son (Genesis 17:16) to Isaac's birth (Genesis 21:1–3).

6:17 God's promises are unchangeable and trustworthy because God is unchangeable and trustworthy. When God promised Abraham a son, he took an oath in his own name. The oath was as good as his name, and his name was as good as his divine nature.

6:18, 19 God embodies all truth, and he therefore cannot lie. Because God is truth, you can be secure in his promises; you don't need to wonder if he will change his plans. For the true seeker who comes to God in belief, God gives an unconditional promise of acceptance. When you ask God in all openness, honesty, and sincerity of heart to save you from your sins, *he will do it*. This assurance should give you courage and hope.

6:19, 20 The veil (the curtain) referred to in the text hung across the entrance from the Holy Place to the Holy of Holies, the two innermost chambers of the Tabernacle. This curtain prevented anyone from entering, gazing into, or even getting a fleeting

souls, connecting us with God himself behind the sacred curtains of heaven, [20]where Christ has gone ahead to plead for us from his position as our High Priest, with the honor and rank of Melchizedek.

Melchizedek compared to Abraham

7 This Melchizedek was king of the city of Salem, and also a priest of the Most High God. When Abraham was returning home after winning a great battle against many kings, Melchizedek met him and blessed him; [2]then Abraham took a tenth of all he had won in the battle and gave it to Melchizedek.

Melchizedek's name means "Justice," so he is the King of Justice; and he is also the King of Peace because of the name of his city, Salem, which means "Peace." [3]Melchizedek had no father or mother and there is no record of any of his ancestors. He was never born and he never died but his life is like that of the Son of God—a priest forever.

[4]See then how great this Melchizedek is:

(a)]Even Abraham, the first and most honored of all God's chosen people, gave Melchizedek a tenth of the spoils he took from the kings he had been fighting. [5]One could understand why Abraham would do this if Melchizedek had been a Jewish priest, for later on God's people were required by law to give gifts to help their priests because the priests were their relatives. [6]But Melchizedek was not a relative, and yet Abraham paid him.

(b)]Melchizedek placed a blessing upon mighty Abraham, [7]and as everyone knows, a person who has the power to bless is always greater than the person he blesses.

[8]*(c)]The Jewish priests, though mortal, received tithes; but we are told that Melchizedek lives on.*

[9]*(d)]One might even say that Levi himself (the ancestor of all Jewish priests, of all who receive tithes), paid tithes to Melchizedek through Abraham.* [10]For although Levi wasn't born yet, the seed from which he came was in Abraham when Abraham paid the tithes to Melchizedek.

[11]*(e)]If the Jewish priests and their laws had been able to save us, why then did God need to send Christ as a priest with the rank of Melchizedek, instead of sending someone with the rank of Aaron—the same rank all other priests had?*

[12, 13, 14]And when God sends a new kind of priest, his law must be changed to permit it. As we all know, Christ did not belong to the priest-tribe of Levi, but came from the tribe of Judah, which had not been chosen for priesthood; Moses had never given them that work.

Christ is like Melchizedek

[15]So we can plainly see that God's method changed, for Christ, the new High Priest who came with the rank of Melchizedek, [16]did not become a priest by meeting the old requirement of belonging to the tribe of Levi, but on the basis of power flowing from a life that cannot end. [17]And the Psalmist points this out when

6:20 *from his position as our High Priest,* literally, "having become our high priest." **7:3** *Melchizedek had no father or mother.* No one can be sure whether this means that Melchizedek was Christ appearing to Abraham in human form or simply that there is no *record* of who Melchizedek's father and mother were, no *record* of his birth or death.

---

glimpse of the interior of the Holy of Holies (see also 9:1–8). The High Priest could enter the Holy of Holies only once a year to stand before God's presence and atone for the sins of the entire nation. But Christ is in God's presence at all times, not just once a year, as the High Priest who can continually plead for us.

7:1 *Melchizedek* means "king of righteousness," and *Salem* means "peace."

7:2 The writer of Hebrews uses this story to show that there is someone greater even than Abraham, father of the Jewish nation, and Levi (Abraham's descendant). Therefore, the Jewish priesthood (made up of Levi's descendants) was inferior to Melchizedek's priesthood (a type of Christ's priesthood).

7:3–10 Melchizedek was a priest of the most high God (see note on Genesis 14:18 and his Profile in Genesis 15). He is said to be a priest forever (Psalm 110:4) because his priesthood has no record of beginning or end—he was a priest of God in Salem (Jerusalem) long before the nation of Israel and the levitical system began.

7:11–16 Jesus' high-priestly role was superior to that of any priest of Levi, because the Messiah was a priest of a higher rank (Psalm 110:4). The animal sacrifices had to be repeated, and they offered only temporary forgiveness; Christ's sacrifice was offered once, and it offers total and permanent forgiveness. Under the new covenant, the levitical priesthood was canceled in favor of Christ's role as High Priest.

6:20
Heb 4:14; 5:6
9:24

7:1
Gen 14:17-20
Ps 110:4
Heb 5:6,10

7:4
Gen 14:20

7:5
Num 18:21,26

7:6
Rom 4:13
Gal 3:16

7:8
Heb 5:6

7:11
Gal 2:21
Heb 7:17,18

7:14
Gen 49:10
Isa 11:1
Mt 1:3
Lk 3:33
Rom 1:3
Rev 5:5

7:17
Ps 110:4

he says of Christ, "You are a priest forever with the rank of Melchizedek." | **7:18**
Rom 8:3
Gal 4:9
Heb 7:11

18Yes, the old system of priesthood based on family lines was canceled because it didn't work. It was weak and useless for saving people. 19It never made anyone really right with God. But now we have a far better hope, for Christ makes us acceptable to God, and now we may draw near to him. | **7:19**
Acts 13:39
Rom 3:20; 5:2
Gal 2:16

20God took an oath that Christ would always be a Priest, 21although he never said that of other priests. Only to Christ he said, "The Lord has sworn and will never change his mind: You are a Priest forever, with the rank of Melchizedek." 22Because of God's oath, Christ can guarantee forever the success of this new and better arrangement. | **7:20**
Heb 6:18; 9:9
10:19-22
7:21
Num 23:19
Ps 110:4
Heb 7:28
7:22
Heb 8:6

23Under the old arrangement there had to be many priests, so that when the older ones died off, the system could still be carried on by others who took their places. | **7:24**
Isa 9:6,7
Jn 12:34
Rev 1:18

24But Jesus lives forever and continues to be a Priest so that no one else is needed. 25He is able to save completely all who come to God through him. Since he will live forever, he will always be there to remind God that he has paid for their sins with his blood. | **7:25**
Rom 8:34
1 Tim 2:5
1 Jn 2:1

26He is, therefore, exactly the kind of High Priest we need; for he is holy and blameless, unstained by sin, undefiled by sinners, and to him has been given the place of honor in heaven. 27He never needs the daily blood of animal sacrifices, as other priests did, to cover over first their own sins and then the sins of the people; for he finished all sacrifices, once and for all, when he sacrificed himself on the cross. 28Under the old system, even the high priests were weak and sinful men who could not keep from doing wrong, but later God appointed by his oath his Son who is perfect forever. | **7:26**
2 Cor 5:21
1 Pet 2:22
7:27
Lev 9:7
16:6,11,15
Rom 6:10
Eph 5:2
Heb 5:3; 9:7,12
7:28
Heb 2:10; 5:1,2

← 4. The new covenant is greater than the old

Christthe High Priest of the new covenant

8 What we are saying is this: Christ, whose priesthood we have just described, is our High Priest, and is in heaven at the place of greatest honor next to God himself. 2He ministers in the temple in heaven, the true place of worship built by the Lord and not by human hands. | **8:1**
Col 3:1
Heb 1:3; 2:17
8:2
Ex 33:7
Heb 9:11; 10:11

3And since every high priest is appointed to offer gifts and sacrifices, Christ must make an offering too. 4The sacrifice he offers is far better than those offered by the | **8:3**
Eph 5:2
Heb 5:1

7:18, 19 The law was not intended to save people, but to point out sin (see Romans 3:20; 5:20) and to point toward Christ (see Galatians 3:24, 25). Salvation comes through Christ, whose sacrifice brings forgiveness for our sins.

7:22–24 This new arrangement is also called the new covenant or new testament. It is new in allowing us to go directly to God through Christ, no longer having to rely on sacrificed animals and priests to gain God's forgiveness. This new arrangement is better because, while priests died, Christ lives forever. Priests and sacrifices could not save people, but Christ truly saves.

7:25 What does it mean that Jesus is able to save completely? No one else can add to what Jesus did to save us; our past, present, and future sins are all forgiven, and Jesus is with the Father as a sign that our sins are forgiven. If you are a Christian, remember that Christ has paid the price for your sins once and for all. (See also 9:25, 26.)

7:25 As our High Priest, Christ is our advocate, the mediator between us and God. The Old Testament High Priest went before God once a year to plead for the forgiveness of the nation's sins; Christ makes perpetual intercession before God for us. Christ's presence in heaven with the Father assures us that our sins have been paid for and forgiven (see Romans 8:33, 34; Hebrews 2:17, 18; 4:15, 16).

7:27 In Old Testament times when animals were sacrificed, they were cut into pieces, the parts were washed, the fat was burned, the blood was sprinkled, and the meat was boiled. Blood was

demanded as atonement for sins, and God accepted animal blood to cover the people's sins (Leviticus 17:11). Because of the sacrificial system, the Israelites were generally aware that sin costs and that they themselves were sinful. One problem with the world today is that most people don't realize how costly it was for Jesus to secure our forgiveness—it cost him his blood (1 Peter 1:18, 19).

7:27 Because Christ died *once* and *for all*, he finished all sacrifices. He forgave sins—past, present, and future. The Jews did not need to go back to the old system because Christ, the perfect sacrifice, completed the work of redemption. You need not look for another way to have your sins forgiven—Christ was the final sacrifice for you.

7:28 These verses help explain why Jesus had to die. As we better understand the Jewish sacrificial system, we see that Jesus' death served as the perfect atonement for our sins. His death brings us eternal life. How callous, how cold, how stubborn are those who refuse to accept this death, God's greatest gift.

8:4 Under the old Jewish system, priests were chosen only from the tribe of Levi, and sacrifices were offered daily on the altar for forgiveness of sins (see 7:12–14). This system would not have allowed Jesus to be a priest because he was from the tribe of Judah. But his perfect sacrifice ended all need for further priests and sacrifices.

The use of the present tense, "the priests *still follow* the old Jewish system," seems to indicate that this book was written before A.D. 70 when the Temple in Jerusalem was destroyed, ending the sacrifices.

8:5
Ex 25:40
Col 2:17
Heb 9:23

8:6
2 Cor 3:6
Heb 7:22

8:7
Heb 7:11
8:8-11
Jer 31:31-34

8:11
Jn 6:45
1 Jn 2:27

8:13
Heb 12:24

earthly priests. (But even so, if he were here on earth he wouldn't even be permitted to be a priest, because down here the priests still follow the old Jewish system of sacrifices.) 5Their work is connected with a mere earthly model of the real tabernacle in heaven; for when Moses was getting ready to build the tabernacle, God warned him to follow exactly the pattern of the heavenly tabernacle as shown to him on Mount Sinai. 6But Christ, as a Minister in heaven, has been rewarded with a far more important work than those who serve under the old laws, because the new agreement which he passes on to us from God contains far more wonderful promises.

7The old agreement didn't even work. If it had, there would have been no need for another to replace it. 8But God himself found fault with the old one, for he said, "The day will come when I will make a new agreement with the people of Israel and the people of Judah. 9This new agreement will not be like the old one I gave to their fathers on the day when I took them by the hand to lead them out of the land of Egypt; they did not keep their part in that agreement, so I had to cancel it. 10But this is the new agreement I will make with the people of Israel, says the Lord: I will write my laws in their minds so that they will know what I want them to do without my even telling them, and these laws will be in their hearts so that they will want to obey them, and I will be their God and they shall be my people. 11And no one then will need to speak to his friend or neighbor or brother, saying, 'You, too, should know the Lord,' because everyone, great and small, will know me already. 12And I will be merciful to them in their wrongdoings, and I will remember their sins no more."

13God speaks of these new promises, of this new agreement, as taking the place of the old one; for the old one is out of date now and has been put aside forever.

THE OLD AND NEW COVENANTS
Like pointing out the similarities and differences between the photograph of a person and the actual person, the writer of Hebrews shows the connection between the old Mosaic covenant and the new Messianic covenant. He proves that the old covenant was a shadow of a real Christ.

The Old Covenant under Moses	The New Covenant in Christ	Application
Gifts and sacrifices by those guilty of sin	Self-sacrifice by the guiltless Christ	Christ died for you
Focused on a physical building where one goes to worship	Focuses on the reign of Christ in the hearts of believers	God is directly involved in your life
A model	A reality	Not temporal, but eternal
Limited promises	Limitless promises	We can trust God's promises to us
Failed agreement by people	Faithful agreement by Christ	Christ has kept the agreement where people couldn't
External standards and rules	Internal standards—a new heart	God sees both actions and motives—we are accountable to God, not rules
Limited access to God	Unlimited access to God	God is personally available
Based on fear	Based on love and forgiveness	Forgiveness keeps our failures from destroying the agreement
Legal cleansing	Personal cleansing	God's cleansing is complete
Continual sacrifice	Conclusive sacrifice	Christ's sacrifice was perfect and final
Obey the rules	Serve the living God	We have a relationship, not regulations
Forgiveness earned	Forgiveness freely given	We have true and complete forgiveness
Repeated yearly	Completed by Christ's death	Christ's death can be applied to your sin
Man's effort	God's grace	Initiated by God's love for you
Available to some	Available to all	Available to you

8:7-12 This passage quotes Jeremiah 31:31–34 and compares the new agreement with the old. The old agreement was the covenant of law between God and Israel. The new and better way is the covenant of grace—Christ's offer to forgive our sins and bring us to God through his sacrificial death. This agreement is new in extent—it goes beyond Israel and Judah to all the Gentile nations. It is new in application, since it is written in our hearts and minds. It offers a new way to forgiveness, not through animal sacrifice but through faith. Have you entered into this new agreement and begun walking in the better way?

8:10, 11 Under God's new agreement, God's law is inside us. The Holy Spirit reminds us of Christ's words, quickens our consciences, influences our motives and desires, and makes us want to obey.

Rules for worship under the old covenant

9 Now in that first agreement between God and his people there were rules for worship and there was a sacred tent down here on earth. Inside this place of worship there were two rooms. The first one contained the golden candlestick and a table with special loaves of holy bread upon it; this part was called the Holy Place. ³Then there was a curtain and behind the curtain was a room called the Holy of Holies. ⁴In that room there were a golden incense-altar and the golden chest, called the ark of the covenant, completely covered on all sides with pure gold. Inside the ark were the tablets of stone with the Ten Commandments written on them, and a golden jar with some manna in it, and Aaron's wooden cane that budded. ⁵Above the golden chest were statues of angels called the cherubim—the guardians of God's glory—with their wings stretched out over the ark's golden cover, called the mercy seat. But enough of such details.

⁶Well, when all was ready the priests went in and out of the first room whenever they wanted to, doing their work. ⁷But only the high priest went into the inner room, and then only once a year, all alone, and always with blood which he sprinkled on the mercy seat as an offering to God to cover his own mistakes and sins, and the mistakes and sins of all the people.

⁸And the Holy Spirit uses all this to point out to us that under the old system the common people could not go into the Holy of Holies as long as the outer room and the entire system it represents were still in use.

⁹This has an important lesson for us today. For under the old system, gifts and sacrifices were offered, but these failed to cleanse the hearts of the people who brought them. ¹⁰For the old system dealt only with certain rituals—what foods to eat and drink, rules for washing themselves, and rules about this and that. The people had to keep these rules to tide them over until Christ came with God's new and better way.

Christ is the perfect offering for sin

¹¹He came as High Priest of this better system which we now have. He went into that greater, perfect tabernacle in heaven, not made by men nor part of this world, ¹²and once for all took blood into that inner room, the Holy of Holies, and sprinkled it on the mercy seat; but it was not the blood of goats and calves. No, he took his own blood, and with it he, by himself, made sure of our eternal salvation.

¹³And if under the old system the blood of bulls and goats and the ashes of young cows could cleanse men's bodies from sin, ¹⁴just think how much more surely the blood of Christ will transform our lives and hearts. His sacrifice frees us from the worry of having to obey the old rules, and makes us want to serve the living God.

9:1 Ex 25:8

9:2 Ex 25:23,31 26:1 Lev 24:5

9:3 Ex 26:31,33 40:3

9:4 Ex 16:33 25:10,16 30:1; 31:18 Num 17:10 Deut 10:2 2 Chron 5:10

9:5 Ex 25:18-20 Lev 16:2

9:7 Ex 30:10 Lev 16:11 Num 15:25 Heb 5:3

9:8 Jn 14:6 Heb 10:20

9:9 Gal 3:21,22 Heb 5:1

9:10 Lev 11:2,25 Num 6:3; 19:7 Rom 14:17 Eph 2:15

9:11 Mk 14:58; Heb 8:2; 9:24 10:1

9:12 Lev 4:3 Heb 7:27

9:13 Lev 16:14,15 Num 19:2,9

9:14 Heb 1:3; 6:1 1 Pet 3:18 1 Jn 1:7

9:1 The "sacred tent" refers to the Tabernacle that God instructed Moses to set up (see Exodus 36–40).

9:6–8 The High Priest could enter the Holy of Holies, the innermost room of the Tabernacle, one day each year, the Day of Atonement, to atone for the nation's sins. The Holy of Holies was a small room that contained the ark of the covenant (a gold-covered chest containing the original stone tablets on which the Ten Commandments were written, a pot of manna, and Aaron's rod). The top of the chest served as the "mercy seat" (the altar) on which the blood was sprinkled by the High Priest on the Day of Atonement. The Holy of Holies was the most sacred spot on earth for the Jews. Only the High Priest could enter—the other priests and the common people were forbidden to come into the room. Their only access to God was through the High Priest who offered a sacrifice and used its blood to atone first for his own sins and then for the people's sins (see also 10:19).

9:9–14 Though you know Christ, you may still be trying to make yourself good enough for God. But rules and rituals have never cleansed people's hearts. By Jesus' blood alone (1) our consciences are cleared, (2) we are freed from death and can live

to serve God, and (3) we are freed from sin's power. If you are carrying a load of guilt because you can't be good enough for God, take another look at Jesus' death and what it means for you.

9:12 This imagery comes from the Day of Atonement rituals described in Leviticus 16.

9:13, 14 Through the blood of sacrificed animals, God cleansed people from sin, making them *ceremonially* acceptable according to Old Testament law. But Christ's sacrifice transforms our lives and hearts and makes us clean on the inside. His sacrifice is infinitely more effective than animal sacrifices.

9:14 God required the people to bring perfect animals for sacrifices. Their sins cost them something; they could not dump them on the heads of useless or damaged animals. This pointed to Christ, the unblemished Lamb of God. Because he was sinless, his sacrifice was infinitely valuable.

9:14 If our hearts are not changed, following God's rules is unpleasant and difficult. We rebel against being told how to live. The Holy Spirit, however, gives us new desires. He helps us want to obey God (see Philippians 2:12, 13). With new hearts, we find that serving God is our greatest joy.

9:15
Rom 3:25
1 Tim 2:5
Heb 3:1
1 Pet 3:18

For by the help of the eternal Holy Spirit, Christ willingly gave himself to God to die for our sins—he being perfect, without a single sin or fault. 15Christ came with this new agreement so that all who are invited may come and have forever all the wonders God has promised them. For Christ died to rescue them from the penalty of the sins they had committed while still under that old system.

16Now, if someone dies and leaves a will—a list of things to be given away to certain people when he dies—no one gets anything until it is proved that the person who wrote the will is dead. 17The will goes into effect only after the death of the person who wrote it. While he is still alive no one can use it to get any of those things he has promised them.

9:17
Gal 3:15

9:18
Ex 24:6

9:19
Ex 24:5-8
Lev 14:4
Heb 1:1

9:20
Ex 24:8
Mt 26:28

9:21
Ex 29:12
Lev 8:15

18That is why blood was sprinkled [as proof of Christ's death] before even the first agreement could go into effect. 19For after Moses had given the people all of God's laws, he took the blood of calves and goats, along with water, and sprinkled the blood over the book of God's laws and over all the people, using branches of hyssop bushes and scarlet wool to sprinkle with. 20Then he said, "This is the blood that marks the beginning of the agreement between you and God, the agreement God commanded me to make with you." 21And in the same way he sprinkled blood on the sacred tent and on whatever instruments were used for worship. 22In fact we can say that under the old agreement almost everything was cleansed by sprinkling it with blood, and without the shedding of blood there is no forgiveness of sins.

9:22
Lev 17:11

9:23
Heb 8:5

9:24
Rom 8:34
Heb 6:20; 7:25
8:2; 9:12
1 Jn 2:1

23That is why the sacred tent down here on earth, and everything in it—all copied from things in heaven—all had to be made pure by Moses in this way, by being sprinkled with the blood of animals. But the real things in heaven, of which these down here are copies, were made pure with far more precious offerings.

9:25
Heb 9:2,7

9:26
1 Cor 10:11
Eph 1:10
Heb 7:27; 10:10
1 Pet 3:18

24For Christ has entered into heaven itself, to appear now before God as our Friend. It was not in the earthly place of worship that he did this, for that was merely a copy of the real temple in heaven. 25Nor has he offered himself again and again, as the high priest down here on earth offers animal blood in the Holy of Holies each year. 26If that had been necessary, then he would have had to die again and again, ever since the world began. But no! He came once for all, at the end of the age, to put away the power of sin forever by dying for us.

9:27
Gen 3:19
Eccles 3:20

9:28
Mt 25:34; 26:28
Acts 1:11
Rom 5:15; 6:10
Tit 2:13
Heb 4:15; 5:19
7:27
1 Pet 2:24

27And just as it is destined that men die only once, and after that comes judgment, 28so also Christ died only once as an offering for the sins of many people; and he will come again, but not to deal again with our sins.

This time he will come bringing salvation to all those who are eagerly and patiently waiting for him.

9:18 *as proof of Christ's death,* implied.

9:15 Value, in our human way of thinking, is not measured by how *many* can have something good, but by how *few* can have something good. "Limited edition" means "valuable" because only a few can have it. God's great plan of redemption, however, stands in sharp contrast to this. It is the most valuable of all treasures, yet it is available to all. The more who have it, and the more they use it, the greater its value! Exercise your faith by sharing it and using it to serve God, and so increase its value.

9:15 People in Old Testament times were saved through Christ's sacrifice, although it had not yet happened. In offering unblemished animal sacrifices, they were looking forward to Christ's coming. There was no point in returning to the sacrificial system now that Christ had come and died for sins. Why continue to look toward something that has already happened?

9:22 Why does forgiveness require the shedding of blood? This is no arbitrary decree on the part of a bloodthirsty God, as some have supposed. There is no greater symbol of life than blood; blood keeps us alive. Jesus shed his blood—gave his life—for our sins so that we wouldn't have to experience spiritual death, which is eternal separation from God. Jesus is the source of life, not death, and he offered his own life so that we might live. After

shedding his blood for us, he rose victorious from the grave and proclaimed victory over sin and death.

9:23 In a way we don't fully understand, the earthly Tabernacle was a reflection and symbol of heavenly realities.

9:24 Amidst references to priests, tabernacles, sacrifices, and other ideas unfamiliar to us, we come to this description of Christ as our Friend. We can relate to this role and be encouraged by it. A friend stands with and stands for; Christ is on our side at God's side. He is our Lord and Savior, but do you also know him as your friend?

9:26 The "end of the age" refers to the time of Christ's coming to earth in fulfillment of the Old Testament prophecies. He ushered in the new era of grace and forgiveness. We are still living in the "last days." The day of the Lord has begun and will be completed at Christ's return.

9:27 All people die physically, but Christ died so that we would not have to die spiritually. His death affects our past, present, and future. He has forgiven our past sin; he has given us the Holy Spirit to help us deal with present sin; and he promises to return and raise us to eternal life in a world from which sin is banished.

— *A sacrifice once for all*

10 The old system of Jewish laws gave only a dim foretaste of the good things Christ would do for us. The sacrifices under the old system were repeated again and again, year after year, but even so they could never save those who lived under their rules. ²If they could have, one offering would have been enough; the worshipers would have been cleansed once for all, and their feeling of guilt would be gone.

³But just the opposite happened: those yearly sacrifices reminded them of their disobedience and guilt instead of relieving their minds. ⁴For it is not possible for the blood of bulls and goats really to take away sins.

⁵That is why Christ said, as he came into the world, "O God, the blood of bulls and goats cannot satisfy you, so you have made ready this body of mine for me to lay as a sacrifice upon your altar. ⁶You were not satisfied with the animal sacrifices, slain and burnt before you as offerings for sin. ⁷Then I said, 'See, I have come to do your will, to lay down my life, just as the Scriptures said that I would.' "

⁸After Christ said this, about not being satisfied with the various sacrifices and offerings required under the old system, ⁹he then added, "Here I am. I have come to give my life."

He cancels the first system in favor of a far better one. ¹⁰Under this new plan we have been forgiven and made clean by Christ's dying for us once and for all. ¹¹Under the old agreement the priests stood before the altar day after day offering sacrifices that could never take away our sins. ¹²But Christ gave himself to God for our sins as one sacrifice for all time, and then sat down in the place of highest honor at God's right hand, ¹³waiting for his enemies to be laid under his feet. ¹⁴For by that one offering he made forever perfect in the sight of God all those whom he is making holy.

¹⁵And the Holy Spirit testifies that this is so, for he has said, ¹⁶"This is the agreement I will make with the people of Israel, though they broke their first agreement: I will write my laws into their minds so that they will always know my will, and I will put my laws in their hearts so that they will want to obey them." ¹⁷And then he adds, "I will never again remember their sins and lawless deeds."

10:1
Col 2:17
Heb 7:19; 8:5
9:11

10:3
Lev 16:21
Heb 9:7

10:4
Mic 6:6
Heb 9:12

10:7
Ps 40:6-8; 50:8
Isa 1:11
Jer 6:20
Amos 5:21

10:10
Jn 17:19
Eph 5:26
Heb 7:27; 9:14,28
1 Pet 2:24

10:11
Num 28:3
Heb 5:1

10:12
Col 3:1
Heb 1:3

10:13
Ps 110:1

10:15
Heb 3:7
2 Pet 1:21

10:16,17
Jer 31:33,34

— **10:3** When people gathered for sacrifice on the Day of Atonement, they were reminded of their sins and felt guilty all over again. What they needed was forgiveness—the permanent, powerful, sin-destroying forgiveness we have from Christ. Once we have confessed a sin to him, we need never think of it again. He has forgiven it, and it no longer exists.

10:4 Animal blood could not take away sin; it could only take it out of sight until Jesus came to deal with it permanently. How, then, were people forgiven in Old Testament times? Just as they are forgiven today—through God's grace, which they accepted through faith.

10:5–10 This quotation is not cited in any other New Testament book. The writer of Hebrews applied to Christ the words of the psalmist in Psalm 40:6–8. But all of Psalm 40 does not apply to Christ (for example, verse 12, where the psalmist speaks of his own sins). Christ came to offer his body upon the cross for us as a sacrifice completely acceptable to God.

10:5-10 The costly sacrifice of a valued animal's life impressed upon the sinner the seriousness of his sin before God. Because Jesus shed his own blood for us, his sacrifice is infinitely bigger than any Old Testament offering. Looking at the immeasurable gift he has given us, we should be overwhelmed with desire to obey him.

10:9 Canceling the first system in favor of a far better one means doing away with the system of sacrifices contained in the ceremonial law; it doesn't mean eliminating God's *moral* law. The ceremonial law prepared people for Christ's coming. With Christ's death and resurrection it was no longer needed. Through Christ we

can fulfill the moral law as we let him live in us.

10:11, 12 It was customary for the priests to stand while offering sacrifices. Christ's act of sitting down at God's right hand symbolizes the end of the sacrificial system.

10:12 The Jewish readers of this book were in danger of returning to the old Jewish system, which would be saying that Christ's sacrifice wasn't enough to forgive their sins. But adding anything to his sacrifice or taking anything from it denies its validity. Any system to win God's approval through good works is essentially rejecting the significance of Christ's death and spurning the Holy Spirit's work. Beware of anyone who tells you that Christ's sacrifice was incomplete or that something else is needed to make you acceptable to God, because this can lead you away from right faith and right living.

10:14 We have been made perfect (complete in Christ), but we are being made holy. Through his death and resurrection, Christ once for all made his believers perfect in God's sight. At the same time, he is making them holy in their daily pilgrimage here. We should not be surprised, ashamed, or shocked that we still need perfection. God is not finished with us. We can encourage this growth process by obeying Christ, by appropriating the values of Scripture in all areas of our lives, and by accepting the forgiveness Christ provides.

10:17 The writer concludes his argument with this powerful statement that God will never remember our sins. If, in Christ, forgiveness is complete, there is no need to continue the former sacrificial system. As believers, we can be confident that our sins—past, present, and future—have been forgiven and forgotten.

18Now, when sins have once been forever forgiven and forgotten, there is no need to offer more sacrifices to get rid of them.

B. THE SUPERIORITY OF FAITH (10:19—13:25)

Moving from argument to instruction, the author cites many examples of those who have demonstrated faith throughout history. Living by faith is far better than merely fulfilling rituals and rules. This can challenge us to grow in faith and to live in obedience to God each day.

Living by faith

19And so, dear brothers, now we may walk right into the very Holy of Holies where God is, because of the blood of Jesus. 20This is the fresh, new, life-giving way which Christ has opened up for us by tearing the curtain—his human body—to let us into the holy presence of God.

21And since this great High Priest of ours rules over God's household, 22let us go right in, to God himself, with true hearts fully trusting him to receive us, because we have been sprinkled with Christ's blood to make us clean, and because our bodies have been washed with pure water.

23Now we can look forward to the salvation God has promised us. There is no longer any room for doubt, and we can tell others that salvation is ours, for there is no question that he will do what he says.

24In response to all he has done for us, let us outdo each other in being helpful and kind to each other and in doing good.

25Let us not neglect our church meetings, as some people do, but encourage and warn each other, especially now that the day of his coming back again is drawing near.

26If anyone sins deliberately by rejecting the Savior after knowing the truth of forgiveness, this sin is not covered by Christ's death; there is no way to get rid of it. 27There will be nothing to look forward to but the terrible punishment of God's awful anger which will consume all his enemies. 28A man who refused to obey the laws given by Moses was killed without mercy if there were two or three witnesses to his sin. 29Think how much more terrible the punishment will be for those who have trampled underfoot the Son of God and treated his cleansing blood as though it were common and unhallowed, and insulted and outraged the Holy Spirit who brings God's mercy to his people.

30For we know him who said, "Justice belongs to me; I will repay them"; who also said, "The Lord himself will handle these cases." 31It is a fearful thing to fall into the hands of the living God.

32Don't ever forget those wonderful days when you first learned about Christ. Remember how you kept right on with the Lord even though it meant terrible suffering. 33Sometimes you were laughed at and beaten, and sometimes you

Cross-references

10:19
Heb 9:25

10:20
Jn 10:9; 14:6
Heb 6:19; 9:8

10:21
1 Tim 3:15
Heb 2:17; 3:6

10:22
Ezek 36:25
2 Cor 7:1
Eph 3:12
Jas 1:6
1 Jn 3:21

10:23
1 Cor 1:9; 10:13
Heb 3:6

10:25
Acts 2:42
Heb 3:13
2 Pet 3:9

10:26
Num 15:30
1 Tim 2:4
2 Pet 2:20
1 Jn 5:16

10:27
Ezek 36:5

10:28
Deut 17:2-5

10:29
Mt 12:31
1 Cor 11:29

10:30
Deut 32:35,36
Ps 50:4; 135:14

10:31
2 Cor 5:11

10:32
Gal 3:4

10:33
1 Cor 4:9
Phil 1:7
1 Thess 2:14

Notes

10:19 The Holy of Holies in the Temple was sealed from view by a curtain. Only the High Priest could enter this holy room, and he did so only once a year on the Day of Atonement when he atoned for the nation's sins. But now, Jesus' death has removed the curtain, and all believers may walk into God's presence at any time (see also 6:19, 20).

10:22–25 These are some of the privileges that come with our new life in Christ: (1) we have personal access to God through Christ and can approach him without an elaborate system (10:22); (2) we may grow in faith, overcome doubts and questions, and deepen our relationship with God (10:23); (3) we may enjoy encouragement from each other (10:24); (4) we may worship together (10:25).

10:25 To neglect Christian meetings is to give up the encouragement and help of other Christians. We gather together to share our faith and strengthen each other in the Lord. As we near the end of the age and as we get closer to the day when Christ will return, we may face many spiritual struggles, tribulations, and even persecution. Anti-Christian forces will grow in strength. Difficulties should never be excuses for missing church services. Rather, as difficulties arise, we should make an even greater effort to be faithful in attendance.

10:26 When people deliberately reject Christ's offer of salvation, they reject God's most precious gift. They push away the work of the Holy Spirit, the one who communicates to us God's saving love. This warning was given to Jewish Christians who were tempted to reject Christ for Judaism, but it applies to anyone who rejects Christ for another religion or, having understood Christ's atoning work, deliberately turns away from it (see also Numbers 15:30, 31 and Mark 3:28–30). The point is that there is no other acceptable sacrifice for sin than the death of Christ on the cross. If someone deliberately, intentionally, purposely rejects the sacrifice of Christ after clearly understanding the gospel teaching about it, then there is no other hope of salvation for that person, for God has not provided any other name under heaven by whom we could be saved (see Acts 4:12).

10:31 This judgment is for those who have rejected God's mercy. For those who accept Christ's love and accept his salvation, the coming judgment is no cause for worry. Being saved through his grace, they have nothing to fear (see 1 John 4:18).

watched and sympathized with others suffering the same things. 34You suffered with those thrown into jail, and you were actually joyful when all you owned was taken from you, knowing that better things were awaiting you in heaven, things that would be yours forever.

35Do not let this happy trust in the Lord die away, no matter what happens. Remember your reward! 36You need to keep on patiently doing God's will if you want him to do for you all that he has promised. 37His coming will not be delayed much longer. 38And those whose faith has made them good in God's sight must live by faith, trusting him in everything. Otherwise, if they shrink back, God will have no pleasure in them.

39But we have never turned our backs on God and sealed our fate. No, our faith in him assures our souls' salvation.

Great heroes of faith

11 What is faith? It is the confident assurance that something we want is going to happen. It is the certainty that what we hope for is waiting for us, even though we cannot see it up ahead. 2Men of God in days of old were famous for their faith.

3By faith—by believing God—we know that the world and the stars—in fact, all things—were made at God's command; and that they were all made from things that can't be seen.

4It was by faith that Abel obeyed God and brought an offering that pleased God more than Cain's offering did. God accepted Abel and proved it by accepting his gift; and though Abel is long dead, we can still learn lessons from him about trusting God.

5Enoch trusted God too, and that is why God took him away to heaven without dying; suddenly he was gone because God took him. Before this happened God had said how pleased he was with Enoch. 6You can never please God without faith, without depending on him. Anyone who wants to come to God must believe that there is a God and that he rewards those who sincerely look for him.

7Noah was another who trusted God. When he heard God's warning about the

11:5 *God had said,* implied.

10:34
Mt 5:12
Heb 13:3

10:36
Col 3:24
Heb 9:15

10:37,38
Lk 18:8
Hab 2:3,4

11:1
Rom 8:24
Heb 3:6,14

11:2
Heb 11:3

11:3
Gen 1:1-31
John 1:3
Rom 1:19,20
4:20
Heb 1:2

11:4
Gen 4:3-5

11:5
Gen 5:22-24

11:6
Jn 3:18,36
Heb 7:19
10:19-22

11:7
Gen 6:13-22
Rom 3:22
Phil 3:9

10:34-37 Hebrews encourages believers, though in the midst of persecution and pressures, to persevere in their Christian lives. We don't usually think of suffering as good, but it can be a positive experience. During times of great stress, we may feel God's presence clearly. Knowing that Jesus is with us in our suffering, and expecting him to return soon to put an end to all pain, we grow in our faith and our relationship with him (see Romans 5:3-5).

10:35-38 The writer encouraged his readers not to shrink back from their faith in times of persecution, but to show by their endurance that their faith was real. Faith means resting in what Christ has done for us in the past, but it also means hoping for what he will do for us in the future (see Romans 8:12-25; Galatians 3:10-13).

11:1 Do you remember how you felt when you were younger and your birthday approached? You were excited and anxious. You knew you would certainly receive gifts and other special treats. But some things would be a surprise. Birthdays combined assurance and anticipation, and so does faith! Faith is the conviction based on past experience that God's new and fresh surprises will surely be ours.

11:1 Two words describe our faith: confidence and certainty. These two qualities need a secure beginning and ending point. The beginning point of faith is believing in God's character—he *is* who he says. The end point is believing in God's promises—he will *do* what he says. We believe that God will fulfill his promises even though we don't see those promises materializing *now*—this is true faith (see John 20:24-31).

11:3 God called the universe into being out of nothing; he

declared that it was to be, and it was. Our faith is in the God who created the entire universe by his Word. God's Word has awesome power. When he speaks, do you listen and respond? How can you better prepare yourself to respond to his Word?

11:4 Cain and Abel were Adam and Eve's first two sons. Abel offered a sacrifice that pleased God, while Cain's sacrifice was unacceptable. Abel's Profile is found in Genesis 5. Cain's Profile is in Genesis 6. Abel's sacrifice (a substitutionary animal) was more acceptable to God, both because it was a blood sacrifice, and because of the attitude in which Abel offered it.

11:6 Believing that God exists is only the beginning, even the demons believe that much (James 2:19, 20). God will not settle for your mere acknowledgment of his existence. He wants a personal, dynamic, life-transforming relationship with you. Those who "sincerely look for him," will find that they are rewarded with God's intimate presence.

11:6 Sometimes we wonder about the fate of those who haven't heard of Christ and have not even had a Bible to read. God assures us that all who honestly seek him—who act in faith on the knowledge of God that they possess—will be rewarded. When you tell others about God's Good News, encourage them to be honest and diligent in their search for truth. Those who hear the gospel are responsible for what they have heard (see 2 Corinthians 6:1, 2).

11:7 Noah experienced what it meant to be different from his neighbors. God commanded him to build a huge boat in the middle of dry land, and although God's command seemed foolish, Noah obeyed. Noah's obedience made him appear strange to his neighbors, just as the new beliefs of Jewish Christians made them

future, Noah believed him even though there was then no sign of a flood, and wasting no time, he built the ark and saved his family. Noah's belief in God was in direct contrast to the sin and disbelief of the rest of the world—which refused to obey—and because of his faith he became one of those whom God has accepted.

8Abraham trusted God, and when God told him to leave home and go far away to another land which he promised to give him, Abraham obeyed. Away he went, not even knowing where he was going. 9And even when he reached God's promised land, he lived in tents like a mere visitor, as did Isaac and Jacob, to whom God gave the same promise. 10Abraham did this because he was confidently waiting for God to bring him to that strong heavenly city whose designer and builder is God.

11Sarah, too, had faith, and because of this she was able to become a mother in spite of her old age, for she realized that God, who gave her his promise, would certainly do what he said. 12And so a whole nation came from Abraham, who was too old to have even one child—a nation with so many millions of people that, like the stars of the sky and the sand on the ocean shores, there is no way to count them.

13These men of faith I have mentioned died without ever receiving all that God had promised them; but they saw it all awaiting them on ahead and were glad, for they agreed that this earth was not their real home but that they were just strangers visiting down here. 14And quite obviously when they talked like that, they were looking forward to their real home in heaven.

15If they had wanted to, they could have gone back to the good things of this world. 16But they didn't want to. They were living for heaven. And now God is not ashamed to be called their God, for he has made a heavenly city for them.

17While God was testing him, Abraham still trusted in God and his promises, and so he offered up his son Isaac, and was ready to slay him on the altar of sacrifice; 18yes, to slay even Isaac, through whom God had promised to give Abraham a whole nation of descendants!

19He believed that if Isaac died God would bring him back to life again; and that is just about what happened, for as far as Abraham was concerned, Isaac was doomed to death, but he came back again alive! 20It was by faith that Isaac knew God would give future blessings to his two sons, Jacob and Esau.

21By faith Jacob, when he was old and dying, blessed each of Joseph's two sons as he stood and prayed, leaning on the top of his cane.

11:8
Gen 12:1-4

11:9
Gen 12:8

11:10
Heb 11:16; 12:22
Rev 21:2

11:11
Gen 17:19
21:1-3

11:12
Gen 15:5
Rom 4:19

11:13
Gen 23:4
Mt 13:17
Jn 8:56
Heb 11:39
11:14
Heb 13:14

11:15
Gen 24:6

11:16
Gen 26:24
Ex 3:6,15
Phil 3:20

11:17
Gen 22:1,2
Jas 2:21

11:18
Gen 21:12

11:19
Rom 4:21
11:20
Gen 27:27-29

11:21
Gen 47:31; 48:5

---

stand out. As you obey God, don't be surprised if others consider you different. Your obedience makes their disobedience stand out. Remember, if God asks you to do something, he will give you the necessary strength to carry out that task. For more information on Noah, see his Profile in Genesis 8.

11:8-10 Abraham's life was filled with faith. At God's command, he left home and went to another land—obeying without question (Genesis 12:1ff). He believed the covenant that God made with him (Genesis 12:2, 3; 13:14-16; 15:1-6). In obedience to God, Abraham was even willing to sacrifice his son Isaac (Genesis 22:1-19). Do not be surprised if God asks you to give up the security of the familiar to obey him. For further information on Abraham, see his Profile in Genesis 17.

11:11, 12 Sarah was Abraham's wife. They were unable to have children through many years of their marriage. God promised Abraham a son, but Sarah doubted that she could become pregnant in her old age. At first she laughed, but afterwards, she believed (Genesis 18). For more information on Sarah, see her Profile in Genesis 19.

11:13-16 The people of faith listed here died without receiving all that God had promised, but they never lost their vision of heaven. Many Christians become frustrated and defeated because their needs, wants, expectations, and demands are not immediately met when they believe in Christ. They become impatient and want to quit. Are you discouraged because your goal seems far away? Take courage from these heroes of faith who lived and died without

seeing the fruit of their faith on earth, and yet continued to believe.

11:17-19 Abraham was willing to give up his son when God commanded him to do so (Genesis 22:1-19). God did not let Abraham take Isaac's life, because God gave the command to test Abraham's faith. Instead of taking Abraham's son, God gave him a whole nation of descendants through Isaac. If you are afraid to trust God with your most prized possession, dream, or person, pay attention to Abraham's example. Because Abraham was willing to give up everything for God, he received back more than he could have imagined. What we receive, however, is not always immediate, or in the form of material possessions. After all, material possessions should be among the least satisfying of rewards. Our best and greatest rewards await us in eternity.

11:20 Isaac was the son promised to Abraham and Sarah in their old age. It was through Isaac that God fulfilled his promise to give Abraham countless descendants. Isaac had twin sons, Jacob and Esau. God chose the younger son, Jacob, through whom to continue his promise to Abraham. For more information on Isaac, see his Profile in Genesis 22.

11:21 Jacob was Isaac's son and Abraham's grandson. Jacob's sons became the fathers of Israel's 12 tribes. Even when Jacob (also called "Israel") was dying in a strange land, he believed the promise that Abraham's descendants would be like the sand on the seashore and that Israel would become a great nation (Genesis 48:1-22). True faith helps us see beyond the grave. For more information on Jacob and Esau, see their Profiles in Genesis.

➤ 22And it was by faith that Joseph, as he neared the end of his life, confidently
spoke of God bringing the people of Israel out of Egypt; and he was so sure of it that
he made them promise to carry his bones with them when they left!

23Moses' parents had faith too. When they saw that God had given them an
unusual child, they trusted that God would save him from the death the king
commanded, and they hid him for three months, and were not afraid.

24, 25It was by faith that Moses, when he grew up, refused to be treated as the
grandson of the king, but chose to share ill-treatment with God's people instead of
enjoying the fleeting pleasures of sin. 26He thought that it was better to suffer for
the promised Christ than to own all the treasures of Egypt, for he was looking
forward to the great reward that God would give him. 27And it was because he
trusted God that he left the land of Egypt and wasn't afraid of the king's anger.
Moses kept right on going; it seemed as though he could see God right there with
him. 28And it was because he believed God would save his people that he commanded them to kill a lamb as God had told them to and sprinkle the blood on the
doorposts of their homes, so that God's terrible Angel of Death could not touch the
oldest child in those homes, as he did among the Egyptians.

29The people of Israel trusted God and went right through the Red Sea as though
they were on dry ground. But when the Egyptians chasing them tried it, they all
were drowned.

30It was faith that brought the walls of Jericho tumbling down after the people of
Israel had walked around them seven days, as God had commanded them. 31By
faith—because she believed in God and his power—Rahab the harlot did not die
with all the others in her city when they refused to obey God, for she gave a friendly
welcome to the spies.

32Well, how much more do I need to say? It would take too long to recount the
stories of the faith of Gideon and Barak and Samson and Jephthah and David and
Samuel and all the other prophets. 33These people all trusted God and as a result

11:22
Gen 50:24,25
Ex 13:19

11:23
Ex 1:16; 2:2

11:25
Ex 2:10-12
Ps 84:10

11:27
Ex 10:28; 12:37
Heb 11:1

11:28
Ex 12:1-13,21-30

11:29
Ex 14:13-31

11:30
Josh 6:20

11:31
Josh 2:9; 6:23
Jas 2:25

11:32
Judg 4:6; 6:11
11:1; 13:24
1 Sam 1:20
16:1

11:33
1 Sam 17:34
Dan 6:22

11:22 Joseph, one of Jacob's sons, was sold into slavery by his
jealous brothers (Genesis 37). Eventually, Joseph was sold again,
this time to an officer of the Pharaoh of Egypt. Because of his
faithfulness to God, however, Joseph was given a top-ranking
position in Egypt. Although Joseph could have used that position
to build a personal empire, he remembered God's promise to
Abraham. After he had been reconciled to his brothers, he brought
his family to be near him, and requested that his bones be taken to
the Promised Land when the Jews eventually left Egypt (Genesis
50:24, 25). Faith means trusting in God and doing what he wants,
regardless of the circumstances. For more information on Joseph,
see his Profile in Genesis 37.

11:23 Moses' parents trusted God for their son's life. They were
not merely proud parents, they were believers who had faith that
God would care for him. As a parent, have you trusted God
enough to take care of your children? God has a plan for every
person, and your important task is to pray for and prepare your
children to do the work God has planned for them to do. Faith
allows us to entrust even our children to God.

11:24–28 Moses became one of Israel's greatest leaders, a
prophet and a lawgiver. But when he was born, his people were
slaves in Egypt and the Egyptian officials had ordered that all
Hebrew baby boys were to be killed. Moses was spared, however,
and Pharaoh's daughter raised Moses in Pharaoh's own household
(Exodus 1, 2)! It took faith for Moses to give up his place in the
palace, but he could do it because he saw the fleeting nature of
great wealth and prestige. It is easy to be deceived by the
temporary benefits of wealth, popularity, status, and achievement,
and to be blind to the long-range benefits of God's Kingdom. Faith
helps us look beyond the world's value system to see the eternal
values of God's Kingdom. For more information on Moses, see his
Profile in Exodus 16.

11:31 When Joshua planned the conquest of Jericho, he sent

spies to investigate the fortifications of the city. The spies met
Rahab, who had two strikes against her—she was a Gentile and a
prostitute. But she showed that she had faith in God by welcoming
the spies and by trusting God to spare her and her family when the
city was destroyed. Faith helps us to change and do what is right
regardless of our past or the disapproval of others. For more
information on Rahab, see her Profile in Joshua 2.

11:32–40 These verses summarize the lives of other great men
and women of faith. Some experienced outstanding victories, even
over death. But others were severely mistreated, tortured, and
even killed. Having a steadfast faith in God does not guarantee a
happy, carefree life. On the contrary, our faith almost guarantees
us some form of abuse from the world. While we are on earth, we
may never see the purpose of our suffering. But we know that God
will keep his promises to us. Is your faith based on the assurance
that God will keep his promises to you?

11:33–35 The Old Testament records the lives of various people
who experienced these great victories. Deborah won battles
(Judges 4, 5). Joshua overthrew kingdoms (the book of Joshua).
Nehemiah ruled God's people well (the book of Nehemiah). Daniel
was kept from harm in the den of lions (Daniel 6). Shadrach,
Meshach, and Abednego were kept from harm in the fiery furnace
(Daniel 3). Elijah escaped the swords of evil queen Jezebel's
henchmen (1 Kings 19:2ff). Hezekiah became strong after
sickness (2 Kings 20). Gideon had great power in battle (Judges
7). A widow's son was brought back to life by the prophet Elisha
(2 Kings 4:8–37).

We, too, can experience victory through faith in Christ. Our
victories may be similar to those experienced by the Old
Testament saints, but more likely, each of our victories will be
directly related to our unique circumstances in life. Ultimately our
most important victory will not be that we are saved from physical
torture or death. Those experiences happen to some, but they only

11:34
Judg 7:18-21
1 Sam 14:13
1 Kgs 19:3
2 Kgs 20:7
Job 42:10
Dan 3:25

11:35
1 Kgs 17:22
2 Kgs 4:35
Acts 22:25

11:36
Gen 39:20
Jer 20:2; 37:15

11:37
1 Kgs 19:10
21:13
2 Chron 24:21
Acts 7:58; 14:19

11:38
1 Kgs 18:4

11:40
Rom 11:26
Rev 6:11

won battles, overthrew kingdoms, ruled their people well, and received what God had promised them; they were kept from harm in a den of lions, 34and in a fiery furnace. Some, through their faith, escaped death by the sword. Some were made strong again after they had been weak or sick. Others were given great power in battle; they made whole armies turn and run away. 35And some women, through faith, received their loved ones back again from death. But others trusted God and were beaten to death, preferring to die rather than turn from God and be free—trusting that they would rise to a better life afterwards.

36Some were laughed at and their backs cut open with whips, and others were chained in dungeons. 37, 38Some died by stoning and some by being sawed in two; others were promised freedom if they would renounce their faith, then were killed with the sword. Some went about in skins of sheep and goats, wandering over deserts and mountains, hiding in dens and caves. They were hungry and sick and ill-treated—too good for this world. 39And these men of faith, though they trusted God and won his approval, none of them received all that God had promised them; 40for God wanted them to wait and share the even better rewards that were prepared for us.

God's discipline proves his love

12:1
1 Cor 9:24
Phil 3:12-14

12:2
Ps 110:1
2 Cor 3:18
Heb 2:9,10
1 Pet 1:11

12:3
Jn 15:20

12:4
Heb 10:32

12:5
Job 5:17
Prov 3:11

12 Since we have such a huge crowd of men of faith watching us from the grandstands, let us strip off anything that slows us down or holds us back, and especially those sins that wrap themselves so tightly around our feet and trip us up; and let us run with patience the particular race that God has set before us.

2Keep your eyes on Jesus, our leader and instructor. He was willing to die a shameful death on the cross because of the joy he knew would be his afterwards; and now he sits in the place of honor by the throne of God.

3If you want to keep from becoming fainthearted and weary, think about his patience as sinful men did such terrible things to him. 4After all, you have never yet struggled against sin and temptation until you sweat great drops of blood.

5And have you quite forgotten the encouraging words God spoke to you, his child? He said, "My son, don't be angry when the Lord punishes you. Don't be

---

symbolize the real victory that God has promised. Even though we may physically die, we will live forever because of Christ. In the promised resurrection, even physical death will be defeated and Christ's victory will be made complete.

11:35–38 Many think that pain is the exception in the Christian life. When suffering occurs they say, "Why me?" They feel that God has deserted them, or perhaps he was not as dependable as they thought. In reality, however, we live in an evil world, and life includes much suffering even for believers. But God is still in control. He allows some Christians to become martyrs for the faith, and he allows others to survive persecution. Rather than asking, "Why me?" it is much more helpful to ask, "Why not me?" Your faith and the values of this world are on a collision course. Expect pain and suffering to come, and you will not be shocked when it hits. But we can also take comfort in knowing that Jesus suffered too. He understands our fears, our weaknesses, our disappointments (see 2:16–18; 4:14–16). He has promised never to leave us (Matthew 28:18–20), and he intercedes on our behalf (7:24, 25). In times of pain, persecution, or suffering we should trust confidently in Christ and in him alone.

11:39, 40 Hebrews 11 has been called faith's hall of fame. No doubt the author surprised his readers by this conclusion: these mighty Jewish heroes did not receive God's total reward, because they died before Christ came. In God's plan, they and the Christian believers (who were also enduring much testing) would be rewarded together. Once again Hebrews shows that Christianity supersedes Judaism.

12:1 This "huge crowd" is composed of the people described in chapter 11. Their faithfulness is a constant encouragement to us.

We do not struggle alone and we are not the first to struggle with problems in our lives. Others have run the race and won and their witness stirs us to run and win also. What an inspiring heritage we have!

12:1–4 The Christian life involves hard work. It requires us to give up whatever endangers our relationship with God, to run patiently, and to struggle against sin with the power of the Holy Spirit. To live this life effectively, we must keep our eyes on Jesus. We stumble when we look away from him and at ourselves or the circumstances surrounding us. We are running Christ's race, not our own, and we must always keep him in sight.

12:3 When we face hardship and discouragement, it is easy to lose sight of the big picture. But we're not alone, there is help. Many have already made it through life enduring far more difficult circumstances than we have experienced. Suffering is the training ground for Christian maturity. It develops our patience and makes our final victory sweet.

12:4 This verse can also be translated, "You have not yet resisted to the point of shedding blood." These readers were facing difficult times of persecution, but none of them had yet died for their faith. Because they were still alive, the writer urged them to continue to run their race. Just as Christ did not give up, neither should they.

12:5–11 Who loves his child more—the father who allows the child to do what will harm him, or the one who corrects, trains, and even punishes the child to help him learn what is right? It's never pleasant to be corrected and disciplined by God, but his discipline is a sign of his deep love for you. When God corrects you, see it as proof of his love and ask him what he is trying to teach you.

discouraged when he has to show you where you are wrong. 6For when he punishes you, it proves that he loves you. When he whips you it proves you are really his child.''

12:6
Prov 3:12
Ps 94:12
Jas 1:12
Rev 3:19

7Let God train you, for he is doing what any loving father does for his children. Whoever heard of a son who was never corrected? 8If God doesn't punish you when you need it, as other fathers punish their sons, then it means that you aren't really God's son at all—that you don't really belong in his family. 9Since we respect our fathers here on earth, though they punish us, should we not all the more cheerfully submit to God's training so that we can begin really to live?

12:7
Deut 8:5

12:8
1 Pet 5:9

12:9
Isa 38:16

10Our earthly fathers trained us for a few brief years, doing the best for us that they knew how, but God's correction is always right and for our best good, that we may share his holiness. 11Being punished isn't enjoyable while it is happening—it hurts! But afterwards we can see the result, a quiet growth in grace and character.

12:10
2 Pet 1:4

12:11
1 Pet 1:6

12:12
Isa 35:3

12So take a new grip with your tired hands, stand firm on your shaky legs, 13and mark out a straight, smooth path for your feet so that those who follow you, though weak and lame, will not fall and hurt themselves, but become strong.

12:13
Prov 4:26
Gal 6:1

Warning against refusing to listen

14Try to stay out of all quarrels and seek to live a clean and holy life, for one who is not holy will not see the Lord. 15Look after each other so that not one of you will fail to find God's best blessings. Watch out that no bitterness takes root among you, for as it springs up it causes deep trouble, hurting many in their spiritual lives. 16Watch out that no one becomes involved in sexual sin or becomes careless about God as Esau did: he traded his rights as the oldest son for a single meal. 17And afterwards, when he wanted those rights back again, it was too late, even though he wept bitter tears of repentance. So remember, and be careful.

12:14
Rom 6:22; 14:19

12:15
Deut 29:18
Heb 4:1

12:16
Gen 25:33

12:17
Gen 27:34

18You have not had to stand face to face with terror, flaming fire, gloom, darkness and a terrible storm, as the Israelites did at Mount Sinai when God gave them his laws. 19For there was an awesome trumpet blast, and a voice with a message so terrible that the people begged God to stop speaking. 20They staggered back under God's command that if even an animal touched the mountain it must die. 21Moses himself was so frightened at the sight that he shook with terrible fear.

12:18
Ex 19:12,16

12:19
Ex 20:19

12:20
Ex 19:12

12:22
Ps 68:17
Gal 4:26
Rev 3:12; 14:1
21:2

22But you have come right up into Mount Zion, to the city of the living God, the heavenly Jerusalem, and to the gathering of countless happy angels; 23and to the church, composed of all those registered in heaven; and to God who is Judge of all;

12:23
Phil 3:12
Heb 2:12

12:11 We may respond to discipline in several ways: (1) we can accept it with resignation; (2) we can accept it with self-pity, thinking we really don't deserve it; (3) we can be angry and resent God for it; or (4) we can accept it gratefully as the appropriate response towards a loving Father.

12:12, 13 God is not only a disciplining parent, but also a demanding coach who pushes us to our limits and requires of us a disciplined life. Although we may not feel strong enough to push on to victory, we will be able to continue as we follow Christ and draw upon his strength. Then we can use our growing strength to help those around us who are weak and struggling.

12:12, 13 The word "so" is a clue that what follows is important! We must not live with only our own survival in mind. Others will follow our example, and we have a responsibility to them if we claim to live for Christ. Does your example make it easier for others to believe, follow, and mature in Christ? Or would those who follow you end up confused and misled?

12:14 The readers were familiar with the ceremonial cleansing ritual that prepared them for worship, and they knew they had to be "holy" or "clean" in order to enter the Temple. Sin always blocks our vision of God, so if we want to see God, we must remove it from our lives (see Psalm 24:3, 4). Holiness is coupled with peace—staying out of quarrels. A right relationship with God leads to right relationships with fellow believers. Although we will not

always feel love toward all other believers, we must pursue peace as we become more Christlike.

12:15 Like a small root that grows into a great tree, bitterness springs up in our hearts and overshadows even our deepest Christian relationships. Bitterness brings with it jealousy, dissension, and immorality. When the Holy Spirit fills our lives, however, he leaves no room for bitterness.

12:16, 17 Esau's story shows us that mistakes and sins sometimes have long-lasting consequences (Genesis 25:29-34; 27:36). Even repentance and forgiveness do not always eliminate sins's consequences. How often do you make decisions based on what you want now, rather than on what you need long-term? Evaluate the long-range effects of your decisions and actions.

12:18-24 What a contrast between the people's terrified approach to God at Mount Sinai and their joyful approach at Mount Zion! What a difference Jesus has made! Before he came, God seemed distant and threatening. After he came, God welcomes us through Christ into his presence. Don't neglect to accept his invitation.

12:22 Christians are partakers in the heavenly Jerusalem right now because Christ rules our lives, the Holy Spirit is always with us, and we experience sweet fellowship with other believers. The full and ultimate rewards and reality of the heavenly Jerusalem are depicted in Revelation 21.

12:24
Gen 4:10
Ex 24:8
Heb 9:19; 10:19

and to the spirits of the redeemed in heaven, already made perfect; 24and to Jesus himself, who has brought us his wonderful new agreement; and to the sprinkled blood which graciously forgives instead of crying out for vengeance as the blood of Abel did.

12:25
Num 16
Heb 1:1; 2:2

25So see to it that you obey him who is speaking to you. For if the people of Israel did not escape when they refused to listen to Moses, the earthly messenger, how terrible our danger if we refuse to listen to God who speaks to us from heaven!

12:26
Ex 19:18

12:27
Ps 102:26
Mt 24:35
2 Pet 3:10

26When he spoke from Mount Sinai his voice shook the earth, but, "Next time," he says, "I will not only shake the earth, but the heavens too." 27By this he means that he will sift out everything without solid foundations, so that only unshakable things will be left.

12:28
Dan 2:44

12:29
Ex 24:17
Deut 9:3
Isa 66:15

28Since we have a Kingdom nothing can destroy, let us please God by serving him with thankful hearts, and with holy fear and awe. 29For our God is a consuming fire.

Holy and obedient lives

13:1
Rom 12:10

13:2
Gen 18:1-3
Mt 25:35

13 Continue to love each other with true brotherly love. 2Don't forget to be kind to strangers, for some who have done this have entertained angels without realizing it! 3Don't forget about those in jail. Suffer with them as though you were there yourself. Share the sorrow of those being mistreated, for you know what they are going through.

13:3
Mt 25:36
Col 4:18
Heb 10:34

13:4
1 Cor 7:38

4Honor your marriage and its vows, and be pure; for God will surely punish all those who are immoral or commit adultery.

13:5
Gen 28:15
Ps 37:25

5Stay away from the love of money; be satisfied with what you have. For God has said, "I will never, *never* fail you nor forsake you." 6That is why we can say without any doubt or fear, "The Lord is my Helper and I am not afraid of anything that mere man can do to me."

13:6
Ps 118:6

13:7
Heb 6:12

7Remember your leaders who have taught you the Word of God. Think of all the good that has come from their lives, and try to trust the Lord as they do.

13:8
Jn 8:58

13:9
Eph 4:14
Col 2:16

8Jesus Christ is the same yesterday, today, and forever. 9So do not be attracted by strange, new ideas. Your spiritual strength comes as a gift from God, not from ceremonial rules about eating certain foods—a method which, by the way, hasn't helped those who have tried it!

13:10
1 Cor 10:18

10We have an altar—the cross where Christ was sacrificed—where those who

---

12:27-29 Eventually the world will crumble, and only God's Kingdom will last. Those who follow Christ are part of this Kingdom, and they will withstand the shaking, sifting, and burning. When we feel unsure about the future, we can take confidence from these verses. Whatever happens here, our future is built on a solid foundation that cannot be destroyed. Don't put your confidence in that which will be destroyed; instead, build your life on Christ and his unshakable Kingdom. (See Matthew 7:24-29 for the importance of building on a solid foundation.)

13:1-5 Real love toward others produces tangible actions: (1) kindness to strangers (13:2); (2) sympathy for those who are in prison and those who have been mistreated (13:3); (3) respect for one's marriage vows (13:4); and (4) satisfaction with what you have (13:5). Make sure your love runs deep enough to affect your hospitality, sympathy, fidelity, and contentment.

13:2 Three Bible characters entertained angels without realizing it: (1) Abraham (Genesis 18:1ff), (2) Gideon (Judges 6:11ff), and (3) Manoah (Judges 13:2ff). Some people say they cannot be hospitable because their homes are not large enough or nice enough. But even if you have no more than a table and two chairs in a rented room, there are people who would be grateful to spend time in your home. Are there visitors to your church who would like to share a meal with you? Do you know single people who would enjoy an evening of tea and talk? Is there any way your home could meet the needs of traveling missionaries? Hospitality simply means making other people feel comfortable and at home.

13:3 We are to have sympathy for those in prison, especially for Christians imprisoned for their faith. Jesus said his true followers would visit those in prison as his representatives (Matthew 25:36).

13:5, 6 We are contented when we realize God's sufficiency for our needs. Christians today who become materialistic are saying with their lives that God can't take care of them—or at least won't take care of them the way they want. Insecurity can lead to the love of money, whether we are rich or poor. The only antidote is to trust God to meet all our needs.

13:7 If you are a Christian, you owe much to others who have taught you and modeled for you what you needed to know about the gospel and living the Christian life. Continue following the good examples of those who have invested a part of themselves in you. A part of following their example is to pass on the faith to others—to invest your life through evangelism, service, and Christian education.

13:8 We must keep our eyes on Christ, our ultimate leader, who, unlike human leaders, will never change. He has been and will be the same forever. In a changing world we can trust our unchanging Lord.

13:9 Apparently some were teaching that keeping the Old Testament ceremonial laws and rituals was important to salvation. But these laws were useless for conquering a person's evil thoughts and desires (Colossians 2:23). The laws could influence conduct, but they could not change the heart. Lasting changes in conduct begin when the Holy Spirit comes to live in the heart.

continue to seek salvation by obeying Jewish laws can never be helped. [11]Under the system of Jewish laws the high priest brought the blood of the slain animals into the sanctuary as a sacrifice for sin, and then the bodies of the animals were burned outside the city. [12]That is why Jesus suffered and died outside the city, where his blood washed our sins away.

[13]So let us go out to him beyond the city walls [that is, outside the interests of this world, being willing to be despised] to suffer with him there, bearing his shame. [14]For this world is not our home; we are looking forward to our everlasting home in heaven.

[15]With Jesus' help we will continually offer our sacrifice of praise to God by telling others of the glory of his name. [16]Don't forget to do good and to share what you have with those in need, for such sacrifices are very pleasing to him. [17]Obey your spiritual leaders and be willing to do what they say. For their work is to watch over your souls, and God will judge them on how well they do this. Give them reason to report joyfully about you to the Lord and not with sorrow, for then you will suffer for it too.

Final words

[18]Pray for us, for our conscience is clear and we want to keep it that way. [19]I especially need your prayers right now so that I can come back to you sooner.

[20, 21]And now may the God of peace, who brought again from the dead our Lord Jesus, equip you with all you need for doing his will. May he who became the great Shepherd of the sheep by an everlasting agreement between God and you, signed with his blood, produce in you through the power of Christ all that is pleasing to him. To him be glory forever and ever. Amen.

[22]Brethren, please listen patiently to what I have said in this letter, for it is a short one. [23]I want you to know that Brother Timothy is now out of jail; if he comes here soon, I will come with him to see you. [24, 25]Give my greetings to all your leaders and to the other believers there. The Christians from Italy who are here with me send you their love. God's grace be with you all.

Good-bye.

13:13 *willing to be despised*, implied.

13:11
Lev 4:12,21

13:12
Jn 19:17
Heb 9:12

13:13
1 Pet 4:14

13:14
Heb 10:34; 11:10

13:15
Lev 7:12
Ps 50:14
1 Pet 2:5

13:17
Ezek 3:17
33:2,7
Acts 20:28

13:18
Acts 24:16

13:19
Philem 22

13:20
Isa 40:11
Ezek 31:23
37:24
Zech 9:11
Jn 10:11

13:21
Rom 11:36
Phil 2:13
1 Pet 5:10

13:23
Acts 16:1
1 Thess 3:2

13:13 This verse can also be translated, "Let us go to him outside the camp, and bear the disgrace he endured." The Jewish Christians were being ridiculed and persecuted by Jews who didn't believe in Jesus the Messiah. Most of the book of Hebrews tells them how much greater Christ is than the sacrificial system. Now the writer makes the point of his lengthy argument: It may be necessary to leave the "camp" and suffer with Christ. To be outside the camp meant to be unclean. But Jesus suffered humiliation and uncleanness outside the Jerusalem gates on their behalf. The time had come for Jewish Christians to declare their loyalty to Christ above any other loyalty, to choose to follow the Messiah whatever suffering that might entail. Is there anything holding us back from complete loyalty to Jesus Christ?

13:14 We should not be attached to this world, because all that we are and have here is temporary. Only our relationship with God and our service to him will last. Don't store up your treasures here, store them in heaven (Matthew 6:19–21).

13:15, 16 If these Jewish Christians, because of their witness to the Messiah, could no longer worship with other Jews, they could consider praise their sacrifice—one they could offer anywhere, anytime. This must have reminded them of the prophet Hosea's words, "O Lord, take away our sins; be gracious to us and receive us, and we will offer you the sacrifice of praise" (Hosea 14:2). A sacrifice of praise today would include thanking Christ for his sacrifice on the cross and telling others about it.

13:17 The task of church leaders is to help people mature in Christ. Cooperative followers greatly ease the burden of leadership. Does your conduct give your leaders reason to report joyfully about you?

13:18, 19 The writer recognized the need for prayer. Christian leaders are especially vulnerable to criticism from others, pride if they succeed, depression if they fail, and Satan's constant efforts to nullify their work for God. They desperately need our prayers! For whom should you regularly pray?

13:20, 21 These verses include two significant results of Christ's action in our lives. The writer prayed that God would (1) work in the Christians to produce the kind of *persons* that would please him, and (2) equip the Christians to do the kind of *work* that would please him. Let God change you, then use you.

13:23 We have no record of Timothy's imprisonment, but we learn here that he had been released. For more about Timothy, see his Profile in 1 Timothy.

13:24, 25 Hebrews is a call to Christian maturity. It was addressed to first-century Jewish Christians, but it applies to Christians of any age or background. Christian maturity means making Christ the beginning and end of our faith. To mature, we must center our lives on him, not depending on religious ritual, not falling back into sin, not trusting in ourselves, and not letting anything come between us and Christ.

JAMES

"MIRACULOUS!" . . . "Revolutionary!" . . . "Greatest ever!" We are inundated with a flood of extravagant claims as we flip the television dial or magazine pages. We are assured that these products are "new," "improved," "fantastic," and will change lives. For only a few dollars we can have "cleaner clothes," "whiter teeth," "glamorous hair," "tastier food," happiness, friends, and the good life. And just before an election, no one can match the politicians' promises. But talk is cheap, and we soon realize that the boasts were hollow, quite far from the truth.

Christians also make great claims, and are often guilty of belying them with their actions. Professing to trust God and to be his people, they cling tightly to the world and its values. Possessing all the right answers, they contradict the gospel with their lives.

With energetic style and pointed, well-chosen words, James confronts the unethical practices of his readers head-on. Christianity must not only be *believed*, it must be *lived*. "What's the use of saying that you have faith and are Christians if you aren't proving it by helping others? Will *that* kind of faith save anyone?" (2:14). The proof that our faith is real is a *changed life*.

Genuine faith will inevitably produce good works. This is the central theme of James' epistle, around which he supplies practical advice on living the Christian life.

James begins his epistle outlining some general characteristics of the Christian life (1:1–27). Next, he exhorts Christians to act justly in society (2:1–13). He follows this practical advice with a theological discourse on the relationship between faith and action (2:14–26). Then James shows the importance of controlling one's speech (3:1–12). In 3:13–18, James distinguishes two kinds of wisdom, earthly and heavenly. Then he encourages his readers to turn from evil desires and obey God (4:1–12). James reproves those who trust in their own plans and possessions (4:13—5:6). Finally, James exhorts his readers to be patient with each other (5:7–11), to be straightforward in their promises (5:12), to pray for each other (5:13–18), and to help one another remain faithful to God (5:19, 20).

This epistle could be considered a how-to book on Christian living. Confrontation, challenge, and commitment await you in its pages. Read James and become a *doer* of the Word (1:22–25).

VITAL STATISTICS

PURPOSE:
To expose unethical practices and to teach right Christian behavior

AUTHOR:
James, Jesus' brother, a leader in the Jerusalem church

TO WHOM WRITTEN:
First century Jewish Christians residing in Gentile communities outside Palestine, and to all Christians everywhere

DATE WRITTEN:
Probably A.D. 49, prior to the Jerusalem council held in A.D. 50

SETTING:
This letter expresses James' concern for persecuted Christians who were once part of the Jerusalem church

KEY VERSE:
". . . You say the way to God is by faith alone, plus nothing; well, I say that good works are important too, for without good works you can't prove whether you have faith or not . . ." (2:18).

THE BLUEPRINT

1. Genuine religion (1:1–27)
2. Genuine faith (2:1—3:12)
3. Genuine wisdom (3:13—5:20)

James wrote to Jewish Christians who had been scattered throughout the Mediterranean world because of persecution. In their hostile surroundings they were tempted to let intellectual agreement pass for true faith. This letter can have rich meaning for us as we are reminded that genuine faith transforms lives. We are encouraged to put our faith into action. It is easy to say we have faith, but true faith will produce loving actions toward others.

MEGATHEMES

THEME	EXPLANATION	IMPORTANCE
Living Faith	James wants believers not only to hear the truth, but also to do it. He contrasts empty faith ("claims without conduct") with faith that works. Commitment to love and to serve is evidence of true faith.	Living faith makes a difference. Make sure your faith is more than just a statement—it should also result in action. Be alert to ways of putting your faith to work.
Trials	In the Christian life there are trials and temptations. Successfully overcoming these adversities produces maturity and strong character.	Don't resent troubles when they come. Pray for wisdom; God will supply all that you will need to face persecution or adversity. He will give you patience and keep you strong in times of trial.
Law of Love	We are saved by God's gracious mercy, not by keeping the law. But Christ gave us a special command, "love your neighbor as yourself" (Matthew 19:19). We are to love and serve those around us.	Keeping the law of love shows that our faith is vital and real. To show love to others, we must root out our own selfishness.
Wise Speech	Wisdom shows itself in speech. We are responsible for the destructive results of our talk. The wisdom of God that helps control the tongue can help control all our actions.	Accepting God's wisdom will affect your speech because your words will reveal their godly source. Think before you speak and allow God to give you self-control.
Wealth	James taught Christians not to compromise with worldly attitudes about wealth. Because the glory of wealth fades, Christians should store up God's treasures through sincere service. Christians must not show partiality to the wealthy, nor be prejudiced against the poor.	All of us are accountable for how we use what we have. We should not hoard wealth, but be generous towards others. In addition, we should not be impressed by the wealthy nor look down on those who are poor.

1. Genuine religion

1 *From:* James, a servant of God and of the Lord Jesus Christ.
To: Jewish Christians scattered everywhere. Greetings!

Enduring trials and temptations

²Dear brothers, is your life full of difficulties and temptations? Then be happy, ³for when the way is rough, your patience has a chance to grow. ⁴So let it grow, and don't try to squirm out of your problems. For when your patience is finally in full bloom, then you will be ready for anything, strong in character, full and complete.

⁵If you want to know what God wants you to do, ask him, and he will gladly tell you, for he is always ready to give a bountiful supply of wisdom to all who ask him;

1:2
1 Pet 1:6-8
1:3
Rom 2:7; 5:3-5
1:5
Prov 2:3-13
Mt 7:7-11
Jas 3:17

1:1 The writer of this letter, a leader of the church in Jerusalem (see Acts 12:17; 15:13), was not James the apostle, but James, Jesus' brother. The book of James was one of the earliest epistles, probably written before A.D. 50. After Stephen was martyred (Acts 8:1-3), Christians in Jerusalem were scattered throughout the Roman world. Persecution increased. Because these early believers did not have the support of established Christian churches, James wrote to them as a concerned leader, to encourage them in their faith during that difficult time.

1:2 The word *temptation* as used here refers to trials or testing. It does not mean an enticement to do evil. While God tests us, he never provokes us to commit sin (see 1:12-16).

1:2, 3 James doesn't say *if* the way is rough, but *when* it is rough. He assumes we will have trials and that it is possible to profit from them. James tells us to turn our hardships into times of learning. Rough times can teach us patience. For other passages dealing with patience (also called perseverance and steadfastness), see Romans 2:7; 5:3-5; 8:24, 25; 2 Corinthians 6:3-7; 2 Peter 1:2-9.

1:2-4 We can't really know the depth of our character until we see how we react under pressure. It is easy to be kind when everything is going well, but can we still be kind when others are treating us unfairly? Instead of complaining about our struggles, we should see them as opportunities for growth. Thank God for promising to be with you in rough times. Ask him to help you solve your problems or give you the strength to endure them. Then be patient. God will not leave you alone with your problems; he will stay close by and help you grow.

1:5 The statement, "If you want to know what God wants you to do" can also be translated, "If any of you lacks wisdom." James is not only talking about knowledge, but the ability to make wise decisions in difficult circumstances. If we need wisdom, we can pray to God and he will supply what we need. Christians never need to grope about in the dark, hoping to stumble upon answers. God's wisdom is available to guide our choices.

1:5 When James speaks of wisdom, he means practical discernment. Wisdom begins with respect for God, leads to right

he will not resent it. 6But when you ask him, be sure that you really expect him to tell you, for a doubtful mind will be as unsettled as a wave of the sea that is driven and tossed by the wind; 7. 8and every decision you then make will be uncertain, as you turn first this way, and then that. If you don't ask with faith, don't expect the Lord to give you any solid answer.

9A Christian who doesn't amount to much in this world should be glad, for he is great in the Lord's sight. 10, 11But a rich man should be glad that his riches mean nothing to the Lord, for he will soon be gone, like a flower that has lost its beauty and fades away, withered—killed by the scorching summer sun. So it is with rich men. They will soon die and leave behind all their busy activities.

12Happy is the man who doesn't give in and do wrong when he is tempted, for afterwards he will get as his reward the crown of life that God has promised those who love him. 13And remember, when someone wants to do wrong it is never God who is tempting him, for God never wants to do wrong and never tempts anyone else to do it. 14Temptation is the pull of man's own evil thoughts and wishes. 15These evil thoughts lead to evil actions and afterwards to the death penalty from God. 16So don't be misled, dear brothers.

◄ 17But whatever is good and perfect comes to us from God, the Creator of all light, and he shines forever without change or shadow. 18And it was a happy day

1:18 *happy day for him,* literally, "Of his own free will he gave us," etc.

CHAPTER SUMMARY			
	Chapter 1	Confident Stand	What a Christian has
	Chapter 2	Compassionate Service	What a Christian does
	Chapter 3	Careful Speech	What a Christian says
	Chapter 4	Contrite Submission	What a Christian feels
	Chapter 5	Concerned Sharing	What a Christian gives

---

living, and results in increased ability to tell right from wrong. God is willing to give us this wisdom. To learn God's will, we need to ask him to reveal it to us, and then we must be willing to do what he tells us to do.

1:5–8 If you have ever seen the constant rolling of huge waves at sea, you know how restless they are—subject to the forces of wind, gravity, and tide. Doubt leaves one as unsettled as the restless waves, tossed to-and-fro. If you want to stop being tossed about, believe that God knows what is best for you. Ask him for wisdom, and trust that he will give it to you. Then your decisions will be sure and solid.

1:6 What is a doubtful mind? It is a mind that is not completely convinced that God's way is best. It treats God's Word like any human advice, retaining the option of disobedience. It vacillates between feelings, the world's ideas, and God's commands. The cure for a doubtful mind is wholehearted commitment to God's reliable way. See the note on James 1:5.

1:7, 8 To "ask with faith" is to ask with confidence that God will align our desires with his purposes. For more on this concept, read the note on Matthew 21:22.

1:9 This verse refers to a person of humble circumstances, without status or wealth. Such people are often overlooked, even in our churches today.

1:9–11 If wealth, power, and status mean nothing to God, why do we attribute so much importance to them and honor those who possess them? Do your material possessions give you a sense of purpose and a reason for living? If they were gone, what would be left? What you have in your heart, not your bank account, matters to God and endures for eternity.

1:10, 11 The rich should be glad that wealth means nothing to God, because wealth is easily lost. The poor should be glad riches mean nothing to God, otherwise they would be considered unworthy. True wealth is found in an individual's spiritual life, not his financial assets. God is interested in what is lasting (our souls), not in what is temporary (our money and possessions). See Mark

4:19 for Jesus' words on this subject.

1:12 The world says happiness comes from pleasure, money, location, job, image, and success. These cannot provide lasting happiness, however, because they are temporary and provide no eternal benefits.

1:12–15 Temptation comes from evil desire within, not from God. It begins with an evil thought. It becomes sin when we dwell on the thought and allow it to become an action. Like a snowball rolling downhill, sin's destruction grows the more we let sin have its way. The best time to stop a snowball is before it is too big or moving too fast to control. See Matthew 4:1–11; 1 Corinthians 10:13; and 2 Timothy 2:22 for more about escaping temptation.

1:13–15 It is easy to blame others and make excuses for evil thoughts and wrong actions. Excuses include (1) it's the other person's fault; (2) I couldn't help it; (3) everybody's doing it; (4) it was just a mistake; (5) nobody's perfect; (6) the devil made me do it; (7) I was pressured into it; (8) I didn't know it was wrong. A person who makes excuses is trying to shift the blame from himself to something or someone else. A Christian, on the other hand, accepts responsibility for his wrongs, confesses them, and asks God for forgiveness.

1:13, 14 People who live for God often wonder why they still have temptations. Does God tempt them? God *tests* people, but he does not *tempt* them by trying to seduce them into sin. He allows Satan to tempt them, however, in order to refine their faith and to grow in their dependence upon Christ. We can endure the temptation to sin by turning to God for strength and choosing to act in obedience to his Word.

►**1:17** Scripture often compares goodness with light and evil with darkness. For other passages where God is pictured as light, see Psalm 27:1, Isaiah 60:19–22, John 1:1–14.

1:18 First-century Christians were the first generation to believe in Jesus Christ as Messiah. James calls them "the first children in his God's new family."

for him when he gave us our new lives, through the truth of his Word, and we became, as it were, the first children in his new family.

Listening and doing

19Dear brothers, don't ever forget that it is best to listen much, speak little, and not become angry; 20for anger doesn't make us good, as God demands that we must be.

21So get rid of all that is wrong in your life, both inside and outside, and humbly be glad for the wonderful message we have received, for it is able to save our souls as it takes hold of our hearts.

22And remember, it is a message to obey, not just to listen to. So don't fool yourselves. 23For if a person just listens and doesn't obey, he is like a man looking at his face in a mirror; 24as soon as he walks away, he can't see himself anymore or remember what he looks like. 25But if anyone keeps looking steadily into God's law for free men, he will not only remember it but he will do what it says, and God will greatly bless him in everything he does.

26Anyone who says he is a Christian but doesn't control his sharp tongue is just fooling himself, and his religion isn't worth much. 27The Christian who is pure and without fault, from God the Father's point of view, is the one who takes care of orphans and widows, and who remains true to the Lord—not soiled and dirtied by his contacts with the world.

2. Genuine faith

Do not favor the rich

2 Dear brothers, how can you claim that you belong to the Lord Jesus Christ, the Lord of glory, if you show favoritism to rich people and look down on poor people?

2If a man comes into your church dressed in expensive clothes and with valuable

1:19
Prov 10:19
15:18; 17:27,28
Eph 4:26,31

1:21
Rom 13:12,13
Eph 4:22
1 Pet 1:23

1:22
Mt 7:24;
12:50 28:20
Lk 6:46-49
Jn 13:17

1:25
2 Cor 3:17,18
Gal 5:1
Jas 2:12
1 Pet 2:16

1:26
Prov 13:3; 21:23

1:27
Deut 14:29
24:17-20
Col 3:1-3
Jas 4:4
1 Jn 2:15-17

2:1
Lev 19:15
Deut 16:19
Prov 24:23
28:21
1 Cor 2:8

1:19 When we talk too much and listen too little, we communicate to others that we think our ideas are much more important than theirs. James wisely advises us to reverse this process. Put a mental stopwatch on your conversations and keep track of how much you talk and how much you listen. In your conversations, do others feel that their viewpoints and ideas have value?

1:19, 20 This verse speaks of anger that erupts when our egos are bruised—"*I* am hurt"; "*My* opinions are not being heard." When injustice and sin occur, we *should* become angry because others are being hurt. But we should not become angry when we fail to win an argument, or when we feel neglected. Selfish anger never helps anybody.

1:22–25 It is important to know what God's Word says, but it is much more important to obey it. The effectiveness of our Bible study time can be measured by the effect it has on our behavior and attitudes.

1:25 "God's law for free men" is also called the "law of liberty," or the "perfect law that gives freedom." It seems paradoxical that a law could give us freedom. But God's law points out sin in our lives and gives us opportunity to ask God's forgiveness (see Romans 7:7, 8). As Christians, we are saved by God's grace. Salvation includes freedom from sin's control. We can live a holy life that we could not live otherwise. As believers, we are free to live as we should (as God created us to live). Of course, this does not mean that we are free to do as we please (see 1 Peter 2:14–16).

1:27 In the first century, orphans and widows had very few means of economic support. Unless a family member was willing to care for them, they were reduced to begging, selling themselves as slaves, or starving. By caring for these powerless people, the church put God's Word into practice. Giving with no hope of receiving in return, they showed what it means to serve others. This is what Jesus expects of all true believers.

2:1ff In this chapter James argues for the necessity of good works. He sets forth three truths: (1) Commitment is an essential part of faith. You cannot be a Christian simply by affirming the right doctrines or agreeing with biblical facts. You must commit your mind and heart to Christ (2:19). (2) Good works are the evidence of true faith. A genuine Christian will have a changed life (2:18). (3) Faith without good works doesn't do anybody any good—it is useless (2:14–17). These statements are consistent with Paul's teaching that salvation is by faith alone. Paul emphasizes the purpose of faith—to bring salvation. James emphasizes the results of faith—a changed life.

2:1ff Often we treat a well-dressed, impressive-looking person better than someone who looks poor. We do this because we would rather identify with successful people than with apparent failures. We feel better about ourselves when we associate with people we admire. The irony, as James reminds us, is that the supposed winners may have gained their impressive lifestyle at our expense. In addition, the rich find it hard to identify with the Lord Jesus who came as a humble servant. Are you easily impressed by status, wealth, or fame? Are you partial to the "haves" while ignoring the "have nots"? This prejudice is sin. God views all people as equals, and if he favors anyone, it is the poor and the powerless who cannot help themselves. We should follow his example.

2:2–4 Why is it wrong to judge a person by his economic status? Wealth may indicate intelligence, wise decisions, and hard work. On the other hand, it may mean only that a person had the good fortune of being born into a wealthy family. Or it can even be the sign of greed, dishonesty, and selfishness. By honoring someone just because he dresses well, we are making his appearance more important than his character. We sometimes do this because (1) poverty makes us uncomfortable; we don't want to face our responsibilities to those who have less than we do; (2) we too want to be wealthy, and we hope to use the rich person as a means to

gold rings on his fingers, and at the same moment another man comes in who is poor and dressed in threadbare clothes, ³and you make a lot of fuss over the rich man and give him the best seat in the house and say to the poor man, "You can stand over there if you like, or else sit on the floor"—well, ⁴judging a man by his wealth shows that you are guided by wrong motives.

⁵Listen to me, dear brothers: God has chosen poor people to be rich in faith, and the Kingdom of Heaven is theirs, for that is the gift God has promised to all those who love him. ⁶And yet, of the two strangers, you have despised the poor man. Don't you realize that it is usually the rich men who pick on you and drag you into court? ⁷And all too often they are the ones who laugh at Jesus Christ, whose noble name you bear.

⁸Yes indeed, it is good when you truly obey our Lord's command, "You must love and help your neighbors just as much as you love and take care of yourself." ⁹But you are breaking this law of our Lord's when you favor the rich and fawn over them; it is sin.

¹⁰And the person who keeps every law of God, but makes one little slip, is just as guilty as the person who has broken every law there is. ¹¹For the God who said you must not marry a woman who already has a husband, also said you must not murder, so even though you have not broken the marriage laws by committing adultery, but have murdered someone, you have entirely broken God's laws and stand utterly guilty before him.

¹²You will be judged on whether or not you are doing what Christ wants you to. So watch what you do and what you think; ¹³for there will be no mercy to those who have shown no mercy. But if you have been merciful, then God's mercy toward you will win out over his judgment against you.

Faith results in good works

¹⁴Dear brothers, what's the use of saying that you have faith and are Christians

Marginal references:

2:4 Jn 7:24

2:5 Prov 8:17-21; Mt 5:3; 11:6; Lk 6:20; 12:21; 1 Cor 1:27; 2 Cor 6:10

2:7 Acts 11:26; 1 Pet 4:16

2:8 Lev 19:18; Mt 7:12; Rom 13:8

2:10 Deut 27:26; Mt 5:18,19; Gal 5:3

2:11 Ex 20:13,14; Deut 5:17,18; Mt 19:18

2:12 Jas 1:25

2:13 Mt 18:32-35

SHOWING FAVORITISM
Why it is wrong to show favoritism to the wealthy:

1. It is inconsistent with Christ's teachings.
2. It results from evil thoughts.
3. It belittles people made in God's image.
4. It is a by-product of selfish motives.
5. It goes against the biblical definition of love.
6. It shows a lack of mercy to those less fortunate.
7. It is hypocritical.
8. It is sin.

---

that end; (3) we want the rich person to join our church and help support it financially. All these motives are selfish; none of them sees the rich man or the poor man as a human being in need of fellowship. If we say Christ is Lord of our lives, then we must live as he lived, showing no favoritism and loving all people regardless of their circumstances.

2:2-4 We are often partial to the rich because we mistakenly assume they are rich because they have been blessed by God. But God does not promise earthly rewards or riches; in fact, Christ calls us to be ready to suffer for him and give up everything in order to hold on to eternal life (Matthew 6:19–21; 19:28–30; Luke 12:14–34; Romans 8:15–21; 1 Timothy 6:17–19).

2:5 When James speaks about the poor, he is talking about those who have no money, and also those whose simple values are despised by much of our affluent society. Perhaps they prefer serving to managing, human relationships to financial security, peace to power. This does not mean that the poor will automatically go to heaven and the rich to hell. Poor people, however, are usually more aware of their powerlessness, and thus it is usually easier for them to acknowledge their need for salvation. One of the greatest barriers to salvation for the rich is pride. For the poor, it is bitterness.

2:8, 9 We must treat all people as we would want to be treated. We should not ignore the rich, because then we would be withholding our love. But we must not favor them for what they can do for us, while ignoring the poor because they can offer us little in return. (See also Leviticus 19:18; Matthew 22:37–40; Romans 13:8.)

2:10, 11 It is easy to spot the sins in others while we overlook or rationalize our own. James reminds us that if we've broken just one law, we are sinners. You can't break the law a little bit; if you have broken it at all, you need Christ to pay for your sin. Measure yourself, not someone else, against God's standards. Ask for forgiveness where you need it, and then renew your effort to show your faith by your actions.

2:13 Our sins are forgiven by God's mercy alone. We can't earn forgiveness by forgiving others. But when we withhold forgiveness from others after having received it ourselves, it shows we don't understand or appreciate God's mercy toward us (see Matthew 6:14, 15; Ephesians 4:31, 32).

2:14 Intellectual assent—agreement with a set of Christian teachings—is incomplete faith. True faith transforms our lives. If our lives remain unchanged, we don't truly believe the truths we claim to believe.

if you aren't proving it by helping others? Will *that* kind of faith save anyone? 15If you have a friend who is in need of food and clothing, 16and you say to him, "Well, good-bye and God bless you; stay warm and eat hearty," and then don't give him clothes or food, what good does that do?

17So you see, it isn't enough just to have faith. You must also do good to prove that you have it. Faith that doesn't show itself by good works is no faith at all—it is dead and useless.

18But someone may well argue, "You say the way to God is by faith alone, plus nothing; well, I say that good works are important too, for without good works you can't prove whether you have faith or not; but anyone can see that I have faith by the way I act."

19Are there still some among you who hold that "only believing" is enough? Believing in one God? Well, remember that the demons believe this too—so strongly that they tremble in terror! 20Fool! When will you ever learn that "believing" is useless without *doing* what God wants you to? Faith that does not result in good deeds is not real faith.

21Don't you remember that even our father Abraham was declared good because of what he *did*, when he was willing to obey God, even if it meant offering his son Isaac to die on the altar? 22You see, he was trusting God so much that he was willing to do whatever God told him to; his faith was made complete by what he did, by his actions, his good deeds. 23And so it happened just as the Scriptures say, that Abraham trusted God, and the Lord declared him good in God's sight, and he was even called "the friend of God." 24So you see, a man is saved by what he does, as well as by what he believes.

25Rahab, the prostitute, is another example of this. She was saved because of what she did when she hid those messengers and sent them safely away by a different road. 26Just as the body is dead when there is no spirit in it, so faith is dead if it is not the kind that results in good deeds.

Controlling the tongue

3 Dear brothers, don't be too eager to tell others their faults, for we all make many mistakes; and when we teachers of religion, who should know better, do wrong, our punishment will be greater than it would be for others.

If anyone can control his tongue, it proves that he has perfect control over himself in every other way. 3We can make a large horse turn around and go wherever we want by means of a small bit in his mouth. 4And a tiny rudder makes a huge ship turn wherever the pilot wants it to go, even though the winds are strong.

5So also the tongue is a small thing, but what enormous damage it can do. A great

3:1 *don't be too eager to tell others their faults,* literally, "not many (of you) should become masters (teachers)."

Cross references (right margin):

2:15 Mt 25:35,36
2:16 1 Jn 3:17
2:17 Gal 5:6 / Jas 2:14-16, 20,26 / 1 Pet 1:5-9
2:18 Mt 7:16 / Rom 3:28
2:19 Deut 6:4 / Isa 43:10 / 44:6,8 / Mt 8:28,29
2:20 Gal 5:6 / Jas 2:14,17,26
2:21 Gen 22:16-18
2:22 Heb 11:17
2:23 Gen 15:6 / Isa 41:8 / Jn 15:13-15 / Rom 4:3-5
2:25 Josh 2:4,6,15 / Heb 11:31
2:26 Gal 5:6 / Jas 2:14,17,20
3:1 Mt 23:8-10 / Rom 2:17-2 / Jas 1:26
3:2 Jas 1:4
3:3 Ps 32:9
3:5 Prov 26:20

2:17 Living the way God wants us to live does not earn our way into heaven, but it shows that our commitment to God is real. Godly conduct is not a substitute for, but a verification of our faith in Christ.

2:18 At first glance, this verse seems to contradict Romans 3:28, "we are saved by faith in Christ and not by the good things we do." Deeper investigation, however, shows that the teachings of James and Paul are not at odds. While it is true that our good works can never earn salvation, true faith always results in a changed life and good works. Paul speaks against those who try to be saved by works instead of true faith; James speaks against those who confuse mere intellectual assent with true faith. After all, even demons know who Jesus is, but they don't obey him (2:19). True faith involves a commitment of your whole self to God.

2:21–24 James says Abraham was declared good (righteous) because of what he *did*, and Paul says he was declared good (righteous) because of what he *believed* (Romans 4:1–5). James and Paul are not contradicting, but complementing each other. Belief brings us salvation; active obedience demonstrates that our belief is genuine.

2:25 Rahab lived in Jericho, a city the Israelites conquered as they entered the Promised Land (Joshua 2). When Israel's spies came to the city, she hid them and helped them escape. In this way she demonstrated faith in God's purpose for Israel. As a result, she and her family were saved when the city was destroyed (Joshua 2). Hebrews 11:31, 32 lists Rahab among the heroes of faith.

3:1, 2 Teaching was a highly valued and respected profession in Jewish culture. Many Jews who embraced Christianity wanted to become teachers. James warned that although it is good to aspire to teach, the teachers' responsibility is great because their words affect others' spiritual lives. If you are in a teaching or leadership role, how is your example affecting those you lead?

3:2, 3 What you say and what you *don't* say are both important. Proper speech is not only saying the right words at the right time, but controlling your desire to say what you shouldn't. Examples of wrongly using the tongue include gossiping, putting others down, bragging, manipulating, false teaching, exaggerating, complaining, flattering, and lying. Before you speak, ask, "Is it true, is it necessary, and is it kind?"

3:6
Ps 120:3
Prov 6:12-19
10:11; 16:27
Mt 15:11
Mk 7:15,16

forest can be set on fire by one tiny spark. 6And the tongue is a flame of fire. It is full of wickedness, and poisons every part of the body. And the tongue is set on fire by hell itself, and can turn our whole lives into a blazing flame of destruction and disaster.

3:8
Ps 140:3
Rom 3:13

3:9
Gen 1:26,27; 5:1
1 Cor 11:7

7Men have trained, or can train, every kind of animal or bird that lives and every kind of reptile and fish, 8but no human being can tame the tongue. It is always ready to pour out its deadly poison. 9Sometimes it praises our heavenly Father, and sometimes it breaks out into curses against men who are made like God. 10And so blessing and cursing come pouring out of the same mouth. Dear brothers, surely this is not right! 11Does a spring of water bubble out first with fresh water and then with bitter water? 12Can you pick olives from a fig tree, or figs from a grape vine? No, and you can't draw fresh water from a salty pool.

3:12
Mt 7:16

3. Genuine wisdom
Wisdom from heaven

3:14
Rom 13:13

3:15
Jas 1:17

3:16
1 Cor 3:3

3:17
Lk 6:36
Rom 12:9-11,18
2 Cor 6:6
Phil 1:11
Heb 12:10,11
Jas 2:13; 4:8
1 Jn 3:18-20

13If you are wise, live a life of steady goodness, so that only good deeds will pour forth. And if you don't brag about them, then you will be truly wise! 14And by all means don't brag about being wise and good if you are bitter and jealous and selfish; that is the worst sort of lie. 15For jealousy and selfishness are not God's kind of wisdom. Such things are earthly, unspiritual, inspired by the devil. 16For wherever there is jealousy or selfish ambition, there will be disorder and every other kind of evil.

17But the wisdom that comes from heaven is first of all pure and full of quiet gentleness. Then it is peace-loving and courteous. It allows discussion and is willing to yield to others; it is full of mercy and good deeds. It is wholehearted and straightforward and sincere. 18And those who are peacemakers will plant seeds of peace and reap a harvest of goodness.

3:18
Prov 11:18
Mt 5:9

SPEECH	When our speech is motivated by:	It is full of:
	Satan	Jealousy
		Selfishness
		Earthly concerns and desires
		Unspiritual thoughts and ideas
		Disorder
		Evil
	God and his wisdom	Mercy
		Love for others
		Peace
		Courtesy
		Yielding to others
		Sincerity, straightforwardness
		Quiet gentleness
		Goodness

3:6 James compares the damage the tongue can do to a raging fire—the tongue's wickedness has its source in hell itself. The uncontrolled tongue can do terrible damage. Satan uses the tongue to divide people and pit them against one another. Idle words are damaging because they spread destruction quickly, and no one can stop the results once they are spoken. A few words spoken in anger can destroy a relationship that took years to build. Before you speak, remember that words are like fire—you can neither control nor reverse the damage they can do.

3:7–12 If no human being can control the tongue, why bother trying? Because even if we do not achieve perfect control of it in this life, we can still learn enough control to reduce the damage it can do. It is better to fight a fire than to go around setting new ones! Remember that we are not fighting the tongue's fire in our own strength. The Holy Spirit will give us increasing power to monitor and control what we say. As Christians we are not perfect, but we should never stop growing.

3:9–12 Our contradictory speech often puzzles us. At times it is right and pleasing to God, but at other times it is violent and destructive. Which of these reflects our true identity? The tongue gives us a picture of our basic human nature. We are good—made in God's image; but we are also bad—fallen and sinful. God works to change us from the inside out. As the Holy Spirit purifies our hearts, he also gives us self- control so that we will speak words that please God.

3:13–18 Have you ever known anyone who claimed to be wise, but acted foolishly? True wisdom can be measured by the depth of one's character. As you can identify a tree by the type of fruit it produces, you can evaluate your wisdom by the way you act. Foolishness leads to disorder, but wisdom leads to peace and goodness.

Drawing near to God

4 What is causing the quarrels and fights among you? Isn't it because there is a whole army of evil desires within you? ²You want what you don't have, so you kill to get it. You long for what others have, and can't afford it, so you start a fight to take it away from them. And yet the reason you don't have what you want is that you don't ask God for it. ³And even when you do ask you don't get it because your whole aim is wrong—you want only what will give *you* pleasure.

⁴You are like an unfaithful wife who loves her husband's enemies. Don't you realize that making friends with God's enemies—the evil pleasures of this world—makes you an enemy of God? I say it again, that if your aim is to enjoy the evil pleasure of the unsaved world, you cannot also be a friend of God. ⁵Or what do you think the Scripture means when it says that the Holy Spirit, whom God has placed within us, watches over us with tender jealousy? ⁶But he gives us more and more strength to stand against all such evil longings. As the Scripture says, God gives strength to the humble, but sets himself against the proud and haughty.

⁷So give yourselves humbly to God. Resist the devil and he will flee from you. ⁸And when you draw close to God, God will draw close to you. Wash your hands, you sinners, and let your hearts be filled with God alone to make them pure and true to him. ⁹Let there be tears for the wrong things you have done. Let there be sorrow and sincere grief. Let there be sadness instead of laughter, and gloom instead of joy. ¹⁰Then when you realize your worthlessness before the Lord, he will lift you up, encourage and help you.

¹¹Don't criticize and speak evil about each other, dear brothers. If you do, you will be fighting against God's law of loving one another, declaring it is wrong. But your job is not to decide whether this law is right or wrong, but to obey it. ¹²Only he who made the law can rightly judge among us. He alone decides to save us or destroy. So what right do you have to judge or criticize others?

Trust God in making future plans

¹³Look here, you people who say, "Today or tomorrow we are going to such and

4:2
1 Jn 3:15
4:3
1 Jn 3:22; 5:14
4:4
Jn 15:19
1 Jn 2:15
4:5
1 Cor 6:19
2 Cor 6:16
4:6
Ps 138:6
Prov 3:34; 29:23
Mt 23:12
1 Pet 5:5
4:7
Rom 14:11
Eph 5:21
6:11,12
1 Pet 5:6,8,9
4:8
Ps 73:28
Isa 1:16; 55:6,7
Mt 15:2
1 Pet 3:21
4:9
Lk 6:25
4:11
Mt 7:1
2 Cor 12:20
Eph 4:31
2 Tim 3:3
1 Pet 2:1
4:12
Mt 10:28
Rom 2:1
14:4,13
Jas 5:9

4:1–3 Quarrels among believers are always harmful. James tells us that these quarrels result from evil desires within us—we want more possessions, more money, higher status, more recognition. When we want badly enough to fulfill these desires, we fight in order to do so. Instead of aggressively grabbing what we want, we should ask God to help us get rid of our selfish desires and trust him to give us what we really need.

4:2, 3 James mentions the most common problems in prayer: not asking, asking for the wrong things, asking for the wrong reasons. Do you talk to God at all? When you do, what do you talk about? Do you ask only to satisfy your desires? Do you seek God's approval for what you already plan to do? Our prayers will become powerful when we allow God to change our desires so that they perfectly correspond to his will for us (1 John 3:21, 22).

4:3, 4 There is nothing wrong with wanting a pleasurable life. God gives us good gifts that he wants us to enjoy (1:17; Ephesians 4:7; 1 Timothy 4:4, 5). But it is wrong to seek pleasure at others' expense or at the expense of obeying God. Pleasure that keeps us from pleasing God is sinful; pleasure in God's rich bounty is good.

4:4–6 The cure for evil desires is humility (see Proverbs 16:18, 19; 1 Peter 5:5, 6). Pride makes us self-centered and leads us to conclude we deserve all we can see, touch, or imagine. It creates greedy appetites for far more than we need. The antidote to self-centered desires is to humble ourselves before God, realizing that we need nothing except his approval. When his Holy Spirit fills us, we realize that the things we have coveted are only cheap substitutes for what God has to offer.

4:7 Although God and Satan are at war, we don't need to wait until the end to see who will win. God has *already* defeated Satan (Colossians 2:13–15; Revelation 12:10–12), and when Christ returns, Satan and all he stands for will be eliminated forever

(Revelation 20:10–15). Satan is here now, however, and he is trying to win us over to his evil cause. With the Holy Spirit in our lives, we can resist Satan and he will flee from us.

4:8 How can you draw close to God? James gives five suggestions: (1) "Give yourselves humbly to God" (4:7). Realize that you need his forgiveness, and be willing to follow him. (2) "Resist the devil" (4:7). Don't allow him to entice and tempt you. (3) "Wash your hands" (that is, lead a pure life) and "let your hearts be filled with God" (4:8). Be cleansed from sin, replacing it with God's purity. (4) Let there be tears, sorrow, and sincere grief for your sins (4:9). Don't be afraid to express deep heartfelt sorrow for them. (5) "Realize your worthlessness" (4:10). Humble yourself before God, and he will lift you up (1 Peter 5:6).

4:10 "Realize your worthlessness" can also be translated, "Humble yourselves before the Lord." Humbling ourselves means recognizing that our worth comes from God alone. We do not deserve his favor, but he reaches out to us in love and gives us worth and dignity, despite our human shortcomings.

4:11, 12 Jesus summarized the law as love to God and neighbor (Matthew 22:37–40), and Paul said love demonstrated towards a neighbor fully satisfies the law (Romans 13:6–10). When we fail to love, we are actually breaking God's law. Examine your attitudes and actions toward others. Do you build people up or tear them down? When you're ready to criticize someone, remember God's law of love and say something good about him or her instead. If you make this a habit, your tendency to find fault with others will diminish and your ability to obey God's law will increase.

4:13–16 It is good to have goals, but goals can disappoint us if we leave God out of them. There is no point in making plans as though God does not exist, because the future is in his hands. What would you like to be doing ten years from now? One year

4:14
Ps 102:3

4:16
1 Cor 4:7,8; 5:6

4:17
Lk 12:47,48
Rom 2:17-23

5:1
Prov 11:4,28
Isa 13:6
Zeph 1:18
Mt 19:23,24
Lk 6:24

5:4
Ex 2:23,24
Lev 19:13
Deut 24:14,15
Ps 9:12
Jer 22:13

such a town, stay there a year, and open up a profitable business." 14How do you know what is going to happen tomorrow? For the length of your lives is as uncertain as the morning fog—now you see it; soon it is gone. 15What you ought to say is, "If the Lord wants us to, we shall live and do this or that." 16Otherwise you will be bragging about your own plans, and such self-confidence never pleases God. 17Remember, too, that knowing what is right to do and then not doing it is sin.

Warning to the rich

5 Look here, you rich men, now is the time to cry and groan with anguished grief because of all the terrible troubles ahead of you. 2Your wealth is even now rotting away, and your fine clothes are becoming mere moth-eaten rags. 3The value of your gold and silver is dropping fast, yet it will stand as evidence against you, and eat your flesh like fire. That is what you have stored up for yourselves, to receive on that coming day of judgment. 4For listen! Hear the cries of the field workers whom you have cheated of their pay. Their cries have reached the ears of the Lord of Hosts.

FAITH THAT WORKS

James offers a larger number of similarities to the Sermon on the Mount than any other book in the New Testament. James relied heavily on Jesus' teachings.

Lesson	Reference
When your life is full of difficulties and persecutions, be happy. A reward awaits you.	James 1:2 / Matthew 5:10–12
You are to be perfect, strong in character, full and complete.	James 1:4 / Matthew 5:48
Ask God and he will answer.	James 1:5; 5:15 / Matthew 7:7–12
Those who are humble, who don't amount to much by the world's standards, should be very glad.	James 1:9 / Matthew 5:3
Watch out for your anger . . . it can be dangerous.	James 1:20 / Matthew 5:22
Be merciful to others, as God is merciful to you.	James 2:13 / Matthew 5:7; 6:14
Your faith must prove itself by helping others.	James 2:14–16 / Matthew 7:21–23
Happy are those who strive for peace; peacemakers plant seeds of peace and reap a harvest of goodness.	James 3:17, 18 / Matthew 5:9
You cannot serve God *and* money, pleasures, or evil. Friendship with evil makes you an enemy of God.	James 4:4 / Matthew 6:24
When we humble ourselves and realize our need for God, he will come to us and encourage us.	James 4:10 / Matthew 5:3, 4
Don't criticize or speak evil of others; it works against God's command to love one another.	James 4:11 / Matthew 7:1, 2
Treasures on earth will only erode and disappear—we must store eternal treasures in heaven.	James 5:2 / Matthew 6:19
Be patient in suffering, as God's prophets were patient.	James 5:10 / Matthew 5:12
Be honest in your speech so you can say a simple "yes" or "no" and always be trusted.	James 5:12 / Matthew 5:33–37

from now? Tomorrow? How will you react if God steps in and rearranges your plans? Plan ahead, but hang on to your plans lightly. If you put God's desires at the center of your planning, you will not be disappointed.

4:14 Life is short no matter how long we live. Don't be deceived into thinking you have lots of remaining time to live for Christ, to enjoy your loved ones, or to do what you know you should. Live for God today! Then, no matter when your life ends, you will have fulfilled God's plan for you.

4:17 We tend to think that *doing* wrong is sin. But James tells us that sin is also *not* doing right. (These two kinds of sin are sometimes called sins of commission and sins of omission.) It is a sin to lie; it can also be a sin to know the truth and not tell it. It is a sin to speak evil of someone; it is also a sin to avoid him when you

know he needs your friendship. We should be willing to help as the Holy Spirit guides us. We should also pray that we do not sin by neglecting to do what is good and right.

5:1-6 James proclaims the worthlessness of riches, not the worthlessness of the rich. Today's money will be worthless when Christ returns, so we should spend our time accumulating treasures that will be worthwhile in God's eternal Kingdom. Money itself is not the problem; Christian leaders need money to live and support their families; missionaries need money to help them spread the gospel; churches need money to do their work effectively. It is the *love* of money that leads to evil (1 Timothy 6:10). This is a warning to all Christians who are tempted to adopt worldly standards rather than God's standards (Romans 12:1, 2). Also read Matthew 6:19–21 to see what Jesus says about riches.

⁵You have spent your years here on earth having fun, satisfying your every whim, and now your fat hearts are ready for the slaughter. ⁶You have condemned and killed good men who had no power to defend themselves against you.

5:5
Lk 16:19
5:6
Jas 4:2

Patience in suffering

⁷Now as for you, dear brothers who are waiting for the Lord's return, be patient, like a farmer who waits until the autumn for his precious harvest to ripen. ⁸Yes, be patient. And take courage, for the coming of the Lord is near.

5:7
2 Pet 3:4-13
5:8
Rom 8:25; 13:11
Heb 10:25-37

⁹Don't grumble about each other, brothers. Are you yourselves above criticism? For see! The great Judge is coming. He is almost here. [Let him do whatever criticizing must be done.]

5:9
1 Cor 4:5
Jas 4:12

¹⁰For examples of patience in suffering, look at the Lord's prophets. ¹¹We know how happy they are now because they stayed true to him then, even though they suffered greatly for it. Job is an example of a man who continued to trust the Lord in sorrow; from his experiences we can see how the Lord's plan finally ended in good, for he is full of tenderness and mercy.

5:10
Jer 2:30
Mt 5:11,12
5:11
Job 1:20-22
2:7-10
Rom 2:4

¹²But most of all, dear brothers, do not swear either by heaven or earth or anything else; just say a simple yes or no, so that you will not sin and be condemned for it.

5:12
Mt 5:33-37
23:16-22
5:13
Lk 22:44
Col 3:16,17

Faithful prayer

¹³Is anyone among you suffering? He should keep on praying about it. And those who have reason to be thankful should continually be singing praises to the Lord.

5:14
Mk 6:13
Tit 1:5

¹⁴Is anyone sick? He should call for the elders of the church and they should pray over him and pour a little oil upon him, calling on the Lord to heal him. ¹⁵And their prayer, if offered in faith, will heal him, for the Lord will make him well; and if his sickness was caused by some sin, the Lord will forgive him.

5:15
Mt 21:22
Mk 16:18
Jas 1:6

¹⁶Admit your faults to one another and pray for each other so that you may be

5:16
Mt 18:15-18
1Jn 1:9

5:9 *Let him do whatever criticizing must be done,* implied.

5:6 The defenseless people James mentions here are probably poor laborers. The poor who could not pay their debts were thrown in prison or forced to sell all their possessions, and at times, even sell their family members into slavery. With no opportunity to work off their debts, poor people often died of starvation. God called this murder.

5:7, 8 The farmer must wait patiently for his crops to grow, he cannot hurry the process. But he does not take the summer off and hope that all goes well in the fields. There is much work to do to ensure a good harvest. In the same way, we must wait patiently for Christ's return. We cannot make Christ return any sooner, but while we wait there is much work we can do to advance God's Kingdom. Both the farmer and the Christian must live by faith, looking toward the future reward for their labors. Don't live as if Christ will never come. Work faithfully to build his Kingdom, for the King *will* come when the time is ripe.

5:9 When things go wrong, we tend to blame others for our miseries (see the note on Genesis 3:12, 13). Blaming others is easier than owning our share of the responsibility, but it is both destructive and sinful. Before you judge others for their shortcomings, remember that Christ the Judge will come to evaluate each of us (Matthew 7:1–5). He will not let us get away with shifting the blame to others.

5:10, 11 For more on the topic of suffering, see the notes on Job 1:1ff; 2:10; 3:23–26; 4:7, 8; 23:14; 42:17; and Job's Profile in Job 2.

5:12 A person with a reputation for exaggeration or lying often can't get anyone to believe him on his word alone. Christians should never become like that. Always be honest so that others will believe your simple yes or no. By avoiding lies, half-truths, and omissions of the truth, you will become known as a trustworthy person.

5:14, 15 Here James is talking about someone who is

incapacitated physically. In Scripture, oil was both a medicine (see the parable of the Good Samaritan in Luke 10:30–37) and a symbol of the Spirit of God (as used in anointing kings, see 1 Samuel 16:1–13). Thus oil can represent both the medical and the spiritual spheres of life. Christians should not separate the physical and the spiritual—Jesus Christ is Lord over both the body and the spirit.

5:14, 15 People in the church are not alone. Members of Christ's body should be able to count on others for support and prayer, especially when they are sick or suffering. The elders should be on call to respond to the weakness of any member, and the church should stay alert to pray for the needs of all its members. Prayer, especially corporate prayer, is essential to the life of the church.

5:15 "And their prayer, if offered in faith," does not refer to the faith of the sick person, but to the faith of the church. God heals, faith doesn't, and all prayers are subject to God's will. But our prayers are part of God's healing process. That is why God often waits for our prayers of faith before intervening to heal a person.

5:16 "Admit your faults" can be translated "Confess your sins." Christ has made it possible for us to go directly to God for forgiveness, but confessing our sins to one another still has an important place in the life of the church. (1) If we have sinned against an individual, we must ask him or her to forgive us. (2) If our sin has affected the church, we must confess it publicly. (3) If we need loving support as we struggle with a sin, we should confess it to those who are able to provide that support. (4) If, after confessing a private sin to God, we still don't feel his forgiveness, we may wish to confess that sin to a fellow believer and hear him or her assure us of God's pardon. In Christ's Kingdom, every believer is a priest to other believers (1 Peter 2:9). This means we are charged with helping others come to Christ and telling other's of Christ's words of forgiveness.

healed. The earnest prayer of a righteous man has great power and wonderful results. [17]Elijah was as completely human as we are, and yet when he prayed earnestly that no rain would fall, none fell for the next three and one half years! [18]Then he prayed again, this time that it *would* rain, and down it poured and the grass turned green and the gardens began to grow again.

5:17
1 Kgs 17:1-7
18:36-39
Lk 4:25

Restore wandering believers

5:19
Prov 19:27
Mt 18:15
1 Tim 6:10
2 Pet 3:17

[19]Dear brothers, if anyone has slipped away from God and no longer trusts the Lord and someone helps him understand the Truth again, [20]that person who brings him back to God will have saved a wandering soul from death, bringing about the forgiveness of his many sins.

Sincerely, James

5:16-18 The Christian's most powerful resource is communion with God through prayer. The results are often greater than we thought were possible. Some people see prayer as a last resort to be tried when all else fails. This is backwards. Prayer should come first. Since God's power is infinitely greater than our own, it only makes sense to rely on it—especially because he encourages us to do so.

5:17 For more about the great prophet Elijah, read his Profile in 1 Kings 18.

5:19, 20 Clearly the person who has slipped away is a believer who has fallen into sin—one who is no longer living a life consistent with his beliefs. Christians disagree over whether or not it is possible for people to lose their salvation, but all agree that those who move away from their faith are in serious trouble and need to

repent. James urges Christians to help backsliders return to God. We can do this by taking the initiative, praying for the person, and acting in love to meet the person where he is and bring him back to God.

5:20 The book of James emphasizes faith in action. Right living is the evidence and result of faith. The church must serve with compassion, speak lovingly and truthfully, live in obedience to God's commands, and love one another. The body of believers ought to be an example of heaven on earth, drawing people to Christ through love for God and one another. If we truly believe God's Word, we will *live* it day by day. God's Word is not merely something we read or think about, but something we do. Belief, faith, and trust must have hands and feet—ours!

VITAL STATISTICS

PURPOSE:
To offer encouragement to suffering Christians

AUTHOR:
Peter

TO WHOM WRITTEN:
Jewish Christians who had been driven out of Jerusalem and scattered throughout Asia Minor, and to all believers everywhere

DATE WRITTEN:
About A.D. 62–64 from Rome

SETTING:
Peter was probably in Rome when the great persecution under Emperor Nero began. (Peter was eventually executed during this persecution.) Throughout the Roman Empire, Christians were being tortured and killed for their faith, and the church in Jerusalem was being scattered throughout the Mediterranean world.

KEY VERSE:
"These trials are only to test your faith, to see whether or not it is strong and pure . . ." (1:7).

KEY PEOPLE:
Peter, Silvanus, Mark

KEY PLACES:
Jerusalem, Rome, and the regions of Pontus, Galatia, Cappadocia, Asia Minor, and Bithynia

SPECIAL FEATURES:
Peter used several images that were very special to him because Jesus had used them when he revealed certain truths to Peter. Peter's name (which means "stone") had been given to him by Jesus. Peter's conception of the church—a spiritual house composed of living stones built upon Christ as the foundation—came from Christ. Jesus encouraged Peter to care for the church as a shepherd tending the flock. Thus, it is not surprising to see Peter using living stones (2:5–9) and shepherds and sheep (2:25; 5:2, 4) to describe the church.

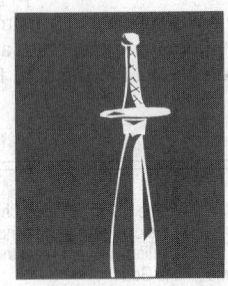

CRUSHED, overwhelmed, devastated, torn—these feelings wash over those who suffer, blinding all vision of hope, threatening to destroy them. Suffering has many forms—physical abuse, debilitating disease, social ostracism, persecution. The pain and anguish tempt one to surrender and give in.

Many first-century Christians suffered because they believed in Jesus Christ. Christians were beaten (Acts 16:16–40), stoned to death (Acts 8:54–60), put in jail and executed (Acts 12:1–5), and many were fed to lions. Apostles were not immune from such suffering. Peter was put in jail and beaten several times (see Acts 4:1–22; 5:12–42).

Peter wrote this epistle to the Jewish Christians scattered throughout Asia Minor who were suffering for their faith in Christ. He comforts them and urges them to remain faithful to Christ in the midst of their trials.

Peter begins by thanking God for salvation (1:2–6). He explains to his readers that trials will refine their faith (1:7–9). They should believe in spite of their circumstances; for many in past ages believed in God's plan of salvation—even the prophets of old who wrote about it, but didn't understand it. But now salvation has been revealed in Christ (1:10–13).

In response to such a great salvation, Peter commands his readers to live holy lives (1:14–16), to reverently fear and trust God (1:17–21), to be honest and loving in their relationships with others (2:1–3a), and to become like Christ (2:3b–4).

Jesus Christ, the "precious Cornerstone" upon whom the church is to be built (2:5, 6), is also the "Stone that was rejected," causing those who "will not listen to God's Word" to fall (2:7, 8). But the church, built upon this Stone, is to be God's holy priesthood (2:9, 10).

Peter then explains how believers should live during difficult times (2:11—4:11). Christians should be above reproach (2:12–17), imitating Christ in all their social roles—masters and servants, husbands and wives, church members and neighbors (2:18—3:17). Jesus Christ should be our model for obedience to God in the midst of great suffering (3:18—4:11).

Peter then outlines the right attitude to have when persecution comes: expect it (4:12), be thankful for the privilege of suffering for Christ (4:13–18), and trust God for deliverance (4:19).

Next, Peter gives some special instructions—elders should feed God's flock (5:1–4), younger men should follow the leadership of the elders (5:5, 6), and everyone should trust God and resist Satan (5:7–11).

Peter concludes by introducing Silvanus and by giving personal greetings from himself, the church in Rome, and Mark (5:12–14).

When you suffer for doing what is right, remember that following Christ is a costly commitment. When you are persecuted for your faith, rejoice that you have been counted worthy to suffer for Christ. He suffered for us; as his followers, we should expect nothing less. As you read 1 Peter, remember that trials will come to refine your faith. When they come, remain faithful to God.

THE BLUEPRINT

1. God's great blessings to his people (1:1—2:10)
2. The conduct of God's people in the midst of suffering (2:11—4:19)
3. The shepherding of God's people in the midst of suffering (5:1–14)

Peter wrote to Jewish Christians who were experiencing persecution for their faith. He wrote to comfort them with the hope of eternal life and to challenge them to continue living holy lives. Those who suffer for being Christians become partners with Christ in his suffering. As we suffer, we must remember that Christ is both our hope in the midst of suffering and our example of how to endure suffering faithfully.

MEGATHEMES

THEME	EXPLANATION	IMPORTANCE
Salvation	Our salvation is a gracious gift from God. God chose us out of his love for us, Jesus died to pay the penalty for our sin, and the Holy Spirit cleansed us from sin when we believed. Eternal life is a wonderful privilege for those who trust in Christ.	Our safety and security are in God. If we experience joy in relationship with Christ now, how much greater will our joy be when he returns and we see him face to face. Such a hope should motivate us to serve Christ with greater commitment.
Persecution	Peter offers faithful believers comfort and hope. We should expect ridicule, rejection, and suffering because we are Christians. Persecution makes us stronger because it refines our faith. We can face persecution victoriously as Christ did, if we rely on him.	Christians still suffer for what they believe. We should expect persecution, but we don't have to be terrified by it. The fact that we will live eternally with Christ should give us the confidence, patience, and hope to stand firm even when we are persecuted.
God's Family	We are privileged to belong to God's family, a community with Christ as the Founder and Foundation. Everyone in this community is related—we are all brothers and sisters, loved equally by God.	Because Christ is the foundation of our family, we must be devoted, loyal, and faithful to him. By obeying him, we show that we are his children. We must accept the challenge to live differently from the society around us.
Family Life	Peter encouraged the wives of unbelievers to submit to their husbands' authority as a means to winning them to Christ. He urged all family members to treat others with sympathy, love, tenderness, and humility.	We must treat our families lovingly. Though it's never easy, willing service is the best way to influence loved ones. To gain the strength we need for self-discipline and submission, pray for God's help.
Judgment	God will judge everyone with perfect justice. We all will face God. He will punish evildoers and those who persecute God's people. Those who love him will be rewarded with life forever in his presence.	Because all are accountable to God, we can leave judgment of others to him. We must not hate or resent those who persecute us. We should realize that we will be held responsible for how we live each day.

1. God's great blessings to his people

1 *From:* Peter, Jesus Christ's missionary.
    To: The Jewish Christians driven out of Jerusalem and scattered throughout
Pontus, Galatia, Cappadocia, Asia minor, and Bithynia.

1:1
Acts 2:9,10
6:9; 16:6,7
Gal 1:2

The hope of eternal life

2Dear friends, God the Father chose you long ago and knew you would become

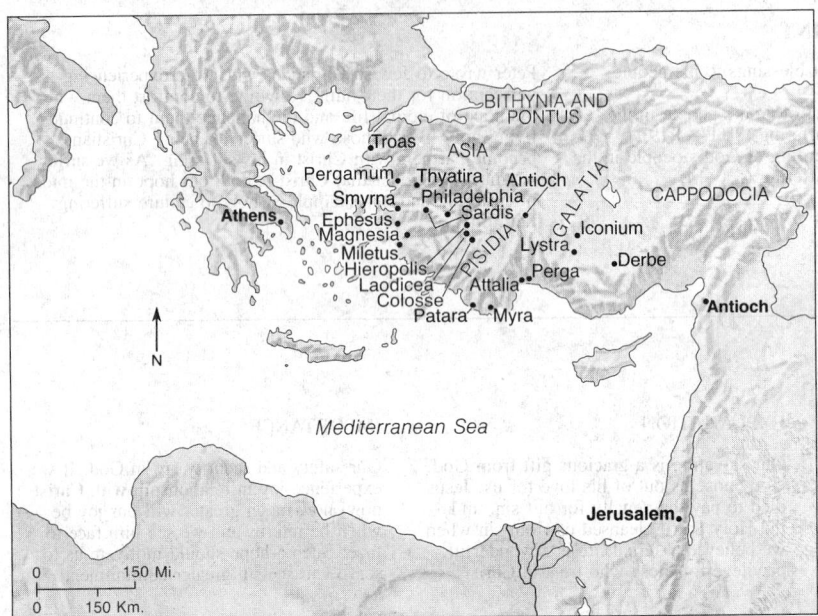

THE CHURCHES OF PETER'S LETTER
Peter addressed his letter to the churches located through Bithynia, Pontus, Asia, Galatia, and Cappadocia. Paul had evangelized many of these areas; others had churches that were begun by the Jews who were in Jerusalem on the day of Pentecost and heard Peter's powerful sermon (see Acts 2:9–11).

1:1 Peter wrote this letter to encourage and strengthen believers who were facing trials and persecution. During most of the first century, persecution was not the rule throughout the Roman Empire. Soldiers were not searching for Christians and torturing them. Christians, however, could expect trials. All would be misunderstood; some would be harassed; a few would be tortured and even put to death. Christians faced persecution from three sources: the Romans, the Jews, and their own families.

The legal status of Christians in the Roman Empire was unclear. Many Romans still thought of Christians as a Jewish sect; and since the Jewish religion was legal, they considered Christianity legal also—as long as Christians went along with the empire's laws. However, if Christians refused to worship the emperor or join the army, or if they were involved in civil disturbances (such as the one in Ephesus recorded in Acts 19:23ff), they might be punished by the civil authorities.

Many Jews did not appreciate being legally associated with Christians. As the book of Acts frequently records, they harmed Christians physically, drove them out of town, or attempted to turn Roman officials against them. Saul, later the great apostle Paul, was an early Jewish persecutor of Christians.

Another source of persecution was the Christian's own family. Under Roman law, the head of the household had absolute authority over all its members. Unless the ruling male became a Christian, the wife, children and servants who were believers might well face extreme hardship. If they were sent away, they would have no place to turn but the church; if they were beaten, no court of law would uphold their interests.

The book of 1 Peter may have been written especially for new Christians and those planning to be baptized. They needed to be warned about what lay ahead, and they needed Peter's

encouraging words to help them face it. This letter is still helpful for new Christians or any Christians facing trials. Many Christians around the world are living under secular governments more repressive than the Roman Empire of the first century. Christians everywhere are subject to misunderstanding, ridicule, and even harassment by unbelieving friends, employers, and family members. And none of us is exempt from catastrophe, pain, illness, and death—trials that, like persecution, make us draw heavily on God's grace. For today's readers, as well as for Peter's original audience, the theme of this letter is *hope*.

1:1 Peter was one of the 12 disciples chosen by Jesus (Mark 1:16–18; John 1:42) and, with James and John, was part of the inner group Jesus singled out for special training and fellowship. Peter was one of the first to recognize Jesus as the Messiah, God's Son; and Jesus gave him a special leadership role in the church (Matthew 16:16–19; Luke 22:31, 32; John 21:15–19). Although during Jesus' trial Peter denied knowing Jesus, he repented and became a great apostle. For more information on Peter, see his Profile in Matthew 27.

1:1 The first believers and leaders of the early church were Jews. When they became Christians, they didn't give up their Jewish heritage, just as we didn't give up our nationalities when we became Christians. Because of persecution, these believers had been scattered throughout the Roman world (this scattering is mentioned in Acts 8:1–4). Persecution didn't quench the gospel; instead, it introduced it to the whole empire. Thus the churches to which Peter wrote probably included Gentile Christians as well.

1:2 Peter encouraged his readers by this strong declaration that they were *chosen* by God the Father and were his children. At one

1:3
Tit 3:5
Jas 1:18
1 Pet 1:13,23
1 Jn 3:3

1:4
Acts 20:32
Col 3:24
2 Tim 4:8
Heb 11:16

1:5
Jn 10:28
Phil 4:7
2 Thess 2:13
1 Pet 4:13

1:6
Mt 5:12
Rom 5:2
Jas 1:2
1 Pet 3:17; 4:12

1:7
Job 23:10
Prov 17:3
Isa 48:10
Jas 1:3

1:8
Jn 20:29
Eph 3:19
1 Jn 4:2

1:10
Gen 49:10
Hag 2:7
Mt 13:17; 26:24
Col 3:4

1:11
Ps 22:6
Mt 26:24
Rom 8:9
2 Pet 1:21

1:12
Acts 2:2-4
Eph 3:10
Heb 11:39

his children. And the Holy Spirit has been at work in your hearts, cleansing you with the blood of Jesus Christ and making you to please him. May God bless you richly and grant you increasing freedom from all anxiety and fear.

³All honor to God, the God and Father of our Lord Jesus Christ; for it is his boundless mercy that has given us the privilege of being born again, so that we are now members of God's own family. Now we live in the hope of eternal life because Christ rose again from the dead. ⁴And God has reserved for his children the priceless gift of eternal life; it is kept in heaven for you, pure and undefiled, beyond the reach of change and decay. ⁵And God, in his mighty power, will make sure that you get there safely to receive it, because you are trusting him. It will be yours in that coming last day for all to see. ⁶So be truly glad! There is wonderful joy ahead, even though the going is rough for a while down here.

⁷These trials are only to test your faith, to see whether or not it is strong and pure. It is being tested as fire tests gold and purifies it—and your faith is far more precious to God than mere gold; so if your faith remains strong after being tried in the test tube of fiery trials, it will bring you much praise and glory and honor on the day of his return.

⁸You love him even though you have never seen him; though not seeing him, you trust him; and even now you are happy with the inexpressible joy that comes from heaven itself. ⁹And your further reward for trusting him will be the salvation of your souls.

¹⁰This salvation was something the prophets did not fully understand. Though they wrote about it, they had many questions as to what it all could mean. ¹¹They wondered what the Spirit of Christ within them was talking about, for he told them to write down the events which, since then, have happened to Christ: his suffering, and his great glory afterwards. And they wondered when and to whom all this would happen.

¹²They were finally told that these things would not occur during their lifetime,

---

time, only the nation of Israel could claim to be God's chosen people; but through Christ, all believers—Jews, former Jews, and Gentiles—belong to God. Our salvation and security rest in the free and merciful choice of the almighty God; no trials or persecutions can rob us of the eternal life he gives to those who believe in him.

1:2 This verse mentions all three members of the Godhead— God the Father, God the Son, and God the Holy Spirit. All three work as one to bring about our salvation. The Father chose us before we chose him (Ephesians 1:4). The Son died for us while we were still sinners (Romans 5:6–10). The Holy Spirit works in our lives to bring us salvation and to set us apart for God's pleasure.

1:3 The term *born again* refers to spiritual birth—the Holy Spirit's act of bringing believers into God's family. Jesus used this term when he explained salvation to Nicodemus (see John 3).

1:3–6 Do you need encouragement? Peter's words offer joy and hope in times of trouble, and he bases his confidence on what God has done for us in Christ Jesus. We're called to *live* in the hope of eternal life (1:3). Our hope is not only for the future: eternal life begins when we believe in God and join his family. The eternal life we now have gives us hope and enables us to live with confidence in God.

1:5 God will help us remain true to our faith, whatever difficult times we must face. The "coming last day" is the Judgment Day of Christ described in Romans 14:10 and Revelation 20:11–15. We may have to endure trials, persecution, or violent death, but our souls cannot be harmed if we have accepted Christ's gift of salvation. We know we will receive the promised rewards.

1:7 Why were Christians the target of persecution? (1) They refused to worship the emperor as a god and thus were viewed as atheists and traitors. (2) They refused to worship at pagan temples, so business for these money-making enterprises dropped wherever Christianity took hold. (3) They didn't support the Roman

ideals of self, power, and conquest; and the Romans scorned the Christian ideal of self-sacrificing service. (4) They exposed and rejected the horrible immorality of pagan culture.

1:7 Peter mentions suffering several times in this letter: 1:6, 7; 3:13–17; 4:12–19; 5:9. When he speaks of trials, he is not talking about natural disasters or God's punishments, but the response of an unbelieving world to people of faith. All believers face such trials when they let their light shine into the darkness. We must accept trials as part of the refining process that burns away impurities, preparing us to meet Christ. Trials teach us patience (Romans 5:3, 4; James 1:2, 3) and help us grow to be the kind of people God wants us to be.

1:7 As gold is heated, impurities float to the top and can be skimmed off. Steel is tempered or strengthened by heating it in fire. Likewise, our trials, struggles, and persecutions strengthen our faith and make us useful to God.

1:10–13 Although the plan of salvation was a mystery to the Old Testament prophets, they still suffered persecution and some died for God. Some Jewish Christians reading Peter's letter, by contrast, had seen Jesus for themselves and knew why he came. They based their assurance on Jesus' death and resurrection. With their firsthand knowledge and personal experience of Jesus, their faith should have been even stronger than that of the Old Testament prophets.

1:11 The Spirit of Christ is another name for the Holy Spirit. Before Jesus left his ministry on earth to return to heaven, he promised to send his Holy Spirit, the Comforter, to teach, help, and guide his followers (John 14:15–17, 26; 16:7). The Holy Spirit would tell them all about Jesus and reveal his glory (John 15:26; 16:14). The Old Testament prophets, writing under the Holy Spirit's inspiration (2 Peter 1:20, 21), described the coming Messiah; the New Testament apostles, through the inspiration of the same Spirit, preached the crucified and risen Lord.

but long years later, during yours. And now at last this Good News has been plainly announced to all of us. It was preached to us in the power of the same heaven-sent Holy Spirit who spoke to them; and it is all so strange and wonderful that even the angels in heaven would give a great deal to know more about it.

13So now you can look forward soberly and intelligently to more of God's kindness to you when Jesus Christ returns.

1:13
1 Cor 1:7
1 Thess 5:6

A call to holy living

14Obey God because you are his children; don't slip back into your old ways—doing evil because you knew no better. 15But be holy now in everything you do, just as the Lord is holy, who invited you to be his child. 16He himself has said, "You must be holy, for I am holy."

1:14
Rom 12:2
Eph 4:18
1 Pet 1:2; 4:2
1:15
2 Cor 7:1
1 Thess 4:7
1 Jn 3:3

17And remember that your heavenly Father to whom you pray has no favorites when he judges. He will judge you with perfect justice for everything you do; so act in reverent fear of him from now on until you get to heaven. 18God paid a ransom to save you from the impossible road to heaven which your fathers tried to take, and the ransom he paid was not mere gold or silver, as you very well know. 19But he paid for you with the precious lifeblood of Christ, the sinless, spotless Lamb of God. 20God chose him for this purpose long before the world began, but only recently was he brought into public view, in these last days, as a blessing to you.

1:16
Lev 11:44,45
1:17
Deut 10:17
Ps 89:26
1:18
Isa 52:3
1:19
Ex 12:5
Jn 1:29
Heb 9:14

21Because of this, your trust can be in God who raised Christ from the dead and gave him great glory. Now your faith and hope can rest in him alone. 22Now you can have real love for everyone because your souls have been cleansed from selfishness and hatred when you trusted Christ to save you; so see to it that you really do love each other warmly, with all your hearts.

1:20
Gal 4:4
2 Tim 1:9,10
1:21
Rom 4:24
1:22
Jn 13:34
Rom 12:10

23For you have a new life. It was not passed on to you from your parents, for the life they gave you will fade away. This new one will last forever, for it comes from Christ, God's ever-living Message to men. 24Yes, our natural lives will fade as grass does when it becomes all brown and dry. All our greatness is like a flower that droops and falls; 25but the Word of the Lord will last forever. And his message is the Good News that was preached to you.

1:23
Jn 1:13; 3:3
1:24
Isa 40:6-8
1:25
Isa 40:8

2 So get rid of your feelings of hatred. Don't just pretend to be good! Be done with dishonesty and jealousy and talking about others behind their backs.

2:1
Eph 4:22,25,31

1:14-16 The God of Israel and of the Christian church is holy—he sets the standard for morality. Unlike the Roman gods, he is not warlike, adulterous, or spiteful. Unlike the gods of the pagan cults popular in the first century, he is not bloodthirsty or promiscuous. He is a God of mercy and justice who cares personally for each of his followers. Our holy God expects us to imitate him by having high moral standards for ourselves. Like him, we should be both merciful and just; like him, we should sacrifice ourselves for others.

1:15, 16 After people commit their lives to Christ, they still feel a pull back to their old ways. Peter tells us to be like our heavenly Father—holy in everything we do. Holiness means being totally devoted or dedicated to God, set aside for his special use, and set apart from sin and its influence. We're to be set apart and different, not blending in with the crowd, yet not being different just for the sake of being different. What makes us different are God's qualities in our lives. Our focus and priorities must be his. All this is in direct contrast to our old ways (1:14). We cannot become holy on our own, but God gives us his Holy Spirit to help us obey and to give us power to overcome sin. Don't use the excuse that our privileged status as God's children gives us freedom to do whatever we want. We should not be spoiled children, but grateful children who love to show respect for our heavenly Father.

1:17 Reverent fear is not the fear of a slave for a ruthless master, but the healthy respect of a believer for the all-powerful God. Because God is the judge of all the earth, we dare not ignore him or treat him casually. We should not assume that our privileged status as God's children gives us freedom to do whatever we want. We should not be spoiled children, but grateful children who love to show respect for our heavenly Father.

1:18, 19 A ransom is money paid to buy freedom for a slave. God paid a ransom to free us from the tyranny of sin (Romans 6:6, 7; 1 Corinthians 6:20; Colossians 2:13, 14; Hebrews 9:12). We could not escape from sin on our own; only the life of God's Son could free us. In Mark 10:45, Jesus says that he is our ransom.

1:20 Christ's sacrifice for our sins was not an afterthought, not something God decided to do when the world got out of control. This plan was set in motion by the all-knowing, eternal God long before the world was created. What a blessing it must have been to Jewish believers to know that Christ's coming and his work of salvation were planned by God long before the world began. This assured them that the law was not being scrapped because it didn't work, but that both the law *and* the coming of Christ were part of God's eternal plan.

1:22 Real love involves selfless giving; therefore, a self-centered person can't truly love. God's love and forgiveness free us to take our eyes off ourselves and to meet others' needs. By sacrificing his life, Christ showed that he truly loved you. Now you can love others by following his example and giving of yourself sacrificially.

1:24, 25 Quoting Isaiah 40:6-8, Peter reminds the believers that everything in this life—possessions, accomplishments, people—will eventually fade away and disappear. Only God's will, Word, and work are permanent. We must stop grasping the temporary and focus our time, money, and energy on the permanent—the Word of God and our new, eternal life in Christ.

2:2
Mt 18:3; 19:14
Eph 4:15
Heb 6:5

2, 3Now that you realize how kind the Lord has been to you, put away all evil, deception, envy, and fraud. Long to grow up into the fullness of your salvation; cry for this as a baby cries for his milk.

Living building stones for God's house

2:4
1 Pet 2:7

2:5
Isa 61:6; 66:21
Eph 2:21
1 Tim 3:15
Heb 13:12
Rev 1:6

2:6
Isa 28:16
Rom 9:32,33
Eph 2:20

2:7
Ps 118:22
Mt 21:42

2:8
Isa 8:14
Lk 2:34,35
1 Cor 1:23
Gal 5:11

2:9
Ex 19:6
Deut 7:6; 10:15
Isa 43:20
Acts 26:18
1 Pet 2:5
Rev 1:6

2:10
Hos 1:10; 2:23
Rom 9:25; 10:19

4Come to Christ, who is the living Foundation of Rock upon which God builds; though men have spurned him, he is very precious to God who has chosen him above all others.

5And now you have become living building-stones for God's use in building his house. What's more, you are his holy priests; so come to him—[you who are acceptable to him because of Jesus Christ]—and offer to God those things that please him. 6As the Scriptures express it, "See, I am sending Christ to be the carefully chosen, precious Cornerstone of my church, and I will never disappoint those who trust in him."

7Yes, he is very precious to you who believe; and to those who reject him, well—"The same Stone that was rejected by the builders has become the Cornerstone, the most honored and important part of the building." 8And the Scriptures also say, "He is the Stone that some will stumble over, and the Rock that will make them fall." They will stumble because they will not listen to God's Word, nor obey it, and so this punishment must follow—that they will fall.

9But you are not like that, for you have been chosen by God himself—you are priests of the King, you are holy and pure, you are God's very own—all this so that you may show to others how God called you out of the darkness into his wonderful light. 10Once you were less than nothing; now you are God's own. Once you knew very little of God's kindness; now your very lives have been changed by it.

2:2, 3 An alternative paraphrase of these verses could read: "If you have tasted the Lord's goodness and kindness, cry for more, as a baby cries for milk. Eat God's Word—read it, think about it—and grow strong in the Lord and be saved."   **2:5** *because of Jesus Christ,* implied.

▬ **2:2, 3** One characteristic all children share is that they want to grow up, to be like the big kids or their parents. When we are born again, we are spiritual babies. If we are healthy, we will yearn to grow. How sad when we are satisfied to stay where we are as months and years roll by. Crying for milk is a natural instinct for a baby; an adult may have to learn to long for spiritual nourishment. Once we see our need and begin to find comfort and fulfillment in Christ, however, our spiritual appetite will increase and we will start to mature. How strong is your desire to grow spiritually? What spiritual food can you take today?

2:4–8 In describing the church as God's building, Peter draws on several Old Testament texts familiar to his Jewish Christian readers: Psalm 118:22; Isaiah 8:14; 28:16. Peter's readers would have understood the chief stone to be Israel; now Peter applies the image to Christ. Once again Peter shows that the church does not cancel the Jewish heritage, but fulfills it.

2:4–8 Peter portrays the church as a living Temple: Christ is the foundation, and each believer is a stone. Paul portrays it as a body: Christ is the head, and each believer is a member (see, for example, Ephesians 4:15, 16). Both pictures emphasize *community.* One stone is not a temple or even a wall; one body part is useless without the others. In our individualistic society, it is easy to forget our interdependence with other Christians. When God calls you to a task, remember that he is also calling others to work with you. Together your individual efforts will be multiplied. Look for those people and join with them to build a beautiful house for God.

2:6 Christians will sometimes face disappointment in this life, but their trust in God is never misplaced. God will not let them down. We can safely put our confidence in him, for the eternal life he promises is certain.

2:6–8 No doubt Peter often thought of Jesus' words to him right after he confessed that Jesus was "the Christ, the Messiah, the Son of the living God": "You are Peter, a stone; and upon this rock

I will build my church; and all the powers of hell shall not prevail against it" (Matthew 16:16–18). What is the stone that really counts in the building of the church? Peter answers: Christ himself. What are the characteristics of Christ, the Cornerstone? (1) He is completely trustworthy; (2) he is precious to believers; (3) and, though rejected by some, he is the most important part of the church.

2:8 Jesus Christ is called "the Stone that some will stumble over." They stumble because they reject him or refuse to believe he is who he says he is. But Psalm 118:22 says that "the stone that was rejected has become the capstone of the arch," the most important part of God's building, the church. In the same way today, people who refuse to believe in Christ have made the greatest mistake of their lives—they have stumbled over the one person who could save them and give meaning to their lives, and they have fallen into God's hands for judgment.

2:9 Christians sometimes speak of "the priesthood of all believers." In Old Testament times, people did not approach God directly. A priest acted as intermediary between God and sinful man. With Christ's victory on the cross, that changed. Now we can come directly into God's presence without fear (Hebrews 4:16), and we are given the responsibility of bringing others to him also (2 Corinthians 5:18–21). When we are united with Christ as members of his body, we join in his work of reconciling God and man. This is what it means to be a priest of the King.

2:9, 10 People often base their self-concept on their accomplishments, but who we are in Christ is far more important than our jobs, our successes, our wealth, or our knowledge. We have been chosen by God as his very own, and we have been called to represent him to others. Remember that your value comes from being one of God's children, not from what you can achieve. You have worth because of what God does, not because of what you do.

2. The conduct of God's people in the midst of suffering

Obey those in authority

¹¹Dear brothers, you are only visitors here. Since your real home is in heaven I beg you to keep away from the evil pleasures of this world; they are not for you, for they fight against your very souls.

¹²Be careful how you behave among your unsaved neighbors; for then, even if they are suspicious of you and talk against you, they will end up praising God for your good works when Christ returns.

¹³For the Lord's sake, obey every law of your government: those of the king as head of the state, ¹⁴and those of the king's officers, for he has sent them to punish all who do wrong, and to honor those who do right.

¹⁵It is God's will that your good lives should silence those who foolishly condemn the Gospel without knowing what it can do for them, having never experienced its power. ¹⁶You are free from the law, but that doesn't mean you are free to do wrong. Live as those who are free to do only God's will at all times.

¹⁷Show respect for everyone. Love Christians everywhere. Fear God and honor the government.

¹⁸Servants, you must respect your masters and do whatever they tell you—not only if they are kind and reasonable, but even if they are tough and cruel. ¹⁹Praise the Lord if you are punished for doing right! ²⁰Of course, you get no credit for being patient if you are beaten for doing wrong; but if you do right and suffer for it, and are patient beneath the blows, God is well pleased.

²¹This suffering is all part of the work God has given you. Christ, who suffered for you, is your example. Follow in his steps: ²²He never sinned, never told a lie,

2:11
Rom 12:1; 13:14
Gal 5:16
Jas 4:1
2:12
Phil 2:15
Tit 2:8
2:13
Rom 13:1
2:14
Rom 13:3,4
2:15
1 Pet 2:12; 3:17
2:16
Jn 8:32
1 Cor 7:22
Jas 1:25
2:17
Rom 12:10; 13:7
1 Pet 1:22
2:18
Eph 6:5
Jas 3:17
2:20
1 Pet 3:14,17
2:21
Mt 11:29; 16:24
Acts 14:22
1 Pet 3:9,18
2:22
Isa 53:9
2 Cor 5:21

2:11 Heaven is an important concept in the Bible, but it is not the pink-cloud-and-harp existence popular in cartoons. In Scripture, heaven is where God dwells. It operates according to God's principles and values, and it is eternal and unshakable. Heaven came to earth in the Jewish sanctuary (the Temple and Tabernacle) where God's presence dwelt. It came in a fuller way in the person of Jesus Christ, "God with us." It permeated the entire world as the Holy Spirit came to dwell in the heart of every believer.

Someday, after God judges and destroys all sin, the Kingdom of Heaven will rule every corner of this earth. We will be with Christ in a way not possible in this life. John saw this day in a vision, and he cried out, "Look, the home of God is now among men, and he will live with them and they will be his people; yes, God himself will be among them" (Revelation 21:3). Our real home, our true loyalty, is not to the things of this earth that will be destroyed. It is to God's truth, his way of life, his perfect creation. Because of this, we often feel like strangers in a world that would prefer to ignore God. In reality, however, we are citizens of the growing Kingdom of Heaven that, at Christ's Second Coming, will last forever.

2:12 Peter's advice sounds like Jesus' in Matthew 5:16: If your actions are above reproach, even hostile feelings will end up praising God. Peter's readers were scattered among Gentiles who were inclined to believe vicious lies about Christians. Attractive, gracious, upright behavior on the part of Christians could show these rumors to be false and could even win some of the unsaved critics to the Lord's side. Don't write off people because they misunderstand Christianity; instead, show them Christ in your life. The day may come when they will praise him with you.

2:12-17 When Peter told his readers to respect the civil government, he was speaking of the Roman Empire under Nero, a notoriously cruel tyrant. Obviously he was not telling believers to compromise their consciences; as Peter had told the High Priest years before, "We must obey God rather than men" (Acts 5:29). But in most aspects of their daily lives, it was possible and desirable for Christians to live according to the law of their land. Today, some Christians live in freedom while others live under

repressive governments. All are commanded to cooperate with the rulers as far as conscience will allow. We are to do this "for the Lord's sake"—so that his Good News and his people will be respected. If we are to be persecuted, it should be for standing for God, and not for breaking moral or civil laws. For more about the Christian and government, see the note on Romans 13:1ff.

2:16 We are free from the law as a means to earning God's approval, but we are still to live, out of gratitude for our free salvation, the kind of moral life required by the Ten Commandments.

2:18-23 Many Christians were household servants. It would be easy for them to submit to masters who were gentle and kind, but Peter encouraged loyalty and persistence even in the face of unjust treatment. In the same way, we should submit to our employers whether they are kind or harsh. By so doing, we may win them to Christ by our good example. Paul gave similar advice in his letters (see Ephesians 6:5–9; Colossians 3:22–25), as did Jesus (Matthew 5:46; Luke 6:32–36).

2:21 There are many reasons for human suffering. Some is the direct result of sin in our lives; some happens because of our foolishness; and some seems to be the result of chance. Peter is writing about yet another category of suffering: that which is part of the work God has given us to do. Christ never sinned, yet he suffered so that we could be set free. When we follow Christ's example and live for others, we too may suffer. Our goal should be to live as Christ lived and to face suffering as he did—with patience, calmness, and confidence that God is in control of the future.

2:21-25 Peter had learned about suffering from Jesus. He knew that Jesus' suffering was part of God's plan (Matthew 16:21- 23; Luke 24:25–27, 44–47) and was intended to save us (Matthew 20:28; 26:28). He also knew that all who follow Jesus must be prepared to suffer (Mark 8:34, 35). Having learned and experienced these truths with Jesus, Peter passes them on to the Jewish Christians and to us.

2:23
Isa 53:7
1 Pet 3:9

2:24
Isa 53:4,5,11

2:25
Heb 13:20
1 Pet 5:4

23never answered back when insulted; when he suffered he did not threaten to get even; he left his case in the hands of God who always judges fairly. 24He personally carried the load of our sins in his own body when he died on the cross, so that we can be finished with sin and live a good life from now on. For his wounds have healed ours! 25Like sheep you wandered away from God, but now you have returned to your Shepherd, the Guardian of your souls who keeps you safe from all attacks.

Wives and husbands

3:1
1 Cor 7:16; 9:19
Eph 5:22
1 Pet 2:18; 3:7

3:3
Isa 3:16-24
1 Tim 2:9

3:4
Ps 45:13
Rom 2:29; 7:22

3:5
1 Tim 5:5
1 Pet 1:3

3:6
Gen 18:12

3:7
Mt 5:23,24
18:19
Eph 5:25
Col 3:19

3 Wives, fit in with your husbands' plans; for then if they refuse to listen when you talk to them about the Lord, they will be won by your respectful, pure behavior. Your godly lives will speak to them better than any words.

3Don't be concerned about the outward beauty that depends on jewelry, or beautiful clothes, or hair arrangement. 4Be beautiful inside, in your hearts, with the lasting charm of a gentle and quiet spirit which is so precious to God. 5That kind of deep beauty was seen in the saintly women of old, who trusted God and fitted in with their husbands' plans.

6Sarah, for instance, obeyed her husband Abraham, honoring him as head of the house. And if you do the same, you will be following in her steps like good daughters and doing what is right; then you will not need to fear [offending your husbands].

7You husbands must be careful of your wives, being thoughtful of their needs and honoring them as the weaker sex. Remember that you and your wife are partners in receiving God's blessings, and if you don't treat her as you should, your prayers will not get ready answers.

➤ **3:6** *offending your husbands*, implied.

2:24 Christ died for *our* sins, in *our* place, so we would not have to suffer the punishment we deserve. This is called *substitutionary atonement.*

3:1ff If a man became a Christian, he usually brought his whole family into the church (see, for example, the story of the conversion of the Philippian jailer, Acts 16:29–33). By contrast, a woman who became a Christian usually came into the church alone. Under Roman law, the husband and father had absolute authority over all members of his household, including his wife. If he disapproved of her new beliefs, she could endanger her marriage by demanding her rights as a free woman in Christ. Peter reassured Christian women married to unbelievers that they did not need to preach to their husbands. Under the circumstances, their best approach would be loving service: they should show their husbands the kind of self-giving love that Christ showed the church. By being exemplary wives, they would please their husbands. At the very least, the men would then allow them to continue practicing their "strange" religion. At best, their husbands would join them and become Christians too.

3:1-7 A changed life speaks loudly and clearly, and it is often the most effective way to influence a family member. Peter instructed Christian wives to develop inner beauty rather than being overly concerned about their appearance. Their husbands would be won by their love rather than by their looks. Live your Christian faith quietly and consistently in your home, and your family will see Christ in you.

3:3 We should not be obsessed by fashion, but neither should we be so unconcerned that we do not bother to care for ourselves. Hygiene, neatness, and grooming are important, but even more important are a person's attitude and spirit. True beauty begins inside.

3:6 Submission is voluntarily cooperating with someone else out

of love and respect for God and for that person. Ideally, submission is mutual ("Honor Christ by submitting to each other"—Ephesians 5:21). Even when it is one-sided, however, it can be an effective Christian tool. Jesus Christ submitted to death so that we could be saved; we may sometimes have to submit to unpleasant circumstances so that others will see Christ in us. (Christian submission never requires us to violate our principles, however; we should never submit to evil.) One-sided submission requires tremendous strength. We could not do it without the power of the Holy Spirit working in us.

3:7 When Peter calls women the "weaker sex" he does not imply moral or intellectual inferiority, but he is recognizing women's physical limitations. Women in his day, if unprotected by men, were vulnerable to attack, abuse, and financial disaster. Women's lives may be easier today, but they are still more vulnerable to criminal attack and family abuse. And in spite of increased opportunities in the workplace, most women still earn considerably less than most men, and the vast majority of the nations' poor are single mothers and their children. A man who honors his wife as a member of the weaker sex will protect, respect, help, and stay with her. He will not expect her to work full-time outside and full-time at home; he will lighten her load wherever he can. He will be sensitive to her needs, and he will relate to her with courtesy, consideration, insight, and tact.

3:7 If a man does not treat his wife kindly, his prayers become ineffective, because a living relationship with God depends on right relationships with others. Jesus said that if you have a problem with a fellow believer, you must make things right with that person before coming to worship (Matthew 5:23, 24). This principle carries over into family relationships. If men use their position to mistreat their wives, their relationship with God will suffer.

Suffering for doing good

⁸And now this word to all of you: You should be like one big happy family, full of sympathy toward each other, loving one another with tender hearts and humble minds. ⁹Don't repay evil for evil. Don't snap back at those who say unkind things about you. Instead, pray for God's help for them, for we are to be kind to others, and God will bless us for it.

¹⁰If you want a happy, good life, keep control of your tongue, and guard your lips from telling lies. ¹¹Turn away from evil and do good. Try to live in peace even if you must run after it to catch and hold it! ¹²For the Lord is watching his children, listening to their prayers; but the Lord's face is hard against those who do evil.

¹³Usually no one will hurt you for wanting to do good. ¹⁴But even if they should, you are to be envied, for God will reward you for it. ¹⁵Quietly trust yourself to Christ your Lord and if anybody asks why you believe as you do, be ready to tell him, and do it in a gentle and respectful way.

¹⁶Do what is right; then if men speak against you, calling you evil names, they will become ashamed of themselves for falsely accusing you when you have only done what is good. ¹⁷Remember, if God wants you to suffer, it is better to suffer for doing good than for doing wrong!

We are partners with Christ in our suffering

¹⁸Christ also suffered. He died once for the sins of all us guilty sinners, although

3:8
Rom 12:16
Eph 4:32
3:9
Lk 6:28
Rom 12:14,17
Heb 6:14; 12:17
3:10-12
Ps 34:12–16
3:13
Prov 16:7
3:14
Isa 8:12,13
3:15
Col 4:6
2 Tim 2:25
1 Pet 1:3,17
3:16
1 Pet 2:12; 3:21
3:17
1 Pet 2:20,21
4:15,19

		SUBMISSION
Functional	a distinguishing of our roles and the work we do	
Relational	a loving acknowledgement of another's value as a person	
Reciprocal	a mutual, humble cooperation with one another	
Universal	an acknowledgement by the church of the all-encompassing lordship of Jesus Christ	

Submission is voluntarily cooperating with anyone out of love and respect for God first, then secondly, love and respect for that person. Submitting to nonbelievers is difficult, but it is a vital part of leading them to Jesus Christ. We are not called to submit to nonbelievers to the point that we compromise our relationship with God, but we must look for every opportunity to humbly serve in the power of God's Spirit.

3:8 Peter lists five key elements that should characterize any group of believers: (1) harmony—pursuing the same goals; (2) sympathy—being responsive to others' needs; (3) love—seeing one another as brothers and sisters; (4) tender hearts—being affectionately sensitive; and (5) humble minds—being willing to encourage one another and rejoice in each other's successes. These five qualities go a long way toward helping believers serve God effectively.

3:8, 9 Peter developed the qualities of tenderness and humility the hard way. In his early days with Christ, these attitudes did not come naturally to his impulsive, strong personality (see Mark 8:31–33; John 13:6–9 for examples of Peter's blustering). But the Holy Spirit changed Peter, turning his strong personality to God's use, and teaching him tenderness and humility.

3:9 In our fallen world, it is often acceptable to tear people down verbally or get back at them if we feel hurt. Peter, remembering Jesus' teaching to turn the other cheek (Matthew 5:39), encourages his readers to pay back wrongs by praying for the offenders. In God's Kingdom, revenge is unacceptable behavior. So is insulting a person, no matter how indirectly it is done. Rise above getting back at those who hurt you. Instead of reacting angrily to these people, pray for them.

3:10 For more about controlling your tongue, see the notes in James 3.

3:11 Too often we see peace as merely the absence of conflict, and we think peacemaking is a passive role. But an effective peacemaker actively pursues peace. He builds good relationships, knowing that peace is a by-product of commitment. He anticipates problems and deals with them before they occur. When conflicts

arise, he brings them into the open and deals with them before they grow unmanageable. Making peace can be harder work than waging war, but it results not in death but in life and happiness.

3:15 Some Christians believe faith is a personal matter that should be kept to oneself. It is true that we shouldn't be boisterous or obnoxious in sharing our faith, but we should always be ready to answer, gently and respectfully, when asked about our faith, our lifestyle, or our Christian perspective. Is your hope in Christ readily observable to others? Are you prepared to tell others what Christ has done in your life?

3:16 You may not be able to keep people from attacking you, but you can at least stop supplying them with ammunition. As long as you do what is right, their accusations will be empty and will only embarrass them. Keep your conduct above criticism!

3:18–20 The meaning of these verses is not completely clear, and commentators have explained them many different ways. The traditional interpretation is that Christ, between his death and resurrection, announced salvation to God's faithful followers who had been waiting for their salvation during the whole Old Testament era. Matthew records that when Jesus died, "many godly men and women who had died came back to life again" (see Matthew 27:52, 53). Other commentators think this passage says that Christ's spirit was in Noah as he preached to those imprisoned by sin. Still others hold that Christ went to Hades to proclaim his victory to the fallen angels imprisoned there since Noah's day (see 2 Peter 2:4). In any case, the passage shows that Christ's Good News is not limited. It has been preached in the past as well as in the present; it has gone to the dead as well as to the living. God has given everyone the opportunity to come to him, but this does

3:19
1 Pet 4:6

3:20
Gen 6:3; 7:1
8:18
Heb 11:7
1 Pet 1:9,22
2:25; 4:19

3:21
Heb 9:14
10:22; 13:18

3:22
Mk 16:19
Rom 8:38
Heb 1:6; 4:14
6:20

he himself was innocent of any sin at any time, that he might bring us safely home to God. But though his body died, his spirit lived on, 19and it was in the spirit that he visited the spirits in prison, and preached to them— 20spirits of those who, long before in the days of Noah, had refused to listen to God, though he waited patiently for them while Noah was building the ark. Yet only eight persons were saved from drowning in that terrible flood. 21(That, by the way, is what baptism pictures for us: In baptism we show that we have been saved from death and doom by the resurrection of Christ; not because our bodies are washed clean by the water, but because in being baptized we are turning to God and asking him to cleanse our *hearts* from sin.) 22And now Christ is in heaven, sitting in the place of honor next to God the Father, with all the angels and powers of heaven bowing before him and obeying him.

4:1
Rom 6:7
Gal 2:20
Col 3:5
1 Pet 2:21

4:2
Rom 6:2,11

4:3
Rom 13:13
Eph 2:2; 4:17

4:4
Eph 5:18
1 Pet 3:16

4:5
Acts 10:42
17:31
Rom 14:10

4 Since Christ suffered and underwent pain, you must have the same attitude he did; you must be ready to suffer, too. For remember, when your body suffers, sin loses its power, 2and you won't be spending the rest of your life chasing after evil desires, but will be anxious to do the will of God. 3You have had enough in the past of the evil things the godless enjoy—sex, sin, lust, getting drunk, wild parties, drinking bouts, and the worship of idols, and other terrible sins.

4Of course, your former friends will be very surprised when you don't eagerly join them any more in the wicked things they do, and they will laugh at you in contempt and scorn. 5But just remember that they must face the Judge of all, living and dead; they will be punished for the way they have lived. 6That is why the Good News was preached even to those who were dead—killed by the flood—so that although their bodies were punished with death, they could still live in their spirits as God lives.

4:7
Rom 13:11-13

4:8
1 Pet 1:22

4:10
Rom 12:6-8

➤ *Continue to love each other in the midst of suffering*

7The end of the world is coming soon. Therefore be earnest, thoughtful men of prayer. 8Most important of all, continue to show deep love for each other, for love makes up for many of your faults. 9Cheerfully share your home with those who need a meal or a place to stay for the night.

10God has given each of you some special abilities; be sure to use them to help

3:21 *In baptism we show that we have been saved from death and doom by the resurrection of Christ,* or "Baptism, which corresponds to this, now saves you through the resurrection." **4:3** *and other terrible sins,* literally, "lawless idolatries." **4:6** *killed by the flood,* implied. See 3:19, 20. **4:8** *for love makes up for many of your faults,* or "love overlooks each other's many faults."

not mean a second chance for those who reject Christ in this life.

3:21 In baptism we identify with Jesus Christ, who separates us from the lost and gives us new life. It is not the ceremony by itself that saves us, but faith in Christ's death and resurrection. Baptism is the symbol of the transformation that happens in the hearts of those who believe (Romans 6:3–5; Galatians 3:27; Colossians 2:12). By identifying themselves with Christ through baptism, Peter's readers could never turn back, even under the pressure of persecution. Public baptism would keep them from the temptation to renounce their faith.

4:1, 2 Some people will do anything to avoid pain. As followers of Christ, however, we should be willing and prepared to do God's will and to suffer for it if necessary. When our bodies are in pain or our lives in jeopardy, our real values show up clearly, and sinful pleasures seem less important.

4:4 A person whose life changes radically at conversion may experience contempt from his old friends. He may be scorned not only because he refuses to participate in certain activities, but also because his priorities have changed and he is now heading in the opposite direction. His very life incriminates their sinful activities.

4:5 The basis of salvation is whether we have believed in Jesus (Acts 16:31), but the basis for judgment is how we have lived. Those who inflict persecution are marked for punishment when they stand before God. Believers have nothing to fear, however, because Jesus will be the final Judge over all (John 5:22).

4:5, 6 Many people in the early church had an unclear idea of life after death. In Thessalonica, Christians worried that loved ones who died before Christ's return might never see him (1 Thessalonians 4:13–18). Peter's readers needed to be reminded that the dead will be judged. The judgment will be perfectly fair, he points out, because even the dead have heard the gospel (see also 3:18, 19). The Good News was first announced when Jesus Christ preached on the earth, but it has been operating since before the creation of the world (Ephesians 1:4), and it affects all mankind, the dead as well as the living.

➤ **4:7–9** Live expectantly, for Christ is coming. Getting ready to meet him involves continually growing in love for God and for others (see Jesus' summary of the law in Matthew 22:37–40). It is important to pray regularly, and it is also important to reach out to needy people. Your possessions, status, and power will mean nothing in God's Kingdom, but you will spend eternity with other people. Invest your time and talents where they will make an eternal difference.

4:10, 11 Some people, well aware of their abilities, believe they have the right to use them as they please. Others feel they have no special talents at all. To both groups Peter addresses these verses. Everyone has some abilities, he says; find yours and use them. All our abilities should be dedicated to others, he points out; none are for our own exclusive enjoyment. Peter mentions preaching and helping. Paul lists these and other abilities in Romans 12:6–8; 1 Corinthians 12:8–11; Ephesians 4:11.

each other, passing on to others God's many kinds of blessings. ¹¹Are you called to preach? Then preach as though God himself were speaking through you. Are you called to help others? Do it with all the strength and energy that God supplies, so that God will be glorified through Jesus Christ—to him be glory and power forever and ever. Amen.

¹²Dear friends, don't be bewildered or surprised when you go through the fiery trials ahead, for this is no strange, unusual thing that is going to happen to you. ¹³Instead, be really glad—because these trials will make you partners with Christ in his suffering, and afterwards you will have the wonderful joy of sharing his glory in that coming day when it will be displayed.

¹⁴Be happy if you are cursed and insulted for being a Christian, for when that happens the Spirit of God will come upon you with great glory. ¹⁵Don't let me hear of your suffering for murdering or stealing or making trouble or being a busybody and prying into other people's affairs. ¹⁶But it is no shame to suffer for being a Christian. Praise God for the privilege of being in Christ's family and being called by his wonderful name! ¹⁷For the time has come for judgment, and it must begin first among God's own children. And if even we who are Christians must be judged, what terrible fate awaits those who have never believed in the Lord? ¹⁸If the righteous are barely saved, what chance will the godless have?

¹⁹So if you are suffering according to God's will, keep on doing what is right and trust yourself to the God who made you, for he will never fail you.

3. The shepherding of God's people in the midst of suffering

5 And now, a word to you elders of the church. I, too, am an elder; with my own eyes I saw Christ dying on the cross; and I, too, will share his glory and his honor when he returns. Fellow elders, this is my plea to you: ²Feed the flock of God; care for it willingly, not grudgingly; not for what you will get out of it, but because you are eager to serve the Lord. ³Don't be tyrants, but lead them by your

4:14 *the Spirit of God will come upon you with great glory,* or "the glory of the Spirit of God is being seen in you."

Cross-references:

4:12 1 Pet 1:6

4:13 Rom 8:17 / 2 Cor 1:5 / Phil 3:10 / 2 Tim 2:12

4:14 Mt 5:11 / Jn 15:21 / 2 Cor 4:10 / Heb 11:26

4:15 1 Thess 4:11 / 2 Thess 3:11 / 1 Tim 5:13

4:16 Acts 5:41; 28:22

4:17 Jer 25:29 / Mal 3:5 / Rom 2:9 / 2 Thess 1:8

4:18 Lk 23:31

4:19 Ps 31:5,6

5:1 Lk 24:48 / Rev 1:9

5:2 Jn 21:16 / Acts 20:28

4:11 How is God glorified when we use our abilities? When we use them as he directs, to help others, they will see Jesus in us and praise him for the help they have received. Peter may have been thinking of Jesus' words, "Let your good deeds glow for all to see, so that they will praise your heavenly Father" (Matthew 5:16).

4:14-16 Again Peter brings to mind Jesus' words: "When you are reviled and persecuted and lied about because you are my followers—wonderful!" (Matthew 5:11). It is never shameful to suffer for Christ, and he will send his Spirit to strengthen those who are persecuted for their faith. This does not mean that all suffering is good, however. Sometimes a person will grumble, "He's just picking on me because I'm a Christian," when it's obvious to everyone else that the person's own unpleasant behavior is the cause of his problems. It may take careful thought or wise counsel to determine the real cause of our suffering. We can be assured, however, that whenever we suffer because of our loyalty to Christ, he will be with us all the way.

4:16 It is not shameful to suffer for being a Christian. When Peter and John were persecuted for preaching the Good News, they rejoiced because such persecution was a mark of God's approval of their work (Acts 5:41). Don't seek out suffering, and don't try to avoid it. Instead, keep on doing what is right regardless of the suffering it might bring.

4:17, 18 This is not final judgment but God's refining discipline (Hebrews 12:7). God often allows the consequences of sin to take their course, even with believers. He does this for several reasons: (1) to show us our potential for sinning, (2) to encourage us to turn from sin and more constantly depend on him, (3) to prepare us to face other, even stronger temptations in the future, and (4) to help us stay faithful and keep on trusting him. If believers need earthly discipline (judgment) from God, how much more will unbelievers receive it? If believers are "barely saved" (only because of God's

mercy, or as some say, barely saved through persecution), what chance do those have who reject Christ?

4:19 God created the world, and he has faithfully ordered it and kept it since the creation. Because we know he is faithful, we can count on him to fulfill his promises to us. If he can oversee the forces of nature, surely he can see us through the trials we face.

5:1 Elders were church officers providing supervision, protection, discipline, instruction, and direction for the other believers. *Elder* simply means "older." Both Greeks and Jews gave positions of great honor to wise older men, and the Christian church continued this pattern of leadership. Elders carried great responsibility, and they were expected to live exemplary lives.

5:1, 2 Peter, one of Jesus' 12 disciples, was one of the three who saw Christ's glory at the transfiguration (Mark 9:1-13; 2 Peter 1:16-18). Often the spokesman for the apostles, he witnessed Jesus' death and resurrection, preached at Pentecost, and became a pillar of the Jerusalem church. But writing to the elders, he identifies himself as a fellow elder, not a superior. He asks them to "feed the flock of God," exactly what Jesus had told him to do (John 21:15-17). Peter was taking his own advice as he worked along with the other elders in caring for God's faithful people. His identification with the elders is a powerful example of Christian leadership, where authority is based on service, not power (Mark 10:42-45).

5:2-5 Peter describes several characteristics of good leaders in the church: (1) they realize they are caring for God's flock, not their own; (2) they lead out of eagerness to serve, not out of obligation; (3) they are concerned for what they can give, not for what they can get; (4) they lead by example, not force. All of us lead others in some way. Whatever your role, your leadership should be in line with these characteristics.

5:4
1 Cor 9:25
Heb 13:20,21

5:5
Prov 3:34
Jas 4:6

5:6
Jas 4:10

5:7
Mt 6:25
Heb 13:5

5:8
Job 1:7
Jas 4:7
1 Pet 1:13

5:9
Acts 14:22
Heb 12:8

5:10
Rom 16:25
2 Thess 2:17
2 Tim 2:10
1 Pet 1:6; 4:10

5:12
Acts 11:23
2 Cor 1:19
Heb 13:22

5:13
Acts 12:12

5:14
Rom 16:16
Eph 6:23

good example, ⁴and when the Head Shepherd comes, your reward will be a never-ending share in his glory and honor.

⁵You younger men, follow the leadership of those who are older. And all of you serve each other with humble spirits, for God gives special blessings to those who are humble, but sets himself against those who are proud. ⁶If you will humble yourselves under the mighty hand of God, in his good time he will lift you up.

⁷Let him have all your worries and cares, for he is always thinking about you and watching everything that concerns you.

⁸Be careful—watch out for attacks from Satan, your great enemy. He prowls around like a hungry, roaring lion, looking for some victim to tear apart. ⁹Stand firm when he attacks. Trust the Lord; and remember that other Christians all around the world are going through these sufferings too.

¹⁰After you have suffered a little while, our God, who is full of kindness through Christ, will give you his eternal glory. He personally will come and pick you up, and set you firmly in place, and make you stronger than ever. ¹¹To him be all power over all things, forever and ever. Amen.

Peter's final greetings

¹²I am sending this note to you through the courtesy of Silvanus who is, in my opinion, a very faithful brother. I hope I have encouraged you by this letter for I have given you a true statement of the way God blesses. What I have told you here should help you to stand firmly in his love.

¹³The church here in Rome—she is your sister in the Lord—sends you her greetings; so does my son Mark. ¹⁴Give each other the handshake of Christian love. Peace be to all of you who are in Christ.

Peter

5:13 *The church here in Rome,* literally, "She who is at Babylon is likewise chosen"; but Babylon was the Christian nickname for Rome, and the "she" is thought by many to be Peter's wife to whom reference is made in Mt 8:14; 1 Cor 9:5, etc. Others believe this should read: "Your sister church here in Babylon salutes you, and so does my son Mark."

5:4 The Head Shepherd is Jesus Christ. This refers to his Second Coming, when he will judge all people.

5:5 Both young and old can benefit from Peter's instructions. Pride often keeps elders from trying to understand young people and young people from listening to their elders. Peter told both young and old to be humble and serve each other. Young men should follow the leadership of older men, who should lead by example. Respect your elders, listen to those younger than you, and be humble enough to admit you can learn from each other.

5:6 We often worry about our position and status, hoping we'll get proper recognition for what we do. But Peter advises us to remember that God's recognition counts more than human praise. God is able and willing to bless us according to his own timing. Obey God regardless of present circumstances, and in his good time—either in this life or in the next—he will lift you up.

5:7 Carrying your worries, stress, and daily struggles by yourself shows that you have not trusted God fully with your life. It takes humility, however, to recognize that God cares, to admit your need, and to let others in his family help you. Sometimes we think that struggles caused by our own sin and foolishness are not God's concern. But when we turn to him in repentance, he will bear the weight even of those struggles. Letting God have your worries is active, not passive. Don't submit to circumstances, but to the Lord who controls circumstances.

5:8, 9 Lions attack sick, young, or straggling animals; they choose victims who are alone or not alert. Peter warns us to watch out for Satan when we are suffering or persecuted. Feeling alone, weak, helpless, and cut off from other believers, so focused on our troubles that we forget to watch for danger, we are especially vulnerable to Satan's attacks. During times of suffering, seek other Christians for support. Keep your eyes on Christ, and resist the devil. Then, says James, "he will flee from you" (James 4:7).

5:10 When we are suffering, we feel as though our pain will never end. Peter shows these faithful Christians the wider perspective. In comparison with eternity, their suffering would last only "a little while." Some of Peter's readers would be picked up, set in place, and strengthened in their own lifetimes. Others would be released from their suffering through death. All of God's faithful followers, however, are assured of Christ's eternal glory—endless, joyful life in which suffering plays no part at all (Revelation 21:4).

5:12 Silvanus, also called Silas, was one of the men chosen to deliver the letter from the Jerusalem council to the church in Antioch (Acts 15:22). He accompanied Paul on his second missionary journey (Acts 15:40—18:11), helped Paul write his letters to the Thessalonians (1 Thessalonians 1:1; 2 Thessalonians 1:1), and ministered with Timothy in Corinth (2 Corinthians 1:19).

5:13 Mark, also called John or John Mark, was known to many of this letter's readers because he had traveled widely (Acts 12:25—13:13; 15:36–51) and was recognized as a leader in the church (Colossians 4:10; Philemon 1:24). Mark was probably with the disciples at the time of Jesus' arrest (Mark 14:51, 52). Tradition holds that Peter was Mark's main source of information when he wrote the Gospel of Mark.

5:14 Peter wrote this letter just before the cruel emperor Nero began persecuting Christians in Rome and throughout the empire. Afraid for his life, Peter had three times denied even knowing Jesus (John 18:15–27); now, having learned how to stand firm in an evil world, he encourages other Christians who are facing persecution for their faith. Peter himself lived by the words he wrote, for he was martyred for his faith. Those who stand for Christ will be persecuted, because the world is ruled by Christ's greatest enemy. But just as the small group of early believers stood against persecution, so we must be willing to stand for our faith with the patience, endurance, and courage that Peter exhibited.

2 PETER

VITAL STATISTICS

PURPOSE:
To warn Christians about false teachers and to exhort them to grow in their faith and knowledge of Christ

AUTHOR:
Peter

TO WHOM WRITTEN:
The church at large

DATE WRITTEN:
About A.D. 67, three years after 1 Peter was written, possibly from Rome

SETTING:
Peter knows that his time on earth is limited (1:13, 14), so he is writing about what is on his heart, warning believers of what will happen when he is gone—especially about false teachers. He reminds them of the unchanging truth of the gospel.

KEY VERSES:
"For as you know him better, he will give you, through his great power, everything you need for living a truly good life: he even shares his own glory and his own goodness with us!" (1:3).

KEY PEOPLE:
Peter, Paul

SPECIAL FEATURES:
The date and destination are uncertain, and the authorship has been disputed. Because of this, 2 Peter was the last book admitted to the canon of the New Testament Scripture. Also, there are similarities between 2 Peter and Jude.

WARNINGS have many forms—lights, signs, sights, sounds, smells, feelings, and written words. With varied focus, their purpose is the same—to warn one of imminent danger. Responses to these warnings will also vary, from disregard and neglect to evasive or corrective action. How a person reacts to a warning is usually determined by the situation and the source of the warning. An impending storm is treated differently than an oncoming automobile, and the counsel of a friend is heeded much more than the flippant remark of a stranger.

Second Peter is a letter of warning—from an authority none other than the courageous, experienced, and faithful apostle. It is the last communication from this great warrior of Christ. Soon thereafter he would die, martyred for the faith.

Previously Peter had written to comfort and encourage believers in the midst of suffering and persecution—an external onslaught. But three years later, in this epistle containing his written message, he wrote to warn them of an internal attack—complacency and heresy. He speaks of holding fast to the nonnegotiable facts of the faith, of growing and maturing in the faith, and of rejecting all who would twist the truth. If his readers heeded Peter's warnings, their lives would be honoring to Christ and their churches would be Christ-centered.

After a brief greeting (1:1), Peter gives the antidote for stagnancy and shortsightedness in the Christian life (1:2–11). He explains that his days are numbered (1:12–15) and that the believers should listen to his messages and the words of Scripture (1:16–21).

Peter then gives a blunt warning about false teachers (2:1–22). They will become prevalent in the last days (2:1, 2), they will do or say anything for money (2:3), they will laugh at the things of God (2:2, 10, 11), they will do whatever they feel like doing (2:12–17), they will be proud and boastful (2:18, 19), and they will be judged and punished by God (2:3–10, 20–22).

Peter concludes his brief letter by explaining why he has written it (3:1–18). He reminds them that God predicted the coming of false teachers, and gives the reasons for the delay in Christ's return (3:1–13), encouraging them to beware of heresies, and to grow in their faith (3:14–18).

Addressed to "all of you who have our kind of faith," 2 Peter could have been written to us. Our world is filled with false prophets and teachers claiming to have the truth and clamoring for attention and allegiance. Listen carefully to Peter's message and heed his warning. Determine to grow in your knowledge of Christ and to reject all those who preach anything but that which is consistent with the revealed Word of God.

THE BLUEPRINT

1. Guidance for growing Christians (1:1-21)
2. Danger to growing Christians (2:1-22)
3. Hope for growing Christians (3:1-18)

While Peter wrote his first letter to teach about handling persecution (trials from without), he wrote this letter to teach about handling heresy (trials from within). False teachers are often subtly deceitful. Believers today must still be vigilant against falling into false doctrine, heresy, and cults. This letter gives us clues to help detect false teaching.

MEGATHEMES

THEME	EXPLANATION	IMPORTANCE
Diligence	If our faith is real, it will be evident in our faithful behavior. If people are diligent in Christian growth, they won't backslide or be deceived by false teachers.	Growth is essential. It begins with faith and culminates in love for others. To keep growing we need to know God, keep on following him, and remember what he taught us. We must remain diligent in faithful obedience and Christian growth.
False Teachers	Peter warns the church to beware of false teachers. These teachers were proud of their position, promoted sexual sin, and advised against keeping the Ten Commandments. Peter countered them by pointing to the Spirit-inspired Scriptures as our authority.	Christians need discernment to be able to resist false teachers. God can rescue us from their lies if we stay true to his Word, the Bible, and reject those who twist the truth.
Christ's Return	One day Christ will create a new heaven and earth where we will live forever. As Christians, our hope is in this promise. But with Christ's return comes his judgment on all who refuse to believe.	The cure for complacency, lawlessness, and heresy is found in the confident assurance that Christ will return. God is still giving unbelievers time to repent. To be ready, Christians must keep on trusting and resist the pressure to give up waiting for Christ's return.

1. Guidance for growing Christians

1 *From:* Simon Peter, a servant and missionary of Jesus Christ.
To: all of you who have our kind of faith. The faith I speak of is the kind that Jesus Christ our God and Savior gives to us. How precious it is, and how just and good he is to give this same faith to each of us.

1:1
Rom 1:1,12
2 Cor 4:13
Eph 4:5
Tit 2:13
1 Pet 1:1,7; 2:7

1:1 First Peter was written around the time that the Roman Emperor Nero began his heavy persecution of Christians. Second Peter was written two or three years later (between A.D. 66-68), after intense persecution had begun. First Peter was a letter of encouragement to the Christians who suffered, but 2 Peter focuses on the church's internal problems, especially the false teachers

who were causing people to doubt and turn away from Christianity. Second Peter combats their heresies by denouncing the evil motives of the false teachers and reaffirming Christianity's truths—the authority of Scripture, the primacy of faith, and the certainty of Christ's return.

Character qualities to develop in life

2Do you want more and more of God's kindness and peace? Then learn to know him better and better. 3For as you know him better, he will give you, through his great power, everything you need for living a truly good life: he even shares his own glory and his own goodness with us! 4And by that same mighty power he has given us all the other rich and wonderful blessings he promised; for instance, the promise to save us from the lust and rottenness all around us, and to give us his own character.

5But to obtain these gifts, you need more than faith; you must also work hard to be good, and even that is not enough. For then you must learn to know God better and discover what he wants you to do. 6Next, learn to put aside your own desires so that you will become patient and godly, gladly letting God have his way with you. 7This will make possible the next step, which is for you to enjoy other people and to like them, and finally you will grow to love them deeply. 8The more you go on in this way, the more you will grow strong spiritually and become fruitful and useful to our Lord Jesus Christ. 9But anyone who fails to go after these additions to faith is blind indeed, or at least very shortsighted, and has forgotten that God delivered him from the old life of sin so that now he can live a strong, good life for the Lord.

10So, dear brothers, work hard to prove that you really are among those God has called and chosen, and then you will never stumble or fall away. 11And God will open wide the gates of heaven for you to enter into the eternal kingdom of our Lord and Savior Jesus Christ.

Paying attention to Scripture

12I plan to keep on reminding you of these things even though you already know them and are really getting along quite well! 13, 14But the Lord Jesus Christ has showed me that my days here on earth are numbered, and I am soon to die. As long as I am still here I intend to keep sending these reminders to you, 15hoping to impress them so clearly upon you that you will remember them long after I have gone.

16For we have not been telling you fairy tales when we explained to you the

Cross-references (margin):

1:2 — 2 Pet 3:18
1:3 — 2 Thess 2:14
1:4 — Jas 1:27; 1 Jn 2:15,16
1:5 — Col 2:3
1:6 — 1 Cor 9:25; Gal 5:22
1:7 — Jn 13:34,35; Rom 12:10; 1 Pet 1:22
1:8 — Jn 15:1-6; Col 1:10; 2 Pet 1:3
1:9 — 2 Cor 4:3,4; 1 Jn 2:11
1:10 — Mt 22:14; Rom 8:28-31; 11:29; 1 Thess 1:4; Jude 24
1:11 — 2 Tim 4:18; 2 Pet 2:20; Rev 3:21
1:13,14 — Jn 13:36; 21:18; 2 Tim 4:6; 2 Pet 1:12; 3:1
1:16 — Mt 17:1-5; 28:18; Mk 13:26; Lk 9:28-32; Eph 4:14; 1 Thess 2:19; 1 Tim 1:4

1:2 Many believers want more of God's kindness and peace, but they are unwilling to put forth the effort to get to know him better. To enjoy the privileges God offers us freely, we have to combine hard work with complete trust.

1:3, 4 The expression "God's goodness" is literally translated "divine nature." The power to grow doesn't come from within us, but from God. Since we don't have the resources to live a "truly good life," God gives us his nature to keep us from sin and help us live for him.

1:5-9 Faith is more than belief in certain facts; it must result in action, or it dies away because it does not demonstrate a truly transformed life (James 2:14-17). Peter lists several of faith's actions: learning to know God better, developing patience, doing God's will, loving others. These actions do not come automatically; they require hard work. They are not optional. All of them must be a continual part of the Christian life. We don't finish one and start on the next, but we work on them all together.

1:6 False teachers were saying that self-control is not needed because works do not help the believer anyway (2:19). It is true that works cannot save us, but it is absolutely false to think they are unimportant. We are saved so that we can grow to resemble Christ and so that we can serve others. God wants to produce his character of active love in us. But to do this, he demands effort from us. To grow spiritually, we must develop self-control.

1:9 Our faith must go beyond what we believe; it must become a dynamic part of our lives, resulting in good works and spiritual maturity. Salvation does not depend on good works, but it results

in good works. A person who claims to be saved while remaining unchanged may not understand faith at all.

1:10 Peter wants to rouse the complacent believers who have listened to the false teachers and believe that because salvation is not based on good works they can live as they want. If you truly belong to the Lord, he says, your hard work will prove it. If you're not working for God, maybe you don't belong to him. If you are the Lord's—and your hard work backs up your claim—you will never be led astray by false teaching or glamorous sin.

1:12-15 Outstanding coaches constantly review the basics of the sport with their teams, and good athletes can execute the fundamentals consistently well. In our spiritual lives we must not neglect the basics of our faith when we go on to study deeper truths. Just as an athlete needs constant practice, we need constant reminders of the fundamentals of our faith and of how we came to believe in the first place. Don't allow yourself to be bored or impatient with messages on the basics of the Christian life. Instead, take the attitude of an athlete who continues to practice and refine the basics even as he learns more advanced skills.

1:13, 14 Many years before, Christ had prepared Peter for the kind of death he would face (see John 21:18, 19). Now Peter knew his death was at hand. Peter was martyred for the faith in about A.D. 68. One tradition says he was crucified upside down, at his own request, because he did not feel worthy to die in the same manner as his Master.

1:16-18 Peter is referring to the transfiguration where Jesus' divine identity was revealed to him and two other disciples (see Matthew 17:1-8; Mark 9:2-8; Luke 9:28-36).

power of our Lord Jesus Christ and his coming again. My own eyes have seen his splendor and his glory: 17, 18was there on the holy mountain when he shone out with honor given him by God his Father; I heard that glorious, majestic voice calling down from heaven, saying, "This is my much-loved Son; I am well pleased with him."

19So we have seen and proved that what the prophets said came true. You will do well to pay close attention to everything they have written, for, like lights shining into dark corners, their words help us to understand many things that otherwise would be dark and difficult. But when you consider the wonderful truth of the prophets' words, then the light will dawn in your souls and Christ the Morning Star will shine in your hearts. 20, 21For no prophecy recorded in Scripture was ever thought up by the prophet himself. It was the Holy Spirit within these godly men who gave them true messages from God.

2. Danger to growing Christians

2 But there were false prophets, too, in those days, just as there will be false teachers among you. They will cleverly tell their lies about God, turning against even their Master who bought them; but theirs will be a swift and terrible end. 2Many will follow their evil teaching that there is nothing wrong with sexual sin. And because of them Christ and his way will be scoffed at.

3These teachers in their greed will tell you anything to get hold of your money. But God condemned them long ago and their destruction is on the way. 4For God did not spare even the angels who sinned, but threw them into hell, chained in gloomy caves and darkness until the judgment day. 5And he did not spare any of the people who lived in ancient times before the flood except Noah, the one man who spoke up for God, and his family of seven. At that time God completely destroyed the whole world of ungodly men with the vast flood. 6Later, he turned the cities of Sodom and Gomorrah into heaps of ashes and blotted them off the face of the earth, making them an example for all the ungodly in the future to look back upon and fear.

7, 8But at the same time the Lord rescued Lot out of Sodom because he was a good man, sick of the terrible wickedness he saw everywhere around him day after day. 9So also the Lord can rescue you and me from the temptations that surround us, and continue to punish the ungodly until the day of final judgment comes. 10He is especially hard on those who follow their own evil, lustful thoughts, and those who are proud and willful, daring even to scoff at the Glorious Ones without so much as trembling, 11although the angels in heaven who stand in the very presence of the Lord, and are far greater in power and strength than these false teachers, never speak out disrespectfully against these evil Mighty Ones.

1:17
Mt 17:5
Heb 1:3

1:19
Ps 119:105
Prov 6:23
Lk 1:78,79
2 Cor 4:6
1 Pet 1:10-12
Rev 22:16
1:20
Rom 12:6
2 Pet 3:3
1:21
Jn 14:26
1 Cor 2:13
2 Tim 3:16

2:1
Deut 13:1-3
Mt 7:15
2 Cor 11:13
1 Tim 4:1
Jude 4

2:3
1 Tim 6:5
Jude 16
2:4
Jude 6
Rev 20:1-3
2:5
Gen 6:13-22
1 Pet 3:20
2 Pet 3:6
2:6
Gen 19:24,25
Mt 10:15; 11:23
Rom 9:29
Jude 7
2:7
Gen 19:5,16,29
2 Pet 3:17
2:9
Jude 6
2:10
Ex 22:28
2 Pet 3:3
Jude 8,16,18
2:11
Jude 9

1:16–21 This section is a strong statement on the inspiration of Scripture. Peter affirms that the Old Testament prophets wrote God's messages, and he puts himself and the other apostles in the same category since they also proclaim God's truth. The Bible is not a collection of fables or of human ideas about God. It is God's very words given *through* people *to* people. Peter emphasizes his authority as an eyewitness as well as the God-inspired authority of Scripture to prepare for his attack on the false teachers. If these wicked men contradict the apostles and the Bible, their message cannot come from God.

2:1 Jesus had told the disciples that false teachers would come (Matthew 24:11; Mark 13:22, 23). Peter had heard these words, and now he was seeing them come true. Just as false prophets had contradicted the true prophets in Old Testament times (see, for example, Jeremiah 23:16–40; 28:1–17), telling people only what they wanted to hear, so false teachers twisted Christ's teachings and the words of his apostles. These teachers belittled the significance of Jesus' life, death, and resurrection. Some claimed he couldn't be God; others claimed he couldn't have been a real man. They allowed and even encouraged all kinds of wrong

and immoral acts, especially sexual sin. Though these false teachers were popular, Peter warned that they would be destroyed.

2:3 Teachers should be paid by the people they teach, but these false teachers were attempting to make more money by distorting the truth and saying what people wanted to hear. They were more interested in making money than in teaching truth. Peter and Paul both condemned greedy, lying teachers (see 1 Timothy 6:5).

2:4–6 If God did not spare angels, or people who lived before the flood, or the citizens of Sodom and Gomorrah, he would not spare these false teachers. Some would have us believe that God will save all people because he is so loving. But we are foolish if we think he will cancel the last judgment. These three examples should warn us clearly that God judges sin and that unrepentant sinners cannot escape.

2:7–9 Just as God rescued Lot from Sodom, so he will rescue us from the temptations of a wicked world. Lot was not sinless, but he put his trust in God and was spared when Sodom was destroyed. For more information on Lot, see his Profile in Genesis 14.

¹²But false teachers are fools—no better than animals. They do whatever they feel like; born only to be caught and killed, they laugh at the terrifying powers of the underworld which they know so little about; and they will be destroyed along with all the demons and powers of hell.

¹³That is the pay these teachers will have for their sin. For they live in evil pleasures day after day. They are a disgrace and a stain among you, deceiving you by living in foul sin on the side while they join your love feasts as though they were honest men. ¹⁴No woman can escape their sinful stare, and of adultery they never have enough. They make a game of luring unstable women. They train themselves to be greedy; and are doomed and cursed. ¹⁵They have gone off the road and become lost like Balaam, the son of Beor, who fell in love with the money he could make by doing wrong; ¹⁶but Balaam was stopped from his mad course when his donkey spoke to him with a human voice, scolding and rebuking him.

¹⁷These men are as useless as dried-up springs of water, promising much and delivering nothing; they are as unstable as clouds driven by the storm winds. They are doomed to the eternal pits of darkness. ¹⁸They proudly boast about their sins and conquests, and, using lust as their bait, they lure back into sin those who have just escaped from such wicked living.

¹⁹"You aren't saved by being good," they say, "so you might as well be bad. Do what you like, be free."

But these very teachers who offer this "freedom" from law are themselves slaves to sin and destruction. For a man is a slave to whatever controls him. ²⁰And when a person has escaped from the wicked ways of the world by learning about our Lord and Savior Jesus Christ, and then gets tangled up with sin and becomes its slave again, he is worse off than he was before. ²¹It would be better if he had never known about Christ at all than to learn of him and then afterwards turn his back on the holy commandments that were given to him. ²²There is an old saying that "A dog comes back to what he has vomited, and a pig is washed only to come back and wallow in the mud again." That is the way it is with those who turn again to their sin.

2:10 *at the Glorious Ones,* or "the glories of the unseen world." **2:12** *the terrifying powers of the underworld,* literally, "the things they do not understand." **2:12** *all the demons and powers of hell,* implied. Literally, "will be destroyed in the same destruction with them."

2:12 Jude 10	
2:13 Rom 13:13 1 Cor 11:21 Phil 3:19 2 Pet 2:15	
2:14 Eph 2:3 2 Pet 2:18; 3:16	
2:15 Num 22:5-7,17 Deut 23:4 Acts 13:10 2 Pet 2:13 Jude 11 Rev 2:14	
2:16 Num 22:21-28	
2:17 Jude 12,13	
2:18 Acts 2:40 Eph 4:17-19 2 Pet 2:2,14,20 Jude 16	
2:19 Jn 8:34 Rom 6:16 Gal 5:13	
2:20 Mt 12:43-45 Lk 11:26 2 Tim 2:4 2 Pet 1:2; 2:18	
2:21 Ezek 18:24 1 Tim 6:14 Heb 6:4; 10:26 Jas 4:17	
2:22 Prov 26:11	

2:10–12 The "Glorious Ones" may be angels, all the glories of the unseen world, or, more probably, fallen angels. A similar passage is found in Jude 1:8–10. Whichever they are, the false teachers scoffed at the spiritual realities they did not understand, taking Satan's power lightly and thinking they had the ability to judge evil. Many in our world today mock the supernatural. They deny the reality of the spiritual world and claim that only what can be seen and felt is real. Like the false teachers of Peter's day, they are fools who will be proven wrong in the end. Don't take Satan and his supernatural powers of evil lightly or feel arrogant about how defeated he will be. Although he will be destroyed completely, he is at work now trying to lure complacent or arrogant Christians over to his side.

2:13, 14 The love feast was part of the celebration of the Lord's Supper. It was a full meal, ending with communion. The false teachers, though living openly sinful lives, took part in the love feasts with everyone else in the church. In one of the greatest of hypocritical acts, they attended a sacred feast designed to promote love and unity among believers, while at the same time they gossiped and slandered those who disagreed with their opinions. As Paul told the Corinthians, "If anyone eats this bread and drinks from this cup of the Lord in an unworthy manner, he is

guilty of sin against the body and blood of the Lord" (1 Corinthians 11:27). These men were guilty of more than false teaching and evil pleasures; they were guilty of leading others away from God's Son, Jesus.

2:15 Balaam was hired by a pagan king to curse Israel. He did what God told him for a while (Numbers 22—24), but eventually his evil motives and desire for money won out (Numbers 25:1–3; 31:16). Like the false teachers of Peter's day, Balaam used religion for personal advancement, a sin God does not take lightly.

2:19 Many believe freedom means doing anything you want. But no one is ever completely free in that sense. If we refuse to follow God, we will follow our own sinful desires and become enslaved to what our bodies want. If we submit our lives to Christ, he will free us from slavery to sin. Christ frees us to serve him, which always results in our ultimate good.

2:20–22 Peter is speaking of a person who has learned about Christ and how to be saved, and has perhaps even been positively influenced by the lives of Christians, but then rejects the truth and returns to his sin. He is worse off than before, because he has rejected the only way out of his sin, the only way of salvation. Like a man sinking in quicksand who refuses to grab the rope thrown to him, the person who turns away from Christ casts aside his only means of escape (see the note on Luke 11:24- 26).

3. Hope for growing Christians

3:1
Acts 3:21
Eph 3:5
2 Pet 1:13

3 This is my second letter to you, dear brothers, and in both of them I have tried to remind you—if you will let me—about facts you already know: facts you learned from the holy prophets and from us apostles who brought you the words of our Lord and Savior.

3:3
1 Tim 4:1
2 Pet 2:10
Jude 18

³First, I want to remind you that in the last days there will come scoffers who will do every wrong they can think of, and laugh at the truth. ⁴This will be their line of argument: "So Jesus promised to come back, did he? Then where is he? He'll never come! Why, as far back as anyone can remember everything has remained exactly as it was since the first day of creation."

3:4
Isa 5:19
Jer 17:15

3:5,6
Gen 1:6,9,10
7:10-12
Ps 24:2; 136:6
Col 1:17
Heb 11:3

⁵, ⁶They deliberately forget this fact: that God did destroy the world with a mighty flood, long after he had made the heavens by the word of his command, and had used the waters to form the earth and surround it. ⁷And God has commanded that the earth and the heavens be stored away for a great bonfire at the judgment day, when all ungodly men will perish.

3:7
Isa 66:15
Mt 10:15
1 Cor 3:13
2 Thess 1:8
Heb 12:29

⁸But don't forget this, dear friends, that a day or a thousand years from now is like tomorrow to the Lord. ⁹He isn't really being slow about his promised return, even though it sometimes seems that way. But he is waiting, for the good reason that he is not willing that any should perish, and he is giving more time for sinners to repent. ¹⁰The day of the Lord is surely coming, as unexpectedly as a thief, and then the heavens will pass away with a terrible noise and the heavenly bodies will disappear in fire, and the earth and everything on it will be burned up.

3:9
Isa 30:18
Rom 2:4; 13:11
1 Tim 2:4
Rev 2:21

3:10
Mt 24:43
1 Cor 1:8
1 Thess 5:2
Rev 3:3

¹¹And so since everything around us is going to melt away, what holy, godly lives we should be living! ¹²You should look forward to that day and hurry it along—the day when God will set the heavens on fire, and the heavenly bodies will melt and disappear in flames. ¹³But we are looking forward to God's promise of new heavens and a new earth afterwards, where there will be only goodness.

3:12
Ps 50:3
Isa 24:19; 34:4
1 Cor 1:7

3:13
Isa 60:21
65:17,25
Rev 21:1,27

¹⁴Dear friends, while you are waiting for these things to happen and for him to come, try hard to live without sinning; and be at peace with everyone so that he will be pleased with you when he returns.

3:14
1 Pet 1:7

3:15
Acts 9:17
Rom 2:4;
Col 1:25-27
Heb 5:11

¹⁵, ¹⁶And remember why he is waiting. He is giving us time to get his message of salvation out to others. Our wise and beloved brother Paul has talked about these same things in many of his letters. Some of his comments are not easy to understand, and there are people who are deliberately stupid, and always demand some unusual interpretation—they have twisted his letters around to mean something

3:16
Isa 28:13
Heb 5:11
2 Pet 3:2

3:13 *where there will be only goodness,* literally, "wherein righteousness dwells."

3:3, 4 Scoffers in the last days would say Jesus was never coming back, but Peter refutes their argument by explaining God's mastery over time. The "last days" are the time between Christ's first and second comings; thus we, like Peter, live in the last days. We must do the work to which God has called us and believe he will return as he promised.

3:7 In Noah's day the earth was judged by water; at the Second Coming it will be judged by fire. This fire is described in Revelation 19:20; 20:10-15.

3:8 God may have seemed slow to these believers as they faced persecution every day and longed to be delivered. But God is not slow; he just is not on our timetable (Psalm 90:4). Jesus is waiting so that more sinners will repent and turn to him. We must not sit and wait for him, but live in the realization that time is short and we have important work to do. Be ready to meet him any time, even today; yet plan your course of service as if he may not return for many years.

3:10, 11 Christ's Second Coming will be sudden and terrible for those who do not believe in him. For other prophetic pictures of the day of the Lord, see Isaiah 34:4; Joel 3:15, 16; Matthew 24; Mark 13; Luke 21; Revelation 6:12-17. Realizing that the earth is going to be burned up, we should put our confidence in what is lasting

and eternal. Do you spend more of your time piling up possessions, or striving to develop Christlike character?

3:12 How can we "hurry" Christ's return? We really can't. He is waiting so more people can repent; thus we should work hard to share the Good News and bring more people to faith in him (see Matthew 24:14).

3:13 God's purpose for mankind is not destruction but re-creation (see Isaiah 6:17; 66:22; Revelation 21, 22). He will purify the heavens and earth with fire, and he will then create them anew. We can joyously look forward to the restoration of God's good world.

3:14 We should not become lazy and complacent because Christ has not yet returned. Instead, our lives should express our eager expectation of his coming. What would you like to be doing when Christ returns? Is that the way you are living each day?

3:15, 16 By the time of Peter's writing, Paul's letters already had a widespread reputation. Notice that Peter speaks of Paul's letters as if they are on a level with "other parts of Scripture." Already the early church was thinking of them as inspired by God.

quite different from what he meant, just as they do the other parts of the Scripture—and the result is disaster for them.

¹⁷I am warning you ahead of time, dear brothers, so that you can watch out and not be carried away by the mistakes of these wicked men, lest you yourselves become mixed up too. ¹⁸But grow in spiritual strength and become better acquainted with our Lord and Savior Jesus Christ. To him be all glory and splendid honor, both now and forevermore.

Good-bye, Peter

3:17
1 Cor 10:12
Eph 4:14
2 Pet 2:18
Rev 2:5

3:18
Rom 11:36
2 Tim 4:18
2 Pet 1:2,8
Rev 1:6

3:15-18 Peter and Paul had very different backgrounds and personalities, and they preached from different viewpoints. Paul emphasized salvation by grace, not law; while Peter preferred to talk about Christian life and service. The two men did not contradict each other, however; and they always held each other in high respect. The false teachers intentionally misused Paul's writings by twisting them to condone lawlessness. No doubt this made them popular, because people always like to have their favorite sins justified, but it totally destroyed Paul's message. Paul may have been thinking of teachers like these when he wrote Romans 6:15: "Does this mean that now we can go ahead and sin and not worry about it? . . . Of course not!" Peter warns his readers

to avoid the mistakes of these wicked teachers by growing in the knowledge of Jesus. The better we know Jesus, the less attractive false teaching will be.

3:18 Peter concludes this brief letter as he began, by urging his readers to get to know God better and better. This is the most important step in refuting false teachers. No matter where we are in our spiritual journey, no matter how mature we are in our faith, the sinful world always challenges our faith in one way or another. We still have much room for growth. If every day we find some way to draw closer to Christ, we will be prepared to stand for truth in all circumstances.

"A GOOD MAN . . . yes . . . perhaps one of the best who ever lived . . . but just a man," say many. Others disagree, claiming that he suffered from delusions of grandeur—a "messiah complex." And the argument continues to rage over Jesus' true identity. Whoever he was, they all agree that Jesus left his mark on history.

Hearing these discussions, even Christians can begin to wonder and doubt. Is Jesus really God? Did he come to save sinners like us?

First John was written to dispel doubts and to build assurance by presenting a clear picture of Christ. Entering into human history through the incarnation, the Son of God became the very embodiment of God in the flesh—seen, heard, and touched by the author of this epistle, John the apostle. John walked and talked with Jesus, saw him heal, heard him teach, watched him die, met him arisen, and saw him ascend. John knew God—he had lived with him and had seen him work.

As the elder statesman in the church, he wrote this letter to his "little children." In it he presents God as light, as love, and as life. He explains in simple and practical terms what it means to have fellowship with God.

At the same time, false teachers had entered the church, denying the incarnation of Christ. John wrote to correct their serious errors. So, John's letter is a model for us to follow as we combat modern heresies.

John opens this letter by giving his credentials as an eyewitness of the incarnation and by stating his reason for writing (1:1–4). He then presents God as "light," symbolizing absolute purity and holiness (1:5–7), and explains how believers can walk in God's light and have fellowship with him (1:8–10) because they have Christ as their advocate (2:1, 2). He urges them to obey Christ fully and to love all the members of God's family (2:3–17). He warns his readers of "antichrists" and the Antichrist who will try to lead them away from the truth (2:18–29).

In the next section, John presents God as love (3:1—4:21). Because God loves us, he calls us his children and makes us like Christ (3:1, 2). This truth should motivate us to live in union with Christ (3:3–6). We can be sure that our fellowship with God is genuine when our lives are filled with good works and love for others (3:7–24). Again, John warns of false teachers who twist the truth. We should reject these false teachers (4:1–6) as we continue to live in God's love (4:7–21).

In the last section, John presents God as "life" (5:1–21). God's life is in his Son. To have life in his Son is to have eternal life.

First John was written to help you know the reality of God in your life, to assure you that you have eternal life through Christ, and to encourage you to have continual fellowship with the God who is light and love. Read of God's love in this letter and with renewed confidence, pass on his love to others.

VITAL STATISTICS

PURPOSE:
To reassure Christians in their faith and to counter false teachings

AUTHOR:
The apostle John

TO WHOM WRITTEN:
The letter is untitled and was written to no particular church. It was sent as a pastoral letter to several Gentile congregations. It was also written to all believers everywhere.

DATE WRITTEN:
Probably between A.D. 85 and 90 from Ephesus

SETTING:
John was an older man and perhaps the only surviving apostle at this time. He had not yet been banished to the island of Patmos where he would live in exile. As an eyewitness of Christ, he wrote authoritatively to give this new generation of believers assurance and confidence in God and in their faith.

KEY VERSE:
"I have written this to you who believe in the Son of God so that you may know you have eternal life" (5:13).

KEY PEOPLE:
John, Jesus

SPECIAL FEATURES:
John is the apostle of love, and love is mentioned throughout this letter. There are a number of similarities between this letter and John's Gospel—in vocabulary, style, and main ideas. John uses brief statements and simple words, and he features sharp contrasts—light and darkness, truth and error, God and Satan, life and death, love and hate.

THE BLUEPRINT

1. God is light (1:1—2:29)
2. God is love (3:1—4:21)
3. God is life (5:1–21)

John wrote about the most vital aspects of faith so readers would know Christian truth from error. He emphasizes the basics of faith so we can be confident in our faith. In our dark world, God is light. In our cold world, God brings the warmth of love. In our dying world, God brings life. When we feel a lack of confidence, these truths bring us certainty.

MEGATHEMES

THEME	EXPLANATION	IMPORTANCE
Sin	Even Christians sin. Sin requires God's forgiveness and Christ's death provides it for us. Determining to live according to God's standards in the Bible shows our lives are being transformed.	We cannot deny our sin nature, maintain that we are "above" sinning, or minimize the consequences of sin in our relationship with God. We must resist the attraction of sin, yet we must confess when we do sin.
Love	Christ commands us to love others as he did. This love is evidence that we are truly saved. God is the Creator of love; he cares that his children love each other.	Love means putting others first, being unselfish. Love is action—showing others we care—not just saying it. To show love we must give sacrificially of our time and money to meet the needs of others.
Family of God	We become God's children by believing in Christ. God's life in us enables us to love our fellow family members.	How we treat others shows who our Father is. Live as a faithful, loving family member.
Truth and Error	Teaching that the body does not matter, false teachers encouraged believers to throw off moral restraints. They also taught that Christ wasn't really a man and that we must be saved by having some special mystical knowledge. The result was that people became indifferent to sin.	God is truth and light, so the more we get to know him the better we can keep focused on the truth. Don't be led astray by any teaching that denies Christ's deity or humanity. Check the message; test the claims.
Assurance	God is in control of heaven and earth. Because his Word is true, we can have assurance of eternal life and victory over sin. By faith we can be certain of our eternal destiny with him.	Assurance of our relationship with God is a promise, but it is also a way of life. We build our confidence by trusting in God's Word and in Christ's provision for our sin.

1. God is light

Jesus Christ is God's Son

1 Christ was alive when the world began, yet I myself have seen him with my own eyes and listened to him speak. I have touched him with my own hands. He is God's message of life. ²This one who is life from God has been shown to us and we guarantee that we have seen him; I am speaking of Christ, who is eternal Life. He was with the Father and then was shown to us. ³Again I say, we are telling

1:1
Jn 1:1,4,14
1 Jn 4:14

1:2
Jn 1:1-4
19:35; 20:30,31
1 Jn 5:11,13,20

1:1 First John was written by John, one of Jesus' original 12 disciples. He was the "disciple Jesus loved" (John 21:20) and, along with Peter and James, had a special relationship with Jesus. This letter was probably written between A.D. 85–90 from Ephesus, before John's exile to the island of Patmos (see Revelation 1:9). Jerusalem had been destroyed in A.D. 70, and Christians were scattered throughout the empire. By the time John wrote this epistle, Christianity had been around for more than a generation. It had faced and survived severe persecution. The main problem confronting the church at this time was seduction: many believers were conforming to the world's standards, failing to stand up for Christ, and compromising their faith. False teachers were plentiful, and they accelerated the church's downward slide away from the Christian faith.

John wrote this letter to put believers back on track, to show the difference between light and darkness, and to encourage the church to grow in genuine love for God and for each other. He also

wrote to assure true believers that they possessed eternal life and to help them know their faith was genuine—so they could enjoy all the benefits of being God's children. For more about John, see his Profile in John 13.

1:1–5 John opens his first letter to the churches much as he opened his Gospel, emphasizing that Christ is eternal, that God came into the world as a man, that he, John, was an eyewitness to Jesus' life, and that Jesus brings light and life.

1:3 As an eyewitness to Jesus' ministry, John was qualified to teach the truth about him. The readers of this letter had not seen and heard Jesus themselves, but they could trust that what John wrote was accurate. We are like those second- and third-generation Christians. Though we have not personally seen, heard, or touched Jesus, we have the New Testament record of his eyewitnesses, and we can trust that they spoke the truth about him.

you about what we ourselves have actually seen and heard, so that you may share the fellowship and the joys we have with the Father and with Jesus Christ his son. [4]And if you do as I say in this letter, then you, too, will be full of joy, and so will we.

Living in the light of God

[5]This is the message God has given us to pass on to you: that God is Light and in him is no darkness at all. [6]So if we say we are his friends, but go on living in spiritual darkness and sin, we are lying. [7]But if we are living in the light of God's presence, just as Christ does, then we have wonderful fellowship and joy with each other, and the blood of Jesus his Son cleanses us from every sin.

[8]If we say that we have no sin, we are only fooling ourselves, and refusing to accept the truth. [9]But if we confess our sins to him, he can be depended on to forgive us and to cleanse us from every wrong. [And it is perfectly proper for God to do this for us because Christ died to wash away our sins.] [10]If we claim we have not sinned, we are lying and calling God a liar, *for he says we have sinned.*

1:9 *Confess our sins to him,* implied. Literally, "if we confess our sins."

1:4
Jn 15:11

1:5
Jn 1:9; 8:12
1 Tim 6:16
1 Jn 3:11
1:6
2 Cor 6:14
1:7
Heb 9:14
1:8
Prov 20:9
1:9
Heb 9:14
1:10
Prov 20:9

1:3, 4 There are three steps to true Christian fellowship. First, it is grounded in the testimony of the Word of God. Without this underlying strength, togetherness is impossible. Second, it is mutual, depending on the unity of believers. Third, it is daily renewed through the Holy Spirit. True fellowship combines the social and the spiritual, and it is made possible only by a living relationship with Christ.

1:5, 6 Light represents what is good, pure, true, holy, and reliable. Darkness represents sin and evil. To say "God is light" means that God is perfectly holy and true, and that he alone can guide us out of the darkness of sin. Light is also related to truth, in that it exposes whatever exists, whether it is good or bad. In the dark, good and evil look alike; in the light, they can be clearly distinguished. Just as darkness cannot exist in the presence of light, sin cannot exist in the presence of a holy God. If we want to have a relationship with God, we must put aside our sinful ways of living. To claim that relationship but live for ourselves is hypocrisy. Christ will expose and judge such deceit.

1:6 False teachers who thought the body was evil or worthless had one of two approaches to behavior: either they insisted on denying bodily desires through rigid discipline, or they approved of gratifying every physical lust because the body was going to be destroyed anyway. Obviously the second approach was more popular! Here John exposes the error in both these approaches. Faith is not real unless it results in changed lives and good works, and people cannot be true believers if they continue living in sin. And the body itself is not evil, for Jesus himself had a human body.

1:7 How does Jesus' blood cleanse us from every sin? In Old Testament times, believers symbolically transferred their sins to the head of an animal, which they then sacrificed (see a description of this ceremony in Leviticus 4). The animal died in their place, ridding them of sin and allowing them to continue living in God's favor. This ceremony taught important truths about sin and forgiveness, but it did not actually remove sin. Real cleansing from sin came with Jesus, the "Lamb of God who takes away the world's sin" (John 1:29). Sin, by its very nature, brings death—that is a fact as certain as the law of gravity. Jesus did not die for his own sins; he had none. Instead, by a transaction we may never fully understand, he died for the sins of the world. When we identify ourselves with him, his death becomes ours. We discover that he has already paid the penalty for our sins; his blood has cleansed us. Just as he rose from the grave, we rise to a new life of fellowship with him (Romans 6:4).

1:8 John here attacks more false teaching. Some were saying they had no natural tendency toward sin, that their sinful nature

had been eliminated, and that they were now incapable of sinning. This is at best self-deception, at worst a lie. They refused to take sin seriously. They wanted to be considered Christians, but they saw no need to confess their sins and repent. The blood of Jesus did not mean much to them, because they didn't think they needed it. Instead of repenting and being cleansed by Christ's blood, they were introducing impurity into the circle of believers. In this life, no Christian will ever be beyond sinning, so no one should dare let down his guard.

1:8–10 The false teachers taught not only that they had no sin in them (1:8), but also that no matter what they did they would not sin (1:10). This is a lie. They forgot one basic truth: we are sinners by nature and by practice. At conversion all our sins are forgiven—past, present, and future. Yet even after we become Christians, we still sin and must confess. This kind of confession is not to gain God's acceptance, but to remove the barrier to fellowship that our sin has put between us and him. It is difficult, however, for many people to admit their faults and shortcomings, even to God. It takes humility and honesty to recognize our weaknesses, and most of us would rather pretend we are strong. But we need not fear revealing our sins to God—he knows them already. He will not push us away, no matter what we've done. Instead he will push away the sins and draw us to himself.

1:9 Confession is supposed to free us to enjoy fellowship with Christ. It should ease our consciences and lighten our cares. But some Christians do not understand how it works. They feel so guilty that they confess the same sins over and over, and then wonder if they might have forgotten something. Other Christians believe God forgives them when they confess, but if they died with unconfessed sins, they would be forever lost. These Christians do not understand that *God wants to forgive us.* He allowed his beloved Son to die just so he could pardon us. When we come to Christ, he forgives all the sins we have committed or will ever commit. We don't need to confess the same sins all over again, and we don't need to fear that he will cast us out if we don't keep our slate perfectly clear at all moments. Of course we want to continue to confess our sins, but not because we think failure to do so will make us lose our salvation. Our hope in Christ is secure. Instead, we confess our sins so we can enjoy maximum fellowship and joy with him.

True confession also involves a commitment not to continue in sin. We are not genuinely confessing our sins before God if we plan to commit the sin again and just want temporary forgiveness. We must pray for strength to defeat the temptation the next time it appears.

2 My little children, I am telling you this so that you will stay away from sin. But if you sin, there is someone to plead for you before the Father. His name is Jesus Christ, the one who is all that is good and who pleases God completely. ²He is the one who took God's wrath against our sins upon himself, and brought us into fellowship with God; and he is the forgiveness for our sins, and not only ours but all the world's.

³And how can we be sure that we belong to him? By looking within ourselves: are we really trying to do what he wants us to?

⁴Someone may say, "I am a Christian; I am on my way to heaven; I belong to Christ." But if he doesn't do what Christ tells him to, he is a liar. ⁵But those who do what Christ tells them to will learn to love God more and more. That is the way to know whether or not you are a Christian. ⁶Anyone who says he is a Christian should live as Christ did.

⁷Dear brothers, I am not writing out a new rule for you to obey, for it is an old one you have always had, right from the start. You have heard it all before. ⁸Yet it is always new, and works for you just as it did for Christ; and as we obey this commandment, *to love one another,* the darkness in our lives disappears and the new light of life in Christ shines in.

⁹Anyone who says he is walking in the light of Christ but dislikes his fellow man,

2:2 *he is the forgiveness for our sins,* or "he is the atoning sacrifice for our sins."

Contrast between:	Passage
Light and darkness	1:5
The new rule and the old commandment	2:7, 8
Loving God and loving the world	2:15, 16
Christ and Antichrist	2:18
Truth and falsehood	2:20, 21
Child of God and child of Satan	3:1–10
Eternal life and eternal death	3:14
Love and hatred	3:15, 16
True teaching and false teaching	4:1–3
Love and fear	4:18, 19
Having life and not having life	5:11, 12

A BOOK OF CONTRASTS One of the distinct features of John's writing style was his habit of noting both sides of a conflict. He wrote to show the difference between real Christianity and anything else. Here are some of his favorite contrasts.

2:1 John uses the address "little children" in a warm, fatherly way. He is not talking down to his readers but is showing affection for them. John, by now a very old man, had spent almost all his life in ministry, and many of his readers were indeed his spiritual children.

2:1, 2 To people who are feeling guilty and condemned, John offers reassurance. They know they have sinned, and Satan (called "the Accuser of our brothers" in Revelation 12:10) is demanding the death penalty. When you feel this way, don't give up hope—the best defense attorney in the universe is pleading your case. Jesus Christ, your advocate, is the Judge's Son. He has already suffered your penalty in your place. You can't be tried again for a case that is no longer on the docket. United with Jesus, you are as safe as he is. Don't be afraid to ask him to plead your case—he has already won it (see Romans 8:33, 34; Hebrews 7:24, 25).

2:2 We sometimes have a difficult time forgiving someone who wrongs us. Imagine how hard it would be to tell everyone we are willing to forgive no matter what they do! This is what God has done in Jesus. No one, no matter what they have done, is beyond hope of forgiveness. All we have to do is turn to Jesus and commit our hearts to him.

2:3–6 How can you be sure you belong to Christ? This passage gives two ways to know: a Christian should do what Christ tells him to do and live as Christ wants him to live. And what does Christ tell us to do? John answers in 3:23: "Believe on the name of his Son

Jesus Christ, and love one another." True Christian faith results in loving behavior; that is why John says our behavior can assure us that we are Christ's.

2:6 Living as Christ did doesn't mean choosing 12 disciples, performing great miracles, or being crucified. We cannot merely copy Christ's life, because much of it had to do with his identity as God's Son, his special role in dying for sin, and the cultural context of the first-century Roman world. To live today as Christ did in the first century, we must follow his example of complete obedience to God and loving service to people.

2:7, 8 The commandment to love is both old and new. It is old because it comes from the Old Testament (Leviticus 19:18), but it is new because Jesus interpreted it in a radically new way (John 13:34, 35). In the Christian church, love goes beyond respect to self-sacrifice and servanthood (John 15:13). In fact, it can be defined as "selfless giving." It reaches beyond friends to enemies and persecutors (Matthew 5:43–48). Love should be the unifying force and the identifying mark of the Christian community. It is the key to walking in the light, because we cannot grow spiritually while we hate others. A growing relationship with God results in growing relationships with others.

2:9–11 Does this mean if you dislike anyone you aren't a Christian? These verses are not talking about disliking a disagreeable Christian brother. There will always be people we will not like as well as others. John's words focus on the attitude that

is still in darkness. 10But whoever loves his fellow man is "walking in the light" and can see his way without stumbling around in darkness and sin. 11For he who dislikes his brother is wandering in spiritual darkness and doesn't know where he is going, for the darkness has made him blind so that he cannot see the way.

2:11
Jn 12:35
2 Cor 4:4
2 Pet 1:9
1 Jn 2:9; 3:15

Do not love this evil world

12I am writing these things to all of you, my little children, because your sins have been forgiven in the name of Jesus our Savior. 13I am saying these things to you older men because you really know Christ, the one who has been alive from the beginning. And you young men, I am talking to you because you have won your battle with Satan. And I am writing to you younger boys and girls because you, too, have learned to know God our Father.

2:12
Lk 24:27
Acts 4:12
1 Cor 6:11
1 Jn 2:1
2:13
1 Jn 1:1; 4:4

14And so I say to you fathers who know the eternal God, and to you young men who are strong, with God's Word in your hearts, and have won your struggle against Satan: 15Stop loving this evil world and all that it offers you, for when you love these things you show that you do not really love God; 16for all these worldly things, these evil desires—the craze for sex, the ambition to buy everything that appeals to you, and the pride that comes from wealth and importance—these are not from God. They are from this evil world itself. 17And this world is fading away, and these evil, forbidden things will go with it, but whoever keeps doing the will of God will live forever.

2:14
Jer 31:33
Eph 6:10
1 Jn 1:1; 1:10
2:13
2:15
Mt 6:24
Rom 12:2
Jas 1:27; 4:4
2:16
Prov 27:20
Rom 13:14
2:17
1 Cor 7:31

Warning against antichrists

18Dear children, this world's last hour has come. You have heard about the

---

JOHN COUNTERS FALSE TEACHINGS		John counters two major strands in the false teachings of the heretics in this epistle:
	1:6, 8	They denied the reality of sin. John says that if we continue in sin, we can't claim to belong to God. If we say we have no sin, we are only fooling ourselves and refusing to accept the truth.
	2:22; 4:1–3	They denied that Jesus was the Messiah—God in the flesh. John said that if we believe that Jesus was God incarnate and trust him for our salvation, we are children of God.

causes us to ignore or despise others, to treat them as irritants, competitors, or enemies. Fortunately, Christian love is not a feeling but a choice. We can choose to be concerned with people's well-being and treat them with respect, whether or not we feel affection toward them. If we choose to love others, God will give us the necessary strength and will show us how to express our love.

2:12, 13 John was writing to believers of all ages, his "little children," who had experienced forgiveness through Jesus. The older men were mature in the faith and had a long-standing relationship with Christ. The younger men had struggled with Satan's temptations and had won. The boys and girls had learned about Christ and were just beginning their spiritual journey. In each stage of life, God's Word is relevant. Each stage of life builds upon the other. As children learn about Christ, they grow in their ability to win battles with temptation. As young adults move from victory to victory, they grow in their relationship with Christ. Older adults, having known Christ for years, have developed the wisdom needed to teach young people and start the cycle all over again. Is your Christian growth appropriate for your stage in life?

2:15, 16 Some people think worldliness has to do with external behavior—the people we associate with, the places we go, the activities in which we participate. This is not entirely accurate, for worldliness begins in the heart. It is characterized by these three attitudes: (1) lust—preoccupation with gratifying physical desires; (2) materialism—craving and accumulating things; and (3) pride—obsession with one's status or importance. When the serpent tempted Eve (Genesis 3:6), he tempted her in these areas. Also, when the devil tempted Jesus in the wilderness, these were

his three areas of attack (see Matthew 4:1–11). By contrast, God values self-control, a spirit of generosity, and humble service. It is possible to avoid "worldly pleasures" while still harboring worldly attitudes in one's heart. It is also possible, like Jesus, to love sinners and spend time with them while maintaining the values of God's Kingdom. What values are most important to you? Do your actions reflect the world's values or God's values? Will you fail like Eve did or be victorious like Jesus was?

2:17 When our attachment to things is strong, it's hard to believe that the things we want will one day pass away. It may be even harder to believe that the person who does the will of God will live forever. But this was John's conviction based on the facts of Jesus' life, death, resurrection, and the promises he made. Knowing that this evil world and its sin will end gives us courage to continue doing God's will.

2:18–21 John is talking about the "last days," the time between Christ's first and second comings. The first-century readers of 1 John lived in the last days, and so do we. During this time, "antichrists" (false teachers who pretend to be Christians and lure weak members away from Christ) will appear. Finally, just before the world ends, one great Antichrist will arise (Revelation 13; 19:20; 20:10). We do not need to fear these evil people, however. The Holy Spirit shows us their errors, so we are not deceived. However, we must teach the Word of God clearly and carefully to the peripheral, weak members among us so they won't fall prey to these teachers "who come disguised as harmless sheep, but are wolves" (Matthew 7:15).

Antichrist who is coming—the one who is against Christ—and already many such persons have appeared. This makes us all the more certain that the end of the world is near. 19These "against-Christ" people used to be members of our churches, but they never really belonged with us or else they would have stayed. When they left us it proved that they were not of us at all.

20But you are not like that, for the Holy Spirit has come upon you, and you know the truth. 21So I am not writing to you as to those who need to know the truth, but I warn you as those who can discern the difference between true and false.

22And who is the greatest liar? The one who says that Jesus is not Christ. Such a person is antichrist, for he does not believe in God the Father and in his Son. 23For a person who doesn't believe in Christ, God's Son, can't have God the Father either. But he who has Christ, God's Son, has God the Father also.

24So keep on believing what you have been taught from the beginning. If you do, you will always be in close fellowship with both God the Father and his Son. 25And he himself has promised us this: *eternal life*.

26These remarks of mine about the Antichrist are pointed at those who would dearly love to blindfold you and lead you astray. 27But you have received the Holy Spirit and he lives within you, in your hearts, so that you don't need anyone to teach you what is right. For he teaches you all things, and he is the Truth, and no liar; and so, just as he has said, you must live in Christ, never to depart from him.

28And now, my little children, stay in happy fellowship with the Lord so that when he comes you will be sure that all is well, and will not have to be ashamed and shrink back from meeting him. 29Since we know that God is always good and does only right, we may rightly assume that all those who do right are his children.

2:19
Mt 24:24
2 Tim 2:19
2:20
Jn 14:26
1 Jn 2:27
2:23
Jn 8:19; 16:3
17:3
1 Jn 4:15; 5:1
2:24
1 Jn 1:3; 2:7
2 Jn 9
2:25
Jn 3:15; 6:40
17:3
2:26
1 Jn 3:7
2 Jn 7
2:27
Jer 31:33
Jn 14:16,26
16:13
1 Cor 2:10-12
1 Thess 4:9
1 Jn 2:20
2:28
Mk 8:38
Lk 17:30
Col 3:4
1 Thess 2:19
1 Jn 3:2,21
2:29
1 Jn 3:7,9; 4:7
5:1,4,18

2:19 The antichrists were not total strangers to the church; they once belonged to it, but they did not continue. John does not say why they left; it is clear that their reasons for joining in the first place were wrong. Today many people are "Christians" for less than the best reasons. Perhaps going to church is a family tradition. Maybe they like the social and business contacts they make there. Or possibly going to church is a long-standing habit, and they have never stopped to ask themselves why they do it. What is your main reason for being a Christian? Unless it is a Christ-centered reason, you may not really belong. You don't have to settle for less than the best. You can become personally acquainted with Jesus Christ and become a loyal, trustworthy follower.

2:20 When you become a Christian you receive the Holy Spirit. One way the Holy Spirit helps the believer and the church is by communicating truth. Jesus is the Truth (John 14:6), and the Holy Spirit guides believers to him (John 16:13). People who are against Christ are also against truth, and the Holy Spirit is not working in their lives. But people who are led by the Spirit are continually growing in their experience of Jesus' truth (see 2:27).

2:23 Apparently the "antichrists" in John's day were attempting to be loyal to God while denying and opposing Christ. This, John firmly said, is impossible. Since Jesus is God's Son and his Messiah, to deny him is to reject God's way of revealing himself to the world. A person who accepts Christ as God's Son, however, accepts God the Father at the same time. The two are one and cannot be separated. Many cultists today call themselves "Christians" but deny that Jesus is divine. We must expose these heresies and oppose such teachings so the weak believers among us do not succumb to their teachings.

2:24 These Christians had heard the gospel, very likely from John himself. They knew that Christ was God's Son, that he died for our sins and was raised to give us new life, and that he would return

and establish his Kingdom in its fullness. But now they were being infiltrated by teachers who denied these basic doctrines of the Christian faith, and some of the believers were in danger of succumbing to false arguments. John encouraged them to hold on to the Christian truth they heard at the beginning of their walk with Christ. It is important to grow in our knowledge of the Lord, to deepen our understanding through careful study, and to teach these truths to others. But no matter how much we learn, we must never abandon the basic truths about Jesus. Jesus will always be God's Son, and his sacrifice for our sins is permanent. No truth will ever contradict these teachings in the Bible.

2:26, 27 Christ promised to send the Holy Spirit to teach his followers and remind them of all that Jesus had taught (John 14:26). As a result, Christians have the Holy Spirit within them to keep them from going astray. In addition, they have the God-inspired Scriptures, against which they can test questionable teachings. Let the Holy Spirit help you discern truth from error. For more about who the Holy Spirit is and what he does, see the notes on John 3:6; Acts 1:5; and Ephesians 1:14.

2:27 Christ lives in us, and we also live in Christ. This means we place our total trust in him and live as he wants us to live. It implies a personal, life-giving relationship. John uses the same idea in John 15:5, where he speaks of Christ as the Vine and his followers as the branches (see also 3:24; 4:15).

2:28, 29 The visible proof of being a Christian is right behavior. Many people do some good things but don't have faith in Jesus Christ. Others claim to have faith but rarely produce good works. A deficit in either faith or right behavior is cause for shame when Christ returns. Because true faith always results in good works, those who claim to have faith *and* who consistently live rightly are true believers. Good works cannot produce salvation (see Ephesians 2:8, 9), but they are necessary proof that true faith has actually occurred (James 2:14-17).

2. God is love

We are God's children

3 See how very much our heavenly Father loves us, for he allows us to be called his children—think of it—and we really *are!* But since most people don't know God, naturally they don't understand that we are his children. ²Yes, dear friends, we are already God's children, right now, and we can't even imagine what it is going to be like later on. But we do know this, that when he comes we will be like him, as a result of seeing him as he really is. ³And everyone who really believes this will try to stay pure because Christ is pure.

⁴But those who keep on sinning are against God, for every sin is done against the will of God. ⁵And you know that he became a man so that he could take away our sins, and that there is no sin in him, no missing of God's will at any time in any way. ⁶So if we stay close to him, obedient to him, we won't be sinning either; but as for those who keep on sinning, they should realize this: They sin because they have never really known him or become his.

⁷Oh, dear children, don't let anyone deceive you about this: if you are constantly doing what is good, it is because you *are* good, even as he is. ⁸But if you keep on sinning, it shows that you belong to Satan, who since he first began to sin has kept steadily at it. But the Son of God came to destroy these works of the devil. ⁹The person who has been born into God's family does not make a practice of sinning, because now God's life is in him; so he can't keep on sinning, for this new life has been born into him and controls him—he has been *born again*.

We must love other Christians

¹⁰So now we can tell who is a child of God and who belongs to Satan. Whoever is living a life of sin and doesn't love his brother shows that he is not in God's family; ¹¹for the message to us from the beginning has been that we should love one another.

¹²We are not to be like Cain, who belonged to Satan and killed his brother. Why did he kill him? Because Cain had been doing wrong and he knew very well that his

3:1ff Verse 1 tells us who we are—members of God's family. Verse 2 tells us who we are becoming—reflections of God. The rest of the chapter tells us what we take with us as we grow to resemble God: (1) victory over sin (3:4–9); (2) love for the brothers (3:10–18); and (3) confidence before God (3:19–24).

3:1 As believers, our self-worth is based on the fact that God loves us and calls us his children. We are his children *now,* not just sometime in the distant future. Knowing that we are his children encourages us to live as Jesus did. For other references on being part of God's family, see Romans 8:14–17; Galatians 3:26,27; 4:6,7.

3:2 The Christian life is a process of becoming more and more Christlike (see Romans 8:29). This process will not be complete until we see him face to face (1 Corinthians 13:12; Philippians 3:21), but knowing that it is our ultimate goal should motivate us to live more and more like Christ each day.

3:4ff There is a difference between committing a sin and remaining in sin. Even the most faithful believers sometimes commit sins, but they do not cherish a particular sin and choose to commit it. A believer who commits a sin repents, confesses, and is forgiven. A person who remains in sin, by contrast, is not sorry for what he is doing. Thus he never confesses and never receives forgiveness. Such a person is against God, no matter what religious claims he makes.

3:5 Under the Old Testament sacrificial system, a lamb without blemish was offered as a sacrifice for sin. Jesus is "the Lamb of God who takes away the world's sin" (John 1:29). Because he lived a perfect life and sacrificed himself for our sins, we can be completely forgiven (1 John 2:2). We can look back to his death for

us and know we need never suffer eternal death (1 Peter 1:18–20).

3:8, 9 We all have areas where temptation is strong and habits are hard to conquer. These weaknesses give Satan a foothold, so we must deal with them. If we are struggling with a particular sin, however, these verses are not directed at us, even if for the time we seem to "keep on sinning." John is not talking about people whose victories are still incomplete; he is talking about people who make a practice of sinning and look for ways to justify it.

Three steps are necessary to find victory over prevailing sin: (1) one must seek the power of the Holy Spirit and the Word of God on a daily basis; (2) one must flee lustful desires; and (3) one needs the help of the body of Christ—accountability to others and the prayers of others.

3:9 We are born again when the Holy Spirit lives in us and gives us Jesus' new life. Being born again is more than a fresh start; it is a rebirth, receiving a new family name based on Christ's death for us. God forgives us and totally accepts us. The Holy Spirit gives us new minds and hearts, lives in us, and begins helping us be like Christ. Our perspective changes too. We have a new mind which is to be renewed day by day by the Holy Spirit (see Romans 12:2; Ephesians 4:22–24). So we must begin to think and act differently. See John 3:1–21 for more on being born again.

3:12, 13 Cain killed his brother, Abel, when God accepted Abel's offering and not Cain's (Genesis 4:1–16). Abel's offering showed that Cain was not giving his best to God, and Cain's jealous anger drove him to murder. People who live good lives expose and shame those who don't. If we live for God, the world will often hate us because we make them painfully aware of their immoral way of living.

brother's life was better than his. ¹³So don't be surprised, dear friends, if the world hates you.

¹⁴If we love other Christians it proves that we have been delivered from hell and given eternal life. But a person who doesn't have love for others is headed for eternal death. ¹⁵Anyone who hates his Christian brother is really a murderer at heart; and you know that no one wanting to murder has eternal life within. ¹⁶We know what real love is from Christ's example in dying for us. And so we also ought to lay down our lives for our Christian brothers.

¹⁷But if someone who is supposed to be a Christian has money enough to live well, and sees a brother in need, and won't help him—how can God's love be within *him*? ¹⁸Little children, let us stop just *saying* we love people; let us *really* love them, and *show it* by our *actions*. ¹⁹Then we will know for sure, by our actions, that we are on God's side, and our consciences will be clear, even when we stand before the Lord. ²⁰But if we have bad consciences and feel that we have done wrong, the Lord will surely feel it even more, for he knows everything we do.

²¹But, dearly loved friends, if our consciences are clear, we can come to the Lord with perfect assurance and trust, ²²and get whatever we ask for because we are obeying him and doing the things that please him. ²³And this is what God says we must do: Believe on the name of his Son Jesus Christ, and love one another. ²⁴Those who do what God says—they are living with God and he with them. We know this is true because the Holy Spirit he has given us tells us so.

3:13	Jn 15:18; 17:14
3:14	Jn 5:24; 13:35
3:15	Mt 5:21,22 Jn 8:44 Gal 5:21
3:16	Jn 3:16; 15:13 Rom 5:8 Eph 5:2,25
3:17	Lk 3:11 Jas 2:15 1 Jn 4:20
3:18	Rom 12:9 1 Jn 3:7
3:19	Jn 18:37 1 Jn 2:21
3:22	Mt 21:22 Jn 8:29; 9:31 Jas 5:16
3:24	Rom 8:9 1 Jn 2:3,5,27

Distinguish truth from false teaching

4 Dearly loved friends, don't always believe everything you hear just because someone says it is a message from God: test it first to see if it really is. For there are many false teachers around, ²and the way to find out if their message is from the Holy Spirit is to ask: Does it really agree that Jesus Christ, God's Son, actually became man with a human body? If so, then the message is from God. ³If not, the

4:1	1 Thess 5:20
4:2	1 Cor 12:3 1 Jn 1:2; 2:23 5:1

3:20 *the Lord will surely feel it even more,* or, perhaps, "the Lord will be merciful anyway." Literally, "If our heart condemns us God is greater than our heart."

3:15 John echoes Jesus' words that one who hates another person is a murderer at heart (Matthew 5:21, 22). Christianity is a religion of the heart; outward compliance alone is not enough. Bitterness against someone who has wronged you is an evil cancer within you and will eventually destroy you. Don't let a "root of bitterness" (Hebrews 12:15) grow in you or your church.

3:16 Real love is an action, not a feeling. It produces selfless, sacrificial giving. The greatest act of love anyone can do is to give himself or herself for others. How can we lay down our lives? Sometimes it is easier to say we'll die for others than to truly live for them, which involves putting others' desires first. Jesus taught this same principle of love in John 15:13.

3:17, 18 These verses give an example of how to lay down our lives for others. Christians must show their love, and one way to do that is to provide money to help meet others' needs. This is strikingly similar to James' teaching (James 2:14–17). How clearly do your actions say you really love others? Are you as generous as you should be with your money, possessions, and time?

3:19, 20 Many are afraid they don't love others as they should. They feel guilty because they think they are not ready or they are unable to show proper love. Their conscience bothers them. John had these people in mind when he wrote this letter. How do we escape the gnawing accusations of our conscience? Not by ignoring them or rationalizing our behavior, but by right actions, says John. If we still feel guilty, we should remind ourselves that God knows our hearts as well as our actions. If we are in Christ, he will not condemn us (Romans 8:1; Hebrews 9:14, 15). So if you are living for the Lord but feel you are not "good enough," remind yourself that God is greater than your conscience. He knows you belong to him, so you can know it too.

3:21, 22 If your conscience is genuinely clear, you can come to God without fear, confident that your requests will be heard. John reaffirms Jesus' promise, "Ask, and you will be given what you ask for" (Matthew 7:7; see also Matthew 21:22; John 9:31; 15:7). You will receive if you obey, because when you obey, you ask in line with God's will. Of course this does not mean you can have anything you want, like instant riches. If you are truly seeking God's will, there are some things you do not request.

3:23 In the Bible, a person's name stands for his character. It represents who he really is. We are to believe not only in Jesus' words, but also in his very person as the Son of God. Moreover, to believe "in his name" means to pattern your life after Christ's, to become more like him by uniting yourself with him.

4:1, 2 There are many ways to test teachers to see if their message is truly from God. One is to check their words with what God says in the Bible. Other tests include their commitment to the body of believers (2:19), their lifestyle (3:23, 24), and the fruit of their ministry (4:6). But the most important test of all, says John, is what they believe about Christ. Do they teach that Jesus is fully God and fully man? Our world is filled with voices claiming to speak for God. Give them these tests to see if they are indeed speaking God's truth.

4:1–3 Some people believe everything they read or hear. Unfortunately, many things printed and taught are not true. Christians should have faith, but they should not be gullible. Verify every message you hear, even if the person who brings it says it's from God. If the message is truly from God, it will be consistent with Christ's teachings.

4:3 The Antichrist will be a person who epitomizes all that is evil, and he will be readily received by an evil world. He is more fully described in 2 Thessalonians 2:3–12 and Revelation 13.

message is not from God but from one who is against Christ, like the "Antichrist" you have heard about who is going to come, and his attitude of enmity against Christ is already abroad in the world.

4:4
Jn 12:31; 14:30
Rom 8:31
1 Jn 2:1,13
3:20

⁴Dear young friends, you belong to God and have already won your fight with those who are against Christ, because there is someone in your hearts who is stronger than any evil teacher in this wicked world. ⁵These men belong to this world, so, quite naturally, they are concerned about worldly affairs and the world pays attention to them. ⁶But we are children of God; that is why only those who have walked and talked with God will listen to us. Others won't. That is another way to know whether a message is really from God; for if it is, the world won't listen to it.

4:5
Jn 15:19
17:14,16

4:6
Jn 8:47; 10:27
14:17
1 Cor 14:37
1 Tim 4:1

— *Love comes from God*

4:7
1 Jn 2:3,29
3:11; 5:1

⁷Dear friends, let us practice loving each other, for love comes from God and those who are loving and kind show that they are the children of God, and that they are getting to know him better. ⁸But if a person isn't loving and kind, it shows that he doesn't know God—for God is love.

4:8
Ex 34:4,5
Mic 7:18
1 Jn 4:7,16

⁹God showed how much he loved us by sending his only Son into this wicked

---

HERESIES

Most of the eyewitnesses to Jesus' ministry had died by the time John composed this epistle. Some of the second- or third-generation Christians began to have doubts about what they had been taught about Jesus. Some Christians with a Greek background had a hard time believing that Jesus was human as well as divine, because in Platonic thought, the spirit was all-important. The body was only a prison from which one desired to escape. Heresies developed from a uniting of this kind of Platonic thought and Christianity.

A particularly widespread false teaching, later called *Docetism* (from a Greek word meaning "to seem"), held that Jesus was actually a spirit who only appeared to have a body. In reality he cast no shadow and left no footprints; he was God, but not man. Another heretical teaching, related to *Gnosticism* (from a Greek word meaning "knowledge"), held that all physical matter was evil, the spirit was good, and only the intellectually enlightened could enjoy the benefits of religion. Both groups found it hard to believe in a Savior who was fully human.

John answers these false teachers as an eyewitness to Jesus' life on earth. He saw Jesus, talked with him, touched him—he knew that Jesus was more than a mere spirit. In the very first sentence of his letter, John establishes that Jesus had been alive before the world began and also that he lived as a man among men. In other words, he was both divine and human.

Through the centuries, many heretics have denied that Jesus was both God and man. In John's day people had trouble believing he was man; today more people have problems seeing him as God. But Jesus' divine-human nature is the pivotal issue of Christianity. Before you accept what religious teachers say about any topic, listen carefully to what they believe about Jesus. To deny either his divinity or his humanity is to consider him less than Christ, the Savior.

4:4 It is easy to be frightened by the wickedness we see all around us. Evil is obviously much stronger than we are. John assures us, however, that God is stronger yet. He will conquer all evil—and his Spirit lives in our hearts!

4:6 False teachers are popular with the world because, like the false prophets of the Old Testament, they tell people what they want to hear. John warns that Christians who faithfully teach God's Word will not win any popularity contests in the world. People don't want to hear their sins denounced; they don't want to listen to demands that they change their lives. Where do you want to be popular?

4:7ff Everyone believes love is important, but we usually think of it as a feeling. In reality, love is a choice and an action, as 1 Corinthians 13:4–7 shows. God is the source of our love: he loved us enough to sacrifice his son for us. Jesus is our example of what it means to love; everything he did in life and death was supremely loving. The Holy Spirit gives us the power to love. God's love always involves a choice and an action, and our love should be like his.

How well is your love for God displayed, in the choices you make and the actions you take?

4:8 John said, "God is love," not "Love is God." Our world, with its shallow and selfish view of love, has turned these words around and contaminated our understanding of love. The world thinks love is what makes you feel good, and it is willing to sacrifice moral principles and others' rights in order to obtain such "love." But that isn't real love; it is love's exact opposite—selfishness. We cannot apply to God the view of love propagated by an evil world. Our definition of love must come from God who is holy, just, and perfect. We must learn to love like God does.

4:9, 10 Love explains (1) why God creates—because he loves, he creates people to love; (2) why God cares—because he loves them, he cares for sinful people; (3) why we are free to choose—he wants a loving response from us; (4) why Christ died—his love for us caused him to seek a solution to the problem of sin; and (5) why we receive eternal life—his love expresses itself to us forever.

world to bring to us eternal life through his death. ¹⁰In this act we see what real love is: it is not our love for God, but his love for us when he sent his Son to satisfy God's anger against our sins.

¹¹Dear friends, since God loved us as much as that, we surely ought to love each other too. ¹²For though we have never yet seen God, when we love each other God lives in us and his love within us grows ever stronger. ¹³And he has put his own Holy Spirit into our hearts as a proof to us that we are living with him and he with us. ¹⁴And furthermore, we have seen with our own eyes and now tell all the world that God sent his Son to be their Savior. ¹⁵Anyone who believes and says that Jesus is the Son of God has God living in him, and he is living with God.

¹⁶We know how much God loves us because we have felt his love and because we believe him when he tells us that he loves us dearly. God is love, and anyone who lives in love is living with God and God is living in him. ¹⁷And as we live with Christ, our love grows more perfect and complete; so we will not be ashamed and embarrassed at the day of judgment, but can face him with confidence and joy, because he loves us and we love him too.

¹⁸We need have no fear of someone who loves us perfectly; his perfect love for us eliminates all dread of what he might do to us. If we are afraid, it is for fear of what he might do to us, and shows that we are not fully convinced that he really loves us. ¹⁹So you see, our love for him comes as a result of his loving us first.

²⁰If anyone says "I love God," but keeps on hating his brother, he is a liar; for if he doesn't love his brother who is right there in front of him, how can he love God whom he has never seen? ²¹And God himself has said that one must love not only God, but his brother too.

3. God is life

5 If you believe that Jesus is the Christ—that he is God's Son and your Savior—then you are a child of God. And all who love the Father love his children too. ²So you can find out how much you love God's children—your brothers and sisters in the Lord—by how much you love and obey God. ³Loving God means doing what he tells us to do, and really, that isn't hard at all; ⁴for every child of God

4:10
Jn 15:16
Rom 5:8,10
Tit 3:4,5
1 Jn 2:2

4:12
Jn 1:18; 14:23
1 Tim 6:16

4:13
Jn 14:20
Rom 8:9
1 Jn 3:24

4:14
Jn 1:14; 3:17
4:42
1 Jn 1:2; 2:2

4:15
Mt 16:16
Jn 6:69
Rom 10:9

4:17
Mt 10:15
Jas 2:13

4:18
Rom 8:15

4:21
Lev 19:18
Mt 5:43; 22:37
Jn 13:34
1 Jn 3:11

5:1
Jn 1:11
8:41,42

5:3
Mic 6:8
Mt 11:30
1 Jn 2:3

4:10 Nothing sinful or evil can exist in God's presence. He is absolute goodness. He cannot overlook, condone, or excuse sin as if it never happened. He loves us, but his love does not make him morally lax. If we trust in Jesus, however, we do not have to bear the penalty for our sins (1 Peter 2:24). We can be acquitted (Romans 5:18).

4:12 Some people love to be with others. They befriend strangers easily and always are surrounded by many friends. Other people are shy or reserved. They have a few friends, but they are uncomfortable talking with people they don't know or mingling in crowds. Shy people don't need to become extroverts in order to love others. John isn't telling us *how many* people to love, but *how much* to love the people we already know. Our job is to faithfully love the people God has given us to love, whether there are two or two hundred of them. If God sees we are ready to love others, he will bring them to us. No matter how shy we are, we don't need to be afraid of the love commandment. God never leads us beyond the sufficiency of his strength.

4:13 When we become Christians, we receive the Holy Spirit. God's presence in our lives is a proof that we really belong to him and gives us the power to love (Romans 5:5; 8:9; 2 Corinthians 1:22). Rely on that power as you reach out to others. If you lack assurance of your salvation, listen to the Holy Spirit within you (see also Romans 8:16).

4:17 The day of judgment is that final day when we will appear before Christ and be held accountable for our lives. With God living in us through Christ, we have no reason to fear this day, because we have been saved from punishment. Instead, we can look forward to the judgment, because it will mean the end of sin

and the beginning of a face-to-face relationship with Jesus Christ.

4:18 If we ever fall prey to fear of eternity, heaven, or God's judgment, we can remind ourselves of God's love. We know he loves us perfectly (Romans 8:38, 39). We can resolve our fears first by focusing on his immeasurable love for us, then by allowing him to love others through us. We can be confident if in this life we have learned to be more like Jesus.

4:19 God's love is the source of all human love, and it spreads like fire. In loving his children, he kindles a flame in their hearts. In turn, they love others, who are warmed by God's love through them.

4:20, 21 It is easy to say we love God when it doesn't cost us anything more than weekly attendance at religious services. But the real test of our love for God is how we treat the people right in front of us—our family members and fellow believers. We cannot truly love God while neglecting to love those who are created in his image.

5:1, 2 When we become Christians, we become part of God's family, with fellow believers as our brothers and sisters. It is God who determines who the other family members are, not us. We are simply called to accept and love them. How well do you treat your fellow members in the family of God?

5:3, 4 Jesus never promised that obeying him would be easy. Hard work, however, can be rewarding if we value its results. Another way of translating the last half of verse 3 is this: "His commands are not burdensome." The hard work and self-discipline of serving Christ is no burden to those who love him. And if our load starts to feel heavy, we can always trust Christ to help us bear it.

5:5
1 Cor 15:57

5:6
Hag 2:5
Mt 18:16
Jn 15:26; 19:34
Rev 19:11,13

5:9
Mt 3:16,17
Jn 5:31-38; 8:18

5:10
Jn 3:18,33
Rom 8:16
Gal 4:6
1 Jn 1:10

5:11
Jn 1:4
1 Jn 2:25; 4:9
5:13,20

5:12
Jn 3:15,36; 5:24
14:6; 17:2,3

5:13
Jn 20:31
1 Jn 3:23

5:14
Mt 7:7
Jn 14:13
15:7
1 Jn 3:21,22

5:16
Num 15:30
Jer 7:16; 14:11
Mk 3:29
Heb 6:4; 10:26
Jas 5:15

5:17
1 Jn 2:1; 3:4

5:18
Jn 10:28,29
1 Jn 2:13; 3:9

can obey him, defeating sin and evil pleasure by trusting Christ to help him. 5But who could possibly fight and win this battle except by believing that Jesus is truly the Son of God? 6, 7, 8And we know he is, because God said so with a voice from heaven when Jesus was baptized, and again as he was facing death—yes, not only at his baptism but also as he faced death. And the Holy Spirit, forever truthful, says it too. So we have these three witnesses: the voice of the Holy Spirit in our hearts, the voice from heaven at Christ's baptism, and the voice before he died. And they all say the same thing: that Jesus Christ is the Son of God. 9We believe men who witness in our courts, and so surely we can believe whatever God declares. And God declares that Jesus is his Son. 10All who believe this know in their hearts that it is true. If anyone doesn't believe this, he is actually calling God a liar, because he doesn't believe what God has said about his Son.

11And what is it that God has said? That he has given us eternal life, and that this life is in his Son. 12So whoever has God's Son has life; whoever does not have his Son, does not have life.

13I have written this to you who believe in the Son of God so that you may know you have eternal life. 14And we are sure of this, that he will listen to us whenever we ask him for anything in line with his will. 15And if we really know he is listening when we talk to him and make our requests, then we can be sure that he will answer us.

16If you see a Christian sinning in a way that does not end in death, you should ask God to forgive him and God will give him life, unless he has sinned that one fatal sin. But there is that one sin which ends in death and if he has done that, there is no use praying for him. 17Every wrong is a sin, of course. I'm not talking about these ordinary sins; I am speaking of that one that ends in death.

18No one who has become part of God's family makes a practice of sinning, for Christ, God's Son, holds him securely and the devil cannot get his hands on him. 19We know that we are children of God and that all the rest of the world around us

5:6-8 *as he was facing death,* literally, "This is he who came by water and blood." See Mt 3:16, 17; Lk 9:31, 35; Jn 12:27, 28, 32, 33. Other interpretations of this verse are equally possible. *as he faced death,* literally, "not by water only, but by water and blood." *and the voice before he died,* literally, "the Spirit, and the water, and the blood." *Jesus Christ is the Son of God,* implied.

5:6-8 The phrase, "a voice from heaven" is a paraphrase of "he . . . came by water and blood" (see textual note). This expression may refer to Jesus' baptism and Jesus' crucifixion. At this time, there was a false teaching in circulation which said that Jesus was God only between his baptism and his death—that is, he was born merely human until he was baptized, at which time "the Christ" then descended upon him, but then later left him before his death on the cross. But if Jesus died only as a man, he could not have taken upon himself the sins of the world, and Christianity would be an empty religion. Only an act of God could take away the punishment we deserve for our sins.

5:9 In the Gospels, God twice clearly declared that Jesus is his Son, once at Jesus' baptism (Matthew 3:16, 17), and once at his transfiguration (Matthew 17:5).

5:12 Whoever believes in God's Son has eternal life. He is all you need. You don't need to *wait,* because eternal life begins today. You don't need to *work* for it, because it is already yours. You don't need to *worry,* because you have been given eternal life by God himself, and it is guaranteed.

5:13 Some people *hope* they will be given eternal life. John says we can *know* we have it. Our certainty is based on God's promise that he has given us eternal life through his Son. This is true whether you feel close to God or distant from him. Eternal life is not based on feelings, but on facts. You can know you have eternal life if you believe God's truth. If you lack assurance as to whether you are a Christian, ask yourself if you have honestly committed your life to him as your Savior and Lord. If so, you know by faith that you are indeed a child of God.

5:14, 15 The emphasis here is on God's will, not our will. When we communicate with God, we don't demand what we want, rather we

discuss with him what *he* wants for us. If we align our prayers to his will, he will listen; and we can be certain that if he listens, he will give us a definite answer. Start praying with confidence!

5:16, 17 Commentators differ widely in their thoughts about what this sin is, and whether the death it causes is physical or spiritual. Paul wrote that some Christians had died because they took communion "in an unworthy manner" (1 Corinthians 11:27-30), and Ananias and Sapphira were struck dead when they lied to God (Acts 5:1-11). Blasphemy against the Holy Spirit results in spiritual death (Mark 3:29), and the book of Hebrews describes the spiritual death of the person who turns against Christ (Hebrews 6:4-6). John was probably thinking of the people who had left the Christian fellowship and joined the "antichrists." By rejecting the only way of salvation, these people were putting themselves out of reach of prayer. In most cases, however, even if we know what the "sin which ends in death" is, we have no sure way of knowing if a certain person has committed it. Therefore we should continue praying for our loved ones and Christian brothers and sisters, leaving the judging up to God. Note that John says, "there is no use praying for him," rather than "You cannot pray about that." He recognized the lack of certainty.

5:18, 19 Christians commit sins, of course, but they ask God to forgive them and then they continue serving him. God has freed them from their slavery to Satan, and he keeps them safe from Satan's continued attacks. The rest of the world does not have the Christian's freedom to obey God. Unless they come to Christ in faith, they have no choice but to obey Satan. There is no middle ground; people either belong to God and obey him, or they live under Satan's control.

is under Satan's power and control. **20**And we know that Christ, God's Son, has come to help us understand and find the true God. And now we are in God because we are in Jesus Christ his Son, who is the only true God; and he is eternal Life.

21Dear children, keep away from anything that might take God's place in your hearts. Amen.

Sincerely, John

5:20
Lk 24:45
Jn 1:1,18; 14:20
15:5; 17:3,21,23
1 Jn 5:5,10
Rev 3:7

5:21
1 Cor 10:7
1 Thess 1:9

5:21 This verse is also translated, "Keep yourself from idols." An idol is anything that substitutes for the true faith, anything that robs Christ of his full deity and humanity, any human idea that claims to be more authoritative than the Bible, anything that replaces God as the center of our lives.

5:21 What we think about Jesus Christ is central to our teaching, preaching, and living. Jesus is the God-man, fully God and fully human at the same time. He came to earth to die in our place for our sins. Through faith in him, we can have eternal life and the power to do his will. What is your answer to the most important question you could ever be asked—who is Jesus Christ?

TRUTH and *love* are frequently discussed in our world, but seldom practiced.

From politicians to salesmen, people conveniently ignore or conceal facts and use words to enhance positions or sell products. Perjury is common, and integrity and credibility are endangered species. It is not surprising that we have to "swear" to tell the truth.

And what about love? Our world is filled with its words—popular songs, greeting cards, media counselors, and romantic novels shower us with notions and dreams of ethereal, idyllic relationships and feelings. Real love, however, is scarce—selfless giving, caring, sharing, and even dying if need be. We yearn to love and be loved, but see few living examples of real love.

Christ is the antithesis of society's prevailing values— falsehood, and self-centeredness—for *he is truth and love* in person. Therefore, all who claim loyalty to him must be committed to these ideals, following and living the truth, and acting with love toward one another.

The apostle John had seen truth and love firsthand—he had been with Jesus. So affected was this disciple that all of his writings (the Gospel of John, the letters of 1, 2, and 3 John, and the book of Revelation) are filled with this theme—truth and love are vital to the Christian and are inseparable in the Christian life. Second John, his brief letter to a dear friend, is no different. John says to follow the truth and obey God (1:4), watch out for false leaders (1:7), and love God and each other (1:6).

Second John will take just a few minutes to read, but its message should last a lifetime. As you reflect on these few paragraphs penned by the wise and aged follower of Christ, recommit yourself to being a person of truth, of love, and of obedience to the Lord.

VITAL STATISTICS

PURPOSE:
To emphasize the basics of following Christ—truth and love—and to warn against false teachers

AUTHOR:
The apostle John

TO WHOM WRITTEN:
To a woman called "Cyria" or "the elect lady" and her household— some think that the greeting refers instead to a local church

DATE WRITTEN:
About the same time as 1 John, around A.D. 90, from Ephesus

SETTING:
Evidently this woman and her family were involved in one of the churches which John was overseeing—they had developed a strong friendship. John was warning her of the false teachers which were becoming prevalent in some of the churches.

KEY VERSE:
"If we love God, we will do what he tells us to. And he has told us from the very first to love each other" (1:6).

KEY PEOPLE:
John, Cyria and her children

THE BLUEPRINT

1. Watch out for false teachers (1:1–11)
2. John's final words (1:12, 13)

False teachers were a dangerous problem for the church to which John was writing. His warning against giving hospitality to false teachers may sound harsh and unloving to many today. Yet these men were teaching heresy that could seriously harm many believers—for eternity.

MEGATHEMES

THEME	EXPLANATION	IMPORTANCE
Truth	Following God's Word, the Bible, is essential to Christian living because God is truth. Christ's true followers consistently obey his truth.	To be loyal to Christ's teaching we must seek to know the Bible, but never twist its message to our own needs or purposes, nor encourage others who misuse it.
Love	Christ's command is for Christians to love one another. This is the basic ingredient of true Christianity.	To obey Christ fully, we must believe his command to love others. Helping, giving, and meeting needs put love into practice.
False Leaders	We must be wary of religious leaders who are not true to Christ's teaching. We should not give them a platform to spread false teaching.	Don't encourage those who are contrary to Christ. Politely remove yourself from association with false leaders. Be aware of what's being taught in the church.

1. Watch out for false teachers

1 *From:* John, the old Elder of the church.

To: That dear woman Cyria, one of God's very own, and to her children whom I love so much, as does everyone else in the church. ²Since the Truth is in our hearts forever, ³God the Father and Jesus Christ his Son will bless us with great mercy and much peace, and with truth and love.

⁴How happy I am to find some of your children here, and to see that they are living as they should, following the Truth, obeying God's command.

⁵And now I want to urgently remind you, dear friends, of the old rule God gave us right from the beginning, that Christians should love one another. ⁶If we love God, we will do whatever he tells us to. And he has told us from the very first to love each other.

⁷Watch out for the false leaders—and there are many of them around—who don't believe that Jesus Christ came to earth as a human being with a body like ours. Such people are against the truth and against Christ. ⁸Beware of being like them, and losing the prize that you and I have been working so hard to get. See to it that you win your full reward from the Lord. ⁹For if you wander beyond the teaching of Christ, you will leave God behind; while if you are loyal to Christ's teachings, you will have God too. Then you will have both the Father and the Son.

¹⁰If anyone comes to teach you, and he doesn't believe what Christ taught, don't even invite him into your home. Don't encourage him in any way. ¹¹If you do you will be a partner with him in his wickedness.

2. John's final words

¹²Well, I would like to say much more, but I don't want to say it in this letter, for I hope to come to see you soon and then we can talk over these things together and have a joyous time.

¹³Greetings from the children of your sister—another choice child of God.

Sincerely, John

1:2
Jn 8:32
14:16,17
2 Cor 4:7,10
1 Jn 1:8; 3:18

1:5
Jn 13:34; 15:12
Eph 5:2
1 Pet 1:22

1:6
Jn 14:15
15:10,14
Rom 13:8
1 Jn 2:7; 4:7-12

1:7
1 Tim 4:1-5
2 Pet 2:1-3
1 Jn 2:18,26
4:1-3

1:8
Phil 3:14; 4:1

1:9
Jn 8:31; 15:7
1 Jn 2:23,24

1:10
Rom 16:17
1 Cor 5:11
Tit 3:10

1:11
1 Tim 5:22
Jude 23

1:1 John was one of Jesus' 12 disciples and the writer of the Gospel of John, three epistles, and the book of Revelation. For more information about him, see his Profile in John 13. This letter was written shortly after 1 John to warn about false teachers. The salutation is literally translated, "To the chosen lady and her children." Although some think this letter was written to a specific woman, it may also refer to a church whose identity is no longer known.

1:2 The "Truth" is the truth about Jesus Christ, as opposed to the lies of the false teachers (see 1 John 2:21-23).

1:5, 6 The love Christians should have for one another is a recurrent New Testament theme. Yet love for one's neighbor is an old command first appearing in the third book of Moses (Leviticus 19:18). We can show love in many ways: by avoiding prejudice and discrimination, by accepting people, by listening, helping, giving, serving, and refusing to judge. But just knowing God's command is not enough. We must put it into practice. (See also Matthew 22:37-39 and 1 John 2:7, 8.)

1:7 In John's day, many false teachers taught that spirit was good and matter was evil; therefore, they reasoned that Jesus could not have been both God and man. In strong terms, John warned against this kind of teaching. There are still many false teachers who promote an understanding of Jesus that is not biblical. They are dangerous because they twist the truth and undermine the foundations of Christian faith. They may use the right words but

change the meanings. The way your teachers live shows a lot about what they believe about Christ. For more on testing teachers, see 1 John 4:1.

1:8 The prize and full reward to which John refers is not salvation but the rewards of loyal service. All who value the truth and persistently hold to it will win their "full reward from the Lord." Those who live for themselves and justify it by teaching false doctrines will lose that reward (see Matthew 7:21-23).

1:10 John instructed the believers not to give hospitality to false teachers. They were to do nothing that would encourage the heretics in their propogation of falsehood. In addition, if believers invited them in, it would show they were approving of what the false teachers said and did. It may seem rude to turn people away, even if they are teaching heresy, but how much better to be faithful to God than merely courteous to people! John is not condemning hospitality to unbelievers, but rather the supporting of those who are dedicated to opposing the true teachings of God. Note that John adds that a person who supports a false teacher in any way shares that teacher's wicked work.

1:13 False teaching is serious business, and we dare not overlook it. It is so serious that John wrote this letter especially to warn against it. There are so many false teachings in our world today that we might be tempted to take them lightly. Instead, we should realize the dangers they pose and actively refuse to give heresies any foothold.

WHEN company arrives at the door, with them comes the promise of soiled floors, dirty dishes, altered schedules, personal expense, and inconvenience. From sharing a meal to providing a bed, *hospitality* costs . . . in time, energy, and money. But how we treat others reflects our true values. Do we see people as objects or inconveniences, or as unique creations of a loving God? And which is more important to God, a person or a carpet? Perhaps the most effective way to demonstrate God's values and Christ's love to others is to invite and welcome guests into our homes.

For Gaius, hospitality was a habit, and his reputation for friendship and generosity, especially to "traveling teachers and missionaries" (1:5) had spread. To affirm and thank him for his Christian lifestyle, and to encourage him in his faith, John wrote this personal note.

John's format for this epistle centers around three men— Gaius, the example of one who follows Christ and loves others (1:1–8); Diotrephes, the self-proclaimed church leader who does not reflect God's values (1:9–11); and Demetrius, who also follows the truth (1:12). John encouraged Gaius to practice hospitality, cling to the truth, and do what is right.

Although this is a personal letter, we can apply its lessons to our lives. As you read 3 John, with which man do you identify? Are you a Gaius, generously giving to others? A Demetrius, loving the truth? Or a Diotrephes, looking out for yourself? Determine to reflect Christ's values in your relationships, opening your home and touching others with his love.

VITAL STATISTICS

PURPOSE:
To commend Gaius for his hospitality and to encourage him in his Christian life

AUTHOR:
The apostle John

TO WHOM WRITTEN:
Gaius, a prominent Christian in one of the churches known to John

DATE WRITTEN:
About A.D. 90, from Ephesus

SETTING:
Church leaders traveled from town to town helping to establish new congregations. They depended on the hospitality of fellow believers. Gaius was one who welcomed them into his home.

KEY VERSE:
"Dear friend, you are doing a good work for God in taking care of the traveling teachers and missionaries who are passing through" (1:5).

KEY PEOPLE:
John, Gaius, Diotrephes, Demetrius

THE BLUEPRINT

1. God's children live by the standards of the gospel (1:1–12)
2. John's final words (1:13–15)

John wrote to commend Gaius who was taking care of traveling teachers and missionaries and to warn against people like Diotrephes, who are proud and refuse to listen to spiritual leaders in authority. If we are to live in the truth of the gospel, we must look for ways to support pastors, Christian workers, and missionaries today. All Christians should work together to support God's work, both at home and around the world.

MEGATHEMES

THEME	EXPLANATION	IMPORTANCE
Hospitality	John wrote to encourage those who were kind to others. Genuine hospitality for traveling Christian workers was needed then and is still important.	Faithful Christian teachers and missionaries need our support. Whenever you can extend hospitality to others, it will make you a partner in their ministry.
Pride	Diotrephes not only refused to offer hospitality, but he set himself up as a church boss. Pride disqualified him as a real leader.	Christian leaders must shun pride and its effects on them. Be careful not to misuse your position of leadership.
Faithfulness	Gaius and Demetrius were commended for their faithful work in the church. They were held up as examples of faithful, selfless servants.	Don't take for granted Christian workers who serve faithfully. Be sure to encourage them so they won't grow weary of serving.

1. God's children live by the standards of the gospel

1 *From:* John, the Elder.
To: Dear Gaius, whom I truly love.

1:1
2 Jn 1

²Dear friend, I am praying that all is well with you and that your body is as healthy as I know your soul is. ³Some of the brothers traveling by have made me very happy by telling me that your life stays clean and true, and that you are living by the standards of the Gospel. ⁴I could have no greater joy than to hear such things about my children.

1:3
2 Jn 4

1:4
1 Cor 4:15
Gal 4:19
1 Jn 2:1

⁵Dear friend, you are doing a good work for God in taking care of the traveling teachers and missionaries who are passing through. ⁶They have told the church here of your friendship and your loving deeds. I am glad when you send them on their way with a generous gift. ⁷For they are traveling for the Lord, and take neither food, clothing, shelter, nor money from those who are not Christians, even though they have preached to them. ⁸So we ourselves should take care of them in order that we may become partners with them in the Lord's work.

1:5
Rom 12:13
Heb 13:2
1 Pet 4:10,11

1:6
Col 1:10
1 Thess 1:12

1:7
Mt 10:9-14
Mk 6:8-13
Lk 9:3-5
10:4-11
Acts 20:33

⁹I sent a brief letter to the church about this, but proud Diotrephes, who loves to push himself forward as the leader of the Christians there, does not admit my authority over him and refuses to listen to me. ¹⁰When I come I will tell you some of the things he is doing and what wicked things he is saying about me and what insulting language he is using. He not only refuses to welcome the missionary travelers himself, but tells others not to, and when they do he tries to put them out of the church.

1:9
Mt 19:30; 20:16
Mk 10:31
Lk 13:30
Phil 2:3

1:10
3 Jn 5

1:11
Ps 34:14
1 Cor 4:16; 11:1
1 Jn 2:29; 3:6,9

¹¹Dear friend, don't let this bad example influence you. Follow only what is good. Remember that those who do what is right prove that they are God's children; and those who continue in evil prove that they are far from God. ¹²But

---

1:1 This letter gives us an important glimpse into the life of the early church. Third John, addressed to Gaius, is about the need for hospitality to traveling preachers and other believers. It also warns against a would-be church dictator.

1:1 John was one of Jesus' 12 disciples and the writer of the Gospel of John, three epistles, and the book of Revelation. For more information about him, see his Profile in John 13. We have no further information about Gaius, but he is someone John loved dearly. Perhaps he had shared his home and hospitality with John at some time during John's travels. If so, John would have appreciated his actions, because traveling preachers depended on hospitality to survive (see Matthew 10:11–16).

1:2 John was concerned for Gaius' physical *and* spiritual well-being. This was in direct contrast to the popular heresy of the day that taught the separation of spirit and matter and despised the physical side of life. Still today, many people fall into this way of thinking. This non-Christian attitude logically leads to one of two responses: neglect of the body and physical health, or indulgence of the body's sinful desires. God is concerned for both your body and your soul. As responsible Christians, we should neither neglect nor indulge ourselves, but care for our physical needs and discipline our bodies so we are at our best for God's service.

1:4 John says "my children" because, as a result of his preaching, he was the spiritual father of many, including Gaius.

1:5 In the church's early days, traveling prophets, evangelists, and teachers were helped on their way by people like Gaius who housed and fed them. Hospitality is a lost art in many churches today. We would do well to invite more people for meals—fellow church members, young people, traveling missionaries, those in need, visitors. This is an active and much-appreciated way to show your love. In fact it is probably more important today. Because of our individualistic, self-centered society, there are many lonely people who wonder if anyone cares whether they live or die. If you find such a lonely person, show him or her that *you* care!

1:7 The traveling missionaries neither asked for nor accepted anything from non-Christians, because they didn't want anyone

questioning their motives for preaching. God's true preachers did not preach in order to make money, but out of love for God. It is the church's responsibility to care for Christian workers; this should never be left to nonbelievers (see 2 Corinthians 12:13).

1:7 When you help someone who is spreading the gospel, you are in a very real way a partner in the ministry. This is the other side of the principle in 2 John 1:10 (see the note there). Not everyone should go to the mission field; those who work for Christ at home are vital to the ministry of those who go and need support. We can support missionaries by praying for them and by giving them our money, hospitality, and time.

1:9 This letter to which John refers was neither 1 or 2 John, but another letter that no longer exists.

1:9, 10 All we know about Diotrephes is that he wanted to control the church. John denounces (1) his refusal to listen to other spiritual leaders, (2) his slander of the leaders, (3) his bad example in refusing to welcome any gospel teachers, and (4) his attempt to excommunicate those who opposed his leadership. Sins such as pride, jealousy, and slander are still present in the church, and when a leader makes a habit of encouraging sin and discouraging godly actions, he must be stopped. If no one speaks up, great harm can come to the church. We must confront sin in the church; if we try to avoid it, it will continue to grow. Some leaders misuse the Old Testament idea of "opposing God's anointed"; but such use is false because that injunction applied to the prophet, not to every church leader. A true Christian leader is a servant, not an autocrat!

1:12 We know nothing about Demetrius except that he probably carried this letter from John to Gaius. The book of Acts mentions an Ephesian silversmith named Demetrius who opposed Paul (Acts 19:24ff), but this is probably another man. In contrast to the corrupt Diotrephes, Demetrius had a high regard for truth. John personified truth as a witness to Demetrius' character and teaching. In other words, if truth itself could speak, it would speak on Demetrius' behalf. When Demetrius arrived, Gaius would have certainly opened his home to him.

everyone, including Truth itself, speaks highly of Demetrius. I myself can say the same for him, and you know I speak the truth.

2. John's final words

1:13
2 Jn 12
1:14
2 Jn 12

13I have much to say but I don't want to write it, 14for I hope to see you soon and then we will have much to talk about together. 15So good-bye for now. Friends here send their love, and please give each of the folks there a special greeting from me.

Sincerely, John

1:15 Whereas 2 John emphasized the need to refuse hospitality to false teachers, 3 John urges continued hospitality to those who teach the truth. Hospitality is a strong sign of support for people and their work. It means giving them of your means so their stay will be comfortable and their work and travel easier. Actively look for creative ways to show hospitality to God's workers. It may be in the form of a letter of encouragement, a "care" package, financial support, an open home, or prayer.

VITAL STATISTICS

PURPOSE:
To remind the church of the need for constant vigilance—to keep strong in the faith and to defend it against heresy

AUTHOR:
Jude, James' brother and Jesus' half-brother

TO WHOM WRITTEN:
Jewish Christians and all believers everywhere

DATE WRITTEN:
About A.D. 65

SETTING:
From the first century on, the church has been threatened by heresy and false teaching—we must always be on our guard.

KEY VERSE:
"Dearly loved friends, I had been planning to write you some thoughts about the salvation God has given us, but now I find I must write of something else instead, urging you to stoutly defend the truth which God gave, once for all, to his people to keep without change through the years" (1:3).

KEY PEOPLE:
Jude, James, Jesus

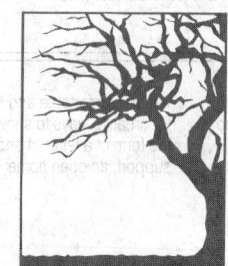

TO protect from harm—to guard from attack—to repulse enemies, for centuries rugged defenders have built walls and waged wars, expending material and human resources in battle to save nations and cities. And with total commitment and courageous abandon, individuals have fought for their families. It is a rule of life that we fight for survival, defending with all our strength what is most precious to us, from every real or imagined attack.

God's Word and the gift of eternal life have infinite value. They have been entrusted to Christ's faithful followers. There are many people who live in opposition to God and his followers. They twist God's truth, seeking to deceive and destroy the unwary. But God's truth stands, carried and defended by those who have committed their lives to God's Son. It is an important task, an awesome responsibility, and a profound privilege to have this commission.

This was Jude's message to Christians everywhere. Opposition would come and godless teachers would arise, but Christians should "stoutly defend the truth" (1:3) by rejecting all falsehood and immorality (1:4–19), remembering God's mighty acts of rescue and punishment (1:5–11, 14–16) and the warnings of the apostles (1:17–19). His readers are to build up their own faith through prayer (1:20), keeping close to Christ (1:21), helping others (1:22, 23), and hating sin (1:23). Then Jude concludes with a glorious benediction of praise to God (1:24, 25).

How much do you value God's Word, the fellowship of the church, and obedience to Jesus Christ? There are many false teachers waiting to destroy your Christ-centered life, the credibility of God's Word, and the unity of the body of Christ. Read Jude and determine to stand firm in your faith and defend God's truth at all costs.

THE BLUEPRINT

1. The danger of false teachers (1:1–16)
2. The duty to fight for God's truth (1:17–25)

Jude wrote to motivate Christians everywhere to action. He wanted them to recognize the dangers of false teaching, to protect themselves and other believers, and to win back those who had already been deceived. Jude was writing against godless teachers who were saying that Christians could do as they pleased without fear of God's punishment. While few teach this heresy openly in the church today, many in the church act as though this were true. This letter contains a warning against living a nominal Christian life.

MEGATHEMES

THEME	EXPLANATION	IMPORTANCE
False teachers	Jude warns against false teachers and leaders who reject the lordship of Christ, undermine the faith of others, and lead them astray. These leaders and any who follow them will be punished.	We must stoutly defend Christian truth. Make sure that you avoid leaders and teachers who change the Bible to suit their own purposes. Genuine servants of God will faithfully portray Christ in their words and conduct.
Apostasy	Jude also warns against apostasy—turning away from Christ. We are to remember that God punishes rebellion against him. We must be careful not to drift away from a firm commitment to Christ.	Those who do not seek to know the truth in God's Word are susceptible to apostasy. Christians must guard against any false teachings that would distract them from the truth preached by the apostles and written in God's Word.

1. The danger of false teachers

1:1
Mt 13:55
1:3
Acts 20:27
1 Cor 15:3-9
1 Tim 6:12
Tit 1:4
2 Pet 3:1,2
Jude 20
1:4
Rom 6:1-4
Gal 6:13
2 Tim 3:6
1 Pet 2:16
2 Pet 2:1-4,10,
18-22
2 Jn 7

1 *From:* Jude, a servant of Jesus Christ, and a brother of James.
To: Christians everywhere—beloved of God and chosen by him. 2May you be given more and more of God's kindness, peace, and love.

3Dearly loved friends, I had been planning to write you some thoughts about the salvation God has given us, but now I find I must write of something else instead, urging you to stoutly defend the truth which God gave, once for all, to his people to keep without change through the years. 4I say this because some godless teachers have wormed their way in among you, saying that after we become Christians we can do just as we like without fear of God's punishment. The fate of such people was written long ago, for they have turned against our only Master and Lord, Jesus Christ.

1:1 The letter of Jude focuses on *apostasy*—when people turn away from God's truth and embrace false teachings. Jude reminds his readers of God's judgment on those who apostasized in the past. This letter is a warning against false teachers—in this case, probably Gnostic teachers (see the note on Colossians 2:4ff, for a description of the Gnostic heresy). Gnostics opposed two of the basic foundations of Christianity—the incarnation of Christ and Christian ethics. Jude wrote to combat these false teachings and to encourage true doctrine and right conduct.

1:1 Jude was a brother of James, who was one of the leaders in the early church. Both of these men were Jesus' half-brothers. Mary was their mother. Joseph was the father of James and Jude, and although Mary was Jesus' true mother, God was Jesus' true Father.

1:3 Jude emphasizes the important relationship between correct doctrine and true faith. The truth of the Bible must not be compromised because it gives us the real facts about Jesus and salvation. Scripture is inspired by God and should never be twisted or changed; when it is, we become confused over right and wrong and lose sight of the only path that leads to eternal life. Before writing about salvation, then, Jude felt he had to set his readers back on the right track, calling them back to the basics of their

faith. Then the way to salvation would be clearer.

1:4 Even some of our churches today have godless (or false) teachers who twist the Bible's teachings to justify their own opinions, lifestyle, or wrong behavior. This may give them temporary freedom to do as they wish, but they will discover that in twisting Scripture they are playing with fire. God will judge them for excusing, tolerating, and promoting sin.

1:4 Because people think theology is dry, they avoid studying the Bible. Those who refuse to learn correct doctrine, however, are susceptible to false teaching because they are not fully grounded in God's truth. We must understand the basic doctrines of our faith so that we can recognize false doctrines and prevent them from hurting us and others.

1:4 Many first-century false teachers taught that Christians could do whatever they liked without fear of God's punishment. They took a light view of God's holiness and his justice. Paul refutes this same kind of false teaching in Romans 6:1–23. Even today, some Christians minimize the sinfulness of sin, believing that how they live has little to do with their faith. They may do well to ask, "Does the way I live show that I am sincere about my faith?" Those who truly have faith will show it by their deep respect for God and their sincere desire to live according to the principles in his Word.

⁵My answer to them is: Remember this fact—which you know already—that the Lord saved a whole nation of people out of the land of Egypt, and then killed every one of them who did not trust and obey him. ⁶And I remind you of those angels who were once pure and holy, but turned to a life of sin. Now God has them chained up in prisons of darkness, waiting for the judgment day. ⁷And don't forget the cities of Sodom and Gomorrah and their neighboring towns, all full of lust of every kind including lust of men for other men. Those cities were destroyed by fire and continue to be a warning to us that there is a hell in which sinners are punished.

⁸Yet these false teachers carelessly go right on living their evil, immoral lives, degrading their bodies and laughing at those in authority over them, even scoffing at the Glorious Ones. ⁹Yet Michael, one of the mightiest of the angels, when he was arguing with Satan about Moses' body, did not dare to accuse even Satan, or jeer at him, but simply said, "The Lord rebuke you." ¹⁰But these men mock and curse at anything they do not understand, and, like animals, they do whatever they feel like, thereby ruining their souls.

¹¹Woe upon them! For they follow the example of Cain who killed his brother; and, like Balaam, they will do anything for money; and like Korah, they have disobeyed God and will die under his curse.

¹²When these men join you at the love feasts of the church, they are evil smears among you, laughing and carrying on, gorging and stuffing themselves without a thought for others. They are like clouds blowing over dry land without giving rain, promising much, but producing nothing. They are like fruit trees without any fruit at picking time. They are not only dead, but doubly dead, for they have been pulled out, roots and all, to be burned.

¹³All they leave behind them is shame and disgrace like the dirty foam left along the beach by the wild waves. They wander around looking as bright as stars, but ahead of them is the everlasting gloom and darkness that God has prepared for them.

¹⁴Enoch, who lived seven generations after Adam, knew about these men and

1:5 Ex 14:21-31
Num 14:20-24
Deut 2:14,15
1 Cor 10:5-10
1:6 2 Pet 2:4,9
Rev 12:9
1:8 2 Pet 2:10
1:9 Deut 34:6
Dan 10:13,20,
21; 12:1
Zech 3:2
Rev 12:7
1:11 Gen 4:3-16
Num 16:1-35
22:20-33
26:5-11; 31:16
Hab 2:6-19
Mt 11:21
23:13-33
2 Pet 2:15-16
1 Jn 3:12
Rev 2:14
1:12 Mt 15:13
1 Cor 11:20-22
Phil 3:19
1 Thess 5:6,7
Jas 5:5
1:13 Isa 57:20
Phil 3:19
2 Pet 2:17
Jude 6
Rev 20:10; 21:8
1:14 Gen 5:18-24
Deut 33:2
1 Chron 1:1-4

1:6 Or, "who abandoned their original rank and left their proper home."

1:5-7 Jude gives three examples of rebellion: (1) the children of Israel—who, although they were delivered from Egypt, refused to trust God and enter the Promised Land (Numbers 14:26- 39); (2) the angels—who, although they were once pure and holy, and living in God's presence, gave in to pride and rebelled against God (2 Peter 2:4); and (3) the cities of Sodom and Gomorrah—which were so full of sin that God wiped them off the face of the earth (Genesis 19:1–29). If the chosen people, angels, and sinful cities were punished, how much more would these false teachers be severely judged?

1:7 Many people don't want to believe that God sentences people to hell (literally, "eternal fire") for rejecting him, but this is clearly taught in Scripture. Sinners who don't seek forgiveness from God will face eternal separation from him. Jude gave this warning to all who rebel against, ignore, or reject God.

1:8 The "Glorious Ones" here probably refer to angels. Just as the men of Sodom insulted angels (Genesis 19), these false teachers whom Jude refers to, scoff at any authority. For more information on the danger of insulting Glorious Ones, see the note on 2 Peter 2:10.

1:9 This incident is not recorded any other place in Scripture. Moses' death is recorded in Deuteronomy 34. Here Jude is making use of an apocryphal book called *The Assumption of Moses*. The book demonstrated that Moses was taken immediately into God's presence after his death. Two other saints in the Old Testament were also taken into God's presence (only they were taken before they died)—Enoch (Genesis 5:21–24) and Elijah (2 Kings 2:1–15). Moses and Elijah appeared with Jesus at the Transfiguration (Matthew 17:1–9).

1:10 False teachers claimed that they possessed secret knowledge which gave them authority. Their "knowledge" of God

was esoteric—mystical and beyond human understanding. In reality, the nature of God *is beyond* our understanding. But God, in his grace, has chosen to reveal himself to us—in his Word, and supremely in Jesus Christ. Therefore, we must seek to know all we can about what he has revealed, even though we cannot fully comprehend God with our finite human minds. Beware of those who claim to have all the answers and who belittle what they do not understand.

1:11 Jude offers three examples of men who did whatever they wanted (1:10)—Cain, who murdered his brother out of vengeful jealousy (Genesis 4:1–16); Balaam, who prophesied to get money, not out of obedience to God's command (Numbers 22—24); and Korah, who rebelled against God's divinely appointed leaders, wanting the power for himself (Numbers 16:1–35). These stories illustrate attitudes that are typical of false teachers—pride, selfishness, jealousy, greed, lust for power, and disregard of God's will.

1:12 When the Lord's Supper was celebrated in the early church, believers ate a full meal before taking part in the communion with the bread and wine. The meal was called a love feast; it was designed to be a sacred time of fellowship to prepare one's heart for communion. In several of the churches, however, this meal had turned into a time of gluttony and drunken revelry. In Corinth, for example, some people hastily gobbled food while others went hungry (1 Corinthians 11:20–22). No church function should be an occasion for selfishness, gluttony, greed, disorder, or other sins which destroy unity or take one's mind away from the real purpose for assembling together.

1:12 The false teachers were "doubly dead." They were useless because they weren't producing fruit; and they weren't even believers, so they were rooted up and burned.

said this about them: "See, the Lord is coming with millions of his holy ones. 15He will bring the people of the world before him in judgment, to receive just punishment, and to prove the terrible things they have done in rebellion against God, revealing all they have said against him." 16These men are constant gripers, never satisfied, doing whatever evil they feel like; they are loudmouthed "show-offs," and when they show respect for others, it is only to get something from them in return.

1:16
Num 14:36-38
Deut 1:27,28
1 Thess 4:3-8
Jas 1:14,15
1 Pet 2:3,10,18
Jude 18

2. The duty to fight for God's truth

1:17
Heb 2:3
2 Pet 3:2

1:18
2 Pet 3:3
Jude 16

17Dear friends, remember what the apostles of our Lord Jesus Christ told you, 18that in the last times there would come these scoffers whose whole purpose in life is to enjoy themselves in every evil way imaginable. 19They stir up arguments; they love the evil things of the world; they do not have the Holy Spirit living in them.

1:19
Prov 18:1
1 Cor 2:14

20But you, dear friends, must build up your lives ever more strongly upon the foundation of our holy faith, learning to pray in the power and strength of the Holy Spirit.

1:20
Acts 9:31
Rom 8:15,26,27
Col 2:7
Jude 3

21Stay always within the boundaries where God's love can reach and bless you. Wait patiently for the eternal life that our Lord Jesus Christ in his mercy is going to give you. 22Try to help those who argue against you. Be merciful to those who doubt. 23Save some by snatching them as from the very flames of hell itself. And as for others, help them to find the Lord by being kind to them, but be careful that you yourselves aren't pulled along into their sins. Hate every trace of their sin while being merciful to them as sinners.

1:21
2 Tim 4:8
Tit 2:13
Heb 9:28

1:23
Rom 11:14
1 Cor 5:5
Rev 3:4

24, 25And now—all glory to him who alone is God, who saves us through Jesus Christ our Lord; yes, splendor and majesty, all power and authority are his from the beginning; his they are and his they evermore shall be. And he is able to keep you from slipping and falling away, and to bring you, sinless and perfect, into his glorious presence with mighty shouts of everlasting joy. Amen.

1:24,25
Jn 10:28,29
Rom 14:4; 16:25
2 Cor 4:14
Eph 3:20
1 Pet 4:13

1:14 Enoch is mentioned briefly in Genesis 5:21–24. This quotation is from a book of the Apocrypha called 1 Enoch.

1:14 Other places where Jesus is mentioned as coming with angels are Matthew 16:27 and 24:31. Daniel 7:10 speaks of God judging mankind in the presence of millions of angels.

1:17 Other apostles also warned about false teachers—see Acts 20:29; 1 Timothy 4:1; 2 Timothy 3:1–5; 2 Peter 2:1–3; 2 John 7.

1:18 The "last times" is a common phrase referring to the time between Jesus' first and second comings. We live in the last times.

1:20 To pray in the power and strength of the Holy Spirit means to be guided by the Holy Spirit who prays for us (Romans 8:26, 27), opens our minds to Jesus (John 14:26), and teaches us about him (John 15:26).

1:21 To stay within the boundaries of God's love means to live close to him and his people, not listening to false teachers who would pull us away from him (John 15:9, 10).

1:22, 23 Effective witnessing saves people from God's judgment. Unbelievers, no matter how successful they seem by worldly standards, are lost and in need of salvation. We should not take witnessing lightly—it is a matter of life and death.

1:23 In trying to find common ground with those to whom we witness, we must be careful not to fall into the quicksand of compromise. When reaching out to others, we must be sure our own footing is safe and secure. Be careful not to become so much

like non-Christians that no one can tell who you are or what you believe. Influence them for Christ—don't allow them to influence you to sin!

1:24, 25 As the epistle begins, so it ends—with assurance. God's power enables believers to keep from falling prey to false teachers. Although false teachers are widespread and dangerous, we don't have to be afraid if we trust God and are rooted and grounded in him.

1:24, 25 To be sinless and perfect (literally, "without blemish") will be the ultimate condition of the believer when he or she finally sees Christ face to face. When we are given our new bodies, we will be like Christ (1 John 3:2). Coming into Christ's presence will be more wonderful than we could ever imagine!

1:24, 25 The audience to whom Jude wrote was susceptible to heresies and temptations toward immoral living. He encouraged the believers to remain firm in their faith and trust in God's promises for their future. This was all the more important because they were living in a time of increased apostasy. We too are living in the last days, much closer to the end than were the original readers of this letter. We too are susceptible to doctrinal error. We too are tempted to give in to sin. Although there is much false teaching around us, we need not fear or give up in despair—God can keep us from falling, and if we remain faithful, he guarantees that he will bring us into his presence and give us everlasting joy.

VITAL STATISTICS

PURPOSE:
To reveal the full identity of Christ and to give warning and hope to believers

AUTHOR:
The apostle John

TO WHOM WRITTEN:
The seven churches in Asia and all believers everywhere

DATE WRITTEN:
About A.D. 95, from Patmos

SETTING:
Most scholars believe that the seven churches of Asia to whom John writes were experiencing the persecution which took place under Emperor Domitian (A.D. 90–95). It seems that the Roman authorities had exiled John to the island of Patmos (off the coast of Asia). John, who had been an eyewitness of the incarnate Christ, has a vision of the glorified Christ. God also reveals to him what is to take place in the future—judgment and the ultimate triumph of God over evil.

KEY VERSE:
"If you read this prophecy aloud to the church, you will receive a special blessing from the Lord. Those who listen to it being read and do what it says will also be blessed. For the time is near when these things will all come true" (1:3).

KEY PEOPLE:
John, Jesus

KEY PLACES:
Patmos, the seven churches, the new Jerusalem

SPECIAL FEATURES:
Revelation is written in "apocalyptic" form—a type of Jewish literature which uses symbolic imagery to communicate hope (the ultimate triumph of God) to those in the midst of persecution. The events are ordered according to literary, rather than strictly chronological patterns.

WITH TINY wrinkles and cries, he entered the world and, wrapped in strips of cloth, took his first nap on a bed of straw. Subject to time and parents, he grew to manhood in Roman-occupied Palestine, his gentle hands becoming strong and calloused in Joseph's woodworking shop. As a man, he walked through the countryside and city, touching individuals, preaching to crowds, and training 12 men to carry on his work. At every step he was hounded by those seeking to rid the world of his influence. Finally, falsely accused and tried, he was condemned to a disgraceful execution by foreign hands. And he died—spat upon, cursed, pierced, and hung heavenward for all to deride. Jesus, the God-man, gave his life completely so that all might live.

At God's appointed time, the risen and ascended Lord Jesus will burst onto the world scene. Then everyone will know that Jesus is Lord of the universe! Those who love him will rejoice, greeting their Savior with hearts overflowing into songs of praise. But his enemies will be filled with fear. Allied with Satan, the enemies of Christ will marshal their legions against Christ and his armies. But who can withstand God's wrath? Christ will win the battle and reign victorious forever! Jesus, the humble suffering Servant, is also the powerful, conquering King and Judge.

Revelation is a book of hope. John, the beloved apostle and eyewitness of Jesus, proclaims that their victorious Lord will surely return to vindicate the righteous and judge the wicked. But Revelation is also a book of warning. Things are not as they should be in the churches, so Christ calls them to commit themselves to live in righteousness.

Although Jesus gave this revelation of himself to John nearly 2,000 years ago, it still stands as a warning to God's people today. We can take heart as we understand John's vision of hope—Christ will return to rescue his people and settle accounts with all who defy him.

John begins this book by explaining how he received this revelation from God (1:1–20). He then records specific messages from Jesus to the seven churches in Asia (2:1—3:22). Suddenly the scene shifts, as a mosaic of dramatic and majestic images burst into view before John's eyes. This series of visions portray the future rise of evil, culminating in the Antichrist (4:1—18:24). This is followed by the triumph of the King of kings, the marriage of the Lamb, the final judgment, and the coming of the new Jerusalem (19:1—22:5). Revelation concludes with the promise of Christ's soon return (22:6–21), and John breathes a prayer which has been echoed by Christians through the centuries, "Amen! Come, Lord Jesus!" (22:20).

As you read the book of Revelation, marvel with John at the wondrous panorama of God's revealed plan. Listen as Christ warns the churches, and root out any sin that blocks your relationship with him. Have hope, knowing that God is in control, Christ's victory is assured, and all who trust him will be saved.

THE BLUEPRINT

A. LETTERS TO THE CHURCHES
(1:1—3:22)

The vision John received opens with instructions for him to write to seven churches. He both commends them for their strength and warns them about their flaws. Each letter was directed to a church then in existence, but also represents conditions in the church throughout history. Both in the church and in our individual lives, we must constantly fight against the temptation to become loveless, immoral, lenient, compromising, lifeless, or casual about our faith. The letters make it clear how our Lord feels about these qualities.

B. MESSAGE FOR THE CHURCH
(4:1—22:21)
1. Worshiping God in heaven
2. Breaking the seven seals
3. Sounding the seven trumpets
4. Observing the great conflict
5. Pouring out the seven plagues
6. Seizing the final victory
7. Making all things new

This revelation is both a warning to Christians who have grown apathetic and an encouragement to those who are faithfully enduring the struggles in this world. It reassures us that good will triumph over evil, gives us hope in difficult times, and direction when we are wavering in our faith. Christ's message to the church is a message of hope for all believers in every generation.

MEGATHEMES

THEME	EXPLANATION	IMPORTANCE
God's sovereignty	God is sovereign. He is greater than any power in the universe. God is not to be compared with any leader, government, or religion. He controls history for the purpose of uniting true believers in loving fellowship with him.	Though Satan's power may temporarily increase, we are not to be led astray. God is all-powerful. He is in control. He will safely bring his true family into eternal life. Because he cares for us, we can trust him with our very lives.
Christ's return	Christ came to earth as a "Lamb," the symbol of his perfect sacrifice for our sin. He will return as the triumphant "Lion," the rightful ruler and conqueror. He will defeat Satan, settle accounts with all those who reject him, and bring his faithful people into eternity.	Assurance of Christ's return gives suffering Christians the strength to endure. We can look forward to his return as King and Judge. Since no one knows the time when he will appear, we must be ready at all times by keeping our faith strong.
God's faithful people	John wrote to encourage the church to resist the demands to worship the Roman emperor. He warns all God's faithful people to be devoted only to Christ. Revelation identifies who the faithful people are and what they should be doing until Christ returns.	You can take your place in the ranks of God's faithful people by believing in Christ. Victory is sure for those who resist temptation and make loyalty to Christ their top priority.
Judgment	One day God's anger toward sin will be fully and completely unleashed. Satan will be defeated with all of his agents. False religion will be destroyed. God will reward the faithful with eternal life, but all who refuse to believe in him will face eternal punishment.	Evil and injustice will not prevail forever. God's final judgment will put an end to these. We need to be certain of our commitment to Jesus if we want to escape this great final judgment. No one who is uncommitted to Christ will escape God's punishment.
Hope	One day God will create a new heaven and a new earth. All believers will live with him forever in perfect peace and security. Those who have already died will be raised to life. These promises for the future bring us hope.	Our great hope is that what Christ promises will be true. When we have confidence in our final destination, we can follow Christ with unwavering dedication no matter what we must face. Those facing oppression can be encouraged by hoping in Christ's return.

A. LETTERS TO THE CHURCHES (1:1—3:22)
Near the end of his life, John received a vision from Christ which he recorded for the benefit of the seven churches in Asia and for Christians throughout history. This is the only book in the Bible that promises a blessing to those who listen to its words and do what it says.

1 This book unveils some of the future activities soon to occur in the life of Jesus Christ. God permitted him to reveal these things to his servant John in a vision; and then an angel was sent from heaven to explain the vision's meaning. ²John wrote it all down—the words of God and Jesus Christ and everything he heard and saw.

³If you read this prophecy aloud to the church, you will receive a special blessing from the Lord. Those who listen to it being read and do what it says will also be blessed. For the time is near when these things will all come true.

John's greetings and praise to God
⁴*From:* John

To: The seven churches in Turkey.

Dear Friends:

May you have grace and peace from God who is, and was, and is to come! and from Jesus Christ before his throne; ⁵and from Jesus Christ who faithfully

1:1
Dan 2:28-45
Jn 12:49; 17:8
Rev 1:9; 5:7
17:1
22:6,8,16

1:2
Rev 1:9; 12:17

1:3
Rev 3:11
22:7,10

1:4
Ex 3:14
Zech 3:9; 4:2-6
Rev 3:14; 17:14

1:5
Rev 3:14; 17:14

1:1 *the life of Jesus Christ,* literally, "the revelation of *(concerning,* or *from)* Jesus Christ." **1:4** *in Turkey,* literally, "in Asia." *the seven-fold Spirit,* literally, "the seven Spirits." But see Isa 11:2, where various aspects of the Holy Spirit are described, and Zech 4:2-6, giving probability to the paraphrase; see also 2:7.

1:1 Revelation is a book about the future *and* about the present. It offers future hope to all believers, especially those who have suffered for their faith, by proclaiming Christ's final victory over evil and the reality of eternal life with him. It also gives present guidance as it teaches us about Jesus Christ and how we should live for him now. With graphic pictures we learn that (1) Jesus Christ is coming again, (2) evil will be judged, and (3) the dead will be raised for judgment, resulting in eternal life or eternal destruction.

1:1 According to tradition, John, the author, was the only one of Jesus' original 12 disciples who was not killed for the faith. He also wrote the Gospel of John and the letters of 1, 2, and 3 John. When he wrote Revelation, John was in exile on the island of Patmos in the Aegean Sea, sent there by the Romans for his witness about Jesus Christ. For more information on John, see his Profile in John 13.

1:1 This verse is also translated, "the revelation *of, concerning,* or *from* Jesus Christ." The book of Revelation unveils Christ's full identity and God's plan for the end of the world; it focuses on Jesus Christ, his Second Coming, his victory over evil, and the establishment of his Kingdom. Don't focus so much on the timetable of these events or the details of John's imagery that you miss the main message—the infinite love, power, and justice of the Lord Jesus Christ.

1:1 The book of Revelation is *apocalyptic* (meaning "uncovered," "unveiled," or "revealed") in style. This is a type of ancient literature that usually featured spectacular and mysterious imagery and was written in the name of an ancient hero. John was acquainted with Jewish apocalyptic works, but his book is different in several ways: (1) he uses his own name rather than the name of an ancient hero; (2) he denounces evil and exhorts people to high Christian standards; (3) he offers hope rather than gloom. John was not a psychic attempting to predict the future; he was a prophet of God describing what God showed him.

1:1 For more about angels, see the note on 5:11.

1:1 Jesus gave his message to John in a vision, allowing him to see and record certain future events so they could be an encouragement to all believers. The vision includes many signs and symbols, because they well convey the essence of what is to happen. What John saw, in most cases, was indescribable, so he was given illustrations to show what it was *like.* When reading this

symbolic language, don't think you have to understand every detail—John didn't. Instead, realize that John's imagery is used to show us that Christ is indeed the glorious and victorious Lord of all.

1:1–3 The book of Revelation reveals future events, but there is not the gloomy pessimism we might expect. The drama of these unfolding events is spectacular, but there is nothing to fear if you are on the winning side. When you think about the future, walk with confidence because Christ, the victor, walks with you.

1:3 Revelation is a book of prophecy that is both *prediction* (foretelling future events) and *proclamation* (preaching about who God is and what he will do). Prophecy is more than telling the future. Behind the predictions are important principles about God's character and promises. Each prophecy in this book has present implications—the reader is urged to trust God more and "conquer" sin (see 2:7, 11, 17, 29; 3:5, 12, 21).

1:3 The usual news reports—filled with violence, scandal, and political haggling—are depressing, and many wonder where the world is heading. God's plan for the future, however, provides inspiration and encouragement, because we know he will intervene in history to conquer evil. John encourages churches to read this book aloud so everyone can hear it and be assured of the fact that God will triumph, and that even though they may experience terrible persecution, God will vindicate them.

1:3 When John says, "the time is near when these things will all come true," he is urging his readers to be ready at all times for the last judgment and the establishment of God's Kingdom. We do not know when these events will occur, but we must always be prepared. They will happen quickly, and there will be no second chance to change sides.

1:4 Jesus told John to write to seven churches who knew and trusted him and who had read his earlier letters. The letters were addressed so that they could be read and passed on in a systematic fashion, following the main Roman road clockwise around the province of Asia (now called Turkey).

1:4 The seven-fold Spirit is another name for the Holy Spirit. The number seven is used throughout the Revelation to symbolize completeness and perfection. For more about the Holy Spirit, see the notes on John 3:6 and Acts 1:5.

1:5 The Trinity—the Father, the Son, and the Holy Spirit—is the source of all truth (John 14:6, 17; 1 John 2:27; Revelation 19:11). Thus we can be assured that God's Word is reliable.

1:6
Ex 19:6
Dan 4:34
Rom 11:36
1 Tim 6:16
1 Pet 2:5,9
Jude 24,25

reveals all truth to us. He was the first to rise from death, to die no more. He is far greater than any king in all the earth. All praise to him who always loves us and who set us free from our sins by pouring out his lifeblood for us. 6He has gathered us into his Kingdom and made us priests of God his Father. Give to him everlasting glory! He rules forever! Amen!

A JOURNEY THROUGH THE BOOK OF REVELATION
Revelation is a complex book which has baffled interpreters for centuries. We can avoid a great deal of confusion by understanding the literary structure of this book. This will allow us to understand the individual scenes within the overall structure of Revelation and keep us from getting unnecessarily bogged down in the details of each vision. John gives hints throughout the book which indicate a change of scene, a change of subject, or a flashback to an earlier scene.

In chapter one, John relates the circumstances which led to the writing of this book (1:1–20). In chapters two and three, Jesus gives special messages to the seven churches of Asia Minor (2:1—3:22).

Suddenly John is caught up into heaven where he sees a vision of God Almighty on his throne. All of Christ's followers and the heavenly angels are worshiping him (4:1–11). John watches as God gives a scroll with seven seals to the Worthy Lamb, Jesus Christ, (5:1–14). The Lamb begins to break the seals one by one. As each seal is broken, a new vision appears.

As the first four seals are broken, riders appear on different color horses—war, famine, disease, and death are in their path (6:1–8). As the fifth seal is broken, John sees those in heaven who have been martyred for their faithfulness to Jesus Christ (6:9–11).

A set of contrasting images appears at the breaking of the sixth seal. On one side, there is a huge earthquake, stars falling from the sky, and the heavens rolling up like a scroll (6:12–17). On the other side, multitudes are before the great throne, worshiping and praising God and the Lamb (7:1–17).

Finally, the seventh seal is broken (8:1–5), unveiling a series of God's judgments announced by seven angels with seven trumpets. The first four angels bring hail, fire, a volcano, and a poisonous star—the sun and moon are darkened (8:6–13). The fifth trumpet announces the coming of locusts with the power to sting (9:1–12). The sixth trumpet heralds the coming of an army of warriors on horses (9:13–21). In chapter 10:1–11, John is given a small scroll to eat. Following this, John is commanded to measure the Temple of God (11:1–3). He sees two prophets who proclaim God's judgment on the earth for three and a half years (11:4–13).

Finally the seventh trumpet blasts, calling the rival forces of good and evil to the final battle. On one side is Satan and his forces, on the other side stands Jesus Christ with his forces (11:14—13:18). In the midst of this call to battle, John sees three angels announcing the final judgment (14:1–13). Two angels begin to reap this harvest of judgment upon the earth (14:14–20). Following upon the heels of these two angels are seven more angels who pour out God's judgment upon the earth from seven bowls (15:1—16:21). One of these angels from the group of seven reveals to John a vision of a Prostitute called Babylon (symbolizing the Roman Empire) riding a scarlet animal (17:1–18). After the defeat of Babylon (18:1–24), "a vast crowd in heaven" shout choruses of praise to God for his mighty victory (19:1–21).

The final three chapters of the book of Revelation catalogue the events which finalize Christ's victory over the enemy: Satan's thousand-year imprisonment (20:1–10), the final judgment (20:11–15), the creation of a new earth and a new Jerusalem (21:1—22:5). An angel then gives John final instructions concerning the visions he has seen and what to do once he has written them all down (22:6–11).

Revelation concludes with the promise of Christ's soon return, an offer to drink of the Water of Life which runs through the main street of the new Jerusalem, and a warning to those who read the book (22:12–21). May we pray with John, "Amen! Come, Lord Jesus!" (22:20).

The Bible ends with a message of warning and hope for men and women of every generation. Christ is victorious and all evil has been done away with. As you read the book of Revelation, marvel at God's grace in the salvation of the saints, his power over the evil forces of Satan, and remember the hope of this victory to come.

1:5 Others had risen from the dead—people whom the prophets, Jesus, and the apostles had brought back to life during their ministries—but later these people died again. Jesus was the first who rose from death *to die no more.*

1:5, 6 Many hesitate to share what Christ has done in their lives because they don't feel the change has been spectacular enough. But you qualify as a witness for Jesus because of what he has done for you, not because of what you have done for him. John assures us that Christ has done specific things for each person that can be shared with others. For example, Christ demonstrated

his great love by "setting us free from our sins" through his death on the cross, guaranteeing us a place in his Kingdom, and making us priests to administer God's love to others. The fact that the all-powerful God has offered eternal life to you is nothing short of spectacular.

1:5–9 Jesus is portrayed as an all-powerful King, victorious in battle, glorious in peace. He is not just a humble earthly teacher, but the glorious God. When you read John's description of his vision, keep in mind it is not just good advice, but truth from the King of Kings. Let it penetrate your life.

7See! He is arriving, surrounded by clouds; and every eye shall see him—yes, and those who pierced him. And the nations will weep in sorrow and in terror when he comes. Yes! Amen! Let it be so!

1:7
Dan 7:13
Zech 12:10
Jn 19:36,37

8"I am the A and the Z, the Beginning and the Ending of all things," says God, who is the Lord, the All Powerful One who is, and was, and is coming again!

1:8
Isa 41:4; 48:12
Rev 21:6; 22:13

The vision of Christ

9It is I, your brother John, a fellow sufferer for the Lord's sake, who am writing this letter to you. I, too, have shared the patience Jesus gives, and we shall share his Kingdom!

1:9
Rom 8:17
2 Thess 3:5
Rev 1:6; 3:10

I was on the island of Patmos, exiled there for preaching the Word of God, and

1:8 *I am the A and the Z,* literally, "I am Alpha and Omega." *is coming again,* literally, "who comes" or "who is to come."

Approach	Description	Challenge	Caution	INTERPRETING THE BOOK OF REVELATION
PRETERIST VIEW	John is writing to encourage Christians in his own day who are experiencing persecution from the Roman Empire.	To gain the same kind of encouragement John's first readers gained from the vivid images of God's sovereignty.	Do not forget that most biblical prophecy has both an immediate and future application.	Over the centuries, four main approaches to interpreting the book of Revelation have developed.
FUTURIST VIEW	Except for the first three chapters, John is describing events which will occur at the end of history.	To see in contemporary events many of the characteristics John describes and realize the end could come at any time.	Do not assume that we have "figured out" the future, since Jesus said no man will know the day of his return before it happens.	Each approach has had capable supporters, but none has proved itself the only way to read this book.
HISTORICIST VIEW	The book of Revelation is a presentation of history from John's day until the Second Coming of Christ and beyond.	To note the consistency of man's evil throughout history and recognize that names may change but the rebellion against God has not.	Be careful before identifying current events or leaders as fulfilling aspects of the book of Revelation.	However, the most basic application question for each approach can be summarized by asking yourself, "Will this help me become a better follower of Jesus Christ today?"
IDEALIST VIEW	The book of Revelation is a symbolic representation of the continual struggle of good and evil. It does not refer to any particular historical events. It is applicable at any point in history.	Read the book to gain insight into the past, prepare for the future, and to live obediently and confidently in the present.	Do not avoid the book because it is difficult. Try to understand Revelation within its broader literary context.	

1:7 John is announcing the return of Jesus to earth (see also Matthew 24; Mark 13; 1 Thessalonians 4:15–18). Jesus' Second Coming will be *visible* and *victorious*. All people will see him arrive (Mark 13:26), and they will *know* it is Jesus. When he comes, he will conquer evil and judge all people according to their deeds (20:11–15).

1:7 "Those who pierced him" could refer to the Roman soldiers who pierced Jesus' side as he hung on the cross or to the Jews who were responsible for his death. John saw this event with his own eyes, and he never forgot the horror of it (see John 19:34, 35; Zechariah 12:10).

1:8 Jesus is the A and the Z (also translated, "the Alpha and Omega," the first and last letters of the Greek alphabet)—the beginning and the end. Jesus is the eternal Lord and Ruler of the past, present, and future (see also 4:8; Isaiah 44:6; 48:12–15). Without him you have nothing that is eternal, nothing that can change your life, nothing that can save you from sin. Is Christ your reason for living, the "first and last" of your life? Honor the One who is the beginning and the end of all existence.

1:9 Patmos was a small rocky island in the Aegean Sea, about 50 miles offshore from the city of Ephesus on the Asia Minor seacoast (see map).

1:9 John describes himself as a "fellow sufferer for the Lord's sake," indicating that the church was undergoing intense persecution as he was writing this letter. The whole church, as the body of Christ, should experience joy and suffering together. Follow John's example in your relationships with other Christians: identify with them, encourage them to be steadfast and faithful, and remind them of their future reward with God (see also Romans 5:2–4).

1:9 The Christian church was facing severe persecution— almost all believers were victims of suffering in some way because of this empire-wide persecution. Some were even being killed for their faith. John was exiled to Patmos because he refused to stop preaching the Word of God. We may not face such persecution for our faith in Jesus, but few of us have the courage even now to share God's Word with others. If we are afraid to share our faith during easy times, how will we do during times of persecution?

1:10
Rev 4:1,2
21:10

1:11
Rev 1:2,19
2:1,18,24
3:1,4,7,14

1:12
Zech 4:2-6

1:13
Dan 10:5,6
Rev 2:1; 14:14

1:14
Dan 7:9,10
Rev 2:18; 19:12

1:15
Dan 10:6

1:16
Rev 1:20; 2:12
10:1; 19:15

for telling what I knew about Jesus Christ. ¹⁰It was the Lord's Day and I was worshiping, when suddenly I heard a loud voice behind me, a voice that sounded like a trumpet blast, ¹¹saying, "I am A and Z, the First and Last!" And then I heard him say, "Write down everything you see, and send your letter to the seven churches in Turkey: to the church in Ephesus, the one in Smyrna, and those in Pergamos, Thyatira, Sardis, Philadelphia, and Laodicea."

¹²When I turned to see who was speaking, there behind me were seven candlesticks of gold. ¹³And standing among them was one who looked like Jesus who called himself the Son of Man, wearing a long robe circled with a golden band across his chest. ¹⁴His hair was white as wool or snow, and his eyes penetrated like flames of fire. ¹⁵His feet gleamed like burnished bronze, and his voice thundered like the waves against the shore. ¹⁶He held seven stars in his right hand and a sharp, double-bladed sword in his mouth, and his face shone like the power of the sun in unclouded brilliance.

1:11 in Turkey, "in Asia." **1:13** like Jesus who called himself the Son of Man, literally, "like unto a Son of Man." **1:14** His hair, literally, "His head—the hair—was white like wool." **1:16** in his mouth, literally, "coming out from his mouth."

THE SEVEN CHURCHES
The seven churches were located on a major Roman road. A letter carrier would leave the island of Patmos (where John was exiled), arriving first at Ephesus. He would travel north to Smyrna and Pergamum (Pergamos), turn southeast to Thyatira, and continue on to Sardis, Philadelphia, and Laodicea—in the exact order in which the letters were dictated.

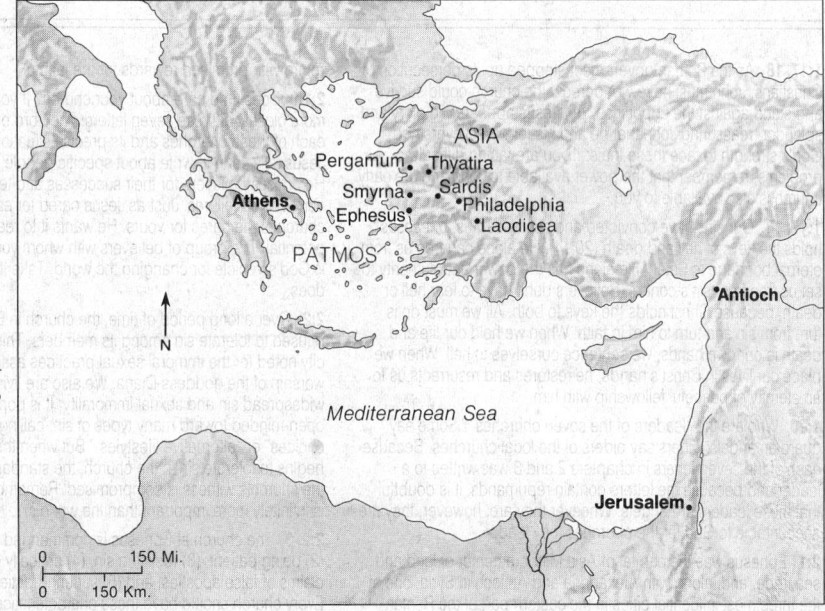

1:13 This man who "looked like Jesus" is Jesus himself. The title *Son of Man* occurs many times in the New Testament in reference to Jesus as the Messiah. John recognized Jesus because he lived with him for three years and had seen him both as the Galilean preacher and as the glorified Son of God at the transfiguration (Matthew 17:1–8). Here Jesus appears as the mighty Son of Man. His white hair indicates his wisdom and divine nature (see Daniel 7:9); his piercing eyes symbolize judgment of all evil; the golden band reveals him as the High Priest who goes into God's presence to plead forgiveness for those who have believed in him.

1:13ff Many of the details in this vision of the Son of Man recur throughout the remainder of the book (especially in the letters to the seven churches, Revelation 2—3). The repetition of these

details reminds the reader that the Son of Man is directly involved in judgment and deliverance.

1:13, 14 The seven candlesticks are the seven churches in Turkey (1:20), and Jesus stands among them. No matter what the churches face, Jesus walks among them with reassuring love and fearsome power. Through his Spirit, Jesus Christ is still among the churches today. When a church faces persecution, it should remember his deep love and care. When a church is wracked by internal strife and conflict, it should remember his concern for purity and his intolerance of sin.

1:16 The sword in Jesus' mouth symbolizes the power and force of his message. His words of judgment are sharp as swords (Isaiah 49:2; Hebrews 4:12).

17, 18When I saw him, I fell at his feet as dead; but he laid his right hand on me and said, "Don't be afraid! Though I am the First and Last, the Living One who died, who is now alive forevermore, who has the keys of hell and death—don't be afraid! 19Write down what you have just seen, and what will soon be shown to you. 20This is the meaning of the seven stars you saw in my right hand, and the seven golden candlesticks: The seven stars are the leaders of the seven churches, and the seven candlesticks are the churches themselves.

1:17,18
Isa 41:4
Ezek 1:27,28
Dan 8:17,18
10:8,9,17-19
Lk 24:5
Rev 2:8
1:20
Zech 4:2
Rev 1:4,11,16
2:1; 3:1

The loveless church

2 "Write a letter to the leader of the church at Ephesus and tell him this:
"I write to inform you of a message from him who walks among the churches and holds their leaders in his right hand.

"He says to you: 2I know how many good things you are doing. I have watched your hard work and your patience; I know you don't tolerate sin among your members, and you have carefully examined the claims of those who say they are apostles but aren't. You have found out how they lie. 3You have patiently suffered for me without quitting.

4"Yet there is one thing wrong; you don't love me as at first! 5Think about those

2:1
Rev 1:11-16
2:2
2 Cor 11:13
1 Jn 4:1
Rev 2:19
2:3
Jn 15:21
Heb 12:1-13
2:4
Jer 2:2
2:5
Hos 14:1
Rev 1:20; 3:3,19

1:20 leaders, literally, "angels." **2:1** leader, literally, "angel" and so also in 2:8; 2:12; 2:18; 3:1; 3:7; 3:14. from him who walks among the churches, literally, "from him who holds the seven stars in his right hand and walks among the golden candlesticks."

1:17, 18 As the Roman government stepped up its persecution of Christians, John must have wondered if the church could survive and stand against the opposition. But Jesus appeared in glory and splendor, reassuring John that he and his fellow believers had God's strength to face these trials. If you are facing difficult problems, remember that the power available to John and the early church is also available to you.

1:17, 18 Our sins have convicted and sentenced us, but Jesus holds the keys of hell and death (20:14). He alone can free us from eternal bondage to Satan. He alone has the power and authority to set us free from sin's control. Believers don't have to fear hell or death, because Christ holds the keys to both. All we must do is turn from sin and turn to him in faith. When we hold our life and death in our own hands, we sentence ourselves to hell. When we place our lives in Christ's hands, he restores and resurrects us to an eternity of peaceful fellowship with him.

1:20 Who are the "leaders of the seven churches"? Some say guardian angels; others say elders of the local churches. Because each of the seven letters in chapters 2 and 3 was written to a leader and because the letters contain reprimands, it is doubtful that these leaders are angels. Whoever they are, however, they are accountable to God for the churches they lead.

2:1 Ephesus was the capital of Asia Minor, a center of land and sea trade, and, along with Alexandria and Antioch in Syria, one of the three most influential cities in the eastern part of the Roman Empire. The Temple to Diana, one of the ancient wonders of the world, was located in this city, and a major industry was the manufacture of idols of this goddess (see Acts 19:21–41). Pau had ministered in Ephesus for three years and had warned the Ephesians that false teachers would come and try to draw people away from the faith (see Acts 20:29–31). False teachers did indeed cause problems in the Ephesian church (see Ephesians 4:14; 1 Timothy 1:3,4), but the church resisted them as we can see from Paul's letter to them. John spent much of his ministry in this city and knew they had resisted false teaching (2:2).

2:1 The one who "walks among the churches" is Jesus (1:11–13). He holds the leaders of the churches "in his right hand," indicating his power and authority over the churches and their leaders. Ephesus had become a large, proud church, and Jesus' message reminds them that he is the head of the body of believers.

2:1ff Each of the letters to the seven churches basically follows a set form: salutation, evaluation (commendation and/or condemnation), exhortation, and a declaration of Christ's

return with promised rewards for the faithful.

2:1ff Does God care about your church? If you don't think so, look more closely at these seven letters. The Lord of the universe knew each of these churches and its precise situation. In each letter, Jesus tells John to write about specific people, places, and events. He praises believers for their successes and tells them how to correct their failures. Just as Jesus cared for each of these churches, he cares for yours. He wants it to reach its greatest potential. The group of believers with whom you worship and pray is God's vehicle for changing the world. Take it seriously—God does.

2:2 Over a long period of time, the church in Ephesus had refused to tolerate sin among its members. This was not easy in a city noted for the immoral sexual practices associated with the worship of the goddess Diana. We also are living in times of widespread sin and sexual immorality. It is popular to be open-minded toward many types of sin, calling them "personal choices" or "alternative lifestyles." But when the body of believers begins to tolerate sin in the church, the standards are lowered and the church's witness is compromised. Remember, God's approval is infinitely more important than the world's.

2:2, 3 The church at Ephesus is commended for (1) working hard, (2) being patient, (3) resisting sin, (4) critically examining the claims of false apostles, and (5) suffering patiently without quitting. Every church should have these characteristics. But these good things should spring from our love for Jesus Christ. The Ephesians had lost their first love, and they may have been in danger of falling into legalism. The spiritual life of the Ephesian church had become sterile. They had lost their "first love." Jesus describes this "first love" in his summary of the law in Matthew 22:37–40, "'Love the Lord your God with all your heart, soul, and mind.' This is the first and greatest commandment." Because the Ephesian Christians had failed to love God above all else, they were under God's condemnation (2:5).

2:4 The church at Ephesus was once commended for its love for God and others (Ephesians 3:17–19), but many of the church founders had died, and the second-generation believers had lost their zeal for God. They were a busy church—they did much to benefit the church and the community—but they were acting for the wrong reasons. Work for God is not lasting unless it is based on love for God and others.

2:4, 5 As when a man and woman fall in love, new believers experience enthusiasm when they realize how important it is to be

2:6
Num 31:15,16
Rev 2:15

2:7
Gen 2:9
3:22-24
Prov 3:18
11:30; 13:12
Rev 22:2,14

times of your first love (how different now!) and turn back to me again and work as you did before; or else I will come and remove your candlestick from its place among the churches.

6"But there is this about you that is good: You hate the deeds of the licentious Nicolaitans, just as I do.

7"Let this message sink into the ears of anyone who listens to what the Spirit is saying to the churches: To everyone who is victorious, I will give fruit from the Tree of Life in the Paradise of God.

~ The persecuted church

2:8
Rev 1:8,11,
17,18

2:9
Rev 1:9
2:13,24

8*"To the leader of the church in Smyrna write this letter:*

"This message is from him who is the First and Last, who was dead and then came back to life.

9"I know how much you suffer for the Lord, and I know all about your poverty

THE NAMES OF JESUS	Reference	Jesus' name		Reference	Jesus' name
	1:8	A to Z, Beginning to End		5:5	Root of David
	1:8	Lord		5:6	Lamb
	1:8	All-Powerful One		7:17	Shepherd
	1:13	Son of Man		12:10	Christ
	1:18	First and Last		19:11	Faithful and True
	1:18	The Living One		19:13	Word of God
	2:18	Son of God		19:16	King of Kings
	3:14	Witness		19:16	Lord of Lords
	4:11	Creator		22:16	The Morning Star
	5:5	Lion of Judah			

Scattered among the vivid images of the book of Revelation is a large collection of names for Jesus. Each one tells something of his character and highlights a particular aspect of his role within God's plan of redemption.

forgiven. But when we lose sight of the seriousness of sin, we begin to lose the thrill of our forgiveness (see 2 Peter 1:9). In the first steps of your Christian life, you may have had enthusiasm without knowledge. Do you now have knowledge without enthusiasm? Both are necessary if we are to keep love for God and others intense and untarnished (see Hebrews 10:32, 35). Do you love God with the same fervor as when you were a new Christian?

2:5 To have the "candlestick" removed from its place among the churches means to cease (1) to be an effective church or (2) to be a church at all. Just as the seven-branched candlestick in the Temple gave light for the priests to see by, the churches were to give light to their surrounding communities. But Jesus warned them that their lights could go out. In fact, Jesus himself would extinguish any light that did not fulfill its purpose.

2:6 The Nicolaitans were believers who compromised their faith in order to enjoy some of the sinful practices of Ephesian society. They falsely called themselves "apostles" (2:2). The name *Nicolaitans,* may have come from the Hebrew word for "Balaamites." Balaam was a prophet who induced the Israelites to carry out their lustful desires (see 2:14 and Numbers 31:15, 16). When we want to take part in something we know is wrong, we often make excuses to justify our behavior, saying that it isn't as bad as it seems or it won't hurt our faith. Are you tempted to compromise your faith in order to be accepted by non-Christians? Christ has strong words for those who look for excuses to sin.

2:6 Through John, Jesus commends the church at Ephesus for hating the wicked deeds of the Nicolaitans. Note that they didn't hate the people, just their sinful actions. Accept and love all people, and refuse to tolerate all evil. God cannot tolerate sin, and he expects us to stand against it. The world needs Christians who will stand for God's truth and point people toward right living.

2:7 To be victorious means to believe, persevere, remain faithful, and live as one who follows Christ. Doing so brings great rewards (21:7).

2:7 In the Garden of Eden were two trees—the Tree of Life and the Tree of Conscience (see Genesis 2:9). Eating from the Tree of Life brought eternal life with God; eating from the Tree of Conscience brought knowledge of good and evil. Adam and Eve ate from the Tree of Conscience, which God had forbidden them to do, so they were excluded from Eden and barred from eating from the Tree of Life. Eventually, evil will be destroyed and believers will be brought into a restored paradise. In the new earth, no Tree of Conscience will tempt people to sin. Instead, everyone will eat from the Tree of Life and will live eternally.

~ **2:8** The city of Smyrna was about 25 miles north of Ephesus. It was nicknamed "Port of Asia" because it had an excellent harbor on the Aegean Sea. The church in this city struggled against two hostile forces: a Jewish population strongly opposed to Christianity, and a non-Jewish population that was loyal to Rome and supported emperor worship. Persecution and suffering were inevitable in an environment like this.

2:9-11 Everyone would like to feel good and live comfortably, but pain is part of life—and it is not easy to suffer, no matter what the cause. Jesus commended the church at Smyrna for their faith in the midst of suffering. He then encouraged them that they need not fear the future if they remained faithful. In fact, Smyrna and Philadelphia were the only churches among the seven to receive completely positive messages. If you are experiencing difficult times, don't let them turn you away from God. Instead let them draw you toward greater faithfulness. Trust him and remember your heavenly reward (see also 22:12-14). God is especially near to those who suffer for him.

(but you have heavenly riches!). I know the slander of those opposing you, who say that they are Jews—the children of God—but they aren't, for they support the cause of Satan. [10]Stop being afraid of what you are about to suffer—for the devil will soon throw some of you into prison to test you. You will be persecuted for 'ten days.' Remain faithful even when facing death and I will give you the crown of life—an unending, glorious future. [11]Let everyone who can hear, listen to what the Spirit is saying to the churches: He who is victorious shall not be hurt by the Second Death.

2:10
Dan 1:12,14
3:16-18
1 Cor 9:25
Jas 1:12
Rev 3:10; 12:11
17:14
2:11
Rev 2:7,29
20:6,14

The lenient church

[12]*"Write this letter to the leader of the church in Pergamos:*

"This message is from him who wields the sharp and double-bladed sword. [13]I am fully aware that you live in the city where Satan's throne is, at the center of satanic worship; and yet you have remained loyal to me, and refused to deny me, even when Antipas, my faithful witness, was martyred among you by Satan's devotees.

[14]"And yet I have a few things against you. You tolerate some among you who do as Balaam did when he taught Balak how to ruin the people of Israel by involving them in sexual sin and encouraging them to go to idol feasts. [15]Yes, you have some of these very same followers of Balaam among you!

[16]"Change your mind and attitude, or else I will come to you suddenly and fight against them with the sword of my mouth.

[17]"Let everyone who can hear, listen to what the Spirit is saying to the churches:

2:12
Rev 1:16; 2:16
2:13
Rev 14:12
2:14
Num 31:16
1 Cor 6:13-20
2 Pet 2:15
Rev 2:20
2:15
Rev 2:6
2:16
2 Thess 2:8
Rev 1:16; 2:5
22:7
2:17
Jn 6:49-58
Rev 2:7; 14:3
19:12

2:10 *an unending, glorious future,* implied.   2:15 *Balaam,* literally, "Nicolaitans," Greek form of "Balaamites."

2:10 Persecution comes from Satan, not from God. Satan, the devil, will cause believers to be thrown into prison and even killed. But believers need not fear death, because it will only result in their receiving the crown of life. Satan may harm their earthly bodies, but he can do them no spiritual harm. "Ten days" means that although persecution will be intense, it will be relatively short. It has a definite beginning and end, and God remains in complete control.

2:10 The message to the church of Smyrna is to remain faithful throughout their suffering because God is in control and his promises are reliable. Jesus never says that by being faithful to him we will avoid troubles, suffering, and persecution. Rather, we must be faithful to him *in* our sufferings. Only then will our faith prove itself genuine. We remain faithful by keeping our eyes on Christ and on what he promises for us now and in the future (see Philippians 3:13, 14; 2 Timothy 4:8).

2:11 Believers and unbelievers alike experience physical death. All people will be resurrected, but believers will be resurrected to eternal life with God while unbelievers will be resurrected to be punished with a Second Death and eternal separation from God (see also 20:14; 21:8, 27; 22:15).

2:12 The city of Pergamos was built on a hill 1,000 feet above the surrounding countryside, creating a natural fortress. It was a sophisticated city, a center of Greek culture and education, with a 200,000-volume library. But it was also the center of four cults, and it rivaled Ephesus in its worship of idols. The city's chief god was a serpent, who was considered the god of healing. People came to Pergamos from all over the world to seek healing from this god.

2:12 Just as the Romans used their swords for authority and judgment, Jesus' sharp, double-bladed sword (1:16) represents God's ultimate authority and judgment. It may also represent God's future separation of believers from unbelievers. Unbelievers cannot experience the eternal rewards of living in God's Kingdom.

2:13 As the center for four idolatrous cults, Pergamos is called "the city where Satan's throne is." Surrounded by Satan worship, the church at Pergamos refused to deny Christ even when Satan's worshipers martyred one of their members. Perhaps the

Nicolaitans taught that it was alright for Christians to participate in these idolatrous rituals on the grounds that "no one believes in it anyway and it is just good citizenship." We, like Pergamos, must "remain loyal" to Christ against similar attempts to rationalize sin. Standing firm against Satan's attractive temptations is never easy, but the alternative is deadly (2:11).

2:14 There is room for differences of opinion among Christians in some areas, but there is no room for heresy and moral impurity. Your town may not participate in idol feasts, but it probably has pornography, sexual sin, cheating, gossiping, and lying. Don't tolerate sin under the pressure to be open-minded.

2:14, 15 It was not easy to be a Christian in Pergamos. Believers experienced great pressure to compromise or leave the faith. Nothing is known about Antipas except that he did *not* compromise. He was faithful, and he died for his faith. Apparently, however, some in the church were tolerating those who taught or practiced what Christ opposed. Compromise can be defined as "blending qualities of two different things," or "a concession of principles." When evil is mixed with good, the good is no longer pure. Don't allow compromise to taint your faith.

2:14–16 Balak was a king who feared the large number of Israelites traveling through his country, so he hired Balaam to pronounce a curse on them. Balaam refused at first, but an offer of money changed his mind (Numbers 22—24). Later he influenced the Israelites to turn to idol worship (Numbers 31:16; also see 2 Peter 2:15; Jude 1:11). Here Christ rebukes the church for tolerating those who, like Balaam, lead people away from God.

2:16 This sword is God's judgment against rebellious nations (19:15, 21) and all forms of sin. See also the note on 2:12.

2:17 "Hidden manna" suggests the spiritual nourishment the faithful believers will receive. As the Israelites traveled toward the Promised Land, God provided manna from heaven for their physical nourishment (Exodus 16:14–18). Jesus, as "the Bread of Life" (John 6:51), provides spiritual nourishment that satisfies our deepest hunger.

2:17 It is unclear what the white stones are or exactly what the names on each will be, but since they are probably related to the

Every one who is victorious shall eat of the hidden manna, the secret nourishment from heaven; and I will give to each a white stone, and on the stone will be engraved a new name that no one else knows except the one receiving it.

The compromising church

18 *"Write this letter to the leader of the church in Thyatira:*

"This is a message from the Son of God, whose eyes penetrate like flames of fire, whose feet are like glowing brass.

19"I am aware of all your good deeds—your kindness to the poor, your gifts and service to them; also I know your love and faith and patience, and I can see your constant improvement in all these things.

20"Yet I have this against you: You are permitting that woman Jezebel, who calls herself a prophetess, to teach my servants that sex sin is not a serious matter; she urges them to practice immorality and to eat meat that has been sacrificed to idols. 21I gave her time to change her mind and attitude, but she refused. 22Pay attention now to what I am saying: I will lay her upon a sickbed of intense affliction, along with all her immoral followers, unless they turn again to me, repenting of their sin with her; 23and I will strike her children dead. And all the churches shall know that I am he who searches deep within men's hearts, and minds; I will give to each of you whatever you deserve.

24, 25"As for the rest of you in Thyatira who have not followed this false teaching ('deeper truths,' as they call them—depths of Satan, really), I will ask nothing further of you; only hold tightly to what you have until I come.

26"To every one who overcomes—who to the very end keeps on doing things that please me—I will give power over the nations. 27You will rule them with a rod of iron just as my Father gave me the authority to rule them; they will be shattered like

2:22 *along with all her immoral followers,* literally, "together with all those who commit adultery with her."

2:18
Rev 1:11,14
2:24

2:19
Rev 2:2
2:20
1 Kgs 16:31
2 Kgs 9:7
2:21
Rev 9:20
2:22
Rev 17:2
2:23
Mt 16:27
Lk 16:15
2:24
Rev 2:18; 3:11
2:25
Rev 3:11
2:26
Dan 7:22
Mt 10:22; 19:28
Lk 22:29,30
1 Cor 6:3,4
Rev 2:7; 3:21
20:4
2:27
Ps 2:8,9
Rev 12:5

---

hidden manna, they may indicate that the individual believer receives eternal "nourishment," or eternal life. In Roman times, stones were given to people to designate a person's right to enter a banquet (similar to our engraved invitations today). The imagery here calls to mind the messianic banquet (19:7). The stones are significant because each will bear the new name of every person who truly believes in Christ. They are the evidence that a person has been accepted by God and declared worthy to receive eternal life. A person's name represented his character. God will give us new names and new hearts.

2:18 Thyatira was a working man's town, with many trade guilds for cloth-making, dyeing, and pottery. Lydia, Paul's first convert in Philippi, was a merchant from Thyatira (Acts 16:14). The city was basically secular, with no focus on any particular religion.

2:19 The believers in Thyatira were commended for growing in good deeds. We should not feel satisfied when we have done one good work, but continue to do more. These are the last days, and there is no time to rest on our laurels.

2:20 A woman in the church in Thyatira was teaching that immorality was not a serious matter for believers. Her name may have been Jezebel, or John may have used the name Jezebel to symbolize the kind of wrong she was doing. Jezebel, a heathen queen of Israel, was considered the most evil woman who had ever lived (see 1 Kings 19:1, 2; 21:1–15; 2 Kings 9:7–10, 30–37; and her Profile in 1 Kings 21).

2:20 Why is sex sin serious? Sex outside marriage always hurts someone. It hurts God because it shows we prefer to follow our own desires instead of God's Word. It hurts others because it violates the commitment so necessary to a relationship. It hurts us because it often brings disease to our bodies and adversely affects our personalities (see 1 Corinthians 6:12–20). Sex sin has tremendous power to destroy families, communities, and even nations, because it destroys the relationships upon which these institutions are built. God wants to protect us from hurting

ourselves and others; thus we are to have no part in sex sin, even if our culture accepts it.

2:20 In heathen temples, meat was often offered to idols. Then the meat that wasn't burned was sold to shoppers in the temple marketplace. Taking meat offered to idols wasn't wrong in itself, but it could violate the principle of sensitivity toward weaker Christian brothers and sisters who would be bothered by it (see 1 Corinthians 8 and the note on Romans 14:2). Jezebel was obviously more concerned about her own selfish pleasure and freedom than about the needs and concerns of fellow believers.

2:21 Obedience to Christ always involves a change of attitudes. When we are converted, a battle begins inside us as Satan tries to keep us from changing. John records this example from Jezebel's life to show the importance of changes in attitude. Our attitudes powerfully influence our behavior. Which of your attitudes would Jesus highlight as needing change? If you're having trouble doing right in an area of your life, perhaps you need a change of attitude.

2:23 The very things we try to hide from God are the sins that need to be confessed to him instead. We cannot hide from Christ, because he knows what is in our hearts. Jesus will judge both our motives and actions.

2:24, 25 Christ told the believers in Thyatira to hold on to their faith and let God's Word be their guide. Likewise, we should hold tightly to the Bible to avoid the many errors set forth as "deeper truths." We can do this by listening carefully to teaching and preaching in church and by reading the Bible daily.

2:26, 27 Christ says that the victorious ones (those who remain faithful until the end and continue to please him) will rule over his enemies and reign with him as he judges evil. We will participate in God's judgment of evil when his enemies are "shattered like a clay pot when it is dashed to the ground" (see also Psalm 2:8, 9; Isaiah 30:14; Jeremiah 19:11; 1 Corinthians 6:2, 3; 12:5; 19:15; 20:3, 4 for more about God's judgment).

a pot of clay that is broken into tiny pieces. 28And I will give you the Morning Star! 29"Let all who can hear, listen to what the Spirit says to the churches.

2:28
2 Pet 1:19
Rev 22:16

The lifeless church

3 *"To the leader of the church in Sardis write this letter:* "This message is sent to you by the one who has the seven-fold Spirit of God and the seven stars.

3:1
Rev 1:4,11,16
3:8,15

"I know your reputation as a live and active church, but you are dead. 2Now wake up! Strengthen what little remains—for even what is left is at the point of death. Your deeds are far from right in the sight of God. 3Go back to what you heard and believed at first; hold to it firmly and turn to me again. Unless you do, I will come suddenly upon you, unexpected as a thief, and punish you.

3:3
Mt 24:42,43
1 Thess 5:2-6
1 Pet 3:10
Rev 2:5; 16:15

3:4
Rev 3:5; 4:4
6:11; 19:14

4"Yet even there in Sardis some haven't soiled their garments with the world's filth; they shall walk with me in white, for they are worthy. 5Everyone who conquers will be clothed in white, and I will not erase his name from the Book of Life, but I will announce before my Father and his angels that he is mine.

3:5
Ps 49:28
Mt 10:32
Lk 10:20; 12:8
Rev 13:8; 17:8
20:12

6"Let all who can hear, listen to what the Spirit is saying to the churches.

3:6
Rev 2:7

The obedient church

7"Write this letter to the leader of the church in Philadelphia.

"This message is sent to you by the one who is holy and true, and has the key of David to open what no one can shut and to shut what no one can open.

3:7
Isa 6:3; 22:22
Mt 16:19

8"I know you well; you aren't strong, but you have tried to obey and have not denied my Name. Therefore I have opened a door to you that no one can shut.

3:8
Acts 14:27
Rev 2:13

9"Note this: I will force those supporting the causes of Satan while claiming to be mine (but they aren't—they are lying) to fall at your feet and acknowledge that you are the ones I love.

3:9
Rev 2:9

3:10
2 Tim 2:12
2 Pet 2:9
Rev 2:10; 3:8

10"Because you have patiently obeyed me despite the persecution, therefore I will protect you from the time of Great Tribulation and temptation, which will come upon the world to test everyone alive. 11Look, I am coming soon! Hold

3:11
Rev 2:10,25
22:7,12,20

3:8 *you have tried to obey,* literally, "you have kept my word." **3:9** *while claiming to be mine,* literally, "say they are Jews but are not." **3:11** *soon,* or, "suddenly," "unexpectedly."

2:28 Christ is called the Morning Star in 2 Peter 1:19 and Revelation 2:28 and 22:16. A morning star appears just before dawn, when things are coldest and darkest. When the world is at its bleakest point, Christ will burst onto the scene, exposing evil with his light of truth and bringing his promised reward.

3:1 The wealthy city of Sardis was actually in two locations. The older section of the city was on the mountain, and, when its population outgrew it, a newer section was built in the valley below.

3:1 The seven-fold Spirit of God is another name for the Holy Spirit (see the note on 1:4).

3:1 The problem in the church of Sardis was not heresy, but spiritual death. In spite of its reputation for being active, Sardis was infested with sin. Its deeds were evil and its garments soiled. The Spirit has no words of commendation for this church that looks good on the outside but is corrupt on the inside.

3:3 The church at Sardis was urged to hold on to the Christian truth they had heard when they first believed in Christ, to get back to the basics of the faith. It is important to grow in our knowledge of the Lord, to deepen our understanding through careful study. But no matter how much we learn, we must never abandon the basic truths about Jesus. Jesus will always be God's Son, and his sacrifice for our sins is permanent. No new truth from God will ever contradict these biblical teachings.

3:5 The Book of Life is where the names of all believers are registered. It symbolizes God's knowledge of who belongs to him. "Clothed in white" means set apart for God and made pure. Christ promises future honor and eternal life to those who stand firm in their faith. They will be guaranteed a listing in the Book of Life and

introduced to the hosts of heaven as ones who belong to Christ.

3:7 Philadelphia was founded by the citizens of Pergamos. The community was built in a frontier area as a gateway to the central plateau of Asia Minor. Philadelphia kept barbarians out of the region and brought in Greek culture and language. The city was destroyed by an earthquake in A.D. 17, and aftershocks kept the people so worried that most of them lived outside the city limits.

3:7 The key of David represents Christ's authority to open the door of invitation into his future Kingdom. After it is open, no one can close it—salvation is assured. Once it is closed, no one can open it—judgment is certain.

3:8 Philadelphia was a small church with little status or influence. However, the Philadelphian church was faithful to God, and he was pleased with them (Smyrna and Philadelphia were the only churches to receive completely positive messages from Christ). God would vindicate them for their faithfulness. If we feel insignificant, we should remember that God wants faithfulness more than worldly success. It isn't what we *accomplish* but what we *are* that really counts with God.

3:10 "I will protect you from the time of Great Tribulation" can also be translated, "I will keep you from failing in the hour of testing." Some believe there will be a future time of great tribulation from which true believers will be spared. Others interpret this to mean that the church will go through the time of tribulation and that God will keep them strong in spite of it. Still others believe this refers to "times of great tribulation" in general, the church's suffering through the ages. Whatever the case, the emphasis is on patiently obeying God through suffering.

tightly to the little strength you have—so that no one will take away your crown.

¹²"As for the one who conquers, I will make him a pillar in the temple of my God; he will be secure, and will go out no more; and I will write my God's Name on him, and he will be a citizen in the city of my God—the New Jerusalem, coming down from heaven from my God; and he will have my new Name inscribed upon him.

¹³"Let all who can hear, listen to what the Spirit is saying to the churches.

The lukewarm church

¹⁴*"Write this letter to the leader of the church in Laodicea:*

"This message is from the one who stands firm, the faithful and true Witness [of all that is or was or evermore shall be], the primeval source of God's creation:

¹⁵"I know you well—you are neither hot nor cold; I wish you were one or the other! ¹⁶But since you are merely lukewarm, I will spit you out of my mouth!

¹⁷"You say, 'I am rich, with everything I want; I don't need a thing!' And you don't realize that spiritually you are wretched and miserable and poor and blind and naked.

¹⁸"My advice to you is to buy pure gold from me, gold purified by fire—only then will you truly be rich. And to purchase from me white garments, clean and pure, so you won't be naked and ashamed; and to get medicine from me to heal your eyes and give you back your sight. ¹⁹I continually discipline and punish everyone I love; so I must punish you, unless you turn from your indifference and become enthusiastic about the things of God.

²⁰"Look! I have been standing at the door and I am constantly knocking. If

3:14 *from the one who stands firm,* literally, *"from the Amen." of all that is evermore shall be,* implied.

Cross-references (left margin):
3:12 1 Kgs 7:21; Jer 1:18; Ezek 48:35; Gal 4:26,27; Eph 3:15; Heb 12:22; Rev 14:1,21; 21:2; 22:4
3:14 Jn 1:3; 2 Cor 1:20; Col 1:15-18; Rev 1:5; 21:6
3:15 Rom 12:11; Rev 3:1
3:17 Hos 12:8; Zech 11:5; Mt 5:3; 1 Cor 4:8
3:18 1 Cor 3:12,13; 1 Pet 1:7; Rev 3:4; 16:15
3:19 Job 5:17; 1 Cor 11:32; Heb 12:6; Rev 2:5

3:11 Christians have differing gifts, abilities, experience, and maturity. God doesn't expect us all to be the same, but he does expect us to persevere in using our assets for him. The Philadelphians are commended for their effort to obey (3:8) and encouraged to hold tightly to whatever strength they have. You may be a new believer and feel that your faith and spiritual strength are small. Use what you have to live for Christ, and God will commend you.

3:12 The New Jerusalem is the future dwelling of the people of God (21:22). Jesus will make us citizens of his holy city, giving us a new identity. We will have a new citizenship in God's future Kingdom. Everything will be new, pure, and secure.

3:14 Laodicea was the wealthiest of the seven cities of Asia, known for its banking industry, manufacture of wool, and a medical school that produced eye salve. But the city always had a problem with its water supply. At one time an aqueduct was built to bring water to the city from hot springs. But by the time the water reached the city, it was neither hot nor refreshingly cool—only lukewarm. The church had become as bland as the tepid water that came into the city.

3:15 Lukewarm water is unpalatable. The church in Laodicea had become lukewarm and thus distasteful and repugnant. The believers didn't stand for anything. Indifference had led them to idleness. By neglecting to do anything for Christ, the church had become hardened and self-satisfied. The church was destroying itself.

3:17 Some believers falsely assume that lots of material possessions are a sign of God's spiritual blessing. Laodicea was a wealthy city, and the church was also wealthy. But what the Laodiceans could see and buy had become more valuable to them than what is unseen and eternal. Wealth, luxury, and ease can make people feel confident, satisfied, and complacent. But no matter how much you possess or how much money you make, you have nothing if you don't have a vital relationship with Christ.

3:18 Laodicea was known for its great wealth—but Christ told the Laodiceans to buy their gold from him. The city was proud of its

cloth and dyeing industries—but Christ told them that they were naked and must purchase white garments from him. Laodicea prided itself on its precious eye salve that healed many eye problems—but Christ told them to get medicine from him to heal their eyes so they could see the truth. Christ was showing the Laodiceans that true value was not in material possessions, but in a right relationship with God. Their possessions and achievements were valueless compared with the everlasting future of Christ's Kingdom.

3:19 God would discipline this lukewarm church unless they turned from their indifference toward him. His purpose in discipline is not to punish, but to bring people back to him. Are you lukewarm in your devotion to God? God may discipline you to help you out of your indifference; but he uses only loving discipline. You can avoid God's discipline by drawing near to him again through confession, prayer, worship, and studying his Word. Just as the spark of love can be rekindled in marriage, so the Holy Spirit can reignite our zeal for God when we allow him to work in our hearts.

3:20 The Laodicean church was complacent and rich. They felt fulfilled, but they didn't have Christ's presence among them. He knocked at the door of their hearts, but they were so busy enjoying worldly pleasures that they didn't notice he was trying to enter. The pleasures of this world—money, security, material possessions—can be dangerous, because their temporary satisfaction makes us indifferent to God's offer of lasting satisfaction. If you find yourself feeling indifferent to church, to God, or to the Bible, you have begun to shut God out of your life. Leave the door of your heart constantly open to God and you won't need to worry about missing his knock. Letting him in is your only hope of lasting fulfillment.

3:20 Jesus is knocking on the door of our hearts every time we sense we should turn to him. He wants to have fellowship with us, and he wants us to open up to him. He is patient and persistent in trying to get through to us—not breaking and entering, but knocking. He allows us to decide whether or not to open our lives to him. Do you intentionally keep his life-changing presence and power on the other side of the door?

anyone hears me calling him and opens the door, I will come in and fellowship with him and he with me. 21I will let every one who conquers sit beside me on my throne, just as I took my place with my Father on his throne when I had conquered. 22Let those who can hear, listen to what the Spirit is saying to the churches."

3:21
Mt 19:28
Rev 5:5; 6:2
17:14; 20:4
3:22
Rev 2:7

B. MESSAGE FOR THE CHURCH (4:1—22:21)

Moving from the conditions within the churches in Asia to the future of the universal church, John sees the course of coming events in a way similar to Daniel and Ezekiel. Many of these passages contain clear spiritual teachings, but others seem beyond our ability to understand. The clear teaching of this book is that God will defeat all evil in the end. We must live in obedience to Jesus Christ, the coming Conqueror and Judge.

1. Worshiping God in heaven

The glorious throne

4 Then as I looked, I saw a door standing open in heaven, and the same voice I had heard before, that sounded like a mighty trumpet blast, spoke to me and said, "Come up here and I will show you what must happen in the future!" 2And instantly I was, in spirit, there in heaven and saw—oh, the glory of it!—a throne and someone sitting on it! 3Great bursts of light flashed forth from him as from a glittering diamond, or from a shining ruby, and a rainbow glowing like an emerald encircled his throne. 4Twenty-four smaller thrones surrounded his, with twenty-four Elders sitting on them; all were clothed in white, with golden crowns upon their heads. 5Lightning and thunder issued from the throne, and there were voices in the thunder. Directly in front of his throne were seven lighted lamps representing the seven-fold Spirit of God. 6Spread out before it was a shiny crystal sea. Four Living Beings, dotted front and back with eyes, stood at the throne's four sides. 7The first of these Living Beings was in the form of a lion; the second looked like an ox; the third had the face of a man; and the fourth, the form of an eagle, with wings spread out as though in flight. 8Each of these Living Beings had six wings, and the central sections of their wings were covered with eyes. Day after day and night after night they kept on saying, "Holy, holy, holy, Lord God Almighty—the one who was, and is, and is to come."

9And when the Living Beings gave glory and honor and thanks to the one sitting on the throne, who lives forever and ever, 10the twenty-four Elders fell down before him and worshiped him, the Eternal Living One, and cast their crowns before the throne, singing, 11"O Lord, you are worthy to receive the glory and the honor and

4:1
Ezek 1:1
Rev 1:10,19
11:12; 19:11
4:2
Isa 6:1
Rev 1:10; 4:9
4:3
Ezek 1:28; 28:13
Rev 10:1
21:11,19,20
4:4
Mt 19:28
2 Tim 2:12
Rev 11:16; 20:4
4:5
Ex 25:31-39
Zech 4:2-6
Rev 1:4; 5:6
4:6
Ezek 1:5-14
10:12,14
Rev 15:7; 19:4
4:7
Ezek 1:10; 10:21
4:9
Dan 4:34; 12:7
Rev 4:2; 10:6
4:10
Rev 4:4
5:8,14; 10:6
4:11
Rev 10:6

3:22 At the end of each letter to these churches, the believers are urged to listen to and take to heart what is written to them. Although a different message is addressed to each church, all the messages contain warnings and principles for everyone. Which letter speaks most directly to your church? Which has the greatest bearing upon your own spiritual condition at this time? How will you respond?

4:1 Chapters 4 and 5 are a glimpse into Christ's glory. Here we see into the throne room of heaven. God is orchestrating all the events that John will record. The world is not spinning out of control; the God of creation will carry out his plans as Christ initiates the final battle with the forces of evil. John shows us heaven before showing us earth so we will not be frightened by future events.

4:1 The "same voice [John] had heard before" was Christ (see 1:10, 11).

4:2 John says he was "in the Spirit" (alternate translation) four times in the book of Revelation (1:10; 4:2; 17:3; 21:10). This expression means the Holy Spirit was giving him a vision—showing him situations and events he could not see with mere human eyesight. All true prophecy comes from God through the Holy Spirit (2 Peter 1:20, 21).

4:4 Who are these 24 elders? Since there were 12 tribes of Israel in the Old Testament and 12 apostles in the New Testament, the 24

elders in this vision probably represent all the redeemed of God for all time (both before and after Christ's death and resurrection). They symbolize all those—both Jews and Gentiles—who are now part of God's family. The 24 elders show us that *all* the redeemed of the Lord are worshiping him.

4:5 In Revelation, lightning and thunder are connected with significant events in heaven. They remind us of the lightning and thunder at Mount Sinai when God gave the people his laws (Exodus 19:16). The Old Testament often uses such imagery to evoke God's power and majesty (Psalm 77:18).

4:5 The "seven-fold Spirit of God" is another name for the Holy Spirit (see the note on 1:4). See also Zechariah 4:2–6, where the seven lamps are equated with the one Spirit.

4:6 Just as the Holy Spirit is seen symbolically in the seven lighted lamps, so the four Living Beings represent the attributes (the qualities and character) of God. These Beings, probably not real animals, guard God's throne, lead others in worship, and proclaim God's holiness. God's attributes symbolized in the animal-like appearance of these four Beings are faithfulness (the ox), majesty and power (the lion), intelligence (the man), and sovereignty (the eagle). The Old Testament prophet Ezekiel saw four similar beings in one of his visions (Ezekiel 1:5–10).

4:11 The point of this chapter is summed up in this verse: all beings in heaven and earth will praise and honor God because he is the Creator and Sustainer of everything.

the power, for you have created all things. They were created and called into being by your act of will."

The scroll and the Lamb

5 And I saw a scroll in the right hand of the one who was sitting on the throne, a scroll with writing on the inside and on the back, and sealed with seven seals. ²A mighty angel with a loud voice was shouting out this question: "Who is worthy to break the seals on this scroll, and to unroll it?" ³But no one in all heaven or earth or from among the dead was permitted to open and read it.

⁴Then I wept with disappointment because no one anywhere was worthy; no one could tell us what it said.

5:4 Then I wept with disappointment, implied.

5:1
Isa 29:11
Ezek 2:9
Dan 12:4
Rev 5:7

5:2
Rev 10:1; 18:21

5:3
Phil 2:10

EVENTS IN REVELATION DESCRIBED ELSEWHERE IN THE BIBLE	Other Reference	Revelation Reference	Event
	Ezekiel 1:22–28	4:2, 3; 10:1–3	Glowing rainbow around God's throne
	Isaiah 53:7	5:68	Christ is pictured as a Lamb
	Psalms 96	5:9–14	New song
	Zechariah 1:7–11; 6:1–8	6:1–8	Horses and horsemen
	Isaiah 2:19–22	6:12; 8:5; 11:13	Earthquake
	Joel 2:28–32; Acts 2:14–21	6:12	Moon turns blood-red
	Mark 13:21–25	6:13	Stars falling from the heavens
	Isaiah 34:1–4	6:14	Heavens rolled up like a scroll
	Zephaniah 1:14–18; 1 Thessalonians 5:1–3	6:15–17	God's inescapable anger
	Jeremiah 49:35–39	7:1	Four winds of judgment
	Luke 8:26–34	9:1, 2; 17:3–8	Bottomless pit
	Joel 1:2—2:11	9:3–11	Plague of locusts
	Luke 21:20–24	11:1–3	Trampling of the holy city of Jerusalem
	Zechariah 4:1–14	11:4–6	Two olive trees as prophets
	Daniel 7	13:1–10	A Creature rising out of the sea
	2 Thessalonians 2:7–14	13:11–15	Wondrous signs and miracles done by evil beings
	Jeremiah 25:15–29	14:9–12	Drinking the cup of God's wrath
	Isaiah 21:1–10	18:2, 3	"Babylon" falls
	Matthew 22:1–14	19:5–8	Wedding banquet of the Lamb
	Ezekiel 38, 39	20:7–10	Conflict with Gog and Magog
	John 5:19–30	20:11–15	Judging of all people
	Ezekiel 37:21–28	21:3	God lives among mankind
	Isaiah 25:1–8	21:4	Our tears will be wiped away forever
	Genesis 2:8–14	22:1, 2	Trees of life
	1 Corinthians 13:11, 12	22:3–5	We will see God face to face
	Daniel 7:18–28	22:5	Believers shall reign with God forever

5:1ff Chapter 5 continues the glimpse into heaven begun in chapter 4.

5:1 In John's day, writing was done on scrolls—pieces of papyrus or vellum up to 30 feet long, rolled up and sealed with clay or wax. The scroll John sees contains the full account of what God has in store for the world, and only Christ can open it (5:3–5). The seven seals indicate the importance of its contents. They are placed throughout the scroll so that as each one is broken, more of the scroll can be read to reveal another phase of God's plan for the end of the world.

⁵But one of the twenty-four Elders said to me, "Stop crying, for look! The Lion of the tribe of Judah, the Root of David, has conquered, and proved himself worthy to open the scroll and to break its seven seals."

⁶I looked and saw a Lamb standing there before the twenty-four Elders, in front of the throne and the Living Beings, and on the Lamb were wounds that once had caused his death. He had seven horns and seven eyes, which represent the seven-fold Spirit of God, sent out into every part of the world. ⁷He stepped forward and took the scroll from the right hand of the one sitting upon the throne. ⁸And as he took the scroll, the twenty-four Elders fell down before the Lamb, each with a harp and golden vials filled with incense—the prayers of God's people!

⁹They were singing him a new song with these words: "You are worthy to take the scroll and break its seals and open it; for you were slain, and your blood has bought people from every nation as gifts for God. ¹⁰And you have gathered them into a kingdom and made them priests of our God; they shall reign upon the earth."

¹¹Then in my vision I heard the singing of millions of angels surrounding the throne and the Living Beings and the Elders: ¹²"The Lamb is worthy" (loudly they sang it!) "—the Lamb who was slain. He is worthy to receive the power, and the riches, and the wisdom, and the strength, and the honor, and the glory, and the blessing."

¹³And then I heard everyone in heaven and earth, and from the dead beneath the earth and in the sea, exclaiming, "The blessing and the honor and the glory and the power belong to the one sitting on the throne, and to the Lamb forever and ever." ¹⁴And the four Living Beings kept saying, "Amen!" And the twenty-four Elders fell down and worshiped him.

5:9 *singing,* literally, "saying," or "said." Also in vss 11, 12.

5:5
Gen 49:9
Isa 11:1,10
Heb 2:10
7:14,25
Rev 22:16
5:6
Isa 53:7
Zech 3:9; 4:10
Dan 8:3
1 Pet 1:19
Rev 1:4; 4:5
5:8
Rev 4:4,10; 5:6,11
8:3,4; 14:2
15:2
5:9
1 Pet 2:6
Rev 4:11; 7:9
14:3; 15:3,4
5:10
Ex 19:6
1 Pet 2:5-9
Rev 1:6; 3:21
20:4
5:11
Deut 33:2
Ps 68:17
Heb 12:22
Rev 4:4,6
5:12
Zech 13:7
Rev 1:6; 4:11
5:13
Phil 2:10,11
5:14
Rev 4:6,10

5:5 The Lion, Jesus, has proved himself worthy to break the seals and open the scroll by living a perfect life of obedience to God, dying on the cross for the sins of the world, and rising from the dead to show his power and authority over evil and death. Only Christ conquered sin, death, hell, and Satan himself; so only he can be trusted with the world's future.

5:5, 6 Jesus Christ is pictured as both a Lion (symbolizing his authority and power) and a Lamb (symbolizing his humble submission to God's will). One of the Elders calls John to look at the Lion, but when John looks he sees a Lamb. It is the Lamb, not the Lion, that becomes the focus in this vision. Christ the Lamb was the perfect sacrifice for the sins of all mankind; therefore, only he can save us from the terrible events revealed by the scroll. Christ the Lamb won the greatest battle of all—defeating all the forces of evil and death by submitting humbly to God's will and dying on the cross, the perfect sacrifice for mankind's sins. Christ the Lion is victorious in battle against Satan (19:19–21). Christ the Lion is victorious because of what Christ the Lamb has already done. We will enjoy the rewards of victory not because of our power and might but through our humble submission to God's will.

5:6 The Lamb's wounds are those inflicted on Jesus' body during his trial and crucifixion (see John 20:24–31). Jesus was called the Lamb of God by John the Baptist (John 1:29). In the Old Testament, lambs were sacrificed to cover sins. The Lamb of God died as the final sacrifice for all sins (see Isaiah 53:7; Hebrews 10:1–12, 18).

5:6 The horns symbolize strength and power (see 1 Kings 22:11; Zechariah 1:18). Although Christ is a sacrificial lamb, he is in no way weak. He was killed, but now he lives in God's strength and power. In Zechariah 4:2–10, the eyes are equated with the seven lamps and the one Spirit.

5:9, 10 People from every nation are praising God before his throne. The gospel is not limited to a specific culture, race, or country. Anyone who comes in repentance and faith is accepted by God and will be part of his Kingdom. Don't allow prejudice or bias to stop you from sharing Christ with others. Christ welcomes all people into his Kingdom.

5:9, 10 The song of the Living Beings and Elders recounts the work of Christ, for which they praise him. He (1) was slain, (2) bought them with his blood, (3) gathered them into a kingdom, (4) made them priests, and (5) appointed them to reign upon the earth. Jesus has already died and paid the penalty for sin. He is now gathering us into his Kingdom and making us priests, and in the future we will reign with him. Worship God and praise him for what he has done, what he is doing, and what he will do for all who trust in him. When we realize the glorious future that awaits us, we will find the strength to face present difficulties.

5:10 The believers' song praises Christ for bringing them into the Kingdom and making them "priests." Christ's death made all believers priests of God—the channels of blessing between God and mankind (1 Peter 2:5–9). While now we are sometimes despised and mocked for our faith, in the future we will reign over all the earth (John 15:17–27).

5:11 Angels are spiritual beings created by God, who help carry out his work on earth. They bring messages (Luke 1:26), protect God's people (Daniel 6:22), offer encouragement (Genesis 16:7ff), give guidance (Exodus 14:19), bring punishment (2 Samuel 24:16), patrol the earth (Ezekiel 1:9–14), and fight the forces of evil (2 Kings 6:16–18; Revelation 20:1). There are both good and evil angels (12:7), but because evil angels are allied with Satan, they have considerably less power and authority. Eventually, the main role of the good angels will be to offer continuous praise to God (see also 19:1–3).

5:14 The scene in chapter 5 shows us that only the Lamb, Jesus Christ, is worthy to open the scroll (the events of history). He holds it, not Satan. Jesus Christ is in control, and he alone is worthy to set into motion the events of the last days of history.

2. Breaking the seven seals

The seals

6:1
Rev 5:1,6

6 As I watched, the Lamb broke the first seal and began to unroll the scroll. Then one of the four Living Beings, with a voice that sounded like thunder, said, "Come!"

6:2
Zech 6:1-3
Rev 10:3,4
14:14; 19:11

2I looked, and there in front of me was a white horse. Its rider carried a bow, and a crown was placed upon his head; he rode out to conquer in many battles and win the war.

6:3
Rev 4:7

3Then he unrolled the scroll to the second seal, and broke it open too. And I heard the second Living Being say, "Come!"

6:4
Zech 1:8; 6:2
Mt 10:34
Jn 19:11

4This time a red horse rode out. Its rider was given a long sword and the authority to banish peace and bring anarchy to the earth; war and killing broke out everywhere.

6:5
Ezek 4:16
Zech 6:2

5When he had broken the third seal, I heard the third Living Being say, "Come!" And I saw a black horse, with its rider holding a pair of balances in his hand. 6And a voice from among the four Living Beings said, "A loaf of bread for $20, or three pounds of barley flour, but there is no olive oil or wine."

6:8
Prov 5:5
Jer 15:2
Hos 13:14
Zech 6:3
Mt 11:23
Rev 1:18; 20:14

7And when the fourth seal was broken, I heard the fourth Living Being say, "Come!" 8And now I saw a pale horse, and its rider's name was Death. And there followed after him another horse whose rider's name was Hell. They were given control of one-fourth of the earth, to kill with war and famine and disease and wild animals.

6:9
Ex 29:12
Lev 4:7
Jn 16:2
Phil 2:17
2 Tim 4:6
Rev 12:17; 20:4

9And when he broke open the fifth seal, I saw an altar, and underneath it all the souls of those who had been martyred for preaching the Word of God and for being faithful in their witnessing. 10They called loudly to the Lord and said, "O Sovereign Lord, holy and true, how long will it be before you judge the people of the earth for what they've done to us? When will you avenge our blood against those living on the earth?" 11White robes were given to each of them, and they were told to rest a little longer until their other brothers, fellow servants of Jesus, had been martyred on the earth and joined them.

6:10
Ps 79:10
Zech 1:12
Lk 18:7
Rev 3:7,10; 19:2

6:11
Dan 12:13
2 Thess 1:7
Heb 4:9; 11:40
Rev 3:5; 14:13

6:6 *A loaf of bread for $20, or three pounds of barley flour,* literally, "A choenix of wheat for a denarius, and three choenix of barley for a denarius. . . ." *there is no olive oil or wine,* literally, "do not damage the oil and wine."

6:1ff This is the first of three seven-part judgments. The trumpets (chapters 8, 9) and the flasks (chapter 16) are the other two. As each seal is broken, Christ the Lamb sets in motion events which will bring about the end of human history. This scroll is not completely opened until the seventh seal is broken (8:1). The contents of the scroll reveal the guilt and depravity of human beings and portray God's authority over the events of human history.

6:2ff Four horses appear as the first four seals are broken. The horses represent God's judgment of peoples' sin and rebellion. God is directing human history—even using his enemies to unknowingly accomplish his purposes. The four horses are a foretaste of the final judgments yet to come. Some view this chapter as a parallel to the Olivet Discourse (see Matthew 24). The imagery of four horses is also found in Zechariah 6:1–8.

6:2-8 Each of the four horses is a different color. Some say the white horse represents victory, and its rider is Christ (because Christ later rides to victory on a white horse—19:11). But since the other three horses relate to judgment and destruction, this white horse and rider may be the Antichrist who rules the world by deception for a short time. The other colored horses represent different kinds of judgment: red for warfare and bloodshed; black for famine and death; pale for disease and wild animal attacks.

6:8 "And there followed after him another horse whose rider's name was Hell," can also be translated, "and hell followed him." It is not clear whether Hell was on a separate horse or merely went along with Death, but the horsemen described in verses 2–8 are commonly referred to as the four horsemen of the apocalypse.

6:8 The four horsemen are given control of one-fourth of the earth,

indicating that God is still limiting his judgment—it is not yet complete. With these judgments there is still time for believers to turn to Christ and away from their sin. In this case, the limited punishment not only demonstrates God's wrath on sin, but also his merciful love in giving people yet another opportunity to turn to him before he brings final judgment.

6:9 The altar represents the altar of sacrifice in the Temple, where animals were sacrificed to atone for sins. Instead of the animals' blood at the foot of the altar, John saw the souls of martyrs who had died for preaching God's Word. These martyrs were told that still more would lose their lives for their belief in Christ (6:11). In the face of warfare, famine, persecution, and death, Christians will be called on to stand firmly for what they believe. Only those who endure to the end will be rewarded by God (Mark 13:13).

6:9-11 The martyrs are eager for God to bring justice to the earth, but they are told to wait. Those who suffer and die for their faith will not be forgotten, nor do they die in vain. Rather, they will be singled out by God for special honor. We may wish for justice immediately, as these martyrs did, but we must be patient. God works on his own timetable, and he promises justice. No suffering for the sake of God's Kingdom, however, is wasted effort.

6:10 Romans 12:19 says, "Dear friends, never avenge yourselves. Leave that to God, for he has said that he will repay those who deserve it." The prayer of the saints here is in keeping with the "imprecatory psalms" which call for God's judgment upon the psalmists' enemies. In both cases, the concern is for God to vindicate his name and his suffering people. Here, and in 8:4, 5, the judgments of God are revealed (in the seals, trumpets, and bowls) in answer to the prayers of the saints.

12I watched as he broke the sixth seal, and there was a vast earthquake; and the sun became dark like black cloth, and the moon was blood-red. 13Then the stars of heaven appeared to be falling to earth—like green fruit from fig trees buffeted by mighty winds. 14And the starry heavens disappeared as though rolled up like a scroll and taken away; and every mountain and island shook and shifted. 15The kings of the earth, and world leaders and rich men, and high-ranking military officers, and all men great and small, slave and free, hid themselves in the caves and rocks of the mountains, 16and cried to the mountains to crush them. "Fall on us," they pleaded, "and hide us from the face of the one sitting on the throne, and from the anger of the Lamb, 17because the great day of their anger has come, and who can survive it?"

6:12
Joel 2:10
Mt 24:29
Rev 16:18
6:13
Rev 8:10; 9:1
6:14
Ps 102:26
Heb 1:10-12
2 Pet 3:10
Rev 16:20; 21:1
6:16
2 Thess 1:7-9
6:17
Isa 13:6; 63:4
Mal 3:2

The 144,000 marked by God

7 Then I saw four angels standing at the four corners of the earth, holding back the four winds from blowing, so that not a leaf rustled in the trees, and the ocean became as smooth as glass. 2And I saw another angel coming from the east, carrying the Great Seal of the Living God. And he shouted out to those four angels who had been given power to injure earth and sea, 3"Wait! Don't do anything yet—hurt neither earth nor sea nor trees—until we have placed the Seal of God upon the foreheads of his servants."

4-8How many were given this mark? I heard the number—it was 144,000; out of all twelve tribes of Israel, as listed here:

7:1
Jer 49:36
Zech 6:5
Mt 24:31
7:2
Rev 9:14
7:3
Ezek 9:4,6
Dan 6:16
Eph 4:30
2 Tim 2:19
Rev 14:1; 22:4
7:4
Rev 9:16
14:1,3

Judah	12,000	Simeon	12,000
Reuben	12,000	Levi	12,000
Gad	12,000	Issachar	12,000
Asher	12,000	Zebulun	12,000
Naphatali	12,000	Joseph	12,000
Manasseh	12,000	Benjamin	12,000

6:13 *appeared to be falling to earth,* literally, "fell to the earth."   **6:14** *the starry heavens disappeared,* literally, "the sky departed."

6:12 The sixth seal changes the scene back to the physical world. The first five judgments were directed toward specific areas, but this judgment is universal. Everyone will be afraid when the earth itself trembles.

6:15-17 At the sight of God sitting on the throne, all human beings great and small, will be terrified, calling for the mountains to fall on them so they will not have to face the judgment of the Lamb. This picture was not intended to frighten believers. For them, the Lamb is a gentle Savior. But those who previously showed no fear of God and proudly flaunted their unbelief will find they were wrong, and in that day they will have to face his wrath. No one who has rejected God can survive the day of his wrath, but those who belong to Christ will receive a reward rather than punishment. Do you belong to Christ? If so, you need not fear these final days.

7:1ff The sixth seal has been opened, and the people of the earth have tried to hide from God, saying, "Who can survive?" (6:12-17). Just when all hope seems lost, four angels hold back the four winds of judgment until God's people are marked as his. Only then will God break the seventh seal (8:1).

7:2 A seal on a scroll or document identified and protected its contents. God places his Great Seal on his followers, identifying them as his own and guaranteeing his protection over their souls. This shows how valuable we are to him. Our physical bodies may be beaten, maimed, or even destroyed, but *nothing* can harm the souls of those marked by God.

7:3 This Seal of God placed on the foreheads of his servants is the exact opposite of the mark of the beast explained in 13:16. These two marks place the people in two distinct categories—those owned by God and those owned by Satan. This

portrays a theme running throughout Revelation—Satan's attempt to imitate the great works of God.

7:4-8 The number 144,000 is 12 x 12 x 1,000, symbolizing completeness—*all* God's followers will be brought safely to him; not one will be overlooked or forgotten. God seals these believers either by withdrawing them from the earth (this is called the Rapture) or by giving them special power to make it through this time of great persecution. If they are to endure persecution, the seal does not necessarily guarantee protection from physical harm—many will die (see 6:11)—but God protects them from spiritual harm. No matter what happens, they will receive their reward in heaven. Their destiny is secure. These believers will not fall away from God even in intense persecution.

This is not saying that 144,000 individuals must be sealed before the persecution comes, but that when it begins, we can know the faithful have already been sealed (marked by God) and will remain true to him until the end.

7:4-8 This is a different list from the usual listing of the 12 tribes in the Old Testament, because it is a symbolic list of God's true followers. (1) Judah is mentioned first because Judah is both the tribe of David and of Jesus the Messiah (Genesis 49:8-12; Matthew 1:1). (2) Levi had no tribal allotment because of the Levites' work for God in the Temple (Deuteronomy 18:1), but here the tribe is given a place as a reward for faithfulness. (3) Dan and Ephraim are not mentioned, because they were known for rebellion and idolatry, traits unacceptable in God's followers (Genesis 49:17). (4) The two tribes representing Joseph (usually called Ephraim and Manasseh, after Joseph's sons) are here called Joseph and Manasseh, because of Ephraim's rebellion. See Genesis 49 for the story of the beginning of these 12 tribes.

The great crowd

7:9
Rev 3:5; 6:11; 5:9

7:10
Rev 5:13;
12:10; 19:1; 22:3

7:11
Rev 4:4,6,10

7:12
Rev 5:12,14

7:13
Rev 7:9

7:14
Rev 6:11; 22:14

7:15
Rev 4:9; 11:19
22:3

7:16
Isa 49:10

7:17
Ps 23:1-5
Isa 25:8; 35:10
Jn 4:14; 10:11
Acts 20:28
1 Pet 5:2
Rev 21:4,6
22:1

9After this I saw a vast crowd, too great to count, from all nations and provinces and languages, standing in front of the throne and before the Lamb, clothed in white, with palm branches in their hands. 10And they were shouting with a mighty shout, "Salvation comes from our God upon the throne, and from the Lamb."

11And now all the angels were crowding around the throne and around the Elders and the four Living Beings, and falling face down before the throne and worshiping God. 12"Amen!" they said. "Blessing, and glory, and wisdom, and thanksgiving, and honor, and power, and might, be to our God forever and forever. Amen!"

13Then one of the twenty-four Elders asked me, "Do you know who these are, who are clothed in white, and where they come from?"

14"No, sir," I replied. "Please tell me."

"These are the ones coming out of the Great Tribulation," he said; "they washed their robes and whitened them by the blood of the Lamb. 15That is why they are here before the throne of God, serving him day and night in his temple. The one sitting on the throne will shelter them; 16they will never be hungry again, nor thirsty, and they will be fully protected from the scorching noontime heat. 17For the Lamb standing in front of the throne will feed them and be their Shepherd and lead them to the springs of the Water of Life. And God will wipe their tears away."

The seventh seal

8:1
Rev 5:1,9
6:1-17

8:3
Eph 5:2
Heb 9:4
Rev 5:8; 6:9

8:4
Ps 141:2

8:5
Lev 16:12
1 Kgs 19:11
Ezek 10:2
Lk 12:49
Rev 16:18

8 When the Lamb had broken the seventh seal, there was silence throughout all heaven for what seemed like half an hour. 2And I saw the seven angels that stand before God, and they were given seven trumpets.

3Then another angel with a golden censer came and stood at the altar; and a great quantity of incense was given to him to mix with the prayers of God's people, to offer upon the golden altar before the throne. 4And the perfume of the incense mixed with prayers ascended up to God from the altar where the angel had poured them out.

5Then the angel filled the censer with fire from the altar and threw it down upon the earth; and thunder crashed and rumbled, lightning flashed, and there was a terrible earthquake.

7:17 *in front of,* literally, "in the center of the throne"; i.e., directly in front, not to one side. An alternate rendering might be, "at the heart of the throne."

7:9 Who is the crowd too numerous to count? While some say it is the martyrs described in 6:9, it may also be the same group as the 144,000 just mentioned (7:4–8). The 144,000 were sealed by God before the great time of persecution; the vast crowd was spared, as God had promised. Before, they were being prepared; now they are victorious. This crowd in heaven is composed of those who remained faithful to God throughout the generations.

7:10 People try many methods to remove the guilt of sin— good works, intellectual pursuits, and even casting blame. The crowd in heaven however, praises God, saying, "Salvation comes from our God upon the throne, and from the Lamb." Salvation from sin's penalty can come only through Jesus Christ. Have you had the guilt of sin removed in the only way possible?

7:11 More information about the Elders is found in the note on 4:4. The four Living Beings are explained further in the note on 4:6.

7:14 It is difficult to imagine how blood could whiten any cloth, but the blood of Jesus Christ is the world's greatest purifier because it removes the stain of sin. White symbolizes sinless perfection or holiness, which can be given to people only by the sacrifice and shed blood of the the sinless Lamb of God. This is a picture of how we are saved by faith (see Isaiah 1:18; Romans 3:21–26).

7:14 The Great Tribulation has been explained in several ways. Some believe it refers to the suffering of believers through the ages; others believe there will be a specific time of intense

tribulation. In either case, these believers come through their times of suffering by remaining loyal to God. If they are faithful, God will give them eternal life with him (7:17).

7:16, 17 God will provide for his children's needs in their eternal home, where there will be no hunger, thirst, or pain, and he will wipe away all tears. When you are suffering or torn apart by sorrow, take comfort in this truth.

7:17 In verses 1–8 we see the believers receiving a seal to protect them through a time of great tribulation and suffering; in verses 9–17 we see the believers finally with God in heaven. All who have been faithful through the ages are singing before God's throne. Their tribulations and sorrows are over: no more tears for sin, for all sins are forgiven; no more tears for suffering, for all suffering is over; no more tears for death, for all believers have been resurrected to die no more.

8:1, 2 When the seventh seal is opened, the seven trumpet judgments are revealed. In the same way, the seventh trumpet will announce the seven flask (bowl) judgments in 11:15 and 16:1–21. The trumpet judgments, like the seal judgments, are only partial. God's final and complete judgment has not yet come.

8:3 A censer filled with live coals was used in Temple worship. Incense was poured on the coals, and the sweet-smelling smoke drifted upwards, symbolizing believers' prayers ascending to God (see Exodus 30:7–9).

3. Sounding the seven trumpets
The trumpets

⁶Then the seven angels with the seven trumpets prepared to blow their mighty blasts.

⁷The first angel blew his trumpet, and hail and fire mixed with blood were thrown down upon the earth. One-third of the earth was set on fire so that one-third of the trees were burned, and all the green grass.

8, 9Then the second angel blew his trumpet, and what appeared to be a huge burning mountain was thrown into the sea, destroying a third of all the ships; and a third of the sea turned red as blood; and a third of the fish were killed.

¹⁰The third angel blew, and a great flaming star fell from heaven upon a third of the rivers and springs. ¹¹The star was called "Bitterness" because it poisoned a third of all the water on the earth and many people died.

¹²The fourth angel blew his trumpet and immediately a third of the sun was blighted and darkened, and a third of the moon and the stars, so that the daylight was dimmed by a third, and the nighttime darkness deepened. ¹³As I watched, I saw a solitary eagle flying through the heavens crying loudly, "Woe, woe, woe to the people of the earth because of the terrible things that will soon happen when the three remaining angels blow their trumpets."

9 Then the fifth angel blew his trumpet and I saw one who was fallen to earth from heaven, and to him was given the key to the bottomless pit. ²When he opened it, smoke poured out as though from some huge furnace, and the sun and air were darkened by the smoke.

³Then locusts came from the smoke and descended onto the earth and were given power to sting like scorpions. ⁴They were told not to hurt the grass or plants or trees, but to attack those people who did not have the mark of God on their foreheads. ⁵They were not to kill them, but to torture them for five months with agony like the pain of scorpion stings. ⁶In those days men will try to kill themselves but won't be able to—death will not come. They will long to die—but death will flee away!

⁷The locusts looked like horses armored for battle. They had what looked like golden crowns on their heads, and their faces looked like men's. ⁸Their hair was long like women's, and their teeth were those of lions. ⁹They wore breastplates that seemed to be of iron, and their wings roared like an army of chariots rushing into

8:7
Joel 2:30
Zech 13:8,9
Mt 7:25-27
8:8
Ex 7:17
Zech 13:8,9
Rev 16:2
8:9
Rev 8:7-12
9:15,18
8:10
Isa 14:12
Rev 6:13; 9:1
12:4; 16:4
8:11
Ex 15:23
Heb 12:15
Rev 9:15
8:12
Ex 10:21
Zech 13:8
Rev 16:8
8:13
Rev 3:10; 9:12
9:1
Isa 14:12
Lk 8:31; 10:18
Rev 3:10;
8:10; 17:8; 20:1
9:2
Joel 2:2,30
9:3
Ex 10:4,5,12-15
Rev 9:5,7,10
9:4
Ex 12:23
Rev 6:6; 7:2,3
9:6
Job 3:21
Rev 6:16
9:7
Joel 2:4
9:8
Joel 1:6
9:9
Joel 2:5

8:9 *turned red as blood*, literally, "became blood." **8:11** *"Bitterness,"* literally, "Wormwood." **9:1** *one who has fallen to earth from heaven.*

8:6 The trumpet blasts have three purposes: (1) to warn that judgment is certain, (2) to call the forces of God and evil to battle, and (3) to announce the return of the King, the Messiah. These warnings urge us to make sure our faith is firmly fixed on Christ.

8:7-12 Since only one-third of the earth is destroyed by these trumpet judgments, this is only a partial judgment from God. His full wrath is yet to be unleashed.

8:13 Habakkuk used the image of an eagle to symbolize swiftness and destruction (see Habakkuk 1:8). The picture here is of a strong, powerful bird flying over all the earth, warning of the terrors yet to come. While both believers and unbelievers experience the terrors described in verses 7–12, the "people of the earth" are the unbelievers who will meet spiritual harm with the next three trumpet judgments. God has guaranteed believers protection from spiritual harm (7:2, 3).

8:13 In 6:10, the martyrs call out to God, "How long will it be before you judge the people of the earth?" As we see the world's wickedness, we too may cry out to God, "How long?" In the following chapters, the judgment comes at last. We may be distressed and impatient, but God has his plan and his timing, and we must learn to trust him to know what is best. Judgment is coming—be sure of that. Thank God for the time he gives you to turn from sin, and work to help others turn as well.

9:1 It is not known whether this "one" who fell from heaven is Satan, a fallen angel, Christ, or a good angel. Most likely it is Satan or an angel, because the key to the bottomless pit is held by Christ (1:17, 18), and it was temporarily given to this other being who fell from heaven. This being, whoever he may be, is still under God's control and authority. The bottomless pit represents the place of the demons and of Satan, the Prince of demons (9:11). See also Luke 8:31 for another reference to the bottomless pit.

9:3 The prophet Joel described a locust plague as a foreshadowing of the "Day of the Lord," meaning God's coming judgment (Joel 2:1–10). In the Old Testament, locusts were symbols of destruction because they destroyed vegetation. Here, however, they symbolize an invasion of demons called to torture people who do not believe in God. The limitations placed on the demons show that they are under God's authority.

9:3ff Some interpreters think these locusts are demons— evil spirits ruled by Satan who tempt people to sin. They were not created by Satan, because God is the Creator of all; rather, they are fallen angels who joined Satan in his rebellion. God limits what they can do; they can do nothing without his permission. Demons' main purpose on earth is to destroy, prevent, or distort people's relationship with God. While it is important to recognize their evil activity so we can stay away from them, we must avoid any curiosity about or involvement with demonic forces or the occult.

9:11
Job 26:6
Prov 15:11
Lk 8:31
Jn 12:31; 14:30
Rev 9:1

9:12
Rev 8:13; 11:14

9:13
Ex 30:2-10
Heb 9:24; 10:21
Rev 8:3

9:14
Gen 2:14; 15:18
Rev 7:1; 16:12

9:15
Rev 9:18; 20:7

9:16
Dan 7:10; 11:40
Rev 5:11; 7:4

9:17
Dan 8:2; 9:21

9:20
Deut 4:28
Ps 115:4-7
Dan 5:23
Mic 5:13
Acts 7:41
1 Cor 10:20
Rev 2:21

9:21
Rev 7:2

10:1
Mt 17:2
Rev 1:15,16;
4:3; 5:2; 18:1

10:3
Ps 29:3-9
Rev 4:5

10:4
Dan 8:26; 12:4
Rev 1:10; 22:10

10:6
Rev 4:9,11; 16:17
21:6

battle. 10They had stinging tails like scorpions, and their power to hurt, given to them for five months, was in their tails. 11Their king is the Prince of the bottomless pit whose name in Hebrew is Abaddon, and in Greek, Apollyon [and in English, the Destroyer].

12One terror now ends, but there are two more coming!

13The sixth angel blew his trumpet and I heard a voice speaking from the four horns of the golden altar that stands before the throne of God, 14saying to the sixth angel, "Release the four mighty demons held bound at the great River Euphrates." 15They had been kept in readiness for that year and month and day and hour, and now they were turned loose to kill a third of all mankind. 16They led an army of 200,000,000 warriors—I heard an announcement of how many there were.

17, 18I saw their horses spread out before me in my vision; their riders wore fiery-red breastplates, though some were sky-blue and others yellow. The horses' heads looked much like lions', and smoke and fire and flaming sulphur billowed from their mouths, killing one-third of all mankind. 19Their power of death was not only in their mouths, but in their tails as well, for their tails were similar to serpents' heads that struck and bit with fatal wounds.

20But the men left alive after these plagues *still refused to worship God!* They would not renounce their demon-worship, nor their idols made of gold and silver, brass, stone, and wood—which neither see nor hear nor walk! 21Neither did they change their mind and attitude about all their murders and witchcraft, their immorality and theft.

The angel with the small scroll

10 Then I saw another mighty angel coming down from heaven, surrounded by a cloud, with a rainbow over his head; his face shone like the sun and his feet flashed with fire. 2And he held open in his hand a small scroll. He set his right foot on the sea and his left foot on the earth, 3and gave a great shout—it was like the roar of a lion—and the seven thunders crashed their reply.

4I was about to write what the thunders said when a voice from heaven called to me, "Don't do it. Their words are not to be revealed."

5Then the mighty angel standing on the sea and land lifted his right hand to heaven, 6and swore by him who lives forever and ever, who created heaven and

9:11 *and in English, the Destroyer,* implied.   **9:14** *four mighty demons,* literally, "(fallen) angels."

9:13 The altar in the Temple had four projections, one at each corner, and these were called "the horns of the altar" (see Exodus 27:2).

9:14 These four unidentified demons will be exceedingly evil and destructive. But note that they do not have the power to release themselves and do their evil work on earth. Instead, they are held back by God and will be released by him at a specific time, doing only what he allows them to do.

9:15 Here one-third of all people are killed. In 6:7, 8, one-fourth of mankind is killed. Thus, over one-half of the people in the world will have been killed by God's great judgments. Even more would have been killed if God had not set limits on the destruction.

9:16 In John's day this number of warriors in an army was inconceivable, but today there are countries and alliances that could easily amass this many soldiers. This huge army, led by the four demons, will be sent out to destroy one-third of the earth's population. But the judgment is still not complete.

9:20, 21 These men were so hardhearted that even plagues did not drive them to God. People don't usually fall into immorality and evil suddenly—they slip into it a little at a time until, hardly realizing what has happened, they are irrevocably mired in their wicked ways. Any person who allows sin to take root in his life can find himself in this predicament. Temptation entertained today becomes sin tomorrow, then a habit the next day, then death and separation from God forever (see James 1:15). To think you could never become this evil is the first step toward a hard heart.

10:1–6 The purpose of this mighty angel is clear—to announce the final judgments on the earth. His right foot on the sea and left foot on the earth (10:2) indicate that his words deal with all creation, not just a limited part as with the seal and trumpet judgments. The seventh trumpet (11:15) will usher in the seven flask judgments, which will bring an end to the present world. When this universal judgment comes, God's truth will prevail.

10:2 We see two scrolls in Revelation. The first contains a revelation of judgments against evil (5:1ff). The contents of the second scroll are not indicated, but it also may contain a revelation of judgment. The prophet Ezekiel had a vision in which he was told to swallow a scroll filled with judgments against the nation of Israel (Ezekiel 3:1ff). It was sweet in his mouth, but its contents brought destruction—just like the scroll John was told to eat (10:9, 10). God's Word is sweet to believers, but bitter to unbelievers who are judged by it.

10:4 Throughout history people have wanted to know what would happen in the future, and God reveals some of it in this book. But John was stopped from revealing certain parts of his vision. An angel also told the prophet Daniel that some things he saw were not to be revealed yet to everyone (Daniel 12:9), and Jesus told his disciples that the time of the end is known by no one but God (Mark 13:32, 33). God has revealed all we need to know to live for him now. In our desire to be ready for the end, we must not place more emphasis on speculation about the last days than on living godly lives while waiting.

everything in it and the earth and all that it contains and the sea and its inhabitants, that there should be no more delay, 7but that when the seventh angel blew his trumpet, then God's veiled plan—mysterious through the ages ever since it was announced by his servants the prophets—would be fulfilled.

10:7
Amos 3:7
Rev 11:15

8Then the voice from heaven spoke to me again, "Go and get the unrolled scroll from the mighty angel standing there upon the sea and land."

10:8
Rev 10:2

9So I approached him and asked him to give me the scroll. "Yes, take it and eat it," he said. "At first it will taste like honey, but when you swallow it, it will make your stomach sour!" 10So I took it from his hand, and ate it! And just as he had said, it was sweet in my mouth but it gave me a stomach ache when I swallowed it.

10:9
Jer 15:16
Ezek 2:8; 3:1-3

11Then he told me, "You must prophesy further about many peoples, nations, tribes, and kings."

10:11
Rev 5:9

The two prophets

11 Now I was given a measuring stick and told to go and measure the temple of God, including the inner court where the altar stands, and to count the number of worshipers. 2"But do not measure the outer court," I was told, "for it has been turned over to the nations. They will trample the Holy City for forty-two months. 3And I will give power to my two witnesses to prophesy 1,260 days clothed in sackcloth."

11:1
Zech 2:1
Rev 21:15

11:2
Ezek 40:17-20
Lk 21:24
Rev 12:6; 13:5

11:3
Rev 2:13; 12:6

4These two prophets are the two olive trees, and two candlesticks standing before the God of all the earth. 5Anyone trying to harm them will be killed by bursts of fire shooting from their mouths. 6They have power to shut the skies so that no rain will fall during the three and a half years they prophesy, and to turn rivers and oceans to blood, and to send every kind of plague upon the earth as often as they wish.

11:4
Zech 4:3,11,14

11:5
2 Kgs 1:10-12

11:6
Ex 7:19

7When they complete the three and a half years of their solemn testimony, the tyrant who comes out of the bottomless pit will declare war against them and conquer and kill them; 8, 9and for three and a half days their bodies will be exposed in the streets of Jerusalem (the city fittingly described as "Sodom" or "Egypt")—the very place where their Lord was crucified. No one will be allowed to bury them, and people from many nations will crowd around to gaze at them. 10And there will be a worldwide holiday—people everywhere will rejoice and give presents to each

11:7
Rev 13:1,7

11:8
Rev 14:8; 16:9
17:5,18; 18:24

11:9
Ps 79:2

11:10
Neh 8:10
Mt 10:22

11:1 *a measuring stick . . . and to count the number of worshipers,* literally, "Rise and measure the temple of God, and the altar, and them that worship therein." 11:2 *forty-two months,* 3½ years, as in Dan 12:7. Also for *1260 days* in vs 3. 11:4 *two olive trees,* Zech 4:3, 4, 11. 11:7 *the bottomless pit,* Rev 9:11.

10:7 When God's plan for human history is completely revealed, all prophecy will be fulfilled. The end of the age will have arrived (see 11:15).

11:1ff This temple is most likely a symbol of the church (all true believers), because there will be no temple in the New Jerusalem (21:22). John measured the temple to show that God is building walls of protection around his people to spare them from spiritual harm, and that there is a place reserved for all believers who remain faithful to God.

11:2 Those worshiping inside the temple (inner court) will be protected spiritually, but those outside (outer court) will face great suffering. This is a way of saying that true believers will be protected through persecution, but those who refuse to believe will be destroyed.

11:3 In the book of Revelation, numbers are likely to have symbolic rather than literal meanings. The 42 months or 1,260 days equal 3 1/2 years. As half of the perfect number, 7, 3 1/2 can indicate incompletion, imperfection, or even evil. Notice the events predicted for this time period: trouble (Daniel 12:7), the Holy City is trampled (11:2), the woman takes refuge in the wilderness (12:6), and the devil-inspired creature controls the earth (13:5). Some commentators link the 3 1/2 years with the period of famine in the days of Elijah (Luke 4:25; James 5:17). Since Malachi predicted the return of Elijah before the last judgment (Malachi 4:5), and since the events in Daniel and Revelation pave the way for the

Second Coming, perhaps John was making this connection. It is possible, of course, that the 3 1/2 years are literal. If so, we will clearly recognize them when they are over! Whether symbolic or literal, however, they indicate that evil's reign will have a definite end.

11:4 These two prophets (witnesses) bear strong resemblance to Moses and Elijah, two of God's mighty prophets. With God's power, Moses called plagues down upon the nation of Egypt (see Exodus 8—11). Elijah prayed for the rain to cease (1 Kings 17). Both of these men appeared with Christ at his transfiguration (see Matthew 17:1–7).

11:7 This tyrant is also called the "beast" and could refer to Satan or an agent of Satan.

11:8, 9 Jerusalem, once the Holy City and the capital of Israel, is now enemy territory. It is compared with Sodom and with Egypt, both well-known for their evil.

11:10 The whole world rejoices at the deaths of these two prophets, who have caused trouble by saying what the people didn't want to hear—words about their sin, their need for repentance, and the coming punishment. Sinful people hate those who call attention to their sin and who urge them to repent. They hated Christ, and they hate his followers (1 John 3:13). When you obey Christ and take a stand against sin, be prepared to draw the world's hatred. But remember that the great reward awaiting you in heaven far outweighs any suffering you face now.

other and throw parties to celebrate the death of the two prophets who had tormented them so much!

11:11
Ezek 37:5,9-14

11:12
2 Kgs 2:11
Mt 17:1-9
Acts 1:9
Rev 4:1

11But after three and a half days, the spirit of life from God will enter them and they will stand up! And great fear will fall on everyone. 12Then a loud voice will shout from heaven, "Come up!" And they will rise to heaven in a cloud as their enemies watch.

11:13
Jn 9:24
Rev 6:12;
16:9,11,18,19

13The same hour there will be a terrible earthquake that levels a tenth of the city, leaving 7,000 dead. Then everyone left will, in their terror, give glory to the God of heaven.

11:14
Rev 8:13; 9:12

14The second woe is past, but the third quickly follows:

The seventh trumpet

11:15
Dan 2:44
7:14,27
Acts 4:26
Rev 8:2; 10:7
12:10; 16:17

15For just then the seventh angel blew his trumpet, and there were loud voices shouting down from heaven, "The Kingdom of this world now belongs to our Lord, and to his Christ; and he shall reign forever and ever."

11:16
Mt 19:28
Rev 4:4,10

16And the twenty-four Elders sitting on their thrones before God threw themselves down in worship, saying, 17"We give thanks, Lord God Almighty, who is and was, for now you have assumed your great power and have begun to reign.

11:17
Rev 1:8; 19:6

11:18
Ps 2:1
Dan 7:10
Acts 10:42
Rev 10:7; 13:16
19:5; 20:12

18The nations were angry with you, but now it is your turn to be angry with them. It is time to judge the dead, and reward your servants—prophets and people alike, all who fear your Name, both great and small—and to destroy those who have caused destruction upon the earth."

11:19
Rev 4:5; 15:5

19Then, in heaven, the temple of God was opened and the ark of his covenant could be seen inside. Lightning flashed and thunder crashed and roared, and there was a great hailstorm and the world was shaken by a mighty earthquake.

4. Observing the great conflict

The woman and the Dragon

12:2
Isa 26:17
66:6-9
Mic 4:9,10

12 Then a great pageant appeared in heaven, portraying things to come. I saw a woman clothed with the sun, with the moon beneath her feet, and a crown of twelve stars on her head. 2She was pregnant and screamed in the pain of her labor, awaiting her delivery.

12:3
Isa 27:1
Rev 13:1,2
17:3,9,12,16

3Suddenly a red Dragon appeared, with seven heads and ten horns, and seven crowns on his heads. 4His tail drew along behind him a third of the stars, which he

11:15 *he shall reign forever and ever*, or "The Lord and his Anointed shall now rule the world from this day to eternity."

11:15 The seventh trumpet is blown, announcing the arrival of the King. There is now no turning back. The coming judgments are no longer partial, but complete in their destruction. God is in control, and he unleashes his full wrath upon the evil world that refuses to turn to him (9:20). When the wrath begins, there will be no escape.

11:16 For more on the 24 Elders, see the note on 4:4.

11:18 In the Bible, God gives rewards to his people according to what they deserve. Throughout the Old Testament, obedience often brought reward in this life (Deuteronomy 28), but obedience and immediate reward are not always linked. If they were, good people would always be rich, and suffering would always be a sign of sin. If we were quickly rewarded for every faithful deed, we would soon think we were pretty good. Before long, we would be doing many good deeds for purely selfish reasons. While it is true that God will reward us for our earthly deeds (see 20:12), our greatest reward is eternal life in his presence.

11:19 In Old Testament days, the ark of the covenant was the most sacred treasure of the Israelite nation. For more information about the ark, see the note on Exodus 37:1.

12:1—14:20 The seventh trumpet (11:15) ushers in the flask judgments (15:1—16:21), but in the intervening chapters (12—14), John sees the conflict between God and Satan. He sees the source of all sin, evil, persecution, and suffering on the earth, and he understands why the great battle between the forces of God and Satan must soon take place. In these chapters the nature of evil is exposed, and Satan is seen in all his wickedness.

12:1–6 The woman represents God's faithful people who have been awaiting the Messiah; the 12 stars on her head represent the 12 tribes of Israel. God set apart the Jews for himself (Romans 9:4, 5), and that nation gave birth to the Messiah. The boy (12:5) is Jesus, born to a devout Jew, Mary (Luke 1:26–33). Evil King Herod immediately tried to destroy the infant Jesus (Matthew 2:13–20). Herod's desire to kill this newborn "king," whom he saw as a threat to his throne, was motivated by Satan (the red Dragon), who wanted to kill the world's Savior. The heavenly pageant of Revelation 12 shows that Christ's quiet birth in the town of Bethlehem had cosmic significance.

12:3, 4 The red Dragon, Satan, has seven heads, ten horns, and seven crowns, representing his power and the kingdoms of the world over which he rules. The stars that plunged to earth with him are usually considered to be the angels who fell with Satan and became his demons. According to Hebrew tradition, one-third of all the angels in heaven fell with Satan. For more on demons, see the note on 9:3ff and Mark 5:1–20.

plunged to the earth. He stood before the woman as she was about to give birth to her child, ready to eat the baby as soon as it was born.

⁵She gave birth to a boy who was to rule all nations with a heavy hand, and he was caught up to God and to his throne. ⁶The woman fled into the wilderness, where God had prepared a place for her, to take care of her for 1,260 days.

⁷Then there was war in heaven; Michael and the angels under his command fought the Dragon and his hosts of fallen angels. ⁸And the Dragon lost the battle and was forced from heaven. ⁹This great Dragon—the ancient serpent called the devil, or Satan, the one deceiving the whole world—was thrown down onto the earth with all his army.

¹⁰Then I heard a loud voice shouting across the heavens, "It has happened at last! God's salvation and the power and the rule, and the authority of his Christ are finally here; for the Accuser of our brothers has been thrown down from heaven onto earth—he accused them day and night before our God. ¹¹They defeated him by the blood of the Lamb, and by their testimony; for they did not love their lives but laid them down for him. ¹²Rejoice, O heavens! You citizens of heaven, rejoice! Be glad! But woe to you people of the world, for the devil has come down to you in great anger, knowing that he has little time."

¹³And when the Dragon found himself cast down to earth, he persecuted the woman who had given birth to the child. ¹⁴But she was given two wings like those of a great eagle, to fly into the wilderness to the place prepared for her, where she was cared for and protected from the Serpent, the Dragon, for three and a half years.

¹⁵And from the Serpent's mouth a vast flood of water gushed out and swept toward the woman in an effort to get rid of her; ¹⁶but the earth helped her by

12:5
Ps 2:9
Rev 2:27; 19:15
12:6
Rev 11:3; 13:5
17:18
12:7
Dan 10:13; 12:1
Jude 9
Rev 12:3
12:9
Gen 3:1
Zech 3:1,2
Mt 4:10
Lk 10:18
Rev 12:3,15
20:2-10
12:10
Rev 7:10; 11:15
12:11
Rev 2:10; 6:9
7:14; 15:2
12:12
Rev 8:13
10:6; 12:9; 13:6
18:20
12:14
Ex 19:4
Dan 7:25; 12:7
Rev 17:3,18
12:15
Hos 5:10

12:14 *for three and a half years,* literally, "a time and times and half a time."

12:6 The wilderness represents a place of spiritual refuge and protection from Satan. By aiding the woman's escape into the wilderness, God offers security to all true believers. Satan always attacks God's people, but God keeps them spiritually secure. Some will experience physical harm, but all will be protected from spiritual harm. God will not let Satan take the souls of his true followers.

12:6 The 1,260 days (3 1/2 years) is the same length of time that the Dragon was allowed to control the earth (13:5) and that the Holy City was trampled (see the note on 11:3).

12:7 This event fulfills Daniel 12:1ff. Michael is a high- ranking angel. One of his responsibilities is to guard God's community of believers. For instance, it was Michael who fought Satan for the body of Moses (Jude 1:9).

12:7ff Much more happened at Christ's birth, death, and resurrection than most people realize. A battle between the forces of good and evil was under way. With Christ's resurrection, Satan's ultimate defeat was assured. Some believe that Satan's fall to earth took place at Jesus' resurrection or ascension and that the 1,260 days (3 1/2 years) is a symbolic way of referring to the time between Christ's first and second comings. Others say that Satan's defeat occurs at the midpoint of a literal seven-year tribulation period, following the rapture of the church and preceding the Second Coming of Christ and the beginning of his thousand-year reign. Whatever the case, we must remember that Christ is victorious—Satan has already been defeated by Christ's death on the cross (12:10-12).

12:9 Satan is not just a symbol or legend, he is very real. Originally he was an angel of God, but through his pride, he became corrupt. Satan is God's enemy and he constantly tries to hinder God's work, but he is limited by God's power and can do only what he is permitted to do (Job 1:6—2:8). The name *Satan*

means "Adversary" or "Accuser" (12:10). He actively looks for people to attack (1 Peter 5:8, 9). He likes to seek out believers who are vulnerable in their faith, who are spiritually weak.

Even though God permits Satan to do his work in this world, God is still in control. And Jesus has complete power over Satan—he defeated Satan when he died and rose again for the sins of mankind. One day Satan will be bound forever, never again to do his evil work (see 20:10).

12:10 Many believe that until this time, Satan still had access to God (see the note on Job 1:7ff). But here his access is forever barred (see also 9:1). He can no longer accuse people before God (see how Satan made accusations about Job before God in Job 1:6ff).

12:11 The critical blow to Satan came when the Lamb, Jesus Christ, shed his blood for our sins. The victory is won by sacrifice—Christ's sacrifice for sin, and the sacrifices we make because of our faith in him. As we face the battle with Satan, we should not fear it or try to escape from it, but loyally serve Christ who alone brings victory (see Romans 8:34–39).

12:12 The devil begins to step up his persecution because he knows that he "has little time." We are living in the last days, and Satan's work has become more intense. Even though Satan is very powerful, as we can see by the condition of our world, he is always under God's control. One of the reasons God allows Satan to work evil and bring temptation is so that those who pretend to be Christ's followers will be weeded out from his true believers. Satan knows that the great confrontation with Jesus is near. He is desperately trying to recruit as great an enemy force as possible for this final battle.

12:17 While the woman (12:1) represents faithful Jews, and the child (12:5) represents Christ, the "rest of her children" could be either Jewish believers or all believers. Most likely it refers to all believers. He who stands waiting on the beach is the Dragon, Satan.

12:17
Rev 1:2; 11:7
13:7; 14:1

opening its mouth and swallowing the flood! 17Then the furious Dragon set out to attack the rest of her children—all who were keeping God's commandments and confessing that they belong to Jesus. He stood waiting on an ocean beach.

The two Creatures

13:1
Dan 7:2-8
Rev 13:4,12
17:12

13:2
Dan 7:4-6
Rev 2:13; 12:3

13:3
2 Thess 2:9-12
Rev 13:12,14
17:8

13:4
Rev 13:2,12

13:5
Dan 7:8,11,20,
25; 11:36
2 Thess 2:3
Rev 11:2

13:6
Rev 7:15; 12:12

13:7
Rev 5:9; 11:7

13:8
Dan 12:1
1 Pet 1:19,20

13 And now, in my vision, I saw a strange Creature rising up out of the sea. It had seven heads and ten horns, and ten crowns upon its horns. And written on each head were blasphemous names, each one defying and insulting God. 2This Creature looked like a leopard but had bear's feet and a lion's mouth! And the Dragon gave him his own power and throne and great authority.

3I saw that one of his heads seemed wounded beyond recovery—but the fatal wound was healed! All the world marveled at this miracle and followed the Creature in awe. 4They worshiped the Dragon for giving him such power, and they worshiped the strange Creature. "Where is there anyone as great as he?" they exclaimed. "Who is able to fight against him?"

5Then the Dragon encouraged the Creature to speak great blasphemies against the Lord; and gave him authority to control the earth for forty-two months. 6All that time he blasphemed God's Name and his temple and all those living in heaven. 7The Dragon gave him power to fight against God's people and to overcome them, and to rule over all nations and language groups throughout the world. 8And all mankind—whose names were not written down before the founding of the world in the slain Lamb's Book of Life—worshiped the evil Creature.

13:7 The Dragon gave him power to fight against God's people, literally, "It was permitted to fight against God's people." **13:8** whose names were not written down before the founding of the world in the slain Lamb's Book of Life, or "those whose names were not written in the Book of Life of the Lamb slain before the founding of the world." That is, regarded as slain in the eternal plan and knowledge of God.

12:17 The apostle Paul tells us we are in a spiritual battle (Ephesians 6:10–12). John says the war is still being waged, but the outcome is already determined. Satan and his followers have been defeated and will be destroyed. Nevertheless, Satan is battling daily to bring more into his ranks and to keep his own from defecting to God's side. Those who belong to Christ have gone into battle on God's side, and he has guaranteed them victory. God will not lose the war, but we must make certain not to lose the battle for our own souls. Don't waver in your commitment to Christ. A great spiritual battle is being fought, and there is no time for indecision.

13:1ff Chapter 13 introduces Satan's two evil accomplices: (1) the Creature that comes out of the sea (13:1ff) and (2) the strange animal that comes out of the earth (13:11ff). Together, the three evil beings form an unholy trinity in direct opposition to the holy Trinity of God the Father, the Son, and the Holy Spirit (see especially 16:13, 14).

When Satan tempted Jesus in the wilderness, he wanted Jesus to show his power by turning stones into bread, to do miracles by jumping from a high place, and to gain political power by worshiping Satan (see Matthew 4:1–11). Satan's plan was to rule the world through Jesus, but Jesus refused to do Satan's bidding. Thus Satan turns to the fearsome creatures described in Revelation. To the Creature from the sea he gives political power. To the strange animal from the earth he gives power to do miracles. And the Creature and the animal work together to capture the control of the whole world. This unholy trinity—the Dragon, the evil Creature, and the false prophet—unite in a desperate attempt to overthrow God, but their efforts are doomed to failure. To find out what becomes of them, read Revelation 19:19–21 and 20:10.

13:1 This Creature was initially identified with Rome because the Roman Empire, in its early days, had an evil lifestyle, persecuted believers, and opposed God and his followers. But the Creature also symbolizes the Antichrist—not Satan, but someone under

Satan's power and control. This Antichrist looks like a combination of the four beasts which Daniel saw centuries earlier in a vision (Daniel 7). As the Dragon is in opposition to God, so the Creature is against Christ and may be seen as Satan's false messiah. The early Roman Empire was strong and also anti-Christ (or against Christ's standards); many other individual powers throughout history have been anti-Christ. Many Christians believe that Satan's evil will culminate in a final Antichrist, one who will focus all the powers of evil against Jesus Christ and his followers.

13:3ff The Antichrist will be a counterfeit of Christ and will even stage a false resurrection (13:14). People will follow and worship him because they are awed by his power and miracles (13:3, 4). He will unite the world under his leadership (13:7, 8), and he will control the world economy (13:16, 17). People are impressed by power and will follow those who display it forcefully or offer it to their followers. But in following the Creature, they are only fooling themselves: he uses his power to manipulate others, to point to himself, and to promote evil plans. God, by contrast, uses his infinitely greater power to love and serve. Don't be misled by claims of great miracles or reports about a resurrection or reincarnation of someone claiming to be Christ. When Jesus returns, he will reveal himself to all believers (Matthew 24:23–28).

13:5 The power given to the Creature is limited by God. He allows the Creature to have it only for a short time. Even while the Creature is in power, God is still in control (11:15; 12:10–12).

13:5–7 The Creature will conquer God's people and rule over them, but he cannot harm them spiritually. He will establish worldwide dominance and demand that everyone worship him. And many will worship him—everyone except true believers (see 2 Thessalonians 2:3, 4). This will result in temporary suffering for God's people, but they will be rewarded with an eternal reward in the end.

13:8 See the note on 3:5 for more information on the Book of Life.

⁹Anyone who can hear, listen carefully: ¹⁰The people of God who are destined for prison will be arrested and taken away; those destined for death will be killed. But do not be dismayed, for here is your opportunity for endurance and confidence.

¹¹Then I saw another strange animal, this one coming up out of the earth, with two little horns like those of a lamb but a fearsome voice like the Dragon's. ¹²He exercised all the authority of the Creature whose death-wound had been healed, whom he required all the world to worship. ¹³He did unbelievable miracles such as making fire flame down to earth from the skies while everyone was watching. ¹⁴By doing these miracles, he was deceiving people everywhere. He could do these marvelous things whenever the first Creature was there to watch him. And he ordered the people of the world to make a great statue of the first Creature, who was fatally wounded and then came back to life. ¹⁵He was permitted to give breath to this statue and even make it speak! Then the statue ordered that anyone refusing to worship it must die!

¹⁶He required everyone—great and small, rich and poor, slave and free—to be tattooed with a certain mark on the right hand or on the forehead. ¹⁷And no one could get a job or even buy in any store without the permit of that mark, which was either the name of the Creature or the code number of his name. ¹⁸Here is a puzzle that calls for careful thought to solve it. Let those who are able, interpret this code: the numerical values of the letters in his name add to 666!

The Lamb and the 144,000

14 Then I saw a Lamb standing on Mount Zion in Jerusalem, and with him were 144,000 who had his Name and his Father's Name written on their foreheads. ²And I heard a sound from heaven like the roaring of a great waterfall or the rolling of mighty thunder. It was the singing of a choir accompanied by harps.

13:10
Mt 26:52
Heb 6:12

13:11
Rev 13:1,4

13:12
2 Thess 2:4
Rev 14:9; 19:20

13:13
Ex 7:11; 19:9-11
Mt 24:24
2 Thess 2:9
2 Tim 3:8
Rev 11:15
16:14; 19:20

13:14
2 Thess 2:9
Rev 12:9
13:3,8,12

13:15
Dan 3:3
7:20,25
Rev 20:4

13:16
Ps 49:2
Rev 14:9
19:17,18

14:1
Dan 12:5
Heb 12:22
Rev 3:12; 5:6
7:4

13:10 *those destined for death will be killed*, or, "If anyone imprisons you, he will be imprisoned! If anyone kills you, he will be killed." 13:18 *666*, some manuscripts read "616."

13:10 In this time of persecution, being faithful to Christ could bring imprisonment and even execution. But all that the Creature and his followers can do to believers is harm them physically; no spiritual harm can come to those whose faith in God is sincere.

13:10 "Destined for prison" and "destined for death" are simply other ways of saying that some believers will be hurt and some killed in this great persecution. But all believers will enter God's presence perfected and purified by the blood of the Lamb (7:9–17).

13:10 The times of great persecution which John saw will be an opportunity for believers to endure and grow. The tough times we face right now are also opportunities for spiritual growth. Don't fall into Satan's trap and turn away from God when hard times come. Instead, use these tough times as opportunities for growth.

13:11ff The first Creature came out of the sea (13:1), but this animal comes out of the earth. Later identified as the False Prophet (16:13; 19:20), he is a counterfeit of the Holy Spirit. He seems to do good, but the purpose of his miracles is to deceive.

13:14 Throughout the Bible we see miracles performed as proofs of God's power, love, and authority. But here we see counterfeit miracles performed to deceive. This is a reminder of Pharaoh's magicians, who duplicated Moses' signs in Egypt (Exodus 7–12). True signs and miracles point us to Jesus Christ, but miracles alone can be deceptive. That is why we must ask of each miracle we see, "Is this consistent with what God says in the Bible?" The Creature here gains influence through the signs and then orders the people to worship a statue (see note on Matthew 24:15, 16)—a direct flouting of the second commandment (Exodus 20:4–6). Allowing the Scriptures to guide our faith and practice will keep us from being deceived by false signs, however convincing they appear. Any teaching that contradicts God's Word is false.

13:16–18 This mark, sometimes translated, "the mark of the beast," is designed to mock the mark God places on his followers (7:2, 3). Just as God marks his people to save them, so Satan's Creature marks his people to save them from the persecution that Satan will inflict upon God's followers. Identifying this mark is not as important as identifying the purpose of the mark. Those who accept it are showing their allegiance to Satan, their willingness to operate within the economic system he promotes, and their rebellion against God. To refuse the mark means committing oneself entirely to God, preferring death to compromising one's faith in Christ.

13:18 The meaning of this number has been discussed more than that of any other part of the book of Revelation. The three sixes have been said to represent many things, including the number of man or the unholy trinity of Satan, the Creature, and the False Prophet (16:13). If the number seven is looked upon as the "perfect number" in the Bible, and if three sevens represent complete perfection, then the number 666 falls completely short of perfection. The first readers of this book probably applied the number to the emperor Nero, who symbolized all the evils of the Roman Empire. (The Greek letters of Nero's name represent numbers which total 666.) Whatever specific application the number is given, it symbolizes the worldwide dominion and complete evil of this unholy trinity designed to undo Christ's work and overthrow him.

14:1ff Chapter 13 described the onslaught of evil that will occur when Satan and his helpers control the world. Chapter 14 gives a glimpse of eternity to show believers what awaits them if they endure. The Lamb is the Messiah. Mount Zion, often another name for Jerusalem, the capital of Israel, is contrasted with the worldly empire. The 144,000 represent believers who have endured persecutions on earth and now are ready to enjoy the eternal benefits and blessings of life with God forever. The three angels contrast the destiny of believers with that of unbelievers.

14:3
Rev 2:17; 4:4,6

14:4
Mt 19:12
2 Cor 11:2
Rev 5:9; 7:13-17

14:5
Heb 9:14
1 Pet 2:22
Jude 24

3This tremendous choir—144,000 strong—sang a wonderful new song in front of the throne of God and before the four Living Beings and the twenty-four Elders; and no one could sing this song except those 144,000 who had been redeemed from the earth. 4For they are spiritually undefiled, pure as virgins, following the Lamb wherever he goes. They have been purchased from among the men on the earth as a consecrated offering to God and the Lamb. 5No falsehood can be charged against them; they are blameless.

The three angels

14:6
Rev 5:9

14:7
Ps 124:8
Dan 8:19
Acts 14:15
Rev 4:11

14:8
Jer 51:7,8
Nah 3:19
Rev 16:19
17:2-5
18:2,3,10

14:9
Rev 13:14,16

14:10
Ps 75:8
Ezek 38:22
Mk 8:38
2 Thess 1:7
Rev 16:19
19:20; 20:15
21:8

14:11
Rev 13:17

14:12
Rev 2:13
12:17; 13:10

6And I saw another angel flying through the heavens, carrying the everlasting Good News to preach to those on earth—to every nation, tribe, language and people.

7"Fear God," he shouted, "and extol his greatness. For the time has come when he will sit as Judge. Worship him who made the heaven and the earth, the sea and all its sources."

8Then another angel followed him through the skies, saying, "Babylon is fallen, is fallen—that great city—because she seduced the nations of the world and made them share the wine of her intense impurity and sin."

9Then a third angel followed them shouting, "Anyone worshiping the Creature from the sea and his statue and accepting his mark on the forehead or the hand, 10must drink the wine of the anger of God; it is poured out undiluted into God's cup of wrath. And they will be tormented with fire and burning sulphur in the presence of the holy angels and the Lamb. 11The smoke of their torture rises forever and ever, and they will have no relief day or night, for they have worshiped the Creature and his statue, and have been tattooed with the code of his name. 12Let this encourage God's people to endure patiently every trial and persecution, for they are his saints who remain firm to the end in obedience to his commands and trust in Jesus."

The harvest of the earth

13And I heard a voice in the heavens above me saying, "Write this down: At last

14:4 *For they are spiritually undefiled, pure as virgins,* literally, "They have not defiled themselves with women, for they are virgins." 14:9 *anyone worshiping the Creature from the sea,* implied. 14:13 *his martyrs,* literally, "those who die in the faith of Jesus." Vs 12 implies death from persecution for Christ's sake.

14:4 These people are "spiritually undefiled" because they are true believers, whose robes have been washed and purified by Christ's blood through his death (see the first note on 7:14). In the Old Testament, idolatry was often portrayed as spiritual adultery (see the book of Hosea). These believers are spiritually pure; they have remained faithful to Christ and they have received God's reward for staying committed to him.

14:6, 7 Some believe this is a final, worldwide appeal to all people to recognize the one true God. No one will have the excuse of never hearing God's truth. Others, however, see this as an announcement of judgment rather than an appeal. The people of the world have had their chance to proclaim their allegiance to God, and now God's great judgment is about to begin. If you are reading this, you have already heard God's truth. You know that God's final judgment will not be put off forever. Have you joyfully received the everlasting Good News? If so, you have nothing to fear from God's judgment. The Judge of all the earth is your Savior!

14:8 Babylon was both an evil city and an immoral empire, a world center for idol worship. Babylon ransacked Jerusalem and carried off the kingdom of Judah into captivity (see 2 Kings 24 and 2 Chronicles 36). Just as Babylon was the Jews' worst enemy, the early Roman Empire was the worst enemy of the early Christians. John, who did not dare speak against Rome openly, applied the name *Babylon* to this enemy of God's people (see also 1 Peter 5:13)—and, by extension, to all God's enemies of all times.

14:9-11 Those who worship the Creature, accept his mark on their foreheads, and operate according to the Creature's world

economic system will ultimately face God's judgment. Our world values money, power, and pleasure over God's leadership. To get what the world values, many people deny God and violate Christian principles. Thus they must drink the cup of God's wrath.

14:11 The ultimate result of sin is unending separation from God. Because human beings were created in God's image with an inborn thirst for fellowship with him, separation from God will be the ultimate torment and misery. Sin always brings misery, but in this life we can choose to repent and restore our relationship with God. In eternity there will no longer be opportunity for repentance. If in this life we choose to be independent of God, in the next life we will be separated from him forever. Nobody is forced to choose eternal separation from God and nobody suffers this fate by accident. Jesus invites all of us to open the door of our hearts to him (3:20). If we do this, we will enjoy everlasting fellowship with him.

14:12 This news about God's ultimate triumph should encourage God's people to remain firm through every trial and persecution. They can do this, God promises, by trusting in Jesus and obeying the commands in his Word. The secret to enduring, therefore, is trust and obedience. Trust God to give you patience to endure even the small trials you face daily; obey him, even when obedience is unattractive or dangerous.

14:13 The old saying, "You can't take it with you," is certainly true of money, fame, and belongings. But God's people can produce fruit that survives even death. God will remember our love, kindness, and faithfulness, and those who accept Christ through our witness will join us in the new earth.

the time has come for his martyrs to enter into their full reward. Yes, says the Spirit, they are blest indeed, for now they shall rest from all their toils and trials; for their good deeds follow them to heaven!" [14]Then the scene changed and I saw a white cloud, and someone sitting on it who looked like Jesus, who was called "The Son of Man," with a crown of solid gold upon his head and a sharp sickle in his hand.

[15]Then an angel came from the temple and called out to him, "Begin to use the sickle, for the time has come for you to reap; the harvest is ripe on the earth." [16]So the one sitting on the cloud swung his sickle over the earth, and the harvest was gathered in. [17]After that another angel came from the temple in heaven, and he also had a sharp sickle.

[18]Just then the angel who has power to destroy the world with fire, shouted to the angel with the sickle, "Use your sickle now to cut off the clusters of grapes from the vines of the earth, for they are fully ripe for judgment." [19]So the angel swung his sickle on the earth and loaded the grapes into the great winepress of God's wrath. [20]And the grapes were trodden in the winepress outside the city, and blood flowed out in a stream 200 miles long and as high as a horse's bridle.

14:14
Ezek 1:26
Dan 7:13
Rev 1:13; 6:2

14:15
Jer 51:33
Joel 3:13
Mt 13:39-41
Mk 4:29
Rev 14:17
15:6; 16:17

14:18
Joel 3:13
Rev 6:9; 8:3
14:15

14:19
Deut 32:32,33
Isa 62:2,3
Rev 16:8; 19:15

14:20
Gen 49:11
Lam 1:15
Ezek 39:17-21
Heb 13:11,12

5. Pouring out the seven plagues
The angels with the last plagues

15 And I saw in heaven another mighty pageant showing things to come: Seven angels were assigned to carry down to earth the seven last plagues—and then at last God's anger will be finished.

[2]Spread out before me was what seemed to be an ocean of fire and glass, and on it stood all those who had been victorious over the Evil Creature and his statue and his mark and number. All were holding harps of God, [3], [4]and they were singing the song of Moses, the servant of God, and the song of the Lamb:

"Great and marvelous
Are your doings,
Lord God Almighty.
Just and true
Are your ways,
O King of Ages.
Who shall not fear,
O Lord,
And glorify your Name?
For you alone are holy.
All nations will come
And worship before you,
For your righteous deeds
Have been disclosed."

15:1
Lev 26:21
Dan 4:2,3
6:27; 12:6-12
Rev 14:10; 15:6
16:1; 21:9

15:2
Rev 4:6; 5:8
12:11

15:3,4
Ex 15:1
Deut 32:3
Ps 86:9
Jer 10:7
Dan 9:11
Rev 5:9; 14:7

14:14 *"The Son of Man,"* literally, "one like a Son of Man." **14:18** *who has power to destroy the world with fire,* literally, "who has power over fire." **15:3, 4** *O King of Ages.* Some manuscripts read, "King of the Nations."

14:14–17 This is an image of judgment: Christ is separating the faithful from the unfaithful like a farmer harvesting his crops. This is a time of joy for the Christians who have been persecuted and martyred—they will receive their long-awaited reward. Christians should not fear the last judgment. Jesus said, "I say emphatically that anyone who listens to my message and believes in God who sent me has eternal life, and will never be damned for his sins, but has already passed out of death into life" (John 5:24).

14:19 A winepress was a large vat or trough where grapes were collected and then smashed. The juice flowed out of a duct that led into a large holding vat. The winepress is often used in the Bible as a symbol of God's wrath and judgment against sin (Isaiah

63:3–6; Lamentations 1:15; Joel 3:12, 13).

15:1 The seven last plagues are also called the seven flask judgments. They actually begin in chapter 16. Unlike the previous plagues, these are universal and will culminate in the abolition of all evil and the end of the world.

15:2 This is probably the "crystal sea" described in 4:6, located before the throne of God. Those who stand on it are victorious over Satan and his evil Creature. They are pure because they have been faithful to God to the end.

15:3, 4 The song of Moses celebrated Israel's deliverance from Egypt (Exodus 15). The song of the Lamb celebrates the ultimate deliverance of God's people from the power of Satan.

15:5
Rev 11:19

15:6
Rev 1:13
14:5; 15:6

15:7
Rev 4:6,9

15:8
Ex 19:18
1 Kgs 8:10
Isa 6:4

⁵Then I looked and saw that the Holy of Holies of the temple in heaven was thrown wide open!

⁶The seven angels who were assigned to pour out the seven plagues then came from the temple, clothed in spotlessly white linen, with golden belts across their chests. ⁷And one of the four Living Beings handed each of them a golden flask filled with the terrible wrath of the Living God who lives forever and forever. ⁸The temple was filled with smoke from his glory and power; and no one could enter until the seven angels had completed pouring out the seven plagues.

The flasks of God's wrath

16:1
Rev 11:19; 15:1

16:2
Ex 9:9-11
Rev 8:7
13:15-17

16:3
Ex 7:17-21
Rev 8:8,9

16:4
Ex 17:7
Rev 8:10; 11:16

16:5
Rev 1:4,8; 4:8
6:10; 11:17

16:6
Deut 32:42,43
2 Kgs 24:4
Isa 49:26

16:7
Rev 1:8; 6:9
14:18; 15:3; 19:2

16:8
Rev 6:12

16:9
Rev 11:13

16:10
Ex 10:21
Rev 8:12;
9:1,2; 13:2

16:11
Rev 2:21

16:12
Dan 11:43-45
Rev 9:13,14

16 And I heard a mighty voice shouting from the temple to the seven angels, "Now go your ways and empty out the seven flasks of the wrath of God upon the earth."

²So the first angel left the temple and poured out his flask over the earth, and horrible, malignant sores broke out on everyone who had the mark of the Creature and was worshiping his statue.

³The second angel poured out his flask upon the oceans, and they became like the watery blood of a dead man; and everything in all the oceans died.

⁴The third angel poured out his flask upon the rivers and springs and they became blood. ⁵And I heard this angel of the waters declaring, "You are just in sending this judgment, O Holy One, who is and was, ⁶for your saints and prophets have been martyred and their blood poured out upon the earth; and now, in turn, you have poured out the blood of those who murdered them; it is their just reward."

⁷And I heard the angel of the altar say, "Yes, Lord God Almighty, your punishments are just and true."

⁸Then the fourth angel poured out his flask upon the sun, causing it to scorch all men with its fire. ⁹Everyone was burned by this blast of heat, and they cursed the name of God who sent the plagues—they did not change their mind and attitude to give him glory.

¹⁰Then the fifth angel poured out his flask upon the throne of the Creature from the sea, and his kingdom was plunged into darkness. And his subjects gnawed their tongues in anguish, ¹¹and cursed the God of heaven for their pains and sores, but they refused to repent of all their evil deeds.

¹²The sixth angel poured out his flask upon the great River Euphrates and it dried up so that the kings from the east could march their armies westward without

16:10 *the Creature from the sea,* implied.

15:5–8 The Holy of Holies was the innermost room in the Temple (see Hebrews 9:1–17), where the ark of the covenant resided, (a symbol of God's presence among his people). This room was closed off from view by a great curtain. Only the High Priest could enter there, and only once a year on the Day of Atonement. The Holy of Holies was thrown open once before—at Christ's crucifixion, when the curtain was ripped from top to bottom (Matthew 27:50–53). The wide open entrance into the Holy of Holies symbolizes the open access to God's very presence which Christians have on the basis of Jesus' shed blood. Those of us who are united with the sinless Christ, our High Priest, can approach God boldly (Hebrews 4:14–16), but unrepentant sinners will be destroyed by his presence (Nahum 1:2–6).

The angels coming out of the temple are clothed in white with golden belts across their chests. Their garments, reminiscent of the High Priest's clothing, show that they are free from corruption, immorality, and injustice. The smoke that fills the Temple is the manifestation of God's glory and wrath. There is no escape from this judgment.

15:8 Our eternal reign with Christ won't begin until all evil is destroyed by his judgment.

16:1ff The flask judgments are God's final and complete

judgments upon the earth. The end has come. There are many similarities between the flask judgments and the trumpet judgments (8:6—11:19), but there are three main differences: (1) these judgments are complete where the trumpet judgments are partial; (2) the trumpet judgments still give unbelievers the opportunity to repent, but the flask judgments do not; and (3) mankind is indirectly affected by several of the trumpet judgments but directly attacked by all the flask judgments.

16:7 This verse can be translated, "I heard the altar cry." The significance of the altar itself crying out is that everyone and everything will be praising God, acknowledging his righteousness and perfect justice.

16:9–21 People knew that these judgments had come from God, because they cursed him for sending them. But they still refused to recognize God's authority and repent of their sins. If you find yourself ignoring God more and more, turn back to him now before your heart becomes too hard to repent (see the note on 9:20, 21 for more on hard hearts).

16:12 The Euphrates River was a natural protective boundary against the empires to the east (Babylon, Assyria, Persia). If it dried up, nothing could hold back invading armies. The armies of the east symbolize unhindered judgment.

hindrance. ¹³And I saw three evil spirits disguised as frogs leap from the mouth of the Dragon, the Creature, and his False Prophet. ¹⁴These miracle-working demons conferred with all the rulers of the world to gather them for battle against the Lord on that great coming Judgment Day of God Almighty.

¹⁵"Take note: I will come as unexpectedly as a thief! Blessed are all who are awaiting me, who keep their robes in readiness and will not need to walk naked and ashamed."

¹⁶And they gathered all the armies of the world near a place called, in Hebrew, Armageddon—the Mountain of Megiddo.

¹⁷Then the seventh angel poured out his flask into the air; and a mighty shout came from the throne of the temple in heaven, saying, "It is finished!" ¹⁸Then the thunder crashed and rolled, and lightning flashed; and there was a great earthquake of a magnitude unprecedented in human history. ¹⁹The great city of "Babylon" split into three sections, and cities around the world fell in heaps of rubble; and so all of "Babylon's" sins were remembered in God's thoughts, and she was punished to the last drop of anger in the cup of the wine of the fierceness of his wrath. ²⁰And islands vanished, and mountains flattened out, ²¹and there was an incredible hailstorm from heaven; hailstones weighing a hundred pounds fell from the sky onto the people below, and they cursed God because of the terrible hail.

6. Seizing the final victory
The Prostitute and the scarlet animal

17 One of the seven angels who had poured out the plagues came over and talked with me. "Come with me," he said, "and I will show you what is going to happen to the Notorious Prostitute, who sits upon the many waters of the world. ²The kings of the world have had immoral relations with her, and the people of the earth have been made drunk by the wine of her immorality."

³So the angel took me in spirit into the wilderness. There I saw a woman sitting on a scarlet animal that had seven heads and ten horns, written all over with blasphemies against God. ⁴The woman wore purple and scarlet clothing and beautiful jewelry made of gold and precious gems and pearls, and held in her hand a golden goblet full of obscenities:

⁵A mysterious caption was written on her forehead: "Babylon the Great, Mother of Prostitutes and of Idol Worship Everywhere around the World."

⁶I could see that she was drunk—drunk with the blood of the martyrs of Jesus she had killed. I stared at her in horror.

16:13
Rev 12:3
13:1,11,14

16:14
Rev 6:17;
17:14; 19:19

16:15
1 Thess 5:2
Rev 3:3,18

16:16
Judg 5:19
Zech 12:10,11
Rev 19:19

16:17
Dan 12:7-13
Rev 11:15; 21:6

16:18
Mt 24:21
Rev 4:5; 6:12

16:19
Rev 14:8,10

16:20
Rev 6:14; 20:11

16:21
Ex 9:18-25
Rev 11:19; 16:9

17:1
Jer 51:13
Rev 17:5,15
19:2; 21:9

17:2
Jer 51:7-9
Rev 14:8; 17:8
18:3,9

17:3
Rev 1:10; 12:3,6
13:1

17:5
2 Thess 2:7
Rev 16:19
17:2,7

17:6
Dan 7:21,25
Rev 6:9; 16:6
12:11

16:13 his False Prophet, described in 13:11-15 and 19:20.   **16:17** It is finished, literally, "It has happened."

16:13, 14 These miracle-working demons that come from the unholy trinity unite the rulers of the world for battle against God. The demons which come from the mouths of the three evil rulers signify the verbal enticements and propaganda that will draw many people to their evil causes. For more about demons, see the note on 9:3ff.

16:15 Christ will return unexpectedly (1 Thessalonians 5:1–6), so we must be ready when he returns. We can prepare ourselves by standing firm in the midst of temptation and by being committed to God's moral standards. In what ways does your life show both your readiness and your lack of preparation for Christ's return?

16:16 This battlefield is near the city of Meggido (southeast of the modern port of Haifa) which guarded a large plain in northern Israel. It is a strategic location near a prominent international highway leading north from Egypt through Israel, along the coast, and on to Babylon. Megiddo overlooked the entire plain southward toward Galilee and westward toward Mount Gilboa.

16:16 Sinful men will unite to fight against God in a final display of rebellion. Many are already united against Christ and his people who stand for truth, peace, justice, and morality. Your personal battle with evil foreshadows the great battle pictured here, where God will meet evil and destroy it once and for all. Be

strong and courageous as you battle against sin and evil: you are fighting on the winning side.

16:17–21 For more information on Babylon and what it represents in Revelation, see the note on 14:8. The city's division into three sections is a symbol of its complete destruction.

17:1ff The destruction of Babylon mentioned in 16:17–21 is now described in greater detail. The Notorious Prostitute, called Babylon, represented the early Roman Empire with its many gods and the blood of Christian martyrs on its hands. The Prostitute represents the seductiveness of the governmental system as it used immoral means to gain its own pleasure, prosperity, and advantage. In contrast to the Prostitute, Christ's bride, the church is pure and obedient (19:6–9). The wicked city of Babylon stands in contrast to the heavenly city of Jerusalem (21:10—22:5). The original readers easily identified Babylon with Rome, but it also symbolizes any system that is hostile to God (see 17:5).

17:3 The scarlet animal is either the Dragon of 12:3, or the Creature from the sea described in 13:1.

17:6 Throughout history people have been killed for their faith. Over the last century, millions have been killed by oppressive governments, and many of these were believers. The woman's drunkenness shows her pleasure in her evil accomplishments and

17:8
Rev 11:7; 13:1-8,
12,14

17:9
Rev 17:3

17:11
Rev 18:19

17:12
Dan 7:20-22
Rev 17:16
18:10,17,19

17:14
Mt 22:14
1 Tim 6:15
1 Pet 2:9
Rev 3:21; 16:14

17:15
Isa 8:7
Jer 47:2
Rev 13:7; 17:1

17:16
Jer 50:41,42
Ezek 16:37
Dan 7:5
Rev 18:8,19

17:17
Rev 10:7; 17:13

17:18
Rev 11:8; 16:19

18:1
Ezek 43:2
Rev 10:1

7"Why are you so surprised?" the angel asked. "I'll tell you who she is and what the animal she is riding represents. 8He was alive but isn't now. And yet, soon he will come up out of the bottomless pit and go to eternal destruction; and the people of earth, whose names have not been written in the Book of Life before the world began, will be dumbfounded at his reappearance after being dead.

9"And now think hard: his seven heads represent a certain city built on seven hills where this woman has her residence. 10They also represent seven kings. Five have already fallen, the sixth now reigns, and the seventh is yet to come, but his reign will be brief. 11The scarlet animal that died is the eighth king, having reigned before as one of the seven; after his second reign, he too, will go to his doom. 12His ten horns are ten kings who have not yet risen to power; they will be appointed to their kingdoms for one brief moment, to reign with him. 13They will all sign a treaty giving their power and strength to him. 14Together they will wage war against the Lamb, and the Lamb will conquer them; for he is Lord over all lords, and King of kings, and his people are the called and chosen and faithful ones.

15"The oceans, lakes and rivers that the woman is sitting on represent masses of people of every race and nation.

16"The scarlet animal and his ten horns—which represent ten kings who will reign with him—all hate the woman, and will attack her and leave her naked and ravaged by fire. 17For God will put a plan into their minds, a plan that will carry out his purposes: They will mutually agree to give their authority to the scarlet animal, so that the words of God will be fulfilled. 18And this woman you saw in your vision represents the great city that rules over the kings of the earth."

The fall of Babylon

18 After all this I saw another angel come down from heaven with great authority, and the earth grew bright with his splendor.

17:8 go to eternal destruction, literally, "go to perdition." dumbfounded at his reappearance after being dead, literally, "dumbfounded at the ruler who was, and is not, and will be present." **17:9** represent a certain city, implied in vs 18.

HOW CAN A PERSON KEEP AWAY FROM THE EVIL SYSTEM?
Here are some suggestions:

1. People must always be more important than products.
2. Keep away from pride in your own programs, plans, and successes.
3. Remember that God's will and Word must never be compromised.
4. People must always be considered above the making of money.
5. Do what is right, no matter what the cost.
6. Be involved in businesses that provide worthwhile products or services—not just things that feed the world's desires.

---

her false feeling of triumph over the church. But every martyr who fell before her sword only strengthened the church.

17:8 In chapter 12 we met the Dragon (Satan). In chapter 13 we saw the Creature from the sea and the power he received from Satan. In chapters 14—16 we see God's great judgments. In this chapter, a scarlet animal similar to the Creature and the Dragon appears as an ally of the Notorious Prostitute. The animal's resurrection symbolizes the persistence of evil. This resurgence of evil power will convince many to join forces with him, but those who choose the side of evil condemn themselves to the devil's fate—eternal torment.

17:8 For more information on the Book of Life, see the note on 3:5.

17:9-14 Here John was almost certainly referring to Rome, the city famous for its seven hills. Many say this city also symbolizes all evil in the world—any person, religion, group, government, or structure that is against Christ. Whatever view is taken of the seven hills and seven kings, this section indicates the climax of Satan's struggle against God. Evil's power is limited and its destruction is on the horizon.

17:12 The ten horns represent kings of nations yet to arise. Rome

will be followed by other powers. Rome is a good example of how the Antichrist's system will work, demanding complete allegiance, and ruling by raw power, oppression, and slavery. Whoever the ten kings are, they will give their power to the Antichrist and will wage war against the Lamb.

17:16 In a dramatic turn of events, the woman's allies turn on her and destroy her. This is how evil operates. Destructive by its very nature, it discards its own adherents when they cease to serve its purposes. An unholy alliance is an uneasy alliance, because each partner puts its own interests first.

17:17 No matter what happens, we must trust that God is still in charge, and his plans will happen just as he says. He even uses people opposed to him to execute his will. Although he allows evil to permeate this present world, the new earth will never know sin.

18:1ff This chapter shows the complete destruction of Babylon, John's metaphorical name for the evil world power, and all it represents. Everything that tries to block God's purposes will come to a violent end. For more information on how the book of Revelation uses the name Babylon, see the note on 14:8.

²He gave a mighty shout, "Babylon the Great is fallen, is fallen; she has become a den of demons, a haunt of devils and every kind of evil spirit. ³For all the nations have drunk the fatal wine of her intense immorality. The rulers of earth have enjoyed themselves with her, and businessmen throughout the world have grown rich from all her luxurious living."

⁴Then I heard another voice calling from heaven, "Come away from her, my people; do not take part in her sins, or you will be punished with her. ⁵For her sins are piled as high as heaven and God is ready to judge her for her crimes. ⁶Do to her as she has done to you, and more—give double penalty for all her evil deeds. She brewed many a cup of woe for others—give twice as much to her. ⁷She has lived in luxury and pleasure—match it now with torments and with sorrows. She boasts, 'I am queen upon my throne. I am no helpless widow. I will not experience sorrow.' ⁸Therefore the sorrows of death and mourning and famine shall overtake her in a single day, and she shall be utterly consumed by fire; for mighty is the Lord who judges her."

⁹And the world leaders, who took part in her immoral acts and enjoyed her favors, will mourn for her as they see the smoke rising from her charred remains. ¹⁰They will stand far off, trembling with fear and crying out, "Alas, Babylon, that mighty city! In one moment her judgment fell."

¹¹The merchants of the earth will weep and mourn for her, for there is no one left to buy their goods. ¹²She was their biggest customer for gold and silver, precious stones, pearls, finest linens, purple silks, and scarlet; and every kind of perfumed wood, and ivory goods and most expensive wooden carvings, and brass and iron and marble; ¹³and spices and perfumes and incense, ointment and frankincense, wine, olive oil, and fine flour; wheat, cattle, sheep, horses, chariots, and slaves—and even the souls of men.

¹⁴"All the fancy things you loved so much are gone," they cry. "The dainty luxuries and splendor that you prized so much will never be yours again. They are gone forever."

¹⁵And so the merchants who have become wealthy by selling her these things shall stand at a distance, fearing danger to themselves, weeping and crying, ¹⁶"Alas, that great city, so beautiful—like a woman clothed in finest purple and scarlet linens, decked out with gold and precious stones and pearls! ¹⁷In one moment, all the wealth of the city is gone!"

And all the shipowners and captains of the merchant ships and crews will stand

18:2
Isa 13:19-22
14:23; 21:8,9
Jer 50:39
Rev 14:8
18:3
Ezek 27:9-25
1 Tim 5:11
Rev 17:2
18:4
Gen 19:12,13
Isa 52:11
Jer 51:6,9,45
2 Cor 6:17
18:5
Jer 51:9
Jonah 1:2
Rev 16:19
18:6
Ps 137:8
Jer 51:24
Rev 17:4
18:7
Isa 47:7,8
18:8
Isa 47:9
Jer 50:31,34
Rev 17:16
18:9
Ps 58:10
Jer 50:46
Ezek 26:16
Dan 4:14
Rev 17:2
18:10
Num 16:34
Amos 5:16
Rev 14:8
18:11
Ezek 27:27
Rev 18:3
18:13
1 Tim 1:10
18:16
Lk 16:19
Rev 17:4
18:17
Isa 47:9
Ezek 27:27-36
Jonah 1:6
Rev 17:16

18:2 *of evil spirit,* literally, "of every foul and hateful bird."   **18:3** *have enjoyed themselves with her,* literally, "have committed fornication with her."

18:2, 3 Businessmen in the Roman Empire grew rich by exploiting the sinful pleasures of their society. Many business people today do the same thing. Businesses and governments are often based on greed, money, and power. Many bright individuals are tempted to take advantage of an evil system to enrich themselves. Christians are warned to stay free from the enchantment of money, status, and the "good life." We are to live according to the values Christ lived by: service, giving, self-sacrifice, obedience, and truth.

18:4–8 Babylon "lived in luxury and pleasure." She boasted, "I am queen upon my throne. . . . I will not experience sorrow." The powerful, wealthy people of this world are susceptible to this same attitude. A person who is financially comfortable often feels invulnerable, secure, and in control, not in need of God or anyone else. This kind of attitude defies God, and his judgment against it is harsh. We are told to avoid "her sins" (18:4). If you are financially secure, don't become complacent and deluded by the myth of self-sufficiency. Use your resources to help others and advance God's Kingdom.

18:9, 10 Those who are tied to the world's system will lose everything when it is taken away. Those who work only for material rewards will have nothing when they die or when their possessions are destroyed. What can we take with us to the new earth? Our faith, our characters, and our good deeds toward others. These

are more important than any amount of money, power, or pleasure.

18:9–19 Those who are in control of various parts of the economic system will mourn at Babylon's fall. The leaders will mourn because they were the overseers of Babylon's wealth and were in a position to enrich themselves greatly. The merchants will mourn because Babylon, the greatest customer for their goods, is gone. The sailors will no longer have anywhere to bring their goods because the merchants have nowhere to sell them. The fall of the evil world system affects all who enjoyed and depended on it. No one remains unaffected by Babylon's fall.

18:11–13 This list of various merchandise illustrates the extreme materialism of this society. Few of these goods are necessities—most are luxuries. The society had become so self-indulgent that people were willing to use evil means to gratify their desires. Even people had become commodities—the "souls of men," slaves, were sold to Babylon. It is amazing to realize that many of these goods, associated with unbelievable luxury in the ancient world, can be found in our homes. In our affluent society it is very easy to leave God out of this part of our lives.

18:11–19 God's people should not live for money. Instead, they should keep on guard constantly against greed, which is always ready to take over their lives. Money will be worthless in eternity, and God calls greed sinful.

18:18
Ezek 27:30,32
Rev 13:4

18:19
Ezek 27:30

18:20
Jer 51:48
Lk 11:49,50
Rev 6:10
12:12; 19:2

18:21
Jer 51:63,64
Dan 11:19

18:22
Ezek 26:13

18:23
Prov 4:18,19
24:20
Jer 7:34; 16:9
Nah 3:4

18:24
Mt 23:35-36
Rev 16:6; 17:6

19:1
Jer 51:48
Jonah 2:9
Mt 6:13
Rev 4:11;
7:10; 12:10

19:2
Rev 6:10;
16:7; 17:1; 18:20

19:3
Isa 34:10
Rev 4:4; 14:11

19:4
Rev 4:10; 5:14

19:5
Rev 11:18

19:6
Rev 11:15

19:7
Ps 45:10-16
Mt 25:1-10
Eph 5:25-32
Rev 21:2

19:8
Ps 45:13; 132:9
Rev 15:4,6
19:14

19:9
Lk 14:15; 22:16
Rev 21:5; 22:6

19:10
Rev 22:8,9

a long way off, ¹⁸crying as they watch the smoke ascend, and saying, "Where in all the world is there another city such as this?" ¹⁹And they will throw dust on their heads in their sorrow and say, "Alas, alas, for that great city! She made us all rich from her great wealth. And now in a single hour all is gone. . . ."

²⁰But you, O heaven, rejoice over her fate; and you, O children of God and the prophets and the apostles! For at last God has given judgment against her for you.

²¹Then a mighty angel picked up a boulder shaped like a millstone and threw it into the ocean and shouted, "Babylon, that great city, shall be thrown away as I have thrown away this stone, and she shall disappear forever. ²²Never again will the sound of music be there—no more pianos, saxophones, and trumpets. No industry of any kind will ever again exist there, and there will be no more milling of the grain. ²³Dark, dark will be her nights; not even a lamp in a window will ever be seen again. No more joyous wedding bells and happy voices of the bridegrooms and the brides. Her businessmen were known around the world and she deceived all nations with her sorceries. ²⁴And she was responsible for the blood of all the martyred prophets and the saints."

19 After this I heard the shouting of a vast crowd in heaven, "Hallelujah! Praise the Lord! Salvation is from our God. Honor and authority belong to him alone; ²for his judgments are just and true. He has punished the Great Prostitute who corrupted the earth with her sin; and he has avenged the murder of his servants."

³Again and again their voices rang, "Praise the Lord! The smoke from her burning ascends forever and forever!"

⁴Then the twenty-four Elders and four Living Beings fell down and worshiped God, who was sitting upon the throne, and said, "Amen! Hallelujah! Praise the Lord!"

⁵And out of the throne came a voice that said, "Praise our God, all you his servants, small and great, who fear him."

The wedding banquet of the Lamb

⁶Then I heard again what sounded like the shouting of a huge crowd, or like the waves of a hundred oceans crashing on the shore, or like the mighty rolling of great thunder, "Praise the Lord. For the Lord our God, the Almighty, reigns. ⁷Let us be glad and rejoice and honor him; for the time has come for the wedding banquet of the Lamb, and his bride has prepared herself. ⁸She is permitted to wear the cleanest and whitest and finest of linens." (Fine linen represents the good deeds done by the people of God.)

⁹And the angel dictated this sentence to me: "Blessed are those who are invited to the wedding feast of the Lamb." And he added, "God himself has stated this."

¹⁰Then I fell down at his feet to worship him, but he said, "No! Don't! For I am a servant of God just as you are, and as your brother Christians are, who testify of

18:22 *no more pianos, saxophones, and trumpets,* literally, "harpers . . . pipers . . . and trumpeters." **19:2** *sin,* literally, "fornication," the word used symbolically throughout the prophets for the worship of false gods. **19:9** *the angel,* literally, "he"; the exact antecedent is unclear. *God himself has stated this,* literally, "These are the true words of God." **19:10** *The purpose of all prophecy and of all I have shown you is to tell about Jesus,* literally, "The testimony of Jesus is the spirit of prophecy."

19:1, 2 The identity of this Great (or Notorious) Prostitute is explained in the note on 17:1.

19:1–8 A "vast crowd in heaven" initiates the chorus of praise to God for his victory (19:1-3). Then the 24 elders (identified in the note on 4:4), join the chorus (19:4). Finally, the great choir of heaven once again praises God—the wedding banquet of the Lamb has come (19:6-8).

19:1–10 Praise is the heartfelt response to God by those who love him. The more you get to know him and realize what he has done, the more you will respond with praise. Praise is at the heart of true worship. Let your praise of God flow out of your realization of who he is and how much he loves you.

19:7 This is the culmination of human history—the judgment of

the wicked and the marriage feast of the Lamb and his bride, the church. The church consists of all faithful believers from all time. The bride's purity stands in stark contrast to the filth of the Notorious Prostitute of chapter 17.

19:7–9 Here the church is pictured as both the bride (19:7, 8) and the guests invited to the wedding feast (19:9). As those given to Christ, we are the bride; as those called to be part of God's Kingdom, we are the invited guests.

19:9, 10 Jesus is the central focus of God's revelation and his redemptive plan (as announced by the prophets). As you read the book of Revelation, don't get bogged down in all the details of the awesome visions; remember that the overarching theme in all the visions is the ultimate victory of Jesus Christ over evil.

their faith in Jesus. The purpose of all prophecy and of all I have shown you is to tell about Jesus."

The rider on the white horse

¹¹Then I saw heaven opened and a white horse standing there; and the one sitting on the horse was named "Faithful and True"—the one who justly punishes and makes war. ¹²His eyes were like flames, and on his head were many crowns. A name was written on his forehead, and only he knew its meaning. ¹³He was clothed with garments dipped in blood, and his title was "The Word of God." ¹⁴The armies of heaven, dressed in finest linen, white and clean, followed him on white horses.

¹⁵In his mouth he held a sharp sword to strike down the nations; he ruled them with an iron grip; and he trod the winepress of the fierceness of the wrath of Almighty God. ¹⁶On his robe and thigh was written this title: "King of Kings and Lord of Lords."

¹⁷Then I saw an angel standing in the sunshine, shouting loudly to the birds, "Come! Gather together for the supper of the Great God! ¹⁸Come and eat the flesh of kings, and captains, and great generals; of horses and riders; and of all humanity, both great and small, slave and free."

¹⁹Then I saw the Evil Creature gathering the governments of the earth and their armies to fight against the one sitting on the horse and his army. ²⁰And the Evil Creature was captured, and with him the False Prophet, who could do mighty miracles when the Evil Creature was present—miracles that deceived all who had accepted the Evil Creature's mark, and who worshiped his statue. Both of them—the Evil Creature and his False Prophet—were thrown alive into the Lake of Fire that burns with sulphur. ²¹And their entire army was killed with the sharp sword in the mouth of the one riding the white horse, and all the birds of heaven were gorged with their flesh.

The 1,000 years

20 Then I saw an angel come down from heaven with the key to the bottomless pit and a heavy chain in his hand. ²He seized the Dragon—that old Serpent, the devil, Satan—and bound him in chains for 1,000 years, ³and threw him into the

19:11
Isa 11:4
Rev 1:14; 3:14
6:2

19:12
Rev 2:17

19:13
Isa 63:1-3
Jn 1:1,14

19:14
Mt 28:3
Rev 3:4; 4:4

19:15
Isa 11:4; 63:3
2 Thess 2:8
Rev 1:16; 2:27
14:19,20

19:16
Rev 2:17; 17:14

19:17
Isa 56:9
Jer 12:9
Ezek 39:17-20

19:19
Rev 13:1
16:14,16; 18:9

19:20
Dan 2:40-45
7:7,11-14
2 Thess 2:8-11
Rev 13:11-16
20:10,14,15
21:8

20:1
Rev 1:18; 9:1

20:2
Rev 12:9

19:12 *A name was written on his forehead,* implied.   **19:13** *The Word of God,* literally, "The Logos," as in Jn 1:1—the ultimate method of God's revealing himself to man.   **19:20** *the False Prophet.* See ch 13, vss 11-16.

19:11 The name "Faithful and True" contrasts with the faithless and deceitful Babylon described in chapter 18.

19:11–21 John's vision shifts again. Heaven opens and Jesus appears; this time not as a Lamb, but as a warrior on a white horse (symbolizing victory). Jesus came first as a Lamb to be a sacrifice for sin, but he will return as a Conqueror and King to execute judgment (2 Thessalonians 1:7–10). His first coming brought forgiveness, his second will bring judgment. The battle lines have now been drawn between God and evil, and the world is waiting for the King to ride onto the field.

19:12 Although Jesus is called the "Faithful and True" (19:11), the "Word of God" (19:13), and the "King of Kings and Lord of Lords" (19:16), this verse implies that no name can do him justice. He is greater than any description or expression the human mind can devise for him.

19:13 For more about the symbolism of Jesus' garments being dipped in blood, see the first note on 7:14.

19:16 This title indicates our God's sovereignty. Most of the world is worshiping the Antichrist, who they believe has all power and authority. Then suddenly out of heaven rides Christ and his army of angels—the "King of Kings and Lord of Lords." His entrance signals the end of the false powers.

19:17 This "supper of the Great God" is a grim contrast to the wedding banquet of the Lamb (19:7). One is a celebration; the other, devastation.

19:19 The Evil Creature is identified in the note on 13:1.

19:19–21 The battle lines are drawn, and the greatest confrontation in the history of the world is about to begin. The Antichrist and the False Prophet have gathered the governments and armies of the earth under the Antichrist's rule (see 16:14). They believe they have come of their own volition; in reality, God has summoned them to battle in order to defeat them. There really is no fight, however, because the victory was won when Jesus died on the cross for sin and rose from the dead. Thus the evil leaders are immediately captured and sent to their punishment, and the forces of evil are all annihilated.

19:20 The Lake of Fire is the final destination of the wicked. It is different from the bottomless pit referred to in 9:1. The Evil Creature and the False Prophet are thrown into the Lake of Fire. Then their leader, Satan himself, is cast there (20:10). Finally Death and Hell are also cast there (20:14). Afterward, everyone whose name is not recorded in the Book of Life will be sent to the same fate (20:15).

20:1 The bottomless pit is explained in the notes on 9:1 and 19:20.

20:2 The Dragon, Satan, is discussed in more detail in the notes on 12:3, 4 and 12:9. The Dragon is not bound in chains for punishment—that occurs in 20:10—but so that he cannot deceive the nations.

20:3 John doesn't say why God once again releases Satan, but it is part of his plan for judging the world. Perhaps it is to expose those who rebel against God in their hearts and confirm those who are truly faithful to God. Whatever the reason, Satan's release

20:4
Dan 7:9,18,
22,27
Mt 19:28
2 Tim 2:12
Rev 3:21
6:9,13

20:5
Ezek 37:2-14
Lk 14:14
Jn 5:28,29
Rom 11:15

20:6
1 Pet 2:9
Rev 1:6; 5:10
20:14; 21:8

20:7
Rev 20:2

20:8
Ezek 38:2
Rev 16:14

20:9
Ps 87:2
Ezek 38:9,22
Lk 9:54; 17:29

20:10
Mt 25:41,46
Rev 14:10; 19:20
20:14,15

20:12
Rom 14:10-12

bottomless pit, which he then shut and locked, so that he could not fool the nations any more until the thousand years were finished. Afterwards he would be released again for a little while.

⁴Then I saw thrones, and sitting on them were those who had been given the right to judge. And I saw the souls of those who had been beheaded for their testimony about Jesus, for proclaiming the Word of God, and who had not worshiped the Creature or his statue, nor accepted his mark on their foreheads or their hands. They had come to life again and now they reigned with Christ for a thousand years.

⁵This is the First Resurrection. (The rest of the dead did not come back to life until the thousand years had ended.) ⁶Blessed and holy are those who share in the First Resurrection. For them the Second Death holds no terrors, for they will be priests of God and of Christ, and shall reign with him a thousand years.

The destruction of Satan

⁷When the thousand years end, Satan will be let out of his prison. ⁸He will go out to deceive the nations of the world and gather them together, with Gog and Magog, for battle—a mighty host, numberless as sand along the shore. ⁹They will go up across the broad plain of the earth and surround God's people and the beloved city of Jerusalem on every side. But fire from God in heaven will flash down on the attacking armies and consume them.

¹⁰Then the devil who had betrayed them will again be thrown into the Lake of Fire burning with sulphur where the Creature and False Prophet are, and they will be tormented day and night forever and ever.

The final judgment

¹¹And I saw a great white throne and the one who sat upon it, from whose face the earth and sky fled away, but they found no place to hide. ¹²I saw the dead, great

20:9 *of Jerusalem*, implied.   **20:11** *they found no place to hide*, literally, "There was no longer any place for them."

---

results in the final destruction of all evil (20:12–15).

20:2–4 The thousand years are often referred to as the *millennium*, (Latin for "one thousand"). Just how and when this thousand years takes place is understood differently among Christian scholars. The three major positions on this issue are called postmillennialism, premillennialism, and amillennialism.

(1) *Postmillennialism* looks for a literal thousand-year period of peace on earth brought in by the church. At the end of the thousand years, Satan will be unleashed once more, but then Christ will return to defeat him and reign forever. Christ's Second Coming does not occur until after the thousand-year period.

(2) *Premillennialism* also views the thousand years as a literal time period, but holds that Christ's Second Coming initiates his thousand-year reign and this reign occurs before the final removal of Satan.

(3) *Amillennialism* understands the thousand-year period to be symbolic of the time between Christ's ascension and his return. This millennium is the reign of Christ in the hearts of believers and in his church; thus it is the same as the church age. This period will end with the Second Coming of Christ.

These different views about the millennium need not cause division and controversy in the church, because each one acknowledges what is most crucial to Christianity—Christ will return, defeat Satan, and reign forever! Whatever and whenever the millennium is, Jesus Christ will unite all believers. We should not let this issue divide us.

20:4 The Creature's mark is explained in the note on 13:16–18.

20:5, 6 Christians hold two basic views concerning this First Resurrection. (1) Some believe the First Resurrection is spiritual, and that the millennium is our spiritual reign with Christ between his first and second comings. During this time, we are priests of God because Christ reigns in our hearts. In this view, the Second Resurrection is the bodily resurrection of all people for judgment.

(2) Others believe the First Resurrection occurs after Satan has been set aside. It is a physical resurrection of believers who then reign with Christ on the earth for a literal 1,000 years. The Second Resurrection occurs at the end of this millennium in order to judge unbelievers who have died.

20:6 The Second Death is spiritual death—everlasting separation from God (see 21:8).

20:7–9 Gog and Magog symbolize all the forces of evil who band together to battle God. Noah's son, Japheth, had a son named Magog (Genesis 10:2). Ezekiel presents Gog as a leader of forces against Israel (Ezekiel 38, 39).

20:9 This is not a typical battle where the outcome is in doubt during the heat of the conflict. Here there is no contest. Two mighty forces of evil—those of the Creature (19:19) and of Satan (20:8)—unite to do battle against God. The Bible uses just two verses to describe each battle—the evil Creature and his forces are captured and thrown into the Lake of Fire (19:20, 21), and fire from God consumes Satan and his attacking armies (20:9, 10). For God, it is as easy as that. There will be no doubt, no worry, no second thoughts for believers about whether they have chosen the right side. If you have chosen God, you will experience this tremendous victory with Christ.

20:10 Satan's power is not eternal—he will meet his doom. He began his evil work in mankind at the beginning (Genesis 3:1–6) and continues it today, but he will be destroyed when he is thrown into the Lake of Fire. Satan was released from the bottomless pit (20:7), but he will never be released from the Lake of Fire. He will never be a threat to anyone again.

20:11–15 At the judgment, the Books are opened. They represent God's judgment, and in them are recorded the deeds of everyone, good or evil. The Book of Life contains the names of those who have put their trust in Christ to save them.

and small, standing before God; and The Books were opened, including the Book of Life. And the dead were judged according to the things written in The Books, each according to the deeds he had done. ¹³The oceans surrendered the bodies buried in them; and the earth and the underworld gave up the dead in them. Each was judged according to his deeds. ¹⁴And Death and Hell were thrown into the Lake of Fire. This is the Second Death—the Lake of Fire. ¹⁵And if anyone's name was not found recorded in the Book of Life, he was thrown into the Lake of Fire.

20:13
Mt 16:27
20:14
1 Cor 15:26; 53
Rev 20:6,10,15
20:15
Rev 3:5; 20:12

7. Making all things new
The new earth

21 Then I saw a new earth (with no oceans!) and a new sky, for the present earth and sky had disappeared. ²And I, John, saw the Holy City, the new Jerusalem, coming down from God out of heaven. It was a glorious sight, beautiful as a bride at her wedding.

³I heard a loud shout from the throne saying, "Look, the home of God is now among men, and he will live with them and they will be his people; yes, God himself will be among them. ⁴He will wipe away all tears from their eyes, and there shall be no more death, nor sorrow, nor crying, nor pain. All of that has gone forever."

⁵And the one sitting on the throne said, "See, I am making all things new!" And then he said to me, "Write this down, for what I tell you is trustworthy and true: ⁶It is finished! I am the A and the Z—the Beginning and the End. I will give to the

21:1
Isa 65:17; 66:22
2 Pet 3:10,13
21:2
Jer 31:23
Heb 11:10; 12:22
21:3
2 Cor 6:16
21:4
Isa 25:8; 35:10
61:3
Rev 7:17
21:5
Isa 43:19
2 Cor 5:17
21:6
Rev 1:8; 22:17

21:3 *be among them;* some manuscripts add, "and be their God."

Genesis	*Revelation*	**THE BEGINNING AND THE END**
The sun is created	The sun is not needed	The Bible records for us the beginning of the world and the end of the world. The story of mankind, from beginning to end—from the fall into sin to the redemption of Christ and God's ultimate victory over evil—is found in the pages of the Bible.
Satan is victorious	Satan is defeated	
Sin enters the human race	Sin is banished	
People run and hide from God	People are invited to live with God forever	
People are cursed	The curse is removed	
Tears are shed, with sorrow for sin	No more sin, no more tears or sorrow	
The Garden and earth are cursed	God's city is glorified, the earth is made new	
The fruit from the Tree of Life is not to be eaten	God's people may eat from the Tree of Life	
Paradise is lost	Paradise is regained	
People are doomed to death	Death is defeated, believers live forever with God	

20:14 Death and Hell are thrown into the Lake of Fire— when God's judgment is finished. The Lake of Fire is the ultimate destination of everything wicked—Satan, the Creature, the False Prophet, the demons, Death, Hell, and all those whose names are not recorded in the Book of Life because they have not placed their faith in Jesus Christ.

21:1 The earth as we know it will not last forever, but after God's great judgment, he will create a new earth (see Romans 8:18–21; 2 Peter 3:7–13). God had also promised Isaiah that he would create a new and eternal earth (Isaiah 65:17; 66:22). We don't know how it will look or where it will be, but God and his followers—those whose names are written in the Book of Life—will be united to live there forever. Will you be there?

21:2, 3 The new Jerusalem is where God dwells among his people. Instead of our going up to meet him, he comes down to be with us, just as God became man in Jesus Christ and lived among us (John 1:14). Wherever God reigns, there is peace, security, and love.

21:3, 4 Have you ever wondered what eternity will be like? The

"Holy City, the new Jerusalem" is described as the place where God "will wipe away all tears." Forevermore, there will be no death, pain, sorrow, or crying. What a wonderful truth! No matter what you are going through, it's not the last word—God has written the final chapter, and it is about true fulfillment and eternal joy for those who love him. We do not know as much as we would like, but it is enough to know that eternity with God will be more wonderful than we can imagine.

21:5 God is the Creator. The Bible begins with the majestic story of his creation of the universe, and it concludes with his creation of a new heaven and earth. This is a tremendous hope and encouragement for the believer. When we are with him, with our sins forgiven and our future secure, we will be like Christ. We will be made perfect like him.

21:6 Just as God finished the work of creation (Genesis 2:1–3) and Jesus finished the work of redemption (John 19:30), so the Trinity will finish the entire plan of salvation by inviting the redeemed into a new creation.

21:6 For more about the Water of Life, see the note on 22:1.

21:7
Rom 8:17,32

21:8
Deut 20:8
Mal 3:5
1 Cor 6:9,10
Gal 5:19-21
Eph 5:5
Rev 2:11

thirsty the springs of the Water of Life—as a gift! 7Everyone who conquers will inherit all these blessings, and I will be his God and he will be my son. 8But cowards who turn back from following me, and those who are unfaithful to me, and the corrupt, and murderers, and the immoral, and those conversing with demons, and idol worshipers and all liars—their doom is in the Lake that burns with fire and sulphur. This is the Second Death."

The new Jerusalem

21:9
Rev 21:2
21:10
Ezek 40:1,2
2 Cor 12:2-4
Rev 1:10; 17:3
21:11
Job 28:17
Isa 60:1
Ezek 48:35
Rev 4:3
21:12
Ezek 48:31-34
Rev 22:14
21:14
Eph 2:20
Heb 11:10
21:15
Ezek 40:3
Zech 2:1,3
Rev 11:1

9Then one of the seven angels, who had emptied the flasks containing the seven last plagues, came and said to me, "Come with me and I will show you the bride, the Lamb's wife."

10In a vision he took me to a towering mountain peak and from there I watched that wondrous city, the holy Jerusalem, descending out of the skies from God. 11It was filled with the glory of God, and flashed and glowed like a precious gem, crystal clear like jasper. 12Its walls were broad and high, with twelve gates guarded by twelve angels. And the names of the twelve tribes of Israel were written on the gates. 13There were three gates on each side—north, south, east, and west. 14The walls had twelve foundation stones, and on them were written the names of the twelve apostles of the Lamb.

15The angel held in his hand a golden measuring stick to measure the city and its gates and walls. 16When he measured it, he found it was a square as wide as it was long; in fact it was in the form of a cube, for its height was exactly the same as its

WHAT WE KNOW ABOUT ETERNITY	Reference	Description
	John 14:2–3	A place prepared for us
	John 20:19, 26	Unlimited by physical properties (1 Corinthians 15:23)
	1 John 3:2	We shall be like Jesus
	1 Corinthians 15:1–58	We will have new bodies
	1 Corinthians 2:9	Our experience will be wonderful
	Revelation 21:1	A new environment
	Revelation 21:3	A new experience of God's presence (1 Corinthians 13:12)
	Revelation 21:4	New emotions
	Revelation 21:4	There will be no more death

The Bible devotes much less space to describing eternity than it does to convincing people that eternal life is available as a free gift from God. Most of the brief descriptions of eternity would be more accurately called hints, since they use terms and ideas from present experience to describe what we cannot fully grasp until we are there ourselves. These references hint at aspects of what our future will be like if we have accepted Christ's gift of eternal life.

21:7,8 *Cowards* are not those who are fainthearted in their faith or who sometimes doubt or question. Rather, they are those who turn away from God and refuse to follow him further. They are not brave enough to stand up for Christ; they are not humble enough to accept his authority over their lives. They are put in the same list with the corrupt, murderers, liars, idolators, the immoral, and those practicing demonic arts.

Conquerors are those who "endure to the end without renouncing" Christ (Mark 13:13). They will receive the blessings God promised: (1) eating from the Tree of Life (2:7), (2) escaping from the Lake of Fire (2:11), (3) having a special name (2:17), (4) having power over the nations (2:26), (5) being included in the Book of Life (3:5), (6) being a pillar in God's spiritual temple (3:12), and (7) sitting with Christ on his throne (3:21). Those who can endure the testing of evil and remain faithful are those whom God will reward.

21:8 The Lake of fire is explained in the notes on 19:20 and 20:14. The Second Death is spiritual death, meaning either eternal torment or destruction. In either case, it is permanent separation from God.

21:10ff The rest of this section (21:9—22:5) is the final vision of

the book, a stunning description of the new city of God. The vision is symbolic and shows us that our new home with God will defy description. We will not be disappointed by it in any way.

21:12–14 The new Jerusalem is a picture of God's place for God's people. The 12 tribes of Israel (21:12) probably represent all the faithful in the Old Testament; the 12 apostles (21:14) represent the church. Thus, both believing Gentiles and Jews who have been faithful to God will live together on the new earth.

21:15–17 The city's measurements are symbolic of a place that will hold all God's people. Given in cubits, these measurements are all multiples of 12. Twelve is the number for God's people—there were 12 tribes in Israel, and 12 apostles who started the church. The walls are 144 cubits across (translated "216 feet across"); there are 12 layers in the walls, and 12 gates in the city; and the height, length, and breadth are all the same, 12,000 stadia (translated "1,500 miles"). The new Jerusalem is a perfect cube, the same shape as the Holy of Holies in the Temple (1 Kings 6:20). These measurements illustrate that this new home will be perfect for us, and the image portrays God as our Holy of Holies—we will live in him forever.

other dimensions—1,500 miles each way. [17]Then he measured the thickness of the walls and found them to be 216 feet across (the angel called out these measurements to me, using standard units).

[18, 19, 20]The city itself was pure, transparent gold like glass! The wall was made of jasper, and was built on twelve layers of foundation stones inlaid with gems: The first layer with jasper; the second with sapphire; the third with chalcedony; the fourth with emerald; the fifth with sardonyx; the sixth layer with sardus; the seventh with chrysolite; the eighth with beryl; the ninth with topaz; the tenth with chrysoprase; the eleventh with jacinth; the twelfth with amethyst.

[21]The twelve gates were made of pearls—each gate from a single pearl! And the main street was pure, transparent gold, like glass.

[22]No temple could be seen in the city, for the Lord God Almighty and the Lamb are worshiped in it everywhere. [23]And the city has no need of sun or moon to light it, for the glory of God and of the Lamb illuminate it. [24]Its light will light the nations of the earth, and the rulers of the world will come and bring their glory to it. [25]Its gates never close; they stay open all day long—and there is no night! [26]And the glory and honor of all the nations shall be brought into it. [27]Nothing evil will be permitted in it—no one immoral or dishonest—but only those whose names are written in the Lamb's Book of Life.

The river of Life

22 And he pointed out to me a river of pure Water of Life, clear as crystal, flowing from the throne of God and the Lamb, [2]coursing down the center of the main street. On each side of the river grew Trees of Life, bearing twelve crops of fruit, with a fresh crop each month; the leaves were used for medicine to heal the nations.

[3]There shall be nothing in the city which is evil; for the throne of God and of the Lamb will be there, and his servants will worship him. [4]And they shall see his face; and his name shall be written on their foreheads. [5]And there will be no night there—no need for lamps or sun—for the Lord God will be their light; and they shall reign forever and ever.

The promise of Jesus' return

[6, 7]Then the angel said to me, "These words are trustworthy and true: 'I am coming soon!' God, who tells his prophets what the future holds, has sent his angel

Marginal references:

21:17 Rev 13:18

21:18-20 Isa 54:11,12 / Rev 4:3,6

21:22 Ps 90:1 / Jn 4:21-24 / 17:23,24

21:23 Isa 60:19,20 / Rev 21:25

21:24 Ps 72:10 / Isa 60:3 / 66:10-14

21:25 Isa 60:11,20 / Rev 22:5

21:26 Ps 72:10 / Isa 49:23

21:27 Isa 52:1 / Rev 3:5 / 22:14,15

22:1 Ezek 47:1,2 / Jn 7:37-39 / Rev 7:17

22:2 Gen 2:9 / Ezek 47:12 / Rev 2:7,22:14

22:3 Rev 7:15

22:4 1 Cor 13:12 / Rev 7:3; 14:1

22:5 Rev 21:23,25

22:6,7 Rev 1:3; 21:5

21:17 *216 feet across . . . using standard units,* literally, "144 cubits by human measurements." A cubit was the average length of a man's arm—not an angel's! The angel used normal units of measurement that John could understand. **21:18-20** *The first layer,* implied. **21:22** *are worshiped in it everywhere,* literally, "are its temple." **22:2** *Trees of life,* literally, "the tree of life"—used here as a collective noun, implying plurality. **22:20** *soon,* or, "suddenly," "unexpectedly."

21:18-21 The picture of walls made of jewels reveals that the new Jerusalem will be a place of purity and durability—it will last forever. The ornate breastplate of the High Priest had twelve precious stones, representing the twelve tribes of Israel (see Exodus 28:15-21).

21:22-24 The Temple, center of God's presence among his people, was the primary place of worship. No temple is needed in the new city because God's presence will be everywhere. He will be worshiped throughout the city, and nothing will hinder us from being with him.

21:25-27 Not everyone will be allowed into the new Jerusalem, "only those whose names are written in the Lamb's Book of Life." (The Book of Life is explained in the notes on 3:5 and 20:11-15.) Don't think you'll get in because of your background, personality, or good behavior. Eternal life is available to you only because of what Jesus, the Lamb, has done. Trust him today to secure your citizenship in his new creation.

22:1 The Water of Life is a symbol of eternal life. Jesus used this same image with the Samaritan woman (John 4:7-14). It pictures the fullness of life with God and the eternal blessings that come when we believe in him and satisfy our spiritual thirst (see 22:17).

22:2 This Tree of Life (see textual note) is like the Tree of Life in the Garden of Eden (Genesis 2:9). After Adam and Eve sinned, they were forbidden to eat from the Tree of Life because they could not have eternal life as long as they were under sin's control. But because of the forgiveness of sin through the blood of Jesus, there will be no evil or sin in this city. We will be able to eat freely from the Tree of Life when sin's control over us is destroyed and our eternity with God is secure. Moreover, this "Tree of Life" bears twelve kinds of fruit so that fruit is available each month. Life in the new Jerusalem will be abundant and never-ending.

22:2 Why would the nations need to be healed if all evil is gone? John is quoting from Ezekiel 47:12, where water flowing from the Temple produces trees with healing leaves. He is not implying that there will be illness in the new earth; he is emphasizing that the Water of Life produces health and strength wherever it goes.

22:8
Rev 1:1-4
22:9
Rev 19:10
22:10
Rev 1:3
22:11
Ezek 3:27
Dan 12:10
22:12
Mt 16:27
Rev 22:7
22:13
Rev 1:8,17; 21:6
22:14
Rev 21:2,12,27
22:15
Gal 5:19-21
Rev 21:8
22:16
Isa 11:1
Mt 1:1; 2:2
Rev 1:1; 2:28
22:17
Jn 7:37-39
Rev 2:7,7:17
21:2,6,9
22:18
Deut 4:2; 12:32
Prov 30:5,6
Rev 15:6-16
22:19
Ex 32:33
Deut 4:2
Rev 3:5
21:10 22:5

to tell you this will happen soon. Blessed are those who believe it and all else written in the scroll."

8I, John, saw and heard all these things, and fell down to worship the angel who showed them to me; 9but again he said, "No, don't do anything like that. I, too, am a servant of Jesus as you are, and as your brothers the prophets are, as well as all those who heed the truth stated in this Book. Worship God alone."

10Then he instructed me, "Do not seal up what you have written, for the time of fulfillment is near. 11And when that time comes, all doing wrong will do it more and more; the vile will become more vile; good men will be better; those who are holy will continue on in greater holiness."

12"See, I am coming soon, and my reward is with me, to repay everyone according to the deeds he has done. 13I am the A and the Z, the Beginning and the End, the First and Last. 14Blessed forever are all who are washing their robes, to have the right to enter in through the gates of the city, and to eat the fruit from the Tree of Life.

15"Outside the city are those who have strayed away from God, and the sorcerers and the immoral and murderers and idolaters, and all who love to lie, and do so.

16"I, Jesus, have sent my angel to you to tell the churches all these things. I am both David's Root and his Descendant. I am the bright Morning Star. 17The Spirit and the bride say, 'Come.' Let each one who hears them say the same, 'Come.' Let the thirsty one come—anyone who wants to; let him come and drink the Water of Life without charge. 18And I solemnly declare to everyone who reads this book: If anyone adds anything to what is written here, God shall add to him the plagues described in this book. 19And if anyone subtracts any part of these prophecies, God

---

22:8, 9 Hearing or reading an eyewitness account is the next best thing to seeing the event yourself. John witnessed the events reported in Revelation and wrote them down so we could "see" and believe as he did. If you have read this far, you have "seen." Have you also believed?

22:8, 9 The first of the Ten Commandments is "You may worship no other god than me" (Exodus 20:3). Jesus said that the greatest command of Moses' laws was "Love the Lord your God with all your heart, soul, and mind" (Matthew 22:37). Here, at the end of the Bible, this truth is reiterated. The angel instructs John to "worship God alone." God alone is worthy of our worship and adoration. He is above all creation, even the angels. Are there people, ideas, goals, or possessions that occupy the central place in your life, crowding God out? Worship *only* God by allowing nothing to distract you from your devotion to him.

22:10, 11 The angel tells John what to do after his vision is over. Instead of sealing up what he has written, as Daniel was commanded to do (Daniel 12:4–12), the scroll is left open to let others see it so that all can read and understand. Daniel's message was sealed because it was not a message for Daniel's time. But the book of Revelation was a message for John's time, and it is equally relevant today. As Christ's return gets closer, there is a greater polarization between God's followers and Satan's followers. We must read the book of Revelation, hear its message, and be prepared for Christ's imminent return.

22:12–14 Those who are washing their robes are those who are seeking to purify themselves from a sinful way of life. They are daily striving to remain faithful and ready for Christ's return. This concept is also explained in the second note on 7:14.

22:14 In Eden, Adam and Eve were barred from the Tree of Life because of their sin (Genesis 3:22–24). In the new earth, God's people will eat from the Tree of Life because their sins have been

removed by Christ's death and resurrection. Those who eat the fruit of this tree will live forever. If Jesus has forgiven your sins, you will have the right to eat from this tree. For more on this concept, see the first note on 22:2.

22:16 Jesus is both David's Root and his Descendant. As the Creator of all, he existed long before David's day. As a human, however, he was one of David's direct descendants (see Isaiah 11:1–5; Matthew 1:1–17). As the Messiah, he is the Morning Star, the light of salvation to all.

22:17 Both the Holy Spirit and the bride, the church, extend the invitation to all the world to come to Jesus and experience the joys of salvation in Christ.

22:17 When Jesus met the Samaritan woman at the well, he told her of the Living Water that he could supply (John 4:10–15). This image is used again as Christ invites anyone to come and drink of the Water of Life. The gospel is unlimited in scope—all people, everywhere, may come. Salvation cannot be earned, but God gives it freely. We live in a world desperately thirsty for Living Water, and many are dying of thirst. But it's still not too late. Let us invite everyone to come and drink.

22:18, 19 This warning is given to those who might purposefully distort the message in this book. Moses gave a similar warning in Deuteronomy 4:1–4. We too must handle the Bible with care and great respect so that we do not distort its message, even unintentionally. We should be quick to put its principles into practice in our lives. No human explanation or interpretation of God's Word should be elevated to the same authority as the text itself.

shall take away his share in the Tree of Life, and in the Holy City just described.

²⁰"He who has said all these things declares: Yes, I am coming soon!"Amen! Come, Lord Jesus!

²¹The grace of our Lord Jesus Christ be with you all. Amen!

22:20
1 Thess 1:10
Heb 9:28
Rev 1:2; 22:7,16
22:21
Rom 16:20

22:20 We don't know the day or the hour, but Jesus is coming soon and at a time when no one will expect him. This is good news to those who trust him, but a terrible message for those who have rejected him and stand under judgment. *Soon* means at any moment, and we must be ready for him, always prepared for his return. Would Jesus' sudden appearance catch you off guard?

22:21 Revelation closes human history as Genesis opened it—in Paradise. But there is one distinct difference in Revelation—evil is gone forever. Genesis describes Adam and Eve walking and talking with God; Revelation describes people worshiping him face to face. Genesis describes a Garden with an evil serpent; Revelation describes a perfect city with no evil. The Garden of Eden was destroyed by sin; but Paradise is re-created in the new Jerusalem.

The book of Revelation ends with an urgent request: "Come, Lord Jesus!" In a world of problems, persecution, evil, and immorality, Christ calls us to endure in our faith (13:10, 11; 14:12). Our efforts to better our world are important, but their results cannot compare with the transformation Jesus will bring about when he returns. He alone controls human history, forgives sin, and will re-create the earth and bring lasting peace.

Revelation is above all a book of hope. It shows that no matter what happens on earth, God is in control. It promises that evil will not last forever. And it depicts the wonderful reward that is waiting for all those who believe in Jesus Christ as Savior and Lord.

This is an index to the notes, charts, maps, and personality profiles in the *Life Application Bible.* Every entry concerning a note has a Bible reference and a page number; every entry concerning a chart, map, or personality profile has a page number. In some instances, a Bible reference is followed by a number in parentheses to indicate that there is more than one note on that particular scripture. For example, Rv 1:1(2) means that the reader should look up the second note with the heading of 1:1 in Revelation. In most cases, the entries follow in biblical/canonical order (i.e., from Genesis to Revelation). In some cases, however, the entries follow a chronological order—this is especially true with important people in the Bible. Following the general index are special indexes: Index to Charts, Index to Maps, and Index to Personality Profiles. Because of the emphasis on application in the *Life Application Bible,* these indexes are helpful guides for personal and group Bible Study, sermon preparation, or teaching.

JETHRO

JEWELRY

JEWISH LEADERS

JEWISH SUPREME COURT

JEWS

JEZEBEL (wife of Ahab)

JEZEBEL (in Thyatira church)

JEZREEL, CITY OF

JEZREEL, VALLEY OF

JOAB

Note: maps concerning Jesus' ministry are given in chronological order—see Harmony of the Gospels.